GW00367026

RECORD COLLECTOR

RARE RECORD PRICE GUIDE 2012

PUBLISHED BY
RECORD COLLECTOR MAGAZINE
THE WORLD'S LEADING PUBLICATION FOR
COLLECTORS OF RARE RECORDS AND MEMORABILIA

RECORD COLLECTOR'S GRADING SYSTEM

In order to assist everyone who buys and sells rare discs, *Record Collector* magazine has originated a set of standards for the condition of second-hand records, cassettes and CDs. Anyone buying or selling records through the magazine must use our conditions to state what amount of wear and tear the disc, its sleeve and/or contents have been subject to. The seven standard condition categories, and a description of what each one means, are listed below:

MINT: The record itself is in brand new condition with no surface marks or deterioration in sound quality. The cover and any extra items such as the lyric sheet, booklet or poster are in perfect condition. Records advertised as Sealed or Unplayed should be Mint.

EXCELLENT: The record shows some signs of having been played, but there is very little lessening in sound quality. The cover and packaging might have slight wear and/or creasing.

VERY GOOD: The record has obviously been played many times, but displays no major deterioration in sound quality, despite noticeable surface marks and the occasional light scratch. Normal wear and tear on the cover or extra items, without any major defects, is acceptable.

GOOD: The record has been played so much that the sound quality has noticeably deteriorated, perhaps with some distortion and mild scratches. The cover and contents suffer from folding, scuffing of edges, spine splits, discoloration, etc.

FAIR: The record is still just playable but has not been cared for properly and displays considerable surface noise; it may even jump. The cover and contents will be torn, stained and/or defaced.

POOR: The record will not play properly due to scratches, bad surface noise, etc. The cover and contents will be badly damaged or partly missing.

BAD: The record is unplayable or might even be broken, and is only of use as a collection-filler.

CDs & CASSETTES: As a general rule, CDs and cassettes either play perfectly — in which case they are in Mint condition — or they don't, in which case their value is minimal. Cassette tape is liable to deteriorate with age, even if it remains unplayed, so care should be taken when buying old tapes. CDs are difficult to grade visually: they can look perfect but actually be faulty, while in other cases they may appear damaged but still play perfectly. Cassette and CD inlays and booklets should be graded in the same way as record covers and sleeves. In general, the plastic containers for cassettes and CDs can easily be replaced if they are broken or scratched, but card covers and digipaks are subject to the same wear as record sleeves.

RECORD COLLECTOR'S GRADING READY RECKONER

This Ready Reckoner will help you work out the value of a record in any condition. For example, if you see a disc which is valued at £10 in Mint condition, but which you consider to be in only Very Good condition, then you can consult the Ready Reckoner and find out the appropriate price for the record — in this case, £5. As very few collectors are interested in records in Poor or Bad condition, we consider that any disc worth less than £10 in Mint condition is effectively worthless in Poor or Bad condition.

MINT	EX	VG	Good	Fair	Poor	Bad
1,000	800	500	300	150	80	25
500	400	250	150	75	40	12
300	240	150	90	45	25	8
250	200	125	75	38	20	6
200	160	100	60	30	15	5
150	120	75	45	25	13	4
125	100	60	38	18	12	3
100	80	50	30	15	8	2.50
75	60	35	22	10	6	2
50	40	25	15	8	4	1.50
40	32	20	12	6	3	1
30	25	15	9	4.50	2.50	—
25	20	12	7.50	3.50	2	—
22	18	11	6.50	3	1.75	—
20	16	10	6	2.50	1.50	—
15	12	8	4.50	2	1	—
12	10	6	3.50	1.75	0.75	—
10	8	5	3	1.50	—	—
8	6	4	2.50	1	—	—
7	5	3.50	2	0.75	—	—
6	4.50	3	1.75	—	—	—
5	4	2.50	1.50	—	—	—
4	3.25	2	1.25	—	—	—
3	2.50	1.50	1	—	—	—
2	1.75	1	—	—	—	—

RRPG 2012 ADVERTISING INDEX

CONTENTS

EDITOR
Ian Shirley

EDITOR IN CHIEF
Alan Lewis

ART & PRODUCTION MANAGER
Val Cutts

ADVERTISEMENT PRODUCTION
Peter Barry

PUBLISHER
Andy McDuff

Published in the United Kingdom 2010 by
Diamond Publishing Ltd. Room 101, 140 Wales Farm Road, London W3 6UG

Founded by Sean O'Mahony in 1987.

ISBN 978-0-9532601-6-4

THE ULTIMATE COLLECTOR'S GUIDE

Welcome to the eleventh edition of the *Rare Record Price Guide*, the largest and most comprehensive book of its kind. Like its predecessors, this volume has been compiled by the expert research team of *Record Collector*, the world's leading magazine in the field.

The goal of this book is simple: to list and value every collectable pop and rock record issued in the UK since 1950. As regular readers will already know, the *Rare Record Price Guide* doesn't just include vinyl singles, EPs and LPs, although they are still very heavily featured. It also provides information about every other way in which recorded music has been sold to the public over the last 50 years or more, from the brittle 78rpm shellac singles of the 1950s, to the latest permutations of digital sound on compact discs and even memory sticks. The only format we don't cover is digital downloads!

Musically, the coverage is equally diverse and thorough. Although the majority of items listed in this book could be at least vaguely described as 'rock' or 'pop', every aspect of music-making outside the specialist classical field is featured in these pages. For over 35 years, record collecting itself has expanded enormously, both in terms of the number of people taking part and the types of music that they are interested in.

Rest assured that no matter how obscure your tastes, you'll find the most sought-after items here whether your particular obsession is 50s rockabilly, 60s MOR, 70s jazz-funk, house, 80s post-punk, hip-hop, reggae, NWOBHM, Northern soul, British jazz, folk, Progressive or today's indie bands. If it's collectable, and it was released in the UK, then you'll find it in the *Rare Record Price Guide*.

WHO SAYS HOW MUCH IT'S WORTH?

The question we're always asked about the prices listed in this book is how we calculate them. The answer is a mix of our 31 years of experience in the field; our ongoing research into the latest prices at record fairs and shops, and in sales both via mail order and online; and the invaluable help of a dedicated and extremely knowledgeable team of consultants and experts, who themselves regularly buy and sell items in their specialist areas.

As we always say, however, there is no *fixed* price for a second-hand record, no matter how rare it is. There are still bargains to be found out there, while in other situations like a feverishly competitive online auction particularly sought-after items can fetch prices way above their 'book' value. The price of a rare record is purely determined by what people are prepared to pay for it.

That said, our close scrutiny of the collecting market since the start of the 1980s allows us to make the best possible judgement about the records in this book. Prices may vary from one part of the country to another, or depending whether a disc is being sold in a shop, via an advert in *Record Collector*, at a major international fair, or on internet sites like 991.com, GEMM, Music Stack or eBay. But we believe that the guide values we list are the most accurate and realistic you'll find anywhere.

The other important point, which can't be repeated often enough, is that anyone selling records to a professional dealer can't expect to raise more than 40-50% of the prices listed here, except in very unusual cases. It doesn't matter whether you're selling rock'n'roll or jewellery, the same basic mark-up applies right across the collecting field, to cover the dealer's costs and profit margin. If you're selling directly to another collector, however, face-to-face or over the internet you can obviously hope to obtain the prices we list or even more, though please remember that all the values in this book are for records in absolutely perfect (or 'Mint') condition. To find out what you should be paying or charging, for a record in less than perfect condition, check the Ready Reckoner printed at the back of this book.

ACROSS THE AGES

Although many of the most valuable items listed in the *Rare Record Price Guide* date back to the 1950s, 1960s and 1970s, don't be fooled into thinking that record collecting is all about the distant past. As you turn the pages, you'll find plenty of releases from the 21st Century as well as the 20th – the latest collectables by major artists, for example, alongside limited edition singles by hot indie bands, and other rarities which were on sale one day and then became fiendishly hard to track down the next.

Check the details of those brand-new collectables, and you'll get some idea which of tomorrow's releases are likely to be sought-after in the future. But there are some things you can't predict, like the next 60s or 70s 7" that is worth £6 today but will be worth £60 in three months time. Or bands who were hot and collectable one year and saw their prices tumbling the next. Also, don't forget that virtually every record listed in this book, even the ones worth thousands of pounds, were once available for a few pounds, or even pence. For all those thousands of releases which have already become collector's items, however, the *Rare Record Price Guide* tells you what they are, what they look like, and how much they're going to cost.

ACKNOWLEDGEMENTS

CONSULTANTS Kingsley Abbot, Billy Albert, Jorn Rune Andersen, Alan Barndale John Barnjum, Neil Baylis, Mikael Billborn, Marco Bonacchi Greg Brooks, Nick Brown (Intoxica), Mark Burgess, Ian Clark, Peter Croxson, Les Hare, Michael De Koningh, Jason Draper, James Ellis, Steve Elphick, John Esplen, Mark Evetts, Leo Feigin, John Fisher, Joe Geesin, Roger Gorbell, Steve Guntrip, Kevin Goulding, Paul Green (Sounds Original), Tim Greenhall, Steve Guntrip, Les Hall, Marco Henning, Sam Hobden, John Hodgson, Dizzy Holmes, Justin Huntley, Max Hooley, Dudley Jaynes, Gordon Johnson, Michael Johnson, Damien Jones, Freek Kinkelaar, Jake Kennedy, Ben Legge, Dave Lewis, Graeme McLagen, John Manship, Haaken Eric Mathiesen, Joel McIver, Lee Medhurst, Richard Morton-Jack, Mike at Elista, Howie Moxon, Pete Nash, Pol O' Maoleoin, Ian Peel, Ray Platt, Edwin Pouncey, Laurence Prangell, Andy Price, Kurt Prinz, J. Rathbone, John Reed, Oscar Richt, Ian Roberts, Dave Sallis, Mike Savage, Barry Smith, Bob Solly, Bob Stoat, Torbjorn Stuhre, Brian Strong, Mitchell Thompson, Jonny Trunk, Audun Tylden, Peter Vickers, J Walton, Jamie, Ward, Ben Watkins, Martin Webb, Barry Winton, Alan Whitaker, Eric White (Out Of Time), Robin Wills, Conrad Zimmer. If I have missed any-one, please let me know!

FINALLY, SPECIAL THANKS to previous editors, contributors, Tomek Klas, Lee Davis, Simon Denison-Smith and the vast numbers of fanzines, websites and fan clubs whose hard work and expertise has helped - and continues - to make the Guide what it is today.

HOW TO USE THE GUIDE

PRICING YOUR RECORDS

Although the *Rare Record Price Guide 2012* contains a comprehensive listing of collectable UK releases, it does NOT list all the recordings made by the artists we've included. More detailed discographies of important artists can be found every month in *Record Collector* magazine.

MINIMUM VALUES FOR INCLUSION

ONLY THOSE RELEASES WHICH ARE CURRENTLY SOLD AT THE MINIMUM VALUES LISTED BELOW HAVE BEEN INCLUDED.
Any other releases obviously sell for less than these prices.

7" SINGLES, MAXI-SINGLES, CASSETTE SINGLES, DOUBLE PACKS & FLEXIDISCS	£5
78s	£10
10" SINGLES	£7
EPs, 12" SINGLES, CASSETTE EPs AND CD SINGLES	£8
LPs	£12
DOUBLE-LPs	£15
CD ALBUMS	£18

NOTE: EPs from the 1950s and 1960s usually sold at around twice the retail price of a 7" single. But most so-called EPs released since 1976 actually retailed at the same price as 7" singles. These records have been included in the Guide if they are worth £5 or more.

CURRENT MINT VALUES

The prices listed in this book are for the original issues of records, cassettes and CDs in MINT condition. Bear in mind that most records which turn up from the 1950s, 60s and even the early 1970s are NOT in Mint condition and their value will be affected accordingly. To find out the value of any item which is in less than Mint condition, consult our Grading System on page 1439 and the Ready Reckoner on page 1440.

ALPHABETICAL ORDER

The artists in this Guide are listed in alphabetical order, from A to Z. After the alphabetical listings, there is a section of Various Artists compilation releases, divided into several sections covering singles and 50s & 60s EPs, 70s, 80s & 90s EPs, LPs, film soundtrack LPs, original cast recordings from theatrical shows and library music.

The alphabetical order within the Guide has been determined by the first letter of a group name or an artist's surname. The word 'The' has not been taken into account when placing artists in alphabetical order; for instance, The Beatles' are listed under 'B', rather than 'T'.

The order follows the usual alphabetical principle of 'reading through' an artist's name or title, so that (for example) 'Peter Gabriel' is listed before 'Gabriel's Angels', and 'Generation X' is listed before 'Gen X'. Names and titles which include numbers appear as if the number was spelt out in full; e.g. the band '23 Skidoo' are listed as if their name was 'Twenty Three Skidoo'.

CHRONOLOGICAL ORDER

Within each artist entry, records are listed in chronological order of release. Singles (including 7", 10", 12", CD, cassette, and double packs) are listed first; then EPs; and finally LPs (including cassette and CD albums).

In the case of long entries, different formats of releases have also been grouped together under separate headers to make them easier to find.

PACKAGING AND INSERTS

All prices refer to records with all their original packaging and inserts (where applicable) intact. Wherever possible, we have provided details of inserts and special items of packaging for each entry – pointing out gatefold sleeves, lyric sheets and other bonus items like posters, for example.

Any record with some or all of these additional items missing will obviously be worth less than the values listed here. The level of depreciation depends on the missing items: in some cases, the value of an album can be dramatically reduced without its collectable insert (as in the case of the Who's *The Who Sell Out* LP, for example), while in others, it is the record itself that is desirable, and the insert is only of secondary importance (as with the Picadilly Line LP, *The Huge World Of Emily Small*).

DOUBLE PRICES: PICTURE SLEEVES

Since 1978, all U.K. 7", 10" and 12" singles have usually been issued in picture sleeves. Before 1978, however, picture covers were definitely the exception rather than the rule.

All those singles which originally appeared in a picture sleeve are listed with the abbreviation '(p/s)'. Where the picture sleeve was only available with the first batch of singles, there are two prices listed: the first refers to the record with its picture sleeve, the second without. If only one price is listed, then the single has to have its picture sleeve intact and in Mint condition to qualify for this value.

Most singles from the 1950s, 1960s and early 1970s were issued in 'company' sleeves, carrying the name and logo of the label which issued the record. Unless a picture sleeve is indicated, the prices listed in this guide are for singles with their company sleeves intact and, like the records themselves, in Mint condition. Many collectors are not too concerned about company sleeves - although in isolated cases (like the cult 60s label Planet), the company sleeves can be harder to find than the records themselves.

Company sleeves don't usually have much effect on a record's value. For example, an original Creation single from 1966, valued at £45, may only be worth £35 without its Planet company sleeve. At the other extreme, no doo-wop collector is going to be bothered if a copy of a rarity like The Penguins' Earth Angel, valued at £2,000, comes in a plain sleeve, or indeed, no sleeve at all - what matters here is that the record is in Mint condition.

DOUBLE PRICES: FREEBIES & INSERTS

Two prices have been listed for those items which were available in more than one form. 'Freebie' singles given away with newspapers and magazines have two values: the first for the record with the publication, the second for the disc itself. Records which were issued only briefly with an insert, like a poster or lyric sheet, are often priced both with and without the extra packaging.

DOUBLE PRICES: CHANGES IN DESIGN

Two or more prices have been given for records which were released more than once with the same catalogue number, but in slightly different form - with a change of label colour or sleeve design (for instance, the substitution of triangular centres by round centres on late 1950s singles), or the manufacture of more recent singles in a variety of different coloured vinyls.

These variations of packaging and presentation can make an enormous difference to the value of a record, which is why we have documented them here. They help collectors identify the first pressing or edition of each release, which is almost always more sought-after than later issues of the same record. One notable example is the first edition of the Beatles' *Please Please Me* LP, which featured the black-and-gold Parlophone label for a few weeks, before the introduction of the more modern-looking yellow-and-black label. Black-and-gold copies of the stereo version of this LP are worth £3,500, whilst standard yellow and black label later pressings are worth between £3,000 and £200.

Occasionally, second pressings can be worth more than the originals, as is the case with early Shadows and Cliff Richard singles. Green label copies of these 45s sold in their millions, while later re-pressings on black labels are much scarcer. So always check which pressing of any record you are buying before parting with your money.

MONO AND STEREO

In the case of EPs and LPs from the 1950s and 1960s, mono and stereo releases often have different values – and different catalogue numbers. Both prices are listed, together with the separate catalogue numbers for the two versions of each release (mono first, then stereo). Where the mono and stereo editions are worth the same amount, only one price has been listed.

The last few years have seen a polarisation in the prices between mono and stereo pressings – increasingly so for those late mono releases from 1968 to 1970, when the single-channelled format was being phased out in favour of the twin-tracked stereo. Similarly, early stereo copies should prove to be sound investments.

UK RELEASES AND EXPORT ISSUES

Only UK releases are included in the *Rare Record Price Guide*, not overseas issues. The exceptions to this rule are a handful of folk releases and U2 singles, all from the Irish Republic, which were heavily imported into Britain, but not officially issued here. The other exceptions are 'Export Releases'. These were manufactured in the UK in the 1950s and 1960s by companies like EMI and Decca for distribution to countries which didn't have their own pressing plants. Because they were pressed in very small quantities, and then distributed to the furthest corners of the globe, export records by artists like the Beatles and the Rolling Stones are often worth many times the values of similar items pressed for the UK.

UK RELEASES PRESSED OVERSEAS

Although the great majority of the records we've listed were manufactured in the UK, not all UK releases were made in this country – or vice versa. For example, a large proportion of the Rolling Stones' US singles on the London label in the 1960s were actually manufactured in Britain. More recently, many British releases by major labels – notably Warners –

have been made in Europe, and sent in identical form to Britain and many other countries. In these cases, the record sleeves often carry many different catalogue numbers, to cater for every country where the records are being distributed.

The problem of identifying the country where a particular record has been issued has grown more difficult with the advent of CDs. In these cases, it is the packaging that helps you identify the origin of a particular CD, rather than the disc itself.

78 rpm RELEASES

The common misconception about 78s is that they are more valuable than 7" singles. In fact, the opposite is true in most cases, as far more 78s were sold in the 1950s than 45 rpm 7" singles.

The last batches of 78s issued from 1958 to 1960 are the main exception to this rule (see Eddie Cochran's entry, for example). As these were often only available in small quantities (as the public switched to 45s), or even by special order, they can prove to be much harder to find than their 45 rpm equivalents.

COMMERCIAL RELEASES, NOT PROMOS

In general, this Guide only includes records which were manufactured for commercial release, or for distribution in some way to the public – as a freebie with a magazine, for example.

Promotional records, demos, acetates and test pressings have not usually been included, apart from exceptional cases where these items actually reached the public, or where (as with artists like the pre-Iron Maiden act, Urchin) one promo single has become so famous among collectors that it would have been misleading for it not to be mentioned. The major exceptions to this rule are artists like the Beatles, and modern artists like The Pet Shop Boys, Kylie Minogue, Depeche Mode and Madonna whose promos – often with extended hard to find remixes – are sometimes more valuable than their commercial releases and highly sought after by their fans. Also, although we have included some CD-R promo releases in this Guide the value of these items usually fluctuate wildly upwards before release and then fall alarmingly once the official album or single is in the shops. Some collectors do want them – especially completists – but we should state that the sale of watermarked and numbered CD-R's is illegal.

Full details of the values of non-commercial rarities like promos, demos, acetates and test pressings can be found in the articles and discographies in *Record Collector* every month.

IMPORTANT NOTE

Every effort has been taken to ensure that the information contained in this Price Guide is as accurate and up-to-date as possible. However, the publishers cannot take any responsibility for any errors or omissions; nor can they be held responsible or liable for any loss or damage to any person acting on the information in this Guide. The publishers welcome any corrections or additions to the Guide, which will be considered for future editions.

ian.shirley@metropolis.co.uk

THE HISTORY OF THE RARE RECORD PRICE GUIDE

RECORD COLLECTOR MAGAZINE

Record Collector was first published in 1979, and the magazine quickly established itself as the bible of pop and rock history. When the magazine was born, record collecting was a small, rather disorganised business, which wasn't making much effort to encourage new people to get involved.

From the start, *Record Collector* set out to provide the information that collectors needed, whether they'd been buying and selling records for years, or were just starting to build up a collection. There were two vital things they wanted to know: what records had been released by their favourite artists, and how much were they worth?

Every issue of *Record Collector* has provided complete discographies (lists of record releases, complete with full catalogue numbers, release dates and current Mint values) for an amazing variety of performers, from pre-rock stars like Frank Sinatra to the latest chart-bound arrivals and cult indie bands, via every imaginable style and genre along the way. Our in-depth features have provided the essential information to help readers get the most out of their music – by explaining the history of the artists and the records.

THE CHANGING FACE OF THE RARE RECORD PRICE GUIDE

In 1987, we published our first price guide - a slim volume which was designed as a quick and easy reference source to records by around 2,000 important artists.

That was only the beginning, though. We soon began work on the first edition of the book you're holding. Published in late 1992, the first *Rare Record Price Guide* filled 960 pages and listed 60,000 rare and collectable records.

The response to that book was tremendous, but we quickly realised that the collecting market was changing so fast that we couldn't rest on our laurels. Every year, thousands of new records reach the shops, in a bewildering variety of formats - everything from 7" singles and cassettes to expensive multi-CD box sets.

A small but sizeable proportion of these new releases became instant collector's items. Over the last 20 years, it's been common for record companies to issue special limited editions – anything from a few hundred to a few thousand copies – which sell out in a few days. The most sought-after of these records can triple or quadruple their value within a few months.

At the same time, interest in vinyl from the past continues to grow. As collectors track down all the records they want in a particular genre, they start to broaden their horizons. As a result, obscure items from the 50s, 60s, 70s and 80s become much-wanted treasures on the collectors' market – and their prices rise to reflect the new demand.

That's why we published a second edition, a year later, which grew to 1152 pages, with 70,000 records listed. And this was expanded again for the 1995 edition (over 75,000 entries and 1252 pages) and 1997/98 edition (85,000 entries and 1440 pages), to take in all the latest collectable releases.

The Millennium Edition ran to 1504 pages; another two years on, the *Rare Record Price Guide 2002* was bigger than ever, the 2004 edition was 1536 pages the RRPG 2006 1504 pages and RRPG 2008 and 2010 1408 pages. Now you're holding the latest edition that runs to 1440 pages, covering more than 50 years of rare and collectable records.

THE BIRTH OF COLLECTING

When the collecting scene was in its infancy in the 1970s, the market was focused on particular artists or genres. All the early attention was concentrated on 1950s rock'n'roll, and 1960s beat music. In addition, major artists like the Beatles, the Rolling Stones, Elvis Presley and David Bowie began to attract specialist collectors. But the whole collecting scene blossomed during the 1980s and it's now true to say that there aren't any musical styles which *aren't* collectable. Folk, jazz, techno, hip-hop, blues, heavy metal, punk, psychedelia, progressive rock, film soundtracks, soul, funk, reggae, disco, mainstream rock and pop, even easy listening - each genre boasts its share of in-demand rarities.

LIMITED EDITIONS

In the late 1970s, the arrival of punk spawned scores of new, independent record labels, which had fresh views about the way to market their releases. It became common for singles to appear in picture sleeves, as they had done overseas since the 1960s.

Records also began to appear on coloured vinyl or as picture discs, in an attempt to attract more buyers. Never slow to cash in on a marketing trend, the major record companies soon joined in. By the early 1980s, they were issuing a bewildering variety of editions of the same record in slightly different formats.

This sudden change in marketing techniques helped to trigger an entirely new development on the collecting scene. For the first time, records were becoming instant collector's items. A limited-edition single could be released one week, and sell for twice its retail price a fortnight later.

That opened the floodgates. No longer were 1950s and 1960s records the only things you'd find in the collector's shops. Now, it was open season, for anything and everything from Tubby Hayes to U2.

COMPACT DISCS

The arrival of CDs in the mid-1980s was greeted with doom and gloom in some quarters. But extensive remastering and reissue programs on CD have helped to increase the market for old vinyl releases.

If you grew up in the 1960s, you probably remember that it was difficult to find records that had been hits only a few years earlier. Now, you can go into most record stores and buy compilations and original albums with bonus tracks from every era of music history. For thousands of collectors, however, owning the music on CD or via download isn't enough – and they track down the original releases of music made and released before they were born.

The CD is now well established as a collectable format – particularly for promotional items, limited edition singles, and some original 80s albums which have yet to be remastered. Although more music is sold through digital downloading than any other format the CD still remains the dominant physical format on which music is released and bought worldwide.

STATE OF THE MARKET

On March 18th 2010 The Rare Record Price Guide went online...

With many collectors and dealers now trading internationally we thought that it was vital that we established an online presence. Also, although this printed Guide contains over 100,000 entries and is published every two years the market is more fluid today than in the past with new collectables coming out of the woodwork almost daily. It was almost impossible to contain them all within one book and market conditions have also seen the value of some 78 rpm, 7", and 12" singles, EPs and LPs fall below the entry prices for the Rare Record Price Guide. Although we have always stressed that the Rare Record Price Guide is not a complete discography we understand that many collectors do use it for this purpose and, for example, want to find out how many singles Bing Crosby released in 1953. Therefore, the online version of the Rare Record Price Guide not only contains every record in this printed guide but will also provide information on records that are no longer in the Guide as well as giving them a price. So, although Michael Holliday's *MIKE SINGS RAGTIME* EP from 1961 is no longer in this edition of the Guide it still lives online with a Guide value of £6. We will, of course, also be adding the latest collectables from new and established bands as well as new discoveries of hot 7" singles from the 60s and 70s that are now being frantically sought out by collectors.

Going forward, our intention to list in our growing online database every record ever released in the U.K. and give it a price from an unloved album by Phil Collins that is worth £6 to the solitary Enough's Enough single from 1968 that is worth £500. We also intend to post, eventually, images of every record sleeve, label, inner sleeve and insert as well as highly detailed information as to what makes record rare from matrix numbers to label variation on different pressings. There will also be regular news items and features on collectable artists as well as a resource for collectors to add their own records to the database that were released in the U.K. and other countries. Indeed, there is already a facility for collectors to establish their own 'collection' with the Rare Record Price Guide Online, grade their record individually and even convert the value of records from pounds sterling into U.S. dollars, Euros and the Japanese Yen. The book will always be an indispensible aid to record collectors of all persuasions and we want to make the Rare Record Price Guide Online as much as a 'bible' and vital resource for collectors as the book has been for over thirty years.

As for the current state of the market, in the last two years the transition to online trading has accelerated at warp speed. The sheer volume of records now offered for sale on sites like eBay, Music Stack, GEMM or dealers own sites is vast giving collectors even more choice than ever before. At the lower end of the market this has driven down prices with buyers being able to snaffle up excellent copies of singles, EPs and albums by the likes of Adam Faith, Peggy Lee, Gene Pitney, The Vibrators, Devo, The Teardrop Explodes, Elvis Presley, The Cure, Depeche Mode and many others at bargain prices. Of course, when it comes to rarities in excellent or mint condition the online bidding is furious with many records fetching prices well in excess of our guide prices. From 7" Beatles demos to factory samples of the Tinkerbell's Fairydust LP our monthly eBay-O-Meter only shows the tip of a vast and ever-growing iceberg. Whilst these high prices are good for collectors and online dealers – with the right stock – the transition to internet trading has further eroded the position of the remaining record shops that have kept their heads above water. Even Beanos has bowed to the inevitable and finally closed down. Ironically, Record Store Day which was started in 2008 to help sustain independent record shops is also becoming an internet phenomenon. On 17th April 2010 literally hours after shops across the country had opened their doors there were dozens of copies of the limited edition singles by artists like Blur, The Pet Shop Boys, The Rolling Stones and the sought after Flaming Lips album *The Dark Side Of The Moon* being offered for sale on eBay. So, Record Store Day is generating an 'instant' collectables market where many people buy to sell on.

As collectors and dealers are aware, the market for rare 60s and early 70s albums is vibrant with prices being paid over Guide for psychedelic, progressive, krautrock, British jazz and rare folk and acid folk albums. To further assist collectors we have also tried to give more details about first pressings from label designs to the distinguishing marks between a Harvest first pressing and a later reissue with the EMI logo on the label. We have also substantially revised upwards the prices for rare records from this period to reflect market conditions as eBay and Popsike are showing that collectors are prepared to pay well over the odds to add mint records from this period to their collections. For example, in the last Guide the rare Wil Malone album was priced at £300 and now it is a more realistic £1500. One interesting development is the widening gulf between what collectors will pay for a mint and excellent record and those that are simply in very good condition. In some respects this is due to collectors having a wider variety of choice with internet sites and dealers from all over the world offering millions of albums all year round. If a record comes up for auction or sale in very good or worse condition, collectors may not bid because – like a bus – another one in better condition might come along minutes, hours, days or weeks later. Saying that, many records – 7" singles, EPs and LPs - that have a mint price of between £12 -£40 in good very good and even excellent condition can be picked up very cheaply at fairs or record shops.

The Beatles remain the most sought-after and collectable artists in the world. Prices for mint Beatles singles, EPs and albums continue to increase with some amazing prices being paid for mint copies of the *Please Please Me* LP with the famed black and gold labels. There is also a new variant of the first stereo issue of the black and yellow label that is also commanding thousands of pounds which you can read about on page 107... As well as the Beatles, other blue chip artists like the Rolling Stones, The Who, Queen, Radiohead, Led Zeppelin The Smiths, Iron Maiden, Jimi Hendrix, David Bowie, Marc Bolan, Pink Floyd, Oasis and others continue to appreciate. Indeed, a mint copy of the first pressing of Led Zeppelin's debut album from 1969 with the turquoise sleeve is now worth in the region of £1000 which is double the price that was listed in the 2006 Guide. Despite his death in 2009, prices for Michael Jackson collectables remain steady although - obviously - autographed material and memorabilia has shot up in price. As for genres, the market for Northern Soul, soul, psychedelic, metal, folk, indie, punk, post-punk, new wave, reggae, jazz, afro-beat, early hip-hop and ska still command strong followings. Indeed, we have taken great pains to add rare boogie, funk, hip-hop, dance as well as digi-dub records in this edition of the guide as well as records by artists across the board from David Whitfield to collectable folk artist Nic Jones.

Finally, one of the most interesting developments is the dramatic increase in prices for albums issued in the 90s. This was the decade where the CD established itself as the most dominant format and as the decade progressed record companies issued less and less albums on vinyl. Thus, as well as a host of collectable albums by indie and metal bands like Pulp, Primal Scream, P.J. Harvey, Spiritualized, Burzum, Iron Maiden, Radiohead, Blur, Oasis, The Cocteau Twins and Mazzy Star, there were only limited edition runs of albums by mainstream artists like David Bowie, Queen, Iron Maiden, Bryan Ferry, The Corrs, Kate Bush, Bob Dylan, Tom Waits, The Rolling Stones and others that are now sought after by collectors. At the other end of the scale although there are bright spots the price for low value 78 rpm singles has fallen alarmingly and due to this we have revised upwards our entry level for 78 rpm singles to £10. It should be stressed that there is a market out there for UK 78rpm singles but it is limited to a small number of collectors. Of course, all those 78rpm singles that were previously in the printed guide are still listed – with prices – online. Although 50s rock and roll is just holding its value there are many artists form the 50s and early 60s whose prices have fallen or stagnated. There is nothing wrong with the music of artists like Keely Smith or Bobby Vee but they are not attracting new collectors and therefore prices for their records have decreased in value. On the subject of value, it was interesting to note that when eBay changed its policy of not allowing dealers to charge postage a glut of records appeared at fairs where it was no longer economical for dealers to list records cheaply and make a profit on postage. It should be stressed that however vibrant the online market, there are still fantastic bargains and deals to be had in record stores and record fairs where albums by the likes of Iggy Pop, Pavement, Neu!, The Fall, The Violent Femmes, Killing Joke, Bob Dylan, John Cale, Oasis, Nirvana, Crass, Wire, Joy Division, the Velvet Underground, Samson, the Clash, Judas Priest, the Beach Boys and many others will always tick over. Also, the face to face contact and haggling over price and condition of a rare record cannot be replaced by the online online experience where you have to play email ping-pong to ascertain the condition of the vinyl and sleeve.

In this latest edition of the Guide we have also made some stylistic changes. Thus, the "see also" information on artists is now directly below the artist name for ease of reference. We have also separated, in most cases, mono and stereo pressings in order to give more details on each. We have also re-established single line entries for 78rpm records as well as DJ promo and demostration singles. Finally, those records that were unissued used to have no price next to them which confused some users of the Guide. We have now replaced this with a 0. This is not to say that these records are worthless, but to indicate that there is no given value for this record as it either not thought to exist or was never released.

In closing we hope that you will find the 2012 Guide an essential tool whether you are a collector or a dealer. Of course, if you disagree with of the values then you can subscribe to the online version - see Page 16 to secure a £30 discount - which is not only going to be updated on a regular basis but allows you to comment with pricing suggestions or additional details on individual records!

We will, in due course, also list all those Frankie Vaughan singles that have been deleted from previous copies of the Guide...

USING THE GUIDE
A BRIEF SUMMARY

ALL PRICES REFER TO RECORDS AND PACKAGING IN MINT CONDITION

(See pages 1439-40 for Grading System and Ready Reckoner)

ARTISTS AND GROUPS are listed in alphabetical order.
Numerical names (e.g. 2.3) are listed as if the numbers are spelt in full (i.e. Two.Three).

ALL RECORDS LISTED ARE U.K. COMMERCIAL RELEASES

with the following exceptions:

(1) Records pressed in the U.K. for export overseas.

(2) Important demo or promo releases.

(3) Records or flexidiscs included as freebies with magazines, books and other records.

In general, promo and demo editions are not included, except when these records contain unique material and/or packaging, or are by major collectable artists.

EACH ENTRY includes:

SINGLES (7" 45s & cassettes) valued at £5 or more
78 rpm singles valued at £10 or more
10" singles valued at £6 or more
EPs, 12" singles & CD singles valued at £8 or more
LPs valued at £12 or more
DOUBLE-LPs valued at £15 or more
CD ALBUMS valued at £18 or more
Records worth less than these prices have not been included.

WITHIN EACH ENTRY, records are listed in chronological order of release, within each of the following categories (where applicable):
78s, SINGLES, EPs, LPs, CDs, PROMOS. The exceptions are major artists like the Beatles, the Rolling Stones and Elvis Presley, where the entry is further divided into originals, reissues and label variations.

Where TWO PRICES are listed for a single item, they refer to

(a) the record with and without a special insert or piece of packaging

(b) mono and stereo editions of EPs and LPs

(c) versions of the same record with different artwork, vinyl colour, etc.

ABBREVIATIONS
USED IN THIS GUIDE

act	actually	mag.	magazine
alt.	alternative	no.	number
b&w	black and white	no'd.	numbered
cass.	cassette	p/s	picture sleeve
cat. no.	catalogue number	pic disc	picture disc
CD	compact disc	pt(s)	part(s)
co.	company	sl.	sleeve
d/pack	double pack	st.	stereo
dble.	double	stkr	sticker
diff.	different	t/p	test pressing
edn.	edition	vers.	version
EP	extended-play record	vol.	volume
ext.	extended	w/.	with
flexi.	flexidisc	w/l	white label
g/f(old)	gatefold sleeve	2-CD or 2xCD	double CD
inst	instrumental	2-LP or 2xLP	double LP
intl.	international	2 x 45	two 45rpm singles
LP	long-playing record	3-LP	triple LP
m/s.	mono/stereo	78.	78rpm single

IMPORTANT RECORD COMPANY ABBREVIATIONS

Amalgam	Amalgamated
B. Banquet	Beggars Banquet
B'full/Brains	Bucketfull Of Brains
Col.	Columbia
Elek	Elektra
Font	Fontana
L.T.T. Slaughter	Lambs To The Slaughter
M. For Nations	Music For Nations
MFP	Music For Pleasure
M. Minor	Major Minor
Parl	Parlophone
PSI	Phil Spector International
Pye Intl	Pye International
R. Digest	Readers Digest
Regal Zono	Regal Zonophone
R. Stones	Rolling Stones
S'side	Stateside
St. Tones	Street Tones
Sweet Folk & C.	Sweet Folk And Country
T. Motown	Tamla Motown
UA	United Artists
W. Bros	Warner Brothers
WRC	World Record Club

IMPORTANT TERMS
USED IN THIS GUIDE

acetate	one-off disc cut by hand in a mastering studio, used for demonstration purposes
adaptor	plastic outer disc clipped onto 3" CDs to make them compatible with 5" CD players
art sleeve	pictorial cover using graphics rather than photographs or drawings
artwork	original design for sleeves or labels
audiophile pressing	high quality pressing for hi-fi enthusiasts
blister pack	shaped outer PVC packaging, usually for 3" CDs
bonus disc	disc given away free with another disc
bootleg	illegal pressing of material
box set	records or CDs in presentation case
budget release	pressing which retailed below full-price
catalogue number	manufacturer's reference number on record labels and sleeves
CD-R	one-off CD, digital equivalent of acetate
CD-ROM	audio/visual computer-compatible CD
CD Video	5" CD containing several audio tracks and (usually) one video track; now obsolete
company sleeve	standard non-picture sleeve for singles, printed with name or logo of label
counterfeit	illegal reproduction of official release (a.k.a. pirates)
DAT	digital audio tape
deleted	no longer commercially available
demo	record issued for demonstration purposes; not commercially available
die-cut sleeve	sleeve with circular hole cut into the centre
digipak	gatefold CD sleeve with plastic inner tray
DJ-only	record issued for radio airplay only
double groove	record with two grooves pressed concentrically on same side
double pack	two singles issued together as one package
DVDAC	digital versatile disc Audio
DVD	digital versatile disc
8-track cartridge	1970s tape format, popular for in-car entertainment; now obsolete
EP	extended play disc, with four or more tracks, usually in a picture sleeve
EPK	electronic press kit; i.e. short promo-only documentary available on video
envelope p/s	large mailing-type cover with envelope-style foldover flap
etched disc	one-sided vinyl record with laser-etched graphics (e.g. group's signatures) on other side
export issue	record or CD pressed in the UK for sale exclusively overseas
factory custom pressing	unofficial record pressed after hours (usually on coloured vinyl) at official pressing plant
flexidisc	thin, flexible record, usually issued free with magazine, etc.
flipback sleeve	LP or EP cover glued together with card flaps from the front folded over onto the back
foldaround/foldout/ foldover sleeve	sleeve which opens out as a poster, etc.
freebie	record given away free of charge
gatefold sleeve	double-size sleeve opening out like a book
import	record or CD pressed abroad but sold in the UK
inlay	printed paper booklet with CD packaging
inner sleeve	protective sleeve inside main cover
insert	loose item included as part of a record's packaging, e.g. postcard, poster, lyric sheet, etc.
interview album	spoken word record, often used as promo

jewel case	standard clear plastic case for cassettes and CDs
jukebox centre	plastic centre inserted into record with large centre hole
jukebox issue	record issued exclusively to jukebox franchise holders
laminated sleeve	cover with high-gloss plastic coating
large centre hole	1.5 inch (3.8 cm) hole in singles
long box	tall, rectangular outer card packaging for CDs
LP	long playing vinyl record; standard album format superseded by CDs
matrix number	master tape number, scratched into the 'land' or run-off groove area; sometimes also found on the record label
maxi-single	early 70s term for an EP, featuring more than two tracks, often in a picture sleeve
megamix	medley of different tracks, often linked by dance beats
mid-price release	record which retails at a discount
mispressing	record or CD pressed with incorrect material
mono	one-channelled playback system
numbered (no'd)	individually numbered, limited edition release
obi	sealed paper strip wrapped around sleeve of disc; originated in Japan where obis were printed with Japanese translations of foreign titles
one-sided	vinyl record which plays on one side only
picture disc	novelty record made by sealing a picture within clear vinyl
picture sleeve	pictorial paper or card sleeve, used specifically for one particular record
plain sleeve	single sleeve without special printing or artwork
premium	record available via a special offer with another product e.g. food or drink
press kit	information pack with photos and biography, used by record companies to promote new releases
private pressing	record issued and distributed by private individuals rather than a company
promo	promotional record or item sent out to the media for publicity purposes
push-out centre	centre of a single connected to the rest of the disc at 3 or 4 points, so it can be pushed out for use on jukeboxes, etc.
quadrophonic	1970s four-channelled playback system, now obsolete
reel-to-reel tape	1960s tape format, superseded by cassette
reissue	re-release of a deleted disc
remix	different version of existing track created by rearranging its component parts
removeable/ replaceable centre	centre which can be removed from a record without damage and later replaced (not to be confused with jukebox or 'spider' centres)
re-pressing	a second run of a record or CD which hasn't been deleted
run-off groove	groove between end of playing surface and record label
sampler	compilation showcasing an artist or label
sealed/shrinkwrapped	machine-wrapped in cellophane
shaped disc	any non-circular record
shellac	brittle material used for 78s
slipcase	small card cover used for some CDs and cassette singles
solid centre	centre of record which cannot be removed, as on LPs
stickered sleeve	sleeve with sticker as an integral part of its packaging
stereo	two-channelled playback system
test pressing	manufacturer's sample record, pressed for quality control
tri-centre	push-out triangular centre on some 1950s singles/EPs
tri-fold	triple fold-out sleeve
uncut picture disc	shaped disc not yet trimmed to proper shape
unissued/unreleased	disc not made commercially available; may or may not have been pressed
vinyl	material from which records are made
warp	buckle in vinyl caused by heat
white label	usually blank, perhaps printed or handwritten labels, often for promo purposes; term also used for demo, promo or test pressing
withdrawn	record deliberately removed from sale by its manufacturer

A

AARDVARK
(see also Home)

70	Deram Nova SDN 17	AARDVARK (LP, mono)	250
70	Deram Nova DN 17	AARDVARK (LP, stereo)	200

A-AUSTR
(see also Bill Nelson)

70	Holy Ground HG 113	A-AUSTR - MUSICS FROM HOLY GROUND (LP, with booklet, 99 only)	400
89	Magic Mixture MM 1	A-AUSTR (LP, reissue, 425 only)	45
95	Holyground 010101LP	A-AUSTR (LP, second reissue, foldover gatefold sleeve)	20

ABACUS

74	York YR 207	Indian Dancer/Be That Way	15
72	Polydor 2371 215	ABACUS (LP)	50

A BAND CALLED DORIS
(see under Doris)

ABBA
(see also Hep Stars, Hootenanny Singers, Agnetha Faltskog, Frida, Northern Lights)

73	Epic EPC 1793	Ring Ring/Rock'N'Roll Band (yellow label)	40
74	Epic EPC 2848	So Long/I've Been Waiting For You (yellow label)	10
79	Epic EPC 7499	Voulez Vous/Angel Eyes (red or yellow vinyl, p/s)	400
80	Epic EPC 12-8835	The Winner Takes It All/Elaine (12", gatefold pop-up p/s)	15
81	Epic EPCA 11-1740	One Of Us/Should I Laugh Or Cry (picture disc)	6
82	Epic EPCA 11-2971	Under Attack/You Owe Me One (picture disc)	20
82	Epic EPCA 2618	GREATEST ORIGINAL HITS (EP)	8
83	Epic A 3894	Thank You For The Music/Our Last Summer (poster p/s)	5
83	Epic WA 3894	Thank You For The Music/Our Last Summer (shaped picture disc)	25
84	Epic ABBA 26	ANNIVERSARY BOXED SET (26 x blue vinyl 7", numbered, 2,000 only)	300
84	Epic ABBA 26	ANNIVERSARY BOXED SET (26 x black vinyl 7")	100
93	Polydor 859 085-2	MORE ABBA GOLD (4-track CD, promo only)	25
94	Polydor 853 891-2	DREAM WORLD (CD, 4-track sampler, promo only)	40
99	No label ABBA 1	MAMMA MIA (4-track CD)	8
99	Polydor 563 286-2	ABBA Singles Collection 1974-1982 (29 CD singles in card sleeves & 1-track CD picture disc, with booklet, in silver tin, 20,000 only)	60
04	Polydor 982054-1	Waterloo/Watch Out (picture disc, 2,000 only, numbered)	25
74	Epic EPC 80179	WATERLOO (LP, yellow label)	15
75	Epic EPC 80835	ABBA (LP, yellow label)	15
76	Epic EPC 69218	GREATEST HITS (LP, gatefold sleeve, yellow label, some with "Fernando" sticker)	15
78	Epic EPC 86052	THE ALBUM (LP, gatefold with sticker)	15
79	Epic EPC 11-86086	VOULEZ VOUS (LP, picture disc)	50
80	Epic ABBOX 1	SUPER TROUPER (LP, box set with book & poster)	15
83	Epic ABBOX 11-2/ABBA-11-10	THE SINGLES - THE FIRST TEN YEARS (2-LP, picture discs, with poster, ticket & booklet in box)	60
83	Epic CDEPC 10022	SUPER TROUPER (CD, original issue)	20
83	Epic CDEPC 10032	THE VISITORS (CD, original issue)	18
84	St. Michael 1361/5704	THE HIT COLLECTION (cassette, with 64-page book Their Story, available via Marks & Spencer)	25
99	Simply Vinyl SVLP103	ABBA (LP, 180 gram pressing)	15

ABBASANI

91	Roots Rock RR 001	Revelation Time/Version	40
91	Roots Rock RR 009	REVELATION TIME (LP)	30

BILLY ABBOTT & JEWELS

63	Cameo Parkway P 874	Groovy Baby/Come On And Dance With Me	30

A.B.H.

78	Music Bank BECK 694	Geoffrey/Colt 45 Rock (no p/s)	20

SHIRLEY ABICAIR

56	Parlophone MSP 6224	Willie Can/Happy Trails	8
57	Parlophone R 4347	Bimini/Where The Sun Always Shines (with Humphrey Lyttleton)	6
64	Piccadilly 7N 35364	I Will Be There/Am I Losing You	10
66	Pye 7N 17119	Flowers Never Bend With The Rainfall/I Know	7
59	Fontana TFE 17123	FOUR FAVOURITES (EP)	8
65	Decca DFE 8640	THE NURSERY BEAT (EP)	8

ABNORMAL/BARBED WIRE

87	Oi Records OIR 010	SKINS 'N' PUNKS VOL. 4 (LP)	12

MICK ABRAHAMS (BAND)
(see also Blodwyn Pig, Jethro Tull, Mighty Flyers)

71	Chrysalis ILPS 9147	(A MUSICAL EVENING WITH) THE MICK ABRAHAMS BAND (LP, g/fold sleeve)	15
72	Chrysalis CHR 1005	AT LAST (LP, first pressing, circular foldout sleeve, Island logo and address in white on green label)	70
75	SRT SRTM 73313	HAVE FUN LEARNING THE GUITAR WITH MICK ABRAHAMS (LP, solo, with typed insert)	20

ABRASIVE WHEELS

81	Abrasive ABW 1	Army Song/Juvenile/So Low (p/s)	10

MINT VALUE £

82	Riot City RIOT 4	VICIOUS CIRCLE (EP, p/s)	6
82	Riot City RIOT 9	Army Song/Juvenile/So Slow (p/s, reissue, red vinyl)	6
82	Riot City RIOT 16	Burn The Schools/Urban Rebels/Burn 'Em Down (p/s)	6
82	Riot City CITY 001	WHEN THE PUNKS GO MARCHING IN (LP)	20
84	Clay CLAY 9	BLACK LEATHER GIRL (LP)	18

ABS

87	Shed 001	GREASE YOUR RALPH (EP, fold-out p/s)	12
89	Link MLP 100	MENTAL ENENA (LP)	12
90	Blasting Youth	NAIL IT DOWN (LP, with insert)	12

MIKE ABSALOM

60s	Sportsdisc ILP 1081	THE MIGHTY ABSALOM SINGS BATHROOM BLUES (LP)	15
69	Saydisc SDL 162	SAVE THE LAST GHERKIN FOR ME (LP)	80
71	Vertigo 6360 053	MIKE ABSALOM (LP, swirl label, poster sleeve)	150
72	Philips 6308 131	HECTOR AND OTHER PECCADILLOS (LP)	35

ABSOLUTE

(see also Erasure)

85	Reset 7REST 5	TV Glare/At The Third Stroke (p/s)	10
85	Reset 12 REST 5	TV Glare/At The Third Stroke (12", p/s)	20
87	Reset 7REST 8	Can't You See/Love In My Heart (release cancelled)	60

ABSOLUTE ELSEWHERE

(see also Bill Bruford)

76	Warner Bros K 16697	Earthbound/Gold Of The Gods (p/s)	5
76	Warner Bros K 56192	IN SEARCH OF ANCIENT GODS (LP, gatefold, die-cut, with booklet)	20

ABSOLUTELY FABULOUS

(see also Pet Shop Boys)

94	Parlophone CDR 6382	Absolutely Fabulous (7" Mix)/(Our Tribe Tongue-In-Cheek Mix)/ Absolutely Dubious/This Wheel's On Fire (CD, card sleeve withdrawn)	8

ABSTRAC & LADY PENELOPE

97	Confetti Records COEP 03	Love In Dub/Dub In Love/Peeper (Part 1) (12")	8
97	Confetti Records COEP 12	10 TIMES A DAY E.P. (12", Promo)	12

ABYSSINIAN BAPTIST CHOIR

63	Philips 847095 BY	ABYSSINIAN BAPTIST CHOIR (LP)	15

ABYSSINIANS

73	Harry J. HJ 6652	Yim Mas Gan/JOHN CROW GENERATION: Crank Shaft	20
75	Grounation GR 2029	Love Comes And Goes/(Version)	6
75	Soundtracs SK1	Tenayistillin Wandimae/Tenayistillin	8
76	Tropical S'tracks TST 109	African Race/Satta A Massagana	8
76	Nationwide NW009	Sweet Feelings/Version	8
77	Klik KL 631	Forward On To Zion/Satta A Massagana	5
78	Different HAVED 7	Sat A Masagana/I & I (12")	30
79	Different HAVE 18	Declaration Of Rights/African Race	8
78	Different GETL 100	FORWARD ON TO ZION (LP)	30
78	Virgin Front Line FL1019	ARISE (LP, with lyric sheet)	15

ACADEMY

(see also Polly Perkins)

69	Morgan Bluetown BTS 2	Rachel's Dream/Munching The Candy (as Academy featuring Polly Perkins)	20
69	Morgan Bluetown BT 5001	POP-LORE ACCORDING TO THE ACADEMY (LP)	200

ACCENT

(see also Rick Hayward)

67	Decca F 12679	Red Sky At Night/Wind Of Change	200

ACCENTS

59	Coral Q 72351	Wiggle, Wiggle/Dreamin' And Schemin'	25

ACCIDENT

(see also Major Accident)

84	Flicknife SHARP 016	A CLOCKWORK LEGION (LP)	20
87	Link LP 12	CRAZY! (LP)	15

ACCIDENTS

80	H. Line 'n' Sinker HOOK 1	Blood Spattered With Guitars/Curtains For You (p/s)	25
80	Hook Line 'n' Sinker	KISS ME ON THE APOCALYPSE (LP, unreleased; test pressings only, White handwritten labels)	150
90s	Detour DRLP04	KISS ME ON THE APOCALYPSE (LP)	15

ACCIDENT ON THE EAST LANCS.

80	Roach RR 1	The Back End Of Nowhere/Rat Race (p/s)	75
80	Roach SPLIFF 001	We Want It Legalised/Tell Me What You Want (no p/s)	75

ACCOLADE

(see also Gordon Giltrap, Wizz Jones, Pauline Filby, Don Partridge)

70	Columbia DB 8688	Natural Day/Prelude To A Dawn	12
70	Columbia SCX 6405	ACCOLADE (LP)	35
72	Regal Zono. SLRZ 1024	ACCOLADE 2 (LP)	45

ACCURSED

80s	Wrek 'Em ACC 3	Going Down (p/s)	8
83	Wrek 'Em ACC 1	AGGRESSIVE PUNK (LP)	20
83	Wrek 'EM ACC 3	UP WITH THE PUNKS (LP)	15
84	Wrek 'EM ACC 4	LAUGHING AT YOU (LP)	15

AC/DC

(see also Geordie, A II Z, Home)

76	Atlantic K 10745	It's A Long Way To The Top (If You Wanna Rock'N'Roll)/ Can I Sit Next To You, Girl? (no p/s)	22

			MINT VALUE £
76	Atlantic K 10805	Jailbreak/Fling Thing (original issue with running times on label, dark label, heavy print, no p/s)	22
76	Atlantic K 10860	High Voltage/Live Wire (in p/s)	120
76	Atlantic K 10860	High Voltage/Live Wire (no p/s)	15
77	Atlantic K 10899	Dirty Deeds Done Dirt Cheap/Big Balls/ The Jack (maxi-single, 'schoolboy' p/s)	75
77	Atlantic K 11018	Let There Be Rock (edit)/Problem Child (initial pressing with small label lettering & 3.06 timing, no p/s)	12
77	Atlantic K 11018	Let There Be Rock (edit)/Problem Child (without small label lettering & 3.06 timing, no p/s)	7
78	Atlantic K 11142	Rock'N'Roll Damnation/Sin City (initially with small label lettering & 3.05 timing, no p/s)	6
78	Atlantic K 11142T	Rock'N'Roll Damnation/Sin City (12", p/s)	15
78	Atlantic K 11207	Whole Lotta Rosie (live)/Hell Ain't A Bad Place To Be (live) (dark labels; later reissued with lighter labels (worth less) ; no p/s)	5
78	Atlantic K 11207T	Whole Lotta Rosie (live)/Hell Ain't A Bad Place To Be (live) (12", no p/s)	15
79	Atlantic K 11321	Highway To Hell/If You Want Blood (You've Got It) ('1979' on p/s)	5
79	Atlantic K 11406	Girl's Got Rhythm/Get It Hot (p/s, initial pressing without 'Elephant Head' motif)	6
79	Atlantic K 11406	Girl's Got Rhythm/Get It Hot (p/s, without 'Elephant Head' motif)	5
79	Atlantic K 11406E	Girl's Got Rhythm/If You Want Blood (You've Got It)/Hell Ain't A Bad Place To Be (live)/Rock'N'Roll Damnation (EP, gatefold envelope p/s)	10
80	Atlantic K 11435	Touch Too Much/Live Wire (live)/Shot Down In Flames (live) (p/s)	5
80	Atlantic K 11435	Touch Too Much/Live Wire (live)/Shot Down In Flames (live) (p/s, misprinted back-to-front)	15
80	Atlantic K 10805	Jailbreak/Fling Thing (reissue, light label, fine print; first pressing initially without 'Elephant Head' motif on p/s)	15
80	Atlantic K 10805	Jailbreak/Fling Thing (reissue, light label, fine print; with 'Elephant Head' motif on p/s)	10
80	Atlantic K 11142	Rock'N'Roll Damnation/Sin City (reissue, initially without 'Elephant Head' motif on p/s)	8
80	Atlantic K 11321	Highway To Hell/If You Want Blood (You've Got It) (reissue, '1980' on p/s)	5
80	Atlantic HM 1	High Voltage/Live Wire (reissue, p/s)	7
80	Atlantic HM 2	Dirty Deeds Done Dirt Cheap/Big Balls/The Jack (reissue, p/s)	7
80	Atlantic HM 3	It's A Long Way To The Top (If You Wanna Rock'N'Roll)/ Can I Sit Next To You? (p/s, reissue)	7
80	Atlantic HM 4	Whole Lotta Rosie (live)/Hell Ain't A Bad Place To Be (live) (p/s, reissue)	7
80	Atlantic K 11600	You Shook Me All Night Long/Have A Drink With Me (p/s)	5
80	Atlantic K 11600	You Shook Me All Night Long/Have A Drink With Me (p/s, mispressing, A-side plays "Shake A Leg")	100
80	Atlantic K 11630T	Rock'N'Roll Ain't Noise Pollution/Hell's Bells (12", p/s, with badge)	8
82	Atlantic SAM 143	For Those About To Rock (We Salute You)/C.O.D. (12", p/s, promo only)	40
83	Atlantic A 9774P	Guns For Hire/Landslide (logo-shaped picture disc)	15
84	Atlantic A 9651P	Nervous Shakedown/Rock'N'Roll Ain't Noise Pollution (live) (shaped picture disc)	15
85	Atlantic A 9532W	Danger/Back In Business (poster p/s)	6
85	Atlantic A 9532P	Danger/Back In Business (fly-shaped picture disc)	20
86	Atlantic A 9474P	Shake Your Foundations/Stand Up (Angus-shaped picture disc)	20
86	Atlantic A 9425P	Who Made Who/Guns For Hire (live) (shaped picture disc)	18
86	Atlantic A 9425TW	Who Made Who (remix)/Guns For Hire (live) (12", stickered p/s & poster)	15
86	Atlantic A 9377P	You Shook Me All Night Long/She's Got Balls (live) (shaped picture disc)	20
88	Atlantic A 9136TP	Heatseeker/Go Zone/Snake Eye (12", picture disc)	12
88	Atlantic A 9098TP	That's The Way I Wanna Rock'N'Roll/Kissin' Dynamite/Borrowed Time (12", picture disc)	8
88	Atlantic A 9098CD	That's The Way I Wanna Rock'N'Roll/Kissin' Dynamite/Shoot To Thrill/ Whole Lotta Rosie (3" CD with adaptor, 5" case)	15
90	Atco B8907T	Thunderstruck/Fire Your Guns/DT/Chase The Ace (12" poster p/s)	8
90	Atco B8907T	Thunderstruck/Fire Your Guns/DT/Chase The Ace (12" coloured test pressings, white, blue, red, clear, yellow, green & marbled swirl pattern	300
91	Atco 8830X	Are You Ready/Got You By The Balls (numbered p/s, with patch)	5
91	Atco 8830W	Are You Ready/Got You By The Balls (numbered 'satchel' p/s)	8
91	Atco B8886T	Money Talks/Mistress For Christmas/Borrowed Time (12" poster p/s)	25
92	Atco B8479CD/X	Highway To Hell (Bonny Intro)/Hell's Bells/The Jack/Highway To Hell/ Hell Ain't A Bad Place To Be/High Voltage (2 x CD, digipak)	12
93	Atco B8396T	Big Gun/Back To Black/For Those About To Rock (12", p/s)	8
95	East West 3BALLCD	Hail Caesar/Hard As A Rock/Ballbreaker (CD, no'd hologram p/s, promo only)	15
76	Atlantic K50257	HIGH VOLTAGE (LP, cartoon sleeve)	15
77	Atlantic K 50366	LET THERE BE ROCK (LP, mispressing, both sides play Side 1)	200
79	Atlantic K50625	HIGHWAY TO HELL (LP)	12
79	Atlantic K 50628	HIGHWAY TO HELL (LP, test pressing in alternative "live" proof sleeve)	300
80	Atlantic K50735	BACK IN BLACK (LP, emobossed sleeve, with inner)	12
81	Atlantic SAM 155	JAPAN TOUR ' 81 (LP, picture disc, promo only, clear rim)	150
81	Atlantic SAM 155	JAPAN TOUR ' 81 (LP, picture disc, promo only, black rim)	120
81	Atlantic 60149	BOX SET (3-LP, including "High Voltage", "Dirty Deeds Done Cheap" & Powerage, promo 7" & poster; export issue)	35
91	Atco WX 364P	THE RAZOR'S EDGE (LP, picture disc with inlay card)	15
95	East West SAM 1693	BALLBREAKER (CD, promo only compilation)	25
95	East West 7559 61780-1	BALLBREAKER (LP)	15
97	East West 7559 62162 2	BONFIRE (CD boxed set)	30
03	Epic 509298-7	ACDCROCKS.com BOX (15 x CD box set)	150
09	Columbia 38377	BLACK ICE (2-LP, gatefold, inner sleeves)	18

ACE

71	Decca F13216	Speed Freak/Ace Of Spades	5

BUDDY ACE

68	Action ACT 4504	Got To Get Myself Together/Darling Depend On Me	20
64	Vocalion VEP 1-70164	BUDDY ACE (EP)	100

MINT VALUE £

CHARLIE ACE

(see also Charles, Paulette & Gee, Gaytones, Phil Pratt Allstars, Maytones, G.G. Allstars, Upsetters, Gaby Wilton & Charlie Ace)

70	High Note HS 051	Creation (Version)/GAYTONES: Creation (Version Three)	15
70	Punch PH 49	Silver And Gold/PHILL PRATT ALLSTARS: Bump And Bore	12
70	Punch PH 53	Book Of Books/WINSTON HARRIS: Musical Dove	12
70	Punch PH 62	Love I Madly/Especially For You (A-side by Charley & Lloyd)	12
70	Punch PH 67	Do Something/MAYTONES: Run Babylon	12
71	G.G. GG 4507	Ontarius Version/G.G. ALL STARS: Ontarius Version 2	10
71	G.G. GG 4518	Do Something/MAYTONES: Groove Me	10
71	Upsetter US 359	The Creeper/UPSETTERS: The Creeper (Version)	25
71	Smash SMA 2325	Need No Whip/Grine Grine	10

JOHNNY ACE

61	Vogue V 9180	Pledging My Love/Anymore	80
61	Vocalion V 9180	Pledging My Love/Anymore (reissue)	25
62	Vogue VE 1-70150	JOHNNY ACE (EP)	100
61	Vocalion VA 160177	THE MEMORIAL ALBUM (LP)	150

RICHARD ACE (& SOUND DIMENSIONS)

(see also Viceroys, Soul Vendors, Gladiators, Ken Boothe)

67	Coxsone CS 7031	Don't Let The Sun Catch You Crying/VICEROYS: Magadown	45
67	Studio One SO 2022	I Need You/SOUL VENDORS: Cool Shade	100
69	Studio One SO 2072	More Reggae (with Sound Dimensions)/GLADIATORS: Hello Carol	40
69	Trojan TR 654	Hang 'Em High (with Sound Dimensions)/BLACK & GEORGE: Candy Lady	35
70	Sugar SU 104	Sound Of The Reggae/Got To Build A Wall	10

ACEN

92	Production House PNT 034	Close Your Eyes (XXX mix)/Close Your Eyes (Vitamin 'E' mix) (12")	20
92	Production... PNT 034 R	Close Your Eyes (Remix I: Optikonfusion!)/ Close Your Eyes (Remix II: The Sequel) (12")	20
93	Production... PNT 034 R-A, PNT 051 A-2	Close Your Eyes (Non Beatles Version Mispress) (12")	90
92	Production... PNT 042	Trip II The Moon (Part 1)/Obsessed (12", die-cut p/s)	25
92	Production... PNT 042R	Trip II The Moon - Part 2 (12", Promo 100 copies)	60
92	Production... PNT 042 R	Trip II The Moon (Part 2, The Darkside)/ The Life And Crimes Of A Ruffneck (12", die-cut p/s)	25
92	Production... PNT 042 RX	Trip II The Moon (Part 3, kaleidoscopiklimax) / Obsessed (part 2, pictures of silence) (12", die-cut p/s)	25
92	Production... PNC 042	Trip II The Moon/Obsessed/Close Your Eyes (XXX Mix) (CD)	15
92	Production... PNC 042R	Trip II The Moon (The Darkside)/The Life And Crimes Of A Ruffneck/ Close Your Eyes (Optikonfusion!) (CD)	15
92	Production... PNC 042RX	Trip II The Moon (Kaleidoscopiklimax)/Obsessed II (Picture Of Silence) (CD)	15
93	Production... PNT 051R	Window In The Sky (DMS Remix)/ Window In The Sky (Nino's Night Remix) (white label 12")	15
93	Production... PNT 051	Krystal Fairground (12", Promo, one-sided)	50
93	Production... PNC 051	Window In The Sky (Kingdom Of Light - Radio Edit)/ Window In The Sky(Monolythikmaniak)/ Window In The Sky (Krystal Fairground)/ Window In The Sky (Kingdom Of Light) (CD)	20

A CERTAIN RATIO

(see also Sir Horatio)

79	Factory FAC 5	All Night Party/The Thin Boys (p/s, 5,000 only, 1,000 with sticker stating ltd. edition on poor quality vinyl)	12
79	Factory FAC 5	All Night Party/The Thin Boys (p/s, 5,000 only, 4,000 without sticker stating ltd. edition on poor quality vinyl)	10
80	Factory FAC 22	Blown Away/Flight/And Then Again (12", p/s, with inner sleeve)	10
81	Factory FAC 52	Waterline/Funaezekea (12", p/s)	8
82	Factory FAC 62-7	Knife Slits Water/Tumba Rumba (p/s)	5
83	Factory FAC 72-7	I Need Someone Tonite (edit)/Don't You Worry 'Bout A Thing (edit) (promo)	5
84	Factory FAC 112P	Life's A Scream (edit)/There's Only This (edit) (promo pack including 7", photo & biography in custom ACR envelope)	10
81	Factory FACT 35	TO EACH (LP)	12
82	Factory FACT 55	SEXTET (LP, textured sleeve with insert)	12
82	Factory FACT 65	I'D LIKE TO SEE YOU AGAIN (LP)	12
85	private label	A CERTAIN RATIO LIVE IN AMERICA (cassette, sold at gigs)	12
86	Factory FACT 166	FORCE (LP)	12

ACES

63	Parlophone R 5094	Wait Until Tomorrow/The Last One	15
64	Parlophone R 5108	I Count The Tears/But Say It Isn't So	15

ACES

(see also Menace)

81	Etc ETC 01	One Way Street/Why Should It Be Mine (p/s)	15

ACHES & PAINS

66	Page One POF 008	There's No Other Like Your Mother/Again And Again	8

ACHILLES & HIS HEELS

61	Fontana H 340	Brigitte Bardot/Acapulco	7

ACHOR

(see also Wine Of Lebanon, Valley Of Achor)

76	Cedar CEDAR 1	END OF MY DAY (LP)	15
78	Dove Tail DOVE 54	HOSANNA TO THE SON OF DAVID (LP)	12

ACID GALLERY

(see also Christie, Epics, Carl Wayne & Vikings, Roy Wood, Outer Limits)

69	CBS 4608	Dance Around The Maypole/Right Toe Blues	55

MINT VALUE £

ACID MOTHERS TEMPLE AND THE MELTING PARAISO UFO

(See also Cotton Casino)

00	Staticresonance 2	MONSTER OF THE UNIVERSE (Monster Of The Universe/Wholly Weary Flashback/Surfin' Paris-Texas/Midnight Mountain Dew (EP, 500 only, p/s 2 x 7" sold on tour, 500 only)	20
01	Staticresonance 5	My Guitar Wants To Kiss Your Mother/NISHINIHON: Super Station (Hell In A Cell Version) (red vinyl, p/s)	10
	Ochre OCH 057	Hello Good Child/You're My Boy (300 on purple vinyl)	6
01	Staticresonance 1	ABSOLUTELY FREAKOUT, (ZAP YOUR MIND) (LP, 1000 only)	20
02	Staticresonance 4	ABSOLUTE FREAK OUT (ZAP YOUR MIND) (2xCD, gatefold card sleeve)	20

DAVID ACKLES

68	Elektra EKSN 45039	La Route A Chicago/Down River	5
69	Elektra EKSN 45054	Laissez Faire/Blue Ribbons	5
70	Elektra EKSN 45079	Subway To The Country/That's No Reason To Cry	5
68	Elektra EKL 4022	DAVID ACKLES (LP, orange label, mono)	40
68	Electra EKS74022	DAVID ACKLES (LP, orange label, stereo)	30
70	Elektra EKS 74060	SUBWAY TO THE COUNTRY (LP, orange label)	25
72	Elektra K 42112	AMERICAN GOTHIC (LP)	15
73	CBS 32466	FIVE AND DIME (LP)	15

BARBARA ACKLIN

(see also Gene Chandler & Barbara Acklin)

68	MCA MU 1038	Love Makes A Woman/Come And See Me Baby	12
69	MCA MU 1071	Am I The Same Girl/Be By My Side	15
69	MCA MU 1102	Love Makes A Woman/Come And See Me Baby (reissue)	5
69	MCA MU 1103	Am I The Same Girl/Be By My Side (reissue)	5
69	MCA MUP(S) 366	LOVE MAKES A WOMAN (LP)	20
71	MCA MUPS 410	SEVEN DAYS OF NIGHT (LP)	15
71	MCA MUPS 416	SOMEONE ELSE'S ARMS (LP)	20

ACME ATTRACTIONS

80	A Trax KICK 007	Anyway/Never Again (p/s)	60
81	Orchid OR1	Eve Of Destruction/It's OK (p/s, with Bonnie Parker)	20

SEPH ACRE & PETS

(see also Pets)

58	Pye International 7N 25001	You Are My Love/Rock And Roll Cha Cha	5

ACT

67	Columbia DB 8179	Cobbled Streets/One Heart	30
67	Columbia DB 8261	Here Come Those Tears Again/Without You	15
68	Columbia DB 8331	Just A Little Bit/The Remedies Of Doctor Brohnicoy	70

ACT

81	Act ACT 001	Dance To Despair/Who Let The Flowers Fall? (p/s and lyric sheet)	7

ACT

(see also Propaganda, Claudia Brucken, Glenn Gregory & Claudia Brucken, Thomas Leer)

87	ZTT 12 XACT 28	Snobbery And Decay (Naked Civil Remix)/Strong Poison/ Theme From Snobbery And Decay (12", gatefold p/s, with poster)	10
87	ZTT CID 28	Emotional Highlights From Snobbery And Decay: Snobbery And Decay (Extended For Stephanie Beecham)/I'd Be Surprisingly Good For You/Poison/ (Theme From) Snobbery And Decay (CD, gatefold card sleeve)	8
87	ZTT CT 01	Snobbery And Decay (Moonlighting Mix)/Instant 1/Instant 2 (12" promo, plain black die-cut sleeve)	20
87	ZTT VIMM 1	Absolutely Immune 2/Bloodrush/States Of Logic (12", p/s)	10
88	ZTT CD IMM 2	I Can't Escape From You (Love And Hate)/Heaven Knows I'm Miserable Now/ Dear Life/I Can't Escape From You (CD)	8
88	ZTT BET 1	Chance/Winner '88 (p/s, withdrawn)	30
88	ZTT BETT 1	Chance (12 To 1 Mix)/Winner '88/Chance (We Give You Another Chance) (12", p/s, withdrawn)	80
88	ZTT BETCD 1	Chance (12 To 1 Mix)/Winner '88/Chance (We Give You Another Chance) (CD, existence unconfirmed)	0
88	ZTT ZQCD 1	LAUGHTER, TEARS AND RAGE (CD)	30

ACRYLIC TONES

	Detour DR010	Girl/Theme From?.../Rainbow Song (p/s)	5

ACTION

(see also Boys, Sandra Barry & Boys, Mighty Baby, Reg King, Stone's Masonry)

65	Parlophone R 5354	Land Of 1000 Dances/In My Lonely Room	60
66	Parlophone R 5410	I'll Keep On Holding On/Hey Sah-Lo-Ney	65
66	Parlophone R 5474	Baby You've Got It/Since I Lost My Baby	75
67	Parlophone R 5572	Never Ever/Twenty Fourth Hour	65
67	Parlophone R 5610	Shadows And Reflections/Something Has Hit Me	90
67	Parlophone R5610 DJ	Shadows And Reflections	90
67	Parlophone R 5410	Shadows And Reflections/Something Has Hit Me (p/s for export to Holland)	150
81	Edsel E 5001	I'll Keep On Holding On/Wasn't It You? (p/s)	10
81	Edsel E 5002	Since I Lost My Baby/Never Ever/Wasn't It You (p/s)	10
82	Edsel E 5003	Shadows And Reflections/Something Has Hit Me (p/s)	10
84	Edsel E 5008	Hey Sah-Lo-Ney/Come On, Come With Me (p/s)	10
80	Edsel ED 101	THE ULTIMATE ACTION (LP, with inner sleeve)	12

ACTION PACT

81	Subversive ANARCHO 1	HEATHROW TOUCHDOWN (EP, 1 side by Dead Man's Shadow)	18
82	Fallout FALL 003	Suicide Bag/Stanwell/Blue Blood (p/s)	10
83	Fallout FALL 010	People/Times Must Change/Sixties Flix (p/s)	10
83	Fallout FALL 019	Question Of Choice/Hook Line & Sinker (p/s)	10
83	Fallout FALL 013	MERCURY THEATRE ON THE AIR (LP)	12
84	Fallout FALL 030	SURVIVAL OF THE FATTEST (LP)	12

MINT VALUE £

ACTION PAINTING!
90 Sarah SARAH 028 These Things Happen/Boy Meets World (wraparound p/s, with insert) 10

ACTIVES
83 Quiet QS001 RIOT (EP) 30
84 Quiet Records QS 004 WAIT & SEE (EP, 12") 25
83 Quiet Records QLP 4 KICK IT DOWN (LP, with insert) 50

ACTRESS
69 CBS 4016 It's What You Give/Good Job With Prospects 175

ROY ACUFF & SMOKY MOUNTAIN BOYS
57 Brunswick 05635 I Like Mountain Music/It's Hard To Love (And Not To Be In Love) 10

AD 1984
80 Grand Prix Records Race To Nowhere/Leisure Crime (with lyric sheet) 12

ADAM & THE ANTS
(see also Adam Ant, Maneaters, Models)
78 Decca F 13803 Young Parisians/Lady (in p/s, original with paper labels) 12
79 Do It DUN 8 Zerox/Whip In My Valise 5
79 Do It RIDE 3 DIRK WEARS WHITE SOX (LP) 12
79 Do It RIDE 3M DIRK WEARS WHITE SOX (cassette with insert) 15
80 CBS 4025361 DIRK WEARS WHITE SOX (cassette reissue) 20
90 Strange Fruit SFRLP 115 PEEL SESSIONS (LP) 15
00 Sony ANTBOX 5007822 ANTBOX (3-CD with book in 7" sized box) 35
06 Sony 88697009032 ADAM & THE ANTS - REMASTERED (7-CD, box set) 40

ADAM, MIKE & TIM
(see also Mike Sedgewick)
65 Decca F 12221 Little Pictures/Summers Here Again 12
66 Columbia DB 7836 Flowers On The Wall/Give That Girl A Break 6
66 Columbia DB 7902 A Most Peculiar Man/Wedding Day 5
64 Decca F 12040 Little Baby/You're The Reason Why 6

ADAMO
63 HMV 7EG 8860 BELGIUMS TOP RECORDING STAR (EP) 8

ALICIA ADAMS
61 Capitol CL 15195 Love Bandit/Oom Dooby Doom Lovey Dovey Sh' Boom 10

ARTHUR K. ADAMS
68 Blue Horizon 57-3136 She Drives Me Out Of My Mind/Gimme Some Of Your Lovin' 25

BILLY ADAMS
60 Capitol CL 15107 Count Every Star/Peggy's Party 10

BILLY ADAMS
69 London HL 10258 I Need Your Love/Why Don't You Believe Me 8

ADAMS (CHRIS AND PAULINE)
75 Charisma CB 244 If Only The Good Die Young/The City At Night 8

CLIFF ADAMS ORCHESTRA
60 Pye International 7N 25056 The Lonely Man Theme/Trigger Happy 8

DANNY ADAMS & CHALLENGERS
64 Philips BF 1346 Bye Bye Baby, Bye Bye/I'm So Proud Of You 5

DERROLL ADAMS
67 Ace Of Clubs ACL 1227 PORTLAND TOWN (LP) 80
72 Village Thing VTS 17 FEELIN' FINE (LP, with inner sleeve) 80
72 Village Thing VTS 17 FEELIN' FINE (LP, without inner sleeve) 50

EDITH ADAMS
55 Brunswick 05406 Ohio (with Rosalind Russell)/A Little Bit In Love 5

EVE ADAMS
61 Qualition PSP 7131 Kookie Talk/My Love Dear 5

FAYE ADAMS
56 London HLU 8339 I'll Be True/Happiness To My Soul (Gold Tri label) 650
56 London HLU 8339 I'll Be True/Happiness To My Soul (Gold label) (78) 50

GAYLE ADAMS
82 Epic A 2167 Baby I Need Your Loving/Don't Jump To Conclusions 20
82 Epic A13 2167 Baby I Need Your Loving/Don't Jump To Conclusions (12") 20

GLADSTON ADAMS
(see also Gladstone Anderson)
69 Trojan TR 659 Dollars And Cents/TOMMY McCOOK: Popcorn Reggay 20

GLEN ADAMS
(see also Glen Adams, Reggae Boys, Roy Shirley, Maxie & Glen, Delroy Wilson, Derrick Morgan, Ernest Wilson, Owen Gray)
67 Island WI 3072 Silent Lover/I Remember 70
67 Island WI 3083 She (actually titled "I'm Shocking")/SONNY BURKE: Some Other Time 50
67 Island WI 3099 Grab A Girl/DELROY WILSON: This Heart Of Mine 50
67 Island WI 3100 Hold Down Miss Winey/VINCENT GORDON: Sounds And Soul 80
67 Island WI 3120 She's So Fine/ROY SHIRLEY: Girlie 45
68 Blue Cat BS 126 She Is Leaving/UNIQUES: Girls Like Dirt 40
68 Trojan TR 621 Rent Too High/Every Time 20
68 Duke DU 58 My Girl/GLADIATORS: You Were To Be 20
68 Bullet BU 414 Cat Woman/PETER TOUCH: Selassie Serenade (B-side actually by Peter Tosh) . 20
68 Collins Downbeat CR 010 King Sized/I'm Gonna Take You Back (B-side actually by Owen Gray) 75
68 Giant GN 33 Lonely Girl/ROY SHIRLEY: Warming Up The Scene 50
69 Amalgamated AMG 837 She's So Fine/ERNEST WILSON: Private Number 100
69 Crab CRAB 21 Mighty Organ/ERNEST WILSON: Just Once 30

			MINT VALUE £
69	Sound Systems SS 105	Down To Earth Reggae/Reggae From Mankind	20
70	Gas GAS 141	Leaving On A Jet Plane/REGGAE BOYS: Phrases	25
71	Big BG 321	Weary Version 3/TONY BREVETT: Hills And Valleys	18
71	Explosion EX 2048	Never Fall In Love/JET SCENE: Jet 747	12

JOHNNY ADAMS (& GONDOLIERS)

59	Top Rank JAR 192	Come On/Nowhere To Go (as Johnny Adams & Gondoliers)	10

JONI ADAMS

64	Columbia DB7320	There's No Time Like Now/My River Of Memories	6
65	Columbia DB7604	Go With Her/Who Am I?	6

JUNE ADAMS

66	King KG 1038	River Keep Movin'/Heavenly Father	30

MARIE ADAMS

(see also Johnny Otis)

59	Capitol CL 14963	A Fool In Love/What Do You Want To Make Those Eyes At Me For	40
59	Capitol CL 14964	A Fool In Love/What Do You Want To Make Those Eyes At Me For (promo copy in picture sleeve)	50

PAUL & LINDA ADAMS

75	S. Folk & Country SFA 27	FAR OVER THE FELL (LP)	15
76	S. Folk & Country SFA 053	COUNTRY HIRINGS (LP)	12

PEPPER ADAMS

58	Vogue LAE 12134	CRITICS CHOICE (LP)	18
59	Pye NLP 28007	COOL SOUND (LP)	15

RAY ADAMS

61	Pye Int. 7N 25117	Soria Maria/Little Rose Marie	5
61	Pye International	Hear My Song Violetta/You Belong To My Heart	6
62	Pye 7N 15481	Gypsy/Brother Bill	5
62	Decca F 11507	Venus In Blue Jeans/He's Got My Sympathy	6

RITCHIE ADAMS

60	London HLU 9200	Back To School/Don't Go My Love, Don't Go	30

RUSH ADAMS

(see also David Rose)

54	Parlophone MSP 6101	I'm Sorry Dear/No One To Cry To	10
55	Parlophone CMSP 33	Then I'll Be Happy/Arizona (with Ace Dooley & Son) (export issue)	5
56	MGM SP 1162	Love Plays The Strings Of My Banjo/Kiss! Kiss! Kiss!	5
56	MGM SP 1176	The Birds And The Bees (with Louie Jean Norman)/My Buddy's Girl	5

WOODROW ADAMS

65	Blue Horizon BH 1001	Baby You Just Don't Know/Wine Head Woman (99 copies only)	200

ADAM'S APPLES

77	Brunswick BR 42	Don't Take It Out On This World/Don't You Want To Take Me Home	12

ADAMS FAMILY

93	Loose LOOSE 02	Frustration/Timewaster (p/s)	6

AD CONSPIRACY

79	Diamond	AD CONSPIRACY (LP)	25

CANNONBALL ADDERLEY

(see also Nancy Wilson, Miles Davis, John Coltrane)

61	Riverside 45414	Things Are Getting Better/Sidewalks Of New York	6
63	Riverside 106911 RIF	Jive Samba/Lillie	12
63	Riverside 10691R RIF	Tengo Tango/Brother John Dix	5
67	Capitol CL 15489	Mercy Mercy Mercy/Games	10
59	Riverside 12-30333	CANNONBALL TAKES CHARGE (LP)	20
62	Riverside RLP 12-311	THE CANNONBALL ADDERLEY QUINTET IN SAN FRANCISCO (LP)	12
62	Riverside RLP 12-318	WORK SONG (LP, actually by Nat Adderley)	20
63	Riverside RLP 433	KNOW WHAT I MEAN (LP, with BILL EVANS)	15
65	Fontana FJL 107	WOW (LP)	15
65	Fontana FJL 117	WHAM! (LP)	15
67	Capitol T2617	WHY AM I TREATED SO BAD? (LP)	20
68	Capitol ST2822	74 MILES AWAY (LP)	15

NAT ADDERLEY

56	London LTZC 15018	NAT ADDERLEY (LP)	20
62	Riverside RLP 12-318	WORK SONG (LP)	20
65	Fontana FJL 118	NATURALLY (LP)	20

ADDICTION

92	Vicious Pumpin' OBS 002	ADDICTION EP (12", stamped white label)	20
92	Vicious Pumpin' VIC 003	MIND PENETRATION EP (12", stamped white label)	25
92	Vicious Pumpin' VIC 003R	MIND PENETRATION (THE REMIXES) EP (12", stamped white label)	40
92	Vicious Vinyl VIC 001	THE CREATIVE DUB EP (12")	15
93	Vicious Pumpin' VIC 013	Wildstyle/Untitled (12")	10

ADDICTS

64	Decca F 11902	That's My Girl/Here She Comes	40

JOHN ADDISON

64	United Artists UP 1053	The Girl With Green Eyes/Love Theme From "Tom Jones"	5

ADDIX

79	Zig Zag ZZ 22002	Too Blind To See/(No Such Thing As A) Bad Boy (p/s)	15

ADDRISSI BROTHERS

59	London HL 8922	Cherrystone/Lilies Grow High (some copies have tri-centre)	25
59	London HL 8922	Cherrystone/Lilies Grow High (78)	10
59	London HL 8973	Un Jarro/Saving My Kisses	10
59	Columbia DB 4370	Back To The Old Salt Mine/It's Love	30

MINT VALUE £

JEAN ADEBAMBO

80s	Ade J ADE 101	Say That You Love Me/Dance Of Love	30

ADELE

07	Pacemaker 1	Hometown Glory/Best For Last (7", 500 only)	15

BOBBY ADENO

66	Vocalion V 9279	The Hands Of Time/It's A Sad World (£60 for demo)	35

ADICTS

(see also ADX)

81	Dining Out TUX 1	LUNCH WITH THE ADICTS (EP, with insert & screen-printed p/s)	40
82	Fall Out FALL 002	Viva La Revolution/Steamroller (p/s)	20
82	Razor RZS 101	Chinese Takeaway/You'll Never Walk Alone (p/s)	7
83	Razor RZS 104	Bad Boy/Shake, Rattle, Bang Your Head (p/s)	10
83	Razor RZLP 104	Bad Boy/Shake, Rattle, Bang Your Head (shaped picture disc)	12
81	Dwed SMT 008	SONGS OF PRAISE (LP)	40
81	Fall Out FALL LP 006	SONGS OF PRAISE (LP, reissue, yellow vinyl, 2,000 only)	20
81	Fall Out FALL LP 006P	SONGS OF PRAISE (LP, reissue, picture disc)	20
82	Razor RAZ 2	SOUND OF MUSIC (LP)	20
85	Razor RAZ15	SMART ALEX (LP)	15
87	Fall Out FALLLP021	THIS IS YOUR LIFE (LP)	18

BETH ADLAM with BUZZ & BOYS

60	Starlite ST45 024	Seventeen/I'll Walk Into The Sea	18

PETER ADLER

64	Decca 12394	I'm Gonna Turn My Life Around/But I Was Cool	25
65	Decca F 12262	Love And Not Hate/You Especially	5

ADLIBS (U.K.)

65	Fontana TF 584	Neighbour Neighbour/Lovely Ladies	45

AD-LIBS (U.S.)

66	Red Bird RB 10-102	The Boy From New York City/Kicked Around	40
66	Red Bird RB 10-102	The Boy From New York City/Kicked Around (DJ Copy)	70
69	Deep Soul DS 9102	Giving Up/Appreciation	30
75	Contempo CS 9029	The Boy From New York City/Johnny My Boy	10
79	Inferno HEAT 1	New York In The Dark/The Boy From New York City (p/s, coloured vinyl)	12

ADMIRAL TIBET

	Live & Love LLD301	Victim of Babylon/GREGORY PECK: Wah Do You (12")	30

ADMIRALS

65	Fontana TF 597	Promised Land/Palisades Park	25

ADMIRALS

75	Angen ANG 102	Natty Should Be Free/ANSEL COLLINS: Far East Special	12

ADMIT YOU'RE SHIT

81	Mortarhate MORT 17	EXPECT NO MERCY (EP)	25

AD NAUSEUM

83	Flicknife FLS 12	BRAINSTORM (EP, p/s)	10
87		THE GREATEST SHOW ON EARTH (Mini-LP)	20

A.D. 1984

79	Voyage VOY 005	The Russians Are Coming/New Moon Falling (p/s)	12
81	Grand Prix GP 003	The Clockwork Generation/Melody In The Key Of Time (p/s)	10

ADVENTURES

61	Philips BBL 7548	CAN'T STOP TWISTIN' (LP)	40

ADVENTURERS

60	Capitol CL 15108	Trail Blazer/Rip Van Winkle	30

ADVERTISING

(see also Secret Affair, Innocents, Simon Boswell)

77	EMI EMI 2710	Lipstick/Lonely Guys (p/s)	5
77	EMI EMI 2754	Stolen Love/Suspender Fun (p/s)	5

ADX

(see also Adicts)

85	Sire U 9070	Falling In Love Again/Come Along (p/s)	5

ANTHONY ADVERSE

86	él GPO 13	Our Fairy Tale/Eine Symphonie Des Grauens (p/s)	5
87	él GPO 29	Imperial Violets/Fountain (p/s)	5

ADVERTS

77	Stiff BUY 13	One Chord Wonders/Quickstep (p/s, 1st pressing with push-out centre)	20
77	Stiff BUY 13	One Chord Wonders/Quickstep (p/s, re-pressing with solid centre)	10
77	Anchor ANC 1043	Gary Gilmore's Eyes/Bored Teenagers (p/s)	8
77	Anchor ANC 1047	Safety In Numbers/We Who Wait (p/s)	8
78	Bright BR 1	No Time To Be 21/New Day Dawning (p/s)	7
78	RCA PB 5128	Television's Over/Back From The Dead (p/s)	6
79	RCA PB 5160	My Place/New Church (p/s)	6
79	RCA PB 5191	Cast Of Thousands/I Will Walk You Home	5
83	Bright BULB 1	Gary Gilmore's Eyes/We Who Wait/New Day Dawning (p/s)	10
87	Strange Fruit SFPS 034	PEEL SESSIONS (12", metallic finish)	8
78	Bright BRL 201	CROSSING THE RED SEA WITH THE ADVERTS (LP, red vinyl, 5,000 only)	25
78	Bright BULB 1	CROSSING THE RED SEA WITH THE ADVERTS (LP, black vinyl second pressing)	15
79	RCA PL 25246	CAST OF THOUSANDS (LP)	15
81	Butt/Bright ALSO 002	CROSSING THE RED SEA WITH THE ADVERTS (LP, reissue, red vinyl)	15

MINT VALUE £

AEROPHONE
71 RPM 357 Sweet Sweet Suzie/Of Tomorrow 15

AEROSMITH
(see also Run DMC, Flame)
73 CBS 1898 Dream On/Somebody 10
76 CBS 4000 Dream On/Somebody (reissue) 5
76 CBS 4452 Last Child/Combination 5
77 CBS 4878 Walk This Way/Uncle Salty 5
77 CBS S AR 2 Draw The Line/Bright, Light, Fright (p/s) 5
78 CBS 6584 Come Together/Kings And Queens 5
80 CBS 8220 Remember (Walking In The Sand)/Bone To Bone (p/s) 5
87 Geffen GEF 29TP Dude (Looks Like A Lady)/Simoriah/Once Is Enough (12", picture disc) 10
88 Geffen GEF 34TP Angel/Girl Keeps Coming Apart (12", picture disc) 8
89 Geffen GEF 68P Janie's Got A Gun/Voodoo Medicine Man (shaped picture disc) 10
90 Geffen GEF 72P Dude (Looks Like A Lady)/Monkey On My Back (shaped picture disc) 8
97 Columbia 664501-7 Hole In My Soul/Nine Lives (live) (picture disc, card insert) 6
98 Columbia 6664087 I Don't Want To Miss A Thing/Taste Of India (picture disc) 10
01 Columbia 670931-7 Jaded (shaped picture disc) 8
73 CBS 32005 AEROSMITH (LP) 12

AEROVONS
69 Parlophone R 5790 The Train/A Song For Jane 50
69 Parlophone R 5804 World Of You/Say Georgia 120

A FAIR SET
65 Decca F 12168 Honey And Wine/Runaround 18

AFEX
67 King KG 1058 She Got The Time/I Never Knew Love Was Like This 100

AFFINITY
(see also Linda Hoyle, Jeff Beck Group, Queen, Ice)
70 Vertigo 6059 007 I Wonder If I Care As Much/Three Sisters 20
70 Vertigo 6360 004 AFFINITY (LP, gatefold sleeve, large swirl label) 200

AFFLICTED
81 Bonk AFF 1 I'm Afflicted/Be Aware (rubber-stamped white labels, p/s, with insert) 45
81 Bonk AFF 1 I'm Afflicted/Be Aware (rubber-stamped white labels, p/s, without insert) 12
82 Bonk AFF 2 All Right Boy/Who Can Tell (with p/s, stamped white labels) 45
82 Bonk AFF 2 All Right Boy/Who Can Tell (without p/s, stamped white labels) 10
82 Bonk AFF 4 One Forty Two/Senseless Whale Stalker (untitled single in stamped striped bag) 20
82 Bonk AFF 3 THE AFFLICTED MAN'S MUSICAL BAG (LP, stamped white label in stamped bag sleeve, some with insert) 25
82 Bonk AFF 6 HIGH SPEED AND THE AFFLICTED MAN - GET STONED (LP) 12

AFFLICTED MAN
80 Human HUM1 I'M OFF MI HEAD (LP) 20

AFI
99 Nitro ADELINE 002 A FIRE INSIDE EP (ps, insert) 10
01 Nitro 15843-2 The Days Of The Phoenix/A Winter's Tale/Wester (CD, 500 only) 25
03 Nitro 450 460-2 Girl's Not Grey/The Hanging Garden (p/s, grey vinyl) 8
03 Nitro 450 462-6 The Leaving Song Pt. II/The Great Disappointment (Demo) (p/s, green vinyl) 8
03 Nitro 450 462-7 The Leaving Song Pt. II/?But Home Is Nowhere (Demo)/ The Leaving Song (Demo) (CD, digipak) 8
03 Nitro 65522300261 SING THE SORROW (2-LP, red vinyl, inner sleeves) 25
03 Universal SING THE SORROW (CD, with DVD in black hardback book 500 only, sold on tour) 40

AFRICAN
72 Sioux SI 006 Cock Mouth Kill Cock/ERROL T.: I Need To Know 20

AFRICAN BEAVERS
65 RCA RCA 1447 Find My Baby/Jungle Fever 20

AFRICAN BROTHER (actually MATUMBI)
77 Mainline ML 1 Gimme Gimmie African Love/PURE ROOTS: Dub 6
79 Greensleeves GRED 14 A Di System/Gimme Gimme African Love (12") 15

AFRICAN MESSENGERS
64 Page One P04043 Highlife Picadilly/Blues For The Messengers 6

AFRICAN MUSIC MACHINE
72 Mojo 2092 046 Black Water Gold (Pearl)/Making Nassau Fruit Drink 15
73 Contempo CR 13 Tropical/The Girl In France 8
73 Contempo CR 25 Never Name A Baby/Dapp 8
74 Contempo CS 2025 Mr Brown/Camel Time 8

AFRICAN PRINCESS
81 Jah Shaka Shaka 809 Jah Jah Children Cry/Jah Jah Dub (12") 40

AFRIQUE
73 Pye International 7N 25616 Soul Makossa/Hot Mud 8
74 Mainstream MSL 1018 SOUL MAKOSSA (LP) 20

AFRO
71 Punch PH 89 Lonely World/ALTON ELLIS ALL STARS: Put It On 20

AFRO AKINO
74 Afrodesia 1001 Hwe Anna/Maria 10

AFRO DIMENSIONS
72 Ackee 535 Dance With Me/Lonely Nights 15
72 Jay Boy BOY 84 If You Don't Want My Love/Just Because 20

MINT VALUE £

AFRO ENCHANTERS
63 Island WI 071 — Peace And Love/Wayward African — 30

AFTERMATH
87 Moshroom MOSH 2001 — DON'T CHEER ME UP (LP) — 12

AFROTONES
(see also Delroy Wilson)
69 Trojan TR 655 — Things I Love/ERIC FATTER: Since You've Been Gone — 20
69 Duke DU 19 — Freedom Sound/BOYS: Easy Sound — 20
69 High Note HS 023 — All For One/BELTONES: Broken Heart — 20

AFTER DARK
81 After Dark AD 001 — Evil Woman/Johnny/Lucy (p/s) — 50
83 Lazer PROMO 1 — Deathbringer/Call Of The Wild (picture disc, promo only) — 50
83 Lazer PROMO 1 — Deathbringer/Call Of The Wild (white label test pressing) — 60

AFTER TEA
(see also Ray Fenwick)
68 Ace Of Clubs SCL-R 1251 — AFTER TEA (LP) — 35

AFTER THE FIRE
(see also Narnia, Waiting For The Sun)
80 Epic EPC 8394 — Love Will Always Make You Cry/Every Mother's Son (p/s, withdrawn) — 5
75 Rapid RR 001 — SIGNS OF CHANGE (LP, with insert) — 25
82 Epic EPC 85135 — BATTERIES NOT INCLUDED (LP, withdrawn version with different sleeve) — 12

AFX
(see under Aphex Twin)

AGENT ORANGE
92 Dog Tag AO 001 — Sounds Flakey To Me (Jungle Mix)/Only You Have The Bass/ Sounds Flakey To Me (Original Mix) (12") — 30
93 Dog Tag AO 002 — TECNOSKA EP: The Nuttiest Ska/Gettin' Rougher (Ska Mix)/ Gettin' Rougher (Kaos Remix) (12") — 20

AGENTS
79 Grapevine GRP 142 — Trouble/The Love I Hold — 15

AGGRESSORS
70 Pye 17889 — Whisky And Soda/Soul Of The Jungle — 15
70 Marble Arch 1260 — REGGAE STEADIE GO (LP) — 15

AGGROVATORS
(see also Dave Barker, Dennis Alcapone, Jerry Lewis [Jamaica], Delroy Wilson, John Holt, Alton Ellis, Cornell Campbell)
70 Jackpot JP 751 — Sex Machine/You Left Me And Gone (both act. by Dave Barker & Aggrovators) — 30
70 Smash SMA 2302 — Big Red Ball Parts 1 & 2 (A-side actually "Big Red Bumble" by Lloyd Tyrell; B-side actually "Big Bumble Version" by Lloyd & Devon) — 20
71 Smash SMA 2312 — One More Bottle Of Beer/Beer Version — 12
73 Smash SMA 2339 — Straight To Jackson Head/You Are My Angel — 12
73 Downtown DT 500 — Dreadlocks Man/Rasta Want Peace (both actually by Rasta Twins) — 12
76 Grounation GROL 507 — RASTA DUB '76 (LP) — 30
78 Live & Love LAP 04 — JAMMIES IN A LION STYLE DUB (LP) — 35
78 Third World TWS 939 — KAYA DUB (LP) — 25
78 Conflict COLP 2006 — RASTA DUB 2000 (LP) — 30

AGGROVATORS AND THE REVOLUTIONARIES
77 Third World TWS 900 — THE AGGROVATORS MEET THE REVOLUTIONARIES AT CHANNEL ONE (LP) — 35
78 Burning Sounds BS 1028 — GUERILLA DUB (LP) — 40

AGINCOURT
(see also Friends, Ithaca, Alice Through The Looking Glass, Tomorrow Come Someday)
70 Merlin HF 3 — FLY AWAY (LP, with insert) — 700

AGNES STRANGE
75 Birdsnest BN 1 — Give Yourself A Chance/Clever Fool — 8
77 Baal BDN 38048 — Can't Make Up My Mind/Johnny B. Goode — 8
75 Birdsnest BRL 9000 — STRANGE FLAVOUR (LP) — 150

AGONY BAG
(see also Pesky Gee, Black Widow)
80 Monza MON 2 — Rabies Is A Killer/Never Never Never (p/s) — 10

AGORA
94 Z Records ZEDD 010 — LATIN CONNECTION EP (12") — 10

AGROS
71 Punch PH 56 — What Do You Fall In Love For/SLICKERS: Too Much — 20

AGRESSORS
70 Pye 17889 — Whisky & Soda/Soul Of The Jungle — 15

A GUY CALLED GERALD
88 Rham RX 8804 — Voodoo Ray/Escape/Rhapsody In Acid/Blow Your House Down (12", p/s) — 25
90 Columbia XPR 1535 — Emotions Electric (Frankie Foncett Remix 1)/Emotions Electric (Frankie Foncett Remix 2)(12", promo in stickered plain sleeve) — 15
92 Juice Box JBOX 001 — Digital Bad Boy/Let It Move You/A Storm Is Coming/Could You Understand? (12", tracks 1 and 4 vocals by MC Tunes) — 12
92 Juice Box JBOX 003 — Cops/The Trak/28 Gun Bad Boy/Paranoia (12") — 40
92 Juice Box JBOX 004 — Ses Makes You Wise/Sunshine/King Of The Jungle/Boase up (12") — 15
92 Juice Box JBOX 005 — The Musical Magical Midi Machine/Let It Go/Like A Drug/Free Africa (12") — 15
92 Columbia XPR 1684 — Cops/The Track/Paranoia/28 Gun Bad Boy (12" white label promo) — 40
93 Juice Box JBOX 009 — Too Fucked To Dance/Darker Than I Should Be/Anything v2.1/The Right Time (12") — 12
93 Juice Box JBOX 014 — The Glok Track/Gerald's Bassline/Ease The Pressure/Take Me (12") — 12
94 Juice Box JBOX 019 — Darker Than I Should Be (Ladies mix)/Gloc (Remix) (12") — 12

MINT VALUE £

A-HA
(see also Phenomena)

84	Warner Bros W 9146	Take On Me/And You Tell Me (silver/blue p/s)	40
84	Warner Bros W 9146T	Take On Me (Extended)/And You Tell Me/Stop And Make Your Mind Up (12", silver/blue p/s, with poster & stickers)	100
84	Warner Bros W 9146T	Take On Me (Extended)/And You Tell Me/Stop And Make Your Mind Up (12", silver/blue p/s, without poster & stickers)	50
85	Warner Bros W 9006T	Take On Me/Love Is The Reason (12", black & white p/s)	10
85	Warner Bros W 9006	Take On Me/Love Is The Reason (reissue, colour p/s with gatefold booklet)	5
86	Warner Bros W 8736P	Train Of Thought (Remix)/And You Tell Me (train-shaped picture disc)	8
86	Warner Bros W 8663TP	Hunting High And Low (Extended)/Hunting High And Low (Remix)/ The Blue Sky (Demo) (12", picture disc)	10
86	Warner Bros W 8500TP	Cry Wolf (Extended)/Cry Wolf (7" Version)/Maybe Maybe (12", picture disc)	10
87	Warner Bros W 8405TP	Manhattan Skyline (Extended Remix)/Manhattan Skyline (LP Version)/ We're Looking For The Whales (12", picture disc)	8
87	Warner Bros W 8305TP	The Living Daylights (Extended)/(7" Remix)/(Instrumental) (12", picture disc)	10
88	Warner Bros W 7936TP	Stay On These Roads (Extended Remix)/Soft Rains Of April (Original Mix) (12", picture disc)	8
88	Warner Bros W 7840TP	The Blood That Moves The Body (Extended)/The Blood That Moves The Body (LP Version)/There's Never A Forever Thing (12", picture disc)	10
88	Warner Bros W 7636TP	You're The One (12" Remix)/You're The One (Instrumental)/ Out Of The Blue Comes Green (12", picture disc)	8

AHAB
(see also Another Pretty Face, Waterboys)

82	Chicken Jazz JAZZ 5	Party Girl/Don't Give Up On Us (p/s)	5

AHAB & WAILERS

63	Pye 7N 15553	Cleopatra's Needle/Neb's Tune	15

A HEADS

82	TW Records	Dying Man (p/s)	12
82	Bluurg FISH 03	Forgotten Hero	8

AIKEN'S DRUM

81	SRTX/CUS 1134	AIKEN'S DRUM (LP)	40

AIM

94	Detour DR 018	Call Your Name/Out On The Streets (p/s,1,000 only, 100 on blue vinyl)	8
94	Detour DR 018	Call Your Name/Out On The Streets (p/s,1,000 only, black vinyl)	6

AIR

98	Source V 2848	MOON SAFARI (LP)	15

AIR

71	Atlantic 2400 148	AIR (LP)	20

AIRBORNE

83	Clubland SJP 844	Burn In Hell/Lord Satan/Temple Of Metal (p/s)	12

AIRCRAFT

79	Lathe TSR1	Here Comes That Sound/Video Romance/White Boys (EP)	12

DEBRAH AIRE
(see also Sharon Tandy)

67	Polydor 56180	This Land Is Mine/What The World Needs Now Is Love	50

AIRHEAD

92	Korova 9030 74679 2	BOING! (LP)	20

AIRMAIL

79	Graffiti GIT 001	No Human Feeling/In A Moment	8

AIRTO
(see also Deodato)

71	Buddah 2318 040	SEEDS ON THE GROUND - THE NATURAL SOUNDS OF AIRTO (LP, gatefold)	20
73	CTI CTI 18	FINGERS (LP)	18
74	CTI CTI 21	IN CONCERT (LP, with Deodato)	15
74	CTI CTI 23	VIRGIN LAND (LP)	15

AISHA

94	Ariwa ARI 153	Only Jah Works/Crisis (12")	15

AITCH

71	Decca F13150	Let It Be Me/Let Me Say This	6

BOBBY AITKEN (& CARIBBEATS)
(see also Caribbeats, Laurel Aitken, Frank Cosmo, Lloyd & Glen)

62	Island WI 028	Baby Baby (actually with Patsy)/Lonely Boy	18
62	Blue Beat BB 93	Never Never (South Virginia)/Isabella (as Bobby Aitken & Buster's Group)	15
63	Blue Beat BB 146	Don't Leave Me/Mom And Dad (as Bobby Aitken & Tinse)	18
63	Rio R 14	I've Told You/Please Go Back	18
63	Rio R 15	It Takes A Friend/LAUREL AITKEN: Sunshine	18
64	Rio R 34	Rolling Stone/LESTER STERLING'S GROUP: Man About Town	40
64	Rio R 40	Garden Of Eden/Whiplash	20
64	Rio R 50	Little Girl/Together	10
65	Rio R 52	Rain Came Tumbling Down/SHENLEY & LUNAN: Something Is On Your Mind	15
65	Rio R 64	Mr Judge/BINZ: Times Have Changed	18
65	Black Swan WI 441	Jerico/LESTER STERLING: Lunch Time	25
66	Ska Beat JB 252	Thunderball/ORIGINATORS: Chelip Chelip	150
67	Doctor Bird DB 1071	Keep On Pushing/You Won't Regret It	30
67	Doctor Bird DB 1072	Let Them Have A Home/Temptation (with Caribbeats)	30
67	Doctor Bird DB 1077	Sweets For My Sweet/How Sweet It Is (with Caribbeats)	50

			MINT VALUE £
67	Island WI 3028	Kiss Bam Bam/CYNTHIA RICHARDS: How Could I	70
67	Giant GN 11	What A Fool/Curfew (with Caribbeats)	50

LAUREL AITKEN (& BLUE BEATS)

(see also Laurel & Owen, Girlie, King Horror, Lorenzo, Ruts, Bobby Aitken, Classics, Beresford Ricketts, Duke Reid, Tommy McCook)

59	Kalypso XX 15	Sweet Chariot/Nebuchnezer	40
59	Kalypso XX 16	Aitken's Boogie/Cherrie	40
60	Kalypso XX 19	Baba Kill Me Goat/Tribute To Collie Smith	40
60	Starlite ST45 011	Boogie In My Bones/Little Sheila	75
60	Starlite ST45 014	Honey Girl (with Caribs)/Drinkin' Whisky (with Bluebeats)	50
60	Melodisc M 1570	Mary Lee/Lonesome Lover (with Bluebeats)	30
60	Blue Beat B 1	Boogie Rock/Heavenly Angel (with the BOOGIE CATS) (white label)	60
60	Blue Beat BB 1	Boogie Rock/Heavenly Angel (with the BOOGIE CATS) (blue label)	40
60	Blue Beat BB 10	Jeannie Is Back/If It's Money You Need	40
60	Blue Beat BB 14	Judgment Day/Yea Yea Baby	25
60	Blue Beat BB 22	Railroad Track/Tell Me Darling (with the Blue Beats)	25
60	Blue Beat BB 25	More Whisky/LLOYD CLARKE: Parapinto Boogie	25
61	Starlite ST45 034	Love Me Baby/Stars Were Made	50
61	Blue Beat BB 40	Bartender/Mash Potato Boogie	25
61	Blue Beat BB 52	Bouncing Woman/Nursery Rhyme Boogie (with Blue Beats)	40
61	Blue Beat BB 70	Mighty Redeemer/Please Don't Leave Me	15
62	Blue Beat BB 84	Brother David/Back To New Orleans (with Blue Beats)	15
62	Blue Beat BB 109	Lucille/I Love You More Everyday	15
62	Blue Beat BB 120	Sixty Days And Sixty Nights/Going To Kansas City (with Les Dawson Trio)	50
62	Blue Beat BB 142	Jenny Jenny/Weary Wanderer (with Bandits and Ruddy & Sketto)	20
62	Dice CC 1	Mabel/You Got Me Rocking (with Hyacinth)	25
63	Dice CC 13	Sweet Jamaica/Bossa Nova Hop	25
63	Blue Beat BB 164	Zion/Swing Low Sweet Chariot	20
63	Blue Beat BB 194	Little Girl/Daniel Saw The Stone (with Ruddy and Sketto)	20
63	Duke DK 1002	Low Down Dirty Girl/Pink Lane Shuffle	30
63	Island WI 092	I Shall Remove/We Got To Move	40
63	Island WI 095	What A Weeping/Zion City Wall	40
63	Island WI 099	In My Soul/One More River To Cross	40
63	Rio R 11	Adam & Eve/BOBBY AITKEN: Devil Woman	20
63	Rio R 12	Mary/Hometown	20
63	Rio R 13	Bad Minded Woman/Life	20
63	Rio R 17	Devil Or Angel/Fire	20
63	Rio R 18	Freedom Train/Peace Perfect Peace	20
64	Rio R 35	Rock Of Ages/The Mule	20
64	Rio R 36	Leave Me Standing/Bagaboo (Bug-A-Boo)	20
64	Rio R 37	John Saw Them Coming/Jericho	20
64	R&B JB 167	Yes Indeed/You Can't Stop Me From Loving You	20
64	R&B JB 170	Pick Up Your Bundle And Go/Let My People Go	20
64	R&B JB 171	Bachelor Life/You Was Up	20
64	Columbia DB 7280	Be Mine/Don't Stay Out Late	15
64	Blue Beat BB 249	This Great Day/I May Never See My Baby	25
64	J.N.A.C. 1	West Indian Cricket Test/3 Cheers For Worrell	25
64	Black Swan WI 401	Lion Of Judah/Remember My Darling (B-side with Cynthia Richards)	40
64	Black Swan WI 411	The Saint/Go Gal Go	40
64	Dice CC 28	Jamaica/I Don't Want No More	25
65	Dice CC 31	We Shall Overcome/You Left Me Standing	25
65	Rio R 53	Mary Don't You Weep/I Believe	20
65	Rio R 54	Mary Lou/Jump And Shout	20
65	Rio R 56	One More Time/Ring Don't Mean A Thing	20
65	Rio R 60	Come And Let Us Go/Lonely Nights	25
65	Rio R 65	Let's Be Lovers/I Need You	25
65	Venus VE 4	How Can I Forget You?/Weeping And Crying	10
65	Island WI 198	Boogie In My Bones/Little Sheila	25
65	Island WI 252	How Can I Forget You/Weeping And Crying (white label, existence unconfirmed)	0
66	Blue Beat BB 340	Clementine/Bongo Jerk	30
66	Blue Beat BB 369	Shame And Scandal/Coconut Woman	30
66	Ska Beat JB 232	Jamboree/Looking For My Baby	60
66	Ska Beat JB 236	Propaganda/Shake	40
66	Ska Beat JB 239	Green Banana/Darling	40
66	Rio R 91	How Can I Forget You/I've Been Weeping And Crying	15
66	Rio R 92	Baby Don't Do It/That Girl	15
66	Rio R 97	We Shall Overcome/Street Of Glory	15
66	Rio R 99	Clap Your Hands/Revival	15
66	Rainbow RAI 101	Don't Break Your Promises/Last Night (with Soulmen)	40
66	Rainbow RAI 106	Voodoo Woman/Bewildered And Blue (B-side with Carols)	40
67	Rainbow RAI 111	Sweet Precious Love/I Want To Love You Forever (with Carols)	40
67	Columbia Blue Beat DB 102	Rock Steady/Blowin' In The Wind	30
67	Columbia Blue Beat DB 106	I'm Still In Love With You Girl/Blue Rhythm	30
67	Fab FAB 5	Never You Hurt/I Need You (as Laurel Aitken & Soulmen)	50
68	Fab FAB 45	For Sentimental Reasons/Last Waltz (as Laurel Aitken & Rainbows)	30
68	Doctor Bird DB 1160	Mr Lee/Birmingham Girl	30
68	Doctor Bird DB 1161	La La La (Means I Love You)/DETOURS: Sunnyside	25
69	Doctor Bird DB 1187	Fire In Your Wire/Quando Quando	30
69	Doctor Bird DB 1190	Rice And Peas/CLASSICS: Worried Over Me	40
69	Doctor Bird DB 1196	Reggae Prayer/Deliverance Will Come	40
69	Doctor Bird/J.J. DB 1197	The Rise And Fall (Of Laurel)/If You're Not Black	40
69	Doctor Bird DB 1202	Haile Haile (The Lion)/SEVEN LETTERS: Call Collect	50
69	Doctor Bird DB 1203	Carolina/Kingston Town	40
69	Junior JR 105	Think Me No Know/RECO: Trombone Man	30
69	Nu Beat NB 024	Woppi King/Mr Soul	25
69	Nu Beat NB 025	Suffering Still (with Girlie)/Reggae '69	30

			MINT VALUE £
69	Nu Beat NB 032	Haile Selassie/Blues Dance	30
69	Nu Beat NB 033	Lawd Doctor (with Girlie)/Big Fight In Hell Stadium	30
69	Nu Beat NB 035	Run Powell Run/RICO RODRIGUEZ: A Message To You	30
69	Nu Beat NB 039	Save The Last Dance/Walk Right Back	20
69	Nu Beat NB 040	Don't Be Cruel/John B.	20
69	Nu Beat NB 043	Shoo Be Doo/Babylon Gone	30
69	Nu Beat NB 044	Landlords And Tenants/Everybody Sufferin'	20
69	Nu Beat NB 045	Jesse James/Freedom	20
69	Nu Beat NB 046	Pussy Price Gone Up/Gimme Back Me Dollar	20
69	Nu Beat NB 047	Skinhead Train/GRUVY BEATS: Kent People	70
70	Nu Beat NB 048	Skinhead Invasion/Benwood Dick (unissued, blank white label demos only)	100
70	Nu Beat NB 048	Mr Popcorn/GRUVY BEATS: Share Your Popcorn	18
70	Nu Beat NB 049	I've Got Your Love/GRUVY BEATS: Blue Mink	15
70	Nu Beat NB 050	Scandal In Brixton Market/Soul Grinder (both sides with Girlie)	20
70	New Beat NB 054	Nobody But Me/Baby Please Don't Go	12
70	New Beat NB 056	I'll Never Love Any Girl/The Best I Can	12
70	New Beat NB 057	Reggae Popcorn/Take Me Back	20
70	New Beat NB 063	Baby I Need Your Loving/Think It Over	20
70	New Beat NB 065	Sex Machine/Since You Left	20
70	New Beat NB 072	Pachanga/Version	20
70	Ackee ACK 104	Pussy Got Thirteen Life/Single Man	25
70	Ackee ACK 106	Sin Pon You/Everynight	25
70	Bamboo BAM 16	Moon Rock/Cut Up Munno	40
70	Pama PM 818	Mary's Boy Child/RUPIE EDWARDS ALLSTARS: Version	12
70	Pama Supreme PS 300	Why Can't I Touch You/Can't Turn Your Back On Me	12
71	Trojan TR 7826	It's Too Late/AITKEN'S BAND: Slow Rock	10
71	New Beat NB 078	True Love/The Best I Can	6
71	New Beat NB 089	I Can't Stop Loving You/El Paso	6
71	Black Swan BW 1408	If It's Hell Below/Just A Little Bit Of Love	40
71	Big Shot BI 595	Dancing With My Baby/Do The Boogaloo	20
72	Big Shot BI 605	Take Me In Your Arms/Two-Timing Woman	8
72	Camel CA 90	Africa Arise/GI GINGRI: Holy Mount Zion	15
72	Columbia DB 8914	Pretty Face In The Market Place/Come Back To My Lonely World	6
75	Camel CA 2007	La Vien En Rose/Spanish Eyes	10
75	Punch PU 121	Fattie Bum Bum/Fattie Bum Bum	5
80	I-Spy SEE 4	Big Fat Man/It's Too Late (as Laurel Aitken & Unitone)	5
80	I-Spy SEE 6	Rudi Got Married/Honey Come Back To Me	5
66	Rio LR 1	SKA WITH LAUREL (LP)	200
67	Doctor Bird DLM 5012	SAYS FIRE (LP)	120
69	Pama PSP 1012	THE HIGH PRIEST OF REGGAE (LP)	100
69	Pama ECO 8	SCANDAL IN BRIXTON MARKET (LP, with Girlie)	100
69	J.J.	RISE AND FALL (LP)	120
73	Count Shelly CSLP1	MORIA SOPHIA (LP)	40

A-JAES

64	Oak RGJ 132	I'm Leaving You/Kansas City	1000

AKA & CHARLATANS

78	Vanity VANE 1	Heroes Are Losers/Lady Of The Night/Perhaps One Day (12", various screen-printed die-cut p/s)	12

AKAPEL

92	Phlange AK001	Pick It Up (vocal)/(Instrumental)/Stick Your Big Dinky In/Background Beats/ Let Me Hear You Say/Keep On/They Won't Believe Me (12")	15

JEWEL AKENS

65	London HLN 9954	The Birds And The Bees/Tic Tac Toe	5
65	London HLN 9969	Georgie Porgie/Around The Corner	5
66	Ember EMB S 219	Dancin' Jenny/A Wee Bit More of Your Lovin'	10
65	London HA-N 8234	THE BIRDS AND THE BEES (LP)	20

AKERCOCKE

05	Earache 7MOSH 322	Eyes Of The Dawn (Demo)/The Fulcrum (transluscent red vinyl, no p/s)	15

AK 47

(see also AK Process, File Under Pop)

81	Output ORR 202	Stop! Dance!/Autobiography/Hilversum-Ao (p/s)	10
91	Rugger Bugger SEEP 004	DON'T CALL ME VANILLA (LP)	12

TOSHIKO AKIYOSHI

58	Columbia 33CX 101101	NEWPORT JAZZ FESTIVAL 1957 (LP)	15

JAN AKKERMAN

(see also Hunters [Holland], Brainbox, Focus)

73	Harvest HAR 5069	Blue Boy/Minstrel-Farmers Dance	6
73	Harvest SHSP 4026	PROFILE (LP)	20
73	Atlantic K40522	TABERNAKEL (LP, gatefold)	15

AK PROCESS

(see also AK 47)

79	Output OPQ 101	Electronic Music: After All Love/Post Town (p/s, white labels)	15

AKRYLYKZ

80	Double R RED 2	Spyderman/Smart Boy (p/s)	6
80	Polydor POSP 128	Spyderman/Smart Boy (reissue, p/s)	5
80	Polydor 2059 253	J.D./Ska'd For Life (p/s)	5

AL ET ALL

80	Arny's Shack As 047	STRANGE AFFAIR (LP)	200

ROLANDO AL

(see under Roland Alphonso)

MINT VALUE £

AL & VIBRATORS
(see also Vibrators, Patsy Todd, Lord Power)

67	Doctor Bird DB 1085	Move Up/Lone Lover	30
69	High Note HS 005	Check Up/I'll Come Back	25
69	High Note HS 007	Move Up Calypso/PATSY: Fire In Your Wire	20

STEVE ALAIMO

62	Pye International 7N 25161	My Friends/Going Back To Marty	8
63	Pye International 7N 25174	Every Day I Have To Cry/(Please Take A Chance On Me) Little Girl	30
63	Pye International 7N 25174	Every Day I Have To Cry/(Please Take A Chance On Me) Little Girl (DJ Copy)	50
63	Pye International 7N 25199	It's A Long Long Way To Happiness/A Lifetime Of Loneliness	8
66	HMV POP 1531	So Much Love/Truer Than True	20
66	HMV POP 1531	So Much Love/Truer Than True (DJ Copy)	30
68	Atlantic 588 227	Watching The Trains Go By/Thank You For The Sunshine Days	8

ALARM
(see also Seventeen)

81	White Cross W 3/4	Unsafe Buildings/Up For Murder (gatefold p/s)	25
82	Illegal ILS 0032	Marching On/Across The Border/Lie Of The Land (p/s)	5
83	I.R.S. PFPC 1023	68 Guns Parts 1 & 2 (p/s, with free cassette: "The Stand"/"Across The Border"/ Marching On/"Lie Of The Land"/"For Freedom" (all live) [CS 70504])	5
84	I.R.S. IRS 103	The Deceiver/Reason 41 (p/s, clear vinyl)	5
84	I.R.S. IRS 103	The Deceiver/Reason 41 (p/s, mispress on mustard vinyl)	45
84	I.R.S. IRSD 103/103A	The Deceiver/Reason 41//Lie Of The Land/Legal Matter (double pack, g/fold p/s)	5

ALBA

77	Rubber RUB 021	ALBA (LP)	12

DAMON ALBARN
(see also Blur, Gorillaz, Monkey, GB & TQ)

03	Honest Johns HJP10	DEMOCRAZY (2x10" white vinyl, picture disc, 5,000 only)	12
03	Honest Johns HJP20	A Rappy Song (Remix)/Original Version (12")	8

ALBATROSS

74	Mooncrest Moon 28	Anything I Want To/Bournemouth Rock	6
74	Mooncrest Moon 29	Rock 'N' Roll Boogie Man/Witchy Witchy Lady	5
75	Gull GULS. 16	Tobacco Road/Let It Roll	5

BILLY ALBERT "THE KID"

56	Vogue Coral Q 72214	Black Jack/The Golden Touch	8

EDDIE ALBERT

55	London HL 8136	I'm In Favour Of Friendship/Come Pretty Little Girl	20
56	London HLU 8241	Little Child (Daddy Dear) (with Sondra Lee)/Jenny Kissed Me	20

MEL ALBERT

59	Top Rank JAR 178	Sugar Plum/Never Let Me Go	15
59	Top Rank JAR 178	Sugar Plum/Never Let Me Go (78)	10

ALBERT EMBANKMENT

71	Decca F23152	As Tears Go By/Cover Me	8

ALBERTO Y LOST TRIOS PARANOIAS
(see also Mothmen, Charlie Parkas)

76	Big T BIG 541	Dread Jaws/De Version	6
77	Stiff LAST 2	SNUFF ROCK EP (12" promo, only 50 pressed)	200
78	Logo GO(D) 323	Heads Down No Nonsense Mindless Boogie/ Thank You Fuck You/Dead Meat (double pack, gatefold p/s)	5
78	Logo GO 340	Juan Lopez (The Lonely Goatherd)/Teenage Paradise/Dead Meat Part III	6
76	Transatlantic TRA 316	ALBERTO Y LOST TRIOS PARANOIAS (LP, with insert)	12
77	Transatlantic TRA 349	ITALIANS FROM OUTER SPACE (LP)	12
78	Logo LOGO 1009	SKITE (LP)	12

AL ALBERTS

58	Coral Q 72344	Things I Didn't Say/God's Greatest Gift	6
58	Coral Q 72352	Willingly (Meudie Perdue)/My Love	6
58	Coral Q 72363	How Soon/Will I Be Seeing You/Taking A Chance On Love	5

ALBINO GORILLA

71	Ember EMBS321	Shake Me, Wake Me/Going To A Go Go	6

ALBION BAND
(see also Shirley Collins, Fairport Convention, Keith Dewhurst & Albion Band)

76	Harvest HAR 5113	Hopping Down In Kent/Merry Sherwood Rangers (as Albion Dance Band)	5
77	Harvest HAR 5128	The Postman's Knock/La Sexte Estample Real (as Albion Dance Band)	5
78	Harvest HAR 5156	Poor Old Horse/Ragged Heroes (p/s)	5
79	Harvest HAR 5175	Pain And Paradise/Lay Me Low (p/s)	5
73	Island HELP 25	BATTLE OF THE FIELD (LP, as Albion Country Band)	20
77	Harvest SHSP 4059	THE PROSPECT BEFORE US (LP, as Albion Dance Band)	15
78	Harvest SHSP 4092	RISE UP LIKE THE SUN (LP)	15

MICHAEL ALBUQUERQUE
(see also Michael D'Albuquerque, E.L.O.)

69	United Artists UP 35037	Better Men Than Me/Burn Burn Burn	8
70	United Artists UP 35098	Roll Him Over/Blind Man	8

DENNIS ALCAPONE
(see also El Paso, Dennis & Lizzy, Mad Roy, D. Smith, Wailing Souls, Innkeepers, GG Allstars, Stranger Cole, Lizzy & Dennis, Lee)

70	Explosion EX 2039	Revelation Version/Marka Version	15
70	Supreme SUP 214	You Must Believe Me (with Niney)/RUPIE EDWARDS ALLSTARS: Funk The Funk	12
70	Big Shot BI 565	Shades Of Hudson/Spanish Amigo	30
71	Treasure Isle TI 7069	The Great Woggie/TOMMY McCOOK & SUPERSONICS: Buttercup Version	22
71	Banana BA 328	Duppy Serenade (as Innkeeper)/Sunshine Version	18

			MINT VALUE £
71	Banana BA 341	(Love Me) Forever Version/I Don't Want To See You Cry	25
71	Upsetter US 373	Well Dread/UPSETTERS: Dread Version	12
71	Upsetter US 377	Alpha And Omega/JUNIOR BYLES: Beat Down Babylon	15
71	Duke DU 125	Medley Version/Version Two	10
71	Prince Buster PB 8	Sons Of Zion/ANSELL COLLINS: Short Circuit	12
71	Prince Buster PB 12	Let It Roll (with Max Romeo)/ANSELL COLLINS: Clear Blue (w/l demos only)	15
71	Jackpot JP 773	Jumping Jack (with John Holt)/AGGROVATORS: King Of The Track	8
71	Jackpot JP 775	Togetherness (Black & White) (with John Holt)/DELROY WILSON: Live Good	8
71	Jackpot JP 776	Tell It Like It Is/DELROY WILSON : Come Along	8
71	Dynamic DYN 421	Horse And Buggy/ROLAND ALPHONSO & DENZIL LAING: Buggy And Horse	12
71	Dynamic DYN 422	Ripe Cherry/INNER CIRCLE: Red Cherry	10
71	Dynamic DYN 427	Alcapones Guns Don't Bark/Alcapones Guns Don't Bark Version	20
71	Camel CA 74	This A Butter/PHIL PRATT ALLSTARS: Version	12
71	Tropical AL 003	False Prophet/MAX ROMEO: Rude Medley	12
72	Tropical AL 019	Worldwide Love (with Twinkle Brothers)/CARL MASTERS: Gable Up	12
72	Ackee ACK 146	Power Version/BLUESBLASTERS: Martie (B-side actually titled «Margie»)	18
72	Prince Buster PB 24	Giant/PRINCE BUSTER: Science	20
72	Upsetter US 381	Wonderman (with Dave Barker, actually by Dave Barker)/ Place Called Africa (with Dave Barker & Junior Byles)	20
72	Upsetter US 388	Master Key/UPSETTERS: Keyhole	20
72	Grape GR 3035	Rasta Dub/UPSETTERS: Rasta Version	20
72	Attack ATT 8027	Fine Style/WINSTON SCOTLAND: On The Track	15
72	Duke DU 131	The Sky's The Limit/HUDSON'S ALLSTARS: Limit Version	12
72	Duke DU 147	Get In The Groove (with Dennis Brown)/DYNAMITES: Version	12
72	Techniques TE 918	Look Into Yourself/TECHNIQUES ALLSTARS: Yourself Version	15
72	Green Door GD 4041	Rub Up A Daughter/TONY'S ALLSTARS: Daughter Version	15
72	Bullet BU 509	Dub Up A Daughter/PRINCE TONY'S ALL STARS: Version	18
73	Downtown DT 508	You Don't Say/TONY'S ALLSTARS: Version	12
73	Treasure Isle TI 7074	Wake Up Jamaica/Version (with Tommy McCook)	18
73	Jackpot JP 808	Cassius Clay/SLIM SMITH: Love And Affection	18
73	Bread BR 1121	Musical Liquidator/Lorna Banana (B-side with Prince Jazzbo)	18
73	G.G. GG 4538	Musical Alphabet/BUCKLEY ALLSTARS: Things Gonna Change (B-side actually by Maytones)	12
73	Pyramid PYR 7008	Belch It Off/Jack Horner	10
74	Harry J HJ 6666	Sorry Harry/Party Time	8
76	Ethnic Fight EF 001	Pressure In A Babylon/ETHNIC FIGHT BAND: Pressure Dub	6
71	Trojan TBL 187	GUNS DON'T ARGUE (LP)	30
73	Magnet MGT 001	KING OF THE TRACK (LP)	30
74	Attack ATLP 1005	BELCH IT OFF (LP)	15
75	Live And Love LALP 104	DREAD CAPONE (LP)	40
77	Third World TWS 801	SIX MILLION DOLLAR MAN (LP)	15
77	Third World TWS 911	INVESTIGATOR ROCK (LP)	15

ALCO

(see under Threads Of Life)

CRAIG ALDEN

60	London HLW 9224	Crazy Little Horn/Goggle-Eye'd	5

STEVE ALDO (& CHALLENGERS)

64	Decca F 12041	Can I Get A Witness/Baby What You Want Me To Do (with Challengers)	60
66	Parlophone R 5432	Everybody Has To Cry/You're Absolutely Right (solo)	200
66	Parlophone R 5432	Everybody Has To Cry/You're Absolutely Right (solo) (DJ Copy)	200

RONNIE ALDRICH

(see also Squadronaires, Joan Regan)

54	Decca F 10248	Coach Call Boogie/Donegal Cradle Song	15
54	Decca F 10274	Wolf On The Prowl/Mudhopper	15
55	Decca F 10494	Ko Ko Mo (I Love You So)/Rock Love (with Squads)	15
55	Decca F 10544	Rock Candy/Boom, Boom Boomerang (with Squads)	20
55	Decca F 10564	Rhythm 'N Blues/Where Ya Gone, Baby? (with Squads)	20
57	Columbia DB 3882	Right Now, Right Now/Rock And Roll Boogie (with Squadronaires)	20
57	Columbia DB 3945	Crazy Bear/The Big Band Beat (with Squadronaires)	15
69	Decca F 12909	Ride My See-Saw/Romance On The North Sea (with London Festival Orch.)	8

URIE ALDRIDGE

(see also John Holt)

71	Harry J. HJ 6634	Set Me Free/LLOYD WILLIS: Free Version	8

ALEANNA

78	Inchecronin INC 7421	ALEANNA (LP)	40

ALEEM

84	Streetwave MKHAN 26	Release Yourself/Dub (12")	15
84	Streetwave MKHAN 61	Get Loose/Release Yourself (12")	15

AKI ALEONG (& HIS LICORICE TWISTERS)

61	Reprise R 20021	Trade Winds, Trade Winds/Without Your Love	5
61	Reprise R 20042	Moon River (Twist)/Tonight (Twist)	6
61	Reprise R 6011	TWISTIN' THE HITS (LP)	12

ALETHIANS

	Myrrh Gold MYR 1002	R.S.V.P. (LP)	40
	Myrrh Gold MST 6506	ONE WAY (LP)	30

ARTHUR ALEXANDER

62	London HLD 9523	You Better Move On/A Shot Of Rhythm And Blues	40
63	London HLD 9566	Where Have You Been/Soldier Of Love	20
63	London HLD 9641	Anna/I Hang My Head And Cry	30
63	London HLD 9667	Go Home Girl/You're The Reason	30
64	London HLD 9899	Black Night/Ole John Amos	30

			MINT VALUE £
66	London HLU 10023	(Baby) For You/The Other Woman	30
76	Buddah BDS 439	Everyday I Have To Cry/Everybody Needs Somebody To Love	20
63	London RE-D 1364	ALEXANDER THE GREAT (EP)	100
63	London RE-D 1401	ARTHUR ALEXANDER (EP)	120
62	London HA-D 2457	YOU BETTER MOVE ON (LP)	150

DAVID ALEXANDER

74	Rare Earth RES112	Love, Love, Love/Missy	6

GOLDIE ALEXANDER

81	Project PRJ 1	Show You My Love/Get Back	12

JEFF ALEXANDER & HIS ORCHESTRA

58	London HA-P 2130	ALFRED HITCHCOCK PRESENTS - MUSIC TO BE MURDERED BY (LP, mono)	50
58	London SH-P 6012	ALFRED HITCHCOCK PRESENTS - MUSIC TO BE MURDERED BY (LP, stereo)	40

LLOYD ALEXANDER REAL ESTATE

68	President PT 157	Gonna Live Again/Watcha Gonna Do	80

LUCIEN ALEXANDER

67	Polydor 56205	Baby, You've Been On My Mind/Play Along (Miss R)	15

TEXAS ALEXANDER

61	Fontana 467 136TE	TREASURES OF NORTH AMERICAN NEGRO MUSIC VOLUME 7 (EP)	10

LOREZ ALEXANDRIA

60	Parlophone PMD 1062	LOREZ SINGS PREZ (LP)	15

ALFI & HARRY

(see also David Seville)

56	London HLU 8242	Trouble With Harry/A Little Beauty (triangular centre, gold lettering on label)	20
57	London HLU 8494	Closing Time/Safari	8

ALFIE

01	Regal (no cat. no.)	Zoom (p/s, 1-track square, 300 only)	15
00	Twisted Nerve TN 011	ALFIE EP: Sure And Simple Time/Ooze A Lullaby/Check The Weight (10")	8

CLEM ALFORD

(see also Sagram, Magic Carpet)

74	Columbia SCX 6571	MIRROR IMAGE - THE ELECTRONIC SITAR OF CLEM ALFORD (LP)	50
75	KPM KPM 1183	INDIA (LP, music library issue, side 2 only)	40

ALFRED & MELMOTH

68	Island WI 3130	I Want Someone/ALFRED BROWN: One Scotch One Bourbon One Beer	20

SANDRA ALFRED

(see also Sandra Barry, Slack Alice)

58	Oriole CB 1408	Rocket And Roll/Six Day Rock	75
58	Oriole CB 1408	Rocket And Roll/Six Day Rock (78)	20

AUGUSTO ALGUERO & HIS ORCHESTRA

71	Polydor 2489 034	LAUGH! LAUGH! (LP)	15

LYNN ALICE

76	K&B KB 5520	(You Keep Me) Hanging On/(You Keep Me) Hanging On	7

ALICE THROUGH THE LOOKING GLASS

(see also Ithaca, Friends, Agincourt, Tomorrow Come Someday, BBC Radiophonic Workshop/Peter Howell)

69	H&F Recording/SNP (no cat. no.)	ALICE THROUGH THE LOOKING GLASS (LP, private pressing, handmade sleeve, by Peter Howell & John Ferdinando)	500
97	Tenth Planet TP 032	ALICE THROUGH THE LOOKING GLASS (LP, reissue, no'd, 1,000 only)	20

ALICE IN CHAINS

92	Columbia 658 888-7	Would?/Man In The Box (picture disc, numbered, PVC sleeve)	10
92	Columbia 658 888-6	Would?/Man In The Box/Brother/Right Turn (12", green vinyl, no'd die-cut slv.)	10
93	Columbia 659 090-6	Them Bones/We Die Young/Got Me Wrong/Am I Inside (12", no'd, blue vinyl)	8
93	Columbia 659 090-7	Them Bones/We Die Young (p/s, numbered poster)	5
93	Columbia 659 365-7	Angry Chair/I Know Somethin' About You (snakeskin wallet sleeve)	5
93	Columbia 659 751-7	Down In A Hole/Rooster (picture disc)	10
93	Columbia 659365-6	Angry Chair/I Know Somethin' ('Bout You)/Bleed The Freak/ It Ain't Like That (12", stickered, die-cut p/s)	8
93	Columbia 659 751-6	Down In A Hole/A Little Bitter/Rooster/Love Hate Love (12", die cut p/s)	8
93	Columbia 659751-6	Down In A Hole/A Little Bitter/Love, Hate, Love (12", die-cut p/s)	8
95	Columbia 662 623-7	Grind/Nutshell (green vinyl, numbered card)	6
96	Columbia 662893-7	Heaven Beside You/Would? (live) (white vinyl, foldover p/s in stickered PVC sleeve)	5
91	Columbia 467201-1	FACELIFT (LP)	15
92	Columbia 472330-1	DIRT (LP)	15
94	Columbia 475713-1	JAR OF FLIES/SAP (LP, yellow vinyl with blue vinyl, 1-sided, etched 12" EP)	40
95	Columbia 481114-1	ALICE IN CHAINS (double LP, gatefold sleeve, inners)	25

ALICE ISLAND BAND

74	Warren WAR 341	SPLENDID ISOLATION (LP, with insert)	200

ALIEN KULTURE

81	RAR LRAR 1	Asian Youth/Culture Crossover (p/s)	40

ALIEN SEX FIEND

(see also Demon Preacher, Demons)

84	Anagram 11 ANA 25	E.S.T. (Trip To The Moon)/Boneshaker Baby/I Am A Product (live) (11", PVC sleeve with insert)	10
90	Windsong 02	ASF BOX (box set, export issue, 4,000 only, with 3 coloured vinyl singles [12", 11" & 10"], poster, T-shirt & imitation dog turd)	25

ALIMANTADO (Dr.)

73	Atra ATRA 007	Return Of Muhummad Ali/Black Love	12
75	Sun & Star ST 003	Best Dress Chicken/She Wreng-EP	15

MINT VALUE £

77 Greensleeves GRE 002 — Born For A Purpose/Reason For Living (with the Rebels) — 10
78 Virgin VOLE 1 — Slavery Let I Go/Find The One (12") — 8
78 Greensleeves GRE 5 — Still Alive/Life All Over (with the Rebels) — 6
78 Greensleeves GRE 13 — Best Dressed Chicken In Town/Can't Conquer Natty Dreadlocks (yellow vinyl) — 15
79 Greensleeves GRED 10 — Born For A Purpose/Reason For Living/Still Alive/Life All Over (12", with the Rebels) — 20
79 Greensleeves GRED 17 — Sitting In The Park/Skanking In The Park (12", with the Rebels) — 10
80 Isda SUS 11 — It Cold In A Babylon/Version (12") — 8
78 Greensleeves GREL 1 — BEST DRESSED CHICKEN IN TOWN (LP) — 20
81 Greensleeves GREL 22 — SONS OF THUNDER (LP) — 20

ALISON, ANN, KEN, BLUE & TAF

72 TEB SLE 50 — SONGS FROM AN OLD BARN (EP) — 25

ALKALINE TRIO

02 B-Unique BUN 007-7 — Stupid Kid/Metro (7" picture disc, stickered PVC sleeve) — 8
02 B-Unique BUN 013-7 — Private Eye/Private Eye (original) (picture disc, stickered PVC sleeve) — 5
03 Universal 9809024 — We've Had Enough/Blue In The Face (live) (picture disc, stickered PVC sleeve) — 8
03 Universal 9811507 — All On Black/This Could Be Love (Acoustic SBN Session) (picture disc) — 8
05 Vagrant VRUK 012LP — CRIMSON (LP, red vinyl, stickered sleeve, inner) — 15

ALKATRAZ

(see also Man, Quicksand)

76 Rockfield UAS 30001 — DOING A MOONLIGHT (LP) — 20

ALL ABOUT EVE

(see also Ghost Dance, Gene Loves Jezebel)

85 Eden EDEN 1 — D For Desire/Don't Follow Me (12", p/s) — 12

ALL BECAUSE THE LADY LOVES

80 Sweet — IF YOU RISK EVERYTHING (EP, with insert) — 25

ALLAH & MR. LONELY

73 Fab FAB 190 — Hide & Seek/CANCER ALL STARS : Version (actually by Allen & Mr. Lonely) — 8

JOHNNIE ALLAN

74 Oval 1001 — Promised Land/SHELTON DUNAWAY: Betty And Dupree — 8
78 Oval Still LOT 1 — Promised Land/PETE FOWLER: One Heart, One Song (p/s) — 5

RICHARD ALLAN

60 Parlophone R 4634 — As Time Goes By/Only One — 30
60 Parlophone R 4711 — Don't Ever Say You're Gonna Leave Me/Poetry In Motion — 6

ALL DAY

73 private pressing — YORK POP MUSIC PROJECT (LP) — 150

BARRY ALLDIS

63 Decca F11642 — Like Lazy/Go Get It — 5

ANNISTEEN ALLEN

55 Capitol CL 14264 — Fujiyama Mama/Wheels Of Love — 250
55 Capitol CL 14264 — Fujiyama Mama/Wheels Of Love (78) — 30
57 Brunswick 05639 — Don't Nobody Move/The Money Tree — 30

BARBARA ALLEN

59 Felsted AF 115 — Tommy's Song/Never Let Me Go — 8

BOBBY ALLEN (& COMMANCHES)

(see also Commanches)

62 Fontana 267252 TF — Your Cheatin' Heart/I'll Forget About You — 5
63 Fontana TF 401 — Here Comes The Bride/Nothing's Impossible — 5
64 Fontana TF 429 — Half As Much As You/So In Love With You (with Commanches) — 5

CLAY ALLEN

62 Starlite ST45 086 — This Time It's Really Goodbye/Broken Home — 6
63 Starlite ST45 096 — I Can't Stop The Blues From Moving/You've Got The Cleanest Mind — 6
63 Starlite ST45 106 — Crazy Crazy World/Just A Stone's Throw Away — 6

DAEVID ALLEN

(see also Gong, Planet Gong, Soft Machine)

75 Virgin VS 123 — Fred The Fish/It's The Time Of Your Life (p/s, promo only) — 8
79 Charly CY 51056 — Much Too Old/I Am A Freud (with New York Gong, p/s with insert) — 5
83 Charly CY 2101 — ALIEN IN NEW YORK (12" EP) — 8
75 Caroline C 1512 — BANANA MOON (LP, black and white 'Twins' label) — 30
76 Virgin V 5024 — GOOD MORNING! (LP, by Daevid Allen & Euterpe) — 25

DEAN ALLEN

58 London HLM 8698 — Rock Me To Sleep/Ooh-Ooh Baby Baby — 25
58 London HLM 8698 — Rock Me To Sleep/Ooh-Ooh Baby Baby (78) — 10

EDGAR J ALLEN

73 Spark SRL 1102 — Happiness Corner/Got You On The Run — 10

JEFF ALLEN

57 HMV JO 477 — That'll Be The Day/Guilty Mind (export issue) — 35

JERRY ALLEN & HIS TRIO

54 Decca F 10248 — S'Posin'/When I Needed You Most — 5
55 Decca F 10443 — Kind/Delaunay's Dilemma — 5

LEE ALLEN (& HIS BAND)

(see also Huey 'Piano' Smith & Clowns)

58 HMV POP 452 — Walkin' With Mr. Lee/Promenade — 40
58 HMV POP 452 — Walkin' With Mr. Lee/Promenade (78) — 20
59 Top Rank JAR 265 — Cat Walk/Creole Alley — 15

			MINT VALUE £
59	Top Rank JKR 8020	WALKIN' WITH MR LEE (EP)	30
62	Ember ELR 3312	MOOD MUSIC LIBRARY (LP, uncredited library issue, generic sleeve)	50

LILY ALLEN

06	No Label LILY 001	LDN/Knock Em Down (500 only, jukebox centre)	30
06	Regal 7REG 135	Smile/Smile (Gutter Mix) (stickered, black, die-cut sleeve)	5
06	Regal REG 137	LDN/Nan, You're A Window Shopper (stickered, black die-cut sleeve)	5
06	Regal REG 140	Littlest Things/Everybody's Changing (stickered, black die-cut sleeve)	5
06	Regal REG 141	Shame On You/Alfie (stickered, black die-cut sleeve)	5
06	Regal 3694931	ALRIGHT, STILL (LP, approx 200 pressed)	30

MAURICE ALLEN

58	Pye 7N 15128	Ooh Baby/Rockhearted	30
58	Pye 7N 15128	Ooh Baby/Rockhearted (78)	10

PATRICK ALLEN

77	Kab KB 5540	Groovy Feeling/Instrumental	40

PETER ALLEN

77	A&M AMLH 63706	IT IS TIME FOR (2 x LP)	40

RED ALLEN

57	RCA RD27045	RID, RED, RIDE IN HI-FI (LP)	12

REX ALLEN

(see also Tex Williams, Patti Page)

54	Brunswick 05341	This Ole House/They Were Doin' The Mambo (with Tex Williams)	15
57	Brunswick 05675	The Little White Horses/Drango	5
57	Brunswick 05677	Wringle Wrangle/Westward Ho The Wagons	5
57	Brunswick 05699	Flower Of San Antone/Money, Marbles And Chalk	5
59	Top Rank JAR 188	One More Sunrise (Morgen)/The Little Old Church In The Valley	5
59	Top Rank JAR 188	One More Sunrise (Morgen)/The Little Old Church In The Valley (78)	12
62	Mercury AMT 1191	Don't Go Near The Indians/Touched So Deeply	10
57	Brunswick OE 9317	WESTWARD HO THE WAGONS (EP)	10
64	Mercury 10011MCE	COUNTRY AND WESTERN ACES (EP)	10

STEVE ALLEN (& HIS ORCHESTRA)

(see also George Cates)

56	Vogue Coral Q 72118	The Ballad Of Davy Crockett/Very Square Dance	10

STEVE ALLEN

79	Creole CR 164	Together We Are Beautiful/All Mine	6
74	M & M FFM10025	Villa Katrina/Singers Song	6

TONY ALLEN

63	Philips BF 1252	That Little Touch Of Magic/On Such A Night As This	6
62	Philips BBE 12522	TIME TO SWING (EP)	8

VERNON ALLEN

64	R&B JB 169	Far I Come/Babylon	250

(VERNON) ALLEN & (MILTON) HAMILTON

66	Blue Beat BB 348	It Is I/Baby What's More	15
66	Blue Beat BB 353	You're The Angel/Someone Like You	15

DAVE ALLENBY

69	RCA 1865	Where Has All The Love Gone/Somewhere In The World	5

ALLENS

75	Mowest MW 3029	High Tide/California Music	6

ALLEY CATS

59	Vogue V 9155	Last Night/Snap-Crackle And Pop	25
59	Vogue V 9155	Last Night/Snap-Crackle And Pop (78)	50
59	Oriole CB 1484	The Whistler And His Dog/Limehouse Blues	6

ALLISON

94	Twinkle NG 544	WAILING (LP)	15

BOBBY ALLISON

64	Solar SRP 103	You've Got Everything/Change Your Mind	5

GENE ALLISON

58	London HLU 8605	Hey, Hey, I Love You/You Can Make It If You Try	150
58	London HLU 8605	Hey, Hey, I Love You/You Can Make It If You Try (78)	50

JERRY ALLISON & CRICKETS

(see also Crickets, Ivan)

65	Liberty LIB 10196	Now Hear This/Everybody's Got A Little Problem	20

LUTHER ALLISON

71	Delmark DS 625	LOVE ME MAMA (LP, blue label)	15

LYNN ALLISON

57	Columbia DB 3867	Mama From The Train (A Kiss, A Kiss)/Song Of The Sparrow	7
57	Columbia DB 3906	If Only/The Sky	5

MOSE ALLISON

61	Fontana H 292	Baby Please Don't Go/Deed I Do	30
64	Columbia DB 7330	I Love The Life I Live/Life Is Suicide	12
59	Esquire EP 214	PARCHMAN FARM (EP)	30
59	Esquire EP 221	BACK COUNTRY SUITE (EP)	20
60	Esquire EP 224	BLUEBERRY HILL (EP)	20
61	Esquire EP 231	THAT MAN MOSE AGAIN (EP)	20
64	Columbia SEG 8353	ALLISON SINGS THE BLUES (EP)	20
59	Esquire 32-051	BACK COUNTRY SUITE (LP)	20
59	Esquire 32-071	LOCAL COLOUR (LP)	20

			MINT VALUE £
59	Esquire 32-083	YOUNG MAN MOSE (LP)	20
60	Esquire 32-094	CREEK BANK (LP)	20
61	Esquire 32-131	AUTUMN SONG (LP)	20
62	Esquire 32-171	RAMBLIN' WITH MOSE (LP)	20
63	London HA-K 8083	SWINGIN' MACHINE (LP, as Mose Allison Jazz Group)	20
64	Columbia SX 6058	V-8 FORD (LP)	20
64	Stateside SL 10106	MOSE ALLISON SINGS (LP)	20
66	Atlantic 587/588 007	MOSE ALIVE (LP, plum and orange label)	15
66	CBS Realm RM(S) 52318	I LOVE THE LIFE I LIVE (LP)	15
66	Atlantic 587/588 031	WILD MAN ON THE LOOSE (LP)	12
67	Transatlantic PR 7189	AUTUMN SONG (LP)	12
68	Transatlantic PR 7279	MOSE ALLISON (LP)	12

ALLISONS (U.K.)

61	Fontana H 304	Words/Blue Tears	6
61	Fontana H 336	What A Mess!/Lorraine (p/s)	15
61	Fontana H 362	Lesson In Love/Oh, My Love	8
62	Fontana 267 231TF	Sweet And Lovely/Sugar Love	7
62	Fontana 267 255TF	I'll Cross My Fingers/You Should Be Sorry	7
61	Fontana TFE 17339	THE ALLISONS (EP)	15
61	Fontana TFL 5135	ARE YOU SURE (LP, mono)	25
61	Fontana STFL 558	ARE YOU SURE (LP, stereo)	30

ALLISONS (U.S.)

(see also Blossoms, Darlene Love)

64	Stateside SS 289	Surfer Street/Money (vocal: Darlene Love)	35

ALL LIVING FEAR

94	FEAR 002CD	JESSICA (CD single, 460 copies)	15

ALLMAN BROTHERS BAND

(see also Gregg Allman, Duane & Gregg Allman, Allman Joys, Hour Glass)

73	Capricorn/Sound For Industry SFI 165	Ramblin' Man/MARSHALL TUCKER BAND: Take The Highway (flexidisc free with Rolling Stone magazine)	8
69	Atco 228 033	THE ALLMAN BROTHERS BAND (LP, gatefold sleeve)	50
71	Atco 2400 032	IDLEWILD SOUTH (LP)	70
71	Atlantic 2402 035	AT FILLMORE EAST (2xLP, gatefold sleeve)	40
72	Capricorn K67501	EAT A PEACH (2-LP, gatefold sleeve with insert)	30
73	Capricorn K47507	BROTHERS AND SISTERS (LP, gatefold sleeve with insert)	15

DUANE & GREGG ALLMAN

(see also Allman Brothers, Gregg Allman)

73	Polydor 2310 235	DUANE & GREGG ALLMAN (LP)	12

GREGG ALLMAN

(see also Allman Brothers, Duane & Gregg Allman)

73	Capricorn K 47508/CP0116	LAID BACK (LP)	12

ALLMAN JOYS

73	Mercury 6398 005	ALLMAN JOYS (LP)	20

ALL NIGHT BAND

79	Contact CON 5	Lovely Ladies/It's My Life	15
79	Contact CON 5	Lovely Ladies/It's My Life (12")	30

ALL NIGHT LONG

62	Fontana H 365	Muy Rapido/Skin Fever	10

TOMMY ALLSUP

65	London HA-U 8218	BUDDY HOLLY SONG BOOK (LP)	40

JOHNNY ALMOND MUSIC MACHINE

(see also Alan Price Set, Zoot Money, Paul Williams Set, John Mayall & Bluesbreakers, Mark-Almond, Jon Mark)

69	Deram DM 266	Solar Level/To R.K.	30
69	Deram DML/SML 1043	PATENT PENDING (LP)	50
70	Deram SML 1057	HOLLYWOOD BLUES (LP)	60

ALMOND LETTUCE

68	Columbia DB 8442	The Tree Dog Song/To Henry With Hope	6
69	Philips BF 1764	Magic Circle/Twenty Weary Miles	10

MARC ALMOND

(see also Soft Cell, Marc & Mambas, Burmoe Brothers, Vicious Pink Phenomena, Flesh Volcano, Annie Hogan, Sally Timms, Gene Pitney)

84	Some Bizzare BZS 2310	The Boy Who Came Back (Extended)/Joey Demento (Extended) (10", p/s)	8
84	Some Bizzare BZS 2410	You Have (Ext.)/Black Mountain Blues/Split Lip (Ext.) (10", p/s, with lyric sheet)	8
84	Some Bizzare BZS 2510	Tenderness Is A Weakness (Extended)/Love For Sale/Pink Shack Blues (live)/ The Heel (live) (10", p/s, with lyric insert)	8
86	Some Bizzare GLOWY 2-10	A Woman's Story/The Heel/A Salty Dog/The Plague/ The Little White Cloud That Cried/For One Moment/Just Good Friends (10" picture disc, stickered PVC sleeve)	8
87	Some Bizzare GLOWD 4	Melancholy Rose/Gyp The Blood//Pirate Jenny/Surabaya Johnny (double pack, gatefold p/s)	6
88	Parlophone PSR 500	Kept Boy (1-sided 7" with etched reverse - intended to be free with THE STARS WE ARE LP - but plans scrapped)	20
92	WEA YZ 638T	Extract From "Trois Chanson De Bilitis"/The Days Of Pearly Spencer/ Dancing In A Golden Cage/Dancing In A Golden Cage	12
84	Gutter Hearts GH 1	BITE BACK + BLUES (fan club-only LP, credited to "Raoul & The Ruined")	30
04	Theatre Of Dreams 005	Sheherezade (Turkish Delight Mix)/Sheherezade (Seven Veils Mix) (p/s, pink vinyl, only available online)	8
05	Theatre Of Dreams 006	Delirious (Demented Deluded Delirious)/Theatre Of Dreams (p/s, blue vinyl, only available online)	8
82	Lyntone LYN 12505	Discipline (as 'Marc Almond & Friends', pink flexidisc with	

			MINT VALUE £
		Flexipop issue 23. Friends are Throbbing Gristle)	20
84	Gutter Hearts LYN 14210	My Death (fan club flexidisc)	12
92	(no label or cat. no.)	Christmas In Vegas (fan club flexidisc)	5
86	(no label or cat. no.)	Your Aura (live) (fan club flexidisc)	8
89	Offbeat 1	Tears Run Rings (la Magia Dance Mix) 3" CD with Offbeat magazine)	8

ALMOND MARZIPAN

70	Trend TNT 53	Open Up Your Heart/Summer Love	15
70	Trend TNT 55	Marie Take A Chance/I'll Forget You	6

ALONE AGAIN OR

(see also Shamen)

84	All One ALG 1	Drum The Beat (In My Soul)/Smartie Edit (p/s)	5

HERB ALPERT (& TIJUANA BRASS)

62	Stateside SS 138	The Lonely Bull/Acapulco 1922	6
67	Pye International 7N 25419	Casino Royale (From The Film)/The Wall Street Rag (unissued)	0
68	A&M AMS 700	Casino Royale (From The Film)/The Wall Street Rag (p/s)	5

ALPHA & OMEGA

90s	A&O 09	KING & QUEEN (LP)	20
90s	A&O 18	OVERSTANDING (LP)	20
90s	A&O 27	WATCH AND PRAY (LP)	15
90s	A&O 93	EVERYDAY LIFE (LP)	15

ORVILLE ALPHANSO

65	Caribou CRC 1	Bellylick/Inspiration	40

ALPHASTONE

90s	Enraptured RAPTLP 18	ELASTICATED WAVEBAND (LP, clear vinyl, 100 only)	15
90s	Enraptured RAPTLP 33	LIFE IS A MOTORWAY EP (2 x 12", gatefold sleeve, limited issue)	10

CARLTON ALPHONSO

67	Pama PM 700	Where In This World/Peace Makers	40
69	Grape GR 3000	Belittle Me/Keep Your Love	30

CLYDE ALPHONSO

69	Studio One SO 2076	Good Enough/Let The Music Play	150

PANCHO ALPHONSO AND THE REVOLUTIONARIES

(see also Alphonso Pancho)

79	Attack ATT TACK 8	Never Give Up In A Babylon/Love Is A Pleasure (12")	25
78	Trojan TRLS 165	NEVER GET TO ZION (LP)	18

ROLAND ALPHONSO (ALIAS ROLAND AL)

(see also Eric Morris, Bob Marley/Wailers, Prince Buster, Hopeton Lewis, Joe White, Johnny Melody, Monty & Roy, Derrick Morgan, Niney, Jackie Opel, Owen & Leon, Kentrick Patrick, Duke Reid, Roy & Millie, Slickers, Lou Sparkles, Jack Sparrow, Austin Faithful, Clancey Eccles, Charmers, Denny & Wilson, Dennis Alcapone, Ken Boothe, Larry Marshall)

61	Blue Beat BB 58	Blackberry Brandy/ALVIN & CECIL: Marjorie	35
62	Blue Beat BB 112	Four Corners Of The World (with Alley Cats)/SHINERS: Romantic Shuffle	30
64	R&B JB 161	Mr President/The MAYTALS: A Man Who Knows	25
64	R&B JB 164	Crime Wave/MAYTALS: Hello Honey	45
65	Island WI 217	El Pussy Cat/LORD BRYNNER: Tiger In Your Tank	40
65	Ska Beat JB 210	Nimble Foot/ANDY & JOEY: Love Is Stronger	65
65	Ska Beat JB 216	Nuclear Weapon (with Baba Brooks)/STRANGER COLE: Love Thy Neighbour	65
65	Rio R 5804	Jazz Ska/HYACINTH: Oh Gee	50
66	Blue Beat BB 356	Just A Closer Walk/Jericho Train	150
66	Island WI 259	James Bond/LEE PERRY: Just Keep It Up	150
66	Doctor Bird DB 1010	From Russia With Love/Cleopatra (with Soul Brothers)	80
66	Doctor Bird DB 1011	Sufferer's Choice (with Soul Brothers)/SOULETTES: I Want To Be	50
66	Doctor Bird DB 1013	WAILERS: Rude Boy/ROLANDO AL & SOUL BROTHERS: Ringo's Theme (This Boy)	90
66	Doctor Bird DB 1017	Sugar And Spice/Get Out Of My Life (with Soul Brothers)	40
66	Doctor Bird DB 1020	Phoenix City (with Soul Brothers)/DEACONS: Men Alone	25
66	Doctor Bird DB 1023	Doctor Ring-A-Ding/FREDDIE & HEARTACHES: Here Is My Heart	80
66	Doctor Bird DB 1035	I Love You/Song Of Love	25
66	Doctor Bird DB 1039	WAILERS: Rasta Put It On/ROLAND AL & SOUL BROTHERS: Ska With Ringo	150
66	Ska Beat JB 231	Rinky Dink (So Good) (with Studio One Orchestra)/ SCRATCH & DYNAMITES: Deacon Johnson	50
67	Pyramid PYR 6003	Middle East/Wise Man	30
67	Pyramid PYR 6004	El Torro/007 (Shanty Town)	20
67	Pyramid PYR 6005	Women Of The World (& Beverley's Allstars)/SPANISHTONIANS: Kisses	25
67	Pyramid PYR 6006	On The Move (& Beverley's Allstars)/DESMOND DEKKER & ACES: It's A Shame	25
67	Pyramid PYR 6007	Jungle Bit (& Beverley's Allstars)/NORMAN GRANT: Somebody Please Help Me	25
67	Pyramid PYR 6008	The Cat/DESMOND DEKKER & ACES: Rudy Got Soul	30
67	Pyramid PYR 6009	Guantanamera Ska (& Beverley's Allstars)/SPANISHTONIANS: Suffer Me Not	30
67	Pyramid PYR 6011	Nothing For Nothing/DESMOND DEKKER & ACES: Rude Boy Train	25
67	Pyramid PYR 6018	Sock It To Me (& Beverley's Allstars)/SPANISHTONIANS: Rudie Gets Plenty	100
68	Pyramid PYR 6022	Whiter Shade Of Pale/On The Move	80
68	Pyramid PYR 6030	Dreamland/MAYTALS: 54-46, That's My Number	30
68	Pyramid PYR 6043	Stream Of Life/MAYTALS: Struggle	60
68	Coxsone CS 7077	Reggae In The Grass/ROY RICHARDS: Get Smart	50
69	Gas GAS 112	A Thousand Tons Of Megaton (actually by Derrick Morgan)/Musical Resurrection	25
70	Punch PH 39	Roll On (& Upsetters)/CARL DAWKINS: True Love	30
71	Banana BA 340	Mellow Mood (Way To My Heart)/MAYTALS: Marching On	20
68	Hi Note BSLP 5001	ABC ROCK STEADY (with the Originals Orchestra)	120

ALPHORAS

78	Junior JR 107	Running Out Of Love/It Pains Me (actually by LEROY SMART)	15

ALPINES

68	Double D DD 110	Get Ready/CARIBBEATS: Come Back Charlie	30

MINT VALUE £

AL QUAFA QUINTETO
76 Pablo PAB 12 — LEBLON BEACH (LP) — 12

ALQUIN
73 Polydor 2480 152 — MARKS (LP) — 15

RITA ALSTON
(see also Rita, Nat Cole)
70 Trojan TR 7751 — Popcorn Funky Reggae/NAT COLE: My Love — 15
70 Trojan TR 7752 — All Kinds Of Everything/CARL LEVEY: Instrumental Version — 6

SHIRLEY ALSTON
(see also Shirelles)
75 London HLA 10506 — I'd Rather Not Be Loving You/Can't Stop Singin' (Bout The Boy I Love) — 15
75 London SHA 8491 — WITH A LITTLE HELP FROM MY FRIENDS (LP) — 25

ALTECS
(see also The Black Dog)
61 London HLU 9387 — Easy/Recess — 18

ALTERATIONS
78 Bead Records BEAD 9 — CUSACK/BERESFORD/DAY/TOOP (LP) — 30

ALTERED STATES
88 Red Rhino CALC 31 — IS ANYONE OUT THERE? (LP) — 60

ALTERN 8
91 Network NWKTR 34 — Frequency (12") — 15
92 Network ST-8 — Full On...Mask Hysteria Megamix (12") — 15
92 Network E-VAPO 38DJ — Evapor 8 (12" Special DJ Edition) — 15
93 Network NWKT 73 — Everybody (12") — 15
93 Network NWKTR 73 — Everybody Remix (12") — 20
91 Network NWKT 24 — VERTIGO EP (12") — 15
92 Network Records A8 PIC 1 — FULL ON?MASK HYSTERIA (LP) — 25
92 Network TOP LP1 — FULL ON?MASK HYSTERIA (LP & 12") — 30

ALTERNATIVE
82 Crass Records 221984/8 — IN NOMINE PATRI (EP) — 10
83 Corpus Christi CHRIST 13 — IF THEY TREAT YOU LIKE SHIT - ACT LIKE MANURE (LP, with lyric insert) — 50

ALTERNATIVE TV
(see also Mark Perry, Good Missionaries, The Door & The Window, Reflections, Jools Holland, Alex Fergusson, Rat & Whale)
77 Sniffing Glue SG 75 RPS — Love Lies Limp (1-sided flexidisc with Sniffing Glue fanzine issue 12) — 20
77 Deptford Fun City DFC 02 — How Much Longer/You Bastard (p/s) — 7
77 Deptford Fun City DFC 02 — How Much Longer/You Bastard (p/s, labelled 'alternate versions') — 7
78 Deptford Fun City DFC 04 — Life After Life/Life After Dub (p/s) — 6
78 Deptford Fun City DFC 06 — Life/Love Lies Limp (p/s) — 7
78 Deptford Fun City DFC 07 — Action Time Vision/Another Coke (live p/s) — 10
79 Deptford Fun City DFC 10 — The Force Is Blind/Lost In Room (Vibing Up The Senile Man) (p/s, last track uncredited) — 5
78 Deptford Fun City DLP 01 — THE IMAGE HAS CRACKED (LP) — 18
78 Deptford Fun City DLP 02 — WHAT YOU SEE IS... WHAT YOU ARE (LP, 1 side by Here & Now) — 12
79 Crystal CLP 01 — LIVE AT THE RAT CLUB (LP) — 15
80 Deptford Fun City DLP 05 — ACTION TIME VISION (LP, with inner sleeve) — 15

ALTERNATORS
78 Energy NRG 001 — No Answers/The Kid Don't Know (no p/s) — 60

ALTERNOMEN UNLIMITED
(see also Spherical Objects)
79 Object OM 06 — Facade/Connections (p/s) — 5

ALTON (Ellis) & EDDY
(see also Alton Ellis)
60 Blue Beat BB 17 — Muriel/CLUE J. & HIS BLUES BLASTERS: Silky — 15
62 Island WI 009 — My Love Divine/Let Me Dream — 20

ALTON & FLAMES
(see under Alton Ellis)

ALVARO
(see also 101'ers)
77 Squeaky Shoes SSRM 1 — DRINKING MY OWN SPERM (LP) — 20

ALVIN'S HEARTBEATS
74 Magnet MAG 24 — Chilli Willi/Chilli Willi (Part 2) — 8

ALVYN
69 Morgan Bluetown MR 18S — You've Gotta Have An Image/Mind The Gap — 15

AMALGAM
69 Transatlantic TRA 196 — A PRAYER FOR PEACE (LP) — 50
73 A Records A 002 — PLAY BLACKWELL & HIGGINS (LP) — 25

AMALGAM
80 Impetus IMPLP 47901 — WIPE OUT (4-LP box set with booklet) — 50

GLEN AMAMS
(see also Glen Adams)
69 Escort ES 804 — Rich In Love/WOODPECKERS: Zumbelly — 15

A MAN CALLED ADAM
(see also Leftfield)
89 Acid Jazz JAZID 15T — Earthly Powers/Techno Powers (12", p/s) — 10

AMAZIAH
74 Sunrise SR 001 — STRAIGHT TALKER (LP, private pressing with insert) — 75

MINT VALUE £

AMAZING BLONDEL
(see also Dimples, Gospel Garden, Methusilah)
72 Island WIP 6153 Alleluia (Cantus Firmus To Counterpoint)/Safety In God Alone 5
70 Bell SBLL 131 THE AMAZING BLONDEL AND A FEW FACES (LP, blue/silver label) 175
70 Island ILPS 9136 EVENSONG (LP, gatefold sleeve) 25
71 Island ILPS 9156 FANTASIA LINDUM (LP, with inner lyric sleeve) 30
71 Island ILPS 9156 FANTASIA LINDUM (LP, without inner lyric sleeve) 15
72 Island ILPS 9327 ENGLAND (LP) 25
73 Island ILPS 9257 BLONDEL (LP, gatefold sleeve) 20
74 DJM DJF 20442 MULGRAVE STREET (LP) 15
75 DJM DJF 20446 INSPIRATION (LP) 15
76 DJM DJLPS 472 BAD DREAMS (LP) 12

AMAZING DANCING BAND
68 Verve VS 567 Deep Blue Train/Simon Smith & His Amazing Dancing Bear 20
67 Verve SVLP 9214 AMAZING DANCING BAND (LP) 20

AMAZING FRIENDLY APPLE
69 Decca F 12887 Water Woman/Magician 90

AMAZING SPACE FROGS
79 Ribbett RIB 1 THE DIRTY HABITS EP 300

AMAZON TRUST
70 Polydor 2058065 Run Baby Run/Sheila Lee 40

AMBASSADOR 277
88 EI GPUT37 Pop Up Man/Malediction (10" p/s) 10

AMBASSADORS OF SWING
92 Kold Sweat KSEP 204 RAP GAME EP 6

AMBER SQUAD
80 Sound Of Leicester ST 1 (I Can't) Put My Finger On You/Tell You A Lie (p/s) 25
80 Dead Good DEAD 17 Can We Go Dancing?/You Should See (What I Do To You In My Dreams) (p/s) 20

AMBERGRIS
70 Paramount SPFL 262 AMBERGRIS (LP) 12

AMBOY DUKES (U.K.)
68 Polydor 56228 Judy In Disguise/Who's Foolin' Who 15
68 Polydor 56243 Simon Says/The Marquis 15

(AMERICAN) AMBOY DUKES
(see also Ted Nugent)
68 Fontana TF 971 Let's Go Get Stoned/It's Not True 20
67 Fontana (S)TL 5468 THE AMBOY DUKES (LP) 75
69 London HA-T/SH-T 8378 JOURNEY TO THE CENTER OF THE MIND (LP, as American Amboy Dukes) 50
69 London HA-T/SH-T 8392 MIGRATION (LP, as American Amboy Dukes) 45
74 Discreet DS 2203 TOOTH, FANG AND CLAW (LP) 15

AMANDA AMBROSE
63 RCA Victor RD 7605 THE AMAZING AMANDA AMBROSE (LP) 12

SAMMY AMBROSE
65 Stateside SS 385 This Diamond Ring/Bad Night 100
65 Stateside SS 399 Monkey See Monkey Do/Welcome To Dreamsville 200
65 Stateside SS 399 Monkey See Monkey Do/Welcome To Dreamsville (DJ Copy) 350

AMBROSE SLADE
(see also Slade, 'N Betweens)
69 Fontana TF 1015 Genesis/Roach Daddy 270
69 Fontana STL 5492 BEGINNINGS (LP, laminated sleeve, black label with silver print; beware of counterfeits with matt sleeve & black & white label) 700
75 Contour 6870 678 BEGINNINGS OF SLADE (LP, reissue, different cover & running order, withdrawn) 70

AMEBIX
82 Spiderleg SDL 6 Who's The Enemy/Carnage/No Gods No Masters (p/s) 30
83 Spiderleg SDL 10 Winter/Beginning Of The End (p/s) 25
82 Spiderleg SDLP 14 NO SANCTUARY (LP) 30
85 Alt. Tentacles VIRUS46 ARISE (LP) 20
87 Heavy Metal HMRLP 99 MONOLITH (LP) 25

LOLA AMECHE
53 Oriole CB 1143 Rock The Joint/Don't Let The Stars Get In Your Eyes (78) 15

AMEN CORNER
(see also Andy Fairweather-Low, Fairweather, Mayfield's Mule, Judas Jump)
67 Deram DM 136 Gin House Blues/I Know (early copies entitled "Gin House" on label) 6
67 Deram 151 The World Of Broken Hearts/Nema 6
68 Deram 172 Bend Me, Shape Me/Satisnek The Jobsworth 6
68 Derman 197 High In The Sky/Run Run Run 6
69 Immediate IM 073 (If Paradise Is) Half As Nice/Hey Hey Girl 6
69 Immediate IM 081 Hello Susie/Evil Man's Gonna Win 5
69 Immediate IM 084 Get Back/Farewell To The Real Magnificent Seven 5
69 Immediate AS 3 So Fine (promo only 'single sampler' for IMSP 023) 20
68 Deram DML/SML 1021 ROUND AMEN CORNER (LP) 20
69 Immediate IMSP 023 THE NATIONAL WELSH COAST LIVE EXPLOSION COMPANY (LP, g/fold sleeve, pink label) 20
69 Immediate IMSP 028 FAREWELL TO THE REAL MAGNIFICENT SEVEN (LP, gatefold sleeve) 20

AMERICAN BREED
67 CBS 2888 Step Out Of Your Mind/The Same Old Thing 10
67 CBS 2972 Step Out Of Your Mind/The Same Old Thing (reissue) 5

MINT VALUE £

68	Stateside SS 2078	Bend Me Shape Me/Mindrocker	10
68	Dot DOT 101	Green Light/Don't It Make You Cry	15
68	Dot DOT 106	Ready, Willing And Able/Take Me If You Want Me	7
67	Dot DOLP 255	AMERICAN BREED (LP)	15
68	Dot (S)LPD 502	BEND ME, SHAPE ME (LP)	15
68	Dot (S)LPD 507	NO WAY TO TREAT A LADY (LP, soundtrack)	20
68	Dot (S)LPD 518	PUMPKIN, POWDER, SCARLET AND GREEN (LP)	15
69	Dot (S)LPD 526	THE LONELY SIDE OF THE CITY (LP)	12

AMERICAN GYPSY

71	CBS 7027	Gypsy Queen Pt 1/Dead & Gone	12
75	BTM SBT 101	Angel Eyes/Lady Eleanor	15
75	BTM BTM 1001	AMERICAN GYPSY (LP)	20

AMERICAN JAM (BAND)

(see also Kansas Hook)

72	Parlophone R5971	American Jam/Natures Child	12
74	Young Blood YB 1059	Jam Jam/Back On The Road	15

AMERICAN MUSIC CLUB

87	Zippo ZONG 0202	ENGINE (LP, with inner sleeve)	15
88	Demon FIEND 134	CALIFORNIA (LP)	12
89	Demon FIEND 151	UNITED KINGDON (LP)	12
93	Virgin V2708	MERCURY (LP)	15

AMERICAN POETS

66	London HLC 10037	She Blew A Good Thing/Out To Lunch (as American Poets)	120
66	London HLC 10037	She Blew A Good Thing/Out To Lunch (as American Poets) (DJ copy)	200
71	United Artists UP 35308	She Blew A Good Thing/Out To Lunch (reissue, as Poets)	20

AMERICAN SPRING

(see also Beach Boys, Honeys)

72	United Artists UP 35376	Good Time/Sweet Mountain	15
72	United Artists UP 35421	Mama Said/Tennessee Waltz	15
73	CBS CBS 1590	Shyin' Away/Falling In Love	20
72	United Artists UAG 29363	AMERICAN SPRING (LP, "Tree" cover)	45
72	United Artists UAG 29363	AMERICAN SPRING (LP, "Tree" gatefold cover with picture of group)	60

AMERICAN YOUTH CHOIR

71	Polydor 2066 013	Together We Can Make It/Keep Your Fine Self Near Me	40

AMES BROTHERS

53	HMV 7M 153	You, You, You/My Life, My Love, My Happiness	10
54	HMV 7M 179	I Can't Believe That You're In Love/Boogie Woogie Maxine	30
54	HMV 7M 209	The Man With The Banjo/Man, Man, Is For The Woman Made	5
54	HMV 7M 253	Hopelessly/One More Time	5
55	HMV 7M 281	The Naughty Lady Of Shady Lane/Addio	7
55	HMV 7M 310	Sweet Brown-Eyed Baby/Sympathetic Eyes	5
55	HMV 7M 322	Wrong Again/Merci Beaucoup	5
55	HMV 7M 331	So Will I/My Bonnie Lassie	5
56	HMV 7M 410	My Love, Your Love/If You Wanna See Mamie Tonight	5
56	HMV 7MC 46	If You Wanna See Mamie Tonight/It Only Hurts For A Little While (export issue)	5
57	RCA RCA 1015	Rocking Shoes/Tammy	10

ED AMES

67	RCA 1577	My Cup Runneth Over/Climb Ev'ry Mountain	5

NANCY AMES

66	Columbia DB 7809	Friends And Lovers Forever/I've Got A Lot Of Love (Left In Me)	20
66	Columbia DB 8039	Cry Softly/I Don't Want To Talk About It	100
66	Columbia DB 8039	Cry Softly/I Don't Want To Talk About It (DJ copy)	150

AMITY

76	Red Rag RRR 001	AMITY (LP)	150

AMM

(see also Eddie Provost Band)

66	Incus EP 1	AT THE ROUNDHOUSE (EP)	100
67	Elektra EUKS 7256	AMM MUSIC (LP)	120
87	Matchless MR13	INEXHAUSTABLE DOCUMENT (LP)	30

ALBERT AMMONS

(see also [Big] Joe Turner)

55	Vogue EPV 1071	ALBERT AMMONS (EP)	20
57	Brunswick OE 9325	BOOGIE WOOGIE STOMP (EP)	20
54	Mercury MG 25012	ALBERT AMMONS (10" LP)	30
62	Storyville SLP 184	BOOGIE WOOGIE TRIO (LP)	20

ALBERT AMMONS & PETE JOHNSON

55	HMV DLP 1011	EIGHT TO THE BAR (10" LP)	25

ALBERT AMMONS, PETE JOHNSON & MEADE 'LUX' LEWIS

(see also Pete Johnson, Meade 'Lux' Lewis)

55	Columbia SEG 7528	SHOUT FOR JOY (EP)	12
63	Riverside RLP 12-106	GIANTS OF BOOGIE WOOGIE (LP)	15

GENE AMMONS (BAND)

60	Starlite ST45 017	Echo Chamber Blues/Ammons' Boogie	40
63	Starlite ST45 097	Anna/Cae' Cae'	10
59	Esquire 32-047	HI FI JAM SESSION (LP)	20
59	Esquire 32-077	FUNKY (LP)	25
60	Esquire 32-097	JAMMIN' WITH GENE (LP)	25
62	Esquire 32-147	BLUE GENE (LP)	20
63	Esquire 32-177	BOSS TENOR (LP)	30
63	Esquire 32-178	BAD! BOSSA NOVA (LP)	30

			MINT VALUE £
72	Prestige PR 24021	JUG & DODO (LP, with Dodo Marmarosa)	15
73	Prestige PR 10019	YOU TALK THAT TALK (LP)	15
73	Prestige PR 10021	BROTHER JUG (LP)	25

AMON DÜÜL

81	Illuminated JAMS 24	HAWK MEETS PENGUIN (LP)	15
85	Illuminated JAMS 27	MEETINGS WITH MENMACHINES (LP)	15

AMON DÜÜL II

(see also Utopia)

70	Liberty LBF 15355	Archangel's Thunderbird/Burning Sister	25
69	Liberty LBS 83279	PHALLUS DEI (LP)	100
70	Liberty LSP 101/LBS 83359	YETI (2-LP, gatefold sleeve)	60
71	United Artists UAD 60003/4	DANCE OF THE LEMMINGS (2-LP, gatefold sleeve)	50
72	Sunset SLS 50257	PHALLUS DEI (LP, reissue)	15
72	United Artists UAG 23927	CARNIVAL IN BABYLON (LP, gatefold sleeve)	30
72	United Artists UAG 29406	WOLF CITY (LP, gatefold sleeve)	25
73	United Artists USP 102	LIVE IN LONDON (LP)	20
73	United Artists UAS 29504	VIVE LA TRANCE (LP, with inner sleeve)	20
74	United Artists UA 29723 G	LEMMINGMANIA (LP)	15
74	Atlantic K 50136	HIJACK (LP)	15

AMORPHOUS ANDROGYNOUS

(see also Future Sound Of London)

93	Quigley LPEBV 1	TALES OF EPHIDRINA (LP)	15

AMORY KANE

68	MCA MU 1036	Reflections Of Your Face/Four Ravens	25
70	CBS 5111	Him Or Me/Forever Waiting	10

ADAM AMOS & NOEL ROCKS

60s	Celtic Music CM 011	CASUAL ON THE BALCONY (LP)	35
60s	Celtic Music CM 026	ADAM AMOS & NOEL ROCKS (LP)	30

AMOS & SARA

(see also Homosexuals)

82	It's War Boys	Go Home Soldier/Enough Is Enough/Surveillance O.H.M.S. (12", screenprint p/s)	8

TORI AMOS

91	East West YZ 618T	ME AND A GUN EP (12")	8
91	East West YZ 618CD	ME AND A GUN EP (CD)	8
91	East West YZ 618T	Silent All These Years/Upside Down/Me And A Gun/Thoughts (12", p/s)	8
91	East West YZ 618CD	Silent All These Years/Upside Down/Me And A Gun/Thoughts (CD)	8
92	East West A 7531T	China/Sugar/Flying Dutchman/Humpty Dumpty (12", p/s)	8
92	East West A 7531CD	China/Sugar/Flying Dutchman/Humpty Dumpty (CD)	8
92	East West A7504DJ	Winter (radio edit)/The Pool (promo 7" in p/s)	15
92	East West A 7479CDX	CRUCIFY LIVE EP (CD, box set, with art prints, sealed)	30
92	East West A 7479CDX	CRUCIFY LIVE EP (CD, box set, with art prints, unsealed)	20
92	East West A 7433	Silent All These Years/Ode To The Banana King Part 1 (p/s)	5
92	East West A 7433CDX	Silent All These Years/Ode To The Banana King Part 1/Song For Eric/ Happy Phantom (CD, digipak, sealed)	35
92	East West A 7433CDX	Silent All These Years/Ode To The Banana King Part 1/Song For Eric/ Happy Phantom (CD, digipak, unsealed)	20
94	East West A 7281CDX	Cornflake Girl/A Case Of You/If 6 Were 9/Strange Fruit (CD, digipak, sealed)	30
94	East West A 7281CDX	Cornflake Girl/A Case Of You/If 6 Were 9/Strange Fruit (CD, picture disc digipak, unsealed)	20
94	Easwest SAM 1418	God - Carl Craig and C.J. Bolland remixes (12" promo)	12
98	East West AT 0045C	Raspberry Swirl (Lip Gloss Version)/(Sticky Extended Vocal Mix)/ (Scarlet Spectrum Feels) (CD, withdrawn)	10
99	Atlantic AT 0077CD2	GLORY OF THE 80s EP (CD, part 2 of 2-CD set, mispressing, plays CD-1 tracks)	12
92	East West 7567 82358-1	LITTLE EARTHQUAKES (LP)	20
92	East West 7567-82358-2	LITTLE EARTHQUAKES ('Wooden box' CD set)	50
06	Epic (No cat no)	THE ORIGINAL BOOTLEGS (12 CD box set, 6 stickers)	150

AMPHETAMEANIES

(see also Belle and Sebastian, Franz Ferdinand)

99	F&J Records SHAG024	Last Night/Suzie The Muppet Ltd (7" p/s 600 pressed)	8

CURTIS AMY

61	Vogue LA12287	GROOVIN' BLUE (LP, with Frank Butler)	25
60s	Fontana 688136ZL	KATANGA (LP)	20
60s	Vogue	THE BLUE MESSAGE (LP, with Paul Bryant)	15
60s	Vogue	MEETIN' HERE (LP, with Paul Bryant)	15

ANAL FLEAS

82	Rectal FLEA 45	Psych/Over the Edge/Landlord/Go Down (p/s, with insert)	80

ANAN

68	Pye 7N 17571	Haze Woman/I Wonder Where My Sister's Gone	60
68	Pye 7N 17642	Madena/Standing Still	20

PETER ANATHAN

66	Fontana TF 705	You Can't Stop Me Loving You/Feel I'm Falling	15

ANATHEMA

94	Peaceville CC 6	WE ARE THE BIBLE EP (purple vinyl, p/s)	25
90	Private Pressing	AN ILLIAD OF WOES EP (4 track demo cassette)	30
91	Private Pressing	ALL FAITH IS LOST EP (4 track demo cassette)	30
93	Peaceville VILE 34	SERENADES (LP)	30
95	Peaceville VILE 52	THE SILENT ENIGMA (LP)	15

ANCIENT GREASE

(see also Eyes Of Blue, Big Sleep, Man, Gary Pickford-Hopkins, Gentle Giant)

71	Mercury 6338 033	WOMAN AND CHILDREN FIRST (LP, black/silver labels)	120

MINT VALUE £

AND ALSO THE TREES
84 Reflex RE 3 — The Secret Sea/Secrecy (p/s) — 8
84 Reflex 12 RE 6 — The Secret Sea/Secrecy/There Were No Bounds/The Tease The Tear/ Midnight Garden/Wallpaper Dying (12", p/s) — 10
84 Reflex FS 9 — Shantell/Wallpaper Dying (p/s) — 5
83 Reflex (no cat. no.) — AND ALSO THE TREES (EP, cassette only) — 15
84 Reflex LEX 1 — AND ALSO THE TREES (LP) — 18

ERIC ANDERSEN
65 Fontana TFL 6061 — TODAY IS THE HIGHWAY (LP) — 50
68 Fontana STFL 6068 — 'BOUT CHANGES AND THINGS TAKE 2 (LP, black/silver label) — 40

LALE ANDERSEN
56 HMV 7EG 8277 — THE ORIGINAL LILI MARLENE (EP) — 10

BILL ANDERSON
62 Brunswick 05879 — Mama Sang A Song/On And On And On — 5
63 Brunswick 05887, 63 — Still/You Made It Easy — 6

CAROL ANDERSON
79 Grapevine GRP 133 — Sad Girl/I'll Get Off At the Next Stop — 15

CHRISTIAN ANDERSON
74 DJM DJS 330 — Supergirl/My Imagination — 6

ERNESTINE ANDERSON
60 Mercury AMT 1103 — A Kiss To Build A Dream On/Come On, Baby, Let's Go — 5
61 Mercury AMT 1137 — A Lover's Question/That's All I Want From You — 15
64 Sue WI 309 — Keep An Eye On Love/Continental Mind — 120
65 Stateside SS 455 — Somebody Told You/How Many Times — 15
65 Mercury MF 912 — Jerk & Twine/You Can't Buy Love — 30
58 Pye Nixa NPT 19025 — BY SPECIAL REQUEST (LP) — 8
59 Mercury MMC 14016 — TOAST OF THE NATIONS CRITICS (LP) — 20
60 Mercury MMC 14037 — THE FASCINATING ERNESTINE (LP) — 12
61 Mercury MMC 14062 — MOANIN' (LP) — 15
64 Sue ILP 911 — THE NEW SOUND OF ERNESTINE ANDERSON (LP, unissued) — 150
67 Columbia S(C)X 6145 — ERNESTINE ANDERSON (LP) — 15

GLADSTONE ANDERSON (& FOLLOWERS)
(see also Stranger & Gladdy, Tommy McCook)
69 Blue Cat BS 172 — Judas/The World Come To An End (with Followers) — 30
74 Ashanti ASH 413 — It May Sound Silly/Gladdy's Workshop — 6
73 Ashanti SHAN 103 — IT MAY SOUND SILLY (LP) — 15

HALEY ANDERSON
83 Magnet 12 MID 5 — All To Myself (Dance Mix)/(7" Version)/(Instrumental) (12") — 30

IAN (A.) ANDERSON
(see also Mike Cooper, Anderson Jones Jackson)
71 Village Thing VTSX 1002 — One More Chance/Policeman's Ball — 18
69 Saydisc EP SD 134 — ALMOST THE COUNTRY BLUES (EP, with Elliot Jackson) — 50
68 Saydisc Matchbox SDM 159 — THE INVERTED WORLD (LP, with Mike Cooper) — 70
69 Liberty LBS 83242E — STEREO DEATH BREAKDOWN (LP, blue label, as Ian Anderson Country Blues Band) — 60
70 Fontana STL 5542 — BOOK OF CHANGES (LP, black/silver labels) — 120
70 Village Thing VTS 3 — ROYAL YORK CRESCENT (LP, with lyric insert) — 35
72 Village Thing VTS 9 — A VULTURE IS NOT A BIRD YOU CAN TRUST (LP) — 35
72 Village Thing VTS 18 — SINGER SLEEPS ON AS BLAZE RAGES (LP) — 60

JAMES ANDERSON
71 Atlantic 2091-055 — Mama Mama/Muskatel Muskatel — 20

JON ANDERSON
(see also Hans Christian, Warriors, Yes, Mike Oldfield, Jon & Vangelis)
76 Atlantic K 10840 — Flight Of The Moorglade/To The Runner — 5
80 Atlantic K 11619 — Some Are Born/Days (p/s) — 5

KIP ANDERSON
67 President PT 163 — You'll Lose A Good Thing/I'm Out Of Love — 10

LEROY ANDERSON
55 Brunswick 05375 — Sandpaper Ballet/Song Of The Bells — 5
55 Brunswick 05485 — Forgotten Dreams/The Last Rose Of Summer — 5

MILLER ANDERSON
(see also Voice, At Last The 1958 Rock'n'Roll Show, Keef Hartley Band, Hemlock, Dog Soldier, Lyn Dobson)
71 Deram DM 337 — Bright City/Another Time, Another Place — 10
71 Deram SDL 3 — BRIGHT CITY (LP, gatefold sleeve) — 70

MOIRA ANDERSON
69 Decca F12989 — The Holy City/Ave Maria — 8

REUBEN ANDERSON
66 Doctor Bird DB 1045 — Christmas Time Again/DESMOND TUCKER: Oh Holy Night — 25

SONNY ANDERSON
60 London HLP 9036 — Lonely Lonely Train/Yes, I'm Gonna Love You — 90

UDELL T. ANDERSON
69 Direction 58-4212 — Love Ain't Love/Funky Walk — 10
69 Direction 58-4459 — Keep On Loving Me/Rainmaker — 10

VICKI ANDERSON
(see also Bobby Byrd, James Brown)
71 Mojo 2001 150 — Super Good/Super Good (Version) — 10
73 Mojo 2093 005 — I'm Too Tough For Mr Big Stuff (Hot Pants)/Sound Funky — 20

MINT VALUE £

74 Mojo 2093 028 Don't Throw Your Love In The Garbage Can/Land Of Milk And Honey/ BOBBY BYRD: Sayin' It And Doin' It Are Two Different Things ... 10

ANDERSON, HARLEY & BATT
(see also Steve Harley, Mike Batt)
88 Epic PEEPS 1 Whatever You Believe/Whatever You Believe (live) (p/s) ... 5

ANDERSON, JONES, JACKSON
(see also Ian A. Anderson, Al Jones)
68 Saydisc 33 SD 125 ANDERSON, JONES, JACKSON (EP) ... 35

ANDERSON'S ALLSTARS
68 Blue Cat BS 133 Intensified Girls/Jump And Shout ... 150

PETER ANDREOLII
77 20th Century BTC 2342 Mind Excursion/When I Open Up My Eyes ... 6

BARBARA ANDREWS
70 Escort ERT 838 Lonesome Feeling/RAINY BOP: Hop Scotch ... 20

BARRY ANDREWS
(see also XTC, Shriekback, Robert Fripp)
80 Virgin VS 378 Rossmore Road (NW1)/Win A Night Out With A Well Known Paranoiac (p/s) ... 6

CATHERINE ANDREWS
(see also Gordon Giltrap, Inner City Unit)
80 Cat Tracks PURR LP 2 FRUITS (LP, with lyric sheet & poster sleeve) ... 50

CHRIS ANDREWS
(see also Chris Ravel & Ravers)
66 Decca F 22365 Something On My Mind/I'll Do The Best I Can ... 8
66 Decca F 22404 Whatcha Gonna Do Now?/Lady Oh Lady ... 6
67 Decca F 22668 Hold On/Easy ... 30
69 Pye International 17727 Pretty Belinda/Make No Mistakes ... 7

DAVE ANDREWS & SUGAR
(see also Heinz)
68 Jewel JL 04 I'm On My Way/Beatin' Of My Heart ... 60

EAMONN ANDREWS
(see also Vernons Girls)
57 Parlophone R 4318 The Ship That Never Sailed/The Magic Tree (with the Vernons Girls) ... 5

ERNIE ANDREWS
60 Vogue V 9166 'Round Midnight/Lover Come Back To Me ... 12
65 Capitol CL 15407 Where Were You/What Do I See In The Girl ... 20
76 Capitol CL 15873 Fine Young Girl/Then I'll Know ... 10

HARVEY ANDREWS
72 Cube BUG 20 Soldier/In The Darkness ... 5
72 Cube BUG 26 Learning The Game/Don't Know The Time ... 5
75 Transatlantic BIG 525 (I'm Resigning) From Today/Darby And Joan (with Graham Cooper) ... 6
65 Transatlantic TRAEP 133 HARVEY ANDREWS (EP) ... 35
70 Decca Nova SDN 9 PLACES AND FACES (LP) ... 40
72 Cube HIFLY 10 WRITER OF SONGS (LP, with lyric insert) ... 20
73 Fly HIFLY 15 FRIENDS OF MINE (LP, gatefold sleeve) ... 20

INEZ ANDREWS & ANDREWETTES
65 Vogue EDVP 1283 INEZ ANDREWS & ANDREWETTES (EP) ... 40

JOHN ANDREWS & LONELY ONES
66 Parlophone R 5455 A Rose Growing In The Ruins/It's Just Love ... 230
66 Parlophone R 5455 A Rose Growing In The Ruins/It's Just Love (DJ copy) ... 250

JULIE ANDREWS
60 Decca F11230 Tom Philby/Lazy Afternoon ... 5

LEE ANDREWS (& HEARTS)
57 London HL 7031 Teardrops/Girl Around The Corner (solo, export issue) ... 300
58 London HLM 8546 Teardrops/Girl Around The Corner (solo) ... 300
58 London HLM 8546 Teardrops/Girl Around The Corner (solo) (78) ... 60
58 London HLU 8661 Try The Impossible/Nobody's Home (as Lee Andrews & Hearts) ... 400
58 London HLU 8661 Try The Impossible/Nobody's Home (as Lee Andrews & Hearts) ... 70

PATTY ANDREWS
(see also Bing Crosby, Jimmy Durante)
55 Capitol CL 14324 Without Love/Where To My Love? ... 10
55 Capitol CL 14374 Suddenly There's A Valley/Booga Da Woog ... 10

ANDREWS SISTERS
57 Capitol CL 14705 Rum And Coca-Cola/No, Baby ... 7
57 Capitol CL 14807 I'm Goin' Home/By His Word ... 7
60 Capitol CL 15170 Rum And Coca-Cola/I'll Be With You In Apple Blossom Time ... 5
53 Brunswick LA 8599 SING SING SING (10" LP) ... 15

TIM ANDREWS
(see also Fleur De Lys, Rupert's People)
67 Parlophone R 5656 Sad Simon Lives Again/You Won't Be Seeing Me Anymore ... 40
68 Parlophone R 5695 Your Tea Is Strong/(Something About) Suburbia ... 40
70 Parlophone R 5824 Tiny Goddess/Josephine ... 40

TIM ANDREWS & PAUL KORDA
(see also Paul Korda)
68 Parlophone R 5714 Smile If You Want To/Makin' Love To Him ... 40

ANDROMEDA
(see Attack, Five Day Week Straw People, Hard Stuff, Atomic Rooster, John Du Cann, Fuzzy Duck)
69 RCA RCA 1854 Go Your Way/Keep Out 'Cos I'm Dying ... 30

			MINT VALUE £
69	RCA SF 8031	ANDROMEDA (LP)	400
90	Reflection MM 06	SEVEN, LONELY STREET (LP, numbered & signed, 500 only)	18
95	Kissing Spell KSLP 9497	LIVE 1967 (LP)	12

AND SO TO BED

78	Stonehouse SH004	THE EP	12

AND THE INDIAN LOGIC

80s	Logic KJR 01	Beggar Man/The Change (p/s)	10

AND THE NATIVE HIPSTERS

79	Heater Volume HVR 003	There Goes Concorde Again?/Stands, Still The Building?/ I Wanna Be Around (several different coloured photocopied foldaround sleeves with insert in ploythene bag)	12
82	Illuminated/Glass HIP 1	TENDERLY HURT ME (Poor Prince/Hang Ten/ Tenderly Hurt Me/Stuck) (12" EP, p/s)	15

ANDWELLA('S DREAM)

(see also David Lewis, David Baxter)

69	CBS 4301	Sunday/Midday Sun (as Andwella's Dream)	35
69	CBS 4469	Mrs. Man/Felix (as Andwella's Dream)	80
69	CBS 4634	Mr. Sunshine/Shades Of Grey (as Andwella's Dream)	40
70	Reflection RS 1	Every Little Minute/Michael Fitzhenry (as Andwella)	10
70	Reflection RS 3	Hold Onto Your Mind/Shadow Of The Night (as Andwella)	20
71	Reflection RS 6	People's People/Are You Ready (as Andwella)	10
69	CBS 63673	LOVE AND POETRY (LP, as Andwella's Dream)	500
70	Reflection REFL 10	WORLD'S END (LP, as Andwella, stickered sleeve with poster)	120
70	Reflection REFL 10	WORLD'S END (LP, without poster)	60
71	Reflection REF 1010	PEOPLE'S PEOPLE (LP, as Andwella)	70

BOB ANDY

(see also Bob & Marcia, Larry & Alvin)

67	Island WI 3040	I've Got To Get Back Home/SONNY BURKE: Rudy Girl	100
68	Studio One SO 2063	Too Experienced/Let Them Stay	40
68	Coxsone CS 7074	Born A Man/MARCIA GRIFFITHS: Mark My Word	40
69	Doctor Bird DB 1183	The Way I Feel/ETHIOPIANS: Long Time Now	45
69	Doctor Bird DB 1191	Games People Play/The Sun Shines For Me	25
69	Studio One SO 2075	I'm Going Home/SOUND DIMENSION: Straight Flush	40
70	Harry J. HJ 6612	Peace Of Mine/Weep	10
71	Trojan TR 7809	Green Green Valley/Peace Of Mind	6
71	Trojan TR 7821	One Woman/You Don't Know (B-side actually "Save Me Version" by Bob Andy Band)	6
71	Trojan TR 7840	One Woman/You Don't Know	6
71	London HLJ 7127	Games People Play/GAYLETTES: Son Of A Preacher Man (export issue)	10
72	Sioux SI 019	Baby I Need Your Loving/CIRCLES: Mammy Blue	6
72	Sioux SI 020	Everyday People/HONG GANG: Smoking Wild	6
72	Green Door GD 4047	Life/HARRY J. ALL STARS: Version	10
73	Green Door GD 4059	You Don't Know/The Border Song	18
73	Horse HOSS 31	One Woman/Second Hand Love	6
75	Fab FAB 241	Feeling Soul/SOUND DIMENSION: Part 2	12
75	Sound Tracs SK2 8	Nyah/Nyah Dub	8
76	Tropical TST 110	Feeling Soul/Rock It Baby	10
86	L ANKA AV0025TLP	RETROSPECTIVE (LP)	12

HORACE ANDY

(see also Jon Cuno, Big Youth)

72	Count Shelley 2	Cha Cha Children/Version	8
72	Attack ATT 8026	Feel Good All Over/PHIL PRATT ALLSTARS: Feel Good (Version)	6
73	Bread BR 1170	Don't Try To Use Me/Goddess Of Love	8
73	Randy's RAN 533	Don't Think About Me (with Earl Flute)/DINO PERKINS: Skin Him Alive	20
73	Atra ATRA 008	Children Of Israel/Part 2	8
74	Ackee ACK 530	Til/IMPACT ALLSTARS: Version	6
75	Attack ATT 8117	Nice And Easy/Version	6
75	Fab FAB 260	Oh Lord Why Lord/SOUND DIMENSION: Part 2	10
75	Morpheus MOR 1010	Got To Get You	6
76	Venture VEN 7706	Skylarking/Version	10
76	Terminal TM 105	Thank The Lord/Part Two (actually the SUNSHOT BAND)	10
77	Serious Business SB 02	Rock To Sleep/Version	25
79	Sufferer's Height SUFF 005	Pure Ranking/The Return Of Jammy's Hi-Fi (Round One)/ TREVOR RANKING: Whip Them Jah Jah (12")	30
84	Music Hawk MHD 13	Confusion/Version (12")	15
85	Rough Trade RTT 172	Get Down/RHYTHM POSSE : Get Down Deeper (12")	50
72	Trojan TBL 197	YOU ARE MY ANGEL (LP)	25
84	Music Hawk MHLP001	CONFUSION (LP)	18

HORACE ANDY & FREDDIE MCKAY

75	Treble 7	Talking Love/Dub	8
64	Port-O-Jam PJ 4009	I Want To Know/My Love Has Gone	40
64	Ska Beat JB 162	You're Wondering Now/You'll Never (copies also exist on R&B label)	30

PATRICK ANDY

78	Grove Music GMDM 3	Woman, Woman, Woman/TOMMY MCCOOK: Lamb's Bread (12")	30

ANDY & BEY SISTERS

59	Fontana H 174	Pretty Baby/Sweeter Than Sweet	5
59	Fontana H 197	Scoubidou/Don't Get Around Much Anymore	5

ANDY & CLYDE

65	Rio R 62	Never Be A Slave/Magic Is Love	12
65	Rio R 69	I'm So Lonesome/WINSTON STEWART: Day After Day	12
65	Rio R 71	We All Have To Part/UPSETTERS: Scandalizing	80

MINT VALUE £

ANDY & JOEY
(see also Roland Alphonso)

62	Island WI 056	Have You Ever/Cross My Heart	20

ANGEL

74	Cube BUG 41	Good Time Fanny/Who D'Ya Think Your Fooling	5
74	Cube BUG 51	Little Boy Blue/Tragedy Queen	5

ANGEL

77	Casablanca CBC 104	Magic Touch/Big Boy	5
76	Casablanca CBC 4007	ANGEL (LP, with insert)	15
76	Casablanca CBC 4010	HELLUVA BAND (LP)	12

JOHNNY ANGEL

60	Parlophone R 4642	Chinese Butterfly/My Very Good Friend The Milkman	10
60	Parlophone R 4679	Too Young To Go Steady/You're Thrilling	10
61	Parlophone R 4750	What Happens To Love/Luna Luna Luna Lu	10
61	Parlophone R 4795	Web Of Love/Trocadero-Double-Nine-One-O	10
62	Parlophone R 4874	Look, Look Little Angel/Jenny From Missouri	10
62	Parlophone R 4948	Better Luck Next Time/The Power Of You	10
63	Parlophone R 5026	A Touch Of Venus/The Two Together	10

MARIAN ANGEL

65	Columbia DB 7537	It's Gonna Be Alright/Tomorrow's Fool	15
65	Columbia DB 7705	You Can't Buy My Love/One Way Only	10
66	CBS 202391	Little Bit Of Sunshine/All The Time In The World	6

ANGELA & HER FANS
(see also Alma Cogan)

66	Pye 7N 17108	Love Ya Illya/I Know You	20

ANGELETTES

72	Decca F 13284	Don't Let Him Touch You/Rainy Day	8

ANGELIC UPSTARTS

78	Dead IS/AU/1024	Murder Of Liddle Towers/Police Oppression (p/s, 1,000 only)	50
78	Rough Trade RT/SW 001	Murder Of Liddle Towers/Police Oppression (reissue, p/s)	5
79	Warner Bros K 17354	I'm An Upstart/Leave Me Alone (green vinyl, no p/s)	5
79	Warner Bros K 17354T	I'm An Upstart/Leave Me Alone (12", p/s)	8
79	Warner Bros K 17426C	Teenage Warning/The Young Ones (red vinyl, no p/s)	5
80	Warner Bros SPZ 2	I'm An Upstart/Never 'Ad Nothin' (cassette single)	6
80	Zonophone Z 7	Last Night Another Soldier/The Man Who Came In From The Beano (p/s)	5
81	Zonophone Z 12	England/Stick's Diary (p/s)	12
83	Anagram ANA 12	The Burglar (p/s, unissued)	0
85	Gas GM 3010	Brighton Bomb/Thin Red Line/Soldier (12", banned 'Maggie Thatcher' p/s)	15
79	Warner Bros K 56717	TEENAGE WARNING (LP)	15
80	Warner Bros K 56806	WE GOTTA GET OUT OF THIS PLACE (LP)	12
81	Zonophone ZEM 102	LIVE (LP, with free live flexidisc: "We're Gonna Take The World"/ Leave Me Alone/"The Young Ones"/"White Riot" [no cat. no.])	15
81	Zonophone ZEM 102	LIVE (LP)	12
83	Anagram GRAM 007	ANGEL DUST (LP)	12
85	Gas GLP 4012	THE POWER OF THE PRESS (LP)	12
85	Razor RAZM 32	LIVE IN YUGOSLAVIA (LP)	15
85	Anagram GRAM004	REASONS WHY (LP, with inner sleeve)	12
90	Link LP 140	LOST & FOUND (LP)	15

ANGELINA

65	Fontana TF 648	I Just Don't Know How/Wishing My Life Away	5

ANGELO & EIGHTEEN

72	RAK RAK 137	Midnight Flight/Flight Two	35

BOBBY ANGELO & TUXEDOS
(see also Innocents [UK], End)

61	HMV POP 892	Baby Sitting/Skinny Lizzie	20
61	HMV POP 982	I Gotta Have You/Don't Stop	30

JERRY ANGELO

59	Parlophone R 4548	Crush Me/Mary Lou	10
59	Parlophone R 4561	If You Change Your Mind/I Love You My Love	10
60	Parlophone R 4656	Maria Elena/Old Man River	10
62	Palette PG 9031	Lonely Hill/Make Her Mine	10
62	Palette PG 9034	Innocent Angel/The Boy Who Walks Alone	10

MICHAEL ANGELO & HIS ORCHESTRA
(see also John Barry)

61	Columbia DB 4705	Rocco's Theme/Spinneree	5
62	Columbia DB 4800	Tears/The Roman Spring Of Mrs Stone	5

MAYA ANGELOU

57	London HA-U 2062	MISS CALYPSO (LP)	20

ANGELS
(see also Beach-Nuts)

62	Pye International 7N 25150	Everybody Loves A Lover/Blow Joe	15
63	Mercury AMT 1211	My Boyfriend's Back/(Love Me) Now	20
63	Mercury AMT 1215	I Adore Him/Thank You And Goodnight	20
64	Philips BF 1312	Wow Wow Wee/Snowflakes And Teardrops	10

ANGEL PAVEMENT
(see also Fortes Mentum, Pussy)

69	Fontana TF 1059	Baby You've Gotta Stay/Green Mello Hill	18
70	Fontana TF 1072	Tell Me What I've Got To Do/When Will I See June Again	20

MINT VALUE £

ANGEL STREET

79	Ellie Jay EJSP 9290	Done It Again/Song For You (500 only)	200

ANGEL WITCH

(see also Tytan)

80	EMI EMI 5064	Sweet Danger/Flight Nineteen (p/s)	10
80	EMI 12EMI 5064	Sweet Danger/Flight Nineteen/Hades Paradise (12", p/s)	20
80	Bronze BRO 108	Angel Witch/Gorgon (p/s)	8
81	Bronze BRO 121	Loser/Suffer/Dr Phibes (p/s)	10
85	Killerwatt KIL 3001	Goodbye/Reawakening (no p/s)	6
80	Bronze BRON 532	ANGELWITCH (LP)	18
85	Killerwatt KILP 4001	SCREAMIN' N' BLEEDIN' (LP)	15

ANGLIANS

(see also Moving Finger)

67	CBS 202489	A Friend Of Mine/Daytime Lover	20

ANGLOS

(see also Spencer Davis Group, Stevie Winwood)

65	Brit WI 004	Incense/You're Fooling Me	80
65	Fontana TF 589	Incense/You're Fooling Me (reissue)	25
67	Sue WI 4033	Incense/You're Fooling Me (unissued)	200
69	Island WIP 6061	Incense/You're Fooling Me (2nd reissue)	10

ANGRY YOUNG MEN

59	Fontana H 187	Big Daddy/Ciribiribin	5

ANIMAL COLLECTIVE

04	Paw PAW 003	Wastered/Wastered (12" one side BLACK DICE, 1,000 only)	20
04	Fat Cat 7FAT 15	Who Could Win A rabbit/Baby Day (p/s)	20
05	Fat Cat 7FAT 19	Grass/Must Be Treeman/Flcle Cycle (p/s)	20
07	Domino RUG 270T	Fireworks (1-sided pink vinyl 10", stickered, die-cut pink sleeve)	10
04	Fat Cat FATSPLP 08	SUNG TONGS (LP)	20
05	Fat Cat FATSLP 11	FEELS (2-LP)	18
06	Domino WIGLP199	STRAWBERRY JAM (2-LP, gatefold with inners)	18
09	Fat Cat FATSP08LPX	SUNG TONGS (2-LP, reissue, 180gm vinyl)	15
09	Fat Cat FATSP11LPX	FEELS (2-LP, gatefold, reissue 180gm vinyl)	15
09	Domino WIGLP216	MERRIWEATHER POST PAVILION (2-LP, gatefold)	15

ANIMAL FARM

84	Rot Records ASS 7	Model Soldier/John And Julie (p/s)	6

ANIMAL MAGNET

81	EMI 12 EMI 5240	Welcome To The Monkey House/Game Over Player 1 (12")	8

ANIMALS

(see also Eric Burdon & Animals, Alan Price, Danny McCullough)

64	Columbia DB 7247	Baby Let Me Take You Home/Gonna Send You Back To Walker	10
64	Columbia DB 7301	The House Of The Rising Sun/Talkin' 'Bout You	6
64	Columbia DB 7354	I'm Crying/Take It Easy	6
65	Columbia DB 7445	Don't Let Me Be Misunderstood/Club-A-Go Go (standard issue, matrix: '2N')	6
65	Columbia DB 7445	Don't Let Me Be Misunderstood/Club-A-Go Go (mispressing, with 'demo' version of A-side, matrix: '1N')	15
65	Columbia DB 7539	Bring It On Home To Me/For Miss Caulker	6
65	Columbia DB 7639	We've Gotta Get Out Of This Place/I Can't Believe It	8
65	Columbia DB 7741	It's My Life/I'm Going To Change The World	6
66	Decca F 12332	Inside Looking Out/Outcast	10
66	Decca F 12407	Don't Bring Me Down/Cheating	10
82	Rak RRP 1	The House Of The Rising Sun/ Don't Let Me Be Misunderstood/I'm Crying (picture disc)	5
63	Graphic Sound ALO 10867	I JUST WANNA MAKE LOVE TO YOU (12" EP, 1-sided, 99 only, as Alan Price Rhythm & Blues Group or as Animals, private pressing, blank white cover, typed label)	450
64	Columbia SEG 8374	THE ANIMALS IS HERE (EP)	25
65	Columbia SEG 8400	THE ANIMALS (EP)	20
65	Columbia SEG 8439	THE ANIMALS NO. 2 (EP)	25
65	Columbia SEG 8452	THE ANIMALS ARE BACK (EP)	30
65	Decca DFE 8643	IN THE BEGINNING THERE WAS EARLY ANIMALS (EP, reissue of Graphic Sound EP)	30
66	Columbia SEG 8499	ANIMAL TRACKS (EP)	35
64	Columbia 33SX 1669	THE ANIMALS (LP, blue/black label with "Sold in the U.K..." label text)	70
64	EMI Regal SREG 1104	THE ANIMALS (LP, export issue)	60
65	Columbia 33SX 1708	ANIMAL TRACKS (LP)	60
66	Columbia SX 6035	THE MOST OF THE ANIMALS (LP)	25
66	Decca LK 4797	ANIMALISMS (LP)	45
71	BARN 2314 104	BEFORE WE WERE RUDELY INTERRUPTED (LP)	15
76	DJM DJSL 069	IN CONCERT FROM NEWCASTLE (LP)	15

ANIMALS & MEN

80	Strange Days DAYS 1	The Terraplane Fixation/Shell Shock (p/s)	5
80	TW HIT 101	Don't Misbehave In The New Age/Machines (p/s)	5

ANIMATED EGG

69	Marble Arch MAL 890	ANIMATED EGG (LP)	25

ANITA & TH' SO AND SO'S

62	RCA RCA 1278	Joey Baby/Rinky Tinky Rhythm	10

PAUL ANKA

(see also Micki Marlo & Paul Anka, Neil Sedaka)

57	Columbia DB 3980	Diana/Don't Gamble With Love (mauve label)	7
57	Columbia DB 3980	Diana/Don't Gamble With Love (re-pressings on green or black label)	10

			MINT VALUE £
57	Columbia DB 4022	I Love You, Baby/Tell Me That You Love Me (mauve or green label)	6
58	Columbia DB 4063	You Are My Destiny/When I Stop Loving You (mauve or green label)	6
58	Columbia DB 4110	Crazy Love/Let The Bells Keep Ringing (mauve or green label)	5
58	Columbia DB 4199	Just Young/So It's Goodbye	5
59	Columbia DB 4241	(All Of A Sudden) My Heart Sings/That's Love	6
59	Columbia DB 4286	I Miss You So/Late Last Night	7
59	Columbia DB 4324	Lonely Boy/Your Love	8
59	Columbia DB 4355	Put Your Head On My Shoulder/Don't Ever Leave Me	10
60	Columbia DB 4390	It's Time To Cry/Something Has Changed Me	8
63	RCA RCA 1340	Remember Diana/At Night (p/s)	10
68	RCA RCA 1676	Can't Get You Out Of My Mind/When We Get There	40
68	RCA RCA 1676	Can't Get You Out Of My Mind/When We Get There (DJ copy)	40
57	Columbia SEG 7747	DIANA (EP)	15
58	Columbia SEG 7801	ANKA AGAIN (EP)	15
59	Columbia SEG 7890	SING SING SING (EP)	15
60	Columbia SEG 7985	SINGS SONGS FROM 'GIRLS' TOWN' AND OTHER SUCCESSES (EP)	15
64	RCA RCX 7127	FLY ME TO THE MOON (EP)	8
64	RCA RCX 7152	FOUR GOLDEN HITS (EP)	8
64	RCA RCX 7170	SYLVIE (EP)	8
58	Columbia 33SX 1092	PAUL ANKA (LP, green label)	40
59	Columbia 33SX 1196	MY HEART SINGS (LP)	20
60	Columbia 33SX 1268	ANKA SWINGS FOR YOUNG LOVERS (LP)	20
60	Columbia 33SX 1282	PAUL ANKA SINGS HIS BIG 15 (LP)	20
60	Columbia 33SX 1287	IT'S CHRISTMAS EVERYWHERE (LP)	20
64	RCA RD 7700	EXCITEMENT ON PARK AVENUE - LIVE AT THE WALDORF ASTORIA (LP)	20

ANNABEL DREAM

	Oak (no cat no)	My Last Date With You/Gary, Won't You Marry Me (Unreleased - acetate only)	50

ANNALISE

99	Boss Tunage BOSTAGE 701	Signposts And Alleyways/Empire Builder (p/s, 1-sided green vinyl with free CD, numbered, 250 copies only)	10

ANNETTE (& AFTERBEATS)

59	Top Rank JAR 137	Lonely Guitar/Wild Willie	15
59	Top Rank JAR 137	Lonely Guitar/Wild Willie (78)	10
59	Top Rank JAR 233	First Name Initial/My Heart Became Of Age (with Afterbeats)	15
60	Top Rank JAR 343	It Took Dreams/O Dio Mio	10
60	Pye International 7N 25061	Pineapple Princess/Luau Cha Cha Cha (with Afterbeats)	10
64	HMV POP 1270	Muscle Beach Party/I Dream About Frankie	30
64	HMV POP 1322	Scrambled Egghead/Merlin Jones	10
65	HMV POP 1447	The Monkey's Uncle (with The Beach Boys)/How Will I Know My Love	45
59	Gala 45XP 1046	TALL PAUL (EP)	20
64	HMV CLP 1782	ANNETTE'S BEACH PARTY (LP)	35
61	Buena Vista BV 3305	DANCE ANNETTE (LP)	20

ANNETTE & KEYMEN

64	King KG 1006	Look Who's Blue/How Can I Tell Him	5

ANNIS

79	GTO GT 266	Don't Play Your Games/After Me	20

ANNIVERSARY

78	Aerco AERE 102	GIVE ME A SMILE (EP)	20

ANN-MARGRET

(see Al Hirt)

61	RCA RCA 1245	I Just Don't Understand/I Don't Hurt Anymore	10
64	RCA RCX 7148	THE VIVACIOUS ONE (EP)	20
62	RCA RD 27239/SF 5116	AND HERE SHE IS (LP, mono/stereo)	20
62	RCA Victor RD/SF 7503	ON THE WAY UP (LP, mono/stereo)	20
63	RCA Victor RD 7580	BYE BYE BIRDIE (LP, mono)	20
64	RCA Victor RD/SF 7632	BEAUTY AND THE BEARD (LP, mono/stereo, with Al Hirt)	12
64	RCA Victor RD/SF 7649	BACHELORS' PARADISE (LP, mono/stereo)	25
64	RCA Victor RD/SF 7591	ANNE MARGRET (LP, mono/stereo)	15

ANNO DOMINO

71	Deram SML-R 1085	ON THIS NEW DAY (LP)	220

ANONYMOUSLY YOURS

69	Trojan TR 680	Get Back/ERNIE SMITH : Not For Sale	15
69	Trojan TR 681	It's Your Thing/69 (B-side actually by Wallace Wilson)	15
69	Duke DU 40	Organism/Itch	12

ANOREXIA

80	Slim SJP 812	Rapist In The Park/I'm A Square/Pets	35

ANOTHER PRETTY FACE

79	New Pleasure Z1	All The Boys Love Carrie/That's Not Enough (green and white foldout p/s)	12
79	New Pleasure Z2	All The Boys Love Carrie/That's Not Enough (red and white p/s)	7
80	Virgin VS 320	Whatever Happened To The West?/Goodbye 1970's (p/s)	10
80	Chicken Jazz JAZZ 1	I'M SORRY THAT I BEAT YOU, I'M SORRY THAT I SCREAMED, FOR A MOMENT THERE I REALLY LOST CONTROL (8-track cassette with fanzine and badge. Some copies exist with tracks of DNV single taped onto the end)	30
81	Chicken Jazz JAZZ 2	Soul To Soul/A Woman's Place/God On The Screen (foldout p/s)	12

ANOTHER SUNNY DAY

88	Sarah SARAH 003	Anorak City (flexidisc free with Are You Scared To Get Happy fanzine (SARAH 004, 1,500 only, must be together)	30
88	Sarah SARAH 007	I'm In Love With A Girl Who Doesn't Know I Exist/Things Will Be Nice/ The Centre Of My Little World (14" x 10" foldout poster p/s)	25
89	Caff CAFF 7	Genetic Engineering/Kilburn Towers (p/s, with inner)	30

MINT VALUE £

89 Sarah SARAH 016 What's Happened?/Can't You Tell It's True?/Impossible (foldover p/s in poly bag, insert) 10
89 Sarah SARAH 022 You Should All Be Murdered/Horseriding/Green (foldover p/s in poly bag, insert) 10
90 Sarah SARAH 035 Rio/The Very Beginning (p/s, insert) 8
92 Sarah SARAH 060 New Year's Honours/I Don't Suppose I'll Get A Second Chance (p/s, insert) 8
92 Sarah SARAH 613 LONDON WEEKEND (LP) 25

ANSEL SCANDAL
76 Dynamic DYN 105 Roots Food/Roots Food - Dub 6

BRETT ANSELL
62 Oriole CB 1701 That's Where Lonesome Lives/The Door Is Open 30
62 Oriole CB 1725 Rosalita/The Outsider 20

ANSELL (Collins) & ELAINE
72 Camel CA 98 Presenting Cheater/RON WILSON: Official Trombone 15

MARK ANSLEY
70 Mother MOT 2 909/Venus 10

ANSWERS
(see also Misunderstood, High Tide)
66 Columbia DB 7847 It's Just A Fear/You've Gotta Believe Me 180
66 Columbia DB 7953 That's What You're Doing To Me/Got A Letter From My Baby 50

ANT
74 Pye 7N 45332 Banana Pie/No Road Goes Your Way 15

ADAM ANT
(see also Adam & The Ants, Maneaters)
85 CBS A 6367 Vive Le Rock/Greta X (p/s, mispressing, both sides play "Vive Le Rock") 5
85 CBS CD 26583 VIVE LE ROCK (CD, with extra track "Human Bondage Den") 20
95 EMI CDEMS370 Beautiful Dream (single version)/Let's Have A Fight/Billy Boy/Wonderful (acoustic) (CD withdrawn, 7 known copies) 70
85 EMI CDEM370 Beautiful Dream (single version)/Shake Your Hips/Antmusic (Acoustic)/Beautiful Dream (Lucas Full Length Mix) (CD, withdrawn, 2 known copies) 80

ANTEEEKS
66 Philips BF 1471 I Don't Want You/Ball And Chain 175

PETER ANTELL
65 Pye International 7N 25329 The Times They Are A-Changin'/Yesterday And Tomorrow 5

ANTHEM
71 Buddah 2359017 ANTHEM (LP) 30

ANTHEM
81 EJSP9576 England/Some Like It Hot/Do You Mind (EP, p/s, 500 only) 150

ANTHILL MOB
92 Anthill ANT 1T Penelope's Theme (12" white label) 35
93 Anthill ANT 2T Antology/Black Rushin'/The hooded claw (tango mix) (12") 30
93 Anthill ANT 3T Antology (The Top Buzz Stonehenge Remix)/Black Rushin' (Anthill Remix) (12") 20

ANTHILL MOB
(see also Mystic matt And The Anthill Mob)
95 Confetti MK 01 Feel It/Deep Down/Untitled/Untitled (white label 12") 30
95 Confetti MK001 MAKESHIFT EP (12") 90
96 Confetti COEP 01 Promise Of... /Was She Ever Mine?/So In Love/Got To Do It (12") 35
96 Confetti COEP 02 Feel The Groove/ANTHILL MOB FEATURING P. PITSTOP - Do you know?/P. PITSTOP - I Know How To Love! (12") 25
97 Confetti COEP 05 Why (Inside The Rise)/Things Just Started (12") 25
97 Confetti COEP 06 Cloudy Day/Agitator (12") 15
97 Confetti CODP 01 Missing/Player/X2C/Flava/Sound/Cuts (2 x 12") 70
97 Confetti COEP 08 Higher/How Ya Feeling (12") 15
97 Love Peace & Unity LOVE 03 Burning (the original mix) (10" picture disc, 500 only, same track both sides) 35
97 Makeshift MR 001 Set You Free/In The Name/Shake The House/Heaven Knows (12") 15
98 Makeshift MR 002 Never Ever Time/Time To Move/Don't Know/Give Me (12") 20
98 Quench QUE 14 Don't Leave Me/Listen (12") 30
00 Confetti COEP 19 ANTHILL MOB EP (12") 25
97 Love Peace & Unity LOVE 04A SPECIAL COLLECTION OF ENCHANTED RHYTHMS (2 x LP) 40

BILLIE ANTHONY
(see also Big Ben Banjo Band)
54 Columbia SCM 5143 This Ole House/Oh, What A Dream 12
54 Columbia SCM 5155 Teach Me Tonight/Don't Let The Kiddygeddin 10
55 Columbia SCM 5164 Butterscotch Hop/No More 10
55 Columbia SCM 5174 Tweedlee Dee/Shake The Hand Of A Stranger 12
55 Columbia SCM 5184 Something's Gotta Give/Boom Boom Boomerang 10
55 Columbia SCM 5191 The Banjo's Back In Town (with Big Ben Banjo Band)/Ten Little Kisses 6
55 Columbia SCM 5210 Bring Me A Bluebird/The Old Pi-anna Rag 6
57 Columbia DB 3874 I Dreamed/The Charge Of The Light Brigade (B-side with ex-R.S.M. Brittain) 5
57 Columbia DB 3935 Rock-A-Billy/A Needle And Thread 15
57 Columbia DB 3970 One/It's Fun Finding Out About London (with Big Ben Banjo Band) 6
56 Columbia SCM 5286 Sweet Old Fashioned Girl/The Treasure Of Love 10

DAVID ANTHONY
(see also Dave Anthony's Moods)
68 Island WI 3148 All Night/Out Of My Mind 40

DAVE ANTHONY'S MOODS
(see also David Anthony)
66 Parlophone R 5438 New Directions/Give It A Chance 75

MINT VALUE £

JIM ANTHONY

72	Satril SAT 4	Sasha/White Rose	5

MARC ANTHONY

63	Stateside SS 210	Let's All Cheer Again/Why Do I Love You	12

MARK ANTHONY & JETS

70	Unity UN 565	More Balls/TONY KING: Bum Ball (Chapter II)	5

MARKE ANTHONY

60	Decca F11242	Why Didn't You Tell Me/Foolishly	6

RAY ANTHONY

(see also Gordon MacRae & Ray Anthony)

55	Capitol CL 14205	I Don't Hurt Anymore/Woman's World	5
55	Capitol CL 14243	Juke Box Special/Heat Wave	10
55	Capitol CL 14275	Baby You/Happy Hornblowers (with Dick Stabile Orchestra)	5
55	Capitol CL 14306	Sluefoot/Something's Gotta Give	5
55	Capitol CL 14321	Learnin' The Blues/Mmmm Mamie	5
55	Capitol CL 14345	Pete Kelly's Blues/DC-7	5
55	Capitol CL 14354	Hernando's Hideaway/The Bunny Hop	10
56	Capitol CL 14525	Flip-Flop/Hurricane Anthony	10
56	Capitol CL 14670	Love Is Just Around The Corner/Dancing Lovers	5
57	Capitol CL 14689	Rock Around The Rock Pile/The Girl Can't Help It	40
57	Capitol CL 14689	Rock Around The Rock Pile/The Girl Can't Help It	12
57	Capitol CL 14703	Plymouth Rock/Calypso Dance	10
57	Capitol CL 14740	The Incredible Shrinking Man/This Could Be The Night	5
57	Capitol CL 14752	The Lonely Trumpet/Cello-phane	5
57	Capitol CL 14769	The Bunny Hop/The Hokey Pokey	8
57	Capitol CL 14775	Drive-In/Show Me The Way To Go Home	5
58	Capitol CL 14929	Peter Gunn/Tango For Two (Mmm Shall We Dance?)	10
59	Capitol CL 15019	The Bunny Hop Rock/Walkin' To Mother's	10
57	Capitol EAP 1-823	THE GIRL CAN'T HELP IT (EP)	40
57	Capitol EAP 1-958	ROCK AND ROLL WITH RAY ANTHONY (EP)	40

RAY ANTHONY

79	Mango Media 23	The Arabian Funk/Time	20

RAYBURN ANTHONY

60	London HLS 9167	Who's Gonna Shoe Your Pretty Little Feet/There's No Tomorrow	40

RICHARD ANTHONY

65	Columbia SCX 3566	RICHARD ANTHONY (LP, stereo)	15

VAL ANTHONY

53	Columbia SCM 5079	Walk With The Wind/No Tears, No Regrets	5
54	Columbia SCM 5103	The Heart Of A Fool/The Portuguese Fishermen	5

ANTHONY & IMPERIALS

(see under Little Anthony & Imperials)

ANTHRAX (U.K.)

83	Small Wonder SMALL 27	THEY'VE GOT IT ALL WRONG (EP, p/s)	10
83	Crass 221984/9	CAPITALISM IS CANNIBALISM (EP, foldout p/s)	12

ANTHRAX (U.S.)

86	Island 12ISP 285	Madhouse/Air/God Save The Queen (12", picture disc)	15
86	Island 12IS 285	Madhouse/Air/God Save The Queen (12", p/s with patch)	12
87	Island ISX 316	I Am The Law (live)/Bud E. Luvbomm And Satan's Lounge Band/ Madhouse (live) (red vinyl, p/s)	15
87	Island ISP 325	Indians/Sabbath Bloody Sabbath (picture disc with sticker)	5
86	Music For Nations MFN62P	SPREADING THE DISEASE (LP, picture disc)	20
87	Music For Nations MFN14P	FISTFUL OF METAL (LP, picture disc)	20
87	Island PILPS 9865	AMONG THE LIVING (LP, picture disc)	25

ANTI ESTABLISHMENT

80	Charnel House CADAV 1	1980/Mechanical Man (p/s)	10
82	Glass GLASS 022	Future Girl/No Trust (p/s)	5
83	Glass GLASS 023	Anti Men/Misunderstood (p/s)	5

ANTILLES

83	Creole CR 12-51	I've Got To Have You/Latin Dream (12")	50

ANTI NOWHERE LEAGUE

81	WXYZ ABCD 1	Streets Of London (1-sided test pressing)	35
82	WXYZ ABCD 1	So What/Streets Of London (p/s, withdrawn)	8
82	WXYZ ABCD 2	I Hate... People/Let's Break The Law (p/s)	6
82	WXYZ ABCD 4	Woman/Rocker (picture disc)	6
87	GWR A1	Crime/Working For The Company (Unreleased Test Pressing)	20
82	WXYZ LMNOP1	WE ARE...THE LEAGUE (LP)	15

ANTI PASTI

90	Dose DOSE1	FORE SORE POINTS (EP, 500 only)	18
81	Rondelet ABOUT 5	LAST CALL (LP)	12

ANTI SECT

84	Endangered Music EDR 4	Out From The Void/Hope Future Poisoned By Fear	25
83	Spiderleg SDL 16	IN DARKNESS THERE IS NO CHOICE (LP)	30
84	Big Top	LIVE IN THE DARKNESS (LP, splattered grey vinyl with insert, 1,000 only)	20
94	Vinyl Japan	PEACE IS BETTER THAN A PLACE IN HISTORY (LP)	20

ANTI SOCIAL

77	Dynamite DRO 1	Traffic Lights/Teacher Teacher (no p/s)	500

MINT VALUE £

ANTI SOCIAL

82	Beat The System BTS 2	Battle Scarred Skinheads/Sewer Rat/Official Hooligan (p/s)	12
82	Beat The System FIT 2	Too Many People/Let's Have Some (p/s)	5
82	Lightbeat SOCIAL 1	MADE IN ENGLAND (EP)	20

ANTI-SOCIAL WORKERS & MAD PROFESSOR

83	Ariwa ARI008LP	POSITIVE STYLE PUNKY REGGAE PARTY (LP)	20

ANTI SYSTEM

83	Reconcilliation RECONCILE 3	Strangelove/Oh My God	25
83	Paragon/Pax PAX 11	DEFENCE OF THE REALM (EP)	25
85	Reconcilliation RECONCILE 1	NO LAUGHING MATTER (LP)	30

ANTOINE

66	Vogue VRS 7009	Les Elucubrations D'Antoine/J'ai Oublié La Nuit	6
66	Vogue VRS 7017	Before The Good Thing/Elephants Looking At Me	6
66	Vogue VRS 7022	Ma Fete Forraine/Only These Few Snowflakes	6
68	Vogue VRS 7028	La Tramontana/Io Voglie Andaré In Guerra	6
69	Vogue VRS 7031	The Football Match/Where Did Everyone Go To	6
68	Vogue VRL 3032	ANTOINE (LP)	20

ANTOINETTE

(see also Toni Daly)

64	Decca F 11820	Jenny Let Him Go/Please Don't Hurt Me Anymore	15
64	Piccadilly 7N 35201	There He Goes (The Boy I Love)/Little Things Mean A Lot	15
65	Piccadilly 7N 35223	Thank You For Loving Me/If You Really Love Me	15
65	Piccadilly 7N 35252	Our House/What's A-Happening To Me	5
66	Piccadilly 7N 35293	Why Don't I Run Away From You/There's No-One In The Whole Wide World	30
66	Piccadilly 7N 35310	Lullaby Of Love/I'm For You	25

REY ANTON

62	Oriole CB 1722	As If I Care/After The Laughter	15
62	Oriole CB 1771	Hey Good Looking/Mary Lou	15
63	Oriole CB 1811	Peppermint Man/Can't Say More Than That (with Batons)	15
63	Oriole CB 1843	How Long Can This Last/If You Don't Want Me Now	20
64	Parlophone R 5132	You Can't Judge A Book By The Cover/It's Cold Outside (with Peppermint Men)	35
64	Parlophone R 5172	Heard It All Before/I Want You (with Peppermint Men)	15
65	Parlophone R 5245	Wishbone/Kingsway (with Peppermint Men)	20
65	Parlophone R 5274	Girl You Don't Know Me/Don't Treat Me Bad (with Peppermint Men)	30
65	Parlophone R 5310	Nothing Comes Easy/Breakout (with Peppermint Men)	15
65	Parlophone R 5358	Premeditation/Now That It's Over (with Pro Form)	30
66	Parlophone R 5420	Don't You Worry Boy/Hold It Babe (with Pro Formula)	15
66	Parlophone R 5487	Things Get Better/Newsboy (with Pro Form)	15

ANTONIOU

(see also Atmosfear)

82	Elite DAZZ 17	Sound On Sound/Street Sound (12" stickered plain sleeve)	8

TONY ANTONIU

84	Spartan 12 SP 12	Send In The Night/(Extended Version) (12")	30

DAVE ANTONY

(see also Dave Anthony['s Moods])

68	Mercury MF 1031	Race With The Wind/Hide And Seek	20

MARK ANTONY & AVENGERS

	Malconi MCD LP 17	MARK ANTONY & THE AVENGERS (LP, private pressing, plain sleeve)	100

MIKI ANTONY

70	RCA 1906	Cinnamon/Easy Rider	7
71	Columbia DB 8759	Sally Sunshine/It's Good To See You	8
72	Bell 1275	If It Wasn't For The Reason I Love You/Try It, You'll Like It	6

ANTS

63	Parlophone R 5082	Christmas Star/Wandering	10

ANVIL FLUTES & CAPRICORN VOICES

68	Deram DML/SML 1026	SOMETHING NEW IS COMING (LP)	25

ANNIE ANXIETY

(see also Crass)

81	Crass Records 32984/3	BARBED WIRE HALO: Cyanide Tears/Hello Horror (7")	8
84	Corpus Christi CHRIST 10	SOUL POSSESSION (LP)	12

AOA

85	COR GURT 4	WHO ARE THEY TRYING TO CON (EP, 12")	20
86	COR GURT 12	UNLIMITED GENOCIDE (Split LP with OI POLLOI, insert)	20
88	ENDANGERED EDR LP 2	SATISFACTORY ARRANGEMENT (LP)	30

APARTMENT

80	Heartbeat PULSE 7	The Car/Winter (p/s)	20

APATCHI BAND

73	President PT 392	Issmak/Crashpad	30

APEX RHYTHM & BLUES ALLSTARS

(see also Ian Hunter)

59	John Lever AP 100	Yorkshire Relish/Caravan	40
60s	John Lever JLEP 1	APEX RHYTHM & BLUES ALLSTARS (EP, no p/s)	350

APHEX TWIN

(see also Caustic Window, Polygon Window, Q-Chastic, Kosmic Kommando)

91	Mighty Force 01	ANALOGUE BUBBLEBATH VOL. 1 (12" EP, label on 1 side only,	

			MINT VALUE £
		other side has white label, some stamped)	20
91	Rabbit City CUT 002	ANALOGUE BUBBLEBATH VOL. 2 (12" EP, stamped white label)	40
92	R&S RSUK 12	Didgeridoo/Analogue Bubblebath 1/Flaphead/Isoprophlex (12", stickered R&S sleeve, 'Isoprophlex' is actually 'Phloam')	10
92	R&S RSUK 12CD	Didgeridoo/Analogue Bubblebath 1/Flaphead/Isoprophlex (CD, 'Isoprophlex' is actually 'Phloam')	50
93	Rephlex CAT 008	ANALOGUE BUBBLEBATH VOL. 3 (12" EP, paper bag sleeve)	15
93	Rephlex CAT 008	ANALOGUE BUBBLEBATH VOL. 3 (CD, bubble wrap sleeve)	18
93	Warp WAP 39	On/73-Yips/D-Scape/Xepha (12", p/s)	8
93	Warp WAP 39R	On (D-Scape Mix)/On (Reload Mix)/On (µ-Ziq Mix)/On (28 Mix) (12", p/s)	10
93	Warp WAP 60	VENTOLIN EP (12", p/s)	15
93	Warp WAP 60R	VENTOLIN EP (THE REMIXES) (12", p/s)	15
93	Warp WAP 60/WAP 60R	VENTOLIN EP (2 x 12", includes both above 12"s, stickered gatefold p/s)	25
94	Rephlex CAT 019 EP	ANALOGUE BUBBLEBATH VOL. 4 (12" EP, p/s with insert, as AFX)	10
94	Rephlex CAT 019 CD	ANALOGUE BUBBLEBATH VOL. 4 (CD, as AFX)	20
95	Warp WAP 63	Donkey Rhubarb/Vaz Deferenz/Icct Hedral (Philip Glass Orchestration)/ Pancake Lizard (12", p/s)	12
95	Warp WAP 67	HANGABLE AUTO BULB EP (12",as AFX)	40
95	Warp WAP 69	HANGABLE AUTO BULB 2 EP (12", as AFX)	40
97	Warp WAP 94P/WAP 94RP	Come To Daddy(Pappy Mix)/Flim/Come To Daddy (Little Lord Faulteroy Mix)/ Bucephalus Bouncing Ball/To Cure A Weakling Child (Contour Regard)/ Funny Little Man/Come To Daddy (Mummy Mix)/IZ-US (2 x promo 12", 500 only)	40
01	Warp DRUKQS 01 54	Cymru Beats (Argonaut Mix)/Cock 10 (Delco Freedom Mix) (12", stickered black sleeve)	10
05	Rephlex ANALORD 10	Fenix Funk 5/XMD 5a (12" in PVC binder with 12 sleeves for the Analord series)	180
05	Rephlex ANALORD 10	Fenix Funk 5/XMD 5a (12", picture disc)	8
92	R&S/Apollo AMBLP 3922	SELECTED AMBIENT WORKS 85-92 (2-LP, 1st issue with no barcode)	25
94	Warp WARPLP 21	SELECTED AMBIENT WORKS VOL. 2 (3-LP, brown vinyl, black and white sleeve with numbered sticker)	50
94	Warp WARPLP 21	SELECTED AMBIENT WORKS VOL. 2 (3-LP, black vinyl, stickered colour sleeve)	30
95	Warp WARPLP 30	I CARE BECAUSE YOU DO (2-LP, stickered sleeve)	15
96	Warp WARPLP 43	RICHARD D. JAMES (LP)	12
02	Warp WARPLP 92X	DRUKQS (4-LP in 12" x 17" numbered box, 1,000 only)	25

APHRODITE'S CHILD

(see also Vangelis, Forminx)

68	Mercury MF 1039	Rain & Tears/Don't Try To Catch A River	15
69	Mercury MF 1079	End Of The World/You Always Stand In My Way	10
69	Polydor 56769	I Want To Live/Magic Mirror	10
69	Polydor 56785	Let Me Love, Let Me Live/Marie Jolie	5
70	Polydor 56791	It's Five O'Clock/Funky Mary	5
72	Vertigo 6032 900	Break/Babylon	15
68	Mercury SMCL 20140	END OF THE WORLD/RAIN AND TEARS (LP, black/silver label, laminated sleeve)	35
69	Polydor 2384 005	IT'S FIVE O'CLOCK (LP, gatefold sleeve)	40
72	Vertigo 6673 001	666 - THE APOCALYPSE OF JOHN (2-LP, swirl labels, gatefold, red laminated sleeve. NB. Sleeve has catalogue number 6673 001 whilst albums have 6333500/6333501 on labels)	400
77	Vertigo 6641 581	666 (2-LP, reissue, as Aphrodite's Child with Demis Roussos & Vangelis, different sleeve, 'spaceship' labels)	30

APOCALYPSE

82	Gate GATE 2	Storm Child/Chosen Few (p/s)	125

APOLLO XI

(see also Orb)

91	Wau! Mr. Modo APOLLO 11	Peace (In The Middle East) (7" Mix 2)/Peace (Sea Of Tranquility Mix)/ Peace (Is This Really The Orb? Mix) (12")	10

APOLLOS

60	Mercury AMT 1096	Rockin' Horses/Just Dreaming	10

APOSTOLIC INTERVENTION

(see also Small Faces, Humble Pie)

67	Immediate IM 043	(Tell Me) Have You Ever Seen Me/Madame Garcia	220

APPALACHIANS

63	HMV POP 1158	Bony Moronie/It Takes A Man	20

APPALACHIANS

65	Mercury MF 930	Look Away/My Broken Heart (this is a different band)	10

APPALOOSA

(see also Global Communications)

94	Recoil RCL 003	UNPLUGGED EP (12", 3-track, die-cut sleeve)	15

DAVE APPELL (& APPLEJACKS)

(see also Applejacks [U.S.], John Zacherle)

55	Brunswick 05396	Smarter/My Heart Will Wait For You (as Dave Appell & Applejacks)	12
57	Columbia DB 3894	Country Dance/Applejack (as Dave Appell & Applejacks)	12
62	Columbia DB 4763	Happy Jose/Noivous (as Dave Appell & Orchestra)	6

APPLE

68	Page One POF 101	Let's Take A Trip Down The Rhine/Buffalo Billy Can	65
68	Page One POF 110	Doctor Rock/The Other Side	75
69	Page One POLS 016	AN APPLE A DAY (LP, textured sleeve, blue/silver labels with 'apple' insert)	900
69	Page One POLS 016	AN APPLE A DAY (LP, without 'apple' insert)	700

GEOFF APPLEBY

76	Virgin VS157	Hey Sadie/Move On Down The Road	8

APPLEJACKS (U.K.)

64	Decca F 11833	Tell Me When/Baby Jane	6

MINT VALUE £

64 Decca F 11916 Like Dreamers Do/Everybody Fall Down 8
64 Decca F 11981 Three Little Words/You're The One For Me 7
65 Decca F 12050 Chim Chim Chiree/It's Not A Game Anymore (export, unissued) 20
65 Decca F 12106 It's Not A Game Anymore/Bye Bye Girl 10
65 Decca F 12216 I Go To Sleep/Make Up Or Break Up 20
65 Decca F 12301 I'm Through/We Gotta Get Together 8
67 CBS 202615 You've Been Cheating/Love Was In My Eyes 30
64 Decca LK 4635 THE APPLEJACKS (LP) 150

APPLEJACKS (U.S.)
(see also Dave Appell)
58 London HLU 8753 Mexican Hat Rock/Stop, Stop Red Light 10
58 London HL 7063 Mexican Hat Rock/Stop, Stop Red Light (export issue) 10
59 London HLU 8806 Rocka-Conga/Am I Blue 15
59 London HLU 8806 Rocka-Conga/Am I Blue 12
60 Top Rank JAR 273 Circle Dance/Love Scene 5

APPLE PIE AND CUSTARD
74 Philips 6006439 Five Sisters/Doctor Fantastic 6
72 Pye 7N 45145 You Could Have Been A Lady/Teacher 6

APPLETREE THEATRE
68 Verve (S)VLP 6018 PLAYBACK (LP) 40

CHARLIE APPLEWHITE
54 Brunswick 05358 No One But You/Parade 5
55 Brunswick 05411 Prize Of Gold/Mister Publisher (Have I Got A Song For You) 5
55 Brunswick 05416 Blue Star - The Medic Theme/A Prayer Was Born 18

APPOLINAIRES
Two Tone 20 TT Feelings Gone/Feelings Back (paper labels) 10

APPRECIATIONS
77 Destiny 1016 I Can't Hide It/Instrumental Version (2 acetates only) 100

APRIL SHOWERS
84 Chrysalis CHS 122787 Abandon Ship/Everytime We Say Goodbye (12", p/s) 70

APRIL WINE
72 Pye 7N 45145 You Could Have Been A Lady/Teacher 25
72 Pye 7N 45163 Bad Side Of The Moon/Believe In Me 10
73 Pye 7N 45624 Weeping Widow/Just Like That 6
76 London HLU 10549 You Won't Dance With Me/Shot Down 8
81 Capitol CL 16184 Just Between You And Me/Big City Girls (P/S) 5

AQUA LEVI & THE ROOTS IMENSION
91 Roots RI 001 His Foundation/His Dub (12") 50
92 Roots RI 003 Gather My Children/Gather My Dub (12") 50

AQUARIAN AGE
(see also Twink, Tomorrow, Clem Cattini Ork, Nicky Hopkins)
68 Parlophone R 5700 10,000 Words In A Cardboard Box/Good Wizard Meets Naughty Wizard 400

AQUARIAN DREAM
(see also Norman Connors)
79 Buddah BDSL 488 Phoenix/East 6th Street (12") 40
76 Buddah DISC 008 NORMAN CONNERS PRESENTS AQUARIAN DREAM (LP) 50

AQUARIANS
(see also Augustus Pablo, Herman)
71 Ackee ACK 135 Circy Cap/Circy Version 12
71 Ackee ACK 137 Rebel/Invasion Version 35

AQUATONES
58 London HLO 8631 You/She's The One For Me 50
58 London HLO 8631 You/She's The One For Me (78) 20

AQUILA
(see also Patrick Campbell-Lyons)
70 RCA SF 8126 THE AQUILA SUITE (LP, gatefold sleeve, orange labels) 70

ARABESQUE
72 Polydor 2058-237 Fariytale/Solace And Jamboree 12

ARABIS
69 Doctor Bird DB 1204 Jump High Jump Low/TONY SHABAZZ: Stool Pigeon 18

ARABS
(see also Prince Far I)
78 Hit Run APLP 9002 CRY TUFF - DUB ENCOUNTER CHAPTER 1 55

ARAB STRAP
96 Chemikal U'nd CHEM 007 The First Big Weekend/Gilded (700 only) 30
99 Chemikal Un'd CHEM 017 Hey! Fever/Girls Of Summer (p/s) 15
98 Too Many Cooks BROTH 001 Live: Packs Of Three/Blood 18
03 Chemikal underground CHEM 0677 THE SHY RETIRER EP : Radio Edit, Dirty Hospital Remix, Why Can't This Be Love, Good Part, New Saturday (12") 10
96 Chemikal U'nd CHEM 010 THE WEEK NEVER STARTS AROUND HERE (LP) 25
98 Chemikal U'nd CHEM 021 PHILOPHOBIA (2-LP) 20
99 Go! Beat 547387 MAD FOR SADNESS (LP, 1000 only) 25
99 Go! Beat 547387 2 MAD FOR SADNESS (CD, 3000 only) 20
02 Private Pressing QUIET VIOLENCE (LP) 30

ARAGORN
81 Neat NEAT 07 Black Ice/Noonday (p/s) 15

MINT VALUE £

A RAINCOAT

76	EMI EMI 2393	It Came In The Night/Morocco	15
75	EMI EMI 2289	I Love You For Your Mind (Not Your Body)/Vote For Me	5

ARANBEE POP SYMPHONY ORCHESTRA

(see also Andrew Oldham Orchestra, Keith Richard[s])

66	Immediate IMLP/IMSP 003	TODAY'S POP SYMPHONY (LP, lilac labels)	100

ARBORS

69	CBS 4640	Motel Overture/Touch Me	7

ARBRE

75	DJM DJS 397	Fallin'/Doin' Alright	10
76	DJM DJS 10716	Senorita/Zero To Four (with promo p/s)	12

ARC

(see also Heavy Jelly, Skip Bifferty, Bell & Arc, Blockheads)

71	Decca SKL-R 5077	ARC . . . AT THIS (LP, blue/silver "boxed" Decca labels)	100

ARC

80	Orchrist ORC 1	Tribute (To Mike Hailwood) (p/s)	75
81	Slipped Disc SD001	War Of The Ring/Ice Cream Theme (p/s)	100

ARCADE FIRE

03	Private Pressing	ARCADE FIRE DEMO EP (CD, p/s Known as Us Kids Now)	35
05	Rough Trade RTRADS225	Neighbourhood #2/My Buddy (p/s)	7
05	Rough Trade RTRADS232	Neighbourhood #2/My Buddy (luminous vinyl, p/s)	7
05	Rough Trade RTRADSX 232	Neighbourhood #3 (live)/Power Out (Live)/This Must Be The Place (Live, featuring David Byrne) (p/s)	8
05	Rough Trade RTRADS 252	Rebellion (Lies)/Rebellion (Lies) (Live) (p/s, white vinyl)	5
05	Rough Trade RTRADLP 219	FUNERAL (LP)	15

ARCADIA

(see also Duran Duran)

85	EMI 12 NSR 1	Election Day (Consensus Mix)/Election Day (7" Version)/She's Moody And Grey She's Mean And She's Restless 12" promo in foil sleeve, sealed)	20
85	EMI 12 NSR 1	Election Day (Consensus Mix)/Election Day (7" Version)/She's Moody And Grey She's Mean And She's Restless 12" promo in foil sleeve, unsealed)	15
85	EMI 12 NSRA 1	Election Day (Cryptic Cut No Voice Mix)/Election Day (7" Mix)/ Election Day (Consensus Mix) (12", p/s)	8
85	EMI 12 NSRX 1	Election Day (The Fact And Story Mix) (12", 1-sided, white label, plain black black sleeve, promo only)	35
85	EMI 12 NSR 2	The Promise (Extended Remix)/Rose Arcana/The Promise 7" version (12" gold cover with sticker and poster insert)	30
86	EMI 12 NSR 3	The Flame (Extended Remix)/Yo Homeboy Mix/Election Day - Early Rough Mix (12" p/s)	12

ARCADIUM

(see also Kingdom Come, 'Middle Earth Sampler' in Various Artists)

69	Middle Earth MDS 102	Sing My Song/Riding Alone	200
69	Middle Earth MDLS 302	BREATHE AWHILE (LP, laminated sleeve)	450

DON ARCHELL

63	Decca F 11749	When I Fall In Love/Stay Away	6

ARCTIC MONKEYS

05	Bang Bang BANGB 71	FIVE MINUTES WITH EP (500 only, p/s)	100
05	Bang Bang BANGBCD	FIVE MINUTES WITH EP (CD, 1000 only)	100
05	Domino RUG 212	I Bet You Look Good On The Dancefloor/ Bigger Boys And Stolen Sweethearts (p/s)	7
07	Domino RUG 258	Matador/Deframe2r (die-cut p/s, white vinyl, 1000 only)	10
07	Domino RUF 279	Death Ramps/Nettles (As DEATH RAMPS, 250 only, stamped labels)	15
06	Domino FAKE 1P	Fake Tales Of San Francisco/From The Ritz To The Rubble (white label promo)	30
09	Domino RUG349CDP2	Cornerstone/Catapult/Sketched/Fright Lined DIning Room (CD promo, jewel case)	25
08	Domino DOMDVD005X	AT THE APOLLO (LP, box set with poster, DVD & stickered sleeve)	35

ARCTURUS

96	Ancient Lore ALC 002 PLP	ASPERA HIEMS SYMFONIA (LP, picture disc, 1000 only)	20

ARDELLS

63	Columbia DB 7138	Eefananny/Lonely Valley	6

TONI ARDEN

55	HMV 7M 314	Beware/I'll Step Aside	8
57	Brunswick 05645	Little By Little/Without Love (There Is Nothing)	10
57	Brunswick 05679	My Empty Heart/Like A Baby	10
58	Brunswick 05745	Padre/All At Once	5

NEIL ARDLEY

(see also Ian Carr, Don Rendell, New Jazz Orchestra, Michael Gibbs)

79	Decca FR 13847	Leap In The Dark/Summer Ice	5
65	Decca SKL 4690	WESTERN UNION (LP)	150
70	Columbia SCX 6414	GREEK VARIATIONS (LP, with Ian Carr & Don Rendell)	250
72	Regal Zono. SLRZ 1028	A SYMPHONY OF AMARANTHS (LP, red/silver labels)	200
74	Argo ZDA 164/5	WILL POWER (2-LP, with Ian Carr, Stan Tracey & Mike Gibbs)	125
75	Gull GULP 1018	KALEIDOSCOPE OF RAINBOWS (LP)	25
78	Decca TXS-R 133	HARMONY OF THE SPHERES (LP, featuring John Martyn)	18

AREA CODE 615

70	Polydor 2066 249	Stone Fox Chase/Always The Same	6

COLIN AREETY

72	Deram DM 370	Holy Cow/Can't Do It For You	8

MINT VALUE £

ARENA TWINS

59 London HL 7071 — Mama, Care Mama/Little Pig (export issue) . . . 20

ARGENT

(see also Zombies, Unit 4 + 2, Roulettes, John Verity Band, Phoenix)

74 Epic SEPC 2849 — Keep On Rollin'/I Am The Dance Of Ages . . . 10
72 Epic S EPC 7786 — Hold Your Head Up/Keep On Rollin' . . . 5
70 CBS 63781 — ARGENT (LP, gatefold sleeve) . . . 50
71 Epic EPC 64190 — RING OF HANDS (LP, gatefold sleeve) . . . 35
72 Epic EPC 64962 — ALL TOGETHER NOW (LP, gatefold sleeve, with booklet) . . . 25
74 Epic EQ 32195/Q 65475 — IN DEEP (LP, quadrophonic) . . . 25
75 Epic EPC 80691 — CIRCUS (LP, with lyric insert) . . . 15
75 RCA RS 1020 — COUNTERPOINTS (LP) . . . 15

ARGONAUTS

(see also Madness)

85 Lyntone LYN 18249/50 — Apeman/Under My Thumb (signed white label, no p/s) . . . 60

ARGOSY

(see also Elton John, Supertramp)

69 DJM DJS 214 — Mr. Boyd/Imagine . . . 100

ARGUS

(see also People Like Us)

84 ABS SRT 4KS258 — Holocaust/The Widow (title sleeve) . . . 250

ARIEL

74 Harvest HAR 5085 — Jamaican Farewell/And I'm Blue . . . 7
74 Harvest HAR 5088 — Yeah Tonite/Laughing Man . . . 20

ARIZONA SWAMP COMPANY

(see also Nashville Teens)

70 Parlophone R 5841 — Train Keeps Rollin'/Tennessee Woman . . . 30

DEE ARLEN

59 Philips PB 950 — Stay/Why Should We Wait Any Longer . . . 8

STEVE ARLEN

58 Melodisc M 1458 — That's Love/Easy 'N' Free . . . 8
60 HMV POP 835 — Suddenly I'm In Love/Happy Days (Hoppahey) . . . 7

DEKE ARLON (& OFFBEATS)

64 HMV POP 1340 — I Need You/I Must Go And Tell Her . . . 10
64 Columbia DB 7194 — I'm Just A Boy/Can't Make Up My Mind . . . 20
65 Columbia DB 7487 — If I Didn't Have A Dime/Gotta Little Girl . . . 5
65 Columbia DB 7753 — Little Piece Of Paper/I've Been Away (solo) . . . 5
66 Columbia DB 7841 — Hard Times For Young Lovers/Little Boy (solo) . . . 10

ARMADA ORCHESTRA/ULTRAFUNK

76 Contempo CX13 — For The Love Of Money/Sting Your Jaws (Part 1) (12") . . . 20

ARMAGEDDON

(see also Keith Relf, Steamhammer, Captain Beyond)

75 A&M AMLH 64513 — ARMAGEDDON (LP, with lyric inner sleeve, silver labels) . . . 40

ARMANDO

00 Trax UK DJTRX 002 — New World Order (Remix) (12", promo) . . . 8

JOAN ARMATRADING

72 Cube HIFLY 12 — WHATEVER'S FOR US (LP) . . . 15

ARMED FORCE

80 Armed Forces AF1 — Popstar/Attack (p/s, 500 only) . . . 20

ARMENIAN JAZZ QUARTET

57 London HLR 8454 — Pretty Girl/Harem Dance . . . 10

ARMENTA

83 Savoir Faire FAIT 005 — I Wanna Be With You/Part 2/Part 3 (12") . . . 15

ARMPIT JUG BAND

75 Cottage COT 201/R — NO SWEAT (LP) . . . 12

RUSSELL ARMS

57 London HLB 8406 — Cinco Robles (Five Oaks)/The World Is Made Of Lisa (gold label) . . . 25
57 London HLB 8406 — Cinco Robles (Five Oaks)/The World Is Made Of Lisa (silver label) . . . 12
57 London HL 7018 — Cinco Robles (Five Oaks)/The World Is Made Of Lisa (export issue) . . . 12

ARMS & LEGS

(see also Joe Jackson)

76 MAM MAM 140 — Janice/She'll Surprise You . . . 8
76 MAM MAM 147 — Heat Of The Night/Good Times . . . 8
77 MAM MAM 156 — Is There Any More Wine/She'll Surprise You . . . 8

CHUCK ARMSTRONG

73 Action ACT 4620 — God Bless The Children/Black Foxy Woman . . . 15

FRANKIE ARMSTRONG (& FRIENDS)

(see also A.L. Lloyd)

79 Action Against Corrie RRFA 001 — We Must Choose/RED RINSE: A Woman's Right To Choose (private pressing) . . 30
72 Topic 12TS 216 — LOVELY ON THE WATER (LP) . . . 30
75 Topic 12TS 273 — SONGS AND BALLADS (LP) . . . 18

JACK ARMSTRONG

57 Beltona SEP 43 — NORTHUMBRIAN PIPE MUSIC (EP) . . . 8
74 Saydisc SDL 252 — CELEBRATED MINSTREL (LP) . . . 20

MINT VALUE £

LORNA ARMSTRONG

74	Ackee 535	Dance With Me/Lonely Nights	15

LOUIS ARMSTRONG

(see also Danny Kaye, Ella Fitzgerald & Louis Armstrong, Nina & Frederik, Bing Crosby, Earl 'Fatha' Hines, Red Onion Jazz Babies)

53	Columbia SCM 5061	King Of The Zulus/Lonesome Blues	5
54	Columbia SCM 5118	Chicago Breakdown/Twelfth Street Rag	5
54	Columbia SCM 5142	I'm Not Rough/Put 'Em Down Blues	5
54	Brunswick 05303	Basin Street Blues (Parts 1 & 2)	5
54	Brunswick 05332	Skokiaan (Parts 1 & 2)	5
54	Brunswick 05347	Muskrat Ramble/Someday You'll Be Sorry (B-side with Commanders)	5
55	Brunswick 05364	Trees/Spooks	5
55	Brunswick 05400	Ko Ko Mo (I Love You So)/Struttin' With Some Barbecue (with Gary Crosby)	7
59	Philips PB 967	Mack The Knife/The Faithful Hussar	6
69	United Artists UP 35059	We Have All The Time In The World/Pretty Little Missy	20
69	United Artists UA 3172	We Have All The Time In The World/Pretty Little Missy (reissue, p/s)	15

LPs

51	Brunswick LA 8528	LOUIS ARMSTRONG CLASSICS (10")	12
51	Brunswick LA 8534	JAZZ CONCERT (10")	12
52	Brunswick LA 8537	NEW ORLEANS DAYS (10")	12
52	Brunswick LAT 8017	SATCHMO AT SYMPHONY HALL	12
52	Brunswick LAT 8018	SATCHMO AT SYMPHONY HALL	12
52	Brunswick LAT 8019	SATCHMO AT PASADENA	12
53	Brunswick LA 8597	LOUIS ARMSTRONG JAZZ - CLASSICS (10")	12
53	London AL 3501	PLAYS THE BLUES (10")	15
53	Columbia 33S 1007	JAZZIN' WITH ARMSTRONG (10")	12
53	HMV DLP 1015	NEW YORK TOWN HALL CONCERT 1947 (10")	12
54	Columbia 33SX 1029	LOUIS ARMSTRONG AND HIS HOT FIVE	12
54	HMV DLP 1036	LAUGHIN' LOUIS (10")	12
54	Columbia 33S 1041	LOUIS ARMSTRONG AND HIS HOT SEVEN (10")	12
54	Brunswick LA 8679	SATCHMO SERENADES (10")	12
54	Brunswick LA 8681	LOUIS ARMSTRONG AND THE MILLS BROTHERS (10")	12
54	Brunswick LA 8691	BASIN STREET BLUES (10")	12
55	Columbia 33S 1058	RENDEZVOUS AT THE SUNSET CAFE (10")	12
55	Columbia 33S 1069	LOUIS ARMSTRONG (10")	12
55	HMV DLP 1105	SATCHMO SESSION (10")	12
55	Brunswick LA 8698	LOUIS' HOT FIVES AND SEVENS (10")	12
55	Brunswick LA 8700	BLUEBERRY HILL (10")	12
58	Fontana TFR 6003	LOUIS ARMSTRONG AND HIS HOT FIVE (10")	12

B.J. ARNAU

72	Mojo 2092 028	I Want To Go Back There Again/I Love You	5

GINNY ARNELL

60	Brunswick 05836	Carnival/We	8
63	MGM MGM 1217	Dumb Head/How Many Times Can One Heart Break	25
63	MGM MGM 1243	I Wish I Knew What Dress To Wear/He's My Little Devil	20
65	MGM MGM 1270	Just Like A Boy/Portrait Of A Fool	15
65	MGM MGM 1283	Little Bit Of Love/B-I-I-I-Why	20

CHICO ARNEZ (& HIS LATIN AMERICAN ORCHESTRA)

59	Pye N 15196	Yashmak/Ain't She Sweet	15
59	Pye N 15196	Yashmak/Ain't She Sweet (78)	10
69	Columbia DB 8642	Hippy Parade/Tina	8
69	Columbia DB 8597	Eso Beso/One For Pancho	6
71	Gemini GMS 019	Leg Box/Reggae Deck	6
68	Columbia SCX6265	FROM CHICO...WITH LOVE (LP)	15
69	Studio 2 TWO 279	CHICO (LP)	18
71	Gemini GM 2006	THIS IS CHICO (LP)	18
72	Contour 2870 153	NEW SOUNDS OF CHICO ARNEZ (LP)	15

CALVIN ARNOLD

68	MGM MGM 1378	Funky Way/Snatchin' Back	12
68	MGM MGM 1449	Mama In Law/Mini Skirt	15

EDDY ARNOLD

54	HMV 7MC 10	Prayer/Robe Of Calvary (export issue)	10
54	HMV 7MC 16	Free Home Demonstrations/If I Never Get To Heaven (export issue)	10
54	HMV 7MC 19	Second Fling/My Everything (export issue)	10
54	HMV 7MC 22	Hep Cat Baby/This Is The Thanks I Get (For Loving You) (export issue)	30
55	HMV 7MC 32	In Time/Two Kinds Of Love (export issue)	10
55	HMV 7M 339	I Walked Alone Last Night/The Richest Man (In The World)	8
57	RCA RCA 1008	Gonna Find Me A Bluebird/Little Bit	7
57	RCA RCA 1017	Scarlet Ribbons/Bayou Baby (A Cajun Lullaby)	6
58	RCA RCA 1057	Little Miss Sunbeam/My Darling, My Darling	6
59	RCA RCA 1138	Tennessee Stud/What's The Good (Of All This Love)	8
60	RCA RCA 1212	Just Out Of Reach/Before This Day Ends	5
66	RCA 1519	I Want To Go With You/Mary Claire Melvina Rebecca Jane	5
66	RCA 1529	If You Were Mine, Mary/Molly Ddarling	5
54	HMV 7EG 8020	EDDY ARNOLD (EP)	15
55	HMV 7EG 8080	CHAPEL ON THE HILL (EP)	10
59	RCA Camden CDN 133	EDDY ARNOLD (LP)	15
59	RCA RD 27155	THEREBY HANGS A TALE (LP)	15

KOKOMO ARNOLD

69	Saydisc Matchbox SDR 163	KOKOMO ARNOLD (LP)	35

PAUL ARNOLD

(see also Overlanders)

67	Pye 7N 17317	Somewhere In A Rainbow/Got A Feeling	7

MINT VALUE £

P.P. ARNOLD

(see also Ikettes, Nice, Small Faces, Spectrum, P.P. & Primes)

66	Immediate IM 040	Everything's Gonna Be Alright/Life Is But Nothin'	120
66	Immediate IM 040	Everything's Gonna Be Alright/Life Is But Nothin' (DJ copy)	250
67	Immediate IM 047	The First Cut Is The Deepest/Speak To Me	20
67	Immediate IM 055	The Time Has Come/If You See What I Mean	18
68	Immediate IM 061	(If You Think You're) Groovy/Though It Hurts Me Badly	18
68	Immediate IM 067	Angel Of The Morning/Life Is But Nothin'	8
69	Immediate IM 079	The First Cut Is The Deepest/The Time Has Come	8
69	Polydor 56350	Bury Me Down The River/Give A Hand, Take A Hand	8
70	Polydor 2058 061	Likely Piece Of Work/May The Winds Blow	5
80	Virgin/NEMS SV 103	Angel Of The Morning/Everything's Gonna Be Alright/ The First Cut Is The Deepest/Groovy/The Time Has Come (doublepack, gatefold p/s)	10
75	Immediate IM 109	First Cut Is The Deepest/King Of Kings (re-issue)	10
67	Immediate IMLP/IMSP 011	THE FIRST LADY OF IMMEDIATE (LP, withdrawn)	400
68	Immediate IMSP 017	KAFUNTA (LP, gatefold sleeve)	60

P.P. ARNOLD & THE JEFF WAYNE SINGERS

	Pepsi Lyntone 2498	We've Got Pepsi (1-sided with Pepsi Company sleeve)	15

AROVANE

99	City Centre BLOCK 1	Occer (plain black sleeve, with inserts, 850 only)	10

ARPADYS

77	Polydor 2933802	ARPADYS (LP)	40

ARRIVAL

69	Decca F 12986	Friends/Don't Turn His Love Away	6
71	CBS S 7617	Family Tree/Part Of My Dream	10
70	Decca SKL 5055	ARRIVAL (LP, blue/silver with 'boxed' Decca logo)	20

ARRIVALS

69	Pye 7N 17761	Scooby Doo/She's About A Mover	12

DON ARROL

61	Decca F 11318	Everybody Likes It/It's Happening Here	6

ARROWS (U.K.)

69	Pye 7N 17756	Mercy/See Saw	5

ARROWS (U.K.)

75	RAK RAK 205	I Love Rock 'n' Roll/Broken Down Heart	18

ARROWS (U.S.)

65	Capitol CL 15386	Apache '65/Blue Guitar	7

CLIVE ARROWSMITH

74	Scratchy CHS 2027	Desire/Almost Gone	8

ARSENAL 1ST TEAM SQUAD

71	Pye 7N 46067	Good Old Arsenal/The Boys From Highbury (in p/s)	7

ARS NOVA

68	Elektra EKSN 45029	Zoroaster/Pavan For My Lady	12
68	Elektra EKSN 45034	Fields Of People/Song To The City	12
68	Elektra EKS 74020	ARS NOVA (LP, orange label, gatefold sleeve)	30
69	Atlantic 588 196	SUNSHINE AND SHADOWS (LP)	30

ART

(see also V.I.P.'s, Baron With His Pounding Piano, Spooky Tooth, Luther Grosvenor, Hapshash & Coloured Coat)

67	Island WIP 6019	What's That Sound (For What It's Worth)/Rome Take Away Three	25
69	Island WIP 6048	Room With A View/SPOOKY TOOTH: Nobody There At All (promo only)	40
75	Island WIP 6224	What's That Sound (For What It's Worth)/Flying Anchors	7
67	Island ILP 967	SUPERNATURAL FAIRY TALES (LP, first pressing, pink label with black/orange circle logo, laminated sleeve)	300
70	Island ILP 967	SUPERNATURAL FAIRY TALES (LP, second pressing, pink label with 'i' logo and factory stamped matrix numbers, those with hand written matrixes are bootlegs, laminated sleeve)	200
75	Island ILP 967	SUPERNATURAL FAIRY TALES (LP, reissue, matt sleeve, 'palm tree' label)	35

ART ATTACKS

(see also Monochrome Set, Tagmemics, Kray Cherubs)

78	Albatross TIT 1	I'm A Dalek/Neutron Bomb (p/s)	20
79	Fresh FRESH 3	First And Last: Punk Rock Stars/Rat City/First And Last (p/s)	20

ART BEARS

(see also Henry Cow, Slapp Happy)

81	Recommended RE 6622	CODA TO "MAN AND BOY" (EP, live, 1-sided clear vinyl, silk-screened p/s, 1,750 only, this price for 500 signed & numbered for subscribers)	12
78	Recommended REC 2188	HOPES AND FEARS (LP, gatefold sleeve with poster & booklet)	15
79	Recommended REC 0618	WINTER SONGS (LP, with booklet)	15
81	Recommended RE 6622	THE WORLD AS IT IS TODAY (LP, 45rpm, with booklet)	18

ARTERY

(see also Mission)

79	Limited Edition TAKE 1	Mother Moon/Pretends/Heinz (p/s)	10
80	Aardvark STEAL 3	Unbalanced/The Slide (p/s, with EP [Perhaps/Turtle/Toytown/Heinz])	8
81	Aardvark AARD 5	Cars In Motion/Life And Death (p/s)	6
81	Armageddon AS 026	Afterwards/Into The Garden (p/s)	6
82	Red Flame RFM 4	OCEANS (LP, with insert)	12
83	Red Flame RF 18	ONE AFTERNOON IN A HOT AIR BALOON (LP)	18
84	Golden Dawn GDLP 01	SECOND COMING (LP)	15
85	Golden Dawn GDLP 02	NUMBER FOUR (LP)	15

MINT VALUE £

DAVE & TONI ARTHUR

70 Trailer LER 1 — Bushes And Briars/Lazio Feher . . . 8
67 Transatlantic TRA 154 — MORNING STANDS ON TIPTOE (LP) . . . 75
69 Topic 12T 190 — THE LARK IN THE MORNING (LP, blue label) . . . 45
71 Trailer LER 2017 — HEARKEN TO THE WITCHES' RUNE (LP, red label) . . . 40

ARTHUR'S MOTHER

71 Polydor 2058093 — On The Dole/Butterfly . . . 8

ARTISTICS

66 Coral Q 72488 — I'm Gonna Miss You/Hope We Have . . . 70
66 Coral Q 72488 — I'm Gonna Miss You/Hope We Have (DJ Copy) . . . 100
67 Coral Q 72492 — Girl I Need You/I'm Glad I Met You . . . 40
67 Coral Q 72492 — Girl I Need You/I'm Glad I Met You (DJ Copy) . . . 100
70 MCA MU 1117 — I'm Gonna Miss You/Hope We Have (reissue) . . . 8
76 Brunswick BR 39 — I'm Gonna Miss You/GENE CHANDLER: There Was A Time . . . 10
66 Columbia — GET MY HANDS ON SOME LOVIN' (LP, unconfirmed existence) . . . 250

ART MOVEMENT

68 Decca F 12768 — I Love Being In Love With You/The Game Of Love . . . 12
68 Decca F 12836 — Loving Touch/Happy Song . . . 7
69 Columbia DB 8602 — Yes Sir . . . No Sir/Sally Goes Round The Moon . . . 5
70 Columbia DB 8651 — For As Long As You Need Me/Nice 'n' Easy . . . 5
70 Columbia DB 8697 — The Sooner I Get To You/Morning Girl . . . 5

ART NOUVEAUX

64 Fontana TF 483 — Extra Terrestrial Visitations/The Way To Play It . . . 30

ART OBJECTS

80 Heartbeat PULSE 10 — Showing Off To Impress The Girls/Our Silver Sister (live) (p/s) . . . 12
81 Fried Egg EGG 007 — Hard Objects/Bibliotheque/Fit Of Pique (p/s) . . . 10
81 Heartbeat HB 5 — BAGPIPE MUSIC (LP) . . . 18

ART OF NOISE

83 ZTT 100 — Beatbox/Moments In Love (12") . . . 10
84 ZTT P ZTPS 01 — Close (To The Edit)/A Time To Hear (Who's Listening) (picture disc) . . . 5
84 ZTT 12 P ZTPS 01 — Edited/A Time To Clear (It Up) (12", picture disc) . . . 8
85 ZTT 12 ZTPS 1 — CLOSE TO THE EDIT (12", stamped green label, unreleased) . . . 10
85 ZTT P ZTPS 02 — Moments In Love/Beatbox (tortoise-shaped picture disc) . . . 6
86 China WOKP 9 — Paranoimia/Why Me (shaped picture disc) . . . 15
91 China CHINX 23 — Art Of Love/(Ambience Of Love Mix) (12", p/s) . . . 10
83 ZTT ZTIS 100 — INTO BATTLE WITH THE ART OF NOISE (12" EP) . . . 8
84 ZTT ZCID Q2 — DAFT (CD) . . . 18

ART SCIENCE TECHNOLOGY

(see also Future Sound Of London, Stakker)

90 Debut DEBTX 3100 — A.S.T./Esus Flow (2 mixes) (12", p/s) . . . 12

ARTWOODS

(see also St. Valentine's Day Massacre, Keef Hartley Band, Jon Lord, Dog Soldier, Lucas & Mike Cotton Sound)

64 Decca F 12015 — Sweet Mary/If I Ever Get My Hands On You . . . 65
65 Decca F 12091 — Oh My Love/Big City . . . 45
65 Decca F 12206 — Goodbye Sisters/She Knows What To Do . . . 45
66 Decca F 12384 — I Take What I Want/I'm Looking For A Saxophonist Doubling French Horn Wearing Size 37 Boots . . . 50
66 Decca F 12465 — I Feel Good/Molly Anderson's Cookery Book . . . 50
67 Parlophone R 5590 — What Shall I Do/In The Deep End . . . 120
66 Decca DFE 8654 — JAZZ IN JEANS (EP) . . . 500
66 Decca LK 4830 — ART GALLERY (LP, red/silver label with 'unboxed' Decca logo and 'FFrr" laminated front sleeve) . . . 500
70 Decca Eclipse ECM 2025 — ART GALLERY (LP, reissue in different sleeve, also stereo [ECS 2025]) . . . 100
73 Spark SRLM 2006 — THE ARTWOODS (LP) . . . 40

ARZACHEL

(see also Egg, Steve Hillage, Khan, Hatfield & the North, National Health, Gong)

69 Evolution Z 1003 — ARZACHEL (LP, blue label, laminated front sleeve) . . . 500

ARZENBOYS

75 DJM — Bump On My Head/Instrumental Version . . . 12

A.S.A.P.

(see under Adrian Smith & Project)

ASGARD

72 Threshold TH 10 — Friends/Children Of A New Born Age . . . 6
73 Threshold TH 15 — In The Realm Of Asgard/Town Cryer . . . 6
72 Threshold THS 6 — IN THE REALM OF ASGARD (LP, white/blue label, gatefold sleeve) . . . 80

ASH

94 La La Land LA LA 001 — Jack Names The Planets/Don't Know (wraparound p/s in poly bag, 5,000 only) . 30
94 Infectious INFECT 13S — Petrol/The Little Pond/A Message From Oscar Wilde And Patrick The Brewer (p/s, 500 only) . . . 15
94 Infectious INFECT 16S — Uncle Pat/Different Today (p/s, 1,000 only) . . . 12
95 Infectious INFECT 21J — Kung Fu/Day Of The Triffids (p/s, 'Japanese' wraparound no'd p/s in poly bag) . . 8
95 Infectious INFECT 21S — Kung Fu (mispressed, 1-sided only, p/s) . . . 6
95 Infectious INFECT 21C — Kung Fu/Kung Fu (red vinyl promo) . . . 6
95 Fantastic Plastic FP 004 — Get Ready/Zero Zero Zero (red vinyl, 1,000 only, mail order only) . . . 20
95 Infectious INFECT 24S — Girl From Mars/Astral (Conversations With Toulouse Lautrec)/Cantina Band (p/s) . . 8
97 Barbie Records KEN 1 — I Only Want To Be With You/Kung Fu (Live) (silver speckled vinyl p/s, fan club 7") . . . 60
94 Infectious INFECT 14LP — TRAILER (LP, with yellow vinyl 7", "Silver Surfer"/"Jazz '59" [INFECT 14S]) . . . 20
98 Infectious INFECT60LP — NU-CLEAR SOUNDS (LP, gatefold, clear vinyl) . . . 18
96 Infectious INFECT 40LP — 1977 (LP, gatefold) . . . 18
01 Infectious INFECT 100LP — FREE ALL ANGELS (LP, gatefold) . . . 15

MINT VALUE £

VIC ASH QUARTET
(see also Maxine Sullivan, Jazz Five)

56	Tempo A 135	Blue Lou/Doxy	10
56	Tempo A 137	Early Morning/Just One Of Those Things	10
55	Jazz Today JTE 100	SESSION FOR FOUR (EP)	25
56	Nixa NJE 1002	HOAGY (EP)	15
56	Nixa NJE 1032	VIC ASH & FOUR (EP)	20
56	Columbia SEG 7634	CLARINET VIRTUOSO (EP)	15
56	Tempo EXA 44	MODERN JAZZ SCENE (EP)	40

IRVING ASHBY & HIS COMBO

58	London HLP 8578	Big Guitar/Motatin'	30
58	London HLP 8578	Big Guitar/Motatin' (78)	10

PEGGY ASHCROFT & MARTIN BEST

72	Argo ZSW 532	SENSE AND NONSENSE (LP)	40

DOUG ASHDOWN

66	CBS 202083	Guess I'm Doing Fine/I Sure Ain't Standing Still	8

ASHER D & DADDY FREDDY

87	Music Of Life NOTE 005	RAGAMUFFIN HIP HOP EP (12")	8

ASHFORD & SIMPSON
(see also Valerie Simpson)

78	Warner Bros. 12K 17096	Don't Cost You Nothing/Let Love Use Me (12")	15
78	Warner Bros. 12K 17237	It Seems To Hang On (12")	15
77	Warner Bros. K17679 (T)	Bourgie Bourgie (with correct mastering) /Love Don't Make It Right (12")	50

ASHKAN
(see also Fleetwood Mac)

70	Decca Nova DN-R 1	IN FROM THE COLD (LP, mono)	150
70	Decca Nova SDN-R 1	IN FROM THE COLD (LP, stereo)	80

MICKEY ASHMAN

60	Pye Jazz NJL 25	TAKING THE MICKEY (LP)	40
61	Pye Jazz NJL 29	THROUGH DARKEST ASHMAN (LP)	60

BUD ASHTON (& HIS GROUP)
(see also Typhoons, Jaybirds)

60	Embassy WB 409	Because They're Young/Apache	5
60	Embassy WB 422	Kommotion/STEVE STANNARD: Rockin' Goose (78)	10
61	Embassy NEP 1058	SWINGIN' GUITARS (EP)	8
63	Embassy NEP 1088	MORE SWINGING GUITARS (EP)	8

MARK ASHTON

72	United Artists UP 353390	Get Up And Groove/Barking Dogs	15

TONY ASHTON

72	Purple PUR 109	Celebration/Sloeback	5

(TONY) ASHTON & (JON) LORD
(see also Ashton Gardner & Dyke, Paice Ashton & Lord, Jon Lord, Deep Purple, Green Bullfrog)

74	Purple PUR 121	We're Gonna Make It/Band Of The Salvation Army Band	7
74	Oyster OYR 101	TONY ASHTON: The Resurrection Shuffle/Ballad Of Mr Giver	6
74	Purple TPS 3507	FIRST OF THE BIG BANDS (LP)	20

ASHTON, GARDNER & DYKE
(see also Ashton & Lord, Remo Four, Creation, Birds, Mike Hurst & Method, Badger, Medicine Head, Family)

69	Polydor 56306	Maiden Voyage/See The Sun In My Eyes	60
70	Capitol CL 15665	The Resurrection Shuffle/Hymn To Everyone	5
69	Polydor 583 081	ASHTON, GARDNER & DYKE (LP)	25
70	Capitol E-ST 563	THE WORST OF ASHTON, GARDNER AND DYKE (LP)	20
72	Capitol EA-ST 22862	WHAT A BLOODY LONG DAY IT'S BEEN (LP, gatefold sleeve)	20

ASIA
(see also Yes, Emerson Lake & Palmer, Steve Howe)o

82	Geffen GEFA 2228	Only Time Will Tell/Ride Easy (picture disc)	8
82	Geffen WA 3580	Don't Cry/True Colours (blue or green logo-shaped picture disc)	10
92	IRS 951.959	AQUA (LP, gatefold sleeve)	12

ED ASKEW

69	Fontana	ED ASKEW (LP)	30

ASLAN

76	Profile GMOR 006	PAWS FOR THOUGHT (LP)	70
77	Profile GMOR 144	SECOND HELPINGS (LP)	70

AS ONE

95	New Electronica Elec 23LP	REFLECTIONS ON REFLECTIONS (2xLP)	25
95	New Electronica Elec 26LP	CELESTIAL SOUL (2xLP)	20

ASPECTS

01	Hombre MEX033	We Get Fowl/Correct English (remix) (12")	12
99	Hombre MEX 010	REVENGE OF THE NERDS (EP)	15
98	Hombre MEX007	2012 (EP)	30

MONICA ASPELUND

77	RCA PB 9044	Lapponia/La-La, Sing A Song	8

RON ASPERY

72	Blakey BLP5989	BACK DOOR (LP)	50

GARY & VERA ASPEY

76	Topic 12TS 299	A TASTE OF HOT POT (LP)	25

MINT VALUE £

ASPHALT RIBBONS

(see also Tindersticks)

88	Tigerlily LILY 002	PASSION, COOLNESS, INDIFFERENCE (12", p/s)	30
89	In Tape IT 063	THE ORCHARD EP (p/s)	25
89	In Tape ITTI 063	THE ORCHARD EP (12", p/s)	30
89	In Tape ITTI 063	THE ORCHARD EP (12", p/s + T-Shirt inset)	35
89	In Tape ITTI 063	THE ORCHARD EP (12", 200 pressed at 48rpm and withdrawn)	30
89	In Tape IT 068	Good Love/Long Lost Uncle/The Day I Turned Bad (p/s)	35
89	In Tape ITTI 068	Good Love/Long Lost Uncle/The Day I Turned Bad (12", p/s)	20
89	In Tape IT 6545 1	Over Again/EVA: Unquenchable (p/s, promo only)	15
91	ETT 101-1	OLD HORSE (LP)	30
91	ETT 101-2	OLD HORSE (CD)	30

MARY ASQUITH

78	Mother Earth MUM 1204	CLOSING TIME (LP)	30

ASSAGAI

71	Vertigo 6059 034	Telephone Girl/I'll Wait For You	40
71	Vertigo 6360 030	ASSAGAI (LP, gatefold sleeve, large swirl label)	100
72	Philips 6308 079	ZIMBABWE (LP, black/silver labels)	90
72	Contour 2870 394	ASSAGAI (LP)	12
70s	Sounds Superb SPR 90054	AFRO ROCK (LP) (Same as Vertigo 6360030)	12

LYS ASSIA

57	Decca F 10930	Through The Eyes Of Love/Scusami	6
57	Decca DFE 6383	FOUR CONTINENTAL HITS (EP)	10

ASSOCIATES

(see also Billy MacKenzie, Jih)

79	Double Hip DHR 1	Boys Keep Swinging/Mona Property Girl (no p/s, 500 only)	60
79	MCA MCA 537	Boys Keep Swinging/Mona Property Girl (no p/s, demos more common, £15)	25
80	Fiction FICS 11	The Affectionate Punch/You Were Young (p/s)	5
81	Fiction FICSX 13	A/Would I... Bounce Back (p/s)	5
81	RSO RSO 78	Kites/A Girl Named Property (p/s, band on A-side credited as "39 Lyon St.")	5
81	RSO RSOX 78	Kites/A Girl Named Property (12", p/s, A-side credited as "39 Lyon St.")	8
82	Lyntone LYN 11649	Even Dogs In The Wild (clear 1-sided flexi free with Flexipop mag, issue 20)	12
82	Beggars Banquet BEG 86	Tell Me Easter's On Friday/Straw Towels (unreleased, white labels only)	30
85	WEA YX 47TE	Take Me To The Girl/Perhaps/God Bless The Child (live)/ Even Dogs In The Wild (live)/ The Boy That Santa Claus Forgot (live) (10", p/s)	10
88	WEA YZ 329T	Country Boy/Heart Of Glass (Dub Mix)/Just Can't Say Goodbye (12" Mix) (12", p/s, unissued, white labels only)	50
88	WEA YZ 329CD	Country Boy/Just Can't Say Goodbye (12" Mix)/Take Me To The Girl/ Heart Of Glass (Dub Mix) (3" CD with adaptor in jewel case, unissued)	50
90	Circa YRCDT 46	Fever (single version)/Groovin' With Mr. Bloe/Fever In The Shadows (CD)	15
90	WEA YZ 534T	POPERETTA (EP) (12", p/s)	10
90	WEA YZ 534CD	POPERETTA (EP) (CD)	10
80	Fiction FIX 05	THE AFFECTIONATE PUNCH (LP)	20
90	Circa CIRCD 11	WILD AND LONELY (CD)	30
82	Beggars Banquet BEGA 43	FOURTH DRAWER DOWN (LP, gatefold sleeve with poster, label credits SITU 2)	15
88	WEA WX 222C	THE GLAMOUR CHASE (unreleased advance cassette only: with extra track Take Me To The Girl)	30

ASSOCIATION

66	London HLT 10054	Along Comes Mary/Your Own Love	10
66	London HLT 10074	Cherish/Don't Blame It On Me	10
66	London HLT 10098	Pandora's Golden Heebie Jeebies/Standing Still	15
67	London HLT 10118	No Fair At All/Looking Glass	8
67	London HLT 10140	Windy/Sometime	10
67	London HLT 10157	Never My Love/Requiem For The Masses	8
68	Warner Bros WB 6113	Everything That Touches You/Requiem For The Masses	6
68	Warner Bros WB 7163	Everything That Touches You/We Love Us	5
68	Warner Bros WB 7195	Time For Livin'/Birthday Morning	5
68	Warner Bros WB 7229	Six Man Band/Like Always	5
69	Warner Bros WB 7267	Goodbye Columbus/The Time It Is Today	8
69	Warner Bros WB 7119	Windy/Never My Love	7
70	Warner Bros WB 7372	Just About The Same/Look At Me, Look At You	6
72	CBS S 8062	Darling Be Home Soon/Indian Wells Woman	6
67	London HA-T 8305	AND THEN . . . ALONG COMES THE ASSOCIATION (LP)	50
67	London HA-T 8313	RENAISSANCE (LP)	35
67	London HA-T/SH-T 8342	INSIGHT OUT (LP)	35
68	Warner Bros W(S) 1733	BIRTHDAY (LP)	30
69	Warner Bros W(S) 1767	GREATEST HITS (LP)	20
69	Warner Bros W(S) 1786	GOODBYE COLUMBUS (LP, soundtrack)	18
69	Warner Bros W(S) 1800	THE ASSOCIATION (LP)	20

FRED ASTAIRE

(see also Judy Garland, Bing Crosby)

57	HMV POP 337	Funny Face/AUDREY HEPBURN: How Long Has This Been Going On	5
57	MGM MGM 964	The Ritz Roll And Rock/JANIS PAIGE: Satin And Silk	5
57	MGM EP 601	SHOES WITH WINGS ON (EP)	10
56	Philips BBL 7052	THE BEST OF FRED ASTAIRE (LP)	12

ASTERIX

70	Decca F 13075	Everybody/If I Could Fly	30

EDWIN/TED ASTLEY (ORCHESTRA)

63	Oriole CB 1880	The World Ten Times Over/Soho	20
65	RCA RCA 1492	Danger Man Theme/Saint Theme	50
66	Decca F 12389	The Baron/Drop Head (as Ted Astley)	30

MINT VALUE £

VIRGINIA ASTLEY
(see also David Sylvian)

82	Why Fi WFI 001	Love's A Lonely Place To Be/Soaring (p/s with lyric insert)	5
82	Why Fi WHY 08	A BAO A QU (10" EP)	10
87	Warner Bros. WEA YZ 107	Some Small Hope/A Summer Long Since Passed (P/s, featuring David Sylvian)	6

ANN ASTON

74	Pye 7N 45403	I Can't Stop Myself From Loving You Babe/Freedom Train	5

ASTON HALL

80	Tamebeat TAME 001	The Daily Sun/Popular People (p/s)	8

ASTON VILLA F.C.

75	Polydor 2058 563	We're Going Up/THE VILLAINS: We're Going Up	6

ASTON & YEN

66	Doctor Bird DB 1064	Skillamy/BABA BROOKS & BAND: Party Time	30

ASTORS

65	Atlantic AT 4037	Candy/I Found Out	80
65	Atlantic AT 4037	Candy/I Found Out (DJ Copy)	120
69	Atlantic 584 245	Candy/I Found Out (reissue)	10

ASTRA NOVA ORCHESTRA

74	Alaska ALA 26	Ev'ry Little Beat Of Your Heart/Soul Sleeper	30

ASTRAL NAVIGATIONS
(see also Bill Nelson, David John & Mood)

71	Holyground HG 114/ NSR 172	ASTRAL NAVIGATIONS (LP, actually by Lightyears Away & Thundermother, poster cover & booklet, 250 copies only, some numbered)	425
89	Magic Mixture MM 2	ASTRAL NAVIGATIONS (LP, reissue with booklet, 425 copies only)	35
90s	Holyground HBG 122/1 CD	ASTRAL NAVIGATIONS (CD)	20

ASTRONAUTS

63	RCA Victor RCA 1349	Baja/Kuk	20
63	RCA Victor RD 7662	ORBIT KAMPUS (LP)	50

ASTRONAUTS

66	Hala Gala HG 9	Before You Leave/Syncopate	5

ASTRONAUTS (U.K.)
(see also Restricted Hours, Syndicate)

79	Bugle BLAST 1	THE ASTRONAUTS EP (All Night Party/Back Soon/Everything Stops The Baby/... Survivors) (p/s)	15
80	Bugle BLAST 5	PRANKSTERS IN REVOLT (EP)	20
81	Bugle GENIUS 001	PETER PAN HITS THE SUBURBS (LP)	50
82	Bugle GENIUS 002	IT'S ALL DONE BY MIRRORS (LP)	40
86	All The Madmen MAD 5	IT'S ALL DONE BY MIRRORS (LP, reissue)	15
86	All The Madmen MAD 11	SOON (LP)	12

A SUDDEN SWAY
(see under Sudden Sway)

ASWAD

76	Island WIP 6312	Back to Africa/Africa	8
76	Island WIP 6338	Three Babylon/Ire Woman	8
78	Grove Music GMDM 9	It's Not Our Wish (That We Should Fight)/Stranger	15
80	Grove Music 12WIP 6575	Rainbow Culture/Covenant (dub) (12")	18
81	Grove Music 12WIP 6693	Babylon/Behold (12")	12
81	Grove Music IPR 2037	Warrior Charge/Dub Charge (12")	30
81	CBS CBSA 13-1653	Ways Of The Lord/Lords Of The Dub (12", p/s)	8
84	Simba SIM 014	Hooked On You/Version	8
79	Grove Music GMLP 6	HULET (LP)	20

ASYLUM

74	Wax SR 2073	It's My Destiny - Lazy Love/Suzy's Back (p/s)	100

ASYLUM CHOIR
(see also Leon Russell)

68	Mercury SMCL 21041	A LOOK INSIDE THE ASYLUM CHOIR (LP)	25

ATACAMA

71	Charisma CAS 1039	ATACAMA (LP, pink/white 'scroll' label)	30
72	Charisma CAS 1060	THE SUN BURNS UP ABOVE (LP, large 'mad hatter' label)	25

ATGYFODIAD

74	Sain SAIN 41	DISGYN MAE'R GLAW (EP)	12

ATHENIANS

64	ESC ESC 1	You Tell Me/Little Queenie (custom sleeve)	50
64	Waverley SLP 532	I've Got Love If You Want It/I'm A Lover Not A Fighter (p/s)	120
64	Waverley SLP 532	I've Got Love If You Want It/I'm A Lover Not A Fighter	60
65	Waverley SLP 533	Thinking Of Your Love/Mercy Mercy (in custom sleeve)	60
65	Waverley SLP 533	Thinking Of Your Love/Mercy Mercy (not in custom sleeve)	30

GLENN ATHENS & TROJANS

65	Spot 7E 1018	GLENN ATHENS & TROJANS (EP)	200

ATHLETE

02	Regal REG 72	Westside/Dungeness/One Of Those Days (p/s, with stencil, 1,000 only)	12
02	Regal REG 72CD	Westside/Dungeness/One Of Those Days (CD, card sleeve, 1,000 only)	12

PETE ATKIN

70	Philips 6006 050	Be Careful When They Offer You The Moon/Master Of The Revels	5
67	Private pressing	WHILE THE MUSIC LASTS (LP, 99 copies)	30
67	Private pressing	THE PARTY'S MOVING ON (LP, 99 copies)	30

MINT VALUE £

70	Fontana 6309 011	BEWARE THE BEAUTIFUL STRANGER (LP, black/silver labels)	30
71	Philips 6308 070	DRIVING THROUGH MYTHICAL AMERICA (LP)	30
73	RCA SF 8336	A KING AT NIGHTFALL (LP)	15
74	RCA LPL1 5014	THE ROAD OF SILK (LP)	12

BENNY ATKINS

60	Mercury AMT 1113	Lipstick On Your Lips/I'm Following You	18

CHET ATKINS

(see also Country Hams, Hank Snow, Mark Knopfler)

59	RCA Victor RCA 1153	Boo Boo Stick Beat/Django's Castle	6
60	RCA Victor RCA 1174	Teensville/One Mint Julep	8
60	RCA Victor RCA 1209	The Dark At The Top Of The Stairs Theme/Hocus Pocus	6
64	RCA Victor RCA 1382	Susie Q/Windy & Warm	10
65	RCA Victor RCA 1441	Cloudy And Cool/Travelin'	5
65	RCA Victor RCA 1464	Yakety Axe/Letter Edged In Black	6
66	RCA Victor RCA 1515	From Nashville With Love/Rhythm Guitar	5
63	RCA Victor RCX 7118	GUITAR GENIUS (EP)	10
60	RCA Victor RD 27168	TEENSVILLE (LP)	20
60	RCA Victor RD 27194	THE OTHER CHET ATKINS (LP)	12
60	RCA Victor RD 27214	CHET ATKINS' WORKSHOP (LP)	12
62	RCA Victor RD 7507	GENIUS WITH CHET ATKINS (LP)	12
63	RCA Victor RD/SF 7529	OUR MAN IN NASHVILLE (LP, mono)	15
63	RCA Victor SF 7529	OUR MAN IN NASHVILLE (LP, stereo)	20
63	RCA Victor RD 7557	TRAVELIN' (LP)	12
63	RCA Victor RD 7602	TEENSCENE (LP, mono)	12
63	RCA Victor SF 7602	TEENSCENE (LP, stereo)	15
63	RCA Victor RD 7647	PROGRESSIVE PICKING (LP, mono)	12
63	RCA Victor SF 7647	PROGRESSIVE PICKING (LP, stereo)	15
66	RCA Victor RD/SF 7813	CHET ATKINS PICKS ON THE BEATLES (LP, mono/stereo)	15

ATLANTIC BRIDGE

71	Dawn DNX 2507	I Can't Lie To You/Hilary Dickson/Childhood Room (p/s)	7
70	Dawn DNLS 3014	ATLANTIC BRIDGE (LP, gatefold sleeve, red/black labels)	40

ATLANTICS

64	Windsor WPS 129	Don't Say No/Send Him To Me	20
64	Oriole CB-1963	Bombora/Greensleeves	12

ATLANTIS

72	Fury FY 302	I Ain't Got Time/Teddy Boyd's Rock 'N' Roll Show	6
73	Vertigo 6360 609	ATLANTIS (LP, small swirl label, sleeve printed in Germany)	30

ATLANTIS RISING

83	CMI CMI700	Tightrope/Reverie: A Vision	20

ATLAS

78	Emerging WIL 001	AGAINST ALL THE ODDS (LP, private pressing)	25

AT LAST THE 1958 ROCK & ROLL SHOW

(see also Ian Hunter, Mott The Hoople, Freddie 'Fingers' Lee, Miller Anderson, Charles Woolfe)

68	CBS 3349	I Can't Drive/Working On The Railroad	25

ATMOSFEAR

(see also Antoniou)

79	Elite DAZZ 1	Dancing In Outer Space/Dancing In Outer Space (Version) (12")	15
79	MCA 12 MCA 543	Dancing In Outer Space/Dancing In Outer Space (Version) (12", co. sleeve)	15
79	Elite DAZZ 4	Journey To The Powerline (Remix)/LEVEL 42: Sandstorm (12", promo)	75
82	Elite/City Sounds LDAZZ 12	Xtra Speical (Dry Mix)/(Wet Mix) (12")	15
81	MCA MCF 3110	ENTRANCE (LP)	15
84	Elite ATM 33-1	FIRST/FOURMOST (mini-LP)	15

ATMOSPHERES

59	London HLW 8977	Kabalo/The Fickle Chicken	30
59	London HLW 8977	Kabalo/The Fickle Chicken (78)	20
60	London HLW 9091	Telegraph/Caravan	30

ATOMIC ROOSTER

(see also Crane/Farlowe, Chris Farlowe, Crazy World Of Arthur Brown, Hard Stuff, Leaf Hound, Andromeda, John Du Cann)

70	B&C CB 121	Friday The 13th/Banstead (initial copies in p/s)	20
70	B&C CB 121	Friday The 13th/Banstead	8
72	Dawn DNS 1027	Stand By Me/Never To Lose	6
72	Dawn DNS 1029	Save Me/Close Your Eyes	6
74	Decca FR 13503	Tell Your Story (Sing Your Song)/O.D. (as Vincent Crane's Atomic Rooster)	8
80	EMI EMI 5084	Do You Know Who's Looking For You/Throw Your Life Away (p/s)	6
80	EMI 12EMI 5084	Do You Know Who's Looking For You (Ext.)/Throw Your Life Away (12", p/s)	10
81	Polydor POSP 334	Play It Again/Start To Live (p/s)	5
81	Polydor POSPX 334	Play It Again/Start To Live/Devil's Answer (live) (12", p/s)	8
82	Polydor POSP 408	End Of The Day/Living Underground (p/s)	5
82	Polydor POSPX 408	End Of The Day/Living Underground/Tomorrow Night (live) (12", p/s)	8
70	B&C CAS 1010	ATOMIC ROOSTER (LP, Matrix CAS +1010 + A/CAS + 1010 + B (Flute Mix)	150
70	B&C CAS 1010	ATOMIC ROOSTER (LP, Matrix CAS +1010 + A2/CAS + 1010 + B2 (Flute Mix)	100
70	B&C CAS 1010	ATOMIC ROOSTER (LP, Matrix CAS +1010 + A1U/CAS + 1010 + B1U (Guitar mix)	50
70	B&C CAS 1026	DEATH WALKS BEHIND YOU (LP, gatefold sleeve)	40
71	Pegasus PEG 1	IN HEARING OF ATOMIC ROOSTER (LP, gatefold sleeve)	30
72	Dawn DNLS 3038	MADE IN ENGLAND (LP, limited 'denim' cover, gatefold, with poster, lilac label)	70
73	Dawn DNLS 3038	MADE IN ENGLAND (LP, re-pressing, standard cover, gatefold insert, lilac label)	30
73	Dawn DNLS 3049	NICE'N'GREASY (LP, lilac label)	40
80	EMI EMC3341	ATOMIC ROOSTER (LP)	15
83	Towerbell TOW LP 4	HEADLINE NEWS (LP)	15

MINT VALUE £

ATOMS

79	Rinka R 23	Max Bygraves Killed My Mother/Beatles Jacket (colour silk-screened p/s in poly bag with inserts)	12

ATORIE

89	Conscious CON001	It's My Time/Peace Of Mind (12")	80

A II Z

(see also AC/DC)

81	Polydor POSP 243	No Fun After Midnight/Treason (no p/s)	10
81	Polydor POSPX 243	No Fun After Midnight/Treason/Valhalla's Force (12", p/s, red vinyl)	15
81	Polydor POSP 314	I'm The One Who Loves You/Ringside Seat (p/s)	12
80	Polydor 2383 587	THE WITCH OF BERKELEY - LIVE (LP, initially sealed with sew-on patch)	20
80	Polydor 2383 587	THE WITCH OF BERKELEY - LIVE (LP)	15

ATTACK (U.K.)

(see also Andromeda, Five Day Week Straw People, Nice)

67	Decca F 12550	Try It/We Don't Know	150
67	Decca F 12578	Any More Than I Do/Hi-Ho Silver Lining	45
67	Decca F 12631	Created By Clive/Colour Of My Mind	100
67	Decca F 12631	Created By Clive/Colour Of My Mind (p/s for export to Holland)	200
68	Decca F 12725	Neville Thumbcatch/Lady Orange Peel	200
72	Decca F 13353	Hi-Ho Silver Lining/Any More Than I Do (reissue, unissued)	0
90	Reflection MM 08	MAGIC IN THE AIR (LP)	15

ATTACK (U.S.)

67	Philips BF 1585	Washington Square/Please Phil Spector	15

ATTACK WAVE PESTREPELLER

98	Prescription DRUG 4	NUG YAR (LP, hand-made sleeve, label, with insert 99 copies only)	18

ATTAK

82	No Future OI 17	Today's Generation: Murder In The Subway/Future Dreams (p/s)	8
83	No Future PUNK 6	ZOMBIES (LP)	12

ATTEMPTED MOUSTACHE

78	Skeleton SKL 003	Superman/No Way Out (folded p/s)	8

ATTRACTION

66	Columbia DB 7936	Stupid Girl/Please Tell Me	50
66	Columbia DB 8010	Party Line/She's A Girl	120

ATTRITION

81	Sound For Industry SFI 671/A.R.R. 002	Fear/Devoid (flexidisc, p/s, with Adventures In Reality fanzine, issue 5)	8
85	Third Mind TMS 04	Shrinkwrap/Pendulum Turns (12", p/s with insert)	10
83	Third Mind TMT 06	ONSLAUGHT (cassette)	15
83	Rabbit RR 003	DENX DEMOS (cassette)	15
83	Air ARR 11	DEATH HOUSE (cassette)	15

ATTRIX

78	Attrix RB 01	Lost Lenore/Hard Times (p/s, stamped white labels)	15
81	Scoff DT 011	Procession/11th Hour (p/s)	10

WINIFRED ATWELL

56	Decca F 10681	Poor People Of Paris (Poor John)/Piano Tuners Boogie	5
56	Decca F 10785	Bumble Boogie/St. Louis Blues	8
57	Decca F 10852	Let's Rock 'N' Roll (medley, both sides)	5
57	Decca F 10886	Spaceship Boogie/Jane Street	5

AUBREY SMALL

(see also Sons Of Man)

72	Polydor 2058 204	Loser/Oh What A Day It's Been	15
71	Polydor 2383 048	AUBREY SMALL (LP, with gatefold insert)	90

AUDACITY

81	Ellie Jay EJSP 9674 STA001-7	AUDACITY EP (EP, p/s)	20

AUDIENCE

(see also Howard Werth & Moonbeams, Stackridge, Hot Chocolate)

71	Charisma CB 126	Belladonna Moonshine/The Big Spell	6
71	Charisma CB 141	Indian Summer/It Brings A Tear/Priestess (p/s)	8
71	Charisma CB 156	You're Not Smiling/Eye To Eye	5
72	Charisma CB 185	Stand By The Door/Thunder And Lightnin'	5
72	Charisma CB 196	Raviole/Hard Cruel World	5
69	Polydor 583 065	AUDIENCE (LP)	200
70	Charisma CAS 1012	FRIEND'S FRIEND'S FRIEND (LP, pink label with 'scroll' logo)	40
71	Charisma CAS 1032	THE HOUSE ON THE HILL (LP, gatefold sleeve with lyric inner sleeve)	30
72	Charisma CAS 1054	LUNCH (LP, gatefold sleeve, with lyric inner sleeve)	30

AUDREY

(see also Dandy)

69	Downtown DT 414	Love Me Tonight/BROTHER DAN ALLSTARS: Show Them Amigo	12
69	Downtown DT 418	Lover's Concerto/HERBIE GREY & RUDIES Along Came Roy	12
69	Downtown DT 436	You'll Lose A Good Thing/DESMOND RILEY: If I Had Wings	10
70	Downtown DT 452	Sweeter Than Sugar/The Way You Move	10
70	Downtown DT 454	Oh I Was Wrong/Let's Try It Again (B-side with Dandy)	10
70	Downtown DT 457	Someday We'll Be Together/MUSIC DOCTORS: Sunset Rock	12
70	Downtown DT 463	How Glad I Am/DANDY & AUDREY: I'm So Glad	8
70	Trend 6099 006	Getting Ready For A Heartache/M Y O B: Leave Me Alone	10
81	Jah Skaka 826	English Girl/African Queen (12")	20

MIKE AUDSLEY

72	Sonet SNTF 641	DARK AND DEVIL WATERS (LP, with insert)	18
74	Sonet SNTF 659	STORYBOARD (LP)	12

MINT VALUE £

HUGHES AUFRAY

66	Fontana TL 5419	EN DIRECT DE L'OLYMPIA (LP)	12

BRIAN AUGER (&) TRINITY

(see also Julie Driscoll Brian Auger & Trinity, Shotgun Express, Jimmy Page, Sonny Boy Williamson)

65	Columbia DB 7590	Fool Killer/Let's Do It Tonight (as Brian Auger Trinity)	70
65	Columbia DB 7715	Green Onions '65/Kiko (as Brian Auger Trinity)	60
67	Columbia DB 8163	Tiger/Oh Baby, Won't You Come Back Home To Croydon, Where Everybody Beedle's And Bo's (solo)	40
67	Marmalade 598 003	Red Beans And Rice Pts 1 & 2	40
68	Marmalade 598 006	I Don't Know Where You Are/A Kind Of Love In (with Julie Driscoll, unissued in favour of "This Wheel's On Fire")	0
69	Marmalade 598 015	What You Gonna Do/Bumpin' On Sunset	18
70	RCA RCA 1947	I Want To Take You Higher/Just Me Just You	10
71	Polydor 2058 119	This Wheel's On Fire/Road To Cairo (as Brian Auger & Julie Driscoll)	8
71	Polydor 2058 133	Marie's Wedding/Tomorrow City (as Brian Auger's Oblivion Express)	6
73	CBS 1444	Inner City Blues/Light Of The Path (as Brian Auger's Oblivion Express)	10
74	CBS 2309	Straight Ahead/Change	6
68	Marmalade 608 004	DON'T SEND ME NO FLOWERS (LP, with Jimmy Page & Sonny Boy Williamson)	100
69	Marmalade 607/608 003	DEFINITELY WHAT! (LP)	100
69	Polydor 2334 004	THE BEST OF BRIAN AUGER, JULIE DRISCOLL & THE TRINITY (LP)	20
70	RCA SF 8101	BEFOUR (LP)	35
71	RCA SF 8170	OBLIVION EXPRESS (LP)	25
71	Polydor 2383 062	BETTER LAND (LP, as Brian Auger's Oblivion Express)	30
72	Polydor 2383 104	SECOND WIND (LP, as Brian Auger's Oblivion Express)	30
73	CBS 65625	CLOSER TO IT (LP)	15
74	CBS 80058	STRAIGHT AHEAD (LP)	15

AU GO-GO SINGERS

(see also Buffalo Springfield, Stephen Stills, Poco)

65	Columbia DB 7493	San Francisco Bay Blues/Pink Polemoniums	8
64	Columbia 33SX 1696	THEY CALL US AU GO-GO SINGERS (LP)	40

NAT AUGUSTIN

83	Debut DEBT 12 6	All Of My Love/Summer Is Here Again (12")	80

AUM

69	London HA-K/SH-K 8401	BLUESVIBES (LP)	35

CLIFF AUNGIER

(see also Royd Rivers & Cliff Aungier)

68	Polydor 56250	Time/Fisherboy	30
68	RCA RCA 1730	My Love And I/Abigail	10
69	Pye 7N 17753	Lady From Baltimore/Back On The Road Again	10
69	Pye NSPL 18294	THE LADY FROM BALTIMORE (LP)	20

AUNTIEPUS

(see also Damned)

79	Septic AUNT 1	Half-Way To Venezuela/Marmalade Freak (p/s)	6

AU PAIRS

80	Human OTO 2	You/Domestic Departure/Kerb Crawler	8
80	Human OTO 4	It's Obvious/Diet	8
81	Human HUM 8	Inconvenience/Pretty Boys (p/s)	8
81	Human HUM 8-12	Inconvenience/Pretty Boys/Headache (For Michelle) (12")	10
81	Human HUMAN 1	PLAYING WITH A DIFFERENT SEX (LP, with iron-on transfer)	15
81	Human HUMAN 1	PLAYING WITH A DIFFERENT SEX (LP)	15
82	Kamera KAM 010	SENSE AND SENSUALITY (LP, with insert)	15
83	AKA AKA 6	LIVE IN BERLIN (LP)	12

AURORA

(see also AC/DC)

83	Aurora RAM 9	I'll Be Your Fantasy/If I Really Knew Her (no p/s)	60

AURRA

82	Battersea BATTL 1	A Little Love/Make Up Your Mind (12")	10

AUSTIN

93	Suburban Base SUBBASE 18	THE AUSTIN EP (12", stamped white label)	30

PATTI AUSTIN

69	United Artists UP 35018	The Family Tree/Magical Boy	8
70	United Artists UP 35097	Your Love Made The Difference In Me/It's Easier To Laugh Than Cry	6
71	CBS 7180	Are We Ready For Love/Now That I Know What Loneliness Is	25
74	Probe PRO 608	Music To My Heart/Love 'Em And Leave 'Em Kind Of Love	12

PETER AUSTIN

(see also Little Freddy, Mr. Foundation)

68	Caltone TONE 125	Your Love/Time Is Getting Harder	120
75	Terminal 108	When You Are Near/Dub	7

REG AUSTIN

65	Pye 7N 15885	My Saddest Day/I'll Find Her	60

SIL AUSTIN

58	Mercury 7MT 220	Don't You Just Know It/Rainstorm	15
58	Mercury 7MT 220	Don't You Just Know It/Rainstorm	15
58	Mercury 7MT 225	Hey, Eula/The Last Time	10
58	Mercury 7MT 225	Hey, Eula/The Last Time	20
58	Mercury MEP 9540	THE BAND WITH THE BEAT (EP)	50

			MINT VALUE £
58	Mercury MEP 9541	GO SIL GO (EP)	50
58	Mercury MPL 6534	SLOW WALK ROCK (LP)	60

AUSTRALIAN CRICKET TEAM

72	Penny Farthing PEN 739	Bowl, Ball, Swing, Bat/Here Come The Aussies	7

AUSTRALIAN PLAYBOYS

(see also Procession, Manfred Mann Earth Band)

67	Immediate IM 054	Black Sheep R.I.P./Sad	800

AUTECHRE

(see also Gescom)

91	Hardcore HARD 003	Cavity Job/Accelera 1 + 2 (12", 1,000 only)	40
94	Warp 10WAP 11	BASSCADET REMIXES (3 x 10" p/s in box)	15
95	Warp WAP64r	ANVIL VAPRE EP (12")	12
96	Warp WAP 72	We R Are Why/Are Y Are We (12", p/s, mail order only)	25
97	Warp WAP96r	CICHLISUITE EP (12")	12
99	Warp WAPEP7.1	EP 7.1 (12")	10
99	Warp WAPE7.2	EP 7.2 (12")	10
99	Warp WAP 112	PEEL SESSION (12")	12
93	Warp LP 17LTD	INCUNABULA (2-LP set, silver vinyl)	35
98	Warp WARPLP66	LP5 (2-LP)	15
08	Warp WARPCD 333X	QUARISTICE (2-CD metal sleeve)	70

AUTEURS

92	Hut HUTCD24	Showgirl/Glad To Be Gone/Staying Power (CD)	10
93	Rough trade 45REV15	Housebreaker/Valet Parking	12
96	Hut HUT LP33	AFTER MURDER PARK (LP)	20
99	Hut HUT LP53	HOW I LEARNED TO LOVE THE BOOTBOYS (LP)	25

AUTOGRAPHS

78	RAK RAK 281	While I'm Still Young/Fabulous (p/s)	15
78	Strawberry Mastering	While I'm Still Young (different version, acetate only)	30

AUTOMATIC DLAMINI

(see also P.J. Harvey)

87	D For Drum DLAM 2	I Don't Know You But... /I've Never Seen That Colour Anywhere Before (p/s, with insert)	5
87	Idea IDEA 009	Me And My Conscience (p/s)	5
87	Idea IDEAT 009	Me And My Conscience (12", p/s)	8
87	Idea IDEALP 001	THE D IS FOR DRUM (LP)	12
92	Big Intl. BOT 04	FROM A DIVA TO A DIVER (LP)	12

AUTOMATIC FINE TUNING

76	Charisma CAS 1122	A.F.T (LP)	25

AUTOMATICS

78	Island WIP 6433	Wakin' With The Radio On/Watch Her Now (unissued)	0
78	Island WIP 6439	When Tanks Roll Over Poland Again/Watch Her Now (p/s)	15

AUTOPSY

89	Peaceville VILE 12	SEVERED SURVIVAL (LP, picture disc)	25
91	Peaceville VILE 25	MENTAL FUNERAL (LP, picture disc)	25

GENE AUTRY

59	London HLU 9001	Nine Little Reindeer/Buon Natale	6

AUTUMN

71	Pye 7N 45090	My Little Girl/Sun Sunshine	7
72	Pye 7N45144	Stood Up/Not The Way She Looks	20

AUTUMN VINE

70	Evolution E 2447	He Ain't No Superman/Maxi Baby	12

AVALANCHE

(see also Norman Haines Band)

71	Parlophone R 5890	Finding My Way Home/Rabbits	40

AVALANCHE

80	Childers AVA 1	The Preacher/Mean Lady (no p/s)	90

AVALON

82	SRTS 82/CUS/1296	Going Thru'/Gypsey Secret (not released in p/s)	130

FRANKIE AVALON

58	HMV POP 453	Dede Dinah/Ooh-La-La	20
58	HMV POP 453	Dede Dinah/Ooh-La-La (78)	15
58	London HL 8636	You Excite Me/Darlin'	30
58	London HL 8636	You Excite Me/Darlin' (78)	30
58	HMV POP 517	Ginger Bread/Blue Betty	15
58	HMV POP 517	Ginger Bread/Blue Betty (78)	25
59	HMV POP 569	I'll Wait For You/What Little Girl?	15
59	HMV POP 569	I'll Wait For You/What Little Girl? (78)	30
59	HMV POP 603	Venus/I'm Broke	10
59	HMV POP 603	Venus/I'm Broke (78)	35
59	HMV POP 636	Bobby Sox To Stockings/A Boy Without A Girl	10
59	HMV POP 636	Bobby Sox To Stockings/A Boy Without A Girl (78)	35
59	HMV POP 658	Just Ask Your Heart/Two Fools	8
59	HMV POP 658	Just Ask Your Heart/Two Fools (78)	35
60	HMV POP 688	Why/Swinging On A Rainbow	6
60	HMV POP 688	Why/Swinging On A Rainbow (78)	40
60	HMV POP 727	Don't Throw Away All Those Teardrops/Talk, Talk, Talk	5
60	HMV POP 742	The Faithful Kind/Gee Whizz - Whilikins - Golly Gee	8
60	HMV POP 766	Where Are You/Tuxedo Junction	8
60	HMV POP 794	Togetherness/Don't Let Love Pass Me By	6

MINT VALUE £

60	HMV POP 816	Green Leaves Of Summer/Here's To The Ladies	7
61	HMV POP 828	A Perfect Love/The Puppet Song	6
61	HMV POP 879	Gotta Get A Girl/Who Else But You	8
61	HMV POP 903	Voyage To The Bottom Of The Sea/The Summer Of '61	7
61	HMV POP 940	True True Love/Married	6
61	HMV POP 951	The Lonely Bit/Sleeping Beauty	6
62	Pye Int. 7N 25171	Dance The Bossa Nova/Welcome Home Baby	6
63	Pye Int. 7N 25183	My Ex-Best Friend/First Love Never Dies	6
63	Pye Int. 7N 25198	Come Fly With Me/The Girl Back Home	7
63	Pye Int. 7N 25203	Cleopatra/Heartbeats	7
58	HMV 7EG 8471	FRANKIE AVALON (EP)	20
58	HMV 7EG 8482	FRANKIE AVALON NO. 2 (EP)	20
58	HMV 7EG 8507	FRANKIE AVALON NO. 3 (EP)	20
60	HMV 7EG 8632	SONGS OF THE ALAMO (EP)	15
59	HMV CLP 1346	SWINGIN' ON A RAINBOW (LP)	25
60	HMV CLP 1423	SUMMER SCENE (LP)	25
60	HMV CLP 1440	YOUNG AND IN LOVE (LP, mono)	20
60	HMV CSD 1358	YOUNG AND IN LOVE (LP, stereo)	30
64	United Artists ULP 1078	MUSCLE BEACH PARTY (LP)	40

AVALONS

66	Island WI 263	Everyday/I Love You	15

AVANT-GARDE

68	CBS 3704	Naturally Stoned/Honey And Gall	12

AVANT GARDENER(S)

77	Virgin VEP 1003	GOTTA TURN BACK (EP)	6
80	Appaloosa AP 013	DIG IT (LP)	12

AVAVA

91	A5 AVA 5555	AVAVA (LP, 500 only)	12

AVENGER

83	Neat NEAT 31	Too Wild To Tame/On The Rocks (p/s, with insert)	8
84	Neat NEAT 1018	BLOOD SPORTS (LP)	15
85	Neat NEAT 1026	KILLER ELITE (LP, with lyric insert)	15

AVENGERS

(see also Vanity Fair)

68	Parlophone R 5661	Everyone's Gonna Wonder/Take My Hand	15

AVENGERS

72	Bullet BU 521	Highjack Plane/Shower Of Rain	5

AVERAGE WHITE BAND

73	MCA MUPS 486	SHOW YOUR HAND (LP, black/silver labels)	25
80	RCA XC 1152	Let's Go Round Again/A Love Of Your Own (12")	12

AVO-8

80	Stroppo STROP 1	Gone Wrong/Target One/No Hesitation (p/s)	7

ALAN AVON & TOY SHOP

(see also Hedgehoppers Anonymous)

70	Concord CON 005	These Are The Reasons/Night To Remember	150

AVON CITIES' JAZZ BAND

(see also Ray Bush)

56	Tempo A 151	Shim-Me Sha-Me Wabble/Hawaiian War Chant	5
60	Tempo A 169	Upper Set/American Patrol	5
56	Tempo LAP 10	AVON CITIES JAZZ BAND (LP)	25
58	Tempo TAP 18	AVON CITIES JAZZ (LP, with Ray Bush)	25

VALERIE AVON

(see also Avons)

67	Columbia DB 8201	He Knows I Love Him Too Much/To Be Let	12

AVONS

(see also Valerie Avon, Avon Sisters)

59	Columbia DB 4363	Seven Little Girls Sitting In The Back Seat/Alone At Eight	6
60	Columbia DB 4413	Pickin' Petals/We Fell In Love	6
60	Columbia DB 4461	We're Only Young Once/I Keep Dreaming	6
60	Columbia DB 4522	Four Little Heels/This Was Meant To Be	7
61	Columbia DB 4569	Rubber Ball/Cool And Cosy	7
61	Columbia DB 4700	Skin Divin'/Little Bo Peep	6
62	Columbia DB 4280	Tonight I Cannot Sleep/Gotta Go	5
62	Columbia DB 4899	A Wonderful Dream/Tonight You Belong To Me	7
63	Decca F 11588	Hey Paula/I Wanna Do It	6
63	Decca F 11641	Love Should Be True/All About You	6
64	Fontana TF 442	I Am The Girl/Once Upon A Summer's Day	6

AVON SISTERS

59	Columbia DB 4236	Jerri-Lee (I Love Him So)/Baby-O	12

AXEGRINDER

89	Peaceville VILE 7	RISE OF THE SERPENT MEN (LP)	30

DAVID AXELROD

(see also Electric Prunes)

68	Capitol ST 2982	SONGS OF INNOCENCE (LP, 'Sold in the U.K...' on label)	45
71	RCA LSP 4636	MESSIAH (LP)	40
73	MCA MUPS 472	THE AUCTION (LP, black/blue hexagon label)	40

AXIS

80	Metal Minded ISAX 1047	Lady/Messiah (p/s)	6

			MINT VALUE £
81	Axis	When You Hold Me	8
81	Neat NEAT 13	You Got It/One Step Ahead (p/s)	5

HOYT AXTON

63	Saga SS503	Greenback Dollar/The Crawdad Song	8
69	CBS 4316	It's All Right Now/Way Before The Time Of Towns	12
64	Stateside SL 10082	GREENBACK DOLLAR (LP)	20
64	Stateside SL 10096	THUNDER 'N' LIGHTNIN' (LP)	20
66	London HA-F/SH-F 8276	THE BEST OF HOYT AXTON (LP)	20

AYERS, CALE, NICO & ENO

(see also Kevin Ayers, John Cale, Nico, Brian Eno)

74	Island ILPS 9291	JUNE 1ST, 1974 (LP)	15

KEVIN AYERS (& WHOLE WORLD)

(see also Soft Machine, Lady June, Lol Coxhill, David Bedford, Mike Oldfield, Bridget St. John)

70	Harvest HAR 5011	Singing A Song In The Morning/Eleanor's Cake Which Ate Her	20
70	Harvest HAR 5027	Butterfly Dance/Puis-Je? (with Whole World)	15
71	Harvest HAR 5042	Stranger In Blue Suede Shoes/Stars (with Whole World)	10
72	Harvest HAR 5064	Oh! Wot A Dream/Connie On A Rubber Band	10
73	Harvest HAR 5071	Caribbean Moon/Take Me To Tahiti (p/s)	20
74	Island WIP 6194	The Up Song/Everybody's Sometimes & Some People's All The Time Blues	6
74	Island WIP 6201	After The Show/Thank You Very Much	6
75	Harvest HAR 5100	Caribbean Moon/Take Me To Tahiti	6
76	Island WIP 6271	Falling In Love Again/Everyone Knows The Song	6
76	Harvest HAR 5107	Stranger In Blue Suede Shoes/Fake Mexican Tourist Blues (possibly in p/s)	20
76	Harvest HAR 5107	Stranger In Blue Suede Shoes/Fake Mexican Tourist Blues	5
76	Harvest HAR 5109	Caribbean Moon/Take Me To Tahiti (reissue)	5
76	Harvest HAR 5109	Caribbean Moon/Take Me To Tahiti (reissue, in different p/s)	20
77	Harvest HAR 5124	Star/The Owl	6
80	Harvest HAR 5198	Money, Money, Money/Stranger In Blue Suede Shoes (p/s)	6
83	Charly/Celluloid CYZ 7107	My Speeding Heart/Champagne & Valium (p/s)	10
86	Illuminated LEV 71	Stepping Out/Only Heaven Knows (no p/s)	10
70	Harvest SHVL 763	JOY OF A TOY (LP, gatefold sleeve, 1st pressing with no EMI box)	80
70	Harvest SHSP 4005	SHOOTING AT THE MOON (LP, with Whole World)	50
72	Harvest SHVL 800	WHATEVERSHEBRINGSWESING (LP, gatefold sleeve)	40
73	Harvest SHVL 807	BANANAMOUR (LP, gatefold sleeve, with booklet)	100
73	Harvest SHVL 807	BANANAMOUR (LP, gatefold sleeve, without booklet)	30
74	Island ILPS 9263	THE CONFESSIONS OF DR. DREAM AND OTHER STORIES (LP, with inner)	20
75	Island ILPS 9322	SWEET DECEIVER (LP, with inner sleeve)	15
75	Harvest SHDW 407	JOY OF A TOY/SHOOTING AT THE MOON (2-LP, reissue, gatefold sleeve)	15
76	Harvest SHSP 2005	ODD DITTIES (LP)	12
76	Harvest SHSP 4057	YES WE HAVE NO MAÑANAS (LP, with inner sleeve)	20
78	Harvest SHSP 4085	RAINBOW TAKEAWAY (LP)	15
86	Illuminated AMA 25	AS CLOSE AS YOU THINK (LP)	25
92	Permanent PERM LP 5	STILL LIFE WITH GUITAR (LP)	15

ROY AYERS (UBIQUITY)

(see also Jack Wilson Quartet)

77	Polydor 2066 842	Running Away/Cincinnati Growl (as Roy Ayers' Ubiquity)	5
80	Polydor POSP 135	Running Away/Can't You See Me	5
80	Polydor POSPX 135	Running Away/Can't You See Me (12")	10
80	Polydor POSPX 186	Sometimes, Believe In Yourself (12")	8
83	Polydor UM 1T	Silver Vibrations/Fast Money (12")	8
87	Urban URBX 6	Can't You See Me/Love Will Bring Us Back Together/Sweet Tears (12", p/s)	15
77	Polydor 2391-256	VIBRATIONS (LP)	15
83	Uno Melodic UMLP 2	DRIVIN' ON UP (LP)	20

ALBERT AYLER

64	Transatlantic TRA 130	SPIRITS (LP)	40
64	Fontana Jazz SFJL 925	GHOSTS (LP)	40
64	Fontana Jazz STJL 927	MY NAME IS (LP)	40
65	Fontana 933 SFJL	SPIRITUAL UNITY (LP)	40
65	Fontana SFJL 925	GHOSTS (LP, reissue)	30
65	Fontana Jazz SFJL 927	MY NAME IS (LP, reissue)	30
67	Polydor 2383089	WITCHES & DEVILS (LP)	25
68	Impulse IMPL 8022	NEW GRASS (LP, gatefold sleeve)	25
69	Impulse SIPL 519	NEW GRASS (LP, reissue, single sleeve)	20
69	Sonet SNTF 604	FIRST RECORDINGS (LP)	15
60s	Freedom 41000 FLP	VIBRATIONS (LP)	15

J AYRES

77	Hawkeye HE 004	Pretty Looks/THE REVOLUTIONARIES - Ugly	6

AYRSHIRE FOLK

74	Deroy DER 1052	AYRSHIRE FOLK (LP, private pressing)	50

AYSHEA

(see also Ayshea Brough, Roy Wood)

65	Fontana TF 627	Eeny Meeny/Peep My Love	20
68	Polydor 56276	Celebration Of The Year/Only Love Can Save Me Now	30
69	Polydor 56302	Another Night/Taking The Sun From My Eyes	12
70	Polydor 2001 029	Mr White's White Flying Machine/Ship Of The Line	10
70	Polydor 2058 074	Who's Gonna Rescue Jesus/The Flowers Are Mine	5
71	MAM MAM 59	Old Fashioned Love Song/Family Of A Man	5
73	Harvest HAR 5073	Farewell/The Best Years Of My Life	8
70	Polydor 2384 026	AYSHEA (LP)	30

CHARLES AZNAVOUR

56	London DEP 95014	AZNAVOUR INVADES	20

MINT VALUE £

AZTEC CAMERA

(see also French Impressionists)

81	Postcard 81-3	Just Like Gold/We Could Send Letters (die-cut sleeve, with card)	30
81	Postcard 81-3	Just Like Gold/We Could Send Letters (die-cut sleeve, without card)	10
81	Postcard 81-8	Mattress Of Wire/Lost Outside The Tunnel (p/s)	15
82	Rough Trade RT 112	Pillar To Post/Queen's Tattoos (p/s)	5
82	Rough Trade RT 112P	Pillar To Post/Queen's Tattoos (picture disc)	8
83	Rainhill ACFC 1	Oblivious (Langer/Winstanley Remix)/Oblivious (Colin Fairley Remix) (fan club issue, no p/s)	20
94	Windsong WHISCD 006	LIVE ON THE TEST (CD)	20

AZUL

77	Venture VEN7778	Babylon Special/Version	10

AZYMUTH

80	Milestone MRC 101	Jazz Carnival/Fly Over The Moon (12")	10
80	Milestone MRC 102	Dear Limmertz/Papasong (12")	25

B

B's

70s	Private Pressing	IN YOUR BONNET (LP)	35

IKE B & CRYSTALS

68	Island WI 3151	Try A Little Merriness/Patricia	25

JOHN B

72	Decca F 13362	Take A Look Around/Run Run Run	6

MEHER BABA

(see also Pete Townshend)

70	Univ. Spiritual League 1	HAPPY BIRTHDAY (LP, with booklet and lyric sheet 6 Pete Townshend tracks, 100 only)	200
70	Univ. Spiritual League 2	I AM (LP, with inserts, features 5 Pete Townshend tracks)	100
76	Univ. Spiritual League 3	WITH LOVE (LP, features 3 Pete Townshend tracks)	100
70s	MBO MBO 1	STAR OF THE SILENT SCREEN . . . MEHER BABA (LP, reissue of "Happy Birthday"without inserts)	20
70s	MBO MBO 2	I AM (LP, reissue, without inserts)	20

BABE RUTH

(see also Jenny Haan, Bernie Marsden, Wild Turkey, Elias Hulk, Liquid Gold)

71	Decca F13234	Rupert's Magic Feather/Flood	6
71	Capitol CL 15869	Elusive/Say No More	8
71	Capitol CL 15869	Elusive/Say No More (DJ Copy)	10
72	Harvest HAR 5087	Wells Fargo/Theme From A Few Dollars More	5
75	Harvest HAR 5090	Private Number/Somebody's Nobody	5
72	Harvest SHSP 4022	FIRST BASE (LP, with lyric insert)	30
74	Harvest SHVL 812	AMAR CABALLERO (LP, gatefold sleeve)	20
75	Harvest SHSP 4038	BABE RUTH (LP)	20

ALICE BABS

63	Fontana TF 409	After You've Gone/St. Louis Blues Twist	6
64	Oriole CB1955	Drip Drop/Droppen Drip Och Droppen Drapp	6

MONTY BABSON

59	London HLJ 8877	All Night Long/The Things Money Cannot Buy	5
60	London HAJ 2212	ALL NIGHT LONG (LP)	12

BABY

69	Spark SRL 1030	Heartbreaker/Michael Blues	15

BABY BIRD

95	Baby Bird LP 1	IF I WAS BORN A MAN (LP, 500 only)	15
95	Baby Bird LP 2	BAD SHAVE (LP, 500 only)	15

BABY D

92	Production House PNT 043RX	Let Me Be Your Fantasy (Acen In Wonderland)/ Fantasy (Ray Keith Remix) (12")	15

BABY DOLLS

60	Warner Bros WB 16	Quiet!/Hey, Baby!	15

BABY FORD

88	Rhythm King BFORD 3CD	FORD TRAX (CD)	20

BABY GRUNTING

71	United Artists UP 35258	Keep The Circle Turning/Way Down The Line	5

BABY HUEY

71	Buddah 2365 001	LIVING LEGEND - THE BABY HUEY STORY (LP)	40

BABY JANE & ROCKABYES

63	United Artists UP 1010	How Much Is That Doggie In The Window/My Boy John	15

BABY LEMONADE

87	Narodnik NRK 004	The Secret Goldfish/Real World (p/s)	8

MINT VALUE £

BABYLON
(see also Carole Grimes)

69	Polydor 56356	Into The Promised Land/Nobody's Fault But Mine (p/s)	35
69	Polydor 56356	Into The Promised Land/Nobody's Fault But Mine (no p/s)	20

BABYLON TIMEWARP

93	Subliminal TENSE 001	Durban Poison/Durban Poison (-32Hz And Dropping Mix)/ Durban Poison (The Kashmir Mix) (12")	40

BABYSHAMBLES
(see also Libertines, Wolfman)

04	Amelia's (no cat no)	What Katie Did (Demo) (1,000 numbered copies of clear flexi, with Annelise's Magazine)	50
04	Amelia's (no cat no)	What Katie Did (Demo) (1,000 numbered copies of clear flexi without Annelise's Magazine)	30
04	High Society HS7IN011	Babyshambles/At The Flophouse (p/s, 1000 only)	30
04	High Society HSCDS003	Babyshambles/At The Flophouse (CD, 1,000 only)	30
04	Rough Trade RTRADS201	Killamanjiro/The Man Who Came To Stay (ltd edn. p/s)	5
05	Rough Trade RTRADS 210	Fuck Forever/Black Boy Lane (p/s)	5
05	Rough Trade RTRADLP240	DOWN IN ALBION (2xLP with side 4 etched)	15

BABY SUNSHINE
(see also Fairy's Moke)

75	Deroy DER 1301	BABY SUNSHINE (LP, with insert)	100

BACCA

73	Grape GR 3048	George Foreman/Version	5

BURT BACHARACH
(see also Tony Middleton, Breakaways)

65	London HLR 9958	Don't Go Breaking My Heart/24 Hours From Tulsa	5
65	London HLR 9968	Trains And Boats And Planes/Wives And Lovers	5
65	London HLR 9983	What's New Pussycat/My Little Red Book (B-side with Tony Middleton)	35
65	London HLR 9958	24 Hours From Tulsa/Don't Go Breaking My Heart	7
69	A&M AMS 702	Bond Street/Alfie	10
67	RCA Victor RD 7874	CASINO ROYALE (LP, soundtrack, mono)	50
67	RCA Victor SF 7874	CASINO ROYALE (LP, soundtrack, stereo)	60

BACHDENKEL

77	Initial IRC 001	LEMMINGS (LP, stickered gatefold sleeve, with bonus EP)	50
77	Initial IRL 001	LEMMINGS (LP)	15
77	Initial IRL 002	STALINGRAD (LP, numbered with lyric insert)	40

JOHNNY BACHELOR

60	London HLN 9074	Mumbles/Arabella Jean	80

BACHELORS (U.K.)

58	Parlophone R 4454	Platter Party/Love Is A Two Way Street	25
59	Parlophone R 4547	Please Don't Touch/Ding Dong	20
60	Decca F 11300	Lovin' Babe/Why Can't It Be Me	20

BACH TWO BACH

71	Mushroom 100 MR 10	BACH TWO BACH (LP)	20

BACK ALLEY CHOIR

72	York SYK 517	Smile Born Of Courtesy/Why Are You Here	40
73	York FYK 406	BACK ALLEY CHOIR (LP, 500 only)	400

BACKBEAT PHILHARMONIC

61	Top Rank JAR 576	Rock And Roll Symphony Parts 1 & 2	8

BACK DOOR
(see also Whitesnake)

72	Blakey BLP 5989	BACK DOOR (LP, sold at gigs)	50
73	Warner Bros K 46231	BACK DOOR (LP)	12

BACKHOUSE JAMES BLUES BAND

68	private pressing	BACKHOUSE JAMES BLUES BAND	400

MIRIAM BACKHOUSE

77	Mother Earth MUM 1203	GYPSY WITHOUT A ROAD (LP)	120

BACKLASH

80	Gargoyle GRGL 777	OFF WITH HIS HEAD (EP)	50

BACK PORCH MAJORITY

65	Columbia DB 7627	Ramblin' Man/Good Time Joe	8

BACKSEAT ROMEOS

80	Future Earth FER 007	Zero Ambition/In The Night (p/s)	35

BACK STREET BAND

69	Ember EMBS 277	This Ain't The Road/Daybreak (p/s)	6

BACK TO ZERO

79	Fiction FICS 004	Your Side Of Heaven/Back To Back	10

JIM BACKUS

58	London HLJ 8674	Delicious (The Laughing Song)/I Need A Vacation	6

BACKYARD BABIES
(see also Hanoi Rocks, Super$hit666, Wildhearts)

98	Coalition COLA 046	Look At You/Powderhead/Can't Find The Door/Wireless Mind (gatefold p/s)	5
98	Coalition COLA 051	Bombed (Out Of My Mind)/Rocker (featuring Michael Monroe) (yellow vinyl, fully-autographed numbered (apart from promos) gatefold p/s, 2000 only)	10
99	Coalition COLA 073	Babylon (featuring "Wildhearted Ginger")/Stars (red vinyl, foldover p/s & insert in poly bag, 1000 copies sold at gigs only)	10

MINT VALUE £

BACKYARD HEAVIES

73	Action ACT 4616	Just Keep On Truckin'/Never Can Say Goodbye	25

BACON FAT

(see also Dirty Blues Band, George 'Harmonica' Smith)

70	Blue Horizon 57-3171	Nobody But You/Small's On 53rd	18
70	Blue Horizon 57-3181	Evil/Blues Feeling	25
70	Blue Horizon 7-63858	GREASE ONE FOR ME (LP)	70
71	Blue Horizon 2431 001	TOUGH DUDE (LP)	90

GAR BACON

58	Felsted AF 107	Mary Jane/Chains Of Love	20
58	Felsted AF 107	Mary Jane/Chains Of Love (78)	40
59	Fontana H 196	Marshal, Marshal/Too Young To Love	30
59	Fontana H 196	Marshal, Marshal/Too Young To Love (78)	40

BAD ACTORS

80	Sophist. Noise SONO 1	Strange Love/Energy Society (p/s)	10
80	Plastic Speech	Love Song/Are They Hostile (p/s)	5

BAD BOYS

64	Piccadilly 7N 35208	The Owl And The Pussycat/That's What'll Do	15

BAD BRAINS

82	Alt. Tentacles VIRUS 13	I Luv Jah/Sailin' On/Big Takeover (12", p/s)	8
83	Food For Thought YUMT101	I And I Survive (An' T'ing)/Destroy Babylon (12", insert, p/s)	20
83	Abstract ABT 007	ROCK FOR LIGHT (LP)	20

BAD COMPANY

98	BC Recordings BCR 001	The Nine/The Bridge (company p/s)	20
99	BC Recordings BCR 002	THE FEAR EP: 4 days/Refuge/The Fear/Jellyfish (2 x 12", p/s)	8
99	Prototype PROUK 001	The Pulse/China Cup (12", die-cut p/s)	10
00	BC R'dings BCRUKLPS 001	DIGITAL NATION ALBUM SAMPLER: Flashback (Tumpa)/Spacewalk (promo 12", stickered black die-cut sleeve, A-side with Trace)	12
01	BC R'dings BCRUKEP 001	BOOK OF THE BAD VOL. 1 EP: The Voice/Numbers/Spider/Believe (2 x 12", p/s)	10
01	BC R'dings BCRUKEP 002	BOOK OF THE BAD VOL. 2 EP: Dogs On The Moon/Grunge/Ladies of Spain/ The Running Man (2 x 12", p/s)	10
01	BC R'dings BCRUKEP 003	BOOK OF TH BAD VOL. 3 EP: Mindgames/Rodeo/Miami flashback/ Storyteller (2 x 12", p/s)	10
01	Prototype PROUK 003	Planet Dust/Speedball (12", p/s)	10
00	BC R'dings BCRLP 001	INSIDE THE MACHINE (5 x 12")	35
00	BC R'dings BCRUKLP 001	DIGITAL NATION (5 x 12")	25

BADFINGER

(see also Iveys, Masterminds, Gary Walker & Rain, Natural Gas, Blue Goose)

70	Apple APPLE 20	Come And Get It/Rock Of All Ages (p/s)	8
70	Apple APPLE 31	No Matter What/Better Days (p/s)	15
71	Apple APPLE 35	Name Of The Game/Suitcase (unreleased)	0
72	Apple APPLE 40	Day After Day/Sweet Tuesday Morning (p/s)	15
72	Apple APPLE 42	Baby Blue/Flying (unreleased in U.K.)	0
74	Apple APPLE 49	Apple Of My Eye/Blind Owl	50
70	Apple SAPCOR 12	MAGIC CHRISTIAN MUSIC (LP)	50
70	Apple SAPCOR 16	NO DICE (LP, gatefold sleeve)	50
72	Apple SAPCOR 19	STRAIGHT UP (LP)	60
73	Warner Bros K 56023	BADFINGER (LP, with insert)	30
74	Apple SAPCOR 27	ASS (LP, with inner sleeve)	60
74	Warner Bros K 56076	WISH YOU WERE HERE (LP, withdrawn)	100
79	Elektra K52129	AIRWAVES (LP, with lyric inner sleeve)	20
91	Apple SAPCOR 12	MAGIC CHRISTIAN MUSIC (LP, reissue, gatefold sleeve with bonus 12"[Sapcor 121])	25
92	Apple SAPCOR 16	NO DICE (LP, reissue, gatefold sleeve with bonus 12"[SAPCOR 161])	25
93	Apple SAPCOR 19	STRAIGHT UP (LP, reissue, gatefold sleeve with bonus 12"[SAPCOR 191])	25
95	Apple SAPCOR 28	COME AND GET IT - THE BEST OF BADFINGER (2-LP, gatefold sleeve)	30

BADGE

81	Metal Minded MM 2	Silver Woman/Something I've Lost (p/s)	25

BADGER

(see also Ashton Gardner & Dyke, Jackie Lomax, Yes, Flash)

74	Epic EPC 2326	White Lady/Don't Pull The Trigger	5
73	Atlantic K 40473	ONE LIVE BADGER (LP, gatefold pop-up sleeve)	40
74	Epic EPC 80009	WHITE LADY (LP)	15

BADGER

81	Noize Gate NG 02	Over The Wall/Faceless Gang (p/s)	40

BADLY DRAWN BOY

(see also Doves)

97	Mo Wax (no cat no)	Nursery Rhyme (with UNKLE, 5"promo 150 only)	70
98	Twisted Nerve TNXL001	Roadmovie/My Friend Cubilas (feat. Doves) (die-cut sleeve, with insert)	8
s	Twisted Nerve (no cat. no.)	I Love You All (one-track musical box, 150 only)	90
98	Twisted Nerve TNXMS1	Donna And Blitzen (1 track on 5 track one-sided red vinyl 7", 195 copies, p/s)	50
01	Twisted Nerve TNXL 011	Donna And Blitzen (p/s, one-sided, 800 only)	8
97	Twisted Nerve TN 001	EP1 (EP, 500 only)	60
98	Twisted Nerve TN 002	EP2: I Love You All/The Treeclimber/I Love You All (I Loop You All Andy Votel Mix)/Thinking Of You (EP, 1,000 only)	30
98	Twisted Nerve XL TN 001T	EP3 (EP, 1,000 only)	10
06	EMI (no cat no)	BORN IN THE UK (3 x 7"200 of each red, blue, green in "chip bag"with Wooden fork, stickered, price is same for each)	15
00	Twisted Nerve TNXLCD 133	THE HOUR OF THE BEWILDERBEAST (LP, 1st pressing, withdrawn, with version of 'Magic In The Air' with the line "Love Is Contagious", and Woody Allen on sleeve	20

MINT VALUE £

BAD NEWS
(see also Brian May)
87 EMI EMC 3535 BAD NEWS (LP, gatefold sleeve) 12
88 EMI EMC 3542 BOOTLEG (LP, 1 track produced by Brian May) 12

BAD TASTE
88 Newgate SRT8KS 1554 Rockin' Girl (p/s, with insert) 30
88 Newgate SRT8KS 1554 Rockin' Girl (p/s, without insert) 10

JOAN BAEZ
(see also Earl Scruggs, Bob Dylan)
65 Fontana TF 564 We Shall Overcome/Don't Think Twice It's All Right 5
65 Fontana TF 587 There But For Fortune/Plaisir D'Amour 5
65 Fontana TF 604 It's All Over Now Baby Blue/Daddy You've Been On My Mind 5
65 Fontana TF 639 Farewell Angelina/Queen Of Hearts 5
60 Fontana (S)TFL 6002 JOAN BAEZ (LP) 15
61 Fontana (S)TFL 6025 JOAN BAEZ 2 (LP) 15

DOC BAGBY
58 Fontana H 106 Dumplin's/Sylvia's Calling (78) 10

DON BAGLEY
58 Pye NPL 28008 JAZZ ON THE ROCKS (LP) 20

BAG-O-WIRE
77 Epic 82133 BAG-O-WIRE (LP) 30

BURR BAILEY (& SIX SHOOTERS)
63 Decca F 11686 San Francisco Bay/Like A Bird Without Feathers (with Six Shooters) 25
64 Decca F 11846 Chahawki/You Made Me Cry 50

CLIVE BAILEY & RICO'S GROUP
62 Blue Beat BB 92 Evening Train/Going Home 15

DEREK BAILEY
(see also Tony Oxley, Springboard, Steve Lacy & Derek Bailey, Anthony Braxton & Derek Bailey, Jamie Muir & Derek Bailey)
70s Incus INCUS 2 SOLO GUITAR (LP) 60
70s Incus INCUS 2R SOLO GUITAR (LP) 60
74 Incus INCUS 12 LOT 74 (LP) 50
80 Incus INCUS 40 AIDA (LP) 35
85 Incus INCUS 48 NOTES (LP) 25
04 Organ Of Corti 10 TAPS (LP, 220gm vinyl, limited issue) 15

DEREK BAILEY & HAN BENNINK
72 Incus INCUS 9 SELECTIONS FROM LIVE PERFORMANCES AT VERITY'S PLACE (LP) 40
76 Incus INCUS 25 COMPANY 3 (LP) 35

DEREK BAILEY, ANTHONY BRAXTON & EVAN PARKER
76 Incus INCUS 23 COMPANY 2 (LP) 30

DEREK BAILEY & TONY COE
79 Incus INCUS 34 TIME (LP) 40

DEREK BAILEY, HUGH DAVIES, JAMIE MUIR, EVAN PARKER
70s Incus INCUS 17 THE MUSIC IMPROVISATION COMPANY 1968-1971 (LP) 30

DEREK BAILEY, BARRY GUY & PAUL RUTHERFORD
(see also Barry Guy)
70 Incus INCUS 3/4 ISKRA 1903 (LP) 45

DEREK BAILEY & TRISTAN HONSINGER
76 Incus INCUS 20 DUO (LP) 40

DEREK BAILEY & EVAN PARKER
(see also Evan Parker)
75 Incus INCUS 16 THE LONDON CONCERT (LP) 35
85 Incus INCUS 50 COMPATIBLES (LP) 35

DEREK BAILEY, EVAN PARKER & HAN BENNINK
70 Incus INCUS 1 THE TOPOGRAPHY OF THE LUNGS (LP) 45

MILDRED BAILEY
57 Parlophone GEP 8600 MILDRED BAILEY AND HER ALLEY CATS (EP) 10
54 Brunswick LA 8692 THE ROCKIN' CHAIR LADY (10"LP) 15

PEARL BAILEY
56 London HLN 8354 That Certain Feeling/Hit The Road To Dreamland 15
56 London REU 1104 THAT CERTAIN FEELING (EP) 10

ROY BAILEY (JAMAICA)
72 Duke DU 146 Run Away Child/Wedding March 7

ROY BAILEY (U.K.)
(see also Leon Rosselson)
71 Trailer LER 3021 ROY BAILEY (LP) 15
76 Fuse AC 262 NEW BELL AWAKE (LP) 15
82 Fuse CF 382 HARD TIMES (LP, with insert) 15

ZEDDIE BAILEY
73 Grape GR 3037 Babylon Gone/TONY KING: Speak No Evil 7

ALY BAIN & MIKE WHELLANS
70s Trailer LER 2022 ALY BAIN & MIKE WHELLANS (LP) 15

BOB BAIN & HIS MUSIC
58 Capitol CL 14912 Wagon Wheels/Strollin' Home 5
58 Capitol T965 ROCKIN' ROLLIN' AND STROLLIN' (LP) 40

MINT VALUE £

ARTHUR BAIRD SKIFFLE GROUP
56 Beltona BL 2669 Union Train/Union Maid . . . 35
56 Beltona BL 2669 Union Train/Union Maid (78) . . . 12

EDDIE BAIRD
(see also Amazing Blondel)
76 DJM DJLP 467 HARD GRAFT (LP) . . . 12

BAJA MARIMBA BAND
63 London HL 9828 Comin' In The Back Door/December Child. . . . 6

CARROLL BAKER
76 RCA PB 9056 It's My Party/Loves Golden Rule. . . . 6
78 RCA PB 9370 I'm Getting High Remembering/If It Wasn't For You . . . 6

CHET BAKER (QUARTET)
(see also Art Pepper, Russ Freeman & Chet Baker Quartet, Gerry Mulligan)
56 Vogue V 2377 My Funny Valentine/But Not For Me . . . 5
56 Vogue V 2381 Just Friends/Daybreak . . . 5
56 Vogue V 2232 Winter Wonderland/This Time The Dream's On Me . . . 5
56 Vogue V 2309 Long Ago And Far Away/Bea's Flat . . . 5
54 Vogue LDE 045 CHET BAKER QUARTET (10"LP) . . . 25
55 Philips BBL 7022 CHET BAKER AND STRINGS (LP) . . . 20
55 Vogue LDE 116 CHET BAKER QUARTET (10"LP) . . . 20
56 Vogue LAE 12018 CHET BAKER SINGS (LP) . . . 20
56 Vogue LDE 159 CHET BAKER SEXTET (10"LP) . . . 25
56 Vogue LDE 163 CHET BAKER ENSEMBLE (10"LP) . . . 25
56 Vogue LDE 182 CHET BAKER SINGS (10"LP) . . . 20
56 Felsted PDL 85008 CHET BAKER QUARTET VOL. 1 (LP) . . . 25
56 Felsted PDL 85013 CHET BAKER QUARTET VOL. 2 (LP) . . . 20
57 Felsted PDL 85036 I GET CHET (LP, as Chet Baker & His Combo) . . . 20
57 Vogue LAE 12044 CHET BAKER QUARTET AT ANN ARBOR (LP) . . . 20
57 Vogue LAE 12076 CHET BAKER AND HIS CREW (LP, mono) . . . 20
58 Vogue LAE 12109 CHET BAKER - PHIL'S BLUES (LP) . . . 20
59 Vogue SEA 5005 CHET BAKER AND HIS CREW (LP, stereo) . . . 15
59 Vogue LAE 12164 CHET BAKER SINGS (LP) . . . 15
59 Vogue LAE 12183 CHET BAKER AND ART PEPPER SEXTET - PLAYBOYS! (LP) . . . 15

DESMOND BAKER & CLAREDONIANS
(see also Claredonians)
66 Island WI 295 Rude Boy Gonna Jail/SHARKS: Don't Fool Me. . . . 25

DOROTHY BAKER
63 Parlophone R5040 A Little Like Lovin'/Try Being Nice To Me . . . 6

ERNEST BAKER
00 Grapevine 2000 110 Alone Again/Do It With Feeling 15

GINGER BAKER('S AIRFORCE)
(see also Graham Bond Organisation, Cream, Blind Faith, Fela Ransome-Kuti [& Africa '70], Harold McNair, Griffin, Denny Laine)
70 Polydor 56380 Man Of Constant Sorrow/Doin' It . . . 5
71 Polydor 2058 107 Atunde! (We Are Here)/Part 2 (as Ginger Baker Drum Choir) . . . 5
70 Polydor 2662 001 GINGER BAKER'S AIRFORCE (2-LP, gatefold sleeve) . . . 50
70 Polydor 2383 029 AIRFORCE II (LP, gatefold sleeve, with insert) . . . 30
72 Polydor 2383 133 STRATAVARIOUS (LP) . . . 20

GLEN BAKER
(see also Enid)
85 The Stand THE STAND 3 BRIEF ENCOUNTER (LP). . . . 20

HYLDA BAKER
59 Decca F 11186 She Knows Y'know/Makin' Love . . . 7
69 Columbia DB 8936 Nearest And Dearest/The More You Laugh . . . 6

JEANETTE BAKER
59 Vogue Pop V 9143 Everything Reminds Me Of You/JEANETTE & DECKY: Crazy With You. . . . 250
59 Vogue Pop V 9143 Everything Reminds Me Of You/JEANETTE & DECKY: Crazy With You (78) . . . 50

JOHN BAKER
08 Trunk JBH 030 LP THE JOHN BAKER TAPES (LP, 500 only). . . . 20

KENNY BAKER
53 Parlophone MSP 6019 Round About Midnight/Afternoon In Paris. . . . 7
53 Parlophone MSP 6057 Hayfoot, Strawfoot/The Continental . . . 7
55 Jazz Today JTL 1 OPERATION JAM SESSION (10"LP, with The Jazz Today Unit). . . . 50
55 Jazz Today JTL 4 KENNY BAKER QUARTET/AFTER HOURS GROUP (10"LP) . . . 30
55 Jazz Today JTL 5 TRIBUTE TO BENNY CARTER
(10"LP, with The Jazz Today Unit, one side by Bertie King Jazz Group). . . . 20
57 Pye Nixa NJL 10 PRESENTS THE HALF DOZEN (LP) . . . 15
57 Pye Nixa NJT 517 BAKER PLAYS McHUGH (LP) . . . 15
59 Columbia 33S1140 BLOWIN' UP A STORM (LP). . . . 20

LAVERN BAKER (& GLIDERS)
55 Columbia SCM 5172 Tweedle Dee/Tomorrow Night (with Gliders) . . . 500
55 Columbia DB 3591 Tweedle Dee/Tomorrow Night (with Gliders) (78) . . . 40
55 London HLA 8199 Play It Fair/That Old Lucky Sun (with Gliders) . . . 300
55 London HLA 8199 Play It Fair/That Old Lucky Sun (with Gliders) (78). . . . 30
56 London HLE 8260 My Happiness Forever (with Gliders)/Get Up! Get Up! (You Sleepy Head) . . . 300
56 London HLE 8260 My Happiness Forever (with Gliders)/Get Up! Get Up! (You Sleepy Head) (78). . . 25
57 Columbia DB 3879 Jim Dandy/Tra La La (with Gliders). . . . 350
57 Columbia DB 3879 Jim Dandy/Tra La La (with Gliders) (78) . . . 25
57 London HLE 8396 I Can't Love You Enough/Still . . . 150
57 London HLE 8396 I Can't Love You Enough/Still (78) . . . 25

			MINT VALUE £
57	London HLE 8442	Game Of Love/Jim Dandy Got Married	250
57	London HLE 8442	Game Of Love/Jim Dandy Got Married (78)	20
57	London HLE 8524	Humpty Dumpty Heart/Love Me Right	150
57	London HLE 8524	Humpty Dumpty Heart/Love Me Right (78)	20
58	London HLE 8638	Learning To Love/Substitute	100
58	London HLE 8638	Learning To Love/Substitute (78)	15
58	London HLE 8672	Whipper Snapper/Harbour Lights	100
58	London HLE 8672	Whipper Snapper/Harbour Lights (78)	20
59	London HLE 8790	I Cried A Tear/St. Louis Blues	50
59	London HLE 8790	I Cried A Tear/St. Louis Blues (78)	20
59	London HLE 8871	I Waited Too Long/You're Teasing Me	30
59	London HLE 8871	I Waited Too Long/You're Teasing Me (78)	25
59	London HLE 8945	So High So Low/If You Love Me (I Won't Care)	30
59	London HLE 8945	So High So Low/If You Love Me (I Won't Care) (78)	25
60	London HLE 9023	Tiny Tim/For Love Of You	35
60	London HLE 9252	Bumble Bee/My Turn Will Come	25
61	London HLE 9300	You're The Boss/I'll Never Be Free (with Jimmy Ricks)	45
61	London HLK 9343	Saved/Don Juan	30
61	London HLK 9468	Hey, Memphis/Voodoo Voodoo	50
63	London HLK 9649	See See Rider/The Story Of My Love (I Had A Dream)	25
65	Atlantic AET 6009	THE BEST OF LAVERN BAKER (EP)	80
58	London HA-E 2107	ROCK 'N' ROLL WITH LAVERN BAKER (LP, with thin card cover)	400
58	London Jazz LTZK 15139	SINGS BESSIE SMITH (LP)	75
61	London HA-K 2422	SAVED (LP)	60
63	London HA-K 8074	SEE SEE RIDER (LP)	50
64	Atlantic ATL 5002	THE BEST OF LAVERN BAKER (LP, plum label)	60
68	Atlantic 587/588 133	SEE SEE RIDER (LP, reissue)	20

MICKEY BAKER
(see also Mighty Flea, Champion Jack Dupree)

70	Major Minor SMLP 67	IN BLUNDERLAND (LP)	30

SALLY BAKER

s	Old Dog PUP 1	IN THE SPOTLIGHT (LP)	50

SAM BAKER

68	Monument MON 1009	I Believe In You/I'm Number One	22

TWO-TON BAKER

55	London HL 8121	Clink, Clank (In My Piggy Bank)/Mr. Froggie (Went A Courtin')	40
55	London HL 8121	Clink, Clank (In My Piggy Bank)/Mr. Froggie (Went A Courtin') (78)	10

VICKY BAKER

64	London HLU 9856	No More Foolish Stories/Darling Say The Word	15

YVONNE BAKER
(see also Sensations, Bobby Paris)

77	London HLU 10553	You Didn't Say A Word/BOBBY PARIS: Night Owl	15

BAKER-GURVITZ ARMY
(see also Ginger Baker, Three Man Army, Parrish & Gurvitz, Gun, Sharks)

75	Mountain TOP 4	The Gambler/Time	5
74	Vertigo 9103 201	BAKER-GURVITZ ARMY (LP)	15

BAKERLOO
(see also Colosseum, Uriah Heep, Humble Pie)

69	Harvest HAR 5004	Driving Backwards/Once Upon A Time	25
69	Harvest SHVL 762	BAKERLOO (LP, gatefold sleeve, no EMI logo on label)	200

BAKER STREET PHILHARMONIC
(see also Mike Vickers)

71	Pye International 7N 25540	The Last One/Theme From 'Love Story'	5
70	Pye Intl. NSPL 28131	BY THE LIGHT OF THE MOON (LP)	15

BAKER TWINS

64	Pye 7N 15628	He's No Good/Words Written On Water	20

BALANCE

81	Portrait PRTA 1477	Breaking Away/It's So Strange	8
73	Incus INCUS 11	BALANCE (LP)	70
73	Private pressing	IN FOR THE COUNT (LP)	20
81	Portrait	BALANCE (LP, reissue)	12
82	Portrait	IN FOR THE COUNT (LP, reissue)	12

BALDHEAD GROWLER

67	Jump Up JU 531	Sausage/Bingo Woman	8

CHRIS BALDO

68	Vogue VRS 7029	Living For Your Love/Arretez - Vous A Saint Michel	15

LONG JOHN BALDRY
(see also Rod Stewart, Alexis Korner, Bluesology)

64	United Artists UP 1056	Up Above My Head (I Hear Music In The Air)/You'll Be Mine (with Rod Stewart)	50
65	United Artists UP 1078	I'm On To You Baby/Goodbye Baby	10
65	United Artists UP 1107	How Long Will It Last/House Next Door	35
66	United Artists UP 1124	Unseen Hands/Turn On Your Lovelight	10
66	United Artists UP 1136	The Drifter/Only A Fool Breaks His Own Heart	50
66	United Artists UP 1158	Cuckoo/Bring My Baby Back To Me	20
67	United Artists UP 1204	Only A Fool Breaks His Own Heart/Let Him Go (And Let Me Love You)	15
65	United Artists UEP 1013	LONG JOHN'S BLUES (EP, with Hoochie Coochie Men)	80
64	United Artists ULP 1081	LONG JOHN'S BLUES (LP, with Hoochie Coochie Men)	70
66	United Artists (S)ULP 1146	LOOKING AT LONG JOHN (LP)	50
68	Pye N(S)PL 18228	LET THERE BE LONG JOHN (LP, unissued)	0
69	Pye N(S)PL 18306	WAIT FOR ME (LP)	15
72	Warner Bros. K46160	EVERYTHING STOPS FOR TEA (LP, gatefold sleeve, green label)	20

MINT VALUE £

THOR BALDURSSON
67 Decca F12653 — Arlene Chateau/Painter 20

BALDWIN
67 Decca F22624 — The Land At Rainbows End/Beautiful Butterfly 20

KEITH BALFOUR
69 Studio One SO 2079 — Dreaming/Tired Of Waiting 20

BALIL
93 Rising High RSN 72 — Parasight/Island/Rosary Pilots/Avidya (12") 20
95 Pure Plastic PP 005 — Nine Open/RUE EAST: Endless Filters (12") 8

CANNON BALL (Carl Bryan) & JOHNNY MELODY (Moore)
69 Big Shot BI 518 — Parapinto/Cool Hand Luke 20

DAVE BALLANTYNE
(see also Just Plain Jones, Esprit De Corps)
66 Columbia DB 7807 — I Can't Express It/Ginger Eyes 6
66 Columbia DB 7896 — Love Around The World/Wonder Full Of Women 6

FLORENCE BALLARD
(see also Supremes)
68 Stateside SS 2113 — It Doesn't Matter How I Say It (It's What I Say That Matters)/Goin' Out Of My Head 75
68 Stateside SS 2113 — It Doesn't Matter How I Say It (It's What I Say That Matters)/Goin' Out Of My Head (DJ Copy) 90

HANK BALLARD (& MIDNIGHTERS)
(see also Midnighters)
59 Parlophone R 4558 — The Twist/Kansas City 50
60 Parlophone R 4682 — Finger Poppin' Time/I Love You, I Love You So-o-o 40
60 Parlophone R 4688 — The Twist/Teardrops On Your Letter 40
60 Parlophone R 4707 — Let's Go, Let's Go, Let's Go/If You'd Forgive Me 40
61 Parlophone R 4728 — The Hoochie Coochie Coo/LITTLE WILLIE JOHN: Walk Slow 40
61 Parlophone R 4762 — Let's Go Again/Deep Blue Sea 50
61 Parlophone R 4771 — The Continental Walk/What Is This I See 30
72 Mojo 2093 010 — Annie Had A Baby/Teardrops On Your Letter 10
80s Urban — From The Loveside/FOSTER SYLVERS: Misdemeanor 10
61 Parlophone PMC 1158 — SPOTLIGHT ON HANK BALLARD (LP) 150
63 London HA 8101 — THE JUMPIN' HANK BALLARD (LP) 100

KAYE BALLARD
55 Brunswick 05376 — Triumph Of Love/Where Were You Last Night? 6
55 Brunswick 05436 — Don't You Tell Pa/In Love And Out Again 5

BALLOON BUSTERS
69 Pye 7N 17748 — Alcock And Brown/Bluer Than Blue (p/s) 8
69 Pye 7N 17748 — Alcock And Brown/Bluer Than Blue (no p//s) 5

BALLOON CORPS
69 Stateside SS8034 — Make It Right/Muddy Water 20

BALLOON FARM
68 London HLP 10185 — A Question Of Temperature/Hurtin' For Your Love 90

BALLS
(see also Denny Laine, Lemon Tree, Trevor Burton, Uglys, Wizzard)
71 Wizard WIZ 101 — Fight For My Country/Janie Slow Down 30

LORI BALMER
68 Polydor 56293 — Treacle Brown/Four Faces West 12

BALTIMORE & OHIO MARCHING BAND
67 Stateside SS 2065 — Lapland/Condition Red 60
67 Stateside SS 2065 — Lapland/Condition Red (DJ copy) 200
68 Stateside (S)SL 10231 — LAPLAND (LP) 30

BAMA WINDS
69 Island ILPS 9096 — WINDY (LP) 22

BAM BAM
88 Desire Records WANTX 7 — Where's Your Child/Spend The Night (12") 10

BAMBI
76 Sol-Doon SDR 019 — Lady Of Lies/Somebody Told Me 15

BAMBIS
64 Oriole CB 1965 — Not Wrong/Handle With Care 45
65 CBS 201778 — Baby Blue/If This Is Love 45

BAMBOO SHOOT
68 Columbia DB 8370 — The Fox Has Gone To Ground/There And Back Again Lane 200

BAMBOOS OF JAMAICA
70 Pye Intl. 7N 25515 — Reggae Man/Candy 6

BANANA BUNCH
(see also Nite People)
71 DJM DJS 252 — Tra-La-La Song/Season Of The Rain 15
70 Page One POF 183 — Tra-La-La Song/Funky Hoe 20

BANANAMEN
83 Big Beat NS 88 — The Crusher/Love Me/Surfin' Bird (p/s) 5

BANANARAMA
85 London NANPD 9 — Do Not Disturb (3- shaped picture discs with plinth) 15
86 London NAN PD 11 — More Than Physical/Venus/Scarlett (picture disc, PVC sleeve) 15

MINT VALUE £

BANBARRA

76	United Artists UP 36113	Shack Up Parts 1 & 2	10
85	Stateside 12STATES 1	Shack Up (Extended)/Shack Up (Part 1)/Shack Up (Part II) (12"p/s)	10

BANCO DE GAIA

95	Bark L 011 S	LAST TRAIN TO LHASA (4-LP, limited edition)	18

THE BAND

(see also Levon & The Hawks, Bob Dylan, Ronnie Hawkins, Robbie Robertson)

68	Capitol CL 15559	The Weight/I Shall Be Released	8
69	Capitol CL 15613	Up On Cripple Creek/The Night They Drove Old Dixie Down	8
69	Capitol CL 15629	Rag Mama Rag/The Unfaithful Servant	5
73	Capitol CL 15767	Ain't Got No Home/Get Up Jake	5
78	Warner Bros K 17187	Theme From The Last Waltz/Out Of The Blue	5
68	Capitol T 2955	MUSIC FROM BIG PINK (LP, black/rainbow label, mono)	50
68	Capitol ST 2955	MUSIC FROM BIG PINK (LP, black/rainbow label, stereo)	40

BAND AKA

81	Epic EPC A13 2376	Grace/Instrumental (12")	12

BANDITS

85	Hosspig HPG1	Treasure Trove/Right In The Head (p/s)	25

BAND OF ANGELS

(see also Mike D'Abo, Manfred Mann)

64	United Artists UP 1049	Not True As Yet/Me	15
64	United Artists UP 1066	Gonna Make A Woman Of You/She'll Never Be You	15
66	Piccadilly 7N 35279	Leave It To Me/Too Late My Love	15
66	Piccadilly 7N 35292	Invitation/Cheat And Lie	70

BAND OF JOY

78	Poydor 2310588	BAND OF JOY (LP, with lyric insert)	25

BAND OF MERCY & SALVATION

69	Duke DU 20	Suffering Stink/BOB MELODY: The Break (B-side actually by Winston Francis)	50

BANDOGGS

(see also Peter & Chris Coe)

78	Transatlantic LTRA 504	BANDOGGS (LP)	18

BANDWAGON

(see under Johnny Johnson & Bandwagon)

BANDY LEGS

(see also Quartz)

74	WWW WWS 01	Ride Ride/Don't Play Games	20
76	Jet JET 783	Bet You Can't Dance/Circles	20

BANG

(see also Quartz)

72	EST 11015	BANG (LP)	35

BANG

72	Capitol CL15722	Questions/Future Shock	20

ED BANGER

(see also Nosebleeds, Slaughter & The Dogs)

78	Rabid TOSH 106	Kinnel Tommy/Baby Was A Baby (p/s)	7
78	EMI International INT 570	Kinnel Tommy/Baby Was A Baby (reissue, numbered p/s)	7
81	Spiv DIV 1	I've Just Had My Car Nicked/P.C. Plod/Sponge (p/s, with photo insert)	8
83	Cloud Nine CNS 01	Poor People/Vicars In The Dark (p/s)	7

BANGOR FLYING CIRCUS

70	Stateside-Dunhill SSL 5022	BANGOR FLYING CIRCUS (LP)	25

DEVENDRA BANHART

05	XL XLLP 185	REJOICING IN THE HANDS/NINO ROJO (2-LP)	25

BESSIE BANKS

64	Red Bird BC 106	Go Now/Sounds Like My Baby	80
64	Red Bird BC 106	Go Now/Sounds Like My Baby(DJ Copy)	100
67	Verve VS 563	I Can't Make It (Without You Baby)/Need You	100
67	Verve VS 563	I Can't Make It (Without You Baby)/Need You (DJ Copy)	100
68	Soul City SC 105	Go Now/Sounds Like My Baby (reissue)	25
75	Contempo CS 2070	Baby You Sure Know How To Get To Me/Try To Leave Me If You Can	35

DARRELL BANKS

66	London HL 10070	Open The Door To Your Heart/Our Love (Is In The Pocket) (demo only)	900
66	Stateside SS 536	Open The Door To Your Heart/Our Love (Is In The Pocket) (1st pressing demo with white/red label)	150
66	Stateside SS 536	Open The Door To Your Heart/Our Love (Is In The Pocket) (1st pressing)	40
66	Stateside SS 536	Open The Door To Your Heart/Our Love (Is In The Pocket) (2nd pressing demo with green/white label)	90
66	Stateside SS 536	Open The Door To Your Heart/Our Love (Is In The Pocket) (2nd pressing)	20
67	Atlantic 5841 120	Angel Baby (Don't You Ever Leave Me)/Look Into The Eyes Of A Fool	50
69	Stax STAX 124	Just Because Your Love Is Gone/I'm The One Who Loves You	120
77	Atlantic K 10879	Angel Baby (Don't You Ever Leave Me)/Look Into The Eyes Of A Fool (reissue)	10
69	Stax SXATS 1011	HERE TO STAY (LP)	50

HOMER BANKS

66	Liberty LIB 12028	A Lot Of Love/Fighting To Win	30
66	Liberty LIB 12028	A Lot Of Love/Fighting To Win (DJ Copy)	60
67	Liberty LIB 12047	60 Minutes Of Your Love/Do You Know What	30
67	Liberty LIB 12047	60 Minutes Of Your Love/Do You Know What (DJ Copy)	60

MINT VALUE £

67	Liberty LIB 12060	Hooked By Love/Lady Of Stone	40
67	Liberty LIB 12060	Hooked By Love/Lady Of Stone (DJ Copy)	75
68	Minit MLF 11004	Round The Clock Lover Man/Foolish Hearts Break Fast	15
68	Minit MLF 11007	60 Minutes Of Your Love/A Lot Of Love	15
69	Minit MLF 11015	Me Or Your Mama/I Know You Know I Know You Know	10
70	Liberty LBF 15392	60 Minutes Of Your Love/I Know You Know I Know You Know	10
72	United Artists UP 35360	Hooked By Love/Lady Of Stone (reissue)	8

LARRY BANKS

67	Stateside SS 579	I Don't Wanna Do It/I'm Coming Home	60
67	Stateside SS 579	I Don't Wanna Do It/I'm Coming Home (DJ Copy)	75

LLOYD BANKS

66	Reaction 591 008	We'll Meet Again/Look Out Girl	18

PETER BANKS

(see also Syndicats, Syn, Neat Change, Yes, Flash, Jan Akkerman, Phil Collins, Steve Hackett)

73	Sovereign SVNA 7256	PETER BANKS (LP, gatefold sleeve)	30

BANNED

77	Can't Eat EAT 1 UP	Little Girl/CPGJ's (stamped white labels, in handmade p/s)	50
77	Can't Eat EAT 1 UP	Little Girl/CPGJ's (stamped white labels)	12

BANSHEES

64	Columbia DB 7361	I Got A Woman/Don't Say Goodnight And Mean Goodbye	25
65	Columbia DB 7530	Big Buildin'/Mockingbird	20
65	Columbia DB 7752	I'm Gonna Keep On Loving You/Yes Indeed	15

BUJU BANTON

94	Jet Star CRT 195R	Champion (Four Mixes) (12", stamped white label, remixed by Tax Dodgers)	15

PATO BANTON

85	Ariwa ARI LP 023	MAD PROFESSOR CAPTURES PATO BANTON (LP)	15

SELWYN BAPTISTE

70	Black Swan BW 1402	Mo' Bay/RECO'S ALL STARS: Going West	10

BARBARA & BRENDA

68	Direction 58-3799	Never Love A Robin/Sally's Party	20

BARBARA & WINSTON

64	Island WI 418	The Dream/I Love You	18

BARBARA ANN

65	Piccadilly 7N 35221	You've Lost That Loving Feeling/Till The Summer Time	15
65	Piccadilly 7N 35244	Black Is The Colour Of My True Love's Hair/Since You've Loved Me	6

BARBARIANS

65	Stateside SS 449	Are You A Boy Or Are You A Girl/Take It Or Leave It	25
66	Stateside SS 497	Moulty/I'll Keep On Seeing You	30

BARBECUE BOB

67	Kokomo K 1002	GEORGIA BLUES NO. 1 (LP, 99 copies only)	100

BARBED WIRE

86	Oi Records OIR 006	THE AGE THAT DIDN'T CARE (LP)	20

JOHN HENRY BARBEE

65	Storyville 670 171	PORTRAITS IN BLUES VOLUME 9 (LP)	25

CHRIS BARBER('S JAZZ BAND)

(see also Ottilie Patterson, Lonnie Donegan, Sonny Terry & Brownie McGhee, Kenneth Washington & Chris Barber, Dickie Bishop & Sidekicks)

SINGLES

54	Columbia SCMC 10	White Christmas/On A Christmas Day (with Lonnie Donegan, export issue)	15
55	Decca F 10492	Bobby Shafto/The Martinique	8
55	Decca F 10666	It's Tight Like That/All The Girls Go Crazy About The Way I Walk	8
56	Tempo A 116	Precious Lord, Lead Me On (with Lonnie Donegan)/Tiger Rag	8
56	Tempo A 132	Saratoga Swing/Ice Cream	5
57	Tempo A 160	Ice Cream/Down By The Riverside	5

LPs

54	Decca LF 1198	NEW ORLEANS JOYS (10", with Lonnie Donegan's Skiffle Group)	25
55	Nixa Jazz Today NJL 1	ECHOES OF HARLEM (with Ottilie Patterson)	20
55	Jazz Today JTL 3	CHRIS BARBER PLAYS VOL. 1 (10")	20
56	Nixa Jazz Today NJT 500	CHRIS BARBER PLAYS VOL. 1 (10", reissue)	15
56	Nixa Jazz Today NJT 502	CHRIS BARBER PLAYS VOL. 2 (10")	15
57	Nixa Jazz Today NJT 505	CHRIS BARBER PLAYS VOL. 3 (10")	15
57	Nixa Jazz Today NJT 508	CHRIS BARBER PLAYS VOL. 4 (10")	15
57	Columbia 33S 1112	JAZZ SACRED AND SECULAR (10", with Lonnie Donegan)	15
57	Nixa Jazz Today NJL 6	CHRIS BARBER IN CONCERT (with Ottilie Patterson)	15
58	Pye Nixa Jazz NJL 15	CHRIS BARBER IN CONCERT VOL. 2 (with Ottilie Patterson)	15
58	Pye Nixa Jazz NJL 17	CHRIS BARBER IN CONCERT VOL. 3 (with Ottilie Patterson)	15
58	Decca LK 4246	BARBER'S BEST	15
59	Columbia 33SX 1158	BAND BOX VOL. 1	15
59	Columbia 33SX 1189	BARBER IN BERLIN VOL. 1 (with Ottilie Patterson)	15
59	Columbia 33SX	BARBER IN BERLIN VOL. 2 (with Ottilie Patterson)	15
60	Columbia 33SX 1245	BAND BOX VOL. 2 - ELITE SYNCOPATIONS (stereo SCX 3319)	15
61	Columbia 33SX 1321	CHRIS BARBER'S AMERICAN JAZZ BAND (also stereo SCX 3376)	15
61	Columbia 33SX 1333	BLUES BOOK (with Ottilie Patterson, also stereo SCX 3384)	15
61	Columbia 33SX 1346	AT THE LONDON PALLADIUM (also stereo [SCX 3392])	15
61	Columbia 33SX 1401	BEST YET!	15
65	Columbia 33SX 1657	GOOD MORNIN' BLUES	25
65	Decca LK 4742	FOLK BARBER STYLE (mono)	15
65	Phase 4 Stereo PFS 4070	FOLK BARBER STYLE (as Chris Barber & His Jazz Band)	15

MINT VALUE £

CHRIS BARBER'S SKIFFLE GROUP

(see also Lonnie Donegan, Johnny Duncan & Blue Grass Boys)

58	Pye Jazz 7NJ 2014	Doin' My Time/Where Could I Go? (with Johnny Duncan)	15
58	Pye Jazz 7NJ 2017	Can't You Line 'Em/Gipsy Dave (with Dickie Bishop)	15
57	Pye Jazz NJE 1025	CHRIS BARBER SKIFFLE GROUP (EP)	20

CHRIS BARBER AND HIS BAND

67	Marmalade 598 005	Catcall/Mercy Mercy Mercy	50
69	Marmalade 558 013	Battersea Rain Dance/Sleepy Joe	20
69	Marmalade 608 009	BATTERSEA RAIN DANCE (LP, as Chris Barber & His Band)	30
69	Polydor 2384 020	BATTERSEA RAIN DANCE (LP) (2nd Pressing)	20

CHRIS BARBER SOUL BAND

(see also Louis Jordan & Chris Barber)

65	Columbia DB 7461	Finishing Straight/Morning Train	18

FRANK BARBER FIVE

(see also Frank & Barbarians)

62	Ember JBS 709	Flyover/Golden Shadows	5
66	Columbia DB 7886	Busy Lizzie/Theme From "Mr Broadway"	5

DAVE BARBOUR & HIS ORCHESTRA

59	Oriole CB 1507	Tough/Bu Bam	10

EDDIE BARCLAY & HIS ORCHESTRA

57	Felsted ESD 3041	JAMES DEAN - MUSIC FROM HIS FILMS (EP)	15

EDDIE BARCLAY & QUINCY JONES

58	Felsted PDL 85056	EDDIE AND QUINCY (LP)	15

RUE BARCLAY & PEGGY DUNCAN

54	London HL 8033	Tongue Tied Boy/River Of Tears	40

TIMOTHY BARCLAY

70	Penny Farthing PEN 740	Catch The Wind/The Girl From Indiana	12

BARCLAY JAMES HARVEST

(see also Bombadil, John Lees, Woolly Wolstenholme)

68	Parlophone R 5693	Early Morning/Mr. Sunshine	30
69	Harvest HAR 5003	Brother Thrush/Poor Wages	15
70	Harvest HAR 5025	Taking Some Time On/The Iron Maiden	15
71	Harvest HAR 5034	Mocking Bird/Vanessa Simmons	10
72	Harvest HAR 5051	I'm Over You/Child Of Man	10
72	Harvest HAR 5058	Thank You/Medicine Man	10
73	Harvest HAR 5068	Rock And Roll Woman/The Joker (BJH logo p/s)	12
74	Polydor 2058 474	Poor Boy Blues/Crazy City	7
74	Polydor (matrix: SH 1041/2)	Negative Earth/RARE BIRD: Diamonds (33rpm flexidisc with Sounds magazine)	10
74	Polydor (matrix: SH 1041/2)	Negative Earth/RARE BIRD: Diamonds (33rpm flexidisc without Sounds magazine)	5
75	Harvest HAR 5094	Mocking Bird/Galadriel	5
91	Swallowtail SWALLOW 2	Too Much On Your Plate (fan club flexi)	5
70	Harvest SHVL 770	BARCLAY JAMES HARVEST (LP, gatefold sleeve, no EMI box on label)	50
71	Harvest SHVL 788	ONCE AGAIN (LP, gatefold sleeve, no EMI box on label)	30
71	Harvest SHVL 794	BARCLAY JAMES HARVEST AND OTHER SHORT STORIES (LP, gatefold sleeve)	25
72	Harvest Q4SHVL 788	ONCE AGAIN (LP, quadrophonic)	40
73	Harvest SHSP 4023	BABY JAMES HARVEST (LP)	20

PETER BARDENS

(see also Cheynes, Peter B's, Shotgun Express, Them, Village, Camel, Steve Tilston)

70	Transatlantic TRA 222	THE ANSWER (LP, white/lilac label with 't' logo)	80
71	Transatlantic TRA 243	PETER BARDENS (LP, gatefold sleeve, side one label is multi-coloured)	50
76	Transatlantic TRASAM 36	VINTAGE '69 (LP, featuring Peter Green, clear vinyl)	25
76	Transatlantic TRASAM 36	VINTAGE '69 (LP, featuring Peter Green)	20

BRIGITTE BARDOT

66	Vogue VRS 7018	Mister Sun/Gang Gang (p/s)	100
66	Vogue VRS 7018	Mister Sun/Gang Gang	30
68	Pye International 7N 25450	Harley-Davidson/Contact (p/s)	100
68	Pye International 7N 25450	Harley-Davidson/Contact	30
63	Philips BL 7561	BRIGITTE BARDOT (LP)	120
64	Philips B 77 984	'BB'	100

BARDS

68	Capitol CL 15536	The Owl And The Pussycat/Light Of Love	25

BARDS OF BARLEYCORN

77	Beet Music BMR 101	WHEN GRANDMA USED TO CALL (LP)	40

BOBBY BARE

(see also Bill Parsons, Skeeter Davis & Bobby Bare)

60	Top Rank JAR 310	I'm Hanging Up My Rifle/That's Where I Want To Be	8
63	RCA RCA 1352	Detroit City/Heart Of Ice	5
63	RCA RCA 1366	500 Miles Away From Home/It All Depends On Linda	5
64	RCA RCX 7139	DETROIT CITY (EP)	10
66	RCA RD 7783	CONSTANT SORROW (LP)	12
68	RCA SF 7918	ENGLISH COUNTRYSIDE (LP, with Hillsiders)	12

BARE FOOT

71	Pye 7N 45110	Frightened/Girl Are You A Woman Now (Promo copies say "Bear Foot")	15

BAREFOOT BLUES BAND

70	Beacon BEA 163	Can't You See/Sunday Morning Barefoot Blues	25
72	Deram DM 353	The Spirit Of Joe Hill/I Believe In Music	8
73	Deram DM 372	Getting Better All The Time/Half Of Me	6

MINT VALUE £

MINOUCHE BARELLI

67	CBS 2806	Boum Badaboum/Let Me Take You	15

MARK BARKAN

67	Stateside SS 2064	A Great Day For The Clown/Pity The Woman	15

BAR-KAYS

(see also Otis Redding)

67	Stax 601 014	Soul Finger/Knucklehead	10
68	Stax 601 036	A Hard Day's Night/I Want Someone	6
69	Atlantic 584 244	Soul Finger/Knucklehead (reissue)	8
69	Stax STAX 135	Midnight Cowboy/A.J. The House Fly	6
70	Stax STAX 146	Sing And Dance/I Thank You	6
78	Stax 12 STAX 505	Holy Ghost/Monster (12")	15
69	Atco 228 030	SOUL FINGER (LP)	30
69	Stax SXATS 1009	GOTTA GROOVE (LP)	25
71	Stax 2362 003	BLACK ROCK (LP)	20
73	Stax 2325 087	DO YOU SEE WHAT I SEE? (LP)	20
76	Stax STX 1033	COLD BLOODED (LP)	15

BUTCH BARKER

75	Creole CR 113	The Joker/Juicie Brucie	8

DAVE BARKER

(see also Glen & Dave, Dave & Ansell Collins, Bobby & Dave, Aggrovators, David Crooks, Dennis Alcapone, Don Drummond, Owen Gary, Lizzy & Dennis, Bob Marley, Lester Sterling, Busty Brown)

70	Duke DU 74	Funkey Reggae/TOMMY McCOOK & SUPERSONICS: I Love You My Baby (B-side actually by Versatiles)	30
70	Punch PH 20	Prisoner Of Love/BUSTY & UPSETTERS: Soul Juice	25
70	Punch PH 22	You Betray Me/Will You Still Love Me Tomorrow?	20
70	Punch PH 25	Shocks Of Mighty Parts 1 & 2	15
70	Punch PH 42	Reggae Meeting/MARTIN ALL STARS: Soul Bone	20
70	Jackpot JP 736	The Fastest Man Alive/NORMAN GRANT: Bloodshot Eyes	15
70	Jackpot JP 742	Wet Version/I Got To Get Away	15
70	Jackpot JP 745	Girl Of My Dreams/On Broadway	40
70	High Note HS 049	She Want It/FIRST GENERATION: Give Him Up	15
70	Randy's RAN 503	October/RANDY'S ALLSTARS: Time Out	15
70	Unity UN 567	Blessed Are The Meek (with Slim Smith)/JEFF BARNES & UNIQUES: The People's Voice	20
70	Techniques TE915	Karatae/Version	20
70	Upsetter US 331	Shocks Of Mighty/Set Me Free (with Upsetters)	15
70	Upsetter US 344	Some Sympathy/UNTOUCHABLES: Tender Love	20
70	Upsetter US 347	Sound Underground/Don't Let The Sun Catch You Crying (features the Wailers)	80
71	Upsetter US 358	Shocks '71/HURRICANES: You've Got To Be Mine	20
71	Upsetter US 362	Groove Me/UPSETTERS: Screwdriver	15
71	Upsetter US 364	What A Confusion/UPSETTERS: Confusion - Version 2	25
71	Ackee ACK 113	Johnny Dollar/Version	15
71	Ackee ACK 119	Life Of A Millionaire/Version	15
71	Trojan TR 7851	Sex Machine/You Left Me And Gone (both sides with Aggrovators)	20
71	Punch PH 69	What A Confusion/BOB MARLEY: Small Axe	45
71	Supreme SUP 228	Double Heavy/Johnny Dollar	20
71	Downtown DT 482	Only The Strong Survive/Only The Strong - Version	15
72	Jackpot JP 803	You'll Be Sorry/Green Grow The Lilacs	12
72	Big Shot BI 614	Are You Sure/I Don't Know Why (B-side actually by Sensations)	6
72	Fab FAB 25	Green Grow The Lilacs/JIMMY RILEY: Keep An Eye (On Your Closest Friend) (white label)	12
76	Trojan TRL 127	PRISONER OF LOVE (LP)	45

RONNIE BARKER

78	EMI EMI 2768	Going Straight/String Bean Queen	6
78	BBC RESL 60	But First The News/Night Night (With Ronnie Corbett)	5
78	Alaska ALA 2015	Pismonunciation/The Vicar of St. Cain and Abel (with p/s)	6
78	Alaska ALA 2015	Pismonunciation/The Vicar of St. Cain and Abel	5

BARLASTON DOWN

73	Decca F13321	Always/Mean Woman Mambo	7

BARLEY BREE

67	Piccadilly 7N 35393	Sometime In The Morning/Save Your Love	20

BARNABY RUDGE

(see also Will Malone)

68	CBS 3262	Joe, Organ & Co./Railway Jim	10

BARNES/ADAMS

60s	Lyntone LYN 1021	When It Comes To The Crunch (It's Smiths Time)/Rhythm And Crunch (flexi, p/s)	15

BARNEY J. BARNES & INTRO.

67	Decca F 12662	It Must Be Love/Can't Stand The Pain	10

BENNY BARNES

60	Mercury AMT 1094	Token Of Love/That-A-Boy Willie	20

DENA BARNES

80	Grapevine GRP 141	If You Ever Walked Out Of My Life/Who Am I	15

JEFF BARNES

(see also Hugh Roy, Dave Barker, Darker Shade Of Blue, Delroy Wilson)

70	Jackpot JP 735	Get In The Groove/JOHN HOLT: A Little Tear	12
70	Unity UN 568	1,000 Tons Of Version/Wake The Nation (B-side with Hugh Roy)	60
70	Pama PM 802	Jeff Barnes Thing/LENNOX BROWN: Lover's Mood	12
71	Smash SMA 2313	Wake The Nation (with Hugh Roy)/1,000 Tons Of Version	40
71	Gas 163	Peoples Version (work Out) (with PAT KELLY)/TONY LEE & PAT KELLY: Too Late	50

MINT VALUE £

J.J. BARNES

67	Polydor 56722	Day Tripper/Deeper In Love	40
69	Stax STAX 130	Baby Please Come Back Home/Easy Living	35
73	Tamla Motown TMG 870	Real Humdinger/Please Let Me In/I Ain't Gonna Do It	12
74	Contempo CS 2009	To An Early Grave/To An Early Grave (Instrumental Version)	5
78	Contempo 2105	She's Mine/Erroll Flynn	15
75	Contempo CLP 520	THE GROOVESVILLE MASTERS (LP)	15
77	Contempo CLP 604	SARA SMILE (LP)	20

J.J. BARNES/STEVE MANCHA

69	Stax SXATS 1012	RARE STAMPS (LP)	50

LLOYD BARNES

64	Blue Beat BB 235	Time Is Hard/BUSTER'S ALLSTARS: Reincarnation	30

RICHARD BARNES

(see also Quiet Five, Tony Hazzard)

70	Philips BF 1840	Take To The Mountains/But It's Now I Need Your Love	7
70	Philips 630 8027	RICHARD BARNES (LP, black/silver label)	45

SIDNEY BARNES

76	Charly CYS 1007	I Hurt On The Other Side/Good Lovin'	15

BARRY BARNETT

58	HMV POP 487	The Book Of Love/All I Have To Do Is Dream	10
58	HMV POP 511	When/Secretly	8
58	HMV POP 521	My Lucky Love/Too Young To Love	8
58	HMV POP 532	Susie Darlin'/Just A Dream	10
59	HMV POP 579	The Diary/Only A Memory	8
59	HMV POP 627	Cuckoo Girl/I'll String Along With You	8
63	HMV POP 1126	The Hit Of The Week/If You Ever Leave Me	5
66	Mercury MF 945	How Can You Explain/If There Wasn't Any You	5

ERIC BARNET(T)

(see also Theo[philus] Beckford)

68	Gas GAS 100	The Horse (actually by Theo Beckford & Group)/Action Line (actually by Versatiles)	12
69	Gas GAS 106	Te Ta Toe (act. by Theo Beckford & Group)/MILTON BOOTHE: Lonely And Blue	12
69	Crab CRAB 37	Quaker City/Double Up (both actually by Theo Beckford & Group)	12
70	Gas GAS 130	Pink Shark/Swing Free (both actually by Theo Beckford & Group)	10
70	Gas GAS 147	Bumper To Bumper/Fat Turkey (both actually by Theo Beckford & Group)	18

BARNFATHER

73	Bell BLL 1341	Clock On The Wall/Hollywood Girls	5

BARNSTORMERS SPASM BAND

(see also Original Barnstormers Spasm Band)

58	Parlophone R 4416	Whistling Rufus/Won't You Come Home, Bill Bailey?	8
58	Parlophone R 4416	Whistling Rufus/Won't You Come Home, Bill Bailey? (78)	15
59	Tempo A 168	Stormin' The Barn/That's All There Is (There Ain't No More)	10
59	Tempo A 168	Stormin' The Barn/That's All There Is (There Ain't No More) (78)	15

H.B. BARNUM

(see also Robins)

61	Fontana H 299	Lost Love/Hallelujah	15
65	Capitol CL 15391	The Record (Baby I Love You)/I'm A Man	40
65	Capitol CL 15391	The Record (Baby I Love You)/I'm A Man (DJ Copy)	80
76	Capitol CL 15851	Heartbreaker/Searchin' For My Soul	10
79	Capitol CL 16067	Heartbreaker/BOBBY PARIS: I Walked Away	10
64	RCA Victor RCX 7147	THE GREAT H.B. BARNUM (EP)	100
62	RCA Victor RD/SF 7500	THE BIG VOICE OF BARNUM . . . H.B., THAT IS (LP, mono/stereo)	15
63	RCA Victor RD/SF 7543	EVERYBODY LOVES H.B. (LP, mono/stereo)	15

CARL BARON & CHEETAHS

63	Columbia DB 7162	This Is Only The Beginning/Beg Borrow Or Steal	15

RIKKY BARON

60	Parlophone R 4706	Angry Young Man/My Lonely Heart	10
63	Parlophone R 4754	Everybody/You're Breaking My Heart	8

BARON WITH HIS POUNDING PIANO

(see also V.I.P.'s)

65	Sue WI 398	Is A Blue Bird Blue/In The Mood	50

BARONS (U.K.)

61	Oriole CB 1608	Cossack/Summertime	12
61	Oriole CB 1620	Samurai/Whirlwind	15

BARONS (U.S.)

57	London HLP 8391	Don't Walk Out/Once In A Lifetime	1700
57	London HLP 8391	Don't Walk Out/Once In A Lifetime (78)	100
71	Jay Boy BOY 45	No More Baby Love/Society Don't Let Us Down	10

BARRABAS

76	Atlantic K 10716	Checkmate/Four Seasons Woman	5

BARRACUDA

73	EMI EMI 2027	Summer Girls/I Feel So Down	10

BARRACUDAS

79	Cells CELLOUT 1	I Want My Woody Back/Subway Surfin' (p/s)	15
80	Zonophone Z 5	Summer Fun/Chevy Baby (p/s, with stickers)	15
80	Zonophone Z 5	Summer Fun/Chevy Baby (p/s, without stickers)	6
80	Zonophone Z 8	His Last Summer/Barracuda Waver/Surfers Are Back (p/s)	6
80	Zonophone Z 11	(I Wish It Could Be) 1965 Again/Rendezvous (p/s)	5

			MINT VALUE £
81	Zonophone Z 17	I Can't Pretend/The KGB (Made A Man Out Of Me) (p/s)	5
80	Zonophone ZONO 103	DROP OUT WITH THE BARRACUDAS (LP)	12

DICKIE BARRETT

58	MGM MGM 976	Smoke Gets In Your Eyes/Remember Me	60

JOE BARRETT

55	Brunswick 05432	I'm Sincere/Why Did You Break My Heart?	8

RICHARD BARRETT & CHANTELS

(see also Chantels)

59	HMV POP 609	Come Softly To Me/Walking Through Dreamland	30

RITCHIE BARRETT

62	London HLK 9552	Some Other Guy/Tricky Dicky	75

'SWEET EMMA' BARRETT

60s	Riverside RLP 364	THE BELL GAL AND HER DIXIELAND BOYS (LP)	15

SYD BARRETT

(see also Pink Floyd)

69	Harvest HAR 5009	Octopus/Golden Hair	150
69	Harvest HAR 5009	Octopus/Golden Hair (Promo with mispelt 'Barratt' and release date 14.11.69)	250
88	Strange Fruit SFPS 043	THE PEEL SESSIONS (12", EP, initial pressing with metallic sleeve)	15
88	Strange Fruit SFPS 043	THE PEEL SESSIONS (12", EP)	12
88	Strange Fruit SFPSCD 043	THE PEEL SESSIONS (CD EP)	10
70	Harvest SHVL 765	THE MADCAP LAUGHS (LP, laminated sleeve, no EMI box on label)	80
70	Harvest SHVL 765	THE MADCAP LAUGHS (LP, matt gatefold sleeve, no EMI box on label)	70
70	Harvest SHSP 4007	BARRETT (LP, laminated sleeve, first pressing with no EMI boxed label)	100
70	Harvest SHSP 4007	BARRETT (LP, textured flipback sleeve, no EMI logo)	45
72	Harvest SHSP 4007	BARRETT (LP, textured non-flipback sleeve, second pressing with EMI boxed logo)	20
74	Harvest SHDW 404	SYD BARRETT (2-LP, reissue of "Madcap"& "Barrett", gatefold sleeve)	25
88	Harvest SHSP 4126	OPEL (LP, gatefold sleeve)	15
93	EMI SYD BOX 1	CRAZY DIAMOND (3-CD box set, with booklet)	25
97	Harvest 7423 855663 18	THE MADCAP LAUGHS (LP, 180gm reissue, heavy quality sleeve)	15
97	Harvest 7423 821450 11	BARRETT (LP, 180gm reissue, heavy quality sleeve)	15
99	Harvest SVLP 153	OPEL (2-LP, 180gm reissue, heavy quality sleeve)	15
99	Simply Vinyl SVLP 153	OPEL (LP 180gm reissue, heavy quality gatefold sleeve)	15
00	Simply Vinyl SVLP 281	BARRETT (LP, 180gm reissue, heavy quality gatefold sleeve)	15
00	Simply Vinyl SVLP 289	THE MADCAP LAUGHS (LP, 180gm reissue, heavy quality gatefold sleeve)	15

WILD WILLY BARRETT

(see also John Otway/Wild Willy Barrett)

77	Logo GO 105	Return Of Kong/Nice To Know You're My Friend (p/s)	5
79	Polydor 2059 067	Let's Play Schools/I Did It Otway (p/s)	5
86	Galvanised DIP 1	ORGANIC BONDAGE (LP, with Stephen Two Names; in wooden sleeve)	15

RAY BARRETTO

63	Columbia DB 7051	El Watusi/Ritmo Sabroso	20
65	Columbia DB 7684	El Watusi/Swingin' Shepherd Blues	20
69	London HL 10262	Acid/Mercy Mercy Baby (withdrawn)	50
67	Island ILP 946	EL WATUSI (LP)	35
69	London HA/SH 8383	ACID (LP)	75

BARRIER

68	Eyemark EMS 1013	Georgie Brown/Dawn Breaks Through (in handmade p/s)	450
68	Eyemark EMS 1013	Georgie Brown/Dawn Breaks Through	250
68	Philips BF 1692	The Tide Is Turning/Place In Your Heart	8
68	Philips BF 1731	Spot The Lights/Uh	70

BARRINO BROTHERS

72	Invictus INV 523	I Shall Not Be Moved/When Love Was A Child	10

BARRON KNIGHTS

72	Penny Farthing PELS 536	ONE MAN'S MEAT (LP)	12
62	Fontana H 368	Let's Face It/Never Miss A Chance	8
63	Columbia DB 7108	Jo-Anne/That's My Girl	5
64	Columbia DB 7188	Comin' Home Baby/Peanut Butter	5
64	Columbia DB 7375	Come To The Dance/Choose Me Tonight	5
64	Columbia DB 7427	The House Of Johann Strauss/She's The One	5
65	Columbia DB 7698	It Was A Very Good Year/Worry And Wonder	5
66	Columbia DB 7884	Round The World Rhythm & Blues/Where There's A Will	5
66	Columbia DB 7933	Doing What She's Not Supposed To Do/Every Night	5
66	Columbia DB 8071	Under New Management Medley (both sides)	5
67	Columbia DB 8161	Lazy Fat People/In The Night	5
67	Columbia DB 8280	Here Come The Bees/It's A Sin	5
68	Columbia DB 8423	I Never Will Marry/Cold In My Nose	5
68	Columbia DB 8485	An Olympic Record/An Olympic Record	5
69	Columbia DB 8612	Love And The World Loves With You/Along Come Those Summer Days	5
69	Columbia DB 8679	Traces/Awake	5
72	Penny Farthnig PEN 786	You're All I Need/Nothin' Doin'	12
64	Columbia SEG 8425	GUYING THE TOP POPS (EP)	8
66	Columbia SEG 8526	THOSE VERSATILE BARRON KNIGHTS (EP)	8
64	Columbia 33SX 1648	CALL UP THE GROUPS (LP)	20
66	Columbia SX 6007	BARRON KNIGHTS (LP)	20
67	Columbia SX 6176	SCRIBED (LP)	20

BARROW POETS

68	Fontana TF 939	Letter In A Bottle (Music "Sleepy Lagoon")/ Dynamite Barbee (Music "Barbee Song")	5
67	Barrow BR 1	AT THE PRINTER'S DEVIL (EP, private pressing)	20

			MINT VALUE £
63	Argo PLP 1072	PRESENT AN ENTERTAINMENT OF POETRY AND MUSIC (LP)	20
68	Fontana STL 5479	FOLK RHYMES TUNES AND VERSES (LP)	15
68	Fontana 6857 003	FINEST FOLK (LP)	18
70	RCA SF 8110	JOKER (LP)	20
72	Argo ZSW 508	OUTPATIENTS (LP)	15
72	Argo ZSW 511	MAGIC EGG (LP)	22

AL BARRY

(see also Desmond Dekker & Aces)

70	Duke DU 81	Ooh Wee/Hold It Baby	5
70	Doctor Bird DB 1502	Morning Sun/MARKONIANS: Over And Over	25
71	Creole 1005	Down We Go/It Pays To Do Good	6

DAVE BARRY & SARA BERNER

56	London HLU 8324	Out Of This World With Flying Saucers Parts 1 & 2 (Tri gold label)	70
56	London HLU 8324	Out Of This World With Flying Saucers Parts 1 & 2 (Tri silver label)	50

DAWN BARRY

71	Phoenix NIX 118	My World Keeps Getting Smaller Evry Day/No Love At All	6

JOE BARRY

61	Mercury AMT 1149	I'm A Fool To Care/I Got A Feeling	15
68	Stateside SS 2127	I Started Loving You Again/California Bound	15
62	Mercury ZEP 10130	A FOOL TO CARE (EP)	100

JOHN BARRY (SEVEN)

(see also Alan Bown, Chad & Jeremy, Adam Faith, Elizabeth Taylor, Desmond Lane, Johnny Pearson, Tony Bennett, Jim Lowe, Lyn Paul, Russ Conway, Lance Fortune, Alan Haven, Countdowns, Johnny De Little, Marion Ryan, Dick Kallman)

SINGLES

57	Parlophone R 4363	Zip Zip/Three Little Fishes (as John Barry & The Seven)	40
57	Parlophone R 4363	Zip Zip/Three Little Fishes (as John Barry & The Seven) (78)	15
58	Parlophone R 4394	Every Which Way/You've Gotta Way (as John Barry Seven)	40
58	Parlophone R 4394	Every Which Way/You've Gotta Way (as John Barry Seven) (78)	15
58	Parlophone R 4418	Big Guitar/Rodeo (as John Barry Seven)	25
58	Parlophone R 4418	Big Guitar/Rodeo (as John Barry Seven) (78)	12
58	Parlophone R 4453	Pancho/Hideaway (as John Barry Seven)	12
58	Parlophone R 4453	Pancho/Hideaway (as John Barry Seven) (78)	12
58	Parlophone R 4488	Farrago/Bee's Knees (as John Barry Seven)	10
58	Parlophone R 4488	Farrago/Bee's Knees (as John Barry Seven) (78)	12
59	Parlophone R 4530	Long John/Snap 'n' Whistle (as John Barry Seven)	10
59	Parlophone R 4530	Long John/Snap 'n' Whistle (as John Barry Seven) (78)	15
59	Parlophone R 4560	Little John/For Pete's Sake (as John Barry Seven)	10
59	Parlophone R 4560	Little John/For Pete's Sake (as John Barry Seven) (78)	15
59	Parlophone R 4582	Twelfth Street Rag/Christella (as John Barry Seven)	7
60	Columbia DB 4414	Hit And Miss/Rockin' Already (as John Barry Seven)	8
60	Columbia DB 4446	Beat For Beatniks/Big Fella (as John Barry Orchestra)	10
60	Columbia DB 4480	Blueberry Hill/Never Let Go (as John Barry Orchestra)	10
60	Columbia DB 4505	Walk Don't Run/I'm Movin' On (as John Barry Seven)	5
60	Columbia DB 4554	Black Stockings/Get Lost Jack Frost (as John Barry Seven)	6
61	Columbia DB 4598	The Magnificent Seven/Skid Row (as John Barry Seven)	5
61	Columbia DB 4659	The Menace/Rodeo (as John Barry Orchestra)	6
61	Columbia DB 4699	Starfire/A Matter Of Who (as John Barry Seven)	6
61	Columbia DB 4746	Watch Your Step/Twist It (as John Barry Seven)	6
62	Columbia DB 4806	Cutty Sark/Lost Patrol (as John Barry Seven & Orchestra)	6
62	Columbia DB 4898	The James Bond Theme/The Blacksmith Blues (with Orchestra) (green or black labels)	10
62	Columbia DB 4941	The Lolly Theme/March Of The Mandarins (as John Barry Seven & Orchestra)	7
63	Columbia DB 7003	The Human Jungle/Onward, Christian Spacemen (in p/s)	18
63	Columbia DB 7003	The Human Jungle/Onward, Christian Spacemen	5
63	Ember EMB S 178	Kinky/Fancy Dance	6
63	Ember EMB S 181	007/From Russia With Love (in p/s)	18
63	Ember EMB S 181	007/From Russia With Love	5
63	Ember EMB S 183	Elizabeth/The London Theme	7
63	Ember EMB S 185	Zulu Stamp/Monkey Feathers (mauve/grey; in p/s)	20
63	Ember EMB S 185	Zulu Stamp/Monkey Feathers (red/yellow label; in p/s)	20
63	Ember EMB S 185	Zulu Stamp/Monkey Feathers (mauve/grey or red/yellow label)	5
63	Lyntone LYN 378	Theme Music From The Ingersoll Trendsetters T.V. Commercial flexidisc with 8-page A4 promo booklet)	35
64	United Artists UP 1060	Seance On A Wet Afternoon/Oublie Ça	10
64	United Artists UP 1068	Goldfinger/Troubador	10
64	Stateside SS 296	Barney's Blues/Theme From The Film "Man In The Middle"(No More)	15
64	Columbia DB 7414	Twenty-Four Hours Ago/Seven Faces	25
65	CBS 201747	A Man Alone (Ipcress File Theme)/Barbara's Theme	10
65	CBS 201822	The Syndicate/What A Question	10
66	CBS 202390	Vendetta/The Danny Scipio Theme	7
66	CBS Special WB 730	James Bond Theme/RAY CONNIFF: Love Is Blue (p/s)	6
67	CBS 202451	Wednesday's Child (Quiller Memorandum)/Sleep Well My Darling	10
67	CBS 2825	You Only Live Twice/The Girl With The Sun In Her Hair	10
67	Ember EMB S 243	007/The Loneliness Of Autumn (in p/s)	15
67	Ember EMB S 243	007/The Loneliness Of Autumn (p/s)	10
69	CBS 3935	The Lion In Winter Parts 1 & 2	10
69	CBS 4468	Midnight Cowboy/Fun City	10
69	CBS 4680	On Her Majesty's Secret Service/We Have All The Time In The World	10
70	Probe PRO 518	The Last Valley/Main Title Theme	5
71	CBS 7469	Theme From "The Persuaders"/The Girl With The Sun In Her Hair	5
72	Polydor 2058 216	This Way Mary/Diamonds Are Forever	7
72	Polydor 2058 275	The Adventurer/Follow Follow	5
80	United Artists UP 634	Midnight Cowboy/Fun City (p/s)	5

MINT VALUE £

EPS

58	Parlophone GEP 8737	THE BIG BEAT (as John Barry Seven)	40
61	Columbia SEG 8069	THE JOHN BARRY SOUND (as John Barry Seven)	20
62	Columbia SEG 8138	BEAT GIRL (as John Barry Seven, with Adam Faith)	30
63	Columbia SEG 8255	JOHN BARRY THEME SUCCESSES	20
63	United Artists UEP 1011	FROM RUSSIA WITH LOVE (soundtrack)	25
64	Ember EMB EP 4544	LONELINESS OF AUTUMN	20
64	United Artists UEP 1012	GOLDFINGER (soundtrack)	25
65	Ember EMB EP 4551	JAMES BOND IS BACK	25
65	United Artists UEP 1015	THUNDERBALL: Thunderball/Death Of Fiona/ Bond Below Disco Volante/ Mr Kiss Kiss Bang Bang (soundtrack)	25
67	CBS WEP 1126	THEMES FROM JAMES BOND FILMS (mail order via Carr's Sport biscuits)	15
67	CBS WEP 1129	BIG THEMES FROM THE BIG SCREEN (mail order via Wall's)	10
67	CBS WEP 1131	GREAT SCREEN THEMES (mail order via Lyon's Bakery)	10

LPs

60	Columbia 33SX 1225	BEAT GIRL (soundtrack, with Adam Faith)	50
61	Columbia 33SX 1358	STRINGBEAT (mono)	30
61	Columbia SCX 3401	STRINGBEAT (stereo)	35
63	United Artists ULP 1052	FROM RUSSIA WITH LOVE (soundtrack, mono)	25
63	United Artists SULP 1052	FROM RUSSIA WITH LOVE (soundtrack, stereo)	35
63	Colpix PXL 459	ELIZABETH TAYLOR IN LONDON (mono)	40
63	Colpix PXL 459	ELIZABETH TAYLOR IN LONDON (stereo)	50
64	Ember NR 5012	ZULU (soundtrack, yellow/orange label, flipback sleeve)	20
64	Stateside S(S)L 10087	MAN IN THE MIDDLE (soundtrack, with Lionel Bart)	30
64	United Artists ULP 1076	GOLDFINGER (soundtrack, mono)	25
64	United Artists SULP 1076	GOLDFINGER (soundtrack, stereo)	30
65	Ember NR 5025	JOHN BARRY PLAYS 007	30
65	Ember NR 56088	FOUR IN THE MORNING (soundtrack, mono)	30
65	Ember NR 56088	FOUR IN THE MORNING (soundtrack, stereo)	35
65	CBS BPG 62598	PASSION FLOWER HOTEL (original cast, mono only)	12
65	CBS BPG 62530	THE IPCRESS FILE (soundtrack, mono only)	30
65	United Artists ULP 1104	THE KNACK (AND HOW TO GET IT) (soundtrack)	30
65	United Artists ULP 1110	THUNDERBALL (soundtrack, mono)	25
65	United Artists SULP 1110	THUNDERBALL (soundtrack, stereo)	30
66	CBS BPG 62665	THE CHASE (soundtrack, mono)	20
66	CBS SBPG 62665	THE CHASE (soundtrack, stereo)	30
66	CBS BPG 62869	THE QUILLER MEMORANDUM (soundtrack, mono)	15
66	CBS SBPG 62869	THE QUILLER MEMORANDUM (soundtrack, stereo)	20
67	United Artists (S)ULP 1168	THE WHISPERERS (soundtrack)	20
67	United Artists (S)ULP 1171	YOU ONLY LIVE TWICE (soundtrack)	20
67	United Artists LAS 29021	THE BEST OF BOND (mono)	15
68	Stateside S(S)L 10263	DEADFALL (soundtrack, Shirley Bassey on 1 track)	35
69	United Artists UAS 29020	ON HER MAJESTY'S SECRET SERVICE (soundtrack, foldout sleeve)	25
69	United Artists UAS 29021	THE BEST OF BOND (stereo reissue)	12
69	CBS 70049	THE LION IN WINTER (soundtrack)	15
69	MCA MUPS 360	BOOM! (soundtrack, with Georgie Fame)	60
71	CBS 64816	THE PERSUADERS (TV soundtrack)	12
71	United Artists UAS 29216	DIAMONDS ARE FOREVER (soundtrack)	20
71	Probe SPB 1027	THE LAST VALLEY (soundtrack, with insert)	25
71	Probe SPB 1027	THE LAST VALLEY (soundtrack, without insert)	18
71	MCA MUPS 441	MARY QUEEN OF SCOTS (soundtrack)	20
72	Ember SE 8008	JOHN BARRY REVISITED (foldout sleeve, initial pressing in 'nude' gatefold sleeve)	25
72	Ember SE 8008	JOHN BARRY REVISITED	20
72	Warner Bros K 56009	ALICE'S ADVENTURES IN WONDERLAND (soundtrack, gatefold sleeve)	15
73	Polydor 2383 156	THE CONCERT JOHN BARRY	12
74	United Artists UAS 29671	THE MAN WITH THE GOLDEN GUN (soundtrack)	15
74	Phase 4 Stereo PFS 4339	THE DAY OF THE LOCUST (soundtrack)	12
83	A&M 394 967-2	OCTOPUSSY (CD, soundtrack, withdrawn)	75

LEN BARRY

(see also Dovells, Electric Indian)

65	Cameo Parkway P 969	Hearts Are Trump/Little White House	30
65	Brunswick 05942	1-2-3/Bullseye	5
65	Brunswick 05942	1-2-3/Bullseye (DJ Copy)	35
66	Brunswick 05949	Like A Baby/Happiness	10
66	Brunswick 05949	Like A Baby/Happiness (DJ Copy)	35
66	Brunswick 05955	Somewhere/It's A Crying Shame	10
66	Brunswick 05955	Somewhere/It's A Crying Shame (DJ Copy)	35
66	Brunswick 05962	It's That Time Of The Year/Happily Ever After	10
66	Brunswick 05962	It's That Time Of The Year/Happily Ever After (DJ Copy)	35
66	Brunswick 05966	I Struck It Rich/Love Is	20
66	Brunswick 05966	I Struck It Rich/Love Is (DJ Copy)	45
67	RCA RCA 1588	The Moving Finger Writes/Our Love	20
67	RCA RCA 1588	The Moving Finger Writes/Our Love (DJ Copy)	30
68	Bell BLL 1022	4-5-6 Now I'm Alone/Funky Night	5
71	Now! NOW 1003	Now I'm Alone/Funky Night	6
72	MCA MU 1172	1-2-3/You Baby	8
73	Paramount PARA 3031	Heaven And Earth/I'm Marching To The Music	15
73	Paramount PARA 3039	It's Time To Fall In Love/Touching, Holding, Feeling	5
66	Cameo Parkway CPE 556	HAVIN' A GOOD TIME (EP)	35
65	Brunswick LAT 8637	1-2-3 (LP)	20
66	Brunswick LAT 8656	IT'S THAT TIME OF YEAR (LP, unreleased, sleeve may not exist)	900
66	Cameo Parkway C 1082	LEN BARRY AND THE DOVELLS (LP)	30
69	Bulldog BDL 1013	MORE FROM THE 1-2-3 MAN (LP)	20
69	RCA Intl. INTS 1027	MY KIND OF SOUL (LP)	12

MINT VALUE £

MARGARET BARRY

60	Top Rank 251020	IRELAND'S QUEEN OF THE TINKERS SINGS (LP)	20

MARGARET BARRY (& MICHAEL GORMAN)

58	Topic 10T 6	STREET SONGS AND FIDDLE TUNES OF IRELAND (10" LP, mid-blue label, later buff/black or dark blue/silver labels)	15

SANDRA BARRY (& THE BOYS)

(see also Boys, Sandra Alfred, Slack Alice)

64	Decca F 11851	Really Gonna Shake/When We Get Married (as Sandra Barry & Boys)	100
65	Pye 7N 15753	The End Of The Line/We Were Lovers	15
65	Pye 7N 15840	Question/You Can Take It From Me	15
66	Pye 7N 17102	Stop! Thief/I Won't Try To Change Your Mind	15

BARRY & THE TAMERLANES

(see also Barry De Vorzon)

63	Warner Bros WB 116	I Wonder What She's Doing Tonight/Don't Go	30
64	Warner Bros WB 124	Roberta/Butterfly	15
64	Warner Bros WM 8145	I WONDER WHAT SHE'S DOING TONIGHT (LP)	80

BARRY SISTERS (U.S.)

(see also Three Barry Sisters)

56	London HLA 8248	Cha Cha Joe/Baby Come A Little Closer	50
56	London HLA 8248	Cha Cha Joe/Baby Come A Little Closer (78)	10
56	London HLA 8304	Till You Come Back To Me/Intrigue	50
56	London HLA 8304	Till You Come Back To Me/Intrigue (78)	10
56	Columbia DB 3843	Sing Me A Sentimental Love Song/The Italian Theme	8
58	Columbia DB 4215	I Hear Bells/I Get Up Ev'ry Morning	8
60	Columbia DB 4562	Misty/Why Don't You Do Right?	8
60	Columbia 33SX 1309	SIDE BY SIDE (LP)	18

LIONEL BART

68	Deram DM 212	Isn't This Where We Came In/May A Man Be Merry	20
61	Decca F11405	Give Us A Kiss For Christmas/How Now Brown Cow	6
59	Decca LF 1324	BART FOR BART'S SAKE (10" LP)	20
68	Deram SML 1028	ISN'T THIS WHERE WE CAME IN (LP, stereo, gatefold sleeve)	40

CHRIS BARTLEY

67	Cameo Parkway P 101	The Sweetest Thing This Side Of Heaven/Love Me Baby	70
67	Cameo Parkway P 101	The Sweetest Thing This Side Of Heaven/Love Me Baby (DJ Copy)	100
68	Bell BLL 1031	I Found A Goodie/Be Mine Forever	30
75	Right On RO 105	I See Your Name/I See Your Name (Instrumental)	10
86	Move MIS 4	Baby I'm For Real/I've Found A Goodie/Truer Words Were Never Spoken/ The Sweetest Thing This Side Of Heaven (12", p/s)	15

BARTOK

(see also Jah Wobble, Damned)

82	On ON 1	Insanity/I Am The Bomb (p/s)	12

RIA BARTOK

64	Columbia DB 7362	See If I Care/I Don't Wanna Leave You	5

EILEEN BARTON

55	Vogue Coral Q 72060	The Year We Fell In Love/I Don't Want To Mambo Polka	10
55	Vogue Coral Q 72075	Fujiyama Mama/I'd've Baked A Cake	100
55	Vogue Coral Q 72075	Fujiyama Mama/I'd've Baked A Cake (78)	10
56	Vogue Coral Q 72122	Cry Me A River/Come Home	20
56	Vogue Coral Q 72122	Cry Me A River/Come Home (78)	10
56	Vogue Coral Q 72148	Teenage Heart/My Social Hot Dog	20
56	Vogue Coral Q 72148	Teenage Heart/My Social Hot Dog (78)	10
56	Vogue Coral Q 72205	Spring It Was/I Have To Tell You	8
57	Vogue Coral Q 72250	Too Close For Comfort/Here I Am In Love Again	5
57	Vogue Coral Q 72270	Without Love/The Scene Of The Crime	10

MARIA BARTON

80	Airship AP 56	RAINFUL DAYS (LP)	100

ROD BARTON (& THE LINCOLNAIRES)

62	Salvo SLO 1812	Dear Old San Francisco/NERVOUS NORVOUS: Does A Chinese Chicken Have A Pigtail	60

DAVE BARTRAM

83	Utopia UTO 2	Black Ice/Excitement (p/s)	5

BASELINE

81	Extrabit EX 1	Suspended Animation/Truth About The Lies (with p/s)	100
81	Extrabit EX 1	Suspended Animation/Truth About The Lies (without p/s)	40

BASEMENT 5

80	Island ILPS9641	1965-80 (LP, with inner, poster and embossed sleeve)	15

BASEMENT JAXX

01	XL XLLP 143X	ROOTY (LP, picture disc, 1000 only)	15

BASEMENT PHIL

91	Basement BRSS 001	Take Me Up (Part 1)/(Part 2)/(Part 3) (12" promo)	25
92	Basement BRSS 002	Bachbeat (Part 1)/I Love You/Bachbeat (Part 2) (12" promo)	12
92	Basement BRSS 009	WE CAN ROCK IT EP (12", as Basement Phil And The Engineers)	10

BASHERS

(see also Mike McGear)

76	Virgin VS 154	The Womble Bashers/Womble Bashers Wock	20

BASHFUL ALLEY

82	Ellie Jay BA 001	Running Blind/My, My, My (p/s, black-and-white or black-and-yellow sleeve)	50
82	Graffiti BA 001	Running Blind/My, My, My (p/s, reissue)	35

MINT VALUE £

ROBBIE BASHO

69	Sonet SNTF 612	FALCONERS ARMS VOL 1. (LP)	20

BASIC BLACK AND PEARL

75	Bus Stop BUS 1030	There'll Come A Time, There'll Come A Day/Right On Baby	15

COUNT BASIE & HIS ORCHESTRA

(see also Joe Williams, Jackie Wilson, Tony Bennett, Lester Young, Ella Fitzgerald)

67	Coral Q 72497	Green Onions/Hang On Sloopy	15
68	MCA MCA 1014	For Your Precious Love/Uptight (with Jackie Wilson)	5
68	Decca AD 1008	For Your Precious Love/Uptight (with Jackie Wilson, export issue)	5
53	Brunswick LA 8589	BASIE'S BEST (10" LP)	15
53	Mercury MG 25015	KANSAS CITY 7/LESTER YOUNG QUARTET (LP, 1 side each)	15
54	Oriole/Mercury MG 25015	COUNT BASIE/LESTER YOUNG (10" LP, 1 side each)	15
55	Columbia 33S 1054	THE COUNT (10" LP)	15
55	Philips BBR 8036	THE OLD AND THE NEW COUNT (10" LP)	15
55	Columbia Clef 33C 9010	THE COUNT BASIE SEXTET (10" LP)	15
61	Columbia SX 1332	STRING ALONG WITH BASIE (LP)	15
65	Verve VLP/SVLP 9082	BASIELAND (LP)	15
66	United Artists (S)ULP 1127	BASIE MEETS BOND (LP)	18
70	Philips 6369 408	AFRIQUE (LP)	18

BASIES

67	Coxsone CS 7030	River Jordan/SOUL VENDORS: Swing Easy	35

BASKIN & COPPERFIELD

70	Decca F 13053	The Long And Winding Road/Beautiful Blue Eyes	10
70	Decca F 23079	I Never See The Sun/Stranger On The Ground	8

BASKING SHARKS

83	RS 001	SHARK ISLAND (LP)	30

ALFIE BASS

60	Pye 7N 15286	Villikens And His Dinah/Rat Catcher's Daughter	6

BILLY BASS

69	Pama PM 761	I Need Your Love So Bad/I'm Coming To	50

FONTELLA BASS

(see also Bobby McClure)

65	Chess CRS 8007	Don't Mess Up A Good Thing (with Bobby McClure)/OLIVER SAIN: Jerk Loose	30
65	Chess CRS 8007	Don't Mess Up A Good Thing/Baby What You Want Me To Do (different B-side, existence unconfirmed)	0
65	Chess CRS 8023	Rescue Me/Soul Of The Man	10
65	Chess CRS 8023	Rescue Me/Soul Of The Man (DJ Copy)	40
66	Chess CRS 8027	Recovery/Leave It In The Hands Of Love	8
66	Chess CRS 8027	Recovery/Leave It In The Hands Of Love (DJ Copy)	35
66	Chess CRS 8032	I Can't Rest/Surrender	30
66	Chess CRS 8032	I Can't Rest/Surrender (DJ Copy)	70
66	Chess CRS 8042	Safe And Sound/You'll Never Know	10
66	Chess CRS 8042	Safe And Sound/You'll Never Know (DJ Copy)	35
69	Chess CRS 8090	Rescue Me/I Can't Rest	10
69	Chess CRS 8090	Rescue Me/I Can't Rest (DJ Copy)	25
69	Chess CRS 8023	Rescue Me/Soul Of The Man (reissue)	6
72	Mojo 2092 032	Who You Gonna Blame/Hold On This Time	8
72	Mojo 2092 045	I Want Everyone To Know/I Need To Be Loved	8
66	Chess CRE 6015	FONTELLA'S HITS (EP)	25
66	Chess CRE 6020	I CAN'T REST (EP)	40
66	Chess CRE 6025	FONTELLA BASS AND BOBBY McCLURE (EP)	40
66	Chess CRL 4517	THE NEW LOOK (LP)	40

SHIRLEY BASSEY

(see also Yello, Nelson Riddle Orchestra, John Barry)

57	Philips JK 1006	The Banana Boat Song/Tra La La (jukebox issue)	20
57	Philips JK 1018	If I Had A Needle And Thread/Tonight My Heart She Is Crying (jukebox issue)	15
57	Philips JK 1034	Puh-leeze! Mister Brown/Take My Love, Take My Love (jukebox issue)	20
58	Philips PB 845	As I Love You/Hands Across The Sea	5
58	Philips PB 860	Kiss Me, Honey Honey, Kiss Me/There's Never Been A Night	5
59	Philips PB 917	Love For Sale/Crazy Rhythm	5
59	Philips PB 917	Love For Sale/Crazy Rhythm (78)	10
59	Philips PB 919	My Funny Valentine/How About You?	5
59	Philips PB 919	My Funny Valentine/How About You? (78)	10
59	Philips PB 975	Night And Day/The Gypsy In My Soul	5
59	Philips PB 975	Night And Day/The Gypsy In My Soul (78)	15
66	United Artists UP 1134	Don't Take The Lovers From The World/Takeaway	20
70	United Artists UAS29100	SOMETHING (LP)	12

BAS-SHEVA

55	Capitol CL 14218	Flame Of Love/I Just Wanna Be Your Loving Baby	10

JOE BATAAN

75	RCA RCA 2457	Latin Strut/Peace, Friendship And Solidarity	12
75	RCA RCA 2553	The Bottle/When You're Down	12
69	London HA/SH 8386	RIOT! (LP)	50

JUNE BATEMAN

64	Sue WI 347	I Don't Wanna/NOBLE 'THIN MAN' WATTS & HIS BAND: Noble's Theme	50

COLIN BATES TRIO

68	Fontana SFJL 913	BREW (LP)	150

JON BATES

65	CBS 202818	Where Were You Last Night/If Anything Goes Wrong	5

MINT VALUE £

MARTYN BATES
(see also Eyeless In Gaza)

82	Cherry Red TRED 38	LETTERS WRITTEN (10" EP)	10
80s	Ambivalent Scale	IMAGINATION FEELS LIKE POISON (CD, with book, 500 only)	20

BATFINKS

89	Link LINK LP 082	WAZZED 'N' BLASTED (LP)	12

BAT FOR LASHES

06	Echo EC 8185	The Wizard/I Saw A Light	18

BATHORY

84	Under One Flag FLAG 8	BATHORY (LP)	15
87	Under One Flag FLAG 11	UNDER THE SIGN OF THE BLACK MARK (LP)	15

BATMAN THEME
(see also Jan & Dean)

88	Bam Caruso NRIC 107	Batman Theme/Batman Theme (Instrumental Mix) (p/s)	15

STIV BATORS
(see also Dead Boys, Lords Of The New Church, Wanderers)

79	London/Bomp HLZ 10575	It's Cold Outside/The Last Year (p/s)	15

BATS

64	Columbia DB 7429	Accept It/Lovers Lie Sleeping	10
66	Decca F 22534	Listen To My Heart/Stop Don't Do It	30
67	Decca F 22568	You Will Now, Won't You?/You Look Good Together	20
67	Decca F 22616	Hard To Get Up In The Morning/Take Me As I Am	10

MIKE BATT
(see also Hapshash & Coloured Coat, Anderson Harley & Batt)

68	Liberty LBF 15093	Mister Poem/Fading Yellow	30
68	Liberty LBF 15122	I See Wonderful Things In You/Mary Goes Round	25
69	Liberty LBF 15210	Your Mother Should Know/Suddenly	25
75	Epic EPC 3460	Summertime City/Children Of The Storm	5
70	Midland Counties Ice Cream RMS1	Liberate A Lolly	10
77	Epic A 3957	Railway Hotel/The Ride To Agadir	8

BATTERED ORNAMENTS
(see also Pete Brown & His Battered Ornaments, Chris Spedding, People Band)

70	Harvest HAR 5013	Goodbye We Loved You (Madly)/CHRIS SPEDDING: Rock'n'Roll Band	10
69	Harvest SHVL 758	MANTLE-PIECE (LP, gatefold sleeve, no EMI box on label)	200

SKIP BATTIN
(see also Skip & Flip, Byrds, Flying Burrito Brothers, Evergreen Blueshoes)

72	Signpost SGP 756	Central Park/St. Louis Browns	6
72	Signpost SG 4255	SKIP (LP)	18

BATTLEAXE

82	Guardian GRC 132	Burn This Town/Battleaxe (no p/s)	50
83	Music For Nations MFN8	BURN THIS TOWN (LP)	15
84	Music For Nations MFN 25	POWER FROM THE UNIVERSE (LP)	12

BAUHAUS
(see also Sinister Ducks, Tones On Tail, David J)

79	Small Wonder TEENY 2	Bela Lugosi's Dead/Boys/Dark Entries (12", p/s, white vinyl)	20
88	Small Wonder TEENY 2P	Bela Lugosi's Dead/Boys/Dark Entries (12", reissue, picture disc)	15
89	Small Wonder TEENY 2	Bela Lugosi's Dead/Boys/Dark Entries (12", reissue, green vinyl, p/s)	15
89	Small Wonder TEENY 2	Bela Lugosi's Dead/Boys/Dark Entries (12", reissue, blue vinyl, p/s)	15
91	Small Wonder TEENY 2	Bela Lugosi's Dead/Boys/Dark Entries (12", reissue, pink, clear or purple vinyl, in corresponding coloured p/s)	10
80	Axis AXIS 3	Dark Entries/Untitled (brown label, p/s)	18
80	Axis AD 3	Dark Entries/Untitled (blue label, p/s)	8
80	4AD BEG 37	Dark Entries/Untitled (p/s, blue 4AD labels, lists BEG 37 on sleeve)	10
80	Beggars Banquet BEG 37	Dark Entries/Untitled (p/s, red Beggars Banquet labels)	10
82	Beggars Banquet AD 3	Dark Entries/Untitled (reissue, 'nudes' label, no contact address on p/s)	7
80	4AD AD 7	Terror Couple Kill Colonel/Scopes/Terror Couple Kill Colonel II (version) (mispressed with 'rejected' version of third track, p/s)	15
81	Beggars Banquet BEG 54T	Kick In The Eye/Satori (12", white label in stamped plain sleeve)	8
82	Beggars Banquet BEG 74T	Kick In The Eye/Poison Pen/Harry/Earwax (12" mispressing, p/s, matrix: A1)	15
82	Beggars Banquet BEG 79	Spirit/Terror Couple Kill Colonel (live) (p/s, mispressed, A-side plays Gary Numan's "We Take Mystery [To Bed]")	10
82	Beggars Banquet BEG 79P	Spirit/Terror Couple Kill Colonel (live) (picture disc in printed PVC sleeve)	8
82	Beggars Banquet BEG 83T	Ziggy Stardust/Party Of The First Part/Third Uncle/Waiting For The Man, 12" p/s, with stickered poster p/s)	8
82	Lyntone LYN 12106	A God In An Alcove (Early Version) (blue flexidisc with Flexipop, issue 23)	12
82	Lyntone LYN 12106	A God In An Alcove (Early Version) (blue flexidisc with Flexipop, issue 23)	6
82	Lyntone LYN 12106	A God In An Alcove (Early Version) (hard vinyl test pressing)	20
83	Lyntone LYN 13777/8	The Sanity Assassin/Spirit In The Sky (fan club freebie, 320 only)	250
84	Beggars Banquet BEG 91P	She's In Parties/Departure (picture disc in PVC sleeve)	5
82	Beggars Banquet BEGA 42	THE SKY'S GONE OUT (LP, with bonus LP "Press The Eject And Give Me The Tape" [BEGA 38] & inner sleeves)	12
83	B. Banquet BEGA 45P	BURNING FROM THE INSIDE (LP, picture disc)	12
85	Beggars Banquet BEGA 64	1979-1983 (2-LP)	20

ART BAXTER

56	Philips PB 652	Jingle Rock/Rock And Roll Rag (78)	10
57	Philips PB 666	Don't Knock The Rock/Rock Rock Rock (78)	10
57	Philips BBR 8107	ROCK YOU SINNERS (10" LP)	150

DAVID BAXTER
(see also David Lewis, Andwella)

70	Reflection REFL 9	GOODBYE DAVE (LP, white/brown label)	80

MINT VALUE £

JOAN BAXTER
58 Parlophone R 4470 — Ich Liebe Dich (I Love You)/The Only One For Me 5

LES BAXTER & HIS ORCHESTRA
(see also Leonard Pennario)

54	Capitol CL 14166	I Love Paris/Manhattan	6
55	Capitol CL 14217	When You're In Love/Romantic Rio	6
55	Capitol CL 14237	Cherry Pink And Apple Blossom White/Play Me Hearts And Flowers	6
55	Capitol CL 14239	Earth Angel/Happy Baby (as Les Baxter & Bombers)	30
55	Capitol CL 14249	I Ain't Mad At You (with Bombers)/Blue Mirage	6
55	Capitol CL 14257	Unchained Melody/Blue Star (The Medic Theme)	8
55	Capitol CL 14344	Wake The Town And Tell The World/I'll Never Stop Loving You	6
54	Capitol LC 6543	RITUAL OF THE SAVAGE (LP, 10")	12
59	Capitol T/ST 1248	WILD GUITARS (LP)	12
60	Capitol (S)T 1355	TEEN DRUMS (LP)	18

RONNIE BAXTER
60 Top Rank JAR 293 — I Finally Found You/Is It Because? 5

B.B. BLUNDER
(see also Reg King & B.B. Blunder, Action, Julie Driscoll Brian Auger & Trinity, Kevin Westlake, Mark Charig, Blossom Toes)

71	United Artists UP 35203	Sticky Living/Rocky Yagbatee Yagbag	6
71	United Artists UP 35204	Little Boy/10,000 Miles	6
71	United Artists UAG 29156	WORKERS' PLAYTIME (LP, gatefold sleeve)	50

BBC RADIOPHONIC WORKSHOP/PETER HOWELL
(see also Dr. Who, Jon Pertwee, Ray Cathode, Radiophonic Workshop, Ithaca, Alice Through The Looking Glass, Agincourt, Blossom Toes, Dudley Simpson & Brian Hodgson)

64	Decca F 11837	Doctor Who/BRENDA & JOHNNY: This Can't Be Love (unboxed Decca logo)	30
72	Decca F 11837	Doctor Who/BRENDA & JOHNNY: This Can't Be Love (reissue, boxed logo)	8
73	BBC RESL 11	Doctor Who/Reg (blue label, credits 'Delia Derbyshire', 'TARDIS' p/s)	10
73	BBC RESL 11	Doctor Who/Reg (white label, credits 'Delia Derbyshire', 'TARDIS' p/s)	6
76	BBC RESL 11	Doctor Who/Reg (reissue, no p/s, silver label)	6
78	BBC RESL 11	Doctor Who/Reg (2nd reissue, in 'TARDIS' p/s, blue label, white rim)	6
80	PRT RESL 80	Doctor Who/The Astronauts ('Tom Baker' p/s, as 'Peter Howell & BBC Radiophonic Workshop')	8
82	PRT RESL 80	Doctor Who/The Astronauts (reissue, 'Peter Davison' p/s)	8
84	PRT RESL 80	Doctor Who/The Astronauts (2nd reissue, 'Colin Baker' p/s)	5
72	BBC REC 93S	TEST CARD MUSIC (LP)	12
73	BBC RED 93 S	FOURTH DIMENSION (LP)	15
76	BBC REC 225	OUT OF THIS WORLD (LP)	15
70s	BBC REC 25 M	BBC RADIOPHONIC MUSIC - WORK BY DELIA DERBYSHIRE (LP)	20
78	BBC REC 316	DOCTOR WHO SOUND EFFECTS No. 19 (LP)	12
04	Rephlex 147 LP	MUSIC FROM THE BBC RADIOPHONIC WORKSHOP (4 x 10")	30

B B & Q BAND
81 Capitol 12CL 202 — On The Beat/Don't Say Goodbye/Lovin's What We Do (12") 15

BEA & DEE
59 Capitol CL 15066 — Jerry/Wishing Time 8

BEACH BOYS
(see also Brian Wilson, Dennis Wilson, Bruce Johnston, Legendary Masked Surfers, American Spring, Annette, Flame, Flames, California Music, Rutles, Moon, Murry Wilson, Mike Love, Survivors)

SINGLES

62	Capitol CL 15273	Surfin' Safari/409	40
63	Capitol CL 15285	Ten Little Indians/County Fair	90
63	Capitol CL 15305	Surfin' USA/Shut Down	25
64	Capitol CL 15339	Fun, Fun, Fun/Why Do Fools Fall In Love	25
64	Capitol CL 15350	I Get Around/Don't Worry Baby	8
64	Capitol CL 15361	When I Grow Up (To Be A Man)/She Knows Me Too Well	8
65	Capitol CL 15370	Dance, Dance, Dance/The Warmth Of The Sun	10
65	Capitol CL 15384	All Summer Long/Do You Wanna Dance	10
65	Capitol CL 15392	Help Me Rhonda/Kiss Me Baby	10
65	Capitol CL 15409	California Girls/Let Him Run Wild	10
65	Capitol CL 15425	The Little Girl I Once Knew/There's No Other (Like My Baby)	15
66	Capitol CL 15432	Barbara Ann/Girl Don't Tell Me	7
66	Capitol CL 15441	Sloop John B/You're So Good To Me	8
66	Capitol CL 15459	God Only Knows/Wouldn't It Be Nice	7
66	Capitol CL 15475	Good Vibrations/Wendy	6
67	Capitol CL 15502	Then I Kissed Her/Mountain Of Love	8
67	Capitol CL 15510	Heroes And Villains/You're Welcome	8
67	Capitol CL 15521	Wild Honey/Wind Chimes	8
68	Capitol CL 15527	Darlin'/Country Air	6
68	Capitol CL 15545	Friends/Little Bird	6
68	Capitol CL 15554	Do It Again/Wake The World	6
68	Capitol CL 15572	Bluebirds Over The Mountain/Never Learn Not To Love	6
69	Capitol CL 15598	Break Away/Celebrate The News	5
70	Capitol CL 15640	Cottonfields/The Nearest Faraway Place (black label)	5
70	Stateside SS 2181	Tears In The Morning/It's About Time	5
71	Stateside SS 2190	Long Promised Road/Deirdre	6
71	Stateside SS 2194	Don't Go Near The Water/Student Demonstration Time	6
71	Stateside SS 2194	Don't Go Near The Water/Student Demonstration Time (demo in p/s)	20
72	Reprise K 14173	You Need A Mess Of Help To Stand Alone/Cuddle Up (p/s)	10
72	Capitol CMS 1	Wouldn't It Be Nice/Fun Fun Fun/California Girls (printed sleeve)	6
72	Capitol CMS 2	Barbara Ann/Dance Dance Dance/You're So Good To Me (printed sleeve)	6
74	Reprise K 14346	California Saga: California/Sail On Sailor/Marcella/ I'm The Pied Piper (printed sleeve)	5
76	Reprise K 14411	Child Of Winter/Susie Cincinnati (withdrawn)	125
76	Reprise K 14440	Rock And Roll Music/The T.M. Song (p/s)	5

			MINT VALUE £
76	EMI PSR 402	Commercial for "20 Golden Greats"/Good Vibrations/ Carl Wilson Interview (promo)	8
77	Reprise K 14481	Mona/Rock And Roll Music/Sail On Sailor/Marcella (p/s)	5
77	Capitol CL 15954	Little Saint Nick/Little Saint Nick (Instr.)/Santa Claus Is Coming To Town	7
78	Capitol CL 15969	Little Deuce Coupe/SUNRAYS: I Live For The Sun/SUPERSTOCKS: Hot Rod High (p/s)	5
79	Caribou 12-7204	Here Comes The Night/(Disco Version)/Baby Blue (12", p/s, blue vinyl)	10
79	Capitol BBP 26	SINGLES COLLECTION (26 x 7" box set)	50

EPs

63	Capitol EAP 1-20540	SURFIN' USA	30
64	Capitol EAP 1-20603	FUN, FUN, FUN	30
64	Capitol EAP 5267	FOUR BY THE BEACH BOYS	25
64	Capitol EAP 4-2198	BEACH BOYS CONCERT	25
64	Capitol EAP 1-20781	THE BEACH BOYS HITS	18
67	Capitol EAP 6-2458	GOD ONLY KNOWS	20

LPs

62	Capitol T 1808	SURFIN' SAFARI (mono only)	45
63	Capitol T 1890	SURFIN' USA (mono)	35
63	Capitol ST 1890	SURFIN' USA (stereo)	45
63	Capitol T 1981	SURFER GIRL (mono)	25
63	Capitol ST 1981	SURFER GIRL (stereo)	35
63	Capitol T 1998	LITTLE DEUCE COUPE (mono)	25
63	Capitol ST 1998	LITTLE DEUCE COUPE (stereo)	35
63	Capitol T 2027	SHUT DOWN VOLUME 2 (mono)	25
63	Capitol ST 2027	SHUT DOWN VOLUME 2 (stereo)	35
64	Capitol T 2164	THE BEACH BOYS' CHRISTMAS ALBUM (mono)	30
64	Capitol ST 2164	THE BEACH BOYS' CHRISTMAS ALBUM (stereo)	25
64	Capitol T 2198	BEACH BOYS CONCERT (mono)	20
64	Capitol ST 2198	BEACH BOYS CONCERT (stereo)	25
64	Capitol T 2110	ALL SUMMER LONG (mono)	20
64	Capitol ST 2110	ALL SUMMER LONG (stereo)	25
65	Capitol T 2398	BEACH BOYS' PARTY! (mono)	20
65	Capitol ST 2398	BEACH BOYS' PARTY! (stereo)	25
65	Capitol T 2269	BEACH BOYS TODAY! (mono)	20
65	Capitol ST 2269	BEACH BOYS TODAY! (stereo)	25
65	Capitol T 2354	SUMMER DAYS (AND SUMMER NIGHTS!!) (mono)	20
65	Capitol ST 2354	SUMMER DAYS (AND SUMMER NIGHTS!!) (stereo)	25
66	Capitol T 2458	PET SOUNDS	50
66	Capitol ST 20856	THE BEST OF THE BEACH BOYS	12
67	Capitol (S)T 1981	SURFER GIRL (reissue, non-flipback sleeve)	12
67	Capitol (S)T 20956	THE BEST OF THE BEACH BOYS VOL. 2	12
67	Capitol (S)T 9001	SMILEY SMILE	45
68	Capitol T 2859	WILD HONEY (mono)	40
68	Capitol ST 2859	WILD HONEY (stereo)	20
68	Capitol T 2895	FRIENDS (mono)	30
68	Capitol ST 2895	FRIENDS (stereo)	18
69	Capitol T 21142	THE BEST OF THE BEACH BOYS VOL. 3 (mono)	15
69	Capitol ST 21142	THE BEST OF THE BEACH BOYS VOL. 3 (stereo)	12
69	Capitol E-T/ 133	20/20 (mono, gatefold sleeve)	22
69	Capitol E-ST 133	20/20 (stereo, gatefold sleeve)	18

(The above LP's were originally issued with flipback sleeves & rainbow-rim black labels; later orange or yellow label copies are worth half the value.)

70	Stateside SSLA 8251	SUNFLOWER (gatefold sleeve)	30
71	Stateside SSL 10313	SURF'S UP (textured sleeve, with gatefold insert)	20
71	Stateside SSL 10313	SURF'S UP (textured sleeve, without gatefold insert)	15
73	Reprise/Brother K 54008	HOLLAND (with insert & bonus EP "Mount Vernon And Fairway" [K 54008/7] in p/s)	30
73	Reprise/Brother K 54008	HOLLAND	12
81	WRC SM 651-657	THE CAPITOL YEARS (7-LP box set)	25

BEACHCOMBER

70	Parlophone R 5850	Surfin' Soul/Nothing To Say	8

BEACHCOMBERS

(see also Pat Wayne)

63	Columbia DB 7124	Mad Goose/You Can't Sit Down	30
64	Columbia DB 7200	Night Train/The Keel Row	30

BEACH-NUTS

(see also Angels, Strangeloves)

65	London HL 9988	Out In The Sun (Hey-O)/Someday Soon	30

BEACON STREET UNION

68	MGM MGM 1416	Blue Suede Shoes/Four Hundred And Five	25
68	MGM MGM-C(S) 8069	THE EYES OF THE BEACON STREET UNION (LP)	60

BEADS

71	Decca F13244	Eeo Eio/Sweetie Peetie	8

CARL BEAN

78	Motown TMG 1108	I Was Born This Way/Instrumental	6
78	Tamla Motown TMG 1108-12	I Was Born This Way (Remix)/Instrumental (12")	12

GEORGE BEAN

(see also Trifle, Bean & Loopy's Lot)

63	Decca F 11762	Secret Love/Lonely Weekends	25
64	Decca F 11808	Will You Be My Lover Tonight?/It Should Be You	10
64	Decca F 11922	A Sad Story/Er Um Er	10
65	Decca F 12228	She Belongs To Me/Why Must They Criticise? (as George Bean & Runners)	15
67	CBS 2801	The Candy Shop Is Closed/Smile From Sequin	25
68	CBS 3374	Bring Back Lovin'/Floatin'	35

MINT VALUE £

BEAN & LOOPY'S LOT
(see also Alan Bown Set)

66	Parlophone R 5458	A Stitch In Time/Haywire	50

BEANO

77	Decca F 13690	Everybody Knows/Clowns Painted Smile (P/S)	6

BEANS

62	Starlite ST45 071	Jumping Beans/Salute To Fitz	12
62	Starlite ST45 076	Hey Janey/Crazy Dog	12

BEAR

68	Verve FTS 3059	GREETINGS CHILDREN OF PARADISE (LP)	35

EDWARD BEAR

72	Capitol CL 15727	Masquerade/Pirate King	6

DEAN BEARD & CREW CATS

57	London HLE 8463	Rakin' And Scrapin'/On My Mind Again	300
57	London HLE 8463	Rakin' And Scrapin'/On My Mind Again (78)	50

BEARDED LADY

74	Young Blood YB 1018	Rock Star/Country Lady	25

BEARS

79	Good Vibrations Intl. GVI 1	Insane/Decisions (p/s)	15
79	Waldo's JS 001	On Me/Wot's Up Mate (p/s, various designs, with insert)	12
86	Tigerbeat GROWL 001	INSANE!! (LP)	20

BEARZ

80	Axis AXIS 2	She's My Girl/Girls Will Do (p/s)	20
84	Occult OCC 1	Darwin/Julie (p/s)	12

BEAS

68	Pama PM 744	Dr. Goldfoot And His Bikini Machine/Where Do I Go From You	40

BEASTIE BOYS
(see also Money Mark)

86	Def Jam A 7055	Hold It, Now Hit It/Acapulco (p/s)	6
86	Def Jam TA 7055	Hold It, Now Hit It/Acapulco (12", p/s)	10
86	Def Jam 650 114 7	She's On It/Slow'n'Low (p/s with 3 badges)	10
86	Def Jam 650 114 6	She's On It/Slow'n'Low/Hold On, Now Hit It (12", p/s)	10
87	Def Jam 650 169 7	It's The New Style/Paul Revere (p/s)	6
87	Def Jam 650 169 6	It's The New Style/It's The New Style (Instrumental)/Paul Revere/ Paul Revere (Instrumental) (12", p/s)	10
87	Def Jam 650 418 7	(You Gotta) Fight For Your Right (To Party)/Time To Get Ill (p/s)	6
87	Def Jam 650 418 6	(You Gotta) Fight For Your Right (To Party)/Time To Get Ill (12", p/s)	10
87	Def Jam BEASTP 1	No Sleep Till Brooklyn/Posse In Effect (plane-shaped picture disc)	15
87	Def Jam BEASTT 1	No Sleep Till Brooklyn/Posse In Effect (12", p/s)	10
87	Def Jam BEASTQ 3	Girls/She's Crafty (logo shaped picture disc)	10
92	Capitol CDCL 665	Jimmy James (Single Version)/The Blue Nun/Jimmy James (Original Original Version)/Drinkin' Wine (CD, slimline jewel case)	15
92	Capitol 12CLS 665	Frozen Metal Head/Jimmy James (Single Version)/So What'cha Want (All The Way Live Freestyle Version)/Jimmy James (Original Original Version) Drinkin' Wine (12" white, p/s)	10
92	Capitol CDCLS 665	Frozen Metal Head/Jimmy James (Single Version)/So What'cha Want (All The Way Live Freestyle Version)/Jimmy James (Original Original Version) Drinkin' Wine (CD)	15
94	Capitol CL 716	Get It Together/Sabotage/Dope Little Song (green vinyl, p/s)	8
94	Capitol 10CL716	Get It Together/(Buck Wild Remix)/(Intrumental)/Sabotage (10" p/s)	8
94	Capitol 7243 8 8173476	Sure Shot/Mullet Head/Sure Shot (Caldato Mix) (red vinyl, p/s)	6
94	Capitol 10CL726	Sure Shot/Mullet Head/Sure Shot (Caldato Mix) (10" p/s)	8
99	Capitol 10CL818	Alive/Start/Alive Bra Remix) (10" p/s)	8
82	Rat Cage MOTR 21	POLLY WOG STEW (EP)	30
82	Rat Cage MOTR 21	POLLY WOG STEW (12" EP)	30
86	Rat Cage MOR 26	COOKY PUSS EP: Cooky Puss/Bonus Batter/Beastie Revolution/ Cookie Puss (Censored Version) (p/s)	8
88	Rat Cage MOTR 21T	POLLY WOG STEW (12" EP, reissue)	12
92	Capitol CDCL 653	PASS THE MIC (Netty's Girl/Something's Got To Give/Pass The Mic [Pt. 2, Skills To Pay The Bills]) (CD, slimline jewel case)	15
87	Def Jam 450 062 1	LICENSED TO ILL (LP, with poster)	15
89	Capitol EST2102	PAUL'S BOUTIQUE (LP)	12
98	Grand Royal GR062	HELLO NASTY (2-LP, orange vinyl)	25

BEAT
(see also Fine Young Cannibals)

79	2-Tone CHS TT 6	Tears Of A Clown/Ranking Full Stop (paper label, company sleeve)	5
80	Go-Feet FEET 1217	Can't Get Used To Losing You (1983 Remix Version)/ Mirror In The Bathroom/ Spar Wid Me (12", p/s)	8
80	Go-Feet BEAT 001	JUST CAN'T STOP IT (LP, with inner)	12

NICKY BEAT & THE BEATNICKS

78	Rigid IS BEAT 1033	I Can Hear Voices/Split Second Love/Starstruck (p/s)	10

BEAT BOYS
(see also Rats)

63	Decca F 11730	That's My Plan/Third Time Lucky	30

BEAT BROTHERS
(see also Tony Sheridan & Beat Brothers, Bobby Patrick Big Six)

63	Polydor NH 52185	Nick Nack Hully Gully/Lantern Hully Gully	25

BEAT CHICS

64	Decca F 12016	Skinny Minnie/Now I Know	20

BEATHOVEN

88	CBS 651 626-7	Socrates/Socrates (withdrawn)	30

MINT VALUE £

THE BEATLES

SINGLES

(Original Parlophone Beatles singles came in a variety of company sleeves, which are referred to here as "Type X", etc., and are depicted in the illustrations on pages 1434 - 1437. When a sleeve is not specified, details are unknown.)

1962

(with "The Parlophone Co. Ltd." in upper-lower case & "Recording first published 1962" label text, without "Sold in UK ..."; all issues before 1967 have push-out centres)

FIRST PRESSING

Parlophone 45-R 4949	Love Me Do/P.S. I Love You (red label, 'Ringo on drums & no tambourine' version; with or without "Made In Great Britain" credit; in sleeve Type A, B, or C)	90

(Note: 1982 red label re-pressing of "Love Me Do" includes the word "mono" & "Produced by George Martin" on the label)

1963

(with "The Parlophone Co. Ltd." in either upper-lower or upper case & "Recording first published 1963" label text, without "Sold in UK ...")

FIRST PRESSINGS

Parlophone 45-R 4983	Please Please Me/Ask Me Why (red label; with or without "Made In Great Britain" credit; in sleeve Type A, B or C)	150
Parlophone R 5015	From Me To You/Thank You Girl (in Type 1 sleeve)	7
Parlophone R 5055	She Loves You/I'll Get You (in Type 1 sleeve)	10
Parlophone R 5084	I Want To Hold Your Hand/This Boy (with "The Parlophone Co. Ltd" in upper-case only; in Type 1 sleeve)	10

KNOWN SECOND PRESSINGS

Parlophone R 4949	Love Me Do/P.S. I Love You (black label, with "The Parlophone Co. Ltd" in upper-lower case, matrix suffixed with '1N' indicating 'Ringo on drums & no tambourine' version)	100
Parlophone 45-R 4983	Please Please Me/Ask Me Why (black label, with "The Parlophone Co. Ltd" in upper-lower case, with "45" prefix)	15

KNOWN THIRD PRESSING

Parlophone R 4983	Please Please Me/Ask Me Why (black label, with "The Parlophone Co. Ltd" in upper-lower case, without "45" prefix)	12

1964

FIRST PRESSINGS

(with "The Parlophone Co. Ltd." in either upper-lower, or upper case, "Recording first published 1964" & "Sold in UK ..." label text)

Parlophone R 5055	She Loves You/I'll Get You	7
Parlophone R 5114	Can't Buy Me Love/You Can't Do That (with "The Parlophone Co. Ltd" in upper case; in Type 1 sleeve)	7
Parlophone R 5160	A Hard Day's Night/Things We Said Today (Type 1B sleeve)	8
Parlophone R 5200	I Feel Fine/She's A Woman (with "The Parlophone Co. Ltd" in upper case; in Type 1B sleeve)	6

KNOWN THIRD PRESSING

Parlophone R 4949	Love Me Do/P.S. I Love You (black label, with "The Parlophone Co. Ltd" in upper case, matrix suffixed with 1N' indicating 'Ringo on drums & no tambourine' version)	50

KNOWN FOURTH PRESSING

Parlophone R 4983	Please Please Me/Ask Me Why (with "The Parlophone Co. Ltd" in upper case)	10

1965

FIRST PRESSINGS

(with "The Parlophone Co. Ltd." in upper case, & "Sold in UK ..." label text)

Parlophone DP 562	If I Fell/Tell Me Why (domestic pressing of export issue; in Type 1B sleeve)	40
Parlophone R 5265	Ticket To Ride/Yes It Is (in Type 2 sleeve)	7
Parlophone R 5305	Help!/I'm Down (in Type 2 sleeve)	7
Parlophone R 5389	We Can Work It Out/Day Tripper (in Type 3 sleeve)	8

KNOWN SECOND PRESSINGS

(with "The Gramophone Co. Ltd" in upper case, & "Sold in UK ..." label text)

Parlophone R 5305	Help!/I'm Down	8
Parlophone R 5389	We Can Work It Out/Day Tripper	8

1966

(with "The Gramophone Co. Ltd" in upper case, & "Sold in UK ..." label text)

FIRST PRESSINGS

Parlophone R 5452	Paperback Writer/Rain (in Type 4 or 5 sleeve)	15
Parlophone R 5493	Yellow Submarine/Eleanor Rigby (in Type 5 or 6 sleeve)	10

1967

(all the pressings listed below have push-out or solid centres, with "The Gramophone Co. Ltd" in upper case & "Sold in UK ..." label text)

FIRST PRESSINGS

Parlophone R 5570	Strawberry Fields Forever/Penny Lane (250,000 only in p/s)	60
Parlophone R 5655	Hello, Goodbye/I Am The Walrus (company sleeve, with "7/- to 50/- " on reverse)	8

KNOWN SECOND PRESSINGS

Parlophone R 5452	Paperback Writer/Rain (solid centre only)	10
Parlophone R 5493	Yellow Submarine/Eleanor Rigby (solid centre only)	10
Parlophone R 5570	Strawberry Fields Forever/Penny Lane (in Type 5, 6 or 7 sleeve)	10
Parlophone R 5620	All You Need Is Love/Baby You're A Rich Man (with reference to "Live World Television Transmission"; most in Type 8 sleeve)	8

1968

FIRST PRESSINGS

Parlophone R 5675	Lady Madonna/The Inner Light (with Fan Club insert; sleeve with "7/- to 50/-" on reverse)	45

(all Apple pressings except for early issues of "Let It Be" come in black, glossy "Apple" sleeves)

Apple R 5722	Hey Jude/Revolution	10

MINT VALUE £

KNOWN SECOND PRESSINGS

Parlophone R 5675	Lady Madonna/The Inner Light (no insert)	12
Parlophone R 5084	I Want To Hold Your Hand/This Boy (solid centre)	25

1969

FIRST PRESSINGS

Apple R 5777	Get Back/Don't Let Me Down (as "The Beatles with Billy Preston")	15
Apple R 5786	Ballad Of John And Yoko/Old Brown Shoe	15
Apple R 5814	Something/Come Together (without "Sold in UK..." label text)	15

KNOWN SECOND PRESSINGS

(without "Sold in UK ..." label text)

Apple R 5722	Hey Jude/Revolution	6
Apple R 5777	Get Back/Don't Let Me Down (as "The Beatles with Billy Preston")	12
Apple R 5786	Ballad Of John And Yoko/Old Brown Shoe	10

KNOWN THIRD PRESSING

Parlophone R 5305	Help!/I'm Down (with "The Parlophone Co. Ltd" label text)	8
Parlophone R 5493	Yellow Submarine/Eleanor Rigby	10
Parlophone R 5570	Strawberry Fields Forever/Penny Lane	10

(later 1970s Parlophone copies of Beatles singles with EMI boxed logos are of nominal value.
add £10 to the value for any singles with a red & white "Factory Sample Not For Sale" sticker)

1970

FIRST PRESSING

Apple R 5833	Let It Be/You Know My Name (Look Up The Number) (scratched-out B-side matrix: APPLES 1002, p/s)	20

KNOWN SECOND PRESSING

Apple R 5833	Let It Be/You Know My Name (Look Up The Number) (scratched-out B-side matrix: APPLES 1002, no p/s)	7

KNOWN THIRD PRESSING

Apple R 5833	Let It Be/You Know My Name (Look Up The Number) B-side matrix: 7YCE 21408, no p/s)	7

EXPORT SINGLES

64	Parlophone DP 562	If I Fell/Tell Me Why (without "Sold in UK..." label text)	40
65	Parlophone DP 563	Yesterday/Dizzy Miss Lizzy	75
66	Parlophone DP 564	Michelle/Drive My Car	125
68	Parlophone DP 570	Hey Jude/Revolution (with or without Swedish p/s)	45/30
70	Parlophone P-R 5833	Let It Be/You Know My Name (Look Up The Number) (no p/s)	60

("Let It Be" was pressed with "Parlophone" label text on one side & "Gramophone" on the other)

70	Apple P-R 5833	Let It Be/You Know My Name (Look Up The Number) (no p/s)	100

FAN CLUB FLEXIDISCS

63	Lyntone LYN 492	The Beatles' Christmas Record (gatefold p/s)	90
64	Lyntone LYN 757	Another Beatles Christmas Record (p/s, with gatefold newsletter insert)	60
65	Lyntone LYN 948	The Beatles' Third Christmas Record (p/s, with gatefold newsletter insert)	60
66	Lyntone LYN 1145	Pantomime: Everywhere It's Christmas (p/s, with 7" x 7" newsletter insert)	75
67	Lyntone LYN 1360	Christmas Time (Is Here Again) (p/s, with 7" x 7" newsletter insert)	60
68	Lyntone LYN 1743/4	The Beatles' Sixth Christmas Record (p/s, some with 'Superpix' sales insert)	50/80
69	Lyntone LYN 1970/1-IL	The Beatles' Seventh Christmas Record (p/s, some with 2 x foolscap fan club newsletters)	50/70

(fan club flexidiscs are worth around £10 less without newsletters, and a third of the listed values without picture sleeves)

DEMO SINGLES

62	Parlophone 45-R 4949	Love Me Do/P.S. I Love You (McCartney misspelt "McArtney", 250 only)	3000
63	Parlophone 45-R 4983	Please Please Me/Ask Me Why	1200
63	Parlophone (45-)R 5015	From Me To You/Thank You Girl (with or without '45-' prefix)	each 500
63	Parlophone R 5055	She Loves You/I'll Get You	500
63	Parlophone R 5084	I Want To Hold Your Hand/This Boy	500
64	Parlophone R 5114	Can't Buy Me Love/You Can't Do That	500
64	Parlophone R 5160	A Hard Day's Night/Things We Said Today (red "A" on both sides)	500
64	Parlophone R 5200	I Feel Fine/She's A Woman (existence unconfirmed)	
65	Parlophone R 5265	Ticket To Ride/Yes It Is	450
65	Parlophone R 5305	Help!/I'm Down (existence unconfirmed)	
65	Parlophone R 5389	We Can Work It Out/Day Tripper (red "A" on both sides)	450
66	Parlophone R 5452	Paperback Writer/Rain	450
66	Parlophone R 5493	Yellow Submarine/Eleanor Rigby (existence unconfirmed)	

(the above demos have white labels with a red "A" on the A-side, unless otherwise stated)

67	Parlophone R 5570	Strawberry Fields Forever/Penny Lane (existence unconfirmed)	
67	Parlophone R 5620	All You Need Is Love/Baby You're A Rich Man	400
67	Parlophone R 5655	Hello, Goodbye/I Am The Walrus	350
68	Parlophone R 5675	Lady Madonna/The Inner Light	350
69	Parlophone R 5814	Something/Come Together	500

(the above 5 demos have green labels with a white "A" on the A-side.
Demos with centres missing are worth half the listed values)

68	Apple (no cat. no.)	Hey Jude/Revolution (green & white Apple 'custom' label, handwritten details)	350
69	Apple R 5777	Get Back/Don't Let Me Down (green and white Apple 'custom' label test pressing, typed details)	400
69	Parlophone R 5786	Ballad Of John And Yoko/Old Brown Shoe (existence unconfirmed)	
70	Parlophone R 5833	Let It Be/You Know My Name (Look Up The Number) (existence unconfirmed)	
76	Parlophone R 6013	Yesterday/I Should Have Known Better (green generic p/s)	6
76	Parlophone R 6016	Back In The U.S.S.R./Twist And Shout (green generic p/s)	6
78	Parlophone R 6022	Sgt. Pepper's Lonely Hearts Club Band/With A Little Help From My Friends/ A Day In The Life (p/s)	6

(the last three demos listed above have silver/black paper labels with a silver "A")

MINT VALUE £

UNIQUE PROMO SINGLES

68	Apple (no cat. no.)	OUR FIRST FOUR (4 x 7" in presentation pack, including "Hey Jude" [R 5722] & "Those Were The Days" by Mary Hopkin [APPLE 2], "Sour Milk Sea" by Jackie Lomax [APPLE 3] & "Thingumybob" by Black Dyke Mills Band [APPLE 4]; each mounted in PVC pocket on printed dayglo card insert, in 10" x 12" card or scarcer plastic outer box)	1000/2500
76	EMI SPSR 401	Medley Of Songs For "Rock'n'Roll Music" (excerpts)	400

80s & 90s SINGLES: REISSUES & PICTURE DISCS

82	Parlophone R 4949	Love Me Do/P.S. I Love You (p/s, red label reissue, with "mono" notice & publishing miscredited to "Ardmore & Beechwood")	6
82	Parlophone RP 4949	Love Me Do/P.S. I Love You (picture disc, with/without publishing miscredit)	each 10
82	Parlophone 12R 4949	Love Me Do/P.S. I Love You/Love Me Do (Original Single Version) (12", p/s)	8
83	Parlophone RP 4983	Please Please Me/Ask Me Why (picture disc)	5
83	Parlophone RP 5015	From Me To You/Thank You Girl (picture disc, some with "Souvenir From Abbey Road Studios" sticker on sleeve)	10/5
83	Parlophone RP 5055	She Loves You/I'll Get You (picture disc)	12
83	Parlophone RP 5084	I Want To Hold Your Hand/This Boy (picture disc)	5
84	Parlophone RP 5114	Can't Buy Me Love/You Can't Do That (picture disc)	5
84	Parlophone RP 5160	A Hard Day's Night/Things We Said Today (picture disc)	12
84	Parlophone RP 5200	I Feel Fine/She's A Woman (picture disc)	5
85	Parlophone RP 5265	Ticket To Ride/Yes It Is (picture disc)	5
85	Parlophone RP 5305	Help!/I'm Down (picture disc)	5
85	Parlophone RP 5389	We Can Work It Out/Day Tripper (picture disc)	5
86	Parlophone RP 5452	Paperback Writer/Rain (picture disc)	15
86	Parlophone RP 5493	Yellow Submarine/Eleanor Rigby (picture disc)	8
87	Parlophone RP 5570	Strawberry Fields Forever/Penny Lane (picture disc, later with slightly larger picture on disc)	each 8
87	Parlophone RP 5620	All You Need Is Love/Baby You're A Rich Man (picture disc)	8
87	Parlophone 12R 5620	All You Need Is Love/Baby You're A Rich Man (12", p/s)	10
87	Parlophone RP 5655	Hello, Goodbye/I Am The Walrus (picture disc)	5
88	Parlophone RP 5675	Lady Madonna/The Inner Light (picture disc, with "Past Masters" insert)	5
88	Apple RP 5722	Hey Jude/Revolution (picture disc, with "Apple" insert)	5
88	Apple 12R 5722	Hey Jude/Revolution (12", p/s)	8
88	Apple 12RP 5722	Hey Jude/Revolution (12", picture disc with "Apple" insert)	12
89	Apple RP 5777	Get Back/Don't Let Me Down (with Billy Preston, picture disc, with "20th Anniversary" insert)	5
89	Apple RP 5786	Ballad Of John And Yoko/Old Brown Shoe (picture disc, with "20th Anniversary" insert)	5
89	Apple RP 5814	Something/Come Together (picture disc, with "20th Anniversary" insert)	5
90	Apple RP 5833	Let It Be/You Know My Name (Look Up The Number) (picture disc, with "20th Anniversary" insert)	5

(all the picture discs listed above were issued in PVC sleeves)

95	Apple R 6422	Free As A Bird/Christmastime Is Here Again (7", p/s)	8
95	Apple CDR 6422	Free As A Bird/I Saw Her Standing There/ This Boy/Christmastime Is Here (5" CD)	10
96	Apple R 6425	Real Love/Baby's In Black (7", p/s)	8
96	Apple CDR 6425	Real Love/Baby's In Black/Yellow Submarine/Here There And Everywhere (5" CD)	10

SINGLES BOX SETS

76	Parlophone/Apple BS 24	THE BEATLES' SINGLES COLLECTION 1962-1970 (24 x 7", each in green p/s, green & white stickered box set)	45
76	Parlophone/Apple/ World Record Club	THE BEATLES' COLLECTION (24 x 7", mail-order black box set; later copies with "Sgt. Pepper's Lonely Hearts Club Band" [R 6022])	45
78	Parlophone/Apple BSC 1	THE BEATLES' SINGLES COLLECTION (26 x 7" blue box set, with insert; some copies include mispressing of "Get Back" [Apple R 5777])	40
82	Parlophone/Apple BSCP 1	THE BEATLES' SINGLES COLLECTION (27 x 7" blue box set, with bonus picture disc "Love Me Do" [RP 4949], export issue)	45
82	Parlophone/Apple BSCP 1	THE BEATLES' SINGLES COLLECTION (27 x 7" blue box set, with mispressed picture disc "Love Me Do"/"Love Me Do" [RP 4949], export issue)	50
89	Parlophone/Apple CDBSC 1	THE BEATLES' SINGLES COLLECTION (22 x 3" CD single box set)	75
89	Parlophone/Apple CDBSCP 1	THE BEATLES' SINGLES COLLECTION (22 x 5" CD single box set)	65

EPs 1963

(unless otherwise indicated, all 60s EPs have push-out centres & laminated, flipback sleeves, with "The Parlophone Co. Ltd." & "Recording first published 1963" label text, but without "Sold in UK ...")

FIRST PRESSINGS

Parlophone GEP 8882	TWIST AND SHOUT	12
Parlophone GEP 8880	THE BEATLES' HITS (without "Recording first published 1963" label text)	12
Parlophone GEP 8883	THE BEATLES (No. 1)	12

KNOWN SECOND PRESSING

Parlophone GEP 8880	THE BEATLES' HITS	12

EPs: 1964

(with "The Parlophone Co. Ltd.", "Recording first published 1964" & "Sold in UK ..." label text)

FIRST PRESSINGS

Parlophone GEP 8891	ALL MY LOVING (without "Sold in UK..." label text)	15
Parlophone GEP 8899	GOLDEN DISCS (unreleased, 2 x 1-sided test pressings [matrices: 7TCE-1N&7TCE-1N] & 1 set of label proofs only; price does not include labels)	1500
Parlophone GEP 8913	LONG TALL SALLY	20
Parlophone GEP 8920	EXTRACTS FROM THE FILM "A HARD DAY'S NIGHT"	20
Parlophone GEP 8924	EXTRACTS FROM THE ALBUM "A HARD DAY'S NIGHT"	30

MINT VALUE £

KNOWN SECOND PRESSING

Parlophone GEP 8882 TWIST AND SHOUT 12
Parlophone GEP 8891 ALL MY LOVING 12

EPs: 1965

(with "The Parlophone Co. Ltd.", & "Sold in UK ..." label text)

FIRST PRESSINGS

Parlophone GEP 8931 BEATLES FOR SALE 25
Parlophone GEP 8938 BEATLES FOR SALE (No. 2) 35
Parlophone GEP 8946 THE BEATLES MILLION SELLERS (with 'Golden Discs' text on labels) 20
(with "The Gramophone Co. Ltd.", & "Sold in UK ..." label text)

KNOWN SECOND PRESSING

(with "The Gramophone Co. Ltd.", & "Sold in UK ..." label text)
Parlophone GEP 8883 THE BEATLES (No. 1) 10

KNOWN THIRD PRESSING

Parlophone GEP 8880 THE BEATLES' HITS 10
Parlophone GEP 8882 TWIST AND SHOUT 10

EPs: 1966

(with "The Gramophone Co. Ltd.", & "Sold in UK ..." label text)

FIRST PRESSINGS

Parlophone GEP 8948 YESTERDAY 70
Parlophone GEP 8952 NOWHERE MAN 70

KNOWN SECOND PRESSING

Parlophone GEP 8946 THE BEATLES' MILLION SELLERS (with "Million Sellers" label text) 15

EPs: 1967

(with "The Gramophone Co. Ltd.", & "Sold in UK ..." label text)

FIRST PRESSING

Parlophone MMT-1 MAGICAL MYSTERY TOUR (2-EP, gatefold sleeve, with booklet & blue lyric sheet; push-out or solid centre; mono) 50
Parlophone SMMT-1 MAGICAL MYSTERY TOUR (2-EP, gatefold sleeve, with booklet & blue lyric sheet; stereo) 70

KNOWN SECOND PRESSINGS

Parlophone GEP 8931 BEATLES FOR SALE (with "The Parlophone Co. Ltd" label text; solid centre) 25
Parlophone GEP 8952 NOWHERE MAN (solid centre) 35
(the above titles with "The Gramophone Co. Ltd.", & label text, but without "Sold in UK..." are 70s re-pressings, and are worth half the listed values. Later copies with "EMI" label text & varnished sleeves are worth approximately one-third the listed values)

EPs: REISSUES & BOX SET

73 Parlophone SMMT-1 MAGICAL MYSTERY TOUR (2-EP, gatefold sleeve, stereo only, with booklet & yellow lyric sheet) 15
81 Parlophone BEP 14 THE BEATLES EP COLLECTION (14-EP box set, with bonus stereo EP [SGE 1]) 50
95 Apple R 6406 Baby It's You/I'll Follow The Sun/Devil In Her Heart/Boys (7" EP) 8
95 Apple CDR 6406 Baby It's You/I'll Follow The Sun/Devil In Her Heart/Boys (5" CD) 10

LPs: 1963

(with "The Parlophone Co. Ltd." label text but without "Sold in UK ...")

FIRST PRESSINGS

Parlophone PMC 1202 PLEASE PLEASE ME (black & gold label, with "Dick James Mus. Co." publishing credit for "Please Please Me", "I Saw Her Standing There", "Misery", "Do You Want To Know A Secret" & "There's A Place"; E. J. Day sleeve; mono) 750
Parlophone PCS 3042 PLEASE PLEASE ME (black & gold label, with "Dick James Mus. Co." publishing credit for "Please Please Me", "I Saw Her Standing There", "Misery", "Do You Want To Know A Secret" & "There's A Place"; E. J. Day sleeve; stereo) 3500
Parlophone PMC 1206 WITH THE BEATLES (black & yellow label, with "Recording first published", & "Jobete" publishing credit for "Money"; G & L or E. J. Day sleeve, with large "mono" on front cover; mono) 120
Parlophone PCS 3045 WITH THE BEATLES (black & yellow label, with "Recording first published", & "Jobete" publishing credit for "Money"; G & L or E. J. Day sleeve, with large "stereo" on front cover; stereo) 180
(above pressings have polythene-lined "Use Emitex" die-cut inner sleeves)

SECOND PRESSINGS

(with "The Parlophone Co. Ltd." label text but without "Sold in UK ...")
Parlophone PMC 1202 PLEASE PLEASE ME (black & gold label, with "Northern Songs" publishing credit for "Please Please Me", "I Saw Her Standing There", "Misery", "Do You Want To Know A Secret" & "There's A Place"; E. J. Day sleeve; mono) 750
Parlophone PCS 3042 PLEASE PLEASE ME (black & gold label, with "Northern Songs" publishing credit for "Please Please Me", "I Saw Her Standing There", "Misery", "Do You Want To Know A Secret" & "There's A Place"; E. J. Day sleeve; stereo) 3500
Parlophone PMC 1206 WITH THE BEATLES (black & yellow label, with "Recording first published", & "Dominion, Belinda" publishing credit for "Money"; G & L or E. J. Day sleeve, with large "mono" on front cover; mono) 70
Parlophone PCS 3045 WITH THE BEATLES (black & yellow label, with "Recording first published", & "Dominion, Belinda" publishing credit for "Money"; G & L or E. J. Day sleeve,with large "stereo" on front cover; stereo) 150

THIRD PRESSINGS

Parlophone PMC 1202 PLEASE PLEASE ME (black & yellow label with 33 1/3 on label, mono) 500
Parlophone PCS 3042 PLEASE PLEASE ME (black & yellow label with 33 1/3 on label, stereo) 3000

MINT VALUE £

FOURTH PRESSINGS

(with "The Parlophone Co. Ltd." label text but without "Recording first published 1963" & "Sold in UK ...")

Parlophone PMC 1202	PLEASE PLEASE ME (with large "mono" on front cover; E. J. Day sleeve; mono)	120
Parlophone PCS 3042	PLEASE PLEASE ME (with large "stereo" on front cover; E. J. Day sleeve; stereo)	200

FIFTH PRESSINGS

(with "The Parlophone Co. Ltd." & "Recording first published 1963", label text but without "Sold in UK ...")

Parlophone PMC 1202	PLEASE PLEASE ME (G & L or E. J. Day sleeve, with large "mono" on front cover; mono)	80
Parlophone PCS 3042	PLEASE PLEASE ME (G & L or E. J. Day sleeve, with large "stereo" on front cover; stereo)	120

LPs: 1964

FIRST PRESSINGS

(with "The Parlophone Co. Ltd.", "Recording first published 1964" & "Sold in UK ..." label text)

Parlophone PMC 1230	A HARD DAY'S NIGHT (G & L or E. J. Day sleeve, mid-sized "mono" on front cover; mono)	80
Parlophone PCS 3058	A HARD DAY'S NIGHT (G & L sleeve, mid-sized "stereo" on front cover; stereo)	140
Parlophone PMC 1240	BEATLES FOR SALE (G & L gatefold sleeve, with outline "mono" on front cover; mono)	80
Parlophone PCS 3062	BEATLES FOR SALE (G & L gatefold sleeve, with outline "stereo" on front cover; stereo)	150

SIXTH PRESSINGS

(with "The Parlophone Co. Ltd.", "Recording first published 1963" & "Sold in UK ..." label text)

Parlophone PMC 1202	PLEASE PLEASE ME (G & L sleeve, with large "mono" on front cover; mono)	50
Parlophone PCS 3042	PLEASE PLEASE ME (G & L sleeve, with large "stereo" on front cover; stereo)	60

LPs: 1965

FIRST PRESSINGS

(with "The Gramophone Co. Ltd.", & "Sold in UK ..." label text)

Parlophone PMC 1255	HELP! (G & L sleeve, with outline "mono" on front cover; mono)	80
Parlophone PCS 3071	HELP! (G & L sleeve, with outline "stereo" on front cover; stereo)	120
Parlophone PMC 1267	RUBBER SOUL G & L or E. J. Day sleeve; mono)	150
Parlophone PCS 3075	RUBBER SOUL (G & L or E. J. Day sleeve; stereo)	200

SECOND PRESSINGS

(with "The Gramophone Co. Ltd.", & "Sold in UK ..." label text)

Parlophone PMC 1230	A HARD DAY'S NIGHT (small "mono" on front cover; mono)	50
Parlophone PCS 3058	A HARD DAY'S NIGHT (small "stereo" on front cover; stereo)	60
Parlophone PCS 3058	A HARD DAY'S NIGHT (outlibe "stereo" on front cover, stereo)	200
Parlophone PCS 3062	BEATLES FOR SALE (outline "stereo" on front gatefold sleeve; stereo)	60
Parlophone PMC 1267	RUBBER SOUL (matrix: [XEX 579-4 or 5]; mono)	70

THIRD PRESSINGS

(with "The Gramophone Co. Ltd..", & "Sold in UK ..." label text)

Parlophone PMC 1206	WITH THE BEATLES (small "mono" on front cover; mono)	50
Parlophone PCS 3045	WITH THE BEATLES (small "stereo" on front cover; stereo)	50

SEVENTH PRESSINGS

(with "The Gramophone Co. Ltd.", & "Sold in UK ..." label text)

Parlophone PMC 1202	PLEASE PLEASE ME (mono, with small "mono" on front cover)	40
Parlophone PCS 3042	PLEASE PLEASE ME (stereo, with small "stereo" on front cover)	50

(above pressings come with tracing-paper-lined ,"Use Emitex" die-cut inner sleeves)

LPs: 1966

FIRST PRESSINGS

(with "The Gramophone Co. Ltd.", & "Sold in UK ..." label text)

Parlophone PMC 7009	REVOLVER Side Two matrix [XEX 606-1], (G & L or E. J. Day sleeve; mono)	350
Parlophone PMC 7009	REVOLVER (G & L or E. J. Day sleeve; mono)	100
Parlophone PCS 7009	REVOLVER (G & L or E. J. Day sleeve; stereo)	100
Parlophone PMC 7016	A COLLECTION OF BEATLES OLDIES (G & L or E. J. Day sleeve; mono)	65
Parlophone PCS 7016	A COLLECTION OF BEATLES OLDIES (G & L or E. J. Day sleeve; stereo)	70

SECOND PRESSINGS

(with "The Gramophone Co. Ltd.", & "Sold in UK ..." label text)

Parlophone PMC 1255	HELP! (G & L sleeve; mono, with small solid black "mono" on front cover)	50
Parlophone PCS 3071	HELP! (G & L sleeve; stereo, with small solid black "stereo" on front cover)	60
Parlophone PMC 7009	REVOLVER (G & L or E. J. Day sleeve; mono)	70

(above pressings come with plain white or sepia "LP advertising" inner sleeves)

LPs: 1967

FIRST PRESSINGS

(with "The Gramophone Co. Ltd.", & " Sold in UK ..." label text)

Parlophone PMC 7027	SGT. PEPPER'S LONELY HEARTS CLUB BAND (G & L laminated gatefold sleeve, with red & white inner & cut-out insert; mono)	130
Parlophone PCS 7027	SGT. PEPPER'S LONELY HEARTS CLUB BAND (G & L laminated gatefold sleeve, with red & white inner & cut-out insert; stereo)	130

LPs: 1968

FIRST PRESSINGS

(with top-opening G & L gatefold sleeve, black inners, poster & 4 colour prints. Dark green label with "Sold in UK ..." text)

Apple PMC/PCS 7067/8	THE BEATLES (mono or stereo, numbered below 0000010)	7,000
Apple PMC/PCS 7067/8	THE BEATLES (mono or stereo, numbered between 0000011 & 0001000)	1200
Apple PMC/PCS 7067/8	THE BEATLES (mono or stereo, numbered between 0001001 & 0010000)	700
Apple PMC 7067/8	THE BEATLES (mono, numbered above 0010000)	250
Apple PCS 7067/8	THE BEATLES (stereo, numbered above 0010000)	200

MINT VALUE £

1969

FIRST PRESSINGS

(with G & L sleeve & black inners. Dark green label with& "Sold in UK ..." text)

Apple PMC 7070	YELLOW SUBMARINE (with red lines above & below rear sleevenote; mono)	200
Apple PCS 7070	YELLOW SUBMARINE (with red lines above & below rear sleevenote; stereo)	80
Apple PCS 7080	GET BACK (LP, unreleased, acetates only)	
Apple PCS 7088	ABBEY ROAD (black or plain white inner sleeve, with Apple logo aligned to Side 1 track listing on rear sleeve; with "Her Majesty" credit on label)	50

SECOND PRESSINGS

(with G & L sleeve. Label text with "The Gramophone Co. Ltd." but without "Sold in UK ...")

Parlophone PCS 3075	RUBBER SOUL (some with E. J. Day sleeve; stereo)	35
Parlophone PCS 7009	REVOLVER (stereo)	35
Parlophone PMC 7016	A COLLECTION OF BEATLES OLDIES (mono)	40
Parlophone PCS 7016	A COLLECTION OF BEATLES OLDIES (stereo)	35
Parlophone PCS 7027	SGT. PEPPER'S LONELY HEARTS CLUB BAND (gatefold sleeve, with white inner & cut-out insert; stereo)	35

(above pressings come with plain white or sepia "LP advertising" inner sleeves with G & L sleeve, black inners. Label text without "Sold in UK ...")

Apple PCS 7067/8	THE BEATLES (top-opening, numbered g/fold sl., poster & 4 colour prints; stereo)	100
Apple PCS 7067/8	THE BEATLES (side opening numbered g/fold sl., poster & 4 colour prints; stereo)	60
Apple PCS 7070	YELLOW SUBMARINE (with red lines above & below rear sleevenote; stereo)	35

THIRD PRESSINGS

(with G & L sleeve. Label text with "The Gramophone Co. Ltd." but without "Sold in UK ...")

Parlophone PMC 1230	A HARD DAY'S NIGHT (small "mono" on front cover; mono)	50
Parlophone PCS 3058	A HARD DAY'S NIGHT (small "stereo" on front cover; stereo)	50
Parlophone PCS 3062	BEATLES FOR SALE (gatefold sleeve; stereo)	40
Parlophone PMC 1255	HELP! (small solid black "mono" on front cover; mono)	50
Parlophone PCS 3071	HELP! (small solid black "stereo" on front cover; stereo)	45
Parlophone PMC 1267	RUBBER SOUL (mono)	40
Parlophone PMC 7009	REVOLVER (mono)	50
Parlophone PMC 7027	SGT. PEPPER'S LONELY HEARTS CLUB BAND (laminated gatefold sleeve, & cut-out insert; mono)	60

(above pressings come with plain white or sepia "LP advertising" inner sleeves)

FOURTH PRESSINGS

(with G & L sleeve. Label text with "The Gramophone Co. Ltd." but without "Sold in UK ...")

Parlophone PCS 3045	WITH THE BEATLES (small "stereo" on front cover; stereo)	50

(above pressings have plain white or sepia "LP advertising" inner sleeves)

SEVENTH PRESSINGS

(with G & L sleeve & sepia "LP advertising" inner. Label has "The Gramophone Co. Ltd." but no "Sold in UK ...")

Parlophone PMC 1202	PLEASE PLEASE ME (small "mono" on front cover; mono)	50
Parlophone PCS 3042	PLEASE PLEASE ME (small "stereo" on front cover; stereo)	40

(Please Please Me, With The Beatles, A Hard Day's Night, Help!, Rubber Soul, Revolver, A Collection Of Beatles Oldies & Yellow Submarine were originally issued with flipback sleeves. Beatles For Sale, Sgt. Pepper's Lonely Hearts Club Band & The Beatles have visible flaps inside gatefold sleeves. Abbey Road has internal flaps)

LPs: 1970

FIRST PRESSINGS

(with G & L sleeve & dark green label)

Apple PXS 1	LET IT BE (box set, dark green label red Apple logo on rear sleeve & white inner, with Get Back book housed in black card tray ['PXS 1' not listed on package])	300
Apple/Lyntone LYN 2154	FROM THEN TO YOU (The Beatles' Christmas Album)	400

EXPORT LPs: ORIGINALS

(with yellow/black labels, unless otherwise stated)

65	Parlophone CPCS 101	SOMETHING NEW (1st pressing, with "Parlophone Co. Ltd." label text)	500
65	Parlophone CPCS 101	SOMETHING NEW (2nd pressing, with "Gramophone Co. Ltd." label text)	325
66	Parlophone CPCS 103	THE BEATLES' SECOND ALBUM	400
66	Parlophone CPCS 104	BEATLES VI	400
68	Parlophone P-PCS 7067/8	THE BEATLES (2-LP, numbered, top opening 'mono' gatefold sleeve with "stereo" sticker & black inners, poster & 4 colour prints)	800
69	Odeon PPCS 7070	YELLOW SUBMARINE (Odeon sticker on rear of Apple sleeve)	2000
69	Parlophone P-PCS 7088	ABBEY ROAD (Parlophone sticker on rear of Apple sleeve)	800
70	Parlophone P-PCS 7096	LET IT BE	650
70	Parlophone CPCS 106	HEY JUDE (silver/black label, large boxed Parlophone label at top and Small EMI boxed logo at bottom, laminated sleeve)	600

EXPORT LPs: REISSUES

(with silver/black labels, unless otherwise stated)

69	Parlophone CPCS 101	SOMETHING NEW (one EMI boxed logo)	125
69	Parlophone CPCS 103	THE BEATLES' SECOND ALBUM (one EMI boxed logo)	150
69	Parlophone CPCS 104	BEATLES VI (one EMI boxed logo)	130
69	Parlophone P-PCS 7088	ABBEY ROAD (Parlophone sticker on rear of Apple sleeve; one EMI boxed logo)	125
69	Apple CPCS 106	HEY JUDE (2nd reissue, dark green label)	75
70	Parlophone P-PCS 7096	LET IT BE (one EMI boxed logo)	150
70	Parl./Apple (P-)PCS 7096	LET IT BE (2nd reissue, Apple label [PCS 7096] in Parlophone sleeve)	35
70	Parlophone CPCS 103	THE BEATLES' SECOND ALBUM (2nd reissue, silver/black labels, two EMI boxed logos)	100
70s	Parl./Apple (P-)CPCS 106	HEY JUDE (Apple label [CPCS 106] in Parlophone sleeve [P-CPSC 106])	35
73	Apple CPCS 106	HEY JUDE (3rd reissue, light green label)	15
78	Parlophone PCTC 255	MAGICAL MYSTERY TOUR (transparent yellow vinyl)	40
78	Apple PCS 7067/8	THE BEATLES (2-LP, white vinyl, gatefold sleeve)	40
78	Apple PCS 7088	ABBEY ROAD (green vinyl)	40
78	Apple PCS 7096	LET IT BE (white vinyl)	40

MINT VALUE £

LPs: 1969 RE-PRESSINGS

(with laminated flipback sleeves & silver/black labels with one boxed EMI logo)

69	Parlophone PMC 1202	PLEASE PLEASE ME (mono)	50
69	Parlophone PCS 3042	PLEASE PLEASE ME (stereo)	30
69	Parlophone PCS 3045	WITH THE BEATLES (stereo only)	30
69	Parlophone PCS 3058	A HARD DAY'S NIGHT (stereo only)	25
69	Parlophone PCS 3062	BEATLES FOR SALE (gatefold sleeve, stereo only)	30
69	Parlophone PMC 1255	HELP! (mono)	150
69	Parlophone PCS 3071	HELP! (stereo)	30
69	Parlophone PCS 3075	RUBBER SOUL (stereo only)	40
69	Parlophone PCS 7009	REVOLVER (stereo only)	40
69	Parlophone PCS 7016	A COLLECTION OF BEATLES OLDIES (stereo only)	25
69	Parlophone PMC 7027	SGT. PEPPER'S LONELY HEARTS CLUB BAND (laminated gatefold sleeve, with cut-out insert, mono)	60
69	Parlophone PCS 7027	SGT. PEPPER'S LONELY HEARTS CLUB BAND (laminated gatefold sleeve, with cut-out insert, stereo)	30
73	Apple PCS 7067/8	THE BEATLES (2-LP, un-numbered, laminated, side-opening gatefold sleeve, with poster & 4 soft card colour prints, stereo only)	35

LPs: 1980s RE-PRESSINGS

(lightweight vinyl with yellow/black labels listing "mono", unless otherwise stated)

82	Parlophone PMC 1202	PLEASE PLEASE ME (mono)	15
82	Parlophone PMC 1206	WITH THE BEATLES (mono)	15
82	Parlophone PMC 1230	A HARD DAY'S NIGHT (mono)	15
82	Parlophone PMC 1240	BEATLES FOR SALE (gatefold sleeve, mono)	12
82	Parlophone PMC 1255	HELP! (mono)	12
82	Parlophone PMC 1267	RUBBER SOUL (mono)	12
82	Parlophone PMC 7009	REVOLVER (mono)	12
82	Parlophone PMC 7027	SGT. PEPPER'S LONELY HEARTS CLUB BAND (gatefold sleeve with cut-out inserts, mono)	12
82	Apple PMC 7067/8	THE BEATLES (2-LP, un-numbered, side-opening gatefold sleeve, with poster & 4 prints, light green Apple label; mono)	30
82	Apple PMC 7070	YELLOW SUBMARINE (light green Apple label; mono)	12

LPs: RETROSPECTIVES

76	Parlophone PCTC 255	MAGICAL MYSTERY TOUR (gatefold sleeve with 24-page stapled insert)	12
77	EMI EMTV 4	THE BEATLES AT THE HOLLYWOOD BOWL (gatefold sleeve, with inner)	12
77	EMI HRL 026	HISTORY OF ROCK VOL.26 THE BEATLES (2-LP gatefold sleeve)	30
77	Parlophone PCSP 721	LOVE SONGS (2-LP, gatefold)	30
78	Apple PCSPR 717	THE BEATLES 1962-1966 (2-LP, red vinyl, gatefold stickered sleeve with lyric inners)	20
78	Apple PCSPB 718	THE BEATLES 1967-1970 (2-LP, blue vinyl, gatefold stickered sleeve with lyric inners)	20
79	Parlophone PCM 1001	RARITIES (LP)	30
79	Parlophone PCS 7184	HEY JUDE (black/silver label with two boxed EMI logos)	12
82	Parlophone EMTVS 34	THE BEATLES' GREATEST HITS (2-LP, unreleased)	
82	Parlophone PCS 7218	REEL MUSIC (with inner & 12-page insert)	12
88	HMV BPM 1	PAST MASTERS VOLUME 1 & 2 (2-LP, gatefold sleeve)	20
94	Apple PCSP 726	LIVE AT THE BBC (2-LP, gatefold sleeve, with inners)	20
95	Apple PCSP 727	ANTHOLOGY 1 (3-LP, gatefold sleeve, with inners)	30
96	Apple PCSP 728	ANTHOLOGY 2 (3-LP, gatefold sleeve, with inners)	30
96	Apple PCSP 729	ANTHOLOGY 3 (3-LP, gatefold sleeve, with inners)	35
99	Apple 521 4811	YELLOW SUBMARINE SONGTRACK (gatefold stickered sleeve)	20
99	Apple 521 4811	YELLOW SUBMARINE SONGTRACK (yellow vinyl, gatefold stickered sleeve)	12
00	Apple 521 4811	THE BEATLES 1 (2-LP, gatefold sleeve, with poster & 4 prints)	35
03	Apple 595 4380	LET IT BE...NAKED (gatefold sleeve PLUS "Fly On The Wall" 7" EP)	30
07	Apple 379 8081	LOVE (2-LP, gatefold sleeve, with inners)	25
00s	Parlophone PCS 3062	BEATLES FOR SALE (gatefold, DMM remaster, mono)	15
00s	Parlophone PCS 3071	HELP! (DMM remaster)	15
00s	Parlophone PCS 7009	REVOLVER (DMM remaster, barcode)	18
00s	Parlophone PCS 7027	SGT. PEPPER'S LONELY HEARTS CLUB BAND (gatefold, insert DMM remaster)	20
00s	Parlophone PCS 7067	THE BEATLES (2-LP, gatefold, 4 postcards, stereo, DMM remaster)	20
00s	Parlophone Apple PCS 7099	ABBEY ROAD (DMM remaster)	15

ALBUM BOX SETS

78	Parlophone BC 13	THE BEATLES COLLECTION (13 x LP, stereo, some with poster)	50
82	Parlophone BMC 10	THE BEATLES MONO COLLECTION (10 x LP, red box)	200

CD ALBUMS & BOX SETS

87	HMV BEACD 25/1	PLEASE PLEASE ME/WITH THE BEATLES/A HARD DAY'S NIGHT/ BEATLES FOR SALE (4 x CD, numbered 12" black box set with Book Of Beatles Lists paperback book)	100
87	HMV BEACD 25/2	HELP!/RUBBER SOUL/REVOLVER (3 x CD, numbered 12" red box set with insert & reprint of Beatles Book Monthly, issue 12)	50
87	HMV BEACD 25/3	SGT. PEPPER'S LONELY HEARTS CLUB BAND (CD, numbered 12" box set with booklet, cut-outs & badge)	18
87	HMV BEACD 25/4	THE BEATLES (2-CD, numbered 12" box set with booklet & badge)	30
87	HMV BEACD 25/5	YELLOW SUBMARINE (CD, numbered 12" box set with insert, cut-outs & badge)	50
87	HMV BEACD 25/6	MAGICAL MYSTERY TOUR (CD, numbered 12" box set with booklet, poster & badge)	20
87	HMV BEACD 25/7	ABBEY ROAD (CD, numbered 12" box set with 2 posters, booklet & badge)	18
87	HMV BEACD 25/8	LET IT BE (CD, numbered 12" box set with booklet & badge)	18

POLYDOR RECORDINGS

SINGLES

(with push-out centres & orange labels, unless otherwise stated)

62	Polydor NH 66833	My Bonnie/The Saints (When The Saints Go Marching In) (as Tony Sheridan & The Beatles; 1st pressing, 'broad' title & "Made In England" label text)	80
63	Polydor NH 66833	My Bonnie/The Saints (When The Saints Go Marching In)	

			MINT VALUE £
		(as Tony Sheridan & The Beatles; 2nd pressing, push-out or solid centre, 'narrow' title & "Made In England" label text)	65
64	Polydor NH 52906	Sweet Georgia Brown/Nobody's Child (German import only, unissued in U.K.)	
64	Polydor NH 52275	Cry For A Shadow (A-side credited to 'Beatles')/ TONY SHERIDAN & THE BEATLES: Why (Can't You Love Me Again) ('scroll' label, with "Made In England" text)	50
64	Polydor NH 52317	Ain't She Sweet (A-side as 'The Beatles, vocal: John Lennon')/If You Love Me, Baby (B-side credited to 'The Beatles with Tony Sheridan, vocal'; 1st pressing, 'scroll' label with "Made In England" text)	45
64	Polydor NH 52317	Ain't She Sweet/If You Love Me, Baby (2nd pressing, red label, with "Made In England" text)	20

EPs

64	Polydor EPH 21 610	TONY SHERIDAN WITH THE BEATLES (1st pressing, German import in U.K. p/s, orange 'scroll' label; "Why" songwriting credit as 'Sheridan' or 'Sheridan-Crompton')	100
64	Polydor EPH 21 610	TONY SHERIDAN WITH THE BEATLES (2nd pressing, German import in U.K. p/s, red label; "Why" songwriting credit as 'Sheridan' or 'Sheridan-Crompton')	40

LPs

64	Polydor Hi-Fi 46 432	THE BEATLES' FIRST (purple/black sleeve, Germany only, unissued in U.K.)	
67	Polydor Special 236 201	THE BEATLES' FIRST (as Tony Sheridan & The Beatles, 1st pressing, without 'stereo' on label or sleeve, 'pop art' sleeve)	50
67	Polydor Special 236 201	THE BEATLES' FIRST (later pressings with 'stereo' on label & sleeve, minor label variations, 'pop art' sleeve)	30

CONTRACT PRESSINGS

(Records were often pressed by non-EMI companies under contract, owing to overwhelming demand. Subtle differences indicating their origin can be detected. Philips pressings (the 'Hey Jude' single only) are the easiest to spot as they alone have three-pronged centres. All the others had four except for the French Pathe-Marconi pressings of 'Hello Goodbye' which have solid centres and 'Made In France' at the foot of the label. The centre of a Decca contract pressing has a ridge 3mm from the perimeter.
Pre-1966 EMI pressings have flat push-out centres. Thereafter many records were produced with a mix of push-out and solid centres. EMI always pressed stamper letters into the vinyl, positioned at 3 o'clock to the matrix number. Up to three letters from the code 'GRAMOPHLTD' were used each representing a number. EMI stamper letters are seldom seen on contract pressings. Controversy has surrounded the origin of the only other known style of pre-1965 Beatles' contract pressings. Previously thought to have been made by PYE they are now believed to have been pressed at the ORIOLE pressing plant before its September 1964 acquisition by CBS. The centres of these pressings have no ridge and are finished with rough edges. They are also thicker and heavier than any of the other pressings. Although released in November 1964 'I Feel Fine' also has these characteristics and is assumed to have come from this source, CBS using the old ORIOLE presses. However, it is thought that PYE actually pressed one Beatles' 45 and one EP after 1964. The centres of these two pressings look very similar to those made by DECCA but have a less prominent ridge. The edges of records made by PHILIPS, ORIOLE and PYE are not straight-cut but are tapered off. The edges of EMI, DECCA and Pathe-Marconi pressings are all straight-cut.)

SINGLES

63	Parlophone R 5055	She Loves You/I'll Get You (Decca pressing)	15
63	Parlophone R 5084	I Want To Hold Your Hand/This Boy (Decca pressing)	15
63	Parlophone R 5084	I Want To Hold Your Hand/This Boy (Pye pressing)	15
64	Parlophone R 5114	Can't Buy Me Love/You Can't Do That (Pye pressing)	15
64	Parlophone R 5200	I Feel Fine/She's A Woman (Decca pressing)	15
64	Parlophone R 5200	I Feel Fine/She's A Woman (Pye pressing)	15
65	Parlophone R 5305	Help!/I'm Down (Decca pressing)	20
67	Parlophone R 5655	Hello Goodbye/I Am The Walrus (Decca pressing)	18
67	Parlophone R 52317	Hello Goodbye/I Am The Walrus (Pathe Marconi pressing)	25
68	Apple R 5722	Hey Jude/Revolution (Decca pressing)	25
68	Apple R 5722	Hey Jude/Revolution (Philips pressing, three-pronged push-out centre)	50
68	Apple R 5722	Hey Jude/Revolution (Pye pressing)	25

EP

66	Parlophone GEP 8946	THE BEATLES MILLION SELLERS (EP, Pye pressing with 'Golden Discs' text on labels)	40

LPs

(Decca contract pressings have no stamper letters (G or D) positioned at 3 o'clock to the matrix number; the label has a circular impression 15mm from the outer edge. Pye pressings are a dark, translucent red when held up to a strong light.)

63	Parlophone PMC 1202	PLEASE PLEASE ME (Decca pressing)	150
63	Parlophone PMC 1206	WITH THE BEATLES (Decca pressing)	120
63	Parlophone PMC 1206	WITH THE BEATLES (Pye pressing)	135
68	Parlophone P-PCS 7067/8	THE BEATLES (export issue, yellow & black labels, Decca pressing)	2000
69	Parlophone P-PCS 7088	ABBEY ROAD (export issue, yellow & black labels, Decca pressing)	1000
69	Parlophone P-PCS 7099	ABBEY ROAD (export issue, silver & black labels, Decca pressing)	500
70s	Apple PCSP 717	THE BEATLES 1962-1966 (2-LP, gatefold sleeve with lyric inners, Pye pressing)	50
84	Parlophone/ Nimbus PCS 7027	SGT. PEPPER'S LONELY HEARTS CLUB BAND (mail-order only, from Practical Hi-Fi Magazine, Nimbus pressing)	500

FRENCH PRESSINGS

SINGLE

67	Parlophone R 5655	Hello Goodbye/I Am The Walrus (Pathé Marconi pressing)	25

LPs

(Parlophone label LPs have 'Made in France' on EMI rim copy. Apple label LPs have 'Made in France by Pathé Marconi EMI' rim copy. All discs are in British-printed sleeves bearing 'Made in France' stickers.)

73	Parlophone PCS 3042	PLEASE PLEASE ME	12
73	Parlophone PCS 3045	WITH THE BEATLES	12
73	Parlophone PCS 3058	A HARD DAY'S NIGHT	12
73	Parlophone PCS 3062	BEATLES FOR SALE (gatefold sleeve)	12
73	Parlophone PCS 3071	HELP!	12
73	Parlophone PCS 3075	RUBBER SOUL	12
73	Parlophone PCS 7009	REVOLVER	12
73	Parlophone PCS 7016	A COLLECTION OF BEATLES OLDIES	12

MINT VALUE £

73	Parlophone PCS 7027	SGT. PEPPER'S LONELY HEARTS CLUB BAND (gatefold sleeve with cut-out insert, some copies with banded vinyl)	15
73	Apple PCS 7067/8	THE BEATLES (2-LP, un-numbered, laminated, side-opening gatefold sleeve, with four colour prints & poster)	25
73	Apple PCS 7070	YELLOW SUBMARINE	15
73	Apple PCS 7088	ABBEY ROAD (some copies with banded vinyl)	15
73	Apple PCS 7096	LET IT BE	12
73	Apple PCSP 717	THE BEATLES 1962-1966 (2-LP, gatefold sleeve with lyric inners)	20
73	Apple PCSP 718	THE BEATLES 1967-1970 (2-LP, gatefold sleeve with lyric inners)	12

MISPRINTS & MISPRESSINGS

SINGLES

63	Parlophone R 4983	Please Please Me/Ask Me Why (A-side actually plays 'Quiet Morning' by the Brian Fahey Orchestra)	50
67	Parlophone R 5620	All You Need Is Love/Baby You're A Rich Man (with no reference to "Live World Television Transmission")	60

EPs

64	Parlophone GEP 8882	TWIST AND SHOUT (label error: "Do You Want A Know A Secret")	20
65	Parlophone GEP 8946	THE BEATLES' MILLION SELLERS (label error: "Beatles Golden Discs")	20

LPs

64	Parlophone PCS 3062	BEATLES FOR SALE (label error: "I'm A Losser")	200
65	Parlophone CPCS 101	SOMETHING NEW (export issue, label error: "Sold in UK")	500
65	Parlophone PCS 3075	RUBBER SOUL (label error: "Norweigian Wood")	350
66	Parlophone CPCS 106	BEATLES VI (export issue, label error: "Sold in UK")	500
66	Parlophone PMC 7009	REVOLVER (copies with side 2 matrix no.: XEX 606-1 have 'Remix 11' of "Tomorrow Never Knows", G & L or E. J. Day sleeve; mono only)	200
67	Parlophone PMC 7027	SGT. PEPPER'S LONELY HEARTS CLUB BAND (label omits "A Day In The Life" credit; G & L laminated gatefold sleeve, with plain white inner & insert,; mono only)	200
68	Apple PCS 7067/8	THE BEATLES (label error: "Rocky Racoon")	200
69	Parlophone PMC 7027	SGT. PEPPER'S LONELY HEARTS CLUB BAND (mono; matrix YEX 637/8; plays stereo)	200
69	Apple CPCS 106	HEY JUDE (label error: "Revolutions")	250
69	Apple PCS 7088	ABBEY ROAD (Apple logo misaligned to Side 1 track listing on rear sleeve; with or without "Her Majesty" credit on label; black or plain white inner sleeve)	60
69	Apple PCS 7088	ABBEY ROAD (label omits "Her Majesty")	35
99	Parlophone PCS 3075	RUBBER SOUL (label error: pressed on Apple)	100

(see also John Lennon, Paul McCartney/Wings, George Harrison, Ringo Starr, Pete Best Four,Quarry Men, Tony Sheridan, George Martin, Billy Preston, Yoko Ono)

BEATMEN

65	Pye 7N 15659	You Can't Sit Down/Come On Pretty Baby	20
65	Pye 7N 15792	Now The Sun Has Gone/Please Believe	15

BEAT MERCHANTS

64	Columbia DB 7367	Pretty Face/Messin' With The Man	80
65	Columbia DB 7492	So Fine/She Said Yeah	70

BEAT SIX

(see also Guys)

64	Decca F 12011	Bernadine/The River And I	15

BEATSTALKERS

65	Decca F 12259	Ev'rybody's Talking 'Bout My Baby/Mr. Disappointed	70
66	Decca F 12352	Left Right Left/You'd Better Get A Better Hold On	60
66	Decca F 12460	A Love Like Yours/Base Line	60
67	CBS 2732	My One Chance To Make It/Ain't No Soul (Left In These Old Shoes)	80
67	CBS 3105	Silver Treetop School For Boys/Sugar Coated Man	60
68	CBS 3557	Rain Coloured Roses/Everything Is For You	60
69	CBS 3936	Little Boy/When I'm Five	70

PAUL BEATTIE

57	Parlophone R 4385	I'm Comin' Home/Nothing So Strange	40
58	Parlophone R 4429	Me, Please Me/Wanderlust	10
58	Parlophone R 4468	A House, A Car, And A Wedding Ring/Banana	20
68	Parlophone R 4664	Slick Chick/The Big Bounce	30

E.C. BEATTY

59	Felsted AF 127	Ski King/I'm A Lucky Man	40

BEAU

(see also Way We Live)

69	Dandelion S 4403	1917 Revolution/Sleeping Town	7
69	Dandelion S 63751	BEAU (LP, black/red/silver label)	50
71	Dandelion DAN 8006	CREATION (LP, with The Way We Live)	40

BEAU BRUMMELS

65	Pye International 7N 25293	Laugh, Laugh/Still In Love With You Baby	6
65	Pye International 7N 25306	Just A Little/They'll Make You Cry	5
65	Pye International 7N 25318	You Tell Me Why/I Want You	5
65	Pye International 7N 25333	Don't Talk To Strangers/In Good Time	10
66	Pye International 7N 25342	Good Time Music/Sad Little Girl (unissued)	0
65	Pye International NPL 28062	INTRODUCING THE BEAU BRUMMELS (LP, mono only)	30

BEAU-MARKS

(see also Del-Tones, Milton De Lugg Orchestra)

60	Top Rank JAR 377	Clap Your Hands/Daddy Said	30

JIMMY BEAUMONT

66	London HLZ 10059	You Got Too Much Going For You/I Never Loved Her Anyway	100
66	London HLZ 10059	You Got Too Much Going For You/I Never Loved Her Anyway (DJ Copy)	180

MINT VALUE £

BEAUTIFUL SOUTH

92	Go! Discs GOD 78	Bell Bottomed Tear/A Thousand Lies/They Used To Wear Black (p/s, postcards)	5
92	Go! Discs GOD 88	36D/Throw His Song Away/Trevor, You're Bizarre (p/s with postcards)	5
94	Go! Discs 828 507-1	MIAOW (LP, withdrawn HMV-style 'dog' sleeve with lyric inner)	30
94	Go! Discs 828 507-1	MIAOW (LP, 'cat' sleeve with lyric inner)	15
96	Go! Discs 828 845-1	BLUE IS THE COLOUR (LP, with lyric inner)	18
07	Mercury 175 252-3	SOUP ('deluxe Fan Edition', in sealed/stickered tin: CD, DVD, T-shirt and mug)	60

BEAVER & KRAUSE

72	Warner Bros K 46130	GANDHARVA (LP)	15
72	Warner Bros K 46184	ALL GOOD MEN (LP)	15

JACKIE BEAVERS

76	Jay Boy BOY 102	Trying To Get Back To You Girl/Trying To Get Back To You Girl (Version)	10

BEAZERS

(see also Chris Farlowe, Little Joe Cook)

64	Decca F 11827	The Blue Beat/I Wanna Shout	45

BE-BOP DELUXE

(see also Bill Nelson, A-Austr, Axe Victim)

73	Smile LAFS 001	Teenage Archangel/Jets At Dawn (mono, 1,000 only)	25
74	Harvest HAR 5081	Jet Silver (And The Dolls Of Venus)/Third Floor Heaven	6
75	Harvest HAR 5091	Between The Worlds/Lights (withdrawn)	50
75	Harvest HAR 5098	Maid In Heaven/Lights	5
76	Harvest HAR 5110	Kiss Of The Light/FUNKY PHASER & HIS UNEARTHLY MERCHANDISE: Shine	5
74	Harvest SHVL 813	AXE VICTIM (LP, gatefold sleeve)	20
77	Harvest SHVL 816	LIVE! IN THE AIR AGE (LP, with bonus EP "Live! In The Air Age" [PSR 412])	20
78	Harvest SHSP 4091	DRASTIC PLASTIC (LP)	12

BE-BOP PRESERVATION SOCIETY

71	Dawn DNLS 3027	THE BE-BOP PRESERVATION SOCIETY (LP, gatefold sleeve, orange label with insert)	25

GILBERT BECAUD

59	HMV POP 574	The Day The Rains Came/Les Marches De Provence	5

BECAUSE

(see also Furniture)

92	Haven HAVEN CD1	MAD, SCARED, DUMB & GORGEOUS (CD)	20

BECK

94	Geffen GFS 67	Loser/Alcohol/Fume (p/s)	8
94	Geffen GFSJB 67	Loser/Loser (jukebox issue, no p/s)	8
94	Geffen GFS 73	Pay No Mind (Snoozer)/Special People (withdrawn)	60
94	Geffen GFST 73	Pay No Mind (Snoozer)/Special People/Trouble All My Days/ Super Golden (Sunchild) (12", p/s, withdrawn - at least 100 pressed up)	50
94	Geffen GFST 73	Pay No Mind (Snoozer)/Special People/Trouble All My Days/ Super Golden (Sunchild) (CD - blue image on CD)	8
94	Geffen GED 21911	Pay No Mind (Snoozer)/Special People/Trouble All My Days/ Super Golden (Sunchild) (CD - pink image on CD)	8
94	Geffen GED 21939	Beercan/Got No Mind/Asskizz Powergrudge (Payback! '94)/Spanking Room/ Loser (Pseudo-Muzak) (unlisted track) (CD)	8
94	Geffen GFS 19235	Beercan/Spanking Room (p/s, 1500 copies)	30
96	Geffen GFS 22183	Devil's Haircut/Lloyd Price Express (Remix By John King) (p/s)	5
96	Geffen GFS 22205	The New Pollution/Electric Music And The Summer People (p/s)	5
97	Geffen GFS 22253	Sissyneck/Feather In Your Cap (p/s)	5
97	Select SELECT 12	Clock/The Little Drum Machine Boy/Totally Confused (with Select mag)	7
97	Geffen GFS 22276	Jack-Ass (Butch Vig Mix)/Strange Invitation/Devil Got My Woman/ Jack-Ass(Lowrider Mix By Butch Vig) Burro Brother (Double 7" gatefold some have Butch Vig Mix with no Lowrider Mix)	6
99	Geffen 497182-7	Sexxlaws/Salt In The Wound (picture disc, stickered p/s)	5
00	Geffen 497312-7	Mixed Bizness/(Dirty Bixin Mizness Remix) (gatefold p/s - 1,500 copies)	5

BECK, BOGERT & APPICE

(see also Jeff Beck, Vanilla Fudge, Cactus)

75	CBS EQ 32140/Q 65455	BECK, BOGERT & APPICE (LP, quadrophonic)	15

GORDON BECK (QUARTET)

(see also Seven Ages Of Man)

68	Morgan MJ 1	GYROSCOPE (LP)	250
69	M. Minor MMLP/SMLP 21	EXPERIMENTS WITH POPS (LP, as Gordon Beck Quartet)	125
69	M. Minor MMLP/SMLP 22	HALF A JAZZ SIXPENCE (LP)	100
69	Major Minor SMLP 88	DR. DOOLITTLE LOVES JAZZ (LP)	35
72	Dire FO 341	BECK-MATTHEWSON-HUMAIR TRIO (LP)	30

JEFF BECK

(see also Yardbirds, Beck Bogert Appice, Donovan, Rod Stewart, Cozy Powell, Honeydrippers, Buddy Guy)

67	Columbia DB 8151	Hi-Ho Silver Lining/Beck's Bolero	10
67	Columbia DB 8227	Tallyman/Rock My Plimsoul	12
68	Columbia DB 8359	Love Is Blue (L'Amour Est Bleu)/I've Been Drinking	12
69	Columbia DB 8590	Plinth (Water Down The Drain)/Hangman's Knee (unissued)	0
72	Epic EPC 7720	Got The Feeling/Situation	8
75	Epic EPC 3334	She's A Woman/It Doesn't Really Matter	10
80	Epic EPC 8806	The Final Peace/Space Boogie	8
80	Epic EPCA 1009	The Final Peace/Scatter Brain/Too Much To Lose/Led Boots (12", p/s)	10
68	Columbia SX 6293	TRUTH (LP, 1st pressing, silver/black labels, boxed Columbia logo, with "Sold in U.K." label text, mono)	100
68	Columbia S(C)X 6293	TRUTH (LP, 1st pressing, silver/black labels, boxed Columbia logo, with "Sold in U.K." label text, stereo)	40
69	Columbia SX 6351	BECK-OLA (LP, 1st pressing, blue/black labels, mono)	70

			MINT VALUE £
69	Columbia S(C)X 6351	BECK-OLA (LP, 1st pressing, blue/black labels, stereo)	30
69	Columbia SCX 6293	TRUTH (LP, 2nd pressing, silver/black labels, mono/stereo)	15
69	Columbia SCX 6351	BECK-OLA (LP, 2nd pressing, silver/black labels, mono/stereo)	15
72	Epic EPC 64619	ROUGH AND READY (LP, yellow label)	15
72	Epic EPC 64899	JEFF BECK GROUP (LP, yellow label)	12
72	Epic EQ 30973	ROUGH AND READY (LP, quadrophonic)	20
74	CBS EQ 31331	JEFF BECK GROUP (LP, quadrophonic)	20

ROBIN BECK

79	Mercury BECK 2	Sweet Talk/Shake It Through The Night (12")	12

BECKETT

73	Raft RA 18506	Little Girl/My Lady	5
74	Raft RA 48502	BECKETT (LP, with lyric insert)	20

HAROLD BECKETT

(see also Graham Collier, Galliard, Ninesense)

71	Philips 6308 026	FLARE UP (LP)	120
72	RCA SF 8225	WARM SMILES (LP)	90
73	RCA SF 8264	THEME FOR FEGA (LP)	40
75	Cadillac SGC 1004	JOY UNLIMITED (LP)	20
76	Ogun OG 800	MEMORIES OF BACARES (LP, as Harry Beckett's Joy Unlimited)	15
70s	Ogun OG 020	GOT IT MADE (LP, as Harry Beckett's Joy Unlimited)	12

JENNY BECKETT

65	Parlophone R 5373	My Love And I/Lock Away Your Love	5

STUART BECKETT

60s	Sherwood SRS 1001	Kariline/Breakthrough	35

(KEE) LYN BECKFORD

68	Island WI 3144	Combination/Hey Little Girl	20
69	Jackpot JP 707	Kiss Me Quick/MRS. MILLER: Feel It	10
69	Big Shot BI 521	Suzie Wong (as K. Beckford)/SWINGING KINGS: Deebo	40
71	G.G. GG 4514	Groove Me/Groove Version (as Keeling Beckford)	10

THEO(PHILUS) BECKFORD

(see also Eric Barnet[t], Maytals, Clue J & His Bluesblasters)

61	Blue Beat BB 33	Jack And Jill Shuffle/Little Lady (as Theophilus Beckford & Clue J. & His Blues Blasters)	12
61	Blue Beat BB 50	Georgie And The Old Shoe/That's Me (as Theo Beckford & City Slickers)	12
62	Blue Beat BB 87	Walking Down King Street/The Clock (B-side actually by Sir D's Group)	12
62	Blue Beat BB 132	Bringing In The Sheep (song actually "Bringing In The Sheaves")/Run Away	12
62	Island WI 026	I Don't Want You (actually by King Edward's All Stars)/Seven Long Years	15
63	Island WI 106	Daphney/Boller Man	12
63	R & B JB 136	Bullo Man/Daphney	25
64	Blue Beat BB 250	She's Gone/Old Flame (as Cotheo Beckford, B-side act. by Frederick Hibbert)	15
64	Blue Beat BB 257	Don't Worry To Cry/Love Me Or Leave Me (as Theophilus Beckford, B-side actually by Lloyd Clarke)	12
64	Blue Beat BB 287	On Your Knees/Now You're Gone (with Yvonne Harrison)	15
65	Blue Beat BB 303	Dig The Dig (as Basil Gabbidon)/Don't Let Me Cry No More	15
65	Black Swan WI 452	Take Your Time/STRANGER COLE: Happy-Go-Lucky	20
65	Island WI 238	Trench Town People/PIONEERS: Sometime	25
65	Island WI 243	You Are The One Girl/Grudgeful People	20
65	Island WI 246	If Life Was A Thing/L. CLARKE: Parro Saw The Light (B-side actually "Pharaoh Saw The Light" by Lloyd Clarke)	12
65	Island WI 248	What A Whoe/Bajan Girl	20
68	Nu Beat NB 009	Easy Snappin'/ERIC MORRIS: My Lonely Days	15
69	Crab CRAB 25	Brother Ram Goat (as T. Beckford)/STARLIGHTS: What A Condition	20

BOB BECKHAM

59	Brunswick 05808	Just As Much As Ever/Your Sweet Love	7
60	Brunswick 05822	Crazy Arms/Beloved	10
60	Brunswick 05835	Mais Oui/Only The Broken Hearted	6
60	Brunswick 05837	Nothing Is Forever/Two Wrongs Don't Make A Right	6
60	Brunswick 05837	Nothing Is Forever/Two Wrongs Don't Make A Right (78)	12
60	Brunswick LAT 8325	JUST AS MUCH AS EVER (LP)	12

BEDASSE & CHIN'S CALYPSO QUINTET

55	Kalypso C 1003	Industrial Fair/Samson & Delilah	12
56	Kalypso C 1008	Big Boy & Teacher/Red Tomato	12
58	Kalypso XX 01	Walk & Talk/Night Food	12

BED BUGS

90	Snake Rattle 01	Haywire/No Safe Haven	15

DAVID BEDFORD

(see also Coxhill/Bedford Trio, Kevin Ayers & Whole World, Mike Oldfield, Roy Harper, Edgar Broughton Band)

70	Argo ZRG 638	MUSIC FOR ALBION MOONLIGHT (LP, 1 side by Elizabeth Lutyens)	25
72	Dandelion 2310 165	NURSE'S SONG WITH ELEPHANTS (LP, gatefold sleeve)	25

BEDLAM

(see also Cozy Powell, Ace Kefford Stand, Big Bertha)

73	Chrysalis CFB 1	I Believe In You/Whiskey And Wine	8
73	Chrysalis CHR 1048	BEDLAM (LP)	20

BEDROCKS

68	Columbia DB 8516	Ob-La-Di-Ob-La-Da/Lucy	10

EDWIN BEE

68	Decca F 12781	I've Been Loving You/Call For My Baby	12

MOLLY BEE

57	London HLD 8400	Since I Met You, Baby/I'll Be Waiting For You	40

			MINT VALUE £
58	Capitol CL 14849	Going Steady (With A Dream)/Magic Mirror	10
58	Capitol CL 14880	Don't Look Back/Please Don't Talk About Me When I'm Gone	7
58	Capitol CL 14949	After You've Gone/Five Points Of A Star	6
64	Liberty LIB 55691	He Doesn't Want You/Our Secret	10
65	MGM MGM 1280	Single Girl Again/Keep It A Secret	7
58	Capitol T1097	YOUNG ROMANCE (LP)	30

BEE BEE CEE

77	Rel RE 48-S	You Gotta Know Girl/We Ain't Listening (p/s, 2,000 only)	70

JOHNNY BEECHER

63	Warner Bros WB89	Sax Fifth Avenue/Jack Sax The City	10

ASHLEY BEEDLE

00	Weekend Inc WKD 999	Untitled (12")	40

BEEFEATERS

(see also Byrds)

64	Pye International 7N 25277	Please Let Me Love You/Don't Be Long	100
70	Elektra 2101 007	Please Let Me Love You/Don't Be Long (reissue)	15

BEE GEES

(see also Barry Gibb, Robin Gibb, Maurice Gibb, Humpy Bong, Fut)

67	Polydor 56727	Spicks And Specks/I Am The World	12
67	Polydor 56161	New York Mining Disaster 1941/I Can't See Nobody	6
67	Polydor 56178	To Love Somebody/Close Another Door	5
67	Polydor 56192	Massachusetts/Barker Of The U.F.O.	5
67	Polydor 56220	World/Sir Geoffrey Saved The World	5
68	Polydor 56229	Words/Sinking Ships	5
68	Polydor 56242	Jumbo/The Singer Sang His Song	5
68	Polydor 56273	I've Gotta Get A Message To You/Kitty Can	5
69	Polydor 56304	Odessa Parts 1 & 2 (unissued)	0
69	Polydor 56304	First Of May/Lamplight	5
69	Polydor 56331	Tomorrow Tomorrow/Sun In The Morning	5
69	Polydor 56343	Don't Forget To Remember/The Lord	5
70	Polydor 56377	I.O.I.O./Sweetheart	7
70	Polydor 2001 104	Lonely Days/Man For All Seasons	5
71	Polydor 2058 115	How Can You Mend A Broken Heart/Country Woman	5
81	RSO SNF 1	Night Fever (promo only 7" with p/s to coincide with ITV showing 'Saturday Night Fever' on Royal Wedding Day)	20
67	Polydor 582/583 012	BEE GEES FIRST (LP)	20
68	Polydor 582/583 020	HORIZONTAL (LP)	18
68	Polydor 236 221	RARE PRECIOUS AND BEAUTIFUL (LP)	15
68	Polydor 236 513	RARE PRECIOUS AND BEAUTIFUL VOL. 2 (LP)	15
68	Polydor 582/583 036	IDEA (LP)	15
69	Polydor 236 556	RARE PRECIOUS AND BEAUTIFUL VOL. 3 (LP)	15
69	Polydor 582 049/050	ODESSA (2-LP, felt cover, gatefold sleeve)	40
70	Polydor 2383 010	CUCUMBER CASTLE (LP)	15
70	Polydor 2310 069	TWO YEARS ON (LP)	15
71	Polydor 2383 052	TRAFALGAR (LP)	20
72	Polydor 2383 139	TO WHOM IT MAY CONCERN (LP)	12

BEEKEEPERS

81	Rundown ACE 40	PLATFORM FIVE EP	10

MARK BEER

81	My China TAO 001	DUST ON THE ROAD (LP)	15

BEES MAKE HONEY

73	EMI EMI 2078	Knee Trembler/Caldonia	5
73	EMI EMC 3013	MUSIC EVERY NIGHT (LP)	25

BEES (UK)

67	Columbia Blue Beat DB 101	Jesse James Rides Again/The Girl In My Dreams	20
68	Columbia Blue Beat DB 111	The Prisoner From Alcatraz/The Ska's The Limit	12

BILLY BEETHOVEN

(see also Graham Bonnet)

75	DJM DJS 10377	Dreams (Out In The Forest)/We're Free	100

BEEZ

79	Edible SNACK 001	Easy/Vagrant (gatefold p/s)	100
78	Edible SNACK 002	THE BEEZ EP: Do The Suicide (no p/s, stickered sleeve)	100

B.E.F. (British Electric Foundation)

(see also Heaven 17, Billy MacKenzie)

91	Ten TEN 386	Free (Edit)/Secret Life Of Arabia (stickered/unstickered p/s, as B.E.F. Featuring Billy MacKenzie, unissued 200 copies only)	40
80	Virgin V 2888	MUSIC FOR STOWAWAYS (cassette)	12
82	Virgin VV 2219	MUSIC OF QUALITY & DISTINCTION VOL. 1 (5 x 7" box set & insert)	20

SI BEGG

97	Mosquito MSQ 010	WORKING ON THE FRONT LINE EP (12")	20
00	Mosquito MSQ 016	BAD DOO DOO (mini-LP)	15

SI BEGG MEETS NEIL LANDSTRUMM

01	Mosquito MSQ 017	TOKYO ASSASSIN (12" EP)	10

BEGGARS FARM

84	White Rabbit WR 1001	THE DEPTH OF A DREAM (LP)	25

BEGGARS HILL

76	Moonshine MS 60	BEGGARS HILL (LP, private pressing)	175

MINT VALUE £

BEGGARS OPERA

70	Vertigo 6059 026	Sarabande/Think	18
72	Vertigo 6059 060	Hobo/Pathfinder	12
73	Vertigo 6059 088	Two Timing Woman/Lady Of Hell Fire	8
74	Vertigo 6059 105	Classical Gas/Sweet Blossom Woman	6
70	Vertigo 6360 018	ACT ONE (LP, large swirl label, gatefold sleeve)	45
71	Vertigo 6360 054	WATERS OF CHANGE (LP, small swirl label, gatefold sleeve)	60
72	Vertigo 6360 073	PATHFINDER (LP, small swirl label, foldout poster cover)	80
73	Vertigo 6360 090	GET YOUR DOG OFF ME! (LP, 'spaceship' label)	20

BEGINNING OF THE END

71	Atlantic 2091 097	Funky Nassau Parts 1 & 2 (initial pressing on red label)	15
71	Atlantic 2091 097	Funky Nassau Parts 1 & 2	8
72	Atlantic 2091166	Monkey Tamarind/Hey Pretty Girl	15
76	Warner Bros. WEA K10021	Funky Nassau (Full Length Version)/Funky Nassau Parts 1 & 2	80
71	Atlantic K 40304	FUNKY NASSAU (LP)	30

BRENDAN BEHAN

60	HMV 7EG 8491	THE HOSTAGE (EP)	8
60	Argo RG 239	THE HOSTAGE (LP)	12

DOMINIC BEHAN

(see also Ewan MacColl)

59	Decca F 11147	The Bells Of Hell/The Captains And The Kings	5
60	Topic STOP 115	The Patriot Game/Erin Go Brath (p/s)	5
64	Piccadilly 7N 35172	Liverpool Lou/Love Is Where You Find It	5
65	Piccadilly 7N 35238	Arkle/Lonely Days	6
68	Major Minor MM 575	Wormwood Scrubs/Rifles Of The IRA	6
58	Collector JEL 3	SONGS OF THE STREETS (EP)	18
60	Topic 12T 35	DOWN BY THE LIFFEYSIDE - IRISH STREET BALLADS (LP)	18
61	Topic 12T 44	EASTER WEEK AND AFTER - SONGS OF "THE TROUBLES" (LP)	18
66	Pye NPL 18134	IRELAND SINGS (LP)	15
69	Marble Arch MAL 1123	ARKLE (LP)	30
67	Major Minor MMLP 6	DOMINIC BEHAN (LP)	15

BIX BEIDERBECKE & HIS GANG

55	Columbia 33S 1035	THE GREAT BIX (10" LP)	12

BEIL TEECS

71	Bullet BU 491	So Far Away/BRUTE FORCE & IGNORANCE: So Far (Version)	8

SVEINBJORN BEINTEINSSON

90	Durtro 005	EDDA (LP, with booklet)	20

HARRY BELAFONTE

(see also Lena Horne)

54	HMV 7M 202	Hold 'Em Joe/Suzanne (Every Night When The Sun Goes Down)	5
54	HMV 7M 224	I'm Just A Country Boy/Pretty As A Rainbow	5
55	Capitol CL 14312	Close Your Eyes/I Still Get A Thrill (Thinking Of You)	5
57	HMV DLP 1147	THE VERSATILE MR. BELAFONTE (10" LP)	12
57	RCA RC 24005	BELAFONTE SINGS OF THE CARIBBEAN (10" LP)	12

BELBORN

01	World Serpent WS7 005	Seelenruhe/Phoenix (picture disc)	5

BEL CANTOS

65	R&B MRB 5003	Feel Aw Right Parts 1 & 2	20

BELFAST GYPSIES

(see also Them, Jackie McAuley, Freaks Of Nature)

66	Island WI 3007	Gloria's Dream/Secret Police	70
77	Sonet SNTF 738	THEM BELFAST GYPSIES (LP)	25

ED 'TEX' BELIN

63	Starlite STEP 39	ED 'TEX' BELIN (EP)	10

ALEXANDER BELL

67	CBS 2977	Alexander Bell Believes/Hymn...With Love	30

ARCHIE BELL & THE DRELLS

68	Atlantic 584 185	Tighten Up/Dog Eat Dog	15
68	Atlantic 584 217	I Can't Stop Dancing/You're Such A Beautiful Child	15
71	Atlantic 2091 156	Tighten Up/I Can't Stop Dancing/(There's Gonna Be A) Showdown	8
72	Atlantic K 10210	Here I Go Again/A World Without Music	8
73	Atlantic K 10263	There's Gonna Be A Showdown/Tighten Up	6
73	President PT 418	Girls Grow Up Faster Than Boys	10
76	Portrait TA 7254	Don't Let Love Get You Down/Where Will You Go When The Party's Over/ The Soul City Walk (12")	8
76	Philly int. 4803	Where Will You Go When The Music's Over?/Part 2	15
86	Nightmare MARE 16	Look Back Over Your Shoulder/Look Back Over Your Shoulder (Dub Mix) (12")	25
68	Atlantic	TIGHTEN UP (LP)	40
72	Atlantic K 40454	HERE I GO AGAIN (LP)	20

BELINDA BELL

73	Columbia DB 8995	If Only You Believe/Stone Valley	5
73	Columbia SCXA 9255	STONE VALLEY (LP, gatefold sleeve)	15
73	One Up OU 2009	MUSIC OF W. GULGOWSKI (LP)	12

BENNY BELL & BLOCK BUSTERS

57	Parlophone R 4372	The Sack Dress/Dr. Jazz	10

CAREY BELL

60s	Delmark DS 622	CAREY BELL'S BLUES HARP (LP)	12

MINT VALUE £

CHARLES BELL & CONTEMPORARY JAZZ QUARTET
63 London HA-K/SH-K 8095 ANOTHER DIMENSION (LP) 25

ERIC BELL BAND
(see also Thin Lizzy, Noel Redding Band)
81 Hobo HOS 016 Lonely Man/Anyone Seen My Baby (p/s) 30

FREDDIE BELL & BELLBOYS
56 Mercury MT 122 Giddy-Up-A Ding Dong/I Said It And I'm Glad 10
57 Mercury MT 141 Hucklebuck/Rompin' And Stompin' (78) 10
57 Mercury MT 146 Teach You To Rock/Take The First Train Out Of Town (78) 10
57 Mercury MT 149 Big Bad Wolf/Rockin' The Polonaise (78) 10
57 Mercury MT 159 Rockin' Is My Business/You're Gonna Be Sorry (78) 18
56 Mercury MEP 9508 ROCK WITH THE BELL BOYS (EP) 30
57 Mercury MEP 9512 ROCK WITH THE BELL BOYS VOL. 2 (EP) 55

FREDRICK BELL
68 Nu Beat NB 004 Rocksteady Cool/CARLTON ALPHONSO: I Have Changed 25

GARY BELL
67 CBS 202234 Is This What I Get For Loving You?/To Keep You 15
67 CBS 2646 Anyway That You Want Me/Leave It To Me 10

GRAHAM BELL
(see also Heavy Jelly, Griffin, Every Which Way, Skip Bifferty, Bell & Arc)
66 Polydor 56067 How Can I Say I Don't Love You/If You're Gonna Go 10
72 Charisma CB 201 Too Many People/Before You're A Man 5
73 Charisma CB 209 You Need A 60 Minute Man/The Whole Town Wants You Hung 5
75 Charisma CB 250 You Need A 60 Minute Man/That's The Way It Is 5
72 Charisma CAS 1061 GRAHAM BELL (LP, large 'mad hatter' label) 15

MADELINE BELL
(see also Seven Ages Of Man, Underground, Ian Green [Revelation])
63 HMV POP 1215 I Long For Your Love/Because You Didn't Care 10
64 Columbia DB 7257 You Don't Love Me No More/Don't Cross Over To My Side Of The Street 20
65 Columbia DB 7512 Daytime/Don't Cry My Heart 10
65 Philips BF 1448 What The World Needs Now Is Love/I Can't Wait To See My Baby's Face 20
66 Philips BF 1501 Don't Come Running To Me/I Got Carried Away 20
66 Philips BF 1526 One Step At A Time/You Won't See Me 15
67 Philips BF 1611 Picture Me Gone/Go Ahead On 20
68 Philips BF 1656 I'm Gonna Make You Love Me/I'm Gonna Leave You 12
68 Philips BF 1688 Thinkin'/Don't Give Your Love Away 5
68 Philips BF 1726 Hold It/What Am I Supposed To Do? 5
69 Philips BF 1799 We're So Much In Love/How Much Do I Love You 5
71 Philips 6006 082 If You Didn't Hear Me The First Time/You Walked Away 5
67 Philips (S)BL 7818 BELLS A POPPIN' (LP) 60
68 Philips SBL 7865 DOIN' THINGS (LP) 25
75 Pye NSPL 18483 THIS IS ONE GIRL 18

PADDIE BELL
(see also Corries)
65 Parlophone R5361 Everytime/The Rose And The Thorn 7

SIMON BELL
78 Pye 7N 46050 Givin' It Plenty/Love Like Lightning 8

WILLIAM BELL
(see also Judy Clay & William Bell)
67 Atlantic 584 076 Never Like This Before/Soldier's Goodbye 10
69 Atlantic 584 259 Everyday Will Be Like A Holiday/Ain't Got No Girl 8
67 Stax 601 019 Eloise (Hang On In There)/One Plus One 10
68 Stax 601 038 A Tribute To A King/Every Man Oughta Have A Woman 8
69 Stax STAX 110 I Forgot To Be Your Lover/Bring The Curtain Down 8
69 Stax STAX 121 My Whole World Is Falling Down/All God's Children Got Soul 10
69 Stax STAX 128 Happy/Johnny I Love You 40
69 Atco 228 003 A TRIBUTE TO A KING (LP) 30
69 Stax SXATS 1016 BOUND TO HAPPEN (LP) 20
71 Stax 2362 009 WOW . . . WILLIAM BELL (LP) 20
72 Stax 2362 027 PHASES OF REALITY (LP) 25

BELLA & ME
67 Columbia DB 8243 Whatever Happened To The Seven Day Week/Help Me Break This Habit 12

GEORGE BELLAMY
(see also Tornados)
65 Parlophone R 5282 Where I'm Bound/How Could I Ever 30
72 Chapter One CH 167 Maman/Come To The Party 7

PETER BELLAMY
(see also Young Tradition)
68 Xtra XTRA 1010 PETER BELLAMY (LP) 25
68 Argo MAINLY NORFOLK (LP) 70
69 Xtra XTRA 1075 FAIR ENGLAND'S SHORE (LP) 40
69 Topic 12T 200 THE FOX JUMPS OVER THE PARSON'S GATE (LP, blue label) 20
70 Argo ZFB 11 OAK, ASH AND THORN (LP) 35
72 Argo ZFB 37 WON'T YOU GO MY WAY (LP) 20
72 Argo ZFB 81 MERLIN'S ISLE OF GRAMARYE (LP) 20
74 Trailer LER 2089 TELL IT LIKE IT IS (LP) 15

BELL & ARC
(see also Skip Bifferty, Arc, Every Which Way, Graham Bell)
71 Charisma CB 170 She Belongs To Me/Dawn 6
71 Charisma CAS 1053 BELL & ARC (LP, gatefold sleeve, pink scroll label) 30

MINT VALUE £

BELL BROTHERS

68	Action ACT 4510	Tell Him No/Throw Away The Key	10

BELLE & SEBASTIAN

(see also Amphetameanies)

97	Jeepster JPR 7001	Dog On Wheels/The State I Am In (p/s, 1,000 only)	8
97	Jeepster JPR 7002	Lazy Line Painter Jane/You Made Me Forget My Dreams (p/s, 1,000 only)	8
97	Jeepster JPR 7003	A Century Of Fakers/Le Pastie De La Bourgeoisie (p/s)	6
96	Elektric Honey EHRLP 5	TIGERMILK (LP, 1,000 only)	80
96	JPRLP001	IF YOU'RE FEELING SINISTER (LP, gatefold)	18
96	Jeepster JPRLP007	TIGERMILK (LP, reissue)	20
98	Jeepster JPRLP003	THE BOY WITH THE ARAB STRAP (LP, gatefold)	18
00	Jeepster JPRLP010	FOLD YOUR HANDS CHILD, YOU WALK LIKE A PEASANT (LP, gatefold)	12
02	Jeepster JPRLP014	STORYTELLING (LP, gatefold)	12
03	My Own Work (No cat. no.)	THE CHRISTMAS ALBUM (CD)	25

BELLES

70	President PT 311	Don't Pretend/Words Can't Explain	10

BELLFIELD

73	Downtown DT 514	Sugar Plum/Sugar Plum Dub	6

BELL NOTES

59	Top Rank JAR 102	I've Had It/Be Mine	12
59	Top Rank JAR 102	I've Had It/Be Mine (78)	12
59	Top Rank JAR 147	Old Spanish Town/She Went That-A-Way	10
59	Top Rank JAR 147	Old Spanish Town/She Went That-A-Way (78)	15
59	Top Rank JAR 201	That's Right/Betty Dear	12

ERROL BELLOT

85	Jah Tubbys JT 012	New Kind Of Sound/Version (12", with the Offbeat Posse)	40
86	Jah Tubbys JT 019	Sound In Fury/Trouble Maker (12", with the Offbeat Posse)	40
00	Jah Tubbys JT 7002	Glory Hallalujah/DUB TEACHER: Glory Dub	15
00	Jah Tubbys JT 7004	Jah Creation/DISCIPLES RIDDIM SECTION: Creation Style	15
01	Jah Tubbys JT 7007	Roots Gone International/OFFBEAT POSSE: International Ridim	15
03	Jah Tubbys JT 014	It's War/Don't Judge (10", with the Offbeat Posse)	30
03	Jah Tubbys JT 10016	Praise H.I.M/New Life (10", with the Offbeat Posse)	30

ERROL BELLOT & DIXIE PEACH

(see also Dixie Peach)

03	Jah Tubbys JT 10011	The Warning/THE OFFBEAT POSSE: Dub Warning (10")	30

BELLS

71	Philips 6006116	Stay Awhile/Simple Song Of Freedom	6
72	Polydor 2121-109	Oh My Love/You, You. You	8

LOUIS BELLSON (ALL STARS/QUINTET/BAND/OCTET)

53	Capitol LC 6568	JUST JAZZ (LP)	15
57	Columbia Clef C 9040	DRUMORAMA (10" LP)	15
58	Columbia Clef CX 10142	AT THE FLAMINGO (LP)	15
59	HMV CLP 1343	THE BRILLIANT BELLSON SOUND (LP)	15
61	Columbia SCX 3418	AROUND THE WORLD IN PERCUSSION (LP)	15
66	HMV CLP/CSD 3558	THUNDERBIRD (LP)	15
67	Studio Two TWO 169	REPERCUSSION (LP, with Eric Delaney)	12
70	Pye NSPL 18349	LOUIE IN LONDON (LP, as Louie Bellson)	15
72	Parlophone PCS 7151	CONVERSATIONS (LP)	12

BELL SOUNDS

59	HMV POP 685	Marching Guitars/Chloe	5

BELL-TONES

62	Columbia DB 4845	Did You Ever See A Dream Walking?/Selina	8

TONY BELLUS

59	London HL 8933	Robbin' The Cradle/Valentine Girl	40
59	London HL 8933	Robbin' The Cradle/Valentine Girl (78)	25

BELMONTS

(see also Dion & Belmonts)

61	Pye International 7N 25094	Tell Me Why/Smoke From Your Cigarette	40
62	Stateside SS 128	Come On Little Angel/How About Me?	35

BELOVED

86	Flim Flam HARP 2	A Hundred Words (Radio Mix)/Slow Drowning (freebie)	5
86	Flim Flam HARP 3	This Means War/If Only (p/s)	5
86	Flim Flam HARP3T	This Means War/Let It Begin/Saints Preserve Us (12")	8
87	Flim Flam HARP 7	Forever Dancing/Surprise Me (p/s)	5
87	Flim Flam HARP 5T	HAPPY NOW: A Kiss Goodbye/If Pennies Came/Righteous Me (12", p/s)	8
87	Flim Flam HARP 7ET	Forever Dancing/Forever Dancing (Remix)/Surprise Me (12", p/s)	8
88	WEA YZ 311T	Loving Feeling (Feeling Lovely Mix)/Acid Love (Love & Ecstasy Mix) (12", p/s)	8

BELT & BRACES ROADSHOW BAND

75	Belt & Braces Roadshow	BELT & BRACES ROADSHOW BAND (LP, with lyric sheet)	15

BELTONES

(see Bop & Beltones, Trevor Shield)

68	Trojan TR 628	No More Heartaches/I'll Follow You	30
69	Duke DU 17	Home Without You/Why Pretend	40
69	High Note HS 017	Mary Mary/Going Away	12
69	High Note HS 023	A Broken Heart/AFROTONES: All For One	20
72	Ackee ACK 150	Wrapped Up In Love/SOUND DIMENSION: Pasero	10

JOHN BELTRAN

96	Peacefrog PF 049	TEN DAYS OF BLUE (2-LP)	18

MINT VALUE £

JESSE BELVIN
59	RCA RCA 1119	Guess Who/Funny	15
59	RCA RCA 1119	Guess Who/Funny (78)	10

BEN
(see also Jonathan Kelly)

71	Vertigo 6360 052	BEN (LP, gatefold sleeve, small swirl label)	700

STEVE BENBOW
65	Columbia DB 7691	The Gallows Pole/I Can't Tell	5
68	L'gue Against Cruel Sports	Tattered Doll (mail-order only)	6
59	Collector	STEVE BENBOW AND THE FOLK FOUR (EP)	10
62	HMV CLP 1603	STEVE BENBOW SINGS (LP)	15
63	HMV CLP 1687	I TRAVEL THE WORLD (LP)	15
67	Decca LK/SKL 4881	OF SITUATIONS AND PREDICAMENTS (LP)	12

DAVID BENDETH
82	Sidewalk 12 SID 113	Feel The Real/Breakdown/Feel The Real (12")	15

BENDY DOG
72	Jam JAM 20	I Wanna Hear/Carry My Mind	10

BENNY BENGIMAN
81	Negus Roots NERT 010	Health And Sorrow/Love A Dub Song	25

TONY BENJAMIN & THE SANE INMATES
83	Ariwa ARILP 009	AFRICAN REBEL (LP)	60

BENNY BENNETT
s	Seeco LDS 024	BENNY BENNETT AND HIS ORCHESTRA (LP)	15

BOBBY BENNETT (U.K.)
67	CBS 202511	Just Say Goodbye/She Believes In Me	7
68	Columbia DB 8435	All My Life Is You/To Give (The Reason I Live)	7
69	Columbia DB 8532	Music Mother Made/You're Ready Now	45

BOBBY BENNETT (U.S.)
69	London HL 10274	Big New York/Baby, Try Me	15

BOYD BENNETT & HIS ROCKETS (WITH BIG MOE)
(see also Moon Mullican)

55	Parlophone MSP 6161	Everlovin'/Boogie At Midnight (with Big Moe)	350
55	Parlophone MSP 6161	Everlovin'/Boogie At Midnight (with Big Moe) (78)	30
55	Parlophone MSP 6180	Seventeen/Little Ole You-All (as Boyd Bennett & His Rockets)	250
55	Parlophone MSP 6180	Seventeen/Little Ole You-All (as Boyd Bennett & His Rockets) (78)	15
56	Parlophone MSP 6203	My Boy - Flat Top/Banjo Rock And Roll (with Big Moe)	250
56	Parlophone MSP 6203	My Boy - Flat Top/Banjo Rock And Roll (with Big Moe) (78)	20
56	Parlophone MSP 6233	Blue Suede Shoes/Oo-Oo-Oo (with Big Moe)	200
56	Parlophone MSP 6233	Blue Suede Shoes/Oo-Oo-Oo (with Big Moe)	20
56	Parlophone R 4214	The Groovy Age/Hit That Jive, Jack (as Big Moe with Boyd Bennett & His Rockets)	300
56	Parlophone R 4214	The Groovy Age/Hit That Jive, Jack (as Big Moe with Boyd Bennett & His Rockets) (78)	30
56	Parlophone R 4252	The Most/Rockin' Up A Storm (as Boyd Bennett & His Rockets)	300
56	Parlophone R 4252	The Most/Rockin' Up A Storm (as Boyd Bennett & His Rockets) (78)	30
58	Parlophone R 4423	Click Clack/Move (as Boyd Bennett & His Rockets)	300
58	Parlophone R 4423	Click Clack/Move (as Boyd Bennett & His Rockets) (78)	30
59	Mercury AMT 1031	Tear It Up/Tight Tights (as Big Moe & His Orchestra)	50
59	Mercury AMT 1031	Tear It Up/Tight Tights (as Big Moe & His Orchestra) (78)	40

BRIAN BENNETT
(see also Shadows, Thunder Company, Wasp, Marty Wilde, Krewcats, Collage, Alan Skidmore, Big Jim Sullivan, Heat Exchange, Julian [Scott])

67	Columbia DB 8294	Canvas/Slippery Jim De Grize	25
74	Fontana 6007 040	Chase Side Shoot-Up/Pegasus	20
76	DJM DJS 10714	Thunderbolt/Clearing Skies (promo in p/s)	12
76	DJM DJS 10714	Thunderbolt/Clearing Skies	5
77	DJM DJS 10756	Saturday Night Special/Farewell To A Friend (promo in p/s)	12
77	DJM DJS 10756	Saturday Night Special/Farewell To A Friend	5
77	DJM DJS 10791	The Girls Back Home/Jonty Jump (as the Brian Bennett Band)	12
78	DJM DJS 10843	Pendulum Force/Ocean Glide	5
82	DJM DJS 10981	Top Of The World/Soul Ice	8
67	Columbia S(C)X 6144	CHANGE OF DIRECTION (LP)	50
69	Col. Studio Two TWO 268	THE ILLUSTRATED LONDON NOISE (LP)	60
77	DJM DJF 20499	ROCK DREAMS (LP, with insert, as the Brian Bennett Band)	20
78	DJM DJF 20532	VOYAGE (LP)	20

BRUCE BENNETT
71	Big BG 311	If You Don't Mind/Lenore (both actually by Dobby Dobson)	7

CAROLE BENNETT
56	Capitol CL 14652	The Little Magician/I Was Your Only Love	5
57	Capitol CL 14692	Play The Music/Miser's Gold	10
57	Capitol CL 14725	Haunted Lover/Let The Chips Fall (Where They May)	25

CLIFF BENNETT & REBEL ROUSERS
61	Parlophone R 4793	You've Got What I Like/I'm In Love With You	30
61	Parlophone R 4836	That's What I Said/When I Get Paid	25
62	Parlophone R 4895	Poor Joe/Hurtin' Inside (Twist)	20
63	Parlophone R 5046	Everybody Loves A Lover/My Old Stand-By	15
63	Parlophone R 5080	You Really Got A Hold On Me/Alright	15
63	Parlophone DP 560	Poor Joe/Hurtin' Inside (Twist) (export issue, black label)	15
63	Parlophone DP 561	When I Get Paid/That's What I Said (export issue, black label)	20

MINT VALUE £

64	Parlophone R 5119	Got My Mojo Working/Beautiful Dreamer	15
64	Parlophone R 5173	One Way Love/Slow Down	10
65	Parlophone R 5229	I'll Take You Home/Do You Love Him?	10
65	Parlophone R 5259	Three Rooms Of Running Water/If Only You'd Reply	15
65	Parlophone R 5317	I Have Cried My Last Tear/As Long As She Looks Like You	7
66	Parlophone R 5406	You Can't Love 'Em All/Need Your Loving Tonight	7
66	Parlophone R 5466	Eyes For You/Hold On I'm Coming	10
66	Parlophone R 5489	Got To Get You Into My Life/Baby Each Day	6
66	Parlophone R 5534	Never Knew Lovin' Could Be So Doggone Good/Don't Help Me Out	6
67	Parlophone R 5565	I'm Sorry/I'll Take Good Care Of You	6
67	Parlophone R 5598	I'll Be There/Use Me	6
65	Parlophone GEP 8923	CLIFF BENNETT AND THE REBEL ROUSERS (EP)	30
65	Parlophone GEP 8936	TRY IT BABY (EP)	30
66	Parlophone GEP 8955	WE'RE GONNA MAKE IT (EP)	30
64	Parlophone PMC 1242	CLIFF BENNETT AND THE REBEL ROUSERS (LP, yellow/black label)	40
66	EMI Regal REG 1039	CLIFF BENNETT (LP, export issue)	20
67	Parlophone PMC/PCS 7017	GOT TO GET YOU INTO OUR LIFE (LP, yellow/black label)	35

CLIFF BENNETT BAND

68	Parlophone R 5666	Take Your Time/House Of A Thousand Dolls	8
68	Parlophone R 5691	You're Breaking Me Up (And I'm Wasting Away)/I Hear Her Voice	10
68	Parlophone R 5711	Lonely Weekends/Good Times	10
68	Parlophone R 5728	One More Heartache/Nobody Runs Forever	10
68	Parlophone R 5749	Back In The USSR/This Man	10
68	Parlophone PMC/PCS 7054	BRANCHES OUT (LP, yellow/black label, with "Sold in the U.K." label text)	40

CLIFF BENNETT

69	Parlophone R 5792	Memphis Streets/But I'm Wrong	10

CLIFF BENNETT'S REBELLION

(see also Charles Hodges, Rebel Rousers, Toefat, Screaming Lord Sutch & Savages)

71	CBS 7231	Amos Moses/Movin' And Travelin' On	5
71	CBS 64487	CLIFF BENNETT'S REBELLION (LP)	18

DICKIE BENNETT

55	Decca F 10595	There, But For The Grace Of God Go I/Stars Shine In Your Eyes	6
56	Decca F 10697	Dungaree Doll/Can't We Be Partners (After The Dance)	12
56	Decca F 10782	You Don't Know Me/Cry Upon My Shoulder	6

DUSTER BENNETT

(see also Fleetwood Mac)

68	Blue Horizon 57-3141	It's A Man Down There/Things Are Changing	20
69	Blue Horizon 57-3148	Raining In My Heart/Jumpin' For Joy	20
69	Blue Horizon 57-3154	Bright Lights, Big City/Fresh Country Jam (with His House Band)	20
69	Blue Horizon 57-3164	I'm Gonna Wind Up Endin' Up Or I'm Gonna End Up Windin' Up With You/ Rock Of Ages, Cleft For Me	20
70	Blue Horizon 57-3173	I Chose To Sing The Blues/If You Could Hang Your Washing Like You Hang Your Lines	10
70	Blue Horizon 57-3179	Act Nice And Gentle/I Want You To Love Me	10
74	Rak RAK 177	Comin' Home/Pretty Little Thing	15
68	Blue Horizon 7-63208	SMILING LIKE I'M HAPPY (LP, with His House Band, i.e. Fleetwood Mac)	60
69	Blue Horizon 7-63221	BRIGHT LIGHTS? (LP, gatefold sleeve)	75
70	Blue Horizon 7-63868	12 DB's (LP, with lyric sheet)	40

JO JO BENNETT

(see also Fugitives, I Roy)

67	Doctor Bird DB 1097	The Lecture/Cantelope Rock (with Fugitives)	35
67	Doctor Bird DB 1116	Rocksteady/Real Gone Loser (with Fugitives)	50
70	Explosion EX 2029	Groovy Jo Jo/Ten Steps To Soul (both actually with Mudie's All Stars)	20
70	Trojan TR 7774	Leaving Rome/In The Nude (both with Mudie's All Stars)	12
71	Moodisc MU 3514	Snowbird/MUDIE'S ALLSTARS: Change The Tide	10
71	Moodisc HME 108	Poison Ivy/MUDIE'S ALLSTARS: Ivy Poison	8
70	Trojan TBL 133	GROOVY JO JO (LP, with Mudie's Allstars)	40

JOE BENNETT & SPARKLETONES

57	HMV POP 399	Black Slacks/Boppin' Rock Boogie	200
57	HMV POP 399	Black Slacks/Boppin' Rock Boogie (78)	25
58	HMV POP 445	Rocket/Penny Loafers And Bobby Socks	200
58	HMV POP 445	Rocket/Penny Loafers And Bobby Socks (78)	25

KIM BENNETT

(see also Roland Shaw)

55	Decca F 10449	Softly Softly/ROLAND SHAW ORCHESTRA: Trumpeter's Lullaby	10
55	Decca F 10460	Melody Of Love/Ding Dong	10
55	Decca F 10599	The Kentuckian Song/Overnight	10
56	Decca F 10706	No, Not Much/You Can't Keep Running	7

LEE BENNETT & SUNLINERS

64	Decca F 12024	Poor Bachelor Boy/Fool, Fool, Fool	6

LORNA BENNETT

72	Blue Mountain BM 1013	Breakfast In Bed/Skank In Bed	15

NICK BENNETT

60	Columbia DB 4516	You Understand Me/Mr. Lonely	7

PETER E, BENNETT

71	RCA SF 8190	THE BALLAD OF GALDWAIN (LP, lyric insert, orange/white label)	20

RAY BENNETT

62	Decca F 11550	Go Away Little Girl/Twistin' To The Blues	5
62	Decca DFE 8516	INTRODUCING RAY BENNETT (EP)	40

ROY BENNETT

68	Blue Cat BS 146	I Dangerous/DEE SET: I Know A Place	40

MINT VALUE £

RUDI BENNETT
68 Decca F 12741 I'm So Proud/WHISTLING JACK SMITH: Havah Nagilah 6

TONY BENNETT
(see also Count Basie, John Barry)
53 Columbia SCM 5048 Congratulations To Someone/Take Me 6
54 Columbia 39745 Here In My Heart/I'm Lost Again 6
57 Philips JK 1008 Whatever Lola Wants/Heart (jukebox issue) 15
59 Philips PB 1079 Till/Ask Anyone In Love 5
57 Columbia B 2582 ONE FOR MY BABY (EP) 8
55 Philips BBR 8051 CLOUD 7 (10" LP) 12
56 Philips BBR 8089 THE VOICE OF YOUR CHOICE (10" LP) 12

VAL BENNETT
(see also Roy Shirley, Max Romeo, Derrick Morgan, Clancy Eccles, Harry J Allstars, George A Penny, Lloyd Terrell,
68 Island WI 3113 Jumping With Mr. Lee/ROY SHIRLEY: Keep Your Eyes On The Road 45
68 Island WI 3146 The Russians Are Coming (Take Five)/LESTER STERLING: Sir Lee's Whip 80
68 Trojan TR 611 Spanish Harlem/ROY SHIRLEY: If I Did Know 15
69 Trojan TR 640 Baby Baby/Barbara 25
69 Crab CRAB 6 Reggae City/CANNON KING: Mellow Trumpet (B-side actually by Carl 'King Cannon Ball' Bryan) 30
69 Camel CA 24 Midnight Spin/SOUL CATS: Money Money 15

JOHNNY BENNINGS & HIS RHYTHM & BLUES BAND
54 Esquire 10-376 Third Degree Blues/Timber (78) 10

MARC BENNO
71 A & M AMS850 Good Year/Second Story Window 10

JON BENNS
(see also The Enid)
80 Aveda AVA 106 BENNS MEANS LAFFS (LP) 15

BENNY & TINA
69 Mercury MF 1133 This Love Is Real/Over My Dead Body 10

BARRY BENSON
66 Parlophone R 5446 Stay A Little While/That's For Sure 35
66 Parlophone R 5484 Not A One Girl Guy/Sunshine Child 25
66 Parlophone R 5544 Always Waitin'/My Friend And I 8
67 Parlophone R 5578 Cousin Jane/Meet Jacqueline 20
67 Page One POF 034 I Can't Wait/Oh No 8

BOBBY BENSON & HIS COMBO
58 Philips PB 854 Taxi Driver, I Don't Care/Gentleman Bobby 6

GARY BENSON
66 Pye 7N 17032 This Man's Got No Luck/I'm So Tired 5
70 Penny Farthing PEN 727 Holly/Oak Tree 5
73 Birth RAB 1002 The Concert/To Kill Another Day 10
70 Penny Farthing PELS 506 THE REUNION (LP) 30
73 Birth RAB 5 THE CONCERT (LP, gatefold sleeve) 25

GEORGE BENSON (QUARTET)
66 CBS (S)BPG 62817 IT'S UPTOWN (LP, flipback sleeve, as George Benson Quartet) 20
67 CBS (S)BPG 62971 THE GEORGE BENSON COOKBOOK (LP) 15
73 CTI 6015 WHITE RABBIT (LP) 12

MARIE BENSON & THE LONDONAIRES
55 Decca F 10452 Mambo Italiano/Mobile 10

MICHAEL BENTINE
(see also Goons)
62 Parlophone 4927 Football Results/The Astronauts 6
72 Polydor 2058294 Home Made Wine/The Olympic Showjumper 7
62 Parlophone PMC 1179 IT'S A SQUARE WORLD (LP, also stereo PCS 3031) 12

BRIAN BENTLEY & THE BACHELORS
60 Philips PB 1085 Wishing Well/Please Make Up Your Mind 25
60 Philips PB 1086 First Flight East/Sunday Break 5
62 Salvo SLO 1813 Caramba/Nellie Dean (99 copies only) 20

JAY BENTLEY & THE JET SET
64 Vocalion VN 9230 Watusi '64/I'll Get You 10

BENTLEY BROTHERS
59 Top Rank JAR 208 Ma (She's Making Eyes At Me)/Yes, We Have No Bananas 5

BROOK BENTON
58 RCA RCA 1044 A Million Miles From Nowhere/Devoted 25
58 Mercury AMT 1014 It's Just A Matter Of Time/Hurtin' Inside 5
59 Mercury AMT 1043 Endlessly/So Close 6
59 Mercury AMT 1043 Endlessly/So Close (78) 10
59 Mercury AMT 1061 Thank You Pretty Baby/With All Of My Heart 8
59 Mercury AMT 1068 So Many Ways/I Want You Forever 6
60 Mercury AMT 1097 The Ties That Bind/Hither And Thither And Yon 5
60 Mercury AMT 1109 Kiddio/The Same One 7
60 Mercury AMT 1121 Fools Rush In/Somebody You'll Want Me To Want You 10
61 Mercury AMT 1134 For My Baby/Think Twice 5
61 Mercury AMT 1148 The Boll Weevil Song/Your Eyes 6
61 Mercury AMT 1157 Frankie And Johnny/It's Just A House Without You 7
61 Mercury AMT 1168 Revenge/Really Really 5
62 Mercury AMT 1172 Walk On The Wild Side/Somewhere In The Used To Be 8
62 Mercury AMT 1178 Hit Record/Thanks To The Fool 6

MINT VALUE £

62	Mercury AMT 1194	Hotel Happiness/Still Waters Run Deep	7
63	Mercury AMT 1212	Two Tickets To Paradise/Don't Hate Me	6
63	Mercury AMT 1217	Baby You Got It Made/Stop Foolin' (with Damita Jo)	10
58	RCA RCX 169	BROOK BENTON (EP, tri centre)	40
58	Fontana TFE 17151	BROOK BENTON AT HIS BEST (EP)	20
59	Mercury ZEP 10023	THE CARESSING VOICE OF BROOK BENTON (EP)	10
60	Mercury ZEP 10046	MAKE A DATE WITH BROOK BENTON (EP)	10
60	Mercury ZEP 10076	I'M IN THE MOOD FOR LOVE (EP)	10
60	Mercury SEZ 19009	WHEN I FALL IN LOVE (EP, stereo)	8
61	Mercury SEZ 19019	WHEN YOU'RE IN LOVE (EP, stereo)	8
61	Mercury SEZ 19024	SO WARM (EP, stereo)	8
60	Mercury CMS 18041	SONGS I LOVE TO SING (LP, stereo)	12
61	Mercury CMS 18060	THE BOLL WEEVIL SONG (LP, stereo)	12
61	Mercury CMS 18068	THERE GOES THAT SONG AGAIN (LP, stereo)	12

BROOK BENTON & DINAH WASHINGTON

60	Mercury AMT 1083	Baby (You've Got What It Takes)/I Do	15
60	Mercury AMT 1099	A Rockin' Good Way/I Believe	15
69	Mercury MF 1100	A Rockin' Good Way/I Do	5
61	Mercury ZEP 10120	A ROCKING GOOD WAY (EP, mono)	15
61	Mercury SEZ 19022	A ROCKING GOOD WAY (EP, stereo)	20
64	Mercury 20069 MCL	THE TWO OF US (LP)	20

HENLEY BENTON

75	Black Wax WAX 6	Jockey Voodoo/Oodoov Version	6

STEVE BERESFORD

75	Incus INCUS 15	TEATIME (LP)	50

BERETS

70	Avant Garde AVS 116	THE MASS FOR PEACE (LP, with insert)	25

BERKELEY KITES

68	Polydor 56742	Hang Up City/Mary-Go-Round	10
69	Polydor 56770	Alice In Wonderland/What Goes Up Must Come Down	10

MILTON BERLE

56	Vogue Coral Q 72197	In The Middle Of The House/Buffalo	5

BERLIN RITZ

80	Big Muff BM 001	Crazy Nights/You're Where I Belong (no p/s)	15

BERMUDAS

64	London HLN 9894	Donnie/Chu Sen Ling	15

BERNADETTE

67	Rim RIM 2	Come Kiss Me Love/Let Me Do The Talking	15
68	Philips 1725	Toys, Toys, Toys/Kiss And Run Away	6

KENNY BERNARD (& WRANGLERS)

(see also Kenny & Wranglers, Wranglers, Cat's Pyjamas)

65	Pye 7N 15920	The Tracker/You Gotta Give (with Wranglers)	20
65	Pye 7N 15920	The Tracker/You Gotta Give (with Wranglers) (DJ Copy)	125
66	Pye 7N 17131	Nothing Can Change This Love/What Love Brings	70
66	Pye 7N 17131	Nothing Can Change This Love/What Love Brings (DJ Copy)	100
67	Pye 7N 17233	Ain't No Soul (Left In These Old Shoes)/Hey Woman	40
67	Pye 7N 17284	I Do/Isn't That A Good Idea	15
67	CBS 2936	Somebody/Pity My Feet	100
67	CBS 2936	Somebody/Pity My Feet (DJ copy)	120
68	CBS 3860	Victim Of Perfume And Lace/A Change Is Gonna Come	20

ROD BERNARD

59	London HLM 8849	This Should Go On Forever/Pardon, Mr. Gordon	25
59	Mercury AMT 1070	One More Chance/Shedding Teardrops Over You	15

AGNES BERNELL

63	HMV 7EG 8696	THE LOST NOISES OFFICE (EP)	20

BERNIE & BUZZ BAND

(see also Pete Kelly's Soulution)

68	Decca F 22829	The House That Jack Built/ PETE KELLY'S SOULUTION: Midnight Confessions (export issue)	18
68	Deram DM 181	When Something's Wrong With My Baby/Don't Knock It	35

ELMER BERNSTEIN

56	Brunswick 05544	Clark Street Parts 1 & 2 (gold print on label)	10
56	Brunswick 05544	Clark Street Parts 1 & 2 (silver print on label)	5
59	Capitol CL 15101	Staccato's Theme/The Jazz At Waldo's	6
63	MGM MGM 1238	Rat Race/Saints & Sinners	20
63	MGM MGM 1238	Rat Race/Saints & Sinners (DJ Copy)	40
66	United Artists UP 1163	The Magnificent Seven/Return Of The Seven	10
60	Capitol EAP1 1287	STACCATO (EP)	10
56	Brunswick LAT 8101	THE MAN WITH THE GOLDEN ARM (LP, soundtrack)	20
57	Brunswick LAT 8195	SWEET SMELL OF SUCCESS (LP, soundtrack)	20
57	London HA-P 2076	MEN IN WAR (LP, soundtrack)	15
58	London HA-D 2074/5	THE TEN COMMANDMENTS (2-LP, soundtrack)	25
58	London HA-D 2111	DESIRE UNDER THE ELMS (LP, soundtrack)	20
58	London HA-T 2125	GOD'S LITTLE ACRE (LP, soundtrack)	25
58	Capitol LCT 6165	KINGS GO FORTH (LP, soundtrack)	15
59	Capitol LCT 6180	SOME CAME RUNNING (LP, soundtrack)	18
62	MGM MGM-C 891	WALK ON THE WILD SIDE (LP, soundtrack)	15
63	MGM MGM-C 934	TO KILL A MOCKINGBIRD (LP, soundtrack)	12
63	United Artists ULP 1041	THE GREAT ESCAPE (LP, soundtrack, mono/stereo)	15

MINT VALUE £

64	MGM MGM-C 984	THE CARPETBAGGERS (LP, soundtrack)	12
64	London HA-A/SH-A 8219	THE CARPETBAGGERS (LP, soundtrack)	12
65	CBS BPG 62558	THE SONS OF KATIE ELDER (LP, mono, soundtrack, feat. Johnny Cash)	20
65	CBS (S)BPG 62558	THE SONS OF KATIE ELDER (LP, stereo, soundtrack, feat. Johnny Cash)	25
67	RCA Victor RD 7792	THE SILENCERS (LP, soundtrack, feat. Vikki Carr)	30
67	Fontana TL 5306	BABY, THE RAIN MUST FALL (LP, soundtrack)	25
68	United Artists (S)ULP 1190	THE SCALPHUNTERS (LP, soundtrack)	15
69	Paramount SPFL 254	WHERE'S JACK? (LP, soundtrack, feat. Mary Hopkin)	12
70	Capitol E-ST 263	TRUE GRIT (LP, soundtrack, feat. Glen Campbell)	15

ROCK BERNTSEN

84	Forest Tracks FT 3017	KELPERS AFTER ALL (LP, with insert)	18

CHUCK BERRY

78s

56	London HLU 8275	Down Bound Train/No Money Down	70
57	London HLN 8375	You Can't Catch Me/Havana Moon	40
57	London HLU 8428	Roll Over Beethoven/Drifting Heart	40
57	Columbia DB 3951	School Day (Ring! Ring! Goes The Bell)/Deep Feeling	30
57	London HLM 8531	Rock And Roll Music/Blue Feeling	40
58	London HLM 8585	Sweet Little Sixteen/Reelin' And Rockin'	30
58	London HLM 8629	Johnny B. Goode/Around And Around	35
58	London HL 8677	Beautiful Delilah/Vacation Time	45
58	London HL 7055	Carol/Hey Pedro (export single)	50
58	London HL 8712	Carol/Hey Pedro	40
58	London HLM 8767	Sweet Little Rock And Roller/Jo Jo Gun	50
59	London HLM 8853	Almost Grown/Little Queenie	80
59	London HLM 8921	Back In The U.S.A./Memphis, Tennessee	80

SINGLES

56	London HLU 8275	No Money Down/Down Bound Train (silver lettering on label, triangular centre)	400
56	London HLU 8275	No Money Down/Down Bound Train (silver lettering on label, round centre)	250
57	London HLN 8375	You Can't Catch Me/Havana Moon (gold lettering on label)	350
57	London HLN 8375	You Can't Catch Me/Havana Moon (silver lettering on label)	150
57	London HLU 8428	Roll Over Beethoven/Drifting Heart	50
57	Columbia DB 3951	School Day (Ring! Ring! Goes The Bell)/Blue Feeling	50
57	London HLM 8531	Rock And Roll Music/Blue Feeling	50
58	London HLM 8585	Sweet Little Sixteen/Reelin' And Rockin'	50
58	London HLM 8629	Johnny B. Goode/Around And Around	25
58	London HL 8677	Beautiful Delilah/Vacation Time	30
58	London HL 8712	Carol/Hey Pedro	40
58	London HL 7055	Carol/Hey Pedro (export issue)	40
58	London HLM 8767	Sweet Little Rock And Roller/Jo Jo Gun	30
59	London HLM 8853	Almost Grown/Little Queenie	30
59	London HLM 8921	Back In The U.S.A./Memphis, Tennessee	25

(The above London 45s were originally issued with triangular centres; later silver top label/round centre Pressings are worth half to two-thirds these values))

60	London HLM 9069	Let It Rock/Too Pooped To Pop	25
60	London HLM 9159	Bye Bye Johnny/Mad Lad	25
61	Pye International 7N 25100	I'm Talkin' 'Bout You/Little Star (blue label)	25
61	Pye International 7N 25100	I'm Talkin' 'Bout You/Little Star (later red/yellow label)	10
63	Pye International 7N 25209	Go Go Go/Come On	10
63	Pye International 7N 25218	Memphis, Tennessee/Let It Rock	7
63	Pye International 7N 25228	Run Rudolph Run/Johnny B. Goode	10
64	Pye International 7N 25236	Nadine (Is It You?)/O Rangutang	10
64	Pye International 7N 25242	No Particular Place To Go/Liverpool Drive	7
64	Pye International 7N 25257	You Never Can Tell/Brenda Lee	10
64	Pye International 7N 25271	Little Marie/Go Bobby Soxer	10
65	Pye International 7N 25285	The Promised Land/The Things I Used To Do	10
65	Chess CRS 8006	I Got A Booking/Lonely School Days	10
65	Chess CRS 8012	Dear Dad/My Little Lovelight	10
65	Chess CRS 8022	It Wasn't Me/It's My Own Business	10
66	Chess CRS 8037	Ramona Say Yes/Lonely School Days	10
66	Mercury MF 958	Club Nitty Gritty/Laugh And Cry	10
67	Mercury MF 994	Back To Memphis/I Do Really Love You	10
68	Mercury MF 1057	St. Louis To Frisco/Ma Dear	10
69	Mercury MF 1102	Back To Memphis/Roll Over Beethoven	10
68	Chess CRS 8075	Johnny B. Goode/Sweet Little Sixteen	5
69	Chess CRS 8089	No Particular Place To Go/It Wasn't Me	5
72	Chess 6145 007	Rock And Roll Music/Johnny B. Goode/School Days	5
73	Chess 6145 020	Reelin' And Rockin' (Live)/I Will Not Let You Go	5
73	Chess 6145 027	South Of The Border (Live)/Bio	5
75	Chess 6145 038	Shake Rattle And Roll/I'm Just A Name	5
79	Atlantic K 11354	Oh What A Thrill/California	5

EPs

56	London REU 1053	RHYTHM AND BLUES WITH CHUCK BERRY (maroon/gold label, tri-centre)	150
56	London REU 1053	RHYTHM AND BLUES WITH CHUCK BERRY (later pressing, maroon/silver label, round centre)	60
60	London REM 1188	REELIN' AND ROCKIN' (maroon and gold label, tri centre)	250
60	London REM 1188	REELIN' AND ROCKIN' (round centre)	100
63	Pye Intl. NEP 44011	CHUCK BERRY	20
63	Pye Intl. NEP 44013	THIS IS CHUCK BERRY	20
64	Pye Intl. NEP 44018	THE BEST OF CHUCK BERRY	20
64	Pye Intl. NEP 44028	CHUCK BERRY HITS	20
64	Pye Intl. NEP 44033	BLUE MOOD	20
65	Chess CRE 6002	THE PROMISED LAND	25
65	Chess CRE 6005	COME ON	25

MINT VALUE £

66	Chess CRE 6012	I GOT A BOOKING	25
66	Chess CRE 6016	YOU CAME A LONG WAY FROM ST. LOUIS	30

LPs

58	London HA-M 2132	ONE DOZEN BERRYS	150
62	Pye Intl. NPL 28019	NEW JUKE BOX HITS	45
63	Pye Intl. NPL 28024	CHUCK BERRY	25
63	Pye Intl. NPL 28027	CHUCK BERRY ON STAGE	30
63	Pye Intl. NPL 28028	MORE CHUCK BERRY	25
64	Pye Intl. NPL 28031	THE LATEST AND THE GREATEST	25
64	Pye Intl. NPL 28039	YOU NEVER CAN TELL	30
65	Chess CRL 4005	CHUCK BERRY IN LONDON	30
65	Chess CRL 4506	FRESH BERRYS	30
66	Golden Guinea GGL 0352	CHUCK BERRY (reissue of NPL 28024)	15
66	Chess CRL 4548	CHUCK BERRY'S GREATEST HITS	15
67	Mercury 20110 (S)MCL	CHUCK BERRY IN MEMPHIS	20
67	Mercury 20112 (S)MCL	LIVE AT THE FILLMORE AUDITORIUM - SAN FRANCISCO	18
69	Mercury 20162 (S)MCL	CONCERTO IN B. GOODE	15
72	Chess 6310 113	BACK HOME	15
72	Chess 6310 115	SAN FRANCISCO DUES	15
72	Chess 6310 122	THE LONDON CHUCK BERRY SESSIONS	12
72	Philips Int. 6619 008	ST. LOUIE TO FRISCO TO MEMPHIS (2-LP)	20
72	Chess 6641 018	GOLDEN DECADE (2-LP, gatefold sleeve)	15

CHUCK BERRY/BO DIDDLEY

(see also Bo Diddley)

63	Pye Intl. NEP 44009	CHUCK AND BO (EP)	20
63	Pye Intl. NEP 44012	CHUCK AND BO, VOL. 2 (EP)	20
64	Pye Intl. NEP 44017	CHUCK AND BO, VOL. 3 (EP)	25
73	Chess 6145 012	BIG DADDIES (LP)	30
64	Pye Intl. NPL 28047	TWO GREAT GUITARS (LP, mono)	35

DAVE BERRY (& CRUISERS)

(see also Cruisers)

63	Decca F 11734	Memphis Tennessee/Tossin' & Turnin' (with Cruisers)	8
63	Decca F 11803	My Baby Left Me/Hoochie Coochie Man (B-side with Cruisers)	8
64	Decca F 11876	Baby It's You/Sweet And Lovely	7
64	Decca F 11937	The Crying Game/Don't Gimme No Lip Child	5
64	Decca F 12020	One Heart Between Two/You're Gonna Need Somebody	10
65	Decca F 12103	Little Things/I've Got A Tiger By The Tail	8
65	Decca F 12188	This Strange Effect/Now	8
65	Decca F 12258	I'm Gonna Take You There/Just Don't Know	10
66	Decca F 12337	If You Wait For Love/Hidden	10
66	Decca F 12435	Mama/Walk, Walk, Talk, Talk	6
66	Decca F 12513	Picture Me Gone/Ann	15
67	Decca F 12579	Stranger/Stick By The Book	7
67	Decca F 12651	Forever/And I Have Learned To Dream	10
68	Decca F 12739	Just As Much As Ever/I Got A Feeling	8
68	Decca F 12771	(Do I Figure) In Your Life/Latisha	15
69	Decca F 12905	Oh What A Life (by Dave Berry & Sponge)/Huma Luma	7
70	Decca F 12999	Change Our Minds/Long Walk To D.C.	7
70	Decca F 13080	Chaplin House/Trees	8
72	CBS 7780	Movin' On (Turn Around)/Don't Bring Me Down	6
88	Flagstaff 002	Out Of Time/Serenade To Alice (p/s, 200 only)	8
64	Decca DFE 8601	DAVE BERRY (EP)	20
65	Decca DFE 8625	CAN I GET IT FROM YOU (EP)	20
64	Decca LK 4653	DAVE BERRY (LP)	30
66	Ace Of Clubs ACL 1218	ONE DOZEN BERRIES (LP, also stereo SCL 1218)	12
66	Decca LK 4823	THE SPECIAL SOUND OF DAVE BERRY (LP)	20
68	Decca LK/SKL 4932	DAVE BERRY '68 (LP)	25

LEN & BARBARA BERRY

60s	Greenwich Village GVR 229	THE PORTWAY PEDDLERS (LP)	50

MIKE BERRY (& THE OUTLAWS)

(see also Outlaws, Le Roys, Shepperton Flames, Innocents [U.K], UK Jones)

61	Decca F 11314	Will You Love Me Tomorrow/My Baby Doll (with The Outlaws)	30
61	HMV POP 912	Tribute To Buddy Holly/What's The Matter (with The Outlaws)	15
62	HMV POP 979	It's Just A Matter Of Time/Little Boy Blue (backing group miscredited as Admirals, actually The Outlaws)	10
62	HMV POP 1042	Every Little Kiss/How Many Times	15
62	HMV POP 1105	Don't You Think It's Time/Loneliness (with The Outlaws) (blue label)	10
62	HMV POP 1105	Don't You Think It's Time/Loneliness (with The Outlaws) (black label)	7
63	HMV POP 1142	My Little Baby/You'll Do It, You'll Fall In Love	10
63	HMV POP 1194	It Really Doesn't Matter/Try A Little Bit Harder	15
64	HMV POP 1257	This Little Girl/On My Mind	10
64	HMV POP 1284	Lovesick/Letter Of Love	10
64	HMV POP 1314	Who Will It Be/Talk (with Innocents)	10
64	HMV POP 1362	Two Lovers/Don't Try To Stand In My Way	10
65	HMV POP 1449	That's All I Ever Wanted From You/She Didn't Care	10
65	HMV POP 1494	It Comes And Goes/Gonna Fall In Love	7
66	HMV POP 1530	Warm Baby/Just Thought I'd 'Phone	10
67	Polydor 56182	Raining In My Heart/Eyes	10
72	York SYK 516	Going Down To Virginia/Love Her	10
72	York SYK 530	Drift Away/Keep Your Eyes On The Road	5
76	Polydor 2058 700	Tribute To Buddy Holly/Dial My Number	20
63	HMV 7EG 8793	IT'S TIME FOR MIKE BERRY (EP, with Outlaws)	25
63	HMV 7EG 8808	A TRIBUTE TO BUDDY HOLLY (EP)	30
72	York FYK 409	AMBUSH (LP)	15
72	York FYK409	DRIFT AWAY (LP)	15

MINT VALUE £

RICHARD BERRY & PHARAOHS
64 Ember EMB EP 4527 RHYTHM AND BLUES VOL. 3 (EP) ... 200

CINDY LEE BERRYHILL
89 awareness AWP 001 Me, Steve, Kirk And Keith/Baby (Should I Have The Baby) p/s ... 6

BERRY STREET STATION
75 Crystal CR 7024 Chocolate Sugar/All I Want Is You ... 10

BERTY B AND DILLINJA
(see also Dillinja, Cybotron Featuring Dillinja)
95 Lionheart BERT1 Lionheart/Art Of Control (12") ... 15

BESHARA
84 Mass Media Music MM121004 Men Cry Too/Version (12") ... 20

ADAM BEST
70 Fontana SFL 13209 WALL OF SOUND (LP) ... 15

JON BEST
65 Decca F 12077 Young Boy Blues/Living Without Love ... 10

PETE BEST FOUR
(see also Beatles, Lee Curtis & All Stars)
64 Decca F 11929 I'm Gonna Knock On Your Door/Why Did I Fall In Love With You? ... 70

RICHARD BESWICK & PHILIPP WACHSMANN
81 Bead Records BEAD 18 HELLO BRENDA! (LP) ... 25

BETA BAND
97 Regal REG 16 CHAMPION VERSIONS EP: Dry The Rain/I Know/B+A/Dog's Got A Bone (12", p/s, 1,000 only) ... 60
98 Regal REG 18 THE PATTY PATTY SOUND EP: Inner Meet Me/The House/ The Monolith/ She's The One (2 x 12", p/s, 1,000 only) ... 40
98 Regal REG 18 THE PATTY PATTY SOUND EP: Inner Meet Me/The House/ The Monolith/ She's The One (CD, card slipcase) ... 25
01 Regal REG 59 HOT SHOTS II (2-LP) ... 20
04 Regal REG 101 HEROS TO ZEROS (2-LP, gatefold sleeve) ... 20

SIR JOHN BETJEMAN
74 Charisma CB 254 Licorice Fields Of Ponterfract/In The Public Gardens ... 12
74 Charisma CAS 1086 BANANA BLUSH (LP) ... 45
75 Charisma CAS 1096 LATE FLOWERING LOVE (LP, with Jim Parker) ... 45

BETTERDAYS
65 Polydor BM 56024 Don't Want That/Here 'Tis ... 130

HAROLD BETTERS
65 Sue WI 378 Do Anything You Wanna (Parts 1 & 2) ... 40

JOHNNY BEV
62 Pye 7N 17030 Tell Her You Love Her/This Love I Lost ... 8
63 Pye 7N 15505 No Peace Of Mind/Summer Romance ... 8
63 Pye 7N 15523 Treat Her Right/For Always ... 8
63 Pye 7N 15576 What Am I To Do/Save All Your Kisses For Me ... 8
65 Columbia DB 7579 You Pass Me By/Leaving My Teardrops Behind ... 8
65 Columbia DB 7767 The World Goes Away/The House ... 8

BEVERLEY
(see also John & Beverley Martyn, Levee Breakers)
66 Deram DM 101 Happy New Year/Where The Good Times Are ... 35
67 Deram DM 137 Museum/DENNY CORDELL TEA TIME ENSEMBLE: A Quick One For Sanity ... 30

BEVERLEY SISTERS
55 Decca F 10539 I Remember Mama/I've Been Thinking ... 5
55 Decca F 10603 Humming Bird/Have You Ever Been Lonely? ... 5
55 Decca F 10641 My Heart Goes A-Sailing/Teddy Bear ... 5
56 Decca F 10705 Willie Can/I've Started Courtin' ... 10
56 Decca F 10729 Rickshaw Boy/You Ought To Have A Wife ... 5
56 Decca F 10770 Born To Be With You/It's Easy ... 8
56 Decca F 10813 Come Home To My Arms/Doodle-Doo-Doo ... 5
57 Decca F 10832 I Dreamed/Mama From The Train (A Kiss, A Kiss) ... 5
57 Decca F 10853 Greensleeves/I'll See You In My Dreams ... 6
57 Decca F 10893 Mr. Wonderful/Blow The Wind Southerly ... 5
57 Decca F 10909 Bye, Bye Love/It's Illegal, It's Immoral, Or It Makes You Fat ... 5
57 Decca F 10943 Riding Down From Bangor/The Young Cavaliero ... 5
58 Decca F 10971 Long Black Nylons/Without You ... 15
55 Philips BBR 8052 A DATE WITH THE BEVS (10" LP) ... 20

BEVERLEY'S ALLSTARS
(see also Clarendoinians, Gaylads, Ken Boothe, Glen Brown, Desmond Dekker, Bob Marley, Maytals, Melodians, Derrick Morgan, Pioneers, Rockstones, Bruce Ruffin, Delroy Wilson)
65 Black Swan WI 449 Go Home/THEO BECKFORD: Ungrateful People ... 20
69 Trojan TR 683 Double Shot/Gimme Gimme Gal (B-side act. "Banana Water" by Mellotones) ... 15
70 Trojan TR 7729 Moon Dust/Fat Cat (both sides actually by Ansell Collins) ... 20

FRANK BEVERLY & BUTLERS
79 Inferno HEAT 4 If That's What You Wanted/Love (Your Pain Goes Deep) (with p/s) ... 15
79 Inferno HEAT 4 If That's What You Wanted/Love (Your Pain Goes Deep) (without p/s) ... 8

BEVERLY HILLBILLIES
66 Starlite GRK 602 THE FABULOUS BEVERLY HILLBILLIES (LP) ... 15

BEVERLY HILLS BLUES BAND
(see also Four Seasons)
76 Warner Bros K 16752 Just Because/If I Can Just Get Through Tonight ... 10

MINT VALUE £

BEVIS FROND
(see also Von Trap Family, Room 13)

88	Freakbeat/Lyntone	African Violets/THE STEPPES: History Hates No Man (flexidisc free with Freakbeat fanzine)	8
88	Freakbeat/Lyntone	African Violets/THE STEPPES: History Hates No Man (flexidisc)	5
88	Bucketfull/Brains BOB 21	High In A Flat/DREAM SYNDICATE: Blind Willie McTell (free with Bucketfull Of Brains issue 27, 33rpm, yellow die-cut sleeve)	12
88	Bucketfull/Brains BOB 21	High In A Flat/DREAM SYNDICATE: Blind Willie McTell (without Bucketfull Of Brains issue 27)	7
90	Clawfist PIS 1	Sexorcist/WALKINGSEEDS: Reflection In A Tall Mirror (p/s, mail-order only)	5
87	Woronzow WOO 3	MIASMA (LP)	12
80s	Reckless RECKLP 13	MIASMA (LP, reissue)	12
87	Woronzow WOO 4	INNER MARSHLAND (LP)	12
80s	Reckless RECKLP 14	INNER MARSHLAND (LP, reissue)	12
87	Woronzow WOO 5 1/2	BEVIS THROUGH THE LOOKING GLASS - THE GREAT MAGNET DISASTER (2-LP, 500 only, originals all signed, with booklet; counterfeits unsigned)	40
80s	Reckless RECKLP 9	BEVIS THROUGH THE LOOKING GLASS (LP, reissue)	12
88	Woronzow WOO 8	TRIPTYCH (LP)	12
80s	Reckless RECKLP 15	TRIPTYCH (LP, reissue)	15
90	Woronzow WOO 13	MAGIC EYE (LP, featuring Twink, 200 only)	12
91	Woronzow WOO 16	NEW RIVER HEAD (2-LP, 1st 500 with EP & insert)	18
91	Woronzow WOO 16	NEW RIVER HEAD (2-LP, without EP & insert)	12
92	Woronzow WOO 18	LONDON STONE (LP)	12
92	Woronzow WOO 26	SUPERSEEDER (2-LP)	15
93	Woronzow WOO 22	SPRAWL (2-LP, gatefold sleeve, with insert)	15
97	Woronzow WOO 406	NORTH CIRCULAR (3-LP, with insert, 750 only, signed & numbered)	25

PAUL BEVOIR
(see also Jetset)

85	Dance Network WORK 2	THE HAPPIEST DAYS OF YOUR LIFE (LP)	12

RODNEY BEWES
(see also Highly Likely)

69	Revolution REV 1003	Remember When/Dear Mother Love Albert	15
70	Revolution Pop REVP 1001	Dear Mother Love Albert/Meter Maid	15

BEYOND THE IMPLODE

79	Diverse DIVE 101	LAST THOUGHTS EP (EP, 250 copies with hand-written labels, numbered, with 'Look Back' Fanzine)	150
80	Diverse DIVE 102	11th HOUR BREAKDOWN EP	70

BEYOND THE WIZARD'S SLEEVE

05	3rd Mynd 02	BEYOND THE WIZARD'S SLEEVE (LP)	15
06	3rd Mynd 03	SPRING (LP)	18
07	3rd Mynd 04	GEORGE (LP, red vinyl)	15
07	3rd Mynd 05	WEST (LP, clear vinyl)	15

B-52'S

79	Island WIP 6527	6060-842/Hero Worship (p/s)	5
79	Island ILPS 9580	THE B-52's (LP, with bonus single "Rock Lobster"/"52 Girls" [PSR 438])	12
80	Island ILPS 9622	WILD PLANET (LP, in plastic bag with badge)	12

B FILM

80	Plastic Records BEE 001	Night Running/Danger Man	12

BG FROM BASS INC

88	Black Steel BS002	Rock The Boat (12")	30

MAURICIO BIANCHI

81	Sterile SR 2	SYMPATHY FOR A GENOCIDE (LP, 200 only)	100
83	Broken BV 3	THE PLAIN TRUTH (LP)	60

GENE BIANCO GROUP

60	Vogue V 9167	Alarm Clock Rock/Harp Rock Boogie	30

BIAS

02	Canteen CR 001	Delerious: Street Of Life/Sunrise	10

BIBBY
(see also B.B. Seaton, Horace Seaton)

65	Blue Beat BB 289	Rub It Down/Wicked Man (actually by Harris Seaton)	20

BIDDU

67	Regal Zonophone RZ 3002	Look Out Here I Come/Daughter Of Love	12

BIFF BANG POW!
(see also Laughing Apple, Times)

84	Creation CRE 003	Fifty Years Of Fun/Then When I Scream (foldaround sprayed p/s in poly bag)	30
84	Creation CRE 007	There Must Be A Better Life/The Chocolate Elephant Man (foldaway p/s in poly bag)	30
90	Caff CAFF 13	Sleep/TIMES: Extase (p/s, with insert)	20
89	Creation CRELP 046	THE ACID HOUSE ALBUM (LP, hand-sprayed sleeve)	12

BIFFY CLYRO

99	Babi Yaga YAGA 001	Iname/All The Way Down (Chapter 2)/Travis Perkins (CD)	100
00	Electric Honey HER 013 CD	Thekidswhopoptodaywillrocktomorrow (CD, 1000 only)	80
01	Beggars Banquet BBQ 352	57/Instruction/Breathe Her (CD)	12
01	Beggars B. BBQ 335	Justboy/Unsubtle/Being Gabriel (p/s)	20
01	Beggars B. BBQ 335CD	Justboy/Being Gabriel/Unsubtle (CD)	10
02	Beggars B. BBQ 361	Joy.Discovery. Invention/Toys Toys Toys Choke/Toys Toys Toys/ All The Way Down Chapter 2 (p/s)	12
02	Beggars B. BBQ 358	57/Kill The Old, Torture Their Young (Evening Session Version) (p/s)	20
02	Beggars B. BBQ 358CD	57/Hope For An Angel/Time As An Imploding Unit/Waiting For Green (CD)	18
02	Beggars B. BBQ 361CD	Toys, Toys, Toys, Choke, Toys, Toys, Toys/Joy. Discovery. Invention/ All The Way Down (Chapter 2) 2002 Version (CD)	18

MINT VALUE £

03	Beggars B. BBQ 365	The Ideal Height/...And With The Scissorkick Is Victorious (p/s)	10
02	Beggars B. BBQLP226	BLACKENED SKY (LP)	25
03	Beggars B. BBQLP233	THE VERTIGO OF BLISS (LP)	18
04	Beggars B. BBQLP238	INFINITY LAND (LP)	18
09	14th Floor 5051865629702	ONLY REVOLUTIONS (LP, 2-CD, DVD box set)	35

BIG AMONGST SHEEP

(see also Inner City Unit, Silverwing)

83	Rock Solid RSS 01	ASTROPOP (12" EP, p/s)	12
82	Rock Solid RSR 2001	TERMINAL VELOCITY (LP)	60

BIG BARON

60	Top Rank JAR 404	Swinging Bells (Oberon Jump)/Romance	15

BIG BERTHA featuring ACE KEFFORD

(see also Cozy Powell, Ace Kefford Stand, Bedlam, Youngblood)

69	Atlantic 584 298	This World's An Apple/Gravy Booby Jamm	30

BIG BLACK

(see also Rapeman)

87	Blast First BFFP 24	He's A Whore/The Model (p/s)	5
85	Homestead HMS 007	RACER-X (12" EP, with insert)	8
87	Blast First BFFP 14T	HEADACHE (12" p/s, 1,000 only, free 45, Heartbeat/ "Things To Do Today"/"I Can't Believe")	12
86	Homestead HMS 044	HAMMER PARTY (LP)	15
86	Blast First BFFP 11	ATOMIZER (LP)	12
87	Blast First BFFP 19	SONGS ABOUT FUCKING (LP)	15
87	NOT 2 (BUT 1)	SOUND OF IMPACT (LP, matt sleeve, numbered up to 1,000, with 8-page booklet)	30
87	NOT 2 (BUT 1)	SOUND OF IMPACT (LP, laminated sleeve, numbered from 1,001-1,500, with 8-page booklet)	20
92	Touch & Go TG 81	PIGPILE (LP, boxed set with video & T-shirt with insert)	30

BIG BOB

59	Top Rank JAR 185	Your Line Was Busy/What Am I	30

BIG BOPPER

58	Mercury AMT 1002	Chantilly Lace/The Purple People Eater Meets The Witchdoctor	20
58	Mercury AMT 1002	Chantilly Lace/The Purple People Eater Meets The Witchdoctor (78)	30
59	Mercury AMT 1017	Big Bopper's Wedding/Little Red Riding Hood	25
59	Mercury AMT 1017	Big Bopper's Wedding/Little Red Riding Hood (78)	30
59	Mercury AMT 1046	It's The Truth, Ruth/That's What I Am Talking About	25
59	Mercury ZEP 10004	THE BIG BOPPER (EP)	200
59	Mercury ZEP 10027	PINK PETTICOATS (EP)	250
58	Mercury MMC 14008	CHANTILLY LACE (LP)	200

BIG BOSS MAN

01	Blow Up BU017	Sea Groove/Sea Groove (Version)	20

BIG BOY BLUE

74	Penny Farthing PEN 844	Getting Hungry/Lonely	6

BIG BOY PETE

(see also Miller, Pete Miller)

68	Camp 602 005	Cold Turkey/My Love Is Like A Spaceship	70
96	Tenth Planet TP 026	HOMAGE TO CATATONIA (LP)	18

BIG BROTHER & HOLDING COMPANY

(see also Janis Joplin, Nick Gravenites)

67	Fontana TF 881	Bye Bye Baby/All Is Loneliness	25
68	CBS 3683	Piece Of My Heart/Turtle Blues (p/s)	20
68	CBS 3683	Piece Of My Heart/Turtle Blues (without p/s)	7
68	London HLT 10226	Down On Me/Call On Me	10
67	Fontana TL 5457	BIG BROTHER & THE HOLDING COMPANY (LP, with Janis Joplin, mono)	45
67	Fontana STL 5457	BIG BROTHER & THE HOLDING COMPANY (LP, with Janis Joplin, stereo)	35
68	CBS 63392	CHEAP THRILLS (LP, with Janis Joplin, laminated single sleeve, mono)	45
68	CBS S63392	CHEAP THRILLS (LP, with Janis Joplin, laminated single sleeve, stereo)	30
69	London HA-T/SH-T 8377	BIG BROTHER & THE HOLDING COMPANY (LP, reissue, mono/stereo)	20
71	CBS S 64118	BE A BROTHER (LP)	25

BIG CARROT

(see also Marc Bolan/T. Rex)

73	EMI EMI 2047	Blackjack/Squint Eye Mangle	40
73	EMI EMI 2047	Blackjack/Squint Eye Mangle (Demo copy)	60

BIG CHARLIE

64	Blue Beat BB 241	Red Sea/You May Not Believe	20

BIG COUNTRY

(see also Skids)

84	Mercury COUNT 5-5	Wonderland/Giant//Lost Patrol (Live - parts 1 & 2) (2 x 7")	10
84	Mercury MERD 185	Where The Rose Is Sown/Belief In The Small Man/ Wonderland (Live)/In A Big Country (Live)/Auld Lang Syne (Live) (2 x 7")	10
91	Vertigo 510230-1	NO PLACE LIKE HOME (LP)	15

BIG DADDY KANE

88	Cold Chillin'	Set It Off (Extended Mix)/Get Into It, Set It Off (12", p/s)	30

BIG DAISY

(see also Wishbone Ash)

80	Elliejay 9428	Fever/Footprints	250

BIG DAVE (Cavanaugh) & HIS ORCHESTRA

54	Capitol CL 14195	Loosely With Feeling/The Cat From Coos Bay (triangular centre)	15
55	Capitol CL 14245	Rock And Roll Party/Your Kind Of Love (triangular centre)	30

MINT VALUE £

BIG FLAME

84	Laughing Gun PLAQUE 001	Sink/The Illness/Sometimes (p/s, with insert)	10

BIGGA DREAD

02	Chariot Cha 001	Batty Dread/Closet Bwoy/Truck Inna Garage/Special Request (10")	30

BIGGLES

71	Philips 6006160	Gimme Gimme Some Lovin'/Can't Buy You	8

BIG IN JAPAN

(see also Pink Industry/Military, Holly, Holly Johnson, Yachts, Bill Drummond, Creatures, Siouxsie & Banshees, Lightning Raiders)

77	Eric's ERICS 0001	Big In Japan/CHUDDIE NUDDIES: Do The Chud (p/s)	10
78	Zoo CAGE 1	FROM Y TO Z AND NEVER AGAIN (EP, foldout p/s)	15

BIG JOE (Joseph Spalding)

73	Chanan Jah 1003	Natty Love/Musical Air Raid	8
73	Atra ATRA 005	Jah Guide/SWEET HARMONY: Student Dub	12
73	Atra ATRA 010	Down Santic Way/Santic Dub	12
74	Dip DL 5007	Selassie Skank/Version	15
74	Dip DL 5008	Weed Specialist/CHERRY & DUB MASTER: Rub A Daughter	12
74	Dip DL 5027	Hog In A Me Minty/Sweet Melody	12
75	Fab FAB 243	American Pum Pum/Tape White Wash	8
76	Bimbo Music BM 4	Zion Dread/D. MORGAN: What A Disturbance	12
76	Burning Sounds BS 008	Natty Dread Don't Bow/CHANNEL ONE: Natty Dubbing	10
77	ATA ATA 1001	Set Your Face At Ease/Version	10
77	Venture VEN7770	Natty Don't Make War/CHANNEL ONE FLYERS: War Dubbing	12
78	Attack ATT 8136	Tubby At The Controls/Dignity And Principle	10
79	Tribesman TM 013	Respect Jah Word (with Rodney)/The Profit Says (12»)	20
77	Live & Love LAP001	KEEP ROCKING AND SWINGING (LP)	30
78	Trojan TRLS 152	AFRICAN PRINCESS (LP)	30

BIG JUMP BAND

73	Decca F 13411	All I Want/Utopia	15

BIG LUCKY, BIG AMOS & DONALD HINES

72	London SHU 8425	RIVER TOWN BLUES (LP)	25

BIG MAYBELLE

57	London HLC 8447	I Don't Want To Cry/All Of Me	50
57	London HLC 8447	I Don't Want To Cry/All Of Me (78)	20
59	London HLC 8854	Baby, Won't You Please Come Home/Say It Isn't So	30
59	London HLC 8854	Baby, Won't You Please Come Home/Say It Isn't So (78)	20
65	London HL 9941	Careless Love/My Mother's Eyes	20
67	CBS 2735	Turn The World Around The Other Way/I Can't Wait Any Longer	30
67	CBS 2926	Mama (He Treats Your Daughter Mean)/Keep That Man	40
68	Direction 58-3312	Quittin' Time/I Can't Wait Any Longer	25
68	Direction 58-3312	Quittin' Time/I Can't Wait Any Longer (DJ Copy)	40
67	CBS 62999	THE PURE SOUL OF BIG MAYBELLE (LP)	60

BIG MOE with BOYD BENNETT & ROCKETS

(see under Boyd Bennett)

BIG MOOSE (Walker)

68	Python PKM 01	Ramblin' Woman/Puppy Howl Blues	50

BIG PINK

08	House Anxiety HA 001	Too Young To Love/Crystal Visions	20

BIG ROY

76	Rockers 6	In The Desert/Natty Judge	6

BIG SLEEP

(see also Eyes Of Blue, Ancient Grease, Gentle Giant, Man, Ritchie Francis, Gary Pickford-Hopkins)

71	Pegasus PEG 4	BLUEBELL WOOD (LP, gatefold sleeve)	70

BIG SPENDERS

70	Gemini GMS 008	If It Feels Good, Do It/Why Don't Ya Tend To Your Business	12
70	Gemini GMS 010	Who's Making Love/Cum Ba Ye	10

BIG STAR

(see also Alex Chilton, Box Tops)

78	Stax STAX 504	September Gurls/Mod Lang	7
78	Aura AUS 103	Kizza Me/Dream Lover (p/s)	7
78	Aura AUS 107	Jesus Christ/Big Black Car	7
78	Stax SXSP 302	RADIO CITY/BIG STAR (2-LP)	25
78	Aura AUL 703	THIRD ALBUM (LP)	12

BIG THREE (U.K.)

(see also Escorts, Paddy Klaus & Gibson, Johnny Gustafson, Faron's Flamingos, Johnny & John)

63	Decca F 11614	Some Other Guy/Let True Love Begin	15
63	Decca F 11689	By The Way/Cavern Stomp	10
63	Decca F 11752	I'm With You/Peanut Butter	10
64	Decca F 11927	If You Ever Change Your Mind/You've Got To Keep Her Under Hand	15
73	Polydor 2058 343	Some Other Guy/Let It Rock/If You Gotta Make A Fool Of Somebody	7
63	Decca DFE 8552	AT THE CAVERN (EP)	40
82	Decca DFE 8552	AT THE CAVERN (EP, reissue)	8
73	Polydor 2383 199	RESURRECTION (LP)	18
82	Edsel ED 111	CAVERN STOMP (LP, with insert)	15

BIG THREE (U.S.)

(see also Mama Cass [Elliot], Mamas & Papas)

68	Roulette RCP 5002	THE BIG THREE FEATURING MAMA CASS (LP)	30

BIG TROUBLE

72	Pye 7N45292	Cyclone Blues/You Said A Bad Word	12

MINT VALUE £

BIG VERN & CHATTERBOX

93	Straight From The Bedroom VOLUME 3 (12", Cat no BED 003)		35

BIG WHEEL

73	Bell Bell 1310	Shake-A-Tail Part 1/Shake-A-Tail Part 2	10

BIG YOUTH

(see also Upsetters, Keith Hudson)

72	Blue Beat BB 424	Chi Chi Run/JOHN HOLT: OK Fred	25
73	Downtown DT 497	Dock Of The Bay/CRYSTALITES: Bass And Drums (Version)	20
73	Gayfeet CS 206	Medicine Doctor/Facts Of Life	15
73	Prince Buster PB 46	Chi Chi Run/Drums And Bass (Version)	12
73	Prince Buster PB 48	Leggo Beast/Leave Your Skeng	12
73	Prince Buster PB 50	Cain And Abel/Cain And Abel (Version)	20
73	Grape GR 3040	Foreman Versus Frazier/Foreman Versus Frazier Round Two	18
73	Grape GR 3044	JA To UK/JA To UK (Version)	12
73	Grape GR 3051	Opportunity Rock/Double Attack	20
73	Grape GR 3061	Concrete Jungle/Screaming Tonight	20
73	Green Door GD 4051	Cool Breeze/CRYSTALITES: Windstorm	20
73	Summit SUM 8542	A So We Say (with Dennis Brown)/WINSTON SCOTLAND: Scarface	8
74	Harry J. HJ 6682	Ride On Ride On/Wild Goose Chase (both with Dennis Brown)	8
75	Action ACT 101	Notty No Jester/Instrumental	10
75	Angem ANG 103	All Nations/ANSEL COLLINS : Stalag 17	12
75	Attack ATT 8096	House Of Dread Locks/GROOVEMASTER: Tangle Locks	8
75	Attack ATT 8104	Mammy Hot And Daddy Cold/GROOVEMASTERS: Some Like It Dread	8
75	Dip DL 5097	Big Youth Dread/Another Version	10
75	Lucky DL 5103	Natty Warning/Version	8
75	Klik KLP 9001	Dread Locks Dread	15
76	Lucky LY 6001	Get Up Stand Up/Version (with Dennis Brown)	8
77	Eji E 011	Strictly Rockers/AUGUSTUS PABLO : No Entry (12")	50
78	Wildflower WF 538	Jah Jah Love Them/Oven Baking	8
72	Fab MS 8	CHI CHI RUN (LP)	45
73	Trojan TRLS 61	SCREAMING TARGET (LP, orange & white label)	20
75	Klik KLP9001	DREAD LOCKS DREAD (LP)	15
76	Trojan TRLS 123	NATTY CULTURAL DREAD (LP)	15
76	Trojan TRLS 137	HIT THE ROAD JACK (LP)	18
78	Virgin Front Line FL1011	ISIAH, FIRST PROPHET OF OLD (LP)	20
80	Trojan TRLS 189	EVERYDAY SKANK (LP)	12

BIG YOUTH & KEITH HUDSON

(see also Keith Hudson)

73	Pyramid PYR 7055	Can You Keep A Secret/HORACE ANDY & EARL FLUTE: Peter And Judas	25

BIJOUX TOO

86	Apex APE 002	Shadows In My Heart/Come On Back (oversized p/s, Welsh-only release)	30

BIKINIS

58	Columbia DB 4149	Bikini/Boogie Rock And Roll	25

BILBO BAGGINS

74	Polydor 2058 479	Saturday Night/Monday Morning Blues	20

(Mr.) ACKER BILK (& HIS PARAMOUNT JAZZ BAND)

(see also Michael London)

60	Melodisc 1547	Goodnight Sweet Prince/East Coast Trot	10

BILL & BUSTER

70	A & M AMS 809	Bend Over Backwards/Going Back In Time	5

BILLIE & EDDIE

59	Top Rank JAR 249	The King Is Coming Back/Come Back, Baby	30

BILLION DOLLAR BABIES

(see also Alice Cooper)

77	Polydor 2391 273	BATTLE AXE (LP)	12

TREVOR BILLMUSS

71	B & C CB 158	English Pastures/Fishing Song	6

BONNIE 'PRINCE' BILLY

99	Domino WIGLP 59	I SEE A DARKNESS (LP)	12

BILLY & ESSENTIALS

63	London HLW 9657	Over The Weekend/Maybe You'll Be There	40

BILLY & LILLIE (& Billy Ford & Thunderbirds)

58	London HLU 8564	La Dee Dah/BILLY FORD'S THUNDERBIRDS: The Monster	40
58	London HLU 8564	La Dee Dah/BILLY FORD'S THUNDERBIRDS: The Monster (78)	10
58	London HLU 8630	Creepin', Crawlin', Cryin'/Happiness (with Billy Ford & Thunderbirds)	40
58	London HLU 8689	The Greasy Spoon/Hangin' On To You (with Billy Ford & Thunderbirds) (78)	15
59	London HLU 8795	I Promise You/Lucky Ladybug	30
59	London HLU 8795	I Promise You/Lucky Ladybug (78)	30
59	Top Rank JAR 157	Bells, Bells, Bells/Honeymoonin' (as Billie & Lillie)	10
59	Top Rank JAR 157	Bells, Bells, Bells/Honeymoonin' (as Billie & Lillie) (78)	18

BIM & BAM

70	Crab CRAB 48	The Pill (with Clover)/TOMMY McCOOK: Spring Fever	15
70	Crab CRAB 49	Immigrant Plight (w/ Clover)/PETER AUSTIN & HORTENSE: Bang Shangalang	15
73	Gayfeet GS 201	Fatty/Landlord	8

BIM, BAM & CLOVER

70	Trojan TR 7754	Party Time Parts 1 & 2	8

UMBERTO BINDI

60	Oriole CB 1577	Il Nostro Concerto/Un Giorno Un Mese Un Anno	7

MINT VALUE £

BINGO

79 Polydor 2066365 We Can't Get Enough/Mumblin' Man 40

SONNY BINNS (& RUDIES)

(see also Rudies)

69 Downtown DT 420 The Untouchables/Lazy Boy 15
69 Downtown DT 424 Wheels/Night Train 12
70 Escort ES 818 Boss A Moon (as S. Binns)/BUNNY LEE ALLSTARS: Brotherly Love 35

TONY BINNS

71 Explosion EX 2044 Love I Madly/Musical Shower 10
71 Explosion EX 2046 Humpty Dumpty/Got To Get A Message 8

BINTANGS

70 Decca F22995 Ridin' On The L And N/Down South Blues 15

BIONIC BOOGIE

(see under Gregg Diamond)

BIOTA

85 Recommended DYS 12 & 13 RACKABONES (LP, with inserts) 30

KEV BIRD

91 Basement BRSS 003 Inside Your Mind (Full Length MIx)/En Bass (Original Mix)/
En Bass (Crash Mix) (12", promo) 20
92 Basement BRSS 006 THE VISIT TO 14B EP (12", with The Wax Doctor) 15
92 Basement BRSS 012 This Is A Trip/Let's Turn It out/Eloquence (12") 10
94 Basement BRSS 031 Kano/Sub Zero (12") 10

BIRD LEGS & PAULINE

66 Sue WI 4014 Spring/In So Many Ways 40

STANLEY & JEFFREY BIRD

60 HMV POP 702 Johnny At The Crossheads/Betty, Betty (Go Steady With Me) 10

BIRDS

(see also Birds Birds, Ron Wood, Faces, Creation, Ashton Gardner & Dyke)

64 Decca F 12031 You're On My Mind/You Don't Love Me (You Don't Care) 100
65 Decca F 12140 Leaving Here/Next In Line 80
65 Decca F 12257 No Good Without You Baby/How Can It Be 80
85 Demon WEST 901 THESE BIRDS ARE DANGEROUS (LP) 12

BIRDS & BRASS

70 Rediffusion ZS 57 SOUNDSATIONAL (LP) 20
74 Rediffusion 0100 171 ...ARE BACK (LP) 20

BIRDS BIRDS

(see also Birds, Gods)

66 Reaction 591 005 Say Those Magic Words/Daddy Daddy 550

BIRDS OF A FEATHER

(see also Chanters)

69 Page One POF 156 Blacksmith Blues/Sing My Song And Pray 10
70 Page One POF 179 All God's Children Got Soul/Get It Together 6
72 Jam JAM 23 You Know Me Better/Summer Has Gone 5
72 DJM DJS 243 Thank You/Baby Don't You Bring Me Down 5
70 Page One POLS 027 BIRDS OF A FEATHER (LP) 60

JANE BIRKIN & SERGE GAINSBOURG

69 Fontana TF 1042 Je T'Aime, Moi Non Plus/Jane B (with p/s) 10
70 Major Minor MM 645 Je T'Aime Moi Non Plus/Jane P 6
72 Philips 6009 201 La Decadanse/Les Langues De Chat 5
74 Antic K 11511 Je T'Aime, Moi Non Plus/Jane B (3rd reissue, 'nude' p/s) 10
69 Fontana STL 5493 JANE BIRKIN AND SERGE GAINSBOURG (LP) 30

BIRMINGHAM

(see also Dave Peace Quartet)

71 Grosvenor GRS 1011 BIRMINGHAM (LP) 80

BIRTH CONTROL

71 Charisma CAS 1036 BIRTH CONTROL (LP, pink/white 'scroll' label) 100

BIRTHDAY PARTY

(see also Nick Cave & Bad Seeds, Roland S. Howard & Lydia Lunch, These Immortal Souls)

80 4AD AD 12 The Friend Catcher/Waving My Arms/Cat Man (p/s) 10
80 Missing Link ML-18 Mr. Clarinet/Happy Birthday (p/s) 60
81 4AD AD 111 Release The Bats/Blast Off (p/s) 10
81 4AD AD 114 Mr. Clarinet/Happy Birthday (p/s) 10
81 (no cat. no.) Mr. Clarinet/Missing Link (sold at gigs only) 50
82 4AD JAD 202 DRUNK ON THE POPE'S BLOOD/THE AGONY IS THE ECSTACY
(12" EP, with Lydia Lunch) 15
82 Masterbag BAG 005 Dead Joe (flexidisc and Masterbag magazine issue 15) 8
82 4AD CAD 207 JUNK YARD (LP) 15
87 Strange Fruit SFSP 020 PEEL SESSIONS 1 (12") 12
88 Strange Fruit SFSP 058 PEEL SESSIONS 2 (12") 12

DICKIE BISHOP & SIDEKICKS

(see also Chris Barber's Skiffle Group)

57 Decca F 10869 Cumberland Gap/No Other Baby 10
57 Decca F 10959 The Prisoner's Song/Please Remember Me 8
58 Decca F 10981 Skip To My Lou/No Other Baby 5
58 Decca F 11028 They Can't Take That Away From Me/Jumpin' Judy 10

TOMMY BISHOP'S RICOCHETS

(see also Rock 'n' Roll Revival Show, Rush, Tinkerbell's Fairydust)

65 Decca F 12238 I Should Have Known/On The Other Hand 15

MINT VALUE £

BISHOPS
(see under Count Bishops)

BITCH

71	B & C CB 151	Laughing/House Where I Live	8
72	Warners K16235	Good Time Coming/At The Party	6

BITCH

79	Hurricane FIRE 5	Big City/Wild Kids (p/s)	20

BITCH

81	Rutland RX 101	First Bite/Maggie (with p/s & promo insert)	20
81	Rutland RX 101	First Bite/Maggie	15

BITCHES SIN

81	Neat NEAT 09	Always Ready For Love/Sign Of The Times (p/s)	8
83	Quiet QT 001	No More Chances/Overnight/Ice Angels (12", p/s)	25
83	Terminal TCAS 21	OUT OF MY MIND (EP, cassette, 6-track)	8
82	Heavy Metal HMRLP 4	PREDATOR (LP, textured sleeve)	20

BITCH MAGNET

91	Caff CAFF 14	Sadie/Ducks And Drakes (p/s, with insert)	8

BITCH SLAPS BITCH

98	Brighton Rock ROK 1	Ladyboy/Locked In a Limo (p/s, 200 only)	5

BITSTREAM

94	City Centre Offices	Crab Nebula (plain sleeve with inserts, 1000 only)	6

BITTER ALMOND

70	Warner Bros WB 8008	In The Morning/Silver	5
71	United Artists UP35197	Loving Each Other/We Need Someone	12

BITTER SUITE

75	Bus Stop BUS 1028	How Married Are You Marianne/Love Is A Friend Of Mine	8

BIZ

93	Warp WARP LP 9	ELECTRO SOMA (LP, orange vinyl)	12

BIZARRE INC

91	Vinyl Sol. STORM 25	Playing With Knives (12")	10
91	Vinyl Sol. STORM 25 RT	Playing With Knives (The Climax) (12")	10
89	Blue Chip BLUE TEC. 1	TECHNOLOGICAL (LP)	15

BJÖRK
(see also Sugarcubes, Kukl)

93	One Little Indian 112TP7	Human Behavior: Underworld Mix/Close To Human Mix/Dom T Mix (12" p/s)	8
93	O. L. Indian 122TP7	Venus As A Boy: Edit/7" Dream Mix	6
96	O. L. Indian 193TP712TD	Possibly Maybe (Calcutta Cyber Café Mix)/I Miss You (Dobie's Rub Part One (12", 1,000 only)	12
96	O.L. Indian 193TP12DM	Enjoy (Beats Mix)/Possibly Maybe (Lucy Mix) (p/s, 1,000 only, numbered)	15
98	Fat Cat 12FAT 022	All Is Full Of Love (FunkstÖrung Remix)/The Shit (12", custom stamped sleeve)	12
96	O. L. Indian 193TP12DM	Enjoy/Possibly Maybe (12", 1,000 only, numbered p/s)	18
96	O. L. Indian 193TP12TD	POSSIBLY MAYBE (12" EP, 1,000 only, numbered p/s)	12
97	O. L. Indian TPLP 81	JOGA (12" triple-pack, inner sleeves, p/s)	12
97	O. L. Indian 20 TP7 BOX	JOGA (CD box set, 3 x CD singles & 1-track video, 3,000 only)	30
97	O. L. Indian 20 TP7 BOX 212TP7BOX	BACHELORETTE (CD box set, 3 x CD singles & 1-track video, 3,000 only)	25
98	O. L. Indian 23TP7BOX	ALARM CALL (3 x CD singles & 1-track video)	25
98	O. L. Indian 222TP7BOX	HUNTER (3 x CD singles & 1-track video)	25
99	O. L. Indian 242TP7BOX	ALL IS FULL OF LOVE (2 x CD singles & 1-track video)	25
08	O. L. Indian 805TP12	EARTH INTRUDERS (CD, DVD & 2 x 12")	20
08	O. L. Indian 837TP12	DECLARE INDEPENDENCE (CD, DVD & 2 x 12")	20
08	O. L. Indian 838TP12	INNOCENCE (CD, DVD & 2 x 12")	20
08	O. L. Indian 853TP12	WANDERLUST (CD, DVD & 2 x 12")	20
93	O. L. Indian TPLP 31L	DEBUT (LP, 5,000 with 16-page lyric booklet)	20
93	O. L. Indian TPLP 31L	DEBUT (LP)	15
94	O. L. Indian 152TP 12	THE BEST MIXES FROM THE ALBUM "DEBUT" FOR THOSE PEOPLE WHO DON'T BUY WHITE LABELS (mini-LP)	20
95	O. L. Indian TPLP 51L	POST (LP, pink vinyl, with inner sleeve)	18
95	O. L. Indian TPLP 51CDL/X	POST (CD, digipak w/poster & lyric book, in PVC purse)	18
95	O. L. Indian TPLP 51CDL/X	POST (CD, digipak w/poster & lyric book)	15
97	O. L. Indian TPLP71	HOMOGENIC (LP)	15
00	O. L. Indian TPLP151	SELMA SONGS (LP)	12
01	O. L. Indian TPLP101	VERSPERTINE (2 x LP, gatefold)	12
02	O. L. Indian TPLP359	GREATEST HITS (2 x LP, gatefold)	15
02	O. L. Indian TPLP365CD	GREATEST HITS & FAMILY TREE (CD x 6 boxed set)	25
03	O. L. Indian TPLP355CDBOX	LIVEBOX (CD x 4, DVD)	25
04	O. L. Indian TPLP358	MEDULLA (2 x LP)	15
06	O. L. Indian TPLP101SACD	SURROUNDED (7 dual disc box-set of all albums)	60
07	O. L. Indian TPLP460H	VOLTA (2 x LP fold-out cover)	20

BLACK

81	Rox ROX 17	Human Features/Electric Church (p/s)	10

BILL BLACK'S COMBO
(see also Elvis Presley)

59	Felsted AF 129	Smokie Parts 1 & 2	18
59	Felsted AF 129	Smokie Parts 1 & 2 (78)	15
60	London HLU 9090	White Silver Sands/The Wheel	10
60	London HLU 9156	Josephine/Dry Bones	10
60	London HLU 9212	Don't Be Cruel/Rollin'	10
61	London HLU 9267	Blue Tango/Willie	7

			MINT VALUE £
61	London HLU 9306	Hearts Of Stone/Royal Blue	7
61	London HLU 9383	Ole Buttermilk Sky/Yogi	7
61	London HLU 9436	Movin'/Honky Train	7
61	London HLU 9479	Twist-Her/My Girl Josephine	10
62	London HLU 9594	So What/Blues For The Red Boy	10
62	London HLU 9645	Joey's Song/Hot Taco	7
63	London HLU 9721	Do It - Rat Now/Little Jasper	7
63	London HLU 9788	Monkey-Shine/Long Gone	7
64	London HLU 9855	Comin' On/Soft Winds	7
64	London HLU 9903	Tequila/Raunchy	7
64	London HLU 9925	Little Queenie/Boo-Ray	25
68	London HLU 10216	Turn On Your Love Light/Ribbon Of Darkness	5
60	London REU 1277	BILL BLACK'S COMBO (EP)	30
63	London REU 1369	THE UNTOUCHABLE SOUND OF BILL BLACK (EP)	30
62	London HA-U 2310	SOLID AND RAUNCHY (LP)	30
62	London HA-U 2427	LET'S TWIST (LP, mono)	20
62	London SAH-U 6222	LET'S TWIST (LP, stereo)	25
62	London HA-U 2433	MOVIN' (LP)	25
63	London HA-U 8080	THE UNTOUCHABLE SOUND OF BILL BLACK (LP)	20
63	London HA-U 8113	GREATEST HITS (LP)	15
64	London HA-U 8187	PLAYS CHUCK BERRY (LP)	15
68	London HA-U/SH-U 8367	BILL BLACK'S BEAT GOES ON (LP)	15
69	London HA-U/SH-U 8373	TURN ON YOUR LOVE LIGHT (LP)	15
69	London HA-U/SH-U 8389	SOULIN' THE BLUES (LP)	15

CILLA BLACK

63	Parlophone R 5065	Love Of The Loved/Shy Of Love	
64	Parlophone GEP 8901	ANYONE WHO HAD A HEART (EP)	8
64	Parlophone GEP 8916	IT'S FOR YOU (EP)	12
67	Parlophone GEP 8967	TIME FOR CILLA (EP)	10
68	Parlophone PCS 7041	SHER-OO (LP, stereo, yellow/black label)	12

'FLIP' BLACK & BOYS UPSTAIRS

59	Capitol CL 15037	For You My Lover/Tell Her Mister Moon	10

FRANK BLACK

(see also Pixies)

93	4AD CADD 3004	FRANK BLACK (LP, die-cut screen-printed sleeve, with lyric inner)	12

IKA BLACK & THE NATIONS CRK

81	I One I IONE 001	Human Life/Better Life (12")	30

JEANNE BLACK

(see also Janie, Jeanne & Janie)

60	Capitol CL 15131	He'll Have To Stay/JEANNE & JANIE: Under Your Spell Again	6
60	Capitol CL 12456	Lisa/ JEANNE & JANIE: Journey of Love	6

LINCOLN BLACK

70	Penny Farthing PEN 712	Famous Last Words/You Built Me Up So High	12

MARY BLACK

92	Grapevine GRALP 005	NO FRONTIERS (LP, audiophile pressing, white sleeve)	30
92	Grapevine GRALP 009	NO FRONTIERS (LP, with lyric inner sleeve)	25
92	Grapevine GRALP 009	NO FRONTIERS (LP, audiophile pressing, red sleeve with different design and inner sleeve)	30
95	Grapevine GRALP 011	THE HOLY GROUND (LP, audiophile pressing)	20
95	Grapevine GRALP 014	CIRCUS (LP, audiophile pressing with lyric inner)	20

BLACK ABBOTTS

70	Chapter One CH 123	She Looked Away/I Don't Mind	7
71	Evolution E 3001	How About Me/Everybody Needs A Little Sunshine	7
71	Evolution E 3004	Love Is Alive/The Painter	20

BLACK ACE

61	XX MIN 701	BLACK ACE (EP)	30
62	Heritage HLP 1006	BLACK ACE (LP, 99 copies only)	120

BLACK AND WHITE LOVERS

86	Guillotine GR 001	Best Years Of Our Lives/Boulevard Of Broken Dreams (p/s)	8

BLACK ANGELS

84	Gull GULP 1041	KICKDOWN (LP)	12

BLACK ARK PLAYERS

80	Black Ark Intl. BALP 4000	BLACK ARK IN DUB (LP)	30

BLACK AXE

80	Metal MELT 1	Highway Rider/Red Lights (in p/s)	15
80	Metal MELT 1	Highway Rider/Red Lights	6

BLACKBEARD

80	More Cut RDC 2002	I WAH DUB (LP)	20

BLACK BEATLES

70	Pama PM 804	Reggae And Shout/LENOX BROWN: The Green Hornet	45

BLACKBIRDS

68	Saga OPP 3	No Destination/Space (company sleeve, possibly promo only)	30
68	Saga FID 2113	NO DESTINATION (LP, black/silver label)	40

BLACK BLOOD

76	Bradleys 1002	Rastafarai/Ewohe Dance	6

BRYAN BLACKBURN AND PETER REEVE

61	Fontana SEBL 636	AT THE BLUE ANGEL (LP)	12

MINT VALUE £

TONY BLACKBURN

65	Fontana TF 562	Don't Get Off That Train/Just To Be With You Again	6
68	MGM 6375	So Much Love/In The Night	7
69	MGM 1467	It's Only Love/Janie	7
69	Polydor 583 082	TONY BLACKBURN (LP)	12

BLACKBYRDS

(see also Donald Byrd)

75	Fantasy FTC 114	Walking In Rhythm/Baby	6
76	Fantasy FTC 122	Rock Creek Park/Flying High	8
78	Fantasy FTCT 194	Rock Creek Park/Don't Know What To Say (12")	20
85	Streetwave SWAVE 3	Rock Creek Park/Walking In Rhythm (12")	15
75	Fantasy FT 9444	BLACKBYRDS (LP)	20
75	Fantasy FT 522	FLYING START (LP)	15
76	Fantasy FTA 3003	CITY LIFE (LP)	12
77	Fantasy FT 534	ACTION (LP)	15
79	Fantasy FT 555	NIGHT GROOVES - THE BEST OF THE BLACKBYRDS (LP)	15

BLACK CAT BONES

(see also Leaf Hound, Brian Short, Free, Foghat)

70	Decca Nova DN 15	BARBED WIRE SANDWICH (LP, mono, blue/silver label)	175
70	Decca Nova SDN 15	BARBED WIRE SANDWICH (LP, stereo, blue/silver label)	120

BLACK COCK

(see also DH Harvey, Ersatz)

97	Black Cock BK 068	Cosmic/Give It Up (12")	35
97	Black Cock BK 076	Luna Party/Frog Scene (12")	50
95	Black Cock BCK 077	FREE RANGE EP (12")	40

BLACK COUNTRY THREE

(see also Jon Raven)

66	W.F.C. WS 100	BLACK COUNTRY SONGS (EP)	250
66	Transatlantic TRA 140	BLACK COUNTRY THREE (LP)	40

BLACK CROWES

91	Def American 7-17580	HARD TO HANDLE (7 x 7" box set, with 2 bonus tracks)	20

BLACK DOG

(see also Alter Ego, Plaid, Repeat, Unexplored Beats, Shiva)

91	GPR GENP(X) 2	PARALLEL EP (12", p/s)	30
92	Black Dog Prods BDP 001	VIRTUAL EP (12", p/s)	80
92	Black Dog Prods BDP 002	AGE OF SLACK (12", p/s)	100
92	Black Dog Prods BDP 003	BLACK DOG EP (12", p/s, 500 only)	125
92	GPR GENP(X) 3	VIR 2 L (12", custom sleeve)	100
92	GPR GENP (R) 03	VIR 2 L (12" remix)	70
92	GPR GENP(X) 9	VANTOOL EP (12", custom sleeve)	100
93	GPR GENP(X) 17	COST II (12", custom sleeve)	15
93	Rising High RSN 046	BLACK DOG PRODUCTIONS (12", 4-track, p/s)	20
91	GPR GPR 004	PARALLEL SQUELCH (LP)	30
92	GPR GPRLP 1	TEMPLE OF TRANSPARENT BALLS (2-LP, with poster)	45
92	GPR GPRLP 1	TEMPLE OF TRANSPARENT BALLS (2-LP, without poster)	30
93	GPR GPRCD 1	TEMPLE OF TRANSPARENT BALLS (CD)	20
95	GPR GPRLP 15	PARALLEL (2-LP)	35
95	GPR GPRCD 15	PARALLEL (CD)	30
95	Warp PUPLP 1	SPANNERS (2-LP)	40
95	Warp WAP LP 8LTD	BYTES (LP, bronze vinyl)	40

BLACK DOG PRODUCTIONS

92	Rising High RSN 46	BLACK DOG PRODUCTIONS EP (12")	25
93	Warp WARP LP 8	BYTES (2xLP)	60

BLACK DOG/SHIVA

92	GRP (no cat no)	VIR 2 L/Shout (12")	70

BLACK DYKE MILLS BAND

68	Apple APPLE 4	Thingumybob/Yellow Submarine	30

BLACK DYNAMITES

60	Top Rank JAR 319	Brush Those Tears/Lonely Cissy	20

BLACK EASTER

82	Illuminated KILL 13	READY TO ROCK (EP, p/s)	10

BLACK FAITH

70	Phillips 6006065	Woman In My Life	10
70	Phillips 6007018	Song For A Dollar/Peace In The Family	10
74	Fresh Air 6121107	The Vow/Stop The World	10

BLACK FLAG

81	Alt. Tentacles VIRUS 9	Six Pack/I've Heard It All Before/American Waste (p/s)	12
84	SST SST 12001	Family Man/I Won't Stick Any Of You Unless And Until I Can Stick All Of You (12", p/s)	10

J.D. BLACKFOOT

71	Mercury 6338 031	THE ULTIMATE PROPHECY (LP)	70

BLACKFOOT SUE

73	DJM DJS 296	Bye Bye Birmingham/Messiah	10
74	DJM DJS 326	You Need Love/Tobago Rose	12
73	Jam JAL 104	NOTHING TO HIDE (LP, gatefold sleeve with poster)	50
73	Jam JAL 104	NOTHING TO HIDE (LP, gatefold sleeve without poster)	20
75	DJM DJLPS 455	GUN RUNNING (LP, withdrawn)	65

BLACK HARMONY

79	Burning Sounds BS 14	I'm Still Waiting/Love Marcus	8
79	Laser LAS 9	Don't Let It Go To your Head/DEB PLAYERS : Don't Let It Go To Your Brain (12")	20

MINT VALUE £

BLACKJACK
(see also Michael Bolotin, Michael Bolton)

80	Polydor POSP 76	Without Your Love/Heart Of Mine (p/s)	18
79	Polydor 2391 411	BLACKJACK (LP)	18
80	Polydor	WORLDS APART (LP)	12

BLACKJACKS
(see also Pat Harris & Blackjacks)

63	Pye 7N 15586	Woo Hoo/Red Dragon	20

BLACK KNIGHTS

65	Columbia DB 7443	I Gotta Woman/Angel Of Love	25

DON BLACKMAN

82	Arista RIST 30	Hearts Desire/Let Your Conscience Be Your Guide (12", EP)	20

HONOR BLACKMAN
(see also Patrick MacNee & Honor Blackman)

68	CBS 3896	Before Today/I'll Always Be Loving You (in p/s)	30
68	CBS 3896	Before Today/I'll Always Be Loving You	10
64	Decca LK/SKL 4642	EVERYTHING I'VE GOT (LP, mono/stereo)	30
60s	Deram 844057-1	KINKY BOOTS (LP)	20

PAUL BLACKMAN

79	Daddy Kool DKR 123	Earth, Wind & Fire/A. Pablo: Ras-Menlik Congo (12")	20

MATT BLACK & THE DOODLEBUGS

76	Punk BCS 0005	Punky Xmas/Nightmare (no p/s)	8

RITCHIE BLACKMORE (ORCHESTRA)
(see also Outlaws, Neil Christian & Crusaders, Deep Purple, [Ritchie Blackmore's] Rainbow, Rally Rounders, Green Bullfrog, Rock Aid Armenia)

65	Oriole CB 314	Getaway/Little Brown Jug (Spelt "Richie" on label)	500

BLACK OAK ARKANSAS

75	Atlantic K 10621	Fancy Nancy/Keep On	7
71	Atlantic 2400 180	BLACK OAK ARKANSAS (LP)	15

BLACK PROPHETZ

91	GTI KICK8	FAX ON WAX (EP)	12

BLACK RADICAL MK II

89	2 The Bone TMS004	Monsoon/B Boys Be Wise II (12")	8
91	Mango 12 MNG 764	Ripping Up The Industry (12")	5
91	Mango 12 MNG 782DJ	Sign Of The Beast (12" - Grey Vinyl/Promo only)	20
93	Copastetic COPDIS8	THIS IS WAR (EP)	8
91	Mango MLPS1070	THE UNDILUTED TRUTH (LP)	12

BLACK RADICAL/SIR NOVA

88	Bass Inc B1001 500	B Boys Be Wise/We Outta Here (12")	30

BLACK REBEL MOTORCYCLE CLUB

02	Virgin VUSLP 224	BLACK REBEL MOTORCYCLE CLUB (LP)	15
03	Virgin VUSLP 245	TAKE THEM ON YOUR OWN (2-LP, gatefold, with inner sleeves)	18
05	Echo ECHLP 67	HOWL (2-LP, with inner sleeves)	30

BLACK RIDERS

85	Plastic Head GILP 555	CHOSEN FEW (LP)	15

BLACK ROOTS

84	Bullet BOL 9	Boys Will Be Boys/Liar (p/s, some with patch)	35
84	Nubian NR 001	Bristol Rock/Tribal War/The Father/The System (12")	20
85	Neat NEAT 4812	Nightmare/Need A Lot Of Lovin'/Rock Me Hard (12", p/s)	8
83	Bullet BOLT 3	BLACK ROSE (12" EP)	8
83	Bullet BOLT 6	WE'RE GONNA ROCK YOU (12" EP)	8
84	BBC REC 555	THE FRONT LINE (LP)	20
84	Bullet BULP 3	BOYS WILL BE BOYS (LP)	12
84	BBC REC 5570	IN SESSION (LP)	20

BLACK ROSE

82	Teesbeat TB 5	Sucker For Your Love/No Point Runnin' (in p/s)	125
82	Teesbeat TB 5	Sucker For Your Love/No Point Runnin'	35

BLACK SABBATH
(see also Ozzy Osborne, Dio, Elf, Cozy Powell, Quartz, Phenomena, Rock Aid Armenia, Brian May)

70	Fontana TF 1067	Evil Woman/Wicked World	100
70	Vertigo V2	Evil Woman/Wicked World (reissue, Vertigo 'swirl' sleeve)	30
70	Vertigo 6059 010	Paranoid/The Wizard (Vertigo 'swirl' sleeve)	20
72	Vertigo 6059 061	Tomorrow's Dream/Laguna Sunrise (Vertigo 'swirl' sleeve)	20
72	Phonogram DJ 005	Children Of The Grave/STATUS QUO: Roadhouse Blues (100 promo copies only)	400
73	WWA WWS 002	Sabbath Bloody Sabbath/Changes (company sleeve)	8
75	NEMS 6165 300	Am I Going Insane? (Radio)/Hole In The Sky (no p/s)	10
78	Vertigo SAB 001	Never Say Die/She's Gone (p/s)	8
78	Vertigo SAB 002	Hard Road/Symptom Of The Universe (purple or black vinyl)	6
80	Vertigo SAB 412	Die Young/Heaven And Hell (extended live) (12", p/s)	8
81	Vertigo SAB 512	Mob Rules/Die Young (live) (12", p/s)	10
82	Vertigo SABP 6	Turn Up The Night/Lonely Is The Word (picture disc)	6
82	Vertigo SABP 612	Turn Up The Night/Lonely Is The Word (12", picture disc)	8
86	Vertigo SABDJ 12	In For The Kill/Turn To Stone/Heart Like A Wheel (12", promo only)	15
87	Vertigo SABAF 1	4 SONGS FROM THE ETERNAL IDOL (12", p/s, promo only)	15
89	I.R.S. EIRS CB 107	Headless Cross (Edit)/Cloak And Dagger (signed label, stickered PVC sleeve)	6
89	I.R.S. EIRSPD 115	Devil And Daughter (1-sided picture disc)	5
89	I.R.S. EIRSB 115	Devil And Daughter (box set, 1-sided disc with stencil, insert & 2 postcards)	8

			MINT VALUE £
92	I.R.S. EIRSDJ 180	Master Of Insanity (edit)/Time Machine/Neon Knights (live)/TV Crimes (live)/ Die (live)/Children Of The Sea (live) (CD, no p/s, promo only)	12
70	Vertigo VO 6	BLACK SABBATH (LP, 1st pressing, with black gatefold sleeve, no composers/ publishers credits on cross; large swirl label with "A Philips record product" text)	150
70	Vertigo VO 6	BLACK SABBATH (LP, 2nd pressing, with white gatefold sleeve and Dunbar credit for 'Warning'; swirl label, with ? allegedly - laminated sleeve)	40
70	Vertigo VO 6	BLACK SABBATH (LP, 2nd pressing, with white gatefold sleeve and Dunbar credit for 'Warning'; swirl label)	200
70	Vertigo 6360 011	PARANOID (LP, gatefold sleeve, 1st press large swirl label)	100
70	Vertigo 6360 011	PARANOID (LP, gatefold sleeve, 2nd press, small swirl label)	50
70	Vertigo 6360 011	PARANOID (LP, gatefold sleeve, 2nd press, small swirl label, laminated sleeve)	60
71	Vertigo 6360 050	MASTER OF REALITY (LP in box cover, swirl label, with poster)	300
71	Vertigo 6360 050	MASTER OF REALITY (LP in box cover, swirl label, without poster)	50
72	Vertigo 6360 071	BLACK SABBATH VOL. 4 (LP, gatefold sleeve with booklet attached, small swirl label)	60
72	Vertigo 6360 071	BLACK SABBATH VOL. 4 (LP, gatefold sleeve with booklet attached, 'spaceship' labell)	125
73	WWA WWA 05	SABBATH BLOODY SABBATH (LP, gatefold with lyric inner)	40
75	NEMS 9119001	SABOTAGE (LP)	12
76	NEMS NEL 6003	PARANOID (LP, reissue)	15
85	Nems BSBLP 001	THE SABBATH COLLECTION (7-LP box set)	50
88	Castle BSBCD 001	THE BLACK SABBATH CD COLLECTION (6-CD box set with badge & book, numbered, 3,000 only)	40
89	IRS EIRSAPD 1002	HEADLESS CROSS (LP, picture disc with extra track)	15
90	IRS EIRSAPD 1038	TYR (LP, picture disc with 2 extra tracks)	12
97	Castle ORRLP 004	BLACK SABBATH (LP, reissue, 5000 only with free 7")	20

BLACK SLATE

76	King George KG 001	Mixed Up Man/Put Your Head On My Shoulder	8
78	Ted TCDD 006	Mind Your Motion/Version	25
78	Ted TCDD 008	Sticks Man (12")	25
78	Slate KG 008	Live Up To Love/Jah In The Ghetto (12")	8
81	TCD TCDLP 02	OGIMA (DUB SLATE) (LP)	60

BLACK STONES

76	Daddy Kool DK 003	We Nah Go Suffer/Unity Dub	6

BLACK SWAN

71	Ember EMBS 303	Echoes And Rainbows/Belong Belong (with p/s)	15
71	Ember EMBS 303	Echoes And Rainbows/Belong Belong (without p/s)	8

BLACK SYMBOL

s	Black Symbol BS 001	Non A Jah Jah Children Passing/Version	35

BLACKTHORN

77	WHM 1921	BLACKTHORN (LP)	60
78	WHM 1923	BLACKTHORN II (LP)	100

BLACK TWANG

95	Sound Of MoneySNM004	What's Going On?/Everyday News (12")	20
95	Sound Of MoneySNM005	Queen's Head/Mr Jam Promota (12")	15
96	Sound Of MoneySNM007	Real Estate (12")	15
96	Sound Of MoneyANTI T3	Dettwork South East/Don't Let Dem Fool You (12")	18
98	Blak Jam BJAM1204	Red Letters (12")	5
99	Blak Jam BJAM1206	Perfect Love Song (12")	5

BLACK UHURU

(See also Don Carlos)

77	Carib Gems CG 015	Sun Is Shining/REVOLUTIONARIES : Version	8
77	Third World TWDIS 009	Natural Mystic/Sorry For The Man (12")	20
79	Warrior WAR 140	Bad Girl/African Love/PRINCE HAMMER - Yogi Bear (12")	15
79	DEB DEB 034	Rent Man/Rent Board/ALTON ELLIS - La La Means I Love You/Version (12")	15
79	DEB DEB 036	Wood For My Fire/EARL CUNNINGHAM/JAH THOMAS - Words of the Father (12")	15
79	D Roy DDR 09	Plastic Smile/Guess Who's Coming To Dinner (12")	20
80	Island 12WIP 6626	Sinsemilla (discomix)/Guess Who's Coming To Dinner (discomix) (12")	8
77	Third World TWS 925	LOVE CRISIS (LP, as Black Sounds Uhro)	40
79	D-Roy DRLP 1003	SHOWCASE (LP)	25
81	Greensleeves GREL 23	BLACK SOUNDS OF FREEDOM (LP)	20

BLACK VELVET

69	Beacon BEA 129	African Velvet/Whatcha' Gonna Do 'Bout It	10
69	Beacon BEA 137	Peace And Love Is The message/Clown	12
70	Beacon BEA 151	Please Let Me In/Clown	20
70	Beacon BEA 162	What Am I To Do/Coal Mine	12
70	Beacon BEA 170	Thought I Had Me A Good Thing/Love Makes The World Go Round	10
71	Mams MAM 47	Make It Better/Tropicana	15
73	Pye 7N 45338	There Must Be A Way/Domestic Man	12
70	Beacon BEAS 16	THIS IS BLACK VELVET (LP)	20
73	Seven Sun SUNLP1	CAN YOU FEEL IT? (LP)	80
72	Pye NSPL 18392	PEOPLE OF THE WORLD (LP)	25

CHARLES BLACKWELL ORCHESTRA

61	HMV POP 977	Taboo/Midnight In Luxembourg	15
62	Columbia DB 4839	Supercar/Persian Theme	15
62	Columbia DB 4919	Freight Train/Death Valley	10
63	Columbia DB 4994	High Noon/For Me And My Gal	7
60	Triumph TRY 4000	THOSE PLUCKING STRINGS (LP, unreleased, test pressings only)	500

OTIS BLACKWELL

58	London HLE 8616	Make Ready For Love/When You're Around	40
58	London HLE 8616	Make Ready For Love/When You're Around (78)	25

MINT VALUE £

RORY BLACKWELL & HIS BLACKJACKS

57	Parlophone R 4326	Bye Bye Love/Such A Shame	20
57	Parlophone R 4326	Bye Bye Love/Such A Shame (78)	10
78	Ellie Jay EJR 604	THE 2 SIDES OF RORY BLACKWELL (LP)	12

SCRAPPER BLACKWELL

67	Collector JEN 7	SCRAPPER BLACKWELL (EP)	10
63	'77' LA 12/4	BLUES BEFORE SUNRISE (LP)	35
60s	Xtra XTRA 5011	MR SCRAPPER'S BLUES (LP)	25

BLACKWELLS (U.K.)

65	Columbia DB 7442	Why Don't You Love Me/All I Want Is Your Love	30

BLACKWELLS (U.S.)

60	London HLW 9135	Unchained Melody/Mansion On The Hill	10
61	London HLW 9334	Love Or Money/Big Daddy And The Cat	10

BLACK WIDOW

(see also Pesky Gee, Agony Bag)

70	CBS 5031	Come To The Sabbat/Way To Power	15
71	CBS 7596	Wish You Would/Accident	15
70	CBS 63948	SACRIFICE (LP, gatefold sleeve)	50
70	CBS 64133	BLACK WIDOW II (LP, gatefold sleeve)	50
72	CBS 64562	BLACK WIDOW III (LP, with inner)	50

BLADE

89	Raw Bass 1202	Lyrical Maniac/The Comin' Is Near/We're Going Independent (12")	20
89	691 Influential 1203	Lyrical Maniac/The Comin' Is Near/We're Going Independent (12")	12
89	691 Influential 1203	Mind Of An Ordinary Citizen/ Forward (12")	18
91	691 Influential 1204	Rough It Up/Whatcha Waitin' For?/You Better Get Yours (12")	18
93	691 Influential 1206	Clear The Way/They Ain't Shit To Me (12", white vinyl, Blade gave this to fans who paid in advance for his THE LION GOES FROM STRENTH TO STRENGTH LP)	35
96	691 Influential SURV 1	Survival Of The Hardest Working (12")	20
97	Bomb 2006	Rhyme Bomb/The Way It Has To Be (12")	12
92	691 Influential 1205	SURVIVAL OF THE HARDEST WORKING (LP)	25
93	691 Influential 1202	THE LION GOES FROM STRENGTH TO STRENGTH (LP)	30
95	691 Influential 1208	PLANNED AND EXECUTED (LP)	15
95	691 Influential 1208	PLANNED AND EXECUTED (LP, limited edition on red vinyl)	30

ANDY BLADE

(see also Eater)

80	SMS SMS 001	Break The News/Girl With The Goods (p/s)	18

BLADE RUNNER

84	Ebony EBON 26	Back Street Lady/Too Far Too Late	6
84	Ebony EBON 21	HUNTED (LP)	15

BLADES

(see also Partisans)

80	Energy NRG 3	Hot For You/The Reunion (p/s; Irish with paper labels)	20
80	Energy NRG 3	Hot For You/The Reunion (p/s; later UK pressing with plastic labels, in plastic sleeve)	15
81	Energy NRG 5	Ghost Of A Chance/Real Emotion (p/s; Irish with paper labels)	20
81	Energy NRG 5	Ghost Of A Chance/Real Emotion (p/s; later UK pressing with plastic labels, in plastic sleeve)	12
84	Reekus RKS 013	The Last Man In Europe (p/s)	12
85	Reekus RKS 15	Those Were The Days (p/s)	10
85	Reekus RKSY 15	Those Were The Days (picture disc)	12
86	Reekus RKS 017	Downmarket/Truth Don't Hurt (as Blades with Paul Cleary)	10
84	Reekus RKLP 1	THE LAST MAN IN EUROPE (LP)	20
86	Reekus RKLP 3	RAY TOWN REVISITED (LP)	20

BLADES OF GRASS

67	Stateside SS 2040	Happy/That's What A Boy Likes	12
68	Stateside SS 2101	Charlie And Fred/You Won't Find That Girl	10

BLAH BLAH BLAH

79	Absurd ABSURD 1	In The Army/Why Diddle? (p/s)	5
80s	Lyntone LYN 17627	Heavenly View/ST. VITUS DANCE: Meet Mohammed (1-sided 33rpm flexidisc with Helden fanzine)	6
80s	Lyntone LYN 17627 Good Vibes H 002	Heavenly View/ST. VITUS DANCE: Meet Mohammed (1-sided 33rpm flexidisc without Helden fanzine)	5
81	Some Bizzare	BLAH BLAH BLAH (LP, unreleased, stickered sleeve, white label test pressings only)	40

HAL BLAINE (& YOUNG COUGARS)

64	RCA RCA 1379	Gear Stripper/Challenger II (with Young Cougars)	35
64	RCA RD 7624	DEUCES, T'S, ROADSTERS AND DRUMS (LP, mono)	40
64	RCA SF 7624	DEUCES, T'S, ROADSTERS AND DRUMS (LP, stereo)	50

VIVIAN BLAINE

53	Brunswick 05137	A Bushell And A Peck/My Time Today/Take Back Your Mink (78)	10
54	Parlophone MSP 6070	Changing Partners/Lonely	5

BLAIR

79	Miracle M4	Night Life/Virgo Princess	8
79	Miracle M4	Night Life/Virgo Princess (12")	30

ARNOLD BLAIR

76	Curtom NEET 1024	Trying To Get Next To You/I Won The Big Deal/House Party (12" with Fred Wesley)	15

MINT VALUE £

BEVERLEY BLAIR
58 Mercury 7MT 209 — With Love We Live/Tony 20

HENRY BLAIR
s Capitol EAP 1-3003 — SPARKY'S MAGIC PIANO (EP) 10

SALLY BLAIR
58 MGM MGM 1000 — Whatever Lola Wants (Lola Gets)/Daddy 25

BARDI BLAISE
80 Din Disc DIN 8 — Trans Siberian Express/Competition Side (p/s) 6

DAVID BLAKE
69 SNB 55-4178 — We'll Meet Again/Now is The Time 5

GARRY BLAKE
66 Columbia DB 7885 — Strawberries And Cream/Look Out Now! 8
66 Columbia DB 7977 — Wait Until Dark/Jungle Juice 8
66 Columbia DB 8074 — The Danny Scipio Theme/Celebration Day 10
66 Studio 2 TWO 124 — MORE SOUNDS LIKE SWINGING (LP) 12
67 Studio 2 TWO 174 — THE IMPACT OF GARY BLAKE (LP) 12

KARL BLAKE
(see also Lemon Kittens, Shock Headed Peters, Underneath, Gland Shrouds, Fur Fur, Sol Invictus)
80 Daark Inc. 1 — TANK DEATH (C-60 cassette) 12
81 Daark Inc. 2 — THE NEW POLLUTION (C-60 cassette) 12
83 Glass GLASS 013 — THE PREHENSILE TAPES (LP) 12
91 Tak Tak Tak TAK 07 — MANDIBLES (cassette, 500 only) 12

KEITH BLAKE
(see also Overtakers, Uniques)
68 Blue Cat BS 102 — Musically/I'm Moving On 60

SONNY BLAKE
64 Ember EMBS 195 — Johnny Janvier/She's Mine 5

TIM BLAKE
(see also Gong, Hawkwind)
78 Barclay Towers BAR 711 — Generator Laserbeam/Woodland Voice (p/s) 8
78 Barclay Towers CLAY 7005 — BLAKE'S NEW JERUSALEM (LP) 12

WINSTON BLAKE & M-SQUAD
69 Crab 40 — Big Thing/RUPIE EDWARDS : Exclusively 15
71 Green Door GD 4003 — Carrol Street/ANSELL COLLINS & M-SQUAD: Carol St. Version 12

ART BLAKEY JAZZ MESSENGERS
(see also Annie Ross)
61 Fontana TFL 5116 — OLYMPIA CONCERT (LP) 15
62 HMV CLP 1532 — ART BLAKEY JAZZ MESSENGERS (LP, also stereo CSD 1423) 15
62 Fontana TFL 5184 — DANGEROUS FRIENDSHIPS (LP, soundtrack) 18
63 United Artists (S)ULP 1017 — THREE BLIND MICE (LP, mono/stereo) 15
64 Riverside RLP 438 — CARAVAN (LP) 15
64 HMV CLP 1760 — A JAZZ MESSAGE (LP) 15
64 Riverside RLP 464 — UGETSU (LP) 30
65 Limelight (S)LML 4000 — 'S MAKE IT (LP) 15
66 Limelight (S)LML 4012 — SOUL FINGER (LP) 15
66 Limelight (S)LML 4021 — BUTTERCORN LADY (LP) 12
66 Fontana FJL 111 — SOUL! (LP) 15
67 Limelight (S)LML 4023 — HOLD ON, I'M COMIN' (LP) 15
67 Atlantic 590 009 — BLUE MONK (LP, with Thelonious Monk) 15
68 Riverside 673013 — KYOTO (LP) 12
69 Polydor 545101 — DRUM THUNDER (LP) 15

ART BLAKEY/MILES DAVIS
(see also Thelonious Monk, Miles Davis)
66 Fontana FJL 135 — L'ASCENSEUR POUR L'ECHAFAUD/FEMME DISPARAISSANTE (LP, soundtrack, 1 side each) 40

ALAN BLAKLEY
75 DJM DJS 367 — Sorry (Lyn's Song)/Windows Are Nice 8

MEL BLANC
58 Capitol CL 14950 — I Taut I Taw A Puddy Cat/K-K-K-Katy 5
60 Warner Bros WB 26 — Tweety's Twistmas Twouble/I Keep Hearing Those Bells 5

BURT BLANCA
60 Zodiac ZR 004 — Texas Rider/Shamash 35

BLANCMANGE
80 Blaah Music MFT-1 — IRENE AND MAVIS (EP, gatefold p/s) 40
82 London SHPD 8552 — HAPPY FAMILIES (LP, picture disc) 12
84 London SHPD 8554 — MANGE TOUT (LP, picture disc) 12

BILLY BLAND
60 London HL 9096 — Let The Little Girl Dance/Sweet Thing 20
71 Atlantic 2091 130 — Let The Little Girl Dance/Chicken Hop 8

BOBBY BLAND
61 Vogue V 9178 — Cry Cry Cry/I've Been Wrong So Long 30
61 Vogue V 9182 — Lead Me On/Hold Me Tenderly 30
61 Vogue V 9188 — Don't Cry No More/St. James Infirmary 30
62 Vogue V 9190 — You're The One (That I Need)/Turn On Your Love Light 30
62 Vogue V 9192 — Blue Moon/Who Will The Next Fool Be? 30
64 Vocalion VP 9222 — Ain't Nothing You Can Do/Honey Child 30
64 Vocalion VP 9229 — After It's Too Late/Share Your Love With Me 30

			MINT VALUE £
65	Vocalion VP 9232	Yield Not To Temptation/How Does A Cheating Woman Feel?	35
65	Vocalion VP 9251	These Hands (Small But Mighty)/Today	40
66	Vocalion VP 9262	I'm Too Far Gone (To Turn Around)/ If You Could Read My Mind	25
66	Vocalion VP 9273	Good Time Charlie/Good Time Charlie (Working His Groove Bag)	35
68	Sue WI 4044	That Did It/A Touch Of The Blues	45
69	Action ACT 4524	Rockin' In The Same Old Boat/Wouldn't You Rather Have Me?	30
69	Action ACT 4538	Gotta Get To Know You/Baby I'm On My Way	25
69	Action ACT 4548	Share Your Love With Me/Honey Child	20
69	Action ACT 4553	Chains Of Love/Ask Me 'Bout Nothing But The Blues	20
74	ABC ABC 4014	Ain't No Love In The Heart Of The City/Twenty Four Blues	10
75	ABC ABC 4030	I Wouldn't Treat A Dog (The Way You Treat Me)/ I Ain't Gonna Be The First To Cry	5
77	ABC ABC 4186	The Soul Of A Man/If I Weren't A Gambler	5
85	Kent Town 108	Shoes/Call On Me/Getting Used To The Blues/Good Time Charlie (EP, p/s)	15
63	Vocalion VEP 170153	YIELD NOT INTO TEMPTATION (EP)	75
64	Vocalion VEP 170157	BOBBY BLAND (EP)	75
60	Vogue VA 160183	TWO STEPS FROM THE BLUES (LP)	150
61	Vocalion VA 160183	TWO STEPS FROM THE BLUES (LP)	70
61	Vogue/Vocalion VAP 8027	AIN'T NOTHING YOU CAN DO (LP)	75
64	Vocalion VAP 8027	AIN'T NOTHING YOU CAN DO (LP)	40
63	Vogue/Vocalion VAP 8034	CALL ON ME/ THAT'S THE WAY LOVE IS (LP)	75
64	Vocalion VAP 8034	CALL ON ME/ THAT'S THE WAY LOVE IS (LP)	40
66	Vocalion VAP 8041	HERE'S THE MAN (LP)	60
68	Island ILP 974	A TOUCH OF THE BLUES (LP)	70
69	Action ACLP 6006	A PIECE OF GOLD (LP)	40
74	Polydor 2383 257	BLUES FOR MR. CRUMP (LP, with tracks by Junior Parker & Howlin' Wolf)	20

MARCIE BLANE

62	London HLU 9599	Bobby's Girl/A Time To Dream	25
63	London HLU 9673	What Does A Girl Do/How Can I Tell Him	25
63	London HLU 9744	Little Miss Fool/Ragtime Sound	25
63	London HLU 9787	You Gave My Number To Billy/Told You So	25
63	London REU 1393	MARCIE BLANE (EP)	140

BLANKS

(see also Destructors)

79	Void SRTS/79/CUS/560	The Northern Ripper/Understand (p/s)	60

BLANK STUDENTS

80	Dexter Discs	We Are Natives/I Want To Be Happy (500 only)	25

BLARNEY SISTERS

67	GO AJ11407	The Greatest Blessing/Golden Band	15

BLAZE

95	Nuphonic NUX 106	THE BLAZE TRACKS (EP)	15
99	Slip And Slide SLIP 99	Wishing You Were Here/(mixes) (2x12")	18

BLAZER, BLAZER

78	Logo GO 362	Cecil B. Devine/Warsaw/Six O'Clock In The Morning (p/s)	10

BLAZERS

58	Fontana TFR 6010	ROCK AND ROLL (10" LP)	80

BLAZING SONS

(see also Phantom)

83	Cool Ghoul COOL 002	Chant Down The National Front/N.F. Dub (no p/s)	10

BLEACH BOYS

78	Tramp THF 002	Chloroform/You've Got Nothing (no p/s, 1,000 only)	60
85	Zombie International ZOMBO 103010	Stocking-Clad Nazi Death Squad Bitches/Death Before Disco/ Gimme That Neutron Taste (12", p/s)	25

BLEAK HOUSE

80s	Buzzard BUZZ 1	Rainbow Warrior/Isandlhwana/Inquisition (in p/s)	100
80s	Buzzard BUZZ 1	Rainbow Warrior/Isandlhwana/Inquisition	30
82	Buzzard BUZZ 2	LIONS IN WINTER (Chase The Wind/No Reply/Down To Zero/ Flight Of The Salamander) (EP, p/s with insert)	90

BLEECHERS

(see also Busty Brown, Upsetters)

69	Trojan TR 679	Ease Up/You're Gonna Feel It	12
69	Upsetter US 314	Come Into My Parlour/MELOTONES: Dry Up Your Tears	15
70	Col. Blue Beat DB 118	Send Me The Pillow (That You Dream On)/Adam And Eve	8
71	Duke DU 118	Put It Good/J.J. ALLSTARS: Good Good Version	10

BLEEDING HEARTS

80	Crazy Plane SP 003	This Is The Way/OK	30

PETER BLEGVAD

(see also Slapp Happy)

80	Recommended RRA 5.75	Alcohol (p/s, 1-sided, other side etched)	5

BLENDELLS

64	Reprise RS 20291	La La La La La La/Huggies Bunnies	20
64	Reprise RS 20291	La La La La La La/Huggies Bunnies (DJ Copy)	40
64	Reprise RS 20340	Dance With Me/Get Your Baby	30
64	Reprise RS 20340	Dance With Me/Get Your Baby (DJ Copy)	40

CARLA BLEY

(see also Jazz Composers Orchestra, Michael Mantler, Jack Bruce)

72	JCOA JT 4001	ESCALATOR OVER THE HILL (3xLP, with Paul Haines & Jack Bruce)	20
74	Watt WATT 1	TROPIC APPETITES (LP, gatefold sleeve)	15

PAUL BLEY TRIO

(see also Bley-Peacock Synthesizer Show, Annette Peacock)

69	Fontana SFJL 929	TOUCHING (LP)	40

MINT VALUE £

BLEY-PEACOCK SYNTHESIZER SHOW
(see also Annette Peacock, Paul Bley)

72	Polydor 2425 043	REVENGE (LP)	200

ARCHIE BLEYER & HIS ORCHESTRA

54	London HL 8035	Amber/Julie's Jump	30
54	London HL 8111	The Naughty Lady Of Shady Lane/While The Vesper Bells Were Ringing	30
55	London HLA 8176	Hernando's Hideaway/S'il Vous Plait	30
56	London HLA 8243	Nothin' To Do/JANET BLEYER: 'Cause You're My Lover	15
56	London HLA 8263	Bridge Of Happiness/You Tell Me Your Dream, I'll Tell You Mine (Gold Tri)	15

B,L&G
(see also Trevor Burton, Denny Laine, Steve Gibbons)

71	Birds Nest BN 3	Live In The Mountains/Janie Slow Down	10

BLIND BLAKE
(see also Paramount Allstars)

50	Tempo R 23	Hey Hey Daddy Blues/Brownskin Mama Blues (78)	15
50	Tempo R 40	Southern Rag/CC Pill Blues (78)	15
54	Jazz Collector L 97	Hot Potatoes/Southbound Rag (78)	15
58	Ristic LP 18	THE LEGENDARY BLIND BLAKE (10" LP)	50
59	Jazz Collector JLP 2001	THE LEGENDARY BLIND BLAKE (10" LP, reissue)	20
67	Riverside RLP 8804	BLUES IN CHICAGO (LP)	20
68	Whoopee 101	BLIND BLAKE 1927-30 (LP)	12

BLIND BLAKE/CHARLIE JACKSON

60s	Heritage HLP 1011	BLIND BLAKE AND CHARLIE JACKSON (LP, 99 only)	70

BLIND BLAKE/RAMBLIN' THOMAS

59	Jazz Collector JEL 4	THE MALE BLUES VOLUME 3 (EP)	10

BLIND FAITH
(see also Stevie Winwood, Ginger Baker, Eric Clapton)

69	Island (no cat. no.)	Change Of Address From June 23rd 1969 (promo issue, 500 only)	300
69	Polydor 583 059	BLIND FAITH (LP, gatefold sleeve, first pressing with single paper on left gatefold stating distribution by Polydor and Island)	70
69	Polydor 583 059	BLIND FAITH (LP, gatefold sleeve, later issue without Polydor and Island distribution credit)	30

BLIND FURY

85	Roadrunner RR 9814	OUT OF REACH (LP)	12

BLINK 182

96	Grilled Cheese GRL 701	They Came To Conquer Uranus/Waggy (blue vinyl, p/s)	12
01	MCA MCS 40264	First Date/Don't Tell Me It's Over (picture disc, printed PVC sleeve)	8
04	Geffen MCS 40400	Always/I Miss You (Live In Minneapolis) (Picture disc)	5
97	Grilled Cheese LPGRL 4	DUDE RANCH (LP, gatefold sleeve)	20

BLINKERS

69	Pye 7N 17752	Original Sin/Dreams Secondhand	60

BLINKY & EDWIN STARR
(see also Edwin Starr)

69	Tamla Motown TMG 720	Oh How Happy/Ooo Baby Baby (unissued, demos only)	400
70	Tamla Motown TMG 748	Oh How Happy/Ooo Baby Baby	10
70	T. Motown (S)TML 11131	JUST WE TWO (LP, as Edwin Starr & Blinky)	25

BLISS

69	Chapter One CH 107	Courtyards In Castile/Lifetime	15

MELVIN BLISS

77	Contempo CS 2013	Reward/Synthetic Substitution	45

BLITZ
(see also Rose Of Victory)

81	No Future OI 1	ALL OUT ATTACK (EP, rubber-stamped labels, 500 only)	25
81	No Future OI 1	ALL OUT ATTACK (EP, reissue, initially with white labels)	15
81	No Future OI 1	ALL OUT ATTACK (EP, reissue, later printed labels)	10
82	No Future OI 6	Never Surrender/Razor In The Night (p/s)	12
82	No Future OI 16	Warriors/Youth (p/s)	12
82	No Future PUNK 1	VOICE OF A GENERATION (LP, with inner sleeve)	25

BLITZ BOYS

80	Told You So TYS 001	Eddy's New Shoes/Eddie's Friend/She Told My Friends (foldover p/s)	100

BLITZKRIEG

81	Neat NEAT 10	Buried Alive/Blitzkrieg (p/s)	60
82	No Future OI 8	LEST WE FORGET (EP)	8
91	Roadrunner R 09302	10 YEARS OF BLITZKRIEG (EP)	10
85	Neat NEAT 1023	A TIME OF CHANGES (LP)	40

BLITZKRIEG BOP

77	Mortonsound MTN 3172/3	Let's Go/Nine Till Five/Bugger Off (p/s, 500 only)	100
77	Lightning GIL 504	Let's Go (re-recorded)/Life Is Just A So-So/Mental Case (p/s)	20
78	Lightning GIL 543	U.F.O./Bobby Joe (p/s)	20

BLIZZARD

71	CBS CBS 7238	Baby Blue/Mama, The Sparrow And The Tree	6

BLOATED TOADS

79	Shattered SHAT 4	Why/Essential In Some Form/Happy Home/Yankee TV Victim (p/s, with insert)	5

BLOC PARTY

04	Trash Aesthetics TA701	She's Hearing Voices/The Marshals Are Dead/The Answer (p/s clear vinyl, 500 only)	70
04	Moshi Moshi MOSHI10	Banquet/Staying Fat (p/s, 500 only)	20

MINT VALUE £

04	Moshi Moshi MOSH110CD	Banquet/Staying Fat (CD, 2000 only)	12
04	Wichita WEBB067S	Little Thoughts/Storm and Stress (Blue vinyl, p/s)	15
05	Wichita WEBB088S	The Pioneers/The Pioneers (Bloc Party vs Mystery Jets) (numbered pic disc)	10
05	Wichita WEBB075LP	SILENT ALARM (LP)	15
05	Wichita WEBB075PD	SILENT ALARM (LP, picture disc)	30
05	Wichita WEBB090LP	SILENT ALARM REMIXED (2-LP)	20
07	Wichita WEBB 120 PD	A WEEKEND IN THE CITY (LP, picture disc)	25

BLOCKHEAD

04	Ninja Tune ZEN 88	MUSIC BY CAVELIGHT (2xLP)	25

BLODWYN PIG

(see also Mick Abrahams, Jethro Tull)

69	Island WIP 6059	Dear Jill/Sweet Caroline	10
69	Island WIP 6069	Walk On The Water/Summer Day	10
70	Chrysalis WIP 6078	Same Old Story/Slow Down	10
69	Island ILPS 9101	AHEAD RINGS OUT (LP, gatefold sleeve, pink label with black/orange circle logo)	60
69	Island ILPS 9101	AHEAD RINGS OUT (LP, gatefold sleeve, 'pink rim palm tree' label)	12
70	Chrysalis ILPS 9122	GETTING TO THIS (LP, gatefold sleeve, island logo and address in white on green label)	25
89	Private release	A TASTE OF THINGS TO COME (cassette, 50 only, sold at gigs)	25

BLOND

(see also Tages)

69	Fontana TF 1040	(I Will Bring You) Flowers In The Morning/I Wake Up And Call	10
69	Fontana STL 5515	THE LILAC YEARS (LP, gatefold sleeve)	125

BLONDE ON BLONDE

69	Pye 7N 17637	All Day All Night/Country Life	40
70	Ember EMB S 279	Castles In The Sky/Circles (in p/s)	20
70	Ember EMB S 279	Castles In The Sky/Circles (some in p/s)	12
72	Ember EMB S 316	Sad Song For An Easy Lady/Happy Families (p/s)	15
79	Pye 7N 46189	Whole Lotta Love/Make Me Smile	6
69	Pye NSPL 18288	CONTRASTS (LP, gatefold sleeve, blue/black label with logo/banner on top)	120
70	Ember NR 5049	RE-BIRTH (LP, gatefold sleeve)	80
71	Ember NR 5058	REFLECTIONS ON A LIFE (LP, gatefold sleeve)	80
70s	Ember LP 7005	BLONDE ON BLONDE (LP, unissued, test pressings only)	200

BLONDIE

(see also Debbie Harry, New York Blondes, Wind In The Willows, Rodney & Brunettes)

77	Private Stock PVT 90	X Offender/In The Sun (unissued, promos or stock copies, no p/s)	900
77	Private Stock PVT 105	In The Flesh/X Offender (no p/s)	20
77	Chrysalis CHS 2180	Rip Her To Shreds/In The Flesh/X Offender (p/s)	8
77	Chrysalis CHS 2180-12	Rip Her To Shreds/In The Flesh/X Offender (12", green labels, '75p' p/s)	8
78	Chrysalis CHS 2204	Denis (Denee)/Contact In Red Square (red/blue p/s)	5
78	Chrysalis CHS 2242	Picture This/Fade Away (And Radiate) (p/s, yellow vinyl)	5
78	Chrysalis CHE 2266	Hanging On The Telephone/Will Anything Happen (p/s, export issue)	6
78	Chrysalis CHE 2275	Heart Of Glass/Rifle Range (p/s, export issue with "pain in the ass" lyrics)	8
80	Flexi FLX 146 Lyntone LYN 10840/1	Speaking From The Studio (Blondie Fan Club flexidisc) Yuletown Throwdown (Rapture) (with Freddie)/ BRATTLES: The Christmas Song/SNUKY TATE: Santa's Agent (33rpm blue or orange vinyl flexi with Flexipop magazine issue 15)	15
89	Chrysalis CHSP 12 3342	Call Me (Remix)/Backfired (Remix)/Call Me (1989) (12", picture disc)	8
98	EMI 12 ATOM 150	ATOMIC 98 (Remixes) (12", p/s, withdrawn)	15
98	EMI CD ATOM 150	ATOMIC 98 (Remixes) (CD, withdrawn)	18
76	Private Stock PVLP 1017	BLONDIE (LP)	18
82	Chrysalis PCDL 1384	THE HUNTER (LP, picture disc)	15
89	Chrysalis CHR 1658	THE 12" MIXES (2-LP)	15
89	Chrysalis CCD 1658	THE 12" MIXES (CD)	18

BLOOBLO

76	Feelgood FLG 104	Please Mister Please/Chaka	12
76	Feelgood FG1	CHAKA (LP)	12
78	Mother & Son	IS THAT YOU (LP)	25

BLOOD

83	No Future OI 22	Megalomania/Calling The Shots/Parasite In Paradise (p/s)	20
83	Noise NOY 1	Stark Raving Normal/Mesrine (p/s)	15
82	Noise NOYZLP 1	FALSE GESTURES FOR A DEVIOUS PUBLIC (LP)	20
85	Conquest QUEST 3	SE PARARE NEX (LP)	15
89	Link Classics CLINK 5	FALSE GESTURES FOR A DEVIOUS PUBLIC (LP, reissue, red vinyl)	15

BARRY BLOOD

75	Alaska ALA 24	Poor Annie/On The Run	50

BLOOD & ROSES

85	Audiodrome ASSAULT	(Some) Like It Hot/Paradise	5

BLOOD DONOR

79	Arista ARIRV 262	Rubber Revolution/Chemical Babies (P/S, red vinyl)	8

BLOOD RED SHOES

06	Jonson Family	Bless His Heart/Don't Always Say Yes/Victory For The Magpie (p/s, insert, 500 only)	40
06	Try Harder	Stitch Me Back/Meet Me At Eight (500 only)	40

BLOODROCK

71	Capitol CL 15670	D.O.A./Children's Heritage	8
71	Capitol E-ST 491	BLOODROCK 2 (LP)	15
71	Capitol E-ST 765	BLOODROCK 3 (LP)	15

MINT VALUE £

BLOOD SISTERS

79	Sound City SCD 002	Ring My Bell/Dub (12")	20
79	Sound City SCD 004	What About Me/I'd Rather Go Blind (12")	15

BLOOD, SWEAT & TEARS

(see also Al Kooper, David Clayton-Thomas)

68	CBS 3563	I Can't Quit Her/House In The Country	20
69	CBS 4116	You've Made Me So Very Happy/The Blues, Part 2	5
69	CBS 4220	Spinning Wheel/More And More	5
74	CBS 2462	Tell Me That I'm Wrong/Rock Reprise	15
68	CBS 63296	CHILD IS THE FATHER TO THE MAN (LP)	18

BOBBY BLOOM

70	Polydor 2001 122	Heavy Makes You Happy/Give 'Em A Hand	5

CLAIRE BLOOM

60s	Caedmon TCP 1279	EDWARD LEARS NONSENSE STORIES & POEMS (LP)	20

ROGER BLOOM'S HAMMER

67	CBS 202654	Out Of The Blue/Life's A Gamble	12
67	CBS 2848	Polly Pan/Fifteen Degree Temperature Rise	8

MIKE BLOOMFIELD

(see also Barry Goldberg Reunion, Stephen Stills, K.G.B.)

69	CBS 63652	IT'S NOT KILLING ME (LP)	20

MIKE BLOOMFIELD & AL KOOPER

(see also Al Kooper, Paul Butterfield Blues Band, Electric Flag)

69	CBS 4094	The Weight/59th Street Bridge Song	10
69	CBS 66216	THE LIVE ADVENTURES OF MIKE BLOOMFIELD AND AL KOOPER (2-LP, mono)	40
69	CBS 66216	THE LIVE ADVENTURES OF MIKE BLOOMFIELD AND AL KOOPER (2-LP, stereo)	18

BLOSSOMS

(see also Darlene Love, Allisons [U.S.])

58	Capitol CL 14833	Move On/He Promised Me	50
58	Capitol CL 14856	Little Louie/Have Faith In Me	40
58	Capitol CL 14947	No Other Love/Baby Daddy-O	40
68	MGM MGM 1435	Tweedle Dee/You Got Me Hummin'	20
71	Pama PM 814	Stand By/Soul And Inspiration	25
73	Mojo 2027 013	Touchdown/It's All Up To You	5

BLOSSOM TOES

(see also B.B. Blunder, Stud, Kevin Westlake, Solid Gold Cadillac)

67	Marmalade 598 002	What On Earth/Mrs Murphy's Budgerigar/Look At Me I'm You (in p/s)	70
67	Marmalade 598 002	What On Earth/Mrs Murphy's Budgerigar/Look At Me I'm You	30
68	Marmalade 598 009	I'll Be Your Baby Tonight/Love Is	30
68	Marmalade 598 012	Postcard/Everyone's Leaving Me Now	30
69	Marmalade 598 014	Peace Loving Man/Up Above My Hobby Horse's Head	30
69	Marmalade 598 022	New Day/Love Bomb (unissued, existence unconfirmed)	0
67	Marmalade 607 001	WE ARE EVER SO CLEAN (LP, mono)	300
67	Marmalade 608 001	WE ARE EVER SO CLEAN (LP, stereo)	400
69	Marmalade 608 010	IF ONLY FOR A MOMENT (LP)	350
88	Decal LIKD 43	COLLECTION (2-LP)	15

MICHAEL BLOUNT

70	CBS 5248	Ryba Jyba/Acorn Street	15
70	CBS 7022	Sometimes/Angelina Baby	5
72	York SYK 519	Beautiful Morning/Feathered Cloud	5
72	York SYK 28	Tackle And Sack/Pretty Face	5
72	York SKY 535	Rosie/Trombone Man	5
71	CBS 64230	PATCHWORK (LP)	20
72	York FYK 401	SOUVENIRS (LP)	20
73	York FYK 414	FANTASIES (LP)	20

BLOWZABELLA

70s	Special Delivery SPD 1028	VANILLA (LP)	40
70s	Plant Life PLR 051	IN COLOUR (LP)	30

BLUE

(see also Poets, Thunderclap Newman)

73	RSO 2090 109	Red Light Song/Look Around	6
73	RSO 2090 114	Little Jody/The Way Things Are	6
73	RSO 2394 105	BLUE (LP)	12

BABBITY BLUE

65	Decca F 12053	Don't Make Me (Fall In Love With You)/I Remembered How To Cry	10
65	Decca F 12149	Don't Hurt Me/Question	10

BARRY BLUE

94	Vinyl Solution STORM85	Cancel Em All Out (12")	8

BOBBY BLUE

70	Duke DU 86	Going In Circles (actually by Lloyd Charmers)/ Doggone Right (actually by Bobby Davis)	8

DAVID BLUE

69	Reprise RS20830	Beautiful Susan/You Don't Need A Thing	8
67	Elektra EKL 4003	DAVID BLUE (LP, red label)	40
72	Asylum SYL 9001	STORIES (LP)	18
73	Asylum SYL 9009	NICE BABY AND THE ANGEL (LP)	18
75	Asylum SYL 9025	COMIN' BACK FOR MORE (LP)	15
76	Asylum K 53056	CUPID'S ARROW (LP)	15

BLUES MASTERS

63	Island WI 078	5 O'Clock Whistle/African Blood (both sides actually by Baba Brooks)	40

MINT VALUE £

PAMELA BLUE
63 Decca F 11761 My Friend Bobby/Hey There Stranger 80

BLUE RONDOS
64 Pye 7N 15734 Little Baby/Baby I Go For You 50
65 Pye 7N 15833 Don't Want Your Lovin' No More/What Can I Do 50

TIMOTHY BLUE
68 Spark SRL 1014 The Room At The Top Of The Stairs/She Won't See The Light 25

BLUE ACES
(see also Riot Squad)
64 Pye 7N 15672 Land Of Love/Love Song Of The Waterfall 10
64 Pye 7N 15713 I Beat You To It/I Just Can't Help Loving You 10
65 Pye 7N 15821 Ain't What You Say/You Don't Care 12
65 Columbia DB 7755 Tell Me What You're Gonna Do/All I Want 100
66 Columbia DB 7954 That's All Right/Talk About My Baby 170

BLUE ANCHOR
79 Workhouse WHR 6 PLENTY LOVE & BACON (LP) 15

BLUE & FERRIS
68 Blue Cat BS 147 You Stole My Money/Tell Me The Reason 40

BLUE ANGEL
(see also Cyndi Lauper)
80 Polydor POSP 212 I'm Gonna Be Strong/Anna Blue (no p/s) 6
81 Polydor POSP 241 I Had A Love/Can't Blame Me 8
84 Polydor POSP 212 I'm Gonna Be Strong/Anna Blue (p/s, reissue) 8
80 Polydor 2391 486 BLUE ANGEL (LP) 25

BLUE AQUARIUS
73 Akashic 998 The Ultimate Train/At The Feet Of The Master 20

BLUE ARSED FLY
(see also Christian Vogel, Neil Landstrumm)
95 Ferox FER 012 IN THE BAG EP (12") 15
96 Mosquito MSQ 04 BLUE ARSED FLY EP (12") 20

BLUE BEARD
71 Ember EMB S 302 Country Man/Sly Willy (in p/s) 30
71 Ember EMB S 302 Country Man/Sly Willy (no p/s) 20
71 Ember LT 7004 BLUE BEARD (LP, unreleased, test pressings only) 200

BLUEBEATERS
64 Piccadilly 7N 35181 Little David/Ain't Got A Care 10
64 Piccadilly 7N 35191 Early In The Morning/There I Go 8

BLUE BEATS
60 Blue Beat 45/BB 20 Baby What You Done Me Wrong/Go Pretty Baby Go 12

BLUEBEATS
64 Ember EMB EP 4525 THE FABULOUS BLUEBEATS VOL. 1 (EP) 40
64 Ember EMB EP 4526 THE FABULOUS BLUEBEATS VOL. 2 (EP) 40

BLUE-BELLES
(see also Patti Labelle)
62 HMV POP 1029 I Sold My Heart To The Junkman/Itty Bitty Twist 25

BLUE BELLS & JAH BERRY
78 Burning Rockers BRD 001 Teacher Teach, Teach The Youth/Golden Rule (12") 30

BLUEBERRIES
66 Mercury MF 894 It's Gonna Work Out Fine/Please Don't Let Me Know 50

BLUE BLOOD
70 Sonet SNTF 615 BLUE BLOOD (LP) 25

BLUE BLUDD
87 Blud Donor no cat. No. LIQUOR 'N' POKER (EP) 20

BLUE CHEER
(see also Leigh Stephens, Group B)
68 Philips BF 1646 Summertime Blues/Out Of Focus 25
68 Philips BF 1684 Just A Little Bit/Gypsy Ball 12
68 Philips BF 1711 Feathers From Your Tree/Sun Cycle 12
69 Philips BF 1778 West Coast Child Of Sunshine/When It All Gets Old 15
71 Philips 6051 010 Pilot/Babaji 10
68 Philips BL 7839 VINCEBUS ERUPTUM (LP, mono) 60
68 Philips SBL 7839 VINCEBUS ERUPTUM (LP, stereo) 30
68 Philips SBL 7860 OUTSIDEINSIDE (LP, gatefold sleeve) 45
69 Philips SBL 7896 NEW! IMPROVED! (LP) 40
69 Philips 6336 001 BLUE CHEER (LP) 40
71 Philips 6336 004 B.C. #5 THE ORIGINAL HUMAN BEING (LP) 45

BLUE CHIPS
65 Pye 7N 15970 I'm On The Right Side/You're Good To Me 30
66 Pye 7N 17111 Some Kind Of Lovin'/I Know A Boy 45
66 Pye 7N 17155 Tell Her/Good Lovin' Never Hurt 30

BLUE DANUBE
80 EMI EMI 5070 You Are A Song (Du Bist Musik)/Let Me Hear That Song Again/Du Bist Musik 10

BLUE DIAMONDS
60 Decca F 21292 Ramona/All Of Me 5

MINT VALUE £

BLUE EPITAPH
(see also Magus)

74	Holyground HG 117	ODE (LP, 99 copies only)	400
91	Holyground HG 117	ODE (LP, reissue, folded gatefold sleeve)	25

BLUE EYES

91	Union Hall001	Pick Up The Mic On A Soul Tip/The Law (12")	40
93	Buback BTT 028	Straight From The UK (12")	10

BLUE FEATHER

81	Mercury MERX 109	Lets Funk Tonight/Its Love (12")	12

BLUE FLAMES
(see also Georgie Fame & Blue Flames)

63	R&B JB 114	J.A. Blues/Orange Street	50
63	R&B JB 126	Stop Right Here/Rik's Tune	50

BLUE GOOSE
(see also Badfinger, Curtis Knight & Zeus, MotÃ¶rhead)

75	Anchor ANC 1015	Loretta/Call On Me	5
75	Anchor ANCL 2005	BLUE GOOSE (LP)	15

BLUE HAZE

72	A&M AMS 891	Smoke Gets In Your Eyes/Anna Rosanna	5

BLUE JEANS
(see also Swinging Blue Jeans, Ray Ennis & Blue Jeans)

69	Columbia DB 8555	Hey Mrs. Housewife/Sandfly	50

BLUE MAXI
(see also Jean-Jacques Burnel & Dave Greenfield)

70	Major Minor MM 705	Here Comes Summer/Famous Last Words	8

BLUE MEN
(see also Joe Meek, Peter Jay & Blue Men, Rodd-Ken & Cavaliers)

60	Triumph RGXST 5000	I HEAR A NEW WORLD (PART ONE) (EP)	300
60	Triumph RGXST 5001	I HEAR A NEW WORLD (PART TWO) (EP, only sleeves exist, this price is for sleeve)	25
60	Triumph TRX ST 9000	I HEAR A NEW WORLD (LP, unreleased, white label demos only)	800

BLUE MINK

74	EMI EMC3021	FRUITY (LP)	12

BLUE MITCHELL

73	Mainstream MSL 1015	THE LAST TANGO = BLUES	18

BLUE MOVIES

79	ROK ROK 9	Mary Jane/THE NOISE: Criminal (company sleeve)	15

BLUE NILE

81	RSO RSO 84	I Love This Life/The Second Act (p/s)	25
84	Linn LKS 1	Stay/Saddle The Horses (white p/s)	8
84	Linn LKS 1-12	Stay/Saddle The Horses (12", white p/s)	8
84	Linn LKS 1	Stay (Remix)/Saddle The Horses (p/s)	5
84	Linn LKSD 1	Stay (Remix)/Saddle The Horses/Tinsel Town In The Rain/ Heatwave (Instrumental) (p/s, double pack)	8
84	Linn LKS 1-12	Stay (Extended Remix)/Saddle The Horses (12", p/s)	8
84	Linn LKS 2	Tinsel Town In The Rain/Heatwave (Instrumental) (p/s)	5
84	Linn LKS 2-12	Tinsel Town In The Rain (Extended)/Regret/Heatwave (Instrumental) (12", p/s)	8

BLUE NOTES

87	OGUN OG 532	BLUE NOTES FOR JOHNNY (LP)	20

BLUENOTES

60	Top Rank JAR 291	I Don't Know What It Is/You Can't Get Away From Love	12

BLUE ORCHIDS
(see also Nosebleeds, Fall)

81	Rough Trade RT 065	Disney Boys/The Flood (p/s)	5
81	Rough Trade RT 067	Work/The House That Faded Out (p/s)	5
82	Rough Trade RT 117T	AGENTS OF CHANGE (12" EP, in carrier bag)	8
84	Rough Trade ROUGH 37	GREATEST HITS (LP)	12

BLUE OX BABES
(see also Dexys midnight Runners)

88	Go! Discs GOLP 14	APPLES AND ORANGES (LP, unissued, test pressings only)	50
88	Go1 Discs ZGOLP 14	APPLES AND ORANGES (cassette, printed inlay, unreleased)	20

BLUE ÖYSTER CULT

76	CBS 4483	(Don't Fear) The Reaper/R U Ready 2 Rock	5
76	CBS 4483	(Don't Fear) The Reaper/Tattoo Vampire (promo with different B-side)	10
78	CBS 5689	Going Through The Motions/Searching For The Celine	5
78	CBS 12-6333	(Don't Fear) The Reaper/R U Ready 2 Rock (12")	8
79	CBS 7763	Mirrors/Lonely Teardrops (clear vinyl, foil p/s)	5
81	CBS A 1453	Burnin' For You/Heavy Metal (p/s)	5
73	CBS 64904	BLUE ÖYSTER CULT (LP)	12

BLUE PHANTOM

72	Kaleidoscope KAL 101	DISTORTIONS (LP, laminated front cover, yellow label)	200

BLUE RIDGE RANGERS
(see also John Fogerty, Creedence Clearwater Revival)

73	Fantasy FTC 105	Hearts Of Stone/Somewhere Listening For My Name	6
73	Fantasy FTC 110	You Don't Own Me/Back In The Hills	6
73	Fantasy FT 511	BLUE RIDGE RANGERS (LP)	18

MINT VALUE £

BLUES BAND

(see also Paul Jones, McGuinness-Flint, Manfred Mann)

80	Blues Band BBBP 101	OFFICIAL BOOTLEG ALBUM (LP, numbered, with autographs, 3000 only)	18

BLUES BENDERS

66	Rio R93	Girl Next Door/Leave Me Out	25

BLUESBREAKERS

(see under John Mayall & Bluesbreakers)

BLUES BUSTERS

59	Limbo XL101	Little Vilma/ Early One Morning	20
61	Starlite ST45 031	The Spiritual/ Lost My Baby	25
61	Blue Beat BB55	Donna/ You're Driving Me Crazy	18
62	Blue Beat BB73	There's Always Sunshine/ You Had It Wrong	15
62	Starlite ST45 072	Your Love/ You Send Me Crazy	25
62	Island WI-023	Behold/ Oh Baby	20
62	Blue Beat BB102	Tell Me Why/ I've Done You Wrong	20
65	Island WI-214	How Sweet It Is/ I Had A Dream	40
65	Island WI-219	Wide Awake In A Dream (actually by Philip James solo)/ MAYTALS: Tell Me The Reason	100
65	Island WI-222	Wings Of A Dove/ BYRON LEE & DRAGONAIRES: Dan Is The Man	25
66	Doctor Bird DB1030	I've Been Trying/ Pretty Girls	40
67	Doctor Bird DB 1078	There's Always Sunshine/ Lovers' Reward	25
71	Dynamic DYN408	Each One Teach One/ Thinking Of You	5
71	Jay Boy BOY 44	I Can't Stop/Inspired To Love You	10
71	Trojan TR7819	Thinking Of You/ Version	5
65	Island ILP-923	BEHOLD! (LP)	60
67	Docto Bird DLM5008	BEST OF THE BLUES BUSTERS (LP)	50
78	Sarge LP1001	TRUTH (LP)	12
78	Sarge LP1003	TRIBUTE TO SAM COOKE (LP)	15
76	Dynamic DYLP 3007	PHILLIP & LLOYD (LP)	20

BLUES BY FIVE

64	Decca F 12029	Boom Boom/I Cried	100

BLUES COUNCIL

65	Parlophone R 5264	Baby Don't Look Down/What Will I Do	100

BLUES 5

64	Studio 36 (no cat. no.)	Hey Baby/When You're In Love	150

BLUES IMAGE

70	Atlantic 2091 009	Ride Captain Ride/Pay My Dues	5

BLUES INCORPORATED

(see under Alexis Korner)

BLUE SKIES

70	Fontana 6007026	Happy/Nightingale	12

BLUES MAGOOS

66	Mercury MF 954	(We Ain't Got) Nothin' Yet/Gotta Get Away	25
67	Fontana TF 848	One By One/Love Seems Doomed	15
71	Probe PRO 522	Can't Get Enough Of You/Sea Breeze Express	5
66	Fontana TL 5402	BLUES MAGOOS (LP, mono)	60
66	Fontana STL 5402	BLUES MAGOOS (LP, stereo)	45
71	Probe SPB 1024	GULF COAST BOUND (LP)	20

BLUESOLOGY

(see also Stu Brown & Bluesology, Elton John, Long John Baldry, Elton Dean, Mark Charig)

65	Fontana TF 594	Come Back Baby/Time's Getting Tougher Than Tough	300
66	Fontana TF 668	Mister Frantic/Everyday (I Have The Blues)	300

BLUES PROJECT

(see also Al Kooper, Tommy Flanders, Seatrain)

67	Verve Forecast VS 1505	I Can't Keep From Crying/The Way My Baby Walks	35
67	Verve (S)VLP 6004	PROJECTIONS (LP)	30

BLUE STARS

65	Decca F 12303	Please Be A Little Kind/I Can Take It	200

BLUE STEAM

78	Rip Off RIP 5	Lizard King/Cortina Cowboys (p/s)	10

BLUE SYSTEM

90	RCA PD 43734	Magic Symphony (7" Mix)/Magic Symphony (Fun Mix)/ Magic Symphony (Power Mix) (CD)	20

BLUETONES

95	Superior Quality TONE 001	Slight Return/The Fountainhead (blue vinyl, plain white sleeve in stickered polythene bag, 2,000 only sold by mail-order or at gigs, some numbered)	8
95	Superior Quality TONE 001	Slight Return/The Fountainhead (red vinyl, foldover p/s in poly bag, 1,000 only, export issue to Japan)	10
96	Superior Qual. BLUE 003X	Slight Return/Don't Stand Me Down (red vinyl, export issue to Japan with Japanese text on rear of p/s)	8

BLUE U

72	York SYK 524	I've Been Looking For So Long/Melinda Marie	10

BLUE VELVET BAND

69	Warner Bros WS 1802	SWEET MOMENTS WITH THE BLUE VELVET BAND (LP, gatefold sleeve)	18

BLUEWATER FOLK

70s	Folk Heritage	BLUEWATER FOLK (LP)	40
70s	Moonraker MOO 1	BUGS, BLACK PUDDINGS AND CLOGS (LP, with insert)	12
70s	Moonraker MOO 2	A LANCASHIRE LIFE (LP, with insert)	12

MINT VALUE £

BLUE YOGURT

70	Penny Farthing PEN 732	Lydia/Umbrella Man	12

COLIN BLUNSTONE

(see also Zombies, Neil MacArthur, Mitchell-Coe Mysteries)

71	Epic EPC 7095	Mary, Won't You Warm My Bed/I Hope I Didn't Say Too Much Last Night	5
71	Epic EPC 7520	Caroline Goodbye/Though You Are Far Away	5
72	Epic EPC 7765	Say You Don't Mind/Let Me Come Closer (p/s)	5
72	Epic EPC 8434	I Don't Believe In Miracles/I've Always Had You	5
73	Epic EPC 1197	How Could We Dare To Be Wrong?/Time's Runnin' Out	5
73	Epic EPC 1775	Wonderful/Beginning	5
74	Epic EPC 2413	It's Magical/Summersong	5
71	Epic EPC 64557	ONE YEAR (LP, textured sleeve)	15
72	Epic EPC 65278	ENNISMORE (LP, textured sleeve)	15

BLUNT INSTRUMENT

78	Diesel DCL 01	No Excuse/Interrogation (p/s)	8

BLUR

(see also Graham Coxon, Gorillaz, Damon Albarn)

90	Food FOOD 26	She's So High (Edit)/I Know (7", p/s)	6
90	Food 12FOOD 26	She's So High (Definitive)/Sing/I Know (Extended) (12", p/s)	12
90	Food CDFOOD 26	She's So High/I Know (Extended)/Down (CD)	20
91	Food FOOD 29	There's No Other Way/Inertia (p/s)	8
91	Food 12FOOD 29	There's No Other Way (Extended)/Inertia/Mr. Briggs/I'm All Over (12", p/s)	15
91	Food 12 FOODX 29	There's No Other Way (The Blur Remix)/Won't Do It/Day Upon Day (live) (12", p/s lists '12 FOODDX 29')	30
91	Food CDFOOD 29	There's No Other Way/Inertia/Mr. Briggs/I'm All Over (CD)	20
91	Food FOOD 31	Bang/Luminous (p/s)	6
91	Food FOOD 31	Bang (Extended)/Explain/Luminous/Uncle Love (12", p/s)	10
91	Food CDFOOD 31	Bang/Explain/Luminous/Beserk (CD)	20
92	Food FOOD 37	Popscene/Mace (p/s)	10
92	Food 12FOOD 37	Popscene/I'm Fine/Mace/Garden Central (12", p/s)	20
92	Food CDFOOD 37	Popscene/Mace/Badgeman Brown (CD)	15
92	Food TCFOOD 37	Popscene/Mace (cassette)	5
92	Food BLUR 6	The Wassailing Song (1-sided 7" gig freebie, no p/s, 500 only)	150
92	Food 12FOOD 40	For Tomorrow (Visit To Primrose Hill Extended)/ Into Another/ Hanging Over/Peach (12", p/s)	10
92	Food CDFOOD 40	For Tomorrow (Visit To Primrose Hill Extended)/Peach/Bone Bag (CD, double jewel case)	10
92	Food CDSFOOD 40	For Tomorrow (Single Version)/When The Cows Come Home/ Beachcoma/For Tomorrow (Acoustic Version) (CD)	10
92	Food TCFOOD 40	For Tomorrow/Into Another/Hanging Over (cassette)	5
93	Food FOODS 45	Chemical World/Maggie May (7" red vinyl, paper labels, p/s)	10
93	Food 12FOOD 45	Chemical World/Es Schmecht/Young And Lovely/My Ark (12", p/s with print)	10
93	Food CDFOODS 45	Chemical World (Reworked)/Never Clever (live)/Pressure On Julian (live)/ Come Together (live) (CD, double jewel case)	10
93	Food CDFOOD 45	Chemical World/Young And Lovely/Es Schmecht/My Ark (CD)	10
93	Food FOODS 46	Sunday Sunday/Tell Me, Tell Me (B-side as "Blur featuring Seymour") (yellow vinyl 7", p/s)	10
93	Food 12FOODS 46	Sunday Sunday/Long Legged/Mixed Up (B-sides as 'Blur featuring Seymour') (12", p/s with print)	10
93	Food CDFOOD 46	Sunday Sunday/Dizzy/Fried/Shimmer (CD, final 3 tracks as B-sides as 'Blur featuring Seymour')	10
93	Food CDFOODX 46	THE SUNDAY SUNDAY POPULAR COMMUNITY SONG CD (Sunday Sunday/Daisy Bell/Let's All Go Down The Strand)	10
94	Food FOODS 47	Girls And Boys/Magpie/People In Europe (7" p/s, numbered)	5
94	Food CDFOOD 50	To The End/Girls And Boys (Pet Shop Boys 7" Remix)/Girls And Boys (Pet Shop Boys 12" Remix) (CD, slimline jewel case)	10
96	Fan Club DEATH 1	Death Of A Party (demo) (CD, 1-track, card p/s, fan club issue, 3250 only)	25
97	Fan Club LOVE 001	I Love Her (CD, card p/s, fan club issue, 3,500 only)	25
99	Fan Club SING 001	Sing (To Me) as 'Blur featuring Seymour') (CD, card p/s, fan club issue)	25
99	Food BLURBOX 10	THE 10 YEAR ANNIVERSARY BOX SET (22xCD singles)	60
02	no label no cat. no.	(red label, bearing Arabic writing which translates as "Don't bomb when you are the bomb"; large centre hole; 1,000 7" were pressed, but many were blown up)	80
02	Fan Club WONT001	B-Sided Gig EP (I'm Fone/Bone Bag/No Monsters/Young & Lovely) (CD, card p/s fan club issue)	25
03	Fan Club COLOURS 01	Colours (CD, card p/s, fan club issue)	25
05	Fan Club SGLAD 01	Some Glad Morning (CD, card wallet, fan club issue)	20
10	Parlophone LCO 3098	Fools Day (1-sided 7", jukebox centre, blue Parlophone sleeve, 1000 only)	30

LPs

91	Food FOODLP 6	LEISURE (LP)	30
93	Food FOODLP 9	MODERN LIFE IS RUBBISH (LP, with inner)	25
94	Food FOODLP 10	PARKLIFE (LP, with inner)	40
95	Food FOODLP 14	THE GREAT ESCAPE (LP, with inner)	25
97	Food CFOODLP19	BLUR (LP)	30
99	Food FOODLP29	13 (2-LP, stickered, gatefold, with inner sleeves)	30
00	Food FOODLPD 33	THE BEST OF (2-LP)	50

PROMOS

90	no cat. no.	Bad Day/Bad Day (version) (white label)	30
91	Food 12BLUR 4	High Cool (Easy Listening Mix)/Bad Day (Leisurely Mix) (12", blue & gold company sleeve, promo, 1,000 only)	15
92	Food 12BLUR5	Popscene (1-sided promo 12" in die cut company sleeve. 1000 only)	20
93	Food 12FOODDJ 40	For Tomorrow (Visit to Primrose Hill extended version/Into Another/ Hanging Over (12" in company die cut sleeve)	15
94	Food CD5 BET BET BET	Girls and Boys/Jubilee/Trouble In The Message Centre/Lot 105 (Live CD promo produced for Mark Radcliffe show)	20

MINT VALUE £

95	Food CDFOODDJ 59	This Is A Low (CD, promo only, plain card sleeve with set of 4 stamps)	15
95	Food 12FOODDJ 69	The Universal/Entertain Me (The Live It! Remix) (12" promo only, die-cut p/s)	10
95	Food 12FOODDJ 63	Country House (12", promo only, 1-sided, die-cut p/s)	10
97	Food 12BLURDJ 7	On Your Own (Crouch End Broadway Mix) (12", 1-sided, promo only)	10
97	Food CDIN 106	BLURB (CD, interview, promo only)	15
97	Food CDFOODDJ 109	Death Of A Party (7" Remix)/(Well Blurred Remix)/(Billy Whiskers Mix)/ (Album Version) (CD, promo only, card p/s)	8
99	Food FOOD CDJX 29	13 (CD in duffelbag with folder, photos, ski-hat and biography, promo only)	50
99	Food 10FOODDJ 117	Tender (10" promo record plays inside to out, foil sealed)	12
99	Food CD FOOD DJ 117	Tender (LP Version)/(Radio Edit) (CD, silver foil pack, promo only)	8
99	Food No Cat No	15ON13 (Interview CD, p/s)	10
00	Food 10FOODDJ 135	Music Is My Radar (12" one-sided w/10" cat. No., white die cut sleeve, stamped label)	10
03	Parlophone THINK 3	Crazy Beat/Brothers And Sisters/Moroccan Peoples Revolutionary Bowls Club/ Gene By Gene (12" sampler, white die-cut sleeve, stamped labels)	10
03	Parlophone THINK1	THINK TANK (CD Promo in card wallet with unique Banksy artwork)	15
03	Parlophone THINK4	THINK TANK INTERVIEW CD (CD in promo p/s, track by track 52 min interview)	18

BLURT

80	Test Pressing TP 1	My Mother Was A Friend Of An Enemy Of The People/Get (p/s)	5
81	Armageddon AS 013	The Fish Needs A Bike/This Is My Royal Wedding Souvenir (p/s)	5

BLUSH

79	Venal Vinyl PMB 117	Everyday/Before We Came Together (no p/s, 200 only)	150

HENRY BLYTHE

56	Oriole MG 20009	AN INVESTIGATION INTO REINCARNATION (LP)	12

JIMMY BLYTHE

54	London AL 3527	SOUTH SIDE BLUE PIANO (10" LP)	15
54	London AL 3529	SOUTH SIDE CHICAGO JAZZ (10" LP)	15

ENID BLYTON

57	HMV 7EG 8260	NODDY STORIES (EP)	8

B-MOVIE

80	Dead Good DEAD 9	TAKE THREE (EP)	20
80	Dead Good BIG DEAD 12	NOWHERE GIRL (12" EP, with insert, 800 only)	20
81	Deram DM 443	Marilyn Dreams/Film Music (Part 1) (p/s)	5
81	Deram DMX 443	Marilyn Dreams/Film Music (Part 1) (12", p/s)	8
88	Wax 12 WAX 3	Nowhere Girl/Remembrance Day (12", p/s, 250 on orange vinyl, numbered)	10
88	Wax 12 WAX 3	Nowhere Girl/Remembrance Day (12", p/s, pink vinyl, numbered)	10
88	Wax 12 WAX 3	Nowhere Girl/Remembrance Day (12", p/s, black vinyl, numbered)	7
88	Wax 12 WAX 4	Polar Opposites/Taxi Driver (12", clear vinyl or picture disc)	8
88	Wax CD WAX 4	Polar Opposites/Taxi Driver (CD)	15
88	Wax WAXLP 1P	THE DEAD GOOD TAPES (LP, picture disc)	12
91	Dead Good GOOD 3	REMEMBRANCE DAYS (LP, with 7" "The Fool"/"Swinging Lights" [CHEAP 1])	12

BMX BANDITS

(see also Soup Dragons, Boy Hairdressers, Teenage Fanclub, Vaselines)

86	53rd & 3rd AGARR 3	Sad?/E102 (p/s, with comic)	10
87	53rd & 3rd AGARR 6	What A Wonderful World/The Day Before Tomorrow (p/s)	6
87	53rd & 3rd AGARR 612	What A Wonderful World/The Day Before Tomorrow/ Johnny Alucard/Sad?/Sandy's Wallet (12", p/s)	8

EDDIE BO

73	Action ACT 4609	Check Your Bucket Parts 1 & 2	30

BO & PEEP

(see also Andrew Oldham Orchestra)

64	Decca F 11968	Young Love/The Rise Of The Brighton Surf	50

HARRY BOARDMAN & DAVE HILLERY

71	Topic 12TS 215	TRANS PENNINE (LP)	15

BOARDS OF CANADA

94	Music 70 THS 012	HOOPER'S BAY (12" EP)	100
94	Music 70 THS 012	HOOPER'S BAY (cassette EP)	25
96	Skam SKA 008	Hi Scores/Turquoise Hexagon Sun/Nlagon/June 9th/ See Ya Later/Everything You Do Is A Balloon (12", p/s)	10
98	Skam KMAS 1	Aquarius/Chinook (p/s, with insert, 500 only)	60
00	Warp Records WAP 144	In A Beautiful Place Out In The Country (12", EP)	20
05	Skam Ska 008	Hi Scores (12" reissue in brail embossed sleeve)	8
95	Music 70 BOARD 1	2ISM (LP, 100 copies only)	400
95	Music 70 BOARD 1	2ISM (Cassette, 100 copies only)	100
98	Warp Records WARP LP 55 P	MUSIC HAS THE RIGHT TO CHILDREN (10", Promo)	40
98	Warp Records, Skam WARP LP 55, SKALP001	MUSIC HAS THE RIGHT TO CHILDREN (2xLP)	50
02	Warp	GEOGADDI (LP, blue vinyl test pressing - etched - 10 only)	200
02	Warp/Music 70	GEOGADDI (3-LP)	45

BOARDWALKERS

(see also Warren Davis)

s	own label J.C. 1	A Miracle/Any Man's Girl	200

BOATMEN

s	Sweet Folk SFA 018	STRAIGHT FROM THE TUNNEL'S MOUTH (LP)	50

BOBALOUIS

81	WEA K18441	Not A Second Chance/City Boys	25

BOB & CAROL

67	CBS 2738	On My Life/Mary Jane	8

MINT VALUE £

BOB (Relf) & EARL (Nelson)
(see also Bob Relf, Jackie Lee, Earl Nelson, Hollywood Flames)

65	Sue WI 374	Harlem Shuffle/I'll Keep Running Back	20
65	Sue WI 393	Baby I'm Satisfied/The Sissy	40
67	Sue WI 4030	Don't Ever Leave Me/Fancy Free	50
69	Island WI 6053	Harlem Shuffle/I'll Keep Running Back (reissue)	5
69	B&C CB 102	Dancin' Everywhere/Baby It's Over	5
69	Warner Bros WB 6059	Everybody Jerk/He's A Playbrother	40
70	Uni UN 519	Pickin' Up Love's Vibrations/Uh, Uh, Naw Naw Naw	5
72	Jay Boy BOY 72	I Can't Get Away/I'll Keep Running Back	15
72	Jay Boy BOY 73	My Little Girl/His & Her Shuffle (as Bob & Earl Band)	15
73	Contempo C 4	Harlem Shuffle/Harlem Shuffle (Instrumental Version)	5
67	Sue ILP 951	HARLEM SHUFFLE (LP)	120
69	Joy JOYS 199	TOGETHER (LP)	15

BOB & JERRY

58	Pye International 7N 25003	Ghost Satellite/Nothin'	20
58	Pye International 7N 25003	Ghost Satellite/Nothin' (78)	15
61	Philips PB 1205	Dreamy Eyes/We're The Guys	10

BOB (Andy) & MARCIA (Griffiths)
(see also Bob Andy, Marcia Griffiths)

70	Bamboo BAM 40	Always Together/BOB ANDY: Desperate Lover	20
70	Harry J. HJ 6605	Young, Gifted And Black/JAY BOYS: Young, Gifted & Black (Instrumental)	6
70	Escort ES 824	Young, Gifted And Black/BARRINGTON BIGGS: My Cheri Amour	12
71	Trojan TR 7818	Pied Piper/Save Me	5
72	Trojan TR 7854	But I Do/I Don't Care	5
70	Trojan TBL 122	YOUNG, GIFTED & BLACK (LP)	20
72	Trojan TRLS 26	PIED PIPER (LP)	15

BOB (ANDY) & TIE (TYRONE EVANS)

69	Coxsone CS 7086	I Don't Care/LASCELLES PERKINS: Little Green Apples	45

BOB(B)ETTES

57	London HLE 8477	Mr. Lee/Look At The Stars	80
57	London HLE 8477	Mr. Lee/Look At The Stars (78)	20
58	London HLE 8597	Come-A Come-A/Speedy	75
58	London HLE 8597	Come-A Come-A/Speedy (78)	20
60	London HLE 9173	I Shot Mr. Lee/Untrue Love	60
60	London HLE 9248	Have Mercy Baby/Dance With Me Georgie	40
60	Pye International 7N 25060	I Shot Mr. Lee/Billy (as Bobettes)	40
72	Action ACT 4603	That's A Bad Thing To Know/All In Your Mind	15
81	Revival 6008	Mr. Lee/I Shot Mr. Lee	5

BOBBIE & VERA

69	Decca F 12897	I Know That He Knows/City Of Dreams	5

BOBBSEY TWINS

57	London HLA 8474	A Change Of Heart/Part-Time Gal	40

BOBBY & DAVE
(see also Dave Barker, Lizzy & Dennis)

71	Ackee ACK 116	Build My World Around You/LIZZY & TONY BOP: Sammy Version	15

BOBBY & JIM

58	Capitol CL 14877	Carry My Books/A Lover Can Tell	10

BOBBY & LAURIE

66	Parlophone R 5480	Hitch Hiker/You'll Come 'Round	20

BOBBY & MIDNITES
(see also Bob Weir, Grateful Dead)

84	CBS 26046	WHERE THE BEAT MEETS THE STREET (LP)	25

BOBBY (ELLIS) & TOMMY (McCOOK)

74	Attack ATLP 1004	GREEN MANGO (LP)	35

BOBCATS

67	Pye 7N 17242	Can't See For Looking/Let Me Get By	15

BOBO MR. SOUL

73	London HLU 10418	Hitch Hiking To Heartbreak/She's My Woman	5

WILLIE BOBO

66	Verve VS 548	Sunshine Super Man/Sockit To Me	12
66	Verve SVLP9134	ELATION (LP)	20
71	A&M AMLS 68034	DO WHAT YOU WANT TO DO (LP)	25

FRIDA BOCCARA

69	Philips BF 1765	Through The Eyes Of A Child/So Fair	15

BOCKY & VISIONS

65	Atlantic AT 4049	I Go Crazy/Good Good Lovin'	40

BODAST
(see also Steve Howe, Tomorrow)

81	Cherry Red BRED 12	THE BODAST TAPES FEATURING STEVE HOWE (LP)	12

J.P. BODDY

73	Columbia DB 89789	Stop Me Spinning (Like A Spinning Top)/Song Without A Word	5

BODGER'S MATE

78	Cottage COT 521	BRIGHTER THAN USUAL (LP)	20

BODIES

79	Waldo's HS 007	Art Nouveau/Machinery (poster p/s, 5 different colours)	5

MINT VALUE £

BODKIN

72 West CSA 104 — BODKIN (LP, private pressing, red label some in posthumously-designed sleeve) ... 800

BODY

81 Recession — THE BODY ALBUM (LP, private pressing with booklet) ... 50

BODY AND SOUL

70 Penny Farthing PEN 720 — Here Comes That Feeling/Go Back To School ... 6

BODYSNATCHERS

80 2-Tone CHS TT 9 — Let's Do Rocksteady/Ruder Than You (paper label, company sleeve) ... 10
80 2-Tone CHS TT 12 — Easy Life/Too Experienced (paper label, company sleeve) ... 10

BODYSNATCHERS

(see also Icepick)

97 Backbone (NO Cat. N0) — GENOCIDE (EP, 30 test copies) ... 400

BOEING DUVEEN & BEAUTIFUL SOUP

68 Parlophone R 5696 — Jabberwock/Which Dreamed It (demos with p/s) ... 200
68 Parlophone R 5696 — Jabberwock/Which Dreamed It (demos without p/s) ... 100

BOFFALONGO

70 United Artists UP 35144 — Dancing In The Moonlight/Endless Questions ... 7
71 United Artists UAG 29130 — BEYOND YOUR HEAD (LP) ... 18

DIRK BOGARDE

65 Fontana TF 615 — Darling/MOVIE SOUNDS: Pavanne For Diane ... 8
60 Decca LK 4373 — LYRICS FOR LOVERS (LP) ... 15

BOGAZ

83 AGR 12 AGR 2 — I've Got Love/I've Got Love (Instrumental) (12") ... 25

BOGDON

(see also Whitesnake, Bernie Marsden)

81 Black Label GB 3 — Oh Eddie/Reet Petite (p/s) ... 10
81 Brilliant HIT 1 — Who Do You Think You Are?/Take Me Back (p/s) ... 10

BOGIES

64 private press (no cat. no.) — THE BOGIES ON CAMPUS (LP) ... 150
64 private press (no cat. no.) — BYE BYE BOGIES (LP) ... 150

ERIC BOGLE

77 Autogram ALLP 211 — LIVE IN PERSON (LP) ... 35
81 Plant Life PLR 033 — PLAIN AND SIMPLE (LP) ... 15
83 Plant Life PLR 046 — SCRAPS OF PAPER (LP) ... 15
85 Topic 12TS 437 — WHEN THE WIND BLOWS (LP) ... 15
88 Plant Life PLR 042 — NOW I'M EASY (LP) ... 15

LEE BOGLE

71 Black Swan BW 1406 — Tomorrow's Dreams/SWANS: Hot Pants Reggae ... 8

BOGUS ORDER

90 Ninja Tune ZEN 01 — ZEB BRAKES (LP) ... 25

BUDDY BOHN

71 Regal Zonophone RX 3040 — Piccalilli Lady/Summer Song ... 10
71 Purple TPSA 7503 — A DROP IN THE OCEAN (LP, gatefold sleeve) ... 30

HOUSTON BOINES

66 Blue Horizon 45 BH 1006 — Superintendent Blues/Monkey Motion (99 copies only, Ike Turner on piano) ... 150

BOLA

95 Skam SKA 5 — Forcasa 3/Krak Jakomo/Metalurg 2/Ballom (12", custom sleeve) ... 50
98 Skam KMAS002 — KS (500 pressed) ... 30
00 33 33Shapes — SHAPES (LP, 3x12") ... 35
01 Skam KMAS 007 — Pae Paoe (1,000 pressed) ... 5

MARC BOLAN

(see also Marc Bolan/T. Rex, Marc Bolan & Gloria Jones, Toby Tyler, John's Children, Big Carrot, Dib Cochran & The Earwigs)

65 Decca F 12288 — The Wizard/Beyond The Rising Sun (some as "Marc Bölan") ... 500
65 Decca F 12288 — The Wizard/Beyond The Rising Sun (demo copy) ... 350
66 Decca F 12413 — The Third Degree/San Francisco Poet ... 500
66 Decca F 12413 — The Third Degree/San Francisco Poet (demo copy) ... 350
66 Parlophone R 5539 — Hippy Gumbo/Misfit ... 650
66 Parlophone R 5539 — Hippy Gumbo/Misfit (demo copy) ... 400
72 Track 2094 013 — Jasper C. Debussy/Hippy Gumbo/The Perfumed Garden Of Gulliver Smith (p/s, withdrawn) ... 50
72 Track 2094 013 — Jasper C. Debussy/Hippy Gumbo/The Perfumed Garden Of Gulliver Smith (white label demo) ... 50
81 Rarn MBFS 001C — Sing Me A Song/Endless Sleep (Extended Version)/The Lilac Hand Of Menthol Dan (12", no p/s, clear vinyl, handwritten labels) ... 10
81 Rarn MBFS 001P — Sing Me A Song/Endless Sleep (Extended Version)/The Lilac Hand Of Menthol Dan (12" picture disc, misprinted with black rim) ... 15
81 Rarn MBFS 001P — Sing Me A Song/Endless Sleep (Extended Version)/The Lilac Hand Of Menthol Dan (12" picture disc, misprinted with white rim) ... 7
81 Rarn MBFS 001P — Sing Me A Song/Endless Sleep (Extended Version)/The Lilac Hand Of Menthol Dan (12", picture disc misprinted back-to-front) ... 15
81 Cherry Red CHERRY 29 — You Scare Me To Death/The Perfumed Garden Of Gulliver Smith (initial copies with bronze label, glossy p/s & free flexidisc [Lyntone LYN 10086]) ... 10
81 Cherry Red CHERRY 29 — You Scare Me To Death/The Perfumed Garden Of Gulliver Smith (later pressing with silver label/matt p/s) ... 5
81 Cherry Red CHERRY 32 — Cat Black/Jasper C. Debussy (p/s) ... 5
82 Cherry Red CHERRY 39 — The Wizard/Beyond The Rising Sun/Rings Of Fortune (p/s) ... 5

			MINT VALUE £
72	Track 2406 101	HARD ON LOVE (LP, unreleased, white label test pressing, 2 copies only)	800
72	Track 2406 009	HARD ON LOVE (LP, unreleased, 2-sided EMIdisc acetate with "swearing intro")	2250
74	Track 2410 201	THE BEGINNING OF DOVES (LP, laminated sleeve, black/silver label)	35
81	Cherry Red PERED 20	YOU SCARE ME TO DEATH (LP, picture disc)	15
81	Cherry Red ERED 20	YOU SCARE ME TO DEATH (LP, gatefold sleeve; early copies with booklet stapled into sleeve; later copies with loose booklet)	12
89	Media Motion MEDIA 2	THE BEGINNING OF DOVES (LP, reissue, 750 only, withdrawn)	25
96	Edsel FBOOK 17	A WIZARD, A TRUE STAR (3-CD Box set)	25

MARC BOLAN & GLORIA JONES

(see also Gloria Jones)

77	EMI EMI 2572	To Know You Is To Love You/City Port	10

MARC BOLAN/T. REX

(see also Marc Bolan, Tyrannosaurus Rex, Dib Cochran & the Earwigs, John's Children, Big Carrot)

SINGLES

70	Octopus OCTO 1	Ride A White Swan/Summertime Blues/Jewel (unreleased, handwritten white label, 2/3 test pressings only)	2500
70	Fly BUG 1	Ride A White Swan/Is It Love/Summertime Blues (p/s, purple labels)	20
70	Fly BUG 1	Ride A White Swan/Is It Love/Summertime Blues (p/s, later pressing with mustard labels)	7
71	Fly	Hot Love/Woodland Rock/King Of The Mountain Cometh (IBC Sound Recordings Studios acetate)	280
71	Fly BUG 6	Hot Love/Woodland Rock/King Of The Mountain Cometh (mustard labels)	10
71	Fly BUG 6	Hot Love/Woodland Rock/King Of The Mountain Cometh (mustard labels, later pressing with 'fly' design)	5
71	Fly BUG 10	Get It On/There Was A Time/Raw Ramp (p/s, black label with silver 'fly' logo)	15
s	Fly BUG 10	Get It On/There Was A Time/Raw Ramp (p/s, black label with white 'fly' or later silver 'fly' text)	6
71	Fly GRUB 1	Electric Warrior Preview Single: Jeepster/Life's A Gas (gig freebie, in pink envelope sleeve)	200
71	Fly GRUB 1	Electric Warrior Preview Single: Jeepster/Life's A Gas (gig freebie, originally in pink envelope sleeve, this price is for later standard paper sleeve)	145
71	Fly BUG 16	Jeepster/Life's A Gas (white 'fly' label)	5
71	Fly BUG 16	Jeepster/Life's A Gas (scarce issue w/out 'GRUB 1A' ref.)	6
72	EMI T REX 101	Telegram Sam/Cadillac/Baby Strange	6
72	Magni Fly ECHO 102	One Inch Rock/The Woodland Bop/The Throat Of Winter (unreleased, rejected 1-sided test pressing for B-side of "Deborah"/"One Inch Rock", stamped white label)	150
72	Magni Fly ECHO 102	Debora/One Inch Rock/The Woodland Bop/Seal Of Seasons (p/s)	6
72	EMI MARC X	Metal Guru (rejected 1-sided test pressing with Marc's annotation 'bad cut')	300
72	EMI MARC 1	Metal Guru/Thunderwing/Lady	6
72	EMI MARC 2	Children Of The Revolution/Jitterbug Love/Sunken Rags	6
72	EMI MARC 3	Solid Gold Easy Action/(5th Dimension track) (mispressing)	15
72	EMI MARC 3	Solid Gold Easy Action/(Partridge Family track) (mispressing)	15
72	EMI SPRS 346	Chariot Choogle/The Slider (promo only, 'T. Rex' picture label)	425
72	EMI SPRS 346	Chariot Choogle/The Slider (promo only, white label)	375
72	Lyntone	Christmas Time/Wanna Spend My Christmas With You/Christmas/Everybody Knows It's Christmas (fan club flexi, with letter in brown envelope)	45
72	Lyntone	Christmas Time/Wanna Spend My Christmas With You/ Christmas/Everybody Knows It's Christmas (fan club flexi, without letter in brown envelope)	30
73	EMI MARC 5	The Groover/Midnight	6
73	EMI MARC 6	Truck On (Tyke)/Sitting Here	6
74	EMI MARC 7	Teenage Dream/Satisfaction Pony (credited to 'Marc Bolan & T. Rex')	6
74	EMI MARC 7	Teenage Dream/Satisfaction Pony (credited to 'Marc Bolan')	5
74	EMI MARC 8	Light Of Love/Explosive Mouth	6
74	EMI MARC 9	Zip Gun Boogie/Space Boss	6
75	EMI MARC 10	New York City/Chrome Sitar	6
75	EMI MARC 11	Dreamy Lady/Do You Wanna Dance?/Dock Of The Bay (as T. Rex Disco Party)	6
75	EMI MARC 12	Christmas Bop/Telegram Sam/Metal Guru (unreleased, A- & B-side paper labels exist, 2 sets only this price is for the labels)	1250
76	EMI MARC 13	London Boys/Solid Baby	6
76	Cube BUG 66	Hot Love/Get It On	6
76	EMI MARC 14	I Love To Boogie/Baby Boomerang	6
76	EMI MARC 15	Laser Love/Life's An Elevator	6
77	EMI MARC 16	The Soul Of My Suit/All Alone	8
77	EMI MARC 17	Dandy In The Underworld/Groove A Little/Tame My Tiger (p/s)	10
77	EMI MARC 18	Celebrate Summer/Ride My Wheels (p/s)	10
78	EMI MARC 19	Crimson Moon/Jason B. Sad (p/s)	10
77	Cube ANT 1	BOLAN'S BEST PLUS ONE (EP, p/s)	8
78	Cube ANT 2	Hot Love/Raw Ramp/Lean Woman Blues (p/s, misprinted Raw Amp, sleeve credits 'Bolan', label credits 'T.Rex')	8
79	Cube ANTS 001	Life's A Gas/Find A Little Wood/Once Upon The Seas Of Abyssinia/ Blessed Wild Apple Girl (12", p/s)	12
81	Cube/Dakota	Christmas Jingle/Sailors Of The Highway (MBFS fan club flexidisc)	6
82	Marc ABOLAN 2	THE CHILDREN OF RARN (10" EP, p/s, 33rpm, gatefold sleeve with 12-page lyric book)	25
82	Marc SBOLAN 13	Mellow Love/Foxy Box/Lunacy's Back (p/s, blue vinyl, as Marc Bolan)	8
82	Rarn MBFS RAP 2	Deep Summer/Oh Baby/One Inch Rock (unreleased version) (12", p/s, blue vinyl)	10
83	Marc SBOLAN 12EP	CHRISTMAS BOP EP (12", p/s, OMBFS only, extra tracks: acoustic versions of "King Of The Rumbling Spires" & "Savage Beethoven")	10
83	Marc SBOLAN 14PD	Think Zinc/Till Dawn/Magical Moon (picture disc)	5
84	Marc On Wax SPS 1	Mister Motion (1-sided, from "Child Of The Revolution - 14 Greats" LP, p/s)	8
84	Cube BUG 99	Sailor Of The Highway/Do You Remember (7" in plain black sleeve)	15

			MINT VALUE £
84	Cube HBUG 99	RARE MAGIC (12" EP)	12
85	Cambra MAIN 1	(Whatever Happened To The) Teenage Dream (Ext.)/Solid Gold Segue (picture disc free with "Mainman" LP)	8
85	Marc PTANX 1	Megarex 1/Megarex 1 (shaped picture disc, with free plinth)	8
87	Strange Fruit SFPS 031	PEEL SESSIONS (12")	15
87	Marc MARCX 1	Children Of The Revolution (remix)/The Slider (remix)/ Tear For The High Star (tribute by Dave Ash-B) (shaped picture disc)	8
94	Edsel MBPROMO 1	T. REX (CD, picture disc, 4-track sampler, tri-fold digipak, promo only)	20
97	Edsel MARC 20-50	20th Century Boy/Carsmile Smith & The Old One/ All My Love/Dandy In The Underworld (CD, gig freebie)	20
07	Edsel BOLAN 1	Metal Guru/The Slider (Acoustic Demo) (Blue vinyl, numbered, 1,000 only)	15
07	Edsel BOLAN 2	Children Of The Revolution/The Leopards (Electric Demo) (Red vinyl, numbered, 1,000 only)	15
07	Edsel BOLAN 3	20th Century Boy/Teenager In Love (Marc & Gloria acoustic duet) (White vinyl, numbered, 1,000 only)	12
07	Edsel TREXMAS 1	Christmas Bop/The Xmas Riff/Xmas Flexi message (7", promo)	60

LPs

70	Fly HIFLY 2	T. REX (semi-gatefold sleeve, white label with 'Fly' logo)	40
71	Fly HIFLY 6	ELECTRIC WARRIOR (unreleased version with "Jeepster" on side 2, 1 test pressing copy only, with Marc's annotations on white sleeve)	700
71	Fly HIFLY 6	ELECTRIC WARRIOR (with poster & inner sleeve, stickered sleeve, white label with 'Fly' logo)	80
71	Fly HIFLY 6	ELECTRIC WARRIOR (with poster & inner sleeve, non-stickered sleeve, white label with 'Fly' logo)	40
72	Fly HIFLY 8	BOLAN BOOGIE (1-sided test pressing with "The Visit" instead of "Jewel")	375
72	Fly HIFLY 8	BOLAN BOOGIE	12
72	EMI BLN 5001	THE SLIDER (with lyric inner sleeve, sleeve with 'sniped' spine edges, flipbacks, blue/red T-Rex label)	30
73	EMI BLN 5002	TANX (with poster & inner sleeve)	20
73	EMI BLN 5003	GREAT HITS (with poster)	12
74	EMI BNLA 7751	ZINC ALLOY AND THE HIDDEN RIDERS OF TOMORROW (with 3-way numbered promo fold-out sleeve & inner, given as competition prize with letter from Pink or Mirabelle magazines, 1,000 only)	250
74	EMI BNLA 7751	ZINC ALLOY AND THE HIDDEN RIDERS OF TOMORROW (with 3-way promo fold-out sleeve & inner, without letter; numbered)	250
74	EMI BNLA 7751	ZINC ALLOY AND THE HIDDEN RIDERS OF TOMORROW (with 3-way promo fold-out sleeve & inner, without letter; unnumbered)	200
74	EMI BNLA 7751	ZINC ALLOY AND THE HIDDEN RIDERS OF TOMORROW (commercial gatefold sleeve with lyric inner sleeve)	18
75	EMI BNLA 7752	BOLAN'S ZIP GUN (diamond-cut laminated sleeve & inner sleeve, blue/red T-Rex label)	20
76	EMI BLNA 5004	FUTURISTIC DRAGON (with lyric inner sleeve)	20
77	EMI BLNA 5005	DANDY IN THE UNDERWORLD (with round-cut sleeve & lyric inner sleeve)	20
78	Cube HIFLD 1	MARC: THE WORDS AND MUSIC OF MARC BOLAN 1947-1977 (2-LP, gatefold sleeve, with free single [BINT 1])	18
81	Marc ABOLAN 1P	T. REX IN CONCERT (picture disc, 2 designs)	15
82	Cube/Dakota ICSX 1004	ACROSS THE AIRWAVES (picture disc)	12
82	Marc ABOLAN 3P	ELECTRIC WARRIOR (picture disc)	12
84	Marc ABOLAN 5	T. REXTASY (with 12" "Jam (live)"/ Elemental Child (live) [ABOLAN 5F], Official Fanclub only)	15
86	Marc On Wax WARRIOR 1/4	HISTORY OF T. REX (4-LP, numbered picture disc set, with free fanclub T-shirt)	45
86	Marc On Wax WARRIOR 1/4	HISTORY OF T. REX (4-LP, numbered picture disc set, without free fanclub T-shirt)	35

FRANCY BOLAND

(see also Kenny Clarke with Francy Boland)

75	Freedom FLP40176	PAPILLON NOIR (LP)	15

TOMMY BOLIN

(see also James Gang, Deep Purple)

76	Nemperor K 10730/NE 4	The Grind/Homeward Strut	10
75	Atlantic K 50208	TEASER (LP, stickered)	18
75	Atlantic K 50208	TEASER (LP, unstickered)	15
76	CBS S 81612	PRIVATE EYES (LP)	12

SIMON BOLIVAR ORCHESTRA

56	London HLG 8245	Meringue Holiday/Shy	10

BOLLARD

72	Satril SAT 1	I Need Your Love/Sunshine In The Morning	6

BOLLARDS

70s	Bumkin Records	BOLLARDS (LP)	15

BOLLWEEVIL

81	Ellie Jay EJSP 9715	Rock Solid/Sands Of Time (p/s)	50

MICHAEL BOLOTIN

(see also Blackjack, Michael Bolton)

75	RCA SF 8451	MICHAEL BOLOTIN (LP)	12

BOLSHOI

86	Beggars BEG 170TD	Books On The Bonfire/A Funny Thing/A Way (live) Billie Jean (live) (2x12", p/s)	8

BOLT THROWER

88	Vinyl Solution SOL 11	IN BATTLE THERE IS NO LAW (LP, with insert)	15
89	Earache MOSH 13	REALM OF CHAOS (LP, picture disc)	15
91	Strange Fruit SFRLP 116	PEEL SESSIONS 19880-90 (12")	20

MINT VALUE £

BOMBADIL

(see also Barclay James Harvest)

72	Harvest HAR 5056	Breathless/When The City Sleeps (p/s)	15
75	Harvest HAR 5095	Breathless/When The City Sleeps (p/s, reissue)	6

BOMBAY DUCKS

80	Complete Control CON 1	Sympathy For The Devil/1-0-6-9 (p/s)	10
80s	United Dairies UD 05	DANCE MUSIC (LP)	18
80s	Eraserhead C-60	ANYONE CAN BE ENO (cassette)	12
80s	Eraserhead C-30	A RETROSPECTIVE LOOK AT THE BOMBAY DUCKS (cassette with mask)	12

ELI BONAPARTE

70	Decca F 13047	Never An Everyday Thing/The Men From Birmingham	8

BON-BONS

55	London HL 8139	That's The Way Love Goes/Make My Dreams Come True	60
55	London HL 8139	That's The Way Love Goes/Make My Dreams Come True (78 rpm)	10
56	London HLU 8262	Circle/Frog On A Log	50

BOBBY BOND

61	Pye International 7N 25081	You're A Livin' Doll/Sweet Love	10
69	Warner Bros WB 7292	One More Mile, One More Town/If You're Leaving Me	5

BRIGITTE BOND

64	Blue Beat BB 212	Oh Yeah Baby/Blue Beat Baby	40

GRAHAM BOND (ORGANISATION)

(see also Jack Bruce, Dick Heckstall-Smith, Ginger Baker, Duffy Power, Who, Don Rendell, Steve York's Camelo Pardalis)

64	Decca F 11909	Long Tall Shorty/Long Legged Baby (as Graham Bond Organization)	50
65	Columbia DB 7471	Wade In The Water/Tammy (as Graham Bond Organisation)	50
65	Columbia DB 7528	Tell Me (I'm Gonna Love Again)/Love Come Shining Through (as Graham Bond Organisation)	45
65	Columbia DB 7647	Lease On Love/My Heart's In Little Pieces (as Graham Bond Organisation)	35
66	Columbia DB 7838	St James Infirmary/Soul Tango (as Graham Bond Organisation)	40
67	Page One POF 014	You've Gotta Have Love Babe/I Love You	55
70	Warner Bros WB 8004	Walking In The Park/Springtime In The City (solo)	15
71	Vertigo 6059 042	Twelve Gates To The City/Water Water (as Graham Bond with Magick)	20
65	Columbia 33SX 1711	THE SOUND OF '65 (LP, 1st pressing, with '33SX' on blue/black label and "Sold in the U.K." label text)	300
65	Columbia 33SX 1750	THERE'S A BOND BETWEEN US (LP, 1st pressing, with '33SX' on blue/black label and "Sold in the UK" label text)	300
66	Columbia SX 1711	THE SOUND OF '65 (LP, 2nd pressing, with 'SX' on blue/black label)	175
66	Columbia SX 1750	THERE'S A BOND BETWEEN US (LP, 2nd pressing, with 'SX' on blue/black label)	110
69	Columbia SX 1711	THE SOUND OF '65 (LP, 3rd pressing, with boxed logo on silver/black label)	60

(All of the above LP's have 33SX on the sleeve, but only 1st pressings have 33SX on the label)

71	Warner Bros WS 3001	SOLID BOND (2-LP, gatefold sleeve, orange label)	50
71	Vertigo 6360 021	HOLY MAGICK (LP, gatefold sleeve, large swirl label, as Graham Bond & Magick)	100
71	Vertigo 6360 042	WE PUT OUR MAGICK ON YOU (LP, gatefold sleeve, swirl label,	100
72	Philips 6382 010	BOND IN AMERICA (2-LP, solo [individual discs: 6499 200/1], unreleased)	30
72	Philips 6382 010	THIS IS GRAHAM BOND (LP, solo)	18

GRAHAM BOND & PETE BROWN

(see also Pete Brown)

71	Greenwich GSS 104	Lost Tribe/Macumbe/Milk Is Turning Sour In My Shoes (maxi-single)	25
72	Chapter One CHS-R 813	TWO HEADS ARE BETTER THAN ONE (LP)	200

ISABEL BOND

68	Major Minor MM 565	Cry/When A Woman Loves A Man (in p/s)	15
68	Major Minor MM 565	Cry/When A Woman Loves A Man	5
69	Major Minor MM 627	Don't Forget About Me/You'll Never Get The Chance Again	10
68	Major Minor MMLP 28	THE HEART AND SOUL OF ISABEL BOND (LP)	30

JACKI BOND

65	Columbia DB 7719	My Sister's Boy/Now I Know	20
66	Strike JH 302	Tell Him To Go Away/Don't You Worry	20
66	Strike JH 320	He Say/Why Can't I Love Him	50

JANE BOND & UNDERCOVER MEN

86	Dreamworld BIG DREAM 1	POLITICALLY CORRECT (LP)	12

JOHNNY BOND

60	London HLU 9189	Hot Rod Jalopy/Five-Minute Love Affair	30
60	London HL 7100	Hot Rod Lincoln/Five-Minute Love Affair (export issue)	20
65	London HLB 9957	Ten Little Bottles/Eleven More Months And Ten More Days (B-side with Cowboy Copas)	10
62	Stateside SL 10008	THAT WILD, WICKED BUT WONDERFUL WEST (LP)	20
63	London HA-B 8098	LIVE IT UP (LP, as Johnny Bond & His Friends On Stage)	20
65	London HA-B 8228	THE SONGS THAT MADE HIM FAMOUS (LP)	15
66	London HA-B 8272	FAMOUS HOT RODDERS I HAVE KNOWN (LP)	15

JOYCE BOND

67	Airborne NBP 0011	It's Alright/Mrs. Soul	90
66	Island WI 3019	Tell Me What It's All About/Tell Me Right Now	50
67	Island WIP 6010	Do The Teasy/Sugar	15
67	Island WIP 6018	This Train/Not So With Me	15
68	Island WIP 6051	Ob-La-Di, Ob-La-Da/Robin Hood Rides Again	10
68	Pama PM 718	Back To School/They Wish	10
69	Pama PM 771	Mr. Pitiful/Let's Get Married (as Joyce Bond & Little John)	12
70	Upfront UPF 5	Wind Of Change/First In Line	7
71	Trojan TR 7837	Help Me Make It Through The Night/Reconsider Our Love	8

			MINT VALUE £
68	Island ILP 968	SOUL AND SKA (LP, mono only)	150
72	Windmill WMD 121	SOUL OF CHANGE (LP)	15

LOUIS BOND

74	Cooltempo 2005	Tell Me When/Instrumental	8

MARGARET BOND

55	Decca F 10506	You'll Always Be My Lifetime Sweetheart/Where Is The One For Me	10
55	Decca F 10555	My Love's A Gentle Man/Mirror, Mirror	10
55	Decca F 10632	There's Always A First Time/Dancing In My Socks	10
57	Parlophone R 4283	Your Love Is My Love/Goodnight My Love, Pleasant Dreams	5
57	Parlophone R 4312	The Wind In The Willow/Young And In Love	5

OLIVER BOND

(see also Oliver Bone)

66	Parlophone R 5476	I Saw You All Alone/Let Me Love You	20

PETER BOND

77	Trailer LER 2108	IT'S ALL RIGHT FOR SOME (LP, yellow label)	15

RONNIE BOND

(see also Troggs)

69	Page One POF 123	Anything For You/Carolyn	20

TONY BOND

(see also Kestrels)

66	Decca SKL 4776	PRESENTING TONY BOND (LP)	20

GARY (U.S.) BONDS

60	Top Rank JAR 527	New Orleans/Please Forgive Me (as U.S. Bonds)	15
61	Top Rank JAR 566	Not Me/Give Me One More Chance (as U.S. Bonds)	12
61	Top Rank JAR 575	Quarter To Three/Time Ole Story (as U.S. Bonds)	10
61	Top Rank JAR 581	School Is Out/One Million Tears	10
61	Top Rank JAR 595	School Is In/Trip To The Moon	10
62	Top Rank JAR 602	Dear Lady Twist/Havin' So Much Fun	10
62	Top Rank JAR 615	Twist Twist Senora/Food Of Love	10
62	Stateside SS 111	Seven Day Weekend/Gettin' A Groove	15
62	Stateside SS 125	Copy Cat/I'll Change That Too	15
63	Stateside SS 144	Mixed Up Faculty/I Dig This Station	15
63	Stateside SS 179	Where Did That Naughty Little Girl Go?/Do The Limbo With Me	15
63	Stateside SS 219	What A Dream/I Don't Wanta Wait	15
64	Stateside SS 271	New Orleans/Quarter To Three	8
64	Stateside SS 308	My Sweet Baby Rose/Ella Is Yella	10
67	Stateside SS 2025	Send Her To Me/Workin' For My Baby	20
75	London HLA 10485	Grandma's Washboard Band/Believing You	7
61	Top Rank 35/114	DANCE 'TIL QUARTER TO THREE WITH U.S. BONDS (LP)	50
62	Stateside SL 10001	TWIST UP CALYPSO (LP)	30
63	Stateside SL 10037	THE GREATEST HITS OF GARY (U.S.) BONDS (LP)	20

OLIVER BONE & SOUNDS MAXIMUM

(see also Oliver Bond)

66	Parlophone R 5527	Knock On Wood/Jugger Tea	30

MATTHEW BONES

71	Pye 7N 45100	I Am A Pixi/Two Sugars	12

BONESHAKER

71	London HLU 10332	Sweetness/Badman Strikes Again	50

BONGO HERMAN (Davis)

70	Songbird SB 1018	True Grit/True Grit Version 2 (both credited with Les Crystalites but actually with Les & Crystalites)	20
71	Songbird SB 1060	BONGO HERMAN & LES BUNNY: Know For I/CRYSTALITES: Version (B-side actually titled 'Know Fari')	15
71	Songbird SB 1066	BONGO HERMAN & LES & BUNNY: Salaam (Peace)/CRYSTALITES: Scraper	12
72	Big BG 332	Eternal Drums/ERROL DUNKLEY: Darling Ooh Wee (both by Hugh Roy Junior)	15
72	Green Door GD 4049	African Breakfast/BONGO HERMAN & LES AND BUNNY: Chairman Of The Board	15
72	Songbird SB 1069	We Are Praying/CRYSTALITES: Version	10

BONGO LES & HERMAN

(see also Heptones, Scotty, Meditators)

71	Songbird SB 1050	Home Sweet Home/Hail I	12
72	Attack ATT 8041	Feel Nice (Version)/WINSTON SCOTLAND: Quick & Slick	8

BON JOVI

84	Vertigo VER 11	She Don't Know Me/Breakout (p/s)	20
84	Vertigo VERX 11	She Don't Know Me/Breakout (12", p/s)	30
84	Vertigo VER 14	Runaway/Breakout (live) (p/s)	20
84	Vertigo VERX 14	Runaway/Breakout (live)/Runaway (live) (12", p/s)	30
85	Vertigo VER 19	In And Out Of Love/Roulette (live) (p/s)	15
85	Vertigo VERP 19	In And Out Of Love/Roulette (live) (picture disc)	45
85	Vertigo VERX 19	In And Out Of Love/Roulette (live)/Shot Through The Heart (live) (12", p/s)	15
85	Vertigo VER 22	The Hardest Part Is The Night/Always Run To You (p/s)	10
85	Vertigo VERDP 22	The Hardest Part Is The Night/Always Run To You//Tokyo Road (live)/ Shot Through The Heart (live) (double pack, gatefold p/s)	15
85	Vertigo VERX 22	The Hardest Part Is The Night/Always Run To You/Tokyo Road (live) (12", p/s)	15
85	Vertigo VERXR 22	Red Hot And Two Parts Live: The Hardest Part Is The Night/ Tokyo Road (live)/In And Out Of Love (live) (12", p/s, red vinyl)	30
86	Vertigo VERP 26	You Give Love A Bad Name/Let It Rock (10", shaped picture disc)	20
86	Vertigo VERX 26	You Give Love A Bad Name/Let It Rock/Borderline (12", p/s with poster)	12
86	Vertigo VERXR 26	You Give Love A Bad Name/Let It Rock/ The Hardest Part Is The Night (live)/ Burning For Love (live) (12", p/s, blue vinyl)	18

			MINT VALUE £
86	Vertigo VERPA 28	Livin' On A Prayer/Wild In The Streets (p/s, with patch, sealed)	20
86	Vertigo VERPA 28	Livin' On A Prayer/Wild In The Streets (p/s, with patch, unsealed)	10
86	Vertigo VERP 28	Livin' On A Prayer/Wild In The Streets (picture disc)	20
86	Vertigo VERXR 28	Livin' On A Prayer/Wild In The Streets/Edge Of A Broken Heart (12", green vinyl, p/s)	10
86	Vertigo VERXG 28	Livin' On A Prayer/Wild In The Streets/Only Lonely (live)/ Runaway (live) (12", gatefold p/s)	12
88	Mercury 080 042-2	Livin' On A Prayer/Borderline/Let It Rock/Wild In The Streets (CD Video)	15
87	Vertigo JOVS 1	Wanted Dead Or Alive/Shot Through The Heart (p/s, with metal stickers)	8
87	Vertigo JOVPB 112	Wanted Dead Or Alive/Shot Through The Heart/Social Disease (12", poster p/s)	15
87	Vertigo JOVR 112	Wanted Dead Or Alive/Shot Through The Heart/Social Disease/ Get Ready (live) (12", p/s, silver vinyl)	12
87	Vertigo JOVR 212	Never Say Goodbye/Raise Your Hands/Wanted Dead Or Alive (Acoustic Version) (12", yellow vinyl, PVC sleeve)	12
87	Vertigo	Never Say Goodbye (CD video)	20
87	Vertigo	Wanted Dead Or Alive (CD video)	20
87	Vertigo 080 042-2	Livin' On A Prayer/Borderline/Let It Rock/Wild In The Streets (CD video)	20
88	Vertigo JOVS 3	Bad Medicine/99 In The Shade (fold-out photofile p/s)	7
88	Vertigo JOVCD 3	Bad Medicine/Lay Your Hands On Me/99 In The Shade (CD, card sleeve)	10
88	Vertigo JOVP 412	Born To Be My Baby/Love For Sale/Wanted Dead Or Alive (live) (12", picture disc)	10
88	Vertigo JOVCD 4	Born To Be My Baby/Love For Sale/Runaway/Livin' On A Prayer (CD)	10
89	Vertigo JOVCD 5	I'll Be There For You/Homebound Train/Borderline/Edge Of A Broken Heart (CD, card sleeve)	10
89	Vertigo JOVS 661	Lay Your Hands On Me/Bad Medicine (live) (red vinyl, stickered PVC sleeve)	5
89	Vertigo JOVS 662	Lay Your Hands On Me/Bad Medicine (live) (white vinyl, stickered PVC sleeve)	5
89	Vertigo JOVS 663	Lay Your Hands On Me/Bad Medicine (live) (blue vinyl, stickered PVC sleeve)	6
89	Vertigo JOVS 661-663	Lay Your Hands On Me/Bad Medicine (live) (3 x 7", red, blue or white vinyl, paper box set)	20
89	Vertigo JOVP 610	Lay Your Hands On Me/Bad Medicine (live)/Blood On Blood (10", picture disc with insert)	8
89	Vertigo JOVCD 6	Lay Your Hands On Me/You Give Love A Bad Name/Let It Rock (CD)	10
89	Vertigo JOVR 712	Living In Sin/Love Is War/The Boys Are Back In Town (12", white vinyl with stickered card insert)	10
89	Vertigo JOVCD 7	Living In Sin/Love Is War/Ride Cowboy Ride/Stick To Your Guns (CD, box set)	15
92	Vertigo JOVCD 8	Keep The Faith/I Wish Everyday Could Be Like Christmas/ Little Bit Of Soul (CD, digipak)	8
92	Vertigo JOVCD 9	Bed Of Roses/Lay Your Hands On Me (live)/Tokyo Road (live)/ I'll Be There For You (live) (CD, slimline jewel case)	8
93	Vertigo JOVMB 10	In These Arms/Bed Of Roses (Acoustic) (cassette, pull-apart outer card slipcase with tour pass)	5
94	Vertigo JOVJB 14	Always (edit)/Always (jukebox issue, no p/s)	5
94	Vertigo JOVP 15	Someday I'll Be Saturday Night/Always (live) (picture disc with insert)	5
94	Vertigo JOVP 16	Please Come Home For Christmas/Back Door Santa (picture disc)	12
88	Vertigo VERHP 38	SLIPPERY WHEN WET (LP, picture disc with poster)	15
88	Vertigo VERHP 62	NEW JERSEY (LP, picture disc, stickered PVC sleeve)	15

JON BON JOVI

90	Vertigo JBJ 212	Miracle/Dyin' Ain't Much Of A Livin'/Interview With Jon Bon Jovi (12", p/s, with poster & numbered sticker)	12
90	Vertigo JBJP 212	Miracle/Dyin' Ain't Much Of A Livin'/Going Back (live) (12", picture disc with insert)	15

JUKE BOY BONNER

69	Blue Horizon 57-3163	Runnin' Shoes/Jackin' In My Plans	35
60s	Jan & Dil JR 451	MORE DOWN HOME BLUES (EP)	50
68	Flyright LP 3501	THE ONE MAN TRIO (LP)	45
69	Liberty LBS 83319	THINGS AIN'T RIGHT (LP)	40

GRAHAM BONNET

(see also Marbles, Rainbow, Cozy Powell, Forcefield, Fut, Michael Schenker Group, Jon Lord)

72	RCA RCA 2230	Rare Specimen/Whisper In The Night	20
73	RCA RCA 2380	Trying To Say Goodbye/Castles In The Air	15
74	DJM DJS 328	Back Row In The Stalls/Ghost Writer In My Eye	8
77	Ring O' 2017 105	It's All Over Now, Baby Blue/Heroes On My Picture Wall (company sleeve)	6
77	Ring O' 2017 106	Danny/Rock Island Line (promo p/s)	10
77	Ring O' 2017 106	Danny/Rock Island Line (company sleeve)	5
77	Ring O' 2017 110	Goodnight And Good Morning/Wino Song (company sleeve)	5
78	Ring O' 2017 114/POSP 2	Warm Ride/10/12 Observation (company sleeve)	5
78	Ring O' POSP 002	Warm Ride/10/12 Observation (12", company sleeve)	8
81	Lyntone LYN 10138/9	Night Games/POLECATS: We Say Yeah/THIN LIZZY: Song For Jimmy/ WAY OF THE WEST: monkey Love (orange flexi with Flexipop magazine, issue 10)	12
81	Lyntone LYN 10138/9	Night Games/POLECATS: We Say Yeah/THIN LIZZY: Song For Jimmy/WAY OF THE WEST: monkey Love (orange flexi without Flexipop magazine, issue 10)	5
81	Vertigo VER 4	That's The Way That It Is/Don't Tell Me To Go (p/s)	6
81	Vertigo VER 1	Night Games/Out On The Water (p/s)	5
81	Vertigo VER 2	Liar/Bad Days Are Gone (p/s)	6
77	Ring O' 2320 103	GRAHAM BONNET (LP, with inner sleeve)	18
81	Vertigo 6302 151	LINE UP (LP, with inner sleeve)	12

GRAHAM BONNEY

(see also Riot Squad)

65	Columbia DB 7773	My Little World Is All Blue/Why Can't We Be Friends	10
66	Columbia DB 7843	Super Girl/Hill Of Lovin'	10
66	Columbia DB 7934	Baby's Gone/Later Tonight	15
66	Columbia DB 8005	No One Knows/Mixed Up Baby Girl	12
67	Columbia DB 8111	Thank You Baby/Briony	7

MINT VALUE £

67	Columbia DB 8142	Happy Together/That Bad Day	7
67	Columbia DB 8283	Papa Joe/My Jenny	7
68	Columbia DB 8338	By The Way I Love You/Devil's Child	7
68	Columbia DB 8382	I'll Be Your Baby Tonight/Back From Baltimore	7
68	Columbia DB 8464	Frenzy/Something I've Got To Tell You	7
69	Columbia DB 8531	Get Ready/Fly Me High Lorelei	15
69	Columbia DB 8592	Leanda Angeline/Mixing The Wine	8
70	Columbia DB 8648	Sign On The Dotted Line/Words We Said	25
70	Columbia DB 8687	When Evelyn Was Mine/Sunny Has Gone	18
66	Columbia SX 6052	SUPER GIRL (LP)	30

BONNIE

67	Ska Beat JB 270	Do You Get The Message/A Man Called Dan	12
69	Jolly JY 014	Loving You/Shoo Be Doo	10

BONNIE & SKITTO

63	Island WI 122	Get Ready (actually by Vikings [alias Maytals])/ DON DRUMMOND: The Rocket	30

BONNIE & TREASURES

65	London HLU 9998	Home Of The Brave/Our Song	40

BONO & GAVIN FRIDAY

(see also U2, Clannad & Bono, The Passengers, Virgin Prunes)

94	Island CID 593	In The Name Of The Father (7" Edit)/(12" Remix)/ (12" Beats Mix)/ (LP Instrumental) (CD)	15
94	Island 12IS593	In The Name Of The Father (7" Edit)/(12" Remix)/ (12" Beats Mix)/ (LP Instrumental) (12" single)	10

BONOBO

00	Tru Thoughts TRU 004	Terrapin (12")	15
01	Tru Thoughts TRU 013	THE SHARK EP (12")	8
00	Tru Thoughts TRU LP 007	ANIMAL MAGIC (2xLP)	15
01	Ninja Tune ZEN 63	ANIMAL MAGIC (2xLP)	20
02	Tru Thoughts TRU LP 031	ONE OFFS?REMIXES & B SIDES (2xLP)	25
03	Ninja Tune ZEN 80	DIAL M FOR MONKEY (2xLP)	15
06	Ninja Tune ZEN 119	DAYS TO COME (2xLP)	20

BONZO DOG (DOO-DAH) BAND

(see also Vivian Stanshall, Neil Innes, Grimms, Roger Ruskin Spear, Topo D. Bill, New Vaudeville Band)

67	Liberty LBL 83056	GORILLA (LP, mono with booklet)	60
66	Parlophone R 5430	My Brother Makes The Noises For The Talkies/ I'm Gonna Bring A Watermelon To My Gal Tonight	30
66	Parlophone R 5499	Alley Oop/Button Up Your Overcoat	30
67	Liberty LBF 15040	Equestrian Statue/The Intro And The Outro	10
68	Liberty LBF 15144	Urban Spaceman/Canyons Of Your Mind (initially pressing with spoken intro to A-side)	10
68	Liberty LBF 15144	Urban Spaceman/Canyons Of Your Mind (later pressing without spoken intro to A-side)	5
69	Liberty LBF 15201	Mr. Apollo/Ready Mades	7
69	Liberty LBF 15273	I Want To Be With You/We Were Wrong	7
70	Liberty LBF 15314	You Done My Brain In/Mr. Slater's Parrot	7
73	United Artists UP 35602	The Intro And The Outro/Hello Mabel	7
74	United Artists UP 35662	Mr. Slater's Parrot/Noises For The Leg	7
92	China WOK 2021	No Matter Who You Vote For The Government Always Gets In/ NEIL INNES: Them (promo only)	15
67	Liberty LBS 83056	GORILLA (LP, stereo with booklet)	40
67	Liberty LBL/LBS 83056	GORILLA (LP, without booklet, blue label)	20
71	Liberty LBL/LBS 83158E	THE DOUGHNUT IN GRANNY'S GREENHOUSE (LP, gatefold sleeve, with booklet, blue label)	50
71	Liberty LBL/LBS 83158E	THE DOUGHNUT IN GRANNY'S GREENHOUSE (LP, gatefold sleeve, without booklet, blue label)	25
69	Liberty LBS 83257	TADPOLES (LP, die-cut sleeve, with insert, blue label)	40
69	Liberty LBS 83257	TADPOLES (LP, die-cut sleeve, without insert, blue label)	25
69	Liberty LBS 83290	KEYNSHAM (LP, gatefold sleeve, blue label)	35
72	United Artists UAS 29288	LET'S MAKE UP AND BE FRIENDLY (LP)	22
74	United Artists UAD 60071/2	THE HISTORY OF THE BONZOS (2-LP, gatefold sleeve with booklet)	25

BETTY BOO

79	Grapevine GRP 125	Say It Isn't So/Say It Isn't So (Instrumental)	20

BLOCK 015

BOOGALOOS

69	President PT 253	Rule Britannia/Love Is Blind	12

JAMES BOOKER

61	Vogue V 9177	Cool Turkey/Gonzo	30
63	Vocalion VEP 170154	GONZO (EP)	50

BOOKER T (Jamaica)

76	Ethnic Fight 2	Eleanor/Version	8

BOOKER T. & THE M.G.s

(see also Mar-Keys, Steve Cropper, Albert King, Judy Clay)

62	London HLK 9595	Green Onions/Behave Yourself	20
63	London HLK 9670	Jelly Bread/Aw' Mercy	12
63	London HLK 9784	Chinese Checkers/Plum Nellie	12
65	Atlantic AT 4033	Boot-Leg/Outrage	12
66	Atlantic AT 4063	Be My Lady/Red Beans And Rice	20
66	Atlantic 584 044	My Sweet Potato/Booker Loo	12
66	Atlantic 584 060	Jingle Bells/Winter Wonderland	12
67	Atlantic 584 088	Green Onions/Boot-Leg	12

			MINT VALUE £
67	Stax 601 009	Hip Hug Her/Summertime (initially dark blue label)	25
67	Stax 601 009	Hip Hug Her/Summertime (later pressing with light blue label)	18
67	Stax 601 018	Groovin'/Slim Jenkins' Place	10
67	Stax 601 026	Chinese Checkers/Plum Nellie (reissue)	10
68	Stax STAX 102	Soul Limbo/Heads Or Tails	7
69	Stax STAX 119	Time Is Tight/Hang 'Em High	7
69	Stax STAX 127	Soul Clap '69/Mrs. Robinson	5
69	Stax STAX 136	The Horse/Slum Baby	8
71	Stax 2025 026	Melting Pot/Kinda Easy Like	10
72	Stax 2025 074	Jamaica This Morning (as the MGs)/Fuquawi	6
63	London REK 1367	R&B WITH BOOKER T (EP)	40
64	Atlantic AET 6002	R&B WITH BOOKER T VOL. 2 (EP)	40
64	London HA-K 8182	GREEN ONIONS (LP, plum label)	60
65	Atlantic ATL 5027	SOUL DRESSING (LP, plum label, 1st pressing with green & white sleeve)	50
66	Atlantic 587/588 033	GREEN ONIONS (LP, reissue, mono/stereo)	15
67	Atlantic 587 047	SOUL DRESSING (LP, reissue, with green & black sleeve)	20
67	Stax 589 002	AND NOW! (LP)	50
68	Stax 589 013	SOUL CHRISTMAS (LP)	18
68	Stax 230 002/231 002	DOIN' OUR THING (LP)	20
68	Stax (S)XATS 1001	SOUL LIMBO (LP)	18
69	Atco 228 004	GET READY (LP)	15
69	Stax (S)XATS 1005	UPTIGHT (LP, soundtrack, with Judy Clay)	15
69	Stax (S)XATS 1015	THE BOOKER T. SET (LP)	15
69	Atco 228 015	THE BEST OF BOOKER T. AND THE M.G.s (LP)	15
70	Stax SXATS 1031	McLEMORE AVENUE (LP)	15
71	Stax 2325 030	MELTING POT (LP)	15

BOOM

91	Music Of Life NOTE049	BOOM EP (12")	8
91	Music Of Life NOTE050	Delivering The Answer (12")	8

BOOMERANGS

64	Fontana TF 507	Rockin' Robin/Don't Let Her Be Your Baby	30
65	Fontana TF 555	Another Tear Falls/Fun Fun Fun	15

BOOMERANGS

66	Pye 7N 17049	Dream World/Upgraded	12

DANIEL BOONE

71	Penny Farthing PEN 764	Daddy Don't You Walk So Fast/Tiger Woman	6
73	Penny Farthing PEN 800	Rock N Roll Bum/Sunday Morning Coming	10

PAT BOONE

(see also Fontane Sisters)

SINGLES

55	London HLD 8172	Ain't That A Shame/Tennessee Saturday Night	35
55	London HLD 8197	At My Front Door/No Arms Can Ever Hold You	25
56	London HLD 8233	Gee Whittakers/Take The Time	20
56	London HLD 8253	I'll Be Home/Tutti Frutti	20
56	London HLD 8291	Long Tall Sally/Just As Long As I'm With You	30
56	London HLD 8303	I Almost Lost My Mind/I'm In Love With You	10
56	London HLD 8316	Two Hearts, Two Kisses/Rich In Love	10
56	London HLD 8346	Friendly Persuasion (Thee I Love)/Chains Of Love	10

(The above 45s were originally issued with gold lettering labels: later silver lettering copies are worth half these values.)

57	London HLD 8370	Don't Forbid Me/Anastasia	5
57	London HLD 8404	Why Baby Why/I'm Just Waiting For You	10
57	London HLD 8445	Love Letters In The Sand/Bernadine	5
57	London HLD 8479	Remember You're Mine/There's A Goldmine In The Sky	5
57	London HLD 8512	April Love/When The Swallows Come Back To Capistrano	5
59	London HLD 8824	There's Good Rockin' Tonight/With The Wind And The Rain In Your Hair	10
59	London HLD 8855	For A Penny/Wang Dang Taffy-Apple Tango	5
59	London HLD 8910	Rock Boll Weevil/Twixt Twelve And Twenty	5
59	London HLD 8974	A Fool's Hall Of Fame/Brightest Wishing Star	5

(The above 45s were originally issued with triangular centres; later round centre copies are worth half to two-thirds of these values)

60	London HLD 9029	Beyond The Sunset/The Faithful Heart	5
60	London HLD 9029	Beyond The Sunset/The Faithful Heart (78)	10
60	London HLD 9067	(Welcome) New Lovers/Words	5
60	London HLD 9067	(Welcome) New Lovers/Words (78 rpm)	10
60	London HLD 9138	Walking The Floor Over You/Spring Rain	5
60	London HLD 9184	Delia Gone/Candy Sweet	5
60	London HLD 9184	Delia Gone/Candy Sweet (78)	20
60	London HLD 9350	Moody River/A Thousand Years	7
62	London HLD 9620	The Main Attraction/Amore Baciami	6
64	Dot DS 16658	Beach Girl/Little Honda	10

EXPORT SINGLES

56	London HL 7007	I'll Be Home/Tutti Frutti	25
56	London HL 7010	Long Tall Sally/Just As Long As I'm With You	25
56	London HL 7012	I Almost Lost My Mind/I'm In Love With You	5
56	London HL 7015	Friendly Persuasion (Thee I Love)/Chains Of Love	5
57	London HL 7019	Love Letters In The Sand/Bernadine	5
58	London HL 7033	A Wonderful Time Up There/It's Too Soon To Know	5
58	London HL 7041	Sugar Moon/Cherie, I Love You	5
58	London HL 7051	If Dreams Came True/That's How Much I Love You	5
58	London HL 7059	Gee, But It's Lonely/For My Good Fortune	5
59	London HL 7070	With The Wind And The Rain In Your Hair/There's Good Rocking Tonight	5
59	London SLD 4002	For A Penny/Wang Dang Taffy-Apple Tango (both tracks stereo)	15
61	London HLD 7112	Moody River/The Exodus Song	5
63	London HL 7118	Send Me The Pillow You Dream On/(You've Got) Personality	5
63	London HLD 7121	Mexican Joe/In The Room	5

MINT VALUE £

EPs

56	London RE-D 1063	PAT BOONE SINGS THE HITS (EP)	15
57	London HA-D 2024	PAT'S BIG HITS (LP)	20
57	London RE-D 1086	PAT BOONE SINGS THE HITS NO. 2 (EP)	10
58	London RE-D 1112	PAT BOONE SINGS THE HITS NO. 3 (EP)	8

LPs

57	London HA-D 2030	HOWDY! (LP)	12
57	London HA-D 2049	PAT! (LP)	20
63	London HA-D 8109	SINGS... GUESS WHO? (LP, mono)	35
63	London SH-D 8109	SINGS... GUESS WHO? (LP, stereo)	40
65	Dot (D)DLP 3594	BOSS BEAT (LP)	20
60	London HAD 2305	THIS AND THAT (LP)	12
61	London HAD 2354	GREAT! GREAT! GREAT! (LP)	12
62	London HAD 2452	I'LL SEE YOU IN MY DREAMS (LP)	12
63	London HAD 8053	I LOVE YOU TRULY (LP, with Shirley Boone)	12

BOONE FAMILY

74	Mowest MW 3022	Please Mr Postman/Friends	5

BOONES FARM

72	CBS 8212	If You Can't Be My Woman/Start Today	20

BOO RADLEYS

91	Rough Trade R3011	LEARNING TO WALK (LP)	15
93	Creation CRELP 149	GIANT STEPS (2-LP)	15

ANTHONY BOOTH

69	Tangerine DP 0008	Till Death Do Us Part/September Days	6

BARRY BOOTH

(see also Monty Python)

68	Pye NPL 18216	DIVERSIONS! (LP, also stereo NSLP 18216))	15

KEN BOOTHE

(see also Stranger & Ken, Keith Hudson, Gaylads, Richard Ace, Lloyd & Ken)

66	Island WI 3020	The Train Is Coming/This Is Me	40
66	Island WI 3035	I Don't Want To See You Cry/Baby I Need You (B-side actually by Wailers)	90
66	Ska Beat JB 248	You're No Good/SOULETTES: Don't Care What The People Say	80
67	Doctor Bird DB 1110	Say You/LYN TAITT & JETS: Smokey Places	50
67	Coxsone CS 7006	Lonely Teardrops/Oowee Baby	100
67	Coxsone CS 7020	Home Home Home/SOUL BROTHERS: Windell	60
67	Caltone TONE 107	The One I Love/You Left The Water Running	75
67	Studio One SO 2000	Feel Good/Mustang Sally	35
67	Studio One SO 2012	Puppet On A String/ROLAND ALPHONSO: Look Away	25
67	Studio One SO 2014	Fatty Fatty (actually Heptones)/Mother Word (actually by Delroy Wilson)	30
67	Studio One SO 2026	Why Did You Leave (actually by Leroy Sibbles)/ Don't Try To Reach Me (actually by Gaylads)	30
68	Studio One SO 2039	When I Fall In Love/HEPTONES: Christmas Time	30
68	Studio One SO 2041	The Girl I Left Behind/TERMITES: My Last Love	30
68	Studio One SO 2053	Tomorrow/Movin' Away	50
68	Fab FAB 63	I Remember Someone/Can't You See?	110
68	Coxsone CS 7041	Everybody Knows/GAYLADS: I'm Free	30
69	Coxsone CS 7094	Sherry/I've Got You	25
69	Studio One SO 2073	You're On My Mind/RICHARD ACE & SOUND DIMENSIONS: Love To Cherish	30
69	High Note HS 003	Lady With The Starlight/LESLIE BUTLER & COUNT OSSIE: Gay Drums	25
69	Bamboo BAM 4	Pleading/SOUND DIMENSION: Call 1143	50
69	Bamboo BAM 8	Be Yourself/SOUND DIMENSION: Rathid	45
70	Trojan TR 7716	Why, Baby Why/Keep My Love From Fading	7
70	Trojan TR 7756	Freedom Street/BEVERLEY'S ALLSTARS: Freedom Version	8
70	Trojan TR 7772	It's Gonna Take A Miracle/Now I Know	10
70	Trojan TR 7780	Drums Of Freedom/BEVERLEY'S ALLSTARS: Version	8
70	Gas GAS 169	Give To Me/Why	8
70	Jackpot JP 748	You Left The Water Running/PHIL PRATT ALL STARS: Cut Throat	20
70	Punch PH 30	Artibella/PRATT ALLSTARS: Version Of Artibella	25
70	Punch PH 33	Morning/Morning (Version)	8
71	Punch PH 70	Stop Your Crying/CONSCIOUS MINDS: Suffering Through The Nation	10
71	Banana BA 352	Original Six (Parts 1 & 2)	15
71	Summit SUM 8518	I Wish It Could Be Peaceful Again/BEVERLEY'S ALLSTARS: Peaceful Version	8
71	Summit SUM 8519	Your Feeling And Mine/BEVERLEY'S ALLSTARS: Your Feeling Version	8
71	Big Shot BI 590	So Nice/So Nice Version	8
71	Green Door GD 4002	Medley Version/Medley Version 2	8
71	Dynamic DYN 411	Hallelujah/Trying To Reach	8
72	Dynamic DYN 453	Tears From My Eyes/CONSCIOUS MINDS: Tears From My Eyes Version	5
72	Pama Supreme PS 369	Look What You've Done/LLOYD CHARMERS: Look What You've Done Version	10
72	Ashanti ASH 403	Make Me Feel Alright (with The Incrowd)/INCROWD: Down On The Corner	8
73	Trojan TR 7893	Is It Because I'm Black/Black, Gold And Green	12
73	Green Door GD 4053	Silver Words/Rasta God Version	8
73	Mirto 100	Is It Because I'm Black?/Just Like A Shelter	15
74	Trojan TR 7920	Everything I Own/Drum Song	5
74	Trojan TR 7944	Crying Over You/Now You Can See Me Again	5
75	Fab FAB 270	Thinking/Moving Away	20
75	Torpedo TOR 54	Say You/You Version	8
79	Attack TACK 6	You're No Good/PRINCE JAMMY: Out Of Order Dub (12")	12
67	Studio One SOL 9001	MR. ROCK STEADY (LP)	200
73	Trojan TRLS 58	BLACK, GOLD AND GREEN (LP)	35
74	Trojan TRLS 83	LETS GET IT ON (LP)	15

BOOTLES

64	Vocalion VN 9216	I'll Let You Hold My Hand/Never Till Now	25

MINT VALUE £

BOOTS

68	CBS 3550	Even The Bad Times Are Good/The Animal In Me	20
68	CBS 3833	Keep Your Lovelight Burning/Give Me One More Chance	25
70	Youngblood YB 1018	You Better Run/A To D	45

DAVE BOOTS

60s	Solent SM 013	GREEN SATIN AND GOLD (LP)	110

BOOTSY'S RUBBER BAND

(see also Parliament, Funkadelic)

77	Warner Bros K 16964T	Pinocchio Theory/Psychoticbumpschool/What's A Telephone (12")	10
78	Warner Bros K 17196T	Bootzilla/Hollywood Squares (12", p/s)	10
76	Warner Bros K 56200	STRETCHIN' OUT IN BOOTSY'S RUBBER BAND (LP)	15
77	Warner Bros K 56302	AHH... THE NAME IS BOOTSY, BABY! (LP, gatefold sleeve)	15
78	Warner Bros K 56424	BOOTSY? PLAYER OF THE YEAR (LP, gatefold sleeve)	12
79	Warner Bros K 56615	THE BOOT IS MADE FOR FONK-N (LP, with inner sleeve)	12
81	Warner Bros K 56998	THE ONE GIVETH, THE COUNT TAKETH AWAY (LP)	12

BOOVER BOYS

70	Torpedo TOR 22	A.G.G.R.O/Sha La La La Lee	30

CHARLIE BOP TRIO

77	Capitol CL 15940	Mr. Big Feet/MERRILL E MOORE: Boogie My Blues Away	6

BOP & BELTONES

(see also Beltones, Soul Vendors, Jackie Mittoo)

67	Coxsone CS 7012	Treat Me Good/PETER TOUCH & WAILERS: Dancing Time (B-side actually by Bop & Beltones)	50

RANNY BOP

70	Gas GAS 155	Pipe Dream/Suck Suck	10

BORE-TOWN BOP

81	Vital VIS001	Try/Surf's Up (p/s)	15

BILLY BORLYNN

60	Philips PB 1031	Baby Listens/Liebelei	5
60	Philips PB 1057	Every Step Of The Way/It Takes Time	7

BORN B.C.

82	Xcentric Noise FIRST 1	THE POWER & THE PRIVILEGE (EP)	8

BOSS

86	Power House (no cat. no.)	One Good Reason/Wake Up Children (p/s, with lyric sheet)	6

BOSS ATTACK

71	Fab FAB 187	Hell-El/TEARDROPS: Let Me Be Free	15

BOSS COMBO

62	Coral LVA 9205	GOLDEN ROCK AND ROLL INSTRUMENTALS (LP)	20

BOSS GUITARS

65	London HA-R/SH-R 8237	PLAY THE WINNERS (LP)	25

BOSS HOG

89	Amphetamine Reptile ARR6/68	DRINKIN', LECHIN' AND LYIN' (LP)	40
99	City Slang 20150	WHITEOUT (LP)	18

EARL BOSTIC (ORCHESTRA)

(see also Bill Doggett, Sonny Carter)

SINGLES

54	Parlophone MSP 6075	Off Shore/What! No Pearls	15
54	Parlophone MSP 6089	Deep Purple/Smoke Rings	15
54	Parlophone MSP 6105	Melancholy Serenade/Don't You Do It	15
54	Parlophone MSP 6110	Jungle Drums/Danube Waves	15
54	Parlophone MSP 6119	Mambolino/Blue Skies	15
54	Parlophone MSP 6131	These Foolish Things/Mambostic	15
54	Parlophone CMSP 8	Cherokee/The Song Is Ended (export issue)	15
55	Parlophone MSP 6162	Melody Of Love/Sweet Lorraine	15
56	Vogue V 2145	Flamingo/Sleep	15
56	Vogue V 2148	Moonglow/Ain't Misbehaving	15
56	Parlophone R 4208	The Bo-Do Rock (with Bill Doggett)/Mean To Me	20
56	Parlophone R 4232	For All We Know/Beyond The Blue Horizon	10
57	Parlophone R 4263	I Hear A Rhapsody/Harlem Nocturne	10
57	Parlophone R 4278	Bubbins Rock/Indiana (with Bill Doggett)	15
57	Parlophone R 4305	Avalon/Too Fine For Crying (B-side with Bill Jones)	10
57	Parlophone R 4370	Temptation/September Song	10
58	Parlophone R 4460	Over The Waves Rock/Twilight Time	10
59	Parlophone DP 553	Barcarolle/My Reverie (export single)	15
62	Ember JBS 708	Tuxedo Junction/Air Mail Special	15
66	Island WI 271	Honeymoon Night/PATSY COLE: Disappointed Bride	25

EPs

54	Parlophone GEP 8506	FLAMINGO	15
55	Parlophone GEP 8513	LINGER AWHILE	15
55	Parlophone GEP 8520	EARL BOSTIC AND HIS ALTO SAX	15
55	Vogue EPV 1010	EARL BOSTIC	15
56	Vogue EPV 1111	VELVET SUNSET	10
56	Parlophone GEP 8539	WRAP IT UP	12
58	Parlophone GEP 8701	BOSTIC BEAT	25
58	Parlophone GEP 8741	ROCKING WITH BOSTIC	25

LPs

54	Vogue LDE 100	EARL BOSTIC AND HIS ORCHESTRA	25

MINT VALUE £

54	Parlophone PMD 1016	EARL BOSTIC AND HIS ALTO SAX	25
56	Parlophone PMD 1040	EARL BOSTIC AND HIS ALTO SAX NO. 2	25
58	Parlophone PMD 1054	BOSTIC MEETS DOGGETT (with Bill Doggett)	30
58	Parlophone PMD 1068	BOSTIC ROCKS	30
59	Parlophone PMD 1071	BOSTIC SHOWCASE OF SWINGING DANCE HITS	20
59	Parlophone PMD 1074	SWEET TUNES OF THE FANTASTIC FIFTIES	20
59	Parlophone PMD 1115	SWEET TUNES OF THE ROARIN' TWENTIES	15
59	Parlophone PMD 1117	SWEET TUNES OF THE SWINGIN' THIRTIES	15
59	Parlophone PMD 1119	SWEET TUNES OF THE SENTIMENTAL FORTIES	15
60	Parlophone PMC 1125	PLAYS THE HIT TUNES OF THE BIG BROADWAY SHOWS (12" LP)	15

BOSTON

76	Epic EPCH 81611	BOSTON (LP, audiophile pressing)	20
76	Epic EPC 81611	BOSTON (LP, picture disc)	12
78	Epic E 9945050	DON'T LOOK BACK (LP, picture disc)	12
86	MCA MCGP 6017	THIRD STAGE (LP, picture disc)	15
94	MCA MCGP	WALK ON (LP, picture disc)	15

BOSTON BOPPERS

74	Penny Farthing PEN 828	Did You Get What You Wanted/Whirlwind Girl	35

BOSTON CRABS

65	Columbia DB 7586	Down In Mexico/Who?	20
65	Columbia DB 7679	As Long As I Have You/Alley Oop	20
66	Columbia DB 7830	Gin House/You Didn't Have To Be So Nice	20

BOSTON DEXTERS

(see also Buzz, Tam White)

64	Contemporary CR 101	Matchbox/La Bamba	200
64	Contemporary CR 102	You've Been Talking About Me/Nothing's Gonna Change Me	150
64	Contemporary CR 103	What Kind Of Girl Are You/I've Got Troubles Of My Own	150
65	Columbia DB 7498	I Believe To My Soul/I've Got Something To Tell You	50
65	Columbia DB 7641	Try Hard/No More Tears	45

JACK ANGLIN BOSTON AND THE SOULITES

69	Ackee ACK 103	Starvation/Slave	15

BO STREET RUNNERS

(see also [Mike] Patto, Timebox, Chicago Line, Cheynes, Fleetwood Mac)

64	Decca F 11986	Bo Street Runner/Tell Me	40
65	Columbia DB 7488	Tell Me What You're Gonna Do/And I Do Just What I Want	50
65	Columbia DB 7640	Baby Never Say Goodbye/Get Out Of My Way	55
66	Columbia DB 7901	Drive My Car/So Very Woman (featuring Mike [Too Much] Patto)	60
64	Oak RGJ 131	BO STREET RUNNERS (EP, 49 copies only)	1000

CONNIE BOSWELL

54	Brunswick 05319	T-E-N-N-E-S-S-E-E (Spells...)/If I Give My Heart To You	10
55	Brunswick 05397	How Important Can It Be?/Fill My Heart With Happiness	10

EVE BOSWELL

53	Parlophone MSP 6006	Sugar Bush/Moon Above Malaya (China Nights)	20
55	Parlophone MSP 6158	Ready, Willing And Able/Pam-Poo-Dey	10
55	Parlophone MSP 6160	The Heart You Break (May Be Your Own)/Tika Tika Tok	10
56	Parlophone MSP 6208	Young And Foolish/Where You Are	10
56	Parlophone MSP 6220	It's Almost Tomorrow/Cookie	10
56	Parlophone MSP 6250	Saries Marias/Come Back My Love	10
56	Parlophone R 4230	True Love/Where In The World Is Billy?	8
57	Parlophone R 4275	Rock Bobbin' Boats/Tra La La	15
57	Parlophone R 4299	Chantez, Chantez/She Said (Aunt Magnolia)	7
57	Parlophone R 4328	With All My Heart/Sugar Candy	7
57	Parlophone R 4341	The Gypsy In My Soul/Stop Whistlin' Wolf	7
57	Parlophone R 4362	Swedish Polka (Chickadee)/Tell My Love	5
58	Parlophone R 4401	(I Love You) For Sentimental Reasons/Bobby	6
58	Parlophone R 4414	I Do/Love Me Again	7
58	Parlophone R 4455	Left Right Out Of Your Heart/Voom-Ba-Voom	8
58	Parlophone R 4479	More Than Ever (Come Prima)/I Know Why	8
58	Parlophone R 4492	Christmas Lullaby/The Christmas Tree	6
59	Parlophone R 4517	If I Had A Talking Picture Of You/Piccaninny	5
59	Parlophone R 4544	Wimoweh Cha Cha/Boegoeberg Se Dam	5
59	Parlophone R 4555	Once Again/You Are Never Far Away From Me	5
60	Parlophone R 4618	Misty/Turnabout Heart	5
69	Morgan MRS 19	This Is My Love/Lonely In A Crowd	5
76	EMI EMI 2517	Sugar Bush '76/This Time	5
57	Parlophone GEP 8601	THE ENCHANTING EVE (EP)	15
58	Parlophone GEP 8690	EVE BOSWELL'S SHOWCASE (EP)	15
58	Parlophone GEP 8717	EVE BOSWELL'S SHOWCASE NO. 2 (EP)	15
56	Parlophone PMD 1039	SUGAR AND SPICE (10" LP)	40
57	Parlophone PMC 1038	SENTIMENTAL EVE (LP)	35
59	Parlophone PMC 1105	FOLLOWING THE SUN AROUND (LP)	35

SIMON BOSWELL

(see also Advertising)

75	Transatlantic TRA 307	MIND PARASITES (LP)	15

BOTHY BAND

76	Polydor 2383 417	OLD HAG YOU HAVE KILLED ME (LP)	15
75	Polydor 2383379	THE BOTHY BAND (LP)	18
77	Polydor 2383456	OUT OF THE WIND, INTO THE SUN (LP)	12

BOULEVARD

79	Chopper CHOP 5D	MAGIC MAN (12", red vinyl, no p/s)	15
81	Boulevard VARD 1	Dawn Raid/Take It Or Leave It (p/s)	60

MINT VALUE £

DENNIS BOVELL
(see also Matumbi, Rama)

78	Tempus TEMLP 001	STRICTLY DUBWISE (LP)	40
78	Ballistic LBR 1031	STRICTLY DUBWISE (LP)	15
81	Fontana 6381047	BRAIN DAMAGE (LP)	15

BOW BELLS
(see also Nola York)

65	Polydor 56030	Not To Be Taken/I'll Try Not To Hold It Against You	5
66	Parlophone R 5520	Belinda/When You're In	5

RICKY BOWDEN

63	HMV POP 1162	Alone To Cry/I'd Be Ashamed	12

JIMMY BOWEN

57	Columbia DB 3915	I'm Stickin' With You/Ever Lovin' Fingers	60
57	Columbia DB 3915	I'm Stickin' With You/Ever Lovin' Fingers (78)	20
57	Columbia DB 3984	Warm Up To Me, Baby/I Trusted You	50
57	Columbia DB 3984	Warm Up To Me, Baby/I Trusted You (78)	15
57	Columbia DB 4027	Cross Over/It's Shameful	30
57	Columbia DB 4027	Cross Over/It's Shameful (78)	15
58	Columbia DB 4184	The Two Step/By The Light Of The Silvery Moon	25
58	Columbia DB 4184	The Two Step/By The Light Of The Silvery Moon (78)	10
65	Reprise RS 23043	The Eagle (demos & some issues list "The Golden Eagle")/Spanish Cricket	20
67	Reprise RS 20592	Raunchy (with Chorus & Orchestra)/It's Such A Pretty World Today (wth Singers)	5
58	Columbia SEG 7757	MEET JIMMY BOWEN (EP)	70
58	Columbia SEG 7793	MEET JIMMY BOWEN NO. 2 (EP)	70

BEN BOWERS

55	Columbia SCM 5192	The Kentuckian Song/The Man From Laramie	10
56	Columbia SCM 5260	To You, My Love/I'm Still A King To You	7
57	Parlophone R 4317	Country Boy (with His Royal Jamaicans)/ Rum And Coconut Water (Rum And Coca-Cola)	5
57	Pye Jazz NJE 1001	BIG BEN BLUES (EP, with His Bluesicians)	8

DAVID BOWIE
(see also Davie Jones & King Bees, Davy Jones & Lower Third, Manish Boys, Arnold Corns, Spiders From Mars, Mick Ronson, Queen, Tao Jones Index, Bing Crosby)

SINGLES

66	Pye 7N 17020	Can't Help Thinking About Me/And I Say To Myself (with Lower Third)	250
66	Pye 7N 17079	Do Anything You Say/Good Morning Girl	250
66	Pye 7N 17157	I Dig Everything/I'm Not Losing Sleep	220
66	Deram DM 107	Rubber Band/The London Boys	250
67	Deram DM 123	The Laughing Gnome/The Gospel According To Tony Day (with inverted matrix number on label)	100
67	Deram DM 135	Love You Till Tuesday/Did You Ever Have A Dream	200
69	Philips BF 1801	Space Oddity/Wild Eyed Boy From Freecloud (unreleased p/s, only 2 or 3 copies known to exist)	3000
69	Philips BF 1801	Space Oddity/Wild Eyed Boy From Freecloud (mono)	15
69	Philips BF 1801	Space Oddity/Wild Eyed Boy From Freecloud (UK pressed stereo 45: unconfirmed)	0
70	Mercury MF 1135	The Prettiest Star/Conversation Piece	200
70	Mercury 6052 026	Memory Of A Free Festival Parts 1 & 2	200
71	Mercury 6052 049	Holy Holy/Black Country Rock	200
72	RCA RCA 2160	Changes/Andy Warhol	10
72	RCA RCA 2199	Starman/Suffragette City (in p/s)	100
72	RCA RCA 2263	John, I'm Only Dancing/Hang Onto Yourself (original pressing with slow 'acoustic guitar' version; later pressings have faster version with saxophone and are worth £4.)	6
72	Pye 7NX 8002	Do Anything You Say/I Dig Everything/ I Can't Help Thinking About Me/ I'm Not Losing Sleep (p/s)	20
72	RCA RCA 2302	The Jean Genie/Ziggy Stardust	5
73	RCA RCA 2352	Drive-In Saturday/Round And Round	5
73	RCA RCA 2316	Life On Mars?/The Man Who Sold The World (in p/s)	30
73	Deram DM 123	The Laughing Gnome/The Gospel According To Tony Day (reissue, matrix number correct way up on label)	5
74	RCA RCA 2424	Sorrow/Amsterdam	5
74	RCA LPBO 5009	Rebel Rebel/Queen Bitch	5
74	RCA LPBO 5021	Rock'N'Roll Suicide/Quicksand	5
74	RCA APBO 0293	Diamond Dogs/Holy Holy	5
74	RCA/Mainman	Bowie's Greatest Hits (excerpts from Knock On Wood/ Lyntone LYN 2929 Space Oddity/The Man Who Sold The World/Life On Mars?/ Starman/Jean Genie/Sorrow/Diamond dogs) 33rpm 1-sided flexidisc with Record Mirror/Popswop magazines)	20
74	RCA/Mainman	Bowie's Greatest Hits (excerpts from Knock On Wood/ Lyntone LYN 2929 Space Oddity/The Man Who Sold The World/Life On Mars?/ Starman/Jean Genie/Sorrow/Diamond dogs) 33rpm 1-sided flexidisc without Record Mirror/Popswop magazines)	6
74	RCA RCA 2466	Knock On Wood/Panic In Detroit	5
75	RCA RCA 2523	Young Americans/Suffragette City	5
75	Decca F 13579	The London Boys/Love You Till Tuesday	12
75	Decca F 13579	The London Boys/Love You Till Tuesday (Demo)	150
75	RCA RCA 2579	Fame/Right	5
75	RCA RCA 2593	Space Oddity/Changes/Velvet Goldmine (p/s)	12
76	RCA RCA 2726	Suffragette City/Stay (p/s)	18
77	RCA PB 0905	Sound And Vision/A New Career In A New Town	5
77	RCA PB 1017	Be My Wife/Speed Of Life	5
77	RCA PB 1121	'Heroes'/V-2 Schneider	5
78	RCA PB 1190	Beauty And The Beast/Sense Of Doubt (with p/s)	6

MINT VALUE £

79	RCA BOW 2	Boys Keep Swinging/Fantastic Voyage (p/s)	5
79	RCA BOW 3	DJ/Repetition (p/s, green vinyl)	20
79	RCA BOW 3	DJ/Repetition (p/s)	5
79	RCA BOW 4	John, I'm Only Dancing (Again)/John, I'm Only Dancing (p/s)	5
79	RCA BOW 12-4	John, I'm Only Dancing (Again) (Extended)/John, I'm Only Dancing (12", p/s)	8
80	RCA BOW 5	Alabama Song/Space Oddity (poster p/s)	5
80	RCA BOW 6	Ashes To Ashes/Move On (with 3 different p/s & 4 different sheets of 9 stamps)	5
81	RCA BOW 8	Scary Monsters/Because You're Young (p/s)	5
81	RCA BOW 9	Up The Hill Backwards/Crystal Japan (p/s)	5
81	RCA BOWC 9	Up The Hill Backwards/Crystal Japan (cassette, card sleeve)	10
82	RCA BOW 11	IN BERTHOLT BRECHT'S "BAAL" (EP, foldout p/s)	5
82	RCA BOW 100	FASHIONS (10 x 7" picture discs in plastic wallet [BOWP 101-110], each £4)	50
83	EMI America EAP 157	China Girl/Shake It (picture disc)	7
83	EMI America 12 EA 158	Modern Love/Modern Love (Live) (12", p/s with poster)	8
84	EMI America EA 187	Tonight/Tumble And Twirl (poster p/s)	6
85	EMI America EAP 195	Loving The Alien (Remixed Version)/Don't Look Down (Remixed Version) (shaped picture disc)	10
85	EMI America 12EAP 195	Living The Alien (Extended Dance Mix)/Don't Look Down (Extended Dance Mix)/ Loving The Alien (Extended Dub Mix) (12" picture disc)	10
86	Virgin VSS 838	Absolute Beginners/Absolute Beginners (Dub Mix) (square picture disc)	6
86	EMI America EAP 216	Underground (Edited Version)/Underground (Instrumental) (shaped picture disc)	8
86	Virgin VSS 906	When The Wind Blows/When The Wind Blows (Instrumental) (shaped pic disc)	8
87	EMI America EAP 237	Time Will Crawl (Single Version)/Girls (Single Edit) (poster p/s)	12
87	EMI America EAP 239	Never Let Me Down/'87 And Cry (picture disc)	12
88	Virgin CDT 20	Absolute Beginners (Full Length Version)/(Dub Mix) (3" CD, card sleeve)	8
88	PRT PYX 6001	I'm Not Losing Sleep/I Dig Everything/Can't Help Thinking/ Do Anything You Say (picture disc)	8
93	BMG Arista 136977	Jump They Say (Radio Edit)/Pallas Athena (Don't Stop Praying Mix) (jukebox issue, no p/s)	5
97	RCA 307031	The Heart's Filthy Lesson (Alternative Mix)/(Bowie Mix)/(Rubber Mix)/ (Simple Text Mix)/(Filthy Mix) (12", picture disc)	8
95	RCA 329407	Strangers When We Meet (Edit)/The Man Who Sold The World (live) (green vinyl, stickered card p/s)	6
95	RCA 353847	Hallo Spaceboy (Remix)/The Heart's Filthy Lesson (Radio Edit) (pink vinyl, stickered card p/s)	6
97	RCA 7432 1475841	Dead Man Walking/Hous/Vigor Mortis/Paradox (plain sleeve, stickered)	6
97	RCA 512347	Seven Years In Tibet (Edit)/Seven Years In Tibet (Mandarin Version) (p/s, clear vinyl)	6
99	Virgin VSP 1767	Survive/Seven (live) (picture disc)	8

ALBUMS

66	Deram DML 1007	DAVID BOWIE (mono)	400
67	Deram SML 1007	DAVID BOWIE (stereo)	500
69	Philips SBL 7912	DAVID BOWIE (gatefold sleeve, black/silver label)	500
70	Decca PA 58	THE WORLD OF DAVID BOWIE (mono)	25
71	Mercury 6338 041	THE MAN WHO SOLD THE WORLD (LP, black/silver labels with 'dress' cover)	500
71	Mercury 6338 041	THE MAN WHO SOLD THE WORLD (cassette, with 'dress' cover)	50
71	RCA SF 8244	HUNKY DORY (orange label with lyric sheet, 1st pressing with laminated sleeve)	200
71	RCA SF 8244	HUNKY DORY (orange label with lyric sheet)	25
72	RCA SF 8287	THE RISE AND FALL OF ZIGGY STARDUST AND THE SPIDERS FROM MARS (1st pressing with with 'Gem Productions' and no 'Mainman' logo on rear sleeve, orange label with lyric inner sleeve)	40
72	RCA LSP 4813	SPACE ODDITY (reissue of SBL 7912 in different sleeve, orange label with lyric inner sleeve & poster)	22
72	RCA LSP 4816	THE MAN WHO SOLD THE WORLD (orange label with inner sleeve & poster)	15
73	RCA RS 1001	ALADDIN SANE (orange label, gatefold sleeve & lyric inner sleeve, with fan club membership folder)	70
73	RCA RS 1001	ALADDIN SANE (orange label, gatefold sleeve & lyric inner sleeve)	25
73	RCA RS 1003	PIN UPS (LP, insert, orange label)	20
74	RCA APLI 0576	DIAMOND DOGS (LP, gatefold sleeve, orange label)	15
74	RCA APL 2-0771	DAVID LIVE (2-LP, gatefold sleeve, orange label, photos on inners)	20
76	RCA APLI 1327	STATION TO STATION (with original colour proof sleeve)	500
76	RCA RS 1055	CHANGESONEBOWIE (with 'sax' version of "John I'm Only Dancing")	25
77	RCA INTS 5065	LOW (red vinyl, semi-official 'factory custom pressing')	500
77	RCA PL12030	LOW (LP, insert, fan club flyer, stickered sleeve)	18
77	RCA PL12030	LOW (LP, insert, stickered sleeve)	12
78	RCA PL 02913	STAGE (2-LP, gatefold sleeve, yellow vinyl)	20
78	RCA PL 02913	STAGE (2-LP, gatefold sleeve)	12
80	RCA BOW LP 2	SCARY MONSTERS (AND SUPER CREEPS) (purple vinyl, semi-official 'factory custom pressing')	600
80	K-Tel NE 1111	THE BEST OF BOWIE (with incorrect tracklisting)	12
81	RCA BL 43606	CHRISTIANE F. WIR KINDER VOM BAHNOF ZOO (soundtrack)	12
83	EMI America AMLP 3029	LET'S DANCE (picture disc)	12
84	RCA BOPIC 1	ALADDIN SANE (picture disc with numbered insert)	18
84	RCA BOPIC 2	HUNKY DORY (picture disc with numbered insert)	18
84	RCA BOPIC 3	ZIGGY STARDUST (picture disc with numbered insert)	18
84	RCA BOPIC 4	PIN-UPS (picture disc with numbered insert)	18
84	RCA BOPIC 5	DIAMOND DOGS (picture disc with numbered insert)	18
90	EMI EMC 3579	ALADDIN SANE (LP, 1990 reissue, gatefold)	12
90	EMI EMC 3571	SPACE ODDITY (LP, 1990 reissue, gatefold with extra tracks)	25
90	EMI EMC 3577	ZIGGY STARDUST (LP, 1990 reissue, gatefold with unreleased tracks)	20
94	MAINMAN GYLP 002	SANTA MONICA LIVE '72 (2xLP, clear vinyl)	40
95	RCA 307021	EXCERPTS FROM OUTSIDE (with 12" booklet & lyric sheet)	40
97	RCA 44949	EARTHLING (gatefold sleeve)	40
97	EMI TVC1	ZIGGY STARDUST (LP, 1997 reissue, EMI Centenary edition)	20
03	EMI 0724359451121	SOUND AND VISION (4-CD box set with booklet)	25

MINT VALUE £

CDs

84	Deram 800 087-2	DAVID BOWIE (withdrawn with white title)	60
84	RCA PD 89002	STAGE (2-CD, withdrawn)	40
84	RCA PD 84234	LODGER (withdrawn)	20
84	RCA PD 83856	LOW (withdrawn)	20
84	RCA PD 83857	'HEROES' (withdrawn)	20
85	RCA PD 84623	HUNKY DORY (withdrawn)	20
85	RCA PD 84654	THE MAN WHO SOLD THE WORLD (withdrawn)	25
85	RCA PD 84702	THE RISE AND FALL OF ZIGGY STARDUST AND THE SPIDERS FROM MARS (withdrawn)	20
85	RCA PD 84813	SPACE ODDITY (withdrawn)	25
85	RCA PD 84653	PIN-UPS (withdrawn)	20
85	RCA PD 83890	ALADDIN SANE (withdrawn)	20
85	RCA PD 80998	YOUNG AMERICANS (withdrawn)	20
85	RCA PD 81327	STATION TO STATION (withdrawn)	25
85	RCA PD 81732	CHANGESONEBOWIE (withdrawn)	35
85	RCA PD 83856	LOW (withdrawn)	25
85	RCA PD 83889	DIAMOND DOGS (withdrawn)	25
86	RCA PD 82743	PETER AND THE WOLF (withdrawn)	20
85	RCA PD 83647	SCARY MONSTERS (AND SUPER CREEPS) (withdrawn)	25
84	RCA PD 84202	CHANGESTWOBOWIE (withdrawn)	30
84	RCA PD 94792	GOLDEN YEARS (withdrawn)	30
84	RCA PD 84919	FAME AND FASHION (ALL TIME GREATEST HITS) (withdrawn)	50
93	Arista 17822-2	THE BUDDHA OF SUBURBIA (special edition in clear plastic case, with novel)	22
93	BBC MMCD 0072	BBC SESSIONS 1969-1972 (CD, picture disc, promo-only, withdrawn)	75
99	Virgin CDVX 2900	'hours...' (hologram sleeve)	15

PROMOS

71	Gem BOWPROMO 1	BOWPROMO (LP, white label only, also known as HUNKY DORY SAMPLER Some with handwritten sleeve or Gem sticker on A-side, B-side features DANA GILLESPIE, 500 only)	1500
77	RCA BOW-1E	From The New Album 'Low" (excerpts from Speed Of Life, Breaking Glass, What In The World, Sound And Vision,	800
83	RCA LIFETIMES 1	LIFETIMES (LP, promo, numbered, with insert)	35
90	BMG BOW 908	SO FAR (CD, 8-track sampler for "Sound & Vision" box set)	50
91	Rykodisc VRCD 0142	BOWIE / ENO: IT'S TIME TO LISTEN (CD, 9-track sampler from Ryko reissues; includes "Sound + Vision", "Be My Wife", "Some Are", "Heroes", "Joe The Lion", Abdulmajid, DJ, Boys Keep Swinging, Look Back in Anger)	15
93	BMG MEAT 1	Pallas Athena (12", white label, no p/s, includes two exclusive Meat Beat Manifesto remixes)	40
93	Back To Basics HOME 1	Night Flights/(B-side by Moodswings) (12")	18
93	EMI BOWIE 1	SELECTIONS FROM THE SINGLES COLLECTION 10-track sampler,card p/s, promo only)	18
95	RCA HALLO 2	Hallo Spaceboy (12" Remix) (12", 1-sided, no p/s)	18
95	BMG SOLO 1	EXCLUSIVE TOUR CD: Strangers When We Meet/ MORRISSEY: The Boy Racer (Outside Tour CD)	90
95	RCA OUT 1	The Heart's Filthy Lesson (12", 1-sided promo)	10
96	RCA SPACE 2	Hallo Spaceboy (12" Remix) (1-sided 12", some copies listed as RCA HALLO 2, no p/s)	25
96	RCA SPACE 3	Hallo Spaceboy (Double Click Mix)/Hallo Spaceboy (Instrumental)/ Hallo Spaceboy (Lost In Space Mix) (12", no p/s)	50
99	Virgin CDVDJ 2900	'hours...' (CD, card sleeve)	20
99	EMI CDLRL 015	ALBUM SAMPLER (CD, 17-track sampler, promo only)	20
99	EMI QUEENWL 28	Under Pressure (Remixes) (with Queen) (12", white label, unreleased mix, promo only)	30
09	Parlophone LCO 299	DAVID BOWIE : Heroes/TV ON THE RADIO : Heroes	40

CANDY BOWMAN

81	RCA RCAT 148	Since I Found You/I Wanna Feel Your Love (12")	15

BOWMAN-HYDE PLAYERS

61	Ember EMB S 141	I Like A Little Honey/Teenage Kiss	8
61	Parlophone PMC 1155	SING ME A SOUVENIR (LP)	15

ALAN BOWN (SET)

(see also Robert Palmer, John Barry Seven, Bronco, Jonesy)

65	Pye 7N 15934	Can't Let Her Go/I'm The One	25
66	Pye 7N 17084	Baby Don't Push Me/Everything's Gonna Be Alright	25
66	Pye 7N 17148	Headline News/Mister Pleasure	80
66	Pye 7N 17192	Emergency 999/Settle Down	80
67	Pye 7N 17256	Gonna Fix You Good (Everytime You're Bad)/I Really Really Care	50
67	Music Factory CUB 1	We Can Help You/Magic Handkerchief (as the Alan Bown!)	12
67	MGM MGM 1355	Toyland/Technicolour Dream	12
68	MGM MGM 1387	Story Book/Little Lesley	25
69	Deram DM 259	Still As Stone/Wrong Idea	10
69	Deram DM 278	Gypsy Girl/All I Can	6
70	Island WIP 6091	Pyramid/Crash Landing	5
75	CBS 3721	Rockford Files/I Don't Know	6
68	Music Factory CUB LM/LS 1	OUTWARD BOWN (LP)	80
69	Deram DML/SML 1049	THE ALAN BOWN! (LP)	50
70	Island ILPS 9131	LISTEN (LP, with inner sleeve)	25
71	Island ILPS 9163	STRETCHING OUT (LP, gatefold sleeve)	25

ALAN BOWN SET/JIMMY JAMES & VAGABONDS

(see also Jimmy James & Vagabonds)

68	Pye N(S)PL 18156	LONDON SWINGS - LIVE AT THE MARQUEE CLUB (LP, 1 side each)	50

ANDREW BOWN

(see also Andy Bown)

70	Parlophone R 5856	Tarot (Theme From 'Ace Of Wands')/Lulli Rides Again	120

MINT VALUE £

ANDY BOWN

(see also Andrew Bown, Herd, Judas Jump, Status Quo, Rossi & Frost, Storyteller)

75	GM GMS 9039	Supersonic/Feeling Better	8
79	EMI EMI 2906	Another Shipwreck/Another Night With You	6
79	EMI EMI 2943	Good Advice/One More Chance	5
81	EMI EMI 5245	Say It Was Magic/One Forward Two Back Again (in p/s)	10
82	EMI EMI 5312	Marianne/One Forward Two Back Again	5
82	EMI EMI 5372	Help Me/Marianne (p/s)	5
72	Mercury 6310 002	GONE TO MY HEAD (LP)	20
73	GM GML 1001	SWEET WILLIAM (LP)	20

BOX CAR RACER

(see also Blink 182)

00s	MCA MCS 40290	I Feel So/Cat Like Thief (picture disc)	8

DAVID BOX

(see also Crickets)

64	London HLU 9874	If You Can't Say Something Nice/Sweet Sweet Day	20
64	London HLU 9924	Little Lonely Summer Girl/No One Will Ever Know	20

BOXER

(see also Patto, Timebox, Koobas, May Blitz)

75	Virgin V 2049	BELOW THE BELT (LP, gatefold sleeve with uncensored full-frontal back cover)	20
76	Virgin V 2073	BLOODLETTING (LP, withdrawn)	100

BOX TOPS

(see also Big Star, Alex Chilton)

67	Stateside SS 2044	The Letter/Happy Times	10
67	Stateside SS 2070	Neon Rainbow/She Knows How	15
68	Bell BLL 1001	Cry Like A Baby/The Door You Closed To Me	8
68	Bell BLL 1017	Choo Choo Train/Fields Of Clover	6
68	Bell BLL 1035	I Met Her In Church/People Gonna Talk	5
69	Bell BLL 1045	Sandman/Sweet Cream Ladies, Forward March	5
69	Bell BLL 1063	I Shall Be Released/I Must Be The Devil	5
69	Bell BLL 1068	Soul Deep/The Happy Song	7
69	Bell BLL 1084	Turn On A Dream/Together	5
70	Bell BLL 1097	You Keep Tightening Up On Me/Come On Honey	5
73	London HLU 10402	Sugar Creek Woman/It's All Over	5
68	Stateside (S)SL 10218	THE LETTER/NEON RAINBOW (LP)	25
68	Bell MBLL/SBLL 105	CRY LIKE A BABY (LP)	25
69	Bell MBLL/SBLL 108	NON-STOP (LP)	20
69	Bell SBLL 120	DIMENSIONS (LP)	20
70	Bell MBLL/SBLL 129	SUPER HITS (LP)	15
70	Bell BELLS 149	BOX TOPS (LP)	18

DENNY BOYCE & HIS ORCHESTRA/RHYTHM

58	Oriole CB 1458	Bad Boy/When Your Hair Has Turned To Silver	10

JUNIOR BOYCE

77	Observer OB 004	Natty Dreadlocks/Sick-More Tree/What Kind Of World/ Sic Easy Stepping (12", with Ranking Buckers)	30

TOMMY BOYCE

65	MGM MGM 1287	Pretty Thing/I Don't Have To Worry 'Bout You	10

TOMMY BOYCE & BOBBY HART

(see also Monkees, Tommy Boyce)

67	A&M AMS 705	Out And About/My Little Chickadee	5
67	A&M AMS 710	Sometimes She's A Little Girl/Love Every Day	5
68	A&M AMS 714	I Wonder What She's Doing Tonight?/Ambushers	5
68	A&M AMS 722	Goodbye Baby/Where Angels Go Trouble Follows	5
68	A&M AMS 729	Alice Long (You're Still My Favourite Girlfriend)/P.O. Box 9847	5
67	A&M AML 907	TEST PATTERNS (LP)	25

EDDIE BOYD

(see also Fleetwood Mac)

66	Blue Horizon 45 BH 1009	It's So Miserable To Be Alone/Empty Arms	150
67	Blue Horizon 57-3137	The Big Boat/Sent For You Yesterday (with Fleetwood Mac)	30
62	Esquire EP 247	BOYD'S BLUES (EP, as Eddie Boyd Blues Combo)	70
65	Fontana SFJL 905	FIVE LONG YEARS (LP)	60
67	Decca LK/SKL 4872	EDDIE BOYD AND HIS BLUES BAND FEATURING PETER GREEN (LP)	120
68	Blue Horizon 7-63202	7936 SOUTH RHODES (LP, with Fleetwood Mac)	70
68	Storyville SLP 4054	IN CONCERT (LP)	25

EDDIE BOYD/BUDDY GUY

(see also Buddy Guy)

66	Chess CRE 6009	WITH THE BLUES (EP, 2 tracks each)	25

FRANKLYN BOYD

57	Nestles NR 01	Bye, Bye Love (78, 1-sided card flexi)	10
57	Nestles NR 05	Teddy Bear (78, 1-sided card flexi)	10

JIMMY BOYD

53	Columbia SCM 5072	I Saw Mommy Kissing Santa Claus/Little Train A-Chuggin' In My Heart	10

CHARLES BOYER

65	London HL 10002	Where Does Love Go/PERRY BOTKIN JR: Theme From Where Love Goes	6
60	London HAT 8268	WHERE DOES LOVE GO (LP)	15

BOY FRIDAY (& GROOVERS)

(see also Dandy & Superboys)

70	Downtown DT 470	Version Girl/Grumble Man	15
71	Downtown DT 471	Music So Good/Right Track (both with Groovers)	8

71	Downtown DT 472	Sounds I Remember/JOAN LONG: Reconsider Our Love	6
71	Downtown DT 473	Take A Message Ruby/Second Note	12
71	Downtown DT 476	There'll Always Be Sunshine/Sunshine Track	7
71	Downtown DT 477	Hot Pants Girl/Raunchy	10
71	Downtown DT 481	El Raunchy/Conversation (as Boy Friday & Collins)	6
71	J-Dan JDN 4416	I Don't Want No War/Third Note Swing	7
71	J-Dan JDN 4418	Situation Version/OUR BAND: Keep Tracking	7

BOYFRIENDS
(see also Vibrators)

78	United Artists UP 36424	I'm In Love Today/Saturday Night (p/s)	10
78	United Artists UP 36442	Jenny/Don't Ask Me To Explain (p/s)	10
78	United Artists UP 36478	Last Bus Home/Romance (p/s)	10

BOYFRIENDS

82	Plastic PRES 001	Boyfriend/Give A Little, Take A Little (p/s)	40

BOY GEORGE
(see also Culture Club, Jesus Loves You)

88	Virgin BOY 105-12	Live My Life/Live My Life (Klub Mix)/Live My Life (12" Club Remix) (12", poster sleeve)	8
88	Virgin BOYT 106	No Clause 28 (Space Face Full Remix)/(Space Face Full Dub)/ (Full Version) (3" CD, in 5" slimline jewel case, with adaptor)	8
88	Virgin BOYCD 106	No Clause 28 (5" CD)	8
98	More Protein PROT 112	Sad (Mixes)/Butterfly (Mixes)	8
98	More Protein (no cat. no.)	Open House With Boy George & Family (CD-ROM, available at selected concerts)	20

BOY HAIRDRESSERS
(see also Teenage Fanclub, BMX Bandits, Clouds)

88	53rd & 3rd AGARR T12	Golden Showers/Tidalwave/The Assumption As An Elevator (12", p/s)	25

BOY KRAZY

91	Polydor PZCD 158	That's What Love Can Do (Extended Version)/One Thing Leads To Another/ That's What Love Can Do (7" version) (CD, p/s)	10
91	Polydor 828 403-2	BOY KRAZY (CD)	20

BILLY BOYLE
(see also Le Roys)

62	Decca F 11503	My Baby's Crazy 'Bout Elvis/Held For Questioning	15
63	Decca F 11709	I'm Coming Home/Sunday's Child	8
63	Columbia DB 7111	Lovers Hill/She's New To You	5
63	Columbia DB 7127	Hootin' In The Kitchen/Lover's Hill	5
64	Columbia DB 7294	Walk, Walk, Walkin'/My Baby Tonight (with Le Roys)	6
70	UPC UPC112	Lookin' For Love/Pisces Man	20

A. BOYNE

70	Punch PH 36	Oh My Darling (actually Audley Rollins)/DENNIS SMITH: Ball Of Confusion	10

BILLY BOYO

82	Greensleeves GRELD 89	Righteousness/Itie Title Girl (12")	15

BOYS (Jamaica)
(see also Harry J. Allstars)

69	Duke DU 19	Easy Sound/AFROTONES: Freedom Sound	20

BOYS (U.K.)

63	Parlophone R 5027	Polaris/Jumpin'	25

BOYS (U.K.)
(see also Sandra Barry & Boys, Action)

64	Pye 7N 15726	It Ain't Fair/I Want You	100

BOYS (U.K.)
(see also Yobs, Rowdies, Hollywood Brats)o

77	NEMS NES 102	I Don't Care/Soda Pressing (p/s)	15
77	NEMS NES 111	First Time/Whatcha Gonna Do/Turning Grey (p/s)	15
78	NEMS NES 116	Brickfield Nights/Teacher's Pet (p/s)	10
79	Safari SAFE 21	Kamikaze/Bad Days (p/s, with booklet)	6
80	Safari SAFE 23	Terminal Love/I Love Me (p/s)	5
80	Safari SAFE 27	You Better Move On/Schoolgirls (p/s)	5
80	Safari SAFE 31	Weekend/Cool (p/s)	5
80	Safari SAFE 33	Let It Rain/Lucy (p/s)	6
77	NEMS NES 6001	THE BOYS (LP)	15
78	NEMS NEL 6015	ALTERNATIVE CHARTBUSTERS (LP, with inner sleeve)	15
79	Safari 1-2 BOYS	TO HELL WITH THE BOYS (LP, with songbook & stickered sleeve)	12
80	Safari BOYS 4	BOYS ONLY (LP)	15
90	Receiver RRLP 135	LIVE AT THE ROXY APRIL '77 (LP)	12

BOYS (U.K.)
(see also Ocean Colour Scene)

88	Cleversounds BOYS 1	Happy Days/Standard Avenue/Learn How To Dance (p/s)	8

BOYS BLUE
(see also Jeff Elroy & Boys Blue)

65	HMV POP 1427	You Got What I Want/Take A Heart	50

BOZ
(see also King Crimson, Bad Company, Alexis Korner)

66	Columbia DB 7832	You're Just The Kind Of Girl I Want/Isn't That So	30
66	Columbia DB 7889	Meeting Time/No (Ah) Body Knows The Blues	30
66	Columbia DB 7941	Pinocchio/Stay As You Are	15
66	Columbia DB 7972	The Baby Song/Carry On Screaming	20
68	Columbia DB 8406	I Shall Be Released/Down In The Flood	20
68	Columbia DB 8468	Light My Fire/Back Against The Wall	15

			MINT VALUE £
JANET BRACE			
55	Brunswick 05272	Teach Me Tonight/My Old Familiar Heartache	10
BRACKEN			
79	Look LKLP 6438	PRINCE OF THE NORTHLANDS (LP, private pressing, with insert)	60
KIM & KELLY BRADEN			
67	Columbia DB 8312	Didn't I/You're Leaving, She's Crying, I'm Laughing	5
68	Columbia DB 8421	Happiness Is/Sing A Rainbow	5
BOBBY BRADFORD			
73	Emanem 302	LOVE'S DREAM (LP)	30
BRADFORD SINGERS			
62	Stateside SL 10026	BLACK NATIVITY (LP)	15
64	Stateside SL 10083	ANGEL ON VACATION (LP)	15
GEORGE BRADLEY & HIS BAND			
65	HMV POP 1459	Breakout/Vendetta	10
JAN BRADLEY			
63	Pye International 7N 25182	Mama Didn't Lie/Lovers Like Me	60
MARTIN BRADLEY			
80	Greenwich Village GVR 205	TIME CAN'T STAND STILL (LP)	15
OWEN BRADLEY (ORCHESTRA/QUINTET)			
56	Brunswick 05528	Theme From "The Threepenny Opera"/Lights Of Vienna (with Orchestra)	5
57	Brunswick 05700	White Silver Sands/Midnight Blues (as Owen Bradley Quintet)	5
58	Brunswick 05736	Big Guitar/Sentimental Dream (as Owen Bradley Quintet)	20
60	Brunswick LAT 8327	THE BIG GUITAR (LP)	30
BRADLEY STRYDER			
92	Rephlex CAT 001	BRADLEY'S BEAT (12" EP, logo sleeve)	20
96	Rephlex CAT 020	BRADLEY'S ROBOT (12" EP, poster p/s)	10
BUDDY BRADSHAW			
(see also Owen Gray)			
59	Capitol CL 15036	Nothing You Can Say/Tonight I Walk Alone	15
DON BRADSHAW-LEATHER			
(supposedly by Robert John Godfrey)			
72	Distance DIST 101	DISTANCE BETWEEN US (2-LP, gatefold sleeve, private pressing)	80
SONNY BRADSHAW (& YOUNG JAMAICA)			
61	Duke DK 1003	Yellow Birds/Festival Jump Up	15
71	Big Shot BI 576	Wig Wam/Peace And Love (as Sonny Bradshaw & Young Jamaica)	12
TINY BRADSHAW & HIS ORCHESTRA			
54	Parlophone CMSP 3	South Of The Orient/Later (export issue)	20
54	Parlophone MSP 6118	The Gypsy/Spider Web	15
55	Parlophone DP 418	Bradshaw Boogie/Walkin' The Chalk Line (78, export issue)	10
55	Parlophone MSP 6145	Overflow/Don't Worry 'Bout Me	20
54	Parlophone GEP 8507	TRAIN KEPT A ROLLING (EP)	50
56	Parlophone GEP 8552	POMPTON TURNPIKE (EP)	30
50s	Parlophone CGEP 2	TINY BRADSHAW (export EP)	25
TINY BRADSHAW ORCHESTRA/WYNONIE HARRIS			
(see also Wynonie Harris)			
70	Polydor 623 273	KINGS OF RHYTHM AND BLUES (LP, 1 side each)	22
BOB BRADY & CONCHORDS			
68	Bell BLL 1025	Everybody's Goin' To The Love-In/It's Been A Long Time Between Kisses	20
70	Bell BLL 1114	Everybody's Goin' To The Love-In/It's Been A Long Time Between Kisses (reissue)	10
MAJELLA BRADY			
65	Rex R11015	Light In My Window/Girl	8
PHIL BRADY & THE RANCH SET			
67	Go AJ 11406	Lonesome For You/Please Come Back	20
VICTOR BRADY			
70	Polydor	BROWN RAIN (LP)	25
BRADY BUNCH			
73	Paramount SPFL 284	MEET THE BRADY BUNCH (LP)	15
AL 'TNT' BRAGGS			
66	Vocalion VP 9278	Earthquake/How Long (Do You Hold On)	20
66	Vocalion VP 9278	Earthquake/How Long (Do You Hold On) (DJ Copy)	60
68	Action ACT 4506	Earthquake/How Long (Do You Hold On) (reissue)	15
69	Action ACT 4526	I'm A Good Man/I Like What You Do To Me	15
65	Vocalion VEP 170163	AL 'TNT' BRAGGS (EP)	110
ERNEL BRAHAM			
(see also Kent Walker)			
66	Rio R 79	Musical Fight/EDWARDS ALLSTARS: Pipeline	30
ROY BRAHAM			
64	R&B 166	Believe Me/Red Sea	30
BRAIN			
(see also Giles Giles & Fripp, Trendsetters Ltd, League Of Gentlemen)			
67	Parlophone R 5595	Nightmares In Red/Kick The Donkey	120
87	Bam Caruso OPRA 63	Nightmares In Red/SRC: Black Sheep (jukebox edition, die-cut company sleeve)	10

MINT VALUE £

BRAINBOX
(see also Jan Akkerman, Hunters, Focus)
69 Parlophone R 5775 Woman's Gone/Down Man 15
70 Parlophone R 5842 So Helpless/To You 10
70 Parlophone PCS 7094 BRAINBOX (LP, black/silver/white boxed Parlophone label) 120

BRAINCHILD
70 A&M AMS 805 Cage/Autobiography 6
70 A&M AMLS 979 HEALING OF THE LUNATIC OWL (LP, brown label) 70

BRAINIAC 5
80 Roach RR 5002 Working/Feel (p/s) 10
78 Roach RREP 5001 MUSHY DOUBT (EP, 33rpm, p/s) 10

BRAINKILLERS
94 3rd Party, Kemet KM3RD#1 BORDER LINE EP (with FAMILY OF INTELLEGENCE) (12") 25
94 3rd Party 3RD#10 Screwface (Remixes) (12") 8

BRAINSTORM
79 Miracle M5 Lovin' Is Really My Game/Stormin' (12", red or black vinyl no p/s) 20

BRAINTAX
92 Low Life Low 2 FAT HEAD (EP 12" - 500 pressed) 60
97 Low Life Low 4 FUTURE YEARS (EP, 12") 35
99 Low Life Low 9 THE TRAVEL SHOW (EP, 12") 20
00 Low Life Low 11 Hardworking/Escuchame/First Joint (12", p/s) 10
06 Low Life Low 44 D90 Rules (Vocal)/D90 Rules (Instrumental) 5
01 Low Life Low 15 BIRO FUNK (2-LP) 15

BRAKES
80 Magnet MAGL FOR WHY YOU KICKA MY DONKEY? (LP) 15

WILFRED BRAMBELL
63 Parlophone R 5058 Secondhand/Ragtime Ragabone Man 15
71 CBS 7062 The Decimal Song/Time Marches On 8

WILFRED BRAMBELL & HARRY H. CORBETT
63 Pye 7N 15588 Steptoe And Son At Buckingham Palace (Parts 1 & 2, in p/s) 8
63 Pye 7N 15588 Steptoe And Son At Buckingham Palace (Parts 1 & 2) 5
63 Pye NEP 24169 THE FACTS OF LIFE (EP) 8
63 Pye NEP 24180 THE WAGES OF SIN (EP) 10
65 Pye NPL 18135 LOVE AND HAROLD STEPTOE (LP) 12
66 Pye NPL 18153 GEMS FROM THE STEPTOE SCRAP HEAP (LP) 12

DELANEY BRAMLETT
(see also Delaney & Bonnie, King Curtis with Delaney & Friends)
64 Vocalion VP 9227 Heartbreak Hotel/You Never Looked Sweeter 15
65 Vocalion VP 9237 Liverpool Lou/You Have No Choice 30
65 Vocalion VP 9237 Liverpool Lou/You Have No Choice (DJ Copy) 50

BRAM STOKER
72 Windmill WMD 117 HEAVY ROCK SPECTACULAR (LP) 40

BILL BRAMWELL
58 Starlite ST45 004 My Old Man/Shoutin' In That Amen Corner 10
60 Decca F 11309 Candid Camera Theme/Frederika 5

BRAN
74 Sain 1038M AIL DDECHRA (LP) 65
74 Gwawr GWA 104 BRAN EP (p/s) 50
75 Sain 1038M AIL-DDECHRA (LP) 300
76 Sain 1070M HEDFAN (LP) 100
78 Sain 1120M GWRACH Y NOS (LP) 40

BRAND
64 Piccadilly 7N 35216 I'm A Lover Not A Fighter/Zulu Stomp 130

BRAND NEW
03 Eat Sleep Jude Law And A Semester abroad/Am I Wrong (p/s) 30

BRAND NEW HEAVIES
91 Acid Jazz JAZID 39P Never Stop (12", company sleeve, withdrawn) 20

BILL BRANDON
73 Mercury 6052 186 I Am Free Of Your Love/(Take Another Little) Piece Of My Heart 10

JOHNNY BRANDON
56 Parlophone MSP 6238 Rock-A-Bye Baby/Lonely Lips 50
56 Parlophone R 4207 Shim Sham Shuffle/I Didn't Know 50
56 Decca F 10778 Glendora/Song For A Summer Night 20
57 Decca F 10858 Nothing Is Too Good For You/A Sort-Of-A-Feeling 10
59 Top Rank JAR 241 Santa Claus Jnr./I Heard A Bluebird Sing 10
55 Pye NEP 24003 JOHNNY BRANDON HITS (EP) 15

KIRK BRANDON & PACK OF LIES
(see also Theatre Of Hate, Spear Of Destiny, Senate, Pack)
87 SS SS1N2/SS2N1 KIRK BRANDON AND THE PACK OF LIES (EP) 8

TONY BRANDON
68 MGM MGM 1401 Candy Kisses/Get Going Baby 5

VERN BRANDON
62 Decca F 11472 Let Me Be The One/Gotta Know The Reason 15

BRAND X
(see also Phil Collins)
79 Charisma CB 340-12 Soho/Dance Of The Illegal Aliens/Noddy Goes To Sweden/
Pool Room Blues (12", p/s) 8

MINT VALUE £

BRANDY BOYS

65	Columbia DB 7507	Gale Winds/Don't Come Knocking At My Door	10

BRANDY WINE BRIDGE

77	Cottage COT 311	THE GREY LADY (LP)	25
78	Cottage COT 321	AN ENGLISH MEADOW (LP, hand-drawn sleeve with insert)	25

BRANDY WINE SINGERS

63	Columbia DB 7156	Funny Face/Will It Last	7
68	President PT 204	Mandy/Two Little Boys	6

LINDA BRANNON

63	Columbia DB 7156	Funny Face/Will It Last	6

JOHNNY BRANTLEY'S ALL STARS

58	London HLU 8606	The Place/Pot Luck	20
58	London HLU 8606	The Place/Pot Luck (78 rpm)	10

BRASS ALLEY

(see under Various Artists EPs)

73	Alaska ALA 11	You Better Run/Be My Friend	20

BRASS CONSTRUCTION

75	United Artists 12 UP 617	Movin'/Changin'	25
79	United Artists 12UP	Movin'/Changin' (12")	40
82	United Artists UAS 29923	BRASS CONSTRUCTION (LP)	15

ANDRÉ BRASSEUR

65	Pye International 7N 25332	Early Bird Satellite/Special 230	10
67	CBS 202557	The Kid/Holiday	20
67	CBS 202557	The Kid/Holiday (DJ Copy)	50
71	CBS 2557	The Kid/Holiday (reissue)	8
66	CBS 62858	TASTY (LP)	15

BRASS INCORPORATED

70	Pye International 7N 25520	At The Sign Of The Swinging Cymbal/Just Like That	18

BRASS MONKEY

71	Philips 6303 025	BRASS MONKEY (LP)	30

BRASS TACKS

68	Big T BIG 110	I'll Keep On Holding On/Let The Sunshine In	35
68	Big T BIG 114	Maxwell Ferguson/Sunshine After The Rain	100

BRASS WYNDS

67	Pye 7N 17255	Music To Watch Girls By/Sugar's Sweet	5

BRATZ

80	A Famous Record AFR 1	The Bratz Are Coming/Coast To Coast/Everyone Wants To Be Elvis (p/s)	6

RICHARD BRAUTIGAN

69	Zapple ZAPPLE 03	LISTENING TO RICHARD BRAUTIGAN (LP, unreleased, acetates exist)	750

CEDRIC BRAVO

65	Ska Beat JB 229	Merry Christmas/Sugar Baby	20

LOS BRAVOS

(see also Mike Kennedy)

66	Decca F 22419	Black Is Black/I Want A Name	5
66	Decca F 22484	I Don't Care/Don't Be Left Out In The Cold	5
66	Decca F 22529	Going Nowhere/Brand New Baby	20
67	Decca F 22615	I'm All Ears/You'll Never Get The Chances Again	8
67	Decca F 22682	Like Nobody Else/Wearing A Smile	5
68	Decca F 22765	Bring A Little Lovin'/Make It Last	12
69	Decca F 22853	Save Me, Save Me/Baby I Love You Because I Need You	5
70	Decca F 13064	People Talking Around/Every Dog Has His Night	5
66	Decca LK 4822	BLACK IS BLACK (LP)	18
68	Decca LK/SKL 4905	LOS BRAVOS (LP)	25

ANTHONY BRAXTON

85	Leo 414/415/416	QUARTET (3-LP box set with insert)	35

ANTHONY BRAXTON & DEREK BAILEY

(see also Derek Bailey)

73	Emanem 601	DUO (2-LP)	30
84	Incus INCUS 43	ROYAL VOLUME 1 (LP)	20

PRISCILLA BRAZIER

74	Dovetail DOVE 9	PRISCILLA BRAZIER (LP)	40
76	Key KL 038	SOMETHING BEAUTIFUL (LP)	35

BREAD

(see also David Gates, Pleasure Fair)

69	Elektra EKSN 45071	London Bridge/Dismal Day	5
70	Elektra 210 010	Making It With You/Why Do You Keep Me Waiting	5
69	Elektra EKS 74044	BREAD (LP)	12

BREAD & BEER BAND

(see also Elton John, Caleb)

69	Decca F 12891	Dick Barton Theme (The Devil's Gallop)/Breakdown Blues	75
72	Decca F 13354	Dick Barton Theme (The Devil's Gallop)/Breakdown Blues (reissue)	40
69	Rubbish (no cat. no.)	THE BREAD AND BEER BAND (LP, 1 copy known to exist)	2000

BREAD, LOVE & DREAMS

(see also Human Beast)

69	Decca F 12958	Virgin Kiss/Switch Out The Sun	20
69	Decca LK/SKL 5008	BREAD, LOVE AND DREAMS (LP, unboxed large Decca on label)	200

MINT VALUE £

70	Decca LK/SKL 5048	THE STRANGE TALE OF CAPTAIN SHANNON AND THE HUNCHBACK FROM GIGHA (LP, small boxed Decca label)	200
71	Decca SKL 5081	AMARYLLIS (LP, small boxed Decca label)	600

BREAKAWAYS
(see also Vernons Girls, Burt Bacharach Orchestra, Mike Patto, Ken Cope, Sharades, De Laine Sisters)

62	Pye 7N 15471	He's A Rebel/Wishing Star	15
63	Pye 7N 15585	That Boy Of Mine/Here She Comes	15
64	Pye 7N 15618	That's How It Goes/He Doesn't Love Me	20
65	Pye 7N 15973	Danny Boy/Your Kind Of Love	20
67	CBS 2833	Sacred Love/Don't Be A Baby	10
68	MCA MU 1018	Santo Domingo/So In Love Are We	10

BREAKDOWN

77	MCP 001	MEET ME ON THE HIGHWAY (LP, private pressing with insert)	25

BREAKERS

81	Riot RS 1001	Radio Love/My Momma Told Me (p/s)	20

BREAKING THE ILLUSION

92	Lowlife LOW 1	WHERE WILL IT END? (EP, 12" p/s, 1000 pressed)	35
93	Lowlife LOW 3	LOSE YOUR ILLUSION (EP)	15

BREAKOUT

81	Guardian GRC 101	Wall Of Solitude/Get Out Fight Back	80

BREAKTHRU'

68	Mercury MF 1066	Ice Cream Tree/Julius Caesar	25

BREAKWATER

86	Arista ARIST 12674	Say You Love Me Girl/Work It Out (12", p/s)	15

BREATHLESS

81	Magnum Force MFEP 005	SOCK HOP BOPPIN' (EP)	25

PATRICIA BREDIN

59	Top Rank JAR 257	'Till The Right Times Comes/I Live To Love You	8

BREEDERS

90	4AD CAD 0006	POD (LP)	12
08	4AD CAD 2803	MOUNTAIN BATTLES (LP, inner sleeve and booklet)	15

JIMMY BREEDLOVE
(see also Cues)

57	London HLE 8490	Over Somebody Else's Shoulder/That's My Baby	100
57	London HLE 8490	Over Somebody Else's Shoulder/That's My Baby (78)	50
62	Pye International 7N 25121	You're Following Me/Fabulous	30
75	Pye Disco Demand DDS 110	I Can't Help Loving You/I Saw You	5

BOBBY BREEN

62	Fontana 373	When The Lights Go Out/Everybody Twist	20

BUDDY BREGMAN & HIS ORCHESTRA

56	HMV 7MC 40	Theme From "Picnic"/Riviera (export issue)	5

JACQUES BREL

62	Fontana SFJL 967	A L'OLYMPIA (LP)	15

BRELLO CABAL
(see also Anita Harris)

67	CBS 3214	Margarine Flavoured Pineapple Chunk/Follow That (as The Brello Cabal)	8

BEVERLEY BREMERS

72	Wand WN 18	Get Smart Girl/Don't Say You Don't Remember	15
72	Wand WN 28	We're Free/Colours Of Love	5
72	Wand WN 34	I'll Make You Music/I Made A Man Out Of You Jimmy	5

BRENDA & TABULATIONS

67	London HL 10127	Dry Your Eyes/The Wash	30
67	London HL 10174	When You're Gone/Hey Boy	25
68	Direction 58-3678	Baby You're So Right For Me/To The One I Love	10
69	Action ACT 4541	That's In The Past/I Can't Get Over Her	30
70	London HL 10325	A Child No One Wanted/'Scuse Uz Y'all	15
71	CBS 7279	Right On The Tip of My Tongue/Always And Forever	8
73	Epic EPC 1361	One Girl Too Late/The Magic Of Your Love	8
69	Action ACLP 6003	DRY YOUR EYES (LP)	50

BUDDY BRENNAN QUARTET

60	London HLU 9049	Big River/The Chase	5

ROSE BRENNAN

55	HMV 7M 299	Ding Dong/Sincerely	15
55	HMV 7M 328	Wake The Town And Tell The People/Ten Little Kisses	10
56	HMV 7M 360	You Are My Love/My Dublin Bay	10
56	HMV 7M 383	Band Of Gold/My Believing Heart	10
57	HMV POP 302	Without Love (There Is Nothing)/Tra La La	10
59	Top Rank JAR 152	Johnny Let Me Go/My Summer Diary	8
61	Philips PB 1193	Tall Dark Stranger/This Girl With The Wistful Eyes	5

WALTER BRENNAN

60	London HLD 9148	Dutchman's Gold/Back To The Farm	12
62	Liberty LIB 55436	Old Rivers/Epic Ride Of John H Glenn	8
62	Liberty LIB 55477	Houdini/The Old Kelly Place	6
63	Liberty LIB 55508	Mama Sang A Song/Who Will Take Gramma	6
64	Liberty LBY 1249	GUNFIGHT AT THE OK CORRAL (LP)	30

TONY BRENT
(see also Coronets)

56	Columbia DB 3844	Cindy Oh Cindy/Two Innocent Hearts	10

MINT VALUE £

57	Columbia DB 3950	Dark Moon/The Game Of Love (A-One and A-Two)	10
57	Columbia DB 4043	Love By The Jukebox Light/We Belong Together	12
58	Columbia DB 4066	The Hours Will Soon Roll By/Don't Save Your Love For Me	10
58	Columbia DB 4177	Girl Of My Dreams/Don't Play That Melody	8
59	Columbia DB 4304	Why Should I Be Lonely/My Little Room	8
58	Columbia SEG 7824	TONY CALLS THE TUNE (EP)	15
58	Columbia SEG 7869	TIME FOR TONY (EP)	15
59	Columbia SEG 8019	OFF STAGE (EP)	15
59	Columbia SEG 8040	OFF STAGE NO. 2 (EP)	15
58	Columbia 33S 1125	OFF STAGE (10" LP)	20
60	Columbia 33SX 1200	TONY TAKES FIVE (LP, also stereo SCX 3288)	15
60	Columbia 33SX 1200	TONY TAKES FIVE (LP, also stereo SCX 3288)	18
60s	Columbia 33SX 5001	TONY'S BIG HITS (LP)	20

TONY BRENT & JULIE DAWN
(see also Julie Dawn)

53	Columbia SCM 5029	Ding Dong Boogie/When Are We Gonna Get Married?	15

BRENT FORD & NYLONS

78	Brumbeat	19th Nervous Breakdown/Big Rock Candy Mountain (handmade foldout p/s)	50

BRENTWOOD ROAD ALLSTARS

70	Bamboo BAM 23	Love At First Sight/MAYTALS: Life Could Be A Dream	30
70	Bamboo BAM 25	Soul Shake/Moon Ride	30

GERRY BRERETON
(see also Eddie Calvert)

53	Parlophone MSP 6056	From Here To Eternity/If You've Never Been In Love	10
54	Parlophone MSP 6081	The Book/Somewhere Someone (Is Saying A Prayer)	10
55	Columbia SCM 5195	A Million Helping Hands/Fair Sets The Wind For Love	10

BERNARD BRESSLAW

58	HMV POP 522	Mad Passionate Love/You Need Feet	5
59	HMV POP 599	Charlie Brown/The Teenager's Lament	5
59	HMV POP 669	Ivy Will Cling/I Found A Hole	5
59	HMV 7EG 8439	I ONLY ARSKED (EP)	15

PAUL BRETT('S SAGE)
(see also Elmer Gantry's Velvet Opera, Fire)

70	Pye 7N 17974	Three D Mona Lisa/Mediterranean Lazy Heat Wave	7
71	Dawn DNX 2508	Reason For Your Askin'/Everlasting Butterfly/Savannah Ladies/ To Everyman (Freedom) (p/s)	10
71	Dawn DNS 1010	Goodbye Forever/Good Old Fashioned Funky Kind Of Music	6
72	Dawn DNS 1021	Dahlia/Cottage Made For Two	6
73	Bradley's BRAD 301	Mr. Custer/Good Times, Hard Times	6
73	Bradley's BRAD 305	Summer Driftin'/Clocks (p/s)	7
70	Pye NSPL 18347	PAUL BRETT SAGE (LP, blue/black label with logo banner on top)	60
71	Dawn DNLS 3021	JUBILATION FOUNDRY (LP, gatefold sleeve, as Paul Brett's Sage, orange label)	40
72	Dawn DNLS 3032	SCHIZOPHRENIA (LP, foldout sleeve, as Paul Brett's Sage, lilac label)	40
73	Bradley's BRADL 1001	PAUL BRETT (LP, envelope sleeve with inner)	30
73	Bradley's BRADL 1004	CLOCKS (LP)	15
75	PF private pressing PF 001	PHOENIX FUTURE (LP, 500 only, numbered on rear sleeve)	30
70s	private pressing	MUSIC MANIFOLD (LP, library issue)	25

STEVE BRETT & MAVERICKS
(see also 'N Betweens, Slade)

65	Columbia DB 7470	Wishing/Anything That's Part Of You	85
65	Columbia DB 7581	Sad, Lonely And Blue/Candy	125
65	Columbia DB 7794	Sugar Shack/Chains On My Heart	100

TONY BREVETT
(see also Melodians, Glen Adams)

71	Supreme SUP 224	Don't Get Weary/BREVETT ALLSTARS: Version	15
71	Bullet BU 497	So Ashamed/GREGORY ISAACS: My Only Lover	10
74	Dip DL 5028	You Don't Love Me/Version	7

BREW
(see also Camel)

60s	Oak LONDON	Crossroads/Play Your Tune (acetate, unreleased, handwritten labels)	150

TERESA BREWER
(see also Snooky Lanson)

SINGLES

54	Vogue Coral Q 2011	Skinny Minnie (Fishtail)/I Had Someone Else Before I Had You	15
54	Vogue Coral Q 2029	Au Revoir/Danger Signs	15
55	Vogue Coral Q 72043	Let Me Go, Lover (with Lancers)/Baby, Baby, Baby	15
55	Vogue Coral Q 72065	How Important Can It Be?/What More Is There To Say?	15
55	Vogue Coral Q 72066	Tweedlee Dee/Rock Love	25
55	Vogue Coral Q 72077	Pledging My Love/I Gotta Go Get My Baby	15
55	Vogue Coral Q 72083	You're Telling Our Secret/Time	15
55	Vogue Coral Q 72098	The Banjo's Back In Town/How To Be Very, Very Popular	10
56	Vogue Coral Q 72130	A Good Man Is Hard To Find/It's Siesta Time	10
56	Vogue Coral Q 72139	Rememb'ring/My Sweetie Went Away	10
56	Vogue Coral Q 72146	A Tear Fell/Bo Weevil	10
56	Vogue Coral Q 72172	A Sweet Old-Fashioned Girl/Goodbye, John	10
56	Vogue Coral Q 72199	Keep Your Cotton Pickin' Paddies Offa My Heart/ So Doggone Lonely	10
56	Vogue Coral Q 72213	Crazy With Love/The Moon Is On Fire	10
57	Vogue Coral Q 72224	Nora Malone/When I Leave The World Behind	8
57	Vogue Coral Q 72239	I'm Drowning My Sorrows/How Lonely Can One Be	8
57	Vogue Coral Q 72251	Empty Arms/The Ricky-Tick Song	8

			MINT VALUE £
57	Vogue Coral Q 72278	Lula Rock-A-Hula/Teardrops In My Heart	15
57	Vogue Coral Q 72292	You Send Me/Born To Love	15
58	Coral Q 72301	Careless Caresses/Mutual Admiration Society	8
58	Coral Q 72320	Saturday Dance/I Think The World Of You	8
58	Coral Q 72336	Pickle Up A Doodle/The Rain Falls On Ev'rybody	8
58	Coral Q 72340	The Hula Hoop Song/So Shy	8
58	Coral Q 72349	I Like Christmas/Jingle Bell Rock	8
58	Coral Q 72349	I Like Christmas/Jingle Bell Rock (78)	10
58	Coral Q 72354	Satellite/The One Rose (That's Left In My Heart)	8
58	Coral Q 72354	Satellite/The One Rose (That's Left In My Heart) (78)	10
59	Coral Q 72364	Heavenly Lover/Fair Weather Sweetheart	8
59	Coral Q 72364	Heavenly Lover/Fair Weather Sweetheart (78)	12
59	Coral Q 72375	Bye Bye Baby Goodbye/Chain Of Friendship	12
59	Coral Q 72375	Bye Bye Baby Goodbye/Chain Of Friendship (78)	12
59	Coral Q 72383	Bill Bailey, Won't You Please Come Home/Mexicali Rose	5
59	Coral Q 72383	Bill Bailey, Won't You Please Come Home/Mexicali Rose (78)	12
60	Coral Q 72386	Peace Of Mind/Venetian Sunset	5
60	Coral Q 72396	How Do You Know It's Love/If There Are Stars In My Eyes	6
60	Coral Q 72405	Anymore/That Piano Man	5
60	Coral Q 72418	Have You Ever Been Lonely/When Do You Love Me	5
60	Coral Q 72447	Pretty Lookin' Boy/Your Cheatin' Heart	6
61	Coral Q 72438	Little Miss Belong To No One/Sea Shell	6
63	Coral Q 72461	Walking The Floor Over You/Jealous Heart	6

EPs

50s	London BEP 6039	TERESA BREWER WITH THE ALL STARS (export issue)	10
50s	London BEP 6041	TERESA BREWER WITH JACK PLEIS AND THE ALL STARS (export issue)	10
59	Coral FEP 2013	HULA HOOP TIME WITH TERESA BREWER	10
59	Coral FEP 2036	WHEN YOUR LOVER HAS GONE PART 1	10
59	Coral FEP 2037	WHEN YOUR LOVER HAS GONE PART 2	10
59	Coral FEP 2038	WHEN YOUR LOVER HAS GONE PART 3	10
60	Coral FEP 2047	TERESA BREWER AND THE DIXIELAND BAND PART 1	10
60	Coral FEP 2048	TERESA BREWER AND THE DIXIELAND BAND PART 2	10
60	Coral FEP 2061	HOW DO YOU KNOW IT'S LOVE	10

LPs

51	London H-APB 1006	SHOWCASE (10")	30
57	Vogue Coral LVA 9020	MUSIC! MUSIC! MUSIC!	30
58	Coral LVA 9075	FOR TEENAGERS IN LOVE	25
58	Coral LVA 9091	AT CHRISTMAS TIME	25
59	Coral LVA 9095	TIME FOR TERESA BREWER	20
59	Coral LVA 9100	WHEN YOUR LOVER HAS GONE (also stereo SVL 3003)	15
59	Coral LVA 9107	TERESA BREWER AND THE DIXIELAND BAND	15
60	Coral LVA 9129	RIDIN' HIGH	15
60	Coral LVA 9131	MY GOLDEN FAVOURITES	15
60	Coral LVA 9138	NAUGHTY NAUGHTY NAUGHTY	15
61	Coral LVA 9145/SVL 3014	SONGS EVERYBODY KNOWS	15
62	Coral LVA 9152	ALOHA FROM TERESA	15
62	Coral LVA 9204	DON'T MESS AROUND WITH TESS	15

BREWER & SHIPLEY

70	Kama Sutra 2013 021	People Love Each Other/Tarkio Road	5
71	Kama Sutra 2013 015	One Toke Over The Line/People Love Each Other	5
70	Kama Sutra 2361 001	TARKIO ROAD (LP)	12
71	Kama Sutra 2361 005	WEEDS (LP)	12
72	Kama Sutra 2319 021	SHAKE OFF THE DEMON (LP)	12

BREWER'S DROOP

(see also McGuinness Flint)

72	RCA RCA 2216	Sweet Thing/Heart Of Stone/It Ain't The Meat - It's The Motion (p/s)	6
72	RCA SF 8301	OPENING TIME (LP, gatefold sleeve, orange label)	30

BRIAR

82	Happy Face MM 142	Rainbow (To The Skies)/Crying In The Rain (p/s)	12
87	PRT BRIART 1	Edge Of A Broken Heart/Don't Forget Me When You're On Your Own (shaped picture disc, with headband)	12
85	Heavy Metal HMRLP 41	TOO YOUNG (LP, with 7" & poster)	12
87	UK UKALP 002	CROWN OF THORNS (LP)	15

DICK BRICE

80s	Sylvan SYL 101R	A FEW ON 'IMS OWN (LP)	50

BRIDGE

85	Atlantic 9565(T)	Baby, Don't Hold Your Love Back/(Instrumental Version) (12")	20

BOBBY BRIDGER

(see also Errol Sobers)

70	Beacon BEA 149	The World Is Turning On/Why Do I Love You	7
70	Beacon BEA 159	Sugar Shaker/You're In Love	12

MARC BRIERLEY

(see also Tractor)

68	CBS 3857	Hold On, Hold On, The Garden Sure Looks Good Spread On The Floor/ Autograph Of Time	8
69	CBS 4191	Stay A Little Longer Merry Ann/Flaxen Hair	7
69	CBS 4632	Lady Of The Light/Sunny Weather	7
70	CBS 5266	Be My Brother/If You Took The Bandage Off	6
60s	Transatlantic TRAEP 147	MARC BRIERLEY (EP)	50
68	CBS 63478	WELCOME TO THE CITADEL (LP, orange label with textured surface)	300
69	CBS 63835	HELLO (LP, gatefold sleeve, stickered sleeve, orange label)	150
69	CBS 63835	HELLO (LP, gatefold sleeve, no sticker, orange label)	130

MINT VALUE £

BRIGANDAGE

84	FO FO 1001	FURG YA MUDDER (cassette only)	10

ANNE BRIGGS

(see also A.L. Lloyd)

63	Topic TOP 94	THE HAZARDS OF LOVE (EP, with leaflet)	160
71	Topic 12TS 207	ANNE BRIGGS (LP)	200
71	CBS 64612	THE TIME HAS COME (LP)	300

DUGGIE BRIGGS

78	It IT 3	Punk Rockin' Granny/I'm A Flasher (p/s)	12
78	It ITEP 5	THE DUGGIE BRIGGS FLASHES ON IT AGAIN (EP)	18

LILLIAN BRIGGS

60	Coral Q 72408	Not A Soul (Blanket Roll Blues)/Smile For The People	8

ANNIE BRIGHT

69	Columbia DB 8587	Concerning Love/Sneakin' Up On You	15

GREG BRIGHT

69	private pressing	ROOM BY GREG (LP)	250

GREGORY BRIGHT

69	Private Pressing	ROOM (LP)	150

LEN BRIGHT COMBO

(see also Wreckless Eric, Milkshakes)

86	Empire LEN 1	Someone Must've Nailed Us Together/Mona (p/s)	6

BRIGHTER

89	Sarah SARAH 019	Around The World In 80 Days (p/s, with inserts)	8

BRIGHT EYES

01	Wichita WEBB 012S	3 NEW HIT SONGS FROM BRIGHT EYES EP (p/s)	8

SARAH BRIGHTMAN

79	Ariola Hansa AHAD 538	The Adventures Of The Love Crusader (Long Version)/Lost In Space (The Nurgon Zone) (12", p/s, red vinyl as Sarah Brightman & Starship Troopers)	10
90	Polydor PZCD 74	Something To Believe In/Brown Eyes/Love Changes Everything (CD single)	30

IAN BRIGHTON

77	Bead Records BEAD 3	MARSH GAS (LP)	50

BRIGHTON HORNS

66	Stateside SS 526	Surf Dell'amore/High Midnight	8

BRIGHTWINTER

70s	Myrrh MYR 1030	A BAND FOR ALL SEASONS (LP)	25

BRILLIANT CORNERS

84	SS20 SS21	She's Got Fever/Black Water (red p/s)	15
84	SS20 SS21	She's Got Fever/Black Water (pink p/s)	30
84	SS20 SS22	Big Hip/Tangled Up In Blue (p/s)	10
88	McQueen MCQ2T	Why Do You Have To Go Out With Him?/Shangri La (12" p/s)	10
88	McQueen MCQLP	SOMEBODY UP THERE LIKES ME (LP, with inner)	15

JOHN BRIMACOMBE

72	Pye 7N 45159	Try A Little Harder/Four Sad Men	10

BRIMSTONE

71	Deram DM 322	Keyhole Jake/The Monkey Song	6
71	Decca DF 13222	If Ever You See Me/Work Out	5

LOS BRINCOS

67	Page One POF 023	Lola/Passport (1st 5,000 in p/s)	35
67	Page One POF 023	Lola/Passport (no p/s)	10
67	Page One POF 031	Nobody Wants You Now/Train	60

BRINDLEY BRAE

(see also Bev Pegg, Away From The Sand)

73	Harmony DB 0002	VILLAGE MUSIC (LP, 50 copies only, private pressing with insert)	120

BRINSLEY SCHWARZ

(see also Kippington Lodge, Hitters, Knees, Limelight, Nick Lowe, Ernie Graham, Rumour, Chilli Willi & Red Hot Peppers, Ducks Deluxe)

70	United Artists UP 35118	Shining Brightly/What Do You Suggest	10
71	Liberty LBY 15419	Country Girl/Funk Angel	15
72	United Artists UP 35312	Country Girl/Funk Angel (reissue)	6
73	United Artists UP 35588	Speedo/I Worry	5
74	United Artists UP 35642	I've Cried My Last Tear/Bringdown	5
74	United Artists UP 35700	(What's So Funny 'Bout) Peace, Love And Understanding/ Ever Since You're Gone	6
75	United Artists UP 35768	Everybody/I Like You, I Don't Love You	6
75	United Artists UP 35812	There's A Cloud In My Heart/I Got The Real Thing	6
70	United Artists UAS 29111	BRINSLEY SCHWARZ (LP, gatefold sleeve, orange/pink label)	50
70	Liberty LBG 83427	DESPITE IT ALL (LP, gatefold sleeve)	35
72	United Artists UAS 29217	SILVER PISTOL (LP, with poster)	30
72	United Artists UAS 29374	NERVOUS ON THE ROAD (LP)	15
73	United Artists UAS 29489	PLEASE DON'T EVER CHANGE (LP)	20
74	United Artists UAS 29641	THE NEW FAVOURITES OF BRINSLEY SCHWARZ (LP)	12
98	Edsel EDCD 546	HEN'S TEETH (CD)	20

LLOYD BRISCO

64	Rio R42	Fabulous Eyes/What You See	20
64	Island WI 187	Jonah The Master/Mr. Cleveland	20

MINT VALUE £

JOHNNY BRISTOL

75	Philips 6006471	Memories Don't Leave Like People Do/It Don't Hurt No More	6
80	Ariola AHA 567	Love No Longer Has A Hold On Me/Till I See You Again	8
80	Ariola AHAD 567	Love No Longer Has A Hold On Me/Till I See You Again (12")	15

BRITISH ELECTRIC FOUNDATION

(see under B.E.F.)

BRITISH LIONS

(see also Mott The Hoople, Medicine Head)

78	Vertigo 6059 192	One More Chance To Run/Booster (p/s)	5
78	Vertigo 6059 201	International Heroes/Eat The Rich	5
78	Vertigo 9102 019	BRITISH LIONS (LP, with inner sleeve)	15

BRITISH SEA POWER

(see also The Wurzels)

01	Golden Chariot BSP 01	Fear Of Drowning/A Wooden Horse (CD, 500 only)	25
01	Rough Trade RTRADE S032	Remember Me/A Lovely Day Tomorrow (p/s, 500 only)	10
02	Rough Trade RTRADE SCD048	The Lonely/Spirit Of St. Louis (CD)	10
02	Rough Trade RTRADES 069	Childhood Memories/Favours In The Beetroot Fields (p/s, 1000 only)	8
03	Rough Trade RTRADE S092	Carrion/Apologies To Insect Life (handdrawn, textured sleeve, 1264 only)	12
03	Rough Trade RTRADES 125	Remember Me/The Scottish Wildlife Experience (hand-drawn sleeve 2003 copies)	15
04	Rough Trade RTRADESCD179	A Lovely Day Tomorrow/Zitra Buke Krasney Den/ Fakir (CD limited edition 1942 copies)	10
05	None	Thirteen Ways To Disappear (CD-R sent to first 13 buyers from BSP web shop)	12
05	Rough Trade RTRADS302	Remember Me/I Am A Cider Drinker (7" limited edition. 1,966 copies)	10

BRITISH WALKERS

65	Pye International 7N 25298	I Found You/Diddley Daddy	30

BRITT

(see also Britt Ekland)

66	Piccadilly 7N 35273	You Really Have Started Something/Leave My Baby Alone	30

MAY BRITT

59	Top Rank JAR 230	Falling In Love Again/Lola-Lola	5

TINA BRITT

65	London HLC 9974	The Real Thing/Teardrops Fell	60
65	London HLC 9974	The Real Thing/Teardrops Fell (DJ Copy)	100

BUDDY BRITTEN & REGENTS

(see also Regents)

62	Piccadilly 7N 35075	My Pride, My Joy/Long Gone Baby	15
62	Decca F 11435	Don't Spread It Around/The Beat Of My Heart	15
63	Oriole CB 1827	If You Gotta Make A Fool Of Somebody/Money	15
63	Oriole CB 1839	Hey There/I'll Cry No More	15
63	Oriole CB 1859	My Resistance Is Low/When I See You Smile	15
63	Oriole CB 1889	Money/Sorrow Tomorrow	20
64	Oriole CB 1911	I Guess I'm In The Way/Zip-A-Dee-Doo-Dah	15
65	Piccadilly 7N 35241	She's About A Mover/Since You've Gone	15
65	Piccadilly 7N 35257	Right Now/Jailer Bring Me Water	7

TERRY BRITTEN

69	Columbia DB8580	2000 Weeks/Bargain Day	80

CHRIS BRITTON

(see also Troggs)

69	Page One POLS 022	AS I AM (LP, gatefold sleeve, blue/silver label)	350

JEFF BRITTON & THE SPITFIRES

76	Decca F 13643	Rub Out/Breakwood	20

MAGGIE BRITTON

80	Piccadilly 7P191	Goodship Earth/No Secrets	6

BRIXTON MARKET

69	Beacon BEA 138	Children Get Ready/Bangarang	15
69	Beacon SBEAB 8	BLACK FUNK (LP)	20

BROADCAST

96	Wurlitzer Jukebox WJ 6	Accidentals/We've Got Time (p/s, some with sticker)	15
96	Wurlitzer Jukebox WJ 6	Accidentals/We've Got Time (p/s, some with sticker)	10
96	Duophonic DS 45-14	Living Room/Phantom (wraparound p/s, 1,500 only)	10
96	Duophonic DS 45-16	THE BOOK LOVERS EP (12", p/s, 2,000)	10
96	Duophonic DS 45-CD 16	THE BOOK LOVERS EP (CD, 2,500 only)	10

BROADSIDE

71	Lincolnshire Ass. LA 4	THE GIPSY'S WEDDING DAY (10" LP)	50
73	Topic 12TS 228	THE MOON SHONE BRIGHT (As The Broadside From Grimsby) (LP, blue label)	40
75	Guildhall GHS 5	SONGS FROM THE STOCKS (LP)	80
75	Guildhall GHS 12	DRIVE THE DARK AWAY (LP)	50

DAVE BROCK

(see also Dr. Technical & Machines, Hawkwind)

83	Flicknife FLS 024	Social Alliance/Raping Robots In The Street (p/s)	5
83	Flicknife FLS 024P	Social Alliance/Raping Robots In The Street (picture disc)	8
84	Flicknife SHARP 018	EARTHED TO THE GROUND (LP)	12
88	Flicknife SHARP 042	AGENT OF CHAOS (LP)	12

NORAH BROCKSTEDT

60	Top Rank JAR 353	Big Boy/Tell Me No Lies	10

MINT VALUE £

PETER BROGGS

79	Hit Run HITDD 13	Higher Field Marshall (Feat. Prince Far I)/I And I A The Chosen One/ PRINCE FAR I & BRIGADIER JAM DOWN : Loved By Everyone (12")	40
80	Cha Cha CHAD 25	Never Forget Jah/CORNWALL CAMPBELL : Rainbow (12")	30
80	Selena SO 006	Jah Golden Throne/DEXTER mCKINTYRE : 144.00 Saints	50

BROKEN BONES

(see also Discharge)

84	Fall Out FALL 020	Decapitated/Problem/Liquidated Brains (p/s)	5
84	Fall Out FALL 025	Crucifix/Fight The Good Fight	5
85	Fall Out FALL 034P	Seeing Through My Eyes/The Point Of Agony/It's Like (picture disc)	5
85	Fall Out FALL 10034	Seeing Through My Eyes/The Point Of Agony/It's Like/ Decapitated/Part 2/ Death Is Imminent (10", p/s)	7
83	Fall Out FALL LP 028	BROKEN BONES (LP)	15
84	Stoned Spliff 1	LIVE AT THE 100 CLUB (LP)	20

BROKEN BOW

87	Sodium	Vagrant/Bite Back	25

BROKEN GLASS

(see also Chicken Shack, Warhorse, Miller Anderson, Bronco)

75	Capitol E-ST 11510	BROKEN GLASS (LP, with insert)	18

BROKEN GLASS

84	Streetwave MKHAN 17	Style Of The Street (12")	30

JOHN BROMLEY

(see also Fleur De Lys, Three People)

68	Polydor 56224	What A Woman Does/My My	30
68	Polydor 56287	And The Feeling Goes/Sweet Little Princess	20
69	Polydor 56305	Melody Fayre/Sugar Love	60
69	Polydor 56340	Hold Me Woman/Weather Man	30
69	Atlantic 584 289	Kick A Tin Can/Wonderland Avenue U.S.A.	30
69	Polydor 583 048	SING (LP)	100

BRONCO

(see also Alan Bown Set)

73	Polydor 2058 395	The Traveller/Steal That Gold	6
70	Island ILPS 9124	COUNTRY HOME (LP, gatefold sleeve, pink 'i' label)	40
70	Island ILPS 9124	COUNTRY HOME (LP, gatefold sleeve, 'pink rim palm tree' label)	15
71	Island ILPS 9161	ACE OF SUNLIGHT (LP, gatefold sleeve, 'pink rim palm tree' label)	25
73	Polydor 2383 215	SMOKIN' MIXTURE (LP, gatefold sleeve)	15

BRONNT INDUSTRIES

05	Static Caravan	KAPITAL BROCKEN (EP) (8" lathe cut, clear vinyl, hand-stamped bag, 100 only)	25

BRONX CHEER

70	Parlophone R 5865	Drive My Car/Foxtrot	8
71	Dawn DNX 2512	Barrelhouse Player/Surprising Find/Whether Or Not/Party For One (p/s)	8
72	Dawn DNS 1019	Hold On To Me/Late Date	6
72	Dawn DNLS 3004	GREATEST HITS VOLUME 3 (LP, gatefold sleeve with insert, lilac label)	20

BRONZ

84	Bronze BRO 178	Send Down An Angel/Tiger (p/s)	5
84	Bronze BROX 178	Send Down An Angel/Tiger/Stranded (12", p/s)	8
80s	Lyntone LYN 14383	Taken By Storm (flexidisc)	5

DAVID BROOK

68	President PT 196	Witchfinder General/Janie	15

MICHAEL BROOK

92	4AD TAD 2011	LIVE AT THE AQUARIUM (CD, digipak)	18

PATTI BROOK (& DIAMONDS)

60	Pye 7N 15300	Since You've Been Gone/That's The Way It's Gonna Be (as Patti Brook & Diamonds)	8
61	Pye 7N 15339	When The Red Red Robin/Look What You've Done To Me	8
61	Pye 7N 15378	Heaven Is Being With You/Your Love Came Into My Heart	6
62	Pye 7N 15422	I Love You, I Need You/Unloved, Unwanted	8

TONY BROOK & BREAKERS

64	Columbia DB 7279	Meanie Genie/Ooh Poo Pah Doo (in p/s)	200
64	Columbia DB 7279	Meanie Genie/Ooh Poo Pah Doo (no p/s)	100
65	Columbia DB 7444	Love Dances On/I Won't Hurt You	10

BROOK BROTHERS

(see also Brooks)

60	Top Rank JAR 349	Green Fields/How Will It End?	20
60	Top Rank JAR 409	Please Help Me, I'm Falling/When Will I Be Loved	20
60	Pye 7N 15298	Say The Word/Everything But Love	6
61	Pye 7N 15333	Warpaint/Sometimes	5
61	Pye 7N 15352	Little Bitty Heart/Tell Her	5
61	Pye 7N 15369	Ain't Gonna Wash For A Week/One Last Kiss	5
61	Pye 7N 15387	Married/I Love Girls	5
62	Pye 7N 15409	He's Old Enough To Know Better/Win Or Lose	8
62	Pye 7N 15415	Too Scared/Tell Tale	5
62	Pye 7N 15441	Just Another Fool/Double Trouble	5
62	Pye 7N 15453	Welcome Home Baby/So Long	5
62	Pye 7N 15463	I Can't Make Up My Mind/Town Girl	6
63	Pye 7N 15498	Trouble Is My Middle Name/Let The Good Times Roll	6
63	Pye 7N 15527	I'm Not Jimmy/Side By Side (with RBQ)	6
63	Pye 7N 15570	Crosswords/Whistle To The Wind	6
61	Pye NEP 24140	BROOK BROTHERS HIT PARADE (EP)	25

			MINT VALUE £
61	Pye NEP 24148	BROOK BROTHERS HIT PARADE VOLUME 2 (EP)	25
62	Pye NEP 24155	BROOK BROTHERS (EP)	25
61	Pye NPL 18067	BROOK BROTHERS (LP)	35

BROOKLYN

80	Rondelet ROUND 3	I Wanna Be A Detective (p/s)	30
81	Rondelet ROUND 6	Hollywood/Late Again (p/s)	20
80	Rondelet ABOUT 3	YOU NEVER KNOW WHAT YOU'LL FIND (LP)	30

BROOKLYN BRIDGE

(see also Johnny Maestro, Crests)

68	Pye International 7N 25473	From My Window I Can See/Little Red Boat By The River	8
69	Buddah 201 029	The Worst That Could Happen/Your Kite, My Kite	10
70	Buddah 2011 010	Free As The Wind/He's Not A Happy Man	6
70	Buddah 2011 034	Down By The River/Look Again	6

BROOKS

(see also Brook Brothers)

64	Decca F 11868	Once In A While/Poor Poor Plan	10

BABA BROOKS

(see also Blues Masters, Eric Brooks, Stranger & Patsy, Riots, Joey Smith, Saints, Richard Brothers, Derrick Morgan, Lord Tanamo, Lord Brisco, Hippy Boys, Roy Panton, Higgs & Wilson, Vinley Gayle, Joe White, Stranger & Patsy)

63	Island WI 078	5 O'Clock Whistle/African Blood (by Blues Masters)	40
63	Island WI 096	Bank To Bank (Parts 1 & 2)	40
63	Island WI 127	Three Blind Mice/BILLY & BOBBY: We Ain't Got Nothing	30
63	R&B JB 125	Water Melon Man/STRANGER COLE: Things Come To Those Who Wait	50
64	Black Swan WI 137	Portrait Of My Love/STRANGER COLE: Goodbye Peggy	20
64	Black Swan WI 412	Jelly Beans/ERIC MORRIS: Sampson	30
64	Black Swan WI 414	Key To The City/ERIC MORRIS: Solomon Grundie	40
64	Black Swan WI 434	Spider/Melody Jamboree	30
64	Black Swan WI 438	Cork Foot/HERSANG COMBO: B.B.C. Channel 2	30
65	Black Swan WI 442	Musical Workshop/DUKE WHITE: Be Wise	35
65	Black Swan WI 444	Bus Strike/DUKE WHITE: Sow Good Seeds	35
65	Black Swan WI 451	Ethiopia/ARCHIBALD TROTT: Promised Land	35
65	Black Swan WI 466	Baby Elephant Walk/DON DRUMMOND: Don's Special	30
65	Ska Beat JB 189	Dr. Decker/OWEN & LEON SILVERA : Woman	15
65	Ska Beat JB 220	One Eyed Giant (with His Band)/DYNAMITES: Walk Out On Me	30
65	Island WI 229	Guns Fever/DOTTY & BONNIE: Don't Do It	45
65	Island WI 233	Independent Ska/STRANGER & CLAUDETTE: Seven Days	30
65	Island WI 235	Duck Soup/ZODIACS: Renegade	150
65	Island WI 239	Vitamin A/ALTON ELLIS: Dance Crasher	50
65	Island WI 241	Teenage Ska/ALTON ELLIS: You Are Not To Blame	90
65	Rio R 061	Shenk I Sheck (& Band)/SHENLEY & HIACYNTH: Set Me Free	50
66	Doctor Bird DB 1042	The Clock (& Band)/LYN TAITT & COMETS & SILVERTONES: Raindrops	40
66	Doctor Bird DB 1046	Jam Session (with His Band)/CONQUERORS: What A Agony	40
67	Ska Beat JB 268	One Eyed Giant (with His Band)/DYNAMITES: Walk Out On Me (reissue)	20

CEDRIC 'IM' BROOKS

73	Tropical AL046	South African Reggae/Part 2	10
78	Water Lily ARCO LP 009	UNITED AFRICA (LP)	25

CHUCK BROOKS

69	Soul City SC 116	Black Sheep/I've Got To Get Myself Together	30
69	Soul City SC 116	Black Sheep/I've Got To Get Myself Together (DJ Copy)	100

D. BROOKS

70	Big BG 304	Oh Me Oh My (actually "Every Time" by Hi-Tals)/ANSEL COLLINS: Staccato (actually "Every Time Version" by Rupie Edwards Allstars)	12

DALE BROOKS

65	King KG 1025	Army Green/Reminds Me Of You	10
66	Stateside SS 553	I Wanna Be Your Girl/Like Other Girls Do	30

DONNIE BROOKS

60	London HLN 9168	Mission Bell/Do It For Me	10
60	London HLN 9168	Mission Bell/Do It For Me (78 rpm)	30
60	London HLN 9253	Doll House/Round Robin	10
61	London HLN 9361	That's Why/Memphis	10
62	London HLN 9572	Oh, You Beautiful Doll/Just A Bystander	10
61	London HA-N 2391	THE HAPPIEST DONNIE BROOKS (LP)	35

ELKIE BROOKS

(see also Dada, Vinegar Joe, Steve York's Camelo Pardalis, Elki & Owen)

64	Decca F 11928	Something's Got A Hold On Me/Hello Stranger	35
64	Decca F 11983	Nothing Left To Do But Cry/Strange Though It Seems	30
65	Decca F 12061	The Way You Do The Things You Do/Blue Tonight	30
65	HMV POP 1431	He's Gotta Love Me/When You Appear	30
65	HMV POP 1431	He's Gotta Love Me/When You Appear (DJ Copy)	40
65	HMV POP 1480	All My Life/Can't Stop Thinking Of You	20
66	HMV POP 1512	Baby Let Me Love You/Stop The Music	25
69	NEMS 56-4136	Come September/If You Should Go	5
74	Island WIP 6187	Rescue Me/Sweet Nuthin's	5
74	Chrysalis CHS 2069	Sacrifice/ALICE COOPER: I'm Flash (p/s, unissued, promo only)	35
84	A & M SCREEN 1	SCREEN GEMS (CD, beware of counterfeit copies!)	50

JOE BROOKS COLLECTIVE

71	CBS 7234	Messing Up The Mind Of A Young Girl/ Before The Sand Has Run Out Of The Hour Glass	12

JULIAN BROOKS

70	Pye 7N17996	Justine/Lazy Guy	15

MINT VALUE £

MIKE BROOKS

79	Hit Run HIT DD 9	Love Is Like A Password/Feeling Of Reggae (12")	25
79	Hit Run HIT DD 23	Long Long Time/Dub In Time	30

NORMAN BROOKS & G-BOYS

54	London L 1166	Hello Sunshine/You're My Baby	30
54	London L 1202	Somebody Wonderful/You Shouldn't Have Kissed Me The First Time	30
54	London L 1228	A Sky-Blue Shirt And A Rainbow Tie/This Waltz With You	35
54	London HL 8015	I'm Kinda Crazy/I'd Like To Be In Your Shoes, Baby	30
54	London HL 8041	I Can't Give You Anything But Love (solo)/GO-BOYS: Johnny's Tune	30
54	London HL 8051	Candy Moon/My 3-D Sweetie	30
55	London HL 8115	Back In Circulation/Lou Lou Louisiana	30
54	London RE-P 1004	PRESENTING NORMAN BROOKS VOLUME 1 (EP)	40
55	London RE-P 1021	BABY MINE (EP)	40

PAM BROOKS

70	Big BG 307	Oh Me Oh My/ANSELL COLLINS: Staccato	18

RAY BROOKS

72	Polydor 2001334	Pictures/On My Own	10

WES BROOKS

77	ATA ATA 1003	Lay Down Your Arms/Version	8

BROOKS & JERRY

68	Direction 58-3267	I Got What It Takes Parts 1 & 2	8
68	Direction 58-3267	I Got What It Takes Parts 1 & 2 (DJ Copy)	30

MARK BROOM

95	Ferox FER 017	SHUFFLE THIS (12" EP)	8

BIG BILL BROONZY/CHICAGO BILL

(see also Chicago Bill)

51	Vogue V 2068	Back Water Blues/Lonesome Road Blues (78)	10
51	Vogue V 2073	In The Evenin'/Low Land Blues (78)	10
51	Vogue V 2074	John Henry/Blues In 1890 (78)	10
51	Vogue V 2075	Big Bill Blues/Hey Hey Baby (78)	10
51	Vogue V 2076	House Rent Stomp/The Moppin' Blues (78)	10
51	Vogue V 2077	Black, Brown And White/Feelin' Low Down (78)	10
52	Vogue V 2078	Make My Getaway/What I Used To Do (78)	10
52	Melodisc 1191	Keep Your Hands Off Her/Stump Blues (78, as Chicago Bill)	10
52	Melodisc 1203	Five Foot Seven/Plough Hand Blues (78, as Chicago Bill)	10
s	private pressing	Keep Your Hand On Your Heart/T For Texas (78)	20
56	Pye Jazz NJ 2012	When Do I Get To Be Called A Man/Mindin' My Own Business (78)	10
57	Pye Jazz NJ 2016	Southbound Train/It Feels So Good (78)	10
58	Vogue V 2351	Guitar Shuffle/When Did You Leave Heaven	25
61	Storyville A 44053	Midnight Special/Black Brown And White	10
55	Vogue EPV 1024	HEY BUD BLUES (EP)	20
56	Vogue EPV 1074	SINGS THE BLUES (EP)	20
56	Vogue EPV 1107	GUITAR SHUFFLE (EP)	20
56	Pye Jazz NJE 1005	MISSISSIPPI BLUES VOLUME 1 (EP)	15
56	Pye Jazz NJE 1015	MISSISSIPPI BLUES VOLUME 2 (EP)	15
56	Melodisc EPM7 65	KEEP YOUR HANDS OFF (EP)	15
57	Pye Jazz NJE 1047	SOUTHERN SAGA (EP)	15
57	Columbia SEG 7674	BIG BILL BROONZY SINGS THE BLUES (EP)	15
57	Tempo EXA 61	BILL BAILEY WON'T YOU PLEASE COME HOME (EP)	15
58	Columbia SEG 7790	BIG BILL BROONZY SINGS THE BLUES NO. 2 (EP)	15
60	Mercury ZEP 10065	WALKIN' DOWN A LONESOME ROAD (EP)	15
60	Mercury ZEP 10093	HOLLERIN' BLUES (EP)	22
60s	Mercury/Emearcy MMB 12003	THE BLUES (LP)	20
62	Storyville SEP 383	BLUES ANTHOLOGY VOLUME 3 (EP)	12
64	Mercury 10003 MCE	BLUES-GOSPEL-SPIRITUAL (EP)	15
57	Vogue LAE 12009	BIG BILL BLUES (LP)	35
57	Philips BBL 7113	BIG BILL BROONZY (LP)	35
58	Vogue LAE 12063	THE BLUES (LP)	35
58	Pye Nixa Jazz NJL 16	TRIBUTE TO BIG BILL (LP)	35
59	Tempo TAP 23	AN EVENING WITH BIG BILL BROONZY (LP)	38
61	HMV CLP 1544	LAST SESSION PART 1 (LP)	25
62	HMV CLP 1551	LAST SESSION PART 2 (LP)	25
62	HMV CLP 1562	LAST SESSION PART 3 (LP)	25
65	Storyville SLP 143	AN EVENING WITH BROONZY (LP)	15
65	Fontana 688 206ZL	TROUBLE IN MIND (LP)	20
66	Mercury 20044 MCL	REMEMBERING BROONZY - THE GREATEST MINSTREL OF THE AUTHENTIC BLUES (LP)	30
66	Storyville SLP 188	BLUES IN EUROPE (LP)	18
67	Storyville 670 154	PORTRAITS IN BLUES VOLUME 2 (LP)	20
69	CBS Realm 52648	BIG BILL'S BLUES (LP)	15
69	Xtra XTRA 1093	SINGS COUNTRY BLUES (LP)	15

BIG BILL BROONZY & PETE SEEGER

(see also Pete Seeger)

64	Xtra XTRA 1006	IN CONCERT (LP)	20
66	Verve Folkways VLP 5006	IN CONCERT (LP, reissue, also stereo SVLP 506)	15

BIG BILL BROONZY/SONNY BOY WILLIAMSON [I]

(see also Sonny Boy Williamson [I])

65	RCA Victor RD 7685	BIG BILL AND SONNY BOY (LP)	45

BIG BILL BROONZY, SONNY TERRY & BROWNIE McGHEE

(see also Sonny Terry & Brownie McGhee, Washboard Sam)

64	Xtra XTRA 1004	BIG BILL BROONZY/SONNY TERRY/BROWNIE McGHEE (LP)	30

MINT VALUE £

BROTH
71 Mercury 6338 032 — BROTH (LP) 40

BROTHER
89 4th & Broadway 12BRW139 — Beyond The 16th Parallel (12") 8
92 Tribal Bass TRIBE 10 — Ghettogedden 8

BROTHER BARON
70s Fab FAB 281 — Your Love/Your Love Version 6

BROTHER BONES & HIS SHADOWS
60 Oriole CB 1030 — Sweet Georgia Brown/Margie 6

BROTHER BUNG
(see also Bob Pearce, Fresh)
68 Avenue BEV 1054 — BLUES CRUSADE (EP) 15

BROTHER D & THE COLLECTIVE EFFORT
80 Island IPR 2005 — How We Gonna Make The Black Nation Rise (12") 10

BROTHER DAN ALLSTARS
(see also Audrey, Pooch Jackson)
68 Trojan TR 601 — Donkey Returns/Tribute To Sir K.B. 20
68 Trojan TR 602 — Eastern Organ/JIVERS: Our Love Will Last 30
68 Trojan TR 603 — Hold Pon Them/OWEN GRAY: Answer Me 18
68 Trojan TR 607 — Read Up/Gallop 15
68 Trojan TR 608 — Another Saturday Night/Bee's Knees 10
68 Trojan TBL 101 — LET'S CATCH THE BEAT (LP) 45
69 Trojan TRL 1 — FOLLOW THAT DONKEY (LP) 60

BROTHER SUSAN
74 EMI EMI 2117 — See My Fingers Fly/Full Blooded Natural Man 12
74 EMI EMI 2174 — Ride Ride Ride/Flash 12

BROTHER TREVOR & U BROWN
(see also Matumbi)
78 Matumbi Music — Skip Away/Selassi I (12") 20

BROTHERHOOD
(see also D2 The K)
69 Philips BF 1766 — Paper Man/Give It To Me Now 12
91 Bite It BITE 1 — DESCENDANTS OF THE HOLOCAUST (EP) 25
91 Bite It BITE 2 — Descendents Of The Holocaust (Remix 12") 8
92 Bite It BITE 6 — Way Of The Wise (12") 8
93 Bite It BITE 7 — XXXIII (EP) 8
95 Bite It BHOODJ2 — Alphabetical Response/One (12", promo) 10

BROTHERHOOD OF BREATH
(see also Chris McGregor's Brotherhood Of Breath, Mark Charig)
74 Ogun OG 100 — LIVE AT WILLISAU (LP, with Chris McGregor) 20
78 Ogun OG 524 — PROCESSION (LP) 15

BROTHERHOOD OF LIZARDS
(see also Gypp, Martin Newall, Cleaners From Venus)
89 Deltic DELT LP5 — LIZARDLAND (LP) 20

BROTHERHOOD OF MAN
(see also Sue & Sunny, Sue & Sunshine, Stockingtops)
69 Deram DM 276 — Love One Another/A Little Bit Of Heaven 6
70 Deram DM 317 — This Boy/You Can Depend On Me 5
71 Deram DM 327 — Reach Out Your Hand/Better Tomorrow 15
74 Dawn DNS 1055 — When Love Catches Up With You/How Can You Love (p/s) 6

BROTHERLY LOVE
73 CBS S CBS 1737 — Public Enemy No.1/Here Stands A Better Man 5

BROTHERS
67 London HLU 10158 — Love Story/The Girl's Alright 6

BROTHERS & SISTERS (U.K.)
68 private pressing — ARE WATCHING YOU (LP) 90

BROTHERS & SISTERS (U.S.)
69 CBS 4583 — Mighty Quinn/Chimes Of Freedom 5
69 CBS 63746 — DYLAN'S GOSPEL (LP) 20

BROTHERS FOUR
60 Philips PB 1009 — Greenfields/East Virginia 6
60 Philips PB 1072 — The Green Leaves Of Summer/Beautiful Brown Eyes 6

BROTHERS GRIMM
65 Decca F 12224 — Lost Love/Make It Or Break It 8
66 Ember EMB 222 — A Man Needs Love/Looky Looky 50

BROTHERS KANE
(see also Sarstedt Brothers, Peter Lincoln, Peter Sarstedt, Clive Sands, Wes Sands, Eden Kane)
66 Decca F 12448 — Walking In The Sand/Won't You Stay Long 10

BROTHERS TWO
68 Action ACT 4513 — Here I Am, In Love Again/I'm Tired Of You Baby 15

BROTHERS WILLIAM
65 Parlophone R 5293 — Linda Jane Blues/Honey Love 8

AYSHEA BROUGH
(see also Ayshea)
71 RCA RCA 2105 — Master Jack/Both Sides Now 7

MINT VALUE £

EDGAR BROUGHTON BAND

69	Harvest HAR 5001	Evil/Death Of An Electric Citizen	10
70	Harvest HAR 5015	Out Demons Out/Momma's Reward	7
70	Harvest HAR 5021	Up Yours!/Officer Dan	8
70	Harvest HAR 5032	Apache Drop Out/Freedom	7
71	Harvest HAR 5040	Hotel Room/Call Me A Liar	8
72	Harvest HAR 5049	Gone Blue/Someone/Mr. Crosby	8
69	Harvest SHVL 757	WASA WASA (LP, gatefold sleeve, no EMI box on label with "Sold in U.K." label text)	150
70s	Harvest SHVL 757	WASA WASA (LP, gatefold sleeve, later issue with EMI box on label)	50
70	Harvest SHVL 772	SING BROTHER SING (LP, gatefold sleeve, with lyric insert, no EMI on label)	60
71	Harvest SHVL 791	THE EDGAR BROUGHTON BAND (LP, textured gatefold sleeve, with "Sold in U.K..." label text on 5 lines)	70
72	Harvest SHTC 252	IN SIDE OUT (LP, multifold gatefold sleeve with lyric sheet)	60
73	Harvest SHVL 810	OORA (LP, wraparound card sleeve in clear artwork plastic bag, inner sleeve)	50
76	Nems NEL 6006	BANDAGES (LP with lyric inner sleeve)	20

AL BROWN (Jamaica)

71	Banana BA 360	No Soul Today/RUFFIANS: Where Did I Go Wrong (B-side actually "Bang Shang Alang" by Peter Austin & Hortense Ellis)	25
71	Fab FAB 186	Ain't Got No Soul/TEARDROPS: I Got A Feeling	20
76	Burning Sounds BS 001	Revival Festival/Version	5

AL BROWN'S TUNETOPPERS (U.S.)

60	Top Rank JAR 374	The Madison/Mo' Madison	6

ARTHUR BROWN (CRAZY WORLD OF)

(see also Kingdom Come, Nick Greenwood, Atomic Rooster, Crane/Farlowe)

65	Lyntone LYN 770/1	You Don't Know (as Arthur Brown & Diamonds)/DIAMONDS: You'll Be Mine (Reading University Rag Week flexidisc)	60
67	Track 604 008	Devil's Grip/Give Him A Flower	12
68	Track 604 022	Fire!/Rest Cure (push-out centre)	6
68	Track 604 022	Fire!/Rest Cure (large centre)	5
68	Track 604 026	Nightmare/What's Happening (some copies list "Music Man" as B-side)	6
74	Gull GULS 4	Gypsies/Dance	5
75	Gull GULS 13	We Gotta Get Out Of This Place/Here I Am	5
77	Gull SIXPACK 4	SIX-PACK/SIX TRACK (EP, picture disc, die-cut sleeve with stand, 5,000 only)	6
68	Track 612 005	THE CRAZY WORLD OF ARTHUR BROWN (LP, mono, black/silver label)	80
68	Track 613 005	THE CRAZY WORLD OF ARTHUR BROWN (LP, stereo, black/silver labels)	70
74	Gull GULP 1008	DANCE (LP)	15
77	Gull GUD 2003/4	THE LOST EARS (2-LP, gatefold sleeve, as Arthur Brown's Kingdom Come)	22

BARRY BROWN

78	Tribesman TM 008	Unity Is Strength/DRUMMIE BENJI: Higher Region (12")	30
79	Justice JUDIS 126	Big Big Politician/No Wicked Shall Enter (12")	30
79	Justice JUDIS 135	We Can't Live Like This/From Creation I Man There (12")	30
79	Sufferer's Heights SUFF 003	I Love Sweet Jah Jah/RANKING JOE : Youthman Promotion (12")	35
80	Daddy Kool DKR 124	Peace And Love (with Ranking Toyan) JAH THOMAS & ROOTS RADICS: Adapter Chapter (12")	30
80	Strong Like Sampson SLSD 07	Natty Dread Nah Run/ANTHONY JOHNSON: Life is not easy (12")	40
80	Strong Like? SLSD 010	Don't You Try/ANTHONY JOHNSON: Hey Mr Rich Man (12")	40
80	Attack TACK 17	Mr. CID/SCIENTIST AND ROOTS RADICAL BAND: King Tubby's Rockers (12")	30
80	Attack TACK 21	Separation/Scientist In A Fine Style (12")	40
80	Attack TACK 23	Living As A Brother/SCIENTIST: Second Hand Girl (12")	30
80	Justice JUDIS 135	We Can't Live Like This/From Creation I Man Free (12")	40
81	City Sounds CSD 003	Warmonger/ROOTS RADICS BAND: Radical Style	25
81	Greensleeves GRED 68	Give Israel Another Try/Sweet Sixteen (12")	30
82	Selena SD004	Them Ha Fi Get A Beatin'/ROOTS RADICS BAND : Stop The Fighting (12")	40
82	Selena SD008	Physical Fitness/HEPTONES : Lovers Feeling (12", blue vinyl)	30
80	Trojan TRLS 191	COOL PON YOUR CORNER (LP)	20
80	Third World TWS 937	SHOWCASE (LP)	40
83	Downbeat DBD 004	Belly Full (with General Saint)/WAYNE WADE: Little Suzie (12")	40

BEN BROWN

67	Polydor 56198	Ask The Lonely/Sidewinder	40

BOOTS BROWN & HIS BLOCKBUSTERS

(see also Shorty Rogers)

58	RCA RCA 1078	Cerveza/Juicy	10
59	RCA RCA 1102	Jim Twangy/Trollin'	10
59	RCA RCA 1102	Jim Twangy/Trollin' (78)	12

BUSTER BROWN

60	Melodisc 1559	Fannie Mae/Lost In A Dream	65
65	Sue WI 368	Fannie Mae/Lost In A Dream (reissue)	40
67	Island WI 3031	My Blue Heaven/Two Women	20
69	Blue Horizon 57-3147	Sugar Babe/I'm Going, But I'll Be Back	40
60s	XX MIN 713	B. AND BUSTER BROWN (EP, with B. Brown)	20

BUSTY BROWN

68	Doctor Bird DB 1158	Here Comes The Night/Don't Look Back	30
69	Upsetter US 304	What A Price/How Can I Forget?	12
69	Upsetter US 308	To Love Somebody/BLEECHERS: Farmer's In The Den	12
69	Punch PH 10	Broken Heart/Tribute To A King	12
70	Punch PH 38	Greatest Love/I Love You Madly	12
70	Escort ES 822	Fight For Your Right/MEDITATORS: Soul Fight (Busty Top A Pop) (B-side actually "Soul Fight" by Busty Brown)	25
70	Escort ES 845	Man Short (with Gaytones)/DAVE BARKER: She Want It	12
70	Gas GAS 154	I Love You Madly/Greatest Love	10

MINT VALUE £

70	High Note HS 048	Man Short (with Gaytones)/GAYTONES: Another Version	12
71	Bullet BU 476	Never Love Another/Version	6
71	Punch PH 72	You Inspire Me/UPSETTERS: Version	6
71	Pama Supreme PS 356	Throw Away Your Gun/TWINKLE BROTHERS: Sad Song	20

CHARLES BROWN (BAND)

(see also Brown Brothers)

56	Vogue V 9061	I'll Always Be In Love With You/Soothe Me	500
56	Vogue V 9061	I'll Always Be In Love With You/Soothe Me (78)	90
57	Vogue V 9065	Confidential/Trouble Blues	500
57	Vogue V 9065	Confidential/Trouble Blues (78 rpm)	90
61	Parlophone R 4848	It's Christmas All Year Round/Christmas Question	25

CLARENCE 'GATEMOUTH' BROWN

65	Vocalion VE 170161	CLARENCE 'GATEMOUTH' BROWN (EP)	80
72	Python PLP 26	CLARENCE 'GATEMOUTH' BROWN VOL. 1: 1948-1953 (LP)	25
72	Python PLP 27	CLARENCE 'GATEMOUTH' BROWN VOL. 2: 1956-1965 (LP)	25

CLIFFORD BROWN (& HIS GROUP)

(see also Art Farmer, Sonny Rollins, Max Roach)

55	Vogue EPV 1027	GIGI GRYCE - CLIFFORD BROWN ORCHESTRA (EP)	10
55	Vogue EPV 1041	CONCEPTION (EP)	10
56	Vogue EPV 1119	CLIFFORD BROWN ENSEMBLE (EP)	10
54	Vogue LDE 042	CLIFFORD "BROWNIE" BROWN QUARTET (10" LP)	25
55	Vogue LDE 121	THE CLIFFORD BROWN SEXTET (10" LP)	25
58	Emarcy EJL 1278	STUDY IN BROWN (LP)	20

DENNIS BROWN

(see also Big Youth & Dennis Brown, Hugh Roy, Big Youth, Sound Dimension)

70	Bamboo BAM 56	Love Grows/SOUND DIMENSION: Less Problem	35
70	Banana BA 309	No Man Is An Island/SOUL SISTERS: Another Night	30
71	Banana BA 336	Never Fall In Love/Make It With You	30
71	Ocean OC 001	Little Green Apples/SOUND DIMENSION: Version	10
72	Duke DU 139	What About The Half/What About The Half Version	30
72	Explosion EX 2068	Black Magic Woman/PHILL PRATT ALL STARS: Black Magic Woman Pt 2	15
72	Pressure Beat PR 5513	Money In My Pocket/JOE GIBBS ALLSTARS: Money Love	15
72	Randy's RAN 526	Cheater/TOMMY McCOOK & IMPACT ALLSTARS: Harvest In The East	15
72	Randy's RAN 528	Meet Me On The Corner (actually unknown instrumental)/ IMPACT ALLSTARS: Version	10
72	Songbird SB 1074	Silhouettes/CRYSTALITES: Version	12
73	Ashanti ASH 402	It's Too Late/Song My Mother Used To Sing	12
73	Jackpot JP 813	He Can't Spell/CRYSTALITES: Acid Version	10
73	Smash SMA 2327	Concentration/Version	12
74	Sydna SYD 5027	No More Shall I Roam/Coming Home	10
77	Observer OBS 999	Jah Is Watching/Hustling/Rock On/Murder Observer Style (12" with DILLINGER)	40
77	Observer OB 003	Tenement Yard/Kill Landlord/HORACE ANDY: Them Never Tell I/ Teacher Gal (12", with Ranking Buckers)	25
77	DEB 0002	Half/Troubled World (12")	15
78	DEB DDDEB 010	Oh What A day/Man Next Door (12")	20
79	Observer OBS 902	Blessed Are The Men (The Pill)/ JUNIOR DELGADO: Cry Cry (12")	20
80	High Times HT 001	Blood City/FREDDIE McGREGOR : Natural Collie (12")	35
80	Pratt PP 30	Black Magic Woman/Version (12")	40
86	Jakki JM 468	Rebel With A Cause/JACKIE MITTOO: Trade Mark (12")	25
73	Trojan TRLS 57	SUPER REGGAE & SOUL HITS (LP)	25
75	Trojan TRLS 107	JUST DENNIS (LP)	15
77	DEB DEBLP 01	WOLF AND LEOPARDS (LP)	25
76	Doctor DR 03	OUT IN THE RAIN (LP)	20
78	Lightning LIP 7	VISIONS OF (LP)	20
78	Laser LASL 1	WORDS OF WISDOM (LP)	20
80	Laser LASL 6	JOSEPH'S COAT OF MANY COLOURS (LP)	18
86	Trojan TRSL 238	THE EXIT (LP)	15

DENNIS BROWN & ASWAD

80	Simba SM003	Promised Land/More Dub (12")	20

DUSTY BROWN

61	Starlite ST45 058	Please Don't Go/Well You Know	40

ERROL BROWN & CHOSEN FEW

(see also Hot Chocolate)

72	Songbird SB 1082	People Make The World Go Round/People Make The World Go Round (Version)	8

FAITH BROWN

(see also Carrolls)

70	CBS 4728	Lock Me In/The Game Of Love	5
71	Penny Farthing PEN 766	Any Way That You Want Me/City Wine	5
72	Regal Zonophone RZ 3063	Take Me With You/If We Only Have Love	5

FAY BROWN

55	Columbia SCM 5185	Unchained Melody/I Was Wrong	15

FRIDAY BROWN

(see also Marianne & Mike, High Society, Manchester Mob, Graham Gouldman)

66	Parlophone R 5396	Getting Nowhere/And (To Me He Meant Everything) (as Friday Browne)	22
66	Fontana TF 736	32nd Love Affair/Born A Woman	150
67	Fontana TF 851	Ask Any Woman/Outdoor Seminar	5
69	Fontana TF 996	Stand By Your Man/I Want To Rain	6
72	Philips 6006 239	Shake A Hand/Everything's Alright	5
73	Philips 6006 324	Groovy Kind Of Love/Salford	5
71	Philips 6308 074	FRIDAY BROWN (LP)	35

MINT VALUE £

FUNKY BROWN

72	Sioux SI 018	African (Indian Reservation)/JUMBO STERLING: Elizabethan Reggae	6

GABRIEL BROWN

77	Policy Wheel PW 4592	GABRIEL BROWN AND HIS GUITAR (LP, withdrawn)	15

GEORGIA BROWN

55	Decca F 10489	My Crazy L'il Mixed Up Heart/Before We Know It	10
55	Decca F 10551	I Love To Dance With You/That's All I Need	10
55	Decca F 10616	I Went To The Village/Wrong Again	10
60	Decca F 11286	Blue Eyed Boy/Milord	8
63	Decca SKL 4586	SINGS GERSHWIN (LP)	25

GLEN BROWN

68	Blue Cat BS 131	Way Of Life (with Joe White & Trevor)/ KARL BRYAN & LYN TAITT: I'm So Proud	120
70	Summit SUM 8502	Collie And Wine/BEVERLEY'S ALLSTARS: Version	10
70	Songbird SB 1021	Love I/CRYSTALITES: Heavy Load	12
72	Songbird SB 1081	Smokey Eyes (with Crystalites)/Smokey Eyes (Version)	20
73	Downtown DT 507	Two Wedding Skank/BARRY SIMPSON: Sugar Down Deh	15
79	Kingley REX 4	Marcus Garvey Words/SLYFORD WALKER: Africa (12")	20

GLENMORE BROWN & HOPETON LEWIS

(see also Hopeton Lewis & Glenmore Brown)

68	Fab FAB 42	Girl You're Cold/Soul Man	100

HENRY BROWN

61	'77' LA 12-5	HENRY BROWN BLUES (LP)	45

HUX BROWN & SCOTTY

71	High Note HS 056	Unbelievable Sounds/GAYTONES: Unbelievable Sounds Version	25

HYLO BROWN (& TIMBERLINERS)

59	Capitol CL 15075	You Can't Relive The Past/Thunder Clouds Of Love	5
60	Capitol CL 15139	I've Waited As Long As I Can/Just Any Old Love	5
63	London HAB/SHB 8094	BLUEGRASS GOES TO COLLEGE (LP)	15

IAN BROWN

(see also Stone Roses)

98	Polydor 571 986-7	My Star/See The Dawn (7", p/s)	5
00	Polydor 561 908-1	Thriller/Billie Jean (12", p/s)	15
09	Fiction 2717752	Stellify/Crowning Of The Poor (red vinyl, 1000 only, numbered)	15
98	Polydor 539 916-1	UNFINISHED MONKEY BUSINESS (LP, gatefold, p/s)	25
99	Polydor 543 141-1	GOLDEN GREATS (LP, yellow vinyl, p/s)	20
01	Polydor 589 126-1	MUSIC OF THE SPHERES (LP)	20
02	Polydor 065 927-1	REMIXES OF THE SPHERES (LP)	20
02	Polydor SPHERE2	REMIXES OF THE SPHERES (2x12" Promo Sampler)	20
05	Fiction 987 287-3	THE GREATEST (2xCD Deluxe Book Edition)	20

IRVING BROWN

(see also Larry Marshall)

70	Bamboo BAM 36	Today/SOUND DIMENSION: Young Gifted And Black Version	15
70	Bamboo BAM 58	I'm Still Around/Run Come	18
70	Bamboo BAM 61	Let's Make It Up (actually by Larry Marshall)/BURNING SPEAR: Free	35
71	Bamboo Now BN 1003	Now I'm Alone/Funky Night	18

JACKIE BROWN

72	High Note HS 057	One Night/GAYTONES: One Night Version	8
72	High Note HS 060	Last Dance/GAYTONES: Last Dance Version	8
75	Black Wax 10	Send Me The Pillow/MIGHTY TWO: Pillow With Strings	6

JAMES BROWN (& FAMOUS FLAMES)

(see also Lyn Collins, JBs, Maceo & All King's Men, Nat Kendrick & Swans)

SINGLES

60	Parlophone R 4667	Think/You've Got The Power (with Famous Flames)	40
60	Fontana H 273	This Old Heart/Wonder When You're Coming Home	30
62	Parlophone R 4922	Night Train/Why Does Everything Happen To Me (with Famous Flames)	50
62	Parlophone R 4952	Shout And Shimmy/Come Over Here (with Famous Flames)	40
63	London HL 9730	Prisoner Of Love/Choo-Choo (Locomotion) (with Famous Flames)	20
63	London HL 9775	These Foolish Things/(Can You) Feel It (Part 1) (with Famous Flames)	20
64	Philips BF 1368	Out Of Sight/Maybe The Last Time (& His Orchestra)	20
64	Sue WI 360	Night Train/Why Does Everything Happen To Me (with Famous Flames)	35
65	London HL 9945	Have Mercy Baby/Just Won't Do Right (with Famous Flames)	18
65	London HL 9990	Papa's Got A Brand New Bag Parts 1 & 2 (with Famous Flames)	20
65	Ember EMB S 216	Tell Me What You're Gonna Do/Lost Someone (p/s)	40
65	Ember EMB S 216	Tell Me What You're Gonna Do/Lost Someone	20
65	Philips BF 1458	Try Me/Papa's Got A Brand New Bag	20
66	Philips BF 1481	New Breed Parts 1 & 2	20
66	Pye International 7N 25350	I Got You (I Feel Good)/I Can't Help It (I Just Do-Do-Do) (with Famous Flames)	22
66	Pye International 7N 25367	Ain't That A Groove Parts 1 & 2 (with Famous Flames)	20
66	Pye International 7N 25371	It's A Man's Man's Man's World/Is It Yes Or Is It No? (with Famous Flames)	15
66	Pye International 7N 25379	Money Won't Change You Parts 1 & 2 (with Famous Flames)	25
66	Pye International 7N 25394	Don't Be A Drop-Out/Tell Me That You Love Me (with Famous Flames)	20
67	Pye International 7N 25411	Bring It Up/Nobody Knows (with Famous Flames)	20
67	Pye International 7N 25418	Kansas City/Stone Fox (with Famous Flames)	20
67	Pye International 7N 25423	Let Yourself Go/Good Rockin' Tonight (with Famous Flames)	15
67	Pye International 7N 25430	Cold Sweat Parts 1 & 2 (with Famous Flames)	20
67	Pye International 7N 25441	Get It Together Parts 1 & 2 (with Famous Flames)	15
68	Polydor 56740	I Can't Stand Myself/There Was A Time	15
68	Polydor 56743	I Got The Feelin'/If I Ruled The World	8
68	Polydor 56744	Licking Stick, Licking Stick Parts 1 & 2	8
68	Polydor 56752	Say It Loud, I'm Black And I'm Proud Parts 1 & 2	10

			MINT VALUE £
68	Polydor 56540	That's Life/Please, Please, Please (with Famous Flames)	15
69	Polydor 56776	Mother Popcorn Parts 1 & 2	8
69	Polydor 56780	The World Parts 1 & 2	8
69	Polydor 56783	Let A Man Come In And Do The Popcorn/Sometimes	10
69	Polydor 56787	There Was A Time/I Can't Stand Myself (When You Touch Me)	15
70	Polydor 56793	Ain't It Funky Now Parts 1 & 2	8
70	Polydor 2001 018	It's A New Day/Georgia On My Mind	8
70	Polydor 2001 071	Get Up, I Feel Like Being A Sex Machine Parts 1 & 2 (paper label)	8
70	Polydor 2001 071	Get Up, I Feel Like Being A Sex Machine Parts 1 & 2 (plastic label)	6
70	Polydor 2001 097	Call Me Super Bad Parts 1, 2 & 3	8
71	Polydor 2001 163	Soul Power Parts 1, 2 & 3	8
71	Polydor 2001 190	I Cried/Get Up, Get Into It, Get Involved	8
71	Polydor 2001 213	Hot Pants (She Got To Use What She Got To Get What She Wants) Parts 1, 2 & 3	8
71	Polydor 2001 223	Make It Funky Parts 1 & 2	8
71	Mojo 2093 006	Hey America!/Brother Rapp (Part 1)	8
71	Polydor 2066 153	I'm A Greedy Man Parts 1 & 2	8
72	Polydor 2066 185	King Heroin/Theme From King Heroin	18
72	Polydor 2066 210	There It Is Parts 1 & 2	7
72	Polydor 2066 216	Honky Tonk Parts 1 & 2	10
72	Polydor 2066 231	Get On The Good Foot Parts 1 & 2	7
72	Polydor 2066 283	What My Baby Needs Now Is A Little More Lovin'/ This Guy's In Love With You (with Lyn Collins)	15
73	Polydor 2066 285	I've Got A Bag Of My Own/I Know It's True	7
73	Polydor 2141 008	Papa's Got A Brand New Bag/Out Of Sight/It's A Man's Man's Man's World (p/s)	5
73	Polydor 2066 296	I Got Ants In My Pants Parts 1, 15 & 16	5
73	Polydor 2066 329	Think/Something	5
73	Polydor 2066 370	Woman Parts 1 & 2	5
74	Polydor 2066 411	Stone To The Bone/Sexy, Sexy, Sexy	5
74	Polydor 2066 485	My Thang/The Payback	5
74	Polydor 2066 513	It's Hell/Papa Don't Take No Mess	5
75	Polydor 2066 520	Funky President (People It's Bad)/Cold Blooded	5
76	Polydor 2066 642	Hot (I Need To Be Loved, Loved, Loved)/Superbad, Superslick (Part 1)	5
76	Polydor 2066 687	Get Up Offa That Thing/Release The Pressure	5
77	Polydor 2066 763	Bodyheat Parts 1, 15 & 16	5
77	Polydor 2066 834	Honky Tonk/Brother Rapp	5
78	Polydor 2066 915	Eyesight/I Never, Never, Never Will Forget	5
78	Polydor 2066 984	Nature Parts 1 & 2	5
79	Polydor POSP 24	For Goodness Sakes, Look At Those Cakes/ Get Up, I Feel Like Being A Sex Machine (red label)	8
79	Polydor POSP 24	For Goodness Sakes, Look At Those Cakes/ Get Up, I Feel Like Being A Sex Machine (silver label)	5
79	Polydor POSPX 24	Get Up, I Feel Like Being A Sex Machine/For Goodness Sakes, Look At Those Cakes (12")	10
79	Polydor POSPX 68	It's Too Funky In Here/Are We Really Dancing? (12")	10
79	Polydor STEP 2	Star Generation/Let The Boogie Do The Rest	5
79	Polydor STEPX 2	Star Generation/Let The Boogie Do The Rest (12")	8
80	Polydor POSP 121	Regrets/Stone Cold Drag	5
80	RCA RCAT 28	Rapp Payback (Where Iz Moses?) (Parts 1 & 2) (12")	8
81	RCA RCAT 44	Stay With Me/Smokin' And Drinkin' (12")	8
81	RCA RCAT 65	Funky Man (Parts 1 & 2)/Mashed Potatoes (12")	8
88	Urban URBX 13	She's The One/Funky President (People It's Bad)/Funky Drummer (9.13)/ Funky Drummer (Bonus Beats Reprise) (12", die-cut title sleeve)	10
88	Urban URBA 13	She's The One (Funky Drummer Remix)/Funky President (People It's Bad)/ Funky Drummer/Funky Drummer (Bonus Beats Reprise) (12")	10
88	Urban URBA17	Payback (Final Mixdown)/Give It Up Or Turn It Loose/Coldsweat (12")	15
88	Urban URBX 17 DJ	Coldcut Meets The Godfather (12" promo, same as "The Payback Mix")	10

EPs

64	London RE 1410	JAMES BROWN AND THE FAMOUS FLAMES	70
64	Ember EMB EP 4549	I DO JUST WHAT I WANT	40
66	Pye Intl. NEP 44059	I GOT YOU	40
66	Pye Intl. NEP 44068	I'LL GO CRAZY	40
67	Pye Intl. NEP 44072	PRISONER OF LOVE	40
67	Pye Intl. NEP 44076	HOW LONG DARLING	40
67	Pye Intl. NEP 44088	BRING IT UP	40
70	Polydor 580 701	TURN IT LOOSE	35

LPs

64	London HA 8177	PURE DYNAMITE! (as James Brown & Famous Flames)	75
64	London HA 8184	LIVE AT THE APOLLO (as James Brown & Famous Flames)	60
64	Ember EMB 3357	TELL ME WHAT YOU'RE GONNA DO	40
64	Philips BL 7630	SHOWTIME	35
65	London HA 8203	UNBEATABLE 16 HITS	65
65	London HA 8231	PLEASE, PLEASE, PLEASE (as James Brown & Famous Flames)	80
65	Philips BL 7664	GRITS AND SOUL	50
65	London HA 8240	JAMES BROWN TOURS THE U.S.A. (with Famous Flames)	50
66	London HA 8262	PAPA'S GOT A BRAND NEW BAG (as James Brown & Famous Flames)	50
66	Philips BL 7697	JAMES BROWN PLAYS JAMES BROWN TODAY AND YESTERDAY	40
66	Pye Intl. NPL 28074	I GOT YOU (I FEEL GOOD)	45
66	Philips BL 7718	JAMES BROWN PLAYS NEW BREED	20
66	Pye Intl. NPL 28079	IT'S A MAN'S MAN'S MAN'S WORLD	35
66	Pye Intl. NPL 28097	THE JAMES BROWN CHRISTMAS ALBUM	60
67	Pye Intl. NPL 28093	MIGHTY INSTRUMENTALS	35
67	Philips (S)BL 7761	HANDFUL OF SOUL	20
67	Pye Intl. NPL 28099	PAPA'S GOT A BRAND NEW BAG (reissue)	20
67	Pye Intl. NPL 28100	MR. EXCITEMENT	30
67	Polydor 582 703	THE JAMES BROWN SHOW (live)	20
67	Pye Intl. NPL 28103	SINGS RAW SOUL	15

			MINT VALUE £
67	Pye Intl. NPL 28104	LIVE AT THE GARDEN	35
68	Philips (S)BL 7823	JAMES BROWN PLAYS THE REAL THING	25
68	Polydor 623 032	MR. DYNAMITE	15
68	Polydor 184 100	MR. SOUL	15
68	Polydor 184 136	I CAN'T STAND MYSELF	20
69	Polydor 184 148	SOUL FIRE	15
69	Polydor 184 159	KING OF SOUL	12
60s	Polydor 2852 002	THE SOUL OF JAMES BROWN (reissue of "I Can't Stand Myself")	15
69	Mercury 20133 SMCL	JAMES BROWN SINGS OUT OF SIGHT	25
69	Polydor 583 729/30	LIVE AT THE APOLLO VOLUME TWO (2-LP)	20
69	Polydor 583 741	SAY IT LOUD - I'M BLACK AND I'M PROUD	20
69	Polydor 583 768	IT'S A MOTHER	20
69	Polydor 643 317	THIS IS... JAMES BROWN	15
70	Polydor 583 742	GETTIN' DOWN TO IT	20
70	Polydor 184 319	THE POPCORN	25
70	Polydor 2343 010	AIN'T IT FUNKY	25
71	Polydor 2625 004	SEX MACHINE (2-LP)	20
71	Polydor 2310 022	SOUL ON TOP	20
71	Polydor 2310 029	IT'S A NEW DAY	20
71	Polydor 2310 089	SUPER BAD	15
72	Polydor 2659 011	REVOLUTION OF THE MIND: RECORDED LIVE AT THE APOLLO VOL. III (2-LP)	25
72	Polydor 2391 033	THERE IT IS	25
73	Polydor 2659 018	GET ON THE GOOD FOOT (2-LP)	25
73	Polydor 2391 057	SOUL CLASSICS (also issued as record club edition [ACB 00222])	18
73	Polydor 2490 117	BLACK CAESAR (soundtrack)	30
73	Polydor 2391 084	SLAUGHTER'S BIG RIP-OFF (soundtrack)	30
74	Polydor 2391 116	SOUL CLASSICS VOLUME TWO	15
74	Polydor 2659 030	THE PAYBACK (2-LP)	30
74	Polydor 2659 036	IT'S HELL (2-LP)	30
75	Polydor 2391 164	REALITY	15
75	Polydor 2391 166	SOUL CLASSICS VOLUME THREE	15
75	Polydor 2391 175	SEX MACHINE TODAY	18
75	Polydor 2391 197	EVERYBODY'S DOIN' THE HUSTLE AND DEAD ON THE DOUBLE BUMP	15
77	Polydor 2391 300	MUTHA'S NATURE (by James Brown & the New J.B,'s)	15

JAMES BROWN (Jamaica)

71	Punch PH 76	Don't Say/TRANS AM ALLSTARS: Don't Say Version	8
72	Ashanti ASH 408	Mama Don't Want To See You/Mama Don't Want To See You Version	7
75	Mango MAN 1001	Stop The War In Babylon/Dub In Peace	15

JANET BROWN

79	Logo GO 366	Iron Lady/The Coming Of The Leader	6
79	Logo MOGO 4006	IRON LADY (LP)	12

JERICHO BROWN

60	Warner Bros WB 14	Don'tcha Know (That I Love You)/Look For A Star	10
64	Warner Bros WB 141	I'm Watching You/Wisdom Of A Fool	5

JIM EDWARD BROWN

(see also Browns)

66	RCA RCX 7179	INTRODUCING JIM EDWARD BROWN (EP)	15

JIM EDWARD (BROWN) & MAXINE BROWN

55	London HL 8123	Itsy Witsy Bitsy Me/Why Am I Falling?	45
55	London HL 8123	Itsy Witsy Bitsy Me/Why Am I Falling? (78)	10
55	London HLU 8166	Your Love Is Wild As The West Wind/Draggin' Mainstreet	45
55	London HLU 8166	Your Love Is Wild As The West Wind/Draggin' Mainstreet (78)	10
55	London HLU 8200	You Thought I Thought/Here Today And Gone Tomorrow (B-side with Bonnie)	45
55	London HLU 8200	You Thought I Thought/Here Today And Gone Tomorrow (B-side with Bonnie) (78)	12
55	London R-EP 1024	COUNTRY SONGS (EP)	25
55	London R-EU 1044	COUNTRY SONGS VOLUME 3 (EP)	25

JOE BROWN (& BRUVVERS)

(see also Vicki Brown)

59	Decca F 11185	People Gotta Talk/Comes The Day (solo, triangular centre)	20
59	Decca F 11185	People Gotta Talk/Comes The Day (78)	25
60	Decca F 11207	Darktown Strutter's Ball/Swagger (solo)	12
60	Decca F 11246	Jellied Eels/Dinah	10
60	Pye 7N 15322	Shine/The Switch	7
61	Piccadilly 7N 35000	Crazy Mixed Up Kid/Stick Around	6
61	Piccadilly 7N 35005	Good Luck & Goodbye/I'm Henery The Eighth I Am	6
62	Piccadilly 7N 35024	What A Crazy World We're Living In/Popcorn	6
62	Decca F 11496	Comes The Day/People Gotta Talk (reissue)	5
64	Piccadilly 7N 35163	You Do Things To Me/Everybody Calls Me Joe	6
62	Decca DFE8500	A PICTURE OF JOE BROWN (EP)	15
62	Picadilly NEP 34025	JOE BROWN HIT PARADE (EP)	15
63	Picadilly NEP 34026	ALL THINGS BRIGHT AND BEAUTIFUL (EP)	10
62	Ace of Clubs ACL 1127	A PICTURE OF JOE BROWN (LP)	20
63	Picadilly MPL 38006	LIVE (LP)	15

JOE BROWN/MARK WYNTER

(see also Mark Wynter)

63	Piccadilly NEP 24167	JUST FOR FUN (EP, soundtrack, 2 tracks each)	10
64	Golden Guinea WO 1	BIG HITS OF JOE BROWN AND MARK WYNTER (EP)	10

JOHNNY BROWN

61	Philips PB 1119	Walkin' Talkin' Kissin' Doll/Sundown	10

KAY BROWN

56	Brunswick 05595	Me 'N' You 'N' The Moon/What Do You Think It Does To Me?	10

MINT VALUE £

KENT BROWN & RAINBOWS
(see also Kent & Jeannie, Sir D's Group)

68	Fab FAB 53	When You Going To Show Me How/Come Ya Come Ya	10

LENNOX BROWN
(see also Jeff Barnes, Peter Tosh)

72	Green Door GD 4023	High School Serenade/WINSTON SCOTLAND: On The Track (1st issue)	7
72	Bullet BU 501	High School Serenade/WINSTON SCOTLAND: On The Track (2nd issue)	7

LEROY BROWN

78	Revue REVD 10	Taxi/Blood A Go Run (12")	40

LES BROWN & HIS BAND OF RENOWN

54	Vogue Coral Q 2034	Ramona/Hot Point	7
54	Vogue Coral Q 2042	St. Louis Blues Mambo/Moon Song	7
55	Vogue Coral Q 72049	The Man That Got Away/Doodle-Doo-Doo	7
55	Capitol CL 14331	Frenesi/Perfidia	6
55	Capitol CL 14350	He Needs Me/Simplicity	6
55	Vogue Coral Q 72107	Lullaby Of Birdland/Bernie's Tune	6
56	Vogue Coral Q 72123	Hong Kong Blues (with Hoagy Carmichael & Band Of Renown)/ It's All Right With Me	10
56	Vogue Coral Q 72215	Flamingo/Midnight Sun	5
56	Capitol CL 14512	Sincerely Yours/Take Back Your Mink	5
56	Capitol CL 14611	That Certain Feeling/Hit The Road To Dreamland	5
56	Capitol CL 14631	Talk About A Party/Ancient History	5
57	Capitol CL 14675	Priscilla/The Best Years Of My Life	5
57	Capitol CL 14706	Original Joe/If I Had The Money	5
57	Vogue Coral Q 72242	Forty Cups Of Coffee/I'm Forever Blowing Bubbles	5

LES BROWN (JR)

60s	Vocalion VA 8011	WILDREST DRUMS YET (LP)	30

MAXINE BROWN
(see also Chuck Jackson & Maxine Brown)

61	London HLU 9286	All In My Mind/Harry, Let's Marry	45
62	HMV POP 1102	Am I Falling In Love/Promise Me Anything	120
63	Stateside SS 188	Ask Me/Yesterday's Kisses	45
64	Pye International 7N 25272	Oh No Not My Baby/You Upset My Soul	30
65	Pye International 7N 25299	It's Gonna Be Alright/You Do Something To Me	25
65	Pye International 7N 25317	One Step At A Time/Anything For A Laugh	40
67	Pye International 7N 25410	I've Got A Lot Of Love Left In Me/Hold On (I'm Comin') (B-side with Chuck Jackson)	35
67	Pye International 7N 25434	Since I Found You/Gotta Find A Way	25
70	Major Minor MM 709	Reason To Believe/I Can't Get Along Without You	25
73	Avco 6105 022	Picked Up, Packed Up And Put Away/Bella Mia	10
75	Pye Disco Demand DDS 117	One In A Million/Let Me Give You My Lovin'	10
90s	Kent TOWN 110	It's Torture/I Got Love	15

NAPPY BROWN (& HIS BAND)

55	London HL 8145	Don't Be Angry/It's Really You	500
55	London HL 8145	Don't Be Angry/It's Really You (78)	30
55	London HLC 8182	Pitter Patter/There'll Come A Day	400
55	London HLC 8182	Pitter Patter/There'll Come A Day (78)	30
57	London HLC 8384	Little By Little/I'm Getting Lonesome (& His Band) (gold lettering on label)	300
57	London HLC 8384	Little By Little/I'm Getting Lonesome (& His Band) (silver lettering on label)	150
57	London HLC 8384	Little By Little/I'm Getting Lonesome (& His Band) (78 rpm)	15
58	London HLC 8760	It Don't Hurt No More/My Baby	75
58	London HLC 8760	It Don't Hurt No More/My Baby (78)	20

NOEL BROWN
(see also Bunny Brown)

50s	Parlophone MP 134	Take Me Back To Africa/Virgin Islands (Get Happy In A Hurry) (78, export)	5
68	Island WI 3149	Man's Temptation/Heartbreak Girl	60
69	Songbird SB 1012	By The Time I Get To Phoenix/Heartbreak Girl	5
70	Bullet BU 423	Phoenix (actually by "By The Time I Get To Phoenix")/Heartbreak Girl	6

OSCAR BROWN JNR

61	Philips PB 1097	But I Was Cool/Dat Dere	5
60	CBS 62229	SIN & SOUL (LP)	18

PAMELA BROWN

70	Joe JRS 8	People Are Running/CRITICS: School Days	15

PATRICK BROWN

82	Kufe EB 003	Fantasy/On The Right Track (12")	40

PETE BROWN('S PIBLOKTO)
(see also Battered Ornaments, Graham Bond & Pete Brown, Deke Leonard, Cream)

69	Parlophone R 5767	The Week Looked Good On Paper/Morning Call (as Pete Brown & His Battered Ornaments, promo p/s)	60
69	Parlophone R 5767	The Week Looked Good On Paper/Morning Call (as Pete Brown & His Battered Ornaments)	25
69	Harvest HAR 5008	Living Life Backwards/High Flying Electric Bird (as Pete Brown & Piblokto!)	20
70	Harvest HAR 5023	Can't Get Off The Planet/Broken Magic (with His Battered Ornaments)	15
70	Harvest HAR 5028	Flying Hero Sandwich/My Last Band (as Pete Brown & Piblokto!)	25
69	Harvest SHVL 752	A MEAL YOU CAN SHAKE HANDS WITH IN THE DARK (LP, as Pete Brown & His Battered Ornaments, with "Sold in U.K..." label text on 4 lines, stereo)	300
70	Harvest SHVL 768	THE ART SCHOOL DANCE GOES ON FOREVER (LP, as Pete Brown & Piblokto!, gatefold sleeve, no EMI on label)	170
70	Harvest SHVL 782	THOUSANDS ON A RAFT (LP, as Pete Brown & Piblokto!, gatefold sleeve, no EMI on label)	150
73	Deram SML 1103	THE NOT FORGOTTEN ASSOCIATION (LP, with Graham Bond)	100

MINT VALUE £

77	Harvest SHSM 2017	MY LAST BAND (LP, as Pete Brown & Piblokto)	20
82	Discs Intl. INTLP 1	PARTY IN THE RAIN (LP, with Ian Lynn, private pressing)	15

PINEY BROWN

54	Esquire 10-330	That's Right Little Girl/EDDIE CHAMBLEE: Blues For Eddie (78)	10

POLLY BROWN

73	Pye NSPL 18396	POLLY BROWN (LP)	18

ROY BROWN

57	London HLP 8398	I'm Sticking With You/Party Doll (gold label print)	600
57	London HLP 8398	I'm Sticking With You/Party Doll (later silver print pressing)	300
57	London HLP 8398	I'm Sticking With You/Party Doll (78)	50
57	London HLP 8448	Saturday Night/Everybody	500
57	London HLP 8448	Saturday Night/Everybody (78)	65

RUTH BROWN (& HER RHYTHMAKERS)

55	London HL 8153	Mambo Baby/Mama (He Treats Your Daughter Mean) (with Rhythmakers)	350
55	London HL 8153	Mambo Baby/Mama (He Treats Your Daughter Mean) (with Rhythmakers) (78)	30
55	London HLE 8210	As Long As I'm Moving/R.B. Blues (with Her Rhythmakers)	350
55	London HLE 8210	As Long As I'm Moving/R.B. Blues (with Her Rhythmakers) (78)	30
56	London HLE 8310	I Want To Do More/Sweet Baby Of Mine	200
56	London HLE 8310	I Want To Do More/Sweet Baby Of Mine (78)	30
57	London HLE 8401	Mom Oh Mom/I Want To Be Loved (But Only By You)	200
57	London HLE 8401	Mom Oh Mom/I Want To Be Loved (But Only By You) (78)	50
57	Columbia DB 3913	Lucky Lips/My Heart Is Breaking Over You	400
57	Columbia DB 3913	Lucky Lips/My Heart Is Breaking Over You (78)	40
57	London HLE 8483	When I Get You Baby/One More Time	100
57	London HLE 8483	When I Get You Baby/One More Time (78)	40
58	London HLE 8552	A New Love/Look Me Up	100
58	London HLE 8552	A New Love/Look Me Up (78)	30
58	London HLE 8645	Just Too Much/Book Of Lies	100
58	London HLE 8645	Just Too Much/Book Of Lies (78)	40
58	London HLE 8757	This Little Girl's Gone Rockin'/Why Me	75
58	London HLE 8757	This Little Girl's Gone Rockin'/Why Me (78)	40
58	London HL 7061	This Little Girl's Gone Rockin'/Why Me (export issue)	75
59	London HLE 8887	Jack O' Diamonds/I Can't Hear A Word You Say	40
59	London HLE 8887	Jack O' Diamonds/I Can't Hear A Word You Say (78)	45
59	London HLE 8946	I Don't Know/Papa Daddy	50
59	London HLE 8946	I Don't Know/Papa Daddy (78)	45
60	London HLE 9093	Don't Deceive Me/I Burned Your Letter	40
61	London HLK 9304	Sure 'Nuff/Here He Comes	30
64	Brunswick 05904	Yes Sir That's My Baby/What Happened To You	20
76	President PT 457	Sugar Babe/Stop Knocking	8
55	London REE 1038	THE QUEEN OF R&B (EP)	200
63	Philips BE 12537	GOSPEL TIME (EP)	50
60	London Jazz LTZ-K 15187	LAST DATE WITH RUTH BROWN (LP)	50
62	Philips 652 012 BL	ALONG COMES RUTH (LP)	50
63	Philips 652 020 BL	GOSPEL TIME (LP)	40
64	Atlantic ATL 5007	THE BEST OF RUTH BROWN (LP, plum label)	100
76	President PTLS 1067	SUGAR BABE (LP)	20

RUTH BROWN/JOE TURNER

56	London REE 1047	THE KING AND QUEEN OF R&B (EP, 2 tracks each)	200

SAMMI BROWN

68	Fontana TF 947	Daydream/Stop The Music	7

SANDY BROWN('S JAZZ BAND)

(see also Wally Fawkes, Sandy & Teachers, Al Fairweather)

58	Tempo A 124	African Queen/Special Delivery (as Sandy Brown's Jazz Band)	5
53	Esquire EP 28	SANDY BROWN'S JAZZ BAND (EP)	10
55	Tempo EXA 13	SANDY BROWN'S JAZZ BAND (EP)	10
55	Tempo EXA 33	SANDY BROWN'S JAZZ BAND (EP)	10
56	Tempo EXA 49	TRADITIONAL JAZZ SCENE '56 (EP)	10
57	Nixa NJE 1054	BLUE McJAZZ (EP)	10
57	Nixa NJE 1056	AFRO McJAZZ (EP)	10
53	Esquire 20-022	SANDY BROWN (10" LP, with Bobby Mickleburgh)	15
56	Tempo TAP 3	SANDY'S SIDEMEN PLAYING COMPOSITIONS BY AL FAIRWEATHER (LP)	40
57	Nixa Jazz Today NJL 9	McJAZZ (LP)	15
66	Fontana TE1 7473	SANDY BROWN ALL STARS (LP)	15
69	Fontana SFJL 921	HAIR AT ITS HAIRIEST (LP, as Sandy Brown & His Gentlemen Friends)	20
71	77 SEU 12/49	WITH THE BRIAN LEMON TRIO (LP)	15

SAVOY BROWN

(see under 'S')

SHIRLEY BROWN

(see also Oliver Sain)

75	Stax STXS 2019	Woman To Woman/Yes Sir, Brother	6
75	Stax STXS 2032	I Can't Give You Up/It Ain't No Fun	20
75	Stax STX 1031	WOMAN TO WOMAN (LP)	20

STU BROWN & BLUESOLOGY

(see also Bluesology, Elton John)

67	Polydor 56195	Since I Found You Baby/Just A Little Bit	300

TEDDY BROWN

61	Starlite ST 45 033	Pretty Little Baby/Genevieve	10

TEDDY BROWN

70	Trojan TR 7793	What Greater Love/Lady Love	6
71	Trojan TR 7827	Walk The World Away/Senorita Rita	6

MINT VALUE £

TINY BROWN
50 Capitol CL 13306 No More Blues/Slow-Motion Baby (78) 12

U BROWN
78 Cancer CAN 702 Starsky And Hutch/Version 6

VIC BROWN COMBO
63 Rio R 7 Swanee River/Robert E. Lee 15

VICKI BROWN
77 Power Exchange PXL 012 FROM THE INSIDE (LP) 15

VINCENT BROWN
70 Gas GAS 128 Look What You're Going To Do/Hold On To What You Have Got 8

WATSON T. BROWN (& EXPLOSIVE)
(see also Explosive)
68 President PT 207 Some Lovin'/Home Is Where Your Heart Lies 6
68 President PT 221 Crying All Night/I Close My Eyes 10
70 Bell BLL 1109 Will You Still Love Me Tomorrow/Save The Last Dance For Me (solo) 6
71 MAM MAM 16 I'm On The Road Again/Feeling Bad 6

WILLIAM BROWN
71 Ackee ACK 128 I'm Alone/BELTONES: Soul People 10

BROWN BROTHERS
(see also Charles Brown)
59 Vogue V 9131 Let The Good Times Roll/You're Right, I'm Left 200
59 Vogue V 9131 Let The Good Times Roll/You're Right, I'm Left (78) 100

DUNCAN BROWNE
68 Immediate IM 070 On The Bombsite/Alfred Bell 25
70 Bell BLL 1119 Resurrection Joe/Final Asylum 12
73 Rak RAK 162 Send Me The Bill/My Only Son 6
78 Logo GO 329 Wild Places/Camino Real 6
68 Immediate IMSP 018 GIVE ME, TAKE YOU (LP, with insert, lilac label with "Sold in U.K..." label text) 400
73 RAK SRKA 6754 DUNCAN BROWNE (LP, gatefold sleeve) 50

GEORGE BROWNE
(see also Humphrey Lyttleton)
54 Parlophone CMSP 6 Calypso Mambo/The Peanut Vendor (export issue) 10
54 Parlophone CMSP 17 Somebody Bad Stole De Wedding Bell (Who's Got De Ding Dong?)/ Matilda, Matilda! (export issue) 7
57 Columbia DB 3940 Sound Barrier/Te-Le-Le 7

JACKSON BROWNE
86 Elektra EKR 35P For America (Edit)/Till I Go Down (Statue Of Liberty-shaped picture disc) 5
86 Elektra EKR 42P In The Shape Of A Heart/Voice Of America (heart-shaped picture disc) 5
74 Asylum K2 43007 LATE FOR THE SKY (LP, quadrophonic) 15

SANDRA BROWNE (& BOYFRIENDS)
63 Columbia DB 4998 By Hook Or By Crook/Johnny Boy (as Sandra Browne & Boyfriends) 15
63 Columbia DB 7109 You'd Think He Didn't Know Me/Mama Never Told Me 15
65 Columbia DB 7465 Knock On Any Door/I Want Love 15

TEDDY BROWN(E)
59 Capitol CL 15059 A Corner In Paradise/The Everglades 8
61 Starlite ST45 033 Pretty Little Baby/Genevieve (as Teddy Brown) 15

THOMAS F. BROWNE
(see also Gary Wright, The Gladiators)
71 Vertigo 6325 250 WEDNESDAY'S CHILD (LP, gatefold sleeve, small swirl label) 175

TOBY BROWNE
64 Parlophone 5192 Play The Music, Keep On Dancing/Child 20

TOM BROWNE
80 Arista ARIST 12357 Funkin' For Jamaica (N.Y.)/Her Silent Smile (12") 8

DUKE BROWNER
(see also Kaddo Strings)
79 Grapevine GRP 145 Crying Over You/Crying Over You (Instrumental) 15

BROWNHILL'S STAMP DUTY
69 Columbia DB 8625 Maxwell's Silver Hammer/My Woman's Back 8

BILL BROWNING
80s Roller Coaster RRC 2003 Wash Machine Boogie/Ramblin' Man (p/s) 8

BROWNS
(see also Jim Edward & Maxine Brown)
59 RCA RCA 1140 The Three Bells/Heaven Fell Last Night (tri centre) 12
59 RCA RCA 1140 The Three Bells/Heaven Fell Last Night 5
59 RCA RCA 1140 The Three Bells/Heaven Fell Last Night (78) 20
59 RCA RCA 1157 Scarlet Ribbons (For Her Hair)/Blue Bells Ring (78) 10
60 RCA RCA 1176 Teen-Ex/The Old Lamplighter 8
60 RCA RCA 1193 Margo (The Ninth Of May)/Lonely Little Robin 8
60 RCA RCA 1218 Send Me The Pillow You Dream On/You're So Much A Part Of Me 5
60 RCA RCX 587 IN THE COUNTRY (EP, mono) 15
60 RCA SRC 7036 IN THE COUNTRY (EP, stereo) 20
59 RCA RD 27153 SWEET SOUNDS BY THE BROWNS (LP, mono) 15
59 RCA RD SF 5052 SWEET SOUNDS BY THE BROWNS (LP, stereo) 20

BROWNS FERRY FOUR
(see also Delmore Brothers, Grandpa Jones, Merle Travis)
54 Parlophone CMSP 11 I Need The Prayers/Through The Pearly Gates (with Clyde Moody, export issue) 25

MINT VALUE £

BROWNS HOME BREW

72	Bell BELL 1211	Billy Come Down/Hit Me Across The Head With A Spoon	5

BROWN SUGAR

70s	Lovers Rock CJ 613	I'm In Love With A Dreadlocks/Version	30

BROWN SUGAR

80	Studio 16 WE 092	Dreaming Of Zion (12")	40
80	Studio 16 WE 106	Confession Hurts (12")	35
80	Studio 16 WE 113	Runaway Love (12")	40
80	African Drums AF 002	Hello Stranger/Black Is The Colour (12")	12
80	Black Roots BRLP 1000	NOT SO LUCKY (LP)	20

ANNETTE (Reis) & VICTOR BROX

(see also Aynsley Dunbar Retaliation)

65	Fontana TF 536	I've Got The World In A Jug/Wake Me And Shake Me	15
74	Sonet SNTF 663	ROLLIN' BACK (LP)	20

DAVE BRUBECK (QUARTET)

(see also Jimmy Rushing, Carmen McRae)

53	Vogue 45-2156	A Foggy Day/Lyons Busy	5
53	Vogue 45-2157	Mam'selle/Me And My Shadow	5
53	Vogue 45-2158	Frenesi/At A Perfume Counter	5
53	Vogue 45-2159	Body And Soul/Let's Fall In Love	5
53	Vogue 45-2160	I'll Remember April/Singin' In The Rain	5
53	Vogue 45-2161	Lullaby In Rhythm/You Stepped Out Of A Dream	5
54	Vogue V 2171	At A Perfume Counter/Me And My Shadow	5
54	Vogue V 2206	Frenesi/Mam'selle	5
60	Philips JAZ 106	I'm In A Dancing Mood/Lover (p/s)	5
54	Vogue LDE 090	DAVE BRUBECK TRIO (10" LP)	15
54	Vogue LDE 095	DAVE BRUBECK QUARTET (10" LP)	15
54	Vogue LDE 104	DAVE BRUBECK QUARTET VOL. 2 (10" LP)	15
55	Vogue LDE 114	DAVE BRUBECK QUARTET VOL. 3 (10" LP)	15
57	Fontana TFL 5017	DAVE DIGS DISNEY (LP)	15
59	Vogue LAE 12008	THE FABULOUS DAVE BRUBECK TRIO AND OCTET (LP)	15
59	Fontana TFL 5071	GONE WITH THE WIND (LP, also stereo STFL 501)	15
60	Vogue LAE 12114	DAVE BRUBECK QUARTET FEATURING PAUL DESMOND (LP)	15

JACK BRUCE

(see also Alexis Korner's Blues Incorporated, Cream, Manfred Mann, Graham Bond Organisation, John Mayall, West Bruce & Laing, Lifetime, Rocket 88, Carla Bley, Duffy Power, Cozy Powell)

65	Polydor BM 56036	I'm Getting Tired (Of Drinking And Gambling)/Rootin' Tootin'	70
71	Polydor 2058 153	The Consul At Sunset/Letter Of Thanks	15
74	RSO 2090 141	Keep It Down/Golden Days	5
69	Polydor 583 058	SONGS FOR A TAILOR (LP, gatefold sleeve)	25
70	Polydor 2343 033	THINGS WE LIKE (LP)	18
71	Polydor 2310 070	THINGS WE LIKE (LP, reissue)	15
71	Polydor 2310 107	HARMONY ROW (LP, gatefold sleeve)	20
74	RSO 2394 143	OUT OF THE STORM (LP, with insert)	12

LENNY BRUCE

69	Transatlantic TRA 195	BERKELEY CONCERT (2-LP)	20

BRUCE & ROBIN ROCKERS

66	Marble Arch MAL 626	THE BATMAN THEME (LP)	12

TOMMY BRUCE (& BRUISERS)

60	Columbia DB 4453	Ain't Misbehavin'/Got The Water Boilin' (with Bruisers)	5
60	Columbia DB 4498	Broken Doll/I'm On Fire (with Bruisers)	8
60	Columbia DB 4532	On The Sunny Side Of The Street/My Little Girl (with Bruisers)	7
61	Columbia DB 4581	You Make Love So Well/I'm Crazy 'Bout My Baby (with Bruisers)	7
61	Columbia DB 4682	Love, Honour And Oh! Baby/I'm Gonna Sit Right Down And Write	10
62	Columbia DB 4776	Babette/Honey Girl, You're Lonely	8
62	Columbia DB 4850	Horror Movies/It's You	12
62	Columbia DB 4927	Buttons And Bows/London Boys	6
63	Columbia DB 7025	Let's Do It, Let's Fall In Love/Two Feet Left	6
63	Columbia DB 7132	Lavender Blue/Sixteen Years Ago Tonight	5
64	Columbia DB 7241	Let It Be Me/No More	5
64	Columbia DB 7387	Over Suzanne/It's Drivin' Me Wild	20
65	Polydor BM 56006	Boom Boom/Can Your Monkey Do The Dog (with Bruisers)	20
66	RCA RCA 1535	Monster Gonzales/I Hate Getting Up In The Morning	25
68	CBS CBS 3405	I've Been Around Too Long/Where The Colour Of The Soil Is Different	5
68	CBS CBS 3937	Heartbreak Melody/The Reason Why	7
61	Columbia SEG 8077	KNOCKOUT (EP)	75

CLAUDIA BRÜCKEN

(see also Propaganda, Act, Glenn Gregory & Claudia Brucken)

90	Island 12ISX 471	Absolut[e] (Bastille Mix)/Absolut[e] (Shooting Star Mix) (12", remix, stickered title sleeve, promo only)	8

HEIDI BRÜHL

60	Philips PB 1095	Ring Of Gold/I'll Belong To You Forever (in p/s)	10
60	Philips PB 1095	Ring Of Gold/I'll Belong To You Forever	5
63	Philips 345 579 BF	Marcel/Talk It Over With Someone	5
69	Philips BF 1768	The Drifter/Berlin	100
69	Philips BF 1768	The Drifter/Berlin (DJ Copy)	200

BRUISERS

(see also [Peter] Lee Stirling & Bruisers)

63	Parlophone R 5042	Blue Girl/Don't Cry	15
63	Parlophone R 5092	Your Turn To Cry/Give It To Me	20

MINT VALUE £

BRUMBEATS

64	Decca F 11834	Cry Little Girl, Cry/I Don't Understand	25

BEAU BRUMMEL ESQUIRE

65	Columbia DB 7447	I Know Know Know/Shoppin' Around	10
65	Columbia DB 7538	The Next Kiss/Come And Get Me	10
65	Columbia DB 7675	A Better Man Than I/Teardrops	10
66	Columbia DB 7878	You Don't Know What You've Got/Take Me Like I Am	10

GEORGE BRUNIS

54	London AL 3536	NEW ORLEANS RHYTHM KINGS (LP)	20

BRUNNING (HALL) SUNFLOWER BLUES BAND

(see also Five's Company, Fleetwood Mac, Leaf Hound)

68	Saga FID 2118	BULLEN STREET BLUES (LP, as Brunning Sunflower Blues Band, with black/silver label)	30
69	Saga EROS 8132	TRACKSIDE BLUES (LP, black/silver labels)	45
70	Saga EROS 8150	I WISH YOU WOULD (LP, as Brunning Sunflower Blues Band, with black/silver labels)	75
71	Gemini GM 2010	THE BRUNNING/HALL SUNFLOWER BLUES BAND (LP, with white/red labels)	120

BRUNO

66	Parlophone R5450	Wonderboy/Window In My Room	20
66	Parlophone R5507	The English Girl/The Driver	20

TONY BRUNO

68	Capitol CL 15534	What's Yesterday/Small Town, Bring Down	50

BRUTE FORCE

69	Apple APPLE 8	King Of Fuh/Nobody Knows (unissued)	800

BRUTUS

75	Purple PUR 126	Payroll/New Deal Princess	7

CARL BRYAN

(see also Cannon Ball & Johnny Melody, King Cannon, Vincent Foster, Hugh Malcolm, King Cannonball, Glen Brown, Shenley Duffas, Alton Ellis, Kid Gungo, Jackie Mittoo, Johnny Moore, Joe White, Royals)

69	Trojan TR 673	Red Ash/SILVERTONES: Bluebirds Flying Over	25
69	Duke DU 13	Soul Pipe/Overproof	15
69	Camel CA 22	Run For Your Life/TWO SPARKS: When We Were Young	12
69	Gas GAS 133	Stagger Back/The Creeper	15
69	Gas GAS 134	Walking The Dead/TREVOR & KEITH: Got What You Want	12

DORA BRYAN

63	Fontana TF 427	All I Want For Christmas Is A Beatle/If I Were A Fairy	5
64	Fontana TF 511	Oh Oh Oh Oh Seven/Because He Loves Me	5

BRYAN & MICHAEL

79	PYE 7P1444	Pinocchio/I Can't Count The Fingers On One Hand	6

FITZVAUGHN BRYAN'S ORCHESTRA

60	Melodisc 45-1560	Evening News/Hold Up Your Head And Smile (with Kenrick Patrick)	10

RAD BRYAN

71	Techniques TE 909	Jumping Jack/ANSELL COLLINS: Point Blank	12
71	Bullet BU 463	Shock Attack/Cuban Waltz	12
71	Big Shot BI 559	Just Do The Right Things/Corporal Jones	10
71	Big Shot BI 591	I'll Be Right There (actually by Techniques)/PLAYBOYS: Hot Pants Rock	12
71	Big Shot BI 592	My Best Girl/My Best Girl Version	12
71	Black Swan BW 1410	Girl You Rock My Soul/Version	15
72	Attack ATT 8040	Standing In The Rain (actually by Neville Grant)/Standing In The Rain Version	8
75	Love 1	Rock Children/Version	7

TIM BRYAN

71	Phillips 6006026	Mary Anne/It's So Easy	8

WES BRYAN

58	London HLU 8607	Lonesome Love/Tiny Spaceman	40
58	London HLU 8607	Lonesome Love/Tiny Spaceman (78)	18
59	London HLU 8978	Honey Baby/So Blue Over You	50
59	London HLU 8978	Honey Baby/So Blue Over You (78)	30

BRYAN & BRUNELLES

65	HMV POP 1394	Jacqueline/Louie Louie	60

ANITA BRYANT

59	London HLL 8983	Six Boys And Seven Girls/The Blessings Of Love	10
59	London HLL 8983	Six Boys And Seven Girls/The Blessings Of Love (78)	15
60	London HLL 9075	Little George (Got The Hiccoughs)/Love Look Away	10
60	London HLL 9114	Paper Roses/Mixed Emotions	5
60	London HLL 9171	In My Little Corner Of The World/Just In Time	5
60	London HLL 9219	One Of the Lucky Ones/The Party's Over	5
60	London HLL 9247	Wonderland By Night/Pictures	5
61	London HLL 9281	Till There Was You/A Texan And A Girl From Mexico	5
61	London HLL 9353	Do-Re-Mi/An Angel Cried	5
61	Philips BF 1182	The Wedding/Seven Kinds Of Lonesome	5
66	CBS 202026	Another Year, Another Love/My Mind's Playing Tricks On Me Again	60
62	CBS AAG 20005	KISSES SWEETER THAN WINE (EP)	20
61	London HA-L 2381	IN MY LITTLE CORNER OF THE WORLD (LP)	50

BOUDLEAUX BRYANT

(see also Bood & Fileece Bryant)

60	Polydor NH 66952	Hot Spot/Touché (with Sparks)	5

MINT VALUE £

DON BRYANT

70	London HA-U/SH-U 8409	PRECIOUS SOUL (LP)	50

JOHN BRYANT

65	Fontana H 625	Tell Me What You See/Poor Unfortunate Me	15

JOHN BRYANT

69	Decca 12894	She's In Need Of Love	25
68	MCA MU 1020	Columbine/I Bring The Sun	20
71	Polydor 2058-145	Back On The Road/I Won't Sleep Tonight/Ain't Got No Woman	6
71	Polydor 2383069	JOHN BRYANT (LP, gatefold sleeve)	20

LAURA K. BRYANT

58	London HLU 8551	Bobby/Angel Tears	40
58	London HLU 8551	Bobby/Angel Tears (78)	20

MARIE/MARGARET BRYANT

61	Kalypso XX 27	Water Melon/Tomato	6
61	Kalypso XX 28	Don't Touch Me Nylon/Little Boy	6
60s	Melodisc MLP 12 132	DON'T TOUCH ME NYLONS (LP, with sleeve)	25

MATT BRYANT & LINDA JOYCE

(see also Maureen Evans, Brian Matthew)

60	Embassy WB 420	Goodness Gracious Me/STEVE STANNARD & HIS GROUP: Man Of Mystery	5

RAY BRYANT TRIO/COMBO

60	Pye International 7N 25052	Little Susie Parts 2 & 4	5
60	Philips PB 1003	Little Susie Parts 1 & 3	5
60	Philips PB 1014	The Madison Time Parts 1 & 2	15
61	Philips BBL 7538	DANCING THE BIG TWIST (LP)	12

RUSTY BRYANT

57	London HB-D 1066	RUSTY BRYANT (10" LP)	60
72	Prestige PRST 10014	FIRE EATER (LP)	15

SANDRA BRYANT

67	Major Minor MM 523	Girl With Money/Golden Hours	10
68	Major Minor MM 553	Out To Get You/There's No Lock Upon My Door	30

GAVIN BRYARS

(see also Brian Eno)

75	Obscure 1	THE SINKING OF THE TITANIC (LP)	15

CALUM BRYCE

68	Condor PS 1001	Lovemaker/I'm Glad	450

BERYL BRYDEN('S BACK-ROOM SKIFFLE)

(see also Alexis Korner, Cyril Davies)

56	Decca F 10823	Casey Jones/Kansas City Blues	40
56	Decca F 10823	Casey Jones/Kansas City Blues (78)	15
57	Decca (no cat. no.)	Rock Me/This Train (test pressing, with Alexis Korner & Cyril Davies)	150
63	Columbia DB 7010	I'm Living With The Blues/Big Daddy	15
56	Melodisc EPM 7-69	BERYL BRYDEN WITH FATTY GEORGE'S JAZZ BAND (EP)	10

BETSY BRYE

59	Columbia DB 4350	Sleep Walk/Daddy Daddy (Gotta Get A Phone In My Room)	25

BRYGADA KRYZYS

82	Fresh Records FRESH 13	BRYGADA KRYZYS (LP)	25

B SIDE

93	B Promo B Side	Rip Piece Off/Can't Slow Me Down (12")	30

B.T.B.

68	Liberty LBF 15067	Do It To 'Em/Sparrows And Daisies	20

B.T. EXPRESS

75	Pye International 7N 25674	Express (Parts 1 & 2)	6
75	Pye International 7N 25682	Once You Get It/This House Is Smokin'	8
75	Pye Intl. NSPL 28207	DO IT (TIL YOU'RE SATISFIED) (LP)	20
75	EMI International INA 1501	NON-STOP (LP)	15

B.T.P. FOLDERS

80	Future Earth FER 005	Radio/All Of A Sudden (p/s)	50

B12

(see also Redcell, Musicology)

93	B12 09 CASSETTE	PRELUDE PART 1 (cassette, 400 only)	20
93	B12 09 CD	PRELUDE PT 1 (CD, 500 only)	25
93	B12 CD 1	REDCELL & STASIS (CD, 1500 only)	20
94	B12 15	B12 (12", 4-track promo only, 10 copies pressed)	40
07	B12 B1215	Practopia (12")	20
93	Warp WAPLP 9LTD	ELECTRO - SOMA (2-LP, orange vinyl)	40

BUBA & SHOP ASSISTANTS

(see also Shop Assistants, Pastels)

85	Villa 21 002	Something To Do/Dreaming Backwards (p/s, with insert in poly bag)	25

BUBBLEGUM

68	Philips BF1677	Little Red Bucket/With The Sun In Your Hair	35

BUBBLEMEN

88	Beggars Banquet BUB1	The Bubblmen Are Coming/B Side (P/S, comic included)	8

BUBBLES

63	Duke DK 1001	The Wasp/Bopping In The Barnyard (matrix: DK 1001A-1, plays Rocking Crickets by Hot Toddy's)	18

MINT VALUE £

BUBBLES

75	Decca F 13583	This Is Where The Hurdie Gurdie Heebie Geebie Greenie Meenie Man Came In/Zap N' Cat	50
78	Rainbow RS 611	Jamias/Night Life	8

BUBBLES & CO

65	Pye 7N 15875	Underneath My Pillow/Just One Girl	15

BUCCA

82	Plant Life PLR 039	THE HOLE IN THE HARPERS HEAD (LP)	20

BUCHANAN BROTHERS

69	Page One POF 139	Medicine Man Part 1/Part 2	7
69	Page One POF 154	Son Of A Lovin' Man/I'll Never Get Enough	5
70	Penny Farthing PEN 725	Rosianna/The Feeling That I Get When Your Near	6

GILLY BUCHANAN

	Toe TOE 002	Me No Mix/PATRICK ANDY: Ain't No Me (12")	80

ROY BUCHANAN

72	Polydor 2066307	Sweet Dreams/John's Blues	6

LINDSAY BUCKINGHAM

81	Mercury MER 85	Trouble/That's How We Do It In L.A. (p/s)	5
82	Mercury MER 96	The Visitor (Bwana)/A Satisfied Mind (p/s)	6
82	Mercury MER 102	Mary Lee Jones/September Song (p/s)	6
83	Mercury MER 150	Holiday Road/Mary Lee Jones (p/s)	8
84	Mercury MER 168	Go Insane/Play In The Rain (p/s)	5
84	Mercury MER 176	Slow Dancing/D.W. Suite (p/s)	8
92	Mercury MER 371	Countdown/This Nearly Was Mine (p/s)	5
92	Mercury MER 380	Soul Drifter/Say You'll Meet Again (p/s)	5

BUCKINGHAM-NICKS

(see also Lindsay Buckingham, Stevie Nicks, Fleetwood Mac)

74	Polydor 2066 398	Don't Let Me Down Again/Races Are Run	15
76	Polydor 2066 700	Don't Let Me Down Again/Crystal	10
73	Polydor 2391 013	BUCKINGHAM-NICKS (LP, with insert, with stickered sleeve)	30
73	Polydor 2391 093	BUCKINGHAM-NICKS (LP, with insert, without stickered sleeve)	35
81	Polydor 2482 378	BUCKINGHAM-NICKS (LP, reissue with insert)	22

BUCKINGHAMS (U.K.)

65	Pye 7N 15848	I'll Never Hurt You No More/She Lied	5
65	Pye 7N 15921	To Be Or Not To Be/I Was Your First Guy	6

BUCKINGHAMS (U.S.)

67	Stateside SS 588	Kind Of A Drag/You Make Me Feel So Good	15
67	CBS 2859	Mercy Mercy Mercy/You Are Gone	12
67	CBS 2995	Hey Baby/And Our Love	15
68	CBS 2640	Don't You Care/Why Don't You Love Me	25
68	CBS 3559	Back In Love Again/You Misunderstand Me	6
69	CBS 3195	Susan/Foreign Policy	12

BOB BUCKLE

70s	Ash ALP 107 S	COME LISTEN TO (LP)	50

JEFF BUCKLEY

95	Columbia 662042 1	Last Goodbye (Edit)/Lover, You Should've Come Over (Live And Acoustic In Japan)/Tongue (Live) (10", p/s, 5000 only)	25
93	Big Cat ABB 61XCD	LIVE AT SIN-E EP (Mojo Pin/Eternal Life/ Je N'en Connais Pas La Fin/The Way Young Lovers Do (CD)	20
95	Columbia 88697098847	Hallelujah/I Know It's Over (Live 1995) (p/s, numbered sleeve, 2,700 only, blue/black vinyl)	25
95	Columbia 661107 2	THE GRACE EP (Grace (Edit)/Tongue/Kanga-Roo/Grace) (CD)	8
94	Columbia 475928	GRACE (LP)	40
98	Columbia 3C 67228	SKETCHES (FOR MY SWEETHEART, THE DRUNK) (3-LP, gatefold sleeve)	40
02	Columbia 4979721	MYSTERY WHITE BOY LIVE 95-96 (LP)	12

SEAN BUCKLEY & BREADCRUMBS

65	Stateside SS 421	It Hurts Me When I Cry/Everybody Knows	70

TIM BUCKLEY

67	Elektra EKSN 45008	Aren't You The Girl/Strange Street Affair Under Blue	12
67	Elektra EKSN 45018	Morning Glory/Knight-Errant	10
68	Elektra EKSN 45023	Once I Was/Phantasmagoria In Two	7
68	Elektra EKSN 45031	Wings/I Can't See You	7
68	Elektra EKSN 45041	Pleasant Street/Carnival Song	10
70	Straight S 4799	Happy Time/So Lonely	20
91	Strange Fruit SFPS082	THE PEEL SESSIONS: Morning Glory/Coming Home To You/ Sing A Song For You/Hallucinations/Troubadour/Once I Was (12", p/s)	10
66	Elektra EKL/EKS 4004	TIM BUCKLEY (LP, orange label)	60
67	Elektra EKL/EKS 318	GOODBYE AND HELLO (LP, orange label, gatefold sleeve)	45
68	Elektra EKS 74045	HAPPY SAD (LP, orange label)	30
69	Straight STS 1060	BLUE AFTERNOON (LP)	60
70	Elektra 2410 005	LORCA (LP)	40
71	Straight STS 1064	STARSAILOR (LP)	60
72	Warner Bros K 46176	GREETINGS FROM L.A. (LP, gatefold sleeve)	18
74	Discreet K 49201	SEFRONIA (LP)	20
74	Discreet K 59204	LOOK AT THE FOOL (LP)	18

VERNON BUCKLEY

73	Grape GR 3057	Mr Softhand/G.G. ALLSTARS: Dub	6
73	Grape GR 3058	Ital Queen/G.G. ALLSTARS: Dub	6

MILT BUCKNER & HIS MUSIC

56	Capitol CL 14662	Night Mist/Good Time Express	6

MINT VALUE £

SID BUCKNER PRODUCTIONS

76	Lyntone/Tropical Sounds DSR SB1008/1009	DUB SENSATION (LP, 50 copies, promo only in stamped white card sleeve)	100

TEDDY BUCKNER & HIS BAND

56	Vogue V 2369	Oh, Didn't He Ramble/Battle Hymn Of The Republic	5
56	Vogue V 2375	When The Saints Go Marching In/West End Blues	5
57	Vogue V 2414	Sweet Georgia Brown/That's My Home	5

BUCKY & STRINGS

62	Salvo SLO 1807	Lolita's On The Loose/Lonely Island (99 copies only)	30

BUD & HIS BUDDIES

58	Starlite ST45 006	June, July And August/Sing A Little Sweeter	5

BUD & TRAVIS

59	London HLU 8965	Bonsoir Dame/Truly Do	10
59	London HLU 8965	Bonsoir Dame/Truly Do (78)	10
60	London HLG 9211	The Ballad Of The Alamo/The Green Leaves Of Summer	10
61	London HA-G 2328	BUD AND TRAVIS IN CONCERT (LP, also stereo SAH-G 6128)	15
61	London HA-G 2328	BUD AND TRAVIS IN CONCERT (LP, also stereo SAH-G 6128)	20

ROY BUDD

65	Pye 7N 15807	Birth Of The Budd/M'Ghee M'Ghee	6
66	Parlophone R 5514	Summer Samba/Bahama Sound	5
67	Pye 7N 17279	Mr Rose/Summer Rain	8
68	Pye 7N 17652	Pavanne/Whizz Ball	5
69	Pye 7N 17773	Tijuana Piano/Lead On	5
70	Pye 7N 17987	Borsalino (Theme)/It Only Goes To Show	5
70	Pye 7N 45051	Carter (Theme)/Plaything (in p/s)	60
70	Pye 7N 45051	Carter (Theme)/Plaything	50
67	Pye N(S)PL 18177	PICK YOURSELF UP - THIS IS ROY BUDD (LP)	15
68	Pye NPL 18212	AT NEWPORT (LP)	15
71	Pye NSPL 18348	PLAYS SOLDIER BLUE AND OTHER THEMES (LP)	20
72	Polydor 2383 102	KIDNAPPED (Roy Budd/Mary Hopkin)	25
72	Pye NSPL 18389	CONCERTO FOR HARRY - SOMETHING TO HIDE (Roy Budd)	35
73	Pye NSPL 18398	FEAR IS THE KEY (LP, soundtrack)	50
76	Bradley's BRADS 8002	DIAMONDS (LP, soundtrack)	50
70s	Pye NSPL 19494	EVERYTHING'S COMING UP (LP)	15

BUDDY & JUNIORS

(see under Buddy Guy)

BUDDY & SKETTO

(see also Father Sketto, Ruddy & Sketto, Sketto Rich)

62	Dice 45/CC 7	Little Schoolgirl/Hush Baby	12

BUDGIE

(see also Tredegar, Phenomena, George Hatcher Band)

71	MCA MK 5072	Crash Course In Brain Surgery/Nude Disintegrating Parachutist Woman	12
72	MCA MK 5085	Whisky River/Guts	8
74	MCA MCA 133	Zoom Club (Edited Version)/Wondering What Everyone Knows	6
75	MCA MCA 175	I Ain't No Mountain/Honey	6
78	A&M AMS 7342	Smile Boy Smile/All At Sea	6
80	Active BUDGE	Wildfire/Wildfire (promo only)	10
80	Active BUDGE 1	IF SWALLOWED DO NOT INDUCE VOMITING (12" EP)	10
80	Active BUDGE 2	Crime Against The World/Hellbender (p/s)	8
81	RCA BUDGE 3	Keeping A Rendezvous/Apparatus (p/s)	5
81	RCA BUDGE 3	Keeping A Rendezvous/Apparatus (picture disc)	5
81	RCA BUDGE 4	I Turned To Stone (Part 1)/I Turned To Stone (Part 2) (orange vinyl)	5
82	RCA RCA 271	Bored With Russia/Don't Cry (poster p/s)	5
82	RCA RCAP 271	Bored With Russia/Don't Cry (picture disc)	5
71	MCA MKPS 2018	BUDGIE (LP, pink/red label, initial pressing with laminated sleeve and poster)	120
71	MCA MKPS 2018	BUDGIE (LP, pink/red label, with no poster)	50
71	MCA MKPS 2018	BUDGIE (LP, later pressing with blue/black label)	15
72	MCA MKPS 2023	SQUAWK (LP, blue/black hexagon label)	30
73	MCA MDKS 8010	NEVER TURN YOUR BACK ON A FRIEND (LP, blue/black label, g/fold sleeve)	25
74	MCA MCF 2546	IN FOR THE KILL (LP, rainbow label)	15
75	MCA MCF 2723	BANDOLIER (LP)	12
75	MCA MCF 2766	THE BEST OF BUDGIE (LP)	12
76	A&M AMLH 68377	IF I WAS BRITANNIA I'D WAIVE THE RULES (LP, silver/green label)	15
78	A&M AMLH 64675	IMPECKABLE (LP)	12
80	Active ACTLP 1	POWER SUPPLY (LP, with insert)	12
81	RCA RCALP 3046	POWER SUPPLY (LP, reissue, with different back sleeve)	20
81	RCA RCALP 6003	NIGHT FLIGHT (LP)	12
82	RCA RCALP 6054	DELIVER US FROM EVIL (LP)	12

DENNIS BUDLIMAR

67	Fontana TL 5307	THE CREEPER (LP)	20

BUENA VISTAS

66	Stateside SS 525	Hot Shot/T.N.T.	25

BUFFALO

81	Heavy Metal HEAVY 3	Battle Torn Heroes/Women Of The Night (p/s)	30
82	Heavy Metal HEAVY 15	Mean Machine/The Rumour (p/s)	25

BUFFALO SPRINGFIELD

(see also Neil Young, Stephen Stills, Poco, Au-Go-Go Singers, Crosby Stills Nash & Young)

67	Atlantic 584 077	For What It's Worth (Stop Hey What's That Sound)/ Do I Have To Come Right Out And Say It	20
67	Atlantic 584 145	Rock'n'Roll Woman/A Child's Claim To Fame	12

			MINT VALUE £
68	Atlantic 584 165	Expecting To Fly/Everydays	15
68	Atlantic 584 189	Uno-Mundo/Merry-Go-Round	10
69	Atco 226 006	Pretty Girl Why/Questions	10
72	Atlantic K 10237	Bluebird/Mr Soul/Rock'n'Roll Woman/Expecting To Fly (p/s)	5
67	Atlantic 587 070	BUFFALO SPRINGFIELD (LP, plum label, mispressing, lists "For What It's Worth" but plays "Baby Don't Scold Me"; matrix no. ends '1' mono)	60
67	Atlantic 588 070	BUFFALO SPRINGFIELD ((LP, plum label, mispressing, lists "For What It's Worth" but plays "Baby Don't Scold Me"; matrix no. ends '1' stereo)	40
67	Atlantic 587 070	BUFFALO SPRINGFIELD (LP, plum label, plays "For What It's Worth", mono)	40
67	Atlantic 588 070	BUFFALO SPRINGFIELD (LP, plum label, plays "For What It's Worth", stereo)	30
68	Atlantic 587 091	BUFFALO SPRINGFIELD AGAIN (LP, plum label, mono)	50
68	Atlantic 588 091	BUFFALO SPRINGFIELD AGAIN (LP, plum label, stereo)	40
69	Atco 228 024	LAST TIME AROUND (LP, plum label, gatefold sleeve)	25
69	Atco 228 012	RETROSPECTIVE (LP, plum label)	15
70	Atlantic 2464 012	EXPECTING TO FLY (LP, plum label)	20
72	Atlantic K 40014	BUFFALO SPRINGFIELD AGAIN (LP, reissue, green & orange label)	15
72	Atlantic K 40077	LAST TIME AROUND (LP, reissue, green & orange label, gatefold sleeve)	12

BUFFALO TOM

89	Caff CAFF 6	Enemy/Deep In The Ground (p/s)	25

BUFF MEDWAYS

00s	Transcopic TRAN 012	A Strange Kind Of Happyness/BILLY CHILDISH: Hound Dog (p/s, 500 only)	8
00s	Transcopic TRAN 015	Troubled Mind/BILLY CHILDISH: Leave My Kitten Alone (p/s, 500 only)	15
01	Gibbet 004	Sally Sensation/Dawn Said What Have I Done	12

BUFFOONS

67	Columbia DB 8317	My World Fell Down/Tomorrow Is Another Day	18

BUG CENTRAL

00	BBP/Yellow Fever BBPV 5	MONEY & RIOTS EP (with inserts)	8
99	Dole Office/DHSS 1	Gotta Get A Real Job/No Free Records (Unreleased, white label test pressings only)	35
99	Helen Of Oi HOO 48	THE MEEK WILL INHERIT NOTHING (LP, with inserts)	15

THE BUGGER ALL STARS

81	Bead Records BEAD 19	THE BUGGER ALL STARS (LP)	20
83	Bead Records BEAD 21	BONZO BITES BACK (LP)	20

BUGGLES

99	Island 562 465-2	Video Killed The Radio Star/Kid Dynamite (CD single)	8

BUGGY

70	Parlophone R5832	The Rolly Pole Coaster/Harry The Keeper	15

SANDY BULL

69	Vanguard 19040	E PLURIBUS UNUM (LP)	25

BULLAMAKANKA

83	BBC REL 454	Dr Who Is Gonna Fix It/Harlequin	8

BULLDOG

72	MCA MU1166	No/Good Times Are Comin'	5

BULLDOG BREED

(see also Flies)

69	Deram DM 270	Portcullis Gate/Halo In My Hair	90
70	Deram Nova DN 5	MADE IN ENGLAND (LP, mono)	200
70	Deram Nova SDN 5	MADE IN ENGLAND (LP, stereo)	150

BULLDOGS

64	Mercury MF 808	John, Paul, George And Ringo/What Do I See	20

BULLET

(see also Hard Stuff, Quatermass, Atomic Rooster)

71	Purple PUR 101	Hobo/Sinister Minister	20

BULLET

(see also Alan Tew)

75	Polydor 2058 548	Hanged Man/The Contract Man	20
75	Contour 2870 437	THE HANGED MAN (LP, TV soundtrack)	30

JOHN BULL BREED

66	Polydor BM 56065	Can't Chance A Breakup/I'm A Man	350

BULLSEYE

80	Kennet K1	No. 10,553/Why Don't You Let Me Know	8

BULLY BOYS BAND

70	Stateside SSL 5032	MOVIE SCENE - HEAVY SOUNDS FROM TODAY'S FILMS (LP)	15

BULLY WEE (BAND)

75	Folksound	BULLYWEE (LP)	20
76	Red Rag RRR 007	THE ENCHANTED LADY (LP)	15
70s	Red Rag RRR 017	SILVERMINES (LP, as Bullywee Band, with insert)	12
81	Jigsaw SAW 1	THE MADMAN OF GOTHAM (LP)	20

B. BUMBLE & STINGERS

(see also Kim Fowley)

61	Top Rank JAR 561	Bumble Boogie/School Day Blues	15
62	Top Rank JAR 611	Nut Rocker/Nautilus	7
62	Stateside SS 113	Apple Knocker/The Moon And The Sea	10
62	Stateside SS 131	Dawn Cracker/Scales	10
63	Stateside SS 192	Baby Mash/Night Time Madness	10

MINT VALUE £

67	Mercury MF 977	Silent Movies/Twelfth Street Rag	10
72	Pye International 7N 25597	Down At Mother's Place/Manhattan Spiritual	10
62	Stateside SE 1001	THE PIANO STYLINGS OF B. BUMBLE (EP)	35

BUMBLE BEE SLIM

s	Fontana 688 138ZL	BEE'S BACK IN TOWN (LP)	35

BUMBLES

72	Purple PUR 107	Beep Beep/Buzz Off (promo only p/s)	25
72	Purple PUR 107	Beep Beep/Buzz Off	8

BUNCH

(see also Peter & The Wolves, Sounds Around, John Pantry)

67	CBS 202506	We're Not What We Appear To Be/You Never Came Home	70
67	CBS 2740	Don't Come Back To Me/You Can't Do This	25
67	CBS 3060	Looking Glass Alice/Spare A Shilling	200
68	CBS 3692	Birthday/Still	30
68	CBS 3709	Birthday/Still (reissue)	15
72	Island ILPS 9189	ROCK ON (LP, with 1-sided flexi attached to die-cut sleeve: "Let There Be Drums" [WI 4002])	70
72	Island ILPS 9189	ROCK ON (LP, without 1-sided flexi: "Let There Be Drums" [WI 4002])	20

BUNCH

69	Beacon BEA 128	Red Rover, Red Rover/Happy Like This	6

BUNCH

(see also Fairport Convention, Sandy Denny, Richard & Linda Thompson, Ashley Hutchings, Trevor Lucas)

72	Island WIP 6130	When Will I Be Loved/Willie And The Hand Jive	8

BUNCH OF FIVES

(see also Viv Prince, Egg, Hullaballoos, Junior's Eyes, Outsiders [U.K.])

66	Parlophone R 5494	Go Home Baby/At The Station	70

BUNDLE

70	Polydor 2058 029	Dirty La Rue/Progressive Underground	15

DAVE BUNDY

72	UK UK 10	Inside A Hole/Nicer Out	8

ROGER BUNN

(see also Pete Browns Pitlokto, Roxy Music)

70	Major Minor SMLP 70	PIECE OF MIND (LP, red/white/black label)	130

BUNNIES

66	Decca F 12350	Thumper/Ja Da	5

BUNNIES (OF LONDON)

68	Decca LK4951	CAUGHT LIVE AT THE PLAYBOY CLUB (LP)	18
69	Decca SKL5026	THE BUNNIES AGAIN SINGIN' AND SWINGIN' AT THE LONDON PLAYBOY CLUB (LP)	18

BUNNY & RICKY

75	Attack ATT 8107	Too Bad Bull (as Bunnie And Rickey)/UPSETTERS: Bad Cow	15
75	Attack ATT 8109	Bushwood Contrash/UPSETTERS: Callying Butt	15

BUNNY & RUDDY

68	Nu Beet NB 007	Rhythm & Soul/MONTY MORRIS: True Romance	25
68	Nu Beat NB 011	On The Town/MONTY MORRIS: Simple Simon	18

BINGY BUNNY

82	Cha Cha CHAD 46	Keep It In The Family (with MORWELLS)/SCIENTIST : Extended Dub/ Me & Jane (with MORWELLS)/SCIENTIST : Extended Dub (12")	40
82	Cha Cha CHAD 48	Street Lover (with MORWELLS)/NICODEMUS : How You Look Girl 'Pon The Street (12")	20
82	Cha Cha CHALP 015	ME & JANE (LP)	20

BINGY BUNNY & BONGO LES

(see also Bongo Les, Mediators)

73	Ackee ACK 506	International Scout/International Scout Version	12

BUNNY BROWN

(see also Noel Brown, Winston Scotland)

72	Songbird SB 1073	Fat Boy/Fat Boy - Version	12

BUNNY LION

79	Starlight SLP 900	RED (LP)	25

BUNNY WAILER

76	Island BUINNY 1	Blackheart Man/Amagideon (12")	20
77	Island IPR 2003	Get up stand up/This train (12")	20
78	Island IPR 2015	Love Fire/Love's Version (12")	15
78	Island IPR 2025	Roots, Radics, Rockers and Reggae/Fig Tree/Armagideon (12")	25
79	Solomonic SM 001	Riding/Version (12")	30
81	Solomonic SM 01	Rise & Shine/Riding	30
81	Solomonic SM07	Rise & Shine/Solomonic Dub (12")	30
83	Solomonic SM 018	Boderation/THE SOLOMONIC PLAYERS - Badder ridim (12")	25

BOB BUNTING

68	Transatlantic TRA 166	YOU'VE GOT TO GO DOWN THIS WAY (LP)	45

VASHTI BUNYAN

(see also Vashti, Fairport Convention, Dave Swarbrick, Robin Williamson)

70	Philips 6308 019	JUST ANOTHER DIAMOND DAY (LP)	900

BUOYS

70	Wand WN7	Timothy/It Feels Good	20
71	Wand MSW 8296	Give Up Your Guns/The Prince Of Thieves	15

MINT VALUE £

VERNON BURCH

79 Casablanca CCSL 3202 Get Up/I Just Want To Be/Sparkle (12", with Cameo) . . . 15

ERIC BURDON (BAND)

75 Capitol E-ST 11359 SUN SECRETS (LP, as Eric Burdon Band) . . . 12
75 Capitol E-ST 11426 STOP (LP, as Eric Burdon Band) . . . 15
78 Polydor 2302 078 SURVIVOR (LP, with 5 inserts with lyrics and drawings) . . . 25
80 Polydor 2344 147 DARKNESS - DARKNESS (LP) . . . 12

ERIC BURDON & THE ANIMALS

(see also Animals, Stud, Zoot Money's Big Roll Band, Family)
66 Decca F 12502 Mama Told Me Not To Come/See See Rider (unreleased) . . . 0
66 Decca F 12502 Help Me Girl/See See Rider (amended issue with new A-side) . . . 8
67 MGM MGM 1340 When I Was Young/A Girl Named Sandoz . . . 8
67 MGM MGM 1344 Good Times/Ain't That So . . . 8
67 MGM MGM 1359 San Franciscan Nights/Gratefully Dead . . . 15
68 MGM MGM 1373 Sky Pilot (Parts 1 & 2) . . . 10
68 MGM MGM 1412 Monterey/Anything . . . 8
69 MGM MGM 1461 Ring Of Fire/I'm An Animal . . . 10
69 MGM MGM 1481 River Deep Mountain High/Help Me Girl . . . 12
67 MGM C(S) 8052 WINDS OF CHANGE (LP, yellow/black label with "Sold in the U.K." label text) . . 70
68 MGM C(S) 8074 THE TWAIN SHALL MEET (LP, yellow black labels with "Sold in the U.K." text) . 70
68 MGM C(S) 8105 LOVE IS (LP, blue/gold labels with "Sold in the U.K." text) . . . 80
71 MGM 2619 002 LOVE IS (2-LP; individual LP nos.: 2354 006/7) . . . 50

ERIC BURDON & WAR

(see also War)
70 Polydor 2001 072 Spill The Wine/Magic Mountain . . . 7
71 Liberty LBF 15434 They Can't Take Away Our Music/Home Cookin' . . . 5
71 United Artists UP 35217 Paint It Black/Spirit . . . 5
70 Polydor 2310 041 ERIC BURDON DECLARES WAR (LP) . . . 35
70 Liberty LDS 8400 BLACKMAN'S BURDON (2-LP, gatefold, with banned track "P.C. 3") . . . 40
70 Liberty LDS 8400 BLACKMAN'S BURDON (2-LP, gatefold, without banned track "P.C. 3") . . . 20
76 ABC ABCL 5207 LOVE IS ALL AROUND (LP) . . . 12

ERIC BURDON & JIMMY WITHERSPOON

(see also Jimmy Witherspoon)
71 United Artists UP 35287 Soledad/Headin' For Home . . . 6
71 United Artists UAG 29251 GUILTY! (LP, gatefold sleeve) . . . 18

DAVE BURGESS (TRIO)

55 London HLB 8175 I Love Paris/Five Foot Two, Eyes Of Blue (Has Anybody Seen My Girl) . . . 25
58 Oriole CB 1413 I'm Available/Who's Gonna Cry? . . . 100
58 Oriole CB 1413 I'm Available/Who's Gonna Cry? (78) . . . 20

SONNY BURGESS

60 London HLS 9064 Sadie's Back In Town/A Kiss Goodnight . . . 250

JIM BURGETT

61 Philips PB 1133 Let's Investigate/The Living Dead . . . 40

ELPEDO BURKE

75 Black Wax WAX 3 Madgie/MIGHTY CLOUD: Madgie Dub . . . 6

KEVIN BURKE

78 Rockburgh ROC 105 IF THE CAP FITS (LP) . . . 15

SOLOMON BURKE

(see also Soul Clan)
61 London HLK 9454 Just Out Of Reach/Be Bop Grandma . . . 45
62 London HLK 9512 Cry To Me/I Almost Lost My Mind . . . 80
62 London HLK 9560 Down In The Valley/I'm Hanging Up My Heart For You . . . 20
63 London HLK 9715 If You Need Me/You Can Make It If You Try . . . 20
63 London HLK 9763 Can't Nobody Love You/Stupidity . . . 35
64 London HLK 9849 He'll Have To Go/Rockin' Soul . . . 20
64 London HLK 9887 Goodbye Baby (Baby Goodbye)/Someone To Love Me . . . 20
64 Atlantic AT 4004 Everybody Needs Somebody To Love/Looking For My Baby . . . 20
64 Atlantic AT 4014 The Price/More Rockin' Soul . . . 15
65 Atlantic AT 4022 Got To Get You Off My Mind/Peepin' . . . 20
65 Atlantic AT 4030 Maggie's Farm/Tonight's The Night . . . 25
65 Atlantic AT 4044 Someone Is Watching/Dance, Dance, Dance . . . 15
65 Atlantic AT 4061 Only Love (Can Save Me Now)/Little Girl That Loves Me . . . 25
66 Atlantic AT 4073 Baby Come On Home/No, No, No, I Can't Stop Lovin' You Now . . . 15
66 Atlantic 584 005 I Feel A Sin Comin' On/Mountain Of Pride . . . 8
66 Atlantic 584 026 Keep Lookin'/Suddenly . . . 10
67 Atlantic 584 100 Keep A Light In The Window Till I Come Home/Time Is A Thief . . . 8
67 Atlantic 584 122 Take Me (Just As I Am)/I Stayed Away Too Long . . . 8
68 Atlantic 584 191 I Wish I Knew (How It Would Feel To Be Free)/It's Just A Matter Of Time . . . 8
68 Atlantic 584 204 Save It/Meet Me In Church . . . 10
68 Bell BLL 1047 Uptight Good Woman/I Can't Stop (No No No) . . . 8
69 Bell BLL 1062 Proud Mary/What Am I Living For . . . 10
74 Anchor ABC 4002 Midnight And You/I Have A Dream . . . 5
63 London REK 1379 TONIGHT MY HEART SHE IS CRYING (EP) . . . 80
65 Atlantic AET 6008 ROCK'N'SOUL (EP) . . . 65
63 London HA-K 8018 SOLOMON BURKE'S GREATEST (LP) . . . 80
64 Atlantic ATL 5009 ROCK'N'SOUL (LP) . . . 55
66 Atlantic 587/588 016 THE BEST OF SOLOMON BURKE (LP) . . . 55
66 Atlantic 590 004 KING OF ROCK'N'SOUL (LP, reissue) . . . 20
68 Atlantic 587 105 KING SOLOMON (LP) . . . 40
68 Atlantic 587/588 117 I WISH I KNEW (LP) . . . 30
69 Bell MBLL/SBLL 118 PROUD MARY (LP) . . . 20
72 MGM 2315 048 THE ELECTRONIC MAGNETISM (LP) . . . 15

MINT VALUE £

SONNY BURKE (U.K.)
(see also Bob Andy, Gaylads, Ken Parker, Eddie Thornton Outfit, Glen Adams, Stranger Cole, Gaylads, Sonny & Yvonne)

62	Island WI 155	Let And Let Live/Our Love Is True	20
64	Black Swan WI 457	I Love You Still/It's Always A Pleasure	15
64	Black Swan WI 458	City In The Sky/Everyday I Love You More	15
65	Black Swan WI 469	Glad/Jeanie	15
65	Black Swan WI 470	Dance With Me/My Girl Can't Cook	15
65	Black Swan WI 471	Wicked People/Good Heaven Knows	15
66	Blue Beat BB 363	Blue Island/You Came And Left	12
67	Blue Beat BB 371	Look In Her Eyes/LLOYD CLARKE: Love Is Strange	12
67	Ska Beat JB272	Have Faith/Guinea Pig	18
68	Island ILP 972	THE SOUNDS OF SONNY BURKE (LP, mono only)	125

SONNY BURKE OUTFIT
(see also Sonny Burke)

68	Instant IN 003	Baby Be My Girl/All You	30

DAVE BURLAND

71	Trailer LER 2029	A DALESMAN'S LITANY (LP, red label)	25
72	Trailer LER 2082	DAVE BURLAND (LP)	20
75	Rubber RUB 012	SONGS AND BUTTERED HAYCOCKS (LP)	18
79	Rubber RUB 036	YOU CAN'T FOOL THE FAT MAN (LP)	15
80	Rubber RUB 012/036	DOUBLE TAKE (2-LP, reissue)	18

SASCHA BURLAND

61	Philips PB 1152	Gorilla Walk/Hole In My Soul	5

BURMOE BROTHERS
(see also Marc Almond, Nick Cave)

85	Wild Blue Yonder WBY 121	Skin/Leber Oder Lippenstift/Under The Blanket Of Love (12", p/s)	15

BURN

00s	Virgin HUTCDP 146	Facing The Music (1-sided, numbered gold-embossed p/s, 1000 only)	20

CHRIS BURN & JOHN BUTCHER

85	Bead Records BEAD 24	FONETIKS (LP)	20

JEAN-JACQUES BURNEL

79	United Artists UP 36500	Freddie Laker (Concorde And Eurobus)/Ozymandias (p/s)	5
80	United Artists BP 361	Girl From The Snow Country/Ode To Joy (live)/ Do The European (live) (p/s, unissued)	350
88	Stranglers Information Service S.I.S. 003	Goebbels, Mosley, God And Ingrams (fan club flexidisc, with issue 27 of Strangled fanzine)	8
88	Stranglers Information Service S.I.S. 003	Goebbels, Mosley, God And Ingrams 5 (fan club flexidisc, without issue 27 of Strangled fanzine)	5

JEAN-JACQUES BURNEL & DAVE GREENFIELD
(see also, Blue Maxi, Stranglers)

84	Epic EPCA 4076	Rain And Dole And Tea/Consequences (p/s)	5

BURNER

84	High Roller 7HRR0132007	Hammer Of The Gods/Time Is On My Side/Old Enough To Know Better (EP, p/s)	10

JOHN BURNESS

69	Columbia DB8536	Theresa/I Don't Want You Anymore	12

FRANCES BURNETT

59	Coral Q 72374	Please Remember Me/How I Miss You So (triangular centre)	70
59	Coral Q 72374	Please Remember Me/How I Miss You So (round centre)	45
59	Coral Q 72374	Please Remember Me/How I Miss You So (78)	15

KING BURNETT

75	Dip DL 5056	I Man Free/UPSETTERS: Version	15
75	Dip DL 5073	Key Card/UPSETTERS: Domino Game	15

REV. J.C. BURNETT/REV. GATES/REV. MOSELEY

60	Fontana TFE 17265	TREASURES OF NORTH AMERICAN NEGRO MUSIC VOLUME 6: PREACHERS AND CONGREGATIONS (EP)	15

DORSEY BURNETTE
(see also Johnny & Dorsey Burnette)

60	London HLN 9047	Juarez Town/(There Was A) Tall Oak Tree	20
60	London HLN 9160	Hey Little One/Big Rock Candy Mountain	30
61	London HLN 9365	(It's No) Sin/Hard Rock Mine	20
65	Tamla Motown TMG 534	Jimmy Brown/Everybody's Angel	200
65	Tamla Motown TMG 534	Jimmy Brown/Everybody's Angel (DJ copy)	250
69	Liberty LBF 15190	The Greatest Love/Thin Little, Simple Little, Plain Little Girl	8
63	London RE-D 1402	DORSEY BURNETTE SINGS (EP)	90
63	London HA-D 8050	DORSEY BURNETTE (LP)	100

JOHNNY BURNETTE (TRIO)
(see also Johnny & Dorsey Burnette)

SINGLES

56	Vogue Coral Q 72177	Tear It Up/You're Undecided (as Johnny Burnette & Rock'N'Roll Trio)	500
56	Vogue Coral Q 72177	Tear It Up/You're Undecided (as Johnny Burnette & Rock'N'Roll Trio) (78)	150
57	Vogue Coral Q 72227	Honey Hush/Lonesome Train (as Johnny Burnette Trio)	500
57	Vogue Coral Q 72227	Honey Hush/Lonesome Train (as Johnny Burnette Trio) (78)	150
57	Vogue Coral Q 72283	Touch Me/Eager Beaver Baby (as Johnny Burnette Trio)	200
57	Vogue Coral Q 72283	Touch Me/Eager Beaver Baby (as Johnny Burnette Trio) (78)	150
60	London HLG 9172	Dreamin'/Cincinnati Fireball	7
60	London HLG 9172	Dreamin'/Cincinnati Fireball (78)	400
60	London HLG 9254	You're Sixteen/I Beg Your Pardon	7
61	London HLG 9315	Little Boy Sad/Pledge Of Love	7
61	London HLG 9388	Girls/I've Got A Lot Of Things To Do	10

			MINT VALUE £
61	London HLG 9453	God Country And My Baby/Honestly I Do (withdrawn)	10
61	London HLG 9458	Settin' The Woods On Fire/I'm Still Dreaming	15
61	London HLG 9473	Big Big World/The Fool	10
62	Liberty LIB 55416	Clown Shoes/The Way I Am	10
62	Liberty LIB 55489	Damn The Defiant/Lonesome Waters	10
66	Liberty LIB 10235	Dreamin'/Little Boy Sad	6
62	Pye International 7N 25158	I Wanna Thank Your Folks/The Giant	10
63	Pye International 7N 25187	Remember Me/Time Is Not Enough	10
63	Capitol CL 15322	All Week Long/It Isn't There	25
64	Capitol CL 15347	Sweet Suzie/Walking Talking Doll	30
96	Cruisin' The 50s CASB 003	The Train Kept A Rollin'/Sweet Love On My Mind (300 copies only) (78)	30

EXPORT SINGLES

60	London HLG 7104	You're Sixteen/Settin' The Woods On Fire	10
61	London HL 7109	Little Boy Sad/I Go Down To The River	10

EPs

60	London RE-G 1263	DREAMING	40
61	London RE-G 1291	LITTLE BOY SAD	50
61	London RE-G 1309	BIG BIG WORLD	40
61	London RE-G 1327	GIRLS	50
63	Liberty LEP 2091	HIT AFTER HIT	40
64	Capitol EAP 20645	FOUR BY BURNETTE	150

LPs

56	Coral LVC 10041	ROCK AND ROLL TRIO (10", as Johnny Burnette Trio)	800
61	London HA-G 2306	DREAMIN'	60
61	London HA-G 2349	YOU'RE SIXTEEN	60
61	London HA-G 2375	JOHNNY BURNETTE SINGS (mono)	100
61	London SAH-G 6175	JOHNNY BURNETTE SINGS (stereo)	120
62	Liberty LBY 1006	BURNETTE'S HITS AND OTHER FAVOURITES	40
64	Liberty LBY 1231	THE JOHNNY BURNETTE STORY	50
66	Ace Of Hearts AH 120	ROCK AND ROLL TRIO (reissue, as Johnny Burnette Trio)	30
68	Coral CP 10	TEAR IT UP (as Johnny Burnette Trio)	30

JOHNNY & DORSEY BURNETTE

(see also Johnny Burnette, Dorsey Burnette)

63	Reprise R 20153	Hey Sue/It Don't Matter Much	60

SMILEY BURNETTE

54	London HL 8071	Lazy Locomotive/That Long White Line	50
54	London HL 8071	Lazy Locomotive/That Long White Line (78)	12
54	London HL 8085	Chuggin' On Down "66"/Mucho Gusto	50
54	London HL 8085	Chuggin' On Down "66"/Mucho Gusto (78)	12

BURNIN' RED IVANHOE

70	Warner Bros WS 3013	BURNIN' RED IVANHOE (LP, green label)	50
72	Dandelion 2310 145	W.W.W. (LP, gatefold sleeve)	60

BURNING SPEAR

(see also Irving Brown, King Cry Cry)

70	Bamboo 50	SOUND DIMENTION : Soul Food/BURNING SPEAR : Door Peeper	50
75	Fab FAB 240	Foggy Road/Version	20
78	Island Pre IPR 2027	Civilised Reggae/Social Living (12")	15
79	Tribesman TM 20	Free The Whole Wide World/Jah Jah No Dead (12")	40
82	Radic 12RIC114	Jah Is My Driver/Driver Dub/Distance/Forever	15
75	Island ILPS 9377	MARCUS GARVEY (LP)	20
76	Island ILPS 9377	GARVEY'S GHOST (LP)	25
76	Island ILPS 9412	MAN IN THE HILLS (LP, gatefold)	15
77	Island MPLS 9431	DRY AND HEAVY (LP)	18

BURNING WITCH

98	Trip 005	CRIPPLED LUCIFER (CD, digipack)	20

JAN BURNNETTE

62	Oriole CB 1716	I Could Have Loved You So Well/The Miracle Of Life	15
62	Oriole CB 1742	All At Once/Does My Heartache Show?	8
62	Oriole CB 1761	Teddy/Trust In Me	15
63	Oriole CB 1807	The Boy I Used To Know/Unimportant Things	15
63	Oriole CB 1841	Till I Hear The Truth From You/Fall In Love	12
64	Oriole CB 1905	Let Me Make You Smile Again/No Regrets	15
64	Oriole CB 1920	Too Young/The Four Winds And The Seven Seas	15
64	Oriole CB 1949	Love, Let Me Not Hunger/The One I Love (Belongs To Somebody Else)	8

DENNIS BURNS

(see Mark Perry)

EDDIE 'GUITAR' BURNS

72	Action ACMP 100	BOTTLE UP AND GO (LP)	30
75	Big Bear BEAR 7	DETROIT BLACKBOTTOM (LP)	20

GEORGE BURNS

80	Mercury MER 6	I Wish I Was Eighteen Again/One Of The Mysteries Of Life	5

GILLIAN BURNS

69	Fontana TF 1044	Hop Skip And Jump/Merry Go Round	12

JACKIE BURNS & BELLES

63	MGM MGM 1226	He's My Guy/I Do The Best I Can	90

JIMMY BURNS

79	Grapevine GRP 118	I Really Love You/I Love You Girl	25
79	Grapevine GRP 118	I Really Love You/I Love You Girl (DJ Copy)	30

LISA BURNS

78	MCA MCF 2849	LISA BURNS (LP)	15

MINT VALUE £

RANDY BURNS
(see also Blue Cheer)

68	Fontana STL 5520	EVENING OF THE MAGICIAN (LP)	45

RAY BURNS
(see also Ruby Murray, Ronnie Harris, Diana Decker, Ray Martin)

53	Columbia SCM 5077	Rags To Riches/Begorrah	15
54	Columbia SCM 5153	I Can't Tell A Waltz From A Tango/Lonely Nightingale	10
56	Columbia DB 3811	Condemned For Life (With A Rock And Roll Wife)/The Mare Piccola	35
57	Columbia DB 3966	Wonderful! Wonderful!/Bernadine	10
58	Columbia DB 4107	Are You Sincere/The Best Dream Of All	10
55	Columbia SEG 7594	RAY BURNS (EP)	20

BURNT OFFERING

94	Misanthropy 001	HVIS LYSET TAR OST (LP)	12
94	Misanthropy 002	DET SOMEGAG VAR (LP)	12

HAROLD BURRAGE

65	Sue WI 353	I'll Take One/A Long Ways Together	50
68	President PT 130	You Made Me So Happy/Take Me Now	20

KENNY BURRELL
(see also Brother Jack McDuff, Jimmy Smith)

61	Esquire 32-140	ALL NIGHT LONG (LP, as Kenny Burrell All Stars)	25
64	Verve VLP 9058	BLUE BLASH (LP, with Jimmy Smith)	20
65	Verve VLP 9099	GUITAR FORMS (LP)	20
67	Transatlantic PR 7315	SOUL CALL (LP)	15
66	Stateside SL 10163	CRASH! (LP, with Brother Jack McDuff)	15
68	Verve (S)VLP 9217	BLUES, THE COMMON GROUND (LP)	20
69	Verve SVLP 9246	NIGHT SONG (LP)	15

WILLIAM S. BURROUGHS

80	Industrial IR 0016	NOTHING HERE NOW BUT THE RECORDINGS (LP)	50

TONY BURROWS

70	Bell BLL 1103	Melanie Makes Me Smile/I'll Get Along Somehow Girl	5
70	Bell BLL 1124	Every Little Move She Makes/I've Still Got My Heart, Joe	6

BUDDY BURTON
(see under Dixie Four)

CHINA BURTON

79	Logo GO(T) 354	You Don't Care (About Our Love) (Long Version)/(Short Version)/(Instrumental Version) (12")	80

GARY BURTON (QUARTET)
(see also Michael Gibbs)

68	RCA Victor SF 7923	LOFTY FAKE ANAGRAM (LP)	18
69	RCA Victor SF 8015	GENUINE TONGUE FUNERAL (LP)	18
71	Atlantic 2400 107	GOOD VIBES (LP)	18
72	Atlantic K 40305	ALONE AT LAST (LP)	12
72	Atlantic K 40378	PARIS ENCOUNTER (LP, with Stefan Grappelli)	12

HAL BURTON

58	Embassy WB 308	Move It/Susie Darling	8

JAMES BURTON
(see also Jim & Joe, Shindogs)

71	A&M AMLS 64293	THE GUITAR SOUNDS OF JAMES BURTON (LP)	50

TOMMY BURTON COMBO

64	Blue Beat BB 237	Lavender Blue/I'm Walking	20

TREVOR BURTON
(see also B,L&G; Uglys, Move, Balls, Denny Laine, Danny King's Mayfair Set, Magic Christians, Idle Race)

71	Wizard WIZ 103	Fight For My Country/Janie Slow Down	30

BURU

83	CSA CSALP 04	BURO (LP)	30

BURZUM

93	Misanthropy Amazon 001	HVIS LYSET TAR OSS (LP, marbled vinyl)	200
94	Misanthropy 001	HVIS LYSET TAR OSS (LP)	20
94	Misanthropy Amazon 002	DET SOM ENGANG VAR (LP, with stickered sleeve, inner sleeve and poster)	200
94	Misanthropy 002	DET SOM ENGANG VAR (LP)	20
95	Misanthropy Amazon 003	BURZUM/ASKE (2-LP, gatefold sleeve)	100
96	Misanthropy Amazon 009	FILOSOFEM (3 - sided etched LP, stickered gatefold sleeve)	100
97	Misanthropy Amazon 013	DAUOI BALDRS (LP, with postcards and booklet, 1,000 only)	25
99	Misanthorpy Amazon 021	HILSSKJALF (LP, booket and insert, 1,000 only)	50

LOU BUSCH & HIS ORCHESTRA
(see also Joe 'Fingers' Carr)

56	Capitol CL 14504	Zambesi/Rainbow's End	7

KATE BUSH
(see also Peter Gabriel & Kate Bush, Lesley Duncan)

78	EMI EMI 2719	Wuthering Heights/Kite (p/s)	30
78	EMI EMI 2806	The Man With The Child In His Eyes/Moving (p/s)	15
79	EMI MIEP 2991	KATE BUSH ON STAGE (EP, gatefold sleeve)	6
79	EMI PSR 442/3	KATE BUSH ON STAGE (EP, double pack, gatefold sleeve, promo only)	60
80	Sound For Industry SFI 562	Selected Highlights from "Never Forever" (flexidisc, black vinyl)	8
80	Sound For Industry SFI 562	Selected Highlights from "Never Forever" (square flexidisc, black vinyl)	8
81	EMI EMI 5201	Sat In Your Lap/Lord Of The Reedy River (p/s)	5
82	EMI EMI 5350	There Goes A Tenner/Ne T'Enfuis Pas (thick card, p/s)	5
84	EMI KBS 1	THE SINGLE FILE (13 x 7" box set with lyric booklet)	70

			MINT VALUE £
85	EMI KB 1	Running Up That Hill/Under The Ivy (gatefold p/s)	10
85	EMI 12 KB 2	Cloudbusting (Organon Mix)/Burning Bridges/My Lagan Love (12", p/s)	8
86	EMI KBP 4	The Big Sky (Single Mix)/Not This Time (picture disc)	8
89	EMI EMPD 119	This Woman's Work/Be Kind To My Mistakes (picture disc, with insert, PVC sl.)	5
90	EMI TRIB02	Rocket Man/Candle In The Wind (poster p/s)	8
93	EMI GIRL 1	Rubberband Girl (CD, 1-track "lyrical teaser", promo only)	15
93	EMI EM 280	Eat The Music/Big Stripey Lie (p/s, picture labels, release cancelled, 17 copies only)	1600
93	EMI 12EMPD 280	Eat The Music/Eat The Music (Madagascan Remix)/Big Stripey Lie (12", picture disc, unissued)	0
93	EMI CDEM 280	Eat The Music/(Madagascan Remix)/Big Stripey Lie (CD, unissued)	0
93	EMI MUSIC 1	Eat The Music (CD, 1-track promo for unissued single, no inlay, withdrawn)	150
93	EMI 12EMP 297	Moments Of Pleasure (Instrumental Version)/Home For Christmas (12" poster p/s)	8
93	EMI CDEMS297	Moments Of Pleasure/December Will Be Magic Again/Experiment IV (CD box set & 4 colour prints)	10
94	EMI EMPD 355	And So Is Love/Rubberband Girl (USA Mix) (picture disc, PVC sleeve, with 60" x 40" poster, unnumbered or 5,000 numbered)	10
94	EMI EMPD 355	And So Is Love/Rubberband Girl (USA Mix) (picture disc, PVC sleeve, with 60" x 40" poster, unnumbered or 5,000 numbered)	6
94	EMI CDEMS355	And So Is Love/Rubberband Girl (U.S. Mix)/Eat The Music (U.S. Mix) CD, with 3 bonus film prints)	8
05	EMI PROMO SAMPLER	KATE BUSH (CD in card sleeve, 9-track promotional back catalogue sampler Sent out prior to release of AERIAL album	20
05	EMI EM674	King Of The Mountain/Sexual Healing (picture disc)	5
78	EMI EMA 787	LIONHEART (LP, gatefold with gold embossed titles)	12
79	EMI EM CP 3223	THE KICK INSIDE (LP, picture disc, stickered sleeve)	50
79	EMI EM CP 3223	THE KICK INSIDE (LP, picture disc, stickered sleeve, second pressing with "manufactured in the U.K. by EMI Records Ltd" wording)	30
79	EMI EM CP 3223	THE KICK INSIDE (LP, picture disc, mispress with same picture both sides)	150
90	EMI KBBX 1	THIS WOMAN'S WORK (9-LP, box set)	120
90	EMI CKBBX 1	THIS WOMAN'S WORK (cassette, box set)	40
90	EMI CDKBBX 1	THIS WOMAN'S WORK (CD, box set)	80
93	EMI 1047	THE RED SHOES (LP)	40
93	EMI (No Cat. No)	THE RED SHOES (CD, video, slide transparency, fountain pen, parchment discography & red ribbon box set, promo)	200
93	EMI 343960-1	AERIAL (2 x LP, gatefold)	20

RAY BUSH & AVON CITIES' SKIFFLE

(see also Avon Cities Jazz Band)

56	Tempo A 146	Hey Hey Daddy Blues/Green Corn	25
56	Tempo A 146	Hey Hey Daddy Blues/Green Corn (78)	10
56	Tempo A 149	Fisherman's Blues/This Little Light Of Mine	25
56	Tempo A 149	Fisherman's Blues/This Little Light Of Mine (78)	10
57	Tempo A 156	How Long, How Long, Blues/Julian Johnson	25
57	Tempo A 156	How Long, How Long, Blues/Julian Johnson (78)	10
57	Tempo A 157	Lonesome Day Blues/I Don't Know	25
57	Tempo A 157	Lonesome Day Blues/I Don't Know (78)	10
57	Tempo EXA 40	RAY BUSH & AVON CITIES' SKIFFLE (EP)	30
57	Tempo EXA 50	RAY BUSH & AVON CITIES' SKIFFLE NO. 2 (EP)	30

BUSH BOYS

59	Capitol CL 15082	A Broken Vow/Never Before	10

BUSHKILLER

92	Danger 001	92 Salute/Bushkiller Draw (12")	25
94	Danger 002	TROUBLEMAKERS (EP)	45

BUSH TETRAS

81	Fetish FET 007	Things That Go Boom In The Night/Das Ah Riot (p/s)	6
82	Fetish FE 15	Can't Be Funky (unissued, stamped white label only, custom plain sleeve)	10
82	Fetish FET 16EP	RITUALS (12" EP)	15

BUSINESS

(see also UK)

81	Secret SHH 123	Harry May/National Insurance Blacklist (p/s)	12
82	Secret SHH 132	SMASH THE DISCOS EP: Day-O (The Banana Boat Song)/Disco Girls/ Smash The Disco (p/s)	10
83	Secret SHH 150	OUT OF BUSINESS (12" EP, unissued, white label promo, 10 copies only)	100
85	Wonderful World Of? 121	Get Out Of My House/All Out Tonight/Foreign Girl/Outlaw (12", p/s)	25
85	Diamond DIA 001	Drinking N Driving/H-Bomb (live) (p/s)	15
85	Diamond DIA 001T	Drinking N Driving/H-Bomb (live)/Hurry Up Harry/Drinking 'N' Driving (original version) (12", p/s)	25
80s	Link LINK 1201	DO A RUNNER (12" EP)	12
83	Secret SEC 11	SUBURBAN REBELS (LP)	20
83	Syndicate SYNLP 2	1980-81 OFFICIAL BOOTLEGS (LP)	15
84	Syndicate SYNLP 6	LOUD, PROUD 'N' PUNK, LIVE (LP)	15
85	Harry May SE 13	SATURDAY HEROES (LP)	20
86	Dojo DOJO LP 35	SINGALONGABUSINESS (LP)	15
80s	Wonderful World WOWDLP 4	OFFICIAL BUSINESS 1980-81 (LP)	20
80s	Link LP 115	SATURDAY'S HEROES (LP)	12
80s	Wonderful World WOWDLP 5	SUBURBAN REBELS/SMASH THE DISCOS - BACK TO BACK VOL 2. (2xLP)	25
88	Link LINK LP 035	WELCOME TO THE REAL WORLD (LP)	12
90	Link LRMO 1	IN AND OUT OF BUSINESS (LP, mail-order, 550 only)	20

BUSKERS

70	RCA 2023	If I Rules The World/Joey Friendship	5
73	Rubber RUB 007	LIFE OF A MAN (LP)	18
75	Hawk HALPX 142	THE BUSKERS (LP)	15

MINT VALUE £

GEORGE HENRY BUSSEY/JIM BUNKLEY
71 Revival RVS 1003 GEORGE HENRY BUSSEY/JIM BUNKLEY (LP) . . . 15

BUSTER
71 Columbia R5881 Pasedena/Priscilla . . . 10

BUSTER
73 Bradley BRAD 310 Motor Machine/Ring Around . . . 25
74 Bradleys BRAD 7401 Superstar/Rainbows & Colours . . . 15

BUSTER
77 RCA PL 25026 BUSTER (LP) . . . 15

BUSTERS
63 Stateside SS 231 Bust Out/Astronauts . . . 25

BUSTER('S) ALLSTARS
(see also Prince Buster, Teddy King, Little Darling, Khandars, Higgs & Wilson, Owen Gray, Charmers, Fitzroy D Long, Maytals, Derrick Morgan, Eric Morris, Personalities, Roy & Millie, Zoot Simms, Spanish Boys, Spanish Town Skabeats)
64 Blue Beat BB 244 Prince Royal/COSMO: One God . . . 50
64 Blue Beat BB 269 The Tickler/COSMO: Rice And Badge . . . 50
65 Blue Beat BB 294 Eye For Eye/South Virginia . . . 35
65 Blue Beat BB 322 Happy Independence 65/STRANGER COLE: When The Party Is Over . . . 25
65 Blue Beat BB 325 Congo Revolution/Little Darlin' - No One . . . 120
65 Blue Beat BB 333 When The Party Is Over/Matilda (with Stranger Cole) . . . 35
66 Blue Beat BB 342 Cincinnatti Kid/Sammy Dead . . . 60
67 Blue Beat BB 372 Sounds And Pressure/My Darling (both actually by Hopeton Lewis) . . . 45
67 Blue Beat BB 384 Take It Easy/Why Must I Cry (both actually by Hopeton Lewis) . . . 30
69 Fab FAB 101 Pum Pum A Go Kill You/Oh Lady Oh . . . 15
70 Fab FAB 124 The Rebel/The Preacher . . . 20

BUSTER'S GROUP
(see also Prince Buster, Rico, Owen Gray)
61 Starlite ST45 052 Buster's Shack/ERIC MORRIS: Search The World . . . 40
65 Blue Beat BB 395 This Gun For Hire/Yes Daddy . . . 60

BUSTY & COOL
62 Blue Beat BB 144 Mr Policeman/What A World . . . 20

TONY BUTALA
62 Salvo SLO 1801 Long Black Stockings/Rumors (99 copies only) . . . 40

BUTCHER
(see also Intestines)
82 Inept INEPT 002 On The Ground/Grow Up Don't Blow Up (p/s) . . . 5
83 Inept INEPT 003 Stand And Fight (p/s, red vinyl) . . . 5

EDDIE BUTCHER
76 Free Reed FRR 003 I ONCE WAS A DAYSMAN (LP, with insert) . . . 12

STAN BUTCHER
67 CBS 63072 SWING LIKE A BASTARD (LP) . . . 30
66 CBS SS62838 HIS BIRDS AND BRASS (LP) . . . 15

SAM BUTERA (& WITNESSES)
(see also Louis Prima)
58 HMV POP 476 Good Gracious Baby/It's Better Than Nothing At All . . . 70
58 HMV POP 476 Good Gracious Baby/It's Better Than Nothing At All (78) . . . 15
58 Capitol CL 14913 Bim Bam/Twinkle In Your Eye (as Sam Butera & Witnesses) . . . 250
59 Capitol CL 14988 Handle With Care/French Poodle . . . 20
64 Prima PR 1003 Skinnie Minnie/Little Liza Jane . . . 18
56 HMV 7EG 8087 SAX SERENADE (EP) . . . 40
60 London HA-D 2288 THE RAT RACE (LP, as Sam Butera & Witnesses) . . . 30

BILLY BUTLER (& ENCHANTERS)
69 Soul City SC 113 The Right Track/Boston Monkey . . . 25
74 Epic S EPC 2508 The Right Track/Can't Live Without Her (Yellow label) . . . 15
74 Epic S EPC 2508 The Right Track/Can't Live Without Her (Orange label) . . . 8

CHAMP BUTLER
56 Vogue Coral Q 72163 The Joshua Tree/Down In Mexico . . . 7

HAROLD BUTLER
77 Charmers 3 GOLD CONNECTION (LP) . . . 50

JERRY BUTLER
(see also Betty Everett & Jerry Butler, Impressions, Gene & Jerry)
58 London HL 8697 For Your Precious Love/Sweet Was The Wine (as Jerry Butler & the Impressions) . . . 200
58 London HL 8697 For Your Precious Love/Sweet Was The Wine (as Jerry Butler & the Impressions) (78 rpm) . . . 100
60 Top Rank JAR 389 I Found A Love/A Lonely Soldier . . . 45
60 Top Rank JAR 531 He Will Break Your Heart/Thanks To You . . . 55
61 Top Rank JAR 562 Find Another Girl/When Trouble Calls . . . 35
61 Columbia DB 4743 Moon River/Aware Of Love . . . 25
62 Stateside SS 121 Make It Easy On Yourself/It's Too Late . . . 25
63 Stateside SS 158 You Can Run But You Can't Hide/I'm The One . . . 30
63 Stateside SS 170 You Go Right Through Me/The Wishing Star . . . 20
63 Stateside SS 195 Whatever You Want/You Won't Be Sorry . . . 20
64 Stateside SS 252 Need To Belong/Give Me Your Love . . . 20
64 Stateside SS 300 Giving Up On Love/I've Been Trying . . . 20
65 Fontana TF 553 Good Times/I've Grown Accustomed To Her Face . . . 20
65 Fontana TF 588 I Can't Stand To See You Cry/Nobody Needs Your Love . . . 15
65 Mercury MF 932 Love (Oh, How Sweet It Is)/Loneliness . . . 15

			MINT VALUE £
66	Sue WI 4003	I Stand Accused/I Don't Want To Hear Anymore	50
66	Sue WI 4009	Just For You/Believe In Me	50
67	Mercury MF 964	I Dig You Baby/Some Kinda Magic	8
67	Mercury MF 1005	Mr. Dream Merchant/'Cause I Love You So	8
68	Mercury MF 1035	Never Give You Up/Beside You	10
68	Mercury MF 1058	Hey Mr Western Union Man (Send A Telegram)/Just Can't Forget About You	10
69	Mercury MF 1078	Are You Happy/Strange I Still Love You	8
69	Mercury MF 1094	Only The Strong Survive/Just Because I Really Love You	10
69	Mercury MF 1122	Moody Woman/Go Away And Find Yourself	20
69	Mercury MF 1122	Moody Woman/Go Away And Find Yourself (DJ copy)	100
69	Mercury MF 1132	A Brand New Me/What's The Use Of Breaking Up	10
70	President PT 299	Make It Easy On Yourself/Moon River	8
72	Mercury 6052 036	One Night Affair/What's So Good About It (You're My Baby)	8
72	Mercury 6052 119	Moody Woman/A Brand New Me	15
72	Mercury 6052 155	I Only Have Eyes For You/Ain't Understanding Mellow	5
72	Mercury 6052 168	One Night Affair/What's So Good About It (You're My Baby) (reissue)	5
63	Stateside SL 10032	HE WILL BREAK YOUR HEART (LP)	100
63	Stateside SL 10050	FOLK SONGS (LP)	40
68	Fontana (S)TL 5246	LOVE ME (LP)	45
68	Mercury 20118 (S)MCL	MR. DREAM MERCHANT (LP)	30
69	Mercury 20144 (S)MCL	SOUL GOES ON (LP)	30
69	Mercury 20154 (S)MCL	THE ICE MAN COMETH (LP)	30

LESLIE BUTLER (& FUGITIVES)

(see also Ken Boothe, Fugitives, Gaylads)

67	Island WI 3069	Hornpipe Rock Steady/You Don't Have To Say You Love Me	35
67	Doctor Bird DB 1083	Winchester Rocksteady (with Fugitives)/ ASTON CAMPBELL & CONQUERORS : Ramona	35
68	High Note HS 008	Top Cat/WEBBER SISTERS: Stars Above	25
68	High Note HS 009	Revival/GAYLADS: Over The Rainbow's End	12
75	Trojan TRLS 112	JA-GAN (LP)	30

BUTLIN'S REDCOAT REVUE

69	Pama SECO 5	BUTLINS'S REDCOAT REVIEW (LP)	12

BUTTERCUPS

68	Pama PM 742	If I Love You/Loving You	15
69	Pama PM 760	Come Put My Life In Order/If I Love You	10

BILLY BUTTERFIELD & HIS ORCHESTRA

(see also John Mayall's Bluesbreakers, Mike Bloomfield)

55	London HLF 8181	The Magnificent Matador/Sugar Blues Mambo	35

PAUL BUTTERFIELD BLUES BAND,

66	London HLZ 10100	Come On In/I Got A Mind To Give Up Living	20
67	Elektra EKSN 45007	All These Blues/Never Say No	8
67	Elektra EKSN 45020	Run Out Of Time/One More Heartache	20
68	Elektra EKSN 45047	Get Yourself Together/Mine To Love	10
69	Elektra EKSN 45069	Where Did My Baby Go/In My Own Dream	10
70	Elektra 2101 012	Love March/Love Disease	6
65	Elektra EKL/EKS 294	PAUL BUTTERFIELD BLUES BAND (LP, with rare gold 'guitar player' label)	200
65	Elektra EKL/EKS 294	PAUL BUTTERFIELD BLUES BAND (LP, orange label)	50
66	Elektra EKL/EKS 315	EAST - WEST (LP, orange label)	50
67	Elek. EKL 4015/EKS 74015	THE RESURRECTION OF PIGBOY CRABSHAW (LP, orange label)	35
68	Elektra EKL 4025	IN MY OWN DREAM (LP, orange label, also stereo EKS 74025)	35
69	Elektra EKS 74053	KEEP ON MOVIN' (LP)	18
71	Elektra EKD 2001	LIVE (2-LP)	20
72	Elektra K 62011	GOLDEN BUTTER (LP, gatefold sleeve)	12

BUTTERFLIES

68	President PT 192	Love Me Forever/He's Got Everything	10

SIMON BUTTERFLY

73	Cherub CHUBS 01	Rain Rain Rain/Rainbow	6

BUTTERFLYS

64	Red Bird RB 10009	Goodnight Baby/The Swim	25

BUTTERSCOTCH

70	RCA 1937	Don't You Know (She Said Hello)/The Closer To You	5
70	RCA 1983	Surprise, Surprise/In This World Of Loving You	5
70	RCA LSA 5000	BUTTERSCOTCH (LP, with insert and music book)	20

BUTTERSCOTCH CABOOSE

68	Bell BLL 1023	Melinda/Let A Little Sunshine In	7

BUTTONDOWN BRASS

(see also Ray Davies & Buttondown Brass)

67	Fontana LPS 16255	HA HA HA (HEE-HEE-HEE) (LP)	15
76	DJM DJS 22046	FUNK IN HELL (LP)	40
76	DJM DJSLM2023	FIREDOG (LP)	15
77	DJM DJS 22076	COPS N'ROBBERS (LP)	15

BUTTONHOLE SURFERS

89	Blast First BFF P41	WIDOWMAKER! (10" EP, with Reading Festival insert)	8
84	Red Rhino RRLEP 2	REMBRANDT PUSSYHORSE (LP)	15
85	Fundamental SAVE 5	PSYCHIC, POWERLESS...ANOTHER MAN'S SAC (LP)	12
91	Rough Trade R 2081 2601	PIOUGHD (LP, with bonus 12")	12

BUTTS BAND

75	ABC ABC4050	Get Up, Stand Up/Mike's Blues	12

SHEILA BUXTON

(see also Craig Douglas)

55	Columbia SCM 5193	Thank You For The Waltz/Just Between Friends	5

MINT VALUE £

57	Columbia DB 3887	Perfect Love/I Love You Baby (My Baby Loves Me)	5
57	Columbia DB 4051	The In-Between Age/Charm	5
59	Top Rank JAR 113	Soldier, Won't You Marry Me?/Li Per Li	6
59	Top Rank JAR 144	The Valley Of Love/The Wonder Of You	5
59	Top Rank JAR 240	All I Do Is Dream Of You/Shakedown	7
60	Top Rank JAR 356	Sixteen Reasons/Goodnight, God I Love You	10

BUY OFF THE BAR

88	Bi-Joopiter BIJOOP 023	PARBOILED (LP, screen printed sleeve with insert)	20

BUZZ

(see also Boston Dexters, Tam White)

66	Columbia DB 7887	You're Holding Me Down/I've Gotta Buzz	300

BUZZ

76	Polydor2058 714	Motorway Madness/Love Games	10

BUZZ

79	Redball RR 06	Insanity/Him Not Me/Sick At Heart (p/s)	30

BUZZ B (MC)

89	Play Hard DEC09	Slap Head/Hard To The Core (12")	5

BUZZ & BUCKY

(see also Ronny & The Daytonas)

65	Stateside SS 428	Tiger A Go Go/Bay City	45

BUZZARD

85	PTO MSPT01	Catch Me Alone/Raven Eyed Queen	45

BUZZCOCKS

(see also Pete Shelley, Things, Stevie's Buzz)

77	New Hormones ORG 1	SPIRAL SCRATCH (EP, plastic labels, p/s doesn't credit Howard Devoto)	40
77	United Artists UP 36316	Orgasm Addict/Whatever Happened To...? (p/s)	7
77	United Artists UP 36316B	Whatever Happened To? (1-sided test pressing)	50
78	United Artists UP36348	What Do I Get/Oh Shit	7
78	United Artists UP36348	What Do I Get?/Oh Shit (Mispress, plays Stranglers Peaches)	75
78	United Artists UP 36433	Love You More/Noise Annoys (p/s)	6
78	United Artists UP 36455	Ever Fallen In Love (With Someone You Shouldn't've?)/ Just Lust (p/s mispressed with Gerry Rafferty track on B-side)	20
78	United Artists UP 36471	Promises/Lipstick (p/s)	7
78	New Hormones ORG 1	SPIRAL SCRATCH (EP, reissue, p/s credits Howard Devoto, paper label)	8
78	United Artists UALP 15	Moving Away From The Pulsebeat (12", 1-sided, die-cut co. sl., promo only)	20
79	United Artists UP 36499	Everybody's Happy Nowadays/Why Can't I Touch It? (p/s, available in 3 different colours)	5
79	United Artists UP 36541	Harmony In My Head/Something's Gone Wrong Again (p/s)	5
80	United Artists BP 365	Why She's A Girl From The Chainstore/Are Everything (p/s)	6
80	United Artists BP 365 DJ	Why She's A girl From The Chainstore/Are Everything (DJ promo)	20
89	EMI EM104	Ever Fallen In Love/Promises/Everybody's Happy Nowdays/ Harmony in My Head (p/s)	8
91	New Hormones ORG 1	SPIRAL SCRATCH (EP, 2nd reissue, promo only 7")	10
95	One Stop Music ONE 7001	Noise Annoys/Isolation (live) (p/s, 1,500 only)	5
95	United Artists ESP001	What Do I Get?/Mad Mad Judy/Raison D'Etre (Demo)	10
87	Strange Fruit SFPS044	PEEL SESSION EP (12")	8
78	United Artists UAG 30159	ANOTHER MUSIC IN A DIFFERENT KITCHEN (LP, black inner sleeve, in printed carrier bag)	30
78	United Artists UAG 30159	ANOTHER MUSIC IN A DIFFERENT KITCHEN (LP)	12
78	United Artists UAG 30159	ANOTHER MUSIC IN A DIFFERENT KITCHEN (LP, mispressing without "I Need")	20
78	United Artists UAG 30197	LOVE BITES (LP, with embossed sleeve with insert)	12
79	United Artists UAG 30260	A DIFFERENT KIND OF TENSION (LP, with inner sleeve)	12
89	Strange Fruit SFRLP 104	PEEL SESSIONS (LP)	15
89	EMI LP PRODT 1	PRODUCT (5xLP boxed set with booklet)	40
89	Absolutely Free FREELP 02	LIVE AT THE ROXY (LP)	15
91	Document DLP 2	TIME'S UP (LP, mock bootleg, with bonus 33rpm interview single [FDLP 2])	20
00	Mute SCRATCH 2	TIMES UP (LP, reissue with poster)	12

BUZZIN CUZZINS

94	Azuli Records AZNY 024	Let Me Show You Love (12")	60

JAKI BYARD

67	Transatlantic PR 7419	LIVE! VOL 1 (LP, white purple label)	20
68	Transatlantic PR 7463	FREEDOM TOGETHER! (LP)	20
68	Transatlantic PR 7550	SUNSHINE OF MY SOUL (LP)	20

DON BYAS & HIS RHYTHM

56	Vogue V 2390	On The Way To Your Heart/The Portuguese Washerwomen	10
64	Realm RM 230	ON 52ND STREET (LP)	15

BYE LAWS

68	Pye 7N 17481	Then You Can Tell Me Goodbye/Come On Over To My Place	8
69	Pye 7N 17701	Run Baby Run/To Sir With Love	12

TREVOR BYFIELD

80	Ethnic Fight EF 086	Jah Guide/TREVOR & CLIVE: Sea Of Love (12")	35

MAX BYGRAVES

(see also Joan Regan)

53	HMV 7M 112	Cowpuncher's Cantata/True Loves And False Lovers	15
53	HMV 7M 113	Little Sir Echo/Bygraves Boogie	15
53	HMV 7M 114	The Travelling Salesman/Ten Bottles Of Gin	8
53	HMV 7M 134	Lovely Dollar Lolly (with Peter Brough & Archie Andrews)/ The Red Robin Cantata	8
53	HMV 7M 145	Time To Dream/The Queen Of Ev'ryone's Heart	8
53	HMV 7M 154	Big 'Ead/Say "Si Si" (B-side with Peter Brough & Archie Andrews)	8

MINT VALUE £

JUNIOR BYLES

(see also King Chubby, Lloyd Terrell, Dennis Alcapone, Upsetters, Bob Marley, Lee & Junior)

71	Bullet BU 499	Beat Down Babylon/UPSETTERS: Version	18
71	Upsetter US 365	Palace Called Africa/UPSETTERS: Earthquake	20
72	Upsetter US 387	Festival Da Da/UPSETTERS: Version	18
72	Pama PM 857	Fever/GROOVERS: Soul Sister (B-side actually by Heptones)	40
72	Dynamic DYN 432	Pharaoh Hiding/UPSETTERS: Hail To Power	10
72	Randy's RAN 523	King Of Babylon/UPSETTERS: Nebuchadnezzer	18
72	Punch PH 109	Pharaoh Hiding/UPSETTERS: Hail To Power	18
73	Pama PM 878	Education Rock/KEN McKAY: Nobody Knows	10
73	Count Shelley CS 31	Break Up To Make Up/YOUTH MAN (DILLINGER): Plat Skank	8
74	Magnet MAG 27	Curly Locks/Now Generation	8
74	Dip DL 5035	Curly Locks/Now Generation	10
75	Dip DL 5074	Long Way/All The Way	12
75	Ethnic ETH 26	Mumbling And Grumbling/King Size Mumble	7
76	Jessus JI 006	Know Where You Are Going/JESSUS EXPERIENCE: Going To Zion	12
76	Ethnic Fight EF 042	Bury O Boy/ THE THING MUSIC CO: Version	6
76	Black Wax WAX 17	Pitchy Patchy/THE JA-MAN ALL STARS: 129 Beat Street	6
72	Trojan TRL 52	BEAT DOWN BABYLON (LP, beware of Canadian imports)	40

JUNIOR BYLES & RUPERT REID

76	Black Wax WAX 15	Chant Down Babylon/THE JA-MAN ALL STARS: Version	12

BOBBY BYRD

(see also JB's, James Brown, Anna King & Bobby Byrd, Vicki Anderson)

71	Mojo 2001 118	I Need Help Parts 1 & 2	12
71	Mojo 2027 003	I Know You Got Soul/If You Don't Work You Can't Eat	12
71	Mojo 2093 004	Hot Pants ? I'm Coming, I'm Coming, I'm Coming/Hang It Up	12
72	Mojo 2093 013	Keep On Doin' What You're Doin'/Let Me Know	12
72	Mojo 2093 017	If You Got A Love You'd Better Keep Hold Of It/ You've Got To Change Your Mind	12
72	Mojo 2093 020	Never Get Enough/My Concerto	12
73	Warner Bros K 16291	Try It Again/I'm On The Move	8
73	Mojo 2093 028	Saying It And Doing It Are Two Different Things/VICKI ANDERSON: Don't Throw Your Love In Garbage/In The Land Of Milk & Honey	20
87	Urban URB 8	I Know You Got Soul/Hot Pants	7
87	Urban URBX 8	I Know You Got Soul/Hot Pants ? I'm Coming, I'm Coming, I'm Coming/ I Know You Got Soul (Version) (12", die-cut company sleeve)	10

C. BYRD & SIR D.'S GROUP

60	Blue Beat BB 49	Baa Baa Black Sheep/LLOYD & CECIL: Come Over Here	12

CHARLIE BYRD

62	Riverside RLP 436	BOSSA NOVA PELOS PASSAROS (LP)	12

DONALD BYRD

(see also Blackbyrds, Art Farmer)

65	Verve VS 532	Boom Boom/See See Rider	8
80	United Artists UP 622	Dominoes/Wind Parade	7
80	Blue Note 12 UP 622	Dominoes/Wind Parade (12")	30
81	Elektra K 12559	Love Has Come Around/Loving You (12")	8
55	Esquire 32-019	BYRD JAZZ (LP, as Donald Byrd Sextet)	300
60s	Esquire 32-039	INFORMAL JAZZ (LP)	25
70s	Blue Note BI 7243187515	KOFI (LP)	20
73	Blue Note BN-LA047	BLACKBYRD (LP)	15
75	Blue Note UAG 20001	PLACES AND SPACES (LP)	30
78	Elektra K52199	DONALD BYRD & 125th STREET (LP)	12

MICHAEL BYRD & COMMERCIALS

(see also Cardiac Arrest, Selecter)

80	Another AN 002	SELL OUT BEFORE THE FALL OUT (EP, gatefold p/s, 500 copies only)	6

RUSSELL BYRD

64	Sue WI 305	Hitch Hike Parts 1 & 2	50

ESTHER BYRDE

79	Survival SUR 1	Touch Me Take Me/Tracks Of Love	50

BYRDS

(see also Beefeaters, Roger McGuinn, David Crosby, Gene Clark, Gram Parsons, Gene Parsons, Skip Battin, Earl Scruggs, Flying Burrito Brothers, Evergreen Blueshoes, Dillard & Clark, Kentucky Colonels)

65	CBS 201765	Mr. Tambourine Man/I Knew I'd Want You	10
65	CBS 201796	All I Really Want To Do/Feel A Whole Lot Better	10
65	CBS 202008	Turn! Turn! Turn! (To Everything There Is A Season)/ She Don't Care About Time	10
66	CBS 202037	Set You Free This Time/It Won't Be Wrong	12
66	CBS 202067	Eight Miles High/Why	12
66	CBS 202259	5D (Fifth Dimension)/Captain Soul	8
66	CBS 202295	Mr Spaceman/What's Happening?!?!	12
67	CBS 202559	So You Want To Be A Rock'n'Roll Star/Everybody's Been Burned	10
67	CBS 2648	My Back Pages/Renaissance Fair	10
67	CBS 2924	Lady Friend/Don't Make Waves	20
67	CBS 3093	Goin' Back/Change Is Now	12
68	CBS 3411	You Ain't Goin' Nowhere/Artificial Energy	8
68	CBS 3752	I Am A Pilgrim/Pretty Boy Floyd	8
69	CBS 4055	Bad Night At The Whiskey/Drug Store Truck Drivin' Man	12
69	CBS 4284	Lay Lady Lay/Old Blue (p/s)	12
69	CBS 4572	Wasn't Born To Follow/Child Of The Universe	8
70	CBS 4753	Jesus Is Just Alright/It's All Over Now Baby Blue	8
71	CBS 5322	Chestnut Mare/Just A Season	7
71	CBS 7253	I Trust/This Is My Destiny	10
72	CBS 7712	America's Great National Pastime/Farther Along (unreleased)	0
73	Asylum AYM 516	Things Will Be Better/For Free (promos in p/s)	12

			MINT VALUE £
73	Asylum AYM 516	Things Will Be Better/For Free (promos in p/s)	6
73	Asylum AYM 517	Full Circle/Long Live The King	6
66	CBS EP 6069	THE TIMES THEY ARE A' CHANGIN' (EP)	22
66	CBS EP 6077	EIGHT MILES HIGH (EP)	30
90	CBS 656544 5	FOUR DIMENSIONS EP (CD, picture disc)	8
65	CBS BPG 62571	MR TAMBOURINE MAN (LP, mono)	45
65	CBS SBPG 62571	MR TAMBOURINE MAN (LP, stereo)	25
66	CBS BPG 62652	TURN! TURN! TURN! (LP, mono)	45
66	CBS SBPG 62652	TURN! TURN! TURN! (LP, stereo)	35
66	CBS BPG 62783	FIFTH DIMENSION (LP, mono)	40
66	CBS SBPG 62783	FIFTH DIMENSION (LP, stereo)	35
67	CBS BPG 62988	YOUNGER THAN YESTERDAY (LP, mono)	40
67	CBS SBPG 62988	YOUNGER THAN YESTERDAY (LP, stereo)	35
68	CBS BPG 63107	THE BYRDS' GREATEST HITS (LP, mono)	15
68	CBS BPG 63169	THE NOTORIOUS BYRD BROTHERS (LP, mono)	40
68	CBS SBPG 63169	THE NOTORIOUS BYRD BROTHERS (LP, stereo)	30
68	CBS 63353	SWEETHEART OF THE RODEO (LP, mono)	30
68	CBS 63353	SWEETHEART OF THE RODEO (LP, stereo)	25
69	CBS 63545	DR BYRDS & MR HYDE (LP, mono)	25

(Original copies of the above LPs were issued with rough-textured, plain orange labels and laminated sleeves; later copies are worth two-thirds these values.)

71	Bumble GEXP 8001	PRE-FLYTE (LP)	25
73	Asylum SYLA 8754	THE BYRDS (LP, gatefold sleeve)	12

JERRY BYRNE

76	Specialty SON 5011	Lights Out/Honey Baby	5

PACKIE BYRNE (& BONNIE SHALJEAN)

69	EFDSS LP 1009	PACKIE BYRNE (LP)	20

EDD/EDWARD BYRNES

(see also Connie Stevens)

60	Warner Bros WB 5	Kookie, Kookie (Lend Me Your Comb) (with Connie Stevens)/You're The Top	8
60	Warner Bros WB 27	Lonely Christmas/Yulesville (as Edd Byrnes)	12
60	Warner Bros WEP 6010	KOOKIE (EP, mono)	15
60	Warner Bros WSEP 2010	KOOKIE (EP, stereo)	20
63	Warner Bros W(S)EP 6108	KOOKIE VOLUME 2 (EP)	20

MARTIN BYRNES

70	Leader LEA 2004	BYRNES (LP)	15

DAVID BYRON

75	Bronze ILPS 9342	TAKE NO PRISONERS (LP, lyric inner sleeve)	15

PAUL BYRON

60	Decca F 11210	Pale Moon/Year Ago Tonight	10

SOL BYRON & IMPACTS

60s	Flamingo PR 5027	Pride And Joy/Thou Shall Not Steal	15

BYSTANDERS

(see also Man)

65	Pylot WD 501	That's The End/This Time	150
66	Piccadilly 7N 35330	(You're Gonna) Hurt Yourself/Have I Offended The Girl	25
66	Piccadilly 7N 35351	My Love - Come Home/If You Walk Away	30
67	Piccadilly 7N 35363	98.6/Stubborn Kind Of Fellow	20
67	Piccadilly 7N 35382	Royal Blue Summer Sunshine Day/Make Up Your Mind	30
67	Piccadilly 7N 35399	Pattern People/Green Grass	15
68	Pye 7N 17476	When Jezamine Goes/Cave Of Clear Light	50
68	Pye 7N 17540	This World Is My World/Painting The Time	15

BYZANTIUM

(see also Ora)

73	A&M AMS 7064	What A Coincidence/My Seasons Changing With The Sun	7
72	A&M AMLH 68104	BYZANTIUM (LP, with poster, brown label)	100
72	A&M AMLH 68104	BYZANTIUM (LP, without poster)	40
73	A&M AMLH 68163	SEASONS CHANGING (LP, poster sleeve, brown labels)	100
74	Private pressing	LIVE AND STUDIO ('BLACK AND WHITE') (LP, 100 only with insert)	300

B.Z.N.

73	Birth RAB 1003	Rolling Round The Band/Superman	12

C

ANDY C

(See also Randall and Andy C.)

92	RAM RAMM 001	SOUR MASH EP (12")	50
93	RAM RAMM 003	BASS LOGIC EP (12")	30
93	RAM RAMM 006	Slip 'N' Slide/Bass Constructor (Sonz Of A Loop Da Loop Era Remix) (12")	25
95	RAM RAMM 12	Cool Down/Roll On (12")	15

FANTASTIC JOHNNY C

67	London HL 10169	Boogaloo Down Broadway/Look What Love Can Make You Do	10
68	London HL 10212	Hitch It To The Horse/Cool Broadway	10
69	Action ACT 4543	Is There Anything Better Than Making Love/New Love	20
75	Island USA 8	Don't Depend On Me (Parts 1 & 2)	8
69	Action ACLP 6001	BOOGALOO DOWN BROADWAY (LP)	45

MINT VALUE £

C & M CONNECTION

90 Blue Chip BLUE c32 — Another Night (12") — 12

ROY C

66 Island WI 273 — Shotgun Wedding/I'm Going To Make It — 25
66 Island WI 273 — Shotgun Wedding/High School Dropout (different B-side) — 15
67 Ember EMB S 230 — Twistin' Pneumonia/Tear Avenue — 15
66 Ember NR 5055 — THE SHOTGUN WEDDING MAN (LP) — 30
75 Mercury 9100 017 — SEX AND SOUL (LP) — 15

CABARET VOLTAIRE

(see also Richard H. Kirk, Hafler Trio, Peter Hope & Richard H. Kirk, Stephen Mallinder, Pressure Co., Eric Random)

78 Rough Trade RT 003 — EXTENDED PLAY EP (paper p/s) — 7
79 Rough Trade RT 018 — Nag Nag Nag/Is That Me (p/s) — 5
79 Rough Trade RT 035 — Silent Command/Chance Versus Causality (p/s) — 5
80 Rough Trade RT 060 — Seconds Too Late/Control Addict (p/s) — 5
79 Rough Trade ROUGH 4 — VOICE OF AMERICA (LP) — 12

CABLES

(see also K. Drummond, Dingle Brothers, Alton Ellis)

68 Coxsone CS 7072 — What Kind Of World?/My Broken Heart — 40
68 Coxsone CS 7082 — Soul Power/HEPTONES: Love Me Alway — 150
68 Studio One SO 2060 — Baby Why?/Be A Man — 30
68 Studio One SO 2071 — Love Is A Pleasure/Cheer Up — 80
69 Studio One SO 2085 — Got To Find Someone/ALEXANDER HENRY: Please Be True — 30
69 Bamboo BAM 12 — So Long/PRESSURE BOYS: More Love — 20
70 Bamboo BAM 19 — How Can I Trust You?/SOUND DIMENSIONS: How Can I Trust You? (Inst.) — 15
70 Trojan TR 7792 — Salt Of The Earth/Ring A Bell — 10
70 Harry J. HJ 6614 — Didn't I/JAY BOYS: Tilly — 10
70 Harry J. HJ 6620 — Feel Alright/Equal Rights — 7
71 Big Shot BI 598 — A Sometime Girl/IN CROWD BAND: A Sometime Girl Version — 6
71 Duke DU 124 — Mixing/IN CROWD BAND: In Orbit — 8
72 Jackpot JP 787 — Come On/Come On Version — 6
73 Attack ATT 8053 — Give Me A Chance/JAH FISH: King Of Zion — 6

CABOOSE

70 Stax STAX 151 — Black Hands, White Cotton/In My Hour Of Need — 6

CACHE

81 Groove G 111 T — Where Is My Sunshine/Jazzin' And Crusin' (12") — 50

CACOPHONY

(see also Marty Friedman, Megadeth)

87 Roadrunner RR 349577 — SPEED METAL SYMPHONY (LP) — 12
88 Roadrunner RR 9577 — GO OFF (LP, as Marty Friedman, Jason Becker & Cacophony) — 12

CACTUS

(see also Vanilla Fudge, Leaf Hound, Beck Bogert Appice, Atomic Rooster)

70 Atco 2400 020 — CACTUS (LP) — 20
71 Atco 2400 114 — ONE WAY ... OR ANOTHER (LP, reissue of above LP) — 20
72 Atlantic K 40307 — RESTRICTIONS (LP) — 12
72 Atlantic K 50013 — 'OT AND SWEATY (LP) — 12

BILL CADDICK

76 Park SHP 102 — ROUGH MUSIC (LP) — 15
77 Leader LER 2097 — SUNNY MEMORIES (LP) — 15
79 Highway SHY 7006 — REASONS BRIEFLY SET DOWN (LP) — 15

ALAN CADDY

(see also Tornados)

64 HMV POP 1286 — Tornado/Workout — 40

CADETS (U.K.)

63 Decca F 11677 — Hello Trouble/Our First Quarrel — 10
64 Pye 7N 15693 — Chapel Of Love/I Gave My Wedding Dress Away — 10
65 Pye 7N 15769 — Are You Teasing Me?/My Heart Skips A Beat — 5
65 Pye 7N 15852 — Jealous Heart/Right Or Wrong — 20
65 Pye 7N 15947 — Baby Roo/Raining In My Heart — 10
66 Pye 7N 17024 — If I Had My Life To Live Over/Best Of All — 5
66 Pye 7N 17167 — At The Close Of A Long Long Day/True Love — 5
69 Pye 7N 17762 — Dying Ranger/Storeen Bawn — 5
66 Marble Arch MAL 643 — THE CADETS (LP) — 12

CADETS (U.S.)

56 London HLU 8313 — Stranded In The Jungle/I Want You (gold label lettering) — 700
56 London HLU 8313 — Stranded In The Jungle/I Want You (silver label lettering) — 300
56 London HLU 8313 — Stranded In The Jungle/I Want You (78) — 45

CADILLAC

86 CBS A 7180 — Valentino/Valentino (p/s) — 8

EARL CADILLAC & HIS ORCHESTRA

59 Vogue V 9133 — Zon, Zon, Zon/Il Suffit D'Une Melodie — 18
59 Vogue V 9133 — Zon, Zon, Zon/Il Suffit D'Une Melodie (78) — 10
59 Vogue V 9138 — The Fish Seller/Tremendo Cha Cha Cha (Plegaria) — 15
59 Vogue V 9138 — The Fish Seller/Tremendo Cha Cha Cha (Plegaria) (78) — 10

VINCE CADILLAC

78 Satric SAT 126 — Memory Lane/Hello — 5

CADILLACS

59 London HLJ 8786 — Peek-A-Boo/Oh, Oh, Lolita — 50
59 London HLJ 8786 — Peek-A-Boo/Oh, Oh, Lolita (78) — 25

MINT VALUE £

BOBBY CADMAN

74	Regal Zonophone RZ3008	A Magic Spell/Own Up Time	40

CADO BELLE

76	anchor 1033	Got To Love/Paper In The Rain	25

SUSAN CADOGAN

74	Dip DL 5030	Hurt So Good/UPSETTERS: Loving Is Good	7
75	Lucky LY 5078	Feeling Right/Congratulations	7
75	Black Wax WAX 2	Love My Life/MR. VIBES: Love Vibes	8
76	Trojan TRLS 122	SUSAN CADOGAN (LP)	20

CAEDMON

78	private pressing	CAEDMON (LP, with insert, with bonus 7": Beyond The Second Mile/"Give Me Jesus")	175
78	private pressing	CAEDMON (LP, with insert, without bonus 7")	100

CAERN

70s	Gem DES 1015	A COLLECTION OF SCOTCH FOLK (LP)	18

CAESAR & CLEO

(see also Sonny & Cher)

65	Reprise R 20419	Love Is Strange/Let The Good Times Roll (in p/s)	25
65	Reprise R 20419	Love Is Strange/Let The Good Times Roll	15
65	Reprise R 30056	CAESAR AND CLEO (EP, 2 tracks each by Caesar & Cleo and Sonny & Cher)	20

CAESARS

65	Decca F 12251	On The Outside Looking In/Can You Blame Me?	15
66	Decca F 12462	Five In The Morning/It's Superman	10

CAFE SOCIETY

(see also Tom Robinson Band, Claire Hamill)

75	Konk KOS 5	Whitby Two-Step/Maybe It's Me	6
75	Konk KONK 102	CAFE SOCIETY (LP, with inner sleeve)	20

BUTCH CAGE/MABEL LEE WILLIAMS

60s	Storyville SLP 129	COUNTRY BLUES (LP)	25

AUBREY CAGLE

62	Starlite ST45 082	Come Along Little Girl/Blue Lonely World	220

CAGLIOSTRO

86	él GPO 22	Libera Me/Madmen And Lovers (p/s)	8

JAMES CAGNEY

81	United Artists UP 36385	Yankee Doodle Dandy/Over There (B-side with Frances Langford) (p/s)	8

JEREMY CAHILL

(see also Shide & Acorn)

70s	Solent	September Blues/Yesterday	15

PATRICIA CAHILL

70	Deram DM 320	Little Altar Boy/Rain	6
71	Deram DM 324	Colm Ban/Eighteen	6
70	Deram Nova SDN 22	SUMMER'S DAUGHTER (LP)	30
72	Rex RPS 104	IRELAND (LP)	15

CAIN

68	Page One POF 054	Her Emotion/Take Me Back One Time	25

CAIN

80s	private pressing	CAIN (2-LP)	30

TUBAL CAINE

70	Attack ATT 8023	I'm A Drifter Part 1/CIMARONS: I'm A Drifter Part 2	7

AL CAIOLA (ORCHESTRA)

(see also Hugo Montenegro)

56	London HLC 8285	Flamenco Love/From The Heart	20
61	London HLT 9294	The Magnificent Seven/The Lonely Rebel	15
61	London HLT 9325	Bonanza/Bounty Hunter	12
61	HMV POP 884	Bonanza/Bounty Hunter (as Al Caiola Orchestra, reissue)	5
61	HMV POP 889	The Magnificent Seven/The Lonely Rebel (as Al Caiola Orchestra)	10
62	Oriole CB 1732	Mambo Jambo/Twistin' At The Woodchoppers Mill	10
62	United Artists UP 1003	Big Guitar/Guns Of Navarone	10
66	United Artists UEP 1018	HIT T.V. THEMES (EP)	15
56	London HA-C 2017	DEEP IN A DREAM (LP)	22
57	London HA-C 2022	SERENADE IN BLUE (LP)	22
62	United Artists ULP 1003	SOLID GOLD GUITAR (LP)	20
62	United Artists ULP 1030	ACAPULCO 1922 AND THE LONELY BULL (LP)	15
62	United Artists ULP 1031	GOLDEN GUITAR (LP)	15
63	United Artists ULP 1065	CITY GUY PLAYS COUNTRY (LP)	15
64	United Artists ULP 1084	ON THE TRAIL (LP)	15
64	United Artists ULP 8053	'CIAO'	20
64	United Artists ULP 1090	TUFF GUITAR (LP)	20
66	United Artists (S)ULP 1115	SOUNDS FOR SPIES AND PRIVATE EYES (LP)	30

CAIRN

70s	GES 1015	A COLLECTION OF SCOTCH FOLK (LP)	15

JOHN CAIRNEY

57	HMV POP 424	Two Strangers/A Certain Girl I Know (with Sammy San)	7
68	Waverley SLP 543	Please/Deep Purple	5

FORRIE CAIRNS

62	Fontana 267240 TF	Salty Dog/Cockles And Mussels	5

MINT VALUE £

CAIRO

80	Absurd ASK 15	Movie Stars/Cuthbert's Birthday Treat (p/s)	5

CAIR PARAVEL

76	Koala KOA PO 16	SOME OTHER MORNING (LP, insert)	400

CAJUN MOON

(see Allan Taylor)

76	Polydor 2058 801	No Honey No Love/Version	6
76	Chrysalis CHR 1116	CAJUN MOON (LP)	12

CAKE

68	MCA MUPS 303	THE CAKE (LP)	18
69	MCA MUPS 390	A SLICE OF CAKE (LP)	18

J.J. CALE

(see also Leathercoated Minds)

66	Liberty LIB 55881	Outside Lookin' In/In Our Time	18
72	A&M AMS 7018	Cajun Moon/Starbound	6
72	A&M AMS 7022	After Midnight/Crazy Mama	6
72	A&M AMLS 68105	NATURALLY (LP, tan label)	12
72	A&M AMLS 68157	REALLY (LP, tan label)	12
79	Shelter ISA 5018	FIVE (LP, with bonus single "Katy Cool"/"Juan And Maria Juarez Blues" [JJ-1]).	15

JOHN CALE

(see also Velvet Underground, Nico, Terry Riley, Ayers Cale Nico & Eno, Judy Nylon)

74	Island WIP 6202	The Man Who Couldn't Afford To Orgy/Sylvia Said	10
77	Illegal IL 006	Jack The Ripper In The Moulin Rouge/Memphis (unissued, test pressings only)	25
81	A&M AMS 8130	Dead Or Alive/Honi Soit	5
83	Ze IS 113	Close Watch/I Keep A Close Watch (p/s)	5
84	Ze IS 157	Caribbean Sunset/(same) (unissued, promo only)	8
84	Ze IS 197	Ooh La La/Magazines (p/s)	5
77	Illegal IL 003	ANIMAL JUSTICE (12" EP)	10
71	CBS 64256	VINTAGE VIOLENCE (LP, orange label)	25
71	CBS 64259	CHURCH OF ANTHRAX (LP, with Terry Riley)	20
72	Reprise K 44212	ACADEMY IN PERIL (LP, die cut 'Warhol' cover)	20
73	Reprise K 44239	PARIS 1919 (LP, with lyric insert)	20
74	Island ILPS 9301	FEAR (LP, pink rim)	15
75	Island ILPS 9317	SLOW DAZZLE (LP)	12
75	Island ILPS 9350	HELEN OF TROY (LP)	20
77	Island ILPS 9459	GUTS (LP)	12
07	EMI 37760	CIRCUS (3-LP with free 7", sealed)	20

CALEB (Quaye)

(see also Mirage, Hookfoot, Bread & Beer Band, Elton John)

67	Philips BF 1588	Baby Your Phrasing Is Bad/Woman Of Distinction (300-500 pressed)	850

CALEDONIANS

(see also Clarendonians, Prince Buster)

69	Fab FAB 103	Funny Way Of Laughing/Don't Please	15

CALENDAR

75	All Platinum 6146 308	Hypertension Parts 1 & 2	5

CALENNIG

80	Greenwich Village GVR 214	SONGS AND TUNES FROM WALES (LP)	15

CALIFORNIA IN-CROWD

66	Fontana TF 779	Questions And Answers/Happiness In My Heart	50

CALIFORNIA MUSIC

(see also Bruce Johnston, Beach Boys)

74	RCA RCA 2488	Don't Worry Baby/Ten Years Harmony	12
76	RCA RCA 2661	Jamaica Farewell/California Farewell	12
78	RSO 014	I Can Hear Music/Love's Supposed To Be That Way (as California)	10

CALIFORNIAN LICENSE

70	Philips 6006052	The Cage/Easter Song	12

CALIFORNIANS

(see also Warren Zevon)

67	CBS 2263	Golden Apples/Little Ship With A Red Sail	75
67	Decca F 12678	Follow Me/What Love Can Do	20
67	Decca F 12712	Sunday Will Never Be The Same/Can't Get You Out Of My Mind	10
68	Decca F 12758	Congratulations/What Is Happy, Baby?	10
68	Decca F 12802	Out In The Sun/The Sound	20
69	Fontana TF 991	Mandy/The Cooks Of Cake And Kindness	100
69	Fontana TF 1052	Sad Old Song/Weep No More	15
69	Chapter One CH 112	You've Got Your Troubles/Early Morning Sun	7

CALLAN & JOHN

69	CBS 4447	House Of Delight/Long Shadow Day	30

CALL GIRLS

88	53rd & 3rd AGAR 001	Primal World/VATICAN SHOTGUN SCARE: Thick Fat Heat Source (p/s)	8

(MISSISSIPPI) JOE CALLICOTT

68	Blue Horizon 7-63227	PRESENTING THE COUNTRY BLUES (LP)	120
71	Revival RVS 1002	DEAL GONE DOWN (LP, as Joe Callicott)	22

TERRY CALLIER

79	Elektra K 12372	Sign Of The Times/Occasional Rain	8
90	Acid Jazz JAZID 27T	I Don't Want To See Myself (Without You)/(If I Could Make You) Change Your Mind (12")	15
78	Elektra K 52096	FIRE ON ICE (LP)	15
79	Elektra K 52140	TURN YOU TO LOVE (LP)	15

MINT VALUE £

CALLIES

71	Rubber RUB 002	ON YOUR SIDE (LP, gatefold sleeve)	15

CALLINAN-FLYNN

72	Mushroom 50 MR 17	We Are The People (The Road To Derry Town)/The Old Man And The Flower	30
72	Mushroom 150 MR 18	FREEDOM'S LAMENT (LP)	190

JO CALLIS

(see also Rezillos, Shake, Human League)

81	Pop: Aural POP 12	Woah Yeah/Sinistrale/Dodo Boys (p/s)	5

CAB CALLOWAY

66	Stateside SS 509	History Repeats Itself/After Taxes	7
58	Gala 45XP 1016	CAB CALLOWAY (EP)	8
60	Fontana TFE 17216	CAB CALLOWAY (EP)	10
70s	Vintage Jazz VEP 22	CABULOUS CALLOWAY (EP)	8
70s	Vintage Jazz VEP 35	CABULOUS CALLOWAY VOL. 2 (EP)	8

CALOOGIE

68	CBS 1095	Bleeker Street/Benedictus	10

GEORGE CALSTOCK

78	Hit Run DD2	The Ungodly (Feat. U Black)/DOCTOR PABLO: Righteous Melody (12")	35

EDDIE CALVERT

(see also Gerry Brereton)

53	Columbia SCM 5003	My Yiddishe Momme/Hora Staccato	8
53	Columbia SCM 5004	Ave Maria/Just A-Wearyin' For You (as Eddie Calvert Orchestra)	8
54	Columbia SCM 5129	My Son, My Son/Sherpa Song	8
55	Columbia SCM 5168	Cherry Pink And Apple Blossom White/Roses Of Picardy	10
56	Columbia SCM 5237	The Man With The Golden Arm/Memories Of You	7
56	Columbia SCM 5277	Moonglow & Theme From "Picnic"/If I Loved You	5
57	Columbia SEG 7710	OH MY PAPA (EP)	10
58	Melodisc EPM 7	MISERLOU (EP)	8
57	Columbia 3351020	THE MAN WITH THE GOLDEN TRUMPET (10" LP)	15

ROBERT CALVERT

(see also Hawkwind, Imperial Pompadours, Catapilla, Adrian Wagner, John Stevens Away)

72	United Artists UP 35543	Ejection/Catch A Falling Starfighter (p/s)	25
79	Wake Up WUR 5	Cricket Star (p/s, 33rpm flexidisc, as Robert Calvert & 1st XI)	10
80	Flicknife FLS 204	Lord Of The Hornets/The Greenfly & The Rose (purple print p/s)	10
81	Flicknife FLS 204	Lord Of The Hornets/The Greenfly & The Rose (reissue, black print p/s)	5
74	United Artists UAG 29507	CAPTAIN LOCKHEED AND THE STARFIGHTERS (LP, embossed gatefold sleeve, with attached booklet and inner sleeve)	40
75	United Artists UAG 29852	LUCKY LIEF AND THE LONGSHIPS (LP, gatefold sleeve)	18
81	A-Side IF 0311	HYPE (SONGS OF TOM MAHLER) (LP)	15
84	Flicknife SHARP 021	FREQ (LP)	12
86	Demi Monde DMLP 1010	TEST TUBE CONCEIVED (LP)	12
86	Harbour (no cat. no.)	THE CELLAR TAPES VOLUME ONE (cassette only)	15
86	Harbour (no cat. no.)	THE CELLAR TAPES VOLUME TWO (cassette only)	15
88	Harbour (no cat. no.)	ROBERT CALVERT READS THE EARTH RITUAL (cassette, limited edition)	15
88	Beat Goes On BGOLP 2	LUCKY LIEF AND THE LONGSHIPS (LP, gatefold sleeve, reissue)	20
88	Beat Goes On BGOLP 5	CAPTAIN LOCKHEED AND THE STARFIGHTERS (LP, gatefold sleeve with booklet, reissue)	12
89	Clear BLACK 1	ROBERT CALVERT AT THE QUEEN ELIZABETH HALL (LP, mail order only, with badge, poster & T-shirt, gatefold sleeve)	40
92	Cyborg (no cat. no.)	REVENGE (cassette only)	12

TABBY CALVIN & ROUNDERS

56	Capitol CL 14640	False Alarm/I Came Back To Say I'm Sorry	10

CAMALEONTI

68	CBS 3968	Applause/Applausi	15

CAMARATA

59	Top Rank JAR 160	Love Theme Sleeping Beauty/ Medley Sleeping Beauty (as Walt Disney Studio Orchestra)	10
60	London HL 9323	Swiss Family Robinson Theme/Trumpeter's Prayer	6
65	London SHU 8257	THINK YOUNG! (LP, as Camarata Orchestra)	15
70	Deram SML 1053	THE VELVET GENTLEMAN: THE MUSIC OF ERIK SATIE (LP)	20

CAMARQUE

83	Clubland SJP 848	Howl Of The Pack/Someone Just Like You (in p/s)	75
83	Clubland SJP 848	Howl Of The Pack/Someone Just Like You	30

CAMBERWELL NOW

(see also This Heat)

86	Ink 19	GHOST TRADE (LP)	18

CAMBODIANS

70	Duke DU 101	Coolie Man/J.J. ALLSTARS: Coolie Version	12

CAMBRIDGE BUSKERS

70s	Polydor 2371984	DOUBLE CONCERTO (LP)	20
70s	Polydor 2371766	ZWISCHEN PINTE UND PODIUM (LP)	20

CAMEL

(see also Pete Bardens, Gong/Camel, Caravan, Hatfield & The North)

73	MCA MUPS 1177	Never Let Go/Curiosity	6
80	Decca FR 13871	Your Love Is Stranger Than Mine/Neon Magic (p/s)	6
84	Decca CAMEL 1	Cloak And Dagger Man/Pressure Point (p/s)	5
73	MCA MUPS 473	CAMEL (LP, black/blue hexagon label)	120
74	Deram SML 1107	MIRAGE (LP, with insert, red/white label, small Deram logo)	25
73	MCA MUPS 473	CAMEL (LP, later rainbow label)	15

MINT VALUE £

75	Decca SKL-R 5207	THE SNOW GOOSE (LP, laminated sleeve, insert)	25
76	Decca TXS-R 115	MOON MADNESS (LP, gatefold sleeve)	15

CAMEL DRIVERS

68	Pye International 7N 25471	Sunday Morning 6 O'Clock/Give It A Try	15

CAMEOS

63	Columbia DB 7092	Powercut/High Low And Lonesomely	40
64	Columbia DB 7201	My Baby's Coming Home/Where E'er You Walk	40

CAMEOS

67	Toast TT 503	A Pretty Shade Of Blue/You Didn't Have To Be So Nice	8
68	Toast TT 508	On The Good Ship Lollipop/The Love Of A Boy	8

CAMERA OBSCURA

80	Small Wonder SMALL 28	Destitution/Race In Athens (p/s)	6

CAMERA OBSCURA

98	Andmoresounds AND 0945	Park And Ride/Swimming Pool	20
98	Andmoresounds AND 1145	Your Sound/Autumn Tides/Annawaltzerpose	20
01	Andmoresounds AND 1733	BIGGEST BLUEST HI-FI (LP)	25

DION CAMERON & THREE TOPS

(see also Dion & Three Tops)

66	Rio R 111	Lord Have Mercy/Get Ready	12

G.C. CAMERON

(see also Detroit Spinners)

76	Tamla Motown TMG 1033	Me And My Life/Act Like A Shotgun	10
80	Flamingo FM-11	Live For Love/If I love You	50

ISLA CAMERON

(see also Ewan MacColl)

64	Transatlantic TRAEP 109	LOST LOVE (EP)	25

JOHN CAMERON (QUARTET)

(see also Frog)

67	Columbia DB 8120	You Owe Me/Walk Small (solo)	8
69	Deram DM 256	Troublemaker/Off Centre	90
67	Columbia SCX 6116	COVER LOVER (LP)	25
69	Deram DML/SML 1044	OFF CENTRE (LP)	70

JOHNNY CAMERON

60	Top Rank JAR 396	I Double Dare You/Fantasy	12

RAY CAMERON

67	Island WIP 6003	Doin' My Time/Getaway, Getaway Car	12

TONY CAMILLO

75	A&M AMLH 63406	BAZUKA (LP)	12

AL CAMPBELL

78	Chanan Jah TUFF 12	Sister Soul/Footstool	30
78	Deb DEB 018	Love The Way It Should Be/Version (12")	20
79	Nigara NADD 103	La-La Means I Love You (12")	40
80	Strong Like Sampson SLSD 14	Jah Shine On Me/SUGAR MINOTT: Halk Of Love (12")	35
80	JB JBD 019	You Jamming/You Jamming (Part 2) (12")	20
81	JB JBD 029	feedback/Part 2 (12")	25
78	ITAL IT001	LOVING MOODS OF (LP)	25
79	Burning Sounds BS 1036	DIAMONDS (LP)	20
79	Hawkeye HLD 03	RAINY DAYS (LP)	50
80	JB JBLP 002	LATE NIGHT BLUES (LP)	30
80	JB JBLP 005	WORKING MAN (LP)	35

AL CAMPBELL & TRINITY

78	Deb DEB 013	Reggae Dance/Dragon Dance/AL CAMPBELL: Roots Man Style (12")	20

ALEX CAMPBELL

(see also Sandy Denny)

65	Transatlantic TRASP 4	Been On The Road So Long/The Night Visiting Song (in p/s)	10
65	Transatlantic TRASP 4	Been On The Road So Long/The Night Visiting Song	6
68	Saga OPP 2	Victoria Dines Alone/Pack Up Your Sorrows	30
63	Society SOC 960	FOLK SESSION (LP)	12
64	Xtra XTRA 1064	ALEX CAMPBELL (LP, with Martin Carthy)	25
65	Polydor 623 035	IN COPENHAGEN (LP)	18
67	Saga ERO 8021	ALEX CAMPBELL AND HIS FRIENDS (LP, with Sandy Denny)	25
71	Ad-Rhythm/Tepee ARPS 1	THIS IS ALEX CAMPBELL VOL. 1 (LP)	30
71	Ad-Rhythm/Tepee ARPS 2	THIS IS ALEX CAMPBELL VOL. 2 (LP)	30
71	Boulevard 4007	16 BEST LOVED SONGS OF BONNIE SCOTLAND (LP)	15
72	Boulevard 4073	AT HIS BEST (LP)	20
76	Look LKLP 6043	NO REGRETS (LP)	12
79	Burlington BURL 002	ALEX CAMPBELL, ALAN ROBERTS AND DOUGIE MACLEAN (LP)	12
87	Sundown SDLP 2048	WITH THE GREATEST RESPECT (2-LP, reissue of "This Is..." Vols. 1 & 2)	18

AMBROSE CAMPBELL

66	Columbia SX 6081	HIGH LIFE TODAY (LP)	75

BILL & PETE CAMPBELL

71	Duke DU 123	Come On Home Girl/You Are Mine	7

CAT CAMPBELL & NICKY THOMAS

72	Pressure Beat PB 5511	Hammering/PETER TOSH: Medicine Man	20

CHOKER CAMPBELL

65	Tamla Motown TMG 517	Mickey's Monkey/Pride And Joy (as Choker Campbell's Big Band)	150

			MINT VALUE £
65	Tamla Motown TMG 517	Mickey's Monkey/Pride And Joy (as Choker Campbell's Big Band) (DJ copy)	250
65	Tamla Motown TML 11011	HITS OF THE SIXTIES (LP, as Choker Campbell & His 16-Piece Band)	125

CORNELL CAMPBELL

(see also Eternals, Don Cornel & Eternals, Clarendonians, Charmers, Stranger & Patsy, GG Allstars)

63	Island WI 039	Rosabelle/Turndown Date (B-side actually "Under The Old Oak Tree")	30
63	Island WI 083	Each Lonely Night/ROLAND ALPHONSO: Steamline	20
64	Port-O-Jam PJ 4008	Jericho Road (with Dimple Hinds)/DON DRUMMOND & GROUP: Roll On Sweet Don	60
64	Rio R 38	Gloria/I'll Be True	25
72	Dynamic DYN 446	My Confession/AGGROVATORS: Version	12
72	Green Door GD 4042	Dearest Darling/Star Dust	15
72	Jackpot JP 801	Queen And The Minstrel/Put Yourself In My Place	12
72	Bullet BU 515	For Once In My Life/Didn't I?	15
73	Jackpot JP 809	Pity The Children/You're No Good	15
73	Jackpot JP 814	Harry Hippy/Just One Kiss	6
73	Green Door GD 4057	Give Me Love/Help Them O Lord	12
73	Duke DU 158	Shotgun Wedding/Girl Of My Dreams	10
73	Duke DU 159	The Very Best I Can/Heading For The Mountains	6
73	Ackee ACK 513	Give Me A Love/SHORTY PERRY: Message Of Love	6
75	Action ACT 102	Natty In A Greenwich Farm/Natty Version	10
75	Angen ANG 101	Talking Love/AGGROVATORS: Gorgon Dub	10
75	Angen ANG 105	The Gorgon Speaks/AGGROVATORS: Version	10
76	Angen ANG 122	A Tear Fell/My True Destination	6
76	Attack ATT 8125	I Will Never Change/Version	6
70s	Rocket VR 001	Many Rivers To Cross/Many Dub	8
76	Daddy Kool DK001	I Heart Is Clean/KING TUBBY AND THE OBSERVERS : Zinc Fence	10
77	Nationwide 1018	Let Me Go Girl/Version	7
77	Terminal TM 104	I Am A King/Watch And Peep	10
78	D-Roy 3	Listen Dread/Version	8
78	Third World 7529	Blessed Are They/New York City (With I ROY)	8
80	Cha Cha CHAD25	Rainbow/PETER BROGGS: Never Forget Jah (12")	30
80s	Live & Love LLDIS0022	Nothing Don't Come Easy/Version (12")	20
80	Papa D PD0167	Rasta Come From Jail (with SASSAFRASS)/100 Pounds of Collie (with PAPA TULLO)	18
72	Trojan TBL 199	CORNELL CAMPBELL (LP)	40
75	Groundnation GROL 503	DANCE IN A GREENWICH FARM (LP)	40
76	Third World	STALOWATT (LP)	25
76	Angen ANGL 03	GORGON (LP)	30
78	Justice JUSLP 09	ROPIN (LP)	25
79	Striker Lee TSL 104	NATTY DREAD IN A GREENWICH FARM (LP)	40
79	Burning Sounds BS 1034	SWEET BABY (LP)	18

DAVID CAMPBELL

67	Transatlantic TRA 141	DAVID CAMPBELL (LP)	25
72	Decca SKL 5139	SUN WHEEL (LP)	18

ERROL CAMPBELL

76	Shebazz SHE 001	Wolves/Follow	30

ETHNA CAMPBELL

64	Mercury MF 804	What's Easy For Two Is Hard For One/Again	20
64	Mercury MF 816	Girls Like Boys/Five Minutes More	10
60s	Philips 6382138	FOR THE GOOD TIMES (LP)	15

GLEN CAMPBELL

(see also Sagittarius, Jimmy Slade)

61	Top Rank JAR 596	Turn Around, Look At Me/Brenda	15
62	Capitol CL 15268	Too Late To Worry, Too Blue To Cry/How Do I Tell My Heart Not To Break?	8
62	Capitol CL 15278	Here I Am/Long Black Limousine	8
63	Capitol CL 15295	Prima Donna/Oh My Darling	8
67	Speciality SPE 1002	Satisfied Mind/Can't You See I'm Trying	7
67	Ember EMB S 249	By The Time I Get To Phoenix/Burning Bridges/Gentle On My Mind (p/s)	8
67	Ember EMB S 249	By The Time I Get To Phoenix/Burning Bridges/Gentle On My Mind	5
68	Ember EMB S 252	I Wanna Live/Hey Little One	5
68	Ember EMB S 255	Dreams Of The Everyday Housewife/Combine	5
68	Ember EMB S 258	Straight Life/That's Not Home	5
69	Ember EMB S 261	Wichita Lineman/Back In The Race (p/s)	8
69	Ember EMB S 261	Wichita Lineman/Back In The Race	5
69	Ember EMB S 263	Galveston/Everytime I Itch I Wind Up Scratching You (p/s)	8
69	Ember EMB S 263	Galveston/Everytime I Itch I Wind Up Scratching You	5
69	Capitol CL 15615	True Grit/Hava Nagila	5
66	London HA-F/SH-F 8291	SWINGING 12-STRING (LP)	15

IAN CAMPBELL (FOLK) GROUP

(see also Dave Swarbrick)

63	Topic STOP 102	The Sun Is Burning/The Crow On The Cradle (in title p/s)	15
63	Topic STOP 102	The Sun Is Burning/The Crow On The Cradle	7
64	Decca F 11802	Marilyn Monroe/The Bells Of Rhymney	7
65	Transatlantic TRASP 2	Kelly From Killane/Boys Of Wexford (with Boys From Wexford)	7
65	Transatlantic TRASP 5	The Times They Are A-Changin'/Across The Hills (in p/s)	20
65	Transatlantic TRASP 5	The Times They Are A-Changin'/Across The Hills	12
66	Transatlantic TRASP 6	Come Kiss Me/The First Time I Ever Saw Your Face (in p/s)	12
66	Transatlantic TRASP 6	Come Kiss Me/The First Time I Ever Saw Your Face	7
66	Transatlantic TRASP 7	Guantanamera/Mary Anne	6
66	Transatlantic TRASP 10	One Eyed Reilly/Snow Is Falling (solo)	6
67	Big T BIG 103	Lover Let Me In/Private Harold Harris (as Ian Campbell Four)	6
69	Major Minor MM 639	Break My Mind/Govan Cross Special (solo)	6
62	Topic TOP 82	SONGS OF PROTEST (EP)	15

			MINT VALUE £
64	Decca DFE 8592	IAN CAMPBELL FOLK GROUP (EP)	15
65	Transatlantic TRAEP 128	SAMPLER (EP)	12
63	Transatlantic TRA 110	THIS IS THE IAN CAMPBELL FOLK GROUP (LP)	40
64	Transatlantic TRA 118	ACROSS THE HILLS (LP)	30
67	Transatlantic TRA 151	NEW IMPRESSIONS (LP)	15
68	Transatlantic TRA 163	THE CIRCLE GAME (LP)	20
68	Xtra XTRA 1074	TAM O'SHANTER (LP, as Ian Campbell & John Dunkerley)	18
69	Transatlantic TRASAM 4	THE IAN CAMPBELL FOLK GROUP SAMPLER (LP)	12
69	Transatlantic TRASAM 12	SAMPLER 2 (LP, as Ian Campbell Folk Four)	12
69	Major Minor 602 204	CAMPBELL COUNTRY 'N' SOUL (LP)	12
69	MFP SMFP 1349	IAN CAMPBELL & FOLK GROUP WITH DAVE SWARBRICK (LP)	12
71	Acorn CF 233	HOPE IS A STAR (LP)	40
71	Argo ZFB 13	THE SUN IS BURNING (LP)	30
72	Pye PKL 5506	SOMETHING TO SING ABOUT (LP)	15

JIMMY CAMPBELL

(see also Kirkbys, 23rd Turnoff, Rockin' Horse)

69	Fontana TF 1009	On A Monday/Dear Marge (in p/s)	10
69	Fontana TF 1009	On A Monday/Dear Marge	6
70	Fontana TF 1076	Lyanna/Frankie Joe	6
70	Fontana 6007 025	Don't Leave Me Now/So Lonely Without You	6
69	Fontana STL 5508	SON OF ANASTASIA (LP, black/silver label)	60
70	Vertigo 6360 010	HALF BAKED (LP, gatefold sleeve, large swirl label)	60
72	Philips 6308 100	JIMMY CAMPBELL'S ALBUM (LP, black/silver label)	80

JO-ANN CAMPBELL

58	London HLU 8536	Wait A Minute/It's True	60
58	London HLU 8536	Wait A Minute/It's True (78)	25
60	HMV POP 776	Bobby, Bobby, Bobby/A Kookie Little Paradise	20
61	HMV POP 873	Motorcycle Michael/Puka Puka Pants	20
62	HMV POP 1003	You Made Me Love You/I Changed My Mind Jack	20
62	Columbia DB 4889	I'm The Girl From Wolverton Mountain/Sloppy Joe	10
62	Cameo Parkway CP 237	Mr Fix It Man/Let Me Do It My Way	12
63	Cameo Parkway CP 249	Mother Please/Waiting For Love	12

JUNIOR CAMPBELL

(see also Marmalade, Clan, Dean Ford & Gaylords)

74	Deram SML 1106	SECOND TIME AROUND (LP)	12

LLOYD CAMPBELL

76	Love LOV 2	FIGHTING DUB (LP)	35

MICHAEL CAMPBELL

(see Dread At The Controls)

PAT CAMPBELL

69	Major Minor MM 648	The Deal/The Mission	6

ROY CAMPBELL (& JAZZBO JASPERS)

68	Giant GN 41	Another Saturday Night/Wonderful World (with Jazzbo Jaspers)	7
68	Jolly JY 003	Suzette/Engine Engine Number Nine	7

CAMPBELL FAMILY

65	Topic 12T 120	THE SINGING CAMPBELLS - TRADITIONS OF AN ABERDEEN FAMILY (LP, blue label)	15

PATRICK CAMPBELL-LYONS

(see also Nirvana [U.K.], Pica, Hat & Tie, Aquila)

73	Sovereign SOV 115	Everybody Should Fly A Kite/I Think I Want Him Too	15
73	Sovereign SOV 119	Out On The Road/Me And My Friend	15
77	Electric WOT 12	That's What My Guru Said Last Night/The Whistling Fiddler	5
73	Sovereign SVNA 7258	ME AND MY FRIEND (LP, gatefold sleeve)	300
81	Public PUBL 1	THE ELECTRIC PLOUGH (LP)	25

RAY CAMPI

74	Injun EP 200	ROCK 'N' ROLL (EP)	12

CAN

73	United Artists UP 35506	Spoon/I'm So Green	15
73	United Artists UP 35596	Moonshake/Future Days (Edit)	12
74	United Artists UP 35749	Dizzy Dizzy (Edit)/Splash (Edit)	10
76	Virgin VS 153	I Want More/... And More	7
76	Virgin VS 166	Silent Night/Cascade Waltz	5
77	Virgin VS 172	Don't Say No/Return	5
78	Lightning LIG 545	Can-Can/Can Be	5
69	United Artists UAS 29094	MONSTER MOVIE (LP, burgundy label)	70
70	United Artists UAS 29283	SOUNDTRACKS (LP)	40
71	Utd. Artists UAD 60009/10	TAGO MAGO (2-LP, flip-top sleeve)	70
72	United Artists UAS 29414	EGE BAMYASI (LP, with inner sleeve)	45
73	United Artists UAS 29505	FUTURE DAYS (LP)	20
74	United Artists UAG 29673	SOON OVER BABALUMA (LP, original silver sleeve)	25
74	United Artists USP 103	LIMITED EDITION (LP)	40
75	Virgin V 2041	LANDED (LP)	15
76	Caroline CAD 3001	UNLIMITED EDITION (2-LP, gatefold sleeve)	20
76	Sunset SLS 50400	OPENER (LP)	15
76	Virgin V2071	FLOW MOTION (LP)	15
77	Virgin V 2079	SAW DELIGHT (LP, with insert)	15
78	United Artists UDM 105/6	CANNABALISM (2-LP, gatefold sleeve)	20
89	Mercury 838883	RITE TIME (LP)	18

CANAAN

73	Dovetail DOVE 3	CANAAN (LP)	25
76	Myrrh MYR 1042	OUT OF THE WILDERNESS (LP, with inner sleeve)	20

MINT VALUE £

LOS CANARIOS
67	Major Minor MM 502	Three Two One Ah/What Can I Do For You	25
67	Major Minor MM 532	Get On Your Knees/Keep On The Right Side	40

CANDIDO
57	HMV DLP 1182	THE VOLCANIC (10" LP)	20

CANDLE FACTORY
70s	CAVS	NIGHTSHIFT (LP, private pressing)	55

CANDLELIGHT
67	CBS 2002507	That's What I Want/The Happy Days Of Summer	20

CANDLEMASS
03	Powerline PRLP 010	DIAMONDS OF DOOM (2-LP, white vinyl, gatefold sleeve with iron-one transfer, 1000 only)	20

CANDLEWICK GREEN
73	Decca FR 13480	Who Do You Think You Are?/Fingers In Your Ears	5

PETER CANDOLI & HIS ORCHESTRA
56	Capitol CL 14615	St. Louis Blues - Boogie/The Big Top (Entry Of The Gladiators)	10
60	Warner Bros WB 2	Sunset Strip Cha-Cha/DON RALKE: 77 Sunset Strip	5

CONTE CANDOLI
56	London Jazz LZ-N 14010	SINCERELY, CONTE (10" LP)	15

CANDY
69	Emerald MD 1119	Little Bit Of Soul/Signs Of Love	10
69	Grape GR 3017	Ace Of Hearts/BILLY JACK: Bet Yer Life I Do	20
70	Big Shot BI 599	Ace Of Hearts/BILLY JACK: Bet Your Life	10

CANDY CHOIR
(see also Summer Set, Barry Ryan)

66	Parlophone R 5472	Silence Is Golden/Shake Hands (And Come Out Crying)	15
67	CBS 3061	Children And Flowers/Marianne	10
68	CBS 3305	Alexander's Ragtime Band/No Grey Skies	10
70	Polydor 56369	Why Do You Cry My Love/Lucky Jim	5

CANDY DATES
65	Pye 7N 15944	A Day Just Like That/Well I Do	10

CANDY FLOSS
72	Polydor 2041360	Delta Queen/Looking Over My Shoulder	8

CANDY & KISSES
65	Cameo Parkway C 336	The 81/Two Happy People	80
65	Cameo Parkway C 336	The 81/Two Happy People (DJ copy)	150
85	Kent TOWN 104	Mr Creator/CHUCK JACKSON: Hand It Over (withdrawn)	50

CANDYMEN
67	HMV POP 1612	Georgia Pines/Movies In My Mind	10

PENNY CANDY
60	Top Rank JAR 328	Come On Over/They Said	10

CANDY ROCK
75	Philips 6006 442	Captain Captain/Pocahontas	6

CANE
78	Lightning GIL 31	3 BY 3 EP (p/s)	15

CANIS MAJOR
(see also Girlschool)

80	Gem GEMLP 109	BUTTERFLY QUEEN (LP)	30

BOB CANN
70s	Topic 12TS 275	WEST COUNTRY MELODEON (LP)	18

CANNED HEAT
(see also Harvey Mandel, John Lee Hooker)

68	Liberty	Rollin' And Tumblin'/Bullfrog Blues (unreleased)	0
68	Liberty LBF 15090	On The Road Again/The World In A Jug	8
69	Liberty LBF 15169	Going Up The Country/One Kind Favour	8
69	Liberty LBF 15200	Time Was/Low Down	8
69	Liberty LBF 15255	Poor Moon/Sic 'Em Pigs	8
69	Liberty LBF 15302	Let's Work Together/I'm Her Man	8
70	Liberty LBF 15350	Sugar Bee/Shake It And Break It	8
70	Pye International 7N 25513	Spoonful/Big Road Blues	8
70	Liberty LBF 15395	Future Blues/Skat	6
70	Liberty LBF 15429	Christmas Blues/Do Not Enter	6
71	Liberty LBF 15439	Wooly Bully/My Time Ain't Long	6
72	United Artists UP 35348	Rockin' With The King (with Little Richard)/I Don't Care What You Tell Me	6
73	United Artists UP 35562	Keep It Clean/You Can Run But You Sure Can't Hide	6
76	United Artists REM 407	CANNED HEAT (EP)	10
67	Liberty LBL/LBS 83059E	CANNED HEAT (LP)	35
68	Liberty LBL/LBS 83103	BOOGIE WITH CANNED HEAT (LP)	30
69	Liberty LDS 84001E	LIVING THE BLUES (2-LP, gatefold sleeve)	30
69	Liberty LBS 83239	HALLELUJAH (LP, gatefold sleeve)	20
70	Pye Intl. NSPL 28129	VINTAGE HEAT (LP)	30
70	Liberty LBS 83303	CANNED HEAT COOKBOOK (LP)	15
70	Liberty LBS 83333	CANNED HEAT '70 CONCERT (RECORDED LIVE IN EUROPE) (LP, g/fold sleeve)	12
70	Liberty LBS 83364	FUTURE BLUES (LP, gatefold sleeve)	18
71	Liberty LPS 103/4	HOOKER'N'HEAT (2-LP, gatefold sleeve, with John Lee Hooker)	35
72	United Artists UAG 29304	HISTORICAL FIGURES AND ANCIENT HEADS (LP, gatefold sleeve)	12
73	United Artists UAS 29455	THE NEW AGE (LP)	12

MINT VALUE £

CANNIBAL & HEADHUNTERS

65	Stateside SS 403	Land Of A Thousand Dances/I'll Show You How To Love Me	30
67	CBS 62942	LAND OF A 1000 DANCES (LP)	40

CANNIBALS

(see also Count Bishops)

78	Big Cock F-UK 1	Good Guys/Nothing Takes The Place Of You (printed paper bag sleeve)	5
85	Hit Records REEBEE 2	Christmas Rock 'n' Roll/New Year's Eve Song (doublepack in stocking)	6

ACE CANNON

62	London HLU 9498	Tuff/Sittin'	7
62	London HLU 9546	Blues Stay Away From Me/Blues In My Heart	7
63	London HLU 9745	Cottonfields/Mildew	7
64	London HLU 9866	Searchin'/Love Letters In The Sand	7
67	London HLU 10105	Wonderland By Night/As Time Goes By	5
70	London HA-U/SH-U 8407	ACE OF SAX (LP)	20

FREDDY CANNON

(see also Danny & Juniors)

59	Top Rank JAR 135	Tallahassee Lassie/You Know	12
59	Top Rank JAR 135	Tallahassee Lassie/You Know (78)	30
59	Top Rank JAR 207	Okefenokee/Kookie Hat	12
59	Top Rank JAR 247	Way Down Yonder In New Orleans/Fractured	6
60	Top Rank JAR 309	California, Here I Come/Indiana	5
60	Top Rank JAR 334	Chattanooga Shoeshine Boy/Boston (My Home Town)	10
60	Top Rank JAR 369	The Urge/Jump Over	8
60	Top Rank JAR 407	Happy Shades Of Blue/Guernavaca Choo Choo	10
60	Top Rank JAR 518	Humdinger/My Blue Heaven	10
61	Top Rank JAR 548	Muskrat Rumble/Two Thousand 88	8
61	Top Rank JAR 568	Buzz Buzz A Diddle It/Opportunity	20
61	Top Rank JAR 579	Transistor Sister/Walk To The Moon	12
61	Top Rank JAR 592	For Me And My Gal/Blue Plate Special	10
62	Top Rank JAR 609	Teen Queen Of The Week/Wild Guy	10
62	Stateside SS 101	Palisades Park/June July And August	8
62	Stateside SS 118	What's Gonna Happen When Summer's Done/Broadway	10
62	Stateside SS 134	If You Were A Rock & Roll Record/The Truth Ruth	20
63	Stateside SS 155	Come On And Love Me/Four Letter Man	10
63	Stateside SS 183	The Ups And Downs Of Love/It's Been Nice	10
63	Stateside SS 201	Patty Baby/Betty Jean	20
63	Stateside SS 220	Everybody Monkey/Oh Gloria	7
64	Stateside SS 260	That's The Way Girls Are/Do What The Hippies Do	7
64	Warner Bros WB 123	Abigail Beecher/All American Girl	7
64	Stateside SS 298	Sweet Georgia Brown/What A Party	7
65	Warner Bros WB 5645	Action/Beechwood City	10
66	Warner Bros WB 5693	The Dedication Song/Come On Come On	8
69	London HLK 10252	Beautiful Downtown Burbank/If You Give Me A Title	7
79	Hot Rock 003	Hey Punk Rocker/At The Disco Down	7
60	Top Rank JKP 2058	THE EXPLOSIVE FREDDY (BOOM! BOOM!) CANNON (EP)	40
60	Top Rank JKP 2066	FOUR DIRECT HITS (EP)	30
61	Top Rank JKP 3010	ON TARGET (EP)	30
62	Stateside SE 1002	BLAST OFF WITH FREDDY CANNON (EP)	40
60	Top Rank 25/018	THE EXPLOSIVE FREDDY CANNON (LP)	30
61	Top Rank 35/106	FREDDY CANNON SINGS HAPPY SHADES OF BLUE (LP)	45
61	Top Rank 35/113	FREDDY CANNON FAVOURITES (LP)	45
63	Stateside SL 10013	BANG ON (LP)	45
64	Stateside SL 10062	STEPS OUT (LP)	50
64	Warner Bros WM/WS 8153	FREDDY CANNON (LP)	30

JUDY CANNON

65	Pye 7N 15900	The Very First Day I Met You/Hello Heartache	50

SEAN CANNON

77	Cottage COT 411	ROVING JOURNEYMAN (LP)	30

CONROY CANNON

69	Pama PM 769	Oh Happy Day/Can't Get Along Without You	8

CANNON BALL & JOHNNY MELODY

(see also Carl Bryan, King Cannon, Johnny Moore, Jackie Mittoo, Royals)

69	Big Shot BI 518	Parapinto/Cool Hand Luke	15

CANNONBALLS

61	Coral Q 72428	Cannonball Caboose/New Orleans Beat	10
61	Coral Q 72431	Lullaby Of Birdland/Calliope Boogie	10

CANNON BROTHERS

65	Brit WI 1003	Turn Your Eyes To Me/Don't Stop Now	18

CANNONS

60	Decca F 11269	I Didn't Know The Gun Was Loaded/My Guy's Come Back	15
61	Columbia DB 4724	Bush Fire/Juicy	20

CANNON'S JUG STOMPERS

66	Tax LP 2	CANNON'S JUG STOMPERS/ CLIFFORD'S LOUISVILLE JUG BAND (LP, 1 side each)	20

CANNY FETTLE

75	Tradition TSR 023	VARRY CANNY (LP)	30
77	Tradition TSR 027	TRIP TO HARROGATE (LP)	18

CANYON

75	RCA RCA 2112	Top Of The World/Boogie Down Broadway	8

MINT VALUE £

CAPABILITY BROWN
(see also Unit 4+2, Tony Rivers & Castaways, Fuzzy Duck)

72	Charisma CB 193	Wake Up Little Sister/Windfall	6
73	Charisma CB 207	Midnight Cruiser/Silent Sounds	6
73	Charisma CB 217	Liar/Keep Death Off The Road (Drive On The Pavement)	6
70s	Charisma BCP 7	War (p/s)	6
72	Charisma CAS 1056	FROM SCRATCH (LP, lyric inner sleeve, pink 'scroll' label)	40
73	Charisma CAS 1068	VOICE (LP, gatefold sleeve, large 'Mad Hatter' label)	25

JIM CAPALDI
(see also Hellions, Traffic)

74	Island WIP 6198	It's All Up To You/Whale Meat Again	5
72	Island ILPS 9187	OH HOW WE DANCED (LP, gatefold sleeve, pink rim label)	25
74	Island ILPS 9254	WHALE MEAT AGAIN (LP, pink rim label)	15
77	Island ILPS 9497	PLAY IT BY EAR (LP)	15

CAPE KENNEDY CONSTRUCTION CO.

69	President PT 265	The First Steps On The Moon/Armageddon	120

CAPERCAILLIE
(see also Etives)

84	Etive/SRT 4KL 178	CASCADE (LP)	12
87	Grampian TV GPN 1001	THE BLOOD IS STRONG (LP, with insert)	12
87	Green Linnet SIF 1077	CROSSWINDS (LP, with insert)	12

CAPES & MASKS

65	Fontana TL 5339	COMIC BOOK HEROES (LP)	50
65	Nevis NEV R005	COMIC BOOK HEROES (LP)	18

CAPES OF GOOD HOPE

66	Stateside SS 577	Winter's Children/If My Monique Could Only Dance	15

CAPITAL LETTERS

77	Greensleeves GRED 2	Smoking My Ganja/Natty Walk (12")	40
79	Greensleeves GRED 16	UK Skanking/Run Run Run (12")	35
79	Greensleeves GREL 7	HEADLINE NEWS (LP)	25

CAPITOL K

99	Planet Mu ZIQ 015	Postcard/JEGA: Untitled (100 in numbered p/s, those un-numbered = £4)	10

CAPITOL SHOWBAND

67	Marble Arch MAL 694	THE CAPITOL SHOWBAND (LP)	12

CAPITOLS (U.K.)

66	Pye 7N 17025	Honey And Wine/Boulavogue	12

CAPITOLS (U.S.)
(see also Three Caps)

66	Atlantic 584 004	Cool Jerk/Hello Stranger	20

CAPOEIRA TWINS

99	Blowpop Records BLOWP 001	4 x 3 (12")	15
00	FFRR FX 385	Four (4x3) (12")	8

ANDY CAPP

69	Treasure Isle TI 7052	Pop-A-Top/RICO: The Lion Speaks	12
70	Duke DU 69	The Law Parts 1 & 2	18
70	Duke DU 71	Poppy Show/Pop-A-Top (Part 2)	12

AL CAPPS

73	Stateside SS 2214	Shangri-La/Magician	10

DANNY CAPRI

55	Capitol CL 14265	Desirable/I Do, I Do	12
55	Capitol CL 14302	Don't Make A Liar Out Of Me/Angelica	15

CAPRICORN
(see also Marty Wilde)

70	MCA MK 5050	Liverpool Hello/How Did You Find Me	6

CAPRIS

61	Columbia DB 4605	There's A Moon Out Tonight/Indian Girl	100

CAPTAIN BEEFHEART & HIS MAGIC BAND
(see also Mu, Frank Zappa, Jack Nitzsche)

SINGLES

68	Pye International 7N 25443	Yellow Brick Road/Abba Zabba	35
68	A&M AMS 726	Moonchild/Who Do You Think You're Fooling	30
73	Reprise K 14233	Too Much Time/My Head Is My Only House Unless It Rains	12
74	Virgin VS 110	Upon The My-Oh-My/Magic Be	5
78	Buddah BDS 466	Sure 'Nuff 'N Yes I Do/Electricity	7
78	MCA MCA 366	Hard Workin' Man (Jack Nitzsche featuring Captain Beefheart)/ JACK NITZSCHE: Coke Machine	6
82	Virgin VS 534	Ice Cream For Crow/Light Reflected Off The Oceans Of The Moon	10

EPs

71	A&M AME 600	DIDDY WAH DIDDY (promo only)	250
79	Virgin SIXPACK 1	SIX-PACK/SIX TRACK (picture disc, die-cut p/s with stand, 5,000 only)	18
82	Virgin VS 534 12	LIGHT REFLECTED OFF THE OCEANS OF THE MOON (12" EP, p/s)	12
84	A&M AMY 226	THE LEGENDARY A&M SESSIONS (12" EP/mini-LP, Diddy Wah Diddy EP plus "Where I Am, I Always Am")	15
86	Edsel BLIMP 902	THE LEGENDARY A&M SESSIONS (12" EP, reissue)	15

LPs

68	Pye Intl. NPL 28110	SAFE AS MILK (mono, flipback sleeve)	80

			MINT VALUE £
68	Liberty LBL 83172	STRICTLY PERSONAL (gatefold sleeve, mono)	45
68	Liberty LBS 83172	STRICTLY PERSONAL (gatefold sleeve, stereo)	35
69	Straight STS 1053	TROUT MASK REPLICA (2-LP, gatefold sleeve)	60
69	Buddah 623171	SAFE AS MILK (LP, reissue, stereo)	40
69	Pye/Marble Arch MAL 1117	SAFE AS MILK (LP, reissue, mono)	40
70	Straight STS 1063	LICK MY DECALS OFF, BABY	60
70	Buddah 2349 002	DROPOUT BOOGIE (stereo reissue of "Safe As Milk")	20
71	Buddah 2365 002	MIRROR MAN (gatefold die-cut sleeve)	35
71	Sunset SLS50208	STRICTLY PERSONAL (LP, reissue)	12
72	Reprise K 44162	THE SPOTLIGHT KID (tan 'riverboat' label, with lyric card insert)	30
72	Reprise K 44162	THE SPOTLIGHT KID (tan 'riverboat' label, without lyric card insert)	15
72	Reprise K 54007	CLEAR SPOT (PVC sleeve with card insert)	30
73	Reprise K 44244	LICK MY DECALS OFF, BABY	18
74	Virgin V 2015	UNCONDITIONALLY GUARANTEED ('two virgins' label)	20
74	Virgin V 2023	BLUEJEANS & MOONBEAMS ('two virgins' label)	20
74	Buddah BDLP 4004	MIRROR MAN	20
75	Reprise K 64026	TROUT MASK REPLICA (2-LP, gatefold sleeve, tan 'riverboat' label, matt sleeve)	30
76	Reprise K 84006	TWO ORIGINALS OF CAPTAIN BEEFHEART (2-LP, reissue of Lick My Decals Off, Baby & "The Spotlight Kid")	20
77	Pye FILD 008	THE FILE SERIES (2-LP, reissue of "Safe As Milk" & "Mirror Man", die-cut sleeve with inners)	18
79	Virgin V 2149	SHINY BEAST (BAT CHAIN PULLER)	20
70s	Reprise K 64026	TROUT MASK REPLICA (2-LP, gatefold sleeve, 2nd re-pressing, tan 'riverboat' label, soft laminated sleeve)	20
80	Virgin V 2172	DOC AT THE RADAR STATION	20
82	Virgin V 2237	ICE CREAM FOR CROW (with inner sleeve)	12
99	Buddah 91751	SAFE AS MILK (2-LP reissue)	20

CAPTAIN BEYOND

(see also Deep Purple)

72	Capricorn K 47503	CAPTAIN BEYOND (LP)	25

CAPTAIN LOCKHEED & THE STARFIGHTERS

(see also Robert Calvert)

73	United Artists UP 35543	Ejection/Catch A Falling Starfighter (p/s)	25
73	United Artists UP 35543	Ejection/Catch A Falling Starfighter (different mix of A-side, no p/s)	10

CAPTAIN MARRYAT

74	Thor THOR 1007 S	CAPTAIN MARRYAT (LP, 200 only)	2000

CAPTAIN ROCK & SKYRIDERS

72	Crystal CR 7028	Luppy Lu/Together	8

CAPTAIN SCARLET

(see under Century 21)

CAPTAIN SINBAD

83	Oak Sound OSLP 002	AGAIN (LP)	30
84	Greensleeves GREL 34	THE SEVEN VOYAGES OF SINBAD (LP)	35

CAPTAIN SKIDLID

72	RCA RCA 2173	Charlie Brown/She Knew Him Too	6

C.A. QUINTET

83	Psycho PSYCHO 12	TRIP THROUGH HELL (LP, reissue of U.S. 60s LP)	15

CARAVAN

(see also Gringo, Matching Mole, Hatfield & The North, Spiro Gyra)

69	Verve VS 1518	A Place Of My Own/Ride	45
70	Decca F 13063	If I Could Do It All Over Again, I'd Do It All Over You/Hello, Hello	20
71	Decca F 23125	Love To Love You (And Tonight Pigs Will Fly)/Golf Girl	20
75	Decca FR 13599	Stuck In A Hole/Lover	5
76	BTM SBT 104	All The Way (With John Wayne's Single-Handed Liberation Of Paris)/ Chiefs And Indians (p/s)	6
77	Arista ARIST 110	Better By Far/Silver Strings	5
80	Kingdom KV 8009	Heartbreaker/It's Never Too Late (p/s)	6
68	Verve VLP 6011	CARAVAN (LP, 'pillar' sleeve, mono, brown/white label, with "Sold in the U.K." text)	350
68	Verve SVLP 6011	CARAVAN (LP, 'pillar' sleeve, stereo)	250
70	Decca SKL 5052	IF I COULD DO IT ALL OVER AGAIN, I'D DO IT ALL OVER YOU (LP, boxed logo)	40
71	Deram SDL-R 1	IN THE LAND OF GREY AND PINK (LP, gatefold sleeve, 1st pressing with brown/white label)	60
71	Deram SDL-R 1	IN THE LAND OF GREY AND PINK (LP, gatefold sleeve, later pressing with red/white label)	20
72	Deram SDL 8	WATERLOO LILY (LP, gatefold sleeve, 1st pressing brown/white large Deram labels. SDL8 on sleeve and label)	80
72	Deram SDL 8	WATERLOO LILY (LP, gatefold sleeve, later pressing with red/white labels and SDL-R 8 on labels and sleeves)	20
72	MGM 2353 058	CARAVAN (LP, reissue)	18
73	Deram SDL-R 12	FOR GIRLS WHO GROW PLUMP IN THE NIGHT (LP, gatefold sleeve, red/white label)	30
74	Deram SML-R 1110	CARAVAN AND THE NEW SYMPHONIA (LIVE AT DRURY LANE) (LP, red/white label)	20
75	Decca SKL-R 5210	CUNNING STUNTS (LP)	20
76	BTM BTM 1007	BLIND DOG AT ST. DUNSTAN'S (LP)	15
80	Kingdom KVL 9003	THE ALBUM (LP, laminated sleeve)	20

CARAVELLES

(see also Lois Lane)

63	Decca F 11697	You Don't Have To Be A Baby To Cry/The Last One To Know	5
63	Decca F 11758	I Really Don't Want To Know/I Was Wrong	5
64	Decca F 11816	Have You Ever Been Lonely?/Gonna Get Along Without Ya Now	5

			MINT VALUE £
64	Fontana TF 466	You Are Here/How Can I Be Sure?	6
64	Fontana TF 509	I Don't Care If The Sun Don't Shine/I Like A Man	6
64	Polydor NH 59034	True Love Never Runs Smooth/Georgia Boy	7
66	Polydor 56137	Hey Mama You've Been On My Mind/New York	10
67	Polydor 56156	I Want To Love You Again/I Had To Walk Home Myself	7
68	Pye 7N 17654	The Other Side Of Love/I Hear A New Kind Of Music	8
63	Decca LK 4565	THE CARAVELLES (LP)	35

GUY CARAWAN
(see also Peggy Seeger & Guy Carawan)

58	Pye Nixa 7N 15132	Old Man Atom (Talking Atomic Blues)/Michael Row The Boat Ashore	8
60	Collector JEA 4	SONGS FROM THE SOUTH (EP)	12
58	Topic 10T 24	MOUNTAIN SONGS AND BANJO TUNES (10" LP)	30
57	77 Records LP8	GUY CARAWAN, HIS BANJO AND GUITAR (10" LP)	50
67	Columbia SX 6065	A GUY CALLED CARAVAN (LP)	30

CARCASS

88	Earache MOSH 06	REEK OF PUTREFACTION (LP)	25
89	Earache MOSH 18	SYMPHONIES OF SICKNESS (LP, picture disc)	25
91	Earache MOSH 42	NECROTICISM - DESCANTING THE INSALUBRIOUS (LP)	30

CARDBOARD ORCHESTRA
(see also Zior, Monument)

69	CBS 4176	Zebady Zak/Mary Tell Me Why	8
69	CBS 4633	Nothing But A Sad Sad Show/Yes I Heard A Little Bird	8

CARDIAC ARREST

79	Another Record AN 1	Running In The Street/T.V. Friends (p/s, 500 only)	20
79	Tortch TOR 002	A BUS FOR A BUS ON A BUS (EP)	20

CARDIACS
(see also Cardiac Arrest)

81	private label	TOY WORLD (cassette)	20
81	private label	THE OBVIOUS IDENTITY (cassette)	20
86	Alphabet ALPH 002	SEASIDE TREATS (12" EP, with poster & lyric insert)	12
87	Alphabet ALPH 006	THERE'S TOO MANY IRONS IN THE FIRE (12" EP, with poster)	10
88	Alphabet ALPH 008	Is This The Life/I'm Eating In Bed (p/s)	8
88	Alphabet ALPHT 008	Is This The Life/Loosefish Goosegash/I'm Eating In Bed (12", p/s)	12
88	Alphabet ALPH 009	Susannah's Still Alive/Blind In Safety And Leafy In Love (p/s)	6
91	Alphabet ALPH 015	DAY IS GONE (12" EP, with lyric sheet)	12
80s	Alphabet ALPH 000	ARCHIVE CARDIACS (cassette, fan club issue, compilation of "Toy World" & "The Obvious Identity")	10
83	Alphabet ALPH 01	THE SEASIDE (13-track cassette, colour inlay)	20
86	Alphabet ALPH 003	MR & MRS SMITH & MR DRAKE (cassette, fan club issue)	10
87	Alphabet ALPH 004	BIG SHIP (mini LP, with lyric insert)	18
87	Alphabet ALPH 005	RUDE BOOTLEG - LIVE AT READING '86 (LP, stamped sleeve with insert)	18
87	Alphabet ALPH MC005	RUDE BOOTLEG - LIVE AT READING '86 (cassette)	12
88	Torso CD 060	A LITTLE MAN AND A HOUSE AND THE WHOLE WORLD WINDOW (CD)	30
88	Alphabet ALPH 009T	Susannah's Still Alive/Blind In Safety And Leafy In Love/ All His Geese Are Swans (12", p/s)	10
89	Alphabet ALPH 011	Baby Heart Dirt/I Hold My Love In My Arms (p/s)	7
88	Night Tracks SFNT 013	RADIO ONE EVENING SESSION: R.E.S./ Buds And Spawn/In A City Lining/ Is This The Life/Cameras (12" EP)	18
88	Alphabet ALPHLP 010	CARDIACS LIVE (LP)	18
88	Alphabet ALPH 012	ON LAND AND IN THE SEA (LP)	18
91	Alphabet ALPHLP 014	SONGS FOR SHIPS AND IRONS (LP)	15
92	Alphabet ALPHLP 017	HEAVEN BORN AND EVER BRIGHT (LP)	15

CARDIGAN BROTHERS

63	London HLU 9740	I Know Know Know/Let's Go To The Movies	7

CARDIGANS

58	Mercury AMT 1007	Poor Boy/Each Other	10
58	Mercury AMT 1007	Poor Boy/Each Other (78)	10

CARDINALS

72	Nelmwood Audio	ON TOP OF THE WORLD (LP)	22

JACK CARDWELL

54	Parlophone CMSP 24	Whiskey, Women And Loaded Dice/Slap-Ka-Dab (export issue)	30
54	Parlophone CMSP 27	Blue Love/Diddle Diddle Dumpling (export issue)	30

CARE
(see also Wild Swans, Lotus Eaters, Lightning Seeds)

83	Arista KBIRD 2	Flaming Sword/Misericorde (picture disc)	5
83	Arista KBIRD 122	Flaming Sword/Misericorde (12" p/s)	10

CAREFREES

63	Oriole CB 1916	We Love You Beatles/Hot Blooded Lover	25
64	Oriole CB 1931	Aren't You Glad You're You/Paddy Wack	15

CARETAKER/ELLIS BAND
(see also Alton Ellis)

80s	Stonehouse 2	Majority Rules/Two Steps Forward	8

DAVE CAREY (JAZZ BAND)

53	Columbia SCM 5030	Broken Wings/Oh, Happy Day (as David Carey)	5
56	Tempo A 122	Kater Street Rag/Kansas City Kitty	10
56	Tempo A 133	I've Found A New Baby/Brown Skin Mama	10
56	Tempo A 138	Sunset Cafe Stomp/Sweet Georgia Brown	10
56	Tempo A 150	Ida, Sweet As Apple Cider/Button Up Your Overcoat	7
61	Philips PB 1158	Bingo (I'm In Love)/Paddlin' Madelin' Home (some in p/s)	5
56	Tempo EXA 38	DAVE CAREY JAZZ BAND (EP)	8

MINT VALUE £

56 Tempo EXA 43 DAVE CAREY JAZZ BAND (EP) . . . 8
56 Tempo EXA 51 DAVE CAREY JAZZ BAND (EP) . . . 10
55 Tempo LAP 4 DAVE CAREY JAZZ BAND (LP) . . . 12
57 Tempo TAP 16 JAZZ AT THE RAILWAY ARMS (LP) . . . 12
72 Grape GR 3025 Come Down Part 1/DYNAMITES: Come Down Part 2 . . . 6

MARIAH CAREY

90 Columbia 655 932-2 Vision Of Love/Sent From Up Above/Medley (CD) . . . 20
90 Columbia 656 364-2 Love Takes Time/Vanishing/You Need Me (CD) . . . 20
90 Columbia 656 364-5 Love Takes Time/Vanishing/You Need Me/Vision Of Love (CD, picture disc) . . . 25
91 Columbia 656 583-2 Someday (7" Jackswing Mix)/(12" Jackswing Mix)/(12" House Mix)(CD) . . . 15
91 Columbia 656 583-5 Someday (7" Jackswing Mix)/Vision Of Love/Love Takes Time/ Alone In Love (CD, picture disc) . . . 20
91 Columbia 656 931-2 There's Got To Be A Way (Album Version)/(12" Remix)/ (ALT Vocal Club Mix) (CD) . . . 15
91 Columbia 656 931-5 There's Got To Be A Way (Album Version)/(7" Remix)/Someday (7" Jackswing Mix)/Vision Of Love (CD, picture disc) . . . 25
91 Columbia 657 403-2 Emotions/Vanishing/Vision Of Love (CD) . . . 8
92 Columbia 657 662-2 Can't Let Go (Edit)/To Be Around You/The Wind (CD, slimline jewel case) . . . 12
92 Columbia 657 941-7 Make It Happen(radio edit)/Emotions (Special Motion Edit) (p/s) . . . 5
92 Columbia 657 941-2 Make It Happen (Radio Edit)/(Ext. Version)/(Dub)/(C&C Classic Mix)/ (LP Version) (CD) . . . 10
92 Columbia 657 662-5 Can't Let Go (Edit)/I Don't Wanna Cry/All In Your Mind (CD) . . . 12
94 Columbia 660 944-5 All I Want For Christmas Is You/Miss You Most (At Christmas Time) Silent Night (CD picture disc) . . . 6
98 Columbia MARIAH 1 12s (10x12" in box) . . . 50

TONY CAREY

(see also Rainbow)

84 MCA MCA 873 Fine Fine Day/Say It's Over (p/s) . . . 6
84 MCA MCFC 3212 SOME TOUGH CITY (LP, with inner sleeve) . . . 12

CAREY & LLOYD

(see also Carey Johnson, Lloyd Young, Lloyd & Carey)

72 Attack ATT 8032 Do It Again (as Carey/Lloyd)/GARY RANGLIN: Watch It . . . 6

HENSON CARGILL

68 Monument MON 1015 Skip A Rope/Very Well-Travelled Man . . . 6
68 Monument SMO 5024 COMING ON STRONG (LP) . . . 12

CARIBBEANS

69 Doctor Bird DB 1181 Let Me Walk By/AMBLINGS: Tell Me Why . . . 20
69 Crab CR 14 Please Please/MATADORS: The Destroyer . . . 15

CARIBBEATS

(see also Bobby Aitken, Itals)

66 Ska Beat JB 246 The Bells Of St. Mary's/WINSTON RICHARDS: Loki . . . 20
67 Double D DD 101 Highway 300/I Think Of You (actually by Merlene McKenzie) . . . 40
67 Double D DD 103 I'll Try/If I Did Look . . . 60
68 Double D DD 111 One Step/HAZEL WRIGHT: Please Help Me . . . 60

CARIBBENN (THE)

65 Pye 7N 15961 Inside Out/Up My Street . . . 10

CARIBOES

71 Bullet BU 479 Let It Be Me/All I Have To Do Is Dream . . . 5

CARIBS

60 Starlite ST45 012 Taboo/Mathilda Cha Cha Cha! . . . 12

CARIFTA ALLSTARS

72 Green Door GD 4040 The Harder They Come (actually by Charlie Ace)/Time Is Still Here . . . 8

CARL & COMMANDERS

61 Columbia DB 4719 Farmer John/Cleanin' Up . . . 22

BELINDA CARLISLE

(see also Go-Go's, Smithereens)

88 I.R.S. DIRM 118 Mad About You/I Never Wanted A Rich Man/Mad About You (Extended Mix) (3" CD) . . . 20
87 Virgin VSCD 1036 Heaven Is A Place On Earth/We Can Change/Heaven Is A Place On Earth (Heavenly Version)/Heaven Is A Place On Earth (Acapella Version) (CD) . . . 15
88 Virgin VSCD 1046 I Get Weak (7" Version)/Should I Let You In/I Get Weak (12" Version) (CD, picture disc) . . . 8
88 Virgin VSTY 1074 Circle In The Sand/(Beach Party Mix)/ (Seaside Groove Mix) (12", picture disc) . . 8
88 Virgin VSX 1114 World Without You (Remix)/Nobody Owns Me (box set, 2 cards & lyric sheet) . . 10
88 Virgin VSCD 1150 Love Never Dies... (Full Length Version)/I Feel Free (live)/Circle In The Sand (live)/Heaven Is A Place On Earth (live) (CD, with prints) . . . 10
89 Virgin VSCD 1210 Leave A Light On (7" Version)/Shades Of Michaelangelo/ Leave A Light On (Extended Mix) (3" CD in card sl., also 5" CD in jewel case [662 719/211], £12) . . . 8
89 Virgin VSCD 1230DJ La Luna/Whatever It Takes (3" CD, picture disc, promo only) . . . 25

BILL CARLISLE & CARLISLES

59 Mercury AMT 1063 Down Boy/Union Suit . . . 40
64 Hickory 45-1254 Shanghai Rooster/Big John Henry's Girl . . . 10

CARLISLE BROTHERS

59 Parlophone GEP 8799 FRESH FROM THE COUNTRY (EP) . . . 30

DON CARLOS ORCHESTRA

54 HMV 7 MC 4 Delicado/Anything Can Happen (export issue) . . . 5
56 HMV 7 MC 48 The Bandit/Mexicana (export issue) . . . 5
60 Top Rank JAR 376 Mustapha/Josita . . . 5
60 Columbia 33SX 1237 CRAZY LATIN (LP) . . . 20

MINT VALUE £

DON CARLOS
(see also Black Uhuru)

78	Dove 511	Plantation/Version	15
80	Pirate PIR 001	Nice Time/Get Up (12")	20
80	Negus Roots NERT003	I Love Jah/I Don't Care (12")	25
81	Negus Roots NERT 004	Gimme Gimme Your Love/PAP TULLO: Gimme More Love (12")	20
82	Negus Roots NERT 015	Magic Man/Magic Dub (12")	12
82	Cha Cha CHAD 52	Can't Waste Time/PAPA BRUCE : No Time To Waste (12")	20
83	Shuttle SH 008	Money & Women (with John Wayne)/ CORNELL CAMPBELL/PURPLEMAN: Keep On Working (12")	20
83	Blacker Dread SCOM 003	From Creation/Versions (12")	30
83	Youth In Progress YP001	Jordan River/LITTLE JOHN: Reasons/LADY ANNE AND SANTANA; Love Life (12")	20
85	Blacker Dread SCOM 020	Strictly Culture (Love We Culture Version)/MIKEY DREAD: Dubuling Mix (12")	25
80s	Rusty International RI 001	Isabel/BILLY BOYO: One Morning/CAPTAIN SINBAD & ROOTS RADICALS: Radication Dehbout (12")	20
81	Blue Moon BM 001	PROPHET (LP)	40
82	Negus Roots NERLP 001	SUFFERING (LP)	40
82	Negus Roots NERLP 005	HARVEST TIME (LP)	60
83	Burning sounds BRD 1053	SPREAD OUT INA DANCEHALL STYLE (LP)	20
84	Saxon International 5550	SAMMY DREAD MEETS DON CARLOS (LP, not released in sleeve)	25

WALTER CARLOS

69	CBS 4296	Brandenburg Concerto/Sinfonia To Cantata	5

DAVE CARLSEN

73	Spark SRLP 110	A PALE HORSE (LP, yellow/blue label)	50

RAY CARLSON

67	MGM MGM 1362	Speak No Sorrow/It's Getting Me Down Girl	6

(LITTLE) CARL CARLTON

68	Action ACT 4501	Competition Ain't Nothin'/Three Way Love	40
68	Action ACT 4514	46 Drums 1 Guitar/Why Don't They Leave Us Alone	15
69	Action ACT 4537	Look At Mary Wonder/Bad For Each Other (as Carl Carlton)	10
75	ABC ABC 4040	Smokin' Room/Signed, Sealed, Delivered, I'm Yours (as Carl Carlton)	6
90s	Kent TOWN 105	Competition Ain't Nothin'/HESITATIONS: I'm Not Built That Way	10

EDDIE CARLTON

76	Cream CRM 5001	It Will Be Done (Parts 1 & 2)	10

CARLTON & HIS SHOES
(see also Lee 'Scratch' Perry, Roy & Enid)

68	Coxsone CS 7065	Love Me Forever/Happy Land	60
68	Studio One SO 2062	This Feeling/You And Me (Love Is A Treasure)	60
70s	Studio One PSOL 003	LOVE ME FOREVER (LP, laminated sleeve)	50

PAUL CARMAN

74	DJM DJS 317	In My World/School Love	6

CARMEN
(see also Jethro Tull)

74	Regal Zonophone RZ 3086	Flamenco Fever/Lonely House	10
74	Regal Zonophone RZ 3090	Bulerias/Stepping Stone	6
73	R. Zonophone SRZA 8518	FANDANGOS IN SPACE (LP, gatefold sleeve, red/silver label)	30
75	R. Zonophone SLRZ 1040	DANCING ON A COLD WIND (LP, with inner sleeve, red/silver label)	45

HOAGY CARMICHAEL

55	Vogue Coral Q 72078	Crazy Otto Rag/Happy Hoagy's Medley	8
55	Vogue Coral Q 72095	Lazy River/I'm Just Wild About Mary	8
56	Vogue Coral Q 72123	Hong Kong Blues/LES BROWN: It's All Right With Me	8
56	Vogue Coral Q 72206	I Walk The Line/Flight To Hong Kong	8
50s	HMV 7EG 8037	STARDUST (EP)	8
54	Brunswick OE 9023	THE STARDUST ROAD (EP)	8
58	Vogue VE 170113	HOAGY CARMICHAEL (EP)	8

IAN CARMICHAEL

57	HMV POP 406	Lucky Jim (How I Envy Him)/Tomorrow, Tomorrow	8
66	Parlophone R 5429	How Would I Do Without You Jeeves?/Bertie's Lucky Day	8
60	HMV 7EG 117	THE HOUSE AT POOH CORNER (EP)	8

CARMITA

58	Fontana H 160	The Crowd/Waterwagon Blues	6
62	Fontana 267222 TF	Far Away/Lazy Lover	6

JEAN CARN

79	Philadelphoa Int. S PIR 13 8840	Was That All It Was/Whats On Your Mind (12")	15

CARNABY

65	Piccadilly 7N 35272	Jump And Dance/My Love Will Stay	100

CARNABY STREET POP ORCHESTRA & CHOIR

69	Carnaby CNLS 6003	THE LONDON THEME (LP)	50

CARNAGE

84	Creative Reality REAL 07	FACE THE FACTS (LP)	12

CARNATIONS

65	Blue Beat BB 285	Mighty Man/What Are You Selling	22

JUDY CARNE

61	Decca F 11347	Late Last Evening (with David Kernan)/A Plea For The Throne (with Betty Marsden & Pip Hinton) ('On The Brighter Side' cast)	5
69	Reprise RS 20680	Right, Said Fred/Sock It To Me	5

MINT VALUE £

CARNEGY HALL
68 Polydor 56224 The Bells Of San Francisco/Slightly Cracked ... 8

CARNIVAL
67 Columbia DB 8255 The Big Bright Green Pleasure Machine/Silver Dreams And Scarlet Memories ... 7
70 Liberty LBF 15252 Son Of A Preacher Man/Walk On By ... 6
70 Liberty LBS 83305 THE CARNIVAL (LP) ... 18

SASHA CARO
68 Decca F12744 Molotov Molotov/Never Play A B Side ... 30

BOBBI CAROL
63 Fontana 267 260TF Will You Love Me Tomorrow/It Doesn't Matter ... 10

CAROL & MEMORIES
66 CBS 202086 Tears On My Pillow/Crying My Eyes Out ... 22

CAROLE & SHERRY
62 Fontana 270 107 TF I Ain't Ready Yet/Like I Gotta Get Away ... 10

CAROLINA SLIM
72 Flyright LP 4702 CAROLINA BLUES AND BOOGIE (LP) ... 20

CAROLINES
65 Polydor BM 56027 Love Made A Fool Of Me/Believe In Me ... 20

CAROLLS
(see also Carrols)
65 Polydor BM 56046 Give Me Time/Darling I Want You So Much ... 20

CAROLS
(see also Carolls)
70 Revolution REV 013 Everyday I Have To Cry Some/FIRE SESSION: Sleeping Reggae ... 6

RENATO CAROSONE
58 Parlophone R 4433 Torero - Cha Cha Cha/Il Piccolo Montanaro (Le Petit Montagnard) ... 10

CAROUSELS
67 Pye 7N 17353 Holiday Romance/The Run Run ... 15

BOB CARPENTER
76 Celtic Music CM 027 SILENT PASSAGE (LP) ... 20

CARPENTER JOE
(See also Doubt)
87 Solo SOLO 2 MAVERICK GENIUS (EP) ... 20

THELMA CARPENTER
61 Coral Q 72422 Yes, I'm Lonesome Tonight/Gimme A Little Kiss Will Ya, Huh? ... 10
61 Coral Q 72442 Back Street/I Ought To Know ... 10

CARPENTER'S APPRENTICE
72 SRS 12107 CHANGES (LP, with insert) ... 100

CARPET BAGGERS
67 Spin SP 2006 Flea Teacher/On Sunday ... 30

CARPETTES
77 Small Wonder SMALL 3 RADIO WUNDERBAR (EP) ... 15
78 Small Wonder SMALL 9 Small Wonder?/2 Ne 1 (p/s, 2,000 only) ... 20
79 Beggars Banquet BEG 27 I Don't Mean It/Easy Way Out (p/s) ... 10
80 Beggars Banquet BEG 32 Johnny Won't Hurt You/Frustration Paradise/Keys To Your Heart/ Total Insecurity (double pack) ... 10
80 Beggars Banquet BEG 47 Nothing Ever Changes/You Never Realise/ Frustration Paradise (live (p/s) ... 10
80 Beggars Banquet BEG 49 The Last Lone Ranger/Love So Strong/Fan Club (p/s) ... 10
79 Beggars Banquet BEGA 14 FRUSTRATION PARADISE (LP) ... 18
80 Beggars Banquet BEGA 21 FIGHT AMONGST YOURSELVES (LP) ... 20

CATHY CARR
56 London HLH 8274 Ivory Tower/Please, Please Believe Me ... 40
56 Vogue Coral Q 72175 Heartbroken/I'll Cry At Your Wedding ... 10
59 Columbia DB 4270 First Anniversary/With Love ... 12
59 Columbia DB 4317 I'm Gonna Change Him/The Little Things You Do ... 12
60 Columbia DB 4408 Little Sister/Dark River ... 12
63 Stateside SS 147 Sailor Boy/The Next Time The Band Plays A Waltz ... 12

IAN CARR
(see under Nucleus)

JAMES CARR
66 Stateside SS 507 You've Got My Mind Messed Up/That's What I Want To Know ... 80
66 Stateside SS 507 You've Got My Mind Messed Up/That's What I Want To Know (DJ Copy) ... 140
66 Stateside SS 535 Love Attack/Coming Back To Me Baby ... 40
66 Stateside SS 535 Love Attack/Coming Back To Me Baby (DJ copy) ... 70
66 Stateside SS 545 You're Pouring Water On A Drowning Man/Forgetting You ... 30
67 Stateside SS 2001 The Dark End Of the Street/Loveable Girl ... 30
67 Stateside SS 2038 Let It Happen/A Losing Game ... 15
67 Stateside SS 2052 I'm A Fool For You/Gonna Send You Back To Georgia ... 25
68 Bell BLL 1004 A Man Needs A Woman/Stronger Than Love ... 12
69 B&C CB 101 Freedom Train/That's The Way Love Turned Out For Me ... 12
69 B&C CB 101 Freedom Train/That's The Way Love Turned Out For Me (DJ Copy) ... 50
72 Mojo 2092 053 Freedom Train/That's What I Want To Know ... 8
67 Stateside SL 10205 YOU GOT MY MIND MESSED UP (LP) ... 100
69 Bell MBLL/SBLL 113 A MAN NEEDS A WOMAN (LP) ... 40

JOE 'FINGERS' CARR
(see also Lou Busch, Vicki Young)
54 Capitol CL 14169 Piccadilly Rag/Fiddle-A-Delphia ... 6

MINT VALUE £

55	Capitol CL 14359	The Barky-roll Stomp/Deep In The Heart Of Texas (with Carr-Hops)	6
55	Capitol CL 14372	Give Me A Band And My Baby/Zig-A-Zig (with Joy-Riders)	6
56	Capitol CL 14581	The Portuguese Washerwoman/Stumbling	6

JOHNNY CARR (& CADILLACS)

64	Decca F 11854	Remember That Night/Respectable	20
65	Fontana TF 600	Do You Love That Girl?/Give Him A Little Time.	15
66	Fontana TF 681	Then So Do I/I'm Just A Little Bit Shy (solo)	10
67	Fontana TF 823	Things Get Better/You Got Me Baby (solo)	35

LEROY CARR

58	Fontana TFE 17051	TREASURES OF NORTH AMERICAN NEGRO MUSIC VOLUME 1 (EP)	15
64	RCA RCX 7168	R.C.A. VICTOR RACE SERIES VOL. 2 (EP)	15
63	CBS BPG 62206	BLUES BEFORE SUNRISE (LP)	50

LINDA CARR

67	Stateside SS 2058	Everytime/Trying To Be Good For You	35

LODY CARR

60	Top Rank 35-111	LADYBIRD (LP)	25

MIKE CARR

62	Decca F11448	That Certain Something/The Girl In The Mountains	10
68	Columbia SCX 6248	UNDER PRESSURE (LP)	20
73	Ad-Rhythm ARPS	MIKE CARR (LP)	18

PETER CARR

69	DJM DJS213	Angel And The Woman/Imagine Yourself	20

ROMEY CARR

70	Columbia DB 8710	These Things Will Keep Me Loving You/Stand Up And Fight	30
70	Columbia DB 8710	These Things Will Keep Me Loving You/Stand Up And Fight (DJ Copy)	50

VALERIE CARR

58	Columbia DB 4083	You're The Greatest/Over The Rainbow	7
58	Columbia DB 4131	When The Boys Talk About The Girls/Padre	10
58	Columbia DB 4225	Bad Girl/Look Forward	7
59	Columbia DB 4365	The Way To My Heart/I'm Only Asking	7
59	Columbia SEG 7860	VALERIE CARR (EP)	10
59	Columbia 33S 1137	VALERIE CARR (10" LP)	18
61	Columbia 33SX 1228	EV'RY HOUR, EV'RY DAY OF MY LIFE (LP, mono)	15
61	Columbia 33SCX 3307	EV'RY HOUR, EV'RY DAY OF MY LIFE (LP, stereo)	18

VIKKI CARR

67	Liberty LBF 15022	There I Go/One More Mountain	10
68	Librety LBF 15166	With Pen In Hand/Can't Take My Eyes Off You	10
64	Liberty LBY 1208	DISCOVERY (LP)	15
65	Liberty LBY 1284	ANATOMY OF LOVE (LP)	10

WYNONA CARR

61	Reprise R 20033	I Gotta Stand Tall/My Faith	15

DAVID CARRADINE

75	Jet JETLP 10	GRASSHOPPER (LP)	12

JOE 'KING' CARRASCO & THE CROWNS

80	Stiff CROWN 1	Bueno/Tuff Enuff (vinyl 78, p/s)	15

CARRIAGE COMPANY

71	CBS 7059	Paint The City Red/Jubilee	12

CARRICK FOLK FOUR

65	Thistle TM 90	Radio Scotland/Blue Nose	7

ANDREA CARROLL

63	London HLX 9772	It Hurts To Be Sixteen/Why Am I So Shy (some copies have Why Am I So Sorry as the B-side)	20

BARBARA CARROLL

59	London HLR 8981	North By Northwest/Far Away	15
59	London HLR 8981	North By Northwest/Far Away (78)	10

BERNADETTE CARROLL

64	Stateside SS 311	Party Girl/I Don't Wanna Know	22

BOB CARROLL

55	MGM SP 1132	I Love You So Much It Hurts/My Dearest, My Darling, My Love	10
56	London HLU 8299	Red Confetti, Pink Balloons And Tambourines/Handwriting On The Wall	25
58	London HLT 8724	Hi Yo Silver/Tonto The Brave	15
58	London HLT 8724	Hi Yo Silver/Tonto The Brave (78)	10
59	London HLT 8888	I Can't Get You Out Of My Heart/Since I'm Out Of Your Arms	10
59	London HLT 8888	I Can't Get You Out Of My Heart/Since I'm Out Of Your Arms (78)	12

CATHY CARROLL

62	Warner Bros WB 72	Poor Little Puppet/Love And Learn	10

DIAHANN CARROLL

59	London HLT 8788	The Big Country/Guiding Light	20
59	London HLT 8788	The Big Country/Guiding Light (78)	10

DON CARROLL

57	Capitol CL 14812	At Your Front Door/The Gods Were Angry With Me	10
58	Capitol CL 14823	In My Arms/The Things I Might Have Been	5

GINA CARROLL

65	Decca F 12297	Bye Bye Big Boy/Down The Street	20

MINT VALUE £

JOHNNY CARROLL & HOT ROCKS

56	Brunswick 05580	Corrine Corrina/Wild Wild Women	800
56	Brunswick 05580	Corrine Corrina/Wild Wild Women (78)	100
56	Brunswick 05603	Crazy, Crazy Lovin'/Hot Rock	800
56	Brunswick 05603	Crazy, Crazy Lovin'/Hot Rock (78)	100
74	UK USA 1	Black Leather Rebel/Be-Bop-A-Lula (as Johnny Carroll & Blue Caps)	10

PAT CARROLL

72	Pye International 7N 25592	To The Sun/Out Of My Mind	7

RONNIE CARROLL

(see also Millicent Martin)

60	Philips PB 1004	Footsteps/Where My True Love Walks	5
62	Philips 326 550 BF	If Only Tomorrow/Think Of Her (p/s)	7
62	Philips 326 550 BF	If Only Tomorrow/Think Of Her	5
56	Philips BBL 7236	RONNIE CARROLL (EP)	8
58	Philips BBL 7236	LUCKY 13 (LP)	12
63	Philips BL 7563	SOMETIMES I'M HAPPY SOMETIMES I'M BLUE (LP)	12

TONI CARROLL

58	MGM MGM 987	Dreamsville/I've Never Felt This Way Before	10
58	MGM EP 689	THIS ONE IS TONI (EP)	20

CARROLLS

(see also Carols, Carolls, Faith Brown, Brotherly Love)

66	Polydor BM 56081	Surrender Your Love/The Folk I Love	25
66	Polydor BM 56081	Surrender Your Love/The Folk I Love (DJ Copy)	50
68	CBS 3710	Ever Since/Come On	5
68	CBS 3875	A Lemon Balloon And A Blue Sky/Make Me Belong To You	10
69	CBS 4401	We're In This Thing Together/We Know Better	15
67	CBS 3414	So Gently Falls The Rain/Nice To See You Darling	10

BEN CARRUTHERS & DEEP

65	Parlophone R 5295	Jack O' Diamonds/Right Behind You	60

CHAD CARSON

63	HMV POP 1156	They Were Wrong/Stop Picking On Me	50

DEL CARSON

59	Decca F 11135	Jean/I Told Myself A Lie	6

JOE CARSON

63	Liberty LIB 55578	I Gotta Get Drunk (And I Shore Do Dread It)/Who Will Buy My Memories	25

JOHNNY CARSON

60	Fontana H 243	Fraulein/I Wish It Were You	8
60	Fontana H 259	The Train Of Love/First Proposal	8
60	Fontana H 277	You Talk Too Much/Now And Always	8
62	Ember EMB S 150	Teenage Bachelor/Are You Anyone's Girl?	8
63	Ember EMB S 161	The Tears Came Rolling Down/One Track Mind	10

KAY CARSON

(see also Kit Carson)

56	Capitol CL 14565	Those Who Have Loved/The Fellow Over There	6
56	Capitol CL 14634	There's A Shadow Between Us/This Man	6

KEN CARSON

55	London HLF 8213	Hawkeye/I've Been Working On The Railroad	40
55	London HLF 8213	Hawkeye/I've Been Working On The Railroad (78)	10
56	London HLF 8237	Let Her Go, Let Her Go/The Song Of Daniel Boone (The Daddy Of Them All)	25

KIT CARSON

(see also Kay Carson)

56	Capitol CL 14524	Band Of Gold/Cast Your Bread Upon The Waters	12

MINDY CARSON

58	Philips PB 822	The Sentimental Touch/I Was Born	5

MINDY CARSON & GUY MITCHELL

(see also Guy Mitchell)

53	Columbia SCM 5022	That's A Why/Train Of Love	30

VINCE CARSON

55	HMV 7M 313	Sweetie, Sweet, Sweet Sue/My Possession	7

CARTE BLANCHE

79	Pye 7NL46193	Get Up On Your Feet/Do It Like You Like It (p/s)	15

ANITA CARTER

58	London HLA 8693	Blue Doll/Go Away Johnnie	20
60	London HLW 9102	Moon Girl/Mama Don't Cry At My Wedding	15

BENNY CARTER

(see also Helen Humes)

54	HMV 7M 189	Blue Mountain/Sunday Afternoon	6
62	HMV CLP 1624/CSD1480	FURTHER DEFINITIONS (LP, mono/stereo)	20
66	HMV CLP/CSD 3576	FURTHER DEFINITIONS (LP, mono/stereo)	20

BETTY CARTER

(see also Ray Charles)

63	London HLK 9748	The Good Life/Nothing More To Look Forward To	10

CAROLINE CARTER

65	Decca F 12239	The Ballad Of Possibilities/We Want Love	12

CAROLYN CARTER

65	London HL 9959	It Hurts/I'm Thru	40

MINT VALUE £

CHRIS CARTER
(see also Throbbing Gristle, Chris & Cosey)

81	Industrial IRC 32	THE SPACE BETWEEN (cassette)	12

CLARENCE CARTER

68	Atlantic 584 154	Thread The Needle/Don't Make My Baby Cry	15
68	Atlantic 584 176	Looking For A Fox/I Can't See Myself (Crying About You)	20
68	Atlantic 584 187	Funky Fever/Slip Away	12
68	Atlantic 584 223	Too Weak To Fight/Let Me Comfort You	12
69	Atlantic 584 248	Snatchin' It Back/Making Love (At The Dark End Of The Street)	12
69	Atlantic 584 272	The Feeling Is Right/You Can't Miss When You Can't Measure	8
70	Atlantic 584 309	Take It Off Him And Put It On Me/The Few Troubles I've Had	8
70	Atlantic 2091 030	Patches/I Can't Leave Your Love Alone	6
71	Atlantic 2091 045	It's All In Your Mind/Willie And Laura Mae Jones	8
71	Atlantic 2091 093	The Court Room/Getting The Bills (But No Merchandise)	8
71	Atlantic 2091 139	Slipped, Tripped And Fell In Love/I Hate To Love And Run	10
68	Atlantic 588 152	THIS IS CLARENCE CARTER (LP)	20
69	Atlantic 588 172	THE DYNAMIC CLARENCE CARTER (LP)	20
69	Atlantic 588 191	TESTIFYIN' (LP)	20
70	Atlantic 2400 027	PATCHES (LP)	20

HAL CARTER FIVE

62	Oriole CB 1709	Come On And Twist Me/Twistin' Time Is Here	10

HERBIE CARTER

68	Duke DU 4	Happy Time (actually by Keble Drummond)/BOYS: Smashville	60

JACK CARTER

70	Penny Farthing PEN 739	Morning/Fanny	8

JEAN CARTER & CENTREPIECES

68	Stateside SS 2114	No Good Jim/And None	15
68	Stateside SS 2114	No Good Jim/And None (DJ Copy)	25

JOHN CARTER & RUSS ALQUIST
(see also Carter-Lewis & Southerners, Ivy League, Flowerpot Men)

68	Spark SRL 1017	The Laughing Man/Midsummer Dreaming	40

LYNDA CARTER

73	EMI 2005	It Might As Well Stay Monday/I Believe In Music	6
80	Motown TMG 1207	The Last Song/What's A Little Love Between Friends (p/s)	7
78	CBS EPC 83052	LYNDA CARTER (aka WONDER WOMAN)	18

MARTIN CARTER

71	Tradition TSR 008	SOMEONE NEW (LP)	
72	Tradition TSR 012	UPS & DOWNS (LP)	35

MEL CARTER

63	Pye International 7N 25212	When A Boy Falls In Love/So Wonderful	12
66	Liberty LIB 66113	Hold Me, Thrill Me, Kiss Me/Sweet Little Girl	20
65	Liberty LIB 66138	(All Of A Sudden) My Heart Sings/When I Hold The Hand Of The One I Love	10
66	Liberty LIB 66148	Love Is All We Need/I Wish I Didn't Love You So	10
66	Liberty LIB 66165	Band Of Gold/Detour	10
66	Liberty LIB 66183	You You You/If You Lose Her	10

MIKE CARTER (& DRAGONFLY)
See also Dragonfly

84	Button BTN 117	My True Love/Talk To Me	6

MOTHER MAYBELLE CARTER

64	London HA-R 8214	QUEEN OF THE AUTOHARP (LP)	15

NEL CARTER

74	RCA 2503	Send Him Back To Me/Dreams	20

RON CARTER

76	CTI 6064	YELLOW AND GREEN (LP, gatefold)	12

SHEILA CARTER & EPISODE SIX
(see also Episode, Episode Six)

66	Pye 7N 17194	I Will Warm Your Heart/Incense	30

SONNY CARTER with EARL BOSTIC & HIS ORCHESTRA
(see also Earl Bostic)

55	Parlophone MSP 6167	There Is No Greater Love/Oh Baby	20
55	Parlophone MSP 6167	There Is No Greater Love/Oh Baby (78)	10

CARTER STEPHENS CHORALE

68	Fontana TF 936	Peace! (Dream Of The Common Man)/The Promised Land	15

SYDNEY CARTER

66	Elektra EPK 801	LORD OF THE DANCE (EP)	15

CARTER FAMILY

55	Brunswick OE 9168	MOUNTAIN MUSIC VOL. 2 (EP)	10

CARTER-LEWIS & SOUTHERNERS
(see also Ivy League, Flowerpot Men, White Plains, John Carter & Russ Alquist, Jimmy Page, Dawn Chorus)

61	Piccadilly 7N 35004	So Much In Love/Back On The Scene	30
61	Ember EMB S 145	Two Timing Baby/Will It Happen To Me?	50
62	Piccadilly 7N 35085	Here's Hopin'/Poor Joe	30
62	Ember EMB S 165	Tell Me/My Broken Heart	50
63	Oriole CB 1835	Sweet And Tender Romance/Who Told You?	20
63	Oriole CB 1868	Your Momma's Out Of Town/Somebody Told My Girl	20
64	Oriole CB 1919	Skinny Minnie/Easy To Cry	40

MINT VALUE £

MARTIN CARTHY

76	Topic STOP 7002	The Bonny Lass Of Anglesey/Palaces Of Gold	6
65	Fontana (S)TL 5269	MARTIN CARTHY (LP, black/silver label)	45
71	Philips 6308 049	LANDFALL (LP, black/silver label)	35
72	Peg PEG 12	SHEARWATER (LP, with insert, purple label)	25
72	Philips 6282 022	THIS IS MARTIN CARTHY (LP)	15
74	Deram SML 1111	SWEET WIVELSFIELD (LP, red/white label)	15

MARTIN CARTHY & DAVE SWARBRICK

(see also Dave Swarbrick, Three City Four, Steeleye Span, Leon Rosselson, Alex Campbell, Nigel Denver)

67	Fontana TE 17490	NO SONGS (EP)	35
66	Fontana STL 5362	SECOND ALBUM (LP, black/silver label)	30
67	Fontana STL 5434	BYKER HILL (LP)	30
68	Fontana STL 5477	BUT TWO CAME BY (LP)	30
70	Fontana STL 5529	PRINCE HEATHEN (LP, black/silver label)	35
71	Pegasus PEG 6	SELECTIONS (LP, gatefold sleeve)	30

BARBARA CARTLAND

78	State STAT 85	If You Were The Only Girl In The World/I'll See You Again	7

CARTOONE

(see also Jimmy Page)

69	Atlantic 584 240	Knick Knack Man/A Penny For The Sun	10
69	Atlantic 588 174	CARTOONE (LP)	18

FLIP CARTRIDGE

66	London HLU 10076	Dear Mrs Applebee/Don't Take The Lovers From The World	12

DAVE CARTWRIGHT

(see also Bev Pegg, Away From The Sand)

73	DJM DJS 10750	Band Of Hope/Queen Of The May (promo)	10
70	Harmony DB 0001	MIDDLE OF THE ROAD (LP, private pressing, 99 only, with insert)	200
72	Transatlantic TRA 255	A LITTLE BIT OF GLORY (LP, with inner sleeve)	20
73	Transatlantic TRA 267	BACK TO THE GARDEN (LP, with lyric inner sleeve)	20
75	Transatlantic TRA 284	DON'T LET YOUR FAMILY DOWN (LP, with lyric insert)	20

DICK CARUSO

60	MGM MGM 1077	Two Long Years/Yes Sir, That's My Baby	8
60	MGM MGM 1099	Pretty Little Dancin' Doll/We've Never Met	8

ALAN CARVELL

(see also Carvells, Five Sapphires, Telegrams)

76	United Artists UP 36124	Georgia On My Mind/Never Give Your Love (To A New York Woman)	5

CARVELLS

(see also Alan Carvell, Five Sapphires, Telegrams)

78	Rocket ROKN 540	Skateboard Queen/Skateboard Surfing	5
78	Rocket ROKN 544	Skateboard Riders/Skateboard King	5
78	Rocket ROLL 15	SKATEBOARD RAMPAGE (LP)	12

CASABLANCA

(see also Trees, Ginger Bakers Airforce)

74	Rocket PIGL 7	CASABLANCA (LP, die-cut sleeve with inner lyric sleeve)	20

CASANOVAS

00s	Singles Society 7STAS 3320	Nasty/Too Cool (numbered die-cut p/s, 500 only)	10

CASCADES

63	Warner Bros WB 88	Rhythm Of The Rain/Let Me Be	7
63	Warner Bros WB 98	Shy Girl/The Last Leaf	7
63	Warner Bros WB 103	I Wanna Be Your Lover/My First Day Alone	7
63	RCA Victor RCA 1358	Cinderella/A Little Like Loving	7
64	RCA Victor RCA 1378	Jeannie/For Your Sweet Love	5
65	Liberty LIB 55822	I Bet You Won't Stay/She'll Love Again	5
66	Stateside SS 515	Cheryl's Goin' Home/Truly Julie's Blues	12
69	Uni UN 508	Maybe The Rain Will Fall/Naggin' Cries	6
63	Warner Bros WEP 6106	RHYTHM OF THE RAIN (EP, mono)	40
63	Warner Bros WSE 6106	RHYTHM OF THE RAIN (EP, stereo)	45
63	Warner Bros WM 8127	RHYTHM OF THE RAIN (LP, mono)	40
63	Warner Bros WSE 8127	RHYTHM OF THE RAIN (LP, stereo)	50

AL CASEY & K.C. ETTES

(see also Sanford Clark, Duane Eddy)

63	Pye International 7N 25215	Surfin' Hootenanny/Easy Picking	20

HOWIE CASEY & SENIORS

(see also Freddie Starr)

62	Fontana H 364	Double Twist/True Fine Mama	25
62	Fontana H 381	I Ain't Mad At You/Twist At The Top	20
63	Fontana TF 403	The Boll Weevil Song/Bony Moronie	20
62	Fontana TFL 5180	TWIST AT THE TOP (LP)	90
65	Wing WL 1022	LET'S TWIST (LP, reissue of "Twist At The Top")	25

ALVIN CASH (& REGISTERS)

65	Stateside SS 386	Twine Time/The Bump (as Alvin Cash & Crawlers)	30
65	Stateside SS 386	Twine Time/The Bump (as Alvin Cash & Crawlers) (DJ Copy)	60
66	Stateside SS 543	Philly Freeze/No Deposits, No Returns (as Alvin Cash & Registers)	25
66	Stateside SS 543	Philly Freeze/No Deposits, No Returns (as Alvin Cash & Registers) (DJ Copy)	40
68	President PT 115	Philly Freeze/No Deposits, No Returns (as Alvin Cash & Registers) (reissue)	5
68	President PT 119	Alvin's Boo-Ga-Loo/Let's Do Some Good Timing (as Alvin Cash & Registers)	10
68	President PT 129	Doin' The Ali Shuffle/Feel So Good	10
68	President PT 147	Charge/Diff'rent Strokes For Diff'rent Folks	10
71	President PT 351	Twine Time/Twine Awhile	8

			MINT VALUE £
72	President PT 383	Barracuda/Do It One More Time (as Alvin Cash & Crawlers)	8
67	President PTL 1000	THE PHILLY FREEZE (LP)	35

JOHNNY CASH

78s

57	London HL 8358	I Walk The Line/Get Rhythm	30
57	London HLS 8427	Train Of Love/There You Go	25
57	London HLS 8461	Next In Line/Don't Make Me Go	25
57	London HLS 8514	Home Of The Blues/Give My Love To Rose	30
58	London HLS 8586	Ballad Of A Teenage Queen/Big River (with Tennessee Two)	25
58	London HLS 8656	Guess Things Happen That Way/Come In, Stranger	20
58	London HLS 8709	The Ways Of A Woman In Love/You're The Nearest Thing To Heaven	30
59	Philips PB 874	All Over Again/What Do I Care	50
59	Philips PB 897	Don't Take Your Guns To Town/I Still Miss Someone	30
59	London HLS 8789	It's Just About Time/I Just Thought You'd Like To Know	30
59	London HLS 8847	Luther Played The Boogie/Thanks A Lot	30
59	Philips PB 928	Frankie's Man, Johnny/You Dreamer You	30
59	London HLS 8928	Katy Too/I Forgot To Remember To Forget	40
59	Philips PB 953	I Got Stripes/Five Feet High And Rising	40
59	London HLS 8979	You Tell Me/Goodbye, Little Darlin', Goodbye	40
59	Philips PB 979	The Little Drummer Boy/I'll Remember You	60

SINGLES

57	London HL 8358	I Walk The Line/Get Rhythm (gold label lettering)	150
57	London HL 8358	I Walk The Line/Get Rhythm (silver label lettering)	60
57	London HLS 8427	Train Of Love/There You Go	50
57	London HLS 8461	Next In Line/Don't Make Me Go	50
57	London HLS 8514	Home Of The Blues/Give My Love To Rose	40
58	London HLS 8586	Ballad Of A Teenage Queen/Big River (with Tennessee Two)	30
58	London HLS 8656	Guess Things Happen That Way/Come In, Stranger (with Tennessee Two)	20
58	London HLS 8709	The Ways Of A Woman In Love/You're The Nearest Thing To Heaven (with Tennessee Two)	20
59	Philips PB 874	All Over Again/What Do I Care	10
59	Philips PB 897	Don't Take Your Guns To Town/I Still Miss Someone	10
59	London HLS 8789	It's Just About Time/I Just Thought You'd Like To Know (with Tennessee Two)	20
59	London HLS 8847	Luther Played The Boogie/Thanks A Lot	30
59	Philips PB 928	Frankie's Man, Johnny/You Dreamer You	10
59	London HLS 8928	Katy Too/I Forgot To Remember To Forget	30
59	Philips PB 953	I Got Stripes/Five Feet High And Rising	10
59	London HLS 8979	You Tell Me/Goodbye, Little Darlin', Goodbye	15
59	Philips PB 979	The Little Drummer Boy/I'll Remember You	6
60	London HLS 9070	Straight A's In Love/I Love You Because	15
60	Philips PB 1017	Seasons Of My Heart/Smiling Bill McCall	7
60	London HLS 9182	Down The Street To 301/Story Of A Broken Heart	18
60	Philips PB 1075	Going To Memphis/Loading Coal	12
61	London HLS 9314	Oh Lonesome Me/Life Goes On	15
61	Philips PB 1148	Forty Shades Of Green/he Rebel - Johnny Yuma	8
61	Philips PB 1200	Tennessee Flat-Top Box/Tall Man	8
63	CBS AAG 159	Ring Of Fire/I'd Still Be There	7
63	CBS AAG 173	The Matador/Still In Town	6
63	CBS AAG 200	Understand Your Man/Dark As A Dungeon	5
65	CBS 201741	Orange Blossom Special/All God's Children Ain't Free	5
65	CBS 201760	It Ain't Me Babe/Time And Time Again	5
65	CBS 201809	Ring Of Fire/Streets Of Laredo	5
66	CBS 202046	The One On The Right Is On The Left/Cotton Pickin' Hands	6
66	CBS 202256	Everybody Loves A Nut/Austin Prison	5
67	CBS 202546	You Beat All I Ever Saw/Put The Sugar To Bed	5
67	CBS 3268	Rosanna's Going Wild/Long-Legged Guitar-Pickin' Man (with June Carter)	5
68	CBS 3438	Certain Kind Of Hurtin'/Another Song To Sing	5
68	CBS 3549	Folsom Prison Blues (live)/The Folk Singer	5
69	CBS 4638	Blistered/See Ruby Fall	5
76	CBS S 4287	One Piece At A Time/Go On Blues	6

EXPORT SINGLES

57	London HL 7020	Next In Line/Don't Make Me Go	35
57	London HL 7023	Home Of The Blues/Give My Love To Rose	35
58	London HL 7032	Ballad Of A Teenage Queen/Big River	25
58	London HL 7053	The Ways Of A Woman In Love/You're The Nearest Thing To Heaven	25
57	London HL 7131	Folsom Prison Blues/I Walk The Line	40

EPs

58	London RES 1120	JOHNNY CASH (triangular centre)	40
58	London RES 1120	JOHNNY CASH (round centre)	20
59	London RES 1193	JOHNNY CASH SINGS HANK WILLIAMS (triangular centre)	40
59	London RES 1193	JOHNNY CASH SINGS HANK WILLIAMS (round centre)	20
59	London RES 1212	COUNTRY BOY (triangular centre)	40
59	London RES 1212	COUNTRY BOY (round centre)	20
59	London RES 1230	JOHNNY CASH NO. 2 (triangular centre)	40
59	London RES 1230	JOHNNY CASH NO. 2 (round centre)	20
60	Philips BBE 12377	THE TROUBADOR	20
60	Philips BBE 12318	GRANDFATHER'S CLOCK	15
60	Philips BBE 12395	SONGS OF OUR SOIL	15
61	Philips BBE 12494	STRICTLY CASH	15
64	CBS AGG 20050	FORTY SHADES OF GREEN	10
64	CBS EP 5576	FABULOUS JOHNNY CASH	10
64	CBS EP 5735	ORANGE BLOSSOM SPECIAL	10
64	CBS EP 5744	EVERYBODY LOVES A NUT	10
64	CBS EP 5964	RING OF FIRE	10
65	CBS EP 6061	IT AIN'T ME BABE	10

			MINT VALUE £
66	CBS EP 6073	MEAN AS HELL! - BALLADS FROM THE TRUE WEST (with Statler Brothers & Carter Family)	10
65	CBS EP 6109	SONGS OF KATIE ELDER	10
65	CBS EP 6147	HAPPINESS IS YOU	10
69	CBS EP 6601	FOLSOM PRISON BLUES	10
72	CBS EP 9155	LITTLE FAUSS AND BIG HALSY	10

LPs

59	London HA-S 2157	SINGS THE SONGS THAT MADE HIM FAMOUS	40
59	London HA-S 2179	WITH HIS HOT AND BLUE GUITAR	40
59	Philips BBL 7298	THE FABULOUS JOHNNY CASH (mono)	20
59	Philips SBBL 554	THE FABULOUS JOHNNY CASH (stereo)	25
59	Philips BBL 7353	SONGS OF OUR SOIL	15
59	Philips BBL 7373	HYMNS BY JOHNNY CASH	15
60	Philips BBL 7358	NOW THERE WAS A SONG! (mono)	18
60	Philips SBBL 580	NOW THERE WAS A SONG! (stereo)	20
60	Philips BBL 7417	RIDE THIS TRAIN	15
61	CBS (S)BPG 62042	THE FABULOUS JOHNNY CASH (mono/stereo)	15
62	CBS (S)BPG 62015	HYMNS FROM THE HEART (mono/stereo)	15
62	CBS (S)BPG 62073	THE SOUND OF JOHNNY CASH (mono/stereo)	15
63	CBS BPG 62119	BLOOD SWEAT AND TEARS	15
63	CBS (S)BPG 62171	RING OF FIRE (mono/stereo)	15
63	CBS (S)BPG 62284	THE CHRISTMAS SPIRIT (mono/stereo)	15
64	CBS (S)BPG 62371	I WALK THE LINE (mono/stereo)	15
64	CBS (S)BPG 62463	BITTER TEARS (mono/stereo)	15
65	CBS (S)BPG 62501	ORANGE BLOSSOM SPECIAL (mono/stereo)	15
65	Fontana FJS 301	JOHNNY CASH'S COUNTRY ROUND-UP (4 tracks only)	12
65	London HA-S 8220	THE ORIGINAL SUN SOUND OF JOHNNY CASH	30
66	London HA-S 8253	LONESOME ME	15
68	CBS LP 63308	LIVE AT FOLSOM PRISON (LP)	15
69	CBS LP 63629	LIVE AT SAN QUENTIN (LP)	15
84	Charley SUN BOX-105	THE SUN YEARS (5-LP box set)	30
91	Mercury 848 051-1	THE MYSTERY OF LIFE (LP, features Bob Dylan on 1 track)	15

CASH CREW

87	Vinyl Lab VL 004	Mission Impossible/Microphone Maniac (12" as Cash Crew (The Force)	40

CASHMAN, PISTILLI & WEST

70	Capitol CL 15633	Goodbye Jo/She Never Looked Better	6

CASH PUSSIES

(see also Sex Pistols)

79	The Label TLR 010	99% Is Shit/Cash Flow (p/s)	6

CASINO

81	Ellie Jay EJSP 9609	More Than Ever/Tonight (p/s)	10

CASINO ROYALES

67	London HLU 10122	When I Tell You That I Love You/Love In The Open Air	6

CASINOS

67	Ember EMB S 241	That's The Way/Too Good To Be True	40
67	President PT 123	Then You Can Tell Me Goodbye/I Still Love You	8
68	President PT 140	To Be Loved/Tailor Made	5
68	President PT 156	When I Stop Dreaming/Please Love Me	5
68	President PTL 1007	THEN YOU CAN TELL ME GOODBYE (LP)	25

TONY CASO

68	London HL 10178	Shadow On The Ground/I Don't Care Who Knows It	7

CASPAR

(see also 10cc)

79	Rock Steady MICK 007	Messin' Around/Make You Feel Like You're Mine (p/s)	20

MAMA CASS

(see under Mama Cass Elliot, Mamas & Papas, Mugwumps, Big Three)

PAUL CASS

75	Rainbow RBW 2000	Mini Marianne/Riverboat Rock	15

CASSANDRA

79	D Roy DRDD 19	Sitting In The Park/D ROY BAND: Hyde Park Dub	30
80	D Roy DRDD 29	my Angel Baby/Thank You For The Many Things You've Done (12")	30
80	D Roy DRDD 31	I Must Be Dreaming/Trading Dub (12")	30

TOMMY CASSELL

70	Injun 114	Rockin' Rock A Rollin' Stone/Go Ahead On	15

CASSETTE

79	1 track CAS 001	THE FAST FORWARD EP: What's The Point/Product/All The Rage	35

CASSETTES

81	Zip ZIP 101	Reverberate/Don't Label Me (die-cut sleeve)	50

DAVID CASSIDY

(see also Partridge Family)

71	Bell BELL 1189	Cherish/All I Wanna Do Is Touch You	5

STEVE CASSIDY

63	Ember EMB S 177	Ecstasy/I'm A Worrying	5

TED CASSIDY

65	Capitol CL 15423	The Lurch/Wesley	20

CASTANARC

74	Peninsula PENCIL 10	JOURNEY TO THE EAST (LP, private pressing)	18

MINT VALUE £

CASTAWAYS

65 London HL 10003 Liar Liar/Sam 40
65 London HL 10003 Liar Liar/Sam (DJ Copy) 70

CASTE

68 President PT 211 Don't Cast Aside/One Step Closer 6

JOEY CASTELL

57 Decca F 10966 I'm Left, You're Right, She's Gone/Tryin' To Get To You 250
57 Decca F 10966 I'm Left, You're Right, She's Gone/Tryin' To Get To You (78) 50

LACKSLEY CASTELL

79 Sufferers Heights SUFF 01 What A great Day/PRINCE JAMMY: Slaughter House 5 (12") 50
79 Soundoff SOFD 003 My Collie tree/RISING SON : Stop Cheating (12") 30
80 Negus Roots NERT 001 African Queen/Queen In Dub (12") 25
80 Negus Roots NERT 003 I Love Jah/Version 40
81 Negus Roots NERT 005 Jah Is Watching You/PAPA TULLO: Sweet Reggae Music (12") 25
80 Black Joy DH 805 Jah Love Is Sweeter/ROCKERS BAND: Sweeter Rockers (12") 50
81 Negus Roots NERT 008 Government Man/P. TULLO: Straight To The Government (12" blue/black vinyl) . 40
82 Negus Roots NERT 013 Speak Softly/Money A The Remedy
(with PAPPA TULLO/ Take This Message To My Woman (12") 25
83 Negus Roots NERT 019 Johnny Brown/Mrs Brown (12") 20
83 Csa SPCSA 12006 Tug A War Game/EARL SIXTEEN: Rise In The Morning (12") 30
82 Negus Roots NERT LP 002 MORNING GLORY (LP) 60
83 Negus Roots NERT LP 008 AFRICAN LADY (LP) 40

CASTELLS

61 London HLN 9392 Sacred/I Get Dreamy 20
62 London HLN 9551 So This Is Love/On The Street Of Tears 25

CASTELLS

67 Masquerade MA 500 Two Lovers/Jerusalem 5

LEE CASTLE & BARONS

64 Parlophone R 5151 A Love She Can Count On/Foolin' 15

ROY CASTLE

60 Philips PB 1087 Little White Berry/Crazy Little Thorn 8
65 CBS 201736 Doctor Terror's House Of Horrors/Voodoo Girl (with Tubby Hayes) 70
68 Olga OLE 12 Wonderful World/For All The World 5
61 Philips BBL 7457 CASTLEWISE (LP, also stereo SBBL 626) 15

CASTLE SISTERS (Jamaica)

66 Ska Beat JB 257 Stop Your Lying/Don't Be A Fool 30

CASTLE SISTERS (USA)

59 Columbia DB 4335 Drifting And Dreaming/Lucky Girl 7

CASTLE TRANCELOT

95 Slate SLATE 19 French Lawyer/Without You (12") 15
95 Slate MMP 001 INDOCTRINATE EP (12") 15

CAST OF THOUSANDS

66 Stateside SS 546 My Jenny Wears A Mini/Girl Do What You Gonna Do 30

CASTON & MAJORS

(see also Radiants)
75 Tamla Motown TMG 938 Child Of Love/No One Will Know 15

JIMMY CASTOR (BUNCH)

66 Philips BF 1543 Hey Leroy, Your Mama's Callin'/Hamhock's Espanol 25
67 Philips BF 1590 Magic Saxophone/Just You Girl 30
71 Mercury 6052 110 Hey Leroy, Your Mama's Callin'/Hamhock's Espanol (reissue) 10
73 RCA Victor APD1 0103 DIMENSION III (LP, quadrophonic) 18

FRANKIE CASTRO

56 Mercury MT 114 Goodbye, So Long, I'm Gone/Too Much (78) 18

CASUAL FOUR

70s Specially Made For Us 102 I Can Tell/Love Potion No. 9 20

CASUALEERS

74 Pye Disco Demand DDS 103 Dance Dance Dance/Something About This Girl 6

CASUALS

(see also American Jam, Kansas Hook)
65 Fontana TF 635 If You Walk Out/Please Don't Hide 10
68 Decca F 12737 Adios Amor (Goodbye My Love)/Don't Dream Of Yesterday 6
68 Decca F 22784 Jesamine/I've Got Something Too 7
68 Decca F 22852 Toy/Touched (p/s) 15
68 Decca F 22852 Toy/Touche 7
69 Decca F 22900 Fools Paradise/7 X 7 5
69 Decca F 22943 Sunflower Eyes/Never My Love 5
69 Decca F 22969 Caroline/Naughty Boy 8
70 Decca F 23027 My Name Is Love/I Can't Say 10
71 Decca F 23112 Someday Rock 'n' Roll Lady/A Letter Every Day 6
72 Parlophone R 5959 Tara Tiger Girl/Nature's Girl 8
74 Dawn DNS 1069 Witch/Good Times 8
69 Decca LK-R/SKL-R 5001 HOUR WORLD (LP, large unboxed logo on label) 35

JOHNNY CASWELL

85 Kent TOWN 106 You Don't Love Me No More/STEINWAYS: You've Been Leading Me On 20

CATAPILLA

(see also Jon Stevens, Liar)
71 Vertigo 6360 029 CATAPILLA (LP, gatefold sleeve, small swirl label) 250
72 Vertigo 6360 074L CHANGES (LP, die-cut gatefold sleeve, small swirl label) 700

MINT VALUE £

CATATONIA

94	Rough Trade 45rev33	Whale/You Can (p/s, 'Singles Club' release)	8
95	Nursery NYS 12L	Bleed/This Boy Can't Swim (red vinyl, numbered p/s, 1,000 only)	8
95	Blanco Y Negro SAM 1746	Blow The Millennium Blow/Beautiful Sailor (p/s, white vinyl Xmas 45, freebie)	5
93	Crai CD 039B	FOR TINKERBELL EP (CD)	8
98	Blanco Y Negro 20834-1	INTERNATIONAL VELVET (LP, 1,000 only, with free 12")	15

CATCH

(see also Tourists, Eurythmics)

77	Logo GO 103	Borderline/Black Blood (company sleeve)	40

CATE BROTHERS

76	Asylum 13062	Where Can We Go/Instrumental	20

CATFISH

70	CBS 64006	GET DOWN (LP, orange label)	15
71	Epic 64408	LIVE CATFISH (LP)	15

CATHEDRAL

92	Earache MOSH 40T	Soul Sacrifice/Autumn Twilight/Frozen Rapture/Golden Blood (Flooding)	12
95	Earache MOSH 152	HOPKINS (THE WITCHFINDER GENERAL) EP (12", p/s)	12
93	Earache MOSH 77C	THE ETHEREAL MIRROR (LP, blue vinyl)	30
94	Rise Above RISE 8	IN MEMORIAM (LP, purple vinyl)	25
95	Earache MOSH 130	THE CARNIVAL BIZARRE (2 x 10" LP, gatefold sleeve)	20

CATHERINE WHEEL

91	Wilde Club WILDE 4	SHE'S MY FRIEND (12", p/s, barcode on sleeve)	10
91	Wilde Club WILDE 5	PAINFUL THING EP (12", p/s)	10
91	Wilde Club WILDE 5CD	PAINFUL THING EP (CD single)	12
93	Fontana CW 512	Crank/Black Metallic/Painful Thing (12", picture disc)	8
92	Fontana 510903-1	FERMENT (LP, initially with free 12")	15
92	Fontana 510903-1	FERMENT (LP, without free 12")	12
93	Fontana 518 039-1	CHROME (LP with inner sleeve)	20

RAY CATHODE (BBC RADIOPHONICS)

(see also BBC Radiophonic Workshop, George Martin)

62	Parlophone R 4901	Time Beat/Waltz In Orbit	10

CAT IRON

69	Xtra XTRA 1087	CAT IRON (LP)	22

CAT MOTHER & ALL NIGHT NEWSBOYS

(see also Jimi Hendrix)

69	Polydor 56543	Good Old Rock'N'Roll/Bad News	8
70	Polydor 2066 026	I Must Be Dreaming/Last Go Round	6
69	Polydor 184 300	THE STREET GIVETH AND THE STREET TAKETH AWAY (LP)	20
70	Polydor 2425 021	ALBION DOO-WAH (LP, gatefold sleeve)	15
72	United Artists UAG 29313	CAT MOTHER & ALL NIGHT NEWS BOYS (LP, gatefold sleeve)	20
73	United Artists UAG 29381	LAST CHANCE DANCE (LP)	15

CATS

69	Baf BAF 1	Swan Lake/Swing Low	10
69	Baf BAF 2	My Girl/The Hog	8
69	Baf BAF 3	The Hig/Blues For Justice	8
69	Baf BAF 4	William Tell/Love Walk Right In	8

CATS

67	Parlophone R 5558	What A Crazy Life/Hopeless Try	7
68	Parlophone R 5663	What Is The World Coming To/How Could I Be So Blind?	10
69	Columbia DB 8524	I Gotta Know What's Going On/Lea	10
69	Columbia DB 8571	Why/Mandy, My Dear	5
70	Columbia DB 8655	Marian/Somewhere Up There	5
71	Columbia DB 8748	I Love You, I Do/Where Have I Been Wrong	5
71	Columbia DB 8816	One Way Mind/Country Woman	5
72	Columbia DB 8850	Dance, Dance, Dance/My Friend Joe	5
72	Columbia DB 8909	Let's Dance/I've Been In Love Before	5
71	Columbia SCX 6459	TAKE ME WITH YOU (LP)	12

CATS EYES

68	Deram DM 190	Smile Girl For Me/In A Fantasy World	10
68	Deram DM 209	I Thank You Marianne/Turn Around	10
69	Deram DM 251	Where Is She Now?/Tom Drum	25
70	MCA MK 5028	Loser/Circus	12
70	MCA MK 5043	Circus/Come Away Melinda	5
70	MCA MK 5056	The Wizard/Hey (Open Your Eyes)	20

CAT'S PYJAMAS

(see also Kenny Bernard)

68	Direction 58-3235	Virginia Waters/Baby I Love You	35
68	Direction 58-3482	Camera Man/House For Sale	35

CLEM CATTINI ORK

(see also Tornados, Aquarian Age, Rumplestiltskin, Spaghetti Head, Sounds Nice)

65	Decca F 12135	No Time To Think/Impact	50

NADIA CATTOUSE

61	Parlophone R 4725	The Boy Without A Heart/Long Time, Boy	7
65	Parlophone R 5420	Port Mahon/A Little More Oil	7
66	Reality RE 503	Beautiful Barbados/Turn Around	8
60s	Church Miss. Soc. LIV/SP/81	The Larder/PAULINE FILBY: I'm Hungry	8
66	Reality RY 1001	NADIA CATTOUSE (LP)	40
70	RCA Victor SF 8070	EARTH MOTHER (LP, orange/white label)	30

MINT VALUE £

CAUSE N EFFECT

90	Foxadelic JTF1	Hype/That's What It Is	20
91	Foxadelic JTF2	Some Bite The Bullet (EP)	12

CAUSTIC WINDOW

(see also Aphex Twin)

92	Rephlex CAT 004	JOYREX J4 EP (12", 6-track)	40
92	Rephlex CAT 005	JOYREX J5 EP (12, 4-track, black vinyl)	50
92	Rephlex CAT 005	JOYREX J5 EP (12, 4-track, white vinyl)	40
93	Rephlex CAT 009 i	JOYREX J9 EP (10", picture disc, with bonus track "HMNA", 300 only)	80
93	Rephlex CAT 009 ii	JOYREX J9 EP (12" 4-track, initial batch in card mailer with bag of "space dust").	60
93	Rephlex CAT 009 ii	JOYREX J9 EP (12" 4-track)	50

CAVALIERS

86	él GPO 11	It's A Beautiful Game/The I.T. Man (p/s)	10
86	él ACME 4	A PERFECT ACTION (LP).	18

EDDIE CAVE & FYX

66	Pye 7N 17161	Fresh Out Of Tears/It's Almost Good	50

NICK CAVE (& BAD SEEDS)

(see also Birthday Party, Annie Hogan, Burmoe Brothers)

84	Mute 7 MUTE 32	In The Ghetto/The Moon Is In The Gutter (p/s)	8
85	Mute 7 MUTE 38	Tupelo/The Six Strings That Drew Blood (p/s).	8
86	Lyntone LYN 18038	Scum (green vinyl flexidisc, with poster, concert freebie)	18
86	Lyntone LYN 18038	Scum (green vinyl flexidisc, without poster, concert freebie)	12
88	Mute MUTE 86	Oh Deanna/The Girl At The Bottom Of My Class (no p/s, DJ-only)	10
88	Mute 12MUTE86	Deanna/The Girl At The Bottom Of My Glass (12". with poster and postcard)	8
92	Mute LMUTE 140	Straight To You/Jack The Ripper (Acoustic Version) (limited issue, p/s)	8
92	Mute MUTE 148	I Had A Dream, Joe/The Good Son (live) (numbered p/s, 7,000 only)	8
94	Mute MUTE 160	Do You Love Me? (Single Version)/Cassiel's Song/Sail Away (silver vinyl, p/s, 1,000 copies)	10
94	Mute MUTE 169	Loverman (Single Version)/(I'll Love You) Till The End Of The World (picture disc, 2,000 only)	10
94	Mute MUTE 172	Red Right Hand/That's What Jazz Is To Me (red vinyl, p/s, with 2 different stickers & labels, 2,000 only)	10
85	Mute STUMM 21	THE FIRSTBORN IS DEAD (LP, with inner sleeve)	15
86	Mute STUMM 28	KICKING AGAINST THE PRICKS (LP).	15
86	Mute STUMM 34	YOUR FUNERAL...MY TRIAL (2-LP, gatefold sleeve, with inner sleeves)	18
88	Mute LSTUMM 52	TENDER PREY (LP, with bonus spoken word 12" And The Ass Saw The Angel [P STUMM 52]: "Autumn"/ Animal Static/Mah Sanctum/Lamentation, 5,000 only)	25
90	Mute LSTUMM 76	THE GOOD SON (LP, with bonus 7" "Acoustic Versions From Tender Prey" [P STUMM 76]: "The Mercy Seat"/"City Of Refuge"/"Deanna")	15
90	Mute STUMM 76	THE GOOD SON (LP, inner sleeve and free 7")	18
90	Mute CDSTUMM 76	THE GOOD SON (CD, with bonus CD "Acoustic Versions From Tender Prey" [P STUMM 76]: "The Mercy Seat"/"City Of Refuge"/"Deanna")	18
92	Mute STUMM 92	HENRY'S DREAM (LP, with inner sleeve).	15
94	Mute LSTUMM 123	LET LOVE IN (LP, with set of postcards or poster).	20
96	Mute STUMM 138	MURDER BALLADS (LP, with insert)	25
01	Mute STUMM 164	NO MORE SHALL WE PART (2-LP, with inner sleeves)	25
04	Mute STUMM 233	ABBATOIR BLUES (2-LP, inner sleeves and insert)	20

ANDY CAVELL

62	HMV POP 1024	Hey There Cruel Heart/Lonely Soldier Boy	40
62	HMV POP 1080	Always On Saturday/Hey There, Senorita	40
63	Pye 7N 15539	Andy/There Was A Boy.	40
64	Pye 7N 15610	Shut Up/Tell The Truth	40

JIMMY CAVELLO & HIS HOUSE ROCKERS

(see also Alan Freed)

57	Vogue Coral Q 72226	Rock, Rock, Rock/The Big Beat	250
57	Vogue Coral Q 72226	Rock, Rock, Rock/The Big Beat (78).	35
57	Vogue Coral Q 72240	Foot Stompin'/Ooh-Wee.	250
57	Vogue Coral Q 72240	Foot Stompin'/Ooh-Wee (78)	35

CAVEMAN

90	Profile PROFT 296	Victory (12").	8
91	Profile PROFT 330DJ	I'm Ready/Pages & Pages/Back To Cause Mayhem (EP)	8
90	Profile PROFT 286	Fry You Like Fish (12").	8
91	Profile FILER 406	POSITIVE REACTION (LP).	12

TERRY CAVENDISH ORCHESTRA

73	Pye NSPL 41023	ALL IN AN AFTERNOON'S WORK (LP)	15

CAVE OF THE LIVING STREAMS

74	Indigo Sound UHC 1	SIXTEEN SONGS (LP, private pressing with booklet).	40

MONTE CAZAZZA

(see also Psychic TV)

79	Industrial IR 0005	To Mom On Mother's Day/Candy Man (p/s, with outer polystyrene sleeve & insert, 2,500 only)	12
80	Industrial IR 0010	SOMETHING FOR NOBODY (EP)	10
81	Industrial IRC 28	LIVE AT LEEDS FAN CLUB (cassette)	10

C.C.S. (Collective Consciousness Society)

(see also Alexis Korner)

73	Rak RAK 154	The Band Played The Boogie/Hang It On Me.	5
70	Rak SRAK 6751	C.C.S. (LP, gatefold sleeve)	20
72	Rak SRAK 503	C.C.S. (LP)	18
73	Rak SRAK 504	THE BEST BAND IN THE LAND (LP)	15

MINT VALUE £

CEDARS
(see also Seaders)

68	Decca F 22720	For Your Information/Hide If You Want To Hide	50
68	Decca F 22772	I Like The Way/I Don't Know Why	50

CELEBRATION FEATURING MIKE LOVE
(see also Beach Boys)

73	MCA 365	Almost Summer/Lookin' Good	8

CELIA & THE MUTATIONS
(see also Stranglers, Tonight)

77	United Artists UP 36262	Mony Mony/Mean To Me (p/s)	6
77	United Artists UP 36318	You Better Believe Me/Round And Around (p/s)	10

CELLOPHANE
(see under Selofane)

CELTIC F.C.

67	Thistle	Celtic Celtic (p/s)	12
73	Polydor 2058332	Celtic Your Favourites In Green/Saturday	5

CELTIC FROST

84	Noise N 0017	MORBID TALES (mini-LP, with poster)	40
84	Noise N 0017	MORBID TALES (mini-LP, without poster)	25
86	Combat MX 8091	TO MEGA THERION (LP, gatefold, with inner sleeve)	18
87	NOIXE NOISE 065	INTO THE PANDEMONIUM (LP, gatefold sleeve, with insert)	18

CENOTAPH CORNER

76	Cottage COT 501	UPS AND DOWNS (LP)	20
79	Cottage COT 031	EVERY DAY BUT WEDNESDAY (LP)	25

CENTIPEDE
(see also Mark Charig, Ian Carr, Elton Dean, Zoot Money, Alan Skidmore, Keith Tippett, Julie Tippetts, Mike Patto, Robert Wyatt)

71	RCA Neon NE 9	SEPTOBER ENERGY (2-LP, gatefold sleeve, black inner sleeve)	70
74	RCA DPS 2054	SEPTOBER ENERGY (2-LP, reissue, different cover)	20

CENTRY

80s	Conscious Sounds DPS 001	Stepping Time/Stepping Dub (12")	10

CENTURION

82	Centurion 0001	Two Wheels/Bitch (private pressing)	50
82	Centurion 0001	Two Wheels/Bitch (private pressing, mislabelled 'Nikki')	30

CENTURY 21 (Gerry Anderson TV spin-offs)
(see also Barry Gray, Dr. Who)

65	Century 21 MA 100	JOURNEY TO THE MOON (EP)	15
65	Century 21 MA 101	INTO ACTION WITH TROY TEMPEST (EP)	12
65	Century 21 MA 102	A TRIP TO MARINEVILLE (EP)	15
65	Century 21 MA 103	INTRODUCING THUNDERBIRDS (EP)	15
65	Century 21 MA 104	MARINA SPEAKS (EP)	15
65	Century 21 MA 105	TV CENTURY 21 THEMES (EP)	15
66	Century 21 MA 106	THE DALEKS (EP)	50
66	Century 21 MA 107	F.A.B. (EP)	18
66	Century 21 MA 108	THUNDERBIRD 1 (EP)	18
66	Century 21 MA 109	THUNDERBIRD 2 (EP)	18
66	Century 21 MA 110	THE STATELY HOME ROBBERIES (EP)	25
66	Century 21 MA 111	LADY PENELOPE & OTHER TV THEMES (EP)	25
66	Century 21 MA 112	THUNDERBIRD 3 (EP)	25
66	Century 21 MA 113	THUNDERBIRD 4 (EP)	25
66	Century 21 MA 114	THE PERILS OF PENELOPE (EP)	30
66	Century 21 MA 115	TOPO GIGIO IN LONDON (EP)	45
67	Century 21 MA 116	GREAT THEMES FROM GERRY ANDERSON'S THUNDERBIRDS (EP)	30
67	Century 21 MA 117	SPACE AGE NURSERY RHYMES (EP)	35
67	Century 21 MA 118	LADY PENELOPE AND PARKER (EP)	35
67	Century 21 MA 119	BRAINS AND TIN TIN (EP)	35
67	Century 21 MA 120	INTERNATIONAL RESCUE (EP)	35
67	Century 21 MA 121	THUNDERBIRDS (EP)	35
67	Century 21 MA 122	LADY PENELOPE (EP)	35
67	Century 21 MA 123	BRAINS (EP)	35
67	Century 21 MA 124	BRINK OF DISASTER (EP)	35
67	Century 21 MA 125	ATLANTIC INFERNO (EP)	35
67	Century 21 MA 126	RICOCHET (EP)	35
67	Century 21 MA 127	TINGHA & TUCKER & THE WOMBAVILLE BAND (EP)	35
67	Century 21 MA 128	ONE MOVE & YOU'RE DEAD (EP)	35
67	Century 21 MA 129	30 MINUTES AFTER NOON (EP)	35
67	Century 21 MA 130	TINGHA & TUCKER IN NURSERY RHYME TIME (EP)	35
67	Century 21 MA 131	INTRODUCING CAPTAIN SCARLET (EP)	30
67	Century 21 MA 132	CAPTAIN SCARLET AND THE MYSTERONS (EP)	30
67	Century 21 MA 133	CAPTAIN SCARLET IS INDESTRUCTIBLE (EP)	25
67	Century 21 MA 134	CAPTAIN SCARLET OF SPECTRUM (EP)	20
67	Century 21 MA 135	CAPTAIN SCARLET VS. CAPTAIN BLACK (EP)	25
67	Century 21 MA 136	THEMES FROM GERRY ANDERSON'S CAPTAIN SCARLET (EP)	25
65	Century 21 LA 100	JOURNEY TO THE MOON (LP)	70
66	Century 21 LA 1	THE WORLD OF TOMORROW (LP)	50
66	Century 21 LA 2	LADY PENELOPE PRESENTS (LP)	50
66	Century 21 LA 3	JEFF TRACY INTRODUCES INTERNATIONAL RESCUE (LP)	50
66	Century 21 LA 4	LADY PENELOPE INVESTIGATES (LP)	50
66	Century 21 LA 5	THE TINGHA & TUCKER CLUB SONG BOOK (LP)	50
67	Century 21 LA 6	FAVOURITE TELEVISION THEMES (LP)	50
68	Marble Arch MAL 770	TV FAVOURITES VOL. 1 (LP)	20
68	Marble Arch MAL 771	TV FAVOURITES VOL. 2 (LP)	20

MINT VALUE £

CEOLBEG

90	Ceolbeg Music CB 001	NOT THE BUNNY HOP (LP)	20

CERTAIN LIONS & TIGERS

70	Polydor 2344 002	SOUL CONDOR (LP)	40

FRANK CHACKSFIELD

56	Decca F10639	In Old Lisbon/Memories Of You	8
56	Decca F 10743	The Donkey Cart/Two Banks Of The Seine	8

CHAD (STUART) & JEREMY (CLYDE)

(see also John Barry, Jeremy Clyde)

64	Ember EMB S 180	Yesterday's Gone/Lemon Tree (as Chad Stuart & Jeremy Clyde)	6
64	Ember EMB S 186	Early In The Morning/Like I Love You Today (as Chad Stuart & Jeremy Clyde)	6
64	United Artists UP 1062	Summer Song/No Tears For Johnnie (as Chad Stuart & Jeremy Clyde)	5
64	United Artists UP 1070	Willow Weep For Me/If She Was Mine	5
65	Ember EMB S 205	If I Loved You/No Tears For Johnnie	5
65	CBS 201769	Before And After/Evil-Hearted Me	5
65	CBS 201814	I Don't Want To Lose You/Pennies	5
66	CBS 202279	Distant Shores/Last Night	5
66	CBS b202397	You Are She/I Won't Cry	12
64	Ember EMB EP 4543	YESTERDAY'S GONE (EP)	12
65	United Artists UEP 1008	CHAD STUART AND JEREMY CLYDE (EP)	15

ERNIE CHAFFIN

57	London HLS 8409	Feelin' Low/Lonesome For My Baby	160
57	London HLS 8409	Feelin' Low/Lonesome For My Baby (78)	60

CHAIN REACTION

77	Gull GULS 43	This Eternal Flame/Never Lose, Never Win	20
77	Gull GULS 53	Why Can't We Be Lovers/Hogtied	18

CHAINSAW

80	Square SQSP 2	Police And Politicians/Hole In The Road (p/s)	45
80	Pot Belly EJSP 9462	Lonely Without You/On The Highway	35
84	GMC CS 001	Long Legged Woman/Midnight Blue	30
84	Thunderbolt THBE 1006	MASSACRE (12" EP)	8

CHAIRMEN OF THE BOARD

(see also Showmen, General Johnson, Norman Johnson)

70	Invictus INV 501	Give Me Just A Little More Time/Since The Days Of Pigtails	8
70	Invictus INV 501	Give Me Just A Little More Time/Since The Days Of Pigtails (DJ Copy)	20
70	Invictus INV 504	You've Got Me Dangling On A String/Patches	6
70	Invictus INV 504	You've Got Me Dangling On A String/Patches (DJ Copy)	20
71	Invictus INV 507	Everything's Tuesday/Bless You	6
71	Invictus INV 507	Everything's Tuesday/Bless You (DJ Copy)	15
71	Invictus INV 511	Pay To The Piper/When Will She Tell Me She Needs Me?	5
71	Invictus INV 511	Pay To The Piper/When Will She Tell Me She Needs Me? (DJ Copy)	15
71	Invictus INV 516	Chairman Of The Board/Hanging On To A Memory	5
71	Invictus INV 516	Chairman Of The Board/When Will She Tell Me She Needs Me? (different B-side)	5
72	Invictus INV 519	Working On A Building Of Love/Try On My Love For Size	5
72	Invictus INV 524	Elmo James/Bittersweet	5
72	Invictus INV 527	I'm On My Way To A Better Place/So Glad You're Mine	5
73	Invictus INV 530	Finders Keepers/Finders Keepers (Instrumental)	5
70	Invictus SVT 1002	CHAIRMEN OF THE BOARD (LP)	20
71	Invictus SVT 1003	IN SESSION (LP)	20
72	Invictus SVT 1006	BITTERSWEET (LP)	20
73	Invictus SVT 1009	GREATEST HITS (LP)	15
74	Invictus 65868	SKIN I'M IN (LP)	20

CHAKACHAS

61	RCA RCA 1264	Twist Twist/Baila La Bamba	8
72	Polydor 2121 093	Jungle Fever/Chaka Cha	10
72	Polydor 2489 050	JUNGLE FEVER (LP)	20
73	Young Blood SYB 3003	CHAKACHAS (LP)	20

GEORGE CHAKIRIS

59	Saga SAG 45-2905	Cool/I Got Rhythm	5
60	Triumph RGM 1010	Heart Of A Teenage Girl/I'm Always Chasing Rainbows	40

BRYAN CHALKER('S NEW FRONTIER)

70	Amity OTS 502	Ned Kelly/Four Girls From The Town Of Boston	6
72	Columbia DB 8883	Daddy Sang Bass/Lot 69	6
72	Chapter One SCH 179	Help Me Make It Through The Night/Eskimo Song	6
73	Chapter One SCH 185	Daisy A Day/Life Gets Tee-jus, Don't It	6
71	Avenue AVE 071	THE HANGING OF SAMUEL HALL (LP, as Bryan Chalker's New Frontier)	15

CHALLENGER

81	CMC CM 0001	So Sure Of Yourself/Out To Kill	20

CHALLENGERS (U.K.)

61	Parlophone R 4773	Cry Of The Wild Goose/Deadline	15

CHALLENGERS (U.S.)

63	Stateside SS 177	Torquay/Bulldog	20
65	Vocalion V 9253	The Man From U.N.C.L.E./The Streets Of London	20
66	Vocalion V 9270	Walk With Me/How Could I	10
63	Stateside SL 10030	SURFBEAT (LP)	70
67	Vocalion VA-N 8069	WIPE OUT (LP, mono)	65
67	Vocalion SAV-N 8069	WIPE OUT (LP, stereo)	75

JUDITH CHALMERS & DAVID JACOBS

74	G&C	SOUNDS BEAUTIFUL (LP)	25

MINT VALUE £

RICHARD CHAMBERLAIN

62	MGM 1173	Love Me Tender/All I Do Is Dream Of You	5
62	MGM EP 776	RICHARD CHAMBERLAIN (EP)	8

CHAMBER POP ENSEMBLE

68	Decca F 12789	Walk Away Renee/59th Street Bridge Song (Feeling Groovy)	6
68	Decca LK/SKL 4933	CHAMBER POP ENSEMBLE (LP)	20

CHAMBERPOT

76	Bead Records BEAD 2	CHAMBERPOT (LP)	50

JAMES CHAMBERS

(see also Jimmy Cliff)

71	Summit SUM 8523	Bongo Man/KEN BOOTHE: Now I Know	10

CHAMBERS BROTHERS

66	Vocalion VL 9267	Love Me Like The Rain/Pretty Girls Everywhere	20
66	Vocalion VL 9276	Call Me/Seventeen	20
67	CBS 202565	All Strung Out Over You/Falling In Love	10
68	Direction 58-3215	Up Town/Love Me Like The Rain	7
68	Direction 58-3671	Time Has Come Today/Dinah	12
68	Direction 58-3760	Time Has Come Today/Dinah (reissue)	8
68	Direction 58-3865	I Can't Turn You Loose/Do Your Thing	8
69	Direction 58-4098	Are You Ready/You Got The Power To Turn Me On	6
69	Direction 58-4318	People Get Ready/No, No, No, Don't Say Goodbye	6
69	Direction 58-4367	Wake Up/Everybody Needs Someone	10
70	Direction 58-4846	Love Peace And Happiness/If You Want Me To	7
70	Direction 58-5033	Let's Do It/To Love Somebody	7
71	CBS 5389	Funky/Love, Peace And Happiness	15
71	CBS 7689	By The Hair On My Chinny Chin Chin/Heaven	6
66	Vocalion VA-L/SAV-L 8058	PEOPLE GET READY (LP)	60
68	Liberty LBS 83272	SHOUT! (LP, blue label)	30
68	Direction 8-63407	THE TIME HAS COME (LP)	30
69	Direction 8-63451	A NEW TIME - A NEW DAY (LP)	30
70	Direction 8-66228	LOVE PEACE AND HAPPINESS (Live At Bill Graham's Fillmore West) (2-LP)	30
70	Liberty LBS 83276	FEELIN' THE BLUES (LP)	15
71	CBS 64156	A NEW GENERATION (LP)	15

CHAMELEON

71	CBS 5428	Who Am I/Coogans Keep	20

CHAMELEONS

(see also Sun & Moon, Reegs)

82	Epic EPCA 2210	In Shreds/Less Than Human (p/s)	15
83	Statik STAT 30	As High As You Can Go/Pleasure And Pain (p/s)	6
83	Statik STAT 3012	As High As You Can Go/Pleasure And Pain/Paper Tigers (12", p/s)	10
83	Statik TAK 6	A Person Isn't Safe Anywhere These Days/Thursday's Child (p/s)	7
83	Statik TAK 6/12	A Person Isn't Safe Anywhere These Days/Thursday's Child/ Prisoners Of The Sun (12", p/s)	8
85	Statik TAK 29	In Shreds/Nostalgia (p/s)	6
85	Statik TAK 29/12	In Shreds/Less Than Human/Nostalgia (12", p/s)	10
85	Statik TAK 35/12	Singing Rule Britannia (While The Walls Close In)/Singing Rule Britannia (Radio 1 'Saturday Live' Session Version) (12", p/s)	8
86	Geffen GEF 4F/SAM 287	Tears/Paradiso//Swamp Thing/Inside Out (double pack, gatefold p/s)	7
90	Glass Pyramid EMC 1	TONY FLETCHER WALKED ON WATER (12" EP)	35
90	Glass Pyramid EMCD 1	TONY FLETCHER WALKED ON WATER (CD EP)	30
90	Glass Pyramid EMC 2	TRIPPING DOGS (LP)	20
85	Statik STATLP 17	SCRIPT OF THE BRIDGE (LP, picture disc)	20
85	Statik STATLP 22	WHAT DOES ANYTHING MEAN? BASICALLY (LP, gatefold sleeve, with insert)	12

TEDDY CHAMES

68	Blue Cat BS 141	I Want It Girl/She Is Gone (actually by Teddy Charmes)	30

CHAMPIONS

63	Oriole CB 1854	Circlorama/Pinky	15

CHAMPIONS OF NATURE

00	White FOFF 1	The Fuck Off Song/An Undercurrent/360/Carpe Diem (EP)	40
00	White FOFF 2	Finalisation/Cold Dessert/Breakfast Of Champions (EP)	40
01	White SALSA001	Salsa Smurph/Jazzy Styles (12")	25
01	Wordplay WORD T020	Salsa Smurph/Jazzy Styles (12")	8

CHAMPS (Jamaica)

64	Blue Beat BB 267	Walk Between Your Enemies/Do What I Say	20

CHAMPS (U.S.)

58	London HLU 8580	Tequila/Train To Nowhere	15
58	London HLU 8580	Tequila/Train To Nowhere (78)	10
58	London HL 8655	Midnighter/El Rancho Rock	15
58	London HL 8655	Midnighter/El Rancho Rock (78)	12
58	London HL 8715	Chariot Rock/Subway	15
58	London HL 8715	Chariot Rock/Subway (78)	20
59	London HLH 8811	Beatnik/Gone Train	12
59	London HLH 8811	Beatnik/Gone Train (78)	20
59	London HLH 8864	Caramba/Moonlight Bay	12
59	London HLH 8864	Caramba/Moonlight Bay (78)	20
60	London HLH 9052	Too Much Tequila/Twenty Thousand Leagues	10
61	London HLH 9430	Cantina/Panic Button	10
62	London HLH 9506	Tequila Twist/Limbo Rock	10
62	London HLH 9539	Experiment In Terror/La Cucaracha	10
62	London HLH 9604	Limbo Dance/Latin Limbo	10
59	London RE 1176	FOUR BY THE CHAMPS (EP)	40

			MINT VALUE £
59	London RE-H 1209	ANOTHER FOUR BY THE CHAMPS (EP)	40
59	London RE-H 1223	STILL MORE BY THE CHAMPS (EP)	40
61	London RE-H 1250	KNOCKOUTS! (EP)	50
58	London HA-H 2152	GO CHAMPS GO! (LP)	60
59	London HA-H 2184	EVERYBODY'S ROCKIN' WITH THE CHAMPS (LP)	60
62	London HA-H 2451	GREAT DANCE HITS (LP, early issue with flipback cover)	40
62	London HA-H 2451	GREAT DANCE HITS (LP)	25

JACQUI CHAN
(see also Simon Dupree & Big Sound)

60	Pye 7N 15273	But No One Knows/Gentlemen Please!	5

ROB CHANCE & CHANCES-R
(see also Chances-R)

67	CBS 3130	At The End Of The Day/I've Got The Power	12

CHANCES ARE

67	Columbia DB 8144	Fragile Child/What Went Wrong	40

CHANCES-R
(see also Ron Chance & Chances-R)

67	CBS 202614	Talking Out The Back Of My Head/I Aimed Too High	20
67	CBS 2940	Do It Yourself/Turn A New Leaf Over	12

CHANCIS

64	Decca F 11860	Everybody's Laughing/Tell Me	15

CHANDELIERS

73	Penny Farthing PEN 809	Can't You Hear My Neartbrek/One Way Street	6

TIM CHANDELL

78	Orbitone 05	Keep Me/Let's Make Love	20

DANY CHANDELLE

65	Columbia DB 7540	Lying Awake/I Love You	30

BARBARA CHANDLER

63	London HLR 9823	Do You Really Love Me Too?/I Live To Love You	30
64	London HLR 9861	I'm Going Out With The Girls/Lonely New Year	35

GENE CHANDLER

62	Columbia DB 4793	Duke Of Earl/Kissing In The Kitchen	30
63	Stateside SS 185	Rainbow/You Threw A Lucky Punch	40
64	Stateside SS 331	Just Be True/A Song Called Soul	25
64	Stateside SS 364	Bless Our Love/London Town	25
65	Stateside SS 388	What Now/If You Can't Be True (Find A Part Time Love)	35
65	Stateside SS 401	You Can't Hurt Me No More/Everybody Let's Dance	25
65	Stateside SS 425	Nothing Can Stop Me/The Big Lie	60
65	Stateside SS 425	Nothing Can Stop Me/The Big Lie (DJ copy)	150
65	Stateside SS 458	Good Times/No One Can Love You (Like I Do)	35
66	Stateside SS 500	(I'm Just A) Fool For You/Buddy Ain't It A Shame	35
66	Chess CRS 8047	I Fooled You This Time/Such A Pretty Thing	40
66	Chess CRS 8047	I Fooled You This Time/Such A Pretty Thing (DJ copy)	80
67	Coral Q 72490	The Girl Don't Care/My Love	20
68	Soul City SC 102	Nothing Can Stop Me/The Big Lie (reissue)	15
69	Action ACT 4551	I Can't Save It/I Can Take Care Of Myself	60
69	President PT 234	Duke Of Earl/Stand By Me	8
70	Mercury 6052 033	Groovy Situation/Not The Marrying Kind	6
71	Mercury 6052 098	You're A Lady/Stone Cold Feeling	15
76	Brunswick BR 39	There Was A Time/ARTISTICS: I'm Gonna Miss You	10
65	Fontana TL 5247	DUKE OF EARL (LP)	100
67	Coral LVA 9236	THE GIRL DON'T CARE (LP)	60
69	MCA MUPS 367	THERE WAS A TIME (LP)	30
69	Action ACLP 6010	LIVE ON STAGE (LP)	50
71	Mercury 6338 037	SITUATION (LP)	20
74	Joy JOYS 136	A GENE CHANDLER ALBUM (LP)	15

GENE CHANDLER & BARBARA ACKLIN
(see also Barbara Acklin, Gene & Jerry)

74	Brunswick BR 30	From The Teacher To The Preacher/Little Green Apples	10

GEORGE CHANDLER

82	Polydor 436	This Could Be The Night/Can't Go Back No More	15

JEFF CHANDLER

54	Brunswick 05264	I Should Care/More Than Anyone	10
55	Brunswick 05380	Everything Happens To Me/Always	10
55	Brunswick 05417	My Prayer/When Spring Comes	10
55	Brunswick 05441	Foxfire/Shaner Maidel	10
55	Brunswick 05465	Only The Very Young/A Little Love Can Go A Long, Long Way	10
57	London HLU 8484	Half Of My Heart/Hold Me	10
58	London HA-U 2100	JEFF CHANDLER SINGS TO YOU (LP)	45

KAREN CHANDLER
(see also Jimmy Wakely)

55	Vogue Coral Q 72091	The Price You Pay For Love/The Man In The Raincoat	10
56	Brunswick 05570	Love Is The $64,000 Question/(I'm Just A) Beginner	10
56	Brunswick 05596	Tonight You Belong To Me/Crazy Arms (with Jimmy Wakely)	10
57	Brunswick 05662	Your Wild Heart/It's An International Language	10
62	Salvo SLO 1803	My Own True Love/You Made Me Love You (99 copies only)	18

KENNY CHANDLER

63	Stateside SS 166	Heart/Wait For Me	15
68	Stateside SS 2110	Beyond Love/Charity	60
68	Stateside SS 2110	Beyond Love/Charity (DJ Copy)	80

MINT VALUE £

LEN CHANDLER

67	CBS 62931	TO BE A MAN (LP)	20

LORRAINE CHANDLER

75	Black Magic BM 105	Love You Baby/What Can I Do	8
77	Kent 6T 13	You Only Live Twice/METROS: My Imagination	30

CHANDONS

68	RCA RCA 1704	Timber/Never Been Loved Before	6

CHANGE

74	EMI EMI 2354	Wildcat/Hold On	5
73	Orange OAS 210	Yaketty Yak, Smacketty Smack/When The Morning Comes	8

CHANGIN' TIMES

65	Phillips BF 1442	Pied Piper/Thank You Babe	25
68	Bell BLL 1009	When The Good Sun Shines/Show Me The Way To Go Home	6

BRUCE CHANNEL

62	Mercury AMT 1171	Hey! Baby/Dream Girl	8
62	Mercury AMT 1177	Number One Man/If Only I Had Known	10
62	Pye International 7N 25137	Run Romance Run/Don't Leave Me	20
63	London HLU 9776	I Don't Wanna/Blue And Lonesome	20
64	London HLU 9841	Going Back To Louisiana/Forget Me Not	15
67	Stateside SS 2066	Mr. Bus Driver/It's Me	15
68	Bell BLL 1010	Keep On/Barbara Allen	7
68	Bell BLL 1030	Try Me/Water The Family Tree	7
62	Mercury MMC 14104	HEY! BABY! (LP)	90
68	Bell MBLL/SBLL 1110	KEEP ON (LP)	30

CHANNEL 4

79	Ripping RIP 1	Vampire/Channel 4 (numbered p/s with insert)	6

CHANNEL 3

82	No Future OI 11	I've Got A Gun/Manzanar/Mannequin (p/s)	10
82	No Future PUNK 2	I'VE GOT A GUN (LP)	12
83	No Future PUNK 7	AFTER THE LIGHTS GO OUT (LP)	12

CHANTAYS

63	London HLD 9696	Pipeline/Move It	10
64	King KG 1018	Beyond/I'll Be Back Someday	20
66	Dot DS 26757	Pipeline/Move It (reissue)	7
63	London RED 1397	PIPELINE (EP)	60
63	London HA-D 8087	PIPELINE (LP, mono)	60
63	London SH-D 8087	PIPELINE (LP, stereo)	75

CHANTELLES

(see also Lana Sisters)

65	Parlophone R 5271	I Want That Boy/London My Home Town	25
65	Parlophone R 5303	The Secret Of My Success/Sticks And Stones	15
65	Parlophone R 5350	Gonna Get Burned/Gonna Give Him Some Love	15
66	Parlophone R 5431	I Think Of You/Please Don't Kiss Me	15
66	Polydor 56119	There's Something About You/Just Another Fool	20
67	CBS 2777	Blue Mood/The Man I Love	25

CHANTELS

(see also Richard Barrett)

58	London HLU 8561	Maybe/Come My Little Baby	400
58	London HLU 8561	Maybe/Come My Little Baby (78)	60
62	London HLL 9428	Look In My Eyes/Glad To Be Back	55
62	London HLL 9480	Well I Told You/Still	60
62	London HLL 9532	Here It Comes Again/Summertime	40
63	Capitol CL 15297	Swamp Water/Eternally	40
70	Roulette RO 514	Maybe/He's Gone	5

CHANTERS

(see also Birds Of A Feather)

66	CBS 202454	Every Night (I Sit And Cry)/Where	30
67	CBS 202616	You Can't Fool Me/All Day Long	20
68	CBS 3400	What's Wrong With You/Right By Your Side	6
68	CBS 3668	My Love Is For You/Mississippi Paddleboat	8

CHANTER

77	Expert ELP 1	SUBURBAN ETHNIA (LP, private pressing)	12

CHANTERS

79	Burning Rockers BRD 011	Mash Down Babylon/I Told You So (12")	25

CHANTS (U.K.)

(see also Real Thing)

63	Pye 7N 15557	I Don't Care/Come Go With Me	25
64	Pye 7N 15591	I Could Write A Book/A Thousand Stars	22
64	Pye 7N 15643	She's Mine/Then I'll Be Home	22
64	Pye 7N 15691	Sweet Was The Wine/One Star	18
66	Fontana TF 716	Come Back And Get This Loving Baby/Love Light	15
67	Decca F 12650	A Lover's Story/Wearing A Smile	25
67	Page One POF 016	Ain't Nobody Home/For You	15
68	RCA Victor RCA 1754	A Man Without A Face/Baby I Don't Need Your Love	100
68	RCA Victor RCA 1754	A Man Without A Face/Baby I Don't Need Your Love (DJ Copy)	130
69	RCA Victor RCA 1823	I Get The Sweetest Feeling/Candy	25
76	Chipping Norton CHIP 2	I've Been Trying/Lucky Old Me	40

CHANTS (U.S.)

58	Capitol CL 14876	Close Friends/Lost And Found	35

MINT VALUE £

CHAOS

79	Chaotic Records VD 1	Summer Of Hate/I Want To Be Left Alone (p/s, 500 only)	100

(originals have a rim around the label - counterfeits have no rim)

CHAOS & JULIA SET

(see also Global Communications)

93	Recoil RCL 001	VOL. 1 ATMOSPHERE EP (12", plain sleeve)	10
93	Recoil RCL 002	VOL. 2 - FEAR OF THE FUTURE (12", plain sleeve)	12

CHAOS U.K.

82	Riot City RIOT 6	BURNING BRITAIN (EP)	8
82	Riot City RIOT 12	LOUD, POLITICAL AND UNCOMPROMISING (EP)	10
85	C.O.R. GURT 1	SHORT SHARP SHOCK (LP)	20
86	Manic Ears ACHE 1	RADIOACTIVE (LP, with inner, split with EXTREME NOISE TERROR)	20
89	Slap Up	THE CHIPPING SODBURY BONFIRE TAPES (LP)	12

CHAOTIC DISCHORD

81	Riot City 12 ROT 30	Don't Throw It Away (12")	15
83	Riot City RIOT RIOT 22	Never Trust A Friend/Are Students Safe? (p/s)	12
82	Riot City RIOT 10	FUCK THE WORLD (EP)	10
83	Beat The System	SAD SOCIETY (EP)	8
83	Riot City CITY 004	FUCK RELIGION, FUCK POLITICS, AND FUCK THE LOT OF YOU (LP)	15
84	Syndicate SYNLP 12	FUCK OFF YOU CUNT WHAT A LOAD OF BOLLOCKS (LP)	15
86	Not Very Nice GRR 2	GOAT FUCKING VIRGIN KILERZ FROM HELL (LP)	12
88	Not Very Nice GRR 3RV	VERY FUCKIN' BAD (LP)	12

CHAOTIC YOUTH

83	Beat The System YOUTH 1	SAD SOCIETY (EP)	35

HARRY CHAPIN

68	Elektra K 62026	LEGENDS OF THE LOST & FOUND (LP)	15
73	Elektra 7E 1012	VERITIES & BALDERDASH (LP)	15
74	Elektra K 42155	SHORT STORIES (LP, gatefold sleeve)	15
75	Elektra K 52089	LIVING ROOM SUITE (LP)	15
70s	Elektra FW 36872	IN SEQUEL (LP)	15
70s	Elektra K 42107	HEADS & TALES (LP)	15
70s	Elektra E1082	ON THE ROAD TO KINGDOM COME (LP)	15
70s	Elektra K 62021	DANCE BAND ON THE TITANIC (2xLP, gatefold sleeve)	20
70s	Ekektra 7E 1041	PORTRAIT GALLERY (LP, gatefold sleeve)	15
70s	Elektra ELK 62017	HARRY CHAPIN GREATEST STORIES LIVE (2xLP)	18

PAUL CHAPLAIN & HIS EMERALDS

60	London HLU 9205	Shortnin' Bread/Nicotine	20

CHARLES CHAPLIN

57	HMV POP 370	The Spring Song/Mandolin Serenade	6

CHAPMAN AND WHITNEY

(see also Family, Streetwalkers)

74	Resprise K54017	STREETWALKERS (LP)	20

COLIN CHAPMAN

60s	CCLP 1001	FOLK SONGS VOL 1 (LP)	15

GENE CHAPMAN

63	Starlite ST45 102	Oklahoma Blues/Don't Come Crying	150

GRADY CHAPMAN

60	Mercury AMT 1107	Sweet Thing/I Know What I Want	30

MICHAEL CHAPMAN

69	Harvest HAR 5002	It Didn't Work Out/Mozart Lives Upstairs	7
69	Harvest SHVL 755	RAINMAKER (LP, gatefold sleeve, with "Sold in U.K..." label text on 4 lines, no EMI on label)	100
69	Harvest SHVL 755	RAINMAKER (LP, gatefold sleeve, later pressing with EMI on label)	40
70	Harvest SHVL 764	FULLY QUALIFIED SURVIVOR (LP, gatefold sleeve, 1st pressing with no EMI on label)	80
70	Harvest SHVL 764	FULLY QUALIFIED SURVIVOR (LP, gatefold sleeve, later pressing with EMI on label)	20
70	Harvest SHVL 786	WINDOW (LP, gatefold sleeve, with no EMI on label)	70
70	Harvest SHVL 786	WINDOW (LP, gatefold sleeve, later pressing with EMI on label)	20
71	Harvest SHVL 798	WRECKED AGAIN (LP, gatefold sleeve, EMI on label)	50
73	Deram SML 1105	MILLSTONE GRIT (LP, red/white label)	18
74	Deram SML 1114	DEAL GONE DOWN (LP)	15
76	Decca SKL-R 5242	SAVAGE AMUSEMENT (LP, with lyric sheet, blue/silver label)	20
70s	Standard ESL 146	GUITARS (LP, library issue)	60

CHAPS

(see also Outlaws)

62	Parlophone R 4979	Poppin' Medley (Parts 1 & 2)	25

CHAPTER FIVE

66	CBS 202395	Anything You Do Is Alright/You Can't Mean It	600
67	CBS 2696	One In A Million/Hey Hey (unissued, demos only)	250
90s	Goldmine/Soul Supply GS 009	You Can't Mean It/One In A Million	8

CHAPTER FOUR (U.K.)

60s	GSP 11009/10	CHAPTER FOUR (EP, no p/s)	90

CHAPTER FOUR (U.K.)

80	Bridge BR 001	HANGING AROUND STERLING (LP)	35

CHAPTER FOUR (U.S.)

(see also Jay & Americans)

66	United Artists UP 1143	In My Life/In Each Other's Arms	250

MINT VALUE £

CHAPTER THREE (U.K.)

67	CBS 2971	Cold And Lonely Hours/Wrecking Crew	7
67	CBS BPG 63007	RAMBLE AWAY (LP)	18

CHAPTERHOUSE

(see also Slowdive)

91	Dedicated STONE 003T	PEARL EP (12")	8
91	Dedicated DEDLP 001	WHIRLPOOL (LP)	20

CHAPTERS

65	Pye 7N 15815	Can't Stop Thinking About Her/Dance Little Lady	50

CHAQUITO & HIS ORCHESTRA

(see also Johnny Gregory)

60	Fontana H 265	Never On Sunday/Song Of Orpheus	10
70	Philips 6006055	The Good The Bad And The Ugly/Revolution	8
72	Philips 6006 225	Hawaii 5-0/Ironside	7

CHARACTERS

86	BEM BEM 101	Love Talk/Where Has All The Love Gone (500 only)	30

ERIC CHARDON

69	Major Minor MM596	One Love One Life/Sorrow Is My Name	8

CHARGE

70	private pressing	Zeugma/Boring Song (art sleeve)	20

CHARGE

73	SRT private pressing	CHARGE (LP, 1 known copy)	750
92	Kissing Spell KSLP 9205	CHARGE (LP, reissue, revised sleeve, 500 only)	12

CHARGE

80	YCAFO Records	You Get What You Deserve/Rather B Crazy/Angel Deceast (foldout p/s)	60
81	Test Pressing	You Deserve More Than A Maybe (p/s, 500 only)	20
82	Test Pressing TP 3	Kings Cross/Brave New World (p/s)	12

CHARGERS

84	Charge BCSK 01	Desperaroes/Are You Out There (p/s)	60

MARK CHARIG

(see also Bluesology, B.B. Blunder, Reg King, Centipede, Keith Tippett, Julie Tippett, Brotherhood Of Breath, Elton Dean, Ninesense)

77	Ogun OG 710	PIPEDREAM (LP)	15

CHARIOT

84	Shades SHADE 2	ALL ALONE AGAIN (EP)	12
84	Shades SHADE 1	THE WARRIOR (LP)	15
86	Shades SHADE 4	BURNING AMBITION (LP)	15

CHARIOTS

62	Piccadilly 7N 35061	Problem Girl/Song Of A Broken Heart	15

CHARLATANS (U.K.)

(see also Electric Crayons, Makin' Time)

89	Dead Dead Good no cat.no	OCTOBER '89 (demo cassette, sold at gigs)	40
90	Dead Dead Good GOOD ONE TWELVE	Indian Rope/You Can Talk To Me/Who Wants To Know (12", 1st issue with barcode on p/s)	8
90	Dead Dead Good SIT 70T	The Only One I Know/Imperial 109 (Edit)/Everything Changed (12", p/s)	8
90	Dead Dead Good SIT 74T	Then/Taurus Moaner/Then (Alternate Take)/Taurus Moaner (Instrumental) (12", p/s)	10
91	Situation Two SIT 84T	Me In Time/Occupation/Monster (12" p/s)	8
90	Situation Two SIT 74T	Then/Taurus Moaner/Then (Alternate Take)/Taurus Moaner (Instrumental) (12", mispressing with vocal version of "Taurus Moaner" on both sides)	8
92	Situation Two SIT 88T	Weirdo/Theme From "The Wish"/Sproston Green (U.S. Version)/ Weirdo (Alternate Take) (12", with art print)	10
93	Dead Dead Good GOOD1CD	Indian Rope/You Can Talk To Me/Who Wants To Know (CD single)	12
93	Beggars Banquet CHAR 7	Subterranean (live) (CD, free with 109 fan club magazine)	12
93	Beggars Banquet CHAR 7	Subterranean (live) (CD, free without 109 fan club magazine)	8
94	Beggars Banquet BBQ 31CD1	I Never Want An Easy Life If Me And He Were Ever To Get There/ Only A Boho/Subterranean/Can't Get Out Of Bed (Demo Version) (CD, oblong box set with 3 postcards, numbered)	12
90	Situation Two SITU 30L	SOME FRIENDLY (LP, 'some friendly edition' in white PVC sleeve with inner)	15
91	Live Live Good CB 2	ISOLATION 21.2.91 (LP, official live bootleg, sold via fan club, 1,000 only)	20
92	Situation Two SITU 37	BETWEEN 10TH AND 11TH (CD, box set with cassette & video, promo only)	20
94	Beggars Banquet BBCD 147	UP TO OUR HIPS (CD, box set with cassette & video, promo only)	25

CHARLATANS (U.S.)

(see also Mike Wilhelm, Tongue & Groove, Dan Hicks & His Hot Licks)

69	Philips SBL 7903	THE CHARLATANS (LP)	90

BOBBY CHARLES

78	Bearsville J 15508	Small Town Talk/Grow Too Old	10
72	Bearsville K 45516	BOBBY CHARLES (LP)	15

BOBBY CHARLES

56	London HLU 8247	See You Later, Alligator/On Bended Knee	2500
56	London HLU 8247	See You Later, Alligator/On Bended Knee (78)	300

DON CHARLES

62	Decca F 11424	Walk With Me My Angel/Crazy Man, Crazy	10
62	Decca F 11464	The Hermit Of Misty Mountain/Moonlight Rendezvous	10
62	Decca F 11528	It's My Way Of Loving You/Guess That's The Way It Goes	20
63	Decca F 11602	Angel Of Love/Lucky Star	20
63	Decca F 11645	Heart's Ice Cold/Daybreak	15
63	HMV POP 1271	Tower Tall/Look Before You Love	7

			MINT VALUE £
64	HMV POP 1307	If You Don't Know I Ain't Gonna Tell Ya/Voice On The Phone	7
64	HMV POP 1332	Big Talk From A Little Man/She's Mine	12
65	HMV POP 1382	Forgetting Me, Loving Him/A Long Time Ago	5
65	HMV POP 1420	Dream On Little Dreamer/We Only Live Once	5
65	HMV POP 1478	I Could Conquer The World/Time Will Tell	5
66	HMV POP 1542	Out Of This Cold/From The Beginning	5
67	Parlophone R 5564	So Let It Be/Bring Your Love To Me	5
67	Parlophone R 5596	Have I Told You Lately/Time Waits For Nobody	5
68	Parlophone R 5659	If I Had The Chance/(I've Got Everything) I've Got You	5
68	Parlophone R 5688	The Drifter/Great To Be Livin'	60
68	Parlophone R 5688	The Drifter/Great To Be Livin' (DJ Copy)	85
68	Parlophone R 5712	Your Name Is On My Heart/How Can I	5
63	Decca DFE 8530	DON CHARLES (EP)	70
67	Parlophone PMC/PCS 7021	HAVE I TOLD YOU LATELY (LP, mono/stereo)	20

GARY CHARLES

71	B & C CB 159	You've Been Away Too Long/Lovely Linda	6

JIMMY CHARLES

60	London HLU 9206	A Million To One/Hop Scotch Hop	25
63	Windsor WPS 120	Pitter Pitter Patter/How You Gonna Treat Me Now	10

JOHN CHARLES

60	Cetra SP 785	Sixteen Tons/Love In Portofino	5
60	Cetra SP 786	La Fine (The End)/Non Dimenticar	5

RAY CHARLES

(see also Raelets, Milt Jackson)

78s

58	London HLE 8768	Rockhouse (Parts 1 & 2)	30
59	London HLE 8917	What'd I Say (Parts 1 & 2)	35
59	London HLE 9009	I'm Movin' On/I Believe To My Soul	40
60	HMV POP 792	Georgia On My Mind/Carry Me Back To Old Virginny	110

SINGLES

58	London HLE 8768	Rockhouse (Parts 1 & 2)	30
59	London HLE 8917	What'd I Say (Parts 1 & 2)	25
59	London HLE 9009	I'm Movin' On/I Believe To My Soul	20
60	London HLE 9058	Let The Good Times Roll/Don't Let The Sun Catch You Cryin'	20
60	HMV POP 774	Sticks And Stones/Worried Life Blues	15
60	London HLK 9181	Tell The Truth/You Be My Baby	15
60	HMV POP 792	Georgia On My Mind/Carry Me Back To Old Virginny	7
60	London HLK 9251	Come Rain Or Come Shine/Tell Me You'll Wait For Me	7
61	HMV POP 825	Ruby/Hard Hearted Hannah	6
61	HMV POP 838	Them That Got/I Wonder	25
61	London HLK 9364	Early In The Mornin'/A Bit Of Soul	15
61	HMV POP 862	One Mint Julep/Let's Go	15
61	HMV POP 935	Hit The Road Jack/The Danger Zone	10
61	London HLK 9435	I Wonder Who/Hard Times	12
62	HMV POP 969	Unchain My Heart/But On The Other Hand Baby	7
62	HMV POP 1017	Hide Nor Hair/At The Club	10
63	HMV POP 1133	Don't Set Me Free/The Brightest Smile In Town	7
63	HMV POP 1161	Take These Chains From My Heart/No Letter Today	6
63	HMV POP 1202	No One/Without Love (There Is Nothing)	6
63	HMV POP 1221	Busted/Making Believe	12
64	HMV POP 1251	That Lucky Old Sun/Mississippi Mud	5
64	HMV POP 1272	Baby Don't You Cry/My Heart Cries For You	6
64	HMV POP 1315	My Baby Don't Dig Me/Something's Wrong	10
64	HMV POP 1333	No One To Cry To/A Tear Fell	5
64	HMV POP 1350	Smack Dab In The Middle/I Wake Up Crying	5
65	HMV POP 1383	Makin' Whoopee/Move It On Over	7
65	HMV POP 1392	Cry/Teardrops From My Eye	5
65	HMV POP 1414	Light Out Of Darkness/Please Forgive And Forget	5
65	HMV POP 1437	I Gotta Woman/Without A Song	5
65	HMV POP 1457	Love's Gonna Live Here/I'm A Fool To Care	5
65	HMV POP 1484	The Cincinnati Kid/That's All I Am To You	5
66	HMV POP 1502	Crying Time/When My Dreamboat Comes Home	5
66	HMV POP 1519	Together Again/You're Just About To Lose Your Clown	5
66	HMV POP 1537	Let's Go Get Stoned/The Train	20
66	HMV POP 1551	I Chose To Sing The Blues/Hopelessly	25
66	HMV POP 1566	Please Say You're Fooling/I Don't Need No Doctor	50
66	HMV POP 1566	Please Say You're Fooling/I Don't Need No Doctor (DJ Copy)	80
67	Atlantic 584 093	What'd I Say/I Got A Woman	10
67	HMV POP 1589	You Win Again/Bye Bye Love	5
67	HMV POP 1595	Somebody Oughta Write A Book About It/Here We Go Again	7
67	HMV POP 1607	In The Heat Of The Night/Something's Got To Change	5
67	Stateside SS 2071	Yesterday/Never Had Enough Of Nothing Yet	5
68	Stateside SS 2120	Eleanor Rigby/Understanding	5
71	Tangerine 6121 001	Booty Butt/Zig Zag	8

EPs

59	London Jazz EZK 19043	THE GREAT RAY CHARLES	15
59	London Jazz EZK 19048	SOUL BROTHERS (with Milt Jackson)	15
61	London REK 1306	WHAT'D I SAY	20
61	London REK 1317	RAY CHARLES AT NEWPORT	15
62	HMV 7EG 8729	HIT THE ROAD JACK	15
62	HMV 7EG 8781	I CAN'T STOP LOVING YOU	15
63	HMV 7EG 8783	THE BALLAD STYLE OF RAY CHARLES	10
63	HMV 7EG 8801	THE SWINGING STYLE OF RAY CHARLES	10
63	HMV 7EG 8807	BABY IT'S COLD OUTSIDE (with Betty Carter)	15

MINT VALUE £

63	HMV 7EG 8812	TAKE THESE CHAINS FROM MY HEART	10
63	London REB 1407	THE ORIGINAL RAY CHARLES VOLUME ONE	15
63	London REB 1408	THE ORIGINAL RAY CHARLES VOLUME TWO	15
63	London REB 1409	THE ORIGINAL RAY CHARLES VOLUME THREE	15
64	HMV 7EG 8841	BUSTED	10
64	HMV 7EG 8861	RAY CHARLES SINGS	10
64	Realm REP 4001	THE YOUNG RAY CHARLES	10
66	HMV 7EG 8932	RAY CHARLES LIVE IN CONCERT	10
66	HMV 7EG 8951	RAY CHARLES SINGS SONGS OF BUCK OWENS	15

LPs

58	London Jazz LTZ-K 15134	THE GREAT RAY CHARLES	50
59	London Jazz LTZ-K 15146	SOUL BROTHERS (with Milt Jackson, mono)	25
59	London Jazz SAH-K 6030	SOUL BROTHERS (with Milt Jackson, stereo)	30
59	London Jazz LTZ-K 15149	RAY CHARLES AT NEWPORT (mono)	25
59	London Jazz SAH-K 6008	RAY CHARLES AT NEWPORT (stereo)	30
59	London HA-E 2168	YES INDEED	50
59	London HA-E 2226	WHAT'D I SAY	40
60	London Jazz LTZ-K 15190	THE GENIUS OF RAY CHARLES	40
60	HMV CLP 1387	THE GENIUS HITS THE ROAD (mono)	18
60	HMV CSD 1320	THE GENIUS HITS THE ROAD (stereo)	25
60	London HA-K 2284	RAY CHARLES IN PERSON	25
61	HMV CLP 1449	DEDICATED TO YOU (mono)	15
61	HMV CSD 1362	DEDICATED TO YOU (stereo)	18
61	HMV CLP 1475	GENIUS + SOUL = JAZZ (mono)	15
61	HMV CSD 1384	GENIUS + SOUL = JAZZ (stereo)	18
62	HMV CLP 1520	RAY CHARLES AND BETTY CARTER (mono)	15
62	HMV CSD 1414	RAY CHARLES AND BETTY CARTER (stereo)	18
62	London Jazz LJZ-K 15238	THE GENIUS SINGS THE BLUES	25
62	HMV CLP 1580	MODERN SOUNDS IN COUNTRY & WESTERN (mono)	20
62	HMV CSD 1451	MODERN SOUNDS IN COUNTRY & WESTERN (stereo)	25
63	HMV CLP 1613	MODERN SOUNDS IN COUNTRY & WESTERN VOL. TWO (mono)	20
63	HMV CSD 1477	MODERN SOUNDS IN COUNTRY & WESTERN VOL. TWO (stereo)	25
63	London HA-K 8022	THE ORIGINAL RAY CHARLES	25
63	London HA-K 8023	THE RAY CHARLES STORY VOL. 1	15
63	London HA-K 8024	THE RAY CHARLES STORY VOL. 2	15
63	London HA-K 8035	THE GENIUS AFTER HOURS	20
63	HMV CLP 1626	GREATEST HITS (mono)	12
63	HMV CSD 1482	GREATEST HITS (stereo)	18
63	London HA-K/SH-K 8045	SOUL MEETING (with Milt Jackson)	25
63	HMV CLP 1678	INGREDIENTS IN A RECIPE FOR SOUL	15
64	HMV CLP 1728	SWEET AND SOUR TEARS (mono)	12
64	HMV CSD 1537	SWEET AND SOUR TEARS (stereo)	15
64	HMV CLP 1795	HAVE A SMILE WITH ME (mono)	12
64	HMV CSD 1566	HAVE A SMILE WITH ME (stereo)	15
65	HMV CLP 1872	LIVE IN CONCERT (mono)	12
65	HMV CSD 1696	LIVE IN CONCERT (stereo)	15
65	HMV CLP 1914	C&W MEETS R&B (mono)	12
65	HMV CSD 1630	C&W MEETS R&B (stereo)	15
65	Summit ATL 4144	THE INCOMPARABLE RAY CHARLES (LP, mono, some tracks by Memphis Slim)	12

ROGER CHARLES

73	Dawn DNS 1038	Understand Each Other/Can't Forget	6

SONNY CHARLES (& CHECKMATES LTD)

(see also Checkmates Ltd)

67	Ember EMB S 240	Mastered The Art Of Love/Please Don't Take My World Away	40
69	A&M AMS 752	Black Pearl/Lazy Susan	10
70	A&M AMS 787	It Takes A Little Longer/Welfare Man	6

TINA CHARLES

69	CBS 4015	Nothing In The World/Millions Of Hearts	15
69	CBS 4307	In The Middle Of The Day/Rich Girl	40
69	CBS 4658	Good To Be Alive/Same Old Story	50

CHARLES, PAULETTE & GEE

(see also Charlie Ace)

71	G.G. GG 4515	Shock And Shake (Version 3)/WINSTON WRIGHT: Roll On (Version 2) (as Charlie, Paulette & Gee)	10
71	G.G. GG 4517	Rock And Shake (Version 3) (actually "Lover's Affair" by Charlie Ace & Maytones)/Roll On (Version 2) (actually "My Love And I" by Winston Wright)	10

DICK CHARLESWORTH (& HIS CITY GENTS)

61	Top Rank JAR 558	Billy Boy/Night Fall	5
61	HMV 7EG 8769	DICK CHARLESWORTH & HIS CITY GENTS (EP)	8
61	Top Rank 35-104	MEET THE GENTS (LP)	25
62	HMV CLP 1495	YES INDEED IT'S THE GENTS (LP)	25

CHARLIE

72	Bumble GE 111	Dream Here/Lament	15
73	Decca F 13451	I Need Your Love/I'm So Happy	20

CHARLIE BOY

(see also Lee Perry/Upsetters)

71	Trojan TR 7823	Funky Strip/UPSETTERS: Mellow Mood	25

CHARLIE & FAY

72	Pama 853	Big 7/YOUTH PROFESSIONAL BAND : Version	15

CHARLIE & MELODIANS

(see under Charlie Ace)

MINT VALUE £

CHARLIE PARKAS
(see also Alberto Y Lost Trios Paranoias)

80 Paranoid Plastics PPS 1 The Ballad Of Robin Hood/Space Invaders (p/s) 5

CHARLIE, PAULETTE & GEE
(see under Charles, Paulette & Gee)

CHARLIES BROTHER
84 Lost Moment LMO 100 Wishing Tree/Further Adventures Of 25

CHARLY & THE BOURBON FAMILY
71 Decca F 23164 Acapulco Gold/Boogachi 8

CHARMER
56 Melodisc MEL 1353 Back To Back, Belly To Belly/Is She Is Or Is She Ain't (78) 12

CHARMERS (Jamaica)
(see also Spanishtown Skabeats, Lloyd & Ken, Lloydie & Lowbites, Lloyd Terrell)

61 Blue Beat BB 42 Lonely Boy/I Am Going Back Home 20
62 Blue Beat BB 114 Crying Over You/Now You Want To Cry 20
63 Blue Beat BB 157 Time After Time/Done Me Wrong (with Prince Buster's Band) 20
60s Blue Beat How Could I Forget/Why Won't You Come Home?
(with Prince Buster's Band) (white label only) 75
63 R&B JB 118 Angel Love/My Heart 20
63 R&B JB 121 Oh Why Baby/ROLAND ALPHONSO: Perhaps 30
64 R&B JB 151 What's The Use/I Am Through 20
64 R&B JB 156 In My Soul/Beware 20
64 Blue Beat BB 204 I'm Back/It's A Dream 20
64 Blue Beat BB 238 Waiting For You/You Are My Sunshine 20
64 Blue Beat BB 251 Dig Then Prince (actually Dip Them Prince)/Girl Of My Dreams (as The Charmer) 25
65 Blue Beat BB 279 Nobody Takes My Baby Away From Me/ BUSTER ALLSTARS: Mules Mules Mules 75
66 Blue Beat BB 345 Oh My Baby/STRANGER COLE: When The Party Is Over 20
66 Ska Beat JB 237 Best Friend/MAYTALS: My Darling 25
66 Rio R 78 You Don't Know/CORNELL CAMPBELL & ROY PANTON: Sweetest Girl 20
68 Coxsone CS 7043 Things Going Wrong/KEN BOOTHE: You Keep Me Hanging On 200
68 Treasure Isle TI 7036 Keep On Going (actually by Lloyd Charmers)/SILVERTONES: Don't Say No 20
70 Duke DU 87 Colour Him Father/Version 30
70 Trojan TR 7773 Sweeter She Is (actually by Lloyd Charmers, Dave Barker & Slim Smith)/
Fire Fire (actually by Lloyd Charmers) 12
70 Explosion EX 2026 Can I Get Next To You?/Big Five 7
70 Explosion EX 2035 Sweet Back/Music Talk (actually by Lloyd Charmers) 7
71 Bullet BU 473 Reggae In Wonderland/Wonder (Version) 6
71 Explosion EX 2045 Skinhead Train/TONY & CHARMERS: Everstrong (B-side with Tony Binns) 40
71 Explosion EX 2055 Reggae In Wonderland/Wonder - Version
(both actually by Byron Lee & Dragonaires) 7
71 Supreme SUP 220 Just My Imagination/Gotta Get A Message To You (actually by Dave Barker) 25
71 Green Door GD 4000 Rasta Never Fails (actually by Lloyd Charmers & Ken Boothe)/
CHARMERS ALL STARS: Rasta Version 7
71 Green Door GD 4001 One Big Unhappy Family/CONSCIOUS MINDS: Africa Is Paradise 12
71 Pama Supreme PS 340 Red Head Duck/Jingle Jangle 6

LLOYD CHARMERS
(see also Charmers, Lloyd Tyrell/Terrell, Ken Boothe, Hippy Boys, Wayne Howard, Martia Riley, Eric Donaldson)

67 Coxsone CS 7023 Time Is Getting Hard/TONY GREGORY: I Sit By The Shore 100
69 Duke DU 15 Cooyah/UNIQUES: Forever 20
69 Duke DU 16 Follow This Sound/Why Pretend 20
69 Duke DU 25 5 To 5/SOUL STIRRERS: Come See About Me 15
69 Duke DU 36 Safari (The Far East)/Last Laugh 15
69 Songbird SB 1001 Ling Ting Tong/LLOYD ROBINSON: Sweet Sweet 12
69 Songbird SB 1007 Duckey Luckey/In The Spirit 20
69 Camel CA 30 Confidential/TOMMY COWAN: House In Session 12
69 Explosion EX 2001 Death A Come/Zylon 30
70 Explosion EX 2032 Vengeance/Look A-Py-Py 10
70 Explosion EX 2034 Ready Talk/There Is Something About You 7
70 Trojan TR 7788 Oh Me Oh My/I Did It 12
70 Bullet BU 435 Dollars And Bonds/Sounds Familiar 40
70 Bullet BU 442 Reggae A Bye Bye/DAVE BARKER:Doctor Jekyll 15
70 Escort ES 820 Soul Of England/Shang I 18
70 Escort ES 836 Hi Shan/Soul At Large 15
70 Smash SMA 2302 Big Red Bum Ball/BUNNIE LEE ALLSTARS: Big Bum Ball Version 7
73 Green Door GD 4064 Save The People (as L. Charmers)/SCOTTY: Salvation Train 10
74 Harry J. HJ 6662 I'm Gonna Love You Just A Little Bit More/Have I Sinned 6
71 Pama Supreme PS 339 Shaft/Harry's Mood 10
71 Pama Supreme PS 346 Show Business/DEBBY & LLOYD: Gloria 8
72 Pama Supreme PS 355 Desiderata/Desiderata Music 8
70 Trojan TTL 25 REGGAE IS TIGHT (LP, orange/white label) 30
70 Trojan TTL 30 REGGAE CHARM (LP) 25
70 Pama SECO 25 HOUSE IN SESSION (LP, with Hippy Boys) 150

CHARMERS (U.S.)
58 Vogue V 9095 He's Gone/Oh! Yes 500
58 Vogue V 9095 He's Gone/Oh! Yes (78) 45

CHARMETTES
63 London HLR 9820 Please Don't Kiss Me Again/What Is A Tear 45

CHARMS (Jamaica)
64 Island WI 154 Carry, Go, Bring Home (actually by Justin Hinds & Dominoes)/
Hill And Gully (actually by L. Reid's Group) 15
66 Rio R 98 Everybody Say Yeah/This World Is Yours 20

MINT VALUE £

CHARMS (U.S.)

(see also Otis Williams & Charms, Tiny Topsy, Harmonizing Four)

55	Parlophone MSP 6155	Hearts Of Stone/Ko Ko Mo (I Love You So)	675
55	Parlophone R3988	Hearts Of Stone/Ko Ko Mo (I Love You So) (78)	60
55	Parlophone DP 412	Hearts Of Stone/Bazoom, I Need Your Lovin' (78) (export issue)	50
55	Parlophone DP 423	Two Hearts/The First Time We Met (78) (export issue)	60

CHARTBUSTERS

64	London HLU 9906	She's The One/Slippin' Thru Your Fingers	15
64	London HLU 9934	Why/Stop The Music	10

CHASE

71	Epic EPC 7301	Get It On In The Morning/River	6

LINCOLN CHASE

57	London HLU 8495	Johnny Klingeringding/You're Driving Me Crazy (What Did I Do)	30
57	London HLU 8495	Johnny Klingeringding/You're Driving Me Crazy (What Did I Do)	10
61	Philips PB 1103	Miss Orangutang/Walking Slowly	25

CHASERS

65	Decca F 12302	Hey Little Girl/That's What They Call Love	50
66	Parlophone R 5451	Inspiration/She's Gone Away	150
67	Philips BF 1546	The Ways Of A Man/Summer Girl	15

CHASERS

(see also Energetic Krusher, Wildhearts)

01	Changes One Changes CD-00	2ONWARDS & UPWARDS EP (CD EP, 1,060 copies only, this price for signed)	18

CHASERS

84	SRT SRT4KS 304	Raiders/Final Stand (300 only)	60

CHATEAUX

83	Ebony EBON 13	CHAINED AND DESPERATE (LP)	20
84	Ebony EBON 18	FIRE POWER (LP)	15
85	Ebony EBON 31	HIGHLY STRUNG (LP)	15

DEBABRATA CHAUDHURI

68	MFP SMFP 2101	SITAR MUSIC MEDITATIONS (LP)	15

ROBERT CHAUVIGNY

59	Top Rank JAR 142	The Bottle Theme/French Rockin' Waltz (Eux)	5

CHEAP BOOTS

70	Fontana 6001 020	Baby I Do Need You/Come And Stay With Me	6

CHEAP TRICK

78	Epic S EPC 6199	So Good To See You/You're All Talk (withdrawn)	20
79	Epic S EPC 7144	Voices/Surrender (withdrawn)	5
79	Epic S EPC 7258	I Want You To Want Me (live)/I Want You To Want Me (studio) (DJ only)	6
79	Epic CT-1	Dream Police/Voice/I'll Be With You Tonight (sampler, promo only)	10

OLIVER CHEATHAM

83	MCA MCAT 828	Get Down Saturday Night/Something About You (12")	20
83	MCA MCAT 846	Bless The Ladies/Just To Be With You (US mix)/ Just To Be With You (Saturday Night Mix) (12")	12

CHEATIN' HEARTS

66	Columbia DB 8048	Zip-Tease/The Bad Kind	15

CHUBBY CHECKER

59	Top Rank JAR 154	The Class/Schooldays, Oh, Schooldays	35
59	Top Rank JAR 154	The Class/Schooldays, Oh, Schooldays (78)	30
60	Columbia DB 4503	The Twist/Toot	12
60	Columbia DB 4541	The Hucklebuck/Whole Lotta Shakin' Goin' On	15
61	Columbia DB 4591	Pony Time/Oh Susannah	12
61	Columbia DB 4652	Good Good Loving/Mess Around	15
61	Columbia DB 4691	Let's Twist Again/Everything's Gonna Be All Right	7
61	Columbia DB 4728	The Fly/That's The Way It Goes	10
62	Columbia DB 4808	Slow Twistin'/The Lose Your Inhibitions Twist	5
62	Columbia DB 4876	Dancin' Party/Gotta Get Myself Together	5
62	Pye International 7N 25160	Dancin' Party/Gotta Get Myself Together (reissue)	5
62	Cameo Parkway P 806	What Do You Say/Something To Shout About	6
62	Cameo Parkway P 824	Let's Twist Again/The Twist	5
62	Cameo Parkway P 849	Limbo Rock/Hitch Hiker	7
63	Cameo Parkway P 862	Let's Limbo Some More/Twenty Miles	5
63	Cameo Parkway P 873	Black Cloud/Birdland	8
63	Cameo Parkway P 879	Twist It Up/Surf Party	8
63	Cameo Parkway P 890	Loddy Lo/Hooka Tooka	8
64	Cameo Parkway P 907	Hey Bobba Needle/Spread Joy	12
64	Cameo Parkway P 920	Lazy Elsie Molly/Rosie	8
64	Cameo Parkway P 922	She Wants T'Swim/You Better Believe It Baby	18
65	Cameo Parkway P 936	Lovely, Lovely/The Weekend's Here	30
65	Cameo Parkway P 949	(At The) Discotheque/Do The Freddie	50
65	Cameo Parkway P 949	(At The) Discotheque/Do The Freddie (DJ copy)	150
65	Cameo Parkway P 959	Everything's Wrong/Cu Ma La Be Stay	40
65	Cameo Parkway P 959	Everything's Wrong/Cu Ma La Be Stay (DJ copy)	120
65	Cameo Parkway P 965	Two Hearts Make One Love/You Just Don't Know (What You Do To Me)	250
65	Cameo Parkway P 989	Hey You Little Boogaloo/Pussy Cat	30
65	Cameo Parkway P 989	Hey You Little Boogaloo/Pussy Cat (DJ Copy)	50
69	Buddah 201 045	Back In the U.S.S.R./Windy Cream	5
71	London HL 10331	Let's Go Down/Goodbye Victoria	5
73	Pye Int 25620	Gypsy/Reggae My Way	25

			MINT VALUE £
76	London HLU 10515	(At The) Discotheque/Slow Twistin'	5
78	London HLU 10557	You Just Don't Know (What You Do To Me)/ Two Hearts Make One Love (reissue)	10
78	London HLU 10557	You Just Don't Know (What You Do To Me)/ Two Hearts Make One Love (reissue) (DJ Copy)	20
61	Columbia 33SX 1315	TWIST WITH CHUBBY CHECKER (LP)	20
61	Columbia 33SX 1341	FOR TWISTERS ONLY (LP)	20
61	Columbia 33SX 1365	IT'S PONY TIME (LP)	20
62	Columbia 33SX 1445	TWIST ALONG WITH CHUBBY CHECKER (LP)	20
63	Cameo Parkway P 7036	CHUBBY CHECKER (LP)	15
71	London SHZ 8419	CHEQUERED (LP)	40

CHUBBY CHECKER & BOBBY RYDELL

62	Columbia DB 4802	Teach Me To Twist/Swingin' Together	10
62	Cameo Parkway C 205	Jingle Bell Rock/What Are You Doing New Year's Eve?	10
64	Cameo Parkway CPE 554	CHUBBY CHECKER AND BOBBY RYDELL IN LONDON (EP)	25
62	Columbia 33SX 1424	CHECKER AND RYDELL (LP)	20
63	Cameo Parkway C 1063	GOLDEN HITS (LP)	15

CHUBBY CHECKER & DEE DEE SHARP

(see also Dream Lovers, Bobby Rydell, Dee Dee Sharp)

62	Cameo Parkway C 1029	DOWN TO EARTH (LP)	50

CHECKERS

54	Parlophone DP 403	Over The Rainbow/CECIL YOUNG QUARTET: Oooh-Diga-Gow (78, export issue)	50

CHECKMATES

(see also Original Checkmates)

61	Piccadilly 7N 35010	Rockin' Minstrel/Pompeii	10
63	Decca F 11603	You've Gotta Have A Gimmick Today/Westpoint	25
64	Decca F 11844	Sticks And Stones/Please Listen To Me	30
65	Decca F 12114	Around/I've Got To Know Now	15
65	Parlophone R 5337	Stop That Music/I've Been In Love Before	15
66	Parlophone R 5402	(You Got) The Gamma Goochie/It Ain't Right	20
66	Parlophone R 5495	Every Day Is Just The Same/I'll Be Keeping The Score	20
61	Pye NPL 18061	THE CHECKMATES (LP)	40

CHECKMATES LTD

(see also Sonny Charles & Checkmates Ltd)

67	Ember EMB S 235	Do The Walk (The Temptation Walk)/Glad For You	10
69	A&M AMS 747	Love Is All I Have To Give/I Never Should Have Lied	5
69	A&M AMS 769	Proud Mary/Spanish Harlem	5
70	Ember NR 5048	LIVE AT CAESAR'S PALACE (LP)	15

CHEE CHEE AND PEPPY

71	Buddah 2011 083	I Know I'm In Love/My Love Will Never Fade Away	5

CHEEKY

80	Woodbine St. WSR 005	Don't Mess Around/Get Outa My 'Ouse (no p/s)	60

CHEERS

(see also Bert Convy [& Thunderbirds])

54	Capitol CL 14189	Bazoom (I Need Your Lovin')/Arrivederci	40
55	Capitol CL 14248	Bernie's Tune/Whadaya Want?	25
55	Capitol CL 14280	Blueberries/Can't We Be More Than Friends	25
55	Capitol CL 14337	I Must Be Dreaming/Fancy Meeting You Here	20
55	Capitol CL 14377	Black Denim Trousers And Motorcycle Boots/Some Night In Alaska	40
56	Capitol CL 14561	Chicken/Don't Do Anything	25
56	Capitol CL 14601	Que Pasa Muchacha/BERT CONVY: Heaven On Earth	20
56	Capitol CL 14601	Que Pasa Muchacha/BERT CONVY: Heaven On Earth (78)	10
56	Capitol EAP1 584	THE CHEERS (EP)	60

CHEETAHS

(see also Carl Wayne & Cheetahs)

64	Philips BF 1362	Mecca/Goodnight Kiss	20
65	Philips BF 1383	Soldier Boy/Johnny	20
65	Philips BF 1412	Goodbye Baby (Baby Goodbye)/That's How It Goes	15
65	Philips BF 1453	Whole Lotta Love/Party	15
66	Philips BF 1499	The Russian Boat Song/Gamble	15

CHEFS

80	Attatrix RB 10	SWEETIE EP	15
81	Graduate GRAD 11	24 Hours/Thrush	12

CHELSEA

77	Step Forward SF 2	Right To Work/The Loner (p/s, original pressing in card p/s)	15
77	Step Forward SF 2	Right To Work/The Loner (p/s)	8
77	Step Forward SF 5	High Rise Living/No Admission (p/s)	10
78	Step Forward SF 8	Urban Kids/No Flowers (p/s)	8
80	Step Forward SF 14	No One's Coming Outside/What Would You Do (p/s)	6
80	Step Forward SF 15	Look At the Outside/Don't Get Me Wrong (p/s)	6
80	Step Forward SF 16	No Escape/Decide (p/s)	6
82	Step Forward SF 22	Stand Out/Last Drink (p/s)	5
84	Chelsea CH 001	Give Me More/Sympathy For The Devil (p/s)	5
79	Step Forward SFLP 2	CHELSEA (LP, with inner sleeve)	25
81	Step Forward SFLP 5	ALTERNATIVE HITS (LP)	20
82	Step Forward SFLP 7	EVACUATE (LP)	15
84	Picasso PIK 003	LIVE AND WELL (LP)	12

CHELSEA SQUAD

72	Penny Farthing PEN 782	Blue Is The Colour/All Sing Together	5
84	W&A YZ 23	Back On The Ball/(Club Mix) (blue vinyl, p/s)	5

MINT VALUE £

CHEMICAL

(see also Two Dark Troopers, DJ Chemistry Meets Jack Smooth)

92	Head Press SRT 92LS 3170	Disturbance/Paranoia (12")	10
92	Head Press HP 002	THE VIRUS EP (12")	12
92	Basement BRSS 017	Hex/Sub Sector (12")	10

CHEMICAL ALICE

(see also Marillion)

81	Acidic GNOME 1	The Judge/Goodnight Vienna/Lands Of Home/Henry The King (12", p/s)	50

CHEMICAL BROTHERS

91	Eastern Bloc	Sea Of Beats/Sea Of Beats (Justin Robertson Mix) (12", p/s, as Ariel)	80
91	Deconstruction PT 44888	Rollercoaster/Mustn't Grumble/Mustn't Grumble (God's Grumble Mix) (12", as Ariel)	30
93	Dust Brothers DB's 333	Song To The Siren (12", as Dust Brothers, no p/s, 500 only)	60
93	Junior Boys Own JBO 10	Song To The Siren/Song To The Siren (Sabres Of Paradise Mixes) (12", p/s)	30
94	Boys Own COLLECT 004	14TH CENTURY SKY EP (12", no p/s, as Dust Brothers)	20
94	Junior Boys Own JBO 20	MY MERCURY MOUTH EP (12", JBO sleeve, as Dust Brothers)	25
95	Junior Boys Own CHEMS TI	Leave Home/Leave Home (Sabres Of Paradise)/Let Me In Mate (12", p/s)	15
95	Junior Boys Own	Leave Home (Underworld Mix One)/Leave Home (Underworld Mix Two) (12", p/s)	15
95	Junior Boys Own XDUSTLP1	EXIT PLANET DUST (2xLP)	15
97	Freestyle Dust XDUST LP2	DIG YOUR OWN HOLE (2-LP, gatefold)	15
99	Freestyle Dust XDUST LP4	SURRENDER (2-LP, gatefold)	15
02	Virgin XDUST LP5	COME WITH US (2-LP)	15

CLIFTON CHENIER

69	Action ACT 4550	Black Gal/Frogs Legs	15
70	Specialty SNTF 5012	BAYOU BLUES (LP)	20
70	Harvest MHSP 4002	CLIFTON CHENIER'S VERY BEST (LP)	50
79	Flyright FLY 539	ZYDECO BLUES (LP, with other artists)	18

CHEQUERED PAST

(see also Steve Jones)

85	Heavy Metal America	CHEQUERED PAST (LP, picture disc, 1,000 only)	30

CHER

(see also Sonny & Cher, Caesar & Cleo, Nilsson)

65	Liberty LIB 66114	All I Really Want To Do/I'm Gonna Love You	5
66	Liberty LIB 66136	Where Do You Go/See See Rider	5
66	Liberty LIB 66160	Bang Bang (My Baby Shot Me Down)/Our Day Will Come	5
66	Liberty LIB 12034	I Feel Something In The Air/Come To Your Window	7
66	Liberty LIB 12038	Sunny/She's No Better Than Me	7
67	Liberty LIB 12046	Mama (When My Dollies Have Babies)/Behind The Door	7
67	Liberty LBF 15038	You Better Sit Down Kids/Elusive Butterfly	7
69	Atlantic 584 278	Walk On Gilded Splinters/Tonight I'll Be Staying Here With You	10
69	Atco 226 003	For What It's Worth/Hangin' On	5
71	MCA MU 1137	Classified 1A/Don't Put It On Me	5
72	MCA MU 1148	The Way Of Love/Fire And Rain	5
72	MCA MU 1158	Living In A House Divided/One Honest Man	5
72	MCA MU 1168	Don't Hide Your Love/First Time	5
75	Phil Spector Intl. 2010 006	A Love Like Yours (with Nilsson)/Hangin' On	20
76	Phil Spector Intl. 2010 013	A Woman's Story/Baby I Love You	18
66	Liberty LEP 4047	THE HITS OF CHER (EP)	15
65	Liberty LBY 3058	ALL I REALLY WANT TO DO (LP, mono)	20
65	Liberty SLBY 3058	ALL I REALLY WANT TO DO (LP, stereo)	25
66	Liberty LBY 3072	THE SONNY SIDE OF CHER (LP, mono)	20
66	Liberty SLBY 3072	THE SONNY SIDE OF CHER (LP, stereo)	25
66	Liberty LBY 3081	CHER (LP, mono)	20
66	Liberty SLBY 3081	CHER (LP, stereo)	25
68	Liberty LBL/LBS 83051	WITH LOVE, CHER (LP)	20
69	Atco 226 026/228 026	3614 JACKSON HIGHWAY (LP, gatefold sleeve, mono/stereo)	15

VIVIENNE CHERING

(see also Flip & Dateliners)

66	Decca F 12360	I'll Do My Crying Tomorrow/Make My Dreams Come True	10

CHEROKEE

71	Probe PRO 550	Girl, I've Got News For You/Write To You	10

CHEROKEES (U.K.)

(see also Lee Diamond)

64	Decca F 11915	You've Done It Again Little Girl/Girl Girl Girl	10
64	Columbia DB 7341	Seven Daffodils/Are You Back In My World Now	15
65	Columbia DB 7473	Wondrous Place/Send Me All Your Love	10
65	Columbia DB 7704	I Will Never Turn My Back On You/Dig A Little Deeper	10
66	Columbia DB 7822	Land Of A 1000 Dances/Everybody's Needs	20

CHEROKEES (U.S.)

61	Pye International 7N 25066	Cherokee/Harlem Nocturne	15

CHERRY

80s	Crashed Records CAR 91	He's A Bum/He Rides With Me	10

DON CHERRY

56	Brunswick 05538	Wanted Someone To Love/The Thrill Is Gone	10
57	Philips JK 1013	The Last Dance/Don't You Worry (jukebox edition)	15

DON CHERRY

73	JCOA/Virgin J2001	RELATIVITY SUITE (LP)	20

CHERRY PEOPLE

68	MGM MGM 1438	And Suddenly/Imagination	40
68	MGM MGM 1438	And Suddenly/Imagination (DJ copy)	60

MINT VALUE £

69 MGM MGM 1472 Gotta Get Back/I'm The One Who Loves You ... 15
69 MGM MGM 1489 Light Of Love/On To Something New ... 8
69 MGM MGM 1489 Light Of Love/I'm The One Who Loves You ... 8
75 Black Magic BM 112 And Suddenly/Imagination (reissue) ... 8

CHERRY PIES
64 Black Swan WI 448 Do You Keep Dreaming/Sweeter Than Cherry Pie ... 20

CHERRY SMASH
67 Track 604 017 Sing Songs Of Love/Movie Star ... 20
68 Decca F 12838 Goodtime Sunshine/Little Old Country Home Town ... 20
69 Decca F 12884 Fade Away Maureen/Green Plant ... 35

FRANKIE CHERVAL
62 MGM MGM 1183 How Come/Tag Along ... 8

CHARLIE CHESTER
61 Pye 7N 15399 The Onion Song/Nellie ... 5

PETE CHESTER
(see also Five Chesternuts)
60 Pye 7N 15305 Ten Swinging Bottles/Whole Lotta Shakin' On The Range (with Consulates) ... 20
61 Pye International 7N 25074 Three Old Maids/Forest Fire (as Pete Chester & Group) ... 20

VIC CHESTER
57 Decca F 10882 Rock-A-Billy/First Date, First Kiss, First Love ... 15

CHESTERFIELDS
86 Household Goods HOLD IT Goodbye Goodbye/Better Smile/Last Train to Yeovil/Hopes for Lauren and Joseph (12") ... 8
86 Subway Org. SUBWAY 7 Completely & Utterly/Girl On A Boat (foldover p/s with insert in poly bag) ... 5
87 Subway Org. SUBORG 003 KETTLE (LP) ... 12
87 Subway Org. SUBORG 005 WESTWARD HO (LP) ... 12

MORRIS CHESTNUT
79 Grapevine GRP 128 Too Darn Soulful/You Don't Love Me Anymore ... 20
79 Grapevine GRP 128 Too Darn Soulful/You Don't Love Me Anymore (DJ Copy) ... 30

MAURICE CHEVALIER
60 London HLP 9297 Breath Of Scandal/ALLESSANDRO CICOGNINI: Prince Phillip Waltz ... 6
58 MGM C 771 YESTERDAY (LP) ... 12
59 MGM C 783 SINGS BROADWAY (LP) ... 12
59 MGM C 826 LIFE IS JUST A BOWL OF CHERRIES (LP) ... 12
60 MGM C 860 THANK HEAVEN FOR GIRLS GIRLS GIRLS (LP) ... 12

CHEVIOT RANTERS
73 Topic 12TS 222 THE CHEVIOT HILLS (LP) ... 18
74 Topic 12TS 245 CHEVIOT BARN DANCE (LP) ... 18

CHEVLONS
66 Pye 7N 17145 Too Long Alone/It's My Problem ... 7

CHEVRONS
60 Top Rank JAR 308 Lullaby/Day After Forever ... 8

CHEVY
80 Avatar AAA 104 Too Much Loving/See The Light (company sleeve) ... 20
80 Avatar AAA 107 The Taker/Life On The Run (p/s) ... 20
81 Avatar AAA 114 Just Another Day/Rock On ... 12
80 Avatar AALP 5001 THE TAKER (LP, with inner sleeve) ... 15

CHEYNES
(see also Peter Bardens, Peter B's, Fleetwood Mac, Mark Leeman Five, Bo Street Runners)
63 Columbia DB 7153 Respectable/It's Gonna Happen To You ... 100
64 Columbia DB 7368 Going To The River/Cheyne-Re-La ... 100
65 Columbia DB 7464 Down And Out/Stop Running Around ... 100

CHEYNES
71 Bell BLL 1144 April Fool/Gotta Get Back ... 6

CHIC
79 Atlantic K11385T My Forbidden Lover/What About Me? (12") ... 12

CHICAGO
69 CBS 4381 Questions 67 And 68/Listen ... 6
69 CBS 4503 I'm A Man (Parts 1 & 2) (withdrawn) ... 20
69 CBS 4715 I'm A Man/Does Anyone Really Know What Time It Is? (promo p/s) ... 25
69 CBS 66221 CHICAGO TRANSIT AUTHORITY (2-LP, orange label) ... 18
71 CBS 66405 IV (AT CARNEGIE HALL) (4-LP, orange label) ... 20

CHICAGO BILL
(see under Big Bill Broonzy)

CHICAGO LINE
(see also Mike Patto, Bo Street Runners, Viv Prince)
66 Philips BF 1488 Shimmy Shimmy Ko Ko Bop/Jump Back ... 150

CHICAGO LOOP
66 Stateside SS 564 (When She Needs Good Lovin') She Comes To Me/This Must Be The Place ... 7

CHICK with TED CAMERON & D.J.'s
60 Pye 7N 15292 Early In The Morning/Cool Water ... 40

CHICKEN SHACK
(see also Errol Dixon, Fleetwood Mac, Christine Perfect, Carmen Macrae, Broken Glass)
67 Blue Horizon 57-3135 It's OK With Me Baby/When My Left Eye Jumps ... 15
68 Blue Horizon 57-3143 Worried About My Woman/Six Nights In Seven ... 15
68 Blue Horizon 57-3146 When The Train Comes Back/Hey Baby ... 15

			MINT VALUE £
69	Blue Horizon 57-3153	I'd Rather Go Blind/Night Life	10
69	Blue Horizon 57-3160	Tears In The Wind/The Things You Put Me Through	15
70	Blue Horizon 57-3168	Maudie/Andalucian Blues	10
70	Blue Horizon 57-3176	Sad Clown/Tired Eyes	15
73	Deram DM 381	Time Goes Passing By/Poor Boy	8
73	Deram DM 396	You Know You Could Be Right/The Loser	8
74	CBS 1832	I'd Rather Go Blind/Sad Clown	5
68	Blue Horizon 7-63203	FORTY BLUE FINGERS FRESHLY PACKED AND READY TO SERVE (LP, 1st pressing with 'stereo' sticker on sleeve)	60
69	Blue Horizon 7-63209	O.K. KEN? (LP, gatefold sleeve, 1st pressing with 'stereo' sticker on sleeve)	60
69	Blue Horizon 7-63218	100 TON CHICKEN (LP, gatefold, 1st pressing with 'stereo' sticker on sleeve)	60
70	Blue Horizon 7-63861	ACCEPT CHICKEN SHACK (LP, gatefold sleeve)	50
72	Deram SDL 5	IMAGINATION LADY (LP, gatefold sleeve, brown/white label with large Deram label)	50
72	Deram SDL 5	IMAGINATION LADY (LP, gatefold sleeve, later pressing with red/white label)	20
73	Deram SML 1100	UNLUCKY BOY (LP)	25

CHICKEN SHED

77	Colby AJ 370	ALICE (LP)	60

CHICKS

63	Oriole CB 1828	What Are Boys Made Of?/Over The Mountain	20

CHICORY TIP

71	CBS 7118	My Girl Sunday/Doctor Man	20
71	CBS 7595	I Love Onions/Don't Hang Jack	20

CHIEFS

58	London HLU 8624	Apache/Dee's Dream	30
58	London HLU 8624	Apache/Dee's Dream (78)	15
58	London HLU 8720	Enchiladas!/Moments To Remember	20
58	London HLU 8720	Enchiladas!/Moments To Remember (78)	15

CHIFFONS

(see also Four Pennies)

63	Stateside SS 172	He's So Fine/Oh! My Lover	10
63	Stateside SS 202	One Fine Day/Why Am I So Shy	10
63	Stateside SS 230	A Love So Fine/Only My Friend	15
64	Stateside SS 254	I Have A Boyfriend/I'm Gonna Dry Your Eyes	18
64	Stateside SS 332	Sailor Boy/When Summer's Through	25
65	Stateside SS 437	Nobody Knows What's Going On (In My Mind But Me)/The Real Thing	30
66	Stateside SS 512	Sweet Talkin' Guy/Did You Ever Go Steady	10
66	Stateside SS 533	Out Of This World/Just A Boy	15
66	Stateside SS 559	Stop, Look And Listen/March	25
67	Stateside SS 578	My Boyfriend's Back/I Got Plenty Of Nuttin'	22
64	Stateside SE 1012	THEY'RE SO FINE (EP)	80
63	Stateside SL 10040	THE CHIFFONS (LP)	100
66	Stateside S(S)L 10190	SWEET TALKIN' GUY (LP)	100
72	London ZGP 125	SWEET TALKING GUY LP, Reissue)	25
75	Philips SON 005	THE CHIFFONS GREATEST HITS (LP)	12
84	Impact Act 002	DOO LANG DOO LANG (LP)	15
85	Impact ACT 007	FLIPS FLOPS & RARITIES (LP)	18

CHILD

77	Pentagram PENT 1	Whats A Nice Girl Like You/Sad One Sided Love Affair	12

ANTHONY CHILD/ANDREW READ

99	Fat Cat 12FAT 031	Speedranch/Jansky Noise (12" EP, 'bullet hole' sleeve)	12

LORRAINE CHILD

64	Decca F 11969	You/Not This Time	10

ALAN CHILDE

76	Epic SEPC 4183	Rainmaker/Mind Blowing Love	6

SONNY CHILDE (& T.N.T.)

65	Decca F 12218	Giving Up On Love/Mighty Nice Of You To Call	150
66	Polydor 56108	Two Lovers/Ain't That Good News	20
66	Polydor 56141	Heartbreak/I Still Love You (as Sonny Childe & T.N.T.)	20
66	Polydor 582 003	TO BE CONTINUED (LP)	40

CHILD HAROLDS

68	Trident TRA 201	Diary Of My Mind/Loophole	30

BILLY CHILDISH

87	Hangman HANG 9-UP	THE 1982 CASSETTES (LP, pink & black sleeve)	25
88	Hangman HANG 16-UP	POEMS OF LAUGHTER & VIOLENCE (LP)	25
91	Hangman 37 UP	50 GREAT ALBUMS (LP)	25

BILLY CHILDISH & THE BLACKHANDS

93	Hangman 53 UP	LIVE IN THE NETHERLANDS (LP)	20

BILLY CHILDISH & THE NATURAL BORN LOVERS

89	Hangman 30 UP	LONG LEGGED BABY (LP)	18

BILLY CHILDISH & SEXTON MING

87	Hangman HANG 05 UP	WHICH DEAD DONKEY DADDY (LP)	12
87	Hangman HANG 10 UP	PLUMP PRIZES & LITTLE GEMS (LP)	15
87	Hangman HANG 12 UP	YPRES 1917 OVERTURE(LP)	15
98	Damaged Goods DAMGOOD 159 LP	CHEEKY CHEESE (LP)	12

MINT VALUE £

BILLY CHILDISH & THE SINGING LOINS

93	Hangmans Daughter SCRAG 1	AT THE BRIDGE (LP)	20

WILD BILLY CHILDISH

87	Hangman HANG 13 UP	I REMEMBER (LP)	25
87	Hangman HANG 2 UP	I'VE GOT EVERYTHING INDEED (LP)	25

WILD BILLY CHILDISH & THE BLACKHANDS

(see also Milkshakes, Thee Mighty Caesars and Billy Childish & entries)

88	Hangman HANG-21 UP	PLAY CAPT'N CALYPSO'S HOODOO PARTY	20

CHI-LITES

(see also Jackie Wilson)

69	Beacon BEA 119	Pretty Girl/Love Bandit	70
71	MCA 1143DJ	What Do I Wish For (1-sided DJ copy)	15
70	MCA MUPS 397	GIVE IT AWAY (LP)	15
71	MCA MUPS 437	(FOR GOD'S SAKE) GIVE MORE POWER TO THE PEOPLE (LP)	15
72	MCA MUPS 457	A LONELY MAN (LP)	15

CHILLIWACK

(see also Collectors, Electric Prunes)

71	London HLU 10327	Everyday/Sundown	5
71	London SHU 8418	CHILLIWACK (LP)	15

CHILLI WILLI & RED HOT PEPPERS

(see also Brinsley Schwarz, Jo-Ann Kelly, Mighty Baby, Savoy Brown, Hapshash And The Coloured Coat, Attractions, Action)

75	Mooncrest MOON 40	Breathe A Little/Friday Song	6
72	Revelation REV 002	KINGS OF THE ROBOT RHYTHM (LP, with lyric insert, inner sleeve and sticker)	60
72	Revelation REV 002	KINGS OF THE ROBOT RHYTHM (LP, with lyric insert, but without inner sleeve and sticker)	30
74	Mooncrest CREST 21	BONGOS OVER BALHAM (LP, with inner sleeve)	25

CHILLS

84	Flying Nun Europe FNE 13	KALEIDOSCOPE WORLD (LP, with free 7")	30
84	Flying Nun Europe FNE 13	KALEIDOSCOPE WORLD (LP, without free 7")	20
90	Slash 828191	SUBMARINE BELLS (LP, with inner sleeve)	15
85	Normal 43	LOST EP (12")	15
92	Slash 828322	SOFT BOMB (LP)	12

CHILLUM

(see also Secondhand)

71	Mushroom 100 MR 11	CHILLUM (LP, with photo insert)	90

ALEX CHILTON

(see also Box Tops, Big Star)

80	Aura AUS 117	Hey! Little Child/No More The Moon Shines Lorena (p/s)	8

CHIMES featuring DENISE (U.K.)

(see also Little Frankie)

63	Decca F 11783	Say It Again/Can This Be Love?	7
64	Decca F 11885	I'll Be Waiting, I'll Be Here/Hello Heartache	7

CHIMES (U.S.)

61	London HLU 9283	Once In A While/Summer Night	35

CHIMNEYS

80	Tagmemics 45-003	Do The Big Baby/Take Your Brain Out For A Walk (p/s, 500 only)	15

TSAI CHIN

62	Decca F 11439	Chinese Charleston/How Shall I Do It	6
63	Decca F 11595	Buttons And Bows/Woa Yaw Nee	6
63	Decca F 11737	School In Cheltenham/Any Old Iron	7
64	Decca F 12039	Tokyo Melody/I Love A Man	6
62	Decca SKL/LK 4501	THE WORLD OF TSAI CHIN (LP)	15

CHINA DOLL

80	Wessex WEX 273	Oysters And Wine/Past Tense (p/s)	200

CHINA DOLLS

(see also Slade, Dummies)

82	Speed FIRED 1	One Hit Wonder/Ain't Love Ain't Bad (p/s)	35

CHINA DRUM

96	Mantra MNTLP1002	GOOSE FAIR (LP)	12
97	Mantra MNTLP1009	SELF MADE MANIAC (LP)	12

CHINA STREET

78	Criminal CRM 1	You're A Ruin/(I Wanna Be) Your M.P. (foldout lyric p/s in poly bag & badge)	10

CHINATOWN

81	Airship AP 138	Short And Sweet/How Many Times (p/s)	60
81	Airship AP 343	PLAY IT TO DEATH (LP)	85

CHINAWITE

83	Future Earth FER 014	Blood On The Streets/Ready To Satisfy (p/s)	30
85	Mausoleum SKULL 8351	RUN FOR COVER (LP)	12

CHRISTINE CHING

64	Decca 12027	Winter's Here Again/Jingle Bells	5

KES CHINS

62	Starlite ST45 089	Annie/Moody	8

CHIPMUNKS

(see under David Seville)

MINT VALUE £

CHIPS

75 Decca FR 13574 Love Matters/Gentle Teacher 5
75 Decca FR 13604 Twice A Week//Reelin In The Years 8

GEORGE CHISHOLM & BLUENOTES

(see also Bert Weedon)

56 Beltona BL 2671 Honky Tonk/D.R. Rock (with Bert Weedon) 10
56 Decca LK 4147 CHIS (LP) 15
61 Philips SBBL 612 TRAD TREAT (LP) 15
64 Wing WL 1043 TRAD SPECIAL (LP) 15
60s 77 SEU 12/43 ALONG THE CHISHOLM TRAIL (LP) 15

CHITINIOUS ENSEMBLE

72 Deram SML 1093 CHITINIOUS ENSEMBLE (LP) 200

CHOC

70 Decca F23106 Way Of Life/I Want You To Be My Girl 30

CHOC ICE

71 Polydor 2056189 Groovy Situation/Instrumental Version 15

CHOCOLATE BOYS

74 Decca F 13556 El Bimbo/Voltaire Pier 40
74 Decca F 13556 El Bimbo/Voltaire Pier (DJ Copy) 50

CHOCOLATE FROG

(see also Fleur De Lys)

68 Atlantic 584 207 Butchers And Bakers/I Forgive You 30

CHOCOLATE MILK

75 RCA RCA 2592 Action Speaks Louder Than Words/Ain't Nothing But A Thing 10
79 RCA RCAT 2592 I'm Your Radio/Actions Speak Louder Than Words (12") 15
77 RCA PL 11830 COMIN' (LP) 20

CHOCOLATE PIER

74 Decca FR 13556 El Bimbo/Voltaire Pier 10

CHOCOLATE WATCH BAND

67 Decca F 12649 The Sound Of The Summer/The Only One In Sight 45
67 Decca F 12704 Requiem/What's It To You 40
84 Big Beat WIK 25 44 (LP) 15

CHOCOLATS

(see also chocolate Boys)

76 Aquarius AQ 1 Voltaire Pier/Brasilia Carnival 50

CHOIR

68 Major Minor MM 537 It's Cold Outside/I'm Going Home 50
68 Major Minor MM 557 When You Were With Me/Changin' My Mind 40

CHOPYN

(see also Ann Odell, Ray Russell, Simon Phillips, C.M.U)

75 Jet LPO 8 GRAND SLAM (LP) 20

CHORALERNA

60s Myrrh MYRRH 1047 LET THERE BE LIGHT (LP) 25
60s Key KL 018 POWER (LP) 20

CHORDETTES

54 Columbia SCM 5158 Mr. Sandman/I Don't Wanna See You Cryin' 250
54 Columbia DB 3553 Mr. Sandman/I Don't Wanna See You Cryin' (78) 20
55 London HLA 8169 Humming Bird/Lonely Lips 80
55 London HLA 8169 Humming Bird/Lonely Lips (78) 10
56 London HLA 8217 Dudelsack Polka/I Told A Lie 60
56 London HLA 8264 Eddie My Love/Our Melody (triangular centre) 75
56 London HLA 8264 Eddie My Love/Our Melody (round centre) 40
56 London HLA 8302 Born To Be With You/Love Never Changes 50
56 London HA 7011 Born To Be With You/Love Never Changes (export issue) 40
56 London HLA 8323 Lay Down Your Arms/Teenage Goodnight 40
57 London HLA 8473 Echo Of Love/Just Between You And Me 40
57 London HLA 8497 Like A Baby/Soft Sands 40
58 London HLA 8566 Baby Of Mine/Photographs 35
58 London HLA 8584 Lollipop/Baby, Come-A-Back-A 20
58 London HLA 8654 Love Is A Two-Way Street/I Don't Know, I Don't Care 15
59 London HLA 8809 We Should Be Together/No Other Arms, No Other Lips 15
59 London HLA 8926 A Girl's Work Is Never Done/No Wheels (B-side with Jeff Crom & Jackie Ertel) 20
61 London HLA 9400 Never On Sunday/Faraway Star 10
62 London HLA 9519 The White Rose Of Athens/Adios (Goodbye My Love) 5
60 London RE-A 1228 THE CHORDETTES (EP) 70
58 London HA-A 2088 THE CHORDETTES (LP) 120
62 London HA-A 2441 THE CHORDETTES SING (LP) 70

CHORDS (U.K.)

(see also Rage)

79 Polydor 2059 141 Now It's Gone/Don't Go Back (p/s) 5
80 Polydor POSP 101 Maybe Tomorrow/I Don't Wanna Know/Hey Girl (p/s) 6
80 Polydor POSP 146 Something's Missing/This Is What They Want (p/s) 5
80 Polydor 2059 258 The British Way Of Life/The Way It's Got To Be (p/s) 6
80 Polydor POSP 185 In My Street/I'll Keep On Holding On (p/s) 6
81 Polydor POSP 270 One More Minute/Who's Killing Who (p/s) 6
81 Polydor POSP 288 Turn Away Again/Turn Away Again (Again) (p/s) 8
80 Polydor Super POLS 1019 SO FAR AWAY (LP, with stickered sleeve & 7" "Now It's Gone"/ Things We Said [KRODS 1]) 20

MINT VALUE £

CHORDS (U.S.)

54 Columbia SCM 5133 Sh-Boom (Life Could Be A Dream)/Little Maiden 2000
54 Columbia DB 3512 Sh-Boom (Life Could Be A Dream)/Little Maiden (78) 200

CHORDS FIVE

(see also Smoke)
67 Island WI 3044 I'm Only Dreaming/Universal Vagrant 100
68 Polydor 56261 Same Old Fat Man/Hold On To Everythin' You've Got 40
69 Jay Boy BOY 6 Some People/Battersea Fair 50

CHOSEN FEW (Jamaica)

70 Songbird SB 1031 Time Is Hard/CRYSTALITES: Time Is Hard Part Two 12
70 Songbird SB 1032 Going Back Home/CRYSTALITES: Going Back Home Part Two 10
70 Songbird SB 1046 Why Can't I Touch You/INNER CIRCLE BAND: Touch You Version 12
71 Songbird SB 1061 Shaft/Shaft (Version) 12
71 Songbird SB 1067 Everybody Just A Stall/Everybody (Version) 10
72 Songbird SB 1070 Do Your Thing/Your Thing (Version) 18
72 Trojan TR 7864 Ebony Eyes/Ebony Eyes (Version) 6
72 Trojan TR 7882 Everybody Plays The Fool/You're A Big Girl Now 12
72 Grape You're A Big Girl Now/Version 12
73 Trojan TR 7894 Am I Black Enough For You/Message From A Blackman 8
73 Duke DU 162 Children Of The Night/LLOYD CHARMERS: For The Good Times 7
73 Duke DU 163 Stoned In Love/MIKE CHUNG & NOW GENERATION: Stoned In Love (Version) 7
73 Duke DU 164 It's Too Late/MIKE CHUNG & NOW GENERATION: It's Too Late (Version) 7
73 Trojan TRLS 56 HIT AFTER HIT (LP) 30
75 Trojan TRLS 106 EVERYBODY PLAYS THE FOOL (LP) 40

CHOSEN FEW (U.K.)

(see also Alan Hull, Lindisfarne, Skip Bifferty)
65 Pye 7N 15905 It Won't Be Around You Anymore/Big City 20
65 Pye 7N 15942 So Much To Look Forward To/Today, Tonight & Tomorrow 20

CHOSEN FEW (U.K.)

74 Action ACT 4623 Funky Butter/Wondering 60
76 Polydor 2058 721 I Can Make Your Dreams Come True/Pretty Face 20
76 Miami MIA401 Night And Day/Funky Buttercup 60
77 Polydor 2058 752 Miracle Worker/Young And Foolish 25
78 Polydor 2058 975 You Mean Everything To Me/It Won't Be Long 30

CHOU PAHROT

79 Klub KEP 101 Buzgo Tram Chorus/Gwizgweela Gwamhnoo/Lemons (p/s) 10
79 Klub KLP 19 LIVE (LP, private pressing) 12

CHRIS AND MAXINE

67 Philips BF 1587 Only A Thousand Times A Day/I've Made You My Mind 15

CHRIS & COSEY/CREATIVE TECHNOLOGY INSTITUTE

(see also Throbbing Gristle, Chris Carter, Eurythmics, Cosey Fanni Tutti)
81 Rough Trade RT 078 October (Love Song)/Little Houses (p/s) 5
81 Rough Trade RTT 078 October (Love Song)/Little Houses (12", p/s) 7
84 Intl. One CTI 002 Conspiracy International/The Gift Of Tongues/The Need (p/s) 7
84 C.T.I. CTI 1 HAMMER HOUSE EP (12") 10
84 C.T.I. CTI 2 GIFT OF TONGUES (12") 10
85 Rough Trade RTT 148 Sweet Surprise 1 (1984)/2 (1985) (12", p/s, with Annie Lennox & Dave Stewart) 8
91 World Serpent WS7 004 Passion (p/s, 1-sided, other side etched) 5
81 Rough Trade ROUGH 34 HEARTBEAT (LP, with insert) 12
81 Rough Trade COPY 008 HEARTBEAT (cassette with 2 bonus tracks) 15
82 Rough Trade ROUGH 44 TRANCE (LP) 12

PETER CHRIS & OUTCASTS

66 Columbia DB 7923 Over The Hill/The Right Girl For Me 40

CHRIS & STUDENTS

61 Parlophone R 4806 Lass Of Richmond Hill/Ducks Away From My Fishin' 15

CHRIST CHILD

78 Barak BAR 5 Let Them Eat Rock/Five Finger Exercise 8

CHRISTIAN

71 Decca F 23137 Other Side Of Life/She 15

CHARLIE CHRISTIAN

50s Philips BBL 7172 CHARLIE CHRISTIAN (LP) 15

FUD CHRISTIAN ALL STARS

71 Big Shot BI 571 Never Fall In Love (actually by Winston Heywood)/Never Fall In Love Version 8

HANS CHRISTIAN

(see also Jon Anderson, Yes)
68 Parlophone R 5676 All Of The Time/Never My Love 80
68 Parlophone R 5698 (The Autobiography Of) Mississippi Hobo/Sonata Of Love 110

LIZ CHRISTIAN

(see also James Royal)
67 CBS 202520 Suddenly You Find Love/Make It Work Out 80
67 CBS 202520 Suddenly You Find Love/Make It Work Out (DJ copy) 100
69 Spark SRL 1004 Call My Name/Think Of You Baby 8

MARIA CHRISTIAN

85 MCA MCA 974 Wait Until The Weekend Comes/(Instrumental) (p/s) 15

NEIL CHRISTIAN (& CRUSADERS)

(see also Christian's Crusaders, Guy Hamilton, Jimmy Page, Ritchie Blackmore, Nicky Hopkins, Miki Dallon, Screaming Lord Sutch)
62 Columbia DB 4938 The Road To Love/The Big Beat Drum 40

			MINT VALUE £
63	Columbia DB 7075	A Little Bit Of Someone Else/Get A Load Of This (with Crusaders)	20
66	Strike JH 301	That's Nice/She's Got The Action	10
66	Strike JH 313	Oops/She Said Yeah	10
66	Strike JH 319	Two At A Time/Wanna Lover	10
67	Pye 7N 17372	You're All Things Bright And Beautiful/I'm Gonna Love You Baby	15
73	Youngblood YB 1044	That's Nice/She's Got The Action	6
76	Satril SAT 106	She's Got The Power/Someone Following Me Around	20
66	Columbia SEG 8492	A LITTLE BIT OF SOMETHING ELSE (EP)	80

CHRISTIAN'S CRUSADERS

(see also Neil Christian & Crusaders)

64	Columbia DB 7289	Honey Hush/One For The Money	50

CHRISTIAN DEATH

88	Jungle JUNG 40T	Church Of No Return/Church Of No Return (Endured) (12")	8
83	No Future FL 2	ONLY THEATRE OF PAIN (LP, with insert)	25
86	Jungle NOS 006	OFFICIAL ANTHOLOGY OF LIVE BOOTLEGS (LP, black & yellow sleeve)	15
86	Jungle NOS 006	OFFICIAL ANTHOLOGY OF LIVE BOOTLEGS (LP, pink vinyl)	12

CHRISTIE

(see also Acid Gallery, Epics, Outer Limits)

71	CBS 9130	Everything's Gonna Be Alright/Freewheelin' Man/Magic Highway (p/s)	6
72	CBS 58403	Fools Gold/Born To Lose	15
70	CBS 64108	CHRISTIE (LP)	15
71	CBS 64397	FOR ALL MANKIND (LP, gatefold sleeve, orange label)	20

DAVE CHRISTIE

68	Mercury MF1028	Love And The Brass Band/Penelope Breedlove	25

JOHN CHRISTIE

74	Polydor 2058 496	4th Of July (written by Paul McCartney)/Old Enough To Know Better (in p/s)	30
74	Polydor 2058 496	4th Of July (written by Paul McCartney)/Old Enough To Know Better	15
74	Polydor 2058 528	Everybody Knows/How Does It Feel (p/s)	6

KEITH CHRISTIE

54	Esquire 20-047	HOMAGE TO THE DUKE (LP)	15

LOU CHRISTIE

63	Columbia DB 4983	The Gypsy Cried/Red Sails In The Sunset	20
63	Columbia DB 7031	Two Faces Have I/All That Glitters Isn't Gold	20
63	Columbia DB 7096	How Many Teardrops/You And I (Have A Right To Cry)	18
66	MGM MGM 1297	Lightnin' Strikes/Cryin' In The Streets	10
66	MGM MGM 1297	Lightnin' Strikes/Cryin' In The Streets (DJ Copy)	40
66	MGM MGM 1308	Rhapsody In The Rain/Trapeze	8
66	MGM MGM 1317	Painter/Du Ronda	12
66	MGM MGM 1325	If My Car Could Only Talk/Song Of Lita	18
66	Colpix PX 735	Merry Go Round/Guitars And Bongos	10
67	King KG 1036	Outside The Gates Of Heaven/All That Glitters Isn't Gold	8
67	CBS 2718	Shake Hands And Walk Away Cryin'/Escape	15
67	CBS 2922	Gina/Back To The Days Of The Romans	10
69	Buddah 201 057	I'm Gonna Make You Mine/I'm Gonna Get Married	6
69	Buddah 201 073	She Sold Me Magic/Are You Gettin' Any Sunshine?	7
70	Buddah 201081	Love Is Over/Generation	5
70	Buddah 2011-052	Indian Lady/Glory River	6
71	Buddah 2011-074	Waco/Lighthouse	7
72	Buddah 2011-111	I'm A Song, Sing Me/Paper Song	7
72	Buddah 2011-127	Why Do Fools Fall In Love/I'm Gonna Get Married	7
72	Buddah 2011-148	Shuffle On Down To Pittsburgh/I'm Gonna Get Married	7
73	CTI Records CTS 4002	Beyond The Blue Horizon/Hey You Cajun	8
75	Elektra K 12188	Summer Days/The One And Only Original Sunshine Kid	7
76	Epic SEPC 4471	Riding In My Van/Summer In Malibu	8
76	Midland International MID 6	You're Gonna Make Love To Me/Fantasies	7
66	MGM MGM-C(S) 8008	LIGHTNIN' STRIKES (LP)	30
66	Colpix PXL 551	STRIKES AGAIN (LP)	25
69	Buddah 203029	I'M GONNA MAKE YOU MINE	12

TONY CHRISTIE (& TRACKERS)

66	CBS 202097	Life's Too Good To Waste/Just The Two Of Us	8
67	MGM MGM 1365	Turn Around/When Will I Ever Love Again?	8
68	MGM MGM 1386	I Don't Want To Hurt You Anymore/Say No More	8
68	MGM MGM 1440	My Prayer/I Need You	8

CHRISTIE BROTHERS STOMPERS

59	Parlophone GEP 8719	TOGETHER AGAIN (EP)	20
60	Esquire EP233	RUM & COCA COLA (EP)	25
60	Esquire EP243	STOMPIN' (EP)	25

CHRISTIEN BROTHERS

69	Major Minor MM 628	I Reached For You/Answer Me	7

DEREK CHRISTIEN

(see also Christien Brothers)

70	Major Minor MM 676	When A Woman Has A Baby/Please Don't Go Away	30
70	Major Minor MM 713	Suddenly There's A Valley/I'll Be Coming Home	100

KEITH CHRISTMAS

(see also Mighty Baby, Magic Muscle)

69	RCA Victor SF 8059	STIMULUS (LP, with Mighty Baby, orange/white label)	150
70	B&C CAS 1015	FABLE OF THE WINGS (LP)	50
71	B&C CAS 1041	PIGMY (LP, gatefold sleeve)	40
74	Manticore K 53503	BRIGHTER DAY (LP. with inner sleeve)	15
76	Manticore K 53509	STORIES FROM THE HUMAN ZOO (LP, with insert)	15

MINT VALUE £

CHRISTOPHER

70	Chapter One CH121	Sharkey/The Race	20

JUNE CHRISTY

(see also Stan Kenton)

55	Capitol CL 14355	Pete Kelly's Blues/Kicks	10
55	Capitol EAP 516	SOMETHING COOL (EP)	8
54	Capitol LC 6682	SOMETHING COOL (10" LP)	18
56	Capitol T 725	JUNE CHRISTY (LP)	20
57	Capitol T 833	JUNE - FAIR AND WARMER (LP)	15
58	Capitol T 902	GONE FOR THE DAY (LP)	15
58	Capitol T 1006	JUNE CHRISTY (LP)	15
59	Capitol (S)T 1076	JUNE'S GOT RHYTHM (LP)	15

CHROME

80	Red RS 12007	READ ONLY MEMORY (12" EP, with poster)	20
80	Red RS 12007	READ ONLY MEMORY (12" EP, without poster)	12
80	Beggars Banquet BEG 36	New Age/Information (p/s)	10
81	D. F. O. T. Mountain Y3	INWORLDS (12")	15
82	D. F. O. T. Mountain Z17	Firebomb/Shadows Of A Thousand Years (p/s)	10
80	Beggars Banquet BEGA 15	RED EXPOSURE (LP, with inner sleeve)	20
80	Beggars Banquet BEGA 18	HALF MACHINE LIP MOVES (LP, with poster insert)	20
80	Beggars Banquet BEGA 18	HALF MACHINE LIP MOVES (LP, without poster insert)	15
81	D. F. O. T. Mountain X6	BLOOD ON THE MOON (LP, with inner sleeve)	18
82	D. F. O. T. Mountain X18	3RD FROM THE SUN (LP, with insert)	15

CHROMING ROSE

90	EMI 5667 93774	LOUIS XIV (LP, some as picture disc)	12

CHRON GEN

81	Gargoyle GRGL 780	PUPPETS OF WAR (EP)	10
81	Gargoyle/Fresh GRGL 780	PUPPETS OF WAR (EP, reissue, silver & black label)	7
81	Step Forward SF 19	Reality/Subway Sadist (p/s)	5
82	Secret SEC 3	LIVING NEXT DOOR TO ALICE (EP, with Chronic Generation Oi magazine No. 1)	8
82	Secret SEC 3	LIVING NEXT DOOR TO ALICE (EP, without Chronic Generation Oi magazine No. 1)	5
82	Secret SHH 129	Jet Boy Jet Girl/Abortions/Subway Sadist (p/s)	5
82	Secret SHH 139	Outlaw/Behind Closed Doors/Disco (p/s)	6
83	Secret SEC 3	CHRONIC GENERATION (LP, with free 7")	15
83	Secret SEC 3	CHRONIC GENERATION (LP without free 7")	12

CHRYSTAL BELLE SCRODD

(see also Nurse With Wound)

86	United Dairies	BELLE DE JOUR (LP with insert)	25

CHUBBY & HONEYSUCKERS

65	Venus VE 3	Come On Home/What Shall I Do?	12
66	Rio R 75	Emergency Ward/LEN & HONEYSUCKERS: One More River	12

CHUBUKOS

73	Mainstream MSS 303	Witch Doctor Bump/House Of The Rising Funk	6

CHUCK & BETTY

59	Brunswick 05815	Sissy Britches/Come Back Little Girl	30
59	Brunswick 05815	Sissy Britches/Come Back Little Girl (78)	15

CHUCK (Josephs) & DOBBY (Dobson)

60	Blue Beat BB 19	Til The End Of Time (as Chuck & Darby)/ DUKE REID & HIS GROUP: What Makes Honey	20
60	Blue Beat BB 23	Cool School/DUKE REID & HIS GROUP: Joker	20
61	Starlite ST45 043	Sad Over You/Sweeter Than Honey	20
61	Starlite ST45 044	Lovey Dovey/Sitting Square	20
61	Blue Beat BB 39	Du Du Wap/I Love My Teacher (with Aubrey Adams & Du Droppers)	18
61	Blue Beat BB 59	Oh Fanny/Running Around	18
64	Blue Beat BB 246	Tell Me/I'm Going Home	15

CHUCK & GARY

58	HMV POP 466	Teenie Weenie Jeanie/Can't Make Up My Mind	60
58	HMV POP 466	Teenie Weenie Jeanie/Can't Make Up My Mind (78)	20

CHUCK & GIDEON

63	Parlophone R 5011	Cherry Berry Lips/The Tender Touch	12

CHUCK & JOE WHITE

(see under Joe White)

CHUCKLES

69	Bullet BU 416	Run Nigel Run/Come On Home	10

CHUCKLES

72	Duke DU 144	Reggae Limbo/ZAP POW: Broken Contract	20

CHUCKS

63	Decca F 11569	Loo Be Loo/Anytime Is The Right Time	8
63	Decca F 11617	Mulberry Bush/That's All I Need	8
63	Decca F 11777	The Hitch Hiker/Humpity Dumpity	8
64	Decca DFE 8562	THE CHUCKS (EP)	40

CHUMBAWAMBA

85	Agit Prop AGIT 1	Revolution EP (booklet p/s)	8
88	Agit Prop AGIT 3	Smash Clause 28/Fight The Alton Bill (with booklet)	6
88	Agit Prop PROP 3	ENGLISH REBEL SONGS 1381-1914 (10" LP, with die-cut sleeve)	15
86	Agit Prop PROP 1	PICTURES OF STARVING CHILDREN SELL RECORDS (LP, with inner)	20
87	Agit Prop PROP 2	NEVER MIND THE BALLOTS... (LP, gatefold)	15

MINT VALUE £

94 One Little Indian TPLP046CD ANARCHY (CD) 20
95 One Little Indian TPLP056 SHOWBUSINESS (LP) 15

MIKIE CHUNG & NOW GENERATION
72 Green Door GD 4032 Breezing/NOW GENERATION: Breezing - Version 5
73 Duke DU 163 Stoned In Love/CHOSEN FEW: Stoned In Love 7
73 Duke DU 164 It's Too Late/CHOSEN FEW: It's Too Late 7

CHUNKY
73 Orange OAS 214 Albatross Baby/Road Runner Girl 25

CHURCH
82 Carrere CAR 212 Unguarded Moment/Bus Driver (p/s) 5
82 Carrere CAR 247 Almost With You/Life Speeds Up (p/s) 5
82 Carrere CAR EP 257 Unguarded Moment/Interlude/Golden Dawn/Sisters (10", p/s) 8
83 Carrere CHURCH R5A Different Man/I Am A Rock (no p/s) 7
83 Carrere CHURCH 5 SING SONGS (12" EP) 10
88 Arista 208895 STARFISH (LP, with bonus 5-track numbered 12") 15

EUGENE CHURCH
59 London HL 8940 Miami/I Ain't Goin' For That (round centre) 75
59 London HL 8940 Miami/I Ain't Goin' For That (78) 20

CHICK CHURCHILL
(see also Ten Years After, Cozy Powell, Jethro Tull, Bernie Marsden)
73 Chrysalis CHR 1051 YOU AND ME (LP) 15

SAVANNAH CHURCHILL
53 Brunswick 05218 Shake A Hand/Shed A Tear (78) 20
60 London HLW 9273 I Want To Be/Time Out For Tears 7

CICCONE YOUTH
(see also Sonic Youth)
88 Blast First BFUS 28P WHITEY ALBUM PROMO (EP, promo only) 12
86 Blast First BFFP 8T Into The Groovey/Burnin' Up (12", p/s) 10

CIGARETTES
78 Dead Good KEVIN 1 THE CIGARETTES (EP, unreleased) 0
79 Company CIGCO 008 They're Back Again, Here They Come/I've Forgot My Number/
All We Want Is Your Money (gatefold p/s, initial pressing with red labels) 70
79 Company CIGCO 008 They're Back Again, Here They Come/I've Forgot My Number/
All We Want Is Your Money (gatefold p/s, later pressing with black labels) 60
80 Dead Good DEAD 10 Can't Sleep At Night/It's The Only Way To Live (Die) (p/s) 40

CIMMARRONS
(see also Reaction, Winston Groovy)
70 Hot Rod HR 105 Grandfather Clock/Kick Me Or I Kick You (as Cimarrons) 12
70 Reggae REG 3003 Bad Day At Black Rock (with Cimmaron Kid)/Fragile 20
71 Big Shot BI 562 Funky Fight/You Turned Me Down 10
71 Spinning Wheel SW 107 Soul For Sale/Bogus-ism 7
71 Downtown DT 486 Oh Mammy Blue/Oh Mammy Blue - Version 6
71 Downtown DT 487 Holy Christmas/Silent Night/White Christmas 6
71 Bullet BU 457 Call Me/Call Me (Part 2) 6
71 Bullet BU 458 Leave Me A Little Love/My Baby 6
74 Trojan TR7919 Over The Rainbow/We Are Not The Same 15
75 Vulcan VUL 1005 Tradition/Wicky Wacky 15
78 Cimarak CR002 Paul Bogle/Greedy Man (12") 30
82 IMP IMPS 50 With A Little Luck/Peggy Sue 5
82 Safari/MPL SAFE 49 Big Girls Don't Cry/How Can I Prove Myself To You? 5
83 MPL/Cimarons CIM 001 Love And Affection 18
83 MPL/Cimarons 12CIM 001 Love And Affection (12", less than 1000 pressed) 60
74 Trojan TRLS 77 IN TIME (LP) 12
78 Polydor 2383512 MAKA (LP, green vinyl) 12

CINDERELLAS
59 Brunswick 05794 Mister Dee-Jay/Yum Yum Yum 40
59 Brunswick 05794 Mister Dee-Jay/Yum Yum Yum (78) 10
60 Philips PB 1012 The Trouble With Boys/Puppy Dog 25

CINDERELLAS
(see also Cookies)
64 Colpix PX 11026 Baby, Baby (I Still Love You)/Please Don't Wake Me 80
64 Colpix PX 11026 Baby, Baby (I Still Love You)/Please Don't Wake Me (DJ Copy) 100

CINDERS
(see also Darlene Love)
63 Warner Bros WB 86 The Cinnamon Cinder/C'mon Wobble 20

CINDY & LINDY
57 HMV POP 409 The Language Of Love/Tell Me Something Sweet 10
59 Coral Q 72368 Saturday Night In Tiajuana/The Wonder That Is You 10
59 Coral Q 72368 Saturday Night In Tiajuana/The Wonder That Is You (78) 10

CINEMATIC ORCHESTRA
99 Ninja Tune ZEN12 084 Channel 1 Suite/Ode To The Big Sea (12") 15
99 Ninja Tune ZEN 45 MOTION (2xLP) 25
00 Ninja Tune ZEN 50 REMIXES 98 - 2000 (2xLP) 20
02 Ninja Tune ZEN 59 EVERY DAY (2xLP) 20
03 Ninja Tune ZEN 78 MAN WITH A MOVIE CAMERA (2xLP) 15
07 Ninja Tune ZEN 122 MA FLEUR (2xLP) 25

CINEMATICS
(see also Razorcuts)
80s Pulsebeat CINE 001 FAREWELL TO THE PLAYGROUND (EP, foldover p/s) 25

MINT VALUE £

CINNAMON

69 Beacon BEA 111 — You Won't See Me Leaving/Leaves Of Love 6
69 President PT 258 — So Long Sam/Broken Hearted Me, Evil Hearted You 6

CINNAMON QUILL

69 Morgan MRS 17 — Girl On A Swing/Take It Or Leave It 20
69 Morgan MRS 21 — Candy/Hello, It's Me 45

GIGLIOLA CINQUETTI

64 Decca F 21882 — Non Ho L'eta' Per Amarti/Sei Un Bravo Ragazzo 6

CIRCLE

60s Circle GR 1 — IN AID OF THE MILLFIELD BUILDING FUND (EP, private pressing) 150

CIRCLES

(see also Plastic Penny, Savages, Tony Dangerfield & Thrills, Screaming Lord Sutch)

66 Island WI 279 — Take Your Time/Don't You Love Me No More 100

CIRCLES

(see also Bob Andy)

72 Sioux SIOUX 017 — Mammy Blue/POOCH JACKSON & HARRY J. ALLSTARS: King Of The Road 7

CIRCLES

79 Graduate GRAD 4 — Opening Up/Billy (p/s) 20
80 Vertigo ANGRY 1 — Angry Voices/Summer Nights (p/s) 12
80 Chrysalis CHS 2418 — Opening Up/Billy (p/s, reissue) 8
85 Graduate GRAD 17 — Circles/Summer Nights (p/s) 25
99 Detour DRLP018 — PRIVATE WORLD (LP) 12

CIRCULUS

05 Rise Above RISE 7/064 — Mirl It Is (Moog UP Mix)/WITCHCRAFT: Chylde Of Fire 10
05 Rise Above RISE 7/065 — Swallow/My Body Is Made Of Sunlight 10
06 Rise Above RISE 7/094 — Song Of Our Despair/Honeycomb (clear, purple or black vinyl) 8
05 Rise Above RISELP 63 — THE LICK ON THE TIP OF MY ENVELOPE YET TO BE SENT (LP, brown vinyl gatefold sleeve, poster) 25
06 Rise Above RISELP 093 — CLOCKS ARE LIKE PEOPLE (LP, white vinyl, free 1-sided 7", "Tapestry", 500 only) 25
06 Rise Above RISELP 093 — CLOCKS ARE LIKE PEOPLE (LP, 700 on blue vinyl, 500 on black vinyl) 18

CIRCUS

(see also Philip Goodhand-Tait, King Crimson)

67 Parlophone R 5633 — Gone Are The Songs Of Yesterday/Sink Or Swim 20
68 Parlophone R 5672 — Do You Dream/House Of Wood 45
69 Transatlantic TRA 207 — CIRCUS (LP, gatefold sleeve, white/lilac label with 'T' logo) 100

CIRCUS MAXIMUS

67 Vanguard VSD 79260 — CIRCUS MAXIMUS (LP) 20
68 Vanguard VSD 79274 — NEVERLAND REVISITED (LP) 20

CIRKUS

80 Guardian GRCA 4 — Melissa/Amsterdam/Pick Up A Phone (EP) 20
73 RCB 1 — CIRKUS ONE (LP, private pressing with gatefold sleeve, black/white label) 200
77 Shock SHOCK 1 — FUTURE SHOCK (LP) 90

CITATIONS

63 Columbia DB 7068 — Moon Race/Slippin' And Slidin' 30

CITY LIMITS

80s Luggage RRP 1003 — Morse Code Signals/If I Had Time/I Just Can't Say (EP) 100

CITY RAMBLERS SKIFFLE GROUP

(see also Henrik Johansen)

57 Tempo A 158 — Ella Speed/2.19 Blues 20
57 Tempo A 161 — Mama Don't Allow/Tom Dooley 20
57 Tempo A 165 — Delia's Gone/Boodle-Am Shake 20
57 Storyville SEP 327 — I WANT A GIRL (EP) 40
57 Storyville SEP 345 — I SHALL NOT BE MOVED (EP) 40
57 Tempo EXA 59 — I WANT A GIRL (EP) 40
57 Tempo EXA 71 — GOOD MORNING BLUES (EP) 40
57 Tempo EXA 77 — DELIA'S GONE (EP) 40

CITY SMOKE

66 Mercury MF 971 — Sunday Morning/A Little Bit Of Love 7

CITY WAITES

74 EMI EMI 2149 — The Fox/One Of My Aunts 5
74 EMI EMC 3027 — A GORGEOUS GALLERY OF GALLANT INVENTIONS (LP) 20
76 Decca SKL 5264 — THE CITY WAITES (LP) 20
81 Hyperion A 66008 — HOW THE WORLD WAGS (LP, gatefold sleeve, some with Hyperion insert) 40

CIVILIANS

79 Arista ARIST 318 — MADE FOR TELEVISION EP 60

CIVILISED SOCIETY?

86 Manic Ears ACHE 2 — SCRAP METAL (LP, with inner) 15
87 Manic Ears ACHE 6 — VIOLENCE SUCKS (LP, with lyric inner) 15

C-JAM BLUES

66 Columbia DB 8064 — Candy/Stay At Home Girl 35

CLAGGERS

71 DJM DJ 5260 — Some-One/Umber Rag 15

CLAGUE

(see also Coyne-Clague, Kevin Coyne, Claque, Siren)

69 Dandelion S 4493 — Mandy Lee/Bottle Up And Go (with Kevin Coyne) 12
69 Dandelion S 4494 — The Stride/I Wonder Where 12

MINT VALUE £

CLAIM
89 Esurient Comms PACE 04 Wait & See/Business Boy/God, Cliffe & Me 12
90 Esurient Comms PACE 07 Losers Corner/Picking Up The Bitter Little Pieces 12
90 Caff CAFF 008 Birth Of A teenager/Mike The Bike 20
91 Esurient Comms PACE 07 Sunday/Sporting Life 12
92 A Turntable Friend TURN 08 Say So/Plastic Grip/Waiting For Jesus. 12
87 Trick Bag CU 0388 THIS PENCIL WAS OBVIOUSLY SHARPENED BY A LEFT-HANDED INDIAN KNIFE THROWER (EP) 18
85 Trick Bag TBR 001 ARMSTRONG'S REVIENGE AND ELEVEN OTHER SHORT STORIES (LP). 30
88 Esurient Comms PACE 003 BOOMY TELLA (LP) 30

CLAN
70 Bullet BU 419 Copycats/BUNNY LEE ALLSTARS: Hot Lead 12

CLAN
(see also Junior Campbell)
72 Deram DM 356 Pretty Belinda/Ode To Karen 7

CLAN OF XYMOX
85 4AD BAD 504 A Day/Stranger (12"). 10

CLANCY'S ALLSTARS
(see also Owen Gray)
68 Pama PM 722 C.N. Express Parts 1 & 2 (B-side actually "You Were Meant For Me" by Lee Perry) 30

CLANDESTINE
86 Market Trader PITCH 1 I'm All Over You (Like Jam On A Scone)/The Valley Of The Larne 6
86 Market Trader PITCH 1-12 I'm All Over You (Like Jam On A Scone)/The Valley Of The Larne/Ben's Men (12") . 10

CLANNAD & BONO
(see also U2, Bono & Gavin Friday, The Passengers)
89 RCA PA42995A In A Lifetime (7" picture disc) 10

JIMMY CLANTON
58 London HLS 8699 Just A Dream/You Aim To Please (as Jimmy Clanton & His Rockets). 25
58 London HLS 8699 Just A Dream/You Aim To Please (as Jimmy Clanton & His Rockets) (78) 20
58 London HL 7066 A Letter To An Angel/A Part Of Me (as Jimmy Clanton & Aces) (export issue). . . 25
59 London HLS 8779 A Letter To An Angel/A Part Of Me (as Jimmy Clanton & Aces) 30
59 London HLS 8779 A Letter To An Angel/A Part Of Me (as Jimmy Clanton & Aces) (78) 20
59 Top Rank JAR 189 My Own True Love/Little Boy In Love. 20
59 Top Rank JAR 189 My Own True Love/Little Boy In Love (78) 20
60 Top Rank JAR 269 Go, Jimmy, Go/I Trusted You 20
60 Top Rank JAR 382 Another Sleepless Night/I'm Gonna Try. 20
60 Top Rank JAR 509 Come Back (To Me)/Wait 20
61 Top Rank JAR 544 What Am I Gonna Do/If I. 12
62 Stateside SS 120 Venus In Blue Jeans/Highway Bound. 12
63 Stateside SS 159 Darkest Street In Town/Dreams Of A Fool 12
65 Stateside SS 410 Hurting Each Other/Don't Keep Your Friends Away 50
69 London HLP 10289 Curly/I'll Never Forget Your Love 5
59 London RES 1224 JUST A DREAM (EP). 100

CLAP
79 SRTS SRTS/79/CUS Hey Little Girl/20 Watts Of Power (p/s). 20

CLAPHAM SOUTH ESCALATORS
(see also Meteors, Escalators, Tall Boys)
81 Upright UP YOUR 1 Get Me To The World On Time/Leave Me Alone/Cardboard Cut Outs (p/s) 12

ERIC CLAPTON
(see also Yardbirds, John Mayall, Cream, Blind Faith, Delaney & Bonnie, Derek & The Dominos, Viv Stanshall, King Curtis, Randy Crawford)
66 Purdah 45-3502 Lonely Years/Bernard Jenkins (with John Mayall, 500 copies only). 400
70 Polydor 2001 096 I Am Yours (unissued) 0
70 Polydor 2001 096 After Midnight/Easy Now 10
74 RSO 2090 139 Willie And The Hand Jive/I Can't Hold Out Much Longer (p/s) 5
76 RSO 2090 208 Hello Old Friend/All Our Pastimes (p/s) 8
80 RSO JON 1 Wonderful Tonight (live)/Further On Up The Road (live) (promo only). 10
80 RSO JONX 1 Wonderful Tonight (live)/Further On Up The Road (live) (12", numbered p/s). . . . 10
81 RSO RSO 75 Another Ticket/Rita Mae (p/s) 5
83 Duck W 9701P The Shape You're In/Crosscut Saw (picture disc). 6
87 Duck W 8461F Behind The Mask/Grand Illusion//Crossroads (live)/White Room (live) (double pack, gatefold p/s) 10
87 Duck W 8397F It's In The Way That You Use It/Bad Influence//Behind The Mask/ Grand Illusion (double pack, shrinkwrapped with sticker) 8
88 Polydor PZCD 8 After Midnight (Extended Version)/I Can't Stand It/Whatcha Gonna Do/ Sunshine Of Your Love (CD, card sleeve) 15
89 BBC CD RSL 178 Edge Of Darkness/Shoot Out/Obituary/Escape From Northmoor/ Oxford Circus/Northmoor (with Michael Kamen, 3" CD with adaptor, 5" case). . . 15
89 Duck W 2644B Bad Love/I Shot The Sheriff (live) (box set with family tree & 2 colour prints) . . . 6
70 Polydor 2383 021 ERIC CLAPTON (LP, laminated sleeve, red label) 25
73 RSO 2479 702 CLAPTON (LP, withdrawn). 60
74 RSO QD 4801 461 OCEAN BOULEVARD (LP, quadrophonic). 18
82 RSO RSDX 3 TIME PIECES (2-LP, unissued) 0
84 Aston PD 20118 TOO MUCH MONKEY BUSINESS (LP, picture disc, with Yardbirds). 15

ALAN CLARE GROUP
62 Parlophone R 4938 Screwball/Love For Sale 5
65 Pye 7N 15764 Dog's Body/Mulligatawny 5
56 Decca DFE 6368 THE IMPROVISATIONS OF... (EP) 30
56 Decca DFE 6391 ALAN CLARE TRIO WITH BOB BURNS (EP). 30
58 Decca LK 4260 JAZZ AROUND THE CLOCK (LP) 30
68 Decca SKL 4965 YOUNG GIRL (LP). 15

MINT VALUE £

KENNY CLARE & RONNIE STEPHENSON

67	Columbia SX 6168	DRUM SPECTACULAR (LP, with Tubby Hayes and Stan Tracey, mono)	30
67	Columbia SCX 6168	DRUM SPECTACULAR (LP, with Tubby Hayes and Stan Tracey, stereo)	40
72	Sounds Superb SPR90057	DRUM SPECTACULAR (LP, reissue with Tubby Hayes and Stan Tracey)	18

CLARENDONIANS

(see also Lee & Clarendonians, Desmond Baker & Clarendonians, Four Aces, Prince Buster, Dennis Walks)

65	Ska Beat JB 219	Muy Bien (My Friend)/You Are A Fool	25
66	Ska Beat JB 261	Doing The Jerk/You Won't See Me	30
66	Island WI 284	Try Me One More Time/Can't Keep A Good Man Down	25
66	Island WI 3005	I'll Never Change/Rules Of Life	25
67	Island WI 3032	Shoo-Be-Doo-Be (I Love You)/Sweet Heart Of Beauty	25
67	Island WI 3041	You Can't Be Happy/Goodbye Forever	25
67	Studio One SO 2004	The Table's Going To Turn/I Can't Go On	40
67	Studio One SO 2007	He Who Laughs Last/GAYLADS: Just A Kiss From You	40
67	Studio One SO 2017	Love Me With All Your Heart/Love Don't Mean Much To Me	40
67	Rio R 112	Rudie Bam Bam/Be Bop Boy	18
67	Rio R 115	Musical Train/Lowdown Girl	18
68	Caltone TONE 114	Baby Baby/Bye Bye Bye	80
69	Duke DU 97	Come Along/Try To Be Happy	10
69	Gas GAS 131	When I Am Gone/She Brings Me Joy	12
70	Trojan TR 7714	Lick It Back/BEVERLEY'S ALLSTARS: Busy Bee	8
70	Trojan TR 7719	Baby Don't Do It/BEVERLEY'S ALLSTARS: Touch Down	50
71	Green Door GD 4009	Seven In One (Medley) (both sides)	6
72	Attack ATT 8039	Bound In Chains/STUD ALLSTARS: Version	6
72	Pama PM 847	This Is My Story/VAL BENNETT: Caledonia	10
73	Pama PM 856	Good Hearted Woman/CORNELL CAMPBELL: What Happens	8
73	Techniques TE 925	Just One Look/Sinner Man	6
73	Dragon DRA 1006	Walking Up A One Way Street/DYNAMITES: Instrumental	30

ALICE CLARK

69	Action ACT 4520	You Got A Deal/Say You'll Never	30

CHRIS CLARK

67	Tamla Motown TMG 591	Love's Gone Bad/Put Yourself In My Place	150
67	Tamla Motown TMG 591	Love's Gone Bad/Put Yourself In My Place (DJ Copy)	200
67	Tamla Motown TMG 624	From Head To Toe/The Beginning Of The End	40
67	Tamla Motown TMG 624	From Head To Toe/The Beginning Of The End (DJ Copy)	80
68	Tamla Motown TMG 638	I Want To Go Back There Again/I Love You	30
68	Tamla Motown TMG 638	I Want To Go Back There Again/I Love You (DJ Copy)	60
68	T. Motown STML 11069	SOUL SOUNDS (LP)	90
68	T. Motown TML 11069	SOUL SOUNDS (LP, mono)	100

CLAUDINE CLARK

62	Pye International 7N 25157	Party Lights/Disappointed	20
63	Pye International 7N 25186	Walk Me Home From The Party/Who Will You Hurt?	20
67	Sue WI 4039	The Strength To Be Strong/Moon Madness	40

DAVE CLARK FIVE

(see also Dave Clark & Friends, Smith D'Abo, Mike Smith, Washington D.C.s)

62	Ember EMB S 156	Chaquita/In Your Heart (grey/pink labels)	40
62	Ember EMB S 156	Chaquita/In Your Heart (red/yellow labels)	30
62	Piccadilly 7N 35088	First Love/I Walk The Line	30
62	Piccadilly 7N 35500	That's What I Said/I Knew It All The Time	30
63	Columbia DB 7011	The Mulberry Bush/Chaquita	20
63	Columbia DB 7112	Do You Love Me/Doo-Dah	10
64	Columbia DB 7291	Can't You See That She's Mine/Because	5
64	Columbia DB 7335	Thinking Of You Baby/Whenever You're Around	6
64	Columbia DB 7377	Any Way You Want It/Crying Over You	6
65	Columbia DB 7453	Everybody Knows/Say You Want Me	10
65	Columbia DB 7503	Reelin' And Rockin'/Little Bitty Pretty One	6
65	Columbia DB 7580	Come Home/Mighty Good Loving (in p/s)	18
65	Columbia DB 7580	Come Home/Mighty Good Loving	7
65	Columbia DB 7625	Catch Us If You Can/Move On	7
65	Columbia DB 7744	Over And Over/I'll Be Yours	10
66	Columbia DB 7863	Try Too Hard/All Night Long	8
66	Columbia DB 7909	Look Before You Leap/Please Tell Me Why	8
66	Columbia DB 8028	Nineteen Days/I Need Love	6
67	Columbia DB 8152	You Got What It Takes/Sitting Here Baby	6
67	Columbia DB 8194	Tabatha Twitchit/Man In A Pin-Striped Suit (in export p/s)	20
67	Columbia DB 8194	Tabatha Twitchit/Man In A Pin-Striped Suit	5
67	Columbia DB 8286	Everybody Knows/Concentration Baby	5
68	Columbia DB 8342	No One Can Break A Heart Like You/You Don't Want My Lovin'	6
68	Columbia DB 8465	The Red Balloon/Maze Of Love	7
68	Columbia DB 8505	Live In The Sky/Children	5
69	Columbia DB 8545	The Mulberry Tree/Small Talk	5
69	Columbia DB 8591	Get It On Now/Maze Of Life (unreleased, acetates exist)	0
69	Columbia DB 8624	Put A Little Love In Your Heart/34-06	6
69	Columbia DB 8638	Good Old Rock'N'Roll Medley (Parts 1 & 2) (in p/s)	5
70	Columbia DB 8660	Everybody Get Together/Darling I Love You	5
70	Columbia DB 8681	Julia/Five By Five	10
70	Columbia DB 8689	Here Comes Summer/Break Down And Cry	6
70	Columbia DB 8724	Play More Good Old Rock'N'Roll Medley (Parts 1 & 2) (in p/s)	6
71	Columbia DB 8749	Southern Man/If You Wanna See Me Cry	5
71	Columbia DB 8791	Won't You Be My Lady/Into Your Life	8
72	Columbia DB 8963	All Time Greats Medley (Glad All Over/Do You Love Me/Bits & Pieces/ Glad All Over)/Wild Weekend (p/s)	15
64	Columbia SEG 8289	THE DAVE CLARK FIVE (EP)	15
65	Columbia SEG 8381	THE HITS OF THE DAVE CLARK FIVE (EP)	20

			MINT VALUE £
65	Columbia SEG 8447	WILD WEEKEND (EP)	25
64	Columbia 33SX 1598	SESSION WITH THE DAVE CLARK FIVE (LP, blue/black label, with "Sold in the U.K..." label text)	35
64	Ember FA 2003	DAVE CLARK FIVE AND THE WASHINGTON D.C.'s (LP)	30
65	EMI Regal REG 2017	IN SESSION (LP, export issue)	35
65	Columbia SX 1756	CATCH US IF YOU CAN (LP, soundtrack, blue/black label)	45
67	Columbia SX 6105	THE DAVE CLARK FIVE'S GREATEST HITS (LP, blue/black label)	15
68	Columbia SX 6207	EVERYBODY KNOWS (LP, blue/black label)	30
69	Columbia SX 6309	5 BY 5 1964-69: 14 TITLES BY THE DAVE CLARK FIVE (LP, blue/black label)	30
70	Columbia SCX 6437	IF SOMEBODY LOVES YOU (LP)	30
72	Columbia SCX 6494	DAVE CLARK AND FRIENDS (LP, boxed logo on label)	20

DEE CLARK

59	London HL 8802	Nobody But You/When I Call On You	30
59	London HL 8802	Nobody But You/When I Call On You (78)	20
59	London HL 8915	Just Keep It Up (And See What Happens)/ Whispering Grass(Don't Tell The Trees)	30
59	London HL 8915	Just Keep It Up (And See What Happens)/ Whispering Grass(Don't Tell The Trees) (78)	20
59	Top Rank JAR 196	Hey, Little Girl/If It Wasn't For Love	30
59	Top Rank JAR 196	Hey, Little Girl/If It Wasn't For Love (78)	30
60	Top Rank JAR 284	How About That/Blues Get Off My Shoulder	15
60	Top Rank JAR 373	At My Front Door/Cling-A-Ling	22
60	Top Rank JAR 501	Gloria/You're Looking Good	12
61	Top Rank JAR 551	Your Friends/Because I Love You	12
61	Top Rank JAR 570	Raindrops/I Want To Love You	18
62	Columbia DB 4768	Don't Walk Away From Me/You're Telling Our Secrets	40
63	Stateside SS 180	I'm A Soldier Boy/Shook Up Over You	22
64	Stateside SS 355	Heartbreak/Warm Summer Breeze	15
65	Stateside SS 400	T.C.B./It's Impossible	20
70	Liberty LBF 15334	Where Did All The Good Times Go?/24 Hours Of Loneliness	10
60	Top Rank BUY 044	HOW ABOUT THAT! (LP)	40
70	Joy JOYS 130	YOU'RE LOOKING GOOD (LP)	15

DOTTY CLARK

61	London HLX 9418	It's Been A Long, Long Time/That's A Step In The Right Direction	10

GENE CLARK

(see also Byrds, Dillard & Clark)

67	CBS 202523	Echoes/I Found You	30
74	Asylum AYM 536	No Other/The True One	6
74	Asylum AYM 540	Life's Greatest Fool/From A Silver Phial	6
88	Bucketfull of Brains BOB 18	Gypsy Rider/SEERS: Flyaway (flexidisc with Bucketfull Of Brains magazine, issue 24)	7
67	CBS 62934	GENE CLARK WITH THE GOSDIN BROTHERS (LP)	60
72	A&M AMLS 64297	WHITE LIGHT (LP)	25
74	Asylum SYL 9020	NO OTHER (LP)	20
77	RSO 2394 175	TWO SIDES TO EVERY STORY (LP)	12
84	Making Waves SPIN 122	FIREBYRD (LP)	12

GUY CLARK

75	RCA Victor APL1-130	OLD NO. 1 (LP)	15
76	RCA Victor RS 1097	TEXAS COOKIN' (LP)	15

JIMMY 'SOUL' CLARK

76	Black Magic BM 115	Sweet Darlin'/Sweet Darlin' (Instrumental)	10

LARENA CLARK

66	Topic 12T 140	A CANADIAN GARLAND (LP)	15

MICHAEL CLARK

66	Liberty LIB 5893	None Of These Girls/Work Out	15

NOBBY CLARK

76	Epic S EPC 4381	Steady Love/Give Me The Heart	10

PAUL CLARK & FRIENDS

77	Myrrh MYR 1054	GOOD TO BE HOME (LP, with inner sleeve)	20
78	Myrrh MYR 1059	HAND TO THE PLOUGH (LP)	20

PETULA CLARK

SINGLES

57	Pye Nixa 7N 15096	With All My Heart/Gonna Find Me A Bluebird	15
57	Pye Nixa 7N 15112	Alone/Long Before I Knew You	8
58	Pye Nixa 7N 15126	Baby Lover/The Little Blue Man	10
58	Pye Nixa 7N 15135	Love Me Again/In A Little Moment	10
58	Pye Nixa 7N 15152	St. Tropez (Sur La Plage)/Devotion	12
58	Pye Nixa 7N 15168	I Wish I Knew/Fibbin'	10
59	Pye Nixa 7N 15182	Ever Been In Love/Lucky Day	8
59	Pye Nixa 7N 15191	Watch Your Heart/Suddenly	8
59	Pye Nixa 7N 15208	Where Do I Go From Here?/Mama's Talking Soft	10
59	Pye Nixa 7N 15220	Adonis/If I Had My Way	10
59	Pye 7N 15244	I Love A Violin/Guitare Et Tambourin	12
60	Pye 7N 15281	Cinderella Jones/All Over Now	10
61	Pye 7N 15337	Something Missing/Isn't This A Lovely Day?	6
61	Pye 7N 15355	Welcome Home/Les Gens Diront	6
62	Pye 7N 15407	I'm Counting On You/Some Other World	6
62	Pye 7N 15448	Ya Ya Twist/Si C'est Oui, C'est Oui	6
62	Pye 7N 15456	Jumble Sale/Too Late	7
62	Pye 7N 15478	The Road/No Love, No Nothin'	6
63	Pye 7N 15517	Valentino/Imagination	7

MINT VALUE £

63	Pye 7N 15551	Let Me Tell You/Be Good To Me	6
63	Pye 7N 15573	Baby It's Me/This Is Goodbye	6
64	Pye 7N 15606	Thank You/Crying Through A Sleepless Night	6
64	Pye 7N 15639	In Love/Forgetting You (J'ai Tout Oublié)	7
64	Pye 7N 15668	True Love Never Runs Smooth/Saturday Sunshine	6
65	Pye 7N 15991	You're The One/Gotta Tell The World (in export p/s)	15
66	Pye 7N 17071	A Sign Of The Times/Time For Love	15
66	Pye 7N 17187	Who Am I/Love Is A Long Journey	5
67	Pye 7N 17377	The Cat In The Window/Fancy Dancin' Man	5
68	Pye 7N 17466	Kiss Me Goodbye/I've Got Love Going For Me	5
71	Pye 7N 45026	The Song Of My Life/For Love	5
71	Pye 7N 45112	I Don't Know How To Love Him/Song Went Wrong	5
72	Polydor 2058 295	Wedding Song (There Is Love)/Song Without End	5
73	Polydor 2058 413	Lead Me On/Taking It On (both with Sacha Distel)	5
74	Polydor 2058 519	Let's Sing A Love Song/I'm The Woman You Need	5
75	Polydor 2058 560	I Am Your Song/Super Loving Lady	5
75	Pye 7N 45473	Wind Of Change (edit)/Memories Are Made Of This	6
75	Pye 7N 45506	What I Did For Love/I Believe In Love	6
EPs			
56	Pye Nixa NEP 24006	CHILDREN'S CHOICE	12
56	Pye Nixa NEP 24016	PETULA CLARK HIT PARADE	12
57	Pye Nixa NEP 24056	PETULA CLARK HIT PARADE NO. 2	10
57	Pye Nixa NEP 24060	YOU ARE MY LUCKY STAR PART 1	12
57	Pye Nixa NEP 24061	YOU ARE MY LUCKY STAR PART 2	12
57	Pye Nixa NEP 24062	YOU ARE MY LUCKY STAR PART 3	12
58	Pye Nixa NEP 24080	PETULA CLARK HIT PARADE NO. 3	10
58	Pye Nixa NEP 24089	PETULA CLARK SINGS IN FRENCH	10
58	Pye Nixa NEP 24094	A CHRISTMAS CAROL (mono)	8
58	Pye Nixa NSEP 85001	A CHRISTMAS CAROL (stereo)	10
59	Pye NEP 24121	ENCORE	10
61	Pye NEP 24137	PETULA CLARK HIT PARADE 4	10
61	Pye NEP 24150	PETULA CLARK HIT PARADE 5	10
62	Pye NEP 24157	PET-OOH-LA-LA	10
65	Pye-Vogue VRE 5004	LES DISQUES D'OR DE LA CHANSON	12
65	Pye-Vogue VRE 5007	PETULA CLARK CHANTE EN ITALIEN	20
66	Pye NEP 24237	CALL ME	10
66	Pye-Vogue VRE 5019	L'AGENT SECRET	10
66	Pye-Vogue VRE 5023	HELLO MISTER BROWN	10
67	Pye-Vogue VRE 5025	C'EST MA CHANSON	10
LPs			
56	Pye Nixa NPT 19002	PETULA CLARK SINGS (10")	60
56	Pye Nixa NPT 19014	A DATE WITH PET (10")	50
57	Pye Nixa NPL 18007	YOU ARE MY LUCKY STAR	50
59	Pye Nixa NPL 18039	PETULA CLARK IN HOLLYWOOD	40
62	Pye NPL 18070	IN OTHER WORDS - PETULA CLARK	30
63	Pye NPL 18098	PETULA	15
64	Pye-Vogue VRL 3001	LES JAMES DEAN	25
65	Pye-Vogue VRL 3010	PETULA '65 (in French)	25
66	Pye-Vogue VRL 3016	HELLO PARIS VOL. 1	20
66	Pye-Vogue VRL 3019	HELLO PARIS VOL. 2	20
66	Pye-Vogue VRL 3022	PETULA '66	15
68	Warner Bros WF(S) 2550	FINIAN'S RAINBOW (soundtrack)	18
68	Pye-Vogue VRLS 3035	PETULA CLARK A PARIS	15

ROY CLARK

59	HMV POP 581	Please Mr. Mayor/Puddin'	150
59	HMV POP 581	Please Mr. Mayor/Puddin' (78)	40
63	Capitol CL 15288	In The Mood/Texas Twist	15
63	Capitol CL 15317	Tips Of My Fingers/Spooky Movies	15
62	Capitol (S)T 1780	THE LIGHTNING FINGERS OF ROY CLARK (LP)	50

SANFORD CLARK

(see also Al Casey)

56	London HLD 8320	The Fool/Lonesome For A Letter (with Al Casey) (gold label print)	200
56	London HLD 8320	The Fool/Lonesome For A Letter (with Al Casey) (later silver print label)	100
56	London HLD 8320	The Fool/Lonesome For A Letter (with Al Casey) (78)	15
56	London HL 7014	The Fool/Lonesome For A Letter (with Al Casey) (export issue)	50
59	London HLW 8959	Run, Boy Run/New Kind Of Fool (triangular centre)	30
59	London HLW 8959	Run, Boy Run/New Kind Of Fool (round centre)	20
59	London HLW 8959	Run, Boy Run/New Kind Of Fool (triangular or round centre) (78)	40
60	London HLW 9026	Son-Of-A-Gun/I Can't Help It (If I'm Still In Love With You)	22
60	London HLW 9095	Go On Home/Pledging My Love	22
68	Ember EMB S 250	Shades/Once Upon A Time	10
57	London RED 1105	PRESENTING SANFORD CLARK (EP)	100
60	London REW 1256	LOWDOWN BLUES (EP)	100
72	Ember CW 131	THEY CALL ME COUNTRY (LP)	15

TERRY CLARK

70	Myrrh MYR 1071	WELCOME (LP)	20

ALLAN CLARKE

(see also Hollies)

72	RCA RCA 2244	You're Losing Me/A Coward By Name	10
75	EMI 2352	Born To Run/Why Don't You Call	5
72	RCA SF 8283	MY REAL NAME IS 'AROLD (LP, lyric insert, orange/white label)	20
73	EMI EMA 752	HEADROOM (LP, gatefold sleeve, lyric inner sleeve)	15
74	EMI EMC 3041	ALLAN CLARKE (LP)	12
76	EMI EMC 3130	I'VE GOT TIME (LP)	12

MINT VALUE £

ANNETTE CLARKE

73	Techniques TE 925	Just One Look/Sinner Man	10

BOB CLARKE

70	CBS 7435	Haunted/Run Colorado	30
72	CBS 17741	Sad/Some Ones Slipping Into My Mind	10

DAVE CLARKE

94	Bush 1012	Red 1 (of 3) (Protective Custody)/Zeno Xero (12", p/s, red vinyl)	15
94	Bush 1015	Red 2 (of 3) (Wisdom To The Wise)/Gonk (12", p/s, red vinyl)	12

ERIC CLARKE

78	Baal BAL 89004	LOVE THAT GROWS AND GROWS BAAL (LP)	60

JAMES CLARK(E) + SOUNDS

68	Fontana TF 918	A Man Of Our Times T.V. Series Theme/Spring Bossa	10
68	Fontana SFJL 966	A MAN OF OUR TIMES (LP)	50

JENNY CLARKE

64	Pye 7N 15661	Spring Will Be A Little Late This Year/Say You Love Me	8

JOHN COOPER CLARKE

79	Epic S EPC 12 7009	¡Gimmix!/I Married A Monster From Outer Space (Third Version) (p/s, triangular disc, orange vinyl)	6
79	Epic S EPC 7982	Splat/Twat/Sleepwalk (double-grooved A-side, p/s, with Epic inner sleeve)	5
78	CBS 83132	DISGUISE IN LOVE (LP)	20
80	Epic EPC 84083	SNAP, CRACKLE [&] BOP (LP, with 48-page book in sleeve pocket)	20
81	Epic EPC 84979	ME AND MY BIG MOUTH (LP)	15

JOHNNY CLARKE

74	Explosion EX 2089	None Shall Escape The Judgement/Every Rasta Is A Star	12
74	Pyramid PYR 7013	My Desire/Lemon Tree	6
74	Lord Koos KOOS42	Enter Into This Gate With Praise/KING TUBBY & THE AGGROVATORS : This Is The Hardest Version	8
74	Atra ATRA019	Everyday Wondering/Julie	7
74	Cactus CTEP32	Jump Back Baby	15
74	Harry J HJ6706	Move Out A Babylon/Move Out A Babylon (Instrumental)	10
74	Explosion EX2089	None Shall Escape The Judgement/Every Rasta Is A Star	12
75	Horse HOSS86	Move out Of Babylon/AGGROVATORS : Version	7
75	Horse HOSS100	Too Much War/AGGROVATORS : Version	8
75	Vulcan VUL 1001	I'm Gonna Put It On/KING TUBBY AND THE AGGROVATORS - Version	6
75	Attack ATT 8100	Rock With Me Baby/KING TUBBYS AND THE AGGROVATORS: A Crabit Version	6
75	Attack ATT 8118	Cold I Up/Cold I Up (Version)	6
76	Virgin VS159	Crazy Baldhead/Version	8
77	Virgin VS173	Roots, Natty Roots, Natty Congo/Version	8
77	Third World TW 70	Age is growing/Version	12
78	Star PTP1009	Every Knee Shall Bow/Version (With U Roy) (12")	25
78	Justice JUDIS 109	Pity Fool Fe Get Wise/Satisfaction (12")	50
78	Third World TW 92	Riding For A Fall/CLINT EASTWOOD AND THE AGROVATORS: Version	8
79	Greensleeves GRED20	Jah Love Is With I/Bad Days Are Going (12")	50
80	Cha Cha CHAD17	Babylon/One Man Live (as J. Clark) (12")	40
81	Chrysalis 122849	Babylon/Than You For The Many Things You've Done - Cassandra (12")	20
81	Art & Craft ACD 007	Can't Get Enough/Version (12')	20
81	Art & Craft ACD 014	Guide Us Jah/Version (12")	20
81	Art & Craft ACD 015	Rude Boy/Version (12")	20
82	Art & Craft ACD 018	You Better Try/Version (12")	20
82	Black Joy DH822	Stop Them Jah/Too Much War	12
82	Cha Cha CHAD 49	Give Me Love/Version (10")	15
83	Top Notch TOP005	Young Rebel/Version (10")	15
89	Jah Shaka SHAKA 876	Rosie/Rosie Dub (12")	12
75	Attack ATLP 1015	ENTER INTO HIS GATES WITH PRAISE (LP)	50
75	Vulcan VULP 001	PUT IT ON (LP)	25
76	Virgin V2076	AUTHORISED VERSION (LP)	12
77	Justice JUSLP 001	GIRL I LOVE YOU (LP)	40
77	Paradise PDLP 001	DON'T STAY OUT LATE (LP)	25
78	Third World TWS 932	KING IN THE ARENA (LP)	40
82	Art and Craft ACDLP001	CAN'T GET ENOUGH (LP)	50
83	Ariwa ARI 007 LP	YARD STYLE (LP)	30
89	Attack ATLP 105	ENTER INTO HIS GATES WITH PRAISE (LP, repressing)	15

KENNY CLARKE

56	London LTZC 15004	KENNY CLARKE SEXTET (LP)	20
56	London LTZC 15008	KENNY CLARKE AND ERNIE WILKINS (LP)	20
57	London LTZC 15038	KENNY CLARKE (LP)	20
57	London LTZC 15047	KENNY CLARKE (LP)	20
57	Vogue LAE 12029	JAZZ INTERNATIONAL (LP)	25

KENNY CLARKE (with Francy Boland Big Band)

(see also Francy Boland, Kenny Clarke)

56	London LTZ C 15047	BOHEMIA AFTER DARK (LP)	15
57	Columbia SEG 7830	KENNY CLARKE QT. (EP)	10
63	London HA-K 8085	JAZZ IS UNIVERSAL (LP, with Francy Boland Big Band)	15
66	CBS SBPG 62567	NOW HEAR OUR MEANIN' (LP)	18
68	Polydor 583726	LATIN KALEIDOSCOPE (LP)	20
69	Polydor 583727	ALL SMILES (LP)	20
69	Polydor 583738	FELLINI 712 (LP)	20
69	Polydor 583054	LIVE AT RONNIE SCOTT'S - THE FIRST SET (LP)	20
69	Polydor 583055	LIVE AT RONNIE SCOTT'S - THE SECOND SET (LP)	20
70	Polydor 583739	FACES (LP)	15
70	Polydor 2310 147	OFF LIMITS (LP, reflective sleeve)	30
71	Polydor 2310 147	OFF LIMITS (LP)	12

MINT VALUE £

LINDA CLARKE

67	Decca F 12709	Your Hurtin' Kinda Love/Send Me The Pillow You Dream On	10
68	Decca F 12787	Society's Child/Rain In My Heart	20

LLOYD CLARKE

(see also Derrick & Lloyd, Theo Beckford, Soulettes, Delroy Wilson, Laurel Aitken, Sonny Burke, Uniques)

62	Blue Beat BB 99	Good Morning/Now I Know A Reason (with Smithie's Sextet)	12
62	Blue Beat BB 104	Fool's Day/You're A Cheat (with Reco's All Stars)	12
62	Island WI 007	Love You The Most/LLOYD ROBINSON: You Said You Loved Me	15
62	Island WI 045	Japanese Girl/He's Coming	15
63	Rio R 16	Love Me/Half As Much	15
64	Rio R 23	Stop Your Talking/A Penny	15
64	Rio R 24	Fellow Jamaican/PATRICK & GEORGE: My Love	15
68	Island WI 3116	Summertime/VAL BENNETT: Soul Survivor	100
68	Blue Cat BS 136	Young Love/UNTOUCHABLES: Wall Flower	40
70	Escort ERT 849	Chicken Thief/STRANGER COLE: Tomorrow	7
71	Black Swan BW 1405	Love You The Most/LOW BITES:Version	12

MICKEY CLARKE

66	HMV 1483	Help Me/For Me	20

PAULA CLARKE

83	Oak Sound OSD 013	University/Didn't I Blow Your mind (12")	40

TERRY CLARKE

72	Polydor 2058191	Lady/Army Captains Daughter	10

TONY CLARKE

64	Pye International 7N 25251	Ain't Love Good, Ain't Love Proud/Coming Back Strong	22
65	Chess CRS 8011	The Entertainer/This Heart Of Mine	25
65	Chess CRS 8011	The Entertainer/This Heart Of Mine (DJ Copy)	50
69	Chess CRS 8091	The Entertainer/Ain't Love Good, Ain't Love Proud	8
74	Chess 6145 030	Landslide/The Entertainer	8

CLARK-HUTCHINSON

(see also Sam Gopal, Vamp, Upp)

68	Decca LK-R 5006	CLARK-HUTCHINSON (LP, one known copy, red Decca labels, no sleeve Matrix: ARL-8968.P-1A/1B	500
70	Decca Nova DN-R 2	A = MH2 (LP, mono)	150
70	Decca Nova DN-R 2	A = MH2 (LP, stereo)	75
70	Deram SML 1076	RETRIBUTION (LP)	60
71	Deram SML 1090	GESTALT (LP)	65

CLARK SISTERS

59	London HLD 8791	Chicago/Opus 1	10
58	London RE-D 1198	SING, SING, SING (EP)	10
58	London HA-D 2128	SING, SING, SING (LP)	20
59	London HA-D 2177	THE CLARK SISTERS SWING AGAIN (LP, mono)	20
59	London SAH-D 6025	THE CLARK SISTERS SWING AGAIN (LP, stereo)	25

CLARO INTELECTO

02	Ai AI 003	PEACE OF MIND (12", first pressings in blue p/s)	15

CLASH

(see also 101'ers, Janie Jones & Lash, Tymon Dogg, Ellen Foley, Futura 2000, Joe Strummer)

77	CBS S CBS 5058	White Riot/1977 (p/s, 'The Clash' or 'The CLASH' on label)	20
77	CBS CL 1	CAPITAL RADIO (EP, NME freebie, p/s)	50
77	CBS S CBS 5293	Remote Control/London's Burning (live) (p/s)	10
77	CBS Promo S CBS 5293	Remote Control/London's Burning (Studio Version) ('A' Label Promo)	50
77	CBS S CBS 5664	Complete Control/The City Of The Dead (p/s)	10
78	CBS S CBS 6383	(White Man) In Hammersmith Palais/The Prisoner (initially green, then pink, blue or yellow die-cut sleeve)	12
78	CBS S CBS 6788	Tommy Gun/1 - 2 Crush On You (p/s)	8
78	CBS S CBS 7082	English Civil War/Pressure Drop (p/s)	8
79	CBS S CBS 7324	THE COST OF LIVING (EP, gatefold p/s & inner sleeve)	8
79	CBS S CBS 8087	London Calling/Armagideon Time (p/s, green or red shaded sleeve, white or yellow/orange label)	10

(All the early Clash singles were re-pressed in 1979 with picture sleeves and sell for around £8 in Mint)

79	CBS 12 8087	London Calling/Armagidion Time/Armagidion Time (version) (12")	15
80	CBS 8323	Bankrobber/Rockers Galore	7
81	CBS A12 1133	The Magnificent Seven/The Magnificent Dance (12", p/s)	15
81	CBS S 2309	Know Your Rights/First Night Back In London (p/s, with free sticker)	10
82	CBS A 2479	Rock The Casbah/Long Time Jerk (p/s, with free stickers)	10
82	CBS A 11 2479	Rock The Casbah/Long Time Jerk (picture disc)	8
82	CBS A 13 2479	Rock The Casbah/Mustapha Dance (12")	18
82	CBS A 2646	Should I Stay Or Should I Go/Straight To Hell (p/s)	10
82	CBS A 11 2646	Should I Stay Or Should I Go/Straight To Hell (picture disc)	8
82	CBS A 12 2646	Should I Stay Or Should I Go/Straight To Hell (12")	12
88	CBS CLASHB 2	London Calling/Brand New Cadillac/Rudie Don't Fail (box set)	12
77	CBS 82000	THE CLASH (LP, 10,000 only with sticker on inner sleeve for free NME Capital Radio EP freebie, most were removed by Clash fans eager for the 7")	50
77	CBS 82000	THE CLASH (LP, 1st issue with orange/yellow labels)	20
78	CBS 82431	GIVE 'EM ENOUGH ROPE (LP, promo-only package with poster in folder)	200
78	CBS 82431	GIVE 'EM ENOUGH ROPE (LP)	15
79	CBS CLASH 3	LONDON CALLING (2-LP, stickered, with inner sleeves, 1st issue with black & white labels)	20
80	CBS FSLN	SANDINISTA (3-LP)	18
82	CBS FMLN2	COMBAT ROCK (LP, inner sleeve and poster)	15
88	CBS 460244 1	THE STORY OF THE CLASH (2-LP)	20

MINT VALUE £

CLASSICS IV
(see also Dennis Yost & Classics IV)

66	Capitol CL 15470	Pollyanna/Cry Baby (issued as if by the "Classics"	40
68	Liberty LBF 15051	Spooky/Poor People	8
69	Liberty LBF 15177	Stormy/Twenty Four Hours Of Loneliness	15
69	Liberty LBF 15196	Traces/Mary, Mary Row Your Boat	5
69	Liberty LBF 15231	Everyday With You Girl/Sentimental Lady	5

CLASSICS (Jamaica)

69	Doctor Bird DB 1190	Worried Over Me/LAUREL AITKEN: Rice And Peas	40
70	New Beat NB 061	Same Old Feeling/So Much Love	8
70	New Beat NB 071	History Of Africa/Honeybee	8
70	Pama PM 830	Sex Education/POWER: Soul Flash	12
71	Punch PH 79	Cheerio Baby/Civilization	8

CLASSICS (U.S.)

61	Mercury AMT 1152	Life Is But A Dream/That's The Way	100
63	Stateside SS 215	Till Then/Enie Minie Mo	40

CLASSMATES

63	Decca F 11736	Let's Get Together Tonight/It's No Game	6
63	Decca F 11779	Go Tell It On The Mountain/Give Me A Girl	6
64	Decca F 11806	In Morocco/I Feel	6
64	Decca F 12047	Go Away/Pay Day	10

CLAUDETTE (& CORPORATION)
(see also Corporation)

69	Jackpot JP 712	Let's Fall In Love/PROPHETS: Purple Moon	30
70	Grape GR 3020	Skinheads A Bash Them (with Corporation)/ CORPORATION: Walkin' Thru Jerusalem	120

CASSIUS CLAY

64	CBS AAG 190	Stand By Me/I Am The Greatest	30
66	CBS 202190	Stand By Me/I Am The Greatest (reissue)	10
63	CBS BPG 62274	I AM THE GREATEST! (LP)	50

JUDY CLAY
(see also Billy Vera & Judy Clay, Booker T. & M.G.'s)

67	Stax 601 022	You Can't Run Away From Your Heart/It Takes A Lotta Good Love	15

JUDY CLAY & WILLIAM BELL
(see also William Bell, Billy Vera & Judy Clay)

68	Stax STAX 101	Private Number/Love, Aye 'Tis	8
69	Stax STAX 115	My Baby Specialises/Left Over Love	10

OTIS CLAY

67	President PT 121	It's Easier Said Than Done/Flame In Your Heart	8
68	President PT 132	I'm Satisfied/I Testify	5
68	President PT 148	That's How It Is/Show Place	10
68	President PT 176	A Lasting Love/Got To Find A Way	5
69	Atlantic 584 282	Baby Jane/You Hurt Me For The Last Time	75
72	London HLU 10397	Trying To Live My Life Without You/Let Me Be The One	10
74	London HLU 10467	You Did Something To Me/It Was Jealousy	10
73	London SH-U 8446	TRYING TO LIVE MY LIFE WITHOUT YOU (LP)	30

TOM CLAY

72	Tamla Motown TMG 801	What The World Needs NowIs Love/The Victors	12

CLAY FAV

79	own label	CONSIGNMENT STOCK (EP, 1,000, 200 with stamped "consignment Stock' sleeve, no p/s)	150
79	own label	CONSIGNMENT STOCK (EP, 1,000, 800 without stamped "consignment Stock' sleeve, no p/s)	50

ALASDAIR CLAYRE

67	Elektra EUK 255	ALASDAIR CLAYRE (LP)	60
76	Acorn CF 252	ADAM AND THE BEASTS (LP)	25

ADAM CLAYTON & LARRY MULLEN
(see also U2)

96	Mother MUM 75	Theme From Mission: Impossible/Theme From Mission: Impossible (Junior's Hard Mix Edit) (jukebox issue, no p/s, promo only)	5

BUCK CLAYTON
(see also Humphrey Lyttelton, Jimmy Rushing)

57	Pye/Vanguard PPT 12006	BUCK MEETS RUBY (10" LP, with Ruby Braff)	15
60s	Fontana 688404ZL	BUCKY & BUDDY (LP, with BUDDY TATE)	18

DOCTOR CLAYTON

65	RCA Victor RCX 7177	RCA RACE SERIES VOLUME 6 (EP)	18
70	RCA Intl. INTS 1176	PEARL HARBOUR BLUES (LP)	20

MERRY CLAYTON
(see also Raelets)

70	A&M AMS 802	Gimme Shelter/Good Girls	20
73	Ode ODS 66301	Acid Queen/Underture (p/s)	15
70	A&M AMLS 995	GIMME SHELTER (LP)	30
72	A&M AMLS 67012	MERRY CLAYTON (LP)	30

PAUL CLAYTON

61	London HLU 9285	Wings Of A Dove/So Long (It's Been Good To Know You)	15
61	London REU 1276	PAUL CLAYTON (EP)	130

STEVE CLAYTON

56	Vogue Coral Q 72200	Two Different Worlds/It Happened Again	6
57	Vogue Coral Q 72253	The Boy With The Golden Kazoo/I Wanna Put My Arms Around You	6
60	London HLU 9033	Let's Tell Them Now/They Say In Time	6

MINT VALUE £

VIKKI CLAYTON
(see also Fairport Convention)
88 Dambuster DAM 021 — LOST LADY FOUND (LP) — 20

CLAYTON SQUARES
(see also Liverpool Scene, Andy Roberts, Mike Hart)
65 Decca F 12250 — Come And Get It/And Tears Fell — 40
66 Decca F 12456 — There She Is/Imagination — 175

DAVID CLAYTON-THOMAS
(see also Blood Sweat & Tears)
72 CBS 64755 — DAVID CLAYTON-THOMAS (LP, plain orange label) — 12
72 CBS 65237 — TEQUILA SUNRISE (LP, plain orange label) — 12
73 RCA SF 8381 — DAVID CLAYTON-THOMAS (LP, gatefold sleeve) — 12

CLAYTOWN TROUPE
92 EMI 12 88007) — SKYBOUND (LP, withdrawn) — 20

CLEAN
89 Flying Nun Europe FNE 29 — IN-A-LIVE (Mini-LP) — 15

CLEANERS FROM VENUS
(see also Gypp, Martin Newall, Brotherhood of Lizards)
87 Ammunition JANGLE 1 — Illya Kurayakin Looked At Me/Black And White And Blue All Over (p/s) — 20
87 Ammunition JANGLE 1T — Illya Kurayakin Looked At Me/Albion's Daughter/Black And White And Blue All Over/Illya Kuryakin Looked At Me (Full Version) (12", p/s) — 15
87 Ammunition JANGLE 2 — Living With VIctoria Grey/Sunday Afternoon (p/s) — 20
87 Ammunition JANGLE 2T — Living With VIctoria Grey/Sunday Afternoon/She's Checking You Out (12", p/s) — 15
88 Ammunition JANGLE 3 — Mercury Girl/Gamma Ray Blues — 20
88 Ammunition JANGLE 3T — Mercury Girl/Gamma Ray Blues/The Iceberg Unicorn (12", p/s) — 15
87 Ammunition CLEAN LP 1 — GOING TO ENGLAND (LP) — 25
88 Ammunition CLEAN LP 2 — TOWN AND COUNTRY (LP) — 20

CLEAR BLUE SKY
70 Vertigo 6360 013 — CLEAR BLUE SKY (LP, gatefold sleeve, large swirl label) — 300
90 Saturn SRLP 101 — DESTINY (LP) — 15

CLEAR LIGHT
67 Elektra EKSN 45019 — Black Roses/She's Ready To Be Free — 10
68 Elektra EKSN 45027 — Night Sounds Loud/How Many Days Have Passed — 20
67 Elektra EKL 4011 — CLEAR LIGHT (LP, orange label, also stereo EKS 74011) — 60
87 Edsel ED 245 — BLACK ROSES (LP, reissue) — 12

CLEARLIGHT
(see also Gong, Steve Hillage)
75 Virgin V 2029 — SYMPHONY (LP, stickered sleeve) — 18
75 Virgin V 2039 — FOREVER BLOWING BUBBLES (LP) — 18

CLEAR SPOT
(see also Stereolab)
98 Duophonic Super 45s — Psycho's Blues/Moonman Bop (33rpm, 300 copies on blue vinyl, p/s) — 10
98 Duophonic Super 45s — Psycho's Blues/Moonman Bop (33rpm, 1700 copies on black vinyl, p/s) — 8

CLEARWAYS
64 Columbia DB 7333 — I'll Be Here/I've Just Got A Letter — 10

JOHN CLEESE (& 1948 CHOIR)
(see also Monty Python)
67 Pye 7N 17336 — The Ferret Song - From 'At Last The 1948 Show'/The Rhubarb Tart Song — 10
67 Parlophone PMC 7024 — I'M SORRY I'LL READ THAT AGAIN (LP) — 20

CLEFS
62 Salvo SLO 1810 — Don't Cry/The Dream Train Special (99 copies only) — 22

CLEFS OF LAVENDER HILL
66 CBS 202230 — Stop, Get A Ticket/ — 20

CLEFTONES
56 Columbia DB 3801 — You Baby, You/Little Girl Of Mine — 500
56 Columbia DB 3801 — You Baby, You/Little Girl Of Mine (78) — 60
61 Columbia DB 4678 — Heart And Soul/How Do You Feel — 150
61 Columbia DB 4720 — (I Love You) For Sentimental Reasons/Deed I Do — 100
63 Columbia DB 4988 — Lover Come Back To Me/There She Goes — 50

PAT CLEMENCE
64 HMV POP 1360 — While I Live/Since I Don't Have You — 6

JACK CLEMENT
58 London HLS 8691 — Ten Years/Your Lover Boy — 150
58 London HLS 8691 — Ten Years/Your Lover Boy (78) — 45

SOUL JOE CLEMENTS
69 Plexium PXM 10 — Smoke And Ashes/Ever, Ever — 150

CLEO
(see also Andrew Oldham Orchestra, This 'N' That)
64 Decca F 11817 — To Know Him Is To Love Him/ANDREW OLDHAM ORCHESTRA: There Are But Five Rolling Stones — 25

CLERKS
80 Rok ROK VIII/VII — No Good For Me/HAZARD: Gotta Change My Life (company sleeve) — 12
84 Puddisc SRT8 KS 1538 — Dancing With My Girl/On The Telephone/All I Want Is You (p/s) — 5

CLEVELANDS
64 Philips BF 1315 — Big Town/Lonely, Weary And Blue — 6
64 Philips BF 1342 — Little Girl In Calico/Everything Is Fine — 6

MINT VALUE £

CLIENTELLE

79	Quest BRS 003	Can't Forget/Skyline (p/s)	125
81	Banana BANANA 505	DESTINATION UNKNOWN (LP, with insert)	120

JIMMY CLIFF

(see also Jackie Edwards & Jimmy Cliff, James Chambers)

62	Blue Beat BB 78	I'm Sorry (with Cavaliers Combo)/BLUE BEATS: Roarin' (with Red Price)	30
62	Island WI 012	Hurricane Hatty/Dearest Beverley	18
62	Island WI 016	Miss Jamaica/Gold Digger	25
62	Island WI 025	Since Lately/I'm Free	25
63	Island WI 062	My Lucky Day/One-Eyed Jacks	25
63	Island WI 070	King Of Kings/SIR PERCY: Oh Yeah	30
63	Island WI 112	Miss Universe/The Prodigal	18
63	Black Swan WI 403	The Man (vocal version)/You Are Never Too Old	20
63	Black Swan WI 403	The Man (Instrumental version)/You Are Never Too Old	20
64	Stateside SS 342	One Eyed Jacks/King Of Kings	18
66	Fontana TF 641	Call On Me/Pride And Passion	12
67	Island WIP 6004	Aim And Ambition/Give And Take	10
67	Island WIP 6011	I Got A Feeling/Hard Road To Travel	10
67	Island WIP 6024	That's The Way Life Goes/Thank You	10
68	Island WIP 6039	Waterfall/Reward	35
69	Trojan TR 690	Wonderful World, Beautiful People/Hard Road To Travel (in p/s)	7
69	Trojan TR 690	Wonderful World, Beautiful People/Hard Road To Travel (no p/s)	5
70	Trojan TR 7722	Vietnam/She Does It Right	5
70	Trojan TR 7745	Suffering/Come Into My Life	5
70	Trojan TR 7745	Those Good Good Old Days/Pack Up Hang Ups	5
70	Trojan TR 7767	You Can Get It If You Really Want/Be Aware	5
70	Island WIP 6087	Wild World/Be Aware	5
70	Island WIP 6097	Synthetic World/I Go To Pieces	5
71	Island WIP 6103	Goodbye Yesterday/Breakdown	5
71	Island WIP 6100	Sitting In Limbo/The Bigger They Come	5
72	Island WIP 6132	Trapped/Struggling Man	5
68	Island ILP 962	HARD ROAD TO TRAVEL (LP)	60
69	Trojan TRLS 16	JIMMY CLIFF (LP)	20
71	Island ILPS 9159	ANOTHER CYCLE (LP)	18
73	EMI EMA 757	UNLIMITED (LP)	12

CLIFF DWELLERS

66	Polydor BM 56707	Hang On Stupid/I'm A Superman For You	15

CLIFFORD

73	Satril SAT 10	Drink Wine Susan/Looking Upon The Day	10

BUZZ CLIFFORD

61	Fontana H 297	Baby Sittin' Boogie/Driftwood	10
61	Fontana H 312	Three Little Fishes/Simply Because	10
62	Columbia DB 4903	More Dead Than Alive/Nobody Loves Me Like You	10
61	Fontana TFL 5147	BABY SITTIN' WITH BUZZ CLIFFORD (LP, mono)	40
61	Fontana STFL 567	BABY SITTIN' WITH BUZZ CLIFFORD (LP, stereo)	50

JOHN & JULIA CLIFFORD

77	Topic 12TS 311	THE HUMOURS OF LISHEEN (LP)	20

LINDA CLIFFORD

78	Curtom K 17163T	If My Friends Could See Me Now/Runaway Love (12")	12

MIKE CLIFFORD

61	Philips PB 1175	Pretty Little Girl In The Yellow Dress/At Last	7
62	United Artists UP 1006	Close To Cathy/She's Just Another Girl	10

CLIFFTERS

62	Philips PB 1242	Django/Amapola (Pretty Little Poppy)	10

BILL CLIFTON

60	Melodisc 1554	You Don't Think About Me/Mail Carrier's Warning	5
63	Decca F 11793	Beatle Crazy/Little Girl Dressed In Blue	5
58	Mercury MEP 9546	BILL CLIFTON AND THE DIXIE MOUNTAIN BOYS (EP)	10
62	London HA-B 8004	CARTER FAMILY MEMORIAL ALBUM (LP)	15
62	London HA-B 8020	THE BLUEGRASS SOUND OF BILL CLIFTON (LP)	15

BILL CLIFTON & JIM EANES

60s	Melodisc EPM 7102	BLUE RIVER HOEDOWN (EP)	10

CLIMAX (CHICAGO) BLUES BAND

(see also Hipster Image)

69	Parlophone R 5809	Like Uncle Charlie/Loving Machine	20
70	Harvest HAR 5029	Reap What I've Sowed/Spoonful	6
71	Harvest HAR 5041	Towards The Sun/Everyday (as Climax Chicago)	6
72	Harvest HAR 5065	Mole On The Dole/Like Uncle Charlie	12
69	Parlophone PMC/PCS 7069	CLIMAX CHICAGO BLUES BAND (LP, yellow/black label, with "Sold in the UK.." text)	100
70	Parlophone PCS 7084	PLAYS ON (LP, yellow/black labels)	200
70	Parlophone PCS 7084	PLAYS ON (LP, later issue with boxed Parlophone logo)	50
70	Harvest SHSP 4009	A LOT OF BOTTLE (LP, no EMI logo on label, fully laminated sleeve)	35
71	Harvest SHSP 4015	TIGHTLY KNIT (LP, with EMI logo on label, flipback sleeve)	30
72	Harvest SHSP 4024	RICH MAN (LP)	18
74	Polydor 2383259	LIVE (LP)	15

CLIMAX INVASION

77	Top Secret TS1	The Advertiser (one-sided)	30

MINT VALUE £

PATSY CLINE

57	Brunswick 05660	A Poor Man's Roses (Or A Rich Man's Gold)/Walkin' After Midnight	90
57	Brunswick 05660	A Poor Man's Roses (Or A Rich Man's Gold)/Walkin' After Midnight (78)	20
61	Brunswick 05855	I Fall To Pieces/Lovin' In Vain	15
61	Brunswick 05861	Crazy/Who Can I Count On	20
62	Brunswick 05866	She's Got You/Strange	7
62	Brunswick 05869	When I Get Through With You/Imagine That	7
62	Brunswick 05874	So Wrong/You're Stronger Than Me	7
62	Brunswick 05878	Heartaches/Why Can't He Be You	6
63	Brunswick 05883	Leavin' On Your Mind/Tra Le La Le La Triangle	7
63	Brunswick 05888	Sweet Dreams/Back In My Baby's Arms	10
63	Decca 31262	Blue Moon Of Kentucky/Faded Love (export)	25
62	Brunswick OE 9490	SWEET DREAMS (EP)	30
62	Brunswick LAT 8394	SHOWCASE (LP)	20
62	Brunswick LAT 8510	SENTIMENTALLY YOURS (LP, mono)	20
62	Brunswick STA 8510	SENTIMENTALLY YOURS (LP, stereo)	22
63	Brunswick LAT 8549	A TRIBUTE TO PATSY CLINE (LP)	20
64	Brunswick LAT 8589	A PORTRAIT OF PATSY CLINE (LP, mono)	20
64	Brunswick STA 8589	A PORTRAIT OF PATSY CLINE (LP, stereo)	22
65	Ember CW 16	IN MEMORIAM (LP)	15
65	Fontana FJL 302	TODAY TOMORROW AND FOREVER (LP)	15
66	Fontana FJL 309	I CAN'T FORGET YOU (LP)	15

CLINIC

97	Aladdin's Cave Of Golf GOLF001	IPC Subeditors Dictate Our Youth/Porno/D.I.Y. (p/s, 500 copies only)	15
98	Aladdin's C.O.G. GOLF002	Monkey On Your Back/D.T. (p/s, 500 copies only)	6
98	Aladdin's C.O.G. GOLF003	Cement Mixer/Kimberley (p/s, 1,000 copies only)	5

BUDDY CLINTON

60	Top Rank JAR 287	Across The Street From Your House/How My Prayers Have Changed	20

DAVY CLINTON

68	NEMS 56-3855	Can I Bring Back Yesterday/The girl With The Sun In Her Hair	6

GEORGE CLINTON

79	ABC ABC 4053	Please Don't Run From Me/Life And Breath	8
79	ABC ABC 4053	Please Don't Run From Me/Life And Breath (DJ Copy)	20

LARRY CLINTON

79	Grapevine GRP 120	She's Wanted In Three States/If I Knew	25
79	Grapevine GRP 120	She's Wanted In Three States/If I Knew (DJ Copy)	40

CLINTONES

73	Ackee ACK 515	Equal Rights/Version	6

CLIQUE (U.K.)

(see also Hammersmith Gorillas)

65	Pye 7N 15786	She Ain't No Good/Time Time Time	100
65	Pye 7N 15853	We Didn't Kiss, Didn't Love, But Now We Do/You've Been Unfair	150
60s	private pressing	THE CLIQUE (EP, no p/s)	550

CLIQUE (U.K.)

94	Detour DR 014	Reggie/She Doesn't Need You Anymore (p/s, red vinyl)	5
94	Detour DR 014	Reggie/She Doesn't Need You Anymore (picture disc, 200 only)	8

CLIQUE (U.S.)

69	London HLU 10286	Sugar On Sunday/Superman	30

JIMMY CLITHEROE

65	Parlophone R 5387	They All Blame Jim/Jim Plays Hookie	10

JOHNNY CLIVE

63	Oriole CB 1820	China Girl/Sue	8

CLIVE & DOREEN

68	Treasure Isle TI 7033	What Can I Do/TOMMY MCCOOK: Black Power	30

CLIVE & GLORIA

63	R&B JB 113	Change Of Plan/Little Gloria	20
64	R&B JB 173	Money Money Money/Have I Told You Lately	20
64	King KG 1004	Do The Ska/You Made Me Cry	20

CLIVE & NAOMI

(see also Desmond Dekker)

65	Ska Beat JB 181	You Are Mine/Open The Door	20

CLOCK DVA

81	Fetish FET 008	Four Hours (Re-mixed)/Sensorium (p/s)	6
85	Fetish FET 008	FOUR HOURS EP (12", p/s)	8
81	Fetish FR 2002	THIRST (LP, with insert)	12
81	Industrial IRC 31	WHITE SOULS IN BLACK SUITS (cassette, with booklet)	20

CLOCKHOUSE

83	Picturesque PIC 1	Vanishing Point/Everyman (p/s)	7

CLOCKWORK CRIMINALS

82	Ace ACE 38	YOUNG AND BOLD (EP)	25

CLOCKWORK ORANGES

66	Ember EMB S 227	Ready Steady/After Tonight	25

CLOCKWORK SOLDIERS

84	Rot ASS 5	Wet Dreams/Suicide/In The Name Of Science (p/s)	15

BETTY CLOONEY

(see also Rosemary Clooney)

55	HMV 7M 311	I Love You A Mountain/Can't Do Without You	10

MINT VALUE £

ROSEMARY CLOONEY
(see also Bing Crosby)

53	Columbia SCM 5019	Half As Much/Botch-A-Me (Ba-Ba-Baciami Piccina)	20
53	Columbia SCM 5027	If I Had A Penny/You're After My Own Heart	10
53	Columbia SCM 5028	On The First Warm Day/If Teardrops Were Pennies	12
53	Columbia SCM 5040	(Remember Me) I'm The One Who Loves You/Lover's Gold	12
53	Columbia SCM 5049	Blues In The Night/Who Kissed Me Last Night?	10
54	Columbia SCM 5093	I Still Feel The Same About You (with Betty Clooney)/Why Fight The Feeling	10
56	Philips JB 100	The Teddy Bear's Picnic/Kitty Kat's Party (78, picture label)	10
57	Philips JK 1010	Mangos/All The Pretty Little Horses (jukebox issue)	25
58	Philips PB 800	I Could Have Danced All Night/I've Grown Accustomed To Your Face	6
59	Philips PB 900	Tonight/Come Rain Or Come Shine	8
59	Coral Q 72357	Diga Me (Deega May-Tell Me)/A Touch Of The Blues	8
59	MGM MGM 1010	Love Eyes/Flattery (B-side with Jose Ferrer)	6
60	Coral Q 72388	Love, Love Away/I Wish I Were In Love Again	5
60	MGM MGM 1062	For You/I Wonder	5
60	RCA RCA 1203	Many A Wonderful Moment/Vaya, Vaya	5
54	Columbia SEG 7552	ROSEMARY CLOONEY AND HARRY JAMES (EP)	10
55	Philips BBE 12004	ROSEMARY CLOONEY (EP)	10
56	Philips BBE 12051	ROSEMARY CLOONEY (EP)	10
60	Coral FEP 2045	SWING AROUND ROSIE VOL. 1 (EP)	10
60	Coral FEP 2046	SWING AROUND ROSIE VOL. 2 (EP)	10
54	Philips BBR 8022	WHITE CHRISTMAS (10" LP)	25
55	Philips BBR 8047	ROSEMARY CLOONEY (10" LP)	20
56	Philips BBR 8073	AT THE LONDON PALLADIUM (10" LP)	20
56	Philips BBL 7090	HEY BABY (LP, with Duke Ellington)	15
57	Philips BBL 7156	RING AROUND ROSIE (LP, with Hi-Lo's)	15
57	Philips BBL 7191	CHILDREN'S FAVOURITES (LP)	15
59	Philips BBL 7301	SHOWCASE OF HITS (LP)	12
59	Coral LVA 9112	SWING AROUND ROSIE (LP)	15
60	MGM ES 3514	SWINGS SOFTLY NO 1 (LP)	20

ROSEMARY CLOONEY & MARLENE DIETRICH
(see also Marlene Dietrich, Betty Clooney, Bob Hope & Rosemary Clooney, Guy Mitchell)

53	Columbia SCM 5010	Too Old To Cut The Mustard/Good For Nothin'	18

CLOSE LOBSTERS

89	Caff CAFF 4	Just Too Bloody Stupid/All The Little Boys And Girls (p/s)	12

CLOSE SHAVE

88	Link LP 056	Oi! KINNOCK GIVE US BACK OUR ROSE (LP)	12

CLOUD

75	Kingsway DOVE 16	FREE TO FLY (LP)	20
77	Kingsway DOVE 44	WATERED GARDEN (LP, gatefold sleeve)	30
78	Dove 62	THE RESTING PLACE (LP)	20
85	Songs Of Fellow. SFR103	THE PROMISE (LP)	15

CLAUDE CLOUD
(see also Sonny Thompson, Sam 'The Man' Taylor)

55	MGM MGM 820	Cloudburst/One Bone (78, as Claude Cloud & Thunderclaps)	20
57	MGM MGM 946	The Beat/Around The Horn (as Claude Cloud & His Orchestra)	15
55	MGM MGM-EP 517	LET'S GO CATSTATIC NO. 1 (EP, as Claude Cloud & Thunderclaps)	45
56	MGM MGM-D 142	ROCK 'N' ROLL (10" LP)	120

CLOUD NINE

90s	Acid Jazz JAZID 87P	I Feel It (12", p/s, promo-only, withdrawn)	18
90s	Acid Jazz JAZID 78	MILLENNIUM (LP, withdrawn)	30

CLOUDS

69	Island WIP 6055	Heritage/Make No Bones About It	20
69	Island WIP 6067	Scrapbook/Carpenter	20
69	Island ILPS 9100	THE CLOUDS SCRAPBOOK (LP, gatefold sleeve, first pressing with black/orange circle logo)	150
69	Island ILPS 9100	THE CLOUDS SCRAPBOOK (LP, second pressing, circle logo)	100
70s	Island ILPS 9100	THE CLOUDS SCRAPBOOK (LP, later pressing 'pink rim palm tree')	25
71	Chrysalis ILPS 9151	WATERCOLOUR DAYS (LP, gatefold sleeve, 'green label with Island logo and Island address in white)	40

CLOUDS
(see also Boy Hairdressers, Teenage Fanclub)

86	Sha La La Ba Ba Ba 001	Throwaway/CLOUDS: Jenny Nowhere (p/s, flexi free with various fanzines)	8
88	Subway Org. SUBWAY 12	Tranquil/Get Out Of My Dream (p/s)	5
88	Subway Org. SUBWAY 12T	Tranquil/Get Out Of My Dream/Village Green (12", p/s)	8

BRIAN CLOUGH

88	MCA MCA 658	You Can't Win 'Em All/It's Only A Game (p/s)	15

CLOUT
(see also Slade)

90	Mooncrest JWL 1000	We'll Bring The House Down/Jim Jam (p/s)	7

CLOVEN HOOF

82	Elemental EM 001	OPENING RITUAL (12" EP)	80
84	Neat NEAT 1013	CLOVEN HOOF (LP)	20
86	Trojan CH 002	FIGHTING BACK (LP, with poster)	25
86	Trojan CH 002	FIGHTING BACK (LP, without poster)	20

CLOVER
(see also Huey Lewis & News)

70	Liberty LBF 15341	Wade In The Water/Stealin'	10
77	Vertigo LYN 4277	There Is No Substitute For Real Magic (flexidisc, promo only)	7

MINT VALUE £

69	Liberty LBS 83340	CLOVER (LP)	30
71	Liberty LBS 83487	FORTY-NINER (LP)	30

CLOVERLEAFS

(see also Art Mooney)

56	MGM MGM 933	Step Right Up And Say Howdy/With Plenty Of Money And You (Gold Digger's Lullaby)	8

CLOVERS

56	London HLE 8229	Nip Sip/If I Could Be Loved By You (gold label lettering)	800
56	London HLE 8229	Nip Sip/If I Could Be Loved By You (silver label lettering)	400
56	London HLE 8229	Nip Sip/If I Could Be Loved By You (78)	40
56	London HLE 8314	Love, Love, Love/Hey, Doll Baby	500
56	London HLE 8314	Love, Love, Love/Hey, Doll Baby (78)	50
56	London HLE 8334	From The Bottom Of My Heart/Your Tender Lips	500
56	London HLE 8334	From The Bottom Of My Heart/Your Tender Lips	50
58	London HL 7048	Wishing For Your Love/All About You (export issue)	250
58	London HL 7048	Wishing For Your Love/All About You (78)	40
58	HMV POP 542	In The Good Old Summertime/Idaho	35
58	HMV POP 542	In The Good Old Summertime/Idaho (78)	30
59	London HLT 8949	Love Potion No. 9/Stay Awhile (triangular centre)	60
59	London HLT 8949	Love Potion No. 9/Stay Awhile (round centre)	40
59	London HLT 8949	Love Potion No. 9/Stay Awhile (78)	40
60	London HLT 9122	Lovey/One Mint Julep	35
60	London HLT 9154	Easy Lovin'/I'm Confessin' (That I Love You)	40
61	HMV POP 883	Honey Dripper/Have Gun	25
68	Atlantic 584 160	Your Cash Ain't Nothin' But Trash/I've Got My Eyes On You	15
69	Atlantic 587 162	LOVE BUG (LP)	60

CLOWN

72	CBS 7906	Lord Of The Ringside/Rumania	40

CLUES

81	Clues CLU 001	NO VACANCIES (EP)	10

CLUTCH

73	EMI 2010	Black Angel/The Frightners	12

CLUTHA (FOLK GROUP)

71	Argo ZFB 18	SCOTIA! (LP, as Clutha Folk Group)	15
74	Topic 12TS 242	SCOTS BALLADS, SONGS AND DANCE TUNES (LP, as Clutha)	12

JEREMY CLYDE

(see also Chad & Jeremy)

65	CBS 201823	I Love My Love/Anytime	5

CLYDE VALLEY STOMPERS

(see also Ian Menzies)

62	Parlophone R 4928	Peter And The Wolf/Loch Lomond	6
60	Pye NJL 23	HAVE TARTAN - WILL TRAD (LP)	12
61	Ace Of Clubs ACL 1075	TRAD PARTY (LP)	12

CMETRIC

94	B12 B1210	Cmetric (12")	30
94	B12 B1210	Cmetric (12")	70

C.M.J.

68	Impression IMP 102	I Can't Do It All By Myself/Nothing At All	45
71	Mother MOT 3	La La La/Step Around It	50
65	Impression EPIM 501	THE C.M.J. TRIO (EP)	50
69	Impression IMPL 1001	C.M.J. LIVE AT THE BANKHOUSE (LP, private pressing)	80

C.M.U. (Contemporary Music Unit)

(see also Chopyn)

72	Transatlantic BIG 508	Heart Of The Sun/Doctor Am I Normal?	10
71	Transatlantic TRA 237	OPEN SPACES (LP, gatefold sleeve, clear plastic with foam inner, this price for mint record that has not reacted/been marked by plastic/foam inner)	150
71	Transatlantic TRA 237	OPEN SPACES (LP, gatefold sleeve, clear plastic with foam inner, this price for mint sleeve with record marked by chemical reaction to plastic/foam inner)	30
72	Transatlantic TRA 259	SPACE CABARET (LP, with lyric insert)	100

COACHMEN

66	Columbia DB 8057	Gabrielle/Seasons In The Sun	8

COACHMEN

59	Vogue V 9154	Those Brown Eyes/Bald Mountain	5
59	Vogue V 9154	Those Brown Eyes/Bald Mountain (78)	10
61	Vogue VAE 170149	HERE COME THE COACHMEN (EP)	10

COACHOUSE RHYTHM SECTION

(see also Eddy Grant)

77	Ice ICE 3 12	Nobody Got Time/Time Warp (12")	20

COASTERS

57	London HLE 8450	Searchin'/Young Blood	75
57	London HLE 8450	Searchin'/Young Blood (78)	10
57	London HL 7021	Searchin'/Young Blood (export issue)	30
58	London HLE 8665	Yakety Yak/Zing! Went The Strings Of My Heart	20
58	London HLE 8665	Yakety Yak/Zing! Went The Strings Of My Heart (78)	20
58	London HLE 8729	The Shadow Knows/Sorry But I'm Gonna Have To Pass	50
58	London HLE 8729	The Shadow Knows/Sorry But I'm Gonna Have To Pass (78)	30
59	London HLE 8819	Charlie Brown/Three Cool Cats	10
59	London HLE 8819	Charlie Brown/Three Cool Cats (78)	20
59	London HL 7073	Charlie Brown/Three Cool Cats (export issue)	15

			MINT VALUE £
59	London HLE 8882	Along Came Jones/That Is Rock And Roll (silver top label)	15
59	London HLE 8882	Along Came Jones/That Is Rock And Roll (silver top label) (78)	30
59	London HLE 8938	Poison Ivy/I'm A Hog For You	15

(The above 45s were originally issued with triangular centres, later round centre copies are worth half these values)

59	London HLE 8938	Poison Ivy/I'm A Hog For You (78)	35
60	London HLE 9020	What About Us/Run Red Run	20
60	London HLE 9020	What About Us/Run Red Run (78)	70
60	London HLK 9111	Besame Mucho (Parts 1 & 2)	30
60	London HLK 9111	Besame Mucho (Parts 1 & 2) (78)	80
60	London HLK 9151	Wake Me, Shake Me/Stewball	20
60	London HLK 9208	Shoppin' For Clothes/The Snake And The Bookworm	30
61	London HLK 9293	Wait A Minute/Thumbin' A Ride	15
61	London HLK 9349	Little Egypt/Keep On Rolling	15
61	London HLK 9413	Girls! Girls! Girls! (Parts 1 & 2)	15
62	London HLK 9493	(Ain't That) Just Like Me/Bad Blood	15
64	London HLK 9863	T'Ain't Nothin' To Me/Speedo's Back In Town	15
66	Atlantic 584 033	She's A Yum Yum/Saturday Night Fish Fry	10
67	Atlantic 584 087	Searchin'/Yakety Yak	8
67	CBS 2749	Soul Pad/Down Home Girl	15
68	Direction 58-3701	She Can/Everybody's Woman	18
71	Parlophone R 5931	Love Potion No. 9/D.W. Washburn	25
72	Stateside SS 2201	Cool Jerk/Talkin' 'Bout A Woman	30
72	London HLZ 10437	Love Potion No. 9/D. W. Washburn	10
59	London REE 1203	THE COASTERS (EP)	60
60	London HA-E 2237	GREATEST HITS (LP)	100
63	London HA-K 8033	COASTIN' ALONG WITH THE COASTERS (LP)	100
66	Atlantic 588 134	COASTIN' ALONG WITH THE COASTERS (LP, reissue)	25
67	Atlantic 590 015	ALL TIME GREATEST HITS (LP)	20
71	Joy JOYS 189	HUNGRY (LP)	20
74	London SHZ 8460	ON BROADWAY (LP)	15

COASTERS (Jamaica)

69	Doctor Bird DB 1182	Stoney Hill/RICK RODRIGUES & JOHNNY MOORE: Continental Shuffle	100

COAST ROAD DRIVE

74	Deram SML 1113	DELICIOUS AND REFRESHING (LP)	60

COAST TO COAST

(see also Status Quo)

82	Polydor POSP 451	The Bell/How Can I Be Sure	8

C.O.B. (Clive's Original Band)

(see also Famous Jug Band, Incredible String Band)

72	Polydor 2058 260	Blue Morning/Bones	20
71	CBS 69010	SPIRIT OF LOVE (LP, gatefold sleeve, orange label)	200
72	Polydor Folk Mill 2383 161	MOYSHE McSTIFF & THE TARTAN LANCERS OF THE SACRED HEART (LP, gatefold sleeve, red label)	450

COBBLERS LAST

79	Banshee BAN 1012	BOOT IN THE DOOR (LP, with insert)	80

COBBS

69	Amalgamated AMG 845	Hot Buttered Corn/COUNT MACHUKI: It Is I	20
69	Amalgamated AMG 849	Space Doctor/LLOYD & DEVON: Baby Reggae	25

JUNIE COBB'S HOMETOWN BAND

59	Collector JDL 38	Chicago Buzz/East Coast Trot	10

BILLY COBHAM

74	Atlantic K50037	CROSSWINDS (LP)	12
73	Atlantic K40506	SPECTRUM (LP, gatefold)	12

COBRA

(see also Speed)

78	Rip Off RIP 3	Graveyard Boogie/Looking For A Lady (p/s)	30

COBRA

87	Ebony EBON 39	BACK FROM THE DEAD (LP)	18

COBWEB

71	Private Pressing SJP 762	You'll Go Far/Broken Web	10

COCHISE

(see also B.J. Cole, Mick Grabham)

70	United Artists UP 35134	Watch This Space/59th St. Bridge Song	6
70	Liberty LBS 15425	Love's Made A Fool Of You/Words Of A Dying Man	6
71	Liberty LBF 15460	Why I Sing The Blues/Jed Colider	6
70	United Artists UAS 29117	COCHISE (LP, gatefold sleeve, orange/pink label)	30
70	Liberty LBS 83428	SWALLOW TALES (LP, black label)	20
72	United Artists UAS 29286	SO FAR (LP)	25

DIB COCHRAN & EARWIGS

(see also Marc Bolan, Tyrannosaurus Rex, Tony Visconti, Rick Wakeman)

70	Bell BLL 1121	Oh Baby/Universal Love	500

EDDIE COCHRAN

78s

57	London HLU 8386	20 Flight Rock/Dark Lonely Street	80
57	London HLU 8433	Sittin' In The Balcony/Completely Sweet	80
58	London HLU 8702	Summertime Blues/Love Again	100
59	London HLU 8792	C'mon Everybody/Don't Ever Let Me Go	150
59	London HLU 8880	Teenage Heaven/I Remember	300
59	London HLU 8944	Somethin' Else/Boll Weevil Song	300

MINT VALUE £

60	London HLW 9022	Hallelujah, I Love Her So/Little Angel	400
60	London HLG 9115	Three Steps To Heaven/Cut Across Shorty	500
95	Cruisin' The 50s CASS 001	Three Steps To Heaven/Cut Across Shorty (reissue, 300 only)	35
96	Cruisin' The 50s CASB 004	Week-End/Cherished Memories (reissue, 400 only)	30

SINGLES

57	London HLU 8386	20 Flight Rock/Dark Lonely Street (triangular centre)	200
57	London HLU 8386	20 Flight Rock/Dark Lonely Street (silver-top label with triangular centre)	125
57	London HLU 8386	20 Flight Rock/Dark Lonely Street (round centre)	50
57	London HLU 8433	Sittin' In The Balcony/Completely Sweet	400
58	London HLU 8702	Summertime Blues/Love Again	25
59	London HLU 8792	C'mon Everybody/Don't Ever Let Me Go	25
59	London HLU 8880	Teenage Heaven/I Remember	35
59	London HL 7082	Teenage Heaven/Boll Weevil Song (export issue)	70
59	London HLU 8944	Somethin' Else/Boll Weevil Song	35
60	London HLW 9022	Hallelujah, I Love Her So/Little Angel (triangular centre)	40

(The above 45s were originally issued with triangular centres, later round centre copies are worth half these values.)

60	London HLW 9022	Hallelujah, I Love Her So/Little Angel (round centre)	25
60	London HLG 9115	Three Steps To Heaven/Cut Across Shorty	15
60	London HLG 9196	Sweetie Pie/Lonely	40
61	London HLG 9362	Weekend/Cherished Memories	20
61	London HLG 9460	Jeannie, Jeannie, Jeannie/Pocketful Of Hearts	25
61	London HLG 9464	Pretty Girl/Teresa	45
61	London HLG 9467	Undying Love/Stockin's 'n' Shoes	50
62	Liberty LIB 10049	Never/Think Of Me	20
63	Liberty LIB 10088	My Way/Rock And Roll Blues	15
63	Liberty LIB 10108	Drive-In Show/I Almost Lost My Mind	15
64	Liberty LIB 10151	Skinny Jim/Nervous Breakdown (black label)	60
66	Liberty LIB 10233	C'mon Everybody/Summertime Blues	15
66	Liberty LIB 10249	Three Stars/Somethin' Else	50
67	Liberty LIB 10276	Three Steps To Heaven/Eddie's Blues	35
68	Liberty LBF 15071	Summertime Blues/Let's Get Together	10
68	Liberty LBF 15109	Somethin' Else/Milk Cow Blues	10
70	Liberty LBF 15366	C'mon Everybody/Mean When I'm Mad	10

EPs

59	London REU 1214	C'MON EVERYBODY (orange sleeve, triangular centre)	100
59	London REU 1214	C'MON EVERYBODY (orange sleeve, round centre)	60
59	London REU 1214	C'MON EVERYBODY (yellow sleeve, silver-top label)	100
59	London REU 1214	C'MON EVERYBODY (yellow sleeve, round centre)	90
60	London REU 1239	SOMETHIN' ELSE (triangular centre)	110
60	London REU 1239	SOMETHIN' ELSE (round centre)	90
60	London REG 1262	EDDIE'S HITS	50
61	London REG 1301	CHERISHED MEMORIES OF EDDIE COCHRAN	50
62	Liberty LEP 2052	NEVER TO BE FORGOTTEN	40
63	Liberty LEP 2090	CHERISHED MEMORIES (VOL.1)	40
63	Liberty LEP 2111	C'MON EVERYBODY (reissue)	20
63	Liberty LEP 2122	SOMETHIN' ELSE (reissue)	20
63	Liberty LEP 2123	CHERISHED MEMORIES OF EDDIE COCHRAN (reissue)	30
63	Liberty LEP 2124	EDDIE'S HITS (reissue)	30
64	Liberty LEP 2165	C'MON AGAIN	35
64	Liberty LEP 2180	STOCKIN'S 'N' SHOES	35

LPs

58	London HA-U 2093	SINGIN' TO MY BABY (initial pressing with laminated rear sleeve)	250
58	London HA-U 2093	SINGIN' TO MY BABY (without laminated rear sleeve)	200
60	London HA-G 2267	THE EDDIE COCHRAN MEMORIAL ALBUM	100
62	Liberty LBY 1109	CHERISHED MEMORIES	50
63	Liberty LBY 1127	THE EDDIE COCHRAN MEMORIAL ALBUM (reissue)	30
63	Liberty LBY 1158	SINGIN' TO MY BABY (reissue)	30
64	Liberty LBY 1205	MY WAY	70
88	Liberty ECB 1	THE EDDIE COCHRAN BOX SET (6-LP box set with booklet)	25

HANK COCHRAN

68	Monument LMO 5020	HEART OF HANK (LP)	15

JACKIE LEE COCHRAN

57	Brunswick 05669	Ruby Pearl (with Jimmy Pruett)/Mama Don't You Think I Know	2500
57	Brunswick 05669	Ruby Pearl (with Jimmy Pruett)/Mama Don't You Think I Know (78)	250

COCK & WOODPECKERS

71	Newbeat 93	Every Day And Every Night/I Fall In Love Everyday	15

BRUCE COCKBURN

71	True North WTN 003	HIGH WINDS WHITE SKY (LP)	15
71	True North TNX 7	SUNWHEEL DANCE (LP)	15

JARVIS COCKER

(see also Pulp)

06	Rough Trade RTRADLP 340	THE JARVIS COCKER RECORD (LP, with bonus one-sided 7")	45

JOE COCKER

(see also Grease Band, Made In Sheffield)

64	Decca F 11974	I'll Cry Instead/Precious Words	100
68	Regal Zonophone RZ 3006	Marjorine/New Age Of The Lily	8
68	Regal Zonophone RZ 3013	With A Little Help From My Friends/Something's Coming On	5
69	Regal Zonophone RZ 3024	Delta Lady/She's So Good To Me	5
70	Regal Zonophone RZ 3027	The Letter/Space Captain	5
70	Fly BUG 3	Cry Me A River/Give Peace A Chance (p/s)	5
71	Fly BUG 9	High Time We Went/Black-Eyed Blues	5
72	Magni Fly ECHO 103	With A Little Help From My Friends/Delta Lady/The Letter (p/s)	5
72	Cube BUG 25	Woman To Woman/Midnight Rider (with Chris Stanton Band)	5

MINT VALUE £

83	Island WIP 6818	Ruby Lee/Talking Back To The Night (export issue)	7
60s	Oak	JOE COCKER (EP, existence unconfirmed)	500
67	Action ACT 002 EP	RAG GOES MAD AT THE MOJO (33rpm EP, 2 tracks by Joe Cocker's Blues Band, in conjunction with Sheffield University rag magazine Twikker)	50
69	Regal Zono. LRZ 1006	WITH A LITTLE HELP FROM MY FRIENDS (LP, mono, red/silver label with "Sold in the U.K..." text)	90
69	Regal Zono. SLRZ 1006	WITH A LITTLE HELP FROM MY FRIENDS (LP, stereo, red/silver label with "Sold in the U.K..." text)	60
69	Regal Zono. SLRZ 1011	JOE COCKER! (LP, red/silver label)	30
70	A&M AMLS 6002	MAD DOG & ENGLISHMEN (2-LP, multifold gatefold sleeve, brown label)	25
71	Fly HIFLY 3	COCKER HAPPY (LP, gatefold sleeve)	20

COCKEREL CHORUS

73	Young Blood YB 107	NICE ONE CYRIL (LP)	12

COCKERSDALE

85	EFDSS ESLP 001	PROSPECT PROVIDENCE (LP)	20

COCKNEY REBEL

(see under Steve Harley/Cockney Rebel)

COCKNEY REJECTS

79	Small Wonder SW 19	Flares'N'Slippers/Police Star/I Wanna Be A Star (p/s)	8
79	EMI EMI 5008	I'm Not A Fool/East End (p/s)	6
80	EMI EMI 5035	Bad Man!/The New Song (p/s)	6
80	Zonophone Z 2	The Greatest Cockney Rip-Off/Hate Of The City (p/s, yellow vinyl)	7
80	Zonophone Z 4	I'm Forever Blowing Bubbles/West Side Boys (p/s)	8
80	Zonophone Z 6	We Can Do Anything/15 Nights (p/s)	6
80	Zonophone Z 10	We Are The Firm/War On The Terraces (p/s)	8
81	Zonophone Z 20	Easy Life/Motorhead/Hang 'Em High (p/s)	6
80	Zonophone ZONO 101	GREATEST HITS VOLUME 1 (LP)	18
80	Zonophone ZONO 102	GREATEST HITS VOLUME 2 (LP, with inner sleeve & poster)	15
81	Zonophone ZEM 101	GREATEST HITS VOLUME 3 (LIVE AND LOUD) (LP)	15

COCKNEYS

64	Philips BF 1303	After Tomorrow/I'll Cry Each Night	15
64	Philips BF 1338	After Tomorrow/I'll Cry Each Night (reissue)	15
64	Philips BF 1360	I Know You're Gonna Be Mine/Oh No You Won't	15

COCK SPARRER

(see also Little Roosters, Guttersnipes)

77	Decca FR 13710	Runnin' Riot/Sister Suzie (demos in p/s)	110
77	Decca FR 13710	Runnin' Riot/Sister Suzie (no p/s)	20
77	Decca FR 13732	We Love You/Chip On My Shoulder (no p/s)	20
77	Decca LFR 13732	We Love You/Chip On My Shoulder (12" p/s, with photo insert, 7,500 only)	25
82	Carrere CAR 255	England Belongs To Me/Argy Bargy (p/s, beware of bootlegs With "fuzzy" looking label logo on sleeve)	30
83	Razor RAZ 9	SHOCK TROOPS (LP)	25
84	Syndicate SYNLP 7	RUNNIN' RIOT IN 84 (LP)	35
86	Razor RAZ 26	TRUE GRIT (LP)	15
87	Link LP 005	LIVE AND LOUD (LP)	12

COCKTAIL CABINET

67	Page One POF 046	Puppet On A String/Breathalyser	18

COCOA TEA

88	Live And Love LLD 87	Lonesome Side/ADMIRAL TIBET: Reality Time (12")	20

COCTEAU TWINS

(see also This Mortal Coil, Felt, Massive Attack, Harold Budd, Lonely Is An Eyesore, The Future Sound Of London)

83	4AD AD 303	Peppermint Pig/Laugh Lines (p/s)	10
88	4AD CAD 807	BLUE BELL KNOLL (LP, tri-foldout sleeve)	12
90	4AD CAD 0012	HEAVEN OR LAS VEGAS (LP)	15
93	Fontana 518259-1	FOUR CALENDAR CAFE (LP)	40
96	Fontana 514-501-1	MILK AND KISSES (LP)	40
05	4AD CTBOX 2	LULLABIES TO VIOLAINE (4-CD box set, tactile cover)	30

CODE 071

92	Reinforced RIVET 1213	A London Sumtin' (12")	20
92	Reinforced RIVET 1230	A London Sumtin' (Remix) (12", with M.A.D)	8

CODENAME JOHN

94	Prototype PRO 001	Deep Inside Of Me/(Inta) The Anthem (12")	12
94	Prototype PRO 002	Kindred/Dreams Of Heaven (Shortys Mix) (12", as John)	10

C.O.D.s

66	Stateside SS 489	Michael (The Lover)/Cry No More	40
66	Stateside SS 489	Michael (The Lover)/Cry No More (DJ copy)	60

CODY

71	Polydor 2058-100	I Belong With You/Wanna Make You Happy	6

JAMIE COE

59	Parlophone R 4600	Summertime Symphony/There's Gonna Be A Day	150
60	Parlophone R 4621	School Day Blues/I'll Go On Loving You	100
61	HMV POP 991	How Low Is Low/Little Dear Little Darling	20
63	London HLX 9713	The Fool/I've Got That Feeling Again	20

PETER & CHRIS COE

(see also Bandoggs)

72	Trailer LER 2077	OPEN THE DOOR AND LET US IN (LP)	25
76	Trailer LER 2098	OUT OF SEASON, OUT OF RHYME (LP)	20
79	Highway SHY 7007	GAME OF ALL FOURS (LP)	15

MINT VALUE £

TONY COE (QUINTET)

61	Philips B 10784L	SWINGIN' TILL THE GIRLS COME HOME (LP)	50
67	Columbia SCX 6170	TONY'S BASEMENT (LP)	70
78	Lee Lambert LAM100	COE-EXISTENCE (LP)	20

TONY COE & BRIAN LEMON TRIO

(see also Robert Farnon & Tony Coe)

68	'77' SEU 12/41	TONY COE AND BRIAN LEMON TRIO (LP)	30

JACK & CHARLIE COEN

77	Topic 12TS 337	THE BRANCH LINE (LP)	22

CARLTON COFFE

78	Justice JUS 110	Chant Away/Version (12")	35

COFFEE

80	Dee Lite DEX 1	I Wanna Be With You/Slip & Dip	8

COFFEE BAR SKIFFLERS

(see also Chas McDevitt Skiffle Group)

58	Embassy WEP 1008	SKIFFLE SESSION (EP)	10

DENNIS COFFEY

72	A&M AMS 7010	Getting It On/Ride Sally Ride	5
70	A&M AMLS 68035	EVOLUTION (LP)	15
71	A&M AMLS 68072	GOIN' FOR MYSELF (LP)	15
74	Sussex LPSX 9	INSTANT COFFEY (LP)	15

ALMA COGAN

(see also Ronnie Hilton, Angela & Fans)

53	HMV 7M 166	Over And Over Again/Isn't Life Wonderful (with Les Howerd)	30
53	HMV 7M 106	I Went To Your Wedding/You Belong To Me	30
53	HMV 7M 107	To Be Loved By You/The Homing Waltz (B-side with Larry Day)	30
54	HMV 7M 173	Ricochet (Rick-O-Shay)/The Moon Is Blue	30
54	HMV 7M 188	Bell Bottom Blues/Love Me Again	40
54	HMV 7M 196	Make Love To Me/Said The Little Moment	30
54	HMV 7M 219	The Little Shoemaker/Chiqui-Chaqui (Chick-ee Chock-ee)	30
54	HMV 7M 228	Little Things Mean A Lot/Canoodlin' Rag	30
54	HMV 7M 239	Skinnie Minnie (Fishtail)/What Am I Going To Do, Ma (The Doo-Ma Song)	45
54	HMV 7M 269	This Ole House/Skokiaan	30
54	HMV 7M 271	I Can't Tell A Waltz From A Tango/Christmas Cards	30
55	HMV 7M 286	Paper Kisses/Softly, Softly	25
55	HMV 7M 293	Chee-Chee-Oo-Chee (Sang The Little Bird)/Tika Tika Tok	25
55	HMV 7M 301	Tweedlee-Dee/More Than Ever Now	25
55	HMV 7M 316	Got'n Idea/Give A Fool A Chance	25
55	HMV 7M 337	Never Do A Tango With An Eskimo/Twenty Tiny Fingers	30
56	HMV 7M 367	Love And Marriage/Sycamore Tree	25
56	HMV 7M 415	Why Do Fools Fall In Love?/ (The Same Thing Happen With) The Birds And The Bees?	40
56	HMV POP 239	Mama Teach Me To Dance/I'm In Love Again	25
56	HMV POP 261	In The Middle Of The House/Two Innocent Hearts	30
57	HMV POP 284	You, Me And Us/Three Brothers	25
57	HMV POP 317	Whatever Lola Wants (Lola Gets)/Lucky Lips	30
57	HMV POP 336	Chantez, Chantez/Funny, Funny, Funny	20
57	HMV POP 367	Fabulous/Summer Love	30
57	HMV POP 392	That's Happiness/What You've Done To Me	20
57	HMV POP 415	Party Time/Please Mister Brown (Mister Jones, Mister Smith)	20
58	HMV POP 433	The Story Of My Life/Love Is	10
58	HMV POP 450	Sugartime/Gettin' Ready For Freddy	15
58	HMV POP 482	Stairway Of Love/Comes Love	15
58	HMV POP 500	Sorry, Sorry, Sorry/Fly Away Lovers	10
58	HMV POP 531	There's Never Been A Night/If This Isn't Love	15
59	HMV POP 573	Last Night On The Back Porch/Mama Says	15
59	HMV POP 608	Pink Shoelaces/The Universe	15
59	HMV POP 670	We Got Love/I Don't Mind Being All Alone	10
60	HMV POP 728	O Dio Mio/Dream Talk	10
60	HMV POP 760	The Train Of Love/The 'I Love You' Bit	10
60	HMV POP 815	Must Be Santa/Just Couldn't Resist Her With Her Pocket Transistor	7
61	Columbia DB 4607	Cowboy Jimmy Joe/Don't Read This Letter	5
61	Columbia DB 4679	With You In Mind/Ja-Da	8
61	Columbia DB 4749	All Alone/Keep Me In Your Heart	8
62	Columbia DB 4794	She's Got You/In The Shade Of The Old Apple Tree	8
62	Columbia DB 4912	Goodbye Joe/I Can't Give You Anything But Love	5
63	Columbia DB 4965	Tell Him/Fly Me To The Moon (Bossa Nova)	5
63	Columbia DB 7059	Hold Out Your Hand You Naughty Boy/Just Once More	5
64	Columbia DB 7233	The Tennessee Waltz/I Love You Too Much	15
64	Columbia DB 7390	It's You/I Knew Right Away	7
65	Columbia DB 7652	Snakes And Snails (And Puppy Dog Tails)/How Many Days, How Many Nights	25
65	Columbia DB 7786	Eight Days A Week/Help!	10
66	Columbia DB 8088	Now That I've Found You/More	10
55	HMV 7EG 8122	THE GIRL WITH A LAUGH IN HER VOICE (EP)	25
55	HMV 7EG 8151	THE GIRL WITH A LAUGH IN HER VOICE NO. 2 (EP)	25
56	HMV 7EG 8169	THE GIRL WITH A LAUGH IN HER VOICE NO. 3 (EP)	25
57	HMV 7EG 8437	SHE LOVES TO SING (EP)	25
58	HMV CLP 1152	I LOVE TO SING (LP)	60
61	HMV CLP 1459	OLIVER! (LP, with others, mono)	30
61	HMV CSD 1370	OLIVER! (LP, with others, stereo)	40
61	Columbia 33SX 1345	ALMA SINGS WITH YOU IN MIND (LP, mono)	40
61	Columbia SCX 3391	ALMA SINGS WITH YOU IN MIND (LP)	50
62	Columbia 33SX 1469	HOW ABOUT LOVE! (LP, mono)	40

			MINT VALUE £
62	Columbia SCX 3459	HOW ABOUT LOVE! (LP, stereo)	50
67	Columbia SX 6130	ALMA (LP)	30

ALMA COGAN & RONNIE HILTON

(see also Ronnie Hilton)

57	HMV 7EG 8352	THE HITS FROM 'MY FAIR LADY' (EP, 1 side each)	10

ALMA COGAN & FRANKIE VAUGHAN

(see also Frankie Vaughan)

54	HMV 7M 226	Do, Do, Do, Do, Do, Do, Do It Again/Jilted	25

DON COGAN

58	MGM MGM 984	The Fountain Of Love/I'm Takin' Over	25

SHAYE COGAN

(see also Buddy Morrow)

58	Columbia DB 4055	Billy Be Sure/Doodle Doodle Doo	15
60	MGM MGM 1063	Mean To Me/They Said It Couldn't Be Done	60

ALAN COHEN BAND

72	Argo ZDA 159	BLACK, BROWN AND BEIGE (LP)	65

LEONARD COHEN

68	CBS 3337	Suzanne/So Long, Marianne	7
69	CBS 4245	Bird On The Wire/Seems So Long Ago, Nancy	7
71	CBS 7292	Joan Of Arc/Diamonds In The Mine	7
74	CBS 2494	Bird On The Wire (live)/Tonight Will Be Fine (live)	7
74	CBS 2699	Lover Lover Lover/Who By Fire	6
76	CBS 4306	Suzanne/Take This Longing	6
77	CBS 5882	Memories/Don't Go Home With Your Hard-On	6
78	CBS 6095	True Love Leaves No Traces/I Left A Woman Waiting	6
72	CBS EP 9162	McCABE AND MRS MILLER (EP, p/s)	8
68	CBS BPG 63241	SONGS OF LEONARD COHEN (LP, orange label, with stickered sleeve; mono)	20
68	CBS (S)BPG 63241	SONGS OF LEONARD COHEN (LP, orange label, with stickered sleeve; stereo)	18
68	CBS 63241	SONGS OF LEONARD COHEN (LP, orange label, re-pressing w/out prefix)	15

COIL

79	North'ton Wood H. HAV 1	Motor Industry/Alcoholic Stork (p/s)	15

COIL

(see also Psychic TV, Throbbing Gristle, Current 93, Thighpaulsandra)

85	F & F/K.422 FFK 512	Panic/Tainted Love/Aqua Regis (12", red vinyl, 'hair'-textured p/s)	25
85	F & F/K.422 FFK 512	Panic/Tainted Love/Aqua Regis (12", black vinyl, 'hair'-textured p/s)	15
86	Force & Form/K.422	The Anal Staircase/Blood From The Air/Ravenous (12", p/s, on clear vinyl)	25
86	Force & Form/K.422 ROTA 121	The Anal Staircase/Blood From The Air/Ravenous (12", p/s)	15
87	Solar Lodge 001	HELLRAISER (10" EP, coloured vinyl [clear or pink, 500 each])	25
87	Solar Lodge 001	HELLRAISER (10" EP, black vinyl)	7
90	Shock SX 002	Wrong Eye/Scope (pink p/s, signed & lettered A-Z, 26 only)	45
90	Shock SX 002	Wrong Eye/Scope (974 with numbered white p/s)	15
90	Shock SX 002	Wrong Eye/Scope (1,000 with un-numbered yellow p/s)	10
90	Shock SX 002	Wrong Eye/Scope (green p/s, 300 only, some with gold/black sticker)	25
92	Clawfist 22	Airborne Bells/Is Suicide A Solution (p/s, 1,250 only)	25
94	Loci S1	Themes From Blue (p/s, 23 on yellow vinyl)	60
94	Loci S1	Themes From Blue (p/s, 1,000 on blue vinyl)	20
94	Eskaton 001	Nasa Arab/First Dark Ride (12", stickered plain black sleeve, 2,500 only)	15
95	Eskaton 003	PHILM (10" EP, with poster, 50 on clear vinyl in handmade p/s)	60
95	Eskaton 003	PHILM (10" EP, with poster, 2,000 only)	12
86	Threshold ROTA 1	HORSE ROTORVATOR (LP, with A5 card insert & stickers)	20
87	Threshold House LOCI 1	GOLD IS THE METAL (LP, red vinyl; with bonus 7": "The Wheel"/ The Wheal, unfinished proof sleeve without writing, 25 only)	200
87	Threshold House LOCI 1	GOLD IS THE METAL (LP, red vinyl [150 only] with inner sleeve and bonus 7": "The Wheel"/"The Wheal")	70
87	Threshold House LOCI 1	GOLD IS THE METAL (LP, clear vinyl [500 only], with inner sleeve and with bonus 7": "The Wheel"/"The Wheal")	50
87	Threshold House LOCI 1	GOLD IS THE METAL (LP, box set with 7", "The Wheel"/"The Wheal", poster & booklet in black linen folder, embossed sleeve, autographed, 55 only)	300
87	Threshold House LOCI CD1	GOLD IS THE METAL (CD, 1,000 only)	20
90	Normal NORMAL 77	GOLD IS THE METAL (LP, black vinyl re-pressing with 7": The Wheel/"Keel Hauler")	18
93	Loci CD 4b	STOLEN AND CONTAMINATED SONGS (CD, 1st edit with different artwork)	20
90s	Loci CD 6	ANGELIC CONVERSATION (CD, gold disc, 1,000 only)	20
95	Eskaton 007	WORSHIP THE GLITCH (2 x 10" LP, as Coil Vs. Elph, with insert, 50 with white optical plastic cover)	55
95	Eskaton 007	WORSHIP THE GLITCH (2 x 10" LP, as Coil Vs. Elph, with insert, 2,000 only)	25
95	Eskaton 006	WORSHIP THE GLITCH (CD, as Coil Vs. Elph, 500 only in black optical plastic)	20
99	Acme/Prescription DRUG8	ASTRAL DISASTER (LP, 99 copies signed and numbered by Balance and Christopherson, with insert, artwork in plastic bag)	100
99	Chalice GRAAL LP002	MUSICK TO PLAY IN THE DARK VOL 1 (LP, 500 only, white vinyl)	50
00	Threshold House LOC114	ASTRAL DISASTER (LP re-issue, 100 copies, grey vinyl signed lyric sheet and art	60
00	Chalice GRAAL LP004	MUSICK TO PLAY IN THE DARK VOL 2 (2 x LP, white vinyl, one side etched)	50
00	Chalice GRAAL LP004	MUSICK TO PLAY IN THE DARK VOL 2 (2 x LP, 100 copies with blue/green vinyl)	50
00	Chalice GRAAL LP004	MUSICK TO PLAY IN THE DARK VOL 2 (2 x LP, translucent purple, 4th side etched with picture of moon and has 'gold leaf' attached, art print on cover, 2 part print inserts - signed - 60 copies only)	300
00	Chalice GRAAL LP004	MUSICK VOL 2 (26 copy "trauma edition" lettered A-Z white sleeves smeared with Balance's blood.)	70
02	Eskaton 28	TIME MACHINES (Coil as Time Machines) (2 x LP, 1,000 only, 55 clear, signed)	50
02	Eskaton 28	TIME MACHINES (Coil as Time Machines) (2 x LP, 1,000 only)	40

COINS

69	Toast TT 513	Love Power/You Can't Get Away From It	6
69	Toast TT 515	Don't You Know It's Just A Game, Love? (actually by Miss White & Mr. Green)/ Crying Over You	6

MINT VALUE £

ALVADEAN COKER

55	London HLU 8191	Do Dee Oodle De Do I'm In Love/We're Gonna Bop	600
55	London HLU 8191	Do Dee Oodle De Do I'm In Love/We're Gonna Bop (78)	60

SANDY COKER & HIS BAND

54	London HL 8109	Meadowlark Melody/Toss Over	70

RIC COLBECK QUARTET

70	Fontana 6383 001	THE SUN IS COMING UP (LP)	60

COLD BLOOD

70	Atlantic 584 319	You Got Me Hummin'/If You Will	8
70	Atlantic 588 218	COLD BLOOD (LP, plum/red label)	25
71	Atlantic 2400 102	SISYPHUS (LP, gatefold sleeve, plum/red label)	18
74	Warner Bros K 56047	LYDIA (LP)	15

COLDCUT

87	Ahead Of Our Time AHED 1201	Beats + Pieces/More Beats (12")	8
87	Ahead Of Our Time CCUT 8 TL	SAY KIDS EP (12", stickered die-cut black sleeve)	8
88	Urban URBX17DJ	Coldcut Meets The Godfather (12")	10
91	Ninja Tune ZEN12 004	Jade (12")	15
99	Ninja Tune ZEN12 012 R	Autumn Leaves (4 Remixes) (12")	8
94	Ninja Tune ZEN 12	PHILOSOPHY (2xLP, promo, different mixes to commercial release)	20
94	Ninja Tune ZEN 12	PHILOSOPHY (2xLP)	15

BEN COLDER

(see also Sheb Wooley)

64	MGM MGM-EP 791	MAKE THE WORLD GO BY (EP)	15

COLD FISH

82	CBS A2779	Love Me Today/Strange Boy	6
82	BK BK 12	Tropicana/Instrumental	12

COLD FLY

73	Bus Stop BUS 1007	Caterpillar/Yesterday Started For Judy	8

COLD HAND BAND

82	BK BK 12	Tropicana/Instrumental	12

COLDPLAY

98	private pressing HGCD 633	SAFETY EP: Bigger, Stronger/No More Keeping My Feet On The Ground/ Such A Rush (CD, 500 only)	500
99	Fierce Panda NING 68	Brothers And Sisters/Easy To Please (wraparound p/s, 1000 only)	45
99	Fierce Panda NING 68CD	Brothers And Sisters/Easy To Please/Only Superstition	15
99	EMI EMI CDR 6528	THE BLUE ROOM EP (Bigger, Stronger/Don't Panic/See You Soon/ High Speed/ Such A Rush) (CD, digipak)	35
99	EMI EMI 12R 6528	THE BLUE ROOM EP (Bigger, Stronger/Don't Panic/See You Soon/ High Speed/ Such A Rush) (12")	35
00	Parlophone R 6536	Shiver/For You/Careful Where You Stand (p/s)	10
00	Parlophone R 6536	Shiver/For You/Careful Where You Stand (CD, digipak)	10
00	Parlophone R 6538	Yellow/Help Is Around The Corner (7" ltd edn. Numbered single p/s)	15
00	Parlophone R 6549	Trouble/Brothers And Sisters (p/s, numbered, stickered poly outer)	10
01	COLDXMAS01	Have Yourself A Merry Little Christmas/Yellow (Alpha Mix) (CD EP, 1000 only, given away with Coldplayground fanzine)	100
01	Parlophone 07243 879080-6-2	Don't Panic/You Only Live Twice (live)/Bigger Stronger (live) (12" p/s, withdrawn)	70
02	Parlophone R 6588	The Scientist/1:36/I Ran Away (p/s)	7
03	Parlophone R 6594	Clocks/Crest Of Waves (p/s)	7
03	Parlophone 12 R 6594	Clocks (Royksopp Trembling Heart Mix)/Royksopp Trembling Heart Instrumental Mix/God Put A Smile Upon Your Face (Def Inc. Remix feat. Mr. Thing) (12", die-cut sleeve, 1000 only)	30
05	Parlophone R6664	Speed Of Sound/Things I Don't Understand/Proof (10", clear vinyl)	8
00	Parlophone 5277831	PARACHUTES (LP)	18
02	Parlophone 540 5041	A RUSH OF BLOOD TO THE HEAD (LP, gatefold sleeve, with inner)	20
05	Parlophone 474 7861	X&Y (LP, gatefold sleeve with slip case and poster)	20
05	Parlophone 474 7862	X&Y (CD, with carrier bag, T shirt, key ring and wrist band)	25
07	Parlophone 3883247	THE SINGLES 1999 - 2006 (15 x 7" box set)	45

PROMOS

98	None	Ode To Deodorant/Brothers And Sisters (2-track cassette sent to concert promoters and radio DJ's. White label, attributed to The Coldplay with "contact Phil" and 0777 mobile no.)	300
99	Parlophone CDRDJ 6528	THE BLUE ROOM EP (Bigger, Stronger/Don't Panic/ See You Soon/High Speed/ Such A Rush) (CD digipak)	35
99	Parlophone 12RDJ 6528	THE BLUE ROOM EP (Bigger, Stronger/Don't Panic/ See You Soon/High Speed/ Such A Rush) (12")	30
00	EMI EMISAMP/13	You're Keeping Me Up All Night (EMI CD sampler with alternative version of Spies)	25
00	Parlophone CDRDJ 6538	Yellow/Help Is Round The Corner/No More Keeping My Feet On The Ground (CD)	8
00	Parlophone 12RDJ 6538	Yellow/Help Is Round The Corner/No More Keeping My Feet On The Ground (12")	20
00	Parlophone 12RDJ 6549	Trouble/Brothers & Sisters/Shiver (12")	10
01	Parlophone PANIC01	Don't Panic (CD)	8
06	Parlophone (No cat no)	Talk (FK Dub Mix) (12" one-sided acetate 10 only DJ copies)	75
06	Parlophone (No cat. no)	Clocks (Royksopp remixes) (12" promo. die-cut sleeve)	15
00	Parlophone CHUTE001	PARACHUTES (CD, blue card sleeve)	30
02	Parlophone COLDADJ001	A RUSH OF BLOOD TO THE HEAD (CD, numbered and sealed card sleeve)	20
02	Parlophone COLDINT001	A RUSH OF BLOOD TO THE HEAD (CD interview disc)	20
03	Parlophone CPLIVE	LIVE (2xCD)	40
05	Parlophone COLDINT2	X&Y (CD interview disc)	20
05	Parlophone (No cat. no)	X&Y (promo, numbered slipcase)	20

MINT VALUE £

COLD TURKEY

72	Pye 7N 45142	Nobody's Fool/Sesame Street	12

B.J. COLE

(see also Cochise)

73	United Artists UAS 29418	NEW HOVERING DOG (LP, laminated front sleeve)	30

BOBBY COLE

68	CBS 3626	Mister Bo Jangles/Bus 22 To Jerusalem	5

CINDY COLE

(see also Jeannie & Big Guys)

65	Columbia DB 7519	A Love Like Yours/He's Sure The Boy I Love	25
66	Columbia DB 7973	Just Being Your Baby (Turns Me On)/Lonely City Blue Boy	35

CLAY COLE

62	London HLP 9499	Twist Around The Clock/Don't Twist With No One Else But Me	10

COZY COLE

58	London HL 8750	Topsy (Parts 1 & 2)	10
58	London HL 7065	Topsy (Parts 1 & 2) (export issue)	10
59	Mercury AMT 1015	St. Louis Blues/Father Co-operates	10
59	London HL 8843	Turvy (Parts 1 & 2)	10
59	London HL 8843	Turvy (Parts 1 & 2) (78)	10
62	Coral Q 72457	Big Noise From Winnetka (Parts 1 & 2)	10
57	MGM MGM-EP 622	COZY COLE ALL STARS (EP)	15

DON COLE & ALLEYNE

65	Fontana TF 522	Gotta Find My Baby/Something's Gotta Hold Of Me	5

JERRY COLE

65	Capitol CL 15397	Every Window In The City/Come On Over To My Place	12

KEITH COLE

71	Big BG 315	Musical Attack/RUPIE EDWARDS ALLSTARS: Shack Attack	8
71	Big BG 316	Music Alone Version 3/RUPIE EDWARDS ALLSTARS: Behold Another Version	8

KING COLE TRIO/QUINTET

(see under Nat 'King' Cole)

LLOYD COLE & COMMOTIONS

84	Welcome To L. Vegas LC 1	Are You Ready To Be Heartbroken?/Down At The Mission (p/s, withdrawn)	30
85	Polydor COLET 5	Lost Weekend (extended)/Big World/Lost Weekend - (7" version) (10" p/s)	8

NAT COLE

(see also Rita Alston)

70	Jackpot JP 717	Pack Of Cards/RITA & NAT COLE: Spread Joy	5
70	Jackpot JP 718	Love Making/SONNY BINNS & RITA: My Love	5
70	Jackpot JP 722	Sugar Sugar/SONNY BINNS & RITA: Sign Off	5
70	Explosion EX 2022	In The Summertime/Apollo Moon Walk	8
70	Creole CR 1002	Me And My Life/Instrumental	5

NAT 'KING' COLE

53	Capitol LC 6569	CAPITOL PRESENTS NAT KING COLE (10" LP)	15
53	Capitol LC 6587	CAPITOL PRESENTS NAT KING COLE AND HIS TRIO VOLUME 1 (10" LP)	15
53	Capitol LC 6593	CAPITOL PRESENTS NAT KING COLE AT THE PIANO (10" LP)	15
53	Capitol LC 6594	CAPITOL PRESENTS NAT KING COLE AND HIS TRIO VOLUME 2 (10" LP)	15
53	Capitol LC 6627	NAT KING COLE SINGS FOR TWO IN LOVE (10" LP)	15
54	Capitol LCT 6003	NAT KING COLE TENTH ANNIVERSARY ALBUM (LP)	12
56	Capitol LC 6818	BALLADS OF THE DAY (10" LP)	12
56	Capitol LC 6830	THE PIANO STYLE OF NAT KING COLE (10" LP	12
56	Brunswick LAT 8123	IN THE BEGINNING (as King Cole Trio) (LP)	15

PATSY COLE

66	Island WI 271	Disappointed Bride/EARL BOSTIC: Honeymoon Night	25

ROCKY COLE

61	Oriole CB 1635	Heaven And Earth/Huey's Song	5

STRANGER COLE

(see also Stranger, Stranger & Gladys, Stranger & Patsy, Stranger & Ken, Rob Walker, Charmers, Lloyd Clarke, Don Drummond, Tommy McCook, Ernest Wilson, Delroy Wilson, Lester Sterling, Baba Brooks, Roland Alphonso)

63	R&B JB 133	Out Of Many/Nothing Tried	25
63	Island WI 110	Stranger At The Door/Conqueror	25
63	Island WI 114	Last Love/STRANGER & KEN: Hush Baby	25
63	Island WI 126	We Are Rolling/Millie Maw	25
64	Island WI 137	Goodbye Peggy (actually plays "Goodbye Peggy Darling" by Roy Panton)/ BABA BROOKS: Portrait Of My Love	25
64	R&B JB 129	Morning Star/Beat Up Your Gum	18
64	Island WI 133	Til My Dying Days/STRANGER & PATSY: I Need You	20
64	Black Swan WI 413	Uno Dos Tres (act. with Ken Boothe)/Look (B-side actually by unknown artist)	20
64	Black Swan WI 415	Summer Day/Loving You Always (both actually by Dottie & Bonnie)	20
64	Black Swan WI 435	Little Boy Blue/ERIC MORRIS: Words Of Wisdom	20
65	Ska Beat JB 192	Pussy Cat/MAYTALS: Sweet Sweet Jenny	25
65	Island WI 169	Koo Koo Doo (with Owen & Leon)/GLORIA & DREAMLETTS: Stay Where You Are	20
65	Island WI 177	Run Joe (with Baba Brooks)/Make Believe	20
65	Blue Beat BB 322	When The Party Is Over/BUSTER'S ALLSTARS: Happy Independence '65	25
65	Blue Beat BB 333	Matilda (actually with Prince Buster)/BUSTER'S ALL STARS: When The Party Is Over	35
66	Doctor Bird DB 1025	We Shall Overcome/Do You Really Love Me (as Stranger Cole & Seraphines)	40
66	Doctor Bird DB 1040	Drop The Ratchet/Oh Yee Mahee (as Stranger Cole & Conquerors)	25
67	Doctor Bird DB 1066	You Took My Love (actually by Patsy Todd)/FUGITIVES: Living Soul	100
68	Island WI 3154	Jeboza Macoo/Now I Know (B-side actually with Gladdy Anderson)	45
68	Amalgamated AMG 801	Just Like A River (as Stranger Cole & Gladdy)/LEADERS: Hope Someday	20

			MINT VALUE £
69	Amalgamated AMG 838	What Mama Na Want She Get/We Two	18
69	Duke DU 27	Glad You're Living/Help Wanted	10
69	Unity UN 501	Last Flight To Reggae City (w/ Tommy McCook)/JUNIOR SMITH: Watch Dem Go	12
69	Unity UN 514	When I Get My Freedom/Life Can Be Beautiful	35
69	Escort ES 810	Pretty Cottage/To Me	10
69	Escort ES 811	Why Did You/Do You Remember	20
69	Escort ES 819	Leana Leana/Na Na Na	7
69	Escort ES 826	Loneliness/Remember	7
70	Escort ES 830	Little Things/Till The Well Runs Dry	6
70	Escort ES 831	Everything With You/Picture On The Wall	6
70	Escort ES 832	Pussy/Let Me In	6
70	Camel CA 54	Everyday Tomorrow/Let Your Head Up High	20
70	Pama PM 790	Come Dance With Me/Dance With Me	10
71	Bullet BU 488	Soul Sop/Stranger Cole Medley	15
71	Camel CA 72	Crying Every Night/DENNIS ALCAPONE & DELROY WILSON: It Must Come	10
71	Escort ERT 849	Tomorrow/SONNY BURKE: Chicken Thief	7
72	Tropical AL 0011	Mail Man (with Charlie Ace)/Mail Man (Version)	7
72	Jackpot JP 791	My Confession/LASCELS & HORTENSE: The Might Organ	6
72	Pama PM 848	The House Where Bombo Lives/Our High School Dance	5

BOBBY COLEMAN

66	Pye International 7N 25365	(Baby) You Don't Have To Tell Me/Pleasure Girl	60
66	Pye International 7N 25365	(Baby) You Don't Have To Tell Me/Pleasure Girl (DJ Copy)	90

FITZROY COLEMAN

61	Starlite ST45 064	Lucilla/Caribbean Sunset	12

LONNIE COLEMAN & JESSE ROBERTSON

56	London HLU 8335	Dolores Diane/Oh Honey, Why Don'tcha	70
56	London HLU 8335	Dolores Diane/Oh Honey, Why Don'tcha (78)	10

ORNETTE COLEMAN

60	Contemporary LAC 12228	TOMORROW IS THE QUESTION (LP)	20
61	London Jazz LTZ-K 15199	CHANGE OF THE CENTURY (LP, mono)	20
61	London Jazz SAH-K 5099	CHANGE OF THE CENTURY (LP, stereo)	25
61	London Jazz LTZ-K 15228	THIS IS OUR MUSIC (LP, mono)	20
62	London Jazz LTZ-K 15241	THE ORNETTE COLEMAN QUARTET (LP, mono)	20
62	London Jazz SAH-K 6235	THE ORNETTE COLEMAN QUARTET (LP, stereo)	25
67	CBS 66023	CHAPPAQUA SUITE (2-LP)	25
68	Polydor 623 246/7	AN EVENING WITH ORNETTE COLEMAN (2-LP)	15
69	Impulse SIPL 518	ORNETTE AT 12 (LP)	20
72	Atlantic K 40278	TWINS (LP)	20
77	Blue Note BNS 40021	AT THE GOLDEN CIRCLE STOCKHOLM (LP, reissue)	12

ROGER COLEMAN

60	Top Rank JAR 311	Nobody's Fool/Endlessly	8

COLENSO PARADE

(see also House Of Love)

86	Fire BLAZE 11T	Fontana Eyes/Here Comes The Night/Anything/Our Man In Havana (12" p/s)	8

COLETTE & BANDITS

65	Stateside SS 416	A Ladies Man/Lost Love	20

COLEY

70s	Coley (Private Pressing)	GOODBYE BRAIN (LP)	35

COLLAGE

(see also Brian Bennett)

73	Studio Two TWO 410	MISTY (LP)	35

COLLECTIVE HORIZONTAL

79	Dolmen DO 1	COLLECTIVE HORIZONTAL EP (gatefold p/s, stickered white labels)	5

COLLECTORS (Canada)

(see also Chilliwack, Electric Prunes)

70	London HLU 10304	I Must Have Been Blind/The Beginning	6
69	Warner Bros WS 1774	GRASS AND WILD STRAWBERRIES (LP)	22

COLLECTORS (U.K.)

80	Central Collection COL 1	Different World/Talking Hands (p/s)	6

COLLEGE BOYS (Jamaica)

64	Blue Beat BB 202	Love Is A Treasure/Someone Will Be There	25

COLLEGE BOYS (U.K.)

64	Columbia DB 7306	I Just Don't Understand/I'm Gonna Cry	20
67	Pye 7N 17294	Good Times/San Antonio Rose	10

GRAHAM COLLIER SEXTET/SEPTET

(see also Harry Beckett)

67	Deram DML/SML 1005	DEEP DARK BLUE CENTRE (LP)	90
69	Fontana SFJL 922	DOWN ANOTHER ROAD (LP)	70
70	Fontana 6309 006	SONGS FOR MY FATHER (LP, as Graham Collier Music featuring Harry Beckett)	50
71	Philips 6308 051	MOSAICS (LP, live, as Graham Collier Music featuring Harry Beckett)	40
72	Saydisc SDL 244	PORTRAITS (LP)	20
75	Cambridge Univ 521205638	JAZZ LECTURE CONCERT (LP)	35

MITTY COLLIER

64	Pye International 7N 25275	I Had A Talk With My Man/Free Girl	25
64	Pye International 7N 25275	I Had A Talk With My Man/Free Girl (DJ Copy)	50

ALBERT COLLINS

69	Liberty LBS 83238	LOVE CAN BE FOUND ANYWHERE (LP)	40
73	Tumbleweed TW 3501	THERE'S GOTTA BE A CHANGE (LP)	30

MINT VALUE £

ANSEL(L) COLLINS

(see also Dave & Ansell Collins, Conquerors, Lloyd Young, Prince Buster, Les Foster, Ethiopians, Eternals, Pam Brooks, Dennis Alcapone, Rad Bryan, Immortals)

69	Trojan TR 699	Night Of Love/DERRICK MORGAN: Copy Cat	12
69	Trojan TR 7712	Cotton Dandy/CARL DAWKINS: Don't Get Weary	12
70	Trojan TR 7729	Moon Dust/Fat Cat	20
70	Trojan TR 7730	Monkey (Version I)/(Version II) (plays "High Voltage"/ "High Voltage Version"; B-side actually by Beverley All Stars)	15
70	J-Dan JDN 4401	Cock Robin/KING DENNIS: Seven Zero	12
70	Techniques TE 907	Top Secret/Crazy Rhythm (both actually by Winston Wright)	15
71	Techniques TE 913	Nuclear Weapon/TECHNIQUES ALL STARS: La, La, La	15

BOOTSY COLLINS

(see under Bootsy's Rubber Band)

CLANCY COLLINS ALL STARS (Actually, Lloyd Chalmers)

71	Smash SMA 2321	Sir Collins Special/Conqueror (Actually, LENNOX BROWN : Heart of Knights)	25

DAVE & ANSELL COLLINS

71	Trojan TBL 162	DOUBLE BARREL (LP)	25

DONIE COLLINS SHOWBAND

68	Pye 7N 17682	Get Down With It/I Can't Help Myself (Sugar Pie Honey Bunch)	10

DOROTHY COLLINS

55	Vogue Coral Q 72111	My Boy - Flat Top/In Love	40
56	Vogue Coral Q 72116	Moments To Remember/Love And Marriage	8
56	Vogue Coral Q 72137	Seven Days/Manuello	25
56	Vogue Coral Q 72173	Treasure Of Love/He's Got Me, Hook, Line And Sinker	25
56	Vogue Coral Q 72193	Love Me As Though There Were No Tomorrow/Rock And Roll Train	40
56	Vogue Coral Q 72198	The Italian Theme/Cool It, Baby	40
56	Vogue Coral Q 72208	The Twelve Gifts Of Christmas/Mr. Santa	15
57	Vogue Coral Q 72232	Baby Can Rock/Would You Ever	25
57	Vogue Coral Q 72252	Mr. Wonderful/I Miss You Already	10
57	Vogue Coral Q 72262	Four Walls/Big Dreams	7
57	Vogue Coral Q 72287	Soft Sands/Sing It, Children, Sing It	5
59	Top Rank JAR 259	Baciare, Baciare/Everything I Have Is Yours	5
60	Top Rank JAR 401	Banjo Boy/Tintarella Di Luna	7
60	Top Rank JAR 523	Unlock Those Chains/I'll Be Yours, You'll be Mine	5
55	London REP 1025	DOROTHY COLLINS SINGS (EP)	30
57	Coral LVA 9058	AT HOME WITH DOROTHY AND RAYMOND (LP)	25

EDWYN COLLINS

(see also Orange Juice, Paul Quinn & Edwyn Collins)

87	Creation CRE 047T	Don't Shilly Shally/If Ever You're Ready (7" white label test pressing only)	40
87	Creation CRE 047T	Don't Shilly Shally/If Ever You're Ready (12", white label test pressing only)	35
87	Elevation ACIDB 6	My Beloved Girl/50 Shades Of Blue (Acoustic Version)/Clouds (Fogging Up My Mind)/What's The Big Idea? (box set with 3 postcards)	6

GLENDA COLLINS

60	Decca F 11280	Take A Chance/Crazy Guy	15
61	Decca F 11321	Oh How I Miss You Tonight/Age For Love	15
61	Decca F 11417	Head Over Heels In Love/Find Another Fool	15
63	HMV POP 1163	I Lost My Heart In The Fairground/I Feel So Good	60
63	HMV POP 1233	If You Gotta Pick A Baby/In The First Place	80
64	HMV POP 1283	Baby It Hurts/Nice Wasn't It	65
64	HMV POP 1323	Lollipop/Everybody's Got To Fall In Love	50
65	HMV POP 1439	Johnny Loves Me/Paradise for Two	50
65	HMV POP 1475	Thou Shall Not Steal/Been Invited To A Party	70
66	Pye 7N 17044	Something I've Got To Tell You/My Heart Didn't Lie	75
66	Pye 7N 17150	It's Hard To Believe It/Don't Let It Rain On Sunday	50
90	Document CSAP LP 108	BEEN INVITED TO A PARTY (LP)	20

JOHNNY COLLINS

75	Tradition TSR 020	JOHNNY'S PRIVATE ARMY (LP)	18

JOHNNY COLLINS & FRIENDS

73	Tradition TSR 014	THE TRAVELLER'S REST (LP)	18

JUDY COLLINS

66	London HLZ 10029	I'll Keep It With Mine/Thirsty Boots	12
67	Elektra EKSN 45011	In My Life/Hard Lovin' Loser	5
67	Elektra EKSN 45043	Both Sides Now/Hey That's No Way To Say Goodbye	6
69	Elektra EKSN 45053	Some Day Soon/My Father	5
69	Elektra EKSN 45073	Chelsea Morning/Pretty Polly	5
69	Elektra EKSN 45077	Turn, Turn, Turn/Mr. Tambourine Man	5
65	Elektra EKL 209	MAID OF CONSTANT SORROW (LP)	20
65	Elektra EKS 7300	FIFTH ALBUM (LP, orange label)	12

LYN COLLINS

(see also James Brown)

64	Sabre SA 0002	What Am I Gonna Do Without You?/When A Girl Meets A Bad, Bad Boy	20
74	Polydor 2066 490	Rock Me Again And Again And Again/Wide Awake In A Dream	20
74	Mojo 2093 029	Think (About It)/Me And My Baby Got Our Own Thing Going	10
88	Urban URBX 15	Yes It's You (by SWEET CHARLES)/Rock Me Again And Again And Again And Again And Again/Think About It (12")	8
72	Polydor 2918 006	THINK (ABOUT IT) (LP)	40

PETER COLLINS

70	Decca F 13048	Get In A Boat/Girl By The Sea	10
70	Decca Nova SDN 21	PETER COLLINS (LP, blue/silver label)	35

MINT VALUE £

PHIL COLLINS

(see also Genesis, Flaming Youth, Brand X, Peter Banks)

81	Virgin VSK 102	In The Air Tonight/The Roof Is Leaking (12-page cartoon booklet p/s)	5

PHIL COLLINS & MARILYN MARTIN

(see also Brand X, Peter Banks, Genesis, Flaming Youth, Marilyn Martin)

85	Virgin VSSD 818	Separate Lives/Only You Know And I Know (2 interlocking picture discs)	5

RODGER COLLINS

67	Vocalion VF 9285	She's Looking Good/I'm Serving Time	25
67	Vocalion VF 9285	She's Looking Good/I'm Serving Time (DJ copy)	60

SHIRLEY COLLINS

60	Collector JEI 1508	SINGS IRISH (EP)	60
60	Collector JEB 3	THE FOGGY DEW (EP)	60
60	Collector JEB 5	ENGLISH SONGS (EP)	60
64	Collector JEB 9	ENGLISH SONGS VOL. 2 (EP, with Robin Hall)	60
63	Topic TOP 95	HEROES IN LOVE (EP)	60
59	Folkways FG 3564	FALSE TRUE LOVERS (LP)	130
60	Argo RG 150	SWEET ENGLAND (LP, blue/silver label)	150
64	Decca LK 4652	FOLK ROOTS, NEW ROUTES (LP, insert, with Davy Graham)	300
67	Topic 12T 170	THE SWEET PRIMROSES (LP, original pressing with blue label)	45
67	Topic 12T 170	THE SWEET PRIMROSES (LP)	25
68	Polydor 583 025	THE POWER OF THE TRUE LOVE KNOT (LP, with Incredible String Band)	250
71	Pegasus PEG 7	NO ROSES (LP, gatefold sleeve, with Albion Country Band)	50
74	Topic 12T 238	ADIEU TO OLD ENGLAND (LP, original pressing with blue label)	35
74	Topic 12T 238	ADIEU TO OLD ENGLAND (LP)	25
75	Deram SML 1117	A FAVOURITE GARLAND (LP)	50
76	Harvest SHSM 2008	AMARANTH (LP)	30
78	Topic 12T 380	FOR AS MANY AS WILL (LP)	15
83	Hannibal HNBL 1327	THE POWER OF THE TRUE LOVE KNOT (LP, reissue)	12
91	Mooncrest CREST 011	NO ROSES (LP, reissue)	15

SHIRLEY & DOLLY COLLINS

(see also Davy Graham, Albion Country Band, Conundrum)

69	Harvest SHVL 754	ANTHEMS IN EDEN (LP, gatefold sleeve, with "Sold in U.K..." text on 4 lines"	150
70s	Harvest SHVL 754	ANTHEMS IN EDEN (LP, gatefold sleeve, later issue with EMI logo on label)	100
70	Harvest SHVL 771	LOVE, DEATH AND THE LADY (LP, gatefold sleeve, no EMI logo on label)	120

SIR COLLINS

(see under 'S')

TOMMY COLLINS

58	Capitol CL 14838	Think It Over Boys/All Of The Monkeys Ain't In The Zoo	12
58	Capitol CL 14894	Let Down/It Tickles	10
59	Capitol CL 15076	Little June/A Hundred Years From Now	10
60	Capitol CL 15118	Wreck Of The Old '97/You Belong In My Arms	10
57	Capitol T 776	WORDS AND MUSIC COUNTRY STYLE (LP)	20
59	Capitol T 1196	THIS IS TOMMY COLLINS (LP)	20

COLLINS BAND & BOB STACKIE

(see also Sir Collins)

68	Collins Downbeat	Bob Stackie In Soho/LORD CHARLES & HIS BAND: Jamaican Bits And Pieces	45

JOE COLMAN

90	Blast First FU10	INFERNAL MACHINE (LP, picture disc, 1,000 only)	18

COLONEL

75	Ring O' 2017 104	Cokey Cokey/Away In A Manger (company sleeve)	10

COLONEL

(see also XTC, Mr. Partridge)

80	Virgin VS 380	Too Many Cooks (In The Kitchen)/I Need Protection (p/s)	6

COLONEL BAGSHOT

71	Parlophone R 5893	Georgia Fireball/Look In Her Eyes	15

JERRY COLONNA

54	Brunswick 05243	Ebb Tide/The Velvet Glove	10
54	Brunswick 05342	It Might As Well Be Spring/Ja-Da	8
55	Parlophone MSP 6165	Let Me Go, Lover/I Want To Love You, Cara Mia	8
55	London HL 8143	Chicago Style/Baffi	20
56	HMV 7M 369	The Shifting, Whispering Sands/Waltz Me Around	15
55	Brunswick LA 8711	MUSIC FOR SCREAMING (10" LP)	30
59	London HA-U 2190	LET'S ALL SING (LP)	15
65	Ace Of Hearts AH 102	JERRY COLONNA AND GROUCHO MARX (LP)	12

COLORADOS

64	Oriole CB 1972	Lips Are Redder On You/Who You Gonna Hurt?	30

COLOR TAPES

79	Wavelength HURT 4	Cold Anger/Leaves Of China (p/s)	6

COLOSSEUM

(see also Bakerloo, Dick Heckstall-Smith, Chris Farlowe, Greenslade, Humble Pie, John Mayall, Howard Riley Trio, Tempest, Mogul Thrash)

69	Fontana TF 1029	Walking In The Park/Those About To Die	10
69	Fontana STL 5510	THOSE WHO ARE ABOUT TO DIE SALUTE YOU (LP, gatefold sleeve)	60
69	Vertigo VO 1	VALENTYNE SUITE (LP, gatefold sleeve, large swirl label with Philips credit & inner bag)	75
70	Vertigo 6360 017	DAUGHTER OF TIME (LP, gatefold sleeve, with large swirl label & bag)	120
70	Vertigo 6360 017	DAUGHTER OF TIME (LP, gatefold sleeve, small swirl label)	25
71	Bronze ICD 1	COLOSSEUM LIVE (2-LP, gatefold, plastic inner)	40
72	Bronze BRNA 214	VALENTYNE SUITE (LP, reissue)	12

MINT VALUE £

COLOURBOX

(see also M/A/R/R/S)

82	4AD AD 215	Breakdown/Tarantula (p/s)	6
82	4AD BAD 215	Breakdown/Tarantula (12", p/s)	8
83	4AD AD 314	Breakdown (Second Version)/Tarantula (Second Version) (different p/s)	5
86	4AD 605	The Official Colourbox World Cup Theme/Philip Glass (p/s)	5
85	4AD CAD 508	COLOURBOX (LP, stickered sleeve, 10,000 only, with bonus LP MAD 509)	18

COLOURED RAISINS

(see also Raisins)

70	Trojan TR 7700	One Way Love/No More Heartaches	7

COLOURFIELD

(see also Specials)

84	Chrysalis COLF D2	Thinking Of You/Wild Flames//Little Things/Thinking Of You (double pack)	5
85	Chrysalis COLF D4	Castles In The Air/Your Love Was Smashing//I Can't Get Enough Of You Baby/Castles In The Air (Instrumental Mix) (double pack, gatefold p/s)	5
87	Chrysalis CCD 1546	DECEPTION (CD)	20
89	Chrysalis CHR 1480	VIRGINS AND PHILISTINES (CD)	40

COLOURFUL SEASONS

68	MGM MGM 1433	Out Of The Blue/It's Gonna Break My Heart	6

COLO(U)RS OF LOVE

68	Page One POF 060	I'm A Train/Up On A Cotton Cloud	8
68	Page One POF 086	Just Another Fly/Twenty Ten	8
69	Page One POF 124	Mother Of Convention/Music Mother Made	8
75	DJM DJS 625	I Can Dream Can't I?/I'll Be Seeing You	6

CHRISTOPHER COLT

68	Decca F 12726	Virgin Sunrise/Girl In The Mirror	40

TONY COLTON('S BIG BOSS BAND)

(see also Poet & One Man Band, Head Hands & Feet, Real McCoy, Peter B's)

64	Decca F 11879	Lose My Mind/So Used To Loving You (solo)	30
65	Pye 7N 15886	I Stand Accused/Further On Down The Track (with Big Boss Band)	200
66	Pye 7N 17046	You're Wrong There Baby/Have You Lost Your Mind	40
66	Pye 7N 17117	I've Laid Some Down In My Time/Run Pony Rider	50
68	Columbia DB 8385	In The World Of Marnie Dreaming/Who Is She? (solo)	25

JOHN COLTRANE

(see also Miles Davis,Thelonious Monk, Cannonball Adderley, Don Cherry, Archie Shepp)

60	Esquire EP 229	SOUL OF 'TRANE (EP)	8
61	Esquire EP 239	BASS BLUES (EP)	8
64	Fontana 469 203TE	WHILE MY LADY SLEEPS (EP)	8
58	Esquire 32-079	THE FIRST TRANE (LP)	25
58	Esquire 32-089	SOUL TRANE (LP)	25
59	Esquire 32-091	TRANEING IN (LP)	25
60	Esquire 32-101	CATTIN' (LP)	25
60	London Jazz LTZ-K 15197	GIANT STEPS (LP)	30
61	Esquire 32-129	LUSH LIFE (LP)	25
61	London Jazz LTZ-K 15219	COLTRANE JAZZ (LP, also stereo SAH-K 6162)	20
62	London Jazz LTZ-K 15232	BAGS AND TRANE (LP, also stereo SAH-K 6192)	20
62	Columbia 33SX 1399	THE BIRDLAND STORY VOL. 1: ECHOES OF AN ERA (LP)	15
62	London Jazz LTZ-K 15239	OLE COLTRANE (LP, mono)	20
62	London Jazz SAH-K 6223	OLE COLTRANE (LP, stereo)	25
62	HMV CLP 1548	AFRICA/BRASS (LP, mono)	25
62	HMV SCD 1431	AFRICA/BRASS (LP, stereo)	30
62	HMV CLP 1590	LIVE AT THE VILLAGE VANGUARD (LP, mono)	20
62	HMV CSD 1456	LIVE AT THE VILLAGE VANGUARD (LP, stereo)	25
63	United Artists (S)ULP 1018	COLTRANE TIME (LP)	15
63	London HA-K/SH-K 8017	COLTRANE PLAYS THE BLUES (LP, as John Coltrane Group)	25
63	Esquire 32-179	STANDARD COLTRANE (LP)	25
63	HMV CLP 1629	COLTRANE (LP, also stereo CSD 1483)	15
63	HMV CLP 1647	BALLADS (LP, also stereo CSD 1496)	15
63	HMV CLP 1657	DUKE ELLINGTON & JOHN COLTRANE (LP, mono)	20
63	HMV CSD 1502	DUKE ELLINGTON & JOHN COLTRANE (LP, stereo)	25
64	HMV CLP 1695	IMPRESSIONS (LP, mono)	25
64	HMV CSD 1509	IMPRRESSIONS (LP, stereo)	30
64	HMV CLP 1700	JOHN COLTRANE WITH JOHNNY HARTMAN (LP)	25
64	Realm RM 157	ON WEST 42ND STREET (LP)	20
64	Realm RM 181	TRANE RIDE (LP)	20
64	HMV CLP 1741	LIVE AT BIRDLAND (LP, also stereo CSD 1544)	20
65	HMV CLP 1799	CRESCENT (LP, mono)	25
65	HMV SCD 1567	CRESCENT (LP, stereo)	30
65	Stateside SL 10124	BLACK PEARLS (LP)	20
65	HMV CLP 1869	A LOVE SUPREME (LP, mono)	25
65	HMV CSD 1605	A LOVE SUPREME (LP, stereo)	30
65	Atlantic ATL/SAL 5022	MY FAVOURITE THINGS (LP)	20
65	Realm RM 52226	TANGANYIKA STRUT (LP)	20
65	HMV CLP 1897	COLTRANE PLAYS (LP, also stereo CSD 1619)	20
66	Stateside SL 10162	BAHIA (LP)	22
66	HMV CLP/CSD 3543	ASCENSION (LP, as John Coltrane Orchestra)	25
66	HMV CLP/CSD 3551	NEW THING AT NEWPORT (LP, with Archie Shepp)	25
66	Atlantic 587/588 004	THE AVANT-GARDE (LP, with Don Cherry)	25
66	HMV CLP 3575	MEDITATIONS (LP, mono)	20
66	HMV CSD 3575	MEDITATIONS (LP, flipback sleeve stereo)	30
67	Atlantic 587/588 039	COLTRANE'S SOUND (LP)	20
67	HMV CLP/CSD 3599	COLTRANE LIVE AT THE VILLAGE VANGUARD AGAIN! (LP)	25
67	HMV CLP/CSD 3617	OM (LP, withdrawn)	40

MINT VALUE £

67	HMV CLP/CSD 3617	KULU SE MAMA (LP)	20
68	Transatlantic PR 7280	DAKAR (LP)	25
68	Transatlantic PR 7378	LAST TRANE (LP)	25
68	Impulse MIPL 502	EXPRESSION (LP, mono)	25
68	Impulse SIPL 502	EXPRESSION (LP, stereo)	18
69	Atlantic 588 139	THREE LITTLE WORDS (LP)	20
69	Impulse MIPL/SIPL 515	COSMIC MUSIC (LP, by Alice & John Coltrane)	30
70	Impulse SIPL 522	SELFLESSNESS (LP)	20
71	Probe SPB 1025	AFRO BLUE (LP)	15
72	Prestige PR 24003	JOHN COLTRANE (2-LP)	15
74	CBS PR 24037	BLACK PEARLS (2-LP)	18

COLTS

65	Pye 7N 15955	San Miguel/Where Has Our Love Gone?	5

COLUMBIA BOYS

68	Pye 7N 17513	Baby Come Back/Born To Lose	8
69	Pye 7N 17763	That's My Pa/She Thinks I Still Care	7

COLUMBUS

70	Deram DM 294	Ev'rybody Loves The U.S. Marshall/Tired	10

RAY COLUMBUS INVADERS

60s	Zodiac AZ/1009	She's A Mod/INVADERS : Cruel Sea	20

COLWELL BROTHERS

56	Philips NBE 11047	COLWELL BROTHERS VOL. 1 (EP)	10
56	Philips NBE 11048	COLWELL BROTHERS VOL. 2 (EP)	10
60	Philips NBE 11117	AFRICA'S GOT THE ANSWER (EP)	10
60	Philips NBE 1118	THERE'LL BE A NEW WORLD (EP)	10

STEVE COLYER

75	Polydor 2058 647	Hey Mary/I Found My Sunshine	6

KEN COLYER('S JAZZMEN)

55	Decca F 10504	Early Hours/Cataract Rag	6
55	Decca F 10519	If I Ever Cease To Love/The Entertainer	6
55	Decca F 10565	It Looks Like A Big Time Tonight/Red Wing	6
56	Tempo A 117	Just A Closer Walk With Thee/Sheik Of Araby	7
56	Tempo A 120	If I Ever Cease To Love You/Isle Of Capri	7
56	Tempo A 126	My Bucket's Got A Hole In It/Wabash Blues	7
56	Tempo A 136	Maryland, My Maryland/The World Is Waiting For The Sunrise	7
56	Decca FJ 10755	All The Girls Go Crazy About The Way I Walk/Dippermouth Blues	6
61	Columbia DB 4676	The Happy Wanderer/Maryland, My Maryland	8
55	Tempo EXA 26	KEN COLYER JAZZMEN (EP)	8
60	Decca DFE 6645	WALKING THE BLUES (EP, also stereo STO 143)	10
60	Columbia SEG 8038	THIS IS JAZZ (EP)	8
61	Storyville SEP 392	TRAD JAZZ SCENE IN EUROPE VOL. 2 (EP)	8
61	Storyville SEP 412	WILDCAT BLUES (EP)	8
61	Columbia SEG 8104	THIS IS JAZZ VOL. 1 NO. 2 (EP)	10
61	Esquire EP 243	STOMPING (EP)	10
62	Columbia SEG 8145	THIS IS JAZZ VOL. 2 (EP)	10
62	Columbia SEG 8180	TOO BUSY (EP)	10
60s	Melodisc EPM7 105	KEN COLYER (EP)	10
66	K.C. KCS 11EP	GREEN CORN (EP)	10
54	Decca LF 1152	NEW ORLEANS TO LONDON (10" LP)	30
54	Decca LF 1196	BACK TO THE DELTA (10" LP, as Ken Colyer's Jazzmen & Skiffle Group)	30
55	Vogue LDE 161	KEN COLYER IN NEW ORLEANS (10" LP)	20
56	Tempo LAP 11	KEN COLYER'S JAZZMEN (10" LP)	20
57	Decca LK 4178	CLUB SESSION (LP)	15
58	Decca LF 1301	IN GLORY LAND (10" LP, as Ken Colyer & His Omega Brass Band)	15
59	Decca LF 1319	COLYER IN HAMBURG (10" LP)	15
59	Decca LK 4294	PLAYS STANDARDS (LP)	15
60	Columbia 33SX 1220	THIS IS JAZZ (LP)	12
61	Columbia 33SX 1297	THIS IS JAZZ VOL. 2 (LP, also stereo SCX 3360)	12
61	Columbia 33SX 1363	THIS IS THE BLUES VOL. 1 (LP)	12
64	77 LEU 12/7	KEN COLYER AND THE ORIGINAL CRANE RIVER BAND (LP)	20
64	77 LEU 12/10	THE REAL KEN COLYER (LP)	20
65	K.C. KCS 1001	WANDERING (LP)	20

KEN COLYER'S SKIFFLE GROUP

(see also Crane Skiffle Group)

55	Decca F 10631	Down By The Riverside/Take This Hammer	20
56	Decca FJ 10711	Streamline Train/Go Down Old Hannah	20
56	Decca FJ 10751	Down Bound Train/Mule Skinner	12
56	Decca FJ 10772	Old Riley/Stack O'Lee Blues	12
57	Decca FJ 10889	The Grey Goose/I Can't Sleep	12
57	Decca FJ 10926	Sporting Life/House Rent Stomp	12
57	Decca FJ 10972	Ella Speed/Go Down Sunshine	12
55	Decca DFE 6286	KEN COLYER'S SKIFFLE GROUP (EP, various coloured sleeves)	20
58	Decca DFE 6444	KEN COLYER'S SKIFFLE GROUP NO. 2 (EP)	20
60	Decca DFE 6563	KEN COLYER'S SKIFFLE GROUP IN HAMBURG (EP)	15

STEVE COLYER

75	Polydor 2058 647	Hey Mary/I Found My Sunshine	6

COMBAT 84

82	Victory VIC 1	ORDERS OF THE DAY (EP, wraparound p/s)	20
83	Victory VIC 2	Rapist/The Right To Choose/Barry Prudom (p/s)	20

PETER COMBE

78	Voyage VOY 001	Music Of The Day (Sing Birds Sing)/You Baby On My Mind	6

MINT VALUE £

COMBINATIONS

72	Punch PH 99	1 2 3 A B C/Zee	6

COME

(see also Whitehouse, New Order)

79	Come Org. WDC 88001	Come Sunday/Shaved Slits	15
79	Come Org. WDC 88203	PRESENT RAMPTON (LP)	80
81	Come Org. WDC 881012	I'M JACK (LP, orange vinyl with insert)	60

COMETS SHOWGROUP

70	LRC SCG 1	COMETS ON LOCATION (LP, private pressing, handmade sleeve)	50

RORY COMMADORE

(see under Tindersticks)

COMMANCHES

(see also Bobby Allen)

64	Pye 7N 15609	Tomorrow/Missed Your Loving	10

COMMANDERS

(see also Louis Armstrong)

55	Brunswick 05366	The Elephants' Tango/Commanders Overture	5
55	Brunswick 05433	The Cat From Coos Bay/Camptown Boogie	5
55	Brunswick 05467	The Monster/Cornball No. 1	5

COMMENDABLES

80s	Lip CC 1	London E1/Decaying House	10

COMMERCIALS

81	Fast Product COM 1	Sixteen Again And Again/The Heroine Dies/Simon (p/s)	8

COMMITTED

79	Ace ACE 006	Crash Victim/British Crimes/Fast Lane/Advertising (500 only)	100

COMMITTEE

68	Liberty LBF 15154	Hard Way/Hey You	15

COMMITTEE

69	Pye 7N 17826	Sleep Tight Honey/Memories Of Melinda	6

COMMODORES

55	London HLD 8209	Riding On A Train/Uranium	1000
55	London HLD 8209	Riding On A Train/Uranium (78)	120
56	London HLD 8251	Speedo/Whole Lotta Shakin' Goin' On	1000
56	London HLD 8251	Speedo/Whole Lotta Shakin' Goin' On (78)	120
69	Atlantic 584 273	Keep On Dancing/Rise Up	30

COMMON ROUND

70s	Galliard GAL 4015	FOUR PENCE A DAY (LP)	15

PERRY COMO

(see also Fontane Sisters, Betty Hutton)

53	HMV 7M 102	The Ruby And The Pearl/My Love And Devotion	15
53	HMV 7M 110	Some Enchanted Evening/Bali Ha'i	15
53	HMV 7M 118	Don't Let The Stars Get In Your Eyes/To Know You (Is To Love You) (B-side with Fontane Sisters)	50
53	HMV 7M 124	Wild Horses/Please Believe Me	10
53	HMV 7M 138	My Lady Loves To Dance/A Bushel And A Peck (B-side with Betty Hutton)	10
53	HMV 7M 149	My One And Only Heart/Say You're Mine Again	10
53	HMV 7M 155	Hello, Young Lovers/We Kiss In A Shadow	10
53	HMV 7M 163	Pa-Paya Mama/Why Did You Leave Me?	10
54	HMV 7M 175	You Alone/Surprising	10
54	HMV 7M 200	Idle Gossip/Look Out The Window	10
54	HMV 7M 215	Wanted/Give Me Your Hand	10
54	HMV 7M 241	Hit And Run Affair/If You Were Only Mine	10
54	HMV 7M 263	There Never Was A Night So Beautiful/Papa Loves Mambo	10
54	HMV 7M 278	Frosty The Snowman/The Twelve Days Of Christmas	10
55	HMV 7M 296	Ko Ko Mo (I Love You So)/You'll Always Be My Lifetime Love	15
55	HMV 7M 305	Door Of Dreams/Nobody	10
55	HMV 7M 326	There's No Place Like Home For The Holidays/Tina Marie	10
56	HMV 7M 366	Fooled/The Rose Tattoo	10
56	HMV 7M 404	Hot Diggity (Dog Ziggity Boom)/My Funny Valentine	15
56	HMV 7MC 39	Hot Diggity (Dog Ziggity Boom)/Juke Box Baby (export issue)	25
56	HMV POP 240	Glendora/More	15
56	HMV 7MC 49	Glendora/More (export issue)	15
56	HMV POP 271	Moonlight Love/Chincherinchee	10
57	HMV POP 304	Somebody Up There Likes Me/Dream Along With Me (I'm On My Way To A star)	10
57	HMV 7MC 51	Somebody Up There Likes Me/Dream Along With Me (I'm On My Way To A Star) (export issue)	10
57	HMV POP 328	Round And Round/My House Is Your House	10
57	RCA RCA 1001	The Girl With The Golden Braids/My Little Baby	10
57	HMV POP 369	Silk Stockings/Childhood Is A Meadow	10
57	HMV POP 394	As Time Goes By/All At Once You Love Her	10
60	RCA RCA 1170	Delaware/I Know What God Is (78)	15
54	HMV DLP 1026	PERRY COMO SINGS (10" LP)	20

LES COMPAGNONS DE LA CHANSON

53	Columbia SCM 5005	The Three Bells (The Jimmy Brown Song)/Ave Maria	10
53	Columbia SCM 5056	The Galley Slave/Dreams Never Grow Old	7

MINT VALUE £

COMPANY
(see also Whitesnake)

79	United Artists BP 326	We Wish You Well/Right Time For Love	30

COMPANY

80	Incus INCUS 36	FABLES (LP)	50
80	Incus INCUS 38	FICTIONS (LP)	50
82	Incus INCUS 46	EPIPHANY (LP)	50
82	Incus INCUS 47	EPIPHANIES (LP)	50
83	Incus INCUS 51	TRIOS (LP)	50

COMPASS

74	MAM 115	No More Whiskey/Maybe She Will	7

COMPLETE CYCLE

70	Jay Boy BOY 23	I'm On The Road Again/Back On The Road Again	6

COMPLEX
(see also Monsoon, Misfits)

70	CLPM 001	COMPLEX (LP, private pressing, 99 copies only)	750
71	Deroy	THE WAY WE FEEL (LP, private pressing, 99 copies only)	600

COMPLEXXION
(see also wavelength)

79	UK Records INT 584	So Much In Love/Weekend (in p/s with bonus floppy gold disc)	8
79	UK Records INT 584	So Much In Love/Weekend	5

COMPROMISE

66	CBS 202050	You Will Think Of Me/Love Minus Zero	7

COMSAT ANGELS

79	Junta JUNTA 1	Red Planet/I Get Excited/Specimen No. 2 (p/s)	6
79	Junta JUNTA 1	Red Planet/I Get Excited/Specimen No. 2 (p/s, later reissue on red vinyl)	8

BOBBY COMSTOCK (& COUNTS)

59	Top Rank JAR 223	The Tennessee Waltz/Sweet Talk	8
60	London HLE 9080	Jambalaya/Let's Talk It Over (as Bobby Comstock & Counts)	20
63	Stateside SS 163	Let's Stomp/I Want To Do It	15
63	Stateside SS 221	Susie Baby/Take A Walk	15
65	United Artists UP 1086	I'm A Man/I'll Make You Glad	20

COMUS
(see also Gong, Henry Cow, Esperanto Rock Orchestra)

71	Dawn DNX 2506	Diana/In The Lost Queen's Eyes/Winter Is A Coloured Bird (p/s)	80
71	Dawn DNLS 3019	FIRST UTTERANCE (LP, gatefold sleeve with lyric sheet, orange label)	400
74	Virgin V 2018	TO KEEP FROM CRYING (LP, twin Virgin label)	40

CON-CHORDS

65	Polydor BM 56059	You Can't Take It Away/Let Me Walk With You	25

CONCORDE

70	Attack ATT 8020	Let Me Out/I Belong To You	12

CONCORDS

66	Emblem JDR 303	SOUL PURPOSE (LP)	30

CONCORDS

69	Blue Cat BS 170	Buttoo/I Need Your Loving	40

CONCRETE SOX

88	C.O.R GURT 10	YOUR TURN NEXT (LP, with insert)	15

CONDEMNED 84

86	RFB SIN 2	Oi Ain't Dead!/Under Her Thumb/Follow The Leader/The Nutter (7", p/s, blue vinyl)	20
86	RFB SIN 2	Oi Ain't Dead!/Under Her Thumb/Follow The Leader/The Nutter (12", p/s, blue vinyl)	25
87	RFB SIN 3	IN SEARCH OF THE NEW BREED (12" EP)	25
88	Oi! OIR 003	BATTLE SCARRED (LP)	22
88	Grade 1	FACE THE AGGRESSION (LP)	22

JEFF CONDON

63	MGM MGM 1221	(Walkin' In) Freddy's Footsteps/Never You Mind	7

HOWIE G. CONDOR

65	Fontana TF 613	Big Noise From Winnetka/The Fix	10

CONEY ISLAND KIDS

55	London HLJ 8207	Baby, Baby You/Moonlight Beach	50

CONFLICT

82	Crass 221984/1	THE HOUSE THAT MAN BUILT (EP, foldout poster p/s)	6
82	Xntrix XN 2001	LIVE AT THE CENTRE IBERICO (EP, with insert)	6
83	Corp. Christi CHRIST IT'S 4	A Nation Of Animal Lovers/Liberate (poster p/s)	6
83	Mortarhate MORT EX001	The Serenade Is Dead (12" with insert)	8
85	Mortarhate MORT 15	The Battle Continues (both sides) (p/s, different colours, with insert)	5
88	FUND 1	FROM PROTEST TO RESISTANCE (LP, mail order, w/l, stickered plain sleeve)	12

CONGO ASHANTI ROY

82	On-U Sound DP 08	Hands & Feet/African Blood (10")	15

CONGOS

77	Black Swan BS 1	Congo Man/Congo Man Chant (12")	40
81	Go-Feet BEAT 2	HEART OF THE CONGOS (LP)	25

CONGREGATION

71	Columbia DB 8830	Softly Whispering I Love You/When Susie Takes The Plane	5

MINT VALUE £

ARTHUR CONLEY
(see also Soul Clan)

67	Atlantic 584 083	Sweet Soul Music/Let's Go Steady	8
67	Atlantic 584 121	Shake, Rattle And Roll/You Don't Have To See Me	8
67	Atlantic 584 143	Whole Lotta Woman/Love Comes And Goes	8
68	Atlantic 584 175	Funky Street/Put Our Love Together	8
68	Atlantic 584 197	People Sure Act Funny/Burning Fire	8
68	Atlantic 584 224	Aunt Dora's Love Soul Shack/Is That You Love	8
69	Atco 226 004	Star Revue/Love Sure Is A Powerful Thing	7
70	Atco 226 011	They Call The Wind Maria/Hurt	5
70	Atlantic 2091 025	All Day Singing/God Bless	5
71	Atlantic 2091 106	Sweet Soul Music/Shake, Rattle And Roll	5
71	Atlantic 2091 120	I'm Living Good/I'm So Glad You're Here	5
72	Capricorn K 17506	Rita/More Sweet Soul Music	5
67	Atlantic 587 069	SWEET SOUL MUSIC (LP)	40
68	Atlantic 587 084	SHAKE, RATTLE AND ROLL (LP)	25
68	Atlantic 587/588 128	SOUL DIRECTION (LP)	25
69	Atco 228 019	MORE SWEET SOUL (LP)	20

CONNARD

68	Spot JW 11	Amadhan/Desdemona	50

BRIAN CONNELL & ROUND SOUND

66	Mercury MF 956	Just My Kind Of Loving/Something You've Got	10
66	Mercury MF 991	The Same Thing's Happened To Me/Mister Porter	10
68	Philips BF 1661	What Good Am I/Just Another Wedding Day	10
68	Philips BF 1718	I Know/Mister Travel Company	35

RAY CONNIFF & ROCKIN' RHYTHM BOYS

55	Vogue Coral QW 5001	Piggy Bank Boogie/Short Stuff	18
68	CBS (S)BPG 63276	HOW TO SAVE A MARRIAGE AND RUIN YOUR LIFE (LP, soundtrack)	12

BILLY CONNOLLY
(see also Humblebums)

72	Transatlantic TRA 258	LIVE! (LP)	12

BRIAN CONNOLLY
(see also Sweet)

82	Carrere CAR 231	Hypnotised/Fade Away (p/s)	18

CHRIS CONNOR

59	London HLE 8869	Hallelujah I Love Him So/I Won't Cry Anymore	15
59	London HLE 8869	Hallelujah I Love Him So/I Won't Cry Anymore (78)	12
60	London HLK 9124	I Only Want Some/That's My Desire	10
56	London EZ-N 19010	CHRIS CONNOR SINGS LULLABYS OF BIRDLAND (EP, with Ellis Larkin Trio)	15
57	London RE-N 1093	LONDON'S GIRL FRIENDS - NO. 2 (EP)	15
56	London HA-K 2030	PRESENTING CHRIS CONNOR (LP, also stereo SAH-K 6032)	20
56	London LZ-N 14007	SINGS LULLABYS FOR LOVERS (10" LP)	15
57	London HB-N 1074	CHRIS (10" LP)	15
57	London HA-K 2066	HE LOVES ME, HE LOVES ME NOT (LP)	15
60	London LZ-N 14036	THIS IS CHRIS (10" LP)	15
60	London LTZ-K 15142	A JAZZ DATE WITH (LP)	15
60	London LTZ-K 15151	CHRIS CRAFT (LP)	15
60	London Jazz LTZ-K 15183	THE BALLAD OF THE SAD CAFÉ (LP)	15
60	London Jazz LTZ-K 15185	WITCHCRAFT (LP)	15
60	London Jazz LTZ-K 15195	CHRIS IN PERSON (LP, also stereo SAH-K 6088)	15
61	London SAH-K 6190	DOUPLE EXPOSURE (LP, with Maynard Ferguson)	15
61	Columbia SX 1377	TWOS COMPANY (LP, with Maynard Ferguson)	12

EDRIC CONNOR

57	Oriole CB 1362	Manchester United Calypso/Yorumba Highlife (78)	10

KENNETH CONNOR

59	Top Rank JAR 138	Rail Road Rock/Ramona	10
61	Fontana H 321	Nearly A Nasty Accident/Smile	8

PAUL CONNOR

71	Polydor 2121045	Little Sparrow/I Don't Love You Any More	35

TIM CONNOR

62	HMV POP 1007	Lost Love/Down	15
62	HMV POP 1096	Take This Message/Maybe	15
62	HMV POP 1056	Without A Shoulder To Cry On/I've Fallen In Love	15

CAROL CONNORS
(see also Teddy Bears)

62	London HLN 9619	Big Big Love/Two Rivers	20

NORMAN CONNORS

74	Buddah BDS 5611	SLEWFOOT (LP)	20
77	Buddah BDLP 4043	AQUARIAN DREAM (LP)	30
77	Buddah BDLP 4043	YOU ARE MY STARSHIP (LP)	18

CONNY

61	HMV POP 867	Midi Midinette/CONNY & REX GILDO: Yes My Darling	15
61	Columbia DB 4714	No One Can Tell Me I'm Too Young/Lovable	20
62	Columbia DB 4845	Gino/Midi-Midinette	20

CONQUERORS
(see also Stranger Cole & Conquerors, Baba Brooks)

67	Doctor Bird DB 1119	Won't You Come Home Now?/Oh That Day	50
67	Treasure Isle TI 7035	Lonely Street/I Fell In Love	40
69	Amalgamated AMG 832	Secret Weapon (actually by Ansell Collins)/Jumpy Jumpy Girl	40

MINT VALUE £

69	High Note HS 016	If You Can't Beat Them/Anywhere You Want To Go	12
69	High Note HS 025	National Dish/Mr D.J.	12
72	Fab FAB 22	You Hold The Handles/SOUL REBELS : Bongo Skank	150

BOB CONRAD

61	Warner Bros WB 54	Bye Bye Baby/Love You	10

JESS CONRAD

(see also Guvners)

60	Decca F 11236	Cherry Pie/There's Gonna Be A Day	8
60	Decca F 11259	Unless You Meant It/Out Of Luck	12
61	Decca F 11315	Mystery Girl/The Big White House	8
61	Decca F 11348	This Pullover/Why Am I Living?	7
61	Decca F 11375	Oh You Beautiful Doll/I See You	6
61	Decca F 11394	Walkaway/Every Breath I Take	6
61	Decca F 11412	Twist My Wrist/Hey Little Girl (some in p/s)	12
61	Decca F 11412	Twist My Wrist/Hey Little Girl (no p/s)	5
62	Decca F 11511	Pretty Jenny/You Can Do It If You Try	12
63	Decca F 11620	It's About Time/As You Like It	6
63	Columbia DB 4969	Take Your Time/I Know You	6
64	Columbia DB 7223	Pussycat/Tempted	6
65	Columbia DB 7561	Things I'd Like To Say/Don't Turn Around	6
65	Pye 7N 15849	Hurt Me/It Can Happen To You	20
69	President PT 269	Other Side Of Life/See The Tinker Ride	5
70	President PT 292	Pussycat/Crystal Ball Dream	5
71	President PT 357	Here She Comes Again/My Idea	5
60	Decca DFE 6666	JESS CONRAD (EP)	20
62	Decca DFE 6702	TWIST MY WRIST (EP)	20
63	Decca DFE 8524	THE HUMAN JUNGLE (EP, with Rhet Stoller)	20
61	Decca LK 4390	JESS FOR YOU (LP)	40

TONI CONRAD & FAUST

(see also Faust)

72	Caroline C 1501	OUTSIDE THE DREAM SYNDICATE (LP)	40

CONSCIOUS MINDS

(see also Ken Boothe, Jamaicans, B.B.Seaton, Charmers)

71	Big BG 318	Jamaican Boy/Brainwash	10
71	Ackee ACK 141	Paul, Marcus And Norman/Version	7
71	Punch PH 97	Paul, Marcus And Norman/Version (reissue)	6
71	Escort ERT 857	Peace Treaty/Brainwash	7

CONSOLERS

67	President PT165	Someone Must Answer/No One	8

CONSORTIUM

68	Pye 7N 17635	All The Love In The World/Spending My Life Saying Goodbye	10
69	Pye 7N 17725	When The Day Breaks/Day The Train Never Came	35
69	Pye 7N 17797	Beggar Man/Cynthia Serenity	18
69	Pye 7N 17841	I Don't Want Her Anymore/The House Upon The Hill	7
70	Trend TNT 52	Melanie Cries Alone/Copper Coloured Years	7

JACK CONSTANZO & ORCHESTRA

61	London HLG 9401	Theme From 'Route 66'/'Naked City' Theme	8

CONSTELLATION ORCHESTRA

78	CBS 6585	Perfect Love Affair/Cosmic Melody	10

CONSTRUCTION

90	White SDT17	Sudden Impact - In A State Of Experimentation	40
90	White SDT30	Transmission/Revenge Of The Dragon (12")	100
91	White SDT37	Change Your Attitude/Time To Get Raw (12")	75

CONSUMATES

68	Coxsone CS 7054	What Is It/ROLAND ALPHONSO: Musical Happiness	35

CONTINENTALS

62	Island WI 010	Going Crazy/Give Me All Your Love	25

CONTINENTALS

79	CBS S 7476	Fizz Pop (Modern Rock)/(I Lost My Love On A) 747	5

CONTINENTAL UPTIGHT BAND

71	Columbia SCX 6454	BEAUTIFUL FRIENDSHIP (LP, black/silver/white boxed Columbia label)	25

CONTINUUM

70	RCA Victor SF 8157	CONTINUUM (LP, gatefold, orange labels)	20
71	RCA Victor SF 8196	AUTUMN GRASS (LP, gatefold sleeve, orange label)	40

CONTOURS

62	Oriole CB 1763	Do You Love Me/Move Mister Man	30
63	Oriole CB 1799	Shake Sherry/You Better Get In Line	60
63	Oriole CB 1831	Don't Let Him Be Your Baby/It Must Be Love	80
64	Stateside SS 299	Can You Do It/I'll Stand By You	50
64	Stateside SS 299	Can You Do It/I'll Stand By You (DJ Copy)	90
65	Stateside SS 381	Can You Jerk Like Me/That Day She Needed Me	55
65	Stateside SS 381	Can You Jerk Like Me/That Day She Needed Me (DJ Copy)	90
65	Tamla Motown TMG 531	First I Look At The Purse/Searching For A Girl	55
65	Tamla Motown TMG 531	First I Look At The Purse/Searching For A Girl (DJ Copy)	120
66	Tamla Motown TMG 564	Determination/Just A Little Misunderstanding	50
66	Tamla Motown TMG 564	Determination/Just A Little Misunderstanding (DJ Copy)	130
67	Tamla Motown TMG 605	It's So Hard Being A Loser/Your Love Grows More Precious Every Day	30
67	Tamla Motown TMG 605	It's So Hard Being A Loser/Your Love Grows More Precious Every Day (DJ Copy)	70
70	Tamla Motown TMG 723	Just A Little Misunderstanding/First I Look At The Purse	10

			MINT VALUE £
70	Tamla Motown TMG 723	Just A Little Misunderstanding/First I Look At The Purse (DJ Copy)	40
65	Tamla Motown TME 2002	THE CONTOURS (EP)	120
63	Oriole PS 40043	DO YOU LOVE ME (LP)	250

CONTRABAND
(see also Mae McKenna)

74	Transatlantic BIG 518	Lady For Today/On The Road	6
74	Transatlantic TRA 278	CONTRABAND (LP, with lyric insert)	18

CONTRAST

69	Orange OAS 202	Hey That's No Way To Say Goodbye/We Can Make It If We Try	10

CONTRASTS featuring BOB MORRISON
(see also Bill Forbes)

64	Parlophone R 5095	I Can't Get You Out Of My Mind/Click When You're In Love	8
64	Parlophone R 5190	Call Me/Come On Let's Go	5
68	Monument MON 1018	What A Day/Lonely Child	10

CONTROLLED BLEEDING

86	Sterile SR 11	HEADCRACK (LP)	20

CONUNDRUM & RICHARD HARVEY
(see also Bert Jansch, Shirley Collins)

78	Streetsong No. 1	Black Birds Of Brittany/SHIRLEY COLLINS & ANNIE POWER: The Mariners Farewell (poster p/s)	18

CONVAIRS

66	HMV POP 1549	Tomorrow Is A Long Time/Midnight Mary	10

BERT CONVY & THUNDERBIRDS
(see also Cheers, Thunderbirds)

55	London HLB 8190	C'mon Back/Hoo Bop De Bow	150
55	London HLB 8190	C'mon Back/Hoo Bop De Bow (78)	40
56	Capitol CL 14601	Heaven On Earth/CHEERS: Que Pasa Muchacha	20
56	Capitol CL 14601	Heaven On Earth/CHEERS: Que Pasa Muchacha (78)	20

CONNIE CONWAY

60	London HA-W 2214	CONNIE CONWAY (LP)	20

STEVE CONWAY

55	Columbia SEG 7573	MEMORIES OF STEVE CONWAY (EP, company sleeve)	12
56	Columbia SEG 7649	MORE MEMORIES OF STEVE CONWAY (EP)	12

JIMMY CONWELL

72	Jay Boy BOY 64	Cigarette Ashes/Second Hand Happiness	10
72	Jay Boy BOY 64	Cigarette Ashes/Second Hand Happiness (DJ Copy)	25

COO-COO RACHAS

59	Capitol CL 15024	Chili Beans/Track Down	15

RY COODER
(see also Captain Beefheart, Don Everly)

71	Reprise RS 23497	How Can A Poor Man Stand Such Times And Live/Goin' To Brownsville	7
71	Reprise RSLP 6402	RY COODER (LP)	15
72	Reprise K 44142	INTO THE PURPLE VALLEY (LP, with lyric sheet)	12

ENGLAND COOK

72	Explosion EX 2063	Samba Girl/NOW GENERATION: Samba (Version)	5

LITTLE JOE COOK (U.K.)
(see also Chris Farlowe, Beazers)

65	Sue WI 385	Stormy Monday Blues (Parts 1 & 2)	50

LITTLE JOE COOK (U.S.)

68	Sonet SON 2002	Don't You Have Feelings?/Hold On To Your Money	20
74	Sonet SON 2041	Hold On To Your Money/Don't You Have Feelings? (reissue, sides reversed)	8

PETER COOK
(see also Peter London)

65	Pye 7N 15847	Georgia/There And Bach Again	40

PETER COOK

65	Decca F 12182	The Ballad Of Spotty Muldoon/Lovely Lady Of The Roses	12
60s	Lyntone LYN 776	Watney's Pale Ale (Flexi, p/s)	10
61	Parlophone PMC 1145	BEYOND THE FRINGE (LP, with other artists)	20
63	Parlophone PMC 1190	BRIDGE ON THE RIVER WYE (LP, with other artists; mono)	20
63	Parlophone PCS 3036	BRIDGE ON THE RIVER WYE (LP, with other artists; stereo)	25
63	Parlophone PMC 1198	PETER COOK PRESENTS THE ESTABLISHMENT (LP, with other artists)	20
65	Decca LK 4722	PETER COOK PRESENTS MISTY MR. WISTY (LP)	25
65	Transatlantic TRA 131	PRIVATE EYE'S BLUE RECORD (LP, with other artists)	25

PETER COOK & DUDLEY MOORE
(see also Dudley Moore Trio)

62	Parlophone R 4969	Excerpts From "Beyond The Fringe": Sitting On The Bench/The End Of The World (with Alan Bennett & Jonathan Miller)	12
65	Decca F 12158	Goodbyeee (& Dudley Moore Trio)/DUDLEY MOORE TRIO: Not Only But Also	10
66	Decca F 12380	Isn't She A Sweetie/Bo Dudley	12
67	Decca F 12551	The L.S. Bumble Bee/The Bee Side	20
67	Decca F 12710	Bedazzled/Love Me	50
65	Parlophone GEP 8940	PETER COOK AND DUDLEY MOORE (EP)	10
65	Decca DFE 8644	BY APPOINTMENT (EP)	10
65	Decca LK 4703	NOT ONLY PETER COOK BUT ALSO DUDLEY MOORE (LP)	15
66	Decca LK 4785	ONCE MOORE WITH COOK (LP)	15
68	Decca SKL 4923	BEDAZZLED (LP, stereo, soundtrack)	90
68	Decca LK 4981	GOODBYE AGAIN (LP, excerpts from TV series)	20
71	Decca LK 5080	NOT ONLY BUT ALSO (LP)	20

MINT VALUE £

COOK COUNTY

77	Barak BAR 5	Space Dancin'/Star Wars	15

PAUL COOKE

71	Ackee ACK 129	That Girl Was Mine/No Harm	5

ROGER (JAMES) COOKE

(see also David & Jonathan)

68	NEMS 56 3719	If I Didn't Have You/I Know It's You	7
68	Columbia DB 8458	Skyline Pigeon/I'm Burning	7
69	Columbia DB 8510	Not That It Matters Anymore/Paper Chase	6
69	Columbia DB 8556	Stop/Someday	6
69	Columbia DB 8596	Smiling Through My Tears/Ain't That A Wonderful Thing (with Eve Graham)	8
70	Columbia DB 8729	Jubilation/Anticipation Grows	6
71	Columbia DB 8761	If You Would Stay/Mama Packed A Picnic Tea	6
71	Columbia DB 8806	People I Gotta Dream/Today I Killed A Man I Didn't Know	6
70	Regal Zonophone	We Will Get By/My Home City (as Roger Cook)	6
73	Regal Zonophone RZ 3074	She/Stay With Me (as Roger Cook)	6
70	Columbia SCX 6388	STUDY (LP, boxed logo on label)	20
72	Regal Zono. SRZA 8508	MEANWHILE ... BACK AT THE WORLD (LP, gatefold sleeve, red/silver label)	30
73	Regal Zono. SLRZ 1035	MINSTREL IN FLIGHT (LP)	20

SAM COOKE

57	London HLU 8506	You Send Me/Summertime	35
57	London HLU 8506	You Send Me/Summertime (78)	20
58	London HLU 8615	That's All I Need To Know/I Don't Want To Cry	50
58	London HLU 8615	That's All I Need To Know/I Don't Want To Cry (78)	30
58	HMV POP 568	Love You Most Of All/Win Your Love For Me	40
58	HMV POP 568	Love You Most Of All/Win Your Love For Me (78)	40
59	HMV POP 610	Everybody Likes To Cha Cha Cha/The Little Things You Do	40
59	HMV POP 610	Everybody Likes To Cha Cha Cha/The Little Things You Do (78)	50
59	HMV POP 642	Only Sixteen/Let's Go Steady Again	10
59	HMV POP 642	Only Sixteen/Let's Go Steady Again (78)	70
59	HMV POP 675	There, I've Said It Again/One Hour Ahead Of The Posse	30
60	London HLU 9046	Happy In Love/I Need You Now	40
60	RCA RCA 1184	Teenage Sonata/If You Were The Only Girl	20
60	HMV POP 754	Wonderful World/Along The Navajo Trail	15
60	RCA RCA 1202	Chain Gang/I Fall In Love Everyday	10
61	RCA RCA 1221	Sad Mood/Love Me	15
61	RCA RCA 1230	That's It, I Quit, I'm Movin' On/What Do You Say	15
61	RCA RCA 1242	Cupid/Farewell, My Darling	8
61	RCA RCA 1260	Feel It/It's Alright	15
62	RCA RCA 1277	Twisting The Night Away/One More Time	5
62	RCA RCA 1296	Bring It On Home To Me/Having A Party	8
62	RCA RCA 1310	Nothing Can Change This Love/Somebody Have Mercy	8
63	RCA RCA 1327	Send Me Some Loving/Baby Baby Baby	20
63	RCA RCA 1341	Another Saturday Night/Love Will Find A Way	8
63	RCA RCA 1361	Frankie And Johnny/Cool Train	8
63	RCA RCA 1367	Little Red Rooster/Shake Rattle And Roll	12
64	RCA RCA 1386	Good News/Basin Street Blues	10
64	RCA RCA 1405	Good Times/Tennessee Waltz	12
64	RCA RCA 1420	Cousin Of Mine/That's Where It's At	15
65	RCA RCA 1436	Shake/A Change Is Gonna Come	30
65	RCA RCA 1452	It's Got The Whole World Shakin'/Ease My Troublin' Mind	20
65	RCA RCA 1476	Sugar Dumpling/Bridge Of Tears	40
65	RCA RCA 1476	Sugar Dumpling/Bridge Of Tears (DJ Copy)	70
68	RCA RCA 1701	Another Saturday Night/DUANE EDDY: Dance With The Guitar Man (w/drawn)	15
63	RCA RCX 7117	HEART AND SOUL (EP)	30
64	RCA RCX 7128	SWING SWEETLY (EP)	40
58	HMV CLP 1261	SAM COOKE (LP, with Bumps Blackwell Orchestra)	130
59	HMV CLP 1273	ENCORE (LP)	100
61	RCA RD 27190	COOKE'S TOUR (LP, mono)	45
61	RCA SF 5076	COOKE'S TOUR (LP, stereo)	60
61	RCA RD 27215	HITS OF THE FIFTIES (LP, mono)	45
61	RCA RD SF 5098	HITS OF THE FIFTIES (LP, stereo)	60
61	RCA RD 27222	SWING LOW (LP)	50
62	RCA RD 27245	MY KIND OF BLUES (LP, mono)	40
62	RCA SF 5120	MY KIND OF BLUES (LP, stereo)	50
62	RCA RD 27263	TWISTIN' THE NIGHT AWAY (LP, mono)	40
62	RCA RD SF 5133	TWISTIN' THE NIGHT AWAY (LP, stereo)	50
63	RCA RDF 7539	MR. SOUL (LP, mono)	40
63	RCA SF 7539	MR. SOUL (LP, stereo)	50
63	RCA RD 7583	NIGHT BEAT (LP, mono)	40
63	RCA SF 7583	NIGHT BEAT (LP, stereo)	60
64	RCA RD 7635	AIN'T THAT GOOD NEWS (LP, mono)	35
64	RCA SF 7635	AIN'T THAT GOOD NEWS (LP, stereo)	45
65	RCA RD 7674	AT THE COPA (LP, mono)	35
65	RCA SF 7674	AT THE COPA (LP, stereo)	45
65	RCA RD 7730	SHAKE (LP, mono)	40
65	RCA SF 7730	SHAKE (LP, stereo)	55
65	London HA-U 8232	THE SOUL STIRRERS FEATURING SAM COOKE (LP)	90
66	RCA RD/SF 7764	TRY A LITTLE LOVE (LP)	40
66	Immediate IMLP 002	THE WONDERFUL WORLD OF SAM COOKE (LP)	50
74	BBC	SAM COOKE AND OTHERS (LP, for radio use)	70

COOKIES

(see also Earl-Jean, Cinderellas, Dorothy Jones)

62	London HLU 9634	Chains/Stranger In My Arms	25

MINT VALUE £

- 63 London HLU 9704 — Don't Say Nothin' Bad About My Baby/Softly In The Night — 25
- 63 Colpix PX 11012 — Will Power/I Want A Boy For My Birthday — 30
- 64 Colpix PX 11020 — Girls Grow Up Faster Than Boys/Only To Other People — 30

COOL

(see also Elastic Band)

- 69 De Wolfe DW/LP 3136 — POP SOUNDS (LP, music library only) — 35

OLIVER COOL

- 60 Columbia DB 4552 — Oliver Cool/I Like Girls — 10
- 61 Columbia DB 4616 — Give Me The Summertime/I Said Yeah — 10

COOL BREEZE

- 71 Patheway PAT 103 — People Ask What Love Is/There'll Be No More Sad Tomorrows — 20
- 72 Decca F 13324 — Summertime Sunshine/Sing Out Your Love — 6
- 75 Bus Stop BUS 1023 — Do It Some More/Citizen Jones — 6
- 75 Bus Stop BUS 1027 — You Gotta Love Me More/Turn On The Sun — 6

COOL CATS

- 68 Jolly JY 007 — What Kind Of Man/HEMSLEY MORRIS: Little Things — 40
- 69 Jolly JY 009 — Hold Your Love/ALVA LEWIS: Hang My Head And Cry — 60

COOLERS

- 73 Bread BR 1112 — The Youth Of Today/TYRONE TAYLOR: Close Observation — 6

EDDIE COOLEY & DIMPLES

- 57 Columbia DB 3873 — Priscilla/Got A Little Woman — 250
- 57 Columbia DB 3873 — Priscilla/Got A Little Woman (78) — 50

SPADE COOLEY & HIS FIDDLIN' FRIENDS

- 51 Brunswick 04812 — Horse Hair Boogie/Down Yonder (78) — 10

COOL HAND FLEX

- 92 De Underground UG 08 — Your Risk/Untitled/Untitled (12", white label) — 12
- 92 Ruff Groove HN 05 — Lock Me Up/I Don't Want No (12", stamped white label) — 10
- 92 Ruff Groove UG 10 — Welcome/Way Back Then/Woman (12") — 10
- 92 In Touch INT 001 — On The Strength/Your Risk/Go Insane (12") — 25

RITA COOLIDGE

- 83 A&M AM 007 — All Time High/All Time High (Extended Instrumental) (p/s) — 6
- 83 Scanlite BOND 1 — All Time High/All Time High (Extended Instrumental) (p/s) — 12

COOLIES

- 77 Electric WOT 14 — Geisha Girl/Calling Out Your Name — 25

JOE COOL & KILLERS

(see also Killers)

- 77 Ariola ARO 165 — I Just Don't Care/My Way — 6

COOL MEN

- 58 Parlophone GEP 8739 — COOL FOR CATS NO. 1 (EP) — 25
- 58 Parlophone GEP 8752 — COOL FOR CATS NO. 2 (EP) — 25

COOL NOTES

- 80 Jama JADC 0008 — Billy The Kid/Kidnap My Baby (12") — 12
- 80 Jama JADC 0024 — My Tune (Re-Mix)/Version (12") — 30
- 84 Sour Grapes SGR 116 — I Wanna Dance (Extended)/Blowin It (12") — 80
- 84 Sour Grapes SG 116 — I Wanna Dance/Blowin It — 25
- 84 Mass Media — Forgot How To Love/Why Can't We Be Friends (12") — 30
- 85 Abstract Dance 12AD 001 — You're Never Too Young/Sound Of Summer (12") — 15
- 84 Mass Media MMLP 2 — DOWN TO EARTH (LP) — 70

COOL SPOON (Jeff Dixon & Alton Ellis)

- 67 Coxsone CS 7031 — Yakety Yak/SOUL VENDORS: Drum Song — 25

COOL STICKY

- 68 Amalgamated AMG 825 — Train To Soulsville/ERIC MONTY MORRIS: Cinderella (actually by Errol Dunkley) — 50

CHRIS COOMBES

- 65 Holyground HG 110 — WHERE IT'S AT (EP, 99 only) — 35

NIGEL COOMBES & STEVE BERESFORD

- 80 Bead Records BEAD 16 — IMPROVISED VIOLIN AND PIANO DUETS (LP) — 25

ALICE COOPER

(see also Billion Dollar Babies)

- 71 Straight W 7209 — Eighteen/Body — 70
- 71 Warner Bros K 16127 — Under My Wheels/Desperado — 8
- 72 Warner Bros K 16188 — School's Out/Gutter Cat (p/s) — 10
- 72 Warner Bros K 16214 — Elected/Luney Tune (p/s) — 10
- 73 Warner Bros/Lyntone LYN 2585/6 — Slick Black Limousine/Extracts From: Unfinished Sweet/Elected/No More Mr Nice Guy/Billion Dollar Babies/I Love The Dead (33rpm flexi free with NME magazine) — 5
- 73 Warner Brothers K16262 — No More Mr. Nice Guy/Raped And Freezin' (possibly export only) — 20
- 74 Warner Bros K 16409 — School's Out/No More Mr. Nice Guy/Elected/Billion Dollar Babies (maxi-45) — 5
- 74 Chrysalis CHS 2069 — I'm Flash/ELKIE BROOKS: Sacrifice (p/s, promo only) — 35
- 75 Anchor ANC 1012 — Department Of Youth/Cold Ethyl (p/s) — 6
- 75 Anchor ANE 7001 — Welcome To My Nightmare/Department Of Youth/Black Widow/Only Women Bleed (EP, p/s) — 7
- 75 Anchor ANE 12001 — Welcome To My Nightmare/Department Of Youth/Black Widow/Only Women Bleed (12" EP, p/s) — 10
- 76 Warner Bros K 16792 — I Never Cry/Got To Hell (p/s) — 5
- 77 Warner Bros K 16935 — (No More) Love At Your Convenience/It's Hot Tonight (p/s, gothic type on label) — 5
- 80 Warner Bros K 17598 — Clones (We're All)/Model Citizen (p/s) — 8
- 86 MCA MCA 1090 — He's Back (The Man Behind The Mask)/Billion Dollar Babies (poster p/s) — 6
- 89 Epic ALICE 3 — Bed Of Nails/I'm Your Gun (p/s, with poster) — 8

MINT VALUE £

89	Epic ALICEP 3	Bed Of Nails/I'm Your Gun/Go To Hell (live) (12", picture disc)	8
69	Straight STS 1051	PRETTIES FOR YOU (LP, purple label, gatefold sleeve)	80
69	Straight STS 1061	EASY ACTION (LP, purple label, gatefold sleeve)	70
71	Straight STS 1065	LOVE IT TO DEATH (LP, purple label, gatefold sleeve)	60
71	Warner Bros K 56005	KILLER (LP, green label, gatefold sleeve with perforated foldout calendar)	30
72	Warner Bros K 56007	SCHOOL'S OUT (LP, green label, 'desktop' gatefold sleeve, with 'paper panties' inner)	60
73	Warner Bros K 56013	BILLION DOLLAR BABIES (LP, green label, gatefold embossed sleeve with attached perforated cards, with $ billion note & inner sleeve)	20
73	Warner Bros K 46177	LOVE IT TO DEATH (LP, reissue, green label, gatefold sleeve)	15
73	Warner Bros K 66021	SCHOOL DAYS (2-LP, gatefold sleeve, reissue of STS 1051 & 1061)	18
74	Warner Bros K 56018	MUSCLE OF LOVE (LP, 'cardboard box' sleeve, with insert & inner sleeve)	15

GARNELL COOPER & KINFOLKS

63	London HL 9757	Green Monkey/Long Distance	30

HENRY COOPER

76	DJM DJS 10734	Knock Me Down With A Feather/Knocked Out For Your Love (p/s)	12
76	DJM DJS 10734	Knock Me Down With A Feather/Knocked Out For Your Love	5

LES COOPER & SOUL ROCKERS

62	Stateside SS 142	Wiggle Wobble/Dig Yourself	20

MARTY COOPER CLAN

63	RCA Victor RD 7596	NEW SOUNDS - OLD GOODIES (LP)	15

MIKE COOPER

(see also Ian A. Anderson, Heron)

70	Dawn DNX 2501	Your Lovely Ways (Parts 1 & 2)/Watching You Fall (Parts 1 & 2) (p/s)	7
71	Dawn DNX 2511	Too Late Now/The Ballad Of Fulton Allen/Good Times (p/s)	7
72	Dawn DNS 1022	Time In Hand/Schwabisch Hall	6
60s	Saydisc SD 137	UP THE COUNTRY BLUES (EP)	80
68	Matchbox SDM 159	THE INVERTED WORLD (LP, with Ian A. Anderson)	70
69	Pye NSPL 18281	OH REALLY!? (LP, blue/black label with logo banner on top)	45
70	Dawn DNLS 3005	DO I KNOW YOU? (LP, gatefold sleeve, orange label)	30
70	Dawn DNLS 3011	TROUT STEEL (LP, with poster insert, gatefold sleeve, orange label)	35
71	Dawn DNLS 3026	PLACES I KNOW (LP, with insert, lilac label)	25
72	Dawn DNLS 3031	THE MACHINE GUN COMPANY (LP, lilac label)	25
74	Fresh Air 6370 500	LIFE AND DEATH IN PARADISE (LP)	20

TOMMY COOPER

61	Palette PG 9019	Don't Jump Off The Roof Dad/How Come There's No Dog Day?	15
67	Pye 7N 17259	Happy Tommy/Tom Tom The Piper's Son	10
78	Pye 7N 46061	We'll Meet Again/The Sheik Of Araby (p/s)	8
78	Pye 7N 46061	We'll Meet Again/The Sheik Of Araby	5

COOPERETTES

70s	Brunswick BR22	Shing A Ling/Don't Trust Him	15

COOPER TEMPLE CLAUSE

00s	Private pressing	The Crayon Demos/Who Needs Enemies?/Let's Kill Music/ Devil Walks In The Sand Demos (CD-R, in hand-crayoned sleeve)	50
01	Morning MORNING 2	THE HARDWARE EP (Way Out West/Sister Soul/ The Devil Walks In The Sand/ Solitude) (2 x 7", 1 black and 1 white vinyl, poly sleeves in box, 500 only)	30
01	Morning MORNING 6	THE WARFARE EP (Panzer Attack/ I'll Still Write/I'll Still Write [Acoustic]/Mansell) (2 x 7", 1 black and 1 white vinyl in box, 1000 only)	15
01	Morning MORNING 8	Let's Kill Music (Dirty Sanchez Mix)/Panzer Attack (Dirty Sanchez Mix) (12")	10
02	Morning MORNING 20	SEE THIS THROUGH AND LEAVE (6 x 7", limited, numbered box set)	12

COWBOY COPAS

(see also Johnny Bond)

54	Parlophone CMSP 10	I Can't Go On/A Wreath On The Door Of My Heart (export issue)	30
54	Parlophone MSP 6079	Tennessee Senorita/If You Will Let Me Be Your Love	30
54	Parlophone MSP 6109	A Heartbreak Ago/The Blue Waltz	30
55	Parlophone MSP 6164	I'll Waltz With You In My Dreams/Return To Sender	30
60	Melodisc M 1566	Alabama/I Can	20
55	Parlophone GEP 8527	FAVOURITE COWBOY SONGS (EP)	15
56	Parlophone GEP 8575	WESTERN STYLE (EP)	15
50s	Parlophone CGEP 3	COWBOY COPAS (EP, export issue)	15
62	Top Rank JKP 3014	COUNTRY MUSIC (EP)	15
63	Stateside SE 1003	COUNTRY HITS (EP)	15
61	Melodisc MLP 12-119	COWBOY COPAS (LP)	30
63	Stateside SL 10035	SONGS THAT MADE HIM FAMOUS (LP)	15
63	London HA-B 8088	COUNTRY ENTERTAINER NO. 1 (LP)	12
64	London HA-B 8180	STARS OF THE GRAND OLE OPRY - COWBOY COPAS (LP)	12

JULIAN COPE

(see also Teardrop Explodes, Rabbi Joseph Gordan)

87	Antar 4503	Interview/Christmas Mourning/Transmitting (fan club box set, with card, biography, membership card, letter, photos & stickers)	7
91	Island JC 1	Safesurfer/If You Love Me At All (33rpm, sold at gigs, stickered white sleeve)	6
94	K.A.K. (no cat. no.)	Paranormal In The West Country (Original Version)/(String Quartet Version)/ (Acoustic Version)/(Krankenhausmusik Version)/(Acoustic Version)/ (Krankenhausmusik Version) (Mail-order only via offer with "Queen Elizabeth" LP)	10
87	Island ILPS 9861	SAINT JULIAN (LP, with free 12" interview LP [JCCLP 1])	12
90	Zippo MoFoCo 1990	DROOLIAN (LP)	15
91	Island ILPSD 9977	PEGGY SUICIDE (2-LP)	20
92	Island ILPSD 9997	JEHOVAHKILL (2-LP, 4th side etched)	20
95	Echo ECHLP5	20 MOTHERS (2-LP)	20

KEN COPE & BREAKAWAYS

(see also Breakaways)

63	Pye 7N 15524	Hands Off, Stop Muckin' About/Why Am I So Shy	7

MINT VALUE £

SUZY COPE

61 HMV POP 941 — Teenage Fool/Juvenile Delinquent — 25
62 HMV POP 1047 — Not Never Not Now/Kisses And Tears — 25
63 HMV POP 1167 — Biggity Big/Doing What You Know Is Wrong — 25
65 CBS 201792 — You Can't Say I Never Told You/And Now I Don't Want You — 25

AL(L)AN COPELAND

57 Vogue Coral Q 72237 — Feeling Happy/You Don't Know — 15
57 Vogue Coral Q 72277 — How Will I Know?/Will You Still Be Mine — 7
59 Pye International 7N 25007 — Flip Flop/Lots More Love (as Allan Copeland) — 25
59 Pye International 7N 25007 — Flip Flop/Lots More Love (as Allan Copeland) (78) — 10

KEN COPELAND

57 London HLP 8423 — Pledge Of Love/MINTS: Night Air — 300
57 London HLP 8423 — Pledge Of Love/MINTS: Night Air (78) — 60

BOB & RON COPPER

63 EFDSS 1002 — BOB & RON COPPER (LP) — 35

COPPER FAMILY

71 Leader LED 2067 — A SONG FOR EVERY SEASON (LP, sampler, tracks from 4-LP set) — 40
71 Leader LEAB 404 — A SONG FOR ALL SEASONS (4xLP) — 70

COPPERFIELD

(see also Quartz)

69 Instant IN 004 — Any Old Time/I'm No Good For Her — 12
69 Parlophone R 5818 — I'll Hold Out My Hand/Far Away Love — 6

JOHNNY COPPIN

87 Rola RO 15 — FOREST & VALE (LP) — 20

COPS 'N ROBBERS

(see also Fairies)

64 Decca F 12019 — St. James Infirmary/There's Gotta Be A Reason — 60
65 Pye 7N 15870 — I Could Have Danced All Night/Just Keep Right On — 25
65 Pye 7N 15928 — It's All Over Now Baby Blue/I've Found Out — 25

COPY CATS

69 Bullet BU 419 — Copy Cat (with Derrick Morgan)/BUNNY LEE ALL STARS: Hot Lead — 12

CORAL

01 Deltasonic DLT 1 — SHADOWS FALL EP (Shadows Fall/The Ballad Of Simon Diamond/A Sparrow's Song) (CD, 1000 only) — 30
01 Deltasonic DLTCD 3 — THE OLDEST PATH EP (The Oldest Path/God Knows/Short Balled/Flys (CD, 1000 only, picture disc) — 20
04 Deltasonic DLTLP014 — MAGIC AND MEDICINE (LP) — 18

CORBAN

78 Acorn AC 002 — A BREAK IN THE CLOUDS (LP, with insert) — 18

HARRY CORBETT

61 Fontana TFE 17367 — SOOTY AND SWEEP (EP) — 10
61 Fontana TFE 17368 — SOOTY AND SWEEP (EP) — 10

HARRY H. CORBETT

(see also Wilfred Brambell, Wilfred Brambell & Harry H. Corbett, Faraway Folk)

67 Decca F 12714 — Flower Power Fred/(I'm) Saving All My Love (with Unidentified Flower Objects) — 25

MIKE CORBETT & JAY HIRSH

(see also Mr. Flood's Party)

71 Atlantic 2091-126 — Gypsey Child/Butterfly Day — 6
71 Atlantic 2400 141 — MIKE CORBETT & JAY HIRSH (LP, gatefold sleeve) — 20

RONNIE CORBETT

68 Columbia DB 8512 — Big Man/Fancy You Fancying Me — 5
70 Philips 6006 070 — It's All Going Up, Up, Up/Put On A Happy Face — 5

CORBY & CHAMPAGNE

66 Pye 7N 17203 — Time Marches On/I'll Be Back — 5

JASON CORD

69 Chapter One CH 102 — I've Got My Eyes On You/I Can't Take No More Of Your Lies — 6
69 Chapter One CH 110 — Why Shouldn't I/Spring Never Came Twice — 6

FRANK CORDELL & HIS ORCHESTRA

56 HMV 7M 397 — Port-Au-Prince/"Double Cross" TV Theme — 10
56 HMV 7M 419 — Sadie's Shawl/Flamenco Love — 10
61 HMV POP 824 — The Black Bear/Darling Charlie — 10
61 HMV POP 852 — Theme From 'The Rebel'/Ou La La — 10
63 HMV CSD 1475 — HERE THIS! (LP) — 15
58 HMV CSD 1251 — THE MELODY LINGERS ON (LP) — 15

PHIL CORDELL

(see also Thursday's Children)

69 Warner Bros WB 8001 — Pumping The Water/Red Lady — 35

CORDES

65 Cavern Sound IMSTL 1 — Give Her Time/She's Leaving — 70

LOUISE CORDET

62 Decca F 11476 — I'm Just A Baby/In A Matter Of Moments (export copy in p/s) — 10
62 Decca F 11524 — Sweet Enough/Someone Else's Fool (export copy in p/s) — 10
63 Decca F 11673 — Around And Around/Which Way The Wind Blows — 15
64 Decca F 11824 — Don't Let The Sun Catch You Crying/Loving Baby — 15
64 Decca F 11875 — Don't Make Me Over/Two Lovers — 20
62 Decca DFE 8515 — THE SWEET BEAT OF LOUISE CORDET (EP) — 70

MINT VALUE £

CORDUROYS

66	Planet PLF 122	Tick Tock/Too Much Of A Woman	45

CHICK COREA (& RETURN TO FOREVER)

(see also Return To Forever)

72	ECM ECM 1018/9	PARIS CONCERT FEBRUARY 1971 (2-LP, as Corea & Braxton & Holland)	15
74	Atlantic K 60081	INNER SPACE (2-LP)	15
74	People PLEO 9	SUNDANCE (LP)	15

PADDY COREA

72	Explosion EX 2066	Soul And Inspiration/STAGS: You Must Be Trying My Faith	6

CORKSCREW

79	Highway SHY 7005	FOR OPENERS (LP)	25

CORNBREAD & JERRY

61	London HLG 9352	L'il Ole Me/Loco Moto	10

DON CORNEL & ETERNALS

70	Moodisc MU 3506	Christmas Joy/WINSTON & RUPERT: Musically Beat	7

CORNELIUS BROTHERS & SISTER ROSE

71	United Artists UP 35218	Treat Her Like A Lady/Over At My Place	8
72	United Artists UP 35378	Too Late To Turn Back Now/Lift Your Love Higher	10
73	United Artists UP 35502	I'm Never Gonna Be Alone Anymore/Let's Stay Together	8

EDDIE CORNELIUS

80	GB Records GB 001	That's Love Making In Your Eyes/Hurry Up	15

DON CORNELL

54	Vogue Coral Q 2013	Hold My Hand/I'm Blessed	25
54	Vogue Coral Q 2037	S'Posin'/I Was Lucky	15
55	Vogue Coral Q 72058	No Man Is An Island/All At Once	10
55	Vogue Coral Q 72070	Give Me Your Love/When You Are In Love	10
55	Vogue Coral Q 72071	Athena/Size 12	10
55	Vogue Coral Q 72073	Stranger In Paradise/The Devil's In Your Eyes	20
55	Vogue Coral Q 72080	Unchained Melody/Most Of All	12
55	Vogue Coral Q 72104	Love Is A Many Splendored Thing/The Bible Tells Me So	10
56	Vogue Coral Q 72132	There Once Was A Beautiful/Make A Wish	12
56	Vogue Coral Q 72144	Teenage Meeting (Gonna Rock It Right)/I Still Have A Prayer	35
56	Vogue Coral Q 72152	Rock Island Line/Na-Ne Na-Na	20
56	Vogue Coral Q 72164	But Love Me (Love But Me)/Fort Knox	15
56	Vogue Coral Q 72203	All Of You/Heaven Only Knows	12
57	Vogue Coral Q 72218	See-Saw/From The Bottom Of My Heart	18
57	Vogue Coral Q 72234	Let's Be Friends/Afternoon In Madrid	15
57	Vogue Coral Q 72257	Sittin' In The Balcony/Let's Get Lost	30
57	Vogue Coral Q 72276	Mama Guitar/A Face In The Crowd	30
57	Vogue Coral Q 72291	There's Only You/Non Dimenticar	12
58	Coral Q 72308	Before It's Time To Say Goodnight/Mailman, Bring Me No More Blues	10
58	Coral Q 72313	I've Got Bells On My Heart/Keep God In The Home	10
59	Pye International 7N 25041	Sempre Amore/Forever Couldn't Be Long Enough	10
59	Pye International 7N 25041	Sempre Amore/Forever Couldn't Be Long Enough (78)	12
59	London HLD 8937	This Earth Of Mine/The Gang That Sang "Heart Of My Heart"	10
59	London HLD 8937	This Earth Of Mine/The Gang That Sang "Heart Of My Heart" (78)	15
54	Vogue Coral LVC 10004	DON CORNELL FOR YOU (10" LP)	30
56	Coral LVA 9037	LET'S GET LOST (LP)	25

JERRY CORNELL

55	London HL 8157	Please Don't Talk About Me When I'm Gone/St. Louis Blues	25

LYN CORNELL

60	Decca F 11227	Like Love/Demon Lover	20
60	Decca F 11260	Teaser/What A Feeling	10
60	Decca F 11277	Never On Sunday/Swain Kelly	5
60	Decca F 11301	The Angel And The Stranger/Xmas Stocking	6
61	Decca F 11326	The Sweet Life (La Dolce Vita)/When Is Someday	6
61	Decca F 11374	Surely In Love/Adios My Love	6
62	Decca F 11430	African Waltz/Moanin'	6
62	Decca F 11469	I Sold My Heart To The Junkman/Step Up And Rescue Me	25
63	Decca F 11750	Sally Go Round The Roses/You Can Kiss Me If You Like	10

CORNFLAKES

62	Fontana 267 227TF	Oh, Listen To The Band/Moonstruck	10

BARRY CORNISH

73	Jam 60	Questions/Stones From The Wishing Well	8

ARNOLD CORNS

(see also David Bowie)

71	B&C CB 149	Moonage Daydream/Hang Onto Yourself (as 'The Arnold Corns')	75
72	B&C CB 189	Hang Onto Yourself/Man In The Middle	60
74	Mooncrest MOON 25	Hang Onto Yourself/Man In The Middle (reissue)	18

CORONADOS

64	London HL 9895	Love Me With All Your Heart/Querida	10
67	Stateside SS 2043	Johnny B. Goode/Shook Me Down	10

CORONETS

(see also Chris Sandford & Coronets, Tony Brent, Ronnie Harris, Benny Hill, Eric Jupp, Lee Lawrence)

54	Columbia SCM 5117	Do, Do, Do, Do, Do, Do, Do It Again/I Ain't Gonna Do It No More	15
56	Columbia SCM 5235	Lizzie Borden/My Believing Heart	10
56	Columbia SCM 5261	There's No Song Like An Old Song/The Magic Touch	10
56	Columbia DB 3827	Someone To Love/The Rocking Horse Cowboy	10
56	Columbia SEG 7603	RHYTHM AND BLUES (EP, as Coronets with Eric Jupp Orchestra)	15

MINT VALUE £

56 Columbia SEG 7621 THE PERFECT COMBINATION (EP, as Coronets with Eric Jupp Orchestra) 10
56 Columbia SEG 7714 SONG SHOW (EP) 10

CORONETS
68 Stresa BEV SP 1104/1105 I Wonder Why/You're Leaving Tomorrow 45

CORPORATION (Jamaica)
(see also Claudette & Corporation, Billy Jack)
70 Grape GR 3022 Sweet Musille/Walking Thru' Jerusalem 22

CORPORATION (U.S.)
69 Capitol E-T/E-ST 175 THE CORPORATION (LP) 25

CORRIE FOLK TRIO/CORRIES
(see also Paddie Bell)
63 Waverley SLP 530 Love Is Teasing/O, Waly Waly (p/s) 8
63 Waverley ELP 129 CORRIE FOLK TRIO (EP) 12
63 Waverley ELP 131 YON FOLK SONGS IS FOR THE BURDS (EP) 12
63 Waverley ELP 132 MORE FOLK SONGS FOR THE BURDS (EP) 10
65 Parlophone GEP 8947 FROSTY WINDS (EP) 8
65 Waverley ZLP 2042 CORRIE FOLK TRIO WITH PADDIE BELL (LP, also stereo SZLP 2043) 15
65 Waverley ZLP 2050 THE PROMISE OF THE DAY (LP) 15

JAY C CORRY
76 Decca FR 13680 Love Me Or Leave Me/House Of Truth 12

CORSAIRS (Jamaica)
70 Unity UN 558 Goodnight My Love/Lover Girl 8

CORSAIRS (U.K.)
67 CBS 202624 Pay You Back With Interest/I'm Going To Shut You Down 20

CORSAIRS (U.S.)
62 Pye International 7N 25142 I'll Take You Home/Sitting On Your Doorstep (with Jay 'Bird' Uzzel) 15

BOB CORT (SKIFFLE GROUP)
(see also Liz Winters & Bob Cort)
57 Decca FJ 10831 It Takes A Worried Man To Sing A Worried Blues/ Don't You Rock Me Daddy-O . 20
57 Decca F 10892 Six-Five Special/Roll Jen Jenkins 20
57 Decca F 10899 Maggie May/Jessamine (with Liz Winters) 8
57 Decca F 10905 Schoolday (Ring! Ring! Goes The Bell)/Ain't It A Shame (To Sing Skiffle On Sunday) 20
57 Decca F 10951 'Bob Cort Skiffle Party' Medley (Parts 1 & 2) 5
58 Decca F 10989 The Ark (Noah Found Grace In The Eyes Of God)/Yes! Suh! 5
59 Decca F 11109 Foggy Foggy Dew/On Top Of Old Smokey (solo) 5
59 Decca F 11145 Waterloo/Battle Of New Orleans (solo) 6
59 Decca F 11160 Kissin' Time/I'm Gonna Get Married (solo) 5
59 William Timpson Ltd The Shop In The Cellar (1-sided 78, 200 only) 15
60 Decca F 11197 El Paso/A Handful Of Gold (solo) 5
60 Decca F 11256 Mule Skinner Blues/The Ballad Of Walter Williams (solo) 12
60 Decca F 11285 The Ballad Of The Alamo/Five Brothers (solo) 6
59 Decca DFE 6630 BARRACK ROOM BALLADS (EP) 10
61 Decca DFE 6686 BOB CORT'S GENTLEFOLK (EP, as Bob Cort's Gentlefolk) 10
57 Decca LK 4222 AIN'T IT A SHAME (LP) 30
59 Decca LK 4301 ESKIMO NELL (LP) 15

DAVE 'BABY' CORTEZ
59 London HLU 8852 The Happy Organ/Love Me As I Love You 12
59 London HLU 8919 The Whistling Organ/I'm Happy 7
60 Columbia DB 4404 Piano Shuffle/Dave's Special 7
60 London HLU 9126 Deep In The Heart Of Texas/You're Just Right 15
62 Pye International 7N 25159 Rinky Dink/Getting Right 20
66 Roulette RK 7001 Countdown/Summertime 10
60 London RE-U 1233 DAVE 'BABY' CORTEZ (EP) 40
64 London HA-U 8142 THE GOLDEN HITS OF DAVE 'BABY' CORTEZ (LP) 30

CORTINAS
77 Step Forward SF 1 Fascist Dictator/Television Families (p/s, first 1,000 in card sleeve) 20
77 Step Forward SF 1 Fascist Dictator/Television Families (p/s) 12
78 Step Forward SF 6 Defiant Pose/Independence (p/s) 12
78 Step Forward SF 6 Defiant Pose/Independence (12", pink die-cut sleeve) 12
78 CBS CBS 6759 Heartache/Ask Mr. Waverley (p/s) 8
78 CBS CBS 82831 TRUE ROMANCES (LP, with photo insert) 20

CORTINAS
(see also Octopus)
68 Polydor 56255 Phoebe's Flower Shop/Too Much In Love 15

LEE CORVETTE
62 Decca The Heart You Break (May Be Your Own)/Tender Love 12

CORVETTES
82 Bitchin BIT 100 Surf, Don't Walk/She'll Be Blonde (p/s) 15
84 Bitchin BIT 101 Girls Cars Girls Sun Girls Surf Girls Fun Girls/The Beach Is Not Enough (p/s) . . 15

LARRY CORYELL
(see also Jazz Composers Orchestra)
69 Vanguard SVRL 19051 LADY CORYELL (LP) 12
69 Vanguard SVRL 19059 CORYELL (LP) 12
71 Vanguard 6359 005 SPACES (LP) 20

BILL COSBY
67 Warner Bros WB 7072 Little Ole Man (Uptight! Everything's Alright)/Don'cha Know (in p/s) 35

MINT VALUE £

COSMIC BABY/VANGELIS
(see also Vangelis)
94 East West SAM 1484 A TRIBUTE TO BLADERUNNER (12", double pack, promo only) . . . 20

COSMIC EYE
72 Regal Zono. SLRZ 1030 DREAM SEQUENCE (LP) . . . 200

COSMO
(see also Cosmo & Dennis, Denzil Dennis)
63 Blue Beat BB 175 Gypsy Woman/Do Unto Others . . . 10
64 Blue Beat BB 244 One God/BUSTER'S ALL STARS: Prince Royal (actually "Reincarnation") . . . 50
64 Blue Beat BB 269 Rice And Badgee/BUSTER'S ALL STARS: The Tickler . . . 50

FRANK COSMO
(see also Two Kings)
63 Island WI 058 Revenge/Laughin' At You (B-side actually with Bobby Aitken) . . . 15
63 Island WI 073 Dear Dreams/Go Go Go . . . 15
63 Island WI 100 Merry Christmas/Greetings From Beverley's . . . 20
63 R&B JB 119 I Love You/DON DRUMMOND: Close Of Play . . . 22
64 Island WI 135 Better Get Right/Ameletia . . . 20
64 Black Swan WI 446 Alone/Beautiful Book . . . 20

COSMO & DENNIS (alias Denzil)
(see also Cosmo)
62 Blue Beat BB 145 Bed Of Roses/Tonight And Evermore (as Cosmo & Denzil) . . . 10
65 Blue Beat BB 296 Sweet Rosemarie/Lollipop I'm In Love . . . 12
65 Blue Beat BB 312 Come On Come On/I Don't Want You (As COSMO & DENZIL) . . . 12

COSMOTHEKA
70s Shy SHY 7001 WINES & SPIRITS (LP) . . . 35
85 Dambuster DAM 1 COSMOTHEKA (LP) . . . 18

DON COSTA, HIS ORCHESTRA & CHORUS
55 London HLF 8186 Love Is A Many Splendoured Thing/Safe In The Harbour . . . 40
59 London HLT 8992 I Walk The Line/Cat Walk . . . 10
60 London HLT 9137 Theme From "The Unforgiven"/Streets Of Paris . . . 6
60 London HLT 9195 Never On Sunday/Sounds of Love . . . 7
60 London HLT 7103 Theme From "The Unforgiven"/ FERRANTE & TEICHER: Theme From "The Apartment" (export issue) . . . 5
60 London HLT 9195 Never On Sunday/The Sound Of Love . . . 7
60 London HLT 9320 The Misfits/Chi Chi . . . 6
61 HMV CLP 1507 THE SOUND OF THE MILLION SELLERS (LP) . . . 12

SAM COSTA
61 Palette PG 9026 I'm Changing My Hat To A Bowler/Oh Dear! . . . 5

JACK COSTANZO
61 London HLG 9401 Theme From Route 66/Naked City Theme . . . 5
60s Sunset SLS 50033E BONGO FEVER (LP) . . . 15

JACK COSTANZO & TUBBY HAYES
(see also Tubby Hayes)
62 Fontana TFL 5190 COSTANZO PLUS TUBBS - EQUATION IN RHYTHM (LP, mono) . . . 60
62 Fontana STFL 598 COSTANZO PLUS TUBBS - EQUATION IN RHYTHM (LP, stereo) . . . 30

CELIA COSTELLO
75 Leader LEE 4054 CELIA COSTELLO (LP, with insert) . . . 20

DANNY COSTELLO
57 Oriole CB 1393 Like A Brook Gets Lost In A River/That's Where I Shine . . . 5

DAY COSTELLO
(see also Ross McManus)
71 Spark SRL 1042 The Long And Winding Road/Free (Unlimited Horizons) . . . 10

ELVIS COSTELLO (& ATTRACTIONS)
(see also Nick Lowe, George Jones, Coward Brothers)
77 Stiff BUY 14 Alison/Welcome To The Working Week (p/s, A-side mispress on white vinyl) . . . 300
77 Stiff BUY 15 Red Shoes/Mystery Dance (p/s, mispress, plays "Dream Tobacco" by Max Wall) . . . 8
(The above singles were later repressed with 'Made In England' on label and are worth £3 each.)
78 Radar ADA 24 Radio Radio/Tiny Steps (12", promo-only, 500 pressed) . . . 15
78 Radar RG 1 Talking In The Dark/Wednesday Week (p/s, gig freebie) . . . 8
80 F-Beat XX 5P New Amsterdam/Just A Memory/Dr Luther's Assistant/Ghost Train (picture disc) . . . 6
80 2-Tone CHS TT 7 I Can't Stand Up For Falling Down/Girls Talk (unreleased) . . . 25
80 2-Tone CHS TT 7 I Can't Stand Up For Falling Down/Girls Talk (unreleased, later a gig freebie, this is more common issue with XX1 in run-off groove, 13,000 pressed) . . . 15
80 Stiff GRAB 3 STIFF SINGLES FOUR PACK (BUY 11, 14, 15 & 20 in clear plastic wallet) . . . 20
81 F-Beat XX 17 A Good Year For The Roses/Your Angel Steps Out Of Heaven (withdrawn p/s) . . . 10
93 Demon ECPROMO 1 TWO AND A HALF YEARS IN 31 MINUTES (CD, fold-out digipak, promo only) . . . 10
94 Demon ECPROMO 2 HIGHLIGHTS FROM ALMOST BLUE AND IMPERIAL BEDROOM (CD, fold-out digipak, promo only) . . . 8
95 Demon ECPROMO 3 SELECTIONS FROM THE KING OF AMERICA (CD, fold-out digipak, promo only) . . 8
78 Radar RAD 3 THIS YEAR'S MODEL (LP, with free 7" "Stranger In The House"/"Neat Neat Neat" (live) [die-cut company sleeve, SAM 83], 50,000 pressed; 1st 5,000 shrinkwrapped and stickered) . . . 25
79 Radar RAD 15 ARMED FORCES (LP, foldout stickered sleeve with free EP Live At Hollywood High [p/s, SAM 90] & postcards) . . . 20
79 Radar RAD 15 ARMED FORCES (LP, mispress, plays "[What's So Funny 'Bout] Peace, Love & Understanding" instead of "Two Little Hitlers"; sticker on insert) . . . 25
86 IMP FIEND CD 21 ARMED FORCES (CD, with 'Peace, Love & Understanding") . . . 18

MINT VALUE £

BILLY COTTON
(see also Alma Cogan)
54 Decca F10299 Friends And Neighbours/The Kid's Last Fight ... 25
61 Columbia 33SX 1383 WAKEY WAKEY (LP) ... 20

GENE COTTON
76 ABC 173 Me And The Elephant/Song For You ... 6

JAMES COTTON (BLUES BAND)
78 Buddah BDS 471 Rock'n'Roll Music/Help Me ... 5
68 Vanguard SVRL 19035 CUT YOU LOOSE! (LP, as James Cotton Blues Band) ... 25

JIMMY COTTON
(see also James Cotton Blues Band, Alexis Korner)
62 Columbia SEG 8141 CHRIS BARBER PRESENTS JIMMY COTTON (EP) ... 25
62 Columbia SEG 8189 CHRIS BARBER PRESENTS JIMMY COTTON NO. 2 (EP) ... 25

JOSEPH COTTON
77 Observer OB 001 Fit And Ready/OBSERVER: Iron Fist (12") ... 40

MIKE COTTON JAZZMEN
61 Columbia DB 4697 Senorita/The Colonel's Tune ... 6
62 Columbia DB 4821 The Cobbler's Song/African Twist ... 6

MIKE COTTON (SOUND)
(see also Lucas & Mike Cotton Sound, Satisfaction)
62 Columbia DB 4910 The Tinker/Zulu Warrior (as the Mike Cotton Jazz Men) ... 10
63 Columbia DB 7029 Swing That Hammer/Heartaches (as Mike Cotton Jazzmen) ... 10
63 Columbia DB 7134 Midnite Flyer/One Mint Julep (as Mike Cotton Band) ... 10
64 Columbia DB 7267 I Don't Wanna Know/This Little Pig ... 50
64 Columbia DB 7382 Round And Round/Beau Dudley ... 50
65 Columbia DB 7623 Make Up Your Mind/I've Got My Eye On You ... 50
66 Polydor BM 56096 Harlem Shuffle/Like That ... 40
62 Columbia SEG 8144 COTTON PICKING (EP) ... 40
63 Columbia SEG 8190 THE WILD AND THE WILLING (EP) ... 40
64 Columbia 33SX 1647 MIKE COTTON SOUND (LP) ... 350

COTTON CASINO
(See also Acid Mothers Temple and the Melting Paraiso UFO)
03 Riot Season REPOSE 701 Fly High/Open The Shine (white vinyl, p/s) ... 8

JOHN(NY) COUGAR
(see also John Cougar Mellencamp)
78 Riva RIVA 14 I Need A Lover/Born Reckless (as Johnny Cougar, p/s) ... 7
78 Riva RIVA 16 Factory/Alley Of The Angels (as Johnny Cougar, p/s) ... 10

COUGARS
63 Parlophone R 4989 Saturday Night At The Duckpond/See You In Dreamland ... 15
63 Parlophone R 5038 Red Square/Fly-By-Nite ... 15
64 Parlophone R 5115 Caviare And Chips/While The City Sleeps ... 20
63 Parlophone GEP 8886 SATURDAY NIGHT WITH THE COUGARS (EP) ... 50
78 EMI NUT 2833 SATURDAY NIGHT WITH THE COUGARS (EP) ... 10

ROGER COULAM QUARTET
67 CBS 52399 ORGAN IN ORBIT (LP) ... 20
70 Fontana 16009 BLOW HOT, BLOW COLD (LP) ... 20

DENIS COULDRY (& SMILE)
(see also Felius Andromeda)
68 Decca F 12734 James In The Basement (solo)/DENIS COULDRY & NEXT COLLECTION: I Am Nearly There ... 40
68 Decca F 12786 Penny For The Wind/Tea And Toast, Mr. Watson? (as Denis Couldry & Smile) ... 20

COULSON, DEAN, McGUINNESS, FLINT
(see also Manfred Mann, McGuinness Flint, Dennis Coulson, Lyle McGuinness Band)
72 DJM DJS 267 Lay Down Your Weary Tune/Tiny Montgomery/I Wanna Be Your lover ... 6
72 DJM DJLPS 424 LO AND BEHOLD (LP, gatefold sleeve) ... 18

DENNIS COULSON
73 Elektra K 42148 DENNIS COULSON (LP, gatefold sleeve) ... 15

PHIL COULTER ORCHESTRA
68 Pye 7N 17511 Congratulations/Gold Rush ... 20

COUNCIL COLLECTIVE
(see also Style Council, Jimmy Ruffin)
84 Polydor MINEX 1 Soul Deep (Club Mix)/Soul Deep (12", stickered black die-cut sleeve) ... 8

COUNT
(see also Cannibals)
74 Purple PUR 122 Gazaroody/The So, So Song ... 10

COUNT BISHOPS
75 Chiswick SW 1 SPEEDBALL (EP, 1st 1,000 in glossy p/s, promos £10) ... 8
78 Chiswick NS 35 Mr Jones/Human Bean/Route 66/Too Much Too Soon (unissued, test pressings only, as Bishops) ... 18
77 Chiswick WIK 1 THE COUNT BISHOPS (LP) ... 12
78 Chiswick CH 7 LIVE AT THE ROUNDHOUSE (10" mini-LP) ... 12

COUNT BUSTY & RUDIES
68 Melody MRC 003 You Like It/The Reggay ... 10

COUNT DOWNE & ZEROS
(see also Peter & Headlines)
64 Ember EMB S 189 Hello My Angel/Don't Shed A Tear ... 35

MINT VALUE £

COUNT FIVE
66 Pye International 7N 25393 — Psychotic Reaction/They're Gonna Get You 50

COUNT HALA
69 Rude Boy RBH 005 — Cut Price Pussy/THE ATTACKERS : Police In Z Cars Blues 75
70 Rude Boy RBH 006 — Gems Of Christies/Cut Price Meow 25

COUNT HOUSE FOLK MUSIC CLUB
65 Own label MSCH 2 — MORE SINGING AT THE COUNT HOUSE (LP, private pressing) 250

COUNT LASHER
59 — Caribou Calabash/Dalvey Girl 20

COUNT OSSIE & HIS MYSTIC REVELATION
(see also Jackie Estick, Gaylads, Soul Defenders)
71 Ashanti ASH 404 — Rasta Reggae/Samia 12
71 Moodisc MU 3515 — Whispering Drums/SLIM SMITH & UNIQUES: Give Me Some More Loving 15
71 Moodisc HM 105 — Whispering Drums/SLIM SMITH & UNIQUES: Give Me Some More Loving 15
74 Ashanti NTI 1301 — GROUNATION (3-LP, with Mystic Revelation Of Rastafari) 60

COUNT OSSIE & THE REVOLUTIONARIES
78 Charmers CH 0012 — Hog Head/TRINITY: Dog Meat (12") 40

COUNT PRINCE
(see under Count Prince Mller)

COUNT STICKY
68 Amalgamated AMG 825 — Train To Soulsville/ERIC MORRIS : Cinderella 40

COUNT SUCKLE
70 Q 2200 — Lavender Blues/Humpty Dumpty 10
70 Q 2201 — Please Don't Go/FREDDIE & THE NOTES: Bread On The Table 12

COUNT VICTORS
62 Coral Q 72456 — Peepin' 'N' Hidin'/Don't Laugh At Me ('Cos I'm A Fool) 25
63 Coral Q 72462 — Road Runner/Lorie 25

COUNTDOWNS
(see also John Barry)
63 United Artists UP 1024 — Mouse On The Moon/The Big Safari 10

COUNTING CROWS
93 Geffen GEF 24528 — AUGUST AND EVERYTHING AFTER (LP) 50

COUNTRY BOY
64 Blue Beat BB 236 — I'm A Lonely Boy (actually by Shenley Duffas)/EDWARD'S ALL STARS: He's Gone Ska 30

COUNTRY FEVER
69 Bell BLL 1052 — Too Much Of othingTears Of Rage 8

COUNTRY FOLK
70s Thule SLP 101 — THE COUNTRY FOLK (LP, private pressing) 180

COUNTRY FUNK
70 Polydor 248 2018 — COUNTRY FUNK (LP) 18

COUNTRY GAZETTE
(see also Flying Burrito Brothers)
72 United Artists UAG 29404 — TRAITOR IN OUR MIDST (LP) 15
73 United Artists UAS 29491 — DON'T GIVE UP YOUR DAY JOB (LP) 12

COUNTRY GENTLEMEN
(see also High Society, Peter Cowap)
63 Decca F 11766 — Greensleeves/Baby Jean 15

COUNTRY HAMS
(see also Paul McCartney/Wings, Chet Atkins, Floyd Cramer)
74 EMI EMI 2220 — Walking In The Park With Eloise/Bridge On The River Suite (p/s, red & brown label) 55
82 EMI EMI 2220 — Walking In The Park With Eloise/Bridge On The River Suite (p/s, reissue, beige label) 15

COUNTRY JOE & THE FISH
(see also Country Joe McDonald)
67 Fontana TF 882 — Not So Sweet Martha Lorraine/Love 12
69 Vanguard VA 3 — Here I Go Again/It's So Nice To Have Love 7
70 Vanguard 6076 250 — I-Feel-Like-I'm-Fixin'-To-Die Rag/Maria 8
67 Fontana TFL 6081 — ELECTRIC MUSIC FOR THE MIND AND BODY (LP, mono, flipback sleeve) 40
67 Fontana STFL 6087 — ELECTRIC MUSIC FOR THE MIND AND BODY (LP, stereo, flipback sleeve) 50
68 Fontana TFL 6086 — I-FEEL-LIKE-I'M-FIXIN'-TO-DIE (LP, flipback sleeve) 40
68 Vanguard SVRL 19006 — TOGETHER (LP) 20
69 Vanguard SVRL 19026 — ELECTRIC MUSIC FOR THE MIND AND BODY (LP, reissue) 20
69 Vanguard SVRL 19029 — I-FEEL-LIKE-I'M-FIXIN'-TO-DIE (LP, reissue) 15
69 Vanguard SVRL 19048 — HERE WE ARE AGAIN (LP) 20
70 Vanguard SVRL 19058 — THE BEST OF COUNTRY JOE AND THE FISH (LP) 12
70 Vanguard 6359 002 — C.J. FISH (LP) 18
73 Vanguard VSD 27/28 — THE LIFE AND TIMES OF (2-LP, gatefold sleeve, quadrophonic) 20
73 Vanguard VSD 27/28 — THE LIFE AND TIMES OF (2-LP, gatefold sleeve, stereo) 15
75 Vanguard VSD 79244 — ELECTRIC MUSIC FOR THE MIND AND BODY (LP, reissue) 15
80 Piccadilly PIC 3009 — THE EARLY YEARS (LP, private pressing, withdrawn) 40
87 Decal LIK 8 — THE FIRST THREE EPS (LP, as Country Joe McDonald, The Mostly Fish Recordings) 12

COUNTRY JUG
(see also Ray Dorset)
72 Decca F 13270 — I'm Sorry/Do You Wanna?/Flying 8

MINT VALUE £

COUNTRYMEN

69	Jayboy BOY 3	After All/White Rose Of Athens	5

COUNTRYMEN

62	Piccadilly 7N 34012	I KNOW WHERE I'M GOING (EP)	8
62	Picadilly NPL 38003	A FLYING VISIT (LP)	12

WAYNE/JAYNE COUNTY (& ELECTRIC CHAIRS)

(see also Mystere Five's)

77	Illegal IL 002	Stuck On You/Paranoia Paradise/The Last Time (p/s)	10
77	Sweet F.A. WC 1	Fuck Off/On The Crest (p/s)	12
78	Safari SAFE 1	Eddie And Sheena/Rock And Roll Cleopatra (p/s, with cartoon insert)	15
78	Safari SAFE 1	Eddie And Sheena/Rock And Roll Cleopatra (p/s, without cartoon insert)	10
78	Safari SAFE 6	I Had Too Much To Dream Last Night/Fuck Off (unissued)	0
78	Safari WC 2	BLATANTLY OFFENZIVE (EP, gold vinyl)	10
78	Safari SAFE 9	Trying To Get On The Radio/Evil Minded Momma (p/s)	5
78	Safari SAFELS 13	Berlin (Long Version)/Waiting For The Marines/Midnight Pal (12", p/s, pink vinyl)	8
79	Illegal IL 005	Thunder When She Walks/What You Got (p/s)	5
83	Safari WCP 3	Fuck Off/Toilet Love (picture disc)	6
78	Safari GOOD 1	STORM THE GATES OF HEAVEN (LP, multicoloured or grey marbled vinyl)	18
79	Safari GOOD 2	THINGS YOUR MOTHER NEVER TOLD YOU (LP)	15

DIANA COUPLAND

60	HMV POP 690	Love Him/I Am Loved	6

COURIERS

(see also William E. Kimber)

66	Ember EMB S 218	Take Away/Done Me Wrong (with p/s)	70
66	Ember EMB S 218	Take Away/Done Me Wrong	20

COURIERS

69	Ash ALP 201	PACK UP YOUR SORROWS (LP)	30

COURTEENERS

07	Loog LOOG 022	Cavorting/No You Didn't, No You Don't (p/s, 750 only)	20
07	Loog LOOG 023	Cavorting/No You Didn't, No You Don't (CD single)	18

TOM COURTENAY

63	Decca F 11729	Mrs. Brown You've Got A Lovely Daughter/Knocking On The Door	5

COURT MARTIAL

82	Riot City RIOT 11	NO SOLUTION (EP)	12

COURTYARD MUSIC GROUP

74	Deroy	JUST OUR WAY OF SAYING HELLO (LP, private pressing)	200

COUSIN EMMY & HER KINFOLK

56	Brunswick OE 9258	KENTUCKY MOUNTAIN BALLADS VOL. 1 (EP)	15
56	Brunswick OE 9259	KENTUCKY MOUNTAIN BALLADS VOL. 2 (EP)	15

COUSINS (U.K.)

64	Decca F 11924	Yes Sir That's My Baby/Two Lovely Black Eyes	5

DAVE COUSINS

(see also The Strawbs)

72	A&M AMS 7032	Going Home/Ways And Means	6
72	A&M AMLS 68118	TWO WEEKS LAST SUMMER (LP, brown label)	45
79	Old School SLURP 1	OLD SCHOOL SONGS (LP, private pressing with Brian Willoughby)	35
80	Passport PVC 8901	OLD SCHOOL SONGS (LP, reissue with different sleeve)	12

DON COVAY (& GOODTIMERS)

(see also Soul Clan)

61	Pye International 7N 25075	Pony Time/Love Boat	25
61	Philips PB 1140	Shake Wid The Shake/Every Which Way	30
62	Cameo Parkway C 239	The Popeye Waddle/One Little Boy Had Money	30
64	Atlantic AT 4006	Mercy, Mercy/Can't Stay Away	10
65	Atlantic AT 4016	Take This Hurt Off Me/Please Don't Let Me Know	10
65	Atlantic AT 4056	See Saw/I Never Get Enough Of Your Love	10
66	Atlantic AT 4078	Sookie Sookie/Watching The Late Late Show	10
66	Atlantic 584 025	You Put Something In Me/Iron Out The Rough Spots	10
66	Atlantic 584 059	See Saw/Somebody's Got To Love You	10
67	Atlantic 584 082	Shingaling '67/I Was There	8
67	Atlantic 584 094	Sookie Sookie/Mercy Mercy	8
67	Atlantic 584 114	40 Days - 40 Nights/The Usual Place	10
70	Atlantic 2091 018	Everything I Do Goin' Be Funky/Key To The Highway	5
65	Atlantic ATL 5025	MERCY! (LP, plum label)	80
67	Atlantic 587 062	SEE-SAW (LP)	30
69	Atlantic K 50225	HOUSE OF BLUE LIGHT (LP)	20
75	Mercury 9100010	HOT BLOOD (LP)	12

DAVID COVERDALE

(see also Coverdale-Page, Whitesnake, Deep Purple, Wizard's Convention, Roger Glover, Jimmy Page)

77	Purple PUR 133	Hole In The Sky/Blindman	8
78	Purple PUR 136	Breakdown/Only My Soul	8
90	Epic 656 292 7	Last Note Of Freedom/HANS ZIMMER: Car Building (poster p/s)	8
90	Epic 656 292 6	Last Note Of Freedom/HANS ZIMMER: Car Building (12", p/s)	8
77	Purple TPS 3509	DAVID COVERDALE'S WHITESNAKE (LP, with inner)	15
77	Purple TPS 3509TC	DAVID COVERDALE'S WHITESNAKE (LP, white label promo, plain sleeve, with insert)	25
78	Purple TPS 3513	NORTHWINDS (LP, with inner sleeve)	15

COVERS

79	Decca FR 13880	Modern Girls/Head Out On The Road	30

MINT VALUE £

JULIEN COVEY & MACHINE

67	Island WIP 6009	A Little Bit Hurt/Sweet Bacon	50
67	Island WIP 6442	A Little Bit Hurt/Sweet Bacon (reissue)	12
87	Sunset	A Little Bit Hurt/Sweet Bacon (reissue)	12

JULIE COVINGTON

(see also Rock Follies)

70	Columbia DB 8649	The Magic Wasn't There/The Way Things Ought To Be	15
70	Columbia DB 8705	Tonight Your Love Is Over/If I Had My Time Again	15
72	RCA RCA 2181	Day By Day/With Me It Goes Deeper	6
71	Columbia SCX 6466	THE BEAUTIFUL CHANGES (LP)	170

COWBOY

71	Atlantic 2466 022	REACH FOR THE SKY (LP)	15
72	Atlantic K 40312	5'LL GETCHA TEN (LP, with insert)	15

COWBOY CHURCH SUNDAY SCHOOL

55	Brunswick 05371	Open Up Your Heart/The Lord Is Counting On You	5
55	Brunswick 05455	Go On By/The Little Black Sheep	5
56	Brunswick 05533	These Bad Bad Kids/A Handful Of Shame	5
56	Brunswick 05598	It Is No Secret/Don't Send Those Kids To Sunday School	5

COWBOYS INTERNATIONAL

(see also Public Image Ltd.)

79	Virgin VS 253	Aftermath/Pt. 2 (orange vinyl, p/s)	10

STANLEY COWELL

72	Freedom FLP40104	BRILLIANT CIRCLES (LP)	20

COWSILLS

67	MGM MGM 1353	The Rain, The Park And Other Things/River Blue	30
68	MGM MGM 1383	We Can Fly/A Time For Remembrance	18
68	MGM MGM 1400	In Need Of A Friend/Mr. Flynn	8
68	MGM MGM 1424	Indian Lake/Newspaper Blanket	6
68	MGM MGM 1441	Poor Baby/Meet Me At The Wishing Well	6
69	MGM MGM 1469	Hair/What Is Happy	6
69	MGM MGM 1484	The Prophecy Of Daniel And John The Divine/Gotta Get Away From It All	6
69	MGM MGM 1490	Love American Style/Silver Threads And Golden Needles	6
71	London HLU 10329	On My Side/There Is A Child	6
67	MGM C/CS 8059	THE COWSILLS (LP)	30
68	MGM CS 8077	WE CAN FLY (LP)	25
68	MGM CS 8095	CAPTAIN SAD AND HIS SHIP OF FOOLS (LP)	20
68	MGM C8111	IN CONCERT (LP)	15

BILLY COX

(see also Jimi Hendrix)

71	Pye Intl. NSPL 25158	NITRO FUNCTION (LP, blue/black label with logo-banner on left)	80

HARRY COX

65	EFDSS LP 1004	ENGLISH FOLK SINGER (LP)	15

IDA COX

(see also Ma Rainey)

59	Fontana TFE 17136	IDA COX (EP)	20
54	London AL 3517	SINGS THE BLUES (10" LP)	50
60s	Riverside RLP 374	BLUES FOR RAMPART STREET (LP)	20
75	Gannet GEN 5371-5376	PARAMOUNT RECORDINGS (6-LP box set)	20

IDA COX/ETHEL WATERS

50s	Poydras 104	IDA COX AND ETHEL WATERS (EP)	25

MICHAEL COX

59	Decca F 11166	Boy Meets Girl/Teenage Love	25
59	Decca F 11166	Boy Meets Girl/Teenage Love (78)	10
59	Decca F 11182	Too Hot To Handle/Serious	30
59	Decca F 11182	Too Hot To Handle/Serious (78)	10
60	Triumph RGM 1011	Angela Jones/Don't Want To Know	20
60	Ember EMB S 103	Angela Jones/Don't Want To Know (export issue)	45
60	HMV POP 789	Along Came Caroline/Lonely Road	20
61	HMV POP 830	Teenage Love/Linda	20
61	HMV POP 905	Sweet Little Sixteen/Cover Girl	25
62	HMV POP 972	Young Only Once/Honey Cause I Love You	15
62	HMV POP 1065	Stand Up/In April	20
63	HMV POP 1137	Don't You Break My Heart/Hark Is That A Cannon I Hear	20
63	HMV POP 1220	Gee What A Party/See That Again	20
64	HMV POP 1293	Rave On/Just Say Hello	25
65	HMV POP 1417	Gypsy/It Ain't Right	15
66	Parlophone R 5436	I Hate Getting Up In The Morning/Love 'Em And Leave 'Em	10
67	Parlophone R 5580	I'll Always Love You/You Never Can Tell (Till You Try)	15

SONNY COX

70	Pama PM 815	Choking Kind/Chocolate Candy	15

WALLY COX

61	Vogue V 9175	I Can't Help It/The Heebie Jeebees	30
74	Pye Disco Demand DDS 105	This Man/I've Had Enough (DJ Copy = £20)	8

LOL COXHILL

(see also Stephen Miller & Lol Coxhill, Kevin Ayers, Steve York's Camelo Pardalis)

78	Chiltern Sound CS 100	MURDER IN THE AIR (12" EP)	35
71	Dandelion DSD 8008	EAR OF THE BEHOLDER (2-LP, gatefold sleeve)	90
71	Dandelion DSD 69001	EAR OF THE BEHOLDER (2-LP, gatefold sleeve)	50

MINT VALUE £

72	Mushroom 150 MR 23	TOVERBAL SWEET (LP)	80
73	Caroline C 1503	COXHILL MILLER (LP, with Stephen Miller)	20
74	Caroline C 1507	THE STORY SO FAR ... OH REALLY? (LP, with Stephen Miller)	18
75	Caroline C 1514	LOL COXHILL & WELFARE STATE (LP)	15
75	Caroline C 1515	FLEAS IN THE CUSTARD (LP)	18
76	Ogun OG 510	DIVERSE (LP)	15
78	Ogun OG 525	THE JOY OF PARANOIA (LP)	15
78	Ictus 0008	MOOT (LP)	25
80	Pipe PIPE 1	SLOW MUSIC (LP)	30

COXHILL BEDFORD DUO

(see also David Bedford, Lol Coxhill)

71	Polydor 2001 253	Pretty Little Girl (Parts 1 & 2)	25
72	Dandelion 2058 214	Mood/WILL DANDY & DANDYLETTES: Sonny Boy/Oh Mein Papa	20

GRAHAM COXON

(see also Blur)

02	Transcopic TRAN020	Escape Song/Mountain Of Regret (p/s)	5
04	EMI R 6632	Freakin' Out/Feel Right (numbered p/s)	8
00	Transcopic 10 RDJ 6541	Oochy Woochy/That's When I Reach For My Revolver (10" promo p/s)	15
07	Regal SCO16	This Old Town (with Paul Weller)/Each New Morning/ Black River (7" die-cut sleeve)	10
09	Transgressive TRANS 101	In The Morning (10", one side etched)	10
98	Transcopic TRANLP 005	THE SKY IS TOO HIGH (LP, inner sleeve, 4 postcards)	20
01	Transcopic TRANLP 010	CROW SIT ON BLOOD TREE (2-LP, with inners & print, signed, 1,000 only)	30
01	Transcopic TRANLP 010	CROW SIT ON BLOOD TREE (2-LP, with inners & print, 1,000 only)	20
02	Transcopic TRANLP 018	THE KISS OF MORNING (2xLP, 10" x 10" picture book)	18
04	EMI 5775191	HAPPINESS IN MAGAZINES (LP)	15
06	Live Here Now (No cat no)	BURNT TO BLITZ : AT THE ASTORIA (2xCD sold at 25/10/06 only)	20

KEVIN COYNE

(see also Clague, Coyne-Clague, Siren, Gordon Smith)

72	Dandelion 2001 357	Cheat Me/Flowering Cherry	7
80	Virgin VGD 3504	SANITY STOMP (EP, double pack)	8
72	Dandelion 2310 228	CASE HISTORY (LP)	120
73	Virgin VD 2501	MARJORY RAZORBLADE (2-LP, gatefold sleeve, black/white label)	40
74	Virgin V 2012	BLAME IT ON THE NIGHT (LP, lyric insert, coloured 'twin Virgin' label)	25
75	Virgin V 2033	MATCHING HEAD AND FEET (LP, laminated sleeve, lyric poster, coloured "twin-Virgin" label)	15
80	Dandelion BUTBOX 1	DANDELION YEARS (3-LP, re-issue of Siren LP's "Siren", "Strange Locomotion" and "Coynes Case History")	25

COYNE-CLAGUE

69	Dandelion S 4494	The Stride/I Wonder Where	8

(see Clague, Kevin Coyne)

CRABBY APPLETON

70	Elektra EKS 74067	CRABBY APPLETON (LP)	18
71	Elektra EKS 74106	ROTTEN TO THE CORE (LP)	18

CRACK

80	JSO EAT 4	Making The Effort/Easy Street	8

CRACK

82	RCA RCA 214	Don't You Ever Let Me Down/I Can't Take It (die-cut 'Battle of the Bands' sleeve)	25
82	RCA RCA 255	Going Out/The Troops Have Landed (p/s)	15
83	RCA CRACK 1	All Or Nothing/I Caught You Out (p/s)	20
83	Link LP073	IN SEARCH OF THE CRACK (LP)	15

CRACKED MIRROR

83	CMLP 001	CRACKED MIRROR (LP, private pressing, 200 only)	80

CRACKERS

(see also Merseys)

69	Fontana TF 995	Honey Do/It Happens All The Time	12

SARAH CRACKNELL

(see also St. Etienne, 50 Year Void, Lovecut D.B.)

87	3 Bears TED 001	Love Is All You Need/Coastal Town (p/s)	10
97	Gut CDGUT 7	Goldie (Radio Edit)/(Original Version)/Empire State High/ Aussie Soap Girl (CD, slimline jewel case, withdrawn)	10

CRACK THE SKY

76	Lifesong ELS 45016	We Want Mine/Invaders From Mars	8
76	Lifesong LSLP 6005	ANIMAL NOTES (LP, with inner sleeve)	15

(BILLY) 'CRASH' CRADDOCK

59	Philips PB 966	Boom Boom Baby/Don't Destroy Me (as 'Crash' Craddock)	30
59	Philips PB 966	Boom Boom Baby/Don't Destroy Me (as 'Crash' Craddock) (78)	20
60	Philips PB 1006	Since She Turned Seventeen/I Want That (as 'Crash' Craddock)	30
60	Philips PB 1092	Good Time Billy (Is A Happiness Fool)/Heavenly Love	20
61	Mercury AMT 1146	How Lonely He Must Be/Truly True	15

CRADLE OF FILTH

94	Cacophonous NIHIL1	THE PRINCIPLE OF EVIL MADE FLESH (LP)	15

CRAIG

65	King KG 1022	Ain't That A Shame/International Blues	18

CRAIG

(see also Galliard)

66	Fontana TF 665	A Little Bit Of Soap/Ready Steady Let's Go	80
66	Fontana TF 715	I Must Be Mad/Suspense	300

MINT VALUE £

CARL CRAIG

94	Open OPENT-001	Throw/Remake Uno (as CARL CRAIG PRESENTS PAPERCLIP PEOPLE) (12")	15
94	Open OPENT-004	Throw (The Remixes) (as CARL CRAIG PRESENTS PAPERCLIP PEOPLE (12")	12
95	Blanco Y Negro EG 80T	Science Fiction (12")	8
04	Carl Craig (White) CCR002	Volume Two (2x12")	25
95	Blanco Y Negro 509-99865-1	LANDCRUISING (2xLP)	15
01	Obsessive EVSLP20	ABSTRACT FUNK THEORY (as CARL CRAIG PRESENTS...) (2xLP)	15

PAUL CRAIG

66	CBS 202406	Midnight Girl/Autumn	10

WENDY CRAIG

68	Philips BF 1704	Hushabye Mountain/Windows Of The World	5

DON CRAINE'S NEW DOWNLINERS SECT

(see also Downliners Sect)

67	Pye 7N 17261	I Can't Get Away From You/Roses	250

FLOYD CRAMER

(see also Country Hams)

54	London HL 8012	Fancy Pants/Five Foot Two Eyes Of Blue	40
54	London HL 8012	Fancy Pants/Five Foot Two Eyes Of Blue (78)	10
54	London HL 8062	Jolly Cholly/Oh! Suzanna	50
54	London HL 8062	Jolly Cholly/Oh! Suzanna (78)	10
55	London HLU 8195	Rag-A-Tag/Aunt Dinah's Quiltin' Party	30
55	London HLU 8195	Rag-A-Tag/Aunt Dinah's Quiltin' Party (78)	12
58	RCA RCA 1050	Flip Flop And Bop/Sophisticated Swing	30
58	RCA RCA 1050	Flip Flop And Bop/Sophisticated Swing (78)	20
60	RCA RCA 1211	Last Date/Sweetie Baby	7
61	RCA 1231	On The Rebound/Mood Indigo	6
61	RCA 1241	San Antonio Rose/I Can Just Imagine	6
62	RCA 1301	Hot Pepper/For Those That Cry	7
55	London REP 1023	PIANO HAYRIDE (EP, with Louisiana Hayride Band)	50
63	RCA RCX 7120	THAT HANDSOME PIANO (EP)	10
61	RCA RD 27221	ON THE REBOUND (LP)	12

FLOYD CRAMER/HOUSTON ROBERTS

65	Fontana FJL 308	FLOYD CRAMER/HOUSTON ROBERTS (LP, one side each)	12

CRAMP

78	Rip Off RIP 7	She Doesn't Love Me/Suzy Lie Down (p/s)	10

CRAMPS

79	Illegal ILS 12013	GRAVEST HITS (12" EP, blue vinyl)	30
79	Illegal ILS 12013	GRAVEST HITS (12" EP, black vinyl)	10
80	Illegal ILS 0017	Fever/Garbage Man (withdrawn 1st 'full band' p/s)	20
80	Illegal ILS 0017	Fever/Garbage Man (p/s; re-pressing in different p/s with 4 separate shots)	15
80	Illegal ILS 0017	Garbage Man/Mystery Plane (Unreleased test pressing)	150
80	Illegal ILS 021	Drug Train/Love Me/I Can't Hardly Stand It (p/s)	10
81	IRS PFS 1003	Goo Goo Muck/She Said (p/s, yellow vinyl)	15
81	IRS PFSX 1008	The Crusher/Save It/New Kind Of Kick (12", p/s)	15
85	Big Beat NS 110	Can Your Pussy Do The Dog?/Blue Moon Baby (p/s, orange see-through vinyl)	8
86	Big Beat NS 115	What's Inside A Girl/Give Me A Woman (p/s, purple vinyl)	8
86	Big Beat NS 115	What's Inside A Girl/Get Off The Road/Give Me A Woman (12", p/s, white vinyl)	12
89	Enigma ENVPD 17	Bikini Girls With Machine Guns/Jackyard Backoff (picture disc)	8
89	Enigma ENV 19	All Women Are Bad/King Of The Drapes/ Teenage Rage/High School Hellcats (12", pic disc)	8
90	Enigma 12ENV22	Creature From The Black Leather Lagoon/Jailhouse Rock/Beat Out My Love (shrinkwrapped inner with sticker)	15
80	Illegal ILP 005	SONGS THE LORD TAUGHT US (LP, white label with "Drug Train" in place of "T.V. Set")	175
80	Illegal ILP 005	SONGS THE LORD TAUGHT US (LP, with "T.V. Set")	20
81	IRS SP 70016	PSYCHEDELIC JUNGLE (LP)	20
83	Illegal ILP 012	OFF THE BONE (LP, white label, with different mix of "Drug Train", around 50 copies pressed, unreleased)	100
83	Illegal ILP 012	OFF THE BONE (LP, with 3-D sleeve & glasses)	40
83	Illegal ILP 012	OFF THE BONE (LP, picture disc with extra track)	15
84	Big Beat NED 6	SMELL OF FEMALE (LP, red see-through vinyl)	20
84	Big Beat BEDP 6	SMELL OF FEMALE (LP, picture disc)	20
84	Big Beat NED 6	SMELL OF FEMALE (LP, 2nd issue, black vinyl)	12
86	Big Beat WIKA 46	A DATE WITH ELVIS (LP, with poster)	20
86	Big Beat WIKA 46	A DATE WITH ELVIS (LP, blue vinyl)	25
91	Big Beat WIKPD 101	LOOK MOM NO HEAD (LP, picture disc)	15
91	Windsong WINDSONG 4	LUX (3 x 12" box set, with poster, T-shirt & book, numbered, withdrawn)	50

CRANBERRIES

91	Xeric XER 014	Uncertain/Nothing Left At All (p/s)	15
91	Xeric XER 014T	Uncertain/Nothing Left At All/Pathetic Senses/Them (12", p/s)	20
91	Xeric XER 014CD	Uncertain/Nothing Left At All/Pathetic Senses/Them (CD)	40
92	Mlah FAN 2	Fields Of Athenry/Little Green Apes (1-sided flexi, with Spudsound fanzine)	7
94	Island ILPS 8029	NO NEED TO ARGUE (LP)	25
99	Mercury/Island 524 644 1	BURY THE HATCHET (2-LP)	40

CRANE/FARLOWE

(see also Atomic Rooster, Crazy World Of Arthur Brown, Chris Farlowe, Katmandu)

73	Dawn DNS 1034	Can't Find A Reason/Moods	7

LES CRANE

71	Warner Bros K16119	Desiderata/A Different Drummer	7

TONY CRANE

(see also Bob Miller, Merseys/Merseybeats)

65	Polydor BM 56008	Ideal Love/Little You	15

MINT VALUE £

66	CBS 202022	Even The Bravest/I Still Remember	20
67	Pye 7N 17337	Anonymous Mr Brown/In This World	15
68	Pye 7N 17517	Scratchin' Ma Head/Patterns In The Sky	15

CRANE RIVER JAZZ BAND

(see also Ken Colyer)

53	Parlophone MSP 6008	Lily Of The Valley/Till We Meet Again	5
57	77 LP/4	ORIGINAL CRANE RIVER JAZZ BAND (LP)	20
57	77 LP/5	ORIGINAL CRANE RIVER JAZZ BAND (LP)	20
57	77 LP/17	ORIGINAL CRANE RIVER JAZZ BAND (LP)	20
57	77 LP/18	ORIGINAL CRANE RIVER JAZZ BAND (LP)	20

CRASH

82	Crash EJSP 9819	FIGHT FOR YOUR LIFE (EP, no p/s)	20

CRASHERS

69	Amalgamated AMG 834	Hurry Come Up/Off Track	35

CRASS

(see also Anne Anxiety, Joy De Vivre, Eve Libertine, Poison Girls)

78	Small Wonder WEENY 2	THE FEEDING OF THE 5000 (12" EP, with 4-page insert & poster)	15
78	Crass 621984	THE FEEDING OF THE 5000 (12" EP, reissue with "Reality Asylum")	8
79	Crass 521984/1	Reality Asylum/Shaved Women (brown cardboard gatefold p/s)	20
79	Crass 521984/1	Reality Asylum/Shaved Women (later pressing in white newspaper foldout sleeve)	6
80	Crass/Xntrix 421984/1	Bloody Revolutions/POISON GIRLS: Persons Unknown (foldout p/s)	8
80	Crass 421984/5	Nagasaki Nightmare/Big A Little A (foldout p/s, with patch)	20
80	Crass 421984/5	Nagasaki Nightmare/Big A Little A (foldout p/s, without patch)	6
81	Crass 421984/6	Rival Tribal Rebel Revel/Bully Boys Out Fighting (flexidisc with Toxic Graffiti fanzine)	20
81	Crass 421984/6	Rival Tribal Rebel Revel/Bully Boys Out Fighting (flexidisc without Toxic Graffiti fanzine)	8
81	Crass 421984/6	Rival Tribal Rebel Revel/Bully Boys Out Fighting (hard vinyl promo, p/s)	40
81	Crass COLD TURKEY 1	Merry Crassmass/Merry Crassmass - Have Fun (p/s)	6
81	Crass 321984/IF flexi	Our Wedding (free flexi sent to readers of Loving - 'for the price of a Stamp'. By Creative Recording And Sound Services - CRASS' with mailer envelope)	300
82	Crass 221984/6	How Does It Feel (To Be The Mother Of 1000 Dead?)/The Immortal Death/ Don't Tell Me You Care (foldout p/s)	8
83	Crass 121984/3	Sheep Farming In The Falklands/Gotcha! (live) (foldout p/s with lyric insert)	6
83	(no label)	Gotcha! (clear flexidisc)	10
83	Crass 121984/4	Who Dunnit? (Parts 1 & 2) (p/s, brown vinyl)	6
79	Crass 521984	STATIONS OF THE CRASS (2-LP, fold-out sleeve, black and white inners, original issue with "Pay no more than £3.00" on sleeve)	15
81	Crass 321984	PENIS ENVY (LP, original pressing with "pay no more than £2.25" on sleeve)	12
82	Crass BOLLOX 2U2	CHRIST THE ALBUM (2-LP, box set with booklet)	20
83	Crass 121984	YES SIR, I WILL (LP, fold-out sleeve, original issue with "Pay no more than £2.75" on sleeve)	12

CRAVATS

(see also Very Things)

78	The Cravats CH 004	Gordon/Situations (p/s)	25
79	Small Wonder SMALL 15	The End/Burning Bridges/I Hate The Universe (p/s)	8
80	Small Wonder SMALL 24	Precinct/Who's In Here With Me? (p/s, some free flexidisc ["Fireman"/ A FLUX IN 3D: Divide])	8
80	Small Wonder SMALL 24	Precinct/Who's In Here With Me? (p/s)	5
80	Small Wonder SMALL 25	You're Driving Me Mad/I Am The Dregs (p/s)	10
81	Small Wonder SMALL 26	Off The Beach/And The Sun Shone On (p/s)	8
82	Crass 221984/2	RUB ME OUT (EP, 21" x 14" poster p/s)	8
85	Reflex 12 RE 10	THE LAND OF THE GIANTS (12" EP)	12
80	Small Wonder CRAVAT 1	THE CRAVATS IN TOYTOWN (LP, with inner sleeve)	18

CAROLYN CRAWFORD

65	Stateside SS 384	When Someone's Good To You/My Heart	150
65	Stateside SS 384	When Someone's Good To You/My Heart (DJ copy)	220

HANK CRAWFORD

63	London HAK 8103	SOUL OF THE BALLAD (LP)	30

JAMES 'SUGARBOY' CRAWFORD

73	Chess 6145 024	Jock-o-mo (Iko Iko)/BOBBY CHARLES: See You Later, Alligator	6

JIMMY CRAWFORD

60	Columbia DB 4525	Long Stringy Baby/Unkind	50
61	Columbia DB 4633	Love Or Money/Does My Heartache Show	15
61	Columbia DB 4717	I Love How You Love Me/Our Last Embrace	6
62	Columbia DB 4841	I Shoulda Listened To Mama/A Boy Without A Girl	15
62	Columbia DB 4895	Thank You/There'll Be No Goodbyes	10
63	Columbia DB 4975	Another Of Your Toys/Young And Afraid	7
63	Columbia DB 7175	Don't Worry About Bobby/Take This Rose	10
70	CBS 4891	I Can Make It With You/I'm Gonna Change The Plans You Made	6

JOHNNY CRAWFORD

62	Pye International 7N 25145	Cindy's Birthday/Patti Ann	10
62	London HL 9605	Your Nose Is Gonna Grow/Something Special	7
62	London HL 9638	Rumors/No One Really Loves A Clown	7
63	London HL 9669	Proud/Lonesome Town	10
64	London HL 9836	Judy Loves Me/Living In The Past	10
62	London RE 1343	JOHNNY CRAWFORD (EP)	30
64	London RE 1416	WHEN I FALL IN LOVE (EP)	30
63	London HA 8060	RUMORS (LP)	40
64	London HA 8197	JOHNNY CRAWFORD - HIS GREATEST HITS (LP)	40

			MINT VALUE £
MICHAEL CRAWFORD			
65	United Artists UP 1095	The Knack/Oh That Girl	7
66	United Artists UP 1127	It's Gonna Take A Little Time/Help Me	8
CRAWFORD BROTHERS			
57	Vogue V 9077	Midnight Mover Groover/Midnight Happenings	250
57	Vogue V 9077	Midnight Mover Groover/Midnight Happenings (78)	50
59	Vogue V 9140	It Feels Good/I Ain't Guilty (triangular or round centre)	275
59	Vogue V 9140	It Feels Good/I Ain't Guilty (78)	50
CRAWLING CHAOS			
80	Factory FAC 17	Sex Machine/Berlin (p/s)	15
CRAYS			
65	Polydor BM 56033	Nancy's Minuet/Don't Pity Me	5
CRAZE			
(see also Skunks, Hard Corps)			
79	Cobra COB 3	Motions/Spartans (p/s)	5
80	Harvest HAR 5200	Motions/Spartans (reissue in different p/s)	5
80	Harvest HAR 5205	Lucy/Stop Living In The Past (p/s)	6
CRAZY CAVAN AND THE RHYTHM ROCKERS			
73	Crazy Rhythm CR 01	Teddy Boy Boogie/Bop Little Baby	8
74	Crazy Rhythm CR 02	Teddy Boy Rock'N'Roll/Rockabilly Star/ Wildest Cat In Town/Little Teddy Girl	10
CRAZY ELEPHANT			
69	Major Minor MM 609	Gimme Gimme Good Lovin'/Dark Part Of My Mind	5
69	Major Minor MM 623	Sunshine Red Wine/Pam	5
70	Major Minor MM 672	There's A Better Day Coming/Space Buggy	5
69	Major Minor SMLP 62	CRAZY ELEPHANT (LP, red/white/black label)	30
CRAZY FEELINGS			
67	Polydor NH 56723	Please Lie/Time Is Running Out	6
CRAZY HORSE			
(see also Neil Young, Nils Lofgren, Jack Nitzsche)			
72	Reprise RSLP 6438	CRAZY HORSE (LP)	22
72	Reprise K 44171	LOOSE (LP, gatefold sleeve)	15
CRAZY PAVING			
70	MCA KM55057	Anytime Sunshine/Sweet Brandy	12
CRAZY ROCKERS			
64	King KG 1001	Third Man Theme/Mama Papa	5
PAPA JOHN CREACH			
(see also Jefferson Airplane)			
71	Grunt FTR 1003	PAPA JOHN CREACH (LP)	12
73	Grunt FTR 1009	FILTHY (LP)	12
CREAM			
(see also Eric Clapton, Jack Bruce, Ginger Baker, Blind Faith)			
66	Reaction 591 007	Wrapping Paper/Cat's Squirrel	20
66	Reaction 591 011	I Feel Free/N.S.U.	12
67	Reaction 591 015	Strange Brew/Tales Of Brave Ulysses	15
68	Polydor 56258	Anyone For Tennis (The Savage Seven Theme)/Pressed Rat And Warthog	10
68	Polydor 56286	Sunshine Of Your Love/SWLABR	7
68	Polydor 56300	White Room/Those Were The Days	7
69	Polydor 56315	Strange Brew/Wrapping Paper (unissued)	0
69	Polydor 56315	Badge/What A Bringdown	7
71	Polydor 2058 120	I Feel Free/Wrapping Paper	6
72	Polydor 2058 285	Badge/What A Bringdown (reissue)	6
66	Reaction 593 001	FRESH CREAM (LP, mono)	70
66	Reaction 594 001	FRESH CREAM (LP, stereo)	50
67	Reaction 593 003	DISRAELI GEARS (LP, sleeve laminated on front & back, mono)	80
67	Reaction 594 003	DISRAELI GEARS (LP, sleeve laminated on front & back, stereo)	60
68	Reaction 593 003	DISRAELI GEARS (LP, sleeve laminated on front only, mono)	40
68	Reaction 594 003	DISRAELI GEARS (LP, sleeve laminated on front only, stereo)	30
68	Polydor 582/583 031/2	WHEELS OF FIRE (2-LP, gatefold sleeve, mono; set no. 2612 001)	70
68	Polydor 582/583 031/2	WHEELS OF FIRE (2-LP, gatefold sleeve, stereo; set no. 2612 001)	50
68	Polydor 582 033	WHEELS OF FIRE - IN THE STUDIO (LP, mono)	40
68	Polydor 583 033	WHEELS OF FIRE - IN THE STUDIO (LP, stereo)	30
68	Polydor 582 040	WHEELS OF FIRE - LIVE AT THE FILLMORE (LP, mono)	40
68	Polydor 583 040	WHEELS OF FIRE - LIVE AT THE FILLMORE (LP, stereo)	30
69	Polydor 583 053	GOODBYE (LP, gatefold sleeve)	18
69	Polydor 583 060	THE BEST OF CREAM (LP)	12
70	Polydor 2383 016	LIVE CREAM (LP)	15
71	Polydor 2855 002	CREAM ON TOP (LP, mail-order compilation)	35
72	Polydor 2383 119	LIVE CREAM VOL. 2 (LP)	12
80	RSO 2658 142	CREAM (7-LP set including "Fresh Cream", "Disraeli Gears", "Wheels Of Fire", Goodbye, "Live Cream" & "Live Cream Vol. 2")	40
92	UFO CR 1	CREAM IN GEAR (96-page book packaged with "Disraeli Gears" CD)	20
CREAMERS			
89	Fierce FRIGHT 045	Sunday Head/Think I'm Gonna Be Sick (p/s)	10
JOAN CREARY			
71	Fab FAB 181	Your Best Friend/Version	7
CREATION (U.K.)			
(see also Mark Four, Birds, Ashton Gardner & Dyke, Kennedy Express, Eddy Phillips, Smiley, Spectrum)			
66	Planet PLF 116	Making Time/Try And Stop Me (with Planet sleeve)	45

			MINT VALUE £
66	Planet PLF 116	Making Time/Try And Stop Me (without Planet sleeve)	35
66	Planet PLF 119	Painter Man/Biff Bang Pow (with Planet sleeve)	45
66	Planet PLF 119	Painter Man/Biff Bang Pow (without Planet sleeve)	35
67	Polydor 56177	If I Stay Too Long/Nightmares	50
67	Polydor 56207	Life Is Just Beginning/Through My Eyes	100
68	Polydor 56230	How Does It Feel To Feel/Tom Tom	75
68	Polydor 56246	Midway Down/The Girls Are Naked	50
73	Charisma CB 213	Making Time/Painter Man	8
77	Raw RAW 4	Making Time/Painter Man (reissue, p/s)	10
84	Edsel E 5006	Making Time/Uncle Bert (p/s)	10
73	Charisma Perspective CS 8	THE CREATION '66-67 (LP)	45
82	Edsel ED 106	HOW DOES IT FEEL TO FEEL (LP, with foldout insert)	15

CREATION (U.S.)

(see also Prophets)

72	Stateside SS 2205	I Got The Fever/Soul Control	15

CREATION REBEL

79	Hit Run HIT DD8	Beware/Natty Conscience Free (12")	40
81	On-U Sound DP3	Independent Man Dub/CREATION REBEL : Dub	30
78	Hit Run APLP 9001	DUB FROM CREATION (LP)	30
79	Hit Run APLP 9004	REBEL VIBRATIONS (LP)	60
81	4D Rhythms 4DLP1	STARSHIP AFRICA (LP)	30
81	Static STATLP 04	PSYCHOTIC JONKANOO	30
82	On-U Sound ON-U LP08	STARSHIP AFRICA (LP)	30
82	Cherry Red BRED 21	THREAT TO CREATION (LP, With the New Age Steppers)	15

CREATIONS

(see also Little Roys)

67	Rio R 133	Meet Me At Eight/Searching	18
68	Amalgamated AMG 818	Holding Out/Get On Up	30
69	Punch PH 2	Mix Up Girl/Qua Kue Shut	35

CREATION STEPPER

(see also Fred Locks)

79	Tribesman TM 22	What You Are Not Supposed To Do/Children Obey Your Parents (12")	15
80	Nationwide NWD 015	Homeward Bound/Version (12")	45
81	Moa Anbassa MA005	Treat Me Unkind/Unkind Dub (12")	15
04	Jah Tuibbys JT 10019	King Nebuchadnezzar (with the Disciples Riddim Section)/ The Nebuchadnezzar Skarock (with the Dread-UK Crew) (12")	30

CREATIVE SOURCE

73	Sussex LPSX6	CREATIVE SOURCE (LP)	20

CREATIVE THIEVES

91	Stress Records 12 STR 02	Nasty Rhythm (12")	8

CREATOR & NORMA

63	Island WI 105	We Will Be Lovers/Come On Pretty Baby	10

CREATORS

96	Blind Side BS002	HAVE A MASTER PLAN (EP)	8

CREATURES

66	CBS 202048	Turn Out The Light/It Must Be Love	12
66	CBS 202350	String Along/Night Is Warm	12
67	CBS 2666	Looking At Tomorrow/Someone Needs You	12

CREEDENCE CLEARWATER REVIVAL

(see also Golliwogs, John Fogerty, Tom Fogerty, Blue Ridge Rangers)

69	Liberty LBF 15223	Proud Mary/I Put A Spell On You (withdrawn)	20
69	Liberty LBF 15223	Proud Mary/Born On The Bayou	6
69	Liberty LBF 15230	Bad Moon Rising/Lodi	7
69	Liberty LBF 15250	Green River/Commotion	6
70	Liberty LBF 15283	Down On The Corner/Fortunate Son	6
70	Liberty LBF 15310	Travellin' Band/Who'll Stop The Rain	8
70	Liberty LBF 15354	Up Around The Bend/Run Through The Jungle (in p/s)	10
70	Liberty LBF 15354	Up Around The Bend/Run Through The Jungle	5
70	Liberty LBF 15384	Long As I Can See The Light/Lookin' Out My Back Door (in p/s)	10
70	Liberty LBF 15384	Long As I Can See The Light/Lookin' Out My Back Door	5
71	Liberty LBF 15440	Have You Ever Seen The Rain/Hey Tonight	5
71	United Artists UP 35261	Sweet Hitch-Hiker/Door To Door	6
72	Fantasy F 676	Someday Never Comes/Tearin' Up The Country	5
72	Fantasy FTC 101	Born On The Bayou/I Put A Spell On You	5
73	Fantasy FTC 104	It Came Out Of The Sky/Side O' The Road	5
69	Liberty LBS 83259	CREEDENCE CLEARWATER REVIVAL (LP)	25
69	Liberty LBS 83261	BAYOU COUNTRY (LP)	20
69	Liberty LBS 83273	GREEN RIVER (LP)	20
70	Liberty LBS 83338	WILLY AND THE POORBOYS (LP)	18
70	Liberty LBS 83388	COSMO'S FACTORY (LP)	18
71	Liberty LBG 83400	PENDULUM (LP, gatefold sleeve)	15

CREEPERS

66	Blue Beat BB 366	Beat Of My Soul/LLOYD ADAMS: I Wish Your Picture Was You	20

CREME CARAMEL

69	Pye International 7N 25495	My Idea/Excursion	5

CRESCENDOS

58	London HLU 8563	Oh Julie/My Little Girl	110
58	London HLU 8563	Oh Julie/My Little Girl (78)	20

CRESCENTS

58	Columbia DB 4093	Wrong/Baby, Baby, Baby	100
58	Columbia DB 4093	Wrong/Baby, Baby, Baby (78)	20

MINT VALUE £

CRESCENTS
64 London HLN 9851 — Pink Dominos/Breakout — 25

CRESSIDA
(see also Uriah Heep, Black Widow)
70 Vertigo VO 7 — CRESSIDA (LP, gatefold sleeve, large swirl label) — 250
71 Vertigo 6360 025 — ASYLUM (LP, gatefold sleeve, large swirl label) — 400

CRESTAS
65 Fontana TF 551 — To Be Loved/When I Fall In Love — 25

CRESTERS
(see also Mike Sagar & Cresters, Richard Harding)
64 HMV POP 1249 — I Just Don't Understand/I Want You — 15
64 HMV POP 1296 — Put Your Arms Around Me/Do It With Me — 10

CRESTS
(see also Johnny Maestro)
59 London HL 8794 — Sixteen Candles/Beside You — 100
59 London HL 8794 — Sixteen Candles/Beside You (78) — 25
59 Top Rank JAR 150 — Flower Of Love/Molly Mae — 25
59 Top Rank JAR 168 — Six Nights A Week/I Do — 25
59 Top Rank JAR 168 — Six Nights A Week/I Do (78) — 25
59 London HL 8954 — The Angels Listened In/I Thank The Moon — 60
59 London HL 8954 — The Angels Listened In/I Thank The Moon (78) — 25
60 Top Rank JAR 302 — A Year Ago Tonight/Paper Crown — 25
60 Top Rank JAR 372 — Step By Step/Gee (But I'd Give The World) — 25
60 HMV POP 768 — Always You/Trouble In Paradise — 25
60 HMV POP 808 — Isn't It Amazing/Molly Mae — 25
61 HMV POP 848 — Model Girl/We've Got To Tell Them — 20
62 HMV POP 976 — Little Miracles/Baby I Gotta Know — 25
63 London HLU 9671 — Guilty/Number One With Me — 25

CREW
69 Plexium PXM 12 — Marty/Danger Signs — 7
70 Decca F 13000 — Cecilia/1970 — 7

CREW-CUTS
56 Mercury 7MT 2 — Angels In The Sky/Seven Days (export issue) — 30
58 RCA RCA 1075 — Hey, Stella!/Forever, My Darling — 30
58 RCA RCA 1075 — Hey, Stella!/Forever, My Darling (78) — 10
56 Mercury MEP 9002 — PRESENTING THE CREW-CUTS (EP) — 60
56 Mercury MPT 7501 — THE CREW-CUTS ON PARADE (10" LP) — 90

BOB CREWE (GENERATION)
60 London HLI 9077 — Water Boy/Voglio Cantare (solo) — 5
64 Stateside SS 356 — Maggie Maggie May/We Almost Made It — 5
67 Stateside SS 582 — Music To Watch Girls By/Girls On The Rocks — 12
67 Stateside SS 2032 — You Only Live Twice/A Lover's Concerto — 10
67 Philips BL 7788 — PLAY THE FOUR SEASONS HITS (LP, as Bob Crewe Orch.) — 25
67 Stateside SL 10210 — MUSIC TO WATCH GIRLS BY (LP) — 35
68 Stateside S(S)L 10260 — BARBARELLA (LP, soundtrack) — 100

BERNARD CRIBBINS
67 Parlophone R 5603 — When I'm Sixty-Four/Oh My Word — 7
62 Parlophone PMC 1186 — A COMBINATION OF CRIBBINS (LP, also stereo [PCS 3035]) — 18

THE CRIBS
(see also The Smiths, Wrinkle)
03 Squirrel No 5 — Baby Don't Sweat/You and I (other 2 tracks by JEN SCHANDE) — 40
03 Wichita WEBB051S — Baby Don't Sweat/Another Number (p/s, yellow vinyl) — 10
04 Wichita WEBB059S — You Were Always The One/Song From Practice 1 (p/s) — 15
04 B-Unique KAISER — Plays Kaiser Chiefs (gig only 7" given away free, stickered sleeve) — 15
04 Wichita WEBB061S — What About Me/Feelin' It (yellow vinyl, p/s) — 7

CRICKETS featuring Buddy Holly
(see also Buddy Holly)

78s
57 Vogue Coral Q 72279 — That'll Be The Day/I'm Lookin' For Someone To Love — 15
57 Coral Q 72298 — Oh Boy!/Not Fade Away — 12
58 Coral Q 72279 — That'll Be The Day/I'm Lookin' For Someone To Love — 12
58 Coral Q 72307 — Maybe Baby/Tell Me How — 20
58 Coral Q 72329 — Think It Over/Fool's Paradise — 25
58 Coral Q 72343 — It's So Easy/Lonesome Tears — 35

SINGLES
57 Vogue Coral Q 72279 — That'll Be The Day/I'm Lookin' For Someone To Love — 25
57 Coral Q 72298 — Oh Boy!/Not Fade Away — 20
58 Coral Q 72279 — That'll Be The Day/I'm Lookin' For Someone To Love (2nd issue) — 20
58 Coral Q 72307 — Maybe Baby/Tell Me How — 20
58 Coral Q 72329 — Think It Over/Fool's Paradise — 20
58 Coral Q 72343 — It's So Easy/Lonesome Tears — 20
(The above 45s were originally issued with triangular centres; later round centre copies are worth around half these values)
68 Decca AD 1012 — Oh, Boy/That'll Be The Day (export issue) — 75

EPs
58 Coral FEP 2003 — THE SOUND OF THE CRICKETS (triangular or round centre) — 30
59 Coral FEP 2014 — IT'S SO EASY (triangular or round centre) — 30
60 Coral FEP 2060 — FOUR MORE BY THE CRICKETS — 35
60 Coral FEP 2062 — THAT'LL BE THE DAY — 35

LPs
58 Vogue Coral LVA 9081 — THE CHIRPING CRICKETS (Vogue-Coral labels & Coral sleeve) — 150
58 Coral LVA 9081 — THE CHIRPING CRICKETS (re-pressing with Coral labels & sleeve) — 100

MINT VALUE £

CRICKETS

(see also Buddy Holly, Jerry Allison & Crickets, Ivan, Sonny Curtis, Earl Sinks, Sinx Mitchell, David Box)

59	Coral Q 72365	Love's Made A Fool Of You/Someone, Someone (78)	75
59	Coral Q 72382	When You Ask About Love/Deborah (78)	100
59	Coral Q 72365	Love's Made A Fool Of You/Someone, Someone	15
59	Coral Q 72382	When You Ask About Love/Deborah	15
60	Coral Q 72395	More Than I Can Say/Baby My Heart	15
61	Coral Q 72417	Peggy Sue Got Married/Don'tcha Know	15
61	Coral Q 72440	I Fought The Law/A Sweet Love	15
61	London HLG 9486	He's Old Enough To Know Better/I'm Feeling Better	15
62	Liberty LIB 55441	Don't Ever Change/I Am Not A Bad Guy	8
62	Liberty LIB 55495	Little Hollywood Girl/Parisian Girl	12
63	Liberty LIB 10067	My Little Girl/Teardrops Fall Like Rain	8
63	Liberty LIB 10092	Don't Try To Change Me/Lost And Alone	8
63	Liberty LIB 10113	Right Or Wrong/You Can't Be In Between	7
64	Liberty LIB 10145	Lonely Avenue/Playboy	7
64	Liberty LIB 55696	(They Call Her) La Bamba/All Over You	8
64	Liberty LIB 10174	I Think I've Caught The Blues/We Gotta Get Together	10
66	Liberty LIB 55603	April Avenue/Don't Say You Love Me	10
68	Liberty LBF 15089	My Little Girl/Lonely Avenue	7
72	United Artists UP 35457	Don't Ever Change/Playboy	5
73	Philips 6006 269	My Rockin' Days/Lovesick Blues	7
73	Philips 6006 294	Hayride/Wasn't It Nice In New York City (in p/s)	20
73	Philips 6006 294	Hayride/Wasn't It Nice In New York City	12
74	Mercury 6008 006	Ooh Las Vegas/Rhyme And Time	5
79	Rollercoaster RRC 2001	Cruise In It/Rock Around With Ollie Vee (1st 2,000 with 'single photo' p/s)	8
79	Rollercoaster RRC 2001	Cruise In It/Rock Around With Ollie Vee (p/s)	6
87	Rollercoaster RRC 2007	Forever In Mind/The Weekend/Your M-M-Memory/ Three-Piece (tri-centre in overprinted p/s)	6
88	MPL/CBS TSH 1	T-Shirt/Hollywould (p/s)	6

EPs

60	Coral FEP 2053	THE CRICKETS (initial trangular centre)	50
60	Coral FEP 2053	THE CRICKETS (later round centre)	30
61	Coral FEP 2064	THE CRICKETS DON'T EVER CHANGE	40
63	Liberty (S)LEP 2094	STRAIGHT NO STRINGS (mono/stereo)	30
64	Liberty LEP 2173	COME ON	40

LPs

61	Coral LVA 9142	IN STYLE WITH THE CRICKETS	50
62	Liberty LBY 1120	SOMETHING OLD, SOMETHING NEW, SOMETHING BLUE, SOMETHING ELSE! (mono)	30
62	Liberty (S)LBY 1120	SOMETHING OLD, SOMETHING NEW, SOMETHING BLUE, SOMETHING ELSE! (stereo)	40
65	Liberty LBY 1258	THE CRICKETS - A COLLECTION	20
71	CBS 64301	ROCKIN' 50's ROCK 'N' ROLL (LP)	15

CRICKETS & BOBBY VEE

(see also Bobby Vee)

63	Liberty LEP 2084	JUST FOR FUN (EP)	25
63	Liberty LEP 2116	BOBBY VEE MEETS THE CRICKETS (EP, mono)	10
63	Liberty SLEP 2116	BOBBY VEE MEETS THE CRICKETS (EP, stereo)	15
63	Liberty LEP 2149	BOBBY VEE MEETS THE CRICKETS VOL. 2 (EP)	15
62	Liberty LBY 1086	BOBBY VEE MEETS THE CRICKETS (LP, mono)	12
62	Liberty SLBY 1086	BOBBY VEE MEETS THE CRICKETS (LP, stereo)	15

JIMMY CRIKIT

70	MCA MK 5047	Isabella/Love Is A See Saw	10

CRIME

80	Punk Products PP 1	Johnny Come Home/Generation Gap (p/s, beware of bootlegs)	100

THE CRIMEWATCH PROJECT

92	Strategic Dance Initiative SDI 004	Boomzabang/Kis My Neck/Friday Night Style (white label 12", stickered paper sleeve)	80

CRIMINAL CLASS

82	Inferno HELL 7	Fighting The System/Soldier (p/s)	15

CRIMINAL JUSTICE

85	Endangered Music EDR 2	HIERARCHY OF HELL (EP)	12

THE CRIMINAL MINDS

90	TCM SRT90L2748	GUILTY AS CHARGED (EP)	150
91	TCM EP002	TALES FROM THE WASTELAND (EP)	120

CRIMSON BRIDGE

72	Myrrh Ms 6224	FILL YOUR HEAD WITH... (LP)	25

GEOFF CRIPPS & LOUISA RUGG

85	Steam Pie SPR 1003S	ICARUS (LP)	12

CRISIS

(see also Death In June, Current 93, Theatre Of Hate)

79	Peckham Action NOTH 1	No Town Hall (Southwark)/Holocaust/P.C. One Nine Eight Four (p/s)	15
79	Ardkor CRI 002	UK '79/White Youth (p/s)	15
80	Ardkor CRI 003	HYMNS OF FAITH (12" EP)	20
81	Ardkor CRI 004	Alienation/Brückwood/Hospital (p/s, with insert)	15
82	Crisis NOTH 1/CRI 002	HOLOCAUST UK (12" EP)	15

CRISIS

70s	private pressing	ANOTHER FINE MESS (LP)	35

MINT VALUE £

CRISP
73	EMI 2050	Sally And Jake/Dimbledale (A Land Not Far Away)	6

MARILYN CRISPELL
83	Leo LR 118	RHYTHMS HUNG IN UNDRAWN SKY (LP)	15
85	Leo LR 126	AND YOUR IVORY VOICE SINGS (LP)	15

CRISPY AMBULANCE
(see also Ram Ram Kino)

79	Aural Assault AAR 001	From The Cradle To The Grave/4 Minutes From The Frontline (glossy p/s)	15
79	Aural Assault AAR 001	From The Cradle To The Grave/4 Minutes From The Frontline (matt p/s)	8
81	Factory FAC 32	Unsightly And Serene: Not What I Expected/Deaf (10", p/s)	8
83	CBST 7	THE BLUE AND YELLOW OF THE YACHT CLUB (cassette)	8
83	CBST 8	OPEN GATES OF FIRE (cassette)	8
89	Temps Moderne LTMV:X	FIN (LP)	12

GARY CRISS
62	Stateside SS 104	Our Favourite Melodies/Welcome Home To My Heart	15
62	Stateside SS 123	My Little Heavenly Angel/The Girl That I Told You About	8
63	Stateside SS 164	Long Lonely Nights/I Still Miss You So	8
63	Stateside SS 265	Sweet, Warm And Soft/Little Joe	8
65	Stateside SS 427	Hands Off Buddy/If This Is Goodbye	8

PETER CRISS
(see also Kiss)

79	Casablanca CAN 139	You Matter To Me/Hooked On Rock And Roll (p/s, green vinyl with mask)	20
79	Casablanca CAN 139	You Matter To Me/Hooked On Rock And Roll (p/s, black vinyl)	8
80	Mercury 6302 065	OUT OF CONTROL (LP)	12

LINDA CRISTAL
59	Coral Q 72350	Strictly For Pleasure (A Perfect Romance)/It's Better In Spanish	6

CRISTINA
80	Ze 12WIP 6560	Is That All There Is/Jungle Love	15

BOBBY CRISTO & REBELS
64	Decca F 11913	The Other Side Of The Track/I've Got You Out Of My Mind	40

MARY CRISTY
76	Polydor 2056 513	Thank You For Rushing Into My Life/We Can't Hide This Time	10

CRITICS & NYAH SHUFFLE
70	Joe JRS 1	Behold/SEXY FRANKIE: Tea, Patty, Sex And Ganja	12

CRITICS GROUP
66	Argo ZDA 46	A MERRY PROGRESS TO LONDON (LP, with insert)	20
68	Argo ZDA 82	THE FEMALE FROLIC (LP, with insert)	20
68	Argo DA 86	WATERLOO PETERLOO (LP, with insert)	20
71	Argo ZDA 138	YE MARINERS ALL (LP)	15

CRITTERS
66	London HLR 10047	Younger Girl/Gone For Awhile	15
66	London HLR 10071	Mr. Dieingly Sad/It Just Won't Be That Way	15
66	London HLR 10101	Bad Misunderstanding/Forever Or No More	25
67	London HLR 10119	Marryin' Kind Of Love/New York Bound	25
67	London HLR 10149	Don't Let The Rain Fall Down On Me/Walk Like A Man Again	18
67	London HA-R 8302	THE CRITTERS (LP)	45

JIM CROCE
72	Vertigo 6073 251	Operator/Rapid Roy	6
72	Vertigo 6360 700	YOU DON'T MESS AROUND WITH JIM (LP, gatefold sleeve, swirl label)	40
72	Vertigo 6360 702	I GOT A NAME (LP)	12
70s	Life Song 135004	LIFE & TIMES (LP, with spiral label)	200
70s	Life Song 135004	LIFE & TIMES (LP)	15
70s	Life Song 135004	GREATEST CHARATOR (LP)	15

CROCHETED DOUGHNUT RING
(see also Force Five, Doughnut Ring, Fingers, Daddy Lindberg)

67	Polydor 56204	Two Little Ladies (Azalea And Rhododendron)/Nice	30
67	Deram DM 169	Havana Anna/Happy Castle	40
68	Deram DM 180	Maxine's Parlour/Get Out Your Rock And Roll Shoes	25

BARRY CROCKER
71	Pye 7N 25567	Love Is A Beautiful Song/Sarah's Coming Home	6

TONY CROCKET
82	Alternative ALT 010	Queen Of Hearts/Plane Jane (12", p/s)	50

CROFT
71	Maple MP 1	The Dream/Henry And His Friends	200

CROFTERS
69	Say Disc SD 113	PILL FERRY (EP)	10
69	Beltona SBE 103	CROFTERS (LP)	15

NICOLE CROISILLE
77	Decca F13708	The Loving Song/Tell Me What I Want To Hear/Telephone Moi	6

TONY CROMBIE
(see also Annie Ross, Ray Ellington, London Jazz Quartet)

54	Decca F 10424	Stop It All/All Of Me (& His Orchestra)	8
55	Decca F 10454	Perdido/Love You Madly (& His Orchestra)	8
55	Decca F 10547	Early One Morning/Flying Home (& His Orchestra)	8
55	Decca F 10592	Flying Hickory/String Of Pearls (& His Orchestra)	8
55	Decca F 10637	I Want You To Be My Baby (with Annie Ross)/Three Little Words	6
55	Decca F 10637	I Want You To Be My Baby (with Annie Ross)/Three Little Words (78)	10

			MINT VALUE £
56	Columbia DB 3822	Teach You To Rock/Short'nin' Bread Rock (as Tony Crombie & Rockets)	45
56	Columbia DB 3822	Teach You To Rock/Short'nin' Bread Rock (as Tony Crombie & Rockets) (78)	10
56	Columbia DB 3859	Sham Rock/Let's You And I Rock (as Tony Crombie & Rockets)	40
57	Columbia DB 3880	Rock, Rock, Rock/The Big Beat (as Tony Crombie & Rockets) (78)	12
57	Columbia DB 3881	Lonesome Train (On A Lonesome Track)/We're Gonna Rock Tonight (78, as Tony Crombie & Rockets)	20
57	Columbia DB 3921	London Rock/Brighton Rock (as Tony Crombie & Rockets)	30
57	Columbia DB 3921	London Rock/Brighton Rock (as Tony Crombie & Rockets) (78)	15
57	Columbia DB 4000	Sweet Beat/Sweet Georgia Brown (as Tony Crombie & His Sweet Beat)	10
57	Columbia DB 4000	Sweet Beat/Sweet Georgia Brown (as Tony Crombie & His Sweet Beat)(78)	10
58	Columbia DB 4076	Dumplin's/Tw'on Special	10
58	Columbia DB 4076	Dumplin's/Tw'on Special (78)	12
58	Columbia DB 4145	Unguaua/Piakukaungchung (as Tony Crombie Men)	6
58	Columbia DB 4189	Rock-Cha-Cha/The Gigglin' Gurgleburp (as Tony Crombie Men)	5
58	Columbia DB 4189	Rock-Cha-Cha/The Gigglin' Gurgleburp (as Tony Crombie Men) (78)	12
59	Columbia DB 4253	Champagne Cha Cha/Shepherd's Cha Cha (as Tony Crombie Men)	5
59	Columbia DB 4253	Champagne Cha Cha/Shepherd's Cha Cha (as Tony Crombie Men) (78)	10
59	Top Rank JAR 182	Man From Interpol Theme/Interpol Cha Cha Cha & Chase (as Tony Crombie Orchestra)	10
59	Top Rank JAR 182	Man From Interpol Theme/Interpol Cha Cha Cha & Chase (as Tony Crombie Orchestra) (78)	20
62	Ember JBS 706	Gutbucket/Just Like Old Times	7
56	Decca DFE 6247	PRESENTING TONY CROMBIE NO. 1 (EP)	15
56	Decca DFE 6281	PRESENTING TONY CROMBIE NO. 2 (EP)	15
57	Columbia SEG 7676	ROCK ROCK ROCK (EP)	90
57	Columbia SEG 7686	LET'S YOU AND I ROCK (EP)	90
61	Decca DFE 6670	FOUR FAVOURITE FILM THEMES (EP)	10
59	Columbia SEG 7882	SWINGIN' DANCE BEAT NO. 1 (EP)	10
59	Columbia SEG 7896	SWINGIN' DANCE BEAT NO. 2 (EP)	10
59	Columbia SEG 7918	ATMOSPHERE (EP, as Tony Crombie & His Men)	10
56	Columbia 33S 1117	TONY CROMBIE & HIS SWEETBEAT (10" LP)	40
57	Columbia 33S 1108	ROCKIN' WITH TONY CROMBIE & ROCKETS (10" LP)	100
58	Columbia SCX 3262	ATMOSPHERE (LP)	30
59	Top Rank 35/043	MAN FROM INTERPOL (LP, TV series music, by Tony Crombie & Band)	25
60	Top Rank BUY 027	DRUMS! DRUMS! DRUMS! (LP, as Tony Crombie & His Band)	20
61	Tempo TAP 30	JAZZ INC. (LP)	100
61	Decca SKL 4114	SWEET WIDE AND BLUE (LP)	25
61	Decca LK 4385	TWELVE FAVOURITE FILM THEMES (LP, also stereo SKL 4127)	15
61	Ember EMB 3336	WHOLE LOTTA TONY (LP)	40

BILL CROMPTON

58	Fontana H 152	A Hoot An' A Holler/The Popocatepetl Beetle	10
59	Fontana H 178	Out Of Sight, Out Of Mind/My Lover	10

CROMWELL

(see also Establishment)

75	Cromwell WELL 006	First Day	20
75	Cromwell WELL 005	AT THE GALLOP (LP, private pressing)	120

LINK CROMWELL (Lenny Kaye)

(see also Patti Smith Group)

66	London HLB 10040	Crazy Like A Fox/Shock Me	25

ANDREW CRONSHAW

77	Trailer LREP 1	CLOUD VALLEY (EP)	10
74	Xtra XTRA 1139	A IS FOR ANDREW, Z IS FOR ZITHER (LP)	15
77	Trailer LER 2104	EARTHED IN CLOUD VALLEY (LP)	15

CROOKED OAK

76	Folkland FL 0102	FROM LITTLE ACORNS GROW (LP, 500 only)	50
79	Eron ERON 019	THE FOOT O'WOR STAIRS (LP)	25

CROOKS

79	Blue Print BLU 2002	Modern Boys/The Beat Goes On (die-cut p/s)	6
80	Blue Print BLU 2006	All The Time In The World/Bangin' My Head (p/s)	10
80	Blue Print BLUP 5002	JUST RELEASED (LP)	12

DAVID CROOKS

(see also Dave Barker)

70	Jackpot JP 759	I Won't Hold It Against You (actually by Dave Barker)/ BOBBY JAMES: King Of Hearts	7

STEVE CROPPER

70	Stax STAX 147	Funky Broadway/Crop Dustin'	10
69	Stax SXATS 1008	WITH A LITTLE HELP FROM MY FRIENDS (LP)	30

STEVE CROPPER & ALBERT KING

(see also Booker T. & M.G.'s, Albert King)

69	Stax SXATS 1020	JAMMED TOGETHER (LP, with Pops Staples)	20

BING CROSBY

(see also Gary Crosby, Louis Armstrong, Bob Hope, Fred Astaire, Peggy Lee)

54	Brunswick 03384	White Christmas/Let's Start The New Year Right	10
54	Brunswick 05224	What A Little Moonlight Can Do/Down By The Riverside (with Gary Crosby)	6

BOB CROSBY & HIS BOBCATS

(see also Modernaires)

59	London HLD 8828	Petite Fleur/Such A Long Night	8
60	London HLD 9228	The Dark At The Top Of The Stairs/Night Theme	7
60	London SAHD 6105	GREAT HITS (LP)	15

DAVID CROSBY

(see also Byrds, Crosby [Stills] Nash [& Young])

93	Atlantic A 7360	Hero/Coverage/Fare Thee Well (CD)	8
71	Atlantic 2401 005	IF I COULD ONLY REMEMBER MY NAME (LP, gatefold sleeve, red/plum label)	30

MINT VALUE £

GARY CROSBY
(see also Bing Crosby, Louis Armstrong)

58	HMV POP 550	Judy, Judy/Cheatin' On Me	50
58	HMV POP 550	Judy, Judy/Cheatin' On Me (78)	10
59	HMV POP 648	The Happy Bachelor/This Little Girl Of Mine	6
57	Vogue VA 160118	GARY CROSBY (LP)	15

CROSBY & NASH

72	Atlantic K 10192	Southbound Train/Whole Cloth	7
72	Atlantic K 50011	GRAHAM NASH & DAVID CROSBY (LP, foldout sleeve)	18

PHIL CROSBY

63	Reprise R 20220	Where The Blue Of The Night (Meets The Gold Of The Day)/Little By Little	8

CROSBY, STILLS & NASH

69	Atlantic 584 283	Marrakesh Express/Helplessly Hoping	10
69	Atlantic 584 304	Suite: Judy Blue Eyes/Long Time Gone	8
69	Atlantic 588 189	CROSBY, STILLS & NASH (LP, gatefold sleeve, with lyric sheet)	22

CROSBY, STILLS, NASH & YOUNG
(see also David Crosby, Stephen Stills [Manassas], Graham Nash, Neil Young)

70	Atlantic 2091 002	Teach Your Children/Country Girl	7
70	Atlantic 2091 010	Woodstock/Helpless	8
70	Atlantic 2091 023	Ohio/Find The Cost Of Freedom	7
70	Atlantic 2091 039	Our House/Deja Vu	10
88	Atlantic A 9003TX	American Dream/Compass/Soldiers Of Peace/Ohio (12", p/s)	8
70	Atlantic 2401 001	DÉJA VU (LP, gatefold sleeve, pasted-on photo on front, plum/red label)	25
71	Atlantic 2657 007	FOUR WAY STREET (2-LP, gatefold sleeve with lyric sheet)	25

CROSS
(see also Roger Taylor, Queen)

87	Virgin VST 1007	Cowboys And Indians (Full Length Version 5.53)/Love Lies Bleeding (She's A Wicked Wily Waitress) (12", p/s)	10
87	Virgin CDEP 10	Cowboys And Indians (4.20)/Cowboys And Indians (Full Length Version 6.12)/ Love Lies Bleeding (She's A Wicked Wily Waitress) (CD, promo only)	35
88	Virgin VST 1062	Heaven For Everyone/Love On A Tightrope (Like An Animal)/Contact (12", p/s)	8
88	Virgin VST 1100	Manipulator (Extended)/Stand Up For Love/Manipulator (7" Version) (12", p/s)	8
90	Parlophone 12R 6251	Power To Love (Extended Version)/Passion For Trash/ Power To Love (7" Version) (12", p/s)	10
90	Parlophone PCS 7342	MAD, BAD AND DANGEROUS TO KNOW (LP)	15
90	Parlophone CDPCS 7342	MAD, BAD AND DANGEROUS TO KNOW (CD)	40

JIMMIE CROSS
(see also T2)

66	Red Bird RB 10042	Super Duper Man/Hey Little Girl	35

(Keith) CROSS & (Peter) ROSS

71	Decca F 13224	Can You Believe It?/Blind Willie Johnson	7
72	Decca F 13316	Peace In The End/Prophets Guiders	7
72	Decca SKL 5129	BORED CIVILIANS (LP, blue/silver labels)	200

CROSSBEATS

67	Pilgrim PSR 7003	Step Aside/Forgive Me (p/s or art sleeve)	8
60s	Pilgrim PSR 7004	Busy Man/Change (p/s)	6
60s	Pilgrim KLP 12	CRAZY MIXED UP GENERATION (LP)	20

CROSS COUNTRY
(see also Tokens)

72	Atlantic K 10353	In The Midnight Hour/A Smile Song	6

ANDRAE CROUCH (& DISCIPLES)

70s	Light LS 7014	JUST ANDRAE (LP)	30
70s	Light LS 7018	DISCIPLES LIVE AT CARNEGIE HALL (LP)	30
70s	Light LS 7019	KEEP ON SINGING (LP)	30
70s	Light LS 7025	TAKE ME BACK (LP)	30
70s	Myrrh MYR 1188	NO TIME TO LOSE (LP)	30
70s	Light LS 7052	I'LL BE THINKING OF YOU (LP)	25
70s	Light LSD 7034	BEST OF (2xLP)	40

CROW

70	Stateside SS 2159	Evil Woman, Don't Play Your Games With Me/Gonna Leave A Mark	6
70	Stateside SS 2171	Slow Down/Cottage Cheese	6
70	Stateside SS 2180	Don't Try To Lay No Boogie Woogie On The King Of Rock And Roll/Satisfied	6
75	Right On R101	Your Autumn Of Tomorrow/Uncle Funk	30
70	Stateside SSL 10301	CROW MUSIC (LP)	18
70	Stateside SSL 10310	CROW BY CROW (LP)	15

SHERYL CROW

93	A&M 580 380-7	Run, Baby, Run/All By Myself (p/s)	5
93	A&M 580 381-2	Run, Baby, Run/All By Myself/The Na-Na Song/Reach Around Jerk (CD)	10
94	A&M 580 462-7	What Can I Do For You (Radio Edit)/Volvo Cowgirl 99 (p/s)	5
94	A&M 580 462-7	What Can I Do For You (Radio Edit)/What Can I Do For You (LP Version)/ Volvo Cowgirl 99/I Shall Believe (CD)	8
94	A&M 580 568-7	Run, Baby, Run/Leaving Las Vegas (Acoustic Version) (p/s)	5
94	A&M 580 569-2	Run, Baby, Run/Leaving Las Vegas (Acoustic Version)/ All By Myself/Reach Around Jerk (CD)	10
94	A&M 581 147-2	Run, Baby, Run/Can't Cry Anymore/Reach Around Jerk/I Shall Believe (CD, 'The Nashville Sessions', box set with poster & numbered 'obi')	15
94	A&M 580 644-7	Leaving Las Vegas/Leaving Las Vegas (Live In Nashville) (p/s, with postcard)	5
96	A&M 581 902-7	If It Makes You Happy (Edit)/All I Wanna Do (jukebox issue, no p/s)	6
96	A&M 580 918-7	Strong Enough/No One Said It Would Be Easy (p/s)	5
95	A&M 540 368-2/	TUESDAY NIGHT MUSIC CLUB (CD, 2nd issue, with patchwork/montage cover and bonus 6-track CD "Sheryl Crow Live" [540 367-2])	25

MINT VALUE £

CROWBAR

84	Skinhead SKIN 1	Hippie Punks/White Riot (p/s)	45

CROWD

79	SRT SRTS/79/CUS 377	Ronnie (Is A Headbanger)/A Little Of What I Fancy/Let's Fly Together (p/s)	6

CROWDED HOUSE

(see also Split Enz, Tim Finn)

87	Capitol CDCL 416	World Where You Live (Extended Version)/Something So Strong/ Don't Dream It's Over/That's What I Call Love (CD, card sleeve)	10
88	Capitol CDCL 498	Better Be Home Soon/Kill Eye/Don't Dream It's Over (live)/ Better Be Home Soon (CD)	15
88	Capitol CDCL 509	Sister Madly/Mansion In The Slums/Something So Strong (live) (CD)	18
91	Capotol CDCD (S) 661	It's Only Natural/It's Only Natural (Live)/Hole In The River (live)/ The Burgular's Song (Medley)/It's Only Natural/Sister Madly (live)/ There Goes God (live)/Chocolate Cake (live) (2xCD single, gatefold wallet sleeve).	12
92	Capitol CDCL 655	Four Seasons In One Day (LP)/Dr. Livingstone/Recurring Dream/ Anyone Can Tell (CD, in collector's box)	10
92	Capitol CH 1/2	LIVE AT THE TOWN AND COUNTRY CLUB, LONDON, NOVEMBER 9 1991 (2-CD, in PVC gatefold wallet & inserts, promo only, autographed)	60
92	Capitol CH 1/2	LIVE AT THE TOWN AND COUNTRY CLUB, LONDON, NOVEMBER 9 1991 (2-CD, in PVC gatefold wallet & inserts, promo only)	40

CROWDY CRAWN

(see under Brenda Wootton)

CROWFOOT

70	Paramount PARA 3008	California Rock 'N' Roll/Maybe I Can Learn To Live	5
70	Paramount SPFL 265	CROWFOOT (LP)	12

DON CROWN & HIS BUSKING BUDGIES

70	Orange OA 5507	Budgerigar Man/Piper Call A Tune	15
71	President PT 340	Mrs Wilson's Budgie/Flying Machines	10

CROWNS

68	Pama PM 725	I Know, It's Alright/I Surrender	25
68	Pama PM 736	Jerking The Dog/Keep Me Going	30
68	Pama PM 745	She Ain't Gonna Do Right/I Need Your Loving	25
68	Pama PM 759	Since You Been Gone/Call Me	25
68	Pama PMLP 6	MADE OF GOLD (LP)	45

CROWS

54	Columbia SCM 5119	Gee/I Love You So	2000
54	Columbia DB 3478)	Gee/I Love You So (78)	150

TREVOR CROZIER'S BROKEN CONSORT

72	Argo AFB 60	PARCEL OF OLD CRAMS (LP)	40

CRUCIFIX

83	Corpus Christi CHRIST ITS 11	DEHUMANISATION (LP)	18

CRUCIFIXION

80	Miramar MIR 4	The Fox/Death Sentence (no p/s)	80
82	Neat NEAT 19	Take It Or Leave It/On The Run (p/s)	5
84	Neat NEAT 37	Green Eyes/Moon Rising/Jailbait (p/s)	5
84	Neat NEAT 3712	Green Eyes/Jailbait/Moon Rising (12", p/s, purple or green vinyl)	18
84	Neat NEAT 3712	Green Eyes/Jailbait/Moon Rising (12", p/s)	8

ARTHUR 'BIG BOY' CRUDUP

64	RCA RCA 1401	My Baby Left Me/I Don't Know It	40
64	RCA RCX 7161	RHYTHM AND BLUES VOL. 4 (EP)	25
69	Blue Horizon 7-63855	MEAN OLE FRISCO (LP)	80
70	Delmark DS 614	LOOK ON YONDERS WALL (LP)	25
71	Delmark DS 621	CRUDUP'S MOOD (LP)	30
72	RCA RD 8224	THE FATHER OF ROCK 'N' ROLL (LP)	30
74	United Artists UAS 29092	ROEBUCK MAN (LP)	30

CRUISERS

(see also Dave Berry, Godley & Creme)

65	Decca F 12098	It Ain't Me Babe/Baby What You Want Me To Do	30

CRUISERS

73	EMI 2202	Schoolgirls/College Collage	5

SIMON CRUM

(see also Ferlin Husky)

58	Capitol CL 14965	Stand Up, Sit Down, Shut Your Mouth/Country Music Is Here To Stay	25
59	Capitol CL 15077	I Fell Out Of Love With Love/Morgan Poisoned The Water Hole	15
61	Capitol CL 15183	Enormity In Motion/Cuzz Yore So Sweet	15

RAY CRUMLEY

77	Magnet MAG 103	It's Uncanny/All The Way In Love With You	15

CRUNCH

72	Youngblood YB 1064	Let's Do It Again/Not Tonight Josephine	8

CRUSADERS

(see also Jazz Crusaders)

71	Rare Earth SRE 3001	OLD SOCKS NEW SHOES (LP)	15
72	Blue Thumb ILPS 9218	CRUSADERS (2-LP)	15
73	Mowest MWS 7004	HOLLYWOOD (LP)	20
75	ABC ABCD 607	SOUTHERN COMFORT (2-LP)	15

BETTYE CRUTCHER

74	Stax STX 1035	LONG AS YOU LOVE ME (LP)	18

MINT VALUE £

CRUX/CRASH

82	No Future OI 18	KEEP ON RUNNING (12" EP)	12

CRY

87	Crazy Flowerpot CFP 001	Party After Dark (with p/s)	80
87	Crazy Flowerpot CFP 001	Party After Dark	15
87	Crazy Flowerpot CFP 002	Give Her An Ice Cream (no p/s)	20

CRYAN' SHAMES

(see under Shames)

CRYER

80	Happy Face MM 124	The Single/Hesitate (p/s, with 2 inserts)	65

BARRY CRYER

58	Fontana H 139	The Purple People Eater/Hey! Eula	15
58	Fontana H 151	Nothin' Shakin'/Seven Daughters	15
59	Fontana H 177	Angelina/Kissin'	10

CRYIN' SHAMES

(see also Paul & Ritchie & Cryin' Shames, Gary Walker & Rain)

66	Decca F 12340	Please Stay/What's News Pussycat	25
66	Decca F 12425	Nobody Waved Goodbye/You	30

CRYING SHAMES

80	Logo GO 385	That's Rock'n'Roll/Too Late (p/s)	12

CRYSTAL CASTLES

07	Merok ME 002	Alice Practice/Air War/Love And Caring (p/s)	20
07	Rough Trade	Pre Untrust/S&MSMS (demo)/Fuck Nicole/And Prolapse (7" given away as 'ticket' to Rough Trade In-Store appearance, 500 only)	8

CRYSTAL MANSION

70	Polydor 2058-070	Carolina in My Mind/If I Live	6

CRYSTALITES

(see also Chosen Few, Scotty, Ramon & Crystalites, Kingstonians, Bongo Herman, Denzil Laing, Derrick Harriot, Ethiopians, Dennis Brown, Glen Brown, Big Youth)

69	Big Shot BI 510	Biafra/Drop Pan	40
69	Nu Beat NB 036	Splash Down/Finders Keepers	70
69	Songbird SB 1015	Musical Madness Parts 1 & 2	12
69	Songbird SB 1016	The Bad Parts 1 & 2	12
69	Explosion EX 2002	Doctor Who (Parts 1 & 2)	12
69	Explosion EX 2003	Barefoot Brigade/Slippery	12
69	Explosion EX 2005	Bombshell/Bag-A-Wire (B-side actually by Bobby Ellis & Crystalites)	15
69	Explosion EX 2006	A Fistful Of Dollars/The Emperor (B-side actually by Bobby Ellis & Crystalites)	45
70	Explosion EX 2010	The Bad/The Bad Version	12
70	Bullet BU 424	A Fistful Of Dollars/BOBBY ELLIS: Crystal	12
70	Songbird SB 1017	The Undertaker/Stop That Man (B-side actually "Easy Ride" by Ike Bennett & Crystalites)	15
70	Songbird SB 1020	Lady Madonna/Ghost Rider	12
70	Songbird SB 1024	Isies/Isies (Version 2)	12
70	Songbird SB 1025	Stranger In Town/Stranger In Town (Version 2)	12
70	Songbird SB 1030	Sic Him Rover/Drop Pon	25
70	Songbird SB 1034	Overtaker (Version I)/Overtaker (Version II)	10
70	Songbird SB 1035	Undertaker's Burial/Ghost Rider	12
70	Songbird SB 1036	Short Story/No Baptism (Version 2)	60
71	Songbird SB 1057	Earthly Sounds/Version	12
73	Grape GR 3050	Blacula/Version	25

CRYSTALS

(see also Darlene Love, Bob B. Soxx & Blue Jeans, Phil Spector)

62	Parlophone R 4867	There's No Other Like My Baby/Oh Yeah Maybe Baby	150
62	London HLU 9611	He's A Rebel/I Love You Eddie	15
63	London HLU 9661	He's Sure The Boy I Love/Walking Along (La-La-La)	15
63	London HLU 9732	Da Doo Ron Ron/Git It	10
63	London HLU 9773	Then He Kissed Me/Brother Julius	8
64	London HLU 9837	Little Boy/Uptown (withdrawn)	125
64	London HLU 9852	I Wonder/Little Boy	45
64	London HLU 9909	All Grown Up/PHIL SPECTOR GROUP: Irving (Jaggered Sixteenths)	15
65	United Artists UP 1110	My Place/You Can't Tie A Girl Down	50
69	London HLU 10239	Da Doo Ron Ron/He's A Rebel	5
74	Warners/Spector K 19010	Da Doo Ron Ron/Then Kissed Me (blue vinyl)	5
76	Phil Spector Intl. 2010 020	All Grown Up/The Twist	5
63	London RE-U 1381	DA DOO RON RON (EP)	75
63	London HA-U 8120	HE'S A REBEL (LP)	160
76	Phil Spector 2307006	SING THEIR GREATEST HITS (LP)	15

CRYTUFF & THE ORIGINALS

79	Hit Run APLP 9006	DUB TO AFRICA (LP)	45

CSA

78	Goat GOAT 001	STOCKADE (LP)	40

C.S.A.

96	Squariel Records SQ003	Don't/'Till I Waltz Again With You (p/s)	6

JOE CUBA SEXTET

66	Pye International 7N 25401	Bang! Bang!/Push, Push, Push	35

CUBAN HEELS

78	Housewives' Choice JY 1/2	Downtown/Do The Smoke Walk (p/s)	30

MINT VALUE £

CUBY & BLIZZARDS

68	Philips BF 1638	Distant Smile/Don't Know Which Way To Go	15
68	Philips BF 1719	Windows Of My Eyes/Checkin' Up On My Baby	10
69	Philips BF 1827	Apple Knocker's Flophouse/Go Down Sunshine	25
69	Philips (S)BL 7874	DESOLATION (LP, black/silver labels)	80
69	Philips SBL 7918	APPLE KNOCKERS FLOPHOUSE (LP)	45

'CUDDLY' DUDLEY (Heslop)

59	HMV POP 586	Lots More Love/Later	20
59	HMV POP 586	Lots More Love/Later (78)	10
60	HMV POP 725	Too Pooped To Pop/Miss In-Between	25
61	Ember EMB S 136	Sitting On A Train/One Thing I Like	12
62	Piccadilly 7N 35090	Monkey Party/The Ferryboat Ride (as Cudley Dudley)	10
64	Oriole International ICB 9	Blarney Blues/Peace On Earth	10
64	Oriole International ICB 10	Way Of Life/When Will You Say You'll Be Mine	15

CUDDLY TOYS

(see also Raped)

80	Fresh FRESH 010	Madman/Join The Girls (p/s)	12
81	Parole PURLE 9	Astral Joe/Slowdown (p/s)	12
81	Fresh FRESH 10	Mothman/Jo In The Girls (p/s, with 5 stickers)	12
81	Fresh FRESH 20	Astral Joe/Slowdown (p/s, reissue)	12
81	Fresh FRESH 25	Someone's Crying/Bring On The Ravers (p/s)	8

CUES

(see also Jimmy Breedlove)

56	Capitol CL 14501	Burn That Candle/O My Darlin'	250
56	Capitol CL 14501	Burn That Candle/O My Darlin' (78)	20
56	Capitol CL 14651	Crackerjack/The Girl I Love (featuring Jimmy Breedlove)	200
56	Capitol CL 14651	Crackerjack/The Girl I Love (featuring Jimmy Breedlove) (78)	20
57	Capitol CL 14682	Prince Or Pauper/Why	200
57	Capitol CL 14682	Prince Or Pauper/Why (78)	20

CUFF-LINKS

69	MCA MU 1101	Tracy/Where Do You Go?	5
70	MCA MU 1112	When Julie Comes Around/Sally Ann (You're Such A Pretty Girl)	6
70	MCA MU 1128	Robin's World/Lay A Little Love On Me	6
70	MCA MUP(S) 398	TRACY (LP)	18

XAVIER CUGAT

54	Columbia SCMC 2	Spanish Dance/The Bells Of San Raquel (export issue)	5
54	Columbia SCMC 4	Yo Ta Namora/Anna Boroco Tinde (export issue)	5
54	HMV 7MC 35	MI Espanan/Society Conga (export issue)	5
63	Mercury AMT 1202	Watermelon Man/Swinging Shepherd Blues	10

CLIVE CULBERTSON

79	Rip Off RIP 9	Time To Kill/Busy Signal (initially came in brown paper bag sleeve)	75
85	Mint Chew 101	I Can't Fight It/You Don't Have A Dream	20

CHRIS CULLEN

82	Zim Zam Z1	Coincidence/I'll See You Later (p/s)	15

JAMIE CULLUM TRIO

99	own label	HEARD IT ALL BEFORE (CD, private pressing, 700 only)	60

CULPEPPER'S ORCHARD

72	Polydor 2480 123	SECOND SIGHT (LP)	120

CULT

(see also Death Cult, Lonesome No More, Theatre Of Hate, Studio Sweethearts)

80s	Beggars Banquet 235H	Sun King/Edie (Ciao Baby)/She Sells Sanctuary (12", holographic plastic sleeve.)	12
84	B. Banquet BEGA 57P	DREAMTIME (LP, picture disc)	12
84	B. Banquet BEGA 57	DREAMTIME (white label test pressing, with unique version of "Go West")	30
80s	Beggars Banquet	ELECTRIC (LP, gatefold sleeve gold vinyl, 5,000 only)	25
91	Beggars Banquet CBOX 1	SINGLES COLLECTION (10-CD box set, picture discs with booklet)	30

CULT FIGURES

(see also Swell Maps)

79	Rather GEAR 4/RT 020	Zip Nolan (Highway Patrolman)/P.W.T. (Playing With Toys)/ Zip Dub (gatefold p/s)	8

CULT HERO

(see also Cure)

79	Fiction FICS 006	I'm A Cult Hero/I Dig You (p/s, 2,000 only)	50

CULT MANIAX

82	Elephant Rock ROCK 001	Blitz/Lucy Looe (p/s)	6
82	Elephant Rock ROCK 002	American Dream/Elephant Rock	15
82	Next Wave NXT 2/BAK 1	Frenzie/The Russians Are Coming/Black Horse/Death March (p/s, withdrawn most have band-inflicted scratch through Black Horse)	45
84	Xcentric SIXTH 1	FULL OF SPUNK! (EP, fold-over p/s in polythene bag)	6

CULTURE

77	Sky Note DD 003	The Cultures Trod On/THE REVOLUTIONARIES, CULTURE AND RANKING TREVOR: Trod On In Dub (A-side as "The Cultures") (12" white pasted sleeve)	25
78	Lightning LIG 515	Jah Pretty Face/Natty Dread Taking Over	5
78	Sky Note SKY LP 016	IN DUB (LP)	40
78	Lightning LIP 1	TWO SEVENS CLASH (LP)	25
78	Virgin FL 1016	HARDER THAN THE REST (LP)	15

CULTURE CLUB

(see also Boy George, Jesus Loves You, The Edge)

82	Virgin VSY 518	Do You Really Want To Hurt Me/Do You Really Want To Hurt Me (Dub Version) (picture disc)	5

MINT VALUE £

82	Virgin (no cat. no.)	I'll Tumble 4 Ya/BLUE RONDO: Change (blue 1-sided flexi with Noise mag)	6
82	Virgin VSY 558	Time (Clock Of The Heart)/White Boys Can't Control It (picture disc)	5
84	Virgin VSY 694	The War Song/La Cancion De Guerra (picture disc, withdrawn)	65
86	Virgin VSX 845	Move Away/Sexuality (5", picture disc, 33rpm, with booklet & gatefold p/s)	5
86	Virgin VSY 861	God Thank You Woman/From Luxury To Heartache (picture disc)	18
82	Virgin VP 2232	KISSING TO BE CLEVER (LP, picture disc, with insert)	12
83	Virgin VP 2285	COLOUR BY NUMBERS (LP, picture disc)	12
84	Virgin VP 2330	WAKING UP WITH THE HOUSE ON FIRE (LP, picture disc, with insert)	12

CULTURE PAUL

80s	Music House MH 2	Mini Van Man (12")	40

CULTURE SHOCK

87	Bluurg FISH 19	GO WILD (LP)	12

CULVER STREET PLAYGROUND

68	President PT 145	Alley Pond Park/A Decent Sort Of Guy	12

CUMBERLAND THREE

(see also John Stewart)

60	Columbia DB 4460	Johnny Reb/Come Along Julie	5
64	Parlophone R 5113	The Cumberland Crew/Chilly Winds	5
61	Columbia 33SX 1302	FOLK SCENE, U.S.A. (LP, also stereo SCX 3364)	12
61	Columbia 33 SX 1325	CIVIL WAR ALABAMA VOL 2 (LP)	15
64	Parlophone PMC 1223	INTRODUCING (LP)	15

BARBARA CUMMINGS

67	London HLU 10110	She's The Woman/There's Something Funny Going On	6

JON CUNDO

(see also Joncuno)

72	Bamboo BAM 69	Love Is Strange/When We Were Children	8

DAVID CUNNINGHAM

80	Piano PIANO 001	GREY SCALE (LP)	12

EARL CUNNINGHAM

79	Hit Run HIT DD 14	Jah Will Lead Us Home/A Fe We Jah (12" in company sleeve)	50
70s	One Top OSM 002	Got To Know That Place/Gates Are Wide Open (12")	30
80	Freedom Sounds FS 0017	Never Give Up/Follow Fashion (12")	25
84	Time TRLP 002	JOHN TOM (LP)	20

H. CUNNINGHAM

71	Tropical AL 004	Ethiopian Son/TROPICAL ALLSTARS: Version 2	5

LARRY CUNNINGHAM

64	King KG 1016	Tribute To Jim Reeves/Take My Hand Precious Lord	6

RUPERT CUNNINGHAM

70	Duke DU 98	Funky/Sugar Cane	5

CUPIDS

58	Vogue V 9102	Now You Tell Me/Lillie Mae	900
58	Vogue V 9102	Now You Tell Me/Lillie Mae (78)	150

CUPID'S INSPIRATION

(see also Gordon Haskell, Paper Blitz Tissue)

68	NEMS 56-3500	Yesterday Has Gone/Dream	7
68	NEMS 56-3702	My World/Everything Is Meant To Be	7
69	Bell BLL 1069	The Sad Thing/Look At Me	7
69	CBS 4509	Boat Trip/Time Only Knows	20
70	CBS 4722	Without Your Love/Different Guy	8
70	CBS 4994	Are You Growing Tired Of My Love/Sunshine	8
74	DJM DJS 300	Yesterday Has Gone/My World	6
69	NEMS 6-63553	YESTERDAY HAS GONE (LP, gatefold, as Cupid's Inspiration Featuring T. Rice-Milton)	20

CUPOL

(see also Wire)

80	4AD BAD 9	Like This For Ages/Kluba Cupol (12", p/s, 45/33rpm)	12

CUPPA T

(see also Overlanders)

67	Deram DM 144	Miss Pinkerton/Brand New World	20
68	Deram DM 185	Streatham Hippodrome/One Man Band	20

CUPS

(see also Gallagher & Lyle)

68	Polydor 56777	Good As Gold/Life And Times	40

MIKE CURB CONGREGATION

70	Polydor 2058 075	Burning Bridges/Sweet Gingerbread Man	5

CURE

(see also Cult Hero, Siouxsie & Banshees, Glove, Fools Dance, Tim Pope, Lockjaw, Obtainers)

SINGLES

78	Small Wonder SMALL 11	Killing An Arab/10.15 Saturday Night (p/s, 15,000 only, beware of counterfeits)	25
79	Fiction FICS 001	Killing An Arab/10.15 Saturday Night (p/s, reissue)	20
79	Fiction FICS 002	Boys Don't Cry/Plastic Passion ('soldier' p/s, typed matrix, 'but Bill does' on A side runout and 'land of 1000 motorhomes' on B)	20
79	Fiction FICS 005	Jumping Someone Else's Train/I'm Cold (p/s, typed matrix)	25
80	Fiction FICS 010	A Forest/Another Journey By Train (p/s)	15
80	Fiction FICS 010	A Forest/Another Journey By Train ('radiophonic' die-cut sleeve)	10
80	Fiction FICSX 010	A Forest (Extended Version)/Another Journey By Train (12", p/s)	25
81	Fiction FICS 012	Primary/Descent (p/s)	15

			MINT VALUE £
81	Fiction FICSX 012	Primary (Extended)/Descent (12", p/s)	25
81	Fiction FICS 014	Charlotte Sometimes/Splintered In Her Head (p/s)	15
81	Fiction FICSX 014	Charlotte Sometimes/Splintered In Her Head/Faith (live) (12", p/s)	18
82	Fiction FICS 015	The Hanging Garden/Killing An Arab (live) (p/s)	10
82	Fiction FICG 015	The Hanging Garden/100 Years//A Forest/Killing An Arab (double pack, gatefold p/s, 5,000 only)	15
82	Lyntone LYN 12011	Lament (1-sided flexidisc, red vinyl)	40
82	Lyntone LYN 12011	Lament (1-sided flexidisc, green vinyl)	15
82	Lyntone LYN 12011	Lament (1-sided flexidisc, red vinyl with Flexipop issue 22)	50
82	Lyntone LYN 12011	Lament (1-sided flexidisc, green vinyl, with Flexipop issue 22)	18
82	Fiction FICSX 017	Let's Go To Bed (Extended)/Just One Kiss (Extended) (12", p/s)	12
83	Fiction FICS 018	The Walk/The Dream (paper labels, poster p/s)	20
83	Fiction FICSP 018	The Walk/The Dream (picture disc)	35
83	Fiction FICSX 018	Upstairs Room/The Dream/The Walk/Lament//Let's Go To Bed (Extended)/ Just One Kiss (Extended) (12" double pack, shrinkwrapped with sticker)	30
83	Fiction FICSP 019	The Lovecats/Speak My Language (picture disc, PVC sleeve)	35
84	Fiction FIXSP 020	The Caterpillar/Happy The Man (picture disc, printed PVC sleeve)	30
85	Fiction 080182-2	In Between Days/The Exploding Boy/A Few Hours After This/ Six Different Ways (live)/Push (live) (CD Video)	45
85	Fiction FICSG 23	Close To Me (Remix)/A Man Inside My Mouth (poster p/s; some copies with blue & white 'Head On The Door' sticker)	15
85	Fiction FICST 23	HALF AN OCTOPUS: Close To Me (Remix)/A Man Inside My Mouth/ New Day/ Stop Dead (10" EP, p/s)	18
85	Fiction 080180-2	Close To Me (12" Remix)/A Man Inside My Mouth/Stop Dead/ New Day (CD Video)	45
87	Fiction FICSG 25	Why Can't I Be You?/A Japanese Dream//Six Different Ways (live)/ Push (live) (numbered double pack, gatefold p/s)	12
87	Fiction FICS 26	Catch/Breathe (p/s, in carrier bag)	8
87	Fiction FICSP 26	Catch/Breathe (clear vinyl, printed PVC sleeve)	18
87	Fiction 080186-2	Catch/Breathe/A Chain Of Flowers/Icing Sugar (Remix) (CD Video)	45
87	Fiction FICS 27	Just Like Heaven/Snow In Summer (p/s, numbered, white vinyl)	8
87	Fiction FICS 27	Just Like Heaven/Snow In Summer (p/s, mispress, A-side plays both sides)	20
87	Fiction FICSP 27	Just Like Heaven/Snow In Summer (picture disc in custom PVC sleeve)	20
87	Fiction FIXCD 27	Just Like Heaven (Remix)/Snow In Summer/Sugar Girl (CD, card sleeve)	25
87	Strange Fruit SFPS 050	PEEL SESSIONS EP (12")	12
88	Fiction FIXCD 28	Hot Hot Hot!!! (Extended Remix)/Hot Hot Hot!!! (Remix)/Hey You!!! (Extended Remix) (CD, card sleeve with insert for 10 Imaginary Years book)	20
89	Fiction FICSG 29	Lullaby (Remix)/Babble (gatefold p/s, numbered with sticker)	8
89	Fiction FICSP 29	Lullaby (Remix)/Babble (clear vinyl, numbered printed 'spider web' PVC sleeve)	18
89	Fiction FICVX 29	Lullaby (Remix)/Babble/Out Of Mind (12", pink vinyl, numbered with stickers)	18
89	Fiction FICCD 29	Lullaby (Remix)/Babble/Out Of Mind/Lullaby (Extended Remix) (3" CD, gatefold p/s)	18
89	Fiction FICSG 30	Lovesong/2 Late ('The Love Box' set with linen print)	12
89	Fiction FICCD 30	Lovesong (7" Mix)/2 Late/Fear Of Ghosts/Lovesong (Extended Mix) (CD)	10
90	Fiction FICPA 34	Pictures Of You (Remix)/Last Dance (live) (p/s, green vinyl, no'd sticker)	6
90	Fiction FICPA 34	Pictures Of You (Remix)/Last Dance (live) (p/s, green vinyl, mispress, plays "Last Dance" both sides)	30
90	Fiction FICPB 34	Pictures Of You (Remix)/Prayers For Rain (p/s, purple vinyl, numbered sticker)	10
90	Fiction FICXA 34	Pictures Of You (Extended Remix)/Last Dance (Live)/ Fascination Street (Live) (12")	18
90	Fiction FICCDA 34	Pictures Of You (Remix)/Last Dance (live)/Fascination Street (live) (CD)	10
90	Fiction FICCDB 34	Pictures Of You (Strange Mix)/Prayers For Rain (live)/Disintegration (live) (CD)	10
90	Fiction FICDP 35	Never Enough (Big Mix)/Harold & Joe/Let's Go To Bed (Milk Mix) (CD, with window sticker, numbered slimline jewel case)	10
90	Fiction 080184-2	Why Can't I Be You? (12" Remix)/A Japanese Dream (5.40 Remix)/Hey You!!! (CD Video)	45
91	Fiction FICDR 36	Close To Me (Closer Mix)/Just Like Heaven (Dizzy Mix)/Why Can't I Be You (12" remix) (CD, with poster, shrinkwrapped with card insert and numbered sticker)	8
92	Fiction FICCD 39	High/This Twilight Garden/Play/High (Higher Mix) (CD, box set)	8
92	Fiction FICCD 42	Friday I'm In Love/Halo/Scared Of You/Friday I'm In Love (Strangelove Mix) (12", p/s, different coloured or marbled vinyl)	25

LPs

79	Fiction FIX 1	THREE IMAGINARY BOYS (with inner sleeve, postcard & badge)	50
79	Fiction FIX 1	THREE IMAGINARY BOYS (LP, with inner sleeve and "Limited edition special price" stamped in gold on cover)	20
80	Fiction FIXD 004	SEVENTEEN SECONDS (LP)	12
80	Fiction FIXC 6	FAITH/CARNAGE VISORS (original double-play cassette, b&w cover, paper labels)	15
82	Fiction FIX D7	PORNOGRAPHY (LP, with inner sleeve)	12
84	Fiction FIXS 9	THE TOP (with badge & poster, green inner sleeve)	20
84	Fiction FIXS 9	THE TOP (with promo plastic snake & top)	35
86	Fiction 815 011-2	BOYS DON'T CRY (CD, original non-picture disc, with "Object" & "World War" & without "So What")	30
86	Fiction FIXH 12	STANDING ON A BEACH - THE SINGLES (LP, gatefold with inner sleeve)	12
87	Fiction FIXH 13/FIXHA 13	KISS ME, KISS ME, KISS ME (with bonus orange vinyl 6-track 12" [FIXHA 13], in custom PVC sleeve)	50
89	Fiction FIXH 14	DISINTERGRATION (LP, with inner sleeve)	12
89	Fiction FIXHP 14	DISINTEGRATION (picture disc, printed PVC sleeve)	30
90	Fiction FIXCD 17	ENTREAT (CD, exclusive to HMV, card p/s, yellow photo)	25
92	Fiction 513 600-0	LIMITED EDITION CD BOX (15 x CD hinged box set, 2,500 only)	200
04	Fiction 981463	JOIN THE DOTS: B-SIDES AND RARITIES 1978-2001 (4-CD box set)	20

PROMOS

79	Fiction	Boys Don't Cry	45
79	Fiction CUR 1	Grinding Halt/Meat Hook (12", stickered sleeve)	70
81	Fiction FICS 12	Primary (1-sided, no p/s)	25

			MINT VALUE £
82	Lyntone LYN 12011	Lament (hard vinyl test pressing, no p/s)	400
82	Fiction CURE 1	One Hundred Years/The Hanging Garden (12", p/s, promo/gig freebie)	70
88	Fiction FICSDJ 28	Hot Hot Hot!!! (Remix)/Hey You!!! (Remix) (die-cut title p/s)	15
84	Fiction KAREN 1	THE TOP (12", 1-sided, 3-track sampler)	55
80s	Fiction FICS DJ 42	Friday I'm In Love (Promo in die-cut Fiction sleeve)	20
89	Fiction DISIN 1	DISINTEGRATION (CD, 4-track sampler)	20
89	Fiction CIFCD 3	STRANGER THAN FICTION (CD, 6-track sampler, 1000 only)	100
90	Fiction CUREPROCD 1	MIXED UP (CD, 4-track sampler)	15
90	Fiction CUREPROCD 3	THE CURE - AN INTERVIEW (CD)	25
92	Fiction CURE 1	CLASSIC CURE: Love Cats/Close To Me (Closer Mix)/Lovesong/ Charlotte Sometimes/Lullaby/Why Can't I Be You/A Forest (CD, sampler, inlay)	25
93	Fiction SHOWPRO 1	SHOWPRO: Just Like Heaven/Doing The Unstuck (CD, 2-track sampler)	20
93	Fiction PARISPRO 01	PARISPRO: Catch/Play For Today (CD, 2-track sampler)	20
94	Fiction FICCS 50	LOST WISHES (cassette, 4-track, mail order only)	70
96	Fiction FICSTX 53	Gone! (Ultraliving Mix) (12", same track both sides, with 'DJ' insert)	12
97	Fiction FICSX 54	Wrong Number (Single Mix)/(ISDN Mix)/(Digital Exchange Mix)/ (Dub Analogue Exchange Mix)/(Crossed Line Mix)/(Engaged Mix)/(P2P Mix) (12", double pack, p/s promo only)	25
97	Fixtion FIXCD.COM 1	FIVE SWING LIVE (CD, 5-track sampler, available via the internet, 5,000 only)	30

MARTIN CURE & PEEPS

(see also Peeps, Rainbows)

67	Philips BF 1605	It's All Over Now/I Can Make The Rain Fall Up	50

CURIOSITY SHOPPE

68	Deram DM 220	Baby I Need You/So Sad	100

JOHNNY CURIOUS & STRANGERS

78	Illegal IL 009	In Tune/Road To Cheltenham/Pissheadsville/Jennifer (p/s)	10
79	Bugle BLAST 2	Someone Else's Home/Backwards In The Night (p/s)	12

CURLEY MOORE

71	Pye 25570	Funky Yeah/Shelly's Rubber Band	20

CURLY

75	EPIC EPC 3145	High Flying Bird/Breakout	6
71	Pye 25570	Funky Yeah/Shelly's Rubber Band	12

CURRANT KRAZE

70	Deram DM 292	Lady Pearl/Breaking The Heart Of A Good Man	5

CURRENT 93

(see also Nurse With Wound, 23 Skidoo, Psychic TV, Crisis, Death In June, Sol Invictus, Steven Stapleton & David Tibet, Tibet & Stapleton)

83	L.A.Y.L.A.H. L.A.Y. 1	Lashtal/Salt/Caresse (12", white p/s)	22
83	L.A.Y.L.A.H. L.A.Y. 1	Lashtal/Salt/Caresse (12", white p/s [reissue from in 1988 with dark p/s and "1988" on label])	18
85	L.A.Y.L.A.H. L.A.Y. 14	NIGHTMARE CULTURE (12" EP, with Sickness Of Snakes [i.e. Coil feat. Boyd Rice]; matt black & red sleeve)	22
87	L.A.Y.L.A.H. L.A.Y. 18	HAPPY BIRTHDAY PIGFACE CHRISTUS (12" EP)	22
87	Maldoror MAL 108	Crowleymass/Christmassacre/Crowleymass (Mix Mix Mix) (12", p/s)	28
88	Yangki 002	FAITH'S FAVOURITES EP (Ballad Of The Pale Girl/NURSE WITH WOUND: Swamp Rat) (12", laminated p/s)	28
88	Maldoror MAL 088	The Red Face Of God/The Breath And The Pain Of God (12", p/s, with insert, 666 only)	40
89	Yangki 003	DEATH OF THE CORN (12" EP, with Sol Invictus; 'art' sleeve)	18
90	Harbinger 001	No Hiding From The Blackbird/NURSE WITH WOUND: Burial Of The Stoned Sardine (p/s, remixed reissue of giveaway 7")	12
90	Shock SX 003	She Is Dead And All Fall Down/God Has Three Faces And Wood Has No Name (folded sleeve in bag, 1,000 only, this price for 26 copies signed/ lettered)	45
90	Shock SX 003	She Is Dead And All Fall Down/God Has Three Faces And Wood Has No Name (folded sleeve in bag, 1,000 only)	22
90	Cerne 004	This Ain't The Summer Of Love (live) (with Sol Invictus, gig freebie, printed labels, this price for 93 copies with ticket)	30
90	Cerne 004	This Ain't The Summer Of Love (live) (with Sol Invictus, gig freebie, printed labels)	20
92	Durtro DURTRO 004	LOONEY RUNES (12", live EP, 2,000 only, with poster)	20
94	Ptolemaic Terrascope POT6	Broken Birds Fly/RANDY CALIFORNIA: The American Society/ The Whale Song (free with Ptolemaic Terrascope mag)	10
94	Ptolemaic Terrascope POT6	Broken Birds Fly/RANDY CALIFORNIA: The American Society/ The Whale Song (without Ptolemaic Terrascope mag)	8
94	Durtro DURTRO 022	THE FIRE OF THE MIND (CD EP, free with book 'Simply Being')	55
95	Durtro DURTRO 025	Tamlin/How The Great Satanic Glory Faded (12", numbered with insert, 2,000 only)	28
95	Durtro DURTRO 025	Tamlin/How The Great Satanic Glory Faded (CD, numbered, 3,000 only)	18
95	Durtro DURTRO 028	Where The Long Shadows Fall (12", 1-sided clear vinyl with insert, 2,000 only)	18
96	Durtro DURTRO 033	The Seven Seals/(various artists) (CD, mail order)	18
84	L.A.Y.L.A.H. LAY 008	DOGS BLOOD RISING (LP; CDs £18)	25
86	Maldoror UDO 22M	IN MENSTRUAL NIGHT (LP, 25 with handmade inserts & cover)	115
86	Maldoror UDO 22M	IN MENSTRUAL NIGHT (LP)	20
86	United Dairies UD 022	IN MENSTRUAL NIGHT (LP, picture disc)	28
87	L.A.Y.L.A.H. LAY 20	SWASTIKAS FOR NODDY (LP, with insert)	25
88	Maldoror MAL 666	CHRIST AND THE PALE QUEENS MIGHTY IN SORROW (3-sided LP, with inserts, 93 copies only)	110
88	Maldoror MAL 777	IMPERIUM (LP, black label, with insert)	28
88	Maldoror MAL 777	IMPERIUM (LP, later pressing with white label)	18
89	Maldoror MAL 093	DAWN (LP)	60
89	Durtro DURTRO 001	LIVE AT BAR MALDOROR (LP, white label, 1,000 only)	55
80s	Maldoror MAL 123	NATURE UNVEILED (LP, with insert & free 7": "No Hiding From The Blackbird/ NURSE WITH WOUND: Burial Of The Sardine")	30

MINT VALUE £

80s	Maldoror MAL 123	NATURE UNVEILED (LP, with insert)	20
90	United Dairies UD 029	EARTH COVERS EARTH (mini-LP)	35
90	Cerne 00123	THE CERNE BOX SET (3-LP set, includes "Horse"; other LPs by Sol Invictus & Nurse With Wound, 2,000 only)	70
90	United Dairies UD 033CD	CROOKED CROSSES FOR THE NODDING DOG (CD)	18
90	NER BADVC 693	1888 (LP, split with Death In June, 500 each on clear & red vinyl)	35
90	NER BADVC 693	1888 (LP, split with Death In June, black vinyl)	25
92	Durtro DURTRO 006	ISLAND (LP, with insert, 2,000 only)	20
92	Durtro DURTRO 011	THUNDER PERFECT MIND (2-LP, with insert)	20
94	Durtro DURTRO 018	OF RUINE, OR SOME BLAZING STARRE (LP, blue vinyl w/insert, 2,000 only)	18
94	Durtrohoho 019	LUCIFER OVER LONDON (LP, red vinyl with insert, 2,000 only)	20
96	Durtro DURTRO 026	ALL THE PRETTY LITTLE HORSES (LP, clear vinyl with insert, 2,000 only)	12
96	United Dairies UDOR 4	WHEN THE MAY RAIN COMES (CD, mail order, free with 'Ultrasonic Seraphim' [2-CD by SAND])	15
01	United Durtro UDOR 8	BRIGHT YELLOW MOON (CD, with Nurse With Wound, first 1,000 with bonus CD)	25

DAVID CURRIE

71	Philips 6006165	I Don't Want To Talk About It/The Question	10

CLIFFORD CURRY

69	Action ACT 4549	She Shot A Hole In My Soul/We're Gonna Hate Ourselves In The Morning	15
69	Pama PM 793	You Turn Out The Light/Good Humour Man	20
69	Pama PM 797	I Can't Get A Hold Of Myself/Ain't No Danger	50

TIM CURRY

74	Ode ODE 66103	Sweet Transvestite/Time Warp (in p/s)	10
74	Ode ODE 66103	Sweet Transvestite/Time Warp	5

CURTAINS

95	Detour DR 025	In My Street/Family Affair (p/s, blue vinyl, 100 only)	7

DAN CURTIN

94	Peacefrog PF 018X	PARALLEL EP (12", sampler, plain sleeve)	10
95	Peacefrog PF 023	PURVEYORS OF FINE FUNK - HEIGHTS TRAX VOL 1 EP (12", plain sleeve)	15
95	Peacefrog PF 024	DREAMS NOT OF TODAY EP (12", plain sleeve)	10
95	Peacefrog PF 032	PURVEYORS OF FINE FUNK - HEIGHTS TRAX VOL 2 EP (12", plain sleeve)	10
96	Peacefrog PF 058	PURVEYORS OF FINE FUNK VOL 3 EP (12", plain sleeve)	10
97	Peacefrog PF 064	PURVEYORS OF FINE FUNK VOL 4 EP (12", plain sleeve)	8
94	Peacefrog PF 018	THE SILICON DAWN (2-LP)	18
95	Peacefrog PF 038	WEB OF LIFE (2-LP)	18

ALLEN CURTIS

64	Hickory 45-1226	Fireball Mail/The Hole He Said He'd Dig For Me	8

CHRIS CURTIS

(see also Searchers)

66	Pye 7N 17132	Aggravation/Have I Done Something Wrong	40

CLEM CURTIS & FOUNDATIONS

(See also the Foundations)

75	Riverdale RS 105	Sweet Happiness/Lady Luck	60
72	Pye 7N 45150	I've Never Found A Girl (To Love Me Like You)/Point Of No Return	40

DENNY CURTIS

68	Plexium PXM 2	Crying Over You/You Don't Love Me No More	6
69	Plexium PXM 6	Message/You Gotta Be Mine	6

JOHNNY CURTIS

66	Parlophone R 5529	Our Love's Disintegrating/(I'd Be) A Legend In My Time	70
67	Parlophone R 5582	Jack And The Beanstalk/Go On Back	30
68	Major Minor MM 564	Pickin' Up Pebbles/Gentle On My Mind	7

KING CURTIS

(see under 'K')

LEE CURTIS (& ALL STARS)

(see also Pete Best Four)

63	Decca F 11622	Little Girl/Just One More Dance (solo)	20
63	Decca F 11690	Let's Stomp/Poor Unlucky Me	25
64	Decca F 11830	What About Me/I've Got My Eyes On You	20
64	Philips BF 1385	Ecstasy/A Shot Of Rhythm And Blues	20

LYNNE CURTIS

64	Decca F11869	House For Sale/My Little Boy	12

MAC CURTIS

57	Parlophone R 4279	The Low Road/You Ain't Treatin' Me Right	2000
57	Parlophone R 4279	The Low Road/You Ain't Treatin' Me Right	275
74	Polydor 2310 293	ROCKABILLY KINGS (LP, with Charlie Feathers)	25
79	Radar RAD 22	ROCKIN' MOTHER (LP)	12

SONNY CURTIS

(see also Crickets)

60	Coral Q 72400	The Red Headed Stranger/Talk About My Baby	40
64	Colpix PX 11024	A Beatle I Want To Be/So Used To Loving You	15
64	Liberty LIB 55710	I Pledged My Love To You/Bo Diddley Bach	20
85	Songworks S1	I Think I'm In Love/A Whole Lot Less To Me Than Meets The Eye	5
85	Songworks S2	Heart Of Gold/Why Did You Say 'I Do' To Me	5
90	Ritz 217	I'm No Stranger To The Rain/Rock Around With Ollie Vee	6
89	Songworks SWX 052089	SONNY CURTIS (EP)	10

MINT VALUE £

DAVE CURTISS & TREMORS

63	Philips BF 1257	You Don't Love Me/Sweet Girl Of Mine	10
63	Philips BF 1285	What Kind Of Girl Are You?/Dreamer's Funfair	10
64	Philips BF 1330	Summertime Blues/I'm A Hog For You Baby	10

CURTISS MALDOON

71	Regal Zonophone 3038	You Make Me Happy (And You Make Me Sad)/Amber Man	5
72	Purple PUR 106	One Way Ticket/Next Time	7
71	Purple TPS 3501	CURTISS MALDOON (LP)	30
73	Purple TPS 3502	MALDOON (LP)	15

ROCKY CURTISS & HARMONY FLAMES

59	Fontana TFE 17172	U.S.A. HIT PARADE (EP)	50

BOBBY CURTOLA (& MARTELLS)

61	Columbia DB 4672	Don't You Sweetheart Me/My Heart's Tongue-Tied (solo)	20
62	London HL 9577	Fortune Teller/Johnny Take Your Time (solo)	20
62	London HL 9639	Aladdin/I Don't Want To Go On Without You (solo)	20
63	Decca F 11670	Gypsy Heart/I'm Sorry	20
63	Decca F 11725	Three Rows Over/Indian Giver	20

CURVE

91	Anxious ANXP 27	Blindfold/Ten Little Girls (picture disc)	8
93	Anxious	FALLING FREE - APHEX TWIN REMIX (12", 1-sided promo only, 500 only)	20
93	Anxious ANXCDS 42	BLACKERTHREETRACKERTWO EP (CD, with Future Sound Of London mix)	10

CURVED AIR

(see also Kirby, Sonja Kristina, [Darryl Way's] Wolf, Trace, Legs, Stretch, Police)

71	Warner Bros WB 8023	It Happened Today/What Happens When You Blow Yourself Up	7
72	Warner Bros K 16164	Sarah's Concern/Phantasmagoria	6
84	Pearl Key PK 07350	Renegade/We're Only Human (p/s)	15
71	Warner Brothers K 16092	Backstreet Luv/Everdance	5
70	Warner Bros K 56004	AIR CONDITIONING (LP, picture disc, with booklet, 10,000 only)	40
70	Warner Bros K 56004	AIR CONDITIONING (LP, picture disc)	15
70	Warner Bros WSX 3012	AIR CONDITIONING (LP, green label, laminated sleeve)	30
70	Warner Bros K 56004	AIR CONDITIONING (LP, green label)	12
71	Warner Bros K 46090	SECOND ALBUM (LP, die-cut 'leaves' fold-out sleeve, green label)	30
72	Warner Bros K 46158	PHANTASMAGORIA (LP, green label, with inner lyric card)	15
73	Warner Bros K 46224	AIR CUT (LP, green label, gatefold sleeve)	18
75	Deram SML 1119	LIVE (LP, red/white label)	20

PETER CUSACK

77	Bead Records BEAD 5	AFTER BEING IN HOLLAND FOR TWO YEARS (LP)	40
84	Bead Records BEAD 22	BIRD JUMPS INTO WOOD (LP, with Clive Bell)	20

CUSTERS TRACK

70	Major Minor MM698	Hello Heaven/On The Run	12

ADGE CUTLER & WURZELS

67	Columbia SEG 8525	SCRUMPY WESTERN (EP)	8
67	Columbia SX6126	ADGE CUTLER & THE WURZELS (LP)	12
67	Columbia SX6165	ADGE CUTLER'S FAMILY ALBUM WITH THE WURZELS (LP)	12
68	Columbia SX6263	CUTLER OF THE WEST (LP)	12
69	Columbia SX6367	CARRY ON CUTLER! (LP)	12

IVOR CUTLER TRIO

67	Parlophone R 5624	I Had A Little Boat/A Great Grey Grasshopper	5
59	Fontana TFE 17144	OF Y'HUP (EP)	20
61	Decca DFE 6677	GET AWAY FROM THE WALL (EP)	20
61	Decca LK 4405	WHO TORE YOUR TROUSERS? (LP)	60
67	Parlophone PCS 7040	LUDO (LP)	70
74	Virgin V2021	DANDRUFF (LP)	35
75	Virgin V2037	VELVET DONKEY (LP)	25
76	Virgin V2056	JAMMY SMEARS (LP)	20
85	Virgin OVED 12	JAMMY SMEARS (LP, reissue)	15

T. TOMMY CUTRER (& GINNY WRIGHT)

(see also Ginny Wright)

54	London HL 8093	Mexico Gal/Wonderful World (B-side with Ginny Wright)	65
54	London HL 8093	Mexico Gal/Wonderful World (B-side with Ginny Wright) (78)	10

CUTTERS

(see also Neville Taylor & Cutters)

59	Decca F 11110	I've Had It/Rockaroo	18

CYAN THREE

66	Decca F 12371	Since I Lost My Baby/Face Of A Loser	20

CYANIDE

78	Pye 7N 46048	I'm A Boy/Do It (p/s)	25
78	Pye 7N 46094	Mac The Flash/Hate The State (demo copies in p/s)	60
78	Pye 7N 46094	Mac The Flash/Hate The State	15
79	Pinnacle PIN 23	Fireball/Your Old Man (p/s)	40
78	Pye NSPL 18554	CYANIDE (LP)	40

CYBERMEN

78	Rockaway AERE 101	THE CYBERMEN (EP, available in 2 different sleeves with info sheet)	100
78	Rockaway AERE 101	THE CYBERMEN (EP, available in 2 different sleeves without info sheet)	40
79	Rockaway LUV 002	You're To Blame/It's You I Want (with inserts)	40

CYBERNETIC SERENDIPITY GROUP

68	ICA ICA 1/2	CYBERNETIC SERENDIPITY MUSIC (LP, private pressing)	100

MINT VALUE £

CYBOTRON FEATURING DILLINJA
(see also Dillinja)

96	Prototype PRO004	Threshold/Got To (12")	10
98	Prototype PRO 010	Light Years/Revelations (12")	10
00	Valve CYBX 001	NASTY WAYZ (EP)	15

CYCLONES

71	Banana BA 338	My Sweet Lord/DENNIS BROWN: Silky (B-side actually by Monty Alexander & Cyclones)	12

CYCLONES

64	Oriole CB 1898	Nobody/Little Egypt	60

CYCLOP'S EYE

72	Phoenix PHO12	Rolling Thunder/Kentucky Freeway	12

CYLOB

95	Rephlex CAT 015	INDUSTRIAL FOLKSONGS (12", initially in polystyrene sleeve)	12

CYMANDE

73	Alaska ALA 4	The Message/Zion I	8
73	Alaska ALA 10	Bras/Ras Tafarian Folk Song	8
74	Contempo CS 2019	Brothers On The Slide/Pon De Dungle	25
73	Alaska ALKA 100	CYMANDE (LP)	20
74	Contempo CLP 508	PROMISED HEIGHT (LP)	20

JOHNNY CYMBAL
(see also Derek)

60	MGM MGM 1106	It'll Be Me/Always, Always	25
63	London HLR 9682	Mr Bass Man/Sacred Lovers Vow	10
63	London HLR 9731	Teenage Heaven/Cinderella Baby	20
63	London HLR 9762	Dum Dum Dee Dum/Surfing At Tijuana	20
64	London HLR 9911	Mitsou/Robinson Crusoe On Mars	20
65	United Artists UP 1093	Go V.W. Go/Sorrow And Pain	25
63	London RER 1375	MISTER BASS MAN (EP)	40
64	London RER 1406	CYMBAL SMASHES (EP)	40

CYMBALINE

65	Pye 7N 15916	Please Little Girl/Coming Home Baby	30
65	Mercury MF 918	Top Girl/Can You Hear Me?	25
66	Mercury MF 961	I Don't Want It/Where Did Love Go Wrong	8
66	Mercury MF 975	Peanuts And Chewy Macs/Found My Girl	8
67	Philips BF 1624	Matrimonial Fears/You Will Never Love Me	70
68	Philips BF 1681	Down By The Seaside/Fire	25
69	Philips BF 1749	Turn Around/Come Back Baby	5

CYMERONS

64	Decca F 11976	I'll Be There/Making Love To Another	15
66	Polydor 56098	Everyday (Will Change)/I Can See You	7

CYNIC

83	Cynic CYN 1	Suicide/No Time At All (no p/s)	130

CYNTHIA & ARCHIE

64	R&B JB 168	Every Beat/DELROY WILSON: Sammy Dead	25

CYRKLE

66	CBS 202064	Red Rubber Ball/How Can I Leave Her	8
66	CBS 202246	Turn Down Day/Big Little Woman	8
67	CBS 202516	Bony Maronie/Please Don't Ever Leave Me	8
67	CBS 202577	I Wish You Could Be There/The Visit (She Was Here)	8
67	CBS 2790	We Had A Good Thing Goin'/Two Rooms	8
67	CBS 2917	Penny Arcade/Words	8
67	CBS 62977	NEON (LP)	30

CZAR
(see also Hungry Wolf)

70	Philips 6006 071	Oh Lord I'm Getting Heavy/Why Don't We Be A Rock'n'Roll Band	25
70	Fontana 6309 009	CZAR (LP, black/silver label, laminated sleeve)	600

HOLGER CZUKAY
(see under Jah Wobble, Can)

D

KIM D
(see also Kim Davis)

65	Pye 7N 15953	The Real Thing/Come On Baby	30

ROB D

95	Mo' Wax MW 037	Clubbed To Death/(Mixes) (12", p/s)	25

TONY D & SHAKEOUTS

64	Piccadilly 7N 35168	Is It True/Never Let Her Go	25

DA BAND

78	Rip Off RIP 2	I Like It/Pirate's Lullaby (p/s)	20

MINT VALUE £

DA BIZ
80 Small Operations SO 002 — On The Beach/This Is No Audition (p/s) ... 10
80 Sire SIR 4045 — On The Beach/This Is No Audition (p/s, reissue) ... 6

DAB HAND
85 Celtic Music CM 025 — HIGH ROCK AND LOWATER (LP) ... 18

MIKE D'ABO
(see also Manfred Mann, Band Of Angels, Gulliver's Travels, Smith & D'Abo)
69 Immediate IM 075 — See The Little People - Gulliver's Travels/ Anthology Of Gulliver's Travels Part 2 (withdrawn) ... 20
70 Uni UNS 525 — Let It Roar/California Line ... 7
70 Bell BLL 1134 — Miss Me In The Morning/Arabella, Cinderella ... 6
72 A&M AMS 7016 — Belinda/Little Miss Understood ... 6
74 A&M AMS 7121 — Fuel To Burn/Hold On Darlin' ... 6
70 Uni UNLS 114 — D'ABO (LP, gatefold sleeve) ... 40
72 A&M AMLH 68097 — DOWN AT RACHEL'S PLACE (LP, with lyric insert) ... 15
74 A&M AMLH 63634 — BROKEN RAINBOWS (LP) ... 15

RITA DACOSTA
75 Contempo CS 2060 — Don't Bring Me Down/No! No! No! ... 8

DADA
(see also Robert Palmer, Elkie Brooks, Paul Korda, Vinegar Joe)
71 Atco 2400 030 — DADA (LP, mustard/blue label) ... 60

DADDY DEWDROP
71 Stateside SS2192 — Foxhunting On The Weekend/March Of The White Corpuscles ... 12

DADDY LONGLEGS
(see also Daylight)
70 Warner Bros WB 8012 — High Again/To The Rescue (Wet Putso) ... 5
70 Warner Bros WS 3004 — DADDY LONGLEGS (LP) ... 30
71 Vertigo 6360 038 — OAKDOWN FARM (LP, gatefold sleeve, swirl label) ... 70
72 Polydor 2371 261 — THREE MUSICIANS (LP) ... 15
73 Polydor 2371 323 — SHIFTING SANDS (LP) ... 25

DADDY MAXFIELD
73 Pye 7N 45266 — Rave 'N' Rock/Smilin' Again ... 30

DADDY-O'S
58 Oriole CB 1454 — Got A Match?/Have A Cigar ... 15

DADDY'S ACT
67 Columbia DB 8242 — Eight Days A Week/Gonna Get You ... 18

DAD'S ARMY PLATOON
71 Columbia DB 8766 — Dad's Army March/What Did You Do In The War? ... 6
72 Columbia DB 8952 — We Stood Alone/Down Our Way (AS DAD'S ARMY CHOIR) ... 6

D.A.F. (Deutsche Amerikanische Freundschaft)
81 Virgin VS 418 — Der Mussolini/Der Räuber Und Der Prinz (co. sleeve, possibly promo only) ... 8
81 Virgin VS 418-12 — Der Mussolini/Der Räuber Und Der Prinz (12", p/s, original issue) ... 10

CALVIN DAFOS
66 Blue Beat BB 347 — Brown Sugar/I'm Gone ... 22
69 Doctor Bird DB 1174 — Lash Them/CDs: Medicine Master ... 20

DAFT PUNK
94 Soma 014 — Alive/The New Wave (12" EP, company sleeve) ... 12
95 Soma 025 — Da Funk/Rollin' And Scratchin' (12" EP, company sleeve) ... 10

DAGABAND
80 Rutland RX 100 — Test Flight/Images (p/s) ... 5
83 MHM A-M 094 — Second Time Around/Reds Under The Beds/I Can See For Miles (p/s) ... 25

DAGGERMEN
(see also James Taylor Quartet)
86 Empire UPW 258J — INTRODUCING THE DAGGERMEN (EP, die-cut company sleeve) ... 10
86 Own Up DAG 001 — DAGGERS IN MY MIND (LP) ... 12

DAILY FLASH
84 Psycho PSYCHO 32 — I FLASH DAILY (LP) ... 15

TONY DAINES
63 Fontana TF 433 — Chapel In The Moonlight/Echo Of Footsteps ... 8
64 Fontana TF 472 — Too Late/I Told You So ... 5

BILLY DAINTY
62 Decca F11499 — Cry Upon My Shoulder/If I'd Known You ... 6

DAISY CHAINSAW
91 Jeva JVA 001 — Get Real Pleasure/Love Your Money (p/s) ... 10

DAISY CLAN
70 Pye Intl. 7N 25532 — Love Needs Love/Glory Be ... 45
71 Decca F23169 — San Francisco China Town/Ridin' A Rainbow ... 35

DAISY PLANET
60s Oak (no cat. no.) — DAISY PLANET (EP, no p/s) ... 60

DAKOTA JIM
(see also Slim Smith)
66 Blue Beat BB 358 — Only Soul Can Tell (actually by Slim Smith)/DAKOTA'S ALLSTARS: Call Me Master (actually by Prince Buster All Stars) ... 150

DAKOTAS
(see also Billy J. Kramer & Dakotas)
63 Parlophone R 5044 — The Cruel Sea/The Millionaire ... 10

MINT VALUE £

63 Parlophone R 5064 Magic Carpet/Humdinger ... 10
64 Parlophone R 5203 Oyeh/My Girl Josephine ... 30
67 Page One POF 018 I'm 'N 'Ardworkin' Barrow Boy/Seven Pounds Of Potatoes ... 25
68 Philips BF 1645 I Can't Break The News To Myself/The Spider And The Fly ... 100
63 Parlophone GEP 8888 MEET THE DAKOTAS (EP) ... 40

MICHAEL D'ALBUQUERQUE

(see also E.L.O., Michael Albuquerque)

74 RCA SF 8383 WE MAY BE CATTLE BUT WE ALL HAVE NAMES (LP, with lyric sheet) ... 18
76 Warner Bros K 56276 STALKING THE SLEEPER (LP) ... 12

DALE & GRACE

63 London HL 9807 I'm Leaving It Up To You/That's What I Like About You ... 15
64 London HL 9857 Stop And Think It Over/Bad Luck ... 15
69 London HL 10249 I'm Leaving It Up To You/Love Is Strange ... 8
64 London RE 1428 DALE AND GRACE NO. 1 (EP) ... 40
64 London RE 1429 DALE AND GRACE NO. 2 (EP) ... 40
64 London RE 1430 DALE AND GRACE NO. 3 (EP) ... 40

ALAN DALE

(see also Johnny Desmond)

55 Vogue Coral Q 72072 Cherry Pink And Apple Blossom White/I'm Sincere ... 8
55 Vogue Coral Q 72089 Sweet And Gentle/You Still Mean The Same To Me ... 8
55 Vogue Coral Q 72105 Rockin' The Cha-Cha/Wham! (There I Go In Love Again) ... 20
56 Vogue Coral Q 72121 Robin Hood/Lisbon Antigua ... 8
56 Vogue Coral Q 72156 Dance On/Mr. Moon ... 8
56 Vogue Coral Q 72166 The Birds And The Bees/I Promise ... 8
56 Vogue Coral Q 72191 Be My Guest/Pardners (with Buddy Hackett) ... 8
56 Vogue Coral Q 72194 The Test Of Time/I Cry More ... 8
57 Vogue Coral Q 72225 Don't Knock The Rock/Your Love Is My Love ... 30
57 Vogue Coral Q 72231 The Girl Can't Help It/Lonesome Road ... 30
58 MGM MGM 986 Volare/Weeping Willow In The Wind ... 6

DICK DALE & HIS DELTONES

63 Capitol CL 15296 Peppermint Man/Surf Beat ... 20
63 Capitol CL 15320 The Scavenger/Wild Ideas ... 20
88 Pulch Wave PSC 666 Pick And Play/The Wedge (p/s) ... 6
63 Capitol T 1886 SURFERS' CHOICE (LP) ... 60
63 Capitol T/ST 1930 KING OF THE SURF GUITAR (LP, mono/stereo) ... 60

GLEN DALE

(see also Fortunes)

66 Decca F 12475 Good Day Sunshine/Make Me Belong To You ... 8
68 Page One POF 059 I've Got You On My Mind/Now I See You ... 5
68 Page One POF 105 I've Got Something Too/Something's Gotten Hold Of My Heart ... 5

JIM DALE

57 Parlophone R 4329 Piccadilly Line/I Didn't Mean It ... 18
57 Parlophone R 4343 Be My Girl/You Shouldn't Do That ... 10
57 Parlophone R 4356 All Shook Up/Wandering Eyes (with Vipers & King Brothers) ... 15
57 Parlophone R 4376 Just Born (To Be Your Baby)/Crazy Dream ... 10
58 Parlophone R 4402 Sugartime/Don't Let Go ... 10
58 Parlophone R 4424 Tread Softly Stranger/Jane Belinda ... 8
59 Parlophone R 4522 Gotta Find A Girl/The Legend Of Nellie D. ... 7
60 Academy AD 001 Somewhere There's A Someone/If You Come Back ... 6
62 Piccadilly 7N 35039 One Boy, One Girl/My Resistance is Low ... 5
63 Piccadilly 7N 35100 Start All Over Again/It's For Them ... 5
65 Columbia DB 7449 Forget Tomorrow/Is It OK? ... 6
65 Columbia DB 7746 My Carousel/Short Time To Go ... 6
66 Columbia DB 7331 This Is Me/What Colour Are You? ... 6
69 Pye 7N 17751 Miss Linda Grey/Of My Life ... 6
69 Pye 7N 17839 Twinky/Plenty More Days ... 7
73 United Artists UA 35483 Milligan's Blues/It's Gonna Be A Good War ... 6
57 Parlophone GEP 8656 JIM DALE (EP) ... 35
58 Parlophone PMD 1055 JIM (10" LP) ... 60
69 Pye NSPL 18289 MEET JIM DALE (LP) ... 15

PAUL DALE BAND

(see also Marseille)

82 KA KA 6/PAUL 1 Alright On The Night/Hold On (p/s, clear vinyl) ... 12
82 KA KA 6/PAUL 1 Alright On The Night/Hold On (p/s) ... 6

SYD DALE ORCHESTRA

65 Decca F 22300 C'mon In/Disc A Go Go ... 8

DALEK I LOVE YOU

79 Vertigo DALEK 1 Freedom Fighters/Two Chameleons (p/s, as Dalek I) ... 6

DALEKS

(Dr. Who variety, see under Century 21)

DALEKS

80 Exterminated EXPS 1 Rejected/Man Of The World/This Life (fold-out, p/s) ... 15

DALE SISTERS

60 HMV POP 781 The Kiss/Billy Boy, Billy Boy ... 12
61 Ember EMB S 140 My Sunday Baby/All My Life ... 20
62 Ember EMB S 151 Secrets/Road To Love ... 10

DÄLEX

81 Dodgy DODGY 1 Juvenile/Action Man Touched (p/s) ... 20

BASIL DALEY

68 Studio One SO 2054 Hold Me Baby/HEPTONES: I Got A Feeling ... 25

MINT VALUE £

JIMMY DALEY & DING-A-LINGS

57	Brunswick 05648	Rock, Pretty Baby/Can I Steal A Little Love	130
57	Brunswick 05648	Rock, Pretty Baby/Can I Steal A Little Love (78)	35

SALVADOR DALI

62	Decca SET 230	DALI IN VENICE (LP, gatefold sleeve with booklet)	75

DALIDA

60	HMV POP 793	Never On A Sunday/MILKO PAPAYAKI: Parle Doucement	7
57	Felsted ESD 3043	DALIDA IS HER NAME (EP)	25
59	Felstead ESD 3077	PARDON MY ENGLISH (EP)	25
57	Felsted SDL 86053	THE GLAMOUROUS DALIDA (10" LP)	40
66	Fontana TL 5348	DALIDA (LP)	15

DALLAS BOYS

(see also Five Dallas Boys)

67	Major Minor MM 534	He Won't Love You (Like I Do)/What Do You Know About Losin'	5

DALLIONS

62	Oriole CB 1794	Teardrops In The Rain/Loop De Loop	15

MIKI DALLON

(see also Neil Christian & Crusaders)

65	RCA RCA 1438	Do You Call That Love?/Apple Pie	20
65	RCA RCA 1478	I Care About You/I'll Give You Love	40
66	Strike JH 306	Cheat And Lie/(I'm Gonna Find A) Cave	30
66	Strike JH 318	What Will Your Mama Say Now?/Two At A Time	8

DAVID & MARIANNE DALMOUR

65	Columbia 33SX 1715	INTRODUCING (LP)	20
66	Columbia SCX 6005	STRANGE ENCHANTMENT (LP)	25

DALTONS

(see also Prince Buster)

67	Fab FAB 30	Never Kiss You Again/RIGHTEOUS FLAMES: When A Girl Loves A Boy	40

ROGER DALTREY

(see also Who, High Numbers, McEnroe & Cash)

73	Track 2094 014	Thinking/There Is Love	6
75	A&M AMS 7206	Orpheus Song/Love's Dream	6
75	Lyntone LYN 3176/7	Wagner's Dream/Love's Theme/RICK WAKEMAN: Count Your Blessings (flexidisc with 19 magazine)	10
77	Polydor 2058 896	One Of The Boys/You Better Put Something Inside Me	6
77	Polydor 2058 948	Say It Ain't So Joe/Satin And Lace (withdrawn, existence unconfirmed)	20
77	Polydor 2121 319	Written On The Wind/Dear John	8
78	Polydor 2058 986	Say It Ain't So Joe/The Prisoner	8
73	Track 2406 101	DALTREY (LP, gatefold sleeve)	20
75	Polydor 2442 135	RIDE A ROCK HORSE (LP, with inner sleeve)	15
80	Polydor POLD 5034	McVICAR (LP, soundtrack, clear vinyl)	18
80	Polydor POLD 5034	McVICAR (LP, soundtrack)	12

GLEN DALY

61	Piccadilly 7N 35017	The Celtic Song/If Only We Had Old Ireland Over Here	7

TONI DALY

(see also Antoinette)

66	Columbia DB 8043	Like The Big Man Said/You Can't Get No Water	8

DALYS

65	Fontana TF 546	Me Japanese Boy/Never Kind Of Love	5
65	Fontana TF 637	She's My Girl/When Love Has Gone	5
66	Strike JH 317	Don't Go Breaking My Heart/Little Stranger	6
67	Fontana TF 809	Sweet Maria/Leaving Time	5
67	Fontana TF 841	A Fistful Of Dollars/Man With No Name	6
68	Fontana TF 907	Let Me Go Lover/A Place In The Sun	5
69	Fontana TF 988	Early Morning Rain/Chanson D'Amour	5

DAMARIS

83	CBS 4172	What About My Love/Hooray For Love (12")	30

DAMASCUS

(see also Thin End Of The Wedge)

80s	private pressing	OPEN YOUR EYES (12" EP, with insert)	100
80s	private pressing	OPEN YOUR EYES (12" EP, later with different back sleeve, with insert)	75

DAMBALA

78	Isis ISIS 001	Rebel/MILITANT BARRY : Version	20
78	Music Hive MH001	Zimbabwe/GUS ANYIA : Visins Of War	35
81	Blank IS 1002	Rally Round/Version (12" p/s)	30

DAMITA JO

54	HMV 7MC 2	I'd Do It Again/Do I, Do I, Do I (B-side with Steve Gibson)(export issue)	20
60	Mercury AMT 1085	Widow Walk/Dearest Darling	5
60	Mercury AMT 1116	I'll Save The Last Dance For You/Forgive	10
60	Mercury AMT 1133	Keep Your Hands Off Him/Hush, Somebody's Calling My Name	5
61	Mercury AMT 1141	Do What You Want/Sweet Georgia Brown	5
61	Mercury AMT 1155	I'll Be There/Love Laid Its Hands On Me	5
61	Mercury ZEP 10118	I'LL SAVE THE LAST DANCE FOR YOU (EP)	18
61	Mercury MMC 14089	I'LL SAVE THE LAST DANCE FOR YOU (LP, mono)	18
61	Mercury CMS 18059	I'LL SAVE THE LAST DANCE FOR YOU (LP, stereo)	25
62	Mercury MMC 14105	LIVE AT THE DIPLOMAT (LP)	15

DAMNED

74	Youngblood YB 1067	Morning Bird/Theta	60

MINT VALUE £

DAMNED

(see also Bartok, Captain Sensible, Rat Scabies, Rat & Whale, Edge, Magic Michael, Maxim's Thrash, Naz Nomad & Nightmares, Auntiepus, Disco Brothers, Phantom Chords, Tank, Eddie & Hot Rods, U.F.O., Tanz Der Youth)

SINGLES

76	Stiff BUY 6	New Rose/Help! (First pressing with push-out centre, 'Street music co' credit on label, 'is this a record' & 'a bilbo boppa' on A side run out, 'Damned Beatles & 'Bilbo master room' on B. Delga' credit on p/s)	25
76	Stiff BUY 6	New Rose/Help! (p/s, later issues)	5
77	Stiff BUY 10	Neat Neat Neat/Stab Yor Back/Singalongascabies (glossy p/s, first pressing solid centre)	20
77	Stiff DAMNED 1	Stretcher Case Baby/Sick Of Being Sick (p/s, NME competition & gig freebie)	75
77	Stiff BUY 18	Problem Child/You Take My Money (p/s, originally with press-out centre)	10
77	Stiff BUY 18	Problem Child/You Take My Money (p/s)	5
77	Stiff BUY 24	Don't Cry Wolf/One Way Love (20,000 on pink vinyl, no p/s)	10
77	Stiff BUY 24	Don't Cry Wolf/One Way Love (black vinyl)	5
78	Dodgy Demo Co. SGS 105	Love Song/Burglar (mail order issue/gig freebie, plain sleeve, stickered labels)	25
79	Chiswick CHIS 112	Love Song/Noise Noise Noise/Suicide (red vinyl, 4 different sleeves)	8
79	Chiswick CHIS 112	Love Song/Noise Noise Noise/Suicide (4 different sleeves)	5
79	Chiswick CHIS 116	Smash It Up/Burglar (p/s)	5
79	Chiswick CHIS 120	I Just Can't Be Happy Today/Ballroom Blitz/The Turkey Song (p/s)	5
79	Chiswick CHIS 120 ADJ-1	I Just Can't Be Happy Today/Ballroom Blitz ('A' Label DJ promo copy)	150
80	Chiswick CHIS 130	White Rabbit/Rabid (Over You)/Seagulls (unissued in U.K., Europe-only, 2 x 1-sided white-label test pressings exist, hand-written labels)	400
80	Chiswick CHIS 135	The History Of The World Part 1/I Believe The Impossible/Sugar And Spite (p/s)	5
80	Chiswick CHIS 12 135	The History Of The World Part 1/I Believe The Impossible/ Sugar And Spite (12", p/s)	8
80	Chiswick CHIS 139	There Ain't No Sanity Clause/Hit Or Miss/Looking At You (live) (p/s)	5
81	NEMS TRY 1	Friday The 13th (EP, p/s)	5
81	Stiff GRAB 2	Four Pack (4 x 7" [BUY 6, 10, 18 & 24], in a plastic wallet)	40
82	Big Beat NS 75	Love Song/Noise Noise Noise/Suicide (3 different sleeves, blue vinyl)	6
82	Big Beat NS 76	Smash It Up/Burglar (p/s, red vinyl)	6
82	Big Beat NS 77	Wait For The Blackout/CAPTAIN SENSIBLE & SOFTIES: Jet Boy, Jet Girl (p/s, red/black 'Damned' labels)	5
82	Big Beat NSP 77	Wait For The Blackout/CAPTAIN SENSIBLE & SOFTIES: Jet Boy, Jet Girl (picture disc)	5
82	Big Beat NS 80	Lively Arts/Teenage Dream (p/s, green vinyl)	10
82	Bronze BRO 149	Lovely Money/Lovely Money (Disco Mix)/I Think I'm Wonderful (p/s)	6
82	Bronze BROP 149	Lovely Money/Lovely Money (Disco Mix)/I Think I'm Wonderful (picture disc)	7
82	Bronze BRO 156	Dozen Girls/Take That/Mine's A Large One, Landlord/Torture Me (p/s)	6
82	Bronze BRO 159	Generals/Disguise/Citadel Zombies (p/s)	8
83	Big Beat NS 85	White Rabbit/Rabid (Over You)/Seagulls (p/s)	5
84	Plus One DAMNED 1P	Thanks For The Night/Nasty (picture disc)	6
84	Plus One DAMNED 1	Thanks For The Night/Nasty (p/s, 1,000 each on red, white & blue vinyl)	7
84	Plus One DAMNED 1T	Thanks For The Night/Nasty/Do The Blitz (12", no'd p/s, multicoloured vinyl)	15
84	Plus One DAMNED 1T	Thanks For The Night/Nasty ('woman'-shaped pic disc w/ plinth, 1,000 only)	25
85	MCA GRIM 1	Grimly Fiendish/Edward The Bear (autographed gatefold p/s, 1,000 only)	8
85	MCA GRIMP 1	Grimly Fiendish/Edward The Bear (picture disc)	5
85	MCA GRIMT 1	Grimly Fiendish (Spic'n'Span Mix)/Edward The Bear (12", autographed p/s)	10
85	MCA GRIM 2/GRIMY 2	Edition Premier: The Shadow Of Love/Nightshift/Let There Be Rats/ Wiped Out (double pack)	5
85	MCA GRIM 3	Is It A Dream (Wild West End Mix)/Street Of Dreams (live) (p/s, with 5 badges)	5
86	MCA GRIMT 4	Eloise/Temptation/Beat Girl (12", p/s, 2,000 on blue vinyl)	8
86	Stiff BUY 6/BUYDJ 6A	New Rose/Help!/I'm So Bored (1-sided) (double pack, stickered PVC sleeve with insert, 1st disc on white vinyl, 2nd disc actually plays "I Fall" [live])	12
86	Stiff BUY 6	New Rose/Help! (reissue, red vinyl, PVC sleeve, with card insert)	8
90s	Sugar & Spite SS 01	History Of The World Part 1 (Psychedelic Mix) (1-sided flexi credited to 'The Dimmed' wraparound p/s free with Sugar & Spite fanzine	12
90s	Sugar & Spite SS 01	History Of The World Part 1 (Psychedelic Mix) (1-sided flexi credited to 'The Dimmed' wraparound p/s free without Sugar & Spite fanzine	8
91	Deltic DELT 7T	Fun Factory/CAPTAIN SENSIBLE: Freedom/Pasties/A Riot On Eastbourne Pier (12" p/s, blue vinyl, mail-order only, 2000 only)	8

LPs

77	Stiff SEEZ 1	DAMNED DAMNED DAMNED (LP, 2,000 with Eddie & Hot Rods photograph on rear sleeve; shrinkwrapped with title sticker)	220
77	Stiff SEEZ 1	DAMNED DAMNED DAMNED (LP, 2,000 with Eddie & Hot Rods photograph on rear sleeve; not shrinkwrapped with title sticker)	100
77	Stiff SEEZ 1	DAMNED DAMNED DAMNED (LP)	20
77	Stiff BA 215	MUSIC FOR PLEASURE (LP)	25
79	Chiswick CWK 3011	MACHINE GUN ETIQUETTE (LP, with inner sleeve)	15
81	Ace DAM 1	THE BEST OF THE DAMNED (LP, red or blue vinyl)	12
82	Ace DAM 2	MACHINE GUN ETIQUETTE (LP, reissue, blue or white/clear vinyl with inner)	12
82	Ace DAM 3	THE BLACK ALBUM (LP, single reissue, 12,000 with lyrics & poster)	12
83	Stiff MAIL 2	DAMNED DAMNED DAMNED/MUSIC FOR PLEASURE (2-LP, reissue, gatefold sleeve, mail-order, 5000 only)	25
83	Damned DAMU 2	LIVE IN NEWCASTLE (LP, 5,000 by mail-order only)	15
83	Damned PDAMU 2	LIVE IN NEWCASTLE (LP, picture disc, 5,000 only)	15
85	MCA MCFW 3275	PHANTASMAGORIA (LP, white vinyl, with inner)	15
86	Stiff GET 4	THE CAPTAIN'S BIRTHDAY PARTY - LIVE AT THE ROUNDHOUSE (mini-LP, 45rpm, blue vinyl, stickered plain white sleeve)	12
86	Stiff MAIL 2	DAMNED, DAMNED, DAMNED/MUSIC FOR PLEASURE (2-LP, reissue, yellow vinyl, 4000 by mail-order only)	25
86	Dojo DOJOPD 46	STRAWBERRIES (LP, reissue picture disc)	12
87	Demon PFIEND 91	DAMNED DAMNED DAMNED (LP, reissue picture disc)	12
87	Demon FIEND 108	MUSIC FOR PLEASURE (LP, reissue, orange vinyl)	12
89	Essential ESCLP 008	FINAL DAMNATION (LP, green vinyl, with poster)	12
92	Reciever RRLP 159	LIVE AT THE LYCEUM (LP, clear vinyl)	12

MINT VALUE £

KENNY DAMON
(see also Kenny Roberts)

65	Mercury MF 907	While I Live/Fountain In Capri	5
66	Mercury MF 936	World Of No Return/You Are Everything That's Beautiful	5
68	Mercury MF 1014	Turn Her Away/Till Then My Love	5
67	Mercury MF 959	Only Your Love/Sold To The Man With The Broken Heart	5

RUSS DAMON

64	Stateside SS 258	Hip Huggers/Heaven Sent	12

STUART DAMON

70	Reflection REF L7	STUART 'CHAMPION' DAMON (LP)	20

DAMON & NAOMI
(see also Galaxie 500)

97	Earworm WORM 3	The Navigator/Awake In A Muddle (p/s)	8

VIC DAMONE
(see also Howard Keel, Easy Riders)

57	MGM MGM 949	And This Is My Beloved (with Howard Keel)/Night Of My Nights	5
57	MGM MGM 950	Stranger In Paradise (with Ann Blyth)/ANN BLYTH:Baubles, Bangles And Pearls	5
58	Philips PB 819	On The Street Where You Live/Arrivederci Roma	6
58	Philips PB 837	The Only Man On The Island/When My Love Smiles	7
68	Ember EMB 268	Don't Let Me Go/For Once In My Life (p/s)	8
68	Ember EMB 268	Don't Let Me Go/For Once In My Life	5
57	Mercury MPT 7514	ALL-TIME SONG HITS (10" LP)	20
57	Philips BBL 7144	THAT TOWERING FEELING! (LP)	12
58	Philips BBL 7259	CLOSER THAN A KISS (LP)	12

DAN

87	All The Madmen MAD LP 09	AN ATTITUDE HITS (mini-LP)	12
87	Meantime COX 002b	WHERE HAVE ALL THE CHILDREN GONE (LP)	12
88	Workers Playtime PLAY LP4	MOTHER WITH CHILD AND BUNNY (LP)	12
89	Meantime COX 013c	KICKING ASS AT TJ'S (LP, with flexi)	15

VIC DANA

62	Liberty LIB 51	I Will/Proud	10
62	Liberty LIB 64	A Very Good Year For The Girls/Looking For Me	6
64	Liberty LIB 92	Warm And Tender/Shangri-La	5
65	Liberty LIB 309	Moonlight And Roses/What'll I Do	5
65	Liberty LIB 313	Crystal Chandelier/What Now My Love (Et Maintenant)	5
66	Liberty LIB 319	I Love You Drops/Sunny Skies	5
66	Liberty LIB 322	Million And One/My Baby Wouldn't Leave Me	5
63	Liberty LBY 1193	MORE (LP)	15

DANCE CHAPTER

80	4AD AD 18	Anonymity/New Dance (p/s, with card insert)	8
80	4AD AD 18	Anonymity/New Dance (p/s)	6
81	4AD BAD 115	CHAPTER II (12" EP, most with mismatched A&B-side labels)	10
85	Pleasantly Surprised PS 10	WHEN THE SPIRIT MOVES THEM (cassette, in bag with inserts)	15

DANCELAND ROCK GROUP

62	Danceland Y 2032	Anytime/Because They're Young	15
63	Danceland Y 2043	William Tell/Last Night Was Made For Love	15

DANCER

75	Dawn DNS 1118	Hate Generator/Love Seeds	8

DANCER, PRANCER & NERVOUS
(see also Singing Reindeer)

59	Capitol CL 15097	The Happy Reindeer/Dancer's Waltz (p/s)	12
59	Capitol CL 15097	The Happy Reindeer/Dancer's Waltz	6

DANCING DID

79	Fruit & Veg F&V 1	Dancing Did/Lorry Pirates (p/s)	18
80	Fruit & Veg F&V 2	The Haunted Tearooms/Squashed Things On The Road (p/s)	10
82	Stiff BUY 136	The Lost Platoon/The Human Chicken (withdrawn 'cavalry' p/s)	8
82	Kamera Records KAM 009	AND DID THOSE FEET (LP, with insert)	25

DANDO SHAFT
(see also Hedgehog Pie)

70	Youngblood YB 1012	Cold Wind/Cat Song	15
72	RCA RCA 2246	Sun Clog Dance/This Gift	10
70	Youngblood SSYB 6	AN EVENING WITH DANDO SHAFT (LP, white/red label)	100
71	RCA Neon NE 5	DANDO SHAFT (LP, gatefold sleeve, black inner sleeve)	150
72	RCA Victor SF 8256	LANTALOON (LP, with poster, orange label)	150
72	RCA Victor SF 8256	LANTALOON (LP, without poster, orange label)	60
77	Rubber RUB 034	KINGDOM (LP)	40

DANDY (& SUPERBOYS)
(see also Bobby Thompson, Sugar & Dandy, Rub A Dubs, Don Martin, Boy Friday, Audrey, Little Sal with Dandy & Superboys)

64	Dice CC 21	Rudie Don't Go/It's Just Got To Be	15
65	Dice CC 24	You Got To Pray/I Got To Have You (as Dandy & Barbara)	15
65	Blue Beat BB 308	To Love You/I'm Looking For Love	20
65	Blue Beat BB 319	Hey Boy Hey Girl/So Long Baby (as Dandy & Del)	20
65	Blue Beat BB 327	My Baby/I'm Gonna Stop Loving You	15
65	Blue Beat BB 336	I Found Love/You've Got Something Nice	15
66	Dice CC 29	The Operation/A Little More Ska	15
66	Ska Beat JB 247	The Fight/Do You Know	25
67	Ska Beat JB 269	One Scotch One Bourbon One Beer/Maximum Pressure	25
67	Ska Beat JB 273	Rudie A Message To You/Til Death Do Us Part	10
67	Ska Beat JB 279	You're No Hustler/No No	18

			MINT VALUE £
67	Giant GN 3	My Time Now/East Of Suez (with Superboys)	18
67	Giant GN 5	Puppet On A String/Have Your Fun (with Superboys)	10
67	Giant GN 7	We Are Still Rude/Let's Do Rocksteady (with Superboys)	10
67	Giant GN 10	Somewhere My Love/My Kind Of Love (with Superboys)	10
67	Giant GN 15	There Is A Mountain/This Music Got Soul (with Superboys)	10
68	Giant GN 20	Charlie Brown/Groovin' At The Cue	10
68	Giant GN 23	Propagandist/Giant March	20
68	Giant GN 27	Sweet Ride/Up The Hill (with Superboys)	10
68	Giant GN 30	Tears On My Pillow/Mad Them (with Superboys)	10
68	Giant GN 36	I'm Back With A Bang Bang/Jungle Walk (with Superboys)	10
68	Trojan TR 618	The Toast/Kicks Out	12
68	Trojan TR 629	Sentence (as Dandy & Lee)/LEE PERRY: You Crummy	18
69	Columbia Blue Beat DB 112	Play It Cool/Rude With Me	8
68	Downtown DT 401	Move Your Mule/Reggae Me This	15
69	Downtown DT 402	Come Back Girl/Shake Me Wake Me	10
69	Downtown DT 404	Tell Me Darling/Cool Hand Luke	10
69	Downtown DT 406	Doctor Sure Shot/Put On Your Dancing Shoes	7
69	Downtown DT 410	Reggae In Your Jeggae/DREAMERS: Reggae Shuffle	5
69	Downtown DT 411	You Don't Care/Tryer (both sides with Audrey)	5
69	Downtown DT 415	Rocksteady Gone/Walking Down	7
69	Downtown DT 416	I'm Your Puppet/Water Boy	7
69	Downtown DT 421	Games People Play/AUDREY: One Fine Day	7
69	Downtown DT 429	People Get Ready/RUDIES: Near East	35
69	Downtown DT 434	Be Natural, Be Proud/Who Do You Want To Run To	7
69	Downtown DT 437	Come On Home/Love Is All You Need	7
69	Downtown DT 442	Everybody Loves A Winner/Try Me One More Time	7
69	Downtown DT 445	Let's Come Together (with Israelites)/JAKE WADE: Music Fever	7
69	Downtown DT 453	Won't You Come Home/Baby Make It Soon	7
70	Downtown DT 456	Raining In My Heart/First Note	7
70	Downtown DT 458	Build Your Love (On Solid Foundation)/Let's Talk It Over (p/s)	7
70	Downtown DT 458	Build Your Love (On Solid Foundation)/Let's Talk It Over	5
70	Downtown DT 462	Morning Side Of The Mountain (as Dandy & Audrey)/AUDREY: Show Me Baby	7
70	Downtown DT 468	How Glad I Am/I'm So Glad (as Dandy & Audrey)	7
70	Trojan TR 7800	Take A Letter Maria/You're Coming Back	6
71	Downtown DT 483	Could It Be True/Your Eyes Are Dreaming (as Dandy & Jackie)	6
71	Downtown DT 484	Daddy's Home/Everyman	6
71	Trojan TR 7816	Same Old Fashioned Way/Out Of Many, One People	6
72	Trojan TR 7857	What Do You Want To Make Those Eyes At Me For/Talking About Sally	6
67	Giant GNL 1000	ROCKSTEADY WITH DANDY (LP)	75
68	Trojan TRL 2	DANDY RETURNS (LP)	30
69	Trojan TRL 17	I NEED YOU (LP, with Audrey)	25
70	Trojan TTL 26	YOUR MUSICAL DOCTOR (LP)	25
70	Trojan TBL 118	MORNINGSIDE OF THE MOUNTAIN (LP, with Audrey)	30

BARBARA DANE

66	Delyce/Envoy EIS 8876	AMERICAN FOLK SONGS ANTHOLOGY (LP)	20

CHRIS DANE

55	London HLA 8165	Cynthia's In Love/My Ideal	45
55	London HLA 8165	Cynthia's In Love/My Ideal (78)	12

JERRY DANE

60	Decca F 11234	You're My Only Girl/Nothing But The Truth	7
60	Decca F 11284	Let's/Awhile In Love	8
63	Windsor WPS 127	Everybody Go Wild/Watcha Want (p/s)	15
63	Windsor WPS 127	Everybody Go Wild/Watcha Want	8

PATRICK DANE

(see also Quiet Five)

65	Columbia DB 7466	In My Baby's Eyes/The Only One (with Quiet Five)	6
65	Columbia DB 7749	Go Out And Get Somebody/Go On Your Way (with Club '69)	6
68	MGM MGM 1403	When You Lose The One You Love/Home (as Patrick Dane & Mark 7)	6

CAL DANGER

(see also Tony Dangerfield)

62	Fontana 267 225 TF	Restless/Teenage Girlie Blues	150

A.P. DANGERFIELD

68	Fontana TF 935	Conversations (In A Station Light Refreshment Bar)/Further Conversations	30

KEITH DANGERFIELD

68	Plexium P 1237	No Life Child/She's A Witch	200

TONY DANGERFIELD & THRILLS

(see also Savages, Circles, Cal Danger)

64	Pye 7N 15695	I've Seen Such Things/She's Too Way Out	60

DANI

74	Pye International 7N 25667	La Vie A 25 Ans/Pour Que Ça Dure (p/s)	6
74	Pye International 7N 25667	That Old Familiar Feeling/Pour Que Ça Dure	12

DANIEL

70	Columbia DB 8732	Goodnight My Little Love/Forget You Ever Saw Me Dust	6

ERROLL DANIEL

69	Paradox PAR 45902	No Excuses/Go Back	20

DANIEL IN THE LION'S DEN

70	Trojan TR 7797	Dancing In The Sun/LION'S DEN: Chick A Bow	6

DANIELLE

66	Philips BF 1532	I'm Gonna Marry The Boy/Magic Carpet Of Love	8
67	Philips BF 1574	Oh Mama/Come A Little Closer	7

MINT VALUE £

BILLY DANIELS

56	Vogue V 2386	I Live For You/Medley: Easy To Love, etc.	7
56	Oriole CB 1087	I Get A Kick Out Of You/Too Marvelous For Words	7
56	Oriole CB 1095	That Old Black Magic/I Concentrate On You	7
60	Vogue V 9172	That Old Black Magic/My Yiddishe Mamma	12
56	Mercury MEP 9001	BILLY DANIELS (EP)	12
60	Mercury ZEP 10066	THAT OLD BLACK MAGIC (EP)	12
53	Oriole/Mercury MG 10003	TORCH HOUR (10" LP, Oriole label with stickered U.S. Mercury sleeve)	20
54	Mercury MG 25103	TORCH HOUR (10" LP, reissue)	18
54	Mercury MG 25163	SONGS AT MIDNIGHT (10" LP)	25
56	Mercury MPT 7505	SONGS AT MIDNIGHT (10" LP, reissue)	12

JULIUS DANIELS

65	RCA RCX 7175	R.C.A. VICTOR RACE SERIES VOL. 4 (EP)	15

MAXINE DANIELS

57	Oriole CB 1366	Coffee-Bar Calypso/Cha-Cha Calypso	10
58	Oriole CB 1402	I Never Realised/Moonlight Serenade	8
58	Oriole CB 1440	You Brought A New Kind Of Love To Me/Somebody Else Is Taking My Place	8
58	Oriole CB 1449	When It's Springtime In The Rockies/My Summer Heart	8
58	Oriole CB 1462	Passionate Summer/Lola's Heart	8

MIKE DANIELS & HIS BAND

57	Columbia 33SX 1256	MIKE ON MIKE (LP)	40

ROLY 'YO YO' DANIELS

60s	Stardisc SD 101	Yo Yo Boy/The Teacher (p/s)	15
61	Parlophone R 4759	Late Last Evening/Bella Bella Marie	7
62	Decca F 11501	Yo Yo Boy/The Teacher (reissue)	8

SAM DANIELS

63	Sway SW 003	Tell Me Baby/ERNIE FAULKENER: Beautiful Girl (both with Planets)	12

JOHNNY DANKWORTH ORCHESTRA

(see also Cleo Laine, Philip Green, Tony Mansell, Kenny Wheeler & Johnny Dankworth)

53	Parlophone MSP 6026	Honeysuckle Rose (with Cleo Laine)/Swingin'	10
53	Parlophone MSP 6032	Moon Flowers/Two Ticks	10
53	Parlophone MSP 6037	I Get A Kick Out Of You (with Frank Holder)/Easy Living (with Cleo Laine)	10
54	Parlophone MSP 6067	S' Wonderful/Younger Every Day	10
54	Parlophone MSP 6077	The Slider/It's The Talk Of The Town	10
54	Parlophone MSP 6083	The Jerky Thing/My Buddy	10
54	Parlophone MSP 6092	Runnin' Wild/Oo-Be-Doop	10
54	Parlophone MSP 6113	Perdido/Four Of A Kind	10
54	Parlophone MSP 6139	Bugle Call Rag/You Go To My Head	10
55	Capitol CL 14285	Singin' In The Rain/Non-Stop London	10
56	Parlophone MSP 6255	Experiments With Mice/Applecake	12
57	Parlophone R 4274	All Clare/Melbourne Marathon	5
57	Parlophone R 4294	Duke's Joke/Coquette	5
57	Parlophone R 4321	Big Jazz Story/Firth Of Fourths	5
58	Parlophone R 4456	The Colonel's Tune/Jim And Andy's	5
59	Top Rank JAR 209	We Are The Lambeth Boys/Duet For 16	5
59	Top Rank JAR 209	We Are The Lambeth Boys/Duet For 16 (78)	10
61	Columbia DB 4695	The Avengers/Chano	15
61	Columbia DB 4751	String Of Camels/Winter Wail	5
62	Columbia DB 4852	Cannonball/S.O. Blues	5
63	Fontana TF 422	The Avengers/Off The Cuff	15
64	Fontana TF 512	Beefeaters/Down A Tone	30
65	Fontana TF 643	Sands Of The Kalahari/Night Thoughts	6
66	Fontana TF 675	Return From The Ashes/Piano Theme	5
66	Fontana TF 700	Modesty Blaise Theme/The Frost Report	10
67	Fontana TF 805	(Ain't That) Just Like A Woman/Accident	10
73	Philips 6006 337	Tomorrows World/Bitter Lemons	10
78	BBC RESL 63	Telford's Change/Serenade For Sylvia (p/s)	8
61	Columbia SEG 8137	AFRICAN WALTZ (EP)	12
58	Parlophone GEP 8653	DANKWORTH WORKSHOP NO. 1 (EP)	20
58	Parlophone GEP 8697	DANKWORTH WORKSHOP NO. 2 - EXPERIMENTS WITH DANKWORTH (EP)	15
60	Columbia SEG 8037	THE CRIMINALS (EP, soundtrack; also stereo ESG 7825)	15
56	Parlophone PMD 1042	JOURNEY INTO JAZZ (10" LP)	20
58	Parlophone PMC 1076	THE VINTAGE YEARS (LP)	20
59	Parlophone PMC 1043	FIVE STEPS TO DANKWORTH (LP)	20
60	Top Rank 30/019	LONDON TO NEWPORT (LP)	40
61	Columbia 33SX 1280	JAZZ ROUTES (LP, also stereo SCX 3347)	30
62	Columbia	COLLABORATION! (LP, with London Philharmonic)	15
63	Columbia 33SX 1572	CURTAIN UP (LP)	15
64	Fontana TL/STL 5203	WHAT THE DICKENS! (LP)	20
64	Encore ENC 165	FROM 7 ON (LP)	20
65	Fontana TL 5229	THE ZODIAC VARIATIONS (LP, mono)	25
65	Fontana STL 5229	THE ZODIAC VARIATIONS (LP, stereo)	30
67	Stateside S(S)L 10213	FATHOM (LP, soundtrack)	40
68	Fontana TL 5445	THE $1,000,000 COLLECTION (LP)	20
69	Fontana LPS 16261	OFF DUTY (LP)	18
72	Philips 6308 122	FULL CIRCLE (LP)	15
73	Philips 6308 169	LIFELINE (LP)	15
83	Sepia RSR 2011	ZODIAC VARIATIONS (LP)	12

DANLEERS

58	Mercury AMT 1003	One Summer Night/Wheelin' And A-Dealin'	200
58	Mercury AMT 1003	One Summer Night/Wheelin' And A-Dealin' (78)	40

DANNY & THE JUNIORS

58	HMV POP 436	At The Hop/Sometimes (When I'm All Alone)	15
58	HMV POP 467	Rock And Roll Is Here To Stay/School Boy Romance	40

			MINT VALUE £
58	HMV POP 467	Rock And Roll Is Here To Stay/School Boy Romance (78)	18
58	HMV POP 504	Dottie/In The Meantime	30
58	HMV POP 504	Dottie/In The Meantime (78)	25
60	Top Rank JAR 510	Twistin' U.S.A./Thousand Miles Away	15
61	Top Rank JAR 552	Pony Express/Daydreamer	15
61	Top Rank JAR 587	Back To The Hop/The Charleston Fish	15
62	Top Rank JAR 604	Twistin' All Night Long/Twistin' England (with Freddy Cannon)	15
63	London HL 9666	Oo-La-La-Limbo/Now And Then	12
68	Stateside SS 2117	At The Hop/LLOYD PRICE: (You've Got) Personality	5

C. DANOVAN (actually DON CARLOS)

73	Randy's RAN 529	Sweet Caroline/IMPACT ALL STARS: Caroline (Version)	5

DANSE MACABRE

88	Wild West/Alchemy 1	THINK ABOUT DEATH EP	20

DANSE SOCIETY

81	Society SOC 3-81	The Clock/Continent (brown, black & white foldout p/s)	15
81	Society SOC 3-81	The Clock/Continent (re-pressing, black & white foldout p/s)	5
81	Pax PAX 2	There Is No Shame In Death/Dolphins/These Frayed Edges (12", p/s, blue vinyl)	20
81	Pax PAX 2	There Is No Shame In Death/Dolphins/These Frayed Edges (12", p/s, black vinyl)	6
82	Pax SOC 5	Woman's Own/We're So Happy (p/s)	8
82	Pax PAX 5	Woman's Own/Continent/We're So Happy/Belief (12", with spined p/s)	10
84	Society SOC V 127	2,000 Light Years From Home (12" blue vinyl, 50-150 pressed)	60

DANSETTE DAMAGE

78	Shoestring LACE 001	New Musical Express/The Only Sound (p/s, Robert Plant on backing vocals)	150
79	Pinnacle PIN 30	20013/4 Approximately/Must Be Love (p/s)	8
94	Shoestring BLOO 2LP	SOLD AS SEEN (LP, gatefold sleeve, 500 only)	25

DANTA

72	Epic EPC 7776	Freeway/Mau Mau	30
73	Epic SEPC 1466	Crossfire/Daddy's Gone	20

DANTALIAN'S CHARIOT

(see also Zoot Money's Big Roll Band)

67	Columbia DB 8260	The Madman Running Through The Fields/The Sun Came Bursting Through My Cloud	120
95	Tenth Planet TP 015	CHARIOT RISING (LP, numbered, 1,000 only)	25

DANTE

61	Brunswick 05857	Bye Bye Baby/That's Why	12

DANTE

71	CBS 7382	Queen Of Sheba/Feelin' The Heat	15

RON DANTE

68	MCA MK5003	It's About Time/Behold	8
70	RCA 1992	Let Me Bring You Up/How Do You Know	8

RONNIE DANTE

64	Stateside SS 351	Don't Stand Up In A Canoe/If You Love Me Laurie	5

TROY DANTE (& INFERNOS)

63	Decca F 11639	The Face/Give Me Some More	8
63	Decca F 11746	It's Alright/Tell Me (as Troy Dante & Infernos)	8
64	Fontana TF 445	Tell Me When/It Had To Be (as Troy Dante & Infernos)	8
64	Fontana TF 477	This Little Girl/Loving Eyes (as Troy Dante & Infernos)	15
64	Fontana TF 498	Baby/Tell Me Now	8
65	Fontana TF 541	I Wish I Knew/Sad Tears	8
66	Polydor NH 56110	I'll Never Know/Security	7
68	Columbia DB 8381	My Friend The Scarecrow/Emma May Kingston	7
69	MCA MK 5003	It's About Time/Behold	8

DANTE & EVERGREENS

60	Top Rank JAR 402	Alley-Oop/The Right Time	20

DAN THE BANJO MAN

73	Rare Earth RES 110	Dan The Banjo Man/Everything Will Rhyme	6

DAPHINE

79	My Records MY 12	The World Is Moving On/Just Another Flirt (p/s)	8

STEVE DARBYSHIRE

65	Decca F 12261	That's The Reason Why/She's Got Quality	10
66	Decca F12512	Trains Trains/Alma Jones	7
67	Decca F 12553	Just A Little Lovin' Changes Things/Holiday In Waikiki	6

JOE DARENSBOURG & HIS DIXIE FLYERS

58	Vogue V 2409	Yellow Dog Blues/Careless Love	6
58	Vogue LAE 12149	JOE DARENSBOURG & HIS DIXIE FLYERS (LP)	15

DARIEN SPIRIT

73	Charisma CAS 1065	ELEGY TO MARILYN (LP, large "Mad Hatter" label, with lip intact!)	30

BOBBY DARIN

(see also Rinky Dinks)

78s

56	Brunswick 05561	Rock Island Line/Timber (as Bobby Darin & Jaybirds)	55
58	London HLE 8666	Splish Splash/Judy Don't Be Moody	30
58	London HLE 8679	Early In The Morning/Now We're One	30
58	London HLE 8737	Queen Of The Hop/Lost Love	50
59	London HLE 8793	Mighty Mighty Man/You're Mine (as Bobby Darin with Rinky Dinks)	55
59	London HLE 8815	Plain Jane/While I'm Gone	55
59	London HLE 8867	Dream Lover/Bullmoose	30

			MINT VALUE £
59	London HLK 8939	Mack The Knife/Was There A Call For Me	40
60	London HLK 9034	La Mer (Beyond The Sea)/That's The Way Love Is	50
60	London HLK 9086	Clementine/Down With Love	55
60	London HLK 9142	Bill Bailey Won't You Please Come Home/Tall Story	65

SINGLES

56	Brunswick 05561	Rock Island Line/Timber (as Bobby Darin & Jaybirds)	150
58	London HLE 8666	Splish Splash/Judy Don't Be Moody	30
58	London HLE 8679	Early In The Morning/Now We're One (as Rinky-Dinks featuring Bobby Darin)	40
58	London HLE 8737	Queen Of The Hop/Lost Love	25
58	London HL 7060	Queen Of The Hop/Lost Love (export issue)	20
59	London HLE 8793	Mighty Mighty Man/You're Mine (as Bobby Darin with Rinky Dinks)	40
59	London HLE 8815	Plain Jane/While I'm Gone	30
59	London HL 7078	Plain Jane/Dream Lover (export issue)	25
59	London HLE 8867	Dream Lover/Bullmoose	5
59	London HLK 8939	Mack The Knife/Was There A Call For Me	6
60	London HLK 9034	La Mer (Beyond The Sea)/That's The Way Love Is	7

(The above 45s were originally issued with trianguar centres, later round centre pressings are worth around two-thirds these values)

60	London HLK 9086	Clementine/Down With Love	6
60	London HLK 9142	Bill Bailey Won't You Please Come Home/Tall Story	6
60	Brunswick 05831	Hear Them Bells/The Greatest Builder	10
60	London HLK 9197	Beachcomber/Autumn Blues (credited to ?Bobby Darin At The Piano')	10
60	Lonson HLK 9215	Somebody To Love/I'll Be There	7
61	London HLK 9303	Lazy River/Oo-Ee-Train	6
61	London HLK 9375	Nature Boy/Look For My True Love	6
61	London HLK 9407	Theme From "Come September"/Walk Bach To Me (with Orchestra)	10
61	London HLK 9429	You Must Have Been A Beautiful Baby/Sorrow Tomorrow	5
61	London HLK 9474	Multiplication (From "Come September")/Irresistible You	5
62	London HLK 9540	What'd I Say/Ain't That Love	8
62	London HLK 9575	Things/Jailer Bring Me Water	5
62	Atlantic HLK 9575	Things/Jailer Bring Me Water	25
62	Capitol CL 15272	If A Man Answers/A True, True Love	8
62	London HLK 9624	Baby Face/You Know How	6
63	London HLK 9663	I've Found A New Baby/Keep A-Walkin'	8
63	Capitol CL 15286	You're The Reason I'm Living/Now You're Gone	8
63	Capitol CL 15306	Eighteen Yellow Roses/Not For Me	15
63	Capitol CL 15328	Be Mad Little Girl/Since You've Been Gone	10
64	Capitol CL 15338	I Wonder Who's Kissing Her Now/As Long As I'm Singing	6
64	Atlantic AT 4002	Milord/Golden Earrings	6
64	Capitol CL 15360	The Things In This House/Wait By The Water	6
65	Capitol CL 15401	When I Get Home/Lonely Road	6
65	Capitol CL 15414	Gyp The Cat/That Funny Feeling	6
65	Atlantic AT 4046	We Didn't Ask To Be Brought Here/Funny What Love Can Do	10
66	Atlantic 584 014	Mame/Walking In The Shadow Of Love	5
66	Atlantic 584 051	If I Were A Carpenter/Rainin'	5
67	Atlantic 584 063	The Girl That Stood Beside Me/Reason To Believe	5
67	Atlantic 584 079	Lovin' You/Amy	5
67	Atlantic 584 105	The Lady Came From Baltimore/I Am	6
67	Atlantic 584 147	At The Crossroads/She Knows	5
68	Bell BLL 1040	Change/Long Line Rider	5
69	Bell BLL 1090	Sugar-Man/Jive	5
70	Major Minor MM 697	Maybe We Can Get It Together/RX-Pyro (Prescription: Fire) (as Bob Darin)	5
74	Mowest MW 3014	Blue Monday/Moritat: Mack The Knife	5

EPs

59	London REE 1173	BOBBY DARIN (tri centre)	60
59	London REE 1173	BOBBY DARIN (round centre)	60
59	London REE 1225	BOBBY DARIN NO. 2 (tri centre)	60
59	London REE 1225	BOBBY DARIN NO. 2 (round centre)	40
60	London REK 1243	THAT'S ALL	25
61	London REK 1286	FOR TEENAGERS ONLY	30
61	London REK 1290	UP A LAZY RIVER	20
61	London REK 1310	TWO OF A KIND (with Johnny Mercer)	30
61	London REK 1321	THE 25TH DAY OF DECEMBER	30
61	London REK 1334	LOVE SWINGS	20
62	London REK 1338	TWIST WITH BOBBY DARIN	20
62	London REK 1342	THINGS!	20
65	Atlantic AET 6013	MILORD	20

ALBUMS

58	London HA-E 2140	BOBBY DARIN	60
59	London HA-E 2172	THAT'S ALL	25
59	London HA-K 2235	THIS IS DARIN (mono)	25
59	London SAH-K 6067	THIS IS DARIN (stereo)	30
60	London HA-K 2291	DARIN AT THE COPA (mono)	20
60	London SAH-K 6103	DARIN AT THE COPA (stereo)	25
60	London HA-K 2311	FOR TEENAGERS ONLY	40
61	London HA-K 2363	TWO OF A KIND (with Johnny Mercer; mono)	30
61	London SAH-K 6164	TWO OF A KIND (with Johnny Mercer; stereo)	40
61	London HA-K 2372	THE BOBBY DARIN STORY	25
61	London HA-K 2394	LOVE SWINGS (mono)	25
61	London SAH-K 6194	LOVE SWINGS (stereo)	35
62	London HA-K 2456	DARIN SINGS RAY CHARLES (mono)	25
62	London SAH-K 6243	DARIN SINGS RAY CHARLES (stereo)	35
62	Capitol T 1791	OH! LOOK AT ME NOW	20
62	London HA-K 8030	THINGS AND OTHER THINGS	30
63	London HA-K 8102	IT'S YOU OR NO-ONE (mono)	30
63	London SH-K 8102	IT'S YOU OR NO-ONE (stereo)	40

			MINT VALUE £
63	Capitol T 1826	EARTHY	15
63	Capitol T 1866	YOU'RE THE REASON I'M LIVING	20
63	Capitol T 1942	EIGHTEEN YELLOW ROSES & 11 OTHER HITS (mono)	25
63	Capitol (S)T 1942	EIGHTEEN YELLOW ROSES & 11 OTHER HITS (stereo)	30
64	Capitol T 2007	GOLDEN FOLK HITS (mono)	25
64	Capitol (S)T 2007	GOLDEN FOLK HITS (stereo)	30
65	Capitol T 2194	FROM HELLO DOLLY TO GOODBYE CHARLIE	15
65	Atlantic ATL 5014	BOBBY DARIN WINNERS	20
65	Capitol T 2322	I WANNA BE AROUND	20
66	Capitol T 2571	THE BEST OF BOBBY DARIN	15
66	Atlantic 587/588 014	SINGS THE SHADOW OF YOUR SMILE	15
66	Atlantic 587/588 020	IN A BROADWAY BAG (MAME)	15
66	Atlantic 587/588 051	IF I WERE A CARPENTER	15
67	Atlantic 587 065	THE BOBBY DARIN STORY	15
67	Atlantic 587 073	SOMETHING SPECIAL	30
67	Atlantic 587 076	INSIDE OUT	15

DARK

72	SIS 0102	DARK ROUND THE EDGES (LP, private pressing, 12 copies with colour gatefold sleeve & booklet)	2000
72	SIS 0102	DARK ROUND THE EDGES (LP, private pressing, 8 copies with black & white gatefold sleeve)	1500
72	SIS 0102	DARK ROUND THE EDGES (LP, private pressing, 40 copies with single black & white sleeve)	1000
90	Swank	DARK ROUND THE EDGES (LP, reissue, U.K. pressing marketed in U.S.)	30
91	Swank/Darkside 001	DARK ROUND THE EDGES (LP, as above, with different insert, 225 only)	25
92	Kissing Spell KSCD 9204	DARK ROUND THE EDGES (CD, with 8-page booklet, 1,500 only)	20
95	Acme AC 8009LP	ARTEFACTS FROM THE BLACK MUSEUM (LP, 500 only, with insert)	15

DARKER SHADE OF BLACK

71	Jackpot JP 758	War/JEFF BARNES: People's Version	8

DARKNESS

02	Must Destroy DUSTY 001CD	I Believe In A Thing Called Love/Love On The Rocks With No Ice/ Love Is Only A Feeling (CD)	40
03	Must Destroy DESTROYER 6	Get Your Hands Off My Woman (Clean Version)/ (Dirty Version)/Best Of Me (p/s, 2000 only)	10
03	Must Destroy DARK 02	Christmas Time (Don't Let The Bells End)/I Love You 5 Times (promo-only box set, in giftwrap, with card)	15

DARKSIDE

(see also Spacemen 3)

90	Situation 2 SITU 29P	ALL THAT NOISE (LP, picture disc, die-cut sleeve)	12

DARK STAR

81	Avatar AAA 105	Lady Of Mars/Rock 'N' Romancin' (company sleeve)	12
81	Steel Strike no cat. no.	Lady Of Mars/Rock 'N' Romancin' (12", 250 pressed)	90
81	Avatar AALP 5003	DARK STAR (LP, with patch)	20
81	Avatar AALP 5003	DARK STAR (LP)	15
87	FM WKFMLP 97	REAL TO REEL (LP)	15

DARKTHRONE

91	Peaceville VILE 22	SOULSIDE JOURNEY (LP, picture disc)	50
92	Peaceville VILE 28	A BLAZE IN THE NORTHERN SKY (LP)	50
93	Peaceville VILE 35	UNDER A FUNERAL MOON (LP)	50
94	Peaceville VILE 43	TRANSILVANIAN HUNGER (LP)	80

DARLETTES

70	President PT 317	Lost/Sweet Kind Of Loneliness	15

DARLING BUDS

87	Darling Buds DAR 1	If I Said/Just To Be Seen (p/s, with insert, 2,000 only)	12
87	Darling Buds DAR 1	If I Said/Just To Be Seen (p/s, without insert, 2,000 only)	6
88	Bonk On 001	Spin/BUBBLEGUM SPLASH track (flexidisc free with So Naive fanzine)	6
90	Native NTV 54	Shame On You/Valentine//It's All Up To You/Spin/Think Of Me/ That's The Reason (triple-pack in envelope sleeve)	6

BILL DARNEL

(see also Frank Weir & His Orchestra)

55	London HLU 8204	My Little Mother/Bring Me A Bluebird (with Frank Weir & His Orchestra)	40
56	London HLU 8234	The Last Frontier/Rock-A-Boogie Baby	50
56	London HLU 8267	Guilty Lips/Ain't Misbehavin'	40
56	London HLU 8292	Tell Me More/Satin Doll	40

GUY DARRELL (& MIDNIGHTERS)

63	Oriole CB 1932	Go Home Girl/You Won't Come Home (as Guy Darrell & Midnighters)	15
64	Oriole CB 1964	Sorry/Sweet Dreams (as Guy Darrell & Midnighters)	15
65	CBS 201806	Stupidity/One Of These Days	10
66	CBS 202033	Somewhere They Can't Find Me/It Takes A Lot To Laugh	10
66	CBS 202082	I've Been Hurt/Blessed	25
66	CBS 202082	I've Been Hurt/Blessed	40
66	CBS 202296	Big Louie/My Way Of Thinking	6
67	CBS 202510	Hard Lovin'/I've Never Had A Love Like That	15
67	CBS 202642	Crystal Ball/Didn't I	6
67	Piccadilly 7N 35406	Evil Woman/What You Do About That	20
67	Pye 7N 17435	Cupid/What's Happened To Our Love	6
68	Pye 7N 17586	Skyline Pigeon/Everything	6
69	Page One POF 120	Turn To Me/What's Her Name	5
69	Page One POF 141	Birds Of A Feather/Keep The Rain From My Door	5
69	Page One POF 155	How Are You/Turtle Turquoise And The Hare (as Guy Darrell Syndicate)	5
73	Santa Ponsa PNS4	I've Been Hurt/Blessed	5
72	CBS 53364	GUY DARRELL (LP)	20

MINT VALUE £

JAMES DARREN
59 Pye International 7N 25019 Gidget/There's No Such Thing (as Jimmy Darren) . . . 12
59 Pye International 7N 25034 Angel Face/I Don't Wanna Lose You (as Jimmy Darren) . . . 15
60 Pye International 7N 25059 Because They're Young/Let There Be Love . . . 8
61 Pye International 7N 25116 Goodbye Cruel World/Valerie . . . 7
62 Pye International 7N 25125 Her Royal Majesty/If I Could Only Tell You . . . 6
62 Pye International 7N 25138 Conscience/Dream Big . . . 6
62 Pye International 7N 25155 Mary's Little Lamb/The Life Of The Party . . . 8
62 Pye International 7N 25168 Hail To The Conquering Hero/Too Young To Go Steady . . . 8
63 Pye International 7N 25170 Pin A Medal On Joey/I'll Be Loving You . . . 8
63 Colpix PX 708 Backstage/Gegetta . . . 8
65 Warner Bros WB 5648 Because You're Mine/Millions Of Roses . . . 7
66 Warner Bros WB 5689 Tom Hawk/I Want To Be Lonely . . . 7
67 Warner Bros WB 5874 All/Misty Morning Eyes . . . 7
59 Pye Intl. NEP 44004 P.S. I LOVE YOU (EP) . . . 25
62 Pye Intl. NEP 44008 JAMES DARREN HIT PARADE (EP) . . . 20
63 Pye Intl. NPL 28021 LOVE AMONG THE YOUNG (LP) . . . 30

JEANNIE DARREN & SECOND CITY SOUND
69 Major Minor MM 611 River Deep, Mountain High/Julie . . . 7

MAXINE DARREN
65 Pye 7N 15796 How Can I Hide It From My Heart/Don't You Know . . . 10

CHRIS DARROW
(see also Kaleidoscope, Nitty Gritty Dirt Band)
73 United Artists UAG 29453 CHRIS DARROW (LP) . . . 15
74 United Artists UAG 29634 UNDER MY OWN DISGUISE (LP) . . . 15

DARTELLS
63 London HLD 9719 Hot Pastrami/Dartell Stomp . . . 20

BARRY DARVELL
60 London HL 9191 Geronimo Stomp/How Will It End? . . . 80

DARWIN'S THEORY
67 Major Minor MM 503 Daytime/Hosanna . . . 40

NITAE DASGUPTA
72 Mushroom 100 MR 22 SONGS OF INDIA (LP) . . . 35

DAS SCHNITZ
79 Ellie Jay EJSP 9249 4 AM (EP, custom sleeve) . . . 70

DATE WITH SOUL
(see also Jack Nitzsche, Brian Wilson, Sonny & Cher, Darlene Love/Blossoms, Jackie De Shannon, the Paris Sisters)
67 Stateside SS 2062 Yes Sir, That's My Baby/PRISCILLA: He Noticed Me . . . 50

DAUGHTERS OF ALBION
69 Fontana STL 5486 DAUGHTERS OF ALBION (LP) . . . 25

DAVE & ANSELL COLLINS
(see also Ansel Collins, Les Foster & Ansell Collins, Dave Barker)
72 Techniques TE 915 Karate/Doing Your Own Thing . . . 8
72 Rhino RNO 106 Keep On Trying/Give Me Some Light . . . 6
73 Rhino RNO 111 Hot Line/Sunshine Rock (label credits 'Dave Collins') . . . 6
73 Trojan TR 7891 Bandwagon/Ton Up Kids . . . 6

DAVE DAVANI & D MEN
63 Columbia DB 7125 Don't Fool Around/She's The Best For Me . . . 15
64 Decca F 11896 Midnight Special/Sho' Know A Lot About Love . . . 20

DAVE DAVANI (FOUR)
65 Parlophone R 5329 Top Of The Pops/Workin' Out . . . 25
66 Parlophone R 5490 Tossin' And Turnin'/Jupe . . . 40
66 Parlophone R 5525 One Track Mind/On The Cooler Side . . . 30
72 Philips 6006 195 King Kong Blues/Come Back Baby (solo) . . . 12
65 Parlophone PMC 1258 FUSED (LP) . . . 90

DAVE & DIAMONDS
(see also Dave Russell)
65 Columbia DB 7692 I Walk The Lonely Night/You Do Love (p/s) . . . 35
65 Columbia DB 7692 I Walk The Lonely Night/You Do Love . . . 15

DAVE & DON
67 Polydor 56212 What A Feeling/That's My Way . . . 6

BOB DAVENPORT (& RAKES)
60 Collector JEB 4 GEORDIE SONGS (EP) . . . 15
62 Topic TOP 83 WOR GEORDIE (EP, with Rakes) . . . 15
66 Columbia SX 1786 BOB DAVENPORT AND THE RAKES (LP, with Rakes) . . . 40
71 Trailer LER 3008 BOB DAVENPORT& THE MARSDEN RATTLERS (LP, red label) . . . 22
73 Trailer LER 2088 PAL OF MY CRADLE DAYS (LP, red label) . . . 18
77 Topic 12TS 318 POSTCARDS HOME (LP, with lyric sheet) . . . 15

D.A.V.E. THE DRUMMER
90s Yolk YOLK 05 Steamliner/Jaws (12", with Jerome Hill) . . . 40
00 Smitten SMTLTD 02 Effective Therapy (1-sided 12", green vinyl) . . . 15

ALAN DAVEY
(see also Hawkwind)
87 Hawkfan HWFB 3/4 THE ELF EP (double pack, 2 x 7" with insert in wraparound p/s in poly bag) . . . 20

(Shaun) DAVEY & (James) MORRIS
(see also Strawbs)
73 York FYK 417 DAVEY AND MORRIS (LP, with insert) . . . 110

			MINT VALUE £
DAVID			
69	Philips BF 1776	Please Mister Postman/Light Of Your Mind	75
69	President PT286	The Who The Why/President	6
70	Fontana TF 1081	I'm Going Back/Selppin	40
ALAN DAVID			
64	Decca F 11956	I Want So Much To Know You/I Can't Go Wrong	10
65	Decca F 12084	Hurt/I Found Out Too Late	50
65	Decca F 12130	Crazy 'Bout My Baby/A Thousand Years Too Late	10
67	Polydor BM 56201	Flower Power/Completely Free	80
69	Page One POF116	Oh What A Naughty Man/I've Got To Know	10
65	Decca LK 4674	ALAN DAVID (LP)	40
DAVID & DAVID			
70	Columbia DB8678	In The City/Good Morning Morning	25
DAVID & EMBERS			
(see also Embers)			
63	Decca F 11717	What Is This/Teddy Bear Special	7
DAVID & GIANTS			
68	Capitol CL 15915	Ten Miles High/Super Love	8
DAVID & GOLIATH			
71	Concord CON 025	Why Do You Pretend/I Wonder Where	8
DAVID & JONATHAN			
(see also Roger Cook, Edison Lighthouse, White Plains)			
66	Columbia DB 7950	Lovers Of The World Unite/Oh My World	5
67	Columbia S(C)X 6031	DAVID AND JONATHAN (LP)	25
DAVID & ROZAA			
(see also David Essex)			
70	Philips 6006 040	Time Of Our Life/We Can Reach An Understanding	20
71	Philips 6006 094	The Spark That Lights The Flame/Two Can Share	20
DIANNE DAVIDSON			
72	Janus 6146 019	Sympathy/All I Wanted	8
72	Janus 6146 021	Ain't Gonna Be Treated This Way/All I Wanted (All The Time)	5
72	Janus 6310 209	BACKWOODS WOMAN (LP)	12
FRANKIE DAVIDSON & HI MARKS			
61	Starlite ST45 5037	You're Driving Me Crazy/I Care For You (B-side with Unicords)	15
61	London HL 9309	Detour/Just For Today	10
64	HMV POP 1256	Lickin' And A-Stickin'/I Love To Shake	15
68	Decca F 22780	Hector The Trash Collector/Somebody Come And Take My Wife	5
TOMMY DAVIDSON			
56	London HLU 8219	Half Past Kissing Time/I Don't Know Yet But I'm Learning	90
56	London HLU 8219	Half Past Kissing Time/I Don't Know Yet But I'm Learning (78)	20
HUTCH DAVIE			
58	London HLE 8667	At The Woodchopper's Ball/Honky Tonk Train Blues (& Honky Tonkers)	10
60	London HLE 9076	Sweet Georgia Brown/Heartaches	5
62	Pye International 7N 25149	But I Do/Time Was (& Orchestra)	5
60	London HA-E 2216	MUCH HUTCH (LP)	20
ALUN DAVIES			
(see also Cat Stevens, Sweet Thursday)			
65	Parlophone R 5384	Girls Were Made To Love And Kiss/Rose Marie	6
68	Mercury MF 1043	One Day Soon/Pretend You Don't See Her	6
72	CBS 65108	DAYDO (LP, gatefold sleeve)	25
BARRY DAVIES			
70	Beacon BEA 114	I Wish It Would Rain/Strange Days	30
BAZ DAVIES			
80	BAT EJSP 9397	Back In 1969/Easy On My Mind	8
BOB DAVIES			
63	London HLU 9767	Rock'N'Roll Show/With You Tonight	25
CYRIL DAVIES (R&B ALLSTARS)			
(see also Alexis Korner, Beryl Bryden)			
63	Pye International 7N 25194	Country Line Special/Chicago Calling	25
63	Pye International 7N 25221	Preachin' The Blues/Sweet Mary	40
69	Pye 7N 17663	Country Line Special/Sweet Mary	15
64	Pye Intl. NEP 44025	THE SOUND OF CYRIL DAVIES (EP)	70
57	'77' LP 2	THE LEGENDARY CYRIL DAVIES (10" LP, 99 only, with Alexis Korner)	300
70	Folklore F-LEAT 9	THE LEGENDARY CYRIL DAVIES (LP, reissue)	75
DAVE DAVIES			
(see also Kinks)			
67	Pye 7N 17356	Death Of A Clown/Love Me Till The Sun Shines	8
67	Pye 7N 17429	Susannah's Still Alive/Funny Face	12
68	Pye 7N 17514	Lincoln County/There's No Life Without Love	20
69	Pye 7N 17678	Hold My Hand/Creeping Jean	20
68	Pye NEP 24289	DAVE DAVIES HITS (EP)	300
FREDDY DAVIES			
67	Major Minor MM 536	Sentimental Songs/Cynthia Crisp	5
IRVING DAVIES & METHOD MEN			
62	Decca F 11456	The Method/ABC The Method	6
JACKIE DAVIES & HIS QUARTET			
(see also Chico Arnez)			
57	Pye Nixa N 15115	Land Of Make Believe/Over The Rainbow (78)	50

MINT VALUE £

MARION DAVIES
(see also Ladybirds)

69	Columbia DB 8589	Walk Out Of My Mind/This Is My Lonely Life	7

MIAR DAVIES

64	Decca F 11805	Ten Good Reasons/I Won't Remember You	10
64	Decca F 11894	I Hear You Knocking/Navy Blue	10

NICOLA DAVIES

68	SNB 55-3627	Infatuation/My Boy	6

RAY DAVIES
(see also Kinks)

86	Virgin VS 865-12	Quiet Life/Voices In The Dark/GIL EVANS: Va Va Voom (12", p/s)	8
86	Virgin VS 865	Quiet Life/Voices In The Dark (p/s)	5

RAY DAVIES & BUTTONDOWN BRASS
(see also Buttondown Brass; this is not Ray Davies of the Kinks)

73	Pye NSPL 41021	I BELIEVE IN MUSIC (LP)	15
74	Philips 6382 103	THEMES FROM THE EXORCIST, FRENCH CONNECTION AND OTHER GREAT FILMS (LP)	15
75	Philips 6382 111	FLASHPOINT (LP)	15

RON DAVIES

70	A & M AMS 799	It Ain't Easy/Silent Song Through The Land	6
70	A&M AMLS 993	SILENT SONG THROUGH THE LAND (LP, green label)	30

TYRONE DAVIES

77	D-Roy FORCE 2012	Mind Blowing Decisions/Trenchtown Skank	12

BARRINGTON DAVIS

72	Montague MONS 2	TRACKS OF MIND (LP, with lyric inner sleeve)	60

BARRY DAVIS

71	Beacon BEA 114	I Wish It Would Rain/Strange Days	25

BETTE DAVIS (& DEBBIE BURTON)

63	London HLU 9711	Whatever Happened To Baby Jane?/ DEBBIE BURTON:I've Written A Letter To Daddy	12
76	EMI 2415	Mother Of The Bride/It Can't Be Wrong (as Miss Bette Davis)	8
76	EMI EMA 778	MISS BETTE DAVIS (LP)	30

BETTY DAVIS

75	Island USA 2011	Shut Off The Light/He Was A Big Freak	6
75	Island ILPS 9329	NASTY GIRL (LP)	25

BILLIE DAVIS
(see also Keith & Billie, Le Roys, Mike Sarne)

63	Decca F 11572	Tell Him/I'm Thankful	7
63	Decca F 11572	Tell Him/I'm Thankful (export copies with p/s)	15
63	Decca F 11658	He's The One/V.I.P.	10
63	Decca F 11658	He's The One/V.I.P. (export copies with p/s)	15
63	Columbia DB 7115	Bedtime Stories/You And I	15
64	Columbia DB 7195	That Boy John/Say Nothin' Don't Tell	15
64	Columbia DB 7246	School Is Over/Give Me Love	15
64	Columbia DB 7346	Whatcha Gonna Do/Everybody Knows (as Billie Davis & Le Roys)	30
65	Piccadilly 7N 35227	Last One To Be Loved/You Don't Know	10
65	Piccadilly 7N 35266	No Other Baby/Hands Off	10
66	Piccadilly 7N 35308	Heart And Soul/Don't Take All Night	10
66	Piccadilly 7N 35350	Just Walk In My Shoes/Ev'ry Day	60
67	Decca F 12620	Wasn't It You?/Until It's Time For You To Go	10
67	Decca F 12696	Angel Of The Morning/Darling Be Home Soon	10
68	Decca F 12823	I Want You To Be My Baby/Suffer	7
69	Decca F 12870	Make The Feeling Go Away/I'll Come Home	10
69	Decca F 12923	I Can Remember/Nobody's Home To Go Home To	20
69	Decca F 12977	Nights In White Satin/It's Over	18
70	Decca F 13049	Venid Con Migo/Love (Spanish export issue)	7
70	Decca F 13085	There Must Be A Reason/Love	12
72	Regal Zonophone RZ 3050	I Tried/Touch My Love	6
76	United Artists UP 36117	Any Way That You Want Me/Somewhere Along The Line	6
76	United Artists UP 46066	I've Been Loving Someone Else/Beyond The Pale	6
78	Magnet MAG 124	Run Joey Run/Easy Come Easy Go	6
70	Decca LK 5029	BILLIE DAVIS (LP, mono)	60
70	Decca SKL 5029	BILLIE DAVIS (LP, stereo)	50

BLIND GARY DAVIS/REVEREND GARY DAVIS

63	'77' LA 12-14	PURE RELIGION AND BAD COMPANY (LP)	30
60s	Fontana 688 303 ZL	HARLEM STREET SINGER (LP)	45
64	Xtra XTRA 1009	REV. GARY DAVIS/SHORT STUFF MACON (LP, 1 side each)	22
66	Xtra XTRA 5014	SAY NO TO THE DEVIL (LP)	25
67	Xtra XTRA 5042	A LITTLE MORE FAITH (LP)	25
69	Fontana SFJL 914	BRING YOUR MONEY HONEY (LP)	25
71	Transatlantic TRA 244	RAGTIME GUITAR (LP)	15
72	Transatlantic TRA 249	CHILDREN OF ZION (LP)	15
77	Kicking Mule SNKF 103	LET US GET TOGETHER (LP)	18

BOBBY DAVIS (Jamaica)
(see also Barbara Dunkley)

71	Banana BA 342	Got To Get Away/We'll Cry Together (with BARBARA DUNKLEY)	12
71	Banana BA 344	Return Your Love/RILEY'S ALLSTARS: Version	10
71	Beacon 114	Strange Days/I Wish It would Rain	12

BOBBY DAVIS (U.S.)

61	Starlite ST45 056	I Was Wrong/Hype You Into Selling Your Head	50

MINT VALUE £

BONNIE DAVIS

55	Brunswick 05507	Pepper-Hot Baby/For Always, Darling	40

CLIFFORD DAVIS

69	Reprise RS 27003	Before The Beginning/Man Of The World	10
70	Reprise RS 27008	Come On Down And Follow Me/Homework	15
71	Reprise K 14282	Before The Beginning/Man Of The World (reissue)	7

DANNY DAVIS ORCHESTRA (U.S.)

(see also Ruby & Romantics, Byron Lee)

58	London HL 8766	Trumpet Cha-Cha-Cha/Lonesome Trumpet	8
65	MGM MGM 1277	Main Theme From "The Saint"/Little Bandits Of Juarez	10
64	London HAR 8204	THEY'RE PLAYING OUR SONG (LP, with Ruby & Romantics)	40

DANNY DAVIS & BYRON LEE

64	MGM 1256	Night Train From Jamaica/Ska Dee Dah	18

DANNY DAVIS (U.K.)

(see also Marauders)

60	Parlophone R 4657	Love Me/You're My Only Girl	20
60	Parlophone R 4796	Talking In My Sleep/Lullaby Of Love	15
61	Pye 7N 15391	Tell All The World/Rumours	10
62	Pye 7N 15427	Rome Wasn't Built In A Day/Tell Me	5
62	Pye 7N 15470	Patches/September In The Rain	5

DEL DAVIS

71	Bread BR-1105	Baby Don't Wake Me/Wishing And Hoping	100
72	Trojan 7870	Baby Don't Wake Me/Sugarloaf Hill	70

EDDIE ('LOCKJAW') DAVIS

(see also Coleman Hawkins, Johnny Griffin)

56	Parlophone GEP 8587	EDDIE 'LOCKJAW' DAVIS TRIO (EP)	10
57	Parlophone GEP 8678	LOCKJAW (EP)	10
58	Parlophone GEP 8685	EDDIE 'LOCKJAW' DAVIS TRIO (EP)	10
59	Esquire EP 217	EDDIE 'LOCKJAW'DAVIS (EP)	10
61	Esquire EP 237	EDDIE 'LOCKJAW' DAVIS QUARTET (EP)	10
60	Esquire 32-104	THE EDDIE 'LOCKJAW' DAVIS COOK BOOK (LP)	20
60	Esquire 32-117	VERY SAXY (LP, with Coleman Hawkins, Arnett Cobb & Bobby Tate)	20
61	Esquire 32-128	JAWS IN ORBIT (LP)	20
64	Stateside SL 10102	THE FIRST SET - LIVE AT MINTONS (LP, with Johnny Griffin)	20

EDWARD H. DAVIS

74	Sain SAIN 1016M	HEN FFORDD GYMREIG O FYW (LP)	20
76	Sain SAIN 1053M	SNEB YN BECSO DAM (LP)	15

JESSE (ED) DAVIS

71	Atlantic 2091 076	Every Night Is Saturday Night/Washita Love Child (as Jesse Davis)	6
71	Atco 2400 106	JESSE 'ED' DAVIS (LP)	18
72	Atlantic K 40329	ULULU (LP)	15

JIMMY DAVIS

66	Bounty BY 6009	MAXWELL STREET (LP)	25

KIM DAVIS

(see also Kim D, Kim & Kinetics)

66	Decca F 12387	Don't Take Your Lovin' Away/Feelin' Blue	20
67	CBS 202568	Tell It Like It Is/Losing Kind	12
68	CBS 3260	Until It's Time For You To Go/I Hold No Grudge	7
69	CBS 4210	Are You Ready For Love/Taste Of Excitement	7

LARRY DAVIS/FENTON ROBINSON

72	Python PLP 24	LARRY DAVIS AND FENTON ROBINSON (LP, 99 copies only)	70

MAXWELL DAVIS

66	Ember FA 2040	BATMAN THEME AND OTHER BAT SONGS (LP)	35

MELVIN DAVIS

69	Action ACT 4531	Save It/This Love Was Meant To Be	35

MILES DAVIS

55	Esquire 20-041	MILES DAVIS QUINTET (10")	30
53	Esquire 20-017	MILES DAVIS PLAYS (10")	30
53	Esquire 20-021	MILES DAVIS ALL STARS (10")	30
53	Vogue LDE 028	MILES DAVIS ALL STARS (10")	30
54	Esquire 20-052	MILES DAVIS ALL STARS (A HIFI MODERN JAZZ JAM SESSION) (10")	30
54	Vogue LDE 064	MILES DAVIS AND HIS ORCHESTRA (10")	30
54	Esquire 20-056	MILES DAVIS ALL STARS (A SECOND HIFI MODERN JAZZ JAM SESSION) (10")	30
54	Capitol LC 6683	CLASSICS IN JAZZ (10")	30
55	Esquire 20-062	MILES DAVIS ALL STARS SEXTET (10")	30
55	Esquire 20-072	MILES DAVIS QUINTET (10")	30
56	Esquire 32-012	THE MUSINGS OF MILES	30
56	Philips BBL 7140	'ROUND ABOUT MIDNIGHT	20
57	Esquire 32-028	CHANGES	20
57	Esquire 32-030	BIRTH OF THE COOL	20
57	Vogue LDE 191	NATURE BOY	30
57	Fontana TFL 5007	MILES AHEAD	20
58	Fontana TFL 5035	MILESTONES	20
58	Esquire 32-048	COOKIN'	30
58	Esquire 32-068	RELAXIN' WITH THE MILES DAVIS QUARTET	30
59	Esquire 32-090	BAGS' GROOVE	25
59	Fontana TFL 5056	PORGY AND BESS (mono)	20
59	Fontana STFL 507	PORGY AND BESS (stereo)	25
60	Fontana TFL 5081	JAZZ TRACK - "L'ANSCENSEUR POUR L'ECHAFAUD"	20

			MINT VALUE £
60	Fontana TFL 5089	THE MOST OF MILES	15
60	Fontana TFL 5072	KIND OF BLUE (mono)	20
60	Fontana STFL 513	KIND OF BLUE (stereo)	25
60s	CBS BPG 62066	KIND OF BLUE (LP, mono)	20
60s	CBS SBPG 62066	KIND OF BLUE (LP, stereo)	30
60	Esquire 32-088	BLUE HAZE	20
60	Esquire 32-098	WALKIN'	20
60	Esquire 32-100	MILES DAVIS AND THE MODERN JAZZ GIANTS VOL. 2	20
60	Esquire 32-108	WORKIN' WITH THE MILES DAVIS QUINTET	20
61	Font. TFL 5100/STFL 531	SKETCHES OF SPAIN	20
61	Esquire 32-118	EARLY MILES	20
61	Esquire 32-138	STEAMIN' WITH THE MILES DAVIS QUINTET	25
61	Fontana TFL 5163	FRIDAY NIGHT AT THE BLACKHAWK, SAN FRANCISCO (VOL. 1) (with Cannonball Adderley & John Coltrane; also stereo STFL 580)	15
61	Fontana TFL 5164	SATURDAY NIGHT AT THE BLACKHAWK, SAN FRANCISCO (VOL. 2) (with Cannonball Adderley & John Coltrane; also stereo STFL 581)	15
62	Fontana TFL 5172	SOMEDAY MY PRINCE WILL COME (also stereo STFL 587)	15
62	Transatlantic PR 7254	THE ORIGINAL QUINTET (LP)	18
63	CBS BPG 62389	MILES AND MONK AT NEWPORT (LP, mono, with Thelonious Monk)	18
63	CBS SBPG 62389	MILES AND MONK AT NEWPORT (LP, stereo, Thelonious Monk)	20
64	Vocalion LAEF 584	BLUE MOODS	20
65	Stateside SL 10111	MILES DAVIS AND JOHN COLTRANE	15
66	Stateside SL 10168	MILES DAVIS PLAYS FOR LOVERS	15
66	Fontana FJL 135	BACK TO BACK	18
69	CBS 63630	IN A SILENT WAY	15
70	CBS 66236	BITCHES BREW (2-LP)	20
70	CBS 70089	A TRIBUTE TO JACK JOHNSON	15
71	CBS 66257	MILES DAVIS AT FILLMORE (2-LP)	20
72	CBS 64575	LIVE-EVIL (2-LP, gatefold)	25
72	CBS 65246	ON THE CORNER	15
72	Prestige PR 24001	MILES DAVIS (2-LP)	15
72	Prestige PR 24012	TALLEST TREES (2-LP)	15
73	CBS CQ 30997/Q 66236	BITCHES BREW (2-LP, quadrophonic)	30
73	CBS GQ 30954/Q 67219	LIVE-EVIL (2-LP, quadrophonic)	30
74	Columbia 88024	BIG FUN (LP, gatefold)	20

MILES DAVIS/ART BLAKEY

(see also Art Blakey, Thelonius Monk, Dizzy Gillespie, Milt Jackson, Cannonball Adderley, Charlie Parker)

66	Fontana FJL 135	L'ASCENSEUR POUR L'ECHAFAUD/LA FEMME DISPARAISSANTE (LP, soundtrack, 1 side each)	40

MILES DAVIS & JOHN COLTRANE

(see under Miles Davis, John Coltrane)

PAT DAVIS

75	Black Wax WAX 8	I'm Just A Girl/SKIN, FLESH & BONES: Girl Version	5

PAUL DAVIS

74	London HLM 19473	Ride'Em Cowboy/I'm The Only Sinner (In Salt Lake City)	5

RONNIE DAVIS

75	Angen ANG 104	The Good News/AGGROVATORS: Version	8
75	Angen ANG 110	Maga Lion/AGGROVATORS: Version	8
75	Attack ATT 8088	I Lost My Lover/MATADOR ALL STARS: Bula Dub	8
75	Attack ATT 8116	Tradition/Tradition (Version)	8
77	Third World TWDIS 005	Anywhere Don't Watch Your Woman (with Dillinger)/ BARRY BROWN : Mr Money Man (12")	25
77	Hawkeye HE 011	Used To Be My Girl/HAWKEYE IN SESSION - My Dub	10
76	Dip DLP 5028	BEAUTIFUL PEOPLE FROM JAMAICA (LP)	40

SAMMY DAVIS (Jnr.)

(see also Dean Martin)

54	Brunswick 05326	Because Of You (Parts 1 & 2)	8
55	Brunswick 05383	The Birth Of The Blues/Love (Your Magic Spell Is Everywhere)	8
55	Brunswick 05389	Six Bridges To Cross/Glad To Be Unhappy	8
55	Brunswick 05409	And This Is My Beloved/The Red Grapes	8
55	Brunswick 05428	Love Me Or Leave Me/Something's Gotta Give	10
55	Brunswick 05450	That Old Black Magic/Give A Fool A Chance	10
55	Brunswick 05469	Hey There/My Funny Valentine	10
55	Brunswick 05478	Backtrack/It's Bigger Than You And Me	6
56	Brunswick 05518	In A Persian Market/The Man With The Golden Arm	10
56	Capitol CL 14562	Azure/Dedicated To You	6
56	Brunswick 05583	Adelaide/I'll Know	5
56	Brunswick 05594	Earthbound/Five	5
56	Brunswick 05611	Frankie And Johnny/Circus	5
56	Brunswick 05617	You're Sensational/Don't Let Her Go	5
56	Brunswick 05629	All Of You/Just One Of Those Things	8
57	Brunswick 05637	The Golden Key/All About Love	5
57	Brunswick 05647	Dangerous/The World Is Mine Tonight	5
57	Brunswick 05668	Too Close For Comfort/Jacques D'Iraque	8
57	Brunswick 05694	Goodbye, So Long, I'm Gone/French Fried Potatoes And Ketchup	8
57	Brunswick 05717	Mad Ball/The Nearness Of You	5
57	Brunswick 05724	Long Before I Knew You/Never Like This	5
58	Brunswick 05732	I'm Comin' Home/Hallelujah, I Love Her	5
60	Brunswick 05830	Happy To Make Your Acquaintance/Baby, It's Cold Outside (with Carmen McRae)	8
62	Reprise R 20048	What Kind Of Fool Am I/Gonna Build A Mountain	6
63	Reprise R 20227	The Shelter Of Your Arms/Falling In Love With You	25
64	Reprise R 20289	Not For Me/Bang Bang	18
69	MCA MK 5016	Rhythm Of Life/Pompeii Club/Rich Man's Frug	30

			MINT VALUE £
76	20th Century BTC 2292	Baretta's Theme/I Heard A Song	10
50	Brunswick OE 9445	BOY MEETS GIRL (EP, with Carmen McRae)	10
56	Capitol EAP1 555	SAMMY DAVIS JNR. (EP)	10
63	Reprise 30028	SAMMY (EP)	20
70	Tamla Motown STML 11160	SOMETHING FOR EVERYONE (LP)	40

SILKIE DAVIS

70	Torpedo TOR 2	Conversations/TWIZZLE & HOT ROD ALL-STARS: Peace & Tranquility	5
70	Torpedo TOR 12	When I Was A Little Girl/I'm So Lonely	5

SKEETER DAVIS

60	RCA Victor RCA 1201	No Never/(I Can't Help You) I'm Falling Too	7
61	RCA Victor RCA 1222	My Last Date With You/Someone I'd Like To Forget	7
63	RCA Victor RCA 1328	The End Of The World/Somebody Loves You	8
63	RCA Victor RCA 1345	I'm Saving My Love/Somebody Else On Your Mind	6
63	RCA Victor RCA 1363	I Can't Stay Mad At You/It Was Only My Heart	8
64	RCA Victor RCA 1384	He Says The Same Things To Me/How Much Can A Lonely Heart Stand	5
64	RCA Victor RCA 1398	Now You're Gone/Gonna Get Along Without You Now	6
65	RCA Victor RCA 1474	Sun Glasses/He Loved Me Too Little	10
64	RCA Victor RCX 7153	SILVER THREADS AND GOLDEN NEEDLES (EP)	20
63	RCA Victor SF 7563	THE END OF THE WORLD (LP, mono)	15
63	RCA Victor SF 7563	THE END OF THE WORLD (LP, stereo)	20
63	RCA Victor RD 7604	CLOUDY, WITH OCCASIONAL TEARS (LP, mono)	15
63	RCA Victor SF 7604	CLOUDY, WITH OCCASIONAL TEARS (LP, stereo)	20
64	RCA Victor RD 7676	LET ME GET CLOSE TO YOU (LP)	15
69	RCA Victor SF 8068	MARY FRANCES (LP)	15

SKEETER DAVIS & BOBBY BARE

(see also Bobby Bare)

65	RCA RD 7711	TUNES FOR TWO (LP)	20

SMILEY DAVIS

53	London L 1189	Big Mamou/Play Girl (78, actually by Smiley Lewis)	130

SPENCER DAVIS (GROUP)

(see also Stevie Winwood, Traffic, Anglos, Blind Faith, Ray Fenwick, Pete York, Hardin & York, Murgatroyd Band, Mirage, Portobello Explosion, Shotgun Express)

64	Fontana TF 471	Dimples/Sittin' And Thinkin'	30
64	Fontana TF 499	I Can't Stand It/Midnight Train	25
65	Fontana TF 530	Every Little Bit Hurts/It Hurts Me So	15
65	Fontana TF 571	Strong Love/This Hammer	20
65	Fontana TF 632	Keep On Running/High Time Baby	7
66	Fontana TF 679	Somebody Help Me/Stevie's Blues	7
66	Fontana TF 739	When I Come Home/Trampoline	15
66	Fontana TF 762	Gimme Some Loving/Blues In F	7
67	Fontana TF 785	I'm A Man/I Can't Get Enough Of It	12
67	Fontana TF 854	Time Seller/Don't Want You No More	15
67	United Artists UP 1203	Mr. Second Class/Sanity Inspector	8
68	United Artists UP 2213	After Tea/Moonshine	8
68	United Artists UP 2226	Short Change/Picture Of Heaven	8
73	Vertigo 6059 076	Catch You On the Rebop/The Edge	7
73	Vertigo 6059 087	Livin' In A Back Street/Sure Need A Helping Hand	6
65	Fontana TE 17444	YOU PUT THE HURT ON ME (EP)	25
65	Fontana TE 17450	EVERY LITTLE BIT HURTS (EP)	30
66	Fontana TE 17463	SITTIN' AND THINKIN' (EP)	35
65	Fontana TL 5242	THEIR FIRST LP (LP, laminated front, black/silver label)	70
66	Fontana TL 5295	THE SECOND ALBUM (LP, laminated front cover, flipbacks, island label on rear)	60
66	Fontana TL 5359	AUTUMN '66 (LP, laminated front sleeve, flipbacks. black/silver label)	60
67	United Artists ULP 1186	HERE WE GO ROUND THE MULBERRY BUSH (LP, soundtrack, with Traffic, mono)	40
67	United Artists SULP 1186	HERE WE GO ROUND THE MULBERRY BUSH (LP, soundtrack, with Traffic, stereo)	35
68	United Artists ULP 1192	WITH THEIR NEW FACE ON (LP, mono, blue/silver label)	50
68	United Artists SULP 1192	WITH THEIR NEW FACE ON (LP, stereo)	25
68	Wing WL 1165	EVERY LITTLE BIT HURTS (LP, reissue of "Their First LP")	15
68	Island ILP 970 9070	THE BEST OF THE SPENCER DAVIS GROUP FEATURING STEVIE WINWOOD (LP, plain pink label, flipback sleeve; sleeve lists "Please Do Something" but plays "Together Till The End Of Time", mono)	30
68	Island ILPS 9070	THE BEST OF THE SPENCER DAVIS GROUP FEATURING STEVIE WINWOOD (LP, plain pink label, flipback sleeve; sleeve lists "Please Do Something" but plays "Together Till The End Of Time", stereo)	15
69	CBS 63842	LETTERS FROM EDITH (LP, unissued, 50 white label test pressings only)	400
71	United Artists UAS 29177	IT'S BEEN SO LONG (LP, solo with Peter Jameson, envelope cover)	15
72	United Artists UAS 29361	MOUSETRAP (LP, solo)	15
73	Vertigo 6360 088	GLUGGO (LP, die cut, gatefold sleeve, 'spaceship' label)	20
74	Vertigo 6360 105	LIVIN' IN A BACK STREET (LP)	12

STEVE DAVIS

68	Fontana TF 922	Takes Time To Know Her/She Said Yeah	50

TYRONE DAVIS

68	Stateside SS 2092	What If A Man/Bet You Win	45
69	Atlantic 584 253	Can I Change My Mind/A Woman Needs To Be Loved	12
69	Atlantic 584 265	Is It Something You've Got?/Undying Love	12
69	Atlantic 584 288	All The Waiting Is Not In Vain/Need Your Lovin' Everyday	12
70	Atlantic 2091 003	Turn Back The Hands Of Time/I Keep Coming Back	15
71	Atlantic 2091 078	Could I Forget You/Just My Way Of Loving You	10
71	Atlantic 2091 131	One Way Ticket/We Got A Love	10
72	Atlantic K 10207	Can I Change My Mind/Turn Back The Hands Of Time/One Way Ticket	8
73	Brunswick BR 4	Without You In My Life/How Could I Forget You	10

MINT VALUE £

73	Brunswick BR 6	There It Is/You Wouldn't Believe	10
74	Brunswick BR 10	I Wish It Was Me/You Don't Have To Beg To Stay	10
76	Brunswick BR 31	Turning Point/Don't Let It Be Too Late	10
77	Brunswick BR 40	Ever Lovin' Girl/Forever	10
70	Atlantic 588 209	CAN I CHANGE MY MIND (LP)	30
71	Atlantic 2465 021	TURN BACK THE HANDS OF TIME (LP)	30
73	Brunswick BRLS 3002	I HAD IT ALL THE TIME (LP)	35
73	Brunswick BRLS 3005	GREATEST HITS (LP)	18

WALTER DAVIS

64	RCA RCX 7169	R.C.A. VICTOR RACE SERIES VOL. 3 (EP)	15
70	RCA Intl. INTS 1085	THINK YOU NEED A SHOT (LP)	15

WARREN DAVIS MONDAY BAND

(see also Boardwalkers)

67	Columbia DB 8190	Wait For Me/I Don't Wanna Hurt You	20
67	Columbia DB 8270	Love Is A Hurtin' Thing/Without Fear	20

BRIAN DAVISON

(see also Habits, Nice, Every Which Way, Refuge)

70	Charisma CAS 1021	BRIAN DAVISON'S EVERY WHICH WAY (LP, pink 'scroll' label)	40

WILD BILL DAVISON

55	Melodisc MLP 501	WILD BILL DAVISON (LP)	15

TIM DAWE

69	Straight ST(S) 1058	PENROD (LP)	25

CARL DAWKINS

(see also Rass Dawkins, Untouchables, Winston Wright, Ansell Collins, Roland Alphonso, West Indians)

67	Rio R 136	All Of A Sudden/Running Shoes	18
67	Rio R 137	Baby I Love You/Hard Time	18
68	Blue Cat BS 114	I Love The Way You Are/DERMOTT LYNCH: I Can't Stand It	20
68	Duke DU 3	I'll Make It Up/J.J. ALL STARS: One Dollar Of Music	20
69	Nu Beat NB 030	Rodney's History/DYNAMITES: Tribute To Drumbage	12
70	Duke DU 93	Get Together/FAMILY MAN: Instalment Plan	8
70	Duke DU 95	This Land/J.J. ALL STARS: Land Version	12
70	Trojan TR 7765	Satisfaction/Things A Get Bad To Worse	7
71	Big Shot BI 570	Perseverence/J.J. ALL STARS: Perseverence (Version)	12
71	Explosion EX 2051	I Feel Good/J.J. ALL STARS: I Feel Good Version Two	10
71	Explosion EX 2059	Make It Great/STONE: What A Day	6
71	New Beat NB 086	Walk A Little Prouder/YOUTH PROFESSIONALS: Walk (Version)	6
72	Duke DU 133	My Whole World/Men A Broken Heart	6

HORRELL DAWKINS

66	Ska Beat JB 240	Cling To Me/Butterfly	25

JIMMY DAWKINS

73	Mojo 2027 011	The Things I Used To Do/Put It On The Hawg	8
71	Delmark DS 623	FAST FINGERS (LP)	22
78	Sonet SNTF 758	TRANSATLANTIC 770 (LP)	15

RASS DAWKINS (& WAILERS)

(see also Bob Marley/Wailers, Carl Dawkins)

71	Upsetter US 368	Picture On The Wall/UPSETTERS: Picture Version	25

DAWN AND CHRISTINE

78	Burning Rockers BRD 002	We Love Collie Weed (with Clint Eastwood)/ LAWES ROCKERS: Collie Weed Version (12")	30

JULIE DAWN

(see also Tony Brent & Julie Dawn, Cyril Stapleton)

53	Columbia SCM 5035	Wild Horses/A Whistling Kettle And A Dancing Cat	10

DAWN TRADER

80	AFE 1980	NO ONE GONNA BETTER ME (EP, private pressing)	40

DAWNBREAKERS

65	Decca F 12110	Let's Live/Lovin' For You	15

DAWN CHORUS

(see also Carter-Lewis)

69	MCA MK 5004	A Night To Be Remembered/Crying All Night	15

DAWN CHORUS

85	Dawn DAWN 1	Teenage Kicks/Dream Lover (p/s)	18

DAWN & DEEJAYS

65	RCA RCA 1470	These Are The Things About You/I Will Think Of You	15

DAWNWATCHER

80	Dawnwatcher DWS 001	Spellbound/Hall Of Mirrors	100
82	Dawnwatcher DWS 002	Backlash (p/s)	20

DAWNWIND

76	Amron ARN 5003	LOOKING BACK ON THE FUTURE (LP, private pressing)	80

DONNA DAWSON

73	Trojan TR 7892	You Can't Buy Me Love/First Cut Is The Deepest	6

LES DAWSON

69	Chapter One CH 106	Send Her Roses/I'm Just Another Sweetheart	6

LES DAWSON SYNDICATE

(see under Johnny Stevens and Les Dawson Syndicate)

LESLEY DAWSON

66	Mercury MF 924	Pastel Shades Of Love/The Time Has Come	5

MINT VALUE £

67	Mercury MF 946	Just Say Goodbye/Just A Passing Phase	8
67	Mercury MF 965	Run For Shelter/I'll Climb On A Rainbow	35

DANIELLE DAX

(see also Lemon Kittens)

83	Initial IRC 009	POP-EYES (LP, with 'Meat Harvest' cover & lyric sheet)	20

DAY

94	Detour DR 019	Another Country/Gospel (p/s, 100 on green vinyl)	7

BING DAY

59	Mercury AMT 1047	I Can't Help It/Mama's Place	100

BOBBY DAY (& SATELLITES)

57	HMV POP 425	Little Bitty Pretty One/When The Swallows Come Back To Capistrano (as Bobby Day & Satellites)	175
57	HMV POP 425	Little Bitty Pretty One/When The Swallows Come Back To Capistrano (as Bobby Day & Satellites) (78)	25
58	London HL 8726	Rockin' Robin/Over And Over	20
58	London HL 8726	Rockin' Robin/Over And Over (78)	20
59	London HL 8800	The Bluebird, The Buzzard And The Oriole/Alone Too Long	50
59	London HL 8800	The Bluebird, The Buzzard And The Oriole/Alone Too Long (78)	40
59	London HL 8964	Love Is A One Time Affair/Ain't Gonna Cry No More	30
59	London HL 8964	Love Is A One Time Affair/Ain't Gonna Cry No More (78)	40
60	London HLY 9044	My Blue Heaven/I Don't Want To	25
61	Top Rank JAR 538	Over And Over/Gee Whiz	20
65	Sue WI 388	Rockin' Robin/Over And Over (reissue)	30

DORIS DAY

(see also Four Lads, Frank Sinatra, Frankie Laine, Howard Keel)

SINGLES

53	Columbia SCM 5038	April In Paris/Your Mother And Mine (with Four Lads)	15
53	Columbia SCM 5039	That's What Makes Paris Paree/I Know A Place	15
53	Columbia SCM 5044	A Bushel And A Peck/If I Were A Bell	15
53	Columbia SCM 5045	The Second Star To The Right (with Four Lads) I'm Gonna Ring The Bell Tonight	12
53	Columbia SCM 5059	The Cherries/Papa, Won't You Dance With Me?	12
53	Columbia SCM 5062	Mister Tap-Toe/Why Should We Both Be Lonely?	12
53	Columbia SCM 5067	We Kiss In A Shadow/Something Wonderful	12
53	Columbia SCM 5075	That's The Way He Does It/Cuddle Up A Little Closer	12
54	Columbia SCM 5087	A Load Of Hay/It Had To Be You	12
55	Columbia SCM 5171	Just One Of Those Things/Sometimes I'm Happy	12
57	Philips JK 1020	Twelve O'Clock Tonight/Today Will Be Yesterday Tomorrow! (jukebox issue)	20
57	Philips JK 1031	The Party's Over/Rickety-Rackety Rendezvous (jukebox issue)	20
58	Philips PB 799	Teacher's Pet/A Very Precious Love	6
59	Philips PB 949	The Tunnel Of Love/Run Away, Skidaddle, Skidoo	7
59	Philips PB 958	Possess Me/Roly Poly	6
63	CBS AAG 183	Move Over Darling/Twinkle Lullaby	6
64	CBS AAG 219	Oowee Baby/The Rainbow's End	10

LPs

54	Columbia 33S 1038	LULLABY OF BROADWAY (10", 2 different sleeve designs)	30
54	Philips BBR 8026	THE VOICE OF YOUR CHOICE (10")	20
55	Philips BBR 8040	YOUNG AT HEART (10", with Frank Sinatra)	20
55	Philips BBL 7047	LOVE ME OR LEAVE ME	20
56	Philips BBR 8094	DORIS DAY FAVOURITES (10")	15
56	Philips BBR 8104	CALAMITY JANE (10", with Howard Keel)	15
57	Philips BBL 7120	DAY DREAMS	20
57	Philips BBL 7137	DORIS AND FRANK (6 tracks each by Doris Day & Frank Sinatra)	20
57	Philips BBL 7142	DAY BY DAY	20
58	Philips BBL 7175	DAY IN HOLLYWOOD	20
58	Philips BBL 7197	THE PYJAMA GAME (with other artists, 5 tracks by Doris Day)	12
58	Philips BBL 7211	DAY BY NIGHT	25
58	Philips BBL 7247	HOORAY FOR HOLLYWOOD VOL. 1	20
58	Philips BBL 7248	HOORAY FOR HOLLYWOOD VOL. 2	15
59	Philips BBL 7296	CUTTIN' CAPERS (also stereo SBBL 540)	12
59	Philips BBL 7297	SHOWCASE OF HITS	12
59	Philips SBBL 519	HOORAY FOR HOLLYWOOD (stereo reissue)	15
59	Philips SBBL 548	DAY BY NIGHT (stereo reissue)	15
60	Philips BBL 7377	WHAT EVERY GIRL SHOULD KNOW (also stereo SBBL 563)	12
60	Philips SBBL 537	IN THE STILL OF THE NIGHT	12
64	CBS (S)BPG 62226	LOVE HIM (mono/stereo)	15

DORIS DAY & JOHNNIE RAY

(see also Johnnie Ray)

53	Columbia SCM 5033	Ma Says, Pa Says/A Full Time Job	25

JACKIE DAY

67	Sue WI 4040	Before It's Too Late/Without A Love	250

JILL DAY

55	Parlophone MSP 6169	Sincerely/Chee-Chee-Oo Chee (Sang The Little Bird)	15
55	Parlophone MSP 6177	Promises/Whistlin' Willie	15
56	HMV 7M 362	I Hear You Knocking/Far Away From Everybody	15
56	HMV 7M 391	A Tear Fell/Holiday Affair	15
56	HMV POP 254	Happiness Street (Corner Sunshine Square)/Somewhere In The Great Beyond	10
57	HMV POP 288	I Dreamed/Give Her My Love When You See Her	10
57	HMV POP 320	Mangos/Cinco Robles (Five Oaks)	10
70	B&C CB117	I'll Think About You/The Way Of Love	7

JOHNNY DAY

69	Stax STAX 111	Stay Baby Stay/I Love Love	20

MINT VALUE £

KENNY DAY
60	Top Rank JAR 339	Teenage Sonata/My Love Doesn't Love Me At All (p/s)	20
60	Top Rank JAR 339	Teenage Sonata/My Love Doesn't Love Me At All	5
61	Top Rank JAR 400	Why Don't We Do This More Often/The Sheik Of Morocco (p/s)	10
61	Top Rank JAR 400	Why Don't We Do This More Often/The Sheik Of Morocco	5

MURIEL DAY
66	Pye 7N 17197	A Petal From A Faded Rose/I Wear His Heart	10
69	CBS 4115	The Wages Of Love/Thinking Of You	15
69	Page One POF 151	Optimistic Fool/Nine Times Out Of Ten	60
69	Page One POF 151	Optimistic Fool/Nine Times Out Of Ten (DJ copy)	100

TANYA DAY & NU-NOTES
64	Polydor NH 52331	His Lips Get In The Way/I Get So Lonely	8

TERRY DAY
(see also Rip-Chords, Rogues)

62	CBS AAG 104	That's All I Want/I Waited Too Long	20

DAY BROTHERS
60	Oriole CB 1575	Angel/Just One More Kiss	20

JOEL DAYDE
71	Barclay BAR 7	Mammy Blue/You've Got Freedom	25

JENNIFER DAYE
80	Arawak ARK DD 018	Together/Version (12")	10

DAYLIGHT
(see also Daddy Longlegs)

71	RCA RCA 2106	Lady Of St. Clare/Wednesday People	10
71	RCA SF 8194	DAYLIGHT (LP, gatefold sleeve, orange label)	50

DAYLIGHTERS
64	Sue WI 343	Oh Mom! (Teach Me How To Uncle Willie)/Hard-Headed Girl	45

DAY N NIGHT
70	DJM DJS 220	I Just Need Somebody/Such A Lot To Talk About	12

DAY OF THE PHOENIX
70	Greenwich GSLP 1002	WIDE OPEN N-WAY (LP)	80
72	Chapter One CHS-R 812	THE NEIGHBOUR'S SON (LP, red/silver label)	50

DAYS OF GRACE
82	DJM DJS 10988	My Life Is A Video/21st Century (p/s)	6

DAYTRIPPERS
71	Trojan TR 7839	The Birds And The Bees/My Family	5

DAZZLE
75	DJM DJS 384	Jim'll Fix It/Leave It Up To Jim	8

DBX
93	Peacefrog PF 015	Alien EP (12", plain sleeve)	12
94	Peacefrog PF 022	Losing Control/Beat Phreak/Live Wire/Spock's Brain (12", plain sleeve)	22
95	Peacefrog PR 025	Losing Control Remixes (12", plain sleeve)	20

D.C. 10's
80	Certain Euphoria ACE 451	Bermuda/I Can See Through Walls	10

DDR
90s	Smitten SMTLTD 05	The Gift (12", 1-sided yellow vinyl, 500 only)	60

BOBBY DEACON
60	Pye 7N 15270	A Fool Was I/Where's My Love?	15
60	Pye 7N 15299	I Love You So/Your Kisses Are Fine	12

GEORGE DEACON & MARION ROSS
73	Xtra XTRA 1130	SWEET WILLIAM'S GHOST (LP, with lyric insert)	65

DEADBEATS
80	Red Rhino RED 3	Choose You/Julie's New Boyfriend (p/s)	8

DEAD BOYS
(see also Stiv Bators, Lords Of The New Church, Wanderers)

77	Sire SRE 1004	Sonic Reducer/Down In Flames (no p/s)	25
77	Sire 6078 609	Sonic Reducer/Little Girl/Down In Flames (12", p/s)	15
78	Sire SRE 1029	Tell Me/Not Anymore/Ain't Nothin' To Do (p/s)	25
77	Sire 9103 329	YOUNG, LOUD & SNOTTY (LP)	25
78	Sire SRK 6054	WE HAVE COME FOR YOUR CHILDREN (LP)	20
87	Line LILP 400200	NIGHT OF THE LIVING DEAD BOYS (LP)	15
99	Rude LP00010	3RD GENERATION NATION (LP, clear vinyl, mail order only)	15

DEAD CAN DANCE
84	4AD BAD 408	GARDEN OF THE ARCANE DELIGHTS EP (12", p/s)	8
96	4AD DCD 2	Nierika/Dedicate Outo/The Snake And The Moon (12", promo red vinyl, PVC sleeve)	12
84	4AD CAD 404	DEAD CAN DANCE (LP)	15
85	4AD CAD 512	SPLEEN AND IDEAL (LP)	15
87	4AD CAD 705	WITHIN THE REALM OF A DYING SUN (LP)	15
88	4AD CAD 808	THE SERPENT'S EGG (LP)	15
90	4AD CAD 0007	AION (LP)	20
93	4AD DAD 3013	INTO THE LABYRINTH (2-LP)	30
94	4AD DAD 4015	TOWARDS THE WITHIN (2-LP)	25
96	4AD DAD 608	SPIRITCHASER (2-LP)	30

MINT VALUE £

DEAD FINGERS TALK

79	Pye 46156	This Crazy World/The Boyfriend (p/s)	20

DEAD KENNEDYS

(see also East Bay Ray, Lard)

80	Fast Products FAST 12	California Uber Alles/Man With The Dogs (p/s, moulded or paper labels)	6
81	Statik STAT EP 2	IN GOD WE TRUST (12" EP, with insert)	10
81	Cherry Red CHERRY 13	Holiday In Cambodia/Police Truck ('digger' p/s)	5
81	Cherry Red CHERRY 13	Holiday In Cambodia/Police Truck ('burning man' p/s, with lyric sheet)	6
81	Cherry Red CHERRY T13	Holiday In Cambodia/Police Truck (12")	10
81	Cherry CHERRY 16	Kill The Poor/In-Sight (p/s)	8
81	Cherry CHERRY 24	Too Drunk To Fuck/The Prey (p/s, with lyric sheet)	5
82	Statik STAT 24	Nazi Punks Fuck Off/Moral Majority (p/s)	5
81	Cherry Red B RED 10	FRESH FRUIT FOR ROTTING VEGETABLES (LP, with insert & 'Heads' picture on rear)	25
80	Cherry Red B RED 10	FRESH FRUIT FOR ROTTING VEGETABLES (LP, with insert & without 'Heads' picture on rear)	20
87	Alternative Tent. VIRUS 57	GIVE ME CONVENIENCE... (LP, with "Buzzbomb From Pasadena" flexidisc)	15
82	Statik/Alternative Tentacles VIRUS 27	PLASTIC SURGERY DISASTERS (LP)	12

DEADLY TOYS

79	Bonhard/Hunt DT 1	Nice Weather/Roll On Doomsday/I'm Logical/Deadly Mess Around (EP, in hand-made gatefold sleeve)	50
79	Bonhard/Hunt DT 1	Nice Weather/Roll On Doomsday/I'm Logical/Deadly Mess Around (EP)	20

DEAD OR ALIVE

(see also Nightmares In Wax, Sisters Of Mercy, Pauline Murray & Invisible Girls, International Chrysis, Mission)

80	Inevitable INEV 005	I'm Falling/Flowers (foldout p/s)	12
81	Inevitable INEV 008	Number Eleven/Name Game (live) (p/s)	8
82	Black Eyes BE 1	It's Been Hours Now/Whirlpool/Nowhere To Nowhere/ It's Been Hours Now (Alternative Mix) (12", p/s)	20
82	Black Eyes BE 2	The Stranger/Some Of That (p/s)	8
83	Epic A 3399	Misty Circles/Misty Circles (Instrumental) (p/s)	8
83	Epic TA 3399	Misty Circles (Dance Mix)/Misty Circles (Dub Mix)/Selfish Side (12", p/s)	10
83	Epic A 3676	What I Want/The Stranger (Remix) (white 'floppy hat' p/s, withdrawn)	35
83	Epic TA 3676	What I Want (Dance Mix)/The Stranger (12", p/s, with poster)	18
83	Epic TA 3676	What I Want (Dance Mix)/The Stranger (12", p/s, without poster)	8
84	Epic A 4069	I'd Do Anything/Anything (Dub) (p/s)	5
84	Epic QA 4069	I'd Do Anything/Anything (Dub)/Give It To Me (10", p/s)	10
84	Epic TA 4069	I'd Do Anything/Misty Circles/What I Want/Give It To Me (12", p/s)	8
84	Epic WA 4271	That's The Way (I Like It)/Keep That Body Strong (That's The Way) (picture disc)	6
84	Epic A 4510	What I Want (Remix)/The Stranger (poster p/s)	15
84	Epic A 4510	What I Want (Remix)/The Stranger (2nd issue, 'dreadlock' p/s)	8
84	Epic TA 4510	What I Want (Dance Mix)/The Stranger (12", p/s)	10
84	Epic XPR 1257	MIGHTY MIX: Wish You Were Here/What I Want/Do It/Misty Circles/ Absolutely Nothing/Sit On It/You Make Me Wanna/That's The Way (I Like It) (12", white label, promo only)	20
84	Epic A4861ADJ	You Spin Me Round (Big Ben Mix) (1-sided, stickered p/s, promo only)	15
84	Epic TX 4861/TA 4510	You Spin Me Round (Like A Record) (Murder Mix)/Misty Circles (Extended Mix)/ What I Want (Dance Mix)/The Stranger (12", p/s, double pack, gatefold p/s)	15
85	Epic A 6086	Lover Come Back To Me/Far Too Hard (blue p/s, withdrawn)	100
85	Epic WA 6086	Lover Come Back To Me/Far Too Hard (fan-shaped picture disc with plinth)	10
85	Epic QTA 6086	Lover Come Back To Me (Extended Remix)/Far Too Hard (12", p/s)	10
85	Epic GA6360	In Too Deep/I'd Do Anything (gatefold p/s)	5
87	Epic BURNSD1	Something In My House (7" double pack, stickered shrinkwrapped sleeve)	8
87	Epic BURNSG1	Something In My House/DJ Hit That Button (gatefold 'pop up' p/s)	6
87	Epic XPR 1328	CLEAN AND DIRTY: Something In My House (Mortevicar Mix)/ Something In My House (Naughty XXX Mix) (12", white label, plain white sleeve)	50
88	Epic BURNSQ 4	Turn Around And Count 2 Ten (I Had A Disco Dream Mix)/Something In My House (Instru-Mental)/Then There Was You/Come Inside (12", p/s autographed)	30
88	Epic BURNSQ 4	Turn Around And Count 2 Ten (I Had A Disco Dream Mix)/Something In My House (Instru-Mental)/Then There Was You/Come Inside (12", p/s)	20
88	Epic BURNSC 4	Turn Around And Count 2 Ten/Something In My House (Instru-Mental)/ Turn Around And Count 2 Ten (I Love BPM Mix)/(Instru-Mental (CD, picture disc)	20
88	Epic BURNSP4	Turn Around And Count 2 Ten/Something In My House (instrumental) (fold-out poster p/s)	8
89	Epic BURNSC5	Come Home With Me Baby (7" version)/(12" Version)/(Deadhouse Dub) (CD)	8

DEAD SEA FRUIT

67	Camp 602 001	Kensington High Street/Put Another Record On	15
68	Camp 602 004	Love At The Hippiedrome/My Naughty Bluebell	15
67	Camp 603 001	DEAD SEA FRUIT (LP)	70

DEAD WEATHER

(see also The Kills/White Stripes/Raconteurs)

09	Third Man TMR 001	Hang You From The Heavens/Are Friends Electric? (luminous vinyl, 'Halloween' cover, 100-only)	200

DEADWOOD

71	Decca F13109	The Turning Of Them All/They Don't Help Me None	40
71	Decca F13179	Me And My Friends/Little Joe	12

DEAD WRETCHED

82	Tempest HELL 2	NO HOPE FOR ANYONE EP	20

BILL DEAL & RHONDELLS

69	MGM MGM 1466	May I/Day By Day My Love Grows Stronger	6
69	MGM MGM 1479	I've Been Hurt/I've Got My Needs	15
69	MGM MGM 1488	What Kind Of Fool Do You Think I Am/Are You Ready For This	10

MINT VALUE £

DEALER

83	Windrush WR 1030	Better Things To Do/Suspected Foul Play (p/s)	100
86	Ebony EBON 42	FIRST STRIKE (LP)	12

DEALERS

76	Private Stock PVT 73	Midnight Dog/Higher Than God's Hat	6

ALAN DEAN

55	MGM SP 1116	The Song From "Desiree"/Tonight, My Love	5
55	MGM SP 1139	Remember Me, Wherever You Go/Love Is All That Matters	5
56	MGM SP 1173	Without You/Take A Bow	5
57	Columbia DB 3932	Rock 'n' Roll Tarantella/Life Is But A Dream	20

ALAN DEAN & HIS PROBLEMS

64	Decca F 11947	The Time It Takes/Dizzy Heights	40
65	Pye 7N 15749	Thunder And Rain/As Time Goes By	60

LITTLE BILLY DEAN

67	Strike JH 325	That's Always Like You/Tic Toc	25

BOBBY DEAN

65	Parlophone R 5254	More And More/Saint James' Infirmary	8

DEREK DEAN & FRESHMEN

(see also Derek & Freshmen)

66	Pye 7N 17037	So This Is Love/King Cole Yenka	8

ELTON DEAN

(see also Bluesology, Soft Machine, Centipede, Ninesense, Julie Tippetts, Hugh Hopper, Mike Hugg, Reg King, Keith Tippett)

71	CBS 64539	ELTON DEAN (LP)	45
77	Ogun OG 610	THE CHEQUE IS IN THE MAIL (LP, with Joe Gallivan & Kenny Wheeler)	15
78	Ogun OG 530	THE BOLOGNA TAPE (LP)	20

EMIL DEAN

(see also Nirvana [UK])

68	Island WIP 6033	This Is Our Anniversary/Lonely Boy	12

HAZELL DEAN

75	Decca F 13613	Our Day Will Come/Instrumental	6
76	Decca F 13668	Got You Where I Want You/You Were There	6
77	Decca F 13683	Look What I've Found At The End Of A Rainbow/Where Are We Going	6
77	Decca F 13736	No One's Ever Gonna Love You (The Way That I Love You)/ Just One More Time	6
77	Decca F 13751	Who Was That Lady (I Saw You With)/One Bad Mistake	6
81	Carlin Music Corp CMC 1004	THE SOUND OF BACHARACH & DAVID (LP, promo only)	25

JIMMY DEAN

59	Philips PB 940	Weekend Blues/Sing Along	6
60	Philips PB 984	There's Still Time, Brother/Thanks For The Dream	6
61	Philips PB 1187	Big Bad John/I Won't Go Hunting With You Jake	5
61	Philips PB 1210	To A Sleeping Beauty/The Cajun Queen	6
62	Philips PB 1223	Smoke Smoke (Smoke) That Cigarette/Dear Ivan	6
62	CBS AAG 107	Steel Men/Little Bitty Big John	7
62	CBS AAG 122	Little Black Book/Please Pass The Biscuits	8
61	Philips BBE 12501	JIMMY DEAN (EP)	15
66	CBS EP 6075	THE BEST OF JIMMY DEAN (EP)	20
61	Philips BBL 7537	BIG BAND JOHN AND OTHER FABULOUS SONGS AND TALES (LP)	20
63	CBS BPG 62152	EVERYBODY'S FAVOURITE (LP)	15
63	CBS BPG 62096	PORTRAIT OF JIMMY DEAN (LP)	15

NORA DEAN

(see also Hugh Roy)

69	Upsetter US 322	The Same Thing You Gave To Daddy/UPSETTER PILGRIMS: A Testimony	80
70	Trojan TR 7735	Barbwire/BRONS: Calypso Mama	20
71	Randy's RAN 508	Want Man/RANDY'S ALL STARS: Man	20
71	High Note HS 050	I Must Get A Man/The Valet	10
71	Bullet BU 472	Peace Begins Within/SLICKERS: Go Back Home	10
71	Gas GAS 165	Greedy Boy/KEITH: Please Stay (B-side actually by Slim Smith)	10
72	Big Shot BI 611	Night Food Reggae/PROPHETS: Jaco	8
73	Bread BR 1117	Mama/Man A Walk And Talk	6
76	Attack ATT 8126	Scorpion/Version	6
79	Nationwide NWLP 007	PLAY ME A LOVE SONG (LP)	12

PAUL DEAN (& SOUL SAVAGES)

(see also Oscar, Thoughts)

65	Decca F 12136	You Don't Own Me/Hole In The Head (as Paul Dean & Thoughts)	18
66	Reaction 591 002	She Can Build A Mountain/A Day Gone By (as Paul Dean & Soul Savages)	15

PAULA DEAN & NYAH SHUFFLE

70	Joe's JRS 2	Since I Met You Baby/Jug Head	15

ROGER DEAN'S LYSIS

77	Mosaic GCM 762	LYSIS LIVE (LP)	15
77	Mosaic GCM 774	CYCLE (LP)	15

TERRI DEAN

59	Top Rank JAR 141	I'm Confessin' (That I Love You)/I Blew Out The Flame	10
59	Top Rank JAR 179	Adonis/You Treat Me Like A Boy	10

TRACEY DEAN

74	Decca FR 13497	Moonshiner/Boy On The Ball	70

DEAN & JEAN

(see also Brenda Lee Jones)

64	Stateside SS 249	Tra La La La Suzy/I Love The Summertime	20

MINT VALUE £

64 Stateside SS 283 Hey Jean Hey Dean/Please Don't Tell Me How 20
64 Stateside SS 313 Thread Your Needle/I Wanna Be Loved 20

DEAN & MARK

(see also Newbeats, Larry Henley)

64 Hickory 45-1227 With Tears In My Eyes/Kissin' Games 10
64 Hickory 45-1249 When I Stop Dreaming/There Oughta Be A Law 10
65 Hickory 45-1294 Just A Step Away/Fallen Star 10

JASON DEANE

(see also Jason Dene)

66 King KG 1049 Make Believe/Don't Ever Want To See You No More.......... 30
67 King KG 1060 Down In The Street/Ain't Got No Love 40

PETER DE ANGELIS

58 London HL 8743 The Happy Mandolin/Holiday In Naples 7

DEANO

65 Columbia DB 7728 Just A Child In This World/Little Miss With-It 12
66 Columbia DB 7898 Starlight, Starbright/I'm So Happy 22
66 Columbia DB 7965 Please Don't Talk To The Lifeguard/When You Wish Upon A Star 12
67 Columbia DB 8233 What's The Matter With The Matador?/Baby, Let Me Be Your Baby 10
65 Columbia SEG 8470 DEANO (EP).......... 40

BLOSSOM DEARIE

66 Fontana TF 719 I'm Hip/Wallflower Lonely, Cornflower Blue.......... 10
67 Fontana TF 788 Sweet Georgie Fame/One Note Samba 10
67 Fontana TF 886 Once I Loved/Sunny 10
67 Fontana TF 934 The Music Played/Discover Who I Am 10
68 Fontana TF 986 Hey John/59th Street Bridge Song 10
67 Fontana TL 5399 SWEET BLOSSOM DEARIE (LP).......... 50
67 Fontana TL 5352 BLOSSOM TIME AT RONNIE'S (LP) 60
67 Fontana STL 5454 SOON IT'S GONNA RAIN (LP) 45
70 Fontana 6309 015 THAT'S THE WAY I WANT IT TO BE (LP) 100

DEARLY BELOVED

66 CBS 202398 Peep Peep Pop Pop/It Is Better.......... 6

DEAR MR. TIME

70 Square SQ 3 Prayer For Her/Light Up A Light 50
71 Square SQA 101 GRANDFATHER (LP, black/white label) 200

DEATH

87 Under One Flag FLAG 12 SCREAM BLOODY GORE (LP, with inner sleeve).......... 12

DEATH ADDICT

83 Stench STN 1 Killing Time/Dead And Buried (p/s).......... 12

DEATH CULT

(see also Cult)

83 Situation 2 SIT 29 God's Zoo/God's Zoo (These Times) (p/s) 5
83 Situation 2 SIT 29 T God's Zoo/God's Zoo (These Times) (12", p/s) 8

DEATH IN JUNE

(see also Crisis, Current 93, Boyd Rice & Friends, Sol Invictus)

84 New European SA 29634 Heaven Street/We Drive East/In The Night Time (12", 2,000 with brown/gold embossed/textured sleeve) 60
84 New European SA 29634 Heaven Street/We Drive East/In The Night Time (12", later pressing of 2,000 with blue/white sleeve) 50
84 New European SA 30634 State Laughter/Holy Water (p/s) 40
84 New European BADVC 6 She Said Destroy/The Calling (p/s).......... 25
84 New European 12BADVC 6 The Calling/She Said Destroy/Doubt To Nothing (12", p/s with insert).......... 35
85 New European BADVC 69 Born Again/The Calling (Mk II)/Carousel (Bolt Mix) (12", p/s) 25
85 New European BADVC 73 ...And Murder Love/A.M.L. (Instrumental) (p/s) 25
85 New European 12BADVC73 Come Before Christ And Murder Love/Torture By Roses (12", p/s) 25
87 New European BADVC 10 To Drown A Rose/Zimmerit/Europa/The Gates Of Heaven (10", p/s).......... 20
88 Cenaz CENAZ 09 Born Again/The Calling (Mk II)/Carousel (Remix) (12" picture disc, 1st pressing with silver print & rim, 970 only) 25
88 Cenaz CENAZ 09 Born Again/The Calling (Mk II)/Carousel (Remix) (12" picture disc, 2nd pressing bronze print & rim) 20
94 Twilight Command NERO I SUNDOGS (Rose Clouds Of Holocaust/13 Years Of Carrion) (p/s with sticker).......... 7
92 New European BADVC 8 CATHEDRAL OF TEARS (12" EP, picture disc with sticker).......... 25
93 New European BADVC 63 PARADISE RISING (12" EP).......... 18
96 Twilight. Command NERO XIII Kapo!/Occidental Martyr (p/s) 18
85 New European BADVC 3 THE GUILTY HAVE NO PRIDE (LP).......... 25
80s Leprosy UBADVC 4 BURIAL (LP, 'quilted' sleeve, brown, pink, white & other coloured vinyl) 35
90s Leprosy UBADVC 4 BURIAL (LP, textured sleeve, various coloured vinyl) 35
92 Leprosy UBADVC 4 BURIAL (LP, standard sleeve, green vinyl) 35
85 New European BADVC 13 NADA (LP, blue sleeve).......... 40
85 New European BADVC 13 NADA (LP, brown sleeve) 25
85 New European BADVC 13 NADA (LP, picture disc) 15
86 New European BADVC 726 LESSON ONE: MISANTHROPY (LP, embossed sleeve with insert).......... 25
87 New European BADVC 11 BROWN BOOK (LP, textured sleeve with inner & insert; export copies with extra inserts & postcards) 35
87 New European BADVC 11 BROWN BOOK (LP, textured sleeve with inner & insert) 25
88 New European BADVC 9 THE WORLD THAT SUMMER (2-LP, gatefold textured sleeve) 30
88 New European BADVC 88 WALL OF SACRIFICE (LP, red sleeve) 70
88 New European BADVC 88 WALL OF SACRIFICE (LP, green/yellow sleeve) 40
89 New European BADVC 93 93 DEAD SUN WHEELS (mini-LP, with Current 93).......... 20
92 Leprosy LEPER 2 NIGHT AND FOG (LP, red vinyl, 1,000 only).......... 30

			MINT VALUE £
93	New European BADVC 36	BUT WHAT ENDS WHEN THE SYMBOLS SHATTER (LP, with inner & insert, 500 on purple vinyl)	40
93	New European BADVC 36	BUT WHAT ENDS WHEN THE SYMBOLS SHATTER (LP, with inner & insert, 3,000 on black vinyl)	20
93	New European BADVCCD 36	BUT WHAT ENDS WHEN THE SYMBOLS SHATTER (CD, gold disc digipak, 5,000 only)	20
93	New European BADVCCD 96	SOMETHING IS COMING (2-CD, digipak, 5,000 only)	25
94	New European BADVC 38	ROSE CLOUDS OF HOLOCAUST (LP, with insert & inner)	12
94	New European BADVCCD 38	ROSE CLOUDS OF HOLOCAUST (CD, digipak, 5,000 only)	20
95	New European BADVC 39	BLACK WHOLE OF LOVE (box set with 12", 10", 7" & CDs with inserts)	30
96	New European BADVC 96	SOMETHING IS COMING (2-LP, textured sleeve with insert)	15

DEATH IN VEGAS

02	Concrete HARD 5112	Leather Girls (Original Mix)/Natja (LAMF Mix)/Natja (Zoo Station) (12", double pack, p/s)	8
03	Concrete	So You Say You've Lost Your Baby (7", pink vinyl, white labels featuring Paul Weller)	15
02	Concrete HARD 5312	SCORPIO RISING (2-LP, gatefold sleeve with inners)	15

DEATH SENTENCE

82	Beat The System DEATH 1	DEATH & PURE DESTRUCTION (EP)	10

DEB MUSIC PLAYERS

78	Deb DEB LP 003	UMOJA - LOVE AND UNITY (LP)	40

DEBONAIRES (U.K.)

66	Pye 7N 17151	A Love Of Our Own/The Night Meets The Dawn	5
66	Pye 7N 17204	Crying Behind Your Smile/Forever More	5

DEBONAIRES (U.S.)

70	Track 604 035	I'm In Love Again/Headache In My Heart	70

DEBONAIRS

63	Parlophone R 5054	That's Right/When True Love Comes Your Way	5

DEBS

65	Mercury MF 888	Sloopy's Gonna Hang On/Under A Street Light	15

DEB-TONES

59	RCA RCA 1137	Knock, Knock - Who's There?/I'm In Love Again	25
59	RCA RCA 1137	Knock, Knock - Who's There?/I'm In Love Again (78)	20

DEBUTANTES

80	Rok ROK XVII/XVIII	Man In The Street/INNOCENT BYSTANDERS: Where Is Johnny	6

DECAMERON

73	Vertigo 6360 097	SAY HELLO TO THE BAND (LP)	15
73	Mooncrest CREST 19	MAMMOTH SPECIAL (LP, lyric insert)	25
75	Transatlantic TRA 304	THIRD LIGHT (LP)	15
76	Transatlantic TRA 325	TOMORROWS'S PANTOMIME (LP)	20

YVONNE DE CARLO

55	Capitol CL 14380	Take It Or Leave It/Three Little Stars	8

PAULO DE CARVALHO

74	Pye International 7N 25647	(And Then) After Love/E Depois Do Adeus (p/s)	10

DE CASTRO SISTERS

54	London HL 8104	Teach Me Tonight/It's Love	40
55	London HL 8137	Boom Boom Boomerang/Let Your Love Walk In	35
55	London HL 8158	I'm Bewildered/To Say You're Mine	35
55	London HLU 8189	If I Ever Fall In Love/Cuckoo In The Clock	25
55	London HLU 8212	Christmas Is A-Comin'/Snowbound For Christmas	25
56	London HLU 8228	Give Me Time/Too Late Now	25
56	London HLU 8228	Give Me Time/Too Late Now (78)	10
56	London HLU 8296	No One To Blame But You/Cowboys Don't Cry	25
58	HMV POP 527	Who Are They To Say?/When You Look At Me	10
59	HMV POP 583	Teach Me Tonight Cha Cha/The Things I Tell My Pillow	10
59	HMV POP 583	Teach Me Tonight Cha Cha/The Things I Tell My Pillow (78)	10
61	Capitol CL 15199	Red Sails In The Sunset/Bells	5

DECEMBER

96	Elfenblut SAG 44	River Of Blood/Venus In Chains (red vinyl, p/s, 1000 only)	10

DECISION

68	MCA MU 1027	In The Shade Of Your Love/Constable Jones	7

DIANA DECKER

(see also Ray Burns, Ruby Murray)

54	Columbia SCM 5083	Oh, My Papa/Crystal Ball	20
54	Columbia SCM 5096	The Happy Wanderer/Till We Two Are One	20
54	Columbia SCM 5120	Jilted/The Man With The Banjo	20
54	Columbia SCM 5123	Kitty In The Basket/Never Never Land	18
54	Columbia SCM 5130	Mama Mia/Percy The Penguin	20
54	Columbia SCM 5145	Sisters/Abracadabra	20
55	Columbia SCM 5166	Open The Window Of Your Heart/The Violin Song	15
55	Columbia SCM 5173	Apples, Peaches And Cherries/Paper Valentine	20
56	Columbia SCM 5246	Rock-A-Boogie Baby/Willie Can	20

DECORATORS

81	New Hormones ORG 5	Twilight View/Reflections (p/s)	5

NINA DECOSTA

80	Rokel ROK 12	Don't Want To Lose You/Instrumental Version (12")	50

MINT VALUE £

DE COURCY'S

65	Egmont EGM 9220	SALUTE TO THE SHADOWS (LP)	15

DE DANAAN

82	Cara CARA 1	Hey Jude/St. Jude's Hornpipe/Trip To Taum Reel/Teetotaller	5
75	Polydor 2904 005	DE DANAAN (LP)	15
77	Decca SKL-R 5287	DE DANAAN - SELECTED JIGS AND REELS (LP)	18
80	Decca SKL 5318	BANKS OF THE NILE (LP)	12

DEDICATED MEN'S JUG BAND

65	Piccadilly 7N 35245	Boodle-Am-Shake/Come On Boys	6
66	Piccadilly 7N 35283	Don't Come Knocking/One Time Blues	6

DEDRINGER

80	DinDisc DIN 10	Sunday Drivers/We Don't Mind (p/s)	5
80	DinDisc DIN 11	Innocent 'Till Proven Guilty/Maxine//Took A Long Time/ We Don't Mind (double pack)	8
81	DinDisc DIN 12	Direct Line/She's Not Ready (p/s)	5
82	Neat NEAT 18	Hot Lady/Hot Licks And Rock'N'Roll (p/s)	5
81	DinDisc DID 7	DIRECT LINE (LP)	12
83	Neat NEAT 1009	SECOND RISING (LP, with inner sleeve)	12

BRIAN DEE

75	Atlantic 2460 255	HAMMOND EXCITEMENT (LP)	12

DAVE DEE

(see also Dave Dee, Dozy, Beaky, Mick & Tich)

70	Fontana TF 1074	My Woman's Man/Gotta Make You Part Of Me	5
70	Fontana 6007 021	Annabella/Kelly	5
70	Philips 6006 061	Everything About Her/If I Believed In Tomorrow	5
71	Philips 6006 100	Wedding Bells/Sweden	5
71	Philips 6006 154	Hold On/Mary Morning, Mary Evening	5
71	Philips 6006 180	Swingy/Don't You Ever Change Your Mind	5

DAVE DEE, DOZY, BEAKY, MICK & TICH

(see also Dozy Beaky Mick & Tich [D,B,M & T], Dave Dee)

65	Fontana TF 531	No Time/Is It Love	25
65	Fontana TF 586	All I Want/It Seems A Pity	25
65	Fontana TF 630	You Make It Move/I Can't Stop	10
67	Fontana TF 798	Touch Me Touch Me/Marina	6
68	Fontana TF 903	The Legend Of Xanadu/Please	5
74	Antic K 11510	She's My Lady/Babeigh	6
67	Fontana TE 17488	LOOS OF ENGLAND (EP)	12
66	Fontana TL 5350	DAVE DEE, DOZY, BEAKY, MICK & TICH (LP)	20
66	Fontana TL 5388	IF MUSIC BE THE FOOD OF LOVE PREPARE FOR INDIGESTION (LP, mono)	25
66	Fontana TL 5388	IF MUSIC BE THE FOOD OF LOVE PREPARE FOR INDIGESTION (LP, stereo)	35
67	Fontana STL 5441	GOLDEN HITS OF DAVE DEE, DOZY, BEAKY, MICK & TICH (LP)	15
68	Fontana (S)TL 5471	IF NO-ONE SANG (LP)	20
69	Fontana SFL 13002	DDDBM&T (LP)	12
70	Fontana SFL 13173	TOGETHER (LP)	12

JAY DEE

74	Warner Bros. 7798	Strange Games And Funky Things/Intrumental	7

JEANNIE DEE

69	Beacon BEA 115	Come Into My Arms/Sun Shine On Me	7
69	Beacon BEA 142	Don't Go Home My Little Darling/Come See About Me	15

JOEY DEE & STARLI(GH)TERS

(see also Young Rascals)

61	Columbia DB 4758	Peppermint Twist (Parts 1 & 2)	10
62	Columbia DB 4803	Hey, Let's Twist/Roly Poly	10
62	Columbia DB 4842	Shout (Parts 1 & 2)	10
62	Columbia DB 4862	Ya Ya/Fanny Mae	10
62	Columbia DB 4905	What Kind Of Love Is This?/Wing Ding	12
63	Columbia DB 4955	I Lost My Baby/Keep Your Mind On What You're Doin'	10
63	Columbia DB 7005	Baby You're Driving Me Crazy/Help Me Pick Up The Pieces	10
63	Columbia DB 7055	Hot Pastrami With Mashed Potatoes (Parts 1 & 2)	10
63	Columbia DB 7102	Dance, Dance, Dance/Let's Have A Party (features Ronettes uncredited)	12
63	Columbia DB 7277	Down By The Riverside/Getting Nearer (features Ronettes uncredited)	12
61	Columbia 33SX 1406	DOIN' THE TWIST LIVE AT THE PEPPERMINT LOUNGE (LP)	25
62	Columbia 33SX 1461	BACK AT THE PEPPERMINT LOUNGE (LP)	25
62	Columbia 33SX 1502	ALL THE WORLD IS TWISTIN' (LP)	25
63	Columbia 33SX 1532	JOEY DEE (LP)	25
63	Columbia 33SX 1607	DANCE DANCE DANCE (LP, with Starlighters, also with Ronettes uncredited)	30

JOHN CHRISTIAN DEE

68	Pye 7N 17566	Take Me Along/The World Can Pack Its Bags And Go Away	10
70	London HLH 10317	Come Forward The Man/Mr. & Mrs. Jones	5
69	Decca F12901	The World Can Pick Up Its Bags And Go Away/Stick To Your Guns	15

JOHNNIE DEE

65	Columbia DB 7612	Frankie's Angel/Everything's Upside Down	7

JOHNNY DEE

(see also John D. Loudermilk)

57	Oriole CB 1367	Sittin' In The Balcony/A-Plus Love	140
57	Oriole CB 1367	Sittin' In The Balcony/A-Plus Love (78)	35

KIKI DEE

(see also Elton John)

63	Fontana TF 394	Early Night/Lucky High Heels	20

MINT VALUE £

63	Fontana TF 414	I Was Only Kidding/Don't Put Your Heart In His Hand	12
64	Fontana TF 443	Miracles/That's Right, Walk On By	18
64	Fontana TF 490	(You Don't Know) How Glad I Am/Baby I Don't Care	12
65	Fontana TF 596	Runnin' Out Of Fools/There He Goes	10
66	Fontana TF 669	Why Don't I Run Away From You?/Small Town	20
67	Fontana TF 792	I'm Going Out (The Same Way I Came In)/We've Got Everything Going For Us	15
67	Fontana TF 833	I/Stop And Think	10
67	Fontana TF 870	Excuse Me/Patterns	10
68	Fontana TF 926	Can't Take My Eyes Off You/Hungry Heart	10
68	Fontana TF 983	Now The Flowers Cry/On A Magic Carpet Ride	200
70	Tamla Motown TMG 739	The Day Will Come Between Sunday And Monday/ My Whole World Ended (The Moment You Left Me)	25
72	Philips 6006 352	Excuse Me/Patterns	8
73	Rocket PIG 2	Lonnie And Josie/The Last Good Man In My Life	7
65	Fontana TE 17443	KIKI DEE (EP)	40
66	Fontana TE 17470	KIKI DEE IN CLOVER (EP)	30
68	Fontana (S)TL 5455	I'M KIKI DEE (LP)	45
70	Tamla Motown STML 11158	GREAT EXPECTATIONS (LP)	60

LENNY DEE

55	Brunswick 05440	Plantation Boogie/Birth Of The Blues	10

RICKY DEE & EMBERS

62	Stateside SS 136	Workout/JOHN MOBLEY: Tunnel Of Love	15

SANDRA DEE

61	Brunswick 05858	Tammy Tell Me True/Let's Fall In Love	10

SIMON DEE

69	Chapter one CH 105	Julie/Whatever Happened To Us	7

TAMMI DEE

71	Downtown DT 479	Val/MUSIC DOCTORS: Bank Raid	12

TOMMY DEE

59	Melodisc 1516	Three Stars/TEEN JONES (TONES): I'll Never Change (tri centre)	75
59	Melodisc 1516	Three Stars/TEEN JONES (TONES): I'll Never Change (round centre)	50
59	Melodisc 1516	Three Stars/TEEN JONES (TONES): I'll Never Change (78)	25

DEE II

93	Kold Sweat KS127	Doggin' Me Around/Break Out The Vaseline (12")	8

DEE & DYNAMITES

60	Philips PB 1081	Blaze Away/South Bound Gasser	12

DEE AND THE QUOTIUM

69	Jay Boy Boy 8	Someday You'll Need Someone/Send Some Flowers To Julie	45

MAURICE DEEBANK

(see also Felt)

84	Cherry Red MRED 61	INNER THOUGHT ZONE (LP)	12

DEEJAY FRIENDLY

96	Deejay Friendly PK 01	Piano Me Softly (12" promo)	8

DEEJAYS

65	Polydor BM 56034	Dimples/Coming On Strong	60
65	Polydor BM 56501	Blackeyed Woman/I Just Can't Go To Sleep	110

ANTHONY DEELEY

68	Pama PM 728	Anytime Man/Don't Change Your Mind About Me	10

ANGELA DEEN

64	Fontana TF 491	There's So Much About My Baby That I Love/Gotta Hand It To The Boy	12

CAROL DEENE

61	HMV POP 922	Sad Movies (Make Me Cry)/Don't Forget	10
62	HMV POP 973	Norman/On The Outside Looking In	6
62	HMV POP 1027	Johnny Get Angry/Somebody's Smiling	10
62	HMV POP 1058	Some People/Kissin'	10
62	HMV POP 1086	James/It Happened Last Night	8
63	HMV POP 1123	Let Me Do It My Way/Growin' Up	10
63	HMV POP 1200	Oh Oh Oh Willie/I Want To Stay Here	10
64	HMV POP 1275	Who's Been Sleeping In My Bed?/Love Is Wonderful	10
64	HMV POP 1337	Very First Kiss/Hard To Say Goodnight	10
65	HMV POP 1405	Most People Do/I Can't Forget Someone Like You	10
65	Columbia DB 7743	He Just Don't Know/Up In The Penthouse	10
66	Columbia DB 7890	Dancing In Your Eyes/Please Don't Be Unfaithful Again	10
67	Columbia DB 8107	Love Not Have I/Time	10
68	CBS 3206	When He Wants A Woman/I'm Not Crying	6
69	Conquest CXT 102	One More Chance/Invisible Tears	6
79	RIM 003	Ready For The Times To Get Better/It's So Easy	6
70	World Records ST 1031	A LOVE AFFAIR (LP)	25

DEEP END

78	private pressing	BEGGED AND BORROWED (LP, listed as CPLP 016)	15

DEEP FEELING

(see also Raw Material)

69	Page One POF 160	Oh Darlin'/Feelin'	40
70	DJM DJS 231	Do You Wanna Dance/The Day My Lady Cried	6
70	Page One POF 165	Do You Love Me/Move On	6
70	Page One POF 177	Skyline Pigeon/We've Thrown It All Away	6
71	DJM DJS 237	Sweet Dust And Red Wine/Turn Around	6
74	Santa Ponsa PN 512	Lets Spend The Night Together/Avalon	8
71	DJM DJLPS 419	DEEP FEELING (LP)	150

MINT VALUE £

DEEP FREEZE

70s	Guardian GRL 43	Keeping You In Furs/Don't Look Back	5

DEEP FREEZE MICE

86	Cordelia ERICAT 002	These Floors Are Smooth/Zoology (500 copies)	15
86	Cordelia ERICAT 016	NEURON MUSIC (12" EP also featuring Mr. Concept, Yung Analysts and Rimarimba)	20
93	Single Farce 042	Slow Shiney Bricks/George Bailey Lassoes A Refrigerator (Remix) (300 numbered copies)	10
79	Mole Embalming MOLE 1	MY GERANIUMS ARE BULLETPROOF (LP, 250 copies with paste-on sleeve, 8-page booklet & various A4 inserts)	120
80s	Cordelia MOLE 1	MY GERANIUMS ARE BULLETPROOF (LP, with printed sleeve, 1500 copies)	30
81	Mole Embalming MOLE 2	TEENAGE HEAD IN MY REFRIGERATOR (LP, 800 copies)	50
81	Mole Emblaming MOLE 3	GATES OF LUNCH (LP, 1,000 copies)	45
82	Mole Embalming MOLE C1	TEENAGE HEAD IN MY REFRIGERATOR/LED ZEPPELIN 2 (cassette, 30 copies reissue on Jarmusic label (Germany) in 90s is worth £20)	50
83	Mole Embalming MOLE 4	SAW A RANCH BURNING LAST NIGHT (LP, 1000 copies)	40
83	Cordelia MOLE 4	SAW A RANCH BURNING LAST NIGHT (LP, 120 copies)	40
83	Lazy Dog LZD 802	SAW A RANCH BURNING LAST NIGHT (LP, 500 copies)	30
84	Cordelia ERICAT 001	I LOVE YOU LITTLE BOBO WITH YOUR DELICATE GOLDEN LIONS (2-LP, 250 in blue sleeve)	60
84	Cordelia ERICAT 001	I LOVE YOU LITTLE BOBO WITH YOUR DELICATE GOLDEN LIONS (2-LP, 500 in brown in sleeve)	60
84	Cordelia MOLE 2	TEENAGE HEAD IN MY REFRIGERATOR (LP, 400 copies)	45
84	Cordelia ERICAT 004	HANG ON CONSTANCE, LET ME HEAR THE NEWS (LP, 120 in wraparound poster sleeve)	25
84	Cordelia ERICAT 004	HANG ON CONSTANCE, LET ME HEAR THE NEWS (LP, 1000 copies)	20
84	Cordelia MOLE 3	GATES OF LUNCH (LP, 150 copies pressed)	55
84	Mole Embalming MOLE C2	MY GERANIUMS ARE BULLETPROOF (cassette, around 30 copies)	50
84	Mole Embalming MOLE C3	TEENAGE HEAD IN MY REFRIGERATOR (cassette, around 30 copies)	50
84	Cordelia/CERICAT 001	I LOVE YOU LITTLE BOBO WITH YOUR DELICATE GOLDEN LIONS (double cassette, around 25 copies)	25
87	Cordelia ERICAT 013	RAIN IS WHEN THE EARTH IS TELEVSION (1000 copies)	20
87	Cordelia ERICAT 024	WAR, FAMINE, DEATH, PESTILENCE & MISS TIMBERLAKE (LP, 1000 copies)	20
88	Cordelia ERICAT 027	THE TENDER YELLOW PONIES OF INSOMNIA (LP, 1000 copies)	20
89	Logical Fish 1	LIVE IN SWITZERLAND (LP, 500 copies)	15

DEEP PURPLE

(see also Ritchie Blackmore, Rainbow, Gillan, [David Coverdale's] Whitesnake, Tommy Bolin, [Sheila Carter &] Episode Six, Jon Lord, Roger Glover, Green Bullfrog, Wizard's Convention, Elf, Maze, M.I. Five, Warhorse, Captain Beyond, John Lawton, Hell Preachers Inc., Glen Hughes, Trapeze, Leading Figures, Paice Ashton & Lord, Silverhead, Pete York Percussion Band)

68	Parlophone R 5708	Hush/One More Rainy Day (in promo-only p/s)	350
68	Parlophone R 5708	Hush/One More Rainy Day	35
68	Parlophone R 5745	Kentucky Woman/Wring That Neck (withdrawn)	50
69	Parlophone R 5763	Emmaretta/Wring That Neck	35
69	Harvest HAR 5006	Hallelujah (I Am The Preacher)/April Part 1 (in promo-only p/s)	250
69	Harvest HAR 5006	Hallelujah (I Am The Preacher)/April Part 1	30
70	Harvest PSR 325	Concerto, 1st Movement (edit)/Concerto, 2nd Movement (edit) (promo, possibly some commercial)	30
70	Harvest HAR 5020	Black Night/Speed King	6
71	Harvest HAR 5033	Strange Kind Of Woman/I'm Alone	6
71	Harvest HAR 5045	Fireball/Demon's Eye	6
72	Purple PUR 102	Never Before/When A Blind Man Cries	6
74	Purple PUR 117	Might Just Take Your Life/Coronarias Redig	8
76	Purple PUR 130	You Keep On Moving/Love Child	8
77	Purple PUR 132	Smoke On The Water/Woman From Tokyo/Child In Time (10,000 with p/s)	7
85	Polydor POSPP 719	Perfect Strangers (edit)/Son Of Alerik (edit) (picture disc)	7
87	Polydor POSPP 843	Call Of The Wild/Strange Ways (12", picture disc)	10
88	Polydor POC 4	Hush ('88 Re-recording)/Dead Or Alive (Live) (black vinyl, p/s)	7
88	Polydor POC 4	Hush ('88 Re-recording)/Dead Or Alive (Live) (blue vinyl, p/s)	5
88	Polydor RX 4	Hush ('88 Re-recording)/Dead Or Alive (Live)/Bad Attitude (12", gatefold p/s)	8
88	Polydor PZCD 4	Hush ('88 Re-recording)Dead Or Alive/Bad Attitude (CD)	8
88	Polydor 080 088-2	Bad Attitude/Black And White/Unwritten Law/Strangeways (CD Video)	15
90	RCA PT 49224	Love Conquers All (Edit)/Truth Hurts (die-cut picture disc, with insert)	7
93	BMG DP 001	Anya/Excerpts of: Time To Kill/The Battle Rages On/Talk About Love (CD single, promo)	15
95	EMI 7243 8 82214 67	Black Night (Remix)/Black Night (Original Mix)/Speed King (12", purple vinyl, numbered limited edition)	8
77	Purple PUR 135	NEW LIVE AND RARE VOL. 1 (EP, 15,000 on purple vinyl)	8
78	Purple PUR 137	NEW LIVE AND RARE VOL. 2 (EP)	8
80	Harvest SHEP 101	NEW LIVE AND RARE VOL. 3 (EP)	8
68	Parlophone PMC 7055	SHADES OF DEEP PURPLE (LP, yellow/black label, mono, with "Sold in U.K..." text)	300
68	Parlophone PCS 7055	SHADES OF DEEP PURPLE (LP, yellow/black label, stereo, with "Sold in U.K..." text)	200
69	Parlophone PCS 7055	SHADES OF DEEP PURPLE (LP, stereo repressing, white/black label)	25
69	Harvest SHVL 751	THE BOOK OF TALIESYN (LP, laminated gatefold sleeve, first pressing with "Sold in U.K." text spread over 4 lines, no EMI logo on label)	120
69	Harvest SHVL 751	THE BOOK OF TALIESYN (LP, laminated sleeve, second pressing with "Sold in U.K." text spread over 5 lines)	70
69	Harvest SHVL 751	THE BOOK OF TALIESYN (LP, laminated sleeve, third pressing without "Sold in U.K." text)	40
70s	Harvest SHVL 751	THE BOOK OF TALIESYN (LP, laminated gatefold sleeve, later pressing with EMI logo on label)	40
69	Harvest SHVL 759	DEEP PURPLE (LP, laminated gatefold sleeve, no EMI logo on label)	60
71	Harvest SHVL 759	DEEP PURPLE (LP, laminated gatefold sleeve, non EMI pressing with indented circular groove around spindle hole)	20
70s	Harvest SHVL 759	DEEP PURPLE (LP, laminated gatefold sleeve, later pressing with EMI logo on label)	20

MINT VALUE £

70	Harvest SHVL 767	CONCERTO FOR GROUP AND ORCHESTRA (LP, laminated gatefold sleeve, no EMI logo on label)	40
70s	Harvest SHVL 767	CONCERTO FOR GROUP AND ORCHESTRA (LP, laminated gatefold sleeve, later pressing with EMI logo on label)	20
70	Harvest SHVL 777	IN ROCK (LP, laminated gatefold sleeve, A1, B1 matrix, no EMI logo on label)	50
70s	Harvest SHVL 777	IN ROCK (LP, laminated gatefold sleeve, later pressing with EMI logo on label)	20
71	Harvest SHVL 793	FIREBALL (LP, textured gatefold sleeve, with lyric insert)	40
72	Purple TPSP 351	MADE IN JAPAN 2-LP, double gatefold sleeve)	20
72	Purple TPSA 7504	MACHINE HEAD (LP, laminated gatefold sleeve, with lyric insert)	20
73	Purple TPSA 7508	WHO DO WE THINK WE ARE (LP, laminated gatefold sleeve, with insert)	12
74	Purple Q4TPS 7504	MACHINE HEAD (LP, laminated gatefold sleeve, quadrophonic)	45
74	Purple TPS 3505	BURN (LP)	15
74	Purple TPS 3508	STORMBRINGER (LP)	15
75	Purple TPSA 7515	COME TASTE THE BAND (LP, gatefold sleeve with inner)	15
78	Harvest SHSM 2026	THE SINGLES A's AND B's (LP, purple vinyl)	15
79	Purple TPS 3514	THE MARK 2 PURPLE SINGLES (LP, purple vinyl)	15
80	Harvest SHSM 2016	SHADES OF DEEP PURPLE (LP, 'dismembered doll-limb' sleeve, withdrawn)	150
84	Polydor POLHP 16	PERFECT STRANGERS (LP, picture disc, with extra track & die-cut sleeve)	15
84	Polydor DEEP 1A	DEEP PURPLE INTERVIEW (LP, 1-sided, promo-only, stickered white sleeve)	18
85	EMI EJ 26 0343 0	IN ROCK (LP, picture disc with poster)	20
85	EMI EJ 34 0344 0	FIREBALL (LP, picture disc with poster)	20
85	EMI EG 26 0345 0	MACHINE HEAD (LP, picture disc with poster)	20
85	EMI PUR 1/E 2606131	DEEP PURPLE - ANTHOLOGY (2-LP, blue vinyl)	25
86	Polydor DEEP 2A	HOUSE OF BLUE LIGHT (interview LP, promo-only, plays same both sides, stickered black sleeve)	15
87	Polydor 831 318-2	HOUSE OF BLUE LIGHT (CD)	20
88	Connoisseur VSOP 125	SCANDINAVIAN NIGHTS (2-LP, gatefold sleeve, with booklet)	18
91	Connoisseur DPVSOPLP 163	IN THE ABSENCE OF PINK - KNEBWORTH 85 (2-LP gatefold)	15
91	EMI 96129	ANTHOLOGY (3-LP)	20
93	BMG 74321 15420-1	THE BATTLE RAGES ON (LP, with inner sleeve)	12
95	EMI 7243 8 34019 18	DEEP PURPLE IN ROCK (2-LP, purple vinyl, gatefold sleeve with inners)	15
97	EMI DEEPP 3	MACHINE HEAD (2-LP, 'EMI 100' remixed anniversary edition, purple vinyl, gatefold sleeve, with insert)	18
97	EMI LPCENT 25	SHADES OF DEEP PURPLE (LP, 'EMI 100', 180gm vinyl edition, yellow/black label)	15
97	EMI DEEPP 2	FIREBALL (2-LP, gatefold sleeve with inners & limited edition print)	15
98	EMI PP 074	VERY BEST OF (2-LP, purple vinyl)	18
98	EMI 7243 8 57864 19	MADE IN JAPAN (2-LP, numbered, purple vinyl, gatefold sleeve with inners)	18
99	Harvest 7243 4 99469 10	BOOK OF TALIESYN (LP, 180gm vinyl, gatefold sleeve in stickered PVC outer)	15

DEEP RIVER BOYS

(see also Fats Waller, Harry Douglass & Deep River Boys)

54	HMV 7M 174	Sweet Mama Tree Top Tall/A Kiss And Cuddle Polka	20
54	HMV 7M 280	Shake, Rattle And Roll/St. Louis Blues	40
56	HMV 7M 361	Rock-A-Beatin' Boogie/Just A Little Bit More!	40
56	HMV POP 263	That's Right/Honey Honey	20
57	HMV POP 395	Whole Lotta Shakin' Goin' On/There's A Goldmine In The Sky	30
58	HMV POP 449	Not Too Old To Rock And Roll/Slow Train To Nowhere	25
58	HMV POP 537	Itchy Twitchy Feeling/I Shall Not Be Moved	10
59	Top Rank JAR 172	Nola/Kissin'	5
59	Top Rank JAR 174	I Don't Know Why (I Just Do)/Timbers Gotta Roll (with Harry Douglass)	10
60	Top Rank JAR 352	Go Galloway, Go/Dum Dum De Dum (with Harry Douglass)	6
62	HMV POP 1081	Settle Down/Ashes Of Roses	5
55	Nixa 45EP 113	GO ON BOARD LITTLE CHILDREN (EP)	10
55	Nixa 45EP 114	SWING LOW SWEET CHARIOT (EP)	10
55	Nixa 45EP 130	WALK TOGETHER CHILDREN (EP)	10
55	Nixa 45EP 131	EZEKIEL SAW THE WHEEL (EP)	10
55	HMV 7EG 8133	DEEP RIVER BOYS (EP)	10
57	HMV 7EG 8321	ROMANCE A LA MODE (EP)	10
57	HMV 7EG 8445	NEGRO SPIRITUALS (EP)	10
54	Nixa XLTY 135	SPIRITUALS SUNG BY THE DEEP RIVER BOYS (10" LP)	20
54	Nixa XLTY 138	SPIRITUALS SUNG BY THE DEEP RIVER BOYS (10" LP)	20
60	Top Rank 35/108	THE BLUE DEEPS (LP)	15

DEEP SET

68	Pye 7N 17594	That's The Way Life Goes/Hello Amy	45
69	Major Minor MM 607	I Started A Joke/Spicks And Specks	8
70	Target 7N 45018	Cinnamon Girl/You'll Never Know	100

DEEP SIX

66	Liberty LIB 55882	Counting/When Morning Breaks	8

DEEP SWITCH

86	SWITCH 1	NINE INCHES OF GOD (LP, private pressing)	20

DEEP TIMBRE

72	Westwood WR 5006	DEEP TIMBRE (LP)	40

DEERHUNTER

07	4AD CAD 2822	MICROCASTLE/WEIRD ERA CONT. (LP)	18

SAM DEES

69	Major Minor MM 655	If It's All Wrong (It's All Right)/Don't Keep Me Hangin' On	30
75	Atlantic K 10676	Fragile, Handle With Care/Save The Love At Any Cost	100
89	RCA PB 43129	After All/Always Something (p/s)	10
75	Atlantic K 50142	THE SHOW MUST GO ON (LP)	50
97	G'mine/Soul Supply GS002X	Lonely For You Baby/SAM FLETCHER: I'd Think It Over (promo)	12
97	G'mine/Soul Supply GS0002	Lonely For You Baby/SAM FLETCHER: I'd Think It Over	10

MINT VALUE £

SAM DEES & BETTYE SWANN
(see also Bettye Swann)

76	Atlantic K 10719	Storybook Children/Just As Sure	30

DEE SET

68	Blue Cat BS 146	I Know A Place/ROY BENNETT: I Dangerous	40

DEF J
(see also Encona Coarse)

92	Kold Sweat KS122	Just Save It (12")	15

DEF LEPPARD
(see also Lucy, Gogmagog)

79	Bludgeon Riffola SRT/CUS/232	THE DEF LEPPARD EP: Ride Into The Sun/Getcha Rocks Off/The Overture (red label, p/s with lyric insert, 150 only)	350
79	Bludgeon Riffola SRT/CUS/232	THE DEF LEPPARD EP: Ride Into The Sun/Getcha Rocks Off/The Overture (red label, with p/s, 850 only)	250
79	Bludgeon Riffola SRT/CUS/232	THE DEF LEPPARD EP: Ride Into The Sun/Getcha Rocks Off/The Overture (red label, without p/s, 850 only)	60
79	Bludgeon Riffola MSB 001	Ride Into The Sun/Getcha Rocks Off/The Overture (reissue, yellow label, 15,000 pressed, no p/s)	18
79	Phonogram 6059 240	Getcha Rocks Off/Ride Into The Sun/The Overture (2nd reissue, no p/s)	10
79	Phonogram 6059 240	Getcha Rocks Off/Ride Into The Sun/The Overture (mispressing, both sides play "The Overture")	40
79	Phonogram 6059 247	Wasted/Hello America (p/s)	12
80	Phonogram LEPP 1	Hello America/Good Morning Freedom (p/s)	12
81	Phonogram LEPP 2	Let It Go/Switch 625 (p/s, 10,000 shrinkwrapped with patch)	15
81	Phonogram LEPP 2	Let It Go/Switch 625 (p/s)	12
82	Phonogram LEPP 3	Bringin' On The Heartbreak/Me And My Wine (p/s)	35
82	Phonogram LEPP 312	Bringin' On The Heartbreak/Me And My Wine/You Got Me Runnin' (12", p/s)	18
83	Phonogram VER 5	Photograph/Bringin' On The Heartbreak (p/s)	10
83	Phonogram VERP 5	Photograph/Bringin' On The Heartbreak (camera-shaped fold-out/pop-up sleeve, 500 only)	25
83	Phonogram VERX 5	Photograph/Bringin' On The Heartbreak/Mirror, Mirror (12", p/s)	20
83	Phonogram VER 6	Rock Of Ages/Action! Not Words (p/s)	7
83	Phonogram VERP 6	Rock Of Ages/Action! Not Words (guitar-shaped picture disc)	35
83	Phonogram VERQ 6	Rock Of Ages/Action! Not Words (foldout 'rock box' cube sleeve, 500 only)	40
83	Phonogram VERX 6	Rock Of Ages/Action! Not Words (12", p/s)	18
83	Phonogram VERDJ 8	Too Late/Foolin' (p/s, DJ-only promo with rear band photo in football kit)	150
83	Phonogram VER 8	Too Late For Love/Foolin' (p/s)	12
83	Phonogram VERX 8	Too Late For Love/Foolin'/High And Dry (12", p/s)	20
84	Phonogram VER 9	Photograph/Bringin' On The Heartbreak (reissue, 'wallet' p/s)	10
84	Phonogram VERG 9	Photograph/Bringin' On The Heartbreak (g/fold printed 'wallet' p/s, 500 only)	35
84	Phonogram VERX 9	Photograph/Bringin' On The Heartbreak/Mirror, Mirror (12", p/s)	15
87	Phonogram LEPC 1	Animal/Animal (Extended Mix)/Tear It Down (12", p/s, red vinyl)	15
87	Phonogram LEPCD 1	Animal/Women/Animal (Extended Mix)/Tear It Down (CD, no'd, 1,000 only)	25
87	Phonogram LEPS 2	Pour Some Sugar On Me/I Wanna Be Your Hero (tri-shaped picture disc in silver 12" foldout p/s with tour dates)	15
87	Phonogram LEPPX 2	Pour Some Sugar On Me (Extended Version)/Pour Some Sugar On Me (Extended)/I Wanna Be Your Hero (12", picture disc, unissued)	0
87	Phonogram LEPS 3	Hysteria/Ride Into The Sun (1987 Version) (p/s, shrinkwrapped with patch)	10
87	Phonogram LEPX 313	Hysteria/Ride Into The Sun (1987 Version)/Love And Affection (live) (12", envelope box sleeve with poster & international discography, 5,000 only)	15
87	Phonogram LEPCD 3	Hysteria/Ride Into The Sun (1987 Version)/Love And Affection (live)/ I Wanna Be Your Hero (CD, 5,000 only with titles in red, numbered)	15
88	Phonogram LEPP 4	Armageddon It! (The Atomic Mix)/Ring Of Fire (poster p/s)	7
88	Phonogram LEPXB 4	Armageddon It!/Armageddon It! (The Atomic Mix)/Ring Of Fire (12", numbered box set with poster, enamel badge & 5 postcards, 5,000 only)	18
88	Phonogram LEPCD 4	Armageddon It! (The Atomic Mix)/Ring Of Fire/Animal/ Pour Some Sugar On Me (CD, picture disc)	15
88	Phonogram LEPG 5	Love Bites/Billy's Got A Gun (live) (no'd gatefold p/s with 8-page lyric book)	8
88	Phonogram LEPXB 5	Love Bites/Billy's Got A Gun (live)/Excitable (Orgasmic Mix) (12", box set with 4 cardboard inserts, 5,000 only)	18
88	Phonogram LEPCD 5	Love Bites/Rocket (The Lunar Mix)/Billy's Got A Gun (live) (CD, card sleeve)	12
89	Phonogram LEPC 6	Rocket/Release Me (foldout ?Brit' pack, envelope sleeve with 3 inserts)	8
89	Phonogram LEPXP 6	Rocket (The Lunar Mix)/(Radio Edit)/Release Me (12", picture disc, numbered)	15
89	Phonogram LEPXP 6	Rocket (The Lunar Mix)/(Radio Edit)/Release Me (12", picture disc, un-numbered)	10
89	Phonogram LEPXC 6	Rocket (The Lunar Mix)/Release Me/Rock Of Ages (live) (12", calendar pack)	15
89	Phonogram LEPCD 6	Rocket (The Lunar Mix)/Rock Of Ages (live)/Release Me (CD)	12
92	Phonogram DEFXP 7	Let's Get Rocked/Only After Dark/Too Late For Love (live) (12", picture disc, with insert)	10
92	Phonogram DEFCD 7	Let's Get Rocked/Only After Dark/Women (live) (CD, picture disc, in box with space for 4 CD's)	10
88	Bludgeon Riffola 080 458-2	Love Bites/Rocket (Lunar Mix)/Billy's Got A Gun (live)/ Love Bites (Video) (CD Video)	20
89	Bludgeon Riffola 080 034-2	Rock Of Ages/Stagefright/Billy's Got A Gun/Too Late For Love/ Rock Of Ages (Video) (CD Video)	20
89	Bludgeon Riffola 080 626-2	Animal (Extended Version)/Animal/Tear It Down/Animal (Video) (CD Video)	20
90	Bludgeon Riffola 080 990-2	Rocket (Radio Edit)/Release Me/Rock Of Ages/Rocket (Video) (CD Video)	20
87	Phonogram HYSPD 1	HYSTERIA (LP, picture disc)	15
89	Phonogram 836 606-2	THE FOUR ALBUMS (4-CD box set, with booklet)	50
92	Phonogram 510 978-1	ADRENALIZE (LP, picture disc, 5,000 only, numbered, die-cut sleeve)	15
94	Phonogram (no cat. no.)	ADRENALIZE - MAHOGANY BOX SET (CD, picture disc, with interview picture CD, 3 booklets, signed/no'd certificate, signed photo & plectrum, 1,000 only)	200
95	Mercury DLINT 3	1980-1995 VAULT - AN INTERVIEW WITH JOE ELLIOT & RICK SAVAGE (CD, promo only)	20

MINT VALUE £

DEF TEX

92	Sound Clash SCR 001	TUTORIAL SESSIONS (EP)	30
92	Sound Clash SCR003	MASTER BLASTER (EP)	60
94	Sound Clash CLASH003	HERBS & VERBS (EP)	10
95	Sound Clash SCR007	MOON MEDITATION (EP)	10
99	Son SON008	Poetic Speech Techniques (12")	15
00	Son SON013	Synchronise (12")	12
01	Son SONCD018	SERENE BUG (LP)	15
01	Monkey Face MF01	Sing Sad Songs (7")	15

DEFECTS

85	WXYZ LMNOP2	DEFECTIVE BREAKDOWN (LP, with insert)	15

DEFENDANTS

80s	Edible EAT 001	Headmaster/Such A Spiv (stickered insert cover & stickered labels)	12

DEFENDERS

(see also Lee Perry)

68	Doctor Bird DB 1104	Set Them Free/Don't Blame The Children (actually by Lee Perry & Sensations)	30

ZION DE GALLIER

(see also Mark Wirtz)

68	Parlophone R 5686	Me/Winter Will Be Cold	25
68	Parlophone R 5710	Dream Dream Dream/Geraldine	18

GLORIA DE HAVEN

55	Brunswick 05369	So This Is Paris/The Two Of Us	10
55	Brunswick 05457	Red Hot Pepper Pot/Won't You Save Me?	15
59	Oriole CB 1524	Dearly Beloved/Life	10

DE-HEMS

72	President PT 388	Don't Cross That Line/Lover Let Me Go	20

DEIGHTON TASK FORCE

(see also Unique 3)

89	White REACT1	Neighbourhood (12")	60

DEIRDRE-WILSON TABAC

69	RCA 1880	Get Back/Angel Baby	6

JACK DE JOHNETTE

70	CBS 64076	COMPLEX (LP)	20

DE JOHN SISTERS

57	Mercury MT 174	What Am I/Where Would I Be	10
60	London HLT 9127	Yes Indeed/Be Anything (But Be Mine)	10

DEK & JERRY

66	Philips BF 1494	What's The Matter With Me?/Don't Waste Your Time	8

DESMOND DEKKER (& ACES)

(see also Al Barry, Skatalites, Maytals)

63	Island WI 054	Honour Your Mother And Father (as Desmond Decker & Beverley's Allstars)/ Madgie ('63) (with Beverley's Allstars)	20
63	Island WI 111	Parents/Labour For Learning (solo)	30
64	Island WI 158	Jeserine/King Of Ska (as Desmond Dekkar & His Cherry Pies)	30
64	Black Swan WI 455	Dracula (as Desmond Dekkar)/DON DRUMMOND: Spitfire	50
65	Island WI 181	Get Up Adine (as Desmond Dekkar, actually with Four Aces)/Be Mine Forever (as Patsy & Desmond; song is act. "Down Down Down" by Clive & Naomi)	35
65	Island WI 202	This Woman (as Desmond Dekker & Four Aces)/ LEE PERRY & UPSETTERS: Si Senora (B-side actually by Ossie & Upsetters)	25
67	Pyramid PYR 6003	Wise Man/ROLAND ALPHONSO: Middle East	30
67	Pyramid PYR 6004	007 (Shanty Town)/ROLAND ALPHONSO: El Torro	20
67	Pyramid PYR 6006	It's A Shame/ROLAND ALPHONSO: On The Move	25
67	Pyramid PYR 6008	Rudy Got Soul/ROLAND ALPHONSO: The Cat	30
67	Pyramid PYR 6011	Rude Boy Train/ROLAND ALPHONSO: Nothing For Nothing	25
67	Pyramid PYR 6012	Mother's Young Girl/SOUL BROTHERS: Confucious	45
67	Pyramid PYR 6017	Unity/Sweet Music	18
67	Pyramid PYR 6020	Sabotage/Pretty Africa	15
67	Pyramid PYR 6020	Sabotage/It Pays	15
67	Pyramid PYR 6026	It Pays/Young Generation	15
68	Pyramid PYR 6031	Beautiful And Dangerous/I've Got The Blues	15
68	Pyramid PYR 6035	Bongo Gal/Shing A Ling	15
68	Pyramid PYR 6037	To Sir, With Love/Fu Manchu	100
68	Pyramid PYR 6044	Mother Pepper/Don't Blame Me	15
68	Pyramid PYR 6045	Try Me/I'm Leaving	15
68	Pyramid PYR 6047	Hey Grandma/Young Generation	15
68	Pyramid PYR 6051	Music Like Dirt (Intensified)/Coconut Water	15
68	Pyramid PYR 6054	It Mek/Writing On The Wall	8
68	Pyramid PYR 6058	Israelites/BEVERLEY'S ALLSTARS: The Man	7
68	Pyramid PYR 6059	Christmas Day/I've Got The Blues	10
69	Pyramid PYR 6068	It Mek/Problems	5
69	J.J. PYR 6058	Israelites/BEVERLEY'S ALLSTARS: The Man (reissue, mis-labelled copy)	5
70	Trojan TR 7777	You Can Get It If You Really Want/Perseverance	5
70	Trojan TR 7802	The Song We Used To Sing/Get Up Little Suzie	5
71	Trojan TR 7847	Lightning Stick/Troubles And Miseries	5
72	Trojan TR 7876	It Gotta Be So/The First Time For A Long Time	5
73	Rhino RNO 115	Sing A Little Song/I'm A Busted Lad	5
67	Doctor Bird DLM 5007	007 SHANTY TOWN (LP)	150
69	Doctor Bird DLM 5013	THE ISRAELITES (LP, solo)	200
69	Trojan TTL 4	THIS IS DESMOND DEKKAR (LP, label credits Dekker)	28
70	Trojan TBL 146	YOU CAN GET IT IF YOU REALLY WANT (LP)	18
73	Trojan TRLD 401	DOUBLE DEKKER (2-LP)	15

MINT VALUE £

GEORGE DEKKER

71	Trojan TR 7879	Time Hard/SYDNEY, GEORGE & JACKIE: Fall In Love	6

HOWARD DEKKER

74	A Rover AR 01	Me Throw Me Corn/On The Fire	12

DELACARDOS

61	HMV POP 890	Hold Back The Tears/Mister Dillon	80

DE LAINE SISTERS

(see also Ladybirds, Breakaways)

62	Piccadilly 7N 35070	It Might As Well Rain Until September/Puppet On A String	10

DEL AMITRI

83	No Strings NOSP 1	Sense Sickness/The Difference Is (p/s)	30
85	Chrysalis CHS 12 2925	Hammering Heart/Lines Running North/Brown Eyed Girl (12", p/s)	12
89	A&M AM 527	Stone Cold Sober/The Return Of Maggie Brown/Talk It To Death (p/s)	10
89	A&M CDEE 515	Kiss This Thing Goodbye/No Holding On/Slowly, It's Coming Back (3" CD, card sleeve)	12
90	A&M AMX 589	Spit In The Rain/Scared To Love/The Return Of Maggie Brown/ Talk It To Death (10", in box with lyric insert)	12

DELANEY & BONNIE (& FRIENDS)

(see also Eric Clapton, Delaney Bramlett, King Curtis with Delaney & Friends, Shindogs)

69	Elektra EKSN 45066	Get Ourselves Together/Soldiers Of The Cross (withdrawn)	20
69	Apple SAPCOR 7	THE ORIGINAL DELANEY & BONNIE (LP, unreleased, no sleeve)	850
69	Elektra EKS 74039	THE ORIGINAL DELANEY & BONNIE - ACCEPT NO SUBSTITUTE (LP, commercial release of above LP)	18
69	Stax SXATS 1029	HOME (LP)	15
70	Atlantic 2400 013	ON TOUR WITH ERIC CLAPTON (LP)	20
71	Atco 2400 029	TO BONNIE FROM DELANEY (LP)	15
72	CBS 64959	TOGETHER (LP)	12

ERIC DELANEY BAND

60	Parlophone R 4646	Bass Drum Boogie/Let's Get Organised	6
62	Parlophone R 4925	Manhattan Spiritual/Down Home	5
57	Pye Nixa NEP	AT THE BBC FESTIVAL (EP)	10
59	Pye NIXA NEP 24115	THESE SWINGIN' JINGLES (EP)	10
56	Pye NIXA NP 19018	HI-FI DELANEY (10" LP)	25

ERIC DELANEY'S BIG BEAT SIX

65	Pye 7N 15782	The Big Beat/Big Noise From Winnetka	6

DEL-CAPRIS

79	Grapevine GRP 112	Hey Little Way Out Girl (actually by Construction)/ EULA COOPER: Beggars Can't Be Choosey (p/s)	10

DELEGATION

77	State 25	The Promise Of Love/It Only Happens	25

DELFONICS

68	Bell BLL 1005	La La Means I Love You/Can't Get Over Losing You	10
68	Bell BLL 1016	Together We Can Make Such Sweet Music/Bad Bad Weather	10
68	Bell BLL 1042	Ready Or Not Here I Come/Somebody Loves You	10
69	Bell BLL 1066	You Can't Be Loving Him/Let It Be Me	15
69	Bell BLL 1073	Funny Feeling/You Got Yours	12
70	Bell BLL 1099	Didn't I (Blow Your Mind This Time)/Down is Up, Up Is Down	10
70	Bell BLL 1467	With These Hands/Let It Be Me	20
68	Bell SBLL 106	LA-LA MEANS I LOVE YOU (LP)	25
69	Bell SBLL 121	THE SOUND OF SEXY SOUL (LP)	20
71	Bell SBLL 137	THE DELFONICS (LP)	15
72	Bell 217	TELL ME THIS IS A DREAM (LP)	20
74	Bell BELLS 245	ALIVE AND KICKING (LP)	15

TERESA DEL FUEGO

81	Satril HH 155	Don't Hang Up/Wonder Wonder (no p/s)	8

DELGADOS

95	Radar SCAN 07	THE LAZARWALKER EP (p/s)	10
96	Chemikal U'grd CHEM 004	Cinecentre/Thirteen Gliding Prices/Mule Emulator (p/s)	5
96	Boa HISS 4	Liquidation Girl/VAN IMPE: Piranha (hand-painted brown paper bag p/s, 500 only)	15

DELICATES

59	London HLT 8953	Ronnie Is My Lover/Black And White Thunderbird	100
59	London HLT 8953	Ronnie Is My Lover/Black And White Thunderbird (78)	30
60	London HLT 9176	Too Young To Date/The Kiss	80

DELICATESSAN

67	Vocalion VN 9286	The Red Baron's Revenge/The Dog Fight (Der Hundtkampf)	10

DE LITE

89	Circa YRTPRX 35	Wild Times (12")	30

DELITES

80	Grapevine GRP 127	Lover/Tell Me Why	25

JOHNNY DE LITTLE

(see also John Barry)

61	Columbia DB 4578	Not Guilty/They	10
62	Columbia DB 4907	Lover/You Made Me Love You	10
63	Columbia DB 7023	Days Of Wine And Roses/Ride On	10
63	Columbia DB 7044	The Wind And The Rain/Unchained Melody	8
65	CBS 201790	The Knack/What To Do With Laurie	8

MINT VALUE £

DELIVERANCE

87	Metalworks VOV 664	DEVIL'S MEAT (LP)	15
89	Metalworks VOV 673	EVIL FRIENDSHIP (LP, lyric inner)	15
90	Metalworks VOV 679	THE BOOK OF LIES (LP)	15

DELIVERANCE

92	European Rhyme ERR001	Serious Public Disorder/Do Not Disturb (12")	25
94	Nut Cracker NUT001	Dead Funny/Up And Down The Country (12")	35
95	Nut Cracker NUT002	INJECT INTELLECT (EP)	15
96	Nut Cracker NUT003	Twisted Mystics/Sedating Your Aims (12")	15

DELKOM

91	Wau! Mr Modo MWS 034R	Superjack - Orbital Infusion 2000/Neutron 9000 Mix (12", 500 only)	12

DENNIS D'ELL

(see also Honeycombs)

67	CBS 202605	It Breaks My Heart In Two/Better Use Your Head (withdrawn)	400
67	CBS 202605	It Breaks My Heart In Two/Better Use Your Head (withdrawn: DJ copy)	300
67	Decca F 12647	A Woman Called Sorrow/The Night Has A Thousand Eyes (as Denny D'ell)	15
76	Polydor 2058 715	Home Is Home/Morning Without You (as Denis D'ell)	7

JIMMY DELL

58	RCA RCA 1066	Teeny Weeny/BARRY DE VORZON: Barbara Jean	70
58	RCA RCA 1066	Teeny Weeny/BARRY DE VORZON: Barbara Jean (78)	40

DEL(L)-VIKINGS

(see also Chuck Jackson)

57	London HLD 8405	Come Go With Me/How Can I Find A True Love (gold label lettering)	150
57	London HLD 8405	Come Go With Me/How Can I Find A True Love (silver label lettering)	50
57	London HLD 8405	Come Go With Me/How Can I Find A True Love (78)	20
57	London HLD 8464	Whispering Bells/Little Billy Boy	60
57	Mercury MT 169	Cool Shake/Jitterbug Mary (78)	30
58	Mercury 7MT 199	The Voodoo Man/Can't Wait	65
58	Mercury 7MT 199	The Voodoo Man/Can't Wait (78)	20
59	Mercury AMT 1027	Flat Tyre/How Could You	60
59	Mercury AMT 1027	Flat Tyre/How Could You (78)	20
62	HMV POP 1072	Kilimanjaro/Confession Of Love	50
63	HMV POP 1145	An Angel Up In Heaven/The Fishing Chant	20
71	Contour 2870 388	COME GO WITH ME (LP)	12

DELLINGER

(see also Dillinger)

77	Carib Gems GG 004	Melting Pot/Version	7

PETE DELLO & FRIENDS

(see also Honeybus, Lace, Red Herring, Leah, John Killigrew, Magic Valley, Grant Tracy & Sunsets, Sunsets)

71	Nepentha 6437 001	INTO YOUR EARS (LP, gatefold sleeve)	500

DELLS

63	Pye International 7N 25178	The (Bossa Nova) Bird/Eternally	25
67	Chess CRS 8066	O-O I Love You/There Is	15
68	Chess CRS 8071	Wear It On Our Face/Please Don't Change Me Now	20
68	Chess CRS 8079	Stay In My Corner/Love Is So Simple	8
68	President PT 223	It's Not Unusual/Stay In My Corner	15
68	Chess CRS 8084	Always Together/I Want My Momma	8
69	Chess CRS 8099	I Can Sing A Rainbow/Love Is Blue-Hallelujah Baby	6
69	Chess CRS 8102	Oh What A Night/Believe Me	7
69	President PT 270	Oh What A Night/Moving On	7
69	Chess CRS 8105	On The Dock Of The Bay/When I'm In Your Arms	7
71	Chess 6145 001	The Love We Had Stays On My Mind/Freedom Means	7
72	Chess 6145 008	It's All Up To You/Oh, My Dear	6
73	Chess 6145 022	Give Your Baby A Standing Ovation/Run For Cover	30
68	Chess CRLS 4554	GREATEST HITS (LP)	25
69	Chess CRLS 4555	LOVE IS BLUE/OH, WHAT A NIGHT (LP)	30
71	Joy JOYS 186	OH WHAT A NIGHT (LP)	15

ELAINE DELMAR

68	CBS 63511	Sneakin' Up On You	50
70	CBS 5329	Hurt So Bad/The Train	5
68	EMI SX6222	LA BELLE ELAINE (LP)	35
68	CBS 63511	SNEAKIN' UP ON YOU (LP)	35

DEL MONAS

80s	Big Beat WIK 35	DANGEROUS CHARMS (LP)	20
80s	Empire SYF 95	5 (LP)	25
88	Hangman HANG 20 UP	5 (LP, reissue)	12
89	Hangman HANG 28 UP	DEL MONAS (LP)	15

DANNY DELMONTE

63	Oriole CB 1894	John Kennedy/Come Summer	7
64	Oriole CB 1958	Worry/Till I'm Back With You Darlin' Again	6

DELMONTES

80s	Rational RATE 3	Don't Cry Your Tears/So It's Not To Be (yellow or blue p/s)	8

DELMONTS

72	Spiral DIT 2	Gimmie Gimmie Your Loving/Now Is The Time For Love	8

DELMORE BROTHERS

(see also Brown's Ferry Four, Grandpa Jones, Merle Travis)

58	Parlophone GEP 8728	COUNTRY AND WESTERN (EP)	20

AL DE LORY

65	London HLU 9999	Yesterday/Traffic Jam	25
70	Capitol CL 15644	Song From MASH/Feeling Of Love	8

MINT VALUE £

DELROY & SPORTY

71	Banana BA 322	Lovers Version/DUDLEY SIBLEY: Having A Party	15

DELROY & TENNORS

71	Camel CA 62	Donkey Shank/MURPHY'S ALL STARS: Donkey Track	10

DELTA CATS

(see also Thrillers)

69	Bamboo BAM 3	I Can't Re-Live (song actually "I Can't Believe")/I've Been Hurt	50

DELTA 5

79	Rough Trade RT 31	Mind Your Own Business/Now That You've Gone (p/s)	10
80	Rough Trade RT 41	Anticipation/You (p/s)	7
81	Rough Trade RT 61	Try/Colour (p/s)	7

DELTA KINGS

61	London RE-R 1318	AT SUNDOWN (EP)	10
61	London Jazz LTZ-R 15204	AT SUNDOWN (LP, mono)	15
61	London Jazz SAH-R 6118	AT SUNDOWN (LP, stereo)	18

DELTA RHYTHM BOYS

54	Brunswick 05353	Mood Indigo/Have A Hope, Have A Wish, Have A Prayer	12
52	Esquire 15-001	DELTA RHYTHM BOYS WITH THE METRONOME ALLSTARS (10" LP)	25

DELTAS

64	Blue Beat BB 265	Georgia/The Party	20
65	Blue Beat BB 275	The Visitor/SKATALITES: Hanging The Beam	50

DELTA SKIFFLE GROUP

58	Esquire EP 162	DELTA SKIFFLE GROUP (EP)	60

DELTONES (Jamaica)

71	Green Door GD 4010	Chopsticks/DES BRYAN: Belmont Street	8
72	Trojan TRM 9001	Chopsticks/I Got It/Put It On	6

DELTONES (U.K.)

70	Columbia DB 8719	Gimme Some Lovin'/Have A Little Talk With Myself	20

DEL-TONES (U.S.)

(see also Beau-Marks)

59	Top Rank JAR 171	Moonlight Party/Rockin' Blues	90
59	Top Rank JAR 171	Moonlight Party/Rockin' Blues (78)	35

DELTRON 3030

(see also Gorillaz, Blur, Damon Albarn)

00	Ark ARK 75	DELTRON 3030 (2-LP)	18

MILTON DE LUGG ORCHESTRA

(see also Beau-Marks)

65	Columbia DB 7474	The Addams Family Theme/The Alfred Hitchcock Theme	15
66	Columbia DB 7762	The Munsters Theme/The Addams Family Theme	15

DELUSION

80s	Wizzo WIZZO 2	Pessimists Paradise/Desert Island (gatefold p/s)	8

LEO DE LYON

54	MGM SP 1087	The Band Played On/Say It Isn't So	7
60	Oriole CB 1561	Rich In Love/The Blue Train	7
60	Oriole MG 20053	LEO DE LYON (LP)	18

ARIN DEMAIN

90s	Goldmine/Soul Supply GS 028	Silent Treatment/PARIS: Sleepless Nights	8

RALPH DE MARCO

59	London HLL 9010	Old Shep/More Than Riches	10
59	London HLL 9010	Old Shep/More Than Riches (78)	25

ERIC DE MARSAN

68	Philips BF 1728	L'Oiseau (The Bird) (Vocal)/L'Oiseau (The Bird) (Instrumental)	5

DEMENSIONS

(see also Wheels, James Brothers, Fox)

60	Top Rank JAR 505	Over The Rainbow/Nursery Rhyme Rock	90
61	Coral Q 72437	Count Your Blessings Instead Of Sheep/Again	30

DEMENTED ARE GO

86	ID NOSE 9	IN SICKNESS AND IN HEALTH (LP)	20
88	ID NOSE 21	KICKED OUT OF HELL (LP)	20
90	Link LRM 05	GO GO DEMENTED (LP, blue vinyl)	15
91	Fury F 3016	ORGASMIC NIGHTMARE (LP, blue vinyl)	15
93	Fury DAGLP 1	TANGENTAL MADNESS ON A PLEASANT SIDE OF HELL (LP, white vinyl)	15
89	Link MLP 084	THE DAY THE EARTH SPAT BLOOD (LP, as the Demon Teds)	15

(ROD) DEMICK & (HERBIE) ARMSTRONG

70	Decca F 13056	We're On The Right Track/Dreaming (as Demick-Armstrong)	6
71	Mam MAM 10	If I Ever Get To You/Girl	5
71	Mam MAM-AS 1001	LITTLE WILLY RAMBLE (LP, black/silver labels)	25
72	A&M AMLH 68908	LOOKIN' THROUGH (LP, inner sleeve, brown label)	50

DEMOB

81	Round Ear ROUND 1	Anti Police/Teenage Adolescence (foldout p/s)	15
81	Round Ear ROUND 1	Anti Police/Teenage Adolescence (later standard p/s)	10
81	Round Ear EAR 3	No Room For You/Think Straight/New Breed (p/s)	15

DEMOLITION

81	Demolition Rock ZEL SPS 296	Hooker Hater/Axeman (p/s)	200

MINT VALUE £

DEMON

81	Clay CLAY 4	Liar/Wild Woman (p/s, red vinyl)	8
82	Carrere CAR 226	One Helluva Night/Into The Nightmare (picture disc)	6
83	Clay CLAY 25	The Plague/The Only Sane Man (p/s)	6
84	Clay CLAY 41	Wonderland/Blackheath (p/s)	6
84	Clay 12CLAY 41	Wonderland/Blackheath/Nowhere To Run (12", p/s)	8
88	Clay CLAY 48D	Tonight (The Hero Is Back)/Hurricane/Night Of The Demon/ Don't Break The Circle (double pack)	5
83	Clay CLAYLP 6	THE PLAGUE (LP, gatefold sleeve, with insert)	15
83	Clay CLAYLP 6P	THE PLAGUE (LP, picture disc)	20
84	Clay CLAYLP 15	BRITISH STANDARD APPROVED (LP)	12
90	Sonic SONICLP 1	NIGHT OF THE DEMON (LP)	15
90	Flametrader LP 1	ONE HELLUVA NIGHT (2-LP)	18

DEMON BOYZ

88	Music Of Life NOTE 013	Northside/Rougher Than An Animal	20
88	Music Of Life NOTE 022	Vibez (12")	12
89	Music Of Life NOTE 26	Recognition/Lyrical Culture (12")	15
90	Mango 12 MNS 738	International Karate (12")	10
92	Tribal Bass Tribe 4	DETT (12")	20
92	Tribal Bass Tribe 9	Glimity Glamity/Junglist (12")	20
89	Music Of Life DEMON 1	RECOGNITION (LP)	18
92	Tribal Bass Tribe 11	ORIGINAL GUIDANCE - THE SECOND CHAPTER (LP)	60

DEMON D

95	Voyager VOD 94	Let The Jazz Take You/Together (12")	8

DEMON FUZZ

70	Dawn DNX 2504	I Put A Spell On You/Message To Mankind/Fuzz Oriental Blues (p/s)	25
70	Dawn DNX 2504	I Put A Spell On You/Message To Mankind/Fuzz Oriental Blues	10
70	Dawn DNLS 3013	AFREAKA! (LP, gatefold sleeve, orange label)	130

DEMON PACT

81	Slime PACT 1	Eaten Alive/Raiders (p/s)	50
81	Slime PACT 2	Escape/Demon Pact (unreleased, labels only)	0

DEMON PREACHER

(see also Demons, Alien Sex Fiend, Fenzyx)

78	Illegal SRTS/CUS/78110	Royal Northern (N7)/Laughing At Me/ Steal Your Love/Dead End Kidz (numbered p/s)	80
78	Small Wonder SMALL TEN	Little Miss Perfect/Perfect Dub (p/s)	10

DEMON ROCKA

82	Unity UN 001	Iron Lady/Stick Together	12

DEMONS (Jamaica)

69	Big Shot BI 523	You Belong To My Heart/Bless You	10

DEMONS (U.K.)

(see also Alien Sex Fiend, Demon Preacher)

80	Crypt Music DEM 1	Action By Example/I Wish I Was A Dog (p/s)	12

DEMONSTRATORS

64	Warner Bros WB 132	Sweet Violets/Ultra Violet	12

JASON DENE

(see also Jason Deane)

66	Parlophone R 5485	Opportunity/It's Me	8

TERRY DENE

57	Decca F 10895	A White Sport Coat/The Man In The Phone Booth	30
57	Decca F 10914	Start Movin'/Green Corn	20
57	Decca F 10938	Come And Get It/Teenage Dream	20
57	Decca F 10964	Lucky Lucky Bobby/Baby, She's Gone	20
58	Decca F 10977	The Golden Age/C'Min And Be Loved	15
58	Decca F 11016	Stairway Of Love/Lover, Lover!	8
58	Decca F 11037	Seven Steps To Love/Can I Walk You Home	15
58	Decca F 11076	Who Baby Who/Pretty Little Pearly	15
59	Decca F 11100	I've Got A Good Thing Going/Bimbombey	12
59	Decca F 11136	There's No Fool Like A Young Fool/I've Come Of Age	12
59	Decca F 11154	Thank You Pretty Baby/A Boy Without A Girl	15
59	Decca F 11154	Thank You Pretty Baby/A Boy Without A Girl (78)	12
60	Oriole CB 1562	Geraldine/Love Me Or Leave Me	20
61	Oriole CB 1594	Like A Baby/Next Stop Paradise	15
63	Aral PS 107	The Feminine Look/Fever (all in p/s)	15
82	Logo GO 412	Paralysed/Lorna (The Girl In The Long Black Dress)	10
88	Charm C 45001	Jingle Bear Rock/Peace In The Valley	8
57	Decca DFE 6427	THE GOLDEN DISC (EP)	30
58	Decca DFE 6459	TERRY DENE NO. 1 (EP)	40
66	Herald ELR 107	TERRY DENE NOW (EP)	20
74	Decca SPA 368	I THOUGHT TERRY DENE WAS DEAD (LP)	15

DENE BOYS

57	HMV POP 374	Bye Bye Love/Love Is The Thing	20
58	HMV POP 455	Skylark/I Walk Down The Street	8

DENE FOUR

(see also Dene Boys)

59	HMV POP 666	Hush-a-bye/Something New	25

DENIGH

80	Ace ACE 16	No Way/Running (no p/s)	80

MINT VALUE £

DENIM
(see also Felt, Go-Kart Mozarts)

92	Boys Own BOIX 12	Middle Of The Road/Ape Hangers/Robin's Nest/ The Great Grape Ape Hangers (12")	12
96	Echo EC 517	It Fell Off The Back Of A Lorry/Snake Bite/Internet Curtains	5
97	DISC009	Summer Smash/Sun's Out (p/s)	5
92	Boys Own 82849	BACK IN DENIM (LP)	30
96	Echo ECH LP8	DENIM ON ICE (LP)	20
97	EMI ADISC 001	NOVELTY ROCK (LP)	15

DENIMS

65	CBS 201807	I'm Your Man/Ya Ya	75

ROGER DENISON

66	Parlophone R 5545	I'm On An Island/I'm Running Out Of Time	12
67	Parlophone R 5566	It Just Doesn't Seem To Be My Day/She Wanders Through My Mind	50

DENIZENS

79	Big SOLD 5	People Of The Night/Ammonia Subway (p/s)	10
80	Citizen	IN THE CROWD EP (with 16-page booklet)	12

CLAUDE DENJEAN

71	Decca PFS 4212	MOOG! (LP)	15

SUE DENNING

65	Columbia DB 7486	Kiss Me Once Again/Goodtime Johnny	20

WADE DENNING & PORT WASHINGTONS

67	MGM MGM 1339	Tarzan's March/Batman	15

D.D. (Denzil) DENNIS
(see also Denzil Dennis)

70	Crab CRAB 53	Rain Is Gonna Fall/This Game Ain't Free	15
70	Crab CRAB 60	Having A Party/Man With Ambition	10
70	Pama Supreme PS 301	My Way/Happy Days	10
71	Punch PH 93	Christmas Message/Cool It Girl	10
71	Pama Supreme PS 330	I'm A Believer/I'll Make The Way Easy	10
74	Pama Supreme PS 391	Women And Money/UPSETTERS: Ten Cent Skank	12

D D DENNIS - BROTHER LLOYD'S ALL STARS

68	Mercury MF 1064	Save The Last Dance For Me/Will You Still Love Me Tomorrow	20

DENZIL DENNIS
(see also D.D. Dennis, Cosmo & Dennis, Denzil & Pat, Denzil & Jennifer, Les & Silkie)

63	Blue Beat BB 181	Seven Nights In Rome/Love Is For Fools (as DENZIL)	15
68	Trojan TR 614	Donkey Train/Down By The Riverside	12
68	Trojan TR 615	Me Nah Worry/Hush Don't You Cry	12
68	Jolly JY 011	Oh Carol/Where Has My Little Girl Gone	8
70	Mary Lyn ML 100	I Guess I'd Better Start Believing/When Will You Ever Learn	12
70	Pama Supreme PS 304	Painful Situation/Nothing Has Changed	5
71	Pama Supreme PS 350	South Of The Border/GRAHAM: Long Island	10
72	Pama Supreme PS 375	Mama We're All Crazy Now/ROY SHIRLEY: A Lady's A Man's Best Friend	7
72	Duke DU 142	I Forgot To Be Your Lover/I've Got To Settle Down	5
73	Grape GR 3059	People Got To Be Friends/Ups And Downs (actually by Pat Rhoden)	5
74	Arrow AR 003	If/How Can I Touch You	8

JACKIE DENNIS

58	Decca F 10992	La Dee Dah/You're The Greatest	5
58	Decca F 11011	Miss Valerie/My Dream	5
58	Decca F 11033	The Purple People Eater/You-Oo	5
58	Decca F 11060	More Than Ever (Come Prima)/Linton Addie	5
58	Decca F 11090	Gingerbread/Lucky Ladybug	5
59	Top Rank JAR 129	Summer Snow/Night Bird	5
58	Decca DFE 6513	JACKIE DENNIS NO. 1 (EP)	40

DENNIS & LIZZY
(see also Dennis Alcapone, Lizzy & Dennis)

70	Camel CA 56	Everybody Bawlin'/Mr Brown	10
73	Pyramid PYR 7002	Ba-Ba-Ri-Ba-Shank/TOMMY McCOOK ALL STARS: Buck And The Preacher	12

DENNISONS

63	Decca F 11691	(Come On) Be My Girl/Little Latin Lupe Lu	20
64	Decca F 11880	Walkin' The Dog/You Don't Know What Love Is	25
64	Decca F 11990	Nobody Like My Babe/Lucy (You Sure Did It This Time)	30

MARTIN DENNY (& HIS ORCHESTRA)

60	London REU 1241	THE EXOTIC SOUNDS OF MARTIN DENNY (EP)	15
58	London HB-U 1079	EXOTICA (10" LP, mono only)	20
58	London SAH-U 6004	FORBIDDEN ISLAND (LP, stereo only)	20
59	London HA-U 2196	AFRO-DESIA (LP, also stereo SAH-U 6048)	20
60	London HA-U 2208	QUIET VILLAGE (LP, also stereo SAH-U 6055)	20
60	London SAH-W 6062	EXOTICA (12" LP, stereo reissue with extra tracks "Busy Port" & "Waipio")	15
60	London HA-G 2253	EXOTICA - VOL. 2 (LP, also stereo SAH-G 6076)	15
60	London HA-W 2239	EXOTICA - VOL. 3 (LP, also stereo SAH-W 6069)	15
60	London HA-G 2281	THE ENCHANTED SEA (LP, also stereo SAH-G 6098)	15

SANDY DENNY
(see also Fairport Convention, Bunch, Strawbs, Fotheringay, Alex Campbell, Trevor Lucas, Richard Thompson)

72	Island WIP 6141	Here In Silence/Man Of Iron (theme from Pass Of Arms film, in p/s)	25
72	Island WIP 6141	Here In Silence/Man Of Iron (theme from Pass Of Arms film)	40
72	Island WIP 6142	Listen Listen/Tomorrow Is A Long Time	6
73	Island WIP 6176	Whispering Grass/Friends (p/s)	6
73	Island WIP 6176	Whispering Grass/Friends	10

			MINT VALUE £
74	Island WIP 6195	Like An Old Fashioned Waltz (unissued)	0
76	Mooncrest MOON 54	Make Me A Pallet On Your Floor/This Train	6
77	Island WIP 6391	Candle In The Wind/Still Waters Run Deep (unissued, promo only)	30
67	Saga EROS 8041	SANDY AND JOHNNY (LP, with Johnny Silvo, black/silver label)	40
70	Saga EROS 8153	SANDY DENNY (LP)	30
71	Island ILPS 9165	THE NORTH STAR GRASSMAN AND THE RAVENS (LP, gatefold sleeve, 'pink rim palm tree' label)	40
72	Island ILPS 9207	SANDY (LP, gatefold sleeve, original pressing with 'pink rim palm tree' label)	40
72	Island ILPS 9207	SANDY (LP, gatefold sleeve)	12
73	Island ILPS 9258	LIKE AN OLD FASHIONED WALTZ (LP, gatefold sleeve, 'pink rim palm tree' label)	40
73	Hallmark SHM 813	ALL OUR OWN WORK (LP, with Strawbs)	15
77	Island ILPS 9433	RENDEZVOUS (LP, with lyric inner sleeve)	25
78	Mooncrest CREST 28	THE ORIGINAL SANDY DENNY (LP)	25
97	Strange Fruit SFRSCD 006	THE BBC SESSIONS 1971-73 (CD, limited edition, withdrawn - beware of bootlegs)	30
85	Island SDSP 100	WHO KNOWS WHERE THE TIME GOES (4-LP, box set with booklet)	50

SUSAN DENNY

65	Melodisc MEL 1596	Don't Touch Me/Johnny	35

DENNY & WILSON

72	Hillcrest HCT 6	Hey Hey Girl/CARLTON ALPHONSO: Girl I Love You	6

DENTISTS

85	Spruck SP 003	Strawberries Are Growing In My Garden (And It's Wintertime)/ Burning The Thoughts From My Skin/Doreen (p/s)	12
85	Spruck SP 004	YOU AND YOUR BLOODY ORANGES (12" EP, p/s)	10
86	Tambourine SP 006	DOWN AND OUT IN PARIS AND CHATHAM (12" EP, brown/white or group p/s)	10
87	Tambourine URINE 3	Writhing On The Shagpile/Just Like Oliver Reed/A Strange Way To Go About Things/Calm You Down/The Turquoise Castle (12", p/s)	10
85	Spruck SPR 001	SOME PEOPLE ARE ON THE PITCH THEY THINK IT'S ALL OVER IT IS NOW (LP)	15

MICKEY DENTON

61	London HLX 9398	The Steady Kind/Now You Can't Give Them Away	12

KARL DENVER

64	Decca F 11903	Love Me With All Your Heart/Am I That Easy To Forget	7
65	Mercury MF 878	Cry A Little Sometimes/Today Will Be Yesterday Tomorrow	7
65	Mercury MF 904	Marta/I'll Never Forget To Remember	7
65	Mercury MF 926	The Tips Of My Fingers/I'm Alone Because I Love You	7
68	Page One POF 063	You've Still Got A Place In My Heart/I Still Miss Someone (as Karl Denver Trio)	8
74	Emerald MD 1181	Sonny Boy/Careless Love	6

NIGEL DENVER

64	Decca DFE 8580	FOLK SINGER (EP)	20
66	Decca LK 4728	MOVIN' ON (LP, featuring Martin Carthy)	50
67	Decca LK 4844	REBELLION (LP)	25
67	Major Minor MMLP 1	SCOTTISH REPUBLICAN SONGS (LP)	25
68	Decca SKL 4943	FOLK OLD AND NEW (LP)	25

DENZIL & JENNIFER

70	Escort ES 824	Young, Gifted And Black/OWEN GRAY: I Am Satisfied	7

DENZIL (Dennis) & PAT (Rhoden)

69	Downtown DT 403	Dream/Sincerely	12

DEODATO

72	CTI CTS4000	Also Sprach Zarathustra (2001)/Spirit Of Summer	5

WILBUR DE PARIS' NEW ORLEANS BAND

59	London HLE 8816	Petite Fleur/Over And Over Again	7

LYNSEY DE PAUL

73	MAM SS 504	SURPRISE (LP)	15
73	MAM MAME 3002	LYNSEY SINGS (LP)	15
74	Jet LP 07	TASTE ME - DON'T WASTE ME (LP, with insert)	15
75	Jet LP 14	LOVE BOMB (LP, with insert)	15

DEPECHE MODE

SINGLES

81	Lyntone LYN 10209	Sometimes I Wish I Was Dead/FAD GADGET: King Of The Flies (red flexidisc free with Flexipop magazine, issue 11)	25
81	Lyntone LYN 10209	Sometimes I Wish I Was Dead/FAD GADGET: I Wish I Was Dead (red vinyl flexidisc without Flexipop magazine, issue 11)	5
81	Lyntone LYN 10209	Sometimes I Wish I Was Dead/FAD GADGET: King Of The Flies (test pressing)	150
81	Mute MUTE 013	Dreaming Of Me/Ice Machine (p/s)	5
83	Mute L12BONG 2	Get The Balance Right/My Secret Garden (live)/See You (live)/ Satellite (live) (12", numbered p/s)	8
83	Mute L12BONG 3	Everything Counts/Boys Say Go (live)/New Life (live)/Nothing To Fear (live)/ The Meaning Of Love (live) (12", numbered p/s)	8
83	Mute L12BONG 4	Love In Itself (2)/Just Can't Get Enough (live)/Photograph Of You (live)/ Shout (live)/Photographic (live) (12", numbered p/s)	8
85	Mute D12BONG 9	It's Called A Heart (Mixes)/Fly On The Windscreen (Mixes) (12", p/s, dbl-pack)	8
87	Mute L12BONG 14	Never Let Me Down Again (Tsangarides Mix)/Pleasure Little Treasure (Join Mix)/To Have And To Hold (Spanish Taster) (12", p/s)	8
87	Mute CDBONG 14	Never Let Me Down Again (Split Mix)/Pleasure Little Treasure (Join Mix)/ To Have And To Hold (Spanish Taster)/Never Let Me Down Again (Aggro Mix) (CD in pouch)	8
87	Mute P12 BONG 14	Never Let Me Down Again (7? Mix)/Pleasure Little Treasure (7" Mix)/Never Let Me Down Again (12" Split Mix) (12")	50
89	Mute 10BONG 16	Everything Counts (Absolute Mix)/(1983 12" Mix)/Nothing (US 7" Mix)	

Year	Label / Cat. No.	Title	MINT VALUE £
		(10", envelope p/s, with 2 postcards & window sticker)	10
89	Mute LCDBONG 16	Everything Counts (Tim Simenon & M. Saunders Remix)/Nothing (Justin Strauss Remix)/Strangelove (Tim Simenon & M. Saunders Remix) (3" CD 'filofax' page- p/s)	15
89	Mute L12BONG 17	Personal Jesus (Mixes)/Dangerous (Hazchemix) (12", p/s)	15
89	Mute LCDBONG 17	Personal Jesus (Pump Mix)/Personal Jesus (Telephone Stomp Mix)/ Dangerous (Hazchemix) (3" CD)	15
90	Mute XL12BONG 18	Enjoy The Silence (The Quad: Final Mix) (12", 1-side etched, p/s)	8
90	Mute L12BONG 20	World In My Eyes (Dub In My Eyes)/(Mode To Joy)/Happiest Girl (The Pulsating Orbital Mix) (12", p/s with inner, in sealed blue PVC pack)	8
90	Mute LCDBONG 20	World In My Eyes (Dub In My Eyes)/World In My Eyes (Mode To Joy)/ Happiest Girl (The Pulsating Orbital Vocal Mix)/Sea Of Sin (Sensoria)/ World In My Eyes (Mayhem Mode)/Happiest Girl (Jack Mix) CD	15
91	Mute DMBX 1	1 (6-CD single box set, with booklet)	15
91	Mute DMBX 2	2 (6-CD single box set, with booklet)	15
91	Mute DMBX 3	3 (6-CD single box set, with booklet)	15
02	Mute MUTE 12BONG 33	Goodnight Lovers (ISAN Falling Leaf Mix)/When The Body Speaks (Acoustic Version)/The Dead Of Night (Electronicat Remix) (12", red vinyl, p/s)	8
LPs			
87	Mute STUMM 47	MUSIC FOR THE MASSES (LP, clear vinyl)	50
87	Mute STUMM 47	MUSIC FOR THE MASSES (LP, with bonus 12" "Strangelove (Maximix)"/ "Never Let Me Down Again (Split Mix)" [HMV1])	40
89	Mute STUMM 101	101 (2-LP, stickered gatefold sleeve, inner sleeves and booklet)	18
97	Mute STUMM 148	ULTRA (LP, inner sleeve with transfer)	15
98	Mute MUTEL 5	SINGLES 86-98 (3-LP box set, numbered, with booklet)	20
98	Mute MUTEL 5	THE SINGLES 86-98 (3-LP, box set with booklet)	25
98	Mute MUTEL 5	THE SINGLES 86-98 (3-LP, box set with booklet)	25
98	Mute P12MUTEL5	REMIXES 86-98 (3-LP)	40
04	Mute MUTEL 8	MUTE REMIXES 81-04 (6 x LP box set, numbered)	45
09	Mute STUMM 300	SOUNDS OF THE UNIVERSE (2-LP)	20
09	Mute BXSTUMM300	SOUNDS OF THE UNIVERSE (4-CD/DVD set)	40
PROMOS			
86	Mute RR BONG 10	Breathing In Fumes/Stripped (Highland Mix) (12", white labels, some stamped)	80
86	Mute 7BONG 12	A Question Of Time (Edited)/Black Celebration (Live) (white label)	40
86	Mute L12 BONG 12	A Question Of Time (New Town Mix)/A Question Of Time (Live)/ Black Celebration (Black Tulip Mix)/More Than A Party (Live) (12", printed labels with stamped number, plain black die-cut sleeve)	30
87	Mute R BONG 13	Strangelove (Radio Edit)/Strangelove (p/s)	80
87	Mute DANCE BONG 13	Strangelove (Blind Mix)/(Fresh Ground Mix) (12", promo-only remix some on blue vinyl)	80
87	Mute CLUB BONG 13	Strangelove (12 Inch Maxi Mix)/Strangelove (Pain Mix) (12", promo)	80
87	Mute BONG 14R	Never Let Me Down Again/Pleasure Little Treasure	40
87	Mute 12BONG 14	Never Let Me Down Again (Split Mix)/Pleasure Little Treasure (Glitter Mix)/ Never Let Me Down Again (Aggro Mix) (12")	40
87	Mute DJBONG 15	Behind The Wheel (DJ Remix)/Behind The Wheel (LP Mix)	120
87	Mute D BONG 15	Behind The Wheel (Shep Mix)/Behind The Wheel (LP Mix)/Route 66 (7" Mix) (12")	30
89	Mute PP12BONG 16	Strangelove (Hijack Mix)/Nothing (12")	18
89	Mute BONG 16R	Everything Counts (Live - Radio Edit)/Nothing (Live Mix) (stickered p/s)	20
89	Mute P12 BONG 16	Everything Counts (Tim Simenon/Mark Saunders Remix)/(Alan Moulder Remix) (12", black die-cut sleeve)	15
89	Mute P12 BONG 17	Personal Jesus (Pump Mix)/Dangerous (Hazchemix) (12", black die-cut sleeve)	15
89	Mute BONG 17	Personal Jesus/Dangerous (censored black rear p/s)	40
90	Mute BONG 18	Enjoy The Silence/Memphisto ('A' label)	25
90	Mute RCDBONG 18	Enjoy The Silence (7")/Memphisto (7") (CD)	20
90	Mute P12 BONG 18	Enjoy The Silence (Bass Line)/(Ricki Tik Tik Mix)/(7" mix) (12", die-cut Mute sleeve)	20
90	Mute R7 BONG 19	Policy Of Truth (Radio Edit)/Kaleid (p/s)	20
90	Mute BONG 19R	Policy Of Truth (7" Version)/Kaleid (Remix) (CD)	20
90	Mute P12 BONG 19	Policy Of Truth (Capitol Mix)/(Pavlov's Dub)/(Trancentral)/Kaleid (Remix) (12", die-cut Mute sleeve)	15
90	Mute 12BONG 20	World In My Eyes (Oil Tank Mix)/Happiest Girl (Kiss-A-Mix)/Sea Of Sin (Sensoria) (12", white label, numbered, stickered sleeve)	30
90	Mute BONG 20R	World In My Eyes (7" Version)/Happiest Girl (Jack Mix)/Sea Of Sin (Tonal Mix) (p/s, 33rpm)	20
90	Mute P12 BONG 20	World In My Eyes (Mayhem Mode Mix)/Happiest Girl (The Pulsating Orbital Mix) (12", die-cut Mute sleeve)	20
93	Mute P12 BONG 21	I Feel You (Throb Mix)/(Seven Inch Mix)/(Babylon Mix)/One Caress (12", die-cut Mute sleeve)	20
93	Mute BONG 22	Walking In My Shoes/My Joy (large centre hole)	30
93	Mute P12 BONG 22	Walking In My Shoes (Grungy Gonads Mix)/(Seven Inch Mix)/My Joy (Seven Inch Mix)/(Slow Slide Mix) (12", die-cut Mute sleeve)	20
93	Mute BONG 23	Condemnation (Paris Mix)/Death's Door (Jazz Mix) (large centre hole)	30
93	Mute PL12 BONG 23	Rush (Spiritual Guidance Mix)/Rush (Amylnitrate Mix)/Rush (Wild Planet Vocal Mix) (12")	40
93	Mute P 12 BONG 23	Condemnation (Paris Mix)/Death's Door (Jazz Mix)/Rush (Spiritual Guidance Mix) (12". die-cut Mute sleeve)	30
94	Mute P12 BONG 24	In Your Room (The Jeep Rock Mix)/Higher Love (Adrenaline Mix)/ In Your Room (Extended Zephyr Mix) (12", die-cut Mute sleeve)	25
97	Mute PL 12 BONG 25	Barrel Of A Gun (One Inch Punch Mix [Version 2])/Painkiller (Original Mix)/ Barrel Of A Gun (3 Phase Mix)/Barrel Of A Gun (Original Mix) (12", p/s)	8
97	Mute BONG 26	It's No Good (Club 69 Future Mix)/It's No Good (Club 69 Future Dub)/ It's No Good (Club 69 Funk Dub) (12")	35
97	Mute PL12BONG 26	It's No Good (Club 69 mixes) (12")	40
97	Mute P12BONG26	It's No Good (Hardfloor Mix)/(Speedy J mix)/(Motor Bass Mix) / (Andrea Parker Mix)/(Dom T Mix) (12")	8

			MINT VALUE £
97	Mute XLCD BONG 26	It's No Good (Live) (CD)	70
97	Mute P12 BONG 27	Home (Jedi Knights Remix [Drowning In Time])/(Air 'Around The Golf? Remix)/(Meant To Be)/(Grantby Mix) (12", 33rpm, die-cut p/s)	12
97	Mute P12 BONG 28	Useless (CJ Bolland Funky Sub Mix)/Useless (the Kruder & Dorfmeister Session) (12", die-cut p/s)	20
98	Mute P12 BONG 29	Only When I Lose Myself (Dan The Automator Mix)/Only When I Lose Myself (Subsonic Legacy Mix)/Painkiller (Kill The Pain - DJ Shadow Vs Depeche Mode) /Headstar (12", die-cut p/s)	8
01	Mute PL12 BONG 30	Dream On (Dave Clarke Club Mix)/Dream On (Bushwacka Blunt Mix) (12", p/s)	8
01	Mute PL12 BONG 30	Dream On (Octagon Man Mix)/(Octagon Man Dub)/(Dave Clarke Acoustic Mix)/(Kid 606 Mix) 12" p/s)	12
01	Mute PXL 12 BONG 31	I Feel Loved (Umek Mix)/(Thomas Brinkman Remix)/(Chamber's Remix) (12", p/s)	10
01	Mute PL12 BONG 32	Freelove (Deep Dish Freedom Mix)/Freelove (Josh Wink Vocal Interpretation)/Freelove (Deep Dish Freedom Dub)/Freelove (Power Productions Remix) (12", doublepack, p/s)	10
87	Mute (no cat. no.)	THE B-SIDES (4-LP test pressings in title box)	800
87	Mute (no cat. no.)	THE B-SIDES (4-cassette set)	200
90	Mute (no cat. no.)	VIOLATOR (LP, CD & cassette in 12" x 12" picture box with insert)	100
90	Mute PSTUMM 64	VIOLATOR (12" EP, 4-track sampler)	30
93	Mute VERBONG 1	SONGS OF FAITH & DEVOTION (interview CD)	50
93	Mute (no cat. no.)	SONGS OF FAITH & DEVOTION (4-CD box set)	300
94	Mute DEPRO 1	DEPRO 1 (13-track compilation CD)	50
97	Mute BXSTUMM 148	ULTRA (box set, with CD, T-shirt, stickers & EPK video, soap box pack)	80
98	Mute (no cat. no.)	THE SINGLES 86>98 (15" x 6" box set, with 3 CDs, video tape & cards)	120
01	Mute IPKSTUMM 190	EXCITER (interview CD with bonus multimedia disc)	30
01	Mute BCDSTUMM 190	EXCITER (interview CD with bonus multimedia disc, in long box)	60
04	Mute P12BONG 34	REMIXES 81 - 04 SAMPLER : Enjoy The Silence (Richard X Extended Mix)/(Ewan Pearson Extended Instrumental)/Timo Maas Extended Remix)/ Ewan Pearson Extended Remix) (2 x 12")	20
04	Mute ACD MUTEL8	REMIXES 81 - 04 (3 x CD, insert & press release)	30
06	Mute DMINT06CD	THE BEST OF VOLUME 1 - Interview Disc CD (p/s)	25
06	Mute PLCDBONG39	REMIXES - THE BEST OF VOLUME 1 CD (p/s)	20

DEPRAVED

86	Children Of Rev. GURT 6	COME ON DOWN (LP, with lyric inner)	12

DEPRESSIONS

77	Barn 2014 112	Living On Dreams/Family Planning (p/s)	10
78	Barn 2014 119	Messing With Your Heart/Street Kid (p/s)	10
78	Barn 2014 122	Get Out Of This Town/Basement Daze (p/s)	10
78	Barn 2314 105	THE DEPRESSIONS (LP)	25

DEPTH CHARGE

89	Vinyl Solution STORM 13	Bounty Killers (12")	5

DEPUTIES

66	Strike JH 305	Given Half A Chance/Where Do People Go	12

DEPUTY DAWG

(see also Luke Slater)

96	Peacefrog P F053	GUN SLINGER EP (12", plain sleeve)	10

DEREK

(see also Johnny Cymbal)

68	London HLZ 10230	Cinnamon/This Is My Story	10

DEREK B

87	Music Of Life NOTE 3	Rock The Beat (12")	8

DEREK & THE DOMINOES

(see also Eric Clapton, Bobby Whitlock)

70	Polydor 2058 057	Tell The Truth/Roll It Over (withdrawn)	80
71	Polydor 2058 130	Layla/Bell Bottom Blues (original, red paper label)	5
74	RSO 2090 104	Why Does Love Got To Be Sad?/Presence Of The Lord	5
82	RSO RSO 87	Layla/ERIC CLAPTON: Wonderful Tonight (p/s)	5
82	RSO RSOX 87	Layla/ERIC CLAPTON: Wonderful Tonight (live) (12", p/s)	8
71	Polydor 2625 005	LAYLA AND OTHER ASSORTED LOVE SONGS (2-LP, gatefold sleeve)	20
73	RSO 2659 020	IN CONCERT (2-LP, gatefold sleeve)	15

DEREK & FRESHMEN

(see also Derek Dean & Freshmen)

65	Oriole CB 305	Gone Away/I Stand Alone	15

FRANK DE ROSA & HIS ORCHESTRA

58	London HLD 8576	Big Guitar/Irish Rock	20

DERRICK (Morgan) & JENNIFER

(see also Derrick Morgan)

70	Crab CRAB 47	Need To Belong/Let's Have Some Fun	10
70	Crab CRAB 54	Rocking Good Way/Wipe These Tears	5

DERRICK (Morgan) & LLOYDS (Clarke)

(see also Derrick Morgan, Lloyd Clarke)

62	Blue Beat BB 135	Love And Leave Me (actually by Lloyd Clarke)/Merry Twist (actually "Whistle Stop Tour" by Roy Richards)	15

DERRICK (Morgan) & NAOMI (Campbell)

(see also Derrick Morgan, Naomi, Don Drummond)

65	Island WI 193	Two Of A Kind/I Want A Lover (credited to Derrick Morgan)	25
65	Ska Beat JB 185	Heart Of Stone/DERRICK MORGAN: Let Me Go	18
65	Ska Beat JB 188	I Wish I Were An Apple/DERRICK MORGAN: Around The Corner	18

DERRICK (Morgan) & PATSY (Todd)

(see also Derrick Morgan, Patsy Todd)

61	Blue Beat BB 57	Feel So Fine/ROLAND ALPHONSO & GROUP: Mean To Me	18

			MINT VALUE £
61	Blue Beat BB 65	Baby Please Don't Leave Me/Let The Good Times Roll	20
62	Blue Beat BB 97	Love Not To Brag/DRUMBAGO'S ALL STARS: Duck Soup	15
62	Blue Beat BB 100	In My Heart (actually by Derrick Morgan)/BELL'S GROUP: Kingston 13	15
62	Blue Beat BB 106	Oh Shirley/BASIL GABIDON'S GROUP: Sam The Fisherman (B-side actually by Roland Alphonso)	18
62	Blue Beat BB 121	Crying In The Chapel/Come Back My Love	15
62	Blue Beat BB 123	Oh My Love/Let's Go To The Party	15
62	Island WI 018	Housewife's Choice/Gypsy Woman	18
63	Blue Beat BB 152	Little Brown Jug/Mow Sen Wa (with Lloyd Clarke)	15
63	Blue Beat BB 160	Trying To Make You Mine (actually "Baby Please Don't Leave Me" by Derrick Morgan)/Hold Me	15
63	Island WI 055	Sea Wave/Look Before You Leap	20
64	Blue Beat BB 207	Lover Boy/The Moon	15
64	Blue Beat BB 224	Steal Away/Money	15
64	Blue Beat BB 247	Troubles/Right (B-side actually "Baby Face")	15
65	Blue Beat BB 291	You I Love/Let Me Hold Your hand (song actually "Steal Away")	15
65	Blue Beat BB 318	Eternity/Want My Baby	15
65	Island WI 224	The National Dance/DESMOND DEKKER & FOUR ACES: Mount Zion	25
66	Island WI 288	I Found A Queen/It's True My Darling	18
68	Nu Beat NB 008	Hey Boy, Hey Girl/Music Is The Food Of Life	12

DERRICK (Morgan) & PAULETT

(see also Derrick Morgan, Paulette)

69	Nu Beat NB 027	I'll Do It/Give You My Love	12

DERRICK (Morgan) & PAULINE (Morgan)

(see also Derrick Morgan, Patsy Todd, Basil Gabbidon)

68	Pyramid PYR 6027	You Never Miss Your Water/DERRICK MORGAN: Got You On My Mind	12
68	Pyramid/J.J. PYR 6063	Don't Say/DERRICK MORGAN: Johnny Pram Pram	15

DERRICK & SOUNDS

68	Pye 7N 17601	Power Of Love/I'll Take You Home	5
69	Pye 7N 17709	My Sly Sadie/I Can't Lose That Girl	5
69	Pye 7N 17801	Morning Papers And Margarine/Winter Of Your Love	12

DERRINGERS

61	Capitol CL 15189	(If You Cry) True Love, True Love/Sheree	20

GLEN DERRY ORCHESTRA

61	Oriole CB 1609	Blue Sax/Beatnik	10

DES (Bryan) ALLSTARS

70	Grape GR 3014	Night Food Reggae/Walk With Des	20
70	Grape GR 3015	If I Had A Hammer/Hammer Reggae	20
70	Grape GR 3016	Henry The Great/Black Scorcher	25

DES & DAVE

66	Columbia DB 7957	That's Us/Gotta Little Gal	10

HENRI DES

70	United Artists UP 35109	Return/Retour	18

SUGAR PIE DE SANTO

(see also Etta James & Sugar Pie De Santo)

64	Pye International 7N 25249	Soulful Dress/Use What You Got	25
64	Pye International 7N 25267	I Don't Wanna Fuss/I Love You So Much	30
66	Chess CRS 8034	There's Gonna Be Trouble/In The Basement (B-side with Etta James)	30
69	Chess CRS 8093	Soulful Dress/There's Gonna Be Trouble	20

MICHAEL DES BARRES

(see also Silverhead, Detective, Phoenix)

74	Purple PUR 123	Leon/New Moon Tonight	8

DESCENDANTS

67	CBS 202545	Garden Of Eden/Lela	50

DESECTORS

70	GAS GAS 137	King Kong/Please Stay	6

DESERT WOLVES

87	Ugly Man UGLY 6T	Love Shattered Lives/Stopped In My Tracks/ Desolation/ Sunday Morning (12", p/s)	10
88	Ugly Man UGLY 9	Speak To Me Rochelle/Besotted (p/s)	8
88	Ugly Man UGLY 9T	Speak To Me Rochelle/Mexico/Besotted/La Petite Rochelle (12", p/s)	15

JACKIE DE SHANNON

(see also Date With Soul)

62	Liberty LIB 55497	You Won't Forget Me/I Don't Think So Much	20
63	Liberty LIB 55563	Needles And Pins/Did He Call Today Mama?	20
64	Liberty LIB 55645	When You Walk In The Room/Till You Say You'll Be Mine	20
64	Liberty LIB 10165	Dancing Silhouettes/Hold Your Head High	12
64	Liberty LIB 10175	Don't Turn Your Back On Me/Be Good Baby	15
65	Liberty LIB 10192	She Don't Understand Him Like I Do/The Prince	12
65	Liberty LIB 10202	What The World Needs Now Is Love/It's Love Baby	7
65	Liberty LIB 12019	A Lifetime Of Loneliness/I Remember The Boy	10
66	Liberty LIB 66171	Come And Get Me/Splendour In The Grass	7
66	Liberty LIB 66202	I Can Make It With You/To Be Myself	7
66	Liberty LIB 66224	Come On Down/Find Me Love	25
68	Liberty LBF 15133	The Weight/Effervescent Blue	7
69	Liberty LBF 15238	Put A Little Love In Your Heart/Always Together	10
70	Liberty LBF 15281	Love Will Find A Way/I Let Go Completely	7
70	Liberty LBF 15324	What The World Needs Now/Keep Me In Mind	5
72	Atlantic K 10184	Vanilla Olay/I Wanna Roo You	5
75	CBS 3669	Let The Sailors Dance/Dreamin' As One	6

MINT VALUE £

72	Atlantic K 10241	Only Love Can Break Your Heart/Would You Like To Learn To Dance	5
65	Liberty LEP 2233	JACKIE (EP)	40
64	Liberty LBY 1182 (S)	THIS IS JACKIE DE SHANNON (LP)	20
65	Liberty LBY 1245	DON'T TURN YOUR BACK ON ME (LP)	20
65	Liberty LBY 3063	THIS IS JACKIE DE SHANNON (LP)	20
66	Liberty (S)BLY 3085	ARE YOU READY FOR THIS? (LP)	25
68	Liberty LBS 83117E	GREAT PERFORMANCES (LP)	20
69	Liberty LBS 83148E	ME ABOUT YOU (LP)	20
70	Liberty LBS 83304	PUT A LITTLE LOVE IN YOUR HEART (LP)	20
72	Atlantic K 40396	JACKIE (LP)	15

DESIGN

70	CBS 5112	Willow Stream/Coloured Mile	7
71	Epic EPC 7119	Jet Song/Minstrel's Theme	12
72	Regal Zonophone RZ 3044	Colour All The World/Lazy Song	7
72	Regal Zonophone RZ 3060	Mayday/Yellow Bird	6
73	Regal Zonophone RZ 3082	One Sunny Day/End Of The Party	6
71	Epic EPC 64322	DESIGN (LP)	15
71	Epic EPC64653	TOMORROW IS SO FAR AWAY (LP, with lyric insert, stickered sleeve)	20
73	Regal Zono. SLRZ 1037	DAY OF THE FOX (LP, red/silver label)	15

DESIGN

86	Dental 12DENT001	I Want You I Need You/Never Gonna Give You Up (12")	20

DESI ROOTS

79	Hawkeye HD 018	Hung-Up/Up-Town Rebel (12")	40
80	Hawkeye HD 025	Weed Fields/Hawkeye All Stars - Burning (12")	50
80	Hawkeye HD 033	Go Deh Right/Revolutionaries Go Right Deh (12")	30
80	Hawkeye HLP 007	DO IT RIGHT (LP)	45

ANDY DESMOND

(see also Gothic Horizon)

74	Konk KOS2	So It Goes/She Can Move Mountains	5
75	Konk KOS4	Beware/Only Child	5

JOHNNY DESMOND

56	Vogue Coral Q 72115	Sixteen Tons/Ballo Italiano	10
57	Vogue Coral Q 72261	A White Sports Coat (And A Pink Carnation)/Just Lookin'	12
57	Vogue Coral Q 72269	Shenandoah Rose/Consideration	5
58	Philips PB 890	Willingly/Apple (when Ya Gonna Fall From The Trees?)	5
58	MGM MGM 994	Hot Cha Cha/I'll Close My Eyes	5
60	Coral Q 72398	The Most Happy Fella/LANCERS: Joey, Joey, Joey	5
60	Philips PB 1044	Hawk/Playing The Field	25
62	Top Rank JAR 612	Twistin' Rose Of Texas/ Hello Honey	10
66	Polydor BM 56703	My Melancholy Baby/The Common Touch	5
56	Vogue Coral LVA 9035	SOUVENIR D'ITALIE (LP)	15

LORRAE DESMOND (& REBELS)

54	Decca F 10375	Hold My Hand/On The Waterfront	10
54	Decca F 10398	Far Away (My Love Is Far Away)/No One But You	10
54	Decca F 10404	I Can't Tell A Waltz From A Tango/For Better, For Worse (with Johnston Brothers)	10
55	Decca F 10461	A Boy On Saturday Night/Why - Oh Why?	10
55	Decca F 10510	Don't/Where Will The Baby's Dimple Be?	10
55	Decca F 10533	Stowaway/Heartbroken (B-side with Johnston Brothers)	8
55	Decca F 10612	You Should Know/Wake The Town And Tell The People	8
56	Parlophone R 4239	Written On The Wind/A House With Love In It	8
57	Parlophone R 4287	You Won't Be Around/Play The Music (as Lorrae Desmond & Rebels)	8
57	Parlophone R 4320	Kansas City Special/Preacher, Preacher (as Lorrae Desmond & Rebels)	8
57	Parlophone R 4361	Ding-Dong Rock-a-billy Weddin'/Cabin Boy (as Lorrae Desmond & Rebels)	15
58	Parlophone R 4400	Two Ships/Little David	8
58	Parlophone R 4430	Down By The River/The Secret Of Happiness	8
58	Parlophone R 4430	Down By The River/The Secret Of Happiness (78)	10
58	Parlophone R 4463	Soda Pop Hop/Blue, Blue Day	20
58	Parlophone R 4463	Soda Pop Hop/Blue, Blue Day (78)	10
59	Parlophone R 4534	Tall Paul/Wait For It	10
60	Parlophone R 4670	Tell Me Again/Get Your Daddie's Car Tonight	10

MIKE DESMOND

57	Columbia DB 3954	Young And In Love/Two Loves (as Michael Desmond)	6
57	Columbia DB 4018	Chances Are/If You're Not Completely Satisfied (as Michael Desmond)	6

PAUL DESMOND

(see also Gerry Mulligan, Dave Brubeck)

60	RCA 1373	Take Ten/Embarcadero	6
65	RCA RS 7701	BOSSA ANTIGUA (LP, label with red spot)	15

DESOLATION ANGELS

84	AM AM 266	Valhalla/Boadicea (p/s)	40
85	Thameside TRR 111	DESOLATION ANGELS (LP)	50

DESPERATE BICYCLES

77	Refill RR 1	Smokescreen/Handlebars (p/s, same tracks both sides)	18
77	Refill RR 2	The Medium Was Tedium/Don't Back The Front (p/s, same tracks both sides)	18
78	Refill RR 4	Occupied Territory/Skill (p/s)	10
78	Refill RR 7	Grief Is Very Private/Obstructive/Conundrum (some copies may be in p/s)	8
80	Refill RR 6	REMORSE CODE (LP)	25

DESSIE & JOHN

69	Downtown DT 440	Boss Sound/Everything Is Alright	10

MINT VALUE £

DESSUS
81 Ellie Jay EJSP 9710 Ghetto Children/Dessus Jammin' (with p/s) ... 25
81 Ellie Jay EJSP 9710 Ghetto Children/Dessus Jammin' (without p/s) ... 12

DESTROY ALL MONSTERS
(see also MC5)
79 Cherry Red CHERRY 3 Bored/You're Gonna Die (p/s, red vinyl) ... 5
79 Cherry Red CHERRY 7 Meet The Creeper/November 22nd 1963 (p/s) ... 5
79 Cherry Red CHERRY 9 Nobody Knows/What Do I Get? (p/s) ... 5

DESTROYER
81 Clean Kill SJP 829 Evil Place/Stand And Deliver (no p/s) ... 50

DESTROYERS
(see also Soul Brothers, Nicky Thomas)
70 Amalgamated AMG 856 Niney Special/Danger Zone ... 15
70 Pressure Beat PR 5505 Pressure Tonic/Machuki's Cooking (B-side actually with Count Machuki) ... 20

DESTRUCTORS
(see also Blanks)
82 No label or Cat no Electronic Church/Khymer Rouge Boogie (rubber-stamped white label, 500 only given away with copies of Forced Exposure punkzine) ... 50
82 Carnage BOOK 2 Meaningless Names/AK 47/Police State/Dachau/Death Squad (p/s) ... 5
82 Carnage Benelux KILL 2 Religion/Soldier Boy/Agent Orange/Corpse Gas (p/s) ... 5
82 Carnage Records BOOK 2 SENSELESS VIOLENCE (EP) ... 12
80s EXORCISE THE DEMONS OF YOUTH (EP, with insert) ... 8
82 Death DEATH 1 MERRY XMAS & FUCK OFF (LP) ... 20
83 Radical Change RCLP 2 ARMAGEDDON IN ACTION (LP) ... 20

DETAILS
80 Energy NRG 2 Keep On Running/Run'ins (p/s) ... 5
80 Energy NRG 002 Keep On Running/Run'ins (12", stickered plain sleeve, promo only) ... 8

FRANK DETAILS
80 Buzz Bomb BB 1 False Pretences/Stranger On A Train (p/s) ... 10

DETECTIVE
(see also Michael Des Barres)
77 Swansong SS K59405 DETECTIVE (LP, with inner) ... 12
78 Swansong SS 8504 IT TAKES ONE TO KNOW ONE (LP, with inner sleeve) ... 12

DETERGENTS
65 Columbia DB 7513 Leader Of The Laundromat/Ulcers ... 15
65 Columbia DB 7591 I Don't Know/The Blue Kangaroo ... 10

DETONATORS
78 Local LR 1 Need Love Tonight/Great Big Ghetto/Shoob Shooby Do/ Give Me A Helping Hand (p/s) ... 6

DETONATORS
79 Burning Rockers BR 1008 GANGSTER (LP) ... 30

DETOURS
(see also Gene Latter)
68 CBS 3213 Run To Me Baby/Hangin' On ... 40
68 CBS 3401 Whole Lotta Lovin'/Pieces Of You ... 150

DETOURS
76 MCA 249 Try To Hold On/Love To ... 5

DETRIUS
90 Under One Flag FLAG 55 PERPETUAL DEFIANCE (LP, with inner sleeve) ... 15

DETROIT with MITCH RYDER
(see also Mitch Ryder)
72 Paramount PARA 3022 It Ain't Easy/Long Neck Goose ... 5
72 Paramount SPFL 277 DETROIT (LP) ... 20

DETROIT EMERALDS
71 Pye International 7N 25544 Do Me Right/Just Now And Then ... 5
71 Janus 6146 004 Wear This Ring/I Bet You Get The One ... 5
72 Janus 6146 007 You Want It, You Got It/Till You Decide To Come Home ... 8
72 Janus 6146 015 Do Me Right/Baby Let Me Take You In My Arms ... 5
72 Janus 6146 020 Feel The Need In Me/And I Love Her ... 5
73 Westbound 6146108 You're Getting A Little Too Smart/Lee ... 10
71 Janus 6310 204 DO ME RIGHT (LP) ... 12
72 Janus 6310 207 YOU WANT IT, YOU GOT IT (LP) ... 12
73 Janus 6309 101 ABE, JAMES AND IVORY (LP) ... 15

DETROIT ESCALATOR CO.
96 Ferox FERLP 2 SOUNDTRACK (313) (LP) ... 20

DETROIT SPINNERS
(see also Spinners, G.C. Cameron)
65 Tamla Motown TMG 514 Sweet Thing/How Can I? (demo credited to 'Spinners') ... 300
65 Tamla Motown TMG 514 Sweet Thing/How Can I? (demo credited to 'Detroit Spinners') ... 225
65 Tamla Motown TMG 514 Sweet Thing/How Can I? (stock copies credited to 'Spinners') ... 400
65 Tamla Motown TMG 523 I'll Always Love You/Tomorrow May Never Come (as 'Spinners') ... 100
65 Tamla Motown TMG 523 I'll Always Love You/Tomorrow May Never Come (as 'Detroit Spinners') ... 75
65 Tamla Motown TMG 523 I'll Always Love You/Tomorrow May Never Come (as 'Spinners' or 'Detroit Spinners' DJ Copy) ... 250
67 Tamla Motown TMG 627 For All We Know/I'll Always Love You (1st pressing with tall, narrow print) ... 25
67 Tamla Motown TMG 627 For All We Know/I'll Always Love You (2nd pressing) ... 18
70 Tamla Motown TMG 755 It's A Shame/Together We Can Make Such Sweet Music (unissued) ... 0
70 Tamla Motown TMG 755 It's A Shame/Sweet Thing (as Motown Spinners) ... 6

MINT VALUE £

71	Tamla Motown TMG 766	Together We Can Make Such Sweet Music/Truly Yours (as Motown Spinners)	7
74	Tamla Motown TMG 871	Together We Can Make Such Sweet Music/Bad Bad Weather	5
80	Atlantic K 11558	Split Decision/Now That You're Mine Again	5
80	Atlantic K 11558	Split Decision/Now That You're Mine Again (12")	12
68	T. Motown TML 11060	THE DETROIT SPINNERS (LP, mono)	50
68	T. Motown STML 11060	THE DETROIT SPINNERS (LP, stereo)	60
71	T. Motown STML 11182	SECOND TIME AROUND (LP, as Motown Spinners)	20

DETROITS

70	Fontana 6438 006	'TIS US OURSELVES (LP)	12

DEUCE

86	1986 Powermetal VB004	Backs To The Ball/Queen Of The Night/Jealousy	10

DEUCE COUP

67	Mercury MF 1013	A Clown In One Town/Angela (some in p/s)	12
67	Mercury MF 1013	A Clown In One Town/Angela (some in p/s)	6

DEUCE OF HEARTS

66	CBS 202345	Closer Together/The Times They Are A Changin'	10

JIMMY DEUCHAR

(see also Victor Feldman)

55	Tempo EXA 18	JIMMY DEUCHAR ENSEMBLE (EP)	40
56	Esquire EP 93	JIMMY DEUCHAR QUARTET (EP)	40
56	Esquire EP 103	JIMMY DEUCHAR QUARTET (EP)	40
58	Tempo EXA 79	OPUS DE FUNK (EP, as Jimmy Deuchar Sextet)	40
58	Tempo EXA 81	SWINGIN' IN STUDIO TWO (EP)	40
59	Tempo EXA 88	WAIL (EP, with Victor Feldman Quintet)	40
54	Esquire 20-059	DIG DEUCHAR, DON'T DANCE (LP)	80
55	Tempo LAP 2	JIMMY DEUCHAR ENSEMBLE (10" LP)	250
56	Tempo TAP 4	TOP TRUMPETS (LP)	250
56	Vogue LDE	SHOWCASE (LP)	60
58	Tempo TAP 20	PAL JIMMY (LP)	400

BIG PETE DEUCHAR/DUKER

63	Fontana 267 278 TF	Google Eye/There's A Hand Leading Me (as Big Pete Deuchar)	10
63	Fontana TF 423	It Comes And Goes/Married By The Bible	10
65	Columbia DB 7763	Goin' In Training/I Saw Your Face In The Moon (as Big Pete Duker)	8

DEUS

94	Island 155981854 018-7	Suds & Soda/Secret Hell (limited edition, numbered)	10
94	Island 1215598854-019-1	Suds & Soda (Extended Version)/Texan Coffee/ Secret Hell/Furniture In The Far West (12")	12
94	Island 15599/854 150 7	Via/Violins And Happy Endings	8
94	Island 1215599/854 131-1	Via/Violins And Happy Endings/Great American Nude/Strip Mix (12")	8
95	Island 15603/854 188-7	Hotel Lounge (Be The Death Of Me)/Jigsaw You (Live) (limited edition, die-cut sleeve)	8
96	Island 630/854 682-7	Theme From Turnpike/Overflow/My Little Contessa (7" picture disc)	10
96	Island 1015630/854 682-0	Theme From Turnpike/Overflow/My Little Contessa (10", gatefold sleeve)	10
96	Island 15645/845726-7	Roses/I Suffer Rock (7" picture disc)	10
99	Island 15750/562-109-7	Sister Dew (Album Version)/Thirteen (Live) (with poster)	8
94	Island ILPS 8028/524-0451	WORST CASE SCENARIO (LP, limited edition with postcard and CD booklet)	80
96	Island ILPS 8052/524 29-1	IN A BAR UNDER THE SEA (LP, with inner sleeve)	40
99	Island ILPS 8082/524 643-1	THE IDEAL CRASH (LP)	40

DEVIANTS

(see also Mick Farren, Pink Fairies, Larry Wallis)

68	Stable STA 5601	You Got To Hold On/Let's Loot The Supermarket	20
67	Underground Imp. IMP 1	PTOOFF! (LP, foldout sleeve, private pressing via IT magazine)	250
68	Stable SLP 007	DISPOSABLE (LP, gatefold sleeve, red/black label)	200
69	Transatlantic TRA 204	THE DEVIANTS (LP, with booklet, white/lilac label with 't' logo)	200
69	Transatlantic TRA 204	THE DEVIANTS (LP, without booklet, white/lilac label with 't' logo)	100
69	Decca LK-R/SKL-R 4993	PTOOFF! (LP, reissue, large unboxed logo on label)	90
84	Psycho PSYCHO 25	HUMAN GARBAGE (LIVE AT DINGWALLS '84) (LP)	15

DEVIL'S HOLE GANG

70s	Slow Burning Fuse SSSS 1	Free The People/Isn't It/Something To Look Forward To (p/s, with insert)	12

JOHNNY DEVLIN (& DETOURS)

64	Pye 7N 15598	Sometimes/If You Want Someone (as Johnny Devlin & Detours)	10
66	CBS 202085	Hung On You/Prove It	8
66	CBS 202339	My Strength; Heart Of Soul/I Can't Get You Off My Mind	8
67	CBS 202452	Tender Lovin' Care/Five O'Clock World	8
67	CBS 2751	Hurtin'/You Gotta Tell Me	7

DEVO

78	Stiff DEV 1	Jocko Homo/Mongoloid (foldout p/s)	5
78	Stiff DEV 2/BOY 1	(I Can't Get No) Satisfaction/Sloppy (I Saw My Baby Getting) (p/s)	5
78	Stiff BOY 2	Be Stiff/Social Fools (clear vinyl)	5
79	Elevator NICE 1	Mechanical Man/Blockhead/Blackout/Auto-Modern (official bootleg, red/yellow stamped sleeves)	8
78	Virgin V 2106	Q: ARE WE NOT MEN? (LP, various coloured vinyl)	12
78	Virgin VP 2106	Q: ARE WE NOT MEN? (LP, picture disc, with 'Flimsy Wrap' 33rpm 1-sided flexidisc [VDJ 27/Lyntone LYN 6260])	15
79	Virgin V2125	DUTY NOW FOR THE FUTURE (LP)	12

DEVON (Russell) & SEDRIC (Myton)

69	Blue Cat BS 158	What A Sin Thing/Short Up Dress	30

DEVON (Russell) & TARTANS

(see also Tartans)

68	Nu Beat NB 021	Let's Have Some Fun/Making Love	10

MINT VALUE £

BARRY DE VORZON
(see also Barry & Tamerlanes, Jimmy Dell)

58	RCA RCA 1066	Barbara Jean/JIMMY DELL: Teeny Weeny	65
58	RCA RCA 1066	Barbara Jean/JIMMY DELL: Teeny Weeny (78)	40
60	Philips PB 993	Betty Betty (Go Steady With Me)/Across The Street	25

DEVOTED

68	Page One POF 076	I Love George Best/United (p/s)	25
68	Page One POF 076	I Love George Best/United	15

DEVOTIONS

64	Columbia DB 7256	Rip Van Winkle/I Love You For Sentimental Reasons	100

JANINE DE WAYLENE & HER MARTENOT

60	Top Rank JAR 363	Faces In The Dark/Martenot Theme/Farewell Christina	7
60	Oriole CB 1576	Faces In The Dark/Martenot Theme/Farewell Christina	8

DEWDROPS

67	Blue Beat BB 381	Somebody's Knocking/By And By	18

BRIAN DEWHURST

75	Folk Heritage FHR 075	THE HUNTER & THE HUNTED (LP)	20

KEITH DEWHURST & ALBION BAND
(see also Albion Band)

80	Charisma CDS 4020	LARK RISE TO CANDLEFORD (A COUNTRY TAPESTRY) (LP, soundtrack)	12

HARRY DE WIT

79	Bead Records BEAD 11	APRIL '79 (LP)	25
79	Bead Records BEAD 12	FOR HARM (LP, with Philipp Wachsmann)	25

DANNY DEXTER

63	London HLU 9690	Sweet Mama/Go On	20

EDDIE DEXTER & HIS BAND

55	Capitol CL 14371	Moonlight/The Verse Of Stardust	8

RAY DEXTER & LAYABOUTS

62	Decca F 11538	The Coalman's Lament/Lonely Weekend	30

DEXYS MIDNIGHT RUNNERS
(see also Killjoys, Kevin Rowland)

85	Mercury DEXYS 13	An Extract From 'This Is What She's Like'/'This Is What She's Like' Finale (p/s)	5
85	Mercury DEXYSD 13	An Extract From 'This Is What She's Like'/'This Is What She's Like' Finale//Marguerita Time/Reminisce Part One (double pack, gatefold p/s)	8
85	Mercury DEXYS 1310	This Is What She's Like/Marguerita Time (10", p/s)	8

TRACEY DEY

64	Stateside SS 287	Go Away/Gonna Get Along Without You Now	18

DEZIGN

84	EN AY DZ 256	Love Myth/Let's Go (no p/s)	10

BOBBY D'FANO

62	Palette PG 9038	Message Of Love/The Kiss That Broke My Heart	10

DHARMA B featuring ACE OF CLUBS

90s	Acid Jazz JAZID 35T	Everything Is Going To The Beat (12", company sleeve)	20

DHARMA BLUES BAND
(see also Hawkwind)

69	Major Minor SMCP 5017	DHARMA BLUES (LP, yellow/white/black label)	90

DIALS (Jamaica)

69	Duke DU 48	Bye Bye Love/It's Love	7
69	Duke DU 49	Love Is A Treasure/DIAMONDS: I Want To Be	7

DIALS (U.K.)

79	Wessex WEX 266	Maxine/Hey Denise (p/s)	7
79	Scene ACT1	All I Hear/Running (p/s)	10

BRIAN DIAMOND & THE CUTTERS

63	Decca F 11724	Jealousy Will Get You Nowhere/Brady Brady	15
64	Fontana TF 452	Shake, Shout And Go/Whatcha Gonna Do Now Pretty Baby	15
65	Pye 7N 15779	Big Bad Wolf/See If I Care	15
65	Pye 7N 15952	Bone Idol/Sands Of Time	15

GREGG DIAMOND'S BIONIC BOOGIE

79	Urban URBX 16	Hot Butterfly/Mess Up The Boogie/When The Shit Hits The Fan (12", p/s)	12
79	Polydor PB 50	Chains/Hot Butterfly (7")	5
79	Polydor POSPX 50	Chains/Hot Butterfly (12")	15
79	Polydor 2391 322	BIONIC BOOGIE (LP)	12

JERRY DIAMOND

57	London HLE 8496	Sunburned Lips/Don't Trust Love	40
57	London HLE 8496	Sunburned Lips/Don't Trust Love (78)	20

LEE DIAMOND (& CHEROKEES)
(see also Cherokees)

61	Fontana H 310	I'll Step Down/Josephine (as Lee Diamond & Cherokees)	18
61	Fontana H 345	Stop Your Crying/You'll Want Me	18

NEIL DIAMOND

66	London HLZ 10049	Solitary Man/Do It	10
66	London HLZ 10072	Cherry, Cherry/I'll Come Running	10
66	London HLZ 10092	I Got The Feelin' (Oh No No)/The Boat That I Row	10
67	London HLZ 10111	You Got To Me/Someday Baby	10
67	London HLZ 10126	Girl, You'll Be A Woman Soon/You'll Forget	8

MINT VALUE £

67	London HLZ 10151	Thank The Lord For The Night Time/The Long Way Home	8
67	London HLZ 10161	Kentucky Woman/The Time Is Now	8
68	London HLZ 10177	New Orleans/Hanky Panky	10
68	London HLZ 10187	Red Red Wine/Red Rubber Ball	8
68	Uni UN 503	Brooklyn Roads/Holiday Inn Blues	5
71	President PT 335	Kentucky Woman/Cherry, Cherry/I Thank The Lord For The Night Time (p/s)	7
66	London HA-Z 8307	THE FEEL OF NEIL DIAMOND (LP)	45

DIAMOND BOYS

(see also Albert Ammons)

62	Parlophone GIB 102	Fool In Love/New Orleans (export issue)	25
63	RCA RCA 1351	Hey Little Girl/What'd I Say	15

DIAMOND HEAD

80	Happy Face MMDH 120	Shoot Out The Lights/Helpless (p/s)	15
80	Media SCREEN 1	Sweet And Innocent/Streets Of Gold (p/s)	15
81	DHM DHM 004	Waited Too Long/Play It Loud (p/s)	7
81	DHM DHM 005	DIAMOND LIGHTS EP (Diamond Lights/ We Won't Be Back/ I Don't Got/It's Electric) (12", p/s)	20
82	MCA DHMT 101	FOUR CUTS (12" EP, with insert)	12
83	MCA DHM 103	Makin' Music/(Andy Peebles Interview) (p/s)	8
83	MCA DHMT 103	Makin' Music/(Andy Peebles Interview) (12", p/s)	15
83	MCA DHM 104	Out Of Phase/The Kingmaker (p/s)	5
83	MCA DHMP 104	Out Of Phase/The Kingmaker (picture disc)	6
83	MCA DHMT 104	Out Of Phase/The Kingmaker/Sucking My Love (live) (12", p/s)	25
92	Bronze	Wild In The Streets (12", p/s, 1 side etched)	8
80	DHM MMDHLP 105	LIGHTNING TO THE NATIONS (LP, plain or printed white labels, plain white sleeve, sold at gigs, signed in blue ink & available via Sounds)	65
80	DHM MMDHLP 105	LIGHTNING TO THE NATIONS (LP, plain or printed white labels, plain white sleeve, sold at gigs)	50
81	MCA DH 1001	LIVING ON BORROWED TIME (LP, gatefold sleeve with inner sleeve, poster & fan club insert)	25
81	MCA DH 1001	LIVING ON BORROWED TIME (LP, gatefold sleeve with inner sleeve only)	15
83	MCA DH 1002	CANTERBURY (LP, with lyric and tour dates sheet, first pressing faulty and jumps)	15
86	Metal Masters METALP 110	BEHOLD THE BEGINNING (LP, remixed reissue of 1st LP)	15
87	FM WKFMLP 92	AM I EVIL (LP, with inner sleeve)	20
93	Bronze/Essential ESSLP 192	DEATH AND PROGRESS (LP)	12

DIAMONDS (Jamaica)

(see also Dymonds, Sir Collins Band)

72	Songbird SB 1079	Mash Up/DYNAMITES: Mash Up (Version)	6
75	Attack ATT 8108	Jah Jah Bless Your Dreadlocks/Version	10
75	Attack ATT 8113	Just Can't Figure Out/Just Can't Figure Out (Version)	8
75	Black Wax WAX 5	Country Living/A Living Version	8
70s	Virgin V2102	PLANET EARTH (LP)	18

DIAMONDS (U.K.)

63	Philips BF 1264	The Lost City/Chasey Chasey	10

DIAMONDS (U.S.)

(see also Pete Rugolo)

55	Vogue Coral Q 72109	Black Denim Trousers And Motorcycle Boots/Nip Sip	50
55	Vogue Coral Q 72109	Black Denim Trousers And Motorcycle Boots/Nip Sip (78)	10
58	Mercury 7MT 187	Silhouettes/Honey Bird	40
58	Mercury 7MT 195	The Stroll/Land Of Beauty	35
58	Mercury 7MT 207	Don't Let Me Down/High Sign	35
58	Mercury 7MT 208	Straight Skirts/Patsy	50
58	Mercury 7MT 233	Where Mary Go?/Kathy-O	8
58	Mercury AMT 1004	Eternal Lovers/Walking Along	8
59	Mercury AMT 1024	She Say (Oom Dooby Doom)/From The Bottom Of My Heart	12
59	Mercury AMT 1024	She Say (Oom Dooby Doom)/From The Bottom Of My Heart (78)	15
60	Mercury AMT 1086	Tell The Truth/Real True Love	25
61	Mercury AMT 1156	One Summer Night/It's A Doggone Shame	15
57	Mercury MEP 9515	PRESENTING THE DIAMONDS (EP)	35
57	Mercury MEP 9523	THE DIAMONDS VOL. 1 (EP)	40
58	Mercury MEP 9527	THE DIAMONDS VOL. 2 (EP)	40
58	Mercury MEP 9530	THE DIAMONDS VOL. 3 (EP)	40
59	Mercury ZEP 10003	DIG THE DIAMONDS (EP)	40
59	Mercury ZEP 10020	THE DIAMONDS MEET PETE RUGOLO (EP)	20
59	Mercury ZEP 10026	DIAMONDS ARE TRUMPS (EP)	40
60	Mercury ZEP 10053	STAR STUDDED DIAMONDS (EP)	40
61	Mercury ZEP 10097	PETE RUGOLO LEADS THE DIAMONDS (EP, mono)	25
61	Mercury SEZ 10912	PETE RUGOLO LEADS THE DIAMONDS (EP, stereo)	35
57	Mercury MPT 7526	THE DIAMONDS (10" LP)	60
60	Mercury MMC 14039	SONGS FROM THE OLD WEST (LP)	18

DIAMOND TWINS

(see also Sonia Kent)

66	HMV POP 1508	Crying The Night Away/Start The World Spinning Again	6

ALENA DIANE

06	Names NAMES 25	SONGS WHISTLED THROUGH WHITE TEETH (EP, 10", 500 only)	12

DIANE & JAVELINS

66	Columbia DB 7819	Heart And Soul/Who's The Girl	55

(PAUL) DI'ANNO

(see also Gogmagog, Iron Maiden)

84	FM VHF 1	Heart User/Road Rat (p/s)	8
84	FM WKFM LP1	DI'ANNO (LP, blue vinyl, stickered sleeve)	15
84	FM WKFM PD1	DI'ANNO (LP, picture disc)	18

MINT VALUE £

DIATONES

61	Starlite ST45 057	Ruby Has Gone/Oh Baby Come Dance With Me	100

DANNY DIAZ & THE CHECKMATES

69	Pye 7N 17690	Solomon Grundy/Goodbye Baby	20

MANU DIBANGO

73	London HL 10423	Soul Makossa/Lily	10
73	London SH 8451	O BOSO (LP)	20
75	Creole CRLP 503	MAKOSSA MUSIC (LP)	15
78	Decca SKL-R 5296	AFROVISION (LP)	12
79	Decca SKL-R 5303	MANU '76 (LP)	12

BILLY DICE & SHENLEY DUFFUS

73	Pama 874	Women Smarter/Standing On The Hill	8

DICE THE BOSS

(see also Pama Dice, Joe The Boss, Ray Martel)

69	Duke DU 50	Brixton Cat Big And Fat/JOPES ALL STARS : Solitude	18
69	Duke/Joe DU 51	Gun The Man Down/JOE MANSANO: The Thief	30
69	Duke/Joe DU 52	But Officer/JOE'S ALL STARS: Reggae On The Shore	50
70	Duke/Joe DU 57	Your Boss D.J./TITO SIMON: Read The News	40
70	Joe's JRS 17	The Informer/Cool It	40
70	Explosion EX 2017	Funky Monkey/JOE'S ALL STARS: Funky Monkey Version	15
70	Explosion EX 2020	Funky Duck/Dunkier Than Duck	15

LLOYD DICE

(see also Trevor Lloyd)

70	Joe JRS 5	Trial Of Pama Dice/JOE: Jughead Returns	25

PAMA DICE

(see also Dice The Boss, Joe The Boss)

69	Jackpot JP 715	Honky Tonk Popcorn/Bongo Man	12
69	Jackpot JP 716	Sin, Sun And Sex/Reggae Popcorn	12

DICEMEN

83	Random MCPS RR1	Number 19/A Year Without You/Sunrise/Today	15

DICK & DEE DEE

61	London HLG 9408	The Mountain's High/I Want Someone	10
62	London HLG 9483	Goodbye To Love/Swing Low	12
65	Warner Bros WB 156	Be My Baby/Room 404	15
65	Warner Bros WB 5671	Use What You've Got/P.S. 1402	6
63	Warner Bros WM 8132	YOUNG AND IN LOVE (LP, mono)	30
63	Warner Bros WS 8132	YOUNG AND IN LOVE (LP, stereo)	40
63	Warner Bros WM 8150	TURN AROUND (LP, mono)	30
63	Warner Bros WS 8150	TURN AROUND (LP, stereo)	40

DICKENS

(see also Ice)

80	Hawkmoon ROCK 101	STANDING OUT (LP, private pressing)	12

CHARLES DICKENS

(see also Habits)

65	Pye 7N 15887	That's The Way Love Goes/In The City	25
65	Pye 7N 15938	I Stand Alone/Hey Little Girl	10
66	Immediate IM 025	So Much In Love/Our Soul Brothers	40

DOLES DICKEN'S BAND

58	London HLD 8639	Piakukaungchung (Pie-ah-coo-ka-ung-chung)/Our Melody	10

LITTLE JIMMY DICKENS

65	CBS 201969	May The Bird Of Paradise Fly Up Your Nose/My Eyes Are Jealous	6
66	CBS BPG 62404	MAY THE BIRD OF PARADISE FLY UP YOUR NOSE (LP)	12

NEVILLE DICKIE

69	Major Minor MM 644	The Robin's Return/Brandon Bounce	5

DICKIES

(see also Chuck Wagon)

78	A&M AMS 7368	Paranoid/I'm OK, You're OK (p/s, milky vinyl)	5
78	A&M AMS 7403	Silent Night/The Sounds Of Silence (p/s, white vinyl)	6
79	A&M AMS 7491	Manny, Moe And Jack/She Loves Me Not (p/s, black vinyl only)	8
80	A&M AMS 7504	Fan Mail/Tricia Toyota (I'm Stuck In A Pagoda) (opaque or translucent red vinyl, poster p/s)	6
80	A&M AMS 7544	Gigantor/Bowling With Bedrock Barney (yellow vinyl, p/s with full colour or b&w reverse)	8
90	Overground OVER 12	Just Say Yes/Ayatollah You So (p/s with lyric sheet, mauve, blue or white vinyl, 2,000 of each colour)	5
95	Plastic Head HOLE 008	Make It So/Oh Baby (p/s, black vinyl, 1,000 only)	5
79	A&M AMLE 64742	THE INCREDIBLE SHRINKING DICKIES (LP, black or yellow vinyl)	12
79	A&M AMLE 64742	THE INCREDIBLE SHRINKING DICKIES (LP, blue vinyl, with black or red-and-black on sleeve)	12
79	A&M AMLE 64742	THE INCREDIBLE SHRINKING DICKIES (LP, orange vinyl, with black or red-and-black on sleeve)	15
79	A&M AMLH 68510	DAWN OF THE DICKIES (LP, blue vinyl)	15
79	A&M AMLH 68510	DAWN OF THE DICKIES (LP, black vinyl)	12

BRUCE DICKINSON

(see also Iron Maiden, Samson, Xero, Rock Aid Armenia)

90	EMI EM 138	Tattooed Millionaire/Ballad Of Mutt (paper label, glossy p/s)	5
90	EMI EMPD 138	Tattooed Millionaire/Ballad Of Mutt (shaped picture disc)	10
90	EMI EMPD 138	Tattooed Millionaire/Ballad Of Mutt (uncut shaped picture disc)	30
90	EMI EMPD 142	All The Young Dudes/Darkness Be My Friend (shaped picture disc with plinth)	10

			MINT VALUE £
90	EMI EMPD 142	All The Young Dudes/Darkness Be My Friend (uncut shaped picture disc)	25
90	EMI EMPD 151	Dive! Dive! Dive!/Riding With The Angels (live)/ Sin City (live)/ Black Night (live) (12", picture disc)	10
94	EMI EM 341	Shoot All The Clowns/Over And Out (p/s, clear vinyl with insert)	5

BARBARA DICKSON

74	RSO 2090 144	Here Comes The Sun/The Long And Winding Road	5
70	Decca SKL 5041	THRO' RECENT YEARS (LP, with Archie Fisher)	40
71	Decca SKL 5058	DO RIGHT WOMAN (LP)	40
72	Decca SKL 5116	FROM THE BEGGAR'S MANTLE FRINGED WITH GOLD (LP)	35
74	RSO 2394 141	JOHN, PAUL, GEORGE, RINGO AND BERT (LP, with London cast)	30

DICK TURPIN

70	Evolution E 2446	If You've Got The Time/Madeline	250

DICTATORS with TONY & HOWARD

(see also Tony & Howard)

63	Oriole CB 1934	So Long Little Girl/Say Little Girl	20

DICTATORS

77	Asylum K 13091	Search And Destroy/Sleepin' With The TV On	5
77	Asylum K 13091	Search And Destroy/Sleepin' With The TV On (12" p/s)	8
75	Epic S EPC 80767	GO GIRL CRAZY (LP)	20
77	Asylum K 53061	MANIFEST DESTINY (LP)	15

BO DIDDLEY

(see also Chuck Berry & Bo Diddley)

59	London HLM 8913	The Great Grandfather/Crackin' Up	60
59	London HLM 8913	The Great Grandfather/Crackin' Up (78)	50
59	London HLM 8975	Say Man/The Clock Strikes Twelve	60
59	London HLM 8975	Say Man/The Clock Strikes Twelve (78)	50
60	London HLM 9035	Say Man, Back Again/She's Alright	75
60	London HLM 9112	Road Runner/My Story	50
62	Pye Intl. 7N 25165	You Can't Judge A Book By The Cover/I Can Tell	25
63	Pye Intl. 7N 25193	Who Do You Love?/The Twister	20
63	Pye Intl. 7N 25210	Bo Diddley/Detour	18
63	Pye Intl. 7N 25216	You Can't Judge A Book By The Cover/I Can Tell (reissue)	12
63	Pye Intl. 7N 25217	Pretty Thing/Road Runner	15
63	Pye Intl. 7N 25227	Bo Diddley Is A Lover/Doin' The Jaguar	15
64	Pye Intl. 7N 25235	Memphis/Monkey Diddle	15
64	Pye Intl. 7N 25243	Mona/Gimme Gimme	18
64	Pye Intl. 7N 25258	Mama Keep Your Big Mouth Shut/Jo-Ann	15
65	Chess CRS 8000	Hey Good Lookin'/You Ain't Bad (As You Claim To Be)	15
65	Chess CRS 8014	Somebody Beat Me/Mush Mouth Millie	18
65	Chess CRS 8021	Let The Kids Dance/Let Me Pass	15
66	Chess CRS 8026	500% More Man/Stop My Monkey	18
66	Chess CRS 8036	We're Gonna Get Married/Easy	18
67	Chess CRS 8053	Ooh Baby/Back To School	15
67	Chess CRS 8057	Wrecking My Love Life/Boo-Ga-Loo Before You Go	18
68	Chess CRS 8078	Another Sugar Daddy/I'm High Again	10
69	Chess CRS 8088	Bo Diddley 1969/Soul Train	12
72	Chess 6145 002	I Said Shut Up Woman/I Love You More Than You'll Ever Know	8
56	London RE-U 1054	RHYTHM AND BLUES WITH BO DIDDLEY (EP, gold label lettering)	200
63	Pye Intl. NEP 44014	HEY! BO DIDDLEY (EP)	25
64	Pye Intl. NEP 44019	THE STORY OF BO DIDDLEY (EP)	30
64	Pye Intl. NEP 44031	BO DIDDLEY IS A LUMBERJACK (EP)	30
64	Pye Intl. NEP 44036	DIDDLING (EP)	30
65	Chess CRE 6008	I'M A MAN (EP)	30
66	Chess CRE 6023	ROOSTER STEW (EP)	25
59	London HA-M 2230	GO BO DIDDLEY (LP)	350
62	Pye Jazz NJL 33	BO DIDDLEY IS A GUNSLINGER (LP)	40
63	Pye Intl. NPL 28025	HEY! BO DIDDLEY (LP)	30
63	Pye Intl. NPL 28026	BO DIDDLEY (LP)	30
63	Pye Intl. NPL 28029	BO DIDDLEY RIDES AGAIN (LP)	30
63	Pye Intl. NPL 28032	BO DIDDLEY'S BEACH PARTY (LP)	30
64	Pye Intl. NPL 28034	BO DIDDLEY IN THE SPOTLIGHT (LP)	30
64	Pye Intl. NPL 28049	16 ALL-TIME HITS (LP)	20
64	Chess CRL 4002	HEY GOOD LOOKIN' (LP)	20
65	Chess CRL 4507	LET ME PASS (LP)	25
67	Chess CRL 4525	THE ORIGINATOR (LP)	25
67	Marble Arch MAL 751	SURFIN' WITH BO DIDDLEY (LP)	12
68	Chess CRL 4529	SUPER BLUES (LP, with Muddy Waters & Little Walter)	45
68	Chess CRL 4537	THE SUPER SUPER BLUES BAND (LP, with Muddy Waters & Howlin' Wolf)	45
71	Chess 6310107	ANOTHER DIMENSION (LP)	30
73	Chess 6499 476	THE LONDON SESSIONS (LP)	15

DIDDY MEN

65	Columbia DB 7782	The Song Of The Diddy Men/Hello Dolly	8

DIDJITS

95	Touch & Go RCRPA 11	Pigs (1-sided white label)	5

DIE ELECTRIC EELS

78	Rough Trade RT 008	Agitated/Cyclotron (p/s)	15

DIE LAUGHING

80	Oceaon OC 003	Hard Living Man/You Got The Power (p/s)	50

DIESEL M

(see also Mµ-Ziq)

94	Choci's Chewns CCB 001	M For Multiple (12", blue vinyl, 666 only)	25
95	Choci's Chewns DDL 001	M For Mangoes (12", red vinyl, 666 only)	25

MINT VALUE £

MARLENE DIETRICH

(see also Rosemary Clooney)

52	Columbia SCM 5010	Too Old To Cut The Mustard/Good For Nothing (with Rosemary Clooney)	18
57	London HLD 8492	Near You/Another Spring, Another Love	18
63	HMV POP 1196	Lili Marlene/Sag Mir Wo Die Blumen Sind?	6
64	London HLR 9883	Such Trying Times/If He Swing By The String	7
65	HMV POP 1379	Where Have All The Flowers Gone?/Blowin' In The Wind	8
65	Pye 7N 15770	Go Away From My Window/Shir Hatan	6
57	HMV 7EG 8257	MARLENE DIETRICH IN 'THE BLUE ANGEL'(EP)	25
58	London RED 1146	MARLENE DIETRICH (EP)	15
64	HMV 7EG 8844	RETURNS TO GERMANY (EP)	10
53	Brunswick LA 8591	SOUVENIR ALBUM (10" LP)	25
54	Philips BBR 8006	AT THE CAFÉ DE PARIS (10" LP, introduced by Noel Coward)	25
59	Philips BBL 7322	LILI MARLENE (LP)	15
60	Philips BBL 7386	DIETRICH IN RIO (LP, also stereo SBBL 571)	15

DIF JUZ

81	4AD BAD 109	HU/RE/MI/CS (12" EP)	10
81	4AD BAD 116	VIBRATING AIR: Heset/Diselt/Gunet/Soarn (12" EP)	15
83	Red Flame RFM 24	WHO SAYS SO (LP)	12
85	Pleasantly Surprised PS 9	TIME CLOCK TURNS BACK (cassette, with inserts)	25

DIGA RHYTHM BAND

(see also Grateful Dead, Mickey Hart, Jerry Garcia)

76	United Artists UAG 29975	DIGA RHYTHM BAND (LP)	22

RICHARD DIGANCE & FRIENDS

78	Chrysalis CHR 1187	AT THE Q.E.H. (LP)	12

STEVE DIGGLE

(see also Buzzcocks, Flag Of Convenience)

80	Faulty Products FEP 7000	Fifty Years Of Comparative Wealth/Shut Out The Light/ Here Comes The Fire Brigade (unreleased)	0

DIGITAL MYSTIKS & LEOFAH

04	DMZ DMZ 002	Lost City/Jah Fire/Horror Show/Dread Commands (EP)	25

DIGITAL PRINCESS

02	Mosquito MSQ 019	LISTEN TO ME TENDER (12" EP)	8

DILLARD & CLARK

(see also Gene Clark, Byrds, Dillards)

69	A&M AMS 764	Radio Song/Why Not Your Baby	15
69	A&M AMLS 939	THE FANTASTIC EXPEDITION OF DILLARD & CLARK (LP)	18
69	A&M AMLS 966	THROUGH THE MORNING, THROUGH THE NIGHT (LP)	18

MOSES & JOSHUA (DILLARD)

67	Stateside SS 2059	My Elusive Dreams/What's Better Than Love (as Moses & Joshua Dillard)	25
67	Stateside SS 2059	My Elusive Dreams/What's Better Than Love (as Moses & Joshua Dillard) (DJ Copy)	40
68	Bell BELL 1018	Get Out Of My Heart/They Don't Want Us Together (as Moses & Joshua)	20
72	Mojo 2092 054	My Elusive Dreams/Get Out Of My Heart	8

DILLARDS

(see also Dillard & Clark)

65	Capitol CL 15420	Nobody Knows/Ebo Walker	6
69	Elektra EKSN 45048	Reason To Believe/Nobody Knows	6
69	Elektra EKSN 45062	She Sang Hymns Out Of Tune/Single Saddle	5
69	Elektra EKSN 45081	Rainmaker/West Montana Hanna	5
66	Bounty BY 6019	BACK PORCH BLUEGRASS (LP)	20
68	Elektra EKS 7265	LIVE!!! ALMOST!!! (LP)	15
68	Elektra EKS 74035	WHEATSHEAF SUITE (LP)	12
70	Elektra EKS 74054	COPPERFIELDS (LP)	12

DILLINGER

(see also David Isaacs)

73	Duke DU 149	Headquarters (as Dellenger)/CHENLEY DUFFAS: Black Girl In My Bed	10
73	Downtown DT 512	Tighten Up Skank/Middle East Rock	10
76	Black Swan WIP 6355	Bionic Dread/Eastman Skank	10
79	Island ISL 976	Cokane In My Brain/Power	5
77	Black Swan WIP 6380	Natty BSc/Buckingham Palace	10
77	Black Swan WIP 6416	Cocaine In My Brain/Buckingham Palace/Ragnampiza	10
77	Black Swan BS 7	Cocaine In My Brain/Buckingham Palace/Ragnampiza (12")	20
79	Jamaica Sound JSD 921	Dread Call Fred/Lamb's Bread (Let Go The Dread) (12", with Sugar Minott)	8
76	Black Swan ILPS 9455	BIONIC DREAD (LP)	50
76	Black Swan ILPS9385	CB200 (LP)	15
77	Magnum DEAD 1001	TALKIN' BLUES (LP)	50
77	Third World TWS 919	TOP RANKING (LP)	20

DILLINGER V TRINITY

78	Burning Sounds BSLP 1003	CLASH (LP)	35

TODD DILLINGHAM

95	Woronzow WOO 25	SGT. KIPPER (2-LP)	15

DILLINJA

(See also Cybotron featuring Dillinja)

93	Cybotron DILL 01	Steal The Way/Forever Fierce (1-sided 12")	20
93	Cybotron DILL 03	From Beyond/Ride It Hard (1-sided 12")	20
93	Cybotron DILL 04	Sine/Dark Science (1-sided 12")	30
93	Tough Toonz TT 02	DILLINJA EP (12", promo only, four untitled tracks)	20
93	Wave Form DIL 08	TEST [2] EP (12", as Dillinger)	15
94	Deadly Vinyl D2	Deadly Ceremonies/Soverign Melody (12")	30

MINT VALUE £

94	Deadly Vinyl D3	Deadly Deep Subs/Calculus Beats (12")	30
94	Logic Productions DM 003	You Don't Know (Remix)/Heavenly Bass (12")	15
94	Deadly Vinyl DIL 06	MAJESTIC B-LINE EP (12")	12
94	IQ IQ 001	3.01 In The Morning/Catch The Vibe (12", as Dillinja And Mr E)	10
94	Logic Productions DM 001	Moods/Deep Love (Remix) (12", as Dillinja And Mystery)	12
94	Logic Productions DM 002	You Don't Know/Warrior (12")	10
94	Heavyweight HW 003	VOL 3 (10", two untitled tracks, as Dillinja And Ruffkut)	12
94	JA 1	South Side (Riffin Mix)/Stompers Delight (12")	8
95	Deadly Vinyl D4	Deadly Deep Subs (Remix)/Perfect Match (12")	12
95	Philly Blunt PB 005	Muthaf*cka/Sky (12")	12
95	Metalheadz MET 006	The Angel Fell/Ja Know Ya Big/Brutal Bass (12")	8

PHYLLIS DILLON

66	Doctor Bird DB 1061	Don't Stay Away (as Phillis Dillon)/ TOMMY McCOOK & SUPERSONICS: What Now	60
67	Trojan TR 006	This Is A Lovely Way/Thing Of The Past (as Phyllis Dellon)	60
67	Treasure Isle TI 7003	This Is A Lovely Way/Thing Of The Past	25
67	Treasure Isle TI 7015	Perfidia/It's Rocking Time	50
68	Treasure Isle TI 7041	I Wear This Ring/Don't Touch Me Tomato	18
69	Trojan TR 651	Love Is All I Had/Boys And Girls Reggae (as Phillis Dylon)	50
69	Trojan TR 671	The Right Track/TOMMY McCOOK & SUPERSONICS: Moonshot	15
69	Trojan TR 686	Lipstick On Your Collar (as Phillis Dillon)/ TOMMY McCOOK & SUPERSONICS: Tribute To Rameses	12
70	Duke Reid DR 2508	This Is Me/Skabuvie (act. "If Your Name Is Andy"/"Ska Vovi" by Dorothy Reid)	12
70	Duke DU 76	Walk Through This World/The Rooster	8
71	Treasure Isle TI 7058	One Life To Live, One Love To Give/TOMMY McCOOK: My Best Dress	15
71	Treasure Isle TI 7070	Midnight Confession/TOMMY McCOOK & SOUL SYNDICATE: Version	15
72	Sioux SI 009	In The Ghetto/NYAH EARTH: Knight Of The Long Knives	12
72	Trojan TRL 41	ONE LIFE TO GIVE (LP)	45

DIMENSIONALS

53	London L 1217	Sleepy Time Gal/DON BAKER/DIMENSIONALS: Drinkin' Pop-Sodee Odee (78)	30

DIMENSIONS

65	Parlophone R 5294	Tears On My Pillow/You Don't Have To Whisper	35

DIMPLES

(see also Gospel Garden, Amazing Blondel)

66	Decca F 12537	The Love Of A Lifetime/My Heart Is Tied To You	40

DIMPLES & EDDIE with RICO's COMBO

62	Planetone RC 3	Fleet Street/Good Bye World	20

D INFLUENCE

90s	Acid Jazz JAZID 30T	I'm The One (12", p/s)	15

DINGER

(see also Erasure)

85	Face Value FVRA 221	Air Of Mystery/I Love To Love (no p/s)	35

DINGLE BROTHERS

71	Dynamic DYN 418	You Don't Know/CABLES: Rich Man, Poor Man	6

MARK DINNING

60	MGM MGM 1053	Teen Angel/Bye Now Baby	12
60	MGM MGM 1069	You Win Again/A Star Is Born (A Love Is Dead)	8
60	MGM MGM 1101	The Lovin' Touch/Come Back To Me (My Love)	8
61	MGM MGM 1125	Top Forty, News, Weather And Sport/Suddenly	20
62	MGM MGM 1148	In A Matter Of Moments/What Will My Mary Say	8
62	MGM MGM 1155	All Of This For Sally/The Pickup	12
65	Hickory 45-1293	Dial Al 1-4883/I'm Glad We Fell In Love	8

DINNING SISTERS

(see also Tennessee Ernie Ford)

55	London HLF 8179	Drifting And Dreaming/Truly	30
56	London HLF 8218	Hold Me Tight/Uncle Joe	30

DINO, DESI & BILLY

65	Reprise R 20367	I'm A Fool/So Many Ways	12
66	Reprise R 23047	Not The Loving Kind/Chimes Of Freedom	12

KENNY DINO

61	HMV POP 960	Your Ma Said You Cried In Your Sleep Last Night/Dream A Girl	15

DINOSAUR JR

88	Blast First BFFP 30	Freak Scene (censored)/Keep The Glove (plain white labels, no p/s, promo only)	5
89	The Catalogue CAT 069/2	Just Like Heaven/LUNACHICKS: Get Off The Road (33rpm square flexidisc with The Catalogue magazine)	7
89	Blast First BFFP 47CD	Just Like Heaven/Throw Down/Chunks (A Last Rites Tune)/Freak Scene (Uncensored Version)/Keep The Glove (CD, picture disc)	10
97	Trade 2 TRDSC 009	I'm Insane (2000 copies pressed)	5
06	Blast First PIL 0713	Been There All The Time/Back To Your Heart	6
89	Blast First BFFP 31	BUG (LP)	15

DIO

(see also Elf, Rainbow, Roger Glover, Black Sabbath, John Lawton)

75	Purple PUR 128	Sitting In A Dream (as Ronnie Dio featuring Roger Glover & Guests)/ JOHN LAWTON: Little Chalk Blue	15
83	Vertigo DIOP 2	Rainbow In The Dark/Stand Up And Shout (live) (picture disc)	7
84	Vertigo DIOP 4	Mystery/Eat Your Heart Out (live) (picture disc)	6
85	Vertigo DIOD 5	Rock'n'Roll Children/Sacred Heart (gatefold p/s)	5
85	Vertigo DIOW 512	Rock'n'Roll Children/We Rock (live)/The Last In Line (live) (12", white vinyl, stickered PVC sleeve)	8

			MINT VALUE £
85	Vertigo DIOFP 6	Hungry For Heaven/King Of Rock And Roll (p/s, with poster & sticker)	5
85	Vertigo DIOP 6	Hungry For Heaven/King Of Rock And Roll (dragon-shaped picture disc)	8
85	Vertigo DIOW 612	Hungry For Heaven/The Message (12", white vinyl)	8
86	Vertigo DIOP 710	THE DIO EP (10", shaped picture disc)	8
86	Vertigo DIO 712	THE DIO EP (12", p/s with family tree)	8
86	Vertigo DIO 712	THE DIO EP (2x7" gatefold sleeve)	8
87	Vertigo DIOP 912	Hey Angel/Why Are They Watching Me?/Rock'n'Roll Children/Mystery (12", picture disc with insert)	8
86	Vertigo VERB 40	INTERMISSION (mini-LP with postcards & discography, stickered sleeve)	12
93	Vertigo 518486-1	STRANGE HIGHWAYS (LP, on 'swirl' label, with inner sleeve)	15

DION (& BELMONTS)

(see also Belmonts)

78s

58	London HL 8646	I Wonder Why/Teen Angel (as Dion & Belmonts)	60
58	London HL 8718	I Can't Go On (Rosalie)/No One Knows (as Dion & Belmonts)	30
59	London HL 8799	Don't Pity Me/Just You (as Dion & Belmonts)	30
59	London HLU 8874	A Teenager In Love/I've Cried Before (as Dion & Belmonts)	30
59	Pye International 7N 25038	A Lover's Prayer/Every Little Thing I Do (as Dion & Belmonts)	60
60	London HLU 9030	Where Or When/That's My Desire (as Dion & Belmonts)	90

SINGLES

58	London HL 8646	I Wonder Why/Teen Angel (as Dion & Belmonts)	60
58	London HL 8718	I Can't Go On (Rosalie)/No One Knows (as Dion & Belmonts)	50
59	London HL 8799	Don't Pity Me/Just You (as Dion & Belmonts)	50
59	London HL 8874	A Teenager In Love/I've Cried Before (mispressing as Dion & Delmonts)	40
59	London HLU 8874	A Teenager In Love/I've Cried Before (as Dion & Belmonts)	35

(The above 45s were originally issued with triangular centre, round-centre re-pressings are worth half these values.)

59	Pye International 7N 25038	A Lover's Prayer/Every Little Thing I Do (as Dion & Belmonts)	50
60	London HLU 9030	Where Or When/That's My Desire (as Dion & Belmonts)	25
60	Top Rank JAR 368	When You Wish Upon A Star/My Private Joy (as Dion & Belmonts)	20
60	Top Rank JAR 503	In The Still Of The Night/Swinging On A Star (as Dion & Belmonts)	20
60	Top Rank JAR 521	Lonely Teenager/Little Miss Blue	20
61	Top Rank JAR 545	Havin' Fun/North-East End Of The Corner	15
61	Top Rank JAR 586	Runaround Sue/Runaway Girl	12
62	HMV POP 971	The Wanderer/The Majestic	12
62	HMV POP 1020	Lovers Who Wander/(I Was) Born To Cry	10
62	Stateside SS 115	Little Diane/Lost For Sure	10
62	Stateside SS 139	Love Came To Me/Little Girl	8
63	CBS AAG 133	Ruby Baby/He'll Only Hurt You	12
63	Stateside SS 161	Sandy/Faith	20
63	CBS AAG 145	This Little Girl/The Loneliest Man In The World	8
63	Stateside SS 209	Come Go With Me/King Without A Queen	15
63	CBS AAG 161	Be Careful Of Stones That You Throw/I Can't Believe (That You Don't Love Me Anymore)	10
63	CBS AAG 169	Donna, The Prima Donna/You're Mine	10
63	CBS AAG 177	Drip Drop/No One's Waiting For Me	10
64	CBS AAG 188	I'm Your Hoochie Coochie Man/The Road I'm On (Gloria)	12
64	CBS AAG 224	Johnnie B. Goode/Chicago Blues	15
65	CBS 201728	Sweet, Sweet Baby/Unloved, Unwanted Me (as Dion Di Mucci)	12
65	CBS 201780	Spoonful/Kickin' Child	12
66	HMV POP 1565	Berimbau (as Dion & Belmonts)/My Girl The Month Of May	25
67	HMV POP 1586	Movin' Man/For Bobbie (as Dion & Belmonts)	12
68	London HLP 10229	Abraham, Martin And John/Daddy Rollin'	6
69	London HLP 10277	Both Sides Now/You Better Watch Yourself (Sonny Boy)	5
70	Warner Bros WB 7356	If We Only Have Love/Natural Man	5
70	Warner Bros WB 7401	Your Own Back Yard/Sit Down, Old Friend	5
71	Warner Bros WB 6120	Close To It All/Windows	5
71	Warner Bros K 16100	Peaceful Place/Sunniland	5
72	Warner Bros K 16132	Sanctuary/Brand New Morning	5
75	Phil Spector Intl. 2101 005	Make The Woman Love Me/Running Close Behind You	6
75	Phil Spector Intl. 2010 012	Born To Be With You/Good Lovin' Man	8

EPs

62	HMV 7EG 8749	SWINGALONG WITH DION	70
63	Stateside SE 1006	DION'S HITS	40

ALBUMS

59	London HA-U 2194	PRESENTING DION AND THE BELMONTS (as Dion & Belmonts)	300
60	Top Rank 25-027	THE TOPPERMOST - VOL. 1 (as Dion & Belmonts, with others)	75
61	HMV CLP 1539	RUNAROUND SUE	100
63	Stateside SL 10034	LOVERS WHO WANDER	80
63	CBS (S) BPG 62137	RUBY BABY (mono/stereo)	25
64	CBS (S) BPG 62203	DONNA THE PRIMA DONNA (mono/stereo)	25
67	HMV CLP 3618	TOGETHER AGAIN (as Dion & Belmonts, also stereo CSD 3618)	40
70	London HA-P/SH-P 8390	DION	12

DION (Cameron) & THREE TOPS

(see also Three Tops)

67	Doctor Bird DB 1101	Miserable Friday/This World Has A Feeling	30
72	Big BG 331	Three Tops Time/UNDERGROUND PEOPLE: Tops (Version)	10

CELINE DION

93	Columbia 474743	COLOUR OF MY LOVE (LP)	25

DIOS MALOS

06	Full Time Hobby FTH 012S	I Want It All/Asshole (p/s, 500 only)	8

DIPLOMATS

(see also Scene)

82	Exchange EX 1	Memories Of You/I'll Keep Holding On (p/s)	7

MINT VALUE £

DIPLOMATS
67 Caltone TONE 108 Meet Me At The Corner/Do It To Me Baby (by Lloyd & Groovers) 25
68 Caltone TONE 109 Going Alone/My Heart My Soul (by Lloyd & Groovers) 30
68 Caltone TONE 112 Strong Man/Listen To The Music (by Lloyd & Groovers) 30
68 Direction 58-3899 I Can Give You Love/I'm So Glad I Found You 20

DIRECT CURRENT MCS
90 Underground Recordz TUBE1 Keep In Step/Gangland Rap (12") 45

DIRECT HITS
(see also Exits)
82 Whaam! WHAAM 007 Modesty Blaise/Sunny Honey Girl (p/s) 15
85 Direct POP 001 Christopher Cooper/She Really Didn't Care (p/s) 7

DIRECTION
93 Detour DR 003 Yesterday/The Kids Wanna New Direction (p/s, 1,000 only) 6

DIRECTIONS
(see also Big Sound Authority)
79 Tortch TOR 004 Three Bands Tonite/On The Train (p/s, with badge) 80
79 Tortch TOR 004 Three Bands Tonite/On The Train (p/s) 75

DIRECTIONS IN JAZZ UNIT
64 Philips BL 7625 DIRECTIONS IN JAZZ (LP) 100

DIRE STRAITS
(see also Mark Knopfler, Notting Hillbillies)
82 Vertigo DSTR 101 Private Investigations/Badges Posters Stickers T-Shirts (10", p/s) 6
84 Vertigo DSTR 610 Love Over Gold (live)/Solid Rock (live) (10", p/s) 6
85 Vertigo DSTR 910 So Far Away/Walk Of Life (10", p/s) 6
85 Vertigo DSTR 1010 Money For Nothing/Love Over Gold (live) (10", p/s) 6
85 Vertigo DSPIC 10 Money For Nothing/Love Over Gold (live) (shaped picture disc with plinth) 12
85 Vertigo DSPIC 11 Brothers In Arms/Going Home - Theme From 'Local Hero' (Live Version) (oblong picture disc in stickered PVC sleeve) 10
85 Vertigo DSTR 1110 Brothers In Arms/Going Home - Theme From 'Local Hero' (Live Version) (10", p/s) 7
85 Vertigo 884 285-2 Brothers In Arms (short)/Going Home (live)/Brothers In Arms (long)/ Why Worry (CD, promo only) 30
88 Vertigo DSCD 15 Sultans Of Swing/Portobello Belle (live)/Romeo And Juliet/ Money For Nothing (CD, card sleeve) 8
88 Vertigo 080 130-2 Money For Nothing (Full Length Version)/One World/So Far Away (CD Video) 15
88 Vertigo 080 134-2 Walk Of Life/Why Worry (LP Version)/Ride Across The River (CD Video) 15
89 Vertigo 080 128-2 Sultans Of Swing/Wild West End/Down The Waterline (CD Video) 15
89 Vertigo 080 132-2 Brothers In Arms (Full Length Version)/Your Latest Trick/ Ride Across The River (CD Video) 15
89 Vertigo 080 136-2 Twisting By The Pool/Two Young Lovers/If I Had You/ Twisting By The Pool (live) (CD Video) 15
91 Vertigo DSHAM 17 Heavy Fuel/Planet Of New Orleans/Kingdom Come (3" CD - Hamburger shape p/s) 8
82 Vertigo HS 6359 034 MAKING MOVIES (LP, half-speed master recording) 15
82 Vertigo HS 9102 021 DIRE STRAITS (LP, half-speed master recording) 15

DIRK & STIG
(see also Rutles, Neil Innes)
78 Ring O' 2017 109/DIB 1 Ging Gang Goolie/Mr. Sheene (unissued) 0
79 EMI EMI 2852 Ging Gang Goolie/Mr. Sheene (p/s, black vinyl) 18
79 EMI EMI 2852 Ging Gang Goolie/Mr. Sheene (p/s, khaki vinyl) 10

DIRT
82 Crass 221984/7 NEVER MIND THE DIRT HERE'S THE BOLLOCKS (LP) 18

DIRTY BLUES BAND
(see also Bacon Fat and Juicy Lucy)
68 Stateside S(S)L 10234 DIRTY BLUES BAND (LP) 35
69 Stateside S(S)L 10268 STONE DIRT (LP) 30

DIRTY DOG
78 Lightning GIL 511 Let Go Of My Hand/Shouldn't Do It/Gonna Quit/Guitar In My Hand (p/s) 25

DIRTY HARRY
73 Unity UN 573 Big Haire/YOUNG DOUG: Skank In Skank 5
76 Treble C CCC 015 Djamballa (with Bobby Ellis)/BIG JOE: Rock Up A Zion 8

DIRTY STRANGERS
(see also Rolling Stones)
89 Thrill TH 3 Bathing Belles/Oh Yeah/Hands Up (p/s, featuring Keith Richards) 8

DIRTY TRICKS
75 Polydor 2383351 DIRTY TRICKS (LP, red label) 30

DISASTER
91 Tone Deaf TONE DEAF 1 WAR CRY (LP) 20

DISASTER
93 Croydon CR 1 Computer Programers Are On E/Not What We Ordered (12") 8

DISCHARGE
(see also Broken Bones)
80 Clay CLAY 1 Realities Of War/They Declare It/But After The Gig/Society's Victim (p/s) 8
80 Clay CLAY 3 Fight Back/War's No Fairy Tale/Always Restrictions/You Take Part In Creating This System/Religion Instigates (p/s) 7
80 Clay CLAY 5 Decontrol/It's No TV Sketch/Tomorrow Belongs To Us (p/s) 10
81 Clay CLAY 6 Never Again/Death Dealers/Two Monstrous Nuclear Stock-Piles (p/s) 7

MINT VALUE £

81	Clay PLATE 2	WHY (12" EP)	10
82	Clay CLAY 14	State Violence, State Control/Doomsday (p/s)	7
83	Clay CLAY 29	Price Of Silence/Born To Die In The Gutter (p/s)	7
82	Clay CLAYLP 3	HEAR NOTHING, SEE NOTHING, SAY NOTHING (LP, original issue has "Pay no more than £3.99" on top right of sleeve)	20
84	Clay CLAYLP 12	NEVER AGAIN (LP, red vinyl)	18

DISCIPLE

69	Parlophone R 5760	Cherie Alamayonaika/Caucasoid Junkie	35

DISCIPLES OF BELIAL

95	Praxis PRAXIS 17	GOAT OF MENDES EP (12")	40
97	Praxis PRAXIS 7	Lucifer We Praise Thee/Sell Your Soul To The Devil/One God (p/s)	50

DISCIPLES RIDDIM SECTION

03	Jah Tubbys JT 10018	Roots Workout/Mission Of Dub (10")	25

DISCO BROTHERS

(see also Nick Lowe, Tartan Horde, Roogalator, Damned, Brinsley Schwartz)

76	United Artists	THE DISCO BROTHERS/THE TARTAN HORDE (EP, p/s)	6

DISCO DUB BAND

76	Movers MO 1	For the Love Of Money/For The Love Of Money Part 2	50

DISCO 2000

(see also J.A.M.s, KLF, Timelords, Bill Drummond, Space)

87	KLF Comms. D 2001	I Gotta CD (7" Edit) (unissued, white labels only)	18
87	KLF Comms. D 2000	I Gotta CD/I Love Disco 2000 (12", p/s)	12

DISCORDS

91	Hangman 41 UP	SECOND TO NO-ONE (LP)	12

DISCO STUDENTS

79	Yeah Yeah Yeah UHHUH 1	South Africa House/Kafkaesque (no p/s)	15
80	Yeah Yeah Yeah UHHUH 2	A Boy With A Penchant For Open-Necked Shirts/Pink Triangles/Credit (no p/s)	15

DISCO ZOMBIES

(see also Steppes, Fifty Fantastics)

79	South Circular SGS 106	Drums Over London/Heartbeats Love (black, white & pink or black, white & green handmade wraparound p/s)	30
79	Uptown/Wizzo WIZZO 1	THE INVISIBLE (EP)	12
81	Dining Out TUX 2	Here Come The Buts/Mary Millington (p/s)	15

DISCS

65	Columbia DB 7477	Not Meant To Be/Come Back To Me	7

BABA DISE

69	Gas GAS 118	Wanted/SENSATIONS: I'll Always Love You	30

DISGUISE

78	Chiswick CHIS 107	Hey Baby/Juvenile Delinquent	10

DISORDER

80	Ace ACE 12	Air Raid/Law And Disorder (1st 100 in custom 'War Book' p/s)	150
80	Ace ACE 12	Air Raid/Law And Disorder	50
80	Durham Book Centre BOOK 1	Reality Crisis/1984 (over sized p/s)	20

DISORDER

81	Disorder ORDER 1	Complete Disorder/Insane Youth/Today's World/Violent Crime (p/s)	6
81	Disorder ORDER 2	Distortion To Deafness/More Than Fights/Daily Life/ You've Got To Be Someone (p/s)	5
82	Disorder 12ORDER 3	PERDITION (12" EP)	8
83	Disorder ORDER 4	MENTAL DISORDER (EP)	6
84	Disorder 12 ORDER 5	THE SINGLES COLLECTION (12" EP)	10
84	Disorder AARGH! 1	UNDER THE SCALPEL BLADE (LP, with poster)	15

DISRUPTERS

85	Radical Change 12 RC 8	ALIVE IN THE ELECTRIC CHAIR (12" EP, with insert)	20
83	Radical Change RCLP1	UNREHEARSED WRONGS (LP)	30
80s	Radical Change RCLP3	PLAYING WITH FIRE (LP)	20

TOM DISSEVELT

65	Philips BL 7681	FANTASY IN ORBIT (LP)	40

DISTANT COUSINS

66	CBS 202352	She Ain't Loving You/Here Today, Gone Tomorrow	18
67	CBS 2800	Mister Sebastian/Empty House	7

DISTINCTIVE DRONE

79	No label, no cat no	The Count/The Count (Version) hand-made cassette single	5
79	No label, no cat no	DISTINCTIVE DRONE (cassette LP)	15

DISTRACTIONS

79	Factory FAC 12	Time Goes By So Slow/Pillow Fight (p/s)	15
79	TJM TJM 2	YOU'RE NOT GOING OUT DRESSED LIKE THAT (12" EP)	12

DISTRAINERS

79	DJ Records BECK 885	Say Goodbye/Spies In Your Eyes (no p/s, 300 only)	125

DISTRIBUTORS

80	Tap TAP 1	TV Me/Wireless (various foldover p/s)	6
81	Red Rhino RED 9	Hold/Get Rid Of These Things/Wages For Lovers (12", p/s)	8

DIVERSIONS

76	Gull GULS 28	But Is It Funky/To Make Us Happy	5

DIVINE

84	Proto ENAT 118	You Think You're A Man/You Think You're A Man (Remix)/Give It Up (12", p/s)	8

MINT VALUE £

DIVINE COMEDY

91	Setanta SET 008	Timewatch/Jerusalem/The Rise And Fall (12", p/s)	10
92	Setanta SET 011	Europop: New Wave/Intifada/Monitor/Timewatch/Jerusalem/ The Rise And Fall (12", p/s)	10
92	Setanta SET 011CD	Europop: New Wave/Intifada/Monitor/Timewatch/Jerusalem/ The Rise And Fall (CD)	15
93	Setanta CAO 008	Lucy/The Pop Singer's Fear Of The Pollen Count/ I Was Born Yesterday (mail order, p/s)	10
93	Setanta CAO 009	Your Daddy's Car (Demo)/THE GLEE CLUB: Free To Believe (33 rpm clear vinyl flexi)	10
93	Setanta DC 001	Indulgence No. 1: Hate My Way/Untitled Melody/Europe By Train (picture disc)	10
94	Setanta DC 002	Indulgence No. 2: A Drinking Song/When The Lights Go Out All Over Europe/ Tonight We Fly (hand-finished wraparound p/s, stamped labels)	15
90	Setanta SETLPM 002	FANFARE FOR THE COMIC MUSE (LP, with inner sleeve)	40
90	Setanta SETCD 002	FANFARE FOR THE COMIC MUSE (CD, beware of counterfeits)	40
94	Setanta SETCD 013	PROMENADE (CD, with bonus 4-track live CD)	20
97	Setanta SETCDL 036	A SHORT ALBUM ABOUT LOVE (numbered boxed digipak, with 3 postcards)	20

DIXIE BELLES

63	London HLU 9797	Down At Papa Joe's/Rock, Rock, Rock	10
64	London HLU 9842	Southtown, U.S.A./Why Don't You Set Me Free?	10
64	London REU 1434	THE DIXIE BELLES (EP)	25
64	London HA-U/SH-U 8152	DOWN AT PAPA JOE'S (LP, with Cornbread & Jerry)	20

DIXIE CUPS

64	Pye International 7N 25245	Chapel Of Love/Ain't That Nice	15
64	Red Bird RB 10006	People Say/Girls Can Tell (some copies on Pye label)	8
64	Red Bird RB 10012	You Should Have Seen The Way He Looked At Me/No True Love	15
64	Red Bird RB 10017	Little Bell/Another Boy Like Mine	15
65	Red Bird RB 10024	Iko Iko/Gee Baby Gee	12
65	Red Bird RB 10032	Gee The Moon Is Shining Bright/I'm Gonna Get You Yet	20
65	HMV POP 1453	Two Way Poc A Way/That's Where It's At	15
66	HMV POP 1524	What Kind Of Fool/Danny Boy	25
66	HMV POP 1557	Love Ain't So Bad (After All)/Daddy Said No	30
71	Buddah 2011 079	Chapel Of Love/People Say	5
65	Red Bird RB 20100	CHAPEL OF LOVE (LP)	60
66	HMV CLP 1916	RIDING HIGH (LP)	50

DIXIE DRIFTER

65	Columbia DB 7710	Soul Heaven/Three Chairs Theme	12

DIXIE FOUR

60s	Rarities RA 3	THE DIXIE FOUR (EP)	25

DIXIE HUMMINGBIRDS

64	Vogue V 2422	Have A Talk With Jesus/In The Morning	15
64	Vogue LAE-P 588	PRAYER FOR PEACE (LP)	25

DIXIELANDERS

63	Vocalion V 9209	Cyclone/Mardyke	35

DIXIELAND JUG BLOWERS

(see also Johnny Dodds)

54	HMV 7M 223	Memphis Shake/Boodle-Am-Shake	15
54	HMV 7M 233	Hen Party Blues/Carpet Alley Breakdown	15

DIXIE PEACH

85	Jah Tubbys JT 005	Just Worries/Pure Worries (12")	100
85	Jah Tubbys JT 014	Spin Spin/Spin Style (12", with the Offbeat Posse)	40
86	Jah Tubbys JT 018	Slaughter/Slaughter Mix (12")	60
86	Y&D YDD 0102	Raggamuffin And Rambo/Ragamuffin Style (12")	40
87	Y&D YDD 0106	Get Up And Skank/LONG MAN AND THE OFFBEAT POSSE: Skank With Me/OFFBEAT POSSE: The Skank (12")	40
87	Y&D YDD 0112	Hold Onto Your Man/Tonight Is The Night (12")	30
88	Y&D YDD 0119	Running Around/Run Come Follow Me Now (12")	30
00	Jah Tubbys JT 7003	Every Step/DISCIPLES RIDDIM SECTION: Step Dub	20
01	Jah Tubbys JT 7008	I Heard Them Bawling/OFFBEAT POSSE: Bawling For Riddim	20
03	Jah Tubbys JT 10013	Sufferers Time/What Am I to Do? (10", with the Offbeat Posse)	30
03	Jah Tubbys JT 10017	Jah Jah Army/Who's Gonna Stop Us? (10", with the Offbeat Posse)	30
06	Jah Tubbys JT 10027	Roots Vibration (with the Roots Squad)/Got To Be Humble (with WD Production)	20

THE DIXIES

64	Parlophone R 5223	Love Made A Fool/Valley Of Tears	15

ERROL DIXON

(see also Chicken Shack)

60	Blue Beat BB 27	Midnight Track/Anytime Anywhere	15
61	Blue Beat BB 46	Mama Shut Your Door/Too Much Whisky	15
62	Blue Beat BB 86	Bad Bad Woman/Early This Morning	15
62	Island WI 017	Morning Train/Lonely Heart	20
63	Island WI 069	I Love You/Tell Me More	20
63	Carnival CV 7001	Oo Wee Baby/Twisting And Shaking	10
63	Carnival CV 7004	Mean And Evil Woman/Tutti Frutti	10
64	Oriole CB 1945	Rocks In My Pillow/Give Me More Time (as Errol Dixon & Bluebeaters)	70
66	Blue Beat BB 337	Gloria/Heavy Shuffle	12
66	Blue Beat BB 344	You're No Good/Midnight Bus	12
66	Rainbow RAI 104	I Need Someone To Love/I Want (as Errol Dixon & Goodtime Band)	35
66	Fab EP 1	I Need Someone To Love/I Want (reissue)	20
67	Ska Beat JB 271	Midnight Party/It Makes No Difference	20
67	Direct DS 5002	I Don't Want/The Hoop	60

			MINT VALUE £
67	Decca F 12613	Six Questions/Not Again	15
67	Decca F 12717	True Love Never Runs Smooth/What Ya Gonna Do (B-side with Judy Kay)	8
68	Decca F 12826	Back To The Chicken Shack (as Big City Blues Of Errol Dixon)/ I Done Found Out.	8
69	Doctor Bird DB 1197	Why Hurt Yourself/She Started To Scream	18
60s	Carnival CU 7002	Crazy Baby/Our First Love (with Maynell Wilson)	10
70	Gas GAS 148	Something On Your Mind/I Need Love	8
72	Transatlantic BIG 503	Let The Love Shine into Your Heart/In A Moment Of Weakness	10
65	Decca DFE 8626	SINGS FATS (EP, with Honeydrippers)	60
68	Decca LK/SKL 4962	BLUES IN THE POT (LP, with Chicken Shack)	100
70	Transatlantic TRA 225	THAT'S HOW YOU GOT KILLED BEFORE (LP)	25

HUGH DIXON

64	London HA-U 8188	FRANTIC GUITARS (LP)	15

JEFF DIXON

67	Coxsone CS 7015	The Rock/HAMBOYS: Harder On The Rock	35
68	Studio One SO 2051	Tickle Me/ENFORCERS: Forgive Me	50

WILLIE DIXON & ALLSTARS

56	London HLU 8297	Walking The Blues/Crazy For My Baby	1500
56	London HLU 8297	Walking The Blues/Crazy For My Baby (78)	150
64	Pye International 7N 25270	Crazy For My Baby/Walkin' The Blues (reissue)	25

TEX DIXSON

70	Ackee ACK 111	Funky Trombone/Crying Horn	10
70	Ackee ACK 112	My Ring/Here I Am	10

DIXXY SISTERS

54	Columbia SCM 5105	Spin The Bottle Polka/The Game Of Broken Hearts	12

DIZZY MANS BAND

70	Warner Bros WB 8015	Tickatoo/My Love	5

DJ B and EZM.

92	Industrial Noize DE 001	Can't Beat Ruff Beats/Shockin' To The Break Of Dawn (12", stamped white label)	35

DJ CHEMISTRY MEETS JACK SMOOTH

(see also Chemistry, Jack Smooth)

94	Homegrown HG 015	Alchemy/Freefall (12")	12

DJ CRYSTL

92	Lucky Spin LSR 001	Suicidal/Drop XTC (12")	20
93	Force Ten FTR 001	The Dark Crystl/Inna Year 3000 (12")	10
93	Dee Jay Recordings DJX 008	Crystalize/Deep Space (12")	15
93	Dee Jay... DJX 010	Meditation/Warpdrive (12")	20
94	Dee Jay... DJX 016	Your Destiny/Sweet Dreamz (12")	8
94	Dee Jay... DJX 020	Let It Roll/Paradise (12")	12
94	Lucky Spin STU 01	Untitled (1-sided, white label 12")	8

DJ CRYSTL & SLIPMASTER J

92	Lucky Spin LSR 004	Frantic Situation/Drop XTC (12")	25

DJ CYCLONE

96	Acid Fever MDMA 9612	909 TRAX EP: Trak 101/Trak 3/4/Trak 303/Trak 23 (12")	20
96	Acid Fever MDMA 9613	Innersense (Hardcore Remix)/Innersense (Original Hardcore Mix)/ Mushroom Of Fire/Non-sense (12")	20
96	Acid Fever MDMA 9614 303	joy Ride/Cycloid Spiral Motion/Circular Motion/ Cycloid Spiral Slow Motion (12")	20
97	Acid Fever MDMA 9703	STATE OF THE PLANET EP (12" two tracks, other two tracks by OCTODRED)	15

DJ DADO

96	Steppin' Out IAN 045T	Face It (Club Mix)/(Radio Edit)/(Alternative Mix)/(Status Mix) (12")	15

DJ EXCEL

91	(No company) EDUC 2	Just When You Thought It Was Safe/Breakbeat 1/ Breakbeat 2/Breakbeat 3 /Breakbeat 4 (12")	30

DJ FOOD

00	Ninja Tune ZEN12 015/021	Classic House Tracks From The Vaults (12")	10
90s	Ninja Tune 106267	REFRIED FOOD LUNCHBOX (3-LP)	15
90	Ninja Tune ZEN 02	JAZZ BRAKES VOL. 1 (LP)	15
91	Ninja Tune ZEN 03	JAZZ BRAKES VOL. 2 (LP)	25
92	Ninja Tune ZEN 04	JAZZ BRAKES VOL. 2 (2-LP)	15
92	Ninja Tune ZEN 05	JAZZ BRAKES VOL. 3 (2-LP)	15
93	Ninja Tune ZEN 06	JAZZ BRAKES VOL. 4 (2-LP)	15
94	Ninja Tune ZEN 10	JAZZ BRAKES VOL. 5 (2-LP)	15

DJ FORCE & EVOLUTION

93	Knifeforce KF 003	Fall Down On Me/The Force Will Be With You/Escape The Feeling/ Mine All Mine (12")	30
93	Knifeforce KF 003	Fall Down On Me/The Force Will Be With You/Escape The Feeling/ Mine All Mine (12", red vinyl, 200 only)	35
93	Knifeforce KF 011	Twelve Midnight/Lost It (12")	20
93	Knifeforce KF 16	Poltergeist/Perfect Dreams (10", some on clear vinyl)	20
93	Knifeforce KF 019	Perfect Dreams (Citadel Of Kaos Remix)/Perfect Dreams (Original Mix)/ Fall Down On Me (Remix) (12")	10
93	Knifeforce KF 024	High On Life/Raining Smiles (12")	15
94	Knifeforce KF 028	Perfect Dreams (Vices & Wishdokta Remix/TIMESPAN: Music (Ramos & Supreme Remix) (12", p/s)	8

DJ GOLLUM

(see also Gollum & Gary D, M-Zone & DJ Gollum)

96	UK 44 UK44 07	Pleasant Experience/Mystic Fusion (12")	30
98	UK 44 UK44 15	The Energy (Trance Mix)/The Energy (Rave Mix)/The Energy (Mix Mix) (12", p/s)	10

MINT VALUE £

DJ HARVEY
(see also Black Cock, Ersatz)

96	Noid Recordings NOID 0066	I Am A Man/MONSIEUR D: Hot Love (12")	20
98	Black Cock Records BK 016	LOVE HOTEL EP (12")	12
00	Black Cock Records BK 017	LOVE HOTEL EP 2 (12")	8
00	Weekend Inc WKD 069	Done Turn Me/Protect And Survive (Fuck Loop) (12")	20

DJ JINX

92	Music Madness MM 003	Devotion/Paradise Project/Paradise Project (Bounty Remix) (12")	40

DJ KRUSH
(see also DJ Shadow)

95	Mo' Wax MW 033	A Whim/89.9 Megamix by DJ SHADOW (12", stickered p/s, Promo 12")	8
95	Mo' Wax MW 033	A Whim/89.9 Megamix by DJ SHADOW (12", DJ Copy)	15
93	Mo' Wax MWLP 001	JAZZ HIP JAP (LP)	30
94	Mo' Wax MWLP 025	STRICTLY TURNTABLIZED (2-LP)	20
97	Mo' Wax MW 077 LP	MILIGHT (2-LP)	20
98	Mo' Wax MW 088 LP	HOLONIC (LP)	25
99	Columbia 492893 1	KAKUSEI (2-LP)	18

DJ MAXI JAZZ

91	Tam Tam TT047	Through The Mirror (12", promo)	8
92	Namu NAMU1	EP (EP)	12
92	Namu NAMU2	More Of What You Need (12")	8
92	Namu NAMU3	Moving Up (EP)	10

DJ MAYHEM
(see also Two Dark Troopers)

92	Basement BRSS 008	Damage/Metrix: The Remix/Signal Generator (12")	15
92	Basement BRSS 016	Storm Trooper/Cold Acid (12")	15

DJ MINK FEAT. 2WICE THE TROUBLE

89	FON T18	Hey Hey Can You Relate (4 Mixes) (12")	30
90	Warp WAR4	Hey Hey Can U Relate (3 Mixes) (12")	12

DJ NUT NUT

93	Virtual Motion VM 001	Forbidden Planet/Set My Mind Free (12")	12
94	Production Hse PNT 058 R	The Rumble (Remixes) (12")	25
94	Production Hse PNT 058	The Rumble/Virtual Reality (10" with PURE SCIENCE)	8
94	Babylon BR 001	Press Up (VIP Mix)/Press Up (Dub Mix) (12", stamped white labels)	15
94	Hard Step HRD 001	Special Dedication (Ladies Mix)/Bloodclart Hour (12")	20
96	London Some 'ting LS 006	Special Dedication (DJ Ron Remix)/Special Dedication (The Dream Team Remix) (12")	10

DJ PESHAY

93	Reinforced RIVET 1248	PROTÉGÉ EP (12")	20

DJ SHADOW
(see also Q-Bert, U.N.K.L.E.)

93	Mo' Wax MW 014	In/ Flux/Hindsight (12", plain sleeve, with obi sticker, with the Groove Robbers)	20
93	Mo' Wax MW 014	In/ Flux/Hindsight (12" picture disc, plastic sleeve, with the Groove Robbers)	30
94	Mo' Wax MW 024	Lost And Found/DJ KRUSH: Kemuri (12", p/s)	8
94	Mo' Wax MW 027	What Does Your Soul Look Like (Parts 1, 3 & 4) (12" p/s)	10
96	Mo' Wax MW 057	Midnight In A Perfect World (Remixes)/Mutual Slump (12", p/s)	8
96	Mo' Wax MW 058	Stem/Red Bus Needs To Leave (p/s)	5
97	Mo' Wax MW 063s	High Noon/Organ Donor (Extended Overhaul) (p/s)	10
97	Mo' Wax MW 063	High Noon/Devil's Advocate/Organ Donor (Extended Overhaul) (p/s)	8
97	Mo Wax MW 084	Q-BERT MIX: Camel Bobsled Race/(Mixes) (12")	8
06	No label	Untitled/Untitled (Acapella) (7", 300 only hand-stamped white label given away At door of London Indig02 gig 2007)	25
98	Mo' Wax MW 059	ENDTRODUCING (2-LP, gatefold, spine opening sleeve)	15
96	Mo Wax MW059LP	ENDTRODUCING (2-LP, gatefold, centre opening sleeve)	20

DJ SIDE PHONE/DJ CYDER CLONE

97	Acid Fever MDMA 9705	ACID FLUFF EP (12", three tracks each)	20

DJ TOKEN PACE & TOXIC KEV

92	Face The Bass FBR 001	Losing You/Dreamers Revenge (12")	40

DJ TOOLZ

93	Ninja Tune TOOL 1	BREAK BEATS 'N' GROOVES VOL. 1 (LP)	12
93	Ninja Tune TOOL 2	BREAK BEATS 'N' GROOVES VOL. 2 (LP)	12
93	Ninja Tune TOOL 3	BREAK BEATS 'N' GROOVES VOL. 3 (LP)	12
95	Ninja Tune TOOL 4	BREAK BEATS 'N' GROOVES VOL. 4 (LP)	12

DJ TRACE

91	Orbital 12 ORBIT 11	Inception/Ain't Gonna Wait No More/Love Dove Sound (12")	20
92	(No company, no number)	Rudeboy Hardcore/Untitled/Untitled (white label 12" with DJ Trace and phone number stamped on labels. A-side samples Orinoco Flow)	10
92	Orbital 12OUT 997	Teach Me To Fly/Inception (After Dark Remix) (12")	18
93	Lucky Spin LSR 003	Lost Entity (London Side)/Lost Entity (New York Side) (12")	20
93	Dee Jay Recordings DJX 007	Never Felt This Way (One Step Ahead)/Never Felt This Way (Intel Mix)	8

DJ TRACE & ED RUSH

93	Lucky Spin LSR 008	Don Bad Man/Clean Gun (12")	10

DJ TREMA & THE AVENGER

93	DBS 22	Untitled/Untitled (12", white label, "DBS 22" etched in run-out groove)	45

DJ VADIM

95	Jazz Fudge JFR 001	ABSTRACT HALLUCINATING GASES (EP)	40
95	Jazz Fudge JFR 002	HEDZ AIN'T READY (EP)	20
96	Ninja Tune ZEN1240	NON LATERAL HYPNOSIS (EP)	10
96	Ninja Tune ZEN 1245	AURAL PROSTITUTION (EP)	20

MINT VALUE £

97	Ninja Tune ZEN1251	CONQUEST OF THE IRRATIONAL (EP)	12
99	Ninja Tune ZEN 1279	Friction/Raps Don't Grow On Trees (12")	8
98	Ninja Tune ZEN 31/2	U.S.S.R. RECONSTRUCTION (2 x 12")	15

D'JURANN JURANN

(see also Paul King, King Earl Boogie Band, Mungo Jerry)

74	Dawn DNS 1068	Streakin'/Oh! Janine	10

JED(RZEZ) DMOCHOWSKI

(see also V.I.P.'s)

83	Whaam! WHAAM 009	Sha-La-La-La (Dance With Me)/Ruined City (with Jed on p/s)	8
83	Whaam! WHAAM 009	Sha-La-La-La (Dance With Me)/Ruined City (without Jed on p/s)	10
82	Whaam! WHAAM 84	STALLIONS OF MY HEART (LP)	12

DMS

91	Production House PNT 032	Exterminate (12")	15
92	Production House PNT 039	Vengeance/Love Overdose (Remix) (12")	15

DNV

(see also Another Pretty Face, Funhouse, Waterboys, TV21)

79	New Pleasures Z2	Mafia/Death In Venice/Goodbye 70s (foldout p/s)	20

D.O.A.

93	Alt. Tentacles VIRUS 120	It's Not Unusual/Dead Men Tell No Tales (yellow vinyl)	5
81	Alt. Tentacles VIRUS 7	POSITIVELY D.O.A. (EP)	7
83	Alt. Tentacles VIRUS 31	BLOODIED BUT UNBOWED - THE DAMAGE TO DATE 1978-84 (12" EP)	8
84	Alt. Tentacles VIRUS 24	WAR ON 45 (12" EP)	8
85	Alt. Tentacles VIRUS 42	DON'T TURN YOUR BACK (ON DESPERATE TIMES) (LP)	12
85	Alt. Tentacles VIRUS 44	LET'S WRECK THE PARTY (LP, with insert & small spy logo)	12

CARL DOBKINS JNR.

59	Brunswick 05804	My Heart Is An Open Book/My Pledge To You	15
59	Brunswick 05811	If You Don't Want My Lovin'/Love Is Everything	25
60	Brunswick 05817	Lucky Devil/(There's A Little Song A-Singing) In My Heart	15
60	Brunswick 05832	Exclusively Yours/One Little Girl	10
60	Brunswick LAT 8329	CARL DOBKINS JNR. (LP)	75

BOBBY DOBSON

(see also Dobby Dobson)

69	Punch PH 4	Strange/Your New Love	10

BONNIE DOBSON

69	RCA RCA 1901	I'm Your Woman/I Got Stung	6
70	RCA SF 8079	BONNIE DOBSON (LP)	35
72	Argo ZFB 79	BONNIE DOBSON (LP)	30
76	Polydor 2383 400	MORNING DEW (LP)	15

DOBBY DOBSON (& DELTAS)

(see also Bobby Dobson, Chuck & Dobby, Bruce Bennett, Ernest Wilson & Freddy)

65	King KG 1008	Cry A Little Cry/Diamonds And Pearls (as Dobby Dobson & Deltas)	15
67	Trojan TR 011	Loving Pauper/TOMMY McCOOK & SUPERSONICS: Sir Don	20
68	Studio One SO 2068	Walking In The Footsteps/SOUL VENDORS: Studio Rock	50
68	Coxsone CS 7058	Seems To Me I'm Losing You/GAYLADS: Red Rose	35
69	Blue Cat BS 171	Strange/Your New Love	25
69	Punch PH 12	The Masquerade Is Over/Love For Ambition	10
70	Success RE 906	Crazy/RUPIE EDWARDS ALL STARS: Your New Love	6
70	Big BG 303	That Wonderful Sound/I Wasn't Born Yesterday	6
70	Big BG 310	Halfway To Paradise/Utopia	5
71	Dynamic DYN 426	Carry That Weight/More Weight	5
69	Pama SECO 33	STRANGE (LP)	50
70	Trojan TBL 145	THAT WONDERFUL SOUND (LP)	35

LYN DOBSON

(see also Manfred Mann, Soft Machine, Miller Anderson)

74	Fresh Air 6370 501	JAM SANDWICH (LP)	30

DOC SCOTT

91	Absolute 2 ABS 001DJR	Surgery (Remix) (12")	8
92	Absolute 2 ABS 006DJ	The N.H.S. EP Vol 2 - The Second Chapter EP (12")	10
92	Absolute 2 ABS 006DJR	The N.H.S. EP Vol 2 - The Second Chapter (Remix) EP (12")	60
92	Absolute 2 ABS 006DJRR	The N.H.S. EP Vol 2 - The Second Chapter (Remix) (12")	8
94	Metalheadz MET 004	Far Away (Fourteen Flavors Of Funk)/It's Yours (12")	20
94	Reinforced RIVET 1256	Last Action Hero EP (12")	15
94	Metalheadz MH 001	Doc Scott/GOLDIE : Unreleased Metal (12")	20
95	Metalheadz METH 015	Drumz '95 (Nasty Habits Remix)/Blue Skies (12")	15

ROY DOCKER

68	Domain D3	Mellow Moonlight/MUSIC THROUGH SIX: Riff Raff	20
69	Pama PM 750	When/Go	20
69	Pama PM 756	Everyday Will Be Like A Holiday/I'm An Outcast	8

DR. ATOMIC

93	Guerilla GRRR42	Schudelfloss (12")	20

DOCTOR BROWN

95	Magic Gnome	ANOTHER REALM (LP, 500 only)	15

DR. CALCULUS

(see also Stephen Tin Tin Duffy)

86	10 DIXCD 45	DESIGNER BEATNIK (CD)	25

DOCTOR DARK

(see also Snivelling Shits)

76	Target TGT 102	Red Hot Passion/Instrumental (no p/s)	7

MINT VALUE £

DOCTOR FATHER

(see also 10cc, Godley & Creme, Hotlegs)

70	Pye 7N 17977	Umbopo/Roll On	7

DR. FEELGOOD & THE INTERNS (U.S.)

(see also Piano Red)

62	Columbia DB 4838	Dr. Feelgood/Mister Moonlight	25
64	Columbia DB 7228	The Doctor's Doogie/Blang Dong	25
66	CBS 202099	Don't Tell Me No Dirty/Where Did You Go	20
68	Capitol CL 15569	Sugar Bee/You're So Used To It	20
64	Columbia SEG 8310	DR. FEELGOOD AND THE INTERNS (EP)	75

DR. FEELGOOD (U.K.)

(see also Wilko Johnson, Lew Lewis, Oil City Sheiks)

74	United Artists UP 35760	Roxette/(Get Your Kicks On) Route 66 (no p/s)	5
75	United Artists UP 35815	She Does It Right/I Don't Mind (no p/s)	5
75	United Artists UP 35857	Back In The Night/I'm A Man	5
77	United Artists UP 36304	She's A Windup/Hi-Rise (p/s)	5
77	United Artists 12UP 36304	She's A Windup/Hi-Rise/Homework (12", die-cut sleeve)	8
77	United Artists UP 36332	Baby Jane/Looking Back	6
77	United Artists 12UP 36332	Baby Jane/Looking Back/You Upset Me Baby (live) (12", p/s)	8
79	United Artists X/Y/ZUP 36506	As Long As The Price Is Right/Down At The (Other) Doctors (p/s, either black, blue, brown or violet vinyl, 3 different p/s designs)	5
86	Stiff BUY 253	Don't Wait Up/Something Good (shrink-wrapped with bonus 45: "Back In The Night"/"Milk And Alcohol" [FBUY 56]) (p/s)	5
75	United Artists UAS 29727	DOWN BY THE JETTY (LP, mono only)	12
75	United Artists UAS 29880	MALPRACTICE (LP)	12
76	United Artists UAS 29990	STUPIDITY (LP, with stickered covers & bonus 7": "Riot In Cell Block No. 9"/"Johnny B. Goode" [FEEL 1])	15
79	United Artists UAK 30239	AS IT HAPPENS (LP, with inner sleeve & bonus 7" "Encore EP": "Riot In Cell Block No. 9"/"The Blues Had A Baby And They Named It Rock'N'Roll"/"Lights Out"/"Great Balls Of Fire" [p/s, FEEL 2], with inner sleeve.	15

DR. HOOK

73	CBS 1037	The Cover Of "Radio Times" (1-sided, promo only, by Dr. Hook & Friends)	50
78	Capitol CL 15992	The Radio/Only Sixteen/I'm A Lamb (p/s)	8
78	Capitol PSLP 314	FOR YOU FROM DR. HOOK (EP, promo only)	10
71	CBS 64754	DR. HOOK AND THE MEDICINE SHOW (LP, plain orange label)	15
71	CBS 65132	SLOPPY SECONDS (LP, plain orange label)	15

DR. JOHN (The Night Tripper)

70	Atco 2091 019	Wash Mama Wash/Mama Roux	12
72	Atlantic K 10158	Iko Iko/Huey Smith Medley	6
72	Atlantic K 10214	Wang Dang Doodle/Big Chief	5
73	Atlantic K 10291	Right Place, Wrong Time/I Been Hoodooed	10
73	Atlantic K 10329	Such A Night/Life	6
68	Atlantic 587/588 147	GRIS GRIS (LP, plum label, mono/stereo)	35
69	Atco 228 018	BABYLON (LP, plum label)	22
70	Atco 2400 015	REMEDIES (LP, plum label)	20
71	Atlantic 2400 161	THE SUN, MOON AND HERBS (LP, plum label, gatefold sleeve with insert)	25
72	Atlantic K 40384	GUMBO (LP, green & orange label, gatefold sleeve)	15
72	Atlantic K 40168	GRIS GRIS (LP, reissue, green & orange label)	15
72	Atlantic K 40250	THE SUN, MOON AND HERBS (LP, reissue, green & orange label, gatefold sleeve with insert)	15
73	Atco K 50017	IN THE RIGHT PLACE (LP, U.K. disc in U.S. stickered 3-way gatefold sleeve)	20
73	CBS 65659	TRIUMVIRATE (LP, with John Hammond & Mike Bloomfield)	15
74	Atlantic K 50035	DESITIVELY BONNAROO (LP)	15
75	DJM DJSLM 2019	CUT ME WHILE I'M HOT (LP)	20
75	United Artists UAG 29902	HOLLYWOOD BE THY NAME (LP, with inner sleeve)	15

DR. K'S BLUES BAND

68	Spark SRLP 101	DR. K'S BLUES BAND (LP, red/silver label)	100

DR. MARIGOLD'S PRESCRIPTION

68	Pye 7N 17493	My Old Man's A Groovy Old Man/People Get Ready	6
69	Pye 7N 17832	You've Got To Build Your Love/My Picture Of Love	6
70	Bell BLL 1096	Breaking The Heart Of A Good Man/Night Hurries On By	6
70	Bell BLL 1126	Sing Along, Sing Along, Sing Along/Father Jim	6
71	Bell BLL 1149	Muddy Water/Come With Me	6

DR. MIX & THE REMIX

79	Rough Trade ROUGH 6	Wall Of Noise (12")	20

DR. OCTAGON

96	Mo' Wax MWLP 046	OCTAGONECOLOGYST (3-LP)	20
96	Mo' Wax MW064LP	INSTRUMENTALYST (OCTAGON BEATS) (LP)	20

DOCTOR ROCKIT

96	Clear CLR 411	Ready To Rockit EP (2 x 10", p/s)	8
96	Clear CLR 416	D For Doktor EP (12", p/s)	12

DR. STRANGELY STRANGE

(see also Sweeney's Men, Gary Moore)

69	Island ILPS 9106	KIP OF THE SERENES (LP, pink label, with black/orange circle logo)	200
69	Island ILPS 9106	KIP OF THE SERENES (LP, later 'palm-tree' label with remix)	100
70	Vertigo 6360 009	HEAVY PETTING (LP, gatefold sleeve, large swirl label; original pressing has machine etched matrix in the run out grooves, beware of counterfeits)	300

DR. TECHNICAL & MACHINES

(see also Dave Brock, Hawkwind)

83	Hawkfan HWFB 1	Zones/Processed (1-sided with insert, mail-order issue, no p/s)	25

MINT VALUE £

DR. WEST'S MEDICINE SHOW & JUNK BAND
(see also Norman Greenbaum)

67	CBS 202492	The Eggplant That Ate Chicago/You Can't Fight City Hall Blues	8
67	CBS 202658	Gondoliers, Shakespeares, Overseers/Daddy I Know	8
68	Page One POF 061	Bullets La Verne/Jigsaw	50
70	Page One POF 176	Gondoliers, Shakespeares, Overseers/Daddy I Know (reissue)	6
69	Page One POLS 017	THE EGGPLANT THAT ATE CHICAGO (LP)	25

DR. WHO
(see also BBC Radiophonic Workshop, Century 21, Jon Pertwee)

76	Argo ZSW 564	DR. WHO AND THE PESCATONS (LP, spoken word, read by Tom Baker & Elizabeth Sladen)	18
79	BBC REC 364	GENESIS OF THE DALEKS (LP, spoken word)	15
81	RNIB	TALKING BOOK (reel-to-reel tape, read by Gabriel Wolf)	20
82	BBC 2LP-22001	DOCTOR WHO COLLECTOR'S EDITION (2-LP, includes "Genesis Of The Daleks" [BBC 22364], "Sound Effects" [BBC 22316], & bonus 7" "Doctor Who"/ "The Astronauts" [RESL 451], with poster)	30

DR. Z

70	Fontana 6007 023	Lady Ladybird/People In The Street	90
71	Vertigo 6360 048	THREE PARTS TO MY SOUL (LP, gatefold sleeve, small swirl label)	1000

PAT DODD

59	Pye International 7N 25030	Stag Party/Odds'n'Dodds	7

DODD'S ALLSTARS

69	Coxsone CS 7096	Mother Aitken (actually by Lord Power)/What A Love (actually by Denzil Laing)	25

JOHNNY DODDS
(see also Dixieland Jugblowers)

53	London AL 3505	JOHNNY DODDS VOLUME 1 (10" LP)	15
54	London AL 3513	JOHNNY DODDS VOLUME 2 (10" LP)	15
55	Vogue Coral LRA 10025	JOHNNY DODDS VOL. 1 (10" LP)	25
55	HMV DLP 1073	JOHNNY DODDS WASHBOARD STOMP (10" LP)	15
56	London AL 3555	JOHNNY DODDS VOLUME 3 (10" LP)	15
57	London AL 3560	JOHNNY DODDS VOLUME 4 (10" LP)	15

MALCOLM DODDS

59	Brunswick 05774	This Is Real (This Is Love)/I'll Always Be With You	5
59	Brunswick 05796	Tremble/Deep Inside	7

NELLA DODDS

65	Pye 7N 25281	Come See About Me/You Don't Love Me Anymore	50
65	Pye 7N 25281	Come See About Me/You Don't Love Me Anymore (DJ Copy)	75
65	Pye 7N 25291	Finders Keepers, Losers Weepers/A Girl's Life	35
65	Pye 7N 25291	Finders Keepers, Losers Weepers/A Girl's Life (DJ Copy)	50

DODGERS

60	Downbeat CHA 2	Let's Make A Whole Lot Of Love/You Make Me Happy	25

DODGERS

70	S & S SC 002	True Love/Baby I Will Be Yours	12

DODO'S

67	Polydor BM 56153	I Made Up My Mind/Can't Make It Out	30

ERNIE K-DOE
(see under 'K')

DOES IT OFFEND YOU, YEAH?

07	Private Pressing	LIVE AT THE FEZ CLUB (12" white label)	20

DOGFEET

71	Reflection HRS 7	Sad Story/On The Road	20
71	Reflection HRS 12	Since I Went Away/Evil Woman	35
70	Reflection REFL 8	DOGFEET (LP, white/brown label)	700
94	Kissing Spell CA 36001	DOGFEET (LP, reissue)	15

TYMON DOGG
(see also Timon, Clash)

81	Ghost Dance GHO 1	Lose This Skin (featuring the Clash)/Indestructible (p/s)	6

DOGGEREL BANK

73	Charisma CAS 1079	SILVER FACES (LP, gatefold sleeve, large "Mad Hatter" label)	20
75	Charisma CAS 1102	MISTER SKILLCORN DANCES (LP, small "Mad Hatter" label)	25

BILL DOGGETT
(see also Ella Fitzgerald, Earl Bostic)

55	Parlophone DP 411	Gumbo/Tara's Theme (78, export issue)	10
55	Parlophone DP 432	Christmas Song/Winter Wonderland (78, export issue)	10
56	Parlophone CMSP 39	Honky Tonk (Parts 1 & 2) (gold label lettering, export issue)	25
56	Parlophone R 4231	Honky Tonk (Parts 1 & 2) (gold label lettering, later silver)	25
57	Parlophone R 4265	Slow Walk/Peacock Alley	15
57	Parlophone R 4306	Ram-Bunk-Shush/Blue Largo	15
57	Parlophone R 4379	Hot Ginger/Soft	18
58	Parlophone R 4413	Leaps And Bounds (Parts 1 & 2)	10
60	Parlophone R 4629	Smokie/Evening Dreams	10
61	Warner Bros WB 32	The Hully Gully Twist/Jackrabbit	10
61	Warner Bros WB 46	You Can't Sit Down (Parts 1 & 2)	15
57	Parlophone GEP 8644	HONKY TONK (EP)	30
57	Parlophone GEP 8674	PLAYS DUKE ELLINGTON (EP)	10
58	Parlophone GEP 8711	BILL DOGGETT (EP)	10
58	Parlophone GEP 8727	RAINBOW RIOT (EP)	10
59	Parlophone GEP 8771	A JOLLY CHRISTMAS (EP)	10

MINT VALUE £

58	Parlophone PMD 1067	DAME DREAMING (10" LP)	30
59	Parlophone PMD 1073	DANCE AWHILE WITH DOGGETT (10" LP)	30
60	Parlophone PMC 1118	DOGGETT'S BIG CITY DANCE PARTY (LP)	25
60	Parlophone PMC 1124	ON TOUR (LP)	20
61	Warner Bros WM 402	3046 PEOPLE DANCED 'TIL 4 A.M. (LP, live, as Bill Doggett & His Combo)	15
62	Parlophone PMC 1165	BACK WITH MORE BILL DOGGETT (LP)	18
62	Warner Bros WM 4056	THE BAND WITH THE BEAT (LP, with His Combo)	15
65	HMV CLP 1884	WOW (LP)	18

DOGGS

71	Chapter 1 CH156	Billy's Gotta Run/Why Do I Lie	5

DOGROSE

72	Satril SAT 2	Paradise Row/Sunday Morning	10
73	Satril SAT 6	All For The Love Of City Lights/All for The Love Of Each Other	6
72	Satril SATL 4002	ALL FOR THE LOVE OF DOGROSE (LP)	22

DOGS

05	Fallout IS874/986	London Bridge/End Of An Era (Custom printed parcel tape label)	5
05	Fallout IS874/986791-8	London Bridge/End Of An Era (CD, custom printed parcel tape sleeve)	8

DOGS D'AMOUR

88	China WOL 7	THE (UN)AUTHORISED BOOTLEG (LP)	30

DOG SOLDIER

(see also Miller Anderson, Keef Hartley)

75	United Artists UA 29769	DOG SOLDIER (LP)	20

THE DOG THAT BIT PEOPLE

(see also Norman Haines, Locomotive)

71	Parlophone R 5880	Lovely Lady/Merry-Go-Round	45
71	Parlophone PCS 7125	THE DOG THAT BIT PEOPLE (LP, black/silver label with boxed logo)	400
95	Shoestring BL003	THE DOG THAT BIT PEOPLE (CD, reissue)	25

DOGWATCH

79	Bridgehouse BHLP 002	PENFRIEND (LP, with insert)	20

NED DOHENY

81	CBS 9481	To Prove My Love/On The Swing Shift (p/s)	8
81	CBS 13-9481	To Prove My Love/On The Swing Shift (12", p/s)	10

JIM DOHERTY TRIO

65	Decca LK 4684	EXECUTIVE SUITE (LP)	40

DOKKEN

82	Carrere CAR 229	We're Illegal/Paris Is Burning (p/s)	5
82	Carrere CAL 136	BREAKIN' THE CHAINS (LP)	12

JOE DOLAN

65	Pye 7N 15902	Don't Ever Let That Little Chance Go By/My Own Peculiar Way	8
67	Piccadilly 7N 35368	House With The Whitewashed Gable/Work Day Blues	6
67	Pye 7N 17354	Tar And Cement/Time Of My Life	6
69	Pye 7N 17738	Make Me An Island/If You Care A Little Bit About Me	5
69	Pye 7N 17833	Teresa/My First Love	6
70	Pye 7N 17891	You're Such A Good Looking Woman/Something Happens	8
76	Pye 7N 45702	I Need You/Caterina Ballerina	7

DAVE DOLBY

73	Bell 1418	Shine A Light/Your Weight Is Your Mind	6

DOLE

78	Ultimate ULT 402	New Wave Love/Hungry Men No Longer Steal Sheep But Are There Hanging Judges? (die-cut p/s)	30

MICKY DOLENZ

(see also Monkees)

67	London HLH 10117	Don't Do It/FINDERS KEEPERS: (We Wear) Lavender Blue	12
67	London HLH 10152	Huff Puff/OBVIOUS: Fate	12
73	MGM 2006 265	Daybreak/Love War	8
74	MGM 2006 392	Ooh She's Young/Love War	8
79	Chrysalis CHS 2297	Love Light/Alicia	6

ANDY DOLL

62	Starlite ST45 068	Wild Desire/Wyat	15
63	Starlite STLP II	ON STAGE (LP, by Andy Doll Band & Guests)	15

LINDA DOLL & SUNDOWNERS

64	Piccadilly 7N 35166	Bonie Maronie/He Don't Want Your Love Anymore	15

DOLLIES

65	CBS 201788	You Touch Me Baby/I Can't Go On	10

DOLLY MIXTURE

83	Dead Good Dolly Platters DMS 1	Remember This/Listening Pleasure/Borinda's Lament (p/s)	10
84	DM 1	DEMONSTRATION TAPES (2-LP, rubber stamped, hand-numbered signed sleeves with insert)	30

DOLPHIN

76	Private Stock PVT 52	Then I Kissed Her/The Glyderes	6
76	Private Stock PVT 67	Goin' Back/Think Ahead	10
77	Private Stock PVT 91	Only Seventeen/Take Care Of The Ocean	5
77	Private Stock PVT 122	Imagination Dancing/The Actress	6
78	Private Stock PVT 154	Carry Me Away/Linda Lovelace	6
80	Gale 5	Hey Joe/Dubby Dubby	5
77	Private Stock PVLP 1055	GOODBYE (LP)	12
80	Gale GALELP 02	MOLECULES (LP)	12

MINT VALUE £

DOLPHINS

65	Stateside SS 375	Hey Da Da Dow/I Don't Want To Go On Without You	15

ERIC DOLPHY

61	Esquire 32-123	THE ERIC DOLPHY QUINTET (LP)	20
64	Esquire 21-123	OUTWARD BOUND (LP)	20
64	Esquire 32-153	OUT THERE (LP)	20
61	Esquire 32-173	AT THE 5 SPOT VOL. 1.(LP)	30
64	Fontana TL5284	LAST DATE (LP)	40
65	Fontana 688521XL	MEMORIAL ALBUM (LP)	20
69	Transatlantic PR 7311	OUTWARD BOUND (LP)	15
67	Xtra 5039	SCREAMING THE BLUES (LP, with Oliver Nelson Sextet)	20

ERIC DOLPHY & BOOKER LITTLE

66	Stateside SL 10160	ERIC DOLPHY AND BOOKER LITTLE MEMORIAL ALBUM (LP)	15

BILLY DOLTON

61	Parlophone R 4733	Winkie Doll/Girls	15

DOME

(see also Wire, Gilbert & Lewis)

81	Dome DOME 3	Jasz (1-sided flexidisc)	6
80	4AD CAD 16	3R4 (12")	8
80	Dome DOME 1	DOME ONE (LP)	15
80	Dome DOME 2	DOME 2 (LP)	15
81	Dome DOME 3	DOME 3 (LP)	12
82	Uniton UO111	WHEN YOU SPEAK THIS WORD (LP, featuring Vince Clarke)	12

DOMINANT FORCE

91	Gangster GAGR001	Criminals/Raptivity (12")	25
92	Ital Juice DOMF 12 002	We're Ready/When We Flex (12")	10

ANNA DOMINO

86	Factory FAC 158	Summer (p/s)	12

FATS DOMINO

78s

54	London HL 8007	Rose Mary/You Said You Love Me	50
54	London HL 8063	Little School Girl/You Done Me Wrong	50
54	London HL 8096	Don't Leave Me This Way/Something's Wrong	45
55	London HL 8124	Love Me/Don't You Hear Me Calling You	40
55	London HL 8133	Thinking Of You/I Know	25
55	London HLU 8173	Ain't That A Shame/La La	10
56	London HLU 8256	Bo Weevil/Don't Blame It On Me	18
56	London HLU 8309	When My Dream Boat Comes Home/So Long	10
56	London HLU 8330	Blueberry Hill/I Can't Go On (Rosalie)	10
57	London HLU 8356	Honey Chile/Don't You Know	10
57	London HLP 8377	Blue Monday/What's The Reason I'm Not Pleasing You	10
57	London HLP 8407	I'm Walkin'/I'm In The Mood For Love	12
57	London HLP 8449	The Valley Of Tears/It's You I Love	10
57	London HLP 8471	What Will I Tell My Heart/When I See You	10
57	London HLP 8519	Wait And See/I Still Love You	10
58	London HLP 8575	The Big Beat (from the film)/I Want You To Know	10
58	London HLP 8628	Sick And Tired/No, No	10
58	London HLP 8663	Little Mary/The Prisoner's Song	10
58	London HLP 8727	Young School Girl/It Must Be Love	15
58	London HLP 8759	Whole Lotta Loving/Coquette	15
59	London HLP 8822	When The Saints Go Marching In/Telling Lies	20
59	London HLP 8865	Margie/I'm Ready	20
59	London HLP 8942	I Want To Walk You Home/I'm Gonna Be A Wheel Some Day (tri centre)	20
59	London HLP 9005	Be My Guest/I've Been Around	40
60	London HLP 9073	Country Boy/If You Need Me	40
60	London HLP 9163	Walking To New Orleans/Don't Come Knockin'	60

SINGLES

55	London HL 8124	Love Me/Don't You Hear Me Calling You	200
55	London HL 8133	Thinking Of You/I Know	150
55	London HLU 8173	Ain't That A Shame/La La	90
56	London HLU 8256	Bo Weevil/Don't Blame It On Me	100
56	London HLU 8280	I'm In Love Again/My Blue Heaven	100
56	London HLU 8309	When My Dream Boat Comes Home/So Long	60
56	London HLU 8330	Blueberry Hill/I Can't Go On (Rosalie)	60
57	London HLU 8356	Honey Chile/Don't You Know	100
57	London HLP 8377	Blue Monday/What's The Reason I'm Not Pleasing You	60

(The above 45s were originally issued with triangular centres & gold lettering labels; later silver-label repressing are worth half these values)

57	London HLP 8407	I'm Walkin'/I'm In The Mood For Love	25
57	London HLP 8449	The Valley Of Tears/It's You I Love	20
57	London HLP 8471	What Will I Tell My Heart/When I See You	20
57	London HLP 8519	Wait And See/I Still Love You	20
58	London HLP 8575	The Big Beat (From The Film)/I Want You To Know	20
58	London HLP 8628	Sick And Tired/No, No	20
58	London HLP 8663	Little Mary/The Prisoner's Song	20
58	London HLP 8727	Young School Girl/It Must Be Love	30
58	London HLP 8759	Whole Lotta Loving/Coquette	25
59	London HLP 8822	When The Saints Go Marching In/Telling Lies	15

(HLP 8407 through to 8822 45s were issued with triangular centres & silver lettering on all-black labels; later copies are worth around half these values.)

59	London HLP 8865	Margie/I'm Ready (triangular centre & silver-top)	15
59	London HLP 8865	Margie/I'm Ready (later round centre)	8

			MINT VALUE £
59	London HLP 8942	I Want To Walk You Home/I'm Gonna Be A Wheel Some Day (round)	10
59	London HLP 9005	Be My Guest/I've Been Around (triangular centre)	40
59	London HLP 9005	Be My Guest/I've Been Around (round centre)	10

(All subsequent London 45s for Fats Domino after London HLP 9005 were issued with round centres & silver-top labels.)

60	London HLP 9073	Country Boy/If You Need Me	10
60	London HLP 9133	Tell Me That You Love Me/Before I Grow Too Old	12
60	London HLP 9163	Walking To New Orleans/Don't Come Knockin'	10
60	London HLP 9198	Three Nights A Week/Put Your Arms Around Me, Honey	12
60	London HLP 9244	My Girl Josephine/Natural Born Lover	10
61	London HLP 9301	What A Price/Ain't That Just Like A Woman	12
61	London HLP 9327	Fell In Love On Monday/Shu-Rah	12
61	London HLP 9374	It Keeps Rainin'/I Just Cry	30
61	London HLP 9415	Let The Four Winds Blow/Good Hearted Man	10
61	London HLP 9456	What A Party/Rockin' Bicycle	10
62	London HLP 9520	Jambalaya/You Win Again	8
62	London HLP 9557	My Real Name/My Heart Is Bleeding	12
62	London HLP 9590	Dance With Mr. Domino/Nothing New (Same Old Thing)	12
62	London HLP 9616	Did You Ever See A Dream Walking/Stop The Clock	12
63	London HLP 9738	You Always Hurt The One You Love/Trouble Blues	10
63	HMV POP 1164	There Goes My Heart Again/Can't Go On Without You	10
63	HMV POP 1197	When I'm Walkin'/I've Got A Right To Cry	8
63	HMV POP 1219	Red Sails In The Sunset/Song For Rosemary	6
63	HMV POP 1265	Just A Lonely Man/Who Cares	8
64	HMV POP 1281	I Don't Want To Set The World On Fire/Lazy Lady	7
64	HMV POP 1303	If You Don't Know What Love Is/Something You Got Baby	40
64	HMV POP 1324	Mary Oh Mary/Packin' Up	8
64	HMV POP 1370	Kansas City/Heartbreak Hill	8
65	Mercury MF 869	(I Left My Heart) In San Francisco/I Done Got Over It	8
65	Mercury MF 873	What's That You Got?/It's Never Too Late	8
65	HMV POP 1421	Why Don't You Do Right?/Wigs	8
67	HMV POP 1582	I'm Livin' Right/I Don't Want To Set The World On Fire	8
67	Liberty LBF 12055	It Keeps Rainin'/Blue Monday	15
67	Liberty LBF 12055	It Keeps Rainin'/Blue Monday (DJ Copy)	30
68	Liberty LBF 15098	Walking To New Orleans/Blueberry Hill	5
68	Reprise RS 20696	Honest Mamas Love Their Papas Better/One For The Highway (withdrawn)	25
68	Reprise RS 20763	Lady Madonna/One For The Highway	10
69	Reprise RS 20810	Everybody's Got Something To Hide Except Me And My Monkey/ So Swell When You're Well	5
69	Liberty LBF 15274	I'm Ready/The Fat Man	5
69	Mercury MF 1104	What's That You Got?/Jambalaya (On The Bayou)	5
78	Sonet SON 2168	Sleeping On The Job/After Hours	5

EXPORT SINGLES

57	London HL 7028	Wait And See/I Still Love You	30
58	London HL 7040	Sick And Tired/No, No	30
58	London HL 7054	The Big Beat (From The Film)/Little Mary	30

EPs

55	London RE-P 1022	BLUES FOR LOVE (1st pressing with gold lettering label)	60
55	London RE-P 1022	BLUES FOR LOVE (2nd pressing with silver lettering label)	40
56	London RE-U 1062	BLUES FOR LOVE VOL. 2 (1st pressing with gold label)	80
56	London RE-U 1062	BLUES FOR LOVE VOL. 2 (2nd pressing with silver label)	50
57	London RE-U 1073	FATS (export issue, plain sleeve)	100
57	London RE-P 1079	HERE COMES FATS VOL. 1	50
58	London RE-P 1080	HERE COMES FATS VOL. 2	50
58	London RE-P 1115	CARRY ON ROCKIN' PART 1	80
58	London RE-P 1116	CARRY ON ROCKIN' PART 2	80
58	London RE-P 1117	BLUES FOR LOVE VOL. 3	50
58	London RE-P 1121	BLUES FOR LOVE VOL. 4	50
58	London RE-P 1138	HERE COMES FATS VOL. 3	40
59	London RE-P 1206	THE ROCKIN' MR. D VOL. 1	40
59	London RE-P 1207	THE ROCKIN' MR. D VOL. 2	40

(The above EPs were originally issued with triangular centres; round-centre re-pressings are worth two-thirds these values.)

60	London RE-P 1261	BE MY GUEST	30
60	London RE-P 1265	THE ROCKIN' MR. D VOL. 3	30
62	London RE-P 1340	WHAT A PARTY	30
64	HMV 7EG 8862	RED SAILS IN THE SUNSET	20
65	Liberty LEP 4026	MY BLUE HEAVEN	20
66	Liberty LEP 4045	ROLLIN'	20

LPs

56	London HA-U 2028	FATS' ROCK AND ROLLIN'	100
56	London HA-P 2041	CARRY ON ROCKIN'	100
57	London HA-P 2052	HERE STANDS FATS DOMINO	100
56	London HA-P 2073	THIS IS FATS DOMINO	70
58	London HA-P 2087	THIS IS FATS	70
58	London HA-P 2135	THE FABULOUS "MR. D"	60
59	London HA-P 2223	LET'S PLAY FATS DOMINO	60
60	London HA-P 2312	A LOT OF DOMINOES!	50
61	London HA-P 2364	I MISS YOU SO	50
61	London HA-P 2420	LET THE FOUR WINDS BLOW	50
61	London HA-P 2426	WHAT A PARTY	50
62	London HA-P 2447	TWISTIN' THE STOMP	50
63	London HA-P 8039	JUST DOMINO	50
63	London HA-P 8084	WALKING TO NEW ORLEANS	50
63	HMV CLP 1690	HERE COMES FATS DOMINO (also stereo CSD 1520)	30
63	HMV CLP 1740	FATS ON FIRE (also stereo CSD 1543)	30
65	Liberty LBY 3033	MILLION SELLERS BY FATS VOL. 1	15

MINT VALUE £

65	Liberty LBY 3046	MILLION SELLERS BY FATS VOL. 2	15
65	HMV CLP 1821	GETAWAY WITH FATS DOMINO (also stereo CSD 1580)	20
65	Mercury (S)MCL 20070	DOMINO '65 (mono/stereo)	15
68	Stateside (S)SL 10240	FANTASTIC FATS	15

DOMINOES (Jamaica)

68	Melody MRC 001	Tears In Your Eyes/Johnny Darling	10
68	Melody MRC 002	A Tribute (actually by Ann Reid)/Hooray (actually by Uniques)	10

DOMINOES (U.K.)

58	Reading Rag LYN 545	Bye Bye Johnny/Yakety Yak	15

DOMINOES (U.S.)

(see also Billy Ward & Dominoes, Clyde McPhatter, Jackie Wilson)

51	Vogue V 9012	Sixty Minute Man/I Can't Escape From You (78)	50
52	Vogue V 2135	Have Mercy, Baby/That's What You're Doing To Me (78)	45
67	Vogue V 212	Sixty Minute Man/I Can't Escape From You	35
56	Vogue EPV 1113	RHYTHM AND BLUES (EP, 2 tracks by Swallows)	300

DON DAVID AND DEAN

64	United Artists UP 1064)	No Need to Cry/Fairy Tales	10

DON, DICK & JIMMY

54	Columbia SCM 5110	Brand Me With Your Kisses/Angela Mia	15
55	London HL 8117	You Can't Have Your Cake And Eat It Too/That's What I Like	30
55	London HL 8144	Make Yourself Comfortable/(Whatever Happened To The) Piano Players (That Played Like This)	15
56	HMV POP 280	That's The Way I Feel/Two Voices In The Night	10
55	London RE-U 1043	DON, DICK AND JIMMY (EP)	30

SAM DONAHUE & HIS ORCHESTRA

55	Capitol CL 14349	Saxaboogie/September In The Rain	15

TROY DONAHUE

63	Warner Bros WB 111	Live Young/Somebody Loves Me	10

MIKE DONALD & BOB SIDDALL

(see also Mike Donald)

74	Tradition Century TSC 2	A BUG'S EYE VIEW (LP, 100 copies only)	30

MIKE DONALD

71	Folk Heritage FHR 021	YORKSHIRE SONGS OF THE BROAD ACRES (LP, first pressing, textured sleeve with black and white photo)	30
71	Folk Heritage FHR 021	YORKSHIRE SONGS OF THE BROAD ACRES (LP, second pressing, laminated sleeve with colour photo)	20
72	Galliard GAL 4020	NORTH BY NORTH EAST (LP)	20
82	Tradition PRS PR 001	THROUGH PEAKS AND DALES (LP, Peak Railway Society Production)	15

ERIC DONALDSON

(see also Prunes, Satchmo)

71	Dynamic DYN 420	Cherry Oh Baby/LLOYD CHARMERS: Sir Charmers Special	5
71	Dynamic DYN 423	Love Of The Common People/DRAGONAIRES: The Dragon's Net	5
71	Dynamic DYN 425	Just Can't (Happen This Way)/Just Can't (Happen This Way) Version	5
72	Dynamic DYN 431	I'm Indebted/I'm Indebted (Version)	5
72	Dynamic DYN 439	Miserable Woman/The Lion Sleeps	5
72	Dynamic DYN 445	Blue Boot/Blue Boot (Version)	5
72	Dynamic DYN 452	Little Did You Know/Little Did You Know (Version)	5
73	Dragon DRA 1017	What A Festival/I ROY & ERIC: Festival Version	5
73	Dragon DRA 1018	The Way You Do The Things You Do/Version	5
73	Dragon DRA 1020	Watch What You're Doing To Me/You Must Believe Me	5
73	Dragon DRA 1027	A Weh We A Go Go/SOUL DEFENDERS: Version	5
72	Trojan TRL 42	ERIC DONALDSON (LP)	15
70s	Dynamic DYLP 3003	KEEP ON RIDING (LP)	18

DON & DENNY

60s	Loop LOO 504	(Ain't That) Just Like Me/Feeling Groovy	40

DON & DEWEY

(see also Dewey Terry)

64	London HL 9897	Get Your Hat/Annie Lee	30
66	Cameo Parkway CP 750	Soul Motion/Stretchin' Out	40
67	Sue WI 4032	Soul Motion/Stretchin' Out (reissue)	30
71	Specialty SNTF 5006	DON AND DEWEY (LP)	15

DON & GOODTIMES

67	Columbia DB 8199	I Could Be So Good To You/And It's So Good	12
67	Columbia DB 8266	Happy And Me/If You Love Her, Cherish Her And Such	8

DON & JUAN

62	London HLX 9529	What's Your Name?/Chicken Necks	30

DON & PETE

66	Columbia DB 7881	And I'm Crying Again/Time Will Tell	5

DONAYS

62	Oriole CBA 1770	Devil In His Heart/Bad Boy	150

LONNIE DONEGAN

(see also Monty Sunshine, Chris Barber, Max Miller)

78s

56	Oriole CB 1329	The Passing Stranger/TOMMY REILLY: The Intimate Stranger	10
56	Columbia DB 3850	On A Christmas Day/Take My Hand, Precious Lord	10
59	Pye N 15237	San Miguel/Talking Guitar Blues	15
60	Pye N 15256	My Old Man's A Dustman/The Golden Vanity	10
60	Pye N 15267	I Wanna Go Home (The Wreck Of The John B)/Jimmy Brown The Newsboy	10
60	Pye N 15327	Lorelei/In All My Wildest Dreams	20

MINT VALUE £

SINGLES

55	Decca F 10647	Rock Island Line/John Henry (as Lonnie Donegan Skiffle Group) (tri-centre)	25
56	Decca FJ 10695	Diggin' My Potatoes/Bury My Body (as Lonnie Donegan Skiffle Group) (tri-centre)	25
56	Columbia DB 3850	On A Christmas Day/Take My Hand, Precious Lord (as Lonnie Donegan with Chris Barber's Jazz Band)	25
57	Pye Nixa 7N 15116	Jack O' Diamonds/Ham 'N' Eggs	10
58	Pye Nixa 7N 15129	The Grand Coolie Dam/Nobody Loves Like An Irishman	8
58	Pye Jazz 7NJ 2006	Midnight Special/When The Sun Goes Down	25
58	Pye Nixa 7N 15148	Sally, Don't You Grieve/Betty, Betty, Betty	10
62	Pye 7N 3109	The Comancheros/Medley (export, p/s)	30
62	Pye 7N 15455	Pick A Bale Of Cotton/Steal Away (in p/s)	6
62	Pye 7N 15493	The Market Song/Tit-Bits (with MAX MILLER)	7
66	Pye 7N 15993	World Cup Willie/Where In This World Are We Going (in p/s)	15
66	Pye 7N 15993	World Cup Willie/Where In This World Are We Going	5
68	Columbia DB 8371	Toys/Relax Your Mind	7
72	Pye 7N 45184	Speak To The Sky/Get Out Of My Life	7
76	Decca F 13669	I've Lost My Little Willie/Censored	6

EPs

56	Decca DFE 6345	THE LONNIE DONEGAN SKIFFLE GROUP (tri-centre)	20
56	Jazz Today JTE 107	BACKSTAIRS SESSION	20
56	Pye Nixa Jazz NJE 1014	BACKSTAIRS SESSION (reissue)	10
56	Pye Nixa Jazz NJE 1017	SKIFFLE SESSION	15

ALBUMS

56	Pye Nixa NPT 19012	LONNIE DONEGAN SHOWCASE (10")	30
57	Pye Nixa NPT 19027	LONNIE (10" LP)	45
58	Pye Nixa NPT 19027	LONNIE (10" LP)	30
62	Pye NPL 18073	SING HALLELUJAH (LP)	25
65	Pye NPL 18126	THE LONNIE DONEGAN FOLK ALBUM	25
70	Decca SKL 5068	LONNIEPOPS (LP)	15

DONKEYS

80	Rhesus GO APE 102	What I Want/Four Letters (yellow or orange label, p/s)	12
80	Rhesus GO APE 103	No Way/You Jane (p/s)	10
80	Rhesus GO APE 105	Don't Go/Living Legends (p/s)	10
80	Back Door DOOR 006	No Way/You Jane (reissue, p/s)	7
80	Deram DM-R 431	What I Want/Four Letters (reissue, p/s)	5
81	MCA MCA 721	Let's Float/Watched By Everyone (p/s)	10
81	MCA MCA 737	Listen To Your Radio/Watched By Everyone (as Donkees) (p/s)	10

JIMMY DONLEY

57	Brunswick 05715	South Of The Border/The Trail Of The Lonesome Pine	20
59	Brunswick 05807	The Shape You Left Me In/What Must I Do	100
59	Brunswick 05807	The Shape You Left Me In/What Must I Do (78)	20

DONNA & FREEDOM SINGERS

70	Bamboo BAM 53	Oh Me Oh My (actually by Jerry Jones)/JACKIE MITTOO: Gold Mine	20

PAUL DONNER

78	Wildfire WRP 22	Yesterday's Roses - No More Baby/Carolina Feel It Burning (p/s)	6

RAL DONNER

61	Parlophone R 4820	You Don't Know What You've Got/So Close To Heaven	15
61	Parlophone R 4859	Please Don't Go/I Didn't Figure On Him	25
62	Parlophone R 4889	I Don't Need You/She's Everything (I Wanted You To Be)	25
62	Stateside SS 109	Bells Of Love/Loveless Life	25
63	Reprise R 20141	I Got Burned/A Tear In My Eye	35
78	Thunder TD 7801	The Day The Beat Stopped/I Got Burned/Run Little Linda (coloured vinyl)	8
60s	Pye NSPL 28269	YOU DON'T KNOW WHAT YOU'VE GOT (LP)	20

DONNIE & DREAMERS

61	Top Rank JAR 571	Count Every Star/Dorothy	50

DONOVAN

(see also Jeff Beck, Open Road)

65	Pye 7N 15801	Catch The Wind/Why Do You Treat Me Like You Do	5
65	Pye 7N 15866	Colours/To Sing For You	5
65	Pye 7N 15984	Turquoise/Hey Gyp (Dig The Slowness)	8
66	Pye 7N 17067	Josie/Little Tin Soldier	5
66	Pye 7N 17088	Remember The Alamo/The Ballad Of A Crystal Man	15
66	Pye 7N 17241	Sunshine Superman/The Trip	7
67	Pye 7N 17267	Mellow Yellow/Preachin' Love	6
67	Pye 7N 17403	There Is A Mountain/Sand And Foam	6
68	Pye 7N 17457	Jennifer Juniper/Poor Cow	6
68	Pye 7N 17537	Hurdy Gurdy Man/Teen Angel	10
68	Pye 7N 17660	To Susan On The West Coast Waiting/Atlantis (unreleased)	0
68	Pye 7N 17660	Atlantis/I Love My Shirt	6
69	Pye 7N 17778	Goo Goo Barabajagal (Love Is Hot)/Bed With Me (with Jeff Beck Group)	12
69	Pye 7N 17778	Barabajagal/Trudi (shortened A-side title & retitled B-side)	10
70	Dawn DNS 1006	Ricki Ticki Tavi/Roots Of Oak (as Donovan with Open Road)	6
70	Dawn DNS 1006	Riki Tiki Tavi (shortened spelling of A-side)/Roots Of Oak (with Open Road)	5
70	Dawn DNS 1007	Celia Of The Seals (with Danny Thompson)/Mr. Wind	6
72	private pressing	The Music Makers (one-sided, paper sleeve, 50 only)	50
73	Epic EPC 1471	I Like You/Earth Sign Man	5
73	Epic EPC 1644	Maria Magenta/Intergalactic Laxative (p/s)	8
73	Epic EPC 1960	Sailing Homeward/Lazy Daze (p/s)	6
74	Epic EPC 1960	Sailing Homeward/Yellow Star (p/s, reissue with different B-side; some copies list both Donovan & Andrew Oldham as producers)	6
75	Epic EPC 2661	Rock'n'Roll With Me/Divine Daze Of Deathless Delight (in p/s)	30

			MINT VALUE £
75	Epic EPC 2661	Rock'n'Roll With Me/Divine Daze Of Deathless Delight	6
75	Epic EPC 3037	Rock And Roll Souijer/Love Of My Life	5
77	Rak RAK 265	The Light/The International Man (p/s)	8
77	Rak RAK 265	The Light/The International Man	5
92	Silhouette MDCDKR 3	Newest Bath Guide/Moira MacCavendish/Brother Sun, Sister Moon (CD)	18
65	Pye NEP 24219	THE UNIVERSAL SOLDIER (EP, incorrectly lists 'Summer 1955' instead of 'Summer 1965' as date on rear sleeve)	10
65	Pye NEP 24219	THE UNIVERSAL SOLDIER (EP)	10
65	Pye NEP 24229	COLOURS (EP)	15
66	Pye NEP 24239	DONOVAN VOL. 1 (EP)	15
68	Pye NEP 24287	CATCH THE WIND (EP)	15
68	Pye NEP 24299	HURDY GURDY DONOVAN (EP)	20
65	Pye NPL 18117	WHAT'S BIN DID AND WHAT'S BIN HID (LP, some with misprinted Side 2 label)	25
65	Pye NPL 18128	FAIRYTALE (LP, some copies with blank rear sleeve)	35
66	World Records ST 951	DONOVAN (LP)	18
67	Pye NPL 18181	SUNSHINE SUPERMAN (LP)	35
68	Pye NPL 20000	A GIFT FROM A FLOWER TO A GARDEN (2-LP, black or navy blue box set, separate halves or with taped hinge; with 12 inserts in folder, mono)	65
68	Pye NSPL 20000	A GIFT FROM A FLOWER TO A GARDEN (2-LP, black or navy blue box set, separate halves or with taped hinge; with 12 inserts in folder, stereo)	50
68	Pye NPL 18237	DONOVAN IN CONCERT (LP, mono)	20
68	Pye NSPL 18237	DONOVAN IN CONCERT (LP, stereo)	18
69	Pye NPL 18283	DONOVAN'S GREATEST HITS (LP, gatefold sleeve with booklet, mono)	12
70	Dawn DNLS 3009	OPEN ROAD (LP, gatefold sleeve)	30
71	Dawn DNLD 4001	H.M.S. DONOVAN (2-LP, gatefold sleeve, with foldout poster)	80
71	Dawn DNLD 4001	H.M.S. DONOVAN (2-LP, gatefold sleeve, without foldout poster)	25
73	Pye 11PP 102	FOUR SHADES ("H.M.S. Donovan"/"Greatest Hits"/"Open Road") (4-LP box set)	50
73	Epic EPC 69550	ESSENCE TO ESSENCE (LP, gatefold sleeve, lyric insert, with sticker)	15
90	Permanent PERMLP 2	DONOVAN RISING (LP, 500 only)	12

DONTELLS

65	Fontana TF 566	In Your Heart/Nothing But Nothing	75
74	President PT 373	In Your Heart/Nothing But Nothing (reissue)	15

DICKY DOO & DON'TS

58	London HLU 8589	Click Click/Did You Cry	30
58	London HLU 8589	Click Click/Did You Cry (78)	20
58	London HLU 8754	Leave Me Alone/Wild, Wild Party (with Orchestra)	40
58	London HLU 8754	Leave Me Alone/Wild, Wild Party (with Orchestra) (78)	30
60	Top Rank JAR 318	Wabash Cannonball/WEST TEXAS MARCHING BAND: The Drums Of Richard A Doo	25

DOOKIE SQUAD

94	Dookie DS 001	6FT Under/Mad Shit (12")	25

DOOLEY SISTERS

55	London HL 8128	Ko Ko Mo (I Love You So)/Heart Throb	50

DOOM

89	Strange Fruit SFPMA 203	DOUBLE PEEL SESSIONS (LP, with insert)	12
88	Peaceville VILE 4	WAR CRIMES INHUMAN BEINGS (LP, white vinyl)	18
89	Peaceville VILE 11	BURY THE DEBT NOT THE DEAD (split LP with NO SECURITY)	18

JOHN DOONAN

72	Leader LEA 2043	FLUTE FOR THE FEIS (LP)	15

DOONICANS

87	Probe Plus PP 23T	THE FISHERMAN'S WAY (12" EP)	10

DOOR & THE WINDOW

(see also Alternative TV)

79	NR NR 1	Subculture/Fashion Slaves/Nostradamus/Don't Kill Colin/Wurst Ban	25
79	NB Records NB 3	He Feels Like A Doris/I Like Sound/Innocent/Dig/Production Line (white label with stickers & insert p/s in poly bag)	5
80	NB Records NB 5	DETAILED TWANG (LP, blank labels)	12
80	NB Records NB 9	MUSIC AND MOVEMENT (live cassette)	12

DOORS

(see also Ray Manzarek)

SINGLES

67	Elektra EKSN 45009	Break On Through (To The Other Side)/End Of The Night	45
67	Elektra EKSN 45012	Alabama Song (Whisky Bar)/Take It As It Comes	25
67	Elektra EKSN 45014	Light My Fire/The Crystal Ship	20
67	Elektra EKSN 45017	People Are Strange/Unhappy Girl	20
67	Elektra EKSN 45022	Love Me Two Times/Moonlight Drive	15
68	Elektra EKSN 45030	We Could Be So Good Together/The Unknown Soldier	15
68	Elektra EKSN 45037	Hello, I Love You/Love Street	10
69	Elektra EKSN 45050	Touch Me/Wild Child	10
69	Elektra EKSN 45059	Wishful Sinful/Who Scared You?	10
69	Elektra EKSN 45065	Tell All The People/Easy Ride	10
70	Elektra 2101 004	You Make Me Real/The Spy	10
70	Elektra 2101 008	Roadhouse Blues/Blue Sunday	10
71	Elektra EK 45726	Love Her Madly/(You Need Meat) Don't Go No Further	6
71	Elektra K 12021	Riders On The Storm/The Changeling	6
72	Elektra K 12036	Tightrope Ride/Variety Is The Spice Of Life	5
72	Elektra K 12048	Ship W/ Sails/In The Eye Of The Sun	5
72	Elektra K 12059	Get Up And Dance/Tree Trunks	5
79	Elektra K 12215/SAM 94	Love Me Two Times/Hello, I Love You// Ghost Song/Roadhouse Blues (double pack)	8
83	Elektra E 9974T	Gloria/Love Me Two Times (12", p/s with poster)	10
91	Elektra EKR 125TW	Light My Fire/People Are Strange/Soul Kitchen (12", p/s, with poster)	8

MINT VALUE £

92	Final Vinyl FV 1/2	INTERVIEW TAPES (2 x 7" box set, with 7 inserts, numbered, 500 only)	10

LPs

67	Elektra EKL 4007	THE DOORS (orange label, mono)	80
67	Elektra EKS 4007	THE DOORS (orange label, stereo)	50
68	Elektra EKL 4014	STRANGE DAYS (textured orange label, inner sleeve, mono)	80
68	Elektra EKS 4014	STRANGE DAYS (textured orange label, inner sleeve, stereo)	50
68	Elektra EKL 4024	WAITING FOR THE SUN (orange label, gatefold sleeve with insert, mono)	65
68	Elektra EKS 4024	WAITING FOR THE SUN (orange label, gatefold sleeve with insert, stereo)	40
69	Elektra EKS 75005	THE SOFT PARADE (orange label, gatefold sleeve, with lyric sheet)	40
70	Elektra EKS 75007	MORRISON HOTEL (orange label, gatefold sleeve)	30
70	Elektra 2665 002	ABSOLUTELY LIVE (2-LP, red label, gatefold sleeve)	25
71	Elektra EKS 74079	13 ('butterfly' label, compilation)	15
71	Elektra K 42090	L.A. WOMAN ('butterfly' label, round-cornered, die-cut PVC 'window' sleeve & yellow inner sleeve)	30
71	Elektra K 42104	OTHER VOICES ('butterfly' label, gatefold sleeve)	15
72	Elektra K 62009	WEIRD SCENES INSIDE THE GOLDMINE (2-LP, 'butterfly' label, gatefold sleeve)	20
72	Elektra K 62116	FULL CIRCLE ('butterfly label', gatefold sleeve)	15
78	Elektra K 52111	AN AMERICAN PRAYER ('butterfly' label, gatefold sleeve, with 8-page booklet)	20
88	HMV C 8816	L.A. WOMAN (CD, HMV box set, 2,500 only, numbered with booklet)	18

DOORS OF PERCEPTION

91	Lizard Nation LN 002	ACID DREAMS (12" EP, includes Jim Morrison sample, withdrawn)	8
91	Lizard Nation LN 001	SO JOIN MR. DREAMS (LP, with inner sleeve and booklet)	15
91	Lizard Nation LN 001	SO JOIN MR. DREAMS (LP, with inner sleeve)	12

DOPE ON PLASTIC

94	Wave DJC 001	Wave Dub/Out Of Time/East A Bit/It's A Dream (12")	100

MIKE DORANE & CIMARONS

71	Ackee ACK 144	Penguin Funk/Ad-Lib	12

DOREEN (Campbell) & ALL STARS

67	Rainbow RAI 114	Rude Girls/Please Stay	15

DOREEN (Shaffer) & JACKIE (Opel)

(see also Jackie & Doreen)

65	Ska Beat JB 208	Welcome Home/You And I	35

KENNY DORHAM & SONNY ROLLINS

58	London LTZU 15133	JAZZ CONTRASTS (LP)	15

DORIAN

70	Ember EMB S 285	Psychedelic Lipstick/Help For My Waiting	6

DORIS

98	EMI/Mr. Bongo MRBLP 010	DID YOU GIVE THE WORLD SOME LOVE TODAY, BABY? (LP, reissue of Swedish 60s LP)	12

DORIS

81	ABCD ABCD 1	Sitting Here Waiting (no p/s)	5
82	ABCD ABCD 3	GYPSY LADY (LP, actually credited to A Band Called Doris)	250

HAROLD DORMAN

60	Top Rank JAR 357	Mountain Of Love/To Be With You	30
61	London HLS 9386	There They Go/I'll Stick By You	40

STACY DORNING

74	Scratchy CHR 1070	STACY DORNING (LP, with Duncan Browne)	12

DOROTHY

80	Industrial IR 0014	I Confess/Softness (p/s)	8

RALPH DORPER

(see also Propaganda)

83	Operation Twilight OPT 18	THE ERASERHEAD EP (12")	20

CHRIS DORS

61	Fontana H 329	That's When Your Heartaches Begin/They Called It Love	10

DIANA DORS

53	HMV B 10613	I Feel So Mmm.../A Kiss And A Cuddle (78)	20
60	Pye 7N 15242	April Heart/Point Of No Return	8
60	Pye N 15242	April Heart/Point Of No Return (78)	15
64	Fontana TF 506	So Little Time/It's Too Late	12
66	Polydor BM 56111	Security/Gary	10
77	EMI EMI 2705	Passing By/It's A Small World	6
82	Nomis NOM 1	Where Did They Go/It's You Again (with Gary Dors)	6
60	Pye NPL 18044	SWINGIN' DORS (LP, foldout sleeve, red vinyl)	100

RAY DORSET (WITH MUNGO JERRY)

(see also Mungo Jerry, Good Earth, County Jug, Macon Jug, Katmandu, Insiders, Panache, Made In England)

72	Dawn DNS 1018	Cold Blue Excursion/I Need It (solo)	5
79	Satellite RAY 001	Forgotten Land/New Way Of Life (solo, unreleased; 100 promos only)	6
72	Dawn DNLS 3033	COLD BLUE EXCURSION (LP, solo; gatefold sleeve with lyric inner, lilac label)	30

DORSETS

65	Sue WI 391	Pork Chops/Cool It	40

GERRY DORSEY

59	Decca F 11108	Mister Music Man/Crazy Bells	15
59	Decca F 11108	Mister Music Man/Crazy Bells (78)	15
59	Parlophone R 4595	I'll Never Fall In Love Again/Every Day Is A Wonderful Day	10
61	Parlophone R 4739	Big Wheel/The Sentimental Joker	10
64	Pye 7N 15622	Baby I Do/Take Your Time	10
65	Hickory 45-1337	Baby Turn Around/Things I Wanna Do	35

MINT VALUE £

JACK DORSEY ORCHESTRA

64	Pye 7N 15730	Ringo's Dog/March Of The Gonks (as BIG BAND)	10
65	Polydor 56020	Dance Of The Daleks/Likely Lads	18
68	Pye 7N 17501	Soul Coaxing/Elizabeth's Waltz	8

LEE DORSEY

62	Top Rank JAR 606	Do-Re-Mi/People Gonna Talk	25
65	Sue WI 367	Do-Re-Mi/Ya Ya	40
65	Stateside SS 441	Ride Your Pony/The Kitty Cat Song	10
65	Stateside SS 465	Work Work Work/Can You Hear Me	10
66	Sue WI 399	Messed Around/When I Meet My Baby	40
66	Stateside SS 485	Get Out Of My Life, Woman/So Long	10
66	Stateside SS 506	Confusion/Neighbour's Daughter	8
66	Stateside SS 528	Working In A Coalmine/Mexico	10
66	Stateside SS 528	Working In A Coalmine/Mexico (yellow vinyl)	50
66	Stateside SS 552	Holy Cow/Operation Heartache	7
67	Stateside SS 593	Rain Rain Go Away/Gotta Find A Job	5
67	Stateside SS 2017	My Old Car/Why Wait Until Tomorrow	5
67	Stateside SS 2055	Go-Go Girl/I Can Hear You Callin'	10
68	President PT 226	Ya Ya/Give Me You	5
68	Bell BLL 1006	Can You Hear Me/Cynthia	5
69	Bell BLL 1051	I'm Gonna Sit Right Down And Write Myself A Letter/Little Baby	5
69	Bell BLL 1060	Ride Your Pony/Get Out Of My Life, Woman	5
69	Bell BLL 1074	Everything I Do Gonna Be Funky/There Should Be A Book	12
71	Mojo 2066 063	Occapella/Yes We Can Part 1	5
72	Mojo 2093 009	Freedom For The Stallion/If She Won't (Find Someone Who Will)	5
66	Stateside SE 1038	RIDE YOUR PONY (EP)	30
66	Stateside SE 1043	YOU'RE BREAKING ME UP (EP)	30
65	Sue ILP 924	THE BEST OF LEE DORSEY (LP)	60
66	Stateside S(S)L 10177	LEE DORSEY - RIDE YOUR PONY (LP)	30
66	Stateside S(S)L 10192	THE NEW LEE DORSEY (LP)	25
71	Polydor 2489 006	YES WE CAN (LP)	25

LEE DORSEY & BETTY HARRIS

(see also Betty Harris)

69	Buffalo BFS 1002	Love Lots Of Lovin'/Take Care Of Your Love	20

TOMMY DORSEY ORCHESTRA

(see also Frank Sinatra, Jo Stafford)

58	RCA RD 27069	FRANKIE AND TOMMY (LP, with Frank Sinatra)	12

D.O.S.E.

(see also Fall)

95	Colosseum TOGA 001TJX	Plug Myself In (with Mark E. Smith) (p/s, numbered, 1-sided, 500 only)	10

JOHNNY DOT & DASHERS

62	Salvo SLO 1805	I Love An Angel/Just For You (99 copies only)	50

DOTTY & BONNIE

(see also Bonnie Frankson, Eric Morris, Don Drummond, Skatalites, Baba Brooks)

64	Rio R 43	I'm So Glad/DOUGLAS BROTHERS: Got You On My Mind	12
64	Island WI 143	Your Kisses/Why Worry	18
64	Island WI 148	Dearest/Tears Are Falling	15
65	Ska Beat JB 183	Foul Play/ROLAND ALPHONSO & GROUP: Yard Broom	35
67	Ska Beat JB 274	I'll Know/Love Is Great	15

DOUBLE FEATURE

67	Deram DM 115	Baby Get Your Head Screwed On/Come On Baby	50
67	Deram DM 165	Handbags And Gladrags/Just Another Lonely Night	18

DOUBLES with GAY BLADES

59	HMV POP 613	Hey Girl!/Little Joe	150

DOUBT

(See also Carpenter Joe)

80	Solo SOLO 1	Fringes/Lookaway/Contrast Disorder/Time Out (EP, no p/s but insert)	20

SUZANNE DOUCET

68	Liberty LBF 15150	Swan Song/Cry My Heart	12

DOUGHNUT RING

(see also Crocheted Doughnut Ring)

68	Deram DM 215	Dance Around Julie/The Bandit	30

JOHNNY DOUGHTY

77	Topic 12TS 324	ROUND RYE BAY FOR MORE (LP, with insert)	15

CARL DOUGLAS (& BIG STAMPEDE)

66	Go AJ 11401	Crazy Feeling/PETER PERRY SOUL BAND: Keep It To Myself	35
67	Go AJ 11408	Let The Birds Sing/Something For Nothing	50
67	United Artists UP 1206	Nobody Cries/Serving A Sentence Of Life	175
67	United Artists UP 1206	Nobody Cries/Serving A Sentence Of Life (DJ Copy)	200
68	United Artists UP 2227	Sell My Soul To The Devil/Good Hard Worker	30
68	Pye 7N 45551	Witchfinder General/Crazy Feeling	20
71	CBS 7101	Do You Need My Love/Lean On Me	60
72	Blue Mountain BM 1007	Somebody Stop This Madness/Ain't No Use (as Karl Douglas)	10
79	Pye 7N 46155	Choose Between Two Lovers/Shame (red vinyl)	6

CHIC DOUGLAS

58	Fontana H 121	I'm Not Afraid Anymore/Jo-Ann	10

CRAIG DOUGLAS

(see also Bert Weedon)

58	Decca F 11055	Nothin' Shakin'/Sitting In A Tree House	25

			MINT VALUE £
58	Decca F 11075	Go Chase A Moonbeam/Are You Really Mine	12
59	Top Rank TR 5004	Battle Of New Orleans/Dream Lover/SHEILA BUXTON: Personality/ Where Were You On Our Wedding Day/BERT WEEDON: I Need Your Love Tonight ('King-Size' 7", special sleeve)	10
61	Top Rank JAR 555	A Hundred Pounds Of Clay/Hello Spring	6
61	Top Rank JAR 556	A Hundred Pounds Of Clay (censored version)/Hello Spring (p/s)	25
61	Top Rank JAR 556	A Hundred Pounds Of Clay (censored version)/Hello Spring	10
62	Top Rank JAR 603	A Change Of Heart/Another You	5
62	Top Rank JAR 610	When My Little Girl Is Smiling/Ring A Ding	5
62	Columbia DB 4854	Our Favourite Melodies/Rainbows	6
63	Decca F 11575	Town Crier/I'd Be Smiling Now	5
63	Decca F 11665	Danke Shoen/Teenage Mona Lisa	5
63	Decca F 11722	I'm So Glad I Found Her/Love Her While She's Young	5
63	Decca F 11763	Counting Up The Kisses/From Russia With Love	5
64	Fontana TF 458	Silly Boy/Love Leave Me Alone	6
64	Fontana TF 475	Come Closer/She's Smiling At Me (as Craig Douglas & Tridents)	12
65	Fontana TF 525	Across The Street/Party Girl	6
65	Fontana TF 580	Around The Corner/Find The Girl	6
69	Pye 7N 17746	How Do You Feel About That/Then	12
59	Top Rank JKR 8033	CRAIG SINGS FOR 'ROXY' (EP)	20
60	Decca DFE 6633	CRAIG (EP)	25
62	Decca DFE 8509	CUDDLE UP WITH CRAIG (EP)	15
63	Columbia SEG 8219	CRAIG MOVIE SONGS (EP)	30
60	Top Rank BUY 049	CRAIG DOUGLAS (LP)	40
61	Top Rank 35-103	BANDWAGON BALL (LP)	40
62	Columbia 33SX 1468	OUR FAVOURITE MELODIES (LP)	60

DEV DOUGLAS

64	Parlophone R5462	What Am I Doing HereI've Got Lovin'	12

DONNA DOUGLAS

58	Fontana H 158	The Shepherd/I'm Dancing With Tears In My Eyes	7
59	Fontana H 223	Six Boys And Seven Girls/Into Each Life Some Rain Must Fall	7
61	Piccadilly 7N 35014	Tammy Tell Me True/Memory Lane	7
62	Piccadilly 7N 35031	The Message In A Bottle/If This Is Love	10
62	Piccadilly 7N 35042	Matelot/All The Other Girls	7
63	Piccadilly 7N 35111	It's A Pity To Say Goodnight/Do I Know	7
63	Piccadilly 7N 35135	He's So Near/Turn Around	7
64	Pye 7N 15654	Blue Star/Java Jones	7

JACK DOUGLAS

68	Columbia DB 8393	Swanee River/Call Alf (Why Does Love Pass Me By)	8

JAN DOUGLAS

64	Vocalion V 9226	More And More/Walkin' In The Rain	10

JOHNNY DOUGLAS (& HIS ORCHESTRA/COMBO)

54	Decca F 10276	Ballet Of The Bells/Solfeggio (as Johnny Douglas & His Orchestra)	5
63	Speyside SK 1501	Ski Jump/Clementine (as Johnny Douglas Combo)	5
65	RCA 1444	Crack In The World/Time	15

KIRK DOUGLAS & MELLOMEN

55	Brunswick 05408	A Whale Of A Tale/And The Moon Grew Brighter And Brighter	15

LEW DOUGLAS & HIS ORCHESTRA

54	MGM SP 1093	Caesar's Boogie/Turn Around Boy	15

MARK DOUGLAS

62	Ember EMB S 166	It Matters Not/Upside Down	75

NORMA DOUGLAS

57	London HLZ 8475	Be It Resolved/Joe He Gone	25

BOBB & DEAN DOUGLAS

67	Deram DM 132	I Can Make It With You/Phone Me	50

DOUGLAS BROTHERS

(see also Dotty & Bonnie)

66	Rio R 57	Valley Of Tears/CHARMERS: Where Do I Turn	15
66	Rio R 63	Down And Out/RONALD WILSON: Lonely Man	100

HARRY DOUGLASS & DEEP RIVER BOYS

(see also Deep River Boys)

60	Top Rank JAR 352	Dum Dum De Dum/Go Galloway, Go	7

RONNIE DOVE

64	Stateside SS 314	Sweeter Than Sugar/I Believed In You	6
64	Stateside SS 346	Say You/Let Me Stay Today	6
64	Stateside SS 366	Right Or Wrong/Baby, Put Your Arms Around Me	6
65	Stateside SS 392	Hello Pretty Girl/Keep It A Secret	6
65	Stateside SS 412	One Kiss For Old Times' Sake/Bluebird	7
65	Stateside SS 436	A Little Bit Of Heaven/If I Live To Be A Hundred	7
65	Stateside SS 462	I'll Make All Your Dreams Come True/I Had To Lose You	6
65	Stateside SS 480	Kiss Away/Where In The World	6
66	Stateside SS 492	When Liking Turns To Loving/I'm Learning How To Smile Again	6
66	Stateside SS 510	Let's Start All Over Again/That Empty Feeling	6
66	Stateside SS 524	Happy Summer Days/Long After	6
66	Stateside SS 542	I Really Don't Want To Know/Years Of Tears	6
66	Stateside SS 571	Cry/Autumn Rhapsody	6
70	Stateside SS 2003	One More Mountain To Climb/All	6
70	Stateside SS 2018	My Babe/Put My Mind At Ease	6
70	Stateside SS 2047	I Want To Love You For What You Are/I Thank You For Your Love	6
70	Stateside SS 2086	Dancin' Out Of My Heart/Back From Baltimore	6

MINT VALUE £

68 Stateside SS 2119 — Mountain Of Love/Never Gonna Cry (The Way I'll Cry Tonight) — 10
65 Stateside SL 10149 — RONNIE DOVE (LP) — 30

DOVELLS

(see also Len Barry)

61 Columbia DB 4718 — The Bristol Stomp/Out In The Cold Again — 20
62 Columbia DB 4810 — Do The New Continental/Mopitty Mope Stomp — 20
62 Columbia DB 4877 — Bristol Twistin' Annie/The Actor — 20
62 Cameo Parkway P 845 — Hully Gully Baby/Your Last Chance — 10
63 Cameo Parkway P 861 — You Can't Run Away From Yourself/Save Me Baby — 10
63 Cameo Parkway P 867 — You Can't Sit Down/Stompin' Everywhere — 20
63 Cameo Parkway P 882 — Betty In Bermudas/Dance The Froog — 12
63 Cameo Parkway P 901 — Be My Girl/Dragster On The Prowl — 25
79 London HAU 8515 — CAMEO PARKWAY SESSIONS (LP) — 15

DOVES

(see also Badly Drawn Boy, Sub Sub, Jane Weaver v Doves)

98 Manchester MANC 9 — Seven Day Smile (with Jane Weaver)/ANDY VOTEL & JANE WEAVER: Gutter Girl (p/s) — 12
98 Manchester MANCCD 9 — Seven Day Smile (with Jane Weaver)/ANDY VOTEL & JANE WEAVER: Gutter Girl/JANE WEAVER: You're Not The Only Person That I Used To Know (CD) — 15
98 Casino CHIP 001 — CEDAR EP: Cedar Room/Rise/Zither (10", wraparound p/s) — 50
99 Casino CHIP 002 — SEA EP (10", p/s) — 30
99 Casino CHIP 002CD — SEA EP (CD, gatefold card sleeve) — 30
99 Casino CHIP 003 — Here It Comes/Meet Me At The Pier/(Acoustic Version) (10", p/s) — 15
00 Heavenly HVN9610 — Catch The Sun/Valley/Down To Sea (10") — 15
02 Heavenly HVN115-10 — Pounding/Satellites (Soulsavers Remix)/M62 (Four Tet Remix) (10") — 15
00 HVNLP 26 — LOST SOULS (2-LP) — 20
02 HVNLP 35 — THE LAST BROADCAST (2-LP) — 20
05 Heavenly HVNLP50 — SOME CITIES (2-LP) — 20
09 Heavenly HVNLP67 — KINGDOM OF RUST (2-LP) — 15

NICK DOW

79 Dingles DIN 306 — BURD MARGARET (LP) — 15

BRENT DOWE

(see also Melodians)

71 Summit SUM 8521 — Knock Three Times/GAYLADS: This Time I Won't Hurt You — 6
71 Summit SUM 8525 — Put Your Hand In The Hand/Miracle (B-side actually "It Took A Miracle Version" by Beverley's All Stars) — 6
71 Summit SUM 8530 — Freedom Train/BEVERLEY'S ALL STARS: Freedom Train (Version) — 6
73 Green Door GD 4061 — Reggae Makossa/No Nola (B-side actually by Melodians) — 8
76 Student STU 1006 — It was Love/Version — 8

JOE DOWELL

61 Mercury AMT 1161 — The Bridge Of Love/Just My Love — 7
62 Mercury AMT 1180 — Little Red Rented Rowboat/The One I Left For You — 7
60s Wing — WOODEN HEART (LP) — 20

DOWLANDS

62 Oriole CB 1748 — Little Sue/Julie (as Dowlands & Soundtracks) — 50
62 Oriole CB 1781 — Big Big Fella/Don't Ever Change — 100
63 Oriole CB 1815 — Break Ups/A Love Like Ours — 50
63 Oriole CB 1892 — Lonely Johnny (song actually titled "Lucky Johnny")/Do You Have To Have Me Blue? — 800
64 Oriole CB 1897 — All My Loving/Hey Sally (as Dowlands & Soundtracks) — 15
64 Oriole CB 1926 — I Walk The Line/Happy Endings — 40
64 Oriole CB 1947 — Wishing And Hoping/You Will Regret It — 80
65 Columbia DB 7547 — Don't Make Me Over/Someone Must Be Feeling Sad — 40

DOWNBEATS

61 Starlite ST45 051 — Thinkin' Of You/Midnight Love — 200

BRUCE DOWNER

71 Summit SUM 8524 — Free The People (actually by Bruce Ruffin)/BEVERLEY'S ALL STARS: Free The People (Version) — 6

ROLAND DOWNER & COUNT OSSIE

68 Doctor Bird DB 1130 — Ethiopian Kingdom/A Ju Ju Wah — 100

BOB DOWNES

(see also Rock Workshop)

70 Vertigo 6059 011 — No Time Like The Present/Keep Off The Grass — 35
70 Philips SBL 7922 — BOB DOWNES' OPEN MUSIC (LP) — 125
70 Vertigo 6360 005 — ELECTRIC CITY (LP, gatefold sleeve, large swirl label) — 90
70 Music For Pleasure MFP 1412 — DEEP DOWN HEAVY (LP, red/silver label) — 20
73 Ophenian BDOM 001 — DIVERSIONS (LP) — 25
74 Ophenian BDOM 002 — EPISODES AT 4AM (LP, with insert) — 22
75 Ophenian BDOM 003 — HELLS ANGELS (LP) — 30

DEIRDRE DOWNES & BROADSIDERS

69 Pye 7N 17781 — Lady Mary/Did He Mention My Name — 5

DOWNHILL

79 Bead Records BEAD 8 — DOWNHILL (LP) — 30

DOWN HOME

70s Lismor Folk LIFL 7011 — FIDDLE MUSIC VOLUME ONE (LP) — 15

BIG AL DOWNING

64 Sue WI 341 — Yes I'm Loving You/Please Come Home — 45

MINT VALUE £

DON DOWNING
73 People PEO 102 — Lonely Days Lonely Nights/I'm So Proud Of You — 6

DOWNLINERS SECT
(see also Don Crane's Downliners Sect)
64 Columbia DB 7300 — Baby What's Wrong/Be A Sect Maniac — 30
64 Columbia DB 7347 — Little Egypt/Sect Appeal — 15
64 Columbia DB 7415 — Find Out What's Happening/Insecticide — 30
65 Columbia DB 7509 — Wreck Of The Old '97/Leader Of The Sect — 30
65 Columbia DB 7597 — I Got Mine/Waiting In Heaven Somewhere — 30
65 Columbia DB 7712 — Bad Storm Coming/Lonely And Blue — 30
66 Columbia DB 7817 — All Night Worker/He Was A Square — 25
66 Columbia DB 7939 — Glendora/I'll Find Out — 65
66 Columbia DB 8008 — The Cost Of Living/Everything I've Got To Give — 25
64 Contrast Sound RBCSP 1 — NITE IN GREAT NEWPORT STREET (EP) — 300
65 Columbia SEG 8438 — THE SECT SING SICK SONGS (EP) — 100
64 Columbia 33SX 1658 — THE SECT (LP) — 150
65 Columbia 33SX 1745 — THE COUNTRY SECT (LP) — 80
66 Columbia SX 6028 — THE ROCK SECT'S IN (LP, mono, black/blue label with "Sold in the U.K..." text) — 100
66 Columbia S(C)X 6028 — THE ROCK SECT'S IN (LP, stereo, blue/black label with "Sold in the U.K..." text) — 140
93 Hangman HANG 42 UP — BIRTH OF SUAVE (LP) — 15

DOWN TO EARTH
71 Downtown DT 485 — Under The Boardwalk/Under The Boardwalk (Version)
(B-side actually "Double Barrel Version") — 7

DOWNTOWN ALL STARS
69 Downtown DT 426 — Everybody Feel Good/RUDIES: Downtown Jump — 8

GENE DOZIER & UNITED FRONT
74 Mercury 6167 007 — Give The Women What They Want/The Best Girl I Ever Had — 20

LAMONT DOZIER
(see also Holland & Dozier)
74 Probe PRO 618 — Trying To Hold On To My Woman/We Don't Want Nobody To Come — 5
74 Anchor ABC 4003 — Fish Ain't Bitin'/Breaking Out All Over — 5
75 Anchor ABC 4056 — All Cried Out/Rose — 5
77 Warner Bros K 16942 — Going Back To My Roots/Going Back To My Roots (Version) — 8
81 CBS A 1235 — To Cool Me Out/Starting Over — 10
74 ABC ABCL 5042 — OUT HERE ON MY OWN (LP) — 15
75 ABC ABCL 5096 — BLACK BACH (LP) — 12

DOZY, BEAKY, MICK & TICH (D.B.M.&T.)
(see also Dave Dee Dozy Beaky Mick & Tich)
69 Fontana TF 1061 — Tonight Today/Bad News — 5
70 Fontana 6007 022 — Mr. President/Frisco Annie (as D.B.M.&T) — 6
70 Fontana 6006 066 — Festival/Leader Of A Rock 'N' Roll Band — 6
70 Philips 6308 029 — FRESH EAR (LP, gatefold sleeve, credited to D.B.M.&T) — 25

DP'S
78 Barn 2314107 — IF YOU KNOW WHAT I MEAN (LP) — 15

DRAGON
76 Acorn CF 268 — DRAGON (LP, gatefold sleeve) — 60

DRAGONFLY
80s Dragonfly DF 001 — SILENT NIGHTS EP (p/s, private pressing) — 200

DRAGONFLY
74 Retreat RTS 257 — Gondola/Almost Abandoned (demo) — 15
75 Retreat RTS 261 — Driving Around The World/Since I Left My Home — 8
74 Retreat RTL 6002 — ALMOST ABANDONED (LP) — 25

DRAGONFLY
80s Dragonfly DF 001 — SILENT NIGHTS EP (p/s, private pressing) — 200

DRAGONS
69 Page One — Heart Transplantation/Hello I Love Maria — 40

DRAGONSFIRE
(see also Spinning Wheel)
82 Belltree BTR 001 — RISING PHOENIX (LP, with insert) — 20

DRAGONSLAYER
83 Cavalier CAV 017 — Broken Hearts/Satan Is Free/I Want Your Life
(Early copies with band name as 'Slayer'. NO STICKER) — 120
83 Cavalier CAV 017 — Broken Hearts/Satan Is Free/I Want Your Life
(Early copies had band name as 'Slayer', these later copies have sticker
with new name 'Dragonslayer' covering it) — 80

DRAG SET
(see also Open Mind)
66 Go AJ 11405 — Get Out Of My Way/Day And Night — 250

DRAGSTER
81 Heavy Metal HEAVY 4 — Ambition/Won't Bring You Back (p/s) — 30

CHARLIE DRAKE
58 Parlophone R 4461 — Splish Splash/Hello, My Darlings — 5
58 Parlophone R 4478 — Volare/Itchy Twitchy Feeling — 5
58 Parlophone R 4496 — Tom Thumb's Tune/Goggle Eye Ghee — 5
59 Parlophone R 4552 — Sea Cruise/Starkle, Starkle Little Twink — 5
60 Parlophone R 4675 — Naughty/Old Mr. Shadow — 5
60 Parlophone R 4701 — Mr. Custer/Glow Worm — 5
61 Parlophone R 4824 — My Boomerang Won't Come Back/She's My Girl — 5

			MINT VALUE £
62	Parlophone R 4875	Tanglefoot/Drake's Progress	5
62	Parlophone R 4918	I Bent My Assigai/Sweet Freddy Green	5
63	Parlophone R 5057	I've Lost The End Of My Yodel/I Can Can't I	5
64	Parlophone R 5143	I'm Too Heavy For The Light Brigade/The Reluctant Tight-Rope Walker	5
64	Parlophone R 5209	Charles Drake 007/Bumpanology (Bump Head Blues)	5
67	Pye 7N 17269	Who Is Sylvia/I Wanna Be In A Group	6
71	Columbia DB 8829	Puckwudgie/Toffee And Tears	5
73	EMI 2079	Someone Opened Watergate And They All Got Wet/'Ello Erf	6
75	Charisma CB 270	You Never Know/I'm Big Enough For Me (produced by Peter Gabriel)	8
76	Sol Doon SDRO 24S	Super Punk/Someone	8
58	Parlophone GEP 8720	HELLO MY DARLINGS (EP)	10
60	Parlophone GEP 8812	NAUGHTY CHARLIE DRAKE (EP)	10
64	Parlophone GEP 8903	HITS FROM THE MAN IN THE MOON (EP)	10

NICK DRAKE

79	Island RSS 7	Introduction/Hazy Jane II/Time Has Told Me/Fruit Tree/Rider On The Wheel ("Fruit Tree" sampler, 1-sided promo only)	200
69	Island ILPS 9105	FIVE LEAVES LEFT (LP, 1st pressing, pink label, black 'circle' logo, g/fold sleeve)	800
69	Island ILPS 9105	FIVE LEAVES LEFT (LP, gatefold sleeve, 2nd pressing, 'pink' rim label, 'palm tree' logo)	150
70	Island ILPS 9134	BRYTER LAYTER (LP, 'pink' rim label, 'palm tree' logo)	300
71	Longman (no cat. No.)	INTERPLAY ONE (2-LP, educational recording for schools, Drake plays guitar on three tracks, 2 booklets and 'teachers' notes)	400
72	Island ILPS 9184	PINK MOON (LP, 'pink' rim label, 'palm tree' logo, gatefold sleeve)	250
79	Island NDSP 100	FRUIT TREE (3-LP, box set with booklet)	70
85	Island ILPS 9826	HEAVEN IN A WILD FLOWER (THE BEST OF NICK DRAKE) (LP)	20
86	Hannibal HNBX 5302	FRUIT TREE (4-LP, expanded reissue with booklet)	75
86	Hannibal HNBL 1318	TIME OF NO REPLY (LP)	20
89	Island ILPS 9105	FIVE LEAVES LEFT (LP, reissue, 'blue with white palm tree' label)	12
89	Island ILPS 9134	BRYTER LAYTER (LP, reissue, 'blue with white palm tree' label)	12
89	Island ILPS 9184	PINK MOON (LP, reissue, 'blue with white palm tree' label)	12
91	Hannibal HNCD 5402	FRUIT TREE (4-CD, with booklet in 12" x 12" box)	70
00	Simply Vinyl SVLP 163	FIVE LEAVES LEFT (LP, 180gm Simply Vinyl repressing)	15
04	Island ILPS 8141	MADE TO LOVE MAGIC (LP, gatefold with inner sleeve)	15
07	Island FRUITCD 1	THE PICK OF THE FRUIT TREE (CD, sampler featuring River Man, Way To Blue, Cello Song, Fruit Tree, Northern Sky, Pink Moon, From The Morning)	15
07	Sunbeam SBR2LP 5041	FAMILY TREE (2-LP)	15

PETE DRAKE

63	Philips BF 1332	Forever/Sleep Walk	10

DRAMATICS

72	Stax 2025 053	Whatcha See Is Whatcha Get/Thankful For Your Love	8
72	Stax 2025 101	In The Rain/Get Up And Get Down	6
73	Stax 2025 117	Toast To A Fool/Your Love Was Strange	12
73	Stax 2025 181	Hey You, Get Off My Mountain/Devil Is Dope	6
76	ABC ABC 4101	You're Fooling You/I'll Make It So Good	6
72	Stax 2362 025	WHATCHA SEE IS WHATCHA GET (LP)	12
74	Stax STX 1021	A DRAMATIC EXPERIENCE (LP)	12
75	ABC ABCL 5121	DRAMATIC JACKPOT (LP, gatefold sleeve)	12
75	ABC ABCL 5150	DRAMA V (LP, gatefold sleeve)	12

BARRY DRANSFIELD

(see also Robin & Barry Dransfield, Dransfields)

72	Polydor Folk Mill 2383 160	BARRY DRANSFIELD (LP, red label)	250
78	Topic 12TS 5386	BOWIN' AND SCRAPIN' (LP)	25

ROBIN DRANSFIELD

(see also Robin & Barry Dransfield, Dransfields)

80	Topic 12TS 414	TIDEWAVE (LP)	15

ROBIN & BARRY DRANSFIELD

(see also Robin Dransfield, Barry Dransfield, Dransfields)

70	Trailer LER 2011	THE ROUT OF THE BLUES (LP yellow label)	60
71	Trailer LER 2026	LORD OF ALL I BEHOLD (LP)	30

DRANSFIELDS

(see also Robin & Barry Dransfield, Robin Dransfield, Barry Dransfield)

76	Transatlantic TRA 322	THE FIDDLER'S DREAM (LP)	20
77	Free Reed 018	POPULAR TO CONTRARY BELIEF (LP)	12
78	Transatlantic TRA 386	BOWIN' AND SCRAPIN' (LP)	12

RUSTY DRAPER

56	Mercury MT 113	Rock And Roll Ruby/House Of Cards (78)	10
56	Mercury MT 128	In The Middle Of The House/Pink Cadillac (78)	10
58	Mercury MT 194	Buzz Buzz Buzz/I Get The Blues When It Rains (78)	10
58	Mercury 7MT 211	Gamblin' Gal/That's My Doll	12
58	Mercury MT 211	Gamblin' Gal/That's My Doll (78)	10
58	Mercury 7MT 229	Chicken-Pickin' Hawk/June, July And August	15
59	Mercury AMT 1019	Shoppin' Around/With This Ring	30
59	Mercury MT 1019	Shoppin' Around/With This Ring (78)	10
59	Mercury AMT 1034	The Sun Will Always Shine/Hey Li Lee Li Lee Li	6
60	Mercury AMT 1101	Mule Skinner Blues/Please Help Me, I'm Falling	7
60	Mercury AMT 1110	Luck Of The Irish/It's A Little More Like Heaven	6
61	Mercury AMT 1127	Jealous Heart/Ten Thousand Years Ago	10
63	London HLU 9786	Night Life/That's Why I Love You Like I Do	10
65	London HLU 9989	Folsom Prison Blues/You Can't Be True, Dear	10
56	Mercury MEP 9506	PRESENTING RUSTY DRAPER (EP)	40

			MINT VALUE £
59	Mercury ZEP 10016	RUSTY DRAPER (EP)	20
60	Mercury ZEP 10059	RUSTY IN GAMBLING MOOD (EP)	20
60	Mercury ZEP 10095	MULE SKINNER BLUES (EP)	25
64	London RE-U 1431	RUSTY DRAPER NO. 1 (EP)	20
64	London RE-U 1432	RUSTY DRAPER NO. 2 (EP)	20
60	Mercury MMC 14040	HITS THAT SOLD A MILLION (LP)	15

MIKEY DREAD (AKA MICKEY CAMPBELL

79	Do It DUNE 24	Heavyweight Style/Rub A Dub (12")	20
79	Warrior WAR 125	Barber Saloon/CARLTON PATTERSON: Wash Wash	10
79	Warrior WAR 125	Barber Saloon/CARLTON PATTERSON: Wash Wash (12")	20
81	Dread At The Controls DATC 003	Warrior Stylee/Israel Stylee (12")	25
82	Dread... DATCD 008	Roots & Culture/Jungle Dread (12")	25
77	Hawkeye HALP 001	DUB (LP)	15
79	Dread...DTCLP 002	AFRICAN ANTHEM - THE MIKEY DREAD SHOW DUBWISE (LP)	20
80	Dread...DTCLP 006	WORLD WAR III (LP)	15
80	Dread...DTLP 001	MASTER SHOWCASE (LP)	30
82	Dread...DATCLP 008	JUNGLE SIGNAL (LP)	30
83	Dread...DTLP 009	DUB MERCHANT (LP)	25

DREAMBOYS

80	St Vitus SV1	Bela Lugosi's Birthday/Outer Limits/Shall We Dance	25

DREAMERS
(see also Freddie & Dreamers)

68	Columbia DB 8340	The Maybe Song/The Long Road	10

DREAMERS

69	Downtown DT 407	Sweet Chariot/Let's Go Downtown	10
69	Downtown DT 408	I Second That Emotion/Dear Love	10

DREAMLETS

65	Ska Beat JB 182	Really Now/SKATALITES: Street Corner	50

DREAMLOVERS
(see also Chubby Checker)

61	Columbia DB 4711	When We Get Married/Just Because	200

DREAM MERCHANTS

67	Decca F 12617	Rattler/I'll Be With You In Apple Blossom Time	10

DREAM POLICE
(see also Average White Band)

70	Decca F 12998	I'll Be Home (In A Day Or So)/Living Is Easy	10
70	Decca F 13078	Our Song/Much Too Much	6
70	Decca F 13105	I've Got No Choice/What's The Cure For Happiness?	6

DREAMS

68	United Artists UP 2249	I Will See You There/A Boy Needs A Girl	35
69	CBS 4247	Baby I'm Your Man/Softly, Softly	25
69	Dolphin 4432	Casatschok/Don't You Ask Me	7
70	CBS 64203	DREAMS (LP)	20
72	CBS 64597	IMAGINE MY SURPRISE (LP)	20

DREAM THEATER

94	East West A 5835	Lie/Space-Dye Vest/To Live Forever/Another Day (live) (p/s)	8
94	East West A 5835 T	Lie/Take The Time (Demo)/Space-Dye Vest (12", p/s)	10
89	MCA MCF 3445	WHEN DREAM AND DAY UNITE (LP)	12
92	Atco 7567 92148 1	IMAGES AND WORDS (LP)	15

DREAMTIMERS

61	London HLU 9368	The Dancin' Lady/An Invitation	25

DREAM WEAVERS

56	Brunswick 05515	It's Almost Tomorrow/You've Got Me Wondering (gold label lettering)	40
56	Brunswick 05515	It's Almost Tomorrow/You've Got Me Wondering (silver label lettering)	25
56	Brunswick 05568	A Little Love Can Go A Long, Long Way/Into The Night (featuring Wade Buff)	25
56	Brunswick 05607	You're Mine/Is There Somebody Else? (featuring Wade Buff)	15

MIKE DRED

90	Machine Codes DH VOL 1	THE MIGHTY DRED EP (12")	12
93	Machine Codes CODE A	FU-CHIN-RA EP (12")	10

DRED & FRED

92	Ironworks D&F 001	Down Too Long/CREATIVE STEPPERS: Creative Version (12")	30

DREGS

79	Disturbing DRO 1	THE DREGS EP (p/s, numbered, stamped sleeve, 500 only)	50

DRESSED IN BLACK

92	Kold Sweat KSEP202	Discretions/Freedom Of Speech (EP)	8

LEN DRESSLAR

56	Mercury 7MT 3	Chain Gang/These Hands (export issue)	15

JOHN DREVAR('S EXPRESSION)

67	MGM MGM 1367	The Closer She Gets/When I Come Home	200
67	MGM MGM 1367	The Closer She Gets/When I Come Home (DJ Copy)	300
68	Polydor BM 56290	What Greater Love/I've Decided (solo)	10

ALAN DREW

63	Columbia DB 7090	Here Comes The Rain/Always The Lonely One	7

PATTI DREW

68	Capitol CL 15557	Workin' On A Groovy Thing/Without A Doubt	15
68	Capitol CL 15575	Hard To Handle/Just Can't Forget About You	8

MINT VALUE £

DREXCIYA

93	Rephlex Cat 017	3 - Molecular Enhancement (12", 4-track)	10
95	Warp WAP 57	The Journey Home (12", company sleeve)	10

DRIFTERS (U.K.)

(see also Shadows, Cliff Richard, Jet Harris, Tony Meehan)

59	Columbia DB 4263	Feelin' Fine/Don't Be A Fool (With Love)	50
59	Columbia DB 4263	Feelin' Fine/Don't Be A Fool (With Love) (78)	65
59	Columbia DB 4325	Driftin'/Jet Black	45

DRIFTERS (U.S.)

(see also Clyde McPhatter, Ben E. King, Bobby Hendricks)

78s

56	London HLE 8344	Soldier Of Fortune/I Gotta Get Myself A Woman	50
58	London HLE 8686	Moonlight Bay/Drip-Drop	40
59	London HLE 8892	There Goes My Baby/Oh, My Love	60
59	London HLE 8988	Dance With Me/True Love, True Love	60
60	London HLE 9081	This Magic Moment/Baltimore	80

SINGLE

56	London HLE 8344	Soldier Of Fortune/I Gotta Get Myself A Woman	1000
58	London HLE 8686	Moonlight Bay/Drip-Drop	200
59	London HLE 8892	There Goes My Baby/Oh, My Love	30
59	London HLE 8988	Dance With Me/True Love, True Love	15
60	London HLE 9081	This Magic Moment/Baltimore	18
60	London HLK 9145	Lonely Winds/Hey Senorita	18
60	London HLK 9201	Save The Last Dance For Me/Nobody But Me	6
61	London HLK 7114	Save The Last Dance For Me/This Magic Moment (export issue)	15
61	London HLK 7115	I Count The Tears/Dance With Me (export issue)	20
61	London HLK 9287	I Count The Tears/Sadie My Lady	25
61	London HLK 9326	Some Kind Of Wonderful/Honey Bee	15
61	London HLK 9382	Please Stay/No Sweet Lovin'	15
61	London HLK 9427	Sweets For My Sweet/Loneliness Or Happiness	10
62	London HLK 9500	Room Full Of Tears/Somebody New Dancin' With You	10
62	London HLK 9522	When My Little Girl Is Smiling/Mexican Divorce	8
62	London HLK 9554	Stranger On The Shore/What To Do	8
62	London HLK 9626	Up On The Roof/Another Night With The Boys	10
63	London HLK 9699	On Broadway/Let The Music Play	15
63	London HLK 9750	Rat Race/If You Don't Come Back	15
63	London HLK 9785	I'll Take You Home/I Feel Good All Over	8
64	London HLK 9848	Vaya Con Dios/In The Land Of Make Believe	8
64	London HLK 9886	One Way Love/Didn't It	10
64	Atlantic AT 4001	Under The Boardwalk/I Don't Want To Go On Without You	12
64	Atlantic AT 4008	I've Got Sand In My Shoes/He's Just A Playboy	12
64	Atlantic AT 4012	Saturday Night At The Movies/Spanish Lace	12
65	Atlantic AT 4019	At The Club/Answer The Phone	12
65	Atlantic AT 4023	Come On Over To My Place/Chains Of Love	15
65	Atlantic AT 4034	Follow Me/The Outside World	15
65	Atlantic AT 4040	I'll Take You Where The Music's Playing/Far From The Maddening Crowd	10
66	Atlantic AT 4062	We Gotta Sing/Nylon Stockings	18
66	Atlantic AT 4084	Memories Are Made Of This/My Island In The Sun	10
66	Atlantic 584 020	Up In The Streets Of Harlem/You Can't Love 'Em All	10
67	Atlantic 584 065	Baby What I Mean/Aretha	25
68	Atlantic 584 152	I'll Take You Where The Music's Playing/On Broadway	6
68	Atlantic 584 195	Still Burning In My Heart/I Need You Now	10
69	Atlantic 584 246	Saturday Night At The Movies/Under The Boardwalk	10
71	Atlantic 2091 064	A Rose By Any Other Name/Be My Lady	10
76	Atlantic K 10700	You Gotta Pay Your Dues/Black Silk	15
77	Arista 94	I'll Know When True Love Really Passes By/A Good Song Never Dies	30
78	Arista 202	Closely Guarded Secret/I Can't Believe It's Over	20
79	Epic EPC 7806	Pour Your Little Heart Out Parts 1 & 2	70

EPs

61	London RE-K 1282	THE DRIFTERS' GREATEST HITS	40
63	London RE-K 1355	THE DRIFTERS	40
63	London RE-K 1385	DRIFTIN'	40
64	Atlantic AET 6003	DRIFTIN' VOL. 2	40
65	Atlantic AET 6012	TONIGHT	30

LPs

60	London HA-K 2318	THE DRIFTERS' GREATEST HITS	60
62	London HA-K 2450	SAVE THE LAST DANCE FOR ME	70
65	Atlantic ATL 5015	OUR BIGGEST HITS	40
65	Atlantic ATL/STL 5023	THE GOOD LIFE WITH THE DRIFTERS (mono/stereo)	40
66	Atlantic ATL/STL 5039	I'LL TAKE YOU WHERE THE MUSIC'S PLAYING (mono/stereo)	40
67	Atlantic 587 038	BIGGEST HITS	20
67	Atlantic 587 061	I'LL TAKE YOU WHERE THE MUSIC'S PLAYING (reissue)	18
67	Atlantic 590 010	SOUVENIRS	25
67	Atlantic 587 063	SAVE THE LAST DANCE FOR ME (reissue)	20
68	Atlantic 587/588 103	THE DRIFTERS' GOLDEN HITS	15
68	Atlantic 587 123	ROCKIN' AND DRIFTIN'	40
68	Atlantic 587 144	GOOD GRAVY (as Clyde McPhatter & Drifters)	45
69	Atlantic 587/588 160	UP ON THE ROOF	20

DRIFTING SLIM

66	Blue Horizon 45-1005	Good Morning Baby/My Sweet Woman (99 copies only)	120

DRIFTWOOD

(see also Neil Harrison)

70	Decca F 13084	Shylock Bay/The Wind Cries Above You	6

MINT VALUE £

71	Decca F 13139	Say The Right Things/Still I'll Stay With You	6
70	Decca SKL 5069	DRIFTWOOD (LP, blue/silver label with boxed logo)	70

JIMMY DRIFTWOOD

60	RCA RCX 191	COUNTRY GUITAR VOL. 13 (EP)	8
60	RCA RCX 193	TALL TALES IN SONG VOL. 1 (EP)	10
60	RCA RCX 195	TALL TALES IN SONG VOL. 2 (EP)	10
60	RCA RCX 198	TALL TALES IN SONG VOL. 3 (EP)	10
59	RCA RD 27144	THE WILDERNESS ROAD (LP)	18
61	RCA RD 27226	BILLY YANK AND JOHNNY REB (LP)	12

JULIE DRISCOLL

63	Columbia DB 7118	Take Me By The Hand/Stay Away From Me	35
65	Parlophone R 5296	Don't Do It No More/I Know You	35
66	Parlophone R 5444	I Didn't Want To Have To Do It/Don't Do It No More	20
67	Parlophone R 5588	I Know You Love Me Not/If You Should Ever Leave Me	20
67	Marmalade 598 005	Save Me Pts 1 & 2	35
71	Polydor 2383077	JULIE DRISCOLL... 1969 (LP)	50

JULIE DRISCOLL, BRIAN AUGER & TRINITY

(see also Brian Auger & Trinity, Working Week, Julie Tippetts, B.B. Blunder)

68	Marmalade 598 006	This Wheel's On Fire/A Kind Of Love In	8
68	Marmalade 598 011	Road To Cairo/Shadows Of You	8
69	Marmalade 598 018	Take Me To The Water/Indian Rope Man	50
67	Marmalade 607002	OPEN (mono, first pressing, with 1-sided insert and non laminated cover produced by "Upton Printing")	100
67	Marmalade 607 002	OPEN (LP, mono)	70
67	Marmalade 608 002	OPEN (LP, stereo)	50
68	M. For Pleasure MFP 1265	JOOLS/BRIAN (LP, tracks shared by Julie Driscoll & Brian Auger)	18
69	Marmalade 608 005/6	STREET NOISE (2-LP, gatefold sleeve)	200
69	Marmalade 608 014	STREET NOISE PART 1 (LP)	35
69	Marmalade 608 015	STREET NOISE PART 2 (LP)	35
70s	Polydor 2334004	BEST OF (LP, 99p series)	20

DRIVE

78	NRG NE 467	Jerkin'/Push'N'Shove (no p/s)	50

DRIVER

79	Rods ROD 1	Like A Mirror/Here I Am (p/s)	20
79	Rods ROD 2	I'm Not Dreaming/So They Say	15
80	Rods HOT 1	YOU BETTER TAKE IT (LP, 300 only)	100

DRIVERS

(see also Nick Van Eede)

83	Greyhound GRK 701	Talk All Night/Sister (p/s)	6
84	Nouveau NMS 5	Things/Stolen Treasure (p/s)	6
83	Greyhound GRK 3301	SHORT CUTS (LP)	12

DRIVESHAFT

80	Undercover DC 02	Cold As Ice/I Know What You Are After (features Noel Redding who also produced the single)	50
82	Undercover DC 03	Heartbreaker/Now That It's Over (p/s)	25

DRIZABONE

94	4th & Broadway 12 BRW 264	Pressure (Roger's Soul Sensation Mix)/Pressure (album version)/Pressure (Bonus Beats Mix)/Pressure (Bone Idol Remix)/Pressure (Nu Solution Mix)/ Pressure (Underground Network Mix) (12", p/s)	15

D-ROK

(see also Brian May)

91	Warhammer DROK 08722	Get Out Of My Way (D-Mix)/Renegade/Get Out Of My Way (Airmix) (12", p/s)	10
91	Warhammer DROK 08710	OBLIVION (LP)	12

DROME

94	Ninja Tune ZEN 11	THE FINAL CORPORATE COLONIZATION OF THE UNCONSCIOUS (2 x LP)	15

FRANK D'RONE

59	Mercury ART 1040	Fascinating Rhythm/Yesterdays	6
60	Mercury AMT 1123	Strawberry Blonde (The Band Rocked On)/Time Hurries By	8
59	Mercury ZEP 10033	FRANK D'RONE SINGS (EP)	15
59	Mercury ZEP 10083	BLUE SERENADE (EP)	10
59	Mercury ZEP 10116	THE BAND ROCKED ON (EP)	20
60	Mercury MMC 14053	AFTER THE BALL (LP)	20

DRONES

77	Valer VRS 1	Bone Idle/I Just Wanna Be Myself (gatefold p/s, made in France)	12
77	Valer VRS 1	Bone Idle/I Just Wanna Be Myself (gatefold p/s, made in England)	6
77	Fifth Avenue CAS 107	Bone Idle/I Just Wanna Be Myself (cassette, flip-open 'cigarette box' sleeve)	30
77	Valer VRSP 1	Be My Baby/Lift Off The Bans (12", white label, unreleased)	50
77	Valer	Be My Baby (Take Two)/The Clique (white label, unreleased, many autographed)	20
77	Ohms GOOD MIX 1	TEMPTATIONS OF A WHITE COLLAR WORKER (EP, different coloured sleeves, some with writing on inner sleeve)	15
80	Fabulous JC 4	Can't See/Fooled Today (p/s)	7
77	Valer VRLP 1	FURTHER TEMPTATIONS (LP)	35

DROWNING CRAZE

81	Situation 2 SIT 3	Storage Case/Damp Bones (p/s)	8
81	Situation 2 SIT 13	Trance/I Love The Fjords (p/s)	8
82	Situation 2 SIT 16	Heat/Replays (p/s)	8

DRUG ADDIX

(see also Kirsty MacColl)

78	Chiswick SW 39	MAKE A RECORD (EP)	12

MINT VALUE £

DRUID
76 EMI SPSR 395 — Barnaby Kestrel/Nothing But Morning — 12
75 EMI EMC 3081 — TOWARDS THE SUN (LP, with inner sleeve) — 20
76 EMI EMC 3128 — FLUID DRUID (LP, with inner sleeve) — 20

DRUID CHASE
67 CBS 3053 — Take Me In Your Garden/I Wanna Get My Hands On You — 30

DRUIDS
63 Parlophone R 5097 — Long Tall Texan/Love So Blue — 20
64 Parlophone R 5134 — It's Just A Little Bit Too Late/See What You've Done — 20
71 Argo ZFB 22 — BURNT OFFERING (LP) — 75

DRUIDS
(see also Giles Farnaby's Dream Band)
73 Argo ZFB 39 — PASTIME WITH GOOD COMPANY (LP) — 45

DRUM CLUB
93 Butterfly BFLT10A — Sound System Volume 1 (12") — 10
93 Big Life DC PROMO 2 — Big Life (2 x 12" promo) — 15

DRUMBAGO
(see also Derrick Patsy, Dennis Walks)
63 Island WI 085 — I Am Drunk (actually by Raymond Harper & Drumbago's Group)/ Sea Breeze (actually by Sammy & Drumbago's Group) — 20
68 Blue Cat BS 145 — Reggae Jeggae (with Blenders)/TYRONE TAYLOR: Delilah — 30
69 Trojan TR 638 — Dulcemania (with Dynamites)/CLANCY ECCLES: China Man — 10

BILL DRUMMOND
(see also Big In Japan, Lori & Chameleons, J.A.M.s, KLF, Disco 2000, Timelords)
87 Creation CRE 039T — King Of Joy/The Manager (12", p/s) — 25

DON DRUMMOND
(see also Joe White, Rhythm Aces, Roy & Millie, Movers, Desmond Dekker, Shenley Duffas, Hi-Tones, Duke Reid, Soul Brothers, Baba Brooks, Bonnie & Skitto, Eric Morris, Pioneers, Stranger & Patsy, Techniques, Winston Wright)
62 Island WI 021 — Schooling The Duke/Bitter Rose (as Don Drummond Orchestra; B-side is actually by Shenley Duffus) — 30
63 Black Swan WI 406 — Scrap Iron/DRAGONAIRE: Prevention — 25
63 Blue Beat BB 179 — Reload/Far East — 30
63 Island WI 094 — Scandal/My Ideal (B-side actually by W. Sparks) — 25
63 R&B JB 103 — Royal Flush/MAYTALS: Matthew Mark — 30
63 R&B JB 105 — The Shock/TONETTES: Tell Me You're Mine — 25
64 Ska Beat JB 178 — Silver Dollar/TOMMY McCOOK: My Business — 30
64 Island WI 149 — Eastern Standard Time/DOTTY & BONNIE: Sun Rises — 25
64 Island WI 153 — Musical Storeroom/STRANGER COLE: He Who Feels — 25
64 Island WI 162 — Garden Of Love/STRANGER COLE: Cherry May — 40
65 Island WI 192 — Stampede (with Drumbago)/JUSTIN HINDS & DOMINOES: Come Bail Me — 25
65 Island WI 204 — Coolie Baby/LORD ANTICS: You May Stray — 25
65 Island WI 208 — Man In The Street/RITA & BENNY: You Are My Only Love — 40
65 Island WI 242 — University Goes Ska/DERRICK & NAOMI: Pain In My Heart — 40
69 Studio One SO 2078 — Heavenless/GLEN BROWN & DAVE BARKER: Lady Lovelight — 45
69 Trojan TR 678 — Memory Of Don/JOHN HOLT: Darling I Love You — 15
69 Coxsone CSL 8021 — IN MEMORY OF DON DRUMMOND (LP) — 60
69 Studio One SO 9008 — THE BEST OF DON DRUMMOND (LP) — 150
69 Trojan TTL 23 — MEMORIAL ALBUM (LP) — 25

DON DRUMMOND JUNIOR
(see also Vincent Gordon)
67 Caltone TONE 104 — Sir Pratt Special/HEMSLEY MORRIS: Love Is Strange — 100
68 Caltone TONE 124 — Dirty Dozen/PHIL PRATT: Reach Out — 100
70 Jackpot JP 710 — Memory Of Don Drummond/TOBIES: Resting — 20

JOHN DRUMMOND
68 Page One POF 084 — Break My Mind/Molly Bye Bye — 7

K. DRUMMOND
(see also Cables)
73 Jackpot JP 810 — Your Pretty Face/Your Pretty Face (Version) — 5

LEE DRUMMOND
66 Fontana TF 728 — Messrs Lindsay, Parker & Flynn/Sitting And Drinking Alone — 8

PETE DRUMMOND & THE VHF BAND
72 Warner Bros K 16232 — Rocking At The BBC/Goodbye (vinyl 78) — 20

DRUNKEN MASTER
(see also SLR)
93 Kold Sweat KSEP209 — DEVIL IN DISGUISE (EP) — 8

ROY DRUSKY
59 Brunswick 05785 — Wait 'N' See/Just About That Time — 10
66 Mercury MF1022 — Teach Me Little Children/Too Much Of You — 6

REGINA DRUTTON
68 CBS 5684 — A Hard Man Is Good To Hold Onto/Tell Me Lies Again — 5

DRY ICE
(see also Pluto)
69 B&C CB 115 — Running To The Convent/Nowhere To Go — 25

DRY RIB
(see also Television Personalities, Times, L'Orange Mechanik)
79 Clockwork COR 001 — THE DRY SEASON (EP, 33rpm, photocopied foldover p/s, screen-printed labels) — 30

MINT VALUE £

DRY WATERS
72 Denby DEN 003 Crystal Ball/The Magic Valley . . . 120

AMANCIO D'SILVA
(see also Cosmic Eye)
69 Columbia S(C)X 6322 INTEGRATION (LP) . . . 300
71 Columbia SCX 6465 REFLECTIONS (LP) . . . 20

D.S.K.F.
92 WG 001 NEW SCIENCE EP (12", stickered white label) . . . 70

D.S.P.
92 FX FXUKT 10 Obsession/Revenge Attack/Intravenus/Kebab (12") . . . 20

D TO THE K
88 BPM BP12004 Hard But Live/Ease Up Your Mind (12") . . . 45

DUALS
61 London HL 9450 Stick Shift/Cruising . . . 25

DUBBING IN THE U.K.
81 Star Light SDLP 902 DUBBING IN THE U.K. (LP) . . . 35

DUBLINERS
67 Transatlantic TRA 158 THE BEST OF (LP) . . . 12
67 Major Minor MMLP 3 A DROP OF THE HARD STUFF (LP) . . . 12
67 Major Minor MMLP 5 MORE OF THE HARD STUFF (LP) . . . 12

DUBS
57 London HLU 8526 Could This Be Magic/Such Lovin' . . . 250
57 London HLU 8526 Could This Be Magic/Such Lovin' (78) . . . 40
58 London HL 8684 Gonna Make A Change/Beside My Love . . . 300
58 London HL 8684 Gonna Make A Change/Beside My Love (78) . . . 30

DUB SYNDICATE
84 On-U Sound ON-U LP 18 POUNDING SYSTEM (LP) . . . 18
86 On-U Sound ON-U LP 38 TUNES FROM THE MISSING CHANNEL (LP) . . . 18

DIANE DUCANE
79 Contact WN 2 Better Late Than Never/One Day . . . 30

JOHN DU CANN
(see also Attack, Andromeda, Five Day Week Straw People, Atomic Rooster, Hard Stuff, Status Quo)
77 Arista ARIST 128 Throw Him In Jail/Street Stutter . . . 5
77 Arista ARIST 145 Where's The Show/Hang Around . . . 5
79 Vertigo 6059 241 Don't Be A Dummy/If I'm Makin' (p/s) . . . 5

DUCHESS OF BEDFORD
56 HMV POP 361 Luck's In Love With You/MRS GERALD LEGGE: I'm In Love . . . 8

DUCKS DELUXE
(see also Motors, Tyla Gang, Brinsley Schwarz)
73 RCA RCA 2438 Coast To Coast/Bring Back That Packard Car . . . 6
75 RCA RCA 2531 I Fought The Law/Cherry Pie . . . 6
74 RCA LPL1 5008 DUCKS DELUXE (LP) . . . 12
74 RCA SF 8402 TAXI TO THE TERMINAL ZONE (LP) . . . 12
82 Blue Moon BMLP 001 LAST NIGHT OF A PUB ROCK BAND (2-LP) . . . 15

DUDLEY
60 Vogue V 9171 Lone Prairie Rock/El Pizza . . . 20

DAVE DUDLEY
63 United Artists UP 1029 Six Days On The Road/I Feel A Cry Coming On . . . 15
67 Mercury MF 1003 Trucker's Prayer/Don't Come Cryin' To Me . . . 8
68 Mercury MF 1037 There Ain't No Easy Run/Why Can't I Be With You? (It's A Shame) . . . 5

ROBERTA DUDLEY
(see also Kid Ory)
50 Tempo R 22 Krooked Blues/When You're Alone (78) . . . 15
51 Poydras 3 Krooked Blues/When You're Alone (shellac 45) . . . 8

DU-ETTES
72 President PT 382 Every Beat Of My Heart/Sugar Daddy . . . 8
72 President PT 398 Please Forgive Me/Lonely Days . . . 8

D DUFFUS
79 Jay Dee JD 009 Is It Just A Dream/Cheaters (12") . . . 50

SHENLEY DUFFAS
(see also Chenley Duffus, Billy Dyce)
62 Island WI 036 Give To Get/What You Gonna Do (as S. Duffas; B-side actually with Millie Small) . . . 20
63 Island WI 063 Fret Man Fret/Doreen . . . 20
63 Island WI 093 What A Disaster/I Am Rich . . . 20
63 Island WI 115 Know The Lord/TOMMY McCOOK: Ska Ba . . . 45
63 Island WI 125 Easy Squeal/Things Ain't Going Right . . . 20
63 R&B JB 134 No More Wedding Bells/Let Them Fret . . . 15
64 R&B JB 146 Big Mouth/FRANKIE ANDERSON: Peanut Vendor . . . 18
64 R&B JB 152 Christopher Columbus/CARL BRYAN ORCHESTRA: Barber Chair . . . 18
64 R&B JB 154 Mother-In-Law/DON DRUMMOND & GROUP: Festival . . . 18
64 Black Swan WI 440 Digging A Ditch/He's Coming Down . . . 18
64 Black Swan WI 443 Gather Them In/Crucifixion . . . 20
64 Rio R 41 I Will Be Glad/Heariso (as Shandly Duffus) . . . 18
65 Island WI 182 La La La/UPCOMING WILLOWS: Jonestown Special . . . 30
65 Island WI 184 You Are Mine/UPCOMING WILLOWS: Red China . . . 30
65 Island WI 186 Rukumbine/One Morning . . . 20

MINT VALUE £

72 Upsetter US 380 — Bet You Don't Know/UPSETTERS: Ring Of Fire . . . 18
72 Dynamic DYN 451 — Peace (with Soul Avengers)/UPSETTERS: Peace ? Version . . . 7
72 Grape GR 3031 — Sincerely/Sincerely ? Version (with Upsetters) . . . 8

CHRIS DUFFIN
76 Deroy ADM LP 864 — HEY SANDY (LP) . . . 250

CHENLEY DUFFUS
(see also Shenley Duffas)
72 Pama PM 859 — At The End/Good Night My Love . . . 8

DUFFY
73 Chapter One SCHR 184 — The Joker/Running Away . . . 18
70 Chapter One CHS-R 814 — SCRUFFY DUFFY (LP, red/silver label) . . . 200

DUFFY
04 Awen REG150 CD — Dim Dealltwriaeth/Hedfan Angel/Cariad Dwi'n Unig (CD single as Aimee Duffy) . 25
07 A&M 175 410-6 — Rockferry/Oh Boy (p/s, 1,500 only) . . . 6

STEPHEN 'TIN TIN' DUFFY
(see also Hawks, Tin Tin, Dr. Calculus, Lilac Time)
85 10 — She Loves Me/She Loves It (p/s, withdrawn) . . . 40
85 10 — Baby Impossible (p/s, withdrawn) . . . 40

DUFFY'S NUCLEUS
(see also Duffy Power, Pentangle, John McLaughlin)
67 Decca F 22547 — Hound Dog/Mary Open The Door . . . 50

DON DUGGAN
68 Pye 7N 17633 — Let Her Dance/Westmeath Bachelor (with Savoys) . . . 6

BILLY DUKE
62 Ember EMB S 153 — Walking Cane/Amen . . . 6
62 Ember EMB S 160 — Ain't She Pretty/Timbuctu . . . 6
64 London HLU 9907 — While The Bloom Is On The Rose/I'm The Lonesomest Guy In Town . . . 7
65 London HLU 9960 — Sugar 'N' Spice/Prisoner Of Love . . . 7

DENVER DUKE & JEFFREY NULL BLUEGRASS BOYS
63 Starlite STEP 33 — DENVER DUKE & JEFFREY NULL BLUEGRASS BOYS (EP) . . . 15

DORIS DUKE
71 Mojo 2092 005 — To The Other Woman/I Don't Care Anymore . . . 8
71 Mojo 2092 017 — If She's Your Wife Who Am I?/It Sure Was Fun . . . 15
73 Mainstream MSS 302 — Business Deal/Nobody But You . . . 8
74 Contempo 7703 — Grasshopper/Please Come Back . . . 8
76 Contempo CX15 — Woman Of The Ghetto/TAMIKO JONES: Let It Flow . . . 5
71 Mojo 2916 001 — I'M A LOSER (LP) . . . 40
71 Mojo 2916 006 — A LEGEND IN HER OWN TIME (LP) . . . 40
75 Contempo CRM 111 — A LEGEND IN HER OWN TIME (LP, reissue) . . . 15
75 Contempo CLP 519 — WOMAN (LP) . . . 30

PATTY DUKE
65 United Artists UP 1103 — Don't Just Stand There/Everything But Love . . . 12
65 United Artists UP 1116 — Say Something Funny/Funny Little Butterflies . . . 8
66 United Artists UP 1131 — Whenever She Holds You/Nothing But You . . . 15
65 United Artists (S)ULP 1123 — DON'T JUST STAND THERE (LP, mono/stereo) . . . 40

DUKE ALL STARS
68 Blue Cat BS 111 — Letter To Mummy And Daddy (Parts 1 & 2) . . . 20

DUKE & DUCHESS
(see also Sir Hubert Pimm)
55 London HLU 8206 — Borrowed Sunshine/Get Ready For Love (with Sir Hubert Pimm) . . . 40

DUKE OF BURLINGTON
71 Decca F23120 — Flash/Slot Machine . . . 10

AGGIE DUKES
57 Vogue V 9090 — John John/Well Of Loneliness . . . 400
57 Vogue V 9090 — John John/Well Of Loneliness (78) . . . 60

DUKES OF ILLYRIA
70 IAMBIG 0001 — Food Of Love/Come Away Death . . . 20

DUKES OF STRATOSPHEAR
(see also XTC, Mr. Partridge)
87 Virgin VSY 982 — You're A Good Man Albert Brown/Vanishing Girl (p/s, 5,000 on multi-coloured vinyl) . . . 8
85 Virgin WOW 1 — 25 O'CLOCK (LP) . . . 18
87 Virgin VP 2440 — PSONIC PSUNSPOT (LP, gatefold sleeve, 5,000 on multi-coloured vinyl) . . . 30

DULCIMER
71 Nepentha 6437 003 — AND I TURNED AS I HAD TURNED AS A BOY (LP, gatefold sleeve) . . . 120
80 Happy Face MMLP 1021 — A LAND FIT FOR HEROES (LP, private pressing) . . . 15

LIZA DULITTLE
(see also Margo & Marvettes)
68 Pye 7N 17590 — I've Got To Get A Grip Of Myself/Did You Hear A Heart Break Last Night? . . . 8

DUM
(see also Mud)
74 RAK RAK 179 — In The Mood/Watching The Clock . . . 5

DUM DUM
72 Philips 6414-318 — Peter Gunn/Cosa Nostra . . . 15

JOHNNY DUMAR
68 CBS 3545 — Illusion/You Went Away . . . 5

MINT VALUE £

DUMB ANGELS
(see also Pooh Sticks)

88	Fierce FRIGHT 033	Love And Mercy/Love And Mercy (p/s, numbered)	55

DUMBELLES
(see also Roxy Music)

80	Polydor POSP 209/EGO 3	Giddy Up/A Christmas Dream (no p/s)	10

JOHN DUMMER (BLUES BAND)
(see also Darts, Nick Pickett, Dave Kelly, Famous Music Band, Tony McPhee)

68	Mercury MF 1040	Travelling Man/40 Days (as John Dummer Blues Band)	20
69	Mercury MF 1119	Try Me One More Time/Riding At Midnight (as John Dummer Blues Band)	15
70	Fontana 6007 027	Happy/Nightingale (unissued in U.K.; France-only)	0
70	Philips 6006 111	Nine By Nine/Going In The Out (credited to either Famous Music Band or John Dummer Band)	15
71	Philips 6006 176	Medicine Weasel/The Endgame (with Nick Pickett)	5
73	Vertigo 6059 074	Ooblee-Dooblee Jubilee/The Monkey Speaks His Mind (as John Dummer Oobleedooblee Band)	5
69	Mercury SMCL 20136	CABAL (LP, black/silver label)	150
69	Mercury SMCL 20167	JOHN DUMMER BAND (LP, black/silver label)	200
70	Philips 6309 008	FAMOUS MUSIC BAND (LP, gatefold sleeve, black/silver labels)	100
72	Philips 6382 039	THIS IS THE JOHN DUMMER BLUES BAND (LP)	20
73	Philips 6382 040	VOLUME II - TRY ME ONE MORE TIME (LP)	20
72	Vertigo 6360 056	BLUE (LP, gatefold sleeve, small swirl label)	300
73	Vertigo 6360 083	OOBLEEDOOBLEE JUBILEE (LP, as John Dummer Oobleedooblee Band, small swirl label)	60

DUMMIES
(see also China Dolls, Slade)

79	Cheapskate FWL 001	When The Lights Are Out/She's The Only Woman (no p/s)	8
80	Pye 7P 163	When The Lights Are Out/She's The Only Woman (no p/s, reissue)	5
80	Cheapskate CHEAP 003	Didn't You Used To Use To Be You?/Miles Out To Sea (p/s)	8
81	Cheapskate CHEAP 014	Maybe Tonite/When I'm Dancin' I Ain't Fightin' (p/s)	10

DUMMY RUN
(see also Stock, Hausen & Walkman)

97	Hot Air BSE LP 002	ICE CREAM HEADACHE (LP)	12

DUNAMIS

79	Daybreak DB 2602	I CAN FLY (LP, signed)	60
79	Daybreak DB 2602	I CAN FLY (LP, un-signed)	15

AYNSLEY DUNBAR (RETALIATION)
(see also John Mayall & Bluesbreakers, Heavy Jelly, Annette & Victor Brox, Excheckers)

67	Blue Horizon 3109	Warning/Cobwebs (in p/s)	60
67	Blue Horizon 3109	Warning/Cobwebs	25
68	Liberty LBF 15132	Watch 'N' Chain/Roamin' And Ramblin'	15
68	Liberty LBL/LBS 83154	AYNSLEY DUNBAR RETALIATION (LP, mono/stereo)	45
68	Liberty LBL/LBS 83177	DR. DUNBAR'S PRESCRIPTION (LP, mono/stereo)	60
69	Liberty LBS 83223	RETALIATION (LP)	60
70	Liberty LBS 83316	REMAINS TO BE HEARD (LP)	60
71	Warner Bros WS 3010	BLUE WHALE (LP, green label)	40

SCOTT DUNBAR

71	Ahura Mazda AMS SDS 1	FROM LAKE MARY (LP)	30

JOHNNY DUNCAN (& BLUE GRASS BOYS)
(see also Chris Barber's Skiffle Group)

57	Columbia DB 3925	Kaw-Liga/Ella Speed (gold label lettering)	25
57	Columbia DB 3925	Kaw-Liga/Ella Speed (silver label lettering)	15
57	Columbia DB 3959	Last Train To San Fernando/Rock-A-Billy Baby (gold label lettering)	20
57	Columbia DB 3959	Last Train To San Fernando/Rock-A-Billy Baby (silver label lettering)	10
57	Columbia DB 3996	Blue, Blue Heartache/Jig Along Home	8
57	Columbia DB 4029	Footprints In The Snow/Get Along Home, Cindy	8
58	Columbia DB 4074	Goodnight Irene/If You Love Me Baby	10
58	Columbia DB 4118	Itching For My Baby/I Heard The Bluebirds Sing	8
58	Columbia DB 4167	All Of The Monkeys Ain't In The Zoo/More And More	8
58	Columbia DB 4179	My Lucky Love/Geisha Girl	8
59	Columbia DB 4282	Rosalie/This Train	8
59	Columbia DB 4311	Kansas City/That's All Right Darlin'	10
60	Columbia DB 4415	Any Time/Yellow, Yellow Moon (solo)	5
61	Pye 7N 15358	Tobacco Road/Sleepy-Eyed John (solo)	5
61	Pye 7N 15380	The Legend Of Gunga Din/Hannah (solo)	5
62	Pye 7N 15420	A Long Time Gone/Waitin' For The Sandman (solo)	5
63	Columbia DB 7164	The Ballad Of Jed Clampett/Will You Be Mine? (as Johnny Duncan & Kingpins)	5
64	Columbia DB 7334	Dang Me/Which Way Did He Go? (solo)	5
66	Columbia DB 7833	My Little Baby/I Thank My Lucky Stars (solo)	5
57	Columbia SEG 7708	JOHNNY DUNCAN AND HIS BLUE GRASS BOYS (EP)	15
57	Columbia SEG 7733	JOHNNY DUNCAN AND HIS BLUE GRASS BOYS NO. 2 (EP)	15
58	Columbia SEG 7753	FOOTPRINTS IN THE SNOW (EP)	15
58	Columbia SEG 7850	TENNESSEE SING SONG (EP)	15
57	Columbia 33S 1122	TENNESSEE SONG BAG (10" LP)	50
58	Columbia 33S 1129	JOHNNY DUNCAN SALUTES HANK WILLIAMS (10" LP)	40
61	Columbia 33SX 1328	BEYOND THE SUNSET (LP)	30

LESLEY DUNCAN (& JOKERS)
(see also Mitchell/Coe Mysteries, Pete Townshend, Phil Lynott, Madeline Bell, Joe Brown & Vicki Brown)

63	Parlophone R 5034	I Want A Steady Guy/Movin' Away (as Lesley Duncan & Jokers)	15
64	Parlophone R 5106	Tell Me/You Kissed Me Boy	15
64	Mercury MF 830	When My Baby Cries/Did It Hurt?	10
65	Mercury MF 847	Just For The Boy/See That Guy	20

MINT VALUE £

65	Mercury MF 876	Run To Love/Only The Lonely And Me	20
65	Mercury MF 939	Hey Boy/I Go To Sleep	10
68	RCA 1746	Lullaby/I Love You, I Love You	6
79	CBS 8061	Sing Children Sing/Rainbow Games (p/s, with Kate Bush)	10
71	CBS 64202	SING CHILDREN SING (LP, gatefold sleeve, orange labels)	20
72	CBS 64807	EARTH MOTHER (LP, gatefold sleeve, orange labels)	15

TOMMY DUNCAN

66	Sue WI 4002	Dance, Dance, Dance/Let's Try It Over Again	40

TOMMY DUNCAN & HIS WESTERN ALL STARS

50	Capitol CL 13261	Gamblin' Polka Dot Blues/Chattanooga Shoe Shine Boy (78)	10

DIANE DUNCANE

79	Contact 2	Better Late Than Never/One Day	15

BARBARA DUNKLEY

71	Banana BA 342	We'll Cry Together/BOBBY DAVIS: Got To Get Away	7

DELROY DUNKLEY

70	Hot Rod HR 109	I Wish You Well/TONY & DELROY: Impossible Love	10

ERROL(L) DUNKLEY

(see also Errol & His Group, Gaynor & Erroll], Mister Versatile, Don Lee, Ken Parker, Bongo Herman)

67	Rio R 109	Love Me Forever/VIETNAM ALLSTARS: The Toughest	100
67	Rio R 131	You're Gonna Need Me/Seek And You'll Find	35
68	Island WI 3150	Once More/I'm Not Your Man	20
68	Amalgamated AMG 800	Please Stop Your Lying/Feel So Fine (B-side actually by Tommy McCook & Band)	35
68	Amalgamated AMG 805	I'm Going Home/I'm Not Your Man	30
68	Amalgamated AMG 807	The Scorcher/Do It Right Tonight	60
68	Amalgamated AMG 820	Love Brother/I Spy	20
69	Fab FAB 117	I'll Take You In My Arms/KING CANNON: Daphney Reggae	10
70	Unity UN 554	My Special Prayer/Never Hurt The One You Love	7
70	Banana BA 302	Satisfaction/CECIL LOCKE: Sing Out Loud	15
71	Big BG 324	Deep Meditation/RUPIE EDWARDS ALL STARS: Meditation Version	20
71	Big BG 327	Three In One/RUPIE EDWARDS ALL STARS: One In Three	6
71	Nu Beat NB 091	Three In One/RUPIE EDWARDS ALL STARS: One In Three	8
71	Explosion EX 2053	O Lord/KEITH with IMPACT ALL STARS: Raindrops (B-side actually "My Baby" by Lloyd Charmers)	6
72	Camel CA 87	Black Cinderella/PHIL PRATT ALLSTARS: Our Anniversary (B-side actually Tropic Shadows)	12
73	Grape GR 3039	Why Did You Do It/One Love	8
73	Count Shelley CS 3039	Girl You Cried/Where Must I Go	6
73	Ackee 507	Keep The Pressure Down/Version	35
76	Daddy Kool DK 002	Eunoch Power/INTIMIDATORS: Straight To Him Chest	6
77	Aries ARI 001	Hard Luck Story/To Hell And Forward (both with Jah Steach, actually Jah Stitch)	15
78	Arawak ARK DD 002	Little Way Different/Differentiah (with Dreadful Julio) (12")	20
82	Success SRLD 014	If You Say So/AFRICAN BROTHERS: Mystery Or Nature	10
70s	Attack AT 1003	YOU NEVER KNOW (LP)	30
73	Attack ATLP 1003	DARLING OOH (LP)	20
79	Black Joy DH 802	DISCO SHOWCASE (LP)	45

GEORGE DUNN

73	Leader LEE 4042	GEORGE DUNN (LP, with insert)	18

TONY DUNNING (& TREMELOS)

60	Palette PG 9006	Seventeen Tomorrow/Be My Girl	10
61	Palette PG 9018	Pretend/Don't Bother To Call	10
61	Palette PG 9027	Under Moscow Skies/Sixteen Candles	10

DUNNO

71	M&M FFMS 100013	Sunday Girl/Magic Beat	20

BLIND WILLIE DUNN'S GIN BOTTLE FOUR with KING OLIVER

(see also Eddie Lang & Lonnie Johnson)

54	Columbia SCM 5100	Jet Black Blues/Blue Blood Blues	25
54	Columbia DB3440	Jet Black Blues/Blue Blood Blues (78)	20

PETE DUNTON

73	Rockfield ROC3	Taking Time/Still Confused	12

DUPARS

76	Contempo 2104	Love Cookin'/Instrumental	30

CHAMPION JACK DUPREE

(see also T.S. McPhee)

51	Jazz Parade B 16	Fisherman's Blues/County Jail Special (78)	30
62	Storyville A 45051	Whiskey Head Woman/Shirley May	20
67	Decca F 12611	Barrelhouse Woman/Under Your Hood	20
67	Blue Horizon 45-1007	Get Your Head Happy/Easy Is The Way (with T.S. McPhee)	115
68	Blue Horizon 57-3140	I Haven't Done No-One No Harm/How Am I Doing It (with Stan Webb)	20
69	Blue Horizon 57-3152	Ba'la Fouche/Kansas City	20
69	Blue Horizon 57-3158	I Want To Be A Hippy/Goin' Back To Louisiana	25
61	Storyville SEP 381	BLUES ANTHOLOGY VOL. 1 (EP)	30
64	RCA RCX 7137	RHYTHM AND BLUES VOL. 1 (EP)	30
64	Decca DFE 8586	LONDON SPECIAL (EP, with Keith Smith Climax Band)	60
65	Ember EMB 4564	JACK DUPREE (EP)	25
59	London Jazz LTZ-K 15171	BLUES FROM THE GUTTER (LP)	65
61	London Jazz LTZ-K 15217	CHAMPION JACK'S NATURAL AND SOULFUL BLUES LP, mono)	80
61	London Jazz SAH-K 6150	CHAMPION JACK'S NATURAL AND SOULFUL BLUES LP, stereo)	100
65	Storyville SLP 145	TROUBLE TROUBLE (LP)	20
65	Xtra XTRA 1028	CABBAGE GREENS (LP)	25

			MINT VALUE £
65	Storyville SLP 161	PORTRAITS IN BLUES (LP)	35
66	Decca LK/SKL 4747	FROM NEW ORLEANS TO CHICAGO (LP)	120
67	Storyville 670 194	CHAMPION JACK DUPREE (LP)	20
67	Decca SKL 4871	CHAMPION JACK DUPREE AND HIS BIG BLUES BAND (LP)	120
68	Blue Horizon 7-63206	WHEN YOU FEEL THE FEELING YOU WAS FEELING (LP)	100
69	Blue Horizon 7-63214	SCOOBYDOOBYDOO (LP)	100

CHAMPION JACK DUPREE/JIMMY RUSHING

(see also Jimmy Rushing)

64	Ember CJS 800	TWO SHADES OF BLUE (LP)	18

CHAMPION JACK DUPREE & KING CURTIS

(see also King Curtis)

73	Atlantic K 40434	BLUES FROM MONTREUX (LP)	12

SIMON DUPREE & BIG SOUND

(see also Moles, Gentle Giant, Jacqui Chan, Shape Of The Rain)

66	Parlophone R 5542	I See The Light/It Is Finished	10
67	Parlophone R 5574	Reservations/You Need A Man	15
67	Parlophone R 5594	Day Time, Night Time/I've Seen It All Before	10
67	Parlophone R 5646	Kites/Like The Sun Like The FIre (with Jacqui Chan)	5
68	Parlophone R 5670	For Whom The Bell Tolls/Sleep	7
68	Parlophone R 5697	Part Of My Past/This Story Never Ends	8
68	Parlophone R 5727	Thinking About My Life/Velvet And Lace	8
69	Parlophone R 5757	Broken Hearted Pirates/She Gave Me The Sun	10
69	Parlophone R 5816	The Eagle Flies Tonight/Give It All Back	10
67	Parlophone PMC/PCS 7029	WITHOUT RESERVATIONS (LP, yellow & black label, with "Sold in the U.K..." text, laminated sleeve)	80

DUPREES

62	HMV POP 1073	You Belong To Me/Take Me As I Am	40
62	Stateside SS 143	My Own True Love/Ginny	15
63	London HLU 9678	I'd Rather Be Here In Your Arms/I Wish I Could Believe You	20
63	London HLU 9709	Gone With The Wind/Let's Make Love Again	20
63	London HLU 9774	Why Don't You Believe Me?/My Dearest One	20
63	London HLU 9813	Have You Heard?/Love Eyes	20
64	London HLU 9843	It's No Sin/The Sand And The Sea	20
65	CBS 201803	Around The Corner/They Said It Couldn't Be Done	20
66	CBS 202028	She Waits For Him/Norma Jean	15
68	MGM MGM 460	My Special Angel/Ring Of Love	10
70	Polydor 2058 077	Check Yourself/The Sky's The Limit	35

DURAN DURAN

(see also Arcadia, Power Station)

81	EMI 12EMI 5137	Planet Earth (Night Version)/Planet Earth/Late Bar (12", p/s)	8
81	EMI 12EMI 5168	Careless Memories/Fame/Khanada (12", p/s)	8
81	EMI 12EMI 5206	Girls On Film (Night Version)/Girls On Film/Faster Than Light (12", p/s)	8
81	EMI 12EMI 5254	My Own Way (Night Version)/Like An Angel/My Own Way (Short Version)(12", p/s)	8
82	EMI 12EMI 5327	Save A Prayer/Hold Back The Rain (12" remix) (12", p/s)	8
82	EMI 12EMI 5346	Rio (Part 1)/Rio (Part 2)/My Own Way (12", p/s)	8
83	Flexi (no cat. no.)	The Smash Hits Interview (flexidisc free with Smash Hits)	5
84	EMI DURANP 2	The Reflex/Make Me Smile (poster p/s)	5
84	EMI 12 DURANP 2	The Reflex (Dance Mix)/Make Me Smile/The Reflex (12", picture disc)	8
87	Parlophone TC TRADE 1	Skin Trade (Stretch Mix)/We Need You/Skin Trade (cassette in 'video' case)	10
88	Parlophone CD YOUR 1	I Don't Want Your Love (7" Mix)/I Don't Want Your Love (Album Version)/ I Don't Want Your Love (Big Mix) (CD, stickered case)	8
88	Parlophone CDDD 11	All She Wants Is (45 Mix)/Skin Trade (Parisian Mix)/I Believe – All I Need To Know (Medley) (3" CD)	10
89	Parlophone CDDD 12	Do You Believe In Shame?/The Krush Brothers LSD Edit/Notorious (live)/ God (London)/This Is How A Road Gets Made (3" CD)	15
89	Parlophone CDDD 13	Burning The Ground/Decadance/Decadance (Extended Mix) (CD, 2,000 only)	20
93	Parlophone CDDDS 16	Ordinary World (Single Version)/Save A Prayer/ Skin Trade/ My Antarctica (CD, fold-out pack)	15

JIMMY DURANTE

(see also Ethel Merman, Groucho Marx)

69	Paramount PARA 3002	Monte Carlo Or Bust/They're Playing Chester's Song	6

ALLISON DURBIN

69	Decca LK-R/SKL-R 4996	I HAVE LOVED ME A MAN (LP)	40

JUDITH DURHAM

(see also Seekers, Keith Potger)

67	Columbia DB 8207	The Olive Tree/The Non Performing Lion Quickstep	6
67	Columbia DB 8290	Again And Again/Memories	12
69	Columbia S(C)X 6374	FOR CHRISTMAS WITH LOVE (LP)	15

JUDITH DURHAM

71	A&M AMS 823	Climb Ev'ry Mountain/What Could Be A Better Way	5
74	Pye 7N 45312	I Wanna Dance To Your Music/Mama's Got The Blues	6
74	Pye NSLP 18431	THE HOTTEST BAND IN TOWN (LP)	15

KENNY DURHAM

58	London LTZU 15133	JAZZ CONTRASTS (LP, with Sonny Rollins)	18

TERRY DURHAM

(see also Storyteller)

69	Deram DML/SML 1042	CRYSTAL TELEPHONE (LP, with insert, red/white label with large logo)	25

DURUTTI COLUMN

(see also Nosebleeds, Gammer & His Familiars, Morrissey)

82	Factory FAC 64	I Get Along Without You Very Well/Prayer (p/s)	7
80	Factory FACT 14	THE RETURN OF THE DURUTTI COLUMN (LP, with sandpaper sleeve, with Martin Hannett's "Testcard" flexidisc [FACT 14C])	200

MINT VALUE £

80 Factory FACT 14 — THE RETURN OF THE DURUTTI COLUMN (LP, with sandpaper sleeve, without Martin Hannett's "Testcard" flexidisc [FACT 14C]) ... 50
82 Factory FACT 44 — LC (LP, with inner) ... 15
83 Factory FACT 74 — ANOTHER SETTING (LP, with perfumed cut-out insert) ... 12
83 VU VINI 1 — LIVE AT THE VENUE LONDON (LP) ... 18
88 Factory FACT 244 — VINI REILLY (LP, with free p/s 7" "I Know Very Well How I Got My Note Wrong" [FAC 244++] by Vincent Gerard & Steven Patrick) ... 45
88 Factory FACD 244 — VINI REILLY (CD, with 3" CD "I Know Very Well How I Got My Note Wrong" [FAC CD 244++] by Vincent Gerard & Steven Patrick) ... 40

IAN DURY (& THE BLOCKHEADS)

(see also Kilburn & The High Roads, Greatest Show On Earth, Loving Awareness)

78 Stiff BUY 2712 — What A Waste/Wake Up (12", plain white sleeve) ... 20
78 Stiff BUY 38 — Hit Me With Your Rhythm Stick/There Ain't Half Been Some Clever Bastards (red vinyl, p/s, one copy known) ... 300
78 Stiff FREEBIE 1 — Sex And Drugs And Rock And Roll/England's Glory/ Two Steep Hills (p/s, free at NME party/competition) ... 8
77 Stiff SEEZ 4 — NEW BOOTS AND PANTIES!! (LP, with bonus track 'Sex And Drugs And Rock And Roll') ... 20
77 Stiff SEEZ 4 — NEW BOOTS AND PANTIES!! (LP, limited edition gold vinyl) ... 25

ANDREW DURYER

75 Real RR 2003 — BALLADS OF A WANDERER (LP) ... 25

JEAN DUSHON

65 Chess CRL 4000 — MAKE WAY FOR JEAN DUSHON (LP) ... 40

DUSK

71 Bell BLL 1167 — I Hear Those Church Bells Ringing/I Cannot See To See You ... 12

PAT DUSKY AND MARINES

67 Stardust STP 1 — I Fall To Pieces/This Can Be The Night ... 6

LA DüSSELDORF

(see also Neu!)

78 Radar ADA 5 — La Düsseldorf/Silver Cloud (unissued, white label promo only) ... 25
81 Albion ION 1025 — Tintarella Di (some might have p/s) ... 10
80 Teldec — Dampfrieman/Individuellos (12", p/s) ... 10
78 Radar RAD 7 — DUSSELDORF (LP) ... 20
80 Albion ALB 107 — INDIVIDUELLOS (LP) ... 20

DUST BROTHERS

(see also Chemical Brothers)

93 Dust Brothers DBS 333 — Song To The Siren (12" single sided) ... 100
93 Dust Brothers DB's 333 — Song To The Siren (12", no p/s, 500 only) ... 120
93 Junior Boys Own JBO 10 — Song To The Siren/Song To The Siren (Sabres Of Paradise Mixes) (12", p/s) ... 25
94 Dust Up Beats NS 1 — Loops Of Fury (12") ... 25
94 Boys Own COLLECT 004 — 14TH CENTURY SKY EP (12", no p/s) ... 15
94 Junior Boys Own JBO 20 — MY MERCURY MOUTH EP (12", JBO sleeve) ... 15

SLIM DUSTY

58 Columbia DB 4212 — A Pub With No Beer/Once When I Was Mustering (with His Country Rockers) ... 8
59 Columbia DB 4294 — The Answer To A Pub With No Beer/Winter Winds (with His Bushlanders) ... 6
60 Columbia SEG 8009 — SLIM DUSTY AND HIS COUNTRY ROCKERS (EP) ... 20
65 Decca LK 4551 — SING SONG (LP) ... 15

DUTCH

68 Phillips — What Is Soul/Down Here ... 12

DUTCH SWING COLLEGE BAND

51 Saturn EGX 106 — Alexander's Ragtime Band/Birthday Blues (78 picture disc) ... 20

DUTCHESS

81 B'kreig Waxworks EJSP 9580 — Your Love/Dead And Gone ... 150

JACQUES DUTRONC

66 Vogue VRS 7015 — Et Moi, Et Moi, Et Moi/Mini-Mini-Mini ... 12
66 Vogue VRS 7021 — Les Cactus/L'Espace D'Une Fille ... 7
66 Vogue VRS 7024 — J'Aime Les Filles/L'Idole ... 6
67 Vogue VRS 7027 — Le Plus Difficile/Les Rois De La Reforme ... 6
67 Vogue VRL 3029 — JACQUES DUTRONC (LP) ... 25

JOSE DUVAL

57 London HLR 8458 — Message Of Love/That's What You Mean To Me ... 25

D & V

83 Crass 121984/1 — THE NEAREST DOOR (EP) ... 10
85 Crass CAT NO 1 — INSPIRATION GAVE THEM MOTIVATION (LP) ... 18

MARK DWAYNE

62 Oriole CB 1712 — Remember Me Huh/Poorest Boy In Town ... 8
62 Oriole CB 1744 — Today's Teardrops/Little Bitty Heart ... 8

JUDY DYBLE

06 Fungus 006 — SONGS FROM THE SPINDLE AND THE WHORL (LP, hand-made sleeves, 250 only, numbered) ... 25

BILLY DYCE

72 G.G. GG 4532 — Be My Guest/HUGH ROY: Way Down South ... 10
72 G.G. GG 4534 — Take Warning/TYPHOON ALL STARS: Warning (Version) ... 8
72 G.G. GG 4537 — Time Is Still Here/G.G. ALL STARS: Time - Version ... 7
72 Pama PM 835 — Be My Guest/HUGH ROY: Way Down South ... 10
73 Pama PM 874 — Woman Smarter/SHENLEY DUFFAS: Standing On The Hill ... 6
73 Bread BR 1115 — You Need Love (with Millions)/G.G. ALL STARS: Love - Dub ... 6

MINT VALUE £

DYKE & BLAZERS

67	Pye International 7N 25413	Funky Broadway (Parts 1 & 2)	20

MICHAEL DYKE

70s	Attack ATT 8112	Saturday Night Special/CHINNA : Saturday Night Version	20

BOB DYLAN

(see also Dick Farina, Band, George Harrison, Traveling Wilburys, Doug Sahm, Earl Scruggs)

SINGLES

65	CBS 201751	The Times They Are A-Changin'/Honey, Just Allow Me One More Chance	8
65	CBS 201753	Subterranean Homesick Blues/She Belongs To Me	8
65	CBS 201781	Maggie's Farm/On The Road Again	8
65	CBS 201811	Like A Rolling Stone/Gates Of Eden	8
65	CBS 201824	Positively 4th Street/From A Buick 6	10
66	CBS 201900	Can You Please Crawl Out Your Window/Highway 61 Revisited	12
66	CBS 202053	One Of Us Must Know (Sooner Or Later)/Queen Jane Approximately	20
66	CBS 202307	Rainy Day Women Nos. 12 & 35/Pledging My Time	10
66	CBS 202258	I Want You/Just Like Tom Thumb's Blues (live)	12

(Some of the above singles were reissued with four-figure catalogue numbers, e.g. CBS 1811, which are worth around £7 each)

66	CBS 2700	Leopard-Skin Pill-Box Hat/Most Likely You Go Your Way And I'll Go Mine (p/s)	45
66	CBS 2700	Leopard-Skin Pill-Box Hat/Most Likely You Go Your Way And I'll Go Mine	10
67	CBS 2476	Mixed Up Confusion/Corrine Corrina (unissued in U.K.)	0
69	CBS 4219	I Threw It All Away/The Drifter's Escape	6
70	CBS 5122	Wigwam/Copper Kettle (The Pale Moonlight)	5
71	CBS 7329	Watching The River Flow/Spanish Is The Loving Tongue	5
71	CBS 7688	George Jackson (Acoustic)/George Jackson (Big Band Version)	8
73	CBS 1158	Just Like A Woman/I Want You (p/s, ?Hall Of Fame Hits' series)	6
74	CBS 2006	A Fool Such As I/Lily Of The West	6
74	Island WIP 6168	On A Night Like This/Forever Young	5
75	CBS 3160	Tangled Up In Blue/If You See Her, Say Hello	6
75	CBS 3665	Million Dollar Bash/Tears Of Rage	6
76	CBS 3878	Hurricane (Part 1)/(Full Version) (some list Pt 1/Pt 2; with p/s)	8
76	CBS 3878	Hurricane (Part 1)/(Full Version) (some list Pt 1/Pt 2; without p/s)	5
76	CBS 3945	Lay Lady Lay/I Threw It All Away (p/s)	5
76	CBS 4859	Stuck Inside Of Mobile With The Memphis Blues Again/Rita May (p/s; demos have "Rita May" as A-side, p/s)	12
76	CBS 4859	Rita May/Stuck Inside Of Mobile With The Memphis Blues Again (demos with "Rita May" as A-side)	8
78	CBS 12-6499	Baby Stop Crying/New Pony (12", p/s)	8
78	CBS 12-6718	Is Your Love In Vain?/We Better Talk This Over (12", p/s)	8
78	CBS 6935	Changing Of The Guard/Sènor	5
81	CBS A 1406	Heart Of Mine/Let It Be Me	5
83	CBS A 3916	Union Sundown/Angels Flying Too Close To The Ground (p/s)	5
84	CBS A 4055	Jokerman/Licence To Kill (p/s, embossed or standard label)	5
84	CBS A 4055	Jokerman (Special Faded Radio Version)/Licence To Kill (p/s, promo only)	15
85	CBS GA 5020	Highway 61 Revisited (live)/It Ain't Me Babe (live) (gatefold p/s)	8
85	CBA TA 6469	When The Night Comes Falling Down (Full Length Version)/Dark Eyes (12", p/s)	8
86	MCA 23633	Band Of The Hand/M. RUBINI: Theme From Joe's Death (12", p/s)	8
87	CBS 651 148-6	The Usual/Got My Mind Made Up/They Killed Him (12", p/s; mispressing, 3rd track plays either "Drifting Too Far From Shore" or "Precious Memories")	8
88	CBS 6514066	Silvio/When Did You Leave Heaven? (p/s)	6
89	CBS 6553588	Everything Is Broken/Dead Man, Dead Man/I Want You (Live) (12" with limited edition album sleeve print)	20
89	CBS 6553587	Everything Is Broken/Death Is Not The End (p/s)	6
90	CBS 6556436	Political World/Ring Them Bells/Silvio/ All Along The Watchtower (Live) (12" p/s)	6
90	CBS 6563047	Unbelievable/10,000 Men (p/s grey shaded not laminated/brown shaded laminated)	6
00	Columbia 6693797	Things Have Changed/Blind Willy McTell (numbered p/s)	6

EPs

64	CBS 6051	DYLAN (Bob Dylan below song titles, solid/push-out centre, designer credits in bottom right corner, p/s)	40
64	CBS 6051	DYLAN (Bob Dylan vertically on left: 'EXTENDED PLAY' on 1 line above 'EP 6051', push out centre - no designer credits, p/s)	45
65	CBS 6051	DYLAN (Bob Dylan vertically on left: 'EXTENDED PLAY' on 2 lines above 'EP 6051', solid centre, no designer credits, p/s)	45
65	Fontana TFE 18009	WITH GOD ON OUR SIDE (Joan Baez and Bob Dylan title track)/PETE SEEGER: The Bells of Rhymney/JOAN BAEZ: Waggoner's Lad, p/s)	75
65	Fontana TFE 18010	BLOWIN' IN THE WIND (BOB DYLAN: Blowin' In The Wind/JOAN BAEZ: Oh Freedom/ PETE SEEGER: Careless Love, p/s)	75
65	Fontana TFE 18011	YE PLAYBOYS AND PLAYGIRLS (Bob Dylan and Pete Seeger title track/ JOAN BAEZ: Te Ador, Te Manha/PETE SEEGER: This Land Is Mine, p/s)	75

(Contrary to popular belief the Fontana EPs were never officially released. On the verge of release with some copies sent to record stores Phonogram cancelled the project as permission from CBS was refused. Planned release date was May 1965 and all tracks were taken live from Newport Folk Festival in July 1963)

66	CBS 6070	ONE TOO MANY MORNINGS (Only EP in Europe with five songs, p/s)	50
66	CBS 6070	MR. TAMBOURINE MAN (length of EP on both sides: 27mm 'EXTENDED PLAY' on 1 line, 'Blossom Music LTD' on both sides. Solid/push-out centre, p/s)	50
66	CBS 6078	MR. TAMBOURINE MAN (length of EP on side 1, 'EXTENDED PLAY' divided over 2 lines, 'Blossom Music' (side 1) 'Bossom Music Ltd' (Side 2),	50

LPs

62	CBS BPG 62022	BOB DYLAN (mono)	50
62	CBS SBPG 62022	BOB DYLAN (stereo)	40
63	CBS BPG 62193	THE FREEWHEELIN' BOB DYLAN (mono)	50
63	CBS SBPG 62193	THE FREEWHEELIN' BOB DYLAN (stereo)	40
63	CBS BPG 62251	THE TIMES THEY ARE A-CHANGIN' (mono)	50

			MINT VALUE £
63	CBS SBPG 62251	THE TIMES THEY ARE A-CHANGIN' (stereo)	40
64	CBS BPG 62429	ANOTHER SIDE OF BOB DYLAN (mono)	50
64	CBS SBPG 62429	ANOTHER SIDE OF BOB DYLAN (stereo)	40
65	CBS BPG 62515	BRINGING IT ALL BACK HOME (mono)	50
65	CBS SBPG 62515	BRINGING IT ALL BACK HOME (stereo)	40
65	CBS BPG 62572	HIGHWAY 61 REVISITED (mono)	50
65	CBS SBGP 62572	HIGHWAY 61 REVISITED (stereo)	40
66	CBS BPG 66012	BLONDE ON BLONDE (2-LP, 8 or 9 photos on inside gatefold sleeve, mono)	60
66	CBS SBPG 66012	BLONDE ON BLONDE (2-LP, 8 or 9 photos on inside gatefold sleeve, stereo)	40
67	CBS BPG 62847	BOB DYLAN'S GREATEST HITS (mono)	18
68	CBS BGP 63252	JOHN WESLEY HARDING (mono)	30
68	CBS SBGP 63252	JOHN WESLEY HARDING (stereo)	15

(The above LPs were originally issued with rough textured labels & flipback sleeves, without CBS Records' credit on rear sleeve & with inner sleeves advertising other CBS albums)

69	CBS (M/S) 63601	NASHVILLE SKYLINE (mono/stereo)	30
69	CBS (M/S) 63601	NASHVILLE SKYLINE (mono/stereo)	15
70	CBS S 64085/6	SELF PORTRAIT	15
71	CBS S 67239	MORE BOB DYLAN GREATEST HITS	15
73	CBS S 69049	DYLAN	15
74	Island ILPS 9261	PLANET WAVES ('pink rim palm tree' label, with inner sleeve)	15
74	Island IDBD-1	BEFORE THE FLOOD	15
75	CBS 69097	BLOOD ON THE TRACKS (orange label, red inner with painting on rear sleeve)	12
75	CBS 69097	BLOOD ON THE TRACKS (orange label, red inner with liner notes on rear sleeve)	15
75	CBS S 88147	THE BASEMENT TAPES	15
76	CBS S 86003	DESIRE	15
76	CBS CBS 86015	HARD RAIN	12
78	CBS CBS 86067	STREET LEGAL	12
79	CBS CBS 96004	AT BUDOKAN	15
01	CBS S 69001	NEW MORNING (2-LP)	18
06	CBS 82876876061	MODERN TIMES (2-LP)	20

(1998, 1999 and 2000 Simply Vinyl 180gm reissued of Bob Dylan,The Freewheelin' Bob Dylan, The Times They Are A Changin', Highway 61 Revisited, Blonde On Blonde, John Wesley Harding, Blood On The Tracks and Nashville Skyline are worth in the region of £15 each)

DYMONDS

71	Big BG 326	Girl You Are Too Young/RUPIE EDWARDS ALL STARS: Version	6

DYNAMETRIX

91	Kold Sweat KS118	Keep The Crowd Dancing (12")	8
92	Kold Sweat KSEP208	Dis One's For You/Class Dismissed (EP)	6

DYNAMIC CONCEPT

74	Power Exchange PX 103	California Part 1/California Part 2	7

DYNAMIC CORVETTES

75	Contempo CS 2059	Funky Music Is The Thing (Parts 1 & 2)	5

DYNAMIC GANG (Bob Andy & Marcia Griffiths)

71	Moodisc MU 3511	I'll Never Believe In You/LLOYD WILLIS: Black Attack	8

DYNAMIC MCS

87	Tuff GrooveTUFF002	I Feel Dynamic (12")	60

DYNAMICS (Jamaica)

68	Blue Cat BS 104	My Friends/NEVILLE IRONS: Soul Glide	50
69	Punch PH 1	The Burner/Juckie Juckie (B-side actually by Tommy McCook & Carl Bryan)	12

DYNAMICS (U.S.)

63	London HLX 9809	Misery/I'm The Man	50
64	King KG 1007	So In Love With Me/Say You Will	25
69	Atlantic 584 270	Ice Cream Song/The Love That I Need	20

DYNAMITES

(see also Clancy Eccles & Dynamites, Baba Brooks, Dennis Alcapone, Diamonds, Joe Higgs, Silvertones, Carl Dawkins, Chris Leon, Hopeton Lewis, Melodians, Cynthia Richards, Soul Twins, Stranger & Gladys, Carey & Lloyd)

69	Duke DU 30	John Public/CLANCY ECCLES: Fire Corner (B-side actually by King Stitt)	10
69	Duke DU 31	I Don't Care (actually by Dingle Brothers)/CLANCY ECCLES: Shoo-Be-Do	8
69	Clandisc CLA 200	Mr. Midnight (Skokiaan)/KING STITT: Who Yeah	10
70	Clandisc CLA 212	Black Beret/BARRY & AFFECTIONS: Love Me Tender	10
70	Clandisc CLA 219	Sha La La La/Pop It Up	10
71	Clandisc CLA 237	Hello Mother/FABULOUS FLAMES: Hi-De-Ho	7
69	Trojan/Clandisc TTL 21	FIRE CORNER (LP, with King Stitt)	20

DYNASTY

72	Top Nix 134	Tutankhamen/Let's Boogie	15

DYNATONES

59	Top Rank JAR 149	Steel Guitar Rag/The Girl I'm Searching For	15
59	Top Rank JAR 149	Steel Guitar Rag/The Girl I'm Searching For (78)	20
66	Pye International 7N 25389	The Fife Piper/And I Always Will	50

RONNIE DYSON

74	CBS 2430	We Can Make It Last Forever/Just A Little Love From Me	10

MINT VALUE £

E

VINCE EAGER (& THE VAGABONDS)

58	Decca F 11023	Tread Softly Stranger & Yea Yea (as Vince Eager & The Vagabonds; unissued, 2 x 1-sided demos only)	30
58	Parlophone R 4482	Five Days, Five Days/No More	35
58	Parlophone R 4482	Five Days, Five Days/No More (78)	12
59	Parlophone R 4531	When's Your Birthday, Baby?/The Railroad Song	20
59	Parlophone R 4531	When's Your Birthday, Baby?/The Railroad Song (78)	25
59	Parlophone R 4550	This Should Go On Forever/No Other Arms, No Other Lips	20
59	Top Rank JAR 191	Makin' Love/Primrose Lane	6
59	Top Rank JAR 191	Makin' Love/Primrose Lane (78)	30
60	Top Rank JAR 275	Why/El Paso	5
60	Top Rank JAR 307	Lonely Blue Boy/No Love Have I	10
61	Top Rank JAR 539	(I Wanna) Love My Life Away/I Know What I Want	7
61	Top Rank JAR 593	The World's Loneliest Man/Created In A Dream	5
63	Piccadilly 7N 35110	Any Time Is The Right Time/Heavenly	6
63	Piccadilly 7N 35157	I Shall Not Be Moved/It's Only Make Believe	6
58	Decca DFE 6504	VINCE EAGER AND THE VAGABONDS NO. 1 (EP)	100
72	Avenue AVE 093	VINCE EAGER PAYS TRIBUTE TO ELVIS PRESLEY (LP)	12
80	Nevis NEV 143	20 YEARS ON (LP)	12

EAGLE

70	Pye International 7N 25530	Kickin' It Back To You/Come In, It's All For Free	15
69	Pye Intl. NSPL 28138	COME UNDER NANCY'S TENT (LP)	40

EAGLES (Jamaica)

(see also Jamaican Eagles, Roy Richards)

69	Songbird SB 1006	Rudam Bam/Prodigal Boy (B-side actually "Any Little Bit" by Crystals)	8
72	Duke Reid DR 2522	Your Enemies Can't Hurt You/Version	7
73	Techniques TE 927	Rub It Down/TOMMY McCOOK ALL STARS: Rub It Down â?? Version	6

EAGLES (U.K.)

(see also Valerie Mountain)

62	Pye 7N 15451	Bristol Express/Johnny's Tune	10
62	Pye 7N 15473	Exodus: The Main Theme/March Of The Eagles	12
62	Pye 7N 15503	The Desperados/Special Agent	10
63	Pye 7N 15550	Come On Baby (To The Floral Dance)/Theme From Station Six Sahara	10
63	Pye 7N 15571	Eagles Nest/Poinciana (unreleased)	0
64	Pye 7N 15613	Andorra/Moonstruck	10
64	Pye 7N 15650	Write Me A Letter/Wishin' And Hopin'	10
62	Pye NEP 24166	NEW SOUND T.V. THEMES (EP)	15
63	Pye NPL 18084	SMASH HITS (LP)	45

EAGLES (U.S.)

72	Asylum AYM 505	Take It Easy/Get You In The Mood (promo only p/s)	8
75	Asylum K 53003	DESPERADO (LP, audiophile pressing, mail-order via Hi-Fi Today mag)	40

SNOOKS EAGLIN

60s	Storyville A 45056	Country Boy/Alberta (some with p/s)	15
60s	Storyville SEP 386	BLUES ANTHOLOGY VOL. 6 (EP)	20
61	Heritage HLP 1002	SNOOKS EAGLIN (LP, 99 only)	100
63	Storyville SLP 119	NEW ORLEANS STREET SINGER (LP)	25
64	Storyville SLP 140	VOL. 2 - BLUES FROM NEW ORLEANS (LP)	15
70s	Storyville 670 146	PORTRAITS IN BLUES VOLUME 1 (LP)	18

JIM EANES

59	Melodisc 1530	Christmas Doll/It Won't Seem Like Christmas	12

EARCANDY

93	Poor Person Prod. PPPR 1	SPACE IS JUST A PLACE (LP, handmade sleeve, 500 only)	12
94	Poor Person Prod. PPPR 2	TIME IS JUST A STATE OF MIND (LP, handmade sleeve)	12
95	Poor Person Prod. PPPR 5	SOUND IS JUST THE WAY YOU EAR IT (LP, handmade sleeve with insert) numbered, 600 only)	12
95	Poor Person Prod. PPPR 8	TASTING 1,2,3, TASTING (LP, handmade sleeve & insert, numbered, 500 only)	12

EARGASM

80	Venture CUT 007	LOVERS DUB (LP)	40
81	Venture EAR 26	This Is Lovers Rock/Name That Tune (as Eargasm, P Pop & Beagle)	20

ROBERT EARL

58	Philips PB 805	I May Never Pass This Way Again/Someone	5
58	Philips PB 867	More Than Ever (Come Prima)/No One But You (In My Heart)	5
59	Philips PB 891	The Wonderful Secret Of Love/The Boulevard Of Broken Dreams	6
58	Philips BBE 12032	ROBERT EARL (EP)	10
59	Philips BBE 12240	THE WONDERFUL SECRET OF LOVE (EP)	10
60	Philips BBL 7394	SHOWCASE (LP)	20
66	Wing WL 1058	WALK HAND IN HAND (LP)	15

CHARLES EARLAND

78	Mercury 9199831	Let The Music Play/Broken Heart (12")	15

EARL & DEAN

66	Strike JH 323	Slowly Goin' Out Of My Head/Little Buddy	7

MINT VALUE £

KENNETH EARLE
60 Decca F 11205 The New Frankie And Johnny/40-30-40 . . . 12
60 Decca F 11224 Standing On The Corner/Put Your Arms Around Me, Honey . . . 5

EARLIES
02 Q2 R 001 Song For 3/Ride Condensed . . . 40

EARL-JEAN
(see also Cookies)
64 Colpix PX 729 I'm Into Somethin' Good/We Love And Learn . . . 30
64 Colpix PX 748 Randy/They're Jealous Of Me . . . 30

JOSEPH EARLOCKS
80s Freedom Sounds FSD014 Free Up The Blackman/JAMAICANS & I DAUGHTER : Country Life (12") . . . 20

EARLS
63 Stateside SS 153 Remember Then/Let's Waddle . . . 40
63 London HL 9702 Never/I Keep-A Tellin' You . . . 50
71 Atlantic 2091 129 Remember Then/I Believe . . . 10

EARLY B
82 Black Solidarity BSI 001 Imitator/Mi Huh Know (with Papa San) . . . 40

EARTH
69 CBS 4671 Resurrection City/Comical Man . . . 40
69 Decca F 22908 Stranger Of Fortune/Everybody Sing The Song . . . 15

EARTH
05 Southern Lord SUNN 48 HEX (OR PRINTING IN THE INFERNAL METHOD) (2xLP) . . . 25

EARTH & FIRE
70 Penny Farthing PEN 741 Mechanical Lover/Ruby Is The One . . . 5
70 Polydor 56790 Seasons/Paradise . . . 15
71 Nepentha 6129 001 Invitation/Wild And Exciting . . . 15
72 Polydor 2001 356 Memories/From The End To The Beginning . . . 8
71 Nepentha 6437 004 EARTH AND FIRE (LP, gatefold sleeve) . . . 350
73 Polydor 2310 262 ATLANTIS (LP) . . . 20

EARTH & STONE
79 Cha Cha CHAD 09 Sweet Africa/Dance With Me (12") . . . 30
79 Cha Cha CHAD 013 False Ruler/Don't Let Them Fool You (12") . . . 50
79 Cha Cha CHAD 015 Slave Driver/Magic Woman (12") . . . 30
77 Different DIFF 105 BACK TO AFRICA (LP) . . . 50
79 Cha Cha CHADLP 007 KOOL ROOTS (LP) . . . 60

EARTH BAND
(see under Manfred Mann's Earth Band)

EARTHBOUND
79 Archway AR 19745 Liberated Lad/Song For South Kensington/Robot (12" p/s) . . . 20

EARTH BOYS
59 Capitol CL 14979 Barbara Ann/Space Girl . . . 25

EARTH LEAKAGE TRIP
91 Moving Shadow SHADOW 1 PSYCHOTRONIC EP (12", p/s) . . . 20
92 Rising High RSN 17 THE VIRTUALITY EP (12") . . . 8
92 Rising High RSN 30 NEOPOLITAN EP (12") . . . 8

EARTHLINGS
65 Parlophone R 5242 Landing Of The Daleks/March Of The Robots . . . 50

EARTH OPERA
(see also Rowan Brothers)
68 Elektra EKSN 45035 Close Your Eyes And Shut The Door/Dreamless . . . 8
69 Elektra EKSN 45049 American Eagle Tragedy/When You Were Full Of Wonder . . . 7
69 Elektra EKSN 45061 Alfie Finney/Home To You . . . 7
68 Elektra EKS 74016 EARTH OPERA (LP, gatefold sleeve) . . . 35
69 Elektra EKS 74038 GREAT AMERICAN EAGLE TRAGEDY (LP) . . . 25

EARTHQUAKE
74 Cloud One HIT 4 Friday On My Mind/Madness (p/s) . . . 10

EARTHQUAKERS
67 Stateside SS 2050 Whistling In The Sunshine/Dreaming In The Moonlight . . . 10

EARTHQUAKES
(see also Sir Collins & Earthquakes)
69 Duke DU 54 Pair Of Wings/I Can't Stop Loving You . . . 12
69 Duke DU 56 Earthquake/Simmering . . . 12

TIM EASLEY
68 Bell BLL 1036 Susie Q (Parts 1 & 2) . . . 8

EAST BAY RAY
(see also Dead Kennedys)
84 Alt. Tentacles VIRUS 34 Trouble In Town/Poison Heart (p/s) . . . 5

EASTER MONDAY
89 SRT TTWW001 EASTER MONDAY EP (numbered foldover p/s, 500 only) . . . 15

EAST MAIN ST. EXPLOSION
69 Fontana TF 1039 Hop, Skip And Jump/Little Jackie Horner . . . 6

EAST OF EDEN
68 Atlantic 584 198 King Of Siam/Ballad Of Harvey Kaye . . . 30
69 Deram DM 242 Northern Hemisphere/Communion . . . 10
70 Deram DM 297 Jig-A-Jig/Marcus Junior . . . 8

			MINT VALUE £
71	Deram DM 338	Ramadhan/In The Snow For A Blow/ Better Git It In Your Soul/ Have To Whack It Up A Bit	10
72	Harvest HAR 5055	Boogie Woogie 'Flu/Last Dance Of The Clown (p/s)	8
73	United Artists UP 35567	Sin City Girls/All Our Yesterdays	5
69	Deram DML 1038	MERCATOR PROJECTED (LP, mono, red/white label with large label)	80
69	Deram SML 1038	MERCATOR PROJECTED (LP, stereo, red/white label with large logo)	60
70	Deram SML 1050	SNAFU (LP, red/white label with small logo)	40
71	Decca SPA 157	WORLD OF EAST OF EDEN (LP)	12
71	Harvest SHVL 792	EAST OF EDEN (LP, gatefold sleeve, early copies with EMI box on side 1 label, but no EMI box on side 2)	50
71	Harvest SHVL 792	EAST OF EDEN (LP, gatefold sleeve)	30
71	Harvest SHVL 796	NEW LEAF (LP, gatefold sleeve, with EMI on label)	40

EASTWOOD

70	SRT SRTS7332	Little Miss Lucy/Living To Learn	200
71	CBS 7076	I Am Free/Gypsy	45
72	CBS 7325	Orphan/Another Day In My Life	25

ALAN JAMES EASTWOOD

72	President PT 379	Closer To The Truth/Strange News	20

BUGSY EASTWOOD

(see also Exception)

68	President PT 209	Blackbird Charlie/My Sun	6

CLINT EASTWOOD

62	Cameo Parkway C 240	Rowdy/Cowboy Wedding Song (in p/s)	12
62	Cameo Parkway C 240	Rowdy/Cowboy Wedding Song	6
62	Cameo SC 1056	COWBOY FAVOURITES... (LP)	40

CLINT EASTWOOD

77	Jamaica Sounds JSLP 0010	JAH LIGHTS SHINING (LP)	15
78	Cha Cha CHALP003	DEATH IN THE ARENA (LP)	45
78	Third World TWS933	AFRICAN YOUTH (LP)	35
79	Burning Vibrations BV 1001	LOVE AND HAPPINESS (LP)	20
80	Greensleeves GREL 17	SEX EDUCATION (LP)	15

EASTWOOD & POWELL

71	President PT 352	Beautiful/Opal Blue Sunday	8

EASYBEATS

(see also Paintbox, Haffy's Whisky Sour, Harry Vanda, Grapefruit)

66	United Artists UP 1144	Come And See Her/Make You Feel Alright (Women)	20
66	United Artists UP 1157	Friday On My Mind/Made My Bed, Gonna Lie In It	8
66	United Artists UP 1175	Who'll Be The One?/Saturday Night	12
67	United Artists UP 1183	Heaven And Hell/Pretty Girl	12
67	United Artists UP 1201	The Music Goes Round My Head/Come In, You'll Get Pneumonia	12
68	United Artists UP 2209	Hello, How Are You?/Falling Off The Edge Of The World	8
68	United Artists UP 2219	The Land Of Make-Believe/We All Live Happily	8
68	United Artists UP 2243	Good Times/Lay Me Down And Die	8
69	Polydor 56335	St. Louis/Can't Find Love	8
70	Polydor 2001 028	(Who Are My) Friends?/Rock'n'Roll Boogie	6
67	United Artists (S)ULP 1167	GOOD FRIDAY (LP)	100
68	United Artists (S)ULP 1193	VIGIL (LP)	60
70	Polydor Special 2482 010	FRIENDS (LP)	60

EASY RIDERS

(see also Terry Gilkyson & Easy Riders, Vic Damone, Frankie Laine)

58	Philips PB 823	Salute To Windjammer/Kari Waits For Me	6
60	London HLR 9204	Young In Love/Saturday's Child	6
60	London HA-R 2323	REMEMBER THE ALAMO (LP, mono)	12
60	London SAH-R 6126	REMEMBER THE ALAMO (LP, stereo)	15

EASY STREET

76	Polydor 2058807	Feels Like Heaven/Shadows On The Wall (no p/s)	10
70s	Muscle Music AP 591	Person To Person/Easy Come Easy Go	30
77	Polydor 2058873	Flying/Blame The Love	12
77	Polydor 2383 444	UNDER THE GLASS (LP)	12

EATER

(see also Andy Blade)

77	The Label TLR 001	Outside View/You (p/s)	10
77	The Label TLR 003	Thinkin' Of The USA/Space Dreamin'/Michael's Monetary System (p/s)	10
77	The Label TLR 004	Lock It Up/Jeepster (p/s)	10
77	The Label TLR 004/12	Lock It Up/Jeepster (12", p/s)	8
78	The Label TLR 007	GET YOUR YO-YO'S OUT (EP, white vinyl; blue, green or red p/s)	8
78	The Label TLR 007	GET YOUR YO-YO'S OUT (12" EP, white vinyl; (blue, green or red p/s)	10
78	The Label TLR 009	What She Wants She Needs/Reaching For The Sky (p/s)	6
78	The Label TLRLP 001	THE ALBUM (LP, with inner sleeve)	30
85	De Lorean EAT 1	THE HISTORY OF EATER (LP, 1,000 each on red, white & blue vinyl, with bonus 7" [EAT FREEBIE 1])	12
85	De Lorean EAT 1	THE HISTORY OF EATER (LP, green vinyl)	12

EATHOPIANS

(see also Ethiopians)

69	Nu Beat NB 038	Buss Your Mouth (actually "Contention" by Ethiopians)/ REGGAE BOYS: Rough Way Ahead (B-side actually by Keith Blake & Hi-Tals)	12
68	Crab 4	Reggie Hit The Town/Ding Dong Bell	10

EAZIE RYDER

78	Graduate GRAD 1	Motorbikin'/City Lights (p/s)	15

EBONIES

68	Philips BF 1648	Never Gonna Break Your Heart Again/Shoeshine Boy	10

MINT VALUE £

EBONY DUBSTERS

03	Ebony EBR 028	EBONY DUBS VOL. 2 (12", p/s one side etched)	20

EBONY KEYES

66	Piccadilly 7N 35358	Sitting In The Ring/If You Knew	7

EBONY SISTERS

(see also Sister)

69	Bullet BU 401	Let Me Tell You Boy/RHYTHM RULERS: Mannix	12
70	Bullet BU 420	Each Time/BUNNY LEE ALLSTARS: Boss Walk	10

BUDDY EBSEN

65	Valiant VS 128	HOWDY HILLBILLIES (LP)	15

KATJA EBSTEIN

70	Liberty LBF 15317	No More Love For Me/Without Love	12

ECCENTRICS

65	Pye 7N 15850	What You Got/Fe Fi Fo Fum	45

CLANCY ECCLES (& DYNAMITES)

(see also Dynamites, Drumbago, Marlene Webber, Westmorelites)

61	Blue Beat BB 34	River Jordan/I Live And I Love (with Hersan & His City Slickers)	20
61	Blue Beat BB 67	Freedom/More Proof	25
63	Island WI 044	Judgement/Baby Please (B-side actually with Paulette)	25
63	Island WI 098	Glory Hallelujah/Hot Rod (B-side actually by Roland Alphonso)	25
65	Ska Beat JB 194	Sammy No Dead/Roam Jerusalem	20
65	Ska Beat JB 198	Miss Ida/KING ROCKY: What Is Katty	20
67	Doctor Bird DB 1156	Feel The Rhythm/Easy Snapping (B-side actually by Theo Beckford)	20
67	Pama PM 701	What Will Your Mama Say/Darling Don't Do That	25
67	Pama PMB 703	Western Organ/Mother's Advice (actually by The Clancy Set)	20
68	Pama PM 712	The Fight/Great	20
68	Nu Beat NB 006	Festival '68/I Really Love You	25
69	Trojan TR 639	Sweet Africa/Let Us Be Lovers	30
69	Trojan TR 647	Bangarang Crash/DYNAMITES: Rahthid	50
69	Trojan TR 648	Constantinople/Deacon Sun	30
69	Trojan TR 649	Demonstration/VAL BENNETT: My Girl	30
69	Trojan TR 658	Fattie Fattie/SILVERSTARS: Last Call	30
69	Duke DU 9	Auntie Lulu/SLICKERS: Bag A Boo	55
69	Duke DU 31	Shoo-Be-Do/DYNAMITES: I Don't Care (B-side actually by Dingle Brothers)	30
69	Clandisc CLA 201	The World Needs Loving/DYNAMITES: Dollar Train (B-side actually by Clancy Eccles)	20
69	Clandisc CLA 206	Dance Beat/KING STITT: The Ugly One	25
70	Clandisc CLA 209	Open Up/HIGGS & WILSON: Agane (B-side actually "Again")	10
70	Clandisc CLA 211	Promises/Real Sweet (both sides with Dynamites)	8
70	Clandisc CLA 212	Black Beret (with Dynamites)/BARRY & AFFECTIONS: Love Me Tender	10
70	Clandisc CLA 213	Phantom/Skank Me (both sides with Dynamites) (B-side actually by Barry & Affections)	12
70	Clandisc CLA 214	Africa/Africa Part Two (both sides with Dynamites)	6
70	Clandisc CLA 221	Unite Tonight/Uncle Joe	6
70	Clandisc CLA 227	Credit Squeeze/DYNAMITES: Credit Squeeze	6
71	Clandisc CLA 231	Sweet Jamaica/DYNAMITES: Going Up West	6
71	Clandisc CLA 232	Rod Of Correction/Rod Of Correction Version	6
71	Clandisc CLA 235	John Crow Skank/KING STITT: Merry Rhythm	10
71	Clandisc CLA 236	Power For The People/DYNAMITES: Power For The People â?? Version	8
71	Pama Supreme PS 332	What Will Your Mama Say/TIGER: United We Stand	10
72	Clandisc CLA 239	Hallelujah, Free At Last/DYNAMITES: Sha-La-La	8
72	Attack ATT 8037	Ganja Free/DYNAMITES: Ganja (Version)	12
69	Clandisc TTL 22	FREEDOM (LP)	30
69	Trojan TTL 22	FREEDOM (LP)	40
70	Clandisc TBL 124	HERBSMAN REGGAE (LP)	40
73	Big Shot BILP 101	TOP OF THE LADDER (LP)	20

JIMMY ECHO

65	Columbia DB 7629	After Tonight/Practise What You Preach	6

ECHO & BUNNYMEN

(see also Ian McCulloch, Will Sergeant)

83	Korova KOW 26	The Cutter/Way Out And Up We Go/Zimbo (12", with bonus Peel Session [KOW 26C])	8
84	Korova KOW 35F/	Seven Seas/All You Need Is Love//The Killing Moon/Stars Are Stars/ Villiers Terrace (numbered double pack, gatefold p/s)	
88	Korova KOW 43P	Bring On The Dancing Horses/Over Your Shoulder ('cow'-shaped picture disc in stickered PVC sleeve)	6
81	Korova KODE 1	CROCODILES (LP, with bonus 7", "Do It Clean"/"Read It In Books" [SAM 128] & inner sleeve)	12
83	Korova KODE 6	PORCUPINE (LP, with bonus Peel Session [KOW 26C])	12
85	Korova KODE 13	SONGS TO LEARN AND SING (LP, with lyric booklet & 7": "The Pictures On My Wall"/"Read It In Books" [p/s, yellow/blue labels, CAGE 004], no "Voodoo Billy" run-off groove message; signed	12

ECHO BASE

(see also Ocean Colour Scene)

84	DEP International DEP 14	Out Of My Reach/Splash Down (p/s)	12
85	DEP International DEP 19	Puppet At The Go Go/Genius + Soul = Jazz (p/s)	12
85	DEP International LPDEP 9	BUY ME (LP)	15

ECHOES (U.K.)

62	Fontana 267254 TF	Cloak And Dagger/Sounds Like Winter	10
62	Fontana TF 392	The Happy Whistler/Sticks And Stones	8
63	Fontana TF 415	The Jog/Marching Thru'	10

			MINT VALUE £
64	Fontana TF 439	My Little Girl/More	10
64	Philips BF 1370	Don't You Believe Them/I'll Get Over You	10
66	Philips BF 1480	Got To Run/Thanks A Lot	10
68	Philips BF 1687	Searchin' For You Baby/Listen To Me Baby	15

ECHOES (U.S.)

60	Top Rank JAR 399	Born To Be With You/My Guiding Light	25
61	Top Rank JAR 553	Baby Blue/Boomerang	22

ECHOES & CELESTIALS (Jamaica)

61	Hornet H 1004	Are You Mine/I'll Love You Forever	18
62	Blue Beat BB 89	Are You Mine/I'll Love You Forever (reissue)	10

BILLY ECKSTINE

(see also Sarah Vaughan & Billy Eckstine)

53	MGM SP 1011	Kiss Of Fire/I Apologise	10
53	MGM SP 1020	Come To The Mardi Gras/Be Fair	8
53	MGM SP 1040	Coquette/A Fool In Love	8
53	MGM SP 1055	I've Never Been In Love Before/I'll Know	8
53	MGM SP 1060	St. Louis Blues (Parts 1 & 2) (as Billy Eckstine & Metronome All Stars)	8
54	MGM SP 1082	Tenderly/Fortune Telling Cards	8
54	MGM SP 1084	Rendezvous/Don't Get Around Much Anymore	7
54	MGM SP 1095	Seabreeze/Sophisticated Lady	7
54	MGM SP 1101	No One But You/I Let A Song Go Out Of My Heart	18
54	MGM SP 1107	Beloved/Olay Olay (The Bullfighter's Song)	7
55	MGM SP 1117	Mood Indigo/Do Nothin' Till You Hear From Me	7
55	MGM SP 1124	What More Is There To Say?/Prelude To A Kiss	7
55	MGM SP 1136	Love Me Or Leave Me/The Life Of The Party	6
55	MGM SP 1140	More Than You Know/La De Do De Do (Honey Bug Song)	5
56	MGM SP 1153	Farewell To Romance/Lost In Loveliness	5
56	MGM SP 1167	Good-bye/You've Got Me Crying Again	5
56	MGM SP 1170	The Show Must Go On/You'll Get Yours	5
56	MGM MGM 925	Solitude/I Got It Bad (And That Ain't Good)	5
57	MGM MGM 948	A Man Doesn't Know/My Fickle Heart	5
57	HMV POP 341	Pretty, Pretty/Blue Illusion	5
57	MGM MGM 970	Bring Back The Thrill/Over The Rainbow	5
59	Mercury AMT 1018	Gigi/Trust In Me	6
65	Tamla Motown TMG 533	Had You Been Around/Down To Earth	100
65	Tamla Motown TMG 533	Had You Been Around/Down To Earth (DJ copy)	150
57	Parlophone GEP 8672	A DATE WITH RHYTHM (EP, with His All Star Band)	10
54	MGM MGM-D 126	TENDERLY (10" LP)	20
56	MGM MGM-D 138	THAT OLD FEELING (10" LP)	20
58	MGM MGM-D 151	A WEAVER OF DREAMS (10" LP)	20
66	T. Motown TML 11025	THE PRIME OF MY LIFE (LP, mono)	50
66	T. Motown STML 11025	THE PRIME OF MY LIFE (LP, stereo)	60
67	T. Motown TML 11046	MY WAY (LP, mono)	50
67	T. Motown STML 11046	MY WAY (LP, stereo)	60
69	T. Motown (S)TML 11101	GENTLE ON MY MIND (LP, mono/stereo)	40

ECLECTION

(see also Fotheringay, Dorris Henderson, Trevor Lucas, Mogul Thrash)

68	Elektra EKSN 45033	Nevertheless/Mark Time	12
68	Elektra EKSN 45040	Another Time, Another Place/Betty Brown	12
68	Elektra EKSN 45042	Please/Saint George And The Dragon	12
68	Elektra EKSN 45046	Please (Mark II)/In The Early Days	10
76	Elektra K 12196	Nevertheless/Please	5
68	Elektra EKL 4023	ECLECTION (LP, gatefold, mono)	50
68	Elektra EKS 4023	ECLECTION (LP, gatefold, stereo)	60

ECOLOGY

92	Vicious Pumpin'	THE COMMUNAL MIND EP (12", stamped white label)	20
92	Vicious Pumpin' OBS 004	ECOLOGY EP (12", stamped white label)	30
92	Vicious Pumpin' VIC 002	THE SMOKIN' JAM EP (12", stamped white label)	20
93	Vicious Pumpin' VIC 010	Vicious House/Take Me Higher (12", stamped white label)	15

ECSTASY CLUB

88	Swordfish DROP 1	JESUS LOVES THE ACID (EP, 12")	15
88	Flim Flam FFR 1207	JESUS LOVES THE ACID (EP, 12")	30
88	Flim Flam FFR 1207	JESUS LOVES THE ACID (EP, 12" picture disc)	80
89	LD Records	JESUS LOVES THE ACID (EP, 12")	30

ECSTASY, PASSION & PAIN

74	Pye International 7N 25641	Don't Burn Your Bridges Behind You/I Wouldn't Give You Up	5
74	Pye International 7N 25660	Good Things Don't Last Forever/Born To Lose You	8
74	Pye International 7N 25669	Ask Me/I'll Take The Blame	5

ECTOMORPH

90s	Woronzow WOO 15	THE FURIOUS SLEEPER (LP, with poster & inserts, 500 only)	20

EDDIE & THE CRAZY JETS

64	King KG 1000	Come On Let's Slop/Down By The Riverside	6

EDDIE & THE HOT RODS

(see also Rods, Rob Tyner & Hot Rods, Lew Lewis)

76	Island WIP 6270DJ	Writing On The Wall/Cruisin' (In The Lincoln) (promos in generic title p/s)	15
76	Island WIP 6270	Writing On The Wall/Cruisin' (In The Lincoln) (in black & white p/s)	15
76	Island WIP 6270	Writing On The Wall/Cruisin' (In The Lincoln)	5
76	Island WIP 6306	Wooly Bully/Horseplay (Weary Of The Schmaltz) (p/s)	8
76	Island WIP 6354	Teenage Depression/Shake	6
77	Island WIP 6388	I Might Be Lying/Ignore Them	6
77	Island 12WIP 6401	Do Anything You Wanna Do/Schoolgirl Love (12", white stickered sleeve)	8

			MINT VALUE £
77	Island IEP 5	AT THE SPEED OF SOUND (12", plain sleeve)	8
77	Island WIP 6411	Quit This Town/Distortion May Be Expected (p/s)	5
77	Island 12WIP 6438	Life On The Line/Do Anything You Wanna Do (live)/(I Don't Know) What's Really Going On (live)/Why Can't It Be (live) (12", p/s)	8
76	Island ILPS 9457	TEENAGE DEPRESSION (LP, with poster)	25

JASON EDDIE & THE CENTREMEN

65	Parlophone R 5388	Whatcha Gonna Do Baby/Come On Baby (as Jason Eddie & the Centremen)	150
66	Parlophone R 5473	Singing The Blues/True To You (as Jason Eddie & the Centremen)	175
69	Tangerine DP 0010	Heart And Soul/Playing The Clown (solo)	50

EDDIE & JERRY

72	Hillcrest HCT 4	Hail Rasta Man Hail/UPSETTERS: Scorcher	8

EDDIE'S CROWD

66	CBS 202078	Baby Don't Look Down/Take It Easy Baby	90

DUANE EDDY (& THE REBELS)

(see also Lee Hazlewood)

78s

58	London HL 8669	Rebel-Rouser/Stalkin'	15
58	London HL 8723	Ramrod/The Walker (as Duane Eddy & Rebels, actually by Al Casey)	15
58	London HL 8764	Cannonball/Mason-Dixon Lion (as Duane Eddy & Rebels)	15
59	London HLW 8821	The Lonely One/Detour	20
59	London HLW 8879	Peter Gunn/Yep!	40
59	London HLW 8929	Forty Miles Of Bad Road/The Quiet Three	30
59	London HLW 9007	Some Kind-A Earthquake/First Love, First Tears	30
60	London HLW 9050	Bonnie Came Back/Movin 'N' Groovin'	40
60	London HLW 9104	Shazam!/The Secret Seven	50
60	London HLW 9162	Because They're Young/Rebel Walk	60

SINGLES

58	London HL 8669	Rebel-Rouser/Stalkin' (initially with triangular centre)	15
58	London HL 8669	Rebel-Rouser/Stalkin' (later round centre)	8
58	London HL 8723	Ramrod/The Walker (as Duane Eddy & Rebels, actually by Al Casey tri-centre centre)	15
58	London HL 8723	Ramrod/The Walker (as Duane Eddy & Rebels, actually by Al Casey round centre)	8
58	London HL 8764	Cannonball/Mason-Dixon Lion (as Duane Eddy & Rebels, tri centre)	15
58	London HL 8764	Cannonball/Mason-Dixon Lion (as Duane Eddy & Rebels, round centre)	8
59	London HLW 8821	The Lonely One/Detour (triangular centre)	15
59	London HLW 8821	The Lonely One/Detour (round centre)	8
59	London HLW 8879	Peter Gunn/Yep! (triangular or round centre)	12
59	London HLW 8929	Forty Miles Of Bad Road/The Quiet Three (triangular centre)	10
59	London HLW 8929	Forty Miles Of Bad Road/The Quiet Three (round centre)	7
59	London HLW 9007	Some Kind-A Earthquake/First Love, First Tears (tri centre)	15
59	London HLW 9007	Some Kind-A Earthquake/First Love, First Tears (round centre)	8
60	London HLW 9050	Bonnie Came Back/Movin 'N' Groovin'	6
60	London HLW 9104	Shazam!/The Secret Seven	6
60	London HLW 9162	Because They're Young/Rebel Walk	5
60	London HLW 9225	Kommotion/Theme For Moon Children	7
61	London HLW 9257	Pepe/Lost Friend	6
61	London HLW 9324	Theme From Dixie/The Battle	7
61	London HLW 9370	Ring Of Fire/Gidget Goes Hawaiian	7
61	London HLW 9406	Drivin' Home/My Blue Heaven	7
61	London HLW 9477	The Avenger/Londonderry Air	7
61	Parlophone R 4826	Caravan (Parts 1 & 2) (actually by Al Casey)	12
62	RCA RCA 1288	Deep In The Heart Of Texas/Saints And Sinners	7
62	RCA RCA 1300	The Ballad Of Paladin/Wild Westerner	7
62	RCA RCA 1316	(Dance With The) Guitar Man/Stretchin' Out (with Rebelettes)	6
63	RCA RCA 1329	Boss Guitar/Desert Rat (with Rebelettes)	7
63	RCA RCA 1344	Lonely Boy, Lonely Guitar/Joshin'	7
63	RCA RCA 1357	You're Baby's Gone Surfin'/Shuckin'	10
63	RCA RCA 1369	My Baby Plays The Same Old Song On His Guitar All Night Long/ Guitar'd And Feather'd	12
64	RCA RCA 1389	The Son Of Rebel Rouser/The Story Of Three Loves	12
64	RCA RCA 1425	Guitar Star/The Iguana	15
65	Colpix PX 779	Trash/South Phoenix	15
65	Colpix PX 788	The House Of The Rising Sun/Don't Think Twice, It's All Right	15
66	Reprise RS 20504	Daydream/This Guitar Was Made For Twangin'	15
67	Reprise RS 20557	Monsoon/Roarin'	15
68	Reprise RS 20690	Niki Hoeky/Velvet Nights (Theme From "Elvira Madigan")	15
68	RCA RCA 1701	Dance With The Guitar Man/SAM COOKE: Another Saturday Night (withdrawn)	15
68	London HLW 10191	Peter Gunn/Rebel-Rouser	6
69	CBS 3962	Break My Mind/Loving Bird	15
75	Target 101	Love Confusion/Love Is A Warm Emotion	8

EXPORT SINGLES

58	London HL 7057	Ramrod/The Walker (as Duane Eddy & Rebels)	20
59	London HL 7072	The Lonely One/Detour	20
59	London HL 7076	Yep!/Three-30-Blues	30
59	London SLW 4001	Peter Gunn/Yep! (stereo)	90
59	London HL 7080	Forty Miles Of Bad Road/The Quiet Three	15
60	London HL 7090	Bonnie Come Back/Lost Island	15
60	London HL 7096	Because They're Young/Rebel Walk	15

EPs

58	London RE 1175	REBEL ROUSER (as Douane Eddy)	22
59	London RE-W 1216	THE LONELY ONE	22
59	London RE-W 1217	YEP!	20
60	London RE-W 1252	BECAUSE THEY'RE YOUNG	15

DUANE EDDY (& THE REBELS)

			MINT VALUE £
60	London RE-W 1257	TWANGY	15
61	London RE-W 1287	PEPE	15
61	London RE-W 1303	DUANE EDDY PLAYS MOVIE THEMES	20
61	London RE-W 1341	TWANGY NO. 2	20
63	RCA RCX 7115	A COUNTRY TWANG	25
63	RCA RCX 7129	MR. TWANG	35
64	RCA RCX 7146	TWANGIN' UP A SMALL STORM	40
65	Colpix PXE 304	COTTONMOUTH	50
LPs			
58	London HA-W 2160	HAVE 'TWANGY' GUITAR, WILL TRAVEL	45
59	London HA-W 2191	ESPECIALLY FOR YOU (mono)	20
59	London SAH-W 6045	ESPECIALLY FOR YOU (stereo with different version of "Tuxedo Junction")	30
60	London HA-W 2236	THE "TWANG'S" THE "THANG!" (mono)	20
60	London SAH-W 6068	THE "TWANG'S" THE "THANG!" (stereo)	30
60	London HA-W 2285	SONGS OF OUR HERITAGE (gatefold sleeve, mono)	25
60	London SAH-W 6119	SONGS OF OUR HERITAGE (gatefold sleeve, stereo)	30
61	London HA-W 2325	A MILLION DOLLARS' WORTH OF TWANG	25
61	London HA-W 2373	GIRLS, GIRLS, GIRLS (mono)	25
61	London SAH-W 6173	GIRLS, GIRLS, GIRLS (stereo)	30
62	London HA-W 2435	A MILLION DOLLARS' WORTH OF TWANG VOL. 2	30
62	RCA RD 27264/SF 5134	TWISTIN' AND TWANGIN' (mono/stereo)	25
62	RCA RD 7510	TWANGY GUITAR - SILKY STRINGS (mono)	15
62	RCA SF 7510	TWANGY GUITAR - SILKY STRINGS (stereo)	20
63	RCA RD 7545	DANCE WITH THE GUITAR MAN (mono)	20
63	RCA SF 7545	DANCE WITH THE GUITAR MAN (stereo)	25
63	RCA RD 7560	TWANG A COUNTRY SONG (mono)	20
63	RCA SF 7560	TWANG A COUNTRY SONG (stereo)	25
63	RCA RD 7568	TWANGIN' UP A STORM (mono)	20
63	RCA SF 7568	TWANGIN' UP A STORM (stereo)	25
64	RCA RD 7621	LONELY GUITAR (mono)	20
64	RCA SF 7621	LONELY GUITAR (stereo)	25
64	RCA RD 7656	WATER SKIING (mono)	25
64	RCA SF 7656	WATER SKIING (stereo)	30
65	RCA RD 7689	TWANGIN' THE GOLDEN HITS (mono)	18
65	RCA SF 7689	TWANGIN' THE GOLDEN HITS (stereo)	20
65	RCA RD 7754	TWANGSVILLE (mono)	25
65	RCA SF 7754	TWANGSVILLE (stereo)	30
65	Colpix PXL 490	DUANE A-GO-GO-GO	25
66	Colpix PXL 494	DUANE EDDY DOES BOB DYLAN	25
67	Reprise RLP 6218	THE BIGGEST TWANG OF THEM ALL (mono)	15
67	Reprise RSLP 6218	THE BIGGEST TWANG OF THEM ALL (stereo)	20
67	Reprise RLP 6240	THE ROARIN' TWANGIES (mono only)	30
67	G. Guinea GGL 10337	DUANE DOES BOB DYLAN (reissue, mono)	15
67	G. Guinea GGSL 10337	DUANE DOES BOB DYLAN (reissue, stereo)	20
70	Valiant VS 108	THE BIGGEST TWANG OF THEM ALL	15
84	Magnum Force MFM 023	REBEL ROUSIN' (Duane Eddy Convention anniversary issue, with overprinted labels, 200 only)	15

PEARL EDDY

54	HMV 7M 262	Devil Lips/That's What A Heart Is For	12

EDDY & TEDDY

61	London HLU 9367	Bye Bye Butterfly/Star Crossed Lovers	15

EDDYSONS

68	Olga OLE 010	Ups And Downs/Sweet Memories	7

DAVID EDE BAND

(see also Oscar Rabin)

60	Pye 7N 15280	Easy Go/The Blue Bird (as David Ede & Rabin Rock)	15
61	Pye 7N 15329	Obsession/Bootnik	12
61	Pye 7N 15370	Last Night/Ding Dong John (as David Ede & Go Man Go Men)	20
61	Pye 7N 15394	Twelfth Street Rag/No Hats On Ilkley	15
62	Pye 7N 15417	Twistin' Those Meeces To Pieces/Twistin' The Trad (as David Ede & Rabin Band)	15

EDEN STREET SKIFFLE GROUP

57	Headquarter & General Stores (no cat. no.)	SKIFFLE ALBUM NO. 1 (10 x 7" 78rpm clear flexidiscs in p/s)	70

TONI EDEN

60	Columbia DB 4409	Teen Street/No One Understands (My Johnny)	25
60	Columbia DB 4458	Grown Up Dreams/Whad'ya Gonna Do	20
60	Columbia DB 4527	Will I Ever/The Waitin' Game	15
61	Decca F 11342	Send Me/Interesting Facts	12

EDEN'S CHILDREN

68	Stateside (S)SL 10235	EDEN'S CHILDREN (LP)	65

EDGE

(see also Damned, Culture Club)

78	Albion ION 4	Macho Man/I'm Cold (p/s)	8
79	Hurricane FIRE 3	Downhill/American Excess (p/s, white vinyl)	8
79	Chiltern Sound CSLP	UNEASY PEACE (LP)	15
80	Hurricane FLAK 102	SQUARE 1 (LP)	15

THE EDGE with SINÉAD O'CONNOR

(see also U2, Jah Wobble)

86	Virgin VS 897	Heroine (Theme From "Captive")/Heroine (Mix II) (p/s)	5
86	Virgin VS 897-12	Heroine (Theme From "Captive")/Heroine (Mix II) (12", p/s)	8
86	Virgin V 2401	CAPTIVE (LP, soundtrack)	12

MINT VALUE £

HARRY 'SWEETS' EDISON SEXTET

60	HMV POP 720	Hollering At The Watkins/K.M. Blues	6
56	Vogue LDE 118	HARRY EDISON QUARTET (10" LP)	15

EDISON LIGHTHOUSE

(see also Flowerpot Men, White Plains, David & Jonathan, First Class)

71	Bell BLL 1136	It's Up To You Petula/Let's Make It Up	5
71	Bell BLL 1153	What's Happening/Take A Little Time	6
72	Bell BLL 1206	Find Mr. Zebedee?/Reconsider, My Belinda	6
81	Greenstone GRS 3441	Endearing Young Charms/Livin' On A Roller	6

EDITORS

04	Kitchenware SKCD77	Bullets/You Are Fading/Dust In The Sunlight (CD, 500 only)	50
04	Kitchenware SKX77	You Are Fading/Dust In The Sunlight (500 only)	50
05	Kitchenware SKX78	Munich/Disappear (Numbered, p/s)	20
07	Kitchenware (no cat no)	Escape The Nest (Demo)/When Anger Shows (Demo) (Fan club 7", 1,000 only)	10

LADA EDMUND JR

75	MCA MU 172	The Larue/Soul Au Go-Go	10
75	MCA MU 172	The Larue/Soul Au Go-Go (DJ Copy)	20

DAVE EDMUNDS (& ROCKPILE)

(see also Image, Human Beans, Love Sculpture, Rockpile, Andy Fairweather-Low)

71	Regal Zonophone RZ 3032	I'm-A Comin' Home/Country Roll	10
71	Regal Zonophone RZ 3037	Blue Monday/I'll Get Along	10
72	Regal Zonophone RZ 3059	Down, Down, Down/It Ain't Easy	10
90	Capitol 10CL 568	King Of Love/Stay With Me Tonight (45rpm)/King Of Love (78 rpm) (10", p/s)	30
90	Capitol 12CL 568	King Of Love/Stay With Me Tonight/Every Time I See Her (12", p/s)	10
72	Regal Zono. SLRZ 1026	ROCKPILE (LP)	35
75	Rockfield RRL 101	SUBTLE AS A FLYING MALLET (LP)	20
82	Arista SPART 1184	DE 7TH (LP, with bonus EP "Live At The Venue" [JUKE 1])	12

EDOUARD

66	CBS 202200	My Name Is Edouard/N'aie Pas Peur Antoinette (p/s)	8

EDSELS

61	Pye International 7N 25086	Rama Lama Ding Dong/Bells	120

EDWARD & HARDING

71	Stateside SS 2196	Mr. Sunlight/Blackbird	10

IAN EDWARD & ZODIACS

(see under Ian & Zodiacs)

ADINA EDWARDS

(see also Coxsone Dodd)

72	Dynamic DYN 454	Talk About Love/Don't Forget To Remember	6
60s	Tabernacle TLP 1005	JESUS IS MINE (LP)	20

BOBBY EDWARDS

61	Top Rank JAR 584	You're The Reason/I'm A Fool Loving You	15

BRENT EDWARDS

63	Pye International 7N 25197	Pride/Over The Weekend	12

C EDWARDS & SYMBOLIC

80	Symbolic BS 02	Loving Jah/Loving One & All (12")	80

CHUCK EDWARDS

68	Soul City SC 104	Downtown Soulville/I Need You	20
68	Soul City SC 104	Downtown Soulville/I Need You (DJ Copy)	100

DEVON EDWARDS

82	CF 12	Bad Boy Lay Down Flat/JAH RUBAL : Burst Shot	35

GARY EDWARDS (COMBO)

62	Oriole CB 1700	Twist Or Bust/The Franz Liszt Twist (as Gary Edwards Combo)	10
62	Oriole CB 1717	The Method/Twistful Thinkin'	10
62	Oriole CB 1733	Africa/One Fifteen A.M.	10
62	Oriole CB 1759	Hopscotch/Theme For A Broken Dream	15

IDIATER EDWARDS

85	Pressure HAVE 2	Loving Sweet Devotion/Version	70

(WILFRED) JACKIE EDWARDS

(see also Wilfred & Millicent, Wilfred & Millie, Jackie & Millie, Jackie's Boys)

60	Starlite ST45 016	We're Gonna Love/Your Eyes Are Dreaming (as Wilfred Edwards & Caribs)	30
60	Starlite ST45 026	I Know/Tell Me Darling (as Wilfred Edwards)	30
61	Starlite ST45 046	Whenever There's Moonlight/Heaven Just Knows (as Wilfred Edwards)	30
61	Starlite ST45 062	More Than Words Can Say/I Love You No More (as Wilfred Edwards)	30
62	Starlite ST45 076	Little Bitty Girl/Never Go Away (as Wilfred Edwards)	30
62	Island WI 008	All My Days/Hear Me Cry (as Wilfred Jackie Edwards)	22
62	Island WI 019	One More Week/Tears Like Rain (as Wilfred Edwards)	22
62	Decca F 11547	Lonely Game/Suddenly	15
63	Black Swan WI 404	Why Make Believe/Do You Want Me (as Wilfred Jackie Edwards & Velvetts)	15
64	Black Swan WI 416	The Things You Do/Little Smile (as Wilfred Jackie Edwards)	15
64	Black Swan WI 426	Why Make Believe/Do You Want Me Again	22
64	Fontana TF 465	Sea Cruise/Little Princess	15
64	Sue WI 329	Stagger Lee/Pretty Girl	40
65	Aladdin WI 601	He'll Have To Go/Gotta Learn To Love Again	12
65	Aladdin WI 605	Hush/I Am In Love With You No More (p/s)	12
65	Aladdin WI 611	The Same One/I Don't Know	15
65	Island WI 255	White Christmas/My Love And I	20
66	Island WI 270	Sometimes/Come On Home	20
66	Island WI 274	L-O-V-E/What's Your Name	60

			MINT VALUE £
66	Island WI 287	Think Twice/Oh Mary	30
66	Island WI 3006	I Feel So Bad/I Don't Want To Be Made A Fool Of	250
66	Island WI 3018	Royal Telephone/It's No Secret	15
67	Island WI 3030	Only A Fool Breaks His Own Heart/The End	15
67	Island WIP 6008	Come Back Girl/Tell Him You Lied	25
68	Island WIP 6026	Julie On My Mind/If This Is Heaven	15
68	Island WI 3157	You're My Girl/Heaven Only Knows	15
69	Direction 58-4096	Why Must I Be Alone/I'm Gonna Make You Cry	6
69	Direction 58-4402	Too Experienced/Someone To Love	6
69	Direction 58-4630	Oh Manio/Here We Go Again	6
70	CBS 5147	Tell Me Why Say Goodbye/Walter Walter	6
71	Horse HOSS 1	I Must Go Back/Baby I Want To Be Near You (in p/s)	20
71	Horse HOSS 1	I Must Go Back/Baby I Want To Be Near You	15
71	Bread BR 1107	Johnny Gunman/JACKIE'S BOYS: Johnny Gunman Version	10
72	Bread BR 1108	I Do Love You/Who Told You So?	8
66	St. Mary's IEP 701	SACRED HYMNS VOL. 1 (EP, in p/s)	40
66	St. Mary's IEP 701	SACRED HYMNS VOL. 1 (EP, no p/s)	15
66	St. Mary's IEP 702	SACRED HYMNS VOL. 2 (EP, with St. Mary's label, in p/s)	40
66	St. Mary's IEP 702	SACRED HYMNS VOL. 2 (EP, with St. Mary's label, no p/s)	15
66	St. Mary's IEP 702	SACRED HYMNS VOL. 2 (EP, with red-and-white Island label; in p/s)	40
66	St. Mary's IEP 702	SACRED HYMNS VOL. 2 (EP, with red-and-white Island label, no p/s)	15
66	Island IEP 708	HUSH! (EP)	45
64	Island ILP 906	THE MOST OF WILFRED JACKIE EDWARDS (LP)	60
64	Island ILP 912	STAND UP FOR JESUS (LP)	60
66	Island ILP 931	COME ON HOME (LP)	60
66	Island ILP 936	THE BEST OF JACKIE EDWARDS (LP)	60
66	Island ILP 940	BY DEMAND (LP)	60
67	Island ILP(S) 960	PREMATURE GOLDEN SANDS (LP)	40
69	Island IWP 4	PUT YOUR TEARS AWAY (LP)	50
69	Direction 8-63977	LET IT BE ME (LP)	25
70	Trojan TTL 40	THE MOST OF WILFRED JACKIE EDWARDS (LP, as Wilfred Jackie Edwards)	25
70	Trojan TTL 45	COME ON HOME (LP)	25
70	Trojan TTL 46	BY DEMAND (LP)	25
70	Trojan TTL 57	PREMATURE GOLDEN SANDS (LP, reissue)	25

JACKIE EDWARDS & JIMMY CLIFF

(see also Jackie & Millie, Millie, Jimmy Cliff, Wilfred & Millie, Jackie's Boys)

68	Island WIP 6036	Set Me Free/Here I Come	10
68	Island WIP 6042	You're My Girl/Heaven Only Knows	10

JIMMY EDWARDS (& PROFILE)

(see also Time U.K., Pretenders, Sham 69)

79	Warner Bros K 17415	Nora's Diary/Call Me A Fraud (features Sham 69) (p/s)	20
79	Warner Bros K 17464	Twentieth Century Time/Seven Hail Marys (features Pretenders) (p/s)	6
80	Polydor 2059 240	Toys/Hard Heart (p/s)	5
80	Polydor 2059 256	Cabaret/Drag It Back (p/s, solo)	5
81	Polydor POSP 240	In The City/Five Minute Girl (p/s, solo)	5

JIMMY EDWARDS (U.S.)

58	Mercury 7MT 193	Love Bug Crawl/Honey Lovin'	550
58	Mercury MT 193	Love Bug Crawl/Honey Lovin' (78)	70

JONATHAN & DARLENE EDWARDS

(see also Gordon MacRae, Jo Stafford)

60	Philips BBL 7412	JONATHAN & DARLENE EDWARDS IN PARIS (LP, also stereo SBBL 590)	12

MILL EDWARDS

73	Action ACT 4617	I Found Myself/Don't Forget About Me	20

NOKIE EDWARDS

(see also Ventures)

77	Cream CR 9006	NOKIE (LP)	15

O.G. EDWARDS

88	Dance Yard YARDT 4	Only You (Know What I Like)/Only You (Know What I Like) (Extended Version) (12")	40

PAUL EDWARDS

76	Cottage COT 301	LONGSTONE FARM (LP)	18

R. EDWARDS & SOCIAL EAGLES

73	Dip DL 5014	One Sunday Morning/Version Sunday Morning (with Allstars)	6
73	Dip DL 5014	One Sunday Morning/AFRICAN BROTHERS: Mysterious Nature (2nd issue, different B-side)	10

RUPIE EDWARDS (ALL STARS)

(see also R. Edwards & Social Eagles, Gaylads, Heptones, Ethiopians, Dymonds, Dobby Dobson, Keith Cole, Country Boy, Keith Cole, Laurel Aitken, Dennis Alcapone, Gregory Isaacs, Itals, Hugh Roy, Kingstonians, Little George, Mediators, Max Romeo, I Roy, B. B Seaton, Soul Kings. Joe White)

62	Blue Beat BB 90	Guilty Convict/Just Because (as Rupert Edwards & Smithie's Sextet)	25
68	Doctor Bird DB 1163	I Can't Forget/I'm Writing Again	25
69	Crab CRAB 35	Long Lost Love/Uncertain Love	12
70	Crab CRAB 41	Sharp Pan Ya Machete/Redemption	12
70	Explosion EX 2030	Full Moon/Baby	20
70	Explosion EX 2031	Love At First Sight/I Need Your Care	8
70	Success RE 902	Grandfather Clock/Promoter's Grouse	25
70	Success RE 905	Handicap/If You Can't Beat Them	15
70	Success RE 909	Pop Hi (as Rupie Edwards All Stars)/ VAL BENNETT AND BUNNY LEE ALL STARS: High Tide	15
71	Bullet BU 494	I'm Gonna Live Some Life/RUPIE EDWARDS ALLSTARS: Rock 'In'	6
71	Nu Beat NB 082	Black Man/Tell The People	10
71	Nu Beat NB 091	One In Three/ERROLL DUNKLEY: Three In One	8

			MINT VALUE £
71	Big BG 320	Soulful Stew/Soulful Stew â?? Version Two (as Rupie Edwards Allstars)	10
71	Big BG 324	Deep Meditation (version)/ERROLL DUNKLEY: Deep Meditation	20
71	Big BG 327	One In Three/ERROLL DUNKLEY: Three In One	6
71	Bullet BU 462	My Love (actually by Gaylads)/Stronger Love (both as Rupie Edwards All Stars)	8
72	Big BG 333	Press Along/Press Along - Version (as Rupie Edwards Allstars)	6
72	Big BG 335	Jimmy As Job Card (actually titled "Jimmy Has A Job Card")/ Riot (as Rupie Edwards Allstars)	15
72	Big BG 337	Christmas Parade (actually by Rupie Edwards Allstars)/ UNDERGROUND PEOPLE: Santa	5
78	Success SLD 016	Oh Black People/NOEL TEMPO : It's Time To Be Free (12")	30
75	Cactus CTLP 106	IRE FEELING (LP)	25
75	Cactus CTLP 107	DUB BASKET (LP)	60
76	Cactus CTLP 117	DUB BASKET CHAPTER 2 (LP)	40
76	Cactus CTLP 120	JAMAICA SERENADE (LP)	40
77	Success SUCLP	101 DUB CLASSICS (LP)	80

SAMUEL EDWARDS

69	Blue Cat BS 159	Want It Want It/SPARKERS: Israel	35

TOM EDWARDS

57	Vogue Coral Q 72236	What Is A Teen Age Girl?/What Is A Teen Age Boy?	6

TOMMY EDWARDS

53	MGM SP 1030	(Now And Then, There's) A Fool Such As I/Take These Chains From My Heart	10
56	MGM SP 1168	Baby, Let Me Take You Dreaming/MARION SISTERS: Life Could Not Be Better	10
58	MGM 989	It's All In The Game/Please Love Me Forever	6
59	MGM MGM-C 774	IT'S ALL IN THE GAME (LP)	20
59	MGM MGM-C 791	FOR YOUNG LOVERS (LP)	20
60	MGM MGM-C 824	YOU STARTED ME DREAMING (LP)	20

TYRONE EDWARDS

74	Invictus S INV 2542	Can't Get Enough Of You/You Took Me From A World Outside	8

VINCE EDWARDS (U.K.)

67	United Artists UP 1179	I Can't Turn Back Time/The Lively One	20
68	United Artists UP 2230	County Durham Dream/It's The Same Old Song	6
68	United Artists UP 2236	Aquarius/Hair	5

VINCE EDWARDS (U.S.)

58	Capitol CL 14825	Widget/Lollipop	10
62	Brunswick 05872	Don't Worry About Me/And Now	8
64	Colpix PX 771	No Not Much/See That Girl (p/s)	10

WEBLEY EDWARDS

60	Capitol ST1033	FIRE GODDESS (LP)	20

WILFRED EDWARDS

(see under Jackie Edwards)

EDWARDS HAND

(see also Picadilly Line)

71	RCA SF 8154	STRANDED (LP, orange label)	20
73	Regal Zono. SRZA 8513	RAINSHINE (LP, unissued, demos only)	100

WINSTON EDWARS

75	Fay FLP 2004	NATTY LOCKS DUB (LP)	170

EDWICK RUMBOLD

66	CBS 202393	Specially When/Come Back	120
67	Parlophone R 5622	Shades Of Grey/Boggle Woggle	200

EEK A MOUSE

81	Love Linch LL019	No Wicked/Trying To Be Free (12")	60
82	Greensleeves GRED 88	Do You Remember/TOYAN : Strictly The Dread (12")	15
81	Greensleeves GREL 31	WA-DO-DEM (LP)	12
82	Greensleeves GREL 41	SKIDIP! (LP)	15

EELS

96	Dreamworks DRLP 50001	BEAUTIFUL FREAK (LP)	40

E.F. BAND

80	Rok ROK XI/XII	Another Day Gone/SYNCHROMESH: October Friday (die-cut co. sleeve)	30
80	Aerco/EF Band EF 1	Night Angel/Another Day Gone (p/s)	30
80	Aerco/EF Band EF 1	Night Angel/Another Day Gone	15
80	Redball RR 026	Self Made Suicide/Sister Syne (with wraparound p/s)	30
80	Redball RR 026	Self Made Suicide/Sister Syne	7
80	Redball RR 036	The Devil's Eye/Comprende (with wraparound p/s)	25
80	Redball RR 036	The Devil's Eye/Comprende	7
82	Bullet CULP 2	DEEP CUT (LP)	15

WALTER EGAN

77	United Artists UP 36321	When I Get My Wheels/Waitin'	5

WILLIE EGANS

70s	Flyright LP 6000	ROCKS, BOOGIES AND ROLLS (LP)	15

JULIE EGE

71	CBS 5431	Love/In One Of Your Weaker Moments	10

JOSEPH EGER

70	Charisma CAS 1008	CLASSICAL HEADS (LP, gatefold sleeve, "pink scroll" label)	25

EGG

(see also Hatfield & The North, Arzachel, Bunch Of Fives, Khan)

69	Deram DM 269	Seven Is A Jolly Good Time/You Are All Princes	25
70	Deram Nova (S)DN 14	EGG (LP, red/silver labels, with sticker on rear sleeve correcting credits)	100

MINT VALUE £

70 Deram Nova (S)DN 14 — EGG (LP, red/silver labels) — 60
71 Deram SML 1074 — THE POLITE FORCE (LP, red/white label with small logo) — 70
74 Caroline C 1510 — THE CIVIL SURFACE (LP, red/white/red "twin" label) — 70

EGGY

69 Spark SRL 1024 — Hookey/You're Still Mine — 45

EGYPT

(see also Paul Samson)

88 HTD 7HTD 1 — Crazy Horses /Got No Fear (p/s) — 10
88 HTD HTD LP 1 — EGYPT (LP, with inner) — 15

EGYPTIAN EMPIRE

91 Fokus FKFR 1 — The Horn Track (Original Mix)/The Horn Track (Mickey Finn Fog Horn Mix) (12") — 25
92 FFRR TABX 115 — The Horn Track (Original Mix)/The Horn Track (Foghorn Mix)/The Horn Track (Toxic 2 Mix) (12") — 15

EIFFEL TOWER

69 Chappell LPC 1032 — THE EIFFEL TOWER (LP, library edition) — 25

8-EYED SPY

(see also Lydia Lunch)

82 Fetish FE 19 — Diddy Wah Diddy/Dead You Me B Side (p/s) — 12
81 Fetish FR 2003 — 8-EYED SPY (LP, with inner sleeve) — 20

808 STATE

(see also Hit Squad)

88 Creed STATE 003 — Let Yourself Go (303 Mix)/Let Yourself Go (D50 Mix)/Deepville (12", plain stickered sleeve) — 8
89 ZTT ZANG 1TX — Pacific - 909 (Mellow Birds Mega Edit)/Bonus Bird Beats/ Cobra Bora (12", plain stickered sleeve) — 8
89 ZTT ZANG 2CD — THE EXTENDED PLEASURES OF DANCE EP (CD, withdrawn) — 30
93 ZTT SAM 933 — 10 X 10 (Vox Mix)/10 X 10 (Beats Version) (12", promo only) — 8
88 Creed STATE 002 — NEWBUILD (LP) — 12

EIGHTH DAY

71 Invictus INV 514 — She's Not Just Another Woman/I Can't Fool Myself — 6
72 Invictus INV 521 — Eeny Meeny Miny Mo/Rocks In My Head — 6

EIGHTH WONDER

(see also Pet Shop Boys, Rock Aid Armenia)

88 CBS SCARE Y1 — I'm Not Scared/I'm Not Scared (Disco Mix)/ J'ai Pas Peur (10", p/s, with Pet Shop Boys) — 15

EIGHTIES LADIES

(see also Roy Ayers)

86 Music Of Life MOLIF 6 — Turned On To You/Sing Me/And I Knew That Love 12", p/s) — 20

EINSTÜRZENDE NEUBAUTEN

85 Some Bizzare BART 12 — Yu-Gung/Seelebrennt/Sand (12", p/s) — 10

EIRE APPARENT

(see also Ernie Graham, Henry McCulloch)

67 Track 604 019 — Follow Me/Here I Go Again — 20
69 Buddah 201 039 — Rock'N'Roll Band/Yes I Need Someone — 20
72 Buddah 2011 117 — Rock'N'Roll Band/Yes I Need Someone (reissue) — 10
69 Buddah 203 021 — SUN RISE (LP, featuring Jimi Hendrix, black/silver labels) — 100

EJECTED

82 Riot City RIOT 14 — HAVE YOU GOT 10p? (EP) — 10
82 Riot City RIOT 19 — NOISE FOR THE BOYS (EP) — 10
83 Riot City RIOT 28 — PRESS THE BUTTON (EP) — 8
82 Riot City CITY 003 — A TOUCH OF CLASS (LP) — 25
83 Riot City CITY 007 — THE SPIRIT OF REBELLION (LP) — 25

BRITT EKLAND

(see also Britt)

79 Jet JET 161 — Do It To Me (Once More With Feeling)/Private Party (gatefold p/s) — 5
79 Jet JETP 161 — Do It To Me (Once More With Feeling)/Private Party (picture disc) — 10
79 Jet Jet 12 161 — Do It To Me (Once More With Feeling)/Private Party (12" gatefold) — 10

EKSEN TRICK BRICK BAND

78 Aerco AERL 17 — SKY STORY (LP, with insert) — 30

EKSEPTION

70 Philips 318 992 BF — Air/Dharma For One — 5
72 Philips 6012 219 — Ava Maria/Dharma For One — 5
69 Philips 6314 001 — BEGGAR JULIAN'S TIME TRIP (LP) — 15
70 Philips 6314 005 — EKSEPTION (LP) — 18
71 Philips 6423 005 — EKSEPTION III (LP) — 15
72 Philips 6423 019 — 00.04 (LP) — 15
72 Philips 6423 042 — V (LP) — 15
74 Philips 6423 079 — CLASSICS IN POP (LP) — 12

EL PAS(S)O

(see also Dennis Alcapone)

71 Big Shot BI 572 — Out De Light, Baby/Mosquito I (both actually by Dennis Alcapone) — 15
71 Punch PH 61 — Mosquito One/Out De Light (reissue) — 12

MARGARET ELAINA

73 Bullet BU 522 — Ben/RICHIE & NOW GENERATION: Laughing Stock Version — 5

ELAINE

63 Columbia DB 7091 — I Never Wonder Where My Baby Goes/Look But Don't Touch — 12

ELAINE & DEREK

63 Piccadilly 7N 35105 — Hey Paula/Goodbye Twelve-Hallo Teens — 7

			MINT VALUE £
64	Decca F 11914	All The Sheep In The World/The Boy I'm Gonna Marry	6
65	Decca F 12054	Invisible Tears/Come On Now	6
61	Parlophone GEP 8868	HYMNS FOR LITTLE CHILDREN (EP)	8
63	Picadilly NEP 34014	WESTERING HOME (EP)	10
61	Parlophone PMC 1160	ELAINE & DEREK (LP)	20

ELASTICA
(see also Suede)

93	Deceptive BLUFF 003	Stutter/Pussycat (numbered die-cut sleeve, 1,500 only)	20
93	Deceptive BLUFF 003	Stutter/Pussycat (White label test pressing)	15
94	Deceptive BLUFF 004	Line Up/Vaseline (numbered die-cut sleeve, 1,500 only)	5
94	Deceptive BLUFF 010	Connection/See That Animal (numbered die-cut sleeve, 3,000 only)	5
95	Deceptive BLUFF 014LP	ELASTICA (LP, with flexidisc & booklet, no'd & stickered sleeve, 5,000 only)	30
95	Deceptive BLUFF 014LP	ELASTICA (LP, with flexidisc & booklet, no'd & stickered sleeve, 5,000 only, mispressed labels)	40
95	Decepetive BLUFF 014LP	ELASTICA (LP)	12

ELASTIC BAND
(see also Mayfield's Mule, Sweet, Andy Scott, Love Affair, Northwind)

68	Decca F 12763	Think Of You Baby/It's Been A Long Time Baby	28
68	Decca F 12815	Do Unto Others (From "Mr. Rose" T.V. Series)/81/2 Hours Of Paradise	45
69	Decca Nova DN 6	EXPANSIONS ON LIFE (LP, mono)	100
69	Decca Nova SDN 6	EXPANSIONS ON LIFE (LP, stereo)	70

ELASTICK BAND

67	Stateside SS 2056	Spazz/Papier Mache (unissued, demos only)	300

ELASTIC OZ BAND
(see under Bill Elliott)

DONNIE ELBERT

58	Parlophone R 4403	Let's Do The Stroll/Wild Child	100
58	Parlophone R 4403	Let's Do The Stroll/Wild Child (78)	40
65	Sue WI 377	A Little Piece Of Leather/Do Wat'cha Wanna	35
65	Sue WI 396	You Can Push It (Or Pull It)/Lily Lou	30
67	CBS 2807	Get Ready/Along Came Pride	20
68	Polydor BM 56234	In Between The Heartaches/Too Far Gone	20
68	Polydor BM 56265	This Old Heart Of Mine (Is Weak For You)/Run Little Girl	10
68	New Wave NW 001	Baby Please Come Home/Without You	8
69	Deram DM 235	Without You/Baby Please Come Home (reissue)	8
69	R&B UP 2000	Without You/(different B-side) (white label test pressing only)	8
72	Epic EPC 7943	Get Ready/Alone Came Pride	5
72	Mojo 2092 040	This Old Heart Of Mine (Is Weak For You)/Good To Me	5
72	Jay Boy BOY 70	Half As Old/Baby Let Me Love You Tonite	5
73	London HLU 10370	A Little Piece Of Leather/If I Can't Have You	6
79	Echo EC 7001	Are You Ready (Willing And Able)/You Keep Me Crying (With Your Lying)	8
97	Joe Boy JBV 1	So Soon/Can't Get Over Losing You (p/s with numbered certificate, 300 only)	20
69	Polydor 236 560	TRIBUTE TO A KING (LP)	50
73	Ember EMB 3421	THE ROOTS OF DONNIE ELBERT (LP)	20

ELBOW

98	Soft Records Softrec 001	NOISEBOX EP: Powder Blue/Red/George Lassoes The Moon (Original version)/ Theme From Munroe Kelly/Can't Stop (CD, 200 copies - 150 numbered)	200
98	Soft Records Softrec 001	NOISEBOX EP: Powder Blue/Red/George Lassoes The Moon (Original version)/ Theme From Munroe Kelly/Can't Stop (CD, 200 copies - 50 un-numbered)	100
00	Uglyman UGLY 20 CD	NEWBORN EP (CD, jewel case)	20
01	Uglyman UGLY 25	ANY DAY NOW EP (10", p/s)	10
05	V2 VVR 5032547	Forgot Myself/McGregor (mispress A side plays Madness' 'Shame and Scandal')	10
01	V2 VVR 1015881	ASLEEP IN THE BACK (2-LP)	50
03	V2 VVR 102181-1	CAST OF THOUSANDS (LP)	30
05	V2 VVR 103255-1	LEADERS OF THE FREE WORLD (LP)	15

ELCORT

66	Parlophone R 5447	Tammy/Searchin'	25

ERIC ELDER

70	Philips 6006 081	San Tokay/Sunflower	5

ELDORADOS (Jamaica)

70	Bullet BU 428	Savage Colt/The Clea Hog	25

ELDORADOS (Rhodesia)

63	Decca DFE 8543	THE ELDORADOS (EP)	100

ELDORADOS (U.S.)

72	Mojo 2092 050	Loose Booty (Parts 1 & 2)	10

ROY ELDRIDGE QUINTET

58	Columbia/Clef SEB 10085	DIXIELAND BLUES (EP)	10
60	HMV 7EG 8682	SWINGING ON THE TOWN (EP)	10
55	Columbia/Clef 33C 9005	ROY ELDRIDGE QUINTET (LP)	15

ROY ELDRIDGE & CLAUDE BOLLING

56	Vogue V 2373	Wild Man Blues/Fireworks	15

ELECAMPANE

75	Dame Jane ODJ 1	WHEN GOD'S ON THE WATER (LP, private pressing with insert)	50
78	Dame Jane ODJ 2	FURTHER ADVENTURES OF MR PUNCH (LP, private pressing with booklet)	20

MINT VALUE £

ELECTRIC BANANA
(see also Pretty Things, Zac Zolar & Electric Banana)

67	De Wolfe DW/LP 3040	ELECTRIC BANANA (LP, 10", original issue, tricolour label)	100
67	De Wolfe DWLP 3040	ELECTRIC BANANA (LP, second issue, with other artists)	30
68	De Wolfe DWLP 3069	MORE ELECTRIC BANANA (LP)	100
69	De Wolfe DWLP 3123	EVEN MORE ELECTRIC BANANA (LP)	40
73	De Wolfe DWLP 3284	HOT LICKS (LP)	40
76	De Wolfe DWLP 3381	THE RETURN OF THE ELECTRIC BANANA (LP)	25
79	Butt NOTT 001	THE SEVENTIES (LP)	18
80	Butt NOTT 003	THE SIXTIES (LP)	18
97	Tenth Planet TP 031	THE ELECTRIC BANANA BLOWS YOUR MIND (LP, numbered, 1,000 only)	15

ELECTRIC CHAIRS
(see under Wayne/Jayne County)

ELECTRIC CIRCUS

	White Label Only	Rhythm & Rhyme/Time	10

ELECTRIC CRAYONS
(see also Charlatans)

89	Emergency MIV 3	Hip Shake Junkie/Happy To Be Hated (p/s)	20

ELECTRIC EELS (U.S.)
(see under Die Electric Eels)

ELECTRIC FLAG
(see also Mike Bloomfield, Buddy Miles, Barry Goldberg)

68	CBS 3584	Groovin' Is Easy/Over-Lovin' You	7
69	CBS 4066	Sunny/Soul Searchin'	7
68	CBS 62394	A LONG TIME COMIN' (LP)	18
69	CBS 63462	THE ELECTRIC FLAG - AN AMERICAN MUSIC BAND (LP)	15
71	CBS 64337	THE BEST OF ELECTRIC FLAG (LP)	12

ELECTRIC FRANKENSTEIN

98	One Louder LOUDER 24	ACTION HIGH (LP)	12

ELECTRICIANS
(see also Don Harper)

67	Columbia DB 8228	Champion House Theme/DON HARPER & ELECTRICIANS: Shin Bone	7

ELECTRIC INDIAN
(see also Len Barry)

69	United Artists UP 35039	Keem-O-Sabe/Broad Street	7

ELECTRIC JOHNNY

61	London HLU 9384	Black-Eyes Rock/Johnny On His Strings	40

ELECTRIC LIGHT ORCHESTRA (E.L.O.)
(see also Idle Race, Jeff Lynne, Move, Roy Wood, Michael D'Albuquerque, Wilson Gale & Co., Tandy-Morgan)

72	Harvest HAR 5053	10538 Overture/1st Movement (Jumping Biz)	6
72	Harvest HAR 5063	Roll Over Beethoven/Manhattan Rumble (49th Street Massacre) (with withdrawn B-side)	10
72	Harvest HAR 5063	Roll Over Beethoven/Queen Of The Hours	5
73	Harvest HAR 5077	Showdown/In Old England Town (Boogie 2) (Instrumental)	8
81	Jet ELO 2	Mr Blue Sky/Across The Border/Telephone Line/Don't Bring Me Down (withdrawn, in p/s)	8
81	Jet ELO 2	Mr Blue Sky/Across The Border/Telephone Line/Don't Bring Me Down (withdrawn)	5
81	Jet JETP 12018	Ticket To The Moon/Here Is The News (12" picture disc)	12
71	Harvest SHVL 797	ELECTRIC LIGHT ORCHESTRA (gatefold sleeve, with inner sleeve & lyric insert)	50
72	Harvest SHVL 806	ELO 2 (LP, gatefold sleeve with EMI box on label)	15
73	Harvest Q4SHVL 797	ELECTRIC LIGHT ORCHESTRA (quadrophonic, promo only)	80
76	Jet JETLP 19	OLE ELO (withdrawn)	15
77	Jet UAG 30091	ON THE THIRD DAY (new mix, new sleeve & inner sleeve)	15
78	Jet JETBX 1	THREE LIGHT YEARS (3-LP, boxed set of "On The Third Day", "Eldorado" & "Face The Music", with booklet & inserts)	18
78	Jet JETLP 200	A NEW WORLD RECORD (red vinyl, with inner sleeve)	12
78	Jet JETLP 201	FACE THE MUSIC (green vinyl, with inner sleeve)	12
78	Jet JETLP 202	ON THE THIRD DAY (clear vinyl, with inner sleeve)	12
78	Jet JETLP 203	ELDORADO (yellow vinyl, with inner sleeve)	12
78	Jet JETDP 400	OUT OF THE BLUE (2-LP, clear or dark blue vinyl, with inner sleeves, with cut-out spaceship, poster & insert)	25

ELECTRIC PRUNES

66	Reprise RS 20532	I Had Too Much To Dream (Last Night)/Luvin'	30
67	Reprise RS 20564	Get Me To The World On Time/Are You Lovin' Me More (But Enjoying It Less)	30
67	Reprise RS 20607	The Great Banana Hoax/Wind-Up Toys	20
67	Reprise RS 23212	A Long Day's Flight/The King Is In His Counting House	18
68	Reprise RS 20652	Everybody Knows You're Not In Love/You Never Had It Better	30
73	Elektra K 12102	I Had Too Much To Dream (Last Night)/KNICKERBOCKERS: Lies	7
79	Radar ADA 16	I Had Too Much To Dream (Last Night)/Luvin' (p/s)	8
67	Reprise R(S)LP 6248	THE ELECTRIC PRUNES (LP, mono/stereo)	75
68	Reprise R(S)LP 6275	MASS IN F MINOR (LP, mono/stereo)	55
68	Reprise RSLP 6316	RELEASE OF AN OATH (LP)	55
73	Reprise K 34003	MASS IN F MINOR (LP, reissue)	12
97	Heartbeat HB 67	STOCKHOLM '67 (LP, gatefold sleeve with booklet)	20

ELECTRIC TOILET

83	Psycho PSYCHO 8	IN THE HANDS OF KARMA (LP, reissue of U.S. LP)	15

ELECTRIC WIZARD

95	Rise Above RISE 11	Demon Lung/OUR HAUNTED KINGDOM: Aquatic Fanatic (blue vinyl, p/s)	20
98	Bad Acid TRIP 1	Supercoven/Burnout (12", p/s)	20
08	Rise Above RISE 12/116	The Processean (Procession) (1-sided 12", 500 only sold at Rise Above 20th Anniversary Gig, ULU London 13th December 2008)	60

			MINT VALUE £
08	Rise Above RISE 12/116	The House On The Border/REVEREND BIZARRE: The Gates Of Nanna (12", 500 clear, 500 purple, 500 silver and 500 black vinyl, censored p/s)	20
08	Rise Above RISE 12/116	The House On The Border/REVEREND BIZARRE: The Gates Of Nanna (12", 350 red vinyl, uncensored p/s, poster)	50
95	Rise Above RISE 009	ELECTRIC WIZARD (LP, green vinyl)	50
04	Rise Above RISELP 48	WE LIVE (2-LP, purple vinyl)	50
04	Rise Above RISELP 52	DOPELTHRONE (2-LP, white vinyl, reissue, first issued on CD in 2000)	70
06	Rise Above RISELP 48	WE LIVE (2-LP, gatefold sleeve, reissue with 1-sided 7" "The Llving Dead At Manchester Morgue")	50
07	Rise Above RISELP 74	LET US PREY (2-LP, 100 clear vinyl, reissue of CD album released in 2002)	60
07	Rise Above RISELP 74	LET US PREY (2-LP, 500 dark red, 500 black vinyl, reissue of CD album released in 2002)	40
07	Rise Above RISELP 100	WITCHCULT TODAY (2-LP, 200 green vinyl, foil gatefold sleeve, poster, patch)	50
07	Rise Above RISELP 100	WITCHCULT TODAY (2-LP, 500 silver vinyl, foil gatefold sleeve, poster, patch)	40

ELECTRIX

79	ELX 001	HOLLAND (EP)	6

ELECTRO HIPPIES

87	Strange Fruit SFPS 042	PEEL SESSIONS (12", metallic finish with insert)	8
89	Peaceville VILE 13	LIVE (LP, clear vinyl)	12

ELECTRONIC

(see also New Order, Smiths, Pet Shop Boys)

89	Factory FAC 257	Getting Away With It (Full Length Version)/Getting Away With It (Inst.) (12", p/s)	8
93	Parlophone 10RD 6311	Disappointed (7" Mix)/Disappointed (12" Remix) (10", promo only)	8
99	Parlophone 12R651	Late At Night/Make It Happen (Original Version)/Make It Happen (Darren Price Mix) (12" withdrawn)	12

ELECTRONIC EXPERIENCED

93	Basement BRSS 025	V-10 Overload/No. 303 (12")	25
94	Basement BRSS 032	I.Q./I.Q. More (12")	25

ELECTROSCOPE

97	Wurlitzer Jukebox WJ 19	THE VANISHING PLANET PULSAR EP (p/s)	8
97	Wurlitzer Jukebox WJ 23	SOMMERSON EP (p/s)	8

ELECTROTUNES

80	Cobra COS 5	If This Ain't Love/Bodywork (p/s)	5

ELEGANTS

58	HMV POP 520	Little Star/Getting Dizzy	20
58	HMV POP 520	Little Star/Getting Dizzy (78)	20
58	HMV POP 551	Please Believe Me/Goodnight	60
58	HMV POP 551	Please Believe Me/Goodnight (78)	30

ELEGY

94	ART ART 6	APPLIED RHYTHM TECHNOLOGY (12" EP)	8

ELEKTRAS

63	United Artists UP 1027	All I Want To Do Is Run/It Ain't Easy	30

ELEKTRIC MUSIC

(see also Kraftwerk)

93	East West YZ 755	TV/Television (p/s)	8
93	East West YZ 755T	TV/Television (12", p/s)	8
93	East West SAM 1252	Lifestyle (Edit-Style Mix)/(Club-Style Mix)/(Phoneme-Style Mix) (10", promo)	20

ELENA

65	Columbia DB 7598	Evening Time/Road Of Love	20

ELEPHANT BAND

72	Mojo 2092 036	Stone Penguin/Groovin' At The Apollo	45

ELEPHANT'S MEMORY

(see also John Lennon, Yoko Ono)

69	Buddah 201055	Crossroads Of The Stepping Stones/Yoghurt Song	6
69	Buddah 201067	Old Man Willow/Jungle Gym At The Zoo	15
70	CBS 5207	Mongoose/I Couldn't Dream	15
72	Apple APPLE 45	Power Boogie/Liberation Special	20
69	Buddah 203 022	ELEPHANT'S MEMORY (LP)	25
72	Apple SAPCOR 22	ELEPHANT'S MEMORY (LP, gatefold sleeve with inner sleeve)	30

ELERI, JANET & DIANE

70s	Fanfare FR 2196	THE ANSWER (LP)	100

ELEVATORS

80	Koala KOA 401	Your I's Are Too Close Together/That's My Baby	60

11.59

74	Dovetail DOVE 4	THIS IS OUR SACRIFICE OF PRAISE (LP, with insert)	40

ELF

(see also Roger Glover, Dio, Rainbow, Deep Purple, Black Sabbath)

74	Purple PUR 118	L.A. 59/Ain't It All Amusing	10
74	Purple TPS 3506	CAROLINA COUNTRY BALL (LP)	25

ELFLAND ENSEMBLE

(see also Mary Hopkin)

77	Chrysalis CHS 2151	Too Much Magic (feat. Derek Brimstone)/Lizarel (featuring Mary Hopkin) (p/s)	6
77	Chrysalis CHS 2193	Beyond The Fields We Know/Alveric's Journey	6

STEVE ELGIN

74	Dawn DNS 1093	Don't Leave Your Lover Lying Around (Dear)/Seductress	10

ELGINS

66	Tamla Motown TMG 551	Put Yourself In My Place/Darling Baby	120
66	Tamla Motown TMG 551	Put Yourself In My Place/Darling Baby (DJ Copy)	150

			MINT VALUE £
66	Tamla Motown TMG 583	Heaven Must Have Sent You/Stay In My Lonely Arms	75
66	Tamla Motown TMG 583	Heaven Must Have Sent You/Stay In My Lonely Arms (DJ Copy)	120
67	Tamla Motown TMG 615	It's Been A Long Long Time/I Understand My Man	30
67	Tamla Motown TMG 615	It's Been A Long Long Time/I Understand My Man (DJ Copy)	50
68	Tamla Motown TMG 642	Put Yourself In My Place/Darling Baby (reissue)	25
71	Tamla Motown TMG 771	Heaven Must Have Sent You/Stay In My Lonely Arms (reissue)	7
71	Tamla Motown TMG 787	Put Yourself In My Place/It's Gonna Be Hard Times	7
68	T. Motown (S)TML 11081	DARLING BABY (LP, mono/stereo)	100

ELIAS HULK

(see also Babe Ruth)

70	Youngblood SSYB 8	UNCHAINED (LP, laminated front cover, red/white label)	350

ELIGIBLES

59	Capitol CL 15067	Faker, Faker/24 Hours (Till My Date With You)	10
59	Capitol CL 15098	The Little Engine/My First Christmas With You	10
60	Capitol CL 15203	Young Is My Lover/East Of West Berlin	8
60	Capitol (S)T 1310	ALONG THE TRAIL (LP)	20
61	Capitol (S)T 1411	LOVE IS A GAMBLE (LP)	20

ELIJAH

71	Ackee ACK 121	Selassie High/Mount Zion	6

ELIMINATORS

66	Pye NPL 18160	GUITARS AND PERCUSSION (LP, pink black label)	30

ELIXIR

(see also Iron Maiden)

85	Elixir ELIXIR 1	Treachery (Ride Like The Wind)/Winds Of Time (folded p/s with insert)	80
86	Elixir ELIXIR 2	THE SON OF ODIN (LP, private pressing with insert)	60
90	Sonic SONICLP 9	LETHAL POTION (LP, features Clive Burr)	15

ELIZABETH

73	Paramount PARA 3032	Stop Killing Me With Kindness/Oh Bird	6
68	Vanguard SVRL 19010	ELIZABETH (LP)	60

ELKI & OWEN & RIM RAM BAND

(see also Elkie Brooks, Owen Gray)

69	Revolution REV 004	Groovie Kinda Love	8

JIMMY ELLEDGE

62	RCA RCA 1274	Swanee River Rocket/Funny How Time Slips Away	15
65	Hickory 45-1363	Pink Dally Rue/(I'd Be) A Legend In My Time	10
64	RCA RCX 7132	FUNNY HOW TIME SLIPS AWAY (EP)	30

ELLI

67	Parlophone R 5575	Never Mind/I'll Be Looking Out For You	20

YVONNE ELLIMAN

71	MCA MK 5063	I Don't Know How To Love Him/Jesus Christ Superstar Overture	7
73	Purple PUR 114	I Can't Explain/Hawaii	25
73	Purple TPS 3504	FOOD OF LOVE (LP)	15

DUKE ELLINGTON & HIS (FAMOUS) ORCHESTRA

53	HMV 7M 156	Otto Make That Riff Staccato/Time's A-Wastin'	10
54	HMV 7MC 1	Flamingo/Jump For Joy (export issue)	15
54	HMV 7MC 9	In A Sentimental Mood/I Let A Song Go Out Of My Heart (export issue)	10
54	HMV 7M 170	The Flaming Sword/BARNEY BIGARD ORCHESTRA: A Lull At Dawn	10
54	Capitol CL 14186	Smile/If I Give My Heart To You	10
55	Capitol CL 14229	Twelfth Street Rag (Mambo)/Chile Bowl	8
55	Capitol CL 14260	Tyrolean Tango/All Day Long	8
55	Columbia SCM 5182	Brown Betty/Ting-A-Ling	8
59	Philips PB 946	Anatomy Of A Murder/Flirtibird	8
59	Philips PB 243	Skin Deep (Parts 1 & 2) (with Louis Bellson)	10
53	HMV DLP 1007	ELLINGTON'S GREATEST (10")	12
53	Columbia 33SX 1022	MASTERPIECES	12
53	Vogue LDE 035	DUKE ELLINGTON AND THE CORONETS (10")	12
53	Capitol LC 6616	PREMIERED BY ELLINGTON (10")	12
54	Capitol LC 6670	THE DUKE PLAYS ELLINGTON (10")	12
54	HMV DLP 1025	GREAT ELLINGTON SOLOISTS (10")	12
54	HMV DLP 1034	ELLINGTON HIGHLIGHTS, 1940 (10")	12
54	Columbia 33S 1044	JAZZ COCKTAIL (10")	25
54	Capitol LCT 6008	ELLINGTON '55	12
54	Philips BBL 7003	ELLINGTON UPTOWN	12
55	HMV DLP 1070	PERFUME SUITE/BLACK BROWN AND BEIGE (10")	12
55	HMV DLP 1094	SATURDAY NIGHT FUNCTION (10")	12
55	Vogue Coral LRA 10027	DUKE ELLINGTON AND HIS ORCHESTRA VOL. 1 (10")	12
55	Vogue Coral LRA 10028	DUKE ELLINGTON AND HIS ORCHESTRA VOL. 2 (10")	12
55	Philips BBR 8044	MOOD ELLINGTON (10")	12
56	London AL 3551	THE DUKE - 1926 (10")	12
56	London Jazz LTZ-N 15029	HISTORICALLY SPEAKING - THE DUKE	12
60	Philips SBBL 514	ANATOMY OF A MURDER (soundtrack)	12

MARC ELLINGTON

(see also Fairport Convention, Matthews Southern Comfort)

68	Philips BF 1665	I Shall Be Released/Mrs. Whittle	8
69	Philips BF 1742	Did You Give The World Some Love Today Baby/Bless The Executioner	8
69	Philips BF 1779	Four In The Morning/Peggy Day	8
71	Charisma CB 161	Alligator Man/Song For A Friend	8
69	Philips (S)BL 7883	MARC ELLINGTON (LP, black/silver labels)	100
71	Charisma CAS 1033	RAINS, REINS OF CHANGES (LP, envelope cover with lyric insert)	50
72	Philips 6308 120	A QUESTION OF ROADS (LP, gatefold sleeve, black/silver label)	100

			MINT VALUE £
72	Xtra XTRA 1154	MARC TIME (LP, with Fairport Convention)	40
73	Philips 6308 143	RESTORATION (LP, blue/silver label)	100

RAY ELLINGTON QUARTET

(see also Tony Crombie, Marion Ryan)

53	Columbia SCM 5050	The Little Red Monkey/Kaw-Liga	20
54	Columbia SCM 5088	All's Going Well (My Lady Montmorency) (with Marion Ryan)/Ol' Man River	20
54	Columbia SCM 5104	Rub-A-Dub-Dub/The Owl Song	15
54	Columbia SCM 5147	A.B.C. Boogie/Christmas Cards	30
55	Columbia SCM 5177	Ko Ko Mo (I Love You So)/Woodpecker	30
55	Columbia SCM 5187	Play It Boy, Play/The Irish Were Egyptians Long Ago	20
55	Columbia SCM 5199	Cloudburst/Pet	15
56	Columbia SCM 5250	Hold Him Tight/Who's Got The Money?	10
56	Columbia SCM 5274	Keep The Coffee Hot/Lucky 13	10
56	Columbia DB 3821	Stranded In The Jungle/Left Hand Boogie	30
56	Columbia DB 3838	Giddy-Up-A Ding Dong/The Green Door	30
57	Columbia DB 3905	Marianne/That Rock 'N' Rollin' Man	30
57	Columbia DB 4013	Don't Burn Me Up/Swaller-Tail Coat	10
58	Columbia DB 4057	Living Doll/Long Black Nylons (solo)	20
58	Pye Nixa 7N 15159	The Sultan Of Bezaaz/You Gotta Love Somebody	8
59	Pye Nixa 7N 15189	Chip Off The Old Block/Charlie Brown	15
59	Oriole CB 1512	Carina/I Was A Little Too Lonely	10
60	Ember EMB S 102	The Madison/Jump Over (with Tony Crombie Orchestra) (p/s with insert)	15
60	Ember EMB S 114	Tres Jolie/Dracula's Three Daughters	8
63	Ember EMB S 172	Too Old To Cut The Mustard/She Lied	8
64	Ember EMB S 188	Rhythm Of The World/If You Can't Say Something Nice	8
59	Pye Nixa NPL (NSPL) 83011	THAT'S NICE (LP, with Judd Proctor)	25

ELLINGTONS

79	Grapevine GRP 114	(I'm Not) Destined To Become A Loser/MILLIONAIRES: You've Got To Love Your Baby	10
79	Grapevine GRP 114	(I'm Not) Destined To Become A Loser/MILLIONAIRES: You've Got To Love Your Baby (DJ Copy)	20

BILL ELLIOT & ELASTIC OZ BAND

(see also Splinter, John Lennon/Yoko Ono)

71	Apple APPLE 36	God Save Us/Do The Oz (initially with p/s)	45
71	Apple APPLE 36	God Save Us/Do The Oz	20

DEREK & DOROTHY ELLIOT

72	Trailer LER 2023	DEREK & DOROTHY ELLIOT (LP)	15
76	Tradition TSR 025	YORKSHIRE RELISH (LP)	15

MAMA CASS (ELLIOT)

(see also Mamas & Papas, Big Three, Dave Mason & Cass Elliot, Mugwumps)

68	RCA Victor RCA 1726	Dream A Little Dream Of Me/Midnight Voyage (as Mama Cass)	6
68	Stateside SS 8002	California Earthquake/Talkin' To Your Toothbrush	5
69	Stateside SS 8014	I Can Dream Can't I?/Move A Little Closer Baby	5
69	Stateside SS 8021	It's Getting Better/Who's To Blame? (as Mama Cass)	5
69	Stateside SS 8031	Make Your Own Kind Of Music/Lady Love	5
70	Stateside SS 8039	New World Coming/Blow Me A Kiss	5
70	Stateside SS 8057	A Song That Never Comes/I Can Dream, Can't I?	5
71	Probe PRO 512	Good Times Are Comin'/Welcome To The World	6
71	Probe PRO 519	Easy Come, Easy Go/Ain't Nobody Else Like You	6
68	Stateside S(S)L 5004	DREAM A LITTLE DREAM (LP)	20
69	Stateside S(S)L 5014	BUBBLEGUM, LEMONADE AND SOMETHING FOR MAMA (LP)	18
72	RCA SF 8306	THE ROAD IS NO PLACE FOR A LADY (LP)	15

ELLIOT MANSIONS

71	President PT 323	Float On Up/Shades And Shadows	12

BERN ELLIOTT (& FENMEN)

(see also Fenmen)

63	Decca F 11770	Money/Nobody But Me	10
64	Decca F 11852	New Orleans/Everybody Needs A Little Love	10
64	Decca F 11970	Good Times/What Do You Want With My Baby (as Bern Elliott & Klan)	10
65	Decca F 12051	Guess Who/Make It Easy On Yourself (solo)	12
65	Decca F 12171	Lipstick Traces/Voodoo Woman (solo)	15
64	Decca DFE 8561	BERN ELLIOTT AND THE FENMEN (EP)	30

DAVID ELLIOTT

72	Atlantic K40374	DAVID ELLIOTT (LP, with lyric insert)	20

JACK ELLIOTT

(see also Elliotts Of Birtley)

69	Leader LEA 4001	JACK ELLIOTT OF BIRTLEY (LP, with booklet)	20

(RAMBLIN') JACK ELLIOTT

56	Topic TRC 98	Talking Miner Blues/Pretty Boy Floyd (78)	25
57	Topic TRC 103	Old Blue/Rambling Blues (78)	25
57	Topic TRC 104	Streets Of Laredo/Boll Weevil (78)	25
65	Fontana TF 575	More Pretty Girls/Roll On Buddy (as Ramblin' Jack Elliott)	6
65	Columbia DB 7593	Rusty Jigs And Sandy Sam/Rocky Mountain Belle (as Ramblin' Jack Elliott)	6
58	77 Records EP/1	JACK ELLIOTT SINGS Vol 1. (EP)	150
58	77 Records EP/2	JACK ELLIOTT SINGS Vol. 2. (EP)	150
60	Columbia SEG 8046	KID STUFF (EP)	20
61	Collector JEA 5	RAMBLING JACK ELLIOTT (EP)	20
64	Collector JEA 6	BLUES AND COUNTRY (EP)	20
55	Topic T 5	WOODY GUTHRIE'S BLUES (8" mini-LP)	40
57	Topic 10T 15	JACK TAKES THE FLOOR (10" LP)	40
59	Columbia 33SX 1166	RAMBLIN' JACK ELLIOT IN LONDON (LP)	40

			MINT VALUE £
62	Encore ENC 194	IN LONDON (LP, reissue of Columbia 33SX 1166)	20
60	Columbia 33SX 1291	RAMBLIN' JACK ELLIOTT SINGS WOODY GUTHRIE & JIMMIE RODGERS (LP)	40
61	77 LP 1	JACK ELLIOT SINGS (10" LP, spelt 'Elliot' on sleeve)	200
65	Fontana TFL 6044	JACK ELLIOTT (LP)	20
65	Stateside SL 10143	JACK ELLIOTT COUNTRY STYLE (LP)	20
66	Stateside SL 10167	SINGS THE SONGS OF WOODY GUTHRIE (LP)	20
68	Reprise RSLP 6284	YOUNG BRIGHAM (LP)	15
70	Reprise RSLP 6387	BILL DURHAM SACKS AND RAILROAD SACKS (LP)	15
57	Topic 10T 14	THE RAMBLING BOYS (10" LP, stickered Topic sleeve, insert)	60
63	Topic 12T 105	THE RAMBLING BOYS (LP, reissue of above with 2 extra tracks)	50
67	Bounty BY 6036	ROLL ON BUDDY - THE JACK ELLIOTT AND DERROLL ADAMS STORY VOL. 1 (LP)	55

MARI ELLIOTT

(see also Poly Styrene, X Ray Spex)

76	GTO GT 58	Silly Billy/Half Past One	15

MIKE ELLIOTT

72	Ackee ACK 151	Milk And Honey/Burst A Shirt	7

PETER ELLIOTT

57	Parlophone R 4355	To The Aisle/All At Once (You Love Her)	5
58	Parlophone R 4457	Devotion/No Fool Like An Old Fool	5
59	Parlophone R 4514	Call Me/Flamingo	5
59	Parlophone R 4529	The Young Have No Time/Over And Over	5
61	Top Rank JAR 390	Waiting For Robert E. Lee/Toot Toot Tootsie	5
61	Fontana 325	Three Little Peggies/The Devil's Workshop	5
66	Strike JH 311	Thinking/Song Is Love	5

SHAWN ELLIOTT

71	London HLK 10347	Child Is Father To The Man/Any Dream Will Do	12

SHAWN ELLIOTT

62	Stateside SS 124	Goodbye My Lover/Ain't That A Shame	5
63	Stateside SS 174	Sincerely And Tenderly/Why Don't You Love Me Anymore	5
64	Rio R 51	Shame And Scandal In The Family/My Girl	5
64	Columbia DB 7418	My Girl/Shame And Scandal In The Family (reissue)	5

SIDNEY ELLIOTT

71	CBS 7683	Desperation/Came To See Me Yesterday	8

ELLIOTTS OF BIRTLEY

(see also Jack Elliott)

69	Xtra XTRA 1091	A MUSICAL PORTRAIT OF A DURHAM MINING FAMILY (LP)	15

ELLIOTT'S SUNSHINE

68	Philips BF 1649	Is It Too Late/'Cos I'm Lonely	8

ELLIS

72	Epic SEPC 1052	El Doomo/Your Game	6

ALTON ELLIS (& FLAMES)

(see also Alton & Eddy, Hortense Ellis, Hortense & Alton, Flames [Jamaica], Righteous Flames,Tony Gordon)

65	Island WI 239	Dance Crasher (with Flames)/BABA BROOKS: Vitamin A	50
65	Island WI 241	You Are Not To Blame/BABA BROOKS: Teenage Ska	90
66	Doctor Bird DB 1044	Blessings Of Love/Nothing Sweeter (as Alton & Flames)	60
66	Doctor Bird DB 1049	The Preacher (as Alton & Flames)/LYNN TAITT & COMETS: Tender Loving Care	40
66	Doctor Bird DB 1055	Shake It (with Flames)/SILVERTONES: Whoo Baby	45
66	Doctor Bird DB 1059	Girl I've Got A Date (with Flames)/LYN TAITT & TOMMY McCOOK: The Yellow Basket	40
67	Island WI 3046	Cry Tough (with Flames)/TOMMY McCOOK & SUPERSONICS: Mr Solo	50
67	Treasure Isle TI 7004	Rocksteady (with Flames)/TOMMY McCOOK & SUPERSONICS: Wall Street Shuffle	40
67	Treasure Isle TI 7010	Duke Of Earl/All My Tears (with Flames)	35
67	Treasure Isle TI 7016	Ain't That Loving You/TOMMY McCOOK/SUPERSONICS: Tommy's Rocksteady	25
67	Treasure Isle TI 7030	Oowee Baby/How Can I (with Flames)	25
67	Treasure Isle TI 7044	Willow Tree/I Can't Stop Now	25
67	Trojan TR 004	Ain't That Loving You (with Flames)/TOMMY McCOOK & SUPERSONICS: Comet Rocksteady	25
67	Trojan TR 009	Wise Birds Follow Spring/TOMMY McCOOK & SUPERSONICS: Soul Rock	25
67	Studio One SO 2028	I Am Just A Guy/SOUL VENDORS: Just A Little Bit Of Soul	40
67	Studio One SO 2033	Only Sixteen/Baby (both actually by Heptones)	35
68	Studio One SO 2037	Live And Learn/HEPTONES: Cry Baby Cry	35
68	Trojan TR 630	I Can't Stand It/Trying To Reach My Goal	25
68	Trojan TR 642	Breaking Up/Party Time	18
68	Nu Beat NB 010	I Can't Stand It/Tonight	45
68	Nu Beat NB 013	Bye Bye Love/MONTY MORRIS: My Lonely Days	12
68	Nu Beat NB 014	La La Means I Love You/Give Me Your Love	15
68	Pama PM 707	The Message/Some Talk	15
68	Pama PM 717	My Time Is The Right Time/JOHNNY MOORE: Tribute To Sir Alex	15
68	Coxsone CS 7071	A Fool/SOUL VENDORS: West Of The Sun	50
69	Studio One SO 2084	Change Of Plans/CABLES: He'll Break Your Heart (B-side act. by Mad Lads)	40
69	Gas GAS 105	Diana/Some Talk	10
69	Bamboo BAM 2	Better Example/DUKE MORGAN: Lick It Back	70
69	Duke DU 14	Diana/Personality	25
70	Duke DU 72	Remember That Sunday/TOMMY McCOOK & SUPERSONICS: Last Lick	40
70	Gas GAS 151	Suzie/Life Is Down In Denver (some copies credit Alton Ellis & Flames)	10
70	Gas GAS 161	Deliver Us/NEVILLE HINDS: Originator	10
70	Duke Reid DR 2501	What Does It Take To Win Your Love/TOMMY McCOOK: Reggae Meringue	12
70	Duke Reid DR 2512	You Made Me So Very Happy/TOMMY McCOOK & SUPERSONICS: Continental	25
70	Bamboo BAM 29	Tumbling Tears/SOUND DIMENSION: Today Version	15

			MINT VALUE £
70	Techniques TE 903	It's Your Thing/TECHNIQUES ALL STARS: Get Left	8
70	Techniques TE 905	I'll Be Waiting/TECHNIQUES ALL STARS: I'll Be Waiting Version	8
71	Banana BA 318	Sunday Coming/CARL BRYAN: Sunday Version	12
71	Banana BA 330	Bam Bye/Keep On Yearning	12
71	Banana BA 347	Hey World/Harder And Harder	12
71	Gas GAS 164	Back To Africa/NEVILLE HINDS: Originator	10
71	Fab FAB 165	Good Good Loving/Since I Fell For You	40
71	Bullet BU 466	Black Man's Pride/LEROY PALMER: Groove With It	15
71	Bullet BU 485	Don't Care/True Born African	12
71	Smash SMA 2319	A Little Loving/DELROY WILSON & ALTON ELLIS: Loving Version	7
71	Smash SMA 2320	I'll Be There/ITALS: Rude Boy Train	7
71	Big Shot BI 589	Be True/Be True â?? Version	5
72	Big Shot BI 602	I'm Trying/Luna's Mood	15
72	Spur SP 3	All That We Need Is Love/KEITH HUDSON: Better Love	30
72	Grape GR 3029	Big Bad Boy/HUDSON'S ALLSTARS: Big Bad Version	7
72	Ackee ACK 145	Oppression/Oppression Version (both with Zoot Simms)	45
72	Ackee ACK 148	Let's Stay Together/Version	15
72	Ackee ACK 502	Too Late To Turn Back Now/IMPACT ALLSTARS: Version	10
72	Jackpot JP 796	Play It Cool/AGGROVATORS: King Of The Zozas	10
72	Camel CA 94	Wonderful World/FAB DIMENSION: Wonderful Version	6
72	Pama PM 840	Girl I've Got A Date/Eat Bread	5
72	Pama Supreme PS 347	Moon River/I Can't Find Out	7
72	Pama Supreme PS 361	Working On A Groovy Thing/HARLESDEN SKANKERS: Version	8
73	Ackee ACK 511	Alton's Official Daughter/Aquarius Dub (both with Herman)	15
73	Harry J. HJ 6653	Deliver Us To Africa/Nyah Medley	5
73	A&M AMS 7093	Shoo BeDoo Be Doo/I Love You True	12
73	Pyramid PYR 7003	Truly/LLOYD COXSONE SIX: Cruising	5
77	Venture VEN7709	Confusion/Version	10
83	Fashion FAD 013	Too Late To Turn Back Now/Party Mix (12")	12
67	Coxsone CSL 8008	SINGS ROCK AND SOUL (LP)	130
69	Coxsone CSL 8019	THE BEST OF ALTON ELLIS (LP)	60
71	Bamboo BDLPS 214	SUNDAY COMING (LP)	80
73	Count Shelly SSLO 02	ALTON ELLIS'S GREATEST HITS (LP)	40
80	Cha Cha	MR. SKABEANA (LP)	20

ALTON ELLIS & THE HEPTONES

80	Cha Cha CHAD 21	Mr. Ska Beana/ALTON ELLIS: Ain't No Music (12")	25

BOBBY ELLIS

(see also Jerry Lewis, Derrick Harriot, Rudy Mills, Crystalites, Keith & Tex, Eric Morris, Roy Richards, Soul Vendors)

68	Island WI 3136	Dollar A Head (with Crystalites)/RUDY MILLS: I'm Trapped	25
74	Dragon DRA 1033	Up Park Camp/Verse 4	6

DAVE ELLIS

72	Sonet SNTF 646	ALBUM (LP)	25

ELLIS DEE PROJECT

92	Ellis Dee Project LSD 001	Do You Want Me/Rock To The Max (12")	20
92	Ellis Dee Project LSD 003	Dance Factor (1-sided 12")	20
92	Ellis Dee Project LSD 004	Dance Factor (Rennie P Remix)/Don't Stop Rocking (12")	10
92	Ellis Dee Project LSD 005	Desire/Renegade (12")	10

DON ELLIS (ORCHESTRA)

69	CBS 4518	Eli's Comin'/House In The Country	5
68	Liberty LBL 83060E	LIVE IN THREE QUARTER TIME (LP)	20
68	CBS 63230	ELECTRIC BATH (LP)	30
68	CBS 63356	SHOCK TREATMENT (LP)	15
69	CBS 63680	THE NEW DON ELLIS BAND GOES UNDERGROUND (LP)	15
71	CBS 66261	DON ELLIS AT FILLMORE (2-LP)	15

HERB ELLIS-JIMMY GIUFFRE ALL STARS

60	HMV POP 721	Goose Grease/My Old Flame	6

HORTENSE ELLIS

(see also Hortense & Alton, Hortense & Delroy, Hortense & Jackie, Alton Ellis, Duke Reid, Three Tops, Jackie Opal)

63	R&B JB 101	I'll Come Softly/I'm In Love (with Alton Ellis)	20
65	Blue Beat BB 295	I've Been A Fool/Hold Me Tenderly	25
67	Fab FAB 20	Somebody Help Me (with Buster's All Stars)/ PRINCE BUSTER & ALL STARS: Rock & Shake	60
70	Bullet BU 427	Last Date/PAT SATCHMO: Cherry Pink	45
70	Gas GAS 160	To The Other Man/MUSIC BLENDERS: Raindrops	7
70	Techniques TE 908	To The Other Man/TECHNIQUES ALL STARS: To The Other Man Version	7
71	Gas 166	I Shall Sing/Stand By Your Man	15
72	Green Door GD 4035	Bringing In The Sheaves (with Stranger Cole)/Version	6
73	Tropical AL20	Woman Of the Ghetto/Woman Of The Ghetto (Version)	20
76	Third World TWS 918	JAMAICA'S FIRST LADY OF SONG (LP)	20

JAMES ELLIS

62	Philips PB 1230	Johnny Todd/Trottin' To The Fair	7

JO-JO ELLIS

72	Fury FY 302	The Fly/Perdona Mia	30

LARRY ELLIS

58	Felsted AF 110	Buzz Goes The Bee/Nothing You Can Do	15

MATTHEW ELLIS

(see also Procol Harum, Chris Spedding)

71	Regal Zonophone RZ 3033	Avalon/You Are	15
71	Regal Zonophone RZ 3039	Birthday Song/Salvation	10
72	Regal Zonophone RZ 3045	Palace Of Plenty/Two By Two	12
71	Regal Zono. SRZA 8501	MATTHEW ELLIS (LP, gatefold sleeve, red/silver labels)	25
72	Regal Zono. SRZA 8505	AM I...? (LP, gatefold sleeve, red/silver labels)	30

MINT VALUE £

SHIRLEY ELLIS
(see also Love Affair, Widowmaker, Zoot Money, Peter Bardens)

63	London HLR 9824	The Nitty Gritty/Give Me A List	8
65	London HLR 9946	The Name Game/Whisper To Me Wind	5
65	London HLR 9961	The Clapping Song/This Is Beautiful	5
65	London HLR 9973	The Puzzle Song/I See It, I Like It, I Want It	5
66	London HLR 10021	Ever See A Diver Kiss His Wife While The Bubbles Bounce About Above The Water?/Stardust	8
67	CBS 202606	Soul Time/Waitin'	35
67	CBS 202606	Soul Time/Waitin' (DJ copy)	60
67	CBS 2817	Sugar Let's Shing-A-Ling/How Lonely Is Lonely	15
71	CBS 7463	Soul Time/Waitin' (reissue)	15
77	CBS 4901	Soul Time/Waitin' (2nd reissue, blue coloured vinyl)	10
67	CBS (S)BPG 63044	SOUL TIME WITH SHIRLEY ELLIS (LP)	60

(STEVE) ELLIS

70	CBS 4992	Loot/More More More	90
70	CBS 5199	Evie/Fat Crow	5
71	CBS 7037	Take Your Love/Jingle Jangle Jasmine	5
71	CBS 7411	Hold On/Goody Goody Dancing Shoes	5
72	Epic EPC 64878	RIDING ON THE CREST OF A SLUMP (LP, as Ellis)	20
73	Epic EPC 65650	WHY NOT? (LP, as Ellis)	20

ANDY ELLISON
(see also John's Children, Jet, Radio Stars)

68	Track 604 018	It's Been A Long Time/JOHN'S CHILDREN: Arthur Green	70
68	CBS 3357	Fool From Upper Eden/Another Lucky Lie	45
68	S.N.B. 55-3308	You Can't Do That/Casbah	75
68	S.N.B. 55-3308	You Can't Do That/Cornflake Zoo (second issue, different B-side)	85

LORRAINE ELLISON

66	Warner Bros WB 5850	Stay With Me/I Got My Baby Back	10
66	Warner Bros WB 5850	Stay With Me/I Got My Baby Back (1969 re-pressing)	6
68	Warner Bros WB 2094	Try (Just A Little Bit Harder)/In My Tomorrow	8
70	Warner Bros WB 7394	You've Really Got A Hold On Me/You Don't Know Anything About Love	8
71	Mercury 6052 073	Call Me Anytime You Need Some Lovin'/Please Don't Teach Me To Love You	30
70	Warner Bros WS 1821	STAY WITH ME (LP)	40

ELMER HOCKETT'S HURDY GURDY
(see also Mood Mosaic, Mark Wirtz)

68	Parlophone R 5716	Fantastic Fair/MOOD MOSAIC: The Yellow Spotted Capricorn	8

IAN ELMS

82	Squid Marks SMT 013	GOOD NIGHT (LP, with insert)	180

ELOY

83	Heavy Metal HMINT 1	Fools/Heartbeat (p/s)	5
83	Heavy Metal HMPD 1	Fools/Heartbeat (picture disc)	6
83	Heavy Metal HMPD 1	Fools/Heartbeat (clear vinyl)	6
82	Heavy Metal HMILP 1	PLANETS (LP, clear vinyl with inner sleeve)	15
82	Heavy Metal HMIPD 1	PLANETS (LP, picture disc)	18
82	Heavy Metal HMILP 3	TIME TO TURN (LP, clear vinyl with inner sleeve)	12
82	Heavy Metal HMIPD 3	TIME TO TURN (LP, picture disc)	18
83	Heavy Metal HMIPD 12	PERFORMANCE (LP, picture disc)	15
84	Heavy Metal HMIPD 21	METROMANIA (LP, picture disc)	18
89	FM Revolver REV PD120	RA (LP, picture disc)	15

JEFF ELROY & BOYS BLUE
(see also Boys Blue)

66	Philips BF 1533	Honey Machine/Three Woman	30

ELTI-FITS

80	Worthing Street WSEF 1	GOING STRAIGHT (EP, various foldover picture sleeves)	10

ELVES

70	MCA MU 1114	Amber Velvet/West Virginia	7

CAROL ELVIN

63	Columbia DB 7095	'Cos I Know/C'mon Over	10
65	Parlophone R 5228	Don't Leave Me/'Cos I Love You	10

LEE & JAY ELVIN
(see also Jerry Lordan)

59	Fontana H 191	So The Story Goes/When You See Her	20
59	Fontana H 191	So The Story Goes/When You See Her (78)	15

EMANON

77	Clubland SJP 777	Raging Pain/Rip A Bough (stamped sleeve)	30

BOBBIE EMBER

65	Polydor BM 56062	Why Can't You Bring Me Home/When Love Isn't There	10

EMBERS
(see also David & Embers, Three's A Crowd)

63	Decca F 11625	Chelsea Boots/Samantha	20

EMBRACE

96	Fierce Panda NING 29	All You Good Good People/My Weakness Is None Of Your Business (p/s, 1,300 only, not numbered)	10
96	Fierce Panda NING 29	All You Good Good People/My Weakness Is None Of Your Business (p/s, 1,300 only, numbered)	15
98	Hut HUTLH 128 103	My Weakness Is None Of Your Business/Feelings Through You Shared (Jukebox issue)	5
98	BBC BOX SET	EMBRACE EP'S (6 x 12"s in black box, numbered, 100 only)	100
99	Hut HUTDX 103/CD 109	ABBEY ROAD SESSIONS (2xCD gatefold, one CD mail-order from fanclub)	30

MINT VALUE £

EMBRYO
(see also Jump Squad)

80	Rampant RAM 001	I'm Different/You Know He Did (p/s)	15

EMCEE 5

62	Columbia SEG 8153	LET'S TAKE FIVE (EP)	150
62	Alpha International DB 92	VOLUME ONE (EP)	150

EMERALDS (U.K.)

65	Decca F 12096	Don't Listen To Your Friends/Say You're Mine	7
65	Decca F 12304	King Lonely The Blue/Someone Else's Fool	40

EMERALDS (U.S.)

64	London HL 9839	Donkey Kick Back/Sittin' Bull	10

EMERGENCY

83	Riot City RIOT 21	POINTS OF VIEW (EP)	5

KEITH EMERSON
(see also Emerson Lake & Palmer, Nice, V.I.P.'s, Rock Aid Armenia)

76	Manticore K 13513	Honky Tonk Train Blues/Barrel House Shake Down (p/s)	6
80	Atlantic K 11612	Taxi Ride (Rome)/Mater Tenebrarum (p/s)	6
81	MCA MCA 697	I'm A Man/Nighthawks Main Title Theme (p/s)	7

EMERSON, LAKE & PALMER
(see also Emerson Lake & Powell, Nice, Keith Emerson, Greg Lake, Shame, Asia, King Crimson, Stray Dog, Atomic Rooster)

73	Lyntone/Manticore LYN 2762	Brain Salad Surgery/(excerpts from "Brain Salad Surgery" LP) (flexidisc in gatefold p/s free with NME, £2 without)	15
74	Manticore K 13503	Jerusalem/When The Apple Blossoms Bloom In The WIndmills Of Your Mind, I'll Be Your Valentine (with p/s)	8
77	Atlantic K 10946	Fanfare For The Common Man/Brain Salad Surgery (p/s)	5
77	Atlantic K 10946T	Fanfare For The Common Man (Album Version)/Brain Salad Surgery (12", p/s)	12
70	Island ILPS 9123	EMERSON, LAKE AND PALMER (LP, pink label)	50
70	Island ILPS 9123	EMERSON, LAKE AND PALMER (LP, later 'pink rim palm tree' label)	15
71	Island ILSP 9155	TARKUS (LP, gatefold sleeve, 'pink rim palm tree' label)	20
71	Island HELP 1	PICTURES AT AN EXHIBITION (LP, gatefold sleeve)	15
73	Manticore K 53501	BRAIN SALAD SURGERY (LP, fold-out die cut sleeve with poster)	25
72	Island ILPS 9186	TRIOLOGY (LP, gatefold sleeve. pink rim label)	15

EMERSON, LAKE & POWELL
(see also Emerson Lake & Palmer, Cozy Powell)

86	Polydor POSP 804	Touch And Go/Learning To Fly (p/s)	5
86	Polydor POSPX 804	Touch And Go/Learning To Fly/The Locomotion (12", p/s)	8

DICK EMERY

72	Pye 7N 45202	You Are Awful/Dance Dance	6
69	Pye NPL (NSPL) 18277	DICK EMERY SINGS (LP)	12

KATHLEEN EMERY

97	Jazzman JM001	Sometimes I Feel Like A Motherless Child/Evil Ways	25

EMF

92	Parlophone 12RXDJ 6327	It's You/They're Here (Remixes) (12" promo)	10

ÉMIGRÉ

79	Chrysalis CHS 2291	Poison/Trouble Shooter	6

EMILY

87	Sha La La 007	The Old Stone Bridge/REMEMBER FUN: Hey Hey Hate (flexidisc, p/s)	7
87	Big Fun BIG FUN 001	The Old Stone Bridge/What The Fool Said (flexidisc)	7

EMJAYS

59	Top Rank JAR 145	All My Love All My Life/Cross My Heart	50
59	Top Rank JAR 145	All My Love All My Life/Cross My Heart (78)	20

ENDAF EMLYN

71	Parlophone R 5929	Paper Chains/Madryn	7
72	Parlophone R 5954	Goodbye Cherry Lill/All Of My Life	10

DAVID EMMANUEL

83	White Lodge WLT 1	Giving It Up For Love/Stir It Around (12")	50

EMMET SPICELAND

68	Page One POF 089	Lowlands Low/Bunclody	7
69	Page One POF 143	So Long Marianne/In Search Of Franklin	7
68	Page One POLS 011	THE FIRST (LP, with stickered sleeve, blue/silver labels)	60
68	Page ONe POLS 011	THE FIRST (LP, without sticker on sleeve, blue/silver labels)	50
77	Hawk HALP 166	THE EMMET SPICELAND ALBUM (LP, reissue of above LP)	35

EMMETT

65	Columbia DB 7582	Baby Ain't No Lie/Hard Travelling	7
65	Columbia DB 7695	Nancy/Kilkenny Mountains	6

FRED EMNEY

58	Decca TRI DFE 6554	FRED EMNEY (EP)	20

E-MOTIONS

90s	Slammin 1	E-MOTIONS (EP)	20

EMOTIONS

69	Downtown DT 446	Give Me Love/HORACE FAITH: Daddy's Home	10

EMOTIONS (Jamaica)
(see also Romeo & Emotions, Horace Faith)

66	Ska Beat JB 263	Rude Boy Confession/Heartbreaking Gypsy	35
67	Caltone TONE 100	A Rainbow/TONY & DOREEN: Just You And I	50
68	Caltone TONE 118	Soulful Music/No Use To Cry	30

MINT VALUE £

68	Caltone TONE 129	Careless Hands/TOMMY McCOOK & SUPERSONICS: Caltone Special	50
69	High Note HS 018	The Storm/Easy Squeeze	10
69	High Note HS 026	Rum Bay/PATSY: Find Someone	8
70	Supreme SUP 209	Halleluiah/MATADOR ALLSTARS: Boat Of Joy	6

EMOTIONS (U.K.)

65	Polydor BM 56025	Lonely Man/Line Shooter	5

EMOTIONS (U.S.)

62	London HLR 9640	Echo/Come Dance Baby	50
63	London HLR 9701	L-O-V-E/A Million Reasons	60
63	Stateside SS 237	A Story Untold/One Life One Love One You	40

EMOTIONS (U.S.)

69	Stax STAX 123	So I Can Love You/Got To Be The Man	7
69	Stax STAX 134	I Like It/Best Part Of A Love Affair	8
69	Deep Soul DS 9104	Somebody New/Brushfire	30
75	Stax STXS 2020	Baby I'm Through/I Wanna Come Back	6
70	Stax SXATS 1030	SO I CAN LOVE YOU (LP)	20

EMPEROR (Norway)

93	Candlelight 002	EMPEROR (LP)	15
95	Candlelight 008	IN THE NIGHTSIDE ECLIPSE (LP)	15
98	Candlelight 023	ANTHEMS TO THE WELKIN AT DUSK (LP, gatefold sleeve)	15
99	Candlelight 035	IX :EQUILIBRIUM (LP, gatefold sleeve)	15
01	Candlelight 052	EMPERIAL VINYL PRESENTATION (Numbered box set with 5 picture disc LPs and booklet. 3000 only)	60

EMPERORS

66	Stateside SS 565	Karate/I've Got To Have Her	30
68	Pama 786	I've Got To Have Her/Karate	25

EMPEROR'S NEW CLOTHES

90s	Acid Jazz JAZID 128T	Dark Light (12", company sleeve)	20

EMPIRE

(see also Generation X)

81	Dinosaur DE 004	Hot Seat/All These Things (p/s)	10
80	White Line DE 001	EXPENSIVE SOUND (LP)	12

EMU

72	Columbia DB 8903	A Friend Like Me/Emu	6

ENCHANTED FOREST

68	Stateside SS 2080	You're Never Gonna Get My Lovin'/Suzanne	20

ENCHANTERS

67	Warner Bros WB 2054	We Got Love/I've Lost All Communications	25

ENCONA COURSE (Featuring Def J)

91	Edutainment EDUT001	Rhyme Grenade/Taste Of The Future/Hit Men (EP)	45
92	White (No Cat. No.)	VIA COARSEVILLE (EP)	30

THE END

(see also Tucky Buzzard, Bill Wyman, Innocents, Bobby Angelo, Tuxedo)

65	Philips BF 1444	I Can't Get Any Joy/Hey Little Girl	30
68	Decca F 22750	Shades Of Orange/Loving, Sacred Loving	40
69	Decca LK-R/SKL-R 5015	INTROSPECTION (LP, large unboxed logo on label)	250
96	Tenth Planet TP 025	IN THE BEGINNING ... THE END (LP, gatefold sleeve, numbered, 1,000 only)	15
97	Tenth Planet TP 033	RETROSPECTION (LP, numbered, 1,000 only)	15

ENDEVERS

68	Decca F 12817	Remember When We Were Young/Taking Care Of Myself	30
68	Decca F 12859	She's My Girl/She's That Kind Of Girl	30
69	Decca F 12939	Sunny And Me/I Really Hope You Do	10

ENDGAMES

83	Virgin VS 640	Miracle In My Heart/Ecstacy (12")	30

SERGIO ENDRIGO

68	Pye International 7N 25502	Marianne/Il Dolce Paese	10

ENDVRA

97	Elfenblut SAG V	GREAT GOD PAN (CD box with 11 tarot cards)	18

MELVIN ENDSLEY

57	RCA RCA 1004	I Like Your Kind Of Love/Is It True?	40
57	RCA RCA 1004	I Like Your Kind Of Love/Is It True? (78)	15
58	RCA RCA 1051	I Got A Feelin'/There's Bound To Be	40
58	RCA RCA 1051	I Got A Feelin'/There's Bound To Be (78)	20

ENEMY

07	Stiff BUY 265	40 Days And 40 Nights/Dancin' All Night (numbered sticker on die-cut Stiff sleeve, with free sticker)	20

ENEMY

81	Tin Tin NM 1	50,000 Dead/Society's Fool/Neutral Ground (p/s)	8
82	Fallout FALL 001	Fallen Hero/Tomorrow's Warning/Prisoner Of War (p/s, with inner)	7
82	Fallout FALL 004	Punks Alive/Piccadilly Sidetracks/Twist And Turn (p/s, orange vinyl)	7
83	Fallout FALL 014	Last Rites/Why Not (p/s)	5
84	Rot ASS 9	Last But Not Least/Images (live) (p/s)	6
83	Fallout FALL LP 015	THE GATEWAY TO HELL (LP)	18

ENERGETIC KRUSHER

(see also Chasers, Wildhearts)

89	Vinyl Solution SOL 17	PATH TO OBLIVION (LP, with insert, features Danny McCormack)	20

MINT VALUE £

ENERGY

83	Aros AROS 11233	Nowhere To Hide/Fight For Your Freedom (no p/s)	75
81	GRN 1	CONQUER THE WORLD: Conquer The World/Make It/Law Breaker (EP, no p/s)	100
80	BIPS BECK 927	ENERGISED (EP)	50

ENERGY IQ

80	Optimistic OPT 008	THROUGH THE PLUGHOLE (EP)	6

SCOTT ENGEL

(see also Scott Walker, Walker Brothers)

58	Vogue V 9125	Blue Bell/Paper Doll	400
58	Vogue V 9125	Blue Bell/Paper Doll (78)	80
59	Vogue V 9145	The Livin' End/Good For Nothin' (with Count Dracula & Boys)	450
59	Vogue V 9145	The Livin' End/Good For Nothin' (with Count Dracula & Boys) (78)	100
59	Vogue V 9150	Charlie Bop/All I Do Is Dream Of You	300
59	Vogue V 9150	Charlie Bop/All I Do Is Dream Of You (78)	75
66	Liberty LEP 2261	SCOTT ENGEL (EP)	50

SCOTT ENGEL & JOHN STEWART

(see also Scott Walker, Walker Brothers)

66	Capitol CL 15440	I Only Came To Dance With You/Greens	45

ENGINE

87	Beak BEAK 1	Getting Away From It All (p/s)	5
88	BH SIXFIFTY 1	WELL OILED (LP)	12

ENGLAND

76	Deroy DER 1356	ENGLAND (LP, private pressing)	350

ENGLAND

77	Arista ARIST 88	Pariffinalea/Nanagram	6
77	Arista ARTY 153	GARDEN SHED (LP, allegedly with booklet)	60
77	Arista ARTY 153	GARDEN SHED (LP, without alleged booklet)	40

ENGLAND FOOTBALL SQUAD

70	Pye 7N 17920	Back Home/Cinnamon Stick	7
70	Pye 7N 17920	Back Home/Cinnamon Stick (some with 'football centre)	15
70	Pye 7N 17920	Back Home/Cinnamon Stick (with 'football centre and p/s)	25
70	Pye 7N 17920	Back Home/Cinnamon Stick (in promo 'BOAC' sleeve)	200
70	Pye NSPL 18337	THE WORLD BEATERS SING THE WORLD BEATERS (LP, round fold-out sleeve)	30
82	Event EV 002	ENGLAND IN THE WORLD CUP 1982 (LP, gatefold sleeve)	12

ENGLAND'S GLORY

(see also Only Ones)

73	Venus VEN 105	ENGLAND'S GLORY (LP, private pressing, pink label, 25 copies only; beware of white label counterfeits)	250
87	Five Hours Back TOCK 4	ENGLAND'S GLORY (LP, stickered sleeve)	12

ENGLAND SISTERS

60	HMV POP 710	Heartbeat/Little Child	60

ENGLISH

81	Albion ION 1008	Hooray For The English/When You Fly (p/s)	10

ENGLISH COUNTRY BLUES BAND

83	Rogue FMSL 2004	HOME AND DERANGED (LP)	15

ENGLISH DOGS

83	Clay PLATE 6	MAD PUNX AND ENGLISH DOGS (12")	10
83	Clay LP 10	INVASION OF THE PORKY MEN (LP)	15

ERROL(L) ENGLISH

(see also Junior English, Errol & Champions)

70	Big Shot BI 547	I Don't Want To Love You/Love Is Pure	6
70	Big Shot BI 548	Once In My Life/Rabbit In A Cottage	6
70	Torpedo TOR 8	Open The Door To Your Heart/That Will Do	6
70	Torpedo TOR 9	Where You Lead Me/Hitchin' A Ride	6
70	Torpedo TOR 16	Sad Girl/Welcome Me Back Home	6
70	Torpedo TOR 22	Sha La La La Lee/BOVVER BOYS: A.G.G.R.O.	50
71	Duke DU 99	Sometimes (with Champions)/Sugar Cane	6

JUNIOR ENGLISH

(see also Errol English)

69	Camel CA 35	Nobody Knows (with Tony Sexton)/Somewhere	6
71	Pama PM 828	Jesamine/SYDNEY ALL STARS: The Flash	8
72	Pama PM 841	Miss Playgirl/Once In My Life	8
72	Pama PM 866	I Don't Want To Die/Land Of Sea And Sand	8
72	Pama PM 869	Daniel/Perfidia	8
72	Banana BA 368	Anniversary/Girls Like You	8
73	Pama Supreme PS 381	Garden Party/Version	8
79	Burning Rockers BRD 004	Love And Key/Key Down (12", red vinyl)	20
79	Burning Rockers BRD 009	Natural High/In Loving You (12")	12
74	Cactus CTLP 102	THE DYNAMIC (LP)	40
75	Horse HRLP 707	THE GREAT (LP)	15

ENGLISH ROSE

(see also Neat Change, Love Affair)

70	Polydor 2058 040	Yesterday's Hero/To Jackie	10

ENGLISH SUBTITLES

79	Small Wonder SMALL 22	Time Tunnel/Sweat/Reconstruction (p/s)	5
82	Glass 007/10 SEC 21	Tannoy/Cars On Fire (folded p/s in bag with insert)	6
82	Glass GLASS LP 013	ORIGINAL DIALOGUE (LP, with inner sleeve)	12

MINT VALUE £

ENID

(see also Robert John Godfrey, Godfrey & Stewart, William Arkle, Glen Baker, Kim Wilde)

76	Buk BUK 3002	The Lovers/In The Region Of The Summer Stars	8
77	EMI International INT 540	Golden Earrings/Omega (p/s)	6
79	Pye 7P 106	Dambusters March - Land Of Hope And Glory/The Skye Boat Song (p/s, blue vinyl)	6
80	Pye 7P 187	Fool/Tito (p/s)	6
80	EMI EMI 5109	Golden Earrings/665 The Great Bean (p/s)	6
81	Bronze BRO 127	When You Wish Upon A Star/Jessica (p/s)	6
81	Bronze BRO 134	Heigh Ho/Twinkle Twinkle Little Star (p/s)	6
82	Rak RAK 349	And Then There Were None/Letter From America (p/s)	5
76	Buk BULP 2014	IN THE REGION OF THE SUMMER STARS (LP, 1st issue, white label, with insert, without mention of "Enid" on front cover; distributed by Decca)	20
77	Buk BULP 2014	IN THE REGION OF THE SUMMER STARS (2nd issue, black label, with "Enid" on front cover)	12
84	The Stand LE 1	"THE LIVERPOOL ALBUM" (untitled mini-album, sold at gigs, 800 only)	20
84	The Stand THE STAND 1	THE STAND (fan club issue, 5,000 only, autographed)	25
84	The Stand THE STAND 1	THE STAND (fan club issue, 5,000 only, some autographed)	15
85	The Stand THE STAND 2	THE STAND 1985-1986 (fan club issue, 2,000 only, autographed)	12
85	The Stand THE STAND 2	THE STAND 1985-1986 (fan club issue, 2,000 only)	15

ETHEL ENNIS

64	RCA SF 7654	ONCE AGAIN (LP)	15

RAY ENNIS & BLUE JEANS

(see also Swinging Blue Jeans, Blue Jeans)

68	Columbia DB 8431	What Have They Done To Hazel?/Now That You've Got Me (You Don't Seem To Want Me)	25

SEAMUS ENNIS

68	Ember FA 2054	THE BONNY BUNCH OF ROSES (LP, reissue)	12
70	Leader LEA 2003	SEAMUS ENNIS (LP)	12

BRIAN ENO

(see also Ayers Cale Nico & Eno, Roxy Music, Passengers, Robert Fripp, Lady June, David Toop, Gavin Bryars, Toto)

74	Island WIP 6178	Seven Deadly Finns/Later On	10
75	Island WIP 6233	The Lion Sleeps Tonight (Wimoweh)/I'll Come Running	6
78	Polydor 2001 762	The King's Lead Hat/R.A.F. (B-side with Snatch)	6
83	EG EGO 12	Silver Morning/Deep Blue (with Daniel Lanois & Roger Eno, with wraparound promo p/s with Eno notes on back)	8
89	Virgin CDT 41	Another Green World/Dover Beach/Deep Blue Day (3" CD, g/fold card sleeve)	8
74	Island ILPS 9268	HERE COME THE WARM JETS (LP)	20
74	Island ILPS 9309	TAKING TIGER MOUNTAIN (BY STRATEGY) (LP, gatefold sleeve)	20
75	Island ILPS 9351	ANOTHER GREEN WORLD (LP)	20
75	Island HELP 22	EVENING STAR (LP, as Fripp & Eno)	20
75	Obscure OBS 3	DISCREET MUSIC (LP)	15
76	Editions EG EGM 1	MUSIC FOR FILMS (LP, private pressing)	100
77	Polydor 2302 071	BEFORE AND AFTER SCIENCE (LP, with 4 Peter Schmidt prints)	30
83	EG EGBS 002	WORKING BACKWARDS 1983-1973 (9-LP box set with "Music For Films, Vol. 2" LP & "Rarities" 12")	60
90s	SML ESL 003CD	TEXTURES (CD)	30

BRIAN ENO & DAVID BYRNE

(see also David Byrne, Talking Heads)

81	EG EGO 1	The Jezebel Spirit/Regiment (p/s)	10
81	EG EGLP 48	MY LIFE IN THE BUSH OF GHOSTS (LP)	15

ENORMOUS ROOM

86	Sharp CAL 5	100 Different Words/Sylvia's Children/Melanie And Martin/You Wrote A Book (12", p/s)	8
86	Medium Cool MC 001	I Don't Need You/Melanie And Martin (flexidisc, p/s)	6

ENOS & SHEILA

(see also Enos McLeod)

68	Blue Cat BS 138	Tonight You're Mine/UNTOUCHABLES: Your Love	30

ENOUGH'S ENOUGH

68	Tattoo TT 101	Please Remember/Look Around You Baby	500

EN ROUTE

79	Barn BARN 006	Break Down Your Defences/Rusty Capri	30

ENSLAVED

90s	Candlelight 001MLP	HORDANES LAND (EP)	70

ENTICERS

72	Atlantic 2091 136	Calling For Your Love/Storyteller	35

JIMI ENTLEY SOUND

(see also Portishead)

02	Espionage Disk ESP 001	Apache/Charlie's Theme	8

ENTOMBED

89	Earache MOSH 21P	LEFT HAND PATH (LP, picture disc)	20
91	Earache MOSH 37	CLANDESTINE LP, embossed sleeve, insert)	15

JOHN ENTWISTLE('S OX)

(see also Who, Rigor Mortis)

71	Track 2094 008	I Believe In Everything/My Size	10
75	Decca FR 13567	Mad Dog/Cell No.7 (as John Entwistle's Ox)	8
81	WEA K 79249P	Too Late The Hero/I'm Coming Back (picture disc, some autographed)	10
81	WEA K 79249P	Too Late The Hero/I'm Coming Back (picture disc, some autographed)	6
71	Track 2406 005	SMASH YOUR HEAD AGAINST THE WALL (LP, gatefold, black/silver label)	30

MINT VALUE £

72 Track 2406 104 WHISTLE RYMES (LP, gatefold sleeve, black/silver labels) 25
75 Decca TXS 114 MAD DOG (LP, as John Entwistle's Ox, with poster, lyric insert) 25
75 Decca TXS 114 MAD DOG (LP, as John Entwistle's Ox, without poster, lyric insert) 15

ENYA

87 BBC RESL 201 I Want Tomorrow/The Celts Theme (p/s) 7
87 BBC CDRSL 201 I Want Tomorrow/The Celts Theme/To Go Beyond I/To Go Beyond II (3" CD). . . . 25
88 WEA YZ 312 CD Orinoco Flow/Smaotin.../Out Of The Blue (3" CD). 12
88 WEA YZ 356 CD Evening Falls/Oiche Chiun (Silent Night)/Morning Glory (3" CD) 15
89 WEA YZ 368 CD Storms In Africa (Part II)/Storms In Africa (Part I) (3" CD, card sleeve) 15
89 WEA YZ 368 CDX Storms In Africa (Part II)/The Celts/Aldebaran/Storms In Africa (Part I) (5" CD, picture disc) 15
91 WEA YZ 580 CD Exile/On Your Shore/Watermark/River (CD, slimline jewel case). 8
91 WEA YZ 604 CDX Caribbean Blue/Orinoco Flow/As Baile/Oriel Window (CD, digipak). 10
91 WEA YZ 635 T How Can I Keep From Singing/O'che Chi'n (Silent Night) (12", metallic p/s) 10
92 WEA YZ 640 CDX Book Of Days/Watermark/On Your Shore/Exile (CD, box set with 4 prints). 12
92 WEA YZ 705 CDX The Celts/O'che Chi'n (Silent Night)/Storms In Africa (Pt. II)/ Eclipse (CD, with 4 prints). 8
87 BBC REB 605 ENYA (LP) 15
87 BBC BBCCD 605 ENYA (CD) 25

JAY EPAE

61 Mercury AMT 1132 Putti Putti/Hawaiian Melody. 8

EPICS (Jamaica)

70 Bamboo BAM 37 Your Love/Driving Me Crazy 15

EPICS (U.K.)

(see also Acid Gallery, Christie, T. Rex)

65 Pye 7N 15829 There's Just No Pleasing You/My Little Girl 10
66 Pye 7N 17053 Just How Wrong Can You Be/Blue Turns To Grey 10
68 CBS 3564 Travelling Circus/Henry Long 20

EPILEPTICS

(see also Licks, Flux Of Pink Indians)

80 Stortbeat/Mirror BEAT 8 1970'S EP (black & white p/s, stencilled white labels). 20
81 Spiderleg SDL 1 1970'S EP (re-recorded, printed labels, folded different printed b&w p/s). 15
81 Spiderleg SDL 2 LAST BUS TO DEBDEN (EP, hand-written labels & photocopied p/s) 12

EPISODE

(see also Episode Six)

68 MGM MGM 1409 Little One/Wide Smiles. 30

EPISODE FOUR

86 Lenin & McCarthy LENM 001T STRIKE UP MATCHES EP (p/s with insert, 500 only, many destroyed) 80

EPISODE SIX

(see also Episode, Sheila Carter & Episode Six, Neo Maya, Roger Glover, Jon Lord, Gillan, Deep Purple, Quatermass)

66 Pye 7N 17018 Put Yourself In My Place/That's All I Want. 25
66 Pye 7N 17110 I Hear Trumpets Blow/True Love Is Funny That Way 20
66 Pye 7N 17147 Here, There And Everywhere/Mighty Morris Ten. 20
67 Pye 7N 17244 Love, Hate, Revenge/Baby Baby Baby. 40
67 Pye 7N 17330 Morning Dew/Sunshine Girl. 18
67 Pye 7N 17376 I Can See Through You/When I Fall In Love 40
68 Chapter One CH 103 Lucky Sunday/Mr. Universe. 20
69 Chapter One CH 104 Mozart Versus The Rest/Jak D'Or. 18
87 PRT PYL 6026 PUT YOURSELF IN MY PLACE (LP) 12
97 RPM RPM 178 THE RADIO ONE CLUB SESSIONS LIVE 1968/69 (CD). 25

MINNIE EPPERSON

68 Action ACT 4503 Grab Your Clothes (And Get On Out)/No Love At All 50

PRESTON EPPS

(see also Sandy Nelson)

59 Top Rank JAR 140 Bongo Rock/Bongo Party 15
59 Top Rank JAR 180 Bongos In Pastel/Doin' The Cha Cha Cha 10
60 Top Rank JAR 345 Bongo Boogie/Flamenco Boogie 15
60 Top Rank JAR 413 Bongo Bongo Bongo/Hully Gully Bongo. 12
60 Top Rank JAR 522 Bongola/Blue Bongo 8
70 President PT 294 Bongo Rock/SANDY NELSON: Teen Beat 6
60 Top Rank JKP 2060 RUSHING FOR PERCUSSION (EP, with Sandy Nelson) 30

EQUA

83 Mr Fox FOX 1 In The Red/City Dub 20
83 Mr Fox FOX 1 In The Red/City Dub (12") 60

EQUALS

(see also Little Grants & Eddie, Pyramids, Hickory, Little Brother Grant, Zappata Schmitt, Seven Letters/Syramip, Thirty-Second Turn-Off)

67 President PT 117 I Won't Be There/Fire 8
67 President PT 135 Baby, Come Back/Hold Me Closer 6
67 President ZAM 2 I'm A Poor Man/Can't Find A Girl To Love Me (Export only) 30
67 President PT 158 Give Love A Try/Another Sad And Lonely Night 7
68 President PT 180 I Get So Excited/The Skies Above 6
68 President PT 200 Laurel And Hardy/The Guy Who Made Her A Star. 6
68 President PT 222 Softly Softly/Lonely Rita 6
69 President PT 240 Michael And The Slipper Tree/Honey Gum 6
69 President PT 260 Viva Bobby Joe/I Can't Let You Go. 6
69 President PT 275 Rub A Dub Dub/After The Lights Go Down Low 6
70 President PT 288 Soul Brother Clifford/Happy Birthday Girl 6
70 President PT 303 I Can See But You Don't Know/Gigolo Sam. 70
70 President PT 325 Black Skin Blue Eyed Boys/Ain't Got Nothing To Give You. 6

MINT VALUE £

70	President PT 345	Help Me Simone/Love Potion	6
72	CBS 7874	Stand Up And Be Counted/What Would You Do To Survive	6
73	President PT 405	Honey Bee/Put Some Rock & Roll In Your Soul	6
73	President PT 414	Diversion/Here Today Gone Tomorrow	15
74	President PT 422	Hang Up My Rock & Roll Shoes/She Lives For Today	6
75	President PT 436	Georgetown Girl/We've Got It All Worked Out	6
76	Mercury 6007 104	Kaiwana Sunshine Girl/Soul Mother	6
76	Mercury 6007 106	Funky Like A Train/If You Didn't Miss Me	8
76	Mercury 6007 107	Funky Like A Train/If You Didn't Miss Me (12")	10
77	Mercury 6007 139	Irma La Douce/Ar'e Harry	6
77	President PT 464	Beautiful Clown/Daily Love	6
78	Ice GUY 5	Red Dog/Something Beautiful	6
88	Club JAB 58	Funky Like A Train/Born Ya!/Funky Like A Train (extended) (reissue)	7
88	Club JABX 58	Funky Like A Train/Born Ya!/Funky Like A Train (extended) (12", reissue)	20
68	President PTE 1	BABY COME BACK (EP)	20
68	President PTE 2	THE EQUALS (EP)	20
67	President PTL 1006	UNEQUALLED EQUALS (LP)	22
68	President PTL 1015	EQUALS EXPLOSION (LP)	20
68	President PTL(S) 1020	SENSATIONAL EQUALS (LP)	20
68	President PTL(S) 1025	SUPREME (LP)	18
69	President PTLS 1030	THE EQUALS STRIKE AGAIN (LP)	18
69	President PTLS 1050	BEST OF THE EQUALS (LP)	18
70	President PTLS 1038	AT THE TOP (LP)	18
76	Mercury 9109 601	BORN YA! (LP)	25
78	Ice ICEL 1002	MYSTIC SISTER (LP)	25

EQUATIONS

69	Fontana TF 1035	Waiting On The Shores Of Nowhere/You Stood Beside Me	8

EQUINOX

73	Boulevard BLVD 4118	HARD ROCK (LP, black/silver labels)	25

EQUIPE 84

67	Major Minor MM 517	Auschwitz/Twenty Ninth Of September	20

ERASMUS CHORUM

73	Alaska ALA 13	Jungle/That Is Why	25

ERASMUS CHORUS

72	Chapter 1 SCM173	Oh Lord, The Holy House On Sunday/Mary Jane	15

ERASURE

(see also Depeche Mode, Dinger)

SINGLES

85	Mute L12MUTE 40	Who Needs Love (Like That) (Mexican Mix)/Push Me Shove Me (Tacos Mix) (12", p/s)	20
85	Mute L12MUTE 42	Heavenly Action (Yellow Brick Mix)/Don't Say No (Ruby Red Mix) (12", p/s, L12 cat. no. must be listed on sleeve & label)	40
85	Mute DMUTE 42	Heavenly Action/Don't Say No (Ruby Red Mix)//Who Needs Love (Like That) (Mexican Mix)/Push Me Shove Me (Tacos Mix) (12" shrinkwrapped double pack)	20
86	Mute 12MUTE 45	Oh L'Amour/March On Down The Line/Gimme! Gimme! Gimme! (12", 'Thomas The Tank Engine' p/s, withdrawn)	15
87	Mute CDMUTE 56	It Doesn't Have To Be/Sometimes/Oh L'Amour/Heavenly Action/Who Needs Love (Like That)/Gimme! Gimme! Gimme!/In The Hall Of The Mountain King (CD, 7" sized 'tray' p/s)	10
88	Mute LCDMUTE 93	Crackers International II: Stop! (Mark Saunders Remix)/Knocking On Your Door (Mark Saunders Remix)/God Rest Ye Merry Gentlemen (3" CD, Xmas pack with card and gift label 6" x 3" sleeve)	20
90	Mute XL12MUTE 99	Supernature (Mark Saunders Remix)/You Surround Me (Gareth Jones Remix)/ Supernature (Daniel Miller & Phil Legg Remix) (12", envelope p/s)	10
90	Mute XL12MUTE 109	Blue Savannah (Der Deutsche Mix II)/Blue Savannah (Der Deutsche Mix I) (12", 1-sided, numbered envelope p/s)	10
94	Mute MUTE 166	I Love Saturday/Dodo/Because You're So Sweet (unreleased, p/s only)	30

LPs

99	Mute EBX 1	ERASURE 1 (5-CD box set)	30
99	Mute EBX 2	ERASURE 2 (5-CD box set)	30

PROMOS

86	Mute P12MUTE 45	Oh L'Amour/March On Down The Line/Gimme! Gimme! Gimme! (12", plain white sleeve, dark blue vinyl)	20
89	Mute (no cat. no.)	WILD (CD, promo-only box set, with LP, 12",stickers, postcard, photo & info sheet)	100
90	Mute ERAS 1	Push Me Shove Me (Moonbeam Mix)/(Catatonic Mix)/Senseless (Avalon Mix) (12", p/s)	20
90	Mute ERAS 2	ERAS 2: Who Needs Love Like That (Winnie Cooper Mix)/ Ship Of Fools (Orbital South Seas Isles Of Holy Beats Mix) (12" die-cut title sleeve)	18
90	Mute ERAS 3	Sometimes (Danny Rampling Mix) (12", die-cut title sleeve)	20
90s	Mute P12MUTE 195	Don't Say Your Love Is Killing Me (Tall Paul Mix)/(John Pleased Wimmin Flashback Vox) Oh L'Amour (Tin Tin Out Remix)/(Matt Darey Mix) (12", white label test pressing with press release & release sheet, 10 copies only)	70
91	Mute CDSTUMM 95	CHORUS (promo CD, with booklet)	60
92	Mute (no cat. no.)	POP! THE FIRST 20 HITS (CD, promo-only box set, with T-shirt, info sheets, 2-LP, video tape, &)	100
94	Mute PL12 MUTE 166	Ghost (12", 1-sided)	15
92	Mute ERAS 5 EARS5CD	POP (CD, 19-track compilation, without "Take A Chance On Me" & "Who Needs Love Like That [Hamburg Mix]", numbered, promo only)	20
92	Mute CRERASINT 1	POP (CD, interview disc)	20
96	Mute ERAS SAY 1	I SAY I SAY I SAY I SAY (CD, interview disc)	20

MINT VALUE £

96	Mute ERAS SAY 2	ERASURE (CD, interview disc)	20
96	Mute ERAS SAY 3	COWBOY (CD, interview disc)	20

ERAZERHEAD

81	Test Pressing TP 4	Ape Man/Wipeout/Rock And Roll Zombie (p/s)	5
82	Flicknife FLS 208	Shell Shock/She Can Dance (p/s)	5
82	Flicknife FLS 210	Teenager In Love/All For Me (p/s)	5
84	Flicknife SHARP 025	SHELL SHOCKED - BEST OF (LP)	12

EREHWON

(see also Patrick Campbell-Lyons)

81	Harvest HAR 5213	Tiny Goddess/The Hero (p/s)	5

ERIC (Sykes) & HATTIE (Jacques)

(see also Eric Sykes & Hattie Jacques)

63	Decca LK 4507	ERIC, HATTIE AND THINGS (LP)	12

ERIC HYSTERIC & ESOTERICS

80	Wasted Vinyl WASTE 1	Tropical Vision/Dance And Sing (p/s)	5

ERIC & THE VIKINGS

86	Kool Kat 5	Hurting/My Baby Ain't No Play Thing (red vinyl)	25

ROKY ERICKSON (& THE ALIENS)

(see also 13th Floor Elevators)

77	Virgin VS 180	Bermuda/The Interpreter (p/s)	10
80	CBS 8888	Creature With The Atom Brain/The Wind And More (with The Aliens)	8
80	CBS 9055	Mine Mine Mind/Bloody Hammer (Acoustic Version) (p/s, with The Aliens)	8
87	B'full Of Brains BOB 13	Don't Shake Me Lucifer (live) (flexidisc free with Bucketfull Of Brains mag)	6
87	Five Hours Back TOCK 7P	CASTING THE RUNES (LP, picture disc)	25

ERIK

93	PWL PWLT 270	The Devil & The Deep Blue Sea (mixes) (12", p/s, withdrawn)	8
93	PWL PWCD 270	The Devil & The Deep Blue Sea (mixes) (CD, withdrawn)	12

ERNIE & ED

72	Jay Boy BOY 58	Beautiful World/Indication	50

ERROL (English) & CHAMPIONS

(see also Errol English)

70	Jackpot JP 732	Lonely Boy/Da Boo	7
70	Jackpot JP 738	Lonely Boy/TONY & CHAMPIONS: All Of My Life	8

ERROL (Dunkley) & HIS GROUP

(see also Errol Dunkley)

65	Blue Beat BB 284	Gypsy/Miss May (actually by Errol Dunkley & Roy Shirley)	25

ERROL (Dunkley) & U ROY

72	Punch PH 105	Darling Ooh Wee/GOD SONS: Merry Up Version	12

ERSATZ

(see also DJ Harvey)

81	Raw RAW 35	Motorbody Love/One Good Reason/Gimme A Chance (poster p/s)	6
81	Leisure Sounds SRS 32	Smile In Shadow/House Of Cards (p/s)	6

BOOKER ERVIN

61	Parlophone PMC 1170	THE BOOK (LP)	35

DEE ERVIN

72	Signpost SG 4356	DEE ERVIN SINGS (LP)	20

BLUEGRASS ERWIN

59	Top Rank JAR 252	I Won't Cry Alone/I Can't Love You	7

ESCALATORS

(see also Clapham South Escalators, The Meteors)

83	Big Beat NS 86	Something's Missing/The Edge (p/s)	8
83	Big Beat NS 87	The Munsters Theme/Monday (p/s)	6
83	Big Beat WIKM15	MOVING STAIRCASES (LP)	18

ESCORTS (Jamaica)

(see also Sensations)

70	Big Shot BI 535	I'm So Afraid/Mother Nature	30
74	Fab FAB 245	Sixpense/Loving Feeling	15

ESCORTS (U.K.)

(see also Big Three, Paddy Klaus & Gibson, Swinging Blue Jeans, Terry Sylvester)

64	Fontana TF 453	Dizzy Miss Lizzy/All I Want Is You	25
64	Fontana TF 474	The One To Cry/Tell Me Baby	30
64	Fontana TF 516	I Don't Want To Go On Without You/Don't Forget To Write	20
65	Fontana TF 570	C'Mon Home Baby/You'll Get No Lovin' That Way	25
66	Fontana TF 651	Let It Be Me/Mad Mad World	25
66	Columbia DB 8061	From Head To Toe/Night Time	35

ESCORTS (U.S.)

63	Coral Q 72458	Submarine Race Watching/Somewhere	22

ESCORTS (U.S.)

75	Contempo CLP 521	ALL WE NEED IS ANOTHER CHANCE (LP)	15

ESCORTS & KAY JUSTICE

54	Columbia SCM 5132	If You Took Your Love From Me/Yes, Indeed	15

ESCOURTS

76	Alaska ALA 1014	Disrespect Can Wreck/Bam A Lam A Boogie	8

ESG

81	Factory FAC 34	You're No Good/UFO (p/s)	30

MINT VALUE £

ESOTERIC/ESOTERIK
(See also Spiral Tribe)

96	Club Craft OR 100	Dancing With The Devil/Esoteric Vs. Hybrid (12")	50
96	Club Craft OR 200	Ultimate Straightness/Playing With Voices (12")	40
96	Club Craft OR 300	Elegant Panning/3 After That One (12")	30
96	Club Craft OR 400	Odd Sins/Odd Sins (12")	80
96	Crowd Control CROWD 005T	Desert Planet/Mayhem (12", as Esoterik)	80
96	Utmostfear UTMOST 1301	Falling, Floating, Flying/Ultimate Straightness (12")	40
96	Utmostfear UTMOST 1302	Curley And Ramon/Mad Strings (12")	40
97	Crowd Control CROWD 006	Mayhem/Purdey's Effect/In The Hills (12", as Esoterik)	80
98	Utmostfear UTMOST 1303	Untitled/Untitled (12", label bears legend "Curley Truly Unique 1973-1998")	40

ESP

89	Radical DJ INT 14	It's You (12")	80

ESPERANTO ROCK ORCHESTRA
(see also Keith Christmas, Comus)

73	A&M AMLH 68175	ESPERANTO ROCK ORCHESTRA (LP, gatefold sleeve, brown label)	25
74	A&M AMLH 63624	DANCE MACABRE (LP, as Esperanto, silver/gold labels)	20
75	A&M AMLS 68294	LAST TANGO (LP, as Esperanto, silver/brown labels)	30

ESPERS

03	Wichita WEBB084LP	ESPERS (LP)	50

ESPRIT DE CORPS
(see also David Ballantyne, Just Plain Smith, Just Plain Jones)

73	Jam JAM 24	If (Would It Turn Out Wrong)/Picture On The Wall	15
73	Jam JAM 32	Lonely/Do You Remember Me (Like I Remember You)	10

ESPRIT DE CORPS

80s	Come 0001	Anxiety/The Tea Cup Song (hand-made silk-screened sleeve)	10

ESQUERITA

58	Capitol CL 14938	Rockin' The Joint/Esquerita And The Voola	100
72	Specialty SPE 6603	WILDCAT SHAKEOUT (LP)	35

ESQUIRES

67	Stateside SS 2048	Get On Up/Listen To Me	25
68	Stateside SS 2077	And Get Away/Everybody's Laughing	25
73	Action ACT 4618	My Sweet Baby/Henry Ralph	45
68	London HA-Q/SH-Q 8356	GET ON UP AND GET AWAY (LP)	35

ESQUIVEL

63	Reprise R 6046	MORE OF OTHER WORLDS, OTHER SOUNDS (LP)	15

ESSENTIAL LOGIC
(see also X-Ray Spex)

78	Cells SELL ONE	Aerosol Burns/World Friction (p/s)	8
79	Rough Trade RT29	Popcorn Boy/Flora Force (p/s)	12
80	Rough Trade RT50	Eugene (p/s)	10
81	Rough Trade RT74	Fanfare In The Garden/The Captain (p/s)	7

ESSEX

63	Columbia DB 7077	Easier Said Than Done/Are You Going My Way	25
63	Columbia DB 7122	A Walkin' Miracle/What I Don't Know Won't Hurt Me (with Anita Humes)	20
63	Columbia DB 7178	She's Got Everything/Out Of Sight, Out Of Mind	20
63	Columbia 33SX 1593	EASIER SAID THAN DONE (LP)	60
64	Columbia 33SX 1613	A WALKIN' MIRACLE (LP)	60

DAVID ESSEX
(see also David & Rozaa, Us)

65	Fontana TF 559	And The Tears Came Tumbling Down/You Can't Stop Me Loving You	50
65	Fontana TF 620	Can't Nobody Love You/Baby I Don't Mind	45
66	Fontana TF 680	This Little Girl Of Mine/Brokenhearted	45
66	Fontana TF 733	Thigh High/De Boom Lay Boom	40
68	Uni UN 502	Love Story/Higher Than High	20
68	Pye 7N 17621	Just For Tonight/Goodbye	20
69	Decca F 12935	That Takes Me Back/Lost Without Linda	40
69	Decca F 12967	The Day The Earth Stood Still/Is It So Strange?	30
79	Vertigo 6059 233	M.O.D./M.O.D. (2) (as M.O.D., songwriting credited to D. Cook, p/s, allegedly mispressed on 2-Tone label)	75
79	Vertigo 6059 233	M.O.D./M.O.D. (2) (as M.O.D., songwriting credited to D. Cook, p/s)	7

ESSJAY

71	DJM DJS 254	Twins Of Evil/Fastback	15

ASTON ESSON

80	Studio 16 STD 01	Woman Of My Dreams/Version (12")	30

NEVILLE ESSON

61	Blue Beat BB 37	Lover's Jive/Wicked And Dreadful (with Clue J. & His Blues Busters)	18

ESTABLISHMENT
(see also Cromwell)

81	Foetain	BAD CATHOLICS (LP)	30

'SLEEPY' JOHN ESTES

66	Delmark DJB 3	SLEEPY JOHN'S GOT THE BLUES (EP)	40
63	Esquire 32-195	THE LEGEND OF SLEEPY JOHN ESTES (LP)	60
63	'77' LA 12-27	TENNESSEE JUG BUSTERS - BROKE AND HUNGRY (LP)	40
65	Storyville SLP 172	PORTRAITS IN BLUES VOLUME 10 (LP)	22
72	Delmark DS 619	ELECTRIC SLEEP (LP)	20
71	Delmark DS 613	BROWNSVILLE BLUES (LP)	25

MINT VALUE £

JOHN ESTES/FURRY LEWIS/WILL SHADE

71	Revival RVS 1008	OLD ORIGINAL TENNESSEE BLUES (LP)	20

JACKIE ESTREK

61	Blue Beat BB 64	Boss Girl/COUNT OSSIE & GROUP: Cassavubu	30
63	Island WI 042	Since You've Been Gone/Daisy I Love You	15
66	Ska Beat JB 256	The Ska/Daisy I Love You	18

DEON ESTUS

(see also George Michael)

89	Mika MIKCD 2	Heaven Help Me/It's A Party/Love Can't Wait/Me Or The Rumours (Instrumental) (CD, card p/s)	12

ETCETERAS

64	Oriole CB 1950	Where Is My Love/Bengawan Solo	15
64	Oriole CB 1973	Little Lady/Now I Know	20

ETERNAL

90	Sarah SARAH 031	Sleep/Breathe/Take Me Down (p/s)	8

ETERNALS (Jamaica)

(see also Don Cornel & Eternals)

69	Coxsone CS 7091	Queen Of The Minstrels/Stars	40
70	Moodisc MU 3506	Christmas Joy/WINSTON & RUPERT: Musically Beat	7
71	Moodisc MU 3507	Push Me In The Corner/MUDIE'S ALL STARS: Mudie's Madness (B-side actually by Ansell Collins)	12
71	Moodisc MU 3508	Keep On Dancing/HAZEL WRIGHT: My Jealous Eyes	10

ETERNALS (U.S.)

59	London HL 8995	Rockin' In The Jungle/Rock 'N' Roll Cha-Cha (triangular centre)	150
59	London HL 8995	Rockin' In The Jungle/Rock 'N' Roll Cha-Cha (round centre)	100
59	London HL 8995	Rockin' In The Jungle/Rock 'N' Roll Cha-Cha (78)	35

ETERNAL TRIANGLE

69	Decca F 12979	I Guess The Lord Must Be In New York City/Perfumed Candle	8
69	Decca F 12954	Turn To Me/Window	7

ETERNITY'S CHILDREN

68	Capitol CL 15558	Mrs Bluebird/Little Boy	25

ETHEL THE FROG

80	Best SRTSFMR 014	Eleanor Rigby/Fight Back	60
80	EMI EMI 5041	Eleanor Rigby/Fight Back (reissue)	10
80	EMI EMC 3329	ETHEL THE FROG (LP, with Terry Hopkinson & Doug Sheppard)	18

ETHIOPIAN IRATION BLOOD RELATIVE & IDREN

79	Greensleeves GRED 21	This Foundation/Elders and Deacons/How Can A Man/Jah Children Come (12")	40

ETHIOPIANS

(see Eathopians, Soul Brothers, Soul Vendors, Hamliins)

66	Ska Beat JB 260	Live Good (credited to the Etheopians)/SOUL BROTHERS: Soho	50
66	Island WI 3015	I Am Free/SOUL BROTHERS: Shanty Town	80
67	Rio R 110	Owe Me No Pay Me/SHARKS: I Wouldn't Baby	20
67	Rio R 114	I'm Gonna Take Over Now/JACKIE MITTOO: Home Made	35
67	Rio R 123	What To Do/JACKIE MITTOO: Got My Bugaloo	100
67	Rio R 126	Dun Dead A'Ready/BOB ANDY: Stay In My Lonely Arms	50
67	Rio R 130	Train To Skaville/You Are The Girl (B-side actually by Gladiators)	25
67	Doctor Bird DB 1092	I Need You/Do It Sweet	35
67	Doctor Bird DB 1096	The Whip/Cool It, Amigo	45
67	Doctor Bird DB 1103	Stay Loose, Mama/The World Goes Ska	50
68	Doctor Bird DB 1141	Come On Now/Sh'Boom	35
68	Doctor Bird DB 1147	Engine 54/Give Me Your Love	150
68	Doctor Bird DB 1148	Train To Glory/You Got The Dough	55
68	Doctor Bird DB 1169	Everything Crash/I'm Not Losing You	25
68	Crab CRAB 2	Fire A Muss Tail/Blacker Black (B-side actually by Count Ossie)	40
68	Crab CRAB 5	Reggie Hit The Town/Ding Dong Bell	50
69	Crab CRAB 7	I Am A King/What A Big Surprise	30
69	Doctor Bird DB 1172	Not Me/Cut Down	20
69	J J Records DB 1185	Hong Kong Flu/Clap Your Hands	18
69	J J Records DB 1186	What A Fire/You	20
69	Doctor Bird DB 1199	Everyday Talking/Sharing You	20
69	Trojan TR 666	Woman Capture Man/One	10
69	Trojan TR 697	Well Red/J.J. ALLSTARS: R.F.K.	10
69	Nu Beat NB 031	My Testimony/J.J. ALL STARS: One Dollar Of Soul	10
69	Nu Beat NB 038	Buss Your Mouth/GLEN ADAMS (Actually REGGAE BOYS) Rough Way Ahead	30
69	Duke DU 35	My Girl/ANSELL COLLINS: Bigger Boss	40
70	Duke DU 61	Mek You Go On So/WINSTON WRIGHT & J.J. ALL STARS: Neck Tie	10
70	Duke Reid DR 2507	Mother's Tender Care/TOMMY McCOOK: Soldier Man	5
70	Bamboo BAM 26	Walkie Talkie/SOUND DIMENSION: Moan And Groan	20
70	Bamboo BAM 38	You'll Want To Come Back/JACKIE MITTOO: Baby Why (Instrumental) (B-side actually by Sound Dimension)	30
70	J.J. JJ 3302	Wreck It Up/Don't Go	8
70	J.J. JJ 3303	Hong Kong Flu/Everything Crash	20
70	Gas GAS 142	Satan Girl/MATADORS: The Pum	6
70	High Note HS 042	Praise For I (actually "Praise Fari")/GAYTONES: Charrie Part II	8
70	Songbird SB 1040	No Baptism/CRYSTALITES: No Baptism (Version Two)	20
70	Songbird SB 1047	Good Ambition/CRYSTALITES: Ambition Version	6
71	Randy's RAN 509	Mi Want Girl/RANDY'S ALL STARS: Girl - Version	7
71	Randy's RAN 510	True Man, Free Man/RANDY'S ALL STARS: Truthful - Version	7
71	Randy's RAN 512	Mr. Tom/Sad News	7
71	Fab FAB 180	Monkey Money/Version	8
71	Treasure Isle TI 7067	Pirate/TOMMY McCOOK & SOUL SYNDICATE: Depth Charge	8

MINT VALUE £

Year	Label / Cat. No.	Title	Value
71	Songbird SB 1059	What A Pain/CRYSTALITES: Pain Version	6
71	Songbird SB 1062	Lot's Wife/DERRICK HARRIOTT: Slave	6
71	Songbird SB 1064	Best Of Five (Parts 1 & 2)	6
71	Big Shot BI 569	He's Not A Rebel/J.J. ALL STARS: He's Not A Rebel - Version	15
71	Big Shot BI 574	The Selah/Don't Let Me Go	6
71	Duke DU 102	Drop Him/J.J. ALL STARS: Drop Him Version	6
71	Duke DU 108	Rim Bim Bam/RANDY'S ALL STARS: Rim Bim Bam Version	7
71	Explosion EX 2050	Starvation/TROJAN ALL STARS: Starvation Version	6
71	G.G. GG 4519	Love Bug/Sound Of Our Forefathers	7
71	Supreme SUP 221	Love Bug/Sound Of Our Forefathers	8
71	Supreme SUP 226	Starvation/MAXIE & GLEN: Jordan River	8
71	Big BG 330	Solid As A Rock/RUPIE EDWARDS ALL STARS: Solid As A Rock Version	6
71	Punch PH 96	Solid As A Rock/RUPIE EDWARDS ALL STARS: Solid As A Rock Version	6
72	G.G. GG 4533	Israel Want To be Free/TYPHOON ALL STARS: Israel (Version)	6
72	Prince Buster PB 38	You Are For Me/Playboy	8
72	Techniques TE 919	Promises/TIVOLIS: Promises - Version	6
73	Harry J. HJ 6646	The Word Is Love/The Word Is Love - Version	5
74	Harry J. HJ 6663	Buy You A Ring/Pray Muma	5
74	Cactus CT 37	Better Man/Skanking Man	6
74	Cactus CT 46	Conquering Lion/Lion Head	8
75	Dragon DRA 1032	Knowledge Is Power/Power Version	5
75	Tropical ALO54	Another Moses/Moses	10
76	Attack ATT 8131	Another Moses/SYLFORD WALKER: I Can't Understand	10
78	Sensation SSD015	Hail Rasta/Version (12")	15
68	Doctor Bird DLM 5011	THE ETHIOPIANS GO ROCK STEADY/ENGINE 54 (LP, this is a UK pressing in a Jamaican sleeve)	400
69	Trojan TTL 10	REGGAE POWER (LP)	40
70	Trojan TBL 112	WOMAN CAPTURE MAN (LP)	45

ETHNIC FIGHT BAND

75	Ethnic Fight EF 4416	OUT OF ONE MAN COMES MANY DUBS (LP)	60
77	Ethnic Fight EF 4444	MUSIC EXPLOSION DUB (LP)	70

ETIVES

(see also Capercaillie)

81	Ayrespin AYRC 106	A BREATH OF FRESH AIR (cassette)	20
84	Ayrespin AYRC 015	AN GAOL A THUG MI OG (MY LOVE OF EARLY DAYS) (LP)	20
84	Ayrespin AYRC 015	AN GAOL A THUG MI OG (MY LOVE OF EARLY DAYS) (cassette)	12

ETTA (James) & HARVEY (Fuqua)

(see also Etta James, Moonglows, Harvey & Moonglows)

60	London HLM 9180	If I Can't Have You/My Heart Cries	50

JACK EUBANK'S ORCHESTRA

61	London HLU 9312	What'd I Say/Chiricahua	10
62	London HLU 9501	Searchin'/Take A Message To Mary	8

EUGENE & BURST

71	Supreme SUP 225	Let It Fall/DENZIL & BURST: Can't Change	6

EUGENIUS

(see also Teenage Fanclub)

93	Creation CAUG 005	Caesar's Vein (p/s)	7

EUPHOREAL

91	Ninja Tune ZEN 12 005	THE JUNGLE TEKNO EP (12")	12

EUROPEANS

79	Heartbeat PULSE 2	Europeans/Voices (p/s)	5

EUROPEANS

(see also Marillion)

83	A&M AMLX 68558	VOCABULARY (LP)	12
84	A&M SCOT 1	LIVE (LP)	12
84	A&M AMA 5034	RECURRING DREAMS (LP)	12

EURYTHMICS

(see also David A. Stewart, ACatch, Tourists, Chris & Cosey, Stewart & Harrison)

81	RCA RCA 68	Never Gonna Cry Again/Le Sinistre (p/s)	8
81	RCA RCAT 68	Never Gonna Cry Again (Extended)/Le Sinistre (Extended) (12", p/s)	25
81	RCA RCA 115	Belinda/Heartbeat, Heartbeat (p/s)	15
82	RCA RCA 199	This Is The House/Home Is Where The Heart Is (p/s)	15
82	RCA RCAT 199	This Is The House/Your Time Will Come (live)/Never Gonna Cry Again/ 4/4 In Leather (live)/Take Me To Your Heart (live) (12", p/s)	35
82	RCA RCA 230	The Walk/Step On The Beast/The Walk (Part 2) (p/s)	12
82	RCA RCAT 230	The Walk/Invisible Hands/Dr Trash/The Walk (Part 2) (12", printed die-cut sleeve)	35
82	RCA DAP 1	Love Is A Stranger/Monkey, Monkey (picture disc)	5
82	RCA DAT 1	Love Is A Stranger/Let's Just Close Our Eyes/Monkey, Monkey (12", blue p/s)	8
83	RCA DAP 2	Sweet Dreams (Are Made Of This)/I Could Give You (A Mirror) (picture disc)	6
83	RCA DAT 2	Sweet Dreams (Are Made Of This)/I Could Give You (A Mirror)/ Baby's Gone Blue (12", p/s)	8
83	RCA DAP 3	Who's That Girl?/You Take Some Lentils ... And You Take Some Rice (picture disc)	7
83	RCA DAT 3	Who's That Girl?/You Take Some Lentils ... And You Take Some Rice/ ABC (Freeform) (12", p/s)	8
83	RCA DA 4/EUC 001	Right By Your Side/Right By Your Side (Party Mix) (stickered p/s with free shrinkwrapped (RCA EUC 001)	25
83	RCA DAP 4	Right By Your Side/Right By Your Side (Party Mix) (picture disc)	6
83	RCA DAT 4	Right By Your Side/Right By Your Side (Special Mix)/ Plus Something Else (12", p/s)	8
84	RCA DAP 5	Here Comes The Rain Again/Paint A Rumour (picture disc)	5

MINT VALUE £

84	RCA DAT 5	Here Comes The Rain Again/This City Never Sleeps (live)/ Paint A Rumour (Long Version) (12", p/s)	8
84	Virgin VSY 728-12	Sexcrime (1984) (Extended Mix)/Sexcrime (1984) (Single Version)/ I Did It Just The Same (12" picture disc)	10
85	Virgin VSY 734	Julia/Ministry Of Love (picture disc in pop-up p/s)	8
85	RCA PB 40375	It's Alright (Baby's Coming Back)/Conditioned Soul ('video still' p/s)	5
85	RCA PB 40375/PB 40101	It's Alright (Baby's Coming Back)/Conditioned Soul//Would I Lie To You?/ Here Comes That Sinking Feeling (double pack, with free coloured vinyl 7")	12
85	RCA PB 40376/PB 40102	It's Alright (Baby's Coming Back)/Conditioned Soul/Tous Les Garcons Et Les Filles//Would I Lie To You? (E.T. Mix)/Would I Lie To You? (Extended Remix)/ Here Comes That Sinking Feeling (12", double pack, gatefold PVC sleeve; 2nd on yellow, red or blue vinyl)	10
85	RCA BYTI 100	I Love You Like A Ball And Chain (mono)/I Love You Like A Ball And Chain (stereo) (promo only)	8
86	RCA DA 8	Thorn In My Side/In This Town (p/s, with shrinkwrapped enamel badge)	10
86	RCA DA 9P	The Miracle Of Love/When Tomorrow Comes (live) (shaped picture disc)	8
87	RCA DAT 14P	Shame (Dance Mix)/I've Got A Lover (Back In Japan)/Shame (12", p/s & print)	8
88	RCA DA 15X	I Need A Man/I Need You/There Must Be An Angel (Playing With My Heart) (live)/ Missionary Man (live) (10", p/s)	8
88	RCA DA 15CD	I Need A Man/Missionary Man (Live Version)/I Need You/I Need A Man (Macho Mix) (CD, picture disc in numbered metal tin)	8
83	Lyntone LYN 13916	A CHRISTMAS MESSAGE (fan club flexidisc, no p/s)	8
84	Lyntone LYN 15292	A YULETIDE MESSAGE TO ALL OUR PALS (fan club flexidisc, no p/s)	8
87	Lyntone (no cat. no.)	DAVE AND ANNIE'S CHRISTMAS MESSAGE '87 (fan club flexidisc, no p/s)	8
89	Flexi FLX 880	DAVE AND ANNIE'S CHRISTMAS MESSAGE '89 (fan club flexidisc, foldout p/s)	10
90	Flexi FLX 1000	DAVE AND ANNIE'S CHRISTMAS MESSAGE '90 (fan club flexidisc, foldout p/s)	10
83	RCA RCALP 6063	SWEET DREAMS (LP, picture disc)	12
84	RCA PLP 70109	TOUCH (LP, picture disc)	30

JOHN EVAN BAND

(see also Jethro Tull)

90	A New Day NRS/CD 1	THE JOHN EVAN BAND LIVE '66 (CD, 500 only)	50

BARBARA EVANS

59	RCA RCA 1122	Souvenirs/Pray For Me, Mother (triangular centre)	25
59	RCA RCA 1122	Souvenirs/Pray For Me, Mother (triangular centre) (78)	10
61	Mercury AMT 1151	Charlie Wasn't There/Nothing You Can Do	5

BILL EVANS

59	Riverside 12-315	PORTRAIT IN JAZZ (LP)	15

BRIAN EVANS

71	CBS 5392	We're Going Wrong/Paradise Lost	50
71	CBS 7293	This Is My Woman/If You Still Want Me (as Bryan Evans)	10

BRYAN EVANS

72	Columbia DB 8911	Turnaround Sunday/Re-United	8

CHRISTINE EVANS

65	Philips BF 1406	Growing Pains/Someone In Love	5
66	Philips BF 1496	Somewhere There's Love/Right Or Wrong	6
67	Melodisc MEL 1620	I'm Gonna Tell Tony/Someone In Love	10

DALE EVANS & ROY ROGERS

73	Word WDS 3002	IN THE SWEET BY AND BY (LP)	20

DAVE EVANS

71	Village Thing VTS 6	THE WORDS IN BETWEEN (LP)	40
72	Village Thing VTS 14	ELEPHANTASIA (LP)	45
74	Kicking Mule SNKF 107	SAD PIG DANCE (LP, with booklet)	20
74	Kicking Mule SNKF 122	TAKE A BITE OUT OF LIFE (LP)	18

GIL EVANS ORCHESTRA

60	Vogue EPV 1266	GREAT JAZZ STANDARDS (EP)	8
60	Vogue LAE 12234	GREAT JAZZ STANDARDS (LP)	18
61	HMV CLP 1456	OUT OF THE COOL (LP)	15

JOHN EVANS

62	Palette PG 9040	Melodie Pour Madame/Cry Me A River	10

LARRY EVANS

56	London HLU 8269	Crazy 'Bout My Baby/Henpecked	750
56	London HLU 8269	Crazy 'Bout My Baby/Henpecked (78)	75

MAUREEN EVANS

(see also Matt Bryant & Linda Joyce)

58	Embassy WB 300	Carolina Moon/Stupid Cupid	10
58	Embassy WB 303	Fever/Born Too Late	10
58	Embassy WB 309	The Hula Hoop Song/Hoopa Hoola	8
58	Embassy WB 313	I'll Get By/Someday (You'll Want Me To Want You)	8
58	Embassy WB 316	The Day The Rains Came/You Always Hurt The One You Love	8
58	Embassy WB 319	To Know Him Is To Love Him/Kiss Me, Honey Honey, Kiss Me	10
59	Embassy WB 344	Goodbye Jimmy, Goodbye/May You Always	10
59	Embassy WB 348	Lipstick On Your Collar/What A Diff'rence A Day Made	10
59	Embassy WB 356	Broken-Hearted Melody/Plenty Good Lovin'	6
59	Embassy WB 371	Among My Souvenirs/Happy Anniversary	10
59	Oriole CB 1517	Don't Want The Moonlight/The Years Between	10
60	Oriole CB 1533	The Big Hurt/I Can't Begin To Tell You	10
60	Oriole CB 1533	The Big Hurt/I Can't Begin To Tell You (78)	10
60	Oriole CB 1540	Love, Kisses And Heartaches/We Just Couldn't Say Goodbye	10
60	Oriole CB 1550	Paper Roses/Please Understand	10
60	Oriole CB 1550	Paper Roses/Please Understand (78)	10

MINT VALUE £

61	Oriole CB 1563	Mama Wouldn't Like It/My Little Corner Of The World	7
61	Oriole CB 1578	As Long As He Needs Me/Where Is Love?	6
61	Oriole CB 1581	Till/Why Don't You Believe Me	6
61	Oriole CB 1613	My Foolish Heart/Oh Gypsy Oh Gypsy	6
62	Oriole CB 1743	Never In A Million Years/We Had Words	6
62	Oriole CB 1760	Like I Do/Starlight Starbright	5
63	Oriole CB 1804	Pick The Petals/Melancholy Me	6
63	Oriole CB 1806	Tomorrow Is Another Day/Acapulco Mexico	10
63	Oriole CB 1851	What A Difference A Day Made/Oh What A Guy	6
63	Oriole CB 1875	Like You Used To Do/As You Love Her	6
64	Oriole CB 1906	I Love How You Love Me/John John	6
64	Oriole CB 1939	He Knows I Love Him Too Much/Don't Believe Him	6
64	Oriole CB 1969	Get Away/I've Often Wondered	10
65	CBS 201733	All The Angels Sing/Speak Sugar Speak	12
65	CBS 201752	Never Let Him Go/Poco Sole	12
67	CBS 202621	Somewhere There's Love/It Takes A Little Time	12
68	CBS 3222	I Almost Called Your Name/Searching For Home	12
63	Oriole EP 7076	MELANCHOLY ME (EP)	30
63	Oriole PS 40046	LIKE I DO (LP)	30

MILL EVANS

01	Kent 6T 17	Ain't You Glad/MILLIONAIRES: I'm The One Who Loves You	20

PAUL EVANS (& CURLS)

59	London HLL 8968	Seven Little Girls Sitting In The Back Seat/Worshipping An Idol (with Curls)	10
59	London HLL 8968	Seven Little Girls Sitting In The Back Seat/Worshipping An Idol (78)	20
60	London HLL 9045	Midnite Special/Since I Met You, Baby	30
60	London HLL 9129	Happy-Go-Lucky Me/Fish In The Ocean	12
60	London HLL 9183	Brigade Of Broken Hearts/Twins	10
60	London HLL 9239	Hushabye Little Guitar/Blind Boy	18
62	London HLR 9636	The Bell That Couldn't Jingle/Gilding The Lily	8
63	London HLR 9770	Even Tan/Ten Thousand Years	10
63	London RE-R 1349	PAUL EVANS (EP)	70
60	London HA-L 2248	PAUL EVANS SINGS THE FABULOUS TEENS (LP)	100

ROGER EVANS & SWANSEA CITY FOOTBALL CLUB

79	Rotor Pro 001	Swansea City/The Ballad Of Swansea Jack	8

RUSSELL EVANS & NITEHAWKS

66	Atlantic 584 010	Send Me Some Cornbread/The Bold	25

TOMMY EVANS

02	YNR YNR007	The 4 Horsemen/Not Nice (12", stickered black die-cut sleeve)	8
02	YNR YNR10	Me/You/Silent Mobius (12", p/s, 3 mixes of each track)	8
00	YNR YNR003	THE TIME CAPSULE (12", EP, stickered white sleeve)	12
01	YNR YNR005	THE 4 ELEMENTS (12", EP, stickered black die-cut sleeve)	8

EVEN AS WE SPEAK

90	Sarah SARAH 37	Nothing Ever Happens/Blue Suburban Skies/Bizarre Love Triangle/ Goes So Slow/A Stranger Calls (p/s, insert)	10
91	Sarah SARAH 49	One Step Forward/Must Be Something Else/Best Kept Secret (p/s, insert)	6
91	Sarah SARAH 59	Beautiful Day/Nothing Much At All (p/s, insert)	6
93	Sarah SARAH 79	(All You Find Is) Air/Getting Faster/Blue Eyes Deceiving Me (p/s, insert)	6
93	Sarah SARAH 79	(All You Find Is) Air/Getting Faster/Blue Eyes Deceiving Me (CD)	8

EVEN DOZEN JUG BAND

(see also Lovin' Spoonful, John Sebastian)

66	Bounty BY 6023	THE EVEN DOZEN JUG BAND (LP)	25

EVENSONG

73	Philips 6006 276	I Was Her Cowboy/Gypsy	15

EVER RED

88	Supertone STR 007	Dem No Ruff Like We/Hot Number (12")	40

BETTY EVERETT

64	Stateside SS 259	You're No Good/Chained To Your Love	15
64	Stateside SS 280	It's In His Kiss (The Shoop Shoop Song)/Hands Off	15
64	Stateside SS 321	I Can't Hear You/Can I Get To Know You	20
64	Fontana TF 520	Getting Mighty Crowded/Chained To A Memory	20
64	King KG 1002	Happy I Long To Be/Your Loving Arms	20
65	Sue WI 352	I've Got A Claim On You/Your Love Is Important To Me	60
68	President PT 215	It's In His Kiss (The Shoop Shoop Song)/Getting Mighty Crowded	8
69	President PT 251	You're No Good/Hands Off	8
69	MCA Soul Bag BAG 3	I Can't Say No To You/Better Tomorrow Than Today	8
69	MCA MU 1055	There'll Come A Time/Take Me	8
70	Uni UN 517	Sugar/Hold On	8
71	Liberty LBF 15428	I Got To Tell Somebody/Why Are You Leaving Me	15
72	President PT 372	Trouble Over The Weekend/The Shoe Doesn't Fit	10
65	Fontana TL 5236	IT'S IN HIS KISS (LP)	60
68	Joy JOYS 106	IT'S IN HIS KISS (LP, reissue)	15
69	Uni UNLS 109	THERE'LL COME A TIME (LP)	25

BETTY EVERETT & JERRY BUTLER

(see also Jerry Butler)

64	Stateside SS 339	Let It Be Me/Ain't That Lovin' You Baby	10
65	Fontana TF 528	Smile/Love Is Strange	8
68	President PT 214	Let It Be Me/Smile	5
69	President PT 252	Our Day Will Come/Just Be True	6
65	Fontana TL 5237	DELICIOUS TOGETHER (LP)	45
68	Joy JOYS 123	DELICIOUS TOGETHER (LP, reissue)	12

MINT VALUE £

KENNY EVERETT

68	MGM 1421	It's Been So Long/Without Her	10
77	DJM DJS 10810	Captain Kremmen (Retribution)/Retribution	5

ROY EVERETT

70	Parlophone R 5857	Turn On You Own Heat/Look At That Old Bird	10

VINCE EVERETT

65	Fontana TF 606	Bless You/'Til I Lost You	10
67	Fontana TF 818	Endlessly/Who's That Girl?	10
68	Fontana TF 915	Every Now And Then/Barbarella	10

EVERGREEN BLUES

67	Mercury MF 1012	Midnight Confessions/(Yes) That's My Baby	10
68	Mercury MF 1025	Laura (Keep Hangin' On)/Yesterday's Coming	6
68	Mercury 20122 SMCL	7 DO ELEVEN (LP)	20

EVERGREEN BLUESHOES

(see also Skip Battin, Byrds)

69	London HA-U/SH-U 8399	THE BALLAD OF THE EVERGREEN BLUESHOES (LP)	20

EVERLY BROTHERS

(see also Don Everly, Phil Everly)

78s

57	London HLA 8440	Bye Bye, Love/I Wonder If I Care As Much	10
57	London HLA 8498	Wake Up Little Susie/Maybe Tomorrow	10
58	London HLA 8554	Should We Tell Him/This Little Girl Of Mine	15
58	London HLA 8618	All I Have To Do Is Dream/Claudette	10
58	London HLA 8685	Bird Dog/Devoted To You	12
58	London HLA 8781	Problems/Love Of My Life	15
59	London HLA 8863	Poor Jenny/Take A Message To Mary	20
59	London HLA 8934	('Til) I Kissed You/Oh, What A Feeling	30
60	London HLA 9039	Let It Be Me/Since You Broke My Heart	60
60	Warner Bros WB 1	Cathy's Clown/Always It's You	90
60	London HLA 9157	When Will I Be Loved/Be-Bop-A-Lula	60
60	Warner Bros WB 19	Lucille/So Sad (To Watch Good Love Go Bad)	200

SINGLES

57	London HLA 8440	Bye Bye, Love/I Wonder If I Care As Much (triangular centre)	20
57	London HLA 8440	Bye Bye, Love/I Wonder If I Care As Much (round centre)	8
57	London HLA 8498	Wake Up Little Susie/Maybe Tomorrow (triangular centre)	20
57	London HLA 8498	Wake Up Little Susie/Maybe Tomorrow (round centre)	10
58	London HLA 8554	Should We Tell Him/This Little Girl Of Mine (triangular centre)	20
58	London HLA 8554	Should We Tell Him/This Little Girl Of Mine (round centre)	8
58	London HLA 8618	All I Have To Do Is Dream/Claudette (triangular centre)	7
58	London HLA 8685	Bird Dog/Devoted To You (triangular centre)	7
58	London HLA 8781	Problems/Love Of My Life (triangular centre)	7
59	London HLA 8863	Poor Jenny/Take A Message To Mary (triangular centre)	8
59	London HLA 8934	('Til) I Kissed You/Oh, What A Feeling (triangular centre)	8
60	London HLA 9039	Let It Be Me/Since You Broke My Heart (triangular centre)	18

(Unless otherwise listed, all round centre repressings of the above singles are worth £3)

60	Warner Bros WB 1	Cathy's Clown/Always It's You	7
60	London HLA 9157	When Will I Be Loved/Be-Bop-A-Lula	10
60	Warner Bros WB 19	Lucille/So Sad (To Watch Good Love Go Bad)	6
60	London HLA 9250	Like Strangers/Leave My Woman Alone	6
61	Warner Bros WB 33	Walk Right Back/Ebony Eyes	5
61	Warner Bros WB 42	Temptation/Stick With Me Baby	6
61	Warner Bros WB 50	Muskrat/Don't Blame Me	6
62	Warner Bros WB 56	Crying In The Rain/I'm Not Angry	5
62	Warner Bros WB 67	How Can I Meet Her?/That's Old Fashioned	5
62	Warner Bros WB 79	No One Can Make My Sunshine Smile/Don't Ask Me To Be Friends	5
63	Warner Bros WB 94	So It Will Always Be/Nancy's Minuet	8
63	Warner Bros WB 99	It's Been Nice/I'm Afraid	8
63	Warner Bros WB 109	The Girl Sang The Blues/Love Her	10
64	Warner Bros WB 129	Ain't That Lovin' You Baby/Hello Amy	10
64	Warner Bros WB 135	The Ferris Wheel/Don't Forget To Cry	10
64	Warner Bros WB 143	You're The One I Love/Ring Around My Rosie (withdrawn)	20
64	Warner Bros WB 146	Gone, Gone, Gone/Torture	10
65	Warner Bros WB 154	You're My Girl/Don't Let The Whole World Know	10
65	Warner Bros WB 158	That'll Be The Day/Give Me A Sweetheart	10
65	Warner Bros WB 161	The Price Of Love/It Only Costs A Dime	5
65	Warner Bros WB 5628	The Price Of Love/It Only Costs A Dime (reissue)	6
65	Warner Bros WB 5639	I'll Never Get Over You/Follow Me	6
65	Warner Bros WB 5649	Love Is Strange/Man With Money	10
66	Warner Bros WB 5682	It's All Over/I Used To Love You (unissued)	0
66	Warner Bros WB 5743	(You Got) The Power Of Love/Leave My Girl Alone	10
66	Warner Bros WB 5754	I've Been Wrong Before/Hard Hard Year	15
67	Warner Bros WB 7520	Bowling Green/I Don't Want To Love You	12
67	Warner Bros WB 7062	Mary Jane/Talking To The Flowers	12
67	Warner Bros WB 7088	Love Of The Common People/A Voice Within	12
68	Warner Bros WB 7192	It's My Time/Empty Boxes	12
68	Warner Bros WB 7226	Milk Train/Lord Of The Manor	15
69	Warner Bros WB 6056	Cathy's Clown/Walk Right Back	5
70	Warner Bros WB 6074	Good Golly, Miss Molly/Oh, Boy!	8
70	Warner Bros WB 7425	Yves/Human Race	10
72	RCA Victor RCA 2232	Ridin' High/Stories We Could Tell	10
73	RCA Victor RCA 2286	Not Fade AwayLay It Down	7
77	Warner Bros K 17004	Silent Treatment/Dancing On My Feet	5
80	Old Gold SET 1	THE EVERLY BROTHERS SINGLES SET (15 x p/s 7", box set with book)	20

MINT VALUE £

EPs

58	London RE-A 1113	THE EVERLY BROTHERS	25
58	London RE-A 1148	THE EVERLY BROTHERS - NO. 2	25
58	London RE-A 1149	THE EVERLY BROTHERS - NO. 3	20
59	London RE-A 1174	THE EVERLY BROTHERS - NO. 4	20
59	London RE-A 1195	SONGS OUR DADDY TAUGHT US PART 1	25
59	London RE-A 1196	SONGS OUR DADDY TAUGHT US PART 2	25
59	London RE-A 1197	SONGS OUR DADDY TAUGHT US PART 3	25
60	London RE-A 1229	THE EVERLY BROTHERS - NO. 5	30

(Prices for the above EPs refer to the original triangular centre labels, round-centre editions are worth half to two-thirds this value.)

61	Warners WEP 6034	ESPECIALLY FOR YOU (mono)	25
61	Warners WSEP 6034	ESPECIALLY FOR YOU (stereo)	30
61	London RE-A 1311	THE EVERLY BROTHERS - NO. 6	30
62	Warners WEP 6049	FOREVERLY YOURS (mono)	25
62	Warners WSEP 6049	FOREVERLY YOURS (stereo)	30
62	Warners WEP 6056	IT'S EVERLY TIME (mono)	25
62	Warners WSEP 6056	IT'S EVERLY TIME (stereo)	30
63	Warners WEP 6107	A DATE WITH THE EVERLY BROTHERS VOL. 1 (mono)	25
63	Warners WSEP 6107	A DATE WITH THE EVERLY BROTHERS VOL. 1 (stereo)	30
63	Warners WEP 6109	A DATE WITH THE EVERLY BROTHERS VOL. 2 (mono)	25
63	Warners WSEP 6109	A DATE WITH THE EVERLY BROTHERS VOL. 2 (stereo)	30
63	Warners WEP 6111	INSTANT PARTY VOL. 1 (mono)	25
63	Warners WSEP 6111	INSTANT PARTY VOL. 1 (stereo)	30
63	Warners WEP 6113	INSTANT PARTY VOL. 2 (mono)	25
63	Warners WSEP 6113	INSTANT PARTY VOL. 2 (stereo)	30
63	Warners WEP 6115	BOTH SIDES OF AN EVENING - FOR DANCING VOL. 1 (mono)	25
63	Warners WSEP 6115	BOTH SIDES OF AN EVENING - FOR DANCING VOL. 1 (stereo)	30
64	Warners WEP 6117	BOTH SIDES OF AN EVENING - FOR DREAMING VOL. 2 (Mono)	25
64	Warners WSEP 6117	BOTH SIDES OF AN EVENING - FOR DREAMING VOL. 2 (stereo)	30
64	Warners WEP 6128	THE EVERLY BROTHERS SING GREAT COUNTRY HITS VOL. 1	25
64	Warners WEP 6131	THE EVERLY BROTHERS SING GREAT COUNTRY HITS VOL. 2	25
64	Warners WEP 6132	THE EVERLY BROTHERS SING GREAT COUNTRY HITS VOL. 3	25
65	Warner Bros WEP 6138	BOTH SIDES OF AN EVENING - FOR FUN VOL. 3	20
65	Warner Bros WEP 604	THE PRICE OF LOVE	25
65	Warner Bros WEP 608	ROCK'N'SOUL VOL. 1	25
65	Warner Bros WEP 609	ROCK'N'SOUL VOL. 2	25
66	Warner Bros WEP 610	LOVE IS STRANGE	25
66	Warner Bros WEP 612	PEOPLE GET READY	25
66	Warner Bros WEP 618	WHAT AM I LIVING FOR?	25
67	Warner Bros WEP 622	LEAVE MY GIRL ALONE	25
67	Warner Bros WEP 623	SOMEBODY HELP ME	25
72	Warner Bros K 16209	CRYING IN THE RAIN	8
74	Warner Bros K 16407	WAKE UP LITTLE SUSIE	8

LPs

58	London HA-A 2081	THE EVERLY BROTHERS	40
58	London HA-A 2150	SONGS OUR DADDY TAUGHT US	40
60	Warner Bros WM 4012	IT'S EVERLY TIME (mono)	30
60	Warner Bros WS 8012	IT'S EVERLY TIME (stereo)	35
60	London HA-A 2266	THE FABULOUS STYLE OF THE EVERLY BROTHERS	30
60	Warner Bros WM 4028	A DATE WITH THE EVERLY BROTHERS (mono)	30
60	Warner Bros WS 8028	A DATE WITH THE EVERLY BROTHERS (stereo)	35
61	Warner Bros WM 4052	BOTH SIDES OF AN EVENING (mono)	30
61	Warner Bros WS 8052	BOTH SIDES OF AN EVENING (stereo)	35
62	Warner Bros WM 4061	INSTANT PARTY (mono)	30
62	Warner Bros WM 8061	INSTANT PARTY (stereo)	35
62	Warner Bros WS 8108	THE GOLDEN HITS OF THE EVERLY BROTHERS (stereo)	12
62	Warner Bros WM 8116	CHRISTMAS WITH THE EVERLY BROTHERS AND THE BOYS TOWN CHOIR (mono)	35
62	Warner Bros WS 8116	CHRISTMAS WITH THE EVERLY BROTHERS AND THE BOYS TOWN CHOIR (stereo)	45
63	Warner Bros WM 8138	SING GREAT COUNTRY HITS (mono)	30
63	Warner Bros WS 8138	SING GREAT COUNTRY HITS (stereo)	40
65	Warner Bros WM 8169	GONE GONE GONE (mono)	25
65	Warner Bros WS 8169	GONE GONE GONE (stereo)	30
65	Warner Bros WM 8171	ROCK 'N' SOUL (mono)	25
65	Warner Bros WS 8171	ROCK 'N' SOUL (stereo)	30
65	Warner Bros WS 1578	ROCK 'N' SOUL (reissue, stereo)	15
65	Warner Bros WS 1605	BEAT 'N' SOUL	25
65	Warner Bros W 1620	IN OUR IMAGE (mono)	25
65	Warner Bros WS 1620	IN OUR IMAGE (stereo)	30
67	Warner Bros W 1646	TWO YANKS IN ENGLAND (mono)	25
67	Warner Bros WS 1646	TWO YANKS IN ENGLAND (stereo)	30
67	Warner Bros W1676	THE HIT SOUND OF THE EVERLY BROTHERS (mono)	25
67	Warner Bros WS 1676	THE HIT SOUND OF THE EVERLY BROTHERS (stereo)	30
67	Warner Bros W 1708	THE EVERLY BROTHERS SING (mono)	25
67	Warner Bros WS 1708	THE EVERLY BROTHERS SING (stereo)	30
70	Warner Bros WS 1858	THE EVERLY BROTHERS SHOW (2-LP)	20

DON EVERLY

74	Ode ODS 66046	Warmin' Up The Band/Evelyn Swing	5

PHIL EVERLY

(see also Cliff Richard)

73	RCA RCA 2409	The Air That I Breathe/God Bless Older Ladies	5
74	Pye 7N 45398	Invisible Man/It's True	5
74	Pye 7N 45415	Sweet Music/Goodbye Line	5

MINT VALUE £

EVERREADY'S
80 Taaga TAG 3 — Don't Do It Again/Martian Girl (gatefold p/s) 15

LENNY EVERSONG
57 Vogue Coral Q 72255 — Jezebel/Jealousy 10

EVERYBODY
70 Page One POF 163 — The Shape Of Things To Come/Do Like The Little Children Do 12

EVERYBODY'S CHILDREN
70 Fontana TF 1070 — The Time Is Now/Abide With Me 5

EVERY MOTHER'S SON
67 MGM MGM 1341 — Come And Take A Ride In My Boat/I Believe In You 25
67 MGM MGM 1350 — Put Your Mind At Ease/Proper Four Leaf Clover 25
67 MGM MGM 1372 — Pony With The Golden Mane/Dolls In The Clock 8
67 MGM C(S) 8044 — EVERY MOTHER'S SON (LP) 40
68 MGM C(S) 8061 — EVERY MOTHER'S SON'S BACK (LP) 35

EVERYONE
(see also Andy Roberts)
71 Charisma CB 146 — Trouble At The Mill/Radio Lady 5
71 Charisma CAS 1028 — EVERYONE (LP, gatefold sleeve, attached envelope with booklet) 40

EVERYONE ELSE
79 Woodbine St WSR 001 — Schooldays/Brainwashed/Out Of My Mind/Don't Call Us (p/s) 100

EVERYONE INVOLVED
72 Arcturus ARC 3 — The Circus Keeps On Turning/Motor Car Madness 30
72 Arcturus ARC 4 — EITHER OR (LP, private pressing, embossed plain white sleeve with inserts) .. 200

EVERYTHING BUT THE GIRL
(see also Ben Watt, Marine Girls, Tracey Thorn)
82 Cherry Red CHERRY 37 — Night And Day/Feeling Dizzy/On My Mind (yellow p/s) 5
83 Cherry Red 12CHERRY 37 — Night And Day/Feeling Dizzy/On My Mind (12", p/s) 8

EVERYTHING IS EVERYTHING
69 Vanguard VA 1 — Witchi Tai To/Oooh Baby 15
68 Vanguard SVRL 19036 — EVERYTHING IS EVERYTHING (LP) 18

EVERY WHICH WAY
(see also Brian Davison, Griffin, Heavy Jelly, Skip Bifferty, Graham Bell, Bell & Arc)
70 Charisma BD 1 — Go Placidly/The Light 12

EVIL ED
01 YNR YNR4 — THE TOURNAMENT ROUND 1 (12", EP stickered black die-cut sleeve) 10
02 Hidden Identity HID1 — THE TOURNAMENT ROUND 2 (12" EP) 10

EVOLUTION
90 Positive Vinyl PV 001 — Came Outa Nowhere (12") 20
91 Positive Vinyl PV 002 — Metropolis (12") 20

EWAN (McDermott) & DENVER
67 Giant GN 17 — I Want You So Bad/ERIC McDERMOTT: I'm Gonna Love You 10

EWAN (McDermott) & JERRY (McCarthy)
67 Blue Beat BB 385 — Oh Babe/Dance With Me (with Carib Beats) 18
67 Giant GN 5 — The Right Track/We Got To Be One 10
67 Giant GN 10 — Rock Steady Train/My Baby Is Gone 10
67 Giant GN 14 — Tennessee Waltz/You've Got Something 15

DON EWELL
(see also Mama Yancey/Don Ewell)
57 Tempo TAP 7 — PIANO SOLOS OF KING OLIVER CREOLE JAZZ BAND TUNES (LP) 15

TERRY EWERS
68 Polydor 583028 — ANOTHER WANTED MAN (LP) 12

EX
86 Ron Johnson ZRON 11 — '1936' THE SPANISH REVOLUTION (double pack with book) 20

EX/ALERTA
84 CNT CNT 017 — THE RED DANCE PACKAGE (12", split EP) 15

EXCALIBUR
88 Clay PLATE 1 — HOT FOR LOVE (Hot For Love/Early In The Morning/ Come On And Rock/ Death's Door (12" EP) 15
90 Active 12ATV 101 — Carole Ann/Early In The Morning/Sick & Tired (12", p/s) 8
85 Conquest QUEST 5 — THE BITTER END (mini-LP) 18

EXCEL
79 ARSS XL1 — If It Rains/Rolling Home/She's One Of The Boys/Rock Show (EP, p/s) 100
80 Polydor POSP 110 — What Went Wrong?/Junita (p/s) 8

EXCELS
67 Atlantic 584 133 — California On My Mind/The Arrival Of Mary 25

EXCELSIOR SPRING
69 Instant IN 002 — Happy Miranda/It 20

EXCEPTIONS
(see also Orchids)
65 Decca F 12100 — What More Do You Want?/Soldier Boy 25

EXCEPTION(S)
(see also Bugsy Eastwood, Fotheringay, Fairport Convention)
67 CBS 202632 — The Eagle Flies On Friday/Girl Trouble 70
67 CBS 2830 — Gaberdine Saturday Night Street Walker/Sunday Night At The Prince Rupert ... 20
68 President PT 181 — Rub It Down/It's Snowing In The Desert 6

MINT VALUE £

68 President PT 205 — Helicopter/Back Room — 6
68 President PT 218 — Tailor Made Babe/Turn Over The Soil — 6
69 President PT 236 — Jack Rabbit/Keep The Motor Running — 8
69 President PT 271 — Pendulum/Don't Torture Your Mind — 12
69 President PTLS 1026 — THE EXCEPTIONAL EXCEPTION (LP, yellow/black labels) — 40

EXCHANGE MART
72 President PT 385 — Yeah My Friend/I Know That I'm Dreaming — 20

EXCHECKERS
(see also Aynsley Dunbar Retaliation)
64 Decca F 11871 — All The World Is Mine/It's All Over — 20

EXCITERS
63 United Artists UP 1011 — Tell Him/Hard Way To Go — 20
63 United Artists UP 1017 — He's Got The Power/Drama Of Love — 20
63 United Artists UP 1026 — Get Him/It's So Exciting — 18
64 United Artists UP 1041 — Do-Wah-Diddy/If Love Came Your Way — 25
65 Columbia DB 7479 — I Want You To Be My Boy/Tonight, Tonight — 25
65 Columbia DB 7544 — Just Not Ready/Are You Satisfied — 20
65 Columbia DB 7606 — Run Mascara/My Father — 20
66 London HLZ 10018 — A Little Bit Of Soap/I'm Gonna Get Him Someday — 20
66 London HLZ 10038 — You Better Come Home/Weddings Make Me Cry — 40
69 United Artists UP 2274 — Do Wah Diddy Diddy/Hard Way To Go — 10
71 Jay Boy BOY 38 — Soul Motion/You Know It Ain't Right — 20
65 United Artists UEP 1005 — DO WAH DIDDY DIDDY (EP) — 80
64 United Artists ULP 1032 — THE EXCITERS (LP) — 100

EXCURSION
69 Gemini GMX 5029 — NIGHT TRAIN (LP) — 18

EXECUTIVE(S)
64 Columbia DB 7323 — March Of The Mods/Why, Why, Why — 10
64 Columbia DB 7393 — Strictly For The Beat/No Room For Squares — 8
65 Columbia DB 7573 — It's Been So Long/You're For Me (as Executives) — 8
65 Columbia DB 7770 — Return Of The Mods/How Sad — 10
66 Columbia DB 7919 — Lock Your Door/In My Arms (as Executives) — 8

EXECUTIVE(S)
67 CBS 202652 — Smokey Atmosphere/Sensation — 20
67 CBS 3067 — Ginza Strip/I'll Always Love You — 30
68 CBS 3431 — Tracy Took A Trip/Gardena Dreamer (as Executive, with promo only p/s) — 40
68 CBS 3431 — Tracy Took A Trip/Gardena Dreamer (as Executive) — 30
69 CBS 4013 — I Ain't Got Nobody/To Kingdom Come (as Executive) — 30

EXECUTIVES
80 Attrix RB 05 — Shy Little Girl/Never Go Home/JOHNNIE & LUBES: I Got Rabies/Terror In The Parking Lot (p/s) — 7

EXECUTIVE SUITE
74 Cloud One HIT 1 — When The Fuel Runs Out/When The Fuel Runs Out — 10
74 Polydor 2310400 — EXECUTIVE SUITE 1 (LP) — 30

EXHIBIT A
(see also Doof)
80 Irrelevant Wombat DAMP 1 — NO ELEPHANTS THIS SIDE OF THE WATFORD GAP (EP, with insert) — 25
80 Irrelevant Wombat DAMP 2 — DISTANCE (EP) — 15

EXILE
77 Boring BO 1 — DON'T TAX ME (EP, 1,000 only p/s) — 40
78 Charly CYS 1033 — The Real People/Tomorrow Today/Disaster Movie (p/s) — 15

EXILES
66 Topic 12T 143 — FREEDOM, COME ALL YE (LP) — 15
67 Topic 12T 164 — THE HALE AND THE HANGED (LP) — 15

EXITS
78 Way Out WOO 1 — YODELLING (EP, numbered, gatefold p/s, hand-stamped labels) — 60

EXITS
(see also Direct Hits)
78 Red Lightning GIL 519 — The Fashion Plague/Cheam (p/s, labels on wrong sides) — 100

EXIT STANCE
84 Morterhate MORT 11 — WHILE BACKS ARE TURNED (LP, with insert) — 20
84 Fight Back FIGHT 4 — CRIME AGAINST HUMANITY (EP) — 15

EXIT STANCE
84 Exit Stance ES 002 — Esthetics/Conspiracy Of Silence — 30

EXOCET
86 Exocet EXO 1PS12 — STALEMATE (EP) — 50

EXODUS (Jamaica)
71 Duke DU 103 — Pharaoh's Walk/Little Caesar — 8
72 Sioux SI 001 — Pharaoh's Walk No. 9/SAMMY JONES: Worried Over You — 6
72 Sioux SI 010 — Julia Sees Me/LLOYD THE MATADOR: The Train (Engine 54) — 8

EXORDIUM
70s Face To Face FTF 1001 — TROUBLE WITH ADAM (LP, private pressing) — 20

EXOTIC GUITARS
69 London SHD 8382 — THOSE WERE THE DAYS (LP) — 12

EXOTICS
64 Decca F 11850 — Cross My Heart/Ooh La La — 10
68 Columbia DB 8418 — Don't Lead Me On/You Can Try — 25

MINT VALUE £

EXOTICS

70	Pye 7N 17925	I Don't Want Nobody (To Lead Me On)/Driftaway	6

EXPELAIRES

(see also Mission)

79	Zoo CAGE 007	To See You/Frequency (p/s)	5

EXPELLED

82	Riot City RIOT 8	Dreaming/No Life, No Future/What Justice (p/s)	6
82	Riot City RIOT 17	Government Policy/Make It Alone (p/s)	6
84	Riot City 12RIOT 33	THE SINGLES (12" EP)	8

EXPERIMENTS WITH ICE

81	United Dairies EX 001	EXPERIMENTS WITH ICE (LP)	20

EX PISTOLS

84	Cherry Red/ Virgina Pistol 76p	Land Of Hope And Glory/The Flowers of Romansk (Picture disc)	10

EXPLICIT CORPSE

81	Gistol	That Day Before.../I Gotta Gistol (stickered white labels, plastic gatefold p/s)	5

EXPLOITED

81	Exploited EXP 001	Army Life/Fuck The Mods/Crashed Out (p/s)	8
81	Exploited EXP 002	Exploited Barmy Army/I Believe In Anarchy/What You Gonna Do? (p/s)	8
81	Exploited EXP 003	EXTRACTS FROM EDINBURGH NITE CLUB (EP)	6
81	Secret SHH 110	Dogs Of War/Blown To Bits (live) (p/s)	5
81	Secret SHH 112	Army Life/Fuck The Mods/Crashed Out (p/s, reissue)	5
81	Secret SHH 120	Dead Cities/Hitler's In The Charts Again/Class War (p/s)	5
83	Blurg/Pax PAX 15	Rival Leaders/Army Style/Singalongabushell (p/s)	6
81	Exploited EXP 1001	PUNK'S NOT DEAD (LP)	12
81	Exploited EXP 1002	ON STAGE (LP)	12

EXPLORER

84	Rock Shop RSR 006	EXPLODING (LP)	40

EXPLOSIVE

(see also Watson T. Browne & Explosive)

68	President PT 221	Crying All Night/I Close My Eyes	6
69	President PT 244	Cities Make The Country Colder/Step Out Of Line	20
69	President PT 262	Who Planted Thorns In Miss Alice's Garden?/I Get My Kicks From Living	15
70	President PT 286	I'm Gonna Use What I Got To Get What I Need/Am I A Fool? (with Del Taylor)	6
70	President PT 302	This Ain't The Road To Freedom/Today Is Today	6
71	Plexium PXM 20	Hey Presto, Magic Man/Get It Together	60
71	Plexium PXM 24	Love Doesn't Come Easy/See You In The Morning	6

EXPORT

79	Atlantic K 11344	Julie Bitch/Nice To Know You	15
80	His Master's Vice VICE 2	You've Got To Rock/Wheeler Dealer (title sleeve)	18
80	His Master's Vice VICE 1	EXPORT (LP)	18

EXPOSURE

80	Ahgular Music ACUTE 1	Style & Fashion/Video Eyes (p/s)	10

EXPOZER

80	Hit Hard HARD 1	Rock Japan/On My Knees (p/s)	12
80	Hit Hard	EXPOSED AT LAST (LP)	12

EXTERNAL MENACE

82	Beat The system!! MENACE 1	YOUTH OF TODAY (EP)	15
83	Beat The System!! MENACE 2	NO VIEWS (EP)	15

EXTREEM

66	Strike JH 326	On The Beach/Don't You Ignore Me	15

EXTREME NOISE TERROR

88	Head Eruption HURT 1	A HOLOCAST IN YOUR HEAD (LP, with inner)	20

EXTREME NOISE TERROR/CHAOS U.K.

86	Manic Ears ACHE 01	EAR SLAUGHTER - RADIOACTIVE (LP)	15
87	Strange Fruit SFPS 048	PEEL SESSIONS (12", metallic finish with insert)	8

EXUMA

72	Kama Sutra 2013 053	Monkberry Moon Delight/Obeah Man Come Back	8
70	Mercury 6338 018	EXUMA (LP)	12

EYE FULL TOWER

67	Polydor BM 56734	How About Me?/Carol Cartoon	7

EYEHATEGOD

00	People Like You 772521	SOUTHERN DISCOMFORT (LP, white vinyl with inner)	20

EYELESS IN GAZA

(see also Martyn Bates)

80	Ambivalent Scale ASR 2	Kodak Ghosts Run Amok/China Blue Vision/The Feeling's Mutual (wraparound p/s)	15
81	Cherry Red CHERRY 20	Invisibility/Three Kittens/Plague Of Years (p/s, with insert)	5
81	Cherry Red CHERRY 31	Others/Jane Dancing/Ever Present/Avenue With Trees (p/s)	5
82	Cherry Red CHERRY 47	Veil Like Calm/Taking Steps (p/s)	8
81	Cherry Red BRED 18	CAUGHT IN THE FLUX (LP, with bonus 12" EP [12 BRED 18], with inner)	12
82	Cherry Red BRED 36	DRUMMING THE BEATING HEART (LP)	12

EYES

(see also Pupils)

65	Mercury MF 881	When The Night Falls/I'm Rowed Out	210

MINT VALUE £

66	Mercury MF 897	The Immediate Pleasure/My Degeneration	150
66	Mercury MF 910	Man With Money/You're Too Much	175
65	Mercury MF 934	Good Day Sunshine/Please Don't Cry	100
66	Mercury 10035 MCE	THE ARRIVAL OF THE EYES (EP)	350
84	Bam Caruso KIRI 028	BLINK (LP, 2 different sleeves)	18
87	Bam Caruso MARI 038	SCENE BUT NOT HEARD (mini-LP)	15

EYES

78	RAW 29	Once In A Lifetime/Hello I Love You	5

EYES OF BLUE

(see also Ancient Grease, Big Sleep, Man, Ritchie Francis, Gary Pickford-Hopkins, Gentle Giant)

66	Deram DM 106	Heart Trouble/Up And Down	60
67	Deram DM 114	Supermarket Full Of Cans/Don't Ask Me To Mend Your Broken Heart	45
68	Mercury MF 1049	Largo/Yesterday	12
69	Mercury SMCL 20134	THE CROSSROADS OF TIME (LP, black/silver labels with 'Mercury' logo)	100
69	Mercury SMCL 20164	IN FIELDS OF ARDATH (LP, black/silver label with Mercury logo)	100

EYNESBURY GIANT

78	Ultimate URL 602	FROM THE CASK (LP, with insert)	20

WILL EZELL

(see also Paramount Allstars)

54	London AL 3539	GIN MILL JAZZ (10" LP)	25

EZY MEAT

84	Electric Storm ES 0001	NOT FOR WIMPS (LP, with insert, Irish only)	50
86	Electric Storm ES 0002	ROCK YOUR BRAINS OUT (LP, with insert, Irish only)	40

EZY RIDER

82	English Steel	POWER (LP)	150

F

SHELLEY FABARES

(see also Paul Peterson & Shelley Fabares)

62	Pye International 7N 25132	Johnny Angel/Where's It Gonna Get Me? (blue label)	10
62	Pye International 7N 25132	Johnny Angel/Where's It Gonna Get Me? (later yellow label)	10
62	Pye International 7N 25133	She Can't Find Her Keys/Very Unlikely (with Paul Peterson)	10
62	Pye International 7N 25151	Johnny Loves Me/I'm Growing Up	10
62	Pye International 7N 25166	The Things We Did Last Summer/Breaking Up Is Hard To Do	10
63	Pye International 7N 25184	Telephone (Won't You Ring)/Big Star	10
65	Fontana TF 592	My Prayer/Pretty Please	10

FABIAN

59	HMV POP 587	I'm A Man/Hypnotized	30
59	HMV POP 587	I'm A Man/Hypnotized (78)	35
59	HMV POP 612	Turn Me Loose/Stop Thief!	30
59	HMV POP 643	Tiger/Mighty Cold (To A Warm, Warm Heart)	15
59	HMV POP 659	Got The Feeling/Come On And Get Me	15
60	HMV POP 695	Hound Dog Man/This Friendly World	15
60	HMV POP 724	String Along/About This Thing Called Love	10
60	HMV POP 778	I'm Gonna Sit Right Down And Write Myself A Letter/ Strollin' In The Springtime	12
60	HMV POP 800	Tomorrow/King Of Love	12
60	HMV POP 810	Kissin' And Twistin'/Long Before	12
61	HMV POP 829	You Know You Belong To Somebody Else/Hold On	10
61	HMV POP 869	Grapevine/David And Goliath	10
61	HMV POP 934	You're Only Young Once/The Love That I'm Giving To You	10
82	Revival 6017	Tiger/Turn Me Loose	8
59	HMV CLP 1301	HOLD THAT TIGER (LP)	60
60	HMV CLP 1345	THE FABULOUS FABIAN (LP)	50
61	HMV CLP 1433	YOUNG AND WONDERFUL (LP, mono)	40
61	HMV CSD 1352	YOUNG AND WONDERFUL (LP, stereo)	60

FABIAN (Jamaica)

78	Tribesman TM 08	Prophecy/JIMMY LINSAY : Easy (12")	80
77	Tribesman TM 004	Prophecy/Prophecy Dub	30

FABIONS

69	Bullet BU 410	V. Rocket/Smile (B-side actually "My Baby" by Tennors)	25

FABLE

(see also Trapeze, Uriah Heep)

70	Penny Farthing PEN 725	Minstrel Song/She Said Yes	5
71	Penny Farthing PEN 751	With A Boy Like You/She Said Yes	5
74	Magnet MAG 5002	FABLE (LP, gatefold sleeve, white/red labels)	20

BENT FABRIC

61	Columbia DB 4153	The Alleycat/Markin' Time	6

GREGORY FABULOUS

03	Jah Tubbys JT 10015	Get Up/Moving To Zion (10", with the Offbeat Posse)	20
04	Jah Tubbys JT 10022	Love Jah/Tra-La-La (10", with Prof. Natty)	20

MINT VALUE £

FABULOUS COUNTS

71	Mojo 2092 021	Get Down People/Lunar Funk	8

FABULOUS DIALS

63	Pye International 7N 25200	Bossa Nova Stomp/Forget Me Not	30

FABULOUS FIVE INC.

73	Ahanti SHAN 104	FABULOUS FIVE INC. (LP)	25

FABULOUS FLAMES

(see also Dynamites)

70	Clandisc CLA 224	Holly Holy/LORD CREATOR: Kingston Town	12
71	Trojan TR 7822	Growing Up/Lovitis	6

FABULOUS IMPACT

90	Kent 6T 6	Baby Baby, I Want You/HAMPTONS: No No No No No No Not My Girl (100 Club 6Ts all-nighter anniversary disc)	30

FABULOUS SHADES

71	Tropical AL 005	Lonely Man/Version 2	6

FABULOUS SWINGTONES

58	HMV POP 471	Geraldine/You Know Baby	350
58	HMV POP 471	Geraldine/You Know Baby (78)	60

FABULOUS TALBOT BROTHERS

50s	Melodisc M 1507	Bloodshot Eyes/She's Got Freckles	20
50s	Melodisc M 1507	Bloodshot Eyes/She's Got Freckles (78)	10

FACES

(see also Small Faces, Rod Stewart, Ronnie Lane & Slim Chance, Ron Wood, Jeff Beck Group, Kenney Jones)

70	Warner Bros WB 8005	Flying/Three-Button Hand-Me-Down	10
70	Warner Bros WB 8014	Wicked Messenger/Nobody Knows (unissued)	0
70	Warner Bros WB 8018	Had Me A Real Good Time/Rear Wheel Skid	10
73	Warner Bros K 16247	Cindy Incidentally/Skewiff (Mend The Fuse) (with lyric insert, no p/s)	10
73	Warner Bros K 16281	Borstal Boys (withdrawn)	0
73	NME SF1 139	Dishevelment Blues/Ooh La La Preview (flexidisc free with NME)	15
73	NME SF1 139	Dishevelment Blues/Ooh La La Preview (flexidisc without NME)	5
74	Warner Bros K 16494	You Can Make Me Dance, Sing Or Anything/As Long As You Tell Him (credited to Rod Stewart and the Faces, p/s)	8
77	Riva RIVA 8	THE FACES (EP, p/s)	8
70	Warner Bros WS 3000	FIRST STEP (LP, orange label, gatefold sleeve)	50
71	Warner Bros WS 3011	LONG PLAYER (LP, blue & silver label, stitched die-cut '78rpm' style sleeve)	40
71	Warner Bros K 46053	FIRST STEP (LP, reissue, green label, gatefold sleeve)	20
71	Warner Bros K 56006	A NOD IS AS GOOD AS A WINK ... TO A BLIND HORSE (LP, green label, with poster)	40
71	Warner Bros K 56006	A NOD IS AS GOOD AS A WINK ... TO A BLIND HORSE (LP, green label, without poster)	12
72	Warner Bros K 46064	LONG PLAYER (LP, reissue, blue & silver label, stitched die-cut '78rpm'-style sleeve)	20
73	Warner Bros K 56011	OOH-LA-LA (LP, green label, 'Faces' sleeve with lyric poster)	30
74	Warner Bros K 46053	FIRST STEP (LP, 2nd reissue, 'Burbank' label, gatefold sleeve)	12
74	Warner Bros K 56006	A NOD IS AS GOOD AS A WINK ... TO A BLIND HORSE (LP, reissue, 'Burbank' label)	15
74	Warner Bros K 56011	OOH-LA-LA (LP, 'Burbank' label, 'Faces' sleeve, with lyric poster)	18
74	Warner Bros K 56011	OOH-LA-LA (LP, 'Burbank' label, 'Faces' sleeve, without lyric poster)	12
75	Warner Bros K 66027	TWO ORIGINALS OF . . . (2-LP, reissue of "First Steps" & "Long Player", gatefold sleeve)	20

FACTION

83	Bluurg FISH 7	YOU'VE GOT THE FIRE EP (fold-out p/s)	5

FACTORY

(see also Peter & Wolves, Norman Conquest, John Pantry, Velvet Hush)

68	MGM MGM 1444	Path Through The Forest/Gone	900
69	CBS 4540	Try A Little Sunshine/Red Chalk Hill	800
70	OAK RGJ718	Time Machine/Castle On The Hill (99 copies only)	350

FACTORY

82	Future Earth FER 011	You Are The Music/History Of The World (silver die-cut sleeve)	20

FACTOTUMS

65	Immediate IM 009	In My Lonely Room/Run In The Green And Tangerine Flaked Forest	30
65	Immediate IM 022	You're So Good To Me/Can't Go Home Anymore My Love	30
66	Piccadilly 7N 35333	Here Today/In My Room	22
66	Piccadilly 7N 35355	I Can't Give You Anything But Love/Absolutely Sweet Marie	20
67	Pye 7N 17402	Cloudy/Easy Said, Easy Done	15
69	CBS 4140	Mr And Mrs Regards/Driftwood	20

FADELA

88	Factory FAC 197	N'sel Fik/Ateni Bniti (12")	10

FADERS

79	Rip Off RIP 8	Cheatin'/Library Book (in bag p/s)	50

FAD GADGET

81	Lyntone LYN 10209	King Of The Flies/DEPECHE MODE: Sometimes I Wish I Was Dead (red vinyl flexidisc free with Flexipop magazine, issue 11)	25
81	Lyntone LYN 10209	King Of The Flies/DEPECHE MODE: Sometimes I Wish I Was Dead (red vinyl flexidisc free without Flexipop magazine, issue 11)	5

FADING COLOURS

(see also Orange Seaweed)

66	Ember EMB S 229	(Just Like) Romeo And Juliet/Billy Christian	20
67	Ember EMB S 237	Be With Me/You're No Use	7

MINT VALUE £

FAERIE SYMPHONY

77	Decca F13735	Dance Of The Enashee (Da Oine Sidhe)/The Unseelie Court	8

DONALD FAGIN

82	Warners W3696	THE NIGHTFLY (LP)	18

BRIAN FAHEY (& HIS ORCHESTRA)

59	Parlophone R 4655	Street Of A Thousand Bongos/Waltz For Beatniks	8
60	Parlophone R 4686	At The Sign Of The Swingin' Cymbal/The Clanger	20
62	Parlophone R 4909	At The Sign Of The Swingin' Cymbal/The Clanger (reissue, as Brian Faye)	12
65	Parlophone R 5262	Gidian's Way/Love Theme From "In Harm's Way"	12
65	United Artists UP 1115	Twang/You Can't Catch Me	8
67	Parlophone R 5615	The Plank/Stay On the Island	10
68	Columbia DB 8447	Late Night Extra/Oh The Pity Of It All	12
69	Major Minor MM 656	Open House/Countdown	25
67	Studio Two TWO 175	TIME FOR TV (LP)	20

JOHN FAHEY

(see also Leo Kottke)

67	Transatlantic TRA 173	THE TRANSFIGURATION OF BLIND JOE DEATH (LP, with booklet)	35
67	Transatlantic TRA 173	THE TRANSFIGURATION OF BLIND JOE DEATH (LP, without booklet)	20
68	Vanguard SVRL 19033	YELLOW PRINCESS (LP)	25
68	Vanguard SVRL 19055	REQUIA (LP)	30
69	Takoma SNTF 607	BLIND JOE DEATH (LP)	15
69	Takoma SNTF 608	DEATH CHANTS, WALTZES & MILITARY BREAKDOWNS) (LP)	18
72	Sonet SNTF 628	AMERICA (LP)	20
72	Reprise K 44213	OF RIVERS AND RELIGION (LP)	18
73	Reprise K 44246	AFTER THE BALL (LP)	18
74	Takoma SNTF 675	JOHN FAHEY, PETER LANG AND LEO KOTTKE (LP)	15

JAD FAIR

(see also Half Japanese)

80	Armageddon AEP 003	THE ZOMBIES OF MORA-TAU (EP, die-cut p/s with insert)	15

JAD FAIR & PASTELS

(see also Pastels)

91	Paperhouse PAPER 013T	THIS COULD BE THE NIGHT EP (12", p/s)	15
92	Paperhouse PAPER 018CD	HE CHOSE HIS COLOURS WELL (CD EP)	10

WERLY FAIRBURN & DELTA BOYS

56	London HLC 8349	I'm A Fool About Your Love/All The Time	1000
56	London HLC 8349	I'm A Fool About Your Love/All The Time (78)	150

JOHNNY FAIRE

58	London HLU 8569	Bertha Lou/Till The Law Says Stop	600
58	London HLU 8569	Bertha Lou/Till The Law Says Stop (78)	150

FAIRFIELD PARLOUR

(see also Kaleidoscope [U.K.], I Luv Wight)

70	Vertigo 6059 003	Bordeaux Rosé/Chalk On The Wall	20
70	Vertigo 6059 008	Just Another Day/Caraminda/I Am All The Animals/Song For You	40
76	Prism PRI 1	Bordeaux Rosé/Baby Stay For Tonight	10
70	Vertigo 6360 001	FROM HOME TO HOME (LP, gatefold sleeve, large swirl label)	200
91	UFO BFTP 003	FROM HOME TO HOME (LP, reissue)	30

FAIRIES

(see also Twink, Cops 'N Robbers)

64	Decca F 11943	Don't Think Twice, It's Alright/Anytime At All	100
65	HMV POP 1404	Get Yourself Home/I'll Dance	200
65	HMV POP 1445	Don't Mind/Baby Don't	100

FAIRPORT CONVENTION

(see also Richard Thompson, Ian Matthews, Dave Swarbrick, Sandy Denny, Ashley Hutchings,Trevor Lucas, Albion Band. Bunch, Fotheringay. Vashti Bunyan, Trader Horne, Thieves, Allan Taylor, Krysia, Marc Ellington, Brian Maxine, Steeleye Span, Vikki Clayton)

SINGLES

67	Track 604 020	If I Had A Ribbon Bow/If (Stomp)	75
68	Island WIP 6047	Meet On The Ledge/Throwaway Street Puzzle (pink label)	20
69	Island WIP 6064	Si Tu Dois Partir/Genesis Hall	6
70	Island WIP 6089	Now Be Thankful/Sir B. McKenzie's Daughter's Lament	10
70	Polydor 2058 014	If (Stomp)/Chelsea Morning	12
71	Island WIP 6128	John Lee/The Time Is Near (in p/s)	12
71	Island WIP 6128	John Lee/The Time Is Near	6
73	Island WIP 6155	Rosie/Knights Of The Road	6
75	Island WIP 6241	White Dress/Tears (in p/s)	12
75	Island WIP 6241	White Dress/Tears	6
78	Hawk HASP 423	Jam's O'Donnell's Jig/The Last Waltz (Irish-only)	15
79	Simons PMW 1	Rubber Band/The Bonny Black Hare	12
86	Sunrise Bong 1	Quazi B Goode/MIKE SILVER: Where Would You Rather Be Tonight	10
87	Island 12IF 324	Meet On The Ledge (Re-recorded)/John Barleycorn (live)/ Sigh Bheg Sigh Mhor (live) (12", p/s, with poster)	10
87	Island 12IF 324	Meet On The Ledge (Re-recorded)/John Barleycorn (live)/ Sigh Bheg Sigh Mhor (live) (12", p/s, without poster)	8

POLYDOR/ISLAND ALBUMS

68	Polydor 582 035	FAIRPORT CONVENTION (mono, laminated sleeve)	120
68	Polydor 583 035	FAIRPORT CONVENTION (stereo, laminated sleeve)	90
69	Island ILPS 9092	WHAT WE DID ON OUR HOLIDAYS (1st pressing, pink label with orange/black 'circle')	120
69	Island ILPS 9092	WHAT WE DID ON OUR HOLIDAYS (2nd pressing, pink label with black 'block' logo)	60

			MINT VALUE £
69	Island ILPS 9092	WHAT WE DID ON OUR HOLIDAYS (3rd pressing, pink label with 'i' logo)	50
70	Island ILPS 9092	WHAT WE DID ON OUR HOLIDAYS (4th pressing, pink rim label with 'palm tree' logo)	20
69	Island ILPS 9102	UNHALFBRICKING (1st pressing, pink label with black 'circle' logo)	90
69	Island ILPS 9102	UNHALFBRICKING (2nd pressing, pink label with black 'block' logo)	60
69	Island ILPS 9102	UNHALFBRICKING (3rd pressing, pink label with 'i' logo)	45
70	Island ILPS 9102	UNHALFBRICKING (4th pressing, pink rim label with 'palm tree' logo)	20
69	Island ILPS 9115	LIEGE AND LIEF (gatefold sleeve, 1st pressing, pink label with 'i' logo)	75
70	Island ILPS 9115	LIEGE AND LIEF (gatefold sleeve, 2nd pressing, pink rim label with 'palm tree' logo)	20
70	Island ILPS 9130	FULL HOUSE (white label test pressing, with "Poor Will & The Jolly Hangman")	225
70	Island ILPS 9130	FULL HOUSE (1st pressing, gatefold sleeve lists "Poor Will & The Jolly Hangman")	50
70	Island ILPS 9130	FULL HOUSE (2nd pressing, gatefold sleeve without reference to "Poor Will & The Jolly Hangman")	25
70	Island ILPS 9130	FULL HOUSE (gatefold sleeve, 3rd pressing, pink rim label with 'palm tree' logo)	15
71	Island ILPS 9162	ANGEL DELIGHT (gatefold sleeve with 'stuck-on' photos, pink rim label)	15
71	Island ILPS 9176	BABBACOMBE LEE (gatefold sleeve, with inner sleeve and booklet, with sticker, pink rim label)	35
71	Island ILPS 9176	BABBACOMBE LEE (gatefold sleeve, with inner sleeve and booklet, without sticker)	18
72	Island ICD 4	THE HISTORY OF FAIRPORT CONVENTION (2-LP, with 12-page booklet & blue ribbons)	20
72	Island ICD 4	THE HISTORY OF FAIRPORT CONVENTION (2-LP, later pressing with book & green, red or light blue ribbons)	18
73	Island ILPS 9208	ROSIE	15
73	Island ILPS 9246	FAIRPORT NINE (gatefold sleeve)	18
74	Island ILPS 9285	LIVE CONVENTION (with insert)	15
75	Island ILPS 9313	RISING FOR THE MOON (with insert, 'palm tree' label)	15
75	Island ISS 2	FAIRPORT TOUR SAMPLER (free in NME competition, 500 only)	120
76	Island ILPS 9389	GOTTLE O' GEER	15
76	Island HELP 28	LIVE AT THE L.A. TROUBADOR 1974	30

OTHER ALBUMS

77	Vertigo 9102 015	BONNY BUNCH OF ROSES (gatefold sleeve)	18
78	Vertigo 9102 022	TIPPLER'S TALES (with lyric insert)	15
79	Woodworm BEAR 22	FAREWELL FAREWELL (gatefold sleeve)	20
79	Simons GAMA 1	FAREWELL FAREWELL (reissue, gatefold sleeve)	18
82	Woodworm WR 001	MOAT ON THE LEDGE - LIVE 1981	12
83	Woodworm WRC 1	AT 2 (AIRING CUPBOARD TAPES 2) (cassette)	15
84	Woodworm (no cat. no.)	THE BOOT (2- in video box, 1,000 only)	20
87	Hannibal HNBL	HEYDAY - LIVE AT THE BBC (LP, 2 different issues with alternative versions of 'Reno Nevada)	12
87	Woodworm (no cat. no.)	THE OTHER BOOT (2 cassetes in video box, 1,000 only)	20
88	Woodworm (no cat. no.)	THE THIRD LEG (2 cassettes in video box, 1,000 only)	20
89	BGO BGOCD 72	TIPPLER'S TALES (CD)	20
92	Vertigo 512882	BONNY BUNCH OF ROSES/TIPPLERS TALES (CD)	25

FAIR WARNING

87	Areba ERA 2	Rocking At The Speed Of Light EP (12", p/s)	30

FAIRWAYS (featuring Gary Street)

69	Mercury MF 1116	Yoko Ono/I Don't Care	12

FAIR WEATHER

(see also Andy Fairweather-Low, Amen Corner, Wynder K. Frog)

70	RCA RCA 1977	Natural Sinner/Haven't I Tried (To Be A Good Man)	6
70	RCA RCA 2040	Road To Freedom/Tutti Frutti	8
71	RCA Neon NE 1000	Lay It On Me/Looking For The Red Label Pt 2	12
71	RCA Neon NE 1	BEGINNING FROM AN END (LP, gatefold sleeve, black inner sleeve)	30

AL FAIRWEATHER

(see also Sandy Brown, Henrik Johansen, Albert Nicholas)

57	Columbia SEG 7653	AL FAIRWEATHER'S JAZZ BAND (EP)	8
58	Tempo EXA 63	AL FAIRWEATHER'S JAZZMEN (EP, with Henrick Johansen)	10
58	Nixa NJT 511	FAIRWEATHER FRIENDS (LP)	15
60	Columbia 33SX 1159	AL AND SANDY (LP)	15
60	Columbia 33SX 1221	AL'S PALS (LP)	15
61	Columbia 33SX 1306	DOCTOR McJAZZ (LP, also stereo SCX 3367, with Sandy Brown)	20
63	Columbia 33SX 1509	THE INCREDIBLE McJAZZ (LP, with Sandy Brown's All Stars)	20

ANDY FAIRWEATHER-LOW

(see also Amen Corner, Fair Weather, Gary Pickford-Hopkins & Friends, Dave Edmunds & Rockpile)

86	Stiff BUY 252	Bossa Nova/House Of Blue Light (p/s)	5

FAIRY'S MOKE

(see also Baby Sunshine)

75	Deroy 1175	FAIRY'S MOKE (LP, private pressing, actually various artists LP)	75

FAIRYTALE

67	Decca F 12644	Guess I Was Dreaming/Run And Hide	110
67	Decca F 12665	Lovely People/Listen To Mary Cry	60

ADAM FAITH (& ROULETTES)

(see also Roulettes, John Barry)

SINGLES

58	HMV POP 438	(Got A) Heartsick Feeling/Brother Heartache And Sister Tears	130
58	HMV POP 438	(Got A) Heartsick Feeling/Brother Heartache And Sister Tears (78)	50
58	HMV POP 557	High School Confidential/Country Music Holiday	150
58	HMV POP 557	High School Confidential/Country Music Holiday (78)	50
59	Top Rank JAR 126	Ah, Poor Little Baby!/Runk Bunk (blue label/orange label)	30

MINT VALUE £

59	Top Rank JAR 126	Ah, Poor Little Baby!/Runk Bunk (blue label/orange label) (78)	50
59	Parlophone R 4591	What Do You Want?/From Now Until Forever	5
59	Parlophone R 4591	What Do You Want?/From Now Until Forever (78)	30
60	Parlophone R 4623	Poor Me/The Reason (78)	40
60	Parlophone R 4665	Made You/When Johnny Comes Marching Home	5
60	Parlophone R 4665	Made You/When Johnny Comes Marching Home (78)	40
65	Parlophone R 5289	Someone's Taken Maria Away/I Can't Think Of Anyone Else (with Roulettes)	7
65	Parlophone R 5349	I Don't Need That Kind Of Lovin'/I'm Used To Losing You	7
66	Parlophone R 5398	Idle Gossip/If You Ever Need Me	7
66	Parlophone R 5412	To Make A Big Man Cry/Here's Another Day	7
66	Parlophone R 5516	Cheryl's Goin' Home/Funny Kind Of Love	7
67	Parlophone R 5556	What More Can Anyone Do/You've Got A Way With Me	7
67	Parlophone R 5635	Cowman Milk Your Cow/Daddy, What'll Happen To Me	20
67	Parlophone R 5649	To Hell With Love/Close The Door	7
68	Parlophone R 5673	You Make My Life Worth While/Hey Little Lovin' Girl	4

EPs

60	Parlophone GEP 8811	ADAM'S HIT PARADE	8
60	Parlophone GEP 8824	ADAM NO. 1 (mono)	8
60	Parlophone SGE 2014	ADAM NO. 1 (stereo)	12
60	Parlophone GEP 8826	ADAM NO. 2 (mono)	8
60	Parlophone SGE 2015	ADAM NO. 2 (stereo)	12
60	Parlophone GEP 8831	ADAM NO. 3 (mono)	8
60	Parlophone SGE 2018	ADAM NO. 3 (stereo)	12
61	Parlophone GEP 8841	ADAM'S HIT PARADE VOL. 2	10
62	Parlophone GEP 8851	ADAM FAITH NO. 1	15
62	Parlophone GEP 8852	ADAM FAITH NO. 2	15
62	Parlophone GEP 8854	ADAM FAITH NO. 3 (with John Barry)	15
62	Columbia SEG 8138	BEAT GIRL (2 Faith tracks, with John Barry Orchestra)	20
62	Parlophone GEP 8862	ADAM'S HIT PARADE VOL. 3	12
63	Parlophone GEP 8877	ADAM'S LATEST HITS	12
64	Parlophone GEP 8893	TOP OF THE POPS (with Roulettes)	15
64	Parlophone GEP 8904	FOR YOU - ADAM	12
65	Parlophone GEP 8929	A MESSAGE TO MARTHA - FROM ADAM	12
65	Parlophone GEP 8939	SONGS AND THINGS	20

LPs

60	Columbia 33SX 1225	BEAT GIRL (soundtrack, with John Barry Orchestra)	50
60	Parlophone PMC 1128	ADAM (mono)	15
60	Parlophone PCS 3010	ADAM (stereo)	20
61	Parlophone PMC 1162	ADAM FAITH (mono)	15
61	Parlophone PCS 3025	ADAM FAITH (stereo)	20
62	Parlophone PMC 1192	FROM ADAM WITH LOVE (mono)	12
62	Parlophone PCS 3038	FROM ADAM WITH LOVE (stereo)	20
63	Parlophone PMC 1213	FOR YOU - ADAM (mono)	15
63	Parlophone PMC 1213	FOR YOU - ADAM (stereo)	20
64	Parlophone PMC 1228	ON THE MOVE (with Roulettes)	40
65	Parlophone PMC 1249	FAITH ALIVE! (with Roulettes)	40
60	EMI Regal (S)REG 1033	ADAM (mono/stereo export issue in different sleeve)	15

AUSTIN FAITH

(see also Austin Faithful)

71	Dynamic DYN 407	634 5789/DYNAMIC BOYS: Warm And Tender Love	7

GEORGE FAITH

77	Island IPR 2034	Diana/To Be A Lover (12")	15
77	Black Swan BS 2	To Be A Lover/UPSETTERS: Rastaman Shuffle (12")	20
77	Black Swan BS 3	I've Got The Groove/Diana (12")	20
77	Black Swan BS 4	Midnight Hour/Turn Back The Hands Of Time (12")	20
77	Black Swan BS 5	All The Love I've Got/So Fine (12")	20
79	Warrior WAR 134	Don't Be Afraid/BUNNY SCOTT : What's The Use/Never Had It So Good (act. Jimmy Riley) (12")	10
77	Black Swan ILPS 9504	TO BE A LOVER (LP)	30

HORACE FAITH

69	B&C CB 104	Spinning Wheel/Like I Used To Do	10
69	Downtown DT 446	Daddy's Home/EMOTIONS: Give Me A Love	10
70	Trojan TR 7766	Susie Is Sorrow/DERRICK PEPPER: Don't Go	8
70	Trojan TR 7790	Black Pearl/Help Me Help Myself	7
70	A&M AMS 817	Shame And Scandal In The Family/REGGAE STRINGS: Reggae Strings	6
76	DJM DJS 10687	I Can't Understand It/Gimme Good Lovin'	30

AUSTIN FAITHFUL

(see also Austin Faith)

68	Blue Cat BS 140	Uncle Joe/Can't Understand	80
68	Pyramid PYR 6016	I'm In A Rocking Mood/ROLAND ALPHONSO: Stream Of Life	80
69	Pyramid PYR 6028	Eternal Love/ROLAND ALPHONSO: Goodnight My Love	120
69	Pyramid PYR 6042	Ain't That Peculiar?/Miss Anti-Social	25

FAITHFUL DAWN

94	Dawn 001	The Sequel (Original mix)/Dark Beat Mix (12", white label - 300 only	20

MARIANNE FAITHFULL

64	Decca F 11923	As Tears Go By/Greensleeves	7
64	Decca F 12007	Blowin' In The Wind/The House Of The Rising Sun	10
65	Decca F 12075	Come And Stay With Me/What Have I Done Wrong?	8
65	Decca F 12162	This Little Bird/Morning Sun	6
65	Decca F 12193	Summer Nights/The Sha La La Song	7
65	Decca F 12268	Yesterday/Oh Look Around You	7
66	Decca F 12408	Tomorrow's Calling/That's Right Baby	10
66	Decca F 12443	Counting/I'd Like To Dial Your Number	15

			MINT VALUE £
66	Decca F 22524	Is This What I Get For Loving You?/Tomorrow's Calling	15
69	Decca F 12889	Something Better/Sister Morphine (withdrawn)	55
75	NEMS NES 004	Dreamin' My Dreams/Lady Madalene	10
76	NEMS NES 013	All I Wanna Do In Life/Wrong Road Again	10
77	NEMS NES 014	Wrong Road Again/The Way You Want Me To Be	10
78	NEMS NES 117	The Way You Want Me To Be/That Was The Day (Nashville)	10
79	Island WIP 6491	The Ballad Of Lucy Jordan/Brain Drain	10
80	Island 12WIP 6542	Broken English/Why D'Ya Do It? (12", p/s)	10
80	Decca F 13890	As Tears Go By/Come And Stay With Me/This Little Bird/Summer Nights (p/s)	6
65	Decca DFE 8624	GO AWAY FROM MY WORLD (EP)	40
65	Decca LK 4688	COME MY WAY (LP)	65
65	Decca LK 4689	MARIANNE FAITHFULL (LP)	65
66	Decca LK 4778	NORTH COUNTRY MAID (LP)	75
67	Decca LK/SKL 4854	LOVEINAMIST (LP)	100
69	Decca (S)PA 17	THE WORLD OF MARIANNE FAITHFULL (LP)	15
76	NEMS NEL 6007	DREAMIN' MY DREAMS (LP)	15
78	NEMS NEL 6012	FAITHLESS (LP)	12

FAITH, HOPE & CHARITY

70	Crewe CRW 3	So Much Love/Life Won't Be The Same Without You	6
70	Crewe CRW 3	So Much Love/Let's Try It Over	6
75	RCA 2632	Just One Look/Disco Dan	5

FAITH NO MORE

88	Slash LASH 17	We Care A Lot/Spirit (p/s)	12
88	Slash LASHX 17	We Care A Lot/Spirit/Chinese Arithmetic (Radio Mix) (12", p/s)	12
88	Slash LASH 18	Annie's Song (Remix)/Greed (p/s)	12
88	Slash LASHP 18	Annie's Song (Remix)/Greed (picture disc)	12
88	Slash LASHX 18	Anne's Song (Remix)/Greed (12", p/s)	15
89	Kerrang! FIEND 3	Sweet Emotion/(Balaam & The Angel track) (flexidisc with Kerrang! Mag)	15
90	Slash LASPD 21	Epic/War Pigs (live) (shaped picture disc)	12
90	Slash LASCD 21	Epic/War Pigs (live)/Surprise You're Dead (live)/Chinese Arithmetic (live) (CD, card sleeve)	15
90	Slash LASCD 24	From Out Of Nowhere/Woodpecker From Mars (live)/The Real Thing (live)/ Epic (live) (CD, card sleeve)	10
90	Slash LASPD 26	Epic/Falling To Pieces (live) (shaped picture disc, 12" insert in PVC sleeve)	10
90	Slash LASPD 26	Epic/Falling To Pieces (live)/Epic (live)/As The Worm Turns (live) (CD)	10
90	London/Slash 850 228	KING FOR A DAY, FOOL FOR A LIFETIME (7 x 7" box set)	35
89	Slash 828 217-1	THE REAL THING (LP, picture disc)	20

FAKES

79	Deep Cuts DEEP TWO	Production/Look-Out (p/s)	5

TAV FALCO'S PANTHER BURNS

(see under Panther Burns)

EDDIE FALCON

60	Columbia DB 4420	The Young Have No Time To Lose/My Thanks To You	8
61	Columbia DB 4646	Linda Rose/If Ever I Should Fall In Love	8

FALCONS (U.K.)

64	Philips BF 1297	Stampede/Kazutzka	20

FALCONS (U.S.)

(see also Wilson Pickett, Eddie Floyd)

59	London HLT 8876	You're So Fine/Goddess Of Angels	120
59	London HLT 8876	You're So Fine/Goddess Of Angels (78)	80
62	London HLK 9565	I Found A Love/Swim (some labels credit B-side as "Swin")	50

THE FALL

(see also D.O.S.E.)

78	Step Forward SF 7	Bingo-Masters' Breakout! (EP)	15
78	Step Forward SF 9	It's The New Thing/Various Times (p/s)	15
79	Step Forward SF 11	Rowche Rumble/In My Area (p/s)	12
80	Step Forward SF 13	Fiery Jack/Second Dark Age/Psykick Dancehall 2 (black-and-white p/s)	10
80	Step Forward SF 13	Fiery Jack/Second Dark Age/Psykick Dancehall 2 (yellow p/s)	10
80	Rough Trade RT 048	How I Wrote Elastic Man/City Hobgoblins (p/s)	10
80	Rough Trade RT 056	Totally Wired/Putta Block (p/s)	10
81	Rough Trade RT 071	SLATES (10" EP, 33rpm)	18
81	Kamera ERA 001	Lie Dream Of A Casino Soul/Fantastic Life (p/s)	10
82	Kamera ERA 004	Look, Know/I'm Into C.B. (p/s)	10
82	Rough Trade RT 133	The Man Whose Head Expanded/Ludd Gang (p/s)	10
82	Kamera ERA 014	Marquis Cha Cha/Papal Visit (p/s, B-side plays "Room To Live", withdrawn)	30
83	Rough Trade RT 143	Kicker Conspiracy/Wings//Container Drivers/New Puritan (g/fold double pack)	12
84	Beggars Banquet BEG 116	C.R.E.E.P./Pat-Trip Dispenser (p/s)	6
84	Beggars Banquet BEG 116T	C.R.E.E.P./(Extended Version)/Pat-Trip Dispenser (12", p/s, green vinyl)	8
84	B. Banquet BEG 116TP	C.R.E.E.P./(Extended Version)/Pat-Trip Dispenser (12", p/s, with art print)	8
84	B. Banquet BEG 120E	CALL FOR ESCAPE ROUTE (7"/12" double pack EP)	8
85	B. Banquet BEG 150	Cruiser's Creek (p/s)	6
85	B. Banquet BEG 150T	Cruiser's Creek (12", p/s)	8
87	B. Banquet BEG 187H	There's A Ghost In My House/Haf Found Bormann (hologram p/s)	5
87	B. Banquet BEG 200P	Hit The North (Parts 1 & 2) (picture disc, printed PVC sleeve)	5
87	B. Banquet BEG 200T	Hit The North (Parts 1 & 2) (12", gatefold sleeve)	8
87	B. Banquet BEG 206B	Victoria/Tuff Life Boogie (box set with inserts & badge)	5
88	B. Banquet FALL 2B	Jerusalem (Remix)/Acid Priest 2088 (Remix)//Big New Prinz (Remix)/ Wrong Place Right Time No. 2 (Remix) (double pack box set, with postcard)	5
90	Cog Sinister SINR 5	Popcorn Double Feature/Zandra (p/s)	6
94	Permanent 10SPERM 14	15 Ways (10", p/s)	10
79	Step Forward SFLP 1	LIVE AT THE WITCH TRIALS (LP)	18
79	Step Forward SFLP 4	DRAGNET (LP, with insert)	18

MINT VALUE £

80	Rough Trade ROUGH 10	TOTALE'S TURNS (IT'S NOW OR NEVER) (LP)	18
80	Rough Trade ROUGH 18	GROTESQUE (AFTER THE GRAMME) (LP)	20
81	Step Forward SFLP 6	THE EARLY YEARS 1977-79 (LP)	20
82	Kamera KAM 005	HEX EDUCATION HOUR (LP)	18
83	Rough Trade 062	PERVERTED BY LANGUAGE (LP)	15
84	Beggars Banquet BEGA 58	WONDERFUL AND FRIGHTENING WORLD OF (LP)	12
84	Beggars Banquet BEGA 75	BEND SINISTER (LP)	12
85	Beggars Banquet BEGA 67	THIS NATIONS SAVING GRACE (LP, gatefold with inner sleeve)	15
85	Situation 2 SITU 13	HIP PRIEST AND KAMERADAS (LP)	12
88	Beggars Banquet BEGA 96	I AM A KURIOUS ORANGE (LP, gatefold)	15
90	Cog Sinister 842204	EXTRICATE (LP)	12
91	Cog Sinister 848594	SHIFT-WORK (LP)	12
93	Permanent PERMLP 12	INFOTAINMENT SCAM (LP)	12
05	BBC CMXBX982	COMPLETE PEEL SESSIONS (6-CD box set)	30

FALLEN ANGELS (U.S.)

67	London HL 10166	I Don't Want To Fall/Most Children Do	10
68	London HA-Z/SH-Z 8359	THE FALLEN ANGELS (LP)	50

JOHNNY FALLIN

59	Capitol CL 15043	Party Kiss/The Creation Of Love	45
59	Capitol CL 15091	Wild Streak/If I Could Write A Love Song	50

FALLING LEAVES

65	Parlophone R 5233	She Loves To Be Loved/Not Guilty	70
66	Decca F 12420	Beggar's Parade/Tomorrow Night	40

FALLOUT

83	Mouth Too Small To F. F2	SALAMI TACTICS (EP)	5
84	I FLP 2	BUTCHERY (10" EP, with lyric inner)	8
83	Own Label F3 LP 1	HOME COOKED MEAT (LP, with 2 inserts)	12

FALLOUT

90	Azuli AZ001	The Morning After (12")	20

FALLOUT CLUB

79	Secret SHH104	The Falling Years/The Beat Boys (p/s)	15
81	Happy Birthday UR3	Dream Soldiers/Pedestrian Walk Way (p/s)	15

FALSE IDOLS

78	Old Knew Wave BOG 005	Broken Judy/Marbled Hands/H-Brain (tri-fold p/s)	5
78	Old Knew Wave BOG 007	Ego Wino/Good Night (p/s, pink vinyl)	5

AGNETHA FALTSKOG

(see also Abba)

82	Epic EPC A 2824	Never Again/Just For The Fun (p/s, with Tomas Ledin)	12
83	Epic EPC A 3436	The Heat Is On/Man (p/s)	6
83	Epic EPC WA 3436	The Heat Is On/Man (picture disc)	30
83	Epic EPC A 3622	Wrap Your Arms Around Me/Take Good Care Of The Children (p/s)	6
83	Epic EPC TA 3622	Wrap Your Arms Around Me/The Heat Is On/ Take Good Care Of The Children (Extended) (12", p/s)	12
83	Epic EPC A 3812	Can't Shake Loose/To Love (p/s)	6
83	Epic EPC A 3812	Can't Shake Loose/To Love (poster p/s)	15
83	Epic EPC WA 3812	Can't Shake Loose/To Love (picture disc)	25
85	Epic EPC A 6133	I Won't Let You Go/You're There (p/s)	6
85	Epic EPC TA 6133	I Won't Let You Go (Extended)/You're There (12", p/s)	12
86	Sonet SON 2317	The Way You Are/Fly Like The Eagle (p/s, with Ola Hanansson)	10
88	WEA YZ 170	The Last Time/Are You Gonna Throw It All Away (p/s)	6
88	WEA YZ 170T	The Last Time (Extended Remix)/The Last Time/ Are You Gonna Throw It All Away (12", p/s)	12
88	WEA YZ 177	I Wasn't The One (Who Said Goodbye)/If You Need Somebody Tonight (p/s, with Peter Cetera)	6
88	WEA YZ 177T	I Wasn't The One (Who Said Goodbye) (Extended Version)/(Yo No Fui [Quien Dijo Adios])/If You Need Somebody Tonight (12", p/s, with Peter Cetera)	12
88	WEA YZ 300	Let It Shine/Maybe It Was Magic (p/s)	8
88	WEA YZ 300T	Let It Shine (Extended)/('Bright' Mix)/Maybe It Was Magic (12", p/s)	12
98	Polydor POLPROCD 2	The Queen Of Hearts (Nar Du Tar Mej I Din Fam) (CD, promo only)	30
74	Embassy EMB 31094	AGNETHA (LP)	70

GEORGIE FAME (& THE BLUE FLAMES)

(see also Blue Flames, Jimmy Nicol, Perry Ford & Sapphires, Annie Ross)

SINGLES

64	Columbia DB 7193	Do The Dog/Shop Around	25
64	Columbia DB 7255	Green Onions/Do-Re-Mi	18
64	Columbia DB 7328	Bend A Little/I'm In Love With You (solo)	22
64	Columbia DB 7428	Yeh Yeh/Preach And Teach (some copies list "Yeah, Yeah" on label)	8
64	Columbia DB 7428	Yeh Yeh/Preach And Teach (99 promo copies only with p/s)	75
65	Columbia DB 7494	In The Meantime/Telegram	10
65	Columbia DB 7633	Like We Used To Be/It Ain't Right	12
65	Columbia DB 7727	Something/Outrage	10
66	Columbia DB 7946	Getaway/El Bandido	15

(All of the above singles credited to Georgie Fame & Blue Flames unless stated; the singles listed below were solo)

66	Columbia DB 8015	Sunny/Don't Make Promises	7
66	Columbia DB 8096	Sitting In The Park/Many Happy Returns	10
67	CBS 202587	Because I Love You/Bidin' My Time (p/s)	7
67	CBS 2945	Try My World/No Thanks (p/s)	7
67	CBS 3124	The Ballad Of Bonnie And Clyde/Beware Of The Dog (p/s)	5
68	CBS 3526	By The Time I Get To Phoenix/For Your Pleasure	5
69	CBS 4295	Peaceful/Hideaway (with John Barry)	6
69	CBS 4659	Seventh Son/Fully Booked	8
70	CBS 5035	Entertaining Mr. Sloane/Somebody Stole My Thunder	75

			MINT VALUE £
70	CBS 5131	Fire And Rain/Someday Man	5
77	Island WIP 6384	Daylight/Three Legged Mule	40
77	Island WIP 6384	Daylight/Three Legged Mule (12")	30
EPs			
64	Columbia SEG 8334	RHYTHM AND BLUEBEAT	50
64	Columbia SEG 8382	RHYTHM AND BLUES AT THE FLAMINGO	40
64	Columbia SEG 8393	FAME AT LAST	30
65	Columbia SEG 8406	FATS FOR FAME	35
65	Columbia SEG 8454	MOVE IT ON OVER	35
66	Columbia SEG 8518	GETAWAY	30
67	CBS EP 6363	KNOCK ON WOOD	30
LPs			
64	Columbia 33SX 1599	RHYTHM AND BLUES AT THE FLAMINGO	100
64	Columbia 33SX 1638	FAME AT LAST	35
66	Columbia SX 6043	SWEET THINGS	25
66	Columbia SX 6076	SOUND VENTURE	50
67	Columbia SX 6120	HALL OF FAME	20
67	CBS (S)BPG 63018	TWO FACES OF FAME	20
68	CBS (S) 63293	THE THIRD FACE OF FAME (mono/stereo)	15
69	CBS (S) 63650	GEORGIE DOES HIS OWN THING WITH STRINGS (mono/stereo)	12
69	CBS S 63786	SEVENTH SON	15
69	Regal Starline SRS5002	GEORGIE FAME AND THE BLUE FLAMES	20
71	CBS S 64350	GOING HOME	15
72	Reprise K 44183	ALL ME OWN WORK (LP, gatefold sleeve)	20
73	Embassy EMB 31033	BONNIE & CLYDE	12
74	Island ILPS 9293	GEORGIE FAME	20

GEORGIE FAME & ANNIE ROSS

81	Bald Eagle	Drip Drop/One Morning In May (12" p/s 50 copies only)	40

FAMILY

(see also Farinas, Stud, Mogul Thrash, Hellions, Ashton Gardner & Dyke, Revolution, Streetwalkers)

67	Liberty LBF 15031	Scene Thru The Eye Of A Lens/Gypsy Woman (mispress, B-side plays "Let Me Be Good To You" by Otis Redding)	140
67	Liberty LBF 15031	Scene Thru The Eye Of A Lens/Gypsy Woman	200
68	Reprise RS 23270	Me My Friend/Hey Mr. Policeman	15
68	Reprise RS 23315	Second Generation Woman/Home Town	15
69	Reprise RS 27001	No Mule's Fool/Good Friend Of Mine (p/s)	15
69	Reprise RS 27001	No Mule's Fool/Good Friend Of Mine	5
70	Reprise RS 27005	Today/Song For Lots (p/s)	15
70	Reprise RS 27005	Today/Song For Lots	5
70	Reprise RS 27009	The Weaver's Answer/Strange Band/Hung Up Down (in p/s)	5
71	Reprise K 14090	In My Own Time/Seasons (in p/s)	5
71	Reprise SAM 1	Larf And Sing/Children (promo only)	15
73	Raft RA 18501	Boom Bang/Stop This Car	7
73	Raft RA 18503	Sweet Desiree/Drink To You	7
68	Reprise RLP 6312	MUSIC IN A DOLL'S HOUSE (LP, with insert, mono)	150
68	Reprise RSLP 6312	MUSIC IN A DOLL'S HOUSE (LP, with insert, stereo)	100
69	Reprise RLP 6340	FAMILY ENTERTAINMENT (LP, mono, with poster)	80
69	Reprise RSLP 6340	FAMILY ENTERTAINMENT (LP, stereo, with poster)	60
(The above LPs were originally issued with 'steamboat' label designs, later pressings with same cat. no. are worth around £30 less)			
70	Reprise RSLP 9001	A SONG FOR ME (LP, with lyric sheet, later copies without boat label, £15)	35
70	Reprise RSX 9005	ANYWAY (LP, custom polythene sleeve)	25
71	Reprise RMP 9007	OLD SONGS NEW SONGS (LP)	15
71	Reprise K 54003	FEARLESS (LP, multi gatefold sleeve, lyric insert)	30
72	Reprise K 54006	BANDSTAND (LP, 'window' die-cut sleeve, lyric inner)	30
73	Raft RA58501	IT'S ONLY A MOVIE (LP, lyric inner and 'banger' insert)	40
73	Raft RA 58501	IT'S ONLY A MOVIE (LP, lyric inner and no 'banger' insert)	15

FAMILY CAT

(see also P.J. Harvey)

89	Bad Girl BGRIFC 01	Tom Verlaine (Demo Version) (gig freebie flexidisc, hand-sprayed p/s & insert)	5
91	Bad Girl BGRLT 009T	Color Me Grey/I Must Have Been Blind/Great Ugly Place (12", p/s)	8
78	Union UN 005	Used To Be My Girl/Long Time	10

FAMILY CIRCLE

69	Attack AT 8001	Phoenix Reggae/BIG L: Music Box	8
69	Attack AT 8002	Reggae Krishna/Official	20
69	JJ DB 1300	Give Peace A Chance/GEORGE LEE: Reggae Groove	8

FAMILY DOGG

(see also Steve Rowland, Christine Holmes, Albert Hammond)

67	MGM MGM 1360	Family Dogg/The Storm	15
68	Fontana TF 921	I Wear A Silly Grin/Couldn't Help It	15
68	Fontana TF 968	Brown-Eyed Girl/Let It Rain	7
69	Bell BLL 1055	A Way Of Life/Throw It Away	7
69	Bell BLL 1077	Arizona/The House In The Heather	6
70	Bell BLL 1100	When Tomorrow Comes Tomorrow/This Unhappy Heart Of Mine	6
69	Bell SBLL 122	A WAY OF LIFE (LP, with members of Led Zeppelin, gatefold)	25
72	Buddah 2318 061	THE VIEW FROM ROWLAND'S HEAD (LP, gatefold, lyric insert)	20

FAMILY FODDER

79	Parole/Fresh PURL 4	Playing Golf/My Baby Takes Valium (p/s)	5
79	Fresh Records FRESH 9	SUNDAY GIRLS (12")	15
82	Fresh 42	The Big Dig/Plant Life (p/s)	10

FAMILY MAN (Aston Barrett)

(see also Hippy Boys, Upsetters, Bob Marley & Wailers, Carl Dawkins)

70	Escort ERT 834	Midnight Sunshine/GREGORY & STICKY: You Are My Sunshine	8
72	Downtown DT 491	Herb Tree/STUDIO SOUND: Holy Poly (reissue)	8

MINT VALUE £

FAMILY QUEST
84 Jungle Rhythm SWE-T2 Outerspace 84 Rap 25
86 Streetwave MKHAN74 Sleepwalking (12") 20

FAMOUS ECCLES & MISS FREDA THING
(see also Spike Milligan, Goons)
56 Parlophone R 4251 My September Love/JIM MORIARTY: You Gotta Go Oww! (with The Alberts) 15

FAMOUS JUG BAND
(see also Incredible String Band, C.O.B.)
69 Liberty LBF 15224 The Only Friend I Own/A Leaf Must Fall 10
69 Liberty LBS 83263 SUNSHINE POSSIBILITIES (LP, blue labels) 70
70 Liberty LBS 83355 CHAMELEON (LP, blue labels) 80

FAMOUS MUSIC BAND
(see also John Dummer)
69 Philips 6006 111 Nine By Nine/Going In The Out (with John Dummer) 10

FAMOUS PLAYERS
80 Page 45 AH 1001 Who's Kissing You (p/s) 70

FANATICS
(see also Ocean Colour Scene)
89 Chapter 22 12 CHAP 38 SUBURBAN LOVE SONGS (12" EP) 18

FAN-CLUB
(see also Transvision Vamp)
78 M&S SJP 791B Avenue/Night Caller (p/s, photocopied insert) 15

FANCY
(see also Ray Fenwick, Judas Priest)
73 Sticky STY 3 Starlord/Brother John 25
76 Arista ARIST 32 Music Maker/Bluebird 8
74 Antic K11514 Touch Me/I Don't Need Your Love 8

FANDANGO
73 York SYK 562 High Class Girl/Sha La La 12

FANNY
70 Reprise RSLP 6416 FANNY (LP) 12
72 Reprise K 44144 CHARITY BALL (LP) 12

FANS
79 Fried Egg EGG 3 Giving Me That Look in Your Eyes/Stay The Night/He'll Have To Go (p/s) 45
79 Albion ION 0004 True (dayglo inner, inc bonus 7" & lyric sheet) 20
80 Albion FAN 01 Cars And Explosions/Dangerous Goodbyes (p/s) 20
81 Fried Egg EGG 10 You Don't Live Here Anymore/Following You (p/s) 30

FANTASIA
67 Stateside SS 2031 Gotta Get Away/She Needs My Love 10

FANTASTIC BAGGYS
(see also Jan & Dean, Bruce Johnston)
76 United Artists UP 36142 Summer Means Fun/JAN & DEAN: Surf City/Sidewalk Surfin' 15

FANTASTIC FOUR
68 Tamla Motown TMG 678 I Love You Madly/I Love You Madly (Instrumental) 15
68 T. Motown TML 11105 THE FANTASTIC FOUR (LP, mono) 55
69 T. Motown STML 11105 THE FANTASTIC FOUR (LP, stereo) 50

FANTASTIC JOHNNY C
(see under 'C')

FANTASTIC PUZZLES
76 Right On 106 Come Back/Come Back Part 2 30

FANTASTICS
(see also Velours)
68 MGM MGM 1434 Baby Make Your Own Sweet Music/Who Could Be Lovin' You 20
68 MGM MGM 1434DJ Baby Make Your Own Sweet Music/ Who Could Be Lovin' You (DJ promo) 30
69 Deram DM 264 Face To Face With Heartache/This Must Be My Rainy Day 6
70 Deram DM 283 Waiting Round For Heartaches/Ask The Lonely 20
71 Deram DM 334 For Old Times Sake/Exodus Main Theme 6
71 Mojo 2027 004 Baby Make Your Own Sweet Music/Who Could Be Lovin' You? (reissue) 5

FANTASY
73 Polydor 2058 405 Politely Insane/I Was Once Aware 30
73 Polydor 2383 246 PAINT A PICTURE (LP, gatefold sleeve, red label) 450

BARRY FANTONI
66 Fontana TF 707 Little Man In A Little Box/Fat Man 25
67 Columbia DB 8238 Nothing Today/The Spanish Lady Tango 8

FAPARDOKLY
(see also Mu)
83 Psycho PSYCHO 5 FAPARDOKLY (LP, 300 only) 20

FARAWAY FOLK
(see also Harry H. Corbett)
70s Tabitha TAB 3 Shadow Of A Pie/Folsom Prison Blues/Rent A Man/Soulful Shade Of Blue 12
70s RA EP 7001 INTRODUCING THE FARAWAY FOLK (EP) 25
70s RA LP 6006ST LIVE AT THE BOLTON (LP) 30
72 RA LP 6012ST TIME AND TIDE (LP) 30
73 RA LP 6019 ON THE RADIO (LP) 30
74 RA LP 6022 ONLY AUTHORISED EMPLOYEES TO BREAK BOTTLES (LP, with Harry H. Corbett) 22
75 RA LP 6029 SEASONAL MAN (LP, gatefold sleeve with insert) 60
80s RA BATTLE OF THE DRAGONS (cassette) 15

MINT VALUE £

FAR CRY

69	Vanguard SVRL 19041	THE FAR CRY (LP)	25

DON FARDON

(see also Sorrows)

67	Pye International 7N 25437	(The Lament Of The Cherokee) Indian Reservation/Dreamin' Room	10
68	Pye International 7N 25475	(The Lament Of The Cherokee) Indian Reservation/Dreamin' Room (reissue)	5
69	Pye International 7N 25483	We Can Make It Together/Coming On Strong	5
69	Pye International 7N 25486	Good Lovin'/Ruby's Pictures On My Wall	6
69	Young Blood YB 1003	I'm Alive/Keep On Loving Me	40
69	Young Blood YB 1007	It's Been Nice Loving You/Let The Love Live	7
70	Young Blood YB 1010	Belfast Boy/Echoes Of The Cheers	30
70	Young Blood YB 1013	Delta Queen/Hometown Baby	5
70	Young Blood YB 1015	Indian Reservation/Hudson Bay	5
71	Young Blood YB 1021	Girl/Sandiago	6
71	Young Blood YB 1027	Follow Your Drum/Get Away John	6
70	Young Blood SYB 4	I'VE PAID MY DUES! (LP)	20
70	Young Blood SSYB 13	RELEASED (LP)	18

FAR EAST FAMILY BAND

75	Vertigo 6370 850	NIPPONJIN (LP)	40

DICK FARINA & ERIC VON SCHMIDT

(see also Bob Dylan, Richard & Mimi Farina, Four For Fun)

63	Folklore F-LEUT/7	DICK FARINA & ERIC VON SCHMIDT (LP, featuring 'Blind Boy Grunt')	70

RICHARD & MIMI FARINA

(see also Dick Farina & Eric Von Schmidt)

65	Fontana STFL 6060	CELEBRATIONS FOR A GREY DAY (LP)	30
65	Fontana STFL 6075	REFLECTIONS IN A CRYSTAL WIND (LP)	30
73	Vanguard VSD 21/22	THE BEST OF RICHARD & MIMI FARINA (2-LP)	15

FARINAS

(see also Family)

64	Victor Buckland Sound Studio	Bye Bye Johnny/All You Gotta Do/Twist And Shout (as James King & Farinas)	500
64	Fontana TF 493	You'd Better Stop/I Like It Like That	75

ALEXANDER FARIS ORCHESTRA

76	BBC RESL 37	Wings/The Sussex Lad (p/s)	6

CHRIS FARLOWE (& THUNDERBIRDS)

(see also Thunderbirds, Beazers, Little Joe Cook, Crane/Farlowe, Atomic Rooster, Colosseum, Dave Greenslade, Spectrum)

62	Decca F 11536	Air Travel/Why Did You Break My Heart?	60
63	Columbia DB 7120	I Remember/Push Push (as Chris Farlowe & Thunderbirds)	30
64	Columbia DB 7237	Girl Trouble/Itty Bitty Pieces (as Chris Farlowe & Thunderbirds)	30
64	Columbia DB 7311	Just A Dream/What You Gonna Do? (as Chris Farlow & Thunderbirds)	30
64	Columbia DB 7379	Hey, Hey, Hey, Hey/Hound Dog (as Chris Farlow & Thunderbirds)	20
65	Columbia DB 7614	Buzz With The Fuzz/You're The One (withdrawn, as Chris Farlow & Thunderbirds, demos more common £100)	200
65	Immediate IM 016	The Fool/Treat Her Good	15
66	Immediate IM 023	Don't Just Look At Me/Think	25
66	Immediate IM 035	Out Of Time/Baby Make It Soon	6
66	Columbia DB 7983	Just A Dream/Hey, Hey, Hey, Hey	15
66	Immediate IM 038	Ride On Baby/Headlines	15
67	Immediate IM 041	My Way Of Giving/You're So Good To Me	15
67	Immediate IM 049	Yesterday's Papers/Life Is But Nothing	8
67	Immediate IM 056	Moanin'/What Have I Been Doin'?	8
67	Immediate IM 065	Handbags And Gladrags/Everyone Makes A Mistake	10
68	Immediate IM 066	The Last Goodbye/Paperman Fly In The Sky (B-side with Thunderbirds)	12
68	Immediate IM 071	Paint It Black/I Just Need Your Lovin'	12
69	Immediate IM 074	Dawn/April Was The Month	12
70	Polydor 2066 017	Black Sheep Of The Family/Fifty Years	6
70	Polydor 2066 046	Put Out The Light/Questions (as Chris Farlowe & Hill)	5
75	Polydor 2066 650	We Can Work It Out/Only Women Bleed	5
78	Beeb BEEB 022	Gangsters (as Chris Farlowe & Dave Greenslade)/ DAVE GREENSLADE'S GANGSTERS: Sarah Gant Theme	6
65	Decca DFE 8665	CHRIS FARLOWE (EP)	100
65	Immediate IMEP 001	FARLOWE IN THE MIDNIGHT HOUR (EP)	50
66	Immediate IMEP 004	CHRIS FARLOWE HITS (EP)	40
66	Island IEP 709	STORMY MONDAY (EP)	120
66	Music For Pleasure MFP 1186	STORMY MONDAY (LP, reissue of Chris Farlowe & Thuunderbirds LP)	30
66	Columbia SX 6034	CHRIS FARLOWE AND THE THUNDERBIRDS (LP, black/blue labels with "Sold in the U.K..." text)	150
66	Immediate IMLP 005	14 THINGS TO THINK ABOUT (LP, lilac label)	50
66	Immediate IMLP 006	THE ART OF CHRIS FARLOWE (LP, mono, lilac label)	70
66	Immediate IMSP 006	THE ART OF CHRIS FARLOWE (LP, stereo, lilac label)	100
67	EMI Regal REG 2025	CHRIS FARLOWE (LP, export issue)	35
68	Immediate IMCP 010	THE BEST OF CHRIS FARLOWE VOLUME ONE (LP, lilac label)	30
69	Immediate IMLP 021	THE LAST GOODBYE (LP, pink label with "Sold in U.K..." text)	100
70	Polydor 2425 029	FROM HERE TO MAMA ROSA (LP, as Chris Farlowe & Hill, gatefold sleeve, insert)	60
75	Polydor 2469 259	THE CHRIS FARLOWE BAND LIVE (LP)	12

FARM

74	Spark SRL1105	Fat Judy/Gysy Mountain Woman	40

ART FARMER

(see also Clifford Brown, Benny Golson, Donald Byrd)

54	Esquire 20-033	ART FARMER SEXTET - WORK OF ART (10" LP)	40
55	Esquire 32-037	MUSIC FOR THAT WILD PARTY (LP)	30
56	Esquire 32-072	TWO TRUMPETS (LP, with Donald Byrd)	30

MINT VALUE £

59 London SAH-T 6028 MODERN ART (LP) ... 20
60 London Jazz LTZ-T 15184 BRASS SHOUT (LP) ... 20
60 London Jazz LTZ-T 15198 THE AZTEC SUITE (LP) ... 20
60 Pye Jazz NJL 45 MEET THE JAZZTET (with Benny Golson) ... 20
61 Esquire 32-120 EARTHY (LP) ... 30
64 London HA-K/SH-K 8135 INTERACTION (LP, as Art Farmer Quartet featuring Jim Hall) ... 20

JULES FARMER

59 London HLP 8967 Love Me Now/Part Of Me (Is Still With You) ... 15
59 London HLP 8967 Love Me Now/Part Of Me (Is Still With You) (78) ... 10

MYLENE FARMER

89 Polydor 080 360-2 Ainsi Soit Je. . . (Maxi Remix)/Ainsi Soit Je. . . (Lamentations)/
Ainsi Soit Je. . . (Classic Bonus Beats) (CD Video, export only) ... 45

FARMLIFE

82 Dining Out TUX 19 Susie's Party/Simple Men ... 6
83 Whaam! WHAAM 13 Big Country 1 & 2 (unreleased; Echantillan test pressings only) ... 40

GILES FARNABY'S DREAM BAND

(see also Druids)

73 Argo AFW 112 Newcastle Brown/29th Of May ... 12
73 Argo ZDA 158 GILES FARNABY'S DREAM BAND (LP) ... 45

FARNBOROUGH FIREWORK FACTORY

72 Decca F13290 Too Many People/She's Against The Law ... 8

ROBERT FARNON ORCHESTRA

(see also Jack Saunders)

56 Decca F 10818 Westminister Waltz/Poodle Parade ... 10
72 MCA MCA 117 Colditz March/That Italian Summer ... 5
58 Decca DFE 6470 JOURNEY INTO MELODY (EP) ... 8
55 Decca LK 4119 CANADIAN IMPRESSIONS (LP) ... 20
56 Vogue Coral LVA 9003 GENTLEMEN MARRY BRUNETTES (LP, soundtrack) ... 30
60 Delyse ECB 3157/DS 6057 CAPTAIN HORATIO HORNBLOWER (LP, soundtrack, mono) ... 40
60 Delyse DS 6057 CAPTAIN HORATIO HORNBLOWER (LP, soundtrack, stereo) ... 50
68 Philips SBL 7867 SHALAKO (LP, soundtrack) ... 15

ROBERT FARNON & TONY COE

(see also Tony Coe)

70 Chapter One CHS 804 POP MAKES PROGRESS (LP) ... 30

FARON'S FLAMINGOS

(see also Big Three, Mojos)

63 Oriole CB 1834 Do You Love Me?/See If She Cares ... 25
63 Oriole CB 1867 Shake Sherry/Give Me Time ... 30

WAYNE FARO'S SCHMALTZ BAND

69 Deram DM 222 There's Still Time/Give It Time ... 50

FARQUAHAR

71 Elektra EK45713 Hanging On By A Thread/Start Living ... 6
71 Elektra EKS 74088 FARQUAHAR (LP) ... 12

GARY FARR (& THE T-BONES)

(see also T-Bones, Richard Thompson, Mighty Baby, Meic Stevens, Kevin Westlake & Gary Farr)

65 Columbia DB 7608 Give All She's Got/Don't Stop And Stare (as Gary Farr & T-Bones) ... 50
68 Marmalade 598 007 Everyday/Green (with Kevin Westlake) ... 12
69 Marmalade 598 017 Hey Daddy/The Vicar And The Pope ... 18
71 CBS 5430 Revolution Of The Seasons/Old Man Boulder ... 8
65 Columbia SEG 8414 DEM BONES, DEM BONES, DEM T-BONES (EP) ... 100
69 Marmalade 608 013 TAKE SOMETHING WITH YOU (LP) ... 200
71 CBS 64138 STRANGE FRUIT (LP, with Richard Thompson & Mighty Baby) ... 100

MARY ANN FARRAR & SATIN SOUL

76 Brunswick BR 38 Stoned Out Of My Mind/Living In The Footsteps Of Another Girl ... 10

BILLY FARRELL

58 Philips PB 828 Yeah Yeah/Someday (You'll Want Me To Want You) ... 22

DO & DENA FARRELL

57 HMV POP 427 Young Magic/New Love Tonight ... 15

MICK FARREN

(see also Deviants, Twink)

78 Logo GO 321 Half Price Drinks/I Don't Want To Go This Way ... 6
78 Stiff LAST 4 ALL SCREWED UP (EP, as Mick Farren & Deviants) ... 8
70 Transatlantic TRA 212 MONA (THE CARNIVOROUS CIRCUS) (LP, lilac label with "t" logo) ... 100
78 Logo LOGO 2010 VAMPIRES STOLE MY LUNCH MONEY (LP, with lyric insert) ... 20
84 Psycho PSYCHO 20 MONA (THE CARNIVOROUS CIRCUS) (LP, reissue) ... 18

FARRIERS

76 Broadside BRO 119 KEMPION BRUMMAGEM BALLADS (LP, featuring Dick Brice) ... 50

MIA FARROW

68 Dot DOT 116 Lullaby From Rosemary's Baby (Parts 1 & 2) ... 8

FARTZ

82 Alt. Tentacles VIRUS 17 WORLD FULL OF HATE (12" EP with poster) ... 25

FASCINATIONS

67 Stateside SS 594 Girls Are Out To Get You/You'll Be Sorry ... 75
67 Stateside SS 594 Girls Are Out To Get You/You'll Be Sorry (DJ copy) ... 150
68 Sue WI 4049 Girls Are Out To Get You/You'll Be Sorry (reissue) ... 40
71 Mojo 2092 004 Girls Are Out To Get You/You'll Be Sorry (2nd reissue) ... 8
71 Mojo 2092 018 I'm So Lucky He Loves Me/Say It Isn't So ... 8

MINT VALUE £

FASCINATORS

58 Capitol CL 14942 — Chapel Bells/I Wonder Who — 350
59 Capitol CL 15062 — Oh, Rose Marie/Fried Chicken And Macaroni — 150

FASCINATORS

81 Penthouse PENT 9 — Blue Movies/Monochrome Moon (p/s) — 70

FASHION

79 Fashion FM 001 — Steady Eddie Steady/Killing Time (p/s) — 5
79 Fashion FM 002 — Citinite/Wastelife (p/s) — 5
80 Fashion FM 003 — Silver Blades/Silver Blades (A Deeper Cut) (p/s) — 5
81 Arista 12440 — Move On/Mutant Dance Move (p/s) — 10
79 FML001 — PRODUCT PERFECT (LP) — 12

FASHIONS

68 Stateside SS 2115 — I.O.U. (A Lifetime Of Love)/When Love Slips Away — 15
69 Evolution E 2444 — I.O.U. (A Lifetime Of Love)/He Gives Me Love — 8

FAST BREEDERS & RADIO ACTORS

(see also Radio Actors)
78 Nuke NUKE 235 — Nuclear Waste/Digital Love (in p/s, with insert) — 18
78 Nuke NUKE 235 — Nuclear Waste/Digital Love — 10

FAST CARS

79 Streets Ahead SA 3 — The Kids Just Wanna Dance/You're So Funny (1,000 only, p/s) — 250

FAST EDDIE

88 Westside DJINT 04 — Acid Thunder (12") — 25
88 Westside PROMO 18 — My Melody/Halloween House (12") (with Slick Master Rick) — 20

FAST EDDIE

82 Well Suspect BLAM 001 — My Babe/Help Me/Sweet Sensations (p/s) — 8

FAST SET

80 Axis AXIS 1 — Junction One/Children Of The Revolution (p/s) — 20

FAT

71 RCA LSA 3009 — FAT (LP) — 40

FATAL CHARM

79 Company CR 005 — Paris/Glitterbit/Out Of My Head — 8

FATAL MICROBES

(see also Pete Fender)
79 Small Wonder SMALL 20 — Violence Grows/Beautiful Pictures/Cry Baby (p/s) — 5

FATAL MICROBES/POISON GIRLS

(see also Poison Girls)
79 Small Wonder WEENY 3 — FATAL MICROBES MEET THE POISON GIRLS (12" EP, with insert) — 8

FATHEAD

83 Greensleeves GRED 118 — Champion/Stop All The Fight (12") — 20

FATHER BROWN

70 Decca F23059 — Maybe/The Yellow Moon Is High — 20

FATHER'S ANGELS

68 MGM MGM 1459 — Don't Knock It/Bok To Bach — 250
68 MGM MGM 1459 — Don't Knock It/Bok To Bach (DJ Copy) — 300
75 Black Magic BM 103 — Back To Bach/Disco Trucking — 6

FATMAN VERSUS JAH SHAKA

80 Live & Love LAP12 — DUB CONFRONTATION (LP) — 15

FAT MATTRESS

(see also Noel Redding Band, Jimi Hendrix Experience, Flowerpot Men, Juicy Lucy)
69 Polydor 56352 — Naturally/Iridescent Butterfly — 10
69 Polydor 56367 — Magic Forest/Bright New Way — 15
70 Polydor 2058 053 — Highway/Black Sheep Of The Family — 15
69 Polydor 582/583 056 — FAT MATTRESS (LP, open-out sleeve, red label) — 40
70 Polydor 2383 025 — FAT MATTRESS II (LP, red label) — 40

FATS & CHESSMEN

62 Pye International 7N 25122 — Big Ben Twist/Old Macdonald Had A Twist — 6

ERIC FATTER

(see also Eric Fratter, Afrotones)
69 Camel CA 20 — Since You've Been Gone (actually Eric Fratter)/WINSTON HINES: Cool Down (B-side actually by Winston Hinds) — 12

FAT TULIPS

88 Sweet William BILLY 001 — You Opened My Eyes/ROSEHIPS: Ask Johnny Dee (33rpm flexi, p/s w/insert) — 10

ERNIE FAULKNER

63 Sway SW 003 — Beautiful Girl/SAM DANIELS: Tell Me Baby (both with The Planets) — 10

FAUST

(see also Toni Conrad & Faust)
72 Faust/Polydor 2001-299 — It's A Bit Of A Pain/So Far — 10
79 Recommended RR 2.5 — It's A Bit Of A Pain/So Far (p/s, reissue) — 5
96 Die Stadt 011 — Right Between Yr Eyes (p/s, Uberschall Festival single, with Stereolab and Foetus) — 20
90 Chemical Imbalance CI 08 — Live In Hamburg (issued free with Chemical Imbalance magazine) — 25
97 CRDC 11 — Mikrowaves, Magic Brew And R Be Yr Ey (10", p/s) — 8
79 Recommended RR 1.5 — EXTRACTS FROM FAUST PARTY 3: Extract 1 / Extract 4 (EP) — 8
80 Recommended RR 6.5 — EXTRACTS FROM FAUST PARTY 3: Extract 2 / Extract 6 (EP) — 8
71 Polydor 2310 142 — FAUST (LP, initial pressing on clear vinyl, with clear sleeve & clear insert) — 80

MINT VALUE £

71	Polydor 2310 142	FAUST (LP)	20
72	Polydor 2310 196	SO FAR (LP, with 9 prints in wallet)	70
73	Virgin VC 501	THE FAUST TAPES (LP)	25
73	Virgin V 2004	FAUST IV (LP)	20
79	Recommended R.R. 2	SO FAR (LP, reissue, with 10 insert prints, numbered, 600 only)	20
80	Recommended RR 6	THE FAUST TAPES (LP, plastic bag cover)	15
90	Table Of The Elements 26	CONCERTS 1: LIVE IN HAMBURG (CD)	30
94	Table Of The Elements 27	CONCERTS 2: LIVE IN LONDON (CD)	30

FAVOURITES

80	4 Play FOUR 002	S.O.S./Favourite Shoes (p/s)	15
80	4 Play FOUR 003	Angelica/Cold (p/s)	15

FAVOURITE SONS

65	Mercury MF 911	That Driving Beat/Walkin' Walkin' Walkin'	150

WALLY FAWKES (& HIS TROGLODYTES)

(see also Sandy Brown)

57	Decca FJ 10855	Petite Fleur/Baby Brown (with Sandy Brown Quintet)	10
57	Decca FJ 10936	Sent For You Yesterday And Here You Came Today/Why Can't You Behave	10
58	Decca F 11002	The Pilot Fish And The Whale/Pale Blues	10
57	Decca DEF 6407	AND HIS TROGLODYTES (EP)	12
60	Decca DFE 6600	FLOOK DIGS JAZZ (EP)	12
61	Decca STO 136	A NIGHT AT THE SIX BELLS (EP)	15
56	Decca LF 1214	TAKIN' IT EASY (LP, with Bruce Turner)	20
58	Decca LF 312	FAWKES ON HOLIDAY (LP)	20

CHARLIE FAWN

80	Warner Bros K 17566	Always Something There To Remind Me/Poet For A Generation	8

BILL FAY

67	Deram DM 143	Some Good Advice/Screams In The Ears	60
70	Deram Nova SDN 12	BILL FAY (LP)	150
71	Deram SML 1079	TIME OF THE LAST PERSECUTION (LP, red/white label)	500

FAY & BITTER SWEET

74	A Rover AR 02	You're A Pirate Lover/Message To You	8

ALMA FAYE

78	Flamingo FM 6	I Believed/Instrumental	30

BRIAN FAYE & ORCHESTRA

(see under Brian Fahey)

FRANCIS FAYE

61	Vogue V 9186	I Wish I Could Shimmy Like My Sister Kate/Night And Day	10
61	Verve VLP 9007	SWINGING ALL THE WAY (LP)	15
65	Stateside SL 10129	YOU GOTTA GO! GO! GO! (LP)	25

FAZE ACTION

95	Nuphonic NUX 102	Full Motion (12")	10
00	Nuphonic NUX 150	Samba (12")	10
99	Nuphonic NUX 139	MOVING CITIES (2xLP)	15

FAZED IDJUTS

00	U Star USR 002	Dust Of Life (12")	20

FAZE ONE

86	Streetwave ELCST 15S	Layin' Down A Beat (Remix)/The Man	10

F.B.I. (FOLK BLUES INC.)

73	A&M AMS 7050	I Wonder What She's Doing Tonight/Boogaloo Boo-Boo	10
76	Good Earth GD 6	F.B.I./The Time Is Right To Leave The City	25
77	Good Earth GDS 802	F.B.I. (LP)	50
66	Eyemark EMS 1006	Don't Hide/When The Ship Comes In	25

FEARN'S BRASS FOUNDRY

68	Decca F 12721	Don't Change It/John White	50
68	Decca F 12835	Now I Taste The Tears/Love, Sink And Drown	25

FEAR OF FALLING

83	Excellent XL 7	Like A Lion/You My Prodigal Son (p/s)	20

CHARLIE FEATHERS

76	Charley CEP 116	CHARLIE FEATHERS (EP)	8

CHARLIE FEATHERS/MAC CURTIS

(see also Mac Curtis)

74	Polydor 2310 293	ROCKABILLY KINGS (LP, withdrawn)	25

FEATURES

77	Progress PR 01	Drab City/Job Satisfaction	60

FEATURES

80	Double D DDEE 3	Go Now/Make Me Wanna	10
80	ASM HIT 06	She Makes Me Blue/Don't Let Them Know	20
81	AFM PET 01	Monday-Friday/Cue The Next Army	20

FEDERALMEN

70	London HLU 10303	Soul Serenade/Scorcher	8

FEDERALS (Jamaica)

67	Island WI 3126	Penny For Your Song/I've Passed This Way Before	30
68	Island WI 3152	Shocking Love/By The River	25
69	High Note HS 024	Wailing Festival/Me And My Baby (B-side actually "By The River")	15
70	Camel CA 40	In This World/You Better Call On Me (B-side actually "Shocking Love")	10

MINT VALUE £

FEDERALS (U.K.)

(see also Winston's Fumbs, Yes)

63	Parlophone R 4988	Brazil/In A Persian Market	15
63	Parlophone R 5013	Boot Hill/Keep On Dancing With Me	15
64	Parlophone R 5100	The Climb/Dance With A Dolly	15
64	Parlophone R 5139	Marlena/Please Believe Me	15
64	Parlophone R 5193	Twilight Time/Lost And Alone	15
65	Parlophone R 5320	Bucket Full Of Love/Leah	20

FEEDER

96	Echo ECS 13	TWO COLOURS: Pictures Of Rain/Chicken On A Bone (p/s, clear vinyl)	50
96	Echo ECSCD 13	TWO COLOURS: Pictures Of Rain/Chicken On A Bone (CD, 1,000 only)	50
96	Echo ECS 27	Stereo World/My Perfect Day (p/s)	30
97	Echo ECS 32	Tangerine/Rhubarb (die-cut p/s)	15
97	Echo ECS 36	Cement/Pictures Of Pain (red vinyl, p/s)	8
97	Echo ECS 42	Crash/Here In The Bubble (clear vinyl, numbered p/s)	8
97	Echo ECS 44	High/Wishing For The Sun (sky blue vinyl, p/s)	7
98	Echo ECS 052	Suffocate/Eclipse (purple vinyl, p/s)	7
99	Echo ECS 75	Day In Day Out/Dance To Disco/Honeyfuzz (white vinyl, p/s)	7
01	Echo ECS 116	Turn/Come Back Around (purple vinyl, p/s)	7
01	Echo ECS 121	Just A Day/Early (orange vinyl, p/s)	7
01	Echo	Turn/Bad Hair Day (6-12 white label promo competition prizes. 7" die-cut sleeve)	20
04	Echo ECS157A/B -1	Tumble and Fall/Victoria (12" white label promos auctioned for Warchild charity)	20
96	Echo ECHLP 9	SWIM (LP)	15
97	Echo ECHLP15	POLYPHENE (LP, re-issue with free High 7")	20
04	Echo ECHLP52	PICTURE OF PERFECT YOUTH (3xLP)	25
04	Echo ECHCD52	PICTURE OF PERFECT YOUTH (CD, internet only release - deleted)	25

FEELIES

79	Stiff (no cat. no.)	Fa Ce La/The Boy With Perpetual Nervousness/ Everybody's Got Something To Hide (Except Me And My Monkey) (flexidisc, promo only, free with Be Stiff fanzine issue 6, 5,000 only)	6
79	Rough Trade RT 24	Fa Ce La/Raised Eyebrows (p/s)	7
80	Stiff BUY 65	Everybody's Got Something To Hide/Original Love (p/s)	7

FELDER'S ORIOLES

(see also V.I.P.s, Mike Patto)

65	Piccadilly 7N 35247	Down Home Girl/Misty	40
65	Piccadilly 7N 35269	Sweet Tasting Wine/Turn On Your Lovelight	20
66	Piccadilly 7N 35311	I Know You Don't Love Me No More/Only Three Can Pay	20
66	Piccadilly 7N 35332	Back Street/Something You Got	25

VICTOR FELDMAN BIG BAND/QUARTET

(see also Dizzy Reece, Tubby Hayes)

56	Tempo A 142	Big Top/Cabaletto	10
57	Tempo A 154	Jackpot/You Are My Heart's Desire	10
62	Fontana 267233	A Taste Of Honey/Valerie	10
55	Tempo EXA 29	BIG BAND (EP)	50
57	Tempo EXA 57	VICTOR FELDMAN IN LONDON -- THE QUARTET VOLUME 1 (EP)	60
57	Tempo EXA 67	VICTOR FELDMAN IN LONDON VOLUME 2 (EP)	60
58	Tempo EXA 85	MUTUAL ADMIRATION (EP, with Dizzy Reece)	55
53	Esquire EP 43	MODERN JAZZ QUARTET (EP)	40
53	Esquire EP 54	MODERN JAZZ QUARTET (EP)	20
53	Esquire EP 64	MODERN JAZZ QUINTET/SEXTET (EP)	25
53	Esquire EP 84	MODERN JAZZ QUARTET/SEXTET (EP)	20
54	Esquire EP 104	MODERN JAZZ QUARTET (EP)	40
54	Esquire EP 114	VIC FELDMAN ENCORE (EP)	15
54	Esquire 20 - 046	MULTIPLE TALENTS (LP)	50
55	Esquire 20 - 064	EXPERIMENT IN TIME (LP)	40
55	Tempo LAP 5	VICTOR FELDMAN'S SEXTET (10" LP)	180
56	Tempo LAP 6	VICTOR FELDMAN MODERN JAZZ QUARTET (10" LP)	160
57	Tempo TAP 8	VICTOR FELDMAN IN LONDON VOL. 1 (LP)	130
57	Tempo TAP 12	VICTOR FELDMAN IN LONDON VOL. 2 (LP)	120
58	Tempo TAP 19	TRANSATLANTIC ALLIANCE (LP)	240
59	Contemporary LAC 12172	THE ARRIVAL OF VICTOR FELDMAN (LP)	15
80s	Jasmine JASM 2002	TRANSATLANTIC ALLIANCE (LP, reissue)	12
80s	Jasmine JASM 2023	IN LONDON VOL. 1 (LP, reissue)	12
80s	Jasmine JASM	IN LONDON VOL. 2 (LP, reissue)	12

VICTOR FELDMAN, TERRY GIBBS & LARRY BUNKER

60	Top Rank 30/007	VIBES TO THE POWER OF THREE (LP)	20

JOSE FELICIANO

67	RCA RCA 1608	My Foolish Heart/Only Once	10
68	RCA RCA 1715	Light My Fire/California Dreamin'	6
68	RCA RCA 1769	Hi Heel Sneakers/Hitchcock Railway	5
69	RCA RCA 1871	And The Sun Will Shine/Rain	5
70	RCA RCA 1998	Destiny/Susie-Q	5
74	RCA RCA PB10094	Golden Lady/Virgo	15
71	RCA 2071	Shake A Hand/There's No One About	6

FELIUS ANDROMEDA

(see also Denis Couldry)

67	Decca F 12694	Meditations/Cheadle Heath Delusions	50

FELIX & HIS GUITAR

59	London HLU 8875	Chili Beans/Puerto Rican Riot	10

JULIE FELIX

70	RAK 101	If I Could/Alone	5
71	RAK 106	Snakeskin/Watching Waiting	50

			MINT VALUE £
72	RAK 14	Clothos Web/Windy Morning	25
65	Decca DFE 8613	SINGS BOB DYLAN & WOODY GUTHRIE (EP)	10
66	Fontana TE 17474	SONGS FROM THE FROST REPORT (EP)	10
64	Decca LK 4626	JULIE FELIX (LP)	18
65	Decca LK 4683	SINGS DYLAN AND GUTHRIE (LP)	18
65	Decca LK 4724	SECOND ALBUM (LP)	12
67	Fontana (S) TL 5437	FLOWERS (LP)	12

MIKE FELIX
(see also Migel 5)

66	Pye 7N 17058	You Belong To Me/Booga Dee	25
67	Decca F 12701	Blueberry Hill/I Don't Think You Want Me Anymore	8

RORY FELLOWES

68	S n B 55-3877	Nuina/Endlessly Friendlessly Blue	20

FELT
(see also Denim, Versatile Newts, Maurice Deebank, Cocteau Twins)

79	Shanghai S79/CUS 321	Index/Break It (p/s, early copies have notes on rear sleeve)	60
79	Shanghai S79/CUS 321	Index/Break It (p/s, no notes on rear sleeve)	50
81	Cherry Red CHERRY 26	Something Sends Me To Sleep/Red Indians/Something Sends Me To Sleep (Version)/Red Indians (p/s)	15
82	Cherry Red CHERRY 45	My Face Is On Fire/Trails Of Colour Dissolve (p/s)	12
83	Cherry Red CHERRY 59	Penelope Tree/A Preacher In New England (p/s)	10
83	Cherry Red 12CHERRY 59	Penelope Tree/A Preacher In New England/ Now Summer's Spread Its Wings Again (12", p/s)	12
84	Cherry Red CHERRY 78	Mexican Bandits/The World Is As Soft As Lace (p/s)	8
84	Cherry Red CHERRY 81	Sunlight Bathed The Golden Glow/Fortune (p/s)	15
84	Cherry Red 12CHERRY 81	Sunlight Bathed The Golden Glow/Fortune/Sunlight Strings (12", p/s)	12
85	Cherry Red 12CHERRY 89	Primitive Painters/Cathedral (12", p/s, with Liz Frazer)	10
86	Creation CRE 027	Ballad Of The Band/I Didn't Mean To Hurt You (p/s)	8
86	Creation CRE 032	Rain Of Crystal Spires/I Will Die With My Head In Flames (p/s)	8
88	Cherry Red CDCHERRY 89	Primitive Painters/Cathedral (reissue, picture CD)	10
88	Creation CRE 060	Space Blues/Tuesday's Secret (ltd. ed. die-cut company sleeve)	6
82	Cherry Red MRED 25	CRUMBLING THE ANTISEPTIC BEAUTY (LP)	15
84	Cherry Red MRED 57	THE SPLENDOUR OF FEAR (LP)	20
84	Cherry Red BRED 63	STRANGE IDOLS PATTERN (LP)	12
87	Cherry Red BRED 79	GOLD MINE TRASH (LP)	15
90	Creation CRELP 069	BUBBLEGUM PERFUME (LP)	12

FEMININE TOUCH featuring DUKE DURRELL

76	Paladin PAL 11	You Make Me Come Alive/You Make Me Come Alive (Instrumental)	5

JAYMES FENDA & VULCANS

64	Parlophone R 5210	Mistletoe Love/The Only Girl	12

FREDDY FENDER

74	ABC 4045	Before The Next Teardrop Falls/Waiting For Your Love	6

JAN FENDER

71	Prince Buster PB 5	Sea Of Love/PRINCE BUSTER: Heaven Help Us All	15
71	Fab FAB 164	Sweet P/CLIFF & ORGANIZERS: Mr Brown	25
71	Fab FAB 166	Holly Holy Version/Old Kentrone Version (as Jal Fender)	12

PETE FENDER
(see also Fatal Microbes, Omega Tribe)

81	Xntrix 2002	FOUR FORMULAS (EP, in 8" silk-screened book p/s)	30
81	Xntrix 2002	FOUR FORMULAS (EP, p/s)	8

FENDER BENDERS

79	Sticky SL 001	Big Green Thing/Hillman Hunter Paranoia (textured p/s, various colours)	6

FENDERMEN

60	Top Rank JAR 395	Mule Skinner Blues/Torture	15
60	Top Rank JAR 513	Don't You Just Know It/Beach Party	20

FENMEN
(see also Bern Elliott & Fenmen, Pretty Things, Zac Zolar & Electric Banana)

64	Decca F 11955	Rag Doll/Be My Girl	20
65	Decca F 12269	I've Got Everthing You Need Babe/Every Little Day Now	15
66	CBS 202075	California Dreamin'/Is This Your Way?	12
66	CBS 202236	Rejected/Girl Don't Bring Me Down	25

PETER FENTON

66	Fontana TF 748	Marble Breaks, Iron Bends/Small Town	20
67	Fontana TF 789	I Was Lord Kitcheners Valet/Walking In Circles	15

SHANE FENTON (& FENTONES)
(see also Fentones)

61	Parlophone R 4827	I'm A Moody Guy/Five Foot Two, Eyes Of Blue	10
62	Parlophone R 4866	Walk Away/Fallen Leaves On The Ground	10
62	Parlophone R 4883	It's All Over Now/Why Little Girl	10
62	Parlophone R 4921	Cindy's Birthday/It's Gonna Take Magic	7
62	Parlophone R 4951	Too Young For Sad Memories/You're Telling Me	7
63	Parlophone R 4982	I Ain't Got Nobody/Hey Miss Ruby	10
63	Parlophone R 5020	A Fool's Paradise/You Need Love (solo)	10
63	Parlophone R 5047	Don't Do That/I'll Know (solo)	10
64	Parlophone R 5131	Hey, Lulu/I Do, Do You?	12
72	Fury FY 305	Eastern Seaboard/Blind Fool	20
74	Contour 2870 409	GOOD ROCKIN' TONIGHT (LP)	20
77	EMI NUT 2696	SHANE FENTON & THE FENTONES (EP)	10

FENTONES
(see also Shane Fenton)

62	Parlophone R 4899	The Mexican/Lover's Guitar	10
62	Parlophone R 4937	The Breeze And I/Just For Jerry	20

MINT VALUE £

FENWAYS

65	Liberty LIB 66082	Walk/Whip And Jerk	20

RAY FENWICK

(see also Spencer Davis Group, After Tea, Fancy, Ian Gillan Band, Wizard's Convention, Murgatroyd Band, Marlon, Forcefield, Syndicats, South Coast Ska Kings, Rupert's People)

78	Mercury 6007 176	Queen Of The Night/I Wanna Boogie	6
71	Decca SKL 5090	KEEP AMERICA BEAUTIFUL, GET A HAIRCUT (LP, blue/silver label with small logo)	60

FENWYCK

68	ERA ERA 100	State Of Mind/Away	50

FERDIA

78	Polydor 2904 012	A SIGH FOR OLD TIMES (LP)	15

FERDINAND & DILL

70	Pama PM 805	Take Back Your Nicklet/Blueberry Hill	8

WINSTON FERGUS

78	Arawak ARK DD 001	Fly Natty Dread/Loving Pauper (12")	40

H-BOMB FERGUSON

54	Esquire 10-372	Feel Like I Do/My Love (78)	25

HELENA FERGUSON

67	London HLZ 10164	Where Is The Party?/My Terms	50

JESSIE LEE FERGUSON & OUTER LIMITS

69	Pye International 7N 25492	New Shoes/Puttin' It On, Puttin' It Off	8

JOHNNY FERGUSON

60	MGM MGM 1059	Angela Jones/Blue Serge And White Lace	12
61	MGM MGM 1119	No One Can Love You/The Valley Of Love	7

MAYNARD FERGUSON ORCHESTRA

58	Emarcy EJL 1270	JAM SESSION (LP)	15
58	Emarcy EJL 1275	AROUND THE HORN (LP)	15
58	Emarcy EJL 1287	DIMENSIONS (LP)	15
59	Columbia 33SX 1146	MESSAGE FROM NEWPORT (LP)	15
60	Mercury MMC 14050	THE BOY WITH LOTS OF BRASS (LP, also stereo CMS 18034)	15
60	Columbia 33SX 1210	MESSAGE FROM BIRDLAND (LP, also stereo SCX 3245)	12
60	Columbia 33SX 1270	JAZZ FOR DANCING (LP, also stereo SCX 3338)	15
61	Columbia 33SX 1301	NEWPORT SUITE (LP, also stereo SCX 3368)	15
62	Columbia 33SX 1439	MAYNARD 62 (LP)	15
66	Fontana TL 5274	BLUES ROAR (LP)	18
66	Fontana TL 5293	COLOR HIM WILD (LP)	15
67	Fontana TL 5310	SEXTET (LP)	20
68	Atlantic 2464008	FREAKY (LP)	20
69	CBS 63514	BALLAD STLYE OF MAYNARD FERGUSON (LP)	20
70	CBS 64101	WORLD OF (M.F. HORN) (LP)	12
71	CBS 64432	ALIVE AND WELL IN LONDON (LP)	20
72	CBS 65027	M.F. HORN 2 (LP, gatefold)	15
73	CBS 65589	M.F. HORN 3 (LP)	20
73	CBS 65952	M.F. HORN 4 (LIVE AT JIMMYS) (LP)	20

ALEX FERGUSSON

(see also Alternative TV, Psychic TV)

92	Private Pressing AF 001	ALEX FERGUSSON (LP, white label, 500 copies, no sleeve)	25

FERKO STRING BAND

55	London HL 8140	Alabama Jubilee/Sing A Little Melody	25
55	London HLF 8183	Ma (She's Making Eyes At Me)/You Are My Sunshine	25
55	London HLF 8215	Happy Days Are Here Again/Deep In The Heart Of Texas	25
58	London HL 7052	Happy Days Are Here Again/Alabama Jubilee (export issue)	18
56	London RE-F 1041	PHILADELPHIA MUMMERS PARADE VOL. 1 (EP)	10
56	London RE-F 1052	PHILADELPHIA MUMMERS PARADE VOL. 2 (EP)	10
57	London HB-C 1064	THE FERKO STRING BAND VOL. 1 (10" LP)	15

FERMENA

71	Pama PM 839	Come What May/Version (B-side with Ranny)	8
73	Pama PM 879	Wonderful Dreams/Version	8

PHIL FERNANDO

58	Pye Nixa 7N 15142	Blonde Bombshell/Make Ready for Love	12
62	Palette PG 9029	(Come On And) Do The High Life/High Life Girl	8

ANDY FERNBACH

(see also Groundhogs)

69	Liberty LBL/LBS 83233	IF YOU MISS YOUR CONNEXION (LP, blue label)	150

MAJA FERNICK

72	Philips 6006 196	Give Me Your Love Again/Flowers In The City	30

FERRANTE & TEICHER

60	London HLT 9164	Theme From The Apartment/Lonely Room	7
61	HMV/Utd. Artists 7EG 8700	EXODUS (EP)	10

DIANE FERRAZ & NICKY SCOTT

(see also Nicky Scott, Ferris Wheel)

66	Columbia DB 7824	Me And You/Don't Pretend	8
66	Columbia DB 7897	You've Got To Learn/Like You As You Are	5
66	Columbia DB 7963	Sh-Boom, Sh-Boom/Allah Mobish	5

JOE FERRER & HIS DEVILS BOYS

61	Oriole CB 1629	Rockin' Crickets/Blue Guitar	20

MINT VALUE £

EUGENE FERRIS

66	Planet PLF 112	There Was A Smile In Your Eyes/Soft Moonlight	30

GEORGE FERRIS

71	Ackee ACK 117	With Every Dream/Diana	6

FERRIS WHEEL

(see also Linda Lewis, West Five)

67	Pye 7N 17387	I Can't Break The Habit/Number One Guy	25
68	Pye 7N 17538	Let It Be Me/You Look At Me	8
68	Pye 7N 17631	The Na Na Song/Three Cool Cats	8
69	Polydor 56366	Can't Stop Now/I Know You Well	6
67	Pye NPL 18203	CAN'T BREAK THE HABIT (LP)	40
70	Polydor 583 066	FERRIS WHEEL (LP, lyric insert, red label)	25

BRYAN FERRY

(see also Roxy Music)

73	Island IDJ 1	These Foolish Things/Sympathy For The Devil/Baby I Don't Care/ Loving You Is Sweeter Than Ever (promo)	30
74	Island WIP 6196	The 'In' Crowd/Chance Meeting (in p/s)	8
75	Island WIP 6234	You Go To My Head/Re-Make, Re-Model (DJ copies in generic promo p/s)	20
78	Polydor PPSP 10	Hold On I'm Coming/Take Me To The River (12", unissued, promo only, numbered stamped p/s)	20
73	Island ILPS 9239	THESE FOOLISH THINGS (LP, unissued gatefold sleeve)	400
76	Island ILPS 9367	LET'S STICK TOGETHER (LP, original issue)	15
78	Polydor POLD 5003	THE BRIDE STRIPPED BARE (LP, original with A//3 P matrix, includes 'Broken Wings', white label test pressings only)	200
94	Virgin V2751	MAMOUNA (LP)	30

CATHERINE FERRY

76	Barclay BAR 42	One, Two, Three/1, 2, 3	12

FESTIVAL

78	Nevis NEV 107	Something In Your Smile/Let's Make Love	45

FEVER TREE

68	MCA MU 1043	San Francisco Girls/Come With Me	10
68	Uni UNLS 102	FEVER TREE (LP)	80
68	MCA MUPS 347	ANOTHER TIME, ANOTHER PLACE (LP)	50

FICKLE FINGER

(see also Matchmakers, Mark Wirtz)

69	Page One POF 150	Fickle Lizzie-Anne/Cellophane Mary Jane	10

FICKLE PICKLE

70	Fontana TF 1069	Millionaire/Sam And Sadie	15
70	Philips 6006 038	Maybe I'm Amazed/Sitting On A Goldmine	6
72	B & C CB 178	California Calling/Doctor Octopus	8

FIDD

69	Polydor 56320	Guai Guai (From the film 'Baby Love')/Happy Walk	25

FI-DELS

72	Jay Boy BOY 69	Try A Little Harder/You Never Do Right	15
72	Jay Boy BOY 69	Try A Little Harder/You Never Do Right (DJ Copy)	30
70s	DJM DJS 689	Try A Little Harder/KEYMAN STRINGS: Instrumental Version (DJ copy p/s, £20)	10

KEITH FIELD

68	Polydor 56278	The Day That War Broke Out/Stop Thief	30

ALAN FIELDING

61	Decca F 11404	Scatter Brain/I've Got To Learn To Forget	8
62	Decca F11518	Too Late To Worry, Too Blue To Cry/You Reap Just What You Sow	6

FENELLA FIELDING

66	Columbia DB 8086	Big Bad Mouse/Later	7

JERRY FIELDING & HIS ORCHESTRA

54	London HL 8017	When I Grow Too Old To Dream/Button Up Your Overcoat	30
55	London HL 7001	Faintly Reminiscent/Blues Serenade (export issue)	15
55	London HL 7002	Pea-nut Vendor/Can't Help Lovin' Dat Man (export issue)	15
55	London HL 7003	Tea For Two/Here In My Arms (export issue)	15
55	London HL 7004	I'm In Love/Blue Prelude (export issue)	15
55	Brunswick 05399	The Gypsy In My Soul/The Glory Of Love	10
55	London RE-P 1026	DANCE DATE VOL. 1 (EP)	15
54	London H-APB 1022	FAINTLY REMINISCENT (10" LP)	15
54	London H-APB 1027	PLAYS A DANCE CONCERT (10" LP)	15
58	Brunswick LAT 8244	FIELDINGS ESRMULA (LP)	15

FIELD MICE

88	Sarah SARAH 012	Emma's House/When You Sleep/Fabulous Friend/The Last Letter (p/s)	10
89	Caff CAFF 2	I Can See Myself Alone Forever/Everything About You (foldaround p/s in poly bag with insert)	25
80s	Waaaaah BULL 40	Burning Word (1-sided flexi)	6
90	Sarah SARAH 024	Autumn Store Pt. 1/If You Need Someone/World In Me (p/s)	10
90	Sarah SARAH 025	Autumn Store Pt. 2/Anyone Else Isn't You/Bleak (p/s)	10
88	Sarah SARAH 18	Sensitive/When Morning Comes To Town/Penguins (foldout p/s, with poster)	12
91	Sarah SARAH 44	September's Not So Far Away/Hello And Goodbye (p/s, with insert)	20

FIELDS

69	Uni UNLS 104	FIELDS (LP)	60

FIELDS

(see also Rare Bird, Greenslade)

71	CBS 7555	Friends Of Mine/Three Minstrels	15
71	CBS 69009	FIELDS (LP, with poster)	70
71	CBS 69009	FIELDS (LP, without poster)	30

MINT VALUE £

BILLY FIELDS
55	MGM SP 1126	Sincerely/Thrilled	6
59	Mercury AMT 1067	The Greatest Love In The World/No Other Love	10

ERNIE FIELDS & HIS ORCHESTRA
59	London HL 8985	In The Mood/Christopher Columbus (with tri-centre)	8
59	London HL 8985	In The Mood/Christopher Columbus (78)	20
60	London HL 9100	Chattanooga Choo Choo/Workin' Out	10
60	London HL 9227	Raunchy/My Prayer	10
60	London RE 1260	SAXY (EP)	50
60	London HA 2263	IN THE MOOD (LP)	50

GRACIE FIELDS
57	Columbia DB 3953	Around The World/Far Away	6
59	Columbia DB 4360	Little Donkey/The Carefree Heart	7

IRVING FIELDS TRIO & ORCHESTRA
54	Parlophone CMSP 9	Mr. Piano Player/Cuban Carnival (export issue)	10

KANSAS FIELDS & MILTON SEALEY
56	Ducretet DEP 95017	KANSAS FIELDS & MILTON SEALEY (EP)	10

FIELDS OF THE NEPHILIM
84	Tower N1	BURNING THE FIELDS (12" EP, red/black p/s)	30
85	Tower N1/Jung. JUNG 28T	BURNING THE FIELDS (12" EP, green p/s with insert & band photo label)	8
85	Tower N1/Jung. JUNG 28T	BURNING THE FIELDS (12" EP, green & other coloured vinyl export issue)	8
86	Situation 2 SIT 42	Power/Secrets (7", white label promos only, stickered plain sleeve)	15
87	Situation 2 SIT 46	Preacher Man/Laura II (p/s, swith Beggars Banquet sticker)	35
87	Situation 2 SIT 46	Preacher Man/Laura II (p/s)	25
87	Situation 2 SIT 48	Blue Water/In Every Dream Home A Heartache (p/s)	10
87	Situation 2 SIT 48T	Blue Water (Electrostatic)/In Every Dream Home A Heartache (live)/ Blue Water (Hot Wire) (12", p/s, with poster)	15
87	Situation 2 SIT 48T	Blue Water (Electrostatic)/In Every Dream Home A Heartache (live)/ Blue Water (Hot Wire) (12", p/s, without poster)	8
87	House Of Dolls HOD 15	Dawnrazor (on free EP with House Of Dolls magazine, issue 15)	8
87	House Of Dolls HOD 15	Dawnrazor (on free EP without House Of Dolls magazine, issue 15)	6
89	Situation 2 SIT 57	Psychonaut/Celebrate (Second Seal) (blue/green p/s)	6
90	Beggars Banquet BEG 250	Sumerland/Phobia (live) (no p/s)	5
88	Situation 2 SITU 22	THE NEPHILIM (LP, gatefold sleeve, with inner)	12
88	Situation 2 SITU 22L	THE NEPHILIM (LP, 2 x 45rpm 12", gatefold sleeve, numbered)	20

FIEND
84	Endangered EDR 1	STAND ALONE EP	12

FIESTAS
59	London HL 8870	So Fine/Last Night I Dreamed	45
59	London HL 8870	So Fine/Last Night I Dreamed (78)	35
71	Atlantic 2091 121	So Fine/Broken Heart	8

FIFE REIVERS
69	Columbia SCX 6371	FIFE REIVERS (LP)	15

FIFTH AVENUE
(see also Denny Gerrard, Warm Sounds)

65	Immediate IM 002	The Bells Of Rhymney/Just Like Anyone Would Do	30

FIFTH AVENUE BAND
69	Reprise RSPL 6369	FIFTH AVENUE BAND (LP)	35

FIFTH COLUMN
(see also Gerry Rafferty)

66	Columbia DB 8068	Benjamin Day/There's Nobody There	35

5TH DIMENSION
67	Liberty LIB 12051	Go Where You Wanna Go/Too Poor To Die	30
67	Liberty LIB 12051	Go Where You Wanna Go/Too Poor To Die (DJ Copy)	45
67	Liberty LIB 12056	Another Day, Another Heartache/Rosecrans Blvd.	8
67	Liberty LBF 15014	Up Up And Away/Pattern People	8
68	Liberty LBF 15052	Carpet Man/Magic Garden	18
68	Liberty LBF 15072	Stoned Soul Picnic/Sailboat Song	10
68	Liberty LBF 15081	Ticket To Ride/Orange Air	6
68	Liberty LBF 15130	California Soul/It'll Never Be The Same	12
68	Liberty LBF 15143	Sweet Blindness/Good News	5
69	Liberty LBF 15180	California Soul/I'll Never Be The Same Again	5
69	Liberty LBF 15193	Aquarius - Let The Sun Shine In/Don'tcha Hear Me Callin' To Ya	5
69	Liberty LBF 15288	Wedding Bell Blues/Let It Be Me	7
69	Liberty LBF 15308	Blowing Away/Skinny Man	6
70	Liberty LBF 15356	I'll Be Lovin' You Forever/Train Keep On Movin'	25
67	Liberty LBL/LBS 83038	UP UP AND AWAY (LP)	18
68	Liberty LBL/LBS 83098E	MAGIC GARDEN (LP)	18
68	Liberty LBL/LBS 83155E	STONED SOUL PICNIC (LP)	20
68	Liberty SBL 135	PORTRAITS (LP)	12
69	Liberty LBS 83205	AGE OF AQUARIUS (LP)	15
70	Liberty LBS 83228	THE FANTASTIC 5th DIMENSION (LP)	12

FIFTH ESTATE
67	Stateside SS 2034	Ding Dong The Witch Is Dead/Rub A Dub	10
67	Stateside SS 2068	Heigh Ho/It's Waiting There For You	10
68	Stateside SS 2105	Do Drop In/That's Love	7
69	Stateside SS 2125	Coney Island Sally/Tomorrow Is My Turn	10

FIFTY FANTASTICS
(see also Steppes, Disco Zombies)

79	South Circular SGS 108	God's Got Religion/STEPPES: The Beat Drill (white label)	10
80	Dining Out TUX 5	God's Got Religion/The Beat Drill (reissue, foldout p/s, hand-made labels)	10

MINT VALUE £

FIFTY FOOT HOSE
69 Mercury SLML 4030 — CAULDRON (LP) — 140

50 YEAR VOID
(see also St. Etienne, Sarah Cracknell)
92 BLADE 1 — Blade's Love Machine (1-sided 12", white label promo, 100 only) — 30

FIGGY DUFF
80 Dingles DIN 326 — FIGGY DUFF (LP) — 40
85 Celtic CM 023 — AFTER THE TEMPEST (LP, with insert) — 30

NESTOR FIGUERAS, DAVID TOOP & PAUL BURWELL
77 Bead Records BEAD 6 — NESTOR FIGUERAS, DAVID TOOP & PAUL BURWELL (LP) — 40

PAULINE FILBY
(see also Narnia, Accolade, Gordon Giltrap)
60s Church Miss. Soc. LIV/SP/81 — I'm Hungry/NADIA CATTOUSE: The Larder — 8
68 Herald ELR 1081 — MY WORLD BY PAULINE FILBY (EP) — 20
69 Herald LLR 567 — SHOW ME A RAINBOW (LP) — 90

PHILIP JOHN FILBY
71 Dart ART2007 — David McKenzie/Close My Eyes And Stick With Me — 12

FILE UNDER POP
(see also AK Process)
79 Rough Trade RT 011 — Heathrow/Corrugate/Heathrow SLB (p/s) — 6

FILMCAST
84 True Friends Music TF004 — The Distant Heart/World Of Light — 25

FILTHY PHIL & FAST EDDIE
(see also Motorhead)
89 Receiver RRLP 124 — NAUGHTY OLD SANTA'S CHRISTMAS CLASSICS (LP) — 15

FILTHY RICH
(see also Trident)
87 JM TR 102 — She's 17/Love Ain't A Fool (p/s) — 20

FINAL CONFLICT
89 Futuresound VFS 001 — My England/Across The Room (stickered white sleeve) — 20
86 Futuresound FS 001 — EP (EP) — 10
86 Futuresound FS 002 — THE TIME HAS ARRIVED (EP, with 22-page booklet) — 10

FINAL PROGRAM
81 Program FINAL 001 — PROTECT AND SURVIVE (EP) — 6

FINAL TOUCH
70s Myrrh MYR 1188 — LOVE SONG (LP) — 25

FINCH
78 Rockburgh ROC 103 — GALLEONS OF PASSION (LP) — 18

FINDERS KEEPERS (U.K.)
(see also Trapeze, Glenn Hughes, News)
66 CBS 202249 — Light/Power Of Love (withdrawn, promos may exist) — 60
66 CBS 202249 — Light/Come On Now — 15
67 Fontana TF 892 — On The Beach/Friday Kind Of Monday — 35
68 Fontana TF 938 — Sadie (The Cleaning Lady)/Without Her — 18

FINDERS KEEPERS (U.S.)
67 London HLH 10117 — Lavender Blue/MICKEY DOLENZ: Don't Do It — 12

JEM FINER
00s no cat. no. — LONGPLAYER (LP, with book) — 15

FINGERS
(see also Crocheted Doughnut Ring, Legend)
66 Columbia DB 8026 — I'll Take You Where The Music's Playing/My Way Of Thinking — 20
67 Columbia DB 8112 — All Kinds Of People/Circus With A Female Clown — 35

FINGERS INC.
87 Jack Trax 12 J TRAX 8 — Distant Planet Club Mix/Distant Planet Dub MIx (12", stickered die-cut company sleeve) — 45
88 Desire WANTX 6 — Can You Feel It/My House (Acapella) (12", die-cut p/s) — 30
88 Jack Trax JTX 20 — Can You Feel It (4 Mixes) (12", p/s) — 25
88 Jack Trax JTX 8 — Distant Planet (Remix, 4 Mixes) (12") — 60
89 Jack Trax JTX 2 — Never No More Lonely/Music Takes Me Up/DIstant Planet (Club MIx) (12") — 30
88 Jack Trax FING 1 — ANOTHER SIDE (2-LP, gatefold sleeve) — 30

FINI TRIBE (101)
84 Finiflex LT 1001 — CURLING & STRETCHING EP (12", p/s, original issue) — 10
88 Finiflex FT 002 — DESTIMONY EP (12", p/s) — 10
91 Finiflex/One Little Indian — 101: Sonic Shuffle (Edit)/101: 303 (3D Bass Edit) (promo only, plain stickered sleeve) — 5

FINK BROTHERS
(see also Madness)
85 Zarjazz JAZZ S2 — Mutants IN Mega-City One/Mutant Blues (shaped picture disc) — 10
85 Zarjazz JAZZ2-12 — Mutants IN Mega-City One/Mutant Blues (12", p/s with poster) — 12

LEE FINN & RHYTHM MEN
63 Starlite ST45 103 — High Class Feelin'/Pour Me A Glass Of Wine — 100

MICKEY FINN & BLUE MEN
(see under 'M')

FINN MACCUILL
77 Private pressing — SINK YE SWIM YE (LP) — 80

MINT VALUE £

SIMON FINN

70	Mushroom 100 MR 2	PASS THE DISTANCE (LP, with lyric insert, white/brown labels)	300

TIM FINN

(see also Split Enz, Crowded House)

83	Epic A 3932	Fraction Too Much Friction/Below The Belt (p/s)	5

LARRY FINNEGAN

62	HMV POP 1022	Dear One/Candy Lips	20
62	London HLU 9613	Pretty Suzy Sunshine/It's Walkin' Talkin' Time	20
65	Ember EMB S 207	The Other Ringo (A Tribute To Ringo Starr)/When My Love Passes By (p/s)	20
65	Ember EMB S 207	The Other Ringo (A Tribute To Ringo Starr)/When My Love Passes By	10

MIKE FINNIGAN

78	CBS 6656	Just One Minute More/Blood Is Thicker Than Water	20

FIRE

(see also Strawbs, Paul Brett's Sage)

68	Decca F 12753	Father's Name Is Dad/Treacle Toffee World	400
68	Decca F 12856	Round The Gum Tree/Toothie Ruthie	40
70	Pye NSPL 18343	THE MAGIC SHOEMAKER (LP, blue/black labels with logo banner at top)	400
97	Tenth Planet TP 029	UNDERGROUND AND OVERHEAD: THE ALTERNATE FIRE (LP, gatefold sleeve, numbered, 1,000 only)	18

FIREBALL XL5

(see under Century 21)

FIREBALLS

(see also Jimmy Gilmer, Buddy Holly)

59	Top Rank JAR 218	Torquay/Cry Baby	20
60	Top Rank JAR 276	Bulldog/Nearly Sunrise	18
60	Top Rank JAR 354	Foot-Patter/Kissin'	15
60	Top Rank JAR 507	Vaquero (Cowboy)/Chief Whoopin'-Koff	15
61	Pye International 7N 25092	Quite A Party/Gunshot	15
62	Stateside SS 106	Rik-A-Tik/Yacky Doo	10
63	Stateside SS 151	Carioca/Find Me A Golden Street	10
65	Stateside SS 417	Baby What's Wrong/Yummie Yama Papa	10
67	Stateside SS 2095	Bottle Of Wine/Ain't That Rain	6
68	Stateside SS 2106	Goin' Away/Groovy Motions	6
69	Stateside SS 2134	Come On, React!/Woman Help Me	6
69	London HLZ 10260	Long Green/Light In The Window	6
61	Top Rank 35/105	VAQUERO (LP)	100
68	Stateside S(S)L 10237	BOTTLE OF WINE (LP)	20
69	London HA/SH 8396	COME ON, REACT! (LP)	20

FIREBIRD

74	Bell Bell 1370	Two Wheels/Side Tracking	5

FIREBIRD

79	Rat SRTS79/CUS576	Change/Nightride	40

FIREBRAND

85	What WR 71	Never Felt This Way Before/I'm Leaving (p/s)	75

FIRECLOWN

83	Fireclown FC 1001	INVASION EP (Magic/Poor Man/Invasion) (10", no p/s)	12

FIRE ENGINES

80	Codex Comms. CDX 01	Get Up And Use Me/Everything's Roses (p/s)	15
81	Pop:Aural POP 010	Candy Skin/Meat Whiplash (foldout p/s in poly bag)	12
81	Pop:Aural POP 013	Big Gold Dream/Sympathetic Anaesthetic (p/s)	6
81	Pop:Aural POP 01312	Big Gold Dream/Sympathetic Anaesthetic/New Thing In Cartons (12", non-gatefold p/s; gatefold p/s £5)	7
81	Accessory ACC 001	LUBRICATE YOUR LIVING ROOM (LP, in plastic bag)	12

FIRE EXIT

79	Time Bomb Explosion 1	Timewall/Talkin' About Myself (p/s, stamped labels)	10

FIREFLIES

59	Top Rank JAR 198	You Were Mine/Stella Got A Fella	20
59	Top Rank JAR 198	You Were Mine/Stella Got A Fella (78)	20
60	London HLU 9057	I Can't Say Goodbye/What Did I Do Wrong	50

FIRE KINGS

77	Terminal TM 107	Poor Man Cry/Version	8

FIREMAN

(see also Paul McCartney, Youth)

99	Hydra HYPRO 12 008	Fluid (12", p/s, promo only)	35
99	Hydra HYPRO CD 008	Fluid (CD, promo only)	20
93	Parlophone FIRE 1	STRAWBERRIES OCEANS SHIPS FOREST (2-LP, clear vinyl, numbered white sleeve, with inners, promo only)	50
93	Parlophone PCSD 145	STRAWBERRIES OCEANS SHIPS FOREST (2-LP, clear vinyl, red sleeve, with inners)	50
98	HYPRO CD007	RUSHES (CD 3-track album promo)	20
98	Hydra 4970551	RUSHES (LP)	40

FIRE SESSION

70	Revolution REV 10	Souvenir/Bad Girl	6
70	Revolution REV 13	Sleeping Reggae/CAROLS: Everyday I Have To Cry Some	6
70	Revolution REV 14	Death Of The Ugly One/Big Feet	6

FIRESIGN THEATRE

68	CBS 65129	WAITING FOR THE ELECTRICIAN OR SOMEONE LIKE HIM (LP)	12
68	CBS 65130	HOW TO BE IN TWO PLACES AT ONCE WHEN YOU'RE NOT ANYWHERE AT ALL? (LP)	12
72	CBS CQ 30737	FIRESIGN THEATRE (LP, quadrophonic)	15

MINT VALUE £

FIRESTONES
62 Decca F 11436 Party Twist (Medley) (Parts 1 & 2) ... 6

FIRING SQUAD
64 Parlophone R 5152 A Little Bit More/Bull Moose ... 30

FIRKIN THE FOX
84 Woodworm WR 005 BEHIND BARS (LP) ... 25

FIRM
(see also Jimmy Page, Rock Aid Armenia)
85 Atlantic A 9586P Radioactive/Together (shaped picture disc) ... 8

FIRST AID
77 Decca TXS 117 NOSTRADAMUS (LP) ... 40

FIRST CHOICE
73 Pye International 7N 25613 This Is The House Where Love Died/One Step Away (unissued, demos may exist, this price for acetate) ... 400
74 Bell BLL 1376 The Player (Parts 1 & 2) ... 8
73 Bell BELLS 229 ARMED AND EXTREMELY DANGEROUS (LP) ... 20

FIRST CLASS
(see also White Plains, Edison Lighthouse, Brotherhood Of Man, Carter-Lewis & Southerners, Ivy League)
74 Sunny EON 102 Beach Baby/Surfer Queen ... 6
74 UK UKAL 1008 THE FIRST CLASS (LP) ... 18
76 UK UKAL 1022 S.S.T. (LP) ... 18

FIRST DOWN
90 Cobden Capers FD1 Jaw Warfare/From Now On/Dedication ... 70
93 Ill Gotten Gains FD002 LET THE BATTLE BEGIN (EP) ... 50
94 Blitz Vinyl EFA61008 MAD DOGS AND ENGLISHMAN (EP) ... 15
94 Blitz Vinyl EFA61009 WORLD SERVICE (LP) ... 40

FIRST EDITION
(see also Kenny Rogers)
68 Reprise RS 20655 Just Dropped In (To See What Condition My Condition Was In)/Shadow In The Corner Of Your Mind ... 30
68 Reprise RS 20693 Charlie The Fer'de Lance/Look Around I'll Be There ... 5
69 Reprise RS 20799 But You Know I Love You/Homemade Lies ... 5
68 Reprise RSLP 6276 THE FIRST EDITION (LP) ... 15

FIRST FRONTAL ASSAULT
91 Music Of Life NOTE 56 Blood Fire Assault (12") ... 8
91 Music Of Life NOTE 60 Atomic Air Raid (12") ... 8

FIRST GEAR
64 Pye 7N 15703 A Certain Girl/Leave My Kitten Alone ... 200
65 Pye 7N 15763 The 'In' Crowd/Gotta Make Their Future Bright ... 50

FIRST IMPRESSION
67 Saga SOC 1045 BEAT CLUB (LP) ... 12

FIRST IMPRESSION/GOOD EARTH
(see also Good Earth, Mungo Jerry)
68 Saga FID 2117 SWINGING LONDON (LP) ... 25

FIRST IMPRESSIONS
(see also Legends)
65 Pye 7N 15797 I'm Coming Home/Looking For Her ... 25

FIRST LIGHT
82 Oval FLIGHT 22/12 Don't Be Mistaken/Horse With No Name (12" p/s) ... 8

FIRST NATIONAL NOTHING (featuring J Marks)
70 CBS 5120 Purple Song/I Got The Answer (purple vinyl) ... 8

FIRST OFFENCE
88 Metal Other OTH 11 FIRST OFFENCE (LP, with insert) ... 30
88 Metal Other OTH 11 FIRST OFFENCE (LP, without insert) ... 25

FIRST OFFENCE
90 Blip Blip 3T Tell Em What You Like (12") ... 8
91 Blip Blip 5T Just Try Me (12") ... 8
91 Corona CRNT4 Round And Round/Three Steps (12") ... 10

FIRST STEPS
80 English Rose ER I The Beat Is Back/She Ain't In Love/Let's Go Cuboids (p/s, with insert) ... 20
81 English Rose ER III Anywhere Else But Here/Airplay/I Got The News (p/s) ... 20

CLARE FISCHER
62 Fontana 688124 ZL FIRST TIME OUT (LP) ... 15

WILD MAN FISCHER
(see also Frank Zappa)
69 Reprise RSLP 6332 AN EVENING WITH WILD MAN FISCHER (gatefold sleeve) ... 60

FISCHERMAN'S FRIEND
91 EG OP 51 Money (12", with "Orb Clubmix", 500 only) ... 12

FISH
(see also Marillion)
89 EMI 12EMPD 109 State Of Mind/The Voyeur (I Like To Watch)/State Of Mind (Presidential Mix) (12", picture disc) ... 8

F F & Z (FISHBAUGH FISHBAUGH & ZORN)
72 CBS 8163 Everybody Got Out Of Bed/Spaced On Happy ... 20

MINT VALUE £

ARCHIE FISHER
(see also Barbara Dickson)

68	Xtra XTRA 1070	ARCHIE FISHER (LP)	25
70	Decca SKL 5057	ORFEO (LP)	35
82	Celtic Music CM 007	ARCHIE FISHER (LP, reissue)	20

ARCHIE FISHER, BARBARA DICKSON & JOHN MacKINNON

69	Trailer LER 3002	THE FATE O' CHARLIE: SONGS OF THE JACOBITE REBELLIONS (LP, first pressing, white label)	60
69	Trailer LER 3002	THE FATE O' CHARLIE: SONGS OF THE JACOBITE REBELLIONS (LP, second pressing, red label)	30

CHIP FISHER

59	Parlophone R 4604	Poor Me/No One	15
59	RCA RCX 143	AT THE SUGAR BOWL (EP)	80

CILLA FISHER & ARTIE TREZISE

79	Kettle KAC 1	FOR FOUL DAY AND FAIR (LP)	15
76	Trailer LER 2100	BALCANQUHAL (LP, yellow label)	15

EDDIE FISHER

53	HMV 7M 101	I'm Yours/That's The Chance You Take	10
53	HMV 7M 115	Everything I Have Is Yours/You'll Never Know	10
53	HMV 7M 116	Trust In Me/Forgive Me	10
53	HMV 7M 117	Outside Of Heaven/Lady Of Spain	20
53	HMV 7M 125	Even Now/If It Were Up To Me	10
53	HMV 7M 126	Downhearted/Am I Wasting My Time On You	10
53	HMV 7M 133	I'm Walking Behind You (with Sally Sweetland)/Hold Me	10
53	HMV 7M 146	Just Another Polka/When I Was Young (Yes, Very Young)	8
53	HMV 7M 159	Wish You Were Here/A Fool Was I	10
53	HMV 7M 168	Many Times/With These Hands	8
54	HMV 7M 172	Oh My Papa/(I Never Missed You) Until You Said "Goodbye"	10
54	HMV 7M 185	How Deep Is The Ocean?/That Old Feeling	6
54	HMV 7M 201	April Showers/Just To Be With You	6
54	HMV 7M 212	I'm In The Mood For Love/A Girl, A Girl	6
54	HMV 7M 235	May I Sing To You?/My Friend	6
54	HMV 7M 242	How Do You Speak To An Angel?/My Arms, My Heart, My Love	6
54	HMV 7M 251	I Need You Now/Heaven Was Never Like This	6
54	HMV 7M 257	They Say It's Wonderful/Green Years	6
54	HMV 7M 266	Count Your Blessings Instead Of Sheep/White Christmas	6
56	HMV 7M 374	Dungaree Doll/If It Hadn't Been For You	10
56	HMV POP 273	Cindy, Oh Cindy/Fanny	10

FAYE FISHER

65	Columbia DB 7575	Our Love/I Just Don't Know What To Say	7
65	Columbia DB 7732	Oh Heartache You're Bothering Me/It's You	7

MATTHEW FISHER
(see also Procol Harum, Green Bullfrog)

73	RCA SF8380	JOURNEY'S END (LP)	15

RAY FISHER

72	Trailer LER 2038	THE BONNY LASS (LP, red label)	25
72	Trailer LER 2038	THE BONNY LASS (LP, later yellow label)	12

SONNY FISHER

77	Ace NST 59	Rockin' Daddy/I Can't Lose (78)	20

TONI FISHER

60	Top Rank JAR 261	The Big Hurt/Memphis Belle	8
60	Top Rank JAR 341	How Deep Is The Ocean/Blue, Blue, Blue	10
62	London HLX 9564	West Of The Wall/What Did I Do	10

FISHER BROTHERS

64	London HLN 9928	Big Round Wheel/By The Time You Read This Letter	10

FISHER FAMILY

60s	Topic TOP 67	FAR OVER THE FORTH (EP)	8
66	Topic 12T 137	THE FISHER FAMILY (LP)	15

FISHERFOLK

78	Celebration CR 1007	WORSHIP WITH THE FISHERFOLK (LP)	12
80	Celebration CR 1025	THE SUN'S GONNA SHINE (LP)	12
82	Celebration CR 1028	JOY IN THE MORNING (LP)	12
82	Celebration CR 1030	WILLING TO ROW (LP)	12

FISH TURNED HUMAN

79	Sequel PART 1	TURKEYS IN CHINA (EP)	15

FIST

80	Neat NEAT 04	Name Rank And Serial Number/You'll Never Get Me In One Of Those (p/s, with poster insert)	10
80	Neat NEAT 04	Name Rank And Serial Number/You'll Never Get Me In One Of Those (p/s)	8
80	MCA MCA 615	Name Rank And Serial Number/You'll Never Get Me (In One Of Those) (p/s, reissue, with poster insert)	30
80	MCA MCA 615	Name Rank And Serial Number/You'll Never Get Me (In One Of Those) (p/s, reissue, without poster insert)	20
80	MCA MCA 640	Forever Amber/Brain Damage (p/s)	12
81	MCA MCA 663	Collision Course/Law Of The Jungle (p/s)	100
81	MCA MCA 663	Collision Course/Law Of The Jungle	30
82	Neat NEAT 021	The Wanderer/Too Hot (p/s)	10
80	MCA MCF 3082	TURN THE HELL ON (LP)	15
85	Neat NEAT 1003	BACK WITH A VENGEANCE (LP, yellow vinyl)	30
85	Neat NEAT 1003	BACK WITH A VENGEANCE (LP)	15

MINT VALUE £

JOHN FITCH & ASSOCIATES

71	Beacon BEA 117	Romantic Altitude/Stoned Out Of It	75

FITS

82	Rondelet ROUND 13	Think For Yourself: Burial/Straps (p/s)	5
83	Corpus Christi ITS 9	Tears Of A Nation/Bravado/Breaking Point (p/s)	6
84	Trapper FIT 1	Action/Achilles Heel (p/s)	7
85	Trapper FIT 2	Fact Or Fiction/Give Away (p/s)	5
81	Beat The System FIT 1	YOU SAID WE'D NEVER MAKE IT (EP, wraparound p/s)	10
82	Rondelet ABOUT 6	NOTHING AND NOWHERE (LP)	12
82	Rondelet ABOUT 6	YOU'RE NOTHING, YOU'RE NOWHERE (LP)	15

FITZ & COOLERS

68	Nu Beat NB 003	Cover Me/Darling	12

ELLA FITZGERALD

(see also Oscar Peterson, Count Basie, Ink Spots)

SINGLES

54	Brunswick 05324	Who's Afraid (Not I, Not I, Not I)/I Wished On The Moon (with Gordon Jenkins)	8
55	Brunswick 05392	Lullaby Of Birdland/Later	8
55	Brunswick 05427	Moanin' Low/Take A Chance On Love	6
55	Brunswick 05468	Lover, Come Back To Me/Old Devil Moon	6
55	Brunswick 05473	Pete Kelly's Blues/Hard Hearted Hannah	6
55	Brunswick 05477	Soldier Boy/Air Mail Special (with Bill Doggett)	6
56	Brunswick 05514	My One And Only Love/(Love Is) The Tender Trap	6
56	Brunswick 05539	Ella's Contribution To The Blues/Early Autumn	7
56	Brunswick 05584	You'll Never Know/But Not Like Mine	5
56	HMV POP 266	The Silent Treatment/The Sun Forgot To Shine This Morning	5
57	HMV POP 290	A Beautiful Friendship/Too Young For The Blues	5
57	HMV POP 316	Hotta Chocolatta/Stay There	5
57	HMV POP 348	Johnny One Note/To Keep My Love Alive	5
57	HMV POP 373	Ev'ry Time We Say Goodbye/Manhattan	5
57	HMV POP 380	Goody Goody/A Tisket, A Tasket	5
58	HMV POP 486	The Swingin' Shepherd Blues/Midnight Sun	5
58	HMV POP 499	Beale Street Blues/St. Louis Blues	5
58	HMV POP 518	Your Red Wagon/Trav'lin Light	5
59	Brunswick 05783	My Happiness/A Satisfied Mind	5
59	HMV POP 657	But Not For Me/You Make Me Feel So Young	5
59	HMV POP 686	The Christmas Song/You Make Me Feel So Young	5
60	HMV POP 701	Like Young/Beat Me Daddy Eight To The Bar	5
60	HMV POP 719	It's All Right With Me/Don'cha Go Way Mad (with Oscar Peterson)	5
60	HMV POP 736	Mack The Knife/Lorelei	5
60	HMV POP 782	How High The Moon (Parts 1 & 2)	8
60	HMV POP 809	Good Morning Blues/Jingle Blues	5
60	HMV POP 817	We Three Kings Of Orient Are/White Christmas	5
61	HMV POP 849	The Lady Is A Tramp/Misty	5
64	Verve VS 502	Desafinado/Stardust	5
65	Verve VS 519	Can't Buy Me Love/Sweetest Sound	6
65	Verve VS 524	Why Was I Born/All The Things You Are	5
66	Stateside SS 569	These Boots Were Made for Walkin'/Stardust	5
69	Reprise RS 20850	Get Ready/Open Your Window	25
69	Polydor 56767	Hey Jude/Sunshine Of Your Love	10
71	Reprise RS 23507	I Heard It Through The Grapevine/Days Of Wine & Roses	6

LPs

53	Brunswick LA 8581	SOUVENIR ALBUM (10")	20
54	Brunswick LA 8648	ELLA SINGS GERSHWIN (10")	20
55	Brunswick LAT 8056	ELLA - SONGS IN A MELLOW MOOD	15
56	Brunswick LAT 8091	SWEET AND HOT	15
56	Brunswick LAT 8115	LULLABIES OF BIRDLAND	15
56	HMV CLP 1083	THE COLE PORTER SONGBOOK VOLUME 1	12
56	HMV CLP 1084	THE COLE PORTER SONGBOOK VOLUME 2	12
57	Brunswick LAT 8223	ELLA AND HER FELLAS	12
57	HMV CLP 1116	THE RODGERS AND HART SONGBOOK VOLUME 1	12
57	HMV CLP 1117	THE RODGERS AND HART SONGBOOK VOLUME 2	12
58	HMV CLP 1166	LIKE SOMEONE IN LOVE	12
68	Polydor 583737	SUNSHINE OF YOUR LOVE (LP)	20

ELLA FITZGERALD & LOUIS ARMSTRONG

56	HMV CLP 1098	ELLA AND LOUIS (LP)	20

ELLA FITZGERALD/BILLIE HOLIDAY

58	Columbia Clef 33CX 10100	AT NEWPORT (LP)	15

G.F. FITZGERALD

(see also Sam Gopal)

70	Uni UNLS 115	MOUSEPROOF (LP, gatefold sleeve, with insert, yellow swirl label)	150

PATRICK FITZGERALD

77	Small Wonder SMALL 4	SAFETY PIN STUCK IN MY HEART (EP, with lyrics)	7
78	Small Wonder SMALL 6	Buy Me, Sell Me/The Little Dippers/Trendy/The Backstreet Boys (p/s)	8
79	Polydor 2059 091	All Sewn Up/Hammersmith Odeons (p/s)	8
79	Polydor 2059 135	Improve Myself/The Bingo Crowd/My New Family (p/s)	8
78	Small Wonder WEENY ONE	THE PARANOID WARD/THE BEDROOM TAPES (EP, mono/stereo, 33rpm)	7
78	Small Wonder WEENY ONE	THE PARANOID WARD/THE BEDROOM TAPES (12" EP)	10
80s	Final Solution FSEP 001	TONIGHT (EP)	8
79	Polydor 2383 533	GRUBBY STORIES (LP)	12

FITZROY (Sterling) & HARRY

70	Bullet BU 439	Reggae Sounds Are Boss/Goodbye My Love	7
70	Escort ERT 827	Pop A Top Train/Doing The Moonwalk	10

MINT VALUE £

FIVE AMERICANS
66 Pye International 7N 25354 I See The Light/The Outcasts ... 25
66 Pye International 7N 25373 Evol - Not Love/Don't Blame Me ... 20
67 Stateside SS 2012 Western Union/Now That It's All Over ... 8
68 Stateside SS 2036 Sound Of Love/Sympathy ... 7

5 A.M. EVENT
66 Pye 7N 17154 Hungry/I Wash My Hands (In Muddy Water) ... 300

FIVE & A PENNY
68 Polydor 56282 You Don't Know Where Your Interest Lies/Mary Go Round ... 40
68 Polydor 56282 You Don't Know Where Your Interest Lies/Mary Go Round (2nd pressing injection moulded) ... 8

FIVE BLIND BOYS
64 Vocalion EPVP 1276 NEGRO SPIRITUALS (EP, 2 tracks by Spirits Of Memphis) ... 20
64 Vocalion EPVP 1282 FIVE BLIND BOYS (EP) ... 10

FIVE BLOBS
58 Philips PB 881 The Blob/Saturday Night In Tijuana ... 20
58 Philips PB 881 The Blob/Saturday Night In Tijuana (78) ... 12

FIVE BY FIVE
68 Pye International 7N 25477 Fire/Hang Up ... 50

FIVE CARD STUD
67 Philips BF 1567 Beg Me/Once ... 15

FIVE CHESTERNUTS
(see also Shadows, Pete Chester)
58 Columbia DB 4165 Jean Dorothy/Teenage Love ... 200
58 Columbia DB 4165 Jean Dorothy/Teenage Love (78) ... 120

FIVE COUNTS
62 Oriole CBA 1769 Watermelon Walk/Spanish Nights ... 30

FIVE CRESTAS
66 Excel ES SP 288/289 How Sweet It Is (To Be Loved By You)/You Used To Love Me (private pressing) .. 100

FIVE DALLAS BOYS
(see also Dallas Boys)
57 Columbia DB 4005 Shangri-La/By The Fireside ... 5
57 Columbia DB 4041 I Never Had The Blues/All The Way ... 5
58 Columbia DB 4102 26 Miles (Santa Catalina)/Sail Along, Silv'ry Moon ... 5
58 Columbia DB 4154 Big Man/Lonesome Traveller ... 8
58 Columbia DB 4231 Fatty Patty/Do You Wanna Jump Children? ... 8
59 Columbia DB 4313 Morning Papers/I'm Aware ... 7
61 Columbia DB 4599 One Finger One Thumb Keep Movin'/Nice To Know You Care ... 5
60 Columbia SEG 8035 THE FIVE DALLAS BOYS (EP) ... 15

FIVE DAY RAIN
(see also Scots Of St. James, Hopscotch, One Way Ticket, Glencoe)
70 Private pressing FIVE DAY RAIN (LP, no sleeve, 20-30 copies only) ... 800
93 Private pressing FIVE DAY RAIN (LP, re-pressing in signed, numbered sleeve, signed note in run-out groove & letter of authenticity, 25 only) ... 80

FIVE DAY WEEK STRAW PEOPLE
(see also Attack, Andromeda, John Du Cann)
68 Saga FID 2123 FIVE DAY WEEK STRAW PEOPLE (LP, black/silver labels) ... 160

FIVE DE MARCO SISTERS
53 MGM SP 1043 Bouillabasse/I'm Never Satisfied ... 7
54 Brunswick 05349 Love Me/Just A Girl That Men Forget ... 7
55 Brunswick 05425 Dreamboat/Two Hearts, Two Kisses (Make One Love) ... 10
55 Brunswick 05474 The Hot Barcarolle/Sailor Boys Have Talk To Me In English ... 7
56 Brunswick 05526 Romance Me/This Love Of Mine ... 7

FIVE DU-TONES
63 Stateside SS 206 Shake A Tail Feather/Divorce Court ... 20
68 President PT 134 Shake A Tail Feather/Divorce Court (reissue) ... 8

FIVE EMPREES
65 Stateside SS 470 Little Miss Sad/Hey Lover ... 15

FIVE FLEETS
58 Felsted AF 103 Oh What A Feeling/I Been Cryin' ... 200
58 Felsted AF 103 Oh What A Feeling/I Been Cryin' (78) ... 70

FIVE FLIGHTS UP
70 Bell BLL 1123 Do What You Wanna Do/Black Cat ... 6

FIVE GO DOWN TO THE SEA
83 Kabuki KAFIVE 5 KNOT A FISH (EP) ... 6
84 Abstract 12 ABS 027 THE GLEE CLUB (12" EP) ... 8
85 Creation CRE 021T Singing In Braille/Aunt Nelly/Silk Brain Worm/Women (12", p/s) ... 8

FIVE HAND REEL
76 Rubber RUB 019 FIVE HAND REEL (LP, with lyric insert) ... 12
78 RCA PL 25150 EARL O'MORAY (LP) ... 12

FIVE KEYS
54 Capitol CL 14184 Ling, Ting, Tong/I'm Alone ... 500
54 Capitol CL 14184 Ling, Ting, Tong/I'm Alone (78) ... 50
55 Capitol CL 14313 The Verdict/Make Me Um Pow Pow (triangular centre) ... 500
55 Capitol CL 14313 The Verdict/Make Me Um Pow Pow (78) ... 50
55 Capitol CL 14325 (Close Your Eyes) Take A Deep Breath/Doggone It, You Did It(tri centre) ... 450

MINT VALUE £

55	Capitol CL 14325	(Close Your Eyes) Take A Deep Breath/Doggone It, You Did It (78)	40
56	Capitol CL 14545	Gee Whittakers!/'Cause You're My Lover	300
56	Capitol CL 14545	Gee Whittakers!/'Cause You're My Lover (78)	25
56	Capitol CL 14582	She's The Most/I Dreamt I Dwelt In Heaven	250
56	Capitol CL 14582	She's The Most/I Dreamt I Dwelt In Heaven (78)	25
56	Capitol CL 14639	That's Right/Out Of Sight, Out Of Mind	150
56	Capitol CL 14639	That's Right/Out Of Sight, Out Of Mind (78)	20
57	Capitol CL 14686	The Wisdom Of A Fool/Now Don't That Prove I Love You?	150
57	Capitol CL 14686	The Wisdom Of A Fool/Now Don't That Prove I Love You? (78)	25
57	Capitol CL 14736	Four Walls/Let There Be You	100
57	Capitol CL 14736	Four Walls/Let There Be You (78	30
57	Capitol CL 14756	The Blues Don't Care/This I Promise You	150
57	Capitol CL 14756	The Blues Don't Care/This I Promise You (78)	40
58	Capitol CL 14829	From Me To You/Whippety Whirl	150
58	Capitol CL 14829	From Me To You/Whippety Whirl (78)	45
58	Capitol CL 14967	One Great Love/Really-O Truly-O	150
57	Capitol T 828	THE FIVE KEYS ON STAGE! (LP)	180

FIVE MILES OUT

73	Action ACT 4614	Super Sweet Girl Of Mine/Set Your Mind Free	20

FIVE NITES

64	Decca F 11963	With A Loving Kiss/Let's Try Again	15

FIVE OF DIAMONDS

65	Oak RGJ 150 FD	FIVE OF DIAMONDS (EP)	400

FIVE OR SIX

81	Cherry Red CHERRY 19	Another Reason/The Trial (p/s)	5
81	Cherry Red 12CHERRY 23	Polar Exposure (12" EP)	8
82	Cherry Red 12CHERRY 43	FOUR FROM FIVE OR SIX (12" EP)	8
82	Cherry Red FRIZBEE 2	A THRIVING AND HAPPY LAND (LP)	12

FIVE ROYALES

60	Ember EMB S 124	Dedicated To The One I Love/Miracle Of Love	150

FIVE SAPPHIRES

(see also Alan Carvell, Carvells, Telegrams)

78	Rocket ROKN 539	Love Music/Where Did All The Good Times Go	7
79	Warner Bros K 17307	Duke of Earl/Oh My Darlin'	5
79	Warner Bros K 17360	Once In A While/Falling in Love	5

FIVE SATINS

57	London HL 8501	To The Aisle/Wish I Had My Baby	750
57	London HL 8501	To The Aisle/Wish I Had My Baby (78)	150
59	Top Rank JAR 199	Wonderful Girl/Weeping Willow	50
59	Top Rank JAR 239	Shadows/Toni My Love	50
60	MGM MGM 1087	Your Memory/I Didn't Know	68

FIVE SMITH BROTHERS

54	Decca F 10403	A.B.C. Boogie/Veni-Vidi-Vici (with Dennis Wilson Quartet)	20
55	Decca F 10507	Paper Valentine/You're As Sweet Today (As Yesterday)	10
55	Decca F 10527	Don't Worry/I'm In Favour Of Friendship	10
56	Decca F 10698	You Took My Heart (My Only Heart)/The Grass Is Green	8
55	Parlophone GEP 8667	UP NORTH WITH THE FIVE SMITH BROTHERS (EP)	10

FIVE STAIRSTEPS (& CUBIE)

(see also Stairsteps)

68	Pye International 7N 25448	A Million To One/Something's Missing (with Cubie)	8
69	Buddah 201 026	Stay Close To Me/I Made A Mistake (with Cubie)	10
69	Buddah 201 070	We Must Be In Love/Little Young Lovers (with Cubie)	10
70	Buddah 201 083	Dear Prudence/O-o-h Child	15
70	Buddah 2011 036	O-o-h Child/Who Do You Belong To?	8

FIVE STEPS BEYOND

67	CBS 202490	Not So Young Today/Meanwhile Back In My Heart	25
95	Tenth Planet TP 019	FAINT HEARTS AND FAIR MAIDS (LP, 600 only)	15
96	Tenth Planet TP 021	SMILE (LP, with A4 booklet, 600 only)	15

FIVE THIRTY/5.30

87	Other 12 OTH 2	THE CATCHER IN THE RYE EP (12", p/s)	20

FIVE TOWNS

67	Direction 58-3115	It Isn't What You've Got/Advice	10

FIVEPENNY PIECE

72	Columbia SCX 6488	FIVEPENNY PIECE (LP)	15
73	Columbia SCX 6536	MAKIN' TRACKS (LP)	15
75	EMI EMC 3077	WISH YOU WERE HERE (LP)	12
76	EMI EMC 3234	BOTH SIDES OF (LP)	12
77	One Up OU 2050	ON STAGE (LP)	15

FIVER

70s	EMI 2401	When Love Walks Out The Door/I Don't Wanna Be Alone Tonight	6

FIVE'S COMPANY

(see also Brunning Hall Sunflower Blues Band)

66	Pye 7N 17118	Sunday For Seven Days/The Big Kill	12
66	Pye 7N 17162	Some Girls/Big Deal	6
66	Pye 7N 17199	Session Man/Dejection	18
69	Saga FID 2151	THE BALLAD OF FRED THE PIXIE (LP)	18

FIXED PENALTY

92	FPT 001	Man Of Action/All Of Us (12")	15
92	FPT 002	To You/Bubble Up (12")	12
92	FPT 004	Party Rocker (12"	12

MINT VALUE £

FIXER

78	Rainbow RSL 116	Bright And Rosy (no p/s)	40

FIZZARUM

99	City Centre Offices BLOCK 2	Phut Of Plex (clear vinyl, plain black sleeve, with inserts; 650 copies only)	8

FIZZBOMBS

87	Narodnik NRK 003	Sign On The Line/The Lines That (p/s)	8
88	Calculus KIT 002T	THE SURFIN' WINTER EP (12", p/s)	8

ROBERTA FLACK

(see also Donny Hathaway)

69	Atlantic 588 204	FIRST TAKE (LP, with Donny Hathaway)	15
71	Atlantic K 40097	CHAPTER TWO (LP)	15
72	Atlantic K 40297	QUIET FIRE (LP)	15
73	Atlantic K 50021	KILLING ME SOFTLY (LP)	12
75	Atlantic K 50049	FEEL LIKE MAKIN' LOVE (LP)	12

FLACK OFF

80	Sofa	FLACK OFF EP: COCKTAILS AT SIX	20

FLAG OF CONVENIENCE

(see also Steve Diggle, Buzzcocks)

82	Sire SIR 4057	Life On The Telephone/The Other Man's Sin (no p/s)	5

FLAIRS

57	Oriole CB 1392	Swing Pretty Mama/I'd Climb The Hills And Mountains	500
57	Oriole CB 1392	Swing Pretty Mama/I'd Climb The Hills And Mountains (78)	100

LES FLAMBEAUX

65	HMV POP 1456	Cachita/Greensleeves	5
71	Mushroom 100 MR 13	LES FLAMBEAUX (LP, 2 different sleeve designs)	30

FLAME

(see also Aerosmith)

77	RCA PC 12160	QUEEN OF THE NEIGHBOURHOOD (LP)	12

FLAME

(see also Flames [South Africa], Beach Boys)

70	Stateside SS 2183	See The Light/Get Your Mind Made Up	18
71	Stateside SSL 10312	THE FLAME (LP)	30

FLAME 'N' KING & BOLD ONES

79	Grapevine GRP 123	Ho Happy Day/Ain't Nobody Jivin'	20

FLAMES

(see also Maytals, Vikings)

64	Island WI 130	He's The Greatest/Someone Going To Bawl (both actually by the Maytals)	40
64	Island WI 136	Little Flea/Good Idea (both actually by the Maytals)	40
64	Island WI 138	When I Get Home/Neither Silver Nor Gold (both actually by the Maytals)	40
64	Island WI 139	Broadway Jungle/Beat Lied (both actually by the Maytals)	70
64	Blue Beat BB 205	Helena Darling/My Darling (both actually by Plamers)	20

FLAMES

(see also Alton Ellis & Flames, Righteous Flames, Larry Marshall)

68	Nu Beat NB 020	Mini Really Fit Dem/Soul Train (both actually by Alton Ellis & Flames)	10
69	Nu Beat NB 028	You've Lost Your Date/Little Girl	20
73	Ackee ACK 528	Feeling Good/Zig Zag	6

FLAMES (South Africa)

(see also Flame, Beach Boys)

68	Flame FAN 101/1	Streamliner/Follow The Sun (p/s)	20
68	Page One FOR(S) 009	BURNING SOUL (LP)	65

JOHNNY FLAMINGO

57	Vogue V 9089	My Teen-Age Girl/When I Lost You	120
57	Vogue V 9089	My Teen-Age Girl/When I Lost You (78)	40
58	Vogue V 9100	So Long/Make Me A Present Of You	75
58	Vogue V 9100	So Long/Make Me A Present Of You (78)	50

FLAMINGOS

57	London HLN 8373	Would I Be Crying?/Just For A Kick	600
57	London HLN 8373	Would I Be Crying?/Just For A Kick (78)	100
57	Brunswick 05696	The Ladder Of Love/Let's Make Up	500
57	Brunswick 05696	The Ladder Of Love/Let's Make Up (78)	80
59	Top Rank JAR 213	Love Walked In/Yours	50
60	Top Rank JAR 263	I Only Have Eyes For You/I Was Such A Fool	80
60	Top Rank JAR 367	Nobody Loves Me Like You/You, Me And The Sea	40
60	Top Rank JAR 519	Mio Amore/At Night	35
66	Philips BF 1483	Boogaloo Party/Nearness Of You	15
69	Philips BF 1786	Boogaloo Party/Nearness Of You (reissue, in p/s)	15
69	Philips BF 1786	Boogaloo Party/Nearness Of You (reissue)	10
70	Polydor 2066-007	Buffalo Soldier/Fontaineous Combustion	10
69	Philips SBL 7906	HITS NOW AND THEN (LP)	45

FLAMIN' GROOVIES

(see also Mike Wilhelm)

71	Kama Sutra 2013 031	Teenage Head/Evil-Hearted Ada	12
72	Kama Sutra 2013 042	Gonna Rock Tonite/Keep A-Knockin'/SHA NA NA: Rock'n'Roll Is Here To Stay/At The Hop/Duke Of Earl	8
72	United Artists UP 35392	Slow Death/Talahassie Lassie (in promo only p/s)	25
72	United Artists UP 35392	Slow Death/Talahassie Lassie	7
72	United Artists UP 35464	Married Woman/Get A Shot Of Rhythm And Blues	10

			MINT VALUE £
76	Sire 6198 086	Don't You Lie To Me/She Said Yeah/Shake Some Action (p/s)	7
76	Sire 6078 602	Shake Some Action/Teenage Confidential (p/s, 2 different versions of A-side)	6
76	Kama Sutra KSS 707	Teenage Head/Headin' For The Texas Border	5
78	Sire 6078 619	Feel A Whole Lot Better/Paint It Black/Shake Some Action (p/s)	5
78	Sire 6078 619	Feel A Whole Lot Better/Paint It Black/Shake Some Action (12", p/s)	8
76	United Artists REM 406	SLOW DEATH (EP)	10
71	Kama Sutra 2683 003	FLAMIN' GROOVIES (2-LP)	20
77	Sire 9103 251	SHAKE SOME ACTION (LP)	15
78	Sire 9103 333	THE FLAMIN' GROOVIES NOW! (LP)	15

FLAMING LIPS

89	Glitterhouse EFA 40153	Drug Machine In Heaven/Strychnine/What's So Funny (About Peace, Love And Understanding) (p/s)	20
91	City Slang 04063-05	Unconsciously Screamin'/Ma, I Didn't Notice/Let Me Be It/ Lucifer Rising (clear vinyl, hologram sleeve)	8
92	Warners PRO S 5452	Ballrooms Of Mars/MR BUNGLE: Sudden Death (promo, grey vinyl, no p/s)	15
94	Warners SAM 1431	She Don't Use Jelly/Translucent Egg/Turn It On (Bluegrass Version)/ The Process (12" promo)	15
95	Warners W 0322CD	Bad Days (Edit)/She Don't Use Jelly (Primitive Demo)/Girl With Hair Like An Explosion/Giraffe (Demo Version) (CD)	10
95	Warners W 0322CDX	Bad Days (Edit)/Ice Drummer (Suicide Tribute Album Contribution)/When You Smiled (I Lost My Only Idea)/Put The Waterbug In The Policeman's Ear (Ghetto Blaster Recording At The Art School, September 1993) (CD 'squidgy pack')	15
96	Warners WO 370CD	Brainville/Evil Will Prevail (Recorded On 'Brave New World', KCRW, Santa Monica)/Waterbug (Recorded On 'Brave New World', KCRW, Santa Monica)	8
98	Warners PRO CD 9295	The Big Ol' Bug Is The New Baby Now (Stereo Mix) (enhanced CD-Rom, stickered cardboard sleeve)	12
89	Enigma ENVLP523	TELEPATHIC SURGERY (LP)	20
90	City Slang SLANG 005	IN A PRIEST DRIVEN AMBULANCE (2-LP)	18
03	Warner Bros 9362481411	YOSHIMI BATTLES THE PINK ROBOTS (LP, inner sleeve, pink vinyl)	15
06	Warner Bros. WEA 9362 49966-1	AT WAR WITH THE MYSTICS (2-LP, one orange & one turquoise LP)	20
10	Warner Bros. 523541-1	DOING THE DARK SIDE OF THE MOON (LP, green vinyl, CD, insert, 500 only)	40

FLAMING YOUTH

(see also Genesis, Phil Collins, Jackson Heights)

69	Fontana TF 1057	Guide Me Orion/From Now On (Immortal Invisible)	20
70	Fontana 6001 002	Every Man, Every Woman And Child/Drifting	18
70	Fontana 6001 003	From Now On/Space Child	18
69	Fontana STL 5533	ARK II (LP, with laminated multifold plastic window sleeve)	120
69	Fontana STL 5533	ARK II (LP, later pressing with unlaminated multifold plastic window sleeve)	60
69	Fontana STL 5533	ARK II (LP, gatefold sleeve, white front, black/silver labels)	50

FLAMMA-SHERMAN

68	SNB 55-3488	No Need To Explain/Bassa Love	20
68	SNB 55-3769	Love Is In The Air/Super Day	18
69	SNB 55-4142	Move Me/Where Is He	18
69	SNB 55-4142	Move Me/Where Is He (DJ copy)	50

FLANAGAN & ALLEN

57	Columbia SEG 7709	TOGETHER AGAIN (EP)	8
55	Columbia 33S 1010	SUCCESSES (10" LP)	12

BUD FLANAGAN

69	Pye 7N 17854	Who Do You Think You're Kidding Mr. Hitler?/ BERNARD BEDFORD CHORUS: It Ain't Gonna Rain No mo'!	10

TOMMY FLANAGAN

59	Esquire 32-156	THE CATS (LP)	40

FLANAGAN BROTHERS

58	Vogue Coral Q 72342	Salton City/Early One Evening	20
58	Vogue Coral Q 72342	Salton City/Early One Evening (78)	10

TOMMY FLANDERS

(see also Blues Project)

69	Verve SVLP 6020	MOONSTONE (LP)	20

FLARES

61	London HLU 9441	Foot Stompin'/Hotcha Cha-Cha Brown	25
63	London HA-U 8034	FOOT STOMPIN' HITS (LP)	75

FLASH

(see also Peter Banks, Yes)

72	Sovereign SOV 105	Small Beginnings/Morning Haze	7
73	Sovereign SOV 116	Watch Your Step/Lifetime	7
72	Sovereign SVNA 7251	FLASH (LP, gatefold sleeve)	25
72	Sovereign SVNA 7255	FLASH IN THE CAN (LP, in unissued 'band in studio' proof sleeve)	25
72	Sovereign SVNA 7255	FLASH IN THE CAN (LP, gatefold sleeve)	15
73	Sovereign SVNA 7260	OUT OF OUR HANDS (LP, gatefold sleeve)	30

FLASH & BOARD OF DIRECTORS

68	Bell BLL 1007	Busy Signal/Love Ain't Easy	10

FLASH CADILLAC & THE CONTINENTAL KIDS

75	Private Stock PVT 29	Hot Summer Girls/Time Will Tell	6
75	Private Stock PVLP 1002	SONS OF THE BEACHES (LP)	15

FLASHPOINT

87	private pressing FP 01	NO POINT OF REFERENCE (LP)	40

FLAT EARTH SOCIETY

83	Psycho PSYCHO 17	WALEECO (LP)	20

MINT VALUE £

FLATMATES

86	Subway Organisation SUBWAY 6	I Could Be In Heaven/Tell Me Why/So In Love With You (foldaround p/s with insert in poly bag)	6
88	Subway Org. SUBWAY 17T	Shimmer/On My Mind/If Not For You/Bad (12", p/s, with 'flat sharing guide')	8

(Lester) FLATT & (Earl) SCRUGGS

67	Mercury MF 1007	Foggy Mountain Breakdown/My Cabin In Caroline	7
61	Mercury ZEP 10106	C & W TRAIL BLAZERS NO. 4 (EP)	10
64	Mercury 10010 MCE	COUNTRY AND WESTERN ACES (EP)	10

LINDA FLAVELL

66	Decca F 12312	And The Trouble With Me Is You/Over And Over	12

FLAVOUR

68	Direction 58-3597	Sally Had A Party/Shop Around	10

LOS FLECHAZOS

94	Detour Records DRO 13	Try It/You Drove Me Crazy (p/s, 100 red vinyl)	7

(FABULOUS) FLEE-REKKERS/FLEE RAKKERS

60	Triumph RGM 1008	Green Jeans/You Are My Sunshine (as Fabulous Flee-Rakkers)	40
60	Top Rank JAR 431	Green Jeans/You Are My Sunshine (reissue, as Fabulous Flea-Rakkers)	40
60	Pye 7N 15288	Sunday Date/Shiftless Sam	20
60	Pye 7N 15326	Blue Tango/Bitter Rice	15
61	Piccadilly 7N 35006	Lone Rider/Miller Like Wow	20
62	Piccadilly 7N 35048	Stage To Cimarron/Twistin' The Chestnuts	20
62	Piccadilly 7N 35081	Sunburst/Black Buffalo	20
63	Piccadilly 7N 35109	Fireball/Fandango	20
61	Pye NEP 24141	THE FABULOUS FLEE-REKKERS (EP)	75

(PETER GREEN'S) FLEETWOOD MAC

(see also Peter Green, Stevie Nicks, Buckingham-Nicks, Jeremy Spencer, Christine Perfect, Danny Kirwan, John Mayall, Otis Spann, Eddie Boyd, Duster Bennett, Chicken Shack, Shotgun Express, Bo Street Runners, Cheynes, Tramp, Brunning Hall Sunflower Blues Band)

SINGLES

67	Blue Horizon 57-3051	I Believe My Time Ain't Long/Rambling Pony (as Peter Green's Fleetwood Mac, with p/s)	100
67	Blue Horizon 57-3051	I Believe My Time Ain't Long/Rambling Pony (as Peter Green's Fleetwood Mac)	20
68	Blue Horizon 57-3138	Black Magic Woman/The Sun Is Shining	10
68	Blue Horizon 57-3139	Need Your Love So Bad/Stop Messin' Around	10
68	Blue Horizon 57-3145	Albatross/Jigsaw Puzzle Blues	6
69	Immediate IM 080	Man Of The World/EARL VINCE & VALIANTS: Somebody's Gonna Get Their Head Kicked In Tonight	10
69	Blue Horizon 57-3157	Need Your Love So Bad/Black Magic Woman (unissued)	0
69	Blue Horizon 57-3157	Black Magic Woman/No Place To Go (unissued)	0
69	Blue Horizon 57-3157	Need Your Love So Bad/No Place To Go	6
69	CBS 3051	I Believe My Time Ain't Long/Rambling Pony (reissue)	6
69	Reprise RS 27000	Oh Well (Parts 1 & 2)	6
70	Reprise RS 27007	The Green Manalishi (With The Two-Prong Crown)/ World In Harmony (initially with p/s)	30
70	Reprise RS 27007	The Green Manalishi (With The Two-Prong Crown)/ World In Harmony	8
71	Reprise RS 27010	Dragonfly/The Purple Dancer	5
71	CBS/Blue Horizon 3145	Albatross/Jigsaw Puzzle Blues (reissue)	5
72	Reprise K 14194	Spare Me A Little Of Your Love/Sunny Side Of Heaven	6
73	Reprise K 14280	Did You Ever Love Me?/The Derelict	5
73	CBS 1722	Black Magic Woman/Stop Messin' Around	5
73	CBS 8306	Albatross/Need Your Love So Bad (p/s, 'Hall Of Fame Hits' reissue)	5
74	Reprise K 14315	For Your Love/Hypnotised	5
75	Reprise K 14388	Heroes Are Hard To Find/Born Enchanter	5
75	DJM DJS 10620	Man Of The World/DANNY KIRWAN: Second Chapter	5
75	Reprise K 14403	Warm Ways/Blue Letter (with p/s)	6
76	Reprise K 14413	Over My Head (Edit)/I'm So Afraid	5
76	Reprise K 14430	Rhiannon/Sugar Daddy (with p/s)	6

LPs

68	Blue Horizon 7-63200	PETER GREEN'S FLEETWOOD MAC (mono, laminated front cover)	70
68	Blue Horizon 7-63200	PETER GREEN'S FLEETWOOD MAC (stereo, with stereo sticker, laminated front)	60
68	Blue Horizon 7-63205	MR. WONDERFUL (gatefold sleeve)	50
69	Blue Horizon 7-63215	THE PIOUS BIRD OF GOOD OMEN	30
69	Reprise RSLP 9000	THEN PLAY ON (gatefold sleeve, 'steamboat' label)	30
70	Reprise RSLP 9004	KILN HOUSE (gatefold sleeve, with insert)	35
70	Reprise RSLP 9004	KILN HOUSE (gatefold sleeve, without insert)	20
71	CBS Blue Horizon 63875	THE ORIGINAL FLEETWOOD MAC	30
72	Reprise K 44181	BARE TREES	18
77	Reprise K 54043	FLEETWOOD MAC (white vinyl with lyric sheet)	18
77	Warner Bros K 56344	RUMOURS (white vinyl with lyric sheet)	18

FLEETWOODS

59	London HLU 8841	Come Softly To Me/I Care So Much	10
59	London HLU 8841	Come Softly To Me/I Care So Much (78)	25
59	London HLU 4003	Come Softly To Me/I Care So Much (stereo export issue)	25
59	London HLU 8895	Graduation's Here/Oh Lord Let It Be Me	20
59	London HLU 8895	Graduation's Here/Oh Lord Let It Be Me (78)	35
59	Top Rank JAR 202	Mr. Blue/You Mean Everything To Me	15
59	Top Rank JAR 202	Mr. Blue/You Mean Everything To Me (78)	40
60	Top Rank JAR 294	Outside My Window/Magic Star (in p/s)	20
60	Top Rank JAR 294	Outside My Window/Magic Star	10
60	Top Rank JAR 383	Runaround/Truly Do	10
61	London HLG 9341	Tragedy/Little Miss Sad One	15

MINT VALUE £

61 London HLG 9426 He's The Great Imposter/Poor Little Girl 15
62 Liberty LIB 62 They Tell Me It's Summer/Lovers By Night Strangers By Day 10
63 Liberty LIB 75 Goodnight My Love Pleasant Dreams/Jimmy Beware 10
64 Liberty LIB 93 Ruby Red Baby Blue/Lonesome Town 10
65 Liberty LIB 10191 Almost There/Before And After (Losing You) 10
60 Top Rank BUY 028 MR BLUE (LP, with 3 tracks by Little Bill & Bluetones, Frantics and Bonnie Guitar) 30
61 London HA-G 2388 SOFTLY (LP, mono) 50
61 London SAH-G 6188 SOFTLY (LP, stereo) 60
61 London HA-G 2419 DEEP IN A DREAM (LP) 50

HELEN FLEMING

66 Blue Beat BB 341 Eve's Ten Commandments/Don't Take Your Love Away 15

JOY FLEMING

75 Antic K 11518 A Bridge Of Love/Divorcee 10
76 Private Stock PVT 54 Are You Ready For Love/Alabama Standby 20

RAY FLEMING

63 MGM MGM 1196 I'm Glad I Have You/Humpty Dumpty 10

WADE FLEMONS

59 Top Rank JAR 206 Slow Motion/Walkin' By The River 15
60 Top Rank JAR 327 What's Happening?/Goodnight, It's Time To Go 15
60 Top Rank JAR 371 Easy Lovin'/Whoops Now 15

FLESH FOR LULU

86 Dojo DOJOLP39 FRESH FLESH (LP) 12

FLESHEATERS

81 Initial IRC 007 A MINUTE TO PRAY, A SECOND TO DIE (LP) 18

FLESH VOLCANO

(see also Marc Almond, Foetus)

87 Some Bizzare SLUT 1 Slut/The Universal Cesspool/Bruisin' Chain (12", p/s) 10

DARROW FLETCHER

66 London HLU 10024 The Pain Gets A Little Deeper/My Judgement Day 75
66 London HLU 10024 The Pain Gets A Little Deeper/My Judgement Day (DJ copy) 150

DON FLETCHER

66 Vocalion VP 9271 Two Wrongs Don't Make A Right/I'm So Glad 25

GUY FLETCHER

69 Pye 7N 17765 Magic Woman/All Fall Down 6
71 Philips 6303013 GUY FLETCHER (LP, gatefold sleeve, black/silver lables) 20

SAM FLETCHER

59 MGM MGM 1024 Time Has A Way/No Such Luck 6
60 RCA RCA 1255 Tall Hope/You're So Far Away From Home 6

FLEUR-DE-LYS

(see also John Bromley, Terry Durham, Tony & Tandy, Sharon Tandy, Rupert's People, Shyster, Quotations, Bryn Haworth, Chocolate Frog, Gordon Haskell, Waygood Ellis)

65 Immediate IM 020 Moondreams/Wait For Me 250
66 Immediate IM 032 Circles/So Come On 800
66 Polydor 56124 Mud In Your Eye/I've Been Trying 800
67 Polydor 56200 I Can See A Light/Prodigal Son 80
68 Polydor 56251 The Gong With The Luminous Nose/Hammer Head 300
68 Atlantic 584 193 Stop Crossing The Bridge/Brick By Brick (Stone By Stone) 60
69 Atlantic 584 243 Liar/One Girl City 200

FLEVANS

04 Tru Thoughts TRU 069 MAKE NEW FRIENDS EP (12") 8

VIC FLICK SOUND

70 Chapter One CH 136 Hang On/Wonderful World 10
71 Chapter One CH 155 Quest For Love/Clarice 6

FLIES

(see also Bulldog Breed, T2)

66 Decca F 12533 I'm Not Your Stepping Stone/Talk To Me 175
67 Decca F 12594 House Of Love/It Had To Be You 70
68 RCA RCA 1757 The Magic Train/Gently As You Feel 50

MICK FLINN BAND

(see also Mixtures)

78 EMI EMI 2805 Doin' It Right/Do What You Wanna Do 20

SHELBY FLINT

61 Warner Bros WB 30 Angel On My Shoulder/Somebody 12
66 London HLT 10068 Cast Your Fate To The Wind/The Lilly 20

FLINTLOCKS

66 Decca F 12412 What Goes On?/I Walked Right Into A Heaven 10

FLINTSTONES

64 HMV POP 1266 Safari/Work Out 20

BUNNY FLIP

(see also Winston Scotland)

72 Pressure Beat PB 5510 Shanky Dog (actually "Skanky Dog" by Winston Scotland)/ JOE GIBBS & NOW GENERATION: Boney Dog 10

FLIP & DATELINERS

(see also Vivienne Chering)

64 HMV POP 1359 My Johnny Doesn't Come Around Anymore/Please Listen To Me 70

MINT VALUE £

FLIPPER

81	Alt. Tentacles VIRUS 8	Ha Ha Ha/Love Canal (p/s, with insert)	10
82	Subterranean SUB UK1	FLIPPER (LP)	35

FLIPS

62	London HLU 9490	Rockin' Twist/Oh, You Beautiful Doll - Twist	15

FLIPSIDE

84	Pandora PAND 1	Deputy Leader/Beat The Beatrice (p/s)	7

FLIRTATIONS

(see also Pearly Gates, Gypsies)

68	Deram DM 195	Someone Out There/How Can You Tell Me?	10
68	Deram DM 216	Nothing But A Heartache/Christmas Time Is Here Again	20
69	Deram DM 252	What's Good About Goodbye My Love?/Once I Had A Love	8
70	Deram DM 281	Keep On Searchin'/Moma I'm Coming Home	8
70	Deram DM 295	Can't Stop Loving You/Everybody Needs Somebody	8
71	Deram DM 329	Give Me Love/This Must Be The End Of The Line	8
72	Deram DM 351	Need Your Lovin'/I Wanna Be There	8
71	Polydor 2058 167	Little Darlin'/Take Me In Your Arms And Love Me	20
72	Polydor 2058 249	Love A Little Longer/Hold On To Me Babe	8
74	Polydor 2058 295	Dirty Work/No Such Thing As A Miracle	6
73	Mojo 2092 058	Why Didn't I Think Of That?/Oh Mia Bamba	6
98	London Traffic TRAF 1	Nothing But A Heartache (1-sided, reissue promo, 500 only)	8
69	Deram DML/SML 1046	SOUNDS LIKE THE FLIRTATIONS (LP)	40
72	Deram SPA 218	THE WORLD OF THE FLIRTATIONS (LP)	15
75	RCA SF8448	LOVE MAKES THE WORLD GO ROUND (LP)	15

FLO & EDDIE

(see also Turtles, Frank Zappa/Mothers Of Invention)

73	Reprise K 14261	Afterglow/Carlos And De Bull	5
72	Reprise K 44201	THE PHLORESCENT LEECH AND EDDIE (LP)	15
73	Reprise K 44234	FLO AND EDDIE (LP)	15

FLOATING BRIDGE

69	Liberty LBS 83271	FLOATING BRIDGE (LP)	45

FLOCK

(see also Mahavishnu Orchestra)

70	CBS 4932	Tired Of Waiting For You/Store Bought - Store Thought	8
69	CBS 63733	THE FLOCK (LP, orange label)	15
70	CBS 64055	DINOSAUR SWAMPS (LP, orange label, gatefold sleeve)	18

DICK FLOOD

59	Felsted AF 125	The Three Bells/Far Away	7

FLORIBUNDA ROSE

(see also Scrugg, John T. Kongos)

67	Piccadilly 7N 35408	One Way Street/Linda Loves Linda	40

FLOWERPOT MEN

(see also Ivy League, Friends, Carter-Lewis & Southerners, Edison Lighthouse, Fat Mattress, Gordon Haskell, Kestrels, One & One)

67	Deram DM 142	Let's Go To San Francisco (Parts 1 & 2)	5
68	Page One POF 065	Mighty Quinn/Voices From The Sky	10
67	Deram DM 160	A Walk In The Sky/Am I Losing You?	8
68	Deram DM 183	A Man Without A Woman/You Can Never Be Wrong	8
69	Deram DM 248	In A Moment Of Madness/Young Birds Fly	10
88	C5 C5-526	LET'S GO TO SAN FRANCISCO (LP)	12

FLOWERS & FROLICS

77	Free Reed FRR 016	BEES ON HORSEBACK (LP, featuring June Tabor & Bob Davenport)	35

FLOWERS IN THE DUSTBIN

84	All The Madmen MAD 7	FREAKS RUN WILD IN THE DISCO (12" EP)	15
85	Mortarhate MORT 16	Nails Of The Heart/All Fools Day/The Reason Why	12
86	Cold Harbour COLD 1002	Lick My Crazy Colours!/The Continuing Tragedy Of Mr. Smith/ Stranger In A Strange Land	12

LLOYD FLOWERS & RECO'S RHYTHM GROUP

62	Blue Beat BB 88	I'm Going Home/Lover's Town	15

(Lloyd) FLOWERS & ALVIN (Ranglin)

72	Explosion EX 2067	Howdy And Tenky/SHORTY PERRY: Sprinkle Some Water	7
72	Grape GR 3028	In De Pum Pum/MAYTONES: If Loving You Was Wrong	6
72	Bullet BU 512	Howdy And Tenky/SHORTY PERRY: Sprinkle Some Water	7
73	Duke DU 150	Rastaman Going Back Home/LITTLE YOUTH: Barble Dove Skank	6

FLOWER SERMON

92	Rough Trade 45REV 13	Sugar Lullaby (p/s with insert)	8

FLOWER SHOPPE

72	Polydor 2066 096	You've Come A Long Way/Kill The Monster	20

FLOWER TRAVELLING BAND

71	Atlantic 2091 128	Satori (Enlightment) (Parts 1 & 2)	20

BOBBY FLOYD

72	Pama PM 860	Sound Doctor/YOUNG DILLINGER: Doctor Skank	20

EDDIE FLOYD

(see also Falcons, Primettes/Eddie Floyd)

66	Atlantic 584 041	Knock On Wood/Got To Make A Comeback	8
67	Stax 601 001	Raise Your Hand/I've Just Been Feeling Bad (dark blue label)	10
67	Stax 601 001	Raise Your Hand/I've Just Been Feeling Bad (light blue label)	8

			MINT VALUE £
67	London HL 10129	Set My Soul On Fire/Will I Be The One?	10
67	Speciality SPE 1001	Never Get Enough Of Your Love/Bye Bye Baby	10
67	Stax 601 016	Things Get Better/Good Love, Bad Love	15
67	Stax 601 024	On A Saturday Night/Under My Nose	15
68	Stax 601 035	Big Bird/Holding On With Both Hands	15
68	Stax STAX 104	I've Never Found A Girl (To Love Me Like You Do)/I'm Just The Kind Of Fool	15
69	Stax STAX 108	Bring It On Home To Me/Sweet Things You Do	8
69	Stax STAX 116	I've Got To Have Your Love/Girl I Love You	5
69	Stax STAX 125	Don't Tell Your Mama/Consider Me	5
70	Stax STAX 153	My Girl/Laurie	5
72	Polydor 2025 098	Yum Yum Yum/I Want Some/Tears Of Joy	5
74	Stax STXS 2005	Soul Street/The Highway Man	5
81	I-Spy SEE 9	The Beat Song/London ('I-Spy' sleeve)	5
67	Stax 589 006	KNOCK ON WOOD (LP)	40
68	Stax (S)XATS 1003	I'VE NEVER FOUND A GIRL (LP)	30
69	Stax SXATS 1023	YOU'VE GOT TO HAVE EDDIE (LP)	20

FLUFF

70	DJM DJS 215	Make Believe/Love Machine	12

FLUTTERS

	STEW 101	Haunted Staircase/Something For The Children (P/S)	10

FLUX (OF PINK INDIANS)

(see also Epileptics, Licks)

81	Crass 321984/2	NEU SMELL (EP, foldout poster sleeve)	8
85	Spiderleg SDL 16	TAKING A LIBERTY (EP, as Flux, with booklet sleeve)	6
83	Spiderleg SDL 8	STRIVE TO SURVIVE CAUSING THE LEAST SUFFERING POSSIBLE (LP, with booklet)	15
84	Spiderleg SDL 13	THE FUCKING CUNTS TREAT US LIKE PRICKS (2-LP)	18
87	Overground OVER 87	LIVE STATEMENT (LP, 1,000 only)	12

FLY ON THE WALL

79	Next Wave NEXT 1	DEVON DUMB (EP, numbered)	20

FLYING BURRITO BROTHERS

(see also Byrds, Gram Parsons, Gene Parsons, Stephen Stills & Manassas, Rick Roberts, Country Gazette, Skip Battin)

69	A&M AMS 756	The Train Song/Hot Burrito No. 1	8
70	A&M AMS 794	Older Guys/Down In The Churchyard	5
70	A&M AMS 816	Tried So Hard/Lazy Days	5
72	A&M AMS 871	White Line Fever/Colorado	5
69	A&M AML(S) 931	THE GILDED PALACE OF SIN (LP)	25
70	A&M AMLS 983	BURRITO DELUXE (LP)	18
71	A&M AMLS 64295	THE FLYING BURRITO BROTHERS (LP)	15
72	A&M AMLS 64343	LAST OF THE RED-HOT BURRITOS (LP)	15
73	Bumble GEXD 301	LIVE IN AMSTERDAM (2-LP)	12

FLYING CIRCUS

71	Harvest SHSP 4010	PREPARED IN PEACE (LP, no EMI box on label)	40

FLYING LIZARDS

80	Virgin 2473791	FLYING LIZARDS (LP)	20

FLYING MACHINE

(see also Pinkertons, Pinkerton's Assorted Colours, Tony Newman)

69	Pye 7N 17722	Smile A Little Smile For Me/Maybe We've Been Loving Too Long	7
69	Pye 7N 17722	Baby Make It Soon/Smile A Little Smile For Me	6
69	Pye 7N 17811	Send My Baby Home Again/Look At Me, Look At Me	7
70	Pye 7N 17914	Hanging On The Edge Of Sadness/Flying Machine	7
70	Pye 7N 45001	The Devil Has Possession Of Your Mind/Hey Little Girl	25
70	Pye 7N 45093	Yes I Understand/Pages Of Your Life	6
70	Pye NSPL 18328	DOWN TO EARTH WITH THE FLYING MACHINE (LP, blue/black label with logo-banner on top)	30

FLYING SAUCER ATTACK

92	Heartbeat FSA 6	Soaring High/Standing Stone (p/s, 500 only, with autographed postcards)	25
92	Heartbeat FSA 6	Soaring High/Standing Stone (p/s, 500 only, with different designs)	20
93	Heartbeat FSA 61	Wish/Oceans (p/s, 700 only)	15
94	Domino RUG 23	Land Beyond The Sun/Everywhere Was Everything (p/s, hand-painted rear sleeve, 500 only)	6
95	Planet PUNK 008	Beach Red Lullaby/Second Hour (p/s, 1,300 only)	6
96	Enraptured RAPT 4505	At Night/JESSAMINE: From Hereto And Now Otherwise (500 on clear vinyl)	12
96	Enraptured RAPT 4505	At Night/JESSAMINE: From Hereto And Now Otherwise (2500 on black vinyl)	8
98	Earworm WORMSC 1	Land Beyond The Sun (2 -Track Version)/ Instrumental For Silence (green vinyl, 500 only)	6
94	Heartbeat FSA 62	FLYING SAUCER ATTACK (LP, 1,000 only)	30

FLYING SAUCERS

76	Alaska ALA 2003	Keep On Comming/Shadow Walk	6
76	Alaska ALA 2014	Texas Calls You Home/Pretty Baby (p/s)	8
78	Alaska ALA 2014	Texas Calls You Home/Pretty Baby	6
76	Nevis NEV LP 114	PLANET OF THE DRAPES (LP)	12
91	Rawking Music	THE ROCKING SANDY FORD (LP)	25

FLYING SQUAD

(see also Status Quo)

78	Epic S EPC 6375	Drive On/Baltimore Baby	5
78	Epic S EPC 6542	Backroom Boys (Night After Night)/Tell Me What To Do	5
78	Epic EPC 82875	FLYING SQUAD (LP)	12

STEVE FLYNN

(see also Mark Wirtz)

67	Parlophone R 5625	Mr Rainbow/Let's Live For Tomorrow	30
68	Parlophone R 5689	Your Life And My Life/Come Tomorrow	10

MINT VALUE £

FLYS

78	EMI EMI 2747	Love And A Molotov Cocktail/Can I Crash Here?/Civilisation (p/s)	10
78	EMI EMI 2795	Fun City/E.C. 4 (p/s)	10
78	EMI EMIY 2867	Waikiki Beach Refugees/We Don't Mind The Rave (p/s, yellow vinyl)	10
79	EMI EMI 2907	Beverley/Don't Moonlight On Me (p/s)	6
79	EMI EMI 2936	Name Dropping/Fly V Fly (p/s, some on green vinyl)	15
79	EMI EMI 2979	Living In The Sticks/We Are The Lucky Ones (p/s)	8
79	Parlophone R 6030	16 Down/Night Creatures/Lois Lane/Today Belongs To Me (p/s)	5
77	Zama ZA 10 EP	BUNCH OF FIVE (33rpm EP, die-cut p/s)	50
80	Parlophone R 6063	FOUR FROM THE SQUARE (EP, p/s)	7
80	Parlophone R 6063	FOUR FROM THE SQUARE (demo copies)	20
78	EMI EMC 3249	WAIKIKI BEACH REFUGEES (LP)	15

FLYTE REACTION

91	Woronzow W0014	SONGS IN A CIRCLE (LP)	15

FOALS

07	Transgressive TRANS049	FOALS LIVE (12" promo, p/s)	25
06	Try Harder	Try This On Your Piano/Look At My Furrows Of Worry (700 only)	25
07	Transgressive TRANS 050	Hummer/Astronauts And All (p/s, 1000 only)	12
07	Transgressive TRANS 053	Mathletics/Big Big Love (1,500 only)	10
07	Transgressive TRANS 065	Balloons/Dearth (p/s)	5
08	Transgressive TRANS 069	Cassius/The Chronic (p/s)	5
08	Transgressive TRANS 069X	Cassius/A Song For You (p/s)	5

FOCAL POINT

68	Deram DM 186	Love You Forever/Sycamore Sid	60

FO'C'SLE

72	Tradition TSC 1	FROM THE FOREST (LP, 100 copies only)	25

FOCUS

(see also Jan Akkerman, Thijs Van Leer, Brainbox, Robin Lent)

71	Polydor 2001 134	House Of The King/Black Beauty	5
71	Blue Horizon 2094 006	Hocus Pocus/Janis	15
72	Blue Horizon 2096 008	Tommy/Focus II	15
71	Polydor 2344 003	IN AND OUT OF FOCUS (LP, gatefold sleeve)	15
71	Blue Horizon 2096 2931	MOVING WAVES (LP, white/blue labels)	20
72	Polydor 2659 016	FOCUS III (2-LP, gatefold sleeve)	15
76	SHSP 4069	SHIP OF MEMORIES (LP)	12
73	Polydor 2442 118	AT THE RAINBOW (multifold sleeve)	15

FOCUS THREE

67	Columbia DB 8279	10,000 Years Behind My Mind/The Sunkeeper	50

FOETUS ÜBER FRISCO

82	Self Immolation WOMB 125/SUSC 12	Custom Built For Capitalism/1.0.4.5./Birthday (12", p/s)	8
85	Self Immmolation WOMB UNC 7.12	Finely Honed Machine/Sick Minutes (12")	8

FOETUS UNDER GLASS

(see also You've Got Foetus On Your Breath, Philip & His Foetus Vibrations, Scraping Foetus Off The Wheel)

85	Self Imm... WOMB S201	Spite Your Face/OKFM (p/s)	15

FOGCUTTERS

64	Liberty LIB 55793	Cry Cry Cry/You Say	15

JOHN FOGERTY

(see also Creedence Clearwater Revival, Blue Ridge Rangers)

74	Fantasy FTC 111	Comin' Down The Road/Ricochet	5
75	Fantasy FTC 119	Rockin' All Over The World/The Wall	5
75	Fantasy FTC 120	Almost Saturday Night/Sea Cruise	5
76	Fantasy FTC 133	You Got The Magic/Evil Thing	5
75	Fantasy FT 526	JOHN FOGERTY (LP)	12

TOM FOGERTY

(see also Creedence Clearwater Revival, Ruby)

71	United Artists UP 35264	Goodbye Media Man (Parts 1 & 2)	5
72	Fantasy F 680	Cast The First Stone/Lady Of Fatima	5
73	Fantasy FTC 109	Joyful Resurrection/Heartbeat	5
72	Fantasy FAN 9407	TOM FOGERTY (LP)	12

FOGG

74	EMI EMI 2182	Water In My Wine/Just Like Me	8

FOGGY

(see also Strawbs, Foggy Dew-O)

72	York SYK 534	How Come The Sun/Take Your Time	10
73	York SYK 542	Kitty Starr/She's Far Away (p/s)	15
73	York SYK 542	Kitty Star/She's far Away (no p/s)	10
72	York FYK 411	SIMPLE GIFTS (LP, with insert, featuring Strawbs)	30
75	Canon CNN 5759	PATCHWORK (LP)	20

FOGGY DEW-O

(see also Strawbs, Foggy)

68	Decca F 12776	Reflections/Grandfather's Clock	8
71	York SYK 503	Me And Bobby McGee/Feelin' Groovy	6
68	Decca LK/SKL 4940	THE FOGGY DEW-O (LP, blue/silver labels with large unboxed logo)	25
70	Decca LK/SKL 5035	BORN TO TAKE THE HIGHWAY (LP, blue/silver label with small boxed logo)	15

FOGHAT

(see also Black Cat Bones, Savoy Brown, Warren Philips & The Rockets)

72	Bearsville K15501	What A Shame / Hole To Hide In	6

MINT VALUE £

74	Bearsville K15511	Long Way To Go/Ride Ride Ride	6
74	Bearsville K15517	Step Outside (edit)/Mabellene	5
76	Bearsville K15522	Slow Ride (edit)/Save Your Loving	5
77	Bearsville K15537	I Just Want To Make Love To You (live edit)/Fool For The City (live edit)	5
79	Bearsville WIP6582	Third Time Lucky/Somebody's Been Sleeping In My Bed	5
72	Bearsville K 45503	FOGHAT (LP)	20
73	Bearsville K 45514	FOGHAT - ROCK'N'ROLL (LP)	12

ELLEN FOLEY (& CLASH)
(see also Clash)

81	Epic EPC A 9522	The Shuttered Palace/Beautiful Waste Of Time (p/s)	6
81	Epic EPC A 1160	Torchlight/Game Of A Man (p/s)	6
81	Epic SEPC 84809	SPIRIT OF ST. LOUIS (LP, with inner sleeve)	15

RED FOLEY
(see also Roberta Lee)

54	Brunswick 05307	Pin Ball Boogie/Jilted (78)	12
54	Brunswick 05321	Skinnie Minnie (Fishtail)/Thank You For Calling	15
55	Brunswick 05508	Croce Di Oro (Cross Of Gold) (with Betty Foley)/The Night Watch	10
55	Brunswick 05363	Hearts Of Stone/RED FOLEY & BETTY FOLEY: Never	20
60	Brunswick STA 3034	SING ALONG WITH RED FOLEY (LP, stereo)	25

RED FOLEY & ERNEST TUBB
(see also Ernest Tubb)

55	Brunswick OE 9148	COUNTRY DOUBLE DATE (EP, with Minnie Pearl)	10
57	Brunswick LAT 8206	RED AND ERNIE (LP)	20

SIMON FOLEY

77	Look LKLP 6324	TO STRIVE WITH PRINCES (LP, with booklet)	20

FOLKAL POINT

72	Midas MR 003	FOLKAL POINT (LP)	1000

FOLK DEVILS

84	Ganges RAY 1	Hank Turns Blue/Chewin' The Fat (with p/s)	15
84	Ganges RAY 1	Hank Turns Blue/Chewin' The Fat	8

CALVIN FOLKES

63	Rio R 5	Someone/Kentucky Home	10
63	Rio R 8	You'll Never Know/Is It Time?	10
64	Port-O-Jam PJ 4117	My Bonnie/What A Day	12
64	Port-O-Jam PJ 4118	Hello Everybody/IRVING SIX: King's Boogie	12

FOLKLANDERS

60s	Urban PB 001	TWO LITTLE FISHES (EP)	10

FOLK(S) BROTHERS

61	Blue Beat BB 30	Carolina/I Met A Man (original, blue label, as Folks Brothers)	15
60s	Fab BB 30	Carolina (as Folks Brothers)/ERIC 'HUMPTY DUMPTY' MORRIS: Humpty Dumpty	7
70s	Blue Beat BB 30	Carolina/I Met A Man (reissue, white label, as Folk Brothers)	6

FOLK SONG CLUB

65	white label (no cat. no.)	IMPERIAL COLLEGE (LP, private pressing)	100

FOLKWAYS

72	Folk Heritage	NO OTHER NAME (LP)	12

EDDIE FONTAINE

55	HMV 7M 304	Rock Love/All My Love Belongs To You (with Neal Hefti & Excels)	350
55	HMV B 10852	Rock Love/All My Love Belongs To You (with Neal Hefti & Excels) (78)	45
56	Brunswick 05624	Cool It, Baby/Into Each Life Some Rain Must Fall	200
56	Brunswick 05624	Cool It, Baby/Into Each Life Some Rain Must Fall (78)	40
58	London HLM 8711	Nothin' Shakin' (But The Leaves On The Trees)/Don't Ya Know	50
58	London HLM 8711	Nothin' Shakin' (But The Leaves On The Trees)/Don't Ya Know (78)	30

FONTAINE SISTERS

81	Revival 6007	Seventeen/Hearts Of Stone	8

ARLENE FONTANA

59	Pye International 7N 25010	I'm In Love/Easy	10

WAYNE FONTANA & THE MINDBENDERS
(see also Wayne Fontana, Mindbenders)

63	Fontana TF 404	Hello! Josephine/Road Runner	25
63	Fontana TF 418	For You, For You/Love Potion No.9	15
64	Fontana TF 436	Little Darlin'/Come Dance With Me	20
64	Fontana TF 451	Stop Look And Listen/Duke Of Earl	10
64	Fontana TF 497	Um, Um, Um, Um, Um, Um/First Taste Of Love	5
65	Fontana TF 535	The Game Of Love/Since You've Been Gone	5
65	Fontana TF 579	It's Just A Little Bit Too Late/Long Time Comin'	10
65	Fontana TF 611	She Needs Love/Like I Did	8
69	Fontana H 1022	Um, Um, Um, Um, Um, Um/The Game Of Love (p/s)	8
64	Fontana TE 17421	ROAD RUNNER (EP)	55
64	Fontana TE 17435	UM, UM, UM, UM, UM, UM (EP)	20
65	Fontana TE 17449	THE GAME OF LOVE (EP)	18
65	Fontana TE 17453	WALKING ON AIR (EP)	40
64	Fontana TL 5230	WAYNE FONTANA AND THE MINDBENDERS (LP)	60
65	Fontana TL 5257	ERIC, RICK, WAYNE, BOB - IT'S WAYNE FONTANA AND THE MINDBENDERS (LP)	65
67	Wing WL 1166	WAYNE FONTANA AND THE MINDBENDERS (LP, reissue)	15

WAYNE FONTANA
(see also Mindbenders)

65	Fontana TF 642	It Was Easier To Hurt Her/You Made Me What I Am Today	10
66	Fontana TF 684	Come On Home/My Eyes Break Out In Tears	5

		MINT VALUE £
66 Fontana TF 737	Goodbye Bluebird/The Sun's So Hot Today	5
66 Fontana TF 770	Pamela Pamela/Something Keeps Calling Me Back	6
67 Fontana TF 827	24 Sycamore/From A Boy To A Man	5
67 Fontana TF 866	The Impossible Years/In My World	12
67 Fontana TF 889	Gina/We All Love The Human Race	6
68 Fontana TF 911	Storybook Children/I Need To Love You	6
68 Fontana TF 933	The Words Of Bartholomew/Mind Excursion	6
68 Fontana TF 976	Never An Everyday Thing/Waiting For A Break In The Clouds	7
69 Fontana TF 1008	Dayton Ohio 1903/Say Goodbye To Yesterday	7
69 Fontana TF 1054	Charlie Cass/Linda (withdrawn issue)	25
69 Fontana TF 1054	We're Building A Love/Charlie Cass	10
69 Fontana H 1027	Come On Home/Pamela Pamela (p/s)	10
70 Philips 6006 035	Give Me Just A Little More Time/I'm In Love (withdrawn)	150
70 Philips 6006 035	Give Me Just A Little More Time/I'm In Love (withdrawn) (DJ Copy)	100
73 Warner Bros K 16269	Together/One Man Woman	6
66 Fontana (S)TL 5351	WAYNE ONE (LP, black/silver labels)	25
69 Fontana SFL 13144	WAYNE ONE (LP, reissue)	12

FONTANE SISTERS

(see also Pat Boone, Perry Como)

54 London HL 8099	Happy Days And Lonely Nights/If I Didn't Have You	100
54 London HL 8099	Happy Days And Lonely Nights/If I Didn't Have You (78)	12
55 London HL 8113	Hearts Of Stone/Bless Your Heart	100
55 London HL 8126	Rock Love/You're Mine	100
55 London HL 8126	Rock Love/You're Mine (78)	15
55 London HLD 8177	Seventeen/If I Could Be With You	100
55 London HLD 8211	Rolling Stone/Daddy-O	80
55 London HLD 8211	Rolling Stone/Daddy-O (78)	10
56 London HLD 8225	Adorable/Playmates	50
56 London HLD 8225	Adorable/Playmates (78)	10
56 London HLD 8265	Eddie My Love/Yum Yum	50
56 London HL 7009	Eddie My Love/Yum Yum (export issue)	40
56 London HLD 8289	I'm In Love Again/You Always Hurt The One You Love (gold lettering)	40
56 London HLD 8289	I'm In Love Again/You Always Hurt The One You Love (silver lettering)	20
56 London HLD 8289	I'm In Love Again/You Always Hurt The One You Love	12
56 London HLD 8318	Voices (with narration by Pat Boone)/Willow Weep For Me (gold lettering)	40
56 London HLD 8318	Voices (with narration by Pat Boone)/Willow Weep For Me (silver lettering)	20
56 London HLD 8343	Silver Bells/Nuttin' For Christmas	25
57 London HLD 8378	The Banana Boat Song/Lonesome Lover Blues (gold lettering)	15
57 London HLD 8378	The Banana Boat Song/Lonesome Lover Blues (silver lettering)	10
57 London HLD 8415	Please Don't Leave Me/Still	20
57 London HLD 8488	Fool Around/Which Way To Your Heart?	20
58 London HLD 8621	Chanson D'Amour (Song Of Love)/Cocoanut Grove	15
59 London HLD 8861	Billy Boy/Encore D'Amour	15
60 London HLD 9037	Listen To Your Heart/Please Be Kind	10
60 London HLD 9078	Theme From "A Summer Place"/Darling, It's Wonderful	10
55 London RE-D 1029	FONTANE SISTERS NO. 1 (EP)	60
55 London RE-D 1037	FONTANE SISTERS NO. 2 (EP)	50
57 London HA-D 2053	THE FONTANES SING (LP)	100

SAM FONTEYN

66 Parlophone R 5519	Lost In Space/BERNARD SHARPE: Jorrocks	10

BILLY FONTEYNE

63 Oriole CB 1917	Little Child/Look Before You Leap	15

FOO FIGHTERS

95 Roswell CL 753	This Is A Call/Winnebago (p/s)	6
95 Roswell 12CL 753	This Is A Call/Winnebago/Podunk (12", luminous vinyl)	20
95 Roswell CL 757	I'll Stick Around/How I Miss You (red vinyl, p/s)	10
95 Roswell 12CL 757	I'll Stick Around/How I Miss You (12" p/s)	15
95 Roswell CL 762	For All The Cows/Watershed (blue vinyl, p/s)	8
95 Roswell CDCL 762	For All The Cows/(live version)/Watershed (live) (CD)	10
95 Roswell CL 768	Big Me/Floaty/Gas Chamber (white vinyl, p/s)	12
97 Roswell CL 788	Monkey Wrench/Up In Arms (red vinyl, p/s)	10
97 Roswell CL 792	Everlong/Drive Me Wild (blue vinyl, p/s)	15
97 Roswell CL 796	My Hero/Dear Lover (red vinyl, stickered poly sleeve, with insert)	10
99 BMG 749582	GENERATOR (CD EP)	8
00 RCA 74321 79012-7	Breakout/Stacked Actors (live) (p/s)	5
00 RCA 74321 80926-7	Next Year/Big Me (live) (p/s)	5
02 RCA 74321 97315-7	All My Life/Sister Europe (numbered p/s)	5
03 RCA 74321 98955-7	Times Like These/Lack Of Illision (numbered p/s)	5
03 RCA 82876 56370-7	Have It All/Darling Nikki (p/s)	5
03 BMG 82876-52256-7	Low/Never Talking To You Again (Live Version) (numbered p/s, 3,000 only)	10
95 Roswell EST 2266	FOO FIGHTERS (LP)	25
97 Roswell EST 2295	THE COLOUR AND THE SHAPE (LP)	60
99 RCA 07863678921	THERE IS NOTHING LEFT TO LOSE (LP)	20
02 RCA 74321973481	ONE BY ONE (LP)	25
05 BMG 82876680381	IN YOUR HONOUR (4-LP)	40

FOOL

69 Mercury MF 1111	We Are One/Shining Light	10
69 Mercury SMCL 20138	THE FOOL (LP, gatefold sleeve. black/silver labels)	60

FOOLS DANCE

(see also Cure, Stranglers)

87 L. T. T. Slaughter LTS 22	They'll Never Know/Empty Hours (p/s)	10
87 L. T. T. Slaughter LTS 22T	They'll Never Know/The Collector/Empty Hours/The Ring (12", p/s)	15
85 Top Hole Turn TURN 19	FOOLS DANCE (mini-LP)	20
86 Top Hat TH 22	FOOLS DANCE (mini-LP, reissue)	12

MINT VALUE £

FOOT IN COLD WATER

73	Island WIP 6162	(Isn't Love Unkind) In My Life/Deep Freeze	7
74	Elektra K12164	I Know What You Need/Para - Dice	8
74	Elektra K 52011	OR ALL AROUND US (LP)	20

CHUCK FOOTE

62	London HLU 9495	You're Running Out Of Kisses/Come On Back	15

FORBES

77	Power Exchange PX 253	The Beatles/Sweet Kiss Of Fire	7

BILL FORBES

(see also Contrasts)

58	Columbia DB 4232	My Cherie/God's Little Acre	6
59	Columbia DB 4269	Once More/Believe In Me	8
59	Columbia DB 4386	Too Young/It's Not The End Of The World	6
61	Columbia DB 4566	You're Sixteen, You're Beautiful/Backward Child	15
61	Columbia DB 4619	That's It, I Quit, I'm Moving On/Big City Boy	15
61	Columbia DB 4747	Goodbye Cruel World/Next Time	12
62	Columbia DB 4855	Laughter Or Tears/Like A Good Girl Should	7
62	Columbia DB 4945	Poker Face/Marianne	7

SMOKY FORBES

71	Beacon BEA 176	My Kind Of Music/Loves Goes	6

FORCEFIELD

(see also Cozy Powell, Graham Bonnet, Ray Fenwick, Whitesnake)

87	President PT 551	Smoke On The Water/Shine It On Me (p/s)	5
88	President PT 578	Heartache/I Lose Again (Instrumental Version) (p/s)	5

FORCE FIVE

(see also Crocheted Doughnut Ring)

64	United Artists UP 1051	Don't Make My Baby Blue/Shaking Postman	30
65	United Artists UP 1089	Yeah, I'm Waiting/I Don't Want To See You Again	35
65	United Artists UP 1102	Baby Don't Care/Come Down To Earth	35
65	United Artists UP 1118	I Want You Babe/Gee Too Tiger	50
66	United Artists UP 1141	Don't Know Which Way To Turn/Baby Let Your Hair Down	45

FORCE WEST

65	Decca F 12223	I Can't Give What I Haven't Got/Why Won't She Stay	12
66	Columbia DB 7908	Gotta Find Another Baby/Talkin' About Our Love	15
66	Columbia DB 7963	When The Sun Comes Out (Weatherman)/Gotta Tell Somebody	12
67	Columbia DB 8174	All The Children Sleep/Desolation	15
68	CBS 3632	I'll Walk In The Rain/What's It To Be?	8
68	CBS 3798	I'll Be Moving On/Like The Tide, Like The Ocean	8
69	CBS 4385	Sherry/Mister Blue	8

FORD & THE COALITION

94	Shot In The Dark COAL 2616	The Coalition (12")	15

BICK FORD

63	Parlophone R 5018	Cheat Cheat/Sweet And Tender Romance	8

CLINTON FORD

(see also Hallelujah Skiffle Group)

63	Columbia 33SX 1560	THE MELODY MAN (LP) (also stereo SCX 3496)	12
64	Realm RM 147	BY JINGO (LP)	12
65	Columbia 33SX 1689	LISTEN WITH US (LP) (mono)	15
65	Columbia SCX 3529	LISTEN WITH US (LP) (stereo)	20

DEAN FORD (& GAYLORDS)

(see also Gaylords, Marmalade, Junior Campbell)

64	Columbia DB 7264	Twenty Miles/What's The Matter With Me?	25
64	Columbia DB 7402	Mr Heartbreak's Here Instead/I Won't	25
65	Columbia DB 7610	The Name Game/That Lonely Feeling	25
75	EMI EMC 3079	DEAN FORD (LP)	15

DEE DEE FORD

(see also Don Gardner & Dee Dee Ford)

60	London HLU 9245	Good-Morning Blues/I Just Can't Believe	50

EDDIE/EDDY FORD

72	Pressure Beat PB 5512	You Wrong Fe Trouble Joshua/KENNETH POWER: Joshua Row Us Home	7
73	Duke Reid DR 2523	Guess I This Riddle/Riddle Version (as Eddie Ford)	5

EMILE FORD (& THE CHECKMATES)

59	Pye Nixa 7N 15225	What Do You Want To Make Those Eyes At Me For?/Don't Tell Me Your Troubles	5
60	Pye 7N 15245	On A Slow Boat To China/That Lucky Old Sun	5
60	Pye 7N 15268	You'll Never Know What You're Missin' 'Til You Try/Still	10
60	Pye 7N 15279	Red Sails In The Sunset/Afraid	5
60	Pye 7N 15282	Them There Eyes (solo)/Question	5
60	Pye 7N 15314	Counting Teardrops/White Christmas	5
61	Pye 7N 15331	What Am I Gonna Do/A Kiss To Build A Dream On	7
61	Piccadilly 7N 35003	Half Of My Heart/Gypsy Love (solo)	8
61	Piccadilly 7N 35007	After You've Gone/Hush, Somebody's Calling My Name	8
61	Piccadilly 7N 35019	The Alphabet Song/Keep A-Lovin' Me (solo)	6
62	Piccadilly 7N 35033	I Wonder Who's Kissing Her Now/Doin' The Twist (solo)	7
62	Piccadilly 7N 35078	Your Nose Is Gonna Grow/Rains Come	7
63	Piccadilly 7N 35116	Hold Me Thrill Me Kiss Me/Doin' What You Do To Me	10
69	Decca F 12959	Set Me Free/Don't Remind Me (export issue)	12
79	Transdics TR7	Dance With Me/How Can I Live Without You	6
59	Pye NEP 24119	EMILE (EP)	15

MINT VALUE £

60	Pye NEP 24124	EMILE FORD HIT PARADE (EP)	15
60	Pye NEP 24133	EMILE FORD HIT PARADE VOL. 2 (EP)	15
60	Pye NPL 18049	NEW TRACKS WITH EMILE (LP)	25
61	Piccadilly NPL 38001	EMILE (LP)	30

FRANKIE FORD

(see also Huey Piano Smith)

59	London HL 8850	Sea Cruise/Roberta (with Huey 'Piano' Smith & Clowns) (black triangular centre)	60
59	London HL 8850	Sea Cruise/Roberta (with Huey 'Piano' Smith & Clowns) (later silver-top triangular centre)	40
59	London HL 8850	Sea Cruise/Roberta (with Huey 'Piano' Smith & Clowns) (78 rpm)	50
59	Top Rank JAR 186	Alimony/Can't Tell My Heart (What To Do) (with Huey 'Piano' Smith & Clowns)	12
59	Top Rank JAR 186	Alimony/Can't Tell My Heart (What To Do) (78)	70
60	Top Rank JAR 282	Cheatin' Woman/HUEY 'PIANO' SMITH & CLOWNS: Don't You Just Know Kokomo	20
60	Top Rank JAR 299	Time After Time/I Want To Be Your Man	10
60	London HLP 9222	You Talk Too Much/If You've Got Troubles	20
65	Sue WI 366	Sea Cruise/Roberta (with Huey 'Piano' Smith & Clowns) (reissue)	25
65	Sue WI 369	What's Going On?/Watchdog	35

JASON FORD & THE BULLDOGS

62	Piccadilly 7N 35193	Nobody Knows/Am I The One	10

JOHN FORD

73	UK UKR31	It's Alright Bill/Captain Of Your Ship	8

JON FORD

68	Philips BF 1690	Two's Company, Three's A Crowd/Place In Your Heart	7
69	Philips BF 1791	I Know It's Love/Look Before You Leap	6
69	Philips BF 1817	Ice Cream Man/This Was The Time	6
70	Philips BF 1833	Yesterday When I Was Young/Running Around	6
70	Philips 6006 030	You've Got Me Where You Want Me/You're All Alone Tonight	100
70	Philips 6006 030	You've Got Me Where You Want Me/You're All Alone Tonight (DJ Copy)	150

LITA FORD & OZZY OSBOURNE

(see also Ozzy Osbourne, Runaways)

89	Dreamland A 49396	Close My Eyes Forever (Remix)/Under The Gun (p/s)	5
89	Dreamland PA 49396	Close My Eyes Forever (Remix)/Under The Gun/Blueberry (12", picture disc)	8

MIKE FORD & THE CONSULS

63	Piccadilly 7N 35127	Jumping Jeremiah/The Greenman	15

PERRY FORD (& SAPPHIRES)

(see also Ivy League, Georgie Fame)

59	Parlophone R 4573	Bye, Bye Baby, Goodbye/She Came As A Stranger	15
60	Parlophone R 4633	Crazy Over You/Garden Of Happiness	15
60	Parlophone R 4683	Don't Weep (Little Lady)/Little Grown-Up	12
62	Decca F 11497	Baby, Baby (Don't You Worry)/Prince Of Fools (with Sapphires & Blue Flames)	12

RICKY FORD (& TENNESSEANS)

63	Parlophone R 5018	Sweet And Tender Romance/Cheat Cheat	10
64	Parlophone R 5230	You Are My Love/Long Way From Home (with Tennesseans)	7

SIR TED FORD

77	Bark BAR 3	I Wanna Be Near You/Ridin' Too High	10

'TENNESSEE' ERNIE FORD

(see also Dinning Sisters)

54	Capitol CL 14005	Give Me Your Word/River Of No Return	25
54	Capitol CL 14006	Catfish Boogie/Kiss Me Big	25
55	Capitol CL 14261	His Hands/I Am A Pilgrim	10
55	Capitol CL 14273	Losing You/There Is Beauty In Everything	10
56	Capitol CL 14500	Sixteen Tons/You Don't Have To Be A Baby To Cry	25
56	Capitol CL 14506	The Ballad Of Davy Crockett/Farewell	20
56	Capitol CL 14557	That's All/Bright Lights And Blonde-Haired Women	10
61	Capitol CL 15210	Little Red Rockin' Hood/I Gotta Have My Baby Back	15
77	Capitol CL 15923	Shot Gun Boogie/Smoky Mountain Boogie	8
56	Capitol EAP 1014	SIXTEEN TONS (EP)	15
61	Capitol EAP1 20067	ANTICIPATION BLUES (EP)	15
52	Capitol LC 6573	CAPITOL PRESENTS (10" LP)	25
56	Capitol LC 6825	THIS LUSTY LAND (10" LP)	15
58	Capitol T 888	OL' ROCKIN' ERN (LP)	25
60	Capitol T 1380	SIXTEEN TONS (LP)	20

'TENNESSEE' ERNIE FORD & BETTY HUTTON

54	Capitol CL 14133	This Must Be The Place/The Honeymoon's Over (green label)	18

JOHN FORDE

77	EMI EMI 2656	Stardance/Flight Of The jumping Bean (12", p/s, some on blue vinyl)	50

FORD THEATRE

69	Stateside SSL 10288	TIME CHANGES (LP)	15

EDDIE 'BUSTER' FOREHAND

69	Action ACT 4519	Young Boy Blues/You Were Meant For Me	20

FOREHEADS IN A FISHTANK

80	Stuff Records FAB 4	She Loves You, Yeah/Baby Love (p/s)	8

FOREIGN LEGION

86	Rent-A-Racket RRR0001	TRENCHLINE (EP)	12
89	Schlawiner SO5	SURF CITY (EP, 350 copies only, black/green vinyl)	10
90	Venture VR/FL 100	WELOCME TO FORT ZINDERNEUF (LP)	15

MINT VALUE £

JOHN FOREMAN
66 Reality RY 1004 THE 'OUSES IN BETWEEN (LP) 15

FORERUNNERS
60s Key KL 008 THE FORERUNNERS (LP) 18
60s Key KL 004 RUNNING BACK (LP) 18

FORERUNNERS
64 Solar SRP 100 Bony Maronie/Pride 60

FOREST
69 Harvest HAR 5007 Searching For Shadows/Mirror Of Life 20
69 Harvest SHVL 760 FOREST (LP, gatefold sleeve, no EMI logo on label) 200
70 Harvest SHVL 784 FULL CIRCLE (LP, gatefold sleeve, no EMI logo on label) 350
88 Zap! ZAP 3 FULL CIRCLE (LP, reissue) 20

SHARON FORESTER
73 Ashanti ASH 403 Silly Wasn't I?/NOW-GEN: Silly Wasn't I? - Version 6
74 Ashanti SHAN 105 SHARON (LP, with inner sleeve and poster) 20

FOREVER AMBER
69 Advance (no cat. no.) THE LOVE CYCLE (LP, private pressing, 99 copies only) 2000

FOREVER MORE
(see also Scots Of St. James, Hopscotch)
70 RCA RCA 2024 Put Your Money On A Pony/Yours 6
70 RCA SF 8016 YOURS FOREVER MORE (LP, gatefold sleeve, orange label) 40
71 RCA LSA 3015 WORDS ON BLACK PLASTIC (LP) 30

FORK IN THE ROAD
70 Ember EMB 311 I Can't Turn Around/Skeleton In My Closet (test pressing) 150
70 Ember EMB S 311 I Can't Turn Around/Skeleton In My Closet 100

FORMAT
(see also Fourmost)
69 CBS 4600 Maxwell's Silver Hammer/Music Man 10

FORMATIONS
60 Pye 7N 15269 Happy Go Lucky Me/Banjo Boy 7
68 MGM MGM 1399 At The Top Of The Stairs/Magic Melody 120
68 MGM MGM 1399 At The Top Of The Stairs/Magic Melody (DJ Copy) 220
71 Mojo 2027 001 At The Top Of The Stairs/Magic Melody (reissue) 10

FORMERLY FAT HARRY
(see also Country Joe and the Fish)
71 Harvest SHSP 4016 FORMERLY FAT HARRY (LP, with EMI logo on label) 60

FORMINX
(see also Aphrodite's Child, Vangelis)
65 Vocalion V 9235 Jenka Beat/Geronimo Jenka 30

FORMULA
65 HMV POP 1438 Close To Me/If Ever 10

FORMULA 1
65 Warner Bros WB 155 I Just Can't Go To Sleep/Sure Know A Lot About Love 30

FORMULA TWO
72 CBS SCBS 8285 Easy Times/Girl Who Lives Next Door 6

ANDY FORRAY
68 Parlophone R 5715 Sarah Jane/Don't Care Anymore 10
68 Parlophone R 5729 The Proud One/Messin' Round With Me 15
68 Decca F 12733 Epitaph To You/Dream With Me 80
69 Fontana TF 999 Let The Sunshine In/Baby Is Coming 10

HELEN FORREST
56 Capitol CL 14594 Taking A Chance On Love/I Love You Much Too Much 7
56 Capitol LC 6834 VOICE OF THE NAME BANDS (10" LP) 12

JANE FORREST
56 Columbia SCM 5213 Sincerely Yours/A Girl Can't Say 10

FORRESTERS
65 Polydor 56038 Broken Hearted Clown/Lonely Boy 10
65 Polydor 56057 How Can I Tell Her/So Shy 10
66 Polydor 56104 Early Morning Hours/World Is Mine 8
66 Columbia DB 8040 Sometimes When You're Lonely/Today Or Tomorrow (as Forresters) 7
66 Columbia DB 8086 Mr. Smith/Ship On The Sea (as Foresters) 10
67 Columbia DB 8176 Comin' Home In The Evening/Sunshine's On Its Way (as Foresters) 6

THOMAS FORSTNER
89 Ariola 112 298 Song Of Love/Nur Ein Lied (p/s, withdrawn) 5
89 Ariola 662 298 Song Of Love (12" Version)/Nur Ein Lied/Song Of Love (7") (CD, withdrawn) 8

BRUCE FORSYTH
59 Parlophone R4535 I'm In Charge/So Far So Good 6
62 Piccadilly 7N 35086 The Oh-Be-Joyfuls/I Like People 5
64 Piccadilly 7N 35189 The Mysterious People/You've Just Found Out 5
65 Pye 7N 15879 Hush Hush Sweet Charlotte/Don't Say Goodbye 5
68 Mercury MF 1047 Star/Do, Do, Do 5
68 Pye 7N 17460 I'm Backing Britain/There's Not Enough Love In The World (p/s) 6
69 Decca F 12940 When You Gotta Go/By The Fireside 5
60 Parlophone GEP 8807 I'M IN CHARGE (EP) 10
60 Parlophone PMC 1132 MR ENTERTAINMENT (LP, also stereo PCS 3031) 20

MINT VALUE £

FORTES MENTUM
(see also Angel Pavement, Pussy)

68	Parlophone R 5684	Saga Of A Wrinkled Man/Mr. Partridge Passed Away Today	50
68	Parlophone R 5726	I Can't Go On Loving You/Humdiggle We Love You	12
69	Parlophone R 5768	Gotta Go/Marrakesh	12

LANCE FORTUNE

60	Pye 7N 15240	Be Mine/Action (with Johnny Prendy, alias John Barry)	5
60	Pye 7N 15260	This Love I Have For You/All On My Own	8
60	Pye 7N 15297	I Wonder/Will You Still Be My Girl?	8
61	Pye 7N 15347	Who's Gonna Tell Me?/Love Is The Sweetest Thing	12

FORTUNES
(see also Glen Dale)

63	Decca F 11718	Summertime Summertime/I Love Her Still (as Fortunes & Cliftones) (in p/s)	30
63	Decca F 11718	Summertime Summertime/I Love Her Still (as Fortunes & Cliftones)	15
64	Decca F 11809	Caroline/If You Don't Want Me Now	30
64	Decca F 11912	Come On Girl/I Like The Look Of You	15
64	Decca F 11985	Look Homeward Angel/I'll Have My Tears To Remind Me	15
66	Decca F 12321	This Golden Ring/Someone To Care	6
66	Decca F 12429	You Gave Me Somebody To Love/Silent Street	6
66	Decca F 12485	Is It Really Worth Your While?/Am I Losing My Touch	6
67	Decca F 12612	Our Love Has Gone/Truly Yours	6
67	United Artists UP 1188	The Idol/His Smile Was A Lie	10
68	United Artists UP 2218	Loving Cup/Hour At The Movies	6
68	United Artists UP 2239	Seasons In The Sun/Louise	6
69	United Artists UP 35054	Lifetime Of Love/Sad Sad Sad (withdrawn, existence unconfirmed)	0
69	United Artists UP 35054	Books And Films/Sad Sad Sad	7
71	Capitol CL 15671	Here Comes That Rainy Day Feeling Again/Bad Side Of Town	5
65	Decca LK 4736	THE FORTUNES (LP, mono)	35
65	Decca SKL 4736	THE FORTUNES (LP, stereo)	60
72	Capitol ST 21891	THE FORTUNES (LP)	15

48 CHAIRS

79	Absurd Absurd 3	Snap It Around/Psycle Sluts (p/s)	5

45's

79	Chopper CHEAP 5	Couldn't Believe A Word/Lonesome Lane (no p/s)	7
79	Stiff BUY 52	Couldn't Believe A Word/Lonesome Lane (no p/s, reissue)	5
81	45's Records ONE 45	Secrets And Whispers/Driving/Little Honda (p/s)	8

49 AMERICANS

80	No Bad NB 4	THE HIT ALBUM (14-track EP)	6
80	Choo Choo Train CHUG 2	TOO YOUNG TO BE IDEAL (12" EP)	10
80	Choo Choo Train CHUG 1	EL PLURIBUS UNUM (LP)	12

FORUM

67	London HLM 10120	The River Is Wide/I Fall In Love (All Over Again)	15
70	B&C CB 119	The River Is Wide/I Fall In Love (All Over Again) (reissue)	5

FORWARD INTENSE

92	Harm HARM1	Stated/Imply The Calm (12")	40

SHIRLEY FORWOOD

57	London HLD 8402	Two Hearts (With An Arrow Between)/Juke Box Lovers	30

FOSSIL

74	Penninle PSS14	Black Night/For Your Love/Smile On Me/Wishing Well	30

BOBBY FOSTER

70	Bread BR 1101	Tell Me Why You Say Goodbye/YOUTH: I'll Make Him Believe In You	6

FRANK FOSTER

60s	Esquire 32 033	WAIL FRANK WAIL (LP)	18

JACKIE FOSTER

63	Planetone RC 13	Oh Leona/I Fell In Love	15

JOHN FOSTER

66	Island ILP 939	JOHN FOSTER SINGS (LP)	40

LARRY FOSTER & SOUL EXPLOSION
(see also Sugar Simone)

70	Fab FAB 130	Boom Biddy Boom/Next To Me (actually by Sugar Simone)	7

LES FOSTER

70	Torpedo TOR 7	Run Like A Thief/Nobody's Fool	8
69	Wolf WM 02	You And Your Love/Turning Point (actually by D Dennis)	12

LES FOSTER & ANSELL COLLINS
(see also Dave & Ansell Collins, Sugar Simone, Lance Hannibal)

73	Camel CA 102	The Man In Your Life/Version	5

LESLIE FOSTER

69	Jolly JY 022	Muriel/Nowhere To Hide	7

VINCENT FOSTER

69	Escort ES 803	Shine Eye Gal/Who Nest (B-side actually "Who Next" by Carl Bryan)	6

FOTHERINGAY
(see also Sandy Denny, Trevor Lucas, Eclection, Exception[s], Fairport Convention, Mick Greenwood)

70	Island WIP 6085	Peace In The End/Winter Winds	15
70	Island ILPS 9125	FOTHERINGAY (LP, pink label/'i' logo, gatefold sleeve)	70
70	Island ILPS 9125	FOTHERINGAY (LP, later issue, pink rim label/'palm tree' logo, gatefold sleeve)	25

MINT VALUE £

FOUL PLAY

92	Oblivion OR 001	VOLUME 1 EP: The Alchemist/Ragatere/Ricochet/Feel the vibe (12")	25
92	Oblivion OR 002	VOLUME 2 EP: Survival/Dubbing you/Ricochet (No Stopping The Remix)/Feel The Vibe (Again) (12")	25
93	Section 5 SECTION 04	Finest Illusion/Screwface (12" white label)	60
93	Section 5 SECTION 4	Finest Illusion/Screwface (12" printed labels)	50
93	Section 5 SECTION 4	Finest Illusion/Screwface (12" 2nd pressing, no labels at all!)	50
93	Moving Shadow SHADOW 29	VOLUME III EP: Open Your Mind/Murder Most Foul/Survival (Remix)/ Dub in U (remix) (12", p/s)	8
93	Moving Shadow SHAD 29R	VOLUME III REMIXES: Open Your Mind (Tango Remix)/Open Your Mind (Foul Play Remix) (10", p/s)	8
93	Moving Shadow SHAD 29R2	VOLUME III REMIXES PART 2: Open Your Mind (Nookie Remix)/Finest illusion (Legal Mix) (10", p/s)	10

MR FOUNDATION

(see under 'M')

FOUNDATIONS

(see also Pluto)

67	Pye 7N 17366	Baby, Now That I've Found You/Come On Back To Me	7
68	Pye 7N 17417	Back On My Feet Again/I Can Take Or Leave Your Loving	7
68	Pye 7N 17503	Any Old Time (You're Lonely And Sad)/We Are Happy People	8
68	Pye 7N 17636	Build Me Up Buttercup/New Direction	8
69	Pye 7N 17702	In The Bad Bad Old Days/Give Me Love	5
69	Pye 7N 17809	Born To Live, Born To Die/Why Did You Cry	12
69	Pye 7N 17849	Baby I Couldn't See/Penny Sir	10
71	MCA MCA 5075	Stoney Ground/I'll Give You Love	20
70s	Summit SU 100	Where Were You When I Needed Your Love/Love Me Nice 'n Easy	6
78	Psycho P 2603	Closer To Loving You/Change My Life	250
68	Pye NEP 24297	IT'S ALL RIGHT (EP)	25
67	Pye NPL 18206	FROM THE FOUNDATIONS (LP)	20
68	Pye NPL 18227	ROCKING THE FOUNDATIONS (LP)	20
69	Pye N(S)PL 18290	DIGGING THE FOUNDATIONS (LP, gatefold sleeve)	20

FOUNDED

82	Heroes ER 02	Looking For Love/Run To Hell	60

JAMES FOUNTAIN

76	Cream CRM 5002	Seven Day Lover/Malnutrition	6

PETE FOUNTAIN

(see also Brenda Lee)

60	Coral Q 72404	Columbus Stockade Blues/Sentimental Journey (78 rpm = £15)	15

THE 4

64	Decca F 11999	It's Alright/There's Nothing Like It	20

FOUR ACES (Jamaica)

(see also Desmond Dekker)

65	Island WI 178	Hoochy-Koochy-Kai-Po/River Bank Coberly Again	25
65	Island WI 178	Hoochy-Koochy-Kai-Po/SKATALITES: Sucu Sucu (different B-side)	25
65	Island WI 179	Sweet Chariot/Peace And Love	15
65	Island WI 180	Little Girl/CLARENDONIANS: Day Will Come	18

FOUR ACES (U.K.)

60s	Anton/E.R.S. EAG 178/179	Why Do You/Fortune Teller (private pressing)	250

FOUR ACES (U.S.)

(see also Al Alberts)

54	Brunswick 05256	The Gang That Sang "Heart Of My Heart"/Heaven Can Wait	10
54	Brunswick 05308	Three Coins In The Fountain/Wedding Bells (Are Breaking Up This Gang Of Mine)	20
54	Brunswick 05322	It Shall Come To Pass/Dream	10
54	Brunswick 05348	It's A Woman's World/The Cuckoo Bird In The Pickle Tree	8
54	Brunswick 05355	Mister Sandman/(I'll Be With You) In Apple Blossom Time	25
55	Brunswick 05379	Melody Of Love/There Is A Tavern In The Town	8
55	Brunswick 05401	There Goes My Heart/Take Me In Your Arms	6
55	Brunswick 05418	Stranger In Paradise/You'll Always Be The One	15
55	Brunswick 05429	Sluefoot/I'm In The Mood For Love	5
55	Brunswick 05480	Love Is A Many Splendored Thing/Shine On Harvest Moon	15
55	Brunswick 05504	Jingle Bells/The Christmas Song (Merry Christmas To You)	7
56	Brunswick 05562	To Love Again/Charlie Was A Boxer	5
56	Brunswick 05566	The Gal With The Yaller Shoes/Of This I'm Sure	5
56	Brunswick 05573	If You Can Dream/It's The Talk Of The Town	5
56	Brunswick 05589	A Woman In Love/I Only Know I Love You	10
56	Brunswick 05601	Dreamer/Let's Fall In Love	5
56	Brunswick 05613	You Can't Run Away From It/Written On The Wind	5
56	Brunswick 05623	Friendly Persuasion (Thee I Love)/Someone To Love	8
50s	Decca A 73010	I'm Yours/I Understand (export issue)	5
54	Brunswick OE 9090	PRESENTING THE FOUR ACES (EP)	10
57	Brunswick OE 9324	ACES SING FILM TITLES (EP)	10
53	Brunswick LA 8614	JUST SQUEEZE ME (10" LP)	20
59	Brunswick STA 3014	THE SWINGIN' ACES (LP, stereo)	15

4 DEGREES

65	Oak RGJ 187	4 DEGREES (LP, 1-sided, no sleeve)	425

FOUR DOLLS

57	Capitol CL 14778	Three On A Date/Proud Of You	15
58	Capitol CL 14845	Whoop-A-Lala/I'm Following You	15

MINT VALUE £

FOUR ESCORTS

54	HMV 7M 277	Loop De Loop Mambo/Love Me	15

FOUR ESQUIRES

55	London HL 8152	The Sphinx Won't Tell/Three Things (A Man Must Do)	40
56	London HLA 8224	Adorable/Thunderbolt	25
58	London HLO 8533	Love Me Forever/I Ain't Been Right Since You Left	20
58	London HLO 8579	Always And Forever/I Walk Down The Street	12
58	London HL 8746	Hideaway/Repeat After Me	10
58	London HL 8746	Hideaway/Repeat After Me	12
59	Pye Intl. 7N 25012	Non E Cosi/Land Of You And Me	5
59	Pye Intl. 7N 25027	Act Your Age/So Ends The Night	7
60	Pye Intl. 7N 25049	Wouldn't It Be Wonderful/Wonderful One	5

FOUR EVERS

66	CBS 202549	A Lovely Way To Say Goodnight/The Girl I Wanna Bring Home	45

FOUR FOR FUN

(see also Dick Farina, Carolyn Hester)

63	Waverley ELP 113	FOUR FOR FUN (EP)	70

FOUR FRESHMEN

54	Capitol CL 14196	Love Turns Winter To Spring/Mood Indigo	8
55	Capitol CL 14338	Day By Day/How Can I Tell Her	8
56	Capitol CL 14610	Graduation Day/Lonely Night In Paris	6
56	Capitol CL 14633	You're So Far Above Me/He Who Loves And Runs Away	5
54	Capitol LC 6685	VOICES IN MODERN (10" LP)	18

FOUR FULLER BROTHERS

69	MCA MU 1068	Bitter Honey/Groupie	10

FOUR GEES

67	President PT 160	Ethiopia/Rough Rider	7

FOUR GIBSON GIRLS

58	Oriole CB 1447	No School Tomorrow/June, July And August	18
58	Oriole CB 1453	Safety Sue/VARIOUS ARTISTS: Safety Sue	15

FOUR GUYS

(see also Modernaires)

55	Vogue Coral Q 72054	Half Hearted Kisses/Mine	12

4 HERO

98	Reinforced/Talking Loud	TWO PAGES (4x12")	25
95	Reinforced LP 004	PARALLEL UNIVERSE (2-LP)	40

FOUR JACKS

58	Decca F 10984	Hey! Baby/The Prayer Of Love	25
58	Decca DFE 6460	HEY! BABY (EP)	200

FOUR JACKS & A JILL

68	RCA Victor RCA 1669	Master Jack/I Looked Back	7

FOUR JONES BOYS

(see also Jones Boys, Annette Klooger)

55	Decca F 10568	A Real Romance/When I Let You Go	6
55	Decca F 10671	Moments To Remember/Sing-ing-ing-ing	6
56	Decca F 10717	Tutti Frutti/Are You Satisfied?	20
56	Decca F 10789	Happiness Street (Corner Of Sunshine Square)/Someone To Love	6
56	Decca F 10829	Priscilla/It Isn't Right	10

FOUR JUST MEN

(see also Just Four Men, Wimple Winch)

64	Parlophone R 5186	That's My Baby/Things Will Never Be The Same	80

FOUR KENTS

68	RCA RCA 1705	The Moving Finger Writes/Searchin'	20

FOUR KESTRELS

61	Decca F 11333	Sound Off/Can't Say I Do	6

FOUR KINSMEN

(see also Kinsmen)

67	Decca F 22671	It Looks Like The Daybreak/Forget About Him	15

FOUR KNIGHTS

(see also Nat 'King' Cole)

54	Capitol CL 14076	I Get So Lonely/Till Then	25
54	Capitol CL 14154	Easy Street/In The Chapel In The Moonlight	20
54	Capitol CL 14204	I Don't Wanna See You Cryin'/Saw Your Eyes	20
55	Capitol CL 14244	Honey Bunch/Write Me, Baby	30
55	Capitol CL 14290	Inside Out/Foolishly Yours	15
56	Capitol CL 14516	Guilty/You	15
59	Coral Q 72355	Foolish Tears/O' Falling Star	15
59	Coral Q 72355	Foolish Tears/O' Falling Star (78)	10
55	Capitol EAP1 506	THE FOUR KNIGHTS (EP)	30
53	Capitol LC 6604	SPOTLIGHT SONGS (10" LP)	40

FOUR LADS

(see also Johnnie Ray, Frankie Laine, Doris Day)

57	Philips JK 1021	Golly/I Just Don't Know (jukebox issue)	10
60	Philips PB 1000	Standing On The Corner/Sunday	5
55	Philips BBE 12044	MOMENTS TO REMEMBER (EP)	8

FOUR LEAVED CLOVER

65	Oak RGJ 207	Alright Girl/Why	500

MINT VALUE £

FOUR MACS
(see also Sands Of Time)

64	Parlophone R 5204	Come Back Silly Girl/Darlin'	8

FOUR MATADORS

66	Columbia DB 7806	A Man's Gotta Stand Tall/Fast Cars And Money	70

FOURMOST
(see also Format)

63	Parlophone R 5056	Hello Little Girl/Just In Case	5
63	Parlophone R 5078	I'm In Love/Respectable	6
64	Parlophone R 5128	A Little Loving/Waiting For You	6
64	Parlophone R 5157	How Can I Tell Her/You Got That Way	5
64	Parlophone R 5194	Baby I Need Your Loving/That's Only What They Say	5
65	Parlophone R 5304	Everything In The Garden/He Could Never	6
65	Parlophone R 5379	Girls Girls Girls/Why Do Fools Fall In Love?	5
66	Parlophone R 5491	Here, There And Everywhere/You've Changed	10
66	Parlophone R 5528	Auntie Maggie's Remedy/Turn The Lights Down	10
68	CBS 3814	Apples, Peaches, Pumpkin Pie/He Could Never	12
69	CBS 4041	Rosetta/Just Like Before	40
69	CBS 4461	Easy Squeezy/Do I Love You?	20
72	Phoenix SNIX 126	Goodnight Sweet Dreams/Memphis	8
64	Parlophone GEP 8892	THE SOUND OF THE FOURMOST (EP)	50
64	Parlophone GEP 8917	THE FOURMOST (EP)	50
65	Parlophone PMC 1259	FIRST AND FOURMOST (LP)	130
75	Fourmost SOF 001	THE FOURMOST (LP)	15

FOURMYULA

69	Columbia DB 8549	Honey Chile/Come With Me	20

FOUR PALMS

58	Vogue V 9116	Jeanie, Joanie, Shirley, Toni/Consideration	600
58	Vogue V 9116	Jeanie, Joanie, Shirley, Toni/Consideration (78)	150

FOUR PENNIES (U.K.)
(see also Lionel Morton, Fritz Mike & Mo)

63	Philips BF 1296	Do You Want Me To/Miss Bad Daddy	10
64	Philips BF 1322	Tell Me Girl/Juliet	5
64	Philips BF 1322	Juliet/Tell Me Girl (A- & B-sides supposedly flipped after original release)	7
64	Philips BF 1349	I Found Out The Hard Way/Don't Tell Me You Love Me	5
64	Philips BF 1366	Black Girl/You Went Away	5
65	Philips BF 1398	The Way Of Love/A Place Where No-One Goes	5
65	Philips BF 1435	Until It's Time For You To Go/Till Another Day	8
66	Philips BF 1469	Trouble Is My Middle Name/Way Out Love	7
66	Philips BF 1491	Keep The Freeway Open/Square Peg	7
66	Philips BF 1519	No Sad Songs For Me/Cats	10
64	Philips BBE 12561	THE FOUR PENNIES (EP)	20
64	Philips BBE 12562	SPIN WITH THE PENNIES (EP)	20
64	Philips BBE 12570	THE SWINGING SIDE OF THE FOUR PENNIES (EP)	20
64	Philips BBE 12571	THE SMOOTH SIDE OF THE FOUR PENNIES (EP)	15
64	Philips BL 7642	TWO SIDES OF THE FOUR PENNIES (LP)	40
66	Philips BL 7734	MIXED BAG (LP)	90
67	Wing WL 1146	JULIET (LP)	18

FOUR PENNIES (U.S.)
(see also Chiffons)

63	Stateside SS 198	My Block/Dry Your Eyes	35
63	Stateside SS 244	When The Boy's Happy (The Girl's Happy Too)/Hockaday Part 1	30
79	Ensign ENY 23	When The Boy's Happy/CARLO: Little Orphan Girl	7

FOUR + ONE
(see also In Crowd, Tomorrow, Keith West)

65	Parlophone R 5221	Time Is On My Side/Don't Lie To Me	100

FOUR PREPS

57	Capitol CL 14727	Falling Star/Where Wuz You	8
57	Capitol CL 14747	I Cried A Million Tears/Moonstruck In Madrid	8
57	Capitol CL 14768	Again 'n' Again 'n' Again/Promise Me Baby	5
57	Capitol CL 14783	Band Of Angels/How About That?	5
58	Capitol CL 14815	26 Miles (Santa Catalina)/Fools Will Be Fools	5
58	Capitol CL 14873	Big Man/Stop, Baby	5
60	Capitol CL 15128	Got A Girl/(Wait Till You) Hear It From Me	5
61	Capitol CL 15217	More Money For You And Me (Medley)/Swing Down Chariot	8
59	Capitol T 1090	THE THINGS WE DID LAST SUMMER (LP)	15
59	Capitol T 1216	DANCING AND DREAMING (LP)	12
61	Capitol T 1291	DOWN BY THE STATION (LP)	12
61	Capitol T 1566	ON THE CAMPUS (LP)	12

4 SAXOPHONES IN 12 TONES

56	Vogue V 2355	Fantastic/Frankly Speaking	7

FOUR SEASONS
(see also Beverly Hills Blues Band, Frankie Valli, Wonder Who)

SINGLES

62	Stateside SS 122	Sherry/I've Cried Before	5
63	Stateside SS 145	Big Girls Don't Cry/Connie-O	5
63	Stateside SS 169	Walk Like A Man/Lucky Ladybug	5
63	Stateside SS 194	Ain't That A Shame/Soon (I'll Be Home Again)	8
63	Stateside SS 216	Candy Girl/Marlena	10
63	Stateside SS 241	Santa Claus Is Coming To Town/Christmas Tears	15
64	Stateside SS 262	Peanuts/Silhouettes	15

			MINT VALUE £
64	Philips BF 1317	Dawn (Go Away)/No Surfin' Today	7
64	Philips BF 1334	Ronnie/Born To Wander	8
64	Stateside SS 315	Alone/Long Lonely Nights	10
64	Philips BF 1347	Rag Doll/Silence Is Golden	6
64	Stateside SS 343	Since I Don't Have You/Sincerely	15
65	Philips BF 1364	Save It For Me/Funny Face	8
65	Philips BF 1372	Big Man In Town/Little Angel	7
65	Philips BF 1395	Bye Bye Baby (Baby Goodbye)/Searching Wind	7
65	Philips BF 1411	Toy Soldier/Betrayed	8
65	Philips BF 1420	Girl Come Running/Cry Myself To Sleep	10
65	Philips BF 1439	Let's Hang On!/On Broadway Tonight	6
66	Philips BF 1474	Working My Way Back To You/Too Many Memories	5
66	Philips BF 1493	Opus 17 (Don't Worry 'Bout Me)/Beggar's Parade	10
66	Philips BF 1511	I've Got You Under My Skin/Huggin' My Pillow	8
67	Philips BF 1538	Tell It To The Rain/Show Girl	10
67	Philips BF 1556	Beggin'/Dody	12
67	Philips BF 1584	C'mon Marianne/Let's Ride Again	7
67	Philips BF 1600	Around And Around/WONDER WHO: Lonesome Road	10
67	Philips BF 1621	Watch The Flowers Grow/Raven	12
68	Philips BF 1651	Will You Love Me Tomorrow?/Silhouettes	10
68	Philips BF 1685	Saturday's Father/Goodbye Girl	10
69	Philips BF 1743	Electric Stories/Pity	10
69	Philips BF 1763	Rag Doll/Working My Way Back To You (p/s)	7
71	Philips 6051 018	Rag Doll/Let's Hang On/I've Got You Under My Skin (maxi-single)	5
71	Warner Bros K 16107	Whatever You Say/Sleeping Man (withdrawn, 300 only) As Frankie Valli and the...)	45

EPs/LPs

64	Stateside SE 1011	THE FOUR SEASONS SING (EP)	60
63	Stateside SL 10033	SHERRY AND 11 OTHERS	40
63	Stateside SL 10042	AIN'T THAT A SHAME	50
63	Stateside SL 10051	THE FOUR SEASONS' GREETINGS	35
64	Philips BL 7611	BORN TO WANDER	20
64	Philips BL 7621	DAWN (GO AWAY) AND 11 OTHER GREAT SONGS	20
64	Philips BL 7643	RAG DOLL	18
65	Philips BL 7663	ENTERTAIN YOU	20
65	Philips (S)BL 7687	SING BIG HITS BY BURT BACHARACH ... HAL DAVID ... BOB DYLAN	18
65	Philips BL 7699	WORKING MY WAY BACK TO YOU	18
66	Philips (S)BL 7719	GOLD VAULT OF HITS	12
67	Philips (S)BL 7751	SECOND VAULT OF GOLDEN HITS	12
67	Philips (S)BL 7752	LOOKIN' BACK	15
67	Philips (S)BL 7753	CHRISTMAS ALBUM	25
69	Philips (S)BL 7880	THE GENUINE IMITATION LIFE GAZETTE	25

FOUR SENSATIONS

52	London L 1137	Heaven Knows Why/Believing In You (78)	25
52	Melodisc P 216	Raindrops/When Honeymoon Lane Becomes Memory Lane (78)	10

FOUR SIGHTS

64	Columbia DB 7227	But I Can Tell/And I Cry	15

4-SKINS

(see also Plastic Gangsters)

81	Clockwork Fun CF 101	One Law For Them/Brave New World (p/s)	15
81	Secret SHH 125	Yesterday's Heroes/Justice/Get Out Of My Life (p/s)	10
82	Secret SHH 141	Lowlife/Bread Or Blood (p/s)	10
82	Secret SEC 4	THE GOOD, THE BAD AND THE 4-SKINS (LP, with photo inner)	15
83	Syndicate SYN 1	A FISTFUL OF ... 4-SKINS (LP)	12
84	Syndicate SYN LP 5	FROM CHAOS TO 1984 (LP)	20

FOUR SPICES

57	MGM MGM 944	Armen's Theme (Yesterday And You)/Fire Engine Boogie	150
57	MGM MGM 944	Armen's Theme (Yesterday And You)/Fire Engine Boogie (78)	20

FOUR SQUARES

(see also Pink People)

64	Hollick & Taylor HT 1009	FOUR SQUARES (EP)	100

FOURTEEN

68	Olga OLE 002	Through My Door/Meet Mr. Edgar	20
68	Olga OLE 006	Umbrella/Drizzle (Rain)	20
68	Olga OLE 006	Umbrella/Drizzle (Rain) (Demo)	30
68	Olga S 051	Easy To Fool/Frosty Stars On A Window Pane	15

14 ICED BEARS

86	Frank COPPOLA 101	Inside/Blue Suit/Cut (hand-printed paper bag sleeve)	25
87	Frank CAPRA 202	Like A Dolphin/Balloon Song/Train Song/Lie To Choose (12", p/s)	10
87	Penetration	Balloon Song (flexidisc)	8
87	Penetration 001	Lie To Choose/SPLENDOUR IN THE GRASS: Twist Me (flexidisc)	6
88	Sarah SARAH 005	Come Get Me/Unhappy Days/Sure To See (poster p/s)	15
89	Thunderball 7TBL 2	Mother Sleep (7", unreleased, Mayking test pressings only)	25
90s	Thunderball Surfacer 002	Falling Backwards/World I Love/CROCODILE RIDE: Ex-Hipster/Satellite (Speed Mix) (numbered & stickered mailer, 1,000 only)	8

FOUR TET

(see also Fridge)

98	Output OPR 14	THIRTYSIXTWENTYFIVE EP (2 one-sided 12", p/s)	10
02	Domino RUG 139	I'm On Fire (Part 1)/I'm On Fire (Part 2) (p/s)	5
09	Text TEXT 006	Wolf Cub (12", black label, plain black sleeve)	15
99	Output OPR21	DIALOGUE (LP)	20
01	Domino WIGLP94	PAUSE (LP)	20
02	Domino WIGLP126	ROUNDS (2xLP)	20
05	Domino WIGLP 154	EVERYTHING ECSTATIC (2xLP, one sided etched, with bonus CD)	18

MINT VALUE £

FOUR TONES

58	Decca F 11074	Voom Ba Voom/Rickshaw Boy	15

FOUR TOPHATTERS

55	London HLA 8163	Leave-a My Gal Alone/Go Baby Go	300
55	London HLA 8163	Leave-a My Gal Alone/Go Baby Go (78)	35
55	London HLA 8198	Forty Five Men In A Telephone Booth/Wild Rosie	300
55	London HLA 8198	Forty Five Men In A Telephone Booth/Wild Rosie (78)	35

FOUR TOPS

(see also Supremes & Four Tops)

SINGLES

64	Stateside SS 336	Baby I Need Your Lovin'/Call On Me	50
64	Stateside SS 336	Baby I Need Your Lovin'/Call On Me (DJ Copy)	60
65	Stateside SS 371	Without The One You Love (Life's Not Worthwhile)/Love Has Gone	60
65	Stateside SS 371	Without The One You Love (Life's Not Worthwhile)/Love Has Gone (DJ Copy)	130
65	Tamla Motown TMG 507	Ask The Lonely/Where Did You Go?	85
65	Tamla Motown TMG 507	Ask The Lonely/Where Did You Go? (DJ Copy)	150
65	Tamla Motown TMG 515	I Can't Help Myself/Sad Souvenirs	25
65	Tamla Motown TMG 515	I Can't Help Myself/Sad Souvenirs (DJ Copy)	100
65	Tamla Motown TMG 528	It's The Same Old Song/Your Love Is Amazing	25
65	Tamla Motown TMG 528	It's The Same Old Song/Your Love Is Amazing (DJ Copy)	100
68	Tamla Motown TML 11061	FOUR TOPS GREATEST HITS (mono)	20
65	Tamla Motown TMG 542	Something About You/Darling I Hum Our Song	30
65	Tamla Motown TMG 542	Something About You/Darling I Hum Our Song (DJ Copy)	100
66	Tamla Motown TMG 553	Shake Me, Wake Me (When It's Over)/Just As Long As You Need Me)	35
66	Tamla Motown TMG 553	Shake Me, Wake Me (When It's Over)/Just As Long As You Need Me (DJ Copy)	100
66	Tamla Motown TMG 568	Loving You Is Sweeter Than Ever/I Like Everything About You	35
66	Tamla Motown TMG 568	Loving You Is Sweeter Than Ever/I Like Everything About You (DJ Copy)	100
66	Tamla Motown TMG 579	Reach Out, I'll Be There/Until You Love Someone (small print)	15
66	Tamla Motown TMG 579	Reach Out, I'll Be There/Until You Love Someone (later large print)	5
66	Tamla Motown TMG 579	Reach Out, I'll Be There/Until You Love Someone (DJ Copy)	100
67	Tamla Motown TMG 589	Standing In The Shadows Of Love/Since You've Been Gone (small print)	15
67	Tamla Motown TMG 589	Standing In The Shadows Of Love/Since You've Been Gone (later large print)	8
67	Tamla Motown TMG 589	Standing In The Shadows Of Love/Since You've Been Gone (DJ copy)	100
67	Tamla Motown TMG 601	Bernadette/I Got A Feeling	15
67	Tamla Motown TMG 601	Bernadette/I Got A Feeling (DJ Copy)	100
67	Tamla Motown TMG 612	Seven Rooms Of Gloom/I'll Turn To Stone	15
67	Tamla Motown TMG 612	Seven Rooms Of Gloom/I'll Turn To Stone (DJ Copy)	65
67	Tamla Motown TMG 623	You Keep Running Away/If You Don't Want My Love	12
67	Tamla Motown TMG 623	You Keep Running Away/If You Don't Want My Love (DJ Copy)	65
67	Tamla Motown TMG 634	Walk Away Renee/Mame	12
67	Tamla Motown TMG 634	Walk Away Renee/Mame (DJ Copy)	60
68	Tamla Motown TMG 647	If I Were A Carpenter/Your Love Is Wonderful	12
68	Tamla Motown TMG 647	If I Were A Carpenter/Your Love Is Wonderful (DJ Copy)	60
68	Tamla Motown TMG 665	Yesterday's Dreams/For Once In My Life	15
68	Tamla Motown TMG 665	Yesterday's Dreams/For Once In My Life (DJ Copy)	60
68	Tamla Motown TMG 675	I'm In A Different World/Remember When	15
68	Tamla Motown TMG 675	I'm In A Different World/Remember When (DJ Copy)	60
69	Tamla Motown TMG 698	What Is A Man?/Don't Bring Back Memories	12
69	Tamla Motown TMG 698	What Is A Man?/Don't Bring Back Memories (DJ Copy)	70
69	Tamla Motown TMG 710	Do What You Gotta Do/Can't Seem To Get You Out Of My Mind	15
69	Tamla Motown TMG 710	Do What You Gotta Do/Can't Seem To Get You Out Of My Mind (DJ Copy)	70
70	Tamla Motown TMG 736	It's All In The Game/Love (Is The Answer)	7
70	Tamla Motown TMG 736	It's All In The Game/Love (Is The Answer) (DJ Copy)	40
70	Tamla Motown TMG 752	Still Water (Love)/Still Water (Peace)	7
70	Tamla Motown TMG 752	Still Water (Love)/Still Water (Peace) (DJ copy)	40
71	Tamla Motown TMG 770	Just Seven Numbers (Can Straighten Out My Life)/I Wish I Were Your Mirror	7
71	Tamla Motown TMG 770	Just Seven Numbers (Can Straighten Out My Life)/ I Wish I Were Your Mirror (DJ Copy)	30
71	Tamla Motown TMG 785	Simple Game/You Stole My Love	7
71	Tamla Motown TMG 785	Simple Game/You Stole My Love (DJ Copy)	30
72	Tamla Motown TMG 803	Bernadette/I Got A Feeling/It's The Same Old Song	5
72	Tamla Motown TMG 803	Bernadette/I Got A Feeling/It's The Same Old Song (DJ Copy)	30
72	Tamla Motown TMG 829	I'll Turn To Stone/Love Feels Like Fire	10
72	Tamla Motown TMG 829	I'll Turn To Stone/Love Feels Like Fire (DJ Copy)	30
72	Probe PRO 575	Keeper Of The Castle/Jubilee With Soul	5
73	Probe PRO 596	Are You Man Enough/Peace Of Mind	5
74	Probe PRO 612	I Just Can't Get You Out Of My Mind/Am I My Brother's Keeper	15
75	ABC ABC 4057	Seven Lonely Nights/I Can't Hold On Much Longer	5
83	Tamla Motown TMG 1320	Medley/TEMPTATIONS: Papa Was A Rolling Stone	35

EPs

66	Tamla Motown TME 2012	THE FOUR TOPS (EP, flipback sleeve)	30
67	Tamla Motown TME 2018	FOUR TOP HITS	30

LPs

65	Tamla Motown TML 11010	THE FOUR TOPS	80
66	T. Motown TML 11021	SECOND ALBUM (mono)	40
66	T. Motown STML 11021	SECOND ALBUM (stereo)	55
66	T. Motown TML 11037	FOUR TOPS ON TOP (mono)	40
66	T. Motown STML 11037	FOUR TOPS ON TOP (stereo)	50
67	T. Motown TML 11041	FOUR TOPS LIVE! (mono)	30
67	T. Motown STML 11041	FOUR TOPS LIVE! (stereo)	40
67	T. Motown STML 11056	REACH OUT (stereo)	35
68	T. Motown STML 11061	FOUR TOPS GREATEST HITS (stereo)	25
69	T. Motown (S)TML 11087	YESTERDAY'S DREAMS (mono/stereo)	25
69	T. Motown (S)TML 11113	FOUR TOPS NOW (mono/stereo)	25
70	T. Motown TML 11138	SOUL SPIN (mono)	25

			MINT VALUE £
70	Tamla Motown STML 11138	SOUL SPIN (stereo)	25
70	Tamla Motown STML 11149	STILL WATERS RUN DEEP	20
71	Tamla Motown STML 11173	CHANGING TIMES	18
71	Tamla Motown STML 11195	GREATEST HITS VOL. 2	12
72	Tamla Motown STML 11206	NATURE PLANNED IT	12
73	Probe SPB 1064	KEEPER OF THE CASTLE	15
73	Probe SPB 1077	SHAFT IN AFRICA (soundtrack, with Johnny Pate)	25
73	Probe SPBA 6277	MAIN STREET PEOPLE	12
74	Probe SPBA 6283	MEETING OF THE MINDS	15
74	ABC ABCL 5035	SHAFT IN AFRICA (soundtrack, reissue)	15
67	Tamla Motown TML 11056	REACH OUT (mono)	30

FOUR TUNES

54	London L 1231	I Gambled With Love/Marie (78)	40
54	London HL 8050	Do, Do, Do, Do, Do Do It Again/My Wild Irish Rose (78)	20
55	London HL 8151	I Sold My Heart To A Junkman/The Greatest Feeling In The World	120
55	London HL 8151	I Sold My Heart To A Junkman/The Greatest Feeling In The World (78)	35
55	London HLJ 8164	Tired Of Waitin'/L'Amour, Toujours L'Amour (Love Everlasting)	50
55	London HLJ 8164	Tired Of Waitin'/L'Amour, Toujours L'Amour (Love Everlasting) (78)	30

FOURUM

78	Sirius SP 519	FOURUM (LP)	20
81	Guardian GRC 95	SINGING THE DALES (LP)	20

FOUR VOICES

58	Philips PB 864	Tell Me You're Mine/Tight Spot	5

FOUR WINDS

58	London HLU 8556	Short Shorts/Five Minutes More	35

HARRY FOWLER

61	HMV POP 891	Buddies (with Mario Fabrizl)/Flower Flogger	8

KIM FOWLEY

(see also Freaks Of Nature, Hollywood Argyles, Napoleon XIV, B. Bumble & Stingers)

66	Parlophone R 5521	Lights/Something New And Different	25
66	CBS 202243	They're Coming To Take Me Away Ha-Haaa!!/You Get More For Your Money On The Flip Side Of This Record Talking Blues	15
66	CBS 202338	Lights (The Blind Can See)/Something New And Different (reissue)	15
66	Island WI 278	The Trip/Beautiful People	15
72	Action ACT 4606	Born To Make You Cry/Thunder Road	7
73	Capitol CL 15743	International Heroes/E.S.P. Reader	5
77	Island WIP 278	The Trip/Beautiful People (p/s, reissue)	10
78	Mercury 6005 009	Control/Rubber Rainbow	5
79	Illegal ILS 012	Rubber Rainbow/In My Garage (p/s)	5
80	Island WIP 6555	1989: Waiting For The Next Ten Years/1987: Lost Like A Lizard In Snow	5
73	Capitol E-ST 11159	INTERNATIONAL HEROES (LP)	25

(THE) FOX

68	CBS 3381	Mister Carpenter/Seek And You Find	250

FOX

70	Fontana 6007 016	Second Hand Love/Butterfly	25
70	Fontana 6309 007	FOR FOX SAKE (LP, laminated sleeve, black/silver labels)	200

FOX

(see also Wooden Horse, Demick & Armstrong)

75	GTO GTLP 006	TAILS OF ILLUSION (LP)	12

BOB FOX & STU LUCKLEY

78	Rubber RUB 028	NOWT SO GOOD'LL PASS (LP)	15

DON FOX

57	Decca F 10927	Be My Girl/You'll Never Go To Heaven	12
57	Decca F 10955	The Majesty Of Love/Party Time	12
58	Decca F 10983	Pretend You Don't See Her/Wasteland	12
58	Decca F 11057	She Was Only Seventeen/When You're A Long, Long Way Away	10
60	Triumph RGM 1022	T'ain't What You Do/Out There	40
61	Oriole CB 1643	Don't Fool With Love/If You Go	8
60s	Honey Hit TB 125	Three Swinging Chicks/I Found The Girl I Love In My Home Town (in p/s)	15
60s	Honey Hit TB 125	Three Swinging Chicks/I Found The Girl I Love In My Home Town	7
69	B & C CB 110	Once In A While/You Belong To My Heart	6

FOXTROT

74	RCA APBO 0169	Cave Man Billy/These Passing Days	5

FOXX

71	MCA MUPS 419	REVOLT OF EMILY YOUNG (LP)	15

INEZ FOXX

63	Sue WI 301	Mockingbird/He's The One You Love (actually by Inez & Charlie Foxx)	25
64	Sue WI 304	Jaybirds/Broken-Hearted Fool (actually by Inez & Charlie Foxx)	25
64	Sue WI 314	Ask Me/Hi Diddle Diddle (actually by Inez & Charlie Foxx)	25
64	Sue WI 323	Hurt By Love/Confusion (actually by Inez & Charlie Foxx)	25
71	Pye International 7N 25546	You Shouldn't Have Set My Soul On Fire/Live For Today	10
73	Stax 2025 151	You Hurt Me For The Last Time/Watch The Dog (That Brings The Bone)	8

INEZ & CHARLIE FOXX

64	Sue WI 307	Competition/Here We Go Round The Mulberry Bush (as Charlie & Inez Foxx)	30
64	Sue WI 356	La De Da I Love You/Yankee Doodle Dandy	30
65	London HLC 9971	My Momma Told Me/I Feel Alright	10
65	London HLC 10009	Hummingbird/If I Need Anyone (Let It Be You)	10
66	Stateside SS 556	Come By Here/No Stranger To Love	30
67	Stateside SS 586	Tightrope/My Special Prayer	35

			MINT VALUE £
67	Stateside SS 586	Tightrope/My Special Prayer (DJ copy)	75
67	Direction 58-2712	I Ain't Goin' For That/Undecided	10
67	Direction 58-3192	(1, 2, 3, 4, 5, 6, 7) Count The Days/A Stranger I Don't Know	10
68	Direction 58-3816	Come On In/Baby Drop Your Dime	10
69	Direction 58-4042	Baby Give It To Me/You Fixed My Heartache	40
69	London HLC 10250	Mockingbird/Hummingbird (unissued)	0
69	United Artists UP 2269	Mockingbird/Hurt By Love	8
69	United Artists UP 35013	La De Da I Love You/Don't Do It No More	8
71	Pye International 7N 25561	Tightrope/Baby Take It All	10
83	Sue ENS 2	MOCKINGBIRD (EP)	15
64	Sue ILP 911	MOCKINGBIRD (LP)	100
65	London HA-C 8241	INEZ AND CHARLIE FOXX (LP, plum label)	70
65	London HA-C 8241	INEZ AND CHARLIE FOXX (LP, later black label)	40
68	Direction 8-63085	COME BY HERE (LP)	30
68	Direction 8-63281	GREATEST HITS (LP)	20
69	United Artists UA(S) 29025	MOCKINGBIRD (LP)	15
71	Pye PKL 4406	GREATEST HITS (LP)	12

JOHN FOXX

(see also Ultravox)

80	Virgin VS 338	No-One Driving (2.53 DJ Version)/Glimmer//This City/Mr. No (double pack, stickered gatefold p/s, matrix no. VS 338 A5DJ)	15
80	Virgin VS 360	Burning Car/20th Century (picture disc)	5
82	Virgin VS 543	Endlessly/Ghosts On Water//Dance With Me/A Kind Of Wave (double pack)	5
84	Virgin VS 615	Your Dress/Woman On A Stairway//Lifting Sky/Annexe (double pack)	5
84	Virgin VSP 645	Like A Miracle/Wings And A Wind (shaped picture disc)	6
85	Virgin VS 771	The Stars On Fire/What Kind Of Girl (p/s, with bonus single)	5
80	Virgin V 2146	METAMATIC (LP)	12
81	Virgin V 2194	THE GARDEN (LP)	12

FRABJOY & RUNCIBLE SPOON

(see also Godley & Creme, Doctor Father, Hotlegs, Mockingbirds, 10cc)

69	Marmalade 598 019	I'm Beside Myself/Animal Song	30

FRAGILE FRIENDS

83	KC KCT1	NOVELTY WEARS OFF (12" EP)	25
84	KC KC 001	Paper Doll/What I Call Beautiful	35

FRAME

66	RCA RCA 1556	My Feet Don't Fit In His Shoes/She	18
67	RCA RCA 1571	Doctor Doctor/I Can't Go On	65
70	Pye 7N 45213	Rockin' Machine/One More Time	10
74	Seven Sun SSUN 12	Billy The Dreamer/Rocking Machine	20

FRAMED

(see also Girlschool)

82	Thunderbay TBR 021	Into My Life/Wonderland	20

FRAMES

79	Brain Booster BBC 2	False Accusations/69 (no p/s)	6

PETER FRAMPTON

(see also Preachers, Herd, Humble Pie, Frampton's Camel, Moon's Train)

81	A&M AMS 8151	Breaking All The Rules/Night Town	5

FRAN & ALAN

66	Mercury MF 95	Seein' The Right Love Go Wrong/There's A place	5
68	MGM MGM 1428	Such A Pity/Mrs Robinson	8

PETER FRANC

73	Dawn DNS 1033	I'll Move Along/Song For Every Season	6
73	Dawn DNS 1039	Ballad Of the Superstar/Strange Kind Of Woman	6
74	Dawn DNS 1088	Flag Of Convenience/At Home With You	6
73	Dawn DNLS 3043	PROFILE (LP)	12
73	Dawn DNLS 3051	EN ROUTE (LP)	12

FRANCIS

67	Blue Beat BB 379	Warn The People (actually by Willie Francis)/SWINGERS: Simpleton (actually by Peter Tosh & Crackers)	80
72	Fab FAB 182	Rocking Machine/SOUL CLANS: Flying Rhythm	25
73	Fab FAB 251	Locks/Version	12

B. FRANCIS

65	Ska Beat JB 193	Judy Crowned/Who Crunch	15

BOBBY FRANCIS

(see also Winston Francis)

67	Doctor Bird DB 1153	Chain Gang/Venus	150

CLAIRE FRANCIS

66	Polydor 56079	I've Got My Own Thing Going/Here I Go Again	7
67	Polydor 56142	But I Don't Care/If You Don't Know	7

CONNIE FRANCIS

SINGLES

56	MGM SP 1169	My First Real Love (with Jaybirds)/Believe In Me (Crede Mi)	200
56	MGM SP 1169	My First Real Love (with Jaybirds)/Believe In Me (Crede Mi) (78)	40
56	MGM MGM 932	My Sailor Boy/Everyone Needs Someone	70
56	MGM MGM 932	My Sailor Boy/Everyone Needs Someone (78)	20
57	MGM MGM 945	Little Blue Wren/I Never Had A Sweetheart	60
57	MGM MGM 945	Little Blue Wren/I Never Had A Sweetheart (78)	20
57	MGM MGM 962	Eighteen/Faded Orchid	60
57	MGM MGM 962	Eighteen/Faded Orchid (78)	40
58	MGM MGM 975	Who's Sorry Now?/You Were Only Fooling (While I Was Falling In Love)	6

			MINT VALUE £
58	MGM MGM 982	I'm Sorry I Made You Cry/Lock Up Your Heart	6
58	MGM MGM 985	Carolina Moon/Stupid Cupid	5
58	MGM MGM 993	I'll Get By/Fallin'	15
58	MGM MGM 998	You Always Hurt The One You Love/In The Valley Of Love	6
59	MGM MGM 1001	My Happiness/Happy Days And Lonely Nights	5
59	MGM MGM 1001	My Happiness/Happy Days And Lonely Nights (78)	15
59	MGM MGM 1012	If I Didn't Care/Toward The End Of The Day	6
59	MGM MGM 1012	If I Didn't Care/Toward The End Of The Day (78)	20
59	MGM MGM 1018	Lipstick On Your Collar/Frankie	6
59	MGM MGM 1018	Lipstick On Your Collar/Frankie (78)	20
59	MGM MGM 1036	Plenty Good Lovin'/You're Gonna Miss Me	6
59	MGM MGM 1036	Plenty Good Lovin'/You're Gonna Miss Me (78)	20
59	MGM MGM 1046	Among My Souvenirs/Do You Love Me Like You Kiss Me?	5
59	MGM MGM 1046	Among My Souvenirs/Do You Love Me Like You Kiss Me? (78)	30
60	MGM MGM 1060	Valentino/It Would Be Worth It	5
60	MGM MGM 1070	Mama/Teddy (withdrawn; demos more common)	40
60	MGM MGM 1070	Mama/Teddy (withdrawn; demo copy)	30
61	MGM MGM 1121	Where The Boys Are/Baby Roo	6
62	MGM MGM 1151	Don't Cry On My Shoulder/Mr. Twister	6
62	MGM MGM 1165	Vacation/It's Gonna Take Me Some Time	10
62	MGM MGM 1171	Playin' Games/I Was Such A Fool	8
62	MGM MGM 1185	I'm Gonna Be Warm This Winter/Pretty Little Baby	10
62	MGM MGM 1193	Follow The Boys/Tonight's My Night	6
63	MGM MGM 1202	If My Pillow Could Talk/Lollipop Lips	6
63	MGM MGM 1207	Drownin' My Sorrows/Look At Him	6
63	MGM MGM 1212	Your Other Love/Whatever Happened To Rosemary	6
63	MGM MGM 1220	The Summer Of His Years/My Buddy	7
63	MGM MGM 1224	Blue Winter/Souvenirs	7
63	MGM MGM 1236	Be Anything (But Be Mine)/Tommy	8
64	MGM MGM 1253	Don't Ever Leave Me/Waiting For You	6
65	MGM MGM 1265	Forget Domani/I Don't Want To Be No Better Off	6
65	MGM MGM 1271	My Child/No One Ever Sends Me Roses	10
65	MGM MGM 1282	Roundabout/Love Is Me, Love Is You	8
66	MGM MGM 1293	Jealous Heart/Can I Rely On You?	8
66	MGM MGM 1295	The Phoenix Love Theme - Senza Fine/Bossa Nova Hand Dance	6
66	MGM MGM 1305	Love Is Me, Love Is You/I'd Let You Break My Heart All Over Again	6
66	MGM MGM 1320	Somewhere My Love (Lara's Theme)/Letter From A Soldier (Dear Mama)	6
66	MGM MGM 1327	Spanish Nights And You/Games That Lovers Play	5
67	MGM MGM 1334	Another Page/Souvenir D'Italie	5
67	MGM MGM 1336	Time Alone Will Tell/Born Free	10
67	MGM MGM 1347	My Heart Cries For You/If My Friends Could See Me Now (Medley)	8
68	MGM MGM 1381	My World Is Slipping Away/Till We're Together	6
68	MGM MGM 1407	Why Say Goodbye?/Addio Mi Amore	6
68	MGM MGM 1446	Somebody Else Is Taking My Place/Brother Can You Spare A Dime?	6
69	MGM MGM 1471	The Wedding Cake/Overhill Underground	6
69	MGM MGM 1493	Mr. Love/Zingara	10
EPs			
56	MGM MGM-EP 658	A GIRL IN LOVE	20
58	MGM MGM-EP 677	HEARTACHES	20
58	MGM MGM-EP 686	CONNIE FRANCIS	20
59	MGM MGM-EP 697	IF I DIDN'T CARE	20
60	MGM MGM-EP 711	YOU'RE MY EVERYTHING	20
60	MGM MGM-EP 717	ROCK AND ROLL MILLION SELLERS NO. 1	20
60	MGM MGM-EP 720	ROCK AND ROLL MILLION SELLERS NO. 2	20
60	MGM MGM-EP 731	ROCK AND ROLL MILLION SELLERS NO. 3	20
60	MGM MGM-EP 742	FIRST LADY OF RECORD (laminated or matt rear sleeve)	20
61	MGM MGM-EP 756	WHERE THE BOYS ARE	20
61	MGM MGM-EP 759	CONNIE FRANCIS FAVOURITES	20
61	MGM MGM-EP 760	SINGS ITALIAN FAVOURITES	20
63	MGM MGM-EP 769	CONNIE'S AMERICAN HITS	20
63	MGM MGM-EP 773	HEY RING-A-DING	40
63	MGM MGM-EP 775	WHAT KIND OF FOOL AM I?	20
63	MGM MGM-EP 780	MALA FEMMENA	10
63	MGM MGM-EP 783	FROM ITALY ... WITH LOVE	10
65	MGM MGM-EP 789	SINGS FOR MAMA	10
66	MGM MGM-EP 792	JEALOUS HEART	10
LPs			
58	MGM MGM-D 153	WHO'S SORRY NOW? (10")	35
59	MGM MGM-C 782	MY THANKS TO YOU	20
59	MGM MGM-C 786	THE EXCITING CONNIE FRANCIS	20
59	MGM MGM-C 797	CHRISTMAS WITH CONNIE	30
60	MGM MGM-C 804	ROCK AND ROLL MILLION SELLERS NO. 1	45
60	MGM MGM-C 812	COUNTRY AND WESTERN GOLDEN HITS	20
60	MGM MGM-C 819	FUN SONGS FOR CHILDREN	20
60	MGM MGM-C 821	SINGS ITALIAN FAVOURITES (mono)	15
60	MGM MGM-CS 6002	SINGS ITALIAN FAVOURITES (stereo)	20
60	MGM MGM-C 831	CONNIE'S GREATEST HITS	15
60	MGM MGM-C 836	SPANISH AND LATIN AMERICAN FAVOURITES (mono)	12
60	MGM MGM-CS 6012	SPANISH AND LATIN AMERICAN FAVOURITES (stereo)	15
61	MGM MGM-C 845	SINGS JEWISH FAVOURITES (mono)	12
61	MGM MGM-CS 6021	SINGS JEWISH FAVOURITES (stereo)	15
61	MGM MGM-C 854	MORE ITALIAN FAVOURITES (mono)	12
61	MGM MGM-CS6029	MORE ITALIAN FAVOURITES (stereo)	15
61	MGM MGM-C 861	AT THE COPA (mono)	12
61	MGM MGM-CS 6035	AT THE COPA (stereo)	15
61	MGM MGM-C 870	SONGS TO A SWINGIN' BAND (mono)	12

			MINT VALUE £
61	MGM MGM-CS 6044	SONGS TO A SWINGIN' BAND (stereo)	15
61	MGM MGM-C 875	SINGS 'NEVER ON SUNDAY' AND OTHER TITLE SONGS FROM MOTION PICTURES (mono)	12
61	MGM MGM-CS 6047	SINGS 'NEVER ON SUNDAY' AND OTHER TITLE SONGS FROM MOTION PICTURES (stereo)	15
61	MGM MGM-C 879	DO THE TWIST	40
62	MGM MGM-C 883	SINGS FOLK SONG FAVOURITES (mono)	12
62	MGM MGM-CS 6054	SINGS FOLK SONG FAVOURITES (stereo)	15
62	MGM MGM-C 898	SINGS IRISH FAVOURITES (mono)	25
62	MGM MGM-CS 6056	SINGS IRISH FAVOURITES (stereo)	30
62	MGM MGM-C 916	COUNTRY MUSIC CONNIE STYLE (mono)	20
62	MGM MGM-CS 6062	COUNTRY MUSIC CONNIE STYLE (stereo)	25
63	MGM MGM-C 930	SINGS MODERN ITALIAN HITS (mono)	12
63	MGM MGM-CS 6067	SINGS MODERN ITALIAN HITS (stereo)	15
63	MGM MGM-C 931	FOLLOW THE BOYS (mono)	12
63	MGM MGM-CS 6068	FOLLOW THE BOYS (stereo)	15
63	MGM MGM-C 940	SINGS AWARD-WINNING MOTION PICTURE HITS (mono)	12
63	MGM MGM-CS 6070	SINGS AWARD-WINNING MOTION PICTURE HITS (stereo)	15
64	MGM MGM-C 958	GREATEST AMERICAN WALTZES (mono)	12
64	MGM MGM-CS 6075	GREATEST AMERICAN WALTZES (stereo)	15
64	MGM MGM-C 970	16 OF CONNIE'S BIGGEST HITS	12
78	United Artists ULP 30182	WHO'S HAPPY NOW? (withdrawn sleeve with different lettering)	40

CONNIE FRANCIS & MARVIN RAINWATER

(see also Marvin Rainwater)

58	MGM MGM 969	The Majesty Of Love/You My Darling You	50
58	MGM MGM 969	The Majesty Of Love/You My Darling You (78)	30

(KING) JOE FRANCIS

65	Blue Beat BB 323	Wicked Woman/King Joe's Ska (as King Joe Francis)	15
65	Ska Beat JB 184	Waggling Tails/I Don't Want You No More	20
66	Ska Beat JB 262	Scarborough Ska/I Got A Scar (as Joe Francis & Ricky Logan & Snowballs)	20
66	Rio R 90	Have My Body (song actually "Have Mercy Baby")/Everybody's Got To Know (as King Joe Francis & Hijackers)	15
66	Rio R 94	Days Are Lonely/My Baby	25
67	Rainbow RAI 114	My Granny/Pull It Out (as J. Francis & Rico's Boys)	15

JOHNNIE FRANCIS

55	Decca F 10440	Funny Thing/Give Me The Right	5

LEE FRANCIS

(see also Vernons Girls)

65	Decca F 12148	Ciao/If He Wants Me	5

NAT FRANCIS

66	Blue Beat BB 346	Mama Kiss Him Goodnight/Tra La La (with Prince Buster Junior & Sunsets)	20
66	Blue Beat BB 361	Just To Keep You (credited to B. Junior)/You Only Want My Money	18
67	Blue Beat BB 376	Seven Nights Of Love/Feeling Blue	20

PAT FRANCIS

77	Western Kingston WK 506	Rasta Protest/Part 2	8

RITCHIE FRANCIS

(see also Eyes Of Blue, Big Sleep)

72	Pegasus PEG 11	SONGBIRD (LP, gatefold sleeve)	15

STEVE FRANCIS

64	King KG 1012	Watch Your Step/Lovey Dovey	8

WILBERT FRANCIS & VIBRATORS

(see also Little Willie, Vibrators [Jamaica])

66	Ska Beat JB 267	Memories Of You/CHUCK JACQUES: Now That You're Gone	25

WILLIE FRANCIS

(see also Martin Riley)

69	Bullet BU 415	Motherless Children/I Am Not Afraid	20
71	Escort ERT 848	Burn Them/Poor Boy	10
71	Bullet BU 489	Willie's Rouster/Rouster Version	15
71	Pama PM 829	Oh What A Mini/Version	10
74	Magnet MA 38	Quick March/Africa Melody (actually by Charlie Organaire)	10

WINSTON FRANCIS

(see also Bobby Francis, Jerry & Freedom Singers, Zimm & Dee Dee)

69	Coxsone CS 7089	Reggae And Cry/FREEDOM SINGERS: Easy Come Easy Go (B-side actually by Righteous Flames)	35
69	Studio One SO 2086	The Games People Play/ALBERT GRIFFITHS: The Kicks	35
69	Punch PH 5	Too Experienced/JACKIE MINTO: Mule Jerk (B-side actually by Jackie Mittoo)	15
69	Bamboo BAM 10	The Same Old Song/SOUND DIMENSION: Rattle On	45
70	Bamboo BAM 46	Turn Back The Hands Of Time/Soul Bowl	25
70	Bamboo BAM 48	California Dreaming/JACKIE MITTOO & SOUND DIMENSION: Soul Stew	35
72	Camel CA 99	Ten Times Sweeter Than You/Fat Boy	10
72	Rhino RNO 102	A Little Today A Little Tomorrow/Love Thy Neighbour	7
73	Fab FAB 271	Mr Fix It/Version	8
74	Ashanti ASH 415	California Dreaming/SOUND DIMENSION: Soul Food (reissue)	8
70	Bamboo BDLP 207	MR FIX IT (LP)	50
71	Bamboo BDLPS 216	CALIFORNIA DREAMING (LP)	60

CLAUDE FRANCOIS

66	Fontana TF 725	In My Memory/Gone From My Mind	5
77	EMI EMC 3189	HIS HITS IN ENGLISH (LP)	18

FRANCO-LONDON ORCHESTRA

66	Philips BF 1562	Theme From Robinson Crusoe/Adrift	10

MINT VALUE £

JACKSON C. FRANK

65	Columbia DB 7795	Blues Run The Game/Can't Get Away From My Love	100
65	Columbia 33SX 1788	JACKSON C. FRANK (LP)	300
78	B&C BCLP 4	AGAIN (LP, reissue of above LP)	40

STANLEY FRANK

77	Power Exchange PX 247	S'cool Days/On A Line (p/s)	5

FRANK & BARBARIANS

62	Oriole CB 1758	The Bouncer/Concerto In The Stars	15

(see Frank Barber)

FRANKIE & CLASSICALS

67	Philips BF 1586	I Only Have Eyes For You/What Shall I Do?	200
74	Pye Intl. DDS 101	What Shall I Do?/Goodbye Love, Hello Sadness	10

FRANKIE & JOHNNY

(see also Maggie Bell)

66	Decca F 22376	Never Gonna Leave You/I'll Hold You	250
66	Decca F 22376	Never Gonna Leave You/I'll Hold You (DJ Copy)	250
66	Parlophone R 5518	Climb Ev'ry Mountain/I Wanna Make You Understand	25
78	Inferno HEAT 8	I'll Hold You/Never Gonna Leave You (reissue)	10

FRANKIE & LARRY

60	Capitol CL 15153	Not Yet/A Fool For You	12

FRANKIE & THE PHANTOMS

74	RCA LPBO 5013	Rock 'N' Roll Band/Jamburger	6

FRANKIE & TIMEBREAKERS

68	Philips BF 1696	I'll Be Home/Is There Anybody	7

FRANKIE GOES TO HOLLYWOOD

(see also Spitfire Boys)

83	ZTT P ZTAS 1	Relax (Move)/One September Monday (picture disc)	5
83	ZTT 12 ZTAS 1	Relax (Original Mix)/Ferry Across The Mersey/Relax Bonus (Again) (12", ZTT sleeve or standard p/s, some copies play at 33rpm but list 45rpm)	10
83	ZTT 12 ZTAS 1	Relax (Sex Mix [alias 8.20 "New York Mix"])/Ferry Across The Mersey Relax Bonus (Again) (12", p/s, 45rpm, (matrix no.: 1A 2U))	12
83	ZTT 12 ZTAS 1	Relax (Sex Mix)/Ferry Across The Mersey/Relax Bonus (Again) (12", p/s, 45rpm, different 'U.S. chequered' p/s, (matrix no.: 1A 5U))	8
84	ZTT P ZTAS 3	Two Tribes (We Don't Want To Die)/One February Friday (picture disc)	6
84	ZTT P ZTAS 5	The Power Of Love/The World Is My Oyster (picture disc)	5
84	ZTT 12X ZTAS 5	The Power Of Love/The World Is My Oyster/Welcome To The Pleasuredome (Pleasurefix)/The Only Star In Heaven (Starfix) (12", g/fold p/s with 5 photos)	8
84	ZTT CTIS 105	The Power Of Love (Extended Version)/Trapped And Scrapped/Holier Than Thou (, picture 'envelope' box)	8
85	ZTT ZTAS 7	Welcome To The Pleasure Dome (Altered Reel) (actually plays "Video Mix 5.05")/Happy Hi Get It On (p/s, blue label)	5
85	ZTT P ZTAS 7	Welcome To The Pleasure Dome (Alternative Reel ["Fruitiness Mix"])/ Happy Hi/Get It On (apple-shaped picture disc)	8
86	ZTT ZTD 22	Rage Hard/(Don't Lose What's Left) Of Your Little Mind ('pop-up fists' p/s)	5
86	ZTT 12 ZTAX B 22	Rage Hard (++ Mix)/Roadhouse Blues/(Don't Lose What's Left) Of Your Little Mind (extended) (12", in 'action series 22' box)	8
83	ZTT ZTAS 1DJ	Relax " The Last Seven Inches/One September Monday (white label, stamped label, no p/s)	5
84	ZTT XZTAS 3DJ	Two Tribes (Carnage)/Relax (U.S. Mix) (12", ZTT sleeve)	10
84	ZTT XZIP 1	Two Tribes (Hibakusha)/War (Hide Yourself)/Two Tribes/ One February Friday (12", ZTT sleeve)	15
84	ZTT ZTAS 5 DJ-A	The Power Of Love (5.28)/The World Is My Oyster (12")	10
86	ZTT 12 ZTAK 25	Warriors (The Attack Mix) (12", white label, featuring Gary Moore)	10
94	ZTT (no cat no)	Two Tribes (808 State Remix) (10" 1-sided red or blue vinyl)	8

ARETHA FRANKLIN

SINGLES

61	Fontana H 271	Love Is The Only Thing/Today I Sing The Blues (with Ray Bryant Combo)	15
61	Fontana H 343	Rock-A-Bye Your Baby With A Dixie Melody/Operation Heartbreak	10
65	CBS 201732	Can't You Just See Me/You Little Miss Raggedy Anne	20
67	CBS 202468	Cry Like A Baby/Swanee	6
67	CBS 3059	Take A Look/Lee Cross	6
67	Atlantic 584 084	I Never Loved A Man (The Way I Love You)/Do Right Woman - Do Right Man	6
67	Atlantic 584 115	Respect/Save Me	6
67	Atlantic 584 127	Baby I Love You/Going Down Slow	10
67	Atlantic 584 141	(You Make Me Feel Like A) Natural Woman/Never Let Me Go	6
67	Atlantic 584 157	(I Can't Get No) Satisfaction/Night Life (withdrawn B-side)	10
67	Atlantic 584 157	Chain Of Fools/(I Can't Get No) Satisfaction	10
68	Atlantic 584 172	Since You've Been Gone/Ain't No Way	10
68	Atlantic 584 186	Think/You Send Me	8
68	Atlantic 584 206	I Say A Little Prayer/See-Saw	8
69	Atlantic 584 239	Don't Let Me Lose This Dream/The House That Jack Built	6
69	Atlantic 584 252	The Weight/The Tracks Of My Tears	5
69	Atlantic 584 285	Share Your Love With Me/Pledging My Love/The Clock	5
69	Atlantic 584 306	Eleanor Rigby/It Ain't Fair	6
70	Atlantic 584 322	Call Me/Son Of A Preacher Man	8
70	Atlantic 2091 027	Don't Play That Song/The Thrill Is Gone	5
70	Atlantic 2091 042	Border Song (Holy Moses)/You And Me (unissued)	0
70	Atlantic 2091 044	Oh No, Not My Baby/You And Me	5
71	Atlantic 2091 063	You're All I Need To Get By/The Border Song	5
71	Atlantic 2091 111	I Say A Little Prayer/(I Can't Get No) Satisfaction	5
71	Atlantic 2091 127	A Brand New Me/Spirit In The Dark	10
71	Atlantic 2091 168	Rock Steady/Oh Me, Oh My	10

MINT VALUE £

72	Atlantic K 10154	Daydreaming / I've Been Loving You Too Long	8
72	Atlantic K 10224	Rock Steady/All The King's Horses	7

EPs

62	Fontana TE 467217	TODAY I SING THE BLUES	45

LPs

61	Fontana TFL 5173	ARETHA	60
65	CBS (S)BPG 62566	YEAH!!! - IN PERSON	40
67	CBS (S)BPG 62744	SOUL SISTER	40
67	Atlantic 587/588 066	I NEVER LOVED A MAN	15
67	CBS (S)BPG 62969	TAKE IT LIKE YOU GIVE IT	15
67	CBS 63160	LEE CROSS	15
67	Atlantic 587/588 085	ARETHA ARRIVES	12
67	CBS 64536	GREATEST HITS	12
68	Atlantic 587/588 099	LADY SOUL	12
68	CBS 63269	TAKE A LOOK AT ARETHA FRANKLIN	15
68	Atlantic 587/588 114	ARETHA NOW	12
68	CBS 63064	GREATEST HITS VOL. 2	12
68	Atlantic 587/588 149	ARETHA IN PARIS - LIVE AT THE OLYMPIA	15
69	Atlantic 588 169	SOUL '69	12
69	Chess (S)CRL 54550	SONGS OF FAITH	12
70	Atlantic 2400 004	THIS GIRL'S IN LOVE WITH YOU	12
70	Atlantic 2464 007	I SAY A LITTLE PRAYER	12
70	Atlantic 2400 021	DON'T PLAY THAT SONG	12
71	Atlantic 2400 136	LIVE AT THE FILLMORE WEST (gatefold sleeve)	12

CAROLYN FRANKLIN

69	RCA Victor RCA 1851	Boxer/I Don't Want To Lose You	8
70	RCA Victor RCA 2009	All I Want To Be Is Your Woman/You Really Didn't Mean It	5
69	RCA RD/SF 8035	BABY DYNAMITE! (LP)	20

ERMA FRANKLIN

67	London HLZ 10170	Piece Of My Heart/Big Boss Man	15
68	London HLZ 10201	Open Up Your Soul/I Just Ain't Ready For Love	8
68	London HLZ 10220	The Right To Cry/Don't Catch The Dog's Bone	8
69	Soul City SC 118	Don't Wait Too Long/Time After Time	25
69	MCA MU 1073	Gotta Find Me A Lover (24 Hours A Day)/Change My Thoughts From You	15
71	Jay Boy BOY 36	I Just Ain't Ready For Love/The Right To Cry	8
71	Jay Boy BOY 41	Piece Of My Heart/Big Boss Man (reissue)	10
70	MCA MUP MUPS 394	SOUL SISTER (LP)	40

MARIE FRANKLIN

68	MGM MGM 1455	You Ain't Changed/Don'tcha Bet No Money	10

GORDON FRANKS

60	Oriole CB 1541	Inn For Trouble/Twinkle Toes	6

JOHNNY FRANKS

55	Melodisc P 230	Tweedle Dee/Shake, Rattle And Roll (78)	25
56	Melodisc 1355	Rock Candy Baby/Sing-ing-ing (78)	12
58	Melodisc 1459	Good Old Country Music/Cheatin' On Me	7
58	Melodisc 1459	Good Old Country Music/Cheatin' On Me (78)	20

BONNIE (BLUE) FRANKSON

(see also Dotty & Bonnie)

68	Jolly JY 014	Loving You/Shoo Be Do (both with Joe Nolan Band)	12
69	Jolly JY 021	London City/Dearest (both with Joe Nolan & Dynamic Heatwave)	12
69	Columbia Blue Beat DB 114	Dearest/London City	15
70	Ackee ACK 110	I'm So Glad/Lonely Road (both with Dotty)	8
73	Ackee ACK 512	Getting Things Together/Version	6

FRANTIC ELEVATORS

(see also Simply Red)

79	TJM TJM 5	Voice In The Dark/Passion/Every Day I Die (p/s)	40
80	TJM TJM 6	Hunchback Of Notre Dame/See Nothing And Everything/Don't Judge Me (unreleased; demos only)	150
80	Eric's ERIC'S 6	You Know What You Told Me/Production Prevention (p/s)	50
81	Crackin' Up CRAK 1	Searching For The Only One/Hunchback Of Notre Dame (p/s)	20
82	No Waiting WAIT 1	Holding Back The Years/Pistols In My Brain (p/s)	20
87	TJM TJM 101	THE EARLY YEARS (mini-LP)	20
88	Receiver KNOB 2	THE EARLY YEARS (mini-LP, reissue with new sleeve & interview disc, as Mick Hucknall & Frantic Elevators)	15

FRANZ FERDINAND

(see also The Karelia, The Ampheta Meanies)

03	Domino RUG164T	Darts Of Pleasure/Van Tango/Shopping For Blood (12", p/s 500 only)	15
04	Domino RUG172	Take Me Out/Truck Stop (3,000 only, p/s)	5
04	Domino PRINCIPP01	Take Me Out (Naum Gabo Remix) (7" white label promo)	5
04	Domino RUG172T	Take Me Out/Taken Me Out (Morgan Geist re-version) (12", 2500 only, p/s)	5
05	Domino RUG211TP	Do You Want To (Erol Alkan's Glam Racket Mix/Original Version (12" white label)	12
05	New! NEW001	Get Up and Use Me (Franz Ferdinand)/Jacqueline (The Fire Engines) (7" single)	15
03	Chateau CHAT001	LIVE 2003 (LP, 10-track official bootleg/promo 500 copies)	30
04	Domino WIGCD136X	FRANZ FERDINAND (Ltd edn. 2 CD set with live album p/s)	20
09	Domino WIG 205X	TONIGHT: FRANZ FERDINAND (6 x 7", 2 x CD & DVD box set)	40

ANDY FRASER BAND

(see also Free, Sharks)

75	CBS 80731	THE ANDY FRASER BAND (LP)	20
75	CBS 81027	IN YOUR EYES (LP)	12

JOHN FRASER

58	Pye 7N 15118	Trolley Stop/Don't Take Your Love From Me	5
59	Pye 7N 15212	Bye Bye, Baby, Goodbye/Golden Cage	10
58	Pye NEP 24068	PRESENTING JOHN FRASER (EP)	15

MINT VALUE £

PHILLIP FRASER
78 White Rum/Red Stripe 102 Need To Be Loved/Loving Version ... 6

FRATELLIS
06 No Label Cigarillo/Got Ma Nuts From A Hippy (Demo) (gig freebie, 500 only) ... 20

FRATERNITY BROTHERS
59 HMV POP 582 Passion Flower/A Nobody Like Me (B-side with Gil Fields) ... 6

FRATERNITY OF MAN
70 Stateside SS 2166 Don't Bogart Me/Wispy Paisley Skies ... 12

ERIC FRATTER
(see also Eric Fatter)
69 Trojan TR 655 Since You've Been Gone/AFROTONES: Things I Love ... 8

FRAYS
(see also Mike Patto)
65 Decca F 12153 Keep Me Covered/Walk On ... 150
65 Decca F 12229 My Girl Sloopy/For Your Precious Love ... 50

NORMA FRAZER
(see also Sound Dimension, Righteous Homes, Viceroys, Tommy McCook)
65 Ska Beat JB 223 Heartaches/Everybody Loves A Lover ... 120
67 Coxsone CS 7017 The First Cut Is The Deepest/BUMPS OAKLEY: Rag Doll ... 30
67 Studio One SO 2024 Come By Here/WAILERS: I Stand Predominate ... 250
68 Coxsone CS 7060 Respect/Time ... 35

DALLAS FRAZIER
66 Capitol CL 15445 Elvira/That Ain't No Stuff ... 6
66 Capitol CL 15457 Just A Little Bit Of You/Walkin' Wonder ... 5
59 Capitol EAP 1035 DALLAS FRAZIER (EP) ... 20

FRAZIER CHORUS
87 Virgin VSCD 1192 Sloppy Heart/Anarchy In The UK/String/Typical (3" CD in heart-shaped box) ... 12
91 Virgin CDV 2654 RAY (CD, with bonus remix CD) ... 20

FREAKS OF NATURE
(see also Kim Fowley, Belfast Gypsies, Jackie McAuley)
66 Island WI 3017 People! Let's Freak Out/The Shadow Chasers ... 80

FREAKY REALISTIC
93 Polydor 517 919-2 FREALISM (CD) ... 20

STAN FREBERG
54 Capitol CL 14187 Sh-Boom (Life Could Be A Dream) (with The Toads)/C'est Ci Bon ... 30
55 Capitol CL 14316 The Lone Psychiatrist/The Honey-Earthers (with Daws Butler) ... 25
56 Capitol CL 14509 The Yellow Rose Of Texas/Rock Around Stephen Foster ... 20
56 Capitol CL 14571 The Great Pretender/The Quest For Bridey Hammerschlaugen (B-side with June Foray) ... 20
56 Capitol CL 14608 Heartbreak Hotel/Rock Island Line ... 20
57 Capitol CL 14712 Banana Boat (Day-O)/Tele-vee-shun ... 20
58 Capitol CL 14966 Green Chritma (with Daws Butler)/The Meaning Of Christmas (with Jud Conlon Chorale) ... 10
60 Capitol CL 15122 The Old Payola Roll Blues (with Jesse White)/ Sh-Boom (Life Could Be A Dream) ... 15
55 Capitol EAP1 496 ANY REQUESTS (EP) ... 10
56 Capitol EAP1 628 THE REAL SAINT GEORGE (EP) ... 10
61 Capitol EAP1 1101 OMAHA (EP) ... 10
61 Capitol EAP1 20050 THE GREAT PRETENDER (EP) ... 10
61 Capitol EAP1 20115 FREBERG AGAIN (EP, with Daws Butler) ... 10
57 Capitol T 777 A CHILD'S GARDEN OF FREBERG (LP) ... 20
58 Capitol LCT 6170 THE BEST OF THE STAN FREBERG SHOWS (LP) ... 15
58 Capitol LCT 6171 THE BEST OF THE STAN FREBERG SHOWS VOL. 2 (LP) ... 20
61 Capitol W 1573 PRESENTS THE UNITED STATES OF AMERICA (LP) ... 20

FRED BANANA COMBO
78 Warm AWMR 2004 No Destination Blues/Jerk Off All Nite Long (p/s) ... 5

FRED BLOGGS BAND
76 Firebrand DMO 12 Mr Sun/Seaside/Moonrock/The Tribe ... 8

JOHN FRED & HIS PLAYBOY BAND
67 Pye International 7N 25442 Judy In Disguise (With Glasses)/When The Lights Go Out ... 6
68 Pye International 7N 25453 Hey Hey Bunny/No Letter Today ... 20
68 Pye International 7N 25462 We Played Games/Lonely Are The Lonely ... 7
68 Pye International 7N 25470 Little Dum Dum/Tissue Paper ... 7
68 CBS 3475 Shirley/High Heel Sneakers ... 10
69 MCA MU 1088 Silly Sarah Carter/Back In The USSR ... 6
67 Pye Intl. NPL 28111 AGNES ENGLISH (LP) ... 20

FRED LOCKS
78 Tribesman TM 20 Love & Only Love/Stricker Ishion (12") ... 15
78 Revelations FRW 375 Love & Harmony/Joy & Harmony (featuring Brigadier Jerry) (12", p/s) ... 30
78 Lloyd Coxsone LC 001 Voice Of The Poor/LEVI ROOTS: Poor Man's Story (12") ... 12
78 Form FORM 1091 LOVE & HARMONY (LP) ... 30
80 Rev 001 LP NEBUCHADNEZZER KING OF BABYLON (FRED LOCKS MEETS CREATORS) (LP) ... 60
82 Regal RLP 002 LOVE AND ONLY LOVE (LP, with CREATION STEPPERS) ... 45
83 Vulcan VULA 502 BLACK STAR LINER (LP) ... 25

FREDDIE & THE DREAMERS
(see also Freddie Garrity, Dreamers)
63 Columbia DB 7032 If You Gotta Make A Fool Of Somebody/Feel So Blue ... 6
64 Columbia DB 7322 Just For You/Don't Do That To Me ... 5

			MINT VALUE £
65	Columbia DB 7526	A Little You/Things I'd Like To Say	6
65	Columbia DC 763	A Windmill In Old Amsterdam/A Love Like You (export issue)	15
66	Columbia DB 7857	If You've Gotta Minute Baby/When I'm Home With You	6
66	Columbia DB 7929	Playboy/Some Day	15
66	Columbia DB 8033	Turn Around/Funny Over You	8
67	Columbia DB 8137	Hello, Hello/All I Ever Want Is You	5
67	Columbia DB 8200	Brown And Porter's (Meat Exporters) Lorry/Little Brown Eyes	8
68	Columbia DB 8496	Little Big Time/FREDDIE GARRITY: You Belong To Me	8
68	Columbia DB 8517	It's Great/Gaberdine Mac	8
69	Columbia DB 8606	Get Around Downtown Girl/What To Do	8
71	Philips 6006 098	Susan's Tuba/You Hurt Me Girl	10
78	Polydor 2059 041	Here We Go/I Saw Ya	10
63	Columbia SEG 8275	IF YOU GOTTA MAKE A FOOL OF SOMEBODY (EP)	10
63	Columbia SEG 8287	SONGS FROM THE FILM "WHAT A CRAZY WORLD" (EP)	12
64	Columbia SEG 8302	YOU WERE MADE FOR ME (EP)	10
64	Columbia SEG 8323	OVER YOU (EP)	10
64	Columbia SEG 8349	FREDDIE SINGS JUST FOR YOU (EP)	10
65	Columbia SEG 8403	READY, FREDDIE, GO! (EP)	10
65	Columbia SEG 8457	FREDDIE AND THE DREAMERS (EP)	10
67	EMI Regal	SEE YOU LATER ALLIGATOR (Export issue)	35
63	Columbia 33SX 1577	FREDDIE AND THE DREAMERS (LP)	12
64	Columbia 33SX 1663	YOU WERE MAD FOR ME (LP)	12
66	Columbia SX 6069	IN DISNEYLAND (LP, mono)	12
66	Columbia S(C)X 6069	IN DISNEYLAND (LP, stereo)	15
67	Columbia SX 6177	KING FREDDIE AND THE DREAMING KNIGHTS (LP)	15

FREDDIE & THE DREAMERS/PETER & GORDON

(see also Peter & Gordon)

64	Columbia SEG 8337	JUST FOR YOU (EP, 2 tracks each)	20

FREDDIE & FITZY

60s	Dr Bird 1033	Do Good/SOUL BROTHERS: On The Town	30

DOTTY FREDERICK

59	Top Rank JAR 106	Ricky/Just Wait	50
59	Top Rank JAR 106	Ricky/Just Wait (78)	12

TOMMY FREDERICK & HI-NOTES

58	London HLU 8555	Prince Of Players/I'm Not Pretending	50
58	London HLU 8555	Prince Of Players/I'm Not Pretending (78)	20

BILL FREDERICKS

77	Polydor 2058 895	Lovers/It's Just A Matter Of Time	6
78	Polydor 2059 035	Almost/Wind Of Change	6

DOLORES FREDERICKS

56	Brunswick 05540	Cha Cha Joe/Whole Lotta Shakin' Goin' On	30

MARC FREDERICKS

56	London HLD 8281	Mystic Midnight/Symphony To Anne	25

FREE (Holland)

69	Philips BF 1738	Soul Party/Down To The Bone	15
69	Philips BF 1754	Keep In Touch/Taking It Away	40

FREE (U.K.)

(see also Paul Kossoff, Rabbit, Kossoff Kirke Tetsu & Rabbit, Sharks, Andy Fraser Band, Black Cat Bones, Rock Aid Armenia)

69	Island WIP 6054	Broad Daylight/The Worm	60
69	Island WIP 6062	I'll Be Creepin'/Sugar For Mr Morrison	60
70	Island WIP 6082	All Right Now/Mouthful Of Grass (pink label)	8
70	Island WIP 6093	The Stealer/Lying In The Sunshine	5
71	Island WIP 6100	My Brother Jake/Only My Soul	5
72	Island WIP 6129	Little Bit Of Love/Sail On	5
72	Island WIP 6146	Wishing Well/Let Me Show You	5
73	Island WIP 6160	Travellin' In Style/Easy On My Soul	5
76	Island WIP 6351	The Hunter/Worry	5
82	Island PIEP 6	THE FREE EP (12", picture disc)	10
69	Island ILPS 9089	TONS OF SOBS (LP, gatefold sleeve, 1st pressing, pink label/ black & orange 'circle' logo)	150
69	Island ILPS 9089	TONS OF SOBS (LP, gatefold sleeve, 2nd pressing, pink label/black 'block' logo)	70
70	Island ILPS 9089	TONS OF SOBS (LP, gatefold sleeve, 3rd pressing, pink label/'i' logo)	30
71	Island ILPS 9089	TONS OF SOBS (LP, gatefold sleeve, 4th pressing, pink rim label/ 'palm tree' logo)	15
69	Island ILPS 9104	FREE (LP, gatefold sleeve, 1st pressing, pink label/'i' logo)	100
70	Island ILPS 9104	FREE (LP, gatefold sleeve, 2nd pressing, pink rim label/'palm tree' logo)	15
70	Island ILPS 9120	FIRE AND WATER (LP, 1st pressing, pink label/'i' logo)	50
70	Island ILPS 9120	FIRE AND WATER (LP, 2nd pressing, pink rim label/'palm tree' logo)	15
70	Island ILPS 9138	HIGHWAY (LP, pink rim, palm tree label)	20
71	Island ILPS 9160	LIVE (LP, in envelope sleeve with inner, pink rim, palm tree label)	30
72	Island ILPS 9192	FREE AT LAST (LP)	15
72	Island ILPS 9217	HEARTBREAKER (LP, lyric inner sleeve, pink rim, palm tree label)	20
74	Island ISLD 4	THE FREE STORY (2-LP, gatefold, with 4-page booklet, numbered)	25

FREE AGENTS

(see also Pete Shelley, Eric Random)

80	Groovy STP 1	FREE AGENTS (LP, 1000 only, hand-made sleeve)	20

ALAN FREED & HIS ROCK'N'ROLL BAND

(see also Jimmy Cavello)

57	Vogue Coral Q 72219	Teen Rock/Right Now, Right Now (with Alan Freed's Rock'n'Rollers)	100
57	Vogue Coral Q 72219	Teen Rock/Right Now, Right Now (with Alan Freed's Rock'n'Rollers) (78)	20
57	Vogue Coral Q 72230	Rock'n'Roll Boogie/Teener's Canteen (with Alan Freed's Rock'n'Rollers)	100
57	Vogue Coral Q 72230	Rock'n'Roll Boogie/Teener's Canteen (with Alan Freed's Rock'n'Rollers) (78)	20
56	Vogue Coral LVA 9033	ROCK'N'ROLL DANCE PARTY VOL. 1 (LP, featuring Modernaires)	60
57	Vogue Coral LVA 9066	ROCK'N'ROLL DANCE PARTY VOL. 2 (LP, with Jimmy Cavello)	90

MINT VALUE £

FREE DESIGN

69	Project 3	HEAVEN/EARTH (LP)	30

BOB FREEDMAN ORCHESTRA

63	Island ILP 101	MUSIC TO STRIP BY (LP, with free G string)	40
63	Island ILP 101	MUSIC TO STRIP BY (LP, without G string)	12

J.A. FREEDMAN

69	Decca F12963	When You Walked Out Of My Life/Love's Got A Minf Of It's Own	25
69	Decca LK 5021	MY NAME IS J.A. FREEDMAN, I ALSO SING (LP)	50

FREEDOM

(see also Mick Abrahams, Procol Harum, Snafu)

68	Mercury MF 1033	Where Will You Be Tonight/Trying To Get A Glimpse Of You (in p/s)	25
68	Mercury MF 1033	Where Will You Be Tonight/Trying To Get A Glimpse Of You	12
69	Plexium PXM 3	Escape While You Can/Kandy Kay	10
70	Probe PRO 504	Frustrated Woman/Man Made Laws	20
71	Vertigo 6059 051	Thanks/Miss Little Louise	30
70	Probe SPBA 6252	FREEDOM (LP, gatefold sleeve, pink label)	100
71	Vertigo 6360 050	THROUGH THE YEARS (LP, gatefold sleeve, small swirl label)	100
72	Vertigo 6360 072	FREEDOM IS MORE THAN A WORD (LP, die cut gatefold sleeve, small swirl label)	150

FREEDOM GROUP

72	Randy's RAN 525	Sing A Song Of Freedom (actually by Max Romeo)/ IMPACT ALLSTARS: Song Of Freedom (Version)	7

FREEDOM OF CHOICE

70	Wand	Doctor Tom/Rat Man	20

FREEDOM SINGERS (Jamaica)

(see also Winston Francis)

67	Studio One SO 2010	Have Faith/Work Crazy	40
70	Bamboo BAM 21	Give Peace A Chance/SOUND DIMENSION: In Cold Blood	30

FREEDOM SINGERS (U.K.)

70	New Beat NB 059	Election (with Live Stocks)/FLECE & LIVE SHOCKS: Tomorrow's World	10
71	New Beat NB 074	Your Testimony/Train Coming	8

FREED UNIT

99	Out-There OTT 06	MASONIC YOUTH (9" EP, triangular clear vinyl, 100 only)	50
01	Out-There OTT 09	SIX SIDED (9" EP, clear vinyl, 100 only)	25
98	Out-There OTTLP 04	FIELD REPORTS FROM OUT-THERE (LP, clear vinyl)	18
98	Enraptured RAPTLP 19	THINGS ARE LOOKING UP... (LP, orange vinyl)	15
69	CBS 4456	Mary, What Have You Become?/Friend	8
70	CBS 4647	Haverjack Drive/Flying	20

FREEFORM

95	Skam SKA 3	Fane/Recut/Rail/Siamese Telebox/The Brink/Many/Freeform Dub (12")	25
95	Skam SKA 4	FREE EP (12")	25

ALAN FREEMAN AND THE TALMY STONE BAND

62	Decca F 11543	Madison Time/Madison Time	10

ART FREEMAN

66	Atlantic 584 053	Slippin' Around/Can't Get You Out Of My Mind	150

BOBBY FREEMAN

58	London HLJ 8644	Do You Want To Dance?/Big Fat Woman	40
58	London HLJ 8644	Do You Want To Dance?/Big Fat Woman (78)	25
58	London HLJ 8721	Betty Lou Got A New Pair Of Shoes/Starlight	50
58	London HLJ 8721	Betty Lou Got A New Pair Of Shoes/Starlight (78)	35
59	London HLJ 8782	Shame On You Miss Johnson/Need Your Love	50
59	London HLJ 8782	Shame On You Miss Johnson/Need Your Love (78)	40
59	London HLJ 8898	Mary Ann Thomas/Love Me	40
59	London HLJ 8898	Mary Ann Thomas/Love Me (78)	40
60	London HLJ 9031	Sinbad/Ebb Tide (The Sea)	15
60	Parlophone R 4684	(I Do The) Shimmy Shimmy/You Don't Understand Me	20
64	Pye International 7N 25260	C'mon And Swim (Parts 1 & 2)	20
64	Pye International 7N 25280	S-W-I-M/That Little Old Heartbreaker Me	25
66	Pye International 7N 25347	The Duck/Cross My Heart	30
66	Pye International 7N 25347	The Duck/The Devil (2nd issue with different B-side)	10

BUD FREEMAN

66	Fontana TL 5370	BUD FREEMAN ESQ. (LP)	20
68	Fontana TL 5414	FREEMAN & CO (LP)	20
73	Philips 6308 254	SONG OF THE TENOR (LP)	20

CAROL FREEMAN

67	CBS 202579	The Rolling Sea/Leaving You Now	15

ERNIE FREEMAN

57	London HLP 8523	Raunchy/Puddin'	20
57	London HL 7029	Dumplin's/Beautiful Weekend (export issue)	15
58	London HLP 8558	Dumplin's/Beautiful Weekend	15
58	London HLP 8660	Indian Love Call/Summer Serenade	10
60	London HLP 9041	Big River/Night Sounds	7
65	London HLP 9944	Raunchy '65/Jivin' Around	10
56	London RE-U 1059	ERNIE FREEMAN AND HIS RHYTHM GUITAR (EP)	30
59	London RE-P 1210	ERNIE FREEMAN VOL. 2 (EP)	30

EVELYN FREEMAN EXCITING VOICES

69	London HLU 10287	I Heard The Voice/I Dreamed Last Night	5

GEORGE FREEMAN

71	Jay Boy BOY 54	I'm Like A Fish/Why Are You Doing This To Me	25

MINT VALUE £

MARGARET FREEMAN
61 Starlite ST45 040 Forbidden Fruit/Mister Ting A Ling. . . . 15

PAUL FREEMAN
71 Punch PH 82 Don't Give Up/UPSETTERS: Give Up (Version). . . . 12

RUSS FREEMAN & CHET BAKER QUARTET
(see also Chet Baker)
60 Vogue EPV 1255 RUSS FREEMAN & CHET BAKER QUARTET (EP) 12

FREE MOVEMENT
72 CBS 7768 The Harder I Try/Comin' Home 30

FREE 'N EASY
68 Oak RGJ 628 FREE 'N EASY (LP, private pressing [Warren Coley W.C.P. 001]) 110

FREE SOULS
64 Blue Beat BB 264 I Want To Be Free/Angel. . . . 20

FREESTYLE ORCHESTRA
89 SBK 12SBKDJ 7011 Keep On Pumping It Up (12", promo only) 15

FREEWAY
(see also Terry Melcher)
79 Decca F 13824 I Love The Music/Sarah Girl (p/s) 8
79 Decca F 13843 That Was The Greatest Song/Lost In A Dream (p/s) 8
79 Decca TXs 131 FREEWAY (LP). . . . 18

FREEWHEELERS
65 HMV POP 1406 Why Do You Treat Me Like A Fool?/Ad Lib Blues 8

FREEZE
79 A1.A.1.1.A.1 IN COLOUR (EP, p/s). . . . 10
80 A1 A.1.1.S.1 Celebration/Cross-Over 8

ACE FREHLEY
(see also Kiss)
78 Casablanca CAN 135 New York Groove/Snow Blind (p/s, blue vinyl with mask) 30
78 Casablanca CAN 135 New York Groove/Snow Blind (no p/s, black vinyl). . . . 5

DON FRENCH
59 London HLW 8884 Lonely Saturday Night/Goldilocks 80
59 London HLW 8884 Lonely Saturday Night/Goldilocks (78). . . . 50
59 London HLW 8989 Little Blonde Girl/I Look Into My Heart 150
59 London HLW 8989 Little Blonde Girl/I Look Into My Heart (78) 65

RAY FRENCH
66 Pye 7N 17215 Since I Lost My Baby/Gun Me Down 5

FRENCH REVOLUTION
69 Decca F 22898 Nine Till Five/Why?. . . . 100

FRENZ
70 Sugar SU 101 Mee Lei Moi/I Hear Music. . . . 12
71 Sugar ESS 103 It's A Secret/Dusty Shoes. . . . 10

FRENZY
81 Frenzy FRENZY 1 This Is The Last Time/Gypsy Dancer (no p/s) 100
81 Frenzy FRENZY 2 Blackburn Rovers/Up The Rovers. . . . 80
81 Frenzy FRENZY 3 Without You/Thanks For Nothing (no p/s) 150
84 Nervous NEP 002 Robot Riot/All Alone (p/s) 6
84 Nervous 12 NEP 002 Robot Riot/All Alone/Cry Or Die/Torment (12", p/s, 1st 500 on blue vinyl). . . . 10
84 Nervous 12 NEP 002 Robot Riot/All Alone/Cry Or Die/Torment (12", p/s) 8
86 ABC EYE T7 I See Red/Whose Life (p/s). . . . 8
86 ABC EYE T7 I See Red/Who's Life/Don't Give Up (12", p/s). . . . 8
85 Nervous NERD 016 HALL OF MIRRORS (LP, orange vinyl) 12
86 I.D. NOSE 8 CLOCKWORK TOY (LP) 15
87 I.D. NOSE 19 SALLY'S PINK BEDROOM (LP) 15

FRESH
92 Magnet MAG 1008CD Did I Say "Ti Amo" (mixes) (CD) 12

FRESH
(see also Paul Korda, Brother Bung, Fruit Machine)
70 RCA RCA 2003 Stoned In Saigon/Just A Note 7
70 RCA SF 8122 FRESH OUT OF BORSTAL (LP). . . . 20
71 RCA LSA 3027 FRESH TODAY (LP) 18

FRESH AIR
69 Pye 7N 17736 Running Wild/Stop, Look, Listen 200
72 Philips 6006 187 It Takes Too Long/Here Comes Summer 6
72 Columbia DB 8872 Bye Bye Jane/It's All Over 6
71 Philips 6006 163 In The Sun/Too Many Reasons 7

FRESH MAGGOTS
71 RCA RCA 2150 Car Song/What Would You Do. . . . 30
71 RCA SF 8205 FRESH MAGGOTS (LP, orange label). . . . 350

FRESH MEAT
73 Deram DMR 384 Never Mind The Money/Candy Eyes. . . . 7
73 Raft RA 18504 Hobo/If You Can't Live (You're Dead). . . . 12

FRESH SKI & MO ROCK
87 Tuff GrooveTUFF003 Talking Pays/Pick Up On This (12") 50
91 Conscious CON003 THE LONG AWAITED PAROXYSM (EP) 30

FRESH WINDOWS
67 Fontana TF 839 Fashion Conscious/Summer Sun Shines. . . . 160

MINT VALUE £

FRESHIES

(see also Chris Sievey, Going Red?)

78	Razz RAZZXEP 1	BAISER (EP, with Chris Sievey solo tracks, 33rpm, numbered, handwritten labels)	20
79	Razz RAZZXEP 2	STRAIGHT IN AT NO. 2 (EP, handwritten labels with inserts, 1,000 only, numbered, green or orange p/s)	12
79	Razz RAZZ 3	THE MEN FROM BANANA ISLAND WHOSE STUPID IDEAS NEVER CAUGHT ON IN THE WESTERN WORLD AS WE KNOW IT (EP, black & white photocopied p/s or numbered blue p/s)	8
79	Razz RAZZ 5	We're Like You/CHRIS SIEVEY: Hey (p/s)	6
80	Absurd A9	Octopus/Sheet Music	6
80	Razz RAZZ 6	Yellow Spot/If It's News (p/s)	6
80	Razz RAZZ 7	No Money/Oh Girl (p/s)	6
80	Razz RAZZ 8	RED INDIAN MUSIC (EP, with Chris Sievey)	8
80	Razz RAZZ 11	I'm In Love With The Girl On The Virgin Manchester Megastore Checkout Desk/Singalong Version (p/s, with free lyric book)	12
80	Razz RAZZ 12	I'm In Love With The Girl On The Manchester Checkout Desk (Radio Version)/ Singalong Version ('bleeped') (white label radio issue, 200 only)	10
80	Razz RAZZ 13	One To One/House Beautiful (unreleased)	0
81	MCA MCA 693	Wrap Up The Rockets And It's Gonna Get Better/Tell Her I'm Ill	6
81	CV CVS 1	If You Really Love ... Buy Me A Shirt/I Am A Walrus (p/s)	6
81	HANNA 1	Virgin Megastore/Wrap Up The Rockets/Buy Me A Shirt/Tell Her I'm ill/ Frank Talks To Chris (Conversation) (12", white label, stickered sleeve)	6
80	Razz CS-4	ROUGH AND READY (12-track, 1,000 only)	12
81	Razz CS-5	LONDON PLAYS (LP, live & radio sessions, 1,000 only)	12
85	ETS 1	JOHNNY RADAR STORY (LP, 20-track, with bonus Frank Sidebottom 8-track: "Firm Favourites")	12

FRESHMEN

67	Pye 7N 17432	Papa Oom Mow Mow/Let's Dance	12
68	Pye 7N 17592	Go Granny Go/Look At The Sunshine	18
69	Pye 7N 17689	Just To See You Smile/Indian Lake	8
69	Pye 7N 17757	She Sang Hymns Out Of Tune/Mr. Beverly's Heavy Days	8
70	CBS 4842	Halfway To Where/Time Hasn't Changed Her	6
70	CBS 5168	Banquet For The World/Time Hasn't Changed Her	6
71	CBS 7241	One Bad Thing/Everywhere There Is Love	6
72	CBS 7694	Swanee River/Take The Time It Takes	10
68	Pye NPL 18263	MOVIN' ON (LP, mono)	60
68	Pye NSPL 18263	MOVIN' ON (LP, stereo)	70
70	CBS 64099	PEACE ON EARTH (LP)	30

STEPHEN FRETWELL

03	Tape Recordings TAPE 001	Something's Got To Give/Whenforever/Honey	20

FRIDA

(see also Abba)

82	Epic EPC A 2603	I Know There's Something Going On/Threnody (p/s)	8
82	Epic EPC A 2863	To Turn To Stone/I Got Something (p/s)	10
82	Epic EPC A 2863	To Turn To Stone/I Got Something (p/s, clear vinyl)	10
83	Epic EPC A 3435	Here We'll Stay/Strangers (p/s)	8
83	Epic EPC A 3983	Time/I Am A Seeker (p/s, with B.A. Robertson)	8
84	Epic EPC A 4717	Shine/That's Tough (p/s)	8
84	Epic EPC TA 4717	Shine (6.27 Version)/That's Tough (12", p/s)	12
84	Epic EPC A 4886	Heart Of The Country/Slowly (p/s)	10
84	Epic EPC TA 4886	Heart Of The Country/Slowly/I Know There's Something Going On (Extended) (12", p/s)	20

CAROL FRIDAY

65	Parlophone R 5297	Gone Tomorrow/Show Me The Way	10
65	Parlophone R 5369	Everybody I Know/Wasted Days	30
67	Parlophone R 5567	Big Sister/I Look Around Me	10

FRIDAY CLUB

85	2 Tone CHSTT28	Window Shopping/Window Shopping (instrumental) (p/s)	40
85	2 Tone CHSTT1228	Window Shopping (extended version)/Window Shopping (instrumental) 12" (p/s)	45

FRIDAY KNIGHTS

60	Oriole CB 1579	Poor Man's Roses/Don't Open That Door	10

FRIDGES

80	Ink-Ink II 01	Lynn Freeze/Shower Of B's/That's Why I Took Up The Harmonica/ No Room! (p/s, with insert)	5

MARTY FRIEDMAN

(see also Megadeth, Cacophony)

86	Shrapnel RR 95291	DRAGON'S KISS (LP)	12

BRIAN JOSEPH FRIEL

74	Dawn DNLS 3054	BRIAN JOSEPH FRIEL (LP, gatefold sleeve with insert, pink 'sun' label)	20
75	Dawn DNLS 3064	ARRIVERDERCI ARDROSSAN (LP, punk 'sun' label)	12

FRIEND & LOVER

68	Verve VS 1515	Reach Out Of The Darkness/Time Is On Your Side	12

TERRY FRIEND & FRIENDS

(see also Stonefield Tramp)

77	Tramp (no cat. no.)	COME THE DAY (LP, private pressing, 100 only)	40

FRIENDLY FIRES

08	XL XLS 387	Jump In The Pool (one-sided hand-numbered and stencilled sleeve, white labels, 250 only)	15

MINT VALUE £

FRIENDLY HOPEFULS

81 Abstract ABS 004	Tribute To The Punks Of '76/Tribute To The Punks Of '76 (Disco Dub Mix) (p/s, coloured vinyl)	5

FRIENDS

70 United Artists UP 35146	Futz/Costa Del Sol	7

FRIENDS

(see also Ithaca, Alice Through The Looking Glass, Agincourt, Tomorrow Come Someday, BBC Radiophonic Workshop)

74 Merlin HF 4	FRIENDS (LP, white label test pressing, 1 copy only!)	1500

FRIENDS

83 Rock Shop RSR 002	Night Walker/Wasted Time (no p/s)	25

FRIENDS

(see also Flowerpot Men, Ivy League)

68 Deram DM 198	Piccolo Man/Mythological Sunday	30

FRIENDS AGAIN

83 Moonboot MOON 1	Honey At The Core/Lucky Star (p/s)	6
84 Mercury FAEP 1	THE FRIENDS AGAIN EP: Lullaby No. 2 Love On Board/Wand You Wave/ Thank You For Being An Angel/Sunkissed (New Version)/State Of Art (Remix) (double pack, stickered gatefold p/s)	8

FRIENDS O' MINE

(see also Mark Kjeldsen)

72 Westwood WRS 021	FRIENDS O' MINE (LP, 250 copies only)	80

FRIENDS OF DISTINCTION

69 RCA 1838	Grazing In The Grass/I Really Hope You Do	8
69 RCA SF 8032	GRAZIN' (LP)	15

FRIENDSHIP

70 B&C CB 133	The World Is Going To Be A Better Place/Million Hearts	5

FRIGHTY

88 Y & D YDD 0132	Feel So Good (with the Offbeat Posse)/Life (with Colonel Mite) (12")	8
01 Jah Tubbys JT 7009	Call On Jah Name/OFFBEAT POSSE: Call On Dub	15
03 Jah Tubbys JT 10012	Jah Jah Is Coming/Fright Jah Jah Is Coming Version/Dub Is Coming (10", with the Offbeat Posse)	20

FRIJID PINK

70 Deram DM-R 288	The House Of The Rising Sun/Drivin' Blues	5
70 Deram DM 309	Sing A Song Of Freedom/End Of The Line	6
70 Deram DM 321	Heartbreak Hotel/Bye Bye Blues	6
71 Deram DM 332	Music For The People/Sloony	6
71 Deram DM 336	We're Gonna Be There (When Johnny Comes Marching Home)/Shortly Kline	7
71 Deram DM 347	Lost Son/I Love Her	7
70 Deram SML 1062	FRIJID PINK (LP)	40
70 Deram SML 1077	DEFROSTED (LP)	40

(Robert) FRIPP & (Brian) ENO

(see also Giles Giles & Fripp, King Crimson, Brian Eno, Roxy Music)

73 Island HELP 16	NO PUSSYFOOTING (LP, gatefold sleeve, black label with pink 'i' logo)	25
75 Island HELP 22	EVENING STAR (LP, black label with pink 'i' logo)	20

JACKIE FRISCO

63 Decca F 11566	You Can't Catch Me/Sugar Baby	15
63 Decca F 11692	When You Ask About Love/He's So Near	10

VONNIE FRITCHIE

55 London HLU 8178	Sugar Booger Avenue/There I Stood (To Throw Old Shoes And Rice)	50

FRED FRITH

(see also Henry Cow)

74 Caroline C 1508	GUITAR SOLOS (LP)	18
76 Caroline C 1518	GUITAR SOLOS 2 (LP)	18

FRITZ, MIKE & MO

(see also Four Pennies)

65 Philips BF 1427	Somebody Stole The Sun/Let Me Hear Your Voice	10
65 Philips BF 1441	What Colour Is A Man?/So Now You're Gone	8

LEFTY FRIZZELL

63 CBS BPG 62188	THE ONE AND ONLY LEFTY FRIZZELL (LP)	15
66 CBS BPG 62595	THE SAD SIDE OF LOVE (LP)	15

CORNELIA FROBOESS

62 HMV HMV 1671	GERMAN TEENAGERS (LP)	30

FROCK

78 Frock Music FM 7848	SILKIE (LP, 250 only)	40

EDGAR FROESE

(see also Tangerine Dream)

74 Virgin V 2016	AQUA (LP)	12

FROG

(see also John Cameron)

73 Jam JAM 39	Witch Hunt (Theme From Psychomania)/Living Dead (die-cut company sleeve)	150

WYNDER K. FROG

(see under 'W')

67 Island ILP 944	SUNSHINE SUPERFROG (LP, white label, mono)	90
68 Island ILP 982/ILPS 9082	OUT OF THE FRYING PAN (LP, pink label)	40

MINT VALUE £

RAYMOND FROGGATT
(see also Monopoly)

68	Polydor 56249	Callow-La-Vita/Lost Autumn	6
68	Polydor 56274	Just A Little Bit Of Love/ABC Gold Fish	5
68	Polydor 56284	The Red Balloon/Lost Autumn	6
69	Polydor 583 044	THE VOICE AND WRITING OF RAYMOND FROGGATT (LP, gatefold)	18
71	Bell BLL 1156	The Singer/Church Fete	6
72	Bell BELLS 207	BLEACH (LP)	18
74	Reprise K 44257	ROGUES AND THIEVES (LP)	12

FROGMEN

61	Oriole CB 1617	Underwater/Mad Rush (withdrawn)	100

FROGMORTON

76	Philips 6308 261	AT LAST (LP, blue/silver labels)	20

JANE FROMAN

55	Capitol CL 14208	The Song From "Desiree" (We Meet Again)/Mine	6
55	Capitol CL 14209	The Finger Of Suspicion Points At You/My Shining Hour	8
55	Capitol CL 14254	I Wonder/I'll Never Be The Same	10
56	Capitol CL 14658	You'll Never Walk Alone/One Little Candle	6
56	Capitol EAP1 600	JANE FROMAN (EP)	12
56	Capitol EAP1 889	SONGS AT SUNSET (EP)	10
56	Capitol EAP2 889	SONGS AT SUNSET (EP)	10
56	Capitol EAP3 889	SONGS AT SUNSET (EP)	10
52	Capitol LC 6554	WITH A SONG IN MY HEART (10" LP)	15
53	Capitol LC 6605	YOURS ALONE (10" LP)	15

FRONT

77	The Label TLR 005	System/Queen's Mafia (p/s)	8

DOM FRONTIERE & HIS ORCHESTRA

57	London HLU 8385	Jet Rink Ballad/Uno Mas	15
57	London HLU 8385	Jet Rink Ballad/Uno Mas (78)	12

FRONT LINE

65	Atlantic AT 4057	I Don't Care/Got Love	30

FRONTLINE ORCHESTRA

81	Ice ICET 50	Don't Turn You Back On Me/No Entry (12")	40

FROST
(see also Alice Cooper)

69	Vanguard SVRL 19056	ROCK AND ROLL MUSIC (LP)	18
69	Vanguard SVRL 19052	FROST MUSIC (LP)	18

BERNIE FROST
(see also Status Quo, Rossi & Frost, Boz Frost)

74	Vertigo 6059 108	The House/What Do You Want To Hear Today	50

BOZ FROST
(see also Status Quo, Rossi & Frost, Bernie Frost)

73	Vertigo 6059 083	Foreign Lady/Big White Seagull	25

FROST LANE

71	Cutty Wren MM 1	FROST LANE (LP, actually various artists LP)	45

MAX FROST & TROOPERS
(see also Millicent Martin)

68	Capitol CL 15565	Shape Of Things To Come/Free Lovin'	25

FRUGAL SOUND

66	Pye 7N 17062	Norwegian Wood/Cruel To Be Kind	12
66	Pye 7N 17129	Just Outside The Door/I'm On Your Side	6
67	RCA Victor RCA 1556	Backstreet Girl/Reason To Believe	6
67	RCA Victor RCA 1595	Abilene/Love Is A New Face	5
68	RCA Victor RCA 1659	All Strung Out/Miss Mary	5

FRUIT EATING BEARS

78	DJM DJS 857	Door In My Face/Going Through The Motions (company sleeve)	45
78	Raw RAW 9	Chevy Heavy (p/s)	25
78	Lightning GIL 509	Chevy Heavy/Fifties Cowboy (p/s)	40

FRUIT GUMS

70	Fab FAB 138	Sweet Pork/Crying All Night	6

FRUIT MACHINE
(see also Rare Bird)

69	Spark SRL 1003	Follow Me/Cuddly Toy	70
69	Spark SRL 1027	I'm Alone Today/Sunshine Of Your Love (in title p/s)	130
69	Spark SRL 1027	I'm Alone Today/Sunshine Of Your Love	80

FRUMPY
(see also Atlantis)

71	Philips 6003 133	Life Without Pain/Morning	20
71	Philips 6305 067	ALL WILL BE CHANGED (LP, black/silver labels)	90
72	Philips 6305 098	FRUMP 2 (LP, black & blue vinyl)	60

FRUUPP

74	Dawn DNS 1087	Prince Of Heaven/Jaunting Car	10
73	Dawn DNLS 3053	FUTURE LEGENDS (LP, gatefold sleeve)	50
74	Dawn DNLS 3058	SEVEN SECRETS (LP, with lyric insert)	40
74	Dawn DNLH 2	THE PRINCE OF HEAVEN'S EYES (LP, gatefold sleeve, with book)	50
74	Dawn DNLH 2	THE PRINCE OF HEAVEN'S EYES (LP, gatefold sleeve, without book)	20
75	Dawn DNLS 3070	MODERN MASQUERADES (LP, gatefold sleeve, with lyric insert)	30

MINT VALUE £

MARK FRY

06	Sunbeam SBRLPS 028	DREAMING WITH ALICE (LP, 180 gram vinyl reissue of original 1972 Italian pressing)	15

FUCHSIA

71	Pegasus PEG 8	FUCHSIA (LP)	200

FUD (Christian) & DEL

73	Duke DU 165	Beef Sticker/PRINCE HERON: Ten Commandments	6
73	Songbird SB 1086	Dr. Fud/FUD CHRISTIAN ALLSTARS: La-Fud-Del Skank	6

FUD CHRISTIAN ALLSTARS

(see also Linkers, Ansel Linkers)

71	Big Shot BI 571	Never Fall In Love (actually by Winston Heywood)/Never Fall In Love Version	8

FUDGE TUNNEL

91	Earach MOSH 36	HATE SONGS IN E MINOR (LP, with free 7")	15

FUGAZI

93	Dischord DIS 60V	IN ON THE KILL TAKER (LP)	15

FUGI

71	Blue Horizon 2096 005	Red Moon (Parts 1 & 2)	25

FUGITIVE

81	private pressing FMR 050	Need My Freedom	20

FUGITIVES (Jamaica)

(see also Jo Jo Bennett & Fugitives, Two Kings, Jo Jo Bennett, Stranger Cole)

67	Doctor Bird DB 1082	Musical Pressure/LESLIE BUTLER & FUGITIVES: Winchester Rocksteady	30
67	Doctor Bird 1097	Lecture/Canteloupe Rock	40

FUGITIVES (U.S.)

61	Vogue V 9176	Freeway/Fugitive	30

FUGS

68	Big T BIG 115	Crystal Liaison/When The Mode Of The Music Changes	12
68	Transatlantic TRA 180	TENDERNESS JUNCTION (LP, with poster)	50
68	Transatlantic TRA 180	TENDERNESS JUNCTION (LP, without poster)	20
68	Transatlantic TRA 181	IT CRAWLED INTO MY HAND, HONEST (LP)	35
69	Fontana (S)TL 5501	VIRGIN FUGS (LP)	25
69	Fontana (S)TL 5513	THE FUGS ... FIRST ALBUM (LP)	35
69	Fontana (S)TL 5524	FUGS II (LP)	30
69	Reprise RSLP 6359	THE BELLE OF AVENUE A (LP)	15

FULHAM FURIES

(see also Lurkers)

78	GM GMS 9050	These Boots Are Made For Walking/Under Pressure (no p/s)	35

BLIND BOY FULLER

57	Philips BBL 7512	BLIND BOY FULLER 1935-40 (LP)	35
68	Matchbox SDR 143	BLIND BOY FULLER ON DOWN VOLUME 1 (LP)	25
69	Matchbox SDR 168	BLIND BOY FULLER ON DOWN VOLUME 2 (LP)	25
60s	Flyright LP 105	CAROLINA BLUES (LP)	18

BOBBY FULLER FOUR

(see also Randy Fuller)

66	London HLU 10030	I Fought The Law/Little Annie Lou	30
66	London HLU 10041	Love's Made A Fool Of You/Don't You Ever Let Me Know	25
73	President PT 394	Another Sad And Lonely Night/Only When I Dream	10
67	President PTL 1003	MEMORIAL ALBUM (LP)	40

CURTIS FULLER/TOMMY FLANAGAN

58	Pye PYE28009	IT'S MAGIC (LP)	30

GIL FULLER & DIZZY GILLESPIE

(see also Dizzy Gillespie)

66	Fontana 688 147 ZL	MAN FROM MONTEREY (LP)	15

JERRY FULLER

59	London HLH 8982	The Tennessee Waltz/Charlene	12
59	London HLH 8982	The Tennessee Waltz/Charlene (78)	22
61	London HLN 9439	Guilty Of Loving You/First Love Never Dies	8
62	Salvo SLO 1802	Lipstick And Rouge/Mother Goose At The Bandstand (99 copies only)	150

JESSE FULLER

65	Good Time Jazz GV 2426	San Francisco Bay Blues/New Midnight Special	10
67	Good Time Jazz GV 2427	Runnin' Wild/The Monkey And The Engineer	10
67	Fontana TF 821	Going Back To My Old Used To Be/Bye And Bye	10
58	Good Time Jazz LAG 12159	JESSE FULLER (LP)	25
60	Good Time Jazz LAG 12279	LONE CAT (LP)	25
60	Topic 10T 59	WORKING ON THE RAILROAD (10" LP)	35
63	Good Time Jazz LAG 574	SAN FRANCISCO BAY BLUES (LP)	20
65	Stateside SL 10154	JESSE FULLER'S FAVOURITES (LP)	20
66	Fontana TL 5313	SESSION WITH JESSE FULLER (LP)	25
66	Topic 12T 134	MOVE ON DOWN THE LINE (LP)	35
66	Stateside SL 10166	SAN FRANCISCAN BAY BLUES (LP, reissue)	18
60s	Vocalion VRLP 574	SAN FRANCISCO BAY BLUES (LP)	20
60s	Evolution Z 1004	LIVE IN LONDON (LP)	30

JOHNNY FULLER

73	Speciality SON 5017	Haunted House/Swinging At The Creek	5

RANDY FULLER

(see also Bobby Fuller Four)

67	President PT 111	It's Love, Come What May/The Things You Do	10

MINT VALUE £

FULL MOON

87	Luna SRT 7K51283	The Eternal Now/Nemesis	25

FULL TIME MEN

(see also R.E.M.)

86	Shigaku SHIG 1T	I Got Wheels/One More Time/Way Down South (12", p/s)	8

LOWELL FULSON/FULSOM

53	London L 1199	I Love My Baby/The Blues Came Rollin' In (78)	40
65	Sue WI 375	Too Many Drivers/Key To Your Heart	40
66	Sue WI 4023	Talking Woman/Blues Around Midnight	40
66	Outasite 45-502	Stop And Think/Baby (with Leon Blue)	70
66	Polydor 56515	Black Nights/Little Angel	20
67	Fontana TF 795	Tramp/Pico	35
76	Jet JET 770	Do You Love Me?/Monday Morning	8
69	Fontana SFJL 920	SAN FRANCISCO BLUES (LP)	45
69	Polydor 2384 038	IN A HEAVY BAG (LP, as Lowell Fulsom)	25

FUMBLE

72	Sovereign SOV 110	Hullo Mary Lou/Hanging On	5
73	Sovereign SOV 118	Million Seller/Get Up	5
73	Sovereign SOV 121	Alexandra Park (Palisades Park)/Mama I Can't Tell You	6
72	Sovereign SVNA 7254	FUMBLE (LP, gatefold sleeve)	12

FUN AND GAMES

69	MCA MU 1083	We Got To Say Goodbye	8

FUNBOY FIVE

80s	Cool Cat Daddy-O PHUN 1	Life After Death/Compulsive Eater (foldover p/s)	15

FUNERAL FOR A FRIEND

02	Mighty Atom MTY 338	Between Order And Model/Juno/Red Is The New Black (CD)	25
03	Infectious EW 269	Juneau/Getaway Plan (white vinyl, p/s)	15
03	Infectious EW 269CD 1	Juneau/Getaway Plan (CD, card sleeve)	8
03	Warner EW 274	She Drove Me To Daytime TV/Bullet Theory (blue vinyl, p/s)	15
03	Infectious INFEC 126S	Four Ways - This Year's Most Open Heartbreak/She Drove Me To Daytime Television//Kiss And Make Up (All Bets Are Off)/Escape Artists Never Die (2 x 7" red vinyl, gatefold p/s)	20
03	Infectious INFEC 12CDS	Four Ways - This Year's Most Open Heartbreak/She Drove Me To Daytime Television/Kiss And Make Up (All Bets Are Off)/Escape Artists Never Die (CD 2000 only)	15

FUN FOUR

(see also Orange Juice)

80	NMC NMC 010	Singing In The Showers/By Products/Elevator Crush (p/s)	25

FUNGUS

(see also Secondhand, Seventh Wave)

73	Fungus FUN 1	Premonitions Parts 1 & 2 (LP, private pressing)	100

FUNHOUSE

(see also Another Pretty Face, DNV, Waterboys)

82	Ensign ENY 222	Out Of Control/This Could Be Hell (p/s)	6
82	Ensign ENYT 222	Out Of Control (Full Version)/This Could Be Hell (12", p/s)	10

FUNKADELIC

(see also Parliament, Parlet, Bootsy's Rubber Band, Dolby's Cube, P-Funk Allstars)

70	Pye International 7N 25519	I Got A Thing, You Got A Thing, Everybody's Got A Thing/ Fish, Chips & Sweat	15
71	Pye International 7N 25548	You & Your Folks, Me & Mine/Funky Dollar Bill	15
71	Janus 6146 001	Can You Get To That/Back In Our Minds	20
70	Pye Intl. NSPL 28137	FUNKADELIC (LP)	75
71	Pye Intl. NSPL 28144	FREE YOUR MIND AND YOUR ASS WILL FOLLOW (LP)	75
71	Janus 6310 201	MAGGOT BRAIN (LP)	50
75	20th Century W 215	LET'S TAKE IT TO THE STAGE (LP)	20
78	Warner Bros K 56299	HARDCORE JOLLIES (LP)	15
78	Warner Bros K 56539	ONE NATION UNDER A GROOVE (LP, with free 12" "One Nation Under A Groove")	15

FUNK BAND INC.

76	Beeb 12	Get It Off/Part 2	10

FUNKGUS

76	Baal BAL 89002	II (LP)	15

FUNKMASTERS

84	Master Funk MF4	It's Over/(Versions) (12")	12

FUNKY BROWN & INNER CIRCLE

74	Rhino 128	I See You/Song Of The Swallow	10

FINBAR & EDDIE FUREY

68	Transatlantic TRA 168	FINBAR AND EDDIE FUREY (LP, laminated front sleeve, white/lilac labels)	20
69	Xtra XTRA 1077	TRADITIONAL IRISH PIPE MUSIC (LP)	18
69	Transatlantic TRA 191	THE LONESOME BOATMAN (LP)	15
72	Dawn DNLS 3037	THE DAWNING OF THE DAY (LP, with lyric insert, lilac label)	20

FINBAR FUREY & BOB STEWART

76	Crescent ARS 110	TOMORROW WE PART (LP)	12

FUR FUR

(see also Karl Blake, Danielle Dax, Lemon Kittens, Gland Shrouds)

80s	Daark Inc. D.I. 7	FUR FUR (cassette)	12

MINT VALUE £

FURNITURE

(see also Because)

80	Para 1	Shaking Story/Take A Walk Down Town (p/s)	30
84	Survival SUR 12023	Dancing The Hard Bargain (Extended)/Robert Nightmans Story (12", p/s)	12
84	Premonition PREM 12002	Love Your Shoes/Escape Into My Arms/Throw Away The Script (Inst) (12", p/s)	12
85	PREM 3	I Can't Crack/Switch Off/Pause/I Can't Crack (Broken Mix) (12", p/s)	12
86	Stiff BUY 251	Brilliant Mind/To Gus	6
86	Stiff BUYIT 251	Brilliant Mind (Extended)/Brilliant Mind (7" Mix)/To Gus (12", p/s)	10
86	Stiff BUY 254	Love Your Shoes/Turnupspeed	7
86	Stiff BUYIT 254	Love Your Shoes (Extended)/Love Your Shoes (7" Mix)/ Turnupspeed/Me And You And The Name (12", p/s)	10
90	Arista 12844	One Step Behind You/It Continues (p/s)	6
91	Survival SURT 53	Brilliant Mind (Extended)/Brilliant Mind (7" Version)/On A Bus With Peter Nero/Brilliant Strings (12", p/s)	12
83	Premonition PREM 4CA	WHEN THE BOOM WAS ON (Mini-LP)	25
86	Premonition PREM 6	THE LOVEMONGERS (LP)	25
86	Stiff SEEZ 64	THE WRONG PEOPLE (LP)	15
91	Survival SURCD 13	SHE GETS OUT THE SCRAPBOOK (CD)	18

FURRY DICE

80	White Line WHLS 001	Rudi Don't Take Your Love To Town/K.G.B. (p/s)	6

FURRY PHREAKS (Featuring Terra Deva)

98	FSUK FSUKT3P	SOOTHE (2 x 12" promo)	25

TOMMY FURTADO

57	London HLA 8418	Sun Tan Sam/Isabella	40
57	London HLA 8418	Sun Tan Sam/Isabella (78)	10

FURY

77	Arista 150	Miss Demeanor/Stay On Your feet	6

BILLY FURY

(see also Tornados, Gamblers)

78s

59	Decca F 11102	Maybe Tomorrow/Gonna Type A Letter	150
59	Decca F 11128	Margo/Don't Knock Upon My Door	200
59	Decca F 11158	Angel Face/Time Has Come	250
59	Decca F 11189	My Christmas Prayer/Last Kiss	300

SINGLES

59	Decca F 11102	Maybe Tomorrow/Gonna Type A Letter (triangular centre)	25
59	Decca F 11102	Maybe Tomorrow/Gonna Type A Letter (later pressing with round centre)	15
59	Decca F 11128	Margo/Don't Knock Upon My Door (triangular centre)	30
59	Decca F 11128	Margo/Don't Knock Upon My Door (later pressing with round centre)	20
59	Decca F 11158	Angel Face/Time Has Come (triangular centre)	30
59	Decca F 11158	Angel Face/Time Has Come (later pressing with round centre)	20
59	Decca F 11189	My Christmas Prayer/Last Kiss (triangular centre)	40
59	Decca F 11189	My Christmas Prayer/Last Kiss (later pressing with round centre)	25
60	Decca F 11200	Colette/Baby How I Cried (triangular centre)	40
60	Decca F 11200	Colette/Baby How I Cried (later pressing with round centre)	15
60	Decca F 11237	That's Love/You Don't Know (as Billy Fury & Four Jays)	25
60	Decca F 11267	Wondrous Place/Alright, Goodbye	25
60	Decca F 11311	A Thousand Stars/Push Push	15
61	Decca F 11334	Don't Worry/Talkin' In My Sleep (with Four Kestrels)	15
61	Decca F 11349	Halfway To Paradise/Cross My Heart	6
61	Decca F 11384	Jealousy/Open Your Arms	6
61	Decca F 11409	I'd Never Find Another You/Sleepless Nights	6
62	Decca F 11437	Letter Full Of Tears/Magic Eyes	12
62	Decca F 11458	Last Night Was Made For Love/King For Tonight	6
62	Decca F 11485	Once Upon A Dream/If I Lose You	6
62	Decca F 11508	Because Of Love/Running Around	10
63	Decca F 11582	Like I've Never Been Gone/What Do You Think You're Doing Of?	6
63	Decca F 11655	When Will You Say I Love You?/All I Wanna Do Is Cry	6
63	Decca F 11701	In Summer/I'll Never Fall In Love Again	6
63	Decca F 11744	Somebody Else's Girl/Go Ahead And Ask Her	12
63	Decca F 11792	Do You Really Love Me Too?/What Am I Gonna Do?	7
64	Decca F 11888	I Will/Nothin' Shakin' (But The Leaves On The Trees) (some B-sides list "Nothin' Shakin' ")	15
64	Decca F 11939	It's Only Make Believe/Baby What Do You Want Me To Do?	10
64	Decca F 40719	Hippy Hippy Shake/Glad All Over (export-only, with p/s)	80
64	Decca F 40719	Hippy Hippy Shake/Glad All Over (export-only)	50
65	Decca F 12048	I'm Lost Without You/You Better Believe It, Baby	10
65	Decca F 12178	In Thoughts Of You/Away From You	8
65	Decca F 12230	Run To My Lovin' Arms/Where Do You Run?	10
66	Decca F 12325	I'll Never Quite Get Over You/I Belong To The Wind	12
66	Decca F 12409	Don't Let A Little Pride Stand In Your Way/ Didn't See The Real Thing Come Along	12
66	Decca F 12459	Give Me Your Word/She's So Far Out She's In	15
67	Parlophone R 5560	Hurtin' Is Loving/Things Are Changing	30
67	Parlophone R 5605	Loving You/I'll Go Along With It Now	20
67	Parlophone R 5634	Suzanne In The Mirror/It Just Don't Matter Now	40
67	Parlophone R 5658	Beyond The Shadow Of A Doubt/Baby Do You Love Me?	40
68	Parlophone R 5681	Silly Boy Blue/One Minute Woman	40
68	Parlophone R 5723	Phone Box/Any Morning Now	40
68	Parlophone R 5747	Lady/Certain Things	40
69	Parlophone R 5788	I Call For My Rose/Bye Bye	40
69	Parlophone R 5819	All The Way To The U.S.A./Do My Best For You	50
70	Parlophone R 5845	Why Are You Leaving?/Old Sweet Roll (Hi-De-Ho)	50

			MINT VALUE £
70	Parlophone R 5874	Paradise Alley/Well ... All Right	50
72	Fury FY 301	Will The Real Man Please Stand Up/At This Stage	40
74	Warner Bros WB 16402	I'll Be Your Sweetheart/Fascinating Candle Flame	30
76	NEMS NES 018	Halfway To Paradise/Turn My Back On You	12
81	Polydor POSP 355	Be Mine Tonight/No Trespassers (p/s)	5
82	Polydor POSP 488	Love Or Money/Love Sweet Love (p/s)	5
82	Polydor POSP 528	Devil Or Angel/Don't Tell Me Lies ('guitar' p/s)	6
82	Polydor POSP 528	Devil Or Angel/Don't Tell Me Lies ('microphone' p/s)	8
83	Polydor POSP 558	Forget Him/Your Words (p/s)	5
83	Polydor POSP 558	Let Me Go Lover/Your Words (same p/s as above but diff. A-side, 500 only)	35
83	Lyntone LYN 13078/BF 1	Devil Or Angel/Lost Without You (flexi free within memorial concert booklet)	20
83	Lyntone LYN 13078/BF 1	Devil Or Angel/Lost Without You (flexi without memorial concert booklet)	5
83	private pressing	BILLY FURY IN INTERVIEW WITH STUART COLEMAN (10", 500 white label copies only, 1st 200 numbered)	30
83	private pressing	BILLY FURY IN INTERVIEW WITH STUART COLEMAN (10", 500 white label copies only, un-numbered)	20

EPs

59	Decca DFE 6597	MAYBE TOMORROW (triangular centre, orange/red p/s)	100
59	Decca DFE 6597	MAYBE TOMORROW (round centre, orange/red p/s)	80
59	Decca DFE 6597	MAYBE TOMORROW (round centre, yellow p/s)	60
61	Decca DFE 6694	BILLY FURY	60
62	Decca DFE 6699	BILLY FURY NO. 2	70
62	Decca DFE 6708	PLAY IT COOL	30
62	Decca DFE 6708	PLAY IT COOL (export issue, blue/green 'crouching' cover)	100
62	Decca DFE 8505	BILLY FURY HITS	30
63	Decca DFE 8525	BILLY FURY AND THE TORNADOS	30
63	Decca DFE 8558	AM I BLUE	50
65	Decca DFE 8641	BILLY FURY AND THE GAMBLERS	125
73	Ronco MR EP 001	LONG LIVE ROCK (with others, no p/s)	25
83	Decca DFE 8686	MY CHRISTMAS PRAYER	15

LPs

60	Decca LF 1329	THE SOUND OF FURY (10")	200
60	Ace Of Clubs ACL 1047	BILLY FURY	25
61	Ace Of Clubs ACL 1083	HALFWAY TO PARADISE	25
63	Decca LK 4533	BILLY	40
63	Decca LK 4548	WE WANT BILLY! (with Tornados, mono)	40
63	Decca SKL 4548	WE WANT BILLY! (with Tornados, stereo)	45
65	Decca LK 4677	I'VE GOTTA HORSE (soundtrack)	50
67	Ace Of Clubs ACL 1229	THE BEST OF BILLY FURY	25
76	Decca DPA 3033/4	THE BILLY FURY STORY (2-LP)	15
81	Decca LFT 1329	THE SOUND OF FURY (10", reissue)	12
83	Red Bus BUSLP 1003	THE MISSING YEARS	20
84	Magnum Force MFLP 1027	LOVING YOU (LP)	15

FURYS

63	Stateside SS 182	Never More/Zing! Went The Strings Of My Heart	15
72	Jay Boy BOY 61	What Is Soul?/I Lost My Baby	8
72	Jay Boy BOY 68	I'm Satisfied With You/Just A Little Mixed Up	15
72	Jay Boy BOY 68	I'm Satisfied With You/Just A Little Mixed Up (DJ Copy)	30

FURY'S TORNADOES

(see also Billy Fury)

74	Warner Bros K 16442	Telstar '74/I Would Give You Anything	8

F.U.S.E.

93	Warp WAP38	Train Tracs (12", white vinyl, p/s)	10
93	Warp LP12LTD	Dimension Intrusion (2-LP, white vinyl)	15

FUSION

79	Plastic Fantastic PFUL 1104	COLD OUTSIDE EP (12")	8
80	Telephone TEL 101	TILL I HEAR FROM YOU (LP, blue vinyl)	20

FUSION

95	Ferox FER 015	FREESTYLE EP (12")	8
96	Ferox FER 021	GALAXY OF FUTURE VISIONS (12" EP)	10

FUSION ORCHESTRA

73	EMI EMI 2056	When My Mama's Not At Home/Nuthouse Rock	6
73	EMI EMA 758	A SKELETON IN ARMOUR (LP, gatefold sleeve)	60

FUT

(see also Graham Bonnet, Bee Gees, Marbles, Maurice Gibb, Steve & Stevie; this record has NO Beatles involvement)

70	Beacon BEA 160	Have You Heard The Word/Futting Around	30

FUTURE BEAT ALLIANCE

99	Ferox FER 035	ABACO (12" EP)	10

FUTURE BODIES

80	No label or cat no	Terrorist/Science Of Romance (p/s, lyric insert, rubber stamped labels)	40

FUTURE DAYZE

82	Polydor POSP 455	House On The Hill/Silent Room (P/S)	8

FUTURE PAST

91	B12 03	Our Paths Meet/Harmony Park/Your Hand In My Mind/Dance Intellect/ TV People (12", black vinyl)	50

FUTURE SOUND OF LONDON

(see also Amorphous Androgynous, Art Science Technology, Humanoid,

91	Jumpin' & Pumpin' TOT 17	Papua New Guinea/Papua New Guinea (Andrew Weatherall Mix) (p/s)	6
94	Virgin promo 500	Slider/Snake Hips/You're Creeping Me Out/Herd Killing/Live In New York (2 x 12" p/s, promo only, 500 copies, FSOL under different names)	15

			MINT VALUE £
91	Jumpin'... 12TOT 11	PULSE: Bring On The Pulse/In The Mind Of A Child/ Hardhead/Pulse State (first 2 tracks credited to Indo Tribe which is FSOL under an assumed name)	8
91	Jumpin'...12TOT 16	PULSE 3: Tingler/Owl/Bite The Bullet/Calcium	12
91	Jumpin'...12TOT 17	Papua New Guinea (Dali Mix)/(Dumb Child Of Q Mix)/(Qube Mix) (p/s)	12
92	Jumpin'...12TOT 17R	Papua New Guinea (Andrew Weatherall Mix)/(Dub Mix)/(Journey To Pyramid)/ (Monsoon Mix)/(Graham Massey Mix)/(Dumb Child Of Q Mix) (p/s)	8
94	Virgin VST 1540P	Far Out Son Of Lung And The Ramblings Of A Madman/ Snake Hips/ Smokin' Japanese Babe/Amoeba (white vinyl, promo only)	20
95	Virgin SEMTEX DJ 1	Semtex (Part 1)/Semtex (Part 2)/We Have Explosive/Semtex (stamped sleeve, promo only, 500 copies)	15
92	Jumpin'...CDSTOT 17	Papua New Guinea/(Andrew Weatherall Mix)/(Dub Mix)/ (Journey To Pyramid)/(Graham Mix)/(Journey To The Pyramid)/(Graham Mix)/ (Dumb Child Of Q)/Hamish McDonald Mix)	8
93	Virgin VSCDT 1478	Cascade (Part 1)/(Part 2)/(Part 3)/(Part 4)/(Part 5)/Short Form	8
92	Jumpin'...LPTOT 2	ACCELERATOR (2-LP)	15
94	Virgin V 2722	LIFEFORMS (2-LP, stickered gatefold sleeve with inner sleeves)	20
94	Virgin V 2755	ISDN (LP, embossed, fold-out black sleeve with insert)	20
96	Virgin V 2814	DEAD CITIES (2-LP, gatefold sleeve with inners)	20
97	Virgin ISDNSHOW 1	ISDN Show (CD, promo only, no inlay)	25

FUTUREHEADS

01	Private Pressing	The first Demo (4-track CD, handwritten sticker)	50
02	Private Pressing	1-2-3 Nul Demo (5-track CD)	50
02	Project C'naut PCOS 001	Nul Book Standard - Park Inn/Robot/My Rules/Stupid And Shallow (p/s)	25
03	Fantastic Plastic FP7035	1-2-3-NUL! EP: Carnival Kids/Ticket/Cabaret/A Picture Of Dorian Gray (p/s, with sticker and badge)	25
03	Fantastic Plastic FPS035	1-2-3-NUL! EP: Carnival Kids/Ticket/Cabaret/A Picture Of Dorian Gray (CD, p/s)	20
03	Fantastic Plastic FP 7036	First Day/Balsch/Piece Of Crap (red or clear vinyl, p/s, 500 only)	5
03	Private Pressing	Hounds Of Love (1-track white label: gig/fanclub 7")	15
04	Private Pressing	Meantime/Decent Days & Nights Remixes (1000, white label gig/fanclub 7")	8

FUZZ

71	Mojo 2916 010	FUZZ (LP)	20

FUZZ FACE

68	Page One POF 065	Mighty Quinn/Voices From The Sky	5

FUZZTONES

85	ABC S 006	She's Wicked/Epitaph For A Head (p/s)	6

FUZZY DUCK

(see also Andromeda, Greatest Show On Earth, Alvin Lee, Capability Brown, Cockney Rebel))

71	MAM MAM 37	Double Time Woman/Just Look Around You	15
71	MAM MAM 51	Big Brass Band/One More Hour	15
71	MAM AS 1005	FUZZY DUCK (LP, laminated front sleeve, black/silver labels)	400
90	Reflection MM 05	FUZZY DUCK (LP, reissue with booklet & single "Double Time Woman"/ "One More Hour" [MMS 01])	15

FUZZY LOGIC

92	Guerilla GRRR29	Obsession (12")	20

FX

79	Southern Rock SR 4501	THE SOUTH'S GONNA RISE AGAIN (EP, oversized folding p/s)	100

FYNN McCOOL

(see also Shakespears, Grapefruit, Sleepy)

70	RCA RCA 1956	U.S. Thumbstyle/Diamond Lil	8
70	RCA SF 8112	FYNN McCOOL (LP, gatefold sleeve)	100

G

TOMMY G & CHARMS

67	London HLB 10107	I Know What I Want/I Want You So Bad	40

WINSTON G (& WICKED)

65	Parlophone R 5266	Please Don't Say/Like A Baby	35
66	Parlophone R 5330	Until You Were Gone/That Way Too (as Winston G. & Wicked)	18
66	Decca F 12444	Cloud Nine/I'll Make You Cry Tomorrow	18
67	Decca F 12559	Mother Ferguson's Love Dust/Judge And Jury	30
67	Decca F 12623	Riding With The Milkman/Bye Bye Baby	20

B(ASIL) GABBIDON

(see also Derrick Patsy & Basil, Mellow Larks, Derrick Morgan)

61	Blue Beat BB 069-A	Warpaint Baby (miscredited to B. Cabbidon & Buster's Group)/ I Was Wrong (miscredited to Chuck & Dobbie with Buster's Group)	20
62	Blue Beat BB 111-A	Ivoree/Lover Man	20
62	Blue Beat BB 124	Independence Blues/For My Love (as B. Gabbidon)	20
62	Blue Beat BB 129-A	Our Melody/Going Back To Ja (with Randy's All Stars)	20
62	Island WI 033	I Found My Baby (actually by Roy Braham)/No Fault Of Mine	30
63	Island WI 076	I Bet You Don't Know/3 x 7	30
63	Island WI 089	St. Louis Woman/Get On The Ball	40
63	Blue Beat BB 155-A	Eana Mena/Since You Are Gone (with Prince Buster All Stars)	20
63	Blue Beat BB 161	I'll Find Love (with Prince Buster All Stars)/ MELLOW LARKS: What You Gonna Do?	20
65	Blue Beat BB 288	Tick Tock (actually by Theo Beckford)/The Streets Of Glory (actually by Theo Beckford & Yvonne Harrison)	20

MINT VALUE £

PETER GABRIEL

(see also Genesis, Youssou 'Ndour & Peter Gabriel, Colin Scot, Charlie Drake)

77	Charisma CB 301	Solsbury Hill/Moribund The Burgermeister (p/s)	6
77	Charisma CB 302	Modern Love/Slowburn (no p/s, 'nude' picture label, withdrawn)	30
78	Charisma CB 311	D.I.Y./Perspective (p/s, purple label, Irish-only sleeve)	8
78	Charisma CB 311	D.I.Y./Perspective (p/s, silver label, possibly Irish-only sleeve)	8
78	Charisma CB 319	D.I.Y. (Remix)/Mother Of Violence/Teddy Bear (no p/s, withdrawn)	20
78	Sound For Industry SFI 381	Solsbury Hill (live) (1-sided flexidisc, concert freebie)	5
82	Charisma SHOCK 1	Shock The Monkey/Soft Dog (Instrumental) (p/s)	5
82	Charisma SHOCK 1	Shock The Monkey/Shock The Monkey (Instrumental) (same p/s as above)	10
82	Charisma SHOCK 122	Shock The Monkey/Soft Dog (Instrumental) (picture disc)	8
82	Charisma SHOCK 350	Shock The Monkey/Shock The Monkey (Instrumental) (12", same p/s as [SHOCK 12])	15
82	Charisma CB 405	I Have The Touch/Across The River (p/s)	5
83	Charisma GAB 12	I Don't Remember (live)/Solsbury Hill (live)/Kiss Of Life (live) (12", shrinkwrapped stickered double pack, with 12" white label [GAB 122], "Games Without Frontiers"/ Schnappschuss (Ein Familienfoto)", no p/s)	8
88	Charisma/Virgin CDT 33	Solsbury Hill/Moribund The Burgermeister/Solsbury Hill (live) (3" CD, card p/s)	8
92	Virgin PGS 7	Digging In The Dirt/Bashi-Bazouk (black label, jukebox issue)	5
92	Virgin PGSDG 712	Digging In The Dirt/Digging In The Dirt (Instrumental)/Quiet Steam/ Bashi-Bazouk (12", p/s, withdrawn)	8
92	Virgin PGSDX 8	Steam/Games Without Frontiers (Massive DB Mix)/Steam (Oh, Oh, Let Off Steam Mix)/Games Without Frontiers (live) (CD in fold-out house-shaped box)	8
80	Reformation RSR 113	CHROMEDOME (LP)	20

PETER GABRIEL & KATE BUSH

(see also Kate Bush)

86	Charisma/Virgin PGSP 2	Don't Give Up/In Your Eyes (Special Mix) (poster p/s in stickered PVC sleeve)	6

RUSS GABRIEL

(see also Fusion, Too Funk)

93	Ferox FER 002	PEACE EP (12", plain sleeve)	18
94	Ferox FER 006	DARWINIAN EP (12", plain sleeve)	8
95	Input Neuron INMD(X)1	FUTURE FUNK VOL. 1 (12", double pack, p/s)	10

RUSS GABRIEL & AFFIE YUSUF

94	Ferox FER 005	Sian's Tune/Deep Space (12")	18

GABRIEL & ANGELS

63	Stateside SS 150	That's Life (That's Tough)/Don't Wanna Twist No More	20

GABRIELLI BRASS

65	Polydor 56031	Angel Cake/Cat Walk	8
65	Polydor 56047	Ride Your Pony/Anyone Who Had A Heart	10
68	Polydor 56252	'Canterbury Tales' Theme/Working My Way Back To You	15

GABY & CABLES

(see also Gaby & Wilton)

72	Duke DU 129	Only Love Can Make You Smile/Only Love Version	10

GABY & WILTON

(see also Gaby & Cables)

72	Camel CA 92	Only Love/CHARLEY ACE: The Ten Commandments Of Joshua	10

PABLO GAD

77	Caribbean CBN 318	International Dread/International Dub	10
77	Caribbean CBM 320	Kunte Kinte/Jah Jah Say (with The Equators)	10
78	Burning Sounds BDS 009	Bloodsuckers/Jail House Pressure (12", red vinyl)	20
79	Burning Rockers BRD 007	Visions Of Pablo/Tru I De A Jail (12")	20
79	Burning Rockers BRD 008	Natty Loving/Trodding On Home (12")	20
79	Burning Rockers BRD 020	Riddle I Dis/Iration (12")	20
79	Burning Sounds BS 042	Blood Suckers/Blood Suckers Dub	6
79	Burning Sounds BSD 015	Throw Your Dreams/What Makes A Natty Dread Cry (12", red vinyl)	20
79	Burning Rockers BRD 014	Trafalgar Square/Chereene (12", red vinyl)	20
80	Burning Rockers BRD 043	Hard Time/Lighter Shade Of Black (12")	15
80	Burning Rockers BRD 044	Black Before Creation/Reggae Music (12")	15
80	Greensleeves GRED 33	Fly Away Home/Well Insane (12")	20
80	Jis Majesty HMD 012	Oh Jah/Little Young Girl (12")	35
80	FORM D001	Gun Fever/Fever Dub (12")	15
80	FORM D003	Nursery Rhyme/Bubbling Ahead (12")	8
81	FORM D005	P.G. In Love/RANKING SIMEON: Ranking Love (12")	10
81	FORM D017	Beggarman's Child/Poor Man Versus Rich Man Dub (12")	10
86	Jah Sjhaka SHAKA 853	King Of Kings/Lord Of Lords (12")	10
96	Reggae On Top ROT 013	Sha Sha Mane/Dub (12")	10
80	Burning Sounds BS 1038	TRAFALGAR SQUARE (LP)	15
80	Federation Or Reggae FORM LP 1099	HARD TIMES (10" LP, red vinyl)	30

GADGETS

(see also The The, Matt Johnson, Colin Lloyd Tucker, Plain Characters)

79	Final Solution FSLP 001	GADGETREE (LP, with insert, blue or beige picture on sleeve)	20
80	Final Solution FSLP 002	LOVE, CURIOSITY, FRECKLES & DOUBT (LP)	20
83	Glass GLALP 006	THE BLUE ALBUM (LP, with inner sleeve)	12

MEL GADSON

60	London HLX 9105	Comin' Down With Love/I'm Gettin' Sentimental Over You	20

GAGALACTYCA

(see also Bill Nelson, David John & Mood)

90	Holyground HG 1135/ Magic Mixture MM 3	GAGALACTYCA (LP, with booklet, actually by Lightyears Away & Thundermother, 425 only)	40

MINT VALUE £

MAJOR YURI GAGARIN
61 Britone MK 100 — CONQUEST OF SPACE (EP) . . . 20

GAGS
79 Look LKLP 6312 — DEATH IN BUZZARD'S GULCH (LP) . . . 30

LITTLE SAMMY GAHA
73 Decca FR 13436 — Rock 'N' Roll Is Back Again/Come 'N' On Strong . . . 15

DAVID GAHAN
(see also Depeche Mode)
08 Mute STUMM 288 — HOURGLASS (2-LP, gatefold with CD) . . . 15
08 Mute LSTUMM 288 — HOURGLASS REMIXES (2-LP & CD of remixes) . . . 18

BASIL GAIL
70 Bullet BU 454 — I Wish/Black Is Black . . . 8

SLIM GAILLARD (QUARTET/TRIO)
(see also Meade 'Lux' Lewis & Slim Gaillard)
50 Parlophone R 3291 — Jam Man/JOHNNY OTIS: Harlem Nocturne (78) . . . 20
48 MGM MGM 107 — Tip Light/Arabian Boogie (78, as Slim Gaillard and his Trio) . . . 40
50 MGM MGM 265 — Communications/Serenade To A Poodle (78) . . . 30
50 MGM MGM 281 — Organ-Oreenie/to (78, as Slim Gaillard Sextet) . . . 30
56 Parlophone GEP 8595 — SLIM GAILLARD NO. 1 (EP) . . . 15
56 Columbia Clef SEB 10046 — MUSICAL AGGREGATIONS (EP) . . . 15
60 London RED 1251 — SLIM GAILLARD RIDES AGAIN (EP) . . . 25

DONNA GAINES
(see also Donna Summer)
71 MCA MK 5060 — Sally Go Round The Roses/So Said The Man . . . 7

GAINORS
58 London HLU 8734 — The Secret/Gonna Rock Tonite . . . 100
58 London HLU 8734 — The Secret/Gonna Rock Tonite (78) . . . 35

G.A.K.
(see also Aphex Twin)
94 Warp WAP 48 — GAK EP (12") . . . 40
94 Warp WAP 48CD — GAK (CD) . . . 40

GALACTIC FEDERATION
66 Polydor BM 56093 — The March Of The Sky People/Moon Shot . . . 25

GALACTIC SYMPOSIUM
80 Vague VOG 2 — Money/In The Navy (gatefold p/s) . . . 6

GALAHAD
72 Polydor 2058 215 — Let's Dance/Jellyroll . . . 10
73 Bell BLL 1273 — Rocket Summer/Elephant Stomp . . . 20

GALAHAD
87 Private pressing G 1001 — Dreaming From The Inside/The Opiate (p/s, 500 only) . . . 12

DIAMANDA GALAS
82 Y Y 18 — LITANIES DU SATAN (LP) . . . 30
86 Mute STUMM 33 — SAINT OF THE PIT (12" EP, p/s with inner) . . . 8

GALAXIE 500
(see also Damon & Naomi)
89 Chemical Imbalance C 1005 — Oblivious/tracks by other artists (free with issue 8 of Chemical Imbalance magazine) . . . 7
89 Catalogue CAT 075 — Victory Garden/STRAIGHTJACKET FITS: Hail (1-sided flexi free with The Catalogue magazine) . . . 5
90 Caff CAFF 9 — Rain/Don't Let Your Youth Go To Waste (p/s, with insert in bag) . . . 25
89 Schemer 8905 CD — TODAY (CD, with 2 extra tracks) . . . 15
89 Rough Trade ROUGH 146 — ON FIRE (LP) . . . 30
90 Rough Trade ROUGH 156 — THIS IS OUR MUSIC (LP, with sticker and 3 postcards) . . . 15
91 Rough Trade ROUGH 146L — ON FIRE (LP, reissue with shrinkwrapped CD single) . . . 15
96 Rykodisc RCD 10355 — GALAXIE 500 (4-CD box set with booklet) . . . 30

GALAXIES
60 Capitol CL 15158 — The Big Triangle/Until The Next Time . . . 15

EDDIE GALE
69 Blue Note BST 84294 — GHETTO MUSIC (LP) . . . 15

SANDRA GALE
63 Ember EMB S 162 — Hello Heartbreak/If She's Right For You . . . 10

SUNNY GALE
53 HMV 7M 147 — Teardrops On My Pillow/Send My Baby Back To Me . . . 12
54 HMV 7M 243 — Goodnight, Well It's Time To Go/Close To Me . . . 12
55 HMV 7M 344 — C'est La Vie/Looking Glass . . . 12
57 Brunswick 05659 — Two Hearts (With An Arrow Between)/Maybe You'll Be There . . . 10
57 Brunswick 05661 — Come Go With Me/Please Go . . . 10
58 Brunswick 05753 — A Certain Smile/Just Friends . . . 10
61 London HLU 9322 — Please Love Me Forever/Sunny . . . 10

GALE BROTHERS
66 Parlophone R 5535 — Every Day Of My Life/All Strung Out . . . 6

GALENS
63 London HLH 9804 — Baby I Do Love You/Love Bells . . . 35

FRANCE GALL
65 Philips BF 1408 — Poupée De Cire, Poupeé De Son/Le Coeur Qui Jazze . . . 6
88 WEA YZ 316 CD — Ella Elle L'a (CD, slimline jewel case) . . . 15

MINT VALUE £

HUGHIE GALLAGHER
67 Outlet TOL 101 — THE FLAGS ARE OUT FOR CELTIC (LP) — 15

RORY GALLAGHER
(see also Taste, Killing Floor, Joe O'Donnell)
71 Polydor 2383 044 — RORY GALLAGHER (LP) — 30
71 Polydor 2383 076 — DEUCE (LP) — 25
72 Polydor 2383 112 — LIVE! IN EUROPE (LP, gatefold sleeve) — 18
73 Polydor 2383 189 — BLUEPRINT (LP) — 15
73 Polydor 2383 230 — TATTOO (LP) — 15
74 Polydor 2659 031 — IRISH TOUR '74 (2-LP) — 15
87 Capo/Demon XFIEND 98 — DEFENDER (LP, with bonus 7", "Seems To Me"/"No Peace For The Wicked") — 12

GALLAGHER-LYLE
(see also James Galt, McGuinness Flint, Cups)
67 Polydor BM 56170 — Trees/In The Crowd — 18
72 Capitol ST 21906 — GALLAGHER AND LYLE (LP) — 20
73 A&M AMLH 68148 — WILLIE AND THE LAPDOG (LP) — 18
73 A&M AMLS 8207 — SEEDS (LP) — 12

GALLAHADS
55 Capitol CL 14282 — Ooh-Ah/Careless — 15

RONNIE GALLANT
62 Warner Bros WB 61 — In The Night/The Hole In The Wall — 6

GALLANTS
64 Capitol CL 15366 — Happy Beat/Rhino — 7
65 Capitol CL 15408 — Man From U.N.C.L.E. Theme/Vagabond — 15

GALLERY
69 Midas — THE WIND THAT SHAKES THE BARLEY (LP) — 250

GALLIANO
88 Acid Jazz JAZID 1 — Frederick Lies Still/I Love You Baby (1st pressing, with large centre hole) — 20

GALLIARD
(see also Craig)
70 Deram DM 306 — I Wrapped Her In Ribbons/The Hermit And The Knight — 10
70 Deram Nova (S)DN 4 — STRANGE PLEASURE (LP, red/silver labels) — 120
70 Deram SML 1075 — NEW DAWN (LP, white/red labels with small logo) — 250

GALLIARDS
60 Topic STOP 101 — Black And White/Bahnuah — 7

BOB GALLION
59 MGM MGM 1028 — Out Of A Honky Tonk/You Take The Table And I'll Take The Chairs — 10
60 MGM MGM 1057 — Froggy Went A Courtin'/Hey! Joe — 10
65 Hickory 45-1300 — I Don't Have The Right (To Disagree)/Thank The Devil For Hideaways — 7

GALLON DRUNK
93 Clawfist XPIG 21 — Known, Not Wanted/TINDERSTICKS: We Have All The Time In The World ('singles club' release, p/s, 1,400 only) — 15

GALLOW GLASS CEILI BAND
60 Top Rank RX 30314 — COME TO THE CEILI (LP) — 12

GALLOWS
07 Holy Roar HRR 006V — Just Because You Sleep Next To Me Doesn't Mean You're Safe/ Abandon Ship/Will Someone Shoot That Fucking Snake/Swarm Over Death (white vinyl, 500 only) — 15

JAMES GALT
(see also Gallagher-Lyle)
65 Pye 7N 15936 — Comes The Dawn/My Own Way — 12
65 Pye 7N 17021 — With My Baby/A Most Unusual Feeling — 75
65 Pye 7N 17021 — With My Baby/A Most Unusual Feeling (DJ Copy) — 100

GAMBLERS
(see also Billy Fury)
63 Decca F 11780 — You've Really Got A Hold On Me/Can I See You Tonight? — 15
64 Decca F 11872 — Nobody But Me/It's So Nice — 15
65 Decca F 12060 — Now I'm All Alone/Find Out What's Happening — 25
66 Decca F 12399 — Doctor Goldfoot (And His Bikini Machine)/It Seems So Long — 20
67 Parlophone R 5557 — Cry Me A River/Who Will Buy — 30

FREDDIE GAMBRELL
59 Vogue LAE 12205 — FREDDIE GAMBRELL (LP) — 20

GAME
65 Pye 7N 15889 — But I Do/Gotta Keep On Moving Baby — 80
66 Decca F 12469 — Gonna Get Me Someone/Gotta Wait — 200
67 Parlophone R 5553 — The Addicted Man/Help Me Mummy's Gone (withdrawn) — 1000
67 Parlophone R 5553 — The Addicted Man/Help Me Mummy's Gone (withdrawn) (demo copy) — 750
67 Parlophone R 5569 — It's Shocking What They Call Me/Help Me Mummy's Gone — 500

GAMMA
80 Elektra K12480 — Something In The Air/Mayday — 8

GAMMER
77 Pennine (EP) PSS 147 — Market Place - Your Alone/San Diego (p/s) — 12

GAMMER & HIS FAMILIARS
(see also Durutti Column)
84 Gammer GAMMER 5 — Will The New Baby/All Above (12", p/s) — 8

GANDALF THE GREY
80s Heyoka — THE GREY WIZARD AM I (LP, reissue of U.S. LP) — 25

MINT VALUE £

RON GANDERTON

82	Centridge CENT 2	Giggle Amongst The Tears/Smothered In Love (p/s)	8

RON WARREN GANDERTON

(see under Sound Ceremony)

LITTLE JIMMY GANDY

69	Roulette RO 510	Cool Thirteen/I'm Not Like The Others (Existence unconfirmed)	20

GANELIN TRIO

80	Leo LR 102	CATALOGUE, LIVE IN EAST GERMANY (LP)	15
83	Leo LR 112	NEW WINE...(LP)	30

GANGBUSTERS

63	Fontana TF 419	The Memory Of Your Face/When We Met	5

GANG OF ANGELS

(see also Slade)

94	Shotgun CDBOR 012	Hello Goodbye/Jim Jam (CD)	8

GANG OF FOUR

80	Fast Product FAST 5	DAMAGED GOODS (EP, original with b&w labels, with sticker)	15
80	Fast Product FAST 5	DAMAGED GOODS (EP, original with b&w labels, without sticker)	6
79	EMI EMC 3313	ENTERTAINMENT (LP, with inner sleeve)	20
82	EMI EMC 3412	SONGS OF THE FREE (LP, with inner sleeve)	12
86	Strange Fruit SFPS 008	PEEL SESSIONS (12")	10
81	EMI EMC 3364	SOLID GOLD (LP, with insert)	15

GANGSTERS

80	Big Bear BB 25	Rudi The Red Nose Reindeer/White Christmas	5
80	Big Bear BB 28	Wooly Bully/We Are The Gangsters	5

GANGSTERS

79	Stortbeat A45/B45	Harlow Town/Record Company	15
79	Stortbeat BEAT 3	Best Friend/Best Friend Dub (p/s)	8
79	Stortbeat BEAT 2	GANGSTERS (LP)	20

GANIM'S ASIA MINORS

58	London HLE 8637	Daddy Lolo/Halvah	12

ALAN GANLEY QUARTET

58	Pye Nixa NJE 1046	GONE GANLEY (EP)	150

CECIL GANT

74	Flyright LP 4710	ROCK LITTLE BABY (LP)	15
75	Flyright LP 4714	CECIL'S BOOGIE (LP)	15
79	Magpie 1816	KILLER DILLER BOOGIE (LP)	15

CLENTT GANT

60	Starlite ST45 023	I'm Just A Lucky So-And-So/I Need You So	5

DON GANT

65	Hickory 45-1297	Early In The Morning/Don't Ya Even Cry	5

ELMER GANTRY'S VELVET OPERA

(see also Velvet Opera, Stretch, Strawbs, Hudson-Ford, Paul Brett's Sage)

67	Direction 58-3083	Flames/Salisbury Plain	20
68	Direction 58-3481	Mary Jane/Dreamy	20
69	Direction 58-3924	Volcano/A Quick 'B'	20
68	Direction 8-63300	ELMER GANTRY'S VELVET OPERA (LP, laminated front sleeve, yellow/black labels)	110

GANTS

65	Liberty LIB 55829	Road Runner/My Baby Don't Care	35
67	Liberty LIB 55940	I Wonder/Greener Days	15
88	Bam Caruso KIRI 067	I WONDER (LP)	12

GARBAGE

(see also Goodbye Mr. MacKenzine)

95	Discordant CORD 001	Vow/Torn Apart (embossed metal 'G' logo sleeve, with insert, 3,000 pressed [934 issued], stickered, sealed)	30
95	Discordant CORD 001	Vow/Torn Apart (embossed metal 'G' logo sleeve, with insert, 3,000 pressed [934 issued], stickered, unsealed)	40
95	Discordant CORD 001	Vow/Torn Apart (plain black embossed 'G' logo sleeve, with insert in poly bag, 500 only, sealed)	12
95	Discordant CORD 001	Vow/Torn Apart (plain black embossed 'G' logo sleeve, with insert in poly bag, 500 only, unsealed)	15
95	Mushroom SX 1138	Subhuman/1 Crush (embossed rubber 'G' logo sleeve, with SX 1138 insert, some in white 'G' logo carrier bag, 3,000 only; with incorrect insert [S1138])	20
95	Mushroom S 1138	Subhuman/1 Crush (embossed card 'G' logo sleeve, with insert, 2,000 pressed [1,000 issued])	10
95	Mushroom D 1138	Subhuman/1 Crush/Vow (CD, embossed inlay, stickered case, 3,000 only)	10
95	Mushroom SX 1199	Only Happy When It Rains/Girl Can't Come/Sleep (double-grooved B-side, stickered 'hologram prismaboard' 'G' logo sleeve, with inner sleeve & insert; some in blue 'G' logo carrier bag, 5000 only)	5
95	Mushroom SX 1199	Only Happy When It Rains/Girl Can't Come/Sleep (as above, shrinkwrapped)	7
96	Mushroom SX 1271	Stupid Girl/Dog New Tricks (The Pal Mix) (jukebox issue, white label, no p/s)	7
96	Mushroom SX 1271/1237	Stupid Girl/Queer (jukebox issue, white label, stamped 'Garbage' logo, no p/s)	5
96	Mushroom SX 1271	Stupid Girl/Dog New Tricks (The Pal Mix) (10,000 only, stickered blue 'Tak-Tile' cloth 'G' logo sleeve, with stickered shrinkwrap)	8
95	Mushroom L 31450	GARBAGE (LP) (as 2 x 45rpm 12", with inner sleeves)	15
95	Mushroom LX 31450	GARBAGE (LP) (as 6 x 7" singles in box set with 3 inserts [now import only], sealed)	20
95	Mushroom LX 31450	GARBAGE (LP) (as 6 x 7" singles in box set with 3 inserts [now import only], unsealed)	15
01	Mushroom TRASH 27	Androgyny/Androgyny (Neptunes Remix) (12")	15

MINT VALUE £

GARBO

82	Rarn RARN 201	Dancing Strange/Why Don't You Call Me?/Everyday Hallucinations (with p/s)	200
82	Rarn RARN 201	Dancing Strange/Why Don't You Call Me?/Everyday Hallucinations (without p/s)	50

GARBO'S CELLULOID HEROES

78	Big Bear BB 13	Only Death Is Fatal/Won't You Come To My Funeral (p/s)	10

VIN GARBUTT

72	Trailer LER 2078	THE VALLEY OF TEES (LP, red label)	15
75	Trailer LER 2081	THE YOUNG TIN WHISTLE PEST (LP, yellow label)	15
76	Trailer LER 2102	KING GOODEN (LP, yellow label)	15

JERRY GARCIA

(see also Grateful Dead, Diga Rhythm Band, Old & In The Way)

71	Douglas DGL 69013	HOOTEROLL? (LP, with Howard Wales)	15
72	Warner Bros K 46139	GARCIA (LP)	12
74	Round RX 59301	GARCIA (LP)	12
76	United Artists UAG 29921	REFLECTIONS (LP)	12

RUSS GARCIA ORCHESTRA

58	London HAU 2141	FANTASTICA! (LP)	40

GARDEN ODYSSEY (ENTERPRISE)

(see also Graham Gouldman)

69	Deram DM 267	Sad And Lonely/Sky Pilot (8/M/1) (as Garden Odyssey Enterprise)	50
72	RCA RCA 2159	Joker/Have You Ever Been To Georgia (as Garden Odyssey)	6

BORIS GARDINER (& LOVE PEOPLE)

69	High Note HS 010	Lucky Is The Boy/Bobby Sox To Stockings	60
69	Doctor Bird DB 1205	Elizabethan Reggae/Hooked On A Feeling	25
69	Duke DU 21	Never My Love/The Bold One	20
69	Duke 39	Elizabethan Reggae/BYRON LEE: Soul Serenade	15
70	Treasure Isle TI 7056	Hooked On A Feeling/MESSAGE: Turn Around Twice	12
70	Big Shot BI 537	Sweet Soul Special/Memories Of Love (with Love People)	10
70	Big Shot BI 538	Darkness/Watch This Music (B-side actually "Keep Out") (with Love People)	12
70	Big Shot BI 539	Hot Shot/Watch This Music (with Love People)	40
70	Dynamic DYN 404	Commanding Wife/Band Of Gold (as Boris Gardner & Happening)	6
70	Trojan TR 7753	Dynamic Pressure/Reggae Me Dis, Reggae Me Dat	7
70	Trojan TBL 121	REGGAE HAPPENING (LP)	30

PAUL GARDINER

(see also Tubeway Army, Gary Numan)

81	Beggars Banquet BEG 61	Stormtrooper In Drag/Night Talk (p/s)	5
81	Beggars Banquet BEG 61T	Stormtrooper In Drag/Night Talk (12", unreleased, white label promo)	700
84	Numa NU 1	Venus In Furs/No Sense (p/s)	5
84	Numa NUM 1	Venus In Furs (Extended Mix)/No Sense/Venus In Furs (7" Mix) (12", p/s)	10

AVA GARDNER

53	MGM SP 1005	Can't Help Lovin' Dat Man/Bill	10

DAVE GARDNER

58	Brunswick 05740	Hop Along Rock/All By Myself (B-side with Anita Kerr Singers)	30
58	Brunswick 05740	Hop Along Rock/All By Myself (B-side with Anita Kerr Singers) (78)	10

DON GARDNER & DEE DEE FORD

(see also Baby Washington & Don Gardner, Dee Dee Ford)

62	Stateside SS 114	I Need Your Loving/Tell Me	20
62	Stateside SS 130	Don't You Worry/I'm Coming Home To Stay	20
68	Soul City SC 101	Don't You Worry/I'm Coming Home To Stay (reissue)	15

JOANNE GARDNER

70s	Polydor	JOANNE GARDNER (LP)	15

JOHNNY GARFIELD

(see also Simon & Garfunkel, Tom & Jerry)

65	Pye 7N 15758	Stranger In Paradise/Anyone Can Lose A Heart	45

(Art) GARFUNKEL

74	CBS CQ 31474/Q 69021	ANGEL CLARE (LP, quadrophonic)	12

FRANK GARI

60	London HLU 9277	I Ain't Got A Girl/Utopia	10
61	London HL 9371	Lullaby Of Love/Tonight Is Our Last Night	7

JUDY GARLAND

(see also Fred Astaire)

53	MGM SP 1001	A Couple Of Swells/Medley: I Love A Piano/Snooky Ookums/When The Midnight Choo Choo Leaves (with Fred Astaire)	12
56	Brunswick 02886	Over The Rainbow/The Jitterbug (78)	18
56	MGM SP 1157	Look For The Silver Lining/Who?	10
57	Capitol CL 14789	Rock-a-bye Your Baby With A Dixie Melody/After You've Gone	6
57	Capitol CL 14790	I Feel A Song Coming On/Just Imagine	6
57	Capitol CL 14791	By Myself/It's Lovely To Be Back In London	6
57	Capitol CL 17691	It's Lovely To Be Back In London (1-sided 7" given to audience at Gala Premiere of extended engagement at Dominion Theatre (p/s with insert)	15
55	Philips BBE 12012	BORN IN A TRUNK - SELECTIONS FROM A STAR IS BORN (EP)	10
56	MGM MGM-EP 568	IF YOU FEEL LIKE SINGING (EP)	10
56	MGM MGM-EP 672	WORDS AND MUSIC - SOUNDTRACK EXCERPTS (EP, 1 track with June Allyson & Mickey Rooney)	10
55	Brunswick LA 8725	JUDY AT THE PALACE (10" LP)	12
55	MGM MGM-D 134	BORN TO SING (10" LP)	12
59	Capitol (S)T 1188	THE LETTER (LP, with paste-on letter intact)	25
59	Capitol (S)T 1188	THE LETTER (LP, without paste-on letter intact)	12

MINT VALUE £

RED GARLAND

60	Esquire 32- 096	MANTECA (LP)	15
60	Esquire 32-099	ALL MORNING LONG (LP)	15
61	Esquire 32-116	RED IN BLUES VILLE (LP)	25
61	Esquire 32-126	AT THE PRELUDE (LP)	20
61	Esquire 32-136	SOUL JUNCTION (LP)	20
62	Esquire 32-146	ROJO (LP)	20
62	Esquire 32-166	HIGH PRESSURE (LP)	20

BILLY GARNER

00	BGPS 006	Brand New Girl/JACQUELINE JONES: Can't Stop The Show	15

ERROL GARNER

53	Vogue LDE 034	ERROL GARNER TRIO VOLUME ONE (10" LP)	12
54	Felsted EDL 87002	MARGIE (10" LP)	12
54	Philips BBR 8002	PLAYS FOR DANCING (10" LP)	12
55	Philips BBR 8045	SOLO FLIGHT (10" LP)	12
55	Columbia 33S 1050	PIANO MOODS (10" LP)	12
55	Columbia 33S 1059	PIANO GEMS (10" LP)	12
55	Oriole MG 26042	GONE WITH GARNER (10" LP)	12
55	Felsted EDL 87015	PASSPORT TO FAME (10" LP)	12

KAY GARNER

64	Oriole CB 1951	I Still Get Jealous/Squeeze Me	10

REGGIE GARNER

76	Capitol CL 15874	Hot Line/Blessed Be The Name Of My Baby	10

BLIND LEROY GARNET

52	Jazz Collector L 74	Chain 'Em Down/Louisiana Glide (78)	15

COL GARNET

66	Page One POF 002	With A Girl Like You/Monday Monday	12

ALF GARNETT (& FAMILY)

68	Pye NPL 18192	SEX AND OTHER THOUGHTS (LP)	18

GALE GARNETT

64	RCA RCA 1418	We'll Sing In The Sunshine/Prism Song	10
65	RCA RCA 1451	I'll Cry Alone/Where Do You Go To Go Away?	60
65	RCA RCA 1451	I'll Cry Alone/Where Do You Go To Go Away? (DJ Copy)	85
65	RCA RD 7726	MY KIND OF FOLK SONGS (LP)	30
66	RCA RD 7750	LOVIN' PLACE (LP)	20

LAURENT GARNIER

93	Warp WAP 36	A BOUT DE SOUFFLE (12", company sleeve)	8

JESSE GARON & DESPERADOS

(see under 'J')

VERNON GARRETT

67	Stateside SS 2006	If I Could Turn Back The Hands Of Time/You And Me Together	40
67	Stateside SS 2006	If I Could Turn Back The Hands Of Time/You And Me Together (DJ copy)	80
67	Stateside SS 2026	Shine It On/Things Are Lookin' Better	40
67	Stateside SS 2026	Shine It On/Things Are Lookin' Better (DJ copy)	75
68	Action ACT 4508	Shine It On/Things Are Lookin' Better (reissue)	30

DAVID GARRICK

65	Piccadilly 7N 35231	Go/When The World Was Our Own	7
65	Piccadilly 7N 35263	One Little Smile/We Must Be In Love	7
66	Piccadilly 7N 35317	Lady Jane/Let's Go Somewhere	6
66	Piccadilly 7N 35335	Dear Mrs Applebee/You're What I'm Living For	7
67	Piccadilly 7N 35371	I've Found A Love/(You Can't Hide) A Broken Heart	5
67	Piccadilly 7N 35377	A Certain Misunderstanding/I'm Looking Straight At You	5
67	Piccadilly 7N 35402	Don't Go Out In The Rain (You're Gonna Melt, Sugar)/Theme For A Wishing Heart	7
67	Pye 7N 17409	Ave Maria/Please Stay	5
67	Pye 7N 17409	Ave Maria/You Don't Know (different B-side)	5
68	Pye 7N 17509	Rainbow/I'll Be Home	6
68	Pye 7N 17610	A Little Bit Of This (And A Little Bit Of That)/Flutterby Butterfly	6
69	Pye 7N 17685	Maypole Mews/Like To Get To Know You Better	5
69	Pye 7N 17820	Poor Little Me/Molly With The Hair Like Silver	5
69	Columbia DB 8680	Bake Me A Woman/House In The Heather	7
71	Columbia DB 8784	Mary In The Morning/Beautiful People	7
67	Piccadilly NEP 34056	DAVID (EP)	30
66	Piccadilly NPL 38024	A BOY CALLED DAVID (LP, mono)	20
66	Piccadilly N(S)PL 38024	A BOY CALLED DAVID (LP, stereo)	22
67	Piccadilly N(S)PL 38035	DON'T GO OUT INTO THE RAIN, SUGAR (LP)	20
68	Pye NSPL 18223	LIVE! (LP, blue/black label)	30

MICHAEL GARRICK

(see also Ian Carr, Norma Winstone, Joe Harriott, Garrick's Fairground)

65	Argo EAF/ZFA 92	ANTHEM - MICHAEL GARRICK QUINTET (EP, mono/stereo)	60
66	Argo EAF 115	BEFORE NIGHT/DAY (EP)	60
63	Airborne	CASE OF JAZZ (LP)	65
64	Airborne	MOONSCAPE (10" LP)	1000
64	Argo ZDA 26/27	POETRY AND JAZZ IN CONCERT (2-LP, with Norma Winstone)	60
65	Argo (Z)DA 33	OCTOBER WOMAN (LP, as Michael Garrick Quintet, with Joe Harriott)	75
65	Argo (Z)DA 36	PROMISES (LP, as Michael Garrick Sextet, with Ian Carr)	120
68	Argo (Z)DA 88	BLACK MARIGOLDS (LP, as Michael Garrick Septet)	120
68	Airborne NBP 0021	JAZZ PRAISES AT ST. PAULS (LP)	45
69	Argo ZPR 264/5	POETRY AND JAZZ IN CONCERT 250 (2-LP, as Michael Garrick Quintet)	80
70	Argo ZDA 135	HEART IS A LOTUS (LP, as Michael Garrick Sextet with Norma Winstone)	90
72	Argo ZDA 153	COLD MOUNTAIN (LP, as Michael Garrick Trio)	100

MINT VALUE £

72	Argo ZDA 154	HOME STRETCH BLUES (LP, as Michael Garrick Band with Norma Winstone)	120
73	Impulse AS 49	ILLUMINATION (LP, as Michael Garrick Sextet)	40
74	Argo ZDA 163	TROPPO (LP)	65
81	Hep HEP 2011	YOU'VE CHANGED (LP)	20
07	Trunk JBH 022 LP	MOONSCAPE (LP, reissue 500 only)	30

GARRICK'S FAIRGROUND

(see also Michael Garrick)

71	Argo AFW 105	Epiphany/Blessed Are The Peacemakers	10
72	Argo ZAGF 1	MR. SMITH'S APOCALYPSE (LP)	60

FREDDIE GARRITY

(see also Freddie & Dreamers)

68	Columbia DB 8348	Little Red Donkey/So Many Different Ways	6
74	Bus Stop BUS 1017	Hello Kids/It's Good For You	7
74	Bus Stop BUS 1022	The Chicken Song/Pooh Pooh Pooh	7
70	Starline SRS 5019	OLIVER IN THE OVERWORLD (LP, soundtrack)	12

ROBIN GARSIDE & PAUL GOUGH

77	Northern Sound NSR 01	SEA SONGS (LP)	15

MORT GARSON

69	A & M AMLS 960	ELECTRIC HAIRPEICES (LP)	18

ROBIN GARTON & HIS BAND

58	Martello MC 100	Topsy/Jump For Me	5

GARUDA

77	EMI EMC 3174	GARUDA (LP)	40

REX GARVIN & MIGHTY CRAVERS

66	Atlantic 584 028	Sock It To 'Em J.B. (Parts 1 & 2)	15
67	Atlantic 584 097	I Gotta Go Now (Up On The Floor)/Believe It Or Not	15

JOHN GARY

59	Top Rank JAR 177	Let Them Talk/Tell My Love	7
59	Top Rank JAR 177	Let Them Talk/Tell My Love (78)	12
60	Top Rank JAR 392	Little Things Mean A Lot/Ever Since I Met Lucy	7

GARY & ARIELS

(see also Garry Mills)

64	Fontana TF 476	Say You Love Me/Town Girl	15

GARY & STU

(see also Koobas, March Hare)

72	Carnaby 6151 003	Sweet White Dove/Good Lady Fair	12
72	Carnaby 6302 012	HARLAN FARE (LP, white label with 'crab' logo)	50

GAS

80	Polydor POSP 192	It Shows In Your Face/Tomorrow (p/s)	35
81	Polydor POSP 264	Ignore Me/Do It, Don't Tell Me (p/s)	20
81	Polydor POSP 296	Treatment/That's It (12", p/s)	30
81	Polydor POSP 344	The Finger/Knock It Down (p/s)	18
81	Polydor POLE 1052	EMOTIONAL WARFARE (LP)	15

GASKIN

81	Rondelet ROUND 7	I'm No Fool/Sweet Dream Maker (p/s)	25
82	Rondelet ROUND 21	Mony Mony/Queen Of Hams (p/s)	18
81	Rondelet ABOUT 4	END OF THE WORLD (LP, gatefold sleeve)	25
82	Rondelet ABOUT 8	NO WAY OUT (LP, with inner)	20

GASLIGHT

69	Jay Boy BOY 17	Move/And So To Sleep	18
70	SDE 32732	GASLIGHT (2-LP, private pressing, gatefold sleeve with inserts, 2nd disc by Gaslight Choir)	40

GASOLIN

71	CBS 64685	GASOLIN (LP, gatefold sleeve, orange/black label)	40
72	CBS 65229	2 (LP, gatefold sleeve, orange/black label)	30
73	CBS 65798	3 (LP, orange label)	20
75	Epic SEPC 81436	WHAT A LEMON (LP, yellow/black label)	30

GASOLINE BAND

72	Cube HIFLY 9	GASOLINE BAND (LP, cube label)	200

GASPAR NETSCHER ENSEMBLE

68	Pye 7N 17556	Get Out Of My Bed Darling/Until You're Here Beside Me	6

GASS

(see also Hummingbird, Humble Pie, Streetwalkers, Peter Green)

65	Parlophone R 5344	One Of These Days/I Don't Know Why	30
66	Parlophone R 5456	The New Breed/In The City	50
67	CBS 202647	Dream Baby (How Long Must I Dream?)/Jitterbug Sid	20
71	Polydor 2058 147	Something's Got To Change Your Ways/Mr Banana	6
70	Polydor 2383 022	JUJU (LP, featuring Peter Green)	60
70	Polydor 2383 022	JUJU (LP, featuring Peter Green, alternative sleeve, black/gold with Gass logo on front and drawing on rear, record has same matrix as other issue and red Polydor labels)	150
71	Polydor 2383 035	CATCH MY SOUL - THE ROCK-OTHELLO (LP, cast recording featuring Gass)	20

GASS COMPANY

(see also Wake)

68	President PT 170	Everybody Needs Love/Nightmare	50

GAS WORKS

73	Regal Zonophone RZ 3075	Standing Stiff/Keep On Rolling	6
73	Regal Zonophone RZ 3080	God's Great Spaceship/Cider With Rosie	6
73	Regal Zono. SRLZ 1036	GAS WORKS (LP)	15

MINT VALUE £

DAVID GATES
(see also Bread)

60	Top Rank JAR 504	The Happiest Man Alive/The Road That Leads To Love	30

PEARLY GATES
(see also Flirtations, Gypsies)

74	Polydor 2058 443	Johnny And The Juke-Box/They Were Good Times	5
70	MCA MU 1109	Free/Carole's Epic Song	12

RAY GATES

66	Decca F 12502	It's Such A Shame/Have You Ever Had The Blues	40

GATES OF EDEN

66	Pye 7N 17195	Too Much On My Mind/I'm Warning You	25
67	Pye 7N 17252	In Your Love/Snoopy Versus The Red Baron	12
67	Pye 7N 17278	1 To 7/Hey Now	25

GATEWAY SINGERS

57	Brunswick LAT 8176	PUTTIN' ON THE STYLE (LP)	18

GATHERERS

73	Duke DU 153	Words Of My Mouth/UPSETTERS: Version	40

LUCHO GATICA

54	Parlophone CMSP 16	Besame Mucho/Las Muchachas De La Plaza De Espana (export issue)	8

GATOR CREEK

71	Mercury 6052 058	Danny's Song/Take A Look	6
71	Mercury 6338 035	GATOR CREEK (LP)	15

DICK GAUGHAN

72	Trailer LER 2072	NO MORE FOREVER (LP, red label)	25
76	Rubber RUB 019	FIVE HAND REEL (LP)	20
78	Topic 12TS384	GAUGHAN (LP, tan label)	15
81	Topic 12TS419	HANDFUL OF EARTH (LP)	15

GEORGES GAVARENTZ

69	Philips SBL 7898	THEY CAME TO ROB LAS VEGAS (LP, soundtrack)	60

JIMMY GAVIN

57	London HLU 8478	I Sit In My Window/Lonely Chair	80
57	London HLU 8478	I Sit In My Window/Lonely Chair (78)	15

JOHNNY GAVOTTE

60	Parlophone R 4631	It's Not Too Late/Can't Forget	10

ELAINE GAY

54	Parlophone MSP 6140	Love/Instantly	10
55	Parlophone R 3997	Rock Love/Ebony Eyes (78)	10

MAC GAYDEN
(see also Area Code 615)

73	EMI EMA 760	McGAVOCK GAYDEN (LP)	20

MARVIN GAYE

63	Oriole CBA 1803	Stubborn Kind Of Fellow/It Hurt Me Too	120
63	Oriole CBA 1803	Stubborn Kind Of Fellow/It Hurt Me Too (DJ Copy)	200
63	Oriole CBA 1846	Pride And Joy/One Of These Days	120
63	Oriole CBA 1846	Pride And Joy/One Of These Days (DJ Copy)	200
63	Stateside SS 243	Can I Get A Witness?/I'm Crazy 'Bout My Baby	50
63	Stateside SS 243	Can I Get A Witness?/I'm Crazy 'Bout My Baby (DJ Copy)	90
64	Stateside SS 284	You're A Wonderful One/When I'm Alone I Cry	50
64	Stateside SS 284	You're A Wonderful One/When I'm Alone I Cry (DJ Copy)	90
64	Stateside SS 326	Try It Baby/If My Heart Could Sing	40
64	Stateside SS 326	Try It Baby/If My Heart Could Sing (DJ Copy)	70
64	Stateside SS 360	How Sweet It Is (To Be Loved By You)/Forever	30
64	Stateside SS 360	How Sweet It Is (To Be Loved By You)/Forever (DJ Copy)	90
65	Tamla Motown TMG 510	I'll Be Doggone/You've Been A Long Time Coming	45
65	Tamla Motown TMG 510	I'll Be Doggone/You've Been A Long Time Coming (DJ Copy)	120
65	Tamla Motown TMG 524	Pretty Little Baby/Now That You've Won Me	40
65	Tamla Motown TMG 524	Pretty Little Baby/Now That You've Won Me (DJ Copy)	80
65	Tamla Motown TMG 539	Ain't That Peculiar?/She's Got To Be Real	25
65	Tamla Motown TMG 539	Ain't That Peculiar?/She's Got To Be Real (DJ Copy)	90
66	Tamla Motown TMG 552	One More Heartache/When I Had Your Love	35
66	Tamla Motown TMG 552	One More Heartache/When I Had Your Love (DJ Copy)	80
66	Tamla Motown TMG 563	Take This Heart Of Mine/Need Your Lovin' (Want You Back)	35
66	Tamla Motown TMG 563	Take This Heart Of Mine/Need Your Lovin' (Want You Back) (DJ Copy)	80
66	Tamla Motown TMG 574	Little Darlin' (I Need You)/Hey Diddle Diddle	35
66	Tamla Motown TMG 574	Little Darlin' (I Need You)/Hey Diddle Diddle (DJ Copy)	120
67	Tamla Motown TMG 618	Your Unchanging Love/I'll Take Care Of You	20
67	Tamla Motown TMG 618	Your Unchanging Love/I'll Take Care Of You (DJ Copy)	50
68	Tamla Motown TMG 640	You/Change What You Can	18
68	Tamla Motown TMG 640	You/Change What You Can (DJ Copy)	40
68	Tamla Motown TMG 676	Chained/At Last (I Found A Love)	18
69	Tamla Motown TMG 686	I Heard It Through The Grapevine/Need Somebody	7
69	Tamla Motown TMG 705	Too Busy Thinking 'Bout My Baby/Wherever I Lay My Hat	7
69	Tamla Motown TMG 718	That's The Way Love Is/Gonna Keep On Tryin' Till I Win Your Love	8
70	Tamla Motown TMG 734	Abraham, Martin And John/How Can I Forget?	7
71	Tamla Motown TMG 775	What's Going On?/God Is Love	7
71	Tamla Motown TMG 796	Save The Children/Little Darling (I Need You)	8
72	Tamla Motown TMG 802	Mercy Mercy Me/Bad Tomorrows	6
72	Tamla Motown TMG 817	Inner City Blues/Wholly Holy	10
73	Tamla Motown TMG 846	Trouble Man/Don't Mess With Mister 'T'	12
74	Tamla Motown TMG 882	Come Get To This/Distant Lover	15
66	Tamla Motown TME 2016	MARVIN GAYE (EP)	65

			MINT VALUE £
67	Tamla Motown TME 2019	ORIGINALS FROM MARVIN GAYE (EP)	40
64	Stateside SL 10100	MARVIN GAYE (LP)	200
65	Tamla Motown TML 11004	HOW SWEET IT IS TO BE LOVED BY YOU (LP)	60
65	Tamla Motown TML 11015	HELLO BROADWAY (LP)	75
66	T. Motown TML 11022	A TRIBUTE TO THE GREAT NAT KING COLE (LP, mono)	70
66	T. Motown STML 11022	A TRIBUTE TO THE GREAT NAT KING COLE (LP, stereo)	90
66	T. Motown TML 11033	MOODS OF MARVIN GAYE (LP, mono)	50
66	T. Motown STML 11033	MOODS OF MARVIN GAYE (LP, stereo)	60
68	T. Motown TML 11065	MARVIN GAYE'S GREATEST HITS (LP, mono)	20
68	T. Motown STML 11065	MARVIN GAYE'S GREATEST HITS (LP, stereo)	25
69	T. Motown (S)TML 11091	IN THE GROOVE (LP, mono/stereo)	30
69	T. Motown (S)TML 11119	M.P.G. (LP, mono/stereo)	30
69	T. Motown (S)TML 11123	MARVIN GAYE AND HIS GIRLS (LP, with T. Terrell, M. Wells & K. Weston)	25
70	T. Motown (S)TML 11136	THAT'S THE WAY LOVE IS (LP, mono/stereo)	30
71	Tamla Motown STML 11190	WHAT'S GOING ON? (LP, with lyric sheet)	20
72	Tamla Motown STML 11201	THE HITS OF MARVIN GAYE (LP)	12
73	Tamla Motown STML 11225	TROUBLE MAN (LP, soundtrack)	20
78	Tamla Motown TMSP 6008	HERE, MY DEAR (2-LP)	15
76	Tamla Motown STML 12025	I WANT YOU (LP)	12

MARVIN GAYE & TAMMI TERRELL

67	Tamla Motown TMG 611	Ain't No Mountain High Enough/Give A Little Love	30
67	Tamla Motown TMG 611	Ain't No Mountain High Enough/Give A Little Love (DJ Copy)	80
67	Tamla Motown TMG 625	Your Precious Love/Hold Me Oh My Darling	20
67	Tamla Motown TMG 625	Your Precious Love/Hold Me Oh My Darling (DJ Copy)	50
67	Tamla Motown TMG 635	If I Could Build My Whole World Around You/If This World Were Mine	15
67	Tamla Motown TMG 635	If I Could Build My Whole World Around You/If This World Were Mine (DJ Copy)	30
68	Tamla Motown TMG 655	Ain't Nothin' Like The Real Thing/Little Ole Boy, Little Ole Girl	12
68	Tamla Motown TMG 655	Ain't Nothin' Like The Real Thing/Little Ole Boy, Little Ole Girl (DJ Copy)	30
68	Tamla Motown TMG 668	You're All I Need To Get By/Two Can Have A Party	8
69	Tamla Motown TMG 681	You Ain't Livin' Till You're Lovin'/Oh How I'd Miss You	10
69	Tamla Motown TMG 697	Good Lovin' Ain't Easy To Come By/Satisfied Feelin'	8
69	Tamla Motown TMG 715	The Onion Song/I Can't Believe You Love Me	6
69	Tamla Motown TMG 715	The Onion Song/I Can't Believe You Love Me (demo in p/s)	50
68	T. Motown TML 11062	UNITED (LP, mono)	40
68	T. Motown STML 11062	UNITED (LP, stereo)	45
68	T. Motown (S)TML 11084	YOU'RE ALL I NEED (LP, mono/stereo)	40
70	T. Motown (S)TML 11132	EASY (LP, mono/stereo)	20
70	T. Motown (S)TML 11153	GREATEST HITS (LP)	15

MARVIN GAYE & MARY WELLS

64	Stateside SS 316	Once Upon A Time/What's The Matter With You, Baby?	30
64	Stateside SS 316	Once Upon A Time/What's The Matter With You, Baby? (DJ Copy)	80
64	Stateside SL 10097	TOGETHER (LP)	75

MARVIN GAYE & KIM WESTON

(see also Diana Ross, Tammi Terrell, Mary Wells, Kim Weston)

64	Stateside SS 363	What Good Am I Without You?/I Want You Around	35
64	Stateside SS 363	What Good Am I Without You?/I Want You Around (DJ Copy)	80
67	Tamla Motown TMG 590	It Takes Two/It's Got To Be A Miracle (This Thing Called Love)	12
67	Tamla Motown TMG 590	It Takes Two/It's Got To Be A Miracle (This Thing Called Love) (DJ Copy)	70
67	T. Motown TML 11049	TAKE TWO (LP, mono)	40
67	T. Motown STML 11049	TAKE TWO (LP, stereo)	45

GAYLADS

(see also Gaylords, Rockstones, Delano Stewart, Ken Boothe, B.B. Seaton, Brent Dowe, Dobby Dobson, Jackie Mittoo, Heptones, Clarendonians, Soul Vendors)

64	R&B JB 159	There'll Come A Day/BILLY COOKE: Iron Bar	50
64	R&B JB 165	What Is Wrong With Me?/Whap Whap	60
66	Island WI 281	Goodbye Daddy/Your Eyes	30
66	Island WI 291	You Never Leave Him/Message To My Girl	30
66	Island WI 3002	Stop Making Love/They Call Her Dawn	50
66	Doctor Bird DB 1014	Lady With The Red Dress/Dinner For Two	15
66	Doctor Bird DB 1031	You Should Never Do That/WINSTON STEWART: I Don't Know Why I Love You	25
66	Rymska RA 104	You Should Never Do That/TECHNIQUES: So Many Times	35
67	Island WI 3022	Don't Say No/SONNY BURKE: You Rule My Heart	40
67	Island WI 3025	You No Good Girl/Yes Girl	30
67	Studio One SO 2002	Tears From My Eyes/Never Let Your Country Down	100
67	Studio One SO 2009	Won't You Come Home/PETER & HORTENSE: I've Been Lonely	50
67	Studio One SO 2013	I Am Going To Cool It (actually by Little Roy)/ MELODIANS: Let's Join Together	60
67	Studio One SO 2017	Love Me With All Your Heart/I Don't Care	40
67	Studio One SO 2021	IF You Knew/Festival Day	80
67	Rio R 125	Put On Your Style/SOUL BROTHERS: Soul Serenade	25
68	Blue Cat BS 110	Go Away/SOUL VENDORS: Julie On My Mind	30
68	Doctor Bird DB 1124	It's Hard To Confess/I Need Your Loving	40
68	Doctor Bird DB 1145	She Want It/Joy In The Morning	40
68	Fab FAB 62	Looking For A Girl/Aren't You The Guy	100
68	Hi Note HS 001	A B C Rocksteady/LESLIE BUTLER & COUNT OSSIE: Soul Drums	35
69	Trojan TR 688	You Had Your Chance/Wha' She Do Now	12
69	Upsetter US 323	The Same Things/I Wear My Slanders	20
70	Trojan TR 7703	There's A Fire/Last Time	8
70	Trojan TR 7738	That's What Love Will Do/This Time I Won't Hurt You	10
70	Trojan TR 7743	Young, Gifted And Black/BEVERLEY'S ALLSTARS: Moon Glow	10
70	Trojan TR 7763	Tell The Children The Truth/Something Is Wrong Somewhere	8
70	Trojan TR 7771	Soul Sister/BEVERLEY'S ALLSTARS: Soul Version	8
70	Trojan TR 7782	It's All In The Game/BEVERLEY'S ALLSTARS: Version II	8
70	Trojan TR 7799	Fire And Rain/Cold And Lonely Night	6
71	Ackee AC 141	Accept My Apologies (actually by B.B. Seaton & Ken Boothe)/ My Version (actually by Conscious Minds)	6
71	Big BG 319	Can't Hide The Feeling/RUPIE EDWARDS ALLSTARS: Version	6

MINT VALUE £

71	Camel CA 79	Seven In One Medley (Parts 1 & 2)	6
71	Summit SUM 8514	My Jamaican Girl/BEVERLEY'S ALLSTARS: Version	6
71	Bullet BU 462	My Love/Stranger Love	7
74	Dip DL 5009	You Made A Mistake/Shower Of Blessings	6
67	Coxsone CSL 8005	ROCKSTEADY (LP)	150
67	Coxsone CSL 8006	SUNSHINE IS GOLDEN (LP)	75

VINLEY GAYLE

64	Black Swan WI 453	Go-Go/BABA BROOKS: Take Five	30

GAYLETTS

(see also Bob Andy)

68	Island WI 3129	Silent River Runs Deep/You're My Kind Of Man	40
68	Island WI 3141	I Like Your World/Lonely Feeling	25
68	Big Shot BI 502	If You Can't Be Good/Something About My Man	12
69	Big Shot BI 516	Son-Of-A-Preacher-Man/That's How Strong My Love Is	12
70	London HLJ 10302	Son-Of-A-Preacher-Man/I Like Your World	7

GAYLORDS (Jamaica)

(see also Gaylads)

66	Island WI 269	Chipmunk Ska/What Is Wrong? (both actually by Gaylads)	25

GAYLORDS (U.K.)

(see also Dean Ford & Gaylords, Marmalade)

66	Columbia DB 7805	He's A Good Face But He's Down And Out/You Know It Too	15

GAYLORDS (U.S.)

60	Mercury MMC 14032	THAT'S AMORE (LP)	12

WILTON 'BOGEY' GAYNAIR QUARTET

61	Tempo EXA 103	BLUE BOGEY VOLUME ONE (EP)	60
59	Tempo TAP 25	BLUE BOGEY (LP)	500

GAYNOR (Junior English) & ERROL (Dunkley)

(see also Errol Dunkley)

65	Blue Beat BB 286	My Queen/ROLAND ALPHONSO: Roland Plays Prince (B-side actually "Hanging The Beam" by Skatalites)	60

GLORIA GAYNOR

78	Polydor 2066922	For The First Time In My Life/This Love Affair	10

MEL GAYNOR

(see also Oscar Rabin)

55	Decca F 10497	Just A Man/How Important Can It Be?	5
55	Decca F 10542	With You Beside Me/Oh, My Love	5
55	Decca F 10618	Bella Notte/Sweet Kentucky Rose	5

MITZI GAYNOR

59	Top Rank JAR 258	Happy Anniversary/Play For Keeps	5
60	Top Rank JAR 289	I Don't Regret A Thing/The Touch Of Time	5
58	HMV 7EG 8460	MITZI (EP)	10

ROSEMARY GAYNOR

55	Columbia SCM 5196	Ain't That A Shame/A Happy Song	15

PAUL GAYTEN

57	London HL 8503	Yo, Yo, Walk/TUNE WEAVERS: Happy Happy Birthday Baby	200
57	London HL 8503	Yo, Yo, Walk/TUNE WEAVERS: Happy Happy Birthday Baby (78 rpm)	40
59	London HLM 8998	The Hunch/Hot Cross Buns	100
59	London HLM 8998	The Hunch/Hot Cross Buns (78 rpm)	40

GAYTONES (Jamaica)

(see also Righteous Flames, Max Romeo, Ethiopians, Jackie Brown, Jean & Gaytones, Huxbrown & Scotty, Charlie Ace, Delano Stewart, Teddy & Conquerors)

70	High Note HS 037	Target (actually "Musical Fight" by Crashers)/PATSY: Find Someone (song actually "True Love")	30
70	High Note HS 048	Ten To One/Another Version	12
71	High Note HS 055	Heart Of The Knights/One Toke Over The Line (B-side actually by Stranger & Gladdy)	15
71	Green Door GD 4016	Jamaican Hilite (Parts 1 & 2)	8
73	Smash SMA 2330	Blackman Kingdom Come/Swing And Dine (B-side actually by Melodians)	8

GAYTONES (U.S.)

73	Action ACT 4610	Soul Makossa/Soul Makossa (Version)	15

GBH

82	Clay CLAY 8	No Survivors/Self Destruct/Big Women (p/s)	8
82	Clay CLAY 11	Sick Boy/Slit Your Own Throat/Am I Dead Yet? (p/s)	8
82	Clay CLAY 16	Give Me Fire/Mantrap (p/s)	8
82	Clay CLAY 16P	Give Me Fire/Mantrap (picture disc)	8
83	Clay CLAY 22	Catch 23/Hellhole (p/s)	8
84	Clay CLAY 36	Do What You Do/Four Men (p/s)	8
82	Clay CLAYLP 4	CITY BABY ATTACKED BY RATS (LP)	20
81	Clay PLATE 3	LEATHER, BRISTLES, STUDS AND ACNE (LP)	15

G-CLEFS

56	Columbia DB 3851	Ka-Ding Dong/Darla, My Darlin'	750
56	Columbia DB 3851	Ka-Ding Dong/Darla, My Darlin' (78 rpm)	35
61	London HLU 9433	I Understand/Little Girl I Love You	5
62	London HLU 9530	A Girl Has To Know/(There Never Was A Dog Like) Dad	10
62	London HLU 9563	Make Up Your Mind/Call Me Away	15

GEDDES AXE

80	ACS ACS 1	Return Of The Gods/Wildfire/Aftermath (p/s, with insert)	20
81	Steel City AXE 1	Sharpen Your Wits/Rock 'N' Roll (p/s)	50
82	Bullet BOLT 4	Escape From New York/Day The Wells Ran Dry/Six Six Six (12", p/s)	8

MINT VALUE £

MICKEY GEE
77 Sonet SON 2124 — Dr Livingstone/Jodi ... 6

RON GEESIN
(see also Bridget St. John, Pink Floyd, Original Downtown Syncopators, Amory Kane)
65 RRG 319/320 — RON GEESIN (EP, handmade p/s, 100 only) ... 100
67 Transatlantic (S)TRA 161 — A RAISE OF EYEBROWS (LP) ... 50
72 KPM KPM 1102 — ELECTROSOUND (LP, library issue, 1,000 only) ... 50
73 Ron Geesin RON 28 — AS HE STANDS (LP) ... 20
75 KPM KPM 1154 — ELECTROSOUND VOL. 2 (LP, library issue, 1,000 only) ... 45
75 Ron Geesin RON 31 — PATRUNS (LP) ... 15
77 Ron Geesin RON 323 — RIGHT THROUGH (LP) ... 18
77 KPM KPM 1201 — ATMOSPHERES (LP, library issue, 1,000 only) ... 30

RON GEESIN & ROGER WATERS
(see also Roger Waters, Pink Floyd)
70 Harvest SHSP 4008 — MUSIC FROM THE BODY (LP, soundtrack; green labels with Waters/Geesin photos) ... 40

MAX GELDRAY
59 Parlophone GEP 8764 — GOON WITH THE WIND (EP) ... 8

HERB GELLER QUARTET
56 London RE-U 1067 — SENSATIONAL SAX OF HERB GELLER (EP) ... 15

HERB GELLER
75 Atlantic SD 1681 — RHYME & REASON (LP) ... 25

GEMAGE
80 private pressing BGA 1 — Story So Far/Bring Me Death (no p/s) ... 60

GEMINI (Portugal)
78 Philips 6031 070 — Dal-Li-Dou (Falling In Love)/Dal-Li-Dou ... 12

GEMINI (U.K.)
81 Airship AP 345 — COUNTER BALANCE (LP) ... 60

GEMINI (U.K.)
69 President PT 257 — Never Say Die/Something Special ... 6

GEMINI (U.K.)
(see also Tornados)
65 Columbia DB 7638 — Space Walk/Goodbye Joe (demos may credit the 'Original Tornados') ... 50
69 President PT 257 — Something Special/Never Say Die ... 8

GENE
94 Costermonger COST 1 — For The Dead/Child's Body (p/s, 1,994 numbered copies only) ... 10
94 Costermonger COST 2 — Be My Light, Be My Guide/This Is Not My Crime (numbered p/s) ... 5

GENE & DEBBE
67 London HLE 10165 — Go With Me/Torch I Carry ... 8
68 London HLE 10179 — Playboy/I'll Come Running ... 12
68 London HLE 10203 — Lovin' Season/Love Will Give Us Wings ... 8

GENE & EUNICE
56 Vogue V 9062 — I Gotta Go Home/Have You Changed Your Mind? ... 200
56 Vogue V 9062 — I Gotta Go Home/Have You Changed Your Mind? (78) ... 40
57 Vogue V 9066 — Move It Over, Baby/This Is My Story ... 150
57 Vogue V 9066 — Move It Over, Baby/This Is My Story (78) ... 40
57 Vogue V 9071 — Let's Get Together/I'm So In Love With You ... 150
57 Vogue V 9071 — Let's Get Together/I'm So In Love With You (78) ... 60
57 Vogue V 9083 — Doodle Doodle Doo/Don't Treat Me This Way ... 150
57 Vogue V 9083 — Doodle Doodle Doo/Don't Treat Me This Way (78) ... 40
58 Vogue V 9106 — I Mean Love/The Angels Gave You To Me ... 150
58 Vogue V 9106 — I Mean Love/The Angels Gave You To Me (78) ... 65
58 Vogue V 9126 — Strange World/The Vow ... 50
(The above 45s were originally issued with triangular centres; later issues with round centres are worth about half the values listed.)
58 Vogue V 9126 — Strange World/The Vow (78) ... 70
59 Vogue V 9136 — Bom Bom Lulu/Hi Diddle Diddle ... 100
59 Vogue V 9136 — Bom Bom Lulu/Hi Diddle Diddle (78) ... 70
59 London HL 8956 — Poco-Loco/Go-On Kokomo ... 50
59 London HL 8956 — Poco-Loco/Go-On Kokomo (78) ... 120

GENE & GENTS
68 Pye 7N 17532 — C'mon Everybody/Hound Dog ... 10

GENE & JERRY
(see also Gene Chandler, Jerry Butler)
71 Mercury 6052 050 — You Just Can't Win/Sho' Is Groovin' ... 10
71 Mercury 6052 087 — Everybody Is Waiting/Ten And Two ... 8
71 Mercury 6338 051 — ONE AND ONE (LP) ... 25

GENE LOVES JEZEBEL
82 Situation 2 SIT 18T — Shavin' My Neck/Sun & Insanity/Machismo/Glad To Be Alive (12", p/s) ... 8
82 Situation 2 SIT 20 — Screaming (For Emaline) (p/s) ... 8
82 Situation 2 SIT 24 — Bruises/Punch Drunk (p/s) ... 6

GENERAL JOHNSON
(see under 'J')

GENERAL LEVY
92 Fashion FADLP 024 — THE WICKEDER GENERAL (LP) ... 20

GENERAL STRIKE
79 Canal CANAL 01 — Part 1: My Body/Part 2: (Parts Of) My Body (p/s) ... 5

MINT VALUE £

GENERATION GAP

69	Pye 7N 17845	She's Coming Home/Reach The Top	8
70	Pye 7N 17979	Any Old Time You're Lonely And Sad/Rainbows 'N' Sorrows	8

GENERATION X

(see also Billy Idol, Sigue Sigue Sputnik, Empire, Westworld)

77	Generation X GX 101	Your Generation/Listen! (white label test pressing, official bootleg sold at gigs, no p/s)	50
77	Chrysalis CHS 2165	Your Generation/Day By Day (p/s, original copies with 'A' on label with band credits on front)	6
77	Chrysalis CHS 2165	Your Generation/Day By Day (p/s)	5
77	Chrysalis CHS 2165	Your Generation/Day By Day (sleeve only, unissued, featuring 'pre-peroxide' Billy Idol; 1 copy known to exist)	500
77	Chrysalis CHS 2189	Wild Youth/Wild Dub (Version) (p/s)	5
77	Chrysalis CHS 2189	Wild Youth/Wild Dub (Version) (p/s, mispressing, plays "No No No", B-side matrix: CHS 2189 B/1)	40
78	Chrysalis CHS 2207	Ready Steady Go/No No No (p/s)	5
79	Chrysalis CHS(A) 2261	King Rocker/Gimme Some Truth (pink vinyl, Tony James p/s)	5
79	Chrysalis CHS(B) 2261	King Rocker/Gimme Some Truth (red vinyl, Billy Idol p/s)	5
79	Chrysalis CHS(C) 2261	King Rocker/Gimme Some Truth (yellow vinyl, Mark Laff p/s)	7
79	Chrysalis CHS(D) 2261	King Rocker/Gimme Some Truth (orange vinyl, Bob Andrews p/s)	6
79	Chrysalis CHS 2261	King Rocker/Gimme Some Truth (black vinyl, Bob Andrews p/s)	5
79	Chrysalis CHS 2330	Friday's Angels/Trying For Kicks/This Heat (p/s, black vinyl)	15
81	Chrysalis CHS 2488	Dancing With Myself/Untouchables/King Rocker/Rock On (as Gen X, p/s, on clear vinyl)	8
78	Chrysalis CHR 1169	GENERATION X (LP, with 'T-shirt offer' wraparound)	25

GENERATOR (featuring Gary Numan)

(see also Gary Numan)

94	JVO JVOT 001	Are 'Friends' Electric? (Eccentric Mix)/Bring Back The Love/ Going Home (12", p/s)	8

GENESIS

(see also Flaming Youth, Phil Collins, Mike Rutherford, Peter Gabriel, Steve Hackett, Anthony Phillips, Brand X, Quiet World)

SINGLES

68	Decca F 12735	The Silent Sun/That's Me	400
68	Decca F 12735	The Silent Sun/That's Me (promo copy)	325
68	Decca F 12775	A Winter's Tale/One Eyed Hound	375
68	Decca F 12775	A Winter's Tale/One Eyed Hound (promo copy)	350
68	London F12775	A Winter's Tale/One Eyed Hound (export promo single)	500
69	Decca F 12949	Where The Sour Turns To Sweet/In Hiding	400
69	Decca F 12949	Where The Sour Turns To Sweet/In Hiding (promo copy)	375
70	Charisma GS 1/2	Looking For Someone/Visions Of Angels (promo only)	600
71	Charisma CB 152	The Knife (Parts 1 & 2) (in p/s)	450
71	Charisma CB 152	The Knife (Parts 1 & 2)	100
72	Charisma CB 181	Happy The Man/Seven Stones (some belated copies in p/s; beware counterfeits)	450
72	Charisma CB 181	Happy The Man/Seven Stones	100
72	Charisma CB 181	Happy The Man/Seven Stones (promo copy)	150
73	Charisma (no cat. no.)	Twilight Alehouse (1-sided flexidisc free with Zig Zag & later via fan club, with magazine)	35
73	Charisma (no cat. no.)	Twilight Alehouse (1-sided flexidisc free with Zig Zag & later via fan club, without magazine)	20
73	Charisma (no cat. no.)	Twilight Alehouse (black vinyl, white label test pressings)	70
74	Charisma CB 224	I Know What I Like (In Your Wardrobe)/Twilight Alehouse	8
74	Charisma CB 224	I Know What I Like (In Your Wardrobe)/Twilight Alehouse (promos with press release)	95
74	Charisma CB 238	Counting Out Time/Riding The Scree	8
74	Charisma CB 238	Counting Out Time/Counting Out Time (promo)	60
75	Charisma CB 251	The Carpet Crawlers/The Waiting Room (Evil Jam)	25
75	Charisma CB 251	The Carpet Crawlers/The Waiting Room (Evil Jam) (promo copies)	65
76	Charisma CB 277	A Trick Of The Tail/Ripples (purple label)	8
77	Charisma CB 300	Your Own Special Way/It's Yourself	5
78	Charisma CB 309	Follow You, Follow Me/Ballad Of Big (p/s)	5
78	Charisma CB 315	Many Too Many/The Day The Light Went Out/Vancouver (p/s)	5
80	Charisma CB 369	Misunderstanding/Evidence Of Autumn (p/s)	5
81	Charisma CB 39	Keep It Dark/Naminanu (p/s)	5
81	Charisma CB 391-12	Keep It Dark/Naminanu/Abacab (Long Version) (12", p/s)	5
82	Charisma CB 393	Man On The Corner/Submarine (blue label, with p/s)	80
82	Charisma CB 393	Man On The Corner/Submarine (blue label, without p/s)	5
82	Lyntone LYN 11806	The Lady Lies (live) (green flexidisc free with Flexipop mag, issue 21)	10
83	Lyntone LYN 13143	Firth Of Fifth (live edit) (flexidisc, with numbered gatefold p/s)	15
83	Lyntone LYN 13143	Firth Of Fifth (live edit) (flexidisc, without numbered gatefold p/s)	5
83	Charisma/Virgin TATA Y-1	That's All/Taking It All Too Hard (shaped picture disc)	12
84	Charisma/Virgin ALS 1	Illegal Alien/Turn It On Again (live) (shaped picture disc)	12
84	Charisma/Virgin CB 300	Your Own Special Way/It's Yourself (blue label reissue, no p/s)	6
84	Charisma/Virgin CB 356	Turn It On Again/Behind The Lines Part 2 (blue label reissue, no p/s)	6
84	Charisma/Virgin CB 369	Misunderstanding/Evidence Of Autumn (blue label reissue, no p/s)	6
86	Charisma/Virgin	In Too Deep (Unedited)/Do The Neurotic (Unedited) (12" picture disc in stickered sleeve)	8
86	Virgin SNEG 3-12	Land Of Confusion/Land Of Confusion (Extended)/Feeding The Fire/ Do The Neurotic (CD, gatefold p/s)	10
87	Virgin CDEP 1	Tonight, Tonight, Tonight (Edit)/In The Glow Of The Night/ Invisible Touch (12" Remix)/Tonight, Tonight (CD, gatefold p/s)	40
87	Virgin GENS 512	Throwing It All Away (live)/I'd Rather Be You/Invisible Touch (live) (12", p/s)	5
88	Virgin CDT 5	Mama (Long Version)/It's Gonna Get Better (Long Version) (3" CD, card p/s)	8
88	Charisma/Virgin CDT 40	SPOT THE PIGEON EP (Match Of The Day/Pigeons/Inside And Out) (3" CD, card sleeve)	15
88	Charisma/Virgin CDF 40	SPOT THE PIGEON EP (Match Of The Day/Pigeons/Inside And Out) (5" export CD, card sleeve)	15
89	Virgin VVD 359	Domino: (Part 1) In The Glow Of The Night/(Part 2) The Last Domino	

MINT VALUE £

		(3" CD free with "Invisible Touch Tour" video)	15
92	Virgin GENDG 8	Hold On My Heart/Way Of The World/Your Own Special Way (live) (CD, digipak with 4 postcards)	8
92	Virgin GENDX 9	Jesus He Knows Me (Single Mix)/Hearts On Fire/Land Of Confusion (Rehearsal Version) (CD, "Invisible Series" box set with space for other CDs)	8
92	Virgin GENS 10	Invisible Touch (live)/Abacab (live) (no'd gatefold p/s)	8
92	Virgin GENDX 10	Invisible Touch (live)/Abacab (live)/The Brazilian (live) (CD, numbered box with booklet)	8
98	Virgin SOLO2	Live Rehearsal: Mama (live)/Calling All Stations (live)/Invisible Touch (live)/ Follow You, Follow Me (live)/Turn It On Again (live) (CD 5-track promo)	40

ALBUMS

69	Decca LK 4990	FROM GENESIS TO REVELATION (mono, with 'mono' peephole, with red/pink lyric sheet, red/silver unboxed logo)	1000
69	Decca SKL 4990	FROM GENESIS TO REVELATION (stereo, with stereo 'peephole', with lyric sheet, unboxed logo)	400
70	Decca SKL 4990	FROM GENESIS TO REVELATION (stereo, with lyric sheet, blue/silver boxed logo)	70
70	Decca KSKC 4990	FROM GENESIS TO REVELATION (cassette, boxed logo)	35
70	Charisma CAS 1020	TRESPASS (original pink scroll label & gatefold sleeve with lyric sheet)	65
71	Charisma CAS 1052	NURSERY CRYME (original pink scroll label, gatefold sleeve)	50
72	Charisma CAS 1058	FOXTROT (LP, gatefold sleeve, large 'Mad Hatter' logo and BRC credit on label)	30
73	Charisma CAS 1074	SELLING ENGLAND BY THE POUND (LP, insert, large 'Mad Hatter' logo)	25
73	Charisma CLASS 1	LIVE (LP, non laminated sleeve, large 'Mad Hatter' logo)	25
74	Decca SKL 4990	IN THE BEGINNING (reissue of 1st LP, 'snake' sleeve with lyric insert)	20
75	Charisma CGS 102	GENESIS COLLECTION VOLUME ONE (2-LP, boxed set of Trespass & "Nursery Cryme" in original sleeves, with poster)	95
75	Charisma CGS 103	GENESIS COLLECTION VOLUME TWO (2-LP, boxed set of Foxtrot & "Selling England By The Pound", with poster)	95
91	Virgin Edits 1	WE CAN'T DANCE (CD, 6 track promo - tour edition marketed by Volkswagon)	50
91	Virgin GEN CD	WE CAN'T DANCE (CD & tape, housed in custom promo box With three hand numbered watercolours)	90
93	Virgin GENBOX 1	LIVE: THE WAY WE WALK (2xCD in wooden box with certificate & badge (1000 only)	120
97	Virgin GENLP 6	CALLING ALL STATIONS (2xLP fourth sided no tracks but etched with band picture)	15
98	Virgin CDBOX 6	GENESIS ARCHIVE 1967 - 1975 (4 CD Box Set)	30
98	Virgin CDBOX 98	GENESIS ARCHIVE 1967 - 1975 (CD 12-track promo digipack)	30
98	Virgin VCDJBOX98	GENESIS ARCHIVE 1967 - 1975 The Interviews (2xCD promo, p/s)	65
99	Virgin VGP 000270	TURN IT ON AGAIN - THE HITS (CD, in store promo p/s - each song played for 1 min)	50
00	Virgin CDBOX7	GENESIS ARCHIVE 2: 1976 - 1992 (3xCD Box Set)	25
07	EMI CDBOX 12	GENESIS 1976 - 1882 (2007 UK 12 disc set comprising of 6 Hybrid SA CDs)	70
07	EMI CDBOX 13	GENESIS 1983 - 1998 (2007 UK 10 disc set comprising of 5 Hybrid SA CDs)	60

GENEVA

80	Valiant ROUND1	2.30/Geneva Street (p/s)	10

GENEVEVE

66	CBS 202061	Once/Just A Whisper (in p/s)	20
66	CBS 202061	Once/Just A Whisper	20
66	CBS 202096	Nothing In The World/Summer Days	9
67	CBS 202524	That Can't Be Bad/I Love Him, I Need Him	9

GENGHIS KHAN (Germany)

79	CBS 12-7317	Genghis Khan/Desert Land (12", clear vinyl with p/s insert)	8

GENGHIS KHAN (U.K.)

83	Genghis Khan GK 1	DOUBLE DEALIN' (If Heaven Is Hell/Highway Passion//Midnight Rendezvous Mean Streak) (EP, double pack)	80
83	Wabbit WAB 61/63	Love You/Lady Lady/Mongol Nation/Gone For A Drive (double pack)	40

GENOCIDE

79	Safari SAP 2	IMAGES OF DELUSION (EP)	8

GENOCIDE EXIT

80	Slam SEM 016	FUTURE VIBES (EP)	10

GENTILES (Jamaica)

(see also Melodians)

70	High Note HS 046	Your Destiny/Lock Love Away (actually by Melodians)	12

GENTILES (U.K.)

68	Pye 7N 17530	Goodbye Baby/Marlena	8

JOHNNY GENTLE

(see also Darren Young)

59	Philips PB 908	Wendy/Boys And Girls (Were Meant For Each Other)	10
59	Philips PB 945	Milk From The Coconut/I Like The Way	8
60	Philips PB 988	Darlin' Won't You Wait/This Friendly World	8
60	Philips PB 1069	After My Laughter Came Tears/Sonja	7
61	Philips PB 1142	Pick A Star/Darlin'	7
59	Philips BBE 12345	THE GENTLE TOUCH (EP)	50

TIM GENTLE & HIS GENTLEMEN

65	Oriole CB 1988	Without You/Someone's In The Kitchen With Dinah	15

GENTLE GIANT

(see also Simon Dupree & Big Sound, Moles)

73	WWA WWP 1001	In A Glass House/An Inmate's Lullaby	12
74	WWA WWS 017	The Power And The Glory/Playing The Game	12
77	Chrysalis CHS 2160	I'm Turning Around/Just The Same (live)	6

			MINT VALUE £
70	Vertigo 6360 020	GENTLE GIANT (LP, gatefold sleeve, large swirl label)	120
71	Vertigo 6360 041	ACQUIRING THE TASTE (LP, gatefold sleeve, small swirl label)	120
72	Vertigo 6360 070	THREE FRIENDS (LP, gatefold sleeve, small swirl label)	120
72	Vertigo 6360 080	OCTOPUS (LP, gatefold sleeve, small swirl label)	50
73	WWA WWA 002	IN A GLASS HOUSE (LP, silk-screen sleeve, with photo insert & lyric inner)	50
74	WWA WWA 010	THE POWER AND THE GLORY (LP, with insert, sleeve has 2 rounded corners)	40
75	Vertigo 6641 334	GIANT STEPS - THE FIRST FIVE YEARS (2-LP, gatefold sleeve, spaceship label)	15
75	Chrysalis CHR 1093	FREE HAND (LP, lyric insert, green label)	15
76	Chrysalis CHR 1115	INTERVIEW (LP, green label, with lyric inner sleeve)	12
77	Chrysalis CTY 1133	LIVE (PLAYING THE FOOL) (2-LP, with 12-page booklet)	20
77	Chrysalis CHR 1152	THE MISSING PIECE (LP, with inner sleeve)	15
78	Chrysalis CHR 1186	GIANT FOR A DAY (LP, with mask insert & lyric inner sleeve)	15
80	Chrysalis CHR 1285	CIVILIAN (LP, with lyric inner sleeve)	15

GENTLE INFLUENCE

69	Pye 7N 17666	Never Trust In Tomorrow/Easy To Love	15
69	Pye 7N 17743	Always Be A Part Of My Living/Captain Reale	22

GENTLE PEOPLE

67	Columbia DB 8276	It's Too Late/Sea Of Heartbreak	12

GENTLE PEOPLE

95	Rephlex CAT 040R	JOURNEY (12", Aphex Twin Remix)	8

GENTLE POWER OF SONG

67	Polydor 56211	Constant Penelope/A Court Garden Party, Circa 1580	8
67	Polydor 2310 285	CIRCUS (LP)	25

GENTLE RAIN

73	Polydor 2310 285	MOODY (LP)	175

GENTLE RESPITE

90	Sarah SARAH 026	DARKEST BLUE EP: Summer In Me/Darkest Blue/If I Touch (wraparound p/s, with insert)	15

BILL GENTLES

(see also Bill Jentles, Bill Jenties)

69	Gas GAS 104	Long Life/SCHOOLBOYS: O Tell Me	10
70	Pama PM 801	What A Woman/Sleepy Cat	8
70	Punch PH 54	Fight The Good Fight/Fight Beat	8
71	Escort ERT 853	Bachelor Boy/SCORPIONS: Colour Rites	8
72	Bullet BU 506	Pure In Heart/Clean Hands	6

GENTLE TOUCH

65	London HLR 10175	Among The First To Know/Merry Go Round	7
83	Tristar TRI3	Dreams Of You/Dreams Of You (Instrumental)	6

ART GENTRY

72	Mojo 2092 048	Breakthrough/Wonderful Dream	15

BO GENTRY & RITCHIE CORDELL

69	CBS 4299	Stone Go-Getter/Hung Up	5

BOBBIE GENTRY

67	Capitol CL 15511	Ode To Billie Joe/Mississippi Delta	5
67	Capitol (S)T 2830	ODE TO BILLIE JOE (LP)	18
68	Capitol ST2964	LOCAL GENTRY (LP)	18
68	Capitol (S)T 2842	THE DELTA SWEETE (LP)	18
69	Capitol E-(S)T 155	TOUCH 'EM WITH LOVE (LP)	15
70	Capitol ST21609	I'LL NEVER FALL IN LOVE AGAIN (LP)	18
71	Capitol E-ST494	PATCHWORK (LP)	15

GENTRY ICE

88	Jack Trax JTX 15	Do You Wanna Jack/Lost In The Sound (with Adonis) (12")	20

GENTRYS

65	MGM MGM 1284	Keep On Dancing/Make Up Your Mind	20
66	MGM MGM 1296	Brown Paper Sack/Spread It On Thick	25
66	MGM MGM 1312	Everyday I Have To Cry/Don't Let It Be	15
68	Bell BLL 1012	I Can't Go Back To Denver/You Better Come Home	8

GENTS

81	Posh POSH 001	The Faker/The Pink Panther	20
82	Kosmic KOS 6886	Schooldays/True Stories (p/s)	8
83	Posh POSH 007	Revenge/Girl (p/s)	5
85	Posh no cat. no.	Lambs To The Slaughter/Friday On My Mind	5
85	Lambs To The Slaughter GN7	Shout/The Faker (p/s)	5
80s	Posh MEGA 1	Revenge/Over Me/The Gent (p/s)	5
77	GG no cat. no.	HOW IT ALL BEGAN (LP)	12

GEOFFREY

78	Music Bank BECK 694	ABH (Who Wants To Listen To Punk Rock?)/Colt 45 Rock (p/s)	15

GEORDIE

(see also Influence, AC/DC)

72	Regal Zonophone RZ 3067	Don't Do That/Francis Was A Rocker	5
82	EMI EMI 2031	Nutbush City Limits/No Sweat (p/s)	20
73	EMI EMC 3001	HOPE YOU LIKE IT (LP)	25
74	EMI EMA 764	DON'T BE FOOLED BY THE NAME (LP)	25
76	EMI EMC 3134	SAVE THE WORLD (LP)	15
83	Neat NEAT 1008	NO SWEAT (LP)	18

BARBARA GEORGE

62	London HL 9513	I Know (You Don't Love Me No More)/Love (Is Just A Chance You Take)	25
64	Sue WI 316	Send For Me/Bless You	50

MINT VALUE £

EARL GEORGE

73	Count Shelly CS 025	Gonna Give Her All The Love/PRINCE JAZZBO: Wise Shepherd	6
76	Terminal TM 103	Love Depression/Love Is Something	8
76	Terminal TM 106	So Many Ways/Part 2	8

GEORGE GOLDEN

64	R&B JB145	Fire In My Feet/One More Chance	15
64	R&B JB157	Don't You Know/ Nancy Tell Me	15

LLOYD GEORGE

62	London HLP 9562	Lucy Lee/Sing Real Loud	75

GEORGETTES

58	London HL 8548	Love Like A Fool/Oh Tonight	50
58	London HL 8548	Love Like A Fool/Oh Tonight (78)	30
60	Pye International 7N 25058	Down By The River/A Pair Of Eyes	10

GEORGIA SLIM/WALTER ROLAND

59	Jazz Collector JEL 2	THE MALE BLUES VOL. 1 (EP)	20

GEORGIA TOM

(see also Paramount Allstars)

60s	Riverside RLP 8803	GEORGIA TOM AND FRIENDS (LP)	20

GEORGIE'S VARSITY 5

61	Vogue Pop V 9189	When My Sugar Walks Down The Street/Five Foot Two, Eyes Of Blue	10

GERALDINE

71	Beltona Sword SBE 128)	GERALDINE (LP)	120

GERALDO 1969

69	Morgan MRS 22	QE2/Hello Again	8

WESLEY GERMS

72	Upsetter US 390	Whiplash/UPSETTERS: Whiplash Version	12

GERONIMO BLACK

(see also Frank Zappa/Mothers Of Invention)

72	Uni UNLS 126	GERONIMO BLACK (LP)	35

DENNY GERRARD

(see also Warm Sounds, High Tide, Open Road, Fifth Avenue)

70	Deram Nova DN 10	SINISTER MORNING (LP, mono, with High Tide)	150
70	Deram Nova SDN 10	SINISTER MORNING (LP, stereo, with High Tide)	90

GERRY & THE HOLOGRAMS

79	Absurd ABSURD 4	Gerry And The Holograms/Increased Resistance (p/s)	5
79	Absurd ABSURD 5	The Emperor's New Music (unplayable record, glued into p/s)	8

GERRY & THE PACEMAKERS

(see also Gerry Marsden)

63	Columbia DB 4987	How Do You Do It?/Away From You	5
63	Columbia DB 7041	I Like It/It's Happened To Me	5
63	Columbia DB 7126	You'll Never Walk Alone/It's All Right	5
64	Columbia DB 7189	I'm The One/You've Got What I Like	5
64	Columbia DB 7268	Don't Let The Sun Catch You Crying/Show Me That You Care	6
64	Columbia DB 7353	It's Gonna Be Alright/It's Just Because	7
64	Columbia DB 7437	Ferry Cross The Mersey/You You You	5
65	Columbia DB 7504	I'll Be There/Baby, You're So Good To Me	5
65	Columbia DB 7738	Walk Hand In Hand/Dreams	5
66	Columbia DB 7835	La La La/Without You	8
66	Columbia DB 8044	Girl On A Swing/A Fool To Myself	8
74	DJM DJS 298	Remember (The Days Of Rock And Roll)/There's Still Time	8
63	Columbia SEG 8257	HOW DO YOU DO IT? (EP)	12
64	Columbia SEG 8295	YOU'LL NEVER WALK ALONE (EP, initially in misprinted sleeve listing "It's All Right" instead of "Jambalaya" on front)	25
64	Columbia SEG 8295	YOU'LL NEVER WALK ALONE (EP, initially in misprinted sleeve listing "It's All Right" instead of "Jambalaya" on front)	15
64	Columbia SEG 8311	I'M THE ONE (EP)	15
64	Columbia SEG 8346	DON'T LET THE SUN CATCH YOU CRYING (EP)	15
64	Columbia SEG 8367	IT'S GONNA BE ALRIGHT (EP)	20
65	Columbia SEG 8388	GERRY IN CALIFORNIA (EP)	30
65	Columbia SEG 8397	HITS FROM 'FERRY CROSS THE MERSEY' (EP)	30
65	Columbia SEG 8426	RIP IT UP (EP)	35
63	Columbia 33SX 1546	HOW DO YOU LIKE IT? (LP, mono)	20
63	Columbia 33SCX 1546	HOW DO YOU LIKE IT? (LP, stereo)	30
65	Columbia 33SX 1693	FERRY CROSS THE MERSEY (LP, soundtrack, with Cilla Black & Fourmost, mono)	25
65	Columbia 33SCX 1693	FERRY CROSS THE MERSEY (LP, soundtrack, with Cilla Black & Fourmost, stereo)	35
65	EMI Regal REG 2018	YOU'LL NEVER WALK ALONE (LP, export issue)	25

GERVASE

68	Decca F12822	Pepper Grinder/Visions	20

GESCOM

(see also Autechre, Ad Vance Vs Gescom)

94	Skam SKA 2	Dan One/Five/Cicada/Sciew Spo (12", card folder p/s)	35
95	Skam SKA 3	Snackwitch/Mag (12", bubblewrap sleeve with insert)	40
95	Skam SKA 3	Snackwitch/Mag (12", second issue, black sleeve)	20
95	Clear CLR 408	THE SOUNDS OF MACHINES OUR PARENTS USED (12", p/s)	35
96	Warp WAP 88	Keynell/Keynell (12", p/s, remixes by Autechre)	10
96	Skam SKA 7	KEY NELL 1/2/3/4 (12", bubblewrap sleeve)	15
98	Skam SKA010 THAT	THAT (EP) (12", p/s 2 inserts)	15
98	Sakm SKA010 THIS	THIS (EP) (12", p/s)	15

MINT VALUE £

GESTURES

65	Stateside SS 379	Run Run Run/It Seems To Me	25

STAN GETZ (QUARTET/QUINTET)

(see also Dizzy Gillespie, Gil Fuller & Dizzy Gillespie, Astrud Gilberto, Joao Gilberto, Johnny Smith)

62	HMV POP 1061	Disafinado/Jazz Theme From Dr. Kildare	5
64	Verve VS 520	The Girl From Ipanema (with JOAO GILBERTO)/Blowin' In The Wind	5
54	Vogue EPV 1016	STAN GETZ QUARTET (EP)	10
53	Esquire 20-007	STAN GETZ PLAYS (LP, 10")	25
54	Vogue LDE 089	AT STORYVILLE (LP, 10")	25
55	Vogue LDE 147	STAN GETZ QUARTET (LP, 10")	25
55	Columbia Clef 33CX 10000	AT THE SHRINE NO. 1 (LP, as Stan Getz Quintet)	18
55	Columbia Clef 33CX 10001	AT THE SHRINE NO. 2 (LP, as Stan Getz Quintet)	18
62	HMV CLP 1577	FOCUS (LP, also stereo CSD 1448)	12
62	HMV CLP 1577	FOCUS (LP, also stereo CSD 1448)	15
63	Verve VLP 9013	JAZZ SAMBA (LP, with Charlie Byrd, mono)	12
63	Verve (S)VLP 9013	JAZZ SAMBA (LP, with Charlie Byrd, stereo)	15
63	Verve VLP 9024	BIG BAND BOSSA NOVA (LP)	12
63	Verve VLP 9038	JAZZ SAMBA ENCORE! (LP, with Luiz Bonfa, mono)	12
63	Verve (S)VLP 9038	JAZZ SAMBA ENCORE! (LP, with Luiz Bonfa, stereo)	15
64	Verve VLP 9065	GETZ-GILBERTO (LP)	12
65	MGM MGM-C 8001	MICKEY ONE (LP, soundtrack, mono, with booklet)	20
65	MGM MGM-C(S) 8001	MICKEY ONE (LP, soundtrack, stereo, with booklet)	25

G-FORCE

(see also Gary Moore)

80	Jet JET 183	Hot Gossip/Because Of Your Love (p/s)	20
80	Jet JET 194	You/Trust You Lovin' (no p/s)	12
80	Jet JET 7005	White Knuckles/Rockin' And Rollin'/I Look At You (p/s)	15
80	Jet JETLP 229	G-FORCE (LP, with inner sleeve and patch)	20
80	Jet JETPD 229	G-FORCE (LP, picture disc)	18

G.G. ALLSTARS

(see also Paulette & Gee, Billy Dyce, Maytones, Charlie Ace, Monty Morris, Starlights, Lloyd & Carey, Gladdy & Stranger, Heptones, Shorty Perry, Barbara Jones)

70	Explosion EX 2012	Champion/MAYTONES: Funny Man	10
70	Explosion EX 2014	Barabus/This Kind Of Life	10
70	Explosion EX 2023	Man From Carolina/Gold On Your Dress (B-side actually by Slickers)	10
70	Explosion EX 2024	African Melody/Serious Love (B-side actually by Maytones)	8
70	Explosion EX 2025	Ganja Plane/Deep River	8
70	Gas GAS 153	So Alive/Mercy Mr D.J.	8
70	Escort ERT 835	African Melody/Man From Carolina	7
70	G.G. GG 4501	Music Keep On Playing (actually by Cornell Campbell)/ Music Keep On Playing Version	7
71	G.G. GG 4508	Cleanliness Version 2/MAYTONES: Cleanliness	7
71	G.G. GG 4510	Rocking On The G.G. Beat (actually by Maytones)/WINSTON WRIGHT: Rocking On The G.G. Beat Version II	8
71	G.G. GG 4511	Lonely Nights (actually by Eric Donaldson & West Indians)/ MAYTONES: Let The Version Play	8
71	G.G. GG 4513	All One Nation (actually by Maytones)/VAL BENNETT: Judgement Warrant	8
71	G.G. GG 4526	Rod Of Righteousness (actually "Stretch Forth His Hand" by Jah Huntly)/ DENNIS ALCAPONE: King Of Kings (B-side actually "King Of Glory")	6
72	G.G. GG 4530	Donkey Face Version/MAYTONES: Donkey Face	8
72	Pama PM 846	I'm Feeling Lonely Version/MAYTONES: I'm Feeling Lonely	6
73	Bullet BU 528	People Get Funny Version/MAYTONES: People Get Funny	6
70	Trojan TBL 129	MAN FROM CAROLINA (LP)	30

(see also Paulette & Gee, Billy Dyce, Maytones, Charlie Ace, Monty Morris, Starlights, Lloyd & Carey, Gladdy & Stranger, Heptones, Shorty Perry, Barbara Jones)

G.G.F.H.

94	Peaceville CC8	Welcome To The Process/Too Much Punch/Dread (green vinyl, p/s)	15

G.G. RHYTHM SECTION

69	Blue Cat BS 165	T.N.T./MAYTONES: Botheration	30

AMOS GHERKIN QUARTET

70	Parlophone R 5872	Blakey And Me/Theme From An Unmade Silent Movie	8

GHETTO CHILDREN

73	CBS 1450	I Just Gotta Find Somebody To Love Me/Rat-a-tat-tat	10

WESS & DORI GHEZZI

75	Bradleys BRAD 7515	Fallin'/Era	8

GHOST

(see also Velvett Fogg, Shirley Kent, Virginia Tree, Wizzard)

69	Gemini GMS 007	When You're Dead/Indian Maid	30
70	Gemini GMS 014	I've Got To Get To Know You/For One Second	30
70	Gemini GME 1004	WHEN YOU'RE DEAD - ONE SECOND (LP, laminated front cover, with extra track, "I've Got To Get To Know Her")	350
70	Gemini GME 1004	WHEN YOU'RE DEAD - ONE SECOND (LP, laminated front cover, without extra track, "I've Got To Get To Know Her")	250
87	Bam Caruso KIRI 077	FOR ONE SECOND (LP, reissue of "When You're Dead" with extra track)	12

GHOST DANCE

(see also Skeletal Family, All About Eve, Sisters Of Mercy)

86	Karbon KAR 604	The Grip Of Love/Where Spirits Fly (p/s)	8
88	Karbon KAR XL 303	GATHERING DUST (LP)	15

BILL GIANT

61	MGM MGM 1135	Better Let Her Go/When I Grow Too Old To Dream	12

MINT VALUE £

BILLY GIANT

65	Pye 25337	Leave My Girl Alone/Nice Girls	20

GIANT CRAB

68	Uni UN 509	Hot Line Conversation/E.S.P.	15

GIANT HAYSTACKS

83	BSB BSB 01	Baby I Need You/Baby I Need You (Instrumental) (p/s)	7

GIANTS

60s	Polydor LPHM 46426	IN GERMANY (LP, mono)	25
60s	Polydor SLPHM 237626	IN GERMANY (LP, stereo)	30

GIANT SIZE C

93	Afrocentric AFRO3	Hate (12")	15

GIANT SUNFLOWER

67	CBS 2805	February Sunshine/Big Apple	20
67	CBS 3033	Mark Twain/What's So Good About Goodbye?	10

BARRY GIBB

(see also Bee Gees)

70	Polydor 2058 030	I'll Kiss Your Memory/This Time	8

MAURICE GIBB

(see also Bee Gees, Fut)

70	Polydor 2058 013	Railroad/I've Come Back	8

ROBIN GIBB

(see also Bee Gees)

69	Polydor 56337	Saved By The Bell/Alexandria Good Time (withdrawn)	20
69	Polydor 56368	One Million Years/Weekend	8
70	Polydor 56371	August October/Give Me A Smile	7
69	Polydor 583 085	ROBIN'S REIGN (LP)	25

DOUG GIBBONS

65	Decca F 12122	I Got My Tears To Remind Me/Found Out	15

STEVE GIBBONS (BAND)

(see also Uglys, Magic Christians, B,L&G)

71	Wizard WIZ 102	Alright Now/Lay Some Lovin' Down	10
82	RCA RCA 174	Loving Me, Loving You/That Makes It Tough/ No Money Down (picture disc)	5
71	Wizard SWZA 5501	SHORT STORIES (LP, gatefold sleeve, lyric insert, yellow vinyl)	80
77	Polydor 2058 889	Tuland/Now You Know Me	7

CALY GIBBS

(see also Carlton Gibbs)

71	Amalgamated AMG 870	Seeing Is Believing/JOE GIBBS ALLSTARS: Ghost Capturer	30

CARLTON GIBBS

70	Amalgamated AMG 872	Ghost Walk/Joy Stick	30

GEORGIA GIBBS

55	Vogue Coral Q 72088	Ballin' The Jack/I Still Feel The Same About You	10
56	Vogue Coral Q 72182	If I Were A Bell/I'll Know	10
57	RCA RCA 1011	Sugar Candy/I'm Walking The Floor Over You	10
58	RCA RCA 1029	Great Balls Of Fire/I Miss You	35
58	Mercury 7MT 210	Arriverderci Roma/24 Hours A Day	10
58	Columbia DB 4201	The Hula Hoop Song/Keep In Touch	8
59	Columbia DB 4259	The Hucklebuck/Better Loved You'll Never Be	8
60	London HLP 9098	The Stroll That Stole My Heart/Seven Lonely Days	8
65	Stateside SS 423	Let Me Cry On Your Shoulder/Venice Blues	8
55	Mercury EP-1-3265	THE MAN THAT GOT AWAY (EP)	10
56	Mercury MEP 9505	SWEET GEORGIA GIBBS (EP)	10
57	Mercury MEP 9516	SWEET GEORGIA GIBBS VOL. 2 (EP)	10
56	Mercury MPT 7500	SINGS THE OLDIES (10" LP)	20
57	Mercury MPT 7511	HER NIBS MISS GIBBS (10" LP)	20
57	Mercury MPL 6508	SWINGING WITH HER NIBS (LP)	20

JOE GIBBS (& DESTROYERS)

(see also Lizzy, Reggae Boys, Bunny Flip, Destroyers, Dennis Brown, Caly Gibbs, Nicky Thomas)

68	Amslgamated AMG 822	People Grudgeful (as Sir Joe)/Pan-Ya Machete (actually the Pioneers)	60
70	Amalgamated AMG 855	Nevada Joe (act. by Johnny Lover)/Straight To The Head (act. by Destroyers)	60
70	Amalgamated AMG 858	Franco Nero (actually by Count Machuki & Destroyers)/ Version Two (actually by Destroyers)	25
70	Amalgamated AMG 859	Rock The Clock/Version Two	50
70	Amalgamated AMG 860	Let It Be/Turn Back The Hands Of Time (both actually by Nicky Thomas)	18
70	Amalgamated AMG 861	La La/Reggae Fever (as Joe Gibbs All Stars)	40
70	Amalgamated AMG 865	Hijacked/Life Is Down In Denver	35
70	Amalgamated AMG 867	Movements/Caesar	18
70	Amalgamated AMG 869	Perfect Born Yah/Red Red Wine (as Jo Gibs All Stars)	20
70	Amalgamated AMG 868	Gift Of God (actually by Lizzy)/The Rapper	12
70	Pressure Beat PR 5504	News Flash/Version Two	12
72	Pressure Beat DB5513	Money In My Pocket/Money Love	25
73	Jackpot JP 811	Ration/Version (as Joe Gibbs All Stars)	8
78	Lightning LIP 10	AFRICAN DUB ALMIGHTY (LP, with The Professionals)	20

MICHAEL GIBBS

(see also Neil Ardley, Gary Burton)

70	Deram DML/SML 1063	MICHAEL GIBBS (LP)	40
71	Deram SML 1087	TANGLEWOOD '63 (LP)	40

MINT VALUE £

72	Polydor 2683 011	JUST AHEAD (2-LP)	35
74	Polydor 2383 252	IN THE PUBLIC INTEREST (LP, with Gary Burton)	35
70s	Bronze ILPS 9353	ONLY CHROME ... WATERFALL (LP)	15

TERRY GIBBS SEXTET

(see also Terry Gibbs Big Band)

56	Vogue Coral LVA 9013	TERRY (LP)	20
56	Vogue Coral LVA 9009	JAZZTIME USA (LP, as Terry Gibbs Quartet & Sextet)	20

TERRY GIBBS BIG BAND

59	Mercury CMS 18016	LAUNCHING A NEW BAND (LP)	15
61	HMV/Verve CLP 1560	THE EXCITING TERRY GIBBS BIG BAND (LP, mono)	12
61	HMV/Verve CSD 1439	THE EXCITING TERRY GIBBS BIG BAND (LP, stereo)	15

NICK GIBLER

76	Chrysalis CHS 2104	Roxy Roller/Prophet's Tale	6

DON GIBSON

56	MGM SP 1177	Sweet Dreams/The Road Of Life Alone	150
56	MGM SP 909	Sweet Dreams/The Road Of Life Alone (78)	30
58	RCA RCA 1056	Oh Lonesome Me/I Can't Stop Lovin' You	15
58	RCA RCA 1056	Oh Lonesome Me/I Can't Stop Lovin' You (78)	15
58	RCA RCA 1073	Blue Blue Day/Too Soon	20
58	RCA RCA 1073	Blue Blue Day/Too Soon (78)	15
58	RCA RCA 1098	Give Myself A Party/Look Who's Blue	20
58	RCA RCA 1098	Give Myself A Party/Look Who's Blue (78)	10
59	RCA RCA 1110	A Stranger To Me/Who Cares?	18
59	RCA RCA 1110	A Stranger To Me/Who Cares? (78)	20
59	RCA RCA 1150	Don't Tell Me Your Troubles/Heartbreak Avenue	18
59	RCA RCA 1150	Don't Tell Me Your Troubles/Heartbreak Avenue (78)	20
59	RCA RCA 1158	Big Hearted Me/I'm Movin' On	15

(The above RCA 45s were originally issued with triangular centres; later round-centre copies are worth half these values.)

59	RCA RCA 1158	Big Hearted Me/I'm Movin' On (78)	25
60	RCA RCA 1183	Just One Time/I May Never Get To Heaven	12
60	RCA RCA 1200	Far Far Away/A Legend In My Time	10
60	RCA RCA 1217	Sweet Dreams/The Same Street	10
61	RCA RCA 1243	Sea Of Heartbreak/I Think It's Best (To Forget Me)	10
62	RCA RCA 1272	Lonesome Number One/The Same Old Trouble	5
62	RCA RCA 1297	I Can Mend Your Broken Heart/I Let Her Get Lonely	5
63	RCA RCA 1335	Head Over Heels In Love With You/It Was Worth It	5
65	RCA RCA 1456	Again/You're Going Away	5
66	RCA RCA 1524	(Yes) I'm Hurting/My Whole World Is Hurt	5
67	RCA RCA 1626	All My Love/No Doubt About It (as Don Gibson & Jordanaires)	5
68	RCA RCA 1680	Ashes Of Love/Good Morning Dear	5
60	RCA RCX 1050	BLUE AND LONESOME (EP)	18
62	RCA RCX 213	LOOK WHO'S BLUE (EP)	18
62	RCA RCX 214	THAT GIBSON BOY (EP)	18
63	RCA RCX 7122	MAY YOU NEVER BE ALONE (EP)	18
60	RCA RD 27158	THE GIBSON BOY (LP)	100
62	RCA Victor RD/SF 7506	SOME FAVOURITES OF MINE (LP)	15
63	RCA Victor RD/SF 7576	I WROTE A SONG (LP)	15
64	RCA Victor RD 7641	GOD WALKS THESE HILLS (LP)	15

GINNY GIBSON

55	MGM SP 1121	Like Ma-a-d/Once There Was A Little Girl	15
58	MGM MGM 953	Whatever Lola Wants (Lola Gets)/If Anything Should Happen	15

JODY GIBSON & MULESKINNERS

59	Parlophone R 4579	Kissin' Time/Man On My Trail	15
60	Parlophone R 4645	If You Don't Know/So You Think You've Got Troubles	20

LORNE GIBSON TRIO

62	Decca F 11519	Little Black Book/What Kind Of Love Is This?	5
63	Decca F 11684	Some Do, Some Don't (Some Will, Some Won't)/Heaven's Above	5
64	Decca F 11814	Hang Up The Phone/I Think It's Best To Forget Me	5
64	Decca F 12005	The Girl I Loved/Don't Go Near The Indians	5
65	Decca F 12102	Red Roses For A Blue Lady/Talking To Your Picture	5
66	Decca F12450	Roses From A Stranger/Jingle Jangle	20
69	RCA 1917	Eva Magdalena/A Thing Called Love	7

STEVE GIBSON & RED CAPS

57	HMV POP 417	Silhouettes/Flamingo	200
57	HMV POP 417	Silhouettes/Flamingo (78)	30

WAYNE GIBSON (& DYNAMIC SOUNDS)

63	Decca F 11713	Linda Lu/Beachcomber	20
64	Decca F 11800	Come On Let's Go/DYNAMIC SOUNDS: Pop The Whip	20
64	Pye 7N 15680	Kelly/See You Later Alligator	18
65	Pye 7N 15798	Portland Town/Please Baby Please	10
65	Parlophone R 5357	Ding Dong The Witch Is Dead/In The Night	12
65	Columbia DB 7683	One Little Smile/Baby, Baby, Baby Pity Me	30
66	Columbia DB 7911	Under My Thumb/It Always Happens (Icey) (solo)	20
66	Columbia DB 7911	Under My Thumb/It Always Happens (Icey) (solo) (DJ copy)	100
66	Columbia DB 7998	For No One/He's Got The Whole World In his Hands (solo)	10

GIBSONS

65	CBS 202015	Any Time That You're Lonely/Born To Be Free	7
66	CBS 202063	Come Summertime/Summer Affair	7
66	Deram DM 103	Two Kinds Of Lovers/Hey Girl	6
67	Deram DM 119	The Magic Book/You Know I Need Your Lovin'	10
67	Major Minor MM 524	Night And Day/City Life	20

MINT VALUE £

67 Major Minor MM 538 — Lazy Summer Day/She's Not Like Any Girl ... 12
67 Major Minor MM 547 — Only When You're Lonely/Ode To A Dolls House ... 7

GIDEANS LEAGUE

72 Parlophone R 5933 — Hey! Did You Know You've Got Your Face On Upside Down / You've Got A Mind Of Your Own ... 6

GIDIAN (& UNIVERSALS)

(see also Universals, Chris Lamb & Universals)

66 Columbia DB 7826 — Try Me Out/There Isn't Anything ... 20
66 Columbia DB 7916 — Fight For Your Love/See If She Cares ... 8
66 Columbia DB 8041 — Feeling/Don't Be Sentimental (as Gidian & Universals) ... 10
70 UPC UPC 107 — That's Love/We Are The Happiest ... 6

COLIN GIFFIN

69 CBS 4030 — Changes In Our Time/When I Was So Young ... 40

GIFT

81 Venus ORBIT 1 — Crashing Down/It'll End In Tears (p/s) ... 20

GIFT BOX

85 Steed Stted 01 — Steiner's Lament/Worm Purple ... 5

GIFTED CHILDREN

(see also Television Personalities)

81 Whaam! WHAAM 001 — Painting By Numbers/Lichtenstein Girl (p/s) ... 30

GIGGETTY

78 Pye 7N 46136 — Black Country Christmas/Motorway Mess ... 6
75 GE 100 — DAWN TO DUSK IN THE BLACK COUNTRY (LP, with insert) ... 40
77 Bridge GE 101 — TAMBOURINE (LP) ... 30
80 Bridge GE 103 — BLACK COUNTRY TIME (LP, also listed as Revolver REV LP1) ... 30

GIGGLES

74 EMI 2212 — Maria (The Enchildas Song)/Your Mother Wouldn't Like It ... 6
75 EMI EMI 2288 — Glad To Be Alive/High School Girls ... 6
76 EMI EMI 2512 — Just Another Saturday Night In The City/Bazooka (p/s) ... 6
77 EMI EMI 2640 — Reaching Out/Street Dancer ... 5

GILBERTO GIL

71 Famous SFM 1001 — GILBERTO GIL (LP) ... 20

GILBERT

(see also Gilbert O'Sullivan)

67 CBS 3089 — Disappear/You ... 15
68 CBS 3399 — What Can I Do?/You ... 15
69 Major Minor MM 613 — Mister Moody's Garden/I Wish I Could Cry ... 15

GEORGE GILBERT

74 Mime LPMS 7041 — MEDWAY FLOWS SOFTLY (LP, with insert) ... 15

HERSCHEL BURKE GILBERT

63 London HLD 9655 — Dick Powell Theme/Nervous Teaser Theme ... 5

GILBERT & LEWIS

(see also Wire, Dome, Cupol)

81 4AD AD 106 — Ends With The Sea/Hung Up To Dry Whilst Building An Arch (p/s) ... 6
82 Cherry Red BRED 27 — MZUI (LP, PVC cover, insert sleeve) ... 12

ASTRUD GILBERTO

(see also Stan Getz, Stanley Turrentine)

64 Verve VS 520 — Girl From Ipanema (with Stan Getz)/STAN GETZ & JOAO GILBERTO: Blowin' In The Wind ... 5
66 Verve (S)VLP 9163 — A CERTAIN SMILE AND A CERTAIN KIND OF SADNESS (LP) ... 15
69 Verve (S)VLP 9242 — I HAVEN'T GOT ANYTHING BETTER TO DO (LP) ... 15
72 C.T.I. CTL 1 — GILBERTO WITH TURRENTINE (LP, with Stanley Turrentine) ... 15

JOAO GILBERTO

(see also Stan Getz)

61 Parlophone PMC 1248 — BOSSA-FINADO (LP) ... 15

GILDED CAGE

(see also She Trinity)

69 Tepee TPR 1003 — Long Long Road (For The Broken Heart)/Baby Grumpling ... 50

COSMO GILE

60 Top Rank JAR 410 — Bambina D'Amsterdam/Tintarella Di Luna ... 6

GILES, GILES & FRIPP

(see also Brain, Trendsetters Ltd, League Of Gentlemen, King Crimson, Fripp & Eno, McDonald & Giles)

68 Deram DM 188 — One In A Million/Newly-Weds ... 90
68 Deram DM 210 — Thursday Morning/Elephant Song ... 80
68 Deram DML 1022 — THE CHEERFUL INSANITY OF GILES, GILES AND FRIPP (LP, mono) ... 70
68 Deram SML 1022 — THE CHEERFUL INSANITY OF GILES, GILES AND FRIPP (LP, stereo) ... 120
70 Deram SPA 423 — THE CHEERFUL INSANITY OF GILES, GILES AND FRIPP (LP, stereo reissue) ... 22

TOM GILFELLON

72 Trailer LER 2079 — LOVING MAD TOM (LP, red label) ... 15
76 Topic 12TS 282 — IN THE MIDDLE OF THE TUNE (LP, blue label) ... 15

GILGAMESH

(see also Hugh Hopper, Colosseum, Whitesnake)

75 Caroline CA 2007 — GILGAMESH (LP) ... 20

TERRY GILKYSON & EASY RIDERS

(see also Easy Riders)

58 Philips JK 1007 — Marianne/Goodbye Chaquita (jukebox issue) ... 18

			MINT VALUE £
60	Fontana TFE 17326	STROLLING BLUES (EP)	12
60	Fontana TFE 17327	LONESOME RIDER (EP)	10
61	London RER 1333	ROLLIN' (EP)	12
53	Brunswick LA 8618	GOLDEN MINUTES OF FOLK MUSIC (10" LP)	25
61	London HA-R 2301	ROLLIN' (LP, also stereo SAH-R 6111)	15
61	London HA-R 2301	ROLLIN' (LP, also stereo SAH-R 6111)	18

JONATHAN GILL

73	Pye 7N 45206	I've Got To Please You/Isandulu Road	15

(IAN) GILLAN (BAND)

(see also Episode Six, Deep Purple, Ray Fenwick, Split Knee Loons, John McCoy, Johnny Gustafson, Bernie Torme, Thunderstick, Jerusalem, Quatermass, Colin Towns, White Spirit, Zzebra, Rock Aid Armenia)

78	Island R 553-B	Twin Exhausted (live)/Smoke On The Water (live)/ILLUSION: Madonna Blue/Revolutionary (12", promo only, as Ian Gillan Band)	20
78	Island WIP 6423	Mad Elaine/Mercury High (as Ian Gillan Band, company sleeve)	8
79	Acrobat BAT 1212	She Tears Me Down/Puget Sound/Vengeance/Mr. Universe (12", stickered card sleeve, promo only)	20
79	Acrobat BAT 12	Vengeance/Smoke On the Water	7
80	Virgin VS 355	Sleeping On The Job/Higher And Higher (p/s, with free patch)	5
81	Sounds FREEBIE No. 2	I'll Rip Out Your Spine (extract)/PROFESSIONALS: Little Boys In Blue (extract) (33rpm 1-sided flexi, printed die-cut sleeve, with Sounds paper)	7
80	Virgin SS 362	No Easy Way/Handles On Her Hips/Might As Well Go Home (p/s)	5
80	Virgin VS 377	Trouble/Your Sister's On My List//Mr. Universe (live)/Vengeance (live)/Smoke On The Water (live) (7" double pack, gatefold)	5
81	Lyntone LYN 10599	Higher And Higher/Spanish Guitar (1-sided blue flexi with Flexipop magazine 13)	7
81	Lyntone LYN 10599	Higher And Higher/Spanish Guitar (same tracks both sides, hard vinyl test pressing, handwritten white labels)	35
82	Virgin VSY 519	Living For The City/Purple Sky (picture disc, mispressed, B-side plays Breaking Chains, some with explanatory sticker)	8
81	Virgin VSK 103	Mutually Assured Destruction/The Maelstron (gatefold, with booket)	5
82	Virgin VSY 519	Living for The City/Purple Skies (picture disc)	7
88	Virgin TVS 1088	South Africa (extended mix)/South Africa/John (12", p/s, as Ian Gillan)	8
90	Teldec SAM 678	Talking To You/Moonshine/Gut Reaction/No Good Luck (12", clear vinyl promo, in PVC wallet with insert & postcard)	10
91	East West SAM 906	Toolbox/Hang Me Out To Dry/Dirty Dog/Pictures Of Hell (12" promo, die-cut sleeve)	10
76	Polydor/Oyster 2490 136	CHILD IN TIME (LP, gatefold sleeve, as Ian Gillan Band)	15
78	Island ILPS 9545	LIVE AT THE BUDOKAN (LP, unissued)	0
77	Island ILPS 9511DJ	IAN GILLAN BAND SAMPLER (LP, 1-sided promo for "Scarabus", company sleeve)	20
80	Virgin V 2171	GLORY ROAD (LP, with bonus LP "For Gillan Fans Only" [VDJ 32], stickered, embossed sleeve & inner sleeves)	12
82	Virgin VP 2236	MAGIC (LP, picture disc)	12

DANA GILLESPIE

(see also David Bowie)

65	Pye 7N 15872	Donna Donna/It's No Use Saying If	12
65	Pye 7N 15962	Thank You Boy/You're A Heartbreak Man	15
67	Pye 7N 17280	Pay You Back With Interest/Adam Can You Beat That	8
68	Decca F 12847	You Just Gotta Know My Mind/He Loves Me, He Loves Me Not	60
74	RCA RCA 0211	Weren't Born A Man/All Gone	5
74	RCA RCA 2466	Andy Warhol/Dizzy Heights	8
75	RCA RCA 2489	Really Love That Man/Hold Me Gently	5
69	Decca LK 5012	BOX OF SURPRISES (LP, mono)	90
69	Decca SLK 5012	BOX OF SURPRISES (LP, stereo)	150
73	RCA APL1 0354	WEREN'T BORN A MAN (LP)	25
74	RCA APL1 0682	AIN'T GONNA PLAY NO SECOND FIDDLE (LP)	15

DIZZY GILLESPIE (QUINTET)

(see also Miles Davis, Lalo Schifrin)

55	Vogue EPV 1022	DIZZY GILLESPIE (EP)	8
55	Vogue EPV 1049	DIZZY GILLESPIE WITH STRINGS (EP)	8
52	Esquire 20-003	OPERATIC STRINGS (10" LP)	15
53	Vogue LDE 017	DIZZY GILLESPIE PLAYS (10" LP)	15
53	Vogue LDE 033	DIZZY GILLESPIE PLAYS - JOHNNY RICHARDS CONDUCTS (10" LP)	15
54	Vogue LDE 039	PARIS CONCERT (10" LP)	15
54	Vogue LDE 076	DIZZY GILLESPIE AND ORCHESTRA (10" LP)	15
54	HMV DLP 1047	DIZZY GILLESPIE AND HIS ORCHESTRA (10" LP)	15
54	Felsted EDL 87006	DIZZY GILLESPIE'S OPERATIC STRINGS - JEALOUSY (10" LP)	15
55	Vogue LDE 135	DIZZY GILLESPIE AND HIS ORCHESTRA (10" LP)	15
55	Columbia Clef 33CX 10002	DIZZY GILLESPIE AND HIS ORCHESTRA (LP)	15
58	Columbia Clef 33CX 10144	DIZZY IN GREECE (LP)	15
62	HMV CLP 1484	GILLESPIANA (LP, also stereo CSD 1392)	15
71	Pye PKL 4403	SOULED OUT (LP)	15

DIZZY GILLESPIE & STAN GETZ

(see also Stan Getz)

55	Columbia Clef 33C 9009	DIZZY GILLESPIE - STAN GETZ SEXTET (LP)	15
55	Columbia 33C 9027	MORE OF (10" LP)	15

DIZZY GILLESPIE & CHARLIE PARKER

(see also Charlie Parker)

61	Vogue LAE 12252	DIZ 'N BIRD IN CONCERT (LP)	15

HUGH GILLESPIE

78	Topic 12TS 364	CLASSIC RECORDINGS OF IRISH TRADITIONAL FIDDLE MUSIC (LP)	12

DOBIE GILLIS

68	United Artists UP 2212	How Peculiar/I Wish I Was Harry	8

MINT VALUE £

JAZZ GILLUM
66 RCA Victor RD 7816 — JAZZ GILLUM 1938-1947 (LP) 15
70 RCA Intl. INTS 1177 — YOU GOT TO REAP WHAT YOU SOW (LP) 12

JIMMY GILMER & FIREBALLS
(see also Fireballs, Jim & Monica)
62 London HLD 9632 — I'm Gonna Go Walkin'/Born To Be With You (as Chimmy Gilmer) 15
63 London HLD 9789 — Sugar Shack/My Heart Is Free 10
64 London HLD 9827 — Daisy Petal Pickin'/When My Tears Have Dried 10
64 London HLD 9872 — Ain't Gonna Tell Nobody/Young Am I 10
64 London HLD 9898 — Look At Me/I'll Send For You 10
65 Stateside SS 418 — Thunder 'N' Lightnin'/What Do You Do 10
65 Stateside SS 472 — She Belongs To Me/Rambler's Blues 10
68 London HL 10232 — Three Squares/Baby 6
64 London HA-D/SH-D 8150 — SUGAR SHACK (LP) 25
65 Dot DLP 3577 — BUDDY'S BUDDY - BUDDY HOLLY SONGS BY JIMMY GILMER (LP) 40

DAVID GILMOUR
(see also Pink Floyd, Joker's Wild, Rock Aid Armenia, Unicorn)
78 Harvest HAR 5167 — There's No Way Out Of Here/Deafinitely (no p/s) 7
84 Harvest 12HAR 5226 — Blue Light (LP Version)/Cruise (12", p/s) 10
84 Harvest HAR 5229 — Love On The Air/Let's Get Metaphysical (p/s) 5
84 Harvest HARP 5229 — Love On The Air/Let's Get Metaphysical (shaped picture disc) 12
84 Harvest 12HAR 5229 — Love On The Air/Let's Get Metaphysical (12", p/s) 8
06 EMI 696 — Smile/Island Jam (clear vinyl) 5
06 EMI EMIDJ 733 — Take a Breath (1-sided clear vinyl promo) 50
78 Harvest SHVL 817 — DAVID GILMOUR (LP) 15
08 Sony SONLP 34470 — LIVE IN GDANKSK (5-LP box set) 60

JAMES GILREATH
63 Pye International 7N 25190 — Little Band Of Gold/I'll Walk With You 12
63 Pye International 7N 25213 — Lollipops, Lace And Lipstick/Mean Ole River 10

GORDON GILTRAP (BAND)
(see also Accolade, Pauline Filby, Catherine Andrews)
73 Philips 6006 344 — No Way Of Knowing/I See A Road 15
68 Transatlantic TRA 175 — GORDON GILTRAP (LP, lilac label with 't' logo) 50
69 Transatlantic TRA 202 — PORTRAIT (LP) 45
71 MCA MKPS 2020 — A TESTAMENT OF TIME (LP, red/pink 'dogbone' label) 30
73 Philips 6308 175 — GILTRAP (LP, with lyric insert, blue/silver label) 20

GIMMICKS
70 Decca Eclipse ECS-R 2054 — BRAZILIAN SAMBA (LP) 30

GINGER
(see also SilverGinger 5, Super$hit666, Wildhearts)

GINGER ALE
70 Famous FAM 102 — In The Sand/Get Off My Life Woman 8

GINGER JUG BAND
70s GJB 001 — GINGER JUG BAND (LP, private pressing) 20

GINGER SNAPS
65 RCA RCA 1483 — The Sh Down Down Song/I've Got Faith In Him 20

GINGERBREAD
71 Pye 7N 45054 — Pollution/Moody Trudy 8

GINGERBREAD
69 B&C CB 113 — How Are You/Easy Girl 6

GINGRINI
73 Harry J. HJ 6647 — Zion 'lah/Zion 'lah (Version) 6

GINHOUSE
(see also Kestrel. Mouse, Sammy)
71 Charisma CAS 1031 — GINHOUSE (LP, gatefold sleeve) 150

GINO & GINA
58 Mercury 7MT 230 — Pretty Baby/Love's A Carousel 30

ALLEN GINSBERG
(see also Ginsbergs)
60s Cape Goliard — Wales: A Visitation (single issued with book of same title) 15
65 Better Books (no cat. no.) — ALLEN GINSBERG READING AT BETTER BOOKS (LP) 20
65 Love Books Ltd. LB 0001 — ALLEN GINSBERG, LAURENCE FERLINGHETTI, GREGORY CORSO & ANDREI VOZNESENSKY READING AT THE ARCHITECTURAL ASSOCIATION (LP) .. 20
68 Transatlantic TRA 192 — GINSBERG'S THING (LP) 15

GINSBERGS
(see also Allen Ginsberg)
67 Saga Psyche PSY 3002 — THE GINSBERGS AT THE ICA (LP) 15

MARCELLO GIOMBINI
70 United Artists UP 35110 — Sabata - Main Title/Banjo Arrives 10

GIORGIO
(see also Giorgio Moroder, Giorgio & Marco's Men)
66 Page One POF 003 — Full Stop/Believe Me 6
67 Page One POF 028 — How Much Longer Must I Wait/Bla Bla Diddly 12
69 MCA MCA 1094 — Happy Birthday/Looky Looky 5

GIORGIO & MARCO'S MEN
66 Polydor 56101 — Run Run/Girl Without A Heart 7
68 Electratone EP 1003 — Baby I Need You/Maureen 70

MINT VALUE £

GIPSY LOVE
72 BASF BAP 5026 GIPSY LOVE (LP) ... 20

CHUCK GIRARD
60s Myrrh MYR 1025 CHUCK GIRARD (LP) ... 15
60s Myrrh MYR 1065 WRITTEN ON THE WIND (LP) ... 15
60s myrrh MYR 1089 THE STAND (LP) ... 15

MARTINE GIRAULD
92 Opaz OP 001SRH REVIVAL (12" EP, p/s) ... 8

GIRGIO
69 MCA 5023 Stop/Believe Me ... 20

GIRL
(see also Def Leppard, Bernie Torme)
79 Jet JET 159 My Number/My Number (Version) (clear vinyl, PVC sleeve, with 2 stickers) ... 5

GIRLFRIENDS
63 Colpix PX 712 Jimmy Boy/For My Sake ... 60

GIRLIE
(see also Laurel Aitken & Girlie)
69 Treasure Isle TI 7053 Boss Cocky/LOVE SHOCKS: Musical True ... 18
69 Bullet BU 400 Madame Straggae/LAUREL AITKEN: Stupid Married Man ... 12
69 Duke DU 42 African Meeting (as Girlie & Junior)/JOSH: Higher And Higher ... 10
70 Joe JRS 7 Small Change/Mind Your Business (as Girlie & Joe [Mansano]) ... 12
70 Ackee ACK 124 Decimilization/Decimilization Version (as Girlie & Paul) ... 6

GIRLS AT OUR BEST
80 Records RR 001 Getting Nowhere Fast/Warm Girls (p/s) ... 10
81 Rough Trade RT 055 Politics/It's Fashion (p/s) ... 5
81 Happy Birthday UR 4 Go For Gold/I'm Beautiful Now (p/s) ... 8
81 Happy Birthday UR 6 Fast Boyfriends/This Train (p/s) ... 8
81 Happy Birthday RULP 1 PLEASURE (LP, with lyric insert, 1st 10,000 with free 'pleasure bag' with 2 postcards, sticker & stencil) ... 12

GIRLSCHOOL
(see also Motorhead, Killjoys)
79 City NIK 6 Take It All Away/It Could Be Better (p/s, red vinyl, pink p/s, b&w front photo) ... 7
79 City NIK 6 Take It All Away/It Could Be Better (p/s, black vinyl, orange p/s) ... 5
79 Mulligan LUNS 723 Take It All Away/It Could Be Better (Irish version, no p/s, red vinyl) ... 8
84 Bronze BROX176 Burning In The Heat/Surrender (12", p/s + booklet) ... 8
88 GWR GWR14 Head Over Heals/Action (unissued) ... 10
81 Bronze BRON 534 HIT AND RUN (LP, red vinyl) ... 15

GIRL TALK
84 Innervision IVST 4 Can The Rhythm (mixes) (12", p/s) ... 12

GIST
81 Rough Trade RT 58 This Is Love/Yanks (p/s) ... 8
81 Rough Trade RT 85 Love At First Sight/Light Aircraft (p/s) ... 7
83 Rough Trade RT 125 Fool For A Valentine/Fool For A Version (p/s) ... 7

GITS
89 Stig STIG 0019 Too Many People/Happy Song (p/s) ... 10

GITTE
64 Columbia DB 7440 The Heart That You Break (May Be Your Own)/Seems Just Like Old Times ... 10

JIMMY GIUFFRE
(see also Shelly Manne)
55 Capitol LC 6699 JIMMY GIUFFRE (10" LP) ... 20
57 London Jazz LTZK 15059 THE JIMMY GIUFFRE CLARINET (LP) ... 15
58 London Jazz LTZK 15130 JIMMY GIUFFRE (LP) ... 15
58 London Jazz LTZK 15137 TRAV'LIN' LIGHT (LP) ... 15
58 London LTZ-K 15130 JIMMY GIUFFRE 3 (LP) ... 15

GIZMO
75 President PT 443 Just Like Velvet/Jesus Help Me Sleep ... 8

GIZZARDI
03 Pump Hard PUMP 002 Tight Fitting T-Shirt/Supply and Demand (CD) ... 8

GLADDY (Anderson) & FOLLOWERS
(see also Stranger & Glady)
69 Blue Cat BS 172 Judas/The World Come To An End ... 22

GLADDY (Anderson) & STRANGER (Cole)
(see also Gladstone Anderson, Stranger Cole, Stranger & Glady)
73 Pama PM 872 Dedicated To Illiteracy/G.G. ALLSTARS: Dub ... 8

GLADIATORS
(see also Nero & Gladiators)
63 HMV POP 1134 Bleak House/Tovaritch ... 25

GLADIATORS
68 Direction 58-3854 Girl Don't Make Me Wait/Can't Get Away From Heartbreak ... 15
69 Direction 58-4308 Waiting On The Shores Of Nowhere/I'll Always Love You ... 15
69 Direction 58-4507 As Long As I Live/Everything ... 10
69 Direction 58-4660 Twelfth Of Never/Lovin' My Baby Back Home ... 8
69 Studio One SO 2072 Hello Carol/RICHARD ACE: More Reggae ... 40
69 Studio One 2086 Kicks/Games People Play ... 35
69 Doctor Bird DB 1114 The Train Is Coming/So Fine ... 35
69 Bamboo BAM 7 Anywhere/SOUND DIMENSION: Baby Face ... 30
70 Duke DU 58 My Girl (actually by Glen Adams)/You Were To Be ... 20
72 Ackee ACK 149 Sonia/SOUND DIMENSION: Solas ... 15

			MINT VALUE £
70s	Rock Steady Rev. REVR 12	Unusual Reggae/Andue	6
78	Virgin Frontline 1002	PROVERBIAL REGGAE (LP)	18
78	Virgin Frontline FL 1035	NATURALITY (LP)	18
79	Virgin Frontline FL 1048	SWEET SO TILL (LP)	18
81	Virgin VX 1003	VITAL SELECTION (LP)	15

GLADIOLAS
(see also Maurice Williams & Zodiacs)

57	London HLO 8435	Little Darlin'/Sweetheart, Please Don't Go	250
57	London HLO 8435	Little Darlin'/Sweetheart, Please Don't Go (78 rpm)	75

GLASGOW

84	Neat NEAT 40	Stranded/Heat Of The Night (p/s)	15
84	Clydebank CLY 001	GLASGOW'S MILES BETTER (12" EP)	12

LUD GLASKIN

62	UPC 3428	To My Good Friend Jack Cotton, the 'Allo Twist (1-sided private pressing)	25

GLASS

82	Glass GLASS1	New Colours/Sweet Entropy (p/s)	22

PHILIP GLASS
(see also Ray Manzarek)

70s	Chatham Square LP 1001/2	MUSIC WITH CHANGING PARTS (2-LP)	25
70s	Chatham Square LP 1003	MUSIC IN FIFTHS/MUSIC IN A SIMILAR MOTION (LP)	20
70s	Folkways FTS 33902	TWO PAGES (LP)	20
76	Cardine LA 2010	MUSIC IN 12 (PARTS 1 & 2) (LP)	18
78	Shandar SHAN 83515	SOLO MUSIC (LP)	15

GLASS HARP

72	MCA MUPS 431	GLASS HARP (LP)	25
72	MCA MUPS 449	SYNERGY (LP)	22

GLASS HOUSE

70	Invictus INV 506	Stealing Moments From Another Woman's Life/If It Ain't Love, It Don't Matter	8
71	Invictus INV 510	I Can't Be You/He's In My Life	8

GLASS MENAGERIE
(see also Paladin, Toe-Fat)

68	Pye 7N 17518	She's A Rainbow/But That's When I Start To Love Her	12
68	Pye 7N 17568	You Didn't Have To Be So Nice/Let's All Run To The Sun	10
68	Pye 7N 17615	Frederick Jordan/I Said Goodbye To Me	240
69	Polydor 56318	Have You Forgotten Who You Are/Do You Ever Think?	10
69	Polydor 56341	Do My Thing Myself/Watching The World Pass By	25

GLASS OPENING

68	Plexium P 1236	Silver Bells And Cockle Shells/Does It Really Matter	300

GLASVEGAS

06	Waks WAKS 0035	Go Square Go/Legs 'N' Show (400 only, with lyric insert)	50
07	Sane Man SAN 001	Daddy's Gone/Flowers And Football Tops (p/s, 1,000 only, numbered)	30
07	Sane Man SAN 02	It's My Own Cheating Heart That Makes Me Cry/Be My Baby (2,000 only)	10

GLAXO BABIES

79	Heartbeat PULSE5	Christine Keeler/Nova Bossanova (p/s)	10
80	Heartbeat HBM 3	PUT ME ON THE GUEST LIST (LP)	12

CAPTAIN GLEASON'S GARDEN BAND
(see also Jackie Gleason)

55	Capitol CL 14323	In The Good Old Summertime/The Band Played On	5

GLEN (Brown) & LLOYD (Robinson)

66	Ska Beat JB 250	Live And Let Others Die/Too Late	45
67	Doctor Bird DB 1099	Feel Good Now/What You've Got (credited as Lloyd Glen)	45

GLENCOE
(see also Hopscotch, Five Day Rain, Greatest Show On Earth, Loving Awareness)

72	Epic EPC 8383	Look Me In The Eye/Telephonia	6
72	Epic EPC 65207	GLENCOE (LP)	20
73	Epic EPC 65717	SPIRIT OF GLENCOE (LP)	15

DARRELL GLENN

54	HMV 7MC 23	In The Chapel In The Moonlight/Once And Only Once (export issue)	8

GLIDE
(see also Echo & Bunnymen)

95	Ochre OCH 003	EXCERPTS FROM A SPACE AGE FREAK OUT (Part 1) (orange vinyl, p/s)	5
97	Enraptured RAPT 4512	Glide (Yosum Remix)/Grind Theme 3 (wraparound p/s)	5

GLITTERHOUSE

68	Stateside SS 2129	Barbarella/BOB CREWE: An Angel Is Love	15
68	Stateside SS 2129	Barbarella/Love Drags Me Down (different B-side)	18

GLOBAL COMMUNICATIONS
(see also Mystic Institue, Link, Reload, Reload & E621, Chaos & Julia Set, Jedi Knights)

93	Evolution EVO 04	KEONGAKU EP (12", 4-track, plain sleeve)	25
94	Dedicated DEDLP 014L	76: 14 (2-LP, gatefold sleeve with bonus 12" [DEDLP 0145])	30
94	Dedicated DEDLP 014	76: 14 (2-LP, gatefold sleeve)	25
94	Dedicated SESLP 014 DJ	9 25 (1-sided 12")	8
96	Dedicated DED 21LP	REMOTION - THE GLOBAL COMMUNICATIONS REMIX ALBUM (2-LP)	20

GLOBAL METHOD

92	Not On Label GM1	VIBE TRIBE (EP)	110

GLOBAL VILLAGE TRUCKING COMPANY
(see also Byzantium, Man)

76	Caroline C 1516	GLOBAL VILLAGE TRUCKING COMPANY (LP, with lyric insert, b/s & red label, twins logo)	20

MINT VALUE £

GLOBE SHOW
(see also Chris Shakespeare Globe Show)

69	Page One POF 128	Yes Or No/Gettin' On Back	10

GLOBE TROTTERS

54	Parlophone CMSP 18	At Sundown/My Gal Sal (export issue)	15
54	Parlophone GEP 8528	SATURDAY NIGHT HOP (EP)	18

GLOBETROTTERS

70	RCA RCA 2017	Gravy/Cheer Me Up	10
71	RCA SF 8158	THE GLOBETROTTERS (LP)	15

GLOOMYS

68	Columbia DB 8391	Daybreak/Queen And King	12
71	DJM DJS 240	I'm A Bum/Let Me Dream	10

GLORIA

69	Columbia DB 8568	The Last Seven Days/Merry Dance	15

GLORIA MUNDI

78	RCA PB 5068	Fight Back/Do It (p/s)	5
78	RCA PB 5118	Glory To The World/Nothing To Say (p/s)	8
78	RCA PL2 5157	I INDIVIDUAL (LP, with inner sleeve)	12
79	RCA PL2 5244	THE WORD IS OUT (LP, with lyric inner)	12

GLORIES

67	CBS 2786	I Stand Accused (Of Loving You)/Wish They Could Write A Song	25
67	CBS 2786	I Stand Accused (Of Loving You)/Wish They Could Write A Song (DJ Copy)	30
67	Direction 58-3084	Give Me My Freedom/Security	18
68	Direction 58-3300	Sing Me A Love Song/Oh Baby That's Love	15
68	Direction 58-3646	My Sweet Sweet Baby/Stand By (I'm Comin' Home)	10

GLORY LANDERS

69	IBA SECC 1203	VOLUME 1 (LP)	15

GLOVE
(see also Cure, Siouxsie & Banshees, Creatures)

83	Wonderland SHE 3	Like An Animal/Mouth To Mouth (p/s, some sleeves with centre holes)	5
83	Wonderland SHEX 3	Like An Animal (Club, What Club? Mix)/Like Animal/Mouth To Mouth (12", p/s, some sleeves with centre hole)	8
83	Wonderland SHE 5	Punish Me With Kisses/The Tightrope (p/s)	8
83	Wonderland SHELP 2	BLUE SUNSHINE (LP, mispressing with double-printed sleeve)	20

ROGER GLOVER (& GUESTS)
(see also [Sheila Carter &] Episode [Six], Deep Purple, Elf, Eddie Hardin, Whitesnake, Rainbow, Glenn Hughes, John Lawton, Wizard's Convention, Marlon, Green Bullfrog, David Coverdale, Dio)

74	Purple PUR 125	Love Is All/Old Blind Mole/Magician Moth	10
84	Safari SAF EP 1	Love Is All/Sitting In A Dream/Little Chalk Blue/Homeward	5
84	Polydor POSP 678	The Mask/So Remote (p/s, solo)	6
74	Purple TPSA 7514	THE BUTTERFLY BALL (AND THE GRASSHOPPER'S FEAST) (LP, g/fold sleeve)	15
78	Polydor 2391 306	ELEMENTS (LP, solo)	12
84	Polydor POLD 5139	THE MASK (LP, solo, with insert)	12

JEREMY GLUCK
(see also Barracudas)

86	Flicknife SHARP 037	I KNEW BUFFALO BILL (LP)	15

GMP

93	Kold Sweat KSEP 212	HARDCORE WINS AGAIN (EP)	12

GMT

91	Mausoleum BONE 12-83102	One By One (12", p/s)	10

GNAC

98	Earworm WORM 29	The Moustache/Armchair Thriller (p/s, black vinyl)	6

GNANK

99	Gnank GNANK 01	Gnank Gnank/Oi, Gnank (p/s)	8

GNASHER

74	Purple PUR 119	Medina Road/Easy Meat	8

GNIDROLOG
(see also Pork Dukes, Steeleye Span)

72	RCA SF 8261	IN SPITE OF HARRY'S TOE-NAIL (LP, gatefold sleeve, orange label)	100
72	RCA SF 8322	LADY LAKE (LP, with lyric insert)	250
72	RCA SF 8322	LADY LAKE (LP, without lyric insert)	100

GNOMES OF ZURICH

66	Planet PLF 121	Please Mr Sun/I'm Coming Down With The Blues (with custom 'Planet' sleeve)	80
66	Planet PLF 121	Please Mr Sun/I'm Coming Down With The Blues (without custom 'Planet' sleeve)	50
67	CBS 202556	Hang On Baby/Blues For My Baby	60
67	CBS 2694	High Hopes/Pretender	60
67	RCA Victor RCA 1606	Second Fiddle/Publicity Girl	60

G-NOTES

58	Oriole CB 1456	Ronnie/I Would	20
58	Oriole CB 1456	Ronnie/I Would (78 rpm)	15

PETER GOAMBY

75	Magnet MAG 45	You Are Day You Are Night/Captain's Log	6

GOAT

82	Real Kavoom ARK 1	REAL KAVOOM (12" EP)	8

MINT VALUE £

GOBBLEDEGOOKS
64 Decca F 12023 — Now And Again/Where Have You Been ... 15

GOBBLINZ
79 Pinnacle P 8454 — London/Women In Love (p/s) ... 80
80s Bacon SLICE 01 — Love Me Too/All Of This And More (no p/s) ... 80

GO-BETWEENS
80 Postcard 80-4 — I Need Two Heads/Stop Before You Say It (brown label & brown co. sleeve) ... 20
80 Postcard 80-4 — I Need Two Heads/Stop Before You Say It (yellow label & cream co. sleeve) ... 18
80 Postcard 81-9 — Your Turn My Turn/World Weary (company sleeve) ... 8
82 Rough Trade RT 108 — Hammer The Hammer/By Chance (p/s) ... 6
83 Rough Trade RT 124 — Cattle And Cane/Heaven Says (p/s) ... 6
83 Rough Trade RT 114 — Man O'Sand To Girl O'See/This Girl Black Girl (p/s) ... 6
87 Beggars Banquet BEG 183D — Right Here/When People Are Dead/A Little Romance//Don't Call Me Gone/A Little Romance (live) (double pack) ... 6
88 Beggars Banquet BEG 218B — Streets Of Your Town/Wait Until June (box set) ... 8
81 Rough Trade ROUGH 45 — SEND ME A LULLABY (LP) ... 12
82 Rough Trade ROUGH 54 — BEFORE HOLLYWOOD (LP) ... 12

GOBLIN
79 EMI EMC 3222 — SUSPIRIA (LP, soundtrack) ... 35

VIC GODARD (& SUBWAY SECT)
(see also Subway Sect, Spirit Of The Sect)
80 Oddball/MCA 585 — Split Up The Money/Out Of Touch (p/s, with Subway Sect) ... 5
81 Rough Trade RT 068 — Stop That Girl/Instrumentally Scared/Vertical Integration (p/s, w/Subway Sect) ... 5
81 Club Left CLUB 1 — Stamp Of A Vamp/Hey Now (I'm In Love) (p/s, with Subway Sect) ... 5
85 El Benelux EL 4 — Holiday Hymn/Nice On The Ice (p/s) ... 5
85 El Benelux EL 4T — Holiday Hymn/Nice On The Ice/Stop That Girl/Ice On The Volcano/T.R.O.U.B.L.E. (12", p/s) ... 10
93 Postcard DUBH 937 — Won't Turn Back/Won't Turn Back (Version) (p/s, 1,000 only) ... 5
80 Oddball/MCA MCF 3070 — WHAT'S THE MATTER BOY? (LP, with Subway Sect) ... 20
82 London SH 8549 — SONGS FOR SALE (LP, with Subway Sect) ... 18
85 Rough Trade ROUGH 56 — A RETROSPECTIVE (LP, inner sleeve, with Subway Sect) ... 18
85 MCA/El 01 — HOLIDAY HYMN (LP, 10 test pressings only; abandoned issue of "T.R.O.U.B.L.E.") ... 30
86 Rough Trade ROUGH 86 — T.R.O.U.B.L.E. (LP) ... 12
93 Postcard DUBH 936 — END OF THE SURREY PEOPLE (LP) ... 12

KEITH & DONNA GODCHAUX
(see also Grateful Dead)
75 Round RX 104 — KEITH & DONNA GODCHAUX (LP) ... 18

GEOFF GODDARD
61 HMV POP 938 — Girl Bride/For Eternity ... 50
62 HMV POP 1068 — My Little Girl's Come Home/Try Once More ... 50
63 HMV POP 1160 — Saturday Dance/Come Back To Me ... 40
63 HMV POP 1213 — Sky Men/Walk With Me My Angel ... 120

HUGH GODFREY
(see also Soul Brothers)
67 Coxsone CS 7001 — A Dey Pon Dem/SOUL BROTHERS: Take Ten ... 100
67 Studio One SO 2008 — My Time/MARCIA GRIFFITHS: Hound Dog ... 60
67 Studio One SO 2015 — Go Tell Him/MARCIA GRIFFITHS: After Laughter ... 60

RAY GODFREY
78 Grapevine GRP 111 — Come And Get These Memories/I'm The Other Half Of You ... 5

ROBERT JOHN GODFREY
(see also Enid, Godfrey & Stewart, Don Bradshaw)
74 Charisma CAS 1084 — FALL OF HYPERION (LP) ... 40

GODFREY & STEWART
(see also Robert John Godfrey, Enid)
86 The Enid ENID 11 — THE SEED AND THE SOWER (LP) ... 15
80s The Stand HEARTLP — JOINED BY THE HEART (LP, fan club issue, 2,000 only) ... 20
80s The Stand HEARTC — JOINED BY THE HEART (, fan club issue) ... 12

GODIEGO
79 BBC RESL 66 — Ganghara/The Birth Of The Odyssey/Monkey Magic ... 5
78 Satril SATL 4009 — THE WATER MARGIN (LP, TV soundtrack) ... 12

GODLEY & CREME
(see also Mockingbirds, Hotlegs, 10cc, Dave Berry, Frabjoy & Runcible Spoon, Cruisers, Whirlwinds, Doctor Father)
68 Blinkers 1215 — Goodnight Blinkers/Hello Blinkers (die-cut sleeve) ... 30
79 Mercury SAMP 017 — 5 O'Clock/The Flood//Lost Weekend/Honolulu (double pack sampler, promo) ... 10

GODS
(see also Uriah Heep, Shame, Toe-Fat, Birds Birds, Carmen, Jethro Tull)
67 Polydor 56168 — Come On Down To My Boat Baby/Garage Man ... 180
68 Columbia DB 8486 — Baby's Rich/Somewhere In The Street ... 50
69 Columbia DB 8544 — Hey! Bulldog/Real Love Guaranteed ... 40
69 Columbia DB 8572 — Maria/Long Time, Sad Time, Bad Time ... 40
68 Columbia S(C)X 6286 — GENESIS (LP, blue/black label with "sold in U.K..." text) ... 250
70 Columbia SCX 6372 — TO SAMUEL A SON (LP, black/silver labels with boxed logo) ... 250
76 Harvest SHSM 2011 — GODS (LP) ... 25

GOD'S GIFT
79 Newmarket no cat. no. — THESE DAYS (EP) ... 10
81 New Hormones ORG 14 — Soldiers/Anthony Perkins/No God/The Hunger Of Millions (12", p/s) ... 8

GOD SONS
(see also Errol & U Roy, Carl Masters)
71 Philips 6006155 — All Dressed In White/We've Not Made It ... 15
72 Green Door GD 4024 — Merry Up/Merry Up - Version ... 10

MINT VALUE £

GOD SPEED! YOU BLACK EMPEROR

99	Constellation CST 006	SLOW RIOT FOR NEW ZERO KANADA (12" EP)	15
99	Kranky KRANK 034	SLOW RIOT FOR NEW ZERO KANADA (CD EP)	8

GODZ

67	Fontana STL 5500	CONTACT WITH THE GODZ (LP)	25
69	Fontana STL 5512	GODZ II (LP)	25

GOGMAGOG

(see also Iron Maiden, Di'Anno, Def Leppard, Whitesnake, Gillan, White Spirit)

85	F. For Thought YUMT 109	I Will Be There/Living In A Timewarp/It's Illegal, It's Immoral, It's Unhealthy But It's Fun (12", p/s & insert)	35

GO GO THUNDER

75	RCA RCA 2494	The Race/Mrs. Mann	20

GO-GO's (U.K.)

64	Oriole CB 1982	I'm Gonna Spend My Christmas With A Dalek/Big Boss Man (in p/s)	50
64	Oriole CB 1982	I'm Gonna Spend My Christmas With A Dalek/Big Boss Man	30

GO-GO's (U.S.)

(see also Belinda Carlisle, Jane Wiedlin)

80	Stiff BUY 78	We Got The Beat/How Much More (p/s)	5
81	I.R.S. PFP 1007	Our Lips Are Sealed/Surfing And Spying (p/s, pink vinyl)	6
81	I.R.S. GONP 101	Automatic/Tonite (picture disc)	5
90	A&M AMP 712	Cool Jerk/We Got The Beat (picture disc)	5

GOING RED?

(see also Freshies, Chris Sievey, Jilted John)

81	Razz CLEAN 1	Some Boys/Tune Kevin's Strings (p/s)	8
81	MCA MCA 673	Some Boys/Tune Kevin's Strings (reissue, p/s)	5

HERBIE GOINS & NIGHT-TIMERS

(see also Night-Timers, Alexis Korner's Blues Incorporated)

66	Parlophone R 5478	No. 1 In Your Heart/Cruisin'	125
66	Parlophone R 5478	No. 1 In Your Heart/Cruisin' (DJ Copy)	175
66	Parlophone R 5533	The Incredible Miss Brown/Comin' Home To You	70
67	Parlophone PMC 7026	NUMBER ONE IN YOUR HEART (LP)	150

GO-KART MOZARTS

(see also Felt)

99	West Midlands Records BRUM 1	INSTANT WIGWAM AND IGLOO MIXTURE (LP, 1,000 only, with poster and small sealing sticker over opening)	15

DAVID GOLD

97	Fat Cat 10FAT 001	Respect City Police (10")	40

HARRY GOLD with NORRIE PARAMOR ORCHESTRA

(see also Norrie Paramor)

54	Columbia SCM 5144	Be Good To Me/Frou Frou	5

MARTY GOLD

70	Avco Embassy 6466 001	MOOG PLAYS THE BEATLES (LP)	12

BARRY GOLDBERG (REUNION)

(see also Electric Flag, Mike Bloomfield)

68	Pye International 7N 25465	Another Day/Capricorn Blues (as Barry Goldberg Reunion)	7
68	Pye Intl. NSPL 28116	BARRY GOLDBERG REUNION (LP)	20
69	Buddah 203 020	TWO JEWS BLUES (LP, with Mike Bloomfield)	15
71	Buddah 2318 038	BLASTS FROM MY PAST (LP)	12

GOLDEBRIARS

64	Columbia DB 7384	Sea Of Tears/I've Got To Love Somebody	15

GOLDEN APPLES OF THE SUN

65	Decca F 12194	Monkey Time/Chocolate Rolls, Tea And Monopoly (unissued, test pressings only)	80
65	Immediate IM 010	Monkey Time/Chocolate Rolls, Tea And Monopoly	40

GOLDEN CRUSADERS

64	Columbia DB 7232	I'm In Love With You/Always On My Mind	10
64	Columbia DB 7357	Hey Good Lookin'/Come On, Come On	10
65	Columbia DB 7485	I Don't Care/That Broken Heart Is Mine	10

GOLDEN DAWN

88	Sarah SARAH 009	My Secret World/Spring-Heeled Jack/The Railway Track (p/s, with poster)	12
89	Sarah SARAH 017	George Hamilton's Dead (p/s, with poster)	12

GOLDEN EARRING(S)

68	Capitol CL 15552	I've Just Lost Somebody/The Truth About Arthur (as Golden Earrings)	20
68	Capitol CL 15567	Dong Dong Di Ki Di Gi Dong/Wake Up - Breakfast (as Golden Earrings)	10
69	Major Minor MM 601	Just A Little Peace In My Heart/Remember My Friend (as Golden Earrings)	15
69	Major Minor MM 633	It's Alright But It Could Be Better/Where Will I Be (as Golden Earrings)	8
70	Major Minor MM 679	Another Forty-Five Miles/I Can't Get Hold Of Her	15
70	Polydor BM 56514	That Day/Words I Need	18
70	Polydor 2001 073	Back Home/This Is The Time Of Year	8
72	Polydor 2001 346	Buddy Joe/Avalanche	5
73	Track 2094 116	Radar Love/Just Like Vince Taylor	5
74	Track 2094 121	Instant Poetry/From Heaven, From Hell	5
74	Track 2094 126	Candy's Going Bad/She Flies On Strange Wings	5
75	Track 2094 130	Ce Soir/Lucky Number	5
69	Major Minor SMLP 65	EIGHT MILES HIGH (LP)	90
70	Polydor 2310049	GOLDEN EARRING (LP, gatefold sleeve)	50
71	Polydor 2310 135	SEVEN TEARS (LP)	30
72	Polydor 2310 210	TOGETHER (LP)	18

MINT VALUE £

73	Polydor 2482 329	GOLDEN EARRING (LP)	12
73	Track 2406 109	HEARING EARRING (LP, braille sleeve)	18
73	Track 2406 112	MOONTAN (LP, gatefold sleeve with insert)	18
75	Polydor 2480 330	TO THE HILT (LP)	12

GOLDEN FLEECE

67	Decca F 12669	Athens 6 a.m./Girl From Syracuse	6

GOLDEN GATE QUARTET

53	Columbia SCM 5054	Moses Smote The Waters/Bones, Bones, Bones	5
56	Columbia SEG 7700	SINGS GREAT SPIRITUALS (EP)	6
58	Fontana TFR 6009	THAT GOLDEN CHARIOT (10" LP)	20
59	Columbia 33SX 1172	SHOUT FOR JOY! (LP)	15

GOLDEN GATE STRINGS

65	Columbia DB 7634	Mr. Tambourine Man/With God On Our Side	20

GOLDEN HORDE

80s	Hot Wire HWS 855	Young And Happy/Little UFO/Fiona (p/s)	5
85	Hot Wire WAY OUT 1	DIG THAT CRAZY GRAVE (EP)	5
85	Hot Wire/I.D. NOSE 7	THE CHOCOLATE BISCUIT CONSPIRACY (LP)	12

GOLDFRAPP

00	Mute 12MUTE 247	Lovely Head/(Stare Mesto Mix)/(Mis World Mix) (12", p/s)	15
00	Mute 12MUTE 253	Utopia/(New Ears Mix)/(Sunroof Mix) (12", p/s)	10
01	Mute 12MUTE 259	Human/(Calexico Instrumental)/(Massey's Neanderthal Mix) (12", p/s)	10
00	Mute STUMM 188	FELT MOUNTAIN (LP, with inner)	12
03	Mute STUMM 196	BLACK CHERRY (LP)	12
05	Mute STUMM 250	SUPERNATURE (LP)	12

GOLDIE (& GINGERBREADS)

(see also Ten Wheel Drive)

65	Decca F 12070	Can't You Hear My Heartbeat/Little Boy	15
65	Decca F 12126	That's Why I Love You/Skip	15
65	Decca F 12199	Sailor Boy/Please Please	15
66	Immediate IM 026	Goin' Back/Headlines (solo)	30
66	Fontana TF 693	I Do/Think About The Good Times (solo)	15
69	Decca F 12931	Can't You Hear My Heartbeat/That's Why I Love You	5

JOHN GOLDING

74	Cottage 101S	DISCARDED VERSE (LP, 2,000 only)	18

GOLD LEAF

73	Penbrook PEN 1	After The Rain/The Sun	150

VIVIEN GOLDMAN

(see also Public Image Ltd)

81	Window WIN 1	Launderette/Private Armies (gatefold p/s, with PiL)	10
81	Window 12WIN 1	Launderette/Private Armies (12", p/s, with PiL)	20

ANNA GOLDRICK

60s	Polydor 2384030	IT'S HERSELF (LP)	25

GOLDRUSH

73	Decca F13380	For A Few Dollars More/No More - No Less	6

BOBBY GOLDSBORO

63	Stateside SS 193	The Runaround/The Letter	20
63	United Artists UP 1046	See The Funny Little Clown/Hello Loser	10
64	United Artists UP 1054	Whenever He Holds You/If She Was Mine	10
65	United Artists UP 1079	Little Things/I Just Can't Go On Pretending	15
65	United Artists UP 1091	Voodoo Woman/It Breaks My Heart	10
65	United Artists UP 1104	If You Wait For Love/If You've Got A Heart	10
66	United Artists UP 1120	Broomstick Cowboy/Ain't Got Time For Happy	10
66	United Artists UP 1128	It's Too Late/I'm Goin' Home	15
66	United Artists UP 1128	It's Too Late/I'm Goin' Home (DJ copy)	45
66	United Artists UP 1135	I Know You Better Than That/When Your Love Has Gone	5
66	United Artists UP 1146	Take Your Love/Longer Than Forever	25
67	United Artists UP 1156	It Hurts Me/Pity The Fool	10
67	United Artists UP 1166	No Fun At The Fair/Hold On	35
67	United Artists UP 1177	Too Many People/Goodbye To All You Women	50
67	United Artists UP 1177	Too Many People/Goodbye To All You Women (DJ copy)	85
68	United Artists UP 2223	Autumn Of My Life/She Chased Me	10
69	United Artists UP 2264	Love Arrester/Dissatisfied Man	15
69	United Artists UP 35034	Muddy Mississippi Line/Richer Man Than I	8
69	United Artists UP 35053	Letter To Emily/Tomorrow Is Forgotten	5
73	United Artists UP 25558	Summer (The First Time)/Childhood - 1949	5
65	United Artists UEP 1006	LITTLE THINGS (EP)	45
66	United Artists UEP 1016	THE TALENTED BOBBY GOLDSBORO (EP)	45
65	United Artists ULP 1118	I CAN'T STOP LOVING YOU (LP)	35
66	United Artists (S)ULP 1135	IT'S TOO LATE (LP)	35
67	United Artists (S)ULP 1163	SOLID GOLDSBORO - GREATEST HITS (LP)	22
68	United Artists (S)ULP 1195	HONEY (LP, black label)	20
68	United Artists (S)ULP 1206	WORD PICTURES (LP)	20
69	United Artists UAS 29008	TODAY (LP)	18

GOLDSMITH

83	Bedlam BLM 001	Life Is Killing Me/Music Man (p/s)	50

JERRY GOLDSMITH

(see also under Soundtrack LPs)

74	EMI 2118	Theme from Papillon/Survival	6

GOLDTOP

88	Gee Street GOLD 001	My Introduction (12")	8

MINT VALUE £

GOL GAPPAS

86	el GPO 21	West 14/Roman (p/s)	12

GOLGOTHA

84	Golgotha GOTH 002	DANGEROUS GAMES (Dangerous Games/Old England's Green/Air/ THE GREAT DIVIDE (EP, no p/s)	80
90	Communique CMGLP 003	UNMAKER OF WORLDS (EP, p/s)	15

GOLIARD

76	Broadside BRO 127	FORTUNE MY FOE (LP, with booklet)	18

GOLIATH

70	CBS 5312	Port And Lemon Lady/I Heard About A Friend	10
70	CBS 64229	GOLIATH (LP)	150

GOLLIWOGS

(see also Creedence Clearwater Revival)

66	Vocalion VF 9266	Brown-Eyed Girl/You Better Be Careful	50
67	Vocalion VF 9283	Fragile Child/Fight Fire	50
72	Fantasy FAN 5996	GOLLIWOGS (LP, pressed in U.S. for U.K. distribution)	15

GOLLUM & GARY D

(see also DJ Gollum)

97	UK 44 RMX 3	Black Arrows (Lord Of The Rings Mix)/Black Arrows (Poisoned Tip Mix)/ Black Arrows (Original E.D.M. Mix) (12", p/s)	10

BENNY GOLSON

59	Esquire 32-125	GONE WITH GOLSON (LP)	15
60	Esquire 32-105	GROOVIN' WITH GOLSON (LP)	15

BENNY GOLSON & ART FARMER

(see also Art Farmer)

62	Pye International 7N 25120	Blues March/Serenata	5
65	Stateside SL 10150	STOCKHOLM SOJOURN (LP)	12

IAN GOMM

78	Albion ION 5	24 Hour Service/Black And White	6

GONADS

82	Secret SHH 131	PURE PUNK FOR NOW PEOPLE (EP)	8

GONDOLIERS

58	Starlite ST45 001	Fly, Seagull, Fly/God's Green Acres	15

RON GONELLA

60s	Lismor LILP 5017	FIDDLER'S FANCY (LP)	12

GONG

(see also Mother Gong, Gilli Smyth & Mother Gong, Daevid Allen, Steve Hillage, Clearlight, Radio Actors, Sphynx, Tim Blake, Comus)

71	Philips 6332 033	CONTINENTAL CIRCUS (LP, soundtrack)	60
71	Caroline C1520	CAMEMBERT ELECTRIQUE (LP, 'twin' label)	20
73	Virgin V 2002	RADIO GNOME INVISIBLE PART 1 - THE FLYING TEAPOT (LP, gatefold sleeve original pressing with black & white label design)	30
73	Virgin V 2007	RADIO GNOME INVISIBLE PART 2 - ANGEL'S EGG (LP, gatefold sleeve, initially with b&w label; with booklet)	40
73	Virgin V2007	RADIO GNOME INVISIBLE PART 2 - ANGEL'S EGG (LP, gatefold sleeve, initially with b&w label; without booklet)	15
73	Virgin V 2007	RADIO GNOME INVISIBLE PART 2 - ANGEL'S EGG (LP, gatefold sleeve, initially with b&w label; without book)	12
74	Virgin VC 502	CAMEMBERT ELECTRIQUE (LP)	12
74	Virgin V 2019	YOU (LP, with lyric insert, coloured 'twin' label)	15
76	Virgin V 2046	SHAMAL (LP, gatefold)	12
77	Virgin VGD 3501	LIVE ETC. (2-LP, with cut-out cover & inner sleeves)	12

GONG/CAMEL/HENRY COW/GLOBAL TRUCKING COMPANY

(see also Camel, Henry Cow, Global Trucking Company)

73	Greasy Truckers GT 4997	GREASY TRUCKERS (2-LP, 1 side each; with insert)	18

GONKS

(see also Twinkle)

64	Decca F 11984	The Gonk Song/That's All Right, Mamma	30
70s	LISMOR LILP 5017	FIDDLERS FANCY (LP)	12

PAUL GONSALVES

(see also Tubby Hayes & Paul Gonsalves)

64	Vocalion LAE 587	BOOM JACKIE BOOM CHICK (LP)	900
70	Deram SML 1064	HUMMINGBIRD (LP)	60

GONZALEZ

74	EMI EMC 3046	GONZALEZ (LP)	50
75	EMI EMC 3100	OUR ONLY WEAPON IS OUR MUSIC (LP)	18

BELLE GONZALEZ

(see also Mark Wirtz)

72	Columbia DB 8852	Bottles/I Hate Sunday	18
65	Jupiter JEPOC 37	POETS SET IN JAZZ (EP, as Belle Gonzalez & Sextet)	18
66	Jupiter JEPOC 39	CONTEMPORARY POETS SET IN JAZZ (EP)	18
72	Columbia SCX 6484	BELLE (LP)	80

DOUGLAS GOOD & GINNY PLENTY

68	Stateside SS 2104	Sunny And Me/Living In A World Of Make Believe	5

JACK GOOD'S FAT NOISE

60	Decca F 11233	The Fat Washerwoman/The Fat Noise	12

MINT VALUE £

ELMER GOODBODY

76	Charisma CB 279	Do Ya/Mad About You	8

GOODBYE MR. MACKENZIE

(see also Garbage)o

84	Scruples YTS 1	Death Of A Salesman/LINDY BERGMAN: Locked Inside Your Prison (no p/s, 500 only)	25
86	Precious Org. JEWEL 2	The Rattler/Candlestick Park (p/s)	6
86	Precious Org. JEWEL 2T	The Rattler/Candlestick Park/The End (12", p/s)	10
86	Clandestine MACK 1	Face To Face/Secrets/Good Deeds (12", p/s, 1,000 only)	10
90	Parlophone PCS 7345	HAMMER AND TONGS (LP, unreleased, white label test pressings only)	40

GOOD EARTH

(see also First Impression/Good Earth, Mungo Jerry, Ray Dorset)

68	Saga FID 2112	IT'S HARD ROCK AND ALL THAT (LP)	15
70	Saga FID 8157	IN THE SUMMERTIME (LP, with tracks by Macon Jug)	12

GOOD GUYS

(see also Byron Lee & Dragonaires)

70	Duke DU 82	Death Rides/Destruction	10
70	Duke DU 83	Wreck It Up/Dynamic Groove	10
70	Duke DU 84	Happiness/Latissimo	8

PHILIP GOODHAND-TAIT (& STORMSVILLE SHAKERS)

(see also Circus, Larry Williams, Love Affair)

66	Parlophone R 5448	I'm Gonna Put Some Hurt On You/It's A Lie (with Stormsville Shakers)	20
66	Parlophone R 5498	No Problem/What More Do You Want (with Stormsville Shakers)	25
66	Parlophone R 5547	You Can't Take Love/J.C. Greaseburger (solo)	20
70	DJM DJLPS 411	REHEARSAL (LP)	15
71	DJM DJLPS 416	I THINK I'LL WRITE A SONG (LP, gatefold)	15
72	DJM DJLPS 425	SONGFALL (LP, gatefold)	20
76	Chrysalis CHR 1113	OCEANS AWAY (LP)	12
77	Chrysalis CHR 1146	TEACHING AN OLD DOG NEW TRICKS (LP, with insert)	12

JOHNNY GOODISON

(see also Quotations, Johnny B. Great)

70	Deram DM 319	A Little Understanding/One Mistake	20

LEMME B GOOD

65	Mercury MF 874	I Can't Stop Myself/Mother May I	8

GOODLETTSVILLE FIVE

64	London HLW 9854	Eef/Bailey's Gone Eefing	8

JOHN GOODLUCK

74	Tradition TSR 015	SUFFOLK MIRACLE (LP, with insert)	25
75	Sweet Folk/Country SFA 047	SPEED THE PLOUGH: TRADITIONAL SONGS OF SUFFOLK (LP)	25
88	Big Ben FE 065	THE MAN WHO PUT THE ENGINE IN THE CHIP SHOP: MORE RAILWAY SONGS OF DAVE GOULDER (LP)	12

DAVE GOODMAN & FRIENDS

78	The Label TLR 008	Justifiable Homicide/Take Down Your Fences (p/s, 1st 15,000 on red vinyl)	8

(N.B. rumoured copies with 'Steve Jones & Paul Cook' credit on the sleeve DO NOT exist)

GOOD MISSIONARIES

(see also Mark Perry, Alternative TV)

80	Kif KIF'S 1	Good Missionary (Parts 1 & 2) (p/s)	5
80	Unnormality NORM 001	VIBING UP THE SENILE WORLD (The Good Missionary Part 1 [live]/ The Good Missionary Part/Kif Kif's Free Freak Out [live]) (EP, 1,000 only)	5
79	Deptford Fun City DLP 04	FIRE FROM HEAVEN (LP)	15

GOOD RATS

69	London HLR 10237	The Hobo/The Truth Is Gone	6

GOOD SHIP LOLLIPOP

69	Ember EMB S 276	Maxwell's Silver Hammer/How Does It Feel (p/s)	12
69	Ember EMB S 276	Maxwell's Silver Hammer/How Does It Feel	6

GOOD TIME LOSERS

67	Fontana TF 791	Trafalgar Square/Where Did My Heart Go	6

GOODTIMERS

62	Fontana H 360	It's Twistin' Time/Twisting Train	10

GOOD VIBRATIONS

70	Ember EMB S 270	Call Me Lightning/Nantucket Ferry	6

ROD GOODWAY

90	Woronzow WOO 12	ETHEREAL COUNTERBALANCE (LP)	18

RON GOODWIN CONCERT ORCHESTRA

(see also 20th Century Fox Orchestra, Parlophone Pops Orchestra)

53	Parlophone MSP 6035	Limelight/The Song From Moulin Rouge	18
53	Parlophone MSP 6055	Tropical Mirage/The Man Between	12
54	Parlophone MSP 6064	Grand Waltz Of The Flowers And Dragonflies/The Lobster Quadrille	10
54	Parlophone MSP 6103	The Sons Of The High Seas/Guadalcanal March	12
54	Parlophone MSP 6115	Cara Mia/Three Coins In The Fountain	12
54	Parlophone MSP 6136	Midnight Blue/On The Waterfront	12
55	Parlophone MSP 6159	Under The Linded Tree/Last Love	10
56	Parlophone MSP 6221	Concetta/Handyman	10
56	Parlophone 45 R-4235	War And Peace/The Christmas Tree	10
57	Parlophone R 4297	Skiffling Strings (Swinging Sweetheart)/I'll Find You	15
57	Parlophone R 4349	Swedish Polka/Lingering Lovers	12
58	Parlophone R 4391	Colonel Bogey And The River Kwai March/Laughing Sailor	8
58	Parlophone R 4503	Latin Lovers/Blue Grotto	10

			MINT VALUE £
58	Parlophone R 4608	Lolita/All Strung Up	10
59	Parlophone R 4537	The Whirlpool Theme/Herman's Theme From Whirlpool	10
60	Parlophone R 4632	Tracey's Theme/My Girl	10
60	Parlophone R 4663	Love Theme From Ben Hur/Theme From The Unforgiven	10
60	Parlophone R 4687	Walkin' Down To Washington/Sunshine Cruise	10
61	Parlophone R 4821	Murder she Says/Double Scotch	15
63	Parlophone R 5053	Moonstrike/Midsummer Madness	12
64	Parlophone R 5146	633 Squadron/Love Them From Operation Crossbow	10
65	Parlophone R 5239	The Fat Man/Colonel Schmendrick	10
65	Parlophone R 5394	Theme From The Early Birds/Theme From The Alphabet Murders	8
69	United Artists UP 35040	Battle Of Britain Theme/Luftwaffe March	10
54	Parlophone PMD 1014	FILM FAVOURITES (10" LP)	15
56	Parlophone PMD 1038	MUSIC TO SET YOU DREAMING (10" LP)	15
58	Parlophone PCS 3002	MUSIC FOR AN ARABIAN NIGHT (LP)	15
58	Parlophone PCS 3006	OUT OF THIS WORLD! (LP)	15
64	United Artists ULP 1071	633 SQUADRON (LP, soundtrack)	20
65	Stateside SL 10136	THOSE MAGNIFICENT MEN IN THEIR FLYING MACHINES (LP, soundtrack)	20
66	Polydor 582 004	THE TRAP (LP, soundtrack)	40
68	Stateside (S)SL 10259	DECLINE AND FALL ... OF A BIRDWATCHER (LP, soundtrack)	80
69	Paramount SPFL 255	MONTE CARLO OR BUST! (LP, soundtrack)	40
76	EMI EMC 3148	ESCAPE FROM THE DARK (LP, soundtrack)	15

GOOFERS

55	Vogue Coral Q 72051	Hearts Of Stone/You're The One	50
55	Vogue Coral Q 72051	Hearts Of Stone/You're The One (78)	20
55	Vogue Coral Q 72074	Flip, Flop And Fly/My Babe	50
55	Vogue Coral Q 72074	Flip, Flop And Fly/My Babe (78)	20
55	Vogue Coral Q 72094	Goofy Drybones/Nare	30
55	Vogue Coral Q 72094	Goofy Drybones/Nare (78)	15
56	Vogue Coral Q 72124	Sick! Sick! Sick!/Twenty One	25
56	Vogue Coral Q 72124	Sick! Sick! Sick!/Twenty One (78)	15
56	Vogue Coral Q 72171	Tear Drop Motel/Tennessee Rock And Roll	40
56	Vogue Coral Q 72171	Tear Drop Motel/Tennessee Rock And Roll (78)	25
57	Vogue Coral Q 72267	Wow!/Push, Push, Push Cart	25
57	Vogue Coral Q 72267	Wow!/Push, Push, Push Cart (78)	25
57	Vogue Coral Q 72289	The Dipsy Doodle/Take This Heart	25
57	Vogue Coral Q 72289	The Dipsy Doodle/Take This Heart (78)	15

GOOM

72	Pye 7N 25587	Massai Part 1/Massai Part 2	15

DEREK GOOM

80	BBCRESL 84	Julient Bravo/Madelena (p/s)	6

GOONS

(see also Peter Sellers, Spike Milligan, Michael Bentine, Famous Eccles, Eric Sykes)

56	Flexidisc	Barclays Bank (p/s)	10
56	Parlophone R 4251	My September Love/You Gotta Go Oww (with Eric Sykes)	15
56	Decca F 10756	I'm Walking Backwards For Christmas/Bluebottle Blues	15
56	Decca F 10780	The Ying Tong Song/Bloodnok's Rock 'N' Roll Call	15
57	Decca F 10885	Eeh! Ah! Oh! Ooh!/I Love You	15
57	Decca F 10945	A Russian Love Song/Whistle Your Cares Away	10
56	Decca DFE 6396	THE GOONS (EP, tri centre)	12
56	Decca DFE 6396	THE GOONS (EP, round centre)	8
64	Decca LF 1332	UNCHAINED MELODIES (10" LP)	25
59	Parlophone PMC 1108	BEST OF THE GOON SHOWS (LP)	12
60	Parlophone PMC 1129	BEST OF THE GOON SHOWS (NO. 2) (LP)	12

SAM GOPAL

(see also Hawkwind, Motorhead, Vamp, Isaac Guillory, Clark-Hutchinson, G. F. Fitzgerald)

69	Stable STA 5602	Horse/Back Door Man (unissued, existence unconfirmed)	0
69	Stable SLE 8001	Escalator/Angry Faces/Cold Embrace/The Sky is Burning (LP sampler)	70
69	Stable SLE 8001	ESCALATOR (LP, gatefold sleeve, black/silver label)	300
68	Stable SLE 8001	ESCALATOR (LP, gatefold sleeve, label stating "DJ Copy not for resale)	400

RABBI JOSEPH GORDAN

(see under 'R')

PETE(R) GORDENO

61	Fontana H 319	Be My Girl/Haven't Got Time (as Pete Gordeno)	8
62	Parlophone R 4862	I Got Eyes/You're Following Me	8
76	Zoot 1001	WITH FEELING (LP)	12

GORDON

(see under Gordon Waller)

ANITA GORDON

55	Brunswick 05456	Lonesome Like Nobody Knows/His Hands	10

BARRY GORDON

56	MGM MGM 928	I Can't Whistle/The Milkman's Polka	10
56	MGM MGM 935	Rock Around Mother Goose/Nuttin' For Christmas	22

CHANCE GORDON

63	Pye 7N 15475	Instant Love/You Don't Want My Love	20

CHRIS GORDON

68	Derpy ADMLP 390	IN THE EARLY MORNING RAIN (LP)	200

CURTIS GORDON

57	Mercury MT 163	Sixteen/Cry, Cry (78)	20

DEXTER GORDON

(see also Wardell Gray)

60s	Fontana Jazz FJL 907	MASTER SWINGERS (LP, with Wardell Gray)	15

MINT VALUE £

JOE GORDON (FOLK FOUR)

59	HMV POP 600	Gotta Travel On/Ho Ro My Nutbrown Maid	5
59	HMV POP 634	Dream Lover/Dance To Your Daddy	10
60	HMV POP 737	Football Crazy/By The Bright Shining Light Of The Moon	6
59	HMV 7EG 8454	JOE GORDON FOLK HOUR (EP)	15
60	HMV CLP 1379	THE GAY GORDON (LP)	12

NOELE GORDON

67	Music For Pleasure MFP 50236	NOELE GORDON SINGS (LP)	12

PETER GORDON

62	Parlophone R 4931	Down By The Riverside/The Boys Kept Hanging Around	10
65	Decca F 12088	Have You Looked Into Your Heart?/Don't Come To Me	8
68	MCA MU 1009	Born To Be Wanted/Shout It From The Hilltop	5
68	MCA MU 1058	My Girl Maria/I Appreciate So Much	5

PHIL GORDON

55	Brunswick 05481	Get A Load Of That Crazy Walk/Strip Polka	10
56	Brunswick 05545	Down The Road Apiece/I'm Gonna Move To The Outskirts Of Town	40

ROBERT GORDON WITH LINK WRAY

(see also Link Wray)

77	Private Stock PVTS 127	Endless Sleep & The Fool/The Fool (12", B-side plays at 78rpm)	8
77	Private Stock PVLP 1027	ROBERT GORDON WITH LINK WRAY (LP)	15

RONNIE GORDON

63	R&B JB 127	Shake Some Time/Comin' Home	25

ROSCOE GORDON

60	Top Rank JAR 332	Just A Little Bit/Goin' Home (as Rosco Gordon)	30
63	Stateside SS 204	Just A Little Bit/What I Wouldn't Do	25
65	Vocalion V-P 9245	Keep On Doggin'/Bad Dream	30
65	Island WI 256	Surely I Love You/What You Do To Me	25
66	Island WI 272	No More Doggin'/Goin' Home	30

TONY GORDON

(see also Alton Ellis)

73	Grape GR 3056	Be True (actually by Alton Ellis)/Navajo Trail	6

VINCENT GORDON

(see also Don Drummond Junior)

69	Coxsone CS 7085	Soul Trombone/LARRY & ALVIN: Your Cheating Heart	35
69	Duke DU 37	Everybody Bawlin'/SILVERTONES: Come Look Here	15
69	Crab CRAB 16	Walking By/VICEROYS: Promises Promises	12
74	Big Shot BI 630	Come Go With Me/SKIN, FLESH & BONES: Dub Ali Dub	7
75	DIP DLP 5001	MUSICAL BONES (LP, plain sleeve, white label)	40
79	Attack TACK 10	Liquid Horns (as Vin Gordon & Corner Shots)/ JUNIOR & CORNER SHOTS: Liquidator (12")	18
70s	Trojan TRO 9058	Liquid Horns/JUNIOR: Liquidator	10

CHARLIE GORE

(see also Hawkshaw Hawkins, Ruby Wright)

54	Parlophone CMSP 19	I'll Find Somebody/Heaven Sent You To Me (export issue)	25
54	Parlophone DP 379	I'll Find Somebody/Heaven Sent You To Me (78)	10
54	Parlophone CMSP 26	Two Of A Kind/It's A Long Walk Back To Town (export issue)	20
54	Parlophone DP 397	Two Of A Kind/It's A Long Walk Back To Town (78)	10
54	Parlophone CMSP 30	I Didn't Know/Oh! Mis'rable Love (export issue)	20

LESLEY GORE

63	Mercury AMT 1205	It's My Party/Danny	8
63	Mercury AMT 1210	Judy's Turn To Cry/Just Let Me Cry	8
63	Mercury AMT 1213	She's A Fool/The Old Crowd	8
64	Mercury MF 803	You Don't Own Me/Run Bobby Run	10
64	Mercury MF 810	That's The Way Boys Are/That's The Way The Ball Bounces	10
64	Mercury MF 821	I Don't Wanna Be A Loser/It's Gotta Be You	10
64	Mercury MF 829	Maybe I Know/Wonder Boy	7
64	Mercury MF 837	Sometimes I Wish I Were A Boy/Hey Now	10
65	Mercury MF 846	The Look Of Love/Little Girl Go Home	12
65	Mercury MF 862	Sunshine Lollipops And Rainbows/You've Come Back	12
65	Mercury MF 872	My Town, My Guy And Me/Girl In Love	15
65	Mercury MF 889	I Won't Love You Anymore (Sorry)/No Matter What You Do	15
66	Mercury MF 902	Young Love/I Just Don't Know If I Can	12
66	Mercury MF 963	California Nights/I'm Going Out (The Same Way I Came In)	12
66	Mercury MF 984	I'm Fallin' Down/Summer And Sandy	15
68	Mercury MF 1017	Magic Colours/It's A Happening World	10
75	A&M AMS 7184	Immortality/Give It To Me, Sweet Thing	5
64	Mercury 10017 MCE	LESLEY GORE (EP)	40
63	Mercury MMC 14127	I'LL CRY IF I WANT TO (LP)	40
63	Mercury 20001 MCL	SINGS OF MIXED-UP HEARTS (LP)	30
64	Mercury 20020 MCL	BOYS BOYS BOYS (LP)	30
64	Mercury 20033 MCL	GIRL TALK (LP)	30
65	Mercury 20071 MCL	MY TOWN, MY GUY & ME (LP)	30
65	Mercury 20076 MCL	ALL ABOUT LOVE (LP)	30
67	Wing WL 1183	GIRL TALK (LP, reissue)	12

GORGONI, MARTIN & TAYLOR

72	Buddah 2011-137	Toly Toly Guyluesha/I Can Make You Cry	7
72	Buddah 2318 067	GORGONI, MARTIN AND TAYLOR (LP)	15

GORILLAS

(see also Hammersmith Gorillas)

78	Raw RWLP 103	MESSAGE TO THE WORLD (LP, with insert)	20

MINT VALUE £

GORILLAZ
(see also Blur, Damon Albarn)

01	7RDJ 6552	Clint Eastwood/Dracula (33 rpm dinked 7" - cartoon die-cut stickered sleeve)	12
01	Parlophone (no cat no)	Tomorrow Comes Today/Tomorrow Dub (7" white label, stamped promo)	8
02	EMI SMVG 004	L'IL DUB CHEFIN (10" 4-track sampler)	10
05	Parlophone R 6663	Feel Good Inc./68 State (picture disc in die-cut card sleeve)	6
01	Parlophone 724353113810	GORILLAZ (2-LP)	18

GORKY'S ZYGOTIC MYNCI

93	Ankst ANKST/GZM 040	PATIO (10" EP)	20
94	Ankst ANKST 048	Merched Yn Neud Gwallt Eu Gilydd/Bocs Angelica/ When You Laugh At Your Own Garden In A Blazer (p/s)	6
95	Ankst ANKST 053	Pentref Wrth Y Môr/The Game Of Eyes/Cwpwrdd Sadwrn (p/s)	6
95	Ankst ANKST 058	Gewn Ni Gorffen/12 Impressionistic Soundscapes (clear vinyl, die-cut p/s, mail order only, 1,000 copies)	10
96	Ankst ANKST 068	AMBER GAMBLER EP (10", p/s)	8
97	Fontana 534 769	BARAFUNDLE (LP)	15
98	Mercury ANKST GZM 5	Let's Get Together (In Our Minds)/Billy And The Sugarloaf Mountain/ Hwiangerdd Mar (numbered p/s)	7

JOHN GORMAN
(see also Scaffold, Grimms)

73	Island WIP 6151	WPC Hodges/I Remember	5
77	DJM DJF 20491	GO MAN GORMAN (LP)	15

EYDIE GORMÉ
(see also Steve Lawrence)

54	Vogue Coral Q 2014	Frenesi/Climb Up The Wall	10
54	Vogue Coral Q 2027	Tea For Two/Sure	10
55	Vogue Coral Q 72092	Give A Fool A Chance/A Girl Can't Say	10
55	Vogue Coral Q 72103	Soldier Boy/What Is The Secret Of Your Success?	10
56	London HL 8227	Sincerely Yours/Come Home	15
57	HMV POP 400	Kiss In Your Eyes/Your Kisses Kill Me	7
58	HMV POP 432	Love Me Forever/Until They Sail	10
58	HMV POP 493	You Need Hands/The Gentleman Is A Dope	6
58	HMV POP 513	Gotta Have Rain/To You, From Me	6
58	HMV POP 529	Dormi, Dormi, Dormi/Be Careful, It's My Heart	7
59	HMV POP 577	Separate Tables/The Voice Of My Heart	8
59	HMV POP 616	I'm Yours/Don't Take Your Love From Me	6
60	HMV POP 767	The Dance Is Over/Too Young To Know	10
62	CBS AAG 105	Yes, My Darling Daughter/Sonny Boy	8
63	CBS AAG 131	Blame It On The Bossa Nova/Guess I Should Have Loved Him More	7
63	CBS AAG 149	Don't Try To Fight It Baby/Theme From Light Fantastic	10
63	CBS AAG 163	I Want To Stay Here/Ain't Love (as STEVE & EYDIE)	5
63	CBS AAG 170	Everybody Go Home/The Message	10
63	CBS AAG 178	I Can't Stop Talking About You/To The Movies We Go (AS STEVE & EYDIE)	7
67	CBS 202470	Everybody Go Home/The Message (reissue)	5
59	HMV 7EG 8547	LOVE IS A SEASON (EP, also stereo [GES 5789])	8
59	HMV 7EG 8562	I'LL REMEMBER APRIL (EP, also stereo [GES 5795])	8
59	HMV 7EG 8409	EXCITING EYDIE (EP)	8
59	HMV 7EG 8474	FINE AND DANDY (EP)	8
59	HMV 7EG 8515	WHEN YOUR LOVER HAS GONE (EP)	8
64	CBS AGG 20047	THE SWEETEST SOUNDS (EP)	8
57	Coral LVA 9086	EYDIE GORME'S DELIGHT (LP)	15
57	HMV CLP 1170	SWINGS THE BLUES (LP)	12
58	HMV CLP 1201	VAMPS THE ROARING 20's (LP)	12

FRANK GORSHIN

66	Pye International 7N 25402	The Riddler/Never Let Her Go (in p/s)	75
66	Pye International 7N 25402	The Riddler/Never Let Her Go	35

PETER GOSLING

70	Sonet SON 2010	Values/Peace	10

GOSPEL CLASSICS

68	Chess CRS 8080	More Love, That's What We Need/You Need Faith	100
68	Chess CRS 8080	More Love, That's What We Need/You Need Faith (DJ copy)	150

GOSPELFOLK

69	Emblem 7DR 324	PRODIGAL (LP)	200

GOSPEL GARDEN
(see also Dimples, Amazing Blondel)

68	Camp 602 006	Finders Keepers/Just A Tear	30

GOSPEL OAK

70	Uni UNS 527	Recollections Of Jessica/Brown Haired Girl	6
70	Uni UNLS 113	GOSPEL OAK (LP)	70

GOSPEL PEARLS

63	Liberty LBY 1191	THE GOSPEL PEARLS (LP)	25

GOTHIC HORIZON

70	Argo AFW 102	The Jason Lodge Poetry Book/Wilhelmina Before Sunrise	20
71	Argo AFW 104	Marjorie/Song	18
72	Argo AFW 107	If You Can Smile/Thoughts	12
72	Argo AFW 108	Girl With Guitar/Can't Bear To Think About You	12
71	Argo ZFB 26	THE JASON LODGE POETRY BOOK (LP)	65
72	Argo ZDA 150	TOMORROW IS ANOTHER DAY (LP)	60

KEVIN GOULD

70s	Myrrh MYR 1028	TRUE STORIES BY (LP)	12

MINT VALUE £

MORTON GOULD

60 RCA Victor RD 27028 JUNGLE DRUMS (LP) ... 20

TERRY GOULD

69 Sing SING 1001 SEVERAL KINDS OF LOVING (LP) ... 12

DALE GOULDER & LIZ DYER

70 Argo ZFB 10 JANUARY MAN (LP) ... 40
71 Argo ZFB 30 RAVEN & CROW (LP) ... 40

DAVE GOULDER

73 Big Ben BB 0004 REQUIEM FOR STEAM: THE RAILWAY SONGS OF DAVE GOULDER (LP) ... 15

GRAHAM GOULDMAN

(see also 10cc, Whirlwinds, Mockingbirds, High Society, Frabjoy & Runcible Spoon, Manchester Mob, Garden Odyssey Enterprise, Friday Browne, Doctor Father)

66 Decca F 12334 Stop! Stop! Stop! (Or Honey I'll Be Gone...)/Better To Have Loved And Lost ... 150
68 RCA Victor RCA 1667 Upstairs, Downstairs/Chestnut ... 30
69 Spark SRL 1026 Windmills Of Your Mind/Harvey's Theme (as Graham Gouldman Orchestra) ... 15
72 CBS 7739 Nowhere To Go/Growing Older ... 7

GOVE

69 London HLE 10295 Sunday Morning Early/Death Letter Blues ... 12
72 UNI UNs547 Carry On (Till The Band Adjourns)/I've Been Thinking Of You Lately ... 8

JOHN GRAAS SEPTET

54 London RE-P 1003 FRENCH HORN VOL. 1 (EP) ... 10

GRAB GRAB THE HADDOCK

(see also Marine Girls, Tracey Thorne)

84 Cherry Red 12CHERRY 83 THREE SONGS BY GRAB GRAB THE HADDOCK (12" EP) ... 8

MICK GRABHAM

(see also Plastic Penny, Cochise, Procol Harum)

72 United Artists UP 35391 On Fire For You Baby/Sweet Blossom Woman ... 5
72 United Artists UAS 29341 MICK THE LAD (LP) ... 20

GRACE

80 MCA MCA 628 Fire Of London/Beatnik (p/s) ... 5
81 MCA MCA 667 Billy Boy/Ad Mad (p/s) ... 15

GRAME GRACE

75 RCA SF 8418 HAIL ME (LP, with insert) ... 15
76 RCA RCA 2633 Flambouyant Streak/Don't Hang Around Like That ... 6

CHARLIE GRACIE

57 Parlophone R 4290 Butterfly/Ninety-Nine Ways (initially gold lettering on label) ... 50
57 Parlophone R 4290 Butterfly/Ninety-Nine Ways (later pressing with silver lettering on label) ... 25
57 Parlophone R 4313 Fabulous/Just Lookin' (initially gold lettering on label) ... 50
57 Parlophone R 4313 Fabulous/Just Lookin' (later pressing with silver lettering on label) ... 25
57 London HL 8467 Wandering Eyes/I Love You So Much It Hurts (tri-centre) ... 25
57 London HLU 8521 Cool Baby/You Got A Heart Like A Rock (tri-centre) ... 30
57 London HLU 8521 Cool Baby/You Got A Heart Like A Rock (78) ... 10
58 London HLU 8596 Crazy Girl/Dressin' Up (tri-centre) ... 35
58 London HLU 8596 Crazy Girl/Dressin' Up (78) ... 10
59 Coral Q 72362 Doodlebug/Hurry Up, Buttercup (tri-centre) ... 30
59 Coral Q 72362 Doodlebug/Hurry Up, Buttercup (78) ... 30
59 Coral Q 72373 Angel Of Love/I'm A Fool, That's Why (tri-centre) ... 22
59 Coral Q 72373 Angel Of Love/I'm A Fool, That's Why (later round centre) ... 15
59 Coral Q 72373 Angel Of Love/I'm A Fool, That's Why (78) ... 35
59 Coral Q 72381 Oh-Well-A/Because I Love You So ... 25
59 Coral Q 72381 Oh-Well-A/Because I Love You So (78) ... 40
60 Columbia DB 4477 The Race/I Looked For You ... 20
62 London HLU 9603 Pretty Baby/Night And Day, U.S.A. ... 20
65 Stateside SS 402 He'll Never Love You Like I Do/Keep My Love Next To Your Heart ... 70
65 Stateside SS 402 He'll Never Love You Like I Do/Keep My Love Next To Your Heart (DJ copy) ... 150
78 London HLU 10563 Fabulous/Makin' Whoopie/Wow...w (tri centre) ... 10
57 Parlophone GEP 8630 THE FABULOUS CHARLIE GRACIE (EP) ... 50

GRACIOUS!

68 Polydor 56333 Beautiful/What A Lovely Rain ... 35
70 Vertigo 6059 009 Once On A Windy Day/Fugue In D Minor ... 30
70 Vertigo 6360 002 GRACIOUS! (LP, gatefold sleeve, large swirl label) ... 200
72 Philips Intl. 6382 004 THIS IS ... GRACIOUS!! (LP, black/silver labels) ... 125

GRADUATE

(see also Tears For Fears)

80 Precision PAR 100 Elvis Should Play Ska/Julie Julie (p/s) ... 5
80 Precision PAR 104 Ever Met A Day/Shut Up (p/s, 1980 issue PAR 117 with no p/s = £3) ... 6
80 Precision PAR 111 Ambition/Bad Dreams (p/s) ... 5
81 Precision PAR 117 Shut Up/Ever Met A Day (reissue, no p/s) ... 5
80s Blue Hat 5 BHR Mad One/Somebody Put Out The Fire ... 10
80 Precision PART 001 ACTING MY AGE (LP) ... 12

GRADUATES

79 Graduate GRAD 1 If You Want It/Hey Young Girl (p/s) ... 6

GRAFITTI

76 Beeb 19 Dear Prudence/Come Together ... 20

BILLY GRAHAM & ESCALATORS

67 Atlantic 584 073 Ooh Poo Pah Doo/East 24th Avenue ... 15

BOB GRAHAM EXPERIENCE

78 Anchor ANC 1055 Blast Off (Percussion In Space)/Malfunction ... 6

MINT VALUE £

BOBBY/BOBBIE GRAHAM

(see also Outlaws, Jimmy Page)

65	Fontana TF 521	Skin Deep/Zoom Widge And Wag (as Bobbie Graham)	28
66	Fontana TF 667	Teensville/Grotty Drums (as Bobby Graham)	15

CHICK GRAHAM & COASTERS

64	Decca F 11859	Education/I Know	12
64	Decca F 11932	A Little You/Dance Baby Dance	12

DAV(E)Y GRAHAM

68	Decca F 12841	Both Sides Now/Tristano	5
62	Golden Guinea GGL 0224	THE GUITAR PLAYER (LP)	50
64	Decca LK 4649	FOLK, BLUES AND BEYOND (LP)	140
64	Decca LK 4652	FOLK ROOTS, NEW ROUTES (LP, with Shirley Collins)	300
66	Decca LK 4780	MIDNIGHT MAN (LP)	80
68	Decca LK/SKL 4969	LARGE AS LIFE AND TWICE AS NATURAL (LP)	110
69	Decca LK/SKL 5011	HAT (LP)	110
70	Decca SKL 5056	HOLLY KALEIDOSCOPE (LP, as Davy Graham & Holly)	120
70	Decca LK 4649	FOLK, BLUES AND BEYOND (LP, second issue with boxed Decca logo and laminated front cover)	80
70	President PTLS 1039	GODINGTON BOUNDARY (LP, with Holly)	40
76	Eron ERON 007	ALL THAT MOODY (LP, private pressing)	200
81	Righteous GDC 001	FOLK ROOTS, NEW ROUTES (LP, with Shirley Collins, reissue)	20

DAVY GRAHAM/THAMESIDERS

63	Decca DFE 8538	FROM A LONDON HOOTENANNY (EP, 2 tracks each)	18

DAVY GRAHAM & ALEXIS KORNER

(see also Alexis Korner)

62	Topic TOP 70	3/4 A.D. (EP, first pressing in mauve sleeve with cream label)	150
62	Topic TOP 70	3/4 A.D. (EP, later pressings with lilac sleeve and blue label)	90
62	Topic TOP 70	3/4 A.D. (EP, later pressings with bronze sleeve and blue label)	60

ERNIE GRAHAM

(see also Clancy, Eire Apparent, Brinsley Schwarz, Help Yourself, Nick Lowe)

78	Stiff OFF 2	Romeo And The Lonely Girl/Only Time Will Tell (p/s)	7
71	Liberty LBS 83485	ERNIE GRAHAM (LP, textured sleeve, black label)	200

KENNY GRAHAM'S AFRO-CUBISTS

(see also Yolanda)

60	Starlite ST45 013	Bongo Chant/Beguine	10
57	Pye Jazz NJE 1053	PRESENTING KENNY GRAHAM PART 1 (EP)	20
57	Esquire EP 34	CARIBBEAN SUITE (EP)	20
57	Esquire EP 68	KENNY GRAHAM'S AFRO CUBISTS (EP)	20
57	Esquire EP 83	KENNY GRAHAM'S AFRO CUBISTS (EP)	25
56	MGM MGM-C 764	MOONDOG AND SUNCAT SUITES (LP, as Kenny Graham & His Satellites)	100
57	Nixa NJL 12	PRESENTING KENNY GRAHAM (LP)	100
57	Esquire 20-012	KENNY GRAHAM AFRO CUBISTS (LP)	80
57	Esquire 20-023	CARIBBEAN SUITE (LP)	80

LEN GRAHAM

77	Topic 12TS 334	WIND AND WATER (LP)	12

LEO GRAHAM

73	Upsetter US 399	News Flash/UPSETTERS: Flashing Echo	15
73	Summit SUM 8539	Three Blind Mice/UPSETTERS: Mice Skank	12

LOU GRAHAM

58	Coral Q 72322	Wee Willie Brown/You Were Mean Baby	500
58	Coral Q 72322	Wee Willie Brown/You Were Mean Baby (78)	150

LYNDA GRAHAM

62	Philips 326 552BF	As Long As The River Flows/When I'm Sixteen	8
63	Philips BF 1249	Without Your Love/Wait And See	8
64	Philips BF 1308	You'd Better Believe It/That's The Last Thing I'd Do	10

GRAHAM CENTRAL STATION

(see also Sly & Family Stone)

74	Warner Bros K 46206	GRAHAM CENTRAL STATION (LP)	15

RON GRAINER ORCHESTRA

62	Pye 7N 15411	Happy Joe/Old Ned	6
63	Decca F 11597	That Was The week That Was/Petit Louis	7
63	Decca F 11640	Station Six Sahara/Indian Blues	6
64	HMV POP 1366	Not So Much A Programme, More A Way Of Life/Ascot Gavotte	10
67	Pye 7N 17383	A Man In A Suitcase/Andorra (pink label, later blue)	12
67	RCA Victor RCA 1635	The Prisoner/Happening Sunday	75
68	RCA Victor RCA 1698	Love Theme/Detective	5
69	RCA Victor RCA 1898	The Paul Temple Theme/The Jazz Age	18
72	Pye 7N 45141	Steptoe & Son/Counting The Coaster	5
79	RK 1021	Tales Of The Unexpected/Malice Aforethought (p/s)	7
60	Warner Bros WEP 6012	THEME MUSIC FROM "INSPECTOR MAIGRET" (EP)	10
79	Six Of One 6 OF 1	THE PRISONER ARRIVAL (EP, fan club issue)	30
69	RCA Intl. INTS 1020	THEMES LIKE... (LP)	15
78	RK LB 003	TALES OF THE UNEXPECTED (LP)	15

ROSS GRAINER

79	Music Factory MF102	Cardiff Roses/Wind And The Trees	12

COLIN GRAINGER & THE FRANK CORDELL ORCHESTRA

58	HMV POP 484	This I Know/Are You?	7
59	HMV POP 639	Love Only Me/Plain And Simple Girl	7

GLENDA GRAINGER

60s	Audio Fidelity AFSP 007	Mr. Kiss Kiss Bang Bang/Who	12

MINT VALUE £

BILLY GRAMMER

58	London HLU 8752	Gotta Travel On/Chasing A Dream	10
58	London HLU 8752	Gotta Travel On/Chasing A Dream (78)	15
59	Felsted AF 121	Bonaparte's Retreat/The Kissing Tree	7
59	Felsted AF 121	Bonaparte's Retreat/The Kissing Tree (78)	15
59	Felsted AF 128	Willy, Quit Your Playing/It Takes You	8
59	Felsted AF 128	Willy, Quit Your Playing/It Takes You (78)	15
61	Brunswick 05851	Rainbow Round My Shoulder/Columbus Stockade Blues	8
59	Felsted GEP 1005	BILLY GRAMMER HITS (EP)	55
67	Monument LMO 5010	TRAVELIN' ON (LP)	12

GERRY GRANAHAN

58	London HL 8668	No Chemise, Please/Girl Of My Dreams	20
58	London HL 8668	No Chemise, Please/Girl Of My Dreams (78)	20
60	Top Rank JAR 262	It Hurts/RICHIE ROBIN: Strange Dream	15

ROCCO GRANATA

59	Oriole CB 1525	Marina/Manuela	5
59	Oriole CB 1525	Marina/Manuela (78)	15
61	Oriole CB 1564	Julia/Rocco Cha Cha	5

GRANDADDY

03	V2 VVR1012251	SUMDAY (2-LP, with inner sleeves)	20

GRAND FUNK RAILROAD

70	Capitol CL 15632	Heartbreaker/Please Don't Worry	6
70	Capitol CL 15661	Closer To Home/Aimless Lady	5
71	Capitol CL 15668	Inside Looking Out/Paranoid (33rpm)	8
71	Capitol CL 15689	I Can Feel Him In The Morning/ Are You Ready/Mean Mistreater (33rpm maxi-single)	12
71	Capitol CL 15705	People, Let's Stop The War/Save The Land	5
72	Capitol CL 15738	Rock And Roll Soul/Flight Of Phoenix	5
69	Capitol E-ST 307	ON TIME (LP)	35
70	Capitol E-ST 406	GRAND FUNK (LP)	35
70	Capitol E-ST 471	CLOSER THAN HOME (LP)	35
71	Capitol E-SW 764	SURVIVAL (LP)	20
72	Capitol E-AS 853	E PLURIBUS FUNK (LP, circular 'silver coin' sleeve)	20
73	Capitol E-AST 11099	PHOENIX (LP, gatefold sleeve)	18

GRANDISONS

63	RCA RCA 1339	All Right/True Romance	12

GRANDMASTER RICHIE RICH

85	Spin Offs 12off1	Check It Out/Scratch It Out (12")	12
85	Spin Offs 12off2	Don't Be Flash/Flash Scratch (12")	12

GRAND PRIX

(see also McAuley Schenker Group, Praying Mantis, Stratus, Uriah Heep)

80	RCA RCA 7	Thinking Of You/Feels Good (p/s)	15
83	Chrysalis PRIX 2	Shout/Keep On Believing (p/s, with patch)	8
83	Chrysalis PRIXP 2	Shout/Keep On Believing (picture disc)	6
83	Chrysalis PRIXX 2	Shout (12", p/s)	12

GRAND UNION

(see also Enough's Enough)

68	CBS 3956	Slowly But Surely/She Said	80

GERRI GRANGER

63	London HLX 9759	Just Tell Him Jane Said Hello/What's Wrong With Me	15

GRANNIE

71	SRT SRT 71138	GRANNIE (LP, private pressing of 99 copies only, homemade sleeve)	500

GRANNY

73	DJM DJS. 291	Lady/Weirdie Deirdre's Dilemma	18

GRANNY'S INTENTIONS

(see also Gary Moore)

67	Deram DM 158	The Story Of David/Sandy's On The Phone Again	25
68	Deram DM 184	Julie Don't Love Me Anymore/One Time Lovers	18
68	Deram DM 214	Never An Everyday Thing/Hilda The Bilda	25
70	Deram DM 293	Take Me Back/Maybe	20
70	Deram SML 1060	HONEST INJUN (LP, white/red label with small logo)	100

AMY GRANT

70s	Myrrh MYR 1124	AGE TO AGE (LP)	25

CLINTON GRANT

75	Circle 5	I've Been Trying/Second Attempt	10

CY GRANT

62	Melodisc 45-1433	Heavy Weather/Lucky Oyster (tri-centre)	10

EARL GRANT

58	Brunswick 05762	The End/Hunky Dunky Doo	5
60	Brunswick 05824	House Of Bamboo/Two Loves Have I	10
62	Brunswick 05870	Swingin' Gently/Evening Rain	7
59	Brunswick LAT 8297	THE END (LP)	12
60	Brunswick LAT 8332	NOTHIN' BUT THE BLUES (LP)	12
60	Brunswick LAT 8351	THE MAGIC OF EARL GRANT (LP)	12
61	Brunswick LAT 8389	EBB TIDE (LP)	15
62	Brunswick LAT 8502	EARL AFTER DARK (LP)	12

EDDY GRANT

(see also Equals, Coach House Rhythm Section)

74	Torpedo TOR 30	My Queen Tonight/Hello Africa	5
75	Torpedo TOR 53	Nobody's Got Time (Part 1)/Nobody's Got Time (Part 2)	10

MINT VALUE £

ERKEY GRANT & EARWIGS

63	Pye 7N 15521	I'm A Hog For You/I Can't Get Enough Of You	30

GOGI GRANT

(see also Tony Martin)

55	London HLB 8192	Suddenly There's A Valley/Love Is	30
56	London HLB 8257	Who Are We/We Believe In Love	35
56	London HLB 8282	Wayward Wind/No More Than Forever	30
57	London HLB 8364	You're In Love/When The Tide Is High	25
58	London HLB 8550	The Golden Ladder/All Of Me	20
58	RCA RCA 1038	It's A Wonderful Thing To Be Loved/What A Beautiful Combination	5
58	RCA RCA 1047	Bonjour Tristesse/Johnny's Dream	6
59	RCA RCA 1101	Say A Prayer For Me Tonight/TONY MARTIN: She Is Not Thinking Of Me	5
59	RCA RCA 1105	Kiss Me Honey Honey Kiss Me/Two Dreams	6
60	London HLG 9185	Goin' Home/I'm Going To Live The Life	6
56	London REB 1057	GOGI GRANT (EP, export issue)	20
57	London HA-B 2032	SUDDENLY THERE'S GOGI GRANT (LP)	45
58	RCA RD 27054	BOTH ENDS OF THE CANDLE (LP, soundtrack)	15
59	RCA RD 27097	GIGI (LP, with Tony Martin)	15
60	London HA-G 2242	IF YOU WANT TO GET TO HEAVEN - SHOUT! (LP, mono)	20
60	London SAH-G 6072	IF YOU WANT TO GET TO HEAVEN - SHOUT! (LP, stereo)	25

JANIE GRANT

61	Pye International 7N 25093	Triangle/She's Going Steady With You	18
62	Pye International 7N 25148	That Greasy Kid Stuff/Trying To Forget You	18

JULIE GRANT

62	Pye 7N 15430	Somebody Tell Him/Ev'ry Letter You Write	10
62	Pye 7N 15447	So Many Ways/Unimportant Things	10
62	Pye 7N 15461	When You're Smiling/Lonely Sixteen	10
62	Pye 7N 15483	Up On The Roof/When You Ask About Love	8
63	Pye 7N 15508	Count On Me/Then, Only Then	8
63	Pye 7N 15526	That's How Heartaches Are Made/Cruel World	12
63	Pye 7N 15545	Don't Ever Let Me Down/Somebody Cares	10
63	Pye 7N 15590	Hello Love/It's Alright	10
64	Pye 7N 15684	Come To Me/Can't Get You Out Of My Mind	10
64	Pye 7N 15615	Every Day I Have To Cry/Watch What You Do With My Baby	10
64	Pye 7N 15652	You Are Nobody 'Til Somebody Loves You/I Only Care About You	10
65	Pye 7N 15756	Baby Baby (I Still Love You)/My World Is Empty Without You	20
65	Pye 7N 15812	Giving Up/Cause I Believe In You	10
65	Pye 7N 15884	Lonely Without You/As Long As I Know He's Mine	10
65	Pye 7N 15937	Stop/When The Lovin' Ends	15
62	Pye NEP 24171	THIS IS JULIE GRANT (EP)	40

LEE GRANT (& CAPITOLS)

66	Parlophone R 5531	Breaking Point/Don't Cry Baby (with Capitols)	20
70	Decca F 13029	A Little Love And Understanding/I Got To Get You Out Of My Mind (solo)	7

LITTLE BROTHER (GRANT)

(see also Equals)

70	Torpedo TOR 27	Baby Don't Let Me Down/Brother Strong Man (as Little Brother)	7
70	Torpedo TOR 28	Let's Do It Together/Hey Man, Why (as Little Brother Grant & Zapatta Schmidt)	7

NEVILLE GRANT

73	Downtown DT 509	Sick And Tired/PRINCE DJANGO: Hot Tip	20

NORMAN GRANT ORCHESTRA

61	Starlite ST45 060	Jive Medley/Speak Low	7

TOP GRANT

(see also Rhythm Aces)

62	Island WI 034	Searching/David & Goliath	15
62	Island WI 052	Suzie/Jenny	15
63	Island WI 072	Riverbank Coberley (as Top-Grant)/Nancy	15
63	Island WI 074	Money Money Money/Have Mercy On Me	18
63	Island WI 077	War In Africa/The Birds	15

GRAPE

(see also P.J. Harvey)

92	Pencil Toast PENT 001	Baby In A Plastic Bag/Listen To Your Heart (p/s)	25

GRAPEFRUIT

(see also Tony Rivers & Castaways, Easybeats, Fynn McCool, Sleepy)

68	RCA Victor RCA 1656	Dear Delilah/The Dead Boot	8
68	RCA Victor RCA 1677	Elevator/Yes	20
68	RCA Victor RCA 1716	C'mon Marianne/Ain't It Good	6
68	Stateside-Dunhill SS 8005	Someday Soon/Theme For Twiggy	7
69	Stateside-Dunhill SS 8011	Round Going Round/This Little Man	7
69	RCA Victor RCA 1855	Deep Water/Come Down To The Station	7
70	RCA Victor RCA 1907	Lady Godiva/Thunder And Lightning	6
71	Deram DM 343	Universal Party/Sha Sha	6
69	Stateside-Dunhill S(S)L 5008	AROUND GRAPEFRUIT (LP, black/white/red label with "Sold in the U.K..." text)	80
69	RCA Victor SF 8030	DEEP WATER (LP)	60

GRAPEVINE

68	Liberty LBF 15063	Things Ain't What They Used To Be Anymore/Ace In The Hole	8

GRAPHITE

72	Beacon BEA 109	Gimme Your Number/Chestnut Loke (possibly promo only)	15

GRASSROOTS

(see also P.F. Sloan)

66	RCA Victor RCA 1532	Where Were You When I Needed You/These Are Bad Times	10

			MINT VALUE £
67	Pye International 7N 25422	Let's Live For Today/Depressed Feeling	10
67	Pye International 7N 25431	Things I Should Have Said/Tip Of My Tongue	6
68	RCA Victor RCA 1682	Melody For You/Hey Friend	5
68	RCA Victor RCA 1737	Midnight Confessions/Who Will You Be Tomorrow	10
69	Stateside-Dunhill SS 8006	Bella Linda/Hot Bright Lights	5
69	Stateside-Dunhill SS 8012	All Good Things Come To An End/Melody For You	5
69	Stateside-Dunhill SS 8018	The River Is Wide/(You Gotta) Live For Love	5
69	Stateside-Dunhill SS 8023	Who Will You Be Tomorrow/Midnight Confessions	8
69	Stateside-Dunhill SS 8029	I'd Wait A Million Years/Fly Me To Havana	12
71	Probe PRO 515	Temptation Eyes/Keepin' Me Down	8
69	Stateside S(S)L 5005	GOLDEN GRASS (LP)	25
70	Stateside SSL 5012	LEAVING IT ALL BEHIND (LP)	25

GRASS-SHOW

96	Food FOOD 94	Freak Show/Sympathetic Television (picture disc, poster sleeve)	5

GRATEFUL DEAD

(see also Jerry Garcia, Mickey Hart, Kingfish, Robert Hunter, Bob Weir, Keith & Donna Godchaux, Silver [U.S.], Diga Rhythm Band)

67	Warner Bros WB 7186	Born Cross-Eyed/Dark Star	50
70	Warner Bros WB 7410	Uncle John's Band/New Speedway Boogie	12
71	Warner Bros	Truckin'/Johnny B. Goode (unissued)	0
72	Warner Bros K 16167	One More Saturday Night (as Grateful Dead with Bobby Ace)/Bertha	7
73	Atlantic K 19301	Let Me Sing Your Blues Away/Here Comes Sunshine	7
74	United Artists UP 36030	U.S. Blues/Loose Lucy	6
77	Warner Bros SAM 79	Dark Star/Born Cross-Eyed (mail-order issue with Dark Star magazine)	15
79	Arista ARIST 236	Good Lovin'/Stagger Lee	6
87	Arista RIS 35	Touch Of Grey/My Brother Esau (grey vinyl, p/s)	6
67	Warner Bros W 1689	THE GRATEFUL DEAD (LP, mono)	100
67	Warner Bros WS 1689	THE GRATEFUL DEAD (LP, stereo)	60
68	Warner Bros WS 1749	ANTHEM OF THE SUN (LP, stereo)	50
69	Warner Bros WS 1790	AOXOMOXOA (LP)	65
70	Warner Bros WS 1830	LIVE/DEAD (2-LP)	40
70	Warner Bros WS 1869	WORKINGMAN'S DEAD (LP, matt sleeve)	35
71	Warner Bros WS 1893	AMERICAN BEAUTY (LP)	25
71	Warner Bros K 66009	GRATEFUL DEAD LIVE (SKULL AND ROSES) (2-LP)	25
71	Warner Bros. K66002	LIVE DEAD (LP, reissue)	18
72	Polydor 2310 171	HISTORIC DEAD (LP)	25
72	Polydor 2310 172	VINTAGE DEAD (LP)	25
72	Warner Bros K 66019	EUROPE '72 (3-LP, triple fold-out sleeve)	25
73	Warner Bros K 46246	HISTORY OF GRATEFUL DEAD (BEAR'S CHOICE) (LP)	12
73	Warner Bros K 49301	WAKE OF THE FLOOD (LP)	15
74	Warner Bros K 56024	SKELETONS FROM THE CLOSET: THE BEST OF GRATEFUL DEAD (LP)	12
74	Warner Bros K 59302	FROM THE MARS HOTEL (LP)	12
75	United Artists UA 29895	BLUES FOR ALLAH (LP)	12
76	United Artists UAD 60131/2	STEAL YOUR FACE (2-LP, gatefold sleeve, with sampler LP FOR DEAD HEADS ONLY [FREE 2] in inner sleeve)	20
68	Warner Bros W 1749	ANTHEM OF THE SUN (LP, mono)	75

GRAVE

03	Century Media	MORBID WAYS TO DIE (Numbered box set with 6 picture disc LPs and booklet, 2000 only)	60

GRAVEDIGGAZ

94	Gee Street GEEA 14	NIGGAMORTIS (LP, with inner sleeve)	20

NICK GRAVENITES

(see also Big Brother & Holding Company)

69	CBS 63818	MY LABORS (LP)	22

BILLY GRAVES

59	Felsted AF 119	The Shag (Is Totally Cool)/Uncertain (export issue)	70

CARL GRAVES

75	A&M AM 7151	Baby Hang Up The Phone/Walk Softly	5

GRAVY TRAIN

(see also Mandalaband)

71	Vertigo 6059049	Alone In Georgia/Can Anybody Hear Me	30
73	Dawn DNS 1036	Strength Of A Dream/Tolpuddle Episode	8
74	Dawn DNS 1058	Starbright Starlight/Good Time Thing	8
75	Dawn DNS 1115	Climb Aboard The Gravy Train/Sanctuary	8
70	Vertigo 6360 022	GRAVY TRAIN (LP, gatefold sleeve, large swirl label)	150
71	Vertigo 6360 051	BALLAD OF A PEACEFUL MAN (LP, gatefold sleeve, small swirl label)	600
73	Dawn DNLS 3046	SECOND BIRTH (LP)	70
74	Dawn DNLH 1	STAIRCASE TO THE DAY (LP, gatefold sleeve, pink 'sun' label)	70

BARRY GRAY (ORCHESTRA)

(see also Century 21, Mary Jane with Barry Gray, Richard Harvey)

62	Lyntone LYN 249/250	Sabotage/Supercar Song/Supercar Twist (flexi, with p/s may exist)	30
62	Lyntone LYN 249/250	Sabotage/Supercar Song/Supercar Twist (flexi)	15
64	Melodisc MEL 1591	Fireball/Zero G (by Barry Gray & His Spacemakers; in p/s)	55
64	Melodisc MEL 1591	Fireball/Zero G (by Barry Gray & His Spacemakers)	20
65	Pye 7N 17016	Thunderbirds/Parker - Well Done (in p/s)	35
65	Pye 7N 17016	Thunderbirds/Parker - Well Done	15
67	Pye 7N 17391	Captain Scarlet/The Mysterons Theme (in p/s)	35
67	Pye 7N 17391	Captain Scarlet/The Mysterons Theme	15
68	Pye 7N 17625	Joe 90 - Title Theme/Joe 90 - Hijacked (in p/s)	50
68	Pye 7N 17625	Joe 90 - Title Theme/Joe 90 - Hijacked	25
62	Golden Guinea GGL 0106	SUPERCAR - FLIGHT OF FANCY (LP, with Edwin Astley)	60
67	United Artists ULP 1159	THUNDERBIRDS ARE GO! (LP, soundtrack, mono)	100
67	United Artists SULP 1159	THUNDERBIRDS ARE GO! (LP, soundtrack, stereo)	120

MINT VALUE £

BARRY GRAY

04	Trunk JBH 010	UFO: THE ORIGINAL TELEVISION SERIES SOUNDTRACK (LP, clear vinyl, 500 only)	40

DOBIE GRAY

65	London HL 9953	The "In" Crowd/Be A Man	10
65	London HL 9953	The "In" Crowd/Be A Man (DJ Copy)	40
65	Pye International 7N 25307	See You At The Go Go/Walk With Love	25
65	Pye International 7N 25307	See You At The Go Go/Walk With Love (DJ Copy)	50
69	London HL 10268	The "In" Crowd/Be A Man (reissue)	7
73	MCA MU 1184	Drift Away/City Stars	5
73	MCA MU 1221	Now That I'm Without You/Loving Arms	6
75	Black Magic BM 107	Out On The Floor/Be A Man	5
74	Sydna SYD 5028	Good Old Days/Never Ending Love	8

DOLORES GRAY

55	Brunswick 05382	Heat Wave/After You Get What You Want, You Don't Want It	15
55	Brunswick 05407	Rock Love/One	30
55	Brunswick 05407	Rock Love/One (78)	10
57	Capitol CL 14732	There'll Be Some Changes Made/Fool's Errand	10
57	Capitol CL 14770	I'm Innocent/My Mama Likes You	8
63	Philips 326 582BF	Mornin' Train/Our Day Will Come	7

DORIAN GRAY

67	Parlophone R 5612	Behind The Tear/Walking Down A Back Street	5
68	Parlophone R 5667	I've Got You On My Mind/Move On	10
68	Parlophone R 5705	Love Is All That It Should Be/Let Me Go Home	5
68	Parlophone R 5732	Jingle Down A Hill/Get Goin' Baby	5

HERBIE GRAY

(see also Gene Rondo, Owen & Dandy, Tony Tribe)

68	Giant GN 38	We're Staying Here/Life Ska	18

JERRY GRAY & HIS ORCHESTRA

54	Brunswick 05351	The Ooh And Ah Mambo/Kettle Drum Hop	5

JIMMIE GRAY

82	JKO 12JKO 100	The Kool People (Vocal)/The Kool People (Instrumental) (12")	40

JOHNNIE 'THE GASH' GRAY

58	Fontana H 123	Big Guitar/Tequila	20
58	Fontana H 134	Apache/Zach's Tune	20

LES GRAY

(see also Mud)

77	Warner Bros K 16883	A Groovy Kind Of Love/U.S. Style (p/s)	5
77	Warner Bros K 17004	What Do You Want To Make Those Eyes At Me For/Stand Still Stella	5

LORRAINE GRAY

64	Fontana TF 435	Are You Getting Tired Of Your Little Toy?/ The Boy That I Want Doesn't Want Me	10
64	Fontana TF 484	The Little Girl That Cries/Talk To Him	6

MAUREEN GRAY

61	HMV POP 944	I Don't Want To Cry/Come On And Dance	10

OWEN GRAY

(see also Laurel & Owen, Gray Brothers, Elki & Owen, Owen & Milie, Owen & Dandy, Dennis Lowe, Survivors, Denzil & Jennifer, Brother Dan, Glen Adam)

60	Starlite ST45 015	Far Love/Please Let Me Go	50
60	Starlite ST45 019	Jenny Lee/The Plea	50
60	Blue Beat BB 8	Cutest Little Woman/Running Around (with Ken Richards Band)	20
61	Blue Beat BB 43	Sinners Weep/Get Drunk (with Hersan & His City Slickers)	20
61	Starlite ST45 032	Mash It (Parts 1 & 2)	50
62	Starlite ST45 078	I Feel Good/Someone To Help Me	50
62	Starlite ST45 088	Let Me Go Free/In My Dreams	50
62	Blue Beat BB 75	Rockin' In My Feet/Nobody Else (with Jets)	20
62	Blue Beat BB 91	Millie Girl (with Buster's Group)/DERRICK MORGAN: Headache	25
62	Blue Beat BB 103	Lonely Days/No Good Woman (with Sonny Bradshaw Quartet)	18
62	Blue Beat BB 108	Keep It In Mind/Do You Want To Jump (with Les Dawson Combo)	18
62	Blue Beat BB 113	Best Twist/Grandma-Grandpa (B-side with Hersan & His City Slickers)	18
62	Blue Beat BB 127	Pretty Girl/Twist So Fine	18
62	Blue Beat BB 136	They Got To Move/I Love Her	18
62	Blue Beat BB 139	Tree In The Meadow/Lizebella (with Buster's Group)	18
62	Island WI 002	Patricia/Twist Baby	25
62	Island WI 020	Audrey/Dolly Baby (with Ernest Rauglin [sic] Orchestra)	20
62	Island WI 030	Midnight Trail/Time Will Tell	20
62	Island WI 048	I'm Still Waiting/Last Night	10
62	Chek TD 101	Come On Baby/My One Desire	15
62	Dice CC 3	On The Beach/Young Lover	15
63	Blue Beat BB 147	Big Mabel/Don't Come Knocking (with Edwards' Groupe)	15
63	Blue Beat BB 188	Call Me My Pet/Give Me Your Love	15
63	Blue Beat BB 201	Snow Falling/Oowee Baby (as Owen Gray & His Big Brother)	15
64	Blue Beat BB 217	Draw Me Nearer/Daddy's Girl	15
65	Blue Beat BB 290	Daddy's Gone/BUSTER'S ALLSTARS: Johnny Dark	30
65	Aladdin WI 603	Gonna Work Out Fine/Dolly Baby	12
65	Aladdin WI 607	Can I Get A Witness/Linda Lu	12
65	Island WI 252	Shook Shimmy And Shake/I'm Going Back	20
65	Island WI 258	You Don't Know Like I Do/Take Me Serious (with Sound System)	15
65	Venus VE 2	Too Many Heartaches/Baby It's True	10
66	Island WI 267	Paradise/Bye Bye Love	10
66	Blue Beat BB 365	I'm Gonna Say So Long/The Days I'm Living	12

			MINT VALUE £
67	Island WIP 6000	Help Me/Incense	18
67	Collins Downbeat CR 003	Collins Greetings/Rock It Down (with Sir Collins & Band)	60
67	Collins Downbeat CR 004	I'm So Lonely (with Sir Collins & Band)/ EL RECO, SIR COLLINS & J. SATCH: Shock Steady	80
68	Collins Downbeat CR 007	Am Satisfy (with Sir Collins & Band)/ BOB STACKIE & SIR COLLINS & BAND: Sweet Music	120
68	Collins Downbeat CR 009	Grab It, Hold It, Feel It (with Bob Stackie)/DAN SIMMONS: Way Out Sound	65
68	Collins Downbeat CR 010	I'm Gonna Take You Back (with Bob Stackie)/GLEN ADAMS: King Sized	75
68	Coxsone CS 7047	Give Me A Little Sign/Ain't Nobody Home	150
68	Coxsone CS 7053	Give It To Me/Isn't It So	80
68	Blue Cat BS 123	These Foolish Things/This I Promise	30
69	Blue Cat BS 156	I Can't Stop Loving You/Tell Me Darling	30
68	Trojan TR 632	Lovey Dovey/Grooving	15
68	Revolution REV 001	Sitting In The Park/You've Got It	20
69	Fab FAB 90	Three Coins In The Fountain/Tennessee Waltz	10
69	Fab FAB 96	Ay Ay Ay/Let It Be Me (with Rudies)	10
69	Fab FAB 120	Understand My Love/Apollo 12	10
69	Fab FAB 126	Swing Low/Release Me	10
69	Trojan TR 650	I Can't Stop Loving You/Tell Me Darling	8
69	Trojan TR 670	Too Experienced/I Really Loved You Baby	12
69	Duke DU 12	Reggae Dance/I Know	10
69	Duke DU 33	Seven Lonely Days/He Don't Love You Like I Do	8
69	Downtown DT 423	Groovin'/HERBIE GRAY & RUDIES: These Memories	7
69	Downtown DT 428	Lovey Dovey (with Dandy)/HERBIE GRAY & RUDIES: Kitty Wait	5
69	Camel CA 25	Girl What You Doing To Me/Woman A Grumble	8
69	Camel CA 34	Don't Take Your Love Away/Two Lovers	5
69	Camel CA 37	Every Beat Of My Heart/Don't Cry	5
70	Camel CA 50	Don't Sign The Paper/Packing Up Loneliness	5
70	Camel CA 51	Bring Back Your Love/Got To Come Back	5
70	Upfront UPF 3	Dream Lover/Mudda-Granma-Reggae (with Maximum Breed)	7
70	Bamboo BAM 47	I Can Feel It/I Don't Want (To Lose Your Love)	12
70	Crab CRAB 52	Just A Little Loving/DERRICK MORGAN: Take A Letter Maria	5
70	Pama PM 810	Sugar Dumpling/I Don't Know Why	8
70	Pama Supreme PS 299	I Am In Love Again/RANDY WILLIAMS: Version	6
70	Pama Supreme PS 302	Candida/When Will I Find My Way	6
70	Pama Supreme PS 310	You Gonna Miss Me/I Hear You Knocking	6
70	Supreme SUP 206	Surfin'/All The Love	6
70	Ackee ACK 102	No More/Don't Leave Me (both as Owen Gray & Omen)	5
71	Ackee ACK 123	Whispering Bells/CLANCY'S ALLSTARS: Whiplash	10
71	Camel CA 60	Groove Me/No Other One	7
71	Camel CA 73	Nothing Can Separate Us/Girl I Want You To Understand	6
71	Punch PH 87	Sincerely/Hold On I'm Coming	6
71	Pama Supreme PS 325	Summer Sand/Something To Remind Me	6
71	Pama Supreme PS 332	Greatest Hits (Parts 1 & 2)	6
72	Pama Supreme PS 351	Time/GRAHAM: Harlesden High Street	8
72	Pama Supreme PS 358	Hail The Man/I'll Follow You	6
72	Pama Supreme PS 360	Amazing Grace (with Graham Hawk)/SKETTO RICH: Don't Stay Out Late	6
70s	Rock Steady Rev. REV 004	Groovy Kind Of Love (with Elki & Rim Ram Band)/RIM RAM BAND: The Whistler	5
76	Angen ANG 121	Blazing Fire/Version	6
61	Starlite STLP 5	OWEN GRAY SINGS (LP)	120
63	Melodisc MLP 12-153	CUPID (LP)	45
69	Trojan TTL 24	REGGAE WITH SOUL (LP)	30
77	Trojan TRLS 139	FIRE AND BULLETS (LP)	20
78	Trojan TRLS 150	DREAMS OF OWEN GRAY (LP)	15

SHANE GRAY

68	Page One POF 102	Sing Out Loud/Come Back To My Heart Again	10

VERA GRAY

66	HMV CLP3531	LISTEN, MOVE & DANCE 4 (LP)	25

WARDELL GRAY

54	Brunswick LA 8646	THE CHASE (LP, with Dexter Gordon)	25
65	Stateside SL 10144	WARDELL GRAY MEMORIAL ALBUM (VOL. 1) (LP)	15
65	Stateside SL 10145	WARDELL GRAY MEMORIAL ALBUM (VOL. 2) (LP)	15

GRAY BROTHERS

(see also Owen Gray)

68	Blue Cat BS 124	Always/Big Man	30

KATHRYN GRAYSON

53	MGM SP 1002	(All Of A Sudden) My Heart Sings/Jealousy	8
53	MGM SP 1014	Smoke Gets In Your Eyes/The Touch Of Your Hand (B-side with Howard Keel)	8
54	MGM SP 1078	I Hate Men/ANN MILLER & TOMMY RALL: Always True To You In My Way	8
56	MGM EP 636	WANTING YOU (EP)	8

LARRY GRAYSON

72	York SYK 529	Shut That Door/Slack Alice	8
75	United Artists UP 36029	Who's Stuffing Your Turkey This Christmas?/Head Over Heels	6
72	York MYK 602	WHAT A GAY DAY (LP)	15

MILTON GRAYSON

60	London HLU 9068	Forget You/The Puppet	8

RUDY GRAYZELL

54	London HL 8094	Looking At The Moon And Wishing On A Star/The Heart That Once Was Mine	300
54	London HL 8094	Looking At The Moon And Wishing On A Star/ The Heart That Once Was Mine (78)	80

MINT VALUE £

GRAZINA

(see also Lady Murray, Mr & Mrs Murray, Le Roys, Cliff Richard)

62	HMV POP 1094	Lover Please Believe Me/So What	15
63	HMV POP 1149	Don't Be Shy/Another Like You	15
63	HMV POP 1212	Be My Baby/I Ain't Gonna Knock On Your Door	20
64	Giv-A-Disc LYN 568	Stay Awhile/Let Me Go Lover (with magazine)	10

GREASE BAND

(see also Joe Cocker, Wynder K. Frog, Made In Sheffield, Henry McCullough)

72	Harvest HAR 5052	Laughed At The Judge/All I Want To Do/Jesse James	6
75	Goodear EAR 602	New Morning/Pontardawe Hop	5
71	Harvest SHVL 790	THE GREASE BAND (LP, first pressing)	50
72	Harvest SHVL 790	THE GREASE BAND (LP, second pressing with EMI boxed logo)	20
75	Goodear EAR 2902	AMAZING GREASE (LP)	15

JOHNNY B. GREAT (& GOODMEN)

(see also Quotations, Johnny Goodison)

63	Decca F 11740	School Is In/She's A Much Better Lover Than You (with Goodmen)	10
64	Decca F 11804	Acapulco 1922/You'll Never Leave Him (solo)	8

GREAT ACES

72	Fab FAB 191	Gold And Silver/Liberty Rock	7
72	Fab FAB 200	Liberty Rock/Rock My Soul	7
72	Fab FAB 201	I Didn't Mean It/Boots And Shoes	6
72	Fab FAB 202	Baby Girl/Version	6
73	Fab FAB 203	Banana/My Sweet Lord	6

GREAT AWAKENING

69	London HLU 10284	Amazing Grace/Silver Waterfall	6

GREAT BRITISH HEROES (AKA GBH)

78	Lightning GIL 534	Eric Miller/Don't Give A Damn (1 copy only)	1000

GREATEST LITTLE SOUL BAND IN THE LAND

(see also J.J. Jackson)

69	MCA Soul Bag BAG 4	Tenement Halls/Flat, Black And Together	5
69	MCA Soul Bag BAG 6	Something For My People/Win Lose Or Draw	5

GREATEST SHOW ON EARTH

(see also Living Daylights, Ian Dury & Blockheads, Fuzzy Duck, Glencoe, Naturals)

70	Harvest HAR 5012	Real Cool World/Again And Again	20
70	Harvest HAR 5026	Tell The Story/Mountain Song	6
77	Harvest HAR 5129	Magic Touch Woman/Again And Again	8
70	Harvest SHVL 769	HORIZONS (LP, gatefold sleeve, no EMI on label)	90
70	Harvest SHVL 783	THE GOING'S EASY (LP, gatefold sleeve, no EMI logo on label)	80
75	Harvest SHSM 2004	THE GREATEST SHOW ON EARTH (LP)	15

GREAT EXPECTATIONS

72	Polydor 2058241	I'm So Glad I Gotcha/Time And Place	8
73	Polydor 2058348	Devils Gun/Bigger And Better	8
81	Phillips (no cat no)	Midnight Man/Pt. 2	15

GREAT METROPOLITAN STEAM BAND

69	MCA MNP/S 403	THE GREAT METROPLITAN STEAM BAND (LP)	35

GREAT SATURDAY NIGHT SWINDLE

(see also Rosemary Taylor)

77	CBS 82044	GREAT SATURDAY NIGHT SWINDLE (LP, Irish-only issue)	12

GREAT SOCIETY

(see also Jefferson Airplane)

68	CBS 63476	CONSPICUOUS ONLY IN ITS ABSENCE (LP)	35

GREAT UNCLE FRED

67	Strike JH 324	I'm In Love With An Ex-Beauty Queen/Singalong Version	20

JOE GRECH

71	Electro ES 152	Marija L-Maltija/In-Nassab (export issue)	6

BUDDY GRECO

(see also Johnny Desmond)

57	London HLR 8452	With All My Heart/Game Of Love (with B-G Skiffle Band)	6
58	London HLR 8613	I've Grown Accustomed To Her Face/On The Street Where You Live (as Buddy Greco & His Quartet)	5
60	Fontana H 255	The Lady Is A Tramp/Like Young	6
62	Columbia DB 4924	Mr. Lonely/Sentimental Fool	5
65	Columbia DB 7790	Mr. Kiss Kiss Bang Bang/Passing Pastels	5
56	Vogue Coral LVA 9021	AT MISTER KELLY'S (LP)	15

GREEDIES

(see also Professionals, Thin Lizzy, Sex Pistols)

80	Vertigo GREED 1	A Merry Jingle/A Merry Jangle (p/s)	6

AL GREEN

68	Stateside SS 2079	Back Up Train/Don't Leave Me (as Al Greene & Soul Mates)	30
68	Stateside SS 2079	Back Up Train/Don't Leave Me (as Al Greene & Soul Mates) (DJ copy)	60
69	Action ACT 4540	Don't Hurt Me No More/Get Yourself Together (as Al Greene)	20
70	London HLU 10300	You Say It/Gotta Find A New World	7
71	London HLU 10324	I Can't Get Next To You/Ride Sally Ride	7
71	Bell BLL 1188	Back Up Train/Don't Leave Me (as Al Green & Soul Mates, reissue)	12
71	London HLU 10337	Tired Of Being Alone / Right Now, Right Now	5
71	London HLU 10348	Let's Stay Together/Tomorrow's Dream	5
72	London HLU 10369	Look What You've Done For Me/I've Never Found A Girl	5
72	London HLU 10382	I'm Still In Love With You/Old Time Relovin'	5

			MINT VALUE £
72	London HLU 10393	You Ought To Be With Me/What Is This Feeling	5
73	London HLU 10406	Call Me/What A Wonderful Thing Love Is	5
73	London HLU 10419	Love And Happiness/So You're Leaving	5
73	London HLU 10426	Here I Am/I'm Glad You're Mine	5
74	London HLU 10443	Living For You/It Ain't No Fun To Me	5
74	London HLU 10452	Let's Get Married/So Good To Be Here	5
74	London HLU 10470	Sha La La (Make Me Happy)/School Days	5
75	London HLU 10482	L.O.V.E./I Wish You Were Here With Me	5
75	London HLU 10493	Oh Me Oh My/Strong As Death	5
75	London HLU 10511	Full Of Fire/Could I Be The One	5
76	London HLU 10527	Let It Shine/There's No Way	5
76	London HLU 10542	Keep Me Crying/There Is Love	5
77	London STO U 8685	I TRIED TO TELL MYSELF (EP)	10
69	Action ACLP 6008	BACK UP TRAIN (LP)	60
71	London SHU 8424	AL GREEN GETS NEXT TO YOU (LP)	20
72	London SHU 8430	LET'S STAY TOGETHER (LP)	20
72	London SHU 8443	I'M STILL IN LOVE WITH YOU (LP)	15
73	London SHU 8457	CALL ME (LP)	15
74	London SHU 8464	LIVIN' FOR YOU (LP)	15
74	London SHU 8479	EXPLORES YOUR MIND (LP)	15

BARRY GREEN

72	Decca F 13282	Papa Do/Boomerang	8

BARRY GREEN

63	Ember JBS 713	Together/Collective Marriage	20

BRIAN GREEN

68	Fontana SFJL 912	BRIAN GREEN DISPLAY (LP)	40

GARLAND GREEN

69	MCA Soul Bag BAG 9	Jealous Kinda Fella/I Can't Believe You Quit Me	15
75	Polydor 2066 557	Bumpin' And Stompin'/Nothing Can Take You From Me	6

GRANT GREEN

65	Verve VLP 9111	HIS MAJESTY KING FUNK (LP)	20

HUGHIE GREEN

61	Polydor Decca F11317	The Valley Of Peppermint Springs/The Puppet Song	7
66	Columbia DB 8085	Cuddle Up Baby/Clap Your Hands (B-side with Monica Rose)	8
74	EMI 2244	That's Entertainment/Champagne Charlie	5
77	Philips GB 1	Stand Up And Be Counted/Land Of Hope And Glory	5

IAN GREEN (REVELATION)

(see also Madeline Bell, Rosetta Hightower)

67	Polydor 56194	Last Pink Rose/Green Blues (solo)	30
69	CBS 3997	When You Love A Man/Santa Maria	6
69	CBS 4623	Revelation/Groover's Grave	6
70	CBS 63840	REVELATION (LP)	30

JIMMY GREEN

(see also Jimmy London)

73	Duke DU 155	Suspicion/LLOYD'S ALL STARS: Suspicion - Version	7
73	Green Door GD 4062	I'll Be Standing By/LLOYD'S ALL STARS: I'll Be Standing By "Version"	6

KATHE GREEN

69	Deram DM 279	If I Thought You'd Ever Change Your Mind/Primrose Hill	7
69	Deram SML 1039	RUN THE LENGTH OF YOUR WILDNESS (LP, white/red label)	35

KEITH GREEN

60s	Bird 118	NO COMPROMISE (LP)	30

LLOYD GREEN

75	Monument S MNT 81245	STEEL RIDES (LP)	20

PETER GREEN

(see also Fleetwood Mac, Peter B's, Shotgun Express, John Mayall & Bluesbreakers, Gass, Peter Bardens, Katmandu, Gass)

71	Reprise RS 27012	Heavy Heart/No Way Out	15
72	Reprise K 14141	Beast Of Burden/Uganda Woman (with Nigel Watson)	15
78	PVK PV 16	Apostle/Tribal Dance	8
79	PVK PV 24	In The Skies/Proud Pinto (p/s)	5
80	PVK PV 36	Walking In The Road/Woman Don't	5
80	PVK PV 41	Loser Two Times/Momma Doncha Cry	5
81	PVK PV 103	Give Me Back My Freedom/Lost My Love	5
81	PVK PV 112	Promised Land/Bizzy Lizzy	5
70	Reprise RSLP 9006	THE END OF THE GAME (LP, with Nigel Watson)	35
80	PVK PVLS 102	LITTLE DREAMER (LP, with inner sleeve)	12

PHILIP GREEN & PINEWOOD STUDIO ORCHESTRA

60	Top Rank JAR 355	League Of Gentlemen March/"Golden Fleece" Theme	10

SALLY GREEN

62	Philips PB 1243	It Hurts Too Much To Laugh/When's He Gonna Kiss Me	15

TEDDY GREEN

63	Piccadilly 7N 35146	Gee What A Party/Dream Chaser	10
06	Piccadilly 7N 35131	Can I Take You Out Tonight/Talk	8

TOM GREEN

74	Action ACT 4621	Rock Springs Railroad Station/Endless Confusion	100

GREEN ANGELS

65	Parlophone R 5390	Rockin' Red Wing/Let It Happen	15
66	Parlophone R 5512	An Exile's Dream/Hanningan's Hooley	6

MINT VALUE £

NORMAN GREENBAUM
(see also Dr. West's Medicine Show & Junk Band)

70	Reprise RS 20885	Spirit In The Sky/Milk Cow	5
70	Reprise RS 20846	Jubilee/Skyline	8
70	Reprise RS 20919	Canned Ham/Junior Cadillac	8
71	Reprise RS 21008	California Earthquake/Rhode Island Red	8
70	Reprise RSLP 6365	SPIRIT IN THE SKY (LP)	20
70	Page One POLS 017	WITH DR. WEST'S MEDICINE SHOW & JUNK BAND (LP)	22

GREEN BEAN

69	Regal Zonophone RZ 3017	The Garden's Lovely/Sittin' In The Sunshine	7

GREENBEATS

64	Pye 7N 15718	If This World Were Mine/You Must Be The One	5
65	Pye 7N 15843	So Sad/I'm On Fire	5
67	Spin SP 2007	Pretty Woman/Thing	15

GREEN BULLFROG
(see also Deep Purple, Ritchie Blackmore, Roger Glover, Tony Ashton, Matthew Fisher)

72	MCA MKPS 2021	GREEN BULLFROG (LP, black/blue 'hexagon' label)	150

GREEN DAY

94	Reprise W 0247	Longview/On The Wagon (p/s)	8
94	Reprise W 0247 T	Longview/Going To Pasalacqua (Infatuation)/FOD (Live)/ Christy Road (Live) (10", green vinyl, stickered PVC sleeve)	25
94	Reprise W 0257	Basket Case/Tired Of Waiting For You (Green vinyl, numbered p/s)	10
94	Reprise W 0257 CD	Basket Case/Longview (live)/Burnout (live)/ 2000 Light Years Away (live) (CD)	8
94	Reprise W 0257 CD2	Basket Case/On The Wagon/Tired Of Waiting For You/ 409 In Your Coffee Maker (CD, green jewel case, numbered sleeve)	10
94	Reprise W 0269 T	Welcome To Paradise/Chump (Live)/Emenius Sleepus (green vinyl 12", stickered PVC sleeve)	10
95	Reprise W 0279 X	Basket Case/2,000 Light Years Away (Live) (numbered poster p/s, green vinyl)	8
95	Reprise W 0287X	Longview/Welcome To Paradise (live) (2nd issue with sticker sheet, p/s)	10
95	Reprise W 0294X	When I Come Around/She (live) (Ltd. edn picture disc with insert)	8
95	Reprise W 0320 X	Geek Stink Breath/I Want To Be On TV (p/s, red vinyl)	5
95	Reprise W 0327	Stuck With Me/When I Come Around (Live) (p/s)	8
98	Reprise W 0438	Redundant/The Grouch (live) (p/s)	10
94	Reprise 9362 45529 1	DOOKIE (LP, with crowd photo on back cover, green vinyl, numbered sticker)	30
95	Reprise 9362 46046 1	INSOMNIAC (LP, with inner)	30
97	Reprise 9362 46794 1	NIMROD (LP, with inner)	40

CLAUDE 'FATS' GREENE & ORCHESTRA

66	Island WI 290	Fats Shake 'Em Up Parts 1 & 2 (actually with Al Thomas)	18

JACK GREENE

66	Brunswick 05969	There Goes My Everything/The Hardest Easy Thing	6
68	Decca AD 1005	What Locks The Door/My Elusive Dreams (export issue)	8

JEANIE GREENE

69	Atlantic 584 226	Sure As Sin/I've Been A Long Time Loving You	8

KELLIE GREENE

64	Stateside SS 303	Madrigal/Foggy Day	12

LAURA GREENE
(see also Diane Renay)

79	Grapevine GRP 135	Can't Help Loving Dat Man/It's A Good Day For A Parade	5

LORNE GREENE

64	RCA RCA 1428	Ringo/Bonanza	5
63	RCA RD 7566	YOUNG... AT HEART (LP)	15
65	RCA RD 7709	THE MAN (LP)	15

GREENFIELD

71	Philips 6113002	Sweet America/Dorothys Daughter	15

GREENGAGE

78	RCA PB 5069	Rosie/River	8

GREEN GINGER THREE

65	Decca DFE 8623	FROM THE LAND OF GREEN GINGER (EP)	15

LEE GREENLEE

59	Top Rank JAR 226	Cherry, I'm In Love With You/Starlight	7

GREEN MAN

75	private pressing	WHAT AILS THEE? (LP)	100

GREEN RIVER
(see also Mudhoney)

90	Tupelo TUP CD17	DRY AS A BONE EP (CD)	30
85	Homestead HMS 031	COME ON DOWN (LP, with insert)	25

ARTHUR GREENSLADE (& GEE MEN)

61	Decca F 11363	Rockin' Susannah/Eclipse (with Gee Men)	10
66	Columbia DB 7865	Watermelon Man/Serenade To A Broken Jaw	10

ARTHUR GREENSLADE

72	Deram DM 349	Flirt (Pour Un Flirt)/Rainy Day Love	5

DAVE GREENSLADE
(see also Wes Minster Five, Alan Price Set, Geno Washington & Ram Jam Band, Chris Farlowe, Colosseum, Samurai, Web, King Crimson, Stackridge)

73	Warner Bros K 16264	Temple Song/An English Western	5
73	Warner Bros K 46207	GREENSLADE (LP, gatefold sleeve, green label)	25
73	Warner Bros K 46259	BEDSIDE MANNERS ARE EXTRA (LP, gatefold sleeve 'Burbank' label)	20

MINT VALUE £

73 Warner Bros K 56055 SPYGLASS GUEST (LP, gatefold sleeve) . . . 15
75 Warner Bros K 56126 TIME AND TIDE (LP, gatefold sleeve) . . . 12
76 Warner Bros K 56306 CACTUS CHOIR (LP, lyric insert) . . . 15
80 EMI EMSP 332 THE PENTATEUCH OF THE COSMOGONY (2-LP, with 47-page book, as Dave Greenslade) . . . 40

SIDNEY GREENSTREET
55 Brunswick OE 9171 THE CASK OF AMONTILLADO (EP) . . . 12

GREEN TELESCOPE
86 Imaginary MIRAGE 001 Two By Two/Make Me Stay/Thinkin' About Toady (p/s, various designs) . . . 6
86 Wump BIF 4811 Face In The Crowd/Thoughts Of A Madman (p/s) . . . 5

GREEN VELVET
95 Open OPENP 017 Flash (The Relief Remixes) (12") . . . 15

ELLIE GREENWICH
(see also Popsicles, Raindrops [U.S.])
67 United Artists UP 1180 I Want You To Be My Baby/Goodnight, Goodnight . . . 25
68 United Artists UP 2214 Sunshine After The Rain/A Long Time Comin' . . . 10
70 Bell BLL 1105 I Don't Wanna Be Left Outside/Ain't That Peculiar . . . 10
73 MGM 2006 306 Maybe I Know/Goodnight Baby/Baby I Love You . . . 8
73 MGM 2315 243 LET IT BE WRITTEN, LET IT BE SUNG (LP) . . . 30

GREEN WILLOW
80 Cotswold Music SFA 115 COTSWOLD MUSIC (LP) . . . 30

GREEN WINDOWS
73 Decca F 13427 Twenty Years/Story Of A Man . . . 8

MICHAEL GREENWOOD
64 Oriole CB 1943 Buy Your Kid A Guitar/The Bellringer's Nightmare . . . 5

MICK GREENWOOD
(see also Fotheringay)o
71 MCA MDKS 8003 THE LIVING GAME (LP, gatefold sleeve, pink/orange 'dogbone' label) . . . 20
72 MCA MKPS 2026 TO FRIENDS (LP, black/blue 'hexagon' label) . . . 20

NICHOLAS GREENWOOD
(see also Crazy World Of Arthur Brown, Khan, Bryn Howarth)
72 Kingdom KVLP 9002 COLD CUTS (LP) . . . 900

GREENWOOD SINGERS/GREENWOODS
66 London hLR 10048 Please Don't Sell My Daddy No More Wine/Southbound . . . 5

STOCKER GREENWOOD & FRIENDS
79 Changes BILLY + NINE (LP) . . . 20

BIG JOHN GREER
51 HMV JO 360 Woman Is A Five Letter Word/Got You On My Mind (78, export issue) . . . 15

GINNY GREER
57 Brunswick 05673 Five Oranges, Four Apples/Kiss Me Hello (But Never Goodbye) . . . 6

GREG
(see under Greg Bright)

GREGER
66 Polydor 249 1103 IN THE NIGHT (LP) . . . 25

MAX GREGER
70 Polydor 241 8022 SUNSHINE STARSHINE (LP) . . . 12

BOBBY GREGG & FRIENDS
62 Columbia DB 4825 The Jam (Parts 1 & 2) . . . 15

BRIAN GREGORY
65 HMV POP 1412 Give Me Your Word/The Ballad Of Dick Turpin . . . 5

GLENN GREGORY & CLAUDIA BRÜCKEN
(see also Heaven 17, Propaganda, Act)
85 ZTT P ZTAS 15 When Your Heart Runs Out Of Time/(Drumless) (book-shaped picture disc) . . . 5

IA(I)N GREGORY
60 Pye 7N 15295 Time Will Tell/The Night You Told A Lie (as Ian Gregory) . . . 30
61 Pye 7N 15397 Can't You Hear The Beat Of A Broken Heart/Because . . . 25
62 Pye 7N 15435 Mr. Lovebug/Pocketful Of Dreams . . . 35
63 Columbia DB 7085 Yellow Teddy Bear/How Many Times . . . 12

JOHNNY GREGORY & HIS ORCHESTRA
(see also Chaquito)
61 Fontana H 341 Route 66/M Squad . . . 7
61 Fontana TFE 17325 MAVERICK! (EP) . . . 8
61 Fontana TFE 17331 BONANZA (EP) . . . 8
62 Fontana TFE 17389 THE T.V. THRILLERS (EP) . . . 10
72 Philips 6308 111 SPIES AND DOLLS (LP) . . . 20
74 United Artists UAG 29546 A MAN FOR ALL SEASONS (LP) . . . 40
74 United Artists QUAG 29546 A MAN FOR ALL SEASONS (LP, quadrophonic) . . . 75

TONY GREGORY
(see also Lloyd Charmers)
66 Doctor Bird DB 1007 Baby Come On Home/Marie Elena . . . 25
66 Doctor Bird DB 1016 Give Me One More Chance/I've Lost My Love . . . 25
67 Island WI 3029 Get Out Of My Life/SOUL BROTHERS: Sugar Cane . . . 30
67 Coxsone CS 7013 Only A Fool (Breaks His Own Heart)/Pure Soul . . . 25
71 Horse HOSS 3 Bouncing All Over The World/Tell Me . . . 6
67 Coxsone CSL 8011 TONY GREGORY SINGS (LP) . . . 60

MINT VALUE £

GREHAN SISTERS
66 Rex EPR 5005 THE GREHAN SISTERS (EP) ... 10
67 Transatlantic TRA 160 ON GALTYMORE MOUNTAINS (LP) ... 15

STAN GREIG'S JAZZ BAND
59 Tempo EXA 90 STAN GREIG'S JAZZ BAND (EP) ... 25
72 Redeffusion ZS 116 BOOGIE WOOGIE (LP) ... 12
80s Calligraph CLGLP 004 BLUES EVERY TIME (LP) ... 20

GREMLINS
66 Mercury MF 981 The Coming Generation/That's What I Want ... 22
67 Mercury MF 1004 You Gotta Believe It/I Can't Say ... 22

JOYCE GRENFELL
61 Columbia SCD 2160 Narcissis (Laughing Song)/I Don't 'Arf Love You (with Norman Wisdom) (p/s) ... 7
65 HMV POP 1407 Nursery School Flowers/I'm Going To See You Today ... 6
54 Philips BBL 7004 REQUESTS THE PLEASURE (LP) ... 15
62 HMV CLP 1155 JOYCE GRENFELL IN A MISCELLANY (LP) ... 12

JOYCE GRENFELL & STANLEY HOLLOWAY
(see also Stanley Holloway)
59 Caedmon TC 1104 BAB BALLADS & CAUTIONARY TALES (LP) ... 12

JOEL GREY
54 MGM SPC 1 Last Night In The Back Porch/Two-Faced (export issue) ... 18
57 Capitol CL 14779 Everytime I Ask My Heart/Moonlight Swim ... 7
58 Capitol CL 14832 Be My Next/Shoppin' Around ... 20
61 London HLX 9442 Brigitte Bardot/BURT AND THE BACKBEATS: Felicidade ... 6

RONNIE GREY & JETS
55 Capitol CL 14329 Run, Manny, Run/Sweet Baby ... 20

SARAH GREY & ELLIE ELLIS
86 Greenwich Village GVR 231 YOU GAVE ME A SONG (LP, with insert) ... 15

GREYHOUND
(see also Tillermen)
71 Trojan TR 7820 Black And White/Sand In Your Shoes ... 5
71 Trojan TR 7834 Follow The Leader/Funky Jamaica ... 5
71 Trojan TR 7848 Moon River/I've Been Trying/Pressure Is Coming On ... 5
72 Trojan TRLS 27 BLACK AND WHITE (LP) ... 15

GRID
(see also Timothy Leary Meets The Grid)
93 Virgin VSTX 1442 CRYSTAL CLEAR (Orb Mixes) (12", 4-track, clear vinyl) ... 8

GRIDS
80 Kings Head NEW ANTHEMS (EP) ... 20

ROOSEVELT GRIER
68 Action ACT 4515 People Make The World/Hard To Forget ... 22
69 Pama PM 774 Who's Got The Ball ... 15
69 Pama PM 784 C'mon Cupid/High Society Woman ... 20

GRANT GRIEVES
70 Injun 106 Four On The Floor/M1 Automatic ... 10

GRIFFIN
(see also Heavy Jelly, Skip Bifferty, Every Which Way, Bell & Arc, Happy Magazine, Ginger Baker's Airforce)
69 Bell BLL 1075 I Am The Noise In Your Head/Don't You Know ... 30
72 MGM 2006 088 What Happens In The Darkness/Calling You ... 10

GRIFFIN BROTHERS' ORCHESTRA
52 Vogue V 2139 Weepin' And Cryin' (with Tommy Brown)/The Teaser Boogie (78) ... 10

JOHNNY GRIFFIN
69 Polydor 583734 THE MAN I LOVE (LP) ... 35

JOHNNY GRIFFIN BIG SOUL BAND
(see also Eddie 'Lockjaw' Davis)
61 Riverside REP 3203 THE BIG SOUL BAND (EP, with Clark Terry & Bobby Timmons) ... 10
61 Riverside RLP 12-3331 THE BIG SOUL BAND (LP, also stereo [RLP 9331] ... 20

MERV GRIFFIN
61 London HLL 9339 The Charanga/Along Came Joe ... 10

SYLVIA GRIFFIN
88 Rocket BLAST 7 Love's A State Of Mind/Forgive The Girl (p/s, features George Harrison) ... 8
88 Rocket BLAST 712 Love's A State Of Mind/Forgive The Girl/Lonely Heart (12", p/s, features George Harrison) ... 12

VINCENT GRIFFIN
77 Topic 12TS 338 TRADITIONAL FIDDLE MUSIC FROM COUNTY CLARE (LP) ... 12

VIRGIL GRIFFIN
71 Jay Boy BOY 43 La Da Da Da Da/Climbing ... 6

ANDY GRIFFITH
55 Capitol CL 14263 Ko Ko Mo (I Love You So)/Make Yourself Comfortable ... 25
56 Capitol CL 14619 No Time For Sergeants/Make Yourself Comfortable ... 6
57 Capitol CL 14766 Mama Guitar/A Face In The Crowd ... 25
57 Capitol CL 14766 Mama Guitar/A Face In The Crowd (78) ... 15
58 Capitol CL 14936 Midnight Special/She's Bad, Bad Business (with Dixie Seven) ... 15
56 Capitol EAP1 630 ANDY GRIFFITH (EP) ... 15
60 Capitol ST 1105 SHOUTS THE BLUES AND OLD TIMEY SONGS (LP, mono) ... 12
60 Capitol ST 1105 SHOUTS THE BLUES AND OLD TIMEY SONGS (LP, stereo) ... 15

MINT VALUE £

JOE GRIFFITHS

69	Philips SBL 7902	OUT OF THE HEAD OF...(LP, black/silver labels)	20

MARCIA GRIFFITHS

(see also Bob & Marcia, Peter Touch/Tosh, Roy Richards, Soul Vendor, Bob Andy, Della Humphrey, Mr. Foundation, Bob Marley)

66	Island WI 285	Funny/KING SPARROW: Beggars Have No Choice (B-side actually by Leonard Dillon & Wailers; some copies credit Marcia Griffiths on both sides)	50
67	Studio One SO 2008	Hound Dog (actually by Norma Fraser)/HUGH GODFREY: My Time	60
67	Studio One SO 2015	After Laughter/HUGH GODFREY: Go Tell Him	60
68	Coxsone CS 7035	Mojo Girl (actually Nora Dean)/HAMLINS: Tell Me That You Love Me	100
68	Coxsone CS 7055	Feel Like Jumping/HORACE TAYLOR: Thundering Vibrations	70
68	Coxsone CS 7062	Hold Me Tight/BASIES: Home Sweet Home (B-side actually by Basses)	60
68	Studio One SO 2047	Words (as Marcia Griffiths & Jeff Dixon)/SHARKS: How Could I Live	30
68	Studio One SO 2059	Truly/SIMMS & ROBINSON: Drought	40
69	Gas GAS 111	Tell Me Now/STAN HOPE: The Weight	50
69	High Note HS 029	Talk (Parts 1 & 2) (correct title is actually "Toil")	15
69	Escort ES 808	Don't Let Me Down/REGGAEITES: Romper Room (B-side actually by Peter Tosh)	60
69	Trojan TR 693	Put A Little Love In Your Heart/J BOYS: Jay Fever	8
70	Harry J. HJ 6613	Put A Little Love In Your Heart/JAY BOYS: Bah Oop Ah	7
70	Harry J. HJ 6623	Band Of Gold/JAY BOYS: Cowboy (Version II)	7
70	Bamboo BAM 59	Shimmering Star/SOUND DIMENSION: Mun-Dun-Gu (B-side actually Im & David)	35
83	Island 1215112	Electric Boogie/Electric Boogies (12")	8
70	Trojan TRLS 94	SWEET BITTER LOVE (LP)	25
79	Sky Note SKYLP 09	NATURALLY (LP)	18
74	Trojan TRLS94	SWEET BITTER LOVE (LP, orange/white label)	20

VICTOR GRIFFITHS

70	Punch PH 29	I Am Proud Of You/KING VICTOR ALL STARS: Version	10

FERRE GRIGNARD

68	Atlantic 584 158	Yellow You Yellow Me/La Si Do	6
70	Major Minor SMLP 72	CAPTAIN DISASTER (LP)	15

CAROL GRIMES (& DELIVERY)

(see also Uncle Dog, Babylon)

70	B&C CB 129	Harry Lucky/Homemade Ruin (with Delivery)	7
74	Virgin VS 109	You're The Only One/Southern Boogie	7
76	Decca FR 13674	I Betcha Didn't Know/Dynamite	6
70	Charisma CAS 1023	FOOLS MEETING (LP, with Delivery, gatefold sleeve)	200
74	Caroline CA 2001	WARM BLOOD (LP, black/white/red 'twins' labels)	20
75	Decca SKL-R 5268	CAROL GRIMES (LP, blue/silver labels)	15

GRIMMS

(see also Neil Innes, Liverpool Scene, Scaffold, Mike McGear, McGough & McGear, John Gorman, Zoot Money, Patto, Viv Stanshall, Andy Roberts, Bashers)

75	DJM DJS 393	Backbreaker/The Masked Poet	5
76	DJM DJS 679	The Womble Bashers Of Walthamstow/ The Worst Is Yet To Come/Wiggle Waggle (promo)	8
76	DJM DJS 679	The Womble Bashers Of Walthamstow/ The Worst Is Yet To Come/Wiggle Waggle (p/s)	5
73	Island HELP 11	GRIMMS (LP, black/silver label with pink 'i' logo)	15
73	Island ILPS 9248	ROCKIN' DUCK (LP, die cut 'duck' sleeve outside single sleeve, pink rim, palm tree logo)	25

GRIM REAPER

83	Ebony EBON 16	SEE YOU IN HELL (LP)	20
85	Ebony EBON 32	FEAR NO EVIL (LP)	20

GRIN

(see also Nils Lofgren)

71	CBS 5239	We All Sung Together/See What A Love Can Do	5
71	CBS 7405	Everybody's Missin' The Sun/18 Faced Lover	5
76	CBS 4339	Soft Fun/Slippery Fingers	5
71	Epic EPC 64272	GRIN (LP)	12
72	Epic EPC 64652	1 + 1 (LP)	12
73	Epic EPC 65166	ALL OUT (LP)	12

GRINDERSWITCH

76	Capricorn 2089 030	Picking The Blues/The Best I Can	7

JANNY GRINE

70s	Sparrow BIRD 104	FREE INDEED (LP)	25

GRINGO

(see also Caravan)

71	MCA MKS 5067	I'm Another Man/Soft Mud	6
71	MCA MKPS 2107	GRINGO (LP, red/pink 'dogbone' label)	60

JOE GRINNE

69	Coxsone CS 7098	Mr Editor/How I Feel (both sides actually by Melodians)	25

GRISBY DYKE

69	Deram DM 232	The Adventures Of Miss Rosemary La Page/Mary Anne She	25

GRIZZARDS

98	Baban GRIZ 5	Grizzling/The Green Griz (p/s)	8

GROBBERT & DUFF

72	Sunlamp GRA 101	I Am I Think/The Man From Naz	150

PIERRE GROCOLAS

79	Decca FR13852	Flying Love/You're Gonna Dance	12

MINT VALUE £

DEWEY GROOM
62 Starlite ST45 085 Butane Blues/That's All I Want Out Of Life ... 40
63 Starlite ST45 095 You're Tearing My Heart Out Of Me/Walking Papers ... 20
63 Starlite ST45 105 Heartaches For Sale/Sometimes If I'm Lucky ... 15

GROOP
68 CBS 3204 Woman You're Breaking Me/Mad Over You ... 30
68 CBS 3351 Lovin' Tree/Night Life ... 20
69 Bell BLL 1070 A Famous Myth/Tears And Joys ... 15
69 Bell BLL 1080 The Jet Song (When The Weekend's Over)/Nobody At All ... 18

GROOVE
69 Parlophone R 5783 The Wind/Play The Song ... 22

GROOVE
80 Trendy WHIP 1 Heart Complaint/I Wanna Be Your Pygmy ... 15

GROOVE FARM
87 Raving Pop Blast RPBGF 1 SORE HEADS AND HAPPY HEARTS (EP, with insert & handwritten labels) ... 8
87 Raving Pop Blast RPBGF 2 ONLY THE MOST IGNORANT GUTLESS SHEEP-BRAINED POLTROON CAN DENY THEM NOW (EP) ... 8
87 Raving Pop Blast RAVE 20 BAGISM (EP, hand-painted gatefold no'd p/s with insert, home-made labels) ... 5
87 Subway Org. SUBWAY 15T GOING BANANAS WITH THE GROOVE FARM (12" EP) ... 8
88 Subway Organisation SUBWAY 19T The Big Plastic Explosion! (It's Alright, It's Alright) (Dance Mix)/Nancy Sinatra/ Baby Blue Marine/ Riot On Sunset Strip/Red Dress (p/s) ... 6
88 Subway Organisation SUBWAY 22N Driving In Your New Car (Mini Mix)/Expanding Reindeer/ I Can't Dance With You/Epistle To Duppy (10", p/s) ... 5
88 Subway Organisation SUBWAY 22N Driving In Your New Car (Mini Mix)/Expanding Reindeer/I Can't Dance With You/Epistle To Duppy (12", white label promos only, with press release) ... 10
88 Kvatch 001/LYN 18632 Baby Blue Marine/SEA URCHINS: Clingfilm (flexi, 1,000 only, 500 with p/s) ... 6

GROOVE TUNNEL
95 Detour DR 023 Rainy Day/How Do You Feel (p/s, white vinyl) ... 7

GROOVERS
(see also Lloyd & Groovers, Alva Lewis, Junior Byles, Dennis Walks)
71 Camel CA 83 Put Me Down Easy/I Want To Go Back Home ... 6
71 Escort ERT 863 Bend Down Low/The Burning Feeling ... 6

WINSTON GROOV(E)Y
(see also King Horror, Upsetters)
69 Grape GR 3005 Leaving Me Standing/Little Girl ... 12
69 Grape GR 3008 Merry X-mas/I Am Lonely ... 8
69 Nu Beat NB 041 Island In The Sun/Work It Up ... 10
69 Nu Beat NB 042 Josephine/Champagne And Wine ... 8
70 New Beat NB 053 Standing At The Corner/You Send Me ... 6
70 New Beat NB 055 Yellow Bird/For Your Love ... 6
70 New Beat NB 058 Here Is My Heart/Birds And Flowers ... 6
70 New Beat NB 066 Groovin'/Sugar Mama ... 6
70 New Beat NB 073 Tennessee Waltz/Old Man Trouble ... 6
70 Attack ATT 8018 I Can't Go On/Only You ... 10
70 Attack ATT 8019 You Can't Turn Your Back On Me/PAMA DICE: The Worm ... 10
70 Jackpot JP 708 Funky Chicken/CIMARRONS: Part 2 (B-side actually unknown instrumental) ... 10
70 Jackpot JP 709 Funny/CIMARRONS: Funny Version Two ... 10
70 Torpedo TOR 11 Please Don't Make Me Cry/Motion On The Ocean ... 12
70 Crab CRAB 63 I Like The Way/Tell Me Why ... 8
71 Crab CRAB 64 I've Got The Find A Way To Win Mary Back/Wanna Be There ... 8
71 Bullet BU 471 I Wanna Be Loved/Get Back Together ... 8
71 Pama PM 827 Don't Break My Heart/How Long Will This Go On ... 10
71 Pama Supreme PS 323 Free The People/Not Now ... 8
72 Pama Supreme PS 349 What You Gonna Do/Why Did You Leave ... 8
72 Pama Supreme PS 364 Sylvia's Mother/Here Is My Heart ... 8
73 Explosion EX 2086 Nose For Trouble/RHYTHM RULERS: Version ... 8
74 Explosion EX 2088 Please Don't Make Me Cry/So Easy ... 8
69 Pama PMP 2011 FREE THE PEOPLE (LP) ... 40

WALTER GROSS
54 MGM SP 1070 Blue Moon/Tenderly ... 5
54 MGM SP 1071 You Won't Forget Me (with India Adams)/Follow Me ... 5

G.G. GROSSETT
69 Crab CRAB 10 Run Girl Run/DENNIS WALKS: The Drifter ... 20
69 Crab CRAB 33 Greater Sounds/Live The Life I Love ... 12

STEFAN GROSSMAN
(see also John Renbourn)
70 Big T BIG 133 Pretty Little Tune/Little Sally Walker ... 7
71 Big T BIG 140 'Joe Hill' - Themes ... 7
68 Fontana (S)TL 5463 AUNT MOLLY'S MURRAY FARM (LP) ... 25
69 Fontana STL 5485 THE GRAMERCY PARK SHEIK (LP) ... 20
70 Transatlantic TRA 217 YAZOO BASIN BOOGIE (LP) ... 15
71 Transatlantic TRA 246 THOSE PLEASANT DAYS (LP, with lyric insert) ... 15
72 Transatlantic TRA 257 HOT DOGS (LP) ... 12
73 Transatlantic TRA 264 LIVE! (2-LP, gatefold sleeve) ... 15
73 Transatlantic TRA 274 GUITAR INSTRUMENTALS (LP) ... 12

LUTHER GROSVENOR
(see also Hellions, Revolution, Art, Spooky Tooth, Mott The Hoople, Widowmaker)
71 Island WIP 6109 Here Comes The Queen/Heavy Day ... 6
72 Island WIP 6124 All The People/Waiting ... 6
71 Island ILPS 9168 UNDER OPEN SKIES (LP, gatefold sleeve pink rim palm tree logo) ... 40

MINT VALUE £

CARL GROSZMANN

70	Decca F 13065	Thunderbird/Missouri Woman	6
75	Ring O' 2017 103	I've Had It/C'mon And Roll	15
77	Ring O' 2017 107	Face Of A Permanent Stranger/Your Own Affair (promo p/s)	15
77	Ring O' 2017 107	Face Of A Permanent Stranger/Your Own Affair (company sleeve)	10

GROUND ATTACK

81	Ground Attack GAR 001	THE RED LION EP (Red Lion/Every Mother's Son) (gatefold p/s)	100
81	Ground Attack GAR 001	THE RED LION EP (Red Lion/Every Mother's Son) (later pressing without p/s)	20

GROUNDHOGS

(see also John Lee's Groundhogs, Tony McPhee, Herbal Mixture, Home, Andy Fernbach, John Lee Hooker)

68	Liberty LBF 15174	You Don't Love Me/Still A Fool	25
69	Liberty LBF 15263	B.D.D./TONY McPHEE: Gasoline	35
70	Liberty LBF 15346	Eccentric Man/Status People	18
73	W. Wide Artists WWS 006	Sad Go Round/Over Blue	6
74	W. Wide Artists WWS 012	Plea Sing, Plea Sing/TONY McPHEE: Dog Me Bitch	6
76	United Artists UP 36095	Live A Little Lady/Boogie Withus	6
76	United Artists UP 36177	Pastoral Future/Live Right (as Tony McPhee & Groundhogs)	6
68	Liberty LBL 83199E	SCRATCHING THE SURFACE (LP, mono, blue label)	90
68	Liberty LBS 83199E	SCRATCHING THE SURFACE (LP, stereo, blue label)	50
69	Liberty LBS 83253	BLUES OBITUARY (LP, blue label)	65
70	Liberty LBS 83295	THANK CHRIST FOR THE BOMB (LP, gatefold sleeve, 1st pressing blue label)	70
70	Liberty LBS 83295	THANK CHRIST FOR THE BOMB (LP, gatefold sleeve, 2nd pressing black label)	30
71	Liberty LBS 83401	SPLIT (LP, gatefold sleeve, black label)	25
72	United Artists UAG 29347	WHO WILL SAVE THE WORLD... (LP, gatefold sleeve)	30
72	United Artists UAG 29419	HOGWASH (LP, gatefold sleeve)	20
74	United Artists UDF 31	GROUNDHOGS' BEST 1969-1972 (2-LP)	15
74	W. Wide Artists WWA 004	SOLID (LP, with lyric insert)	15
76	United Artists UAG 29917	CROSSCUT SAW (LP)	12
76	United Artists UAG 29994	BLACK DIAMOND (LP)	12
84	Psycho PSYCHO 24	HOGGIN' THE STAGE (2-LP, with EP, stickered gatefold sleeve)	18
85	Landslide LANDLP 102	RAZORS EDGE (LP)	12
87	Demi Monde DMLP 1014	BACK AGAINST THE WALL (LP)	12
89	HTD Records HTDLP 2	NO SURRENDER (LP)	12

GROUP

(see also Neil Innes)

72	Charisma CB 197	Bovver Boys/Piraeus Football Club/An Open Letter To George Best	6

GROUP B

(see also Blue Cheer)

67	Vocalion VF 9284	I Know Your Name Girl/I Never Really Know	20

GROUP 1850

69	Philips SBL 7884	AGEMO'S TRIP TO MOTHER EARTH (LP, gatefold sleeve)	250

GROUP IMAGE

69	Stable SLE 8005	A MOUTH IN THE CLOUDS (LP)	80

GROUP ONE

58	HMV POP 463	She's Neat/Made For Each Other	30
58	HMV POP 492	Chanson D'Amour/Londonderry Air	5

GROUP SIX

59	Oriole CB 1488	Rock-A-Boogie/Rockin' The Blues	25
59	Oriole CB 1488	Rock-A-Boogie/Rockin' The Blues (78)	20

GROUP THERAPY

69	Philips BF 1744	River Deep Mountain High/Remember What You Said	6
69	Philips BF 1792	Can't Stop Lovin' You Baby/I Must Go	6
69	Philips SBL 7883	YOU'RE IN NEED OF GROUP THERAPY (LP)	18

GROUP TWO

68	Columbia DB 8374	It's Raining Outside/Western Man, Eastern Lady	7

GROUP X

63	Fontana 267 274 TF	There Are 8 Million Cossack Melodies - And This Is One Of Them/ Teneriffe (in p/s)	15
63	Fontana 267 274 TF	There Are 8 Million Cossack Melodies - And This Is One Of Them/ Teneriffe	8
63	Fontana TF 417	Roti Calliope/Cross Beat	20

GROUT

78	Urinating Vicar	DO IT YOURSELF (EP) (100 only, sound quality very poor)	400

GRUDGE

73	Black Label BL 002	When Christine Comes Around/I'm Gonna Smash Your Face In	40

GRUMBLE

(see also 10cc)

73	RCA Victor RCA 2384	Da Doo Ron Ron/Pig Bin An' Gone	5

GRUMBLEWEEDS

71	Phillips 78434	Never Before/Fiona McLaughlin	15
73	Decca F 13416	Trees/I Am A Grumbleweed	6

GRUNT FUTTOCK

(see also Move, Roy Wood)

72	Regal Zonophone RZ 3042	Rock 'N' Roll Christian/Free Sole	30

GRUVY BEATS

70	Nu Beat NB 048	Share Your Popcorn/LAUREL AITKEN: Mr. Popcorn	15
70	Nu Beat NB 049	Blue Mink/LAUREL AITKEN: I've Got Your Love	15

MINT VALUE £

GIGI GRYCE

60	Esquire 32-151	SAYIN' SOMETHIN' (LP)	20
60	Esquire	RAT RACE BLUES (LP)	30

GRYPHON

(see also Richard Harvey)

77	Harvest HAR 5125	Spring Song/Fall Of The Leaf	6
73	Transatlantic TRA 262	GRYPHON (LP, gatefold sleeve)	25
74	Transatlantic TRA 282	MIDNIGHT MUSHRUMPS (LP)	12
74	Transatlantic TRA 287	RED QUEEN TO GRYPHON THREE (LP)	15
75	Transatlantic TRA 302	RAINDANCE (LP)	12
77	Harvest SHSP 4063	TREASON (LP, with lyric inner sleeve)	20

G.T.O.'s

(see also Joey & Continentals)

67	Polydor 56721	She Rides With Me/Rudy Vadoo	75

G.T.O.'s (Girls Together Outrageously)

(see also Jeff Beck, Frank Zappa)

70	Straight STS 1059	PERMANENT DAMAGE (LP)	120

G.T.R.

(see also Steve Hackett)

86	Arista GTR 1	When The Heart Rules The Mind/Reach Out (poster sleeve)	6
86	Arista GTRSD 1	When The Heart Rules The Mind/Reach Out (picture disc)	8

GUANA BATZ

84	Big Beat SW 89	You're So Fine/Rockin' In My Coffin/Jungle Rumble/Guana Rock (p/s)	6
84	Big Beat NS 96	The Cave/Werewolf Blues (p/s)	5
85	I.D. NOSE 4	HELD DOWN ... AT LAST (LP)	12

GUARDIANS OF THE RAINBOW

68	President PT 186	What Do You Do When You've Lost Your Love/Cry Alone	6

JOSE GUARDIOLA & ROSE MARY

63	HMV POP 1147	Algo Prodigioso/Di Papa	7

LENNIS GUESS

75	Route RT 11	Just Ask Me/Workin' For My Baby	5

GUESS WHO

65	Pye International 7N 25305	Shakin' All Over/Till We Kissed	25
66	King KG 1044	His Girl/It's My Pride	30
67	Fontana TF 831	This Time Long Ago/There's No Getting Away From You	15
67	Fontana TF 861	Miss Felicity Grey/Flying On The Ground Is Wrong	15
70	RCA 1943	American Woman/No Sugar Tonight	5
70	RCA SF 8037	WHEATFIELD SOUL (LP)	15
70	RCA SF 8107	AMERICAN WOMAN (LP)	15

EARL GUEST

62	Columbia DB 4707	Honky Tonk Train Blues/Winkle Picker Stomp	10
62	Columbia DB 4926	The Girl From The Fair Isle/Twistin' John	5
64	Columbia DB 7212	Begin The Beguine/Foxy	15

GUEST & EDWARDS

72	Phillips 6006231	All Alone/Sing You A Picture	20

REG GUEST SYNDICATE

65	Mercury MF 927	Underworld/Guys, Guns, Dolls And Danger	90
66	Mercury 20089 MCL	UNDERWORLD (LP)	40

GUGGENHEIM

72	Indigo GOLP 7001	GUGGENHEIM (LP, private pressing)	50

GUIDED BY VOICES

99	Creation CRE 325	Teenage FBI/Flying Into Ashes/Tropical Robots (p/s)	10

GUILLEMOTS

05	Fantastic Plastic FPS 050	I SAW SUCH THINGS IN MY SLEEP EP (CD, p/s)	15
05	Fantastic Plastic FPS 050	I SAW SUCH THINGS IN MY SLEEP EP (10", 300 only p/s)	40
05	Fantastic Plastic FPTEN 055	Trains To Brazil/My Chosen One/Go Away (10", 1,000 only, p/s)	8
06	Polydor IC00309	THROUGH THE WINDOWPANE (2-LP, gatefold sleeve, inner sleeves & booklet)	20

ISAAC GUILLORY

(see also Shames, Sam Gopal)

74	Atlantic K 40521	ISAAC GUILLORY (LP)	18

GUILLOTEENS

65	Pye International 7N 25324	I Don't Believe/Hey You	60

BONNIE GUITAR

58	London HLD 8591	A Very Precious Love/Johnny Vagabond	25
59	Top Rank JAR 260	Candy Apple Red/Come To Me, I Love You	10
58	London HA-D 2122	MOONLIGHT AND SHADOWS (LP)	30

GUITAR CRUSHER with JIMMY SPURRILL

(see also Wild Jimmy Spurrill)

69	Blue Horizon 57-3149	Since My Baby Hit The Numbers/Hambone Blues	30

GUITAR RED

63	Pye International 7N 25219	Just You And I/Old Fashioned Love	30

GUITAR SHORTY

72	Flyright LP 500	CAROLINA SLIDE GUITAR (LP)	15

GULLIVER

70	Elektra 2101 011	Every Day's A Lovely Day/Angelina	6
70	Elektra 2101 017	Angelina/Christine	5
70	Elektra 2410 006	GULLIVER (LP)	18

MINT VALUE £

GULLIVER'S PEOPLE

66 Parlophone R 5435 Splendour In The Grass/Took This Land ... 15
66 Parlophone R 5464 Fi Fo Fum/Over The Hills ... 10
68 Parlophone R 5709 On A Day Like This/My Life ... 10
69 Columbia DB 8588 Somehow, Somewhere/I Found Love ... 10

GULLIVER'S TRAVELS

(see also Mike D'Abo, Andrew Oldham)
69 Instant INLP 003 GULLIVER'S TRAVELS (LP, withdrawn, front laminated sleeve, flipbacks) ... 100

GUN

(see also Baker-Gurvitz Army, Parrish & Gurvitz, Rupert's People, Three Man Army, Knack)o
68 CBS 3764 Race With The Devil/Sunshine ... 10
68 CBS 3764 Race With The Devil/3-4 In The Middle (different B-side) ... 10
69 CBS 4052 Drives You Mad/Rupert's Travels ... 7
69 CBS 4443 Hobo/Don't Look Back ... 7
69 CBS 4443 Hobo/Long Hair Wild Man (different B-side) ... 10
70 CBS 4952 Runnin' Wild/Drown Yourself In The River ... 6
69 CBS M63552 GUN (LP, mono, laminated front sleeve, orange label) ... 150
69 CBS 63552 GUN (LP, stereo, laminated front sleeve, orange label) ... 50
69 CBS 63683 GUNSIGHT (LP) ... 45

GUN CLUB

(see also Jeffrey Lee Pierce, Kid Congo Powers)
82 Beggars Banquet BEG 80 Ghost On The Highway/Sex Beat (p/s) ... 10
82 Animal/Chry. CHCAT 2635 The Fire Of Love/Walking With The Beast (p/s) ... 6
83 Animal/Chrysalis GUN 1 Death Party/House On Highland Avenue/The Lie (p/s) ... 8
83 Animal/Chrysalis GUN 12 Death Party/House On Highland Avenue/The Lie/ Light Of The World/ Come Back Jim (12", p/s) ... 10
88 Red Rhino RED 89 The Breaking Hands/Crabdance (p/s) ... 8
88 Red Rhino RED 89 12 The Breaking Hands/Crabdance/Nobody's City (12", p/s) ... 10
90 Fire BLAZE 47T The Great Divide/Crabdance/St. John's Divine Part 2 (p/s) ... 10

JON GUNN

67 Deram DM 133 I Just Made Up My Mind/Now It's My Turn ... 15
67 Deram DM 166 If You Wish It/I Don't Want To Get Hung Up On You Babe ... 15

JO JO GUNNE

(see under 'J')

JIM GUNNER

60 Decca F 11276 Hoolee Jump/Footloose (as Jim Gunner & Echoes) ... 15
61 Fontana H 313 Desperado/Baghdad (as Jim Gunner & His Sidekicks) ... 20

TONY GUNNER

62 London HLU 9492 Rough Road/You Gotta Get Home ... 20

SARAH OGAN GUNNING

67 Topic 12T 171 A GIRL OF CONSTANT SORROW (LP, mono, blue label) ... 20

GUNS FOR HIRE

(see also Main T. Possee)
80 Korova KOW 6 My Girlfriend's Boyfriend/I'm Famous Now (p/s) ... 10

GUNSHOT

90 Vinyl Solution STORM18 Battle Creek Brawl (12") ... 12
91 Vinyl Solution STORM24 Crime Story/No Sell Out (12") ... 10
91 Vinyl Solution STORM40 Clear From Present Danger (12") ... 8
92 Vinyl Solution STORM49 Killing Season/Nobody Move (12") ... 8
93 Vinyl Solution FART6 To Those Who Deserve It (7") ... 20
93 Vinyl Solution STORM61 Children Of A Dying Breed (12") ... 8

GUNS N' ROSES

87 Geffen GEF 22 It's So Easy/Mr Brownstone (p/s) ... 10
87 Geffen GEF 22T It's So Easy/Mr Brownstone/Shadow Of Your Love/Move To The City (12", p/s) .. 12
87 Geffen GEF 22TP It's So Easy/Mr Brownstone/Shadow Of Your Love/ Move To The City (12", picture disc with stickered PVC sleeve) ... 40
87 Geffen GEF 30 Welcome To The Jungle/Whole Lotta Rosie (live) (red p/s) ... 8
87 Geffen GEF 30T Welcome To The Jungle/Whole Lotta Rosie (live)/It's So Easy (live)/ Knockin' On Heaven's Door (live) (12", red p/s) ... 20
87 Geffen GEF 30TW Welcome To The Jungle/Whole Lotta Rosie (live)/It's So Easy (live)/ Knockin' On Heaven's Door (live) (12", poster p/s) ... 10
87 Geffen GEF 30P Welcome To The Jungle/Whole Lotta Rosie (live)/It's So Easy (live)/ Knockin' On Heaven's Door (live) (12", picture disc) ... 40
88 Geffen GEF 43 Sweet Child O' Mine/Out Ta Get Me (p/s, with wraparound sticker) ... 5
88 Geffen GEF 43TE Sweet Child O' Mine/Out Ta Get Me/Rocket Queen (10", revolving p/s) ... 15
88 Geffen GEF 43TV Sweet Child O' Mine/Out Ta Get Me/Rocket Queen (12", metallic p/s) ... 10
88 Geffen GEF 47 Welcome To The Jungle/Nightrain (p/s) ... 5
88 Geffen GEF 47TV Welcome To The Jungle/Nightrain/You're Crazy (Acoustic Version) (12", p/s, with patch) ... 8
88 Geffen GEF 47TP Welcome To The Jungle/Nightrain/You're Crazy (Acoustic Version) (12", picture disc) ... 10
88 Geffen GEF 47CD Welcome To The Jungle/Nightrain/You're Crazy (Acoustic Version) (3" CD with adaptor, 5" case) ... 12
89 Geffen GEF 50P Paradise City/I Used To Love Her (gun-shaped clear picture disc) ... 12
89 Geffen GEF 50P Paradise City/I Used To Love Her (gun-shaped white picture disc) ... 15
89 Geffen GEF 50X Paradise City/I Used To Love Her (p/s, slotted in holster p/s) ... 7
89 Geffen GEF 50T Paradise City/I Used To Love Her/Anything Goes (12", p/s) ... 7
89 Geffen GEF 50CD Paradise City/I Used To Love Her/Anything Goes/Sweet Child O' Mine (3" CD) .. 8
89 Geffen GEF 55W Sweet Child O' Mine (Remix)/Out Ta Get Me (with tattoo) ... 8
89 Geffen GEF 55X Sweet Child O' Mine/Out Ta Get Me (Limited edition sticker pack) ... 10
89 Geffen GEF 55P Sweet Child O' Mine/Out Ta Get Me/Rocket Queen (shaped pic disc & sticker) .. 12

			MINT VALUE £
89	Geffen GEF 55P	Sweet Child O' Mine/Out Ta Get Me/Rocket Queen (12" uncut shaped pic disc)	100
89	Geffen GEF 55T	Sweet Child O' Mine (Remix)/Move To The City/Whole Lotta Rosie (live)/ It's So Easy (live) (12", p/s)	10
89	Geffen GEF 55CD	Sweet Child O' Mine (Remix)/Move To The City/Whole Lotta Rosie (live)/ It's So Easy (live) (3" CD)	10
89	Geffen GEF 56T	Patience/Rocket Queen/W. Axl Rose Interview (12", p/s)	8
89	Geffen GEF 56CD	Patience/Rocket Queen/W. Axl Rose Interview (3" CD, gatefold card sleeve)	12
89	Geffen GEF 60X	Nightrain/Reckless Life (live) (p/s, with patch)	7
89	Geffen GEF 60P	Nightrain/Reckless Life (live) (case-shaped picture disc, stickered PVC sleeve)	12
89	Geffen GEF 60CD	Nightrain/Knockin' On Heaven's Door (live)/Reckless Life (live) (3" CD, gatefold card sleeve)	10
91	Geffen GFSTP 6	You Could Be Mine/Civil War (12", clear vinyl with insert in PVC sleeve)	8
91	Geffen GFST 9	Don't Cry/Don't Cry (Alternate Lyrics)/Don't Cry (Demo) (12", hologram p/s)	8
91	Geffen GFSX 17	Live And Let Die (LP Version)/Live And Let Die (live) (12", yellow/orange vinyl, die-cut p/s)	8
91	Geffen GFSTD 17	Live And Let Die (LP Version)/Live And Let Die (live)/ Shadow Of Your Love (live) (CD, stencil p/s)	8
92	Geffen GFST 18	November Rain/Sweet Child O' Mine (live)/Patience (live) (12", p/s, 1 side etched)	8
87	Geffen 9240 148	APPETITE FOR DESTRUCTION (LP, withdrawn 'robot' sleeve)	25
91	Geffen GEF 24415	USE YOUR ILLUSION I (2 x LP)	25
91	Geffen GEF 24420	USE YOUR ILLUSION II (2 x LP)	25

ARTHUR GUNTER

72	Blue Horizon 2431 012	BLUES AFTER HOURS (LP)	90
70s	Contempo COLP 119	BLACK AND BLUES (LP)	25

HARDROCK GUNTER

(see also Red Foley, Roberta Lee)

55	Brunswick OE 9167	MOUNTAIN MUSIC (EP)	25

GURU GURU

73	Atlantic K 50022	DON'T CALL US WE'LL CALL YOU (LP)	15
74	Atlantic K 50044	DANCE OF THE FLAMES (LP)	15

GURU GURU/ULI TREPTE

80s	United Dairies UDT 07	LIVE 72 & 73 (, 1 side each)	18

GURU JOSH

90	Deconstruction PT 44140	Freaky Dreamer (12")	45

GURUS

66	United Artists UP 1160	Blue Snow Night/Come Girl	30

JOHNNY GUSTAFSON

(see also Big Three, Merseybeats, Quotations, Hard Stuff, Johnny & John, Ian Gillan Band, G-Force)

65	Polydor 56022	Just To Be With You/Sweet Day	20
65	Polydor 56043	Take Me For A Little While/Make Me Your Number One	30

CARL GUSTAV & 84's

81	Convulsive CN 001	I Want To Kill Russians/Through Birds, Through Fire, But Not Through Glass (p/s)	10

ARLO GUTHRIE

67	Reprise RS 20644	Motorcycle Song/Now And Then	8
70	Reprise RS 20877	Alice's Rock'N'Roll Restaurant/Coming In To Los Angeles	5
70	Reprise RS 20951	Valley To Pray/Gabriel's Mother's Hiway Ballad No. 16 Blues (demo-only)	7
67	Reprise RLP 6267	ALICE'S RESTAURANT (LP)	20
68	Reprise RSLP 6269	ARLO (LP)	20
69	Reprise RSLP 6346	RUNNING DOWN THE ROAD (LP)	15
70	Reprise RSLP 6411	WASHINGTON COUNTY (LP)	15

GWEN GUTHRIE

86	4th + Broadway BRW 1252	Seventh Heaven/It Should Have Been You/Getting Hot (12", p/s)	12

SHEILA GUTHRIE

63	Fontana TF 399	Mirror Mirror/It Doesn't Mean A Thing	8

WOODY GUTHRIE

51	Melodisc 1141	Ramblin' Blues/Talkin' Columbia Blues (78)	15
55	Melodisc EPM7 84	HARD AIN'T IT HARD (EP)	20
55	Melodisc EPM7 85	WORRIED MAN BLUES (EP)	20
55	Melodisc EPM7 91	HEY LOLLY LOLLY (EP)	20
55	Melodisc MLP 12-106	MORE SONGS BY GUTHRIE (LP)	40
58	Topic 12T 31	BOUND FOR GLORY (LP)	35
64	RCA RD 7642	DUST BOWL BALLADS (LP)	25
65	Xtra XTRA 1012	WOODY GUTHRIE (LP)	12
66	Xtra XTRA 1064	WOODY GUTHRIE (LP)	12

GUTTERSNIPES

(see also Cocksparrer)

88	Razor GUTT 1	Addicted To Love/Love's Young Dream (p/s)	8
88	Razor RAZ 42	THE POOR DRESS UP (LP)	12

GUTTERSNYPES

94	Liberty Grooves LIB 004	TRIALS OF LIFE (Radio Edits) (12" EP)	18
94	Liberty Grooves LIB 005	TRIALS OF LIFE (12" EP)	8
94	Liberty Grooves LIB 006	TRIALS OF LIFE EP (Instrumentals)	18
94	Liberty Grooves LIB004	The Trials Of Life (Green vinyl radio edit) (12")	15
94	Liberty Grooves LIB005	The Trials Of Life (Blue, Red) (12")	10
94	Liberty Grooves LIB005	The Trials Of Life (White vinyl, promo version, limited edition, personalised by band) (12")	40
94	Liberty Grooves LIB006	The Trials Of Life (Clear vinyl instrumentals) (12")	40

GUV'NERS

(see also Jess Conrad, Dickie Pride, Nelson Keene)

63	Piccadilly 7N 35117	Let's Make A Habit Of This/The Kissing Had To Stop	10

MINT VALUE £

BARRY GUY
(see also Derek Bailey Barry Guy & Paul Rutherford)

76	Incus INCUS 22	STATEMENTS V-XI FOR DOUBLE BASS AND VIOLONE (LP)	50

BUDDY GUY
(see also Junior Wells, Eddie Boyd/Buddy Guy)

65	Chess CRS 8004	Let Me Love You Baby/Ten Years Ago	20
68	Fontana TF 951	Mary Had A Little Lamb/Sweet Little Angel	18
72	Atlantic K 10195	Honey Dripper/Man Of Many Words	6
91	Silvertone ORE 30	Mustang Sally/Trouble Don't Last (with Jeff Beck, p/s)	5
65	Chess CRE 6004	CRAZY MUSIC (EP)	40
68	Vanguard SVRL 19001	COMING AT YOU (LP)	45
68	Vanguard SVRL 19002	MAN AND HIS BLUES (LP)	45
68	Vanguard SVRL 19004	BLUES TODAY (LP)	30
69	Vanguard SVRL 19008	THIS IS BUDDY GUY! (LP)	30
69	Vanguard SVRL 79290	HOT AND COOL (LP)	30
69	Chess CRL(S) 4546	I LEFT MY BLUES IN SAN FRANCISCO (LP)	35
69	Python KM 2	FIRST TIME I MET THE BLUES (LP)	70
70	Harvest SHSP 4006	BUDDY AND THE JUNIORS (LP, with Junior Mance & Junior Wells)	65
70	Red Lightnin' RL 001	IN THE BEGINNING (LP)	15
72	Atlantic K 40240	PLAY THE BLUES (LP, with Junior Wells)	18
73	Vanguard VSD 79323	HOLD THAT PLANE (LP)	18

GUY CANDY

03	Pump Hard PUMP 001	Raining Hard On Snow/Allotment (CD)	8

GUYS
(see also Beat Six)

69	Tepee TPR SP 1001	You Go Your Way/Little Girl	20

GEORGE GUZMAN

68	London SH 8384	INTRODUCING GEORGE GUZMAN (LP)	30

GYGAFO

89	Holyground HG 1155	LEGEND OF THE KINGFISHER (LP, 160 copies only, posthumously designed semi-gatefold sleeve with insert)	60

GYMSLIPS

83	Abstract ABT 006	ROCKING WITH THE RENEES (LP, with insert)	18

GYNAECOLOGISTS

81	Teesbeat TB 2	The Red Pullover/The Offence (p/s)	5

GYPP
(see also Martin Newell, Cleaners From Venus, Brotherhood Of Lizards)

79	Shy Talk AC 1065	YAAH EP: Marigoldz/Titania/Sister Darling (p/s)	20

GYPPO

79	United Artists	High Rise Love/Free Enterprise (possibly, only promo copies exist)	100

GYPSIES
(see also Flirtations, Pearly Gates)

67	CBS 201785	Jerk It/Diamonds, Rubies, Gold And Fame	40

GYPSY
(see also Legay)

71	United Artists UP 35202	What Makes A Man A Man/I Want To Be Beside You	6
71	United Artists UAG 29155	GYPSY (LP)	15
72	United Artists UAS 29420	BRENDA AND THE RATTLESNAKE (LP)	15

GYPSY

84	Private Pressing	We Came To Be Free/Get It Right	50

H

HABIBIYYA
(see also Mighty Baby)

72	Island HELP 7	IF MAN BUT KNEW (LP, with inner sleeve, black/silver label, pink 'i' logo)	25

HABITS
(see also Charles Dickens, Nice, Brian Davison)

66	Decca F 12348	Elbow Baby/Need You	40

HACKENSACK
(see also Megaton, Tiger [U.K.], Nicky Moore Band, Samson)

72	Island WIP 6149	Moving On/River Boat	12
71	Polydor 2383 263	UP THE HARD WAY (LP, with inner sleeve)	80
74	Zel UZ 003	HERE COMES THE JUDGE (LP, private pressing, as Hack & Sack)	100

STEVE HACKETT
(see also Peter Banks, Genesis, GTR, Quiet World)

78	Charisma CB 312	How Can I?/Kim (with Ritchie Havens)	10
78	Charisma CB 318	Narnia (Remix)/Please Don't Touch	7
79	Charisma CB 334	Every Day/Lost Time In Cordoba	5
79	Charisma CB 341	Clocks - The Angel Of Mons/Acoustic Set	5
79	Charisma CB 341-12	Clocks - The Angel Of Mons /Acoustic Set/Tigermoth (12", p/s)	8
80	Charisma CB 357	The Show/Hercules Unchained (p/s)	5
80	Charisma CB 368	Sentimental Institution/The Toast (p/s)	5

MINT VALUE £

83	Charisma CELL 12	Cell 151/Air Conditioned Nightmare/Time Lapse At Milton Keynes (12", p/s; with bonus white label 12" "Clocks - The Angel Of Mons"/ "Acoustic Set"/"Tigermoth" [CELL 13], 2000 only)	8
01	Camino CAMCD 23	LIVE ARCHIVE (4-CD box set)	25
01	Camino CAMCD 23	LIVE ARCHIVE (5-CD box set, limited edition with extra CD)	25

VERNON HADDOCK'S JUBILEE LOVELIES

65	Columbia SX 6011	VERNON HADDOCK'S JUBILEE LOVELIES (LP)	150

HADOUKEN!

07	Surface Noise SN 0102)	That Boy That Girl/Tuning In (mail order only, 500 pressed p/s)	20

HAFFY'S WHISKY SOUR

(see also Easybeats, Paintbox)

71	Deram DM 345	Shot In The Head/Bye Bye Bluebird	10

HAFLER TRIO

(see also Cabaret Voltaire)

84	Doublevision DVR 4	BANG! - AN OPEN LETTER (LP, with insert)	25
86	Charrm 3	THREE WAYS OF SAYING TWO - THE NETHERLANDS LECTURES (LP, stickered sleeve with booklet)	25
86	Touch T 05	THE SEA ORG (10", 'audio/visual' package with booklet)	20

HAGALAZ RUNEDANCE

97	Elfenblut SAG III	When The Trees Were Silenced/A Tale Of Fate (Folkswang Awaits) (p/s, insert)	10

SAMMY HAGAR

(see also Van Halen, Madonna, Montrose)

77	Capitol E-ST 11599	SAMMY HAGAR (LP, red vinyl)	12
79	Capitol E-ST 11983	STREET MACHINE (LP, with free single)	12

EARLE HAGEN

64	Colpix PX 740	Nancy's Theme/New Interns Watusi	5

MERLE HAGGARD & STRANGERS

68	Capitol CL 15540	The Legend Of Bonnie And Clyde/I Started Loving You Again	5
87	Premier PMP 1003	TO ALL THE GIRLS I'VE LOVED BEFORE (LP, withdrawn)	15
77	MCA MCF 2818	MY FAREWELL TO ELVIS (LP)	12

MEL HAGUE

60s	LK/LP 6558	MERRY-GO-ROUND (LP, signed)	18
60s	LK/LP 6558	MERRY-GO-ROUND (LP)	12

JOYCE HAHN

57	London HLA 8453	Gonna Find Me A Bluebird/I Saw You, I Saw You	25

PAUL HAIG

(see also Josef K, Rhythm Of Life, Juggernauts)

81	Rational no cat. no.	DRAMA (cassette)	12
82	Operation Twilight OPT 03	Running Away/Time (p/s)	5
84	Island ISX 198	The Only Truth (U.S. Remix)/Instrumental/Ghost Rider (12", p/s)	8
84	Island ILPS 9742	RHYTHM OF LIFE (LP)	12
85	Operation Afterglow OPA 3	THE WARP OF PURE FUN (LP, inner sleeve)	12

ROBERT HAIGH

(see also SEMA)

85	Laylah LAY 09	JULIET OF THE SPIRITS EP (12")	25
86	Laylah LAY 21	MUSIC FROM THE ANTE CHAMBER EP (12")	25
88	United Dairies UD 026	VALENTINE OUT OF SEASON (LP)	40
89	Le Rey LR 103	A WALTZ IN PLAIN C (CD)	100
87	United Dairies UDT 034	THE BEST OF ROBERT HAIGH (cassette)	20

NORMAN HAINES (BAND)

(see also Avalanche, Brumbeats, The Dog That Bit People, Locomotive)

70	Parlophone R 5871	Daffodil/Autumn Mobile (as Norman Haynes Band)	20
71	Parlophone SPSR 338	Den Of Iniquity/Everything You See (Mr. Armageddon) (promo only)	45
72	Parlophone R 5960	Give It To You Girl/Elaine (as Norman Haines)	20
71	Parlophone PCS 7130	DEN OF INIQUITY (LP, black/silver label with boxed logo)	900
94	Shoestring BL001	DEN OF INIQUITY (LP, reissue)	30
94	Shoestring BL001	DEN OF INIQUITY (CD)	18

HAIR

(see also Alex Harvey, Hairband)

69	Pye NSPL 18314	RAVE UP (LIVE FROM THE SHAFTESBURY THEATRE) (LP)	90

HAIR

70	Columbia SCX 6452	HAIRPIECE (LP, black/silver labels with boxed logo)	250

HAIRBAND

(see also Alex Harvey, Hair)

69	Bell BLL 1076	Big Louis/Travelling Song	18
69	Bell SBLL 69	BAND ON THE WAGON (LP, blue/silver/black label with "Sold in the U.K..." text)	60

HAIRCUT 100

83	Arista CLIP 5	Whistle Down The Wind (withdrawn)	10
82	Arista HCC 101	BLUE HAT FOR A BLUE DAY (LP, withdrawn, test pressings only)	20

HAIRPOWER

70	CBS 4961	Royal International Love-in/Be There, Be Hair	5

HAL

05	Heavenly HVN 147	Keep Love As Your Golden Rule/THE MAGIC NUMBERS: Animla Sola (Double A side tour single - 500 only p/s)	10

I. HALCIDEONS AND I. JARZIF

78	Greensleeves GRED 7	Rise Ethiopians/Signs Of The Messiah (12")	40

MINT VALUE £

DENNIS HALE

(see also Jack Parnell)

55	Parlophone MSP 6153	The Butterscotch Mop/S'posin'	10

TERENCE HOLDERWAY HALE

60	Fontana H 285	Beauty And The Beast/My New Year's Eve	7

BILL HALEY (& HIS COMETS)

(see also Kingsmen, Jodimars, Nick Nantos & His Fireballs)

78s

53	London L 1190	Crazy Man, Crazy/Whatcha Gonna Do (as Bill Haley with Haley's Comets) (gold label lettering)	30
53	London L 1216	Pat-A-Cake/Fractured (as Bill Haley with Haley's Comets, gold label)	30
54	London HL 1190	Crazy Man, Crazy/Whatcha Gonna Do (as Bill Haley with Haley's Comets) (reissue, silver label lettering)	20
54	London HL 1216	Pat-A-Cake/Fractured (reissue, silver label lettering, as Bill Haley with Haley's Comets)	20
54	Brunswick 05338	Shake, Rattle And Roll/A.B.C. Boogie (gold lettering)	10
55	London HL 8142	Green Tree Boogie/Sundown Boogie	20
55	London HLF 8161	Farewell, So Long, Goodbye/I'll Be True	18
55	London HLF 8194	Ten Little Indians/Rocking Chair On The Moon	20
56	Melodisc 1376	I'm Gonna Dry Ev'ry Tear With A Kiss/Why Do I Cry Over You	60
57	London HLF 8371	Rock The Joint/Yes Indeed!	15
57	Brunswick 05658	Forty Cups Of Coffee/Choo Choo Ch'Boogie	12
57	Brunswick 05688	(You Hit The Wrong Note) Billy Goat/Rockin' Rollin' Rover	12
57	Brunswick 05719	Miss You/The Dipsy Doodle	15
58	Brunswick 05735	Mary, Mary Lou/It's A Sin	15
58	Brunswick 05742	Skinny Minnie/How Many	15
58	Brunswick 05752	Lean Jean/Don't Nobody Move	15
58	Brunswick 05766	Whoa Mabel!/Chiquita Linda	25
59	Brunswick 05788	I Got A Woman/Charmaine	30
59	Brunswick 05805	Shaky/Caldonia	30
59	Brunswick 05810	Joey's Song/Ooh! Look-A There, Ain't She Pretty	40

SINGLES

54	Brunswick 05317	(We're Gonna) Rock Around The Clock/Thirteen Women (gold lettering on label)	60
54	Brunswick 05317	(We're Gonna) Rock Around The Clock/Thirteen Women (silver lettering on label)	25
54	Brunswick 05338	Shake, Rattle And Roll/A.B.C. Boogie (gold lettering on label)	40
54	Brunswick 05338	Shake, Rattle And Roll/A.B.C. Boogie (silver lettering on label)	20
55	Brunswick 05373	Happy Baby/Dim, Dim The Lights (I Want Some Atmosphere) (gold lettering on label)	40
55	Brunswick 05373	Happy Baby/Dim, Dim The Lights (I Want Some Atmosphere) (silver lettering on label)	20
55	Brunswick 05405	Birth Of The Boogie/Mambo Rock (gold lettering on label)	40
55	Brunswick 05405	Birth Of The Boogie/Mambo Rock (silver lettering on label)	20
55	London HL 8142	Green Tree Boogie/Sundown Boogie (gold lettering on label)	150
55	London HL 8142	Green Tree Boogie/Sundown Boogie (silver lettering on label)	50
55	Brunswick 05453	Two Hound Dogs/Razzle Dazzle (gold lettering on label)	40
55	Brunswick 05453	Two Hound Dogs/Razzle Dazzle (silver lettering on label)	20
55	London HLF 8161	Farewell, So Long, Goodbye/I'll Be True (gold lettering on label)	100
55	London HLF 8161	Farewell, So Long, Goodbye/I'll Be True (silver lettering on label)	50
55	London HLF 8194	Ten Little Indians/Rocking Chair On The Moon (gold lettering on label)	120
55	London HLF 8194	Ten Little Indians/Rocking Chair On The Moon (silver lettering on label)	60
55	Brunswick 05509	Rock-A-Beatin' Boogie/Burn That Candle (gold lettering on label)	40
55	Brunswick 05509	Rock-A-Beatin' Boogie/Burn That Candle (silver lettering on label)	20
56	Brunswick 05530	See You Later, Alligator/The Paper Boy (On Main Street, USA) (gold lettering on label)	40
56	Brunswick 05530	See You Later, Alligator/The Paper Boy (On Main Street, USA) (silver lettering on label)	20
56	Brunswick 05565	The Saints Rock 'N' Roll/R-O-C-K	15
56	Brunswick 05582	Rockin' Through The Rye/Hot Dog Buddy Buddy	15
56	Brunswick 05615	Rip It Up/Teenager's Mother	15
56	Brunswick 05616	Rudy's Rock/Blue Comet Blues	15
57	Brunswick 05640	Don't Knock The Rock/Calling All Comets	15
57	Brunswick 05641	Hook, Line And Sinker/Goofin' Around	15
57	London HLF 8371	Rock The Joint/Yes Indeed! (gold label)	150
57	London HLF 8371	Rock The Joint/Yes Indeed! (silver label)	75
57	Brunswick 05658	Forty Cups Of Coffee/Choo Choo Ch'Boogie	15
57	Brunswick 05688	(You Hit The Wrong Note) Billy Goat/Rockin' Rollin' Rover	15
57	Brunswick 05719	Miss You/The Dipsy Doodle	15
58	Brunswick 05735	Mary, Mary Lou/It's A Sin	15
58	Brunswick 05742	Skinny Minnie/How Many	20
58	Brunswick 05752	Lean Jean/Don't Nobody Move	15
58	Brunswick 05766	Whoa Mabel!/Chiquita Linda	15
59	Brunswick 05788	I Got A Woman/Charmaine	15
59	Brunswick 05805	Shaky/Caldonia	15
59	Brunswick 05810	Joey's Song/Ooh! Look-A There, Ain't She Pretty	15

(The above 45s were originally issued with triangular centres; later round centres are worth half the value for earlier 45s to two-thirds for later 45s.)

60	Brunswick 05818	Puerto Rican Peddler/Skokiaan	10
60	Warner Bros WB 6	Candy Kisses/Tamiami	10
61	London HLU 9471	Spanish Twist/My Kind Of Woman	10
63	Stateside SS 196	Tenor Man/Up Goes My Love	10
64	Warner Bros WB 133	Rock Around The Clock/Love Letters In The Sand	10
64	Brunswick 05910	Happy Baby/Birth Of The Boogie	15
64	Brunswick 05917	The Green Door/Yeah! She's Evil	15
68	MCA MU 1013	(We're Gonna) Rock Around The Clock/Shake, Rattle And Roll	6
68	Pye International 7N 25455	Crazy Man, Crazy/Dance With A Dolly (With A Hole In Her Stocking)	20

			MINT VALUE £
73	Sonet SON 2016	Me And Bobby McGee/I Wouldn't Have Missed It For The World	6
74	Sonet SON 2043	Crazy Man, Crazy/Lawdy Miss Clawdy	6
79	Sonet SON 2202	God Bless Rock And Roll/So Right Tonight	6

EXPORT SINGLES

54	Decca BM 05317	(We're Gonna) Rock Around The Clock/Thirteen Women	70
55	Decca BM 05405	Birth Of The Boogie/Mambo Rock	50
55	Decca BM 05509	Rock-A-Beatin' Boogie/Burn That Candle	50
56	Decca BM 05530	See You Later Alligator/The Paper Boy (On Main Street, USA)	50
56	Decca BM 31163	The Saints Rock 'N' Roll/R-O-C-K	40
56	Decca BM 31164	Rockin' Through The Rye/Hot Dog Buddy Buddy	40
56	Decca BM 31171	Rip It Up/Teenager's Mother	40
57	Decca BM 31174	Don't Knock The Rock/Choo Choo Ch'Boogie	40
68	Decca AD 1010	(We're Gonna) Rock Around The Clock/Shake, Rattle And Roll	20

EPs

55	Brunswick OE 9129	DIM, DIM THE LIGHTS (gold lettering label, 'stage' p/s, various colours)	40
55	Brunswick OE 9129	DIM, DIM THE LIGHTS (silver lettering label, 'stage' or 'cameo' p/s)	25
55	London REF 1031	ROCK AND ROLL	50
56	London REF 1049	LIVE IT UP PART 1	35
56	London REF 1050	LIVE IT UP PART 2	35
56	Brunswick OE 9214	ROCK AND ROLL WITH BILL HALEY	25
56	Brunswick OE 9250	ROCK AROUND THE CLOCK	20
56	London REF 1058	LIVE IT UP PART 3	35
56	Brunswick OE 9278	ROCK'N'ROLL STAGE SHOW PART 1	25
56	Brunswick OE 9279	ROCK'N'ROLL STAGE SHOW PART 2	25
56	Brunswick OE 9280	ROCK'N'ROLL STAGE SHOW PART 3	25
58	Brunswick OE 9349	ROCKIN' THE OLDIES PART 1	30
58	Brunswick OE 9350	ROCKIN' THE OLDIES PART 2	30
58	Brunswick OE 9351	ROCKIN' THE OLDIES PART 3	40
59	Brunswick OE 9446	ROCKIN' AROUND THE WORLD	60
59	Brunswick OE 9459	BILL HALEY	50

(The above EPs were originally issued with triangular centres, later round-centre copies are worth half to two-thirds these values)

60	Warners WEP 6001	BILL HALEY AND HIS COMETS	40
61	Warners WEP 6025	BILL HALEY'S JUKE BOX (also stereo WSEP 2025)	40
61	Warners WEP 6025	BILL HALEY'S JUKE BOX (also stereo WSEP 2025)	50
64	Warners WEP 6133	BILL HALEY VOLUME 1	40
64	Warners WEP 6136	BILL HALEY VOLUME 2	40

LPs

55	London H-APB 1042	LIVE IT UP (10", gold lettering on label)	100
55	London H-APB 1042	LIVE IT UP (10", silver lettering on label)	60
56	Brunswick LAT 8117	ROCK AROUND THE CLOCK	30
56	Brunswick LAT 8139	ROCK AND ROLL STAGE SHOW	30
57	London HA-F 2037	ROCK THE JOINT	90
57	Brunswick LAT 8219	ROCKIN' THE OLDIES	60
57	Brunswick LAT 8268	ROCKIN' THE JOINT	60
59	Brunswick LAT 8295	BILL HALEY'S CHICKS (mono)	65
59	Brunswick STA 3011	BILL HALEY'S CHICKS (stereo)	85
60	Brunswick LAT 8326	STRICTLY INSTRUMENTAL	60
62	Columbia 33SX 1460	TWISTIN' KNIGHTS AT THE ROUNDTABLE (LIVE!)	30
62	Ace Of Hearts AH 35	ROCKIN' THE OLDIES	15
64	Ace Of Hearts AH 66	BILL HALEY'S CHICKS	15
65	Xtra XTRA 1027	BILL HALEY & THE COMETS	30
65	Warner Bros W 1391	BILL HALEY'S JUKE BOX	50

HALFBREED

75	United Artists UAG 29877	HALFBREED (LP, fold out sleeve)	20

HAL HOPPERS

54	London HL 8107	More Love/Do Nothin' Blues	50
55	London HL 8129	Mother Of Pearl/Baby I've Had It	45

HALF JAPANESE

(see also Jad Fair)

81	Armageddon AS 009	Spy/I Know How It Feels ... Bad/My Knowledge Was Wrong (p/s)	5
81	Armageddon ABOX 1	1/2 GENTLEMEN NOT BEASTS (3-LP box set with poster, booklet & lyric insert)	80
81	Armageddon ARM 7	LOUD (LP)	12

ADELAIDE HALL

60	Oriole CB 1556	Common Sense/Blue Bird On My Shoulder	10

BARBARA HALL

75	EMI INT 514	You Brought It On Yourself/Drop My heart Off At The Door	10

BOB HALL & ALEXIS KORNER

(see also Brunning Hall Sunflower Blues Band, Alexis Korner)

78	Logo GO 331	Pinetop's Boogie Woogie/All I Got Is You	12

CAROLINE HALL

70	Major Minor MM 689	Dream Boy/Julie	5
71	Decca F 13146	Hold My Hand/Put A Light In The Window	6

DARYL HALL & SOUNDS OF BLACKNESS

94	Mercury MERMC 404	Gloryland/(mixes) (picture disc, in poster sleeve)	10

DEREK HALL & MIKE COOPER

60s	Kennet KRS 766	OUT OF THE SHADES (EP)	35

DOLORES HALL

(see also Jackie Lee & Dolores Hall)

72	Jay Boy BOY 77	Good Lovin' Man/W-O-M-E-N	8

MINT VALUE £

DORA HALL
64 King KG 1003 Hello Faithless/You've Got Me Cryin' Again. . . . 5

JIMMY GRAY HALL
74 Epic EPC 2312 Be That Way/Possessed By The Moon. . . . 10

JUANITA HALL
62 Storyville SEP 382 STORYVILLE BLUES ANTHOLOGY VOL. 2 (EP) . . . 10

LANI HALL
83 A&M AM 159 Never Say Never Again/MICHAEL LEGRAND: Un Chanson D'Amour (p/s) . . . 8
74 A&M AMLS 64359 SUNDOWN LADY (LP) . . . 15

LARRY HALL
60 Parlophone R 4625 Sandy/Lovin' Tree . . . 15
62 Salvo SLO 1811 Ladder Of Love/The One You Left Behind (99 copies only). . . . 20

RENE HALL'S ORCHESTRA
58 London HLU 8581 Twitchy/Flippin'. . . . 50

ROBIN HALL (& JIMMY MacGREGOR)
(see also Galliards)
60 Collector JDS 3 Football Crazy/Rosin The Beau (with p/s) . . . 15
60 Collector JDS 3 Football Crazy/Rosin The Beau. . . . 10
60 Decca F 11266 Football Crazy/Rosin The Beau (reissue, p/s) . . . 10

RONNIE HALL
61 Piccadilly 7N 35001 The Code Of Love/Who Cares . . . 8
61 Piccadilly 7N 35015 She's Mine/My Heart Is The Lover . . . 8
62 Piccadilly 7N 35040 My Very First Love/The Day After Forever . . . 6
65 Fontana TF 569 I'll Stand Aside/I'm Getting Nowhere . . . 6

ROY HALL
56 Brunswick 05531 See You Later, Alligator/Don't Stop Now (gold label lettering) . . . 500
56 Brunswick 05531 See You Later, Alligator/Don't Stop Now (78) . . . 100
56 Brunswick 05555 Blue Suede Shoes/Luscious . . . 400
56 Brunswick 05555 Blue Suede Shoes/Luscious (78) . . . 100
56 Brunswick 05627 Diggin' The Boogie/Three Alley Cats . . . 550
56 Brunswick 05627 Diggin' The Boogie/Three Alley Cats (78) . . . 100
70 Injun 105 One Monkey Don't Stop The Shop/Flood Of love . . . 12

TONY HALL
77 Free Reed FRR 012 FIELDVOLE MUSIC (LP, with insert) . . . 20

CHANCE HALLADAY
62 Vogue V 9203 John Henry/Thirteen Women. . . . 25

HALLELUJAH SKIFFLE GROUP
(see also Clinton Ford)
58 Oriole CB 1429 I Saw The Light/A Closer Walk With Thee (with Clinton Ford). . . . 20

HALLIARD
(see also Jon Raven, Nic Jones)
67 Saga SOC 1058 IT'S THE IRISH IN ME (LP) . . . 30
68 Broadside BRO 106 THE HALLIARD AND JON RAVEN (LP). . . . 50

DICK HALLMAN
56 Brunswick 05608 Two Different Worlds/Love Me As Though There Were No Tomorrow . . . 8
60 Vogue V 9162 Born To Be Loved/Just Squeeze Me But Don't Teeze Me . . . 10

GERRY HALLOM
84 Fellside FE 036 A RUN A MINUTE (LP) . . . 15

HALLUCINOGEN
95 Dragonfly BFLLP 15 TWISTED (2xLP, yellow vinyl or one green and one pink or black vinyl). . . . 20

JOHNNY HALLYDAY
62 Philips BF 1238 Shake The Hand Of A Fool/Hold Back The Sun . . . 8
63 Philips 373 012BF Hey Little Girl/Caravan Of Lonely Men. . . . 8
65 Philips BF 1449 Pour Moi Tu Es La Seule/They Call Him A Man . . . 10
62 Philips 432 813BE ROCKING (EP). . . . 150
66 Vogue VRE 5013 JOHNNY HALLYDAY (EP). . . . 120
61 Philips BBL 7556 SINGS AMERICA'S ROCKIN' HITS (LP) . . . 150

HALOS
61 London HLU 9424 Nag/Copycat . . . 40

STUART HAMBLEN
54 HMV 7MC 20 This Ole House/When My Lord Picks Up The 'Phone (export issue) . . . 25
55 HMV 7MC 30 Go On By/Just A Man (export issue) . . . 12
56 HMV 7M 394 Hell Train/A Few Things To Remember . . . 18

BILLY HAMBRIC
79 Grapevine GRP 139 She Said Goodbye/I Found True Love . . . 10

CLAIRE HAMILL
(see also Cafe Society, Gary Numan, Wishbone Ash)
72 Island WIP 6122 When I Was A Child/Alice In The Streets Of Darlington . . . 6
72 Island WIP 6133 Baseball Blues/Smile Your Blues Away . . . 6
81 WEA K 18440 First Night In New York/Ultraviolet Light (B-side with Gary Numan) (p/s) . . . 7
72 Island ILPS 9182 ONE HOUSE LEFT STANDING (LP, lyric inner sleeve) . . . 40
73 Island ILPS 9225 OCTOBER (LP, gatefold sleeve, pink rim palm tree label) . . . 20
74 Konk KONK 101 STAGE DOOR JOHNNIES (LP, gatefold sleeve, blue label) . . . 15
75 Konk KONK 104 ABRACADABRA (LP, featuring Cafe Society, with lyric insert, blue label) . . . 15

BILLY HAMILTON & STRANDSMEN
67 Philips BF 1622 Try To Remember/Don't You Believe It. . . . 7

MINT VALUE £

CHICO HAMILTON QUINTET

65	HMV POP 1451	Carol's Walk/Chic Chic Chico	8
58	Vogue LAE 12045	CHICO HAMILTON QUINTET IN HIFI (LP)	15
64	HMV CLP 1807	MAN FROM TWO WORLDS (LP)	15
68	Solid State USS 7010	THE GAMUT (LP)	12

DAVID HAMILTON

70s	Spectre SP 501	A Special Goodnight To You/Just For The Weekend	8

EDWARD HAMILTON & ARABIANS

80	Grapevine GRP 134	Baby Don't You Weep/I'm Gonna Love You	10

GARY HAMILTON

(see also Hamilton & [Hamilton] Movement)

67	Decca F 12697	Let The Music Play/Don't Ask	12
69	CBS 4674	Easy Rider/Hare Krishna	6

GAVIN HAMILTON

67	King KG 1067	It Won't Be The Same/Turn The Key Softly	150

GEORGE HAMILTON IV

57	London HL 8361	A Rose And A Candy Bar/If You Don't Know (gold label print)	175
57	London HL 8361	A Rose And A Candy Bar/If You Don't Know (later silver label print)	60
57	London HL 8361	A Rose And A Candy Bar/If You Don't Know (78)	20
57	HMV POP 429	Why Don't They Understand/Even Tho'	8
58	HMV POP 474	Now And For Always/One Heart	10
58	HMV POP 505	I Know Where I'm Goin'/Who's Taking You To The Prom?	5
58	HMV POP 534	Your Cheatin' Heart/When Will I Know?	10
60	HMV POP 813	Before This Day Ends/Loneliness Is All Around Us	5
72	Uni UNS 480	Evel Knievel/Boy From The Country	5
58	HMV CLP 1202	ON CAMPUS (LP)	18
59	HMV CLP 1263	SING ME A SAD SONG - A TRIBUTE TO HANK WILLIAMS (LP)	20

GUY HAMILTON

(see also Neil Christian)

65	HMV POP 1418	A Lifetime Of Loneliness/Give The Game Away	15

(KINGSIZE) HAMILTON & PLATTERMEN

66	Emerald MD 1048	Shake/I Got To Know	25

M. HAMILTON

67	Ska Beat JB 265	Something Gotta Ring/DENNIS LYNWARD & HIS GROUP: Jazz Session	20

MILTON HAMILTON

73	Explosion EX 2069	Long Long Road/Version	8
77	Wolf WM 005	Children Are You Ready/Part 2	8

ROY HAMILTON

58	Fontana H 113	Don't Let Go/The Right To Love	25
58	Fontana H 143	Crazy Feelin'/In A Dream	15
59	Fontana H 180	Pledging My Love/My One And Only Love	15
59	Fontana H 193	I Need Your Loving/Somewhere Along The Way	15
59	Fontana H 193	I Need Your Loving/Somewhere Along The Way (78)	10
61	Fontana H 298	You Can Have Her/Abide With Me	15
61	Fontana H 320	You're Gonna Need Magic/To The One I Love	15
63	MGM MGM 1210	Theme From "The VIPs"/The Sinner	15
64	MGM MGM 1251	There She Is/The Panic Is On	300
64	MGM MGM 1251	There She Is/The Panic Is On (DJ copy)	550
65	MGM MGM 1268	A Thousand Tears Ago/Sweet Violet	15
66	RCA RCA 1500	And I Love Her/Tore Up Over You	15
69	Deep Soul DS 9106	Dark End Of The Street/100 Years Ago	40
59	Fontana TFE 17160	WHY FIGHT THE FEELING (EP)	20
60	Fontana TFE 17163	THE MOOD MOVES (EP)	20
61	Fontana TFE 17170	COME OUT SWINGING (EP)	20
63	Columbia 33SX 1473	GREATEST HITS (LP)	40
64	MGM MGM-C 960	WARM SOUL (LP)	60

ROY HAMILTON

83	HBS K CAP 1	Turn Up The Music/Instrumental Version (12", with Capiche)	20

RUSS HAMILTON

58	Oriole EP 7005	RUSS HAMILTON (EP)	15
58	Oriole MG 20031	WE WILL MAKE LOVE (LP)	30

SCOTT HAMILTON

66	Parlophone R 5492	Good Day Sunshine/For No One	8

HAMILTON & MOVEMENT

(see also Gary Hamilton, Paul Stewart Movement)

65	Polydor BM 56026	Really Saying Something/I Won't See You Tonight	80
67	CBS 202573	I'm Not The Marrying Kind/My Love Belongs To You	40

HAMLET

67	Decca F12571	She Won't See The Light/Go Play In Your Own Yard	20

HAMLETT

72	Pye 7N45171	Where'd The Day Go/Vampireman	15

HAMLINS

(see also Minstrels)

67	Coxsone CS 7021	Trying To Keep A Good Man Down/BOB MARLEY/ MARCIA GRIFFITHS: Oh My Darling	90
67	Coxsone CS 7022	Soul And Inspiration/ETHIOPIANS: Let's Get Together	35
68	Coxsone CS 7048	Sentimental Reasons/SOUL VENDORS: Last Waltz	120
68	Blue Cat BS 115	Sugar And Spice/SOUL VENDORS: Mercy Mercy Mercy	150

MINT VALUE £

HAMMER
(see also Holland)
85 Ebony EBON 29 — CONTRACT WITH HELL (LP) — 15

JACK HAMMER
61 Oriole CB 1634 — Young Only Once/Juliette — 15
62 Oriole CB 1645 — Kissin' Twist/Melancholy Boy — 10
62 Oriole CB 1728 — Crazy Twist/Twist Talk — 10
62 Oriole CB 1753 — Don't Let Baby Know/Number 2539 — 15
66 Polydor 56091 — Thanks/Love Ladder — 20
67 Polydor 56158 — Joe Poor Loves Daphne Rich/Ode To A Discotheque — 50
69 United Artists UP 35029 — What Greater Love/The Mason Dixon Line — 40
60s Youngblood B 1023 — Swim/Colour Combination — 60
63 Oriole PS 40020 — HAMMER + BEAT = TWIST (LP) — 70
66 Polydor 582001 — BRAVE NEW WORLD (LP) — 30

HAMMERHEAD
81 Linden Sounds LS 009 — Time Will Tell/Lonely Man (p/s) — 60

HAMMERS
69 President PT 247 — Baby And Me/Little Butterfly — 5
69 President PT 276 — Sugar Baby/Power Of Love — 5

HAMMERS (Jamaica)
(see also Joan Ross)
70 Gas GAS 162 — Hotter Than Scorcher/Someday Could See You — 10

HAMMERSMITH GORILLAS
(see also Gorillas, Helter Skelter)
74 Penny Farthing PEN 849 — You Really Got Me/Leavin' 'Ome — 20
77 Raw RAW 2 — You Really Got Me/Leavin' 'Ome (reissue, company sleeve) — 12

HAMMERSMITH WELSH MALE VOICE CHOIR
69 Pama SECO 1 — WE'LL KEEP A WELCOME (LP, souveneir at the investiture of HRH Prince Charles as the Prince Of Wales) — 12

PETER HAMMILL
(see also Van Der Graaf Generator, Le Orme, Rikki Nadir, Colin Scot)
75 Charisma CB 245 — Birthday Special/Shingle Song — 8
78 Charisma CB 339 — The Polaroid (credited to Ricky Nadir)/The Old School Tie — 10
78 Charisma PH 001 — Crying Wolf/This Side Of The Looking Glass (promo only) — 30
81 Virgin VS 424 — My Experience/Glue (p/s) — 5
82 Naive NAV 3 — Paradox Drive/Now More Than Ever (p/s) — 6
83 Naive NAV 8 — Film Noir/Seven Wonders — 6
84 Charisma CB 414 — Just Good Friends/Just Good Friends (Instrumental) (p/s) — 5
86 Foundry FOUND 3 — Painting By Numbers/You Hit Me Where I Live (p/s) — 5
86 Foundry FOUND 312 — Painting By Numbers (Extended)/You Hit Me Where I Live/Shell (12", p/s) — 8
71 Charisma CAS 1037 — FOOL'S MATE (LP, gatefold sleeve, pink 'scroll' label) — 50
73 Charisma CAS 1067 — CHAMELEON IN THE SHADOW OF THE NIGHT (LP, gatefold sleeve, large 'Mad Hatter' label) — 30
74 Charisma CAS 1083 — THE SILENT CORNER AND THE EMPTY STAGE (LP, gatefold sleeve., with lyric inner, large 'Mad Hatter' label) — 20
74 Charisma CAS 1089 — IN CAMERA (LP, with inner sleeve, small 'Mad Hatter' label) — 18
75 Charisma CAS 1099 — NADIR'S BIG CHANCE (LP, with inner sleeve small 'Mad Hatter' label) — 15
77 Charisma CAS 1125 — OVER (LP, with inner lyric sleeve, small 'Mad Hatter' label) — 15

ALBERT HAMMOND
73 Mums SMUM 1759 — The Peacemaker/Who's For Lunch Today — 7

CLAY HAMMOND
72 Jay Boy BOY 78 — Dance Little Girl/Twin Brother — 5

JOHN HAMMOND
65 Fontana TF 560 — Baby Won't You Tell Me/I Live The Life I Love — 15
68 Atlantic 584 190 — Brown Eyed Handsome Man/Crosscut Saw — 10
64 Fontana TFL 6046 — BIG CITY BLUES (LP) — 60
65 Fontana TFL 6059 — SO MANY ROADS (LP) — 50
71 CBS 64365 — SOURCE POINT (LP) — 22
72 CBS 65051 — I'M SATISFIED (LP) — 22
72 Vanguard VSD 11/12 — THE BEST OF JOHN HAMMOND - SOUTHERN FRIED (2-LP) — 20

CURLEY HAMNER & COOPER BROTHERS
59 Felsted SD 80061 — Twistin' And Turnin'/King And Queen — 10

BILLY HAMON
78 Bronze BRO 58 — Butch Things/Amusement Arcade (p/s) — 30

SUSAN HAMPSHIRE
65 Decca F 12185 — When Love Is True/When The World Was Our Own — 15

LIONEL HAMPTON (& HIS HAMP-TONES)
(see also Sonny Parker)
57 Vogue V 2405 — Flying Home/Perdido (with Just Jazz All Stars) — 10
57 Vogue V 2406 — Hamp's Boogie Woogie/The Blues (with Just Jazz All Stars) — 10
56 MGM MGM-EP 552 — LIONEL HAMPTON & HIS ORCHESTRA (EP) — 8
51 Brunswick LA 8527 — HAMP'S BOOGIE WOOGIE (10" LP) — 12
52 Brunswick LA 8551 — MOONGLOW (10" LP) — 12
53 Vogue LDE 043 — LIONEL HAMPTON'S "JAZZ TIME PARIS" VOLUME 1 (10" LP) — 12
54 Vogue LDE 051 — NEW SOUNDS FROM EUROPE VOLUME 2 - FRANCE (10" LP) — 12
54 Vogue LDE 063 — LIONEL HAMPTON VOLUME 3 (10" LP) — 12
54 Felsted EDL 87007 — THE HAMP IN PARIS IN PARIS VOLUME 1 (10" LP) — 12
54 Felsted EDL 87008 — THE HAMP IN PARIS IN PARIS VOLUME 2 (10" LP) — 12
55 Felsted PDL 85002 — LIONEL HAMPTON AND HIS NEW FRENCH SOUND VOLUME 1 (10" LP) — 12

			MINT VALUE £
55	HMV CLP 1023	HOT MALLETS (LP)	15
55	Columbia Clef 33C 9011	LIONEL HAMPTON QUARTET (10" LP)	12
55	Philips BBL 7015	APOLLO HALL CONCERT 1954 (LP)	12

PAUL HAMPTON

58	Philips PB 787	Play It Cool/Classy Babe (78)	18

SLIDE HAMPTON & HIS BAND

62	London HA-K/SH-K 8008	JAZZ WITH A TWIST (LP)	18
62	London LZT-K 15225	LONDON JAZZ (LP, as Slide Hampton Octet)	18

HAMPTONS

(see under Fabulous Impact)

HERBIE HANCOCK

(see also Headhunters)

63	Blue Note 45-1887	Blind Man, Blind Man (Parts 1 & 2)	20
70	Warner Bros WB 7358	Fat Mama/Wiggle-Waggle	15
74	CBS 2329	Chameleon/Vein Melter	6
75	CBS 3059	Palm Grease/Butterfly	6
71	Warner Bros WS 1834	FAT ALBERT ROTUNDA (LP)	20
71	Warner Bros K 46077	MWANDISHI (LP)	20
72	Warner Bros K 46164	CROSSINGS (LP)	15
74	Warner Bros K 46039	FAT ALBERT ROTUNDA (LP, reissue)	15
74	CBS 80193	THRUST (LP)	20
74	CBS 80546	DEATH WISH (LP, soundtrack)	15
74	CBS 65582	SEXTANT (LP)	12
74	CBS 65928	HEADHUNTERS (LP)	15
75	CBS 69185	MAN CHILD (LP)	12

TONY HANCOCK

(see also Sidney James, Kenneth Williams)

63	Pye 7N 15575	Wing Commander Hancock - Test Pilot/ The Threatening Letters (with Kenneth Williams)	10
63	Piccadilly FTF 38500	FACE TO FACE (LP, interview disc)	40

OWEN HAND

61	Transatlantic TRA 127	SOMETHING NEW (LP)	120
66	Transatlantic TRA	I LOVED A LASS (LP)	100

JOHNNY HANDLE

(see also Louise Killen & Johnny Handle, High Level Ranters)

61	Topic TOP 78	STOTTIN' DOON THE WAAL (EP)	10
75	Topic 12TS 270	THE COLLIER LAD (LP)	15

HANDLEY FAMILY

73	GL 100	Wam Bam/Rum Dum And Baccy	8

HANDSOME BEASTS

81	Heavy Metal HEAVY 1	All Riot Now/Mark Of The Beast (p/s)	25
81	Heavy Metal HEAVY 2	Breaker/One In A Crowd/Crazy (wraparound p/s)	8
82	Heavy Metal HEAVY 11	Sweeties/You're One Your Own (p/s, with card sheet)	8
82	Heavy Metal HMRLP 2	BEASTIALITY (LP)	20

WAYNE HANDY

58	London HL 8547	Say Yeah/Could It Be (B-side with King Sisters)	200
58	London HL 8547	Say Yeah/Could It Be (B-side with King Sisters) (78)	50

PAUL HANFORD

60	Parlophone R 4680	Itsy Bitsy Teenie Weenie Little Polka Dot Bikini/Why Have You Changed Your Mind	10
60	Parlophone R 4694	If You Ain't Got Love/Ev'ry Little Girl	10
61	Parlophone R 4745	Everything/Cigarettes And Coffee Blues	10
61	Parlophone R 4813	Memphis Address/Flutter Flutter	10
62	Oriole CB 1779	Don't Be/Habit Of Loving You	10
63	Oriole CB 1830	Just When I Need You Most/Judy	10
63	Oriole CB 1866	The Minute You're Gone/High School Dance	10

HANGMAN'S BEAUTIFUL DAUGHTERS

87	Dreamworld DREAM 11	Love Is Blue/Popular Trend (p/s)	7
87	Yo Jo Jo 1	Darkside/Pushing Me Too Far (flexidisc, p/s)	8

HANK & MELLOWMEN

(see also Roger Whittaker)

60s	Lyntone LYN 153/154	Santa Anno/Mosology/(other artists) (Bangor University Rag flexidisc)	7
60s	Lyntone LYN 201	So In Love With You/Michael (Bangor University Rag flexidisc)	7

BOBBY HANNA

67	Decca F 12604	Thanks To You/Here I Stand	5
67	Decca F 12695	Blame It On Me/Goin' Where The Lovin' Is	7
68	Decca F 12738	Too Much Love/What Do I Want For Tomorrow	5
68	Decca F 12783	Written On The Wind/Everybody Needs Love	15
68	Decca F 12833	To Wait For Love (Is To Waste Your Life Away)/Is It Wrong	6
69	Decca F 22917	Winter Love (E' L'Amore)/Time	6

GEORGE HANNA & SARAH ANNE O'NEILL

78	Topic 12TS 372	ON THE SHORES OF LOUGH NEAGH (LP)	12

JOSH HANNA

65	Parlophone R 5385	When I Love You/Love Me, Love Me	6
66	Decca F 12532	Shut Your Mouth/Sweet To My Soul	15

HANNA BARBERA (cartoon soundtrack EPs)

66	Hanna Barbera HBE 1	FLINTSTONES - HANSEL AND GRETEL (EP)	15
66	Hanna Barbera HBE 2	UNCLE REMUS - BRER RABBIT AND THE TAR BABY (EP)	15

MINT VALUE £

66	Hanna Barbera HBE 3	FLINTSTONES - GOLDILOCKS, BEAROSAURUS (EP)	15
66	Hanna Barbera HBE 4	SNAGGLEPUSS TALES - WIZARD OF OZ (EP)	15
66	Hanna Barbera HBE 5	YOGI BEAR AND BOO BOO TELL JACK AND THE BEANSTALK (EP)	15
66	Hanna Barbera HBE 6	FRED FLINTSTONE & BARNEY RUBBLE - SONG FROM MARY POPPINS (EP)	15
67	Hanna Barbera HBE 7	TOP CAT - ROBIN HOOD (EP)	15
67	Hanna Barbera HBE 8	YOGI BEAR AND BOO BOO - LITTLE RED RIDING HOOD (EP)	15
67	Hanna Barbera HBE 9	FLINTSTONES - THREE LITTLE PIGS (EP)	15
67	Hanna Barbera HBE 10	AUGIE DOGGY AND DOGGY DADDY - SONGS FROM PINOCCHIO (EP)	15
67	Hanna Barbera HBE 11	PEBBLES AND BAMM BAMM - WE WISH YOU A MERRY CHRISTMAS (EP)	15
68	Hanna Barbera HBE 12	MERRY CHRISTMAS - ORGAN AND CHIMES (EP)	15
68	Hanna Barbera HBE 13	MAGILLA GORILLA AND OGEE - ALICE IN WONDERLAND (EP)	15
68	Hanna Barbera HBE 14	PEBBLES AND BAMM BAMM - SONGS FROM THE GOOD SHIP LOLLIPOP (EP)	15

PAUL HANNAH

94	Ferox FER 007	CONTROL EP (12", plain sleeve)	12
95	Ferox FER 010	ADVENTURES IN TECHNO SOUL (12" EP)	8

ROSS HANNAMAN

67	Columbia DB 8217	Down Thru' Summer/I'll Give All My Love To Southend	5
67	Columbia DB 8288	1969/Probably On A Thursday (with p/s)	50
67	Columbia DB 8288	1969/Probably On A Thursday	40
74	Bellwood BW1	A NIGHT AT FACTOTUM (LP, 100 only, as John and Rosalind)	20

HANNIBAL

(see also Wizzard)

74	B&C HB 1	Winds Of Change/Winter	6
70	B&C CAS 1022	HANNIBAL (LP, gatefold sleeve)	120

LANCE HANNIBAL

(see also Sugar Simone, Les Foster)

69	Blue Cat BS 148	Read The News/RECO & RHYTHM ACES: Return Of The Bullet	20

HANOI ROCKS

(see also Fallen Angels, Dark, Idle Flowers, Urban Dogs, Suicide Twins)

83	Lick LIX 1	Malibu Beach/Rebel On The Run (p/s)	5
83	Lick LIXPD 1	Malibu Beach/Rebel On The Run (picture disc)	8
84	CBS A 4513	Up Around The Bend/Until I Get You (p/s, with free transfer)	8
84	CBS DA 4513	Up Around The Bend/Until I Get You//Under My Wheels/ I Feel Alright/ Train Kept A Rollin' (double pack)	8
84	CBS TA 4513	Up Around The Bend/Back To The Mystery City/Until I Get You/ Mental 84 Beat (12", p/s, with free transfer)	8
84	CBS WA 4732	Underwater World/Shakes/Magic Carpet Ride (12", picture disc)	10
84	CBS WA 4685	Don't You Ever Leave Me/Oil And Gasoline/Malibu Beach (Calypso) (12", 3-D picture disc)	10
82	Lick LICLPPD4	SELF DISTRUCTION BLUES (LP, picture disc)	15
83	Lick LICLP 1	BACK TO THE MYSTERY CITY (LP, white vinyl)	15

ANNETTE HANSHAW

65	VJM VEP 31	THAT'S ALL (EP)	10

HANSON

73	Manticore K43507	NOW HEAR THIS (LP, gatefold sleeve)	20

HANSON & KARLSSON

(see also Bo Hansson)

67	Polydor 184 196	SWEDISH UNDERGROUND (LP)	15
69	Polydor 462 60	MONUMENT (LP)	60
69	Polydor 583 564	MAN AT THE MOON (LP)	60

BO HANSSON

72	Charisma CAS 1059	LORD OF THE RINGS (LP, insert, large 'Mad Hatter' label)	20
78	Charisma CAS 1059	LORD OF THE RINGS (LP, 1978 reissue with different sleeve, same cat no)	12
73	Charisma CAS 1073	MAGICIANS'S HAT (LP, large 'Mad Hatter' label)	15

HAPPENINGS

66	Fontana TF 735	See You In September/He Thinks He's A Hero	8
66	Fontana TF 766	Go Away Little Girl/Tea Time	8
67	Pye International 7N 25501	My Mammy/I Believe In Nothing	7
67	Stateside SS 587	Goodnight My Love/Lillies By Monet	8
67	Stateside SS 2013	I Got Rhythm/You're In A Bad Way	8
67	BT Puppy BTS 45532	Why Do Fools Fall In Love/When The Summer Is Through	7
67	BT Puppy BTS 45530	My Mammy/I Believe In Nothing	5
68	BT Puppy BTS 45538	Music Music Music/When I Lock My Door	6
68	BT Puppy BTS 45540	Randy/Love Song Of Mummy And Dad	8
68	BT Puppy BTS 45543	Breaking Up Is Hard To Do/Anyway	6
68	BT Puppy BTS 45545	Crazy Rhythm/Love Song Of Mummy And Dad	5
69	BT Puppy BTS 45546	Where Do I Go, Go-Be-In (Hare Krishna)/New Day Comin'	5
67	Fontana TL 5383	BYE BYE, SO LONG, FAREWELL ... SEE YOU IN SEPTEMBER (LP)	35
67	BT Puppy BTLP 1003	PSYCLE (LP)	40
68	BT Puppy BTLPS 1004	GOLDEN HITS (LP)	20

HAPPY CONFUSION

69	Penny Farthing PEN 706	Yes Sir/Hereditary Impediment	15

HAPPY FAMILY

(see also Josef K, Momus)

82	4AD AD 204	Puritans/Innermost Thoughts/The Mistake (p/s)	15

HAPPY MAGAZINE

(see also Griffin)

68	Polydor 56233	Satisfied Street/Do Right Woman Do Right Man	20
69	Polydor 56307	Who Belongs To You (Ooby Dooby Doo)/Beautiful Land	10

MINT VALUE £

HAPPY MONDAYS

85	Factory FAC 129	Delightful/This Feeling/Oasis (12" p/s)	40
86	Factory FAC 142	Freaky Dancing (Live)/The Egg (p/s)	12
87	Factory FAC 176	Tart Tart/Little Matchstick Owen's Rap (12", p/s)	10
87	Factory FACT 170	SQUIRREL & G-MAN TWENTY FOUR HOUR PARTY PEOPLE PLASTIC FACE CARNT SMILE (WHITE OUT) (LP, with "Desmond", 5,000 in plastic sleeve)	25
87	Factory FACT 170	SQUIRREL & G-MAN TWENTY FOUR HOUR PARTY PEOPLE PLASTIC FACE CARNT SMILE (WHITE OUT) (LP, with "Desmond")	15
90	Factory FACT 320	PILLS 'N' THRILLS & BELLYACHES (LP)	12

HAPSHASH & THE COLOURED COAT

(see also Tony McPhee, Warm Sounds, Marc Bolan/T. Rex, Art, Mike Batt)

69	Liberty LBF 15188	Colinda/The Wall	20
67	Minit MLS 40001E	FEATURING THE HUMAN HOST AND THE HEAVY METAL KIDS (LP, with Art, red vinyl (MLL 40001) with insert)	150
67	Minit MLS 40001E	FEATURING THE HUMAN HOST AND THE HEAVY METAL KIDS (LP, with Art, later pressing on black vinyl)	40
69	Liberty LBL/LBS 83212R	THE WESTERN FLYER (LP, with Mike Batt, blue label)	70

HARBOUR LITES

65	HMV POP 1426	Come Back Silly Girl/Revenge	10
65	HMV POP 1465	I Would Give All/They Call The Wind Maria	10
66	Fontana TF 682	Run For Your Life/Lonely Journey	12

HARDBACK

86	Streetwave 7 BOSS 3	The Champ/Bust The Champ	6

HARD CORPS

(see also Craze, Skunks, T.U.F.F.)

84	Hard Corps HC 01	Dirty/To Breathe (12", hand-written white labels, numbered)	25
84	Survival SUR 026	Dirty/Respirer (To Breathe) (white or printed labels, stickered plain black sleeve)	10
84	Survival SUR 12 026	Dirty/Respirer (To Breathe) (12", with sticker in plain black sleeve)	12
85	Immaculate 12 IMMAC 2	Je Suis Passée (Extended French Version)/(Extended Club Dub Mix) (12", p/s)	12
85	Polydor HARDX 1	Je Suis Passée (Extended)/(Instrumental Mix)/(Dub Mix) (12", p/s)	8
85	Polydor HARDA 1	Je Suis Passée (Hard Mix)/(French Mix)/(Dub Mix) (12", gatefold PVC sleeve, various colours, with poster)	25
85	Polydor HARD 2	To Breathe/Metal And Flesh (unreleased)	30
85	Polydor HARDX 2	To Breathe/Metal And Flesh/To Breathe (Instrumental) (12", unreleased)	40
87	Rhythm King TYPE 3T	Lucky Charm/Porte-Bonheur/Lucky Charm (The Music) (12", p/s)	8
90	Concrete P. CPPRODLP 011	METAL AND FLESH (LP, clear vinyl)	15
90	Concrete P. CPPRODCD 011	METAL AND FLESH (CD)	25

HARD-FI

05	Necessary HARDFI01	Cash Machine/Dub Machine/Sick Of It All (3-track CD, 1,500 only, p/s)	10
05	Necessary HARDFI01	Cash Machine/Dub Machine (1,500 only, p/s)	8
05	Necessary HARDFI02	Tied Up Too Tight/Seven Nation Army (yellow vinyl, p/s)	10
05	Necessary HARDFI02TE	Tied Up Too Tight/Middle Eastern Holiday (Chicken Lips Dub) (10" p/s)	12
05	Necessary	STARS OF CCTV (Original CD album, 1,000 only, black and white p/s)	15
05	Necessary 5046786911	STARS OF CCTV (2 x LP, HMV special with bonus Middle Eastern Holiday 7")	12

HARDFLOOR

92	Harthouse HARTUK 1	HARDTRANCE ACPERIENCE EP (12", 4-track)	10

HARD HORSE

72	Dark Art 2012	(Get It) Up Down/So Long I'm Moving On	30

EDDIE HARDIN

(see also Hardin-York, Spencer Davis Group, Roger Glover, Wizards Convention)

72	Decca F 13307	Why Does Everybody Put Me Down/Spend Your Money Honey	5
72	Decca TXS 106	HOME IS WHERE YOU FIND IT (LP, gatefold sleeve, green/silver label)	20

(Eddie) HARDIN & (Pete) YORK

(see also Eddie Hardin, Pete York, Spencer Davis Group)

69	Bell BLL 1064	Tomorrow Today/Candlelight (as Hardin-York)	30
69	Bell SBLL 125	TOMORROW TODAY (LP, gatefold sleeve, blue/silver/black label, with "Sold in the U.K..." text)	30
70	Bell SBLL 136	HARDIN & YORK (THE WORLD'S SMALLEST BIG BAND) (LP, gatefold)	30
71	Bell SBLL 141	FOR THE WORLD (LP, existence unconfirmed)	20
71	Decca SKL 5095	FOR THE WORLD (LP, reissue, blue/silver label with boxed logo)	15

RICHARD HARDIN

(see also Cresters, Mike Sagar & Cresters)

61	HMV POP 887	Jezebel/Temptation	25

TIM HARDIN

(see also Eddie Hardin, Pete York, Spencer Davis Group)

66	Verve VS 1504	Hang On To A Dream/A Reason To Believe	12
67	Verve VS 1511	The Lady Came From Baltimore/Black Sheep Boy	10
68	Verve VS 1516	Don't Make Promises/Smugglin' Man	7
69	CBS 4441	A Simple Song Of Freedom/Question Of Birth	5
71	Verve 2009 006	If I Were A Carpenter/Hang On To A Dream	8
66	Verve (S)VLP 5018	TIM HARDIN 1 (LP)	40
67	Verve (S)VLP 6002	TIM HARDIN 2 (LP)	35
67	Atlantic 587/588 082	THIS IS TIM HARDIN (LP, plum label)	25
68	Verve (S)VLP 6010	LIVE IN CONCERT (LP)	30
69	Verve (S)VLP 6016	TIM HARDIN 4 (LP)	25
69	Verve (S)VLP 6019	THE BEST OF (LP)	20
69	CBS (S/M) 63571	SUITE FOR SUSAN MOORE AND DAMIAN (LP, gatefold sleeve, mono/stereo)	18
70	CBS 64335	BIRD ON A WIRE (LP)	15
72	CBS 65209	PAINTED HEAD (LP)	18
74	Verve 2693 048	TIM HARDIN 1/2 (2-LP, gatefold reissue)	20

MINT VALUE £

MIKE HARDING

86	Moonraker M 003	BOMBERS MOON (LP)	20

ROSEMARY HARDMAN (& BOB AXFORD)

69	Folk Heritage no cat. no.	QUEEN OF HEARTS (LP)	125
71	Trailer LER 2075	FIREBIRD (LP)	25
71	Trailer LER 3018	SECOND SEASON CAME (LP, by Rosemary Hardman & Bob Axford)	25
75	Alida Star Cottage	JERSEY BURGER (LP)	120
78	Plant Life PLR 014	EAGLE OVER BLUE MOUNTAIN (LP, with insert)	12
80	Plant Life PLR 023	ROSIE HARDMAN (LP)	12
83	Plant Life PLR 053	THE WEAKNESS OF EVE (LP, with lyric insert)	12

HARD MEAT

69	Island WIP 6066	Rain/Burning Up Years	15
70	Warner Bros WB 8010	Ballad Of Marmalade Emma And Teddy Grimes/Yesterday, Today, Tomorrow	6
70	Warner Bros WS 1852	HARD MEAT (LP, gatefold sleeve with photo insert)	50
70	Warner Bros WS 1879	THROUGH A WINDOW (LP, green label)	70

HARDNOISE

89	White HNX001	Untitled (different recording to Music Of Life version - 300 pressed) (12")	120
90	Music Of Life NOTE40	Untitled (12")	12
91	Music Of Life NOTE48	Serve Tea, Then Murder/Mice In The Presence Of The Lion(12")	18

HARD ROAD

79	Goodstuff LP 1002	NO PROBLEM (LP, private pressing)	15

HARD ROCK SOUL MOVEMENT

85	Elite 43	Do It Any Way You Wanna (12")	8
86	Elite DAZZ56	The Beat Is Mine/Double Def Fresh (12")	8
86	Elite Elite 46	Double Def Fresh/Def Hypnosis (12")	8

HARDSHIP POST

95	Sub Pop SP 295	Watching You/Your Sunshine (red vinyl)	5

HARD STUFF

(see also Andromeda, Atomic Rooster, John Du Cann, Five Day Week Straw People, Johnny Gustafson, Bullet, Quatermass)

72	Purple PUR 103	Jay Time/The Orchestrator	7
73	Purple PUR 116	Inside Your Life/(It's) How Do You Do It!	7
72	Purple TPSA 7505	BULLETPROOF (LP, gatefold sleeve)	60
73	Purple TPSA 7507	BOLEX DEMENTIA (LP, textured gatefold sleeve)	75

HARD TRAVELLIN'

71	Flams Ltd PR 1065	HARD TRAVELLIN' (LP, private pressing)	100

HARDWARE

79	Narc NARC 001	Speed Unit/Wall To Wall/Walking/Fire (folded p/s)	5
79	Narc NARC 002	Rubberface/Face The Flag/The Seven Minutes (p/s)	5

HARDWARE

85	Reset 7REST 7	Dance/Hey (p/s)	8
85	Reset 12REST 7	Dance/Hey (12", p/s)	15

HARDY

71	Ackee ACK 131	Glorious Morning/Hearing's Not Seeing	6

DAVE HARDY

76	Red Rag RRR 008	LEAVING THE DALES (LP)	12

FRANCOISE HARDY

64	Pye 7N 15612	Catch A Falling Star/Only Friends	8
64	Pye 7N 15653	Tous Les Garcons Et Les Filles/L'Amour S'en Va	6
64	Pye 7N 15696	Pourtant Tu M'Aimes/Jaloux	8
64	Pye 7N 15740	Et Meme/Le Temps De L'Amour	8
65	Pye 7N 15802	All Over The World/Another Place	7
66	Vogue VRS 7001	Just Call And I'll Be There/You Just Have To Say The Word	7
66	Vogue VRS 7004	So Many Friends/However Much	10
66	Vogue VRS 7010	This Little Heart/The Rose	7
66	Vogue VRS 7011	La Maison Ou J'ai Grandi/Je Ne Suis La Pour Personne	7
66	Vogue VRS 7014	Autumn Rendezvous/It's My Heart	7
66	Vogue VRS 7020	Si C'est Ca/Je Serai La Pour Toi	7
66	Vogue VRS 7025	Voila/Qui Peut Dire	7
67	Vogue VRS 7026	On Se Quitte Toujours/Les Petits Garcons	8
68	United Artists UP 1208	Now You Want To Be Loved/Tell Him You're Mine	10
68	United Artists UP 2253	Will You Love Me Tomorrow/Loving You	10
69	United Artists UP 35011	Comment Te Dire Adieu/La Mer, Les Etoiles Et Le Vent	10
70	United Artists UP 35070	All Because Of You/Time Passing By	10
70	United Artists UP 35105	Soon Is Slipping Away/The Bells Of Avignon	10
64	Pye NEP 24188	C'EST FAB (EP)	10
64	Pye NEP 24192	FRANCOISE SINGS IN ENGLISH (EP)	10
64	Pye NEP 24193	C'EST FRANCOISE (EP)	10
65	Vogue VRE 5000	FRANCOISE (EP)	10
65	Vogue VRE 5001	FRANCOISE HARDY (EP)	10
65	Vogue VRE 5003	DIS LUI NON (EP)	10
66	Vogue VRE 5008	LE TEMPS DES SOUVENIRS (EP)	10
66	Vogue VRE 5012	CHANTE EN ALLEMAND (EP)	12
66	Vogue VRE 5015	L'AMITIE (EP)	12
66	Vogue VRE 5017	MON AMIE LA ROSE (EP)	12
67	Vogue VRE 5018	AUTUMN RENDEZVOUS (EP)	12
64	Pye NPL 18094	FRANCOISE HARDY (LP)	15
64	Pye NPL 18099	IN VOGUE (LP)	12
65	Vogue VRL 3000	FRANCOISE HARDY (LP)	18
66	Vogue VRL 3021	FRANCOISE HARDY (LP)	18
66	Vogue VRL 3023	LE MEILLEUR DE FRANCOISE HARDY (LP)	15

MINT VALUE £

66	Vogue VRL 3025	SINGS IN ENGLISH (LP)	15
67	Vogue VRL 3028	FRANCOISE (LP)	15
67	Vogue VRL 3031	VOILA! FRANCOISE HARDY (LP)	15
68	United Artists SULP 1191	IL N'Y A PAS D'AMOUR HEUREUX (LP)	20
68	United Artists ULP 1207	EN ANGLAIS (LP)	25
70	United Artists UAS 29046	ONE-NINE-SEVEN-ZERO (LP)	25

LAVELL HARDY

68	Direction 58-3261	Don't Lose Your Groove/Women Of The World	15

COLIN HARE

(see also Honeybus)

70	Penny Farthing PEN 736	Grannie, Grannie/For Where Have You Been	12
71	Penny Farthing PEN 750	Underground Girl/Fighting For Peace	10
72	Warner Bros K 16203	Didn't I Tell You/Seek Not In The Wide World	10
71	Penny Farthing PELS 516	MARCH HARE (LP)	300

WINSTON HAREWOOD

(see also Winston Heywood)

71	Camel CA 64	I Will Never Fall In Love Again (actually by Winston Heywood)/ LA-FUD-DIL ALL-STARS: La-Fud-Dil (actually "La-Fud-Del")	8

RON HARGRAVE

58	MGM MGM 956	Latch On/Only A Daydream	3000
58	MGM MGM 956	Latch On/Only A Daydream (78)	400

HARLAN COUNTY

70	Nashville 6076 002	Dr. Handy's Dandy Candy/Big Heat	8
70	Nashville 6336 002	HARLAN COUNTY (LP, red/black label)	25

HARLEM JONNS RESHUFFLE

(see under 'J')

HARLEM SPEAKEASY

68	Polydor 56270	Aretha/Sight Of Pegasus	15

HARLESDEN MONKS

72	Pama Supreme PS 352	Time/Harlesden High Street	7
72	Pama Supreme PS 352	Rock Me Mister Ping Wing/Breakdown Rock	30

STEVE HARLEY (& COCKNEY REBEL)

(see also Anderson Harley & Batt)

73	EMI EMI 2051	Sebastian/Rock And Roll Parade	5
74	EMI EMI 2191	Psychomodo/Such A Dream (unreleased)	0
74	EMI EMI 2191	Mr Soft/Such A Dream (with 'Orchestrated by Alan Powell' credit)	5
74	EMI EMI 2233	Big Big Deal/Bed In The Corner	5
77	EMI EMI 2922	Someone's Coming/Riding The Waves (For Virginia Woolf)	5

LEE HARMER'S POPCORN

68	Page One POF 053	Love Is Coming/Hello Sunshine	15

HARMONIANS

(see also Tony & Hippy Boys, Winston Shan)

70	Ackee ACK 107	Music Street/Group Of Girls	10

HARMONICA FATS

63	Stateside SS 184	Tore Up/I Get So Tired	40
68	Action ACT 4507	Tore Up/I Get So Tired (reissue)	20

HARMONISERS

69	Duke DU 32	Mother Hen/WINSTON SINCLAIR: Chastise Them	15

HARMONIZING FOUR

(see also Charms)

66	Rymska RA 102	Who Knows/Heart Of Stone (actually by Charms)	18

HARMONY BEACH

83	Surf King SK 1	HARMONY BEACH (EP, private pressing)	18

HARMONY GRASS

(see also Capability Brown, Tony Rivers & Castaways)

68	RCA RCA 1772	Move In A Little Bit Closer Baby/Happiness Is Toy Shaped	8
69	RCA RCA 1828	First Time Loving/What A Groovy Day	7
69	RCA RCA 1885	I Remember/Summer Dreaming	7
70	RCA RCA 1928	Mrs. Richie/Teach Me How (withdrawn)	10
70	RCA RCA 1928	Cecilia/Mrs. Richie	7
70	RCA RCA 2011	Stand On Your Own Two Feet/Sing In The Sunshine	7
70	RCA SF 8034	THIS IS US (LP)	30

HARMONY TRIO

69	Emblem 7DR 323	LET'S FACE IT (LP)	12

JOE HARNELL

62	London HLR 9637	Fly Me To The Moon - Bossa Nova/Harlem Nocturne	6
78	MCA MCA 397	The Incredible Hulk Theme/Love Theme	5

BILLY HARNER

71	Kama Sutra 2013 029	What About The Music/Please Spare Me This Time	20
71	Kama Sutra 2013 029	What About The Music(instrumental)/Please Spare Me This Time	900
72	Blue Horizon 2431 013	TRIGGER FINGER (LP)	20

BUD HARPER

65	Vocalion VP 9252	Mr. Soul/Let Me Love You	60
65	Vocalion VP 9252	Mr. Soul/Let Me Love You (DJ copy)	100

CHARLIE HARPER

(see also U.K. Subs, Long Tall Shorty, Urban Dogs)

80	Gem GEMS 35	Barmy London Army/Talk Is Cheap (p/s, green or yellow vinyl)	5
81	Ramkup CAC 005	Freaked/Jo (p/s)	5

MINT VALUE £

DON HARPER ORCHESTRA
(see also Electricians)

68	Columbia DB 8519	World Of Sport March/England 88	15
73	Columbia DB 9023	World Of Sport/"Dr. Who" Theme (as Don Harper's Homo Electronicus)	25
74	Columbia SCX 6559	HOMO ELECTRONICUS (LP)	40

JANICE HARPER

57	HMV POP 376	Bon Voyage/Tell Me That You Love Me Tonight	10
58	Capitol CL 14899	Devotion/In Time	10
59	Capitol CL 14977	I Was Hoping You'd Ask Me/I'm Making Love To You	8
59	Capitol CL 15026	Let Me Call You Sweetheart/Just Whistle	5
60	Capitol CL 15159	Only Once/Love Me Now, Love Me Never	5
59	Capitol T 1195	WITH FEELING (LP)	20

JESSIE HARPER
(see also Human Instinct)

92	Kissing Spell KSLP 9203	GUITAR ABSOLUTION IN THE SHADE OF A MIDNIGHT SUN (LP, reissue of acetate-only album)	20

JOE 'HARMONICA' HARPER

58	MGM MGM 983	Lazy Train/Her Lips Were Like Velvet	8

MIKE HARPER

70	Concord CON 026	You've Got Too Much Going For You/This Time	15

ROY HARPER
(see also Rory Phare, Per Yarroh, Pink Floyd)

SINGLES

66	Strike JH 304	Take Me Into Your Eyes/Pretty Baby (in wraparound p/s)	45
66	Strike JH 304	Take Me Into Your Eyes/Pretty Baby	25
67	CBS 203001	Midspring Dithering/Zengem	20
68	CBS 3371	Life Goes By/Nobody's Got Any Money In The Summer	22
72	Harvest HAR 5059	Bank Of The Dead (Valerie's Song)/Little Lady (in p/s)	10
72	Harvest HAR 5059	Bank Of The Dead (Valerie's Song)/Little Lady	6
74	Harvest HAR 5080	(Don't You Think We're) Forever/Male Chauvinist Pig Blues	5
74	Harvest HAR 5089	Home (live)/Home (studio)	5
75	Harvest HAR 5096	When An Old Cricketer Leaves The Crease/Hallucinating Light (Acoustic Version) (p/s)	5
75	Harvest HAR 5102	Grown-Ups Are Just Silly Children/Referendum (Legend)	5
75	EMI PSR 407	Referendum/Another Day (live)/Tom Tiddler's Ground (live) (promo only)	8
77	Harvest HAR 5120	One Of Those Days In England/Watford Gap (p/s)	5
77	Harvest HAR 5140	Sail Away/Cherishing The Lonesome (as Roy Harper's Black Sheep)	7
78	Harvest HAR 5160	When An Old Cricketer Leaves The Crease/Home (studio) (p/s)	5
80	Harvest HAR 5203	Playing Games/First Thing In The Morning (p/s)	6
80	Harvest HAR 5207	Short And Sweet/Water Sports (live)/Unknown Soldier (live) (p/s)	6
82	Public PUBS 1001	No One Gets Out Here Alive/Casualty (live) (p/s)	5
83	Public PUBS 1002	I Still Care/Goodbye Ladybird (p/s)	6
85	B. Banquet BEG 131	Elizabeth (Short Version)/Advertisement (Short Version) (p/s)	5
88	Regal Zonophone HR 1	Laughing Inside/Laughing Inside (p/s, promo only; as Harry Rope)	7
88	EMI EM 46	Laughing Inside/Laughing Inside (Acoustic Version) (p/s)	5

ORIGINAL LPS

66	Strike JHL 105	SOPHISTICATED BEGGAR	400
67	CBS BPG 63184	COME OUT FIGHTING GHENGIS SMITH (mono, orange label)	80
67	CBS SBPG 63184	COME OUT FIGHTING GHENGIS SMITH (stereo, orange label)	90
69	Liberty LBL 83231	FOLKJOKEOPUS (mono, blue label)	80
69	Liberty LBS 83231	FOLKJOKEOPUS (stereo, blue label)	70
69	Harvest SHVL 766	FLAT, BAROQUE AND BERSERK (gatefold sleeve; first pressing with "H. Ash" label credit)	50
71	Harvest SHVL 789	STORMCOCK (gatefold sleeve with lyric inner, no EMI logo on label)	40
73	Harvest SHVL 808	LIFEMASK (foldout 'door' sleeve, with insert)	25
74	Harvest SHSP 4027	VALENTINE (initially with lyric booklet)	30
74	Harvest SHSP 4027	VALENTINE (without lyric booklet)	15
74	Harvest SHDW 405	FLASHES FROM THE ARCHIVES OF OBLIVION (2-LP, gatefold sleeve)	30
75	Harvest SHSP 4046	HQ (with lyric inner sleeve, EMI logo on label)	15
77	Harvest SHSP 4060	BULLINAMINGVASE (with inner sleeve & "Watford Gap"; some with 7", Referendum/"Another Day" (live)/"Tom Tiddler's Ground" [PSR 407])	15
77	Harvest SHSP 4060	BULLINAMINGVASE (2nd pressing with "Breakfast With You")	12
77	Harvest SHSP 4077	COMMERCIAL BREAK (unreleased; test pressing with proof sleeve)	300
78	Harvest SHSM 2025	HARPER 1970-1975	12
78	Harvest	HARPER 1970-1975 (6-LP box set)	100
80	Harvest SHVL 820	THE UNKNOWN SOLDIER (with inner sleeve)	12
82	Public TC PUBLP 5001	WORK OF HEART (on 'real time' high quality tape, different sleeve, 250 only)	12
84	Hard Up PUB 5002	BORN IN CAPTIVITY (880 only)	30
92	Hard Up HU 2	BORN IN CAPTIVITY II (LIVE) (cassette)	15

REISSUE ALBUMS

70	Young Blood SSYB 7	RETURN OF THE SOPHISTICATED BEGGAR (LP, with "Hup Hup Spiral" closed run-out groove, different sleeve)	20
73	Birth RAB 3	RETURN OF THE SOPHISTICATED BEGGAR (LP, 2nd reissue, with "Hup Hup Spiral" closed run-out groove, different sleeve)	12
75	Sunset SLS 50373	FOLKJOKEOPUS (LP)	12
77	Big Ben BBX 502	THE SOPHISTICATED BEGGAR (LP, different rear sleeve)	12
77	Embassy EMB 31544	THE EARLY YEARS (LP, reissue of "Come Out Fighting Ghengis Smith", different sleeve)	12
86	Awareness AWL 1002	WORK OF HEART (LP, different sleeve with inner; later pressing with only "No One Gets Out Of Here Alive"/"Casualty (live) [PUBS 1001])	12
86	Awareness AWL 1002	WORK OF HEART (LP, different sleeve with inner; 1st 1,000 with 2 x 7" "No One Gets Out Of Here Alive"/"Casualty (live) [PUBS 1001]) & "Still Care"/ "Goodbye Ladybird" [PUBS2])	15

MINT VALUE £

86	Awareness AWL 1002	WORK OF HEART (LP, different sleeve, 250 only on 'real time' quality tape)	12
93	Hard Up HUCD 003	FLAT, BAROQUE & BERSERK (CD, in box with 40-page booket & poster, signed)	20
71	Harvest SHVL 766	FLAT, BAROQUE AND BERSERK (gatefold sleeve; second pressing with "H. Ash" label credit and boxed EMI logo)	20
71	Harvest SHVL 789	STORMCOCK (gatefold sleeve with lyric inner, with EMI logo on label)	20

TIM HARPER

95	Peacefrog PF 047	I Feel A Groove (12", plain sleeve)	8

HARPER'S BIZARRE

67	Warner Bros WB 5890	59th Street Bridge Song (Feelin' Groovy)/Lost My Love Today	8
67	Warner Bros WB 7528	Come To The Sunshine/The Debutante's Ball	5
67	Warner Bros WB 7063	Anything Goes/Malibu U	7
67	Warner Bros WB 7090	Chattanooga Choo Choo/Hey You In The Crowd	7
68	Warner Bros WB 7172	Cotton Candy Sandman (Sandman's Coming)/Virginia City	5
68	Warner Bros WB 7223	Battle Of New Orleans/Green Apple Tree	5
69	Warner Bros WB 7238	I Love You, Alice B. Toklas!/Look To The Rainbow	5
70	Warner Bros WB 7388	Anything Goes/Virginia City	5
67	Warner Bros W 1693	FEELIN' GROOVY (LP)	20
67	Warner Bros W 1716	ANYTHING GOES (LP)	20
68	Warner Bros W(S) 1739	THE SECRET LIFE OF HARPER'S BIZARRE (LP)	15

SLIM HARPO

(see also Lightnin' Slim)

61	Pye International 7N 25098	Rainin' In My Heart/Don't Start Cryin' Now	25
63	Pye International 7N 25220	Don't Start Cryin' Now/Rainin' In My Heart	25
66	Stateside SS 491	Baby Scratch My Back/I'm Gonna Miss You (Like The Devil)	30
66	Stateside SS 527	Shake Your Hips/Midnight Blues	30
66	Stateside SS 557	I'm A King Bee/I Got Love If You Want It	30
67	Stateside SS 581	I'm Your Breadmaker Baby/Loving You (The Way I Do)	30
67	President PT 164	I'm Gonna Keep What I've Got/I've Got To Be With You Tonight	10
68	Liberty LBF 15176	Something Inside Me/PAPPA LIGHTFOOT: Wine Whisky And Women	20
68	President PT 187	Tip On In (Parts 1 & 2)	15
70	Blue Horizon 57-3175	Folsom Prison Blues/Mutual Friend	30
65	Stateside SL 10135	A LONG DRINK OF THE BLUES (LP, with Lightnin' Slim)	50
68	President PTL 1017	TIP ON IN (LP)	40
70	Blue Horizon 7-63854	HE KNEW THE BLUES (LP)	110
72	Blue Horizon 2431 013	TRIGGER FINGER (LP)	135
76	Flyright LP 520	BLUES HANGOVER (LP)	18
78	Sonet SNTF 769	HE KNEW THE BLUES (LP)	25
80	Flyright FLY 558	GOT LOVE IF YOU WANT IT (LP)	18

GEORGE HARRASSMENT & HOMOSEXUALS

(see also Homosexuals)

80s	Black Noise 12 NO 6	MASAI SLEEP WALKING (LP)	12

HARRIER

84	Black Horse HARR 1T	OUT ON THE STREET EP (Out On The Street/ Nickels And Dimes/Shine On) (12", p/s)	15

DERRICK HARRIOT(T) (& CRYSTALITES)

62	Blue Beat BB 131	I Care/Have Faith In Me (as Derrick Harriott & Vagabonds)	15
63	Blue Beat BB 178	Be True/I Won't Cry	15
64	Island WI 157	What Can I Do (The Wedding)/Leona	15
65	Island WI 170	I Am Only Human (as Derak Harriott)/OWEN AND LEON SILVERA: I Want My Cock (probably withdrawn)	50
65	Island WI 170	I Am Only Human (as Derak Harriott)/ROY PANTON: Good Man	30
65	Island WI 237	My Three Loves/The Jerk	30
65	Island WI 245	Together/Mama Didn't Lie	30
65	Ska Beat JB 199	Monkey Ska/Derrick!	30
66	Doctor Bird DB 1002	Jon Tom/AUDREY WILLIAMS: Solas Market	20
67	Island WI 3063	The Loser/Bless You	80
67	Island WI 3064	Happy Times/You My Everything	35
67	Island WI 3077	Walk The Streets/BOBBY ELLIS: Step Softly (B-side with Desmond Miles Seven)	80
67	Island WI 3089	Solomon/BOBBY ELLIS: The Emperor (B-side with Desmond Miles Seven)	45
68	Island WI 3135	Do I Worry?/BOBBY ELLIS & CRYSTALITES: Shuntin'	80
68	Island WI 3147	Born To Love You/IKE & CRYSTALITES: Alfred Hitchcock	40
68	Island WI 3153	Tang Tang Festival Song/CRYSTALITES: James Ray	40
69	Big Shot BI 505	Standing In/Bumble Bee	50
69	Big Shot BI 511	Another Lonely Night/Been So Long	15
70	Songbird SB 1013	Riding For A Fall/I'm Not Begging	10
70	Songbird SB 1014	Sitting On Top/You Were Meant For Me	10
70	Songbird SB 1022	Go Bye Bye/Laugh It Off	12
70	Songbird SB 1028	Message From A Black Man/(Version II)	10
70	Songbird SB 1029	Psychedelic Train (w/ Chosen Few)/Psychedelic Train (Pt. 2) (with Crystalites)	12
70	Songbird SB 1033	No Man Is An Island/CRYSTALITES: No Man Is An Island Part 2	10
70	Songbird SB 1042	Groovy Situation/CRYSTALITES: The Crystal Groove	10
70	Songbird SB 1043	Psychedelic Train Chapter Three/CRYSTALITES: Groovy Situation Version II	7
71	Songbird SB 1052	Candy/CRYSTALITES: Candy Version	7
71	Songbird SB 1055	Lollipop Girl/CRYSTALITES: Lollipop Version	15
71	Songbird SB 1063	Medley In 5 (Parts 1 & 2)	7
72	Songbird SB 1065	Have You Seen Her/CRYSTALITES: Have You Seen Her - Version	7
72	Songbird SB 1068	Over The River/River (Version)	7
72	Songbird SB 1071	Since I Lost My Baby/Baby (Version)	7
72	Songbird SB 1078	Being In Love/Love (Version)	6
72	Songbird SB 1084	Don't Rock The Boat/Rock (Version)	7
73	Attack ATT 8056	Brown Baby/CRYSTALITES: Brown Baby Version	6
73	Explosion EX 2071	Let Me Down Easy/Let Me Down Easy - Version	7
74	Harry J. HJ 6675	Some Guys Have All The Luck/Some Guys Have All The Luck - Version	6

			MINT VALUE £
65	Island ILP 928	THE BEST OF DERRICK HARRIOTT (LP)	120
67	Island ILP 955	DERRICK HARRIOTT'S ROCKSTEADY PARTY (LP, actually v/a LP)	300
68	Island ILP 983	THE BEST OF VOLUME TWO (LP, as Derrick Harriott & Crystalites)	150
69	Pama SECO 13	SINGS JAMAICA REGGAE (LP)	150
70	Trojan TTL 43	THE BEST OF DERRICK HARRIOTT (LP)	40
70	Trojan TTL 54	ROCKSTEADY PARTY (LP)	55
70	Trojan TBL 114	THE UNDERTAKER (LP, as Derrick Harriott & Crystalites)	25
70	Trojan TBL 141	PSYCHEDELIC TRAIN (LP, as Derrick Harriott & Crystalites)	30

JOE HARRIOTT

(see also Tony Kinsey Trio & Joe Harriott, John Mayer, Michael Garrick)

56	Jazz Today JTE 106	WITH STRINGS (EP)	20
56	Pye Jazz NJE 1003	NO STRINGS (EP)	50
50s	Melodisc EPM7 117	COOL JAZZ WITH JOE (EP)	25
57	Columbia SEG 7665	JOE HARRIOTT QUARTET (EP)	75
59	Columbia SEG 7939	BLUE HARRIOTT (EP)	35
61	Columbia SEG 8070	A GUY CALLED JOE (EP)	25
60	Jazzland JLP 49	FREE FORM (LP)	60
62	Columbia 33SX 1477	ABSTRACT (LP)	120
63	Columbia 33SX 1627	MOVEMENT (LP)	200
64	Columbia 33SX 1692	HIGH SPIRITS (LP)	130
66	Columbia S(C)X 6025	DOUBLE QUINTET (LP, with John Mayer)	45
67	Melodisc SLP 12150	SWINGS HIGH (LP)	75
67	Columbia S(C) 6122	INDO-JAZZ FUSIONS (LP, with John Mayer)	35
68	Columbia S(C)X 6215	INDO-JAZZ FUSIONS II (LP, with John Mayer)	45
68	Columbia S(C)X 6249	PERSONAL PORTRAIT (LP)	50
69	Columbia SCX 6354	HUM-DONO (LP, with Amancio D'Silva)	500
73	One Up OU 2011	MEMORIAL 1973 (LP)	25

JOE HARRIOTT/DON RENDELL QUARTET

(see also Don Rendell)

57	MGM MGM-EP 615	JAZZ BRITANNIA (EP, 2 tracks each)	25

ANITA HARRIS

(see also Brello Cabal)

61	Parlophone R 4830	I Haven't Got You/Mr One And Only	7
64	Vocalion V 9223	Lies/Don't Think About Love	7
65	Decca F 12082	Willingly/At Last Love	6
65	Pye 7N 15868	Trains And Boats And Planes/Upside Down	6
65	Pye 7N 15894	I Don't Know Anymore/When I Look At You	8
65	Pye 7N 15971	London Life/I Run To Hide	7
66	Pye 7N 17069	Something Must Be Done/Funny Kind Of Feeling	10
66	CBS 2724	Just Loving You/Butterfly With Coloured Wings	5
67	CBS 2991	The Playground/B.A.D. For Me	12
68	CBS 3765	Le Blon/Dusty Road	5
67	Pye NEP 24288	ANITA HARRIS (EP)	15
68	CBS EP 6401	DREAM A LITTLE DREAM OF ME (EP)	10
66	CBS BGP/SBPG 62894	SOMEBODY'S IN MY ORCHARD (LP)	15
67	CBS 63182	JUST LOVING YOU (LP)	12
69	CBS 63927	CUDDLY TOY (LP)	12
70	CBS S 64258	ANITA IN JUMBLELAND (LP)	12

ARTIE HARRIS & HIS BOYS

63	Oriole CB 1816	Go Go Gaudeamus/Mexicana	8

BETTY HARRIS

(see also Betty Harris & Lee Dorsey)

63	London HL 9796	Cry To Me/I'll Be A Liar	20
65	Stateside SS 475	What A Sad Feeling/I'm Evil Tonight	20
67	Stateside SS 2045	Nearer To You/12 Red Roses	20
69	Action ACT 4535	Ride Your Pony/Trouble With My Lover	15
69	Action ACLP 6007	SOUL PERFECTION (LP)	75

BRENDA JO HARRIS

69	Roulette RO 503	I Can Remember/Play With Fire	8

EDDIE HARRIS

69	Atlantic 584 218	Listen Here/Theme - In Search Of A Movie	10
69	Atlantic 584 232	It's Crazy/Live Right Now (unissued)	0
74	Atlantic K 10513	Is It In?/Funkarama	8
75	Atlantic K 10561	I Need Some Money/Don't Want Nobody	8
76	Atlantic K 10741	Get On Up And Dance/Why Must We Part	5
62	Stateside SL 10009	BREAKFAST AT TIFFANY'S (LP)	15
63	Stateside SL 10018	MIGHTY LIKE A ROSE (LP)	15
63	Stateside SL 10049	GOES TO THE MOVIES (LP)	15
65	Atlantic SAL 5045	THE IN SOUND (LP)	15
69	Atlantic 588 177	SILVER CYCLES (LP)	15
73	Atlantic K 40220	THE ELECTRIFYING EDDIE HARRIS (LP)	15

HAL HARRIS

78	Ace NS 47	Jitterbop Baby/I Don't Know When	5

JET HARRIS

(see also Shadows, Jet Harris & Tony Meehan, Keith Meehan, Peter Rawes)

62	Decca F 11466	Besame Mucho/Chills And Fever	8
62	Decca F 11488	Main Title Theme (from The Man With The Golden Arm)/Some People	8
64	Decca F 11841	Big Bad Bass/Rifka	10
67	Fontana TF 849	My Lady/You Don't Live Twice	35
75	SRT SRT 75355	Theme For A Fallen Idol/This Sportin' Life (initial pressing)	15
75	SRT SRT 75355	Theme/This Sportin' Life (later pressing with shortened A-side title)	5
78	SRT SRT 77389	Guitar Man/Theme	8

			MINT VALUE £
62	Decca DFE 8502	JET HARRIS (EP)	20
78	Ellie Jay EJSP 8622	INSIDE JET HARRIS - THE LAST CONCERT (LP, 2,500 only)	20
70s	Q LPMM 1038	ANNIVERSARY ALBUM (LP)	20

JET HARRIS & TONY MEEHAN
(see also Shadows, Jet Harris, Tony Meehan, Vipers Skiffle Group)

63	Decca F 11563	Diamonds/Footstomp	5
63	Decca F 11644	Scarlett O'Hara/(Doing The) Hully Gully	5
63	Decca F 11710	Applejack/The Tall Texan	6
80	Decca F 13892	Diamonds/Scarlett O'Hara/Applejack/Man With The Golden Arm (p/s)	5
63	Decca DFE 8528	JET AND TONY (EP)	20
76	Decca REM 1	REMEMBERING (LP)	12

JOHNNY HARRIS

65	Mercury MF 942	Mynah Hop/Here Comes The Boot	6
69	Warner Bros WB 8000	Footprints On The Moon/Lulu's Theme	10
70	Warner Bros WB 8016	Fragment Of Fear/Stepping Stones	10
70	Warner Bros WS 3002	MOVEMENTS (LP)	30
72	Warner Bros K 46054	MOVEMENTS (LP, reissue)	20
73	Warner Bros K 46187	ALL TO BRING YOU MORNING (LP)	15

JUNE HARRIS

65	CBS 201774	Over And Over Again/Stand Back	12

MAX HARRIS

69	Pye 7N 17730	Theme From The Film 'Baby Love'/Robert's Theme From 'Baby Love'	6

OSCAR HARRIS

70	Upfront UPF 6	T.O.P/I Don't Wanna listen	8

PAT HARRIS & BLACKJACKS
(see also Blackjacks)

63	Pye 7N 15567	The Hippy Hippy Shake/You Gotta See Your Mama Ev'ry Night	25

PHIL HARRIS

54	HMV 7M 199	I Know An Old Lady/Take Your Girlie To The Movies	10
54	HMV 7M 231	I Guess I'll Have To Change My Plan/The Persian Kitten	10
55	HMV 7M 289	I Wouldn't Touch You With A Ten-Foot Pole/There's A Lot More	10
70	Buena Vista DF 478	Thomas O'Malley Cat/SCATMAN CROTHERS: Everybody Wants To Be A Cat	5
59	RCA Camden CDN 124	THAT'S WHAT I LIKE ABOUT THE SOUTH (LP)	12

RICHARD HARRIS
(see also Jim Webb)

68	RCA RCA 1699	MacArthur Park/Paper Chase	8
68	Stateside SS 8001	The Yard Went On Forever/Lucky Me	5
70	Stateside SS 8054	Ballad Of 'A Man Called Horse'/ The Morning Of The Mourning Of Another Kennedy	5
71	Probe PRO 540	My Boy/Why Did You Leave Me	7
68	RCA Victor RD/SF 7947	A TRAMP SHINING (LP)	18
68	Stateside (S)SL 5001	THE YARD WENT ON FOREVER (LP)	15

ROLF HARRIS

64	Columbia DB 7349	Ringo For President/Headhunter	7
66	Columbia SEG 8516	JAKE THE PEG (EP)	8
63	SCK 1507	SUN ARISE (LP, stereo)	20

RONNIE HARRIS (& CORONETS)
(see also Coronets, Ruby Murray, Ray Burns, Russ Conway)

54	Columbia SCM 5138	Hold My Hand/No One Can Change Destiny	7
54	Columbia SCM 5139	I Love Paris/I Still Believe	7
55	Columbia SCM 5159	Don't Go To Strangers/Surprisingly (as Ronnie Harris & Coronets)	7
55	Columbia SCM 5176	Stranger In Paradise/I Wonder	7
56	Columbia SCM 5242	I've Changed My Mind A Thousand Times/Come To Me (with Coronets)	7
56	Columbia DB 3836	That's Right/A House With Love In It	12
57	Columbia DB 3877	Armen's Theme (Yesterday And You)/Dancing Chandelier	5
57	Columbia DB 3934	Dear To Me/It's Not For Me To Say (B-side with Russ Conway)	5

ROY HARRIS

72	Topic 12TS 217	THE BITTER AND THE SWEET (LP, blue label)	15
75	Topic 12TS 256	CHAMPIONS OF FOLLY (LP)	12

SCOTT HARRIS

68	Morgan MR7S	Barry Johnson's Sad Eyes Inn/Morning Sun	40

SHAKEY JAKE HARRIS

69	Liberty LBS 83217	FURTHER ON UP THE ROAD (LP)	40
73	Polydor 2391 015	THE DEVIL'S HARMONICA (LP)	28

SUZANNE HARRIS

70	R.F.S. Records RFS 8270	Here Come The Beautiful People/We're Using Up The World (p/s)	20

THURSTON HARRIS (& SHARPS)
(see also Sharps)

57	Vogue V 9092	Little Bitty Pretty One/I Hope You Won't Hold It Against Me (with Sharps)	200
57	Vogue V 9092	Little Bitty Pretty One/I Hope You Won't Hold It Against Me (with Sharps) (78)	35
58	Vogue V 9098	Do What You Did/I'm Asking Forgiveness (as Thurston Harris & Sharps) (78)	55
58	Vogue V 9098	Do What You Did/I'm Asking Forgiveness (as Thurston Harris & Sharps)	250
58	Vogue V 9108	Be Baba Leba/I'm Out To Getcha	250
58	Vogue V 9108	Be Baba Leba/I'm Out To Getcha (78)	55
58	Vogue V 9122	Smokey Joe's/Only One Love Is Blessed	150
58	Vogue V 9122	Smokey Joe's/Only One Love Is Blessed (78)	50
58	Vogue V 9127	Tears From My Heart/Over Somebody Else's Shoulder	100
58	Vogue V 9127	Tears From My Heart/Over Somebody Else's Shoulder (78)	90
59	Vogue V 9139	Purple Stew (as Thurston Harris & Masters)/I Hear A Rhapsody	150

			MINT VALUE £
59	Vogue V 9139	Purple Stew (as Thurston Harris & Masters)/I Hear A Rhapsody (78)	90
59	Vogue V 9144	You Don't Know How Much I Love You/In The Bottom Of My Heart	100
59	Vogue V 9144	You Don't Know How Much I Love You/In The Bottom Of My Heart (78)	90
59	Vogue V 9146	Hey Little Girl/My Love Will Last	150
59	Vogue V 9146	Hey Little Girl/My Love Will Last (78)	90
59	Vogue V 9149	Runk Bunk/Bless Your Heart	200
59	Vogue V 9149	Runk Bunk/Bless Your Heart	90
59	Vogue V 9151	Slip-Slop/Paradise Hill	200
59	Vogue V 9151	Slip-Slop/Paradise Hill (78)	100
66	Sue WI 4016	Little Bitty Pretty One/I Hope You Won't Hold It Against Me (reissue)	50

WEE WILLIE HARRIS

57	Decca F 10970	Rockin' At The Two 'I's/Back To School Again	40
57	Decca F 10970	Rockin' At The Two 'I's/Back To School Again (78)	30
58	Decca F 10980	Love Bug Crawl/Rosie Lee	40
58	Decca F 10980	Love Bug Crawl/Rosie Lee (78)	30
58	Decca F 11044	Got A Match/No Chemise, Please!	40
58	Decca F 11044	Got A Match/No Chemise, Please! (78)	30
60	Decca F 11217	Wild One/Little Bitty Girl	20
63	HMV POP 1198	You Must Be Joking/Better To Have Loved	10
66	Parlophone R 5504	Someone's In The Kitchen With Diana/Walk With Peter And Paul (some A-sides list 'Dina')	10
66	Polydor 56140	Listen To The River Roll Along/Try Moving Baby (writing in black or white)	10
74	Decca F 13516	Together/Rock'n'Roll Jamboree	5
58	Decca DFE 6465	ROCKING WITH WEE WILLIE (EP)	150

WYNONIE 'MR BLUES' HARRIS

51	Vogue V 2006	All She Wants To Do Is Rock/Drinkin' Wine Spo-Dee-O-Dee (78)	30
52	Vogue V 2111	Luscious Woman/Lovin' Machine (78)	25
52	Vogue V 2127	Bloodshot Eyes/Lollipop Mama (78)	15
52	Vogue V 2128	Just Like Two Drops Of Water/Good Mornin' Judge (78)	15
52	Vogue V 2133	Night Train/Do It Again Please (78)	30
52	Vogue V 2134	Rock, Mr. Blues/Put It Back (78)	30
52	Vogue V 2144	Teardrops From My Eyes/Keep On Churnin' (Till The Butter Comes) (78)	30
52	Vogue V 2166	I Like My Baby's Pudding/Adam Come And Get Your Rib (78)	35
56	Vogue V 2127	Bloodshot Eyes/Lollipop Mama (triangular centre)	125
56	Vogue V 2127	Bloodshot Eyes/Lollipop Mama (round centre)	75
56	Vogue EPV 1103	WYNONIE 'MISTER BLUES' HARRIS (EP)	120
61	Blue Beat BBEP 301	BATTLE OF THE BLUES (EP)	80

WYNONIE HARRIS/EDDIE 'CLEANHEAD' VINSON

(see also Tiny Bradshaw/Wynonie Harris, Eddie 'Cleanhead' Vinson)

72	Polydor 2343 048	JUMP BLUES (LP)	22

HARRIS SISTERS

55	Capitol CL 14232	Kissin' Bug/We've Been Walkin' All Night	20

DANNY HARRISON

62	Starlite ST45 77	No One To Love Me/All The World is Lonely	6
62	Starlite ST45 91	Broken Love Affair/Have I Wasted My Life	6
63	Starlite ST45 108	Have You Ever Been Lonely/Mary Ann I'm Lonesome	6
65	Coral Q 72479	Speak Of The Devil/I'm A Rollin' Stone	15
62	Starlite STEP 23	INTRODUCING DANNY HARRISON (EP)	20

EARL HARRISON

67	London HL 10121	Humphrey Stomp/Can You Forgive Me	50
67	London HL 10121	Humphrey Stomp/Can You Forgive Me (DJ Copy)	100

GEORGE HARRISON

(see also Beatles, Traveling Wilburys, Billy Connolly & Chris Tummings, Sylvia Griffin)

SINGLES

71	Apple R 5884	My Sweet Lord/What Is Life (in colour 'head' p/s)	12
71	Apple R 5912	Bangla-Desh/Deep Blue (with rare p/s [beware of new-looking counterfeits!])	80
71	Apple R 5912	Bangla-Desh/Deep Blue	5
73	apple R 5988	Give Me Love (Give Me Peace On Earth)/Miss O'ell	5
74	Apple R 6001	Dark Horse/I Don't Care Anymore (unissued)	0
74	Apple R 6002	Ding Dong, Ding Dong/I Don't Care Anymore (no p/s)	5
75	Apple R 6001	Dark Horse/Hari's On Tour (Express)	10
75	Apple R 6007	You/World Of Stone (p/s)	8
76	Apple R 6012	This Guitar (Can't Keep From Crying)/Maya Love (no p/s)	35
76	Apple R 5884	My Sweet Lord/What Is Life (reissue, black & white 'gnome' p/s)	10
76	Dark Horse K 16856	This Song/Learning How To Love You (issued with U.S. p/s)	10
77	Dark Horse K 16896	True Love/Pure Smokey (no p/s)	6
77	Dark Horse K 16967	It's What You Value/Woman Don't You Cry For Me (no p/s)	6
79	Dark Horse K 17327	Blow Away/Soft Touch (p/s)	5
79	Dark Horse K 17284	Love Comes To Everyone/Soft Hearted Hana	8
79	Dark Horse K 17423	Faster/Your Love Is Forever (with charity stickered plain white die-cut sleeve)	15
79	Dark Horse K 17423	Faster/Your Love Is Forever (picture disc, stickered PVC sleeve with insert)	35
81	Dark Horse K 17807	All Those Years Ago/Writing On The Wall (p/s)	5
81	Dark Horse K 17837DJ	Teardrops (Edited Version)/Save The World (DJ promo only, no p/s)	25
81	Dark Horse K 17837	Teardrops/Save The World (p/s)	10
82	Dark Horse 929 864-7	Wake Up My Love/Greece (p/s)	8
86	Ganga Publishing B.V.	Shanghai Surprise (with Vicki Brown) (unreleased, 1-sided promo only; no catalogue number, matrix: SHANGHAI 1)	800
87	Dark Horse W 8178	Got My Mind Set On You/Lay His Head (p/s, green label)	8
87	Dark Horse W 8178B	Got My Mind Set On You/Lay His Head (box set with 2 postcards)	20
87	Dark Horse W 8178T	Got My Mind Set On You (Extended Version)/Got My Mind Set On You (Single Version)/Lay His Head (12", p/s with poster)	15
87	Dark Horse W 8178TP	Got My Mind Set On You (Extended Version)/Got My Mind Set On You (Single Version)/Lay His Head (12", picture disc)	20

			MINT VALUE £
88	Dark Horse W 8131B	When We Was Fab/Zig Zag (box set with fold-out poster & cut-out)	10
88	Dark Horse W 8131T	When We Was Fab (Unextended Version)/Zig Zag/ That's The Way It Goes (Remix)/ When We Was Fab (Reverse End) (12", p/s)	10
88	Dark Horse W 8131TP	When We Was Fab (Unextended Version)/Zig Zag/That's The Way It Goes (Remix)/When We Was Fab (Reverse End) (12", picture disc)	20
88	Dark Horse W 8131CD	When We Was Fab (Unextended Version)/Zig Zag/That's The Way It Goes (Remix)/When We Was Fab (Reverse End) (3" CD with 5" adaptor, 5" case)	12
88	Dark Horse W 7913	This Is Love/Breath Away From Heaven (p/s)	8
88	Dark Horse W 7913T	This Is Love/Breath Away From Heaven/All Those Years Ago (12", p/s)	15
88	Dark Horse W 7913CD	This Is Love/Breath Away From Heaven/All Those Years Ago/ Hong Kong Blues (3" CD with adaptor, 5" case)	12
89	Dark Horse W 2696	Cheer Down/That's What It Takes (p/s)	8
89	Dark Horse W 2696T	Cheer Down/That's What It Takes/Crackerbox Palace (12", p/s)	15
89	Dark Horse W 2696CD	Cheer Down/That's What It Takes/Crackerbox Palace (3" CD, gatefold card sleeve)	20
88	Genesis SGH 777	SONGS BY GEORGE HARRISON (Limited Edition) (EP, 33rpm, with limited edition book Songs By George Harrison)	900
88	Genesis SGHCD 777	SONGS BY GEORGE HARRISON (CD EP, issued with limited edition book)	800
92	Genesis SGH 778	SONGS BY GEORGE HARRISON VOL. 2 (EP, with limited edition book Songs By George Harrison Vol. 2)	400
92	Genesis SGHCD 778	SONGS BY GEORGE HARRISON VOL. 2 (CD EP, with limited edition book)	600
03	Parlophone R 6601	Any Road/Marwa Blues (p/s)	7

ALBUMS

68	Apple APCOR 1	WONDERWALL MUSIC (soundtrack; with insert, black inner sleeve, mono)	250
68	Apple (S)APCOR 1	WONDERWALL MUSIC (soundtrack; with insert, black inner sleeve, stereo)	90
69	Zapple ZAPPLE 02	ELECTRONIC SOUND (with inner sleeve)	150
71	Apple STCH 639	ALL THINGS MUST PASS (3-LP box set with poster & lyric inner sleeves; initial batch in U.K. Box)	80
71	Apple STCH 639	ALL THINGS MUST PASS (3-LP box set with poster & lyric inner sleeves; later batch in U.S. box)	30
72	Apple STCX 3385	THE CONCERT FOR BANGLA DESH (3-LP box set, orange inside with BMI/ASCAP label credits, with booklet, featuring Bob Dylan)	40
73	Apple PAS 10006	LIVING IN THE MATERIAL WORLD (gatefold sleeve with inner)	18
74	Apple PAS 10008	DARK HORSE (LP, gatefold sleeve, inner sleeve, lyric insert)	20
91	EPIC EPC 468835 1	THE CONCERT FOR BANGLA DESH (3-LP set in single sleeve)	25
92	Apple SAPCOR 1	WONDERWALL MUSIC (reissue, gatefold sleeve with inner sleeve)	20
92	Dark Horse 759926964-1	LIVE IN JAPAN (2-LP in single sleeve)	35
96	Zapple ZAPPLE 02	ELECTRONIC SOUND (reissue, with inner sleeve	20
01	Parlophone 5304741	ALL THINGS MUST PASS (3-LP, reissue)	20
02	Dark Horse 5419691	BRAINWASHED (Gatefold LP with sticker on cover)	20

CDs

87	Dark Horse 9256432	CLOUD NINE	20
87	Parlophone CDS 7466888	ALL THINGS MUST PASS (2-CD, without Apple logo)	20
87	Parlophone CDS 7466888	ALL THINGS MUST PASS (2-CD, with Apple logo)	15
89	Dark Horse K 9257262	THE BEST OF DARK HORSE 1976-1989	40
92	Dark Horse 7599269642	LIVE IN JAPAN (2-CD)	30
02	Dark Horse 580 3450	BRAINWASHED (CD box set)	25

KATHLEEN HARRISON

66	Columbia DB 7871	Mrs. Thursday/Call Round Any Old Time	5

MIKE HARRISON

(see also Art, Spirit, Spooky Tooth)

71	Island ILPS 9170	MIKE HARRISON (LP, gatefold sleeve, pink rim, palm tree label)	25
72	Island ILPS 9209	SMOKESTACK LIGHTNING (LP, laminated sleeve, pink rim, palm tree label)	20
75	Good Ear EAR 7002	RAINBOW RIDER (LP)	15

NEIL HARRISON

(see also Driftwood)

74	Decca F13520	Sad Eyes/Bicycle Driver	10
74	Deram SML 1115	ALL DRESSED UP AND NOWHERE TO GO (LP, white/red label with small logo)	12

NOEL HARRISON

65	Decca F 12001	Trees/To Ramona	6
66	Decca F 12314	A Young Girl Of Sixteen/Tomorrow Is My Turn	6
66	Decca F 12345	It's All Over Now Baby Blue/Much As I Love You	6
67	Reprise RS 20615	Suzanne/Life Is A Dream	6
68	Reprise RS 20758	Windmills Of Your Mind/Leitch On The Beach	8
69	Reprise RS23395	Sparrow/California Weekend	10
69	Decca F 12918	Love Minus Zero/Just Can't Wait	6
57	HMV 7EG 8383	NOEL HARRISON (EP)	15
65	Decca DFE 8616	NOEL HARRISON (EP)	10
65	Decca DFE 8639	TO RAMONA (EP)	12
60	Philips BBL 7399	AT THE BLUE ANGEL (LP)	20
69	Reprise RSLP 6321	THE GREAT ELECTRIC EXPERIMENT IS OVER (LP)	15

REGGIE HARRISON

63	Cameo Parkway P 863	A Lonely Piano/HIPPIES: Memory Lane	20

WILBERT HARRISON

59	Top Rank JAR 132	Kansas City/Listen My Darling	20
59	Top Rank JAR 132	Kansas City/Listen My Darling (78)	30
62	Island WI 031	I'm Broke/Off To School	20
65	Sue WI 363	Let's Stick Together/Kansas City Twist	20
70	London HL 10307	Let's Work Together/Stagger Lee	15
73	Action ACT 4613	Get It While You Can/Amen	8
70	London HA/SH 8415	LET'S WORK TOGETHER (LP)	40

WILBERT HARRISON/BABY WASHINGTON

(see also Baby Washington)

71	Joy JOYS 191	BATTLE OF THE GIANTS (LP, 1 side each)	18

MINT VALUE £

YVONNE HARRISON

67	Caltone TONE 102	The Chase/Take My Hand	70
75	Camel CA 2003	Knotty Screw Face/UNDERGROUND PEOPLE: Face Dub	6

DEBBIE/DEBORAH HARRY

(see also Wind In The Willows, Blondie, New York Blondes)

93	Chrysalis TC-CHS 4900	I Can See Clearly/Standing In My Way (B-side with Joey Ramone) (cassette)	7

HARRY J. ALL STARS

(see also Jay Boys, Bob Andy, John Holt, Lizzy)

69	Harry J. TR 675	Liquidator/GLEN & DAVE: La La Always Stay (green label)	8
69	Harry J. TR 675	Liquidator/GLEN & DAVE: La La Always Stay (white label)	5
70	Harry J. HJ 6601	The Big Three/Lavender (B-side actually "Lavender Blue" by Lloyd Robinson)	6
70	Harry J. HJ 6608	Reach For The Sky/Interrogator	6
70	Harry J. HJ 6621	Return Of The Liquidator (actually "Tons Of Gold" by Val Bennett)/All Day	12
72	Harry J. HJ 6641	Down Side Up/Down Side Up - Version	8
73	Explosion EX 2073	Chirpy Chirpy Cheep Cheep/Chirpy Chirpy (Instrumental)	5
73	Blue Mountain BM 1028	U.F.O./Reggae With The Birds	5
70	Trojan TBL 104	THE LIQUIDATOR (LP)	20

HARRY & RADCLIFFE

69	Camel CA 26	History/Just Be Alone	20
69	Punch PH 8	History/Just Be Alone	6

HARSH REALITY

(see also Matthews Southern Comfort)

68	Philips PB 1710	Tobacco Ash Sunday/How Do You Feel	18
69	Philips PB 1769	Heaven And Hell/Praying For Reprieve	18
69	Philips (S)BL 7891	HEAVEN AND HELL (LP, gatefold sleeve, blue/silver labels)	300

CAJUN HART

69	Warner Bros WB 7258	Got To Find A Way/Lover's Prayer	200
69	Warner Bros WB 7258	Got To Find A Way/Lover's Prayer (DJ Copy)	300

DERRY HART & HARTBEATS

59	Decca F 11138	Come On Baby/Nowhere In This World	25
59	Decca F 11138	Come On Baby/Nowhere In This World (78)	18

MICKEY HART

(see also Grateful Dead, Diga Rhythm Band)

73	Warner Bros. K 46182	ROLLING THUNDER (LP)	15

MIKE HART

(see also Clayton Squares, Liverpool Scene)

70	Dandelion S 4781	Yawney Morning Song/Almost Liverpool 8	7
74	Deram DM 409	Son Son/Bad News Man	6
70	Dandelion 63756	MIKE HART BLEEDS (LP, black/red/silver labels)	50
72	Dandelion 2310 211	BASHER, CHALKY, PONGO AND ME (LP, as Mike Hart & Comrades)	50

TIM HART

(see also Steeleye Span)

79	Chrysalis CHR 2335	Overseas/Hillman Avenger (p/s)	7
79	Chrysalis CHR 1218	TIM HART (LP)	12

TIM HART & MADDY PRIOR

(see also Steeleye Span, Maddy Prior, Silly Sisters)

68	Tepee TPRM 104	FOLK SONGS OF OLDE ENGLAND VOL. 1 (LP, gatefold sleeve)	70
69	Tepee TPRM 105	FOLK SONGS OF OLDE ENGLAND VOL. 2 (LP, gatefold sleeve)	70
69	Ad-Rhythm ARPS 3	FOLK SONGS OF OLDE ENGLAND VOL. 1 (LP, reissue)	25
69	Ad-Rhythm ARPS 4	FOLK SONGS OF OLDE ENGLAND VOL. 2 (LP, reissue)	25
71	Charisma CAS 1035	SUMMER SOLSTICE (LP, gatefold sleeve)	30

FRANK HARTE

67	Topic 12T 172	DUBLIN STREET SONGS (LP)	18

JOHN HARTFORD

69	RCA SF 8039	JOHN HARTFORD (LP)	12

HARTLEPOOL FC

72	United Artists UP 35358	Who Put The Sugar In My Tea/Never Say Die	10

KEEF HARTLEY (BAND)

(see also Rory Storm & Hurricanes, Artwoods, John Mayall's Bluesbreakers, Miller Anderson, Dog Soldier, Henry Lowther, Wynder K. Frog)

69	Deram DM 250	Leave It 'Till The Morning/Just To Cry	12
69	Deram DM 273	Waiting Around/Not Foolish, Not Wise	12
70	Deram DM 316	Roundabout (Parts 1 & 2)	12
73	Deram DM 380	Dance To The Music/You And Me	8
69	Deram DML/SML 1037	HALFBREED (LP, mono, gatefold sleeve, 1st pressing has 'mono/stereo' holes on rear sleeve, white/red label)	80
69	Deram SML 1037	HALFBREED (LP, stereo, gatefold sleeve, 1st pressing has 'mono/stereo' holes on rear sleeve, white/red label)	60
69	Deram DML 1054	THE BATTLE OF N.W.6 (LP mono, gatefold sleeve, 1st pressing with 'mono/stereo' holes on rear sleeve, white/red labels)	60
69	Deram SML 1037	THE BATTLE OF N.W.6 (LP stereo, gatefold sleeve, 1st pressing with 'mono/stereo' holes on rear sleeve, white/red labels)	40
70	Deram SML 1071	THE TIME IS NEAR (LP, with booklet, white/red labels with small logo)	35
70	Deram SML 1071	THE TIME IS NEAR (LP, without booklet, white/red labels with small logo)	20
71	Deram SDL 2	OVERDOG (LP, gatefold sleeve, white/brown labels with small logo)	30
71	Deram SDL 4	LITTLE BIG BAND (LP, gatefold sleeve)	30
72	Deram SDL 9	SEVENTY SECOND BRAVE (LP, gatefold sleeve)	25
73	Deram SDL 13	LANCASHIRE HUSTLER (LP, gatefold sleeve, as Keeg Hartley)	22
74	Deram DPA 3011/2	THE BEST OF (2-LP, gatefold sleeve)	20
70s	Deram SDN 30251/2	THE BATTLE OF N.W.6/THE TIME IS NEAR (2-LP, gatefold sleeve)	20

MINT VALUE £

TREVOR HARTLEY

80	Matumbi MA 006	Skip Away/Selassi (12")	25

HARVESTERS

72	Westwood WRS 015	THE HARVESTERS (LP)	25

HARVEY (Fuqua) & MOONGLOWS

(see also Moonglows, Etta & Harvey)

58	London HLM 8730	Ten Commandments Of Love/Mean Old Blues	300
58	London HLM 8730	Ten Commandments Of Love/Mean Old Blues (78)	85

(SENSATIONAL) ALEX HARVEY (BAND)

(see also Tear Gas, Hairband, Rock Workshop, Nazareth, Michael Schenker Group, Tandoori)

64	Polydor NH 52264	I Just Wanna Make Love To You/Let The Good Times Roll	35
64	Polydor NH 52907	Got My Mojo Working/I Ain't Worried Baby (as Alex Harvey & His Soul Band)	55
65	Polydor BM 56017	Ain't That Just Too Bad/My Kind Of Love (as Alex Harvey & His Soul Band)	45
65	Fontana TF 610	Agent 00 Soul/Go Away Baby	35
66	Fontana TF 764	Work Song/I Can Do Without Your Love	25
67	Decca F 12640	The Sunday Song/Horizon's	40
67	Decca F 12660	Maybe Some Day/Curtains For My Baby	40
69	Fontana TF 1063	Midnight Moses/Roman Wall Blues	50
72	Vertigo 6059 070	There's No Lights On The Christmas Tree Mother, (They're Burning Big Louie Tonight)/Harp	30
75	Vertigo ALEX 001	Delilah (live)/Soul In Chains (p/s)	5
75	Vertigo ALEX 002	Gamblin' Bar Room Blues / Shake That Thing (p/s)	5
76	Mountain PSLP 183	Amos Moses/$25 For A Massage (promo only 12")	12
77	Mountain TOP 32	Mrs Blackhouse /Engine Room Boogie (p/s)	6
64	Polydor LPHM 46424	ALEX HARVEY AND HIS SOUL BAND (LP)	170
64	Polydor LPHM 46441	THE BLUES (LP)	150
69	Fontana (S)TL 5534	ROMAN WALL BLUES (LP)	300
73	Vertigo 6360 081	FRAMED (LP, as The Sensational Alex Harvey Band, gatefold sleeve, small swirl label)	200
73	Vertigo 6360 081	FRAMED (LP, as The Sensational Alex Harvey Band, gatefold sleeve, later spaceship label)	30
73	Vertigo 6360 103	NEXT (LP, as The Sensational Alex Harvey Band, spaceship label)	20
74	Vertigo 6360 112	THE IMPOSSIBLE DREAM (LP, gatefold sleeve, spaceship label)	15
75	Vertigo 9102 003	TOMORROW BELONGS TO ME (LP, gatefold sleeve, spaceship label)	15
77	K-Tel NE 984	ALEX HARVEY PRESENTS THE LOCH NESS MONSTER (LP, withdrawn, gatefold stickered sleeve, with 16-page 'descriptive diary')	30
78	Mountain TOPS 114	ROCK DRILL (with 'No Complaints Department')	35
78	Mountain TOPS 114	ROCK DRILL (later copies with revised track listing stickered on sleeve)	12
79	RCA PL 25257	THE MAFIA STOLE MY GUITAR (LP, as Alex Harvey - The New Band)	12
83	Power Supply AMP 2	THE SOLDIER ON THE WALL (LP, solo)	20
84	Samurai SAH 117PD	S.A.H.B. LIVE (LP, reissue, picture disc)	12

CARL HARVEY MEETS THE DUB MASTER

78	Cancer CANLP 003	ECSTACY OF MANKIND (LP)	50

FREDERIC HARVEY

61	HMV 7EG 8847	SINGS WEST COUNTRY SONGS (EP)	10

JANCIS HARVEY

73	Pilgrim King KLPS 47	DISTANCE OF DOORS (LP)	45
73	Westwood WRS 029	WORDS YOU LEFT BEHIND (LP)	55
74	Westwood WRS 038	JANCIS HARVEY (LP)	55
75	Westwood WRS 054	TIME WAS NOW (LP)	55
76	Westwood WRS 107	A PORTRAIT OF JANCIS HARVEY (LP)	45
79	Westwood WRS 144	FROM THE DARKNESS CAME LIGHT (LP)	40

JANE HARVEY

60	Pye International 7N 25046	I'm Gonna Go Fishin'/Hundred Dreams From Now	6

LANCE HARVEY & KINGPINS

64	Pye 7N 15647	He's Telling You Lies/How Do You Fix A Broken Heart	10
64	Lyntone LYN 509	SINCE YOU WALKED OUT ON ME (Keele Rag flexidisc EP, with The Escorts)	15

PETER HARVEY

62	Columbia DB 4873	Rainin' In My Heart/Please Don't Tell Joe	7
63	Columbia DB 7030	Wishing You The Best Of Luck My Friend/Lovin' Can Be Lonesome	5
64	Columbia DB 7192	Heart Of Ice/Trace Of A Heartache	5
64	Columbia DB 7331	Big Man In A Big House/Date With A Heartache	5

P.J. HARVEY

(see also Automatic Dlamini, Family Cat, Grape, John Parish & Polly Jean Harvey)

90	Private Pressing	P. J. Harvey (3-track demo, 'wooden' p/s includes pictures of P. J. and lyrics to Dress)	70
91	Too Pure PURE 5	Dress/Water (demo)/Dry (demo) (12")	20
92	Too Pure PURECD 5	Dress/Water (demo)/Dry (demo) (CD)	20
92	Too Pure PURES 8	Sheela-Na-Gig/Joe (p/s, 400 only)	45
92	Too Pure PURE 8	Sheela-Na-Gig/Hair (demo)/Joe (demo) (12", p/s)	20
92	Too Pure PURECD 8	Sheela-Na-Gig/Hair (demo)/Joe (demo) (CD)	20
93	Island 12IS 538	50 Ft Queenie/Mansize (demo)/Hook (demo)/Reeling (12", p/s)	12
93	Island 12IS 569	Mansize/Wang Dang Doodle/Daddy (12", p/s)	20
93	Island CID 569	Mansize/Wang Dang Doodle/Daddy (CD)	20
95	Island IS 607	Down By the Water/Lying In The Sun/Somebody's Down Somebody's Name (p/s)	8
95	Island CID 607	Down By The Water/Living In The Sun/Somebody's Down Somebody's Name (CD)	10
95	Island 12IS 614	C'Mon Billy/Darling Be There/Maniac (12", p/s)	10
95	Island IS 610	Send His Love To Me/Long Time Coming (Evening Session) (7" picture disc in 12" poster p/s)	12
95	Island CIDD J610	Send His Love To Me (Promo-only CD, exclusive 'rose dress' sleeve	30
01	Island IS 785	This Is Love/Angline (live) (p/s)	8

MINT VALUE £

04	Island CIDDJ866	Who The Fuck? (CD, unreleased single, promo only)	10
04	Island IS 873	Shame/97 (p/s)	8
04	Island CIDV 873	Shame/The Letter (video)/You Come Through (DVD video)	10
04	Island IS 861	The Letter/Bows And Arrows (p/s)	8
06	Island PJCD6	Tracks from 'Please Leave Quietly' (CD, promo only)	15
07	Island 1747513	When Under Ether/Wait (p/s)	8
07	Island 1753491	The Piano/Heaven (p/s)	8
92	Too Pure PURE(D) 10	DRY (LP, 1st 5,000 with bonus LP, "Demonstrations", inner sleeve and numbered sticker)	60
92	Too Pure PURE 10	DRY (LP with inner but without "Demonstrations")	30
92	Too Pure PUREDCD 10	DRY (CD, 1st 5,000 with additional "Demonstrations" LP tracks)	60
93	Island 5146961	RID OF ME (LP)	35
90s	Island ILPM 2079	4 TRACK DEMOS (LP, with inner)	25
95	Island 524-178 2	THE B-SIDES CD (picture disc CD, 2,000 only, digipak, beware of bootleg copies)	15
95	Island CIDZ 8035	TO BRING YOU MY LOVE & THE B-SIDES CD (2-CD)	30
95	Island PJCD1	INTERVIEW (CD promo)	20
95	Island ILPS 8035	TO BRING YOU MY LOVE (LP, with inner sleeve)	20
98	Island ILPS 8076	IS THIS DESIRE? (LP, with inner)	50
99	Island DESIRE CD1	IS THIS DESIRE? (CD, interview disc, slimline case, promo only)	20
00	Island ILPS 8099	STORIES FROM THE CITY, STORIES FROM THE SEA (LP, with inner)	20
04	Island ILPS 8143	UH HUH HER (LP, with inner)	15
04	Island PJCD3	UH UH HER (CD, interview disc, slimline case, promo only)	20

RICHARD HARVEY

(see also Gryphon, Barry Gray)

83	Anderburr HX 1010	Theme From Terrahawks (3.00)/Variations On The Theme (3.17) (p/.s)	10
83	Anderburr HX 21010	Theme From Terrahawks (4.50)/Variations On The Theme (7.25) (12", p/s with poster)	12
75	Transatlantic TRA 292	DIVISIONS ON A GROUND (LP)	15

TINA HARVEY

73	UK UK 24	Nowhere To Run/Tina's Second Song	15
73	UK UKAL 1002	TINA HARVEY (LP, bule/silver labels)	25

HARVEY BOYS

57	London HLA 8397	Nothing Is Too Good For You/Marina Girl	50
57	London HLM 8730	Nothing Is Too Good For You/Marina Girl (78)	15

HARVEY'S PEOPLE

69	Galliard GAL 4001	LOVING AND LIVING (LP)	15

CHRISTINE HARWOOD

70	Birth RAB 1	NICE TO MEET MISS CHRISTINE (LP, white 'rabbit' child' label)	120

GORDON HASKELL

(see also Fleur-De-Lys, Cupid's Inspiration, Flowerpot Men, King Crimson)

69	CBS 4509	Boat Trip/Time Only Knows	15
70	CBS 4795	Oo-La-Di-Doo-Da-Day/Born To Be Together	15
90	Wilderness WLD 700	Hambledon Hill/Mystical Illusion (p/s)	5
69	CBS 63741	SAILIN' MY BOAT (LP)	100
72	Atlantic K 40311	IT IS AND IT ISN'T (LP, with lyric insert)	30
73	RCA	SERVE AT ROOM TEMPERATURE (LP, unissued)	200

JACK HASKELL (& HONEY-DREAMERS)

57	London HL 8426	Around The World/Away Out West	25
58	Oriole CB 1442	The Night Of The Senior Prom/Hungry For Love (with Honey-Dreamers)	7

MICHAEL HASLAM

65	Parlophone R 5267	There Goes (The Forgotten Man)/My Heart Won't Say Goodbye	6

JOE HASSELVANDER

85	Pentagram DEVIL 3	LADY KILLER (LP)	15

HASSLES

(see also Billy Joel)

67	United Artists UP 1199	You Got Me Hummin'/I'm Thinkin'	20

HASTINGS OF MALAWI

(see also Nurse With Wound)

81	Papal 003	VIBRANT STAPLER OBSCURES CHARACTERISTIC GROWTH (LP, red vinyl)	12

HAT & TIE

(see also Patrick Campbell-Lyons, Nirvana [U.K.])

66	President PT 105	Chance For Romance/California Jazz Club U.S.A.	15
67	President PT 122	Bread To Spend/Finding It Rough (demos credit A-side as "Bread")	150

TONY HATCH ORCHESTRA

(see also Jackie Trent)

59	Top Rank JAR 107	Chick/Side Saddle	5
59	Top Rank JAR 165	Rhoom Ba-Cha/Stetson	5
61	Pye International 7N 25085	Rocking Waltz/Devil's Herd	7
61	Pye International 7N 25068	Tim Frazer's Theme/Girls Of Copenhagen	5
61	Pye International 7N 25109	La Paloma/Theme From Rosemary	6
61	Pye 7N 15316	Two-Some/Last Summer	6
61	Pye 7N 15408	The Ghost Squad/What's That All About	7
62	Pye 7N 15434	Ben Casey Theme/Perry Mason Theme	6
62	Pye 7N 15440	Theme From 'The Naked City'/In Party Mood	6
62	Pye 7N 15460	Out Of This World Theme/Cyril's Tune (in p/s)	10
62	Pye 7N 15460	Out Of This World Theme/Cyril's Tune	5
62	Pye 7N 15494	Theme From The Dick Powell Show/Sharon	6
63	Pye 7N 15537	The Wonderful World Of The Brothers Grimm/Spanish Main Theme	6
63	Pye 7N 15583	Mondo Cane Theme/Girls Of Copenhagen	6

			MINT VALUE £
65	Pye 7N 15754	Crossroads Theme/The Marie Celeste (in p/s)	10
65	Pye 7N 15754	Crossroads Theme/The Marie Celeste	5
65	Pye 7N15972	Man Alive/Crosstown Commuter	8
65	Pye 7N 15930	Maori/Sugar And Spice	6
66	Pye 7N 17169	Crossroads Theme/Round Every Corner (in p/s)	10
66	Pye 7N 17169	Crossroads Theme/Round Every Corner	5
67	Pye 7N 17263	Comedy Tonight/You're Lovely	10
69	Pye 7N 17814	Theme From Who-Dun-It/The Champions	30
69	Pye 7N 17864	The Doctors - Theme/Love Song	6
73	Pye 7N 45210	Memories Of Summer/Best In Football	6
74	Pye 7N 45326	The World At War/Sportsnight	5
78	EMI EMI 2780	Sweeney 2/Regan's Key	12
83	Tube TUBE 003	Airline/The HI-FA	6
65	Pye NPL/NSPL 18124	THE TONY HATCH SOUND (LP)	12
66	Pye NPL 18164	A LATIN HAPPENING (LP)	15

GEORGE HATCHER BAND
(see also Budgie)

77	United Artists UP 36233	Black Moon Rising/Find A New Lover (p/s)	7

HATE

70	Famous SFMA 5752	HATE KILLS (LP, gatefold sleeve, orange labels)	80

BOBBY HATFIELD
(see also Righteous Brothers, Ringo Starr)

68	Verve VS 570	Hang-Ups/Soul Cafe	10
68	Verve VS 576	Only You/The Wonder Of You	10
72	Warner Bros K 16163	Oo-Wee-Baby, I Love You/Rock'n'Roll Woman	12

HATFIELD & THE NORTH
(see also Matching Mole, Egg, Khan, Camel, National Health, Caravan)

74	Virgin VS 116	Let's Eat (Real Soon)/Fitter Stoke Has A Bath	8
74	Virgin V 2008	HATFIELD AND THE NORTH (LP, gatefold sleeve, coloured 'twin' label)	25
75	Virgin V 2030	THE ROTTER'S CLUB (LP, red Virgin inner, coloured 'twin' label)	20
79	Virgin VR 5	AFTERS (LP, withdrawn)	30

DONNY HATHAWAY
(see also Roberta Flack)

70	Atco 226 010	The Ghetto (Parts 1 & 2)	10
72	Atlantic K 10193	The Ghetto (Parts 1 & 2)/Little Ghetto Boy	8
73	Atlantic K 10354	Love Love Love/Someday We'll Be Free	8
71	Atco 2465 019	EVERYTHING IS EVERYTHING (LP)	18
71	Atlantic 2400 143	DONNY HATHAWAY (LP)	15
72	Atlantic K 40369	LIVE (LP)	15
73	Atlantic K 40487	EXTENSION OF A MAN (LP)	15

FAY HAUSER

75	Philips 6006 489	You Bring The Sun In The Morning/(Pt. 2)	5

ALAN HAVEN

62	Fontana 267253	My Mothers's Eyes/Lean Baby	10
64	United Artists UP 1057	Theme From "A Jolly Bad Fellow"/Jee B'ees (with John Barry)	12
65	Fontana TF 542	Image/Romance On The North Sea	12
65	Fontana TF 590	The Knack/Satin Doll (with John Barry)	12
66	Fontana TF 658	Flamingo/Shangri-La	6
67	Fontana TF 835	Image/Romance Of The North Sea (reissue)	10
65	Fontana TL 5232	LENNON & MCCARTNEY (LP)	15
71	CBS S 63900	ST. ELMO'S FIRE (LP)	12

RICHIE HAVENS

69	Big T BIG 119	Oxford Town/My Own Way	5
69	Verve VS 1512	Three Day Eternity/No Opportunity Necessary No Experience Needed	5
69	Verve VS 1519	Lady Madonna/Indian Rope Man	15
68	Verve (S)VLP 6005	SOMETHIN' ELSE AGAIN (LP)	20
68	Verve (S)VLP 6008	MIXED BAG (LP)	20
69	Verve (S)VLP 6014	1983 (LP)	20
69	Verve (S)VLP 6021	STONEHENGE (LP)	15
69	Transatlantic TRA 187	ELECTRIC HAVENS (LP)	15
69	Transatlantic TRA 199	THE RICHIE HAVENS RECORD (LP)	15

HAVENSTREET

76	Rissole (no cat. no.)	THE END OF THE LINE (LP, private pressing with booklet)	50

CYRIL HAVERMANS

73	MGM 2315 261	CYRIL (LP, gatefold sleeve, blue/gold 'lion' label)	20
74	MGM 2315 311	MIND WAVE (LP, blue/gold 'lion' label)	15

PAT HAWES with DAVE CAREY'S RHYTHM

56	Tempo A 141	Snowy Morning Blues/Sheik Of Araby	5
56	Tempo LAP 9	PAT HAWES (10" LP)	20

HAWK & CO.
(see also Shadows)

81	Epic EPC A 1735	Nite Life/Nite Life (Version)	5
82	Epic EPC A 2223	Livin' For The Good Times/Sweet Talker	5

GRAHAM HAWK & OWEN GRAY

72	Pama Supreme PS 360	Amazing Grace/SKETTO RICH: Don't Stay Out Late	5

JACKSON HAWKE

76	CBS 5034	Into The Mystic/Fortune	6

TOMMY HAWKE

60	Top Rank JAR 348	Good Gravy (I'm In Love Again)/Umpteen Years (And A Million Tears)	20

MINT VALUE £

HAWKEYES

57	Capitol CL 14764	Someone Someday/Who Is He?	20

BUDDY BOY HAWKINS/WILLIAM MOORE

(see also Blind Lemon Jefferson)

50s	Heritage RE 102	BUDDY BOY HAWKINS/WILLIAM MOORE (EP)	60

CAROL HAWKINS

73	Polydor 2058 387	Listen/All For One	8

COLEMAN HAWKINS

(see also Hines & Eldridge, Milt Jackson & Coleman Hawkins, Eddie 'Lockjaw' Davis, Sir Charles Thompson)

53	Capitol LC 6580	CLASSICS IN JAZZ (10" LP)	20
53	Capitol LC 6650	CAPITOL PRESENTS COLEMAN HAWKINS AND SONNY GREER (10" LP)	15
54	HMV DLP 1055	TEN COLEMAN HAWKINS' SPECIALS (10" LP)	15
58	London LTZC 15048	COLEMAN HAWKINS GROUP (LP)	18
59	HMC CLP 1293	GENIUS OF COLEMAN HAWKINS (LP)	15
59	Felsted FJA 7005	THE HIGH AND MIGHTY HAWK (LP, also stereo SJA 2005)	15
61	Esquire 32-095	SOUL (LP)	22
61	Esquire 32-102	HAWK EYES (LP)	22
61	Moodsville MV 7	COLEMAN HAWKINS (LP)	18
62	Swingsville SVLP 2001	COLEMAN HAWKINS WITH THE RED GARLAND TRIO (LP)	15
62	Swingsville SVLP 2005	THE COLEMAN HAWKINS ALL STARS (LP)	15
62	Swingsville SVLP 2013	STASCH (LP)	15
63	HMV CLP 1630	DESAFINADO (LP, also stereo CSD 1484)	15
64	Verve VLP 9044	ALIVE! AT THE VILLAGE GATE (LP)	15
64	HMV CLP 1689	TODAY AND NOW (LP)	20
64	CBS BPG 62157	BACK IN BEAN'S BAG (LP, with Clark Terry)	15
64	Fontana FJL 102	SWING' (LP)	15
65	Fontana TL 5273	MEDITATION (LP)	15
66	Fontana SJL 131	CATTIN' (LP)	15

COLEMAN HAWKINS & LESTER YOUNG

65	Stateside SL 10117	CLASSIC TENORS (LP)	12

DALE HAWKINS

57	London HL 8482	Susie-Q/Don't Treat Me That Way	500
57	London HL 8482	Susie-Q/Don't Treat Me That Way (78)	90
58	London HLM 8728	La-Do-Dada/Cross Ties	50
58	London HLM 8728	La-Do-Dada/Cross Ties (78)	40
59	London HLM 8842	Yea-Yea/Lonely Nights	50
59	London HLM 8842	Yea-Yea/Lonely Nights (78)	40
59	London HLM 9016	Liza Jane/Back To School Blues	50
59	London HLM 9016	Liza Jane/Back To School Blues (78)	40
60	London HLM 9060	Hot Dog/Our Turn	50
69	Bell SBLL 127	L.A., MEMPHIS AND TYLER, TEXAS (LP)	15
73	Checker 6467 301	OH! SUSIE Q (LP)	15

ERSKINE HAWKINS QUINTET

60	Brunswick LAT 8374	THE HAWK BLOWS AT MIDNIGHT (LP, also stereo STA 3042)	15

HAWKSHAW HAWKINS

(see also Charlie Gore, Louis Innis)

51	Vogue V 9003	Doghouse Boogie/Yesterday's Kisses (78)	15
51	Vogue V 9027	Slow Coach/Two Roads (78)	12
54	Parlophone CMSP 1	Betty Lorraine/CHARLIE GORE & LOUIS INNIS: Mexican Joe (export issue)	30
50s	Parlophone DP 336	I Hope You're Crying Too/I'm A Lone Wolf (export 78)	10
63	London HL 9737	Lonesome 7-7203/Everything Has Changed	10
58	Parlophone GEP 8742	COUNTRY AND WESTERN (EP)	40
58	Vogue VE 170117	HAWKSHAW HAWKINS - COUNTRY AND WESTERN (EP)	40
64	London HA 8181	THE ALL NEW HAWKSHAW HAWKINS (LP)	20

JUNE HAWKINS

55	Brunswick 05370	Beat Out Dat Rhythm On A Drum/MURIEL SMITH & CARMEN JONES CHORUS: Dat's Love	8

RONNIE HAWKINS (& HAWKS)

(see also Band, Levon & Hawks)

59	Columbia DB 4319	Forty Days (To Come Back Home)/One Of These Days	50
59	Columbia DB 4345	Mary Lou/Need Your Lovin' (Oh So Bad)	50
60	Columbia DB 4412	Southern Love (Whatcha-Gonna' Do)/Love Me Like You Can	20
60	Columbia DB 4442	Clara/Lonely Hours	30
63	Columbia DB 7036	Bo Diddley/Who Do You Love?	30
70	Roulette RO 512	Who Do You Love?/Bo Diddley	5
70	Atlantic 584 320	Down In The Alley/Matchbox	7
70	Atlantic 2091 007	Bitter Green/Forty Days	5
72	Monument MNT 8292	Cora Mae/Ain't That A Shame	5
60	Columbia SEG 7983	ROCKIN' WITH RONNIE (EP, mono)	100
60	Columbia ESG 7792	ROCKIN' WITH RONNIE (EP, stereo)	150
60	Columbia SEG 7988	ROCKIN' WITH RONNIE (EP, mono)	100
60	Columbia ESG 7795	ROCKIN' WITH RONNIE (EP, stereo)	150
60	Columbia 33SX 1238	MR. DYNAMO (LP, mono)	100
60	Columbia SCX 3315	MR. DYNAMO (LP, stereo)	150
60	Columbia 33SX 1295	THE FOLK BALLADS OF RONNIE HAWKINS (LP, mono)	70
60	Columbia SCX 3358	THE FOLK BALLADS OF RONNIE HAWKINS (LP, stereo)	90
70	Roulette RCP 1003	ARKANSAS ROCK PILE (LP, with The Band)	20
70	Atlantic 2400 009	RONNIE HAWKINS (LP)	15
72	Monument MNT 65122	ROCK & ROLL RESURRECTION (LP)	15

SCREAMIN' JAY HAWKINS

(see also Keith Richards)

58	Fontana H 107	I Put A Spell On You/Little Demon (78)	100
65	Columbia DB 7460	The Whammy/Strange	25

			MINT VALUE £
65	Sue WI 379	I Hear Voices/Just Don't Care	40
66	Sue WI 4008	I Put A Spell On You/Little Demon (unissued)	0
69	Direction 58-4097	I Put A Spell On You/Little Demon	20
80	Polydor POSP 183	I Put A Spell On You/Armpit 6 (with Keith Richards)	10
66	Planet PLL 1001	THE NIGHT AND DAY OF SCREAMIN' JAY HAWKINS (LP)	115
69	Direction (S) 8-63481	I PUT A SPELL ON YOU (LP, mono or stereo)	60
69	Mercury SMCL 20178	WHAT THAT IS (LP)	30

HAWKLORDS

(see also Hawkwind)

78	Charisma HL 1	PSI Power/Death Trap (no p/s, promo only)	12
78	Charisma CB 323	PSI Power/Death Trap (no p/s)	8
79	Charisma CB 332	25 Years/(Only) The Dead Dreams Of A Cold War Kid (no p/s)	6
79	Charisma CB 332 12	25 Years/(Only) The Dead Dreams Of A Cold War Kid/PXR 5 (12", grey vinyl)	10
79	Charisma CB 332 12	25 Years/(Only) The Dead Dreams Of A Cold War Kid/PXR 5 (12", mispressed on black vinyl)	12
82	Flicknife FLS 209	Who's Gonna Win The War?/Time Of (p/s)	6
78	Charisma CDS 4014	25 YEARS ON (LP, with inner sleeve, sold with separate tour book)	20
78	Charisma CDS 4014	25 YEARS ON (LP, with inner sleeve)	15

HAWKS

69	Stateside SS 2147	The Grissle/SHEEP: Hide And Seek	12

HAWKS

(see also Lilac Time, Stephen 'Tin Tin' Duffy)

81	Five Believers FB 001	Words Of Hope/Sense Of Ending (p/s)	12

ALAN HAWKSHAW

(see also Shadows)

70	Tangerine DP 0005	Puppet On A String/Everybody Knows	5
79	BBC RESL 64	Grange Hill/Stoned (as Hawkshaw)	20
72	Studio Two TWO 391	27 TOP TV THEMES AND COMMERCIALS (LP)	30
72	KPM 1080	FLUTE FOR MODERNS (with Alan Parker) (LP)	35

JOHNNY HAWKSWORTH (ORCHESTRA)

(see also Johnny's Jazz)

65	Pye 7N 15969	Lunar Walk/It's Murder (as Johnny Hawksworth Orchestra)	15
66	Columbia DB 8059	Goal/"Goal - World Cup 1966" Theme (as Sounds Of Johnny Hawksworth)	6
67	Columbia DB 8129	Wack Wack/On The Tiles	8

HAWKSWORTH-VERRELL JAZZ GROUP

56	Decca FJ 10726	Ring Dem Bells/Always	6

HAWKWIND

(see also Hawklords, Robert Calvert, Michael Moorcock, Inner City Unit, Sphynx, Dave Brock, Steve Swindells, Tim Blake, Huw Lloyd Langton Group, Alan Davey, Motorhead, Sonic Assassins, Dr. Technical & Machines, Sam Gopal, Magic Muscle, Opal Butterfly, Nik Turner, Widowmaker, Adrian Shaw)

SINGLES

70	Liberty LBF 15382	Hurry On Sundown/Mirror Of Illusion	250
72	United Artists UP 35381	Silver Machine/Seven By Seven ('machine' art p/s)	15
73	United Artists (WD 3637)	Sonic Attack (1-sided promo in cloth sleeve)	250
73	United Artists UP 35566	Urban Guerilla/Brainbox Pollution	15
73	United Artists USEP 1	HURRY ON HAWKWIND (EP)	40
74	United Artists UP 35715	The Psychedelic Warlords (Disappear In Smoke)/It's So Easy	8
75	United Artists UP 35808	Kings Of Speed/Motorhead (in p/s)	40
75	United Artists UP 35808	Kings Of Speed/Motorhead	6
76	Charisma CB 289	Kerb Crawler/Honky Dorky	7
77	Charisma CB 299	Back On The Streets/The Dream Of Isis (p/s)	6
77	Charisma CB 305	Quark, Strangeness & Charm/Forge Of Vulcan	7
78	United Artists UP 35381	Silver Machine/Seven By Seven (reissue, black-on-white p/s)	5
78	United Artists 12UP 35381	Silver Machine/Seven By Seven (12", silver p/s)	10
80	Bronze BRO 98	Shot Down In The Night/Urban Guerilla (p/s)	5
80	Bronze BRO 98	Shot Down In The Night/Urban Guerilla (1-sided gold vinyl flexidisc)	30
80	Bronze BRO 109	Who's Gonna Win The War?/Nuclear Toy (p/s, cream labels)	12
80	Bronze BRO 109	Who's Gonna Win The War?/Nuclear Toy (p/s, green labels)	5
81	RCA RCA 137	Angels Of Death/Trans-Dimensional Man (p/s)	5
82	RCA Active RCA 267	Silver Machine/Silver Machine (Full Version)/Psychedelic Warlords (p/s)	5
82	RCA Active RCAP 267	Silver Machine/(Full Version)/Psychedelic Warlords (picture disc)	10
82	Flicknife FLS 005	Motorhead/Valium Ten (p/s)	5
82	Flicknife FLST 005	Motorhead/Valium Ten (extended) (12", p/s)	8
83	United Artists UP 35381	Silver Machine/Seven By Seven (reissue, white-on-black p/s)	5
83	Liberty UPP 35381	Silver Machine/Seven By Seven (picture disc)	12
83	Liberty UPP 35381	Silver Machine/Seven By Seven (mispressed picture disc, plays Beatles' "Ask Me Why")	15
83	Flicknife FLS 214	Hawkwind And Co: Your Last Chance (p/s, sampler with Robert Calvert & Michael Moorcock)	6
83	Flicknife FLS 025	Motorway City/Master Of The Universe (p/s)	5
84	Flicknife FLEP 104	THE EARTH RITUAL PREVIEW (12" EP)	8
85	Flicknife FLS 032	Needle Gun/Arioch (p/s)	5
85	Flicknife FLST 032	Needle Gun (extended)/Arioch (p/s)	8
86	Flicknife FLS 033	Zarozinia/Assault And Battery (live) (p/s)	5
86	Samurai HW 001	Silver Machine/Magnu (motorcycle-shaped picture disc)	15
86	Flicknife FLS 034-A	Motorhead/Hurry On Sundown (p/s with insert)	5
90	Receiver REPLAY 3014	THE EARLY YEARS LIVE (12", p/s, blue vinyl)	12
93	4 Real 4R 1	SPIRIT OF THE AGE (SOLSTICE REMIXES) (12" EP)	12
93	4 Real 4R 2	DECIDE YOUR FUTURE (12" EP)	10
93	4 Real 4R2T	DECIDE YOUR FUTURE EP (12")	8
94	Emerg. Broadcast EBS 110	QUARK, STRANGENESS & CHARM (12" EP, clear vinyl, 200 only)	15

LPs

70	Liberty LBS 83348	HAWKWIND (LP, gatefold sleeve; blue label)	200
70	Liberty LBS 83348	HAWKWIND (LP, gatefold sleeve; black label)	30

			MINT VALUE £
71	United Artists UAG 29202	IN SEARCH OF SPACE (LP in foldout 'door' sleeve, with 'log book')	50
71	United Artists UAG 29202	IN SEARCH OF SPACE (LP in foldout 'door' sleeve, without 'log book')	25
72	United Artists UAG 29364	DOREMI-FASOL-LATIDO (LP, with inner sleeve, with poster)	60
72	United Artists UAG 29364	DOREMI-FASOL-LATIDO (LP, with inner sleeve, without poster)	20
73	United Artists UAD 60037/8	SPACE RITUAL ALIVE (2-LP, foldout sleeve with inners)	40
74	United Artists UAG 29672	HALL OF THE MOUNTAIN GRILL (LP, with inner sleeve)	20
75	United Artists UAG 29766	WARRIOR ON THE EDGE OF TIME (LP, foldout pop-up sleeve with inner)	45
76	United Artists UAK 29919	ROADHAWKS (LP, gatefold sleeve with poster & sticker)	15
76	United Artists UAK 29919	ROADHAWKS (LP, gatefold sleeve)	12
76	Mushroom	THE XENON CODEX (LP, with inner, gatefold sleeve)	12
79	Charisma CDS 4016	P.X.R.5 (LP, with family tree poster, with picture of incorrectly wired plug on rear)	30
79	Charisma CDS 4016	P.X.R.5 (LP, without family tree poster, but with uncensored wired plug on rear)	15
80	Bronze BRON 530	LEVITATION (LP, blue vinyl)	20
81	RCA Active RCALP 6004	SONIC ATTACK (LP, with insert)	12
82	RCA Active RCALP 9004	CHURCH OF HAWKWIND (LP, with lyric booklet)	15
82	RCA Active RCALP 6055	CHOOSE YOUR MASQUES (LP)	12
84	Flicknife PSHARP 014	ZONES (LP, picture disc reissue)	12
84	Liberty SLP 1972921	HAWKWIND (LP, reissue, picture disc, die-cut)	15
84	Flicknife SHARP 022	STONHENGE: THIS IS HAWKWIND DO NOT PANIC (LP, with 12", gatefold sleeve or single sleeve with poster)	15
85	Flicknife SHARP 033	CHRONICLE OF THE BLACK SWORD (LP, with inner sleeve)	12
85	Flicknife SHARP 033CD	CHRONICLE OF THE BLACK SWORD (CD, with 3 extra tracks)	18
86	Hawkfan HWFB 2	HAWKFAN 12 (LP, with poster, sticker insert & carrier bag, 600 only)	70
86	RCA NL 71150	ANGELS OF DEATH (LP)	12
86	Samurai SMR 046	APPROVED HISTORY OF HAWKWIND 1967-1982 (3-LP, pic discs & booklet)	40
87	Flicknife HWBOX 01	OFFICIAL PICTURE LOG BOOK (4-LP box set, [3 picture discs & interview disc] with badge & insert)	35
92	Essential ESSLP 181	ELECTRIC TEPEE (2-LP, 5,000 only, numbered)	35
94	Emerg. Broadcast EBS 111	THE BUSINESS TRIP (2-LP, clear vinyl, 1,500 only)	18
95	Emerg. B/cast EBSLP 118	ALIEN 4 (2-LP, gatefold sleeve)	15
96	Emerg. B/cast EBSLP 120	LOVE IN SPACE (2-LP, gatefold)	25
96	Emerg. B/cast EBSCD20	LOVE IN SPACE (CD)	30
95	Dojo DOJO CD 244	ELECTRIC TEPEE (CD, picture disc, unreleased)	20
99	HAWK VP999	HAWKWIND 1997 (CD, mail-order only to "Hawkwind Passport" holders)	25

DEANE HAWLEY

61	Liberty LIB 55359	Pocketful Of Rainbows/That Dream Could Never Be	10

RICHARD HAWLEY

05	Mute STUMM 251	COLES CORNER (LP)	15

GOLDIE HAWN

72	Reprise K 14211	Carey/I'll Be Your Baby Tonight	6

BRYN HAWORTH

(see also Fleur De Lys, Nicholas Greenwood)

74	Island ILPS 9287	LET THE DAYS GO BY (LP, with inner sleeve)	12
75	Island ILPS 9332	SUNNY SIDE OF THE STREET (LP, pink rim)	12

HAYDEN WOOD

69	NEMS 56-4499	House Beside The Mine/Lady Wants More	25
70	NEMS 56-4803	Sixty Years On/The Last One To Know	25

HAYDOCK'S ROCKHOUSE

(see also Hollies)

66	Columbia DB 8050	Cupid/She Thinks	50
67	Columbia DB 8135	Lovin' You/Mix A Fix	50

BILL HAYES

53	MGM SP 1036	The Donkey Song/My Ever-Lovin'	15
55	London HL 8149	The Berry Tree/Blue Black Hair	30
56	London HLA 8220	Ballad Of Davy Crockett/Farewell	30
56	London HLA 8239	Kwela Kwela/The White Buffalo	20
56	London HLA 8300	Das Ist Musik/I Know An Old Lady	20
56	London HLA 8325	The Legend Of Wyatt Earp/That Do Make It Nice	20
56	London HLA 8325	The Legend Of Wyatt Earp/That Do Make It Nice (78)	12
57	London HL 8430	Wringle Wrangle/Westward Ho The Wagons	20
59	London HLR 8833	Wimoweh/Goin' Down The Road Feelin' Bad (with Buckle Busters)	10
59	London HLR 8833	Wimoweh/Goin' Down The Road Feelin' Bad (with Buckle Busters) (78)	12
56	London RE-A 1051	GREAT PIONEERS OF THE WEST (EP)	40

ISAAC HAYES

69	Stax STAX 133	Walk On By/By The Time I Get To Phoenix	5
70	Stax STAX 154	I Stand Accused/I Just Don't Know What To Do With Myself	5
71	Stax 2025 020	You've Lost That Lovin' Feelin'/Our Day Will Come	5
71	Stax 2025 029	Never Can Say Goodbye/I Can't Help It (If I'm Still In Love With You)	5
72	Stax 2025 069	Theme From "Shaft"/Cafe Regio's	5
72	Stax 2025 089	Let's Stay Together/Ain't That Loving You (For More Reasons Than One) (with David Porter)	5
72	Stax 2025 146	Theme From The Men/Type Thang	5
74	Stax STXS 2004	Title Theme From Tough Guys/Hung Up On My Baby	5
69	Stax SXATS 1028	HOT BUTTERED SOUL (LP)	15
70	Stax SXATS 1032	THE ISAAC HAYES MOVEMENT (LP)	18
70	Stax 2465 016	BLUE HAYES (LP)	18
71	Stax 2325 026	TO BE CONTINUED (LP)	18
71	Stax 2325 014	THE ISAAC HAYES MOVEMENT (LP, reissue)	12
71	Stax 2659 007	SHAFT - ORIGINAL SOUNDTRACK (2-LP, soundtrack, gatefold sleeve)	15
72	MGM 2315 115	SHAFT'S BIG SCORE! (LP, soundtrack)	20
72	Atlantic K 40327	IN THE BEGINNING (LP)	12
72	Stax 2628 004	BLACK MOSES (2-LP, cruciform sleeve)	30

MINT VALUE £

74	Stax 2325 111	JOY (LP)	12
74	Stax STXD 4001/2	TRUCK TURNER (2-LP, soundtrack)	15

LINDA HAYES
(see also Platters)

55	Parlophone MSP 6174	Please Have Mercy (with Platters)/Oochi Pachi (with Tony Williams)	300
55	Parlophone R 4038	Please Have Mercy (with Platters)/Oochi Pachi (with Tony Williams) (78)	50

PETER LIND HAYES
(see also Peter & Mary)

60	Brunswick 05821	Life Gets Tee-jus Don't It/Sing Me A Happy Song	12

TUBBY HAYES
(see also Jack Constanzo & Tubby Hayes, Jazz Couriers, London Jazz Quartet, Dave Lee, Ronnie Scott, Roy Castle)

56	Tempo A 148	Ode To Ernie/No, I Woodyn't	10
62	Fontana H 397	Sally/I Believe In You (as Tubby Hayes Quintet)	20
55	Tempo EXA 14	THE LITTLE GIANT (EP)	60
55	Tempo EXA 17	TUBBY HAYES AND HIS ORCHESTRA (EP)	30
55	Tempo EXA 27	THE SWINGING GIANT NO. 1 (EP, as Tubby Hayes Quartet)	45
56	Tempo EXA 28	THE SWINGING GIANT NO. 2 (EP, as Tubby Hayes Quartet)	45
56	Tempo EXA 36	MODERN JAZZ SCENE (EP, as Tubby Hayes & His Orchestra)	45
57	Tempo EXA 55	AFTER LIGHTS OUT (EP, as Tubby Hayes Quintet)	60
57	Tempo EXA 75	TUBBY HAYES AND THE JAZZ COURIERS (EP)	60
58	Tempo EXA 82	THE EIGHTH WONDER (EP, solo)	60
09	Trunk TTT005	VOODOO SESSION (EP, 666 copies only)	30
57	Tempo TAP 6	AFTER LIGHTS OUT (LP, as Tubby Hayes Quintet)	350
57	Tempo TAP 15	JAZZ COURIERS (LP)	300
60	Tempo TAP 29	TUBBY'S GROOVE (LP, as Tubby Hayes Quartet)	400
61	Fontana TFL 5142	TUBBS (LP, also stereo STFL 562)	120
61	Ember EMB 3337	AN EVENING WITH MR. PERCUSSION (LP, with Tony Kinsey)	70
61	Fontana TFL 5183	TUBBS IN NEW YORK (LP, also stereo STFL 595)	120
63	Fontana 680 998 TL	DOWN IN THE VILLAGE (LP, mono)	300
63	Fontana 886 163TY	DOWN IN THE VILLAGE (LP, stereo)	200
64	Fontana (S)TL 5195	RETURN VISIT! (LP)	140
64	Fontana TL 5200	LATE SPOT AT SCOTT'S (LP)	250
66	Fontana (S)TL 5221	TUBBS' TOURS (LP, with Orchestra)	70
66	Fontana (S)TL 5410	100% PROOF (LP)	70
67	Wing WL 1162	TUBBS IN NEW YORK (LP, reissue)	15
69	Fontana SFJL 911	MEXICAN GREEN (LP)	125
71	Fontana 6309 002	THE TUBBY HAYES ORCHESTRA (LP)	30
72	Philips 6382 041	THIS IS JAZZ - 100% PROOF (LP)	15
81	Mole MOLE 2	MEXICAN GREEN (LP, reissue)	20
81	Mole MOLE 4	TUBBS' TOURS (LP, reissue)	20
80s	Jasmine JASM 2015	AFTER LIGHTS OUT (LP, reissue)	20
90	MMO 79	67 LIVE - FOR MEMBERS ONLY (LP)	20

TUBBY HAYES & CLEO LAINE
(see also Cleo Laine)

61	Fontana TFL 5151	PALLADIUM JAZZ DATE (LP, also stereo STFL 570)	50
65	Wing WL 1088	PALLADIUM JAZZ DATE (LP, reissue)	12

TUBBY HAYES & PAUL GONSALVES ALLSTARS
(see also Paul Gonsalves)

67	Columbia SX 6003	JUST FRIENDS (LP)	110
60s	World Record Club T 631	CHANGE OF SETTING (LP)	120

LOU HAYLES

77	Myrrh MYR 1055	DON'T HIDE AWAY (LP)	22

ROY HAYNES QUARTET

62	HMV CLP 1628	OUT OF THE AFTERNOON (LP)	25

ROY HAYNES, PHINEAS NEWBORN, PAUL CHAMBERS TRIO

61	Esquire 32-103	WE THREE (LP)	12

STEVE HAYNES BAND

78	Black Bear BLA 2005	Back In My Arms Again/Walk On By (p/s)	20
78	Black Bear BLA 2008	Save Me Save Me/Strong Good Lovin' (p/s)	15

HAYSTACK

69	United Artists UP 35024	Letter To Josephine/Love You're Making A Fool Of Me	6
69	United Artists UP 35035	Tahiti Farewell/Pantomime People	6

HAYSTACKS BALBOA

70	Polydor	Spoiler/Bruce's Twist	25
70	Polydor 2489 002	HAYSTACKS BALBOA (LP)	100

JUSTIN HAYWARD
(see also Wilde Three, Moody Blues)

65	Pye 7N 17041	London Is Behind Me/Day Must Come	150
66	Parlophone R 5496	I Can't Face The World Without You/I'll Be Here Tomorrow	200
80	CBS 11-7731	The Eve Of The War/Horsell (12" picture disc)	15

RICK HAYWARD
(see also Accent, Christine Perfect)

71	Blue Horizon 2431 006	RICK HAYWARD (LP)	175

SUSAN HAYWARD

56	MGM MGM-EP 555	I'LL CRY TOMORROW - SOUNDTRACK SELECTION (EP)	15
62	Fontana 267224	You Bet I Would/I Won't Give My Lips To Anyone	10

JOE HAYWOOD

65	Island WI 218	Warm And Tender Love/I Would If I Could	22

LEON HAYWOOD

66	Vocalion VL 9280	Ain't No Use/Hey, Hey, Hey	30
66	Vocalion VL 9280	Ain't No Use/Hey, Hey, Hey (DJ copy)	50

			MINT VALUE £
67	Vocalion VL 9288	Ever Since You Were Sweet Sixteen/Skate Awhile	25
69	MCA Soul Bag BAG 5	Mellow Moonlight/Tennessee Waltz	10
70	Capitol CL 15634	I Wanna Thank You/I Was Sent To Love You	15
73	Pye International 7N 25611	La La Song/There Ain't Enough Hate Around To Make Me Turn Around	5
75	20th Century BTC 2191	Come On And Get Yourself Some/BMF (Beautiful)	5
75	20th Century BTC 2228	I Wanta Do Something Freaky To You/I Know What Love Is	6
78	Fantasy FTC 151	Baby Reconsider/Would I	15
67	Vocalion VAL 8064	SOUL CARGO (LP)	75
69	MCA MUPS 369	IT'S GOT TO BE MELLOW (LP)	20
73	Pye Intl. NSPL 28177	BACK TO STAY (LP)	25
75	20th Century BT 476	COME AND GET YOURSELF SOME (LP)	15

HAZE

74	Haze HAZE 00174	HAZE (LP, 100 only)	70

HAZE

81	Mushroom MUSH 1	The Night/Dig Them Mushrooms	20
85	Gabadon GABS 003	THE EMBER (12" EP)	8
84	Gabadon GABL 001	C'EST LA VIE (LP)	25

HAZEL

93	Sub Pop SP74 241	Jilted (blue vinyl)	5

HAZEL & JOLLY BOYS

67	Doctor Bird DB 1063	Stop Them/Deep Down	20

RONNIE HAZELHURST

78	Polydor 2384 107	SIXTEEN SMALL SCREEN GREATS (LP)	12

HAMMOND HAZLEWOOD

67	Pye 7N 17273	I Can Make The Rain Fall Up/The Hawkmoth And The Flame	12

LEE HAZLEWOOD

(see also Nancy Sinatra & Lee Hazlewood, Duane Eddy)

60	London HLW 9223	Words Mean Nothing/The Girl On Death Row (with Duane Eddy)	35
66	MGM MGM 1310	Sand/My Autumn's Done Come	10
67	MGM MGM 1348	My Baby Cried All Night Long/These Boots Are Made For Walkin'	12
67	Reprise RS 20613	Ode To Billie Joe/Charlie Bill Nelson	7
68	Reprise RS 20667	Rainbow Woman/I Am, You Are	8
72	RCA RCA 2185	Big Red Balloon/Down From Dover (with Nancy Sinatra)	6
73	Stateside SS 2225	Poet/Come Spend The Morning	6
66	MGM MGM-CS 8014	THE VERY SPECIAL WORLD OF LEE HAZLEWOOD (LP)	30
68	Reprise RSLP 6297	LOVE AND OTHER CRIMES (LP)	25
69	London HA-N/SH-N 8398	TROUBLE IS A LONESOME TOWN (LP)	40
72	Reprise K 44161	REQUIEM FOR AN ALMOST LADY (LP)	20
74	Stateside SSL 10315	POET, FOOL OR BUM (LP)	20

OSTERWALK HAZY

72	Jam JAM 22	Oumbalo Oumbalo/Tai Weh	12

HAZZARD

81	Rammy EJSP9600	Snake In The Grass/Kicked To The Ground (p/s)	100

TONY HAZZARD

66	Columbia DB 7927	You'll Never Put Shackles On Me/Calling You Home	6
68	CBS 3452	Sound Of The Candyman's Trumpet/Everything's Gone Wrong	5
69	CBS 63608	TONY HARRARD SINGS (LP, orange label)	60
71	Bronze ILPS 9174	LOUDWATER HOUSE (LP, gatefold sleeve, lyric inner sleeve)	20
73	Bronze ILPS 9222	WAS THAT ALRIGHT THEN? (LP, gatefold sleeve, lyric inner sleeve)	20

HEAD

75	Canon CNN 5970	RED DWARF (LP)	40

HEAD

79	Ellie Jay MB1	Nothing To Do In A Town Like Leatherhead/University '79	60

MICHAEL HEAD & STRANDS

(see also Pale Saints, Shack)

95	Megaphone Music MEGA 01	THE MAGICAL WORLD OF THE STRANDS (LP, gatefold sleeve)	60

MURRAY HEAD

65	Columbia DB 7635	Alberta/He Was A Friend Of Mine	8
65	Columbia DB 7771	The Bells Of Rhymney/Don't Sing No Sad Songs For Me	10
67	Columbia DB 8102	Someday Soon/You Bore Me	8
67	Immediate IM 053	She Was Perfection/Secondhand Monday	70
69	MCA MK 5019	Superstar/John 1941 (p/s, with Trinidad Singers)	7
71	MCA MKS 5019	Superstar/John 1941 (p/s, reissue)	6
73	CBS 65503	NIGEL LIVED (LP, gatefold sleeve and booklet)	30
75	Island ILPS 9347	SAY IT AIN'T SO (LP, gatefold sleeve, blue rim palm tree label)	12

ROY HEAD (& TRAITS)

(see also Traits)

65	Pye International 7N 25340	Just A Little Bit/Treat Me Right	15
65	Vocalion VP 9248	Treat Her Right/So Long, My Love	20
66	Vocalion VP 9254	Apple Of My Eye/I Pass The Day	15
66	Vocalion VP 9269	My Babe/Pain	20
66	Vocalion VP 9274	Wigglin' And Gigglin'/Driving Wheel	20
66	London HLZ 10097	To Make A Big Man Cry/Don't Cry No More	15
70	Stateside SS 8050	Mama Mama/I'm Not A Fool Anymore	7
75	London HLD 10487	The Most Wanted Woman In Town/Gingers Breadman	8
66	Pye Intl. NEP 44053	JUST A LITTLE BIT OF ROY HEAD (EP)	50
70	Stateside SSL 5033	SAME PEOPLE (LP)	25

HEADACHE

77	Lout 001	Can't Stand Still/No Reason For Your Call (p/s)	20

MINT VALUE £

HEAD ARSE FUSION BAND

00	U-Star US 009	UNTITLED EP (12")	50

HEADBANGERS

(see also Biddu, Leaf Hound, Weapon)

HEADCOATEES (THEE)

(see also Milkshakes, Headcoatees)

91	Damaged Goods DAMGOOD 12	Santa Claus/Evil Things (picture disc)	5
91	Hangman HANG 38 UP	GIRLSVILLE (LP)	15

HEADCOATS (THEE)

(see also Milkshakes, Thee Headcoats)

90	Sub Pop SP 71	Time Will Tell/Davey Crockett (Gabba Hey) (p/s)	8
92	Sub Pop SP 151	Ballad Of Hollis Brown/Grizzly Bear (p/s, blue vinyl)	8
89	Hangman HANG 29 UP	HEADCOATS DOWN (LP)	12
90	Hangman HANG 23 UP	THE KIDS ARE ALL SQUARE (LP)	20
91	Hangman HANG 40 UP	W.O.A.H. (LP)	12
01	Hangman HANG 54 UP	LIVE AT THE DIRTY WATER CLUB (LP)	12

HEADHUNTERS

(see also Herbie Hancock)

76	Arista ARTY 116	SURVIVAL OF THE FITTEST (LP)	25
77	Arista SPART 1046	STRAIGHT FROM THE GATE (LP)	12

HEADLESS CHICKENS

(see also Radiohead)

89	Hometown Atrocities 1	THE HOMETOWN ATROCITIES EP (wraparound 'kylie' p/s with 3 inserts)	80
89	Hometown Atrocities 1	THE HOMETOWN ATROCITIES EP (wraparound 'glossy' p/s)	60
89	Maelstrom Storm 1	THE HOMETOWN ATROCITIES EP (repress of above)	30

HEADLINERS

59	Parlophone R 4593	The Bubble Car Song/Andy's Theme	10

HEADLINERS

65	Decca F 12209	That's The Way I Must Go/Four Seasons	8
65	Decca F 12279	What Became Of Love/Even Though	7

HEAD MACHINE

(see also Uriah Heep)

70	Major Minor SMLP 79	ORGASM (LP, laminated front sleeve, red/white/black labels)	225

HEAD OF DAVID

89	Blast First WANT 001	WHITE ELEPHANT (LP, mail-order only)	12

HEADS, HANDS & FEET

(see also Don Everly, Tony Colton, Poet & One Man Band)

71	Island WIP 6115	Warming Up The Band/Silver Mine	5
71	Island ILPS 9149	HEADS, HANDS AND FEET (LP, gatefold, pink rim palm tree label)	25
72	Island ILPS 9185	TRACKS (LP, gatefold, pink rim palm tree label)	22
73	Atlantic K40465	OLD SOLIDERS NEVER DIE (LP, gatefold sleeve, lyric insert)	15

HEADSTONE

74	EMI EMA 766	BAD HABITS (LP, gatefold sleeve)	20
75	EMI EMC 3673	HEADSTONE (LP)	20

HEALEY SISTERS

64	HMV POP 1313	Give Me Back My Heart/After The Party	8

JOE HEANEY

63	Topic 12T 91	IRISH TRADITIONAL SONGS IN GAELIC AND ENGLISH (LP)	12

HEART

76	Arista Arista 80	Crazy On You/Soul Of The Sea	6
77	Arista ARISTA 140	Heartless/Here Song (withdrawn)	8
86	Capitol CLP 406	Nothin' At All (Extended Remix)/The Wolf (heart-shaped picture disc)	6
87	Capitol CLP 457	Who Will You Run To?/Nobody Home (picture disc)	10
87	Capitol CDCL 473	There's The Girl (12" Remix)/Bad Animals/There's The Girl (7" Remix) (CD)	8
88	Capitol CDCL 507	Nothin' At All (Ext. Remix)/I've Got The Music In Me/I Want You So Bad (CD)	8
77	Arista SPART 1024	MAGAZINE (LP, withdrawn)	15
77	Arista SPART 1024	MAGAZINE (LP, picture disc)	15
90	Capitol HGIFT 1	HEART BOX SET (3-LP: "Heart", "Bad Animals" & "Brigade" + 24 page booklet)	18

HEART

78	On U Sound LP 20	NOAH HOUSE OF DREAD (LP)	30

HEART BEATS

80	Red Shadow REDS 2	Talk To Me/Don't Want Romance (p/s)	5
81	Nothing Shaking SHAD 1	Go/One Of The People (p/s, blue vinyl)	15

HEART BOUND

74	Decca F 13510	Baby Ruth/Sailor Man	12

HEARTBREAKERS

(see also New York Dolls, Johnny Thunders)

77	Track 2094 135	Chinese Rocks/Born To Lose (p/s)	8
77	Track 2094 135T	Chinese Rocks/Born To Lose (12", p/s)	12
77	Track 2094 137	One Track Mind/Can't Keep My Eyes On You (live)/Do You Love Me (p/s)	10
77	Track 2094 142	It's Not Enough/Let Go (p/s, withdrawn)	250
79	Beggars Banquet BEG 21	Get Off The Phone (live)/I Wanna Be Loved (live) (p/s)	5
88	Jungle JUNG 38 T	SHE WANTS TO MAMBO (12" EP)	8
77	Track 2409 218	L.A.M.F. (LP)	25
79	Beggars Banquet BEGA 9	LIVE AT MAX'S KANSAS CITY (LP, with insert)	15
81	Jungle FREUD 1	D.T.K. - LIVE AT THE SPEAKEASY (LP, white or pink vinyl)	18

MINT VALUE £

84 Jungle FREUD 4 L.A.M.F. REVISITED (LP, picture disc) 18
84 Jungle FEEUD 4 L.A.M.F. REVISITED (white label with withdrawn test proof sleeve) 150
88 Jungle FREUDP 1 D.T.K. - LIVE AT THE SPEAKEASY (LP, reissue, picture disc) 18

HEARTS (U.K.)

64 Parlophone R 5147 Young Woman/Black Eyes 20

HEARTS (U.S.)

64 Stateside SS 268 Dear Abby/Dear Abby (Instrumental) 25

HEARTS & FLOWERS

67 Capitol CL 15492 Rock'N'Roll Gypsies/Road To Nowhere 12
68 Capitol CL 15549 She Sang Hymns Out Of Tune/Tin Angel 8

HEARTS OF SOUL

70 Columbia DB 8670 Waterman/Fat Jack 20

HEATERS

70 Upsetter US 329 Melting Pot/UPSETTERS: Kinky Mood 12

HEAT EXCHANGE

(see also Brian Bennett)

79 EMI EMI 2988 Shake Down/You're Gonna Love This (p/s) 5
79 EMI 12EMI 2988 Shake Down/You're Gonna Love This (12", p/s) 8
79 EMI EMC 3306 ONE STEP AHEAD (LP) 12

JIMMY HEATH

60 Riverside RLP 333 REALLY BIG (LP) 15

TED HEATH ORCHESTRA

(see also Joan Regan, Bobbie Britton, Johnston Brothers, Annette Klooger)

53 Confectioners' Candy Queen Waltz (with Dennis Lotis)/The Girl On The Candy Box (with Dickie Valentine) (78, promo) 10
54 Decca F 10246 Skin Deep/Walking Shoes 15
56 Decca F 10746 The Faithful Hussar/Siboney 5
58 Decca F 11000 Swingin' Shepherd Blues/Raunchy 6
58 Decca F 11003 Tequila/Little Serenade 7
58 Decca F 11025 Tom Hark/Cha Cha Baby 5
51 Decca LF 1037 TEMPO FOR DANCERS (10") 12
52 Decca LF 1060 LISTEN TO MY MUSIC (10") 12
58 Decca LK 4275 HITS I MISSED (also stereo SKL 4003) 12
58 Decca LK 4280 OLDE ENGLYSHE (LP) 12
59 Decca SKL 4079 BEAULIEU JAZZ FESTIVAL (stereo only) 15
62 Decca PFM 24004 BIG BAND PERCUSSION (also stereo PFS 34004) 15

HEATHCLIFFE

68 Tangerine DP 0001 Holly Bush And Mistletoe/My World 8

HEATHER

65 King KG 1027 I'll Come Softly/No One In The Whole Wide World 7

HEATWAVE

70 Penny Farthing PEN 738 Sister Simon (Funny Man)/Rastus Ravel 30

HEAVEN

71 CBS 66293 BRASS ROCK 1 (2-LP, ornate fold-out sleeve) 150

HEAVENLY

89 Sarah SARAH 30 I Fell In Love Last Night/Over And Over (p/s) 15
91 Sarah SARAH 41 Our Love Is Heavenly/Wrap My Arms Around Him (p/s, insert) 10
91 Sarah SARAH 51 So Little Deserve/I'm Not Scared Of You (p/s, insert) 10
93 Sarah SARAH 81 P.U.N.K. Girl/Hearts And Crosses (p/s, insert) 10
93 Sarah SARAH 82 Atta Girl/Dig Your Own Grave/So? (p/s, insert) 10
96 Wiiija WIJ 58 Space Manatee/You Tore Me Down/Art School (p/s) 10

HEAVEN 17

(see also B.E.F., Human League, Glenn Gregory & Claudia Brucken)

82 Virgin VS 483 Height Of The Fighting (He-La-Hu)/Honeymoon In New York (unissued, no p/s) 15

HEAVY COCHRAN

(see also Lieutenant Pigeon)

78 Psycho P 2611 I've Got Big Balls/Well, Fairly Big 5
79 Psycho P 2619 I've Got A Little Prick/It's 12 Inches Long, But I Don't Use It As A Rule 6

HEAVY DUTY BREAKS

(see also Youth, Killing Joke)

85 Illuminated ILL 5512 Heavy Duty Breaks (Radio Version)/Bonus Beats (12", p/s) 8
85 Illuminated JAMS 49 HEAVY DUTY BREAKS (LP, remixes of other artists) 12

HEAVY FEATHER

71 Penny Farthing Beautiful And Black/Ceilings 10

HEAVY JEFF

74 Harry J HJ 6689 Black Pepper/Pepper Rock 8

HEAVY JELLY

(see also Jackie Lomax, Aynsley Dunbar Retaliation, Skip Bifferty, Griffin, Graham Bell, Arc)

69 Head HDS 4001 Time Out Chewn In/The Long Wait 20
69 Island WIP 6049 I Keep Singing The Same Old Song/Blue 30
70 Island HELP HEAVY JELLY (LP, promo only) 180
84 Psycho PSYCHO 30 TAKE ME DOWN TO THE WATER (LP, reissue of "Heavy Jelly") 12

HEAVY METAL KIDS

(see also Gary Holton, Kids)

74 Atlantic K 50047 HEAVY METAL KIDS (LP, with poster) 15
77 Rak SRAK 523 KITSCH (LP) 15

MINT VALUE £

HEAVY PETTIN'

82	Neat NEAT 17	Roll The Dice/Love Times Love (p/s)	10
83	Polydor HEPP 3	Love Times Love/Shout It Out (shaped picture disc)	8

HEAVYWEIGHT

91	One After D ODE3	The Way Of The Future (12")	45

HEAVYWEIGHTS

69	Spark SRL 1033	Utterly Funky/Shambala	20

BOBBY HEBB

66	Philips BF 1503	Sunny/Bread (Credited to Bobby Herb)	5
66	Philips BF 1522	A Satisfied Mind/Love Love Love	40
67	Philips BF 1541	Love Me/Baby I'm Crazy	10
67	Philips BF 1570	I Love Everything About You/Some Kinda Magic	10
67	Philips BF 1610	Everything Is Coming Up Roses/Bound By Love	8
68	Philips BF 1702	You Want To Change Me/Dreamy	50
72	Philips 6051 023	Love Love Love/Sunny	10
72	Philips 6051 025	Some Kind Of Magic/Good Lovin'	6
66	Philips BL 7740	SUNNY (LP)	40

HEBREW CHILDREN & INNER CIRCLE

73	Ackee ACK 508	Dog And Bone/Version	6

DICK HECKSTALL-SMITH (QUINTET)

(see also Graham Bond Organisation, John Mayall & Bluesbreakers, Alexis Korner, Colosseum, Rocket 88)

57	Pye Jazz NJE 1037	VERY SPECIAL OLD JAZZ (EP, as Dick Heckstall-Smith Quintet)	25
72	Bronze ILPS 9196	DUST IN THE AIR SUSPENDED MARKS THE PLACE ... WHERE A STORY ENDED (LP, gatefold sleeve with lyric inner sleeve)	40

HECTOR

73	DJM DJS 289	Wired Up/Ain't Got Time	30
74	DJM DJS 303	Bye Bye Bad Days/Lady	30

JESSE HECTOR

99	No Hit NO HIT EP 1961	Fast Train To Memphis/My Bucket's Got A Hole In It/ All By Myself/ Nightmares (p/s)	6

HEDGEHOG AFFAIR

92	Purple Heart PH 002	RUSH TILL DAWN PRESENTS THE HEDGEHOG AFFAIR EP (12")	12
92	Basement BRSS 005	RUSH TILL DAWN PRESENTS THE HEDGEHOG AFFAIR PT. 2 EP (12")	12
92	Basement BRSS 010	RUSH TILL DAWN PRESENTS THE HEDGEHOG AFFAIR PT. 3 EP (12")	12
93	Sound Entity SENT 1203	RUSH TILL DAWN PRESENTS THE HEDGEHOG AFFAIR PT. 4 EP (12")	12
94	Sound Entity SENT 1206	RUSH TILL DAWN PRESENTS THE HEDGEHOG AFFAIR PT. 5 EP (12")	20

HEDGEHOG PIE

(see also Dando Shaft)

76	Rubber ADUB 8	Well I Know/Go With The Flow	6
71	Rubber RUB 004	HIS ROUND (LP, with Tony Capstick, first pressing with black label on side 1 and white label on side 2)	20
75	Rubber RUB 009	HEDGEHOG PIE (LP)	25
75	Rubber RUB 014	GREEN LADY (LP)	50
78	Rubber RUB 024	JUST ACT NORMAL (LP, with lyric insert)	20

HEDGEHOPPERS ANONYMOUS

(see also Alan Avon & Toy Shop, Jonathan King, Mick Tinsley)

65	Decca F 12298	Don't Push Me/Please Don't Hurt Your Heart For Me	6
66	Decca F 12400	Baby (You're My Everything)/Remember	10
66	Decca F 12479	Daytime/That's The Time	10
66	Decca F 12530	Stop Press/Little Memories	8

HEFNER

97	Inertia INERT 0004	Car Chase/Remix (12", p/s)	10
97	Boogie Wonderland BWL 023	Lee Remick/Schoolgirls Knees (p/s)	15
98	Sticky STICKY 23	A Hymn For The Alcohol/My Art College Days Are Over (p/s, 500 only)	8
97	Boogie Wonderland BWL020	A BETTER FRIEND EP (7" p/s with two inserts)	15
98	Too Pure PURE 64	THE HEFNER SOUL: Flowers/A Hymn For The Coffee/Broodmare/ The Girl From The Coast/More Christian Girls (10" EP)	10
02	Too Pure PURE 125X	THE HEFNER BRAIN: When The Angels Play Their Drum Machines/ Dark Hearted Discos/The Baggage Reclaim Song/Can't Help Losing You/ All I'll Ever Need (10" p/s)	8

NEAL HEFTI & ORCHESTRA

66	RCA Victor RCA 1521	The Batman Theme/Batman Chase	30
89	RCA PB 49571PD	The Batman Theme (1966 Version)/Batman Chase (picture disc)	8
54	Vogue/Coral LVC 10005	SWINGIN' ON A CORAL REEF (10" LP)	15
65	Warner Bros W 1599	HARLOW (LP, soundtrack)	25
65	United Artists (S)ULP 1098	HOW TO MURDER YOUR WIFE (LP, soundtrack)	25
66	RCA Victor RD 7795	BOEING BOEING (LP, soundtrack)	20
66	United Artists (S)ULP 1141	DUEL AT DIABLO (LP, soundtrack)	18
67	London HA-D 8337	BAREFOOT IN THE PARK (LP, soundtrack)	30
68	Dot (S)LPD 514	THE ODD COUPLE (LP, soundtrack)	30

LUCILLE HEGAMIN

73	VJM VLP 50	BLUE FLAME (LP)	15

DONALD HEIGHT

66	London HLZ 10062	Talk Of The Grapevine/There'll Be No Tomorrow	130
66	London HLZ 10062	Talk Of The Grapevine/There'll Be No Tomorrow (DJ copy)	150
67	London HLZ 10116	Three Hundred & Sixty Five Days/I'm Willing To Wait	100
67	London HLZ 10116	Three Hundred & Sixty Five Days/I'm Willing To Wait (DJ copy)	140
71	Avco Embassy 6105 005	Dancin' To The Music Of Love/Rags To Riches To Rags	75
71	Jay Boy BOY 32	Talk Of The Grapevine/There'll Be No Tomorrow (reissue)	15
72	Jay Boy BOY 51	Three Hundred & Sixty Five Days/I'm Willing To Wait (reissue)	10
72	Jay Boy BOY 60	We Gotta Make Up/I Can't Get Enough	10

MINT VALUE £

RONNIE HEIGHT

59	Decca F 11126	Come Softly To Me/So Young, So Wise	10
59	Decca F 11126	Come Softly To Me/So Young, So Wise (78)	10
60	London HLN 9144	The One Finger Symphony/Mem'ries & Habits	5

HEINZ (& WILD BOYS)

(see also Tornados, Saints)

63	Decca F 11652	Dreams Do Come True/Been Invited To A Party	25
63	Decca F 11693	Just Like Eddie/Don't You Knock At My Door	7
63	Decca F 11768	Country Boy/Long Tall Jack	10
64	Decca F 11831	You Were There/No Matter What They Say	15
64	Decca F 11920	Please Little Girl/For Loving Me This Way	20
64	Columbia DB 7374	Questions I Can't Answer/The Beating Of My Heart	20
65	Columbia DB 7482	Diggin' My Potatoes/She Ain't Comin' Back (with Wild Boys)	40
65	Columbia DB 7559	Don't Think Twice, It's All Right/Big Fat Spider	30
65	Columbia DB 7656	End Of The World/You Make Me Feel So Good	40
65	Columbia DB 7779	Heart Full Of Sorrow/Don't Worry Baby	40
66	Columbia DB 7942	Movin' In/I'm Not A Bad Guy	45
70s	Cargo CPS 010	Country Boy/Just Like Eddie	10
63	Decca DFE 8545	HEINZ (EP)	60
63	Decca DFE 8559	LIVE IT UP (EP)	40
64	Decca LK 4599	TRIBUTE TO EDDIE (LP)	80
76	Decca REM 7	REMEMBERING (LP)	15

HEISENBERG

89	Uncertain HEI 5001	No More Dreams/Rain (p/s)	20

HELDEN

(see also Ultravox)

83	Zica ZICA 01	Holding On/Once Upon A Time In The ... (p/s)	5
83	Zica 12 ZICA 01	Holding On/Once Upon A Time In The ... (12", p/s)	15

HELICOPTER

(see also Galliard)

72	Maple Annie MA 102	I Belong To Yesterday/Lonely Tonight	25

HELL

83	Deadly Weapons DWS 666	Save Us From Those Who Would Save Us/Death Squad	75

RICHARD HELL (& VOIDOIDS)

(see also Neon Boys)

76	Stiff BUY 7	(I Could Live With You In) Another World/(I Belong To The) Blank Generation/ You Gotta Lose (with p/s, numbered, 5,000 only with 4-point press-out centre; later re-pressed for THE STIFF BOX SET & numbered 001)	12
76	Stiff BUY 7	(I Could Live With You In) Another World/(I Belong To The) Blank Generation/ You Gotta Lose (without p/s, 5,000 only with 4-point press-out centre; later re-pressed for THE STIFF BOX SET & numbered 001)	6
77	Sire 6078 608	Blank Generation/Love Comes In Spurts (no p/s)	8
77	Sire 6078 608	Blank Generation/Liars Beware/Who Says? (12", p/s)	10
79	Radar ADA 30	The Kid With The Replaceable Head/I'm Your Man (p/s)	7
94	Overground OVER 36	Another World/Blank Generation/Love Comes In Spurts (p/s, reissue, 2,000 only)	5
96	Codex CODE 3X	GO NOW (10", p/s, 1,000 only, etched yellow vinyl)	8
96	Codex CODE 3	GO NOW (CD, 1,000 only)	8
92	Overground OVER 24	3 NEW SONGS (EP, 134 yellow vinyl copies)	6
77	Sire 9103 327	BLANK GENERATION (LP, with inner sleeve)	20
77	Sire 9103 327	BLANK GENERATION (LP, without inner sleeve)	12
83	I.D. NOSE 2	DESTINY STREET (LP)	12

HELLACOPTERS

(see also Super$hit666)

99	Butcher's Hook HOOK 004	A House Is Not A Motel/POWDER MONKEYS: Destination X (p/s)	5
01	Polar 158 801 2	FLIGHT CASE (enhanced CD EP, box set with patch & insert)	12

HELLANBACH

84	Neat NEAT 1006	NOW HEAR THIS (LP, with inner sleeve)	15
84	Neat NEAT 1019	THE BIG ... H (LP, with insert)	15

HELLHAMMER

84	Noise N 008	APOCALYPTIC RAIDS (12" EP, 45/33rpm)	50
08	Century Media 9977392	DEMON ENTRAILS (3-LP, 180gm vinyl with booklet and poster)	80

DAVE HELLING

65	Stateside SS 409	It Ain't Me Babe/If You're Gonna Leave Me	10
66	Planet PLF 101	Christine/The Bells	40

HELLIONS

(see also Revolution, Traffic, Roaring Sixties, Jim Capaldi, Dave Mason, Luther Grosvenor, Family, Spooky Tooth)

65	Piccadilly 7N 35213	Daydreaming Of You/Shades Of Blue	25
65	Piccadilly 7N 35232	Tomorrow Never Comes/Dream Child	25
65	Piccadilly 7N 35265	A Little Lovin'/Think It Over	25

HELL IS FOR HEROES

00s	Chrysalis CHS 5143	I Can Climb Mountains/Get Low (blue vinyl, p/s)	7
00s	EMI 5515397	Night Vision/Can't You Hear It (clear vinyl, p/s)	6

HELLO

72	Bell BELL 1238	You Move Me/Ask Your Mama	15
72	Bell BELL 1265	C'mon/Wench	5
73	Bell BELL 1333	Another School Day/C'mon Get Together (p/s)	6
76	Bell BELL 5263	KEEP US OFF THE STREETS (LP)	15

HELL PREACHERS INC.

69	Marble Arch MALS 1169	SUPREME PSYCHEDELIC UNDERGROUND (LP)	50

(Rumoured to be Deep Purple))

MINT VALUE £

BOBBY HELMS

57	Brunswick 05711	Fraulein/(Got A) Heartsick Feeling	12
57	Brunswick 05721	My Special Angel/Standing At The End of My World	12
58	Brunswick 05730	No Other Baby/The Magic Song	20
58	Brunswick 05741	Love My Lady/Just A Little Lonesome	20
58	Brunswick 05748	Jacqueline/Living In The Shadow Of The Past	15
58	Brunswick 05754	Schoolboy Crush/Borrowed Dreams	15
58	Brunswick 05765	Jingle Bell Rock/Captain Santa Claus	20
59	Brunswick 05786	Miss Memory/New River Train	12
59	Brunswick 05801	Soon It Can Be Told/I Guess I'll Miss The Prom	12
59	Brunswick 05813	My Lucky Day/Hurry Baby	12
59	Brunswick 05813	My Lucky Day/Hurry Baby (78)	20
61	Brunswick 05852	Sad Eyed Baby/You're The One	8
60	Brunswick OE 9461	BOBBY HELMS (EP)	40
57	Brunswick LAT 8250	SINGS TO MY SPECIAL ANGEL (LP)	50

JIMMY HELMS

63	Pye 7N 45440	Ragtime Girl/Romeo & Juliet	100
73	Capitol CL 15762	My Little Devil/Magnificent Sanctuary Band	6
73	Fly BUG 27	Gonna Make You An Offer You Can't Refuse/Words And Music	6

HELP

71	MCA MWPS 4039	SECOND COMING (LP)	80

HELP YOURSELF

(see also Man, Deke Leonard, Tyla Gang, Wreckless Eric)

71	Liberty LBF 15459	Running Down Deep/Paper Leaves	8
72	United Artists UP 35355	Heaven Row/Brown Lady	8
72	United Artists UP 35466	Mommy Won't Be Home For Christmas/Johnny B. Goode	6
71	Liberty LBS 83484	HELP YOURSELF (LP)	70
72	United Artists UAS 29287	STRANGE AFFAIR (LP, with inner sleeve)	45
72	United Artists UAS 29413	BEWARE OF THE SHADOW (LP)	35
73	United Artists UDG 4001 [UAS 29487/FREE 1]	THE RETURN OF KEN WHALEY/HAPPY DAYS (2-LP set in envelope sleeve with LPs in individual sleeves)	50
73	United Artists UAS 29487	THE RETURN OF KEN WHALEY (LP)	20

HELPLESS HUW

78	US US 001	Still Love You (In My Heart)	5
80	US US 002	Sid Vicious Was Innocent/Going Through The Motions/ Baby We're Not In Love/When You're Weary (p/s in bag)	7

HELTER SKELTER

(see also Gorillas, Hammersmith Gorillas)

77	Sticky STY 102	I Need You/Goodbye Baby	30

HEMLOCK

(see also Miller Anderson, Keef Hartley Band, Dog Soldier)

73	Deram DM 379	Mr Horizontal/Beggar Man	12
73	Deram SML 1102	HEMLOCK (LP, white/red label with small logo)	90

BERTHA HENDERSON/ROSA HENDERSON

60	Jazz Collector JEL 14	THE FEMALE BLUES VOL. 2 (EP)	10

BILL HENDERSON

60	Top Rank JAR 412	Sweet Pumpkin/Joey, Joey, Joey	8

DORRIS HENDERSON

(see also Eclection, John Renbourn)

65	Columbia DB 7567	The Hangman/Leaves That Are Green	15
67	Fontana TF 811	Message To Pretty/Watch The Stars	10
65	Columbia SX 6001	THERE YOU GO (LP, with John Renbourn)	140
67	Fontana (S)TL 5385	WATCH THE STARS (LP, with John Renbourn)	175

EDMONIA HENDERSON

51	Tempo R 43	Mama Don't Want A Sweet Man Any More/Hateful Blues (78)	10

FINIS HENDERSON

83	Motown TMGT 1304	Skip To My Lou/I'd Rather Be Gone/Vina Del Mar (12")	20

FLETCHER HENDERSON

(see also Clara Smith & Fletcher Henderson)

50s	Audubon AAF-AAK	FLETCHER HENDERSON (6 x 10" LP set)	25

JOE HENDERSON

62	London HLU 9553	Snap Your Fingers/If You See Me Cry	12
63	London REU 1376	JOE HENDERSON (EP)	30

LORNA HENDERSON

60	Oriole CB 1549	Lollipops To Lipstick/Steady Eddie	25
60	Oriole CB 1549	Lollipops To Lipstick/Steady Eddie (78)	18
60	Oriole CB 1590	A Thousand Stars/Murray, What's Your Hurry?	10

RUSS HENDERSON & HIS CALYPSO BAND

(see also Marie Bryant)

BOBBY HENDRICKS

(see also Drifters)

58	London HL 8714	Itchy Twitchy Feeling/A Thousand Dreams	60
58	London HL 8714	Itchy Twitchy Feeling/A Thousand Dreams (78)	30
59	Top Rank JAR 193	Little John Green/Sincerely, Your Lover	20
61	Mercury AMT 1163	I'm Coming Home/Every Other Night	10
64	Sue WI 315	Itchy Twitchy Feeling/Thousand Dreams (reissue, as Bobby Henricks)	20

HUGH HENDRICKS & UPSETTERS

70	Spinning Wheel SW 103	Land Of Kinks/O'NEIL HALL: This Man	15

MINT VALUE £

JON HENDRICKS

(see also Dave Lambert)

56	Brunswick 05521	Four Brothers/Cloudburst (with Dave Lambert Singers)	6
68	Verve VS 572	No More/Rainbow's End	5
71	Philips 6006 088	I Got Soul/Slow Train	5
61	Vogue EPV 1268	A GOOD GIT-TOGETHER (EP)	8
60	Vogue LAE 12231	A GOOD GIT-TOGETHER (LP)	12

JIMI HENDRIX (EXPERIENCE)

(see also Eire Apparent, Jayne Mansfield, McGough & McGear, Noel Redding Band, Fat Mattress, Curtis Knight, Billy Cox, Buddy Miles, Riot Squad)

SINGLES

66	Polydor 56139	Hey Joe/Stone Free	15
67	Track 604 001	Purple Haze (1-sided promo, white label with black text)	250
67	Track 604 001	Purple Haze/51st Anniversary (white label)	20
67	Track 604 001	Purple Haze/51st Anniversary (black label)	15
67	Track 604 001	Purple Haze/51st Anniversary (black label, alternative mix, but no way of telling from either label or matrix number))	25
67	Track 604 004	The Wind Cries Mary/Highway Chile	12
67	Track 604 007	The Burning Of The Midnight Lamp/The Stars That Play With Laughing Sam's Dice	10
67	Decca F 22652	How Would You Feel/You Don't Want Me (with Curtis Knight, test pressing, unreleased)	500
67	Track 604 009	How Would You Feel/You Don't Want Me (with Curtis Knight)	12
67	London HL 10160	Hush Now/Flashing (with Curtis Knight; in export p/s)	30
67	London HL 10160	Hush Now/Flashing (with Curtis Knight)	8
68	Track 604 025	All Along The Watchtower/Long Hot Summer Night	12
69	Track 604 029	Crosstown Traffic/Gypsy Eyes	12
69	Track 604 033	Let Me Light Your Fire/The Burning Of The Midnight Lamp	10
70	London HLZ 10321	Ballad Of Jimi/Gloomy Monday (with Curtis Knight)	8
70	London HL 7126	Ballad Of Jimi/Gloomy Monday (with Curtis Knight, export issue)	30
70	Track 2095 001	Voodoo Chile/Hey Joe/All Along The Watchtower (p/s)	15
70	Track 2095 001	Voodoo Chile/Hey Joe/All Along The Watchtower (p/s; later copies with white border on sleeve)	8
70	Track 2095 001	Voodoo Chile/Hey Joe/All Along The Watchtower	6
71	RCA RCA 2033	No Such Animal (Parts 1 & 2) (initially in p/s, with Curtis Knight uncredited)	25
71	RCA RCA 2033	No Such Animal (Parts 1 & 2) (with Curtis Knight uncredited)	6
71	Track 2094 007	Angel/Night Bird Flying	7
71	Track 2094 010	Gypsy Eyes/Remember/Purple Haze/Stone Free (in p/s)	25
71	Track 2094 010	Gypsy Eyes/Remember/Purple Haze/Stone Free	8
72	Polydor 2001 277	Johnny B. Goode/Little Wing	6
73	Reprise K 14286	Hear My Train A-Comin/Rock Me Baby	6
73	Polydor/Sound For Industry SFI 1572	Red House/Spanish Castle Magic (1-sided flexidisc with Rolling Stone)	15
80	Polydor 2608 001	6 SINGLES PACK (6 plain sleeve singles [2141 275-280], open-out card p/s)	20
82	CBS CBS A 2749	Fire/Are You Experienced? (p/s)	5
89	Castle Comms. HENPD 01	Hey Joe/Purple Haze/Radio One Theme (12", picture disc)	8
89	Polydor PO 33	Purple Haze/51st Anniversary (p/s, reissue)	5
89	Polydor PZCD 33	Purple Haze/51st Anniversary/All Along The Watchtower/Hey Joe (CD, card p/s)	8
90	Polydor PO 71	Crosstown Traffic/Voodoo Chile (p/s)	5
90	Polydor PO 100	All Along The Watchtower/Voodoo Chile/Hey Joe (p/s)	5
92	BMG 791 168	JIMI PLAYS BERKELEY (CD EP, available with "Jimi Plays Berkeley" video)	8

TRACK LPS

67	Track 612 001	ARE YOU EXPERIENCED (mono, laminated (front and back) sleeve)	350
67	Track 612 001	ARE YOU EXPERIENCED (mono, matt sleeve)	200
67	Track 612 003	AXIS: BOLD AS LOVE (laminated gatefold sleeve, with gatefold insert mono)	350
67	Track 612 003	AXIS: BOLD AS LOVE (laminated gatefold sleeve, without gatefold insert, mono)	100
67	Track 613 003	AXIS: BOLD AS LOVE (laminated gatefold sleeve, with gatefold insert, stereo)	300
67	Track 613 003	AXIS: BOLD AS LOVE (laminated gatefold sleeve, without gatefold insert, stereo)	120
68	Track 612 004	SMASH HITS (mono)	45
68	Track 613 004	SMASH HITS (stereo)	25
68	Track 612 008/009	ELECTRIC LADYLAND (2-LP, plain white non-gatefold sleeve, labels marked "Test Pressing", mono)	1000
68	Track 613 008/009	ELECTRIC LADYLAND (2-LP, laminated gatefold sleeve, stereo, blue text inside sleeve)	400
68	Track 613 008/009	ELECTRIC LADYLAND (2-LP, laminated gatefold sleeve, stereo, white text inside sleeve)	175
68	Track 613 010	ELECTRIC LADYLAND PART 1 (stereo only)	30
68	Track 613 017	ELECTRIC LADYLAND PART 2 (stereo only)	30
70	Track Super 2406 002	BAND OF GYPSYS (original 'puppet' sleeve)	150
70	Track Super 2406 002	BAND OF GYPSYS (repressing, gatefold 'Isle Of Wight' sleeve)	40
70	Track Super 2406 002	BAND OF GYPSYS (2nd repressing, single sleeve)	20
70	Track 2407 010	BACKTRACK 10: ARE YOU EXPERIENCED? (budget reissue, mono)	20
70	Track 2407 010	BACKTRACK 10: ARE YOU EXPERIENCED? (budget reissue, stereo, but in mono sleeve)	40
70	Track 2407 011	BACKTRACK 11: AXIS: BOLD AS LOVE (budget reissue, stereo)	20
71	Track 2856 002	ELECTRIC JIMI HENDRIX (mail-order only Record Club release)	800
71	Track 2408 101	THE CRY OF LOVE (gatefold sleeve)	30
71	Track 2408 101	THE CRY OF LOVE (red vinyl, factory custom pressing, 3 copies only)	2000
74	Track 603003	ARE YOU EXPERIENCED (LP, stereo with POLYDOR INT. GmbH on label, this is NOT the 1967 Stereo issue of ARE YOU EXPERIENCED)	40
88	Track/HMV C 881-16	ARE YOU EXPERIENCED (LP, box set, ltd. ed. of 2,500, no'd, with certificate)	30

MINT VALUE £

POLYDOR LPS

71	Polydor 2302 016	ISLE OF WIGHT	15
71	Polydor 2302 018	HENDRIX IN THE WEST (gatefold sleeve)	15
72	Polydor 2302 020	WAR HEROES	15
72	Polydor 2302 023	THE CRY OF LOVE (gatefold sleeve, reissue)	12
73	Polydor 2302 268	SMASH HITS (stereo reissue)	12
73	Polydor 2480 005	BAND OF GYPSYS (reissue, different gatefold sleeve)	12
73	Polydor ACB 00219 Super	SMASH HITS (LP, Audio Club Of Great Britain issue)	15
73	Polydor 2657 012	ELECTRIC LADYLAND (2-LP, laminated gatefold sleeve, reissue)	25
73	Polydor 2310 271	ELECTRIC LADYLAND PART 1 (reissue)	12
73	Polydor 2310 272	ELECTRIC LADYLAND PART 2 (reissue)	12
74	Polydor 2310 301	LOOSE ENDS	15
75	Polydor 2310 398	CRASH LANDING	12
75	Polydor 2310 415	MIDNIGHT LIGHTNING	12
78	Polydor 2612 034	THE ESSENTIAL JIMI HENDRIX (2-LP, with bonus 1-sided 33rpm 7" Gloria [JIMI 1] in special bag)	18
78	St. Michael 2102/0102	JIMI HENDRIX (cat. no. also listed as Polydor 2891 139)	50
78	St. Michael/Poly. 2891 139	JIMI HENDRIX (cassette)	20
80	Polydor 2625 040	JIMI HENDRIX (13-LP box set [11 x LP + 1 x 2-LP])	75
80	Polydor POLS 1023	NINE TO THE UNIVERSE	15
84	Polydor SPDLP 3	ELECTRIC LADYLAND (2-LP, non-laminate gatefold sleeve, 2nd reissue)	18
87	Polydor 833 004-1	LIVE AT WINTERLAND (2-LP, with poster)	18
88	Polydor/HMV C88 LP 1-16	ARE YOU EXPERIENCED? (box set sold via HMV stores, 1,500 only)	12
90	Polydor 847 2311	CORNERSTONES: JIMI HENDRIX 1967-1970	12

OTHER LPS

68	London HA/SH 8349	GET THAT FEELING (with Curtis Knight)	30
68	London HA/SH 8369	STRANGE THINGS (with Curtis Knight)	30
71	Ember NR 5057	EXPERIENCE - THE ORIGINAL SOUNDTRACK (gatefold sleeve)	12
71	Reprise K 40430	LIVE AT THE MONTEREY INTERNATIONAL POP FESTIVAL (shared with Otis Redding)	35
71	Reprise K 44159	RAINBOW BRIDGE (matt gatefold sleeve, 'steamboat' label, soundtrack)	20
72	Ember NR 5061	MORE EXPERIENCE (soundtrack)	12
73	Reprise K 64017	SOUNDTRACK RECORDINGS FROM THE FILM JIMI HENDRIX (2-LP)	18
73	Ember NR 5068	IN THE BEGINNING (textured gatefold sleeve)	15
74	Ember EMB 3428	LOOKING BACK WITH JIMI HENDRIX	15
75	DJM DJLMD 8011	FOR REAL (2-LP, gatefold sleeve)	18
89	Castle Comms. HBLP 100	LIVE AND UNRELEASED - THE RADIO SHOW (5-LP)	30

CDs

84	Track 821 993 2	BAND OF GYPSYS	35
88	Polydor/HMV C88 LP 1-11	ARE YOU EXPERIENCED? (box set via HMV stores, 1,500 only)	18
89	Castle Comms. HBCD 100	LIVE AND UNRELEASED - THE RADIO SHOW (3-CD, box set)	30
89	Polydor 831 312-2	HENDRIX IN THE WEST	18
89	Polydor 837 574-2	LOOSE ENDS	18

MARGIE HENDRIX

66	Mercury MF 976	I Call You Lover But You Ain't Nothin' But A Tramp/The Question	25
67	Mercury MF 1001	Restless/On The Right Track	30

TONY HENDRIX

69	Pye Int. 7n 25485	The Grooviest Girl In The World/Majestic World	6

LARRY HENLEY

(see also Newbeats, Dean & Mark)

64	Hickory 45-1272	My Reasons For Living/Stickin' Up For My Baby	12

CHRISTIE HENNESSY

73	Westwood	CHRISTIE HENNESSY (LP)	35

HENNESSYS

69	Cambrian CLP 593	THE ROADS AND THE MILES (LP)	80
60s	Music Factory MF 106	KARDIFF AFTER DARK (LP)	90

ADRIAN HENRI

(see also Liverpool Scene, McGough & McGear)

60s	Charivari	ADRIAN HENRI (LP)	45
60s	Argo PLP 1194	ADRIAN HENRI AND HUGO WILLIAMS (LP)	40

ANN HENRY

60	Top Rank JAR 292	Like Young/Sugar Blues	10

BOB HENRY

(see also Robert Henry)

65	Philips BF 1450	I Need Someone/Built Like A Man	18

CLARENCE ('FROGMAN') HENRY

57	London HLN 8389	Ain't Got No Home/Troubles Troubles (as Clarence Henry) (gold lettering on label)	250
57	London HLN 8389	Ain't Got No Home/Troubles Troubles (as Clarence Henry) (silver lettering on label)	120
57	London HLN 8389	Ain't Got No Home/Troubles Troubles (as Clarence Henry) (78)	60
61	Pye International 7N 25078	(I Don't Know Why) But I Do/Just My Baby And Me	10
61	Pye International 7N 25089	You Always Hurt The One You Love/Little Suzy	10
61	Pye International 7N 25108	Lonely Street/Why Can't You	10
61	Pye International 7N 25115	Standing In The Need Of Love/On Bended Knees	10
62	Pye International 7N 25123	A Little Too Much/I Wish I Could Say The Same	12
62	Pye International 7N 25141	Dream Myself A Sweetheart/Lost Without You	10
62	Pye International 7N 25169	The Jealous Kind/Come On And Dance	15
64	London HLU 9936	Little Green Frog/Have You Ever Been Lonely?	10
66	London HLU 10025	Ain't Got No Home/Baby, Ain't That Love?	10
61	Pye Intl. NEP 44007	CLARENCE 'FROGMAN' HENRY HIT PARADE (EP)	100
61	Pye Intl. NPL 28017	YOU ALWAYS HURT THE ONE YOU LOVE (LP)	80

MINT VALUE £

MILTON HENRY
76 Cactus CT85 — Gypsy Woman/Dub ... 20

PIERRE HENRY
66 Philips 4FE8000 — LE VOYAGE FROM THE TIBETAN BOOK OF THE DEAD (LP) ... 20
66 Philips 4FE 8504 — VARIATIONS FOR A DOOR AND A SIGH (LP, UK record in French sleeve) ... 20
68 Philips 4FE8004 — MASS FOR THE PRESENT TIME (LP) ... 40

RICHARD HENRY
68 Regal Zonophone RZ 3014 — Oh Girl/Lay Your Head Upon My Shoulder ... 6

ROBERT HENRY
(see also Bob Henry)
66 Philips BF 1476 — Walk Away Like A Winner/That's All I Want ... 70

HENRY III
(see also Uniques)
67 Island WI 3078 — Thank You Girl/Take Me Back ... 22
67 Island WI 3081 — I'll Reach The End/Won't Go Away (B-side actually Lee's Special by Don Tony Lee) ... 35
67 RCA RCA 1568 — So Much Love/Sitting In The Park ... 20
70 Dynamic DYN 402 — Out Of Time/VICEROYS: Love For Everyone (both with Hubcap & Wheels) ... 8

HENRY & LIZA
(see also Max Romeo)
73 Dragon DRA 1004 — Hole Under Cratches/TIVOLIS: Hole Under Cratches (Instrumental) (actually "Hole Under Crutches") ... 6

HENRY & LOUIS
80s 2 Kings 2K7001 — Jah Jah Never Fail/Dub Never Fail I ... 15

HENRY COW
(see also Slapp Happy, Art Bears, Fred Frith, Gong/Henry Cow/Global Trucking Company)
73 Virgin V 2005 — THE LEGEND (LP) ... 45
74 Virgin V 2011 — UNREST (LP, gatefold sleeve, black/white 'twin' label) ... 40
75 Virgin V 2027 — IN PRAISE OF LEARNING (LP) ... 25
76 Caroline CAD 3002 — CONCERTS (LP) ... 30
79 Broadcast BC 1 — WESTERN CULTURE (LP) ... 15

HENRY ESSENCE
79 Ellie Jay EJSP9392 — Margarita/14 Year Old Lover (500 only, p/s) ... 150

JUDY HENSKE
66 Reprise RS 20485 — Road To Nowhere/Sing A Rainbow ... 15
65 Reprise RS 6203 — DEATH DEFYING (LP) ... 30

JUDY HENSKE & JERRY YESTER
69 Straight STS 1052 — FAREWELL ALDEBARAN (LP) ... 40

KEN HENSLEY
73 Bronze ILPS 9223 — PROUD WORDS ON A DUSTY SHELF (LP, gatefold sleeve, lyric inner, Island credit on label) ... 20
75 Bronze ILPS 9307 — ESGER TO PLEASE (LP, lyric inner, Island credit on label) ... 15

ROBERT HENRY HENSLEY
68 Polydor 56295 — You're Gonna See Me Cry/Montage ... 8

NICKY HENSON
63 Parlophone R 4976 — Till I See You Cry/What Does It Mean? ... 20

DAVID HENTSCHEL
75 Ring O' 2017 101 — Oh My My/Devil Woman ... 8

NAT HEPBURN
60s Jump Up JU 516 — River/Political Girl ... 6

HEP STARS
(see also Abba)
66 Decca F 22446 — Sunny Girl/No Response ... 45
67 Olga OLE 001 — Wedding/Consolation ... 25
68 Olga OLE 013 — Let It Be Me/Groovy Summertime (withdrawn, supposedly reissued 1969) ... 45
68 Olga OLE 014 — Malaika/It's Nice To Be Back (in export p/s) ... 55
68 Olga OLE 014 — Malaika/It's Nice To Be Back ... 25

HEPTONES
(see also Barry Llewellyn, Soul Vendors, Ronald & Lloyd, Ed Nangle, Love Generation, Alton Ellis, Basil Daley, Ken Boothe, Jackie Mittoo)
66 Rio R 104 — Gunmen Coming To Town/TOMMY McCOOK & SUPERSONICS: Riverton City ... 70
67 Ska Beat JB 266 — We've Got Love/I Am Lonely ... 80
67 Caltone TONE 105 — Schoolgirls/Ain't That Bad? ... 45
67 Studio One SO 2005 — A Change Is Gonna Come/Nobody Knows ... 60
67 Studio One SO 2014 — Fat Girl/DELROY WILSON: Mother Word ... 30
67 Studio One SO 2021 — If I Knew/Festival Day ... 50
67 Studio One SO 2026 — Why Did You Leave?/GAYLADS: Don't Try To Reach Me ... 30
67 Studio One SO 2027 — Why Must I?/SLIM SMITH: Try Again ... 30
67 Studio One SO 2031 — Take Me (actually by The Soul Vendors)/DELROY WILSON: I'm Not A King ... 50
67 Studio One SO 2033 — Only Sixteen/Baby ... 30
68 Studio One SO 2040 — Tripe Girl/DELROY WILSON: Mr. D.J. ... 30
68 Studio One SO 2049 — Cry, Baby, Cry/Mama ... 30
68 Studio One SO 2052 — Dock Of The Bay/KING ROCKY (ELLIS): The Ruler ... 100
68 Studio One SO 2055 — Party Time/Oil In Your Lamp ... 30
68 Coxsone CS 7052 — Love Won't Come Easy/Gee Wee ... 30
68 Coxsone CS 7068 — Equal Rights/Ting-A-Ling ... 30
68 Coxsone CS 7082 — Soul Power/Love Me Always ... 150
69 Coxsone CS 7092 — Sweet Talking/Ob-La-Di ... 30

MINT VALUE £

69	Studio One SO 2083	I Shall Be Released/Love Me Always	20
69	Bamboo BAM 11	I Shall Be Released/Love Me Always (Power) (reissue)	20
70	Bamboo BAM 28	Young, Gifted and Black/SOUND DIMENSION: Joyland	20
70	Bamboo BAM 39	Young Generation/You Turned Away	20
70	Bamboo BAM 43	Message From A Blackman/SOUND DIMENSION: Jamaica Underground	25
70	Upsetter US 339	Hurry Up/Thanks We Get	20
70	Banana BA 311	Be A Man/U ROY: Shock Attack	12
71	Banana BA 325	Suspicious Minds/Haven't You Any Fight Left?	10
71	Banana BA 349	Freedom Line/SOUND DIMENSION: Version	15
72	Green Door GD 4020	Hypocrite/JOHNNY LOVER: Straight To The Head	12
72	Prince Buster PB 37	Our Day Will Come/PRINCE BUSTER: Protection	12
72	Ashanti ASH 411	I'm In The Mood For Love/TOMMY McCOOK & NOW GENERATION: Eight Years After	8
72	Duke DU 143	Save The Last Dance For Me/Be The One	6
72	Pama PM 843	You've Lost That Lovin' Feelin'/RUPIE EDWARDS ALLSTARS: Feeling Version	8
72	Pama Supreme PS 367	Save The Last Dance For Me/Save The Last Dance Version	7
72	Ackee ACK 407	I Miss You (Parts 1 & 2)	5
73	Ackee ACK 414	Let Me Hold Your Hand/Version	5
73	Jaguar JAG 103	Drifting Away/BONGO LES: Zion Drum	10
73	Grape GR 3053	Old Time/G.G. ALLSTARS: Dub	7
73	Smash SMA 2328	Soul Sister/IMPACT ALLSTARS: Soul Sister (Version)	7
73	Count Shelley CS 017	Now I Know/AUGUSTUS PABLO: Version	12
74	Pama Supreme PS 390	Thanks We Get/Oppression (both actually by Delroy Butler)	10
75	Faith FA 012	Party Time/Version	5
76	Cancer CAN 003	Cool Rasta/Rasta Dub	10
67	Studio One SOL 9002	THE HEPTONES (LP)	150
68	Studio One SOL 9010	ON TOP (LP)	200
72	Trojan TBL 183	THE HEPTONES AND THEIR FRIENDS MEET THE NOW GENERATION (LP)	35
75	Island ILPS 9297	BOOK OF RULES (LP)	20
76	Island ILPS 9456	PARTY TIME (LP)	15
76	Island ILPS 9381	NIGHT FOOD (LP)	20

HERB & KAY

54	Parlophone MSP 6127	This Ole House/Angels In The Sky	30
54	Parlophone CMSP 23	This Ole House/Angels In The Sky (export issue)	30
55	Parlophone CMSP 31	Coffee Blues/Juke Box Jig (export issue)	30

HERBAL MIXTURE

(see also Tony McPhee, Groundhogs)

66	Columbia DB 8021	A Love That's Died/Tailor Made	175
66	Columbia DB 8083	Machines/Please Leave My Mind	225

HERBIE & ROYALISTS

68	Saga FID 2121	SOUL OF THE MATTER (LP)	25

HERBIE'S PEOPLE

65	CBS 202005	Sweet And Tender Romance/You Thrill Me To Pieces	25
66	CBS 202058	One Little Smile/You Never Know	20
67	CBS 202584	Residential Area/Humming Bird	12

HERD

(see also Peter Frampton, Humble Pie, Judas Jump, Andy Bown, Preachers)

65	Parlophone R 5284	Goodbye Baby, Goodbye/Here Comes The Fool	50
65	Parlophone R 5353	She Was Really Saying Something/It's Been A Long Time Baby	50
66	Parlophone R 5413	So Much In Love/This Boy's Always Been True	60
67	Fontana TF 819	I Can Fly/Diary Of A Narcissist	12
67	Fontana TF 856	From The Underworld/Sweet William	7
67	Fontana TF 887	Paradise Lost/Come On - Believe Me (in p/s)	20
67	Fontana TF 887	Paradise Lost/Come On - Believe Me	7
68	Fontana TF 925	I Don't Want Our Loving To Die/Our Fairy Tale	7
68	Fontana TF 975	Sunshine Cottage/Miss Jones	8
69	Fontana TF 1011	The Game/Beauty Queen	8
71	B&C CB 154	You've Got Me Hangin' From Your Lovin' Tree/I Don't Wanna Go To Sleep Again	6
72	Bumble GEX 1	From The Underworld/Paradise Lost/On My Way Home (maxi-single)	5
73	Bumble GE 120	I Don't Want Our Loving To Die/The Game	5
68	Fontana (S)TL 5458	PARADISE LOST (LP, flipback sleeve, black/silver labels)	35
72	Bumble GEMP 5001	NOSTALGIA (LP)	25

HERE & NOW

(see also Daevid Allen)

78	Charly CYS 1055	End Of The Beginning/Choke A Koala (p/s)	5
79	Charly CEP 122	A Dog In Hell/Floating Anarchy Radio (p/s)	5
80	Charly NOW 1	Give And Take	5
78	Deptford Fun City DLP 02	WHAT YOU SEE ... IS WHAT YOU ARE (LP, 1 side by Alternative TV)	12
83	Chick CHRL 003	FANTASY SHIFT (LP)	25

HERESY

86	Earache	Thanks (flexidisc, mail-order, 2,000 only [400 each on different coloured vinyl])	8
89	In Your Face FACE 4	WHOSE GENERATION? EP (gatefold p/s)	8

HERESY/CONCRETE SOX

87	Manic Ears MOSH 2	HERESY/CONCRETE SOX (LP, 1 side each)	15

HERETIC

84	Thunderbolt THBE 1004	BURNT AT THE STAKE EP (Water Of Vice/Keep On Telling Those Lies/ Fever Of Love/Watch Me Grow (12", p/s)	25

HERITAGE

81	Rondelet ROUND 8	Strange Place To Be/Misunderstood (p/s)	20
82	Rondelet ABOUT 12	REMORSE CODE (LP, with lyric insert)	35
82	Plant Life PLR 040	LIVING BY THE AIR (LP)	15

MINT VALUE £

HERMAN (Chin-Loy)
(see also Jimbilin)

71	Big Shot BI 573	El Fishy/HERMAN'S ALLSTARS: Nightmare (B-side actually "In The Spirit" by Lloyd Charmers)	12
71	Big Shot BI 577	Tar Baby (actually "Crazy Baby" by U. Roy Jr.)/TOMMY McCOOK: Archie	7
71	Big Shot BI 578	New Love/AUGUSTUS PABLO: The Mood	25
71	Big Shot BI 579	East Of The River Nile Version/AUGUSTO PABLO: East Of The River Nile	40
71	Duke DU 107	To The Fields/HERMAN'S VERSION MEN: Fields Version	12
71	Ackee ACK 133	Dunce Cap/AQUARIANS: Version Cap	8
71	Ackee ACK 140	Youth Man/AQUARIANS: Version	8
71	Explosion EX 2049	Love Brother/Uganda	6
71	Escort ERT 854	Love Brother/Love Brother Version (B-side actually by Tommy McCook)	7
71	Punch PH 55	Hold The Ghost/AQUARIUS SOUL BAND: Duppy Dance	7
71	Punch PH 58	Listen To The Beat/AQUARIANS: Sounds Only	7

PRIEST HERMAN

64	Blue Beat BB 266	We Are Praying/BUSTER'S ALLSTARS: Dallas, Texas	40

WOODY HERMAN
(see also David Rose Orchestra)

54	London HL 8013	Wooftie/Moten Stomp (as Woody Herman & New Third Herd)	20
54	London HL 8031	Fancy Woman/Eight Babies To Mind (as Woody Herman's Woodchoppers)	20
54	Capitol CL 14183	Muskrat Ramble/Woodchopper's Mambo (Woody Herman & His Orchestra)	12
55	London HL 8122	Sorry 'Bout The Whole Darned Thing/Love's A Dog (with New Third Herd)	15
66	CBS 202522	Sidewinder/Greasy Sack Blues	10
69	Chess CRS 8095	Hush/Light My Fire	10

HERMAN'S HERMITS
(see also Peter Noone)

64	Columbia DB 7338	I'm Into Something Good/Your Hand In Mine	5
64	Columbia DB 7408	Show Me Girl/I Know Why	5
65	Columbia DB 7475	Silhouettes/Can't You Hear My Heartbeat?	5
65	Columbia DB 7546	Wonderful World/Dream On	5
65	Columbia DB 7670	Just A Little Bit Better/Take Love, Give Love	5
65	Columbia DB 7791	A Must To Avoid/The Man With The Cigar	6
66	Columbia DB 7861	You Won't Be Leaving/Listen People	7
66	Columbia DB 7947	This Door Swings Both Ways/For Love	6
66	Columbia DB 8012	No Milk Today/My Reservation's Been Confirmed	6
66	Columbia DB 8076	East-West/What Is Wrong, What Is Right?	8
67	Columbia DB 8123	There's A Kind Of Hush (All Over The World)/Gaslite Street	5
67	Columbia DB 8235	Museum/Moonshine Man	6
68	Columbia DB 8327	I Can Take Or Leave Your Loving/Marcel's	5
68	Columbia DB 8404	Sleepy Joe/Just One Girl	5
68	Columbia DB 8446	Sunshine Girl/Nobody Needs To Know	5
68	Columbia DB 8504	Something's Happening/The Most Beautiful Thing In My Life	5
69	Columbia DB 8563	My Sentimental Friend/My Lady	5
68	EMI SLES 15	No Milk Today/There's A Kind Of Hush (promo only, white label)	10
68	EMI SLES 16	London Look (promo only, white label)	8
69	Columbia DB 8626	Here Comes The Star/It's Alright Now	8
70	Columbia DB 8656	Years May Come, Years May Go/Smile Please	5
71	RCA RCA 2135	She's A Lady/Gold Mandala (listed as HERMITS on 7")	6
72	RCA RCA 2265	The Man/Effen Curly	6
74	Buddah BDS 700	Train/Ride On The Water (withdrawn)	30
65	Columbia SEG 8380	HERMANIA (EP)	15
65	Columbia SEG 8440	MRS BROWN YOU'VE GOT A LOVELY DAUGHTER (EP)	12
65	Columbia SEG 8442	HERMAN'S HERMITS HITS (EP)	8
66	Columbia SEG 8477	A MUST TO AVOID (EP)	10
66	Columbia SEG 8503	MUSIC FROM THE SOUNDTRACK "HOLD ON" (EP)	15
67	Columbia SEG 8520	DANDY (EP)	15
65	Columbia 33SX 1727	HERMAN'S HERMITS (LP)	25
65	Columbia SX 6303	MRS BROWN YOU'VE GOT A LOVELY DAUGHTER (LP, soundtrack, mono, with manuscript)	15
65	Columbia S(C)X 6303	MRS BROWN YOU'VE GOT A LOVELY DAUGHTER (LP, soundtrack, stereo, without manuscript)	11
66	Columbia SX 6084	BOTH SIDES OF HERMAN'S HERMITS (LP)	20
67	Columbia S(C)X 6174	THERE'S A KIND OF HUSH ALL OVER THE WORLD (LP)	20
60s	Regal SREG 1117	HERMAN'S HERMITS (LP, export issue)	20
60s	Columbia SCXC 27	THE BEST OF HERMAN'S HERMITS (LP, export issue)	20
60s	Columbia SCXC 32	THE BEST OF HERMAN'S HERMITS VOL. 2 (LP, export issue)	20
60s	Columbia SCXC 34	THERE'S A KIND OF HUSH ALL OVER THE WORLD (LP, export issue)	25
60s	Columbia SCXC 35	BLAZE (LP, export issue)	25

HEROES
(see also Motors)

75	United Artists UP 36016	Grown Up/Losing You	8
80	Polydor POSP 105	Some Kind Of Woman/10% Will Do	8

TED HEROLD

60	Polydor NH 66817	I Don't Know Why/Moonlight	15

HERON
(see also Mike Cooper)

70	Dawn DNS 1015	Take Me Back Home/Minstrel And A King	15
71	Dawn DNX 2509	Bye And Bye/Through Time/Only A Hobo/I'm Ready To Leave (p/s)	25
71	Dawn DNLS 3010	HERON (LP, with insert, some with "this album was recorded live in a field" sticker)	140
72	Dawn DNLS 3025	TWICE AS NICE & HALF THE PRICE (2-LP, with postcard)	200
72	Dawn DNLS 3025	TWICE AS NICE & HALF THE PRICE (2-LP, without postcard)	80

MINT VALUE £

MIKE HERON('S) REPUTATION)
(see also Incredible String Band)

71	Island WIP 6101	Call Me Diamond/Lady Wonder (p/s)	5
75	Neighbourhood NBH 3109	Evie/Down On My Knees After Memphis (as Mike Heron's Reputation)	5
78	Zoom ZUM 5	Sold On Your Love/Portland Rose (p/s)	5
71	Island ILPS 9146	SMILING MEN WITH BAD REPUTATIONS (LP, gatefold sleeve, pink rim, palm tree label)	30
75	Neighborhood 80637	MIKE HERON'S REPUTATION (LP)	15

BERNARD HERRMAN

69	Phase 4 Stereo PFS 4173	THE GREAT MOVIE THRILLERS (LP)	15
75	Phase 4 Stereo PFS 4309	THE FANTASY FILM WORLD OF BERNARD HERRMANN (LP)	15
76	Phase 4 Stereo PFS 4337	THE MYSTERIOUS FILM WORLD OF BERNARD HERRMANN (LP)	15

KRISTIN HERSH
(see also Throwing Muses)

93	4AD KH 2	Velvet Days (Demo)/Houdini Blues (demo) (promo only, no p/s)	5

EVERIT HERTER

60	Capitol CL 15142	Don't Get Serious/Boys Were Made For Girls	10

PAT HERVEY & TIARAS & ART SNIDER

67	President PT 110	Can't Get You Out Of My Mind/Givin' In	7
63	RCA 1332	Tears Of Misery/Brother, Can You Spare A Dime (as Pat Hervey)	7

HERZFELD

93	Duophonic DS45 07	Two Mothers/Who The Scroungers Are (p/s, mail order only)	6

HESITATIONS

69	London HLR 10180	Born Free/Push A Little Bit Harder	20
68	London HLR 10198	The Impossible Dream (The Quest)/Nobody Knows You When You're Down And Out	8
68	London HA-R/SH-R 8360	THE NEW BORN FREE (LP)	20

CAROLYN HESTER
(see also Four For Fun)

65	Dot DS 16750	Ain't That Rain?/Ten Thousand Candles	5
65	Dot DS 16751	Playboys And Playgirls/High Flyin' Bird	5
65	Dot DS 26750	Come On Back/Three Young Men	5
65	Dot DS 26751	What Does It Get You?/Now He's Gone	10
66	CBS 202409	A Reason To Believe/Early Morning Rain	5
65	Dot DLP 3604	THAT'S MY SONG (LP)	15
66	Dot DLP 3638	AT TOWN HALL (LP)	15
66	CBS (S)BPG 62033	CAROLYN HESTER (LP)	30
69	Pye Intl. NSPL 28121	THE CAROLYN HESTER COALITION (LP)	12

JOHN HETHERINGTON

70	RCA 1965	It's Only Me/Dreamboat Avenue	8

HEWETT SISTERS

59	HMV POP 567	Baby-O/Jerri-Lee (I Love Him So)	25
59	HMV POP 567	Baby-O/Jerri-Lee (I Love Him So) (78)	10

BEN HEWITT

59	Mercury AMT 1041	You Break Me Up/I Ain't Givin' Up Nothin'	50
59	Mercury AMT 1055	For Quite A While/Patricia June	35
59	Mercury AMT 1084	I Want A New Girl Now/My Search	50
60	Mercury ZEP 10035	BREAK IT UP WITH BEN HEWITT (EP)	200
84	Bear Family BFX 15150	THEY WOULD CALL ME ELVIS (LP, gatefold)	15

GARTH HEWITT

70s	Myrrh MYR 1051	LOVE SONGS FOR THE EARTH (LP)	30
70s	Myrrh MYR 1078	I'M GRATEFUL (LP)	30

PETER HEWSON

83	Reset RES 2	Take My Hand/Her (p/s)	40
83	Reset REST 2	Take My Hand/Her (12", p/s)	60

HEX

93	Ninja Tune ZEN 05	SOUNDTRACK TO GLOBAL CHAOS (LP)	20
93	Ninja Tune ZEN 07	DIGITAL LOVE (LP)	12

HEXSTATIC

03	Ninja Tune ZEN 10 133	Telemetron (10", clear vinyl, promo)	15

EDDIE HEYWOOD
(see also Hugo Winterhalter)

58	Mercury 7MT 131	Heywood's Bounce/Soft Summer Breeze	8
64	Stateside SS 264	Theme From The Film "The Prize"/Li'l Darlin'	6

WINSTON HEYWOOD (& HOMBRES)
(see also Winston Harewood, Fud Christian All Stars)

71	Dynamic DYN 424	Bam-Sa-Bo/Version	8
72	Dynamic DYN 441	Stop The War/Version	6
72	Dynamic DYN 457	Seek And You'll Find/Version	6
73	Attack ATT 8046	Da Doo Ron Ron/Version	6

LENNIE HIBBERT & COUNT OSSIE BAND
(see also Sound Dimension)

69	Doctor Bird DB 1113	Pure Sole/PATSY: A Man Is Two Faced	120

AL HIBBLER

55	Brunswick 05420	Unchained Melody/Daybreak (gold label)	25
55	Brunswick 05420	Unchained Melody/Daybreak (silver label)	15
55	Brunswick 05454	They Say You're Laughing At Me/I Can't Put My Arms Around A Memory	12

			MINT VALUE £
55	London HL 8184	Now I Lay Me Down To Dream/Danny Boy	35
55	Brunswick 05492	He/Breeze (Blow My Baby Back To Me)	7
56	Brunswick 05523	The Eleventh Hour Melody/Let's Try Again	7
56	Brunswick 05552	After The Lights Go Down Low/Stella By Starlight	7
57	HMV 7EG 8326	AL HIBBLER SINGS LOVE SONGS (EP)	8
56	Brunswick LAT 8140	STARRING AL HIBBLER (LP)	12

EDDIE HICKEY

59	Decca F 11153	Lady May/Cap And Gown	10
60	Decca F 11204	Who Could Be Bluer?/Plain Jane	10
60	Decca F 11241	Another Sleepless Night/Barbara	10

ERSEL HICKEY

59	Fontana H 198	You Threw A Dart/Don't Be Afraid Of Love	70
59	Fontana H 198	You Threw A Dart/Don't Be Afraid Of Love (78)	20

DWAYNE HICKMAN

60	Capitol CL 15164	I'm A Lover, Not A Fighter/I Pass Your House	10

HICKORY

(see also Equals)

68	Lyntone 1928	Scottish Magic (Promo flexi for Tartan Ale, p/s)	20
69	CBS 3963	Green Light/Key	25

HICKORY SIX

64	Oak RGJ 149	Feelin Blue/Hello My Darling	80

COLIN HICKS (& CABIN BOYS)

57	Pye 7N 15114	Wild Eyes And Tender Lips/Empty Arms Blues (with Cabin Boys)	20
57	Pye 7N 15114	Wild Eyes And Tender Lips/Empty Arms Blues (with Cabin Boys) (78)	10
57	Pye 7N 15125	La Dee Dah/Wasteland	15
57	Pye 7N 15125	La Dee Dah/Wasteland (78)	10
58	Pye 7N 15163	Little Boy Blue/Jambalaya	15
58	Pye 7N 15163	Little Boy Blue/Jambalaya (78)	20

DAN HICKS & HIS HOT LICKS

(see also Charlatans (U.S.))

72	Blue Thumb ILPS 9204	STRIKING IT RICH (LP)	15

JIMMY HICKS

72	London HLU 10396	I'm Mr. Big Stuff/Tell Her That I Love You	15

HIDDEN CAMERAS

04	Rough Trade RTRADST 117	PLAY THE CBC SESSIONS EP (10", 2,000 only)	8

HIDDEN IDENTITY

94	Pure RudenessHIDBBB1	BLUNTED BUMPKIN BUSKERS (EP)	20

HIDDEN STRENGTH

76	United Artists UAS 29949	HIDDEN STRENGTH (LP)	15

HIDEAWAYS

69	Action ACT 4544	Hide Out/Jolly Joe	18
71	Jay Boy BOY 29	Hide Out/Jolly Joe (reissue)	6

HI-FI

(see also Ian Matthews)

84	Butt MGLS 003	Louie Louie/Summertime	8

HI-FI FOUR

56	Parlophone MSP 6210	Band Of Gold/Davy, You Upset My Life	175
56	Parlophone MSP 6210	Band Of Gold/Davy, You Upset My Life (78)	10

HI FI'S

63	Piccadilly 7N 35130	Take Me Or Leave Me/I'm Struck	8
64	Pye 7N 15635	Will Yer Won't Yer/She's The One	8
64	Pye 7N 15710	I Keep Forgettin'/Why Can't I Stop Loving You?	35
65	Pye 7N 15788	Baby's In Black/Kiss And Run	15
66	Alp 595 010	It's Gonna Be Morning/I Wanna Hear You Say Yeah	70

ALEX 'HURRICANE' HIGGINS

82	Solid STOP 003	One-Four-Seven/Life's In The Pocket (p/s)	8

LIZZIE HIGGINS

75	Topic 12TS 260	UP AND AWA WI THE LAVEROCK (LP, gatefold sleeve)	12

JOE HIGGS

(see also Higgs & Wilson, Bob Marley/Wailers, Soul Vendors)

67	Coxsone CS 7004	Neighbour Neighbour/MELODIANS: I Should Have Made It Up	80
67	Island WI 3026	I Am The Song/Worry No More	50
68	Island WI 3131	You Hurt My Soul/LYNN TAITT: Why Am I Treated So Bad?	120
70	Clandisc CLA 208	Mademoiselle/DYNAMITES: Lion	12
71	Big BG 312	Burning Fire/RUPIE EDWARDS ALL STARS: Version	6
71	New Beat NB 087	Mother Radio/DAWN SHARON: Little Deeds	6
71	Supreme SUP 215	Burning Fire/RUPIE EDWARDS ALL STARS: Push And Pull	6
72	Sioux SI 005	The World Is Spinning Around/THE REACTION: Hallelujah	6
72	Sioux SI 014	The Wave Of War/JUMBO STERLING: Shaft	6
72	Sioux SI 021	Lay A Foundation/JACKIE ROWLAND: Lay A Foundation (Version)	5
76	Ethnic Fight EF 038	Creation/AUGUSTUS PABLO & SUPER 8 CORPORATION: Creative Version	15
75	Grounation GROL 508	LIFE OF CONTRADICTION (LP)	45
78	1 STOP STOP 1002	UNITY IS POWER (LP)	15

(Joe) HIGGS & (Roy) WILSON

(see also Clancy Eccles)

60	Blue Beat (B)B 3	Manny Oh/When You Tell Me Baby (yellow label/blue writing [B3] or blue label/silver writing [BB 3]) (with Ken Richards & His Comets)	20

MINT VALUE £

61	Starlite ST45 035	Pretty Baby/I Long For The Day	20
61	Starlite ST45 036	Lover's Song/It Is A Day	20
61	Starlite ST45 042	Come On Home/The Robe	20
61	Starlite ST45 053	Sha Ba Ba/Change Of Mind	20
62	Blue Beat BB 95	How Can I Be Sure/Mighty Man	25
63	R&B JB 109	Let Me Know/Bye And Bye	15
63	Blue Beat BB 190	If You Want Pardon/BABA BROOKS BAND: Musical Communion	20
63	Island WI 081	Last Saturday Morning/Praise The Lord	20
64	Rio R 29	Love Is Not For Me/Gone Is Yesterday	15
65	Blue Beat BB 277	Pain In My Heart/BUSTER ALL STARS: Going West	25
70	Clandisc CLA 218	Don't Mind Me/GLEN AND ROY: Angel	8

HIGH

69	CBS 4164	Long Live The High/Beggar Man Dan	20

HIGH & MIGHTY

66	HMV POP 1548	Tryin' To Stop Cryin'/Escape From Cuba	35

HIGH AUTHORITY

91	Optimisim OPT 12005	I'm The Man (12")	20

HIGH BROOM

(see also Leviathan, Mike Stuart Span, Jason Crest, Holy Mackerel)

70	Island WI 6088	Dancing In The Moonlight/Percy's On The Run	15
73	Columbia DB 8969	Dancing In The Moonlight/Percy's On The Run (reissue)	7

HIGHBURY MARCHERS

72	Columbia DB 8930	The Official Arsenal March/Arsenal Boogie	5

HIGH KEYS

63	London HLK 9768	Que Sera Sera/Daddy, Ooh Long Legs	40

HIGH LEVEL RANTERS

68	Topic 12TS 186	NORTHUMBERLAND FOR EVER (LP, blue label, 2 different sleeves)	18
69	Leader/Trailer LER 2007	THE LADS OF NORTHUMBERLAND (LP)	18
70	Trailer LER 2020	KEEP YOUR FEET STILL GEORDIE HINNIE (LP)	12
71	Trailer LER 2030	HIGH LEVEL (LP)	12
75	Topic 2-12TS 271/2	THE BONNY PIT LADDIE (2-LP, blue label)	18
77	Broadside BRO 128	ENGLISH SPORTING BALLADS (LP, 1-side Martin Wyndham-Read, 2,000 only)	25
79	Topic 12TS 388	FOUR IN A BAR (LP)	12

HIGHLY LIKELY

(see also Mike Hugg, Rodney Bewes)

74	BBC RESL 10	Whatever Happened To You? (Likely Lads Theme)/God Bless Everyone	15

HIGH NUMBERS

(see also Who)

64	Fontana TF 480	Zoot Suit/I'm The Face	600
80	Back Door DOOR 4	I'm The Face/Zoot Suit (reissue, picture)	20
92	Fontana TF 480	I'm The Face/Zoot Suit (reissue, die-cut sleeve from Fontana Box)	12

HIGH SOCIETY

(see also Friday Browne, Graham Gouldman, Country Gentlemen, Manchester Mob)

66	Fontana TF 771	People Passing By/Star Of Eastern Street	22

HIGH SOCIETY

70	CBS 4746	Only You Only You/Tell Me Now	15

HIGH TIDE

(see also Hawkwind, Misunderstood, Denny Gerrard, Magic Muscle, Third Ear Band)

69	Liberty LBS 83264	SEA SHANTIES (LP, gatefold sleeve, blue label)	180
70	Liberty LBS 83294	HIGH TIDE (LP, blue label)	120

HIGH TIDE

81	Sunday Morning (No cat. no.)	Baby Dancing/Letter From A Coward (mail-order only)	8

DEAN HIGHTOWER

60	HMV CLP 1360	TWANGY - WITH A BEAT (LP)	50

DONNA HIGHTOWER

60	Capitol ST 1273	GEE BABY (LP)	15

ROSETTA HIGHTOWER

(see also Orlons, Ian Green [Revelation])

68	Toast TT 506	Pretty Red Balloons/How Can You Mistreat (The One You Love)?	25
68	Toast TT 509	I Can't Give Back The Love I Feel For You/Big Bird	35
69	CBS 4584	One Heart For Sale/What Do I Do?	10
70	CBS 4758	April Fools/I'll Hold Out My Hand	6
70	CBS 4988	Persuader/Come Together	6
71	CBS 7068	Go Pray For Tomorrow/Give Me Just A Little More Line	6
73	Philips 6006 291	The Walls Fell Down/Captain's Army	6
71	CBS 64201	HIGHTOWER (LP)	30
71	Rediffusion ZS 88	ROSETTA HIGHTOWER (LP)	15

HIGH TREASON

80	Burlington BURLS 001	Saturday Night Special/Waste My Love (no p/s)	80

HIGHWAY

74	EMI EMC 3019	HIGHWAY (LP)	15
75	EMI EMA 770	SMOKING AT THE EDGE (LP, gatefold sleeve)	18
61	HMV POP 910	Michael/Santiano	5

HIGHWAYMEN

62	United Artists UP 1001	Birdman (with narration from Burt Lancaster)/Cindy Oh Cindy	7
64	United Artists ULP 1083	HOMECOMING (LP)	12

MINT VALUE £

HIGH WINDOWS

68	CBS 3208	Maybe Someday/Your Eyes	8
68	CBS 3437	Anybody Need A Lover/El El Israel	8

HIGSONS

82	Two Tone CHSTT21	Tear The Whole Thing Down/Ylang Ylang (p/s, paper labels)	10
82	Two Tone CHSTT121	Tear The Whole Thing Down/Ylang Ylang (12", p/s)	12
82	Two Tone CHS TT 1	Tear The Whole Thing Down/Ylang Ylang (12" promo shared with Apollinaires)	35
83	Two Tone CHSTT24	Run Me Down/Put The Punk Back Into Funk (p/s, paper labels)	10
83	Two Tone CHSTT 1224	Run Me Down (extended)/Instrumental /Put The Punk Back Into Funk (1 & 2) (12", p/s)	12
81	Waap 1 WAAPLP	ATTACK OF THE CANNIBAL ZOMBIE B MEN (LP)	12

HIJACK

88	Music Of Life NOTE016	Style Wars (12")	15
88	Syndicate 655517 6	The Badman is Robbin'/Hold No Hostage/Doomsday (12" EP)	12
88	Music Of Life NOTE021	Hold No Hostage/Doomsday Of Rap (12")	20
89	Music Of Life NOTE016R	Style Wars Revenge (12")	15
91	Syndicate 0 21751	Daddy Rich/Hijack The Terrorist Group (12")	15
91	Rhyme Syndicate 6555176	HORNS OF JERICHO (LP)	35
96	Reservoir RES 18	THE ORIGINAL HORNS OF JERICHO (LP)	80

HILARY HILARY

(see also Roger Taylor, Queen)

80	Modern STP 2	How Come You're So Dumb/Rich Kid Blues (p/s)	60

RAY HILDEBRAND

70s	Myrrh MST 6508	SPECIAL KIND OF MAN (LP)	30

DIANE HILDEBRANDE

69	Elektra EKSN 45055	Jan's Blues/Early Morning Blues And Greens	10
69	Elektra EKL 4031	EARLY MORNING BLUES AND GREENS (LP)	20

HI-LITERS

58	Mercury AMT 1011	Dance Me To Death/Cha Cha Rock	150
58	Mercury AMT 1011	Dance Me To Death/Cha Cha Rock (78)	75

HI LITES

65	London HL 9967	Hey Baby/Groovey	20

ALEX HILL

(see also Paramount Allstars)

53	Vocalion V 1027	Stompin' 'Em Down/Track Head Blues (78)	18

BENNY HILL

(see also Coronets)

55	Decca F 10442	I Can't Tell A Waltz From A Tango/Teach Me Tonight	15
56	Columbia SCM 5238	Memories Are Made Of This/Who Done It? (as Benny Hill & Coronets)	15
61	Pye 7N 15327	Gather In The Mushrooms/Pepys' Diary	6
61	Pye 7N 15359	Transistor Radio/Gypsy Rock	6
62	Pye 7N 15520	Harvest Of Love/Bamba 3688	5
65	Pye 7N 15974	What A World/I'll Never Know	6
66	Pye 7N 17026	My Garden Of Love/The Andalucian Gypsies	5
92	EMI ERNPD 1	Ernie/Ting A Ling A Loo (shaped picture disc)	5
61	Pye NEP 24144	BENNY HILL PARADE VOL. 1 (EP)	12
61	Pye NEP 24174	THE HARVEST OF LOVE (EP)	10
65	Decca LK 4723	BENNY AT THE BBC (LP)	15
66	Pye NPL 18133	SINGS? (LP)	12

BUNKER HILL & RAYMEN

62	Stateside SS 135	Hide & Go Seek Parts 1 & 2	20

CHIPPIE HILL/HOCIEL THOMAS

72	Collectors Edition 1001	CHIPPIE HILL AND HOCIEL THOMAS (LP)	12

DAVID HILL

57	Vogue V 9076	All Shook Up/Melody For Lovers (with Ray Ellis Orchestra, probably unreleased)	200
57	Vogue V 9076	All Shook Up/Melody For Lovers (78, with Ray Ellis Orchestra)	70
58	RCA RCA 1041	That's Love/Keep Me In Mind (with Joe Relsman's Orchestra & Chorus)	175
58	RCA RCA 1041	That's Love/Keep Me In Mind (78, with Joe Relsman's Orchestra & Chorus)	70

JESSIE HILL

60	London HLU 9117	Ooh Poo Pah Doo Parts 1 & 2	25

MICHAEL HILL

60	Parlophone R 4700	Jukes' Jingle/Joey's Song	7
60	Parlophone R 4700	Beatnik Boogie/Mike's Tune	6
61	Parlophone R 4727	Glory Rock/Blue On Blue	6

RONNI HILL

77	Creole CR 138	You Keep Me Hanging On/I Wouldn't Give You Up	20

VINCE HILL

(see also [Jackie &] Raindrops, Elmer Bernstein)

62	Piccadilly 7N 35043	The Rivers Run Dry/Not Any More	8
62	Piccadilly 7N 35068	There You Go/Just As Long As (You Belong To Me)	5
63	Piccadilly 7N 35108	A Day At The Seaside/Tricks Of The Trade	7
63	Piccadilly 7N 35118	As It Was Written/Is There Anyone At Home	5
63	Piccadilly 7N 35148	Blue Velvet/Like Anything	5
64	Piccadilly 7N 35161	If You Knew/Fools & Lovers	5
64	Piccadilly 7N 35192	It's Only Make Believe/Let The Wind Blow	5
65	Columbia DB 7781	Take Me To Your Heart Again/Push Push	6
66	Columbia SEG 8509	FOUR SIDES OF VINCE HILL (EP)	10
66	Columbia SCX 6046	HEARTACHES (LP)	12

MINT VALUE £

Z.Z. HILL
(see also Intentions)

65	R&B MRB 5005	Someone To Love Me/Have Mercy Someone	30
69	Action ACT 4532	Make Me Yours/What Am I Living For?	75
71	Mojo 2092 019	Faithful And True/I Think I'd Do It	8
75	United Artists UP 35727	I Keep On Loving You/Whoever's Thrilling You	8
77	CBS 5553	Love Is So Good When You're Stealin' It/Need You By My Side	8
66	Sue IEP 711	GIMME GIMME (EP, 2 tracks each by Z.Z. Hill & Intentions; in p/s)	300
66	Sue IEP 711	GIMME GIMME (EP, 2 tracks each by Z.Z. Hill & Intentions)	100
69	Action ACLP 6004	WHOLE LOT OF SOUL (LP)	60
72	Mojo 2916 013	THE BRAND NEW Z.Z. HILL (LP)	20
75	Contempo CLP 515	THE BRAND NEW Z.Z. HILL (LP, reissue)	15

STEVE HILLAGE
(see also Gong, Khan, Arzachel, Clearlight, Radio Actors, System 7)

76	Virgin VS 161	It's All Too Much/Shimmer	10
77	Virgin VS 171	Hurdy Gurdy Man/Om Nama Shivaya	5
77	Virgin VS 197	Not Fade Away/Saucer Surfing	5
77	Virgin VDJ 23	Leylines To Glassdome/GLEN PHILLIPS: Lies (p/s, gig freebie)	6
78	Virgin VS 212	Getting Better/Palm Trees (Love Guitar) (in p/s)	8
78	Virgin VS 212	Getting Better/Palm Trees (Love Guitar)	5
78	Virgin VDJ 25	Getting Better/Palm Trees (Love Guitar) (12", p/s)	12
79	Virgin VS 313	Don't Dither, Do It/Getting In Tune (p/s)	6
82	Virgin VS 551	Alone (p/s)	6
82	Virgin VS 574	Kamikaze Eyes (p/s)	10
79	Virgin SIXPACK 2	SIX PACK/SIX TRACK (EP, picture disc, 5,000 only, die-cut p/s with stand)	8
78	Virgin V 2098	GREEN (LP, green vinyl, with insert)	15
83	Virgin V 2244	FOR TO NEXT (LP, with bonus instrumental LP "And Not Or")	12
75	Virgin V 2031	FISH RISING (LP, lyric insert, coloured 'twin' label)	20

HILLER BROTHERS

60s	Honey Hit TB 124	Little Darlin'/Changin' My Mind (with p/s)	10
60s	Honey Hit TB 124	Little Darlin'/Changin' My Mind	6

JANE HILLERY
(see also Magistrates)

66	Columbia DB 7918	You've Got That Hold On Me/Take Me Away	40

MABLE HILLERY

69	Xtra XTRA 1063	IT'S SO HARD TO BE A NIGGER (LP)	30

GILLIAN HILLS

65	Vogue VRS 7005	Tomorrow Is Another Day/Look At Them	10

HI-LO'S

62	Reprise RS 20095	A Taste Of Honey/My Baby Just Cares For Me	5
57	London HA-U 2026	UNDER GLASS (LP)	15
58	Philips BBL 7154	SUDDENLY IT'S THE HI-LO'S (LP)	12
59	Philips BBL 7288	AND ALL THAT JAZZ (LP)	12

HILLTOPPERS
(see also Sacca, Billy Vaughn)

52	Vogue V 9045	Trying/You Made Up My Mind (featuring Jimmy Sacca) (78)	10
53	London L 1204	P.S. I Love You/I'd Rather Die Young (78)	10
54	London HL 8003	Love Walked In/To Be Alone (78)	15
54	London HL 8026	From The Vine Came The Grape/Time Will Tell	8
54	London HL 8070	Poor Butterfly/Wrapped Up In A Dream	60
54	London HL 8081	Will You Remember?/The Old Cabaret	50
54	London HL 8092	If I Didn't Care/Bettina	50
55	London HL 8116	Time Waits For No One/You Try Somebody Else	50
55	London HLD 8168	The Kentuckian Song/I Must Be Dreaming	30
55	London HLD 8208	Searching/All I Need Is You	50
56	London HLD 8221	Only You (And You Alone)/(It Will Have To Do) Until The Real Thing Comes Along (gold label lettering)	40
56	London HLD 8221	Only You (And You Alone)/(It Will Have To Do) Until The Real Thing Comes Along (silver label lettering)	20
56	London HLD 8255	My Treasure/Last Word In Love	50
56	London HLD 8278	Do The Bop/When You're Alone	140
56	London HLD 8278	Do The Bop/When You're Alone (78)	30
56	London HLD 8298	Tryin'/D-A-R-L-I-N'	30
56	London HLD 8333	So Tired/Faded Rose	30
57	London HLD 8381	Marianne/You're Wasting Your Time	25
57	London HLD 8441	I'm Serious/I Love My Girl	25
57	London HLD 8455	A Fallen Star/Footsteps	25
57	London HLD 8528	The Joker/Chicken, Chicken	40
58	London HLD 8603	You Sure Look Good To Me/Starry Eyes	20
60	London HLD 9038	Alone/The Prisoner's Song	15
55	London RE-P 1012	PRESENTING THE HILLTOPPERS (EP)	30
55	London RE-D 1030	THE HILLTOPPERS VOL. 2 (EP)	30
57	London RE-D 1099	THE HILLTOPPERS VOL. 3 (EP)	30
57	London HA-D 2029	THE TOWERING HILLTOPPERS (LP)	50
57	London HA-D 2071	TOPS IN POPS (LP)	40

NICKY HILTON

65	Decca F 12099	Give Us Your Blessing/Always In My Heart	6

RONNIE HILTON
(see also Alma Cogan)

55	HMV 7M 285	Prize Of Gold/A Blossom Fell	20
55	HMV 7M 303	Just Say You Love Her/My Loving Hands	10
56	HMV 7M 336	Bella Notte/He	10

			MINT VALUE £
56	HMV 7M 358	Young And Foolish/Moments To Remember	10
56	HMV 7M 382	The Last Frontier/Here Comes My Love	6
56	HMV 7M 390	No Other Love/It's All Been Done Before (B-side with Alma Cogan)	10
56	HMV 7M 413	Who Are We/Give Me My Ranch	6
56	HMV POP 248	A Woman In Love/I Just Found Out About Love	6
56	HMV POP 274	Two Different Worlds/Constant And True	6
57	HMV POP 291	The Wisdom Of A Fool/Amore	6
57	HMV POP 307	For Your Love/Once	6
67	HMV POP 1600	If I Were A Rich Man/Laughing Gnome (Bowie-penned B side)	35
55	HMV DLP 1109	BY THE FIRESIDE (10" LP)	15
59	HMV CLP 1295	I'M BEGINNING TO SEE THE LIGHT (LP)	15

HILTONAIRES

67	Coxsone CSL 8004	THE BEST OF THE HILTONAIRES (LP)	80

HIM & THE OTHERS

66	Parlophone R 5510	I Mean It/She's Got Eyes That Tell Lies	850

JUSTIN HINDS/HINES (& DOMINOES)

(see also Lyn Taitt, Skatalites, Don Drummond)

64	Ska Beat JB 176	King Samuel/River Jordan	25
65	Ska Beat JB 187	Mother Banner/DON DRUMMOND & HIS GROUP: Apanga	40
65	Island WI 171	Botheration/Satan (as Justin Hines & Dominoes)	30
65	Island WI 174	Jump Out Of The Frying Pan/Holy Dove (as Justin Hines & Dominoes)	30
65	Island WI 194	Rub Up, Push Up/The Ark	25
65	Island WI 232	Turn Them Back/TOMMY McCOOK: Rocket Ship	50
65	Island WI 236	Peace And Love/Skalarama (B-side actually by Lyn Taitt & Comets)	40
66	Doctor Bird DB 1048	The Higher The Monkey Climbs/Fight For Your Right	40
67	Island WI 3048	On A Saturday Night/Save A Bread	22
67	Treasure Isle TI 7002	Here I Stand/No Good Rudie	20
67	Treasure Isle TI 7005	Carry Go Bring Come/Fight Too Much	20
67	Treasure Isle TI 7014	On A Saturday Night/Save A Bread	20
67	Treasure Isle TI 7017	Once A Man/TOMMY McCOOK & SUPERSONICS: Persian Cat	20
68	Treasure Isle TI 7063	Botheration/VINCENT HINDS: Mouth Trombone	15
68	Treasure Isle TI 7068	Mighty Redeemer (Parts 1 & 2)	15
69	Trojan TR 652	You Should've Known Better/TOMMY McCOOK & SUPERSONICS: Third Figure	12
70	Duke Reid DR 2511	Say Me Say/I Want It	8
70	Duke DU 67	Drink Milk/Everywhere I Go (as Justin Hines & Dominoes)	8
72	Treasure Isle TI 7068	Mighty Redeemer/DUKE REID'S ALL STARS: Version	10
75	Pama PM 4001	Sinners Where You Going To Hide?/If It's Love You Need	8
76	Island ILPS 9416	JEZEBEL (LP)	30

NEVILLE HINDS

(see also Neville Irons & Byron Lee & The Dragonaires, Lloyd Robinson, Marvels, Alton Ellis)

70	Duke Reid DR 2503	Sunday Gravy (as Neville Hines)/JOHN HOLT: Write Her A Letter	20
70	Camel CA 44	London Bridge/SCORCHERS: Things And Time (B-side act. by Wailing Souls)	20
70	Gas GAS 126	I Who Have Nothing/You Send Me	8
71	Explosion EX 2043	Delivered/Specially For You (B-side actually by Blake Boy)	6
72	Upsetter US 384	Blackman's Time/UPSETTERS: Version	10
73	Harry J HJ 6657	Musical Splendour/JOHN CROW GENERATION: Musical Drum & Bass	6

RUPERT HINE

(see also Jon Pertwee, Quantum Jump)

72	Purple PUR 105	Hamburgers/A Varlet Lad T'was Samuel Green (Historical Moments - Part 7)	6
76	Electric WOT 8	Snakes Don't Dance Fast/Hopi Smile	6
71	Purple TPSA 7502	PICK UP A BONE (LP, with David MacIver, textured gatefold sleeve)	35
73	Purple TPSA 7509	UNFINISHED PICTURE (LP, gatefold sleeve)	60

EARL 'FATHA' HINES

(see also Louis Armstrong)

54	Mercury MG 25018	EARL HINES AND HIS ALL STARS (10" LP)	15
55	Vogue Coral LRA 10031	FATS WALLER SONGS (10" LP)	15
55	Columbia 33S 1063	PIANO MOODS (10" LP)	15
56	HMV DLP 1132	GRAND TERRACE SWING (10" LP)	15
60	MGM MGM-C 833	EARL'S PEARLS (LP, as Earl 'Fatha' Hines Quartet)	15

FRAZER HINES

68	Major Minor MM 579	Who's Dr. Who?/Punch And Judy Man	50

HINES, HINES & DAD

68	CBS 3667	Something Extra/Hambone	5

JUSTIN HINES

(see under Justin Hinds)

SONNY HINES

65	King KG 1009	Anytime, Any Day, Anywhere/Nothing Like Your Love	15

HINES & ELDRIDGE

(see also Coleman Hawkins, Earl Hines, Roy Eldridge)

69	Mercury SMWL 21041	HINES AND ELDRIDGE WITH COLEMAN HAWKINS VOLUME 2 (LP)	12

HINGE

68	RCA RCA 1721	The Village Postman/You'd Better Go Home	10

CLIVE HINTON

68	President PT231	HOW COULD I EVER LEAVE (EP)	12

JOE HINTON

64	Vocalion VP 9224	Funny How Time Slips Away/You Gotta Have Love	30
66	Vocalion VP 9258	Just A Kid Named Joe/Pledging My Love	15
66	Vocalion VA-P 8043	FUNNY HOW TIME SLIPS AWAY (LP)	120

HI-NUMBERS

65	Decca F 12233	Heart Of Stone/Dancing In The Street	70

MINT VALUE £

HIPPIES

63	Cameo Parkway P 863	Memory Lane/REGGIE HARRISON: A Lonely Piano	20

HIPPOLYTES

77	Top Deck TD 003	Don't Make The Promises/I Love Sue	7

HIPPY BOYS

(see also Upsetters, Family Man, Danny Williams, Tony, Hippy Boys, Cynthia Richards, Pioneers)

69	Trojan TR 668	Love/The Whole Family	15
69	Trojan TR 669	Michael Row The Boat Ashore/Who Is Coming To Dinner	12
69	Bullet BU 412	Hog In A Me Minte/Lorna Run	25
69	Bullet BU 413	What's Your Excuse?/Tell Me Tell	10
69	Camel CA 29	Cat Nip/Cooyah (both as Hippie Boys)	15
69	High Note HS 021	Doctor No Go/Sailing (B-side actually "Faberge" by Baba Brooks & Band)	18
69	High Note HS 030	Chicken Lickin'/BABA BROOKS: Old Man Flint	12
69	High Note HS 035	Reggae Pressure/SOUL RHYTHMS: It Hurts (B-side actually Soul Rhythms)	15
69	Unity UN 528	Dreams To Remember/Peace Maker	50
70	High Note HS 038	Piccadilly Hop/Nigeria	10
70	Duke DU 92	Cloud Burst/LLOYD CHARMERS: Message From A Black Man	80
70	Explosion EX 2032	Vengeance/Look-Ea-Py-Py	30
71	Big Shot 580	Voodoo/LITTLE ROY: Hard Fighter	10
69	Big Shot BSLP 5005	REGGAE WITH THE HIPPY BOYS (LP, actually on High Note label)	60

HIPSTER IMAGE

(see also Climax Chicago Blues Band)

65	Decca F 12137	Can't Let Her Go/Make Her Mine	500

HIRSCHE NICHT AUFS SOFA

86	United Dairies UD 018	MELCHIOR (LP, with Insert)	30

AL HIRT

(see also Ann-Margret)

63	RCA 1380	Java/I Can't Get Started	6
67	RCA RCA 1590	Theme From "The Monkees"/Tarzan March	5

HI-SPOTS

58	Melodisc 1457	Lend Me Your Comb/I Don't Hurt Anymore	22
58	Melodisc 1473	Secretly/I Got	22
58	Melodisc 1473	Secretly/I Got (78)	10

ALFRED HITCHCOCK

(see Jeff Alexander)

58	London HA-P 2130	MUSIC TO BE MURDERED BY (LP, music by Jeff Alexander Orchestra, mono)	50
58	London SH-P 6012	MUSIC TO BE MURDERED BY (LP, music by Jeff Alexander Orchestra, stereo)	60
60	Wonderland LP 89	ALFRED HITCHCOCK PRESENTS GHOST STORIES FOR YOUNG PEOPLE (LP, read by Peter Allen)	40

ROBYN HITCHCOCK (& THE EGYPTIANS)

(see also Soft Boys, Knox)

81	Armageddon AS 008	The Man Who Invented Himself/Dancing On God's Thumb (p/s, with flexidisc "It's A Mystic Trip"/"Grooving On An Inner Plane" [4 SPURT 1])	8
81	Armageddon AS 008	The Man Who Invented Himself/Dancing On God's Thumb (p/s, without flexidisc "It's A Mystic Trip"/"Grooving On An Inner Plane" [4 SPURT 1])	6
82	Albion ION 103	America/It Was The Night/How Do You Work This Thing? (p/s)	8
82	Albion FREEBIE 1	52 Stations/COSMOPOLITANS: How To Keep Your Husband Happy/ MOTOR BOYS MOTOR: Little Boy And Fat Man/dB's: Amplifier (flexidisc free with GROOVY DECAL LP [ALB 110] or at gigs)	5
82	Midnight Music DING 2	Eaten By Her Own Dinner/Listening To The Higsons/Dr. Sticky (p/s)	7
82	Midnight Music DONG 2	Eaten By Her Own Dinner/Grooving On An Inner Plane/Messages Of The Dark The Abandoned Brain/Happy The Golden Prince (12", p/s)	10
83	Albion 12 ION 1036	Nightride To Trinidad (Long Version)/Kingdom Of Love/Midnight Fish (12", p/s)	10
84	Midnight Music DONG 8	The Bells Of Rhymney/Falling Leaves/Winter Love/ The Bones In The Ground (12", p/s)	8
85	Midnight Music DONG 12	Heaven/Dwarfbeat/Some Body (12", p/s)	8
85	Midnight Music DONG 17	Brenda's Iron Sledge (live)/Only The Stones Remain/ The Pit Of Souls (Part I-IV) (12", p/s)	8
86	Glass Fish OOZE 1	If You Were A Priest/The Crawling (p/s)	5
84	Bucketfull/Brains BOB 8	Happy The Golden Prince (hard vinyl white label test pressing, 20 only)	30
81	Armageddon ARM 4	BLACK SNAKE DIAMOND RôLE (LP)	12

HI-TENSION

77	Island IPR 2007	Hi-Tension/Girl I Bet Cha (12")	8
79	Island WIP 6493	There's A Reason/If It Moves You	5
79	Island 12 WIP 6493	There's A Reason/If It Moves You (12")	20
78	Island ILPS 9564	HI-TENSION (LP, with poster)	15

HI-TONES

62	Island WI 029	Going Steady/Darlin' Elaine	25
62	Wasp W 004	I'm In Love With You/Singing A Song	15
63	Island WI 086	Ten Virgins (actually by Angelic Brothers)/Too Young To Love (actually by Larry Marshall)	25
63	R&B JB 123	You Hold The Key/DON DRUMMOND: Rock Away	50

HIT PACK

65	Tamla Motown TMG 513	Never Say No To Your Baby/Let's Dance	125
65	Tamla Motown TMG 513	Never Say No To Your Baby/Let's Dance (DJ copy)	175

HIT PARADE

84	JSH JSH 1	Forever/Stop (die-cut p/s)	8
84	JSH JSH 2	My Favourite Girl/It Rained On Monday Morning (die-cut p/s)	7
85	JSH JSH 3	The Sun Shines In Gerrards Cross/You Hurt Me Too (die-cut p/s)	6
85	JSH JSH 4	You Don't Love Me Then/Huevo's Mexicana (die-cut p/s with card)	6

			MINT VALUE £
86	JSH JSH 5	See You In Havana/Wipe Away The Tears (die-cut p/s)	5
87	JSH JSH 6	I Get So Sentimental/Sue (die-cut p/s)	5
91	Sarah SARAH 58	In Gunnersbury Park/Harvey (ps, insert)	8

HIT PARADE

82	Crass 221984/12	BAD NEWS (EP)	25
84	Crass 1984/2	PLASTIC CULTURE: Product of The Troubles/Media Son (12")	18
86	Crass No 9	NICK NACK PADDY WHACK (LP, with lyric inner)	25

HIT SQUAD

(see also 808 State)

88	Eastern Bloc EASTERN 01	Wax On The Melt/SPM MC Tunes/Shure.4 (12", white label promo only, plain stickered sleeve)	30

HITTERS

(see also Brinsley Schwarz)

73	United Artists UP 35530	Hypocrite/The Version	22

HMC

93	New Electronica ELEC 03P	Science Funktion (12", promo)	30

HOAX

80	Hologram HOAX 1	ONLY THE BLIND CAN SEE IN THE DARK (EP)	25
81	Hologram HOAX 3	SO WHAT (12" EP, p/s, blue vinyl)	15
82	Hologram HOAX 4	Quiet In The Sixpenny 5 (p/s)	10

HOBBIT

72	Satril SAT 7	Only Friends/Everything's Turning Out Fine	10
71	Deroy	FIRST AND LAST (LP, private pressing)	80

HOBBITS

68	Decca AD 1004	Daffodil Days (The Affection Song)/Sunny Day Girl (export issue)	20
68	MCA MU 1002	Daffodil Days (The Affection Song)/Sunny Day Girl	8
67	MCA MUP 301	DOWN TO MIDDLE EARTH (LP)	35

HOBBS

78	Big SOLD 4	Bop Around The Shop/(You've Got Me In A) Whirl Girl (gatefold p/s & insert)	6

HOBBY HORSE

(see also Mary Hopkin)

72	Bell BELL 1248	Summertime, Summertime/Sweet And Low	10

HOBBY SHOP

68	Columbia DB 8395	Why Must It Be This Way?/Talk To Me	10

LES HOBEAUX

57	HMV POP 377	Oh, Mary Don't You Weep/Toll The Bell Easy	15
57	HMV POP 377	Oh, Mary Don't You Weep/Toll The Bell Easy (78)	10
57	HMV POP 403	Mama Don't Allow/Hey, Hey, Daddy Blues	15
57	HMV POP 403	Mama Don't Allow/Hey, Hey, Daddy Blues (78)	10
58	HMV POP 444	Dynamo/Two Ships	15
58	HMV POP 444	Dynamo/Two Ships (78)	15
57	HMV 7EG 8297	SOHO SKIFFLE (EP)	50

HOBNAIL

72	Bell Bell 1250	She's Just A Friend Of Mine/Boy Scout Jambouree	12

HOBO

76	United Artists UAS 29809	HOBO (LP)	15

HOBOKEN

73	Oak	HOBOKEN (LP, 6 copies only)	300

TREVOR HOCKEY

70s	Beau Brummie TET 120ST	Happy 'Cos I'm Blue/THE BLUES PLAYERS: Keep Right On To The End Of The Road (p/s)	40

EDMUND HOCKRIDGE

(see also Joan Regan)

53	Parlophone MSP 6027	Luck Be A Lady/I'll Know	8
53	Parlophone MSP 6028	I've Never Been In Love Before/My Time Of Day	8

CHRIS HODGE

72	Apple APPLE 43	We're On Our Way/Supersoul (in p/s)	30
72	Apple APPLE 43	We're On Our Way/Supersoul	10
74	RCA LPBO 5007	Beautiful Love/Sweet Lady From The Sky	6
74	DJM DJS 10337	I Love You/Old James Dean	5

MARVA HODGE

70	Polydor 56792	The Ghetto/Sometimes	8

CHARLES HODGES

(see also Outlaws, Cliff Bennett's Rebellion)

69	Major Minor MM 654	Try A Little Love/Someone To Love	20

EDDIE HODGES

(see also Hayley Mills & Eddie Hodges)

61	London HLA 9369	I'm Gonna Knock On Your Door/Ain't Gonna Wash For A Week	10
62	London HLA 9505	Bandit Of My Dreams/Mugmates	15
62	London HLA 9576	(Girls, Girls, Girls) Made To Love/I Make Believe It's You	7
63	MGM MGM 1232	Just A Kid In Love/Avalanche	10
65	Stateside SS 442	New Orleans/Hard Times For Young Lovers	10
65	Stateside SS 469	Love Minus Zero - No Limit/The Water Is Over My Head	10
62	London REA 1353	EDDIE HODGES (EP)	40

JOHNNY HODGES & HIS ORCHESTRA

52	Vogue LD 011	JOHNNY HODGES (10" LP)	15
56	Columbia/Clef C 9051	IN A TENDER MOOD (10"LP)	12
57	Columbia EC CLEF 10098	ELLINGTON ALL STARS (LP)	12

MINT VALUE £

INGFRIED HOFFMAN
67 Polydor 583 015 SOUL BOND (LP) . . . 15

HOFFNER BROTHERS
72 Bullet BU 513 The King Man Is Back/SHALIMAR ALL STARS: Version . . . 5
72 Green Door GD 4039 The King Man Is Back/SHALIMAR ALL STARS: Version (reissue) . . . 5
73 Ackee ACK 521 Open Up The Gates/Version . . . 5
73 Grape GR 3042 Let Me Dream (Parts 1 & 2) . . . 5

GERARD HOFFNUNG
60 Decca LF 1330 AT THE OXFORD UNION (10" LP) . . . 12

ANNIE HOGAN
(see also Marc Almond, Nick Cave, Soft Cell)
85 Doublevision DVR 9 PLAYS KICKABYE (12" EP) . . . 15

CLAIRE HOGAN
(see also Teresa Brewer)
59 Top Rank JAR 161 Sing A Smiling Song/I Wonder . . . 10

SILAS HOGAN
71 Blue Horizon 2431 008 TROUBLE AT HOME (LP) . . . 110
70s Flyright FLY 595 I'M A FREE-HEARTED MAN (LP) . . . 15

HOGARTH
68 Liberty LBF 15156 Suzie's Getting Married/I've Been Dreaming . . . 10

JAMES HOGG
72 Regal Zonophone RZ 3054 Lovely Lady Rock/Happy Sad . . . 20
72 Regal Zonophone RZ 3068 California Blues/Everybody Smile . . . 10

JAMES HOGG BAND
73 Regal Zonophone 3078 Gotta Be A Winner/Everybody Smile . . . 10

SMOKEY HOGG
(see also John Lee Hooker/Lightnin' Hopkins/Smokey Hogg)
64 Realm RM 197 I'M SO LONELY (LP) . . . 25
72 Ember EMB 3405 SINGS THE BLUES (LP) . . . 20
70s Specialty SNTF 5018 U BETTER WATCH THAT JIVE (LP) . . . 15

HOGGS
80 Now 2001 See It Now/Time On The Line (p/s) . . . 20

HOGS
69 Jay Boy BOY 5 It's All Coming To Me Now/Motor Cycle Rider . . . 6

SUZI JANE HOKUM
66 MGM MGM 1323 Need All The Help I Can Get/Home . . . 18

HOKUS POKE
72 Vertigo 6360 064 EARTH HARMONY (LP, die-cut gatefold sleeve, small swirl label) . . . 275

RON HOLDEN
60 London HLU 9116 My Babe/Love You So . . . 70

MARK HOLDER & THE POSITIVES
73 Atlantic K10280 Whatever's Fair/Why Dear Lord . . . 25

RAM HOLDER BROTHERS
(see also Ram Jam Band, Ram John Holder)
66 Parlophone R 5471 Just Across The River/Ram Blues . . . 30

RAM JOHN HOLDER
(see also Ram Jam Band, Ram Holder Brothers, Geno Washington)
67 Columbia DB 8157 I Need Somebody/She's Alright . . . 12
67 Columbia DB 8262 My Friend Jones/It Won't Be Long Before I Love You . . . 25
68 Beacon BEA 108 I Just Came To Get My Baby/Yes I Do . . . 10
69 Upfront UPF 2 Goodwill To All Mankind/BLACK VELVET: Goodwill Sermon . . . 8
70 United Artists UP 35117 Where Do The Dreams Go?/Miracle Happens Every Day . . . 6
63 Melodisc MLP 12-133 RAM BLUES GOSPEL AND SOUL (LP) . . . 60
69 Beacon BEAS 2 BLACK LONDON BLUES (LP, white/black label with "Sold in U.K..." text) . . . 60
70 Beacon BEAS 17 BOOTLEG BLUES (LP, gatefold sleeve with lyric poster, white/black labels) . . . 80
70 Beacon BEAS 17 BOOTLEG BLUES (LP, gatefold sleeve without lyric poster, white/black labels) . 30

HOLE
91 City Slang EFA 04070-45/ Teenage Whore/Drown Soda (p/s, lilac, clear or green vinyl, 500 of each) . . . 20
91 City Slang EFA 04070 Teenage Whore/Drown Soda (12") . . . 8
91 City Slang EFA 04070 CD Teenage Whore/Drown Soda (CD) . . . 8
93 City Slang EFA 04916-45 Beautiful Son/Old Age/20 Years In The Dakota (purple vinyl) . . . 10
93 City Slang EFA 04916-02 Beautiful Son/Old Age/20 Years In The Dakota (12", green vinyl) . . . 12
94 City Slang EFA 04936-7 Miss World/Rock Star (Alternate Mix) (pink vinyl) . . . 8
96 Mirromax 573 164-7 Gold Dust Woman/N.Y. LOOSE: Spit
(gatefold p/s, 2 x 1-sided 7"s, with etched B-sides, 5,000 numbered) . . . 10
91 City Slang SLANG 012 PRETTY ON THE INSIDE (LP, blue vinyl) . . . 25
94 City Slang EFA 04935-1 LIVE THROUGH THIS (LP, 3000 on white vinyl) . . . 25
94 City Slang EFA 04935-1 LIVE THROUGH THIS (LP, black vinyl) . . . 20

BILLIE HOLIDAY
56 Vogue V 2408 Detour Ahead/Blue, Turning Grey Over You . . . 20
59 MGM MGM 1033 Don't Worry About Me/Just One More Chance . . . 10
55 Brunswick OE 9172 LADY DAY VOL. 1 (EP) . . . 10
55 Columbia Clef SEB 10009 BILLIE HOLIDAY SINGS (EP) . . . 8
55 Vogue EPV 1128 BILLIE HOLIDAY (EP) . . . 10
56 Brunswick OE 9199 LADY DAY VOL. 2 (EP) . . . 10
56 Brunswick OE 9251 LADY DAY VOL. 3 (EP) . . . 8
50s Melodisc EPM7 125 EMBRACEABLE YOU (EP) . . . 10

			MINT VALUE £
60	Fontana TFE 17026	BLUE (EP)	8
54	Columbia 33S 1034	BILLIE HOLIDAY (10" LP)	40
54	Brunswick LA 8676	LOVER MAN (10" LP)	40
55	Philips BBR 8032	FAVOURITES (10" LP)	40
56	Columbia Clef 33C 9023	AT JAZZ AT THE PHILHARMONIC (10" LP)	20
56	Columbia Clef 33CX 10019	MUSIC FOR TORCHING (LP)	40
57	Columbia Clef 33CX 10064	VELVET MOOD (LP)	40
57	Columbia Clef 33CX 10076	SOLITUDE (LP)	30
57	Columbia Clef 33CX 10092	LADY SINGS THE BLUES (LP)	30
59	Columbia Clef 33CX 10145	SONGS FOR DISTINGUÉ LOVERS (LP)	30
59	MGM MGM-C 792	BILLIE HOLIDAY (LP)	15
59	Fontana TFL 5032	LADY IN SATIN (LP)	15
60	Fontana TFL 5106	A BILLIE HOLIDAY MEMORIAL (LP)	15
61	HMV CLP 1414	THE UNFORGETTABLE LADY DAY (LP)	15
62	Stateside SL 10007	BILLIE HOLIDAY (LP)	20
66	Island ILP 929	LAST LIVE RECORDING (LP)	40

CHICO HOLIDAY

59	RCA RCA 1117	Young Ideas/Cuckoo Girl	35
59	RCA RCA 1117	Young Ideas/Cuckoo Girl (78)	12
61	Coral Q 72443	God, Country And My Baby/Fools (withdrawn)	30
59	RCA RCX 171	CHICO HOLIDAY (EP)	100

JIMMY HOLIDAY

63	Vocalion POP V 9206	How Can I Forget/Janet	30
64	London HLY 9868	I Lied/Alison	22
66	Liberty LIB 12040	Baby I Love You/You Won't Get Away	20
67	Liberty LIB 12048	Give Me Your Love/The Turning Point	20
67	Liberty LIB 12053	Everybody Needs Help/I'm Gonna Move To The City	20
68	Minit MLF 11008	Give Me Your Love/The Beauty Of A Girl In Love	15
69	Minit MLL/MLS 40010	SPREAD YOUR LOVE (LP)	60

JIMMY HOLIDAY & CLYDIE KING

(see also Clydie King)

67	Liberty LIB 12058	Ready, Willing And Able/We Got A Good Thing Goin'	30
67	Liberty LIB 12058	Ready, Willing And Able/We Got A Good Thing Goin' (DJ copy)	50
72	United Artists UP 35371	Ready, Willing And Able/JIMMY HOLIDAY: Give Me Your Love	10

JOHNNY HOLIDAY

59	London RE 1226	SENTIMENTAL HOLIDAY (EP)	10
59	London RE 1227	HOLIDAY FOR ROMANCE (EP)	10

HOLIDAYMAKERS

89	Woosh WOOSH 4	Cincinnati/Seventh Valley Girl (p/s)	10
89	Maker 00IT	Gay Cowboy (12", p/s)	8

HOLIDAYS

(see also Edwin Starr)

66	Polydor 56720	I'll Love You Forever/Makin' Up Time	125

HOLLAND

(see also Black Rose, Hammer)

84	Ebony EBON 17	EARLY WARNING (LP)	12

BRIAN HOLLAND

74	Invictus INV 2553	I'm So Glad/I'm So Glad (Version)	20

(Brian) HOLLAND & (Lamont) DOZIER

(see also Lamont Dozier, Brian Holland)

72	Invictus INV 525	Why Can't We Be Lovers/Don't Leave Me	8
73	Invictus INV 528	Don't Leave Me Starvin' For Your Love (Parts 1 & 2)	8

EDDIE HOLLAND

62	Fontana H 387	Jamie/Take A Chance On Me	400
63	Oriole CBA 1808	If It's Love (It's All Right)/It's Not Too Late	450

LYNN HOLLAND

(see also Holly)

64	Ember EMB S 198	And The Angels Sing/I Can't Read Your Writing (For My Tears) (in p/s)	12
64	Ember EMB S 198	And The Angels Sing/I Can't Read Your Writing (For My Tears)	6
65	Polydor BM 56035	Oh Darling How I Miss You/Before	5
67	Polydor 56166	One Man In My Life/Wand'rin Boy	20
67	Polydor 56187	Come And Love/May God Help You And Protect You	25
66	Polydor 56129	All The Love In The World/Loneliness	6
71	Pye 7N 45041	The Last Time/In A Railway Carriage	8
67	Polydor 236217	OH DARLING HOW I MISS YOU (LP)	25

MALCOLM HOLLAND

70	Fontana TF 1075	Dawning Of the Day/Windy	10

TONY HOLLAND

63	HMV POP 1135	Sidewalk/Time Goes By	50

MICHAEL HOLLIDAY

(see also Edna Savage)

56	Columbia SCM 5221	Sixteen Tons/The Rose Tattoo	22
56	Columbia SCM 5252	Nothin' To Do/Perfume, Candy And Flowers	20
56	Columbia SCM 5273	Hot Diggity (Dog Ziggity)/The Gal With The Yaller Shoes	20
56	Columbia DB 3813	The Runaway Train/Ten Thousand Miles	20
57	Columbia DB 3871	Yaller Yaller Gold/I Saw Esau	15
57	Columbia DB 3919	Love Is Strange/My House Is Your House	15
57	Columbia DB 3948	Four Walls/Wringle Wrangle	15
57	Columbia DB 3973	All Of You/It's The Good Things We Remember	10
57	Columbia DB 3992	Old Cape Cod/Love You Darlin'	10

MINT VALUE £

58	Columbia DB 4058	The Story Of My Life/Keep Your Heart	7
58	Columbia DB 4087	In Love/Rooney	5
58	Columbia DB 4121	Stairway Of Love/May I?	7
58	Columbia DB 4155	I'll Always Be In Love With You/I'll Be Lovin' You, Too	6
58	Columbia DB 4188	She Was Only Seventeen/The Gay Vagabond	6
58	Columbia DB 4216	My Heart Is An Open Book/Careless Hands	8
60	Columbia DB 4378	Starry Eyed/The Steady Game	6
60	Columbia DB 4437	Skylark/Dream Talk	7
60	Columbia DB 4475	Little Boy Lost/The One Finger Symphony	7
60	Columbia SEG 7986	FOUR FEATHER FALLS (EP, mono)	15
60	Columbia ESG 7793	FOUR FEATHER FALLS (EP, stereo)	20
62	Columbia SEG 8161	HAPPY HOLLIDAY (EP)	8
62	Columbia SEG 8186	MORE HAPPY HOLLIDAY (EP)	15
61	Columbia SEG 8242	MIKE SINGS COUNTRY AND WESTERN STYLE (EP)	10
64	Columbia SEG 8373	MEMORIES OF MIKE (EP)	10
58	Columbia 33S 1114	HI! (10" LP)	25
59	Columbia 33SX 1170	MIKE (LP)	18
60	Columbia 33SX 1262	HOLLIDAY MIXTURE (LP, also stereo SCX 3331)	15
61	Columbia 33SX 1354/SCX 3398	HAPPY HOLLIDAY (LP)	15
62	Columbia 33SX 1426	TO BING FROM MIKE (LP, also stereo SCX 3441)	15
64	Columbia 33SX 1586	THE BEST OF MICHAEL HOLLIDAY (LP)	12

SU(SAN) HOLLIDAY

(see also Susan Singer)

64	Columbia DB 7363	Dark Despair/The Other Side (demos list A-side as "[Street Of] Dark Despair")	15
64	Columbia DB 7403	Any Day Now/Don't Come Knocking At My Door	15
65	Columbia DB 7616	Sometimes/Long Haired Boy	12
65	Columbia DB 7709	Nevertheless (I'm In Love With You)/Moonglow	12
66	Columbia SX 6067	I WANNA SAY HELLO (LP, as Su Holliday)	75

TIM HOLLIER

(see also Amory Kane)

70	Fontana TF 1080	In This Room/Love Song	6
71	Philips 6006 130	Circle Is Small/In A Corner Of My Life/Time Stood Still	6
68	United Artists (S)ULP 1211	MESSAGE TO A HARLEQUIN (LP, laminated front sleeve, blue/silver labels)	60
70	Fontana 6309 003	TIM HOLLIER (LP, laminated sleve, black/silver labels)	200
71	Philips 6308 044	SKY SAIL (LP, laminated sleeve, black/silver labels)	30

HOLLIES

(see also Allan Clarke, Graham Nash, Terry Sylvester, Haydock's Rockhouse, Peter Sellers & Sophia Loren)

SINGLES

63	Parlophone R 5030	(Ain't That) Just Like Me/Hey, What's Wrong With Me	15
63	Parlophone R 5052	Searchin'/Whole World Over	12
63	Parlophone R 5077	Stay/Now's The Time	10
64	Parlophone R 5104	Just One Look/Keep Off That Friend Of Mine	7
64	Parlophone R 5137	Here I Go Again/Baby That's All	7
64	Parlophone R 5178	We're Through/Come On Back	6
65	Parlophone R 5232	Yes I Will/Nobody	6
65	Parlophone R 5287	I'm Alive/You Know He Did	6
65	Parlophone R 5322	Look Through Any Window/So Lonely	7
65	Parlophone R 5392	If I Needed Someone/I've Got A Way Of My Own	8
66	Parlophone R 5409	I Can't Let Go/Running Through The Night	6
66	Parlophone R 5469	Bus Stop/Don't Run And Hide	7
66	United Artists UP 1152	After The Fox (with Peter Sellers)/BURT BACHARACH: The Fox-Trot	35
66	Parlophone R 5508	Stop! Stop! Stop!/It's You	6
67	Parlophone R 5562	On A Carousel/All The World Is Love	6
67	Parlophone R 5602	Carrie Anne/Signs That Will Never Change	6
67	Parlophone R 5637	King Midas In Reverse/Everything Is Sunshine	10
68	Parlophone R 5680	Jennifer Eccles/Open Up Your Eyes	6
68	Parlophone R 5733	Listen To Me/Do The Best You Can	7
69	Parlophone R 5765	Sorry Suzanne/Not That Way At All	7
69	Parlophone R 5806	He Ain't Heavy, He's My Brother/'Cos You Like To Love Me	7
70	Parlophone R 5837	I Can't Tell The Bottom From The Top/Mad Professor Blyth	5
70	Parlophone R 5862	Gasoline Alley Bred/Dandelion Wine	5
71	Parlophone R 5905	Hey Willy/Row The Boat Together	5
72	Polydor 2058 199	The Baby/Oh Granny	7
72	Parlophone R 5939	Long Cool Woman (In A Black Dress)/Cable Car	10
72	Polydor 2058 289	Magic Woman Touch/Indian Girl	6
73	Polydor 2058 403	The Day That Curly Billy Shot Down Crazy Sam McGee/Born A Man	6
74	Polydor 2058 435	The Air That I Breathe/No More Riders	5
74	Polydor 2058 476	Son Of A Rotten Gambler/Layin' To The Music	6
74	Polydor 2058 533	I'm Down/Hello Lady Goodbye	6
75	Polydor 2058 595	Sandy (Fourth Of July, Asbury Park)/Second-Hand Hangups	6
75	EMI EMI 2353	Long Cool Woman In A Black Dress/Carrie Anne	5
76	Polydor 2058 694	Boulder To Birmingham/Crocodile Woman (She Bites)	6
76	Polydor 2058 719	Star/Love Is The Thing	8
76	Polydor 2058 779	Daddy Don't Mind/C'mon	8
76	Polydor 2058 799	Wiggle That Wotsit/Corrine	8
76	Polydor 2058 880	Hello To Romance/48 Hour Parole	8
77	Polydor 2058 906	Amnesty/Crossfire	8
78	EMI EMI 2813	Look Through Any Window/I'm Alive/Just One Look (p/s)	6
79	Polydor POSP 35	Something To Live For/Song Of The Sun	6
79	Polydor POSPX 35	Something To Live For/Song Of The Sun/The Air That I Breathe (12", p/s)	12
80	Polydor 2059 246	Soldier's Song/Draggin' My Heels	10
80	Polydor POSP 175	Heartbeat/Take Your Time	8
87	Columbia 12DB 9146	This Is It/You Gave Me Strength/You're All Woman (12", p/s)	10

MINT VALUE £

87	Columbia DB 9151	Reunion Of The Heart/Too Many Hearts Get Broken (p/s)	5
90	SRT 90LS 2407	Purple Rain/Naomi/Two Shadows (12", p/s, available only at gigs)	8

EPs

64	Parlophone GEP 8909	THE HOLLIES	40
64	Parlophone GEP 8911	JUST ONE LOOK	35
64	Parlophone GEP 8915	HERE I GO AGAIN	35
64	Parlophone GEP 8927	WE'RE THROUGH	35
65	Parlophone GEP 8934	IN THE HOLLIES STYLE	50
65	Parlophone GEP 8942	I'M ALIVE	35
66	Parlophone GEP 8951	I CAN'T LET GO	35

LPs

64	Parlophone PMC 1220	STAY WITH THE HOLLIES (mono)	70
64	Parlophone PCA 3054	STAY WITH THE HOLLIES (stereo, large 'stereo' on sleeve)	100
65	Parlophone PMC 1235	IN THE HOLLIES STYLE (mid-sized mono on front sleeve, "Sold in U.K..." text)	80
65	Parlophone PMC 1261	THE HOLLIES (small mono on front sleeve, "Sold in U.K..." text)	80
66	Parlophone PMC 7008	WOULD YOU BELIEVE? (mono, with "Sold in U.K..." text)	40
66	Parlophone PCS 7008	WOULD YOU BELIEVE? (stereo, "Sold in U.K..." text)	60
66	Parlophone PMC 7011	FOR CERTAIN BECAUSE (gatefold sleeve, mono, with "Sold in U.K..." text)	35
66	Parlophone PCS 7011	FOR CERTAIN BECAUSE (gatefold sleeve, stereo, with "Sold in U.K..." text)	45
67	Parlophone PMC 7022	EVOLUTION (mono, with "Sold in U.K..." text)	50
67	Parlophone PCS 7022	EVOLUTION (stereo, with "Sold in U.K..." text)	60
67	Parlophone PMC 7039	BUTTERFLY (mono, with "Sold in U.K..." text)	40
67	Parlophone PCS 7039	BUTTERFLY (stereo, with "sold in U.K..." text)	70
67	EMI Regal SREG 2024	THE HOLLIES (export compilation)	20
67	World Records ST 979	THE VINTAGE HOLLIES (stereo reissue of "In The Hollies Style")	35
68	World Records ST 1035	STAY WITH THE HOLLIES (record club reissue)	25
68	Parlophone PMC/PCS 7057	THE HOLLIES' GREATEST	15
69	Parlophone PMC 7078	THE HOLLIES SING DYLAN (mono, with "Solid in U.K..." text)	30
69	Parlophone PCS 7078	THE HOLLIES SING DYLAN (stereo, with "Sold in U.K..." text)	25
69	Parlophone PCS 7092	HOLLIES SING HOLLIES (gatefold sleeve)	18

(The above Parlophone LPs were originally issued with yellow/black labels; 1970s pressings with silver/black labels are worth £8)

70	Parlophone PCS 7116	CONFESSIONS OF THE MIND (with colour insert)	18
71	Parlophone PAS 10005	DISTANT LIGHT (gatefold sleeve)	15
71	Regal Starline SRS 5013	STOP! STOP! STOP! (reissue of "For Certain Because")	12
72	Parlophone PCS 7148	THE HOLLIES' GREATEST HITS VOL. 2	12
72	Polydor 2383 144	ROMANY (gatefold sleeve)	12
74	Polydor 2383 262	HOLLIES (with lyric insert)	12
75	Polydor 2442 128	ANOTHER NIGHT (gatefold sleeve)	12
76	Polydor 2442 141	WRITE ON (with lyric inner)	12
76	Polydor 2383 421	RUSSIAN ROULETTE (with lyric inner)	12
78	Polydor 2383 474	A CRAZY STEAL (with lyric inner)	12
78	Parlophone PMC 7174	THE BEST OF THE HOLLIES' EPs	12
78	Parlophone PMC 7176	THE OTHER SIDE OF THE HOLLIES	15
79	Polydor 2442 160	FIVE THREE ONE - DOUBLE SEVEN O FOUR (with lyric insert)	12
79	St. Michael 2102/0101	UP FRONT (sold through Marks & Spencer in conjunction with Polydor)	18

HOLLINGWORTH

71	Columbia DB 8808	Jump On My Wagon/This Town	18

BRENDA HOLLOWAY

64	Stateside SS 307	Every Little Bit Hurts/Land Of A Thousand Boys	50
64	Stateside SS 307	Every Little Bit Hurts/Land Of A Thousand Boys (DJ Copy)	130
65	Tamla Motown TMG 508	When I'm Gone/I've Been Good To You	90
65	Tamla Motown TMG 508	When I'm Gone/I've Been Good To You (DJ copy)	200
65	Tamla Motown TMG 519	Operator/I'll Be Available	75
65	Tamla Motown TMG 519	Operator/I'll Be Available (DJ copy)	150
66	Tamla Motown TMG 556	Together Till The End Of Time/Sad Song	100
66	Tamla Motown TMG 556	Together Till The End Of Time/Sad Song (DJ copy)	150
66	Tamla Motown TMG 581	Hurt A Little Everyday/Where Were You (demos credit Brenda Holiday)	80
66	Tamla Motown TMG 581	Hurt A Little Everyday/Where Were You (demos credit Brenda Holiday) (DJ copy)	100
67	Tamla Motown TMG 608	Just Look What You've Done/Starting The Hurt All Over Again	50
67	Tamla Motown TMG 608	Just Look What You've Done/Starting The Hurt All Over Again (DJ copy)	100
67	Tamla Motown TMG 622	You've Made Me So Very Happy/I've Got To Find It	40
69	Tamla Motown TMG 700	Just Look What You've Done/You've Made Me So Very Happy	18
68	T. Motown (S)TML 11083	THE ARTISTRY OF BRENDA HOLLOWAY (LP, mono/stereo)	100

LOLEATTA HOLLOWAY

71	United Artists UP 35273	Bring It On Up/Rainbow '71'	8
96	Kent 6T 11	This Mans Arms/JOHN EDWARDS: Ain't That Good Enough	25

PATRICE HOLLOWAY

66	Capitol CL 15484	Love And Desire/Ecstasy	150
66	Capitol CL 15484	Love And Desire/Ecstasy (DJ Copy)	250

STANLEY HOLLOWAY

(see also Joyce Grenfell & Stanley Holloway, Charles Penrose)

59	Decca F 11140	Dark Girl Dressed In Blue/Growing Old	6
60	Columbia SEG 8034	ADVENTURES WITH ALBERT (EP)	8
56	Columbia 33S 1093	FAMOUS ADVENTURES WITH OLD SAM & THE RAMSBOTTOMS (10" LP)	15
58	Philips BBL 7237	'ERE'S 'OLLOWAY (LP)	12
60	Pye NPL 18056	JOIN IN THE CHORUS (LP)	12
65	Columbia SCX 3528	STANLEY, I PRESUME (LP)	12
75	ARGO ZDA 170	LIFE IN THE OLD DOG YET (LP)	12

HOLLOW GROUND

80	Guardian GR/HG C57	FLYING HIGH EP (Flying High/Warlord/ Rock On/Don't Chase The Dragon) (in p/s)	150
80	Guardian GR/HG C57	FLYING HIGH EP (Flying High/Warlord/Rock On/Don't Chase The Dragon)	30

MINT VALUE £

HOLLY

(see also Lynn Holland)

65	Fontana TF 980	On With The Game/Paradise Lost	8

HOLLY

(see also Frankie Goes To Hollywood, Big In Japan)

79	Eric's ERIC'S 003	Yankee Rose/Treasure Island/Desperate Dan (p/s)	25
79	Eric's ERIC'S 007	Hobo Joe/Stars Of The Bars (p/s)	20

BUDDY HOLLY

(see also Crickets, Fireballs)

78s

56	Brunswick 05581	Blue Days - Black Nights/Love Me	350
57	Vogue Coral Q 72293	Peggy Sue/Everyday	150
58	Coral Q 72293	Peggy Sue/Everyday	15
58	Coral Q 72288	Listen To Me/I'm Gonna Love You Too	25
58	Coral Q 72325	Rave On/Take Your Time	30
58	Coral Q 72333	Early In The Morning/Now We're One	35
58	Coral Q 72346	Heartbeat/Well ... All Right	50
59	Coral Q 72360	It Doesn't Matter Anymore/Raining In My Heart	40
59	Brunswick 05800	Rock Around With Ollie Vee/Midnight Shift	200
59	Coral Q 72376	Peggy Sue Got Married/Crying, Waiting, Hoping	200
60	Coral Q 72392	Heartbeat/Everyday	400

SINGLES

56	Brunswick 05581	Blue Days - Black Nights/Love Me	800
57	Vogue Coral Q 72293	Peggy Sue/Everyday	50
58	Coral Q 72293	Peggy Sue/Everyday	20
58	Coral Q 72288	Listen To Me/I'm Gonna Love You Too	25
58	Coral Q 72325	Rave On/Take Your Time	25
58	Coral Q 72333	Early In The Morning/Now We're One	25
58	Coral Q 72346	Heartbeat/Well ... All Right	25
59	Coral Q 72360	It Doesn't Matter Anymore/Raining In My Heart	10
59	Brunswick 05800	Rock Around With Ollie Vee/Midnight Shift	45
59	Coral Q 72376	Peggy Sue Got Married/Crying, Waiting, Hoping	25

(The above 45s were originally issued with triangular centres; reissues with round centres are worth half to two-thirds these values)

60	Coral Q 72392	Heartbeat/Everyday	20
60	Coral Q 72397	True Love Ways/Moondreams	15
60	Coral Q 72411	Learning The Game/That Makes It Tough	12
61	Coral Q 72419	What To Do/That's What They Say	15
61	Coral Q 72432	Baby I Don't Care/Valley Of Tears	10
61	Coral Q 72445	Look At Me/Mailman, Bring Me No More Blues	15
62	Coral Q 72449	Listen To Me/Words Of Love	15
62	Coral Q 72455	Reminiscing/Wait Till The Sun Shines, Nellie	10
63	Coral Q 72459	Brown-Eyed Handsome Man/Slippin' And Slidin'	10
63	Coral Q 72463	Bo Diddley/It's Not My Fault	10
63	Coral Q 72466	Wishing/Because I Love You	10
63	Coral Q 72469	What To Do/Umm Oh Yeah	15
64	Coral Q 72472	You've Got Love/An Empty Cup (as Buddy Holly & The Crickets)	25
64	Coral Q 72475	Love's Made A Fool Of You/You're The One	20
66	Coral Q 72483	Maybe Baby/That's My Desire	40
68	Decca AD 1009	Rave On/Peggy Sue (p/s, export reissue)	75
68	MCA MU 1012	Peggy Sue/Rave On (reissue)	5
69	MCA MU 1059	Love Is Strange/You're The One	10
69	MCA MU 1081	It Doesn't Matter Anymore/Maybe Baby (reissue)	5
70	MCA MU 1116	Rave On/Umm Oh Yeah (Dearest)	5
73	MCA MMU 1198	That'll Be The Day/Well All Right/Every Day	5
74	MCA MCA 119	It Doesn't Matter Anymore/True Love Ways/Brown Eyed Handsome Man	5
75	MCA MCA 207	Oh Boy!/Every Day (as Buddy Holly & Crickets)	5
76	MCA MCA 252	True Love Ways/It Doesn't Matter Anymore/Raining In My Heart/Moondreams (p/s)	5
76	MCA MCA 253	Peggy Sue/Rave On/Rock Around With Ollie Vee/Midnight Shift (p/s)	5
76	MCA MCA 254	Maybe Baby/Think It Over/That'll Be The Day/It's So Easy (p/s, as Buddy Holly & Crickets)	5
78	MCA MCA 344	Wishing/Love's Made A Fool Of You (p/s)	5
83	MCA HR 001	That'll Be The Day/True Love Ways (as Buddy Holly & Crickets) (with/without The History Of Rock issue 1; "Made in France" on label)	7
83	MCA HR 001	That'll Be The Day/True Love Ways (as Buddy Holly & Crickets) (with/without The History Of Rock issue 1; "Made In Gt. Britain" on label)	5
84	MCA BHB 1	THAT'LL BE THE DAY (10 x 7" box set, comprising BH1-10 in p/s)	40
89	MCA MCAV 1368	Oh Boy!/Well ... All Right/Mailman Bring Me No More Blues/Everyday (10", p/s)	8

EPs

58	Coral FEP 2002	LISTEN TO ME (brown cover, sleeve shows Holly without glasses; disc credits title as "Buddy Holly")	400
58	Coral FEP 2002	LISTEN TO ME (re-pressing, various shades of green/brown p/s, shows Holly with glasses; disc credits title as "Buddy Holly")	40
58	Coral FEP 2005	RAVE ON (various shades of green/brown p/s)	40
59	Coral FEP 2014	IT'S SO EASY	40
59	Coral FEP 2015	HEARTBEAT	40
59	Coral FEP 2032	BUDDY HOLLY	40
59	Brunswick OE 9456	BUDDY HOLLY NO. 1	75
59	Brunswick OE 9457	BUDDY HOLLY NO. 2	75

(The above EPs were originally issued with triangular centres; later pressings with round-centres are worth between half and two thirds these values)

60	Coral FEP 2044	THE LATE GREAT BUDDY HOLLY (tri centre)	60
60	Coral FEP 2044	THE LATE GREAT BUDDY HOLLY (round centre)	25
64	Coral FEP 2065	BUDDY - BY REQUEST	45
64	Coral FEP 2066	THAT TEX-MEX SOUND	60
64	Coral FEP 2067	WISHING	55

			MINT VALUE £
64	Coral FEP 2068	SHOWCASE VOLUME 1	65
64	Coral FEP 2069	SHOWCASE VOLUME 2	65
65	Coral FEP 2070	BUDDY HOLLY SINGS	70

LPs

58	Vogue Coral LVA 9085	BUDDY HOLLY (Vogue-Coral labels & Coral sleeve)	120
58	Coral LVA 9085	BUDDY HOLLY	50
59	Coral LVA 9105	THE BUDDY HOLLY STORY ('High Fidelity Coral' logo on sleeve)	30
60s	Coral LVA 9105	THE BUDDY HOLLY STORY (reissue, different 'roll-neck sweater' sleeve with small 'Coral' logo)	50
60	Coral LVA 9127	THE BUDDY HOLLY STORY VOL. II	25
61	Ace Of Hearts AH 3	THAT'LL BE THE DAY	20
63	Coral LVA 9212	REMINISCING	30
64	Coral LVA 9222	SHOWCASE	30
65	Coral LVA 9227	HOLLY IN THE HILLS (with Bob Montgomery, withdrawn mispressing, sleeve & label list "Wishing", plays "Reminiscing"; matrix no's end with 1B both sides)	50
65	Coral LVA 9227	HOLLY IN THE HILLS (corrected edition, with Bob Montgomery, plays "Wishing", matrix numbers end with 1B on one side & 2B on other)	70
68	MCA MUP 320	WISHING (mono only, reissue of "Holly In The Hills")	20
69	MCA MUPS 371	GIANT	20

(The above MCA albums were originally issued with yellow labels; later variations exist with various twin-toned designs.)

75	World Records SM 301/5	THE BUDDY HOLLY STORY (5-LP box set)	20
79	MCA Coral CDMSP 807	THE COMPLETE BUDDY HOLLY (6-LP box set with sepia-tinted book)	35
80	Marks & Spencer IMP 114	HEARTBEAT	30
83	MCA MCM 1002	FOR THE FIRST TIME ANYWHERE	15
86	Rollercoaster ROLL 2013	SOMETHING SPECIAL FROM BUDDY HOLLY	15

STEVIE HOLLY

66	Planet PLF 107	A Strange World/Little Man	30

HOLLY & JOEY

(see also Ramones, Deborah Harry)

82	Virgin VS 478	I Got You Babe/HOLLY & THE ITALIANS: One More Dance (p/s)	12

HOLLY & THE ITALIANS

80	Oval OVAL 1016	Tell That Girl To Shut UP/Chapel Of Love (p/s)	5
81	Virgin VS 411	I Wanna Go Home/Fanzine (p/s)	15
81	Virgin VS 429	Just For Tonight/Baby Gets It All (p/s)	7
81	Virgin V 2186	THE RIGHT TO BE ITALIAN (LP, with lyric insert)	15

HOLLYRIDGE STRINGS

61	Capitol CL 15233	The Guns Of Navarone/Moon River	6
61	Capitol CL 15237	The Comancheros/A Thunder Of Drums	6

HOLLYWOOD ARGYLES

(see also Kim Fowley, Skip & Flip, Gary Paxton)

60	London HLU 9146	Alley Oop/Sho' Know A Lot About Love	15
60	London HLU 9146	Alley Oop/Sho' Know A Lot About Love (78)	12
60	Top Rank JAR 530	Gun Totin' Critter Called Jack/GARY PAXTON: Bug-Eye	20

HOLLYWOOD BRATS

80	Cherry Red A RED 6	HOLLYWOOD BRATS (LP)	12

HOLLYWOOD FLAMES

57	London HL 7030	Buzz Buzz Buzz/Crazy (export issue)	50
58	London HL 8545	Buzz Buzz Buzz/Crazy	75
58	London HL 8545	Buzz Buzz Buzz/Crazy (78)	20
59	London HLW 8955	Much Too Much/In The Dark	75
59	London HLW 8955	Much Too Much/In The Dark (78)	50
60	London HLE 9071	If I Thought You Needed Me/Every Day Every Way	50

HOLLYWOOD FREEWAY

(see also Tony Rivers)

72	Deram DM 359	I've Been Moved/Cool Calamares	6
73	Pye 7N 45273	You're The Song (That I Can't Stop Singing)/ This Feeling Called Love	8

HOLLYWOOD HURRICANES

64	Prima PR 1009	Beavershot/Have Love Will Travel	6

KENNY HOLLYWOOD

62	Decca F 11546	Magic Star/The Wonderful Story Of Love	25

HOLLYWOOD KILLERS

78	Rollerball	Goodbye Suicide/Tramp	50

HOLLYWOOD VINES

61	Capitol CL 15191	When Johnny Comes Slidin' Home/Cruisin'	25

MIKE HOLM

70	Major Minor MM 659	Mendocino/Cutey Girl	6

PETER HOLM

67	Major Minor MM504	This Is Not The Way/You Will Be Mine	20

BILL HOLMAN OCTET

54	Capitol KC 65000	Cousin Jack/Plain Folks	8

EDDIE HOLMAN

65	Cameo Parkway P 960	This Can't Be True/A Free Country	50
69	Action ACT 4547	I Love You/I Surrender	70
70	Stateside SS 2160	(Hey There) Lonely Girl/It's All In The Game	10
70	Stateside SS 2170	Since I Don't Have You/Don't Stop Now	8
77	Salsoul SZ 2026	This Will Be A Night To Remember/Time Will Tell	6

MINT VALUE £

CHRISTINE HOLMES
(see also Family Dogg)

64	Mercury MF 813	This Is My Prayer/My Dream	10
64	Mercury MF 819	Play Me A Sad Song (Mr DJ)/Doesn't He Know	10
64	Mercury MF 831	Goodbye Boys Goodbye/Is It Love	10
65	Mercury MF 851	Many Things From Your Window/You'd Better Believe It	7
65	Mercury MF 887	Goin' Where The Lovin' Is/Where There's Smoke There's Fire	7

DAVID HOLMES
(see also Mogwai)

97	Go Beat GOB 6	Don't Die Just Yet (Mogwai Mix)/Holiday Girl (Arab Strap Mix) (p/s, 500 only)	12
02	13 Amp APM 001LP	COME GET IT I GOT IT (2-LP)	30

ELDRIDGE HOLMES

68	Pama PM 746	Beverley/Wait For Me Baby	18

IVAN HOLMES

67	Columbia DB 8119	The Light, The Love And The Life/Cocaine	7

JAKE HOLMES

69	Polydor 56547	How Are You (Parts 1 & 2)	5
70	Ember EMB S 269	Saturday Night/Diner Song	20
70	Polydor 2066 040	So Close/Django And Friend	5
70	Polydor 583 579	JAKE HOLMES (LP)	25
70	Polydor 2425 036	SO CLOSE SO VERY FAR TO GO (LP)	22
72	CBS 64905	HOW MUCH TIME (LP)	20

JOE HOLMES & LEN GRAHAM

79	Topic 12TS 401	AFTER DAWNING (LP)	12

LEROY HOLMES & ORCHESTRA

59	MGM 1044	Sweet Leicani/Alice Blue Gown	6
59	MGM 1058	Theme From A Summer Place/Indiscreet	6
68	United Artists UP 2222	The Good, The Bad And The Ugly/Live For Life	5

RICHARD 'GROOVES' HOLMES

66	CBS 202240	Misty/Groove's Groove	7
67	Transatlantic PR 7435	SOUL MESSAGE (LP)	25
68	Transatlantic PR 7493	RICHARD 'GROOVES' HOLMES (LP)	18

HOLOCAUST

80	Phoenix PSP 1	Heavy Metal Mania/Only As Young As You Feel (p/s)	20
80	Phoenix 12 PSP 1	Heavy Metal Mania/Love's Power/Only As Young As You Feel (12", p/s)	30
80	Phoenix 12 PSP 2	Smokin' Valves/Friend Or Foe (p/s)	10
80	Phoenix 12 PSP 2	Smokin' Valves/Friend Or Foe/Out My Book (12", p/s)	30
81	Phoenix PSP 3P	HOLOCAUST LIVE (EP)	25
82	Phoenix 12 PSP 4	Comin' Through/Don't Wanna Be A Loser/Good Thing Going (12", p/s)	30
81	Phoenix PSLP 1	THE NIGHTCOMERS (LP)	40
83	Phoenix PSPLP 4	LIVE (HOT CURRY AND WINE) (LP)	25
84	Phoenix PSPLP 5	NO MAN'S LAND (LP)	20

HOLOGRAM

82	Phoenix PSPLP 2	STEAL THE STARS (LP)	12

HOLOSADE

88	Powerstation AMP 16	HELL HOUSE (LP)	12

ERROL HOLT

77	Lior ROAR 111	Come Rock Me/Congo Dread (12")	20
78	Star Time EHLF 427	I Am Not A King (with PRINCE FAR I)/Version (12")	40
79	Hit Run HIT DD25	Sweet Reggae Music/PRINCE FAR I: Hairdressing Salon	90
70s	Dread DDLP 102	VISION OF AFRICA (LP)	30

JOHN HOLT
(see also Jay & Joya, Little John, Neville Hinds, Jeff Barnes, Danny Simpson, Hugh Roy, U Roy Junior, Don Drummond, Interns)

63	Island WI 041	I Cried A Tear/I'll Stay	30
68	Trojan TR 643	Tonight/Oh How It Hurts (B-side actually by Paragons)	25
69	Trojan TR 661	Ali Baba/I'm Your Man	35
69	Trojan TR 674	What You Gonna Do Now/Have You Ever Been To Heaven	12
69	Trojan TR 694	Have Sympathy/HARRY J ALLSTARS: Spyrone	15
69	Trojan TR 7702	Wooden Heart/All My Life	10
70	Duke Reid DR 2506	Come Out Of My Bed/WINSTON WRIGHT: Hide And Seek	12
70	Duke DU 73	Stealing, Stealing/WINSTON WRIGHT: Stealing, Stealing (Volume 2)	20
70	Duke DU 77	The Working Kind/Open Jaw	15
70	Jackpot JP 735	A Little Tear/JEFF BARNS: Get In The Groove	12
70	Bamboo BAM 44	A Love I Can Feel/JOHNNY LAST: Long Liver Man (B-side act. by Hugh Black)	12
70	Bamboo BAM 55	A Stranger In Love/WAILERS: Jailhouse (Good Rudy)	70
70	Bamboo BAM 62	Holly Holy/Do You Love Me?	12
70	Banana BA 314	Why Can't I Touch You/SOUND DIMENSION: Touching Version	10
70	Smash SMA 2303	My Heart Is Gone/PHIL PRATT ALL STARS: Version	6
70	Smash SMA 2305	I Had A Talk With My Woman/MAXINE: Life Is Not The Same Anymore	6
70	Supreme SUP 212	Share My Rest/AL BROWN: Allways	40
70	Unity UN 548	Sometimes/BUNNY LEE ALL STARS: Lash-La-Rue	30
70	Unity UN 549	Sea Cruise/LEE'S ALL STARS: Niney's Hop	8
70	Unity UN 552	Walking Along/LEE'S ALL STARS: Warfare	15
70	Unity UN 556	Give Her All The Love/BUSTY BROWN: Nobody But You	6
70	Success RE 903	Fat Girl, Sexy Girl/Man And Woman	20
71	Banana BA 340	O.K. Fred/Fancy Make-Up	12
71	Banana BA 345	Build Our Dreams/LEROY SIBBLES: Love In Our Nation	15
71	Treasure Isle TI 7061	Let's Build Our Dreams/TOMMY McCOOK & SUPERSONICS: Testify Version	18
71	Treasure Isle TI 7065	Sister Big Stuff/TOMMY McCOOK & SUPERSONICS: Black River	20
71	Treasure Isle TI 7066	Paragons Medley/TOMMY McCOOK & SUPERSONICS: Medley Version	18

			MINT VALUE £
71	Ashanti ASH 401	Again/MUDIES ALL STARS: Ten Steps To Soul Version	7
71	Camel CA 78	Linger A While/Version	7
71	Escort ERT 847	Knock On Your Door/URIEL ALDRIDGE: Set Me Free	6
71	Jackpot JP 772	Stick By Me/It's A Pleasure	6
71	Jackpot JP 774	It's A Jam In The Streets/A Man Needs A Woman	6
71	Jackpot JP 784	Anymore/Lost Love	6
71	Moodisc MU 3513	It May Sound Silly/MUDIE ALL STARS: Instrumental	6
71	Moodisc HM 105	It May Sound Silly/MUDIE ALL STARS: Instrumental (reissue)	10
71	Punch PH 60	Strange Things/WINSTON WRIGHT: Want Money (B-side act. G.G. All Stars)	12
71	Smash SMA 2324	Mother And Father Love/AGGROVATORS: Mother Love Version	6
72	Blue Beat BB 424	O.K. Fred/BIG YOUTH: Chi Chi Run	20
72	Prince Buster PB 40	Close To Me/Version	7
72	Prince Buster PB 41	Get Ready/Version	7
72	Prince Buster PB 42	Rain From The Skies/Version	7
72	Prince Buster PB 43	The First Time/Version	7
72	Prince Buster PB 49	For Your Love/Version	7
72	G.G. GG 4529	Keep It Up/A Love Like Yours	6
72	Fab FAB 188	A Little Happiness/DELROY WILSON: Diamond Rings	10
72	Jackpot JP 790	Don't You Know/Riding For A Fall	6
72	Jackpot JP 807	Looking Back/I'll Be There	6
72	Pama PM 845	I'll Always Love You/SLIM SMITH: 3 x 7 Rock And Roll	7
72	Pama PM 852	Pledging My Love/I Will Know What To Do	7
73	Fab FAB 224	Let's Go Dancing/Version	7
73	Fab FAB 244	Let's Go Dancing/Version (reissue)	7
73	Attack ATT 8045	Time And The River/Version	5
73	Smash SMA 2329	Don't Break Your Promise/I've Been Admiring You	8
73	Ackee ACK 513	Ecstacy/Version	6
83	Greensleeves GRED 120	Police In Helicopter/Youth Pon The Corner (12")	20
70	Bamboo BDLP 210	A LOVE I CAN FEEL (LP)	60
70s	Melodisc MLP 12170	GREATEST HITS (LP)	40
70s	Melodisc MLP 12180	OK FRED (LP)	45
70s	Melodisc MLP 12191	JOHN HOLT & FRIENDS (LP)	45
71	Trojan TRL(S) 37	STILL IN CHAINS (LP)	15
72	Trojan TRL(S) 43	HOLT (LP)	12
72	Trojan TBL 184	PLEDGING MY LOVE (LP)	12
73	Trojan TRLS 55	THE FURTHER YOU LOOK (LP)	12
74	Attack ATLP 1010	A LOVE I CAN FEEL (LP)	15

GARY HOLTON

(see also Heavy Metal Kids, Kids, Slade)

84	Magnet GARY 2	Catch A Falling Star/Angel (star-shaped picture disc)	8

ROOSEVELT HOLTS

68	Blue Horizon 7-63201	PRESENTING THE COUNTRY BLUES (LP)	85

HOLY MACKEREL

(see also Jason Crest, High Broom)

72	CBS 8447	Rock-A-Bye/New Black Shoes	6
72	CBS 65297	HOLY MACKEREL (LP)	20
93	Tenth Planet TP 005	CLOSER TO HEAVEN (LP, numbered, 500 only)	15

HOLY MODAL ROUNDERS

68	Elektra EKL 4026	THE MORAY EELS EAT THE HOLY MODALS (LP, mono)	35
68	Elektra EKS 74026	THE MORAY EELS EAT THE HOLY MODALS (LP, stereo)	35
70	Transatlantic TRA 7451	HOLY MODAL ROUNDERS (LP)	35
70	Transatlantic TRA	HOLY MODAL ROUNDERS 2 (LP)	30

HOM BRU

82	Celtic Music CM 009	OBADEEA: MUSIC FROM SHETLAND AND BEYOND (LP)	12

HOMBRES

67	Verve VS 1510	Let It Out (Let It All Hang Out)/Go Girl Go	15

HOME

(see also Groundhogs, AC/DC, Wlshbone Ash, Blue Rondos)

72	CBS 7809	Fancy Lady, Hollywood Child/Shady Lady	6
72	(No Cat No)	You'll Get A Helping Hand At Barclays/Dreamer (p/s)	15
71	CBS 64365	PAUSE FOR A HOARSE HORSE (LP, gatefold sleeve)	35
72	CBS 64752	HOME (LP)	20
73	CBS 65550	THE ALCHEMIST (LP)	25

HOMER & JETHRO

54	HMV 7M 211	Swappin' Partners/Crazy Mix-Up Song	12
54	Parlophone CMSP 2	Don't Let Your Sweet Love Die/ When It's Long Handle Time In Tennessee (export issue)	10
59	RCA RCA 1148	Waterloo/The Battle Of Kookamonga	6
59	Parlophone GEP 8791	WANTED FOR MURDER OF THE STANDARDS (EP)	10
70	RCA LSA 3172	COUNTRY COMEDY (LP)	12

HOME SERVICE

84	Coda NAT 001	THE MYSTERIES (LP)	15

HOMESICK JAMES

64	Sue WI 319	Crossroads/My Baby's Sweet	60
65	Sue WI 330	Set A Date/Can't Afford To Do It	40

HOMESICK JAMES/SNOOKY PRYOR

74	Caroline C 1502	HOMESICK JAMES AND SNOOKY PRYOR (LP)	18

HOMESTEAD

68	Road R3946	She/Will You Leave	15

MINT VALUE £

HOMOSEXUALS

(see also George Harrassment & Homosexuals, Ice La Bas, Amos & Sara, Nancy Sesay & Melodaires, L-Voag, Sir Alick & Phraser)

78	L'Orelei PF 151	Hearts In Exile/South South Africans (p/s, with insert)	12
79	Black Noise F12 No. 2	Divorce Proceedings/Mecho Madness (12", plain sleeve with sticker)	10
81	Black Noise BN 1	BIGGER THAN THE NUMBER YET MISSING THE DOT (EP, clear vinyl, fold-around hand-painted sleeve)	8
84	Recommended RR 18	THE HOMOSEXUALS RECORD (LP, with inserts)	20

MINAKO HONDA

87	Columbia DB 9153	Golden Days (English Version)/Crazy Nights (English Version) (p/s, features Brian May)	35

HONDELLS

64	Mercury MF 834	Little Honda/Hot Rod High	25
65	Mercury MF 925	Younger Girl/All American Girl	25
66	Mercury MF 967	Cheryl's Goin' Home/Show Me Girl	25

HONEST MEN

69	Tamla Motown TMG 706	Cherie/Baby	50
69	Tamla Motown TMG 706	Cherie/Baby (DJ Copy)	50

HONEYBOY

71	Trojan TR 7835	Jamaica/ITALS: Sea Wave	7
72	Banana BA 375	Homeward Bound/Peace In The Land	70
75	B & C BC 002	Darlin' Coming Home/SIR COLLINS: We A Come Dread	25
74	Cactus CTLP 101	IMPOSSIBLE LOVE (LP)	25

HONEYBUS

(see also Pete Dello, Colin Hare, Lace, Magic Valley, Red Herring)

67	Deram DM 131	Delighted To See You/The Breaking Up Scene	12
67	Deram DM 152	Do I Figure In Your Life?/Throw My Love Away	12
68	Deram DM 182	I Can't Let Maggie Go/Tender Are The Ashes	5
68	Deram DM 207	Girl Of Independent Means/How Long	12
69	Deram DM 254	She Sold Blackpool Rock/Would You Believe	25
70	Deram DM 289	Story/The Right To Choose	7
72	Bell BLL 1205	She Is The Female To My Soul/For Where Have You Been	6
73	Warner Bros K 16250	For You/Little Lovely One	8
76	Decca F 13631	I Can't Let Maggie Go/Julie In My Heart	5
70	Deram DML/SML 1056	STORY (LP)	120
73	Warner Bros K 46248	RECITAL (LP, withdrawn, test pressings only)	300
79	See For Miles SEE 264	AT THEIR BEST (LP)	15

HONEYCOMBS

(see also Lemmings, Dennis D'Ell, Martin Murray)

64	Pye 7N 15664	Have I The Right/Please Don't Pretend Again	5
64	Pye 7N 15705	Is It Because/I'll Cry Tomorrow	8
64	Pye 7N 15736	Eyes/If You've Got To Pick A Baby	12
65	Pye 7N 15781	Don't Love You No More/I'll See You Tomorrow (withdrawn, promo only)	110
65	Pye 7N 15827	Something Better Beginning/I'll See You Tomorrow	10
65	Pye 7N 15890	That's The Way/Can't Get Through To You	6
65	Pye 7N 15979	This Year, Next Year/Not Sleeping Too Well Lately	10
66	Pye 7N 17089	Who Is Sylvia?/How Will I Know	15
66	Pye 7N 17138	It's So Hard/I Fell In Love	15
66	Pye 7N 17173	That Loving Feeling/Should A Man Cry	18
69	Pye 7N 17741	Have I The Right/Please Don't Pretend Again (stereo reissue)	6
65	Pye NEP 24230	THAT'S THE WAY (EP)	45
64	Pye NPL 18097	THE HONEYCOMBS (LP)	60
65	Pye NPL 18132	ALL SYSTEMS GO! (LP)	80
66	Golden Guinea GGL 0350	THE HONEYCOMBS (LP, reissue in different sleeve)	15

HONEYCONE

70	Hot Wax HWX 103	While You're Out Looking For Sugar/The Feeling's Gone	8
71	Hot Wax HWX 105	Girls It Ain't Easy/Take Me With You	6
71	Hot Wax HWX 107	Want Ads/We Belong Together	10
72	Hot Wax HWX 111	One Monkey Don't Stop No Show/Stick Up	6
72	Hot Wax HWX 112	The Day I Found Myself/When Will It End	6
72	Hot Wax HWX 116	Sittin' On A Time Bomb/It's Better To Have Loved And Lost	10
71	Hot Wax SHW 5002	HONEYCONE (LP)	15
71	Hot Wax SHW 5004	SWEET REPLIES (LP)	15
72	Hot Wax SHW 5005	SOULFUL TAPESTRY (LP)	15
73	Hot Wax SHW 5010	LOVE, PEACE AND SOUL (LP)	18

HONEYCRACK

(see also Jellys, Wildhearts)

95	PPP1	King Of Misery/5 Minutes (numbered p/s, 1500 only sold at gigs)	5
95	PPPCD1	King Of Misery/5 Minutes (numbered card p/s, 1500 only sold at gigs)	5
96	Epic 484230 0	PROZAIC (LP, with inner sleeve, white vinyl, 2000 only)	12

HONEYDEW

70	Argo AFW 101	Part Of This Game/To Make You Mine	20
70	Argo	HONEYDEW (LP)	120

HONEYDRIPPERS

(see also Robert Plant)

84	Es Paranza SAM 220	Sea Of Love/Rickin' At Midnight (7" radio promo)	10
84	Es Paranza 790 220-1	THE HONEYDRIPPERS VOL. ONE (10" LP)	8

HONEYEND

72	Spark SRL 1072	Heartbreaker/Beautiful Downtown	20

MINT VALUE £

HONEYS
(see also American Spring, Beach Boys)

63	Capitol CL 15299	Surfin' Down The Swanee River/Shoot The Curl	60

HONEYTONES

58	London HLX 8671	Don't Look Now, But.../I Know, I Know	60
58	London HLX 8671	Don't Look Now, But.../I Know, I Know (78)	35

HONEYTREE

70s	Myrrh MYR 1039	EVERGREEN (LP)	20

HONG GANG
(see also Bob Andy)

72	Sioux SI 004	Reggae Mento/MONTEGO MELON: Swan Lake	5
73	Sioux SI 025	Smoking Wild/ROOSEVELT SINGERS: Heavy Reggae	5

HOOD

92	Fluff HONEY 4	Sirens/Fault/Your Sixth Sense (p/s, 500 only)	12
93	Fluff HONEY 6	I Didn't Think You Were Going To Hit Me In The Face/In The Trap Of Doing/ Choosing A Grimace (wraparound p/s, 500 only)	1
94	Hedonist Prods. 002 F	57 White Bread: My Last August/Experimental Film-Making (flexidisc, p/s, 1000 only)	5
95	Orgasm ORGASM 08	A Harbour Of Thoughts/Disappointed/Uneven Conversation Should Point To Cause/Forced By The Reasoning Hand/John Clyde-Evans/Silo Crash (p/s)	7
95	555 Recordings 555 01	LEE FAUST'S MILLION PIECE ORCHESTRA: Biochemistry Revision Can Wait/ England's Fine Fields/Rocck? I Can't Even Spell The Word/ Stricken Office Worker (EP, 1,000 copies only)	8
96	Earworm WORM 1	SECRETS NOW KNOWN TO OTHERS: Forhead/Crow Blown West/Beware! Falling Ox/I'm Turning Into A Cart/Further Woodland/20X/Visions Of Old Machinery/Sometimes Doomed/You Should Never Feel Alone In This World/ Crushed By Life (EP, p/s, 1,000 only)	8
96	Love Train PUBE 11	I've Forgotten How To Live/The Weather Side Of The Stone Mill Tower/ Dimensions TBA	8
98	Rocket Racer ROCKET 04	The Year Of Occasional Lull/Fog Projections (1000 only, numbered, this price for 20 with red artwork)	10
98	Rocket Racer ROCKET 04	The Year Of Occasional Lull/Fog Projections (1000 only, numbered, this price for 980 with black artwork)	5
98	Happy Go Lucky HGL 12	Filmed Initiative/As Evening Changed The Day (different photo on each p/s)	12
98	555 Recordings 555 13	(The) Weight/Fallen Farmer/We Are Not Promote/Impossible Calm/Feel The Rush (Coming In From The Avant Garde)/I Know What To Squander/Mast-On-Hill/ Collapsing Climate Soul (p/s)	6
94	Fluff ARC 01	CABLED LINEAR TRACTION (LP, 200 only)	40

ROBBIN HOOD

56	MGM SP 1178	The Rock-A-Bye Blues/Beautiful, Beautiful Love	15

HOODOO RHYTHM DEVILS

78	Fantasy FTC 147	Gotta Lot Of Love In My Soul/MDR Of Love	15

HOOK

68	Uni UN 507	In The Beginning/Show You The Way	10

MARCUS HOOK ROLL BAND

72	Regal Zonophone RZ 3061	Natural Man/Boogalooing Is For Wooing	10
73	Regal zonophone RZ 3072	Louisina Lady/Ghoochie Coochie Har Kau	8

EARL HOOKER
(see also John Lee Hooker)

69	Blue Horizon 57-3166	Boogie Don't Blot/Funky Blues	30
70	Blue Horizon 7-63850	SWEET BLACK ANGEL (LP)	90
70	Stateside SSL 10298	DON'T HAVE TO WORRY (LP)	60

JOHN LEE HOOKER
(see also Canned Heat, Carlos Santana & Buddy Miles, John Lee's Groundhogs)

78s

52	Vogue V 2102	Hoogie Boogie/Whistlin' And Moanin' Blues	50
54	London HL 8037	Need Somebody/Too Much Boogie	50

SINGLES

63	Stateside SS 203	Boom Boom/Frisco Blues	25
64	Stateside SS 297	Dimples/I'm Leaving	20
64	Stateside SS 341	I Love You Honey/Send Me Your Pillow	18
64	Pye International 7N 25255	High Priced Woman/Sugar Mama	18
64	Polydor NH 52930	Shake It Baby/Let's Make It Baby	18
65	Sue WI 361	I'm In The Mood/Boogie Chillun	40
66	Chess CRS 8039	Let's Go Out Tonight/In The Mood	20
66	Planet PLF 114	Mai Lee/Don't Be Messing With My Bread (with Groundhogs)	45
70	President PT 295	Dimples/Boom Boom	8

EPs

60	Riverside REP 3202	WEDNESDAY EVENING	25
60	Riverside REP 3207	DEMOCRAT MAN	25
64	Stateside SE 1019	THE BLUES OF JOHN HOOKER	30
64	Stateside SE 1023	I'M JOHN LEE HOOKER	30
64	Ember EP 4561	THINKING BLUES	40
65	Pye Intl. NEP 44034	LOVE BLUES	35
65	Chess CRE 6000	DOWN AT THE LANDING	35
65	Atlantic AET 6010	JOHN LEE HOOKER	35
66	Chess CRE 6007	WALKING THE BOOGIE	30
66	Chess CRE 6014	THE JOURNEY	30
66	Chess CRE 6021	REAL FOLK BLUES VOL. 3	30
73	Impulse 9103	SERVES YOU RIGHT TO SUFFER	15

MINT VALUE £

LPs

60	Advent LP 2801	JOHN LEE HOOKER AND HIS GUITAR	80
62	Riverside RLP 12-838	THE FOLK BLUES OF JOHN LEE HOOKER	45
62	Stateside SL 10014	THE FOLK LORE OF JOHN LEE HOOKER	50
63	London HA-K 8097	DON'T TURN ME FROM YOUR DOOR	80
64	Stateside SL 10053	THE BIG SOUL OF JOHN LEE HOOKER	65
64	Stateside SL 10074	I WANT TO SHOUT THE BLUES	60
64	Pye Intl. NPL 28042	HOUSE OF THE BLUES	60
64	Fontana 688 700 ZL	THE FOLK-BLUES OF HOOKER	45
65	Fontana FJL 119	BLUE!	70
65	Ember EMB 3356	SINGS THE BLUES	35
65	Riverside RLP 008	BURNING HELL	35
65	Chess CRL 4500	JOHN LEE HOOKER PLAYS AND SINGS THE BLUES	60
66	HMV CLP 5032	IT SERVES YOU RIGHT TO SUFFER (mono)	45
66	HMV CSD 3542	IT SERVES YOU RIGHT TO SUFFER (stereo)	50
66	Ember (ST)EMB 3371	DRIFTIN' THROUGH THE BLUES	25
67	Chess CRL 4527	THE REAL FOLK BLUES	40
67	HMV CLP/CSD 3612	LIVE AT THE CAFE A GO GO	40
67	Atlantic Special 590 003	DRIFTIN' BLUES	18
68	Joy JOY(S) 101	I'M JOHN LEE HOOKER	15
68	Joy JOY(S) 124	BURNIN'	15
68	Stateside (S)SL 10246	URBAN BLUES	40
69	Joy JOYS 129	TRAVELIN'	12
69	Joy JOYS 133	THE FOLKLORE OF JOHN LEE HOOKER	15
69	Stateside (S)SL 10280	SIMPLY THE TRUTH	45
69	Joy JOYS 142	CONCERT AT NEWPORT	15
69	Joy JOYS 147	THE BIG SOUL OF JOHN LEE HOOKER	15
69	Storyville 673 005	YOU'RE LEAVIN' ME BABY	15
69	Joy JOYS 152	IN PERSON	15
70	Storyville 673 020	TUPELO BLUES	30
70	Stax SXATS 1025	THAT'S WHERE IT'S AT	15
71	Probe SPB 1016	IF YOU MISS 'IM . . . I GOT 'IM (with Earl Hooker)	30
71	Probe SPB 1034	ENDLESS BOOGIE	15
71	Stax 2362 017	THAT'S WHERE IT'S AT!	20
71	Xtra XTRA 1114	JOHN LEE HOOKER	40
71	United Artists UAS 29235	COAST TO COAST BLUES BAND	22
72	Probe SPB 1057	NEVER GET OUT OF THESE BLUES ALIVE	18
73	Green Bottle GN 4002	JOHNNY LEE	18
75	ABC ABCL 5059	FREE BEER AND CHICKEN	15
85	Virgin VPBLP 22	CHILL OUT (LP)	25

JOHN LEE HOOKER/LIGHTNIN' HOPKINS/SMOKEY HOGG

(see also Lightnin' Hopkins, Smokey Hogg)

73	Specialty SNTF 5013	HOOKER HOPKINS HOGG (LP)	20

STEVE HOOKER & HEAT

77	Takeaway TAKE 1/ EJR 577	If You Don't Do The Business/Rock & Roll Doctor/I'm Hooked/ Marionette (stamped white sleeve with insert)	8

HOOKFOOT

(see also Elton John, Loot, Caleb, Soul Agents)

69	Page One POF 144	Way Of The Musician/Hookfoot	6
72	DJM DJS 265	Sweet Sweet Funky Music/The Opener	8
71	DJM DJLPS 413	HOOKFOOT (LP, gatefold sleeve)	30
72	DJM DJLPS 422	GOOD TIMES A' COMIN' (LP, gatefold sleeve)	25
73	DJM DJLPS 428	COMMUNICATION (LP, gatefold sleeve)	20
73	DJM DJLPS 435	ROARING (LP)	12
75	DJM DJLMD 8013	HEADLINES (2XLP)	18

MARSHALL HOOKS & CO.

71	Blue Horizon 2096 002	I Want The Same Thing Tomorrow/Hookin' It	20
71	Blue Horizon 2431 003	MARSHALL HOOKS & CO. (LP)	90

HOOKY

72	RCA Victor SF 8247	THE COLLECTED TALES OF HOOKY NO.1 (LP, gatefold sleeve)	20

HOOTEN(ANNY) SINGERS

(see also Abba, Hep Stars, Northern Lights)

64	United Artists UP 1082	Gabrielle/Darling (most copies list artist as Hooten Singers)	35

BOB HOPE

(see also Bing Crosby, Rosemary Clooney)

58	London HLU 8593	Paris Holiday/Nothing In Common (with Bing Crosby)	15
59	RCA RCA 1139	Ain't A-Hankerin'/Protection (with Rosemary Clooney)	6
63	United Artists UP 1023	Call Me Bwana/The Flipside	6

LYN(N) HOPE

57	Vogue V 9081	Blue Moon/Blues For Anna Bacca	40
57	Vogue V 9081	Blue Moon/Blues For Anna Bacca (78)	18
57	Vogue V 9082	Eleven Till Two/Blues For Mary	40
58	Vogue V 9115	Temptation/The Scrunch (78)	30
60	Blue Beat BB 21	Shockin'/Blue And Sentimental	20
57	Vogue VE 170103	LYNN HOPE AND HIS TENOR SAX (EP)	80
60	Vogue VE 170146	LYNN HOPE AND HIS TENOR SAX (EP)	100

PETER HOPE & RICHARD H. KIRK

(see also Cabaret Voltaire, Richard H. Kirk)

85	Doublevision DVR 15	Leather Hands (Master Mix)/(Radio Mix)/(Crash Mix) (12", p/s)	8

HOPE STREET

71	Parlophone R5982	Wait Until Tomorrow/Ladies At The Bottom Of the Garden	12

MINT VALUE £

HOPE & KEEN

71	Excello XLO2	Crazy House/You Can Go My Way	12

HOPE OF THE STATES

00s	Seeker SEEK 001	Black Dollar Bills/Everything For Everyone (Demo)/Sts'Ikel (Demo) (CD, numbered & signed, 1000 only)	25

HOPETOWN (Lewis) & GLENMORE (Brown)

68	Fab FAB 43	Skinny Leg Girl/Live Like A King	30

MARY HOPKIN

(see also Hobby Horse, Sundance, Oasis, Elfland Ensemble, Bob Johnson & Pete Knight, Roy Budd, Elmer Bernstein)

68	Apple APPLE 2	Those Were The Days/Turn Turn Turn (later copies credit Mary Hopkins)	6
68	Apple APPLE 2	Those Were The Days/Turn Turn Turn (blank Apple label on A-side)	12
69	Apple APPLE 7	Lontana Dagli Occhi/Game (Europe-only, unreleased in U.K.)	0
69	Apple APPLE 9	Prince En Avignon/The Game (France-only, unreleased in U.K.)	0
69	Apple APPLE 10	Goodbye/Sparrow	6
69	Apple APPLE 16	Que Sera Sera/Fields Of St. Etienne (unreleased)	0
69	Cambrian CSP 703	Aderyn Llwyd/Y Blodyn Gwyn (p/s)	18
70	Cambrian CSP 712	Pleserau Serch/Tyrd Yn Ôl (p/s)	18
70	Apple APPLE 22	Temma Harbour/Lontano Dagli Occhi (black or green lettering on p/s)	6
70	Apple APPLE 26	Knock, Knock Who's There?/I'm Going To Fall In Love Again (p/s)	6
70	Apple APPLE 27	Que Sera Sera/Fields Of St. Etienne (unreleased in U.K., acetates only)	0
70	Apple APPLE 30	Think About Your Children/Heritage (p/s)	6
71	Apple APPLE 34	Let My Name Be Sorrow/Kew Gardens (p/s)	18
71	Apple APPLE 39	Water, Paper And Clay/Jefferson (p/s)	20
72	Regal Zonophone RZ 3070	Mary Had A Baby/Cherry Tree Carol	6
76	Good Earth GD 2	If You Love Me (I Won't Care): (some copies list "If You Love Me")/Tell Me Now	6
77	Good Earth GD 11	Wrap Me In Your Arms/Just A Dreamer (p/s)	10
68	Cambrian CEP 414	LLAIS SWYNOL MARY HOPKIN (EP)	15
69	Cambrian CEP 420	MARY AC EDWARD (EP, with Edward Morris Jones)	15
69	Apple APCOR 5	POST CARD (LP, with black or white inner sleeve, mono)	30
69	Apple SAPCOR 5	POST CARD (LP, with black or white inner sleeve, stereo)	20
71	Apple SAPCOR 21	EARTH SONG - OCEAN SONG (LP, gatefold sleeve, 'Apple' inner sleeve)	30
72	Apple SAPCOR 23	THOSE WERE THE DAYS (LP, with 'Apple' inner sleeve)	70
77	Decca SPA 546	THE WELSH WORLD OF MARY HOPKIN (LP)	25
89	Trax Modem 1045	SPIRIT (LP)	20
91	Apple SAPCOR 5	POST CARD (LP, reissue, gatefold sleeve with bonus 12" [SAPCOR 52])	20
92	Apple SAPCOR 21	EARTH SONG/OCEAN SONG (LP, reissue, gatefold sleeve with inner)	20

ANTHONY HOPKINS

86	Juice AA 5	Distant Star/Ordinary Man (p/s)	7

JOEL & LIGHTNIN' HOPKINS

(see also Lightnin' Hopkins)

60	Heritage H 1000	BLUES FROM EAST TEXAS (LP, 99 copies only)	120

LIGHTNIN' HOPKINS

(see also Sonny Terry & Brownie McGhee, Joel & Lightnin' Hopkins, Lightnin' Hopkins & John Lee Hooker, Big Joe Williams)

61	Bluesville BVLP 1019	LIGHTNIN' HOPKINS (LP)	80
62	'77' LA 12/1	SAM LIGHTNIN' HOPKINS - THE ROOSTER CROWED IN ENGLAND (LP 99 copies only)	100
63	Stateside SL 10031	LIGHTNIN' STRIKES (LP)	70
63	Realm RM 128	LIGHTNIN' HOPKINS SINGS THE BLUES (LP)	30
63	Realm RM 171	DIRTY HOUSE BLUES (LP)	30
64	Stateside SL 10076	BLUES HOOT (LP, some tracks by Sonny Terry & Brownie McGhee)	40
65	Stateside SL 10110	HOOTIN' THE BLUES (LP)	40
65	Stateside SL 10155	DOWN HOME BLUES (LP)	40
65	Fontana AH 183	THE BLUES (LP)	35
65	Fontana 688 301 ZL	LAST NIGHT BLUES (LP)	35
65	Fontana 688 801 ZL	BURNIN' IN L.A. (LP)	35
66	Fontana 688 803 ZL	BLUE BIRD BLUES (LP)	35
66	Fontana 688 807 ZL	BLUES PARTY (LP)	35
66	Ember EMB 3389	A TIME FOR BLUES (LP)	25
66	Ember EMB 3416	LIVE AT THE BIRD LOUNGE (LP)	22
67	Ember EMB 3423	I'VE BEEN BUKED AND SCORNED (LP)	22
66	Verve (S)VLP 5003	ROOTS OF HOPKINS (LP)	25
66	Verve (S)VLP 5014	LIGHTNIN' STRIKES (LP, reissue)	18
66	Saga ERO 8001	LIGHTNIN' HOPKINS (LP)	15
67	Xtra XTRA 5036	BLUES IN MY BOTTLE (LP)	18
68	Xtra XTRA 5044	GOT TO MOVE YOUR BABY (LP, reissue of Fontana 688 301 ZL)	20
68	Minit MLL/MLS 40006	EARTH BLUES (LP)	40
69	Liberty LBL 83254	KING OF DOWLING STREET (LP)	30
69	Joy JOY(S) 115	LIGHTNIN' STRIKES (LP, 2nd reissue)	15
69	Polydor 545 019	THAT'S MY STORY (LP)	25
70	Ace Of Hearts (Z)AHT 183	THE BLUES (LP)	15
70	Poppy PYS 11000	LIGHTNIN'! VOLUME 1 (LP)	15
70	Poppy PYS 11002	LIGHTNIN'! VOLUME 2 (LP)	15
71	Liberty LBS 83293	THE CALIFORNIA MUDSLIDE (AND EARTHQUAKE) (LP)	30
71	Mayfair AMLB 4000 1/2	LIGHTNIN' STRIKES (2-LP)	18
71	Blue Horizon 2431 005	LET'S WORK AWHILE (LP)	120
71	Xtra XTRA 1127	THE ROOTS OF LIGHTNIN' HOPKINS (LP)	18
71	Boulevard BLVD 4001	LIGHTNIN' HOPKINS (LP)	12
72	Carnival 2941 005	LONESOME LIGHTNIN' (LP)	18

LIGHTNIN' HOPKINS & JOHN LEE HOOKER

(see also John Lee Hooker/Lightnin' Hopkins/Smokey Hogg)

69	Storyville 616 001	THERE'S GOOD ROCKIN' TONIGHT! (LP)	35
72	Storyville SLP 174	LIGHTNIN' HOPKINS AND JOHN LEE HOOKER (LP)	35

MINT VALUE £

LINDA HOPKINS

61 Coral Q 72423 I Diddle Dum Dum/All In My Mind ... 20
62 Coral Q 72448 Mama's Doin' The Twist/My Mother's Eyes ... 20

LINDA HOPKINS & JACKIE WILSON

(see also Jackie Wilson)
63 Coral Q 72464 Shake A Hand/Say I Do ... 15
65 Coral Q 72480 Yes Indeed/When The Saints Go Marching In ... 15

NICKY HOPKINS

(see also Aquarian Age, Neil Christian & Crusaders, Cyril Davies R&B All-Stars, Poet & One Man Band, Quicksilver Messenger Service, Sweet Thursday)
66 CBS 202055 Mr Big/Jenni ... 18
67 Polydor 56175 Mister Pleasant/Nothing As Yet ... 18
68 MGM MGM 1419 Top Pops No. 1 (Medley)/(Part 2) ... 8
68 Fontana TF 906 High On A Hill/Trumpet Serenade (actually by Nigel Hopkins) ... 6
73 CBS CBS 1328 Speed On/Sundown In Mexico ... 5
66 CBS (S)BPG 62679 THE REVOLUTIONARY PIANO OF NICKY HOPKINS (LP) ... 60
73 CBS 65416 THE TIN MAN WAS A DREAMER (LP, gatefold sleeve) ... 40

WASH HOPKINS SINGERS

69 Action ACT 4546 He's Got Blessing/Rock In A Weary Land ... 20

HOPKIRK AND LEE

98 Gallery GAL001CD Beneath The Apple Tree (CD, EP, 1000 copies) ... 10
98 Rough Trade/For Us 001 Beneath The Apple Tree (7" 1,000 copies) ... 15

HUGH HOPPER

(see also Caravan, Elton Dean, Gilgamesh, Isotope, Matching Mole, Ninesense, Soft Machine)
73 CBS 65466 1984 (LP) ... 30
76 Compendium FIDARDO 4 CRUEL BUT FAIR (LP) ... 15
77 Compendium FIDARDO 7 HOPPERTUNITY BOX (LP) ... 15
78 Ogun OG 527 ROGUE ELEMENT (LP, as Hopper, Dean, Gowen, Sheen - 'Soft Heap') ... 20

HOPSCOTCH

(see also Scots Of St. James, Five Day Rain, Forever More, Glencoe)
69 United Artists UP 2231 Look At The Lights Go Up/Same Old Fat Man ... 120
69 United Artists UP 35022 Long Black Veil/Easy To Find ... 10

HORACE & IMPERIALS

68 Nu Beat NB 012 Young Love/Days Like These ... 15

HORATIO

70 Penny Farthing PEN 729 I've Gotta Have You/A Sad Song With A Happy Soul ... 5

HORDEN RAIKES

73 Folk Heritage FHR 042 KING COTTON (LP) ... 15
72 Folk Heritage FHR 042 KING COTTON (LP) ... 20
72 Folk Heritage FHR 026 HORDEN RAIKES (LP) ... 20

HORIZON

81 SRT SRTS 81432 Stage Struck/Remember The Bad Boys ... 10

HORIZON

(see also Mungo Jerry)
83 Orbit TRIP 4 Sunshine Reggae/Nightlife ... 6

PAUL HORN

68 Liberty LBL 83084E COSMIC CONSCIOUSNESS (LP) ... 18

KENNETH HORNE

69 Pye NPL 18291 ROUND THE HORNE (LP) ... 15

LENA HORNE

(see also Harry Belafonte)
55 HMV 7M 309 Love Me Or Leave Me/I Love To Love ... 10
55 HMV 7M 319 It's All Right With Me/It's Love ... 6
56 HMV 7M 423 If You Can Dream/What's Right For You (Is Right For Me) ... 6
56 MGM MGM 917 Can't Help Lovin' Dat Man/The Man I Love ... 7
59 RCA RCA 1120 A New Fangled Tango/Honeysuckle Rose ... 5
65 United Artists UP 1101 The Sand And The Sea/It Had Better Be Tonight ... 25
71 Buddah 2011 078 Maybe I'm Amazed/Feels So Good ... 12
57 RCA RD 27021/SF 5007 AT THE WALDORF ASTORIA (LP, mono/stereo) ... 12
58 RCA RD 27063 STORMY WEATHER (LP) ... 12
59 RCA RD 27098/SF 5019 GIVE THE LADY WHAT SHE WANTS (LP, mono/stereo) ... 12
59 RCA RD 27141 A FRIEND OF YOURS (LP) ... 12
64 Stateside S(S)L 10081 HERE'S LENA (LP) ... 12

HANK HORNSBY

57 MGM MGM 955 Pots And Pans/Cotton ... 6
58 MGM MGM 972 The Legend Of The Birds And Bees/Girls Girls Girls ... 6

HORNSEY AT WAR

70s War WAR 001 DEAD BEAT REVIVAL (EP, numbered p/s) ... 8

HORRORCOMIC

77 Lightning/B&C BVZ 0007 I'm All Hung Up On Pierrepoint/The Exorcist/Sex In The Afternoon (p/s) ... 40
78 Lightning GIL 512 I Don't Mind/England 77 (p/s) ... 80
79 B&C BCS 18 Jesus Crisis/Cut Your Throat (p/s) ... 400

HORRORS

06 Loog LOOG 015 Sheena Is A Parasite/Jack The Ripper (p/s, insert, 500 only) ... 25
06 Loog LOOG 016 Death At The Chapel/Crawdaddy Simone (p/s, 500 only with sticker) ... 15

HORSE

(see also Saturnalia, Atomic Rooster)
70 RCA Victor SF 8109 HORSE (LP) ... 250

MINT VALUE £

HORSEPOWER

79	Square SQS 2	Outrageous/Highway Robbery	10

HORSLIPS

73	Oats OAT 1	High Reel/Furniture	5
73	Oats OAT 2	Dearg Doom/The Shamrock Shore	5
73	Oats MOO 3	HAPPY TO MEET ... SORRY TO PART (LP, booklet octagonal sleeve)	45
74	Oats MOO 5	THE TAIN (LP, gatefold sleeve)	20
75	RCA Victor SF 8432	THE UNFORTUNATE CUP OF TEA (LP, orange label)	15
76	DJM DJF 20498	THE BOOK OF INVASION - A CELTIC SYMPHONY (LP, with insert)	12

HORTENSE (Ellis) & ALTON (Ellis)

(see also Hortense Ellis, Alton Ellis, Mr. Foundation)

65	Island WI 230	Don't Gamble With Love/Something You Got (B-side actually by Alton Ellis & Flames)	25

HORTENSE (Ellis) & DELROY (Wilson)

(see also Hortense Ellis, Delroy Wilson)

66	Rio R 119	We're Gonna Make It/SOUL BROTHERS: Ska Shuffle	25

HORTENSE (Ellis) & JACKIE (Opel)

(see also Hortense Ellis, Jackie Opel)

64	R&B JB 138	Stand By Me/JACKIE OPEL: Solid Rock	35

JOHNNY HORTON

59	Philips PB 932	The Battle Of New Orleans/All For The Love Of A Girl	8
59	Philips PB 932	The Battle Of New Orleans/All For The Love Of A Girl (78)	25
59	Philips PB 951	Sal's Got A Sugar Lip/Johnny Reb	12
59	Philips PB 951	Sal's Got A Sugar Lip/Johnny Reb (78)	25
59	Philips PB 976	Take Me Like I Am/I'm Ready If You're Willing	10
60	Philips PB 995	Sink The Bismarck!/The Same Old Tale The Crow Told Me	10
60	Philips PB 1062	North To Alaska/The Mansion You Stole	10
61	Philips PB 1130	When It's Springtime In Alaska/Mr. Moonlight	10
61	Philips PB 1132	Sleepy Eyed John/They'll Never Take Her Love From Me	15
61	Philips PB 1170	Miss Marcy/Ole Slew Foot	10
62	Philips PB 1226	Words/Honky Tonk Man	15
63	CBS AAG 132	All Grown Up/I'm A One Woman Man	12
60	Mercury ZEP 10074	THE FANTASTIC JOHNNY HORTON (EP)	45
64	Mercury 10008 MCE	COUNTRY AND WESTERN ACES (EP)	30
60	Philips BBL 7464	THE SPECTACULAR JOHNNY HORTON (LP)	30
61	Philips BBL 7536	HONKY TONK MAN (LP)	40
63	London HA-U 8096	DONE ROVIN' (LP)	40
63	CBS SBPG 62186	GREATEST HITS (LP)	15
65	Fontana FJL 306	VOICE OF JOHNNY HORTON (LP)	15
66	CBS Realm RM 52362	THE SPECTACULAR JOHNNY HORTON (LP, same cover as Phillips 7464 but 3 different tracks)	20

ROBERT HORTON

60	Pye 7N 15285	(Roll Along) Wagon Train/Sail Ho!	6
61	Pye 7N 15357	The Girl That I Marry/Time After Time	5
66	Pye 7N 17031	Shenadoah/Maria	6

WALTER 'SHAKEY' HORTON

70	London HAK/SHK 8405	SOUTHERN COMFORT (LP, as Shakey Horton)	125
74	Xtra XTRA 1135	WALTER 'SHAKEY' HORTON WITH HOT COTTAGE (LP)	30
74	Sonet SNTF 677	BIG WALTER HORTON (LP, with Carey Bell)	22

LA/THE HOST

84	Orbitone	THE HOST EP (cassette)	5
85	Quiet QU 1	The Big Sleep/Just Breaking Away (p/s)	8

HOT BUTTER

72	Pye International 7N 25583	Popcorn/At The Movies	5
73	Pye International NSPL 28169	POPCORN (LP)	15
73	Pye International NSPL 28181	MORE HOT BUTTER (LP)	15

HOT CHIP

00	Victory Garden VG14	MEXICO EP (CD)	20
05	No label or cat no	ALL KILLER, NO FILLER! (tour-only CD-R 7-track)	30
06	EMI 094634741811	THE WARNING (2-LP with free 7", Won't Wash/Bally)	20

HOT CHOCOLATE (BAND)

(see also Errol Brown & Chosen Few, Tony Wilson)

69	Apple APPLE 18	Give Peace A Chance/Living Without Tomorrow (as Hot Chocolate Band)	50
70	Rak RAK 103	Love Is Life/Pretty Girls (with promo p/s)	5
73	Rak RAK 139	You Could Have Been A Friend/Go Go Girl	15
79	Rak RAK 29	Mindless Boogie/Don't Turn It Off (12" p/s)	8

HOT CITY

71	London HLU 10344	Leaving/I Believe In Life	15

HOT CLUB

(see also Rich Kids, Spectres)

82	RAK 346	The Dirt That She Walks On Is Sacred Ground To Me/Heat (p/s)	12
82	RAK 346	The Dirt That She Walks On Is Sacred Ground To Me/Heat (12", p/s)	10

HOTFOOT GALE

78	Charly SYS 1044	Washin' Machine Boogie/Everybody's Feelin' Allright	5

HOTLEGS

(see also 10cc, Mindbenders, Godley & Creme, Tristar Airbus, Ramases)

70	Fontana 6007 019	Neanderthal Man/You Didn't Like It Because You Didn't Think Of It	5
71	Philips 6006 140	Lady Sadie/The Loser	8
71	Philips 6308 047	THINKS: SCHOOL STINKS (LP, gatefold sleeve, black/silver label)	40
71	Philips 6308 080	SONG (LP, gatefold sleeve, black/silver label)	50

MINT VALUE £

HOT POTATO

73	PMTB 1	HOT POTATO (LP, private pressing)	25

HOT RATS

(see also Supergrass)

09	No label or cat no	Damaged Goods/Fight For Your Right To Party (tour 7", 150-only, die-cut sleeve, signed)	20

HOT ROCKS

73	Bell Bell 1326	Chopper/Roly Poly	6

HOT ROCKS & JAH LOXLEY

80s	Gemini GSM 025	Jah Jah No Parcial/Badda Badda	20

HOT ROD

73	President PT 397	I Want You (All Night Long)/Love Is All Right (Hey)	10

HOT ROD

69	Joe's DU 41	The Judge/RON: Soul Of Soul Of Joel	12

HOT ROD ALLSTARS

(see also Setters, Betty Sinclair)

69	Duke DU 59	Lick A Pop/Treasure	20
70	Duke DU 65	Paint Your Wagon/Organ Man	130
70	Duke DU 66	Return Of The Bad Man/Caysoe Reggae	20
70	Trojan TR 7732	Strong Man/Sentimental	20
70	Trojan TR 7733	Virgin Soldier/Brixton Reggae Festival	50
70	Torpedo TOR 1	Pussy Got Nine Life/BOSS SOUNDS: Lick It Back	70
70	Torpedo TOR 5	Skinheads Don't Fear/Ten Commandments From The Devil	100
70	Torpedo TOR 10	Moonhop In London/Skinhead Moondust	100
70	Torpedo TOR 14	Control Your Doggy/Follow The Stars	30
70	Hot Rod HR 104	Skinhead Speaks His Mind/CARL LEVEY: Carnaby Street	100
70	Hot Rod HR 107	Strictly Invitation/PATSY & PEGGY: Dog Your Woman	100
70	Hot Rod HR 108	Beautiful World/Shocks Of A Drugs Man	15

HOTRODS

65	Columbia DB 7693	I Don't Love You No More/Ain't Coming Back No More	55

HOT SPRINGS

66	Columbia DB 7821	It's All Right/All I Know About Love	20

HOT THUMBS O'RILEY

73	Charisma CAS 1071	HOT THUMBS O'RILEY (LP, gatefold sleeve, large 'Mad Hatter' label)	30

HOT-TODDYS

(see also Rockin' Rebels)

59	Pye International 7N 25020	Rockin' Crickets/Shakin' And Stompin'	30
59	Pye International 7N 25020	Rockin' Crickets/Shakin' And Stompin' (78)	35

HOT TUNA

(see also Jefferson Airplane)

72	Grunt 65-0502	Keep On Truckin'/Water Song	5
76	Grunt RCG 1002	It's So Easy/I Can't Be Satisfied	5
70	RCA SF 8125	HOT TUNA (LP)	15
71	RCA LSP 4550	ELECTRIC LIVE (FIRST PULL UP, THEN PULL DOWN) (LP)	12
72	Grunt FTR 1004	BURGERS (LP, with purple inner sleeve)	12

HOT VULTURES

(see also Ian (A) Anderson)

77	Red Rag RRR 015	THE EAST STREET SHAKES (LP)	20
70s	Plant Life PLR 018	UP THE LINE (LP)	20

HOT WATER

78	Duff DWR 100	Different Morning/Premium Bondage	8
79	Duff DWR 101	Get Lost!/Bird's Eye View (p/s)	7

HOUGHTON WEAVERS

78	Folk Heritage FHR 106	SIT THI DOWN (LP)	15
79	Folk Heritage FHR 111	CLATTER O' CLOGS (LP)	15
80	EMI HW 1001	UP YOUR WAY (LP)	15
80	EMI HW 1002	ALIVE & KICKING (LP)	15
83	EMI HW 1003	IN THE RARE OLD TIMES (LP)	15
85	Folk Heritage FHR 128	KEEP FOLK SMILING (LP)	12
86	Folk Heritage FHR 129	IT'S GOOD TO SEE YOU (LP)	12

HOUNDHEAD HENRY/FRANKIE JAXON

60	Jazz Collector JEL 10	THE MALE BLUES VOLUME 6 (EP)	18

HOUR GLASS

(see also Allman Brothers)

68	Liberty LBL/LBS 83219E	THE HOUR GLASS (LP)	30
74	United Artists USD 303/4	THE HOUR GLASS (2-LP)	18

SON HOUSE

(see under 'S')

HOUSE CREW

91	Production House PNT 029	Keep The Fire Burning/Get On Up (12")	12
91	Production Hse PNT 029R	Keep The Fires Burning (remixes) (12")	20
92	Production Hse PNT 035	We Are Hardcore/Maniac (Hypermix) (12")	15
92	Production Hse PNT 035R	We Are Hardcore/Maniac (Remixes) (12")	15
93	Production Hse PNT 047	The Theme/Euphoria (12")	25
93	Production Hse PNT 047R	The Theme/Euphoria (Remixes) (12")	25
94	Production Hse PNT 060	Superhero (My Knight) (12")	15
94	Production Hse PNT 060R	Superhero (Remixes) (12")	15
94	Production Hse PNT 060RX	Superhero (Remixes II) (12")	15

MINT VALUE £

HOUSEHOLD

67	United Artists UP 1190	I Guess I'll Learn How To Fly/Nothing You Can Do But Cry	6
68	United Artists UP 2210	Twenty First Summer/Winter's Coming On	6

HOUSEHOLD NAMES

81	Blue Chip BC 104	White Light/Much Too Young To Love	7

HOUSEMARTINS

(see also Beautiful South)

85	Go! Discs GOD 7	Flag Day/Stand At Ease (p/s)	5
85	Go! Discs GOD 7/GOD 9	Flag Day/Stand At Ease//Sheep/Drop Down Dead (shrinkwrapped double pack)	6
85	Go! Discs GODX 7	Flag Day/Stand At Ease/Coal Train To Hatfield Main (12", p/s)	8
86	Go! Discs GODP 9	Sheep/I'll Be Your Shelter/Drop Down Dead (picture disc)	5
86	Go! Discs GODP 11	Happy Hour/The Mighty Ship (shaped picture disc)	5
86	Go! Discs GODP 13	Think For A Minute/Who Needs The Limelight (shaped picture disc)	5
86	Go! Discs GODP 16	Caravan Of Love/When I First Met Jesus (rectangular picture disc)	5
86	Go! Discs GODB 16	THE HOUSEMARTINS' CHRISTMAS BOX SET (4 singles in foldout sleeve, signed)	25
07	Mercury 175 252-3	SOUP ('deluxe Fan Edition', in sealed/stickered tin: CD, DVD, T-shirt and mug)	60

HOUSEMASTER BALDWIN

88	Koolkat KOOLT 21	DELTA HOUSE (12", p/s)	10
88	Koolkat KOOLT 22	DON'T LEAD ME (12", p/s)	10

HOUSE OF LORDS

69	B&C CB 112	In The Land Of Dreams/Ain't Gonna Wait Forever	25

HOUSE OF LOVE

87	Creation CRE 043T	Shine On/Love/Flow (12", p/s, 4,000 only)	20
87	Creation CRE 044T	Real Animal/Plastic/Nothing To Me (12", p/s, 4,000 only)	20
88	Creation CRE 053	Christine/Loneliness Is A Gun (die-cut '99p' sleeve)	5
88	Creation CRE 057	Destroy The Heart/Blind (p/s)	5
88	Creation CRE 057T	Destroy The Heart/Blind/Mr Jo (12", p/s)	10
89	Fontana HOLR212	I Don't Know Why I Love You/Clothes/Secrets/The Spy	5
89	Fontana HOLG4	The Beatles & The Stones/Love IV (fold-out flower p/s, numbered & poster)	5
92	Love 1	ROYAL ALBERT HALL EP (10" gig freebie, stickered)	25
88	Creation CRELP 034	HOUSE OF LOVE (LP, with free 7", "Shine On/Christine", matt sleeve)	20

HOUSESHAKERS

72	Contour 2870160	DEMOLITION ROCK (LP)	12

CISCO HOUSTON

60	Top Rank 30/028	THE CISCO SPECIAL (LP)	50
62	Fontana TFL 6007	CISCO SPECIAL! (LP)	25
62	Fontana TFL 6014	SINGS SONGS OF WOODY GUTHRIE (LP)	20
68	Fontana FJL 412	I AIN'T GOT NO HOME (LP)	15
69	Ember CW 135	CISCO HOUSTON AND WOODY GUTHRIE (LP)	15

CISSY HOUSTON

(see also Sweet Inspirations)

70	Major Minor MM 700	He/I Believe/I'll Be There	5
70	Major Minor MM 716	The Long And Winding Road/Be My Baby	5
70	Pye International 7N 25537	I Just Don't Know What To Do With Myself/This Empty Place	40
71	Pye International 7N 25545	The Long And Winding Road/Be My Baby (reissue)	5
71	Janus 6146 003	Darling Take Me Back/Hang On To A Dream	5
72	Janus 6146 027	Midnight Train To Georgia/I'm So Glad I Can Love Again	5
70	Major Minor SMLP 80	PRESENTING CISSY HOUSTON (LP)	30

DAVID HOUSTON

55	London HL 8147	Blue Prelude/I'm Sorry I Made You Cry	50
55	London HL 8147	Blue Prelude/I'm Sorry I Made You Cry (78)	10
63	Columbia DB 7159	Mountain Of Love/Poor Little Angeline	7
66	Columbia DB 7997	Almost Persuaded/We Got Love	7

DAVID HOUSTON & TAMMY WYNETTE

67	Columbia DB 8246	My Elusive Dreams/Marriage On The Rocks	8

SAM HOUSTON

65	Island WI 172	My Mother's Eyes/Danny Boy	12

THELMA HOUSTON

69	Stateside SS 8026	Jumpin' Jack Flash/Sunshower	5
72	Tamla Motown TMG 799	I Want To Go Back There Again/Pick Of The Week	12
72	Mowest MW 3001	No One's Gonna Be A Fool Forever/What If	8
73	Mowest MW 3004	Black California/I'm Letting Go (withdrawn)	60
69	Stateside (S)SL 5010	SUNSHOWER (LP)	12
73	Mowest MWS 7003	THELMA HOUSTON (LP)	15

LARRY HOVIS

58	Capitol CL 14843	Do I Love You/We Could Have Lots Of Fun	5
59	Capitol CL 15083	My Heart Belongs To Only You/I Want To Fall In Love	5

BRIAN HOWARD & SILHOUETTES

62	Columbia DB 4914	Somebody Help Me/Young And Evil	25
63	Columbia DB 7067	The Worryin' Kind/Come To Me	25
64	Fontana TF 464	Back In The U.S.A./Hooked	20

JAN HOWARD

60	London HL 7088	The One You Slip Around With/I Wish I Could Fall In Love Again (export issue)	25

JOHN HOWARD

75	CBS 80473	KID IN A BIG WORLD (LP, with insert)	25

JOHNNY HOWARD BAND

60	Decca F 11298	Up The Wall/Orbit	5
62	Decca F 11423	Mind Reader/Spanish Gipsy Dance	8

MINT VALUE £

64	Decca F 11925	Rinky Dink/Java	8
65	Decca F 12065	El Pussy Cat/A Tune Called Harry	5
65	Decca LK 4735	THE EASY BEAT SOUND (LP)	20
67	Deram DML/SML 1001	THE VELVET TOUCH OF JOHNNY HOWARD (LP)	12
67	Deram SHL 1012	LOVE IS THE SWEETEST THING (LP)	12

KEITH HOWARD
(see also Victory)

80	Rods HOT 2	LOOKING FOR YOU (LP, some sleeves contain Driver artwork on opposite sides of sleeve)	35

LES HOWARD

53	HMV 7M 127	Love Evermore/I Lived When I Met You	10
53	HMV 7M 171	Rags To Riches/From Here To Eternity	10

NOAH HOWARD

69	Polydor Super 2383093	THE BLACK ARK (LP)	40

ROLAND S. HOWARD & LYDIA LUNCH
(see also Lydia Lunch, Birthday Party)

86	4AD BAD 210	Some Velvet Morning/I Fell In Love With A Ghost (12", p/s, with postcard)	12

WAYNE HOWARD

70	Explosion EX 2042	All Kinds Of Everything/Cool And Easy (B-side actually by Lloyd Charmers)	7

JACK HOWARTH

71	Fontana 6438042	OW DO (LP)	12

CATHERINE HOWE

71	Reflection HRS 11	Nothing More Than Strangers/It Comes With The Breezes	20
71	Reflection REFL 11	WHAT A BEAUTIFUL PLACE (LP, laminated front sleeve 'correction' sticker on rear sleeve)	700
75	RCA Victor SF 8407	HARRY (LP)	20
70s	RCA Victor ARL 5013	DRAGONFLY DAYS (LP)	12

STEVE HOWE
(see also Yes)

75	Atlantic K50151	BEGINNINGS (LP, gatefold sleeve)	15

EDDIE HOWELL
(see also Queen, Gary Moore, Brian May, Freddie Mercury)

76	Warner Bros K 16701	Man From Manhattan/Waiting In The Wings (features members of Queen)	15
77	Warner Bros K 16866	Sweet On You/Miss Amerika (features Gary Moore)	8

EDDY HOWELL

69	Parlophone R5756	Easy Street/Judy's Good	45

PETER HOWELL
(see under Friends, Ithaca, Alice Through The Looking Glass, Agincourt, Tomorrow Come Someday, BBC Radiophonic Workshop)

FRANKIE HOWERD

54	Decca F 10420	(Don't Let The) Kiddy Geddin/Abracadabra	10
58	Columbia DB 4230	It's All Right With Me/Song And Dance Man	10
64	Decca F 12028	Last Word On The Election/Last Word On The Election (Part 2)	7
70	Pye 7N 45061	Up Je T'Aime/All Through The Night	5
71	Columbia DB 8757	Up Pompeii/Salute!	5
63	Decca LK 4556	AT THE ESTABLISHMENT (LP)	15
60s	Pye NPL	SOMETHING FUNNY HAPPENED ON THE WAY TO THE FORUM (LP)	15

CHRIS HOWLAND

58	Columbia DB 4114	Mama (Ma, He's Making Eyes At Me)/Fraulein	7
59	Columbia DB 4194	Susie Darlin'/The Rain Falls On Ev'rybody	10

HOWLIN' WOLF
(see also Hubert Sumlin)

61	Pye International 7N 25101	Little Baby/Down In The Bottom	25
63	Pye International 7N 25192	Just Like I Treat You/I Ain't Superstitious	25
64	Pye International 7N 25244	Smokestack Lightnin'/Going Down Slow ('Slow' on B-side label)	25
64	Pye International 7N 25244	Smokestack Lightnin'/Going Down Slow (''South' on B-side label)	20
64	Pye International 7N 25269	Little Girl/Tail Dragger	22
64	Pye International 7N 25283	Love Me Darling/My Country Sugar Mama	22
65	Chess CRS 8010	Killing Floor/Louise	15
65	Chess CRS 8016	Ooh Baby/Tell Me What I've Done	15
69	Chess CRS 8097	Evil/Tail Dragger	15
56	London REU 1072	RHYTHM AND BLUES WITH HOWLIN' WOLF (EP)	220
63	Pye Intl. NEP 44015	SMOKESTACK LIGHTNIN' (EP)	35
64	Pye Intl. NEP 44032	TELL ME (EP)	30
66	Chess CRE 6017	REAL FOLK BLUES (EP)	30
64	Chess CRL 4006	MOANIN' IN THE MOONLIGHT (LP)	80
65	Chess CRL 4508	POOR BOY (LP)	45
66	Ember EMB 3370	BIG CITY BLUES (LP)	25
69	Chess CRLS 4543	THE HOWLIN' WOLF ALBUM (LP)	25
71	Syndicate Chapter SC 003	GOING BACK HOME (LP)	20
71	Chess 6310 108	MESSAGE TO THE YOUNG (LP)	22
71	Rolling Stones COC 49101	THE LONDON SESSIONS (LP)	20
71	Python PLP 13	HOWLIN' WOLF (LP)	60

HOWLIN' WOLF/JUNIOR PARKER/BOBBY BLAND

74	Polydor 2383 257	BLUES FOR MR. CRUMP (LP)	30

HOWLIN' WOLF, MUDDY WATERS & BO DIDDLEY
(see also Muddy Waters, Bo Diddley)

68	Chess CRL 4537	THE SUPER SUPER BLUES BAND (LP)	45

MINT VALUE £

LINDA HOYLE
(see also Affinity, Nucleus)

70	Vertigo 6059 018	Eli's Coming/United States Of Mind (as Linda Hoyle & Affinity)	40
71	Vertigo 6360 060	PIECES OF ME (LP, gatefold sleeve, small swirl label)	500

H.P. LOVECRAFT

67	Philips BF 1620	Wayfarin' Stranger/The Time Machine	7
68	Philips BF 1639	The White Ship (Parts 1 & 2) (unissued)	0
68	Philips BF 1639	The White Ship/I've Been Wrong Before	15
67	Philips (S)BL 7830	H.P. LOVECRAFT (LP)	60
68	Philips SBL 7872	H.P. LOVECRAFT II (LP, without watermark at start of each side)	40
68	Philips SBL 7872	H.P. LOVECRAFT II (LP, with watermark at start of each side)	15
72	Philips 6336 210	THIS IS H.P. LOVECRAFT (LP)	25
72	Philips 6336 213	H.P. LOVECRAFT VOL. 2 (LP)	20

HQ SQUAD

89	Music Of Life NOTE33	Burial Proceedings In The Course Of Three Knights/Onslaught (12")	18

HRATCH

70	Decca F13007	Beautiful Bare Back Rider/Ain't It Tough	10

HT

66	Polydor 56127	You & Me/Love Can Wait	10

H2O

81	Spock PARA 2	Hollywood Dream/Children (with lyric insert)	6
66	Polydor 56127	You & Me/Love Can Wait	10

HUBCAP & WHEELS
(see also Byron Lee & Dragonaires)

70	Dynamic DYN 403	One Pound Weight/VICEROYS: Come Dance	6

WENDY HUBER

65	Philips BF 1446	Come Away Melinda/I Belong To The Wind	10

ROY HUDD

66	Polydor 56136	The Day We Won The Cup/Ramsey's Men	8
67	Pye 7N 17434	Artificial Jumping Spider Seller/Sir Rhubarb Tansy	6
77	BBC RESL 47	Standing Outside The Palace/I'm Gonna Let Them Get Me Down	5

HUDDERSFIELD TRANSIT AUTHORITY

72	Polydor 2001-284	Runaway/Bayou Farm	15
72	Polydor 2001344	A Different Drum/One Of The Old Time Greats	6

JACK HUDSON

72	Folk Heritage FHR 041	SUMMER DAYS AND YOU (LP)	20

JOHNNY HUDSON & TEENBEATS

63	Decca F 11679	Charms/Makin' Up Is So Much Fun	10

KEITH HUDSON (& CHUCKLES)
(see also Big Youth, Alton Ellis, Hugh Roy, Delroy Wilson)

69	Big Shot BI 528	Tambourine Man/Old Fashioned Way (both actually by Ken Boothe)	20
70	Smash SMA 2311	Don't Get Me Confused/D. SMITH: Ball of Confusion (B-side actually by Dennis Alcapone)	20
71	Smash SMA 2526	Light Of Day/I Thought You Knew	20
72	Spur SP 1	Darkest Night On A Wet Looking Road/Version	40
72	Duke DU 145	Satan Side (with Chuckles)/DON T. JUNIOR: Evil Spirit	35
72	Downtown DT 492	True True To My Heart/BIG YOUTH: Ace 90 Skank	15
73	Summit SUM 8541	Melody Maker/Uncover Me	15
75	Atra AT28	Lost All Sense Of Direction/Jah Jah	8
75	Faith FA 025	Blackbelt Jones/Version	20
77	Tunde TR 1000	I Wanna Be Where You Are/Still Water (12")	25
78	Greensleeves GRED 8	Bloody Eyes/Dub	20
79	Greensleeves GRED 26	Nuh Skin Up/Felt We Felt The Strain (12")	25
75	Magnet MGT 007	ENTER THE DRAGON (LP)	220
75	Mamba KH 1	FLESH OF MY SKIN, BLOOD OF MY BLOOD (LP)	200
75	Mamba MAM 002	TORCH OF FREEDOM (LP)	40
75	Atra LP1001	TORCH OF FREEDOM (LP, same as Mamba issue)	50
75	ATRA ATLP 1002	PICK A DUB (LP)	55
76	Virgin V 2056	TOO EXPENSIVE (LP)	25
77	BRD 001	BRAND (LP)	50
88	Atra LP 1004	FLESH OF MY FLESH (LP)	20

KEITH HUDSON & FAMILY MAN

70s	Mamba MAM 003	PICK A DUB (LP)	50

KEITH HUDSON & I ROY
(see also I Roy)

73	Randy's RAN 534	Silver Platter/Jean You Change Everything	20

ROCK HUDSON

59	Brunswick 05816	Pillow Talk/Roly Poly	6
70	Warner Bros WB 8006	Gone With The Cowboys/Meantime	5

HUDSON BROTHERS

75	Rocket PIG 18	Rendezvous/Medley: These Things We Do/Home and four others	6

HUDSON-FORD
(see also Strawbs, Monks, Elmer Gantry's Velvet Opera)

73	A&M AMS 7078	Pick Up The Pieces/This Is Not The Way (To End A War Or Die)	5
74	A&M AMS 7096	Burn Baby Burn/Angels (p/s)	5
73	A&M AMLH 68208	NICKELODEON (LP, lyric insert, brown label)	15
77	Arnakata ARN 5001	REPERTOIRE (LP, for publishers' use)	20

MINT VALUE £

HUDSON PEOPLE
78 Hithouse HIT 1 — Trip To Your Mind/Power To The Hour (12") — 60
79 Ensign ENY 2712 — Trip To Your Mind/Power To The Hour (12", different mix) — 40

HUEYS
69 London HLU 10264 — Coo-Coo Over You/You Ain't No Hippie — 12

HUG
(see also Mike Hugg)
75 Polydor 2058 553 — Keep Pushing On/City — 6
75 Polydor 2383 330 — NEON DREAM (LP) — 20

MIKE HUGG
(see also Manfred Mann, Hug, Highly Likely, Elton Dean)
72 Polydor 2058 265 — Blue Suede Shoes Again/Fool No More — 5
73 Polydor 2058 359 — Stress And Strain/Tonight — 5
72 Polydor/Sound For Industry SFI 122 — Bonnie Charlie/SLADE: The Whole World's Going Crazee (33rpm flexidisc free with Music Scene magazine) — 7
72 Polydor 2383 140 — SOMEWHERE (LP, gatefold sleeve) — 20
73 Polydor 2383 213 — STRESS AND STRAIN (LP) — 20

HUGGY BEAR
93 PUSS 002 — February 14th/Into The Mission (1-sided gig freebie, w/l, plain black sleeve) — 5

BOBBY HUGHES EXPERIENCE
99 Ultimate Diler UDRLP 008 — FUSA RIOT (2xLP) — 20

CAROL HUGHES
58 Columbia DB 4094 — Lend Me Your Comb/First Date — 15

DANNY HUGHES
(see also Orange Machine)
69 Pye 7N 17750 — Hi Ho Silver Lining/I Washed My Hands In Muddy Water — 15

DAVID HUGHES
59 Top Rank JAR 205 — Teach Me (How To Love Him)/You Would Have Done The Same — 5
55 Philips BBE 12020 — DAVID HUGHES (EP) — 8
55 Delyse EDP 205 — CHRISTMAS WITH DAVID HUGHES (EP) — 8

FRED HUGHES
65 Fontana TF 583 — Oo Wee Baby I Love You/Love Me Baby — 25
76 Brunswick BR 37 — Baby Boy/JOHNNY JONES & KING CASUALS: Purple Haze — 10
76 DJM DJS 10717 — Oo Wee Baby I Love You/My Cries Oh — 6

GLENN HUGHES
(see also Deep Purple, News, Finders Keepers, Trapeze, Roger Glover, Hughes-Thrall)
79 Safari SAFE 14 — I Found A Woman/L.A. Cut Off (p/s) — 5
77 Safari LONG 2 — PLAY ME OUT (LP) — 15

JIMMY HUGHES
63 London HL 9680 — I'm Qualified/My Loving Time — 30
64 Pye International 7N 25254 — Steal Away/Lollipops, Lace And Lipstick — 25
66 Sue WI 4006 — Goodbye My Love/It Was Nice — 40
66 Atlantic 584 017 — Neighbour, Neighbour/It's A Good Thing — 20
67 Atlantic 584 135 — Hi-Heel Sneakers/Time Will Bring You Back — 15
69 Stax STAX 117 — Sweet Things You Do/Let 'Em Down Baby — 8
69 Stax STAX 126 — I'm Not Ashamed To Beg Or Plead/Chains Of Love — 12
67 Atlantic 587 068 — WHY NOT TONIGHT? (LP) — 75
69 Stax SXATS 1010 — SOMETHING SPECIAL (LP) — 30

NIA HUGHES
70 Penny Farthing PEN 724 — Turn On The Sun/The Wind — 8

RHETTA HUGHES
70s Polydor 184 223 — RELIGHT MY FIRE (LP) — 80

HUGHES-THRALL
(see also Glenn Hughes)
82 Epic EPC 25052 — HUGHES-THRALL (LP, with inner sleeve) — 12

HUGO & LUIGI
57 Columbia DB 3978 — Rockabilly Party/Shenandoah Rose — 15

ALAN HULL
(see also Lindisfarne, Chosen Few, Radiator)
70 Big T BIG 129 — We Can Swing Together/Obadiah's Grave — 10
75 Warner Brothers K16599 — One More Bottle Of Wine/Squire — 6
73 Charisma CAS 1069 — PIPEDREAM (LP, gatefold sleeve, booklet, large 'Mad Hatter' label) — 20
75 Warner Bros K56121 — SQUIRE (LP, 'Burbank' label) — 15

HULLABALLOOS
(see also Bunch Of Fives)
64 Columbia DB 7392 — I'm Gonna Love You Too/Why Do Fools Fall In Love — 10
65 Columbia DB 7558 — I'll Show You How To Love/Did You Ever — 10
65 Columbia DB 7626 — Don't Stop/I Won't Turn Away Now — 10

GEORGE HULTGREEN
70 Warner Bros WB 8017 — Say Hello/Before You Say Goodbye — 6

HUMAN BEANS
(see also Love Sculpture, Dave Edmunds)
67 Columbia DB 8230 — Morning Dew (Take Me For A Walk)/It's A Wonder — 65

HUMAN BEAST
(see also Bread Love & Dreams)
70 Decca LK/SKL 5053 — VOLUME ONE (LP) — 500

MINT VALUE £

HUMAN BEINZ

67	Capitol CL 15529	Nobody But Me/Sueno	50
67	Capitol CL 15529	Nobody But Me/Sueno (DJ Copy)	85
68	Capitol CL 15542	Turn On Your Lovelight/It's Fun To Be Clean	25

HUMAN INSTINCT

(see also Jessie Harper)

65	Mercury MF 951	Can't Stop Around/I Want To Be Loved By You My Friend	40
66	Mercury MF 972	The Rich Man/Illusions	70
67	Mercury MF 990	Go-Go/I Can't Live Without You	35
68	Deram DM 167	A Day In My Mind's Mind/Death Of The Seaside	150
68	Deram DM 177	Renaissance Fair/Pink Dawn	50

HUMAN LEAGUE

(see also Heaven 17, Men, Respect, Jo Callis)

78	Fast Product FAST 4	Being Boiled/Circus Of Death (p/s, original issue with b&w picture labels)	15
79	Fast Product FAST 10	THE DIGNITY OF LABOUR (12" EP, with spoken-word flexidisc [F10x/VF 1])	15
79	Virgin VS 294	Empire State Human/Introducing (p/s)	5
80	Virgin SV 105	HOLIDAY '80 (EP, double pack, purple & blue labels, 10,000 only)	8
80	Virgin VS 351	Empire State Human/Introducing//Only After Dark/Toyota City (Long Version) (double pack, p/s, shrinkwrapped)	20
80	Virgin VS 351	Only After Dark/Toyota City (Long Version) (p/s)	5
80	Virgin VS 351	Empire State Human/Introducing (p/s, reissue)	5
80	Virgin VS 351-12	Empire State Human/Introducing (12", p/s)	8
81	Virgin VS 395	Boys And Girls/Tom Baker (gatefold or non-gatefold p/s)	5
81	Virgin SV 105	HOLIDAY '80 (EP, reissue double pack, green/red labels, gatefold p/s)	7
81	Virgin SV 105-12	HOLIDAY '80 (12", 5-track EP, withdrawn)	20
79	Virgin V 2133	REPRODUCTION (LP)	12
80	Virgin V 2160	TRAVELOGUE (LP)	12

HUMANOID

(see also Future Sound Of London, Art Science Technology)

88	Westside WSR 7	Stakker Humanoid (Part 1)/Stakker Humanoid (Part 2) (p/s)	8
88	Westside Human 1989	GLOBAL (LP)	12

HUMANTE & RABBIT IN THE MOON

95	Rising High RSN 106	East (The Remixes) (12")	15

HUMBLEBUMS

(see also Gerry Rafferty, Billy Connolly)

69	Big T BIG 122	Saturday Roundabout Sunday/Bed Of Mossy Green	6
69	Big T BIG 127	Coconut Tree/Her Father Didn't Like Me Anyway	6
70	Big T BIG 130	Shoeshine Boy/My Apartment	6
69	Transatlantic TRA 186	THE FIRST COLLECTION OF MERRY MELODIES (LP)	12
69	Transatlantic TRA 201	THE NEW HUMBLEBUMS (LP, lilac/white label with 't' logo)	20
70	Transatlantic TRA 218	OPEN UP THE DOOR (LP)	15
74	Transatlantic TRA 288	THE COMPLETE HUMBLEBUMS (3-LP, box set of above albums)	20

HUMBLE PIE

(see also Steve Marriott, Small Faces, Peter Frampton, Herd, Natural Gas)

69	Immediate IM 082	Natural Born Bugie/Wrist Job	15
69	Immediate IM 082	Natural Born Bugie/Wrist Job (later pressing in p/s)	10
70	A&M AMS 807	Big Black Dog/Strange Days	7
71	A&M AMS 862	I Don't Need No Doctor/A Sonig For Jennie	7
72	A&M AMS 7003	Hot'n'Nasty/You're So Good For Me	5
73	A&M AMS 7052	Black Coffee/Say No More	5
73	A&M AMS 7070	Get Down To It/Honky Tonk Woman	5
73	A&M AMS 7090	Oh La De Da/Outcrowd	5
75	A&M AMS 7185	Rock'n'Roll Music/Scored Out	5
80	Jet JET 180	Fool For A Pretty Face/You Soppy Pratt (p/s)	5
69	Immediate IMSP 025	AS SAFE AS YESTERDAY IS (LP, lyric inner sleeve, pink label)	50
69	Immediate IMSP 027	TOWN AND COUNTRY (LP, lyric inner sleeve, pink label)	50
70	A&M AMLS 986	HUMBLE PIE (LP, textured gatefold sleeve, brown label)	60
71	A&M AMLS 2013	ROCK ON (LP)	20
71	A&M AMLH 63506	PERFORMANCE - ROCKIN' THE FILLMORE (2-LP)	18
72	A&M AMLS 64342	SMOKIN' (LP)	15
73	A&M AMLD 6004	EAT IT (2-LP, gatefold sleeve, booklet, brown label)	20
74	A&M AMLH 63611	THUNDERBOX (LP)	12
75	A&M AMLS 68282	STREET RATS (LP)	12
79	Jet LP231	ON TO VICTORY (LP)	20
80	Atco SD 38 131	GO FOR THE THROAT (LP)	20

HUMBUG

70	CBS 4811	Groovin' With Mr Bloe/Marianna	5
70	CBS 5208	I Got A Feeling (Vocal)/I Got A Feeling (Instrumental)	20

HELEN HUMES

(see also Benny Carter, Jimmy Witherspoon/Helen Humes)

53	Brunswick 05193	I Cried For You/Mean Way Of Loving (78)	10
56	Vogue V 2048	Million Dollar Secret/If I Could Be With You One Hour Of The Day	10
56	Vogue V 2048	Million Dollar Secret/If I Could Be With You One Hour Of The Day (78)	10
59	Contemporary CV 2415	When The Saints Come Marching In/Bill Bailey, Won't You Please Come Home (with Benny Carter's All-Stars)	5
59	Contemporary CV 2415	When The Saints Come Marching In/Bill Bailey, Won't You Please Come Home (with Benny Carter's All-Stars) (78)	10
61	Contemporary LAC 12245	HELEN HUMES AND THE BENNY CARTER ALL STARS (LP)	15

BOBBI HUMPHREY

75	Blue Note UAG 20003	FANCY DANCER (LP)	12

MINT VALUE £

DELLA HUMPHREY
69	Action ACT 4525	Don't Make The Good Girls Go Bad/Your Love Is All I Need	25
72	Fab FAB 183	Dreamland (actually by Marcia Griffiths)/Version	35

HUMPY BONG
(see also Bee Gees, Jonathan Kelly, Morgan)
70	Parlophone R 5859	Don't You Be Too Long/We're Alright 'Till Then	30

HUNGER
84	Psycho PSYCHO 14	STRICTLY FROM HUNGER (LP, reissue of U.S. LP)	15

HUNGRY WOLF
(see also Czar, Alan Parker, Ugly Custard)
70	Philips 6308 009	HUNGRY WOLF (LP, laminated sleeve, black/silver labels)	150

GERALDINE HUNT
69	Roulette RO 515	Never Never Leave Me/Push Sweep	20
75	EMI EMI 2275	You/It's All For You	6

MARSHA HUNT
69	Track 604 030	Walk On Gilded Splinters/Hot Rod Poppa	15
69	Track 604 034	Desdemona/Hippy Gumbo	20
70	Track 604 037	Keep The Customer Satisfied/Lonesome Holy Roller	10
73	Vertigo 6059 080	Beast Day/Somebody To Love (as Marsha Hunt's 22)	20
76	Electric WATT 1	C'est La Vie/Do You Really Believe In Voodoo	10
71	Track 2410 101	WOMAN CHILD (LP)	80

TOMMY HUNT
(see also Ivorys)
62	Top Rank JAR 605	The Door Is Open/I'm Wondering	20
68	Direction 58-3216	I Need A Woman Of My Own/Searchin' For My Baby Looking Everywhere	30
72	Polydor 2058 236	Mind, Body & Soul/One More Mountain To Climb	5
74	Pye 7N 45325	Sleep Tight Honey/Time Alone Will Tell	5
75	Spark SRL 1132	Crackin' Up/Get Out	5
76	Spark SRL 1146	Living On The Losing Side/Sunshine Girl	5
76	Spark SRL 1148	One Fine Morning/Sign On The Dotted Line/Loving You Is	5
85	Kent TOWN 103	The Work Song/IVORYS: Please Stay	25

WILLIE AMOS HUNT
67	Camp 602 003	Would You Believe/My Baby Wants To Dance	50

HUNT & TURNER
72	Village Thing VTS 11	MAGIC LANDSCAPE (LP)	60

CAROL HUNTER
73	Purple PUR 115	Look Out Cleveland/5/4 March	7
73	Purple TPS 3503	THE NEXT VOICE YOU HEAR (LP)	15

DANNY HUNTER (& GIANTS)
60	HMV POP 722	Make It Up/Little Girl (as Danny Hunter & Giants)	20
60	HMV POP 775	Who's Gonna Walk Ya Home?/Lonely And Blue	20
61	Fontana H 300	Lost Weekend/Age For Love	15

DAVE HUNTER
68	RCA RCA 1766	She's A Heartbreaker/Love Me A Lifetime	15
69	RCA RCA 1841	Don't Throw Your Love To The Wind/Hitchcock Railway	6
65	Oriole CB 1985	Evergreen/ Tree/Too Late	15

GREG HUNTER
66	Parlophone R 5483	Five O'Clock World/Away From Happiness	10

IAN HUNTER
(see also Mott The Hoople, At Last The 1958 Rock & Roll Show, Apex Rhythm & Blues All Stars, Mick Ronson, Roger Taylor)
75	CBS 3486	Who Do You Love/Boy	5
76	CBS 4268	All American Alien Boy (Version)/Rape	5
76	CBS 4479	You Nearly Did Me In/A Letter From Britannia To The Union Jack	15
77	CBS 5229	Justice Of The Peace/The Ballad Of Little Star (as Ian Hunter's Overnight Angels)	8
77	CBS 5497	England Rocks/Wild 'N' Free (as Ian Hunter's Overnight Angels)	5
79	Chrysalis CHS 2324	When The Daylight Comes/Life After Death (p/s, white vinyl with mask)	5
79	Chrysalis CHS 2346	Ships/Wild East (p/s)	5
79	Chrysalis CHS 2390	Cleveland Rocks/Bastard (p/s)	5
80	Chrysalis CHS 2434	We Gotta Get Out/Medley: Once Bitten Twice Shy/Bastard/Cleveland Rocks/ Sons And Daughters/One Of The Boys (live double pack, gatefold p/s)	5
81	Chrysalis CHS 2542	Lisa Likes Rock 'N' Roll/Noises (p/s, clear vinyl)	5
83	CBS A 3541	All Of The Good Ones Are Taken/Death 'N' Glory Boys (p/s)	5
83	CBS TA 3541	All Of The Good Ones Are Taken/Death 'N' Glory Boys/Traitor (12", p/s)	8
83	CBS A 3855	Somethin's Goin' On/All Of The Good Ones Are Taken (Slow Version) (p/s)	5
83	CBS A 3855	Somethin's Goin' On (Radio Edit)/All Of The Good Ones Are Taken (Slow Version) (promo only, no p/s)	5
77	CBS	YOU'RE NEVER ALONE WITH A SCHIZOPHRENIC (LP, unissued; later issued on Chrysalis CHR 1214)	12

IVORY JOE HUNTER
50	MGM MGM 271	I Almost Lost My Mind/S.P. Blues (78, with Orchestra)	20
56	London HLE 8261	A Tear Fell/I Need You By My Side	300
56	London HLE 8261	A Tear Fell/I Need You By My Side (78)	20
57	Columbia DB 3872	Since I Met You, Baby/You Can't Stop This Rockin' And Rollin'	250
57	Columbia DB 3872	Since I Met You, Baby/You Can't Stop This Rockin' And Rollin' (78)	20
57	London HLE 8486	Love's A Hurting Game/Empty Arms	150
57	London HLE 8486	Love's A Hurting Game/Empty Arms (78)	20
61	Capitol CL 15220	I'm Hooked/Because I Love You	30
61	Capitol CL 15226	You Better Believe It, Baby/May The Man Win	30

MINT VALUE £

ROBERT HUNTER
(see also Grateful Dead)

74	Round RX 101	TALES OF THE GREAT RUM RUNNERS (LP)	15
75	Round RX 105	TIGER ROSE (LP)	12
80	Dark Star DSLP 8001	JACK O'ROSES (LP)	15

SUSAN HUNTER

55	Brunswick 05458	Not Yet/Was That The Right Thing To Do?	8

TAB HUNTER

57	London HLD 8380	Young Love/Red Sails In The Sunset (gold label)	25
57	London HLD 8380	Young Love/Red Sails In The Sunset (silver label)	10
57	London HLD 8410	Ninety-Nine Ways/I Don't Get Around Much Anymore	15
58	London HLD 8535	Don't Let It Get Around/I'm Alone Because I Love You	20
60	Warner Bros WB 8	(What Can I Give) My Only Love/(I'll Be With You) In Apple Blossom Time	6
60	Warner Bros WB 20	Waitin' For The Fall/Our Love	6
61	London HLD 9381	The Wild Side Of Life/My Devotion	8
62	London HLD 9559	Born To Lose/I Can't Stop Lovin' You	8
58	London RE-D 1134	TAB HUNTER (EP)	20
61	Warner Bros WEP 6023	TAB HUNTER (EP, mono)	15
61	Warner Bros WSEP 2023	TAB HUNTER (EP, stereo)	20
60	Warner Bros WS 4008	TAB HUNTER (LP, mono)	25
60	Warner Bros WS 8008	TAB HUNTER (LP, stereo)	40
61	London HA-D 2401	YOUNG LOVE (LP, mono)	25
61	London SAH-G 6201	YOUNG LOVE (LP, stereo)	35

HUNTER MUSKETT

73	Bradleys BRAD 303	John Blair/Silver Coin (p/s)	6
70	Decca Nova SDN 20	EVERY TIME YOU MOVE (LP, blue/silver labels)	300
73	Bradleys BRADL 1003	HUNTER MUSKETT (LP, lyric inner sleeve)	35

HUNTERS (Holland)
(see also Jan Akkerman, Brainbox)

66	RCA RCA 1541	Russian Spy And I/Spring	20

HUNTERS (U.K.)
(see also Dave Sampson & Hunters, Maisie McDaniel)

60	Fontana H 276	Teen Scene/Santa Monica Flyer	25
61	Fontana H 303	Golden Ear-rings/Tally Ho	15
61	Fontana H 323	The Storm/How's M'Chicks?	20
64	Fontana TF 514	Teen Scene/Someone Else's Baby	15
61	Fontana TFL 5140	TEEN SCENE: THE HUNTERS PLAY THE BIG HITS (LP, mono)	45
61	Fontana STFL 561	TEEN SCENE: THE HUNTERS PLAY THE BIG HITS (LP, stereo)	50
62	Fontana TFL 5175	HITS FROM THE HUNTERS (LP, mono)	45
62	Fontana STFL 572	HITS FROM THE HUNTERS (LP, stereo)	50

HUNTING LODGE

85	Sterile SER 04	NOMAD SOULS (LP)	20

HURDY GURDY

72	CBS 64781	HURDY GURDY (LP, gatefold sleeve)	200

RED HURLEY

77	EMI 2575	Listen To The Children/Just A Little Love	6

RED VINCENT HURLEY

76	Pye 7N 45583	When/Just A Little Love (p/s)	7

HURRICANE STRINGS

63	Columbia DB 7027	Venus/In The Carrick	15

HURRICANES
(see also Dave Barker)

71	Upsetter US 363	Got To Be Mine/UPSETTERS: Version	12

MIKE HURST (& METHOD)
(see also Springfields, Remo Four, Ashton Gardner & Dyke, Sundance)

63	Philips BF 1295	The Banjo Song/Any Chance For Me	5
64	Philips BF 1319	Carol Anne/Anytime That You Want Me	5
64	Philips BF 1353	Half Heaven Half Heartache/Look In Your Eyes	5
65	Philips BF 1389	The Last Time You'll Walk Out On Me/Something Told Me	6
65	Philips BF 1424	Show Me Around/I'm Running Away	7
71	Capitol CL 15681	Show Me The Way To Georgia/Over Again	6

MISSISSIPPI JOHN HURT

65	Vanguard SVRL 19005	THE IMMORTAL MISSISSIPPI JOHN HURT (LP)	35
66	Vanguard SVRL 19032	MISSISSIPPI JOHN HURT (LP)	35
67	Fontana TFL 6079	MISSISSIPPI JOHN HURT (LP)	35
71	Spokane SPL 1001	THE ORIGINAL 1928 RECORDINGS (LP)	50
71	Vanguard VSD 19/20	THE BEST OF MISSISSIPPI JOHN HURT (2-LP)	18
73	Vanguard VSD 79327	LAST SESSIONS (LP)	20
72	Vanguard VSD 79220	TODAY (LP)	20

HUSH

68	Fontana TF 944	Elephant Rider/Grey	425

HüSKER Dü

84	SST SST 025	Eight Miles High/Masochism World (live) (p/s)	12
85	SST 051	Makes No Sense At All/Love Is All Around (p/s)	5
86	Warner Bros W 8746	Don't Want To Know If You're Lonely/All Work And No Play (p/s)	5
86	Warner Bros W 8746T	Don't Want To Know If You're Lonely/All Work And No Play/ Helter Skelter (live) (12", p/s)	10
86	Warner Bros W 8612	Sorry Somehow/All This I've Done For You (p/s)	5
86	Warner Bros W 8612	Sorry Somehow/All This I've Done For You//Celebrated Summer (Acoustic)/ Flexible Flyer (double pack, gatefold sleeve)	8

			MINT VALUE £
86	Warner Bros W 8612T	Sorry Somehow/All This I've Done For You/Celebrated Summer (Acoustic)/Flexible Flyer/Fattie (12", p/s)	8
87	Warner Bros W 8456	Could You Be The One/Everytime (p/s)	5
87	Warner Bros W 8456T	Could You Be The One/Everytime/Charity, Chastity, Prudence, Hope (12", p/s)	10
87	Warner Bros W 8276	Ice Cold Ice/Gotta Lotta (p/s)	5
87	Warner Bros W 8276T	Ice Cold Ice/Gotta Lotta/Medley (12", p/s)	10
82	Bespoke BES 03 LP	EVERYTHING FALLS APART (LP)	20
83	SST SST 020	METAL CIRCUS (LP)	20
84	SST SST 027	ZEN ARCADE (2-LP)	20
86	Warner Bros WX40	CANDY APPLE GREY (LP)	15
87	Warner Bros WB 925544	WAREHOUSE SONGS & STORIES (2-LP)	18
09	Rhino 8122798853	CANDY APPLE GREY (LP, reissue, 180gm vinyl)	12

HUSKY

75	Anchor ANC 1026	Give It Up/Silence Of Dreams	6
76	Anchor ANC 1030	Pretty Little Linda/Make It Turn Out Right	6

FERLIN HUSKY (& HIS HUSH PUPPIES)

(see also Simon Crum)

57	Capitol CL 14702	Gone/Missing Persons (as Ferlin Husky & His Hush Puppies)	15
57	Capitol CL 14702	Gone/Missing Persons (as Ferlin Husky & His Hush Puppies) (78)	10
57	Capitol CL 14753	A Fallen Star/Prize Possession	20
57	Capitol CL 14785	This Moment Of Love/Make Me Live Again	5
57	Capitol CL 14785	This Moment Of Love/Make Me Live Again (78)	10
58	Capitol CL 14824	Wang Dang Doo/What'cha Doin' After School	20
58	Capitol CL 14824	Wang Dang Doo/What'cha Doin' After School (78)	12
58	Capitol CL 14883	Slow Down Brother/The Drunken Driver (& His Hush Puppies)	10
58	Capitol CL 14916	I Feel That Old Heartache Again/I Saw God	8
58	Capitol CL 14922	The Kingdom Of Love/Terrific Together	7
58	Capitol CL 14954	I Will/All Of The Time	5
60	Capitol CL 15160	Wings Of A Dove/Next TO Jimmy	6
57	Capitol EAP1 718	SONGS OF THE HOME AND HEART (EP)	12
57	Capitol EAP1 837	FERLIN HUSKY HITS (EP)	15
57	Capitol EAP1 921	COUNTRY MUSIC HOLIDAY (EP)	15
59	Parlophone GEP 8795	COUNTRY ROUND UP (EP)	15
60	Capitol EAP1 1280	FERLIN'S FAVOURITES (EP)	10
60	Capitol EAP3 1280	FERLIN'S FAVOURITES (EP)	10
58	Capitol T 880	BOULEVARD OF BROKEN DREAMS (LP)	20
59	Capitol T 976	SITTIN' ON A RAINBOW (LP)	20
65	Fontana FJL 304	OLE OPRY FAVOURITES (LP)	15

JACQUES HUSTIN

74	EMI EMI 2143	Fleur De Liberté/Freedom For The Man	15

HUSTLER

74	Firefly AMS501	Get Outa My 'Ouse/Happy Days	5
74	A&M AMLS 68276	HIGH STREET (LP)	12
75	A&M AMLH 33001	PLAY LOUD (LP)	12

HUSTLERS

63	Philips BF 1275	Gimme What I Want/Not Much	7
64	Mercury MF 807	Be True To You/You Can't Sit Down	7
64	Mercury MF 817	Sick Of Giving/Easy To Find	20

WILLIE HUTCH

73	Tamla Motown TMG 862	Brother's Gonna Work It Out/I Choose You	15
73	Tamla Motown STMA 8003	THE MACK (LP, soundtrack)	15
73	Tamla Motown STML 11247	FULLY EXPOSED (LP)	15
74	Tamla Motown STML 11269	FOXY BROWN (LP, soundtrack)	15
74	Tamla Motown STML 11280	THE MARK OF THE BEAST (LP)	20
75	Tamla Motown STML 12015	ODE TO MY LADY (LP)	20
76	Tamla Motown STML 12023	CONCERT IN BLUES (LP)	15

ASHLEY HUTCHINGS

(see also Albion Band, Fairport Convention, Steeleye Span, Bunch)

72	Island HELP 5	MORRIS ON (LP, actually by various folk artists)	18
76	Island HELP 24	RATTLEBONE AND ROUGHJACK (LP)	25
76	Harvest SHSM 2012	SON OF MORRIS ON (LP, actually by various folk artists)	18
77	Harvest SHSP 4073	KICKIN' UP THE SAWDUST (LP)	12

HUTCH HUTCHINS

77	Goodwood GM 12324	FEELS LIKE RAIN (LP)	35

SAM HUTCHINS

69	Bell BLL 1044	Dang Me/I'm Tired Of Pretending	10

LEROY HUTSON

75	Warner Bros K 16536	All Because Of You Parts 1 & 2	10
74	Buddah BDLP 4013	THE MAN (LP)	20
75	Warner Bros K 56139	HUTSON (LP)	50

J.B. HUTTO & HIS HAWKS

73	Delmark DS 617	HAWK SQUAT (LP)	30

BETTY HUTTON

(see also Hutton Sisters, Perry Como, 'Tennessee' Ernie Ford)

53	HMV 7M 103	Somebody Loves Me/Jealous (B-side with Pat Morgan)	10
56	Capitol CL 14568	Sleepy Head/Hit The Road To Dreamland	8
54	Capitol LC 6639	CAPITOL PRESENTS BETTY HUTTON (10" LP)	25

DANNY HUTTON

(see also Three Dog Night)

66	MGM MGM 1314	Funny How Love Can Be/Dreamin' Isn't Good For You	15
65	Pye International 7N 25325	Roses And Rainbows/Monster Shindig	5

MINT VALUE £

HUTTON SISTERS (Betty & Marion)
(see also Betty Hutton)

55	Capitol CL 14250	Ko Ko Mo (I Love You So)/Heart Throb	25

CHARLIE HYATT

65	Island IEP 707	RASS! (EP, as Bam & Charlie Hyatt)	30
66	Island ILP 932	KISS ME NECK (LP)	35

LEON HYATT

76	Nationwide NW 1014	40 Days And Nights/Third World Affairs	15

HYDRA

74	Capricorn 2089 008	Glitter Queen/It's So Hard	5
74	Capricorn 2429 120	HYDRA (LP)	12

HYGRADES

65	Columbia DB 7734	She Cared/We're Through	15

BRIAN HYLAND

60	London HLR 9161	Itsy Bitsy Teeny Weeny Yellow Polka Dot Bikini/Don't Dilly Dally, Sally (78)	200
60	London HLR 9113	Rosemary/Library Love Affair	20
60	London HLR 9161	Itsy Bitsy Teeny Weeny Yellow Polka Dot Bikini/Don't Dilly Dally, Sally	8
60	London HLR 9203	Four Little Heels/That's How Much	8
61	London HLR 9262	Lop Sided, Over Loaded/I Gotta Go ('Cause I Love You)	8
61	HMV POP 915	Let Me Belong To You/Let It Die	7
61	HMV POP 955	The Night I Cried/I'll Never Stop Wanting You	6
62	HMV POP 1013	Ginny Come Lately/I Should Be Gettin' Better	8
62	HMV POP 1051	Sealed With A Kiss/Summer Job	8
62	HMV POP 1079	Warmed Over Kisses/Walk A Lonely Mile	5
63	HMV POP 1113	I May Not Live To See Tomorrow/It Ain't That Way At All	5
63	HMV POP 1143	If Mary's There/Remember Me	6
63	HMV POP 1169	Somewhere In The Night/I Wish Today Was Yesterday	6
63	HMV POP 1188	I'm Afraid To Go Home/Save Your Heart For Me	6
63	HMV POP 1237	Let Us Make Our Own Mistakes/Nothing Matters But You	6
64	Philips BF 1326	Here's To Our Love/Two Kinds Of Girls	6
65	Philips BF 1429	Stay Away From Her/I Can't Keep A Secret	6
65	Philips BF 1486	3,000 Miles/Sometimes They Do	6
66	Philips BF 1508	The Joker Went Wild/I Can Hear The Rain	20
66	Philips BF 1528	Run Run Look And See/Why Did You Do It	8
66	Philips BF 1555	Hung Up In Your Eyes/Why Mine	6
67	Philips BF 1569	Holiday For Clowns/Yesterday I Had A Girl	8
69	Dot 124	A Million To One/It Could All Begin Again (in You)	10
67	Philips BF 1601	Get The Message/Kinda Groovy	6
70	Uni UN 530	Gypsy Woman/You And Me	7
72	Uni UN 540	I Love Every Little Thing About You/With My Eyes Wide Open	7
62	HMV 7EG 8780	SEALED WITH A KISS (EP)	30
61	London HA-R 2289	THE BASHFUL BLONDE (LP)	90
62	HMV CLP 1553	LET ME BELONG TO YOU (LP)	70
63	HMV CLP 1759	COUNTRY MEETS FOLK (LP)	50
66	Philips BL 7762	THE JOKER WENT WILD (LP)	25
68	Fontana SFL 13008	HERE'S TO OUR LOVE (LP)	20

C. HYMAN

65	Ska Beat JB 200	The Ska Rhythm/The Ska Is Moving On	18

DICK HYMAN TRIO

67	Command SCMD 105	BRAZILIAN IMPRESSIONS (LP)	15
69	Command SCMD 508	MOOG - THE ELECTRIC ECLECTICS OF DICK HYMAN (LP)	20
70	Command SCMD 946	THE AGE OF ELECTRONICUS (LP)	30
56	MGM SP 1164	Theme From The Threepenny Opera/Baubles, Bangles And Beads	6

PHYLLIS HYMAN

79	Arista ARIST 323	You Know How To Love Me/Give A Little More (12", p/s)	15

HYPA KONCEPT

91	No LAbel L8 001	Party People (Come Together) (3 Mixes) (12", hand-written labels)	20
92	Club State CSR 12001	Love Addict (4 Mixes) (12", stamped white label)	40

HYPER ON EXPERIENCE

94	Moving Shadow SHADOW 40	THE FAMILY WE NEVER HAD (12" picture disc)	50
93	Moving Shadow SHADOW 40	THE FAMILY WE NEVER HAD EP (12", p/s, as Hyper-On Experience)	15
93	Moving Shadow SHADOW 30	DEAF IN THE FAMILY EP (12", white labe stamped with cat. no. only as Hyper On Exp.)	60
93	Moving Shadow SHADOW 30	DEAF IN THE FAMILY EP (12", p/s as Hyper-On Experience)	40

I

I AM KLOOT
(see also Johnny Dangerously)

99	Ugly Man AH18299	Titanic/To You (7", 1,000 only in brown paper sleeve)	12

JANIS IAN

67	Verve Folkways VS 1503	Society's Child (Baby I've Been Thinking)/Letter To Jon	20
67	Verve Folkways VS 1506	Society's Child (Baby I've Been Thinking)/Letter To Jon (reissue)	5
68	Verve Folkways VS 1513	Sunflakes Fall, Snowrays Call/Insanity Comes Quietly To The Structured Mind	10
67	Verve F'ways (S)VLP 6001	JANIS IAN (LP)	30
67	Verve Forecast (S)VLP 6003	FOR ALL THE SEASONS OF YOUR MIND (LP)	30

MINT VALUE £

68	Verve Forecast (S)VLP 6009	THE SECRET LIFE OF J. EDDY FINK (LP)	20
70	Verve Folkways SVLP 6023	WHO REALLY CARES? (LP)	25
71	Capitol E-ST 683	PRESENT COMPANY (LP)	20

IAN (EDWARD) & ZODIACS

(see also Koppykats, Wellington Wade)

63	Oriole CB 1849	Beechwood 4-5789/You Can Think Again	45
65	Fontana TF 548	Just The Little Things/This Won't Happen To Me (as Ian Edward with Zodiacs)	30
66	Fontana TF 708	No Money, No Honey/Where Were You?	30
66	Fontana TF 753	Wade In The Water/Come On Along, Girl	65
65	Wing WL 1074	GEAR AGAIN - 12 HITS (LP)	30

IAN (Meeson) & BELINDA (Gillet)

(see also Brian May)

89	Odeon ODO 112	Who Wants To Live Forever?/Who Wants To Live Forever? (Instrumental) (p/s, feat. Brian May)	7
89	Odeon 12ODO 112	Who Wants To Live Forever?/Who Wants To Live Forever? (Instrumental)/ Who Wants To Live Forever? (Original Demo) (12", p/s, feat. Brian May)	10

IAN & SYLVIA

63	Fontana TF 426	Four Strong Winds/Long Lonesome Road	7
65	Fontana TFL 6053	EARLY MORNING RAIN (LP)	30
68	Vanguard SVRL 19004	THE BEST OF IAN & SYLVIA (LP)	12

I BENJAHMAN

83	Lion Kingdom LKLP 01	INTRODUCING A FRACTION OF JAH ACTION (LP)	35

IBM 7090 COMPUTER & DIGITAL TO SOUND TRANSCUDER

62	Brunswick STA 8523	MUSIC FOR MATHEMATICS (LP)	30

RAS IBUNA

85	Studio Now SNT 01	Diverse Doctrine/Version/COOL BREEZE: Wi Nuh Want Nun A Dat (12")	12

ICARUS

(see also Soft Machine)

69	Spark SRL 1012	The Devil Rides Out/You're In Life	175
72	Pye Int. NSPL 28161	THE MARVEL WORLD OF ICARUS (LP, laminated sleeve, blue/black labels)	150

ICE

(see also Affinity)

67	Decca F 12680	Anniversary (Of Love)/So Many Times	70
68	Decca F 12749	Ice Man/Whisper Her Name (Maria Laine)	120

ICE

(see also Dickens)

79	Storm SR 3307	SAGA OF THE ICE KING (LP, private pressing with booklet)	80

ICE CREAM

74	Fontana 6007 039	Shout It Out/Hold Yourself Tight	25

ICED EARTH

02	Century Media	DARK GENESIS (5-CD box set, initial issues with mispressed labels)	25

ICE LA BAS

80s	Storm SR 12 NO 4	ICE LA BAS (12" EP, with booklet)	10

ICEPICK

(see also Bodysnatchers)

97	Backbone BR971AA	Phenomenal Criminal/Brixtonites Pt 1 (12")	20
98	Backbone ICEEP1 BB002	The ICEPICK (EP)	15
99	Ruf RUF 027	Dungeon Funk (12")	8

ICICLE WORKS

(see also Ian McNabb, Melting Bear)

82	Troll Kitchen WORKS 1	Nirvana/Love Hunt/Scirocco (p/s)	5

ICONS OF FILTH

83	Corpus Christi CHRIST ITS 7	USED, ABUSED, UNAMUED EP (fold-out p/s)	10
84	Mortarhate MORT 10	BRAIN DEATH EP (p/s with insert)	10
85	Mortarhate MORT 18	THE FILTH AND THE FURY EP (Fold-out p/s)	10
97	BBP/Yellow Fever BBPV3/YF1	SHOW US YOU CARE EP (fold-out p/s, inserts)	6
97	BBP/Yellow Fever BBPV3/YF1	SHOW US YOU CARE EP (12 test pressings with red fold-out p/s and inserts)	25
84	Mortarhate MORT 5	ONWARD CHRISTIAN SOLDIERS (LP)	20

IDEALS

61	Pye International 7N 25103	Knee Socks/Mary's Lamb	40

DAVID IDEMA

72	Buddah 2011 130	House On Holy Road/Dream Weaver	6

IDES OF MARCH

(see also Survivor)

66	London HLU 10058	You Wouldn't Listen/I'll Keep Searching (as I'des Of March)	12
68	London HLU 10183	Hole In My Soul/Girls Don't Grow On Trees	12
70	Warner Bros WB 7378	Vehicle/Lead Me Home, Gently	6
70	Warner Bros WB 7403	Superman/Home	6
70	Warner Bros WS 1863	THE IDES OF MARCH (LP)	20

IDIOTS

(see also Tone Deaf & Idiots)

80s	Blue Angle BLI 2	Operation Julie/(Why Does Politics Turn Men Into) Toads (p/s)	5

IDJUT BOYS

94	U Star US 003	PHANTOM SLASHER EP (12")	40
00	U Star US 001	IDJUT BOY EP (12")	50
98	Noid NOIDLP 001	NOID LONG PLAYER (2-LP)	50
96	Noid NOID ONE	Girth Soup/Crouton Bonus/DJ HARVEY: Keep On Trying/Drums in 6 Twelve (12")	15

MINT VALUE £

IDJUT BOYS & DJ HARVEY

96	Noid NOID ONE	Untitled (12")	25

IDJUT BOYS & LAJ

95	U Star US 004	Not Reggae (12")	40
95	U Star US 006	Foolin' (12")	20
95	U star US 007	BEARD LAW (EP)	15

ERIC IDLE & NEIL INNES

76	BBC REB 233	THE RUTLAND WEEKEND SONGBOOK (LP)	12

IDLE FLOWERS

(see also Hanoi Rocks)

84	Miles Ahead AHEAD 1	All I Want Is You/Fizz Music (p/s)	8

IDLE RACE

(see also Mike Sheridan & Nightriders, Nightriders, Mike Sheridan's Lot, Lemon Tree, Jeff Lynne, Move, E.L.O., Trevor Burton, Steve Gibbons Band, Wizzard)

67	Liberty LBF 15026	The Imposters Of Life's Magazine/Sitting In My Tree	35
68	Liberty LBF 15054	The Skeleton And The Roundabout/Knocking Nails Into My House	25
68	Liberty LBF 15101	The End Of The Road/The Morning Sunshine	15
68	Liberty LBF 15129	I Like My Toys/The Birthday (unissued)	0
69	Liberty LBF 15218	Days Of Broken Arrows/Warm Red Carpet (B-side act. "Worn Red Carpet")	20
69	Liberty LBF 15242	Come With Me/Reminds Me Of You	22
71	Regal Zonophone RZ 3036	Dancing Flower/Bitter Green	12
76	United Artists UP 36060	The Skeleton And The Roundabout/Morning Sunshine	5
68	Liberty LBL 83132	THE BIRTHDAY PARTY (LP, mono)	70
68	Liberty LBS 83132	THE BIRTHDAY PARTY (LP, stereo)	50
69	Liberty LBS 83221	THE IDLE RACE (LP)	80
71	Regal Zono. SLRZ 1017	TIME IS (LP)	170
73	Sunset SLS 50354	ON WITH THE SHOW (LP)	15
76	Sunset SLS 50381	THE BIRTHDAY PARTY (LP, reissue)	15

IDLEWILD

97	Human Condition HC 0017	Queen Of The Troubled Teens/Faster/Self Healer (p/s, 1,000 only)	70
97	Fierce Panda NING 42	Chandelier/I Want To Be A Writer (p/s)	20
97	Deceptive BLUFF 057	Satan Polaroid/House Alone (die-cut p/s, numbered, 1,500 only)	15
98	Deceptive BLUFF 058CD	CAPTAIN EP (Self Healer/Annihilate Now!/Last Night I Missed All The Fireworks/ Satan Polaroid/You Just Have To Be Who You Are) (CD)	15
98	Food FOOD 111	A Film For The Future/Mince Showercap Part 1 (wraparound p/s, stickered poly outer sleeve)	5
98	Food FOOD 113	Everyone Says You're So Fragile/Mince Showercap Part 2 (wraparound p/s, stickered poly outer sleeve)	5
98	Food FOOD 114	I'm A Message/Mince Showercap Part 3 (p/s)	5
02	Parlophone 5402431	THE REMOTE PART (LP, with inner sleeve)	18

BILLY IDOL

(see also Generation X)

82	Chrysalis CHS 12 2543	Mony Mony/Baby Talk/Untouchables/Dancing With Myself (12", p/s)	8
82	Chrysalis CHSP 2625	Hot In The City/Dead On Arrival (picture disc)	5

IDOLS

(see also Mike Sax & Idols)

65	Mercury MF 840	Don't Walk Away/You Don't Care	20

IDOLS

(see also New York Dolls)

79	Ork NYC 2	You/Girl That I Love (p/s)	8

IF

(see also Ferris Wheel, Terry Smith)

70	Island WIP 6083	Raise The Level Of Your Conscious Mind/I'm Reaching Out On All Sides	10
71	United Artists UP 35263	Far Beyond/Forgotten Roads	6
72	United Artists UP 35356	You In Your Small Corner/Waterfall	6
70	Island ILPS 9129	IF (LP, 1st pressing, pink label/'i' logo)	45
71	Island ILPS 9129	IF (LP, 2nd pressing, pink rim label/'palm tree' logo)	25
71	Island ILPS 9137	IF2 (LP, pink label, pink rim label/'palm tree' logo)	30
71	United Artists UAG 29158	IF3 (LP, gatefold sleeve)	30
72	United Artists UAG 29315	IF IV (LP, gatefold sleeve with inner)	30
75	Gull GULP 1007	TEA BREAK OVER - BACK ON YOUR 'EADS (LP)	12
74	Gull GULP 1004	NOT JUST ANOTHER BUNCH OF PRETTY FACES (LP, with inner sleeve)	15

KRIS IFE

(see also Quiet Five, Judd)

67	MGM MGM 1369	Hush/The Spectator	40
68	MGM MGM 1390	This Woman's Love/I Gotta Feeling	12
68	Music Factory CUB 3	Give And Take/Sands Of Time	20
68	Parlophone R 5741	Imagination/I'm Coming 'Round	20
69	Parlophone R 5770	Haven't We Had A Good Time?/Will I Ever Fall In Love Again?	10
73	Bumlade GE122	Wherever You Are/The Sun, The Sea, The Sand And The Wine	25

I GAD

92	Nuff Tuff TUF 006	Brutality/ENHANCERS: Brutal Dub/Wicked Man/MANDINKA: Rootsman Corner/ENHANCERS: Wicked Dub (12")	50

'IGGINBOTTOM

(see also Soft Machine)

69	Deram DML/SML 1051	'IGGINBOTTOM'S WRENCH (LP)	200

IGGY & STOOGES

(see under Stooges, Iggy Pop)

MINT VALUE £

IGNERANTS
79	Rundown ACE 008	Radio Interference/Wrong Place, Wrong Time (p/s)	30

I.G.s
75	RCA RCA 2560	Show And Tell/I Can't Get You Out Of My Mind	15

IGUANA
72	Polydor 2383 108	IGUANA (LP, gatefold sleeve)	25

IGUANAS
65	RCA RCA 1484	This Is What I Was Made For/Don't Come Runnin' To Me	40

I JAH MAN (LEVI)
76	Lucky LY 6016	Jah Heavy Load/Heavy Dub	70
76	Concrete CJ 756	I Am Levi/Part 2	100
77	Ghetto Rocker PRE 1	Africa/Afrodub (handwritten labels)	35
78	Island WIP 6458	Heavy Load/I'm A Levi	20
85	Jahmani JM1 501	Moulding/Jah Is Coming Again (12")	40

I-JOG & TRACKSUITS
78	Tyger TYG 1	Red Box/Worrying Man (p/s)	6

IKE (B) & CRYSTALITES
68	Island WI 3134	Illya Kuryakin/Anne Marie (B-side miscredited to Bobby Ellis & Crystalites)	60
68	Island WI 3151	Try A Little Merriness/Patricia (as Ike B & Crystalites)	20

IKETTES
(see also Ike & Tina Turner, P.P. Arnold)

62	London HLU 9508	I'm Blue/Find My Baby	25
65	Stateside SS 407	Peaches'N'Cream/The Biggest Players	35
65	Stateside SS 434	(He's Gonna Be) Fine Fine Fine/How Come	25
65	Sue WI 389	Prisoner In Love/Those Words	40
66	Polydor 56506	I'm So Thankful/Don't Feel Sorry For Me	20
66	Polydor 56516	(Never More) Lonely For You/Sally Go Round The Roses	20
66	London HLU 10081	What'cha Gonna Do?/Down, Down	80
67	Polydor 56533	I'm So Thankful/Don't Feel Sorry For Me (reissue)	8
73	Mojo 2092 063	Peaches'N'Cream/Sally Go Round The Roses	8
65	Stateside SE 1033	FINE FINE FINE (EP)	125

ILANIT
77	Pye International 7N 25739	I'm No One (If You Leave Me)/I Can't Say I Love You (p/s)	10

I LIFE
64	R&B JB 140	Kiss You Gave Me/No More	18

ILLUSION
69	Dot DOT 122	Did You See Her Eyes?/Falling In Love	8
70	Dot DOT 133	Together/Don't Push It	5
70	Dot DOT 137	Let's Make Each Other Happy/Beside You (unissued)	0
70	Paramount PARA 3007	Let's Make Each Other Happy/Beside You	5
69	Dot (S)LPD 531	ILLUSION (LP)	25
70	Dot SLPD 537	TOGETHER (AS A WAY OF LIFE) (LP)	22
70	Paramount SPFL 264	IF IT'S SO (LP, originally planned for Dot SLPD 539)	15

ILLUSIONS
83	Zella ZEL LPS 405	ILLUSIONS (LP, 100 only, with insert)	50

ILLUSIVE DREAM
(see also Christine Perfect)

69	RCA Victor RCA 1791	Electric Garden/Back Again	30

SOLOMON ILORY
63	Blue Note 45-1899	Yabe E (Farewell) (Parts 1 & 2)	12

ERIK ILOTT, SHANTYMAN
73	Folk'sle FOR 7	SHIPSHAPE & BRISTOL FASHION (LP, card foldout sleeve, pasted on photo & 25-page booklet)	40

I LUDICRIOUS
87	Kaleidoscope KSLP 004	IT'S LIKE EVERYTHING ELSE (LP)	12

I LUV WIGHT
(see also Kaleidoscope, Fairfield Parlour)

70	Philips 6006 043	Let The World Wash In/Mediaeval Masquerade (in p/s)	90
70	Philips 6006 043	Let The World Wash In/Mediaeval Masquerade	35

IMAGE
(see also Dave Edmunds)

65	Parlophone R 5281	Come To The Party/Never Let Me Go	40
65	Parlophone R 5352	Home Is Anywhere/I Hear Your Voice Again	40
66	Parlophone R 5442	I Can't Stop Myself/Let's Make The Scene	40

IMAGES
65	Polydor 56011	I Only Have Myself To Blame/Head Over Heels	30

IM & COUNT OSSIE
71	Banana CA 357	So Long Rastafari Calling/Give Me Back My Language & Culture	40

IM (Cedric Brooks) & DAVID
70	Bamboo BAM 57	Candid Eye/SOUND DIMENSION: Federated Backdrop	40

NATALIE IMBRUGLIA
98	RCA 74321 52799-2	Torn/Contradictions/Diving In The Deep End (CD, withdrawn)	12

IMITATIONS
71	Crystal CR 7013	Walking Up A One Way Street/One Way Street - Version	6

IMMEDIATE
05	Fierce Panda NING161	Never Seen/Say This (p/s)	7

MINT VALUE £

IMMORTALS

69 Amalgamated AMG 851 — Bongo Jah/ANSELL COLLINS: My Last Waltz ... 60

IMMORTALS

(see also Queen)

86 MCA MCA 1057 — No Turning Back/No Turning Back (The Chocks-Away Mix) (p/s) ... 30
86 MCA MCAT 1057 — No Turning Back (Joy Stick Mix)/No Turning Back/No Turning Back (The Chocks-Away Mix) (12", p/s) ... 35

IMPAC

66 CBS 202402 — Too Far Out/Rat Tat Ta Tat ... 110

IMPACT

83 Cyanide — PUNK CHRISTMAS EP ... 20

IMPACT ALL STARS

(see also Randy's All Stars, Alton Ellis, Gregory Issacs, Errol Dunkley, C. Danovan, Heptones, Dennis Brown, Horace Andy)

71 Bullet BU 483 — Dandy Shandy Version 4/Go Back Version 3 ... 7
71 Randy's RAN 519 — Go Back Version 4/Version 3 ... 7
71 Supreme SUP 223 — Go Back/Version ... 8

IMPALAS

59 MGM MGM 1015 — Sorry (I Ran All The Way Home)/Fool, Fool, Fool ... 25
59 MGM MGM 1015 — Sorry (I Ran All The Way Home)/Fool, Fool, Fool (78) ... 40
59 MGM MGM 1031 — Oh, What A Fool/Sandy Went Away ... 35
60 MGM MGM 1068 — Peggy Darling/'Bye Everybody ... 35
59 MGM MGM-EP 696 — SORRY (I RAN ALL THE WAY HOME) (EP) ... 450

IMPERIAL POMPADOURS

(see also Inner City Unit, Robert Calvert)

80 Pompadour POMP 001 — ERSATZ (LP, actually Inner City Unit with Robert Calvert & Barney Bubbles) ... 40

IMPERIALS

68 Nu Beat NB 012 — Young Love/Days Like These ... 25

IMPERIALS

72 Key KL 012 — TIME TO GET IT TOGETHER (LP) ... 18
74 Key KL 025 — FOLLOW THE MAN WITH THE MUSIC (LP) ... 15

IMPERIALS (Jamaica)

69 Bullet BU 417 — Black Is Soul/Always With You ... 12

IMPERSONATORS

(see also Moffat Allstars)

69 Big Shot BI 524 — Make It Easy On Yourself/I've Tried Before ... 12

IMPOSSIBLE DREAMERS

80 Merciful Release MR 1 — Books Books Books/Not A Love Song/Waiting For The Girl/What Can You Do When You See Someone As Beautiful As You? ... 8

IMPOSSIBLE YEARS

85 Dreamworld DREAM 1 — SCENES WE'D LIKE TO SEE (12" EP) ... 12

IMPOSTERS

69 Mercury MF 1080 — Apache '69/Q Three ... 20

IMPRESSIONS

(see also Curtis Mayfield, Jerry Butler)

58 London HL 8697 — For Your Precious Love/Sweet Was The Wine (as Jerry Butler & Impressions) ... 220
58 London HL 8697 — For Your Precious Love/Sweet Was The Wine (78, as Jerry Butler & Impressions) ... 80
61 HMV POP 961 — Gypsy Woman/As Long As You Love Me ... 40
63 HMV POP 1129 — I'm The One Who Loves You/I Need Your Love ... 40
63 HMV POP 1226 — It's Alright/You'll Want Me Back ... 20
64 HMV POP 1262 — Talkin' About My Baby/Never Too Much Love ... 22
64 HMV POP 1295 — I'm So Proud/I Made A Mistake ... 18
64 HMV POP 1317 — Keep On Pushing/I Love You (Yeah) ... 18
64 HMV POP 1343 — You Must Believe Me/See The Real Me ... 18
65 HMV POP 1408 — People Get Ready/I've Been Trying ... 18
65 HMV POP 1429 — Woman's Got Soul/Get Up And Move ... 18
65 HMV POP 1446 — A Meeting Over Yonder/I Found That I've Lost ... 18
65 HMV POP 1472 — I Need You/Never Could You Be ... 18
65 HMV POP 1492 — Amen/Long Long Winter ... 15
66 HMV POP 1498 — You've Been Cheatin'/Just One Kiss From You ... 30
66 HMV POP 1498 — You've Been Cheatin'/Just One Kiss From You (DJ Copy) ... 75
66 HMV POP 1516 — Since I Lost The One I Love/Falling In Love With You ... 15
66 HMV POP 1526 — Too Slow/No One Else ... 15
66 HMV POP 1545 — Can't Satisfy/This Must End ... 40
66 HMV POP 1545 — Can't Satisfy/This Must End (DJ Copy) ... 75
67 HMV POP 1581 — You Always Hurt Me/Little Girl ... 22
68 Stateside SS 2083 — We're A Winner/You've Got Me Runnin' ... 18
68 Buddah 201 021 — Fool For You/I'm Loving Nothing ... 10
69 Stateside SS 2139 — Can't Satisfy/You've Been Cheatin' ... 20
69 Buddah 201 062 — Choice Of Colors/Mighty Mighty Spade And Whitey ... 15
70 Buddah 2011 030 — Check Out Your Mind/Can't You See? ... 10
70 Buddah 2011 045 — (Baby) Turn On To Me/Soulful Love ... 6
71 Buddah 2011 068 — Ain't Got Time/I'm So Proud ... 6
71 Buddah 2011 087 — Love Me/Do You Want Me To Win ... 6
71 Buddah 2011 099 — Inner City Blues/Amen/Keep On Pushin' ... 6
72 Buddah 2011 124 — Our Love Goes On And On/This Love's For Real ... 6
73 Probe PRO 584 — People Get Ready/We Be Rolling On ... 8
65 HMV 7EG 8896 — IT'S ALL RIGHT (EP) ... 60
66 HMV 7EG 8954 — SOULFULLY (EP) ... 60
64 HMV CLP 1743 — THE NEVER ENDING IMPRESSIONS (LP) ... 80

MINT VALUE £

65 HMV CLP 1935 BIG SIXTEEN (LP, mono) . . . 40
65 HMV CSD 1642 BIG SIXTEEN (LP, stereo) . . . 50
66 HMV CLP/CSD 3548 RIDIN' HIGH (LP) . . . 50
67 HMV CLP/CSD 3631 THE FABULOUS IMPRESSIONS (LP) . . . 50
68 Stateside (S)SL 10239 WE'RE A WINNER (LP) . . . 30
68 Joy JOYS 104 FOR YOUR PRECIOUS LOVE (LP, with Jerry Butler) . . . 15
69 Buddah 203 012 THIS IS MY COUNTRY (LP) . . . 20
69 Stateside (S)SL 10279 BIG SIXTEEN (VOL. 2) (LP) . . . 20
70 Buddah 2359 003 THE YOUNG MOD'S FORGOTTEN STORY (LP) . . . 30
70 Buddah 2359 009 AMEN (LP) . . . 18
71 Buddah 2318 017 CHECK OUT YOUR MIND (LP) . . . 18
72 Buddah 2318 059 TIMES HAVE CHANGED (LP) . . . 18
75 ABC ABCL 5104 BIG SIXTEEN (LP, reissue) . . . 15

IMPS

58 Parlophone R 4398 Dim Dumb Blonde/Let Me Lie . . . 22
58 Parlophone R 4398 Dim Dumb Blonde/Let Me Lie (78) . . . 15

INADEQUATES

59 Capitol CL 15051 Pretty Face/Audie . . . 28

IN-BE-TWEENS

(see under 'N Betweens)

INCAS

65 Lyntone LYN 765/6 KEELE RAG RECORD (EP, flexidisc, with 3 other bands) . . . 40
66 Parlophone R 5551 One Night Stand/I'll Keep Holding On . . . 60

INCOGNITO

80 Ensign ENY 4412 Parisienne Girls/Summers Ended (12") . . . 12
81 Ensign ENVY 504 JAZZ FUNK (LP) . . . 12

INCREDIBLE BONGO BAND

73 MGM 2006 161 Bongo Rock/Bongolia . . . 12
72 MGM 2315 255 BONGO ROCK (LP) . . . 30
76 DJM DJS 20452 BONGO ROCK (LP, reissue) . . . 15

INCREDIBLE HOG

73 Dart ART 2026 Lame/Tadpole . . . 12
73 Dart 65372 VOLUME 1 (LP, laminated sleeve, pink/white/black label) . . . 200

INCREDIBLE KIDDA BAND

78 Psycho P 2608 Everybody Knows/No Nerve (a few in p/s) . . . 50
78 Psycho P 2608 Everybody Knows/No Nerve (a few in p/s) . . . 30
79 Carrere CAR 119 Fighting My Way Back/Saturday Night Fever (as KIDDA BAND) . . . 130

INCREDIBLES

67 Stateside SS 2053 There's Nothing Else To Say/Heart And Soul . . . 150
67 Stateside SS 2053 There's Nothing Else To Say/Heart And Soul (DJ copy) . . . 200
74 Contempo CS 9008 There's Nothing Else To Say/Another Dirty Deal . . . 10
74 Contempo CLP 512 HEART AND SOUL (LP) . . . 25

INCREDIBLE STRING BAND

(see also Robin Williamson, Mike Heron, Famous Jug Band, C.O.B., Shirley Collins)

SINGLES

67 Elektra EKSN 45013 Way Back In The 1960s/Chinese White (white-label promo) . . . 50
68 Elektra EKSN 45028 Painting Box/No Sleep Blues . . . 10
69 Elektra EKSN 45074 Big Ted/All Writ Down . . . 10
70 Elektra 2101 003 This Moment/Black Jack Davy . . . 6
72 Island WIP 6145 Black Jack David/Moon Hang Low . . . 5
73 Island WIP 6158 At The Lighthouse Dance/Jigs . . . 5

ORIGINAL ALBUMS

66 Elektra EUK 254 THE INCREDIBLE STRING BAND (1st pressing, white label, green logo, black lettering) . . . 200
67 Elektra EUK 257 THE 5000 SPIRITS OR THE LAYERS OF THE ONION (mono, orange label) . . . 90
67 Elektra EUKS 7257 THE 5000 SPIRITS OR THE LAYERS OF THE ONION (stereo, orange label) . . . 60
68 Elektra EUKS 7258 THE HANGMAN'S BEAUTIFUL DAUGHTER (mono, orange label, with lyric insert) . 45
68 Elektra EUKS 7258 THE HANGMAN'S BEAUTIFUL DAUGHTER (stereo, orange label, with lyric insert) . . . 60
68 Elektra EKL 4036/7 WEE TAM/THE BIG HUGE (2-LP, red label, gatefold sleeve, with insert; also stereo EKS 74036/7) . . . 45
69 Elektra EKS 74057 CHANGING HORSES (red/white label, gatefold sleeve) . . . 40
70 Elektra 2665 001 U (2-LP, red/white label, gatefold sleeve, with foldover lyric insert) . . . 30
70 Elektra 2665 001 U (2-LP, red label, gatefold sleeve, without foldover lyric insert) . . . 25
70 Elektra 2469 002 I LOOKED UP (red/white label) . . . 30
70 Island ILPS 9140 BE GLAD FOR THE SONG HAS NO ENDING (pink rim label/'palm tree' logo) . . . 18
71 Island ILPS 9172 LIQUID ACROBAT AS REGARDS THE AIR (gatefold sleeve, with inner, pink rim label/'palm tree' logo) . . . 18
72 Island ILPS 9211 EARTHSPAN (with lyric inner sleeve, pink rim label/'palm tree' logo) . . . 15
73 Island ILPS 9229 NO RUINOUS FEUD (with inner sleeve, pink rim label/'palm tree' logo) . . . 15
74 Island ILPS 9270 HARD ROPE AND SILKEN TWINE (with inner sleeve, pink rim label/'palm tree' logo) . . . 15
76 Island ISLD 9 SEASONS THEY CHANGE (2-LP, gatefold sleeve) . . . 25

REISSUE ALBUMS

66 Elektra EUK 254 THE INCREDIBLE STRING BAND (2nd pressing, orange label) . . . 50
68 Elektra EKL 254 THE INCREDIBLE STRING BAND (3rd pressing, red label) . . . 20
68 Elektra EKS 7257 THE 5000 SPIRITS OR THE LAYERS OF THE ONION (red label) . . . 20
68 Elektra EKL 4036 WEE TAM (red label, also stereo EKS 74036) . . . 15
68 Elektra EKL 4037 THE BIG HUGE (red label, also stereo EKS 74037) . . . 15
72 Elektra K 62002 U (2-LP, 'butterfly' label, gatefold sleeve, with foldover lyric insert) . . . 15

(All other 'butterfly' label reissues £8-£10 each)

MINT VALUE £

IN CROWD (Jamaica)
71 Spinning Wheel SW 105 Bush Jacket/Soul Face. . . 20
78 Savannah SVN 12-1 Riding High/Version (12"). . . 12
78 Cactus CT 111 Back A Yard/Yard (12") . . . 15

IN CROWD (U.K.)
(see also Tomorrow, Keith West, Steve Howe, Four + One)
65 Parlophone R 5276 That's How Strong My Love Is/Things She Says . . . 80
65 Parlophone R 5328 Stop! Wait A Minute/You're On Your Own . . . 65
65 Parlophone R 5364 Why Must They Criticize?/I Don't Mind . . . 55

INCROWD (U.K.)
69 Deram DM 272 Where In The World/I Can Make Love To You . . . 15

INCUBUS
84 Guardian GRC 2165 TO THE DEVIL A DAUGHTER (LP) . . . 18

INDECENT EXPOSURE
84 Index IS A1 Riots (Single Version)/A Matter Of Time (no p/s). . . 7

INDIAN SUMMER
(see also Badfinger, Ross)
71 RCA Neon NE 3 INDIAN SUMMER (LP, gatefold sleeve). . . 80

INDO-BRITISH ENSEMBLE
69 MFP 1307 CURRIED JAZZ (LP) . . . 20

INDO JAZZMEN
68 Saga FID 2145 RAGAS AND REFLECTIONS (LP) . . . 15

INERTIA
80s Inertial ERT 1 The Screen/4 Submarine (p/s). . . 5

INFANTES JUBILATE
68 Music Factory CUB 5 Exploding Galaxy/Take It Now. . . 60

INFA RIOT
(see also Infas)
81 Secret SHH 117 Kids Of The 80s/Still Out Of Order (p/s). . . 10
82 Secret SHH 133 The Winner/School's Out (p/s) . . . 6
82 Secret SEC 7 STILL OUT OF ORDER (LP). . . 15

INFAS
(see also Infa Riot)
84 Panache PAN 101 Sound And Fury/Triffic Spiff Ya O.K. (p/s) . . . 8
84 Panache PANLP 501 SOUND AND FURY (LP) . . . 12

INFERNAL BLUES MACHINE
76 London SHU 8496 ADIOS AMIGOS (LP). . . 15

INFINITY PROJECT
89 Fabulous FABU 004 HYPERACTIVE (12" EP, sponged cover) . . . 10
90 Fabulous FABU 005 UPHOLD THE LAW (12" EP) . . . 10
90 Fabulous FABU 016 TRIBADELIC MELTDOWN (12" EP). . . 8

IN FLAMES
72 Pama PM 842 Rocket Man/I'm All Broke Up. . . 6

INFLUENCE
(see also John Miles, Geordie, Smokestack Crumble)
69 Orange OAS 201 I Want To Live/Driving Me Wild . . . 20

INFORMATION
69 Beacon BEA 121 Orphan/Oh Strange Man . . . 30
70 Evolution E 2461S Face To The Sun/Lovely To See You . . . 20

NICK INGHAM
75 EMI EMI 2452 American Pie/Brass Knuckles/Terminator . . . 12
75 Studio Two TWOX 1045 TERMINATOR (LP) . . . 25

RED INGLE
59 Capitol EAP 20052 CIGAREETS, WHUSKY AND WILD WILD WOMEN (EP) . . . 12

JORGEN INGMANN
61 Fontana H 311 Cherokee/Anna . . . 6
61 Fontana H 333 Milord/Oceans Of Love. . . 7
61 Fontana H 353 Hear My Song - Violetta/Pinetop's Boogie Woogie . . . 8
62 Fontana 267 237 TF Africa/Johnny's Tune . . . 6
63 Columbia DB 7013 I Loved You (Dansevise)/Little Boy (as Grethe & Jorgen Ingmann) . . . 6
64 Columbia SEG 8340 DRINA (EP) . . . 10

INGRAM
83 Streetwave WAVE 3 DJ's Delight/Smoothin Groovin (12") . . . 12
83 Streetwave WAVLP 001 WOULD YOU LIKE TO FLY (LP, with bonus 12"). . . 30
83 Streetwave WAVLP 001 WOULD YOU LIKE TO FLY (LP, without bonus 12") . . . 20

LUTHER INGRAM
70 Stax STAX 142 My Honey And Me/Puttin' Game Down. . . 8
70 Stax STAX 148 Home Don't Seem Like A Home/Ain't That Lovin' You? . . . 8
72 Koko KOS 2202 IF LOVING YOU IS WRONG I DON'T WANT TO BE RIGHT (LP, photo insert) . . . 20

I 'N' I ONENESS MEETS UK PLAYERS
97 Jah Works JW 018S Further/Further Into Dub (12"). . . 20

INITIALS
64 London HLR 9860 School Day/Song Is Number One . . . 18

INK SPOTS
(see also Ella Fitzgerald)
54 Parlophone MSP 6063 Here In My Lonely Room/Flowers, Mister Florist, Please. . . 15

MINT VALUE £

54	Parlophone MSP 6074	Ebb Tide/If You Should Say Goodbye	15
54	Parlophone MSP 6126	Planting Rice/Yesterdays	15
55	Parlophone MSP 6152	Melody Of Love/Am I Too Late?	15
55	Brunswick OE 9158	SWING HIGH SWING LOW VOL. 1 (EP)	10
56	Brunswick OE 9427	THEY SOLD A MILLION NO. 11 (EP)	8
57	HMV 7EG 8410	CHARLIE FUQUA'S INK SPOTS (EP)	8
57	Parlophone GEP 8673	YESTERDAYS (EP)	10
50s	Britone LP 1003	THE INK SPOTS (10" LP)	15

AUTREY INMAN

63	Decca DFE 8571	AMERICAN COUNTRY JUBILEE NO. 1 (EP)	15

JOHN INMAN

75	DJM DJS 602	Are You Being Served, Sir?/We All Love Captain Ginger	6
75	DJM DJS 645	Teddy Bears Picnic/Sun Signs	5

INMATES

79	Soho SH 7	Dirty Water/Danger Zone (gatefold p/s)	8
79	Radar ADA 47	The Walk/Talkin' Woman (p/s)	5
81	Radar ADA 63	(I Thought I Heard A) Heartbeat/Tallahassie Lassie (p/s)	5

INNER CITY UNIT

(see also Hawkwind, Sphynx, Radio Actors, Imperial Pompadours, Catherine Andrews, Big Amongst Sheep, Nik Turner)

79	Riddle RID 001/ICU 45	Solitary Ashtray/So Try As Id (Dub Version) (plain sleeve with colour insert)	8
79	Riddle RID 003	Paradise Beach/Amyl Nitrate (company die-cut sleeve)	8
81	Avatar AAA 113	Beer, Baccy, Bingo And Benidorm/In The Mood (Nude) (red vinyl, no p/s)	6
82	Avatar AAA 119	Bones Of Elvis/Sid's Song (no p/s)	5
85	Jettisoundz JZ 5	BLOOD AND BONE (12" EP, p/s)	8
79	Riddle RID 002	PASS OUT (THE 360° PSYCHO DELERIA SOUND) (LP)	15
81	Avatar AALP 5004	THE MAXIMUM EFFECT (LP, with insert)	12

INNER MINDS

70	New Beat NB 067	Witchcraft Man/Night In Cairo	7
70	New Beat NB 069	Pum Pum Girl/Freedom	7
71	Bullet BU 465	Arawak Version/Cuffy Cuffy	7
71	Shades SHA 11	Dreams Of Yesterday/Never Over The Land	8
72	Shades SHA 12	Jesse James Hits Back/Let Me In	10

NEIL INNES

(see also Grimms, Bonzo Dog [Doo Dah] Band, Rutles, World, Dirk & Stig, Group)

72	United Artists UP 35358	Slush/Rawlinson's End (this is a different version from that on the Vivian Stanshall LP)	30
73	United Artists UP 35495	How Sweet To Be An Idiot/The Age Of Desperation	7
73	United Artists UP 35639	Momma B/Immortal Invisible	7
74	United Artists UP 35676	Re-cycled Vinyl Blues/Fluff On The Needle	7
74	United Artists UP 35745	Lie Down And Be Counted/Bandwagon	7
75	United Artists UP 35772	What Noise Annoys An Oyster/Oo-Chuck-A-Mao-Mao	7
77	Arista ARISTA 106	Lady Mine/Crystal Balls	6
77	Arista ARISTA 123	Silver Jubilee (A Tribute)/Drama On A Saturday Night	6
78	Warner Bros K 17182	Protest Song/The Hard-To-Get	6
79	Polydor 2059 247	Kenny And Liza/Human Race	6
82	MMC MMC 100	Them/Rock Of Ages	6
82	MMC MMC 103	Mr. Eurovision/Ungawa	6
73	United Artists UAG 29492	HOW SWEET TO BE AN IDIOT (LP)	30
82	MMC MMC 001	OFF THE RECORD (2-LP)	20

INN KEEPERS

(see also WInston Matthews)

71	Banana BA 328	Duppy Serenade/Sunshine Version (actually by Dennis Alcapone)	18

INNOCENCE

66	Kama Sutra KAS 203	There's Got To Be A Word!/I Don't Wanna Be Around You	10
66	Kama Sutra KAS 206	Mairzy Doats And Dozy Doats/Lifetime Of Lovin' You	10

INNOCENT BYSTANDERS

80	Rok ROK XVII/XVIII	Where Is Johnny?/DEBUTANTES: The Man In The Street (company sleeve)	6

INNOCENTS (U.K.)

(see also Woodentops, Advertising, Secret Affair)

80	Kingdom KV 8010	One Way Love/Every Wednesday Night At Eight (p/s)	10

INNOCENTS (U.K.)

(see also Mike Berry, Innocents & Leroys)

63	Columbia DB 7098	Stepping Stones/Grazina	15
63	Columbia DB 7173	A Fine, Fine Bird/Spanish Holiday	15
64	Columbia DB 7314	Stick With Me Baby/Not More Than Everything	10

INNOCENTS (U.S.)

(see also Kathy Young)

60	Top Rank JAR 508	Honest I Do/My Baby Hully Gullys	30
61	Top Rank JAR 541	Gee Whiz/Please Mr Sun	40

INNOCENTS & LEROYS

(see also Innocents [U.K.], Le-Roys)

64	Regal Zonophone RZ 502	HOT SIX: Don't Throw Your Love Away/My Girl Lollipop/I Love You Because; Not Fade Away/Tell Me When/I Believe (maxi-single, plain sleeve)	10

INQUISITIVE PEOPLE

67	Decca F 12699	Big White Chief/Rhapsody Of Spring	10

INSANE

82	Insane INSANE 1	Why Die?/War And Violence (p/s)	15
82	Riot City RIOT 3	Politics/Dead And Gone/Last Day (p/s)	10
82	No Future OI 10	El Salvador/Nuclear War/Chinese Rock (p/s)	10

MINT VALUE £

INSANE MACBETH

00	Insane LP1	THE RETARDATION PROJECT (LP, 100 only)	90
01	Insane 1203	True Heart (12")	20

INSECT TRUST

69	Capitol E-(S)T 109	THE INSECT TRUST (LP)	90

INSIDE OF A ROUGH TRADE SHOP

98	For Us/Out-There FU 005/ OV 003	CARNAGE: LIVE EP (CD, 50 only, numbered, with full-colour back tray art)	30
98	For Us/Out-There FU 005/OV 003	CARNAGE: LIVE EP (CD, 50 only, numbered, without full-colour back tray art)	20

INSIDE OV A COFFIN

(see also Freed Unit)

98	Out-There OTT 1	Banking On Death (7", existence unconfirmed)	0
98	Out-There OTT CD 1	Banking On Death (CD, 50 only, in hand-made sleeve with fake dollar bill)	20
98	Out-There OTT CD 2	Banking On Death - Carnage (CD, 50 only, numbered hand-made sleeve with fake dollar bill)	20

INSIDERS

(see also Ray Dorset)

80	Satellite SATS 1002	Rollin' & Strollin'/She Had To Go (features Ray Dorset)	10

INSPIRAL CARPETS

80s	own label	SONGS OF SHALLOW INTENSITY (p/s, demo)	20
80s	own label	WAITING FOR OURS (p/s, demo)	20
80s	own label	COW (p/s, demo)	20
88	Playtime AMUSE 2	Keep The Circle Around/Theme From Cow (p/s)	15
88	Playtime AMUSE 4	Butterfly/You Can't Take The Truth (unreleased, white label promos only)	8
88	Playtime AMUSE 4T	TRAIN SURFING (12" EP, unreleased, white label test pressings only)	15
94	Mute LDUNG 25	DEVIL HOPPING (LP, with free red vinyl 10" EP)	12

INSPIRATIONS (Jamaica)

(see also Untouchables, Niney)

69	Camel CA 11	Down In The Park/Love Oh Love	25
69	Camel CA 21	Wonder Of Love/Cinderella	30
70	Amalgamated AMG 857	Take Back Your Duck/Nothing For Nothing	12
70	Amalgamated AMG 861	La La/Reggae Fever	15
70	Amalgamated AMG 862	The Train Is Coming/Man Oh Man	10
71	Upsetter US 355	Confusion/THE UPSETTERS: Confusion version	25
70	Trojan TTL 27	REGGAE FEVER (LP)	50

INSPIRATIONS (U.S.)

67	Polydor 56730	Touch Me, Kiss Me, Hold Me/What Am I Gonna Do With You?	200

INSTANT AGONY

83	Flicknife FLS 022	No Sign Of Life/Taste Of Power (p/s)	5
83	Flicknife FLS 028	Nicely Does It/We Don't Need You (p/s)	5

INSTANT AUTOMATONS

80	Deleted DEP 001	PETER PAINTS HIS FENCE EP (2x7", numbered, fold-out sleeve with inserts and stickers)	15

INSTANT SUNSHINE

68	Page One POF 085	Here We Go Again/Methylated	7
68	Page One POL 007	LIVE AT TIDDY DOLS (LP, blue/silver labels)	15

INSTITUTE OF FORMAL RESEARCH

(see also Mick Taylor, Chris Spedding)

97	Bubblehead BH 005	VOLUME ONE: FILE UNDER SUBCONSCIOUS (CD, features Zoot Horn Rollo)	20

INSYNC VS MYSTERON

95	Peacefrog PF 033	AUDIBLE ILLUSION EP (12", plain sleeve)	10
97	Fat Cat 12FAT 004	TALES FROM THE CRYPT (12", custom sleeve)	15

INTELLIGENT COMMUNICATIONS

(see also Future Sound Of London)

91	Jumpin' & Pumpin' 12TOT 15	PRINCIPLES OF MOTION EP (12", p/s)	10

INTENSE DEGREE

88	Earache MOSH 9	WAR IN MY HEAD (LP, with inner)	12

INTENSITY

73	Eden EDEN LP 68	TURN ABOUT INSIDE OUT PLASTIC COATED HUMANS (LP)	150

INTENSIVE CARE

84	Punishment Block CELL 1	COWARDS EP (p/s)	8
87	Back To Back BTB 001	REBBELS, ROCKETS AND RUBBERMEN (12", p/s)	12

INTENTIONS (U.K.)

72	Pye 7N 45123	There's Nobody I'd Sooner Love/Hurry On Home	5

INTENTIONS (U.S.)/Z.Z. HILL

66	Sue IEP 711	GIMME GIMME (EP, 2 tracks each by Intentions & Z.Z. Hill; 2 tracks mistakenly credited to Jackie Day on sleeve; in p/s)	300
66	Sue IEP 711	GIMME GIMME (EP, 2 tracks each by Intentions & Z.Z. Hill; 2 tracks mistakenly credited to Jackie Day on sleeve; no p/s)	100

INTERGALACTIC TOURING BAND

77	Charisma CB 306	Lone Station/Space Command	6

INTERNATIONAL CHRYSIS

(see also Dead Or Alive)

94	PWL PWLT 303	Rebel Rebel (The Hole Mix)/Rebel Rebel (Extended Mix) (12", promo only)	15

INTERNATIONAL PENPALS

03	Radical RADWAL 001	Day They Ate Ronald Reagan (p/s)	12

MINT VALUE £

INTERNS (Jamaica)
(see also Viceroys, Bob Marley & Wailers)
70 Jackpot JP 729 — See You At Sunrise/LITTLE WONDER: Out Of Reach (B-side actually "Just Out Of Reach" by John Holt) — 8

INTERNS (U.K.)
(see also Shadows)
64 Philips BF 1320 — Don't You Dare/Here There Everywhere — 15
64 Philips BF 1345 — Cry To Me/There's Love For You — 15
66 Parlophone R 5479 — Is It Really What You Want?/Just Like Me — 50
67 Parlophone R 5586 — Ray Of Sunshine/Please Say Something Nice — 10

INTERPOL
00 CHEM 047CD — fukd i.d #3 PDA: Precipitate/Roland/5 (CD, stickered card sleeve, 1,000 only) — 60
02 Matador OLE 546-7 — PDA/Specialist (p/s) — 25
02 Matador OLE 546-2 — PDA/NYC/Specialist (CD, digipak, with slipcase) — 8
02 Matador OLE 570-2 — Obstacle 1/PDA (Morning Becomes Electric Session)/ Hands Away (Peel Session) (CD) — 10
07 Capitol/Parlophone CL 894 — The Heinrich Maneuver/Concert Introduction (p/s) — 8
07 Capitol/Parlophone CLS 894 — The Heinrich Maneuver/Wrecking Ball (p/s) — 8
04 Matador (No. cat. no) — ANTICS (5 x 7" box set, only from Interpol Space Art Gallery, London) — 30
00s Matador OLE 5827 — Say Hello To The Angels/NYC (p/s) — 8
00s Matador OLE 582-2 — Say Hello To The Angels/NYC/NYC (Demo Version) (CD) — 8
00s Matador OLE 5949 — Obstacle 1 (Video)/Specialist (Black Session)/Leif Erikson (Black Session) (DVD) — 10
07 Capitol/Parlophone 0946 3 96248 1 — OUR LOVE TO ADMIRE (2-LP) — 20

INTERSTATE ROAD SHOW
69 President PT 249 — Grindy Grind/All I Want To Do Is To Love You — 8

INTESTINES
81 Alternative Capitalists AC51 — Life In A Cardboard Box/New Recruit (p/s) — 25

IN THE NURSERY
84 Paragon VIRTUE 5 — Witness To A Scream/1984 (p/s) — 15
85 New European BADVC 55 — Sonority - A Strength (12" EP) — 10
83 Paragon VIRTUE 2 — WHEN CHERISHED DREAMS COME TRUE (mini-LP, silk-screened g/fold p/s) — 25

IN THE WOODS...
96 Misanthropy OVL 69 — White Rabbit/Mourning The Death Of Aase (p/s) — 10
98 Misanthropy OVL 68 — Let There Be More Light/Child Of Universal Tongue (p/s) — 10
95 Misanthropy AMAZON 004 — HEART OF THE AGES (LP, with booklet) — 70
97 Misanthropy AMAZON 11 — OMNIO (LP, gatefold sleeve, 1-sided etched disc) — 40

INTIMATE STRANGERS
75 Alaska ALA 1005 — Love Sounds/The Track — 50

INTRA VEIN
(see also Veins)
79 Bum FP 001 — Speed Of The City/Sick (printed PVC sleeve) — 40
79 Bum FP 001 — Speed Of The City/Sick (stamped plain sleeve) — 30

INTRIGUE
82 Pressure PRESS D 1003 — I Like It (Vocal)/I Like It (Instrumental) (12") — 30
84 Music Power MPR(T) 1 — No Turning Back/Call Of The Heart (12") — 25
86 Intrigue INT 12-001 — One Touch/Touch Down (12") — 15

INTRIGUES
69 London HL 10293 — In A Moment/Scotchman Rock — 15
72 Janus 6146 008 — To Make A World/Mojo Hanna — 6

INTROZE
82 Monarch MON 037 — Doin' The Lambeth Walk/Kids In Uniform — 50

INTRUDERS
59 Top Rank JAR 158 — Frankfurters And Sauerkraut/Creepin' — 10

INTRUDERS
66 London HL 10069 — Up And Down The Ladder/United — 40
69 Action ACT 4523 — Slow Drag/So Glad I'm Yours — 15
69 Ember EMB S 254 — Cowboys To Girls/Turn Back The Hands Of Time — 15
72 Ember EMB S 325 — Cowboys To Girls/GOOD VIBRATIONS: Shake A Hand — 7

INTURNS
79 Burning Rockers BR 1003 — DETOUR (LP) — 30

INVADERS (Jamaica)
67 Columbia Bluebeat DB 105 — Limbo Girl/Soul Of The Jungle — 10
68 Columbia Bluebeat DB 109 — Stop Teasing/Invaders At The Carnival — 10
68 Studio One SO 2044 — Soulful Music/SOUL VENDORS: Happy Organ — 70
71 G.G. GG 4527 — Got To Go Home/PAULETTE & GEE: How Long Will You Stay? — 7

INVADERS (U.K.)
70s Jovian ZIT 2 — Launderama/Plastic Nose — 5

INVICTAS
64 United Artists UP 1013 — Green Bow Tie/Touch Of Orchid — 7

INVISIBLE MAN
92 Timeless DJ 005 — On A Mission/Twisted/Intro (Think About It)/ The End (Drug Induced Psychosis Mix)/Bonus Turbo Cut (12") — 30
93 Timeless DJ 006 — The Beginning/The End (12") — 20
93 Timeless DJ 007 — Skyliner/Power (12") — 20
93 Timeless DJ 008 — Skyliner (Remix)/MYSTERON: U Don't Know (12") — 20
95 Timeless DJ 010 — Skyliner (Top Buzz's 95 VIP Mix)/The Beginning (Innerspace Remix) (12") — 10

MINT VALUE £

INVITATIONS (Jamaica)

71	Crab CRAB 66	Birmingham Cat/Now You're On Your Own	8

INVITATIONS (U.S.)

65	Stateside SS 453	Hallelujah/Written On The Wall	75
65	Stateside SS 478	What's Wrong With My Baby?/Why Did My Baby Turn Bad?	150
65	Stateside SS 478	What's Wrong With My Baby?/Why Did My Baby Turn Bad? (DJ copy)	300
70	Jay Boy BOY 24	How'd We Ever Get This Way?/Picking Up	40
72	Mojo 2092 055	What's Wrong With My Baby?/Why Did My Baby Turn Bad? (reissue)	8
74	Polydor 2066 366	Let's Love And Find Together/Love Has To Grow	10

INXS

81	RCA RCA 89	Just Keep Walking/Scratch	10
83	Mercury INXS 1	Don't Change/You Never Used To Cry (p/s)	8
83	Mercury INXS 121	Don't Change/You Never Used To Cry/Golden Playpen (12", p/s)	12
83	Mercury INXS 2	The One Thing/The Sax Thing (p/s)	8
83	Mercury INXS 212	The One Thing (6.10)/Black And White (12", p/s)	12
84	Mercury INXS 3	Original Sin/Jan's Song (live)/To Look At You (live) (p/s)	5
84	Mercury INXS 312	Original Sin/Original Sin (Extended Version)/Jan's Song (live)/ To Look At You (live) (12", p/s)	8
84	Philips PH 2	I Send A Message/Mechanical (p/s, in envelope pack with postcard & biography)	15
84	Philips PH 2	I Send A Message/Mechanical (p/s)	5
84	Philips PH 212	I Send A Message (Long Distance)/Mechanical/I Send A Message (Local Call) (12", p/s)	15

IONA

78	Silver Scales	CUCKOO (LP)	35
70s	Celtic Music CM 001	IONA (LP)	35

I.O.W. CHEROKEES

66	69 69EP 001	I.O.W. CHEROKEES (EP, private pressing)	40

DON IPPOLITO ORCHESTRA

55	Parlophone MSP 6187	Camptown Racer Mambo/Can't Do It Mambo	5

IPSISSIMUS

69	Parlophone R 5774	Hold On/Lazy Woman	60

IQ

(see also Niadem's Ghost)

84	Jim White/IQ PROMO 101	Awake And Nervous/Through The Corridors (12", no p/s, 500 only)	30
84	IQFREEB 1	Hollow Afternoon (1-sided, Marquee gig freebie)	30
86	STAL Other Boxer 1	Nomzamo (Demo) (1-sided fan club single)	18
86	Sahara IQSD 1	It All Stops Here/Intelligence Quotient (shaped picture disc)	18
87	RLOG Another Boxer 1	Fascination/The Bold Grenadier Pt. 1 (fan club single)	18
88	RLOG One More Boxer 1	A Different Magic Roundabout (Honest!)/The Big Balls Of Bert Christ (fan club single)	12
92	MIMP 00000001	BLUBA NEENY NOO: Last Human Gateway (Acoustic Middle Section)/ A Bit Of Love Lost (CD, fan club single, 361 copies only)	18
85	STAL BOXER 1	NINE IN A POND IS HERE (2-LP, 1,000 copies only)	20

IQ PROCEDURE (ROOTS MANUVA)

94	Bluntly Speaking PHAT2	Run Tings/Can U Get With This/Big Up (12")	25

IQ ZERO

79	Object Music OM 9	(Everybody Kills) Insects/Electromotion/Quirky Pop Music (p/s)	20
79	Logo GO 374	She's So Rare/Crazy Dolls (p/s)	15

IRATION STEPPAS

94	Iration Steppa BS 159	Scud Missile/High Rise Vibrations (12")	30
03	Tandori Space TS 012	Too Much War/Stop The War Dub/What's Wrong/What's Wrong Dub (10")	25

IRATION STEPPAS & TENA STELIN

(see also Tena Stelin)

01	Tandori Space TSR 001	War Inna Babylon/Dub Version	20
01	Tandori Space TSR 002	Jungle Jungle/Dub Version	20

IRELAND'S FREEMEN

75	Polydor 2908 017	SEAN SOUTH (LP)	15

IRISH MIST

75	SRT/Custom 012	ROSIN THE BOW (LP)	15

IRISH ROVERS

67	Brunswick STA 8679	FIRST OF THE IRISH ROVERS (LP)	12
68	MCA MUPS 310	THE UNICORN (LP)	12
69	MCA MUPS 353	LIVERPOOL LOU (LP)	12

IRISH TRADITION

79	Green Linnet SIF 1016	THE CORNER HOUSE (LP)	15

IRONBELLY

70	Parlophone R5864	Woha! Buck/Wild About My Loving	6

IRON BUTTERFLY

(see also Ramatam)

68	Atlantic 584 188	Possession/Unconscious Power	15
69	Atlantic 584 254	Soul Experience/In The Crowds	12
70	Atlantic 2091 024	In-A-Gadda-Da-Vida/Termination	10
68	Atco 2465 015	HEAVY (LP)	22
68	Atlantic 587/588 116	IN-A-GADDA-DA-VIDA (LP)	30
69	Atco 228 011	BALL (LP, gatefold sleeve)	25
70	Atlantic 2400 014	LIVE (LP)	18
71	Atlantic 2401 003	METAMORPHOSIS (LP)	20

MINT VALUE £

IRON CROSS

72	Spark 1079	Little Bit Of Soul/Sunshine	8
74	Spark 1112	Everybody Rock On/All The Time	5

IRON HORSE

71	Bell BLL1148	The Obeah Man/Magic Love	40

IRON MAIDEN

70	Gemini GMS 006	Falling/Ned Kelly	30

IRON MAIDEN

(see also Bruce Dickinson, A.S.A.P., Di'Anno, Gogmagog, Samson, Urchin, Xero, Lionheart, Pat Travers, Stratus, Nicko McBrain, Money, White Spirit, McEnroe & Cash)

SINGLES

80	EMI EMI 5032	Running Free/Burning Ambition (p/s)	25
80	EMI EMI 5032 DJ	Running Free (1-sided 7" DJ copy)	50
80	EMI EMI 5065	Sanctuary/Drifter (live)/I've Got The Fire (live) (uncensored p/s)	35
80	EMI EMI 5065	Sanctuary/Drifter (live)/I've Got The Fire (live) (censored p/s)	15
80	EMI EMI 5065	Sanctuary/Drifter (live)/I've Got The Fire (live) (DJ copy, censored p/s)	50
80	EMI EMI 5105	Women In Uniform/Invasion (p/s)	15
80	EMI 12EMI 5105	Women In Uniform/Phantom Of The Opera (live)/Invasion (12", p/s)	15
81	EMI EMI 5145	Twilight Zone/Wrathchild (p/s)	15
81	EMI EMI 5145	Twilight Zone/Wrathchild (p/s, red or clear vinyl)	25
81	EMI EMI 5145	Twilight Zone/Wrathchild (p/s, red or clear vinyl)	30
81	EMI EMI 5145	Twilight Zone/Wrathchild (p/s, brown vinyl mispressing)	750
81	EMI TCEMI 5145	Twilight Zone/Wrathchild ()	8
81	EMI EMI 5184	Purgatory/Genghis Khan (p/s)	30
82	EMI EMI 5263	Run To The Hills/Total Eclipse (p/s)	6
82	EMI EMIP 5263	Run To The Hills/Total Eclipse (picture disc, mispressed with B-side picture on both sides)	30
82	EMI EMIP 5263	Run To The Hills/Total Eclipse (picture disc)	15
82	EMI EMI 5287	The Number Of The Beast/Remember Tomorrow (live) (p/s)	5
82	EMI EMI 5287	The Number Of The Beast/Remember Tomorrow (live) (p/s, red vinyl)	12
83	EMI EMI 5378	Flight Of Icarus/I've Got The Fire (p/s)	5
83	EMI 12EMIP 5378	Flight Of Icarus/I've Got The Fire (12", picture disc)	20
83	EMI EMI 5397	The Trooper/Cross-Eyed Mary (p/s)	5
83	EMI EMIP 5397	The Trooper/Cross-Eyed Mary (soldier-shaped picture disc)	25
83	EMI EMIP 5397	The Trooper/Cross-Eyed Mary (uncut shaped picture disc)	200
84	EMI EMI 5489	2 Minutes To Midnight/Rainbow's Gold (p/s)	5
84	EMI 12EMI 5489	2 Minutes To Midnight/Rainbow's Gold/Mission From 'Arry (12", picture disc)	15
84	EMI EMI 5502	Aces High/King Of Twilight (p/s)	8
84	EMI EMI 5502	Aces High/King Of Twilight (mispress, A-side label on both sides)	10
84	EMI 12EMIP 5502	Aces High/King Of Twilight/The Number Of The Beast (live) (12", picture disc)	18
85	EMI EMI 5532	Running Free (live)/Sanctuary (live) (poster p/s)	7
85	EMI 12EMIP 5532	Running Free (live)/Sanctuary (live)/Murders In The Rue Morgue (live) (12", picture disc)	18
85	EMI EMI 5542	Run To The Hills (live)/Phantom Of The Opera (live) (with Xmas card)	8
85	EMI 12EMIP 5542	Run To The Hills (live)/Phantom Of The Opera (live)/ Losfer Words (The Big 'Orra) (live) (12", picture disc)	18
86	EMI EMIP 5583	Wasted Years/Reach Out (computer-shaped picture disc)	15
86	EMI EMI 5589	Stranger In A Strange Land/That Girl (foldout poster p/s)	6
86	EMI 12EMIP 5589	Stranger In A Strange Land/That Girl/Juanita (12", picture disc)	18
88	EMI EMS 49	Can I Play With Madness/Black Bart Blues (p/s, with sticker & transfer)	5
88	EMI EMP 49	Can I Play With Madness/Black Bart Blues (shaped picture disc)	18
88	EMI EMP 49	Can I Play With Madness/Black Bart Blues (uncut shaped picture disc)	75
88	EMI CDEM 49	Can I Play With Madness/Black Bart Blues/Massacre (CD)	12
88	EMI EMP 64	The Evil That Men Do/Prowler '88 (gatefold p/s)	5
88	EMI EMP 64	The Evil That Men Do/Prowler '88 (shaped picture disc)	10
88	EMI EMP 64	The Evil That Men Do/Prowler '88 (uncut shaped picture disc)	75
88	EMI 12EMS 64	The Evil That Men Do/Prowler '88/Charlotte The Harlot '88 (12", poster p/s)	8
88	EMI CDEM 64	The Evil That Men Do/Prowler '88/Charlotte The Harlot '88 (CD, picture disc)	10
88	EMI EMS 79	The Clairvoyant (live)/The Prisoner (live) (clear vinyl, poster p/s)	6
88	EMI EMP 79	The Clairvoyant (live)/The Prisoner (live) (shaped picture disc)	15
88	EMI EMP 79	The Clairvoyant (live)/The Prisoner (live) (uncut shaped picture disc)	60
88	EMI CDEM 79	The Clairvoyant (live)/The Prisoner (live)/Heaven Can Wait (live) (CD, picture disc)	8
89	EMI EM 117	Infinite Dreams (live)/Killers (live) (with free patch)	5
89	EMI EMPD 117	Infinite Dreams (live)/Killers (live) (shaped picture disc with insert)	7
89	EMI EMPD 117	Infinite Dreams (live)/Killers (live) (uncut shaped picture disc)	50
89	EMI 12EM 117	Infinite Dreams (live)/Killers (live)/Still Life (live) (12", poster p/s)	8
89	EMI 12EM 117	Infinite Dreams (live)/Killers (live)/Still Life (live) (CD)	8
90	EMI EMDJ 153	Holy Smoke (1-sided 7" DJ copy)	50
90	EMI 12EMPD153	Holy Smoke/All In Your Mind/Kill Me Ce Soir (12" picture disc with insert)	12
90	EMI 12EMP 153	Holy Smoke/All In Your Mind/Kill Me Ce Soir (12", gold vinyl test pressing, promo only)	150
90	EMI EM 171	Bring Your Daughter ... To The Slaughter/I'm A Mover (Clear or white vinyl Test pressing for 12" picture disc)	10
90	EMI EM 171	Bring Your Daughter ... To The Slaughter/I'm A Mover (1-sided etched, p/s)	6
90	EMI EMPD 171	Bring Your Daughter ... To The Slaughter/I'm A Mover (picture disc 'brain' pack)	6
90	EMI 12EMP 171	Bring Your Daughter ... To The Slaughter/I'm A Mover (12", calendar pack)	10
90	EMI 12EMPD 171	Bring Your Daughter ... To The Slaughter/I'm A Mover/ Communication Breakdown (12", picture disc, die-cut sleeve)	12
90	EMI CDEM 171	Bring Your Daughter...To The Slaughter/I'm A Mover (UK pressed CD single)	100
92	EMI 12EMP 229	Be Quick ...Or Be Dead/Nodding Donkey Blues/Space Station No.5 (12" picture disc, with insert)	10
92	EMI EMPD 240	From Here To Eternity/I Can't See My Feeling (shaped picture disc with insert)	10
92	EMI EMPD 240	From Here To Eternity/I Can't See My Feeling (uncut shaped picture disc)	50
92	EMI EMP 263	Fear Of The Dark (live)/Tailgunner (live) (poster p/s)	5

MINT VALUE £

92	EMI EMPD 263	Fear Of The Dark (live)/Hooks In You (live) (shaped picture disc, with insert)	10
92	EMI EMPD 263	Fear Of The Dark (live)/Hooks In You (live) (uncut shaped picture disc)	50
92	EMI EMPD 263	Fear Of The Dark (live)/Hooks In You (live) (shaped picture disc, with mispressed B-side "Tailgunner" [live])	18
95	EMI 12EM 398	Man On The Edge/I Live My Way (12", picture disc, with poster, die-cut sleeve)	15
95	EMI CDEMS 398	Man On The Edge/The Edge of Darkness/Judgement Day/ Blaze Bailey interview (CD)	25
95	EMI CDMAN 1	Man On The Edge (CD 1-track promo, slim jewel case)	12
95	EMI CDMAN 2	Man On The Edge/The Edge Of Darkness/Sign Of The Cross (CD)	50
96	EMI CDEMDJ 443	Virus (CD, 1-track single edit, jewel case)	12
97	EMI CDINPROF 001	In Profile (CD, 31-track edit band history picture disc custom sleeve)	30
98	EMI CDPP 044	Virtual XI Advance Listening CD custom sleeve jewel case	15
98	EMI VIRTCDXI 001	An Introduction To Virtual XI (CD, 3-track Futureal/ The Angel And The Gambler/ Lightning Strikes Twice custom card sleeve)	20
98	EMI VIRTCDXI 002	The Angel And The Gambler (CD, 1-track edit version in custom card sleeve)	15
98	EMI VIRTCDXI 003	Futureal (CD, 1-track in custom card sleeve)	25
98	EMI VIRTCDXI 004	Futureal (CD, 1-track in custom card sleeve)	15
98	EMI 8860690	Futureal/ The Evil That Men Do(live)/ Man On The Edge(live)/ The Angel And The Gambler (video) (CD digi-pack Fan Club only issue with poster)	45
98	EMI HELLROM001	Maiden Hell promotional CD-Rom in full colour custom card sleeve	25
98	EMI EM 507	The Angel And The Gambler/Blood On The World's Hands (Live) (picture disc)	6
00	EMI no cat. no.	Tommy Vance Previews: The Wicker Man/Ghost Of The Navigator/ Brave New World/Dream Of Mirrors/The Nomad (CD-R with Thomas The Vance intros)	50
00	EMI CDEMDJ 568	The Wicker Man (CD, 1-track promo in slim jewel case)	10
00	EMI CDEMDJ 576	Out Of The Silent Planet (CD, 3 tracks in slim jewel case)	12
02	EMI CDEMDJ 612	Run To The Hills/Run To The Hills Live (CD, custom card sleeve)	10
03	EMI CDEMDJ 633	Rainmaker (CD, 1-track promo in custom card sleeve)	10
03	EMI DODRAD001	Dance Of Death (CD, promo interview, slim jewel case)	20
03	EMI CDEMDJ627	Wildest Dreams (CD, 1-track promo in custom card sleeve)	10
04	EMI CDEMDJ 636	No More Lies (CD, 1-track promo in custom card sleeve)	15
04	EMI CDEM 636	No More Lies/ Paschendale/Journeyman/No More Lies video (Tour CD box set)	15
04	EMI CDEMDJ 653	The Number Of The Beast/The Number Of The Beast (Priceless edit) (CD)	12
04	BMG PUB049	Int Iron Maiden 10 track promo CD in custom sleeve	50
05	EMI CDEMDJ 662	The Trooper/The Trooper (live) (Promo CD, gatefold card sleeve)	12
05	EMI 12EM 662	The Trooper (live)/The Trooper/Murders In The Rue Morgue (live) (12", picture disc)	12
06	EMI 3749682	A Matter Of Life And Death (CD promo interview in custom sleeve slim jewel case)	15
06	EMI 3738012	A Matter Of Life And Death (CD, 4-track in custom sleeve slim jewel case)	15
06	EMI CDEMDJ 703	The Reincarnation Of Benjamin Breeg (CD, 2-track in custom card sleeve)	15
06	EMI CDEMDJ 714	Different World/ Different World video (CD/DVD, custom gatefold sleeve)	10

EPs

79	Rock Hard ROK 1	THE SOUNDHOUSE TAPES (EP, p/s; Matrix ROK-1A EG SA LYN 7627-1T/ ROK-1B EG SA LYN 7628-1T. Counterfeits have slightly glossier sleeves. Any with different p/s and colour vinyl are also counterfeit)	150
81	EMI 12EMI 5219	MAIDEN JAPAN EP (12" EP, p/s)	15
93	EMI 12EMP 288	HALLOWED BE THY NAME EP (12", picture disc)	12

ALBUMS

80	EMI EMC 3330	IRON MAIDEN (LP, with poster)	35
80	EMI EMC 3330	IRON MAIDEN (LP, without poster)	15
82	EMI EMCP 3400	THE NUMBER OF THE BEAST (LP, picture disc, with inner)	40
84	EMI POWERP 1	POWERSLAVE (LP, picture disc)	40
88	EMI EMDP 1006	SEVENTH SON OF A SEVENTH SON (LP, picture disc, with banner)	35
90	EMI EMPD 1017	NO PRAYER FOR THE DYING (LP, picture disc, die cut sleeve)	20
90	EMI (no cat. no.)	NO PRAYER FOR THE DYING (CD, with interview , photos & bio, promo only)	100
90	EMI (no cat. no.)	THE FIRST TEN YEARS - UP THE IRONS (10 x 12" double packs, box set available by mail-order with tokens from records)	75
90	EMI (no cat. no.)	THE FIRST TEN YEARS - UP THE IRONS (10 x CD, box set available by mail order with tokens from CDs)	100
92	EMI (no cat. no.)	FEAR OF THE DARK (CD, interview , EPK video, colour booklet, A4 poster in luminous flip-top box)	150
93	EMI DON 1	LIVE AT DONINGTON (3-LP, numbered)	60
93	EMI EMD 1042	A REAL LIVE ONE (LP, gatefold sleeve with inner sleeve)	15
93	EMI EMD 1048	A REAL DEAD ONE (LP, gatefold sleeve and inner sleeve)	15
95	EMI 724383581917	THE X FACTOR (2-LP, clear vinyl, gatefold with poster)	50
96	EMI (no cat. No.)	THE STORY SO FAR (5-CD box set, 1000 copies only)	300
96	EMI EMDX 1097	BEST OF THE BEAST (4-LP box set, with inners, book and bonus tracks)	100
96	EMI BEST 001	BEST OF THE BEAST (CD, Steve Harris interview disc, commercial CD, video, in 40cm x 30cm, flip-up 3D presentation box with 60-page book, 2 photographs, biography, promo only)	200
97	EMI LPCENT 7	THE NUMBER OF THE BEAST (LP, reissue, 180gm vinyl)	30
98	EMI LPCENT 35	IRON MAIDEN (LP, reissue, 180gm vinyl)	30
98	EMI 4979990	EDDIE'S HEAD (13 CD boxset, plastic skull with flashing eyes)	175
98	EMI 4939151	VIRTUAL XI (2-LP gatefold, with inner sleeves)	60
99	EMI EDHUNTER 666	ED HUNTER DEMO (CD-Rom, card p/s with booklet, press info and photo)	40
00	EMI CDBWDJ001	BRAVE NEW WORLD (5-track sampler CD)	20
00	EMI 526 6051	BRAVE NEW WORLD (2-LP, picture disc, gatefold, inner sleeves)	25
00	EMI CDIN 130	BRAVE NEW WORLD (promo interview CD)	25
02	EMI EDDIE 001	EDWARD THE GREAT (5-track promo sampler CD)	18
02	EMI IMRIODJ 001	ROCK IN RIO (5-track 'Regal Sampler' sampler CD)	15
02	EMI RIOINTCD 001	ROCK IN RIO (Promo interview CD, with colour booklet)	50
02	EMI 538 6431	ROCK IN RIO (3-LP, picture discs, trifold sleeve)	25
02	EMI 544 2772	EDDIE'S ARCHIVE (6-CD, tin box with insert, shot glass, pewter ring and parchment. 1st issue blue lining)	120
02	EMI 544 2772	EDDIE'S ARCHIVE (6-CD, tin box with insert, shot glass, pewter ring and Parchment. 2nd issue red lining)	80

			MINT VALUE £
02	EMI CDSP255	EDDIE'S ARCHIVE (CD, 8-track sampler in card sleeve)	70
03	EMI DODUKDJ001	DANCE OF DEATH (5-track sampler CD, card sleeve)	18
03	EMI 592 3401	DANCE OF DEATH (2-LP, picture disc, gatefold sleeve and inner sleeves)	25
05	EMI 336 4371	DEATH ON THE ROAD (2-LP, picture disc gatefold)	20
06	EMI 372 3211	A MATTER OF LIFE AND DEATH (2-LP, picture disc, gatefold, inner sleeves	20

NEVILLE IRONS
(see also Neville Hinds)

68	Blue Cat BS 104	Soul Glide/DYNAMICS: My Friends	40

IRON VIRGIN

74	Deram DM 408	Jet/Midnight Hitcher	10
74	Deram DM 416	Rebels Rule/Ain't No Clown	22

I ROY
(see under 'R')

IRRESTIBLE FORCE

98	Ninja Tune ZEN 38	IT'S TOMORROW ALREADY (2-LP)	15

ANDY IRVINE

80	Tara 3002	RAINY SUNDAYS, WINDY DREAMS (LP)	15

ANDY IRVINE & PAUL BRADY
(see also Dr. Strangely Strange)

76	Mulligan LUN 008	ANDY IRVINE & PAUL BRADY (LP)	25

WELDON IRVINE

75	Strata East SES 19749	IN HARMONY (LP)	12

LONNIE IRVING

60	Melodisc MEL 1546	Pinball Machine/I Got Blues On My Mind	40

IRVING 6

70s	Port O Jam PJ4116	Ossie's Special/Trouble	20

(BIG) DEE IRWIN

64	Stateside SS 261	Donkey Walk/Someday You'll Understand Why	10
64	Colpix PX 11040	Heigh-ho/It's My Birthday	8
64	Colpix PX 11050	Personality/It's Only A Paper Moon	8
65	Stateside SS 450	You Satisfy My Needs/I Wanna Stay Right Here With You	125
65	Stateside SS 450	You Satisfy My Needs/I Wanna Stay Right Here With You (DJ copy)	200
68	Minit MLF 11013	I Can't Stand The Pain/My Hope To Die Girl (as Dee Irwin)	15

BIG DEE IRWIN & LITTLE EVA
(see also Little Eva, Suzi & Big Dee Irwin)

63	Colpix PX 11010	Swinging On A Star/Another Night With The Boys (Little Eva uncredited)	6
64	Colpix PX 11021	I Wish You A Merry Christmas/Christmas Song	6
63	Colpix PXE 301	SWINGING ON A STAR (EP)	22
65	Golden Guinea GSGL 10497	SWINGING ON A STAR (LP)	15

DAVID ISAACS
(see also Upsetters)

66	Island WI 261	I'd Rather Be Lonely/See That Man	50
68	Trojan TR 616	Place In The Sun/UPSETTER ALL STARS: Handy-Cap	15
69	Upsetter US 302	Good Father/SLIM SMITH: What A Situation	12
69	Upsetter US 305	I've Got Memories/I'm Leaving	12
69	Upsetter US 311	He'll Have To Go/Since You're Gone	12
69	Upsetter US 319	Who To Tell/BUSTY BROWN: I Can't See Myself Cry	12
69	Punch PH 6	I Can't Take It Anymore/LLOYD DOUGLAS: Anyway	10
71	Punch PH 84	You'll Be Sorry/Knock Three Times	8
71	Bullet BU 459	Just Enough/ROY PATIN: Standing (B-side actually by Roy Panton)	8
71	Tropical AL 006	Love Has Join Us/MAX ROMEO: Cross Over The Bridge (correct title for A-side is 'Love Has Joined Us')	5
73	Upsetter US 400	Stranger On The Shore/DILLINGER: John Devour	40
73	Bread BR 1118	Just Enough/We Are Neighbours	5
79	Attack TACK 13	Just Like A Sea (with Jah Thomas)/ WITTY'S ALL STARS: Just Like A Sea (Version) (12")	18

GREGORY ISAACS

70	Escort ERT 833	While There Is Life/HARRY YOUNG: Come On Over	15
70	Success RE 914	Too Late/KINGSTONIANS: You Can't Wine	25
70	Bullet BU 448	Set Back/SYDNEY'S ALLSTARS: Version II	15
71	Big Shot BI 584	Lonely Man/RUPIE EDWARDS ALL STARS: Lonely Man Version	12
73	Ackee ACK 522	I'm Coming Home/Version	5
73	Green Door GD 4054	Lonely Soldier/IMPACT ALL STARS: Version	12
74	Pyramid PYR 7012	Innocent People Cry/Version	8
74	Attack ATT 8066	Love Is Overdue Part 1/Love Is Overdue Part 2	8
74	Attack ATT 8081	Don't Go/Dubwise	8
74	Stop Points DL 0022	End Of The World/Gregory Shuffle	10
75	Black Wax WAX 9	Sunshine For Me/Version	8
75	Attack ATT 8095	Bad Da/Ad Dab	8
75	Attack ATT 8106	Fly Little Silver Bird/Dub	8
75	Camel CA 2008	Lonely Days/Version	8
75	Bullet BU 555	Lonely Days/Version	8
76	Third World TW 032	Look Before You Leap/K. SMILEY: Sata	15
76	Morpheus MOR 1017	Black Kill A Black/Version	25
77	Observer OBMM-1000	Soul On Fire/CHRISTINE: Saturday Night/TYRONE TAYLOR: Sufferation/ In Style (12")	40
78	Observer	Rock On/Murder Observer Style/DENNIS BROWN & DILLINGER: Jah Is Watching/Hustling (12")	60
78	DEB DEB 004	Mr Know It All/OSSIE HIBBERT & REVOLUTIONARIES: War Of The Stars (12")	30
78	Hawkeye HE 008	John Public/LEGGO ALL STARS: Enemy No 1	8

			MINT VALUE £
78	Star PTP 1002	Lonely Days/U ROY: Nanny Skank (12")	15
79	Front Line FLS 12112	Soon Forward/Uncle Joe/ Come Off Mi Toe (Feat. Prince Far I) (12")	15
80	African Museum (no cat.)	If You See My Mary/Mary's Special (12", blue vinyl)	20
85	African Museum AF 0050	G.P./Version (12")	25
80	Solomonic SM 002	Sunday Morning/DENNIS BROWN: Running Around (12")	25
88	Greensleeves GRED 221	Rumours/More Rumours (12")	30
88	Greensleeves GRED 225	Rough Neck/Version (12" with the Mighty Diamonds)	30
89	Greensleeves GRED 256	Report To Me/Report To Me (continued) (12")	30
75	Trojan TRLS 102	IN PERSON (LP)	15
76	Trojan TRLS 121	ALL I HAVE IS LOVE (LP)	15
76	Shack BITE 200	EXTRA CLASSIC (LP)	20
78	Burning Sounds BS1010	SLUM - GREGORY ISAACS IN DUB (LP)	30
78	DEB DEB LP 04	MR ISAACS (LP)	30
78	Virgin Front Line FL 1020	COOL RULER (LP)	20
79	Virgin Front Line FL1044	SOON FORWARD (LP)	30
82	Island 9721	NIGHT NURSE (LP, with poster)	18
83	Burning Sounds BS 1051	SLUM DUB (LP)	25
83	Pre PREX1	THE LONELY LOVER (LP)	15

IKE ISAACS

74	Decca Eclipse ECS 2163	FOURTEEN GREAT T.V. THEMES (LP)	15

ISCA FAYRE

76	Candle CAN 761	THEN AROUND ME YOUNG AND OLD (LP)	15

ISH

79	TKS TKR 7540	Faster Than A Speeding Bullet/Don't Stop	6

JON ISHERWOOD

70	Decca LK/SKL 5051	A LAUGHING CRY (LP)	15

ISHMAEL & ANDY

73	Myrrh MYR 1005	READY SALTED (LP)	20

ISLANDERS

59	Top Rank JAR 215	The Enchanted Sea/Pollyanna	8
60	Top Rank JAR 305	Blue Train/Tornado	6

ISLANDERS

65	Fontana TF 577	It Ain't Me Babe/Four Strong Winds	10
65	Fontana TF 605	Walkin' Away/Roberta Let Your Hair Hang Down	5

JIMMY ISLE

59	London HLS 8832	Diamond Ring/I've Been Waiting	70
59	London HLS 8832	Diamond Ring/I've Been Waiting (78)	25
60	Top Rank JAR 274	Billy Boy/Oh Judy	15

ISLEY BROTHERS

59	RCA RCA 1149	Shout (Parts 1 & 2) (tri centre)	30
59	RCA RCA 1149	Shout (Parts 1 & 2) (round centre)	25
59	RCA RCA 1149	Shout (Parts 1 & 2) (78)	200
60	RCA RCA 1172	Respectable/I'm Gonna Knock On Your Door	20
60	RCA RCA 1190	How Deep Is The Ocean/He's Got The Whole World In His Hands	20
60	RCA RCA 1213	Tell Me Who/Say You Love Me Too	20
62	Stateside SS 112	Twist And Shout/Spanish Twist	15
62	Stateside SS 132	Twistin' With Linda/You Better Come Home	15
63	Stateside SS 218	Nobody But Me/I'm Laughing To Keep From Crying	20
63	United Artists UP 1034	Tango/She's Gone	15
64	United Artists UP 1050	Shake It With Me Baby/Stagger Lee	20
64	Atlantic AT 4010	The Last Girl/Looking For A Love	40
66	Tamla Motown TMG 555	This Old Heart Of Mine (Is Weak For You)/There's No Love Left (1st press with narrow print on label)	20
66	Tamla Motown TMG 555	This Old Heart Of Mine (Is Weak For You)/There's No Love Left (2nd re-press - 1968 - with wider print)	10
66	Tamla Motown TMG 566	Take Some Time Out For Love/Who Could Ever Doubt My Love	35
66	Tamla Motown TMG 572	I Guess I'll Always Love You/I Hear A Symphony (1st pressing with "Sold subject to" on centre piece)	30
67	Tamla Motown TMG 606	Got To Have You Back/Just Ain't Enough Love	25
68	Tamla Motown TMG 652	Take Me In Your Arms (Rock Me A Little While)/Why When Love Is Gone	30
69	Tamla Motown TMG 683	I Guess I'll Always Love You/It's Out Of The Question	8
69	Tamla Motown TMG 693	Behind A Painted Smile/One Too Many Heartaches	7
69	Major Minor MM 621	It's Your Thing/Don't Give It Away	10
69	Tamla Motown TMG 708	Put Yourself In My Place/Little Miss Sweetness	7
69	Major Minor MM 631	I Turned You On/I Know Who You Been Socking It To	6
69	Tamla Motown TMG 719	Take Some Time Out For Love/Who Could Ever Doubt My Love (reissue)	7
70	Stateside SS 2162	Was It Good To You?/I Got To Get Myself Together	6
71	Stateside SS 2188	Warpath/I Got To Find Me One	6
71	Stateside SS 2193	Love The One You're With/He's Got Your Love	10
73	Tamla Motown TMG 877	Tell Me It's Just A Rumour, Baby/Save Me From This Misery	8
73	Epic EPC 1980	The Highways Of My Life/Don't Let Me Be Lonely Tonight	5
74	Epic EPC 2803	Need A Little Taste Of Love/If You Were There	5
76	DJM DJS 640	Twist And Shout/Time After Time (reissue)	5
79	RCA PC 9411	Shout/Respectable/Tell Me Who (12", p/s)	8
64	RCA RCX 7149	THE ISLEY BROTHERS (EP)	80
60	RCA RD 27165	SHOUT (LP, mono)	60
60	RCA SF 7055	SHOUT (LP, stereo)	100
64	United Artists ULP 1064	THE FAMOUS ISLEY BROTHERS - TWISTING AND SHOUTING (LP)	80
66	Tamla Motown TML 11034	THIS OLD HEART OF MINE (IS WEAK FOR YOU) (LP, mono)	30
66	Tamla Motown STML 11034	THIS OLD HEART OF MINE (IS WEAK FOR YOU) (LP, stereo)	40
68	T. Motown TML 11066	SOUL ON THE ROCKS (LP, mono)	30

MINT VALUE £

68	T. Motown STML 11066	SOUL ON THE ROCKS (LP, stereo)	40
69	Major Minor SMLP 59	IT'S OUR THING (LP)	25
69	T. Motown TML 11112	BEHIND A PAINTED SMILE (LP, mono)	25
69	T. Motown STML 11112	BEHIND A PAINTED SMILE (LP, stereo)	25
70	Stateside SSL 10300	THE BROTHERS: ISLEY (LP)	22

ISOLATION

73	Riverside HASLP 2083	ISOLATION (LP, private pressing with insert)	300

ISOTOPE

(see also Brian Auger, Hugh Hopper)

74	Gull GULP 1002	ISOTOPE (LP)	15
74	Gull GULP 1006	ILLUSION (LP)	15
75	Gull GULP 1017	DEEP END (LP)	15

ISRAELITES

(see also Music Doctors)

69	Downtown DT 413	Moma Moma/Melody For Two	8
69	Downtown DT 421	Games People Play/AUDREY: One Fine Day	20
69	Downtown DT 433	Seven Books/Chaka Beat	8
70	J-Dan JDN 4410	Can't Help From Crying/Can't Get Used To Losing You	8

ISRAEL VIBRATION

78	Harvest HAR 184	The Same Song/Weep And Moan	15
79	Harvest 12 HAR 5189	Crisis/Crisis Dub (12", feat. Augustus Pablo)	30
79	Harvest SHSP 4099	THE SAME SONG (LP, black and red Harvest label)	25

ITALS (Jamaica)

(see also Alton Ellis, Honeyboy)

67	Giant GN 8	New Loving (with Soul Brothers)/I Told You Little Girl	30
67	Giant GN 12	Don't Throw It Away/Make Up Your Mind (both with Carib-Beats)	35
71	Big BG 325	Ba-Da-Doo-Ba-Dey/RUPIE EDWARDS ALL STARS: Version	10

ITALS (U.K.)

71	Black Swan BW 1404	Dawn Patrol/Whiskey Bonga (DJ and Rhythm)	12
71	Black Swan BW 1407	Judgement Rock (actually by Charlie Ace)/Night West	12

ITHACA

(see also Friends, Alice Through The Looking Glass, Agincourt, Tomorrow Come Someday, BBC Radiophonic Workshop)

73	Merlin HF 6	A GAME FOR ALL WHO KNOW (LP, with insert)	750
93	Background	A GAME FOR ALL WHO KNOW (LP, reissue)	15

IT'S A BEAUTIFUL DAY

69	CBS 4457	White Bird/Wasted Union Blues	8
70	CBS 4933	Soapstone Mountain/Do You Remember The Sun	15
73	CBS 1625	Ain't That Lovin' You Baby/Time	5
69	CBS 63722	IT'S A BEAUTIFUL DAY (LP, gatefold sleeve)	25
70	CBS 64065	MARRYING MAIDEN (LP)	20
72	CBS 64314	CHOICE QUALITY STUFF - ANYTIME (LP)	20

IT'S IMMATERIAL

84	Eternal JF 4	A Gigantic Raft In The Philipines/The Mermaid (p/s)	10

IVAN

(see also Jerry Allison, Crickets)

58	Coral Q 72341	Real Wild Child/Oh, You Beautiful Doll	250
58	Coral Q 72341	Real Wild Child/Oh, You Beautiful Doll (78)	100

IVAN D. JUNIORS

63	Oriole CB 1874	Catch You If I Can/On My Mind	20

IVANS MEADS

65	Parlophone R 5342	A Little Sympathy/The Sins Of A Family	70
66	Parlophone R 5503	We'll Talk About It Tomorrow/The Bottle	40

BURL IVES

54	Columbia SCMC 5	I've Got No Use For Women/River Of Smoke (export issue)	10
56	Brunswick 05510	Ballad Of Davy Crockett/Goober Peas	10
56	Brunswick 05551	Dying Stockman/Click Go The Shears	10
56	Brunswick 05604	The Bus Stop Song/That's My Heartstrings	10
61	Brunswick 05863	A Little Bitty Tear/Shanghied	5
61	Brunswick 05868	Funny Way Of Laughin'/Mother Wouldn't Do That	5
63	HMV POP 1178	Ugly Bug Ball/On The Front Porch	6
56	Decca BM 31183	Marianne/Pretty Girl (with Trinidadies) (export issue)	10
70	Coral CP 31	CORONATION CONCERT (LP, reissue)	12

IVEYS

(see also Badfinger, Pleasure Garden)

68	Apple APPLE 5	Maybe Tomorrow/And Her Daddy's A Millionaire	55
69	Apple APPLE 14	Dear Angie/No Escaping Your Love (unreleased; Europe & Japan only)	0
92	Apple SAPCOR 8	MAYBE TOMORROW (LP, reissue, gatefold sleeve & bonus 12" [SAPCOR 82])	25

IVOR & SHEILA

81	Eron 027	CHANGING TIMES (LP, with insert)	30

IVORIES

(see also Tommy Hunt)

85	Kent TOWN 103	Please Stay/TOMMY HUNT: The Work Song	15

JACKIE IVORY

66	Atlantic AT 4075	Hi-Heel Sneakers/Do It To Death	20
65	Atlantic ATL 5046	SOUL DISCOVERY (LP)	60
65	Atlantic ATL 5046	SOUL DISCOVERY (LP, 1966 reissue)	18

MINT VALUE £

IVY LEAGUE
(see also Carter-Lewis, White Plains, Edison Lighthouse, Flowerpot Men, Kestrels, One & One, Johnny Shadow, Perry Ford, First Class, Friends, Warm Sensations)

64	Piccadilly 7N 35200	What More Do You Want?/Wait A Minute	10
65	Piccadilly 7N 35228	That's Why I'm Crying/A Girl Like You	5
65	Piccadilly 7N 35267	Our Love Is Slipping Away/I Could Make You Fall In Love	6
66	Piccadilly 7N 35294	Running Round In Circles/Rain Rain Go Away	5
66	Piccadilly 7N 35326	Willow Tree/One Day	5
66	Piccadilly 7N 35348	My World Fell Down/When You're Young	10
67	Piccadilly 7N 35365	Four And Twenty Hours/Arrivederci Baby	5
67	Piccadilly 7N 35397	Suddenly Things/Tomorrow Is Another Day	6
67	Pye 7N 17386	Thank You For Loving Me/In The Not Too Distant Future	8
65	Piccadilly NEP 34038	FUNNY HOW LOVE CAN BE (EP)	20
65	Piccadilly NEP 34042	TOSSING AND TURNING (EP)	20
65	Piccadilly NEP 34046	THE HOLLY AND THE IVY LEAGUE (EP)	12
66	Piccadilly NEP 34048	OUR LOVE IS SLIPPING AWAY (EP)	30
65	Piccadilly NPL 38015	THIS IS THE IVY LEAGUE (LP)	30

IVY THREE

60	London HLW 9178	Yogi/Was Judy There	22

DAFYDD IWAN

69	Welsh Teldisc WD 904	Croeso/Chwedeg Nain (p/s)	8

IWASACUBSCOUT

06	Fear And (No Cat. No.)	We Were Made To Love/That's Not A Crate, It's A Box Of Heaven Part Two (500 only, p/s)	6

IZZY POUND

69	Plexium PXM 9	Pumpkin Miny/Na Na Na Na	50

J

CLUE J. & HIS BLUES BLASTERS

60	Blue Beat BB 15	Easy Snappin'/Goin' Home (with vocal by Theophilus Beckford)	12
61	Blue Beat BB 37	Lovers' Jive/Wicked And Dreadful (actually with Neville Esson)	12
61	Blue Beat BB 60	Little Willie/Pine Juice	12

DAVID J. (& J. WALKERS)
(see also Bauhaus)

81	4AD AD 112	Nothing/Armour (as David Jay & René Halkett) (p/s, with lyric sheet)	5
84	GLASS 12032	V For Vendetta: This Viscious Cabaret/V's Theme/Incidental/V's Theme (12" p/s)	8

HARRY J. ALL STARS
(see under 'H')

TONY J.

75	Stonehouse 001	Telephone Line/Telephone Version	5

JABBERWOCK

77	MCA MCA 264	Sneakin' Snaky/Fortune Teller	20

JOY JACINTH

83	Zebratone ZTD 93	Baby Boy/Red Lights (12")	15

JACK (Bernard) & BEANSTALKS
(see also Kingstonians)

69	Supreme SUP 203	Work It Up/Chatty Chatty	12

BILLY JACK (& CIMARONS)
(see also Candy)

70	Grape GR 3018	Let's Work Together/CORPORATION: Jam Monkey	10
70	Big Shot BI 558	Once A Man/Soul Mood (as Billy Jack & Cimarons)	7
70	Big Shot BI 559	Bet Your Life I Do/CANDY & CIMARONS: Ace Of Hearts	7

BOBBY JACK

59	Top Rank JAR 190	Tempting Me/Early Mornin'	8

JACKAL

74	BASF BA 1009	The Year Of The Tiger/Big Star	10

JACKAL
(see also Renegade Soundwave)

86	Crim. Damage CRI 12-134	Underneath The Arches/Thunder Machine (12", p/s)	15

JACKIE

78	Fashion FAD 002	It's Too Late Baby/Fashion On Fine Style (12")	20

JACKIE & BRIDIE
(see also Jacqueline & Bridie)

68	Major Minor MM 562	Come Me Little Son/We Only Needed Time	6
64	Fontana TL 5212	HOLD BACK THE DAWN (LP)	25
70	Concord CONS 1002	FOLK WORLD OF JACKIE AND BRIDIE (LP)	15
71	Galliard GAL 4009	THE PERFECT ROUND (LP)	15
70s	Nevis NEV LP 102	HELLO FRIEND (LP, as Jacqui & Bridie)	12
77	J & B CNN 5939	COME DAY GO DAY (LP)	12
77	J & B CNN 5949	HOW CAN YOU KEEP FROM SINGING WITH... (LP)	12

MINT VALUE £

JACKIE & DOREEN

(see also Doreen Shaffer, Jackie Opel)

64	Ska Beat JB 168	Every Beat Of My Heart	20
65	Ska Beat JB 209	The New Vow/Adorable You	50

JACKIE (Edwards) & MILLIE (Small)

(see also Wilfred & Millicent, Jackie Edwards, Millie)

65	Island WI 253	This Is My Story/SOUND SYSTEM: Never Again	40
66	Island WI 265	My Desire/MILLIE: That's How Strong My Love Is	15
67	Island WIP 6012	In A Dream/Ooh Ooh	20
67	Island ILP 941	PLEDGING MY LOVE (LP, as Jackie Edwards & Millie Small)	90
68	Island ILP 963	THE BEST OF JACKIE AND MILLIE VOLUME TWO (LP)	80
70	Trojan TTL 52	THE BEST OF JACKIE AND MILLIE VOLUME TWO (LP, reissue)	20
70	Trojan TBL 155	JACKIE & MILLIE (LP)	20

JACKIE & RAINDROPS

(see under Jackie Lee & Raindrops)

JACKIE & ROY

58	Vogue V 9101	You Smell So Good/Let's Take A Walk Around The Block	40
58	Vogue V 9101	You Smell So Good/Let's Take A Walk Around The Block (78)	20
59	Vogue VE 1-70131	JACKIE AND ROY (EP)	30
58	Vogue VA 1-60111	JACKIE AND ROY (LP)	40

JACKPOTS

69	Sonet SON 2006	Jack In The Box/Henbanes Sacrifice	25

ALEXANDER JACKSON & TURNKEYS

65	Sue WI 386	The Whip/Tell It Like It Is (actually "Flea Pot"/"Sweetie Lester" by Lala Wilson)	100

BULLMOOSE JACKSON & HIS ORCHESTRA

53	Vogue V 2129	Nosey Joe/I Know Who Threw The Whisky In The Well (78)	20

CHRIS JACKSON

69	Soul City SC 112	I'll Never Forget You/Forever I'll Stay With You	35
70	444 Label	Since There's No Doubt/We Will Be Together (unissued, acetate only - 2 known copies)	0

CHUBBY JACKSON'S BIG BAND

60	Top Rank TR 5015	A Ballad For Jai/Hail, Hail, The Herd's All Here	5

CHUCK JACKSON

(see also Del[l]-Vikings)

61	Top Rank JAR 564	I Don't Want To Cry/Just Once	40
62	Top Rank JAR 607	The Breaking Point/My Willow Tree	40
62	Stateside SS 102	Any Day Now/The Prophet	30
62	Stateside SS 127	I Keep Forgettin'/Who's Gonna Pick Up The Pieces	25
63	Stateside SS 171	Tell Him I'm Not Home/Getting Ready For The Heartbreak	25
64	Pye International 7N 25247	Beg Me/For All Time	25
64	Pye International 7N 25276	Any Day Now/The Prophet (reissue)	20
65	Pye International 7N 25287	Since I Don't Have You/Hand It Over	100
65	Pye International 7N 25287	Since I Don't Have You/Hand It Over (DJ Copy)	150
65	Pye International 7N 25301	I Need You/Chuck's Soul Brothers Twist	20
65	Pye International 7N 25321	If I Didn't Love You/Just A Little Bit Of Your Soul	22
66	Pye International 7N 25384	Chains Of Love/I Keep Forgettin'	100
66	Pye International 7N 25384	Chains Of Love/I Keep Forgettin' (DJ copy)	150
67	Pye International 7N 25439	Shame On Me/Candy	25
68	Tamla Motown TMG 651	Girls, Girls, Girls/(You Can't Let The Boy Overpower) The Man In You	25
70	Tamla Motown TMG 729	Honey Come Back/What Am I Gonna Do Without You	20
73	Probe PRO 595	I Only Get The Feeling/Slowly But Surely	20
74	Probe PRO 617	I Can't Break Away/Just A Little Tear	10
75	All Platinum 6146 310	I've Got The Need/Beautiful Woman	10
75	Disco Demand DDS 116	These Chains Of Love/Any Day Now	10
85	Kent TOWN 104	Hand It Over/CANDY & KISSES: Mr Creator (withdrawn)	30
80s	Inferno SIN 1	Chains Of Love/Good Things Come To Those Who Wait/ Hand It Over/ Any Day Now	20
92	Kent 8	What's With This Loneliness	20
66	Pye Intl. NPL 28082	TRIBUTE TO RHYTHM AND BLUES (LP)	50
68	T. Motown (S)TML 11071	CHUCK JACKSON ARRIVES! (LP, mono/stereo)	50
69	T. Motown (S)TML 11117	GOIN' BACK TO CHUCK JACKSON (LP, mono/stereo)	50
72	Probe SPB 1084	THROUGH ALL TIMES (LP)	25
74	Anchor ABCL 5040	THROUGH ALL TIMES (LP, reissue)	12

CHUCK JACKSON & MAXINE BROWN

(see also Maxine Brown, Tammi Terrell)

65	Pye International 7N 25308	Something You Got/Baby Take Me	20
65	Pye Intl. NPL 28091	SAYING SOMETHING (LP)	50

DEON JACKSON

66	Atlantic AT 4070	Love Makes The World Go Round/You Said You Loved Me	40
66	Atlantic 584 012	Love Takes A Long Time Growing/Hush Little Baby	25
68	Atlantic 584 159	Ooh Baby/All On A Sunny Day	30
76	Contempo CS 9031	Love Makes The World Go Round/I Can't Go On	20

EARL JACKSON

76	ABC ABC 4110	Soul Self Satisfaction/Looking Thru' The Eyes Of Love	15

GEORGE JACKSON

69	Capitol CL 15605	Find 'Em, Fool 'Em And Forget 'Em/My Desires Are Getting The Best Of Me	25
72	London HLU 10373	Aretha, Sing One For Me/I'm Gonna Wait	12
73	London HLU 10413	Let 'Em Know You Care/Patricia	12

MINT VALUE £

GORDON JACKSON
(see also Hellions, Jane Relf, Traffic)

69	Marmalade 598 010	Me And My Zoo/A Day At The Cottage	20
69	Marmalade 598 021	Song For Freedom/Sing To Me Woman	25
69	Marmalade 608 012	THINKING BACK (LP)	200

HAROLD JACKSON & TORNADOES

58	Vogue V 9105	Move It On Down The Line Parts 1 & 2	120
58	Vogue V 9105	Move It On Down The Line Parts 1 & 2 (78)	60

JACKIE JACKSON
(see also Jacksons, Jackson 5)

74	T. Motown STML 11249	JACKIE JACKSON (LP)	15

JANET JACKSON

87	Breakout USAD 601	Let's Wait A While/Nasty (Cool Summer Mix Pt. 1)/Nasty (Original Mix)/ Control/Let's Wait A While (Remix)/Nasty (Cool Summer Mix Part 1 Fade) (picture disc/clear vinyl double pack in PVC foldout sleeve)	8
90	Breakout USAB 681	Come Back To Me (7" I'm Beggin' You Mix)/Alright (7" R&B mix) (box set with metal badge & foldout poster)	5
90	Breakout USAS 693	Alright (House Mix)/Vuelve A Mi (Come Back To Me) (shaped picture disc with plinth in printed PVC sleeve)	8

JANET JACKSON & CLIFF RICHARD
(see also Cliff Richard)

84	A&M AM 210	Two To The Power Of Love/JANET JACKSON: Rock'n'Roll (p/s)	5
84	A&M AMX 210	Two To The Power Of Love/JANET JACKSON: Rock'n'Roll/ Don't Mess Up This Good Thing (12", p/s)	8

JERMAINE JACKSON
(see also Jacksons, Jackson 5, Michael Jackson)

84	Epic JMJDJ 1	Tell Me I'm Not Dreamin' (Too Good To Be True) (with Michael Jackson)/ Come To Me/Oh Mother (promo only)	10

JERRY JACKSON

63	London HLR 9689	Gypsy Eyes/Turn Back	40
66	Cameo Parkway P 100	It's Rough Out There/I'm Gonna Paint A Picture	175
66	Cameo Parkway P 100	It's Rough Out There/I'm Gonna Paint A Picture (DJ copy)	275

JIM JACKSON

66	RCA RCX 7182	R.C.A. VICTOR RACE SERIES VOL. 7 (EP)	10

JIMMY JACKSON('S ROCK 'N' ROLL SKIFFLE)

57	Columbia DB 3898	California Zephyr/I Shall Not Be Moved	20
57	Columbia DB 3937	Sittin' In The Balcony/Good Morning Blues	25
57	Columbia DB 3957	River Line/Lonely Road	15
57	Columbia DB 3988	White Silver Sands/Build Your Love (On A Strong Foundation) (solo)	5
58	Columbia DB 4085	Love-A Love-A Love A/Photographs (solo)	10
58	Columbia DB 4153	Swing Down, Sweet Chariot/This Little Light Of Mine (solo)	5
58	Columbia SEG 7750	ROCK 'N' SKIFFLE (EP)	75
58	Columbia SEG 7768	COUNTRY AND BLUES (EP)	75

J.J. JACKSON (& Greatest Little Soul Band In The Land)
(see also Greatest Little Soul Band)

67	Polydor 56718	But It's Alright/Do The Boogaloo	20
67	Strike JH 329	Come See Me/Try Me	15
67	Warner Bros WB 2082	Sho Nuff (Got A Good Thing Going)/Here We Go Again	15
68	Warner Bros WB 2090	Down, But Not Out/Why Does It Take So Long?	15
68	Warner Bros WB 6029	Courage Ain't Strength/You Do It 'Cause You Wanna	15
69	Warner Bros WB 7276	Ain't Too Proud To Beg/But It's Alright	10
70	RCA RCA 1924	Bow Down To The Dollar/Indian Thing (as J.J's DILEMMA)	20
71	Mojo 2092 014	But It's Alright/Do The Boogaloo	10
67	Strike JLH 104	J.J. JACKSON WITH THE GREATEST LITTLE SOUL BAND (LP)	30
69	MCA SKA 100	GREATEST LITTLE SOUL BAND (LP)	25
70	RCA Victor SF 8093	J.J. JACKSON'S DILEMMA (LP)	30

J.J. JACKSON/LINDA JONES

77	Loma/Warners K 56271	THIS IS LOMA - VOL. 7 (LP, 1 side each)	15

LEVI JACKSON
(see also Solomon King)

71	Columbia DB 8807	This Beautiful Day/Don't You Be A Sinner	100
71	Columbia DB 8807	This Beautiful Day/Don't You Be A Sinner (DJ copy)	150

LLOYD JACKSON

71	Pama Supreme PS 308	Cracklin' Rosie/Little Deeds Of Kindness (B-side with Scorpions)	5

MAHALIA JACKSON

55	Philips BB 2005	A Rusty Old Halo/The Treasures Of Love (78, export issue)	12
58	Philips PB 869	For My Good Fortune/Have You Any Rivers	5
59	Philips PB 933	Trouble Of The World/Tell The World About This	5
60	Philips PB 1040	Onward Christian Soldiers/The Lord's Prayer	5
60	Vogue V 2418	The Lord's Prayer/Bless This House	5
60	Top Rank JKP 2038	IN THE UPPER ROOM VOLUME 1 (EP)	8
60	Top Rank JKP 2048	IN THE UPPER ROOM VOLUME 2 (EP)	8
52	Vogue LDE 005	MAHALIA JACKSON (10" LP)	20
59	Philips BBL 7289	NEWPORT 1958 (LP, also stereo SBBL 547)	12
60	Top Rank 30/006	JUST AS I AM (LP)	12
60	Philips BBL 7362	GREAT GETTIN' UP MORNING (LP)	12
60	Philips BBL 7391	THE POWER AND THE GLORY (LP, also stereo SBBL 576)	12
60	Philips BBL 7435	COME ON CHILDREN LET'S SING (LP)	12
61	Philips BBL 7456	I BELIEVE (LP, also stereo SBBL 610)	12

MINT VALUE £

MICHAEL JACKSON

(see also Jackson 5, Diana Ross & Michael Jackson, Paul McCartney, Jacksons, Jermaine Jackson)

SINGLES

79	Epic S EPC 7135	You Can't Win (Part 1)/You Can't Win (Part 2) (picture disc)	10
79	Epic 12EPC 7135	You Can't Win (Part 1)/You Can't Win (Part 2) (12")	10
79	Epic 12EPC 7763	Don't Stop 'Til You Get Enough/I Can't Help It (12")	8
79	Epic 12EPC 8206	Rock With You/Get On The Floor/You Can't Win (Extended) (12")	8
81	Motown TMG 977	We're Almost There/We've Got A Good Thing Going (p/s)	5
81	Motown TMGT 977	We're Almost There (Album Version)/We've Got A Good Thing Going (12")	8
82	Epic EPCA 11-2729	The Girl Is Mine (with Paul McCartney)/ Can't Get Outta The Rain (picture disc)	15
83	Epic EPC 2906	GREATEST ORIGINAL HITS: Don't Stop 'Til You Get Enough/ She's Out Of My Life/Off The Wall/Rock With You (EP)	10
83	Epic EPCA 40-2906	GREATEST ORIGINAL HITS: Don't Stop 'Til You Get Enough/ She's Out Of My Life/Off The Wall/Rock With You (EP,)	8
72	Tamla Motown TMG 797	Got To Be There/Maria (You Were The Only One)	6
83	Motown TMG 986	Happy (Love Theme From 'Lady Sings The Blues')/We're Almost There (poster p/s)	8
83	Motown EPCA 112729	Happy (Love Theme From 'Lady Sings The Blues')/We're Almost There (picture disc)	10
83	Epic EPCA 3643	Thriller/JACKSONS: Things I Do For You (live) (poster p/s)	8
83	Epic TA 3643	Thriller (Album Version)/Thriller (Remix Short Version)/JACKSONS: Things I Do For You (live) (12", 'calendar' p/s)	50
83	Epic MJ 1 (1-9)	MICHAEL JACKSON'S 9 SINGLES PACK (9 x 7", p/s, each on red vinyl, in PVC foldout wallet)	35
87	Epic 650 202-0	I Just Can't Stop Loving You (with Siedah Garratt)/Baby Be Mine (poster p/s)	10
87	Epic 650 202-6	I Just Can't Stop Loving You (with Siedah Garratt)/Baby Be Mine (12", p/s with poster)	15
87	Epic 651 155-6	Bad (Dance Extended Mix With False Fade)/Bad (7" Single Mix)/Bad (Dance Radio Edit)Bad (Dub)/Bad (A Cappella) (12", p/s, red vinyl)	8
87	Epic 651 275-7	The Way You Make Me Feel/The Way You Make Me Feel (Instrumental) (p/s, with competition leaflet, stickered sleeve)	5
87	Epic 651 275-3	The Way You Make Me Feel (7" Mix)/(A Cappella)/(Dance Radio Edit)/ (Dub)/(Get Into The Groove - Put Either Side On The Turntable, Lower The Arm And See Which Your Needle Pix) (12", p/s double-groove)	12
87	Epic 651 275-9	The Way You Make Me Feel (Dance Extended Mix)/The Way You Make Me Feel (Dub Version)/The Way You Make Me Feel (A Cappella) (CD, card p/s)	12
88	Epic 651 388-9	Man In The Mirror (Single Mix)/Man In The Mirror (Instrumental) (square-shaped picture disc)	15
88	Epic 651 388-2	Man In The Mirror (4.55)/Man In The Mirror (Album Mix)/ Man In The Mirror (Instrumental) (CD, card sleeve)	10
88	Epic 651 388-2	Man In The Mirror/Man In The Mirror (Album Mix)/Man In The Mirror (Instrumental) (3" CD with adaptor, card sleeve)	12
88	Epic 651 546-7	Dirty Diana/Dirty Diana (p/s, with 13" cardboard figure)	12
88	Epic 652 864-6	Dirty Diana/Dirty Diana (Instrumental)/Bad (Extended Dance Mix With False Fade) (12", with tour poster p/s)	15
88	Epic 651 546-9	Dirty Diana (4.42)/Dirty Diana (Instrumental)/Bad (Dance Extended Mix Includes "False Fade") (CD, card p/s)	10
88	Epic 651 546-2	Dirty Diana (4.42)/Dirty Diana (Instrumental)/Dirty Diana (Album Version) (3" CD with adaptor, card p/s)	12
88	Epic MJ 5	THE MICHAEL JACKSON BAD SOUVENIR SINGLES PACK (5 x 7" square picture discs in foldout PVC wallet, with lyric book)	40
88	Epic 652 844-9	Another Part Of Me/(Instrumental) (p/s, with Bad tour backstage pass)	12
88	Epic 652 844-0	Another Part Of Me/Another Part Of Me (Instrumental) (poster p/s)	8
88	Epic 652 844-2	Another Part Of Me (Extended Dance Mix)/(Radio Edit)/(Drum Mix)/ (A Capella) (CD, card p/s)	10
88	Epic 652 844-3	Another Part Of Me (Extended Dance Mix)/(Radio Edit)/(Dub Mix)/ (Instrumental) (3" CD with adaptor, card p/s)	12
88	Epic 653 004-2	Another Part Of Me (Extended Dance Mix)/Another Part Of Me (Radio Edit) Another Part Of Me (Drum Mix)/Another Part Of Me (A Cappella) (CD, pic disc)	12
88	Epic 653 026-0	Smooth Criminal/Smooth Criminal (Instrumental) (pack with 4 postcards)	15
88	Epic 653 170-6	Smooth Criminal (Extended Dance Mix)/ Smooth Criminal Extended (Dance Mix Dub Mix)/Smooth Criminal (A Cappella) (12" with "Moonwalker" advert calendar)	20
88	Epic 653 026-2	Smooth Criminal (Extended Dance Mix)/Smooth Criminal ("Annie" Mix)/ Smooth Criminal (A Cappella) (CD, card p/s)	10
89	Epic 654 672-0	Leave Me Alone/Human Nature (pop-up p/s)	15
89	Epic 654 672-2	Leave Me Alone (4.40)/Don't Stop 'Til You Get Enough (3.55)/Human Nature (4.05)/Wanna Be Startin' Something (Extended 6.30) (CD, card sleeve)	10
89	Epic 654 672-3	Leave Me Alone (4.40)/Don't Stop 'Til You Get Enough (6.04)/ Human Nature (4.05) (3" CD, gatefold card sleeve)	18
89	Epic 654 947-9	Liberian Girl (Edit)/Girlfriend (star mobile foldout card pack)	15
89	Epic 654 947-2	Liberian Girl (Edit 3.39)/Girlfriend/The Lady In My Life/Get On The Floor (CD, card p/s)	10
89	Epic 654 947-3	Liberian Girl (Edit 3.39)/Get On The Floor/Girlfriend (3" CD, g/fold card p/s)	10
92	Epic MJ 4 (658 281-1/4)	TOUR SOUVENIR PACK (CD, 4-picture disc, box set with booklet)	40
92	Epic 658 360-7	Jam (7" Edit)/Beat It (Moby's Sub Mix) ('picture frame' pack with 2 prints)	5
95	Epic 662 022	Scream (Single Edit)/Childhood (p/s, with 2 page lyric insert)	5
95	Epic 662 127	Scream (Def Radio Mix)/Scream (Single Edit) (limited edition poster sleeve)	5
97	Epic 665 130 6	Smile/It It Scary (Deep Dish Dark And Scary Remix)/Is It Scary (Eddie's Rub-a-Dub Mix)/Is It Scary (Eddie's Love Mix)/Off The Wall (Junior Vasquez Remix) (12" p/s withdrawn. Beware of counterfeits with poor print quality on label, sleeve and especially the barcode)	200

PROMOS

92	Epic XPR 1733	Remember The Time: (12" Main Mix)/(New Jack Mix)/(New Jack Main Mix)/ (Silky Soul 12" Mix)/(Silky Soul Dub)/(E-Smoov's Late Nite Mix) (12" company sleeve)	8

			MINT VALUE £
92	Epic XPR 1814	Jam: (More Than Enuff Mix)/(Roger's Club Mix)/(E-Smoov Jazzy Jam)/(Atlanta Techno Mix)/(Roger's Underground Mix)/(Silky 12")/(More Than Enuff Dub)/(Maurice's Jammin' Dub Mix)/(Roger's Club Dub)/(Atlanta Techno Dub)/(Roger's Slam Jam Mix)/(Silky Dub)/(A C	15
92	Epic XPR 1797	Who Is It (Patience Mix)/(Patience Beats)/(Most Patient Mix)/(HIS Mix)/(The P-Man Dub) (12", company sleeve)	10
95	Epic XPR 2265	The Classic Remix Series: Wanna Be Startin' Something (Brothers In Rhythm Mix)/(Tommy D's Main Mix) (12", plain sleeve, sealed with title sticker)	10
95	Epic XPR 2266	DMC Megamix (15.40)/(11.18) (12", custom sleeve)	12
95	Epic XPR 2229	The Classic Remix Series: Rock With You (Frankie's Favorite Club Mix)/(The Masters At Work Remix) (12", plain sleeve, sealed with title sticker)	12
95	Epic XPCD 7222	The Classic Remix Series: Rock With You (Frankie's Favorite Club Mix Radio Edit)/(Frankie's Favorite Club Mix) (CD)	20
95	Epic XPR 2184	Scream: (Classic Club Mix)/(DM R&B Extended Mix)/(Def Radio Mix)/(Naughty Main Mix)/(Naughty Main Mix No Rap)/(Dave 'Jam' Hall's Extended Urban Remix)/(Pressurised Dub Part 1)/(Pressurised Dub Part 2)/(Album Version)/(Single Edit No. 2)/(Naughty Pretty-P	20
96	Epic XPR 2207	Mj Club Megamix (MJ Mega Remix)/(MJ Urban Megamix) (12", blue & purple title sleeve)	15
96	Epic XPR 3020	They Don't Care About Us (The Love To Infinity Mixes): Classic Paradise Mix/Anthem Of Love/Classic Dub/Anthem Of love Dub/Hacienda Mix (12", p/s)	8
96	Epic XPR 3030	They Don't Care About Us (The R&B Mixes): Track Masters Remix/Dallas Austin Main Mix/Charles' Full Dirty Mix/LP Edit/Love To Infinity's Walk in The Park/Track Master's Instrumental (12" p/s)	10
96	Epic XPR 3033	The Classic Remix Series: Don't Stop Til You Get Enough (Roger's Underground Solution Mix)/Beat It (Moby's Sub Mix) (12", plain sleeve sealed with title sticker)	8
97	Epic XPCD 2176	HIStory (Mix 1)/Ghosts/(HIStory (Mix 2) HIStory (Mix 3)/HIStory (Mix 4) (CD)	8
97	Epic XPR 3125	Blood On The Dancefloor (TM's Switchblade Mix)/(TM's O-Postive Dub) (12", blue title p/s)	8
97	Epic XPR 3136	Blood On The Dancefloor (Refugee Camp Mix)/(7" Version) (12", green title p/s)	8
97	Epic XPR 3149	HIStory (Marks! Philly Vocal)/(Marks! Future Dub) (12", yellow title sleeve)	8
97	Epic XPR 3159	HIStory (Tony Moran's HIStory Lesson)/(Tony Moran's HIStorical Dub) Is It Scary (Eddie's Love Mix)/(Eddie's Rub-A-Dub Mix)/(Eddie's Love Mix)/ (Radio Edit) (12", white embossed title p/s)	20
97	Epic XPR 3169	HIStory (Ummah Urban Mix)/(Ummah Radio Mix)/(Tony Moran's 7" HIStory Lesson Edit)/(Ummah DJ Mix) (12", green title sleeve)	8
97	Epic XPR 3196	Is It Scary (Deep Dish Dark & Scary Remix)/(Deep Dish Double-O-Jazz Dub)/(Deep Dish Dark & Scary Remix)/(Radio Edit) (12", black embossed title p/s)	35
97	Epic XPCD 2989	Cheater (1-track promo CD)	15
03	Epic XPR 3744	Twelves (7 x 12" p/s in box with insert)	60

ALBUMS

79	Epic EPC 83458/83468	OFF THE WALL (LP, gatefold sleeve, with 7" picture disc "You Can't Win (Parts 1)/(Part 2)" [S EPC 7135], some with information sheet)	25
79	Epic SXPR 1207	EPIC HITS FROM THE JACKSONS & MICHAEL JACKSON (LP, promo only, stickered sleeve)	12
82	Epic EPC 11-85930	THRILLER (LP, picture disc in PVC sleeve)	25
83	MCA MCA 70000	E.T. - THE EXTRA TERRESTRIAL (LP, box set with booklet & poster, narration & "Someone In The Dark", with music by John Williams)	30
87	Epic 450 290-0	BAD (LP, picture disc)	20
87	Epic 450 290-8	BAD GIFT PACK (cassette pack, with note pad, highlighter pen & calendar)	15
87	Epic 450 290-9	BAD (CD, picture disc, sealed in long PVC blister pack)	45
87	Epic 450 290-9	BAD (CD, picture disc, unsealed in long PVC blister pack)	25
92	Epic 465 802-9	DANGEROUS (CD, gold disc, 10"x10" pop-up 'Collectors Edition First Printing')	15
08	Sony 88697233441	THRILLER (2-LP 25th Anniversary special edition)	20
09	Sony 88697616541	THIS IS IT (4-LP box set with 36 page book, numbered)	45

MILLIE JACKSON

(see also Elton John)

72	Mojo 2093 011	A Child Of God/You're The Joy Of My Life	15
72	Mojo 2093 015	Ask Me What You Want/I Just Can't Stand It	8
72	Mojo 2093 022	My Man, A Sweet Man/I Gotta Get Away (From My Own Self) (paper label)	10
73	Polydor 2066 317	Breakaway/Strange Things	5
75	Polydor 2066 536	If Loving You Is Wrong/The Rap	5
75	Polydor 2006 612	Loving Arms/Left Over	5
76	Spring 2066 713	A House For Sale/There You Are	20
72	Mojo 2918 005	MILLIE JACKSON (LP)	20

MILT JACKSON

(see also Ray Charles, Modern Jazz Quartet, Stanley Turrentine, Miles Davis/Art Blakey, Coleman Hawkins)

53	Vogue LDE 044	MILT JACKSON AND HIS NEW GROUP (10" LP)	20
55	Esquire 20-042	MILT JACKSON QUINTET (10" LP)	20
55	London Jazz LZ-C 14006	MILT JACKSON QUARTET (10" LP)	20
57	London Jazz LTZ-K 15064	BALLADS AND BLUES (LP)	12
57	London Jazz LTZ-K 15074	THE JAZZ SKYLINE (LP)	12
57	London Jazz LTZ-K 15091	JACKSONSVILLE (LP)	12
57	Vogue LAE 12046	WIZARD OF THE VIBES (LP)	12
59	London Jazz LTZ-K 15141	PLENTY, PLENTY SOUL (LP)	12
59	London Jazz LTZ-T 15172	BAGS' OPUS (LP, also stereo SAH-T 6049)	12
60	London Jazz LTZ-T 15177	BAGS AND FLUTES (LP)	12
60	London Jazz LTZ-K 15196	BEAN BAGS (LP, also stereo SAH-K 6095; with Coleman Hawkins)	12
61	London Jazz LTZ-K 15220	THE ARTISTRY OF MILT JACKSON (LP, also stereo SAH-K 6163)	12
61	London Jazz LTZ-K 15232	BAGS AND TRANE (LP, with John Coltrane; also stereo SAH-K 6192)	12
61	Philips BBL 7459	MILT JACKSON (LP)	12
62	Esquire 32-134	MILT JACKSON MODERN JAZZ QUARTET/QUINTET (LP)	12
62	Riverside RLP (9)407	BAGS MEETS WES (LP, with Wes Montgomery)	12
63	Realm RM 119	THE MILT JACKSON QUARTET (LP)	12

			MINT VALUE £
63	HMV CLP 1589	STATEMENTS (LP, also stereo CSD 1455)	12
63	Realm RM 156	ROLL 'EM BAGS (LP)	12
64	HMV CLP 1888	JAZZ 'N' SAMBA (LP, featuring Joe E. Ross)	15
64	Atlantic ATL/SAL 5012	VIBRATIONS (LP)	12
65	Mercury LML/SML 4008	IN A NEW SETTING (LP)	12
65	Mercury LML/SML 4016	AT THE MUSEUM OF MODERN ART (LP)	12
66	Mercury LML/SML 4028	BORN FREE (LP)	12
73	CTI CTL 8	CHERRY (LP, with Stanley Turrentine)	12

PAPA CHARLIE JACKSON

(see also Paramount Allstars, Blind Blake)

50	Tempo R 30	Long Gone Lost John/I'm Looking For A Woman Who Knows How To Treat Me Right (78)	15
60	Heritage R 100	PAPA CHARLIE JACKSON (EP, 99 only)	80
60	Heritage HLP 1011	PAPA CHARLIE JACKSON (LP, 99 only)	100

POOCH JACKSON

(see also Circles)

72	Sioux SI 013	You Just Gotta Get Ready/BROTHER DAN: Django's Valley	5
72	Sioux SI 016	Once Bitten (with Harry J. Allstars)/KING REGGAE: Slave Driver	5

PYTHON LEE JACKSON

(see under 'P')

RALPH 'SOUL' JACKSON

69	Atlantic 584258	'Cause I Love You/Sunshine Of Your Love	7

RAY JACKSON

(see also Lindisfarne)

76	EMI EMI 2514	Take Some Time/Working On	5
80	Mercury MER 3	In The Night/Waiting For The Time (p/s)	5
80	Mercury MER 8	Little Town Flirt/Make It Last (p/s)	5
80	Mercury 9109 831	IN THE NIGHT (LP, with inner sleeve)	12

ROOT & JENNY JACKSON

(see also Roots and Jenny Jackson)

69	Beacon BEA 136	Let's Go Somewhere/If I Didn't Love You	10

SHIRLEY JACKSON

63	Decca F 11612	Don't Play Me A Love Song/You Gotta Love And Be Loved	7
63	Decca F 11661	THe Boy Of The Year/I Miss You Most Of All	10
63	Decca F 11788	Broken Home/No Greater Love Than Mine	7

SHOVELVILLE K. JACKSON

60s	Melodisc MEL 1683	Be Careful Of Stones That You Throw/Kentucky Blues	12

SIMONE JACKSON

62	Piccadilly 7N 35087	Pop Pop Pop Pie/He Ain't Got No Time For Love	12
63	Piccadilly 7N 35124	Ain't Gonna Kiss Ya/Slow Motion	12
63	Piccadilly 7N 35149	Tell Me What To Do/Done What You Know Is Wrong	12

TONY JACKSON (& VIBRATIONS)

(see also Searchers)

64	Pye 7N 15685	Bye Bye Baby/Watch Your Step	25
64	Pye 7N 15745	This Little Girl Of Mine/You Beat Me To The Punch	40
65	Pye 7N 15766	Love Potion No. 9/Fortune Teller	55
65	Pye 7N 15876	Stage Door/That's What I Want (as Tony Jackson Group)	35
66	CBS 202039	You're My Number One/Let Me Know (as Tony Jackson Group)	40
66	CBS 202069	Never Leave Your Baby's Side/I'm The One She Really Thinks A Lot Of (solo)	40
66	CBS 202297	Follow Me/Walk That Walk (solo)	65
66	CBS 202408	Anything Else You Want/Come On And Stop (solo)	40
91	Strange Things STZ 5005	JUST LIKE ME (LP)	15

VIVIAN JACKSON & THE PROPHETS

(See also Yabby U.)

78	Nationwide PRO 001	CHANT DOWN BABYLON KINGDOM (LP)	70

WALTER JACKSON

65	Columbia DB 7620	Welcome Home/Blowin' In The Wind	40
66	Columbia DB 7949	Tear For Tear/It's An Uphill Climb To The Bottom	75
66	Columbia DB 7949	Tear For Tear/It's An Uphill Climb To The Bottom (DJ copy)	125
66	Columbia DB 8054	A Corner In The Sun/Not You	30
67	Columbia DB 8154	Speak Her Name/They Don't Give Medals (To Yesterday's Heroes)	30
70	Atlantic 584 311	Any Way That You Want Me/Life Has Its Ups And Downs	8
73	Brunswick BR 5	Easy Evil/I Never Had It So Good	8

WANDA JACKSON

59	Capitol CL 15033	You're The One For Me/A Date With Jerry	20
59	Capitol CL 15090	Reaching/I'd Rather Have You	20
60	Capitol CL 15147	Let's Have A Party/Cool Love	25
61	Capitol CL 15176	Mean Mean Man/Honey Bop	30
61	Capitol CL 15223	Right Or Wrong/Funnel Of Love	15
62	Capitol CL 15234	In The Middle Of A Heartache/I'd Be Ashamed	10
62	Capitol CL 15249	If I Cried Every Time You Hurt Me/Let My Love Walk In	10
58	Capitol EAP1 1041	WANDA JACKSON (EP)	75
62	Capitol EAP1 20353	A LITTLE BITTY TEAR (EP)	60
58	Capitol T 1041	WANDA JACKSON (LP)	150
60	Capitol T 1384	ROCKIN' WITH WANDA (LP)	120
61	Capitol T 1511	THERE'S A PARTY GOIN' ON (LP, mono)	80
61	Capitol ST 1511	THERE'S A PARTY GOIN' ON (LP, stereo)	100
61	Capitol T 1596	RIGHT OR WRONG (LP, mono)	50
61	Capitol ST 1596	RIGHT OR WRONG (LP, stereo)	60
62	Capitol T 1776	WONDERFUL WANDA (LP)	30
64	Capitol T 2030	TWO SIDES OF WANDA (LP, mono)	50

			MINT VALUE £
64	Capitol (S)T 2030	TWO SIDES OF WANDA (LP, stereo)	60
64	Capitol (S)T 2306	BLUES IN MY HEART (LP)	15
66	Capitol (S)T 2438	SINGS COUNTRY SONGS (LP, black label)	15
67	Capitol (S)T 2606	SALUTES THE COUNTRY MUSIC HALL OF FAME (LP, black label)	15
67	Capitol (S)T 2812	YOU'LL ALWAYS HAVE MY LOVE (LP)	15
69	Capitol (S)T 2976	CREAM OF THE CROP (LP, with Party Timers)	15
73	Word WST 9514	COUNTRY GOSPEL (LP)	15

JACKSON & SMITH

65	Polydor 56051	Ain't That Loving You Baby/Every Day I Have The Blues	10
66	Polydor 56086	Party '66/And That's It	10

JACKSON BROTHERS

59	London HLX 8845	Tell Him No/Love Me	25
59	London HLX 8845	Tell Him No/Love Me (78)	20

JACKSON 5

(see also Michael Jackson, Jermaine Jackson, Jacksons)

SINGLES

70	Tamla Motown TMG 724	I Want You Back/Who's Loving You	6
70	Tamla Motown TMG 738	ABC/The Young Folks (promo only p/s)	60
70	Tamla Motown TMG 738	ABC/The Young Folks	6
70	Tamla Motown TMG 746	The Love You Save/I Found That Girl	6
70	Tamla Motown TMG 758	I'll Be There/One More Chance	6
71	Tamla Motown SFI 66	Chartbusters Volume 5: Going Back To Indiana (flexidisc)	8
71	Tamla Motown TMG 769	Mama's Pearl/Darling Dear (promo only p/s)	60
71	Tamla Motown TMG 769	Mama's Pearl/Darling Dear	6
71	Tamla Motown TMG 778	Never Can Say Goodbye/She's Good	7
72	Tamla Motown TMG 809	Sugar Daddy/I'm So Happy	5
72	Tamla Motown TMG 825	Little Bitty Pretty One/Maybe Tomorrow	5
72	Tamla Motown TMG 833	Lookin' Through The Windows/Love Song (promo only p/s)	15
72	Tamla Motown TMG 833	Lookin' Through The Windows/Love Song	5
72	Tamla Motown TMG 837	THE CHRISTMAS EP: Santa Claus Is Coming To Town/ Someday At Christmas/Christmas Won't Be The Same This Year	12
73	Tamla Motown TMG 842	Doctor My Eyes/My Little Baby	5
73	Tamla Motown TMG 856	Hallelujah Day/To Know	5
73	Tamla Motown TMG 865	Skywriter/Ain't Nothin' Like The Real Thing (promo only p/s)	20
73	Tamla Motown TMG 865	Skywriter/Ain't Nothin' Like The Real Thing	5
73	Tamla Motown TMG 878	Get It Together/Touch	5
74	Tamla Motown TMG 895	The Boogie Man/Don't Let Your Baby Catch You	5
74	Tamla Motown TMG 904	Dancing Machine/It's Too Late To Change The Time	5
74	Tamla Motown TMG 927	The Life Of The Party/Whatever You Got I Want	5
74	Lyntone LYN 2639	Talk And Sing Personally To Valentine Readers (33rpm flexidisc free with 'Valentine' magazine)	15
74	Lyntone LYN 2639	Talk And Sing Personally To Valentine Readers (33rpm flexidisc without 'Valentine' magazine)	5
75	Rice Krispies (no cat. no.)	Sugar Daddy/Goin' Back To Indiana/Who's Loving You/Mama's Pearl/ ABC/ The Love You Save (6 different Rice Krispies cut-out card discs, price is for each)	
30			
75	Tamla Motown TMG 942	I Am Love (Part 1)/I Am Love (Part 2)	5
75	Tamla Motown TMG 1001	Forever Came Today/I Can't Quit Your Love	5
77	Motown TMG 1081	JUKEBOX GEMS: Skywriter/I Want You Back/The Love You Save (EP)	8
80	Motown SPTMG 2	THE MOTOWN 20TH ANNIVERSARY SINGLES BOX (15 x 7")	30

LPs

70	Tamla Motown TML 11142	DIANA ROSS PRESENTS THE JACKSON 5 (flipback sleeve, mono)	25
70	T. Motown STML 11142	DIANA ROSS PRESENTS THE JACKSON 5 (flipback sleeve, /stereo)	20
70	T. Motown TML 11156	ABC (flipback sleeve, mono)	40
70	T. Motown STML 11156	ABC (flipback sleeve, stereo)	30
70	T. Motown STML 11168	THE JACKSON 5 CHRISTMAS ALBUM (flipback sleeve)	25
71	T. Motown STML 11174	THIRD ALBUM (original with flipback sleeve)	20
71	T. Motown STML 11188	MAYBE TOMORROW	20
72	T. Motown STML 11214	LOOKIN' THROUGH THE WINDOWS	20
73	T. Motown STML 11231	SKYWRITER	12
73	T. Motown STML 11243	GET IT TOGETHER (with photo insert)	18
74	T. Motown STML 11275	DANCING MACHINE	18
75	T. Motown STML 11290	MOVING VIOLATIONS	18
76	Motown STML 12046	JOYFUL JUKEBOX MUSIC	12
77	Tamla Motown TMSP 6004	THE JACKSON 5 ANTHOLOGY (2-LP, original issue)	15
77	Motown STMX 6006	MOTOWN SPECIAL - THE JACKSON 5	15
79	MFP MFP 50418	ZIP-A-DEE-DOO-DAH	15
81	Motown PR 84	JACKSON 5: HISTORY OF MOTOWN (4-LP box set, with 1 Michael Jackson LP)	30
82	Motown/Pickwick TMS 3505	THE JACKSON 5	12

JACKSON HEIGHTS

(see also Nice)

70	Charisma JH 1	Doubting Thomas/Insomnia	6
72	Vertigo 6059 068	Maureen/Long Time Dying	25
70	Charisma CAS 1018	KINGS PROGRESS (LP, pink 'scroll' label)	40
72	Vertigo 6360 067	5TH AVENUE BUS (LP, gatefold sleeve, swirl label)	150
72	Vertigo 6360 077	RAGAMUFFIN'S FOOL (LP, swirl label, with poster)	150
72	Vertigo 6360 077	RAGAMUFFIN'S FOOL (LP, swirl label, without poster)	50
73	Vertigo 6360 092	BUMP AND GRIND (LP, 'spaceship label')	30

JACKSONS

(see also Jackson 5, Michael Jackson, Jermaine Jackson)

77	Epic S EPC 5063	Enjoy Yourself (Extended Version 5.48)/Style Of Life (12", p/s)	12
80	Epic EPC 12-9391	Heartbreak Hotel (Album Version)/Different Kind Of Lady (12")	12
81	Epic EPC A 1294	Walk Right Now/Your Ways (picture disc)	10
79	Epic S XPR 1207	EPIC HITS FROM THE JACKSONS & MICHAEL JACKSON (LP, promo only)	20

MINT VALUE £

84	Epic EPC 86303	VICTORY (LP, picture disc)	30
85	Epic SAI 7561	A TASTE OF VICTORY (LP, picture disc, promo only via Kelloggs offer)	50

JACKSON SISTERS

73	Mums SMUM 1591	(Why Can't We Be) More than Just Friends/Rockin' On My Porch	10
73	Mums SMUM 1829	I Believe In Miracles/Day In The Blue	50
87	Urban URB 4	I Believe In Miracles/Boy You're Dynamite	8
87	Urban URBX 4	I Believe In Miracles/Boy You're Dynamite (12", p/s)	20
87	Urban URBX 4	I Believe in Miracles/MACEO & THE MACS: Across The Tracks/ URBAN ALL STARS: It All Began In Africa (12" promo)	25

JACKSON SISTERS

00	Fab FAB 004	Rocksteady/STOVELLS: Hang On In There	5

JACK THE LAD

(see also Lindisfarne)

73	Charisma CB 206	One More Dance/Draught Genius (Polka) (p/s)	6
73	Charisma CB 218	Why Can't I Be Satisfied/Make Me Happy	5
75	Charisma CB 242	Home Sweet Home/Big Ocean Liner	5
75	Charisma CB 253	Gentleman Soldier/Oakey Strike Evictions	5
75	Charisma CB 264	My Friend The Drink/Rocking Chair	5
74	Charisma CAS 1085	IT'S JACK THE LAD (LP, small 'Mad Hatter' label)	15
74	Charisma CAS 1094	OLD STRAIGHT TRACK (LP, with lyric sheet, Charsima inner)	15
75	Charisma CAS 1110	ROUGH DIAMONDS (LP)	12

JACKY

(see also Jackie & Raindrops, Raindrops, Jackie Lee, Emma Rede, Vince Hill)

68	Philips BF 1647	White Horses/Too Many Chiefs (Not Enough Indians)	10
68	Philips BF 1689	We're Off And Running/Well That's Loving You	6
69	Page One POF 122	Love Is Now/Never Will I Be	7
68	Philips SBL 7851	WHITE HORSES (LP)	35

DICK JACOBS (& HIS ORCHESTRA)

56	Vogue Coral Q 72147	Saxophone/Never Come Sunday	6
56	Vogue Coral Q 72154	The Man With The Golden Arm Theme/Butternut	8
56	Vogue Coral Q 72204	Petticoats Of Portugal/East Of Eden	6
57	Vogue Coral Q 72245	The Big Beat/The Tower Trot	15
57	Vogue Coral Q 72260	Rock-a-billy Gal/The Golden Strings	12
57	Vogue Coral Q 72260	Rock-a-billy Gal/The Golden Strings (78)	10
57	Vogue Coral LVA 9076	THE SKIFFLE SOUND (LP, as Dick Jacobs & His Skiffle Group)	30
59	Coral LVA 9102	THEMES FROM HORROR MOVIES (LP)	25

HANK JACOBS

64	Sue WI 313	So Far Away/Monkey, Hips And Rice	40
83	Sue ENS 5	SO FAR AWAY EP: So Far Away/Out Of Sight/Hank's Groove/Summertime	10

JIMMY JACOBS & NITESPOTS

60s	Gargoyle ADV 305011	SWINGIN' SOHO - JIMMY SINGS, THE NITESPOTS SWING (LP)	15

JACQUELINE & BRIDIE

(see also Jackie & Bridie)

64	Fontana TF 473	Roses/Roving Jack	6
64	Fontana TL 5212	HOLD BACK THE DAWN (LP)	20

CHUCK JACQUES & LYNN TAITT & COMETS

(see also Wilbert Francis & Vibrators)

67	Ska Beat JB 264	Dial 609/VIBRATORS & TOMMY McCOOK & COMETS: Wait For Me	20

HATTIE JACQUES

71	Avenue NUE 143	THE BUNGLES OF BOJUM (EP)	10

ILLINOIS JACQUET & HIS ORCHESTRA

56	Vogue V 2387	Blow Illinois Blow/Destination Moon	6
53	Vogue LDE 026	ILLINOIS JACQUET (10" LP)	15
56	Columbia Clef 33C 9018	ILLINOIS JACQUET (10" LP)	15
57	Columbia Clef 33CX 10085	GROOVIN' WITH JACQUET (LP)	12
50s	Melodisc MLP 12-301	JAZZ AT THE PHILHARMONIC (LP)	12

JADE

70	DJM DJS 227	Alan's Song/Amongst Anemones	15
70	DJM DJLPS 407	FLY ON STRANGE WINGS (LP, gatefold sleeve)	130

JADE WARRIOR

(see also July, Joe O'Donnell)

72	Vertigo 6059 069	The Demon Trucker/Snake	15
78	Island JAD 1	Way Of The Sun/Sun Ra	5
71	Vertigo 6360 033	JADE WARRIOR (LP, gatefold sleeve, swirl label)	100
71	Vertigo 6360 062	RELEASED (LP, multi-poster sleeve, small swirl label)	300
72	Vertigo 6360 079	LAST AUTUMN'S DREAM (LP, gatefold sleeve, swirl label)	110
74	Island ILPS 9290	FLOATING WORLD (LP, pink rim palm tree label)	20
75	Island ILPS 9318	WAVES (LP, pink rim palm tree label)	20
76	Island ILPS 9393	KITES (LP)	18
78	Island ILPS 9552	WAY OF THE SUN (LP)	12
79	Butt BUTT 001	REFLECTIONS (LP)	18

JADIS

84	private pressing	BABOON ENQUIRIES (cassette)	12
87	private pressing DEM 1	G13/Out Of Reach (cassette)	8
88	private pressing DEM 2	Don't Keep Me Waiting/In The Dark (cassette)	8
89	private pressing	Lost For Words/This Changing Face (cassette)	8
90	Back Beat 004-12	THE JADIS ALBUM (LP, numbered)	15

MAX JAFFA (& HIS ORCHESTRA)

56	Columbia SCM 5226	China Boogie/Slap Happy	5

MINT VALUE £

CHRIS JAGGER

73	GM GMS 3	Something New/Joy Of The Ride	6
73	GM GML 1003	CHRIS JAGGER (LP)	15

MICK JAGGER

(see also Rolling Stones, Jacksons, Jack Nitzsche)

70	Decca F 13067	Memo From Turner/Natural Magic (in export p/s)	40
70	Decca F 13067	Memo From Turner/Natural Magic	12
84	CBS TA 4431	State Of Shock/Your Ways (picture disc)	6
87	CBS 651028-0	Let's Work/Catch As Catch Can (poster p/s)	6
87	CBS THROW P1	Throwaway/Peace For The Wicked (picture disc)	10
70	United Artists UAS 29108	NED KELLY (LP, soundtrack)	35
70	Warner Bros WS 2554	PERFORMANCE (LP, first pressing, orange label, soundtrack)	45
70	Warner Bros WS 2554	PERFORMANCE (LP, second pressing, green label, soundtrack)	30

JAGO

72	Duke DU 134	Rebel Train/Babylon Version	10

JAGS

61	Decca F 11397	The Hunch/Cry Wolf	8

JAGS

79	Island WIP 6501	Back Of My Hand/Double Vision (p/s)	6
79	Island 12SWIP 6501	Back Of My Hand/Double Vision/Single Vision/What Can I Do? (12", p/s)	8
80	Island WIP 6531	Woman's World/Dumb Blonde (p/s)	8
80	Island WIP 6587	Party Games/She's So Considerate (p/s)	10
80	Island WIP 6666	I Never Was A Beach Boy/Tune Into Heaven (p/s)	18
80	Island WIP 6683	The Sound Of G-O-O-D-B-Y-E/The Hurt (no p/s)	10
79	Island ILPS 9603	EVENING STANDARDS (LP)	12
81	Island ILPS 9655	NO TIE LIKE A PRESENT (LP)	12

JAGUAR

81	Heavy Metal HEAVY 10	Back Street Woman/Chasing The Dragon (p/s)	40
82	Neat NEAT 16	Axe Crazy/War Machine (p/s)	20
83	Neat NEAT 1007	POWER GAMES (LP, some on purple vinyl)	30
83	Neat NEAT 1007	POWER GAMES (LP, black vinyl)	18
84	Roadrunner RR 9851	THIS TIME (LP)	15

JAGUARS

(see also Dave Mason)

63	Impression IMP 101	Opus To Spring/The Beat (1,000 only)	35
65	Contest RGJ 152	We'll Live On Happily/Now You Wonder Why	300

JAH BUNNY

80	White Label	DUBBS INTERNATIONAL (LP)	40

JAH FATTA & THE BLACK BROTHERS

79	Rite Sound RS DD 002	Free Rasta Free/BLACK BROTHER ALL STARS: Free Dub (12")	60

JAH FISH

72	Grape GR 3034	Vampire Rock/MOD STARS: El-Sisco Rock	8

JAH FRANKIE JONES

77	Third World TWS 916	SATTA & PRAISE JAH (LP)	35

JAH FREE

93	Jah Free	Lightning Clap/Lightning Dub/Jubilation/Jubilation Dub (12")	20

JAH LION

(see also Jah Lloyd)

83	Congo COS 2	Melody For Negus/MAKKA BEES : Fire	15
76	Island ILPS 9386	COLUMBIA COLLY (LP)	25

JAH LLOYD

(see also Jah Lion)

73	Jaguar JAG 102	Channel One (with Douglas Boothe)/SOUL SYNDICATES:Channel Two	6
73	Jaguar JAG 104	Psalm Two/SOUL SYNDICATES: Channel Two	6
75	Treble C CCC 02	Once Bitten/CHARLEY ACE & INSWINGS: Real Red	6
76	Attack ATT 8121	World Class/World Class (Version)	6
74	DIP PL DL 1001	HERBS OF DUB...MORE HERBS (LP)	30
70s	His Majesty MH 1004	REGGAE STICK (LP)	20
70s	His Majesty MH 1003	DREAD LION DUB (LP)	50

JAH RUBY

77	Dynamic DYLP 3011	DREAD AFFAIR (LP)	25

JAH SCOUSE

85	Better Things BETS 1	Merge/Vegan Mix (foldout p/s)	5

JAH SHAKA

82	Jah Shaka 821	Revelation 18/Revelation Dub (12", red vinyl)	15
82	Jah Shaka 823	Jah Children (with Sister Pat)/SHAKA RIDIM SECTION : Jah Works (12")	30
82	Jah Shaka 828	Lion Youth/MAD PROFESSOR : Beyond The Realms (12")	20
82	Jah Shaka LP 824	THE COMMANDMENTS OF DUB (LP)	15
82	Rough trade ROUGH 50	COMMANDMENTS OF DUB (LP)	15
83	Jah Shaka 833	REVELATION SONGS (LP)	15
84	Jah Shaka 847	COMMANDMENTS OF DUB PART 2 (LP)	15
84	Ariwa SALP 84	JAH SHAKA MEETS MAD PROFESSOR (LP)	15
85	Jah Shaka	COMMANDMENTS OF DUB PART 3 (LP)	12
85	Jah Shaka 850	JAH SHAKA MEETS ASWAD (LP)	12
89	Mango MPLM 1001	PRESENTS DUB MASTERS VOL. 1 (LP)	15
94	Jah Shaka SHAK 947	JAH SHAKA MEETS HORACE ANDY (LP)	12

JAH SHAKA VS FATMAN

80	Live & Love LP 10	LIVE (LP)	30

MINT VALUE £

JAH STITCH

78	Aries PFUS 6000	Combination Three/Combine Version	8
75	Third World TWS 401	NO DREAD CAN'T DEAD (LP)	40
78	Cancer CANSLP 002	MY PRECIOUS LOCKS (LP)	25

JAH THOMAS

78	Greensleeves GRE 12	Stop Yu Loafin'/Bicycle Skank	10
78	Greensleeves GREL 3	STOP YU LOAFIN' (LP)	25
80	Daddy Kool DKLP 16	DANCE HALL STYLEE (LP)	20
83	Silver Camel SCLP 03	DANCE HALL CONNECTION (LP)	15

JAH WALTON

81	Music Force MFLP 02	TOUCH HERE WHERE SHE WANT IT MOST (LP)	80

JAH WOBBLE

(see also Bartok)

78	Virgin VOLE 9	Dreadlock Don't Deal In Wedlock/Pthilius Pubis (p/s)	5
78	Virgin 12VOLE 9	Dreadlock Don't Deal In Wedlock/Pthilius Pubis (12", p/s)	8
80	Virgin VS 337	Betrayal/MR. X: Battle Of Britain (p/s)	5
80	Virgin VS 337-12	Betrayal/MR. X: Battle Of Britain (12", p/s)	8
82	Jah Wobble JAH 1	Fading/Nocturnal (p/s, as Jah Wobble With Animal)	5
82	Jah Wobble JAH 2	Long Long Way/Nocturnal (12", p/s)	8
78	Virgin VS 239-12	STEEL LEG MEETS THE ELECTRIC DREAD (12 EP, p/s)	8
92	East West OVAL 103 T	VISIONS OF YOU (12" EP, some with p/s)	8
80	Virgin V 2158	THE LEGEND LIVES ON (mini-LP)	12

JAH WOBBLE, THE EDGE & HOLGER CZUKAY

(see also Don Letts & Jah Wobble, Dan MacArthur, Joolz, Public Image Ltd, The Edge, Orb, Can)

83	Island WOB 1	Snake Charmer/Hold On To Your Dreams (p/s)	5

JAH WOOSH

74	Cactus CT 39	Judy Drownded/Crooked Skank	8
75	Lucky DL 5096	Don't Do That/That Dub	5
75	Lucky DL 5094	Rocking Blues/Version	5
75	Tropical AL 057	Iffie This Life/Iffie Version	8
76	Sunshot SS002	Religious Dread/Religious Dub	8
76	Sunshot SS005	Ital Feast/Dub Feast	8
76	Angen ANG 116	Set Up Yourself Dread/Version	8
76	Attack ATT 8124	I'm Alright/Version	8
76	Attack ATT 8129	Show I The Way/Show I The Way (Version)	8
77	Sunshot SS009	Whip Them Jah/Version	8
78	Grove Music GMDM 7	Pay Them Dues/Diverse Doctrine (with Ras Ibuna) (12")	15
78	Freedom Sounds FSD 001	Ales Skank/Different Style (12")	15
78	Attack ATT 8137	Marcus Say/Take Heed	8
79	Yard International YI 02	Jah Is The Ruler/Ruling Power/Jammys At The Control (12")	15
76	Black Wax WAX LP2	PSALMS OF WISDOM (LP)	100
74	Cactus CTLP 103	JAH WOOSH (LP)	25
76	Student STULP 1003	CHALIS BLAZE (LP)	25
77	K&B KBLP 002	LICK HIM WITH THE DUSTBIN (LP)	25
78	Trojan TRLS 157	RELIGIOUS DREAD (LP)	18
76	Cactus CTLP 116	JAH JAH DEY DEY (LP)	25
79	Dread & Dread 002	GATHERING ISRAEL (LP, multi-coloured vinyl)	35

JAH YOUTH

76	Caribbean CBN 307	Little Natty Dread/Little Natty Dread Version	6

JAHFA CULTURE & THE OFFBEAT POSSE

86	Jah Tubbys JT 017	Listen To We/Listen Mix (12")	100

JAILCELL RECIPIES

91	First Strike	POULTON ROAD EP (marbled grey vinyl)	6
91	First Strike FST 006	TWO YEARS OF TOOTHACHE (LP)	12

JAILHOUSE

(see also Hamlett)

72	Pye 7N 45172	Ya Hoo Hoo/Bad End	12

JAKE & FAMILY JEWELS

70	Polydor 2425 027	JAKE AND THE FAMILY JEWELS (LP)	15

JAKLIN

69	Stable SLE 8003	JAKLIN (LP, laminated sleeve, black/silver labels)	350

JAM

(see also Style Council, Paul Weller, Bruce Foxton, Time U.K., Sharp)

73	Fanfare	Some Kinda Lovin'/Making My Way Back Home (acetate 6 copies only)	2500

ORIGINAL SINGLES

77	Polydor 2058 866	In The City/Takin' My Love	5
77	Polydor 2058 903	All Around The World/Carnaby Street	5
77	Polydor 2058 945	The Modern World/Sweet Soul Music/Back In My Arms Again/ Bricks And Mortar (Part) (B-sides live at 100 Club 11.9.77)	5
78	Polydor 2058 995	News Of The World/Aunties And Uncles (Impulsive Youths)/Innocent Man	5
78	Polydor 2059 054	David Watts/A Bomb In Wardour Street (double-A-sided 7"; plastic moulded label, those with white paper labels are worth £8)	5
78	Polydor 2059 054	David Watts/A Bomb In Wardour Street (double-A-sided 7"; A-side songwriter miscredited as "Ray Davis" without an "e")	15
78	Polydor POSP 8 (2059 068)	Down In The Tube Station At Midnight/So Sad About Us/The Night (7"; misprinted with erroneous B-side ref. to All Mod Cons)	15
78	Polydor POSP 8 (2059 068)	Down In The Tube Station At Midnight/So Sad About Us/The Night	5
79	Polydor POSP 83	The Eton Rifles/See Saw	5

(The above singles were reissued in 1980 in their picture sleeves; early originals have curved edges on sleeve openings whereas reissues are straight. Lettering on the reissues tends to be fatter, reissues are worth £2-3.)

MINT VALUE £

80	Polydor 2059 266	Start/Liza Radley	5
80	Polydor POSPJ 113 2816 024	Going Underground/The Dreams Of Children/Away From The Numbers/ The Modern World/Down In The Tube Station At Midnight	8
82	Polydor POSPX 400	Town Called Malice (Live at Hammersmith Palais 14.12.81)/Precious (Extended Version) (12", double A-side, striped die-cut sleeve)	7
82	Polydor POSPX 540	Beat Surrender/Shopping/Move On Up/Stoned Out Of My Mind/War (12")	8

Note: All 7" singles prior to 'Beat Surrender' were re-pressed on 14th January 1983 in their picture sleeves, the second reissue for singles prior to 'Going Underground'.

FLEXIDISCS

80	Lyntone LYN 9048/ Flexipop 002	Boy About Town/Pop Art Poem (yellow flexi with issue 2 of Flexipop magazine)	5
80	Lyntone LYN 9048...	Boy About Town/Pop Art Poem (green flexi with issue 2 of Flexipop magazine)	6
80	Lyntone LYN 9048/...	Boy About Town/Pop Art Poem (blue flexi with issue 2 of Flexipop magazine)	7

Note: add £4 if stuck to front of magazine & another £5 if also with mailer.

80	Lyntone LYN 9048	Boy About Town/Pop Art Poem (hard vinyl white label test pressing, same tracks both sides, with mailer, 1980)	50
80	Lyntone LYN 9048	Boy About Town/Pop Art Poem (hard vinyl white label test pressing, same tracks both sides, without mailer, 1980)	40
80	Lyntone (no cat. no.)	When You're Young (live) (1-sided fan club flexi)	25
82	Lyntone (no cat. no.)	Tales From The Riverbank (re-recorded) (1-sided fan club flexi)	15
82	Polydor PAOLO 100	Move On Up (live) (flexi with Melody Maker music paper; with Melody Maker)	7

REISSUES & RETROSPECTIVE SINGLES

83	Polydor 2059 482/POSP 482	That's Entertainment/Down In The Tube Station At Midnight (Live Version) (UK reissue of earlier import)	5
83	Polydor POSP 483	Just Who Is The 5 O'Clock Hero/The Great Depression (UK reissue of earlier import)	5
89	Old Gold OG 9894	Town Called Malice/Absolute Beginners (in p/s)	7
89	Old Gold OG 9894	Town Called Malice/Absolute Beginners	5
89	Old Gold OG 9895	Beat Surrender/The Bitterest Pill (I Ever Had To Swallow) (generic Old Gold sleeve)	5
89	Old Gold OG 9896	The Eton Rifles/Down In The Tube Station At Midnight (in p/s)	7
89	Old Gold OG 9896	The Eton Rifles/Down In The Tube Station At Midnight	5
89	Old Gold OG 9897	Going Underground/Start! (in p/s)	7
89	Old Gold OG 9897	Going Underground/Start!	5
90	Strange Fruit SFPS 080	THE PEEL SESSIONS (12" EP)	5
91	Polydor PZ 155	That's Entertainment/Down In The Tube Station At Midnight (live)/ Town Called Malice (live) (12")	5
91	Polydor PZCD 155	That's Entertainment/Down In The Tube Station At Midnight (live)/ Town Called Malice (live) (CD, 17th June 1991)	8
92	Polydor PO 199	The Dreams Of Children/Away From The Numbers (live)	6
92	Polydor POCS 199	The Dreams Of Children/Away From The Numbers (live) (, withdrawn)	6
92	Polydor PZ 199	The Dreams Of Children/Away From The Numbers (live)/ The Modern World (live) (12")	8
92	Polydor PZCD 199	The Dreams Of Children/Away From The Numbers (live)/ The Modern World (live) (CD)	10
99	Polydor 561479-2	Going Underground/The Dreams Of Children (CD, reissue, 1999)	8

ALBUMS

82	Polydor POLD 5055	THE GIFT (LP, 12/3/82, initially in pink/white striped paper bag)	12
91	Receiver RRLP 141	LIVE AT THE ROXY (LP, unreleased, white label test pressings exist with printed proof sleeve shelved before release as the recording was only half a show from the 100 club 11/9/77)	150
93	Polydor 519 667-1	LIVE JAM (2-LP, single sleeve with picture inners)	20
83	Polydor SNAP 1/SNAPL 45	SNAP! (2-LP, gatefold sleeve, with bonus 7" EP: Live! Wembley Arena 2 & 3.12.82 [SNAPL 45])	18
92	Polydor 513 177-1	EXTRAS (2-LP, single sleeve with picture inners)	25
96	Polydor 531 493-1	THE JAM COLLECTION (2-LP, single sleeve, picture inners)	15
02	Simply Vinyl SVLP 108	ALL MOD CONS (LP, 180g vinyl, PVC sleeve, 2002)	18
02	Simply Vinyl SVLP 209	SETTING SONS (LP, 180g vinyl, PVC sleeve, 2002)	18
06	Polydor 9877182	SNAP! (3-CD, limited edition with bonus live EP [9818340])	18

PROMOS

78	Polydor 2059 054DJ	David Watts/A Bomb In Wardour Street	25
82	Polydor POSP 400	Precious (1-sided 7", company sleeve)	25
82	Polydor DEN 1	Town Called Malice (Live at Hammersmith Palais 14.12.81)/Precious (Extended Version) (12", white label promo)	30
82	Polydor PODJ 540	Beat Surrender (Censored)/Shopping (7", radio promo)	15
82	Polydor POSPX 540	Beat Surrender/Shopping/Move On Up/Stoned Out Of My Mind/War (12", white label promo)	15
83	Polydor SNAPL 45	LIVE! WEMBLEY ARENA (bonus Snap! EP, white label promo)	30
97	Polydor 2058 266/	In The City (1-sided 7", "20th anniversary party invite", co. sleeve; with 'tax disc'-style card invite (ADMITS 1)	25
97	Polydor 2058 266/ ADMITS 1	In The City (1-sided 7", "20th anniversary party invite", co. sleeve; without 'tax disc'-style card invite (ADMITS 1)	15
02	Polydor JAMPCD 1	THE COMPLETE JAM: 3-TRACK CD SAMPLER (card sleeve)	15
02	Polydor JAMBBC 1	A SELECTION FROM ... THE JAM AT THE BBC (CD)	20
02	Polydor JAMDVD 1	THE COMPLETE JAM (2-DVD)	25

MISPRESSINGS

78	Polydor 2058 995	News Of The World/Aunties And Uncles (Impulsive Youths)/ Innocent Man (plays B-side on both sides)	40
78	Polydor POSP 6	Sandy/Can't Let You Go (by John Travolta, B-side mispressed with "So Sad About Us")	30
78	Polydor POSP 8	Down In The Tube Station At Midnight/So Sad About Us/ The Night (A-side plays John Travolta's "Sandy")	30
79	Polydor POSP 69	When You're Young/Smithers-Jones (plays B-side both sides)	40
80	Polydor 2059 266	Start!/Liza Radley (A-side plays Village People's "Can't Stop The Music")	10
82	Polydor POSP 400	Town Called Malice/Precious (7", both sides play "Precious")	30

MINT VALUE £

JAM ON THE MUTHA

90	Wau!/Polydor MAGXR 3	Hotel California (Orb In Cali Mix 1)/(Like Joe Never Left Mix)/(Orbitally Ambient Mix) (12", p/s)	10

JAM TODAY

80s	Stroppy Cow SCJT 1	Stereotyping/Song About Myself (p/s, with insert)	50

JAMAICA BAND

73	Action ACT 4611	Sticky Fingers Part 1/Part 2	10

JAMAICA FATS

(see also Al T. Joe)

66	Blue Beat BB 368	Jacqueline/Please Come Home (actually by Al T. Joe & Celestials)	22

JAMAICA JUBILEE STOMPERS

67	Amusicon AMU 1002	Give Your Love To Me/I Cry To My Heart	15

JAMAICAN ACTIONS

68	Coxsone CS 7070	Catch The Quinella/JACKIE MITTOO: Songbird	35

JAMAICAN EAGLES

(see also Eagles)

73	Harry J HJ 6661	Country Living/Country Living (Version)	5

JAMAICAN FOUNDATIONS

68	Coxsone CS 7036	Take It Cool/VICEROYS: Try Hard To Leave	150

JAMAICANS

(see also Norris Weir & Jamaicans, Tommy Cowan)

66	Doctor Bird DB 1109	Cool Night/Ma And Pa	60
67	Trojan TR 007	Dedicated To You/The Things I Said To You	35
67	Treasure Isle TI 7007	Things You Say You Love/I've Got A Pain	35
67	Treasure Isle TI 7012	Baba Boom (Festival Song 1967) (actually by Baba Boom)/TOMMY McCOOK & SUPERSONICS: Real Cool	20
67	Treasure Isle TI 7037	Peace And Love/Woman Gone Home	35
69	Escort ES 806	Early In The Morning/Mr. Lonely	12
70	Harry J. HJ 6604	Fire Parts 1 & 2	10
71	Dynamc DYN 410	Love Uprising/My Love For You	7
71	Dynamic DYN 417	Mary/CONSCIOUS MINDS: Soldier Boy	7
71	New Beat NB 084	Mary/CONSCIOUS MINDS: Soldier Boy	7
72	Dynamic DYN 430	I Believe In Music/Music (Version)	5
72	Dynamic DYN 442	Are You Sure/Are You Sure (Version)	5
72	Dynamic DYN 456	Sunshine Love/Sunshine Version	5
74	Dragon DRA 1029	My Heart Just Keeps On Breaking/My Heart Just Keeps On Breaking (Inst'l)	5

JAMAICAN SHADOWS

67	Coxsone CS 7005	HUGH GODFREY: Have Mercy/Blending Love	40
69	Upsetter US 320	Dirty Dozen (actually by Upsetters)/Crying Too Long	40

JAMAICA'S OWN VAGABONDS

(see also Vagabonds, Jimmy James & Vagabonds)

64	Decca DFE 8588	BEHOLD (EP)	60
64	Decca LK 4617	SKA TIME (LP)	80

AHMED JAMAL

59	London Jazz LTZ-M 15162	BUT NOT FOR ME (LP)	15
59	London Jazz LTZ-M 15170	AHMED JAMAL (LP)	20
62	Pye Jazz NJL 38	ALHAMBRA (LP)	15
62	Pye Jazz NJL 47	ALL OF YOU (LP)	15
63	Pye Jazz NJL 50	Q (LP)	15
63	Pye Jazz NJL 50	MACANUDO (LP)	15
63	Pye Jazz NJL 52	POINCIANA (LP)	15
64	Chess CRL 4001	NAKED CITY THEME (LP)	15

JAMES

86	Sire JIM 3	Chain Mail/Hup Springs (p/s)	10
86	Sire JIM 4	So Many Ways/Withdrawn (p/s)	10
86	Sire JIM 4T	So Many Ways/Just Hipper/Withdrawn (12", p/s)	18
88	Blanco Y Negro NEG 26	Yaho/Mosquito (p/s)	6
88	Blanco Y Negro NEG 26T	Yaho/Mosquito/Left Out Of Her Will/New Nature (12", p/s)	12
88	Blanco Y Negro NEG 31	What For/Island Swing (p/s)	6
88	Blanco Y Negro NEG 31T	What For (Climax Mix)/Island Swing/Not There (12", p/s)	15
88	Blanco Y Negro NEG 31C	What For (Climax Mix)/Island Swing/Not There (cassette in video-style box)	10
89	Rough Trade RT 225	Sit Down/Sky Is Falling (p/s)	8
89	Rough Trade RTT 225	Sit Down/Goin' Away/Sky Is Falling (12", p/s, 1st 500 with postcard)	12
89	Rough Trade RTT 225	Sit Down/Goin' Away/Sky Is Falling (12", p/s, without postcard)	8
89	Rough Trade RTT 225 CD	Sit Down/Goin' Away/Sky Is Falling (3" CD, card sleeve)	12
89	Rough Trade RT 245	Come Home/Promised Land (p/s)	6
89	Rough Trade RTT 245	Come Home (Long Version)/Come Home (7" Version)/Promised Land/Slow Right Down (Demo Version) (12", p/s)	10
90	Fontana JIMM 512	How Was It For You?/How Was It For You? (Different Mix)/Lazy/Undertaker (12", p/s, with stencil)	12
90s	Lyntone	Weather Change (Demo Version) (flexidisc, with tour programme)	12
90s	Lyntone	Weather Change (Demo Version) (flexidisc, without tour programme)	6
84	Factory FAC 78	JIMONE EP: What's The World/Fire So Close/Folklore (p/s)	12
85	Factory FAC 138	VILLAGE FIRE: What's The World/Fire So Close/Folklore/Hymn From A Village/If Things Were Perfect (12" EP)	12
85	Factory FAC 119	JAMES II: Hymn From A Village/If Things Were Perfect (p/s)	12
86	Sire JIM 3T	SIT DOWN EP: Chain Mail/Uprising/Hup Springs (12", p/s)	15
91	Fontana JIM 812	SIT DOWN (12" EP, recorded live at G-Mex)	10
89	Rough Trade ONEMAN 1LP	ONE MAN CLAPPING (LP, with inner sleeve)	18
94	Fontana 5228271	WAH WAH (LP)	25
94	Fontana 5228272	WAH WAH (CD, digipak)	20

MINT VALUE £

BARNABY JAMES

71	Decca F 13198	Feeling Alright/Gone Fishing	6

B.B. JAMES

70	Upsetter US 328	Consider Me/Consider Me Version	12

BOB JAMES

75	CTI CTI 6043	BOB JAMES ONE (LP)	12
75	CTI CTI 6057	BOB JAMES TWO (LP)	12

BOBBY JAMES & DAVE (Barker)

71	Smash SMA 2314	You Said It/AGGRO BAND: Hot Sauce	50

BRIAN JAMES

68	Olga OLE 005	Come Back Silly Girl/It Just Happened That Way	8

CALVIN JAMES

65	Columbia DB 7516	Some Things You Never Get Used To/Remember	25

(pseudonym for George Underwood; see also Davie Jones & King Bees)

COL JAMES

62	Oriole CB 1736	Doesn't Anybody Make Short Movies/(Oooh Looka There) Ain't She Pretty	5

DANNY JAMES

72	Southern Sound BT 100	Your Gravy Train/Devil Made Me Say That	7

DICK JAMES

53	Parlophone MSP 6039	Mother Nature And Father Time/Don't You Care	8
53	Parlophone MSP 6047	The Joker/Guessing	10
55	Parlophone MSP 6170	Unchained Melody/Come Back (Come Back To Me)	7
55	Parlophone MSP 6190	He/So Must I Love You	5
56	Parlophone MSP 6199	Robin Hood/The Ballad Of Davy Crockett	20
56	Parlophone MSP 6230	Summer Sing-Song Medley	5
56	Parlophone R 4220	I Only Know I Love You/Mirabelle	5
56	Parlophone R 4241	Sing Song Time (No. 3) Medley	5
57	Parlophone R 4255	The Garden Of Eden/I Accuse	10
57	Parlophone R 4314	Westward Ho The Wagons!/The Gay Cavalier	5
57	Parlophone R 4375	Skiffling Sing Song Medley	10
58	Parlophone R 4498	Daddy's Little Girl/When You're Young	6
59	Parlophone R 4606	There But For Your Love Go I/Minus One Heart	5
64	Parlophone R 5212	Sing A Song Of Beatles With Dick James Medley (Parts 1 & 2)	8

ELMORE JAMES

64	Sue WI 335	Dust My Blues/Happy Home (as Elmore James & Broom Dusters)	45
65	Sue WI 383	It Hurts Me Too/Bleeding Heart	40
65	Sue WI 392	Knocking At Your Door/Calling The Blues (B-side actually by Junior Wells & Earl Hooker)	120
66	Sue WI 4007	I Need You/Mean Mistreating Mama	40
65	Sue ILP 918	THE BEST OF ELMORE JAMES (LP)	65
65	Sue ILP 927	THE ELMORE JAMES MEMORIAL ALBUM (LP)	65
68	Bell MBLL/SBLL 104	SOMETHING INSIDE OF ME (LP)	45
68	Ember EMB 3397	THE LATE FANTASTICALLY GREAT ELMORE JAMES (LP)	22
70	United Artists UAS 29109	THE LEGEND OF ELMORE JAMES (LP)	50
70	Blue Horizon 7-66230	TO KNOW A MAN (2-LP)	50
70	Blue Horizon 7-63204	TOUGH (LP, with 4 tracks by John Brim)	65
73	Polydor 2383 200	COTTON PATCH HOTFOOTS (LP, shared with Walter Horton)	20
75	DJM DJLMD 8008	ALL THEM BLUES (2-LP)	18
83	Ace CH 68	KING OF THE SLIDE GUITAR (LP, yellow vinyl)	12

ETTA JAMES

(see also Etta & Harvey)

60	London HLM 9139	All I Could Do Was Cry/Tough Mary	50
60	London HLM 9234	My Dearest Darling/Girl Of My Dreams	30
61	Pye International 7N 25079	At Last/I Just Want To Make Love To You	35
61	Pye International 7N 25080	Trust In Me/Anything To Say You're Mine	20
61	Pye International 7N 25113	Dream/Fool That I Am	20
62	Pye International 7N 25131	Something's Got A Hold On Me/Waiting For Charlie To Come Home	30
62	Pye International 7N 25162	Stop The Wedding/Street Of Tears	20
63	Pye International 7N 25205	Pushover/I Can't Hold It In Any More	22
65	Sue WI 359	Roll With Me Henry/Good Rockin' Daddy	50
67	Chess CRS 8052	I Prefer You/I'm So Glad (I Found Love In You)	20
67	Chess CRS 8063	Tell Mama/I'd Rather Go Blind	25
67	Chess CRS 8069	Security/I'm Gonna Take What He's Got	15
68	Chess CRS 8076	I Got You Babe/I Worship The Ground You Walk On	15
68	Chess CRS 8082	You Got It/Fire	15
72	Chess 6145 016	Tell Mama/I'd Rather Go Blind/I Found A Love	15
74	Chess 6145 033	Out On The Streets Again/Come A Little Closer	8
78	Warner Brothers K 17173	Piece Of My Heart/Lovesick Blues	8
65	Chess CRL 4502	ETTA JAMES ROCKS THE HOUSE (LP)	75
67	Chess CRL 4524	AT LAST (LP)	70
68	Ember EMB 3390	THE SOUL OF ETTA JAMES (LP)	40
68	Chess CRL 4536	TELL MAMA (LP)	40
73	Chess 6671 003	PEACHES (2-LP)	25

ETTA JAMES & SUGAR PIE DeSANTO

(see also Sugar Pie DeSanto)

65	Chess CRS 8025	Do I Make Myself Clear/Somewhere Down The Line	25

GARY JAMES

68	Polydor 56134	Nicole/You're Gone	20
67	Polydor S6208	Teddy Bear/In The Rain	15

MINT VALUE £

GRAHAM JAMES

63	Columbia DB 7128	You Could Have Fooled Me/Why Can't You See It My Way?	8

HARRY JAMES & HIS ORCHESTRA

(see also Rosemary Clooney)

65	Dot DS 16729	Love Theme From In Harm's Way/Green Onions	5

JASON JAMES

67	CBS 2705	Miss Pilkington's Maid/Count Me Out	40

JERRY JAMES & BANDITS

64	Solar SRP 101	Sweet Little Sixteen/Three Steps To Heaven	15

JESSE JAMES

54	Vocalion V 1037	Southern Casey Jones/Lonesome Day Blues (78)	20
71	Mojo 2092 016	Don't Nobody Want To Get Married/(Pt. 2)	5

JIMMY JAMES (& THE VAGABONDS)

62	Dice CC 4	Bewildered And Blue/I Don't Want To Cry (solo)	20
63	R&B JB 112	Jump Children/Tell Me (solo)	25
64	Black Swan WI 437	Thinking Of You/Shirley (solo)	30
65	Columbia DB 7653	Shoo Be Doo You're Mine/We'll Never Stop Loving You	20
66	Ska Beat JB 242	Your Love/Someday (solo)	20
66	Piccadilly 7N 35298	I Feel Alright/I Wanna Be Your Everything (p/s)	75
66	Piccadilly 7N 35298	I Feel Alright/I Wanna Be Your Everything	30
66	Piccadilly 7N 35320	Hi Diddley Dee Dum Dum (It's A Good Good Feelin')/Come To Me Softly	20
66	Piccadilly 7N 35331	This Heart Of Mine/I Don't Wanna Cry (p/s)	100
66	Piccadilly 7N 35331	This Heart Of Mine/I Don't Wanna Cry	75
66	Piccadilly 7N 35349	Ain't Love Good, Ain't Love Proud/Don't Know What I'm Gonna Do	20
67	Piccadilly 7N 35360	I Can't Get Back Home To My Baby/Hungry For Love (solo)	12
67	Piccadilly 7N 35374	No Good To Cry/You Showed Me The Way	12
68	Pye 7N 17579	Red Red Wine/Who Could Be Loving You	10
69	Pye 7N 17719	Close The Door/Why (solo)	5
71	Trojan TR 7806	Help Yourself/Why	25
72	Bamboo BAM 67	Riverboat Jenny/If I Wasn't Black	5
72	Stateside SS 2209	A Man Like Me/Survival	15
72	Stateside SS 2209	A Man Like Me/Survival (DJ copy)	35
75	Pye 7N 45524	Whatever Happened To The Love We Knew/Let's Have Fun	5
75	Pye 7N 45472	Hey Girl/I Am Somebody	50
66	Piccadilly NEP 34053	JIMMY JAMES AND THE VAGABONDS (EP)	40
66	Piccadilly NPL 38027	THE NEW RELIGION (LP)	40
68	Marble Arch MAL 823	THIS IS JIMMY JAMES AND THE VAGABONDS (LP)	12
68	Pye N(S)PL 18231	OPEN UP YOUR SOUL (LP)	25
70	Marble Arch MAL 1244	THE NEW RELIGION (LP, reissue)	12

JIMMY JAMES & THE VAGABONDS/ALAN BOWN SET

(see also Vagabonds, Jamaica's Own Vagabonds, Alan Bown Set)

67	Pye N(S)PL 18156	LONDON SWINGS - LIVE AT THE MARQUEE CLUB (LP, 1 side each)	60

JOHN JAMES

70	Transatlantic TRA 219	MORNING BRINGS THE LIGHT (LP)	20
71	Transatlantic TRA 242	JOHN JAMES (LP)	20
72	Transatlantic TRA 250	SKY IN MY PIE (LP)	12
75	Transatlantic TRA 305	HEAD IN THE CLOUDS (LP)	12
76	Kicking Mule SNKF 128	DESCRIPTIVE GUITAR INSTRUMENTALS (LP)	15
78	Kicking Mule SNKF 136	LIVE IN CONCERT (LP)	18
84	Stoptime STOP 101	ACOUSTICA ECLECTICA (LP, signed)	35
84	Stoptime STOP 101	ACOUSTICA ECLECTICA (LP)	20

JONI JAMES

53	MGM SP 1013	Why Don't You Believe Me?/Wishing Ring	15
53	MGM SP 1025	Have You Heard/Purple Shades	8
53	MGM SP 1026	Your Cheatin' Heart/I'll Be Waiting For You	8
53	MGM SP 1041	Almost Always/Is It Any Wonder?	8
53	MGM SP 1064	I'll Never Stand In Your Way/Why Can't I	8
54	MGM SP 1081	I Need You Now/You're Nearer	8
54	MGM SP 1089	I'll Be Seeing You/Am I In Love	8
54	MGM SP 1094	You're My Everything/Maybe Next Time	8
54	MGM SP 1100	In A Garden Of Roses/Every Day	8
54	MGM SP 1105	Pa Pa Pa/Mama, Don't Cry At My Wedding	8
55	MGM SP 1125	This Is My Confession/How Important Can It Be?	8
55	MGM SP 1135	When You Wish Upon A Star/Is This The End Of The Line?	8
56	MGM SP 1149	You Are My Love/My Believing Heart	8
57	MGM MGM 918	Give Us This Day/How Lucky You Are	8
57	MGM MGM 954	Only Trust Your Heart/I Need You So	8
58	MGM MGM 973	My Funny Valentine/My Darling, My Darling	7
58	MGM MGM 978	Never 'Till Now/Love Works Miracles	7
58	MGM MGM 991	There Goes My Heart/Funny	10
59	MGM MGM 1002	There Must Be A Way/I'm Sorry For You, My Friend	10
54	MGM MGM-EP 504	JONI JAMES (EP)	10
55	MGM MGM-EP 518	SINGS TO YOU (EP)	8
56	MGM MGM-EP 530	LITTLE GIRL BLUE (EP)	8
56	MGM MGM-EP 558	LOVE LETTERS (EP)	8
60	MGM MGM-EP 728	THE SONGS OF HANK WILLIAMS (EP, mono)	10
60	MGM MGM-ES 3501	THE SONGS OF HANK WILLIAMS (EP, stereo)	12
54	MGM MGM-D 127	LET THERE BE LOVE (10" LP)	25
59	MGM MGM-C 777	ONE HUNDRED SONGS AND JONI (LP)	20
59	MGM MGM-C 785	JONI SINGS SONGS OF HANK WILLIAMS (LP)	20
60	MGM MGM-C 809	TI VOGLIO BENE (I LOVE YOU SO) (LP)	20
60	MGM MGM-C 823/CS 6005	SINGS IRISH FAVOURITES (LP, mono/stereo)	15

MINT VALUE £

60	MGM MGM-C 825	SWINGS SWEET (LP)	15
61	MGM MGM-C 839	100 STRINGS AND JONI IN HOLLYWOOD (LP, mono)	15
61	MGM MGM-CS 6015	100 STRINGS AND JONI IN HOLLYWOOD (LP, stereo)	20
63	MGM MGM-C 933	AFTER HOURS (LP)	15

MARK JAMES

67	Liberty LIB 55953	Bimbo Knows/I Can't Let You Go	5

NICKY JAMES (MOVEMENT)

(see also Move)

65	Columbia DB 7747	Stagger Lee/I'm Hurtin' Inside (as Nicky James Movement)	30
67	Philips BF 1566	I Need To Be Needed/So Glad We Made It	7
68	Philips BF 1635	Would You Believe/Silver Butterfly	18
68	Philips BF 1694	Lookin' Through Windows/Nobody But Me	7
69	Philips BF 1755	Time/Little Bit Of Paper	8
69	Philips BF 1804	Reaching For The Sun/No Life At All	7
72	Threshold TH 12	Why/Foreign Shore	6
73	Threshold TH 16	Black Dream/She Came To Me	6
73	Threshold TH 17	I Guess I've Always Loved You/My Style	8
71	Philips 6308 069	NICKY JAMES (LP, black/silver labels)	150
73	Threshold THS 10	EVERY HOME SHOULD HAVE ONE (LP, gatefold sleeve)	30
76	Threshold THS 19	THUNDERTHROAT (LP)	15

OSCAR JAMES

64	Carnival CV 7007	Louisa/Go 'Way	7

PHILIP JAMES & BLUES BUSTERS

(see also Blues Busters)

65	Island WI 219	Wide Awake In A Dream/MAYTALS: Tell Me The Reason	100

RICKY JAMES

57	HMV POP 306	Knee Deep in The Blues/Bluer Than Blue	30
57	HMV POP 334	Party Doll/Ninety-Nine Ways	30

ROGER JAMES

71	Chapter One CHS 807	RIDING FREE (LP, red/silver labels)	25

ROGER JAMES FOUR

65	Columbia DB 7556	Letter From Kathy/Leave Me Alone	10
66	Columbia DB 7813	Better Than Here/You're Gonna Come Home Cryin' (withdrawn)	70
66	Columbia DB 7829	Better Than Here/You're Gonna Come Home Cryin'	45

RUBY JAMES

69	Fontana TF 1051	Gettin' Mighty Crowded/Don't Play That Song	20

SALLY JAMES

74	Philips 6006 418	Isn't It Good/Wake Me When It's Over (p/s)	7

SIDNEY JAMES (& DEAN ROGERS/LIZ FRASER)

(see also Tony Hancock)

61	Decca F 11328	The Ooter Song/Double Bunk (with Liz Fraser)	5
61	HMV POP 886	Kids/One Last Kiss (with Dean Rogers)	5
73	Pye 7N 4528	Our House/She's Gone (solo) (p/s)	5

SKIP JAMES

65	Vanguard VSD 79219	SKIP JAMES TODAY (LP)	40
67	Private PR3	1964-67 (LP, 99 copies only)	80
68	Vanguard VSD 79273	DEVIL GOT MY WOMAN (LP)	45
70	Spokane SPL 1003	THE ORIGINAL 1930/31 RECORDINGS (LP)	50
78	Vanguard VDP 20001	I'M SO GLAD (LP)	20
70s	Storyville 670 185	THE GREATEST OF THE DELTA BLUES SINGERS (LP)	15

SONNY JAMES

56	Capitol CL 14635	The Cat Came Back/Hello Old Broken Heart	25
56	Capitol CL 14664	Twenty Feet Of Muddy Water/For Rent (One Empty Heart)	15
57	Capitol CL 14683	Young Love/You're The Reason I'm In Love	15
57	Capitol CL 14708	First Date, First Kiss, First Love/Speak To Me	15
57	Capitol CL 14742	Dear Love/Lovesick Blues	10
57	Capitol CL 14788	Love Conquered (Love Came, Love Saw)/A Mighty Lovable Man	15
57	Capitol CL 14814	Uh-Huh-Mm/Why Can't They Remember?	30
57	Capitol CL 14814	Uh-Huh-Mm/Why Can't They Remember? (78)	10
58	Capitol CL 14848	Kathaleen/Walk To The Dance	15
58	Capitol CL 14879	Are You Mine/Let's Play Love	5
58	Capitol CL 14915	You Got That Touch/I Can See It In Your Eyes	6
58	Capitol CL 14952	I Can't Stay Away From You/Let Me Be The One To Love You	5
59	Capitol CL 14991	Yo-Yo/Dream Big	15
59	Capitol CL 14991	Yo-Yo/Dream Big (78)	20
59	Capitol CL 15022	Talk Of The School/The Table	5
59	Capitol CL 15046	Pure Love/This Love Of Mine	5
59	Capitol CL 15079	Red Mud/Who's Next In Line	5
60	London HL 9132	Jenny Lou/Passin' Through	10
65	Capitol CL 15377	You're The Only World I Know/Tying The Pieces Together	5
57	Capitol EAP1 827	YOUNG LOVE (EP)	20
64	Capitol EAP1 20654	YOU'RE THE ONLY WORLD I KNOW (EP)	10
57	Capitol T 779	SOUTHERN GENTLEMAN (LP)	15
57	Capitol T 867	SONNY (LP)	15
63	London HA-D 8049	YOUNG LOVE (LP)	30

STU(ART) JAMES (& MOJOS)

(see also Mojos)

65	Decca F 12231	Wait A Minute/Wonder If She Knows (as Stu James & Mojos)	12
74	Bradleys BRAD 7406	I Only Wish I Had The Time/Back To Basingstoke (Part 1)	5
76	Bradleys BRAD 7614	I'm In The Mood/Firefly (as Stuart James)	8

MINT VALUE £

SULLIVAN JAMES BAND

66	Parlophone R 5465	Goodbye Mr. Heartache/We're Gonna Make It	10

TOMMY JAMES & SHONDELLS

66	Roulette RK 7000	Hanky Panky/SHONDELLS: Thunderbolt	15
66	Pye International 7N 25398	It's Only Love/Ya! Ya!	10
67	Major Minor MM 511	I Think We're Alone Now/Gone Gone Gone	12
67	Major Minor MM 548	Out Of The Blue/Love's Closing In On Me	5
68	Major Minor MM 558	Wish It Were You/Get Out Now	8
68	Major Minor MM 567	Mony Mony/One, Two, Three And I Fell	7
68	Roulette RO 500	Do Something To Me/Somebody Cares	8
69	Roulette RO 502	Crimson And Clover/Some Kind Of Love	10
69	Roulette RO 506	Sweet Cherry Wine/Breakaway	5
69	Roulette RO 507	Crystal Blue Persuasion/I'm Alive	12
69	Roulette RO 511	Ball Of Fire/Makin' Good Time	5
70	Roulette RO 513	She/Loved One	5
70	Roulette RO 516	Come To Me/Talkin' And Signifyin'	5
70	Roulette RO 518	Ball And Chain/Candy Makers (solo)	5
68	Major Minor MMLP/SMLP 27	SOMETHING SPECIAL (LP)	35
68	Roulette RRLP/SRLP 1	MONY MONY (LP)	30
68	Roulette RRLP/SRLP 2	CRIMSON AND CLOVER (LP)	40
69	Roulette RRLP/SRLP 3	CELLOPHANE SYMPHONY (LP)	20
72	Roulette 2432 002	THE BEST OF TOMMY JAMES & THE SHONDELLS (LP)	15
72	Roulette 2432 005	MY HEAD, MY BED AND MY RED GUITAR (LP, solo)	12

TONY JAMES

68	Jolly JY 002	Treat Me Right/Me Donkey's Dead	12

WINSTON JAMES

70	Hot Rod HR 106	Prison Sentence/JANET FERRON: Darling I Need You	12
70	Torpedo TOR 6	I May Never/Longest Day	25
70	Torpedo TOR 4	Gal You Think You Nice/White Silver Sands	10

JAMES BOYS

68	Direction 58-3721	The Mule (Instrumental)/The Horse (Vocal)	15
73	Penny Farthing PEN 806	Over And Over/Same Old Way	7

JAMES BROTHERS

(see also Wheels)

68	Page One POF 077	I Forgot To Give You Love/The Truth About It	8
68	Page One POF 088	Does It Have To Be Me/You Don't Really Love Me	8
74	Penny Farthing PEN 857	Up until Now/Pick A Bale Of Cotton	6

JAMES GANG

(see also Tommy Bolin)

70	Stateside SS 2158	Funk No. 48/Collage	15
70	Stateside SS 2173	Stop/Take A Look Around (withdrawn)	15
70	Probe PRO 502	Funk 49/Thanks	6
71	Probe PRO 533	Walk Away/Yadig?	5
70	Stateside SSL 10295	YER' ALBUM (LP)	20
70	Probe SPB 6253	RIDES AGAIN (LP)	18
71	Probe SPB 1038	THIRDS (LP)	15
71	Probe SPB 1045	LIVE IN CONCERT (LP)	15
72	Probe SPB 1056	STRAIGHT SHOOTER (LP)	12
73	Probe SPB 1065	PASSIN' THRU (LP)	12

BOBBY JAMESON

64	Decca F 12032	All I Want Is My Baby/Each And Every Day	40
64	London HL 9921	I Wanna Love You/I'm So Lonely	30
65	Brit WI 1001	Rum-Pum/Please Mr. Mailman	20
69	Joy JOYS 193	TOO MANY MORNINGS (LP)	90

STEPHEN JAMESON

70	Pye 7N 45189	Margie Make It March/Happiness Road	5
73	Dawn DNS 1035	Don't Say/Back Together Once Again	5
73	Dawn DNLS 3044	STEPHEN JAMESON (LP)	15

JAMESON RAID

80	Blackbird BRAID 001	The Hypnotist/The Raid/Gettin' Hotter/Straight From The Butchers (p/s)	40
81	GBH GBH 1	Seven Days Of Splendour/It's A Crime/Catcher In The Rye (p/s, with lyric sheet, white sleeve)	35
81	GBH GBH 1	Seven Days Of Splendour/It's A Crime/Catcher In The Rye (p/s, with lyric sheet, later pressing with black sleeve)	30

JAMIE JON & JERRY

67	Decca F12642	You've Still Got A Place In My Heart/One Time Lover (All Time Fool)	6

JAMIES

58	Fontana H 153	Summertime Summertime/Searching For You	45
62	Columbia DB 4885	Summertime Summertime/Searching For You (reissue)	20

JAMIROQUAI

93	Acid Jazz JAZID 46	When You Gonna Learn/Too Young To Die (p/s)	10
93	Acid Jazz JAZID 46T	When You Gonna Learn/Didgin' Out (12", p/s)	15
96	Sony 4839991	TRAVELLING WITHOUT MOVING (2-LP with bonus track, Do You Know Where You're Coming From?)	25

JAMME

70	Stateside-Dunhill SSL 5024	JAMME (LP)	25

JOE JAMMER

(see also Mitchell/Coe Mysteries)

73	Regal Zono. SRZA 8514	BAD NEWS (LP, gatefold sleeve, red/silver labels)	25

MINT VALUE £

J.A.M.s
(see under Justified Ancients Of Mu Mu)

JAN & ARNIE
(see also Jan & Dean)

58	London HL 8653	Jennie Lee/Gotta Getta Date	50
58	London HL 8653	Jennie Lee/Gotta Getta Date (78)	35

JAN & DEAN
(see also Legendary Masked Surfers, Fantastic Baggys, Jan & Arnie)

59	London HLN 8936	Baby Talk/Jeanette, Get Your Hair Done	30
59	London HLN 8936	Baby Talk/Jeanette, Get Your Hair Done (78)	70
59	London HLU 8990	There's A Girl/My Heart Sings	25
59	London HLU 8990	There's A Girl/My Heart Sings (78)	70
60	London HLU 9063	Clementine/You're On My Mind	20
61	London HLH 9395	Heart And Soul/Midsummer Night's Dream	20
62	Liberty LIB 55397	A Sunday Kind Of Love/Poor Little Puppet	20
63	Liberty LIB 55531	Linda/When I Learn How To Cry	18
63	Liberty LIB 55580	Surf City/She's My Summer Girl	10
63	Liberty LIB 55613	Honolulu Lulu/Someday You'll Go Walkin' By	10
64	Liberty LIB 55641	Drag City/Schlock Rod Pt 1	15
64	Liberty LIB 55672	Dead Man's Curve/The New Girl In School	10
64	Liberty LIB 55704	The Little Old Lady From Pasadena/My Mighty GTO	10
64	Liberty LIB 55724	Ride The Wild Surf/The Anaheim, Azusa And Cucamonga Sewing Circle, Book Review And Timing Association	10
65	Liberty LIB 55727	Sidewalk Surfin'/When It's Over	10
65	Liberty LIB 55766	(Here They Come) From All Over The World/Freeway Flyer	10
65	Liberty LIB 55792	You Really Know How To Hurt A Guy/It's As Easy As 1, 2, 3	10
65	Liberty LIB 55833	I Found A Girl/It's A Shame To Say Goodbye	10
66	Liberty LIB 10225	Norwegian Wood/A Beginning From An End	20
66	Liberty LIB 55860	Batman/Bucket 'T'	25
66	Liberty LIB 10244	Popsicle/The Joker Is Wild	25
66	Liberty LIB 55923	The New Girl In School/School Day (Ring Ring Goes The Bell)	8
66	Liberty LIB 10252	Tennessee/Horace The Swinging School Bus Driver	12
67	CBS 202630	Yellow Balloon/A Taste Of Rain	30
65	Liberty LEP 2213	SURF 'N' DRAG HITS (EP)	35
66	Liberty LEP 2258	THE TITANIC TWOSOME (EP)	40
76	United Artists REM 402	REMEMBER JAN & DEAN (EP)	10
63	Liberty LBY 1163	SURF CITY AND OTHER SWINGING CITIES (LP)	35
64	Liberty LBY 1220	DEAD MAN'S CURVE/NEW GIRL IN SCHOOL (LP)	50
64	Liberty LBY 1229	RIDE THE WILD SURF (LP)	45
65	Liberty LBY 1279	GOLDEN HITS (LP)	20
65	Liberty LBY 1304	FOLK 'N' ROLL (LP)	40
66	Liberty LBY 1309	JAN AND DEAN MEET BATMAN (LP)	40
66	Liberty LBY 1339	FILET OF SOUL (A LIVE ONE) (LP)	35
67	Liberty LBS 83016	GOLDEN HITS (LP)	15

JAN & KELLY

62	Philips 326 567 BF	Ooh! 'E Didn't/Prepare To Meet Your Fate Mate	5
62	Philips BF 1253	I Could Have Died/Make Me A Doormat	5
63	Philips BF 1265	Ooh! I Can't/Write Me A Letter	5
64	Philips BF 1323	And Then He Kicked Me/My Country And Western Lover	5
64	Philips BF 1377	There Was A Girl/There Was A Boy/And Then There Was Nothing	5
63	Philips BE 12536	TIME FOR A LAUGH (EP)	12

JAN & KJELD

59	Pye International 7N 25013	Buona Sera/Tiger Rag	6
60	Ember EMB S 101	Banjo Boy/Don't Raise A Storm (in p/s)	20
60	Ember EMB S 101	Banjo Boy/Don't Raise A Storm	10
60	Qualiton PSP 7127	Sweet Sue/Oh! Mein Papa (as Jan & Keld)	6
60	Ember EMB S 109	Down By The Riverside/I Shall Not Be Moved	6
60	Ember EMB 3312	THE KIDS FROM COPENHAGEN (LP, label states "The Boys From Copenhagen")	15

BRUCE JANAWAY

78	Deep Range SRT/CUS/216	PURITANICAL ODES (LP, with insert)	35

JAN DUKES DE GREY
(see also Noy's Band)

70	Decca Nova (S)DN 8	SORCERERS (LP)	200
71	Transatlantic TRA 234	MICE AND RATS IN THE LOFT (LP, g/f sleeve, plastic inner/foam opening)	200

JANE'S ADDICTION

88	WEA W 7520	Mountain Song/Jane Says (p/s)	6
88	WEA W 7520T	Mountain Song/Jane Says/Had A Dad (live) (12", p/s)	8
91	WEA W 0031TP	Classic Girl/No One's Leaving (live)/Ain't No Right (live) (12", picture disc, die-cut sleeve)	8

PETER JANES

67	CBS 203004	Emperors And Armies/Go Home Ulla (in p/s)	10
67	CBS 203004	Emperors And Armies/Go Home Ulla	6
68	CBS 3299	Do You Believe/For The Sake Of Time	20

BUSTER JANGLES' FLYING MATTRESS

72	RCA RCA 2112	Love Has Taken Over My Brain/The Little World I Knew	40

JANIE
(see also Jeanne Black)

61	Capitol CL 15180	You Better Not Do That/Only Girls Can Tell	12

JANIE
(see also Janie Jones)

70	President PT 309	Back On My Feet Again/Psycho	20

MINT VALUE £

JANINE

81	Stiletto JAN 001	Crazy On You/Candy (p/s)	170

JOHNNY JANIS

58	London HLU 8650	The Better To Love You/Can This Be Love	15
60	Philips PB 1090	Gina/If The Good Lord's Willin'	6
58	HMV 7EG 8365	JOHNNY JANIS (EP)	30
66	London HA-U 8270	ONCE IN A BLUE MOON (LP)	20

BERT JANSCH

67	Big T BIG 102	Life Depends On Love/A Little Sweet Sunshine	12
73	Reprise K 14234	Oh My Father/The First Time Ever I Saw Your Face	7
74	Charisma CB 240	In The Bleak Midwinter/One For Jo.	6
75	Charisma CB 267	Dance Lady Dance/Build Another Band	5
79	Kicking Mule SCK 44	Time And Time/Una Linea Di Dolcezza (as Bert Jansch Conundrum)	5
82	Logo GO 409	Heartbreak Hotel/Up To The Stars (p/s)	5
66	Transatlantic EP 145	NEEDLE OF DEATH (EP)	40
65	Transatlantic TRA 125	BERT JANSCH (LP)	50
65	Transatlantic TRA 132	IT DON'T BOTHER ME (LP)	45
66	Transatlantic TRA 143	JACK ORION (LP)	50
67	Transatlantic TRA 157	NICOLA (LP)	35
69	Transatlantic TRA 179	BIRTHDAY BLUES (LP)	30
69	Vanguard VSD 79292	STEPPING STONES (LP)	30
69	Transatlantic TRASAM 10	THE BERT JANSCH SAMPLER (LP)	15
71	Transatlantic TRA 235	ROSEMARY LANE (LP)	25
72	Transatlantic TRASAM 27	BOX OF LOVE - THE BERT JANSCH SAMPLER VOL. 2 (LP)	20
73	Reprise K 44225	MOONSHINE (LP, with lyric insert)	15
74	Charisma CAS 1090	L.A. TURNAROUND (LP, with lyric insert)	35
75	Charisma CAS 1107	SANTA BARBARA HONEYMOON (LP)	15
77	Charisma CAS 1127	A RARE CONUNDRUM (LP)	15
79	Charisma CLASS 6	AVOCET (LP)	12
80	Kicking Mule SNKF 162	THIRTEEN DOWN (LP, as Bert Jansch Conundrum)	30
85	Konexion KOMA 788006	FROM THE OUTSIDE (LP, 500 only)	12

BERT JANSCH & JOHN RENBOURN

(see also Conundrum, Pentangle, John Renbourn)

66	Transatlantic TRA 144	BERT AND JOHN (LP)	50

LITTLE JOHN ANTHONY

60	Ember EMB 3302	TEENAGE DANCE PARTY (LP)	20

JANUARY

69	CBS 4465	It Sings For Me/Julie	10

JAPAN

(see also David Sylvian)

78	Ariola Hansa AHA 510	Don't Rain On My Parade/Stateline (solid or press-out centre, no p/s)	15
78	Ariola Hansa AHA 525	The Unconventional/Adolescent Sex (with p/s)	20
78	Ariola Hansa AHA 525	The Unconventional/Adolescent Sex	6
78	Ariola Hansa AHA 529	Sometimes I Feel So Low/Love Is Infectious (p/s, initial pressing on blue vinyl)	10
78	Ariola Hansa AHA 529	Sometimes I Feel So Low/Love Is Infectious (p/s)	8
79	Ariola Hansa AHA 540	Life In Tokyo (Short Version)/Life In Tokyo Pt 2 (p/s, red vinyl)	8
79	Ariola Hansa AHAD 540	Life In Tokyo (Long Version)/(Short Version) (12", p/s, red vinyl)	12
80	Ariola Hansa AHA 559	I Second That Emotion/Quiet Life (dull red vinyl, card p/s)	8
80	Ariola Hansa AHA 559	I Second That Emotion/Quiet Life (dull red vinyl, paper p/s)	6
80	Virgin VS 379	Gentlemen Take Polaroids/The Experience of Swimming (fully autographed by band, p/s)	75
80	Virgin VS 379	Gentlemen Take Polaroids/The Experience of Swimming//The Width Of A Room/Burning Bridges (double pack, gatefold p/s)	12
82	Virgin VSY 472	Ghosts/The Art Of Parties (Version) (picture disc, stickered PVC cover)	5
88	Virgin CDT 11	Ghosts/The Art Of Parties (Version)/Visions Of China (3" CD, card sleeve)	8
88	Virgin CDT 32	Gentlemen Take Polaroids/Cantonese Boy (12" Version)/Methods Of Dance (12" Version) (3" CD, gatefold card sleeve)	8
80	Virgin V 2180	GENTLEMEN TAKE POLAROIDS (LP, with misprinted sleeve with sticker, Some Kind Of Fool listed instead of "Burning Bridges")	12

JOHNNY JAPES & HIS JESTICLES

(see also XTC, John Otway, Mr. Partridge)

87	Viz VIZ 1	Bags Of Fun With Buster/Scrotal Scratch Mix (p/s)	5

JIMMY JAQUES

58	Fontana H 131	In My Life/Never Let You Go	6

JARMELS

61	Top Rank JAR 560	She Loves To DanceLittle Lonely One	30
61	Top Rank JAR 580	A Little Bit Of Soap/The Way You Look Tonight	40

COOK E. JARR

69	RCA RCA 1820	Pledging My Love/If I Were A Carpenter	5

JEAN-MICHEL JARRE

78	Polydor POSP 20	Equinoxe 5/Equinoxe 1 (p/s, with etched autograph on run-off)	8
79	Polydor 2001 896	Equinoxe 4 (Remix)/Equinoxe 3 (p/s)	6
80	Polydor 2001 968	Jarre At The Concorde: Equinoxe 7 (live)/Equinoxe 8 (live) (p/s)	10
81	Polydor POSP 292	Magnetic Fields 2 (Remix)/Magnetic Fields 1 (Excerpt) (p/s)	5
81	Polydor POSP 363	Magnetic Fields 4 (Remix)/Magnetic Fields 1 (Excerpt) (p/s)	10
82	Polydor POSP 430	Orient Express/Fishing Junks At Sunset (p/s)	8
84	Polydor POSPX 718	Zoolook (Remix)/Wooloomooloo/Zoolook (Extended)/Zoolook (Effects) (12", p/s)	15
85	Polydor POSP 740	Zoolookologie (Remix)/Ethnicolor 2 (p/s)	8
85	Polydor POSPG 740	Zoolookologie (Remix)/Ethnicolor 2//Oxygene 4/Oxygene 6 (double pack)	12
85	Polydor POSPX 740	Zoolookologie (Extended Remix)/(Remix)/Ethnicolor 2 (12", p/s)	15
86	Polydor POSPX 788	Rendezvous 4 (Special Remix)/Rendezvous 4/Moon Machine (12", 'face' or 'city skyline' p/s)	20

MINT VALUE £

88	Polydor PZ 25	Revolutions (Extended Mix)/Revolutions (LP Mix)/Industrial Revolution 2 (12", p/s)	8
88	Polydor PZCD 25	Revolutions (Extended Mix)/Revolutions/Revolutions (Single Remix) (CD, jewel case)	20
88	Polydor PZCD 32	London Kid (Full Version) (featuring Hank Marvin)/ Industrial Revolution 3/ Revolutions (Remix) (CD, card sleeve)	20
89	Polydor PZCD 55	Oxygene IV (Single Version)/Industrial Revolution Overture/ Oxygene IV (live)/September (CD, card sleeve)	15
90	Polydor PZ 84	Calypso (Extended)/Calypso/Calypso Pt 2 (12", p/s)	10
87	Polydor 833 737-2	THE JEAN-MICHEL JARRE 10TH ANNIVERSARY CD BOX SET (7-CD, 5,000 only)	40
88	Polydor C88 1-3	OXYGENE (LP, HMV-only box set with booklet, 3,300 only)	15
88	Polydor C88-1-3	OXYGENE (CD, HMV-only box set with booklet, 3,500 only)	20

MAURICE JARRE

63	Pye Intl. NPL 28023	LAWRENCE OF ARABIA (LP, soundtrack)	12
65	Fontana (S)TL 5259	THE COLLECTOR (LP, soundtrack)	25
66	MGM MGM-CS 8037	GRAND PRIX (LP, soundtrack)	12
66	CBS (S)BPG 62843	IS PARIS BURNING? (LP, soundtrack)	18
67	RCA RD 7848	NIGHT OF THE GENERALS (LP, soundtrack)	30
67	RCA Victor RD/SF 7876	THE PROFESSIONALS (LP, soundtrack)	50
68	Dot (S)LPD 515	VILLA RIDES (LP, soundtrack)	15
71	MGM 2315 028	RYAN'S DAUGHTER (LP, soundtrack, gatefold sleeve)	12
76	EMI SLCW 1033	THE MESSAGE (LP, soundtrack, gatefold sleeve)	12
77	Pye NSPH 28504	JESUS OF NAZARETH (LP, soundtrack, gatefold sleeve)	15

WAYNE JARRETT

80	Greensleeves GRED 41	Saturday Night Jamboree (12")	20
81	Greensleeves GRED 61	Chip In/You Were On My Mind (12")	12
82	Echo ECHO 011	Satta Dread/Sadat (12")	35
81	Greensleeves GREL 28	CHIP IN (LP)	12
82	Wackies W 191	BUBBLE UP (LP)	25

WINSTON JARRETT

77	Carib Gems CG 012	Sleepers/Sleepers Version (with the Righteous Flames)	6
78	Write Sounds WTS 1002	Spanish Town Road/Version	8
80	Warrior WAR 144	Wise Man/I Shen Galore (12")	20

MARIAN JARVIS

75	Chelsea 2005 038	A Penny For Your Thoughts/A Good Man To Wake Up To	30

JASMIN T

69	Tangerine DP 13	Some Other Guy/Evening (with p/s)	50
69	Tangerine DP 13	Some Other Guy/Evening	20

JASON & THE SCORCHERS

85	EMI EA 200	Shop It Around/Change The Tune (p/s)	5
85	EMI 12EA 200	Shop It Around/Absolutely Sweet Marie/Change The Tune (12", p/s)	8

JASON CREST

(see also Holy Mackerel, High Broom)

68	Philips BF 1633	Turquoise Tandem Cycle/Good Life (in export p/s)	160
68	Philips BF 1633	Turquoise Tandem Cycle/Good Life	60
68	Philips BF 1650	Juliano The Bull/Two By The Sea	40
68	Philips BF 1687	(Here We Go Round) The Lemon Tree/Patricia's Dream	50
69	Philips BF 1752	Waterloo Road/Education	30
69	Philips BF 1809	A Place In The Sun/Black Mass	180

JASON'S GENERATIONS

66	Polydor BM 56042	It's Up To You/Insurance Co.'s Are Very Unfair	80

JASPER

69	Spark SRLP 103	LIBERATION (LP, laminated front sleeve, blue/silver labels)	400

JAVELLS

77	Pye Disco Demand DDS 2003	Goodbye Nothin' To Say/Nothin' To Say	6

JAWBONE

(see also Mirage, Portobello Explosion)

70	Carnaby CNS 4007	How's Ya Pa?/Mister Custer	10
70	Carnaby CNS 4020	Way Way Down/Bulldog Goes West	10
72	B&C CB 190	Gotta Go/Automobile Blues	6
70	Carnaby CNLS 6004	JAWBONE (LP)	150

BOB JAXON (& HI-TONES)

55	London HL 8156	Ali Baba/Why Does A Woman Cry (as Bob Jaxon & Hi-Tones)	45
55	London HL 8156	Ali Baba/Why Does A Woman Cry (as Bob Jaxon & Hi-Tones) (78)	20
57	RCA RCA 1019	Beach Party/(Gotta Have Something In The) Bank Frank	80
57	RCA RCA 1019	Beach Party/(Gotta Have Something In The) Bank Frank (78)	20

FRANKIE JAXON/HOUNDHEAD HENRY

60	Jazz Collector JEL 10	THE MALE BLUES VOLUME 6 (EP)	10

JAY (Black)

(see also Jay & The Americans)

64	Coral Q 72471	I Rise, I Fall/How Sweet It Is	35
67	United Artists UP 1174	What Will My Mary Say/Return To Me (as Jay Black)	10

ABNER JAY

63	London HLN 9791	Cleo/Thresher	30

DAVID JAY

(see under David J.)

ERIC JAY

59	London HL 9004	The Little Drummer Boy/Blue Champagne Cha Cha	8
59	London HL 9004	The Little Drummer Boy/Blue Champagne Cha Cha (78)	15

MINT VALUE £

LAURIE JAY COMBO
(see also Nero & Gladiators)

62	Ember JBS 710	Shades Of Red/Nevada Sunsets	8
63	HMV POP 1234	Teenage Idol/Think Of Me	15
64	HMV POP 1300	Love In My Heart/'Til You're Mine	8
64	HMV POP 1335	Maybe/Be Good To Me	8
65	Decca F 12083	A Song Called Soul/Just A Little Bit	25

LONNIE JAY & JAYNES

63	Stateside SS 197	Around And Around We Go/Somewhere	10

PETER JAY (& BLUE MEN)
(see also Blue Men)

60	Triumph RGM 1000	Just Too Late/Friendship (as Peter Jay & Blue Men)	40
60	Pye 7N 15290	Paradise Garden/Who's The Girl?	45

PETER JAY & JAYWALKERS
(see also Terry Reid, Miller, Big Boy Pete)

62	Decca F 11531	Can Can '62/Redskins	5
63	Decca F 11593	Totem Pole/Jaywalker	5
63	Decca F 11659	Poet And Peasant/Oo La La	10
63	Decca F 11757	Kansas City/The Parade Of Tin Soldiers	10
64	Decca F 11840	You Girl/If You Love Me	10
64	Piccadilly 7N 35199	Where Did Our Love Go/Caroline	8
64	Piccadilly 7N 35212	Tonight You're Gonna Fall In Love/Red Cabbage	10
65	Piccadilly 7N 35220	Parchman Farm/What's Easy For Two Is So Hard For One	20
65	Piccadilly 7N 35259	Before The Beginning/Solitaire	15

JAY (John Holt) & JOYA (Landis)
(see also John Holt, Joya Landis)

68	Trojan TR 633	I'll Be Lonely/SUPERSONICS: Second Fiddle	12

JAY & TECHNIQUES

67	Philips PB 1597	Apples, Peaches, Pumpkin Pie/Stronger Than Dirt	25
67	Philips PB 1618	Keep The Ball Rollin'/Here We Go Again	15
67	Mercury 6052 302	Apples, Peaches, Pumpkin Pie/Contact	7
68	Philips PB 1644	Strawberry Shortcake/Still (In Love With You)	12
68	Mercury MF 1034	Baby Make Your Own Sweet Music/Help Yourself To All My Lovin'	12
75	Polydor 2066 473	I Feel Love Comin' On/This World Of Mine	10
71	Mercury MCF 127360	Baby Make Your Own Sweet Music/Help Yourself To All My Lovin' (reissue)	6
67	Philips (S)BL 7834	APPLES, PEACHES, PUMPKIN PIE (LP)	30

JAY & THE AMERICANS
(see also Jay, Chapter Four)

62	HMV POP 1009	She Cried/Dawning	40
63	United Artists UP 1002	This Is It/It's My Turn To Cry	8
63	United Artists UP 1018	What's The Use/Strangers Tomorrow	8
64	United Artists UP 1039	Come Dance With Me/Look Into My Eyes Maria	18
64	United Artists UP 1069	Come A Little Bit Closer/Goodbye Boys Goodbye	8
65	United Artists UP 1075	Let's Lock The Door (And Throw Away The Key)/I'll Remember You	10
65	United Artists UP 1088	Think Of The Good Times/If You Were Mine Girl	8
65	United Artists UP 1094	Cara Mia/When It's All Over	10
65	United Artists UP 1108	Some Enchanted Evening/Girl	8
66	United Artists UP 1119	Sunday And Me/Through This Doorway	12
66	United Artists UP 1129	Why Can't You Bring Me Home/Baby Stop Your Crying	20
66	United Artists UP 1132	Crying/I Don't Need A Friend	8
66	United Artists UP 1142	Livin' Above Your Head/She's The Girl (That's Messing Up My Mind)	40
66	United Artists UP 1162	(He's) Raining In My Sunshine/Reason For Living	7
67	United Artists UP 1178	You Ain't As Hip As All That Baby/Nature Boy	10
67	United Artists UP 1191	(We'll Meet In The) Yellow Forest/Got Hung Up Along The Way	60
68	United Artists UP 2211	French Provincial/Shanghai Noodle Factory	18
69	United Artists UP 2268	This Magic Moment/Since I Don't Have You	10
69	United Artists UP 35008	When You Dance/So Much In Love	10
69	United Artists UP 35026	Hushabye/No I Don't Know Her	6
70	United Artists UP 35074	Walkin' In The Rain/For The Love Of A Lady	12
65	United Artists UEP 1003	COME A LITTLE BIT CLOSER (EP)	50
66	United Artists UEP 1017	LIVING WITH JAY AND THE AMERICANS (EP)	50
66	United Artists (S)ULP 1117	JAY AND THE AMERICANS (LP)	45
66	United Artists (S)ULP 1128	SUNDAY AND ME (LP)	40
67	United Artists (S)ULP 1150	LIVIN' ABOVE YOUR HEAD (LP)	55
67	United Artists (S)ULP 1164	TRY SOME OF THIS (LP)	40

JAYBIRDS

66	Sue WI 4013	Somebody Help Me/The Right Kind	150

JAYBIRDS (U.K.)
(see also Ray Pilgrim & Beatmen)

64	Embassy WB 663	All Day And All Of The Night/Google Eye	7

JAY BOYS
(see also Roy Panton, Bob & Marcia, Cables)

69	Trojan TR 665	Splendour Splash/TREVOR SHIELD: Please	40
70	Harry J. HJ 6602	The Dog (Parts 1 & 2)	8
70	Harry J. HJ 6607	Jack The Ripper/Don't Let Me Down	8
70	Harry J. HJ 6609	Jay Moon Walk/Elcong	8
70	Harry J. HJ 6610	Je T'Aime/It Ain't Me Babe	8
70	Harry J. HJ 6617	Del Gago/Killer Version	40
70	Harry J. HJ 6618	Can't Get Next To You/(Part 2) (both actually by Charmers)	5
71	Harry J. HJ 6628	The Arcade Walk/The Arcade Walk Vers. II	6
72	Harry J. HJ 6644	African People/HARRY J. ALL STARS: African (Version)	8
72	Ashanti AHS 407	Rough Road/TREVOR SHIELD: Rough Road	12

MINT VALUE £

JERRY JAYE
67 London HLU 10128 — My Girl Josephine/Five Miles From Home — 40

JAYE SISTERS
59 London HLT 9011 — Sure Fire Love/G-3 — 60
59 London HLT 9011 — Sure Fire Love/G-3 (78) — 30

JAYHAWKS
56 Parlophone R 4228 — Stranded In The Jungle/My Only Darling — 700
56 Parlophone R 4228 — Stranded In The Jungle/My Only Darling (78) — 140

JAYHAWKS
92 Def American512.986-1 — HOLLYWOOD TOWN HALL (LP, with inner) — 100

JAYLADS
(see also Melodians)
71 Punch PH 95 — Royal Chord (actually by Melodians)/Version (actually "In The Spirit" by Lloyd Charmers) — 12

JAYNETTS
63 Stateside SS 227 — Sally Go Round The Roses/Sally Go Round The Roses (Instrumental) — 20

JAYS
63 Parlophone R 4764 — Shock A Boom/Across The Sea — 10

JAYWALKERS
76 Cream CRM 5003 — Can't Live Without You/Heartbroken Memories — 10

JAZZ BUTCHER
83 Glass GLASS 027 — Southern Mark Smith/Jazz Butcher Meets Count Dracula (p/s) — 20
85 Glass GLASS 12041 — Real Men/The Jazz Butcher V The Prime Minister/ Southern Mark Smith (Original) (12", p/s) — 20
86 Glass HMMM 001 — Christmas With The Pygmies (p/s, promo freebie, given away at gigs) — 10

JAZZ COMPOSERS ORCHESTRA
(see also Carla Bley, Mike Mantler, Don Cherry, Larry Coryell)
74 JCOA/Virgin JDA 311 — JAZZ COMPOSERS ORCHESTRA (2-LP, gatefold sleeve) — 15

JAZZ COURIERS
(see also Tubby Hayes, Ronnie Scott)
50s (no cat. no.) — Top Spot Blues/Monk Was Here/Last Minute Blues (square flexi) — 100
57 Tempo EXA 75 — JAZZ COURIERS (EP) — 60
59 Tempo EXA 87 — JAZZ COURIERS (EP) — 60
58 Tempo TAP 22 — IN CONCERT (LP) — 400
59 Tempo TAP 26 — THE LAST WORD (LP) — 350
60 London Jazz LTZ-L 15188 — THE COURIERS OF JAZZ! (LP) — 200
67 M. For Pleasure MFP 1072 — IN CONCERT (LP) — 15
80s Jasmine JASM 2004 — THE JAZZ COURIERS (LP, reissue) — 20
80s Jasmine JASM 2024 — THE LAST WORD (LP, reissue) — 15

JAZZ CRUSADERS
(see also Crusaders)
66 Fontana 688 149 ZL — THE THING (LP) — 20
66 Fontana 688 117 ZL — LOOKIN' AHEAD (LP) — 18

JAZZ DEFEKTORS
87 Factory FACT 205 — THE JAZZ DEFEKTORS (LP) — 15

JAZZ FIVE
(see also Vic Ash Quartet, Harry Klein Quartet)
61 Tempo TAP 32 — THE FIVE OF US (LP) — 300

JAZZ HIP TRIO
67 Major Minor MMLP 8 — JAZZ IN RELIEF (LP) — 80

JAZZ MAKERS
66 Ember FA 2023 — SWINGIN' SOUNDS (LP) — 20

JAZZ MODES
60 London Jazz LTZ-K 15191 — THE MOST HAPPY FELLA (LP) — 20

JAZZ ROCK EXPERIENCE
70 Deram Nova SDN 19 — JAZZ ROCK EXPERIENCE (LP) — 70

JAZZATEERS
83 Rough Trade RT 138 — Sixteen Reasons/Show Me The Door (p/s) — 5
84 Rough Trade ROUGH 46 — JAZZATEERS (LP, with insert) — 12

J & B
(see also State Of Micky & Tommy, Foreigner)
66 Polydor 56095 — Wow Wow Wow/There She Goes — 50

J BLAST & 100% PROOF
92 Geek Street GEEK666 — 2 The Break Of Dawn (12") — 30

J.B.'s
(see also Fred Wesley & JB's, James Brown, Bobby Byrd)
71 Mojo 2001 155 — These Are The J.B.'s (Parts 1 & 2) — 8
71 Mojo 2027 002 — The Grunt (Parts 1 & 2) — 8
72 Mojo 2093 007 — Gimme Some More/The Rabbit Got The Gun — 8
72 Mojo 2093 016 — Hot Pants Road/Pass The Peas — 8
72 Mojo 2093 021 — Givin' Up Food For Funk (Parts 1 & 2) — 8
72 Mojo 2918 004 — PASS THE PEAS (LP) — 30
72 Polydor 2391 034 — FOOD FOR THOUGHT (LP) — 30
74 Polydor 2391 087 — DOING IT TO DEATH (LP) — 30
75 Polydor 2391 194 — HUSTLE WITH SPEED (LP) — 30
76 Polydor 2391 204 — GIVIN' UP FOOD FOR FUNK - THE BEST OF THE JB's (LP) — 30

MINT VALUE £

J.B.'s ALLSTARS

85	2 Tone CHSTT29	The Alphabet Army/Al arm (p/s)	30
85	2 Tone CHSTT1229	The Alphabet Army (extended mix)/The Alphabet Army (string mix)/ The Alphabet Army/Al Arm (12" p/s)	35

JC001/DJ D ZIRE

88	Furious Fish FFDJD 001	No MC No Comment (12")	12
88	Furious Fish FFJC001	I Dis Therefore I Am (12")	20
89	Furios Fish FFD002	Bad Place To Get Hit (12")	10
91	White JCDZ001	Favourite Breaks (12")	50
92	Anxious ANX1002	Sea Of MCs (12")	8

J.D. (THE ROC)

(see also Jeff Dixon)

72	Sioux SI 008	Superbad/MONTEGO MELON: Lucky Dip	8

BOBBI JEAN

65	Mercury MF 921	Dry Your Tears/Pity The Man	10

JEAN & GAYTONES

71	Trojan TR 7817	I Shall Sing (actually by Judy Mowatt & Gaytones)/GAYTONES: Target	12

LANA JEAN

63	Pye International 7N 25214	It Hurts To Be Sixteen/Bad Boy	25

CATHY JEAN & ROOMATES

61	Parlophone R 4764	Please Love Me Forever/Canadian Sunset	60

JEAN & STATESIDES

64	Columbia DB 7287	Putty In Your Hands/One Fine Day	40
64	Columbia DB 7439	You Won't Forget Me/Cold, Cold Winter	30
65	Columbia DB 7651	Mama Didn't Lie/Just Let Me Cry	30

JEAN-ETTES

59	Pye 7N 15185	May You Always/I Saw A Light	10
59	Pye 7N 15185	May You Always/I Saw A Light (78)	10

JEANNE & JANIE

(see also Jeanne Black)

60	Capitol CL 15146	Journey Of Love/JEANNE BLACK: Lisa	6
60	Capitol CL 15165	Sleep Walkin'/JEANNE BLACK: You'll Find Out	6

JEANNIE (& BIG GUYS)

(see also Cindy Cole)

63	Piccadilly 7N 35147	Don't Lie To Me/Boys (as Jeannie & Big Guys)	15
64	Piccadilly 7N 35164	I Want You/Sticks And Stones (as Jeannie & Big Guys)	15
65	Parlophone R 5343	I Love Him/With Any Other Girl	10

JEANNIE & REDHEADS

(see also Andrew Oldham Orchestra)

64	Decca F 11829	Animal Duds/ANDREW OLDHAM GROUP: Funky And Fleopatra	30

AUDREY JEANS

56	Decca F 10768	Ticky Ticky Tick (I'm Gonna Tell On You)/Will You, Willyum	15
56	Decca F 10788	It's Better In The Dark/The Bus Stop Song (A Paper Of Pins)	10
58	Decca F 11035	Send A Letter To Jeanette - Yet!/Bad Pianna Rag	7
61	HMV POP 876	How Lovely To Be A Woman/What Did I See In Him	6

JEDDAH

83	Death RIP 2001	Eleanor Rigby/Ghosts (with poster, no p/s)	25

JEDI KNIGHTS

(see also Global Communications)

95	Clear CLR 406	MAY THE FUNK BE WITH YOU (12" EP, p/s)	10
95	Clear CLR 406X	MAY THE FUNK BE WITH YOU (12" EP, clear vinyl, embossed sleeve)	15

JEEPS

66	Strike JH 308	He Saw Eesaw/The Music Goes Round	15
66	Strike JH 315	Ain't It A Great Big Laugh/I Put On My Shoes	15

JEFFERSON

(see also Rockin' Berries, Sight & Sound)

68	Pye 7N 17634	Montage/Did You Hear A Heartbreak Last Night	15
69	Pye 7N 17706	The Colour Of My Love/Look No Further	8
69	Pye 7N 17810	Baby Take Me In Your Arms/I Fell Flat On My Face	8
69	Pye 7N 17855	Love And All The World/I've Got To Tell Her	8
71	Pye 7N 45022	Spider/Can't Get You Out Of My Mind	30
75	Alaska ALA 1016	Workin' My Way Back To You/Baby You've Got Everything I Need	10
69	Pye NSPL 18316	THE COLOUR OF MY LOVE (LP)	15
70	Deram DM 314	Mucky Duck/Pycho's On The Run	15
73	Philips 6308 166	I LOVE YOU THIS MUCH (LP, blue/silver labels)	20

BLIND LEMON JEFFERSON

(see also Paramount Allstars)

50	Tempo R 38	Weary Dog Blues/Change My Luck Blues (78)	25
50	Tempo R 39	Lock Step Blues/Hangman's Blues (78)	25
51	Tempo R 46	Shuckin' Sugar Blues/Rabbit Foot Blues (78)	25
52	Tempo R 54	Gone Dead On You Blues/One Dime Blues (78)	25
53	Jazz Collector L 91	Shuckin' Sugar Blues/Rabbit Foot Blues (78)	20
53	Jazz Collector L 103	Jack O'Diamonds Blues/Clock House Blues (78)	20
54	Jazz Collector L 126	Gone Dead On You Blues/One Dime Blues (78)	20
50s	Poydras 99	BLIND LEMON JEFFERSON (10" LP)	50
53	London Jazz AL 3508	FOLK BLUES OF BLIND LEMON JEFFERSON (10" LP)	50
55	London Jazz AL 3546	PENITENTIARY BLUES (10" LP)	50
57	London Jazz AL 3564	SINGS THE BLUES (10" LP)	50

			MINT VALUE £
69	CBS 63738	THE IMMORTAL (LP)	20
70s	Roots Matchbox RL 301	BLIND LEMON JEFFERSON VOLUME 1 (LP)	20
70s	Roots Matchbox RL 306	BLIND LEMON JEFFERSON VOLUME 2 (LP)	18
70s	Roots Matchbox RL 331	BLIND LEMON JEFFERSON VOLUME 3 (LP)	18

BLIND LEMON JEFFERSON/ED BELL

60	Jazz Collector JEL 13	THE MALE BLUES VOLUME 7 (EP)	10

BLIND LEMON JEFFERSON/BUDDY BOY HAWKINS

59	Jazz Collector JEL 8	THE MALE BLUES VOLUME 5 (EP)	10

BLIND LEMON JEFFERSON/LEADBELLY

61	Jazz Collector JEL 24	THE MALE BLUES VOLUME 8 (EP)	10

BLIND LEMON JEFFERSON & RAMBLING THOMAS

50s	Heritage HLP 1007	BLIND LEMON JEFFERSON AND RAMBLING THOMAS (LP, 99 only)	100

EDDIE JEFFERSON

67	Stateside SS 591	Some Other Time/When You Look In The Mirror	20

GEORGE PAUL JEFFERSON

68	Fontana TF 923	Looking For My Mind/Out Of Place	12

MARSHALL JEFFERSON

88	ffrr FFRX 18	Open Your Eyes (Celestial Mix)/(Spiritual Mix)/ (Marshall's Elevated Dub) (12", p/s)	15

JEFFERSON AIRPLANE

(see also Jefferson Starship, Great Society, Paul Kantner, Grace Slick, Papa John Creach, Hot Tuna)

67	RCA Victor RCA 1594	Somebody To Love/She Has Funny Cars	15
67	RCA Victor RCA 1631	White Rabbit/Plastic Fantastic Lover	15
67	RCA Victor RCA 1647	Ballad Of You And Me and Pooneil/Two Heads	10
68	RCA Victor RCA 1711	Greasy Heart/Share A Little Joke (With The World)	12
68	RCA Victor RCA 1736	If You Feel Like China Breaking/Triad	10
70	RCA RCA 1933	Volunteers/We Can Be Together	6
70	RCA RCA 1964	Somebody To Love/White Rabbit	8
70	RCA RCA 1989	Mexico/Have You Seen The Saucers?	6
72	Grunt 65-0500	Pretty As You Feel/Wild Turkey	7
72	Grunt 65-0506	Long John Silver/Milk Train	5
67	RCA Victor RD 7889	SURREALISTIC PILLOW (LP, black label, mono)	60
67	RCA Victor SF 7889	SURREALISTIC PILLOW (LP, black label, stereo)	40
68	RCA Victor RD 7926	AFTER BATHING AT BAXTERS (LP, black label, mono)	60
68	RCA Victor SF 7926	AFTER BATHING AT BAXTERS (LP, black label, stereo)	40
68	RCA Victor RD 7976	CROWN OF CREATION (LP, black label, mono)	60
68	RCA Victor SF 7976	CROWN OF CREATION (LP, black label, stereo)	30
69	RCA RD/SF 8019	BLESS ITS POINTED LITTLE HEAD (LP)	18
69	RCA Victor SF 7889	SURREALISTIC PILLOW (LP, repressing, orange label)	25
69	RCA Victor SF 7926	AFTER BATHING AT BAXTERS (LP, repressing, orange label)	20
69	RCA Victor SF 7976	CROWN OF CREATION (LP, repressing, orange label)	20
70	RCA SF 8076	VOLUNTEERS (LP, gatefold sleeve)	12
71	RCA SF 8164	THE WORST OF JEFFERSON AIRPLANE (LP, textured sleeve)	12
71	Grunt FTR 1001	BARK (LP, bag cover with lyric sheet & brown inner sleeve)	15
71	RCA SF 8195	JEFFERSON AIRPLANE TAKES OFF (LP)	18
72	Grunt FTR 1007	LONG JOHN SILVER (LP, open-out box cover with inner lyric sleeve)	15
73	Grunt FTR 0147	30 SECONDS OVER WINTERLAND (LP, with inner sleeve)	12

JEGA

96	Skam SKA 6	Phlax/Nortom Midgate/Bluette/Ionic/Evil Lee Kirtcele/ Steel Drum/In With The In (12", custom sleeve)	45
97	Skam SKA 9	Card Hore/Oak Hanger/Nausicaa/Stainless Steel Drum/Star/ Houdini (12", p/s)	10
98	Planet Mu ZIQ 001	TYPE XERO EP (12")	20
99	Planet Mu ZIQ 009	Unity Gain/KID SPATULA: Hard Love (12", clear vinyl, p/s)	8
00	Planet Mu ZIQ 012	GEOMETRY (2-LP)	20

JEHST

99	Y n R Productions YNR 001	PREMONITIONS EP: (12", stickered (white die-cut sleeve, first pressing blue text on label)	40
99	Y n R YNR 1	PREMONITIONS (EP, second pressing black text on label)	15
01	Lowlife LOW 12	THE HIGH PLAINS DRIFTER (EP, p/s)	15
01	Lowlife LOW 12 PRO	The Trilogy Remix (1-sided 12", 2 mixes 500 pressed)	40
02	Y n R YNR008	Alcoholic Author/Night Breed (12", p/s)	20
02	Lowlife LOW 18	The Return Of The Drifter/People Under The Weather (12", p/s, 3 mixes each)	8
04	White B8080 1	Stand Up/Wake Up (12")	10
03	Lowlife LOW30	FALLING DOWN (LP)	12

JELLY

72	Mother MOT9	I'll Meet YOu Half Way/Chicago Calling	40

JELLYBEAN

(see also Madonna)

84	EMI America 12EAX 210	Sidewalk Talk (featuring Madonna)/Was Dog A Doughnut/Sidewalk Talk (featuring Madonna)/Was Dog A Doughnut (12" remix, p/s)	10

JELLY BEANS

64	Pye International 7N 25252	I Wanna Love Him So Bad/So Long	30
64	Red Bird RB 10011	The Kind Of Boy You Can't Forget/Baby Be Mine	30
75	Right On R 102	You Don't Mean Me No Good/I'm Hip To You	25

JELLYBREAD

69	Blue Horizon 57-3162	Chairman Mao's Boogaloo/No One Else	12
70	Blue Horizon 57-3169	Comment/Funky Wasp	12
70	Blue Horizon 57-3174	Rockin' Pneumonia And The Boogie-Woogie Flu/Readin' The Meters	12

MINT VALUE £

70	Blue Horizon 57-3180	Old Man Hank/Faded Grace	15
71	Blue Horizon 2096 001	Creepin' And Crawlin'/The Loser/The Clergyman's Daughter	12
72	Blue Horizon 2096 006	Down Along The Cove/Sister Lucy	15
72	Liphook 1	JELLYBREAD (mini-LP)	300
69	Blue Horizon 7-63853	FIRST SLICE (LP)	70
71	Blue Horizon 2431 002	SIXTY-FIVE PARKWAY (LP, with lyric insert)	100
71	Blue Horizon 2431 002	SIXTY-FIVE PARKWAY (LP, without lyric insert)	60
72	Blue Horizon 2931 004	BACK TO THE BEGINNING AGAIN (LP, gatefold sleeve)	150

JELLYS

(see also Honeycrack, Wildhearts)

98	Mission Impossible MIRVL1	WELCOME TO OUR WORLD (LP, with inner sleeve, mail-order only)	12

DIANNE JENKINS

76	Crystal CR 7025	Tow-A-Way-Zone/Anniversary	20

JOHNNY JENKINS

69	Atco 226 009	The Voodoo In You/Backside Blues	10
71	Atco 2400 033	TON-TON MACOUTE (LP)	25

JENNIFER (WARNES)

69	London HLU 10278	Let The Sun Shine In/Easy To Be Hard	7
70	London HLU 10312	Cajun Train/Old Folks (Les Vieux)	8

JENNIFERS

(see also Supergrass)

92	Nude NUD 2T	Just Got Back Today/Rocks And Boulders/Danny's Song/ Tomorrow's Rain (12")	30
92	Nude NUD 2CD	Just Got Back Today/Rocks And Boulders/Danny's Song/ Tomorrow's Rain (CD)	40

BILL JENNINGS

55	Parlophone MSP 6146	Stuffy/Solitude (as Bill Jennings-Leo Parker Quintet)	6
55	Parlophone MSP 6156	Soft Winds/What's New? (as Bill Jennings Quartet)	6

WAYLON JENNINGS

69	RCA RCA 1866	The Days Of Sand And Shovels/Delia's Gone	5
80	RCA PB 9561	The Dukes Of Hazzard Theme/Storms Never Last (p/s)	5

JENNORS

(see also Tennors)

67	Coxsone CS 7024	Pressure And Slide (actually by Tennors)/SOUL BROTHERS: One Stop	25

KRIS JENSEN

62	Fontana 267 241 TF	Torture/Let's Sit Down	20
63	Fontana 267 267 TF	Don't Take Her From Me/Claudette	15
64	Hickory 45-1224	Donna Donna/Big As I Can Dream	20
64	Hickory 45-1243	Lookin' For Love/In Time	12
64	Hickory 45-1256	Come Back To Me/You've Only Got Me To Lose	10
65	Hickory 45-1285	The Little Wind-Up Doll/Somebody's Smiling While I'm Crying	10
65	Hickory 45-1311	What Should I Do/That's A Whole Lotta Love	10

KRIS JENSEN/SUE THOMPSON

(see also Sue Thompson)

65	Hickory LPE 1507	INTRODUCING KRIS JENSEN AND SUE THOMPSON (EP, 2 tracks each)	12

PAUL JENSEN & CAR THIEVES

78	Albatross TIT 3	Holiday In Spain/Always Arrive On Time (p/s)	6

JENSENS

(see also Tempus Fugit)

68	Philips BF 1686	Deep Thinking/Marguerite	12

BILL JENTIES

(see also Bill Gentles/Bill Jentles)

70	Smash SMA 2307	Stop Them (actually by Bill Gentles)/MAXINE: I Don't Care	6

BILL JENTLES

(see also Bill Jenties)

70	Pama PM 809	True True Train/JEFF BARNES: Give And Take	15

JERICHO (JONES)

71	A&M AMS 833	Time Is Now/Freedom	5
72	A&M AMS 883	Don't Let Me Down/Mona Mona	10
72	A&M AMS 7017	Hey Man/Champs	10
72	A&M AMS 7037	Mama's Gonna Take You Home/So Come On	10
71	A&M AMLH 68050	JUNKIES, MONKEYS & DONKEYS (LP, as Jericho Jones, gatefold, brown label)	150
72	A&M AMLS 68079	JERICHO (LP, beware of counterfeits with slightly thicker sleeves)	170

JERKS

78	Underground URA 1	Get Your Woofing Dog Off Me/Hold My Hand (p/s)	35
78	Lightning GIL 549	Cool/Jerkin' (p/s)	20
80	Laser LAS 25	Come Back Bogart (I Wish You Would)/Are You Strong Enough?/ The Strangest Man Of All (p/s)	15

JERMZ

78	One Way EFP 1	Power Cut/Me And My Baby (with p/s)	200
78	One Way EFP 1	Power Cut/Me And My Baby (without p/s)	80

JERRY JEROME

55	MGM SP 1118	Honey/In A Little Spanish Town	5

JERONIMO

70	Major Minor MM695	Hey Ya/Na Na Hey Hey Kiss Him Goodbye	8

JERRY & THE BLUEBELLS

75	Torpedo TOR 44	Girls/Girls Version	15

MINT VALUE £

JERRY & FREEDOM SINGERS
(see also Winston Francis)
70 Banana BA 308 — It's All In The Game (pseudonym for Winston Francis)/ IM: The Way To My Heart (pseudonym for Cedric Brooks) . . . 60

JERRY O
67 London HLZ 10162 — Karate Boo-ga-loo/The Pearl . . . 12
71 Jay Boy BOY 33 — Karate Boo-ga-loo/The Pearl (reissue) . . . 6
72 Jay Boy BOY 62 — Dance What 'Cha Wanna/Afro-Twist Time . . . 8

JERUSALEM
(see also Pussy, Ian Gillan)
72 Deram DM 358 — Kamakazi Moth/Frustration . . . 40
72 Deram SDL 6 — JERUSALEM (LP, gatefold sleeve, white/brown label with large 'Deram' logo). . 250
72 Deram SDL 6 — JERUSALEM (LP, gatefold sleeve, later red/white label) . . . 100

JERUSALEM
79 Praise PLP 4 — JERUSALEM (LP, with insert) . . . 12
80 Myrrh MYR 1097 — VOLUME 2 (LP, with insert) . . . 12
82 Myrrh MYR 1113 — WARRIOR (LP). . . 12

JESS & JAMES
68 MGM MGM 1389 — Move/What Was I Born For . . . 25
68 MGM MGM 1420 — Something For Nothing/I Let The Day Go By (with J.J. Band) . . . 20
68 MGM MGM 1454 — Thank You Show Biz/Motherless Child. . . 10

STEVE JESSE
60s President PT 502 — Shifting Sands/Post Hall Life. . . 6

JESSUP
72 Beacon BEA 108 — Little Friend/On The Run . . . 15

JESTERS
62 R&L RL 15/16 — Little Girl/Casa Pedro (early labels blue and white) . . . 30

JESTERS
73 Jam JAM 35 — Fool For A Day/Can't Live Without You . . . 15

JESUS & MARY CHAIN
(see also Acid Angels, Primal Scream, Meat Whiplash)
84 Creation CRE 012 — Upside Down/Vegetable Man (black & white wraparound p/s in poly bag with address on rear & name in red) 20
84 Creation CRE 012 — Upside Down/Vegetable Man (red & white wraparound p/s in poly bag with address on rear & name in black). . . 20
84 Creation CRE 012 — Upside Down/Vegetable Man (pink, blue or yellow wraparound p/s in poly bag; with small T-shirt offer insert) . . . 12
84 Creation CRE 012 — Upside Down/Vegetable Man (pink, blue or yellow wraparound p/s in poly bag; without small T-shirt offer insert) . . . 8
86 Creation CRE 012 — Upside Down/Vegetable Man (reissue, different printed p/s). . . 5
86 Creation CRE 012T — Upside Down/Vegetable Man/Upside Down (demo) (12" white label, no sleeve). . 60
85 Blanco Y Negro NEG 008 — Never Understand/Suck (p/s). . . 5
85 Blanco Y Negro NEG 17F — Just Like Honey/Head//Inside Me/Just Like Honey (Demo Oct 84) (double pack, gatefold p/s) . . . 8
87 Blanco Y Negro NEGB 25 — Happy When It Rains/Everything Is Alright When You're Down (box set with postcards) . . . 7
89 Blanco Y Negro NEG 41TE — Blues From A Gun/Shimmer/Penetration/Break Me Down (10", gatefold p/s) . . . 8
89 Blanco Y Negro NEG 42/XB/Y/Z — Head On/Terminal Beach//Head On/Deviant Slice//Head On/ I'm Glad I Never/Head On/In The Black (4 x 7" box set; each sold separately) . . . 12
85 Fierce FRIGHT 004 — RIOT (EP, with 'LSD bar' & badge; 2 different sleeves) . . . 25
92 Blanco Y Negro NEG 57T — Almost Gold/Teenage Lust (Acoustic Version)/Reverberation (Doubt)/Don't Come Down (12") . . . 8
85 Blanco Y Negro BYN 7 — PSYCHOCANDY (LP, with inner) . . . 20
87 Blanco Y Negro BY 11 — DARKLANDS (LP, with inner) . . . 12
89 Blanco Y Negro BYN 20W — AUTOMATIC (LP, gatefold sleeve). . . 12

JESUS IS
70s Myrrh MYR 1049 — JESUS IS (LP) . . . 12

JESUS LIZARD
(see also Nirvana)
92 own label — Gladiator (Marquee gig freebie). . . 10
93 Touch & Go TG 83 — Puss/NIRVANA: Oh, The Guilt (p/s, blue vinyl, with poster) . . . 25
93 Touch & Go TG 83 — Puss/NIRVANA: Oh, The Guilt (p/s, blue vinyl, without poster). . . 12
93 Touch & Go TG 83 — Puss/NIRVANA: Oh, The Guilt (p/s, black vinyl) . . . 18
93 Touch & Go TG 83CD — Puss/NIRVANA: Oh, The Guilt (CD, card wallet) . . . 15
93 Touch & Go TG 128 — Fly On The Wall/White Hole (green vinyl). . . 5

JESUS LOVES YOU
(see also Boy George, Culture Club)
89 More Protein PROCD 2 — After The Love (10 Glorious Years Edit)/After The Love (10 Glorious Years Mix)/ After The Love (Orbital House Mix) (3" CD, card sleeve). . . 8

JET
(see also Andy Ellison,John's Children, Nice, Radio Stars, Sparks)
75 CBS S CBS 3317 — Nothing To Do With Us/Brian Damage . . . 8
75 CBS S CBS 3143 — My River/Quandary. . . 10
75 CBS 80699 — JET (LP, with lyric insert). . . 20

JET (Australia)
03 Warner Bros 7559 628861 — DIRTY SWEET EP: Take It Or Leave It/Cold Hard Bitch/ Move On/Rollover DJ (12", p/s). . . 10
03 Elektra 7559-62956-1 — GET BORN (2xLP, white vinyl, stickered, gatefold with inners) . . . 18

MINT VALUE £

JETHRO TULL

(see also Mick Abrahams, Blodwyn Pig, Wild Turkey, The John Evans Band)

SINGLES

68	MGM MGM 1384	Sunshine Day/Aeroplane (miscredited to 'Jethro Toe'; counterfeits credit 'Jethro Tull')	500
68	Island WIP 6043	A Song For Jeffrey/One For John Gee	40
68	Island WIP 6048	Love Story/A Christmas Song (2 different pink label designs)	10
68	Island WIP 6048	Love Story/A Christmas Song (mispressing, B-side or both sides credited to Ian Henderson)	18
69	Island WIP 6056	Living In The Past/Driving Song (2 different pink labels)	15
69	Chrysalis WIP 6070	Sweet Dream/17 (push-out or large centre hole)	7
70	Chrysalis WIP 6077	The Witch's Promise/Teacher (in p/s)	20
70	Chrysalis WIP 6077	The Witch's Promise/Teacher	15
70	Chrysalis WIP 6081	Inside/Alive And Well And Living In	10
71	Chrysalis WIP 6098	Lick Your Fingers Clean/Up To Me (unissued)	0
71	Chrysalis WIP 6106	Life Is A Long Song/Up The 'Pool/Dr. Bogenbroom/From Later/Nursie (EP, p/s)	8
74	Chrysalis CHS 2054	Bungle In The Jungle/Back Door Angels	6
75	Chrysalis CHS 2075	Minstrel In The Gallery/Summerday Sands	5
76	Chrysalis CHS 2086	Too Old To Rock'n'Roll: Too Young To Die/Rainbow Blues	5
76	Chrysalis CXP 2275	Ring Out Solstice Bells/March The Mad Scientist/A Christmas Song/ Pan Dance (EP)	8
77	Chrysalis CHS 2135	The Whistler/Strip Cartoon (some in p/s)	25
77	Chrysalis CHS 2135	The Whistler/Strip Cartoon (some in p/s)	8
78	Chrysalis CHS 2214	Moths/Life Is A Long Song (p/s)	10
78	Chrysalis CHS 2260	A Stitch In Time (3.30 Version)/Sweet Dream (p/s, white vinyl)	12
78	Chrysalis CHS 2260	A Stitch In Time (3.30 Version)/Sweet Dream (p/s, black vinyl)	8
78	Chrysalis CHS 2260	A Stitch In Time (4.20 Version)/Sweet Dream (p/s, white vinyl)	12
78	Chrysalis CHS 2260	A Stitch In Time (4.20 Version)/Sweet Dream (p/s, black vinyl)	8
79	Chrysalis CHS 2378	North Sea Oil/Elegy (p/s)	10
79	Chrysalis CHS 2394	Home/King Henry's Madrigal (Theme From Mainstream)/Warm Sporran (p/s)	12
79	Chrysalis CHS 2443	Ring Out Solstice Bells/March The Mad Scientist/A Christmas Song/ Pan Dance (EP, reissue)	7
79	Chrysalis CHS 2468	Working John, Working Joe/Flyingdale Flyer (p/s)	8
80	Chrysalis CHS 2619	Broadsword/Fallen On Hard Times (p/s)	6
80	Chrysalis CHSP 2619	Broadsword/Fallen On Hard Times (picture disc)	12
84	Chrysalis TULLD 1	Lap Of Luxury/Astronomy//Automotive Engineering/Tundra (double pack, gatefold p/s)	10
84	Chrysalis TULL X 1	Lap Of Luxury/Astronomy/Automotive Engineering/Tundra (12", p/s)	10
86	Chrysalis TULL 2	Coronach (with David Palmer)/Jack Frost And The Hooded Crow (p/s)	7
86	Chrysalis TULLX 2	Coronach (with David Palmer)/Jack Frost And The Hooded Crow/ Living In The Past/Elegy (12", p/s)	40
87	Chrysalis TULLP 3	Steel Monkey/Down At The End Of Your Road (die-cut picture disc)	20
87	Chrysalis ZTULL 3	Steel Monkey/Down At The End Of Your Road/Too Many Too/I'm Your Gun (cassette, numbered edition of 3,000 with competition pack & badge)	15
87	Chrysalis TULLX 3	Steel Monkey/Down At The End of Your Road/Too Many Too/ I'm Your Gun (12", p/s)	10
88	Chrysalis TULLX 4	Said She Was A Dancer/Dogs In The Midwinter/The Waking Edge (p/s)	8
88	Chrysalis TULLP 4	Said She Was A Dancer/Dogs In The Midwinter (shaped picture disc)	10
88	Chrysalis TULLX 4	Said She Was A Dancer/Dogs In The Midwinter (12", p/s)	8
88	Chrysalis TULLCD 4	Said She Was A Dancer/Dogs In The Midwinter/ Down At The End Of The Road/ Too Many Too (CD, picture disc, limited issue)	25
88	Chrysalis TULPCD 1	Part Of The Machine (Edit)/Stormy Monday Blues (live)/Lick Your Fingers Clean/ Minstrel In The Gallery (live)/Farm On The Freeway (live) (CD, picture disc)	15
89	Chrysalis TULL 5	Another Christmas Song (p/s)	10
89	Chrysalis TULLCD 5	Another Christmas Song/Intro - A Christmas Song (live)/Cheap Day Return - Mother Goose (live)/Outro - Locomotive Breath (live) (CD)	10
89	Chrysalis TULLX5	Another Christmas Song/Intro-A Christmas Song/Cheap Day Return-Mother Goose/Outro-Locomotive Breath (12" p/s)	20
91	Chrysalis TULLX 6	This Is Not Love/Night In The Wilderness/Jump Start (12", p/s)	8
92	Chrysalis TULLCD 7	Rocks On The Road/Jack-A-Lynn (Home Demo)/Tall Thin Girl (live)/ Fat Man (live)/Rocks On The Road/Bouree (live)/Mother Goose-Jack-A-Lynn (live)/ Aqualung-Locomotive Breath (live) (2-CD boxed)	8
92	Chrysalis TULLX 7	Rocks On The Road/Jack-A-Lynn (home demo)/ Aqualung-Locomotive Breath (live) (12", picture disc)	10
93	Chrysalis 12CHS 3970	Living In The Past (Club Mix)/Living In The Past (7" Mix) Living In The Past (Dub Ravey Master)/Living In The Past (Dub N.Y. Mix) (12", p/s)	10
93	Chrysalis 23970/1	Living In The (Slightly More Recent) Past (live)/Silver River Turning/ Rosa On The Factory Floor/I Don't Want To Be Me/Living In The Past/ Truck Stop Runner/Piece Of Cake/Man Of Principle (2-CD set)	8
99	Papillon BTFLYS 0001	Bends Like A Willow (edit)/Dot Com (edit)/It All Trickles Down (CD)	15

PROMOS

76	Chrysalis CHS 3 PDJ	Ring Out/Solstice Bells/March, The Mad Scientist/Christmas Song/ Pan Dance (12", p/s)	25
79	Chrysalis CHS018-PDJ	Dark Ages (Special edited version) 12" promo	15
84	Chrysalis AS 1967	Under Wraps#1 (electric)/Under Wraps#2 (acoustic) (12" promo)	12
87	Chrysalis VAS 1039	Budapest (Special Radio Edit) (12" promo with illustrated sticker)	12
87	Chrysalis VAS 2796	Steel Monkey (12" promo)	12
87	Chrysalis VAS 2866	Farm On The Freeway (Special Rock Radio Edit) (12" promo)	15
88	Chrysalis VAS 1170	Part Of The Machine/Part Of The Machine (Edit) (12" promo with tour dates sticker)	18
89	Chrysalis DPRO 23418	Kissing Willy (CD, 1-track promo)	8
89	Chrysalis DPRO 04657	A Christmas Song (CD, 1-track promo)	8
95	Chrysalis CD Ian DJ1	Rare And Precious Chain/This Free Will (CD)	8
99	Roadrunner RR Promo 456	Dot.Com (CD, 1-track promo)	8
99	Fuel 2000 FLDPRO 1119	Bends Like A Willow (Radio Edit) (CD, 1-track promo)	10
03	RandM RR Promo 743	'Live In Europe 2003' With You There To Help Me (live)/ Someday The Sun Won't Shine For You (live) (CD)	12

MINT VALUE £

LPs

68	Island ILP 985	THIS WAS (1st pressing, pink label/black & orange 'circle' logo, mono)	300
68	Island ILPS 9085	THIS WAS (1st pressing, pink label/black & orange 'circle' logo, stereo, flipback sleeve, some sleeves as mono issues with stereo stickers)	120
69	Island ILPS 9103	STAND UP (1st pressing, gatefold sleeve pop-up inside, pink label/black & orange 'circle' logo)	80
70	Chrysalis ILPS 9123	BENEFIT (green Chrysalis or Island pink rim label)	80
70	Chrysalis ILPS 9123	BENEFIT (Island pink rim label 'palm tree' logo)	45
71	Island ILPS 9145	AQUALUNG (with gatefold sleeve & inner bag)	30
72	Chrysalis CHR 1003	THICK AS A BRICK (fold-out newspaper sleeve)	30
72	Chrysalis CJT 1	LIVING IN THE PAST (2-LP, with hard sleeve & booklet)	25
73	Chrysalis CHR 1040	A PASSION PLAY (with theatre booklet)	18
74	Chrysalis CHR 1067	WARCHILD (with lyric inner sleeve)	12
76	Chrysalis CHR 1111	TOO OLD TO ROCK 'N' ROLL	12
77	Chrysalis CJT 4	LIVE - BURSTING OUT (2-LP, gatefold sleeve with inners)	15

(First pressings of the above Chrysalis LPs have a white 'I' logo on the label. Second pressings without this are worth slightly less)

84	Chrysalis CDLP 1461	UNDER WRAPS (picture disc)	15
88	Chrysalis TBOX 1	20 YEARS OF JETHRO TULL (5-LP box set with 24-page booklet)	75
88	Chrysalis TBOX CD1	20 YEARS OF JETHRO TULL (3-CD box set with 24-page booklet)	50
89	Chrysalis CHRP 1708	ROCK ISLAND (Picture disc)	18
91	Chrysalis DCHR 1886	CATFISH RISING (Ltd edn. With 3-track 12" and lyric sheet inner sleeve)	20
93	Chrysalis CDCHR 6004	JETHRO TULL 25th ANNIVERSARY (4-CD cigar box set with 48-page booklet)	55

LP RE-PRESSINGS

68	Island ILP 985	THIS WAS (pink label/'i' logo, mono)	40
69	Island ILPS 9085	THIS WAS (pink label/black 'block' logo, 1st mix)	22
70	Island ILPS 9085	THIS WAS (pink label/'i' logo)	20
70	Chrysalis ILPS 9103	STAND UP (pop-up sleeve, pink label/black 'block' logo or pink label/'I' logo)	15

JETLINERS

66	Blue Beat BB 367	Meditation (actually by Sugar & Dandy)/GIRL SATCHMO: Nature Of Love (actually with Jetliners)	35

JETS

73	Cube BUG 35	Yeah!/Rusty Corinthian Pillar	15

JETS

78	Soho SH 3	Rockabilly Baby/James Dean	5

JET SET

62	Delta DW 5001	VC 10/Cruising 600 (some in p/s)	15

JET SET

(see also Liza & Jet Set, Soulmates)

64	Parlophone R 5199	You Got Me Hooked/True To You	20

JETSET

(see also Paul Bevoir)

80s	Shadows And Reflections	What Can I Say (Demo)/Christmas Greeting (flexidisc free with fanzine)	6
80s	Shadows And Reflections	What Can I Say (Demo)/Christmas Greeting (flexidisc without fanzine)	5
84	Dance Network NET 1	BEST OF THE JETSET (EP)	10
85	Dance Network NET 3	APRIL, MAY, JUNE AND THE JETSET (12" EP)	12
85	Dance Network WORK 1	THERE GOES THE NEIGHBOURHOOD (LP, pink sleeve)	20
86	Dance Network WORK 4	4 GO BANANAS (LP, with lyric insert)	20

JETSTREAMS

59	Decca F 11149	Bongo Rock/Tiger	20
59	Decca F 11149	Bongo Rock/Tiger	30

JEVUTSHTA

78	Zel-La JHSPS 226	Fight Your Way Out/Stomp	20

JEWELLS (Jamaica)

77	Observer OB 005	Black is The Highest Culture (Culture Version)/One Little Lick Version (12")	25
77	Observer OB 1101	Jah I/LEROY SMART: Jah Is My Light/I-ROY: Wicked Eat Dirt (12")	25

JEWELS

64	Colpix PX 11034	Opportunity/Gotta Find A Way	30
65	Colpix PX 11048	But I Do/Smokey Joe	18

JIGSAW

68	Polydor 56241	I Need Your Love/I've Gotta Get Me Some Money (as Jig-Saw Band)	15
68	Music Factory CUB 4	Mister Job/Great Idea	12
68	Music Factory CUB 6	Let Me Go Home/Tumblin'	80
68	MGM MGM 1410	One Way Street/Then I Found You	100
70	Philips 6006 112	One Way Street/Coffucious Confusion	70
70	Fontana 6007 017	Lollipop And Goody Man/Seven Fishes	40
71	Philips 6006 131	Jesu Joy Of Man's Desiring/No Questions Asked	7
71	Philips 6006 182	Keeping My Head Above Water/It's Nice But It's Wrong	7
74	BASF BA 1002	I've Seen The Film I've Read The Book/Mention My Name	7
75	BASF BA 1013	Baby Don't Do It/Stand Next To Me	7
75	Splash CP 1	Sky High/Brand New Love Affair	6
71	Philips 6308 033	LETHERSLADE FARM (LP)	60
72	Philips 6308 072	AURORA BOREALIS (LP)	40
73	BASF 29106-5	BROKEN HEARTED (LP, gatefold sleeve)	15
74	BASF BAP 5051	I'VE SEEN THE FILM, I'VE READ THE BOOK (LP)	12
75	Splash CPLP 1001	SKY HIGH (LP)	12

JIH

(see also Associates)

88	Jungle JUNG 32T/BOV 3	Take Me To The Girl/Come Summer Come Winter/Wake Up (12", unissued, Mayking test pressings only, white proof p/s)	20
88	Jungle JUNG 32T/BOV 3	Take Me To The Girl/Come Summer Come Winter/Wake Up (12", 'small photos' p/s)	10
88	Jungle JUNG 32T/BOV 3	Take Me To The Girl/Come Summer Come Winter/Wake Up (12", later blue art p/s)	7

MINT VALUE £

JILL & BOULEVARDS

62	Columbia DB 4823	And Now I Cry/Eugene	25

JILL & Y'VERNS

60s	Oak RGJ 503	My Soulful Dress/Anything He Wants Me To Do	100

JILTED JOHN

(see also Going Red?)

78	Rabid TOSH 105	Jilted John/Going Steady (p/s)	12
78	EMI International INT 567	Jilted John/Going Steady (p/s, reissue)	6
78	EMI International INT 577	True Love/I Was A Pre-Pubescent (p/s)	7
78	EMI International INT 587	The Birthday Kiss/Baz's Party (p/s)	7
78	EMI Intl. INS 3024	TRUE LOVE STORIES (LP, with board game insert)	18
78	EMI Intl. INS 3024	TRUE LOVE STORIES (LP)	12

JIMBILIN

71	Bamboo BAM 68	Human Race/Let Love In (both actually by Herman Chin-Loy & Aquarians)	15
75	Ashanti ASH 421	Balaclava/Tacku	12

JIM & JEAN

68	Verve Folkways VLP 5017	CHANGES (LP)	40

JIM & JOE

(see also James Burton)

64	London HL 9831	Fireball Mail/Daisy Mae	20

JIM & MONICA

(see also Jimmy Gilmer & Fireballs)

64	Stateside SS 266	Slippin' And Slidin'/Sing Along Without Jim & Monica	20

JOSE JIMINEZ

61	London HLR 9434	The Astronaut Part 1/Part 2	6

JIMMIE & NIGHT HOPPERS

59	London HLP 8830	Cruisin'/Night Hop	30
59	London HLP 8830	Cruisin'/Night Hop (78)	30

JIMMY AND THE DIMENSIONS

(see also Jimmy Powell & Red Alligator)

69	Youngblood YB 1008	Sugar Man/Slow Down	12

JIMMY J & CRU-L-T

94	Knifeforce KF 027	Take Me Away (Slipmatt Remix)/FUTURE PRIMITIVE: Life Me Up (Slammin' Vinyl Remix) (12", p/s)	15

JIVA

75	Dark Horse AMLH 22003	JIVA (LP, with inner sleeve)	12

JIV-A-TONES

58	Felsted AF 101	Flirty Gertie/Fire Engine Baby	200
58	Felsted AF 101	Flirty Gertie/Fire Engine Baby (78)	70

JIVE FIVE

61	Parlophone R 4822	My True Story/When I Was Single	150
62	Stateside SS 133	What Time Is It?/Begging You Please	100
65	United Artists UP 1106	I'm A Happy Man/Kiss Kiss Kiss	45

JIVERS (Jamaica)

(see also Brother Dan Allstars)

68	Trojan TR 604	Wear My Crown/Down On The Beach	8

JIVERS (U.S.)

56	Vogue V 9060	Little Mama/Cherie	650
56	Vogue V 9060	Little Mama/Cherie (78)	150
57	Vogue V 9068	Ray Pearl/Dear Little One	650
57	Vogue V 9068	Ray Pearl/Dear Little One (78)	150

JIVING JUNIORS

(see also Duke Reid)

60	Blue Beat BB 4	Lollipop Girl/Dearest Darling	40
60	Blue Beat BB 5	My Heart's Desire/I Love You	40
60	Starlite ST45 028	Lovers Line/Tu-Woo-Up-Tu-Woo	50
61	Starlite ST45 049	Slop & Mash/My Sweet Angel	50
61	Blue Beat BB 36	Over The River/Hip Rub (with Hersan & His City Slickers)	30
62	Island WI 003	Sugar Dandy/Valerie	25
62	Island WI 027	Andrea/Don't Leave Me	25
63	Island WI 129	Sugar Dandy/Valerie (reissue)	20
73	United Artists UP 35494	Stay/Call Me	5

J.J. ALLSTARS

(see also Lloyd Young, Bleechers, Ethiopians)

68	Duke DU 3	One Dollar Of Music/CARL DAWKINS: I'll Make It Up	20
69	Trojan TR 691	Memphis Underground (Parts 1 & 2)	20
70	Duke DU 94	Collecting Coins/Cabbage Leaf	15
70	Duke DU 95	This Land (actually by Carl Dawkins)/Land Version	12
70	Escort ES 821	Mango Tree/The Removers (both actually by Winston Wright & J.J. All Stars)	20
71	Big Shot BI 570	Perseverence Version/CARL DAWKINS: Perseverance	12
71	Explosion EX 2051	I Feel Good (Version 2)/CARL DAWKINS: I Feel Good	10
71	Duke DU 135	Soup/Soup (Version)	10

J.J. BAND

71	CBS S 64396	THE J.J. BAND (LP)	25

JJ72

99	Lakota LAK 70015	Long Way South/Snow (Acoustic)/Earthy Delights (p/s)	8
00	Lakota LAK 70018	October Swimmer/Guidance (p/s)	8

MINT VALUE £

01	Lakota LAK 70019	Snow/Wounded (p/s)	8
00	Lakota LAKLP 0017	JJ72 (LP)	25

JJ'S POWERHOUSE

83	Sillysybin COX 1657	Running For The Line/Blackrods (no p/s)	250

DAMITA JO

(see under 'D')

MARCY JO & EDDIE RAMBEAU

(see also Eddie Rambeau)

63	Stateside SS 235	Lover's Medley/When You Wore A Tulip	10

JOANIE, JOHNNY & HAL

60	Capitol CL 15126	When You Lose The One You Love/Miracles Are Always Happening	6

ANTONIO CARLOS JOBIM

70	Paramount SPFL 260	THE ADVENTURERS (LP, soundtrack)	12
72	CTI CTL 3	STONE FLOWER (LP)	12

JOBRIATH

73	Elektra K 12129	Take Me I'm Yours/Earthling	5
74	Elektra K 12156	Ooh La La/Gone Tomorrow	5
74	Elektra K 12156	Ooh La La/Gone Tomorrow (demo)	20
73	Elektra EKS 75070	JOBRIATH (LP)	15
74	Elektra K 42163	CREATURES OF THE STREET (LP)	15

JO'BURG HAWK

72	Charisma CB 194	Orang Utang/Dark Side Of The Moon	5
73	Charisma CAS 1064	JO'BURG HAWK (LP, gatefold sleeve, large 'Mad Hatter' label)	20

JOCELYNE JOCYA

69	CBS 4177	I Have Loved Me A Man/Time	60
69	CBS 4177	I Have Loved Me A Man/Time (DJ copy)	150

JODEY

79	Elliejay EJSP 9242	The Rocker/Front Man	150

JODIMARS

(see also Bill Haley & Comets)

56	Capitol CL 14518	Well Now, Dig This/Let's All Rock Together	75
56	Capitol CL 14518	Well Now, Dig This/Let's All Rock Together (78)	20
56	Capitol CL 14627	Rattle My Bones/Lotsa Love	75
56	Capitol CL 14627	Rattle My Bones/Lotsa Love (7)	20
56	Capitol CL 14641	Rattle Shakin' Daddy/Eat Your Heart Out Annie	75
56	Capitol CL 14641	Rattle Shakin' Daddy/Eat Your Heart Out Annie (78)	20
56	Capitol CL 14642	Dance The Bop/Boom, Boom My Bayou Baby	75
56	Capitol CL 14642	Dance The Bop/Boom, Boom My Bayou Baby (78)	20
56	Capitol CL 14663	Midnight/Clarabella	75
56	Capitol CL 14663	Midnight/Clarabella (78)	20
57	Capitol CL 14700	Cloud 99/Later	80
57	Capitol CL 14700	Cloud 99/Later (78)	25
70s	Bulldog BD 16	Well Now, Dig This/Dance The Bop	5
72	Specialty SPE 6608	WELL NOW DIG THIS (LP)	20

JODY GRIND

(see also Vinegar Joe, Hummingbird, Heads, Hands & Feet)

69	Transatlantic TRA 210	ONE STEP ON (LP, gatefold sleeve, lilac label with 't' logo)	100
70	Transatlantic TRA 221	FAR CANAL (LP, white/lilac label with 't' logo)	100

JODY ST

81	Lips LIPS 1	Fight Back/Granny Did It (private pressing)	150
81	Private Pressing	STREET (LP, private pressing)	75

AL T. JOE (& CELESTIALS)

(see also Jamaica Fats)

62	Dice CC 9	Rise Jamaica/I'm On My Own	15
62	Blue Beat BB 126	You Cheated On Me/This Heart Of Mine (as Al T. Joe & Celestials)	12
63	Blue Beat BB 166	Goodbye Dreamboat/Please Forgive Me	12
63	Blue Beat BB 169	Fatso/Slow Boat	12
70	Duke DU 70	It's A Shame/Desertion	8
72	Duke DU 148	Vision/Young And Unlearned	5
72	Dynamic DYN 429	Oh What A Price/The Prisoners Song	5

JOE & ANN

65	Black Swan WI 468	Gee Baby/Wherever You May Be	20

BILLY JOE & CHECKMATES

61	London HLU 9502	Percolator/Round & Round & Round & Round	8

CALYPSO JOE

69	Escort ES 801	Adults Only/Calalue	8

JOE COOL (& THE KILLERS)

77	Ariola ARO 105	I Just Don't Care/My Way (p/s)	25

JOE & DELLA

65	Doctor Bird DB 1043	So Close/BABA BROOKS: Eight Games	20

JOE & EDDIE

59	Capitol CL 15038	Green Grass/And I Believed	5
64	Vocalion V 9215	There's A Meetin' Here Tonight/Lonesome Traveller	5
65	Vocalion V 9238	Gabrielle/He's Got The Whole World In His Hands	5
65	Vocalion V 9242	Depend On Yourself/With You In Mind	5
65	Vocalion V-N 9246	Farewell/Hey Nelly Nelly	5
65	Vocalion V-P 9250	Walkin' Down The Line/It Ain't Me Babe	12
65	Vocalion VAN 8046	WALKIN' DOWN THE LINE (LP)	40

MINT VALUE £

BILLY JOEL
(see also Hassles)

72	Philips 6078 001	She's Got A Way/Everybody Loves You Now	8
74	Philips 6078 018	The Ballad Of Billy The Kid/If I Only Had The Words (To Tell You) (in p/s)	35
74	Philips 6078 018	The Ballad Of Billy The Kid/If I Only Had The Words (To Tell You)	25
79	CBS 7150	Honesty/Root Beer Rag (withdrawn)	20
72	Philips 6369 150	COLD SPRING HARBOR (LP)	15
73	Philips 6369 160	PIANO MAN (LP, withdrawn)	20
73	Philips 6078 018	BALLAD OF BILLY THE KID (LP)	12
78	CBS H 82311	THE STRANGER (LP, half-speed master version)	15

JOE 9T & THUNDERBIRDS
(see also They Must Be Russians)

80s	Gemme JOE 9T/LYN 6526	Joe 9T Theme/THEY MUST BE RUSSIANS: Psycho Analysis (p/s, stamped white label)	7

JOE 90

92	Full Effect FERT 112	Good Times/New Found Strength (12")	20

JOE PUBLIC

70s	Wavelength HURT 3	Herman's Back/Travelling With Raymond/Like It (p/s)	8

JOE PUBLIC
(see also Long Tall Shorty)

85	Capital CLA 55	Anti CND	20

JOE (Mansano) THE BOSS
(see also Joe's Allstars, Joe Mansano, Dice The Boss, Pama Dice)

70	Joe JRS 6	Son Of Al Capone/All My Enemies	25
70	Joe JRS 10	If Life Was A Thing/LLOYD KINGPIN: Daisy Bothering	15

JOE'S ALLSTARS
(see also Joe The Boss, Dice The Boss, King Horror, Pattie La Donne)

69	Joe/Duke DU 24	Hey Jude/Musical Feet	15
69	Joe/Duke DU 28	Battle Cry Of Biafra/Funky Reggae Part 1	15
69	Joe/Duke DU 50	Brixton Cat/Solitude	15
70	Joe JRS 9	Tony B's Theme/JOE THE BOSS: Skinhead Revolt	100
72	Sioux SI 012	Tony B's Theme/RAY MARTELL: She Caught The Train	12
70	Trojan TBL 106	BRIXTON CAT (LP)	35

JOE SOAP

73	Polydor 2383 233	KEEP IT CLEAN (LP, laminated sleeve, correction sticker on rear)	30

JOEY & CONTINENTALS
(see also G.T.O.'s)

70	Polydor 56520	She Rides With Me/Rudy Vadoo	85

JOEY & GENTLEMEN

64	Fontana TF 444	Like I Love You/I'll Never Let You Go	10
64	Fontana TF 485	Dummy Dum Song/Goodbye Little Girl	6

JOHANNE & JIMMY

64	Fontana TF 447	Everybody Knows/I Still Love you	8

HENRIK JOHANSEN'S JAZZ BAND
(see also City Ramblers Skiffle Group, Al Fairweather)

55	Tempo EXA 23	THE TRADITIONAL DANES (EP)	10
57	Tempo EXA 64	HENRIK JOHANSEN'S JAZZ BAND (EP)	10

JOHN

71	Capitol CL 15678	The Ten Lost Tribes Of Israel/Good Morning Old Man Time	10

ALEXSANDER JOHN

70s	Myrrh MYR 1010	DAYS GO BY (LP)	18

ANDREW JOHN

71	CBS 7017	Streets Of London/Rick Rack	10
72	CBS 64835	THE MACHINE STOPS (LP)	20

BASIL JOHN

60s	Planetone RC 12	Drink And Drive/MIKE ELLIOTT: J.K. Shuffle	10

CLIVE JOHN
(see also Man)

75	United Artists UAS 29733	YOU ALWAYS KNOW WHERE YOU STAND WITH A BUZZARD (LP)	25

DAVID JOHN & MOOD
(see also Gagalactyca, Astral Navigations, Little Free Rock)

64	Vocalion V 9220	To Catch That Man/Pretty Thing	200
65	Parlophone R 5255	Bring It To Jerome/I Love To See You Strut	230
65	Parlophone R 5301	Diggin' For Gold/She's Fine	230

ELTON JOHN
(see also [Stu Brown &] Bluesology, Bread & Beer Band, Neil Sedaka, Kiki Dee, Aretha Franklin, Dionne Warwick Radio Heart, Argosy)

SINGLES

68	Philips BF 1643	I've Been Loving You/Here's To The Next Time	250
69	Philips BF 1739	Lady Samantha/All Across The Havens	50
69	DJM DJS 205	It's Me That You Need/Just Like Strange Rain (in p/s)	90
69	DJM DJS 205	It's Me That You Need/Just Like Strange Rain	50
70	DJM DJS 217	Border Song/Bad Side Of The Moon	25
70	DJM DJS 222	Rock And Roll Madonna/Grey Seal	30
71	DJM DJS 233	Your Song/Into The Old Man's Shoes	5
71	DJM DJS 244	Friends/Honey Roll	10
72	DJM DJX 501	Rocket Man/Holiday Inn/Goodbye (gatefold p/s)	10

			MINT VALUE £
72	DJM DJX 501	Rocket Man/Holiday Inn/Goodbye (plain p/s)	5
72	DJM DJS 269	Honky Cat/Lady Samantha/It's Me That You Need	6
72	DJM DJS 271	Crocodile Rock/Elderberry Wine	5
73	DJM DJS 275	Daniel/Skyline Pigeon	5
73	DJM DJX 502	Saturday Night's Alright For Fighting/Jack Rabbit/Whenever You're Ready (We'll Go Steady Again) (p/s)	8
73	DJM DJS 290	Step Into Christmas/Ho! Ho! Ho! (Who'd Be A Turkey At Christmas)	8
73	DJM DJS 10705	Benny And The Jets/Rock 'N' Roll Madonna	6
74	DJM DJS 297	Candle In The Wind/Benny And The Jets	5
74	DJM DJS 302	Don't Let The Sun Go Down On Me/Sick City	5
74	DJM DJS 322	The Bitch Is Back/Cold Highway	5
74	DJM DJS 340	Lucy In The Sky With Diamonds (featuring Dr. Winston O'Boogie [John Lennon] & His Reggae Guitars)/One Day At A Time	5
75	DJM DJS 354	Philadelphia Freedom/I Saw Her Standing There (as Elton John Band; B-side featuring John Lennon with Muscle Shoals Horns) (p/s)	6
75	DJM DJS 610	Island Girl/Sugar On The Floor (p/s)	6
77	DJM DJR 18001	FOUR FROM FOUR EYES (EP)	8
78	DJM DJS 10902	Your Song/Border Song (p/s)	5
78	DJM DJS 10903	Honky Cat/Sixty Years On (p/s)	5
78	DJM DJS 10904	Country Comfort/Crocodile Rock (p/s)	5
78	DJM DJS 10905	Rocket Man/Daniel (p/s)	5
78	DJM DJS 10908	Candle In The Wind/I Feel Like A Bullet (In The Gun Of Robert Ford) (p/s, limited edition)	10
78	DJM DJS 10910	Island Girl/Saturday Night's Alright For Fighting (p/s, limited edition)	5
78	DJM DJS 10911	Philadelphia Freedom/Lucy In The Sky With Diamonds (reissue)	5
78	DJM DJS 10912	Pinball Wizard/Benny And The Jets (p/s)	5
78	DJM EJ 12	THE ELTON JOHN SINGLES COLLECTION (12 x 7" box set [DJS 10901-12])	50
78	DJM DJT 15000	FUNERAL FOR A FRIEND (12" EP)	10
80	DJM DJS 10961	Harmony/Mona Lisas And Mad Hatters (glossy p/s)	8
81	DJM DJS 10965	I Saw Her Standing There/Whatever Gets You Thru The Night/Lucy In The Sky With Diamonds (EP, p/s, featuring John Lennon & Muscle Shoals Horns)	7
77	Rocket GOALD 1	The Goaldigger Song/Jimmy, Brian, Elton, Eric (mail-order, signed, 500 only)	250
77	Rocket RU 1	Bite Your Lip (Get Up And Dance) (Remix)/KIKI DEE: Chicago (12", p/s)	7
79	Rocket XPRES 20	Mama Can't Buy You Love/Strangers (p/s; withdrawn, misspelt "Mamma")	350
79	Rocket XPRES 21	Victim Of Love/Strangers (p/s)	7
79	Rocket XPRES 2412	Johnny B. Goode/Thunder In The Night (12", p/s)	10
80	Rocket XPRES 45	Dear God/Tactics (company sleeve)	40
80	Rocket ELTON 1	Dear God/Tactics//Steal Away Child/Love So Cold (double pack, p/s)	6
82	Rocket XPPIC 77	Empty Garden/Take Me Down To The Ocean (picture disc)	6
82	Rocket XPRPO 88	All Quiet On The Western Front/Where Have All The Good Times Gone (poster p/s)	10
83	Rocket XPRES 91	That's Why They Call It The Blues/Lord Choc Ice Goes Mental ('raised musical note' sleeve with shorter A-side title)	15
83	Rocket EJPIC 1	I'm Still Standing/Earn While You Learn (piano-shaped picture disc)	15
83	Rocket EJS 2/FREEJ 2	Kiss The Bride/Dreamboat//Ego/Song For Guy (double pack, p/s)	10
83	Rocket EJS 3/2	Cold As Christmas/Crystal//Don't Go Breaking My Heart/Snow Queen (double pack, gatefold p/s, 2nd 45 with Kiki Dee)	12
84	Rocket PHPIC 7	Sad Songs (Say So Much) /Simple Man (hat-shaped picture disc)	5
85	Rocket EJS 8	Act Of War (Part 1)/(Part 2) (with Millie Jackson, 'concertina pack' of video stills)	8
85	Rocket EJS 10/EJS 9	Wrap Her Up/Restless (live)//Nikita/The Man Who Never Died (double pack, stickered gatefold PVC wallet with 2 separate p/s)	10
85	Rocket EJSP 10	Wrap Her Up/Restless (live) (with George Michael, oblong-shaped picture disc, with pictures on wrong sides)	25
85	Rocket EJS 1012/ELTON 1	Wrap Her Up (Extended Remix) (with George Michael)/Restless (live)/ Nikita/Cold As Christmas (12", double pack in stickered PVC sleeve)	10
86	Rocket EJSP 13	Slow Rivers (with Cliff Richard)/Billy & The Kids (picture disc)	10
86	Rocket EJS 13-12	Slow Rivers (with Cliff Richard)/Billy & The Kids/Lord Of The Flies (12", p/s)	12
88	Rocket EJSP 15	Candle In The Wind (live)/Sorry Seems To Be The Hardest Word (live) (picture disc)	8
88	Rocket EJS 1512	Candle In The Wind (live)/Sorry Seems To Be The Hardest Word (live)/ Your Song (live)/Don't Let The Sun Go Down On Me (live) (12", p/s)	12
88	Rocket EJSCD 15	Candle In The Wind (live)/Sorry Seems To Be The Hardest Word (live)/ Your Song (live)/Don't Let The Sun Go Down On Me (live) (CD, card sleeve)	18
88	Rocket EJSIP 16	I Don't Wanna Go On With You Like That/Rope Around A Fool/ (Radio 1 interview) (33rpm, poster sleeve)	10
88	Rocket EJS 1612	I Don't Wanna Go On With You Like That (Remix)/(7" Version)/ Rope Around A Fool (12", blue vinyl factory custom pressing, no p/s)	150
90	Rocket EJS 21	Club At The End Of The Street/Give Peace A Chance (p/s, withdrawn)	100
90	Rocket EJSCD 21	Club At The End Of The Street/Give Peace A Chance/ I Don't Wanna Go On With You Like That (Live in Verona) (CD withdrawn with "Made In England" credit)	20
97	Rocket EJSCD 41	Something About The Way You Look Tonight (Edited Version)/ I Know Why I'm In Love/No Valentines/Something About The Way You Look Tonight (Album Version) (CD, card sleeve, unreleased)	40
97	Rocket EJSCX 41	Something About The Way You Look Tonight (Edited Version)/ I Know Why I'm In Love/You Can Make History (Young Again)/Something About The Way You Look Tonight (Album Version) (CD, digipak, unreleased)	75

LPs

69	DJM DJLP 403	EMPTY SKY (gatefold sleeve, mono)	150
69	DJM DJLPS 403	EMPTY SKY (gatefold sleeve, stereo, with 'stereo' sticker on sleeve)	20
70	DJM DJLPS 406	ELTON JOHN (textured gatefold sleeve)	18
70	DJM DJLPS 406	ELTON JOHN (later smooth gatefold sleeve)	15
70	Warlock Music WMM 101/2	WARLOCK MUSIC SAMPLER (untitled publishing sampler, 7 tracks by Elton, 4 by Linda Peters)	1000
73	DJM DJLPD 1001	GOODBYE YELLOW BRICK ROAD (2 x LP, gatefold)	15
76	DJM DJLPH 473	HERE AND THERE (with inner)	12

MINT VALUE £

76 DJM DJE 29001 GOODBYE YELLOW BRICK ROAD (2-LP, yellow vinyl, triplefold sleeve) 20
78 DJM DJV 2300 CAPTAIN FANTASTIC AND THE BROWN DIRT COWBOY (picture disc) 40
78 DJM LSP 14512 ELTON JOHN (5-LP, box set) 40
91 Rocket 848 236-2 TO BE CONTINUED ... THE VERY BEST OF ELTON JOHN (4-CD, 12" x 8" box set with large colour booklet) 100
93 Happenstance HAPP 001 PLAYS THE SIRAN (CD, private pressing, 50 only) 1000
93 Happenstance HAPP 002 THE FISHING TRIP (4-CD set, private pressing, 100 only, existence unconfirmed) 700
97 Rocket ELTON 50 CELEBRATING ELTON JOHN'S 50TH BIRTHDAY (CD, promo only) 50
99 Mercury ADV 1999/1 AIDA (with Sir Tim Rice) (box set with wallet, plinth stand, interview CD, booklet and calender cards, promo only) 50
99 Mercury ADV 1999/1 AIDA PRESS KIT (card box set with wallet, plinth stand, interview CD, booklet, calender cards, scented candle and broadcast CD-R, promo only) . 30
99 Rocket STAR 3 ELTON JOHN'S AIDA (export CD, card p/s, promo only) 20

JOHN LEE'S GROUNDHOGS

(see also Groundhogs, Tony McPhee)

66 Planet PLF 104 Over You Baby/I'll Never Fall In Love Again 120

LITTLE WILLIE JOHN

56 Parlophone DP 510 All Around The World/Don't Leave Me Dear (78, export issue) 30
56 Parlophone R 4209 Fever/Letter From My Darling 150
56 Parlophone R 4209 Fever/Letter From My Darling (78) 50
58 Parlophone R 4396 Uh, Uh, Baby/Dinner Date (With His Girl Friend) 50
58 Parlophone R 4396 Uh, Uh, Baby/Dinner Date (With His Girl Friend) (78) 45
58 Parlophone R 4432 Talk To Me, Talk To Me/Spasms 50
58 Parlophone R 4432 Talk To Me, Talk To Me/Spasms (78) 45
58 Parlophone R 4472 Let's Rock While The Rockin's Good/You're A Sweetheart 70
58 Parlophone R 4472 Let's Rock While The Rockin's Good/You're A Sweetheart (78) 55
59 Parlophone R 4571 Leave My Kitten Alone/Let Nobody Love You 60
60 Parlophone R 4674 Heartbreak (It's Hurtin' Me)/Do You Love Me 30
60 Parlophone R 4699 Sleep/There's A Difference 30
61 Parlophone R 4728 Walk Slow/HANK BALLARD: The Hoochie Coochie Coo 40
59 Parlophone PMC 1163 SURE THINGS (LP) 200
64 London HA 8126 COME ON AND JOIN LITTLE WILLIE JOHN (LP) 100

MABLE JOHN

66 Atlantic 584 022 It's Catching/Your Good Thing (Is About To End) 15
67 Stax 601 010 Same Time Same Place/Bigger And Better (dark blue label) 15
67 Stax 601 010 Same Time Same Place/Bigger And Better (light blue label) 10
68 Stax 601 034 Able Mable/Don't Get Caught 15

ROBERT JOHN

68 CBS 3436 If You Don't Want My Love/Don't 15
68 CBS 3730 Don't Leave Me/Children 5
68 A&M AMS 835 Raindrops Love And Sunshine/When The Party Is Over 50

SAMMIE JOHN

67 Stateside SS 585 Little John/Boss Bag 25

JOHN & JOHNNY

63 Decca F 11719 I Want You To Be My Girl/It's You 6

JOHN & PAUL

65 London HLU 9997 People Say/I'm Walkin' 15

JOHN AND ROSALIND

(see under Ross Hannaman)

JOHNNIE & JOE

58 London HLM 8682 Over The Mountain, Across The Sea/My Baby's Gone, On, On 350
58 London HLM 8682 Over The Mountain, Across The Sea/My Baby's Gone, On, On (78) 75

JOHNNY DANGEROUSLY

(see also I Am Kloot)

90 Village (no cat no) Introducing Jane/Tear It Down/Subway Life (12" p/s) 20
89 Village (no cat no) YOU, ME AND THE ALARM CLOCK (mini LP p/s with photo insert, 1,000 only) .. 35

LITTLE JOHNNY JONES

(see also Johnny Lover)

73 Pressure Beat PB 5515 More Dub/More Dub - Chapter Two 8

JOHNNY (Osborne) & ATTRACTIONS

67 Doctor Bird DB 1118 Young Wings Can Fly/DUDLEY WILLIAMSON: I'm Moving On 60
68 Doctor Bird DB 117 Coming On The Scene/Anything You Want 150

JOHNNY & THE ATTRACTIONS

68 Doctor Bird DB 1118 Young Wings Can Fly/DUDLEY WILLIAMSON: I'm Moving On 100

JOHNNY (STEVENS) & THE BLUE BEATS

64 Blue Beat BB 229 Shame/Ball And Chain 15

JOHNNY & CHARLEY

65 Pye Int. 7N 25326 La Yenka/Baila La Yenka 10

JOHNNY & CHAZ & GUNNERS

61 Decca F 11365 Bobby/Out Of Luck 22

JOHNNY & THE COPYCATS

(see also My Dear Watson)

64 Norco AB 102 I'm A Hog For You Baby/I Can Never See You 60

JOHNNY & THE HURRICANES

59 London HL 8899 Crossfire/Lazy (triangular-centre) 20
59 London HL 8899 Crossfire/Lazy (later round centre) 10
59 London HL 8899 Crossfire/Lazy (78 rpm) 50

			MINT VALUE £
59	London HL 8948	Red River Rock/Buckeye (triangular-centre)	10
59	London HL 8948	Red River Rock/Buckeye (later round centre)	5
59	London HL 8948	Red River Rock/Buckeye (78)	40
59	London HL 9017	Reveille Rock/Time Bomb (triangular-centre)	10
59	London HL 9017	Reveille Rock/Time Bomb (later round centre)	5
59	London HL 9017	Reveille Rock/Time Bomb (78)	50
60	London HLI 9072	Beatnick Fly/Sand Storm	7
60	London HLI 9072	Beatnick Fly/Sand Storm (78)	50
60	London HLX 9134	Down Yonder/Sheba	7
60	London HLX 9134	Down Yonder/Sheba (78)	100
60	London HLX 9190	Rocking Goose/Revival	7
60	London HLX 9190	Rocking Goose/Revival (78)	100
60	London HL 7099	The Hep Canary/Catnip (export issue)	45
61	London HLX 9289	Ja-Da/Mr. Lonely	8
61	London HLX 9378	High Voltage/Old Smokie	10
62	London HLX 9491	Farewell, Farewell/Traffic Jam	10
62	London HLX 7116	You Are My Sunshine/Farewell, Farewell (export issue)	30
62	London HLX 9536	Salvation/Misirlou	18
62	London HLX 9617	Minnesota Fats/Come On Train	15
63	London HLX 9660	Whatever Happened To Baby Jane/Greens And Beans	10
68	London HLX 10199	Rocking Goose/Beatnik Fly (reissue)	5
64	Stateside SS 347	Money Honey/That's All	15
61	London REX 1284	ROCKING GOOSE (EP)	30
62	London REX 1347	JOHNNY AND THE HURRICANES (EP)	30
64	London REX 1414	JOHNNY AND THE HURRICANES VOL. 2 (EP)	30
60	London HA 2227	RED RIVER ROCK (LP, plum label)	50
60	London HA-I 2269	STORMSVILLE (LP)	35
61	London HA-X 2322	THE BIG SOUND OF JOHNNY AND THE HURRICANES (LP)	40
61	London HA 2227	RED RIVER ROCK (LP, reissue, black label)	25

JOHNNY & JACK

54	HMV 7MC 21	Honey, I Need You/Goodnight, Well It's Time To Go (export issue)	20
55	HMV JO 440	Beware Of "It"/Kiss Crazy Baby (78, export)	10
56	HMV JO 456	Weary Moments/S.O.S. (78, export)	10
59	RCA RCA 1145	Sailor Man/Wild And Wicked World	6
59	RCA RCA 1145	Sailor Man/Wild And Wicked World (78)	22
59	RCA RCX 176	COUNTRY GUITAR VOL. 10 (EP)	12

JOHNNY & JAMMERS

(see also Johnny Winter)

79	Big Beat NS 55	School Day Blues/You Know I Love You (p/s)	5

JOHNNY & JOHN

(see also Johnny Gustafson, Big Three)

66	Polydor 56087	Bumper To Bumper/Scrape My Boot	20

JOHNNY & JUDY

(see also John Walker)

59	Vogue Pop V 9128	Bother Me Baby/Who's To Say	650
59	Vogue Pop V 9128	Bother Me Baby/Who's To Say (78)	150

JOHNNY & THE SELF ABUSERS

(see also Simple Minds)

77	Chiswick NS 22	Saints And Sinners/Dead Vandals (p/s)	25

JOHNNY & VIBRATONES

63	Warner Bros WB 107	Bird Stompin'/Movin' The Bird	12

JOHNNY F & KLM

92	Liberty Grooves LIB003	TAKIN' LIBERTIES VOL 1 (LP)	20

JOHNNY MOPED

(see also Slime, Maxim's Trash)

76	Chiswick PROMO 3	BASICALLY, THE ORIGINAL JOHNNY MOPED TAPE (33rpm, no p/s)	20
77	Chiswick S 15	No-One/Incendiary Device (p/s)	7
78	Chiswick NS 27	Darling, Let's Have Another Baby/Something Else/It Really Digs (p/s)	6
78	Chiswick NS 41	Little Queenie/Hard Lovin' Man (p/s)	8
78	Chiswick WIK 8	CYCLEDELIC (LP, with free single [PROMO 3])	30
78	Chiswick WIK 8	CYCLEDELIC (LP, without free single [PROMO 3])	12
90	Deltic DELTLP 6	THE SEARCH FOR XERTES (LP)	20

JOHNNY'S BOYS

59	Decca F 11156	Sleep Walk/Ciao Ciao Bambina	10

JOHNNY'S JAZZ

(see also Johnny Hawksworth)

56	Decca FJ 10663	R.J. Boogie/Get Happy (featuring Johnny Hawksworth)	6

JOHN'S CHILDREN

(see also Marc Bolan, Andy Ellison, Radio Stars, Jook, Tyrannosaurus Rex)

66	Columbia DB 8030	The Love I Thought I'd Found/Strange Affair (very few in p/s)	500
66	Columbia DB 8030	The Love I Thought I'd Found/Strange Affair	300
67	Columbia DB 8124	Just What You Want - Just What You'll Get/But She's Mine	160
67	Track 604 003	Desdemona/Remember Thomas A'Beckett (in p/s)	150
67	Track 604 003	Desdemona/Remember Thomas A'Beckett	60
67	Track 604 005	Midsummer Night's Scene/Sara Crazy Child (withdrawn)	4000
67	Track 604 005	Come And Play With Me In The Garden/Sara Crazy Child (in p/s)	200
67	Track 604 005	Come And Play With Me In The Garden/Sara Crazy Child	90
67	Track 604 010	Go Go Girl/Jagged Time Lapse	80
82	Cherry Red BRED 31	ORGASM (LP, with inner)	15
87	Bam Caruso KIRI 095	MIDSUMMER NIGHT'S SCENE (LP)	30

MINT VALUE £

GLYN JOHNS

62	Decca F 11478	January Blues/Sioux Indian	5
63	Decca F 11753	Old Deceiver Time/Dancing With You	5
65	Immediate IM 013	Mary Anne/Like Grains Of Yellow Sand	25
65	Pye 7N 15818	I'll Follow The Sun/I'll Take You Dancing	5
60s	Westcot LYN 827/828	Today You're Gone/Such Stuff Of Dreams (freebie with jeans offer)	5

GLYNIS JOHNS

54	Columbia SCM 5149	I Can't Resist Men/Always You	8

LYNDON JOHNS (& ISRAELITES)

69	Downtown DT 444	Don't Gamble With Love/Song Bird	5
69	Downtown DT 451	Oh Mama Oh Papa/Bring Back The Night (with The Israelites)	5

AL JOHNSON & JEAN CARN

(see also Jean Carn)

80	CBS 8545	I'm Back For More/You Are My Personal Angel	10

ALEC JOHNSON

(see also Nightwing)

79	RFP RFP 001	Busman's Holiday (no p/s)	12

ANTHONY JOHNSON

81	Greensleeves GRED 76	Let Go This One/BILLY BOYO: One Spliff A Day (12")	20
83	Rusty RILP 003	I'M READY (LP)	25
82	Midnight Rock MRLP 002	GUN SHOT (LP)	30

BETTY JOHNSON

56	London HLU 8307	I'll Wait/Please Tell Me Why	40
56	London HLU 8326	Honky Tonk Rock/Say It Isn't So, Joe	175
56	London HLU 8326	Honky Tonk Rock/Say It Isn't So, Joe (78)	50
57	London HLU 8365	I Dreamed/If It's Wrong To Love You	40
57	London HLU 8432	1492/Little White Lies	25
57	London HLU 8432	1492/Little White Lies (78)	12
58	London HLE 8557	Little Blue Man/Song You Heard When You Fell In Love	25
58	London HLE 8557	Little Blue Man/Song You Heard When You Fell In Love (78)	12
58	London HLE 8678	Dream/How Much	15
58	London HLE 8678	Dream/How Much (78)	20
58	London HLE 8701	There's Never Been A Night/Mr. Brown Is Out Of Town	40
58	London HLE 8701	There's Never Been A Night/Mr. Brown Is Out Of Town (78)	25
58	London HLE 8725	Hoopa Hoola/One More Time	25
58	London HLE 8725	Hoopa Hoola/One More Time (78)	25
59	London HLE 8839	Does Your Heart Beat For Me?/You And Only You	20
59	London HLE 8839	Does Your Heart Beat For Me?/You And Only You (78)	30
59	London RE-E 1221	DREAM (EP)	75
59	London HA-E 2163	THE SONG YOU HEARD WHEN YOU FELL IN LOVE (LP)	50

BLIND WILLIE JOHNSON

50s	Square M1	Dark Was The Night, Cold Was The Ground/ Lord I Just Can't Keep From Crying (78)	10
58	Fontana TFE 17052	TREASURES OF NORTH AMERICAN NEGRO MUSIC NO. 2 (EP)	20
70	Xtra XTRA 1098	BLIND WILLIE JOHNSON (LP)	20

BOB JOHNSON & PETE KNIGHT

(see also Steeleye Span, Mary Hopkin)

77	Chrysalis CHR 1137	THE KING OF ELFLAND'S DAUGHTER (LP, lyric insert, green label)	15

BOBBY JOHNSON & ATOMS

67	Ember EMB S 245	Do It Again A Little Bit Slower/Tramp (in p/s)	20
67	Ember EMB S 245	Do It Again A Little Bit Slower/Tramp	10

BROWNIE JOHNSON

62	Longhorn BLH 0004	Best Dressed Beggar/Just Pretending	30

BRYAN JOHNSON

60	Decca F11213	Looking, High, High, High/Each Tomorrow	6

BUBBER JOHNSON

57	Parlophone R 4259	Confidential/Have A Little Faith In Me	35
57	Parlophone R 4259	Confidential/Have A Little Faith In Me (78)	12

BUDDY JOHNSON

55	Mercury MB 3231	Upside Your Head/ELLA JOHNSON: Crazy About A Saxophone (78)	12
59	Mercury ZEP 10009	BUDDY JOHNSON WAILS (EP, with Ella Johnson)	80
57	Mercury MPT 7515	ROCK AND ROLL (10" LP, with Ella Johnson)	175

BUNK JOHNSON (& HIS NEW ORLEANS BAND)

55	HMV 7M 141	When The Saints Go Marching In/Darktown Strutters' Ball	5
50s	Melodisc EPM 7 52	ONE YOU LOVE (EP)	10
52	Jazz Man no cat. no.	MANDADISC (LP, with the Original Superior Band)	15
54	Goodtime Jazz LDG 110	BUNK JOHNSON AND THE YERBA BUENA JAZZ BAND (10" LP)	15
59	Melodisc MLP 12-112	BUNK JOHNSON AND HIS NEW ORLEANS JAZZ BAND (LP, with George Lewis)	15

CAREY JOHNSON

72	Banana BA 369	Correction Train/SOUL DEFENDERS: Version	18

DANIEL JOHNSON

65	Island WI 250	Come On My People/Brother Nathan	15

DOMINO JOHNSON

72	Green Door GD 4045	Summertime/SWANS: Grazing	5

DOMINO JOHNSON & CHAMPIONS

70	Duke DU 89	You Broke My Heart/TONY & CHAMPIONS: Tell Me The Reason	8

MINT VALUE £

GENERAL JOHNSON

(see also Norman Johnson, Showmen, Chairmen Of The Board)

73	Invictus INV 531	Only Time Will Tell/Only Time Will Tell (Instrumental Version)	8
76	Arista ARIST 45	All In The Family/Ready, Willing And Able	6
73	Invictus SVT 1008	GENERALLY SPEAKING (LP)	20

GINGER JOHNSON AND HIS AFRICAN MESSENGERS

67	Masquerade SM 02001	AFRICAN PARTY (LP)	150

HOWARD JOHNSON

71	Jay Boy BOY 47	The Slide/That Magic Touch Can Send You Flying	15

JAMES P. JOHNSON

54	Columbia SCM 5127	Feeling Blues/Riffs	8
57	HMV 7EG 8215	LOUISIANA SUGAR BABIES (EP, with Fats Waller)	8
54	London AL 3511	EARLY HARLEM PIANO (10" LP)	15
55	London AL 3540	EARLY HARLEM PIANO VOLUME 2 (10" LP)	15

JIMMY JOHNSON

65	Sue WI 387	Don't Answer The Door Parts 1 & 2	30

J.J. JOHNSON

(see also Sonny Stitt)

55	Vogue LDE 124	J.J. JOHNSON SEXTET (10" LP)	15
55	Vogue LDE 162	J.J. JOHNSON QUINTET (10" LP)	15
60	Fontana TFL 5041	J.J. IN PERSON (LP)	12
61	Fontana TFL 5137	BLUE TROMBONE (LP, also stereo STFL 559)	12
73	United Artists UAS 29451	ACROSS 110TH STREET (LP, soundtrack, with Bobby Womack)	20

(JOHNNY JOHNSON &) THE BANDWAGON

68	Direction 58-3520	Baby Make Your Own Sweet Music/On The Day We Fall In Love (as Bandwagon)	6
68	Direction 58-3670	Breaking Down The Walls Of Heartache/Dancin' Master (as Bandwagon)	6
69	Direction 58-3923	You/You Blew Your Cool And Lost Your Fool	6
69	Direction 58-4180	Let's Hang On/I Ain't Lying (withdrawn)	12
69	Direction 58-4180	Let's Hang On/Don't Let It In	6
70	Bell BLL 111	Sweet Inspiration/Pride Comes Before A Fall	5
72	Stateside SS 2207	Honey Bee/I Don't Know Why	20
74	EMI EMI 2114	Strong Love, Proud Love/Fast Running Out Of World	25
69	Direction 8-63500	JOHNNY JOHNSON AND THE BANDWAGON (LP)	30
70	Bell SBLL 138	SOUL SURVIVOR (LP)	25

JUDI JOHNSON (& PERFECTIONS)

64	HMV POP 1371	My Baby's Face/Make The Most Of It (solo)	15
65	HMV POP 1399	How Many Times/A Way Out (as Judi Johnson & Perfections)	20

LARRY JOHNSON

70	Blue Horizon 7-63851	PRESENTING THE COUNTRY BLUES (LP)	150

LAURIE JOHNSON ORCHESTRA

(see also Polka Dots)

56	HMV 7MC 47	Buttercup/Lullaby Of The Leaves (export issue)	10
57	HMV POP 404	The Moonraker/Call Of The Casbah	7
60	Pye 7N 15251	No Hiding Place/The Deputy	6
64	Pye 7N 15599	Dr Strangelove Theme/Nevada	6
64	Pye 7N 15715	Call Me Irresponsible/The Beauty Jungle	6
65	Pye 7N 15933	Latin Quarter/M1 (in p/s)	8
65	Pye 7N 15933	Latin Quarter/M1	6
65	Pye 7N 17015	The Avengers/Minor Bossa Nova (in p/s)	50
65	Pye 7N 17015	The Avengers/Minor Bossa Nova	30
69	MGM MGM 1457	There Is Another Song/Caesar Smith	20
71	Columbia DB 8826	The Jason King Theme/There Comes A Time	50
76	EMI EMI 2562	The New Avengers Theme/A Flavour Of The Avengers (in p/s)	10
76	EMI EMI 2562	The New Avengers Theme/A Flavour Of The Avengers	6
80	Unicorn Kachana MCPS 5	The Professionals Main Title/On Target/The New Avengers Main Title (p/s, by Laurie Johnson & London Studio Orchestra)	6
57	Parlophone GEP 8604	THE GOOD COMPANIONS (EP)	15
58	Pye Nixa NEP 24083	OPERATION ORCHESTRA (EP)	8
58	Pye Nixa NPL 18017	SONGS OF THREE SEASONS (LP)	15
63	Pye NPL 18088	THE NEW BIG SOUND OF THE LAURIE JOHNSON ORCHESTRA (LP)	20
65	Pye NPL 18103	THE BIG NEW SOUND STRIKES AGAIN (LP)	20
66	Pye NPL 18136	TWO CITIES SUITE (LP)	12
67	Marble Arch MAL 695	THE AVENGERS AND OTHER FAVOURITES (LP)	25
68	Columbia S(C)X 6206	SOMETHING'S COMING (LP, mono/stereo)	12
69	MGM C(S) 8104	THEMES AND ... (LP)	20
70	Columbia SCX 6412	LAURIE JOHNSON/LONDON JAZZ ORCHESTRA - SYNTHESIS (LP, with Joe Harriott, Tubby Hayes, Stan Tracey & Tony Coe)	50
71	Columbia SCX 6464	CONQUISTADORS (LP)	12
73	Ronco RR 2006	THE BELSTONE FOX (LP, soundtrack, gatefold sleeve)	12
80	Unicorn Kachana KPM 7009	MUSIC FROM THE AVENGERS, THE NEW AVENGERS AND THE PROFESSIONALS (LP, gatefold sleeve, with London Studio Orchestra)	20

LINTON KWESI JOHNSON

78	Virgin VX 1002	DREAD BET AN' BLOOD (LP)	15
79	Island ILPS 9566	FORCES OF VICTORY (LP, with inner sleeve)	15
80	Island ILPS 9505	BASS CULTURE (LP)	15

LONNIE JOHNSON

(see also Eddie Lang & Lonnie Johnson)

51	Vogue V 2015	Drunk Again/Jelly Roll Baker (78)	30
51	Vogue V 2079	Happy New Year/Little Rockin' Chair (78)	30
51	Melodisc MEL 1138	Rocks In My Bed/Solid Blues (78)	30
51	Melodisc MEL 1186	Blues For Everybody/In Love Again (78)	30

			MINT VALUE £
52	Melodisc MEL 1221	Blues In My Soul/Keep What You Got (78)	30
57	Parlophone GEP 8635	LONESOME ROAD (EP)	30
57	Parlophone GEP 8663	LONNIE'S BLUES (EP)	30
58	Parlophone GEP 8693	LONNIE'S BLUES NO. 2 (EP)	30
64	Storyville SLP 162	PORTRAITS IN BLUES VOL. 6 (LP)	30
64	Storyville 616 010	SEE SEE RIDER (LP, with Otis Spann)	40
60s	Xtra XTRA 1037	LONNIE JOHNSON (LP)	25

LOU JOHNSON

63	London HLX 9805	Reach Out For Me/Magic Potion	50
63	London HLX 9805	Reach Out For Me/Magic Potion (DJ copy)	100
64	London HLX 9917	(There's) Always Something There To Remind Me/Wouldn't That Be Something	25
64	London HLX 9929	A Message To Martha (Kentucky Bluebird)/The Last One To Be Loved	15
65	London HLX 9965	Please Stop The Wedding/Park Avenue	20
65	London HLX 9994	A Time To Love, A Time To Cry/Unsatisfied	80
65	London HLX 9994	A Time To Love, A Time To Cry/Unsatisfied (DJ copy)	150
69	London HLX 10269	(There's) Always Something There To Remind Me/Message To Martha	10
64	London REX 1438	THE MAGIC POTION OF LOU JOHNSON (EP)	150

LUTHER 'GEORGIA BOY SNAKE' JOHNSON

69	Transatlantic TRA 188	THE MUDDY WATERS BLUES BAND (LP, credits Muddy Waters on label)	30

MARV JOHNSON

59	London HLT 8856	Come To Me/Whisper	100
59	London HLT 8856	Come To Me/Whisper	75
59	London HLT 9013	You Got What It Takes/Don't Leave Me	12
59	London HLT 9013	You Got What It Takes/Don't Leave Me (tri centre)	25
59	London HLT 9013	You Got What It Takes/Don't Leave Me (78)	65
60	London HLT 9109	I Love The Way You Love/Let Me Love You	20
60	London HL 7095	I Love The Way You Love/Let Me Love You (export issue)	22
60	London HLT 9165	Ain't Gonna Be That Way/All The Love I've Got	20
60	London HLT 9187	(You've Got To) Move Two Mountains/I Need You	20
61	London HLT 9265	Happy Days/Baby, Baby	20
61	London HLT 9311	Merry-Go-Round/Tell Me That You Love Me	45
65	Tamla Motown TMG 525	Why Do You Want To Let Me Go/I'm Not A Plaything	110
69	United Artists UP 35010	I Love The Way You Love/You Got What It Takes	6
68	Tamla Motown TMG 680	I'll Pick A Rose For My Rose/You Got The Love I Love	8
69	Tamla Motown TMG 713	I Miss You Baby (How I Miss You)/Bad Girl	10
70	Tamla Motown TMG 737	So Glad You Chose Me/I'm Not A Plaything	10
60	London HA-T 2271	MARVELLOUS MARV JOHNSON (LP)	150
69	T. Motown (S)TML 11111	I'LL PICK A ROSE FOR MY ROSE (LP, mono/stereo)	25

MATT JOHNSON

(see also Gadgets, The The)

81	4AD CAD 113	BURNING BLUE SOUL (LP, original 'psychedelic eye' cover)	18

MIRRIAM JOHNSON

61	London HLW 9337	Lonesome Road/Young And Innocent	15

NORMAN JOHNSON (& SHOWMEN)

(see also General Johnson, Chairmen Of The Board, Showmen)

69	Action ACT 4529	You're Everything/Our Love Will Grow	50
69	Action ACT 4545	Take It Baby/In Paradise	50
71	Action ACT 4601	You're Everything/Our Love Will Grow (reissue)	30

PETE JOHNSON

(see also Joe Turner & Pete Johnson, Albert Ammons & Meade Lux Lewis)

51	Vogue V 2007	J.J. Boogie/Yancey Special (78, red label)	10
51	Vogue V 2007	J.J. Boogie/Yancey Special (78, orange label)	12
51	Vogue V 2008	Swanee River Boogie/St. Louis Boogie (78, red label)	12
51	Vogue V 2008	Swanee River Boogie/St. Louis Boogie (78, red orange label)	15
51	Vogue V 2019	Hollywood Boogie/Central Avenue Drag (78, orange label)	15
56	Vogue V 2007	J.J. Boogie/Yancey Special	35
56	Vogue V 2008	Swanee River Boogie/St. Louis Boogie	30
55	Vogue EPV 1039	PETE JOHNSON (EP)	30
59	Top Rank JKR 8009	ROLL 'EM BOY (EP)	25
55	London AL 3549	JUMPIN' WITH PETE JOHNSON (10" LP)	50
55	Vogue Coral LRA 10016	BOOGIE WOOGIE MOOD (LP)	30

PLAS JOHNSON (ORCHESTRA)

57	Capitol CL 14772	The Big Twist/Come Rain Or Come Shine	20
57	Capitol CL 14816	Swanee River Rock/You Send Me	20
58	Capitol CL 14836	Popcorn/Hoppin' Mad	20
58	Capitol CL 14903	Little Rockin' Deacon/Dinah	20
59	Capitol CL 14973	Robbins Nest Cha Cha/Plaz Jazz	10
57	London HB-U 1078	BOP ME DADDY (10" LP)	60

PROFESSOR JOHNSON & HIS GOSPEL SINGERS

51	Vocalion V 1013	Give Me That Old Time Religion/Where Shall I Be (78)	20
58	Brunswick OE 9352	PROFESSOR JOHNSON AND HIS GOSPEL SINGERS (EP)	20

RAY JOHNSON

57	Vogue V 9073	If You Don't Want Me Baby/Calypso Joe	55
57	Vogue V 9073	If You Don't Want Me Baby/Calypso Joe (78)	20
58	Vogue V 9093	Calypso Blues/Are You There	45
58	Vogue V 9093	Calypso Blues/Are You There (78)	20

ROBERT JOHNSON

62	Philips BBL 7539	ROBERT JOHNSON 1936-1937 (LP)	100
65	CBS BPG 62456	KING OF THE DELTA BLUES SINGERS (LP)	45
67	Kokomo K 1000	ROBERT JOHNSON (LP)	80
60s	Smokestack SS/LP 1	BLUES LEGEND 1936-1937 (LP)	50
70	CBS 64102	KING OF THE DELTA BLUES SINGERS VOL. 2 (LP)	30

MINT VALUE £

ROY LEE JOHNSON

69	Action ACT 4518	So Anna Just Love Me/Boogaloo No. 3 (red label)	35
69	Action ACT 4518	So Anna Just Love Me/Boogaloo No. 3 (yellow label)	30

RUBY JOHNSON

67	Stax 601 020	If I Ever Needed Love (I Sure Do Need It Now)/Keep On Keeping On	25

SPIDER JOHNSON & POPEYE BAND

63	Riverside RIF 106904	Doin' The Popeye/The Gospel Truth	5

SYL JOHNSON

(see also Lula Reed)

73	London HL 10403	We Did It/Anyway The Wind Blows	10
73	London HL 10438	Back For A Taste Of Your Love/Wind Blow Her Back My Way	6
75	London HL 10476	Let Yourself Go/Please Don't Give Up On Me	6

T J JOHNSON

83	Switch DSW 003	I Can Make It/Good For You (12")	50

TEDDY JOHNSON & PEARL CARR

57	Pye Nixa NEP 24112	MEET TEDDY & PEARL (EP)	10
64	Columbia SEG 8325	THE ROMANTIC DUETTISTS (EP)	10

THEO JOHNSON

65	Aladdin WI 604	Masters Of War/The Water Is Wide	15

TOMMY JOHNSON

60s	Saydisc SDM 224	THE LEGACY OF TOMMY JOHNSON (LP)	20

WILKO JOHNSON & SOLID SENDERS

(see also Dr. Feelgood, Solid Senders, Ian Dury & Blockheads)

78	Virgin V 2105	SOLID SENDERS (LP, with free LP "Live" [VDJ 26])	12

BRUCE JOHNSTON

77	CBS 5324	(Meet You On A) Rendezvous/I Write The Songs	6
77	CBS 5514	Pipeline/Disney Girls	7
77	CBS 5703	Deirdrie/Thank You Baby	6
77	CBS 61854	GOING PUBLIC (LP, with insert)	20

BRUCE JOHNSTON COMBO

(see also Beach Boys, California Music, Fantastic Baggys, Sagittarius)

63	London HL 9780	Original Surfer Stomp/Pajama Party	55

DANIEL JOHNSTON

92	Seminal Twang TWANG 13	Laurie/The Monster Inside Of Me/Whiz Kid/The Lennon Song (p/s)	10

KEVIN JOHNSTON

74	UK UKR 84	Rock And Roll (I Gave You The Best Years Of My Life)/Life Is What You Make It	5

JOHNSTON BROTHERS

(see also Dennis Lotis, Vera Lynn, Joan Regan, Lita Roza, Suzi Miller, Ted Heath, Keynotes)

54	Decca F 10234	The Creep/Crystal Ball	19
54	Decca F 10286	Oh Baby Mine I Get So Lonely/My Love, My Life, My Own	10
54	Decca F 10302	The Bandit/KEYNOTES: A Dime And A Dollar	15
54	Decca F 10364	Sh-Boom (Life Could Be A Dream)/Crazy 'Bout Ya Baby	15
54	Decca F 10401	Mambo In The Moonlight/Papa Loves Mambo (with Ted Heath Music)	5
54	Decca F 10414	Join In And Sing Medley (both sides)	5
55	Decca F 10451	Majorca/Heartbroken	5
55	Decca F 10490	The Right To Be Wrong/Hot Potato Mambo	5
55	Decca F 10513	Chee Chee-Oo Chee (Sang The Little Bird)Hubble Bubble	5
55	Decca F 10526	Dreamboat/Jim, Johnny And Jonas	5
55	Decca F 10608	Hernando's Hideaway/Hey There	20
55	Decca F 10636	Join In And Sing Again Medley (both sides)	12
56	Decca F 10721	No Other Love/Flowers Mean Forgiveness	12
56	Decca F 10747	How Little We Know/The Street Musician	6
56	Decca F 10781	In The Middle Of The House (with Keynotes)/Stranded In The Jungle	10
56	Decca F 10814	Join In And Sing, No. 3 Medley (both sides)	10
56	Decca F 10828	Give Her My Love (When You Meet Her)/A Rose And A Candy Bar	10
57	Decca F 10860	Whatever Lola Wants (Lola Gets)/Heart	10
57	Decca F 10939	I Like Music - You Like Music/Seven Bar Blues	7
57	Decca F 10962	Join In And Sing, No. 4 Medley (both sides)	5
56	Decca DFE 6249	JOIN THE JOHNSTON BROTHERS (EP)	8
56	Decca DFE 6311	JOIN IN AND SING WITH THE JOHNSTON BROTHERS (EP)	8
57	Decca DFE 6458	JOIN AND SING AGAIN (EP)	8
58	Decca DFE 6503	EASY NO. 1 (EP)	8
58	Decca LK 4266	EASY (LP)	15

JOHNSTONS

(see also Adrienne Johnston)

68	Transatlantic TRA 169	THE JOHNSTONS (LP)	22
68	Transatlantic TRA 184	GIVE A DAMN (LP)	18
68	Transatlantic TRA 185	THE BARLEYCORN (LP)	18
70	Transatlantic TRA 211	BITTER GREEN (LP)	20
71	Transatlantic TRA 231	COLOURS OF THE DAWN (LP)	15
72	Transatlantic TRA 251	IF I SANG MY SONG (LP, gatefold sleeve)	12

JOHN THE POSTMAN

78	Bent BIG BENT 2	PUERILE (12" EP, stamped brown paper bag p/s, with inserts)	12
78	Bent BIG BENT 4	PSYCHEDELIC ROCK'N'ROLL FIVE SKINNERS (12" EP, white label, foldover p/s in bag)	12

JOINER, ARKANSAS, JUNIOR HIGH SCHOOL BAND

60	London HLG 9147	Big Ben/National City	7

MINT VALUE £

JO JO GUNNE (U.K.)

68	Decca F 12807	Every Story Has An End/Should Live Like That	7
69	Decca F 12906	Beggin' You Baby/Bad Penny	7

JO JO GUNNE (U.S.)

(see also Spirit)

72	Asylum AYM 501	Run Run Run/Shake That Fat (withdrawn)	10
72	Asylum AYM 507	Shake That Fat/I Make Love	5
73	Asylum AYM 518	Ready Freddy/Wait A Lifetime	5
73	Asylum AYM 521	Rock Around The Symbol/Take Me Down Easy	5
74	Asylum AYM 528	I Wanna Love You/Neon City	5
74	Asylum AYM 534	Where Is The Show/Single Man	5

JOKER

84	Lost Moment LM 018	Back On The Road/Pusher (p/s)	10

JOKER

(see also Skanna)

93	Skanna 06	The Joker/Roots (12")	40

JOKERS

62	Salvo SLO 1806	Blue Moonbeam/Dog Fight (99 only)	35

JOKER'S WILD

(see also Dave Gilmour, Pink Floyd)

66	Regent Sound RSR 0031	Don't Ask Me/Why Do Fools Fall In Love (handwritten labels, 50 only)	500
66	Regent Sound RSLP 007	JOKER'S WILD: Don't Ask Me/Why Do Fools Fall In Love/You Don't Know What I Know/That's How Strong My Love Is (12", 1-sided, 50 copies only)	1000

JOHN JOLLIFFE

79	Rocket XPRESS 9	Follow The Wind/Dream Love	6

JOLLIVER ARKANSAS

(see also Leslie West, Mountain)

69	Bell SBLL 119	HOME (LP)	30

JOLLY BOYS

70	Moodisc MU 3504	On The Water/MUDIES ALL STARS: Cash Register	15

JOLLY BROTHERS

78	Ballistic FORCE 2002	Conscious Man/PRODIGAL CREATOR: Life (actually dub to Lee Perry's Ne Jah Go Run) (12")	15

JOLT

77	Polydor 2058 936	You're Cold/All I Can Do (p/s)	12
78	Polydor 2059 008	What'cha Gonna Do About It/Again And Again (die-cut p/s)	12
78	Polydor 2059 039	I Can't Wait/Route 66 (p/s)	12
79	Polydor 2229 215	Maybe Tonight/I'm In Tears/See Saw/Stop Look (p/s)	12
79	Polydor 2229 215DJ	Maybe Tonight/See Saw (promo only, no p/s)	12
78	Polydor 2383 504	THE JOLT (LP)	30

JON

(see also Titus Groan, Still Life)

67	Parlophone R 5604	So Much For Mary/Polly Sunday (in p/s)	30
67	Parlophone R 5604	So Much For Mary/Polly Sunday	12
67	Columbia DB 8249	Is It Love/Sing Out	150

JON & ALUN

63	Decca LK 4547	RELAX YOUR MIND (LP, mono)	22
63	Decca SKL 4547	RELAX YOUR MIND (LP, stereo)	30

JON & DAVE

97	Earworm SS 1	Land Beyond The Sun/Instrumental For Silence (p/s, pale green vinyl, 500 copies only)	8

JON & JEANNIE

68	Beacon 3-105	Lover's Holiday/Something You Got	10
69	Beacon BEA 113	Don't Sign The Papers/We Got Lovin'	10

JON & ROBIN & IN-CROWD

67	Stateside SS 2027	Do It Again A Little Bit Slower/If I Need Someone It's You	15

JON & VANGELIS

(see also Jon Anderson, Vangelis)

81	Polydor JV 1	I'll Find My Way Back Home/Back To School	5
81	Polydor POSPX 323	State Of Independence/Beside (12", in blue plastic film canister, promo only)	40
84	Polydor JV 5/POSP 246	State Of Independence/The Friends Of Mr. Cairo/Chariots Of Fire/Eric's Theme (p/s doublepack, stickered shrinkwrapped p/s)	6
81	Polydor POLD 5039	THE FRIENDS OF MR. CAIRO (LP, promo issue with b&w sleeve, raised figures & logo in left corner)	15

JONAH

85	MW MW 7853	Tough/This Is Love (no p/s)	280

JONATHAN & CHARLES

69	Herald LLR 566	ANOTHER WEEK TO GO (LP)	30

JONCUNO(O)

(see Juncuno)

A JONES

04	Jah Tubbys JT 10020	Jah Bless I/MA-KAYA CREW: Iron Dub	25

AL JONES

58	HMV POP 451	Mad, Mad, World/Lonely Traveller	200
58	HMV POP 451	Mad, Mad, World/Lonely Traveller (78)	40

MINT VALUE £

AL JONES
(see also Anderson, Jones, Jackson)
69 Parlophone PMC/PCS 7081 ALUN ASHWORTH JONES (LP, black/yellow label with "Sold in U.K..." text) . . . 150
72 Village Thing VTS 19 JONESVILLE (LP) . . . 140

ALLAN JONES
53 HMV 7M 111 Why Do I Love You/Make Believe . . . 7
53 HMV 7M 135 I Believe/I Talk To The Trees . . . 7
53 HMV 7M 161 Poppa Piccolino/Why? . . . 7

BARBARA JONES
72 Bullet BU 516 Sad Movies/SIR HARRY: Deejay Version . . . 8
74 Count Shelley CS 045 Baby I'm Yours/Don't Turn Your Back On Me . . . 5
74 attack ATT 8077 Changing Partners/Part 2 . . . 6
75 Dip DL 5085 Where Do I Turn/G.G. ALL STARS: Version . . . 5

BETTY HALL JONES
50 Capitol CL 13266 This Joint's Too Hip For Me/You've Got To Have What It Takes (78) . . . 15

BEVERLEY JONES (& PRESTONS)
63 HMV POP 1109 The Boy I Saw With You/When It Comes To Love . . . 12
63 HMV POP 1140 Why Do Lovers Break Each Other's Heart/I'm Just An In-Between . . . 20
63 HMV POP 1201 Wait 'Til My Bobby Gets Home/A Boy Like You . . . 15
64 Parlophone R 5189 Heatwave/Hear You Talking (with Prestons) . . . 25

B-LOU JONES & HIS JUPITERS
61 London HLU 9373 Anchors Aweigh (Parts 1 & 2) . . . 10

BRENDA LEE JONES
(see also Dean & Jean)
75 UK USA 8 You're The Love Of My Life/Thread Your Needle (paper label) . . . 10

BRIAN JONES
(see under Pipes Of Pan, Rolling Stones)

CARMELL JONES
62 Fontana 688 125 ZL BUSINESS MEETIN' (LP) . . . 12

CAROL JONES
60 Triumph RGM 1012 The Boy With The Eyes Of Blue/I Gave Him Back His Ring . . . 125

CASEY JONES & THE ENGINEERS
63 Columbia DB 7083 One Way Ticket/I'm Gonna Love . . . 35

CASEY JONES & THE GOVERNERS
(see also Casey Jones & The Engineers)
64 Golden 12LP 106 DON'T HA HA (LP) . . . 60

CURTIS JONES
66 RCA RCX 7184 R.C.A. VICTOR RACE SERIES VOL. 9 (EP) . . . 15
64 Decca LK 4587 CURTIS JONES IN LONDON (LP) . . . 100
68 Blue Horizon 7-63207 NOW RESIDENT IN EUROPE (LP) . . . 60

DAVEY JONES
65 Philips BF 1410 For Your Love/Love Bug . . . 10

DAVIE JONES & THE KING BEES
(see also David Bowie, Davy Jones, Manish Boys, Calvin James)
64 Vocalion Pop V 9221 Liza Jane/Louie, Louie Go Home (beware of counterfeits without centres) . . . 1000
78 Decca F 13807 Liza Jane/Louie, Louie Go Home (reissue) . . . 25

DAVY JONES (U.K.)
(see also David Bowie)
65 Parlophone R 5315 You've Got A Habit Of Leaving/Baby Loves That Way . . . 800

DAVY JONES (U.K.) & THE LOWER THIRD/MANISH BOYS
(see also David Bowie, Davie Jones & King Bees, Manish Boys, Calvin James)
79 EMI EMI 2925 You've Got A Habit Of Leaving/Baby Loves That Way/MANISH BOYS: I Pity The Fool/Take My Tip (p/s) . . . 12
82 Charly CYM 1 You've Got A Habit Of Leaving/Baby Loves That Way/MANISH BOYS: I Pity The Fool/Take My Tip (10", p/s) . . . 20

DAVY JONES (U.K.)
(see also Davy Jones & Micky Dolenz, Monkees)
65 Colpix PX 784 What Are We Going To Do/This Bouquet . . . 8
67 Pye 7N 17302 It Ain't Me Babe/Baby It's Me (in p/s) . . . 10
67 Pye 7N 17302 It Ain't Me Babe/Baby It's Me . . . 5
67 Pye 7N 17380 Theme For A New Love/Dream Girl (in p/s) . . . 10
67 Pye 7N 17380 Theme For A New Love/Dream Girl . . . 5
67 Pye International 7N 25432 Theme For A New Love/Dream Girl (reissue, withdrawn) . . . 20
71 Bell BLL 1163 Rainy Jane/Welcome To My Love . . . 5
77 MCA MCA 348 Life Line/It's A Jungle Out There/Gotta Get Up (from 'The Point') (p/s, last track with Micky Dolenz) . . . 5
78 Warner Bros K 17161 (Hey Ra Ra) Happy Birthday Mickey Mouse/You Don't Have To Be A Country Boy To Sing A Country Song (p/s) . . . 5
83 J.J. 2001 I'll Love You Forever/When I Look Back On Christmas . . . 12
67 Pye NPL 18178 DAVY JONES (LP) . . . 20

DAVY JONES (U.K.) & MICKY DOLENZ
(see also Monkees, Davey Jones)
71 Bell BLL 986 Do It In The Name Of Love/Lady Jane . . . 12

DAVY JONES (U.S.)
(see also Thelonious Monk)
60 Pye 7N 15254 Amapola/Mighty Man . . . 10
61 Pye 7N 15318 Shenandoah/Scenery . . . 25

MINT VALUE £

61 Pye International 7N 25072 Model Girl/Scarlet Woman ... 12
61 Pye International 7N 25095 Bonnie Banks/Baby Baby ... 10
62 Piccadilly 7N 35038 Jezebel/Don't Come Crying To Me ... 10

DILL JONES TRIO

56 Jazz Today JTE 104 PIANO MOODS VOL. 2 (EP) ... 25
56 Pye Jazz NJE 1024 PIANO MOODS VOL. 5 (EP) ... 25
57 Columbia SEG 7764 TOP OF THE POLL (EP) ... 10
59 Columbia SEG 7893 DILL JONES PLUS FOUR (EP) ... 8
60 Columbia 33SX 1336 JONES THE JAZZ (LP) ... 60

DOROTHY JONES

(see also Cookies)

61 Philips 322 794 BF Takin' That Long Walk Home/It's Unbearable ... 30

GARY JONES

62 Piccadilly 7N 35084 It's Over/Little Miss Nose In The Air ... 8

GEORGE JONES

(see also Gene Pitney, Elvis Costello)

59 Mercury AMT 1021 The Treasure Of Love/If I Don't Love You (Grits Ain't Groceries) ... 20
59 Mercury AMT 1021 The Treasure Of Love/If I Don't Love You (Grits Ain't Groceries) (78) ... 10
59 Mercury AMT 1036 White Lightning/Long Time To Forget ... 50
59 Mercury AMT 1058 Who Shot Sam/Into My Arms Again ... 30
59 Mercury AMT 1078 Big Harlan Taylor/Money To Burn ... 15
60 Mercury AMT 1100 Sparkling Brown Eyes/Accidentally On Purpose ... 15
61 Mercury AMT 1124 Candy Hearts/The Window Up Above ... 15
62 United Artists POP 1037 She Thinks I Still Care/Geronimo ... 15
63 United Artists UP 1015 I Saw Me/Not What I Had In Mind (as George Jones with Jones Boys) ... 10
64 United Artists UP 1044 Your Heart Turned Left (And I Was On The Right)/My Tears Are Overdue ... 10
65 United Artists UP 1080 The Race Is On/She's So Lonesome Again ... 15
69 Stateside SS 2145 If My Heart Had Windows/Taggin' Along ... 8
71 Pye International 7N 25547 It's Been A Good Year For The Roses/Let A Little Come In ... 7
80 Epic EPC 8560 Stranger In The House (with Elvis Costello)/A Drunk Can't Be A Man (p/s) ... 6
59 Mercury ZEP 10036 GEORGE JONES (EP) ... 100
60s Melodisc EPM7 109 COUNTRY SONG HITS (EP) ... 40
64 Mercury 10009 MCE C & W ACES (EP) ... 20
64 Ember EMB 4548 THE BEST OF AMERICAN COUNTRY MUSIC VOL. 4 (EP) ... 15
62 United Artists ULP 1007 THE NEW FAVOURITES OF GEORGE JONES (LP) ... 20
63 United Artists ULP 1014 MY FAVOURITES OF HANK WILLIAMS (LP) ... 20
63 Ember CW 101 THE CROWN PRINCE OF COUNTRY MUSIC (LP, original pressings have grey & orange label) ... 20
63 United Artists ULP 1037 HITS OF HIS COUNTRY COUSINS (LP) ... 15
64 United Artists ULP 1050 I WISH TONIGHT WOULD NEVER END (LP) ... 15
64 London HA-B 8125 GEORGE JONES SINGS HIS GREATEST HITS (LP) ... 15
64 United Artists ULP 1070 WHAT'S IN OUR HEARTS (LP, with Melba Montgomery) ... 18
64 Ember CW 109 THE FABULOUS COUNTRY MUSIC SOUND OF JONES (LP, original pressings have grey & orange label) ... 15
65 Stateside SL 10147 GEORGE JONES AND GENE PITNEY (LP, with Gene Pitney) ... 18
66 Stateside SL 10173 IT'S COUNTRY TIME AGAIN (LP, with Gene Pitney) ... 15

GEORGE JONES/JIMMIE SKINNER

59 Mercury ZEP 10012 COUNTRY AND WESTERN (EP, 2 tracks each) ... 30

GLORIA JONES

(see also Marc Bolan & Gloria Jones)

66 Capitol CL 15429 Heartbeat (Parts 1 & 2) ... 45
66 Stateside SS 555 Finders Keepers/Run One Flight Of Stairs ... 70
74 Tamla Motown TMG 910 Tin Can People/So Tired ... 10
76 EMI EMI 2437 Get It On/Get It On (Version) ... 6
76 EMI EMI 2522 I Ain't Going Nowhere/Simplicity Blues ... 10
77 EMI EMI 2570 Go Now/Drive Me Crazy ... 6
77 EMI EMI 2720 Bring On The Love/Cry Baby ... 6
74 Tamla Motown STML 11254 SHARE MY LOVE (LP) ... 25
76 EMI EMC 3159 VIXEN (LP) ... 20

GRANDPA JONES

(see also Brown's Ferry Four)

57 Brunswick 05676 Eight More Miles To Louisville/Dark As A Dungeon ... 25
59 Brunswick OE 9455 MOUNTAIN MUSIC VOL. 3 (EP) ... 15
57 Parlophone GEP 8666 MEET GRANDPA JONES (EP) ... 20
58 Parlophone GEP 8766 COUNTRY AND WESTERN (EP) ... 15
59 Parlophone GEP 8781 COUNTRY ROUND UP (EP) ... 15
64 London RE-U 1417 GRANDPA SINGS JIMMIE RODGERS (EP) ... 15
62 London HA-U/SH-U 8010 MAKES THE RAFTERS RING (LP) ... 25
64 London HA-U/SH-U 8119 YODELLING HITS (LP) ... 25

HUW JONES

69 Welsh Teldisc WD 912 Y Ffoadur/Dewch I Ganu (La, La, La) (p/s) ... 10
69 Sain SAIN 1 Dwr/Fy Ngwlad Fy Hun ... 20
70 Sain SAIN 3 Paid Digalonni/Ffoi (p/s) ... 10

INDIGO JONES

70 Columbia DB 8744 Noel Highway/Prodigal Son ... 12

JACK JONES

62 London HLR 9525 Lillipops And Roses/Julie ... 5
63 London HLR 9806 Wives And Lovers/Toys In The Attic ... 5
65 London HLR 9956 The Race Is On/I Can't Believe I'm Losing You ... 5
79 Polydor POSP 92 The Love Boat/Wives And Lovers ... 6
58 Capitol CL 14969 Laffin' At Me/Deeply Devoted ... 10

MINT VALUE £

JAKE JONES

71	MCA MVPS 432	JAKE JONES (LP)	25

JANET JONES

74	Midas MR 005	SING TO ME LADY (LP)	200
74	Midas MFHR 059	JANET JONES (LP, released on Folk Heritage label)	200

JANIE JONES (& LASH)

(see also The Clash, Janie)

65	HMV POP 1495	Witches Brew/Take-A My Tip	20
66	HMV POP 1514	Gunning For You/Go Go Away From Me	15
67	Columbia DB 8173	Tickle Me Tootsie Wootsies/High And Dry	12
68	Pye 7N 17550	Charlie Smith/Nobody's Perfect	10
68	Major Minor MM 577	The Girl's Song/I've Never Met A Boy Like You	10
70	President PT 309	Back On My Feet Again/Psycho	10
83	Big Beat NS 91	House Of The Ju-Ju Queen/Sex Machine (as Janie Jones & Lash, p/s)	6

JERRY JONES

70	Banana BA 316	Still Waters (Love)/SOUND DIMENSION: Wig Wam	18
71	Bamboo BAM 65	Still Waters (Love)/SOUND DIMENSION: Wig Wam (reissue)	15
71	Bamboo BALPS 213	LIVE AT THE KINGSTON HOTEL, JAMAICA (LP)	50

JIMMY JONES

60	MGM MGM 1051	Handy Man/The Search Is Over	7
60	MGM MGM 1051	Handy Man/The Search Is Over (78)	80
60	MGM MGM 1078	Good Timin'/Too Long Will Be Too Late	7
60	MGM MGM 1078	Good Timin'/Too Long Will Be Too Late (78)	80
60	MGM MGM 1091	I Just Go For You/That's When I Cried	12
60	MGM MGM 1103	Ready For Love/For You	15
61	MGM MGM 1123	I Told You So/You Got It	15
61	MGM MGM 1133	Dear One/I Say Love	12
61	MGM MGM 1146	Mr Music Man/Holler Hey	15
62	MGM MGM 1168	You're Much Too Young/Nights Of Mexico	12
65	Columbia DB 7592	Walkin'/Pardon Me	30
65	Cameo Parkway P 988	Don't You Just Know It	15
67	Stateside SS 2041	39-21-46/Personal Property	18
60	MGM MGM-EP 745	JIMMY HANDYMAN JONES (EP)	60
61	MGM MGM-EP 787	ORIGINAL HITS (EP)	40
60	MGM MGM-C 832	GOOD TIMIN' (LP)	75

JO JONES TRIO

59	Top Rank 25/039	JO JONES (LP)	18

JOE JONES

60	Columbia DB 4533	You Talk Too Much/I Love You Still	15

JOHN PAUL JONES

(see also Led Zeppelin, Tony Meehan, Andrew Oldham Orchestra)

64	Pye 7N 15637	Baja/A Foggy Day In Vietnam (B-side by Andrew Oldham Orchestra, white label promo)	150
64	Pye 7N 15637	Baja/A Foggy Day In Vietnam (B-side actually by Andrew Oldham Orchestra)	150
99	DGM DGMJPJ 1	ZOOMA (CD, advance promo 4-track sampler)	8

JOHNNY JONES & KING CASUALS

68	MCA MU 1031	Soul Poppin'/Blues For The Brothers	20
76	Cream CRM 5004	Purple Haze/Horsing Around	15
76	Brunswick BR 37	Purple Haze/FRED HUGHES: Baby Boy	10
80	Sonet SNTF 821	JOHNNY JONES WITH BILLY BOY ARNOLD (LP)	12

JONAH JONES (QUARTET)

58	Capitol CL 14939	Night Train/Lots Of Luck Charley	7
59	Capitol 15085	I Dig Chicks/Cherry	5
62	Ember JBS 704	Down By The Riverside/Stars Fell On Alabama	7

JUSTIN JONES

61	London HLU 9463	Dance By Yourself/Love	150

KEN JONES (& HIS ROCK'N'ROLLERS)

60	Parlophone R 4628	Two Way Stretch/Paper Chase	8
61	Parlophone R 4763	Bluesville/On The Rebound	7
61	Parlophone R 4788	Joxville/Just Rollin'	6
58	Embassy WEP 1004	ROCK'N'ROLL TIME (EP, as Ken Jones & His Rock'n'Rollers)	15

KENNEY JONES

(see also Small Faces, Faces, Who)

74	GM GMS 027	Ready Or Not/Woman Trouble	8

LESLIE JONES

59	Pye NSEP 85004	FOUR FARNON FAVOURITES (EP, stereo)	10
59	Pye NSPL 83008/9	THE MUSIC OF ROBERT FARNON (2-LP)	20

LINDA JONES

67	Warner Bros WB 2070	Hypnotised/I Can't Stop Lovin' My Baby	50
72	London HLU 10368	For Your Precious Love/Don't Go	15
75	Warner Bros WB 16621	I Just Can't Live My Life/My Heart Will Understand	20

LINDA JONES/J.J. JACKSON

77	Loma/Warners K 56271	THIS IS LOMA - VOL. 7 (LP, 1 side each)	15

LLOYD JONES

70	Bullet BU 429	Rome/RHYTHM RULERS: Version	30

LOUIS JONES ROCK & ROLL BAND

50s	Vogue VE1 70111	ROCK AND ROLL (EP)	100

MINT VALUE £

MAGGIE JONES

70	VJM VLP 23	COLUMBIA RECORDINGS IN CHRONOLOGICAL ORDER VOL. 1 (LP)	15
70	VJM VLP 25	COLUMBIA RECORDINGS IN CHRONOLOGICAL ORDER VOL. 2 (LP)	15

NIC JONES

(see also Jon Raven, Halliard)

70	Trailer LER 2014	BALLADS AND SONGS (LP, white label)	50
70	Trailer LER 2014	BALLADS AND SONGS (LP, red label)	40
70	Trailer LER 2014	BALLADS AND SONGS (LP, later pressing with 'highway' label)	15
71	Trailer LER 2027	NIC JONES (LP, red label)	35
77	Trailer LER 2091	NOAH'S ARK TRAP (LP)	35
77	Trailer LER 2019	NOAH'S ARK TRAP (LP, reissue with Highway label)	15
78	Transatlantic LTRA 507	FROM THE DEVIL TO A STRANGER (LP)	30
80	Topic 12TS 411	PENGUIN EGGS (LP)	30

NIGEL MAZLYN JONES

76	Isle Of Light IOL 666/1	SHIP TO SHORE (LP)	50
78	Avada AVA 105	SENTINEL (LP, with inner sleeve, b/w picture label)	20
82	Isle Of Light IOL 0230	BREAKING COVER (LP)	20
91	Isle Of Light 1OL 0232 LP	MAZLYN JONES (LP)	20

PALMER JONES

68	Direction 58-3603	The Great Magic Of Love/Dancing Master	25

PATSY JONES

67	RCA 1600	Colours Of Love/There's A time And Place For Everything	7

PAUL JONES

(see also Manfred Mann, Blues Band)

66	HMV POP 1554	High Time/I Can't Hold On Much Longer	5
67	HMV POP 1576	I've Been A Bad Bad Boy/Sonny Boy Williamson	5
67	HMV POP 1602	Thinkin' Ain't For Me/Softly (La Vita)	5
67	HMV PSR 5307	Privilege (1-sided demo)	20
67	Columbia DB 8303	Sons And Lovers/Three Sisters	8
68	Columbia DB 8379	And The Sun Will Shine/The Dog Presides	15
68	Columbia DB 8417	When I Was Six Years Old/You Have No Idea	10
68	Columbia DB 8514	Aquarius/Pisces	6
69	Columbia DB 8567	It's Getting Better/Not Before Time	8
71	Vertigo 6059 053	Life After Death/The Mighty Ship	8
73	Philips 6006 282	Perfect Roadie/Mouth Organ	6
78	RSO RSO 003	Sheena Is A Punk Rocker/Pretty Vacant (p/s)	5
67	HMV 7EG 8974	PRIVILEGE (EP)	20
66	HMV CLP 3586	MY WAY (LP, mono)	25
66	HMV CSD 3586	MY WAY (LP, stereo)	30
67	HMV CLP 3602	LOVE ME, LOVE MY FRIENDS (LP, mono)	25
67	HMV CSD 3602	LOVE ME, LOVE MY FRIENDS (LP, stereo)	30
67	HMV CLP/CSD 3623	PRIVILEGE (LP, soundtrack, with George Bean Group & Mike Leander)	40
69	Columbia SX/SCX 6347	COME INTO MY MUSIC BOX (LP, mono/stereo)	18
71	Vertigo 6360 059	CRUCIFIX IN A HORSESHOE (LP, gatefold sleeve, swirl label)	70
70	President PTLS 1068	DRAKE'S DREAM (LP, soundtrack)	25

POPPA JONES

66	Parlophone R 5404	Birthday Cake Walk/The Street Parade	6

QUINCY JONES

(see also Annie Ross, Eddie Barclay & Quincy Jones, Diana Ross & Quincy Jones, John & Joan Shakespeare)

62	Mercury AMT 1195	Soul Bossa Nova/On The Street Where You Live	20
65	Mercury MF 844	Seaweed/Golden Boy Theme	5
69	RCA RCA 1850	MacKenna's Gold/Soul Full Of Gold	5
70	A&M AMS 781	Killer Joe/Oh Happy Day	5
72	A&M AMS 888	Ironside/Cast Your Fate To The Wind	5
72	Reprise K 14150	Money Runned	8
72	Atlantic K 10172	Listen To The Melody/Hot Rock Theme	5
60	Mercury ZEP 10047	BIG BAND BASH (EP)	10
61	Mercury ZEP 10109	THE BIRTH OF A BAND (EP, mono)	10
61	Mercury SEZ 19017	THE BIRTH OF A BAND (EP, stereo)	15
61	Columbia SEG 8088	DOUBLE SIX MEET QUINCY JONES (EP)	12
61	Mercury ZEP 10119	THE BIRTH OF A BAND PT. 2 (EP, mono)	10
61	Mercury SEZ 19021	THE BIRTH OF A BAND PT. 2 (EP, stereo)	12
60	Mercury MMC 14038	THE BIRTH OF A BAND (LP, mono)	12
60	Mercury CMS 18026	THE BIRTH OF A BAND (LP, stereo)	15
60	Mercury MMC 14046	THE GREAT WORLD OF QUINCY JONES (LP, mono)	12
60	Mercury CMS 18031	THE GREAT WORLD OF QUINCY JONES (LP, stereo)	15
61	Mercury MMC 14080	I DIG DANCERS (LP, also stereo CMS 18055)	15
62	HMV CLP 1581	THE QUINTESSENCE (LP, also stereo CSD 1452)	15
62	Mercury MMC 14098	AROUND THE WORLD (LP, also stereo CMS 18064)	15
63	Mercury MMC 14125	BIG BAND BOSSA NOVA (LP, also stereo CMS 18080)	15
63	Mercury MMC 14128	PLAYS HIP HITS (LP)	15
64	Mercury MCL 20016	EXPLORES THE MUSIC OF HENRY MANCINI (LP, also stereo SMCL 20016)	15
65	Columbia 33SX 1637	QUINCY'S HOME AGAIN (LP)	15
65	Mercury 20047 MCL	GOLDEN BOY (LP)	15
65	Mercury 20063 SMCL	THE PAWNBROKER (LP, soundtrack)	30
66	Mercury 20072 (S)MCL	MIRAGE (LP, soundtrack)	25
66	Mercury 20073 (S)MCL	PLAYS FOR PUSSYCATS (LP)	15
66	Mercury 20078 (S)MCL	QUINCY'S GOT A BRAND NEW BAG (LP)	15
66	Fontana FJL 127	FAB! (LP)	15
67	Mercury SMWL 30003	TRAVELLIN' ON THE QUINCY JONES BANDWAGON (LP)	15
68	RCA Victor RD/SF 7931	IN COLD BLOOD (LP, soundtrack)	15
68	United Artists (S)ULP 1181	IN THE HEAT OF THE NIGHT (LP, soundtrack, with Ray Charles)	25
69	Uni UNLS 103	LOST MAN (LP, soundtrack)	25

			MINT VALUE £
69	Paramount SPFL 256	THE ITALIAN JOB (LP, soundtrack, with Matt Monro)	100
69	RCA Victor SF 8017	MACKENNA'S GOLD (LP, soundtrack, with Jose Feliciano)	12
70	United Artists UAS 29128	THEY CALL ME MISTER TIBBS (LP, soundtrack)	60
71	A&M AMLS 63037	SMACKWATER JACK (LP)	12
72	WEA K 44168	THE HEIST (LP, soundtrack, with Little Richard)	15
72	Atlantic K 40371	HOW TO STEAL A DIAMOND IN FOUR UNEASY LESSONS (LP, soundtrack)	15

RICK JONES

72	Argo AFW106	Theme From The Aeronauts/Lovebug	10
73	Argo ZDA 156	HIYA MAYA (LP)	15

ROBIN JONES & HIS QUINTET

71	Apollo Sound APPS 5012	DENGA (LP)	40
71	Apollo Sound	EL MAJA (LP)	50

RONNIE JONES

(see also Night-Timers)

64	Decca F 12012	Let's Pin A Rose On You/I Need Your Loving (B-side with Night Timers)	20
65	Decca F 12066	My Love/It's All Over	20
65	Decca F 12146	Anyone Who Knows What Love Is/Nobody But You	20
65	Parlophone R 5326	You're Lookin' Good/I'm So Clean (with Blue Jays)	40
67	CBS 2699	Little Bitty Pretty One/Put Your Tears Away	18
67	Polydor 56222	In My Love Mind/Mama Come On Home	15
68	CBS 3304	Without Love (There Is Nothing)/Little Bitty Pretty One	12

SALENA JONES

66	Columbia DB 7818	A Walk In The Black Forest (Our Walk Of Love)/As Long As I Live	7
66	Columbia DB 7991	I Am Yours/I Only Know I Love You	7
67	Columbia DB 8212	When I Tell You (That I Love You)/Respect	8
67	Decca F 12708	I've Got The Blues/The Glory Of Love	25
70	CBS 4767	This Is Love/Everybodys Talkin'	6
73	Indigo GOPOP	Live And Let Die/Some Other World (in p/s)	15
73	Indigo GOPOP	Live And Let Die/Some Other World	6
75	DJM DJS 381	In Love Like You And Me/Tell It Like It Is	6
69	CBS 63613	THE MOMENT OF TRUTH (LP)	35
70	CBS 63901	EVERYBODY'S TALKIN' ABOUT SALENA JONES (LP)	35
73	RCA Victor SF 8335	ALONE & TOGETHER (LP)	20
74	RCA LPL 1 5025	THIS'N'THAT (LP)	20
71	CBS 64435	PLATINUM (LP)	25

SALINA JONES

65	Polydor 56012	Longing/Too Late	7

SAM JONES

60	Riverside 12-324	SOUL SOCIETY (LP)	20

SAMANTHA JONES

(see also Vernons Girls, Krimson Kake)

65	United Artists UP 1072	It's All Because Of You/I Woke Up Crying	15
65	United Artists UP 1087	Don't Come Any Closer/Just Call And I'll Be There	15
65	United Artists UP 1105	Chained To A Memory/Just For Him	10
66	United Artists UP 1139	That Special Way/Somebody Else's Baby	10
67	United Artists UP 1185	Surrounded By A Ray Of Sunshine/How Do You Say Goodbye	80
67	United Artists UP 1185	Surrounded By A Ray Of Sunshine/How Do You Say Goodbye (DJ Copy)	150
67	United Artists UP 1200	Why Can't I Remember/Live For Life	8
68	United Artists UP 2248	Lonely Lonely Man/Doll On A Music Box	10
68	United Artists UP 2258	And Suddenly/Go Ahead And Love Me	50
80	Ford SLE 19	Ford Leads The Way/Go Ahead And Love Me (p/s, Ford cars promo disc)	25
69	Penny Farthing PEN 703	Today (Without You)/The Feelin' That I Get	10
69	Penny Farthing PEN 708	Do I Still Figure In Your Life?/I'm Sorry, But I Think I Love You	10
70	Penny Farthing PEN 734	My Way/Darling Be Home Soon	10
70	Penny Farthing PEN 746	Best Of Both Worlds/Guilty Of Loving You	10
68	United Artists	CALL IT SAMANTHA (LP)	25
72	Contour 2870 003	MY WAY (LP)	15

SAMMY JONES

70	Gas GAS 123	You're My Girl/HONEYBOY MARTIN: Unchained Melody	10
72	Sioux SI 002	Mendicino/RUM RUNNERS: Sugar Brown	5
72	Sioux SI 003	Little Caesar/TWINKLE BROTHERS: Happy Song	5
72	Sioux SI 011	You're My Girl/HONEYBOY MARTIN: Unchained Melody	8

SANDIE JONES

72	Polydor 2058 223	Music Of Love/Ceol An Ghra	12

SOLOMON JONES

70	Bullet BU 452	Be Strong/Version	5
70	Pama PM 812	Here Comes The Night/RECO RODRIQUEZ: Jaded Ramble	8

SPIKE JONES

53	HMV 7M 121	Hot Lips/Hotter Than A Pistol (as Spike Jones & His Country Cousins)	10
53	HMV 7M 160	I Saw Mommy Kissing Santa Claus/Winter (as Spike Jones & His City Slickers)	10
54	HMV 7MC 3	Deep Purple/Dragnet (as Spike Jones & His City Slickers, export issue)	10
54	HMV 7MC 17	I Wanna Go Back To West Virginia/Little Bo-Peep Has Lost Her Sheep (as Spike Jones & His City Slickers, export issue)	10
55	HMV 7M 324	Secret Love/I'm In The Mood For Love (as Spike Jones & His City Slickers)	10
61	Warner Bros WB 34	Monster Movie Babe/Teenage Brain Surgeon	6
57	HMV 7EG 8286	FUN IN HI FI (EP)	10
59	RCA RCX 1030	SPIKE JONES NO. 1 (EP)	10
59	RCA RCX 1037	SPIKE JONES NO. 2 (EP)	10
60	London HAG 2270	OMNIBUST (LP)	15
60	Warner Brothers WM 4004	IN HI-FI (LP)	15
60	Warner Bros. EB 8004	SPIKE JONES IN STEREO (LP)	20
61	London SAHG 6109	SIXTY YEARS OF MUSIC AMERICA HATES BEST (LP)	15

MINT VALUE £

STAN JONES

58	Pye Disneyland DPL 39000	CREAKIN' LEATHER (LP)	15

STEVE JONES

(see also Sex Pistols, Professionals)

87	MCA MCA 1184	Mercy/Through The Night (p/s)	5
89	MCA MCAT 1371	Freedom Fighter/Gimme Love/Suffragette City (12", p/s)	6
87	MCA MCF 3384	MERCY (LP)	12

STEVE JONES (2)

84	P flight PFD 01	I Need You (12")	80

TAMIKO JONES

76	Contempo CX 15	Let It Flow/DORIS DUKE: Woman Of The Ghetto	5

THAD JONES

58	Nixa Jazz NJL 13	LEONARD FEATHER PRESENTS MAD THAD (LP, with others)	15

THELMA JONES

68	Sue WI 4047	Stronger/Never Leave Me	50
69	Soul City SC 110	The House That Jack Built/Give It To Me Straight	30
76	CBS 4711	Salty Tears/You're The Song	15

THUNDERCLAP JONES

56	Oriole CB 1320	Hurricane Boogie/The Laughing Rag (78)	12
56	Oriole CB 1328	Sound Barrier Boogie/Ask For Joe (78)	12

TOM JONES

64	Decca F 11966	Chills And Fever/Breathless	60
65	Columbia DB 7566	Little Lonely One/That's What We'll All Do	20
65	Decca F 12191	With These Hands/Untrue	5
65	Decca F 12203	What's New Pussycat?/Rose	6
65	Columbia DB 7733	Lonely Joe/I Was A Fool	20
65	Decca F 12292	Thunderball/Key To My Heart	10
66	Decca F 12315	To Make A Big Man Cry/I'll Never Let You Go (export issue)	10
66	Decca F 12349	Stop Breaking My Heart/Never Give Away Love	10
66	Decca F 12390	Once There Was A Time/Not Responsible	6
66	Decca F 12461	This And That/City Girl	15
66	Decca F 12516	Green, Green Grass Of Home/If I Had You (export issue)	5
67	Decca F 22555	Detroit City/If I Had You	5
67	Decca F 22563	Detroit City/Ten Guitars (export issue)	10
68	Decca F 12854	A Minute Of Your Time/Looking Out My Window	15
71	Decca FR 13236	Till//The Sun Died (export issue)	5
71	Decca FR 13237	Till/One Day Soon (export issue)	10
65	Columbia SEG 8464	TOM JONES (EP)	20
65	Decca DFE 8668	WHAT A PARTY (EP)	15

U.K. JONES

(see also Mike Berry)

69	Deram DM 231	Let Me Tell Ya/And The Rains Came Down	15
70	Ember EMB S 298	Take Me For What I Am/Love Is Here To Stay	6

VIVIAN JONES

79	White Rum/ Red Stripe 101 PROOF	Jah Music/Vibes (as V. Jones)	10
87	Jah Shaka SHAKA 861	JAH WORKS (LP)	15

WINSTON JONES

73	Gayfeet GS 208	You Make Me Cry/Version	6

WIZZ JONES

(see also Pete Stanley & Wizz Jones, Accolade)

69	United Artists (S)ULP 1209	WIZZ JONES (LP)	150
70	Village Thing VTS 4	LEGENDARY ME (LP)	100
72	CBS 64809	RIGHT NOW (LP)	100
74	Village Thing VTS 24	WHEN I LEAVE BERLIN (LP)	90
77	Plant Life PLR 009	MAGICAL FLIGHT (LP, with insert)	25

JONES BOYS

(see also Four Jones Boys)

57	Columbia DB 4046	Cool Baby/Rock-A-Hula Baby (Ukulele Lady)	15
58	Columbia DB 4170	A Certain Smile/Kathy-O	5
58	Columbia DB 4217	The Day The Rains Came/Hideaway	5
59	Columbia DB 4278	Dream Girl/Straight As An Arrow	6

JONES BROTHERS

69	Pye Intl. 7N 25696	Lucky Lady/Good Old Days	120

JONES GIRLS

82	Philadelphia Intl. PIR 2031	Nights Over Egypt/Love Don't Ever Say Goodbye	8
82	Phil. Intl. PIR 12-2031	Nights Over Egypt/Love Don't Ever Say Goodbye (12")	15
79	Phil. Intl. PIR 83831	THE JONES GIRLS (LP)	15

JONESY

(see also Alan Bown, Ray Thomas)

73	Dawn DNS 1030	Ricochet/Every Day's The Same	20
72	Dawn DNLS 3042	NO ALTERNATIVE (LP, gatefold sleeve)	60
73	Dawn DNLS 3048	KEEPING UP (LP, with lyric insert, lilac label)	70
73	Dawn DNLS 3048	KEEPING UP (LP, without lyric insert, lilac label)	50
73	Dawn DNLS 3055	GROWING (LP, gatefold sleeve, with lyric insert, pink 'sun' label)	65
73	Dawn DNLS 3055	GROWING (LP, gatefold sleeve, without lyric insert, pink 'sun' label)	50

JONIE D

89	Positive Beat PBEP 001	WHICH BASE (EP)	15

MINT VALUE £

HARLEM JONNS RESHUFFLE

68	Fontana TF 970	You Are The One I Love/Good Lovin'	30
69	Fontana TF 1004	Everything Under The Sun/Let Love Come Between Us	20
69	Fontana (S)TL 5509	HARLEM JONNS RESHUFFLE (LP)	40

JONSTON McPHILBRY

66	Fontana TF 663	She's Gone/Woke Up At Eight	90

JOOK

(see also John's Children, Sparks)

72	RCA RCA 2279	Alright With Me/Do What You Can	15
73	RCA RCA 2344	Shame/City And Suburban Blues	12
73	RCA RCA 2368	Oo-Oo-Rudi/Jook's On You	15
73	RCA RCA 2431	King Capp/Rumble	12
74	RCA RCA 5024	Bish Bash Bosh/Crazy Kids	12
78	Chiswick SW 30	Watch Your Step/La La Girl/Aggravation Place/ Everything I Do (EP)	5

JANIS JOPLIN

(see also Big Brother & Holding Company)

69	CBS 3683	Turtle Blues/Piece Of My Heart (withdrawn)	30
71	CBS 7019	Me And Bobby McGee/Half Moon	6
71	CBS 7217	Cry Baby/Mercedes Benz	6
71	CBS 9136	Move Over/Cry Baby/Try/Piece Of My Heart (maxi-single)	8
72	CBS 8241	Down On Me/Bye Bye Baby	6
76	CBS 3960	Piece Of My Heart/Kozmic Blues (p/s)	7
69	CBS 63546	I GOT DEM OL' KOZMIC BLUES AGAIN, MAMA! (LP)	25
74	CBS CQ 30322/Q 64188	PEARL (LP, quadrophonic)	25

DANNY JORDAN

61	Mercury AMT 1159	Jeannie/Boom Ditty Boom	10

DICK JORDAN

(see also Don Duke)

60	Embassy WB 384	Let It Be Me/Running Bear (78)	10
60	Embassy WB 394	Cathy's Clown/Don't Throw All Those Teardrops (78)	10
60	Oriole CB 1534	Hallelujah, I Love Her So/Sandy	50
60	Oriole CB 1534	Hallelujah, I Love Her So/Sandy (78)	30
60	Oriole CB 1548	Little Christine/I'll Love You Forever	35
60	Oriole CB 1548	Little Christine/I'll Love You Forever (78)	30
60	Oriole CB 1566	Garden Of Eden/Alive, Alive Oh!	10
60	Oriole CB 1591	Angel On My Shoulder/The Next Train Home	15
61	Piccadilly 7N 35035	Some Of These Days/I Want Her Back	75
62	Piccadilly 7N 35057	Fortune Teller/My Angel	10
63	Columbia DB 7016	Stop The Music/Dream Chaser	10
66	Parlophone R5475	Progress/Something's Going On In There	25

EARL JORDAN

72	Sovereign SVN 6501	JORDAN (LP, textured sleeve with flipbacks)	60

FRED JORDAN

66	Topic 12T 150	SONGS OF A SHROPSHIRE FARM WORKER (LP, blue label)	15

JACK JORDAN - HIS MUSIC

60	Parlophone R 4677	Golden Girl/Beauty And The Beach	7

LOUIS JORDAN & CHRIS BARBER'S BAND

(see also Chris Barber)

63	Melodisc 45-1616	Is She Is Or Is She Ain't Your Baby/Fifty Cents	18

LOUIS JORDAN (& HIS TYMPANY FIVE)

(see also Louis Armstrong)

54	Melodisc 1031	Dad Gum Ya Hide Boy/Whiskey Do Your Stuff (78)	15
56	Melodisc 1349	Messy Bessy/I Seen What'cha Done (78)	20
60	Downbeat CHA 3	Ooo-Wee/I'll Die Happy	20
50s	Melodisc EPM7 66	LOUIS JORDAN (EP, as Louis Jordan Tympany Five, 3 different sleeves)	90
57	Mercury MPT 7521	SOMEBODY UP THERE DIGS ME (10" LP, with Tympany Five)	100
58	Mercury MPL 6541	MAN, WE'RE WAILIN' (LP, with Tympany Five)	50
64	HMV CLP 1809	HALLELUJAH, LOUIS JORDAN IS BACK (LP)	40

JORDANAIRES

(see also Elvis Presley, Patsy Cline, Don Gibson, Marty Robbins)

57	Capitol CL 14687	Sugaree/Baby, Won't You Please Come Home?	80
57	Capitol CL 14687	Sugaree/Baby, Won't You Please Come Home? (78)	15
57	Capitol CL 14773	Summer Vacation/Each Day	20
57	Capitol CL 14773	Summer Vacation/Each Day (78)	18
58	Capitol CL 14921	Little Miss Ruby/All I Need Is You	25
63	Capitol CL 15281	Don't Be Cruel/Don't Worry	18
71	Ember EMB S 313	Kentucky/Teach The World To Sing	6
62	Capitol T 1742	SPOTLIGHT ON THE JORDANAIRES (LP)	65

JORDAN BROTHERS

59	London HLW 8908	Never, Never/Please Tell Me Now	30
59	London HLW 8908	Never, Never/Please Tell Me Now (78)	25
60	London HLW 9235	Things I Didn't Say/Polly Plays Her Kettle Drum	10
61	London HLW 9308	No Wings On My Angel/Living For The Day	10

JORGE

69	Aurora 7984	Everybody Wants To Be Loved/Tic Tac Toe	10

JOSEF K

(see also Orange Juice, Paul Haig, Happy Family, Rhythm Of Life)

79	Absolute ABS 1	Chance Meeting/Romance (p/s, 1,000 only)	30

MINT VALUE £

80	Postcard 80-3	Radio Drill Time/Crazy To Exist (live) (hand-coloured foldaround p/s, blue labels)	20
80	Postcard 80-3	Radio Drill Time/Crazy To Exist (live) (brown sleeve & labels)	10
80	Postcard 80-3	Radio Drill Time/Crazy To Exist (live) (cream/yellow sleeve & labels)	8
80	Postcard 80-5	It's Kinda Funny/Final Request (p/s in poly bag, with picture insert)	15
80	Postcard 80-5	It's Kinda Funny/Final Request (p/s in poly bag, without picture insert)	8
81	Postcard 81-5	Chance Meeting/Pictures (die-cut sleeve, with postcard)	15
81	Postcard 81-5	Chance Meeting/Pictures (die-cut sleeve, without postcard)	8
81	Postcard 81-4/TWI 023	Sorry For Laughing/Revelation (p/s)	10
87	Supreme Intl. Edit. 87-7	Heaven Sent/Radio Drill Time/Heads Watch/Fun'n'Frenzy (12", p/s)	8
81	Postcard 81-7	THE ONLY FUN IN TOWN (LP, with inner sleeve)	30
87	Supreme Intl. Edit. 87-6	YOUNG AND STUPID (LP)	15
90	Supreme Intl. Edit.	YOUNG AND STUPID (CD)	18

IRVING JOSEPH

60	London HLT 9027	I Left My Love/Lorena	8

MARGIE JOSEPH (& BLUE MAGIC)

72	Stax 2025 052	Medicine Bend/Same Thing	15
74	Atlantic K 10460	Sweet Surrender/My Love	6
75	Atlantic K 10649	What's Come Over Me/You And Me (as Margie Joseph & Blue Magic)	6
72	Stax 2362 008	MAKES A NEW IMPRESSION (LP)	12
73	Atlantic K 40462	MARGIE JOSEPH (LP)	12

JOSH

(see also Girlie)

69	Duke DU 41	Judge/RON: Soul Of Joemel	10
70	Hot Rod HR 111	Leaving Everything/HOT ROD ALL STARS: Psychedelic Bird	20

JOSH & HERBIE

60s	Kalypso AB 107	I'm Nobody's Child/How Can I Believe In You	6

JOSHUA

73	Key KL 014	JOSHUA (LP)	140

MARVA JOSIE

66	Polydor 56711	Crazy Stockings/I'll Get By	15

JOURNEY

82	CBS CBS 11A 1728	Don't Stop Believin'/Natural Thing (12", picture disc)	8
92	Columbia 4728102	TIME3 (3-CD)	25

JOY & DAVID/DAVE

58	Parlophone R 4477	Whoopee!/My Oh My! (as Joy & David)	40
58	Parlophone R 4477	Whoopee!/My Oh My! (78, as Joy & David)	30
59	Decca F 11123	Rocking Away The Blues/If You Pass Me By (as Joy & David)	40
59	Decca F 11123	Rocking Away The Blues/If You Pass Me By (78, as Joy & David)	35
60	Triumph RGM 1002	Let's Go See Gran'ma/Believe Me (as Joy & Dave)	45
60	Decca F 11291	My Very Good Friend The Milkman/Doopey Darling (as Joy & Dave)	25
61	Parlophone R 4855	Joe's Been A-Gittin' There/They Tell Us Not To Love (as Joy & Dave)	20
61	Parlophone R 4855	Joe's Been A-Gittin' There/They Tell Us Not To Love (demo copies with alternate take of B-side)	45

RODDIE JOY

65	Red Bird RB 10021	Come Back Baby/Love Hit Me With A Wallop	60

JOHNNY JOYCE

(see also Velvet Opera, Levee Breakers)

76	Freedom FLP 99003	JOYCE'S CHOICE MIXTURE (LP)	22

JOYCE'S ANGELS

(see also Chris White)

67	Major Minor MM 526	Flowers For My Friends/Rodney Reginald Smithfield Harvey Jones	10

JOY DE VIVRE

(see also Crass)

81	Crass CR & SS ENVY 1	Our Wedding (flexidisc, white vinyl, no p/s, with mailer)	300
81	Crass CR & SS ENVY 1	Our Wedding (flexidisc, white vinyl, no p/s, without mailer)	200

JOY DIVISION

(see also New Order)

78	Enigma PSS 139	AN IDEAL FOR LIVING (Warsaw/No Love Lost/Leaders Of Men/Failures) (EP, 1,000 only, foldout p/s; beware of counterfeits)	1000
78	Anonymous ANON 1	AN IDEAL FOR LIVING (Warsaw/No Love Lost/Leaders Of Men/Failures) (12" EP reissue, 1,200 only)	500
79	Factory FAC 13	Transmission/Novelty (p/s)	10
80	Factory FACUS T2	She's Lost Control/Atmosphere	15
80	Factory FAC 23	Love Will Tear Us Apart/These Days	8
80	Factory FAC23.12	Love Will Tear Us Apart/These Days (12", with flexi)	15
80	Factory FAC 28	Komakino/Incubation/As You Said (flexi)	5
82	Factory FAC 13 12	Transmission/Novelty (12")	12
79	Factory FACT 10	UNKNOWN PLEASURES (LP with inner sleeve, textured sleeve, 1st press slightly transluscent when held up to light)	50
80	Factory FACTUS 6	CLOSER (LP, hard textured sleeve & inner)	40
81	Factory FACT 40	STILL (2-LP, hessian sleeve, card inners & white ribbon)	70
80	Factory FAC 40	STILL (2-LP, gatefold)	30
87	Strange Fruit SFPS 033	PEEL SESSIONS (12" EP)	15
88	Factory FACT 250	SUBSTANCE (LP)	25
07	London 2564699291	JOY DIVISION (4-LP boxed set, 500 only)	70

COL JOYE & JOYBOYS

59	Brunswick 05806	(Rockin' Rollin') Clementine/Bye Bye Baby Goodbye	25
59	Brunswick 05806	(Rockin' Rollin') Clementine/Bye Bye Baby Goodbye (78)	20
60	Top Rank JAR 529	Be My Girl/Yes Sir, That's My Baby	10

MINT VALUE £

JOYFUL SINGERS (with Lynn Tait on Organ)

(see also Lyn[n] Tait)

67	Master Time MT 001	Jesus Christ Is Risen/BELIEVERS: Honey In The Rock	6
67	Master Time MT 002	Happy Days/He Watches Over Me	6

JOYFUL SOUND

73	SRT SRT 73278	IT WILL BE WORTH IT ALL (LP)	300

JOY GUESSING

70	Crimson N 034	The Blue Midget/Officer Bud Babe	6

JOY OF COOKING

72	Capitol E-ST 11050	CASTLES (LP)	12

JOYRIDE

69	RCA SF 8027	FRIEND SOUND (LP)	20

JOY UNLIMITED

69	Page One POF 147	Daytime Night Time/Mister Pseudonym	20
69	Page One POF 160	Oh Darlin'/Feeling	10
70	Page One POLS 028	TURBULENCE (LP)	750

J P SUNSHINE

95	Uncle Glitch Records UG 1	UNCLE GLITCH PRESENTS (LP, 500 only)	30

J.S.D. BAND

73	Cube BUG 29	Sarah Jane/Paddy Stacks (p/s)	6
71	Regal Zono. SRLZ 1018	COUNTRY OF THE BLIND (LP, textured sleeve, first press with flipbacks)	80
71	Regal Zono. SRLZ 1018	COUNTRY OF THE BLIND (LP, textured sleeve, later press without flipbacks)	40
72	Cube HIFLY 11	J.S.D. BAND (LP)	15
73	Cube HIFLY 14	TRAVELLING DAYS (LP)	15

JUAN & JUNIOR

67	CBS 2949	The Chase/Nothing	6
68	CBS 3223	To Girls/Andurina	15

JUBILEE STOMPERS

70	Trojan TR 7725	Luciana/I Really Like It	6

JUDAS JUMP

(see also Herd, Amen Corner, Andy Bown)

70	Parlophone R 5828	Run For Your Life/Beer Drinking Woman	7
70	Parlophone R 5838	This Feelin' We Feel/Hangman's Playing	8
70	Parlophone R 5873	Beer Drinking Woman/I Have The Right	6
70	Parlophone PAS 10001	SCORCH (LP, gatefold sleeve, black/silver label with boxed logo)	40

JUDAS PRIEST

(see also Trapeze, Fancy)

74	Gull GULS 6	Rocka-Rolla/Never Satisfied	25
76	Gull GULS 31	The Ripper/Island Of Domination	25
77	CBS S CBS 5222	Diamonds And Rust/Dissident Aggressor	7
78	CBS S CBS 6077	Better By You, Better Than Me/Invader	5
78	CBS S CBS 6794	Before The Dawn/Rock Forever	5
79	CBS S CBS 12-6915	Take On The World/Starbreaker/White Heat Red Hot (12", p/s)	8
79	CBS S CBS 7312	Evening Star/Beyond The Realms Of Death	5
79	CBS 12-7312	Evening Star/The Green Manalishi/Beyond The Realms Of Death (12", clear vinyl with picture insert)	8
79	Gull GULS 71	The Ripper/Victims Of Change	8
79	Gull GULS 7112	The Ripper/Never Satisfied/Victim Of Changes (12", p/s)	12
80	CBS TA 4298	United/Grinder (poster p/s)	10
81	CBS A12 1153	Hot Rockin'/Steeler/You Don't Have To Be Old To Be Wise (12", no p/s)	8
82	CBS A 112611	You've Got Another Thing Comin'/Exciter (live) (picture disc)	6
82	CBS A 2822	(Take These) Chains/Judas Priest Audio File (p/s)	5
83	Gull GULS 7612	Tyrant/Rocka-Rolla/Genocide (12", p/s, white vinyl)	15
84	CBS TA 4298	Some Heads Are Gonna Roll/Green Manalishi (live)/Jawbreaker (12", p/s)	8
86	CBS QTA 7144	Locked In (Extended)/Reckless/Desert Plains (live)/ Freewheel Burning (live) (12", poster p/s)	10
88	Atlantic A 9114CD	Johnny B. Goode/Rock You All Around The World (live)/Turbo Lover (live)/ Living After Midnight (live) (3" CD, with adaptor in 5" case)	8
90	Columbia 656273 6	Painkiller/United/Better By You, Better Than Me (12" red vinyl, p/s)	8
91	Columbia 656589 0	A Touch Of Evil/Between The Hammer And The Anvil (shaped disc)	12
91	Columbia 656589 6	A Touch Of Evil/Between The Hammer And The Anvil/ You've Got Another Thing Coming (live) (12", p/s, with giant poster)	8
74	Gull GULP 1005	ROCKA ROLLA (LP, original issue, 'bottle top' sleeve)	30
76	Gull GULP 1015	SAD WINGS OF DESTINY (LP)	15
76	Gull PGULP 1015	SAD WINGS OF DESTINY (LP, picture disc)	20
77	CBS 82008	SIN AFTER SIN (LP)	12
78	CBS 82430	STAINED CLASS (LP)	15
78	Gull PGULP 1026	THE BEST OF JUDAS PRIEST (LP, picture disc)	12
78	CBS 83135	KILLING MACHINE (LP, red vinyl)	15
79	CBS 83852	UNLEASHED IN THE EAST (LP, with free single "Rock Forever"/ Hell Bent For Leather/"Beyond The Realms Of Death" [SJP 1])	25
79	CBS 66357	BOX SET (3-LP, reissue of "Sin After Sin"/"Stained Class"/"Killing Machine")	25
80	CBS 84160	BRITISH STEEL (LP)	12
86	Shanghai PGLP 1026	JUDAS PRIEST (LP, picture disc)	12
93	CBS 473050	METAL WORKS (2-LP, gatefold sleeve)	18
98	SPV 0891 8542	98 LIVE MELTDOWN (2-LP)	18
04	Sony 5128933	METALOGY (4-CD, DVD, booklet, leather studded box set)	45

JUDD

(see also Kris Ife)

70	Penny Farthing PEN 709	Snarlin' Mumma Lion/Stronger Than A Man	6
70	Penny Farthing PELS 504	JUDD (LP, die-cut sleeve, insert, red/black/yellow labels)	150

MINT VALUE £

JUDGE HAPPINESS
(see also Mock Turtles)

85	Mynah SCS 8501	Hey Judge/Pig In Pink (very few with p/s)	25
85	Mynah SCS 8501	Hey Judge/Pig In Pink	10

TERRY JUDGE & THE BARRISTERS

63	Oriole CB 1896	Hey Look At Her/Kind Of Girl You Can't Forget	15
64	Oriole CB 1938	I Don't Care/Try To Forget	15
65	Fontana TF 599	Come With Me And Love Me/Waitin' For The Night To Come	15

JUGGERNAUTS
(see also Paul Haig)

84	Supreme Int. Editions 84-2	Come Throw Yourself/My First Million (p/s)	10

JUICE ON THE LOOSE

81	Juice JJOS 1	JUICE ON THE LOOSE (LP)	12

JUICY LUCY
(see also Misunderstood, Van Der Graaf Generator, Ray Owen, Paul Williams' Big Roll Band)

70	Fontana TF 1068	Who Do You Love/Walking Down The Highway (unissued)	0
70	Vertigo V1/6059 001	Who Do You Love/Walking Down The Highway	10
70	Vertigo 6059 015	Pretty Woman/I'm A Thief	18
72	Polydor 2001 279	It Ain't Easy/Promised Land	7
69	Vertigo VO 2	JUICY LUCY (LP, first press with 'Philips' credit on large swirl label, gatefold sleeve)	120
69	Vertigo VO 2	JUICY LUCY (LP, later press without 'Philips' credit on large swirl label, gatefold sleeve)	70
70	Vertigo 6360 014	LIE BACK AND ENJOY IT (LP, large swirl label, gatefold poster sleeve)	80
71	Bronze ILPS 9157	GET A WHIFF OF THIS (LP, textured sleeve, Island credit on label)	30
72	Polydor 2310 160	PIECES (LP)	25

JIMMY JUKEBOX
(see also Kim Fowley)

75	Sonet SON 2057	Motorboat/25 Hours A Day	15
77	Sonet SON 2057	Motorboat/25 Hours A Day (1977 re-issue with new Savage Pencil p/s but original 1975 records inside)	20

JULIAN (Scott)
(see also Brian Bennett)

59	Pye Nixa 7N 15236	Sue Saturday/Can't Wait	30
59	Pye Nixa N 15236	Sue Saturday/Can't Wait (78)	20

JULIAN (Judy Mowatt) & CHOSEN FEW

71	High Note HS 054	Joy To The World/Joyful Version	8

JULIAN (Judy Mowatt) & GAYTONES

72	High Note HS 059	She Kept On Talking/Version	15

JULIAN'S TREATMENT
(see also Julian Jay Savarin)

70	Young Blood YB 1009	Phantom City/Alda, Dark Lady Of The Outer Worlds	25
70	Young Blood SYB 2/3	A TIME BEFORE THIS (2-LP, laminated gatefold sleeve, white/red labels)	250

JULY
(see also Jade Warrior, Tom Newman, Tomcats)

68	Major Minor MM 568	My Clown/Dandelion Seeds	200
68	Major Minor MM 580	Hello, Who's There?/The Way	100
68	Major Minor MMLP 29	JULY (LP, laminated front sleeve, red/white/black labels)	800
87	Bam Caruso KIRI 097	DANDELION SEEDS (LP, reissue of above LP with extra tracks/different sleeve)	22
95	Essex 1011LP	JULY (LP, reissue with bonus 7": "Hello Who's There?"/"The Way" [p/s, 10117])	20

JUMBLE LANE

71	Holyground HG 115	JUMBLE LANE (LP, 99 copies only)	600

JUMP

80	Caveman CLUB 1	Shake Up/All In Vain (p/s)	25

JUMPIN' JACKS

58	HMV POP 440	My Girl, My Girl/Tried And Tested	25

JUMPLEADS

82	Ock OC 001	THE STAG MUST DIE (LP, with insert)	15

JUMP SQUAD
(see also Embryo)

81	101 UR 2	Lord Of The Dance/Debt (p/s)	20

JUNCO PARTNERS

65	Columbia DB 7665	As Long As I Have You/Take This Hammer	70
79	Rigid JUNK 1028	Swinging Sixties Boys/Peepin' And Hidin'	6
81	Energy NRG 4	Tall Windows/Noizez In My Head (p/s)	5
81	Energy NRGX 4	Tall Windows (Extended)/Noizez In My Head (Extended) (12", stickered white label, plain sleeve, promo only)	10
71	Philips 6308 032	JUNCO PARTNERS (LP, laminated sleeve, black/silver labels)	120

JUNCTION 32

75	Holyground HGS 119	JUNCTION 32 (LP, 100 copies only)	650

JUNCUNO
(see also Jon Cundo)

71	Banana BA 361	The End (as Joncuno)/HORACE ANDY: See A Man's Face	30

ROSANNE JUNE

56	London HLU 8352	The Charge Of The Light Brigade/Broken Windows	15
56	London HLU 8352	The Charge Of The Light Brigade/Broken Windows (78)	10
58	Oriole CB 1430	When A Woman Cries/The Great Chicago Fire	8

MINT VALUE £

JUNE BRIDES
(see also Phil Wilson)

84	Pink PINKY 1	In The Rain/Sunday To Saturday (p/s)	10
84	Pink PINKY 2	Every Conversation/Disneyland (die-cut sleeve, with insert)	8
84	Pink PINKY 2	Every Conversation/Disneyland (die-cut sleeve)	7

JUNG COLLECTIVE

02	Nanny Tango NT 1	Injustice/Street Preacher (Plaid Mix) (clear vinyl, poly sleeve w/sticker insert)	20

JUNGLE JIM

71	Pye 7N 4509	Big Fat Oranguman/Neasden Melody	5
72	Pye 7N 4518	Linda Love/Baby Go Down/Baby Go Down	8

JUNIOR (Simpson)

68	Giant GN 18	I'm Gonna Leave You Girl/I Love You I Love You	8
68	Giant GN 25	Come Cure Me/I Want Your Loving	8

JUNIOR B

92	Eastern Sher ES 001	Meditation/Black And White (12")	25

JUNIOR BROWN

78	Tempus TEMD 01	Jah Find Babylon Guilty (feat. Ranking Ruben)/Dub (12")	15
80	Jah Shaka 829	Fly Me Away/Travelling Dub (12")	30

JUNIOR DELGADO

78	Deb DEB 019	Trickster/CARLTON & HIS SHOES: Better Days (12")	12
79	Greensleeves GRED 15	Love Tickles Like Magic/PRINCE JAMMY & AGGROVATORS : Prince Jammy's Magic (12")	20
79	Burning Sounds BRD 005	Raiders/Warrior	20
80	Niagra NIADD 108	Fort Augustus/Escape Prisioners (12")	25
86	Incredible IM001	Poverty/Version (12")	40
88	Mango IS 368	Hanging Tree/Hey Good Looking (12")	20
89	Fashion FAD 066	Dub School/We A Blood (12")	25
82	Incredible Jux HBLP 001	BUSHMAN REVOLUTION (LP)	40
95	Incredible Music IMLP 001	TREAURE FOUND (LP)	12

JUNIOR DISPROL

01	SFDB AO27658	Fight Club/Junq Waffle	25

JUNIOR ENGLISH

79	Ethnic Fight ETH 1328	Keep On Trying/HORSEMOUTH: Herb Vendor (12")	20

JUNIOR'S EYES
(see also David Bowie, Tickle, Bunch Of Fives, Outsiders)

69	Regal Zonophone RZ 3009	Mr. Golden Trumpet Player/Black Snake	30
69	Regal Zonophone RZ 3018	Woman Love/White Light Part 2 (withdrawn B-side)	30
69	Regal Zonophone RZ 3018	Woman Love/Circus Days	20
69	Regal Zonophone RZ 3023	Star Child/Sink Or Swim	20
69	Regal Zono. SLRZ 1008	BATTERSEA POWER STATION (LP, laminated front, flipbacks, "Sold in U.K..." label text)	100

JUNIOR GEE

83	MasterfunkMF005	Caveman Rock/Scratch The Rock (12")	20
83	Masterfunk MF 005	Caveman Rock (12")	10
86	Scorcher 1032	The Truth (12")	25

JUNIOR GEE & THE CAPITAL BOYS

84	Tai Wan 1948	Check Us Out/The Break (12")	25

JUNIOR GEE/JUST US

87	Pana 2009	We Want Justice (12")	8

HUGH ROY JUNIOR
(see also U Roy Junior)

71	Big BG 329	Papcito/RUPIE EDWARDS: I'm Gonna Live Some Life	8
71	Supreme SUP 211	Double Attack/MURPHY'S ALL STARS: Puzzle	12
72	Ashanti ASH 405	King Of The Road/ROOSEVELT ALL STARS: Version	10
72	Jackpot JP 806	Two Ton Guletto/Version	10

JUNIOR MURVIN

68	Doctor Bird DB 1112	Miss Cushie/LYNN TAITT & JETS: Dr. Paul	30
68	Big Shot BI 503	Chattie Chattie/The Magic Touch	25
69	Big Shot BI 527	The Hustler/The Magic Touch	30
70	Gayfeet GS 205	Jennifer/Slipping	8
77	Island IPR 2001	Tedious/Memories	30
77	Island 12WIP 2010	Upsetter Revue Feat. Junior Murvin: Dread Locks In Moonlight/Closer Together (12")	12
82	Dread/Controls DATCD 009	Bad Man Posse/Riddim Request To All Posse Smoker Posse (12")	20
86	Greensleeves GRED 199	Apartheid/Jack Slick (12")	15
77	Island MLPS 9499	POLICE AND THIEVES (LP)	12
82	Dread At The Controls	BADMAN POSSE (LP)	30
84	Greensleeves GREL 70	MUGGERS IN THE STREET (LP)	20

JUNIOR REID

80	Negus Roots NERT 02	Sister Dawn/Dub Version (12")	20
81	Negus Roots NERT 09	IF I/Versions (12")	40

JUNIOR ROOTS

81	Black Roots BR 24	Natty Dread Time/BLACK TRAP: Into The Light (12")	12

TREVOR JUNIOR

84	Tonos TON 002	Ghetto Living/Have Faith In Jah (12")	50

U ROY JUNIOR
(see also Hugh Roy Junior, U Roy)

72	Attack ATT 8030	This Is A Pepper/JOHN HOLT: Justice	8

Year	Label / Cat. No.	Title	MINT VALUE £
72	Sioux SI 024	The Wedding/LLOYD'S ALL STARS: Buttercup	8
73	Randy's RAN 532	Froggie/RHYTHM RULERS: Version	10
73	Techniques TE 928	Aunt Kereba/DON RECO: Waterloo Rock (B-side actually by Reco Rodriquez)	12

JUNIOR WILSON

89	Blue Trac BTRD 035	Speak Softly (with T. Sparks and Mystic Man)/CONROY SMITH: Problems (12")	40

JUNIORS

64	Columbia DB 7339	There's A Pretty Girl/Pocket Size	55

JUNIPER GREEN

71	Columbia DB 8809	Dreams In The Sky/Cascade Of Ice	20

LENA JUNOFF

68	Olga OLE 8	Yesterday Has Gone/Good Kind Of Hurt	40

JUNO'S CLAW

79	MPA EMP 081	Barbara/The Master/Big City (EP, no p/s)	90

JUPITER

72	Parlophone R 5967	The Meteor Song/Life Is Getting Better Every Day	10

ERIC JUPP & HIS ORCHESTRA

(see also Coronets, Rockin' Strings)

53	Columbia SCM 5070	Jog Trot/Doina Voda	7
54	Columbia SCM 5081	Ooop De Ooh (Lazy Mambo)/Footsteps In The Fog	7
54	Columbia SCM 5140	They Were Doin' The Mambo/Skokiian (with Coronets)	7
56	Columbia DB 3817	Theme From 'East Of Eden'/When The Lilac Blooms Again	7
57	Columbia DB 4030	Bleep! Bleep!/Three-Two-One-Zero!	12
55	Columbia SEG 7589	ERIC JUPP AND HIS ORCHESTRA (EP)	10
56	Columbia SEG 7603	RHYTHM AND BLUES (EP)	10

MICKEY JUPP

(see also Rossi & Frost, Legend)

83	A&M AM 128	Stormy Sunday Lunchtime/Reading Glasses	5
83	A&M AM 145	Boxes And Tins/Reading Glasses (p/s)	5

JUS BADD

87	Tuff GrooveTUFF001	Freestyle/Proud (12")	100

JUST BROTHERS

80s	Soul City SC 127	Carlena/IVORIES: Please Stay (die-cut company sleeve)	8

SAMANTHA JUSTE

66	Go AJ 11402	No One Needs My Love Today/If Trees Could Talk	20

JUST FOUR MEN

(see also Wimple Winch, Four Just Men, Pacific Drift)

64	Parlophone R 5186	That's My Baby/Things Will Never Be The Same (withdrawn, as Four Just Men)	80
64	Parlophone R 5208	That's My Baby/Things Will Never Be The Same	60
65	Parlophone R 5241	There's Not One Thing/Don't Come Any Closer	60

JUST FRANK

80	Rok ROK III/IV	You/SPLIT SCREENS: Just Don't Try (die-cut company sleeve)	35

JIMMY JUSTICE

60	Pye 7N 15301	I Understand Just How You Feel/Bloodshot Eyes (as Jimmy Justice & Jury)	25
61	Pye 7N 15351	When Love Has Left You/The Teacher	25
61	Pye 7N 15376	A Little Bit Of Soap/Little Lonely One	15
62	Pye 7N 15443	Ain't That Funny/One (with p/s)	12
62	Pye 7N 15443	Ain't That Funny/One	5
62	Pye 7N 15457	Spanish Harlem/Write Me A Letter	5
62	Pye 7N 15469	Parade Of Broken Hearts/Dawning	5
63	Pye 7N 15502	The World Of Lonely People/I Wake Up Crying	5
63	Pye 7N 15509	Little Cracked Bell/Lighted Windows	5
63	Pye 7N 15528	The Guitar Player/Don't Let The Stars Get In Your Eyes	5
63	Pye 7N 15558	You're Gonna Need My Lovin'/Since You've Been Gone (with Exchequers)	5
63	Pye 7N 15601	Don't Say That Again/Green Leaves Of Summer	5
69	Decca F 12899	Running Out Of Time/There Goes My World	5
65	Pye 7N 15963	Only Heartbreak For Me/Everything In The Garden	6
68	RCA Victor RCA 1681	I'm Past Forgetting You/Walking Away With My Heart	25
72	B&C CB 172	English Rose/Burgundy Port And Wine	10
63	Pye NEP 24159	HIT PARADE (EP)	20
62	Pye NPL 18080	TWO SIDES OF JIMMY JUSTICE (LP)	40
62	Pye NPL 18085	SMASH HITS (LP)	30

JUSTIFIED ANCIENTS OF MU MU (J.A.M.s)

(see also KLF, Timelords, Disco 2000, Space, Orb, Bill Drummond)

87	KLF Comm. JAMS 23	All You Need Is Love (Original) (12", white label, 1-sided, 500 only)	50
87	KLF Comm. JAMS 23(s)	All You Need Is Love (Me Ru Con Mix)/(Ibo Version) (1,000 only, plain sleeve)	10
87	KLF Comm. JAMS 23T	All You Need Is Love/Ivum Naya/Rap, Rhyme And Scratch Yourself (12", 'James Anderton' p/s, 5,000 only)	15
87	KLF Comm. JAMS 24T	Whitney Joins The JAMs (120 bpm) (12", 1-sided, 'Scottish' issue, 500 only)	15
87	KLF Comm. JAMS 25T	1987 - The 45 Edits (12", p/s)	15
87	KLF Comm. JAMS 26T	BURN THE BEAT (12" EP, 5,000 for export only)	10
87	KLF Comm. JAMS 27	Down Town/118 BPM 27 (p/s)	8
87	KLF Comm. JAMS 27	Down Town (A-side Mix) (12", 1-sided, white label, 500 only)	12
87	KLF Comm. JAMS 27	Down Town (B-side Mix) (12", 1-sided, white label, 500 only)	12
87	KLF Comm. JAMS 27	Down Town (A-side Mix)/(B-side Mix) (12", white label)	12
87	KLF Comm. JAMS 27T	Down Town (118 bpm)/Down Town (12", JAMs label, generic sleeve)	10
87	KLF Comm. JAMS 27T	Down Town (118 bpm)/Down Town (12", mispressed 'album' label, generic sleeve)	15
88	KLF Comm. JAMS 28T	It's Grim Up North (Original Vocal Mix) (12", grey vinyl, 1-sided, 350 only)	100
87	KLF Comm. JAMS DS 1	Deep Shit (flexidisc, unreleased)	150
91	KLF Comm. JAMS 028R	It's Grim Up North (Original Vocal Mix) (12", black vinyl, 1-sided promo)	8

MINT VALUE £

88	Fierce FRIGHT 34(T)	20 GREATEST HITS (12" EP; not actually by J.A.M.s!)	12
87	KLF Comm. JAMS LP 1	1987 (WHAT THE FUCK IS GOING ON?) (LP, withdrawn)	100
87	KLF Comm. JAMS LP 1	1987 (WHAT THE FUCK IS GOING ON?) (cassette, withdrawn)	20
88	KLF Comm. JAMS LP 2	WHO KILLED THE JAMS? (LP, stickered sleeve with insert)	20
89	KLF Comm. JAMS DLP 3	SHAG TIMES (2-LP)	50
89	KLF Comm. JAMS CD 3	SHAG TIMES (CD)	40

DAVE JUSTIN

67	Polydor 56221	Everybody's Gone Home/Lincoln Green	12
68	Polydor 56253	You Outside/Thinking Twice	12

JAY JUSTIN

60	HMV POP 801	Nobody's Darlin' But Mine/Sweet Sensation	7
63	HMV POP 1183	Proud Of You/Love, Love Me, Baby Darling	6
68	Columbia DB 8439	I Sell Summertime/Time (withdrawn)	8

JUSTIN & KARLSSON

66	Piccadilly 7N 35295	Somewhere They Can't Find Me/What More Do You Want	8

JUSTIN CASE

80	Rok ROK XIX	TV/STRAIGHT UP: One Out All Out (die-cut company sleeve)	40

JUSTINE

69	Dot DOT 121	Leave Me Be/Clown	20
69	Buffalo BFS 1001	Right Now/Place Where Sorrow Hides	20
70	Uni UNS 528	She Brings Back The Morning With Her/Back To Boulder	12
70	Uni UNLS 111	JUSTINE (LP)	120

JUSTINS

71	Punch PH 65	Cholera/LLOYD ALL STARS: Black Bird	8

BILL JUSTIS & HIS ORCHESTRA

57	London HLS 8517	Raunchy/The Midnight Man	25
57	London HLS 8517	Raunchy/The Midnight Man (78)	10
58	London HLS 8614	College Man/The Stranger (B-side with Spinners)	25
58	London HLS 8614	College Man/The Stranger (B-side with Spinners) (78)	10
63	Mercury AMT 1201	I'm Gonna Learn To Dance/Tamoure	10
69	Sun 6094 003	Raunchy/Flip, Flop And Bop	10

JUST JACK

06	JUSTDJ4	Writers Block (hand-stamped 7")	5

JUST PLAIN JONES

(see also Just Plain Smith, Dave Ballantyne, Esprit De Corps)

71	CBS CBS 7480	Crazy, Crazy/Should Have Stayed With Mary	25

JUST PLAIN SMITH

(see also Just Plain Jones, Esprit De Corps)

69	Sunshine SUN 7702	February's Child/Don't Open Your Mind (with p/s)	135
69	Sunshine SUN 7702	February's Child/Don't Open Your Mind	60

JUST US

66	CBS 202068	I Can't Grow Peaches On A Cherry Tree/I Can Save You	7

JUST WILLIAM

68	spark SRL 1018	I Don't Care/Cherrywood Green	30

JUVENILES

66	Pye International 7N 25349	Bo Diddley/Yes I Believe	100

JYNX

64	Columbia DB 7304	How/Do What They Don't Say	60

K

CAROLINE K

87	Earthly Delights EARTH 1	NOW WAIT FOR LAST YEAR (LP, 1,500 only)	15

MOSES K & PROPHETS

(see also Them)

65	Decca F 12244	I Went Out With My Baby Tonight/So Long	25

SIMON K

69	B&C CB 111	You Know I Do/Bring Your Love Back	40

KABBALA

82	Red Flame RF 1211	Ashewo Ara/Voltan Dance (12")	25

KABUKI

82	Kabaret Noir KAB 1	I Am A Horse/My Hair (p/s)	30

KADDO STRINGS

(see also Duke Browner, Tartans)

80	Grapevine GRP 146	Nothing But Love/Crying Over You	15

KADENZA

82	PRT 12P 247	Let's Stay Together (Night Club Mix)/Let's Stay Together (Vocal 2)/Instrumental Version (12")	30

KADETTES

82	Blank GET 1	Fireball XL5/Mission Impossible	8

MINT VALUE £

BERT KAEMPFERT

66	Brunswick LAT/STA 8651	A MAN COULD GET KILLED (LP, soundtrack)	22

KAINE & ABEL

66	Philips BF 1472	Then You Must Know My Love/Crying In The Rain	8

KAISER CHIEFS

(see also Parva)

04	Drowned In Sound DIS0003	Oh My God/Born To Be A Dancer/Caroline, Yes (CD, 500 only)	35
04	B-Unique BUN088-7	I Predict A Riot/Take My Temperature (p/s)	6
04	B-Unique BUN088-7	I Predict A Riot/Take My Temperature (150 signed 7" with p/s)	25
05	KAISERCRIBS001	KAISER CHIEFS: Another Number/THE CRIBS: Modern Way (Double 'A' Side sold at gigs during 2005 tour dates. 1000 copies)	20
05	No Label or cat no.	You Can Have It All (1-sided Xmas 2005 single sent out to first 2000 website subscribers. Christmas card fold-out sleeve. B-side with 'I predict Some Quiet' label	15
07	No Label or cat no.	The Angry Mob/The Angry Mob (Paul Emmanuel Off The Streets Mix) (mail-order only, with poster, 1,000 only)	15

KAISERS

94	No Hit Records NO HIT 14	IN STEP WITH THE KAISERS (LP)	15
93	No Hit NO HIT 012	SQUAREHEAD STOMP! (LP)	18

KAJANUS/PICKETT

72	Signport SGA 5001	HI HO SILVER (LP, sleeve with cut flap)	20

KAKKO

90	CBS 656023	What Kind Of Fool (mixes)/I Pledge You My Heart (12", p/s)	12
90	CBS 655 710 6	We Should Be Dancing (mixes) (12", p/s)	12
90	CBS 655 710 8	We Should Be Dancing (mixes) (12", p/s)	18
90	CBS 655 710 2	We Should Be Dancing (mixes) (CD)	20

KALA

(see also Quintessence)

73	Bradleys BRAD 302	Travelling Home/Still Got Time	5
73	Bradleys BRADL 1002	KALA (LP)	15

ALAN KALANI

59	Vogue V 9147	A Touch Of Pink/SURFERS: Mambo Jambo	20
59	Vogue V 9147	A Touch Of Pink/SURFERS: Mambo Jambo (78)	20

KALASANDRO!

60	Warner Bros WB 13	Chi Chi/Forbidden City	12

KALEIDOSCOPE (U.K.)

(see also Fairfield Parlour, I Luv Wight)

67	Fontana TF 863	Flight From Ashiya/Holidaymaker (in p/s)	100
67	Fontana TF 863	Flight From Ashiya/Holidaymaker	60
68	Fontana TF 895	A Dream For Julie/Please Excuse My Face	40
68	Fontana TF 964	Jenny Artichoke/Just How Much Are You	35
69	Fontana TF 1002	Do It Again For Jeffrey/Poem	50
69	Fontana TF 1048	Balloon/If You So Wish	110
67	Fontana (S)TL 5448	TANGERINE DREAM (LP, unlaminated sleeve, flipbacks, black/silver label)	400
69	Fontana STL 5491	FAINTLY BLOWING (LP, laminated gatefold sleeve; without watermark on beginning of each side)	600
69	Fontana STL 5491	FAINTLY BLOWING (LP, laminated gatefold sleeve; with watermark on beginning of each side)	200
87	5 Hours Back TOCK 005	TANGERINE DREAM (LP, stereo reissue)	18
87	5 Hours Back TOCK 006	FAINTLY BLOWING (LP, reissue, single sleeve)	18

KALEIDOSCOPE (U.S.)

70	CBS 64005	BERNICE (LP, as American Kaleidoscope)	30
76	Island ILPS 9462	WHEN SCOPES COLLIDE (LP)	12

KALIN TWINS

58	Brunswick D5751	When/Three O'Clock Thrill	5
58	Brunswick 05759	Forget Me Not/Dream Of Me (some B-side labels list "Dream Of You")	8
59	Brunswick 05775	Oh! My Goodness/It's Only The Beginning	8
59	Brunswick 05797	Cool/When I Look In The Mirror	8
59	Brunswick 05803	Moody/Sweet Sugar Lips	8
59	Brunswick 05814	The Meaning Of The Blues/Why Don't You Believe Me?	10
59	Brunswick 05814	The Meaning Of The Blues/Why Don't You Believe Me? (78)	15
60	Brunswick 05826	Chicken Thief/Loneliness	10
60	Brunswick 05844	Zing! Went The Strings Of My Heart/No Money Can Buy	10
61	Brunswick 05848	Momma Poppa/You Mean The World To Me	12
61	Brunswick 05862	One More Time/I'm Forever Blowing Bubbles	12
58	Brunswick OE 9383	WHEN (EP)	30
59	Brunswick OE 9449	THE KALIN TWINS (EP)	30

KITTY KALLEN

54	Brunswick 05261	Are You Looking For A Sweetheart/In The Chapel In The Moonlight	20
54	Brunswick 05287	Little Things Mean A Lot/I Don't Think You Love Me Anymore	20
54	Brunswick 05357	Heartless Heart/The Spirit Of Christmas	20
54	Brunswick 05359	I Want You All To Myself/(Don't Let The) Kiddy Geddin'	12
55	Brunswick 05394	A Little Lie/Take Everything But You	7
55	Brunswick 05402	Polly Pigtails/I'm A Lonely Little Petunia (In A Potato Patch)	7
55	Brunswick 05431	Kitty Who?/By Bayou Bay	7
55	Brunswick 05447	Forgive Me/Lonely	7
55	Brunswick 05475	Let's Make The Most Of Tonight/Just Between Friends	6
55	Brunswick 05494	How Lonely Can I Get?/Sweet Kentucky Rose	6
56	Brunswick 05536	Go On With The Wedding (with Georgie Shaw)/Only Forever	6
56	Brunswick 05612	True Love/Will I Always Be Your Sweetheart?	6

MINT VALUE £

57 Brunswick 05705 — Long Lonely Nights/Lasting Love | 6
58 Brunswick 05734 — Crying Roses/I Never Was The One | 5
59 Philips PB 971 — If I Give My Heart To You/The Door That Won't Open | 5

DICK KALLMAN

56 Brunswick 05608 — Two Different Worlds/Love Me As Though There Were No Tomorrow | 6
60 Vogue V 9162 — Born To Be Loved/Just Squeeze Me But Don't Teeze Me | 10
63 HMV POP 1118 — Say It Isn't So/From This Day On (A-side with John Barry & His Orchestra) | 5
63 HMV CLP 1642 — SPEAK SOFTLY (LP) | 20

BOBBY KALPHAT

68 Nu Beat NB 007 — Rhythm And Soul/BUNNY & RUDDY: True Romance | 12
74 Faith FA 008 — Zion Hill/Dub Hill | 10
73 Tropical AL 049 — Natty Rock/Natty Dub | 10

BOBBY KALPHAT & PHIL PRATT

76 Terminal TERM 001 — ZION HILL DUB (LP) | 200

CAROL KALPHAT

78 Hit Run HIT DD 1 — African Land (featuring Clint Eastwood)/ DOCTOR PABLO AND THE CRYTUFF ALLSTARS - African Melody (12", title sleeve) | 60

KAMARAS

69 CBS 4199 — Let This Moment Pass Away/I Just Can't Break Away From This Lovin' | 18

KANDAHAR

74 Sounds Superb 4M048-97401 — LONG LIVE THE SLICED HAM (LP) | 40

AMORY KANE

(see also Ron Geesin)

70 UNI UNS 518 — You Were On My Mind/All The Best Songs And Marches | 6
68 MCA MUP(S) 348 — MEMORIES OF TIME UNWOUND (LP, with insert) | 45
70 CBS 63849 — JUST TO BE THERE (LP) | 30

EDEN KANE

(see also Brothers Kane, Sarstedt Brothers)

60 Pye 7N 15284 — Hot Chocolate Crazy/You Make Love So Well | 25
61 Decca F 11353 — Well I Ask You/Before I Lose My Mind | 6
61 Decca F 11381 — Get Lost/I'm Telling You | 6
62 Decca F 11418 — Forget Me Not/A New Kind Of Lovin' | 6
62 Decca F 11460 — I Don't Know Why/Music For Strings | 6
62 Decca F 11504 — House To Let/I Told You | 5
63 Decca F 11568 — Sounds Funny To Me/Someone Wants To Know | 5
63 Fontana TF 398 — Tomorrow Night/I Won't Believe You (some in p/s) | 5
63 Fontana TF 413 — Like I Love You/Come Back (with Earl Preston's TTs) | 8
64 Fontana TF 508 — Hangin' Around/Gonna Do Something About You | 10
65 Fontana TF 582 — If You Want This Love/Have I Done Something Wrong | 10
66 Decca F 12342 — Magic Town/The Whole World Was Crying | 20
69 Fontana TF 1023 — Boys Cry/Don't Come Cryin' To Me (p/s, reissue) | 5
70 Bell BLL 1102 — Reason To Believe/I Played It Like A Fool | 8
62 Decca DFE 6696 — WELL I ASK YOU! (EP) | 20
62 Decca DFE 8503 — HITS (EP) | 20
64 Decca DFE 8567 — SIX GREAT NEW SWINGERS (EP) | 25
64 Fontana TFE 17424 — IT'S EDEN (EP) | 20
62 Ace Of Clubs ACL 1133 — EDEN KANE (LP) | 20
64 Fontana TL 5211 — IT'S EDEN (LP) | 30

GARY KANE

67 Pye 7N 17334 — Too Good To Miss/Guilty Of Dreaming | 5

HELEN KANE

55 MGM EP 549 — THE BOOP BOOP A DOOP GIRL (EP) | 25

JEFF KANE

69 Tangerine DP 0006 — Pretty Young Lady/On My Darkest Day | 20

JON KANE

69 Warner Bros WB 8003 — Soulful Lady/In Ancient Times (Jerusalem) | 20

LEE KANE

55 Capitol CL 14297 — Ev'ry Day/How Would You Have Me? | 8
55 Capitol CL 14328 — Around And Around/Merci Beaucoup | 8

MARIA KANE

65 Decca F 12184 — Love Is Slipping Away/Love Is Strange | 10

STEPHANIE KANE

64 Oriole CB1908 — It's Love/Think Of Me | 25

KAN KAN

80 Kabaret Music TRAIN 1 — Film Noir/The Watchmaker | 20

KANSAS

76 Epic SEPC 4932 — Carry On Wayward Son/Questions Of My Childhood | 6

KANSAS HOOK

70 UNI UNI 5515 — Echo Park/Manhattan Woman | 10
71 Decca F13117 — Nervous Shaking/Mr. Universe | 50

PAUL KANTNER

(see also Jefferson Airplane/Starship)

71 RCA Victor SF 8163 — BLOWS AGAINST THE EMPIRE (LP, gatefold sleeve with booklet, as Paul Kantner & Jefferson Starship) | 20
71 Grunt FTR 1002 — SUNFIGHTER (LP, gatefold sleeve with booklet & inner sleeve; as Paul Kantner, Grace Slick & Jefferson Starship) | 15
73 Grunt BFL 1 0148 — BARON VON TOLBOOTH (LP, with Grace Slick & David Freiberg) | 12

MINT VALUE £

PANDIT KANWAR SAIN TRIKHA
70 Mushroom 100MR7 — THREE SITAR PIECES (LP) — 45

KAPLAN
68 Philips BF 1636 — Do You Believe In Magic/I Like — 18
68 Philips BF 1699 — I Love It/Trousers Down — 6

KAPT. KOPTER & FABULOUS TWIRLY BIRDS
(see also Spirit)
73 Epic EPC 65381 — KAPT. KOPTER & THE FABULOUS TWIRLY BIRDS (LP) — 15

ANTON KARAS
60 Decca F 9235 — The "Harry Lime" Theme/The Cafe Mozart Waltz — 5
55 Decca DFE 6035 — ANTON KARAS ZITHER SOLOS (EP) — 10
51 Decca LF 1053 — ANTON KARAS (10" LP) — 15

KAREEM
97 Exploding Plastic EXP8 — Never Give Up On Love/Restless Soul (Peaktime Radio Mix)/Hipster Mix — 30

THE KARELIA
(see also Franz Ferdinand, The Amphetameaniest)
97 The All Blacks B.V RR88232 — DIVORCE AT HIGH NOON (CD, 2005 reissue has different p/s) — 40

KENNY KAREN
61 Philips PB 1213 — Oh Susie Forgive Me/The Light In Your Window — 15

KARIBS
70s Karibs KA1 — Aching Heart/Sugar Lips — 8

KARINA
71 United Artists UP 35205 — Tomorrow I'm Coming Your Way/Something — 10

KARLINS
66 Parlophone R5457 — You Mean Nothing To Me/Walkin' Away — 6
66 Parlophone R5550 — The Spinning Wheel/It's Good To Be Around — 6
67 Parlophone R5607 — The Hawk Moth And The Flame/Water Or The Wine — 6
68 Columbia DB8394 — Everybody Wants To Go To Heaven/Stay On The island — 7
73 Enterprise ENTM 503 — OUR KIND OF MUSIC (LP) — 12

BILLY KARLOFF (& EXTREMES)
(see also Tom Robinson Band, Stiff Little Fingers)
78 Wanted CULT-45-001 — Crazy Paving/Back Street Billy (p/s) — 8
81 Warner Bros K 17753 — Headbangers/Don't Keep Me Down (p/s) — 5

BORIS KARLOFF
60 Caedmon CAL 102/1 — HANS CHRISTIAN ANDERSEN (LP) — 15
67 Brunswick LAT 8678 — AN EVENING WITH BORIS KARLOFF AND FRIENDS (LP) — 50

KARMA SUTRA
87 Paradoxical PARODY 1 — DAYDREAMS OF A PRODUCTION LINE WORKER (LP, with booklet) — 40

STEVE KARMEN BIG BAND
(see also Jimmy Radcliffe)
75 United Artists UP 35770 — Breakaway/Breakaway (Vocal Version) (featuring Jimmy Radcliffe) — 10

KAROO
65 Oak RGJ 193 — Mamma's Out Of Town/Lonely Weekend — 200

KARRIER
84 Unit TRANS 101 — I'm Back/Dreaming (no p/s) — 30
86 Status JEMS 101 — Poor Little Rich Girl/Endless Shadow — 30
85 Unit — WAY BEYOND THE NIGHT (LP) — 15

KARYN KARSH
66 RCA Victor RCA 1740 — I Wasn't Born To Follow/Musty Dusty — 5

KARYOBIN
(see under Spontaneous Music Ensemble)

KASABIAN
03 BMG Paradise 02 — Processed Beats (10" 45 rpm screen print sleeve with elastic bands) — 25
04 BMG Paradise 04 — Reason Is Treason (10" p/s 1,000 only) — 20
04 BMG Paradise 06 — Club Foot (Jagz Kooner mix) (12", with man-shaped hole sleeve) — 8
04 BMG Paradise 09 — Club Foot/(Jagz Kooner Vocal Mix)/(Paradise Mix) (with poster p/s) — 10
04 BMG Paradise 15 — L.S.F (Lost Souls Forever)/Club Foot (Live @ Cabinet War Rooms)/(Jagz Kooner Mix (Full Version) (10" poster p/s) — 12
04 BMG Paradise 22 — Processed Beats/Ovary Stripe(Remix)/Processed Beats (Afrika Bambaata Remix)(10") — 8
07 No label — Fast Fuse/Fast Fuse (10" 200 only die-cut sleeve, stamped labels given away at Somerset House gig, 2007) — 30
04 BMG Paradise 18 — KASABIAN (LP, 2 x 10") — 15

MURRAY KASH
68 RCA 1767 — Sleeping Beauty/Everything's OK — 6

AL KASHA
60 Coral Q 72410 — Teardrops Are Falling/No Matter Where You Are — 5

KATATONIA
96 Misanthropy AMAZON 010 — Scarlet Heavens/PRIMORDIAL: To Enter Pagan MCMXCVI (10", p/s) — 12

KATCH-22
66 Fontana TF 768 — Major Catastrophe/Hold Me — 70
67 Fontana TF 874 — Makin' Up My Mind/While We're Friends — 15
68 Fontana TF 930 — The World's Gettin' Smaller/Don't Bother — 20
68 Fontana TF 984 — Pumpkin Mini/100,000 Years — 25

			MINT VALUE £
69	Fontana TF 1005	Out Of My Life/Baby Love	15
69	CBS 4644	It's The Sunshine/Mrs. Jones	20
68	Saga EROS 8047	IT'S SOFT ROCK & ALLSORTS (LP, with insert, Daga inner sleeve)	25

KATCH 22

90	Kold Sweat KS 105	Hip Hop Pocrisy/Enter The Dope Zone/2½ Years (12")	12
91	Kold Sweat KS 113	Diary Of A Blackman Living In The Land Of The Lost/Right And Exact (12")	10
92	Kold Sweat KSEP 206	RETURN TO THE FUNDAMENTALS (EP)	12
93	Kold Sweat KSEP 213	DARK EPOCH (EP)	10
91	Kold Sweat KSLP 1	DIARY OF A BLACKMAN LIVING IN THE LAND OF THE LOST (LP)	12
93	Kold Sweat KSLP 4	DARK TALE OF TWO CITIES (LP)	12

KATE

(see also Viv Prince, Pretty Things)

68	CBS 3631	Strange Girl/I Don't Make A Sound	70
68	CBS 3815	Hold Me Now/Empty World	20
69	CBS 4123	Shout It/Sweet Little Thing	60

KATHY

69	Morgan MR 14	Bonjour Monsieur/Long Night	5

KATINA

72	Cactus CT 3	Don't Stroke My Pussy/Don't Stroke My Pussy (Version)	5

KATMANDU

(see also Peter Green, Ray Dorset, Crane/Farlowe)

86	Nightflite NTFL 2001	A CASE FOR THE BLUES (LP)	12

KATZ

60s	Tetlow TET 118	LIVE AT THE RUM RUNNER (EP)	75

ARTHUR KAY'S ORIGINALS

80	Red Admiral NYMPH 1	Ska-Wars/Warska (p/s)	8
80	Red Admiral NYMPH 2	Sooty Is A Rudie/Play My Record (p/s)	10
88	Skank MLP 105	RARE 'N' TASTY (mini-LP)	12

BARBARA KAY

65	Columbia DB 8009	The Power And The Glory/I Wanna Walk In Your Sun	5
65	Pye 7N 15774	That's What Angels Are For/What's The Good Of Loving	6
65	Pye 7N 15914	Yes I'm Ready/Someone Has To Cry	20
66	Pye 7N 15997	Chips With Everything/A Lot About Love	5

JANET KAY

78	Arawak ARK DD 003	Silly Games/Dangerous (12")	10

JANET K(AY)

78	Bushays BFM 108	Silhouette (with Rico)/PRINCE JAZEBO & RICO: Silhouette Gone Clear (12")	20

JOHN KAY

(see also Steppenwolf)

72	Probe SPB 1054	FORGOTTEN SONGS AND UNSUNG HEROES (LP)	12
73	Probe SPBA 6274	MY SPORTIN' LIFE (LP)	12

KATHIE KAY

59	HMV 7EG 8424	SONGS FOR MY AIN FOLK (EP)	8
74	Philips 6382 082	WALK SOFTLY ON THE BRIDGE (LP)	12

CAB KAYE

61	Melodisc MEL 1584	Everything Is Go/Don't You Go Away	5

DANNY KAYE

(see also Bing Crosby, Groucho Marx)

59	Brunswick 05031	The Ugly Duckling/The king's New Clothes	10

DANNY KAYE & LOUIS ARMSTRONG

(see also Louis Armstrong)

60	London HL 7092	The Five Pennies Saints/Bill Bailey Won't You Please Come Home (export issue)	5

DAVE KAYE (& DYKONS)

64	Decca F 11866	A Fool Such As I/It's Nice Isn't It (as Davy Kaye)	35
65	Decca F 12073	In My Way/All The Stars In Heaven (as Dave Kaye)	25
69	Major Minor MM 641	Yesterday When I Was Young/Say You Love Me (as Dave Kaye & Dykons)	12

KATHIE KAY(E)

55	HMV 7M 335	Suddenly There's A Valley/Teddy Bear	8
56	HMV 7M 363	Jimmy Unknown/Dreams Can Tell A Lie	8
57	HMV POP	We Will Make Love/Wind In The Willow	8

LINDA KAYE

66	Columbia DB 7915	I Can't Stop Thinking About You/When We Meet Again	25

PETER KAYE

60s	Aral PS 116	Do Me A Favour/You Doll (in p/s)	10
60s	Aral PS 116	Do Me A Favour/You Doll	5

SHIRLEY KAYE

68	Trojan TR 015	Make Me Yours/We Have Happiness	75

STUBBY KAYE

61	Polydor NH 66827	My Wife's A Striptease Dancer/Lydia The Tattooed Lady	6

TONY KAYE & HEARTBEATS

67	Pye International 7N 25412	Hey, Hey Little Orphan Annie/Dream World	8

KAYES

(see also Kaye Sisters)

67	Major Minor MM 515	It's No Secret/Remember Me	8

MINT VALUE £

KAYE SISTERS

(see also Three Kayes/Three Kaye Sisters, Kayes, Frankie Vaughan)

58	Philips PB 806	Are You Ready, Freddy?/The Pansy	15
58	Philips PB 832	Stroll Me/Torero	10
59	Philips PB 892	Jerri-Lee (I Love Him So)/Deeply Devoted	10
60	Philips PB 1024	Paper Roses/If Only You'd Be Mine (in p/s)	8
60	Philips PB 1088	Come To Me/A Whole Lot Of Lovin' (in p/s)	5
57	Philips BBE 12166	PRESENTING THE KAYE SISTERS (EP)	8
59	Philips BBE 12256	THE KAYES AT THE COLONY (EP)	8

KAY GEES

76	Polydor 2310 467	HUSTLE WIT' EVERY MUSCLE (LP)	15

LAINIE KAZAN

69	MGM MGM 1476	Window Of My Mind/It's You	30

KCF & SKELLA TON

91	Kold Sweat KS112	Taken To Heart/In Session (12")	12

ERNIE K-DOE

61	London HLU 9330	Mother-In-Law/Wanted, $10,000.00 Reward	15
61	London HLU 9390	Te-Ta-Te-Ta-Ta/Real Man	20
62	London HLU 9487	I Cried My Last Tear/A Certain Girl	25
65	Vocalion VP 9233	My Mother In Law (Is In My Hair Again)/Looking Into The Future	20
68	Action ACT 4502	Dancing Man/Later For Tomorrow	25
68	Action ACT 4512	Gotta Pack My Bags/How Sweet You Are	25

PHIL KEAGGY BAND

70s	Myrrh MYR 1046	WHAT A DAY (LP)	20
70s	Myrrh MYR 1066	EMERGING (LP)	20
70s	Underground Bird 151	PRIVATE COLLECTION VOL 1 (LP)	20

KEANE

00	Zoomorphic (No cat. no)	Call Me What You Like/Rubbernecking/Closer Now (CD, 500 only)	100
01	Zoomorphic ZOO12101	Wolf At The Door/Call Me What You Like/She Has No Time (CD, 50 only p/s)	100
03	Fierce Panda NING 133CD	Everybody's Changing/Bedshaped/The Way You Want It (CD, 1,500 only)	30
03	Fierce Panda NING 147CD	This Is The Last Time/Can't Stop Now/Allemande (CD, 4,000 only)	20
04	Island CID 849	Somewhere Only We Know/Snowed Under (numbered, p/s)	8
05	Island KEANE 2	The Sun Ain't Gonna Shine Anymore/Your Eyes Open (Fan club issue 1000 only p/s)	30
06	Island (no cat no)	Nothing In My Way (512MB USB stick, 1500 only, numbered in title sleeve)	20
06	Island (no cat no)	A Bad Dream (512MN USB stick, 1500 only, numbered in title sleeve)	20
07	Island 123058	A Bad Dream/She Sells Sanctuary (with fold-out sleeve, numbered)	15
04	Island ILPS 8145	HOPES AND FEARS (LP, 1000 only, numbered)	35
04	Island (no cat no)	HOPES AND FEARS (CD promo, 200 only, numbered)	35
04	Island (no cat no)	HOPES AND FEARS (DVD sampler, jewel case, promo)	25
05	Island	SINGLES BOX SET (1000 only, 5x7" from HOPES AND FEARS LP)	100
06	Island (no cat no)	THE VIDEOS (Fan club issue only)	50
06	Island (no cat no)	UNDER THE IRON SEA (CD promo and A5 lyric booklet)	22

SHAKE KEANE

(see also Marie Bryant)

55	HMV 7MC 38	Akinla/Fire, Fire (export issue)	5
62	Columbia SEG 8140	IN MY CONDITION (EP)	40
65	Decca SKL 4720	SHAKE KEANE WITH THE KEATING SOUND (LP)	20
66	Ace Of Clubs ACL 1219	THAT'S THE NOISE (LP)	25
69	Phase 4 Stereo PFS 4154	DIG IT (LP, with Ivor Raymonde Orchestra)	40
70	Pama SECO 30	RISING STARS AT EVENING TIME (LP with Gordon Langford and Hastings Girl Choir)	30

JOHNNY KEATING ORCHESTRA

62	Piccadilly 7N 35033	Theme From Z Cars/Lost Patrol	5
62	Piccadilly NEP 34011	Z-CARS (EP, with Z-Men)	8
63	Picadilly 7N 35113	The Preacher/Whoop Up (with the Z men)	10
57	Oriole MG 20011	BRITISH JAZZ (LP)	75
58	London LTZ-15122	SWINGIN' SCOTS (LP)	25
64	Ace Of Clubs ACL 1160	SIXTEEN HITS FOR YOUR DANCE PARTY (LP)	20
64	Decca PFS 4038	SWING REVISITED (LP)	25
64	Decca PFS 4078	STRAIGHT AHEAD (LP)	30
72	Studio Two Q4 TWO 393	SPACE EXPERIENCE (LP, quadrophonic)	25
75	Studio Two TWOX 1044	SPACE EXPERIENCE 2 (LP)	15

KEEFERS KIDS

67	King KG 1068	Millions Of Hearts/KEEFERS: Lonely Hill	5

KEELE ROW & KEELE UNIVERSITY STUDENTS

64	Flexi	STANLEY MATTHEWS (EP, flexi)	20

JOHN KEEN

(see also Speedy Keen, Thunderclap Newman)

72	Track 2094 103	Old Fashioned Girl/That's The Way It Is	8
73	Track 2094 108	Let Us In/Keep On The Grass	8

SPEEDY KEEN

(see also John Keen, Thunderclap Newman)

71	Track 2406 105	PREVIOUS CONVICTIONS (LP)	15

MARION KEENE

56	HMV 7M 395	Fortune Teller/A Dangerous Age	7
57	HMV POP 375	In The Middle Of An Island/It's Not For Me To Say	6

NELSON KEENE

(see also Guv'ners)

60	HMV POP 771	Image Of A Girl/Ocean Of Love	15

MINT VALUE £

60	HMV POP 814	Keep Loving Me/Teenage Troubles	15
61	HMV POP 916	Miracles Are Happening To Me/Poor Little Rich Boy	15

REX KEENE

56	Columbia DB 3831	Rebel In Town/Happy Texas Ranger	10

KEETY ROOTS

94	Black Legacy BL 003	African Blood/TENASTELIN: Spirit of	200

ACE KEFFORD STAND

(see also Move, Cozy Powell, Young Blood, Big Bertha, Bedlam, Carl Wayne)

69	Atlantic 584 260	For Your Love/Gravy Booby Jam (small centre hole)	40
69	Atlantic 584 260	For Your Love/Gravy Booby Jam (large centre hole)	35

KEITH

66	Mercury MF 940	Ain't Gonna Lie/It Started All Over Again	8
67	Mercury MF 955	98.6/The Teeny Bopper Song	10
67	Mercury MF 968	Tell Me To My Face/I Can't Go Wrong	8
67	Mercury MF 989	Daylight Savin' Time/Happy Walking Around	15
67	Mercury MF 1002	Sugar Man/Easy As Pie (in p/s)	12
67	Mercury MF 1002	Sugar Man/Easy As Pie	6
67	Mercury MCL 20103	98.6/AIN'T GONNA LIE (LP)	30

BRIAN KEITH

(see also Plastic Penny)

68	Page One POF 072	The Shelter Of Your Arms/C'est La Vie	7
68	Page One POF 103	When The First Tear Shows/When My Baby Smiles At Me	8
69	Page One POF 152	Till We Meet Again/Lady Butterfly	7

BRYAN KEITH

63	London HLU 9707	Sad Sad Song/Mean Woman	20

RON KEITH

76	A&M AMS 7217	Party Music/Gotta Go By What You Tell Me	100

KEITH & BILLIE

(see under Keith Powell & Billie Davis; see also Keith Powell, Billie davis)

KEITH (Stewart) & ENID (Cumberland)

60	Blue Beat BB 6	Worried Over You/Everything Will Be Alright	10
60	Blue Beat BB 11	Send Me/TRENTON SPENCE GROUP: People Will Say We're In Love	10
61	Starlite ST45 047	Never Leave My Throne/Only A Pity (as Keith & Enid with Caribs)	12
61	Starlite ST45 067	You're Gonna Break My Heart/What Have I Done	12
62	Blue Beat BB 125	When It's Spring/True Love (with Sonny Bradshaw Orchestra)	10
63	Dice CC 14	Sacred Vow/My Dreams	8
63	Dice CC 20	Just A Closer Walk/Don't Yield To Temptation	8
64	Black Swan WI 429	Lost My Love/I Cried	10
63	Island ILP 901	KEITH & ENID SING (LP)	60
70	Trojan TTL 37	KEITH & ENID SING (LP, reissue)	15

KEITH (Poppin) & IMPACT ALL STARS

71	Randy's RAN 515	Down By The Riverside/IMPACT ALL STARS: Version Two	6

KEITH (Lyn) & KEN (Lazarus)

65	London HA-R/SH-R 8229	YOU'LL LOVE JAMAICA (LP)	40

KEITH (Rowe) & TEX (Dixon)

67	Island WI 3085	Tonight/LYN TAIT & JETS: You Have Caught Me	100
68	Island WI 3091	Stop That Train/BOBBY ELLIS: Feeling Peckish (with Desmond Miles Seven)	150
68	Island WI 3137	Hypnotizing Eyes/Lonely Man	60
70	Explosion EX 2008	Tighten Up Your Gird/Look To The Sky	12

KEITHY

77	Xamayca XAD 002	Struggling In A Babylon (with Imperial Hudson)/XAMAYCA BAND: Togetherness	25

JERRY KELLER

59	London HLR 8890	Here Comes Summer/Time Has A Way (triangular centre)	10
59	London HLR 8890	Here Comes Summer/Time Has A Way (round centre)	5
59	London HLR 8890	Here Comes Summer/Time Has A Way (78)	20
59	London HLR 8980	If I Had A Girl/Lovable	8
59	London HLR 8980	If I Had A Girl/Lovable (78)	20
60	London HLR 9106	Now, Now, Now/Lonesome Lullaby	10
60	London HA-R 2261	HERE COMES JERRY KELLER (LP, mono)	40
60	London SAH-R 6083	HERE COMES JERRY KELLER (LP, stereo)	60

PAT KELL(E)Y

(see also Wonder Boy)

68	Giant GN 37	Little Boy Blue/You Are Not Mine (as Pat Kelley & Uniques)	60
68	Island WI 3121	Somebodies Baby (as Pat Kelly)/BEVERLY SIMMONS: Please Don't Leave Me	45
69	Gas GAS 110	The Workman Song/Never Give Up (as Pat Kelly)	10
69	Gas GAS 115	How Long/Try To Remember (as Pat Kelly)	5
69	Gas 115	How Long Will It Take/Try To remember	12
69	Gas GAS 124	Festival Time (Parts 1 & 2) (as Pat Kelley)	8
69	Gas GAS 125	If It Don't Work Out/I Am Coming Home (as Pat Kelley)	5
70	Gas GAS 144	Tammy/I Am Not Your Guy (as Pat Kelley)	15
70	Gas GAS 145	Striving For The Right/When A Boy Fall In Love (as Pat Kelley)	7
70	Gas GAS 157	I Just Don't Know What To Do With Myself/What's He Got That I Ain't Got (B-side actually titled 'Lorna') (as Pat Kelley)	8
70	Jackpot JP 734	I Just Don't Know What To Do With Myself/Lorna (as Pat Kelley)	8
71	Camel CA 65	Talk About Love (as Pat Kelley)/PHIL PRATT ALL STARS: Version	10
71	Gas GAS 171	Love/With All Your Heart (as Pat Kelley)	6
71	Punch PH 88	Soulful Love (as Pat Kelly)/HUGH ROY & PARAGONS: One For All	10
72	Pama Supreme PS 353	I'm Gonna Give Her All The Love I've Got (as Pat Kelley)/MAYTONES: As Long As You Love Me	8

MINT VALUE £

73 Pama Supreme PS 379 Twelfth Of Never (as Pat Kelley)/JERRY LEWIS: 5000 Watts ... 6
73 Pama Supreme PS 384 I Wish It Could Rain (as Pat Kelley)/PAT KELLY SINGERS: Hallelujah ... 6
75 Black Wax WAX 1 Sunshine/Sunshine Version ... 6
77 Rainbow Stepper RK 231 Carefree Girl/Version ... 8
69 Pama PMLP 12 PAT KELLEY SINGS (LP) ... 45
71 Pama PMP 2013 COOL BREEZING (LP) ... 60
77 Burning Rockers BR 007LP SO PROUD (LP) ... 25
78 Burning Sounds BS1001 LONELY MAN (LP) ... 20

PETER KELLEY
71 Polydor 2310 119 DEALIN' BLUES (LP) ... 20

MURRAY KELLUM
64 London HLU 9830 Long Tall Texan/GLEN SUTTON: I Gotta Leave This Town ... 15

KELLY
66 RCA RCA 1507 Be My Man/Here Comes My Baby ... 6
69 Deram DM 277 Mary Mary/Reverend Richard Baily ... 35

CHARLIE KELLY
68 Island WI 3155 So Nice Like Rice/STRANGER & GLADDY: Over Again ... 25

DAVE KELLY
(see also John Dummer Blues Band, Brunning-Hall Sunflower Blues Band)
69 Mercury 20151 SMCL KEEPS IT IN THE FAMILY (LP, laminated sleeve, black/silver labels) ... 200
71 Mercury 6310 001 DAVE KELLY (LP, with Jo-Ann Kelly & Brunning-Hall Sunflower Band) ... 250

FRANK KELLY & HUNTERS
62 Fontana 267 242 TF Send Me The Pillow That You Dream On/'Cept Me ... 15
63 Fontana 267 261 TF I Saw Linda Yesterday/Good And True ... 15
63 Fontana 267 277 TF What Do You Wanna Do/She Loves Me So ... 15
64 Fontana TF 454 Some Other Time/Why Baby Why ... 15
(this is not the same group as [Dave Sampson &] Hunters, also on Fontana)

GENE KELLY
53 MGM SP 1012 Singin' In The Rain/All I Do Is Dream Of You ... 5
53 MGM SP 1015 'S Wonderful (with Georges Guetary)/I Got Rhythm (with Children's Choir) ... 5
57 MGM MGM-EP 671 SINGING IN THE RAIN EXCERPTS (EP, with Donald O'Connor/Debbie Reynolds) 10
53 MGM MGM-D 117 SONG AND DANCE MAN (10" LP) ... 18
55 MGM MGM-D 133 S'WONDERFUL (10" LP) ... 18

JO-ANN KELLY
(see also Chilli Willi & Red Hot Peppers, Dave Kelly, Tramp)
64 GW EP 1 BLUES AND GOSPEL (EP, live at the Bridge House Club) ... 110
66 Harlequin HAL 1/HW 349 NEW SOUNDS IN FOLK (LP, with other artists) ... 65
69 CBS 63841 JO-ANN KELLY (LP, laminated front sleeve) ... 200
76 Red Rag RRR 006 DO IT (LP, with Peter Emery) ... 35

JO-ANN KELLY & TONY McPHEE
(see also Tony McPhee, Dave Kelly)
72 Sunset SLS 50209 THE SAME THING ON THEIR MINDS (LP) ... 30

JONATHAN KELLY
(see also John Ledingham)
69 Parlophone R 5805 Denver/Son John ... 10
70 Parlophone R 5830 Make A Stranger Your Friend/Daddy Don't Take Me Down Fishing No More ... 10
70 Parlophone R 5851 Don't You Believe It?/Billy (Eric Clapton on guitar) ... 40
70 Parlophone PCS 7114 JONATHAN KELLY (LP, black/silver labels with boxed logo) ... 100
72 RCA SF 8262 TWICE AROUND THE HOUSES (LP) ... 30
73 RCA SF 8353 WAIT TILL THEY CHANGE THE BACKDROP (LP, gatefold sleeve) ... 30

KEITH KELLY
60 Parlophone R 4640 (Must You Always) Tease Me/Ooh-La-La ... 20
60 Parlophone R 4676 Listen Little Girl/Uh-Huh ... 30
60 Parlophone R 4713 With You/You'll Break My Heart ... 15
61 Parlophone R 4797 Cold White And Beautiful/When You First Fall In Love ... 15
65 CBS 201794 Laurie/Save Your Love For Me ... 10

MIKE KELLY
73 Decca F 13397 Catalina/You Made My World ... 6

MONTY KELLY
60 London HLL 9035 Summer Set/Amalia (as Monty Kelly Orchestra) ... 6

PAT KELLY
(see under Pat Kelley)

PAUL KELLY
65 Atlantic AT 4053 Chills And Fever/Only Your Love ... 40
67 Philips BF 1591 Sweet Sweet Lovin'/Cryin' For My Baby ... 25
72 Atlantic K 10272 Chills And Fever/Only Your Love (reissue) ... 10

PETE KELLY'S SOULUTION
(see also Bernie & Buzz Band, Rhythm & Blues Inc.)
68 Decca F 12755 Midnight Confessions/If Your Love Don't Swing ... 25
68 Decca F 22829 Midnight Confessions/BERNIE & BUZZ BAND: The House That Jack Built (export issue) ... 20

PETER D KELLY
74 DJM DJS 333 Rock To The Juke Box/Brotherhood Within (promo p/s) ... 10
74 DJM DJS 333 Rock To The Juke Box/Brotherhood Within ... 6

SALLY KELLY
59 Decca F 11175 Little Cutie/Come Back To Me ... 10

SEYMOUR KELLY
68 Columbia DB8445 Indian Scene/Worlds Apart ... 25

MINT VALUE £

STAN KELLY
60s	Transatlantic TRASP 21	The Ballad Of Armagh Jail/Kelly The Boy From Killang	5
60	Topic TOP 27	LIVERPOOL PACKET (EP)	10
60	Topic TOP 60	SONGS FOR SWINGING LANDLORDS TO (EP, with Leon Rosselson)	10

WYNTON KELLY TRIO
65	Verve VLP 9103	UNDILUTED (LP)	15

KELLY BROTHERS
67	Sue WI 4034	Falling In Love Again/Crying Days Are Over	80
68	President PT 143	You Put Your Touch On Me/Hanging In There	25
70	Blue Horizon 57-3177	That's What You Mean To Me/Comin' On In	30
68	President PTL 1019	SWEET SOUL (LP)	100

REV. (Samuel) KELSEY (& CONGREGATION)
(see also Sister Rosetta Tharpe)

56	Brunswick OE 9256	REV. KELSEY (EP)	20

WAYNE KEMP
66	Atlantic 584 006	Watch That First Step/Little Home Wrecker	10

KEMPION
77	Broadside BRO 123	KEMPION (LP)	18
77	Sweet Folk & C. SFA 044	CAM YE O'ER FRAE FRANCE (LP)	15

BOB KEN
80	Square S2SP	Keep Me Warm This Winter/More Than Life	6

KEN & NEW ESTABLISHMENT
73	Fab FAB 264	Soul Mood/Golden Locks	10

KEN & STEPPING TONY
78	Rama RMD 005	Sticks Man Affair/ROCKA & DAVE & GIRL WONDER: Skip-A Dip (12")	50

JOHNNY KENDALL & HERALDS
64	RCA RCA 1416	St. James Infirmary/Little Girl	10

KENDALL SISTERS
58	London HLM 8622	Won't You Be My Baby/Yea, Yea	40
58	London HLM 8622	Won't You Be My Baby/Yea, Yea (78)	25

GRAHAM KENDRICK
73	Key KL 011	FOOTSTEPS ON THE SEA (LP)	12
73	Key KL 016	BRIGHT SIDE UP (LP)	12
74	Key KL 024	PAID ON THE NAIL (LP)	12

LINDA KENDRICK
66	Polydor 56076	It's The Little Things/When Your Love Is Warm	30
66	Polydor 56076	It's The Little Things/When Your Love Is Warm (DJ copy)	50
69	Philips BF 1750	I Will See You There/Inside My Heart	8
69	Philips BF 1816	Hold On/Fa La La La La La Le	8
71	Philips 6006-078	Generation (Light Up The Sky)/Come With The Beautiful People	8
70	Philips SBL 7921	LINDA KENDRICK (LP)	15

NAT KENDRICK & SWANS
(see also James Brown)

60	Top Rank JAR 351	(Do The) Mashed Potatoes Parts 1 & 2	25
60	Top Rank JAR 387	Dish Rag Parts 1 & 2	20

EDDIE KENDRICKS
83	Tamla Motown TMG 985	Keep On Truckin' Part 1/Part 2	25

KENICKIE
95	Slampt U.O. SLAMPT 1	CATSUIT CITY (EP)	20
96	Fierce Panda NING 16	SKILLEX (EP)	8
97	EMI CDDISCS 007	PUNKA EP (2-CD, with postcards)	8

CALUM KENNEDY
62	Ember EMB 5167	The Celtic Chorus/Danny Boy	25

CHERYL KENNEDY
67	Columbia DB 8271	Thoroughly Modern Millie/Cradle Song	5

DOUG KENNEDY
65	Columbia DB 7707	Julie/Jailbreak Man	5

GENE KENNEDY
65	Hickory 45-1314	You Better Take Home/Stand In Line	5

JOHN F. KENNEDY
64	Stateside SL 10064	THE PRESIDENTIAL YEARS 1960-1963 (LP)	15

JON KENNEDY
01	Tru Thoughts TRU LP 017	WE'RE JUST WAITING FOR YOU NOW (2xLP)	15

LOU KENNEDY
55	Columbia SCM 5198	Stars Shine In Your Eyes/The Kentuckian Song	10
56	Columbia SCM 5216	Whisper/Sincerely Yours	10

MIKE KENNEDY
(see also Los Bravos)

69	Major Minor MM 614	I'll Never Forget/I'll Never Get You	6
69	Major Minor MM 629	Johnny Rebel/Golden Memories	6
72	Youngblood YB 1035	Louisiana/Look Up In The Sky	20

CHRIS KENNER
61	London HLU 9410	I Like It Like That Parts 1 & 2	30
65	Sue WI 351	Land Of 1,000 Dances/That's My Girl	30
66	Atlantic 587 008	LAND OF 1000 DANCES (LP)	40

MINT VALUE £

JAMES KENNEY

58	Pye 7N 15150	The Shrine On The Second Floor/Expresso Party	10

TONY KENNY & SANDS SHOWBAND

(see also Sands)

67	Major Minor MM 555	Help Me Rhonda/Some Enchanted Evening	5
68	Major Minor MM 573	Yummy Yummy Yummy/Peanuts	5
71	Hit HIT 1	Knock Three Times/See You In September	5

KENNY (Everett) & (Dave) CASH

65	Decca F 12283	Knees/The B Side	6

KENNY & DENY

(see also Jimmy Page, Tony Rivers & The Castaways, Harmony Grass, Capability Brown)

65	Decca F 12138	Try To Forget Me/Little Surfer Girl	70

KENNY & WRANGLERS

(see also Kenny Bernard & Wranglers)

64	Parlophone R 5224	Somebody Help Me/Who Do You Think I Am?	25
65	Parlophone R 5275	Doobie Doo/Moonshine	25

JERRI BO KENO

75	Phil Spector Intl. 2010 001	Here It Comes (And Here I Go)/I Don't Know Why	20

AL KENT

67	Track 604 016	You Got To Pay The Price/Where Do I Go From Here	50
71	Mojo 2092 015	You Got To Pay The Price/Where Do I Go From Here (unissued)	0

BILL KENT

58	Decca F 10975	The Prettiest Girl In School/Hasty Words	5
58	Decca F 10997	Oh-Oh, I'm Falling In Love/In Love	5

CINDY KENT

73	York FYK 418	I AM YOUR SERVANT (LP)	150

ENOCH KENT

59	Top Rank JAR 238	The Ballad Of Johnny Ramensky/The Bonny Lass Of Fyvie	5
60	Top Rank JAR 386	The Smashing Of The Van/Sean South Of Garryowen	5
62	Topic TOP 81	SINGS THE BUTCHER BOY AND OTHER BALLADS (EP)	10

KLARK KENT

78	Kryptone KK 1	Don't Care/Thrills/Office Girls (p/s, green or rarer black vinyl)	5
78	Kryptone KMS 7390	Too Kool To Kalypso/Theme For Kinetic Ritual (p/s, green vinyl)	5

PAUL KENT

71	B&C CB 165	Do You/Helpless Harry	6
70	RCA SF 8083	P.C. KENT (LP)	40
71	B&C CAS 1044	PAUL KENT (LP)	30

RICHARD KENT STYLE

66	Columbia DB 7964	No Matter What You Do/Go, Go Children	200
66	Columbia DB 8051	You Can't Put Me Down/All Good Things	150
67	Columbia DB 8182	Marching Off To War/I'm Out	120
68	MCA MU 1032	Love Will Shake The World Awake/Crocodile Tears	40
69	Mercury MF 1090	A Little Bit O' Soul/Don't Tell Lies	40

SHIRLEY KENT

(see also Ghost, Virginia Tree)

80	Tadpole TAD 001	My Dad/Marianne	6
66	Keele University 103	THE MASTER SINGERS AND SHIRLEY KENT SING FOR CHAREC 67 (EP)	35
89	Magic Spell 0001	FOREVER A WILLOW (LP)	12

SONIA KENT

(see also Diamond Twins)

66	Parlophone R 5401	This Is My Wonderful Day/Somebody Must Care	7

KENT (Brown) & DIMPLE (Hinds)

63	Island WI 046	Day Is Done/Linger A While	20

KENT (Brown) & JEANNIE with City Slickers

(see also Kent Brown & Rainbows)

62	Blue Beat BB 98	Daddy/Hello Love	20

RIK KENTON

(see also Woody Kern, Roxy Music)

74	Island WIP 6214	Bungalow Love/Lay It On You (no p/s)	5
76	EMI EMI 2443	The Libertine/Messin' Round	6

KEN-TONES

(see also Benny Lee)

56	Parlophone MSP 6229	Get With It/In Port Afrique	12
57	Parlophone R 4257	I Saw Esau/Yaller, Yaller Gold	8

KENTUCKY BOYS

55	HMV 7M 312	Don't Fetch It/A Little Fella Like Me	12

KENTUCKY COLONELS

(see also Byrds)

74	United Artists UAS 29514	THE KENTUCKY COLONELS (LP)	18

BILL KENWRIGHT (& RUNAWAYS)

67	Columbia DB 8239	I Want To Go Back There Again/Walk Through Dreams (with Runaways)	10
68	MGM MGM 1430	Giving Up/Love's Black And White (solo)	6
69	MGM MGM 1463	Tiggy/House That Fell On Its Face	5
69	MGM MGM 1478	Baby I Could Be So Good At Loving You/A Boy And A Girl	6
69	Fontana TF 1065	Sugar Man/Epitaph (When Times Were Good)	6

MINT VALUE £

MOIRA KERR			
69	Beltona MBE 102	FOLK WARM AND GENTLE (LP, also stereo [SBE 102])	15
71	Beltona SBE 118	SHADOWS OF MY CHILDHOOD (LP)	15
PATRICK KERR			
65	Decca F 12069	Magic Potion/It's No Trouble To Love You	30
RICHARD KERR			
66	Decca F12478	Concrete Jungle/You Got Nothing To Loose	12
66	Decca F12538	Hard Lovin'/Auntie's Insurance Policy	15
67	Deram DM 138	Happy Birthday Blues/Mother's Blue-Eyed Angel	20
69	RCA RCA 1785	Colour My World/For The Rest Of My Life	5
RICHARD KERR			
73	Warner Bros K 46206	FROM NOW UNTIL THEN (LP, foldout lyric insert)	15
75	Epic SEPC 3662	Somewhere In The Night/In The End	5
JOHN KERRUISH			
70	A&M AMS 604	Time To Wander/Today, Tonight And Tomorrow Morning	60
CHRIS KERRY			
65	Mercury MF 957	Seven Deadly Sins/The Place	20
66	Mercury MF 985	Watermelon Man/I've Got My Pride	20
DOUG KERSHAW			
(see also Rusty & Doug)			
69	Warner Bros WB 7304	Feed It To The Fish/You Fight Your Fight (I'll Fight Mine)	6
70	Warner Bros WB 7413	Orange Blossom Special/Swamp Rat	6
71	Warner Bros WS 1906	DOUG KERSHAW (LP)	12
73	Warner Bros K 46196	DEVIL'S ELBOW (LP)	12
MARY & HARVEY KERSHAW			
76	Topic 12TS 302	LANCASHIRE SINGS AGAIN! (LP)	12
KEN KESEY			
83	Psycho PSYCHO 4	THE ACID TEST (LP, 300 only)	30
BARNEY KESSEL			
(see also Rick Nelson)			
69	Polydor 56765	Frank Mills/Quail Bait	5
54	Vogue LDE 085	BARNEY KESSEL (10" LP)	20
55	Contemporary LDC 153	BARNEY KESSEL VOLUME 2 (10" LP)	20
59	Contemporary LAC 12206	SOME LIKE IT HOT (LP)	12
59	Contemporary LAC 12214	BARNEY KESSEL PLAYS CARMEN (LP)	12
77	Phil Spector Intl. 2307 011	SLOW BURN (LP)	15
LARRY KESSLER			
96	Lissey's LISS 5S	Radar Eyes/Godz Mix (p/s)	10
KESTREL			
(see also Spiders From Mars)			
75	Cube HIFLY 19	KESTREL (LP)	300
KESTRELS			
(see also Ivy League, Flowerpot Men, White Plains)			
59	Pye 7N 15234	There Comes A Time/In The Chapel In The Moonlight	8
60	Pye 7N 15248	I Can't Say Goodbye/We Were Wrong	6
61	Decca F 11391	All These Things/That's It	6
62	Piccadilly 7N 35056	Wolverton Mountain/Little Sacka Sugar	6
62	Piccadilly 7N 35079	Don't Want To Cry/Love Me With All Your Heart	6
63	Piccadilly 7N 35104	Walk Right In/Moving Up The King's Highway	7
63	Piccadilly 7N 35126	There's A Place/Little Star	7
63	Piccadilly 7N 35144	Love Me With All Your Heart/Lazy River	6
60s	Donegal MAU 500	THE KESTRELS (EP)	25
63	Piccadilly NPL 38009	SMASH HITS (LP)	25
KEY CHAINS			
66	London HLU 10055	Morgan's Song/Scruggs	5
EBONY KEYES			
66	Piccadilly 7N 35358	Sitting In The Ring/If You Knew	100
67	Piccadilly 7N 35375	Cupid's House/If Our Love Should End	10
67	Piccadilly 7N 35390	Country Girl/How Many Times	10
67	Piccadilly 7N 35407	Don't/Sweet Mary (Sweeter Than A Rose)	12
KAROL KEYES			
(see also Volunteers)			
64	Fontana TF 517	You Beat Me To The Punch/No-One Can Take Your Place (in p/s)	30
64	Fontana TF 517	You Beat Me To The Punch/No-One Can Take Your Place	20
67	Fontana TF 846	Can't You Hear The Music/The Sweetest Touch	12
66	Columbia DB 7899	A Fool In Love/The Good Love, The Bad Love	20
66	Columbia DB 8001	One In A Million/Don't Jump	75
TROY KEYES			
68	Stateside SS 2087	Love Explosions/I'm Crying (Inside)	20
69	Stateside SS 2149	Love Explosions/I'm Crying (Inside) (reissue)	10
KEY LARGO			
71	Blue Horizon 57-3178	Voodoo Rhythm/As The Years Go Passing By	20
70	Blue Horizon 7-63859	KEY LARGO (LP)	50
KEY MASSIVE			
89	Hat Music HT 001	Oh Girl/Sweet Sensi (12")	25
97	Wild Bunch WBRTDJ8	Rising Son/Instrumental/Single Mix/Neanderthal Mix/Darren Emerson Mix/Underdog Mix/Underdog Instrumental (2 x 12", clear vinyl promo)	18

MINT VALUE £

KEYMEN
59	HMV POP 584	Gazackstahagen/Miss You	6
62	Columbia DB 4902	Five Weeks In A Balloon/Secretly	8
57	Vogue Coral LVA 9048	THE VOCAL SOUNDS OF THE KEYMEN (LP)	15

KEYNOTES
(see also Bobbie Britton, Johnston Brothers, Dave King, Suzi Miller)

54	Decca F 10302	A Dime And A Dollar/JOHNSTON BROTHERS: Bandit	10
55	Decca F 10643	Relax-Ay-Voo/Steam Heat	10
56	Decca F 10745	Let's Go Steady/Chincherinchee	8

KEYNOTES
63	Planetone 14	I'm In Love/In The Valley	15

KEYS
64	Oriole CB 1968	Sleep Sleep My Baby/Colour Slide	25
65	CBS 201804	Go Get Her/My Everything	10

KEYS
81	A & M	THE KEYS ALBUM (LP)	15

BOBBY KEYS
75	Ring O' Records 2017 102	Gimmie The Key/Honky Tonk	7
72	Warner Bros K 46141	BOBBY KEYS (LP)	25

EBONY KEYS
71	Parlophone R 5909	Brother Joe/Under The Apple Tree	8

KEYTONES
85	Keytone KEY 3	Good To Be Alive/Now's The Time	15

KEYWI
83	Virgin VS 623	Lets Get It Right/Dub Version/Short Version (12")	15

K GROOVE
91	The White Label KG 1	The Future/On FB/10 To 10/BYS (12")	60

KHAN
(see also Steve Hillage, Egg, Nick Greenwood, Arzachel, Hatfield & The North)

72	Deram SDL 11	SPACE SHANTY (LP, gatefold, white/red label, small logo)	60
72	Deram SDL 11	SPACE SHANTY (LP, gatefold, white/red label, small logo, later stickered sleeve)	30

ASHISH KHAN
68	Liberty LBL 83083E	ASHISH KHAN (LP)	15
73	Elektra K 42129	JUGAL BANDI (LP, with John Barham)	12

USTAD ALI AKBAR KHAN
(see also Ravi Shankar)

69	HMV ASD 2367	MUSIC FROM INDIA NO. 5 (LP)	15
69	Transatlantic TRA 183	DHUN PALAS KAFI (LP)	20
71	Mushroom 100 MR 14	THE PEACEFUL MUSIC OF USTAD ALI AKBAR KHAN (LP)	35

USTAD VILAYET KHAN
69	RCA SF 8025	THE GURU (LP, soundtrack)	12
70	Transatlantic TRA 239	RAGA TILAKKAMOD (LP)	15

KHANDARS
65	Blue Beat BB 332	Don't Dig A Hole For Me/BUSTER'S ALL STARS: Skara	60

KHANS
62	London HLU 9555	New Orleans, 2 AM/Blue Mist	18

KHARTOMB
83	Whaam! WHAAM 14	Swahili Lullaby/Teekon Warriors	6

KICKS
80	Carrere CAR 138	Get Off The Telephone/Big Boys Don't Cry (p/s)	30
81	Blue Chip BC 102	If Looks Could Kill/Don't She Look Fab	70

KICK
84	Footwear FWR 01	Let's Get Back Together/A Shot In The Dark/Don't Ever Change (p/s)	6
86	Countdown VAIN 03	I Can't Let Go/Armchair Politician (p/s)	8

KID DYNAMITE
73	Pye 7N 45274	Call Me Sunshine Superman/Breaking The Ice	15

KID GUNGO
69	Escort ES 801	Hold The Pussy/KING CANNON: Wha Pen (B-side actually by Carl Bryan)	7

KID KOALA
00	Ninja Tune Zen 10 93	Emperor's Main Course In Cantonese (10")	8
00	Ninja Tune Zen 10 KK	Scratchhappyland (10" promo, 500 only)	10
00	Ninja Tune ZEN 34	CARPAL TUNNEL SYNDROME (2xLP)	15
06	Ninja Tune ZEN 127	YOUR MOM'S FAVOURITE DJ (LP)	12

EDDIE KIDD
77	Decca FR 13722	Motorbike Kid/Big Jump At Picket's Lock	6

JOHNNY KIDD (& PIRATES)
(see also Pirates)

59	HMV POP 615	Please Don't Touch/Growl	40
59	HMV POP 674	Feelin'/If You Were The Only Girl In The World (solo)	25
60	HMV POP 698	You Got What It Takes/Longin' Lips	18
60	HMV POP 753	Shakin' All Over/Yes Sir, That's My Baby	15
60	HMV POP 790	Restless/Magic Of Love	18
61	HMV POP 853	Linda Lu/Let's Talk About Us	20
61	HMV POP 919	Please Don't Bring Me Down/So What	20
62	HMV POP 978	Hurry On Back To Love/I Want That (with The Mike Sammes Singers)	25

			MINT VALUE £
62	HMV POP 1088	A Shot Of Rhythm And Blues/I Can Tell (blue or black label)	20
63	HMV POP 1173	I'll Never Get Over You/Then I Got Everything	5
63	HMV POP 1228	Hungry For Love/Ecstasy	10
64	HMV POP 1269	Always And Ever/Dr. Feelgood	10
64	HMV POP 1309	Jealous Girl/Shop Around	15
64	HMV POP 1353	Whole Lotta Woman/Your Cheatin' Heart	20
65	HMV POP 1397	The Birds And The Bees/Don't Make The Same Mistake As I Did	20
65	HMV POP 1424	Shakin' All Over '65/Gotta Travel On	25
65	HMV POP 1520	It's Got To Be You/I Hate To Get Up In The Morning (solo)	30
66	HMV POP 1559	Send For That Girl/The Fool	40
60s	HMV JO 674	Feelin'/If You Were The Only Girl In The World (export issue, black label)	40
97	Cruisin' 50 CASB 005	Shakin' All Over/Please Don't Touch (78rpm, 300 only)	30
60	HMV 7EG 8628	SHAKIN' ALL OVER (EP)	40
64	HMV 7EG 8834	JOHNNY KIDD AND THE PIRATES (EP)	70
71	Starline SRS 5100	SHAKIN' ALL OVER (LP)	15

KIDDA BAND

79	Carrere CAR 119	Fighting My Way Back/Saturday Night Fever	70

KID 'N' PLAY

88	Cooltempo COOLXR 175	2 Hype (12" promo)	40

KIDROCK

73	Youngblood YB 1058	Ice Cream Man/Dream Dream	35

KIDS

(see also Heavy Metal Kids, Gary Holton)

75	Atlantic K 50143	ANVIL CHORUS (LP, with inner, stickered sleeve)	25

KIDS NEXT DOOR

65	London HLR 9993	Inky Dinky Spider/Goodbye Don't Cry	7

KIDZ NEXT DOOR

79	Warner Bros K 17492	What's It All About?/The Kidz Next Door (p/s)	50

KILBURN & HIGH ROADS

(see also Ian Dury & Blockheads, 999, Nine Days Wonder)

74	Dawn DNS 1090	Rough Kids/Billy Bentley	10
75	Dawn DNS 1102	Crippled With Nerves/Huffety Puff	12
78	Warner Bros K 17225	Bentley/Pam's Moods	8
75	Dawn DNLS 3065	HANDSOME (LP, pink 'sun' label)	40

ROY KILDARE

64	Blue Beat BB 226	I Won't Leave/What About It	12

JUDY KILEEN

56	London HLU 8328	Just Walking In The Rain/A Heart Without A Sweetheart	45
56	London HLU 8328	Just Walking In The Rain/A Heart Without A Sweetheart (78)	15

KILFENORA CEILI BAND

74	Transatlantic TRS 108	KILFENORA CEILI BAND (LP)	12

MERLE KILGORE

54	London HL 8103	Seeing Double, Feeling Single/It Can't Rain All The Time	250
54	London HL 8103	Seeing Double, Feeling Single/It Can't Rain All The Time (78)	50
57	London HLP 8392	Ernie/Trying To Find (Someone Like You)	200
57	London HLP 8392	Ernie/Trying To Find (Someone Like You) (78)	70
60	Melodisc MEL 1545	Dear Mama/Jimmie Bring Sunshine	15
62	Mercury AMT 1193	42 In Chicago/A Girl Named Liz	15
65	London HA-B 8244	THERE'S GOLD IN THEM THAR HILLS (LP)	20

THEOLA KILGORE

67	Sue WI 4035	I'll Keep Trying/He's Coming Back To Me	40

KILLA INSTINCT

(see also Total Fiasco)

92	Music Of Life NOTE061	The Bambi Murders (12")	12
92	Music Of Life NOTE063	Den Of Thieves/Un-united Kingdom (12")	10
93	European Rhyme ERR02	WHISPERS OF HATRED (EP)	30
94	Move MOVE7013 1	ESCAPISM (EP)	15
96	Move MOVE7017 5	THE PENULTIMATE SACRIFICE (EP)	12

LOUIS KILLEN

62	Topic TOP 75	NORTHUMBRIAN GARLAND (EP)	10
66	Topic 12T 126	BALLADS AND BROADSIDES (LP, blue label)	20

LOUIS KILLEN & JOHNNY HANDLE

(see also Johnny Handle)

62	Topic TOP 74	THE COLLIER'S RANT (EP)	10
65	Topic 12T 122	TOMMY ARMSTRONG OF TYNESIDE (LP, with Colin Ross & Tom Gilfellon, blue label with booklet)	15
68	Topic 12T 189	ALONG THE COALY TYNE (LP, with Colin Ross, blue label with booklet)	20

KILLER

77	Ariola ARL 5003	KILLER (LP)	35

KILLERHERTZ

91	Evasion EVA 1	The Enforcer/X.XS (12", p/s)	12
92	FX FXUKT 9	Distant Dream (X-Static Mix)/Love Byte (Apocalypse Mix)/Love Byte (Stronthium Mix)/Distant Dream (Flying Fader Mix) (12")	40

KILLERMETERS

79	Psycho P 2620	Why Should It Happen To Me/Cardiac Arrest (in p/s)	100
79	Psycho P 2620	Why Should It Happen To Me/Cardiac Arrest	30
80	Gem GEMS 22	Twisted Wheel/SX 225 (p/s, demo copies £50)	90
97	Detour DRLP 013	METRIC NOISE (2xLP, gatefold, 'sparkly' clear vinyl)	18
98	Detour DR 065	ARE YOU READY (EP, blue vinyl, 100 only)	8

MINT VALUE £

KILLERS

(see also Joe Cool & The Killers)

78	Satril SAT 129	Killer (On The Dancefloor)/No Surrender (no p/s)	5

KILLERS

03	Lizard King LIZARD007	Mr Brightside/On Top/Smile Like You Mean It/Who Let You Go (CD)	30
03	Lizard King LIZARD007X	Mr Brightside/Smile Like You Mean It (white vinyl, 500 only p/s)	25
04	Lizard King LIZARD009	Somebody Told Me/The Ballad Of Michael Valentine/ Under The Gun (CD, 5000 only)	8
04	Lizard King LIZARD009X	Somebody Told Me/The Ballad Of Michael Valentine (pink vinyl, 2,000 only, p/s and poster)	10
04	Lizard King LIZARD010X	Mr Brightside/Who Let You Go (red vinyl, p/s and poster)	20
04	Lizard King LIZARD 010CD2	Mr Brightside/Somebody Told Me (Remix)/Midnight Show (live)/Video (CD single)	12
04	Lizard King LIZARD 012X	All These Things That I've Done/Andy, You're A Star (Radio 1 session) (2000 only, with poster)	25
05	Lizard King LIZARD 014X	Somebody Told Me (Mylo Remix)/Somebody Told Me (Glimmers Mix) (12")	15
05	Lizard King LIZARD 015X	Smile Like You Mean It/Ruby, Don't Take Your Love To Town (Radio 1 Session) (p/s, red vinyl)	8
05	Lizard King LIZARD 015Y	Smile Like You Mean It (Remix)/Mr Brightside (Dub Mix) (12")	15
05	Lizard King LIZARD 015	Smile Like You Mean It/Get Trashed (CD single)	10
06	Vertigo 170 672-1	When You Were Young/Where The White Boys Dance (numbered p/s)	6
07	Vertigo 17245686	Read My Mind/Steve Bays Remix (numbered p/s)	10
07	Island 60251750356	Don't Shoot Me Santa/Video (CD single)	8
05	Lizard King	HOT FUSS : SINGLES BOX SET (5,000 only. 11 x 7" album box set)	45

KILLER WATT

87	Raglan RGS 312	DEATH (EP)	25

JOHN KILLIGREW

(see also Pete Dello)

71	Penny Farthing PELS 513	JOHN KILLIGREW (LP, with Pete Dello, red/black/yellow labels)	150

KILLING FLOOR

(see also Rory Gallagher)

70	Penny Farthing PEN 745	Call For The Politicians/Acid Bean	20
69	Spark (S)RLP 102	KILLING FLOOR (LP, blue/silver labels)	300
70	Penny Farthing PELS 511	OUT OF URANUS (LP, gatefold sleeve, red/black/yellow label)	200
73	Spark Replay SRLM 2004	ORIGINAL KILLING FLOOR (LP, reissue)	30

KILLING JOKE

(see also Youth, Peyr, Heavy Duty Breaks)

79	Malicious Damage MD 410	Nervous System/Turn To Red/Are You Receiving (10" EP in bag, with picture & 4 cards)	20
79	Malicious Damage MD 410	Nervous System/Turn To Red/Are You Receiving (10" EP in bag, without picture & 4 cards)	10
80	Island WIP 6550	Turn To Red/Nervous System (p/s)	5
80	Island WIP 6550	Turn To Red/Nervous System ('A' label)	15
80	Island 12 WIP 6550	Almost Red/Nervous System/Are You Receiving/Turn To Red (12", p/s)	10
80	Malicious Damage MD 540	Wardance/Psyche (p/s, with 'call up paper' insert)	15
80	Malicious Damage MD 540	Wardance/Psyche (p/s, without 'call up paper' insert)	5
80	Malicious Damage MD 540	Wardance/Psyche (Mispressed B-side plays 'unknown artist', p/s)	25
80	E.G. EGMD 1.00	Requiem/Change (p/s)	5
80	E.G. EGMX 1.00	Requiem/Change/Change/Requiem (12", stamped sleeve)	10
80	E.G. EGMX 1.00	Requiem/Change/Change/Requiem (12", later pressing in p/s)	8
81	E.G. EGMDX 1.01	Follow The Leaders/Follow The Leaders - Dub/Tension (10", p/s)	7
82	E.G. EGOX 10	Birds Of A Feather/Flock The B-Side (12", p/s)	8
83	E.G. EGOD 14/KILL 1/2	Me Or You/Wilful Days//Feast Of Blaze (double pack, gatefold p/s)	5
83	E.G. EGOXD 14	Me Or You/Feast Of Blaze/Wilful Days//Let's All Go (To The Fire Dances)/ The Fall Of Because (live)/Dominator (Version) (12", sealed double pack)	15
84	E.G. EGOX 16	Eighties (Serious Dance Mix)/Eighties/Eighties (Coming Mix) (12", p/s)	8
84	E.G. DJ17	A New Day/Dance Day (DJ promo)	12
85	E.G. EGOY 20	Love Like Blood (Gestalt Mix)/Love Like Blood/Blue Feather (12", p/s)	10
85	E.G. EGOY 21	Kings And Queens (Knave Mix) (12", p/s)	10
85	E.G. EGOX 21	Kings And Queens (The Right Royal Mix)/The Madding Crowd/ Kings And Queens (12", different withdrawn p/s)	10
86	E.G. EGOD 27	Adorations/Exile//Ecstasy/Adorations (Instrumental Mix) (double pack)	5
88	E.G. EGOT 43	My Love Of This Land/Follow The Leaders (Dub)/Sun Goes Down (10", p/s, B-side matrix no. EGOT 43B; last track plays "The Gathering")	7
90	ODIC1	Beautiful Dead (1-sided fan club flexi)	10
80	E.G. EGMD 5.45	KILLING JOKE (LP)	15
81	E.G. EGMD 5.50	WHAT'S THIS FOR? (LP)	12
82	E.G. EGMD 3	REVELATIONS (LP)	12
83	E.G. EGMD 5	FIRE DANCES (LP)	12
90	AG 30405415	EXTREMITIES DIRT AND VARIOUS REPRESSED EMOTIONS (2-LP)	15

KILLJOYS

(see also Girlschool)

77	Raw RAW 3	Johnny Won't Get To Heaven/Naive (p/s, 4 different label designs)	30
91	Dam. Goods FNARR LP10	NAIVE (LP, green vinyl)	20

KILLJOYS

82	Clay CLAY 18	This Is Not Love/In Your Light (p/s)	5

KILLS

(see also Dead Weather)

02	Rug RUG 158	Fuck The People (1-sided, stamped card sleeve, 500 only)	15
05	Domino WIGLP 140	NO WOW (LP, with DVD)	18

KILOWATTS

(see also West Indians)

68	Doctor Bird DB 1140	Bring It On Home/What A Wonderful World	20

MINT VALUE £

PAT KILROY
67 Elektra EKL 311 — LIGHT OF DAY (LP) — 45

KILTIES
56 Beltona BL 2666 — Teach You To Rock/Giddy-Up-A Ding Dong — 20
56 Beltona BL 2666 — Teach You To Rock/Giddy-Up-A Ding Dong (78) — 12

ANDY KIM
69 Dot DOT 125 — Baby I Love You/Gee Girl — 12

KIM & KINETICS
(see also Kim Davis)
60s Mortonsound 3032/3033 — Without A Song/Stormy Monday — 60
60s Mortonsound 3036/3033 — Wee Wee Hours/Stormy Monday — 60

WILLIAM KIMBER
56 EFDSS LP 1001 — WILLIAM KIMBER (LP, with booklet) — 15
74 Topic 12T 249 — THE ART OF WILLIAM KIMBER (LP, with booklet) — 15

WILLIAM E. KIMBER
(see also E William)
68 Parlophone R 5690 — Shilo/Emptiness — 5
68 Parlophone R 5735 — Kilburn Towers/Goodbye (withdrawn) — 8
69 Parlophone R 5796 — Black Sheep Boy/And The Sun Began To Shine — 6

STEVIE KIMBLE
66 Decca F 12378 — Some Things Take A Little Time/All The Time In The World — 18

MAX KIMINSKY
59 Melodisc MLP 12-126 — DIXIELAND HORN (LP) — 15

KINCADE
72 Penny Farthing PEN 796 — Dreams Are Ten A Penny/Counting Trains — 6

KINESPHERE
76 Kinesphere KIN 5001 — ALL AROUND YOU (LP) — 100

KINETIC EFFECT
93 Insane 1201 — Borderin' Insanity/Beyond The Parameters (12" green vinyl, 500 pressed) — 30
93 Insane 1201 — Borderin' Insanity/Beyond The Parameters (12") — 18
97 Insane 1202 — Man Bites Dog/The Effect Of Fear (12") — 20

AL KING
68 Sue WI 4045 — Think Twice Before You Speak/The Winner — 40

ALBERT KING
(see also Steve Cropper & Albert King)
67 Atlantic 584 099 — Crosscut Saw/Down Don't Bother Me — 15
67 Stax 601 015 — Born Under A Bad Sign/Personal Manager — 10
68 Stax 601 029 — Cold Feet/You Sure Drive A Hard Bargain — 10
68 Stax 601 042 — (I Love) Lucy/You're Gonna Need Me — 8
73 Stax 2025 162 — Breaking Up Somebody's Home/Little Brother (Make A Way) — 5
67 Polydor 2343 026 — TRAVELLIN' TO CALIFORNIA (LP) — 30
68 Stax (S)XATS 1002 — LIVE WIRE - BLUES POWER (LP) — 40
69 Atlantic 588 173 — KING OF THE BLUES GUITAR (LP) — 40
69 Stax SXATS 1017 — KING DOES THE KING'S THINGS (LP) — 30
69 Stax SXATS 1022 — YEARS GONE BY (LP) — 30
71 Stax 2363 003 — LIVE WIRE - BLUES POWER (LP, reissue) — 15
71 Stax 2325 042 — LOVEJOY (LP) — 20
73 Stax 2325 089 — I'LL PLAY THE BLUES FOR YOU (LP) — 18
74 Stax STX 1003 — I WANNA GET FUNKY (LP) — 18

ALLAN KING
73 Duke DU 151 — Africa Wants Us All/JOE GIBBS: Liberation (B-side actually by Joe Gibbs' All Stars) — 6

ANNA KING
(see also Bobby Byrd)
65 Philips BF 1402 — If Somebody Told You/Baby, Baby, Baby (as Anna King & Bobby Byrd) — 15
65 Philips BBE 12584 — BACK TO SOUL (EP) — 40
65 Philips (S)BL 7655 — BACK TO SOUL (LP) — 60

ANTHONY KING
70s Peer Intl. — ELECTRICAL BAZAAR - SYNTHESIZERS UNLIMITED (LP, library issue) — 25

B.B. KING
(see also U2)
62 HMV POP 1101 — Tomorrow Night/Mother's Love — 25
64 Ember EMB S 196 — Rock Me Baby/I Can't Lose — 25
65 Sue WI 358 — The Letter/You Never Know — 30
66 HMV POP 1568 — Don't Answer The Door Parts 1 & 2 — 12
67 HMV POP 1580 — Night Life/Waitin' On You — 12
67 HMV POP 1594 — I Don't Want You Cuttin' Your Hair/Think It Over — 15
67 Polydor 56735 — Jungle/Long Gone Baby — 10
68 Stateside SS 2112 — Paying The Cost To Be The Boss/Having My Say — 10
68 Blue Horizon 57-3144 — The Woman I Love/Blues For Me — 20
69 Stateside SS 2141 — Don't Waste My Time/Get Myself Somebody — 6
69 Blue Horizon 57-3161 — Everyday I Have The Blues/Five Long Years — 20
70 Stateside SS 2161 — The Thrill Is Gone/You're Mean — 8
70 Stateside SS 2169 — So Excited/Confessin' The Blues — 5
70 Stateside SS 2176 — Hummingbird/Ask Me No Questions — 5
71 Probe PRO 516 — Chains And Things/King's Special — 5
71 Probe PRO 528 — Ask Me No Questions/Help The Poor/Humming Bird — 5
71 Probe PRO 546 — Ain't Nobody Home/Alexis' Boogie (with Alexis Korner) — 10

			MINT VALUE £
72	Probe PRO 573	Summer In The City/Found What I Need	5
65	HMV CLP 1870	LIVE AT THE REGAL (LP)	50
66	HMV CLP 3514	CONFESSIN' THE BLUES (LP)	40
67	HMV CLP 3608	BLUES IS KING (LP)	30
67	Ember EMB 3379	THE R&B AND SOUL OF B.B. KING (LP)	20
68	Stateside (S)SL 10238	BLUES ON TOP OF BLUES (LP)	35
68	Blue Horizon 7-63216	THE B.B. KING STORY CHAPTER 1 (LP)	60
69	Stateside (S)SL 10272	LUCILLE (LP)	30
69	Stateside SSL 10284	HIS BEST - THE ELECTRIC B.B. KING (LP)	25
69	Blue Horizon 7-63226	THE B.B. KING STORY CHAPTER 2 - BEALE STREET BLUES (LP)	75
70	Stateside SSL 10297	LIVE AND WELL (LP)	25
70	Stateside SSL 10299	COMPLETELY WELL (LP)	25
70	Probe SPBA 6255	INDIANOLA MISSISSIPPI SEEDS (LP)	15
71	Blue Horizon 2431 004	TAKE A SWING WITH ME (LP)	80
71	Probe SPB 1032	LIVE IN COOK COUNTY JAIL (LP)	20
71	Probe SPB 1041	IN LONDON (LP)	15

B.B. KING & BOBBY BLAND

(see also Bobby Bland)

74	ABC ABCD 605	TOGETHER FOR THE FIRST TIME (2-LP)	18

KING BEE

90	Big One RUFF6X	Back By Dope Demand/Oral Excitement (12")	15
90	1st Bass RUFF6R	Back By Dope Demand/Feel The Flow (12")	15

BEN E. KING

(see also Drifters, Soul Clan)

61	London HLK 9258	Spanish Harlem/First Taste Of Love	10
61	London HLK 9358	Stand By Me/On The Horizon	15
61	London HLK 9416	Amor, Amor/Souvenir Of Mexico	10
61	London HLK 9457	Here Comes The Night/Young Boy Blues	15
62	London HLK 9517	Ecstasy/Yes	10
62	London HLK 9544	Don't Play That Song (You Lied)/The Hermit Of Misty Mountain (later copies have Atlantic labels instead of London Atlantic, this price is for both pressings)	10
62	London HLK 9586	Too Bad/My Heart Cries For You	15
63	London HLK 9631	I'm Standing By/Walking In The Footsteps Of A Fool	15
63	London HLK 9691	How Can I Forget/Gloria, Gloria	15
63	London HLK 9778	I (Who Have Nothing)/The Beginning Of Time	10
63	London HLK 9819	I Could Have Danced All Night/Gypsy	15
64	London HLK 9840	Around The Corner/Groovin'	20
64	Atlantic AT 4007	It's All Over/Let The Water Run Down	20
65	Atlantic AT 4018	Seven Letters/River Of Tears	20
65	Atlantic AT 4025	The Record (Baby I Love You)/The Way You Shake It	20
65	Atlantic AT 4043	Cry No More/(There's) No Place To Hide	30
66	Atlantic AT 4065	Goodnight My Love, Pleasant Dreams/Tell Daddy	10
66	Atlantic AT 4065	Goodnight My Love, Pleasant Dreams/I Can't Break The News To Myself (demos with blank label on different B-side)	600
66	Atlantic 584 008	So Much Love/Don't Drive Me Away	10
66	Atlantic 584 046	I Swear By The Stars Above/Get In A Hurry	10
67	Atlantic 584 069	What Is Soul?/They Don't Give Medals To Yesterday's Heroes	15
67	Atlantic 584 090	Save The Last Dance For Me (as Ben E. King & Drifters)/Stand By Me	10
67	Atlantic 584 106	Tears, Tears, Tears/A Man Without A Dream	15
68	Atlantic 584 149	Seven Letters/Goodnight My Love	10
68	Atlantic 584 184	Don't Take Your Love From Me/Forgive This Fool	25
68	Atlantic 584 205	It's Amazing/Where's The Girl	10
69	Atlantic 584 238	'Till I Can't Take It Any More/It Ain't Fair	10
70	Crewe CRW 2	Goodbye My Old Gal/I Can't Take It Like A Man	5
71	Atlantic 2091 100	It's Amazing/Tears, Tears, Tears	10
71	CBS 7397	White Moon/All Of Your Sorrows	6
72	CBS 7785	Take Me To The Pilot/I Guess It's Goodbye	6
75	Atlantic K 10565	Supernatural Things (Parts 1 & 2)	10
75	Atlantic K 10618	Happiness Is Where You Find It/Drop My Heart Off	10
63	London REK 1361	BEN E. KING (EP)	40
63	London REK 1386	I'M STANDING BY (EP)	40
64	Atlantic AET 6004	WHAT NOW MY LOVE (EP)	40
61	London HA-K 2395	SPANISH HARLEM (LP, mono)	50
61	London SAH-K 6195	SPANISH HARLEM (LP, stereo)	70
62	London HA-K 8012	DON'T PLAY THAT SONG! (LP)	50
63	London HA-K 8026	SONGS FOR SOULFUL LOVERS (LP, cover credits Sings For Soulful Lovers; mono)	50
63	London SH-K 8026	SONGS FOR SOULFUL LOVERS (LP, cover credits Sings For Soulful Lovers; stereo)	70
65	Atlantic ATL 5016	GREATEST HITS (LP, plum label)	40
65	Atlantic ATL 5024	SEVEN LETTERS (LP)	50
66	Atlantic 587/588 055	SONGS FOR SOULFUL LOVERS (LP, cover credits Sings For Soulful Lovers; reissue)	18
67	Atlantic 590 001	SPANISH HARLEM (LP, reissue)	12
67	Atlantic 587 072	WHAT IS SOUL? (LP)	25
68	Atlantic 588 125	SEVEN LETTERS (LP, reissue)	12
70	Crewe CRWS 203	ROUGH EDGES (LP)	15

BOB KING & THE COUNTRY KINGS

59	Oriole CB 1497	My Petite Marie/Hey Honey	100
59	Oriole CB 1497	My Petite Marie/Hey Honey (78)	30

BRENTON KING

73	Downtown DT 505	Why Do People Have To Cry/Version	6

MINT VALUE £

BUZZY KING
60 Top Rank JAR 278 Schoolboy Blues/Your Picture 25

CANNON BALL KING
(see also Carl Bryan, King Cannon, Cannon Ball & Johnny Melody)
69 Camel CA 14 Danny Boy/Reggae Happiness 10
70s Junior JR 103 Reggay Got Soul/Land Of Love (actually by Soul Cats) 10

CARL KING
66 CBS 202407 Out Of My Depth/Keep It Coming 20
67 CBS 202553 You And Me/Satin Doll 8

CAROLE KING
62 London HLU 9591 It Might As Well Rain Until September/Nobody's Perfect 7
66 London HLU 10036 Road To Nowhere/Some Of Your Lovin' 40
71 A&M AMS 849 It's Too Late/I Feel The Earth Move 5
72 Ode ODS 66031 Been To Canaan/Bitter With The Sweet 5
70 A&M AMLS 996 WRITER - CAROLE KING (LP) 15
72 Ode ODE 77016 RHYMES AND REASONS (LP) 12

CLAUDE KING
61 Philips PB 1173 Big River Big Man/Sweet Loving 7
61 Philips PB 1199 The Comancheros/I Can't Get Over The Way You Got Over Me 7
62 CBS AAG 108 Wolverton Mountain/Little Bitty Heart 10
62 CBS AAG 119 Burning Of Atlanta/Don't That Moon Look Lonesome 7
65 CBS EP 6067 TIGER WOMAN (EP) 15
62 CBS BPG 62114 MEET CLAUDE KING (LP) 15

CLYDIE KING
(see also Jimmy Holiday & Clydie King, Raelets)
69 Minit MLF 11014 One Part, Two Part/Love Now Pay Later 7

KING COLE TRIO
(see under Nat King Cole)

DANNY KING('S MAYFAIR SET)
(see also Trevor Burton, Lemon Tree, Roy Wood)
64 Columbia DB 7276 Tossin' And Turnin'/Young Blood 35
65 Columbia DB 7456 Pretty Things/Outside Of My Room 40
65 Columbia DB 7792 Amen (My Teenage Prayer)/It's Such A Shame (as Danny King's Mayfair Set) ... 25

DAVE KING
56 Decca F 10684 Memories Are Made Of This (& Keynotes)/I've Changed My Mind A 1000 Times . 10
56 Decca F 10720 You Can't Be True To Two/A Little Bit Independent 10
56 Decca F 10741 The Birds And The Bees/Hot Chocolatta (with Keynotes) 10
56 Decca F 10791 Christmas And You/You Make Nice 6
57 Decca F 10865 Love Is A Golden Ring/If Your Heart Wants To Dance 5
57 Decca F 10910 With All My Heart/Red Shutters 5
57 Decca F 10947 Shake Me I Rattle/Chances Are 5
58 Decca F 10973 The Story Of My Life/I'll Buy You A Star 6

DAVE KING REGGAE BAND
70 Attack ATT 8014 Hey Little Girl/Why Don't You Try Me 6

DEE KING
66 Piccadilly 7N 35316 Sally Go Round The Roses/It's So Fine 12

DENNIS KING
(see also King Brothers)
77 EMI EMI 2578 Regan's Theme From The Film 'Sweeney'/F.J.'s Tune 20
74 EMI 2247 Galloping Home/Within These Walls/Screen Scene 6

DR. MARTIN LUTHER KING
68 Pama PM 732 I Have A Dream/Top Of The Mountain 15
68 Tamla Motown TML 11076 THE GREAT MARCH TO FREEDOM (LP) 80
68 Hallmark CHM 631 IN THE STRUGGLE FOR FREEDOM (LP) 15

EARL (CONNELLY) KING
56 Parlophone DP 511 Gratefully/Don't Take It So Hard (78, export issue) 20

EDDIE KING
65 Columbia DB 7572 Always At A Distance/If You Wish 8
65 Columbia DB 7654 I Wanna Love Her So Bad/If All You Need 10

KING FLOYD
71 Atlantic 2091-051 Groove Me/What Our Love Needs 8

FREDDY/FREDDIE KING
(see also Lula Reed & Freddy King)
61 Parlophone R 4777 Hideaway/I Love The Woman 40
65 Sue WI 349 Driving Sideways/Hideaway 40
69 Atlantic 584 235 Play It Cool/Funky 15
73 A&M AMS 7076 Woman Across The River/Help Me Through The Day 5
69 Atlantic 588 186 FREDDIE IS A BLUES MASTER (LP) 45
69 Polydor 2343 009 KING OF R&B VOL. 2 (LP) 15
69 Python PLP-KM 5 FREDDY KING VOLUME 1 (LP, 99 copies only) 90
69 Python PLP-KM 7 FREDDY KING VOLUME 2 (LP, 99 copies only) 90
69 Python PLP-KM 11 FREDDY KING VOLUME 3 (LP, 99 copies only) 90
(Pre-1970 releases are usually credited to Freddy King, post-1970 releases to Freddie King.)
72 Polydor 2343 047 HIS EARLY YEARS VOLUME 1 (LP) 12
72 A&M AMLS 68113 TEXAS CANNONBALL (LP) 15
72 Black Bear 904 LIVE PERFORMANCES VOLUME 1 (LP) 15
72 Black Bear 905 LIVE PERFORMANCES VOLUME 2 (LP) 15
73 A&M AMLS 68919 WOMAN ACROSS THE RIVER (LP) 12

MINT VALUE £

HAMILTON KING
64 HMV POP 1289 Not Until/I Wanna Live ... 10
64 HMV POP 1356 Ain't It Time/Money, Money ... 20
65 HMV POP 1425 Bird Without Wings/Shoppin' ... 20
69 Toast TT 511 This Love Of Mine/The Cup Is Fuller ... 5

HANK KING
63 Starlite STEP 41 COUNTRY AND WESTERN (EP) ... 25
66 Starlite GRK 510 COUNTRY AND WESTERN (EP, reissue) ... 10

JAY W. KING
66 Stateside SS 505 I'm So Afraid/I Don't Have To Worry (Not Anymore) ... 22

JONATHAN KING
(see also Weathermen, Hedgehoppers Anonymous, Pleasure Garden)
65 Decca F12187 Everyone's Gone To The Moon/Summer's Coming ... 6
67 Decca LK/SKL 4908 OR THEN AGAIN... (LP) ... 15
72 Decca SKL 5127 TRY SOMETHING DIFFERENT (LP) ... 12

MORGAN KING
93 OM Records 12OM006 I Am Free (12" promo) ... 10
93 OM Records OM006 I Am Free (12") ... 10
93 OM Records 12OM0006 T I Am Free (8 Mixes) (2-12") ... 40

KING OLIVER
53 London AL 3510 PLAYS THE BLUES (10" LP) ... 15
53 Columbia 33S 1065 KING JOE (10" LP) ... 15
55 Vogue/Coral LRA 10020 DIXIE SYNCOPATORS (10" LP) ... 15

P. KING
(see also Paul King)
83 Red Bus RBUS 79 Hey Rosalyn/Lyin' Again ... 6

P. RUFUS KING
(see also Paul King, Mungo Jerry)
73 Dawn DNS 1031 Look At Me Now/Nobody Knows ... 12

PAUL KING
(see also Mungo Jerry, P. King, P. Rufus King, King Earl Boogie Band, D'Jurann Jurran, Jigilo Jug Band, Russian Roulette)
72 Dawn DNS 1023 Whoa Buck/Zoe ... 7
72 Dawn DNLS 3035 BEEN IN THE PEN TOO LONG (LP, textured sleeve with lyric insert) ... 40

PEE WEE KING & HIS BAND
(see also Hank Snow)
54 HMV 7MC 14 Bimbo/Changing Partners (export issue) ... 10

PETE KING CHORALE & ORCHESTRA
61 London HLR 9437 Hey! Look Me Over/Tall Hope ... 5

PETER KING
68 Crab CRAB 3 Reggae Limbo/DERRICK MORGAN: River To The Bank ... 8

PETER KING
75 Orbitione OTLP 007 MILIKI SOUND (LP) ... 75
76 Orbitone OTLP 010 OMU LEWA (LP) ... 100

PETER KING
78 Miles Music MM 076 BROTHER BERNARD (LP, with Alan Skidmore) ... 20

PETER KING
85 Fashion FAD 029 Step On The Gas/Ten Commandments Of An MC (12") ... 60
85 Fashion FAD 045 Bad Memory/Rewind/Jack It Up (12") ... 30

RAMONA KING
64 Warner Bros WB 125 It's In His Kiss/It Couldn't Happen To A Nicer Guy ... 25

RAY KING SOUL BAND
67 Piccadilly 7N 35394 Behold/Soon You'll Be Gone ... 20
68 Direction 8-63394 LIVE AT THE PLAYBOY CLUB (LP) ... 20

REG KING
(see also Action, Andy Leigh, B.B. Blunder, Mark Charig, Elton Dean, Mighty Baby)
71 United Artists UP 35204 Little Boy/10,000 Miles (as Reg King & B.B. Blunder) ... 25
71 United Artists UAG 29157 REG KING (LP) ... 80

ROBERT KING
(see also Scars)
82 Charisma PRE 23 Paper Heart/Theme For Love ... 10

SAMMY KING (& VOLTAIRS)
64 HMV POP 1285 What's The Secret/Great Balls Of Fire (as Sammy King & Voltairs) ... 10
64 HMV POP 1330 Rag Doll/We're Through ... 8
65 HMV POP 1384 Only You (And You Alone)/A Kiss, A Promise ... 10
66 HMV POP 1540 If You Can Find Someone To Love You/Past Caring (with Voltairs) ... 8

SID KING & FIVE STRINGS
56 Philips PB 589 Booger Red/Oobie-Doobie (78) ... 100

SOLOMON KING
(see also Levi Jackson)
67 Columbia DB 8306 She Wears My Ring/Try Try (withdrawn B-side) ... 10
70 Columbia DB 8676 Say A Prayer/This Beautiful Day ... 100
70 Columbia DB 8676 Say A Prayer/This Beautiful Day (demo copy) ... 150
72 Polydor 2058258 When You Gotta Go/Life Child ... 30
68 Columbia S(C)X 6250 SHE WEARS MY RING (LP) ... 18
71 Columbia SCX 6458 YOU'LL NEVER WALK ALONE (LP) ... 15

MINT VALUE £

SONNY KING
60 Pye Intl. NPL 28001 — FOR LOSERS ONLY (LP) 12

TEDDI KING
(see also George Shearing)
56 Vogue Coral Q 72142 — My Funny Little Lover/I'll Never Be The Same 5
57 Vogue EPV 1204 — STORYVILLE PRESENTS MISS TEDDI KING (EP) 12
55 Vogue LDE 142 — MISS TEDDI KING WITH RUBY BRAFF (10" LP) 15
57 Vogue VA 160109 — NOW IN VOGUE (LP) 15

TEDDY KING & BUSTER'S ALLSTARS
67 Fab FAB 27 — Mexican Divorce/SOUL TOPS: Baby I Got News 18

TOBY KING
75 President PT 430 — First Man To Die From The Blues/Country Bump 6

TONY KING (& HIPPY BOYS)
(see also Maytals)
69 Trojan TR 667 — Proud Mary/My Devotion (as Tony King & Hippy Boys) 6
70 Gas GAS 156 — Daddy, Daddy Don't Cry/I Like It 6

TONY KING SOUND
75 BBC Records REC 201 — MUSIC THROUGH MIDNIGHT (LP) 15

KINGBEES
66 Tempo TPO 103 — I'm A Kingbee/My Little Red Book (Irish-only, in p/s) 350
66 Tempo TPO 103 — I'm A Kingbee/My Little Red Book (Irish-only) 250

KING BISCUIT BOY
(see also Bobby Bland)
70 Paramount SPFL 270 — OFFICIAL MUSIC (LP) 18
71 Paramount SPFA 7001 — GOODUNS (LP) 18

KING BROTHERS
(see also Jim Dale, Dennis King)
57 Parlophone R 4288 — Marianne/Little By Little 10
57 Parlophone R 4310 — A White Sport Coat (And A Pink Carnation)/Minne-Minnehaha! 8
57 Parlophone R 4338 — In The Middle Of An Island/Rockin' Shoes 10
57 Parlophone R 4367 — Wake Up Little Susie/Winter Wonderland 10
58 Parlophone R 4438 — Torero/Moonlight And Roses 6
58 Parlophone R 4469 — Sitting In A Tree House/Father Time 5
59 Parlophone R 4513 — Leaning On A Lamp-Post/Thank Heaven For Little Girls 5
59 Parlophone R 4554 — Hop, Skip And Jump/Civilization (Bongo, Bongo, Bongo) 10
59 Parlophone R 4577 — Makin' Love/Caribbean 6
61 Parlophone R 4825 — The Next Train Out Of Town/Sabre Dance 6
61 Parlophone R 4861 — The Language Of Love/Got Tell Her For Me 7
64 Oriole CB 1978 — Real Live Girl/Every Time It Rains 6
58 Parlophone PMC 1060 — THREE KINGS AND AN ACE (LP) 15

KING CANNON
(see also Cannon Ball & Johnny Melody, Carl Bryan, Max Romeo, Lester Sterling, Kid Gungo, Erroll Dunkley)
69 Trojan TR 663 — Soul Scorcher/GLEN & DAVE: Lucky Boy 15
69 Harry J TR 664 — Soul Special/TREVOR SHIELD: Moon Is Playing Tricks On Me 30
69 Crab CRAB 6 — Mellow Trumpet/VAL BENNETT: Reggae City 12
71 Hillcrest HCT 2 — Reggay Got Soul/SOUL CATS: Land Of Love 7
71 Moodisc HME 109 — Raw Deal (as King Cannon Allout; actually by Carl Bryan)/ MUDIE'S ALL STARS: Shirley's Hide Out 6

KING CANNON (BALL)
68 Trojan TR 636 — Thunderstorm/BURT WALTERS: Honey Love 40

KING CHUBBY
(see also Junior Byles)
70 Pama Supreme PS 297 — What's The World Coming To/Live As One 10
70 Supreme PS 297 — What's The World Coming To/Live As One (reissue) 10

KING CRIMSON
(see also Giles Giles & Fripp, Fripp & Eno, Andy Summers & Robert Fripp, Gordon Haskell, Shame, McDonald & Giles, Emerson Lake & Palmer, Uriah Heep, Boz, Trendsetters Ltd., Pete Sinfield)
69 Island WIP 6071 — The Court Of The Crimson King (Parts 1 & 2) 20
70 Island WIP 6080 — Cat Food/Groon (in p/s) 25
70 Island WIP 6080 — Cat Food/Groon 10
74 Island WIP 6189 — The Night Watch/The Great Deceiver 7
76 Island WIP 6274 — 21st Century Schizoid Man/Epitaph (in p/s) 30
76 Island WIP 6274 — 21st Century Schizoid Man/Epitaph 10
96 Virgin VSCDG 1597 — SCHIZOID MAN (CD, EP, digipak) 8
69 Island ILPS 9111 — IN THE COURT OF THE CRIMSON KING (LP, 1st pressing, pink label/'i' logo) 450
70 Island ILPS 9111 — IN THE COURT OF THE CRIMSON KING (LP, 2nd pressing, pink rim label/'palm tree' logo) 30
70 Island ILPS 9127 — IN THE WAKE OF POSEIDON (LP, 1st pressing, pink label/'i' logo) 100
70 Island ILPS 9127 — IN THE WAKE OF POSEIDON (LP, 2nd pressing, pink rim label/'palm tree' logo) 30
70 Island ILPS 9141 — LIZARD (LP, pink rim label/'palm tree' logo) 50
71 Island ILPS 9175 — ISLANDS (LP, pink rim label/'palm tree' logo, gatefold sleeve with inner) 40
72 Island HELP 6 — EARTHBOUND (LP, black/pink label) 30
73 Island ILPS 9230 — LARKS' TONGUES IN ASPIC (LP, pink rim label/'palm tree' logo, with inner) 30
74 Island ILPS 9275 — STARLESS AND BIBLE BLACK (LP, pink rim label/'palm tree' logo, with inner) 45
74 Island ILPS 9308 — RED (LP, pink rim label/'palm tree' logo, with inner sleeve) 45
75 Island ILPS 9316 — U.S.A. (LP, pink rim label/'palm tree' logo, with inner) 12
76 Island ISLP 7 — A YOUNG PERSON'S GUIDE (2-LP, with booklet) 18
95 EG/Virgin CDVKCX 13 — THRAK (CD, in metal box, with tour programme) 20
81 EG EGLP 49 — DISCIPLINE (LP) 20
82 EG EGLP51 — BEAT (LP) 20

MINT VALUE £

KING CRY CRY (Prince Far I)
71 Banana BA 356 I Had A Talk/BURNING SPEAR: Zion Higher 25

KING CURTIS
(see also Champion Jack Dupree, Eric Clapton)
62 London HLU 9547 Soul Twist/Twistin' Time (as King Curtis & Noble Knights) 20
64 Capitol CL 15346 Soul Serenade/More Soul 20
67 Atlantic 584 109 Good To Me/Hold On I'm Comin' 10
67 Atlantic 584 134 Memphis Soul Stew/Blue Nocturne 15
68 Speciality SPE 1000 Wiggle Wobble/Night Train 8
69 Atlantic 584 287 Little Green Apples/La Jeanne 8
70 Atco 2091 012 Teasin'/Soulin' (as King Curtis & Delaney Bramlett, Eric Clapton & Friends) 15
60 London RE-K 1307 HAVE TENOR SAX, WILL BLOW (EP) 40
60 London HA-K 2247 HAVE TENOR SAX, WILL BLOW (LP) 60
62 RCA RD 27252 ARTHUR MURRAY'S MUSIC FOR DANCING - THE TWIST (LP) 30
62 Esquire 32-161 THE NEW SCENE OF KING CURTIS (LP) 40
67 Atlantic 587 067 PLAYS THE GREAT MEMPHIS HITS (LP) 20
68 Ember SPE/LP 6600 SOUL SERENADE (LP) 18
68 Atlantic 587 093 KINGSIZE SOUL (LP, as King Curtis & Kingpins) 18
68 Atlantic 587/588 115 SWEET SOUL (LP) 18
69 Atco 228 002 BEST OF KING CURTIS (LP) 12
69 Atco 228 027 INSTANT GROOVE (LP) 15

KING CURTIS, OLIVER NELSON & JIMMY FORREST
63 Esquire 32-189 SOUL BATTLE (LP) 30

KING DIAMOND
89 Road Runner RR 94616 CONSPIRACY (LP, picture disc) 20

KINGDOM
70 United Artists UP 35145 All I Need/Nothing Could Be Better 25

BOBBY KINGDOM/BLUE BEATS
61 Bluebeat BB 44 Honey Please/BLUE BEATS: That's My Girl 25
62 Blue Beat 45/BB/77 Spanish Town Twist/Brand New Automobile 12

KINGDOM COME (U.K.)
(see also Arcadium. Arthur Brown, Kiki Dee, Spirit Of John Morgan, Arcadium)
71 Polydor 2001 234 Eternal Messenger/I D Side To B Side The C Side 5
72 Polydor 2001 416 Spirit Of Joy/Come Alive 5
72 Polydor 2310 130 GALACTIC ZOO DOSSIER (LP, gatefold sleeve, with poster) 50
72 Polydor 2310 130 GALACTIC ZOO DOSSIER (LP, gatefold sleeve, without poster) 20
72 Polydor 2310 178 KINGDOM COME (LP) 25
73 Polydor 2310 254 JOURNEY (LP) 20

KING-EARL BOOGIE BAND
(see also Mungo Jerry, Paul King, Skeleton Crew)
72 Dawn DNS 1024 Plastic Jesus/If The Lord Don't Get You 6
72 Dawn DNS 1028 Starlight/Goin' To Germany 6
72 Dawn DNLS 3040 TROUBLE AT MILL (LP, with poster) 30
72 Dawn DNLS 3040 TROUBLE AT MILL (LP, without poster) 20

KING EDWARDS ALL STARS
66 Rio R 077 North Coast/Kingston 11 150

(KING) EDWARDS GROUP
63 Island WI 040 Dear Hearts/Oh Mary (B-side actually by Ransford Barnett) 25
63 Island WI 047 Russian Roulette (actually by King Edwards All Stars)/You're Mine (actually by Douglas Brothers) 30
63 Island WI 082 He Gave You To Me/Kings Priests And Prophets (both actually by The Schoolboys) 20
63 Island WI 087 Hey Girl/Skies Are Grey (both actually by Ransford Barnett) 18

KING FIGHTER
60s Jump Up JU 518 People Will Talk/Same Thing 8

KINGFISH
(see also Grateful Dead, Bob Weir)
76 United Artists UAG 29922 KINGFISH (LP) 12
77 United Artists UAG 30080 LIVE AND KICKIN' (LP) 12

KING GEORGE
67 RCA RCA 1573 Drive On James/I'm Gonna Be Somebody Someday 30

KING HARVEST
73 Pye NSPL 28174 DANCING IN THE MOONLIGHT (LP) 15

KING HORROR
(see also Laurel Aitken)
69 Joe/Duke DU 34 Dracula Prince Of Darkness/JOE'S ALL STARS: Honky 30
69 Grape GR 3003 Cutting Blade/Vampire 45
69 Grape GR 3006 The Hole/WINSTON GROOVY: Lover Come Back 25
69 Grape GR 3007 Lochness Monster/VISIONS: Zion I. 25
69 Jackpot JP 713 Wood In The Fire/The Naked City 15
69 Jackpot JP 714 Police/PAMA DICE: Honky Tonk Popcorn 30
70 Nu Beat NB 051 Frankenstein/WINSTON GROOVY: I Can't Stand It 60
70 Reggae REG 3005 Slave Driver 20

KING KONG
86 Greensleeves GRED 206 Paro Them Paro/BUBBLERS COMPUTER STARS : Paranoia (12") 30
85 Now Generation NG 013 Predominant/Version (12") 12

KING KOSS
69 Polydor 56329 Spinning Wheel/Louisiana 8

MINT VALUE £

KING KURT
82 Thin Sliced TSR 2 — Zulu Beat/Rockin' Kurt (various coloured p/s) 10

KINGLY BAND
69 Decca F 12926 — The Bitter And The Sweet/Standing At The Crossroads 7

KING MIGUEL
73 Bullet BU 524 — The Word Is Black/Town Talk 10

KING OF LUXEMBOURG
86 él GPO 14 — Valleri/Sketches Of Luxembourg (p/s) 12

KINGPINS (U.K.)
65 Oriole CB 1986 — Two Right Feet/That's The Way It Should Be 35

KINGPINS (U.S.)
58 London HLU 8658 — Ungaua Parts 1 & 2 15
58 London HLU 8658 — Ungaua Parts 1 & 2 (78) 10

KING ROCK & WILLOWS
67 Caltone TONE 111 — You Are The One/ALVA LEWIS: Return Home 55

KING ROCKY
(see also Leroy & Rocky, Clancy Eccles, Heptones)
68 Studio One SO 2045 — The King Is Back/THREE TOPS: Vex Till Yuh Buss 40

KINGS IV
59 London HLT 8914 — Some Like It Hot/The World Goes On 12
59 London HLT 8914 — Some Like It Hot/The World Goes On (78) 15

KING SCRATCH
(see also Lee Perry/Upsetters, Skatalites)
70s Ethnic ETH 16 — Spiritual Whip/Version 20
70s Ethnic ETH 30 — Mash Finger/Version 20

KING'S HENCHMEN
59 Coral FEP 2025 — ALAN FREED PRESENTS VOL. 1 (EP) 150

KING SISTERS
57 Capitol CL 14711 — While The Lights Are Low/In Hamburg (When The Nights Are Long) 10
57 Capitol CL 14729 — Imagination/You're My Thrill 5
57 Capitol CL 14777 — Easy To Love/That Old Feeling 5
58 Capitol CL 14865 — Deep Purple/Unbelievable 5
58 Capitol CL 14893 — What's New?/The Thrill Was New 5
58 Capitol CL 14934 — Autumn In Pleasant Grove/The Guy In The Foreign Sports Car 5
59 Capitol CL 15012 — Keep Smiling (Keep Laughin', Be Happy)/The Maids Of Cadiz 5
59 Capitol CL 15069 — Lovin' Up A Storm/What Would I Do Without You 5
59 Capitol CL 15096 — Over The River (And Through The Woods)/Holiday Of Love (with Their Family) 5
57 Capitol EAP1 919 — IMAGINATION (EP) 8

PADDY KINGSLAND
74 EMI 2110 — Spinball/Wobulator Rock 6
74 Studio 2 TWOX 1024 — SUPERCHARGED (LP) 20

CHARLES KINGSLEY CREATION
65 Columbia DB 7758 — Summer Without Sun/Still In Love With You 70

EVELYN KINGSLEY & TOWERS
(see also Towers)
58 Capitol CL 14944 — To Know Him Is To Love Him/FRANK PERRY & TOWERS: Let Me Be The One 20

KINGSMEN
(see also Bill Haley & Comets)
58 London HLE 8735 — Better Believe It/Week-End 30
58 London HLE 8735 — Better Believe It/Week-End (78) 20
59 London HLE 8812 — Conga Rock/The Cat Walk 30
59 London HLE 8812 — Conga Rock/The Cat Walk (78) 30
59 London REE 1211 — THE KINGSMEN (EP) 100

KINGSMEN
(see also Touch)
63 Pye International 7N 25231 — Louie Louie/Haunted Castle 30
64 Pye International 7N 25262 — Little Latin Lupe Lu/David's Mood 15
64 Pye International 7N 25273 — Death Of An Angel/Searching For Love 10
65 Pye International 7N 25292 — The Jolly Green Giant/Long Green 8
65 Pye International 7N 25311 — The Climb/Waiting 10
65 Pye International 7N 25322 — Annie Fanny/Something's Got A Hold On Me 10
66 Pye International 7N 25366 — Little Latin Lupe Lu/Louie Louie 15
66 Pye International 7N 25370 — Killer Joe/Little Green Thing 10
67 Pye International 7N 25406 — Daytime Shadows/Trouble 10
71 Wand WN 14 — Louie Louie/If I Needed Someone 8
64 Pye Intl. NEP 44023 — THE KINGSMEN (EP) 30
65 Pye Intl. NEP 44040 — MOJO WORKOUT (EP) 30
66 Pye Intl. NEP 44063 — FEVER (EP) 30
63 Pye Intl. NPL 28050 — THE KINGSMEN IN PERSON (LP, live) 25
64 Pye Intl. NPL 28054 — THE KINGSMEN VOLUME II (LP) 25
65 Pye Intl. NPL 28068 — THE KINGSMEN ON CAMPUS (LP) 25
66 Pye Intl. NPL 28085 — 15 GREAT HITS (LP) 25
68 Marble Arch MAL 829 — THE KINGSMEN'S GREATEST HITS (LP) 15

KING SOUNDS
78 Grove Music GMDM5 — Spend One Night In Babylon (feat. Trinity)/Keep Us Down In Poverty (feat. Jah Woosh) (12") 25
79 Grove Music GMDM 11 — They That Hate Us (wrongfully)/Ungrateful Bretheren (12") 15
79 Grove Music GMDM 20 — Kill Them Dead/Look Into Youself (12") 15
82 Grove ILPS 9663 — FORWARD (LP, with the Israelites) 12

MINT VALUE £

KING SPARROW
(see also Mighty Sparrow, Sparrow)

58	Melodisc MEL 1447	Leading Calypsonians/BILLY MOORE: Love Is Everywhere	10
58	Melodisc MEL 1475	Familysize Cokes/Clara Honey Bunch	10
59	Melodisc MEL 1491	Goaty/I Confess	10
59	Melodisc MEL 1491	Goaty/I Confess (78)	12
66	Island WI 285	Beggars Have No Choice (actually by Leonard Dillon & Wailers)/ MARCIA GRIFFITHS: Funny	50

KING SPORTY

70	Banana BA 321	Inspiration/Choice Of Music	12
70	Banana BA 322	Lover's Version (as Sporty & Wilson)/DUDLEY SIBLEY: Having A Party	22
70	Punch PH 44	For Our Desire/WINSTON WRIGHT: Version	15
71	Banana BA 323	D.J. Special/RICHARD & MAD: Creation Version	12
73	Green Door GD 4063	Yearful Of Sundays/Version	6

KING STITT
(see also Kurass)

69	Clandisc CLA 200	Who Yea/DYNAMITES: Mr Midnight	12
69	Clandisc CLA 202	Vigerton Two/On The Street	12
69	Clandisc CLA 203	On The Street/CYNTHIA RICHARDS: Foolish Fool	15
69	Clandisc CLA 206	The Ugly One/CLANCY ECCLES: Dance Beat	25
70	Clandisc CLA 207	Herbsman Shuffle (with Andy [Capp])/HIGGS & WILSON: Don't Mind Me	12
70	Clandisc CLA 223	King Of Kings/DYNAMITES: Reggaedelic	12
71	Clandisc CLA 235	Merry Rhythm/CLANCY ECCLES: John Crow Skank	10
71	Banana BA 332	Back Out Version/VEGETABLES: Holly Rhythm	15
71	Banana BA 334	Rhyming Time/Reality	12

KINGS COUNTY CARNIVAL

69	United Artists UP 2267	Don't Vote For Luke McCabe/The Proof Of The Pudding	18

KINGSTON ALLSTARS

66	Dice CC 25	Happy Hunter/LITTLE NORMA: Ten Commandments Of Woman	25

KINGSTONIANS
(see also Jack (Bernard) & Beanstalks, Gregory Isaacs)

67	Rio R 140	Winey Winey/I Don't Care	30
68	Coxsone CS 7066	Mother Miserable/I Make A Woman	150
68	Doctor Bird DB 1120	Put Down Your Fire/Girls Like Dirt	100
68	Doctor Bird DB 1123	Mummy And Daddy/False Witness	100
68	Doctor Bird DB 1126	Fun Galore/Crime Don't Pay	100
68	Trojan TR 627	Mix It Up/I'll Be Around	40
69	Big Shot BI 508	Sufferer/Kiss A Little Finger	40
69	Big Shot BI 526	Nice Nice/I'll Be Around	30
69	Crab CRAB 19	Hold Down/BARRY YORK: Who Will She Be	50
69	Bullet BU 409	I Am Just A Minstrel/Yesterday	25
69	Songbird SB 1011	The Clip/BRUCE ANTHONY: Little Miss Muffett	20
70	Songbird SB 1019	Singer Man/CRYSTALITES: Version	15
70	Songbird SB 1041	Rumble Rumble/CRYSTALITES: Version	20
70	Songbird SB 1045	Out There/CRYSTALITES: Out There Version II	20
70	Trojan TR 7708	I'll Need You Tomorrow/I'm Gonna Make It	10
70	Duke DU 88	You Can't Wine/RUPIE EDWARDS ALLSTARS: Bee Sting	15
72	Duke DU 126	Lion's Den/Version	15
70	Trojan TBL 113	SUFFERER (LP)	50

KINGS OF LEON

03	Handmedown HMD 28	Molly's Chambers/Holy Roller Novocaine (10", limited issue, numbered p/s)	20
03	Handmedown HMD 31	Wasted Time/Molly's Hangover (10", silver vinyl, numbered p/s)	15
03	Handmedown HMD 20	HOLY ROLLER NOVOCAINE EP: Molly's Chambers/California Waiting/ Holy Roller Novocaine (10", clear red vinyl, numbered p/s, 1000 only)	50
03	Handmedown HMD 21	HOLY ROLLER NOVOCAINE EP (CD, digipak, 1000 only)	20
03	Handmedown HMD 22	WHAT I SAW EP: Red Morning Light/Wicker Chair (10", blue vinyl, numbered p/s)	20
03	Handmedown HMD 24	What I Saw/Red Morning Light/Introducing The Band (audio/visual DVD single)	20
04	Handmedown HMD 43	The Bucket/Trani (Live) (numbered p/s)	8
05	Handmedown HMD 47	Four Kicks/Head To Toe (numbered p/s)	8
05	Handmedown HMD 50	King Of The Rodeo/Soft (Live) (numbered p/s)	8
07	Handmedown HMD 51	On Call/My Third House (p/s)	8
07	Handmedown HMD 53	Fans/Woo Hoo (p/s)	8
07	Handmedown HMD 54	Charmer/My Party (Chad Hugo/Kenna Remix) (p/s)	8
08	RCA 88697 36890 7	Sex On Fire/Beneath The Surface (p/s)	8
03	Handmedown HMD	YOUTH & YOUNG MANHOOD (2 - 10", p/s with picture inners)	50
04	Handmedown HMD 40	AHA SHAKE HEARTBREAK (2-LP, 10" white vinyl, gatefold sleeve)	18

KINGSTON JOE

64	Blue Beat BB 253	Time Is On My Friend (actually by Lloyd Barnes)/Wear And Tear (B-side actually by Lascelles Perkins)	30

KINGSTON PETE & BUSTER'S ALL STARS
(see also Larry Marshall)

67	Blue Beat BB 403	Little Boy Blue/I'm A Lover Try Me (actually by Larry Marshall)	90

KINGSTON TRIO
(see also John Stewart)

58	Capitol CL 14918	Scarlet Ribbons/Three Jolly Coachmen	5
58	Capitol CL 14951	Tom Dooley/Ruby Red	5
59	Capitol CL 14985	Raspberries, Strawberries/Sally	5
59	Capitol CL 15002	The Tijuana Jail/Oh Cindy	5
59	Capitol CL 15073	San Miguel/A Worried Man	7
63	Capitol CL 15287	Greenback Dollar/The New Frontier	7
64	Capitol EAP 1-20460	GREENBACK DOLLAR (EP)	8

MINT VALUE £

KING TRUMAN

(see also Style Council, Paul Weller)

89	Acid Jazz JAZID 9T	Like A Gun (Safe Sax Mix)/(Dub Version)/(Radio Edit) (12", p/s)	75

KING TUBBY & THE AGGROVATORS

82	Black Music BMLP 804	DUBBING IN THE BACKYARD (LP)	25

KING TUBBY & LEE PERRY

75	Live & Love LALP 02	MEETS THE AGROVATORS AT THE DUB STATION (LP)	75
76	Prophets (no. cat. no.)	PROPHECY OF DUB (LP, in plain sleeve)	120
76	Fay FMLP 307	SURROUNDED BY DREAD AT THE NATIONAL ARENA (LP)	55
76	Klik KLIP 9002	SHALOM DUB (LP)	40
77	Fay Music FMLP 304	KING TUBBY MEETS THE UPSETTER AT THE GRASS ROOTS OF DUB (LP)	25
78	Studio 16 WE 102	SURROUNDED BY DREAD AT THE NATIONAL ARENA (LP, re-issue)	35
79	Star PTLP 1029	MAJESTIC DUB (LP)	25
81	Live & Love LAP 015	UPSETS THE UPSETTER (LP)	35

KING TUBBY MEETS ROOTS RADICS

81	Copasetic COPLP 5002	DANGEROUS DUB (LP)	20

KING TUBBY, PRINCE JAMMY & SCIENTIST

81	K&G Imperial KGLP 002	FIRST, SECOND AND THIRD GENERATION OF DUB (LP)	35

KINKS

(see also Dave Davies, Ray Davies, Maple Oak, Leapy Lee, Phoenix)

PYE SINGLES

64	Pye 7N 15611	Long Tall Sally/I Took My Baby Home	120
64	Pye 7N 15611	Long Tall Sally/I Took My Baby Home (Demo copy)	100
64	Pye 7N 15636	You Still Want Me/You Do Something To Me)	170
64	Pye 7N 15636	You Still Want Me/You Do Something To Me (Demo copy)	110
64	Pye 7N 15673	You Really Got Me/It's All Right	10
64	Pye 7N 15714	All Day And All Of The Night/I Gotta Move	10
65	Pye 7N 15759	Tired Of Waiting For You/Come On Now	8
65	Pye 7N 15813	Everybody's Gonna Be Happy/Who'll Be The Next In Line	10
65	Pye 7N 15854	Set Me Free/I Need You	8
65	Pye 7N 15919	See My Friend/Never Met A Girl Like You Before	8
65	Pye 7N 15981	Till The End Of The Day/Where Have All The Good Times Gone	8
66	Pye 7N 17064	Dedicated Follower Of Fashion/Sittin' On My Sofa	8
66	Pye 7N 17125	Sunny Afternoon/I'm Not Like Everybody Else	8
66	Pye 7N 17222	Dead End Street/Big Black Smoke (some labels list "Deadend")	8
67	Pye 7N 17321	Waterloo Sunset/Act Nice And Gentle	8
67	Pye 7N 17400	Autumn Almanac/Mr. Pleasant	10
68	Pye 7N 17468	Wonderboy/Polly	15
68	Pye 7N 17573	Days/She's Got Everything	15
69	Pye 7N 17724	Plastic Man/King Kong	15
69	Pye 7N 17776	Drivin'/Mindless Child Of Motherhood	25
69	Pye 7N 17812	Shangri-La/Last Of The Steam-Powered Trains (unissued, acetates only)	0
69	Pye 7N 17812	Shangri-La/This Man He Weeps Tonight	25
69	Pye 7N 17865	Victoria/Mr Churchill Says	12
70	Pye 7N 17961	Lola/Berkeley Mews	6
70	Pye 7N 45016	Apeman/Rats	8
71	Pye PMM 100	You Really Got Me/Set Me Free/Wonder Boy/Long Tall Shorty (maxi-single, p/s)	8
71	Pye 7NX 8001	PERCY (33rpm 4-track maxi-single, p/s)	20
74	Pye 7N 45313	Where Have All The Good Times Gone/Lola (p/s)	20
79	Arista ARIS 12240	I Wish I Could Fly Like Superman/Low Budget	5
83	PRT KPD 1	You Really Got Me/Misty Water (picture disc)	10
84	PRT KIS 003	All Day And All Of The Night/I Gotta Move (picture disc)	10

EXPORT SINGLES

65	Pye 7N 15981	Till The End Of The Day/Where Have All The Good Times Gone (export p/s)	150
66	Pye 7N 17100	Well Respected Man/Milk Cow Blues	110
67	Pye 7N 17314	Mr. Pleasant/This Is Where I Belong	90
67	Pye 7N 17405	Autumn Almanac/David Watts	90
71	Pye 7N 8001	God's Children/Moments (in p/s)	60
71	Pye 7N 8001	God's Children/Moments	30

RCA SINGLES

72	RCA RCA 2211	Supersonic Rocket Ship/You Don't Know My Name	6
72	RCA RCA 2299	Celluloid Heroes/Hot Potatoes	8
73	RCA RCA 2387	Sitting In The Midday Sun/One Of The Survivors	8
73	RCA RCA 2418	Sweet Lady Genevieve/Sitting In My Hotel	8
74	RCA RCA 5015	Mirror Of Love/Cricket	12
74	RCA RCA 5042	Mirror Of Love/He's Evil	12
74	RCA RCA 2478	Holiday Romance/Shepherds Of The Nation	10
75	RCA RCA 2546	Ducks On The Wall/Rush Hour Blues	10
75	RCA RCA 2567	You Can't Stop The Music/Have Another Drink	10
76	RCA RCM 1	No More Looking Back/Jack The Idiot Dunce/The Hard Way (p/s)	12

ARISTA SINGLES

77	Arista ARIST 153	Father Christmas/Prince Of The Punks (p/s)	10
78	Arista ARIST 189	A Rock'n'Roll Fantasy/Artificial Light	8
78	Arista ARIST 210	Black Messiah/Misfits (p/s)	8
79	Arista ARIST 300	Moving Pictures/In A Space (p/s)	8
80	Arista ARIST 404	Lola (live)/Celluloid Heroes (live) (export only)	12
81	Arista ARIST 415	Better Things/Massive Reductions (p/s)	10
81	Arista ARIST 415/KINKS 1	Better Things/Massive Reductions//Lola (live)/David Watts (live) (double pack, gatefold p/s)	8
81	Arista ARIPD 426	Predictable/Back To Front (picture disc)	8
83	Arista ARIST 524	Don't Forget To Dance/Bernadette (p/s)	7
83	Arista ARIST 524	Don't Forget To Dance/Bernadette//Predictable/Back To Front (shrinkwrapped with free picture disc)	12

MINT VALUE £

OTHER SINGLES

84	Music Week	How Are You (freebie with Music Week magazine)	7
86	London LON 119	How Are You/Killing Time (p/s)	12
87	London LONX 132	Lost And Found/Killing Time (p/s, shrinkwrapped with bonus 7" The Official Ray Davies Interview/"Extracts From The LP 'Think Visual' ")	12
88	London LON 165	The Road (7" Edit)/Art Lover (p/s)	8
89	London LONCD 239	Down All The Days (Til 1992)/You Really Got Me (live)/Entertainment (CD)	12
89	London LON 239	Down All The Days (Til 1992)/You Really Got Me (live) (p/s)	6
90	London LONCD 250	How Do I Get Close/War Is Over (CD, card sleeve)	10
90	London LON 250	How Do I Get Close/War Is Over (p/s)	6
91	Columbia COL 657593-2	Did Ya/Gotta Move (live)/New World/Days/ Look Through Any Doorway (1991) (CD)	12
94	Konk Grapevine KNKD 2	Waterloo Sunset 94/You Really Got Me (live)/Elevator Man/On The Outside (CD)	8

EPs

64	Pye NEP 24200	KINKSIZE SESSION	30
64	Pye NEP 24203	KINKSIZE HITS	40
65	Pye NEP 24221	KWYET KINKS	45
66	Pye NEP 24258	DEDICATED KINKS	120
68	Pye NEP 24296	THE KINKS	275
75	Pye AMEP 1001	THE KINKS ('Yesteryear' export issue, red or blue vinyl)	22

PYE ALBUMS

64	Pye NPL 18096	THE KINKS (mono)	150
64	Pye NSPL 83021	THE KINKS (stereo, export only)	225
65	Pye NSPL 18096	THE KINKS (stereo, export only, reissue)	260
65	Pye NPL 18112	KINDA KINKS	100
65	Pye NPL 18131	THE KINK KONTROVERSY	100
65	Pye NSPL 18131	THE KINK KONTROVERSY (reprocessed stereo with stickered catalogue number, export only)	270
66	Pye NPL 18149	FACE TO FACE (mono)	120
66	Pye NSPL 18149	FACE TO FACE (stereo, stickered sleeve "export only")	200
66	Pye ZCP 18149	FACE TO FACE (, original issue)	18
67	Golden Guinea GGL 0357	THE KINKS (reissue, mono)	12
67	Golden Guinea GGGL 10357	THE KINKS (reissue, stereo)	15
67	Pye NPL 18191	LIVE AT KELVIN HALL (mono)	100
67	Pye NSPL 18191	LIVE AT KELVIN HALL (stereo)	150

(The above Pye LPs were originally issued with laminated flipback sleeves, pink labels & light blue labels)

67	Pye NPL 18193	SOMETHING ELSE BY THE KINKS (mono)	175
67	Pye NSPL 18193	SOMETHING ELSE BY THE KINKS (stereo)	140
68	Pye N(S)PL 18233	THE KINKS ARE THE VILLAGE GREEN PRESERVATION SOCIETY (unissued, 12-track version, 2 test pressings only)	800
68	Pye NPL 18233	THE KINKS ARE THE VILLAGE GREEN PRESERVATION SOCIETY (15-track version, mono)	200
68	Pye NSPL 18233	THE KINKS ARE THE VILLAGE GREEN PRESERVATION SOCIETY (15-track version, stereo)	150
69	Pye NPL 18317	ARTHUR (mono, gatefold sleeve "Quiien Victoria" insert)	150
69	Pye NSPL 18317	ARTHUR (stereo, gatefold sleeve "Quiien Victoria" insert)	50
70	Pye NPL 18326	THE KINKS (2-LP, gatefold sleeve)	20
70	Pye NSPL 18359	THE KINKS PT 1 - LOLA VS POWERMAN & THE MONEY-GO-ROUND (gatefold sleeve)	22
71	Pye NSPL 18365	SOUNDTRACK FROM THE FILM 'PERCY' (soundtrack)	40
73	Pye 11PP 100	ALL THE GOOD TIMES (4-LP, box set)	50
83	PRT KINK 1	GREATEST HITS (with bonus 10" EP of unreleased material)	40

OTHER ALBUMS

71	RCA SF 8243	MUSWELL HILLBILLIES (gatefold sleeve)	40
72	RCA DPS 2035	EVERYBODY'S IN SHOWBIZ, EVERYBODY'S A STAR (2-LP, gatefold sleeve)	22
73	RCA SF 8392	PRESERVATION ACT 1	20
74	RCA LPL2 5040	PRESERVATION ACT 2 (2-LP, gatefold sleeve)	25
75	RCA SF 8411	SOAP OPERA (gatefold sleeve)	15
75	RCA RS 1028	SCHOOLBOYS IN DISGRACE	12
76	RCA RS 1059	CELLULOID HEROES	15
93	Sony 472489-1	PHOBIA (omits 2 tracks from CD)	35
94	Konk Grapevine KNK LP 1	TO THE BONE (LP)	12

TONY KINSEY (QUARTET)

55	Decca F 10548	She's Funny That Way/Fascinatin' Rhythm	20
55	Decca F 10606	Close Your Eyes/Pierrot	15
55	Decca F 10648	Hey! There/Ballet	25
56	Decca F 10708	Stompin' At The Savoy/China Boy (with Dill Jones)	6
56	Decca F 10709	Moonglow/One O'Clock Jump	6
56	Decca FJ 10725	Starboard Bow/Body And Soul	6
56	Decca FJ 10760	Lullaby Of The Leaves/Isolation	12
56	Decca FJ 10773	In A Ditch/A Smooth One	6
57	Decca FJ 10851	Mean To Me/Supper Party	12
57	Decca F 10952	The Midgets/Blue Eyes	6
62	Ember JBS 707	Girl In Blue/Weber The Great	20
56	Decca DFE 6282	PRESENTING THE TONY KINSEY QUARTET NO. 1 (EP)	40
56	Decca DFE 6285	PRESENTING THE TONY KINSEY QUARTET NO. 2 (EP)	40
58	Decca DFE 6461	MY FAIR LADY (EP)	15
59	Parlophone SGE 2004	RED BIRD - JAZZ AND POETRY (EP, mono [GEP 8765]/stereo, with Christopher Logue)	25
59	Parlophone SGE 2008	FOURSOME (EP, stereo)	15
57	Decca LK 4186	INTRODUCING THE QUINTET (LP)	100
57	Decca LK 4207	JAZZ AT THE FLAMINGO (LP)	75
58	Decca LK 4274	TIME GENTLEMEN PLEASE (LP)	80
61	Ember EMB 3337	AN EVENING WITH ... (LP)	70
63	Decca LK 4534	HOW TO SUCCEED IN BUSINESS WITHOUT REALLY TRYING (LP, with Gordon Beck)	50

MINT VALUE £

TONY KINSEY TRIO & JOE HARRIOTT
(see also Joe Harriott)

54	Esquire EP 36	TONY KINSEY TRIO & JOE HARRIOTT (EP)	40
54	Esquire EP 52	TONY KINSEY TRIO & JOE HARRIOTT (EP)	40
54	Esquire EP 82	TONY KINSEY TRIO & JOE HARRIOTT (EP)	40

KINSMEN
(see also Four Kinsmen)

68	Decca F 22724	Glasshouse Green, Splinter Red/It's Started To Rain Again	30
68	Decca F 22777	It's Good To See You/Always The Loser	10

KIPPER FAMILY

84	Dambuster DAM 005	SINCE TIME IMMORAL (LP)	12

KIPPINGTON LODGE
(see also Brinsley Schwartz, Nick Lowe)

67	Parlophone R 5645	Shy Boy/Lady On A Bicycle	40
68	Parlophone R 5677	Rumours/And She Cried	35
68	Parlophone R 5717	Tell Me A Story/Understand A Woman	40
68	Parlophone R 5750	Tomorrow Today/Turn Out The Light	40
69	Parlophone R 5776	In My Life/I Can See Her Face	90
78	EMI NUT 2894	KIPPINGTON LODGE (EP)	12

KIRBY
(see also Curved Air, Stretch)

76	Anchor ANC 1031	Love Letters/Flasher	12
78	Hot Wax WAX 1/ANCHO 1	Bottom Line/That's Some Dream	10
78	Hot Wax HW 2	COMPOSITION (LP)	75
94	Backtrack Archive HW 2	COMPOSITION (LP, reissue)	30

KATHY KIRBY

60	Pye 7N 15313	Love Can Be/Crush Me	15
61	Pye 7N 15342	Danny/Now You're Crying	15
62	Decca F 11506	Big Man/Slowly	12
63	Decca F 11682	Dance On/Playboy	5
63	Decca F 11759	Secret Love/You Have To Want To Touch Him	5
64	Decca F 11832	Let Me Go, Lover!/The Sweetest Sounds	5
64	Decca F 11892	You're The One/Love Me Baby	5
64	Decca F 11992	Don't Walk Away/No Regrets	5
65	Decca F 12177	The Way Of Love/Oh Darling, How I Miss You	5
65	Decca F 12280	Where In The World?/That Wonderful Feeling Of Love	5
66	Decca F 12338	Spanish Flea/Till The End Of Time	5
66	Decca F 12432	The Adam Adamant Theme/Will I Never Learn?	30
67	Columbia DB 8139	No One's Gonna Hurt You Anymore/My Yiddishe Momme	5
67	Columbia DB 8192	In All The World/Time	6
67	Columbia DB 8302	Turn Around/Golden Days	5
68	Columbia DB 8400	I Almost Called Your Name/Let The Music Start	8
68	Columbia DB 8521	Come Back Here With My Heart/Antonio	8
69	Columbia DB 8559	I'll Catch The Sun/Please Help Me I'm Falling	8
69	Columbia DB 8634	Is That All There Is?/Knowing When To Leave	8
70	Columbia DB 8682	Wheel Of Fortune/Lucky	8
70	Columbia DB 8721	My Way/Little Green Apples	8
71	Columbia DB 8795	So Here I Go/Yes - I've Got (A-side titled "Here I Go Again" on demos)	8
71	Decca F 13228	Bill/Can't Help Lovin' Dat Man	8
72	Columbia DB 8910	Do You Really Have A Heart/Dream On, Dreamer	8
73	Columbia DB 8965	Little Song For You/Here, There And Everywhere	8
73	Orange OAS 216	Singer With The Band/Hello Morning	60
76	President PT 455	My Prayer/Nobody Loves Me Like You Do	10
81	President PT 491	He/Nobody Loves Me Like You	8
63	Decca DFE 8547	KATHY KIRBY (EP)	15
65	Decca DFE 8596	KATHY KIRBY VOL. 2 (EP)	15
65	Decca DFE 8611	A SONG FOR EUROPE (EP)	15
67	Decca LK 4746	MAKE SOMEONE HAPPY (LP)	30
67	Ace Of clubs ACL 1235	BEST OF (LP)	15
68	Columbia S(C)X 6259	MY THANKS TO YOU (LP)	60

LARRY KIRBY & ENCORES

59	Top Rank JAR 143	My Baby Don't Love Me/My Rose Of Kentucky	15

PAT KIRBY

56	Brunswick 05560	Happiness Is A Thing Called Joe/Don't Tell Me Not To	7
56	Brunswick 05575	What A Heavenly Night For Love/Greensleeves	7
57	Brunswick 05697	Tammy/Don't Keep Silent	7
58	Brunswick 05731	Sayonara/Please Be Gentle With Me	7

BASIL KIRCHIN (BAND)
(see also Basil Kirchin, London Studio Group)

57	Parlophone R 4344	White Silver Sands/Waiting For The Robert E. Lee	5
58	Parlophone R 4511	Cha Cha Bells/Oh Dear What Can The Cha Cha Be (with Rock-A-Cha Cha Band)	5
59	Parlophone R 4527	Rock-A-Conga/Skin Tight (as Basil Kirchin Band)	6
71	Columbia SCX 6463	A WORLD WITHIN WORLDS (LP)	275
74	Island HELP18	A WORLD WITHIN WORLDS (not a reissue but second LP)	50
03	Trunk JBH 003 LP	QUANTUM LP, hand numbered, 500 only)	30
04	Trunk JBH 005 LP	CHARCOAL SKETCHES/STATES OF MIND (LP, 500 only)	50
05	Trunk JBH 012 LP	ABSTRACTIONS OF THE INDUSTRIAL NORTH (LP)	20
06	Trunk JBH 021 LP	PARTICLES (LP)	20

(IVOR & BASIL) KIRCHIN BAND

54	Parlophone MSP 6144	Mambo Macoco/Tangerine (as Kirchin Band)	10
55	Decca F 10434	Minor Mambo/Mother Goose Jumps (as Kirchin Band)	15
56	Parlophone R 4222	The Roller/St. Louis Blues (as Ivor & Basil Kirchin)	7

MINT VALUE £

56 Parlophone R 4237 Rockin' & Rollin' Thru The Darktown Strutters' Ball/Ambush 20
57 Parlophone R 4266 Rock Around The World Medley (with Shani Wallis) 18
57 Parlophone R 4284 Calypso!!/Jungle Fire Dance (as Ivor & Basil Kirchin with Wendy Windows) 5
57 Parlophone R 4335 Teenage World/So Rare (as Kirchin Band & Bandits) 10
55 Parlophone GEP 8531 KIRCHIN BANDBOX (EP) 15
56 Parlophone GEP 8569 THE IVOR AND BASIL KIRCHIN BAND (EP) 30

DEE KIRK
62 Salvo SLO 1809 I'll Cry/My Used To Be (99 copies only) 15

KEVIN KIRK
62 Columbia DB 4909 Sweet/Don't Waste Your Tears On Him 6
62 Columbia DB 4863 Teenage Heartache/Midnight 7

RICHARD H. KIRK
(see also Cabaret Voltaire, Peter Hope & Richard H. Kirk)
81 Industrial IRC 34 DISPOSABLE HALF TRUTHS (cassette) 20

(RAHSAAN) ROLAND KIRK
64 Mercury 10015 MCE THE KIRK QUARTET MEETS THE BENNY GOLSON ORCHESTRA (EP) 10
65 Mercury 10016 MCE ROLAND SPEAKS (EP, with Benny Golson Orchestra) 10
62 Esquire 32-164 KIRK'S WORK (LP, with Jack McDuff) 25
63 Mercury MMC 14126 WE FREE KINGS (LP) 25
64 Mercury MCL 20002 THE KIRK QUARTET MEETS THE BENNY GOLSON ORCHESTRA (LP) 20
64 Mercury MCL 20021 KIRK IN COPENHAGEN (LP) 20
64 Mercury SMWL 21020 GIFTS & MESSAGES (LP) 15
65 Mercury MCL 20037 WE FREE KINGS (LP, reissue) 12
65 Mercury MCL 20045 DOMINO (LP) 20
65 Fontana FJL 114 HIP! (LP) 20
66 Mercury (S)LML 4005 I TALK WITH THE SPIRITS (LP) 15
66 Mercury (S)LML 4015 RIP, RIG AND PANIC (LP) 15
67 Mercury (S)LML 4019 SLIGHTLY LATIN (LP) 20
67 Verve 9193 NOW PLEASE DON'T YOU CRY BEAUTIFUL EDITH (LP) 18
71 Atlantic 2400 110 RAHSAAN, RAHSAAN (LP, as Rahsaan Roland Kirk) 12
72 Atlantic K 40358 BLACKNUSS (LP) 12
73 Atlantic K 40457 MEETING OF THE TIMES (LP, with Al Hibbler) 12
70 Atlantic 588178 LEFT & RIGHT (LP) 20
69 Atlantic 588 207 VOLUNTEERED SLAVERY (LP) 20

KIRKBYS
(see also 23rd Turnoff, Jimmy Campbell, Rockin' Horse, Merseybeats)
66 RCA RCA 1542 It's A Crime/I've Never Been So Much In Love 150

KEN KIRKHAM
56 Columbia SCM 5244 It's Almost Tomorrow/No Not Much 10
58 Columbia DB 4116 Now And For Always/Cathy 6

JOHN KIRKPATRICK (& SUE HARRIS)
(see also Jon Raven)
72 Trailer LER 2033 JUMP AT THE SUN (LP, with Sue Harris) 25
76 Topic 12TS 295 AMONG THE MANY ATTRACTIONS AT THE SHOW WILL BE A REALLY HIGH-CLASS BAND (LP, with Sue Harris) 20
76 Free Reed FRR 010 PLAIN CAPERS (LP, with booklet) 12
77 Topic 12TS 355 SHREDS AND PATCHES (LP, with Sue Harris) 12

JULIAN KIRSCH
69 Columbia DB 8541 Clever Little Man/The Adventures Of A Young Cuckoo 40

DANNY KIRWAN
(see also Fleetwood Mac, Tramp)
75 DJM DJS 10783 Hot Summer's Day/Love Can Always Bring You Happiness (demo in p/s) 8
75 DJM DJS 10783 Hot Summer's Day/Love Can Always Bring You Happiness 6
75 DJM DJLPS 454 SECOND CHAPTER (LP, gatefold sleeve) 15

KISS
(see also Gene Simmons, Ace Frehley, Peter Criss, Paul Stanley)

SINGLES
75 Casablanca CBX 503 Nothin' To Lose/Love Theme From Kiss 25
75 Casablanca CBX 510 Rock And Roll All Nite/Anything For My Baby 20
76 Casablanca CBX 516 Shout It Out Loud/Sweet Pain 15
76 Casablanca CBX 519 Beth/God Of Thunder 18
77 Casablanca CAN 102 Hard Luck Woman/Calling Dr Love/Beth (in p/s) 35
77 Casablanca CAN 102 Hard Luck Woman/Calling Dr Love/Beth 10
77 Casablanca CAN 110 Then She Kissed Me/Hooligan/Flaming Youth 15
77 Casablanca CANL 110 Then She Kissed Me/Hooligan/Flaming Youth (12", company sleeve) 10
78 Casablanca CAN 117 Rocket Ride/Love Gun (live) 8
78 Casablanca CANL 117 Rocket Ride/Detroit Rock City (live)/Love Gun (live) (12", company sleeve) 12
78 Casablanca CAN 126 Rock And Roll All Nite/C'Mon And Love Me (in p/s) 25
78 Casablanca CAN 126 Rock And Roll All Nite/C'Mon And Love Me 8
79 Casablanca CAN 152 I Was Made For Lovin' You/Hard Times 8
79 Casablanca CANL 152 I Was Made For Lovin' You (extended)/Charisma (12", p/s) 18
79 Casablanca CAN 163 Sure Know Something/Dirty Livin' (no p/s) 6
80 Casablanca NB 1001 2000 Man/I Was Made For Lovin' You/Sure Know Something (p/s) 15
80 Casablanca NBL 1001 2000 Man/I Was Made For Lovin' You/Sure Know Something (12", co. sleeve) . . . 12
80 Casablanca MER 19 Talk To Me/She's So European (p/s) 10
80 Casablanca KISS 1 What Makes The World Go 'Round/Naked City (p/s) 10
81 Casablanca KISS 2 A World Without Heroes/Mr Blackwell (p/s) 5
81 Casablanca KISSP 002 A World Without Heroes/Mr Blackwell (picture disc) 8
82 Casablanca KISS 3 Killer/I Love It Loud (pull-out tongue p/s) 12
82 Casablanca KISS 312 Killer/I Love It Loud/I Was Made For Lovin' You (12", p/s) 15
82 Casablanca KISS 4 Creatures Of The Night/Rock And Roll All Nite (live) (p/s, picture label) 10

			MINT VALUE £
82	Casablanca KISS 4	Creatures Of The Night/Rock And Roll All Nite (live) (p/s, silver label)	8
82	Casablanca KISS 412	Creatures Of The Night/War Machine/Rock And Roll All Nite (live) (12", p/s)	15
82	Casablanca KISSD 4	Creatures Of The Night/Rock And Roll All Nite (live) (12", double groove, autographs engraved on 1 side)	20
83	Vertigo KISS 5	Lick It Up/Not For The Innocent (p/s)	5
83	Vertigo KISSP 5	Lick It Up/Not For The Innocent (poster p/s)	12
83	Vertigo KPIC 5	Lick It Up/Not For The Innocent (tank-shaped picture disc)	20
83	Vertigo KISS 512	Lick It Up/Not For The Innocent/I Still Love You (12", p/s)	8
84	Vertigo VER 12	Heaven's On Fire/Lonely Is The Hunter (p/s)	5
84	Vertigo VERX 12	Heaven's On Fire/Lonely Is The Hunter/All Hell's Breakin' Loose (12", p/s with poster)	10
84	Vertigo VERX 12	Heaven's On Fire/Lonely Is The Hunter/All Hell's Breakin' Loose (12", p/s with poster)	8
88	Mercury 080 100-1	EXPOSED (12" CD video)	20
89	Mercury 080 044-2	Lick It Up/Dance All Over Your Face/Gimme More/Fits Like a Glove (CD video)	15
89	Vertigo 080 059-2	Tears Are Falling/Anyway You Slice It/Who Wants To Be Lonely/ Secretly Cruel (CD Video)	15

LPs

75	Casablanca CBC 4003	KISS (blue 'Bogart' label)	20
75	Casablanca CBC 4004	DRESSED TO KILL (blue 'Bogart' label, embossed sleeve)	20
76	Casablanca CBC 4008	DESTROYER (blue 'Bogart' label with inner sleeve)	20
76	Casablanca CBC 4011/2	ALIVE! (2-LP, blue 'Bogart' label, gatefold sleeve with insert, sleeve also lists CBSP 401)	20
77	Casablanca CALH 2001	ROCK AND ROLL OVER ('lovegun' label, red vinyl)	40
77	Casablanca CAL 2006	KISS (reissue, 'lovegun' label, red vinyl)	40
77	Casablanca CAL 2007	HOTTER THAN HELL ('lovegun' label, red vinyl)	40
77	Casablanca CAL 2008	DRESSED TO KILL (reissue, 'lovegun' label, red vinyl)	40
77	Casablanca CAL 2009	DESTROYER (reissue, different sleeve, 'lovegun' label, red vinyl)	40
77	Casablanca CALD 5001	ALIVE! (2-LP, reissue, 'lovegun' label, red vinyl)	50
77	Casablanca CALH 2017	LOVE GUN ('lovegun' label, with picture inner sleeve)	12
77	Casablanca CALH 2017	LOVE GUN ('lovegun' label, red vinyl with picture inner sleeve)	40
77	Casablanca CALD 5004	KISS ALIVE II (2-LP, 'lovegun' label, with colour booklet & transfer sheet)	25
77	Casablanca CALD 5004	KISS ALIVE II (2-LP, 'lovegun' label, red vinyl with colour booklet)	50
78	Casablanca CALD 5005	DOUBLE PLATINUM (2-LP, 'lovegun' label, silver foil embossed sleeve & insert; sleeve & insert pressed in U.S. with U.K. cat. no. sticker)	18
79	Casablanca CALH 2051	DYNASTY ('lovegun' label, black vinyl, colour inner sleeve & poster)	12
80	Mercury 6302 032	UNMASKED (with poster)	15
81	Casablanca 6302 163	(MUSIC FROM) THE ELDER (single sleeve)	12
82	Casa. CANL 4/6302 219	CREATURES OF THE NIGHT ('make-up' sleeve)	12
87	Vertigo 832 903-1	CRAZY NIGHTS (picture disc in stickered PVC wallet)	12
98	Mercury PLP 31453 8137-2	PSYCHO CIRCUS (LP, promo only picture disc)	30

KISSING SPELL

93	Essex DELUJO 1001LP	LOS PAJAROS (LP, reissue of Chilean LP, 500 only)	12

KATIE KISSOON

(see also Peanut, Marionettes, Rag Dolls [U.K.])

69	Columbia DB 8525	Don't Let It Rain/Will I Never See The Sun	6

MAC KISSOON

(see also Marionettes, Rag Dolls [U.K.])

60s	Boulevard (no cat. no.)	Wear It On Your Face/In A Dream	10
69	Youngblood YB 1005	Wear It On Your Face/In A Dream (reissue)	5

KIT KATS

(see also New Hope)

66	London HLW 10075	Won't Find Better Than Me/That's The Way	18

EARTHA KITT

54	HMV 7M 191	Under The Bridges Of Paris/Lovin' Spree	12
54	HMV 7M 198	Somebody Bad Stole De Wedding Bell/Sandy's Tune	10
54	HMV 7M 234	Santa Baby/Let's Do It (Let's Fall In Love)	15
54	HMV 7M 246	Easy Does It/Mink Shmink	10
55	HMV 7M 282	Monotonous/African Lullaby	10
55	HMV 7M 288	C'est Si Bon (with Henri René)/Senor	10
56	HMV 7M 422	Honolulu Rock-A-Roll-A/Je Cherche Un Homme (I Want A Man)	25
56	MGM SP 1153	Please Do It/Lady Loves	10
56	MGM SP 1178	Diamonds Are A Girl's Best Friend/Good Little Girls	12
57	HMV POP 309	Just An Old-Fashioned Girl/If I Can't Take It With Me When I Go (gold label)	15
57	HMV POP 309	Just An Old-Fashioned Girl/If I Can't Take It With Me When I Go (silver label)	10
57	HMV POP 346	There Is No Cure For L'Amour/Hey Jacque	10
58	RCA RCA 1037	Take My Love/Proceed With Caution	6
58	RCA RCA 1093	I Want To Be Evil/Oh John!	7
63	London HL 7119	Shango/In The Evening (When The Sun Goes Down) (export issue)	15
70	Spark SRL 1039	Hurdy Gurdy Man/Catch The Wind	20
71	CBS 7626	A Knight For My Nights/Summer Storm	5
55	HMV DLP 1067	THAT BAD EARTHA (10" LP)	15
55	HMV DLP 1087	DOWN TO EARTHA (10" LP)	15
58	RCA RD 27076	ST. LOUIS BLUES (LP)	15

KITTENS

64	Decca F 12036	Round About Way/Don't Stop Now	15

KLAN

62	Palette PG 9052	Fifi The Fly/Already Mine	15

KLAXON 5

86	él GPO 20	Never Underestimate The Ignorance Of The Rich/Great Railway Journeys (p/s)	8

KLAXONS

06	Angular ARC 012	Gravity's Rainbow/The Bouncer (500, white label, numbered)	18
06	Merok ME 001	Atlantis To Interzone/4 Horsemen of 1012 (p/s)	8

MINT VALUE £

06	Merok ME 003/4	Atlantis To interzone (Remixes) (6 x mixes on 12" and one 7", white labels)	15
07	Dim Mak DM 111	Gravity's Rainbow (Soulwax Remix) (12" 1-sided, etched)	8

SUSIE KLEE

66	Polydor BM 56082	Mr Zero/Punch And Judy Girl	15

KLEEER

80	Atlantic K11560	Get Tough/Hypnotised	6
84	Atlantic 7801451	INTIMATE CONNECTION (LP)	20

KLEENEX

(see also Liliput)

79	Rough Trade/Sunrise RT 9	Ain't You/Hedi's Head (poster p/s)	12
79	Rough Trade RT 014	You/U (p/s)	10

ALAN KLEIN

(see also New Vaudeville Band)

62	Oriole CB 1719	Striped Purple Shirt/You Gave Me The Blues	15
62	Oriole CB 1737	Three Coins In The Sewer/Danger Ahead	15
65	Parlophone R 5292	It Ain't Worth The Lonely Road Back/I've Cried So Many Tears	5
65	Parlophone R 5370	Age Of Corruption/I'm Counting On You	5
69	Page One POF 119	Honey Pie/You Turned A Nightmare Into A Dream	8
70	Decca F 13033	Dinner's In The Ice Box/Here I Am, There You Are	7
64	Decca LK 4621	WELL, AT LEAST IT'S BRITISH (LP)	30

HARRY KLEIN QUARTET

(see also Jazz Five)

56	Jazz Today JTE 105	BRASH BARITONE (EP)	25
56	Nixa NJE 1009	NEW SOUND (EP)	25
56	Nixa NJE 1022	HARRY KLEIN QUARTET (EP)	25
57	Columbia SEG 7647	BARITONE SAX (EP)	15

KLEPTOMANIA

92	Hypno-Genesis HG 001	Amadeus (Martini Mix)/Amadeus (Stringi Wingi Mix)/ Morf (Plastascene Mix)/ Morf (Scratchi Waxi Mix) (12")	70

DEAN KLEVATT

74	Decca F 13495	Don't Bury Molly/The Story Of His Life	10

KLF

(see also J.A.M.s, Timelords, Disco 2000, Bill Drummond, Space, Orb)

89	KLF Comms. KLF 004T	What Time Is Love? (Trance Mix)/What Time Is Love? (Mix 2) (12", 'Pure Trance 1', original issue with black/green p/s)	12
89	KLF Comms. KLF 004R	What Time Is Love? ('89 Primal Remix)/What Time Is Love? (Techno Slam)/ What Time Is Love? (Trance Mix 1) (12", stickered p/s)	12
90	KLF Comms. KLF 004P	What Time Is Love? (Live At Trancentral)/Wandafull Mix (12", w/l, 1,500 only)	10
90	KLF Comms. KLF 004X	What Time Is Love? (Live At Trancentral)/Techno Gate Mix (12", p/s, mispressing, B-side actually plays "Wandafull Mix", matrix no.: KLF 004X-B)	25
90	KLF Comms. KLF 004CD	What Time Is Love? (Radio)/(Live At Trancentral)/(Trance Mix 1) (CD, mispressing playing part of Knebworth '90 live CD)	15
90	KLF Comms. KLF 005R	3AM Eternal 'Single Edit'/Blue Danube Orbital Mix/Moody Boys Version/ 3PM Electro (12", original issue with stickered p/s)	10
91	KLF Comms. KLF 005S	3AM Eternal (Live At The S.S.L.) (Radio Freedom Edit) (white label, 500 only)	12
91	KLF Comms. KLF 005	3AM Eternal (Live At The S.S.L.)/Guns Of Mu Mu (12" promo)	8
91	KLF Comms. KLF 005Y	3AM Eternal (Moody Boys mixes) (12", white label, promo only)	8
92	KLF Comms. KLF 5 TOTP	3AM Eternal (Xmas Top Of The Pops Version) (1-sided, w/Extreme Noise Terror, mail-order only, with insert & mailing envelope; beware of bootlegs!)	30
92	KLF Comms. KLF 5 TOTP	3AM Eternal (Xmas Top Of The Pops Version) (1-sided, w/Extreme Noise Terror, mail-order only, without insert & mailing envelope; beware of bootlegs!)	8
89	KLF Comms. KLF 008R	Last Train To Trancentral (Remixes 1 & 2) (12", p/s, 'Pure Trance 5', 2,000 pressed, some warped, price is for unwarped copy)	40
89	KLF PROMO 2	Kylie Said To Jason (Full Length)/Kylie Said Trance (12", promo & press sheet)	15
89	KLF Comms. KLF 010(S)	Kylie Said To Jason (Edit)/Kylie Said Trance (p/s)	8
89	KLF Comms. KLF 010T	Kylie Said To Jason (Full Length)/Kylie Said Trance (12", stickered p/s & pstr)	15
89	KLF Comms. KLF 010R	Kylie Said To Jason (Trance Kylie Express)/Kylie In A Trance/ Kylie Said Harder (12" remix, p/s, export issue)	15
89	KLF Comms. KLF 010RR	Kylie In A Trance/Kylie Said Mu (12", p/s, export edition, 500 only, shrinkwrapped with KLF 010R)	70
89	KLF Comms. KLF 010RR	Kylie In A Trance/Kylie Said Mu (12", p/s, export edition, 500 only)	40
89	KLF Comms. KLF 010CD	Kylie Said To Jason (Full Length)/Madrugada Eterna/Kylie Said Trance (CD)	40
89	KLF Comms. KLF 006T	Love Trance/What Time Is Love (12", p/s, 3 copies known)	500
90	KLF Comms. KLF 011T	Madrugada Eterna (Club Mix)/Madrugada Eterna (Edit)/Madrugada Eterna (Ambient House Mix) (12", 20 only, beware of counterfeits!)	150
90	KLF Comms. ETERNA 1	Madrugada Eterna (Club Mix) (12", 1-sided, white label, 6 pressed, beware of counterfeits!)	200
91	KLF Comms. CHOC ICE 1	Justified And Ancient (All Bound For Mu Mu Land)/Justified And Ancient (Make Mine A '99') (12", white label promo)	8
91	KLF Comms. CHOC ICE 2	Justified And Ancient (Stand By The J.A.M.s)/Justified And Ancient (Let Them Eat Ice Cream) (12", white label promo)	12
91	KLF Comms. CHOC ICE 3	Justified And Ancient (Anti-Acapella Version) (12", 1-sided, w/l, 200 only)	50
91	KLF Comms. LP PROMO 1	Make It Rain/No More Tears (12", promo only, 1,729 pressed)	20
91	KLF Comms. 92PROMO 1	America: What Time Is Love/America No More (12", white label)	8
91	KLF Comms. 92PROMO 2	America: What Time Is January? (12", 1-sided, white label promo, 250 only)	100
91	KLF Comms. 3AM 1	3AM Eternal (feat. Extreme Noise Terror) (p/s, mail order only)	20
92	KLF Comms. 92PROMO 3	What Time Is Love (Acid Mix) (12", 1-sided, w/l promo, perhaps 20 only)	200
92	KLF Comms. USA 4X/ CHOC ICE 2	Justified And Ancient/America: What Time Is Love? (12", 'longboat' picture disc, export edition, 4,000 only)	30
97	KLF Comms.	Fuck The Millennium (4-track CD, in white carrier bag Fuck The Millennium kit, with T-shirt, window sticker, certificate)	50
89	KLF Comms. JAMS LP 4	THE WHAT TIME IS LOVE STORY (LP)	20

MINT VALUE £

89	KLF Comms. JAMS CD 4	THE WHAT TIME IS LOVE STORY (CD)	30
89	KLF Comms. JAMS LP 5	CHILL OUT (LP)	20
89	KLF Comms. JAMS CD 5	CHILL OUT (CD)	20
89	KLF Comms. JAMS LP 6	(TUNES FROM) THE WHITE ROOM (LP, 9-track white label, unreleased, promo only, beware of counterfeits!)	50
89	KLF Comms. JAMS MC 6	(TUNES FROM) THE WHITE ROOM (, cassette, 10-track promo, beware of counterfeits!)	40

TONY KLINGER & MICHAEL LYONS

72	Deram SML 1095	EXTREEMS (LP, soundtrack)	30

PETER KLINT (QUINTET)

66	Mercury MF 997	Walkin' Proud/Shake	20
68	Atlantic 584 208	Hey Diddle Diddle/Just Holding On (solo)	15

ANNETTE KLOOGER

(see also Four Jones Boys, Ted Heath Orchestra)

56	Decca F 10701	The Rock And Roll Waltz/Rock Around The Island (with Ted Heath Music)	15
56	Decca F 10733	The Magic Touch/We'll Love Again (with Four Jones Boys)	15
56	Decca F 10738	Why Do Fools Fall In Love?/Lovely One (with Four Jones Boys)	15
56	Decca F 10776	Mama, Teach Me To Dance/Mama, I Long For A Sweetheart (with Edmundo Ros Orchestra)	12
57	Decca F 10844	The Wisdom Of A Fool/Tra La La	10

KLUBS

68	Cam CAM 681	I Found The Sun/Ever Needed Someone	200

KNACK (U.K.)

(see also Gun, Sky)

65	Decca F 12234	She Ain't No Good/Who'll Be The Next In Line	60
65	Decca F 12278	It's Love Baby (24 Hours A Day)/Time Time Time	50
66	Piccadilly 7N 35315	Did You Ever Have To Make Up Your Mind?/Red Hearts	15
66	Piccadilly 7N 35322	Stop! (Before You Get Me Going)/Younger Girl	15
66	Piccadilly 7N 35347	Save All My Love For Joey/Take Your Love	15
67	Piccadilly 7N 35367	(Man From The) Marriage Guidance And Advice Bureau/ Dolly Catch Her Man	15

KNACK (U.S.)

79	Capitol E-ST 11948	GET THE KNACK (LP, limited white cover, unissued)	12

BERNIE KNEE QUARTETTE

(see also Bernie Nee)

55	HMV 7M 306	Chocolate Whiskey And Vanilla Gin/Scrape Off De Bark	7

KNEES

(see also Brinsley Schwarz)

74	United Artists UP 35773	Day Tripper/Slow Down	10

KNICKERBOCKERS

66	London HLH 10013	Lies/The Coming Generation	20
66	London HLH 10035	One Track Mind/I Must Be Doing Something Right	20
66	London HLH 10061	High On Love/Stick With Me	30
66	London HLH 10093	Rumours, Gossip, Words Untrue/Love Is A Bird	15
67	London HLH 10102	Can You Help Me/Please Don't Love Him	15
73	Elektra K 12102	Lies/ELECTRIC PRUNES: I Had Too Much To Dream (Last Night)	5
66	London HA-H 8294	THE FABULOUS KNICKERBOCKERS (LP)	60

KNIFE EDGE

80	No Hessle F001	Favourite Girl/Say You Will	75

BAKER KNIGHT

66	Reprise RS 20465	Would You Believe It/Tomorrow's Good Time Girl	12

CURTIS KNIGHT (& ZEUS)

(see also Jimi Hendrix, Blue Goose)

69	RCA RCA 1888	Fancy Meeting You Here/Love In	12
70	RCA RCA 1950	Down In The Village/No Point Of View	12
74	Dawn DNS 1049	Devil Made Me Do It/Oh Rainbow	7
74	Dawn DNS 1065	People Places And Things/Mysterious Lady	7
74	Dawn DNLS 3060	THE SECOND COMING (LP, laminated sleeve, lyric insert, pink 'sun' label)	100
74	Dawn DNLS 3060	THE SECOND COMING (LP, laminated sleeve, no lyric insert, pink 'sun' label)	45

GLADYS KNIGHT (& PIPS)

(see also Pips, Dionne Warwick)

SINGLES

64	Stateside SS 318	Giving Up/Maybe Maybe Baby	25
64	Stateside SS 352	Lovers Always Forgive/Another Love	25
65	Sue WI 394	Letter Full Of Tears/You Broke Your Promise	40
66	Tamla Motown TMG 576	Just Walk In My Shoes/Stepping Closer To Your Heart	50
66	Tamla Motown TMG 576	Just Walk In My Shoes/Stepping Closer To Your Heart (DJ copy)	150
67	Tamla Motown TMG 604	Take Me In Your Arms And Love Me/Do You Love Me Just A Little Honey	15
67	Tamla Motown TMG 619	Everybody Needs Love/Stepping Closer To Your Heart (demo-only B-side)	90
67	Tamla Motown TMG 619	Everybody Needs Love/Since I've Lost You	15
67	Tamla Motown TMG 629	I Heard It Through The Grapevine/It's Time To Go Now	25
68	Tamla Motown TMG 645	The End Of Our Road/Don't Let Her Take Your Love From Me	15
68	Tamla Motown TMG 660	It Should Have Been Me/You Don't Love Me No More	18
68	Tamla Motown TMG 674	I Wish It Would Rain/It's Summer	15
69	Tamla Motown TMG 714	The Nitty Gritty/Got Myself A Good Man	10
70	Tamla Motown TMG 728	Didn't You Know (You'd Have To Cry Sometime)/Keep An Eye	10
70	Tamla Motown TMG 756	Friendship Train/You Need Love Like I Do (Don't You)	10
71	Tamla Motown TMG 765	If I Were Your Woman/The Tracks Of My Tears	8
72	Tamla Motown TMG 805	Make Me The Woman That You Go Home To/I Don't Want To Do Wrong	15
72	Tamla Motown TMG 813	Just Walk In My Shoes/I'm Losing You	10
73	Ember EMB S 326	Every Beat Of My Heart/Room In Your Heart	6

MINT VALUE £

73	Tamla Motown TMG 844	The Look Of Love/You're My Everything	6
73	Tamla Motown TMG 864	Take Me In Your Arms And Love Me/No One Could Love You More	60
74	Contempo CS 2021	Why Don't You Leave Me/Maybe Baby	6
75	Tamla Motown TMG 945	You've Lost That Loving Feeling/This Child Needs A Father	15
89	MCA MCASP 1339	Licence To Kill/MICHAEL KAMEN: Pain (p/s with postcards & lyric sheet)	6
89	MCA MCAT 1339	Licence To Kill (Extended Version)/MICHAEL KAMEN: Pain (12", picture sleeve)	8

LPs

67	Music F. Pleasure MFP 1187	GLADYS KNIGHT AND THE PIPS	15
67	T. Motown TML 11058	EVERYBODY NEEDS LOVE (mono)	35
67	T. Motown STML 11058	EVERYBODY NEEDS LOVE (stereo)	40
68	Bell MBLL 103	TASTIEST HITS	40
68	T. Motown TML 11080	FEELIN' BLUESY (mono)	35
68	T. Motown STML 11080	FEELIN' BLUESY (stereo)	40
69	T. Motown STML 11100	SILK'N'SOUL (stereo)	35
69	T. Motown TML 11135	THE NITTY GRITTY (mono)	30
69	T. Motown (S)TML 11135	THE NITTY GRITTY (stereo)	25
70	Tamla Motown STML 11148	GREATEST HITS (original with flipback sleeve)	20
71	Tamla Motown STML 11187	IF I WERE YOUR WOMAN	20

JASON KNIGHT

67	Pye 7N 17399	Love Is Getting Stronger/Standing In My Shoes	120
67	Pye 7N 17399	Love Is Getting Stronger/Standing In My Shoes (DJ copy)	200
73	Pye 7N 45287	Love Is Getting Stronger/Standing In My Shoes (reissue)	10

JEAN KNIGHT

71	Stax 2025 049	Mr Big Stuff/Why Do I Keep Living These Memories	8
72	Stax 2025 103	Carry On/Do You Think You're Hot Stuff	5
73	Stax 2025 161	Do Me/Save The Last Kiss For Me	5
72	Stax 2362 022	MR. BIG STUFF (LP)	20

MARIE KNIGHT

(see also Sister Rosetta Tharpe & Sister Marie Knight)

61	Fontana H 354	Nothing/Come Tomorrow	20
65	Stateside SS 419	Cry Me A River/Comes The Knight	18
85	Kent TOWN 102	That's No Way To Treat A Girl/JACK MONTGOMERY: Dearly Beloved	15
57	Brunswick OE 9283	GOSPEL SONGS VOL. 1 (EP, with Sam Price Trio)	12
64	Mercury 10001 MCE	THE STORM IS PASSING OVER (EP)	12
64	Mercury 10034 MCE	SONGS OF THE GOSPEL (EP)	10
58	Mercury MPL 6546	SONGS OF THE GOSPEL (LP)	15

PETER KNIGHT & KNIGHT RIDERS

61	Pye 7N 15388	Lucky Stars/Double Trouble	7
64	Pye 7N 15687	Wonderful Day Like Today/It Isn't Enough	8

PETER KNIGHT ORCHESTRA/SINGERS

55	Parlophone MSP 6183	Twenty Minutes South (Medley) (both sides, as Peter Knight Singers)	6
67	Mercury SML 30023	SGT. PEPPER'S LONELY HEARTS CLUB BAND (LP)	15

ROBERT KNIGHT

62	London HLD 9496	Free Me/The Other Half Of Man	30
68	Monument MON 1008	Everlasting Love/Somebody's Baby	15
68	Monument MON 1016	Blessed Are The Lonely/It's Been Worth It All	8
68	Monument MON 1017	The Power Of Love/Love On A Mountain Top	30
68	Bell BLL 1029	Isn't It Lonely Together/We'd Better Stop	8
68	Monument LMO/SMO 5015	EVERLASTING LOVE (LP)	30
71	Monument MNT 65956	LOVE ON A MOUNTAIN TOP (LP)	18

SONNY KNIGHT

57	London HLD 8362	Confidential/Jail Bird (gold label print)	350
57	London HLD 8362	Confidential/Jail Bird (silver label print)	100
57	London HLD 8362	Confidential/Jail Bird (78 rpm)	60
57	London HL 7016	Confidential/Jail Bird (export issue)	100
59	Vogue Pop V 9134	But Officer/Dear Wonderful God	250
59	Vogue Pop V 9134	But Officer/Dear Wonderful God (78)	100

TERRY KNIGHT & PACK

(see also Grand Funk Railroad)

66	Cameo Parkway C 102	I (Who Have Nothing)/Numbers	75

TONY KNIGHT

64	Decca F 11989	Did You Ever Hear The Sound?/I Feel So Blue (as Tony Knight & Live Wires)	40
65	Decca F 12109	How Sweet/Surfer Street (as Tony Knight's Chessmen)	35

KNIGHT BROTHERS

65	Chess CRS 8015	Sinking Low/Temptation 'Bout To Get Me	30
66	Chess CRS 8046	That'll Get It/She's A1	30

KNIGHTRIDER

87	Omega KS 1299	Shout Out Loud	25

KNIGHTS OF THE ROUND TABLE

68	Pama PM 734	Lament To Bobby Kennedy/If You Were My Girl	7

K9's

79	Dog Breath WOOF 1	The K9 Hassle/Idi Amin/Sweeney Todd (1st issue in numbered blue p/s, with insert, 1000 only; reissue in white p/s with insert, 500 only)	40

KNOCKER JUNGLE

70	Ember EMB S 293	I Don't Know Why/Reality (p/s)	6
71	Ember NR 5052	KNOCKER JUNGLE (LP, gatefold sleeve)	50

KNOCKOUTS

60	Top Rank JAR 279	Riot In Room 3C/Darling Lorraine	25

MINT VALUE £

MARK KNOPFLER

(see also Dire Straits, Randy Newman, Chet Atkins)

84	Vertigo DSDJ 7	Joy (from 'Comfort And Joy') (unissued, 1-sided promo only)	12
84	Vertigo DSTR 712	Joy (from 'Comfort And Joy')/Fistful Of Ice Cream (12", p/s)	12
84	Vertigo MARK ONE	Comfort And Joy (12", 1-sided promo)	25
02	Mercury 063292	THE RAGPICKERS DREAM (2-LP, numbered)	60

KNOPOV'S POLITICAL PACKAGE

(see also Mission)

80	white label	Misadventure/You're In The Army Now	6

KNOTT SISTERS

58	London HLX 8713	Undivided Attention/SHADES with KNOTT SISTERS: Sun Glasses	40
58	London HLX 8713	Undivided Attention/SHADES with KNOTT SISTERS: Sun Glasses (78)	10

KNOWLEDGE

78	A&M AMLH 68500	HAIL DREAD (LP)	25

SONNY KNOWLES

72	Rex RH079	Do I Love You/I'm Just A Country Boy	7

BUDDY KNOX

57	Columbia DB 3914	Party Doll/My Baby's Gone (gold label print)	100
57	Columbia DB 3914	Party Doll/My Baby's Gone (gold label print) (78)	20
57	Columbia DB 3952	Rock Your Little Baby To Sleep/Don't Make Me Cry (as Lieutenant Buddy Knox, gold label print)	100
57	Columbia DB 3952	Rock Your Little Baby To Sleep/Don't Make Me Cry (as Lieutenant Buddy Knox, gold label print) (78)	25
57	Columbia DB 4014	Hula Love/Devil Woman	40
57	Columbia DB 4014	Hula Love/Devil Woman (78)	25
58	Columbia DB 4077	Swingin' Daddy/Whenever I'm Lonely	40
58	Columbia DB 4077	Swingin' Daddy/Whenever I'm Lonely (78)	25
58	Columbia DB 4180	Somebody Touched Me/C'mon Baby	30
58	Columbia DB 4180	Somebody Touched Me/C'mon Baby (78)	25
59	Columbia DB 4302	To Be With You/I Think I'm Gonna Kill Myself	20
61	London HLG 9268	Lovey Dovey/I Got You	15
61	London HLG 9331	Ling Ting Tong/The Kisses (They're All Mine)	15
61	London HLG 9472	Three-Eyed Man/All By Myself	12
62	Liberty LIB 55411	Chi-Hua-Hua/Open Your Loving Arms	15
62	Liberty LIB 55473	She's Gone/Now There's Only Me	20
63	Liberty LIB 55592	Shadaroom/Tomorrow Is Coming	10
64	Liberty LIB 55694	All Time Loser/Good Loving	10
69	United Artists UP 35019	God Knows I Love You/Night Runners	7
70	United Artists UP 35100	Party Doll/God Knows I Love You	5
57	Columbia SEG 7732	ROCK-A-BUDDY KNOX (EP)	100
62	Liberty LBY 1114	GOLDEN HITS (LP)	25
71	Sunset SLS 50206	ROCK REFLECTIONS (LP)	15

KNUCKLEHEAD

93	Saucerman ART 01	Red Eye, Dead Eye/Spirit Matter (p/s, hand-painted label, 150 copies only)	15

FRANKIE KNUCKLES

89	FFRR FX 102	Tears (12")	20
89	Radical Records TRAXT 3	Your Love/ Baby Wants To Ride (12")	20
90	World Dance DJLTD1	Move Your Body (12")	15

KOBALT 60

91	Music Of Life NOTE57	Chaos From Order/Concrete Show (12")	20

KOCK

83	Hard ON 11	One-Eyed Giant/Hickory Dickory Kock (p/s)	6

KODIAKS

69	Decca F 12942	All Because You Wanna See Me Cry/Tell Me Rhonda	20

(SPIDER) JOHN KOERNER

67	Elektra EKSN 45005	Won't You Give Me Some Love/Don't Stop	25
69	Elektra EKSN 45063	Friends And Lovers/Magazine Lady (with Willie Murphy)	10
65	Elektra EKL 290	SPIDER BLUES (LP)	50
68	Elek. EKL 4041/EKS 74041	RUNNING JUMPING STANDING STILL (LP, with Willie Murphy)	30
71	Elektra K 42026	RUNNING JUMPING STANDING STILL (LP, reissue)	12

MOE KOFFMAN

58	London HLT 8549	Swingin' Shepherd Blues/Hambourg Sound	10
74	CBS S 73245	FOUR SEASONS IN ROCK (LP)	15

KOKOMO

60	London HLU 9305	Asia Minor/Roy's Tune	7

KOLETTES

64	Pye International 7N 25278	Who's That Guy?/Just How Much	50
73	Chess 6145 021	Who's That Guy?/Just How Much (reissue)	10

BONNIE KOLOC

72	London HLO 10377	Jazz Man/Got To Get What You Can	6
72	London HLO 10392	Burgundy Wine/We Are Ships	6
72	London SHO 8432	AFTER ALL THIS TIME (LP)	25
72	London SHO 8440	HOLD ON TO ME (LP)	20

JIMMIE KOMACK

54	Vogue Coral Q 2031	Cold Summer Blues/The Nic-Name Song	10
55	Vogue Coral Q 72061	Wabash 4-7473/An Old Beer Bottle	10
55	Vogue Coral Q 72087	Rock-A-Bye Your Baby With A Dixie Melody/This Is The Place	10

CHRISTOPHER KOMEDA

66	Polydor 580001	CUL DE SAC (soundtrack EP)	300
68	Dot (S)LPD 519	ROSEMARY'S BABY (LP, as Kryzstophe Komeda)	35

MINT VALUE £

JOHN (T.) KONGOS

(see also Scrugg, Floribunda Rose)

66	Piccadilly 7N 35341	I Love Mary/Goodtime Party Companion (as John T. Kongos)	10
69	Dawn DNS 1002	Flim Flam Pharisee/Blood	6
71	Fly BUG 8	He's Gonna Step On You Again/Sometimes It's Not Enough	5
69	Dawn DNLS 3002	CONFUSIONS ABOUT A GOLDFISH (LP, with sticker)	40
69	Dawn DNLS 3002	CONFUSIONS ABOUT A GOLDFISH (LP, without sticker)	30
71	Fly HIFLY 7	KONGOS (LP, gatefold sleeve, Fly label)	25

V. KONGS

63	Halagala HG 18	Tomorrow Will Soon Be Here/Pretty Little Girl	20

KONRADS

65	CBS 201812	Baby It's Too Late Now/I'm Over You	50

KONSTRUKTIVITS

(see also Whitehouse)

80s	Third Mind TM 02	PSYKO GENETIKA (LP)	20
86	Sterile SR 10	GLENACAUL (LP)	20

KOOBAS

(see also Kubas, Van Der Graaf Generator, Gary & Stu, Juicy Lucy, March Hare)

65	Pye 7N 17012	Take Me For A Little While/Somewhere In The Night	50
66	Pye 7N 17087	You'd Better Make Up Your Mind/A Place I Know	60
66	Columbia DB 7988	Sweet Music/Face	60
67	Columbia DB 8103	Sally/Champagne And Caviar	35
67	Columbia DB 8187	Gypsy Fred/City Girl	30
68	Columbia DB 8419	The First Cut Is The Deepest/Walking Out	55
69	Columbia S(C)X 6271	THE KOOBAS (LP, black/silver label, boxed logo, "Sold in U.K..." text)	900
88	Bam Caruso KIRI 047	BARRICADES (LP)	18

KOOGA

(see also Skin)

88	Kooga KO 001	Don't Break My Heart/Lay Down Your Love (p/s, private pressing)	8

KOOKS

05	Private Pressing	Slave To The Game (1-sided, stamped label, tour single, 500 only)	10

KOOL

67	CBS 203003	Look At Me, Look At Me/Room At The Top	15
69	CBS 2865	Step Out Of Your Mind/Funny (What A Fool A Man Can Be)	30
69	MCA MU 1085	Lovin'/Baby's Out Of Reach	12

KOOL KEITH/PHAROE MONCH/AKINYELLE

95	Liberty Grooves	Freestyle Frenzy/Gotta Go Down (7")	45

KOOL & THE GANG

70	London HLZ 10308	Kool And The Gang/Raw Hamburgers	15
71	Mojo 2027 005	Funky Man/Kool And The Gang/Let The Music Take Your Mind	10
71	Mojo 2027 006	Love The Life You Live/The Penguin	10
72	Mojo 2027 009	Music Is The Message (Parts 1 & 2)	10
73	Polydor 2001 474	Funky Stuff/More Funky Stuff	6
74	Polydor 2001 500	Jungle Boogie/North, South, East, West	6
71	Mojo 2347 001	LIVE AT P.J.'S (LP)	30
71	Mojo 2347 002	THE BEST OF KOOL AND THE GANG (LP)	20
72	Mojo 2347 003	LIVE AT THE SEX MACHINE (LP)	15
73	Mojo 2347 004	MUSIC IS THE MESSAGE (LP)	15
74	Polydor 2310299	WILD AND PEACEFUL (LP)	15

AL KOOPER

(see also Blues Project, Blood Sweat & Tears, Shuggie Otis)

65	Mercury MF 885	Parchman Farm/You're The Lovin' End (as Alan Kooper)	20
69	CBS 4011	You Never Know Who Your Friends Are/Soft Landing On The Moon	6
69	CBS 4160	Hey Western Union Man/I Stand Alone	8
71	CBS 5146	Brand New Lady/The Landlord (Love Theme)	5
71	CBS 7376	John The Baptist/Back On My Feet	5
72	CBS 8084	Monkey Time/Bended Knees (Please Don't Let Me Down)	10
69	CBS 63538	I STAND ALONE (LP, orange label)	22
69	CBS 63651	YOU NEVER KNOW WHO YOUR FRIENDS ARE (LP, orange label)	20
70	CBS 63797	KOOPER SESSION - WITH SHUGGIE OTIS (LP, orange label)	20
70	CBS 66252	EASY DOES IT (2-LP, orange label)	18
71	United Artists UAS 29120	THE LANDLORD (LP, soundtrack, with Staple Singers & Lorraine Ellison)	20
71	CBS 64340	NEW YORK CITY (YOU'RE A WOMAN) (LP, gatefold sleeve, orange label)	15
72	CBS 64208	A POSSIBLE PROJECTION OF THE FUTURE/CHILDHOOD'S END (LP, orange label)	15
73	CBS 65193	NAKED SONGS (LP)	15

AL KOOPER, MIKE BLOOMFIELD & STEPHEN STILLS

(see also Mike Bloomfield & Al Kooper, Stephen Stills)

68	CBS 3770	Season Of The Witch/Albert's Shuffle	12
68	CBS 63396	SUPER SESSION (LP)	20
73	CBS CQ 30991	SUPER SESSION (LP, quadrophonic)	25

KOPPYKATS

(see also Ian [Edward] & Zodiacs)

68	Fontana SFT 13052/3	BEATLES' BEST (2-LP)	40

TAMARA KORAN WITH PERCEPTION

68	Domain D 7	Veils Of Mourning Lace/Don't Throw Our Love Away	200

TOMMY KÖRBERG

69	Sonet SON 2005	Dear Mrs. Jones/Bird You Must Fly	8

PAUL KORDA

(see also Tim Andrews & Paul Korda, Dada, Fresh)

66	Columbia DB 7994	Go On Home/Just Come Closer To Me	30

MINT VALUE £

69	Parlophone R 5778	Seagull (West Coast Oil Tragedy Of '68)/Night Of The Next Day	5
71	MAM MAM 20	Between The Road/English Country Garden	5
71	MAM AS 1003	PASSING STRANGER (LP, gatefold sleeve)	75

KORN

96	Epic 6638450	No Place To Hide/Proud (white vinyl, 7,500 only)	8

ALEXIS KORNER (BLUES INCORPORATED)

(see also Cyril Davies, C.C.S., Bob Hall & Alexis Korner, Herbie Goins, Duffy Power, Long John Baldry, Rocket 88, Davy Graham, Beryl Bryden, Jimmy Cotton, Ken Colyer, Jack Bruce, Snape & Little Brother Montgomery)

58	Tempo A 166	I Ain't Gonna Worry No More/County Jail (as Alexis Korner Skiffle Group)	100
58	Tempo A 166	I Ain't Gonna Worry No More/County Jail (78)	50
63	Lyntone LYN 299	Blaydon Races/Up-Town (as Blues Incorporated with Alexis Korner, free with women's magazine Trio)	100
63	Parlophone R 5206	I Need Your Loving/Please Please Please (as Alexis Korner's Blues Inc.)	30
65	Parlophone R 5247	Little Baby/Roberta (as Alexis Korner's Blues Inc.)	25
65	King KG 1017	See See Rider/Blues A La King(as Alexis Korner's All Stars)	45
66	Fontana TF 706	River's Invitation/Everyday (I Have The Blues)	25
67	Fontana TF 817	Rosie/Rock Me	25
75	CBS 3520	Get Off My Cloud/Strange'n'Deranged	10
76	CBS 3877	Ain't That Peculiar/Tree Top Fever	8
58	Tempo EXA 76	BLUES FROM THE ROUNDHOUSE VOL. 1 (EP, as Alexis Korner Skiffle Group)	175
59	Tempo EXA 102	BLUES FROM THE ROUNDHOUSE VOL. 2 (EP, as Alexis Korner's Blues Inc.)	220
62	Topic TOP 70	3/4 A.D. (EP, with Davy Graham, first pressing in mauve sleeve with cream label)	225
62	Topic TOP 70	3/4 A.D. (EP, with Davy Graham, later pressing with lilac sleeve and blue label)	125
62	Topic TOP 70	3/4 A.D. (EP, with Davy Graham, later pressings with bronze sleeve and blue label)	100
57	'77' LP/2	BLUES FROM THE ROUNDHOUSE (10" LP, 99 only, as Alexis Korner Breakdown Group)	1500
62	Ace of Clubs ACL 1130	R&B FROM THE MARQUEE (LP, claret labels, with Long John Baldry)	120
64	Transatlantic TRA 117	RED HOT FROM ALEX (LP, with Herbie Goins)	150
64	Oriole PS 40058	AT THE CAVERN (LP, live, with Herbie Goins, laminated sleeve with flipbacks)	375
65	Ace of Clubs ACL 1187	ALEXIS KORNER'S BLUES INCORPORATED (LP)	100
65	Spot JW 551	SKY HIGH (LP, featuring Duffy Power)	400
67	Fontana TL 5381	I WONDER WHO (LP, mono)	150
67	Fontana STL 5381	I WONDER WHO (LP, stereo)	200
67	Polydor Special 236 206	BLUES INCORPORATED (LP, 1st issue, listing 4 tracks on Side A on sleeve/label)	80
67	Polydor Special 236 206	BLUES INCORPORATED (LP, 2nd issue, listing 5 tracks on Side A on sleeve/label)	50
68	Liberty LBL/LBS 83147	A NEW GENERATION OF BLUES (LP)	90
69	Transatlantic TRASAM 7	ALEXIS KORNER'S ALL STAR BLUES INCORPORATED (LP, reissue of "Red Hot From Alex", different cover)	30
71	Rak SRAK 501	ALEXIS KORNER (LP, textured sleeve)	45
72	Rak SRAKSP 51	BOOTLEG HIM! (2-LP, with booklet)	55
73	Transatlantic TRA 269	ACCIDENTALLY BORN IN NEW ORLEANS (LP, as Snape)	35
75	CBS 69155	GET OFF MY CLOUD (LP)	25

ARTIE KORNFELD'S TREE

72	Neighbourhood NBH 3	Island Song/Feel	5
70	Probe SPB 1022	A TIME TO REMEMBER (LP)	20

KORPERAYSHUN

89	BPM BP12007	K Factor/Non Stop (12")	40
91	Kold Sweat KS 111	Monkey See Monkey Do (12")	8
91	Kold Sweat KS 116	Microphone Nutter (12")	8

KOSMIC KOMMANDO

(see also Aphex Twin)

94	Rephlex CAT 007EP	Cat 007 (I)/Cat 007 (II)/Cat 007 (III)/Cat 007 (IV) (12", clear vinyl)	20

PAUL KOSSOFF

(see also Free, Kossoff Kirke Tetsu & Rabbit, Creepy John Thomas)

73	Island ILPS 9264	BACK STREET CRAWLER (LP, pink rim palm tree label)	15
83	St. Tunes SDLP 0012PD	MR. BIG/BLUE SOUL (LP, picture disc)	12

KOSSOFF, KIRKE, TETSU & RABBIT

(see also Paul Kossoff, Rabbit, Free)

71	Island ILPS 9188	KOSSOFF, KIRKE, TETSU AND RABBIT (LP, gatefold sleeve, pink rim palm tree label)	50

CHIM KOTHARI

66	Deram DM 108	Sitar'N'Spice/Indian Bat	12
66	Deram DML 1002	SOUND OF THE SITAR (LP)	20

LEO KOTTKE

(see also John Fahey)

72	Sonet SNTF 629	LEO KOTTKE & HIS 6 & 12-STRING GUITAR (LP)	12
71	Capitol EST 682	MUDLARK (LP)	12

KOUMBA

82	Greensleeves GRED 105	We Are Leggo/Billy (12")	10

JENNIFER KRAAL

69	NEMS 56-4200	The Men In My Life/Sinful Davey	8

KRACKER

73	Rolling Stones RS 19106	A Song For Polly/Medicated Goo	12
74	Rolling Stones COC 49102	KRACKER BRAND (LP, gatefold sleeve)	20

MINT VALUE £

KRAFTWERK
(see also Organisation, Elektric Music)

SINGLES

75	Vertigo 6147 012	Autobahn/Kometenmelodie 1	8
75	Vertigo 6147 015	Comet Melody 2/Kristallo	15
76	Capitol CL 15853	Radio Activity/Antenna (in p/s)	15
76	Capitol CL 15853	Radio Activity/Antenna	8
77	Capitol CL 104	Showroom Dummies/Europe Endless	8
77	Capitol CLX 104	Showroom Dummies/Europe Endless (12", 'train station' p/s)	18
77	Capitol CL 15917	Trans-Europe Express/Franz Schubert	10
78	Capitol CL 15981	The Robots/Spacelab (foldout p/s)	15
78	Capitol CL 15981	The Robots (Alternative Mix)/Spacelab (foldout p/s)	30
78	Capitol CL 15998	Neon Lights/Trans-Europe Express/The Model	8
78	Capitol 12CL 15998	Neon Lights/Trans-Europe Express/The Model (12", luminous vinyl, dayglo sleeve)	35
78	Capitol 12CL 16098	Showroom Dummies/Spacelab/Europe Endless (12", reissue, 'red shirts' p/s)	15
81	EMI EMI 5175	Pocket Calculator/Dentaku (p/s)	8
81	EMI TCEMI 5175	Pocket Calculator/Numbers/Dentaku ('cigarette'-pack style box)	35
81	EMI 12EMI 5175	Pocket Calculator/Numbers/Dentaku (12", p/s)	12
81	Vertigo VER 3	Kometenmelodie 2/Vom Himmel Hoch (p/s)	12
81	EMI EMI 5207	Computer Love/The Model (p/s, original issue)	5
81	EMI 12EMI 5207	Computer Love/The Model (12", p/s, original issue)	12
82	EMI EMI 5272	Showroom Dummies/Numbers (p/s, some with mispressed B-side "The Model")	8
82	EMI EMI 5272	Showroom Dummies/Numbers (p/s)	5
82	EMI 12EMI 5272	Showroom Dummies/Numbers/Pocket Calculator (12", p/s)	12
83	EMI EMI 5413	Tour De France/Tour De France (Instrumental) (p/s, red or yellow labels)	8
83	EMI TCEMI 5413	Tour De France/Tour De France (Short Version)/ Tour De France (2" Etape) (cassette)	15
83	EMI 12EMI 5413	Tour De France (Long Version)/(7" Version)/(2" Etape) (12", p/s, red or yellow labels)	20
84	EMI EMI 5413	Tour De France (Kevorkian Remix)/Tour De France (Original 7" Version) (reissue, 'Breakdance' p/s)	7
84	EMI 12EMI 5413	Tour De France (Kevorkian Remix)/Tour De France (Different Extended Version)/ Tour De France (Original 7" Version) (12", reissue, 'Breakdance' p/s)	18
86	EMI EMI 5588	Musique Non-Stop/Musique Non-Stop (Different Version) (p/s)	5
86	EMI 12EMI 5588	Musique Non-Stop (6.15)/Musique Non-Stop (7" Version) (12", p/s)	15
87	EMI EMI 5602	The Telephone Call/Der Telefon Anruf (p/s)	6
87	EMI 12EMI 5602	The Telephone Call (Remix)/House Phone/Der Telefon Anruf (12", p/s)	20
91	EMI EM 192	The Robots (re-recorded version)/Robotronik (p/s, red/black or white/black song title box)	5
91	EMI 12EM 192	Robotronik/The Robots (Single Mix)/The Robots (Album Version) (12", p/s, red/black or white/black song title box)	8
91	EMI CDEM 192	Robotronik/Robotnik/The Robots (Single Edit) (CD, white/black song title box)	18
91	EMI EM 201	Radioactivity (Francois Kevorkian Remix)/(William Orbit Mix) (p/s)	6
91	EMI 12EM 201	Radioactivity (Francois Kevorkian 12" Remix)/ (Francois Kevorkian 7" Remix)/ (William Orbit 12" Remix) (12", p/s)	8
91	EMI CDEM 201	Radioactivity (Francois Kevorkian 7" Remix)/ (Francois Kevorkian 12" Remix)/ (William Orbit 12" Remix) (CD)	20
97	EMI KLANG BOX 101	KRAFTWERK (4 x 12" box set, including "Trans Europe Express", "Numbers", Musique Non Stop & "Homecomputer"; without T-shirt, promo only)	200
97	EMI KLANG BOX 101	KRAFTWERK (4 x 12" box set, including "Trans Europe Express", "Numbers", "Musique Non Stop" & "Homecomputer"; with separate white or black T-shirt, promo only)	300

LPs

72	Vertigo 6641 077	KRAFTWERK (2-LP, gatefold sleeve, small 'swirl')	250
72	Vertigo 6641 077	KRAFTWERK (2-LP gatefold sleeve, 'spacecraft' labels)	60
74	Vertigo 6360 616	RALF AND FLORIAN (gatefold sleeve, 'spacecraft' label)	110
74	Vertigo 6360 616	RALF AND FLORIAN ('spacecraft' label, no gatefold sleeve)	50
74	Vertigo 6360 620	AUTOBAHN (embossed blue sleeve)	25
75	Vertigo 6360 629	EXCELLER 8 (some with stickered sleeve)	30
76	Capitol EST 11457	RADIOACTIVITY (with insert)	25
77	Capitol E-ST 11603	TRANS-EUROPE EXPRESS (LP)	15
78	Capitol E-ST 11728	MAN MACHINE (LP)	15
81	EMI EMC 3370	COMPUTER WORLD (LP)	15
81	Vertigo 6449 006	ELEKTROKINETIK (LP)	25
83	EMI EMC 3407	TECHNOPOP (unissued, sleeves only)	0
91	EMI EM 1408	THE MIX (2-LP, with inner sleeves)	20
03	EMI EMI 591 708 1	TOUR DE FRANCE SOUNDTRACKS (2-LP, single stickered sleeve with inners)	15
04	EMI KLANG BOX 001	THE CATALOGUE (8-CD, in card box, 1,000 only)	250

KRAFTY KUTS

99	Southern Fried ECB17	Gimme The Funk (12")	20

KRAKEN

80	Knave EJSP 9370	FANTASY REALITY (EP, no p/s)	50

BILLY J. KRAMER

66	Parlophone R 5482	You Make Me Feel Like Someone/Take My Hand	8
67	Parlophone R 5552	Sorry/Going Going Gone	10
67	Reaction 591 014	Town Of Tuxley Toymakers/Chinese Girl	35
68	CBS 56-3396	1941/His Love Is Just A Lie	10
68	NEMS 56-3635	A World Without Love/Going Through It	8
69	MGM MGM 1474	The Colour Of My Love/I'm Running Away	10
73	Decca F 13426	A Fool Like You/I'll Keep You Satisfied	7
73	Decca F 13442	Darlin' Come To Me/Walking	7
74	BASF BA 1006	Stayin' Power/Blue Jean Queen	7
77	EMI EMI 2661	San Diego/Warm Summer Rain	6

MINT VALUE £

78	EMI EMI 2740	Ships That Pass In The Night/Is There Anymore At Home Like You	6
79	Hobo HOS 010	Blue Christmas/Little Love (p/s, blue vinyl)	10
80	JM JM 1005	Silver Dream/Lonely Lady	5
82	Runaway BJK 1	Rock It/Dum Dum	6
83	Rak RAK 359	You Can't Live On Memories/Stood Up (p/s)	5
63	Parlophone PMC 1209	LISTEN (LP, stereo)	25

BILLY J. KRAMER & THE DAKOTAS

(see also Dakotas)

63	Parlophone R 5049	Bad To Me/I Call Your Name	5
64	Parlophone R 5156	From A Window/Second To None	5
65	Parlophone R 5285	Trains And Boats And Planes/That's The Way I Feel	6
65	Parlophone R 5362	Neon City/I'll Be Doggone	10
66	Parlophone R 5408	We're Doing Fine/Forgive Me	10
63	Parlophone GEP 8885	THE BILLY J. KRAMER HITS (EP)	20
63	Parlophone GEP 8895	I'LL KEEP YOU SATISFIED (EP)	20
64	Parlophone GEP 8907	LITTLE CHILDREN (EP)	20
64	Parlophone GEP 8921	FROM A WINDOW (EP)	25
65	Parlophone GEP 8928	BILLY J. PLAYS THE STATES (EP)	50
63	Parlophone PMC 1209	LISTEN (LP, mono)	20
65	Regal REG 1057	BILLY J (LP, export only)	30

WAYNE KRAMER

(see also MC5)

78	Stiffwick DEA/SUK 1	Ramblin' Rose/Get Some (numbered p/s)	8
79	Radar ADA 41	The Harder They Come/East Side Girl (p/s)	6

KRAY CHERUBS

(see also Art Attacks, Savage Pencil)

88	Fierce FRIGHT 014	No (p/s, 1-sided)	20
89	Snakeskin SS 002	Rot In Hell Mom/SAUCERMAN: Motor Drag (numbered black p/s, 300 only)	12
89	Snakeskin SS 002	Rot In Hell Mom/SAUCERMAN: Motor Drag (later reissue in purple p/s)	8
89	Forced Exposure FE 18	Teen Camel/I Hate My Job (p/s)	15

BILL KRENZ & HIS RAGTIMERS

56	London HLU 8258	There'll Be No New Tunes On This Old Piano/Goofus	30
56	London HLU 8258	There'll Be No New Tunes On This Old Piano/Goofus (78)	12

KREW KATS

(see also Shadows, Brian Bennett)

61	HMV POP 840	Trambone/Peak Hour	20
61	HMV POP 894	Samovar/Jack's Good	30

KREWMEN

91	Lost Moment LMLP 023	FINAL ADVENTURES OF THE KREWMEN (LP)	12

KRIMSON KAKE

(see also Samantha Jones, Vernons Girls)

69	Penny Farthing PEN 707	Feelin' Better/Waiter	20

KRISPY 3

90	K3 K3001	Comin' Thru Clear (12")	8
91	K3 K3002	Destroy All Stereotypes (12")	8
91	Gumh 003	Don't Be Mislead (12")	8
91	Gumh 005	Hard Times (12")	10
93	Kold Sweat KS126	We Don't Go Pop Like Bubblegum (12")	8

DAVE KRISS

80s	private pressing	EMIGRATING (2-LP)	15

KRISSI K

74	People PEO110	Stick Up/Who Do You Think You Are?	10

SONJA KRISTINA

(see also Curved Air)

68	Polydor 56299	Let The Sunshine In/Frank Mills	15
80	Chopper CHOP 101	St Tropez/Mr Skin (p/s)	10
80	Chopper CHOPE 5	SONJA KRISTINA (LP)	35

KROKODIL

69	Liberty LBS 83306	KROKODIL (LP)	50
70	Liberty LBS 83417	SWAMP (LP)	50

KROME & TIME

92	Suburban Base SUBBASE 011	This Sound Is For The Underground/Manic Stampede (12", p/s)	40
92	Suburban Base SUBBASE 11R	This Sound Is For The Underground (E.5 Remix)/Manic Stampede (DJ Hype's Sandringham Road Mix) (12")	20
93	Suburban Base SUBBASE 26	The Slammer/Into The Night (12", p/s as DJ Krome & Mr Time)	20

KRONSTADT UPRISING

80s	Spider SDL 12	The Unknown Revolution (p/s)	5

HARDY KRUGER

59	Top Rank TR 5005	Blind Date (I'm A Lonely Man)/PINEWOOD ORCHESTRA: Blind Date (p/s)	8

GENE KRUPA (& HIS ORCHESTRA)

60	HMV POP 750	Cherokee/Indiana Montage	6
59	HMV 7EG 8595	DRUM BOOGIE (EP)	10
58	Columbia/Clef CX 10133	KRUPA ROCKS (LP)	15
61	Verve VLP/SVLP 9005	PERCUSSION KING (LP)	15

MINT VALUE £

GENE KRUPA & BUDDY RICH
64 Verve VS 503 Perdido/Night Train. 5
62 Verve SVLP 9014 BURNIN' BEAT (LP) 12

KRYPTON TUNES
78 Black & Red FIRE 1 Behind Your Smile/Coming To See You (p/s). . . . 12
78 Lightning GIL 546 Limited Vision/All In Jail 12

KRYSIA (Kocjan)
(see also Natural Acoustic Band, Fairport Convention)
74 RCA LPL1 5052 KRYSIA (LP). . . . 18

KRYSTAL GENERATION
72 Mercury 6052 120 Wanted Dead Or Alive/Every Man Seems To Be For Himself. . . . 10

BOB KUBAN & INMEN
66 Stateside SS 488 The Cheater/Try Me Baby. . . . 60
66 Stateside SS 488 The Cheater/Try Me Baby (DJ copy). . . . 110
66 Stateside SS 514 The Teaser/All I Want 20
68 Bell BLL 1027 The Cheater/Try Me Baby (reissue). . . . 12

KUBAS
(see also Koobas)
65 Columbia DB 7451 I Love Her/Magic Potion. . . . 60

DAVE KUBINEC
69 Parlophone R5762 Schopi/The Lady Loves 12

KUF-LINX
58 London HLU 8583 So Tough/What'cha Gonna Do 100
58 London HLU 8583 So Tough/What'cha Gonna Do (78). . . . 50

LENNY KUHR
69 Philips BF 1777 The Troubadour/Oh No Monsieur 10

KUKL
(see also Sugarcubes)
84 Crass 1984/1 THE EYE (LP, foldout sleeve) 20
85 Crass No. 4 HOLIDAYS IN EUROPE (LP, with inner sleeve) 20

KULT
69 CBS 4276 No Home Today/Mister Number One 300

PRAMOD KUMAR
72 Philips 6460 854 THIS IS THE MUSIC OF INDIA (LP) 12

CHARLIE KUNZ
54 Decca F 10419 Charlie Kunz Piano Medley, No. 114. . . . 10

KURASS
70 Escort ES 825 Stampede/KING STITT: You Were Meant For Me (B-side actually by Lee Perry). . 30

FELA RANSOME KUTI (& AFRICA '70)
(see also Ginger Baker)
72 Regal Zonophone RZ 3052 Chop And Quench/Egbe Mi O (with Africa '70 & Ginger Baker) 10
72 Regal Zono. SLRZ 1023 FELI RANSOME-KUTI & THE AFRICA '70 WITH GINGER BAKER LIVE! (LP). . . . 50
73 Regal Zono. SLR2 103Y AFRODISIAC (LP, red/silver labels with EMI boxed logo) 200
75 Decca/Aphrodisia DWAPS 2005 UPSIDE DOWN (LP) 25
75 Creole CRLP 501 SHAKARA (LP, with Africa '70). . . . 20
77 Creole CRLP 511 ZOMBIE (LP, with Africa '70). . . . 20
78 Phase 4 Stereo PFS 4412 YELLOW FEVER (LP). . . . 20
79 Creole CRLP 502 GENTLEMEN (LP). . . . 20
79 Creole CRLP 509 EVERYTHING SCATTER (LP) 20
81 Arista SPART 1167 BLACK PRESIDENT (LP). . . . 20
82 Arista SPART 1177 ORIGINAL SUFFERHEAD (LP) 30

JIM KWESKIN JUG BAND
65 Fontana TFL 6036 JIM KWESKIN JUG BAND (LP) 20
67 Fontana (S)TFL 6080 SEE REVERSE SIDE FOR TITLE (LP). . . . 18
68 Vanguard SVRL 19046 WHATEVER HAPPENED TO THOSE GOOD OLD DAYS AT CLUB 47 (LP) 18

KYDD
75 Dart ASRT 2052 Voodoo Magic/You Need Love Love Love 5

(THE) KYDDS
69 NEMS 56-4095 The Sun Is A Laughing Child/Touch Of The Sun. . . . 15

CHARLES KYNARD
73 Mainstream MSL 1017 YOUR MAMA DON'T DANCE (LP). . . . 25

KYODS
70 President PT 289 Judas In Blue/Where Did I Go Wrong. . . . 6

KYTES
66 Pye 7N 17136 Blessed/Call Me Darling. . . . 10
66 Pye 7N 17179 Frosted Panes/I'll Give You Better Love. . . . 30
68 Island WI 6027 Running In The Water/The End Of The Day. . . . 70

KYTTOCK KYND
70 Dorian 4782 KYTTOCK KYND (LP). . . . 40

MINT VALUE £

L.A.
(see also Elastic Band, Love Affair)
70 CBS 5017 Speak Of Peace, Sing Of Joy/Brings My Whole World Tumbling Down 7
70 CBS 64109 NEW DAY (LP) 30

PATTI LA BELLE (& BLUE BELLES)
(see also Blue-Belles)
64 Sue WI 324 Down The Aisle/C'est La Vie 30
65 Cameo Parkway P 935 Danny Boy/I Believe 20
65 Atlantic AT 4055 All Or Nothing/You Forgot How To Love (as Patty La Belle & Her Belles) 20
66 Atlantic AT 4064 Over The Rainbow/Groovy Kind Of Love (as Patty La Belle & Her Belles) 12
66 Atlantic 584 007 Patti's Prayer/Family Man (as Patti La Belle & Her Belles) 10
67 Atlantic 584 072 Take Me For A Little While/I Don't Want To Go On Without You (solo) 10
66 Atlantic 587 001 OVER THE RAINBOW (LP) 40

LABRADFORD
96 Duophonic DS45-12 Scenic Recovery (10") 10

LACE
(see also Universals, Pete Dello, Honeybus, Red Herring, Gary Walker & Rain)
68 Columbia DB 8499 People People/The Nun 25
69 Page One POF 135 I'm A Gambler/Go Away 10

DAVE LACEY & CORVETTES
65 Philips BF 1419 That's What They All Say/I've Had Enough 10

LACKEY & SWEENEY
73 Village Thing VTS 23 JUNK STORE SONGS FOR SALE (LP) 15

LACK OF KNOWLEDGE
81 LOK LOK 1 The Uninvited/Ritual (with A4 photocopied inserts) 20
83 Crass Records 121984/6 GREY (EP) 15
85 Chainsaw TEXT 7 SENTINEL (EP) 10
84 Corpus Christi CHRIST 15 SIRENS ARE BACK (LP) 20

JUNIOR LACY
70s Aries ARI 003 You Will See Jah Light/Jah Love Version (12") 25

STEVE LACY
72 Emanem 301 SOLO (LP) 25
73 Emanem 304 THE CRUST (LP) 25

STEVE LACY & DEREK BAILEY
(see also Derek Bailey)
76 Incus 26 COMPANY 4 (LP) 25

LADDERS
83 Statik TAK 2 Gotta See Jane/Krugerrands (p/s) 6
83 Statik TAK 2-12 Gotta See Jane/Krugerrands (12", p/s) 10

LADD'S BLACK ACES
56 London AL 3556 LADD'S BLACK ACES (10" LP) 15

LA-DE-DA BAND
69 Parlophone R 5810 Come Together/Here Is Love 18

LADIES
80s Music Of Life MOLIS 6 Turned On To You/I Knew That Love (12") 15

TOMMY LADNIER
(see also Ma Rainey)
54 London AL 3524 BLUES AND STOMPS VOLUME ONE - TOMMY LADNIER (10" LP) 30
55 London AL 3548 PLAYS THE BLUES WITH MA RAINEY & EDMONIA HENDERSON (10" LP) 30

PATTIE LA DONNE
69 Joe/Duke DU 23 Friends And Lovers/JOE'S ALLSTARS: Hot Line 12

LADYBIRDS
(see also Sharades, Russ Loader, Marion Davies, De Laine Sisters)
64 Columbia DB 7197 Lady Bird/I Don't Care Any More 10
64 Columbia DB 7250 The White Cliffs Of Dover/It's Not The Same Without A Boy 10
64 Columbia DB 7351 Memories/Try A Little Love 10
65 Columbia DB 7523 I Wanna Fly/O.K. Fred 10
70 Decca F13014 Love As High As A Mountain/Stand Up And Be Counted 18

LADY JANE
84 Schizoid SCHIZ 01 For You Tonight/Out For The Count/Whisky And Leather (private pressing) 50

LADY JANE & VERITY
59 Pye International 7N 25036 The Slow Look/Cry Baby 8

LADY JUNE
(see also Kevin Ayers, Eno)
74 Caroline C 1509 LADY JUNE'S LINGUISTIC LEPROSY (LP, with perforated lyric sheet) 35

LADY LEE
64 Decca F 11961 I'm Into Something Good/When Love Comes Along 12
65 Decca F 12147 99 Times Out Of 100/I Can Feel It 8
65 Columbia DB 7121 My Whole World (Seems To Be Tumbling Down)/Girl 10

MINT VALUE £

LADY LUCK & LULLABIES

62	Philips PB 1245	Young Stranger/Dance	5

LADYTRON

00s	Telstar 7STAS 3311	Blue Jeans (Single Version)/Blue Jeans (Interpol Remix) (p/s, 1000 only)	8
02	Telstar 12STAR 3284	Seventeen (Soulwax Remixes) (12" die-cut sleeve)	10

LAFAYETTES

62	RCA RCA 1299	Life's Too Short/Nobody But You	10
62	RCA RCA 1308	Caravan Of Lonely Men/I Still Do	8

MARIE LAFORET

66	Ember NR 5034	THE GIRL WITH THE GOLDEN EYES (LP)	15

FRANCIS LAI

67	United Artists SULP 1155	A MAN AND A WOMAN (LP, soundtrack)	12
67	United Artists (S)ULP 1185	VIVRE POUR VIVRE (LIFE FOR LIFE) (LP, soundtrack)	12
67	Brunswick LAT/STA 8689	I'LL NEVER FORGET WHAT'S 'ISNAME (LP, soundtrack)	40
69	United Artists SULP 1231	HANNIBAL BROOKS (LP)	30
69	Philips SBL 7876	MAYERLING (Francis Lai)	20
70	United Artists UAS 29137	RIDER IN THE RAIN (LP)	20
71	M. F. Pleasure MFP 50034	THE LEGEND OF FRENCHIE KING (LP)	12
76	Warner Bros K 56231	EMMANUELLE 2 (LP)	15
77	Warner Bros K 56375	BILITIS (LP, gatefold sleeve)	15

LAIBACH

84	L.A.Y.L.A.H. LAY 002	Boji/Sila/Brat Moj (12", p/s)	12
84	East West 12 EWS 3	Panarama/Decree (12", p/s)	10
85	Cherry Red 12CHERRY 91	Die Liebe/Die Liebe Ist Grösste Kraft, Die Alles Schafft (12", p/s)	10
87	Mute MUTE 62	Life Is Life/Germania (p/s)	5
88	Mute PMUTE 80T	SYMPATHY FOR THE DEVIL (12" EP, picture disc)	10
86	Side Effects SER 08	OCCUPIED EUROPE TOUR '85 (LP)	15
92	Mute STUMM 82	KAPITAL (LP)	12
94	NSK NSK 2CDX	OCCUPIED EUROPE NATO TOUR (EPK, in numbered box, with CD, video & booklet)	20
96	Mute STUMM 136	JESUS CHRIST SUPERSTARS (LP)	15
98	Mute STUMM 121	MCMXCIV (LP, with poster and inner)	15

CLEO LAINE

(see also Johnny Dankworth, Tubby Hayes & Cleo Laine)

54	Parlophone MSP 6107	I Got Rhythm/I Know You're Mine (with Johnny Dankworth Orchestra)	10
55	Parlophone MSP 6147	Ain't Misbehavin'/I Got It Bad, And That Ain't Good (with Johnny Dankworth Orchestra)	10
57	Pye Jazz 7NJ 2013	I'm Beginning To See The Light/Jeepers Creepers	5
58	Pye 7N 15143	Hand Me Down Love/They Were Right	5
60	Fontana H 269	Let's Slip Away/Thieving Boy	10
61	Columbia DB 4723	It Was A Lover And His Lass/O Mistress Mine	7
61	Fontana H 326	You'll Answer To Me/I Only Have Eyes For You	6
62	Fontana TF 267257	You Gotta Have Love/I Can Dream, Can't I?	6
65	Fontana TF 532	Little Boat/The Exciting Mr. Fitch	5
65	Fontana TF 622	If We Live On The Top Of A Mountain/Don't You Pass Me By	5
66	Fontana TF 759	There Is Nothing Left To Say/Life Is A Wheel	5
70	Philips 6006 016	It Will Soon Be Spring/Feeling Good	5
71	Philips 6006 077	Model City's Programme/Night Owl	10
57	Parlophone GEP 8613	I GOT RHYTHM (EP)	10
57	Pye Nixa Jazz NJE 1010	CLEO LAINE (EP)	10
57	Pye Nixa Jazz NJE 1026	THE APRIL AGE (EP, as Cleo Laine & Dave Lee Quintet)	20
57	Esquire EP 102	CLEO LAINE (EP, as Cleo Laine & Keith Christie Quintet)	20
57	Esquire EP 122	CLEO LAINE (EP, as Cleo Laine & Keith Christie Quintet)	20
59	Columbia SEG 7938	CLEO SINGS ELIZABETHAN (EP)	10
61	Fontana TFE 17381	THE FABULOUS CLEO (EP)	10
64	Fontana TFE 17404	CLEO (EP)	15
55	Esquire 15-007	CLEO LAINE (10" LP)	40
58	Pye Nixa NPT 19024	CLEO'S CHOICE (10" LP)	40
58	MGM MGM-C 765	SHE'S THE TOPS (LP)	25
62	Fontana 680 992 TL	ALL ABOUT ME (LP, also stereo 886 159 TY)	20
64	Fontana (S)TL 5209	SHAKESPEARE & ALL THAT JAZZ (LP)	20
66	Fontana (S)TL 5316	WOMAN TALK (LP)	15
68	Fontana STL 5483	SOLILOQUY (LP)	15

DENNY LAINE

(see also Moody Blues, Paul McCartney/Wings, Balls, Trevor Burton, Magic Christians, Ginger Baker's Airforce, BL&G)

67	Deram DM 122	Say You Don't Mind/Ask The People	15
68	Deram DM 171	Too Much In Love/Catherine's Wheel	30
69	Deram DM 227	Say You Don't Mind/Ask The People (reissue)	10
73	Wizard WIZ 104	Find A Way Somehow/Move Me To Another Place	15
77	Palladin PAL 5014	Caroline/Blues	6
73	Wizard SW2 2001	AHH...LAINE (LP, yellow labels)	20

FRANKIE LAINE

(see also Jo Stafford & Frankie Laine, Four Lads, Doris Day, Easy Riders)

SINGLES

53	Columbia SCM 5016	The Ruby And The Pearl/The Mermaid	20
53	Columbia SCM 5017	Jealousy/The Gandy Dancers' Ball	20
53	Columbia SCM 5031	I'm Just A Poor Bachelor/Tonight You Belong To Me	20
53	Columbia SCM 5064	September In The Rain/Chow Willy	10
53	Columbia SCM 5073	The Swan Song/My Ohio Home	10
54	Columbia SCM 5085	Tomorrow Mountain/I'd Give My Life	10
56	Philips JK 1000	Moonlight Gambler/Only If We Love (jukebox issue)	10
57	Philips JK 1009	Love Is A Golden Ring (with Easy Riders)/There's Not A Moment To Spare	10

			MINT VALUE £
57	Philips JK 1017	Lonely Man/Without Him (jukebox issue)	10
57	Philips JK 1032	The Greater Sin/East Is East (jukebox issue)	10
58	Philips PB 797	Shine/Annabel Lee	5
58	Philips PB 821	The Lonesome Road/My Gal And A Prayer	5
58	Philips PB 836	Lovin' Up A Storm/A Kiss Can Change The World	5
58	Philips PB 848	Choombala Bay/I Have To Cry	5
58	Philips PB 886	When I Speak Your Name/Cottage For Sale	6
59	Philips PB 905	That's My Desire/In My Wildest Dreams	5
59	Philips PB 965	Rawhide/Journey's End	5
59	Philips PB 965	Rawhide/Journey's End (78)	10
60	Philips PB 1064	And Doesn't She Roll/Seven Women	7
61	Philips PB 1135	Gunslinger/Wanted Man	5
63	CBS AAG 144	Don't Make My Baby Blue/The Moment Of Truth	7
74	Warner Bros. K 16414	Blazing Saddles/I'm Tired	6
EP			
54	Columbia SEG 7505	JEZEBEL (company die-cut sleeve)	10
LPs			
52	Oriole/Mercury MG 10001	MR RHYTHM SINGS (10", stickered U.S. "Mr Rhythm" sleeve)	25
52	Oriole/Mercury MG 10002	SONGS BY FRANKIE LAINE (10")	20
54	Mercury MG 25097	MR. RHYTHM SINGS (10", reissue)	20
54	Mercury MG 25098	SONGS BY FRANKIE LAINE (10", reissue)	20
54	Columbia 33S 1047	ONE FOR MY BABY (10")	20
54	Philips BBR 8014	THE VOICE OF YOUR CHOICE (10")	20
55	Philips BBR 8068	MR. RHYTHM (10")	12
56	Mercury MPT 7007	CRY OF THE WILD GOOSE (10")	20
56	Philips BBL 7080	JAZZ SPECTACULAR (with Buck Clayton & His Orchestra)	15
57	Philips BBL 7155	ROCKIN'	30

FRANKIE LAINE & JOHNNIE RAY

(see also Johnnie Ray)

57	Philips JK 1026	Up Above My Head, I Hear Music In The Air/ Good Evening Friends (jukebox issue)	10
57	Philips BBE 12153	FRANKIE AND JOHNNIE (EP, 1 track each, 2 together)	10

LINDA LAINE (& SINNERS)

(see also Sinners)

64	Columbia DB 7204	Doncha Know, Doncha Know, Doncha Know/Ain't That Fun	18
64	Columbia DB 7370	Low Grades And High Fever/After Today	18
65	Columbia DB 7549	Don't Do It Baby/All I Want To Do Is Run	18

SCOTT LAINE

63	Windsor WB 114	Tearaway Johnnie/John Silver	40

DENZIL LAING

(see also Soul Vendors, Dennis Alcapone)

71	Songbird SB 1054	Medicine Stick/CRYSTALITES: Short Cut	12

LAKE

76	CBS 5015	Do I Love You/Key To The Rhyme	6

ALAN LAKE

70	Ember EMB S 278	Good Times/Got To Have Tenderness (p/s)	15

BONNIE LAKE & HER BEAUX

(see also Jack Pleis)

56	Brunswick 05622	Thirteen Black Cats/The Miracle Of Love	20
56	Brunswick 05622	Thirteen Black Cats/The Miracle Of Love (78)	10

GREG LAKE

(see also Emerson Lake & Palmer, King Crimson, Asia, Pete Sinfield, Gary Moore, Shy Limbs)

75	Manticore K 13511	I Believe In Father Christmas/Humbug (p/s)	6
77	Atlantic K 10990	C'est La Vie/EMERSON, LAKE & PALMER: Jeremy Bender (p/s)	6
78	Atlantic K 11061	Watching Over You/EMERSON, LAKE & PALMER: Hallowed Be Thy Name (p/s)	6
81	Chrysalis CHS 2553	Love You Too Much/Someone (p/s)	5
82	Chrysalis CHS 2567	It Hurts/Retribution Drive	5
81	Chrysalis CHR1357	GREG LAKE (LP + inner sleeve)	12
83	Chrysalis CHR1392	MANEOVRES (LP)	12

LEE LAMAR & HIS ORCHESTRA

57	London HLB 8508	Teenage Pedal Pushers/Sophia	75
57	London HLB 8508	Teenage Pedal Pushers/Sophia (78)	30

ANNABEL LAMB

83	A&M AMLH 68555	ONCE BITTEN (LP)	12

CHRIS LAMB & UNIVERSALS

(see also Universals, Gidian)

65	Decca F 12176	Mysterious Land/If You Ask Me	15

KEVIN LAMB

70	Concord CON 23	Who Is The Hero?/The Road To Antibes	6
73	Birth RAB 1004	Who Is The Hero?/Who Stole The Ice	5
72	Birth RAB 4	WHO IS THE HERO? (LP, white label with 'rabbit' child logo)	40

LAMB LANCE

95	Long LENGTH 8	THE JOY OF JOUSTING (LP)	12

LAMBCHOP

00	City Slang 20174-2	THE QUEEN'S ROYAL TRIMMA (CD EP, sold at gigs)	15
02	Virgin/City Slang	IS A WOMAN (2xLP with bonus CD EP)	25

JEANNIE LAMBE

67	CBS 202636	Miss Disc/Montano Blues (with Gordon Beck Orchestra)	25
67	CBS 2731	Day After Day After Day/City At Night	20
67	CBS 3000	This Is My Love/Where Have All The Endings Gone (as Jeanne Lam)	8

MINT VALUE £

DAVE LAMBERT, JON HENDRICKS & ANNIE ROSS
(see also Jon Hendricks, Annie Ross)

60 Philips BBL 7368 DAVE LAMBERT, JON HENDRICKS & ANNIE ROSS (LP, stereo SBBL 562) 15

DAVE LAMBERT & BUDDY STEWART
51 Vogue V 2039 Bopelbaby/Bopelground (78, with Al Haig) 9

TREVOR LAMBERT
72 Duke DU 132 Bald Head Teacher (act. by Max Romeo)/HEADMASTERS: Bald Head Version . . . 5

LAMBRETTAS
79 Rocket XPRES 23 Go Steady/Listen Listen/Cortinas (p/s) 8
80 Rocket XPRES 25 Poison Ivy/Runaround (with '2-Stroke' die-cut sleeve & label) 12
80 Rocket XPRES 25 Poison Ivy/Runaround (with ROCKET die-cut sleeve & label) 12
80 Rocket XPRES 333 Da-a-a-ance/(Can't You) Feel The Beat (picture disc; shades, red, white & blue) . . . 5
80 Rocket XPRES 333 Da-a-a-ance/(Can't You) Feel The Beat (picture disc; shades, pink, white & blue) . . 8
80 Rocket XPRES 36 Page 3/Steppin' Out (Of Line) (withdrawn; one copy known to exist with p/s) 500
80 Rocket XPRES 36 Page 3/Steppin' Out (Of Line) (withdrawn) 300
80 Rocket XPRES 36 Another Day (Another Girl)/Steppin' Out (Of Line) ('emergency' p/s) 5
81 Rocket XPRES 48 Good Times/Lamba Samba (p/s) 5
81 Rocket XPRES 52 Anything You Want/Ambience (Rocket die-cut sleeve) 6
81 Rocket XPRES 62 Decent Town/Da-a-a-ance (p/s) 6
81 Rocket XPRES 6212 Decent Town/Da-a-a-ance/Total Strangers/Young Girls (12", p/s) 12
82 Rocket XPRES 74 Somebody To Love/Nobody's Watching Me (p/s) 8
82 Rocket XPRES 74 Somebody To Love/Nobody's Watching Me (p/s, mispressing, crediting Leap Before You Look on label & sleeve) 8
80 Rocket TRAIN 10 BEAT BOYS IN THE JET AGE (LP, with inner) 18

LAMMELA
Direct DO B1 Wasting Your Time/When Julie Dances 6

TONI LAMOND
68 Philips BF 1722 Silent Voices/They Don't Give Medals (To Yesterday's Heroes) 15

DUNCAN LAMONT
67 Studio Two TWO 159 LATIN A LA LAMONT (LP) 12
68 Morgan MRSAM 2 THIS GUY (LP) 15

LAMPLIGHTERS
(see also Thurston Harris)

55 Parlophone DP 416 Salty Dog/Ride Jockey Ride (78, export issue) 80

LAMP SISTERS
68 Sue WI 4048 A Woman With The Blues/I Thought It Was All Over 40

LANA SISTERS
(see also Al Saxon, Dusty Springfield, Chantelles)

58 Fontana H 148 Ring-A My Phone/Chimes Of Arcady 25
58 Fontana H 148 Ring-A My Phone/Chimes Of Arcady (78) 10
59 Fontana H 176 Buzzin'/Cry, Cry, Baby 25
59 Fontana H 176 Buzzin'/Cry, Cry, Baby (78) 25
59 Fontana H 190 Mister Dee-Jay/Tell Him No 25
59 Fontana H 190 Mister Dee-Jay/Tell Him No (78) 18
59 Fontana H 221 (Seven Little Girls) Sitting In The Back Seat (with Al Saxon)/ Sitting On The pavement) 20
59 Fontana H 221 (Seven Little Girls) Sitting In The Back Seat (with Al Saxon)/ Sitting On The Sidewalk) (78) 28
60 Fontana H 235 My Mother's Eyes/You've Got What It Takes 20
60 Fontana H 235 My Mother's Eyes/You've Got What It Takes (78) 28
60 Fontana H 252 Someone Loves You, Joe/Tinatarella Di Luna 15
60 Fontana H 283 Two-some/Down South 15

CYNTHIA LANAGAN
54 Columbia SCMC 8 Body And Soul/I Can't Believe You're In Love With Me (export issue) 10
57 Parlophone R 4316 Jamie Boy/Silent Lips (as Cynthia Lanigan) 10
57 Parlophone R 4383 I'm Available/(Don't Stop, Don't Stop) Tell Me More 10

LANCASHIRE FAYRE
80 Folk Heritage FHR 113 LANCASHIRE FAYRE (LP) 20

STEVE LANCASTER
67 Polydor 56215 San Francisco Street/Miguel Fernando San Sebastian Brown 15

ALAN LANCASTER'S BOMBERS
(see also Status Quo)

96 P.J. Rocks PJR002CD THE MATCHSTICKMEN EP (CD, 4 tracks, card p/s) 15

LANCASTRIANS
64 Pye 7N 15732 We'll Sing In The Sunshine/Was She Tall 25
65 Pye 7N 15791 Let's Lock The Door (And Throw Away The Key)/If You're Goin' To Leave Me 7
65 Pye 7N 15846 There'll Be No More Goodbyes/Never Gonna Come On Home 7
65 Pye 7N 15927 Lonely Man/I Can't Stand The Pain 7
66 Pye 7N 17043 The World Keeps Going Round/Not The Same Anymore 40
66 Pye 7N 17072 The Ballad Of The Green Berets/My Little Rose 5

MAJOR LANCE
63 Columbia DB 7099 The Monkey Time/Mama Didn't Know 30
63 Columbia DB 7099 The Monkey Time/Mama Didn't Know (DJ copy) 50
63 Columbia DB 7168 Hey Little Girl/Crying In The Rain 25
64 Columbia DB 7205 Um, Um, Um, Um, Um, Um/Sweet Music 20
64 Columbia DB 7271 The Matador/Gonna Get Married 30
64 Columbia DB 7365 Rhythm/Please Don't Say No More 25
65 Columbia DB 7463 I'm So Lost/Sometimes I Wonder 25
65 Columbia DB 7527 Come See/You Belong To Me, My Love 30

MINT VALUE £

65	Columbia DB 7609	Pride And Joy/I'm The One	50
65	Columbia DB 7688	Too Hot To Hold/Dark And Lonely	75
65	Columbia DB 7787	Everybody Loves A Good Time/I Just Can't Help It	30
65	Columbia DB 7787	Everybody Loves A Good Time/I Just Can't Help It (DJ Copy)	75
66	Columbia DB 7967	Investigate/Little Young Lover	75
66	Columbia DB 7967	Investigate/Little Young Lover (DJ copy)	125
67	Columbia DB 8122	Ain't No Soul (Left In These Ole Shoes)/You'll Want Me Back	60
67	Columbia DB 8122	Ain't No Soul (Left In These Ole Shoes)/You'll Want Me Back (DJ copy)	100
69	Atlantic 584 277	Follow The Leader/Since You've Been Gone	15
69	Atlantic 584 302	Sweeter As The Days Go By/Shadows Of A Memory	15
69	Soul City SC 114	The Beat/You'll Want Me Back	25
70	Buddah 2011 046	Gypsy Woman/Stay Away From Me	15
72	Stax 2025 124	I Wanna Make Up/That's The Story Of My Life	15
72	Epic EPC 8404	Um, Um, Um, Um, Um, Um/Sweet Music (reissue)	6
73	Contempo C 1	The Right Track/Um, Um, Um, Um, Um, Um	6
73	Contempo C 9	Ain't No Soul (Left In These Ole Shoes)/Investigate	8
73	Contempo C 26	Dark And Lonely/My Girl	20
73	Warner Bros K 16334	Sweeter/Wild & Free	8
74	Warner Bros K 16385	Without A Doubt/Open The Door To Your Heart	15
74	Contempo CS 2017	Gimme Little Sign/How Can You Say Goodbye	25
74	Contempo CS 9015	The Right Track/Ain't No Soul (Left In These Ole Shoes)	6
75	Contempo CS 2045	Don't You Know I Love You (Parts 1 & 2)	20
75	Pye 7N 45487	You're Everything I Need (Parts 1 & 2)	10
76	Pye International 7N 25705	Nothing Can Stop Me/Follow The Leader	10
64	Columbia SEG 8318	UM UM UM UM UM UM (EP)	100
65	Columbia 33SX 1728	THE RHYTHM OF MAJOR LANCE (LP)	170
73	Contempo COLP 1001	GREATEST HITS LIVE AT THE TORCH (LP, colour photo of Major Lance sitting under a tree on cover, first pressing)	40
73	Contempo COLP 1001	GREATEST HITS LIVE AT THE TORCH (LP, second pressing with 'negative' b/w cover)	20
76	Epic EPC 81519	THE BEST OF MAJOR LANCE (LP)	15
78	Tamla Motown STML 12094	NOW ARRIVING (LP)	12

RICK LANCELOT & SEVEN KNIGHTS

66	RCA RCA 1502	Say Girl/Live Like A Lion	15

LANCERS

54	London HL 8027	Stop Chasin' Me Baby/Peggy O'Neil	40
54	London HL 8079	So High, So Low, So Wide/It's You, It's You I Love	40
54	Vogue Coral Q 2038	Mister Sandman/The Little White Light	25
55	Vogue Coral Q 72062	Timberjack/C-r-a-z-y Music	15
55	Vogue Coral Q 72081	Get Out Of The Car (as Lancers & Georgie Auld)/Close Your Eyes	20
55	Vogue Coral Q 72100	Jo-Ann/The Bonnie Banks Of Loch Lomon'	10
56	Vogue Coral Q 72128	Alphabet Rock/Rock Around The Island	40
56	Vogue Coral Q 72128	Alphabet Rock/Rock Around The Island (78)	15
56	Vogue Coral Q 72157	Little Fool/A Man Is As Good As His Word	8
56	Vogue Coral Q 72183	The First Travelling Saleslady/Free	5
57	Vogue Coral Q 72220	Never Leave Me/I Came Back To Say I'm Sorry	5
57	Vogue Coral Q 72254	It Happened In Monterey/Ramona/Freckled-Face Sara Jane	5
57	Vogue Coral Q 72282	Charm Bracelet/And It Don't Feel Bad	10
58	Coral Q 72300	The Stroll/Don't Go Near The Water	8
58	Coral Q 72300	The Stroll/Don't Go Near The Water (78)	15
60	Coral Q 72398	Joey, Joey, Joey/JOHNNY DESMOND: The Most Happy Fella	5
61	Warner Bros WB 39	Young In Love/Lonesome Town	5
55	London REP 1027	PRESENTING THE LANCERS (EP)	25
54	London H-APB 1029	OH SWEET MAMA (10" LP)	40
61	London HA-P 2307	CONCERT IN CONTRASTS (LP)	15

ELSA LANCHESTER

58	Vogue VA 160126	SONGS FOR A SMOKE-FILLED ROOM (LP, with Charles Laughton)	20
59	Vogue VA 160139	SONGS FOR A SHUTTERED PARLOUR (LP, with Charles Laughton)	20

BILLY LAND

62	Oriole CB 1750	I Go Walking/You're Too Much	10

HAROLD LAND

58	Contemporary LAC 12178	HAROLD IN THE LAND OF JAZZ (LP)	15

BOB LANDER & SPOTNICKS

(see also Spotnicks)

62	Oriole CB 1784	Midnight Special/My Old Kentucky Home	15

BILL & BRETT LANDIS

59	Parlophone R 4516	Since You've Gone/Bright Eyes	15
59	Parlophone R 4516	Since You've Gone/Bright Eyes (78)	10
59	Parlophone R 4551	By You, By You/Forgive Me	10
59	Parlophone R 4570	Baby Talk/Love Me True	15

JERRY LANDIS

(see also Paul Simon)

62	Oriole CB 1930	Carlos Dominquez/He Was My Brother	40

JOYA LANDIS

(see also Jay & Joya, Hugh Roy)

68	Trojan TR 620	Kansas City/Out The Light	10
68	Trojan TR 622	Angel Of The Morning/ALTON PHYLIS: Love Letters	15
69	Trojan TR 641	Moonlight Lover/I Love You True	12

LANDLORD

90	Debut DEBTX 3084	I Like It (12")	10

MINT VALUE £

HOAGY LANDS

67	Stateside SS 2030	The Next In Line/Please Don't Talk About Me When I'm Gone	250
67	Stateside SS 2030	The Next In Line/Please Don't Talk About Me When I'm Gone (DJ copy)	400
68	Stateside SS 2085	I'm Yours/Only You	25
72	Action ACT 4605	Why Didn't You Let Me Know/Do You Know What Life Is All About	25
75	UK USA 13	Friends And Lovers Don't Go Together/True Love At Last	30
75	UK USA 14	The Next In Line/I'm Yours	10

NEIL LANDSTRUMM

(see also Blue Arsed Fly)

95	Mosquito MSQ 02	PASCAL EP (12", custom sleeve)	20

DES(MOND) LANE

(see also Cyril Stapleton, John Barry)

56	Decca F 10821	Penny-Whistle Rock/Penny-Whistle Polka	8
57	Decca F 10847	Rock Mister Piper/Plymouth Rock	10
59	Top Rank JAR 203	Moonbird/The Clanger March (as Des Lane Orchestra, with John Barry)	6
68	Pye 7N 17546	Sadie/No More Wild Oats (as Des Lane)	5

GARY LANE & GARRISONS

61	Fontana H 338	Start Walking Boy/How Wrong Can You Be	15
62	Fontana 267221 TF	I'm A Lucky Boy/A Love Like You	15

LOIS LANE

(see also Caravelles)

67	RCA RCA 1570	One Little Voice/Sing To Me	6
68	Mercury MF 1042	Punky's Dilemma/Lazy Summer Day	6
69	Mercury MF 1092	Brontasaurus Named Bert/Windmills Of Your Mind	5
69	Mercury MF 1115	Lovin' Time/Winds Of Heaven	6
70	Philips BF 1829	Putting My Baby To Sleep/Far From The Madding Crowd	5
70	DJM DJS 2280	Day By Day/Cloud Of Blue	5
68	Mercury SMCL 20125	LOIS LANE (LP)	25

MICKEY LEE LANE

64	Stateside SS 354	Shaggy Dog/Oo Oo	18
65	Stateside SS 456	Hey Sah-Lo-Ney/Of Yesterday	75
65	Stateside SS 456	Hey Sah-Lo-Ney/Of Yesterday (DJ copy)	150

PENNY LANE

68	Columbia DB 8377	Loving Or Losing You/Deep Down Inside	6
68	CBS 3718	The Boy Who Never Grew Up/I'm Going Back	6
70	CBS 4749	Bouzouki/Make Up Or Break Up	6
70	CBS 4905	Heartbreak House/He's Got A Hold Of My Heart	6
70	CBS 5311	Rock Me In The Cradle (Of Your Loving Arms)/I'm Free	10

RONNIE LANE & SLIM CHANCE

(see also Small Faces, Faces, Pete Townshend & Ronnie Lane)

73	GM GMS 011	How Come/Tell Everyone/Done This One Before (p/s)	8
77	Polydor 2058 944	Street In The City/Annie (with Pete Townshend)	6
77	Polydor 2058 944	Street In The City/Annie (12", with Pete Townshend)	8
79	Gem GEMS 12	Kuschty Rye/You're So Right (p/s)	8
74	GM GMS 024	The Poacher/Bye & Bye (Gonna See The King)	5
74	GM GMS 033	Roll on Babe/Anymore For Anymore	5
74	Island WIP 6216	What Went Down (That Night With You)/Lovely	7
75	Island WIP 6229	Brother Can You Spare A Dime/Ain't No Lady	7
76	Island WIP 6258	Don't Try And Change My Mind/Well, well, Hello (The Party)	7
80	GEM GEMS 19	One Step/Lad's Got Money	5
74	GML 1013	ANYMORE FOR ANYMORE (LP)	25
75	Island ILPS 9321	RONNIE LANE AND SLIM CHANCE (LP)	18
75	Island ILPS 9366	ONE FOR THE ROAD (LP)	15
76	Atlantic K 50308	MAHONEY'S LAST STAND (LP, with Ron Wood, soundtrack)	15
77	Polydor 2442 147	ROUGH MIX (LP, with Pete Townshend)	12
80	Gem GEMLP 107	SEE ME (LP, with insert)	12
88	Thunderbolt THBL 067P	MAHONEY'S LAST STAND (LP, reissue, picture disc)	12

ROSEMARY LANE

60	Philips PB 1041	Down By The River/My First Love Letter	8

TONY LANE & DELTONES

64	Sabre SA-45-5	It's Great/Now She's Mine	25

LANE BROTHERS

60	London HLR 9150	Mimi/Two Dozen And A Half	10

LANE SISTERS

61	Columbia DB 4671	Peek A Boo Moon/Birmingham Rag	10

DON LANG (& HIS "FRANTIC" FIVE)

(see also Gordon Langhorn)

55	HMV POP 115	Coludburst/Seventeen (78)	10
56	HMV 7M 354	Four Brothers/I Want You To Be My Baby (solo)	30
56	HMV 7M 381	Rock Around The Island/Jumpin' To Conclusions (solo)	30
56	HMV 7M 416	Rock And Roll Blues/Stop The World I Wanna Get Off (solo)	30
56	HMV POP 260	Sweet Sue - Just You/Lazy Latin (solo)	20
56	HMV POP 260	Sweet Sue - Just You/Lazy Latin (solo) (78)	10
57	HMV POP 289	Rock Around The Cookhouse/Rock Mister Piper	30
57	HMV POP 289	Rock Around The Cookhouse/Rock Mister Piper (78)	12
57	HMV POP 335	Rock-A-Billy/Come Go With Me (B-side with Skifflers)	30
57	HMV POP 335	Rock-A-Billy/Come Go With Me (B-side with Skifflers) (78)	12
57	HMV POP 350	School Day (Ring! Ring! Goes The Bell)/Six-Five Special	30
57	HMV POP 350	School Day (Ring! Ring! Goes The Bell)/Six-Five Special (78)	12
57	HMV POP 382	White Silver Sands/Again 'N' Again 'N' Again	15

			MINT VALUE £
57	HMV POP 414	Red Planet Rock/Texas Tambourine	25
57	HMV POP 414	Red Planet Rock/Texas Tambourine (78)	12
58	HMV POP 434	Ramshackle Daddy/6-5 Hand Jive	25
58	HMV POP 434	Ramshackle Daddy/6-5 Hand Jive (78)	12
58	HMV POP 465	Tequila/Junior Hand Jive	25
58	HMV POP 465	Tequila/Junior Hand Jive (78)	15
58	HMV POP 488	Witch Doctor/Cool Baby Cool	10
58	HMV POP 510	Hey Daddy!/The Bird On My Head	10
58	HMV POP 510	Hey Daddy!/The Bird On My Head (78)	15
58	HMV POP 547	Queen Of The Hop/La-Do-Da-Da (solo)	15
58	HMV POP 547	Queen Of The Hop/La-Do-Da-Da (solo) (78)	20
59	HMV POP 585	Wiggle Wiggle/(You Were Only) Teasin' (solo)	15
59	HMV POP 585	Wiggle Wiggle/(You Were Only) Teasin' (solo) (78)	25
59	HMV POP 623	Percy Green/Phineas McCoy (solo)	15
59	HMV POP 623	Percy Green/Phineas McCoy (solo) (78)	30
59	HMV POP 649	A Hoot An' A Holler/See You Friday	8
59	HMV POP 649	A Hoot An' A Holler/See You Friday (78)	25
59	HMV POP 682	Reveille Rock/Frankie And Johnny	15
60	HMV POP 714	Sink The Bismarck!/They Call Him Cliff (solo)	30
60	HMV POP 805	Time Machine/Don't Open That Door	15
62	Decca F 11483	Wicked Women/Play Money (as Don Lang & Boulder Rollers)	10
57	HMV 7EG 8208	ROCK 'N' ROLL (EP)	100
57	HMV DLP 1151	SKIFFLE SPECIAL (LP, 10", by Don Lang & His Skiffle Group)	120
58	HMV DLP 1179	INTRODUCING THE HAND JIVE (LP, 10")	150
62	Ace Of Clubs ACL 1111	TWENTY TOP-TWENTY TWISTS (LP)	20

EDDIE LANG & LONNIE JOHNSON

(see also Blind Willie Dunn's Gin Bottle Four)

67	Parlophone PMC 7019	BLUE GUITARS (LP)	30
70	Parlophone PMC 7106	BLUE GUITARS VOLUME 2 (LP)	30

K.D. LANG

88	Sire W 7841	Sugar Moon/Honky Tonk Medley (p/s)	20
88	Sire W 7841T	Sugar Moon/Honky Tonk Medley/I'm Down To My Last Cigarette (12", p/s)	30
88	Sire W 7697	Our Day Will Come/Three Cigarettes In An Ashtray (live) (p/s)	20
88	Sire W 7697T	Our Day Will Come/Three Cigarettes In An Ashtray (live)/ Johnny Get Angry (live) (12", p/s)	30
90	Warner Brothers W 9535	Ridin' The Rails (with Take Six)/DARLENE LOVE: Mr Fix-It (with p/s)	20
90	Warner Brothers W 9535	Ridin' The Rails (with Take Six)/DARLENE LOVE: Mr Fix-It	15
92	Sire W 0100T	Constant Craving (Edit)/Barefoot (Rhythmic Version)/ Season Of Hollow Soul (12", p/s)	8
92	Sire W 0100CD	Constant Craving (Edit)/Barefoot (Rhythmic Version)/ Season Of Hollow Soul (CD)	12

RAY LANG & JAMAICAN ROOM ORCHESTRA

57	Brunswick 05683	Last Train (Biddi-Biddi Bum-Bum)/Keetch (Hey! Bernice)	10
57	Brunswick 05683	Last Train (Biddi-Biddi Bum-Bum)/Keetch (Hey! Bernice) (78)	10

STEVIE LANGE

81	RCA RCA 152	Remember My Name/I Don't Want To Know (1st issue, p/s)	8
81	RCA LIM 1	Remember My Name/I Don't Want To Know (2nd issue, p/s)	6

GORDON LANGHORN

(see also Don Lang, Cyril Stapleton)

55	Decca F 10591	Give A Fool A Chance/Don't Stay Away Too Long	15

MARY LANGLEY

(see also Perpetual Langley)

67	CBS 2862	Stay In My World/Summer Love	12
67	CBS 3032	It Always Rains On Sunday/All My Life Is You	6

PERPETUAL LANGLEY

(see also Mary Langley)

66	Planet PLF 110	We Wanna Stay Home/So Sad	30
66	Planet PLF 115	Surrender/Two By Two	30

(HUW) LLOYD LANGTON (GROUP)

(see also Hawkwind, Widowmaker)

83	Flicknife FLS 021	Wind Of Change/Outside The Law (as Lloyd Langton Group, p/s)	5
83	Flicknife SHARP 015	OUTSIDE THE LAW (LP, 1,000 only bonus 7": "Working Time"/ I See You [FREE 001], as Huw Lloyd Langton)	15
83	Flicknife SHARP 015	OUTSIDE THE LAW (LP, 1,000 only without bonus 7": "Working Time"/ I See You [FREE 001], as Huw Lloyd Langton)	12
86	Gas GAS 4014	LIKE AN ARROW (THROUGH THE HEART) (LP)	12

PHIL LANGTON TRIO

60s	Holyground	PHIL LANGTON TRIO (LP)	18

LESTER LANIN & HIS ORCHESTRA

62	Columbia 33SX 1442	TWISTIN' IN HIGH SOCIETY! (LP)	12

SNOOKY LANSON

(see also Teresa Brewer)

50	London L 555	The Old Master Painter/Did You Ever See A Dream Walking? (78)	10
50	London L 682	Roses/Where Are You Gonna Be When The Moon Shines (78)	10
56	London HLD 8223	It's Almost Tomorrow/Why Don't You Write	100
56	London HLD 8223	It's Almost Tomorrow/Why Don't You Write (78)	12
56	London HLD 8236	Stop (Let Me Off The Bus)/Last Minute Love	200
56	London HLD 8236	Stop (Let Me Off The Bus)/Last Minute Love (78)	20
56	London HLD 8249	Seven Days/Tippity Top	200
56	London HLD 8249	Seven Days/Tippity Top (78)	20
56	London HL 7005	Seven Days/Tippity Top (export issue)	80

MINT VALUE £

MARIO LANZA
58 RCA 1090 — Drinking Song/Serenade — 7
60 RCA 1210 — Be My Love/Only A Rose — 6

LANZON & HUSBAND
75 Bradley's BRAD 7508 — Do You Still Love Me/Ecstacy Express — 6
75 Bradley's BRADL 1007 — NOSTALGIA (LP) — 15

JENNIFER LARA
79 Hitrun HIT DD 14 — Jah Will Lead Us Home/RANKING PURPLE: Ah Fi We Jah (12") — 50

PHILIP LARKIN
58 Mervell Press — LESS DECEIVED (LP, 100 only, numbered) — 125
68 Listen — LESS DECEIVED (LP) — 40
75 Argo PLP 1202 — HIGH WINDOWS (LP) — 25

LARKS
64 Pye International 7N 25284 — The Jerk/Forget Me — 50
64 Pye International 7N 25284 — The Jerk/Forget Me (DJ copy) — 80

LARKS
86 Exalation 12 LARX 2 — All Or Nothing Girl/Whatever You Say/Teachers: Parents/Heartless (12", p/s) — 12

SAM LARNER
61 Folkways FG 3507 — NOW IS THE TIME FOR FISHING (LP) — 15
74 Topic 12T 244 — A GARLAND FOR SAM (LP, blue label) — 15

LARO
60 Kalypso XX 21 — Jamaican Referendum Calypso/Wrong Impressions Of A Soldier — 8

WINSTON LARO
70 Downtown DT 461 — Goodnight My Love/BOYSIE: I Don't Want To Be Hurt — 5

JULIUS LA ROSA
55 London HL 8154 — Mobile/Pass It On — 25
55 London HLA 8170 — Domani/Mama Rosa — 25
55 London HLA 8193 — Suddenly There's A Valley/Everytime I Kiss Carrie — 20
56 HMV 7M 384 — Lipstick And Candy And Rubber-Sole Shoe/Winter In New England — 10
56 London HLA 8272 — No Other Love/Rosanne — 20
56 London HLA 8353 — Jingle Bells (Campanelle)/Jingle Dingle — 12
58 RCA RCA 1063 — Torero/Milano — 5
60 London HLR 9092 — Green Fields/Caress Me (Accaressama) — 5
54 London RE-P 1005 — SINGS (EP) — 10
57 London HA-A 2031 — JULIUS LA ROSA (LP) — 20

LARRY'S ALL STARS
(see also Larry Lawrence, Delroy Wilson, Hugh Roy, Sensations)
71 Ackee ACK 125 — In The Fields/Teardrops Got The Feeling — 10
71 Ackee ACK 130 — Pre-Fight/The Prayer — 5

LARRY (Marshall) & ALVIN
(see also Larry Marshall, Sound Dimension, Vincent Gordon)
68 Studio One SO 2065 — Nanny Goat/Smell You Crep — 20
68 Studio One SO 2067 — Can't You Understand/Hush Up — 50
69 Studio One SO 2080 — Lonely Room (No One To Give Me Love)/You Mean To Me — 40
69 Coxsone CS 7081 — Love Got Me/BOB ANDY: Lady With The Bright Light (both sides actually by Glen [Brown] & Dave [Barker]) — 25
70 Bamboo BAM 22 — Girl Of My Dream/SOUND DIMENTION: Give It Away — 50

LARRY & JOHNNY
(see also Larry Williams & Johnny 'Guitar' Watson)
65 Outasite 45 501 — Beatle Time Parts 1 & 2 (99 copies only) — 130

LARRY & LINDA
70 Beacon BEA 146 — Most Peculiar Girl/Magnificent Opupouring — 10

LARRY & TOMMY
68 Polydor 56741 — You've Gotta Bend A Little/Yo-Yo — 6

KIM LARSEN & JUNGLE DREAMS
82 CBS A 2232 — Rock 'N' Roll City/Time Bomb — 20

JACK LARSON
61 Top Rank JAR 573 — I Love The Way She Laughs/The Hammer Bell Song — 8

LA'S
(see also Cast)
87 Go! Discs GOLAS 1 — Way Out/Endless (p/s) — 15
87 Go! Discs GOLAS 112 — Way Out/Knock Me Down/Endless (12", red & silver p/s) — 20
87 Go! Discs GOLAR 112 — Way Out/Knock Me Down/Endless/Liberty Ship (Demo)/Freedom Song (Demo) (12", blue & silver stickered p/s listing 4 tracks) — 15
87 Go! Discs GOLAR 112 — Way Out/Knock Me Down/Endless/Liberty Ship (Demo)/Freedom Song (Demo) (12", blue & silver stickered p/s listing 5 tracks) — 15
88 Go! Discs GOLAS 2 — There She Goes/Come In Come Out (red p/s) — 10
88 Go! Discs LASEP 2 — There She Goes/Way Out/Who Knows/Come In Come Out (EP, blue p/s, 5,000 only) — 18
88 Go! Discs GOLAS 212 — There She Goes/Come In Come Out/Who Knows/ Man I'm Only Human (12", red sleeve) — 15
88 Go! Discs LASCD 2 — There She Goes/Come In Come Out/Who Knows/Man I'm Only Human (CD) — 15
89 Go! Discs GOLAS 3 — Timeless Melody/Clean Prophet (p/s, unissued; 10 test pressings only) — 60
89 Go! Discs LASEP 3 — Timeless Melody (10", unissued) — 0
89 Go! Discs LASDJ 312 — Timeless Melody/Clean Prophet/All By Myself/Rider Yer Camel (12", promo, 500 only) — 40
89 Go! Discs GOLAS 4 — Timeless Melody/Clean Prophet (blue p/s) — 7
89 Go! Discs GOLAS 412 — Timeless Melody/Clean Prophet/Knock Me Down/Over (12", purple p/s) — 10

			MINT VALUE £
89	Go! Discs LASCD 4	Timeless Melody/Clean Prophet/Knock Me Down/Over (CD, orange card p/s)	10
90	Go! Discs GOLAB 5	There She Goes/Freedom Song (numbered box set with badge & 3 stickers)	8
90	Go! Discs GOLAS 5	There She Goes/Freedom Song (reissue, white sleeve)	5
90	Go! Discs GOLAS 512	There She Goes/Freedom Song/All By Myself (12", reissue, white p/s)	10
90	Go! Discs LASCD 5	There She Goes/Freedom Song/All By Myself (CD)	15
91	Go! Discs GOLAS 6	Feelin'/Doledrum (p/s)	8
91	Go! Discs GOLAB 6	Feelin'/IOU (Alternate Version)/Feelin' (Alternate Version)/Doledrum (numbered box set with badge & 3 stickers)	12
91	Go! Discs 828 202-1	THE LA'S (LP)	30

DENISE LASALLE

71	Janus 6310206	TRAPPED BY A THING CALLED LOVE (LP)	15

COUNT LASHER

60s	Kalypso 100 AB	Calypso Cha Cha Cha/Perseverance	5
60s	Kalypso 105 AB	Slide Mongoose/Miss Constance	5

LASSIES & RAY CHARLES SINGERS

56	Brunswick 05571	Sleepy Head/This I Offer You	5

LAST BANDITS

(see also Swell Maps, Nikki Sudden)

89	Solid ROK 722	The Angels Are Calling/The Dalkey Rake (p/s)	5

LAST CHANT

(see also Waterboys)

81	Chicken Jazz JAZZ 4	Run Of The Dove/Strength Alone/Tradition (p/s)	8

LAST EXIT

(see also Newcastle Big Band, Police, Sting)

75	Wudwink WUD 01	Whispering Voices/Evensong (no p/s)	35
75	Wudwink WUD.C.101	FIRST FROM LAST EXIT (cassette only, pink card insert, sold at gigs, only 3 copies known to exist)	500

LAST FLIGHT

81	Heavy Metal HEAVY 5	Dance To The Music/I'm Ready (p/s)	8

LAST MAN IN EUROPE

85	Cocteau CO 22	A Certain Bridge/TV Addict (p/s)	15

LAST POETS

72	Douglas DGL 69012	THIS IS MADNESS (LP)	40

LAST RESORT

78	Red Meat RMRS 01	Having Fun?/F.U.2 (die-cut printed paper sleeve)	20

LAST RESORT

81	Own label	Violence In Our Minds/Help Hostage/Soul Boys (cassette; 4-track issue)	20
81	Own label	Violence In Our Minds/Help Hostage (cassette; 3-track issue)	20
82	Last Resort LR 1	SKINHEAD ANTHEMS (LP, red vinyl)	30
82	Last Resort LR 1	SKINHEAD ANTHEMS (LP, white vinyl)	30
82	Last Resort LR 1	SKINHEAD ANTHEMS (LP, blue vinyl)	30
82	Last Resort LR 1	SKINHEAD ANTHEMS (LP, black vinyl)	40

LAST RITES

83	Flicknife FLS 219	We Don't Care/Step Down (p/s)	10
84	Essential 004	FASCISM MEANS WAR (EP, gatefold p/s)	12
84	Essential 001	THIS IS THE REACTION (LP)	30

LAST ROUGH CAUSE

85	LRC 001	THE VIOLENT FEW (EP, with lyric sheet)	40

LAST STAND

81	Silly Symbol SJP 825	Just A Number/Caviare (p/s)	30

LAST STRAW

78	Solent SS 049	Oh Lady/Fly By Night (p/s)	50

LAST WORD

74	Polydor 2066 429	Keep On Bumping Before You Run Out Of Gas/Funky And Some	8

LAST WORDS

79	Rough Trade RT 022	Animal World/No Music In The World Today (p/s)	8
79	Remand REMAND 2	Todays Kidz/There's Something Wrong (p/s)	6
81	Armageddon ARM 2	THE LAST WORDS (LP)	12

BILL LASWELL

88	Venture VE12	HEAR NO EVIL (LP)	25

LATE OF THE PIER

07	Wow 02	Space And The Woods/Heartbeat, Flicker, Line (7", 500 only)	10

LATE SHOW

78	Decca F 13777	Drop Dead/Ain't Gonna Stamp On His Face (p/s)	15
79	Decca F 13822	BRISTOL STOMP EP (p/s)	8

YUSEF LATEEF

58	Esquire 32-069	THE SOUNDS OF YUSEF (LP)	30
58	Columbia Clef 33CX 10124	BEFORE DAWN (LP)	50
59	Esquire 32-139	CRY! TENDER (LP)	40
64	Transatlantic PR 7319	EASTERN SOUND (LP)	30
64	Realm RM 228	FABRIC OF JAZZ (LP)	20
72	Atlantic K 40359	GENTLE GIANT (LP)	12
73	Prestige PR 24007	YUSEF LATEEF (LP)	15
74	Atlantic K 50041	PART OF THE SEARCH (LP)	12
74	Milestone ML 47009	THE MANY FACES OF YUSEF LATEEF (LP)	12
76	Impulse IMPL 8013	CLUB DATE (LP)	15

MINT VALUE £

LATIMORE
73 President PTLS 1058 S.T. (LP) . . . 20
74 President PTLS 1062 MORE MORE MORE (LP) . . . 20

LATIN QUARTER
89 Arista SWIMMING AGAINST THE STREAM (CD) . . . 25

MARCEL LATOUR
69 United Artists UP 350058 Women In Love/Kes . . . 8

GENE LATTER
(see also Detours)
66 Decca F 12364 Just A Minute Or Two/Dream Lover . . . 30
66 Decca F 12397 Mother's Little Helper/Please Come Back To Me Again . . . 25
67 CBS 202483 Something Inside Me Died/Don't Go. . . . 8
67 CBS 202655 Always/A Woman Called Sorrow. . . . 8
67 CBS 2843 A Little Piece Of Leather/Funny Face Girl . . . 30
67 CBS 2843 A Little Piece Of Leather/Funny Face Girl (DJ copy) . . . 50
67 CBS 2986 With A Child's Heart/Ways . . . 10
68 Direction 58-3245 A Tribute To Otis/Bring Your Love Home . . . 10
68 Spark SRL 1015 My Life Ain't Easy/Angie (as Gene Latter & Detours). . . . 6
69 Spark SRL 1022 Sign On The Dotted Line/I Love You. . . . 15
69 Spark SRL 1031 The Old Iron Bell/Holding A Dream. . . . 170
69 Parlophone R 5800 Help Me Judy, Help Me/On The Highway . . . 7
69 Parlophone R 5815 Tiger Bay/We Can Make Out . . . 7
70 Parlophone R 5853 Someday You'll Need My Love/Come On Home . . . 6
71 Parlophone R 5896 Catch My Soul/Happiness . . . 10
71 Parlophone R 5913 Sing A Song Of Freedom/Too Busy Thinking About My Baby. . . . 10

STANLEY LAUDAN
58 Oriole CB 1434 Two Guitars/Blue Shawl . . . 10
57 Oriole CB 1397 Marushka/Bucharest. . . . 6

THE LAUGHING APPLE
(see also Biff Bang Pow!, Revolving Paint Dream)
81 Autonomy AUT 001 HA HA HEE HEE (EP) . . . 8
81 Autonomy AUT 002 Participate!/Wouldn't You? (foldover p/s) . . . 6
82 Essential ESS 001 Precious Feeling/Celebration (p/s) . . . 8
83 Creation Artefact LYN 12903 Wouldn't You?/THE PASTELS: I Wonder Why! (live) (33rpm flexidisc, initially free with The Legend! 7" "'73 In '83" [CRE 001]) . . . 8

LAUGHING GAS
70 RCA RCA 2006 All Shapes And Sizes/Opus No. 1 . . . 6

CYNDI LAUPER
(see also Blue Angel)
84 Portrait WA 4290 Time After Time/I'll Kiss You (picture disc) . . . 6
84 Portrait WA 4620 She Bop/Witness (Cyndi-shaped picture disc) . . . 5

LAUREL & HARDY
75 United Artists UAG 29676 THE GOLDEN AGE OF HOLLYWOOD COMEDY (LP, gatefold) . . . 12

LAUREL (Aitken) & OWEN (Gray)
(see also Laurel Aitken, Owen Gray)
62 Blue Beat BB 149 She's Going To Napoli/Have Mercy Mr Percy . . . 10

LAURELS
68 RCA Victor RCA 1741 Sunshine Thursday/Threepence A Tune . . . 12
69 RCA Victor RCA 1836 Making It Groovy/Rainmaker . . . 25
70 Pye 7N 17980 Shame Shame/Make Believe . . . 10
71 Pye 45034 The Devil's Well/Underground. . . . 60

ROD LAUREN
59 RCA RCA 1165 If I Had A Girl/No Wonder. . . . 10
59 RCA RCA 1165 If I Had A Girl/No Wonder (78) . . . 10

ZACK LAURENCE (ORCHESTRA)
61 Parlophone R 4802 Teenage Concerto/Saratoga . . . 5
63 Parlophone R 5000 Tempo Seven/Sleeve Shaker . . . 7
66 HMV 7EG 8968 BEATLE CONCERTO (EP) . . . 8

JOHN LAURENZ
55 London HL 8138 Goodbye, Stranger, Goodbye/Red Roses . . . 30
55 London HL 8138 Goodbye, Stranger, Goodbye/Red Roses (78). . . . 10
65 Decca F 12147 99 Times Out Of 100/I Can Feel It . . . 5

LAURI
78 Thelopian THEO1 If We Can't Have It Neither Can You/Reconciling Trades (p/s). . . . 6

LAURIE
66 Decca F 12347 He Understands Me/Fools Never Learn . . . 10
66 Decca F 12424 I Love Onions/I Want Him . . . 5

CY LAURIE JAZZ BAND
55 Esquire 20-037 CY LAURIE JAZZ BAND (10" LP) . . . 20
50s Esquire 32-008 CY LAURIE JAZZ BAND (LP). . . . 15

LINDA LAURIE
59 London HL 8807 Ambrose/Ooh, What A Lover. . . . 12
60 Top Rank JAR 277 Stay With Me/All Winter Long . . . 6

LAURIE SISTERS
60 MGM MGM 1083 Don't Forget (To Sign Your Name With A Kiss)/I Surrender Dear . . . 5
61 MGM MGM 1128 Live It Up/Lonesome And Sorry . . . 5

MISS LAVELL
65 Vocalion VP 9236 Everybody's Got Somebody/The Best Part Of Me . . . 30

MINT VALUE £

JUNE LAVERICK
(see also Dickie Henderson & June Laverick, Johnny Webb)

60	Oriole CB 1537	Stop/JOHNNY WEBB: Concertino	10
60	Oriole CB 1537	Stop/JOHNNY WEBB: Concertino (78)	12

ROGER La VERN & MICRONS
(see also Tornados)

63	Decca F 11791	Christmas Stocking/Reindeer Ride	45
75	SRT SRTS/CUS/042	Sing-A-Long Piano Party Parts 1 & 2 (maxi-single, p/s)	8

BETTY LAVETTE

67	Stateside SS 2015	I Feel Good All Over/Only Your Love Can Save Me	60
67	Stateside SS 2015	I Feel Good All Over/Only Your Love Can Save Me (DJ copy)	75
68	Pama PM 748	Only Your Love Can Save Me/I Feel Good All Over (reissue)	40
70	Polydor 56786	He Made A Woman Out Of Me/Nearer To You	10
72	Mojo 2092 030	Let Me Down Easy/I Feel Good All Over/What I Don't Know Won't Hurt Me	10
73	Atlantic K 10299	Your Turn To Cry/Soul Tambourine	10
78	Atlantic K 11198	Doin' The Best I Can Parts 1 & 2	6

DALIAH LAVI

70	Pye Intl. 7N 25533	Won't You Join Me/Karriere	5
71	Pye Intl. 7N 25582	I'm Leaving/Here's To You	6
70	Pye Intl. NSPL 28141	DALIAH LAVI (LP)	15
72	Pye Intl. NSPL 28167	WOULD YOU FOLLOW ME (LP)	12

PETER LAW

67	Major Minor MM 522	Lingering On/Memories Of You	6

LAW (THE)

79	Smile SR011	Be My Girl/Dead City Kicks/I Just Want Your Body (500 pressed)	50

GASPAR LAWAL

80	Cap	AJOMASE (LP)	20

AZIE LAWRENCE

59	Mezzotone ME 7001/7002	West Indians In England/Jump Up	10
59	Mezzotone ME 7004	Love In Every Land/No Dice	8
60	Starlite ST45 022	West Indians In England/Jump Up (with Carib Serenaders)	15
61	Starlite ST45 041	No Dice/Love In Every Land	10
61	Melodisc M 1563	Jamaica Blues/Come Rumble & Tumble With Me	8
61	Melodisc M 1572	You Didn't Want To Know	8
61	Blue Beat BB 71	So Far Apart/Palms Of Victory (with Melobeats)	12
64	Blue Beat BB 222	Pempelem/Lovers Understand	300

DIANE LAWRENCE

67	Doctor Bird DB 1075	I Won't Hang Around Like A Hound Dog/Read It Over	35
68	Jolly JY 005	Treat Me Nice/I'll Be Loving You	12

EDDIE LAWRENCE

59	Coral Q 72361	The Salesman's Philosopher/Mother Philosopher	5

ELLIOTT LAWRENCE BAND

51	Vogue V 9024	Sixty-Minute Man/Quick (78)	10
58	Vogue LAE 12057	PLAYS GERRY MULLIGAN ARRANGEMENTS (LP)	12

GENE LAWRENCE

67	Jump Up JU 505	Longest Day Meringue/Bachelor Boy	6
67	Jump Up JU 510	Meringue Triniana/Devil Woman	6

LARRY LAWRENCE (Jamaica)
(see also Larry's Allstars, McBean Scott & Champions)

63	Island WI 091	Garden Of Eden/DERRICK MORGAN: Sendin' This Message	12

LARRY LAWRENCE (U.S.)

59	Pye International 7N 25042	Goofin' Off/Bongo Boogie (as Larry Lawrence & Band Of Gold)	10
59	Pye International 7N 25042	Goofin' Off/Bongo Boogie (as Larry Lawrence & Band Of Gold) (78)	10
60	Ember EMB S 106	Squad Car Theme/Jug-A-Roo (with Beatniks, in art p/s)	15
60	Ember EMB S 106	Squad Car Theme/Jug-A-Roo (with Beatniks)	10

LEE LAWRENCE (& CORONETS)

54	Decca F 10285	The Little Mustard Seed/My Love For You	10
54	Decca F 10367	The Story Of Tina/For You My Love	10
54	Decca F 10408	The Things I Didn't Do/You Still Mean The Same To Me	6
55	Decca F 10422	My Own True Love (Tara's Theme)/Beware Now!	6
55	Decca F 10438	Lights Of Paris/A Love Like Ours	6
55	Decca F 10485	Wedding Bells And Silver Horse-Shoes/Will You Be Mine Alone?	7
55	Columbia SCM 5175	Beyond The Stars/Give Me Your Word	6
55	Columbia SCM 5181	My World Stood Still/Don't Worry	6
55	Columbia SCM 5190	More Than A Millionaire/Overnight	7
55	Columbia SCM 5201	Suddenly There's A Valley/Mi Muchacha (Little Girl)	15
56	Columbia SCM 5228	Young And Foolish/Don't Tell Me Not To Love You	7
56	Columbia SCM 5254	We Believe In Love/Welcome To My Heart	7
56	Columbia SCM 5283	Come Back, My Love/Valley Valparaiso	6
56	Columbia DB 3830	From The Candy Store On The Corner/High Upon A Mountain	6
57	Columbia DB 3855	Rock 'n' Roll Opera/Don't Nobody Move	10
57	Columbia DB 3885	Your Love Is My Love/By You, By You, By You	5
57	Columbia DB 3922	Sold To The Man With The Broken Heart/Chapel Of The Roses	5
57	Columbia DB 3981	His Servant/Lonely Ballerina	5
58	Columbia SEG 7780	LEE LAWRENCE (EP)	15
53	Decca LF 1132	PRESENTING LEE LAWRENCE (10" LP)	25

STEVE LAWRENCE

53	Parlophone MSP 6038	Say It Isn't True/This Night (Madalena) (as Steve & Bernie Lawrence)	20
54	Parlophone MSP 6080	Remember Me (You Taught Me To Love)/Too Little Time	20

			MINT VALUE £
54	Parlophone MSP 6106	You Can't Hold A Memory In Your Arms/King For A Day	20
55	Vogue Coral Q 72114	Open Up The Gates Of Mercy/My Impression Of Janie	15
56	Vogue Coral Q 72133	Speedo/The Chicken And The Hawk	22
56	Vogue Coral Q 72133	Speedo/The Chicken And The Hawk (78)	10
57	Vogue Coral Q 72228	The Banana Boat Song/If You Would Say You're Mine	10
57	Vogue Coral Q 72243	Party Doll/Pum-Pa-Lum (The Bad Donkey)	20
57	Vogue Coral Q 72264	Fabulous/Can't Wait For The Summer (with Dick Jacobs Band)	20
57	Vogue Coral Q 72281	Fraulein/Blue Rememberin' You	15
57	Vogue Coral Q 72286	Never Mind/Long Before I Knew You	15
58	Coral Q 72304	Geisha Girl/I Don't Know	6
58	Coral Q 72335	Those Nights At The Round Table (with Guinevere)/Stranger In Mexico	6
59	Coral Q 72353	These Things Are Free/I Only Have Eyes For You	7
59	Coral Q 72353	These Things Are Free/I Only Have Eyes For You (78)	15
59	HMV POP 604	Only Love Me (Angelina)/Loving Is A Way Of Living	6
60	HMV POP 689	Pretty Blue Eyes/You're Nearer	6
60	HMV POP 689	Pretty Blue Eyes/You're Nearer (78)	15
60	HMV POP 726	Footsteps/You Don't Know	6
60	HMV POP 726	Footsteps/You Don't Know (78)	15
60	Top Rank JAR 416	Say It Isn't True/My Shawl	6
60	HMV POP 763	Why, Why, Why/You're Everything Wonderful	5
60	London HLT 9166	Girls, Girls, Girls/Little Boy Blue	15
60	HMV POP 795	Going Steady/Come Back, Silly Girl	5
61	HMV POP 914	In Time/Oh How You Lied	5
61	HMV POP 950	Somewhere Along The Way/While There's Still Time	5
62	CBS AAG 127	Go Away Little Girl/If You Love Her Tell Her So	5
63	CBS AAG 150	Poor Little Rich Girl/More	5
63	CBS AAG 166	Walking Proud/House Without Windows	5
59	Coral FEP 2010	HERE'S STEVE LAWRENCE NO. 1 (EP)	15
59	Coral FEP 2012	HERE'S STEVE LAWRENCE NO. 2 (EP)	15
60	HMV CLP 1326	SWING SOFTLY WITH ME (LP)	25
60	Top Rank BUY 033	STEVE LAWRENCE (LP)	18
61	HMV CLP 1462	THE STEVE LAWRENCE SOUND (mono)	15
61	HMV CSD 1374	THE STEVE LAWRENCE SOUND (stereo)	18
62	HMV CLP 1504	PORTRAIT OF MY LOVE (mono)	15
62	HMV CSD 1404	PORTRAIT OF MY LOVE (stereo)	18
63	United Artists (S)ULP 1022	LAWRENCE GOES LATIN (LP)	15

STEVE LAWRENCE & EYDIE GORMÉ

(see also Eydie Gorme)

55	Vogue Coral Q 72044	Make Yourself Comfortable/EYDIE GORME: Chain Reaction	8
55	Vogue Coral Q 72085	Besame Mucho/Take A Deep Breath	8
61	London HLT 9290	The Facts Of Life/I'm A Girl, You're A Boy	5
63	CBS AAG 163	I Want To Stay Here/Ain't Love (in p/s)	8
63	CBS AAG 163	I Want To Stay Here/Ain't Love	5
59	Vogue Coral FEP 2017	STEVE LAWRENCE AND EYDIE GORME (EP)	10
60	HMV CLP 1372/CSD 1310	STEVE AND EYDIE - WE GOT US (LP)	15

VALERIE ANN LAWRENCE

65	DECCA F 12273	My Love Loves Me/12A Heartache Square	7

VICKI LAWRENCE

73	Stateside SS 2210	The Night The Lights Went Out In Georgia/Dime A Dance	7

BILLY (M.) LAWRIE

69	Polydor 56363	Roll Over Beethoven/Come Back Joanna (as Billy M. Lawrie)	25
73	RCA RCA 2439	Rock And Roller/Shalee Shala	6
73	RCA SF 8395	SHIP IMAGINATION (LP)	25

JULIET LAWSON

(see also Trees)

72	Sovereign SOV 111	Only A Week Away/Weeds In The Yard	7
72	Sovereign SVNA 7257	BOO (LP, textured gatefold sleeve)	200

SHIRLEY LAWSON

68	Soul City SC 108	The Star/One More Chance	150

LAWSON-HAGGART ROCKIN' BAND

59	Brunswick OE 9451	BOPPING AT THE HOP (EP)	50
53	Brunswick LA 8576	JELLY ROLL'S JAZZ (10" LP)	15
53	Brunswick LA 8580	BLUES ON THE RIVER (10" LP)	18
53	Brunswick LA 8593	KING OLIVER'S JAZZ (10" LP)	15
54	Brunswick LA 8635	RAGTIME JAMBOREE (10" LP)	15
54	Brunswick LA 8639	WINDY CITY JAZZ (10" LP)	15
55	Brunswick LA 8703	SOUTH OF THE MASON-DIXON LINE (10" LP)	15
59	Brunswick STA 3010	BOPPING AT THE HOP (LP)	60

JOHN LAWTON featuring Roger Glover & Guests

(see also Roger Glover, Ronnie Dio, Deep Purple, Uriah Heep, Lucifer's Friend)

75	Purple PUR 128	Little Chalk Blue/RONNIE DIO: Sitting In A Dream	10

LOU LAWTON

67	Ember EMB S 232	Doin' The Philly Dog/I Am Searching	30
68	Speciality SPE 1005	I'm Just A Fool/Wrapped In A Dream	30

LAXTON & OLIVER

69	Blue Cat BS 168	Wickeder/Stay In My Arms	20

OSSIE LAYNE

65	R&B MRB 5006	Come Back/Never Answer That 'Phone	35

EDDIE LAYTON

58	Mercury 7MT 221	Over The Waves/Bright Lights Over Brussels	5
59	Mercury AMT 1064	Duck Walk/Doodles	10

MINT VALUE £

PAUL LAYTON
68 Paradox PAR 45901 — Mister Mister/Sing Sadman Sing (p/s) . . . 25

TEDDY LAYTON JAZZ BAND
58 Parlophone R 4411 — Down By The Riverside/Wooden Joe's Weary Blues . . . 5

KEN LAZ(A)RUS (& CREW)
65 Island WI 220 — Funny (as Ken Lazrus & Byron Lee Orchestra)/ BYRON LEE ORCHESTRA: Walk Like A Dragon . . . 15
70 London HLJ 10301 — Monkey Man/Bongo Nyah . . . 5
71 Explosion EX 2056 — Girl/TOMORROW'S CHILDREN: Sister Big Stuff . . . 8
72 Explosion EX 2064 — Hail The Man/Where Do I Go . . . 7
72 London HLH 10379 — Hail The Man/Where I Go . . . 6
70 London LGJ/ZGJ 102 — REGGAE SCORCHER (LP) . . . 12
70 London ZGJ 107 — REGGAE - GREATEST HITS VOL. 1 (LP) . . . 20

PETER LAZONBY
96 Brainiak BRAINK 40R — Wavespeech (12") . . . 30

LAZY LATINS
67 Morgan MR 110 P — LAZY LATIN (LP) . . . 15

LAZY SMOKE
80s Heyoka — CORRIDOR OF FACES (LP, reissue of U.S. LP) . . . 15

LCD SOUNDSYSTEM
02 Output OPRDFA004 — Give It Up/Tired (promo, p/s 1000 only) . . . 7
05 DFA DFAEMI2138LP — LCD SOUNDSYSTEM (2xLP) . . . 15

BARBARA LEA
56 London HB-U 1058 — A WOMAN IN LOVE (10" LP) . . . 20
56 Esquire 32/043 — NOBODY ELSE BUT ME (LP) . . . 12
57 Esquire 32/063 — IN LOVE (LP) . . . 12

JIMMY LEA
(see also Slade)
85 Trojan KANE 001 — Citizen Kane/Poland (p/s) . . . 15

LEADBELLY (HUDDIE LEDBETTER)
78s
50 Capitol CL 13282 — Eagle Rock Rag/Backwater Blues . . . 12
51 Melodisc 1140 — How Long/Good Morning Blues . . . 20
51 Melodisc 1151 — Goodnight Irene/Ain't You Glad . . . 20
51 Melodisc 1187 — On A Monday/John Henry . . . 20
54 Jazz Collector L 108 — New Black Snake Moan/Fore Day Worry Blues . . . 20
55 Jazz Collector L 124 — Pig Meat Papa/Becky Beem . . . 20
55 HMV MH 190 — Alabama Bound/Pick A Bale Of Cotton . . . 20
EPs
56 Melodisc EPM7 63 — HOW LONG BLUES . . . 20
58 Melodisc EPM7 77 — LEADBELLY . . . 20
58 Melodisc EPM7 82 — SEE SEE RIDER . . . 20
59 Melodisc EPM7 87 — PARTY PLAYS AND SONGS . . . 20
59 RCA RCX 146 — ROCK ISLAND LINE . . . 15
61 Capitol EAP1 1821 — HUDDIE LEDBETTER'S BEST NO. 1 . . . 15
61 Capitol EAP4 1821 — HUDDIE LEDBETTER'S BEST NO. 2 . . . 15
61 Capitol EAP1 20111 — LEADBELLY . . . 15
61 Storyville SEP 337 — LEADBELLY . . . 15
62 Storyville SEP 387 — STORYVILLE BLUES ANTHOLOGY VOL. 7 . . . 15
LPs
53 Capitol LC 6597 — LEADBELLY SINGS CLASSICS IN JAZZ (10") . . . 30
57 Melodisc MLP 511 — LEADBELLY VOL. 1 (10", green & silver labels) . . . 25
57 Melodisc MLP 512 — LEADBELLY VOL. 2 (10", green & silver labels) . . . 25
58 Melodisc MLP 515 — LEADBELLY VOL. 3 (10", green & silver labels) . . . 25
58 Melodisc MLP 517 — PLAYS PARTY SONGS (10", green & silver labels) . . . 25
58 Melodisc MLP 12-107 — THE SAGA OF LEADBELLY (green & silver or blue & black labels) . . . 20
59 Melodisc MLP 12-113 — LEADBELLY'S LAST SESSIONS VOLUME 2 PART 1 . . . 25
59 Melodisc MLP 12-114 — LEADBELLY'S LAST SESSIONS VOLUME 2 PART 2 . . . 20
62 Storyville SLP 124 — A DEMON OF A MAN - BLUES ANTHOLOGY . . . 18
63 Storyville SLP 139 — LEADBELLY 2 - T.B. BLUES . . . 18
63 Capitol T 1821 — HIS GUITAR, HIS VOICE, HIS PIANO: HUDDIE LEDBETTER'S BEST . . . 15
63 RCA Victor RD 7567 — GOOD MORNING BLUES . . . 20
65 Verve (S)VLP 5002 — TAKE THIS HAMMER . . . 20
66 Elektra EKL 301/2 — THE LIBRARY OF CONGRESS RECORDINGS (3-LP) . . . 30
67 Verve (S)VLP 5011 — KEEP YOUR HANDS OFF HER . . . 22
69 Xtra XTRA 1046 — LEADBELLY SINGS FOLK SONGS . . . 20
69 Xtra XTRA 1126 — SHOUT ON . . . 20

LEADBELLY & BLIND LEMON JEFFERSON
(see also Blind Lemon Jefferson)
61 Jazz Collector JEL 124 — THE MALE BLUES VOLUME 8 (EP) . . . 10

HARRY LEADER BAND
65 Parlophone R 5386 — Dragon Fly/Rush Hour . . . 5

LEADERBEATS
60 Top Rank JAR 405 — Dance, Dance, Dance/Washington Square . . . 12

LEADERS (Jamaica)
(see also Pioneers, Stranger Cole, Versatiles)
68 Amalgamated AMG 804 — Tit For Tat (actually by Lynn Taitt & Jets)/MARVETTS: You Take Too Long . . . 25

LEADERS (U.K.)
65 Fontana TF 602 — Night People/Love Will Find A Way . . . 10

MINT VALUE £

LEADING FIGURES
(see also Jon Lord, Deep Purple)

Year	Label	Title	£
67	Deram DML/SML 1006	OSCILLATION 67! (LP)	30
67	Ace Of Clubs SCL 1225	SOUND AND MOVEMENT (LP)	35

LEAF HOUND
(see also Brunning Sunflower Blues Band, Black Cat Bones, Atomic Rooster, Cactus)

Year	Label	Title	£
71	Decca SKL-R 5094	GROWERS OF MUSHROOM (LP)	2500

LEAGUE OF GENTLEMEN

Year	Label	Title	£
65	Columbia DB 7666	Each Little Falling Tear/And I Do Now	70
66	Planet PLF 109	How Can You Tell/How Do They Know (with Planet company sleeve)	70

LEAGUE OF GENTLEMEN
(see also Giles Giles & Fripp, Brain)

Year	Label	Title	£
80	EG/Virgin EGEDS 1	Heptaparaparshinokh/Marriagemuzic	6

LEAH
(see also Pete Dello, Red Herring)

Year	Label	Title	£
73	GM GMS 10	Arise Sir Henry/Uptight Basil	7

JOE LEAHY (ORCHESTRA)

Year	Label	Title	£
55	Parlophone MSP 6149	Desiree/Milano	5
55	Parlophone MSP 6168	Green Fire/Secretly Mine	5
57	London HBZ 1072	LOVELY LADY (10" LP)	12

JOE LEAHY

Year	Label	Title	£
65	Capitol CL 15417	Life/Pink Powder Puff	8

MIKE LEANDER ORCHESTRA

Year	Label	Title	£
69	MCA MUPS 383	MIGRATION (LP)	12

VICKY LEANDROS
(see also Vicky)

Year	Label	Title	£
72	Philips 6000 025	I Am/Love Tell Me Where Is Your Home	8
71	Philips 6303 019	I AM VICKY LEANDROS (LP)	12

BOB LEAPER

Year	Label	Title	£
65	Pye 7N 15700	High Wire (Theme From 'Danger Man')/The Lost World	40
64	Decca LK 4639	BIG BAND, BEATLE SONGS (LP)	20

LEAPERS CREEPERS SLEEPERS

Year	Label	Title	£
66	Island WI 275	Precious Words/Ba Boo	30

KEVIN 'KING' LEAR

Year	Label	Title	£
67	Polydor 56203	Count Me Out/Pretty Woman	40
68	Page One POF 087	Power Of Love/Mr. Pearly	20
68	Page One POF 109	Cry Me A River/Shoe Shine Sam	20
69	Page One POF 132	The Snake/Man In The Funnies	20

TIMOTHY LEARY MEETS THE GRID
(see also the Grid)

Year	Label	Title	£
90	Evolution EVO 1	Origins Of Dance (Electronic Future Mix)/(Hi-Tec Pagan Mix) (12")	10

LEATHERCOATED MINDS
(see also J.J. Cale)

Year	Label	Title	£
67	Fontana (S)TL 5412	A TRIP DOWN THE SUNSET STRIP (LP)	80

LEATHERFACE
(see also Frankie Stubbs)

Year	Label	Title	£
90	Meantime COXEP 3	BEERPIG (EP, with insert)	30
90	Roughneck HYPE 6T	SMOKEY JOE (12" EP)	10
91	Roughneck HYPE 9T	NOT SUPERSTITIOUS (12" EP)	10
92	Roughneck HYPE 17T	COMPACT AND BIJOU (10" EP)	10
89	Meantime COX 017	CHERRY KNOWLE (LP)	18
90	Roughneck NECKLP 1	FILL YOUR BOOTS (LP, with insert)	20
91	Roughneck NECKLP 5	MUSH (LP)	25
93	Roughneck NECKLP 11	MINX (LP)	18

LEATHERHEAD

Year	Label	Title	£
74	Philips 6006 371	Gimme Your Money Please/Epitaph (die-cut 'Leatherhead' sleeve)	15

LEATHER NUN

Year	Label	Title	£
79	Industrial IR 0006	SLOW DEATH (EP)	10
84	Subterranean SUB 40	Prime Mover/F.F.A. (p/s)	5
79	Industrial IRC 27	THE LEATHER NUN AT THE SCALA CINEMA (cassette)	12

LEA VALLEY SKIFFLE GROUP

Year	Label	Title	£
57	Esquire 10-508	Streamline Train/Railroad Bill (78)	10
58	Esquire 10-518	I'm Gonna Walk And Talk With Jesus/Oh Mary, Don't You Weep (78)	10
58	Esquire EP 163	LEA VALLEY SKIFFLE GROUP (EP)	40

LEAVES

Year	Label	Title	£
66	Fontana TF 713	Hey Joe/Funny Little World	40

OTIS LEAVILL(E)

Year	Label	Title	£
70	Atlantic 2091 015	I Love You/I Need You	8
70	Atlantic 2091 035	Love Uprising/Glad I Met You	8
71	Atlantic 2091 160	There's Nothing Better/I'm So Jealous	8

LE CHEILE

Year	Label	Title	£
78	Inchecronin INC 7423	AIRIS (LP)	12
78	Inchecronin INC 7424	LORD MAYO (LP)	12

LECUONDA CUBAN BOYS

Year	Label	Title	£
55	Columbia 33S 1075	BENEATH THE CUBAN MOON (10" LP)	15

MINT VALUE £

JOHN LEDINGHAM

(see also Jonathan Kelly)

68	Pye 7N 17488	Love Is A Toy/Thank You Mrs. Gilbert	6

LED ZEPPELIN

(see also Jimmy Page, Robert Plant, John Paul Jones, Dansette Damage, Listen, Family Dogg, Ian Whitcomb, P.J. Proby, Lord Sutch, Yardbirds)

SINGLES

69	Atlantic 584 268	Good Times, Bad Times (unissued, 1-sided EMIdisc and LDC acetates only)	2000
69	Atlantic 584 269	Communication Breakdown/Good Times, Bad Times (unissued, promo only)	600
69	Atlantic/Emidisc	Whole Lotta Love (Edit)/Whole Lotta Love (Edit) (Acetate)	2000
69	Atlantic 584 309	Whole Lotta Love (Edit)/Livin' Lovin' Maid (She's A Woman) (withdrawn, large centre hole, clean label or "5th Dec 1969" stamp on label)	500
69	Atlantic 584 309	Whole Lotta Love (Edit)/Llvln' Lovin' Maid (She's A Woman) (withdrawn, solid centre with small centre hole, 1 copy known)	1500
69	Atlantic 584 309	Whole Lotta Love (Edit)/Living Loving Maid (She's A Woman) (withdrawn, large centre hole, mispressing with Living Loving Maid labels on both sides)	600
70	Emidisc	Immigrant Song (unissued 1-sided acetate, scheduled to be released as Atlantic 2091 043 on 27th November 1970)	3000
73	Trident	D'Yer Mak'er (Unissued one sided acetate)	1200
73	Atlantic K 10296	D'Yer Mak'er/Over The Hills And Far Away (unreleased, promo only)	350
75	Swan Song DC 1	Trampled Underfoot/Black Country Woman (white label test pressing)	350
75	Swan Song DC 1	Trampled Underfoot/Black Country Woman (Red label test pressing)	500
75	Swan Song DC 1	Trampled Underfoot/Black Country Woman (Limited edition dealer incentive promo, die-cut title sleeve)	25
75	Swan Song SSK 19403	Trampled underfoot/Black Country Woman (withdrawn first pressing)	150
75	Swan Song SSK 19403	Trampled Underfoot/Black Country Woman (push mispressed cat. no.)	150
79	Swan Song SSK 19421	Wearing And Tearing/Darlene (cancelled Knebworth 45, existence unconfirmed)	0
90	Atlantic LZ 3	Stairway To Heaven/Whole Lotta Love (white label test pressing)	350
90	Atlantic LZ 2	Stairway To Heaven/Immigrant Song/Whole Lotta Love/ Good Times Bad Times (10", p/s, promo only)	30
90	Atlantic LZ 2	Stairway To Heaven/Immigrant Song/Whole Lotta Love/ Good Times Bad Times (10", test pressing, white labels)	350
90	Atlantic CD LZ 1	Stairway To Heaven/Immigrant Song/Whole Lotta Love/ Good Times Bad Times (CD, promo only, in Zeppelin-design long box)	30
90	Atlantic LZ 3	Stairway To Heaven/Whole Lotta Love (with East West Records internal memo, 150 copies only, promo)	150
90	Atlantic LZ 3 LC	Stairway To Heaven/Whole Lotta Love (jukebox single, push-out centre)	30
97	Atlantic PRCD 923	BBC SESSIONS SAMPLER: The Girl I Love/Whole Lotta Love/ Communication Breakdown (CD, promo only)	20
97	Atlantic AT 0031CD	Whole Lotta Love (Edit)/Baby Come On Home/Travelling Riverside Blues (CD, numbered digipak)	10
97	Atlantic AT 0031LC	Whole Lotta Love (Edit)/Whole Lotta Love (Edit) (jukebox issue, with pushout centre)	15
03	Warner Vision PR 03945	What Is And What Should Never Be/In My Time Of Dying/Rock And Roll (DVD, promo sampler)	25

LPs

69	Atlantic 588 171	LED ZEPPELIN (LP, 1st pressing, red/maroon label, turquoise sleeve lettering, "Superhype" publishing credit)	1000
69	Atlantic 588 171	LED ZEPPELIN (LP, 2nd pressing, red/maroon label, orange sleeve lettering, "Warner Bros" publishing credit)	80
69	Atlantic 588 171	LED ZEPPELIN (LP, 2nd pressing, red/maroon label, orange sleeve lettering, "Superhype" publishing credit)	60
69	Atlantic 588 198	LED ZEPPELIN II (LP, 1st pressing, red/maroon label, with "Living Loving Wreck" miscredit, light brown gatefold sleeve with blue-green edge)	250
69	Atlantic 588 198	LED ZEPPELIN II (LP, 1st pressing, red/maroon label, with "The Lemon Song" credit, light brown gatefold sleeve with blue-green edge)	60
70	Atlantic 588 198	LED ZEPPELIN II (LP, light brown sleeve, 2nd pressing, credits "Killing Floor" instead of "The Lemon Song" on label)	40
70	Atlantic Deluxe 2401 002	LED ZEPPELIN III (LP, first pressing, red/maroon label, gatefold rotating wheel sleeve, "Do What Thou Wilt" in run off side 1. "Produced by Jimmy Page" and "Executive Producer Peter Grant" on top of label. Catalogue number 2401002 without a break on the label)	120
70	Atlantic Deluxe 2401 002	LED ZEPPELIN III (LP, second pressing, red/maroon label, gatefold rotating-wheel sleeve, second pressing, no "Peter Grant" credit and catalogue number separated 2401 002 on label)	40
71	Atlantic Deluxe 2401 012	LED ZEPPELIN IV (FOUR SYMBOLS) (LP, gatefold sleeve, red/maroon label with Peter Grant credit, 'Led Zeppelin' at bottom)	200
71	Atlantic Deluxe 2401 012	LED ZEPPELIN IV (FOUR SYMBOLS) (LP, gatefold sleeve, red/maroon label without Peter Grant credit, 'Led Zeppelin' at top)	70
73	Atlantic K 50014	HOUSES OF THE HOLY (LP; original pressings have an 'obi' around the sleeve)	12
75	Swan Song SSK 89400	PHYSICAL GRAFFITI (2-LP, die-cut sleeve, inner sleeve, folded insert)	35
76	Swan Song SSK 59402	PRESENCE (LP, shrinkwrapped gatefold sleeve)	12
78	Atlantic K 50008	LED ZEPPELIN IV (FOUR SYMBOLS) (LP, purple vinyl testpressing or mispressing of lilac vinyl reissue)	250
76	Swan Song SSK 89402	THE SONG REMAINS THE SAME (2-LP, textured gatefold sleeve with booklet)	30
78	Atlantic K 50008	LED ZEPPELIN IV (FOUR SYMBOLS) (LP, lilac vinyl reissue)	50
79	Swan Song SSK 59410 A-F	IN THROUGH THE OUT DOOR (LP, 6 different covers with inner sleeves; set labelled 'A' to 'F', each in individual paper outer; available separately with paper outer £25 each)	300
88	Atlantic K 50008/C 88 1-4	FOUR SYMBOLS (LP, HMV 'Classic Collection' box set, with booklet, numbered)	25
88	Atlantic 250008/C 88 1-4	FOUR SYMBOLS (CD, HMV 'Classic Collection' box set, with booklet, numbered)	30
90	Atlantic ZEP 1	REMASTERS (3-LP, triple gatefold sleeve)	18
90	Atlantic 7567 82144-1	LED ZEPPELIN (5-LP, box set)	50
97	Atlantic 7567 83061-1	BBC SESSIONS (4-LP, box set)	70

			MINT VALUE £
99	Atlantic 7567 83268-1	EARLY DAYS - THE BEST OF LED ZEPPELIN VOLUME 1 (LP)	15
00	Atlantic 7567 83278-1	LATTER DAYS - THE BEST OF LED ZEPPELIN VOLUME 2 (LP)	15
08	Rhino/Atlantic/ Swan Song 8122799489	SOUNDTRACK FROM 'THE SONG REMAINS THE SAME' (4-LP. 180gm expanded edition)	50
08	Rhino/Atlantic/ Swan Song 8122799489	SOUNDTRACK FROM 'THE SONG REMAINS THE SAME' (4-LP 180 gm expanded edition, white vinyl, 200 only)	600
08	Rhino/Atlantic/ Swan Song 8122799513	MOTHERSHIP (4-LP, 180gm vinyl)	50

ALVIN LEE

(see also Ten Years After)

74	Chrysalis CHS 2020	The World Is Changing/Riffin' (with Myron Le Fevre)	6
73	Chrysalis CHR 1054	ON THE ROAD TO FREEDOM (LP, with Myron Le Fevre)	20
75	Chrysalis CHR 1094	PUMP IRON! (LP)	12
78	Chrysalis CHR 1190	LET IT ROCK (LP)	12

ARTHUR LEE

(see also Love)

72	A&M AMLS 64356	VINDICATOR (LP)	20

BENNY LEE (& KEN-TONES)

(see also Ken-Tones)

56	Parlophone MSP 6214	Love Plays The Strings Of My Banjo (with Ken-Tones)/Born To Sing The Blues	6
56	Parlophone MSP 6252	Sweet Heartaches/How Long Has This Been Going On?	6
56	Parlophone R 4245	Rock 'N' Rollin' Santa Claus/Life Was Made For Livin' (with Ken-Tones)	25

BRENDA LEE

78s

56	Brunswick 05628	I'm Gonna Lasso Santa Claus/Christy Christmas (as Little Brenda Lee)	40
57	Brunswick 05685	Dynamite/Love You Til I Die	40
57	Brunswick 05720	Ain't That Love/One Teenager To Another	50
58	Brunswick 05755	Ring-A-My-Phone/Little Jonah (Rock On Your Little Steel Guitar)	50
59	Brunswick 05780	Bill Bailey, Won't You Please Come Home/Hummin' The Blues Over You	40
60	Brunswick 05819	Sweet Nuthin's/Weep No More My Baby	70

SINGLES

56	Brunswick 05628	I'm Gonna Lasso Santa Claus/Christy Christmas (triangular centre)	200
57	Brunswick 05685	Dynamite/Love You Til I Die (with Anita Kerr Singers, triangular centre)	150
57	Brunswick 05720	Ain't That Love/One Teenager To Another (with Anita Kerr Singers, tri-centre)	150
58	Brunswick 05755	Ring-A-My-Phone/Little Jonah (Rock On Your Little Steel Guitar) (tri-centre)	150
58	Decca BM 31186	Fairyland/One Step At A Time (export issue, triangular centre)	50
59	Brunswick 05780	Bill Bailey, Won't You Please Come Home/Hummin' The Blues Over You (triangular centre)	20
59	Brunswick 05780	Bill Bailey, Won't You Please Come Home/Hummin' The Blues Over You (round centre)	10
60	Brunswick 05819	Sweet Nuthin's/Weep No More My Baby (round centre)	15
60	Brunswick 05823	Let's Jump The Broomstick/Rock-A-Bye Baby Blues	10
60	Brunswick 05833	I'm Sorry/That's All You Gotta Do	5
60	Brunswick 05839	I Want To Be Wanted/Just A Little	5
61	Brunswick 05847	Emotions/I'm Learning About Love	8
61	Brunswick 05854	Dum Dum/Eventually	6
62	Brunswick 05864	Break It To Me Gently/So Deep	8
62	Brunswick 05867	Speak To Me Pretty/Lover, Come Back To Me	6
62	Brunswick 05871	Here Comes That Feeling/Everybody Loves Me But You	6
62	Brunswick 05876	It Started All Over Again/Heart In Hand	5
62	Brunswick 05880	Rockin' Around The Christmas Tree/Papa Noel	5
63	Brunswick 05886	Losing You/He's So Heavenly	6
63	Brunswick 05896	Sweet Impossible You/The Grass Is Greener	5
64	Brunswick 05903	Think/The Waiting Game	5
64	Brunswick 05915	Is It True/What'd I Say	10
66	Brunswick 05957	Too Little Time/Time And Time Again	35
66	Brunswick 05963	Ain't Gonna Cry No More/It Takes One To Know One	10
66	Brunswick 05967	Coming On Strong/You Keep Coming Back To Me	15
67	Brunswick 05970	Ride, Ride, Ride/Lonely People Do Foolish Things	5
67	Brunswick 05976	Where's The Melody?/Born To Be By Your Side	20
68	Decca AD 1003	That's All Right/Baby, Won't You Please Come Home (export issue)	5

EPs

59	Brunswick OE 9462	ROCK THE BOP (green p/s & tri-centre)	90
59	Brunswick OE 9462	ROCK THE BOP (blue p/s & round centre)	50
62	Brunswick OE 9482	PRETEND	30
62	Brunswick OE 9488	SPEAK TO ME PRETTY	30
63	Brunswick OE 9492	ALL ALONE AM I	15
64	Brunswick OE 9499	BRENDA LEE'S TRIBUTE TO AL JOLSON	15
65	Brunswick OE 9510	FOUR FROM '64	20

LPs

59	Brunswick LAT 8319	GRANDMA WHAT GREAT SONGS YOU SANG	50
60	Brunswick LAT 8347	MISS DYNAMITE	40
61	Brunswick LAT 8360	THIS IS BRENDA	40
61	Brunswick STA 3044	EMOTIONS (stereo)	15
61	Brunswick STA 3048	ALL THE WAY (stereo)	15
61	Brunswick STA 3056	SINCERELY (stereo)	15
62	Brunswick LAT/STA 8516	BRENDA, THAT'S ALL (mono/stereo)	18
65	Brunswick LAT/STA 8603	TOP TEEN HITS (mono/stereo)	15

BUNNY LEE ALLSTARS

(see also Lloyd Charmers, Sonny Binns & Rudies, Copy Cats, John Holt, Lloyd & Doreen, Delroy Wilson)

70	Camel CA39	Three Stooge/Isle Of Love	20

MINT VALUE £

70	Pama PM 803	Annie Pama/Mr Magoo	12
71	Smash SMA 2304	Stanley (Parts 1 & 2) (as Bunnie Lee Allstars)	10
78	Jamaica Sound JS 013	SUPER DUB DISCO STYLE (LP, with the Aggrovators)	50

BYRON LEE & DRAGONAIR(E)S

(see also Mighty Avengers, Ken Lazarus, Hopeton Lewis, Danny Davis Orchestra, Good Guys, Neville Hinds, Hubcaps & Wheels, Mighty Sparrow, Blues Busters)

60	Blue Beat B 2	Dumplin's/Kissin' Gal (vocal: Buddy Davidson) (white label, blue print)	20
60	Blue Beat BB 2	Dumplin's/Kissin' Gal (vocal: Buddy Davidson) (2nd pressing, blue label, silver print)	15
61	Blue Beat BB 28	Mash! Mr. Lee/Help Me Forget (vocal: Keith Lyn)	15
61	Starlite ST45 045	Joy Ride/Over The Rainbow	12
64	Parlophone R 5124	River Bank/Musical Communion	15
64	Parlophone R 5125	Sour Apples/Hanging Up My Heart	15
64	Parlophone R 5140	Sammy Dead/Say Bye Bye (both actually by Eric Morris with Byron Lee)	15
64	Parlophone R 5177	Beautiful Garden/Too Late	15
64	Parlophone R 5182	Come Back/Jamaica Ska	18
64	MGM MGM 1256	Night Train From Jamaica/Ska Dee Wah (with Danny Davis)	18
66	Doctor Bird DB 1003	Sloopy/Gold Finger	20
67	Pyramid PYR 6015	Sloopy/Gold Finger (reissue)	10
68	Trojan TR 624	Soul Limbo/The Whistling Song	8
68	Trojan TR 631	Mr Walker/Sunset Jump Up	8
69	Major Minor MM 615	Every Day Will Be Like A Holiday/Oh What A Feeling	7
70	Trojan TR 7731	Squeeze Up (Parts 1 & 2)	12
70	Trojan TR 7736	Birth Control/Love At First Sight	6
70	Trojan TR 7747	Bond In Bliss/Musical Scorcher	6
70	Trojan TR 7761	Julianne/We Five	5
70	Duke DU 39	Elizabethan Reggae/Soul Serenade	10
70	Duke DU 91	Cashbox/WINSTON WRIGHT: Strolling Thru' The Park	6
71	Dynamic DYN 405	Hitching A Ride/Hitching A Ride Version	8
71	Dynamic DYN 409	My Sweet Lord/Shock Attack	7
71	Dynamic DYN 414	Way Back Home/Version	6
72	Dynamic DYN 435	Make It Reggae/DENNIS ALCAPONE: Go Johnny Go	8
73	Dragon DRA 1008	In The Mood/Black On	6
65	Atlantic AET 6014	SKA TIME (EP, as Byron Lee Ska Kings)	40
64	Island ILP 905	CARIBBEAN JOY RIDE (LP)	40
66	Atlantic 587018	JUMP UP (LP)	40
69	Trojan TTL 5	ROCKSTEADY EXPLOSION (LP)	40
69	Major Minor Sm 53	BYRON LEE & THE DRAGONAIRES (LP)	20
70	Trojan TRLS 18	REGGAE WITH BYRON LEE (LP)	18

CHRISTOPHER LEE

74	Studio Two TWOA 500	HAMMER PRESENTS DRACULA (LP, gatefold sleeve)	20
74	Studio Two TWOA Q4 500	HAMMER PRESENTS DRACULA (LP, gatefold sleeve, quadrophonic)	20

C.P. LEE

(see also Alberto Y Lost Trios Paranoias)

80	New Hormones	RADIO SWEAT (cassette, with booklet & stickers in plastic 'radio' bag)	12

CURTIS LEE

60	Top Rank JAR 317	With All My Heart (I Love You)/Pure Love	60
61	London HLX 9313	Pledge Of Love/Then I'll Know	25
61	London HLX 9397	Pretty Little Angel Eyes/Gee How I Wish You Were Here	20
61	London HLX 9445	Under The Moon Of Love/Beverly Jean	25
62	London HLX 9533	A Night At Daddy Gee's/Just Another Fool	22
67	CBS 2717	Get My Bag/Everybody's Going Wild (as Curtis Lee & K.C.P.s)	40
67	CBS 2717	Get My Bag/Everybody's Going Wild (as Curtis Lee & K.C.P.s) (DJ copy)	70
72	Stateside SS 2208	Under The Moon Of Love/Beverly Jean (reissue)	6

DAVE LEE (& STAGGERLEES)

63	Decca F 11600	Take Four/Five To Four On	15
63	Oriole CB 1864	Dance Dance Dance/Love Me (as Dave Lee & Staggerlees)	15
63	Oriole CB 1907	Sweet & Lovely/Forever And Always (as Dave Lee & Staggerlees)	15
66	Fontana TF 723	Adam Adamant/Georgie's Theme (as Dave Lee & His Orchestra)	20

DAVE LEE

(see also Tubby Hayes)

66	Colpix PXL 550	OUR MAN CRICHTON (LP, with Tubby Hayes)	80

DAVID H. LEE

65	Pye 7N 15809	Heaven With No Angel	8
69	Morgan MR 1	Johnny's Eyes/You're The Only One	7

DEBBIE LEE

64	Decca F 11931	For Every Man There's A Woman/Can't You See	8

DEREK LEE

66	Parlophone R 5468	Girl/You've Done Something To My Heart	10

DICK LEE

53	Columbia SCM 5066	All I Want Is A Chance/The Show Is Ended	10
53	Columbia SCM 5078	I Thought You Might Be Lonely/Happy Bells	10
54	Columbia SCM 5094	Book/Stay In My Arms Cinderella	10

DICKIE/DICKEY LEE

59	MGM MGM 1013	A Penny A Kiss - A Penny A Hug/Bermuda (as Dick Lee)	7
62	Mercury AMT 1190	Patches/More Or Less	15
62	Mercury AMT 1196	I Saw Linda Yesterday/The Girl I Can't Forget	15
62	Mercury AMT 1200	Don't Wanna Think About Paula/Just A Friend	10
65	Stateside SS 433	Laurie (Strange Things Happen)/Party Doll (as Dickey Lee)	10
65	Stateside SS 464	The Girl From Peyton Place/A Girl I Used To Know (as Dickey Lee)	7

MINT VALUE £

DINAH LEE

65	Aladdin WI 606	I'll Forgive You Then Forget You/Nitty Gritty	30
65	Aladdin WI 608	I Can't Believe What You Say/Pushin' A Good Thing Too Far	40

DON (TONY) LEE

68	Big Shot BI 504	It's Reggae Time (as Don Tony Lee)/ERROL DUNKLEY: The Clamp Is On	30
68	Doctor Bird DB 1106	Lee's Special (as Don Tony Lee)/LLOYD & GROOVERS: My Heart And Soul	30
68	Island WI 3160	It's Reggae Time (as D. Tony Lee)/ERROL DUNKLEY: The Clamp Is On	30
69	Unity UN 519	Peyton Place/Red Gal In The Ring (as Don Tony Lee)	12
70	Gas 163	Work Out/Too Long (as Donald Lee)	25

EDNA LEE

68	President PT 175	I Really Think I'm Crying 'Cause I Love You/ Don't Let My Friends See What You Do	7

(Freddie) 'FINGERS' LEE (& UPPER HAND)

(see also At Last The 1958 Rock & Roll Show)

65	Fontana TF 619	The Friendly Undertaker/Little Bit More (as 'Fingers' Lee)	25
66	Fontana TF 655	I'm Gonna Buy Me A Dog/I Can't Drive (as 'Fingers' Lee)	25
66	Columbia DB 8002	Bossy Boss/Don't Run Away (as Fingers Lee & Upper Hand)	25

GEORGE LEE (& MUSIC DOCTORS)

(see also Desmond Riley)

69	Downtown DT 443	Talking Boss/Jungle Fever (solo)	8
70	J-Dan JDN 4407	Johnny Dollar/Tough Of Poison (with Music Doctors)	8

HUBERT LEE

73	Ackee ACK 504	I Love Verona/Version	5
73	Downtown DT 498	Something On Your Mind/IMPACT ALL STARS: Mind Version	8
73	Green Door GD 4050	High School Dance/PRINCE TONY'S ALL STARS: Version	5
74	Ackee ACK 524	Tonight Will You Still Love Me/IMPACT ALL STARS: Version	6

JACKIE LEE (U.K.) (Female)

(see also Jacky, Jackie Lee & Raindrops, Emma Rede)

55	Decca F 10550	I Was Wrong/For As Long As I Live	12
65	Decca F 12068	I Cry Alone/Cause I Love Him	12
65	Columbia DB 7685	Lonely Clown/Love Is Gone	12
66	Columbia DB 7860	I Know, Know, Know I'll Never Love/So Love Me	10
66	Columbia DB 8052	The Town I Live In/You Too	12
67	Decca F 12663	Born To Lose/Saying Goodbye	10
69	Pye 7N 17829	Love Is a Gamble/Something Borrowed, Something Blue	10
70	Pye 7N 45003	Rupert/Going To The Circus	6

JACKIE LEE & RAINDROPS (U.K.) (Female)

(see also Jacky, Jackie Lee [U.K.], Raindrops [U.K], Emma Rede)

62	Oriole CB 1702	I Was The Last One To Know/There's No One In The Whole World	10
62	Oriole CB 1727	There Goes The Lucky One/I Built My Whole World Around You	12
62	Oriole CB 1757	Party Lights/Midnight	15
63	Oriole CB 1800	The End Of The World/Goodbye Is Such A Lonely Word	10
63	Philips BF 1283	Down Our Street/My Heart Is Your Heart (as Jackie & Raindrops)	12
64	Philips BF 1328	Here I Go Again/Come On Dream Come On (as Jackie & Raindrops)	10

JACKIE LEE (U.S.) (Male)

60	Top Rank JAR 286	Rancho/Like Sunset	10

JACKIE LEE (U.S.) (Male)

(see also Bob & Earl, Earl Nelson, Jackie Lee & Delores Hall)

65	Fontana TF 646	The Duck/Let Your Conscience Be Your Guide	40
66	Jay Boy BOY 28	Would You Believe/You're Everything	10
68	London HLM 10233	The Duck/Dancing In The Street	15
70	Jay Boy BOY 26	Do The Temptation Walk/The Shotgun And The Duck	10
72	Jay Boy BOY 66	Oh! My Darlin'/Don't Be Ashamed	15
72	Jay Boy BOY 66	Oh! My Darlin'/Don't Be Ashamed (DJ copy)	30
72	Jay Boy BOY 76	African Boo-Ga-Loo/Bring It Home	8
73	Contempo CR 5	The Duck (Parts 1 & 2)	5
85	Kent TOWN 107	Darkest Days/EDDIE BISHOP: Call Me	25
67	London HA-M 8336	THE DUCK (LP)	50
71	Joy JOYS 192	THE DUCK (LP, reissue)	20

JACKIE LEE & DELORES HALL

(see also Jackie Lee [U.S.], Delores Hall)

69	B&C CB 105	Whether It's Right Or Wrong/Baby I'm Satisfied	10
72	Jay Boy BOY 52	Whether It's Right Or Wrong/Baby I'm Satisfied (reissue)	6

JAMIE LEE & ATLANTICS

63	Decca F 11571	In The Night/Little Girl In Blue	45

JIMMY LEE

61	Starlite ST45 059	All My Life/Chicago Jump	40

JOHN LEE'S GROUNDHOGS

(see under 'J')

JOHN LEE

72	Explosion EX 2060	Stagger Lee/Musical Version (both sides actually by John Holt)	5

JOHNNIE LEE

59	Pye 7N 15201	Echo/It's-A Me, It's-A Me, It's-A Me My Love	8
59	Pye 7N 15233	I'm Finally Free/I Fell (with The King's Men)	8
60	Fontana H 257	They're Wrong/Cindy Lou	8
60	Fontana H 280	Poetry In Motion/Let It Come True	10
61	Fontana H 306	Lonely Joe/Nobody	8
67	CBS 202591	Kiss Tomorrow Goodbye/Love No Longer Sounds	5
67	CBS 2802	I Forgot What It Was Like/Lonely Is The Willow	5
67	CBS 3112	Because You're Mine/I'll Not Forget	5

MINT VALUE £

JULIA LEE (& HER BOYFRIENDS)

50	Capitol CL 13321	Nobody Knows You When You're Down And Out/Decent Woman Blues (78)	10
50	Capitol CL 13323	Cold Hearted Daddy/Snatch And Grab It (78)	10
51	Capitol LC 6535	PARTY TIME (10" LP, 2 different sleeves)	50

LAURA LEE (U.K.)

60	Triumph RGM 1030	Tell Tommy I Miss Him/I'm Sending Back Your Roses	50
62	Decca F 11513	Too Young To Be In Love/Brand New Heartbeat	15
68	Columbia DB 8495	Love In Every Room/Master Jack	12
71	Columbia DB 8770	Someone To Love Me/Look Left-Look Right	8

LAURA LEE (U.S.)

67	Chess CRS 8062	Dirty Man/It's Mighty Hard	10
68	Chess CRS 8070	As Long As I Got You/A Man With Some Backbone	10
72	Tamla Motown TMG 831	To Win Your Heart/So Will I	15
72	Tamla Motown TMG 831	To Win Your Heart/So Will I (DJ copy)	30
72	Hot Wax HWX 115	Rip Off/Two Lovely Pillows	8
73	Hot Wax HWX 118	Wedlock Is A Padlock/Since I Fell For You	7
73	Hot Wax HWX 119	You've Got The Love To Save Me/Crumbs Off The Table	15
74	Invictus INV 2654	I Need It Just As Bad As You/If I'm Good Enough To Love	7
71	Hot Wax SHW 5006	WOMEN'S LOVE RIGHTS (LP)	20
73	Hot Wax SHW 5009	TWO SIDES OF LAURA LEE (LP)	20

LEAPY LEE

65	Pye 7N 17001	It's All Happening/In The Meantime	5
66	Decca F 12369	King Of The Whole Wide World/Shake Hands (featuring the Kinks)	65
67	CBS 202550	The Man On The Flying Trapeze/My Mixed-Up Mind	5
68	Pye 7N 17619	It's All Happening/It's Great	5
68	MCA MU 1028	Little Arrows/Time Will Tell	5
69	MCA MK 5021	Good Morning/Teresa	5

LITTLE MR. LEE & CHEROKEES

66	Vocalion VP 9268	Young Lover/I Don't Want To Go	40

MANDY LEE

69	Dandelion S 4494	Bottle Up And Go (Parts 1 & 2)	6

MICHELLE LEE

68	CBS 3350	L. David Sloan/Everybody Loves My Baby	6

MICKEY LEE

73	Smash SMA 2332	Hello My Little Queen/AUGUSTUS PABLO: African Queen	10

NICKIE LEE

69	Deep Soul DS 9103	And Black Is Beautiful/Faith Within	25

NORMA LEE

67	CBM CBM 002	Hurt/Rollin' On	6

PEGGY LEE

(see also Bing Crosby, George Shearing)

SINGLES

54	Brunswick 05286	Johnny Guitar/I Didn't Know What Time It Was	15
54	Brunswick 05345	Love, You Didn't Do Right By Me/Sisters	15
55	Brunswick 05360	Let Me Go, Lover/Bouquet Of Blues	15
55	Brunswick 05368	Straight Ahead/It Must Be So (with Mills Brothers)	10
55	Brunswick 05421	Baubles, Bangles And Beads/Summer Vacation	10
55	Brunswick 05435	I Belong To You/How Bitter, My Sweet	10
55	Brunswick 05461	Ooh That Kiss/Oh! No! (Please Don't Go)	10
55	Brunswick 05471	Sugar/What Can I Say After I Say I'm Sorry	10
55	Brunswick 05472	He Needs Me/Sing A Rainbow	12
55	Brunswick 05482	He's A Tramp (with Pound Hounds)/The Siamese Cat Song (with Oliver Wallace)	15
55	Brunswick 05483	Bella Notte/La La Lu	10

(The above 45s were originally issued with gold label lettering; silver reissues are worth half to two-thirds these values.)

56	Brunswick 05549	Three Cheers For Mister Magoo/Mister Magoo Does The Cha Cha Cha (with Jim Backus)	7
56	Brunswick 05554	The Come Back/You've Got To See Mama Every Night	7
56	Brunswick 05593	That's All Right Honey/Love You So	7
56	Brunswick 05625	We Laughed At Love/They Can't Take That Away From Me	7
57	Brunswick 05671	Mr. Wonderful/The Gypsy With Fire In His Shoes	8
57	Brunswick 05714	I Don't Know Enough About You/Where Flamingo's Fly	8
57	Capitol CL 14741	Baby, Baby Wait For Me/Every Night	6
65	Capitol CL 15394	Bewitched/Sneakin' Up On You	7
69	Capitol CL 15614	Is That All There Is?/I'm A Woman (2nd pressing with different A-side)	10

EPs

55	Brunswick OE 9153	PETE KELLY'S BLUES NO. 1	10
55	Brunswick OE 9154	PETE KELLY'S BLUES NO. 2	0
56	Brunswick OE 9282	PRESENTING PEGGY LEE	10

ALBUMS

53	Capitol LC 6584	CAPITOL PRESENTS PEGGY LEE (10")	20
53	Brunswick LA 8629	BLACK COFFEE (10")	20
55	Brunswick LA 8717	SONGS IN AN INTIMATE STYLE (10")	20
55	Brunswick LAT 8078	PETE KELLY'S BLUES (with Ella Fitzgerald)	20
56	Brunswick LA 8731	SONGS FROM 'LADY AND THE TRAMP' (10")	20
56	Capitol LC 6817	MY BEST TO YOU (10")	15

ROBERTA LEE

(see also Red Foley, Hardrock Gunter)

53	Brunswick 05076	Sixty Minute Man (with Hardrock Gunter)/RED FOLEY: Hot Toddy (78)	15
54	HMV 7M 261	True Love And Tender Care/When The Organ Played At Twilight	10
55	Brunswick 05388	Ridin' To Tennessee/I'll Be There If Ever You Want Me	10

MINT VALUE £

ROBIN LEE
62 Reprise R 20068 Gamblin' Man/An Angel With A Broken Wing 18

ROY LEE
61 Decca F 11406 Two Initials/Honey Lies 6

TONY LEE
68 Doctor Bird DB 1106 Lee's Special/LLOYD & GROOVERS: My Heart My Soul 40

TONY LEE TRIO
71 Contour 2870142 ELECTRIC PIANO (LP) 15
76 Lambert 3416 TONY LEE TRIO (LP) 15
79 Lambert LAM105 STREET OF DREAMS (LP) 15

VINNY LEE & RIDERS
61 HMV POP 856 Mule Train/Gambler's Guitar 15

WARREN LEE
69 Pama PM 762 Underdog Backstreet/Come Put My Life In Order 15

WILMA LEE & STONEY COOPER
64 Hickory 45-1257 Big John's Wife/Pirate King 7

LEE & CLARENDONIANS
72 Green Door GD 4038 Night Owl/Night Owl Version 10

LEE (Perry) & JIMMY (Riley)
75 Dip DL 5075 Rasta Train/Yagga Yagga 18

LEE (Perry) & JUNIOR (Byles)
75 Dip DL 5060 Dreader Locks/Militant Rock 12

LEE & PAUL
59 Philips PB 912 The Chick/Valentina, My Valentina 7

BRAD LEEDS
60 Pye International 7N 25050 A Teenage Love Is Born/I'm Walking Behind You 6

PHIL LEEDS
66 London HLR 10044 Would You Believe It?/FRANK GALLOP: The Ballad Of Irving 8

LEEDS UNITED FOOTBALL CLUB
72 Chapter 1 SCH 168 Leeds United/Leeds, Leeds, Leeds 5

MARK LEEMAN FIVE
(see also Cheynes)
65 Columbia DB 7452 Portland Town/Gotta Get Myself Together 20
65 Columbia DB 7648 Blow My Blues Away/On The Horizon 25
66 Columbia DB 7812 Forbidden Fruit/Goin' To Bluesville 25
66 Columbia DB 7955 Follow Me/Gather Up The Pieces 20

THOMAS LEER
(see also Act, Robert Rental)
78 Oblique ER 101 Private Plane/International (folded photocopied p/s, hand-stamped labels) 15
78 Company/Oblique OBCO 1 Private Plane/International (reissue, printed p/s) 8
82 Cherry Red CHERRY 52 All About You/Saving Grace (p/s) 5
82 Cherry Red 12CHERRY 52 All About You/Saving Grace (12", p/s) 8
82 Cherry Red ERED 26 CONTRADICTIONS EP (12", double pack) 8
79 Industrial IR 0007 THE BRIDGE (LP, with Robert Rental) 30

JOHN LEES
(see also Barclay James Harvest)
74 Polydor 2058 513 Best Of My Love/You Can't Get It 15
77 Harvest HAR 5132 Child Of The Universe/Kes (A Major Fancy) 5
73 Harvest SHVL 811 A MAJOR FANCY (LP) 12

RAYMOND LEFEVRE & HIS ORCHESTRA
68 Major Minor MM 559 Soul Coaxing (Ame Caline)/When A Man Loves A Woman 8

JACK LE FORGE
65 Stateside SS 444 Our Crazy Affair/Bossa Bossa Nova (withdrawn) 25

LEFT BANKE
66 Philips BF 1517 Walk Away Renee/I Haven't Got The Nerve 15
67 Philips BF 1540 Pretty Ballerina/Lazy Day 15
67 Philips BF 1575 Ivy Ivy/And Suddenly 10
67 Philips BF 1614 Desiree/I've Got Something On My Mind 7
87 Bam Caruso OPRA 023 Walk Away Renee/Ivy Ivy (DJ/jukebox issue) 6
67 Philips (S)BL 7773 WALK AWAY RENEE/PRETTY BALLERINA (LP) 70

LEFTFIELD
(see also A Man Called Adam, Curve)
90 Outer Rhythm FOOT 9R More Than I Know (10K Remix)/(More Mix)/(Even More Mix) (12") 18
91 Outer Rhythm FOOT 009 More Than I Know (12" Mix)/Not Forgotten (Hard Hands Mix) (12") 20
92 Hard Hands HAND 001T Release The Pressure/Release The Pressure (Instrumental)/ Release The Pressure (with Earl Sixteen) (12") 12
92 Hard Hands HAND 001R Release The Dubs (Dub 1)/(Dub 2)/(Dub 3)/(Dub 4) (12") 15
99 Hard Hands HANDLP4T RHYTHM AND STEALTH (5 x 10" box set, limited edition) 40

LEFT HAND DRIVE
79 Bankrupt BAN 012 Who Said Rock & Roll Is Dead/I Know Where I Am (p/s) 5

LEFT-HANDED MARRIAGE
(see also Queen)
67 private pressing ON THE RIGHT SIDE OF THE LEFT-HANDED MARRIAGE (LP) 500
96 Tenth Planet TP 022 ON THE RIGHT SIDE OF THE LEFT-HANDED MARRIAGE (LP, reissue, gatefold sleeve) 15

MINT VALUE £

LEFT SIDE

69	Columbia DB 8575	Welcome To My House/This Little Village	6

LANCE LE GAULT

68	United Artists UP 2255	Billie/Louisiana Swamp Fox	5

LEGAY

(see also Gypsy)

69	Fontana TF 904	No-One/The Fantastic Story Of The Steam Driven Banana	160

LEGEND

(see also Procol Harum, Fingers, Mickey Jupp)

69	Bell BLL 1048	National Gas/Wouldn't You	18
69	Bell BLL 1082	Georgia George Part 1/July	15
70	Vertigo 6059 021	Life/Late Last Night	15
71	Vertigo 6059 036	Don't You Know/Someday	15
69	Bell MBLL/SBLL 115	LEGEND (LP, blue/silver labels with "Sold in U.K..." text)	120
71	Vertigo 6360 019	LEGEND ('RED BOOT') (LP, gatefold sleeve, large swirl label)	150
72	Vertigo 6360 063	MOONSHINE (LP, gatefold sleeve, small swirl label)	200

LEGEND

81	Legend LEG 1	Hideaway/Heaven Sent (p/s)	70

LEGEND

82	Workshop WR 3478	FRONTLINE EP (Frontline/Sabre & Chatila/ Stormers Of Heaven/Open The Skies (12")	25
81	Workshop WR 2007	LEGEND (LP)	90
82	Workshop WR 3477	DEATH IN THE NURSERY (LP, with insert)	20

LEGEND!

83	Creation CRE 001/ Lyntone LYN 12903	'73 In '83/You (Chunka Chunka) Were Glamorous (foldaround p/s in poly bag, with 33rpm flexidisc "I Wonder Why! (live)" by The Pastels/"Wouldn't You? By Laughing Apple)	15
84	Creation CRE 010	The Legend Destroys The Blues/Arrogant Bastards (foldaround p/s in poly bag)	6

TOBI LEGEND

78	RK RK 1004	Time Will Pass You By/DEAN PARRISH: I'm On My Way/ JIMMY RADCLIFFE: Long After Tonight Is All Over (with p/s)	10
78	RK RK 1004	Time Will Pass You By/DEAN PARRISH: I'm On My Way/ JIMMY RADCLIFFE: Long After Tonight Is All Over	6

LEGENDARY LONNIE

81	Nervous NER 002	Constipation Shake/Devil's Guitar (p/s)	6

LEGENDARY MASKED SURFERS

(see also Beach Boys, Jan & Dean)

73	United Artists UP 35542	Gonna Hustle You/Summertime, Summertime	18

LEGENDARY PINK DOTS

81	Mirrordot MD 01	ONLY DREAMING (cassette, around 10 copies, all different hand-made covers)	100
81	Mirrordot MD02/03	CHEMICAL PLAYSCHOOL 1/2 (double cassette, 24 copies all different handmade covers)	120
81	Cassetteking CK04	DOTS ON THE EYE (cassette)	45
82	Mirrordot MD 02-03	CHEMICAL PLAYSCHOOL 3 / 4 (double cassette, 120 copies, different covers)	75
82	Mirrordot MD 03/II	CHEMICAL PLAYSCHOOL 2 EDITION 2 (cassette, 9 copies, different handmade covers)	120
82	Mirrordot MD 04	KLEINE KRIEG (cassette, 120 copies, individual hand-made covers)	80
82	In Phaze 4	BRIGHTER NOW (cassette, 300 copies, different mixes on some tracks)	45
82	In Phaze IPNER 1	BRIGHTER NOW (LP, around 1000 copies)	25
82	Flowmotion FMC 09	PREMONITION (cassette, around 60 copies)	45
83	Third Mind TMT 08	BASILISK (cassette, 1000 copies)	30
83	In Phaze PHA 2	CURSE (LP, 2500 copies)	20
84	In Phaze PHA 3	THE TOWER (LP, 2500 copies)	20

LEGENDS

(see also First Impressions)

65	Pye 7N 15904	I've Found Her/Something's Gonna Happen	20
67	Parlophone R 5581	Tomorrow's Gonna Be Another Day/Nobody Laughs Anymore	40
67	Parlophone R 5613	Under The Sky/Twenty-Four Hours A Day	20

B. LEGGS

(see also Morgan's All Stars)

71	Green Door GD 4004	Drums Of Passion/Love And Emotion (Version)	6

LEGO FEET

91	Skam SKAM 1	Untitled1/Untitled 2 (12", black die cut sleeve)	100

MICHEL LEGRAND

73	Tamla Motown TMG 848	Love Theme From "Lady Sings The Blues"/Any Happy Home (with Gil Askey)	5
73	Tamla Motown TMG 848	Love Theme From "Lady Sings The Blues"/Any Happy Home (demo in p/s)	15
58	Philips SBBL 510	LEGRAND JAZZ (LP)	12
64	Philips BL 7605	PLAYS RICHARD ROGERS (LP)	12
64	Mercury SML 30020	VIOLENT VIOLINS (LP)	12
66	Philips (S)BL 7792	THE YOUNG GIRLS OF ROCHEFORT (LP, soundtrack)	25
68	United Artists SULP 1218	THE THOMAS CROWN AFFAIR (LP, soundtrack)	35
68	Sunset SLS 50519	THE THOMAS CROWN AFFAIR (LP, reissue)	20
68	CBS (S)BPG 63276	HOW TO SAVE A MARRIAGE AND RUIN YOUR LIFE (LP, soundtrack)	12
69	MGM MGM-C(S) 8101	ICE STATION ZEBRA (LP, soundtrack)	12
70	United Artists UAS 29084	THE HAPPY ENDING (LP, soundtrack)	20
73	Bell BELLS 235	THE THREE MUSKETEERS (LP, soundtrack)	18

LE GRIFFE

83	Bullet BOL 1	Fast Bikes/Where Are You? (p/s)	8
83	Bullet BOLT 1	Fast Bikes/Where Are You?/The Actor (12", p/s)	15

MINT VALUE £

84	Bullet BOL 7	You're Killing Me (p/s)	8
83	Bullet BOLT 7	You're Killing Me/E.T.A. (12", p/s)	15
84	Bullet BULP 2	BREAKING STRAIN (mini-LP)	20

LEGS
(see also Curved Air, Stretch)

74	Warner Bros K 16317	So Many Faces/You Bet You Have	15

TOM LEHRER

60	Decca F 11243	Poisoning Pigeons In The Park/The Masochism Tango (in p/s)	10
66	Reprise RS 23049	Pollution/Folk Song Army	5

LEIBER-STOLLER ORCHESTRA

62	United Artists 1050	Cafe Expresso/Blue Baion	25

LEIBSTANDARTE SS MB

81	Come Organisation WDC 881015	TRIUMPH OF THE WILL (LP, 500 only)	80
81	Come Organisation WDC 881018	WELTANSCHAUUNG (LP)	80

ANDREW LEIGH
(see also Reg King, Spooky Tooth)

70	Polydor 2343 034	MAGICIAN (LP)	60

BERNIE LEIGHTON

63	Pye International 7N 25177	Lawrence Of Arabia Theme/The Wonderful World We Live In (in p/s)	8

LEISURE ADDICTS

80	Addictive ADIC 1	Subway Suicide/Prefab 13 (no p/s)	20

LE MAT

82	Whaam 008	Waltz For A Fool/Every Dream	10

GARY LeMEL

67	London HLM 7124	Beautiful People/Take Me With You (export issue)	20

JOHN LE MESURIER

76	Reprise K54080	WHAT IS GOING TO BECOME OF US ALL (LP)	20

LEMMINGS
(see also Honeycombs, Martin Murray)

65	Pye 7N 15837	Out Of My Mind/My Little Girl	20
65	Pye 7N 15899	You Can't Blame Me For Trying/Bring Your Heart With You	20

LEMMY & UPSETTERS with MICK GREEN
(see also Motorhead, Rockin' Vickers, Sam Gopal)

90	Sunnyside STYLE 777	Blue Suede Shoes/Paradise (p/s)	6

LEMON DIPS

69	De Wolfe DW/LP 3114	WHO'S GONNA BUY? (10" LP, library issue)	60

LEMONHEADS

91	Atlantic A 7709	Gonna Get Along Without Ya Now/Half The Time (p/s, withdrawn)	8

LEMON INTERRUPT
(see also Underworld)

93	Jnr. Boys Own JBO 12002	Eclipse/Bigmouth (12")	15
93	Junior Boys Own JBO 712	Dirty/Minneapolis/Minneapolis (Airwaves) (12")	15

LEMON JELLY

01	Soft Rock SOFTROCK 001	Soft/Rock (blue vinyl, denim sleeve with condom, 1000 only)	50
02	XL IFXLT 147P	Space Walk/Return To Patagonia (10", leather title sleeve, 3000 only)	30
03	Rolled Oats RO 01	Rolled/Oats (gold vinyl, hessian sleeve, 1200 only)	15
98	Impotent Fury IF 001	THE BATH EP: In The Bath/Nervous Tension/A Tune For Jack (10", 1000 only, stickered cardboard sleeve, 1st 250 hand-printed p/s)	150
98	Impotent Fury IF 001	THE BATH EP: In The Bath/Nervous Tension/A Tune For Jack (10", 1000 only, stickered)	50
99	Impotent Fury IF 002	THE YELLOW EP: His Majesty King Raam/The Staunton Lick/Homage To Patagonia (10", 1000 only, stickered cardboard sleeve, 1st 240 in hand-printed p/s)	120
99	Impotent Fury IF 002	THE YELLOW EP: His Majesty King Raam/The Staunton Lick/Homage To Patagonia (10", 1000 only, stickered cardboard sleeve)	40
00	Impotent Fury IF 003	THE MIDNIGHT EP: Kneel Before Your God/Page One/Come (10", 1000 only, stickered cardboard sleeve, 1st 350 in hand-printed p/s)	70
00	Impotent Fury IF 003	THE MIDNIGHT EP: Kneel Before Your God/Page One/Come (10", 1000 only, stickered cardboard sleeve)	25
00	XL IXXLLP 139	KY (2-LP gatefold sleeve with insert)	50
02	XL IFXLLP 160	LOST HORIZONS (2-LP, gatefold sleeve, with booklet)	20

LEMON KITTENS
(see also Danielle Dax, Shock Headed Peters, Underneath, Gland Shrouds, Karl Blake, Fur Fur)

79	Step Forward SF 10	SPOONFED AND WRITHING (EP)	25
81	United Dairies UD 07	CAKE BEAST (12" EP, with inner sleeve & insert)	25
80	United Dairies UD 02	WE BUY A HAMMER FOR DADDY (LP, with inner sheet)	35
83	Illuminated JAMS 131	THE BIG DENTIST (LP)	35

LEMON LINE

67	Decca F 12688	For Your Precious Love/You Made Me See The Light	15

LEMON MEN

69	Polydor 56365	I've Seen You Cut Lemons/Lemon Strip/Lemon Walk	7

LEMON PIPERS
(see also Ram Jam)

68	Pye International 7N 25444	Green Tambourine/No Help From Me	7
68	Pye International 7N 25454	Rice Is Nice/Blueberry Blue	10
68	Pye International 7N 25464	Jelly Jungle (Of Orange Marmalade)/Shoeshine Boy	6

			MINT VALUE £
68	Pye Intl. NPL 28112	GREEN TAMBOURINE (LP)	30
68	Pye Intl. NSPL 28118	JUNGLE MARMALADE (LP)	20
69	Marble Arch MAL 1120	THE LEMON PIPERS (LP)	15

LEMON PIPERS/1910 FRUITGUM CO.

(see also 1910 Fruitgum Co.)

68	Pye Intl. NEP 44091	PRESENTING ... (EP, 1 side each)	15

LEMON TREE

(see also Idle Race, Uglys, Danny King's Mayfair Set, Balls)

68	Parlophone R 5671	I Can Touch A Rainbow/William Chalker's Time Machine	40
68	Parlophone R 5739	It's So Nice To Come Home/Come On Girl	40

LEN & HONEYSUCKERS

66	Rio R 75	One More River/Emergency Ward	10

FREDDIE LENNON

(see also Loving Kind)

66	Piccadilly 7N 35290	That's My Life (My Love And My Home)/The Next Time You Feel Important	50

JIMMY LENNON & ATLANTICS

64	Decca F 11825	Louisiana Mama/I Learned To Yodel	35

JOHN LENNON/PLASTIC ONO BAND

(see also Beatles, Yoko Ono, Bill Elliott/Elastic Oz Band, Elephant's Memory, Musketeer Gripweed, Elton John)

SINGLES

69	Apple APPLE 13/R 5795	Give Peace A Chance/Remember Love (p/s, as Plastic Ono Band; with Parlophone catalogue number, dark green label)	18
69	Apple APPLE 13/R 5795	Give Peace A Chance/Remember Love (p/s, as Plastic Ono Band)	10
69	Apple APPLES 1001	Cold Turkey/Don't Worry Kyoko (Mummy's Only Looking For A Hand In The Snow) (p/s, as Plastic Ono Band)	15
69	Apple APPLES 1002	You Know My Name (Look Up The Number)/What's The New Mary Jane? (as Plastic Ono Band, unreleased; vinyl test pressings only with typed Apple 'Custom Recording' labels & hand written catalogue number)	3000
70	Apple APPLES 1003	Instant Karma!/Who Has Seen The Wind? (p/s, as Lennon/Ono with Plastic Ono Band)	12
71	Apple R 5892	Power To The People/YOKO ONO & PLASTIC ONO BAND: Open Your Box (p/s, full apple label both sides or full/half apple label)	15
72	Apple R 5970	Happy Xmas (War Is Over) (as John & Yoko/Plastic Ono Band with Harlem Community Choir)/YOKO ONO & PLASTIC ONO BAND: Listen, The Snow Is Falling (p/s green vinyl)	15
72	Apple R 5953	Woman Is The Nigger Of The World/Sisters O Sisters (unreleased, test pressings only)	2500
73	Apple R 5994	Mind Games/Meat City (p/s)	6
74	EMI PSR 369	Interview With John Lennon By Bob Mercer And Message To The Salesmen/ Whatever Gets You Thru' The Night (promo only)	2000
75	Apple R 6003	9 Dream (Edited Version)/What You Got (demo only)	80
75	Apple R 6009	Imagine/Working Class Hero (p/s)	12
80	WEA Geffen K 79186	(Just Like) Starting Over/ YOKO ONO : Kiss Kiss Kiss (Green vinyl, promo)	500
81	WEA K 79207	Watching The Wheels/YOKO ONO: I'm Your Angel (Pink vinyl "in house" promo)	500
84	Polydor PODJ 700	Nobody Told Me (1-sided white label promo)	60
84	Polydor PODJ 701	Borrowed Time (Edited Version)/YOKO ONO: Your Hands (promo only)	25
84	Polydor POSP 712	Every Man Has A Woman Who Loves Him/SEAN ONO LENNON: It's Alright (p/s, with poster)	10
84	Polydor POSP 712	Every Man Has A Woman Who Loves Him/SEAN ONO LENNON: It's Alright (p/s)	5
88	Parlophone RP 6199	Imagine/Jealous Guy (picture disc)	15
88	Parlophone 12R 6199	Imagine/Jealous Guy/Happy Xmas (War Is Over) (12" p/s)	18
97	Parlophone IMAGINE 001	Imagine (CD, 1-track, card p/s, promo only)	10
97	Parlophone IMAGINE 002	Happy Xmas (War Is Over) (CD, 1-track, card p/s, promo only)	10
98	Parlophone LENNON 002	Happy Xmas (War Is Over) (rough mix)/Be Bop A Lula (CD, card p/s, promo only)	15

LPs

68	Apple APCOR 2	UNFINISHED MUSIC NO. 1: TWO VIRGINS (with Yoko Ono, mono; black inner, no track listing, with "Merrie In England..." blurb on front sleeve)	3000
68	Apple SAPCOR 2/ Track 613 012	UNFINISHED MUSIC NO. 1: TWO VIRGINS (with Yoko Ono, stereo; black inner, with track listing & "Merrie In England..." blurb on back sleeve & Track Reccords logo on label, dark green label, "Sold in U.K..." "Mfd in UK" label text))	500
69	Zapple ZAPPLE 01	UNFINISHED MUSIC NO. 2: LIFE WITH THE LIONS (with Yoko Ono, with inner sleeve, dark green label, "Sold in U.K..." "Mfd in UK" label text)	250
69	Apple SAPCOR 11	WEDDING ALBUM (with Yoko Ono; gatefold sleeve in box set, includes wedding certificate glued to inside box lid, press booklet, poster, white 'Bagism' bag, passport photographs, postcard & picture of wedding cake)	400
69	Apple CORE 2001	LIVE PEACE IN TORONTO 1969 (as Plastic Ono Band, with stapled calendar, sealed, 1st pressing with rough surface label and Apple publishing credit on side 2, dark green label with "Sold in U.K..." text)	150
69	Apple CORE 2001	LIVE PEACE IN TORONTO 1969 (as Plastic Ono Band, with stapled calendar, unsealed)	40
70	Applie PCS 7124	JOHN LENNON : PLASTIC ONO BAND (LP, with inner)	25
72	Apple PAS 10004	IMAGINE (LP, with inner sleeve, poster & postcard, 1st pressing with laminated sleeve/'sniper' spine edges)	40
72	Apple PAS 10004	IMAGINE (LP, with inner sleeve, without poster & postcard)	20
72	Applie PCSP 716	SOMETIME IN NEW YORK CITY (2-LP, gatefold, inner sleeve & postcard)	30
72	Apple PCSP 716	SOMETIME IN NEW YORK CITY (2-LP, gatefold, inner sleeve & without postcard)	20
72	Apple Q4PAS 10004	IMAGINE (LP, quadrophonic, with inner sleeve, poster & postcard)	150
74	Apple PCTC 253	WALLS AND BRIDGES (LP, gatefold, with booklet and inner sleeve)	12
81	Parlophone JLB 8	THE JOHN LENNON BOX (9-LP set, with insert)	100
84	Polydor POLH P5	MILK AND HONEY (picture disc, original pressing, thin vinyl, 2,000 only)	40

		MINT VALUE £
84 Polydor POLH P5	MILK AND HONEY (picture disc, 2nd pressing, thicker vinyl, 1,000 only)	50
86 Parlophone PCS 7301	LIVE IN NEW YORK CITY (LP, with inner)	15
86 Parlophone PCS 7308	MENLOVE AVENUE (LP, with inner)	20
88 Parlophone PCSP 722	IMAGINE : JOHN LENNON (2xLP with inner)	20
90 Parlophone CDS 79 5220	LENNON (4 x CD set)	70
97 Parlophone 8 21954 2	LENNON LEGEND (2 x LP with inner)	15
98 Parlophone 8306142	ANTHOLOGY (4-CDR, jewel cases with Abbey Road studio inlays, incorrect track listing and missing "Grow Old With Me" from CD4, promo only)	80
99 Capirol 497 6391	WONSAPONEATIME (2 x LP with inner)	30

JOHN LENNON & BLEECHERS (Jamaica)

70 Punch PH 23	Ram You Hard/UPSETTERS: Soul Stew	20

LENNON SISTERS

56 Vogue Coral Q 72176	Graduation Day/Toy Tiger	8
57 Vogue Coral Q 72259	Young And In Love/Teenage Waltz	8
57 Vogue Coral Q 72285	Shake Me I Rattle/Pocohontas	8
61 London HLD 9417	Sad Movies/I Don't Know Why	15

MIKE LENNOX

68 Decca F 12736	Images Of You/Words I Like	7

J.B. LENOIR (& AFRICAN HUNCH RHYTHM)

65 Sue WI 339	I Sing Um The Way I Feel/I Feel So Good (with His African Hunch Rhythm)	50
65 Bootleg 503	Man Watch Your Woman/Mama Talk To Your Daughter (99 copies only)	60
66 Blue Horizon 45-1004	Mojo Boogie/I Don't Care What Nobody Say (99 copies only)	125
68 Python PLP 25	J.B. LENOIR (LP, 99 copies only)	75
70 Polydor 2482 014	CRUSADE (LP)	40
75 Rarity LP 2	J.B. LENOIR (LP)	25
70s CBS 62593	ALABAMA BLUES (LP)	40

ROBIN LENT

(see also Focus, Jan Akkerman)

71 Nepentha 6347 002	SCARECROW'S JOURNEY (LP, gatefold sleeve, with Focus)	100

VAL LENTON

65 Immediate IM 008	Gotta Get Away/You Don't Care	80

LEON (Silvera) & OWEN (Gray)

(see also Owen & Leon, Owen & Millie)

62 Blue Beat BB 117	Murder (with Drumbago All Stars)/ROY PANTON: Forty Four	15

CHRIS LEON

72 Dynamic DYN 450	(Last Night) I Didn't Get To Sleep At All/DYNAMITES: Instrumental Version	5

DEKE LEONARD

(see also Man, Marty Wilde, Help Yourself, Pete Brown's Piblokto, Gary Pickford-Hopkins & Friends)

73 United Artists UAS 29464	ICEBERG (LP, gatefold sleeve)	15
74 United Artists UAG 29544	KAMIKAZE (LP, gatefold sleeve)	15

LEONARD FAMILY

72 Beacon BEA 186	Once You Understand/It Won't Happen Again	6

ANN LEONARDO

57 Capitol CL 14723	Straws In The Wind/Travelling Stranger	15
57 Capitol CL 14755	Lottery/One And Only	10
57 Capitol CL 14797	Three Time Loser/I'll Wait Till Monday	5

LEONIE & JOE NOLAN BAND

68 Jolly JY 015	Move And Groove/Don't Let Me Do It	8

LE ORME

73 Charisma CAS 1072	FELONA AND SORONA (LP, gatefold sleeve, large 'Mad Hatter' label)	50

LEO'S SUNSHIPP

79 Grapevine RED 3	Give Me The Sunshine/I'm Back For More	8
79 Grapevine REDC 3	Give Me The Sunshine/I'm Back For More (12")	10

LEPRECHAUN

81 Excalibur EXC 508	Loc It Up/Party Freaks (12")	8

LE RITZ

77 Breaker BS 2001	Punker/What A Sucker (p/s)	15

MIKE LEROY

64 Columbia DB 7316	Five Hundred Miles/The Big City	6

LEROY & ROCKY (Ellis)

(see also King Rocky)

68 Studio One SO 2042	Love Me Girl/WRIGGLERS: Reel Up	30

LE ROYS

(see also Mike Sarne, Simon Scott, John Leyton, Mike Berry, Grazina, Billie Davis, Billy Boyle, Don Spencer)

64 Give A Disc LYN 504/505	Money/Swinging On A Star (flexidisc, with magazine)	5
64 HMV POP 1274	Gotta Lotta Love (Ciribiribin)/Don't Cry Baby	10
64 HMV POP 1312	Chills/Lost Out On Love	15
64 HMV POP 1368	I Come Smiling On Through/California GL 903	10

LES & MITCH

63 Fontana 267265 TF	Why Can't We Love/Don't Wake Me Up	6

LES & SILKIE

70 Torpedo TOR 13	I Don't Want To Tell You/DENZIL DENNIS: Come On In	5

BILL LE SAGE

(see also Ronnie Ross)

60s Philips BL 7625	DIRECTIONS IN JAZZ (LP)	15
64 World Records	PRESENTING THE BILL LESAGE/RONNIE ROSS QUARTET (LP)	40

MINT VALUE £

LORNE LESLEY

59	Parlophone R 4518	Some Of These Days/When Love Has Let You Down	5
59	Parlophone R 4567	Warm/You Ought To Be Mine	6
59	Parlophone R 4581	So High, So Low/I Don't Know	5
60	Polydor NH 66928	Take All My Love/Ritroviamoci (Till We Meet Again)	10
60	Polydor NH 66956	Bloodshot Eyes/We're Gonna Dance	5
65	Philips BF 1403	Someone Like You/Where My Heart Never Wandered	5
65	Philips BF 1434	Rainy Days Were Made For Lonely People/Fire Down Below	5
66	Philips BF 1487	Somebody's Gonna Be Sorry/(I'm Afraid) The Masquerade Is Over	5

DESMOND LESLIE

05	Trunk JBH 014 LP	MUSIC OF THE FUTURE (LP)	20

JOHN & CHRIS LESLIE

76	Cottage COT 901	THE SHIP OF TIME (LP)	15

MICHAEL LESLIE

65	Pye 7N 15835	Momma Didn't Know/I Don't Wanna Know	6
65	Pye 7N 15908	Penny Arcade/Bye Bye Baby	12
65	Pye 7N 15959	Make Up Or Break Up/She Can't See Me	25
66	Decca F 12531	Right Or Wrong/Office Girl (credited to Michael Leslie)	5

LES RITA MITSOUKO

(see under 'R')

LES SAUTERELLES

(see under 'S')

LESTER & DENWOOD

73	Atlantic K10381	America (What Have You Done)/Song For Joanne	10

HEDDY LESTER

77	Sonet SON 2013	The World Keeps Turning/Never Saw Him Laughing (p/s)	6

KETTY LESTER

62	London HLN 9527	Love Letters/I'm A Fool To Want You	7
62	London HLN 9574	But Not For Me/Moscow Nights	10
62	London HLN 9608	You Can't Lie To A Liar/River Of Salt	7
62	London HLN 9635	This Land Is Your Land/Love Belongs To Everyone	5
63	London HLN 9698	A Warm Summer Day/I'll Never Stop Loving You	7
64	RCA Victor RCA 1394	Some Things Are Better Left Unsaid/The House Is Haunted	60
64	RCA Victor RCA 1394	Some Things Are Better Left Unsaid/The House Is Haunted (DJ copy)	100
64	RCA Victor RCA 1403	Roses Grow With Thorns/Please Don't Cry Anymore	40
64	RCA Victor RCA 1421	I Trust You Baby/Theme From "The Luck Of Ginger Coffey"	15
65	RCA Victor RCA 1460	Looking For A Better World/Pretty Eyes	7
65	Capitol CL 15427	West Coast/I'll Be Looking Back	30
66	Capitol CL 15447	When A Man Loves A Woman/We'll Be Together Again	8
62	London RE-N 1348	KETTY LESTER (EP)	40
63	London HA-N 2455	LOVE LETTERS (LP)	60
64	RCA Victor RD 7669	THE SOUL OF ME (LP)	40
65	RCA Victor RD 7712	WHERE IS LOVE (LP)	40
67	Stateside S(S)L 10196	WHEN A MAN LOVES A WOMAN (LP)	80

LAZY LESTER

64	Stateside SS 277	I'm A Lover Not A Fighter/Sugar Coated Love	35
71	Blue Horizon 2431 007	MADE UP MY MIND (LP)	150
77	Flyright FLYLP 526	THEY CALL ME LAZY (LP)	15
79	Flyright FLYLP 544	POOR BOY BLUES (LP)	15

ROBIE LESTER

62	Polydor NH 66963	Ballad Of Cheating John/Miracle Of Love	5

LES YPER SOUND

67	Fontana TF 880	Too Fortiche/Psyche Rock	60
69	Philips TFE 8004	MASS FOR THE PRESENT TIME (LP)	80

JOE LETHAL

78	Lethal CI 200526	Don't Come Back/You Ain't Free (no p/s)	35

LETTERMEN

61	Capitol CL 15222	The Way You Look Tonight/That's My Desire	5
68	Capitol CL 15526	Goin' Out Of My Head/Can't Take My Eyes Off You - I Believe	5
69	Capitol CL 15609	Hurt So Bad/Traces	5
61	Capitol EAP 41669	THE LETTERMEN (EP)	8
62	Capitol (S)T 1669	A SONG FOR YOUNG LOVE (LP)	12

LETTERMEN

74	Stag SG 10075	FIRST CLASS (LP, private pressing)	90

LETTERS

79	Heartbeat PULSE 9	Nobody Loves Me/Don't Want You Back (p/s)	90

DON LETTS & JAH WOBBLE

(see also Jah Wobble, PiL)

79	Virgin VS 239	Steel Leg: Stratetime & The Wide Man/Electric Dread: Haile Unlikely (p/s)	10
79	Virgin VS 239-12	Steel Leg: Stratetime & The Wide Man/Electric Dread: Haile Unlikely (12", p/s)	12

LEVEE BREAKERS

(see also Beverley, Johnny Joyce)

65	Parlophone R 5291	Babe I'm Leaving You/Wild About My Loving	25

LEVEE CAMP MOAN

69	County	LEVEE CAMP MOAN (LP, private pressing)	750
69	County	PEACOCK FARM (LP, private pressing)	750

MINT VALUE £

LEVEL 42
79 Elite DAZZ 4 Sandstorm/Journey To The Powerline (Remix) (12", white label test pressing, no p/s) ... 75
80 Elite DAZZ 5 Love Meeting Love/Instrumental Love (7", unreleased) ... 0
80 Elite DAZZ 5 Love Meeting Love/Instrumental Love (12", company die-cut stickered sleeve) . 25
91 Polydor 511 635-2 THE COMPLETE LEVEL 42 (9-CD box set) ... 40

LEVELLERS
89 Hag HAG 005 Carry Me/What's In The Way/The Last Days Of Winter/England My Home (12" EP; first 1,000 copies with Brighton contact address on p/s) ... 12
89 Hag HAG 005 Carry Me/What's In The Way/The Last Days Of Winter/England My Home (12" EP; no Brighton contact address on p/s) ... 10
89 Hag HAG 006 Outside Inside/I Have No Answers (500 promo copies only, no p/s) ... 6
91 On The Fiddle OTF EP 1 Police On My Back/Where The Hell Are We Going To Love?/Travelogue (4am Mix) (12", fan club issue, p/s) ... 12
92 On The Fiddle OTF LP 2 LIVE 1992 (LP, fan club issue, 2,000 only) ... 15

GERRY LEVENE (& AVENGERS)
(see also Moody Blues)
64 Decca F 11815 It's Driving Me Wild (solo)/Dr. Feelgood ... 40

ANNABEL LEVENTON
69 Morgan MR 20 Easy To Be Hard/My Dear Friend ... 6

LEVERS
79 Bead Records BEAD 10 LEVERS (LP) ... 25

CARL LEV(E)Y & CIMARRONS
(see also Hot Rod Allstars, Rita Alston, Peggy)
70 Hot Rod HR 100 Walk The Hot Street/PEGGY & CIMARRONS: You Say You Don't Love Me ... 25
70 Hot Rod HR 101 Remember Easter Monday/PEGGY & JIMMY: Pum Pum Lover ... 20

IJAHMAN LEVI
76 Concrete CJ 756 I Am A Levi/Part 2 ... 60
76 Lucky LY 6016 Jah Heavy Load/Version ... 40
80s Jahmani JMI 304 Moulding (as Ijahman)/HIS MAJESTERIANS: Jah Is Coming Again (12") ... 50
85 Jahmani JMI 501 Moulding/Africa (12") ... 50
78 Island ILPS 9521 HAILE I HYMN (LP) ... 18

LEVIATHAN
(see also Mike Stuart Span, High Broom)
68 Elektra EKSN 45052 Remember The Times/Second Production ... 40
69 Elektra EKSN 45057 The War Machine/Time ... 25
69 Elektra EKSN 45052/45057 (WAY IN) THE FOUR FACES OF LEVIATHAN (Remember The Times/ Second Production/The War Machine/Time)(2 x 7" press pack, A4 folder sleeve, some overprinted with 'Harrods' logo, with bio & photo, promo, some commercial) ... 250
69 Elektra EKSN 45075 Flames/Just Forget Tomorrow ... 30
69 Elektra EKS 74046 LEVIATHAN (2-LP, unissued, acetates only, 1 copy known) ... 1000
90s (no cat.no.) ELEKTRA DAZE (CD EP, private pressing) ... 25

HANK LEVINE ORCHESTRA
61 HMV POP 947 Image (Parts 1 & 2) ... 8
65 HMV POP 1390 Image (Parts 1 & 2) (reissue) ... 5

LEVITTS
69 ESP Disk/Fontana STL 5518 WE ARE THE LEVITTS (LP) ... 25

LEVON & HAWKS
(see also Band)
65 Atlantic AT 4054 The Stones I Throw/He Don't Love You ... 50

BARRINGTON LEVY
79 JB JBD Call You On The Phone/RANKING TOYAN: London Girl (12") ... 10
79 Burning Rockers BRD 029 Hunting Man (with Jah Thomas)/LAWES ROCKERS: Hunter Dub (12") ... 20
79 Bushays BFM 128 Sister Debby/Blacksin Dub (12", with Jah Thomas) ... 20
70s Burning Vibrations BVD 003 A Ya We Deh/Give Thanks And Praise (12", with Trinity) ... 20
79 Burning Rockers BRD 033 Shine Eye Gal/Dub version (12". Jah Thomas toasts on A-side but is uncredited) ... 15
79 Burning Sounds BRD 029 Hunting Man (feat. Jah Thomas)/Hunting Dub (12") ... 25
79 Greensleeves GRED 27 Lose Respect (feat. Trinity)/ROMAN STEWART & TRINITY: Since You're Gone (12") . 15
80 Greensleeves GRED 40 Crucifixion/Eventide Fire A Disaster (red vinyl 12") ... 15
80 Cha Cha CHAD 22 Warm and Sunny Day/GENERAL SAINT - DJ cut (12") ... 50
80 His Majesty HMD 004 Shaolin Temple/Version (12") ... 20
80 Strong Like Sampson SLSD8 Wicked Intention/ROD TAYLOR (12") ... 40
80 Lovelinch LL 03 Skylarking/HORTENSE ELLIS - You Done Me Wrong (12") ... 40
82 Greensleeves GRED 80 Tomorrow Is Another Day/PAPA TULLO: Delaware (12") ... 20
82 Oak Sounds OSD 008 Open Book/Open version (12") ... 20
84 Greensleeves GRED 136 Prison Oval Rock (Master Mix)/Prison Oval Rock (Dub Plate Mix) (12") ... 12
84 Greensleeves GRED 145 Pon Your Toe/Girl I Love You (12") ... 15
87 Live & Learn LLD014 Juggling Soldier/Version (12") ... 15
87 Time I TR 026 Living Dangerously/Version ... 8
87 Time I 7TR 0200 Struggler/Version ... 8
79 Greensleeves GREL 9 ENGLISHMAN (LP) ... 30
79 Burning Sounds BS 1039 SHINE EYE GAL (LP) ... 30
80 JB JBLP 01 DOH RAY ME (LP) ... 40
80 Jah Guidance JA CC 14 ROBIN HOOD (LP) ... 40
83 GG's GG 0032 BARRINGTON LEVY'S LIFE STYLE (LP) ... 40
83 Burning Sounds BS 1050 HUNTER MAN (LP) ... 20
85 Time Records TRLP 003 HERE I COME (LP) ... 20

BEN LEVY
66 Ska Beat JB 245 Doren/Never Knew Love ... 10
66 Ska Beat JB 255 I'll Make You Glad/Keep Smiling ... 10

MINT VALUE £

JONA LEWIE
(see also Brett Marvin & Thunderbolts)

74	Sonet SON 2048	Piggy Back Sue/Papa Don't Go	6
75	Sonet SON 2056	The Swan/Custer's Last Stand	5
76	Sonet SON 2081	Hallelujah Europe Parts 1 & 2	5
77	Sonet SON 2117	Rocking Yobs/After We Swum	5

CARL LEWIN

71	Bullet BU 456	Knock Three Times/SIDNEY ALL STARS: The Whealing Mouse	8
71	Punch PH 98	Nobody Told Me/WING: Don't Play That Song Again (version)	7

ALVA (REGGIE) LEWIS
(see also Reggae Boys, Webber Sisters, Lester Sterling, Cool Cats)

67	Caltone TONE 111	Return Home/KING ROCK & WILLOWS: You Are The One	60
67	Island WI 3080	I'm Indebted/GROOVERS: You've Got To Cry	35
68	Jolly HY 009	Hang My Head And Cry/COOL CATS: Hold Your Love	50
72	Upsetter US 391	Natty Natty (as Alva Reggie Lewis)/UPSETTERS: Version	12

ANDY LEWIS & KENI BURKE

90s	Acid Jazz AJX 147S	(Love Is Alive) In Your Heart (pink vinyl, p/s)	12

ANDY LEWIS & PAUL WELLER

97	Acid Jazz AJX 193S	Are You Trying To Be Lonely?/Tell Me Once Again You Love Me (7", blue vinyl, numbered blue-ish p/s, 1,000 only)	15
97	Acid Jazz AJX 193P	Are You Trying To Be Lonely?/Tell Me Once Again You Love Me (7" promo, A-label in Acid Jazz sleeve, 50 copies only)	45

BARBARA LEWIS

63	London HLK 9724	Hello Stranger/Think A Little Sugar	25
63	London HLK 9724	Hello Stranger/Think A Little Sugar (DJ Copy)	60
63	London HLK 9779	Straighten Up Your Heart/If You Love Her	25
64	London HLK 9832	Snap Your Fingers/Puppy Love	20
64	Atlantic AT 4013	Pushin' A Good Thing Too Far/Come Home	40
65	Atlantic AT 4031	Baby I'm Yours/Hello Stranger	15
65	Atlantic AT 4041	Make Me Your Baby/Love To Be Loved	15
66	Atlantic AT 4068	Don't Forget About Me/It's Magic	20
66	Atlantic 584 037	Make Me Belong To You/Girls Need Loving Care	15
67	Atlantic 584 061	Baby What Do You Want Me To Do/I Remember The Feeling	50
68	Atlantic 584 153	Hello Stranger/Baby I'm Yours (reissue)	8
68	Atlantic 584 174	Sho Nuff (It's Got To Be Your Love)/Thankful For What I Got	20
71	Atlantic 2091 143	Someday We're Gonna Love Again/Baby I'm Yours	15
72	Atlantic K 10128	Someday We're Gonne Love Again/Baby I'm Yours (reissue)	10
65	Atlantic AET 6015	SNAP YOUR FINGERS (EP)	80
66	Atlantic ATL 5042	BABY I'M YOURS (LP)	50
66	Atlantic 587 002	IT'S MAGIC (LP, mono)	60
66	Atlantic 588 002	IT'S MAGIC (LP, stereo)	70
70	Stax SXATS 1035	THE MANY GROOVES OF BARBARA LEWIS (LP)	50

BOBBY LEWIS

61	Parlophone R 4794	Tossin' And Turnin'/Oh Yes, I Love You	20
61	Parlophone R 4831	One Track Mind/Are You Ready	25
62	Stateside SS 126	I'm Tossin' And Turnin' Again/Nothin' But The Blues	25

CAPPY LEWIS
(see also Olympics)

61	Vogue V 9184	Bullfight/OLYMPICS: Little Pedro	20

DAVE LEWIS

66	Pye Intl. NEP 44057	GIVIN' GAS (EP)	35
64	Pye Intl. NPL 28053	LITTLE GREEN THING(LP)	25

DAVE LEWIS

76	Polydor 2383 420	FROM TIME TO TIME (LP, with lyric sheet)	18

DAVID LEWIS
(see also Andwella['s Dream], David Baxter)

70	AX 1	SONGS OF DAVID LEWIS (LP, private pressing, paste-on sleeve)	400

FURRY LEWIS
(see also John Estes)

69	Blue Horizon 7-63228	PRESENTING THE COUNTRY BLUES (LP)	80
70	Matchbox SDR 190	IN MEMPHIS (LP)	30
71	Xtra XTRA 1116	FURRY LEWIS (LP)	20
71	Spokane SPL 1004	THE EARLY YEARS 1927-1929 (LP)	30

GARY LEWIS & PLAYBOYS

65	Liberty LIB 10187	This Diamond Ring/Tijuana Wedding	15
65	Liberty LIB 55778	Count Me In/Little Miss Go-Go	15
65	Liberty LIB 55809	Save Your Heart For Me/Without A Word Of Warning	10
65	Liberty LIB 55818	Everybody Loves A Clown/Time Stands Still	7
66	Liberty LIB 55846	She's Just My Style/I Won't Make That Mistake Again	20
66	Liberty LIB 55865	Sure Gonna Miss Her/I Don't Wanna Say Goodnight	8
66	Liberty LIB 55880	Green Grass/I Can Read Between The Lines	8
66	Liberty LIB 55898	My Heart's Symphony/Tina	20
66	Liberty LIB 55914	(You Don't Have To) Paint Me A Picture/Looking For The Stars	10
67	Liberty LIB 55933	Where Will The Words Come From/The Best Man	7
67	Liberty LIB 55949	Loser (With A Broken Heart)/Ice Melts In The Sun	7
67	Liberty LIB 55971	Girls In Love/Let's Be More Than Friends	7
67	Liberty LBF 15025	Jill/Needles And Pins	10
68	Liberty LBF 15131	Sealed With A Kiss/Pretty Thing	5
70	Liberty LBF 15335	Orangutan/Something Is Wrong	5
75	United Artists UP 35780	My Heart's Symphony/I Won't Make That Same Mistake Again (reissue)	6
65	Liberty LBY 1259	THIS DIAMOND RING (LP)	40
66	Liberty LBY 1322	JUST OUR STYLE (LP)	30

MINT VALUE £

GEORGE LEWIS & HIS NEW ORLEANS STOMPERS/BAND

56	Vogue V 2051	Climax Rag/Deep Bayou Blues	8
56	Vogue V 2052	Millenberg Joys/Two Jim Blues	8
56	Vogue V 2053	Just A Closer Walk With Thee/Just A Little While To Stay Here	8
56	Vogue V 2054	Fidgety Feet/Dauphine Street Blues	8
56	Vogue V 2055	Don't Go 'Way Nobody/Careless Love Blues	8
60	HMV POP 707	South Rampart Street Parade/Chinatown My Chinatown (with Band)	7
52	Vogue LDE 012	GEORGE LEWIS AND HIS NEW ORLEANS ALLSTARS (10" LP)	15
54	Vogue LDE 082	GEORGE LEWIS JAM SESSION (10" LP)	15
55	Vogue LAE 12005	GEORGE LEWIS AND HIS NEW ORLEANS STOMPERS (LP)	20
57	Tempo TAP 13	GEORGE LEWIS RAGTIME BAND (LP)	20
50s	'77' LA 12/28	SMILE, DARN YA, SMILE (LP, as George Lewis with Barry Martyn's Band)	20

GEORGE LEWIS/FREDDIE KOHLMAN

53	Brunswick LA 8627	NEW ORLEANS JAZZ CONCERT (10" LP)	15

HOPETON LEWIS

(see also Glenmore Brown & Hopeton Lewis)

67	Island WI 3054	Rock Steady/Cool Collie	150
67	Island WI 3055	Finder's Keepers/ROLAND ALPHONSO: Shanty Town Curfew	30
67	Island WI 3056	Let Me Come On Home/Hardships Of Life (with Merritone All Stars)	30
67	Island WI 3057	Run Down/Pick Yourself Up	30
67	Island WI 3059	Let The Little Girl Dance/This Music Got Soul	50
67	Island WI 3068	Rock A Shacka/I Don't Want Trouble	75
68	Island WI 3076	Everybody Rocking/Stars Shining So Bright	50
68	Fab FAB 43	Skinny Leg Girl/Live Like A King (as Hopetown Lewis & Glenmore Brown)	25
70	Duke Reid DR 2505	Boom Shaka Lacka/TOMMY McCOOK QUINTET: Dynamite	15
70	Duke Reid DR 2516	Testify/TOMMY McCOOK: Super Soul	15
71	Duke DU 112	Grooving Out Of Life (with Byron Lee & Dragonaires) (actually titled Grooving Out On Life)/BYRON LEE & DRAGONAIRES: Fire Fire	8
71	Treasure Isle TI 7060	To The Other Man/TOMMY McCOOK: Stampede	12
72	Treasure Isle TI 7071	Judgement Day (actually by Hopeton Lewis & Dennis Alcapone)/ EARL LINDO: Version Day	10
72	Attack ATT 8035	Starting All Over Again/DYNAMITES: Instrumental Version	5
72	Dynamic DYN 436	Come Together/Going Back To My Hometown	5
72	Dynamic DYN 447	Good Together/Version	5
73	Dragon DRA 1001	City Of New Orleans/The Wind Cries Mary	5
73	Dragon DRA 1011	Groovin' Out On Life/God Bless Whoever Sent You	5
67	Island ILP 957	TAKE IT EASY: ROCKSTEADY WITH HOPETON LEWIS (LP)	160
71	Trojan TRL 36	GROOVING OUT ON LIFE (LP)	30

HUGH X. LEWIS

66	London HLR 10032	Looking In The Future/Too Late	10
66	London HA-R 8293	THE HUGH X. LEWIS ALBUM (LP)	15
67	London HA-R 8303	JUST BEFORE DAWN (LP)	15

JENNIFER LEWIS & ANGELA STRANGE

65	Columbia DB 7662	Bring It To Me/You Know	10
66	Columbia DB 7814	I've Heard It All Before/Bad Storm Coming	12

JERRY LEWIS

(see also Dean Martin)

56	Capitol CL 14626	Buckskin Beauty/Pardners (with Dean Martin)	5
57	Brunswick 05636	Rock-A-Bye Your Baby With A Dixie Melody/Come Rain Or Come Shine	8
53	Capitol LC 6591	CAPITOL PRESENTS JERRY LEWIS (10" LP)	15

JERRY LEWIS (Jamaica)

(see also I Roy)

72	Pama PM 862	The Godfather/ALTON ELLIS: Some Day	15
73	Explosion EX 2077	Rhythm Pleasure/AGGROVATORS: Doctor Seaton	12

JERRY LEE LEWIS

(see also Nashville Teens)

78s

57	London HLS 8457	Whole Lotta Shakin' Goin' On/It'll Be Me	18
57	London HLS 8529	Great Balls Of Fire/Mean Woman Blues	15
58	London HLS 8559	You Win Again/I'm Feelin' Sorry	20
58	London HLS 8592	Breathless/Down The Line	30
58	London HLS 8700	Break-Up/I'll Make It All Up To You	35
59	London HLS 8780	High School Confidential/Fools Like Me	50
59	London HLS 8840	Lovin' Up A Storm/Big Blon' Baby	50
59	London HLS 8941	Let's Talk About Us/The Ballad Of Billy Joe	60
59	London HLS 8993	Little Queenie/I Could Never Be Ashamed Of You	100
96	Cruisin' The 50s CASB 002	Wild One/Old Black Joe (numbered, 300 only)	35

SINGLES

57	London HLS 8457	Whole Lotta Shakin' Goin' On/It'll Be Me	30
57	London HLS 8529	Great Balls Of Fire/Mean Woman Blues	20
58	London HLS 8559	You Win Again/I'm Feelin' Sorry	25
58	London HLS 8592	Breathless/Down The Line	20
58	London HLS 8700	Break-Up/I'll Make It All Up To You	20
59	London HLS 8780	High School Confidential/Fools Like Me	20
59	London HLS 8840	Lovin' Up A Storm/Big Blon' Baby	20
59	London HLS 8941	Let's Talk About Us/The Ballad Of Billy Joe (no triangular centre)	20
59	London HLS 8993	Little Queenie/I Could Never Be Ashamed Of You (no triangular centre)	20

(The above 45s were originally issued with triangular centres; round-centre pressings are worth half to two-thirds of these values.)

60	London HLS 9083	I'll Sail My Ship Alone/It Hurt Me So	20
60	London HLS 9131	Baby, Baby, Bye Bye/Old Black Joe	20
60	London HLS 9202	John Henry/Hang Up My Rock And Roll Shoes	20

			MINT VALUE £
61	London HLS 9335	What'd I Say?/Livin' Lovin' Wreck	10
61	London HLS 9414	It Won't Happen With Me/Cold Cold Heart	10
61	London HLS 9446	As Long As I Live/When I Get Paid	10
62	London HLS 9526	I've Been Twistin'/Ramblin' Rose	10
62	London HLS 9584	Sweet Little Sixteen/How's My Ex Treating You	10
63	London HLS 9688	Good Golly Miss Molly/I Can't Trust Me (In Your Arms Anymore)	10
63	London HLS 9722	Teenage Letter/Seasons Of My Heart (B-side with Linda Gail Lewis)	10
63	Mercury AMT 1216	Hit The Road Jack/Pen And Paper	10
64	Philips BF 1324	I'm On Fire/Bread And Butter Man	10
64	London HLS 9867	Lewis Boogie/Bonnie B	20
65	Philips BF 1371	Hi-Heel Sneakers/You Went Back On Your Word	7
65	Philips BF 1407	Baby Hold Me Close/I Believe In You	8
65	Philips BF 1425	Rockin' Pneumonia And The Boogie Woogie Flu/This Must Be The Place	10
65	London HLS 9980	Carry Me Back To Old Virginia/I Know What It Means	5
66	Philips BF 1521	Memphis Beat/If I Had It All To Do Over	10
67	Philips BF 1594	It's A Hang-Up Baby/Holdin' On	8
67	Philips BF 1615	Turn On Your Love Light/Shotgun Man	10
68	Mercury MF 1020	Another Place, Another Time/Walking The Floor Over You	6
69	Mercury MF 1088	To Make Love Sweeter For You/Let's Talk About Us	5
69	Mercury MF 1105	Long Tall Sally/Jenny, Jenny (some in p/s)	10
69	Mercury MF 1105	Long Tall Sally/Jenny, Jenny (some in p/s)	5
69	Mercury MF 1110	Great Balls Of Fire/Whole Lotta Shakin' Goin' On (some in p/s)	10
69	Mercury MF 1110	Great Balls Of Fire/Whole Lotta Shakin' Goin' On (some in p/s)	5
72	Mercury 6052 14 1	Chantilly Lace/Think About It Darlin'	7
73	Mercury 6052 260	Drinking Wine Spo Dee O Dee/Rock And Roll Medley	6
73	Mercury 6052 378	(Taking My) Music To The Man/Jack Daniels (Old No. 7) (in p/s)	8
73	Mercury 6052 378	(Taking My) Music To The Man/Jack Daniels (Old No. 7)	6
79	Elektra K 12374	Rocking My Life Away/Rita May (p/s)	8
80	Elektra K 12399	Everyday I Have To Cry/Who Will The Next Fool Be	5
80	Elektra K 12432	Rockin' Jerry Lee/Good Time Charles Got The Blues	5

EXPORT SINGLES

58	London HL 7050	High School Confidential/Fools Like Me	20
62	London HL 7117	Save The Last Dance For Me/Hello Josephine	30
63	London HL 7120	Good Golly Miss Molly/I Can't Trust Me (In Your Arms Anymore)	20
63	London HL 7123	In The Mood/I'm Feelin' Sorry	40

EPs

58	London RE-S 1140	JERRY LEE LEWIS - NO. 1 (with triangular centre)	50
58	London RE-S 1140	JERRY LEE LEWIS - NO. 1 (with round centre)	40
59	London RE-S 1186	JERRY LEE LEWIS - NO. 2 (with triangular centre)	50
59	London RE-S 1186	JERRY LEE LEWIS - NO. 2 (with round centre)	40
59	London RE-S 1187	JERRY LEE LEWIS - NO. 3 (with triangular centre)	50
59	London RE-S 1187	JERRY LEE LEWIS - NO. 3 (with round centre)	40
61	London RE-S 1296	JERRY LEE LEWIS - NO. 4	35
62	London RE-S 1336	JERRY LEE LEWIS - NO. 5	30
63	London RE-S 1351	JERRY LEE LEWIS - NO. 6	30
63	London RE-S 1378	FOUR MORE FROM JERRY LEE LEWIS	30
66	Philips BE 12599	COUNTRY STYLE	30
84	Sun JLL EP 001	THE FABULOUS JERRY LEE LEWIS VOL. 1 (Fan Club issue)	15
84	Sun JLL EP 002	THE FABULOUS JERRY LEE LEWIS VOL. 2 (Fan Club issue)	15

ALBUMS

59	London HA-S 2138	JERRY LEE LEWIS	100
62	London HA-S 2440	JERRY LEE'S GREATEST	50
64	Philips (S)BL 7622	GOLDEN HITS	20
65	Philips (S)BL 7646	LIVE AT THE STAR CLUB, HAMBURG (with Nashville Teens)	25
65	Philips BL 7650	THE GREATEST LIVE SHOW ON EARTH	15
65	Philips BL 7668	THE RETURN OF ROCK	15
65	London HA-S 8251	WHOLE LOTTA SHAKIN' GOIN' ON	50
66	Philips BL 7688	COUNTRY SONGS FOR CITY FOLKS	15
66	Philips (S)BL 7706	MEMPHIS BEAT	15
67	London HA-S 8323	BREATHLESS	30

(The above London LPs were originally issued with plum labels; later black label reissues are worth £10-£20.)

69	Mercury 21047 SMCL	SHE STILL COMES AROUND (TO WHAT'S LEFT OF ME) (stereo only)	12
84	Sun SUN 102	THE SUN YEARS (12-LP, box set with booklet)	40

JIMMY LEWIS

68	Minit MLF 11002	The Girls From Texas/Let Me Know	20

JOE 'CANNONBALL' LEWIS

51	MGM MGM 430	Train Whistle Nightmare/Trust Me Again (78)	10

JOHN LEWIS

(see also Modern Jazz Quartet)

60	London Jazz LTZ-K 15186	IMPROVISED MEDITATIONS AND EXCURSIONS (LP)	15
61	London Jazz LTZ-K 15218	THE GOLDEN STRIKER (LP, also stereo SAH-K 6152)	15

JOHN LEWIS AND SACHA DISTEL

59	UK Oriole MG20036	AFTERNOON IN PARIS (LP)	25

LEW LEWIS (REFORMER)

(see also Oil City Sheiks, Dr. Feelgood, Eddie & the Hot Rods)

76	Stiff BUY 5	Caravan Man/Boogie On The Street (p/s, with Dr. Feelgood)	5
77	United Artists UP 36217	Out For A Lark/Watch Yourself	5
78	Lew Lewis LEW 1	Lucky Seven/Night Talk (500 only, plain white sleeve)	8

LINDA LEWIS

(see also Ferris Wheel)

67	Polydor 56173	You Turned My Bitter Into Sweet/Do You Believe In Love	80
71	Reprise K 14096	We Can Win/Hampstead Way	6
72	Reprise K 14209	Old Smokey/It's The Frame	6

MINT VALUE £

75	Arista ARIST 17	It's In His Kiss/Walk About (p/s)	6
73	Raft RA 18502	Rock A Doodle Doo/Reach For The Truth	6
71	Reprise K 44130	SAY NO MORE (LP)	20
72	Reprise K 44208	LARK (LP)	15
73	Raft RA 48501	FATHOMS DEEP (LP)	12
79	Ariola ARL 5033	HACIENDA VIEW (LP)	12

MARGARET LEWIS

62	Starlite ST45 081	Somethings Wrong Baby/John De Lee	40

MEADE 'LUX' LEWIS

(see also Albert Ammons, [Big] Joe Turner)

50	Melodisc 1130	Boogie Tidal/Yancey's Pride (78)	10
50	Melodisc 1136	Glendale Glide/Denapas Parade (78)	10
51	Melodisc 1153	Randini's Boogie/Lux's Boogie (78)	10
52	Vogue V 2123	Blues Whistle/Chicago Flyer (78)	10
54	Vogue V 2229	Six Wheel Chaser Boogie/Bass On Top Boogie (78)	10
55	Vogue EPV 1065	MEADE 'LUX' LEWIS (EP)	20
56	Melodisc EPM7 107	BOOGIE WOOGIE AND BLUES (EP)	20
56	Columbia Clef SEB 10030	BOOGIE WOOGIE PIANO AND DRUMS NO. 1 (EP)	10
56	Columbia Clef SEB 10052	BOOGIE WOOGIE PIANO AND DRUMS NO. 2 (EP)	10
57	Columbia Clef 33CX 10094	YANCEY'S LAST RIDE (LP)	12
57	HMV DLP 1176	OUT OF THE ROARING TWENTIES (10" LP)	12

MEADE 'LUX' LEWIS & SLIM GAILLARD

(see also Slim Gaillard)

56	Columbia Clef 33C 9021	JAZZ AT THE PHILHARMONIC (10" LP)	20

MIA LEWIS

65	Decca F 12117	Wish I Didn't Love Him/This Is The End	12
65	Decca F 12240	It's Goodbye Now/The Luckiest Girl	12
66	Parlophone R 5526	Nothing Lasts Forever/(Baby) I'm Feeling Good	20
67	Parlophone R 5585	No Time For Lovin'/Onion	6
67	Parlophone R 5617	Woman's Love/You Won't Get Away	6

MICHAEL LEWIS

73	United Artists UP 35569	Theatre Of Blood Theme/Edwina's Theme	22

MONICA LEWIS

56	Parlophone R 4224	I Wish You Love/Stay After School	5

NIGEL LEWIS

86	Media Burn MB10	WHAT I FEEL NOW (LP)	20

PATTI LEWIS

56	Columbia DB 3825	Earthbound/Happiness Street (Corner Sunshine Square)	10
57	Columbia DB 3923	Your Wild Heart/A Poor Man's Roses (Or A Rich Man's Gold)	8
57	Columbia DB 3967	Pull Down De Shade/Speak For Yourself John	8

PHILLIPPA LEWIS

65	Decca F 12152	Just Like In The Movies/Get Along Without You	10

RAMSEY LEWIS (TRIO)

(see also Young-Holt Unlimited)

65	Chess CRS 8020	The 'In' Crowd/Since I Fell For You (as Ramsey Lewis Trio)	15
65	Chess CRS 8024	Hang On Sloopy/Movin' Easy (as Ramsey Lewis Trio)	8
66	Chess CRS 8029	A Hard Day's Night/'Tout A Doubt (as Ramsey Lewis Trio)	8
66	Chess CRS 8031	Hi-Heel Sneakers (Parts 1 & 2) (as Ramsey Lewis Trio)	10
66	Chess CRS 8041	Wade In The Water/Ain't That Peculiar (as Ramsey Lewis Trio)	40
66	Chess CRS 8041	Wade In The Water/Ain't That Peculiar (as Ramsey Lewis Trio) (DJ copy)	120
66	Chess CRS 8044	Uptight (Everything's Alright)/Money In The Pocket	10
67	Chess CRS 8051	Day Tripper/Hurt So Bad	20
67	Chess CRS 8055	1-2-3/Down By The Riverside	8
67	Chess CRS 8058	Function At The Junction/Hey Mrs. Jones	10
67	Chess CRS 8060	Saturday Night After The Movies/China Gate	8
67	Chess CRS 8061	Girl Talk/Dancing In The Street	8
67	Chess CRS 8064	Soul Man/Struttin' Lightly	10
69	Chess CRS 8096	Cry Baby Cry/Wade In The Water	20
69	Chess CRS 8096	Cry Baby Cry/Wade In The Water (DJ copy)	45
70	Chess CRS 8104	Julia/Do What You Wanna	10
72	Chess 6145 004	Wade In The Water/Ain't That Peculiar (paper label)	15
72	Chess 6145 013	The 'In' Crowd/Soul Man	6
72	CBS 8280	Slipping Into Darkness/Collage	8
66	Chess CRE 6019	A HARD DAY'S NIGHT (EP, as Ramsey Lewis Trio)	30
65	Pye Jazz NJL 55	AT THE BOHEMIAN CAVERNS (LP)	20
65	Chess CRL 4511	THE 'IN' CROWD (LP)	25
65	Chess CRL 4518	CHOICE! THE BEST OF RAMSEY LEWIS (LP)	25
66	Chess CRL 4520	HANG ON RAMSEY! (LP)	20
66	Chess CRL 4522	WADE IN THE WATER (LP)	40
67	Chess CRL 4528	GOIN' LATIN (LP)	25
67	Chess CRL 4531	THE MOVIE ALBUM (LP)	20
68	Chess CRL(S) 4533	DANCIN' IN THE STREET (LP)	25
68	Chess CRLS 4535	UP POPS RAMSEY LEWIS (LP)	25
68	Chess CRLS 4539	MAIDEN VOYAGE (LP)	25
69	Chess CRLS 4545	MOTHER NATURE'S SON (LP)	30
68	Fontana SFJL 962	DOWN TO EARTH (LP)	20
72	Chess 6310 106	BACK TO THE ROOTS (LP)	15
72	Chess 6310 114	THE BEST OF RAMSEY LEWIS (LP)	15
72	Chess 6310 124	TOBACCO ROAD (LP)	15
72	CBS 64718	UPENDO NI PAMOJA (LP)	12
73	CBS 65307	FUNKY SERENITY (LP)	20
73	CBS CQ 31096	UPENDO NI PAMOJA (LP, quadrophonic)	15
74	CBS S80677	SUN GODDESS (LP)	18

MINT VALUE £

RICHARD LEWIS & HIS BAND

60	Downbeat CHA 1	Hey, Little Girl/Hey, Little Boy	40

SHIRLEY LEWIS

83	High Energy	Loves Warming Up/Dub Mix (12")	15

SMILEY LEWIS

53	London L 1189	Big Mamou/Play Girl (78, some copies miscredited to Smiley Davis)	100
56	London HLU 8312	One Night/Ain't Gonna Do It	800
56	London HLU 8312	One Night/Ain't Gonna Do It (78)	100
56	London HLU 8337	Down Yonder We Go Ballin'/Don't Be That Way (Please Listen To Me)	800
56	London HLU 8337	Down Yonder We Go Ballin'/Don't Be That Way (Please Listen To Me) (78)	100
57	London HLP 8367	Shame, Shame, Shame/No, No (gold lettering)	500
57	London HLP 8367	Shame, Shame, Shame/No, No (silver lettering)	400
57	London HLP 8367	Shame, Shame, Shame/No, No (78)	70
70	Liberty LBF 15337	I Hear You Knocking/Play Girl	10
70	Liberty LBS 83308	SHAME, SHAME, SHAME (LP)	25
78	United Artists UAS 30167	I HEAR YOU KNOCKING (LP)	15

STEVIE LEWIS

65	Mercury MF 871	Take Me For A Little While/My Whole World Seems To Be Tumbling Down	22
65	Mercury MF 919	Sometimes When You're Lonely/Under The Smile Of Love	5
65	Polydor 56003	Heard It All Before/Wild	7
69	RCA RCA 1840	Take A Little Warning/I Can Try	5

TAMALA LEWIS

79	Destiny DS 1010	You Won't Say Nothing/If You Can Stand Me	8
79	Destiny DS 1010	You Won't Say Nothing/If You Can Stand Me (DJ)	15

TINY LEWIS

60	Parlophone R 4617	Too Much Rockin'/I Get Weak	150

VIC LEWIS

63	HMV POP 1127	Bossa Nova Scotia/Vic's Tune	5
62	Columbia SEG 8202	SWINGS NELSON RIDDLE (EP)	8
55	Decca LF 1216	PROGRESSIVE JAZZ (10" LP)	20
62	HMV CLP 1641	PLAY BOSSA NOVA HOME AND AWAY (LP)	25
70	Ember CJS 807	AT THE BEAULIEU FESTIVAL (LP)	25
60s	Ember SE 8018	BIG BAND EXPLOSION (LP)	30
70s	DJM SPECB 103	MY LIFE MY WAY (LP)	15

LEWIS & CLARKE EXPEDITION

67	RCA 1633	Blue Revelations/I Feel Good (I Feel Bad)	20

LEWIS SISTERS

65	Tamla Motown TMG 536	You Need Me/Moonlight On The Beach	110
65	Tamla Motown TMG 536	You Need Me/Moonlight On The Beach (DJ Copy)	150

DAVE LEWRY

72	Westwood WRS 019	ALL I WANT TO DO IS PLAY GUITAR (LP)	35

MONIQUE LEYRAC

68	SNB 55-3309	Time Time/Love Is Blue	7

JOHN LEYTON

(see also Le Roys)

60	Top Rank JAR 426	Tell Laura I Love Her/Goodbye To Teenage Love	40
60	HMV POP 798	The Girl On The Floor Above/Terry Brown's In Love With Mary Dee	70
61	Top Rank JAR 577	Johnny Remember Me/There Must Be	5
61	Top Rank JAR 585	Wild Wind/You Took My Love For Granted	5
61	HMV POP 956	Son This Is She/Six White Horses	5
62	HMV POP 992	Lone Rider/Heart Of Stone	10
62	HMV POP 1014	Lonely City/It Would Be Easy	10
62	HMV POP 1054	Down The River Nile/I Think I'm Falling In Love	15
62	HMV POP 1076	Lonely Johnny/Keep On Loving You	10
63	HMV POP 1122	Cupboard Love/Land Of Love	5
63	HMV POP 1175	I'll Cut Your Tail Off/The Great Escape	10
63	HMV POP 1204	On Lover's Hill/Lovers Lane	8
63	HMV POP 1230	I Guess You Are Always On My Mind/Beautiful Dreamer	8
64	HMV POP 1264	Make Love To Me/Missing You (as John Leyton & Le Roys)	15
64	HMV POP 1338	Don't Let Her Go Away/I Want A Love I Can See	10
64	HMV POP 1374	All I Want Is You/Every Day Is A Holiday (with Grazina Frame & Mike Sarne)	10
73	York SYK 551	Dancing In The Graveyard/Riversong	10
74	York YR 210	Rock 'N' Roll/Highway Song	10
62	Top Rank JKP 3016	JOHN LEYTON (EP)	40
62	HMV 7EG 8747	HIT PARADE (EP)	20
64	HMV 7EG 8843	BEAUTIFUL DREAMER (EP)	20
64	HMV 7EG 8854	TELL LAURA I LOVE HER (EP)	40
61	HMV CLP 1497	THE TWO SIDES OF JOHN LEYTON (LP)	40
62	HMV CLP 1664	ALWAYS YOURS (LP, with Charles Blackwell's Orchestra)	50
73	York FYK 416	JOHN LEYTON (LP)	30

LEYTON BUZZARDS

78	Small Wonder SMALL 7	19 And Mad/Villain/Youthanasia (p/s)	6
79	Chrysalis CHS 2288	Saturday Night Beneath The Plastic Palm Trees/Trough With You (p/s)	5
79	Chrysalis CHS 2328	I'm Hanging Around/I Don't Want To Go/No Dry Ice (p/s, green vinyl)	5
79	Chrysalis CHR 1213	JELLIED EELS TO RECORD DEALS (LP, as Buzzards)	12

L.F.O.

90	Warp WAP 5	L.F.O. (The Leeds Warehouse Mix)/L.F.O. (Track 4)/Probe (The Cuba Edit) (12", p/s)	12

MINT VALUE £

LG & LOPEZ

01	Sit Tight STR001	Life Long/Tempered Waters/Storming (EP)	12
02	Sit Tight STR002	Rocket Fuel/City Breaks (EP)	12

LIAISON

82	Catweazle CR 001	Play It With A Passion/Caught In A ... (grey p/s)	35
82	Catweazle CR 001	Play It With A Passion/Caught In A ... (yellow p/s)	10
83	Liaison LIC 101	LOOKING AFTER NUMBER ONE (EP)	5
84	Liaison LSN 0020	Only Heaven Knows/Ease The Pain Away (p/s)	5

LIAR

79	Bearsville K 55524	SET THE WORLD ON FIRE (LP, picture disc)	15

LIARS

05	Mute MUTE 39	It Fit When I Was A Kid/Don't Techno For An Answer Mix (7", picture disc in p/s, 500 only)	25

SVEN LIBAEK

06	Trunk JBH 020 LP	INNER SPACE: THE LOST FILM MUSIC OF SVEN LIBAEK (LP)	20

LIBERACE

56	Columbia DB 3834	I Don't Care (As Long As You Care For Me)/As Time Goes By	8

LIBERATION SUITE

75	Myrrh MYR 1027	LIBERATION SUITE (LP)	15

LIBERATORS

(see also Pinkerton's Assorted Colours)

65	Stateside SS 424	It Hurts So Much/You Look So Fine	15

EVE LIBERTINE & CRASS

(see also Crass)

84	Crass 1984/4	ACTS OF LOVE (LP, with book)	15

LIBERTINES

(see also Babyshambles, Wolfman)

02	Rough Trade RTRADES 054	What A Waster/I Get Along (p/s, 2000 only)	35
02	Rough Trade RTRADESCD 054	What A Waster/I Get Along (CD)	30
02	Rough Trade RTRADES 064	Up The Bracket/Boys In The Band (p/s)	10
03	Rough Trade RTRADES 074	Time For Heroes/The 7 Deadly Sins (demo version) (p/s)	10
03	Rough Trade RTRADS 119	Don't Look Back Into The Sun/Death On The Stairs (blue vinyl, fold-out poster sleeve in PVC slipcase, 3000 only)	30
04	Rough Trade RTRADS 163	Can't Stand Me Now/The Tide That Left Never Came Back/(I've Got) Sweets (p/s)	8
02	Rough Trade RTRADELP 065	UP THE BRACKET (LP)	20
04	Rough Trade RTRADELPX166	THE LIBERTINES (2xLP, gatefold 3000 only)	30
04	Rough Trade RTRADELP166	THE LIBERTINES (White label test pressing, 10 only)	80

RAY LIBERTO

61	HMV CSD 1435	MOTION PICTURE THEMES A LA DIXIELAND (LP)	12

LIBERTY

80s	Mortarhate MORT 19	Our Voices Tomorrow's Hope	12
80s	Mortarhate MORT 25	THE PEOPLE WHO CARE ARE ANGRY (LP)	25

LIBERTY BELLES

71	Jay Boy BOY 40	Shing-A-Ling Time/Just Try Me	10

LICKS

(see also Epileptics, Flux Of Pink Indians)

79	Stortbeat BEAT 8	1970S EP	15

JAMIE LIDELL

97	Mosquito MSQ 08	FREAKIN' THE FRAME (12" EP)	20

BUNNY LIE LIE

81	Greensleeves GRED 52	Babylonian/WAYNE WADE: Poor And Humble (12")	20

LIEUTENANT BUDDY KNOX

(see under 'K')

LIEUTENANT PIGEON

(see also Shel Naylor, Stavely Makepeace, Heavy Cochran)

78	SMA 1501	Disco Bells/Steam Train Stag	8
73	Decca SKL 5154	MOULDY OLD MUSIC (LP)	20
73	Decca SKL 5174	PIGEON PIE (LP)	20
74	Decca SKL 5196	PIGEON PARTY (LP)	25

LIFE

69	Polydor 56778	Hands Of The Clock/Ain't I Told You Before	22
74	Polydor 2058 500	Woman/Bless My Soul	6
74	Polydor 2383 295	LIFE AFTER DEATH (LP)	60

LIFE

73	Philips 6006 280	Cats Eyes/Death In The Family (paper label)	20
73	Philips 6006 280	Cats Eyes/Death In The Family (moulded label)	10

LIFE AFTER LIFE

85	Timetrack SRTSKL 453	LIFE AFTER LIFE (LP, private pressing)	120

LIFE 'N' SOUL

67	Decca F 12659	Ode To Billy Joe/Peacefully Asleep	35
68	Decca F 12851	Here Comes Yesterday Again/Dear Paul	15

MINT VALUE £

LIFE SUPPORT

79	Slug SLUG 1	Leader Deceiver/Confusion (p/s, white labels)	6

LIFETIME

(see also Tony Williams [Lifetime], Jack Bruce, John McLaughlin)

70	Polydor 2066 050	One Word/Two Worlds	20

JOE LIGES

(see also Delroy Wilson)

63	Blue Beat BB 172	Spit In The Sky/Tell Me What (both actually by Delroy Wilson)	25

JOE LIGGINS & HONEYDRIPPERS

50	Parlophone R 3309	I've Got The Right To Cry/Blue Moods (78)	30
76	Specialty SDN 5006	Pink Champagne/Honey Dripper	5

(THE) LIGHT

96	AAA Recordings TRIP 002	Dusk (12")	15

BEN LIGHT

56	HMV 7M 350	Bring Me A Bluebird/You	10

ENOCH LIGHT

59	Top Rank JAR 134	With My Eyes Wide Open/I Cried For You (as Enoch Light & Light Brigade)	5
59	Top Rank JAR 234	Scarlet Ribbons/Greensleeves (as Enoch Light & His Vibrant Strings)	5
69	Studio Two TWO 312	SPACED OUT (LP)	25
70	Project 3	PERMISSIVE POLYPHONICS (LP)	25
65	Pye Command PCLS 873	DISCOTHEQUE (LP)	20

LIGHT FANTASTIC

73	MAM R 105	Love Is Everywhere/Gone Are The Days	10
73	RCA RCA 2331	Jeanie/You Don't Care	20
74	Blue Jean BJS 701	Take Me, Shake Me/Don't Let Go	8
75	Blue Jean BJS 704	We Are The Song/Raining	6

J.J. LIGHT

69	Liberty LBF 15228	Heya/On The Road Now	10

LIGHT OF THE WORLD

82	EMI EMC 3410	CHECK US OUT (LP)	20
80	Ensign ENVY 14	ROUND TRIP (LP)	12

GORDON LIGHTFOOT

62	Decca F 11527	(Remember Me) I'm The One/Daisy-Doo (as Gord Lightfoot)	20
63	Fontana 267 275TF	Negotiations/It's Too Late, He Wins (as Gordie Lightfoot)	5
63	Fontana TF 405	The Day Before Yesterday/Take Care Of Yourself (as Gordie Lightfoot)	5
65	United Artists UP 1109	Just Like Tom Thumb's Blues/Ribbon Of Darkness	5
66	Warner Bros WB 5621	I'm Not Sayin'/For Lovin' Me	5
68	President PT 138	Adios Adios/Is My Baby Blue Tonight (as Gordie Lightfoot)	5
68	United Artists UP 2216	Black Day In July/Pussy Willow's Cat Tails	5
69	United Artists UP 2272	The Circle Is Small/Does Your Mother Know	5
69	United Artists UP 35020	Bitter Green/May I	5
70	Reprise RS 20974	If You Could Read My Mind/Poor Little Alison	5
68	United Artists SULP 1199	DID SHE MENTION MY NAME (LP)	12
69	United Artists SULP 1239	BACK HERE ON EARTH (LP)	12

PADDY LIGHTFOOT

50s	Melodisc EPM7 100	PADDY LIGHTFOOT (EP)	10

PAPA (GEORGE) LIGHTFOOT

69	Liberty LBF 15176	Wine Whiskey And Woman/SLIM HARPO: Something Inside Me	20
60s	Jan & Dil JR 451	MORE DOWN HOME BLUES (EP)	35
71	Liberty LBS 83353	NATCHEZ TRACE (LP, as Papa George Lightfoot)	30

TERRY LIGHTFOOT'S (NEW ORLEANS) JAZZMEN

61	Columbia DB 4696	True Love/Black Bottom Stomp	5
61	Columbia SCD 2165	King Kong/Riverside Blues (with p/s)	5
62	Columbia DB 4822	Tavern In The Town/My Maryland	5
65	Columbia DB 7534	Alley Cat/Petite Fleur	5
61	Columbia 33SX 1290	TRAD PARADE (LP, with New Orleans Jazzmen, also stereo SCX 3354)	12
61	Columbia 33SX 1353	WORLD OF TRAD (LP)	15
62	Columbia 33SX 1449	LIGHTFOOT AT LANSDOWNE (LP)	12

LIGHTHOUSE

69	RCA RCA 1884	Eight Miles High/If There Ever Was A Time	7
70	RCA RCA 1982	The Chant (Nam Myo-Ho Renge' Kyo)/Could You Be Concerned	10
71	Vertigo 6073 150	Hats Off (To The Strangers)/Sing Sing Sing	12
72	Philips 6073 152	One Fine Morning/Little Kind Words	12
72	Philips 6073 153	Take It Slow/Sweet Lullaby	20
70	RCA SF 8103	SUITE FEELING (LP)	15
70	RCA SF 8121	PEACING IT ALL TOGETHER (LP)	12
71	Vertigo 6342 010	ONE FINE MORNING (LP, gatefold sleeve, swirl label)	80
71	Vertigo 6342 011	THOUGHTS OF MOVIN' ON (LP, gatefold sleeve, swirl label)	80

LIGHTNIN' SLIM

(see also Slim Harpo)

72	Blue Horizon 2096 013	Just A Little Bit/You're Old Enough To Understand/Mind Your Own Business	30
65	Stateside SL 10135	A LONG DRINK OF BLUES (LP, with Slim Harpo)	70
69	Python PLP 8	THE DOWNHOME BLUES PART 1 (LP, 99 copies only)	60
70	Blue Horizon 7-63863	ROOSTER BLUES (LP)	85
72	Blue Horizon 2931 005	LONDON GUMBO (LP)	130
78	Flyright FLYLP 533	TRIP TO CHICAGO (LP)	18
79	Flyright FLYLP 583	THE FEATURE SIDES 1954 (LP)	15
80	Flyright FLYLP 612	WE GOTTA ROCK TONIGHT (LP)	18

MINT VALUE £

LIGHTNING LEON

60s	Jan & Dil JR 450	DOWN HOME BLUES - SIXTIES STYLE (EP)	35

LIGHTNING RAIDERS
(see also Pink Fairies, Professionals)

80	Arista ARIST 341	Psychedelik Musik ('adult' version)/Views (p/s)	18
80	Arista ARIST 341DJ	Psychedelik Musik ('censored' version)/Views (promo only, no p/s)	35
81	Revenge REVS 200	Criminal World/Citizens (p/s)	10
81	Revenge RSS 39	Sweet Revenge/Rowdies/Addiction/Soul Rescue (12", promo only)	45

LIGOTAGE

84	Picasso PIKM005	FORGIVE AND FORGET (LP, lyric insert)	15

LIKE A SONG

73	De Wolfe DW/LP 3273	LIKE A SONG (LP, library issue)	18

LIL LOUIS

89	Rough TOUGH 4	Frequency (Remix) (12", 3,000 copies)	15

LILAC TIME
(see also Hawks, Stephen Duffy)

88	Swordfish LILAC 1	Return To Yesterday/Trumpets From Montparnasse (no p/s)	8
88	Swordfish 12 LILAC 1	Return To Yesterday/Railway Bazaar/Trumpets From Montparnasse/ Reunion Ball (12", p/s)	12
88	Fontana LILCD 2	Return To Yesterday/Rooftrees/Gone For A Burton/ Reunion Ball (CD, card sleeve)	12
88	Fontana LILCD 3	You've Got To Love/Railway Bazaar/Trumpets From Montparnasse (CD, card sleeve)	8
88	Fontana LILAC 4	Black Velvet/Black Dawn (p/s in Xmas card folder)	5
88	Fontana LILCD 4	Black Velvet/Tiger Tea/Street Corner/Black Dawn (CD)	8
89	Fontana LILCD 5	American Eyes/Shepherd's Plaid/The World In Her Arms/ Crossing The Line (CD)	8
89	Fontana LILCD 6	The Days Of The Week/The Queen Of Heartless/Spin A Cavalu (CD)	8
89	Fontana LILCD 7	The Girl Who Waves At Trains/If The Stars Shine Tonight (Acoustic Version)/ Ounce Of Nails/American Eyes (Acoustic Version) (CD)	8
90	Caff CAFF 12	Madresfield/Bird On The Wire (p/s, with insert)	25
88	Swordfish SWF LP 6	THE LILAC TIME (LP, original issue)	15
88	Swordfish SWF CD 6	THE LILAC TIME (CD, original issue)	40

LILIPUT
(see also Kleenex)

80	Rough Trade RT 047	Spilt/Die Matrosen (p/s)	8
81	Rough Trade RT 062	Eisiger Wind/When The Cat's Away Then The Mice Will Play	10

BEATRICE LILLIE

61	Decca F 11377	Typically English/Mr Perfect	6
56	Brunswick OE 9091	PRESENTING (EP)	8
61	Decca DFE 6697	WHAT'S NEW WITH BEA LILLIE? (EP)	8

LILYS

96	Che CHE 51	Returns Every Morning/Touch The Water (white vinyl, p/s, 500 only)	6
96	Che CHE 65	A Nanny In Manhattan/More Than Is Deserved (coffee-coloured vinyl, p/s, 500 only)	6

LIMELIGHT
(see also Brinsley Schwarz)

75	United Artists UP 35779	I Should Have Known Better/Tell Me Why	12

LIMELIGHT

80	Future Earth FER 006	Metal Man/Hold Me Touch Me (p/s)	12
82	Future Earth FER 010	Ashes To Ashes/Knife In Your Back (p/s, with insert)	12
82	Future Earth FER 010	Ashes To Ashes/Knife In Your Back (p/s, some with insert)	10
80	Future Earth FER 008	LIMELIGHT (LP)	22
81	Avatar AALP 5005	LIMITED LIMELIGHT (LP, with bonus single)	20
81	Avatar AALP 5005	LIMITED LIMELIGHT (LP)	15
84	Mausoleum SKULL 9309	ASHES TO ASHES (LP)	12

LIMELITERS
(see also Glenn Yarbrough)

62	RCA RD/SF 7513	SING OUT (LP)	12

LIMEYS

65	Pye 7N 15820	I Can't Find My Way Through/Don't Cry (My Love)	8
65	Pye 7N 15909	Some Tears Fall Dry/Half Glass Of Wine	8
66	Decca F 12382	Cara-Lin/Feel So Blue	30
66	Decca F 12466	The Mountain's High/Lovin' Yourself	8

LIMIT

78	Private Stock PVT 156	Please Please Me/My World At Night (company sleeve)	30

LIMMIE

78	Psycho P 2604	Saturday Night's The Night/Party	50

PETER LINCOLN
(see also Peter Sarstedt, Sarstedt Brothers, Brothers Kane)

67	Major Minor MM 520	In The Day Of My Youth/My Monkey Is A Junkie	30

PHILAMORE LINCOLN

68	NEMS 56-3711	Running By The River/Rainy Day	60
70	CBS 5007	The County Jail Band/You're The One	30

LINCOLN TURNPIKE

71	Polydor 2058109	Green On The Other Side Of The Mountain/You Can Call Everybody Your Friend	8

LINCOLN X

63	Oriole CB 1823	Heartaches And Happiness/Stand In For Her Past	5

MINT VALUE £

LINCOLNS

66	Parlophone R 5418	Mister Loneliness/Only Love Will Break Your Heart	6

BOB LIND

66	Fontana TF 670	Elusive Butterfly/Cheryl's Goin' Home	5
66	Fontana (S)TL 5340	DON'T BE CONCERNED (LP)	15
66	Verve F'ways (S)VLP 5015	THE ELUSIVE BOB LIND (LP)	15

LINDA & FUNKY BOYS

76	Spark SRL 1149	Climbing The Steps Of Love/Baby Are You Satisfied	8

ROSA LINDA

53	London L 1215	Flight 88/Taboo (78)	12

DADDY LINDBERG

(see also Crocheted Doughnut Ring, Fingers)

67	Columbia DB 8138	Shirl/Wade In The Shade	120

ANITA LINDBLOM

62	Fontana 267223 TF	Uptown/Mr Big Wheel	10

DENNIS LINDE

73	Elektra K 42149	DENNIS LINDE (LP)	12
74	Elektra K 52013	TRAPPED IN THE SUBURBS (LP)	12

KATHY LINDEN

58	Felsted AF 102	Billy/If I Could Hold You In My Arms	8
58	Felsted AF 105	You'd Be Surprised/Why Oh Why	8
58	Felsted AF 108	Oh! Johnny, Oh! Johnny Oh!/Georgie	10
58	Felsted AF 111	Kissin' Conversation/Just A Sandy Haired Boy Called Sandy	8
59	Felsted AF 122	Goodbye Jimmy, Goodbye/Heartaches At Sweet Sixteen	6
59	Felsted AF 124	So Close To My Heart/You Don't Know Girls	8
60	Felsted AF 130	Think Love/Mary Lou Wilson And Johnny Brown	8
59	Felsted GEP 1001	KATHY (EP)	15
59	Felsted GEP 1002	KATHY'S IN LOVE VOLUME ONE (EP)	15
59	Felsted GEP 1004	KATHY'S IN LOVE VOLUME TWO (EP)	12

LINDISFARNE

(see also Alan Hull, Jack The Lad, Chosen Few, Radiator, Ray Jackson)

70	Charisma CB 137	Clear White Light Part II/Knackers Yard Blues	12
71	Charisma CB 153	Lady Eleanor/Nothing But The Marvellous Is Beautiful (with p/s)	8
71	Charisma CB 153	Lady Eleanor/Nothing But The Marvellous Is Beautiful	5
70	Charisma CAS 1025	NICELY OUT OF TUNE (LP, pink 'scroll' label)	25
70	Charisma CAS 1025	NICELY OUT OF TUNE (LP, 'mad hatter' label)	12
71	Charisma CAS 1050	FOG ON THE TYNE (LP, gatefold sleeve, pink 'scroll' label)	20
71	Charisma CAS 1050	FOG ON THE TYNE (LP, gatefold sleeve, later 'Mad Hatter' label)	12
72	Charisma CAS 1057	DINGLY DELL (LP, with inner sleeve & poster)	12

JIMMY LINDSAY

77	Black Swan BS 8	Easy/FABIAN: Prophecy (12")	15
78	Music Hive MH002	Ain't No Sunshine/EXODUS : Take Six/DIMBALA : And Ting (12")	30
82	Music Hive MH004	Turn Out The Lights/Dole Queue (12")	30

MARK LINDSAY

(see also Paul Revere & Raiders)

69	CBS 4699	Arizona/Man From Houston	10
70	CBS 5055	Silver Bird/So Hard To Leave You	8
70	CBS 5219	And The Grass Won't Pay No Mind/Funny How Little Men Care	8
71	CBS 5408	Problem Child/Bookends	8
71	CBS 7330	Been Too Long On The Road/All I Really See Is You	8
71	CBS 7551	Are You Old Enough/Don't You Know	8
71	CBS 7690	Something Big/Pretty Pretty	8

TERRY LINDSEY

69	President PT 232	It's Over/One Day Up, Next Day Down	15

DAVID LINDUP ORCHESTRA

66	Columbia DB 7979	Informer Theme/Blue Mountain	10
66	Polydor 56106	Survival Theme/New Forest	20
70	Aristocrat AR 1021	WHEN THE SAINTS GO (LP)	20

LINDYS

60	Decca F 11253	The Train Of Love/You Know How Things Get Around	15
60	Decca F 11272	Boy With The Eyes Of Blue/Someone Else's Roses	15

LINES

78	Linear SJP 782	White Night/Barbican (p/s)	7
79	Illegal ILS 0011	White Night/Barbican (p/s, reissue)	5
80	Red Linear RL 007	Nerve Pylon/Over The Brow (screen-printed p/s)	5
80s	Red Linear RL12 005	COOL SNAP EP (12")	15

LING FAMILY

77	Topic 12TS 292	SINGING TRADITIONS OF A SUFFOLK FAMILY (LP)	12

BUZZY LINHART

72	Kama Sutra 2013049	You Got What It Takes/Tell Me True	5
69	Philips SBL 7885	BUZZY (LP, laminated gatefold sleeve, black/silver labels)	40
71	Kama Sutra 2319011	THE TIME TO LIVE IS NOW (LP, textured gatefold sleeve, yellow/red labels)	25

LINK

(see also Reload, Global Communications, Mystic Institute)

92	Evolution EVO 05	THE FIRST LINK EP (12", plain sleeve)	30
93	Symbiotic SYM 001	THE LINK EP (12", plain sleeve, no credits on label)	8
95	Warp WAP 59	ANTACID EP (12", p/s)	15
95	Warp WAP 59R	ANTACID REMIXES EP (12", p/s as Link & E621)	10

MINT VALUE £

LINKERS
(see also Links)
71 Big Shot BI 567 Bongo Man/FUD CHRISTIAN ALLSTARS: Creation Version 6

ANSEL LINKERS & FUD CHRISTIAN ALL STARS
(see also Links)
73 Summit SUM 8540 Memories By The Score/FUD CHRISTIAN ALL STARS: Scorer 7

LINKS
72 Tropical AL 0010 Sing A Song Of Freedom/TROPICAL ALL STARS: Love Rhythm (A-side actually by Linkers) 6

LINN COUNTY
68 Mercury SMCL 20142 PROUD FLESH SOOTHSEER (LP) 25
69 Mercury SMCL 20165 FEVER SHOT (LP) 20
70 Philips SBL 7923 TILL THE BREAK OF DAWN (LP) 18

ELMO LINN
63 Starlite ST45 101 Another Man's Arms/Sam Houston 18

LINOLEUM
96 Lino Vinyl LINO 001 Dissent/Twisted (lino sleeve, sealed, 1,000 only) 10
96 Lino Vinyl LINO 001 Dissent/Twisted (lino sleeve, unsealed, 1,000 only) 7
96 Lino Vinyl LINO 002 Smear/Tired (lino sleeve, sealed, 2,000 only) 7
96 Lino Vinyl LINO 002 Smear/Tired (lino sleeve, unsealed, 2,000 only) 5

JOE LINTHECOME
50s Poydras 87 Pretty Mama Blues/Hummingbird Blues 15

LION (& His Calypso Cubs)
51 Sagomes SG 117 Ugly Woman/The Lost Watch (78) 10
52 Parlophone MP 114 Mary Ann/Little Mary Had No Lamb (export 78) 10
52 Parlophone MP 115 Tick! Tick!/Ugly Woman (export 78) 10
53 Melodisc 1236 Coronation Of Elizabeth 2/Crosby Cavalcade (78, with Caribbean Rhythm) 10
54 Parlophone MP 129 The Royal Tour/The Weather Man (export 78) 10
54 Parlophone MP 132 I Ain't Gonna Do It No More/Trinidad, The Land Of Calypso (export 78) 10
55 Parlophone MP 135 Bananas/The Devil Fly (export 78, with His Calypso Cubs) 10

LIONHEART
(see also Iron Maiden, Wildfire)
85 Epic A 5001 Die For Love/Dangerous Games (p/s) 7
84 Epic EPC26214 HOT TONIGHT (LP) 12

LIONROCK
92 M.E.R.C. 002 Roots'n'Culture (Part One)/Lionrock (12", original issue) 10
92 De Construction 74321124381 Lionrock - The Remixes: (Most Excellent Mix)/ (Roots 'n' Culture)/ (A Trumpet Jamboree In Edinburgh)/(A Dubtastic Jamboree In Edinburgh) (12") 10
93 De Construction 74321144371 Packet Of Peace (Prankster Sound System Mix)/(Instrumental)/ (No More Fucking Trumpets) (12") 8
93 Distort & Cavort Dub Plate No. 1 (12") 10
94 De Construction DUB PLATE 1 The Guide/Don't Be Foolish (12") 8
98 Concrete HARD 3112 Rude Boy Rock/Best Foot Forward/Push Button Cocktail (p/s) 8

LIONS
69 Polydor 56757 Twisted Nerve/My Friend The Blackbird 30

LIONS (JAMAICA)
77 Truth & Right L 001 Natty Congo 1/Version 12

LIONS OF JUDAH
69 Fontana TF 1016 Our Love's A Growin' Thing/Katja 20

LION TAMERS
68 Polydor 56283 Speak Your Mind/Light 30

LION YOUTH
81 Virgo Stomach VG104 Rat Cut A Bottle/Rub A Dub (12") 15
81 Virgo Stomach VGLP 001 LOVE COMES AND GOES (LP) 18

LIP MOVES
79 Tichonderoga HP 1 Guest/What Is (p/s with insert, stickered white labels, signed) 35
79 Tichonderoga HP 1 Guest/What Is (p/s with insert, stickered white labels) 30

JOE LIPMAN ORCHESTRA
54 MGM SP 1108 Looking Back To See/Stop 5

LIQUID CRYSTAL
91 Bizarre BIZZ 2 Inner Sense/Dischord (12") 25
92 Bizarre BIZZ 3 The Power Within/Let It Go/Inner Sense ('92 remix) (12") 25
92 Bizarre BIZZ 3R T The Power Within (remix)/Radiate/Inner Sense (original) (12", p/s) 25
92 Ruff On Wax ROWT 1 CHROMATIC EP(12", stickered plain sleeve) 70
92 Ruff On Wax ROWTR 1 CHROMATIC 2 EP: (12", stickered plain sleeve) 60

LIQUID SMOKE
75 Pye Int. 7N 25677 Dance Dance Dance/Where Is Our Love 8
70 Avco Embassy 646 6003 LIQUID SMOKE (LP) 25

DAVID LISBON
61 Philips PB 1136 Deer Stalker/Almost Grown Up 7
61 Philips PB 1163 Joy Ride/Swiss Miss 7
61 Philips BBE 12469 LIKE LISBON (EP) 8

LISTEN
(see also Robert Plant, Led Zeppelin)
65 CBS 202456 You'd Better Run/Everybody's Gonna Say 250

MONI LITER ORCHESTRA
61 Fontana H 295 Willow Waltz/Girl Form Corsica 6

MINT VALUE £

LITTER

69	Probe CLPS 4504	EMERGE (LP)	60

'BIG' TINY LITTLE

57	Vogue Coral Q 72263	School Day/That's The Only Way To Live	40
57	Vogue Coral Q 72263	School Day/That's The Only Way To Live (78)	20
60	Coral FEP 2058	HONKY TONK PIANO VOL. 1 (EP)	10
60	Coral FEP 2059	HONKY TONK PIANO VOL. 2 (EP)	10

KENNY LITTLE & LITTLE PEOPLE

65	United Artists UP 1074	A Shot In The Dark/Never On A Sunday	5

SHARON LITTLE

78	One Love (no number)	Don't Mash Up Creation/Version (12")	80

LITTLE ANGELS

87	Little Angels LAN 001	LITTLE ANGELS '87 (12" EP)	30
89	Polydor LTLCD 2	THE BIG BAD EP (CD)	10
87	Powerstation AMP 14	TOO POSH TO MOSH (mini-LP)	18

LITTLE ANN

98	Kent TOWN 111	What Should I Do/O.C. TALBOT: I'm Shooting High (I Reach For The Sky)	15
99	Kent TOWN 112	Who Are You Trying To Fool/I Got To Have You	20

LITTLE ANTHONY & IMPERIALS

58	London HLH 8704	Tears On My Pillow/Two People In The World	50
58	London HLH 8704	Tears On My Pillow/Two People In The World (78)	45
59	London HL 8848	So Much/Oh Yeah	50
59	London HL 8848	So Much/Oh Yeah (78)	40
59	Top Rank JAR 256	Shimmy, Shimmy, Ko-Ko Bop/I'm Still In Love With You	30
60	Top Rank JAR 366	My Empty Room/Bayou, Bayou, Baby	25
64	United Artists UP 1065	I'm On The Outside Looking In/Please Go	20
64	United Artists UP 1073	Goin' Out Of My Head/Make It Easy On Yourself	20
65	United Artists UP 1083	Hurt So Bad/Reputation	25
65	United Artists UP 1098	Take Me Back/Our Song	20
65	United Artists UP 1112	I Miss You/Get Out Of My Life	15
66	United Artists UP 1126	Hurt/Never Again	40
66	United Artists UP 1137	Better Use Your Head/The Wonder Of It All	80
66	United Artists UP 1137	Better Use Your Head/The Wonder Of It All (DJ copy)	150
66	United Artists UP 1151	Gonna Fix You Good (Every Time You're Bad)/You Better Take It Easy Baby	75
67	United Artists UP 1189	My Love Is A Rainbow/You Only Live Twice	8
68	United Artists UP 2260	Let The Sunshine In/The Gentle Rain (as Anthony & Imperials)	10
69	United Artists UP 35017	Anthem/Goodbye Goodtimes (as Anthony & Imperials)	8
72	United Artists UP 35345	Gonna Fix You Good (Every Time You're Bad)/ You Better Take It Easy Baby (reissue)	10
76	United Artists UP 36118	Better Use Your Head/Gonna Fix You Good (Every Time You're Bad)	10
76	United Artists REM 405	Goin' Out Of My Head/I'm On The Outside Looking In/Hurt So Bad/ Gonna Fix You Good (Every Time You're Bad)	10
65	United Artists UEP 1004	LITTLE ANTHONY AND THE IMPERIALS (EP)	140
64	United Artists ULP 1089	I'M ON THE OUTSIDE LOOKING IN (LP)	150
66	United Artists ULP 1100	GOIN' OUT OF MY HEAD (LP)	100

LITTLE ARCHIE

68	Atlantic 584 209	I Need You/I Am A Carpet	40

LITTLE BEAVER

72	President PTLS 1060	JOEY (LP)	25

LITTLE BEVERLEY

(see also Beverley Simmons)

68	Pama PM 731	What A Guy/You're Mine	5

LITTLE BIG HORN

70	Polydor 2058042	Another Man's Song/Just A Game	100

LITTLE BILL & BLUE NOTES

(see also Blue Notes)

59	Top Rank JAR 176	I Love An Angel/Bye, Bye Baby	25
59	Top Rank JAR 176	I Love An Angel/Bye, Bye Baby (78)	25

LITTLE BIRD

84	Magus MGB 1	Zola/Reaching Out For Gold (p/s)	5

LITTLE BO BITCH

79	Cobra COB 1	It's Only Love/I'm Confused (p/s)	5
80	Cobra COB 4	Take It Easy (Lights Out Over London)/Lorraine, Lorraine (p/s)	5
79	Cobra CBR 1002	LITTLE BO BITCH (LP)	12

LITTLE BOOTS

08	50 Bones 4BONES	Meddle/Meddle (Toddla T & Ross Orton Mix) (green vinyl with tattoo set, 500 only)	40

LITTLE BOY BLUE

69	Jackpot JP 701	Dark End Of The Street/MR VERSATILE: Apple Blossoms	15

LITTLE BROTHER

(see under Little Brother Grant)

LITTLE CLARKIE & THE OFFBEAT POSSE

86	Jah Tubbys JT 015	Selector Him Good/COLONEL MITE: Bless The Selector/ JAH TUBBY: Select The Rhythm (12")	80
86	Jah Tubbys JT 20	Live Stock Party/Bounty Hunter (12")	50
87	Y&D YDD 0107	Bubble-N-Rock/Cowboy Stylee (12")	50
88	Y&D YDD 0134	Can't Come A Dance And Stand Up/Never Give You Up (12")	30

MINT VALUE £

LITTLE DARLING

65 Blue Beat BB 325 — No One/BUSTER'S ALL STARS: Congo Revolution 120

LITTLE DARLINGS

65 Fontana TF 539 — Little Bit O' Soul/Easy To Cry 100

LITTLE DES

70 J-Dan JDN 4400 — Somebody's Baby/Spy Man 7

LITTLE DIPPERS

60 Pye International 7N 25051 — Forever/Two By Four 12
61 London HLG 9269 — Lonely/I Wonder, I Wonder, I Wonder 25

LITTLE ESTHER

(see under Little Esther Phillips)

LITTLE EVA

(see also Big Dee Irwin & Little Eva)

62 London HL 9581 — The Locomotion/He Is The Boy 8
62 London HLU 9633 — Keep Your Hands Off My Baby/Where Do I Go 8
63 London HLU 9687 — Let's Turkey Trot/Old Smokey Locomotion 8
63 Colpix PX 11013 — The Trouble With Boys/What I Gotta Do (To Make You Jealous) 12
63 Colpix PX 11019 — Please Hurt Me/Let's Start The Party Again 15
64 Colpix PX 11035 — Run To Her/Making With The Magilla 15
65 Stateside SS 477 — Stand By Me/That's My Man 18
82 London LOCOX1 — The Locomotion (Extended Version)/He Is The Boy/Keep Your Hands Off/ Let's Turkey Trot (12" p/s) 8
63 London HA-U 8036 — L-L-L-L-LOCO-MOTION (LP, original with plum label & laminated sleeve) 50
72 London SH-U 8437 — L-L-L-L-LOCO-MOTION (LP, stereo reissue, plum label, boxed label logo) 20

LITTLE FISH

72 Plant Life PLR 011 — HERTFORDSHIRE FOLK SONGS (LP, with insert) 50

LITTLE FOLK

71 Studio Republic CR 1001 — LEAVE THEM A FLOWER (LP) 18

LITTLE FRANKIE (& COUNTRY GENTLEMEN)

(see also Chimes featuring Denise)

65 Columbia DB 7490 — The Kind Of Boy You Can't Forget/I'm Not Gonna Do It 20
65 Columbia DB 7578 — Make-A-Love/Love Is Just A Game (with Country Gentlemen) 20
65 Columbia DB 7681 — It Doesn't Matter Anymore/Happy, That's Me 20

LITTLE FREDDY (McGregor)

(see also Freddie McGregor, Ernest Wilson)

70 Unity UN 551 — Why Did My Little Girl Cry/PETER AUSTIN: Change Partners 8

LITTLE FREE ROCK

(see also David John & Mood)

69 Transatlantic TRA 208 — LITTLE FREE ROCK (LP, laminated sleeve, white/lilac labels, 't' logo) 150

LITTLE GEORGE

64 Rio R 45 — Mary Anne/EDWARDS ALLSTARS: Blue Night 18

LITTLE GRANT

(see also Equals, Pyramids, Eddy Grant)

70 Torpedo TOR 27 — Baby Don't Let Me Down/Brother Strong Man 20

LITTLE GRANTS & EDDIE (Grant)

(see also Equals, Pyramids, Eddy Grant)

67 President PT 159 — Rudy's Dead/Everything's Alright 10
67 President PT 172 — Rock Steady '67/Bingo 7

LITTLE HANK

66 London HLU 10090 — Mr. Bang Bang Man/Don't You Know (withdrawn) 150
66 London HLU 10090 — Mr. Bang Bang Man/Don't You Know (withdrawn) (DJ copy) 150
70 Monument MON 1045 — Mr. Bang Bang Man/Don't You Know (reissue) 15

LITTLE HOWIE

85 Look to Africa LTAF 03 — Original Love Me/EARL ANTHONY Sensi Man Rock (12") 70

LITTLE JOE (Jamaica)

(see also Sexy Girls)

70 Torpedo TOR 15 — Bad Blood/Maxi-Mini War 6

LITTLE JOE (& THRILLERS)

57 Philips PB 759 — Peanuts/Lilly Lou (78) 15
60 Fontana H 281 — Stay (as Little Joe & Thrillers)/Cherry 25
63 Reprise R 20142 — Peanuts/No No I Can't Stop 20

LITTLE JOEY & FLIPS

62 Pye International 7N 25152 — Bongo Stomp/Lost Love 12

LITTLE JOHN

(see also John Holt)

67 Pama PM 702 — Let's Get Married/Around The World 6
70 Unity UN 561 — No Love/A Little Tear (both sides actually by John Holt) 8
84 Greensleeves GRELD 139 — Form A Line/YELLOWMAN: Rub & Go Down (12") 15

LITTLE JOHN

84 Vista VSLP 4061 — UNITE (LP) 20

LITTLE JOHN & BILLY BOYO

82 Greensleeves GRELD 86 — Connection/BILLY BOYO: Little Girl (12") 18
82 Greensleeves GRELD 92 — Janet Sinclair/Agony Column Dub (12") 25

LITTLE JOHNNY & THREE TEENAGERS

58 Decca F 10990 — Baby Lover/Rickety Rackety Rendezvous 20

MINT VALUE £

LITTLE KIRK

70s	Ruddys RM 004	Ghetto People Broke/Version (12")	30
70s	Ruddys RM 001	Weed Them Out/Version (12")	50

LITTLE LEMMY & BIG JOE

58	Decca F 11054	Little Lemmy Kwela/Kwela No. 5 (78)	10

LITTLE LULU

72	FAB FAB 21	Love & Obey/AL CAMPBELL & FREDDIE MCGREGOR: Free Man	200

LITTLE LUMAN

64	Rio R 44	Hurry Harry/R. ALPHONSE: Hucklebuck (B-side actually by Roland Alphonso)	15

LITTLE LUTHER

64	Pye International 7N 25266	Eenie Meenie Minie Moe/Twirl	70

LITTLE MACK & BOSS SOUNDS

66	Atlantic 584 031	In The Midnight Hour/You Can't Love Me (In The Midnight Hour)	10

MARIE LITTLE

71	Argo ZFB 19	FACTORY GIRL (LP)	150
73	Trailer LER 2084	MARIE LITTLE (LP)	50
87	private pressing	MY ELDORADO (LP)	12

LITTLE MILTON

65	Pye International 7N 25289	Blind Man/Blues In The Night	15
65	Chess CRS 8013	We're Gonna Make It/Can't Hold Back The Tears	15
65	Chess CRS 8013	We're Gonna Make It/Can't Hold Back The Tears (demo copy)	35
65	Chess CRS 8018	Who's Cheating Who?/Ain't No Big Deal On You	15
66	Sue WI 4021	Early In The Morning/Bless Your Heart (actually by Roy Milton)	40
69	Chess CRS 8087	Grits Ain't Groceries/I Can't Quit You Baby	25
69	Chess CRS 8100	Let's Get Together/I'll Always Love You	15
72	Stax 2025 095	That's What Love Will Make You Do/I'm Living Off The Love You Give	8
74	Stax STXS 2003	Behind Closed Doors/Bet You I Win	8
75	Stax STA 100	If That Ain't A Reason/Mr. Mailman	6
69	Chess CRLS 4552	GRITS AIN'T GROCERIES (LP)	80
72	Chess 6310 120	GOLDEN DECADE (LP)	15
74	Stax STX 1013	BLUES 'N' SOUL (LP)	25

LITTLE NELL

75	A&M AMS 7351	Do The Swim/Stilettos And Lipstick/Tropical Isle (red vinyl, p/s)	8

LITTLE RICHARD

(see also Canned Heat, Sister Rosetta Tharpe, Buck Ram's Ramrocks)

78s

56	London HLO 8336	Rip It Up/Ready Teddy	18
57	London HLO 8366	Long Tall Sally/Tutti Frutti	18
57	London HLO 8382	The Girl Can't Help It/She's Got It	18
57	London HLO 8446	Lucille/Send Me Some Lovin' (as Little Richard & His Band)	18
57	London HLO 8470	Jenny, Jenny/Miss Ann (as Little Richard & His Band)	18
57	London HLO 8509	Keep A Knockin'/Can't Believe You Wanna Leave	15
58	London HLU 8560	Good Golly Miss Molly/Hey-Hey-Hey-Hey	25
58	London HLO 8647	Ooh! My Soul/True, Fine Mama	30
58	London HLU 8770	Baby Face/I'll Never Let You Go	20
59	London HLU 8831	By The Light Of The Silvery Moon/Early One Morning	30
59	London HLU 8868	Kansas City/She Knows How To Rock	60
60	London HLU 9065	Baby/I Got It	100

SINGLES

56	London HLO 8336	Rip It Up/Ready Teddy (gold label print)	150
56	London HLO 8336	Rip It Up/Ready Teddy (later pressing with silver label print)	50
50s	London HLO 8336	Rip It Up/Ready Teddy (repressing, silver-top label, round centre)	25
57	London HLO 8366	Long Tall Sally/Tutti Frutti (gold label print)	150
57	London HLO 8366	Long Tall Sally/Tutti Frutti (later silver label print)	40
50s	London HLO 8366	Long Tall Sally/Tutti Frutti (repressing, silver-top label, round centre)	20
57	London HLO 8382	The Girl Can't Help It/She's Got It (gold label print)	150
57	London HLO 8382	The Girl Can't Help It/She's Got It (later silver label print)	40
50s	London HLO 8382	The Girl Can't Help It/She's Got It (repressing, silver-top label, round centre)	20
57	London HLO 8446	Lucille/Send Me Some Lovin' (as Little Richard & His Band)	30
57	London HLO 8470	Jenny, Jenny/Miss Ann (as Little Richard & His Band)	30
57	London HLO 8509	Keep A Knockin'/Can't Believe You Wanna Leave	30
58	London HLU 8560	Good Golly Miss Molly/Hey-Hey-Hey-Hey	30
58	London HLO 8647	Ooh! My Soul/True, Fine Mama	15
58	London HLU 8770	Baby Face/I'll Never Let You Go	10
59	London HLU 8831	By The Light Of The Silvery Moon/Early One Morning	10
59	London HLU 8868	Kansas City/She Knows How To Rock	15

(The above 45s were originally issued with triangular centres; later round-centres are worth around half to two-thirds these values.)

60	London HLU 9065	Baby/I Got It	15
61	Mercury AMT 1165	Joy Joy Joy (Down In My Heart)/He's Not Just A Soldier	8
62	Mercury AMT 1189	He Got What He Wanted (But He Lost What He Had)/ Why Don't You Change Your Ways?	10
63	London HLK 9708	Crying In The Chapel/Hole In The Wall	8
63	London HLK 9756	Travelin' Shoes/It Is No Secret	8
64	London HL 9896	Bama Lama Bama Loo/Annie's Back	10
64	Fontana TF 519	Blueberry Hill/Cherry Red	10
64	Stateside SS 340	Whole Lotta Shakin' Goin' On/Goodnight Irene	10
64	Mercury MF 841	Joy, Joy, Joy (Down In My Heart)/Peace In The Valley	10
66	Fontana TF 652	I Don't Know What You've Got But It's Got Me (Parts 1 & 2)	30
66	Stateside SS 508	Holy Mackeral/Baby, Don'tcha Want A Man Like Me?	20
66	Sue WI 4001	Without Love/Dance What You Wanna	40
66	Sue WI 4015	It Ain't Watcha Do (It's The Way How You Do It)/Crossover	40

MINT VALUE £

66	Columbia DB 7974	Poor Dog/Well	25
66	Columbia DB 8058	I Need Love/The Commandments Of Love	20
67	Columbia DB 8116	Get Down With It/Rose Mary	25
67	Columbia DB 8240	A Little Bit Of Something/Money	50
67	Columbia DB 8240	A Little Bit Of Something/Money (DJ copy)	75
67	Columbia DB 8263	I Don't Want To Discuss It/Hurry Sundown	50
67	Columbia DB 8263	I Don't Want To Discuss It/Hurry Sundown (DJ copy)	85
68	MCA MU 1006	She's Together/Try Some Of Mine	10
68	London HLU 10194	Good Golly Miss Molly/Lucille	10
68	President PT 201	Whole Lotta Shakin' Goin' On/Lawdy Miss Clawdy	8
69	Action ACT 4528	Baby What Do You Want Me To Do (Parts 1 & 2)	10
70	Reprise RS 20907	Dew Drop In/Freedom Blues	10
71	President PT 329	Without Love/Talkin' 'Bout Soul	5
71	Reprise K 14124	Green Power/Dancing In The Street	10
72	Reprise K 14150	Money Is/Money Runner	5

EXPORT SINGLES

57	London HL 7022	Jenny, Jenny/Miss Ann (as Little Richard & His Band)	30
58	London HL 7049	Ooh! My Soul/True, Fine Mama	15
58	London HL 7056	Baby Face/I'll Never Let You Go	15
59	London HL 7074	She Knows How To Rock/Early One Morning	20
59	London HL 7079	By The Light Of The Silvery Moon/Kansas City	20
59	London HL 7085	Whole Lotta Shakin' Goin' On/All Around The World	40
68	Decca AD 1006	She's Together/Try Some Of Mine	25

EPs

57	London RE-O 1071	LITTLE RICHARD AND HIS BAND VOL. 1 (gold tri-centre)	50
57	London RE-O 1071	LITTLE RICHARD AND HIS BAND VOL. 1 (later silver label)	30
57	London RE-O 1074	LITTLE RICHARD AND HIS BAND VOL. 2 (lgold tri-centre)	40
57	London RE-O 1074	LITTLE RICHARD AND HIS BAND VOL. 2 (later silver label)	20
57	London RE-O 1103	LITTLE RICHARD AND HIS BAND VOL. 3	30
57	London RE-O 1106	LITTLE RICHARD AND HIS BAND VOL. 4	30
59	London RE-U 1208	LITTLE RICHARD AND HIS BAND VOL. 5	30
60	London RE-U 1234	LITTLE RICHARD AND HIS BAND VOL. 6	40
60	London RE-U 1235	LITTLE RICHARD AND HIS BAND VOL. 7	45

(The above EPs were originally issued with triangular centres; later round-centre pressings are worth two-thirds of silver values.)

62	Summit LSE 2049	FOUR DYNAMIC NUMBERS (2 each by Little Richard & Brock Peters)	10
63	London REK 1400	HE'S BACK	40
64	Vocalion VEP 170155	MEMPHIS SLIM AND LITTLE RICHARD	80
66	Stateside SE 1042	DO YOU FEEL IT	50

LPs

57	London HA-O 2055	HERE'S LITTLE RICHARD (flipback, rear sleeve in gloss red)	100
57	London HA-O 2055	HERE'S LITTLE RICHARD (flipback)	50
57	London HA-O 2055	HERE'S LITTLE RICHARD (small flipback sleeve)	55
57	London HA-O 2055	HERE'S LITTLE RICHARD (non-flipback sleeve)	35
58	London HA-U 2126	LITTLE RICHARD VOL. 2 (flipback sleeve)	75
58	London HA-U 2126	LITTLE RICHARD VOL. 2 (non-flipback sleeve)	40
59	RCA Camden CDN 125	LITTLE RICHARD (8 tracks only; others by Buck Ram Orchestra, picture of Richard in "frame" on sleeve, brown wooden effect is first pressing)	25
59	London HA-U 2193	THE FABULOUS LITTLE RICHARD (flipback sleeve)	75
59	London HA-U 2193	THE FABULOUS LITTLE RICHARD (non-flipback sleeve)	40
60	Top Rank 25/025	PRAY ALONG WITH LITTLE RICHARD VOL. 1: A CLOSER WALK WITH THEE (plain white sleeve, mail-order only)	40
60	Top Rank 25/026	PRAY ALONG WITH LITTLE RICHARD VOL. 2: I'M QUITTING SHOW BUSINESS (plain white sleeve, mail-order only)	80
64	Stateside SL 10054	SINGS GOSPEL	25
64	Coral LVA 9220	COMING HOME	25
65	Mercury MCL 20036	IT'S REAL	15
65	Fontana TL 5235	IS BACK!	25
67	Columbia SX/SCX 6136	THE EXPLOSIVE LITTLE RICHARD	40
68	Fontana SFL 13010	KING OF THE GOSPEL SINGERS	15
70	Reprise RSLP 6406	THE RILL THING	15

LITTLE ROOSTERS

(see also Cocksparrer, Alison Moyet)

79	Pye 7P 152	She Cat Sister Floozie/Roostering With Intent (p/s)	6
80	Ami AIS 101	That's How Strong My Love Is/Suspicious (p/s)	6
80	Ami AIS 107	I Need A Witness/The Age Of Reason (p/s)	6

LITTLE ROY

70	Bullet BU 445	Keep Trying/Version (actually by the Matadors)	10
81	Copasetic COP 5001	COLUMBUS SHIP (LP)	20

LITTLE ROYS

(see also Little Roy, Hippy Boys)

69	Camel CA 36	Bongonyah/CREATIONS: Dad Name (B-side actually "Bad Name")	10
70	Camel CA 42	Gold Digger (actually by Wailing Soul)/MATADORS: The Mine	15
70	Camel CA 57	Selassie Want Us Back/ROY AND JOY: Make It With You	10

LITTLE SAL with DANDY & SUPERBOYS

(see also Dandy & Superboys, Superboys)

68	Giant GN 19	I'm In The Mood/I'm A Lover	8

LITTLE SISTERS

63	MGM MGM 1192	Goin' To Boston/Where Does It Lead	7

LITTLE SONNY

71	Stax 2363 005	NEW KING OF THE BLUES HARMONICA (LP)	20

LITTLE SUZIE

61	Warner Bros WB 35	Young Love/The Boy I Left Behind	12

MINT VALUE £

LITTLE TONY

75	RCA 2638	Shakin' All Over/Together	6

LITTLE TONY & HIS BROTHERS

59	Durium DC 16639	Who's That Knockin'/The Beat	25
59	Durium DC 16639	Who's That Knockin'/The Beat (78)	40
59	Durium DC 16657	Four An' Twenty Thousand Kisses/Bella Marie	20
59	Decca F 11164	I Can't Help It/Arrivederci Baby	10
59	Decca F 11164	I Can't Help It/Arrivederci Baby (78)	60
59	Decca F 11169	The Hippy Hippy Shake/Hey Little Girl	10
59	Decca F 11169	The Hippy Hippy Shake/Hey Little Girl (78)	50
59	Decca F 11190	Too Good/Foxy Little Mama	8
59	Decca F 11190	Too Good/Foxy Little Mama (78)	50
60	Decca F 21218	I Love You/The Magic Of Love	8
60	Decca F 21223	Princess/I Love You	8
60	Decca F 21247	Teddy Girl/Kiss Me, Kiss Me	8
61	Durium DC 16657	Bella Marie/Four An' Twenty Thousand Kisses	8
66	Durium DRS 54008	Let Her Go/What Did I Do	8
67	Durium DRS 54012	Long Is The Lonely Night/People Talk To Me About You (as Little Tony)	8
58	Durium U 20058	PRESENTING LITTLE TONY AND HIS BROTHERS (EP)	40
65	Durium DRL 50006	I SUCCESSI DI LITTLE TONY (LP)	15

LITTLE WALTER

60	London HLM 9175	My Babe/Blue Midnight	50
64	Pye International 7N 25263	My Babe/You Better Watch Yourself	20
56	London RE-U 1061	LITTLE WALTER AND HIS JUKES (EP)	200
64	Pye Intl. NPL 28043	LITTLE WALTER (LP)	65
67	Chess CRL 4529	SUPER BLUES (LP, with Bo Diddley & Muddy Waters)	45
68	Marble Arch MAL 815	LITTLE WALTER (LP, reissue)	15
69	Python PLP-KM 20	LITTLE WALTER AND HIS DUKES (LP, 99 copies only)	55

LITTLE WILBUR (& PLEASERS)

(see also Wilbur Whitfield)

57	Vogue V 9091	Plaything/I Don't Care	500
57	Vogue V 9091	Plaything/I Don't Care (78)	100
58	Vogue V 9097	Heart To Heart/Alone In The Night (solo)	600
58	Vogue V 9097	Heart To Heart/Alone In The Night (solo) (78)	170

LITTLE WILLIE (Francis)

(see also Wilbert Francis & Vibrators)

63	Blue Beat BB 151	Settle Down/I'm Ashamed	8

LIVE HUMAN

98	Fat Cat 12FAT 005	IMPROVISESSIONS (12" EP, custom sleeve)	8
99	Fat Cat 12FAT 019	ORANGEBUSHMONKEYFLOWER (12" EP, custom sleeve)	8

LIVELY ONES

63	London HA 8082	SURF DRUMS (LP)	70
63	London HA 8107	SURF RIDER (LP, mono)	70
63	London SH 8107	SURF RIDER (LP, stereo)	85

LIVELY SET

65	Pye 7N 15880	Don't Call My Name/What Kind Of Love	6
66	Capitol CL 15472	Let The Trumpets Sound/The Green Years	6

LIVERPOOL ECHO

(see also Mandrake Paddle Steamers)

73	Spark	LIVERPOOL ECHO (LP)	20

LIVERPOOL EXPRESS

76	Warner Brothers K 56281	TRACKS (LP)	15

LIVERPOOL F.C.

78	Logo GO 339	Hail To The Kop/We Are Liverpool (p/s)	5
80	no label	Liverpool's FA Cup Finals (gold flexi)	10
83	Mean MEAN 102	Liverpool We're Never Gonna Stop/Liverpool Anthem (red vinyl)	5
77	State STAT 50	LIVERPOOL FOOTBALL TEAM 76/77 (EP)	10
65	Seddon SED 100	EE AYE ADDIO: SEVENTY YEARS WAITING (LP)	50
84	Extra-Terrestrial KOP 1	CONQUERING LIONS OF ANFIELD (LP, picture disc, gatefold sleeve, with booklet, stickers & photographs)	25

LIVERPOOL F.C. & LIVERPOOL SUPPORTERS

72	Penny Farthing PEN 794	Sing A Song For Liverpool/Liverpool, Liverpool	8

LIVERPOOL FISHERMEN

71	Mushroom 150 MR 9	SWALLOW THE ANCHOR (LP)	50

LIVERPOOL SCENE

(see also Clayton Squares, Adrian Henri, Brian Patten, Mike Hart, Andy Roberts, Grimms)

68	RCA RCA 1762	Son Son/Baby	6
69	RCA RCA 1816	The Woo-Woo/Love Is	6
67	CBS BPG 63045	THE INCREDIBLE NEW LIVERPOOL SCENE (LP)	40
68	RCA SF 7995	THE AMAZING ADVENTURES OF THE LIVERPOOL SCENE (LP)	20
68	RCA SF 7995	THE AMAZING ADVENTURES OF THE LIVERPOOL SCENE (LP, unlaminated cover)	20
69	RCA SF 8057	BREAD ON THE NIGHT (LP)	20
70	RCA SF 8100	ST. ADRIAN AND CO. BROADWAY & 3RD (LP)	20
70	RCA SF 8134	HEIRLOON (LP)	20
72	Charisma CS 3	RECOLLECTIONS (LP)	12

LIVERPOOL SPINNERS

(see also Spinners [U.K.])

61	Topic TOP 69	SONGS SPUN IN LIVERPOOL (EP)	10

RICKY LIVID & TONE DEAFS

(see also Bill Oddie)

64	Parlophone R 5136	Tomorrow/Nuts And Bolts	8

MINT VALUE £

LIVING DAYLIGHTS
(see also Greatest Show On Earth, Naturals)
67 Philips BF 1561 Let's Live For Today/I'm Real (B-side actually titled "It's Real") 40
67 Philips BF 1613 Always With Him/Baila Maria 40

LIVING DAYLIGHTS
79 E.S.R. S/79/CUS 523 HEARTSTOP EP (Personality Changes/Outdoor Girl/Don't Fit/ Let Me Know (331/3, die-cut p/s, also listed as ESR 3) 45

DANDY LIVINGSTONE
72 Horse HOSS 16 Suzanne Beware Of The Devil/Right On Brother 6
80 Mint Music MMD2 Fever/Righteous Man (12") 40
72 Trojan TRLS 45 DANDY LIVINGSTONE (LP) 12

J C LIVINGSTONE
73 Penny Farthing Pen 808 Let's Spend The Summer Together/Viva La Eva 6
73 Penny Farthing P 824 Momma Was A Steamroller Lady/Oo La La Me 25

R D LIVINGSTONE
76 B&C CB 291 Roots Man/Mo' Roots 10

LIZA & JET SET
(see also Liza Strike, Jet Set)
65 Parlophone R 5248 How Can I Know?/Dancing Yet 15

LIZZARD
76 Attack ATT 8130 Fight Down/Jah Jah Bless I 8
76 Black Wax WAX 14 Satta I/I And Eye 10

LIZZIE & DELROY WILSON
71 Jackpot JP 771 Double Attack/AGGRAVATORS: The Sniper 8

LIZZY
70 Harry J HJ 6625 More Heartaches/HARRY J ALL STARS: Version 8
70 Pressure Beat PB 5508 Ten Feet Tall (actually "Wear You From The Ball"/ JOE GIBBS & DESTROYERS: Chapter (actually "Harmony Hall" by Mr Nigel) 10
73 Duke DU 161 Love Is A Treasure/FREDDIE McKAY: Love Is A Treasure 7

LIZZY & DENNIS (Alcapone)
70 Ackee ACK 114 Happy Go Lucky Girl/BOBBY & DAVE: Sammy 12

LIZZY & PARAGONS
71 Ackee ACK 118 On The Beach/DAVE BARKER: Maria 15

LJ IV
(see also London Jazz Four)
69 CBS 63512 AN ELIZABETHAN SONGBOOK (LP) 150

LLAN
(see also Vogues)
66 CBS 202405 Realise/Anytime 40

BARRY LLEWELLYN
(see also Heptones, Sound Dimension)
73 Downtown DT 515 Meaning Of Life/MORWELL ESQ: Version Of Life 20

A.L. LLOYD
(see also Frankie Armstrong, Anne Briggs)
62 Topic TOP 71 A.L. LLOYD EWAN MACCOLL (EP) 12
57 Topic T7 A.L. LLOYD EWAN MACCOLL (8" LP with insert) 25
57 Topic T8 THE BLACK BALL LINE (8" EP, insert, with Ewan MacColl) 25
60 Topic 12T 51 OUTBACK BALLADS (LP, blue label) 40
64 Topic 12T 103 ENGLISH AND SCOTTISH FOLK BALLADS (LP, with Ewan MacColl, with blue label & booklet) 30
64 Topic 12T 103 ENGLISH AND SCOTTISH FOLK BALLADS (LP, with Ewan MacColl) 20
65 Topic 12T 135 BIRD IN THE BUSH (LP, with Anne Briggs & Frankie Armstrong, blue label) 75
66 Topic 12T 118 FIRST PERSON (LP, blue label) 30
67 Topic 12T 174 LEVIATHAN! (LP, blue label with booklet) 35

A.L. LLOYD & MARTYN WYNDHAM-READ
(see also Ewan MacColl, Peggy Seeger, Martin Wyndham-Read)
71 Topic 12TS 203 THE GREAT AUSTRALIAN LEGEND (LP, blue label with booklet) 65

CHARLES LLOYD (QUARTET)
67 Atlantic 584 125 Sombrero Sam (Parts 1 & 2) 5
66 Atlantic 588025 DREAMWEAVER (LP) 20
67 Atlantic 587/588 077 LOVE-IN (LP) 20
68 Atlantic 587/588 101 JOURNEY WITHIN (LP) 20
68 Atlantic 588 108 IN EUROPE (LP) 12
71 Atlantic 2400 108 IN THE SOVIET UNION (LP) 20

FRED LLOYD
65 Polydor BM 56055 Girl From Chelsea/You Kissed Him 8

IAN LLOYD
74 Kama Sutra KSS 702 Another Love/THE STORIES: Love Is In Motion 6

JIMMY LLOYD
(see also Jimmy Logsdon)
58 Philips PB 795 The Prince Of Players/Ever Since I Met Lucy 10
58 Philips PB 827 Witch Doctor/For Your Love 8
58 Philips PB 871 The End/Street In The Rain 6
59 Philips PB 909 I Kneel At Your Throne/Sapphire 12
59 Philips PB 978 That's Why I Dream/Take A Giant Step 8
60 Philips PB 1010 Teenage Sonata/Falling 8
60 Philips PB 1055 I Double Dare You/Just For A Thrill 8

			MINT VALUE £
61	Philips PB 1120	Pony Time/Three Handed Woman	10
61	Philips PB 1201	I'm Coming Home/You Are My Sunshine	5
62	Philips 326 527 BF	True Love/Mother Nature And Father Time	5
63	Philips 326 568 BF	Call On Me/Humma Humma Humma Humming Bird	5
59	Philips BBE 12186	FOCUS ON JIMMY LLOYD (EP)	12
62	Philips BBE 12509	YOU ARE MY SUNSHINE (EP)	12

LLOYD & JOY

71	Explosion EX 2047	Back To Africa (actually by Alton Ellis)/Born To Lose	15

KATHY LLOYD

54	Decca F 10386	It Worries Me/Tomorrow Night	6
54	Decca F 10418	Teach Me Tonight/It's A Woman's World	6
55	Decca F 10464	Our Future Has Only Begun/Unsuspecting Heart	6
55	Decca F 10567	Experience Unnecessary/This Must Be Wrong (with Ted Heath Music)	6

PEGGY LLOYD

55	London RE-P 1017	DIXIELAND HONKY-TONK (EP, with Bill Stegmeyer & His Orchestra)	15

RUE LLOYD

(see also Joe White)

72	Green Door GD 4033	Loving You/Version	7
72	Green Door GD 4036	Cheer Up/Version	7

TREVOR LLOYD

70	Explosion EX 2018	Chinee Brush/DICE & CUMMIE: Real Colley	10
70	Explosion EX 2019	Give Me Back Your Love/Hold Me	5

LLOYD ALEXANDER REAL ESTATE

67	President PT 157	Whatcha Gonna Do/Gonna Live Again	100

LLOYD & BARBARA

73	Grape GR 3045	Dear Lonely Hearts/LLOYD BANTAM: I Tried To Love You	6

LLOYD & CAREY WITH G.G. ALL STARS

(see also Carey & Lloyd, Pat Satchmo)

72	Attack ATT 8029	Scorpion/MAYTONES: Hands And Feet	5

LLOYD & CLAUDETTE

70	Big Shot BI 546	Queen Of The World/PROPHETS: Top Of The World	25

LLOYD (Robinson) & DEVON (Russell)

(see also Cobbs, Derrick Morgan)

69	Punch PH 14	Love Is The Key/VIRTUES: High Tide	30
69	Blue Cat BS 151	Out Of The Fire/Can't Understand (B-side actually by Austin Faithful)	75

LLOYD & DOREEN

(see also Lloyd Clarke/Doreen Shaeffer)

71	Jackpot JP 762	Midnight/BUNNY LEE'S ALL STARS: Midnight - Version	7

LLOYD (Robinson) & GLEN (Brown)

67	Coxsone CS 7011	That Girl/You Got Me Wrong	100
67	Doctor Bird DB 1058	Jezebel/TOMMY McCOOK & SUPERSONICS: Jam Session	45
67	Doctor Bird DB 1071	Keep On Pushing/BOBBY AITKEN & CARIBBEATS: You Won't Regret (B-side actually by Lloyd & Glen)	45
67	Doctor Bird DB 1099	Feel Good Now/What You've Got	25
68	Doctor Bird DB 1105	Successful Man/I'll Give You Love	30

LLOYD (Jackson) & GROOVERS

(see also Groovers, Don Lett, Tony Lee)

67	Caltone TONE 108	Do It To Me Baby/DIPLOMATS: Meet Me At The Corner	25
68	Caltone TONE 109	My Heart My Soul/DIPLOMATS with TOMMY McCOOK & SUPERSONICS: Going Along	30
68	Caltone TONE 112	Listen To The Music/DIPLOMATS: Strong Man	30

LLOYD & JOHNNY

(see also Lloyd Terrell)

68	Island WI 3158	My Argument (actually by Lloyd Terrell)/JOHNNY MELODY: Foey Man (actually by George Dekker)	80

LLOYD & KEN

(see also Lloyd Charmers/Ken Boothe)

72	Punch PH 110	Have I Sinned/Version	7

LLOYD & LARRY

70s	New Beat NB 080	Monkey Spanner/LLOYD & LARRY'S ALL STARS: Version	6

LLOYD & THE PROPHETS

(see also Prophets [Jamaica], Patrick & Lloyd)

70	Big Shot BI 553	Bush Beat/PATRICK & PROPHETS: Please Come Come	10
70	Big Shot BI 556	Jaco/Soul Reggae	10

LLOYD, DICE & THE BARRISTER

70	Joe JRS 14	Appeal Of Pama Dice/BOSS ALL STARS: Young And Strong Version 2	20

LLOYD, DICE & HIS MUM

70	Joe JRS 5	Trial Of Pama Dice/NYAH SHUFFLE: Jughead Returns Version 1	20

LLOYD (Campbell) THE MATADOR

72	Sioux SI 010	The Train/Julia Sees Me (Exodus)	8

LLOYDIE & LOWBITES

(see also Lloyd Tyrell/Charmers)

73	Harry J HJ 6660	Pussy Cat/Skanky Pussy	6
71	Lowbite LOW 001	CENSORED! (LP, green/silver label)	20

LLOYD'S ALLSTARS

(see also Justins, U Roy Junior, Jimmy Green, Victors)

69	Doctor Bird DB 1178	Love Kiss Blue/UNIQUES: Secretly	45

MINT VALUE £

LLYGOD FFYRNIG

78	Pwdwr PWDWR 1	N.C.B./Sais/Cariad Y Bus Stop (p/s, stamped labels)	100
78	Pwdwr PWDWR 1	N.C.B./Sais/Cariad Y Bus Stop (p/s, printed white labels)	130

LOADED FORTY-FOURS

81	X-S TL 44/1	Thunderbirds (Are Go!)/T.V. Child (p/s)	5

DICKIE LOADER

61	Palette PG 9015	Heatwave/Happiness	25

RUSS LOADER

(see also Mark Wirtz)

65	Columbia DB 7522	When Your Heart Is Broken/That Girl Of Mine (with Breakaways Orchestra)	10
65	Columbia DB 7643	Just Lies/Mona Lisa	8
65	Columbia DB 7696	Count The Stars/Triyng Too Hard (with Ladybirds)	10
66	Columbia DB 7839	Too Soon/Just A Little Step To Heaven	10
69	Conquest CXT 2	Just Lies/Take Me Tonight	5

EDU LOBO

71	A&M AMLS63035	SERGIO MENDES PRESENTS (LP)	20

LOCKETS

63	Pye International 7N 25232	Don't Cha Know/Little Boy	40

LOCKJAW

(see also the Cure)

77	Raw RAW 8	Radio Call Sign/The Young Ones (p/s)	20
78	Raw RAW 19	Journalist Jive/I'm A Virgin/A Doonga Doonga (p/s, beware of counterfeits)	80

HANK LOCKLIN

60	RCA RCA 1188	Please Help Me, I'm Falling/My Old Home Town	20
60	RCA RCA 1188	Please Help Me, I'm Falling/My Old Home Town	6
61	RCA RCA 1252	You're The Reason/Happy Birthday To Me	7
62	RCA RCA 1273	From Here To There To You/This Song Is Just for You	6
62	RCA RCA 1305	We're Gonna Go Fishin'/Welcome Home, Mr. Blues	6
63	RCA RCA 1336	Flyin' South/Behind The Footlights	5
66	RCA 1510	I Feel A Cry Coming On/Insurance	6
67	RCA 1641	The Country Hall Of Fame/Evergreen	6
58	RCA RCX 115	COUNTRY GUITAR VOL. 3 (EP)	10
62	RCA RCX 217	SEVEN DAYS (EP)	10
63	Parlophone GEP 8875	ENCORES (EP)	15
63	RCA RCX 7116	WALTZ OF THE WIND (EP)	8
64	RCA RCX 7150	IRISH SONGS COUNTRY STYLE (EP)	8
61	RCA RD 27201	PLEASE HELP ME, I'M FALLING (LP)	15

GERRY LOCKRAN

69	Decca F 12873	Hey Jude/This Train	6
69	Decca F 12919	Standing On Your Own/You're Not There	20
67	Planet PLL 1002	HOLD ON, I'M COMING (LP)	160
68	Waverley ZLP 2091	BLUES VENDETTA (LP)	60
69	Spark SRLP 104	THE ESSENTIAL GERRY LOCKRAN (LP)	50
72	Polydor 2383 122	WUN (LP)	60
76	Decca SKL-R 5257	RAGS TO GLADRAGS (LP)	40
80	BML 2536	ACROSS THE TRACKS (LP)	15

ANNA LOCKWOOD

70	Tangent TGS 104	THE GLASS WORLD OF ANNA LOCKWOOD (LP)	40

MALCOLM LOCKYER ORCHESTRA

54	Decca F 10304	I'm Gonna Rock, Rock, Rock/Changing Partners (78, as Malcolm Lockyer & His Strict Tempo Music For Dancing)	10
61	HMV POP 929	The Pursuers T.V. Theme/Stranger Than Fiction	10
65	Columbia DB 7552	The Intelligence Men/Brighton Run	15
65	Columbia DB 7663	The Eccentric Dr. Who/Daleks And Thals	50
75	Contour 2870 439	TOP TV THEMES (LP)	12

LOCOMOTIVE

(see also Norman Haines Band, Dog That Bit People, Steam-Shovel)

67	Direction 58-3814	Rudy A Message To You/Broken Heart	20
68	Parlophone R 5718	Rudi's In Love/Never Set Me Free	20
69	Parlophone R 5758	Mr. Armageddon/There's Got To Be A Way (in promos p/s)	30
69	Parlophone R 5758	Mr. Armageddon/There's Got To Be A Way	15
69	Parlophone R 5801	I'm Never Gonna Let You Go/You Must Be Joking	20
70	Parlophone R 5835	Movin' Down The Line/Roll Over Mary	10
71	Parlophone R 5915	Rudi's In Love/You Must Be Joking	20
69	Parlophone PCS 7093	WE ARE EVERYTHING YOU SEE (LP, laminated front sleeve)	375
95	Shoestring BL004	WE ARE EVERYTHING YOU SEE (CD reissue)	25

NILS LOFGREN

(see also Grin, Crazy Horse, Bruce Springsteen)

79	A&M AMS 7455	Shine Silently/Kool Skool (p/s, coloured or black vinyl)	5

LOFT

(see also Weather Prophets, Wishing Stones)

84	Creation CRE 009	Why Does The Rain/Like (foldaround p/s in poly bag)	10
85	Creation CRE 015	Up The Hill And Down The Slope/Lonely Street (foldaround p/s in poly bag)	6

CRIPPLE CLARENCE LOFTON

59	Vogue EPV 1209	CRIPPLE CLARENCE LOFTON (EP)	50
54	London AL 3531	A LOST RECORDING DATE (10" LP)	50
55	Vogue LDE 122	JAZZ IMMORTALS NO. 1 (10" LP)	50

LOGIC CONTROLS

90	Conscious CONN2	High Pursuit/Gangster Trip (12")	20

MINT VALUE £

JIMMY LOGSDON
54 Brunswick 05226 Pa-Paya Mama/In The Mission Of St. Augustine (78) ... 10

L.O.K.
79 Fetish FET 001 Fun House/Starlet Love/Tell Me (p/s) ... 7

LOLA PAYOLA
81 Epic EPC 1499 Schoolgirl Song/I Got Married To A Man From Space (p/s) ... 6

LOLITA
60 Polydor NH 66818 Sailor (Your Home Is The Sea)/La Luna (Quanda La Luna) ... 10

LOLITA STORM
99 Rabid Badger NANG 09 Goodbye America/Get Back (I'm Evil) (p/s) ... 5

LOLLIPOP SHOP
85 Big Beat WIK36 JUST COLOUR (LP) ... 15

LOLLIPOPS
71 Atlantic 2091 114 Nothing's Gonna Stop Our Love/I Believe In Love ... 10

LAURIE LOMAN
54 London HL 8101 Whither Thou Goest/I Was The Last One To Know (gold triangular centre) ... 50
54 London HL 8101 Whither Thou Goest/I Was The Last One To Know (78) ... 10

ALAN LOMAX (& RAMBLERS)
56 Decca F 10787 Dirty Old Town/Hard Case (as Alan Lomax & Ramblers) ... 10
56 Decca DFE 6367 OH LULA (EP) ... 10
58 Pye Jazz NJE 1055 SINGS (EP, with Dave Lee's Bandits) ... 12
58 Pye Jazz NJE 1062 MURDERER'S HOME PT. 1 (EP) ... 12
58 Pye Jazz NJE 1063 MURDERER'S HOME PT. 2 (EP) ... 12
58 Pye Jazz NJE 1064 MURDERER'S HOME PT. 3 (EP) ... 12
58 Pye Jazz NJE 1065 MURDERER'S HOME PT. 4 (EP) ... 12
59 Melodisc EPM7 88 SONGS FROM TEXAS (EP) ... 12
57 Nixa Jazz NJL 8 PRESENTS BLUES IN THE MISSISSIPPI NIGHT (LP, with others + insert) ... 15
57 Nixa Jazz NJL 11 MURDERER'S HOME (LP) ... 15
58 Pye Nixa NPL 18013 PRESENTS AMERICAN SONG TRAIN VOLUME ONE (LP) ... 12
58 HMV CLP 1192 GREAT AMERICAN BALLADS (LP, with Alexis Korner & Guy Carawan) ... 25

JACKIE LOMAX
(see also Lomax Alliance, Undertakers, Takers, Heavy Jelly, Badger)
68 CBS 2554 Genuine Imitation Life/One Minute Woman ... 20
68 Apple APPLE 3 Sour Milk Sea/The Eagle Laughs At You ... 18
69 Apple APPLE 11 New Day/I Fall Inside Your Eyes ... 15
70 Apple APPLE 23 How The Web Was Woven/Thumbin' A Ride (in p/s) ... 30
70 Apple APPLE 23 How The Web Was Woven/Thumbin' A Ride ... 15
69 Apple APCOR 6 IS THIS WHAT YOU WANT (LP, with inner sleeve, mono) ... 75
69 Apple (S)APCOR 6 IS THIS WHAT YOU WANT (LP, with inner sleeve, stereo) ... 60
91 Apple SAPCOR 6 IS THIS WHAT YOU WANT (LP, reissue, gatefold sleeve with bonus 12" [SAPCOR 62]) ... 18

LOMAX ALLIANCE
(see also Jackie Lomax)
67 CBS 2729 Try As You May/See The People ... 50

GUY LOMBARDO (& ROYAL CANADIANS)
55 Brunswick 05372 No More/Pupalina ... 5
55 Brunswick 05412 Softly Softly/(I'm Always Hearing) Wedding Bells ... 5
55 Brunswick 05413 Hey, Mr. Banjo/Blue Mirage ... 5
55 Brunswick 05443 Cherry Pink And Apple Blossom White/Marty ... 5
56 Capitol CL 14585 Charleston Parisien/Rinka Tinka Man ... 5

AL LOMBARDY & HIS ORCHESTRA
54 London HL 8076 The Blues/The Boogie ... 40
55 London HL 8127 In A Little Spanish Town/Flying Home ... 20

LONDON
77 MCA MCA 305 Everyone's A Winner/Handcuffed ... 5
77 MCA MCA 336 Animal Games/Us Kids Cold ... 5
77 MCA MCA 319 SUMMER OF LOVE (EP, p/s) ... 6
77 MCA 12 MCA 319 SUMMER OF LOVE (12" EP, p/s) ... 10
78 MCA MCF 2823 ANIMAL GAMES (LP) ... 15

EDDIE LONDON & CHIMES
57 Decca F 10859 Song Of The Moonlight/I'll Thank You ... 5

FRANCO LONDON ORCHESTRA
66 Philips BF 1470 Theme From Robinson Crusoe/Adrift ... 15

JIMMY LONDON
(see also Jimmy Green, The Inspirations)
71 Randy's RAN 514 Shake A Hand/CARL MURPHY: Lick I Pipe ... 6
71 Randy's RAN 517 Bridge Over Troubled Waters/RANDY'S ALLSTARS: War ... 8
71 Randy's RAN 518 Hip Hip Hooray/IMPACT ALLSTARS: Version ... 5
71 Randy's RAN 520 A Little Love/IMPACT ALLSTARS: Version ... 8
72 Randy's RAN 521 It's Now Or Never/IMPACT ALLSTARS: Version ... 5
72 Randy's RAN 527 Jamaica Festival '72 (with Rocking Horse)/IMPACT ALLSTARS: Version ... 5
73 Explosion EX 2080 I'll Never Find Another You/IMPACT ALLSTARS: Version ... 5
73 Dragon DRA 1010 Jennie/I Wonder If I Care As Much (as Jimmi London) ... 5
74 Dragon DRA 1019 No Letter Today/The Road Is Rough ... 5
74 Ackee ACK 531 Till I Kiss You/Version ... 5
75 Black Wax WAX 4 Am I That Easy To Forget/100 Years Of Dub ... 8
72 Trojan TRL 39 BRIDGE OVER TROUBLED WATERS (LP) ... 20
80 JB JBLP 03 CHILDREN CRYING IN THE GHETTO (LP) ... 20

MINT VALUE £

JOE LONDON

59	London HLW 9008	Lonesome Whistle/It Might Have Been	15

JULIE LONDON

SINGLES

56	London HLU 8240	Cry Me A River/S'Wonderful (gold label print)	80
56	London HLU 8240	Cry Me A River/S'Wonderful (later silver label print)	30
56	London HLU 8240	Cry Me A River/S'Wonderful (78)	15
56	London HLU 8279	Baby, Baby All The Time/Shadow Woman (gold label print)	40
56	London HLU 8279	Baby, Baby All The Time/Shadow Woman (78)	15
57	London HLU 8394	The Meaning Of The Blues/Now! Baby, Now! (gold label print)	30
57	London HLU 8394	The Meaning Of The Blues/Now! Baby, Now! (later silver label print)	15
57	London HLU 8394	The Meaning Of The Blues/Now! Baby, Now! (78)	10
57	London HLU 8414	The Boy On A Dolphin/Tall Boy	15
58	London HLU 8602	Saddle The Wind/It Had To Be You	10
58	London HLU 8657	My Strange Affair/It's Easy	10
58	London HLU 8769	Man Of The West/Blue Moon	10
58	London HLU 8769	Man Of The West/Blue Moon (78)	15
59	London HLU 8891	Come On-A My House/Must Be Catchin'	15
59	London HLU 8891	Come On-A My House/Must Be Catchin' (78)	35
61	London HLG 9360	Sanctuary/Every Chance I Get	7
63	Liberty LIB 10078	There'll Be Some Changes Made/Love On The Rocks	7
63	Liberty LIB 55605	I'm Coming Back To You/When Snowflakes Fall In The Summer	8
64	Liberty LIB 55666	I Want To Find Out For Myself/Guilty Heart	6
65	Liberty LIB 10189	Send For Me/Bye Bye Blackbird	6
65	Liberty LIB 10205	Charade/Wives And Lovers	10
67	Liberty LIB 10274	Girl Talk/The Mickey Mouse March	6

EPs

57	London RE-U 1076	JULIE SINGS FILM SONGS (gold label print, silver print labels £10)	20
57	London RE-N 1092	LONDON'S GIRL FRIENDS VOL. 1	20
58	London RE-U 1151	MAKE LOVE TO ME - PART ONE	10
58	London RE-U 1152	MAKE LOVE TO ME - PART TWO	10
58	London RE-U 1153	MAKE LOVE TO ME - PART THREE	10
59	London RE-U 1180	JULIE - PART ONE	10
59	London RE-U 1181	JULIE - PART TWO	10
59	London RE-U 1182	JULIE - PART THREE	10
63	Liberty LEP 2103	DESAFINADO	10
66	Liberty LEP 2260	ALL THROUGH THE NIGHT	10

ALBUMS

56	London HA-U 2005	JULIE IS HER NAME	30
57	London HA-U 2038	CALENDAR GIRL	30
58	London HA-U 2083	MAKE LOVE TO ME	30
58	London HA-U 2091	ABOUT THE BLUES	30
58	London HA-U 2112	JULIE	30
59	London HA-U 2171	LONDON BY NIGHT	25
59	London HA-U 2186	JULIE IS HER NAME VOL. 2 (also stereo SAH-U 6042)	30
60	London HA-W 2225	SWING ME AN OLD SONG	20
60	London HA-W 2229	YOUR NUMBER PLEASE	20
60	London HA-G 2280	JULIE AT HOME (mono)	18
60	London SAH-G 6097	JULIE AT HOME (stereo)	20
61	London HA-G 2299	AROUND MIDNIGHT	20
61	London HA-G 2353	SEND FOR ME (mono)	18
61	London SAH-G 6154	SEND FOR ME (stereo)	20
62	London HA-G 2405	WHATEVER JULIE WANTS (mono)	18
62	London SAH-G 6205)	WHATEVER JULIE WANTS (stereo)	20
62	Liberty (S)LBY 1083	LOVE LETTERS	12
63	Liberty (S)LBY 1113	LOVE ON THE ROCKS	15
63	Liberty (S)LBY 1136	SINGS LATIN IN A SATIN MOOD	20
66	Liberty (S)LBY 1281	FEELING GOOD (with Gerald Wilson Big Band)	12
66	Liberty (S)LBY 1300	ALL THROUGH THE NIGHT	12
67	Liberty (S)LBY 1334	FOR THE NIGHT PEOPLE	12
67	Liberty (S)LBY 1364	NICE GIRLS DON'T STAY FOR BREAKFAST	12
69	Liberty LBL/LBS 83183E	YUMMY, YUMMY, YUMMY	15

LAURIE LONDON

57	Parlophone R 4359	He's Got The Whole World In His Hands/The Cradle Rock	10
57	Parlophone R 4388	Handed Down/She Sells Sea Shells	5
58	Parlophone R 4408	The Gospel Train/Boomerang	5
58	Parlophone R 4426	I Gotta Robe/Casey Jones	5
58	Parlophone R 4450	Basin Street Blues/Joshua (Fit The Battle Of Jericho)	5
58	Parlophone R 4474	My Mother/Darktown Strutters' Ball	5
58	Parlophone R 4499	Up Above My Head/Three O'Clock	7
59	Parlophone R 4557	Pretty-Eyed Baby (with Gitte)/Boom-Ladda-Boom-Boom	8
59	Parlophone R 4601	Old Time Religion/God's Little Acre	5
60	Parlophone R 4662	Banjo Boy/Hear Them Bells	7
61	Parlophone R 4747	Todays Teardrops/Darling Sue	8
57	Parlophone GEP 8664	LAURIE LONDON (EP)	15
58	Parlophone GEP 8689	LITTLE LAURIE LONDON No. 2 (EP)	30

MARK LONDON

65	Pye 7N 15825	Stranger In The World/Moanin'	15

MICHAEL LONDON

62	HMV POP 1026	Miracles Sometimes Happen/Stranger On The Shore (with Acker Bilk)	8
62	HMV POP 1085	Mutiny On The Bounty Love Song/For The Very Young	5

PETER LONDON

(see also Peter Cook)

65	Pye 7N 15957	Bless You/Baby I Like The Look Of You	50

MINT VALUE £

LONDONAIRES
66 Decca F12379 Dearest Emma/Bugles A Go-Go 15

LONDON BALALAIKA ENSEMBLE
68 Deram DML/SML 712 LONDON BALALAIKA ENSEMBLE (LP) 15

LONDON & BRIDGES
66 CBS 202056 It Just Ain't Right/Leave Her Alone 40

LONDON FUNK ALLSTARS
96 Ninja Tune ZEN 24 FLESH EATING DISCO ZOMBIES VERSUS THE BIONIC HOOKERS FROM MARS (3xLP) 30

LONDON HOSPITAL
60s Private Pressing WAD 9-1 LONDON HOSPITAL CHRISTMAS FACTOR (EP) 60

LONDON JAZZ CHAMBER GROUP
(see also Ken Moule's London Jazz Chamber Group, Ken Moule Seven)
72 Ember CJS 823 ADAM'S RIB SUITE (LP) 20

LONDON JAZZ COMPOSERS ORCHESTRA
70s Incus 7 ODE (LP, with insert) 50

LONDON JAZZ FOUR
(see also London Jazz Quartet, LJ IV)
66 Polydor 56092 Norwegian Wood/I Feel Fine 25
67 Polydor 56214 It Strikes A Chord/Song For Hilary 30
67 Polydor 582 005 TAKE A NEW LOOK AT THE BEATLES (LP) 60

LONDON JAZZ QUARTET
(see also London Jazz Four, Tubby Hayes, Tony Crombie)
60 Tempo TAP 28 LONDON JAZZ QUARTET (LP, with Tubby Hayes & Tony Crombie) 350
60s Ember EMB 3306 LONDON JAZZ QUARTET (LP) 150

LONDON POPS ORCHESTRA
68 Pye 7N 17630 Eleanor Rigby/If I Only Had Time 6
68 Pye NSPL 18241 THE LONDON POPS ORCHESTRA (LP) 15

LONDON POSSE
88 JusticeJT003 Money Mad (12") 30
87 Big LifeBLR2T London Posse/My Beatbox Reggae Style (12") 20
89 Mango 12 MNG 735 Live Like The Other Half Do/Money Mad (12") 8
90 Mango 12 MNG 752 Tell Me Something/Original London Style (12") 8
91 Mango 12 MNG 774 Jump Around/Gangster Chronicle (12") 8
93 Bullet BULT2 How's Life In London?/Shut The Fuck Up/How I Make Papes (12") 15
94 Bullet BULT3 Here Comes The Rugged One/Super Model (12") 10
90 Mango MLPS1066 GANGSTER CHRONICLE (LP) 15

LONDON PX
80 New Puritan NP 1 Orders/Eviction (p/s) 25
82 Terrapyn SYD 1 Arnold Layne/Indian Summer (1-sided flexidisc) 12

LONDON RHYME SYNDICATE
88 Rhyme & Reason 12LRS001 Hard To The Core (12") 10
88 Rhyme & Reason 12LRS002 London Rhyme Syndicate/Poetry/Armed And Extremely Dangerous (EP) 8

LONDON STRING CHORALE
72 Polydor 2058 280 Galloping Home/Vicky 6

LONDON STUDIO GROUP
(see also Ivor & Basil Kirchen Band)
66 De Wolfe DW/LP 2974 THE WILD ONE (10" LP, tricolour label) 30

LONDON UNDERGROUND
82 On-U Sound ON-U 4 WATCHING WEST INDIANS IN THE COLD (10" EP) 8
83 On-U Sound ON-U 5 STRANGE (10" EP) 8
83 On-U Sound LP 22 AT HOME WITH THE LONDON UNDERGROUND (LP) 20

LONDON WAITS
66 Immediate IM 030 Softly Softly/Serenadio 30

LONDON ZOO
80 Gramaphone STB 80 Who's Driving This Car?/You And Your Great Ideas (stamped white labels, no p/s) 6
80 Zoom ZUM 12 Receiving End/London Zoo (p/s) 5

LONELY HEARTS
84 Tenacity TROIA FM Fantasy/Young Girl (p/s) 10

LONE PIGEON
(see also Beta Band)
00s Bad Jazz/Fence BEBOP 31 TOUCHED BY TOMOKO EP: Summertime Beeswing/Touched By Tomoko/Empty Town/The Mean Old Mind Of Man/Waterfall 8

LONE RANGER
79 Island WIPDJ 6517 Barnabus Collins/Dub Part 2 8
82 Greensleeves GRED 85 Johnny Make You Bad So/TAXI GANG: Outside Right (12") 12

LONESOME DRIFTER
70 Injun 104 Eager Boy/Teardrop Valley 10

JOHNNY LONESOME
61 HMV POP 837 Marie Marie/Doctor Heartache 20

LONESOME PINE FIDDLERS
64 London HA-B 8143 MORE BLUEGRASS (LP) 15

LONESOME STONE
(see also Sheep)
73 Reflection RL 306 LONESOME STONE (LP, stage production recording) 18

MINT VALUE £

LONESOME SUNDOWN

71	Blue Horizon 7-63864	LONESOME LONELY BLUES (LP)	100
70s	Flyright LP 529	BOUGHT ME A TICKET (LP)	18
70s	Flyright LP 587	LONESOME WHISTLER (LP)	18

LONESOME TRAVELLERS

70	Tradition TSR 004	THE LONESOME TRAVELLERS (LP)	25
70s	Nebula NEB 100	THE LOST CHILDREN (LP)	15

LONE WOLF

80	Wolf Music LW 001	Cash For Candy/Pipedream Mary (p/s)	150
82	Guardian GRC 144	Leave Me Behind/High Class Hooker	20
84	Neat NEAT 44-12	Nobody's Move/Town To Town/Leave Me Behind (12")	20

LONE WOLF

81	Kai KR 02	Fighting For Sommerlund/Vonotar The Traitor (p/s)	15

FITZROY D. LONG & BUSTER ALL STARS

(see also Larry Marshall)

68	Fab FAB 32	Get A New Girl/BUSTER'S ALL STARS: Come And Do It With Me	18

SHORTY LONG

(see also Art Mooney)

65	Tamla Motown TMG 512	Out To Get You/It's A Crying Shame	120
65	Tamla Motown TMG 512	Out To Get You/It's A Crying Shame (DJ copy)	200
66	Tamla Motown TMG 573	Function At The Junction/Call On Me	45
66	Tamla Motown TMG 573	Function At The Junction/Call On Me (DJ copy)	60
67	Tamla Motown TMG 600	Chantilly Lace/Your Love Is Amazing	20
68	Tamla Motown TMG 644	Night Fo' Last (Vocal)/Night Fo' Last (Instrumental)	25
68	Tamla Motown TMG 663	Here Comes The Judge/Sing What You Wanna	18
68	T. Motown (S)TML 11086	HERE COMES THE JUDGE (LP)	60
70	T. Motown STML 11144	THE PRIME OF SHORTY LONG (LP)	35

LONG & SHORT

64	Decca F 11964	The Letter/Love Is A Funny Thing	35
64	Decca F 12043	Choc Ice/Here Comes The Fool	35

LONG BLONDES

04	Thee Sheffield SPC 005	New Idols/Long Blonde (p/s pink vinyl, playing card & newsletter insert)	40
04	Angular ARC 007	Giddy Stratospheres/Polly/Darts (p/s blue vinyl, 500 only)	30
05	Angualr ARC 009	Appropriation (By Any Other Name)/Lust In The Movies (p/s, numbered)	20
07	Rough Trade RTRADST 409	Fulwood Babylon/Five Ways To End It (The Erol Alkan Mixes) (12", 600 only)	10

LONGBOATMEN

66	Polydor 56115	Take Her Any Time/Only In Her Home Town	500

LONG COLD STARE

90	Rise Above RISE 3	TIRED EYES (LP)	12

LONGDANCER

74	Rocket PIG 11	Puppet Man/Cold Love	15
73	Rocket PIGL 1	IF IT WAS SO SIMPLE (LP, gatefold sleeve)	15
77	Rocket PIGL 6	TRAILER FOR A GOOD LIFE (LP, die cut gatefold sleeve)	15

CLAUDINE LONGET

67	A&M AMS 708	Good Day Sunshine/The Look Of Love	8
67	A&M AML 903	CLAUDINE (LP)	20

LONG HELLO

(see also Van Der Graaf Generator)

73	private pressing	THE LONG HELLO (LP, mail-order only, numbered white sleeve)	20

LONG TALL SHORTY

(see also Case, Joe Public, Rage, Charlie Harper)

79	Warner Bros K 17491	By Your Love/1970's Boy (p/s, withdrawn)	100
81	Dr Creation LYN 9904	If I Was You/That's What I Want (flexidisc)	12
81	Ramkup CAC 007	Win Or Lose/Ain't Done Wrong (p/s)	100
85	Diamond DIA 002	On The Streets Again/I Fought The Law/Promises (p/s, with poster)	25
85	Diamond DIA 002	On The Streets Again/I Fought The Law/Promises (p/s, without poster)	12
86	Diamond DIA 005	What's Going On/Steppin' Stone/Win Or Lose/England (p/s)	15
88	No label or cat. no.	ROCKIN' AT THE SAVOY (LP, official bootleg, with poster)	18
88	No label or cat. no.	ROCKIN' AT THE SAVOY (LP, official bootleg, without poster)	15

LONG TALL TEXANS

89	Razor RAZZ 44	FIVE BEANS IN THE WHEEL (LP)	12

LOOKING GLASS

72	Epic 65041	LOOKING GLASS (LP)	20

LOOP

86	Head HEAD 5	16 Dreams/Head On/Burning World (12", p/s)	18
87	Head HEAD 7L	Spinning Parts 1 & 2 (large centre, plain black die-cut sleeve)	15
87	Head HEAD 7	Spinning/Deep Hit/I'll Take You There (12", p/s)	20
88	Chapter 22 12 CHAP 27	COLLISION EP (12")	10
88	Chapter 22 12 CHAP 32	BLACK SUN EP (12")	8
88	Chapter 22 CAT 065	Torched (flexidisc, with The Catalogue magazine no. 65)	12
88	Chapter 22 CAT 065	Torched (flexidisc, without The Catalogue magazine no. 65)	7
89	Situation 2 SIT 64T	ARC LITE EP (12", p/s)	8
89	Situation 2 SIT 64CD	ARC LITE EP (CD)	8
87	Head HEAD LP 1	HEAVEN'S END (LP, with inner sleeve)	15
88	Chapter 22 CHAPLLP 34	FADE OUT (LP, 2 x 45rpm 12", gold stickered gatefold sleeve, signed)	30
88	Chapter 22 CHAPLLP 34	FADE OUT (LP, 2 x 45rpm 12", gold stickered gatefold sleeve)	20
90	Situation 2 SITU 27	A GILDED ETERNITY (2-LP with free 7")	15
91	Reactor REACTORLP 3	WOLF FLOW - JOHN PEEL SESSIONS 1987-90 (2-LP)	18
92	Reactor LP 5	DUAL (LP, blue vinyl)	20
92	Reactor CD5	DUAL (CD)	25

LOOSE ENDS

66	Decca F 12437	Send The People Away/I Ain't Gonna Eat My Heart Out Anymore	40
66	Decca F 12476	Taxman/That's It	90

LOOSE TALK

82	Jet JET 7025	Dan Dare/Home Planet (p/s)	8

LOOT

(see also Soul Agents, Hookfoot)

66	Page One POF 013	Baby Come Closer/Baby	15
67	Page One POF 026	I've Just Gotta Love You/You Need Someone To Love	20
67	CBS 2938	Whenever You're Ready/I Got What You Want	18
68	Page One POF 095	She's A Winner/Radio City (withdrawn B-side)	30
68	Page One POF 095	She's A Winner/Save Me	22
68	CBS 3231	Don't Turn Around/You Are My Sunshine Girl	25
69	Page One POF 115	Try To Keep It A Secret/Radio City	40

LINDA LOPEZ MAMBO ORCHESTRA

55	Parlophone MSP 6179	Limehouse Blues Mambo/Nursery Mambo	7

TRINI LOPEZ

63	London HL 9808	Jeanie Marie/Love Me Tonight	10
64	London HA 8132	TEENAGE LOVE SONGS (LP)	12
64	London HA 8160	MORE OF TRINI LOPEZ (LP)	12
65	Stateside SE 1013	SINNER NOT A SAINT (EP)	30

DENISE LOR

54	Parlophone MSP 6120	If I Give My Heart To You/Hallo Darling	10
55	Parlophone MSP 6148	Every Day Of My Life/And One To Grow On	12

KENNY LORAN

59	Capitol CL 15081	Mama's Little Baby/Magic Star	30

L'ORANGE MECHANIK

(see also Times)

86	Art Pop POP 44	Symphony/Intermezzo (Sprechstimme)/Scherzo (p/s)	15

BOBBY LORD/BOB LUMAN

(see also Bob Luman)

64	Hickory LPE 1501	HICKORY SHOWCASE VOL. 2 (EP, 1 side each)	10
64	Hickory LPE 1504	HICKORY SHOWCASE VOL. 3 (EP, 1 side each)	10

JON LORD

(see also Artwoods, Deep Purple, [Paice] Ashton & Lord, Bernie Marsden, Wizard's Convention, Episode Six, Leading Figures, Whitesnake, Cozy Powell)

76	Purple PUR 131	Bourée/Aria	7
82	Harvest HAR 5220	Bach Onto This/Going Home (p/s)	6
84	Safari SAFE60	The Country Diary Of An Edwardian Lady (main theme)/Love Theme (p/s)	7
71	Purple TPSA 7501	GEMINI SUITE (LP, textured gatefold sleeve)	22
74	Purple TPSA 7513	WINDOWS (LP, gatefold sleeve)	15
76	Purple TPSA 7516	SARABANDE (LP, die-cut sleeve)	15

TONY LORD

66	Planet PLF 102	World's Champion/It Makes Me Sad	25

JERRY LORDAN

(see also Lee & Jay Elvin)

59	Parlophone R 4588	I'll Stay Single/Can We Kiss	8
60	Parlophone R 4627	Who Could Be Bluer?/Do I Worry?	10
60	Parlophone R 4653	Sing Like An Angel/Ev'ry Time	12
60	Parlophone R 4695	Ring, Write Or Call/I've Still Got You	12
61	Parlophone R 4748	You Came A Long Way From St. Louis/Let's Try Again	15
62	Parlophone R 4903	One Good Solid 24 Carat Reason/Second Hand Dress	15
70	CBS 5057	The Old Man And The Sea/Harlequin Melodies	30
61	Parlophone PMC 1133	ALL MY OWN WORK (LP, mono)	90
61	Parlophone PCS 3014	ALL MY OWN WORK (LP, stereo)	120

LORD BEGINNER

(see also Lord Kitchener)

50	Melodisc 1131	Joe Louis Calypso/Trinidad Blues (78)	10
50	Melodisc 1133	Victory Test Match - Calypso/Sergeant Brown (78)	10
50	Melodisc 1134	Straight Hair Girl/Calinda (78)	10
51	Melodisc 1164	Gold Coast Victory/Family Scandal (78)	10
51	Melodisc 1167	Family Scandal/Gold Coast Champion (78)	10
51	Melodisc 1183	Jamaica Hurricane/Pretty Woman (78)	10
51	Melodisc 1193	John Goddard Calypso/Some Girl (78)	10
51	Parlophone MP 112	Federation/Rum, More Rum (78, export)	10
51	Melodisc 1211	Australia V. West Indies/One Morning (78)	10
51	Esquire 5-034	Randolph Turpin's Victory/West Indians And The Steel Band (78, with Kenny Graham's Afro-Cubists)	15
51	Esquire 5-041	Fifty Women To One Man/1951 Festival Of Britain (78, with Kenny Graham's Afro-Cubists)	15
53	Esquire 5-091	England Regains The Ashes/Nobody Wants To Grow Old (78)	15
54	Melodisc 1333	Sir Winston Churchill Calypso/Rhythm Dance (78)	15
54	Melodisc 1334	She Walks Like You/Tambourine (78)	12
50s	Parlophone MP 144	Africa/Syncopation (export 78)	12
60s	Melodisc CAL 1	Victory Test Match - Calypso/Sergeant Brown (reissue)	10

LORD BRISCO(E)

64	Rio R42	Fabulous Eyes/What You See	20
64	Black Swan WI 447	Spiritual Mambo/BABA BROOKS: Fly Right	25
64	Black Swan WI 450	My Love Has Come/BABA BROOKS: Sweet Eileen	25
64	Black Swan WI 454	Trojan/I Am The Least	12
64	Island WI 131	Praise For I/Tell You The Story	15
65	Island WI 187	Jonah (The Master)/Mr. Cleveland	15

MINT VALUE £

LORD BRYNNER & SHEIKS
(see also Roland Alphonso)

66	Island WI 266	Congo War/Teach Me To Ska	18

LORD BUCKLEY

62	Fontana 688 010ZL	IN CONCERT (LP)	30
67	Fontana TL 5396	BLOWING HIS MIND (AND YOURS, TOO) (LP)	30
70	Elektra 2410 002	THE BEST OF LORD BUCKLEY (LP)	18

LORD BURGESS & HIS SUN ISLANDERS

67	Pye Intl. NPL 28109	CALYPSO GO-GO (LP)	12

LORD CHARLES & HIS BAND

70s	Sound Of Jamaica JA 1	Jamaican Bits And Pieces/JA Island Soul	8

LORD COMIC
(see also Sir Lord Comic)

70	Bamboo BAM 66	Rhythm Rebellion/ROY RICHARDS: Reggae Children	20
70	Pressure Beat PR 5507	Jack Of My Trade/CYNTHIA RICHARDS: United We Stand	18

LORD CREATOR
(see also Kentrick Patrick, Fabulous Flames)

62	Island WI 001	Independant [sic] Jamaica Calypso/Remember (B-side is actually Remember Your Mother And Father)	20
63	Kalypso XX 24	Peeping Tom/Second Hand Piano	18
64	Port-O-Jam PJ 4005	Rhythm Of The Blues/Simple Things	12
64	Port-O-Jam PJ 4119	Jamaica's Anniversary/Mother's Love	22
64	National Calypso NC 2001	Drive With Care/Sweet Jamaica	20
65	Blue Beat BB 292	Evening News/Good For Creator	35
65	Black Swan WI 463	Wicked Lady/MAYTALS: My Little Ruby	25
66	Doctor Bird DB 1029	Obeah Wedding/BERTRAM ENNIS COMBO: Part Two	10
67	Jump Up JU 503	Jamaica Jump Up/Laziest Man	8
67	Jump Up JU 524	Big Bamboo/Marjorie And Harry	8
76	Island WIP 6344	Big Pussy Sally/UPSETTERS: Big Pussy Dub	6

LORD CRISTO

67	Jump Up JU 515	Dumb Boy And The Parrot/General Hospital	8
67	Jump Up JU 517	Election War Zone/Bad Luck Man	8

LORD DANIEL

60s	Kalypso XX 26	Small Island Gal	6

LORD FLEA & HIS CALYPSONIANS

57	Capitol CL 14704	The Naughty Little Flea/Shake Shake Senora	5

LORD GANDA

57	Melodisc MEL 1417	Everybody Is Rockin' & Rollin'/Landlady Don't Steal My Clothes (78)	15

LORD KITCHENER
(see also Lord Beginner)

50	Parlophone MP 102	Nora/LORD BEGINNER: The Dollar And The Pound (export 78)	12
50	Parlophone MP 103	Underground Train/LORD BEGINNER: I Will Die A Bachelor (export 78)	12
52	Melodisc MEL 1160	Kitch/Food From The West Indies (78)	10
52	Melodisc MEL 1222	Two Timing Josephine/The Tongue Mopsie (78)	10
53	Lyragon J 717	Alec Bedser Calypso/Mistress Jacob (78)	10
55	Melodisc MEL 1325	My Wife's Nightie/Sweet Home (78)	10
56	Melodisc MEL 1400	Rock 'n' Roll Calypso/Life Begins At Forty (78)	10
56	Melodisc MEL 1401	Romeo/Kitch's Calypso Medley (78)	10
59	Melodisc MEL 1498	Black Puddin'/Piccadilly Folk	7
59	Melodisc MEL 1538	If You're Brown/Come Back In The Morning	7
60	Melodisc MEL 1577	Jamaica Turkey/Edna What You Want	7
63	Melodisc CAL 2	Kitch/Rebound Wife	6
63	Melodisc CAL 3	Muriel And The Bug/Nora And The Yankee	6
63	Melodisc CAL 4	Kitch Take It Easy/Redhead	6
63	Melodisc CAL 5	Drink A Rum/Your Wife	15
63	Melodisc CAL 6	Too Late Kitch/Saxophone Number Two	6
63	Melodisc CAL 7	Wife And Mother/Mango Tree	6
64	Melodisc CAL 10	Kitch Mambo Calypso/Ghana	6
64	Melodisc CAL 11	Life Begins At Forty/Short Skirts	6
64	Melodisc CAL 12	Romeo/Kitch Calypso Medley	6
64	Melodisc CAL 14	Federation/Alfonso In Town	6
64	Melodisc CAL 19	Black Puddin'/Piccadilly Folk	6
64	Melodisc CAL 21	Come Back In The Morning/If You're Brown	6
64	Melodisc CAL 22	Jamaica Turkey/Edna What You Want	6
64	Melodisc CAL 23	Carnival/More Rice	6
60s	Jump Up JU 504	Love In The Cemetery/Jamaica Woman	6
60s	Jump Up JU 506	Road/Neighbour	6
64	Jump Up JU 511	Dr. Kitch/Come Back Home Meh Boy	5
65	Jump Up JU 530	Kitch You So Sweet/Ain't That Fun	6
65	Aladdin WI 612	Dr. Kitch/Come Back Home Meh Boy (reissue)	8
71	Duke DU 115	Dr. Kitch/Love In The Cemetary	5
55	Melodisc MLP 500	KITCH - KING OF CALYPSO (10" LP)	22
57	Melodisc MLP 510	KING OF CALYPSO VOL. 2 (10" LP)	22
60s	Melodisc 12-129	CALYPSOS TOO HOT TO HANDLE (LP)	30
60s	Melodisc 12-130	CALYPSOS TOO HOT TO HANDLE VOL. 2 (LP)	20
60s	Melodisc 12-199	CALYPSOS TOO HOT TO HANDLE (LP, reissue with extra tracks)	20
60s	Melodisc 12-200	CALYPSOS TOO HOT TO HANDLE VOL. 2 (LP, reissue with extra tracks)	20

LORD KITCHENER/FITZROY COLEMAN BAND

56	no label	City And United 1956/The Manchester Football Double (78)	60

MINT VALUE £

LORD LARGE (Featuring DEAN PARRISH)

06	Acid Jazz AJX 185S	Left Right & Centre/Sun In The Sands (7", co. sleeve)	6

LORD LEBBY

58	Kalypso RL 101	Dr Kinsey Report/Ethiopia	15
58	Kalypso XX 05	Sweet Jamaica/Mama Want No Rice No Peas	10
60	Starlite ST45 018	Caldonia/One Kiss For My Baby	100

LORD MELODY

58	Melodisc MEL 1440	The Devil/No, No	6
58	Melodisc MEL 1440	The Devil/No, No (78)	10
58	Melodisc MEL 1449	Robbery/Men Company	8
58	Melodisc MEL 1449	Robbery/Men Company (78)	10
58	Melodisc MEL 1474	Do Able/Happy Holiday	6
58	Melodisc MEL 1474	Do Able/Happy Holiday (78)	12
59	Melodisc MEL 1491	I Confess/MIGHTY SPARROW: Goaty	8
59	Melodisc MEL 1503	Tom Dooley/Jealous Woman	6
59	Melodisc MEL 1504	Romeo/Knock On Any Door	6
60	Kalypso XX 14	Rock 'N' Roll Calypso/Bo Bo Man	5
60s	Melodisc CAL 16	Happy Holiday/Do Able	5

LORD NELSON

63	Stateside SS 189	I Got An Itch/Problems On My Mind	12
64	Stateside SS 281	It's Delinquency/Proud West Indian	15
68	Direction 58-3909	Michael/No Hot Summer	8
64	Stateside SE 1024	PROUD WEST INDIAN (EP)	30

LORD POWER

57	Kalypso XX 02	Chambolina/Penny Reel (78)	12
58	Maracas M 20001	Special Amber Calypso/Mambo La-La (78)	12
69	Coxsone CS 7079	Temptation/AL & VIBRATORS: Change Everything	45

LORD RIGBY

60s	Kalypso XX 29	The Milkman/Old Veterans	6
64	National Calypso NC 1001	Carnival Jamiacia/Music Teacher	20

LORD ROCKINGHAM'S XI

(see also Robinson Crew, Harry Robinson)

58	Decca F 11024	The Squelch/Fried Onions	10
58	Decca F 11059	Hoots Mon/Blue Train	7
59	Decca F 11104	Wee Tom/Lady Rockingham, I Presume?	12
59	Decca F 11139	Ra-Ra Rockingham/Farewell To Rockingham	15
59	Decca F 11139	Ra-Ra Rockingham/Farewell To Rockingham (78)	15
62	Decca F 11426	Newcastle Twist/Rockingham Twist	15
58	Decca DFE 6555	OH BOY! (EP)	40
68	Columbia S(C)X 6291	THE RETURN OF LORD ROCKINGHAM'S XI (LP, mono/stereo)	40

LORD ROSE

60s	Kalypso XX 25	Independent Jamaica/Twistin' Uncle	40

LORDS

67	Columbia DB 8121	Don't Mince Matters/No One Knows	140
68	Columbia DB 8367	Gloryland/Gypsy Boy	18

LORDS OF RAP

92	Mad Dog MADDOG001	STIX 'N' STONES (EP)	12

LORD SITAR

68	Columbia SX/SCX 6256	LORD SITAR (LP)	50

LORD SPOON

70	Escort ERT 839	Woman A Love In The Night Time/World On A Wheel	6

LORD TANAMO

60	Kalypso XX 20	Blues Have Got Me Down/Sweet Dreaming	20
64	Rio R 21	I Had A Dream/OSBOURNE GRAHAM: Be There	12
64	Ska Beat JB 177	Night Food Ska/My Business	20
65	Ska Beat JB 217	Mattie Rag/BABA BROOKS BAND: Mattie Rag	30
65	Ska Beat JB 224	I'm In The Mood For Ska/You Never Know	100
66	Ska Beat JB 243	Mother's Love/Downtown Gal	20
60s	Caribou CRC 3	I Love You Truly/If You Were Only Mine	80
70	Bamboo BAM 45	Rainy Night In Georgia/KEN PACKER: When You're Gone	15
71	Banana BA 319	Keep On Moving/JACKIE MITTOO: Totaly [sic] Together	70

LORELEI

74	CBS 2048	S.T.O.P. (Stop)/I'll Never Let You Down	15

SOPHIA LOREN

(see also Peter Sellers & Sophia Loren)

58	Philips PB 857	Love Song From "Houseboat"/Bing! Bang! Bong!	6
71	Warner Bros WB 8126	Anyone/There Is A Star	5

LORENZO

(see also Laurel Aitken)

69	Harry J HE 6687	Saturday Vocal Night/Instro	10
69	Beacon BEA 134	I Ain't Afraid/Beggar	25
71	New Beat NB 094	I Will Never Let You Down/This Magic Moment	5

LORI & CHAMELEONS

(see also Teardrop Explodes, Bill Drummond)

78	Zoo CAGE 006	Touch/Love On The Ganges (p/s)	5
81	Korova KOW 20T	Touch/The Lonely Spy/Love On The Ganges (12", p/s)	8

GARY & JOHN LORRAINE

65	Pye 7N 15836	I'm Not To Blame/Alone Again	10

MINT VALUE £

MYRNA LORRIE

55	London HLU 8187	Underway/I'm Your Man, I'm Your Gal (B-side with Buddy DeVal)	30
56	London HLU 8294	Life's Changing Scene/Listen To My Heartstrings	30

LORRIES

79	Redball RR 016	The Night/Steal You Anyway/Pushover/Idiot Dances (p/s)	6

DICK LORY

56	London HLD 8348	Cool It Baby/Ball Room Baby	600
56	London HLD 8348	Cool It Baby/Ball Room Baby (78)	100
61	London HLG 9284	My Last Date/Broken Hearted	30
62	Liberty LIB 55415	Handsome Guy/The Pain Is Here	10
63	Liberty LIB 55529	Welcome Home Again/I Got Over You	10

LOS BRAVOS

(see under 'B')

LOS DOURADOS

70	EMI Regal/Starline SRS 5018	INTRODUCING LOS DOURADOS (LP)	15

JOE LOSS (& HIS ORCHESTRA)

66	HMV POP 1500	Thunderbirds Theme/"The Avengers" Theme	15
66	HMV POP 1517	The England World Cup March/Auld Lang Syne (March)	10

LOST CHEREES

83	Riot RIOT 3	NO FIGHTING NO WAR (EP)	10
84	Mortarhate MORT 3	A MAN'S DUTY ... A WOMAN'S PLACE (EP)	8
85	Mortarhate MORT 12	UNWANTED CHILDREN (12" EP, with inner)	10
84	Fight Back FIGHT 6	ALL PART OF GROWING UP (LP, with lyric inner)	12

LOST DOG

71	Phoenix SNIX 143	Latch Key Child/One More Time	60

LOST JOCKEY

82	Operation Twilight OPT 11	Professor Slack/Rise And Fall/Animal/Behaviour And Crude Din (p/s)	8

LOTHAR & THE HAND PEOPLE

69	Capitol CL 15610	Sdrawkcab (Backwards)/Today Is Only Yesterday's Tomorrow	20
69	Capitol E-ST 247	SPACE HYMN (LP)	60

DENNIS LOTIS

(see also Johnstone Brothers)

54	Decca F 10287	Such A Night/Cuddle Me (with Ted Heath Music & Johnston Brothers)	25
54	Decca F 10392	Honey Love/Manhattan Mambo (with Ted Heath Music)	20
55	Decca F 10469	Face Of An Angel, Heart Of A Devil/The Golden Ring	10
55	Decca F 10471	Chain Reaction/Go, Go, Go (with Ted Heath Music)	10
56	Pye 7N 15053	Green Grows The Grass/No Other Love Can Take Your Place	7
57	Columbia DB 3993	Tammy/I Complain	7
57	Columbia DB 4056	Valentina/Good Mornin' Life	7
58	Columbia DB 4090	I May Never Pass This Way Again/Gretna Green	7
58	Columbia DB 4158	The Only Man On The Island/Guessing What The Neighbours'll Say	6
68	Polydor 56266	Funny One/One Man's Life	20
68	Polydor 56298	Celebration/Why Do They Have To Fall In Love	30
68	Polydor 56346	One Woman Man/The Finger Points At you	30
56	Pye NEP 24017	PRESENTING DENNIS LOTIS (EP)	10
57	Pye NEP 24043	LET'S BE HAPPY (EP)	10
57	Pye NEP 24046	HOW ABOUT YOU (EP)	10
57	Pye NEP 24053	HOW ABOUT YOU PT. 2 (EP)	10
57	Pye NEP 24055	HOW ABOUT YOU PT. 3 (EP)	10
59	Columbia SEG 7955	HALLELUJAH IT'S DENNIS LOTIS (EP)	10
57	Nixa NPL 18002	HOW ABOUT YOU (LP)	25
58	Columbia 33SX 1089	BIDIN' MY TIME (LP)	25

PETER LOTIS

60	Ember EMB S 110	Doo-Dah/You're Singing Our Love Song To Somebody Else (with p/s)	6

LOT 39 (STRANGERS)

60s	Eyemark EMS 1004	I'll Get Over You/I Still Love You	12

LOTUS CRUISE

83	Armbury ARM 603	Billy's Got A Gun/Tonight	50

LOTUS EATERS

(see also Wild Swans, Care)

84	Sylvan SYL 2	You Don't Need Someone New/Two Virgins Tender (picture disc)	5
84	Sylvan SYL 4	Out Of Your Own/Endless (picture disc)	5
85	Arista FS 5	It Hurts/Evidence//The Soul In Sparks/Church At Llanbadrig (double pack)	5
84	Sylvan 206 263	NO SENSE OF SIN (LP)	12

BONNIE LOU

53	Parlophone MSP 6021	Seven Lonely Days/Dancin' With Someone	50
53	Parlophone MSP 6036	Hand-Me-Down Heart/Scrap Of Paper	50
53	Parlophone MSP 6048	Tennessee Wig Walk/Just Out Of Reach	50
53	Parlophone MSP 6051	Pa-Paya Mama/Since You Said Goodbye	40
54	Parlophone MSP 6072	The Texas Polka/No Heart At All	30
54	Parlophone MSP 6095	Don't Stop Kissing Me Goodnight/The Welcome Mat	30
54	Parlophone MSP 6108	No One/Huckleberry Pie	30
54	Parlophone MSP 6117	Blue Tennessee Rain/Wait For Me, Darling	30
54	Parlophone MSP 6132	Two Step - Side Step/Please Don't Laugh When I Cry	30
55	Parlophone MSP 6151	Tennessee Mambo/Train Whistle Blues	35
55	Parlophone MSP 6157	Tweedle Dee/The Finger Of Suspicion Points At You	45
55	Parlophone MSP 6173	Drop Me A Line/Old Faithful And True Love	25
55	Parlophone MSP 6178	The Barnyard Hop/Tell The World	20

			MINT VALUE £
55	Parlophone MSP 6188	Dancin' In My Socks/Daddy-O	40
56	Parlophone MSP 6223	Darlin' Why/Miss The Love (That I've Been Dreaming Of)	20
56	Parlophone MSP 6234	Bo Weevil (A Country Song)/Chaperon	20
56	Parlophone MSP 6253	Lonesome Lover/Little Miss Bobby Sox	25
56	Parlophone R 4215	No Rock 'N' Roll Tonight/One Track Love	25
57	Parlophone R 4350	Teenage Wedding/Runnin' Away	25
58	Parlophone DP 545	I'm Available/Waiting In Vain (export issue)	20

BONNIE LOU & RUSTY YORK

58	Parlophone R 4409	Let The School Bell Ring Ding-A-Ling/La Dee Dah	80
58	Parlophone R 4409	Let The School Bell Ring Ding-A-Ling/La Dee Dah (78)	30

BUBBA LOU & THE HIGHBALLS

81	Stiff BUY 114	Love All Over The Place/Over You (Unissued)	30
81	Silent SSH3	Love All Over The Place/Over You (reissue)	15

LOU & KEVIN

(see also Rusty York)

78	Bushays BFM 103	Reunited/Reunited Stepping Out (12")	10

JOHN D. LOUDERMILK

(see also Johnny Dee)

61	RCA RCA 1269	The Language Of Love/Darling Jane	10
62	RCA RCA 1287	Thou Shalt Not Steal/Mister Jones	8
62	RCA RCA 1323	Angela Jones/Road Hog	10
68	RCA RCA 1761	Sidewalks/The Odd Folks Of Okracoke	7
62	RCA RD 27248/SF 5123	THE LANGUAGE OF LOVE (LP)	30
62	RCA Victor RD/SF 7515	TWELVE SIDES OF JOHN D. LOUDERMILK (LP)	30
67	RCA Victor RD/SF 7890	SINGS A BIZARRE COLLECTION OF SONGS (LP)	30
70	RCA LSA 3159	THE BEST OF JOHN D. LOUDERMILK (LP)	12

LOUDNESS

84	Music For Nations MFN 22	DISILLUSION (LP)	12

(THE) LOUDWATER TURN

68	Morgan MR 6S	Senorita/I'll Be Where You Are	40

JOE HILL LOUIS

(see also Willie Nix)

65	Bootleg 502	Heartache Baby/I Feel Like A Million (99 copies only)	40
67	Advent LP 2803	MEMPHIS BLUES AND BREAKDOWNS (LP)	60
74	Polydor 2383 214	BLUE IN THE MORNING (LP)	25

LOUISIANA RED

64	Columbia DB 7270	Keep Your Hands Off My Woman/Don't Cry	40
64	Sue WI 337	I Done Woke Up/I Had A Feeling	40
64	Columbia 33SX 1612	LOWDOWN BACK PORCH BLUES (LP)	45
72	Atlantic K 40436	SINGS THE BLUES (LP)	20
72	Carnival 2941 002	THE SEVENTH SON (LP)	20

LOUISIANA SUGAR BABIES

57	HMV 7EG 8215	LOUISIANA SUGAR BABIES (EP, with Fats Waller & James P. Johnson)	12

LOUVIN BROTHERS

59	Capitol CL 14989	Knoxville Girl/I Wish It Had Been A Dream (withdrawn)	20
59	Capitol CL 15078	You're Learning/My Curly Headed Baby	10
56	Capitol EAP1 769	TRAGIC SONGS OF LIFE (EP)	15
58	Capitol EAP1 910	IRA AND CHARLIE (EP)	15
59	Capitol EAP1 1106	COUNTRY LOVE BALLADS (EP)	10

LOVABLES

68	Stateside SS 2108	You're The Cause Of It/Beautiful Idea	20

LOVE

(see also Arthur Lee)

SINGLES

66	London HLZ 10053	My Little Red Book/Hey Joe	40
66	London HLZ 10073	7 And 7 Is/No. Fourteen	35
67	Elektra EKSN 45010	She Comes In Colours/Orange Skies	30
67	Elektra EKSN 45016	Softly To Me/The Castle	30
68	Elektra EKSN 45024	Alone Again Or/Bummer In The Summer	20
68	Elektra EKSN 45026	The Daily Planet/Andmoreagain	20
68	Elektra EKSN 45038	Laughing Stock/Your Mind And We Belong Together	30
70	Elektra EKSN 45086	I'm With You/Robert Montgomery	15
70	Harvest HAR 5014	Stand Out/Doggone	10
70	Harvest HAR 5030	The Everlasting First/Keep On Shining	15
70	Elektra 2101 019	Alone Again Or/Bummer In The Summer (reissue, red label)	10
73	Elektra K 12113	Alone Again Or/Andmoreagain	6
75	RSO 2090 151	Time Is Like A River/You Said You Would	6

ORIGINAL LPs

66	Elek. EKL 4001/EKS 74001	LOVE (LP, gold label, U.K disc in U.S. sleeve)	100
67	Elek. EKL 4005/EKS 74005	DA CAPO (LP, orange label, with U.K. or U.S. sleeve)	75
67	Elek. EKL 4005/EKS 74005	DA CAPO (LP, with U.K. printed sleeve laminated front and back)	80
67	Elek. EKL 4013	FOREVER CHANGES (LP, mono orange label)	130
67	Elek. EKS 74013	FOREVER CHANGES (LP, stereo orange label)	100
69	Elektra EKL 4049	FOUR SAIL (LP, orange label, mono, existence unconfirmed)	40
69	Elektra EKS 74049	FOUR SAIL (LP, orange label, stereo)	45
70	Harvest SHDW 3/4	OUT HERE (2-LP, gatefold sleeve)	45
71	Harvest SHVL 787	FALSE START (LP, gatefold sleeve)	40
71	Elektra 2469 009	LOVE REVISITED (LP, gatefold sleeve)	18
73	Elektra K 32002	LOVE MASTERS (LP)	15
74	RSO 2394 145	REEL TO REAL (LP)	15

MINT VALUE £

RE-PRESSINGS

67	Elek. EKL 4001/EKS 74001	LOVE (LP, orange label, with U.K. or U.S. sleeve)	60
72	Elektra K 42068	LOVE (LP, 'butterfly' label)	25
71	Elektra EKS 74005	DA CAPO (LP, 'butterfly' label)	18
72	Elektra K 42011	DA CAPO (LP, 'butterfly' label)	15
72	Elektra K 42015	FOREVER CHANGES (LP, 'butterfly' label)	20
72	Elektra K 42030	FOUR SAIL (LP, 'butterfly' label)	15

LOVE

90	Fierce FRIGHT 036	Welsh Girl (1-sided, p/s in bag, hand-finished labels, mail-order only)	20

CHRISTOPHER LOVE

69	London HLU 10263	The Curse Goes On/You May Be The Next	18

DARLENE LOVE

(see also Bob B. Soxx & Blue Jeans, Crystals, Phil Spector, Blossoms, Allisons [U.S.], Date With Soul, Cinders)

63	London HLU 9725	(Today I Met) The Boy I'm Gonna Marry/Playing For Keeps	40
63	London HLU 9765	Wait 'Til My Bobby Gets Home/Take It From Me	40
63	London HLU 9815	A Fine Fine Boy/Marshmallow World	50
69	London HLU 10244	Wait 'Til My Bobby Gets Home/(Today I Met) The Boy I'm Gonna Marry	15
74	Warner Bros/Spector K 19011	Christmas (Baby Please Come Home)/ Not Sure - Wait Till My Bobby Comes Home (blue vinyl)	6
77	Phil Spector Intl. 2010 019	Lord If You're A Woman/Johnny Baby Please Some Home	20
77	Phil Spector Intl. 2010 019	Lord If You're A Woman/Johnny Baby Please Come Home (12", some copies 1-sided)	15
88	CBS 6529357	He's Sure The Man I Love (New Version)/Everybody Needs (p/s)	5
88	CBS 6529356	He's Sure The Man I Love/My Heart Is A clock/Everybody Needs (12" p/s)	8
90	Warner Brothers W 9535	Mr Fix-It/K.D. LANG with TAKE SIX: Ridin' The Rails (with p/s)	25
90	Warner Brothers W 9535	Mr Fix-It/K.D. LANG with TAKE SIX: Ridin' The Rails	20
64	London RE-U 1411	WAIT TILL MY BOBBY GETS HOME (EP)	250

GARFIELD LOVE & JIMMY SPRUILL

69	Blue Horizon 57-3150	Next Time You See Me/Part Time Love	35

GEOFF LOVE ORCHESTRA

(see also Mandingo, Manuel & Music Of The Mountains)

61	Columbia DB 4627	Coronation Street Theme/Sophia	6
62	Columbia DB 4881	Steptoe And Son/Over The Backyard Fence	5
70	Columbia DB 8707	Coronation Street Theme/ALIRIO DIAZ: Aranjuez Mon Amour (Rodgigo)	5
74	EMI EMI 2105	Match Of The Day/Bless This House	6

MARY LOVE

65	King KG 1024	You Turned My Bitter Into Sweet/I'm In Your Hands	250
67	Stateside SS 2009	Lay This Burden Down/Think It Over Baby	75
67	Stateside SS 2009	Lay This Burden Down/Think It Over Baby (DJ copy)	125
68	Stateside SS 2135	The Hurt Is Just Beginning/If You Change Your Mind	15
82	Kent TOWN 501	You Turned My Bitter Into Sweet/SWEETHEARTS: This Couldn't Be Me	10

MIKE LOVE

(see also Beach Boys)

83	Creole CR 61	Jingle Bell Rock/Let's Party (p/s)	8

PRESTON LOVE

00s	Beat Goes Public BGPS 009	Cissy Popcorn/BRENDA GEORGE: I Can't Stand It	8

RONNIE LOVE

61	London HLD 9272	Chills And Fever/Pledging My Love	50
78	Grapevine GRP 108	Let's Make Love/Nothing To It	8

WILLIE LOVE/WILLIE NIX

(see also Willie Nix)

66	Highway 51 H 700	THE TWO WILLIES FROM MEMPHIS (LP, 99 copies only)	75

LOVE AFFAIR

(see also L.A., Ellis, Steve Ellis, Elastic Band, Widowmaker, Morgan, Phillip Goodhand-Tait, English Rose, Rainbow Ffolly)

67	Decca F 12558	She Smiled Sweetly/Satisfaction Guaranteed	50
67	CBS 3125	Everlasting Love/Gone Are The Songs Of Yesterday	6
68	CBS 3366	Rainbow Valley/Someone Like Us (in p/s)	20
68	CBS 3366	Rainbow Valley/Someone Like Us	8
68	CBS 3674	A Day Without Love/I'm Happy	6
69	CBS 3994	One Road/Let Me Know	8
69	CBS 4300	Bringing On Back The Good Times/Another Day	8
69	CBS 4631	Baby I Know/Accept Me For What I Am	15
70	CBS 4780	Lincoln County/Sea Of Tranquility	15
70	Pye 7N 45218	Let Me Dance/Love's Looking Out At You	8
71	Parlophone R 5887	Wake Me I Am Dreaming/That's My Home	12
71	Parlophone R 5918	Help (Get Me Some Help)/Long Way Home	12
72	CBS 5017	Speak Of Peace Speak Of Joy/Brings My Whole Life Tumbling Down	10
73	CBS 1144	Everlasting Love/Bringing On Back The Good Times (p/s, 'Hall Of Fame Hits' series)	5
77	Creole CR 146	Private Lives/Let A Little Love Come In	6
68	CBS 63416	THE EVERLASTING LOVE AFFAIR (LP, mono/stereo)	30
70	CBS 64109	NEW DAY (LP)	20

LOVE & UNITY

80	Studio 16 (no. Cat. No.)	Put It On/(feat Ranking Bogart)/Dub	40
80	Studio 16 WE N1	Just Don't Care/Cut From The Master Tape (12")	30
80	Studio 16 WEA 347	I Adore You/CAPTAIN DESMOND : Lover In Dance (12")	25
79	Studio 16 WE 0014	Can't Let You Go/Dub Version (12")	30

LOVE AND WAR

80s	SRT SRT9KS 2323	Touch Of Class (p/s)	100

MINT VALUE £

LOVE CHILDREN
69 Deram DM 268 Easy Squeezy/Every Little Step 15
70 Deram DM 303 Paper Chase/My Turkey Snuffed It 20

LOVE COMMITTEE
76 Ariola AA 105 Can't Win For Losing/Love Wins Every Time 8

LOVE CONNECTION
77 Strong Like Sampson SLS01 It's My House/Fall In Love (12") 20

LOVECUT D.B.
(see also Sarah Cracknell, St. Etienne)
91 Suburbs Of Hell SOH 009EP Heartspin/Heartspin (Dripping Clock Mix)/(Marisco Disco Mix)/ (Porn Cable Mix) (12", p/s) 10
92 Suburbs Of Hell SOH 011EP JOURNEY TO THE CENTRE OF LOVE EP (12") 10

LOVE DIMENSION
79 Black Bear BLA 2010 You Stepped Into My Life/The Game 15

LOVE GENERATION (Jamaica)
73 Grape GR 3046 Money Raper/HEPTONES: The Magnificent Heptones 3 In One 6
73 Grape GR 3041 Warrika Hill/Battlefield (Third And Fourth Generation) 6

LOVE GENERATION (U.S.)
67 Liberty LBF 15018 She Touched Me/The Love In Me 15
68 Liberty LBL/LBS 83121E LOVE GENERATION (LP) 30

JOY LOVEJOY
72 Chess 6145 010 In Orbit/Uh! Hum (paper label/moulded label) 20

LOVELACE GREEN
69 Concord CON 003 Sister George/Pauper Millionaire 20

LOVELITES
78 Grapevine GRP 107 Get It Off My Conscience/Oh, What A Day 8

LOVE OF LIFE ORCHESTRA
(see also David Byrne)
80 Infidelity JMB 227 EXTENDED NICETIES (12" EP) 8

JOHNNY LOVER
(see also Little Johnny Jones, Heptones)
70 Amalgamated AMG 871 Pumpkin Eater/Version 15
70 Amalgamated AMG 873 Two Edged Sword/Version 20

LOVERS
58 Vogue Pop V 9111 Let's Elope/I Wanna Be Loved 500
58 Vogue Pop V 9111 Let's Elope/I Wanna Be Loved (78) 150

LOVERS DUB
(see also Tradition)
80 Venture CUT 7 (LP) (actually by Eargasm) 40

LOVE SCULPTURE
(see also Human Beans, Dave Edmunds)
68 Parlophone R 5664 River To Another Day/Brand New Woman 20
68 Parlophone R 5731 Wang-Dang-Doodle/The Stumble 20
68 Parlophone R 5744 Sabre Dance/Think Of Love 5
69 Parlophone R 5807 Seagull/Farandole 15
70 Parlophone R 5831 In The Land Of The Few/People People 20
68 Parlophone PMC 7059 BLUES HELPING (LP, 1st pressing, yellow/black label, mono) 70
68 Parlophone PCS 7059 BLUES HELPING (LP, 1st pressing, yellow/black label, stereo) 40
69 Parlophone PCS 7090 FORMS AND FEELINGS (LP, 1st pressing, yellow/black label) 44
70 Parlophone PCS 7059 BLUES HELPING (LP, 2nd pressing, silver/black label) 15
70 Parlophone PCS 7090 FORMS AND FEELINGS (LP, 2nd pressing, silver/black label) 12

EDDIE LOVETTE
69 Big Shot BI 519 You're My Girl/Let Them Say 8
70 London HLU 10298 Boomerang/Together 5
70 London HLJ 10311 Too Experienced/Little Blue Bird 10
70 London LGJ/ZGJ 103 TOO EXPERIENCED (LP) 12

LENE LOVICH
76 Polydor 2058 812 I Saw Mommy Kissing Santa Claus/The Christmas Song (Merry Christmas To You)/Happy Christmas 10
78 Stiff BUYJ 32 I Think We're Alone Now (Japanese)/Lucky Number (mail-order promo only) 10

LOVIN'
(see also Nerve)
67 Page One POF 035 Keep On Believing/I'm In Command 35
67 Page One POF 041 All I've Got/Do It Again 55

LOVIN' SPOONFUL
(see also John Sebastian, Mugwumps, Zalman Yanovsky, Even Dozen Jug Band)
65 Pye International 7N 25327 Do You Believe In Magic?/On The Road Again 12
66 Pye International 7N 25344 You Didn't Have To Be So Nice/My Gal 15
66 Pye International 7N 25361 Daydream/Night Owl Blues 7
66 Kama Sutra KAS 200 Summer In The City/Bald Headed Lena 8
66 Kama Sutra KAS 201 Rain On The Roof/Warm Baby 5
67 Kama Sutra KAS 204 Nashville Cats/Full Measure 10
67 Kama Sutra KAS 207 Darling Be Home Soon/Darlin' Companion 12
67 Kama Sutra KAS 208 Six O'Clock/The Finale 12
67 Kama Sutra KAS 210 She Is Still A Mystery/Only Pretty, What A Pity 8
67 Kama Sutra KAS 211 Money/Close Your Eyes 8
68 Kama Sutra KAS 213 Never Going Back/Forever 10

MINT VALUE £

66 Kama Sutra KEP 300 DID YOU EVER HAVE TO MAKE UP YOUR MIND (EP) 20
66 Kama Sutra KEP 301 JUG BAND MUSIC (EP) 20
66 Kama Sutra KEP 302 SUMMER IN THE CITY (EP) 20
67 Kama Sutra KEP 303 DAY BLUES (EP) 20
67 Kama Sutra KEP 304 NASHVILLE CATS (EP) 25
67 Kama Sutra KEP 305 LOVIN' YOU (EP) 30
67 Kama Sutra KEP 306 SOMETHING IN THE NIGHT (EP) 30
65 Pye Intl. NPL 28069 DO YOU BELIEVE IN MAGIC? (LP) 25
66 Pye Intl. NPL 28078 DAYDREAM (LP) 35
67 Kama Sutra KLP 401 HUMS OF THE LOVIN' SPOONFUL (LP) 18
67 Kama Sutra KLP 402 YOU'RE A BIG BOY NOW (LP, soundtrack) 18
67 Kama Sutra KLP 403 THE BEST OF THE LOVIN' SPOONFUL (LP) 12
68 Kama Sutra KLP 404 EVERYTHING PLAYING (LP) 15
68 Kama Sutra K(S)LP 405 THE BEST OF THE LOVIN' SPOONFUL VOL. 2 (LP) 12
69 Kama Sutra 602 009 REVELATION: REVOLUTION '69 (LP) 12

LOVING AWARENESS

(see also Glencoe, Skip Bifferty, Ian Dury)

76 More Love ML 001 LOVING AWARENESS (LP, gatefold sleeve with 2 posters) 15

LOVING KIND

(see also Noel Redding Band, Freddie Lennon)

66 Piccadilly 7N 35299 Accidental Love/Nothing Can Change This Love 15
66 Piccadilly 7N 35318 I Love The Things You Do/Treat Me Nice 18
66 Piccadilly 7N 35342 Ain't That Peculiar/With Rhyme And Reason 25

LOW

01 Tugboat TUGLP 027 THINGS WE LOST IN THE FIRE (2 x LP, 4th side etched with lyrics) 25

BRUCE LOW

56 HMV JO 464 Just Walking In The Rain/Cindy Oh Cindy (export issue) 20

LOW NOISE

81 Happy Birthday UR 5 Jungle Line/Urban Tribal/Jungle Line (Instrumental) (12", p/s) 8

LOW NUMBERS

79 Warner Brothers K 17493 Keep In Touch/Nine All Out (p/s) 25

LOW PROFYLE

80 Ellie Jay EJSP 9434 Hangin' Around/Substitute (p/s) 50

LOWBITES

70 Black Swan BW 1403 I Got It/I Got It (Version) 6
80 Black Joy DH 800 Can I Go With You?/BOBBY DODSON & TRINITY: Having My Baby (12") 15

DENNIS LOWE

70 Downtown DT 465 What's Your Name/MUSIC DOCTORS: Mr Locabe 10
70 Downtown DT 468 Stand Up For The Sound/OWEN & DENNIS: Old Man Trouble 6

JEZ LOWE

80 Fellside FE 034 JEZ LOWE (LP, textured sleeve, light green label, large 'Rams Horn' logo) 15
83 Fellside FE 044 THE OLD DURHAM ROAD (LP) 15
85 Fellisde FE 049 GALLOWAYS (LP, with lyric insert) 15
86 Fellside FE 055 TWO A ROUE (LP, with Jake Walton, lyric insert) 12

JIM LOWE

(see also John Barry Seven)

55 London HLD 8171 Close The Door/Nueva Laredo (gold label print) 60
55 London HLD 8171 Close The Door/Nueva Laredo (gold label print) (78) 15
56 London HLD 8276 Blue Suede Shoes/Maybellene (silver label print) 100
56 London HLD 8276 Blue Suede Shoes/Maybellene (silver label print) (78) 30
56 London HLD 8288 Love Is The $64,000 Dollar Question/Rene La Rue (gold label print) 75
56 London HLD 8288 Love Is The $64,000 Dollar Question/Rene La Rue (gold label print) (78) 15
56 London HLD 8317 The Green Door/The Little Man In Chinatown (as Jim Lowe & High Fives, gold label print) 50
56 London HLD 8317 The Green Door/The Little Man In Chinatown (as Jim Lowe & High Fives, later silver print label) 25
57 London HLD 8368 I Feel The Beat/By You, By You, By You (gold label print) 45
57 London HLD 8368 I Feel The Beat/By You, By You, By You (later silver print label) 30
57 London HLD 8431 Four Walls/Talkin' To The Blues 30
58 London HLD 8538 Roc-A-Chicka/The Bright Light (with Billy Vaughan's Orchestra) 125
58 London HLD 8538 Roc-A-Chicka/The Bright Light (with Billy Vaughan's Orchestra) (78) 20
60 London HLD 9043 He'll Have To Go/(This Life Is Just A) Dress Rehearsal 12
65 United Artists UP 1096 Mr Moses/Make Your Back Strong 5
58 London HA-D 2108 SONGS THEY SING BEHIND THE GREEN DOOR (LP) 50
59 London HA-D 2146 WICKED WOMEN (LP) 30

LOWLIFE

88 LOLIF DEMO 1 THE DEMOS (LP, white label test pressings only, hand-written white sleeve) 18

LOW/PIANO MAGIC/TRANSIENT WAVES

98 Rocket Girl RGIRL 4 Sleep At The Bottom/TRANSIENT WAVES: Green Acres (p/s) 6

PHILIP LOWRIE

63 Ember EMB S 179 I Might Have Known (Before)/I Might Have Known (After) 12

ART LOWRY

54 Columbia SCMC 1 The Curse Of An Aching Heart/Heart Of My Heart (export issue) 10

HENRY LOWTHER BAND

(see also Manfred Mann, John Mayall & Bluesbreakers, Keef Hartley Band, Ricotti & Albuquerque)

70 Deram SML 1070 CHILD SONG (LP) 125

MARK LOYD

65 Parlophone R 5277 I Keep Thinking About You/Will It Be The Same 10

			MINT VALUE £
65	Parlophone R 5332	Everybody Tries/She Said No	60
66	Parlophone R 5423	When Evening Falls/When I'm Gonna Find Her	200
66	Parlophone R 5423	When Evening Falls/When I'm Gonna Find Her (DJ copy)	300

L7

94	Slash 8576531	Andres/The Bomb/Interview (12" poly sleeve, green vinyl)	10
92	Slash L30780	BRICKS ARE HEAVY (LP, green marbled vinyl)	18

JEREMY LUBBOCK

58	Parlophone R 4399	Catch A Falling Star/The Man Who Invented Love	7
58	Parlophone R 4421	Lemon Twist/Tonight	10
58	Parlophone R 4473	Odd Man Out/Too Bad You're Not Around	5
58	Parlophone GEP 8745	JUST FOR THE FUN OF IT (EP)	10

LUCAS (& MIKE COTTON SOUND)

(see also Mike Cotton Sound, Artwoods)

66	Polydor 56114	I Saw Pity In The Face Of A Friend/Dance Children Dance (solo)	20
67	Pye 7N 17313	Step Out Of Line/Ain't Love Good, Ain't Love Proud	50
68	MGM MGM 1398	Soul Serenade/We Got A Thing Going Baby	40
68	MGM MGM 1427	Jack And The Beanstalk/Mother-In-Law	20

BUDDY LUCAS BAND

53	London L 1181	Organ Grinder's Swing/Laura (78, as Buddy Lucas & His Orchestra)	20
60	Pye International 7N 25045	I Want To Know/Deacon John	18
60	Pye International 7N 25045	I Want To Know/Deacon John (78)	15

TREVOR LUCAS

(see also Eclection, Fotheringay, Fairport Convention, Bronco, Bunch, Sandy Denny)

66	Reality RE 505	Waltzing Matilda/It's On	30
66	Reality RY 1002	OVERLANDER (LP)	275

LUCID DREAM

91	Euphoric E 9999T	DRIPPY EP (12", p/s)	8

JON LUCIEN

74	RCA ALP1-0493	MINDS EYE (LP)	30

LUCIFER

71	Lucifer L 001	Don't Care/Hypnosis	15
72	Lucifer L 003/004	Fuck You/Bad	8
72	Lucifer L 005/006	Prick/Want It	8
72	Lucifer L 005/006/L 003/004	Prick/Want It/Fuck You/Bad (double pack, black box set)	40
73	Lucifer L007	Mr Jack/Mr Jack	50
72	Lucifer LLP 1	BIG GUN (LP, private pressing, with poster/inserts, sold via Oz mag)	100
72	Lucifer LLP 1	BIG GUN (LP, private pressing, without poster/inserts, sold via Oz mag)	60
72	Lucifer LLP 2	EXIT (LP, private pressing, with poster, sold via Oz magazine)	140
72	Lucifer LLP 2	EXIT (LP, private pressing, without poster, sold via Oz magazine)	70

LUCIFER'S FRIEND

(see also John Lawton, Uriah Heep)

71	Philips 6003 092	Ride The Sky/Horla	15
71	Philips 6305 068	LUCIFER'S FRIEND (LP)	100

JOHNNY LUCK

58	Fontana H 110	Play Rough/Buzz, Buzz, Buzz (78)	20

LUCY

69	Major Minor MM667	Georgie/With Him	8

LUCY

(see also Def Leppard)

77	Lightning GIL 516	Never Never/Feel So Good (p/s)	20
78	B&C BCS 8	Really Got Me Goin'/Oy (p/s)	10

TOM LUCY

(see also Wasted Youth)

82	Bridgehouse BHS 15	Paris, France/Man Found Dead In Graveyard (no p/s)	6

LUCY SHOW

83	Shout XS 007	Leonardo Da Vinci/Kill The Beast (p/s)	5
85	A&M AMY 261	Ephemeral/White Space (12", p/s)	20

LUDDITES

83	Xcentric Noise SECOND 1	STRENGTH OF YOUR CRY (EP, black foldout p/s)	15
83	Xcentric Noise SECOND 1	STRENGTH OF YOUR CRY (EP, pink foldout p/s)	10

LUDLOWS

(see also Jim McCann)

61	Pye NEP 24252	THE SEA AROUND US (EP)	20
66	Pye NPL 18150	THE WIND AND THE SEA (LP)	18

LUDUS

80	New Hormones ORG 4	The Visit/Lullaby Cheat/Unveil (12", p/s with insert)	8
81	New Hormones ORG 8	My Cherry Is In Sherry/Anatomy Is Not Destiny (p/s)	5
81	New Hormones CAT 1	PICKPOCKET (C-30 cassette pack with A4 book & button in PVC bag)	12
81	New Hormones ORG 12	Mother's Hour/Patient (p/s, with poster)	5
81	New Hormones ORG 16	THE SEDUCTION (2 x 12" EP, each in p/s; whole package in poly bag)	12
80s	New Hormones	LINDER SINGS BARDOT (cassette)	12
82	New Hormones ORG 20	DANGER CAME SMILING (LP)	12

LUGWORM

97	Guided Missile GUIDE 11	Rococo Negro/BIS: Pop Song (p/s)	5

LUKE & BLAKE

66	CBS 202467	Just You/Wandering Man	8

MINT VALUE £

ROBIN LUKE

58	London HLD 8676	Susie Darlin'/Living's Loving You	12
58	London HLD 8676	Susie Darlin'/Living's Loving You (78)	10
58	London HLD 8771	Chicka Chicka Honey/My Girl	30
58	London HLD 8771	Chicka Chicka Honey/My Girl (78)	20
59	London RED 1222	ROBIN LUKE (EP)	100

LULU (& LUVVERS)

(see also Luvvers, Scotland World Cup Squad)

64	Decca F 11884	Shout/Forget Me Baby (as Lulu & Luvers)	8
64	Decca F 11965	Can't Hear You No More/I Am In Love	15
64	Decca F 12017	Here Comes The Night/That's Really Some Good	15
65	Decca F 12128	Satisfied/Surprise Surprise (as Lulu & Luvers)	18
65	Decca F 12169	Leave A Little Love/He Don't Want Your Love Anymore	10
65	Decca F 12214	Try To Understand/Not In This Whole World	8
65	Decca F 12254	Tell Me Like It Is/Stop Fooling Around	20
66	Decca F 12326	Call Me/After You	7
66	Decca F 12491	What A Wonderful Feeling/Tossin' And Turnin'	12
67	Columbia DB 8169	The Boat That I Row/Dreary Days And Nights	8
67	Columbia DB 8221	Let's Pretend/To Sir With Love	10
67	Columbia DB 8295	Love Loves To Love/You And I	8
68	Columbia DB 8358	Me, The Peaceful Heart/Lookout	5
68	Columbia DB 8425	Boy/Sad Memories	10
68	Columbia DB 8500	I'm A Tiger/Without Him	5
69	Columbia DB 8550	Boom Bang-A-Bang/March!	5
69	Atco 226 008	Oh Me, Oh My (I'm A Fool For You Baby)/Sweep Around Your Own Backyard	10
65	Decca DFE 8597	LULU (EP)	35
65	Decca LK 4719	SOMETHING TO SHOUT ABOUT (LP)	60
67	Ace Of Clubs ACL 1232	LULU! (LP)	20
67	Fontana (S)TL 5446	TO SIR, WITH LOVE (LP, soundtrack, with Ron Grainer & Mindbenders)	60
67	Columbia S(C)X 6201	LOVE LOVES TO LOVE LULU (LP)	35
69	Columbia S(C)X 6365	LULU'S ALBUM (LP)	25
69	Atco 228 031	NEW ROUTES (LP)	25
70	Atco 2400	MELODY FAIR (LP)	15

LULU BELLE & SCOTTY

50	London L 833	Have I Told You Lately That I Love You/Schrudle Du (78)	10
65	London HA-B 8277	SWEETHEART STILL (LP)	15

BOB LUMAN

(see also Sue Thompson & Bob Luman)

60	Warner Bros WB 12	Dreamy Doll/Buttercup	25
60	Warner Bros WB 18	Let's Think About Livin'/You've Got Everything	10
60	Warner Bros WB 28	Why, Why, Bye, Bye/Oh, Lonesome Me	15
61	Warner Bros WB 37	The Great Snow Man/The Pig Latin Song	15
61	Warner Bros WB 49	Private Eye/You Turned Down The Lights	10
62	Warner Bros WB 60	Louisiana Man/Rocks Of Reno (unissued)	0
62	Warner Bros WB 75	Hey Joe/The Fool	12
64	Hickory 45-1238	The File/Bigger Men Than I	10
64	Hickory 45-1266	(Empty Walls) A Lonely Room/Run On Home Baby Brother	6
64	Hickory 45-1277	Old George Dickel/Fire Engine Red	6
65	Hickory 45-1289	Bad Bad Day/Tears From Out Of Nowhere	10
65	Hickory 45-1410	Come On And Sing/It's A Sin	6
68	CBS 3602	Ain't Got Time To Be Unhappy/I Can't Remember To Forget	10
61	Warner Bros WEP 6046	LET'S THINK ABOUT LIVIN' (EP, mono)	40
61	Warner Bros WSEP 2046	LET'S THINK ABOUT LIVIN' (EP, stereo)	45
62	Warner Bros WEP 6055	LET'S THINK ABOUT LIVIN' NO. 2 (EP, mono)	35
62	Warner Bros WSEP 2055	LET'S THINK ABOUT LIVIN' NO. 2 (EP, stereo)	40
62	Warner Bros WEP 6102	LET'S THINK ABOUT LIVIN' NO. 3 (EP, mono)	35
62	Warner Bros WSEP 2102	LET'S THINK ABOUT LIVIN' NO. 3 (EP, stereo)	40
60	Warner Bros WM 4025	LET'S THINK ABOUT LIVIN' (LP, mono)	40
60	Warner Bros WS 8025	LET'S THINK ABOUT LIVIN' (LP, stereo)	60
64	Hickory LPM 124	LIVIN' LOVIN' SOUNDS (LP)	35

BOB LUMAN/BOBBY LORD

(see also Bobby Lord)

64	Hickory LPE 1501	HICKORY SHOWCASE VOL. 2 (EP, 1 side each)	10
64	Hickory LPE 1504	HICKORY SHOWCASE VOL. 3 (EP, 1 side each)	10
64	Hickory LPM 121	CAN'T TAKE THE COUNTRY FROM THE BOYS (LP, 1 side each)	15

RUFUS LUMLEY

66	Stateside SS 516	I'm Standing/Let's Hide Away (Me And You)	250
66	Stateside SS 516	I'm Standing/Let's Hide Away (Me And You) (DJ copy)	375
78	EMI International INT 556	I'm Standing/Let's Hide Away (Me And You) (reissue)	15

LUNA C

93	Knifeforce KF 001	THE LUNA C PROJECT EP (12")	40
93	Knifeforce KF 002	LUNA C PROJECT 2 - MISSION OF MADNESS (12")	40
93	Knifeforce KF 012	Death Of A Psychopath/Bass Drum Jungle Music (12")	10
94	Knifeforce KF 025	Piano Progression (Double Whopper Mix)/Onward (Extra Pepperami Mix) (12")	10

LUNACHICKS

89	Blast First BFFP 44	SUGAR LUV EP (7" double pack)	8

LUNAR TWO

60s	Spot JWS 551	Get It Take It/Don't Ever Leave Me	20

LUNATIC FRINGE

82	Resurrection	Keep In Touch	8
84	COR 1	CRINGE WITH THE FRINGE (EP)	12

MINT VALUE £

LYDIA LUNCH
(see also Eight-Eyed Spy, Roland S. Howard, No Trend)

91	UFO UFOPF 1	Spooky (mono)/Spooky (stereo) (no p/s, promo only)	6
93	Clawfist X-PIG 19	Unearthly Delights/Busted (p/s)	8
82	Situation 2 SITU 6	13.13 (LP, with inner sleeve)	20
84	Doublevision DVR 5	IN LIMBO (LP, red vinyl with inner sleeve)	20
86	Widowspeak SWP 01/07	THE INTIMATE DIARIES OF THE SEXUALLY INSANE (cassette, box set with book, signed)	25
87	Widowspeak WSP 8	HYSTERIE (2-LP, with inners and poster)	20

ART LUND

53	MGM SP 1042	If I Were A Bell/JOHNNY DESMOND: A Bushel And A Peck	5
65	United Artists UP 1100	Branded/Gonna Have A Little Talk	7
57	Vogue Coral LVA 9056	THIS IS ART (LP)	20

TED LUNE
(see also Michael Medwin 8 Army Game Cast)

60	Philips PB 1068	Mr Custer/Time Machine	6

LARRY LUREX
(see also Queen)

73	EMI EMI 2030	I Can Hear Music/Goin' Back (demo)	300
73	EMI EMI 2030	I Can Hear Music/Goin' Back (press-out centre; beware of solid-centered counterfeits)	200

LURKERS
(see also Pete Stride & John Plain, Fulham Furies, Rowdies)

77	Beggars Banquet BEG 1	Free Admission Single: Shadow/Love Story (p/s, black vinyl)	10
77	Beggars Banquet BEG 1	Free Admission Single: Shadow/Love Story (p/s, reissue, red, blue or white vinyl)	12
77	Beggars Banquet BEG 2	Freak Show/Mass Media Believer (p/s)	8
78	Beggars Banquet BEG 6	Ain't Got A Clue/Ooh Ooh I Love You (p/s, 15,000 with gold flexidisc, 'Chaos Brothers Fulham Fallout Firty Free' [BEG 61/2])	6
78	Beggars Banquet BEG 6	Ain't Got A Clue/Ooh Ooh I Love You (p/s)	5
78	Beggars Banquet BEG 6	Ain't Got A Clue/Ooh Ooh I Love You (reissue, different p/s, with clear vinyl picture flexidisc)	5
79	Beggars Banquet BACK 1	Shadow/Love Story//Freak Show/Mass Media Believer (reissue double pack)	5
79	Beggars Banquet BACK 3	I Don't Need To Tell Her/Pills//Just Thirteen/Countdown (double pack)	5
82	Clay CLAY 17P	Drag You Out/Heroin (It's All Over) (picture disc)	5
78	Beggars Banquet BEGA 2	FULHAM FALLOUT (LP, gatefold sleeve, some with picture disc flexi 'Chaos Brothers Fulham Fallout Firty Free' [BEG 6 ½] & stickered sleeve)	20
78	Beggars Banquet BEGA 2	FULHAM FALLOUT (LP, gatefold sleeve)	12
79	Beggars Banquet BEGA 8	GOD'S LONELY MEN (LP, with inner)	12
85	Sin 006	FEAR AND WHISKEY (LP)	12
89	Link LP 103	LIVE & LOUD! (LP)	12

LUSH

90	4AD CAD 0013	SWEETNESS AND LIGHT EP (12")	8
90	4AD CAD 0017	GALA (2-LP)	18

DON LUSHER BAND

55	Decca F 10560	Rock 'n' Roll/On With The Don	20
56	Decca F 10740	Fast And Furious/Let's Do It	8
67	CBS 62883	FROM LUSHER WITH LOVE (LP)	15

LUSTMØRD

82	Sterile SR 3	LUSTMØRD (LP, with odorous label)	35

NELLIE LUTCHER (& HER RHYTHM)

54	Brunswick 05352	Blues In The Night/Breezin' Along With The Breeze	15
55	Brunswick 05437	It's Been Said/Please Come Back	10
55	Brunswick 05497	Whose Honey Are You?/If I Didn't Love You Like I Do	10
60	Capitol CL 15106	My Mother's Eyes/The Heart Of A Clown	6
60	Capitol EAP 20066	REAL GONE (EP)	30
56	Philips BBE 12045	NELLIE LUTCHER (EP)	30
51	Capitol LC 6500	REAL GONE! (10" LP)	50
57	London HA-U 2036	OUR NEW NELLIE (LP)	50

CLAUDE LUTER ORCHESTRA

59	Vogue V 9132	The Day That The Rains Came/La Grande Coco	10

FRANK LUTHER

60	Decca F 9050	The Little Red Hen (Song Story) (both sides)	5
60	Decca F 9051	The Three Billy Goats Gruff (Song Story) (both sides)	5

LUTHER & LITTLE EVA

57	Parlophone R 4292	Love Is Strange/Ain't Got No Home	400
57	Parlophone R 4292	Love Is Strange/Ain't Got No Home (78)	140

LUV BUG

86	Roxy!-Ritz TEASE 2	You Can Count On Me/You Can't Have It (p/s)	7

LUV MACHINE

71	Polydor 2058 080	Witches Wand/In The Early Hours	30
71	Polydor 2460 102	LUV MACHINE (LP)	200

LUVVERS
(see also Lulu)

66	Parlophone R 5459	The House On The Hill/Most Unlovely	70

MICK LUVZIT

66	Decca F 12421	Long Time Between Lovers/Though I Still Love You	20

MINT VALUE £

GARY LUX

85	Global LUX 2	Children Of The World/Movies (p/s)	5

L-VOAG

(see also Homosexuals)

79	Sesame Songs MOVE 1	MOVE (EP, p/s with handmade labels & insert)	30
81	Axis No. 9	THE WAY OUT (LP, with booklet & poster)	40

LYDS

96	Dig The Fuzz DIG 014	Fly Away With Me/Seperations (p/s)	15

ARTHUR LYMAN GROUP

61	Vogue V 9183	Yellow Bird/Havah Magila	6
59	Vogue VEH 70166	GREATEST HITS VOL. 1 (EP)	6
59	Vogue VA 160142	TABOO VOL. 1 (LP, mono)	15
59	Vogue SAV 8002	TABOO VOL. 1 (LP, stereo)	18
61	Vogue VA 160174	TABOO VOL. 2 (LP, also stereo SAV 8003)	15

FRANKIE LYMON (& TEENAGERS)

56	Columbia SCM 5265	Why Do Fools Fall In Love?/Please Be Mine (as Teenagers featuring Frankie Lymon)	60
56	Columbia SCM 5285	I Want You To Be My Girl/I'm Not A Know It All	50
56	Columbia SCM 5285	I Want You To Be My Girl/I'm Not A Know It All (78)	12
56	Columbia DB 3819	Who Can Explain?/I Promise To Remember	50
56	Columbia DB 3819	Who Can Explain?/I Promise To Remember (78)	10
56	Columbia DB 3858	Share/The A.B.C.'s Of Love	50
56	Columbia DB 3858	Share/The A.B.C.'s Of Love (78)	12
57	Columbia DB 3878	I'm Not A Juvenile Delinquent/Baby, Baby	40
57	Columbia DB 3910	Teenage Love/Paper Castles	40
57	Columbia DB 3910	Teenage Love/Paper Castles (78)	10
57	Columbia DB 3942	Miracle In The Rain/Out In The Cold Again	40
57	Columbia DB 3942	Miracle In The Rain/Out In The Cold Again (78)	12
57	Columbia DB 3983	Goody Goody/Creation Of Love	20
57	Columbia DB 4028	My Girl/So Goes My Love	25
57	Columbia DB 4028	My Girl/So Goes My Love (78)	15
58	Columbia DB 4073	Thumb Thumb/Footsteps (solo)	30
58	Columbia DB 4073	Thumb Thumb/Footsteps (solo) (78)	15
58	Columbia DB 4134	Mama Don't Allow It/Portable On My Shoulder (solo)	20
58	Columbia DB 4134	Mama Don't Allow It/Portable On My Shoulder (solo) (78)	18
59	Columbia DB 4245	Melinda/The Only Way To Love (solo)	20
59	Columbia DB 4245	Melinda/The Only Way To Love (solo) (78)	30
59	Columbia DB 4295	Up Jumped A Rabbit/No Matter What You've Done (solo)	22
60	Columbia DB 4499	Little Bitty Pretty One/Creation Of Love (solo)	30
66	King KG 1042	Why Do Fools Fall In Love?/I'm Not A Juvenile Delinquent	7
57	Columbia SEG 7662	TEENAGE ROCK (EP)	50
57	Columbia SEG 7694	THE TEENAGERS FEATURING FRANKIE LYMON (EP)	60
57	Columbia SEG 7734	FRANKIE LYMON AND THE TEENAGERS (EP)	60
58	Columbia 33S 1127	FRANKIE LYMON IN LONDON (10" LP, solo)	100
58	Columbia 33S 1134	ROCKIN' WITH FRANKIE LYMON (10" LP, solo)	500
75	Pye International NSPL 28251	WHY DO FOOLS FALL IN LOVE (LP)	15

LEWIS LYMON & TEENCHORDS

58	Oriole 45-CB 1419	Too Young/Your Last Chance	500
58	Oriole CB 1419	Too Young/Your Last Chance (78)	100

DERMOTT LYNCH

(see also Trevor, Carl Dawkins, Joe White)

68	Blue Cat BS 101	Hot Shot/I've Got Your Number	60
68	Blue Cat BS 122	I Got Everything/Echo	40
68	Doctor Bird DB 1115	Adults Only/Cool It	40

E D LYNCH

66	Fontana TF688	Sad Songs/Shoe Of True Love	15

JOE LYNCH

69	Spectrum SP 107	King Child/Johnny Appleseed	5

KENNY LYNCH

60	HMV POP 751	Mountain Of Love/Why Do You Treat Me This Way?	10
60	HMV POP 786	Slowcoach/You Make Love So Well	6
61	HMV POP 841	So/Love Me	6
61	HMV POP 900	The Story Behind My Tears/Steady Kind	6
61	HMV POP 985	There's Never Been A Girl/Doll Face	6
62	HMV POP 1005	It Would Take A Miracle/Strolling Blues	6
62	HMV POP 1057	Puff/Happy That's Me	10
62	HMV POP 1090	Up On The Roof/Jump On Your Broomstick	6
63	HMV POP 1136	Misery/Shut The Door	8
63	HMV POP 1165	You Can Never Stop Me Loving You/Crazy Crazes	5
63	HMV POP 1229	For You (There's Not A Thing I Wouldn't Do)/With Somebody	6
63	HMV POP 1260	Shake And Scream/Harlem Library	7
64	HMV POP 1280	Stand By Me/Baby It's True	7
64	HMV POP 1321	That's What Little Girls Are Made For/What Am I To You?	6
64	HMV POP 1367	My Own Two Feet/So Much To Love You For	30
65	HMV POP 1430	I'll Stay By You/For Loving You Baby	8
65	HMV POP 1476	Nothing But The Real Thing/Don't Ask Me To Stop Loving You	6
65	HMV POP 1496	Get Out Of My Way/One Look At You	10
66	HMV POP 1534	The World I Used To Know/Come On Come On	7
67	HMV POP 1577	I Just Wanna Love You/It's Too Late	8
67	HMV POP 1604	Movin' Away/Could I Count On You	150
68	Columbia DB 8329	Mister Moonlight/The Other Side Of Dreamland	15
68	Columbia DB 8498	Along Comes Love/Sweet Situation	15

			MINT VALUE £
69	Columbia DB 8599	The Drifter/Did I Stay Too Long?	40
70	Columbia DB 8703	In Old Kentucky/Loving You Is Sweeter Than Ever	15
63	HMV 7EG 8820	HEY GIRL (EP)	15
64	HMV 7EG 8855	KENNY LYNCH (EP)	15
65	HMV 7EG 8881	WHAT AM I TO YOU (EP)	15
63	HMV CLP 1635	UP ON THE ROOF (LP, mono)	45
63	HMV CSD 1489	UP ON THE ROOF (LP, stereo)	50

LEE LYNCH (& BLUE ANGELS)

66	Decca F 12375	You Won't See Me/You Know There's Me (as Lee Lynch & Blue Angels)	10
69	Ember EMB S 262	Stay Awhile/Bad Time To Stop Loving Me (p/s)	10
70	Ember EMB S 271	Sweet Woman/Can't Take My Eyes Off You (p/s)	10
70	Ember EMB S 282	Joe Poor Loves Daphne Elizabeth Rich/It's Love (p/s)	10
67	Pye 7N 17363	I'll Hold You In My Heart/Looking Through My Teardrops	10

LINDA LYNDELL

68	Stax 601 041	Bring Your Love Back To Me/Here I Am	50

BARBARA LYNN

64	London HLW 9918	Oh! Baby (We Got A Good Thing Goin')/Unfair	35
65	Immediate IM 011	You Can't Buy My Love/That's What A Friend Will Do	45
66	London HLU 10094	You Left The Water Running/Until I'm Free	35
67	Sue WI 4028	Letter To Mommy And Daddy/Second Fiddle Girl	50
67	Sue WI 4038	You'll Lose A Good Thing/Lonely Heartaches	55
71	Atlantic 2091 133	Take Your Love And Run/(Until Then) I'll Suffer	20
75	Oval OVAL 1006	Letter To Mommy And Daddy/You'll Lose A Good Thing	10
67	Sue ILP 949	THE BARBARA LYNN STORY (LP)	200

BOBBI LYNN

68	Stateside SS 2088	Earthquake/Opportunity Street	45
68	Stateside SS 2088	Earthquake/Opportunity Street (DJ copy)	75
71	Bell BLL 1168	Earthquake/Opportunity Street (reissue)	8

CHERYL LYNN

84	Streetwave KHAN 23	Encore/Got To Be Real (12")	10
79	CBS CBS 12-6967	Got To Be Real/Come In From The Rain (12")	10

DONNA LYNN

64	Capitol CL 15359	Silly Girl/There Goes The Boy I Love With Mary	6

KARI LYNN

61	Oriole CB 1632	Yo Yo/Summer Day	15
61	Oriole CB 1644	You've Got To See Mamma Every Night/Lonesome And Sorry	15

LORETTA LYNN

(see also Conway Twitty)

68	MCA MUP 338	LORETTA LYNN (LP)	12

PATTI LYNN

62	Fontana H 370	I See It All Now/Someone Else's Valentine	15
62	Fontana H 391	Johnny Angel/Tonight You Belong To Me	15
62	Fontana 267 247 TF	Tell Me Telstar/Big Big Love	20
62	Fontana TFE 17392	PATTI (EP)	40

TAM(M)I LYNN

66	Atlantic AT 4071	I'm Gonna Run Away From You/The Boy Next Door	60
66	Atlantic AT 4071	I'm Gonna Run Away From You/The Boy Next Door (DJ Copy)	100
71	Mojo 2092 001	I'm Gonna Run Away From You/The Boy Next Door (reissue)	10
71	Mojo 2092 012	That's Understanding/Never No More	6
75	Contempo CS 9026	I'm Gonna Run Away From You/The Boy Next Door (2nd reissue)	6
71	Mojo 2916 007	LOVE IS HERE AND NOW YOU'RE GONE (LP)	25

VERA LYNN

(see also Johnstone Brothers, Frank Weir & His Orchestra)

52	Decca F 9927	Auf Wiederseh'n, Sweetheart/From The Time You Say Goodbye	10
54	Decca F 10372	My Son, My Son/Our Heaven On Earth (with Frank Weir & His Saxophone)	10
56	Decca F 10715	Who Are We?/I'll Be True To You	5
56	Decca F 10799	A House With Love In It/Little Lost Dog	5

GLORIA LYNNE

64	London HLY 9846	I Wish You Love/Through A Long And Sleeping Night	8
64	London HLY 9888	I Should Care/Indian Love Call	8
69	Fontana TF 1017	Problem Child/I've Got To Be Someone	6
59	Top Rank JKP 2024	MEET GLORIA LYNNE (EP, with Wild Bill Davis)	22
60	Top Rank BUY 031	LONELY AND SENTIMENTAL (LP)	25
64	London HA-Y 8112	AT THE LAS VEGAS THUNDERBIRD (LP, with Herman Foster Trio)	15
65	Fontana TL 5315	INTIMATE MOMENTS (LP)	15
72	Mojo 2916 016	HAPPY AND IN LOVE (LP)	25

SUE LYNNE

68	RCA Victor RCA 1724	Reach For The Moon/All Alone	10
69	RCA Victor RCA 1822	You/Don't Pity Me	150
69	RCA Victor RCA 1822	You/Don't Pity Me (DJ copy)	200
69	RCA Victor RCA 1874	Baby Baby Baby/You Lose Again	7

PHIL LYNOTT

(see also Thin Lizzy, Gary Moore & Phil Lynott, John Sykes, Rockers)

80	Vertigo LYNT 1	King's Call/Yellow Pearl (12", p/s)	8
80	Vertigo SOLO 2	King's Call/Ode To A Black Man (p/s)	5
81	Vertigo SOLO 3	Yellow Pearl/Girls (p/s, clear vinyl)	5
85	Vertigo SOLO 5	Old Town/Beat Of The Drum (p/s)	6

MINT VALUE £

85	Polydor POSPD 777	19/19 (Dub Version)//THIN LIZZY: Whiskey In The Jar (live) (double pack, 2nd disc 1-sided)	8
80	Vertigo PHIL 1	SOLO IN SOHO (LP, picture disc, die-cut sleeve)	15

JACKIE LYNTON
(see also Savoy Brown Blues Band)

61	Piccadilly 7N 35012	Over The Rainbow/High In The Sky	10
62	Piccadilly 7N 35055	Don't Take Away Your Love/Wishful Thinking	10
62	Piccadilly 7N 35064	All Of Me/I'd Steal	7
63	Piccadilly 7N 35107	I Believe/The Girl In The Wood	7
63	Piccadilly 7N 35140	Jeannie With The Light Brown Hair/Teddy Bear's Picnic	7
63	Piccadilly 7N 35156	I'm Talkin' About You/Lawdy Miss Clawdy	7
64	Piccadilly 7N 35177	Little Child/Never A Mention	7
64	Piccadilly 7N 35190	Laura/Ebb Tide	7
65	Decca F 12052	Three Blind Mice/Corrina Corrine	6
67	Columbia DB 8097	He'll Have To Go/Only You	10
67	Columbia DB 8180	Decision/Sporting Life	10
67	Columbia DB 8224	Answer Me/I Never Loved A Girl Like You	25
79	Thumb TR003	Dan (The Hedgehog Song)/Farting With The Famous	8
74	WWA WWA 012	THE JACKIE LYNTON ALBUM (LP)	15

LYNX

78	ST Products SRTS/78/CUS 112	See The Light/C.I.A. (no p/s, 500 only)	100

LYNYRD SKYNYRD

74	MCA MCA 136	Don't Ask Me No Questions/Take Your Time	5
74	MCA MCA 160	Sweet Home Alabama/Take Your Time	5
75	MCA MCA 199	Saturday Night Special/Made In The Shade	5
76	MCA MCA 229	Double Trouble/Roll Gypsy Roll	5
76	MCA MCA 251	Free Bird/Sweet Home Alabama/Double Trouble (p/s)	8
76	MCA MCA 275	Free Bird (Edit)/Gimme Three Steps (p/s)	8
74	MCA MCG 3502	PRONOUNCED LEH-NERD SKIN-NERD (LP, gatefold sleeve)	18
77	MCA MCG 3525	STREET SURVIVORS (LP, gatefold sleeve with tour dates on inner sleeve)	15

BARBARA LYON

55	Columbia SCM 5186	I Love To Dance With You/Yes You Are	10
55	Columbia SCM 5207	Whisper/Where You Are	10
56	Columbia SCM 5232	Band Of Gold/Such A Day	8
56	Columbia SCM 5276	Puppy Love/The Birds And The Bees	8
56	Columbia DB 3826	It's Better In The Dark/A Heart Without A Sweetheart	6
56	Columbia DB 3865	Falling In Love/Letter To A Soldier	15
57	Columbia DB 3931	C'est La Vie/Fire Down Below	5
57	Columbia DB 4026	Thanks For The Loan Of A Dream/Third Finger - Left Hand	5
58	Columbia DB 4137	Red Was The Moon/Ring On A Ribbon	5
60	Triumph RGM 1027	My Charlie/Tell Me	40
56	Columbia SEG 7640	MY FOUR FRIENDS (EP)	20

RICHARD LYON

59	Fontana H 206	All My Own/Private Eye	22
59	Fontana H 206	All My Own/Private Eye (78)	12

LYON ST.
(see under Associates)

SUE LYON
(See also Leroy Holmes)

62	MGM 1159	Lolita Ya Ya/LEROY HOLMES : Main Theme From Lolita	10

LYONS & MALONE

69	Jay Boy BOY 9	Doctor Gentle/She's Alright	60

LYRICS
(see also Randy's All Stars, Viceroys, Jackie Mittoo, Fred Locks)

67	Coxsone CS 7003	A Get It/KEN PARKER: How Strong	50
68	Coxsone CS 7067	Music Like Dirt/TONETTES: I Give It To You	60
70	Randy's RAN 504	Give Thanks And Praises/TOMMY McCOOK: Get Ready	15
71	Randy's RAN 511	Give Thanks/RANDY'S ALL STARS: Give - Version	15

LYRICS BORN & THE POETS OF RHYTHM

99	Mo Wax MWR 114S	I Changed My Mind (Andy Votel Remix)/(Andy Votel Instrumental)/(Poets Remix)/(DJ Spinna Remix) (double pack, gatefold sleeve)	12

LARS LYSTEDY SEXTET

64	Realm REP 4004	LARS LYSTEDY SEXTET (EP)	10

JIMMY LYTELL

59	London HL 8873	Hot Cargo/A Blues Serenade	10

JOHNNY LYTLE

68	Minit MLF 11006	Gonna Get That Boat (Parts 1 & 2)	12

HUMPHREY LYTTELTON (& HIS BAND)
(see also Shirley Abicair, Sidney Bechet, George Brown, Buck Clayton, Helen Shapiro, Radiohead)o

SINGLES

51	Saturn EGX 105	When The Saints Go Marching In/Careless Love (78, picture disc)	60
53	Parlophone MSP 6001	Out Of The Gallion/The Old Grey Mare	10
53	Parlophone MSP 6023	Muskrat Ramble/Mamzelle Josephine (as Lyttelton Paseo Band, B-side with George Brown)	5
53	Parlophone MSP 6033	Maryland, My Maryland/Blue For Waterloo	5
53	Parlophone MSP 6034	Shake It And Break It/Jail Break	10
54	Parlophone MSP 6076	East Coast Trot/Breeze	10
54	Parlophone MSP 6093	Just Once For All Time/Joshua, Fit The Battle Of Jericho	5

			MINT VALUE £
54	Parlophone MSP 6097	Mainly Traditional/Oh! Dad (with 'Melody Maker' All Stars)	5
54	Parlophone MSP 6128	Mezzy's Tune/Jelly Bean Blues	5
56	Tempo A 10	When The Saints Go Marching In/Careless Love	8
57	Parlophone R 4333	Early Call (Bermondsey Bounce)/Creole Serenade	10
58	Parlophone CMSP 41	Bad Penny Blues/Baby Doll (export issue)	20
58	Decca F 11058	La Paloma/Bodega	5
59	Parlophone R 4519	Saturday Jump/The Bear Steps Out	8
59	Parlophone R 4519	Saturday Jump/The Bear Steps Out (78)	10
EPs			
55	Tempo EXA 1	HUMPHREY LYTTELTON & HIS BAND (EP)	10
LPs			
53	Parlophone PMD 1006	JAZZ CONCERT (10" LP)	30
54	Parlophone PMC 1012	HUMPH AT THE CONWAY (LP)	30
55	Parlophone PMD 1032	JAZZ AT THE ROYAL FESTIVAL HALL (10" LP)	20
56	Parlophone PMD 1035	JAZZ SESSION WITH HUMPH (10" LP)	15
56	Parlophone PMD 1044	HUMPH SWINGS OUT (10" LP)	25
57	Parlophone PMD 1049	HERE'S HUMPH (10" LP)	15
58	Parlophone PMD 1052	KATH MEETS HUMPH (10" LP, with Kathy Stobart)	30
58	Parlophone PMC 1070	HUMPH IN PERSPECTIVE (LP)	25
58	Decca LK 4276	I PLAY AS I PLEASE (LP)	20
59	Parlophone PMC 1110	TRIPLE EXPOSURE (LP)	60
54	Esquire 32-007	HUMPHREY LYTTELTON AND HIS BAND (LP)	20
60	Columbia 33SX 1239	BLUES IN THE NIGHT (LP)	25
60	Columbia 33SX 1305	HUMPH PLAYS STANDARDS (LP)	25
60	Columbia 33SX 1364	HUMPH MEETS CAB (LP)	50
61	Columbia 33SX 3382	HUMPH RETURNS TO THE CONWAY (LP)	20
62	Columbia 33SX 1484	LATE NIGHT FINAL (LP)	20
69	Polydor 2460 140	DUKE ELLINGTON CLASSICS (LP)	15
69	Polydor 2661 001	21 YEARS ON (LP)	15

M

M
(see also Robin Scott)

79	MCA MCAT 413	Pop Musik/M Factor (12", p/s, double groove)	8

MABEL

78	Sonet SON 2147	Boom Boom/FBI On The Nail (p/s)	6

MABEL JOY

75	Real RR 2004	MABEL JOY (LP)	20

MOMS MABLEY

69	Mercury MF 1127	Abraham, Martin And John/Sunny	8
71	Mercury 6052 109	That's Pops/I Surrender Dear	6

WILLIE MABON

64	Sue WI 320	Got To Have Some/Why Did It Happen To Me	45
65	Sue WI 331	Just Got Some/That's No Big Thing	45
65	Sue WI 382	I'm The Fixer/Some More	45

MABRAK

78	Different GET A101	DRUM TALK (mixed by King Tubby) (LP)	100

SPENCER MAC

70	Penny Farthing PEN 723	Blues Up In Down Town/Ka Ka Kabya Mow Mow	90
70	Penny Farthing PEN 742	Commuter/Better By You - Better By Me	45

MACABRE

87	Vinyl solution SOL 18	GRIM REALITY (LP, with insert)	18

GLO MACARI

65	Piccadilly 7N 35218	He Knows I Love Him Too Much/I've Lost You	15
71	Columbia DB 8821	Looking For Love/People Like You	15

DAN MacARTHUR
(see also Jah Wobble, PiL)

79	Virgin VS 275-12	DAN MacARTHUR (12" EP)	8

NEIL MacARTHUR
(see also Colin Blunstone, Zombies)

69	Deram DM 225	She's Not There/World Of Glass	25
69	Deram DM 262	Don't Try To Explain/Without Her	15
69	Deram DM 275	It's Not Easy/12.29	15

MACARTHUR PARK
(see also Shadows)

70	Columbia DB 8683	Taffeta Rose/Sammy	12
71	Philips 6006 086	Lottie Lottie/Love Is Coming	6

MACATTACK

86	Baad! Records 12HIP1AZ	ART OF DRUMS (12" EP)	15

DAVID MACBETH

59	Pye Nixa 7N 15231	Mr. Blue/Here's A Heart	7
60	Pye 7N 15250	Tell Her From Me/Livin' Dangerously	5

MINT VALUE £

62	Piccadilly 7N 35072	Have I Told You Lately That I Love You/A Brother Like You	6
63	Piccadilly 7N 35092	A Very Good Year For Girls/Broken Hearts	5

MACC LADS

89	Renegade RS 1	Jingle Bells/Even Uglier Women (p/s)	5
90	FM Revolver VHF 42	Barrels Round/Jingle Bells (p/s)	5
86	Hectic House HHS 1	EH UP! MACC LADS (EP)	5
85	FM Revolver FMLP 56	BEER AND SEX AND CHIPS'N'GRAVY (LP, white vinyl)	15
88	FM Revolver WKFMLP 115	LIVE AT LEEDS (LP, blue vinyl)	15

EWAN MacCOLL

(see also A.L. Lloyd)

58	Topic 10T 26	BARRACK ROOM BALLADS (10" LP)	30
58	Topic 10T 36	BOLD SPORTSMEN ALL (10" LP, with A.L. Lloyd)	30
58	Topic 10T 50	STILL I LOVE HIM (10" LP with booklet, with Isla Cameron)	35
60	Topic 12T 41	STREETS OF SONG (LP, with Dominic Behan, with booklet and original blue label)	20
61	PRE 13004	THE BEST OF EWAN MacCOLL (LP)	12
62	Topic 12T 79	THE JACOBITE REBELLIONS (LP, with original blue label)	18
64	Topic 12T 103	ENGLISH AND SCOTTISH FOLK BALLADS (LP, with A.L. Lloyd, initial pressing with blue label & booklet)	30
64	Topic 12T 103	ENGLISH AND SCOTTISH FOLK BALLADS (LP, with A.L. Lloyd)	20
67	Topic 12T 130	BUNDOOK BALLADS (LP, originally with blue label)	18
67	Argo ZFB 12	SOLO FLIGHT (LP; reissued 1972)	30
67	Xtra 1052	BLOW BOYS BLOW - SONGS OF THE SEA (LP, with A.L. Lloyd)	15
68	Argo (Z)DA 85	THE WANTON MUSE (LP, with booklet)	25
72	Argo (Z)DA 85	THE WANTON MUSE (LP, reissue)	12

EWAN MacCOLL & PEGGY SEEGER (& CHARLES PARKER)

(see also Peggy Seeger, A.L. Lloyd, Isla Cameron)

60s	AUEW AUEW 1	We Are The Engineers/I'm Gonna Be An Engineer (p/s)	6
57	Topic 10T 13	SHUTTLE AND CAGE (10" LP)	40
61	Topic 12T 16	CHORUS FROM THE GALLOWS (LP, original pressing with blue label, insert)	20
61	Topic 12T 16	CHORUS FROM THE GALLOWS (LP)	15
64	Topic 12T 104	STEAM WHISTLE BALLADS (LP, blue label)	20
64	Topic 12T 104	STEAM WHISTLE BALLADS (LP, later reissue with booklet)	15
65	Argo RG 474	THE BALLAD OF JOHN AXON (LP, by Ewan MacColl & Charles Parker)	25
67	Topic 12T 147	THE MANCHESTER ANGEL (LP, original pressing with blue label)	18
67	Topic 12T 147	THE MANCHESTER ANGEL (LP)	12
67	Argo DA 140	THE BIG HEWER - A RADIO BALLAD BY EWAN MacCOLL, PEGGY SEEGER, CHARLES PARKER (LP, documentary with music)	30
67	Argo (Z)DA 66	LONG HARVEST 1 (LP)	15
67	Argo (Z)DA 67	LONG HARVEST 2 (LP)	15
67	Argo (Z)DA 68	LONG HARVEST 3 (LP)	15
67	Argo (Z)DA 69	LONG HARVEST 4 (LP)	15
67	Argo RG 502	SINGING THE FISHING (LP, with Charles Parker)	25
67	Argo DA 142	SINGING THE FISHING (LP, reissue, with Charles Parker)	18
68	Argo (Z)DA 70	LONG HARVEST 5 (LP)	15
68	Argo (Z)DA 71	LONG HARVEST 6 (LP)	15
68	Argo (Z)DA 72	LONG HARVEST 7 (LP)	15
68	Argo (Z)DA 73	LONG HARVEST 8 (LP)	15
68	Argo (Z)DA 74	LONG HARVEST 9 (LP)	15
68	Argo (Z)DA 75	LONG HARVEST 10 (LP)	15
68	Argo (Z)DA 84	THE AMOROUS MUSE (LP)	15
68	Argo (Z)DA	THE ANGRY MUSE (LP)	15
69	Argo (Z)DA 98	THE PAPER STAGE 1 (LP, with booklet)	15
69	Argo (Z)DA 99	THE PAPER STAGE 2 (LP)	15
60s	XTRA 1054	SCOTS BALLADS (LP)	35
60s	Folkways FW 8958	SONGS OF ROBERT BURNS (LP)	45
70	Argo SPA-A 102	THE WORLD OF EWAN MacCOLL & PEGGY SEEGER (LP)	20
70	Argo SPA-A 216	THE WORLD OF EWAN MacCOLL & PEGGY SEEGER VOL. 2 - SONGS FROM THE RADIO BALLADS (LP)	15
70	Argo DA 133	THE TRAVELLING PEOPLE (LP, with Charles Parker)	25
71	Argo DA 136	ON THE EDGE (LP)	15

KIRSTY MacCOLL

(see also Drug Addix)

79	Stiff BUY 47	They Don't Know/Motor On (p/s)	8
79	Stiff PBUY 47	They Don't Know/Motor On (picture disc)	8
79	Stiff BUY 57	You Caught Me Out/Boys (with Boomtown Rats, unreleased, demos only)	6
81	Polydor POSP 225	Keep Your Hands Off My Baby/I Don't Need You (p/s)	7
81	Polydor POSP 368	You Still Believe In Me/Queen Of The High Teas (p/s)	15

FINN MacCUILL

79	Radio Edinburgh REL 460	SINK YE - SWIM YE (LP)	200

GALT MaCDERMOT

73	Decca SKLR 5164	TWO GENTLEMEN OF VERONA (LP)	30

AIMI MacDONALD

70	Philips 6308 011	WHAT'S LOVE ALL ABOUT (LP)	20

GAVIN MACDONALD

(see also Country Joe & Fish)

72	Regal Zono. SLRZ 1027	LINES (LP, red/silver label)	20

MACEO & ALL THE KING'S MEN

(see also Maceo & The Macks, James Brown)

72	Pye International 7N 25571	Got To Get 'Cha/Thank You For Letting Me Be Myself Again (Part 1)	15
72	Mojo 2916 017	FUNKY MUSIC MACHINE (LP)	30
75	Contempo CRM 114	FUNKY MUSIC MACHINE (LP, reissue)	15

MINT VALUE £

BIG MACEO
62 RCA RCX 203 KINGS OF THE BLUES (EP) . . . 20

MACEO & THE MACKS
(see also Maceo & All The King's Men, James Brown)
87 Urban URB 1 Cross The Tracks (We Better Go Back)/Soul Power (printed die-cut sleeve) . . . 8
87 Urban URBX 1 Cross The Tracks (We Better Go Back) (Extended Version)/Party Part 1/ Soul Power (12", printed die-cut sleeve) . . . 15
74 Polydor 2391 122 US (LP) . . . 30

TEO MACERO
57 Esquire 32-113 TEO (LP) . . . 30

MACEYS WINDOW
72 Parlophone R 5893 It's Getting Harder/Pray For Sister Sunshine . . . 40

MACHINE
(see also Swinging Soul Machine)
69 Polydor 56760 Spooky's Day Off/Nobody Wants You . . . 20

MACHINE
67 Granta GR 7STD Stupidity/Please Stay (private pressing) . . . 40

MACHINES
78 Wax EAR 1 True Life/Everything's Technical/You Better Hear/Evening Radio (stamped p/s, white labels) . . . 100

MACHITO
57 Columbia SEB 10012 MACHITO JAZZ (EP) . . . 10
58 Columbia SEB 10069 MACHITO JAZZ NO. 2 (EP) . . . 10
50s Columbia KENYA (LP) . . . 15

ALURA MACK
50s Poydras 84 Everybody's Man Is Mine/Monkey Blues . . . 8

JOHNNY MACK
70 Columbia Blue Beat DB 116 Reggae All Night Long/A Million Marvellous Feelings . . . 12

LONNIE MACK
63 Stateside SS 207 Memphis/Down In The Dumps . . . 25
63 Stateside SS 226 Wham!/Susie-Q . . . 25
64 Stateside SS 312 Lonnie On The Move/Say Something Nice To Me . . . 15
65 Stateside SS 393 Sa-Ba-Hoola/Chickin' Pickin' . . . 20
67 President PT 127 Where There's A Will/Baby What's Wrong? . . . 7
67 President PT 142 Save Your Money/Snow On The Mountain . . . 7
68 President PT 198 Soul Express/I Found A Love . . . 10
69 Elektra EKSN 45044 Memphis/Why (Edited Version) . . . 10
69 Elektra EKSN 45060 Save Your Money/In The Band . . . 8
71 Elektra EK 45715 Lay It Down/She Even Woke Me Up To Say Goodbye . . . 6
67 President PTL 1004 THE WHAM OF THAT MEMPHIS MAN (LP) . . . 30
69 Elektra EKL 4040 GLAD I'M IN THE BAND (LP, orange label, also stereo EKS 74040) . . . 30
69 Elektra EKS 74050 WHATEVER'S RIGHT (LP, orange label) . . . 30
70 Elektra 2410 007 FOR COLLECTORS ONLY (LP, reissue of "The Wham Of That Memphis Man") . . 12
72 Elektra K 42097 THE HILLS OF INDIANA (LP) . . . 12

WARNER MACK
58 Brunswick 05728 Roc-A-Chicka/Since I Lost You (with Anita Kerr Quartet) . . . 200
58 Brunswick 05728 Roc-A-Chicka/Since I Lost You (with Anita Kerr Quartet) (78) . . . 70
58 Decca Roc-A-Chicka/Since I Lost You (export issue, with Anita Kerr Quartet) . . . 90
62 London HA-R/SH-R 8002 GOLDEN COUNTRY HITS (LP) . . . 15
63 London HA-R/SH-R 8025 GOLDEN COUNTRY HITS VOL. 2 (LP) . . . 15

ANDY MACKAY
(see also Roxy Music, Rock Follies)
75 Island WIP 6243 Wild Weekend/Walking The Whippet (in promo p/s) . . . 6

MAHNA MACKAY
69 Parlophone R 5808 Mah Na Mah Na/Daydream . . . 6

RABBIT MacKAY
68 MCA MU 1041 Hard Time Woman/Candy . . . 8
68 MCA MUPS 351 BUG CLOTH (LP) . . . 12

BILLY MacKENZIE
(see also Associates, Orbidoig, Yello, B.E.F., Sweden Through The Ages)
01 Rhythm Of Life ROL 006 Wild Is The Wind/Mother Earth/Baltimore/Give Me Time (Version) (CD, internet- only release) . . . 75
92 Circa CIRCD 22 OUTERNATIONAL (CD) . . . 75

GISELE MacKENZIE
55 HMV 7M 318 Hard To Get/Boston Fancy . . . 8

MACKENZIE JET COMBO
70 Torpedo TOR 18 Milkman's Theme/Capadulah Recipe . . . 8

JUDY MacKENZIE
70 Key KL 005 JUDY (LP) . . . 22
71 Key KL 009 PEACE AND LOVE AND FREEDOM (LP, with poster) . . . 22

MACKERAL
66 Columbia DB 8013 Funny Fish/This Is Mine . . . 5
68 Columbia DB 8388 Trying Again/White Man's Burden . . . 5

KEN MACKINTOSH (& HIS ORCHESTRA)
56 HMV 7M 343 Creeping Tom/Lovers In The Dark . . . 10
56 HMV 7M 359 Start Walking/Curtain Call . . . 10

			MINT VALUE £
56	HMV 7M 379	Blues In The Night/Come Next Spring (B-side with Kenny Bardell)	10
56	HMV 7M 403	Sleepwalker/The Berkeley Hunt	5
56	HMV 7M 417	Dizzy Fingers/The Policeman's Holiday	5
56	HMV POP 270	Soft Summer Breeze/Highway Patrol	5
57	HMV POP 287	The Buccaneers/Regimental Rock	10
57	HMV POP 300	Apple-Jack/Slow Walk	15
57	HMV POP 327	Almost Paradise/Rock Man Rock	15
57	HMV POP 358	Poni Tail/Keep It Movin'	10
57	HMV POP 396	Marching Along To The Blues/Six-Five Blues	8
57	HMV POP 426	Raunchy/Mojo	10
58	HMV POP 441	The Stroll/The Swingin' Shepherd Blues	8
58	HMV POP 464	Big Guitar/Squatty	10
58	HMV POP 506	The Swivel/Muchacha	5
58	HMV POP 543	Ulterior Mofif/That Old Cha Cha Feeling	5
59	HMV POP 592	Rock-A-Conga/Hampden Park	5
59	HMV POP 656	Sleep Walk/Morgen (One More Sunrise)	7
60	HMV POP 713	No Hiding Place/Tally Ho!	6
56	HMV 7EG 8170	TEENAGER'S SPECIAL (EP)	15
55	HMV DLP 1093	KEN MACKINTOSH (10" LP)	15
58	HMV DLP 1178	ONE NIGHT STAND (10" LP)	18

MACK SISTERS

56	London HLU 8331	Long Range Love/Stop What You're Doing	60

PETE MacLAINE & CLAN

63	Decca F 11699	Yes I Do/U.S. Mail	15

DOUGIE MacLEAN

(see also Alan Roberts)

80	Plant Life PLR 022	SNAIGOW (LP, with lyric insert)	12
88	Dunkeld DUN 008	REAL ESTATE (LP)	20

JOHN MacLEOD SOUND

60s	Transatlantic TRASP 12	Russian Roulette/West Wind	6

JOHN MacLEOD'S FIRST XI

66	Fontana TF 696	Don't Shoot The Ref/Tomato Crisps	15

ANGUS MacLISE

87	Fierce FRIGHT 010	Trance (1-sided, with 'Dopechoc' & badge)	10

PATRICK MacNEE & HONOR BLACKMAN

(see also Honor Blackman)

64	Decca F 11843	Kinky Boots/Let's Keep It Friendly	35

FLORA MacNEIL

77	Tangent TGS 124	CROABH NAN UBHAL (LP, with insert)	12

MADELINE MacNEIL

60s	Skyline DD 103	PATCHWORK (LP)	30

MACON JUG

(see also Ray Dorset, Mungo Jerry)

70	Saga FID 8157	IN THE SUMMERTIME (LP, with tracks by Good Earth)	12
72	Boulevard BLVD 4078	RAY DORSET'S BEST (LP, 4 tracks by Good Earth, 6 tracks by Macon Jug)	12

UNCLE DAVE MACON

63	RCA RCX 7112	UNCLE DAVE MACON NO. 1 (EP)	15
63	RCA RCX 7113	UNCLE DAVE MACON NO. 2 (EP)	15

GORDON MacRAE

(see also Jo Stafford, Ray Anthony, Jonathan & Darlene Edwards)

54	Capitol CL 14168	How Do You Speak To An Angel?/C'est Magnifique	8
54	Capitol CL 14193	Count Your Blessings Instead Of Sheep/Never In A Million Years	8
55	Capitol CL 14222	Here's What I'm Here For/Love Can Change The Stars	8
55	Capitol CL 14276	Stranger In Paradise/High On A Windy Hill	8

JOSH MACRAE

60	Top Rank JAR 290	Talkin' Army Blues/Talkin' Guitar Blues	8
60	Pye 7N 15306	Original Talkin' Blues (Talkin' Southern Blues)/Talkin' Thro' The Mill	7
60	Pye 7N 15307	Let Ramensky Go/Sky High Joe	7
60	Pye 7N 15308	Wild Side Of Life/Dear John	7
61	Pye 7N 15319	Messing About On The River/High Class Feeling	7
61	Pye 7N 15360	Arkansas Rambler/Never Never Man	7
61	Pye 7N 15384	Do It Yourself/Special Place Of Yorn	7
60	Pye NEP 24131	WALKIN', TALKIN', SINGIN' (EP)	12
60	Top Rank JKP 2061	JOSH MACRAE (EP)	12
66	Transatlantic TRA 150	JOSH MACRAE (LP)	15
66	Golden Guinea GGL 0335	MESSING ABOUT ON THE RIVER (LP)	12

MAD DOG

74	Chappell LPC 1053	POP SOUNDS (LP, library edition)	30

MAD DOG

85	Brainy CUTN 1	Sheriff (p/s)	50

JOHNNY MADARA

57	HMV POP 389	Be My Girl/Lovesick	10

JOHNNY MADDOX (& HIS ORCHESTRA)

55	London MSD 1503/1504	Nickelodeon Tango/Solitude (unissued, demos only)	50
55	London HL 8134	The Crazy Otto - Medley/Humoresque	25
55	London HLD 8203	Do, Do, Do/When You Wore A Tulip (And I Wore A Big Red Rose)	15
56	London HLD 8277	Hop Scotch Boogie/Hands Off	30
56	London HLD 8277	Hop Scotch Boogie/Hands Off (78)	10

MINT VALUE £

56 London HLD 8347 Heart And Soul/Dixieland Band . . . 18
58 London HLD 8540 Yellow Dog Blues/Sugar Train . . . 15
59 London HLD 8826 The Hurdy Gurdy Song/Old Fashioned Love . . . 10
59 London HLD 8826 The Hurdy Gurdy Song/Old Fashioned Love (78) . . . 12
55 London RE-P 1020 PRESENTING JOHNNY MADDOX AND THE RHYTHMASTERS (EP) . . . 18
55 London RE-P 1040 PRESENTING JOHNNY MADDOX AND THE RHYTHMASTERS NO. 2 (EP) . . . 18
58 London RE-D 1150 HONKY TONK JAZZ (EP) . . . 15
61 London RE-D 1270 OLD FASHIONED LOVE (EP) . . . 8
56 London HB-D 1060 JOHNNY MADDOX PLAYS (10" LP, with His Rhythmasters) . . . 15
58 London HAD 2101 MY OLD FLAME (LP) . . . 12

ROSE MADDOX

59 Capitol CL 15023 Gambler's Love/What Makes Me Hang Around . . . 10

MADE IN BRITAIN

91 White MIB001 Break The Crunch/Mellow Infection (12") . . . 25

MADE IN ENGLAND

81 Gargoyle GARG 1 Dance Of The Warriors/The Quest (p/s) . . . 40

MADE IN ENGLAND

(see also Ray Dorset)

86 Red Bus RBUS 2208 Prospects/Stay Sharp (A-side with Ray Dorset, p/s) . . . 6

MADE IN SHEFFIELD

(see also Joe Cocker, Grease Band, Chris Stainton)

67 Fontana TF 871 Amelia Jane/Right Satisfied . . . 30

MADE IN SWEDEN

69 Sonet SLP 71 MADE IN SWEDEN (LP) . . . 40
69 Sonet SLP 2504 SNAKES IN A HOLE (LP) . . . 30
70 Sonet SLP 2506 LIVE AT THE GOLDEN CIRCLE (LP) . . . 30
70 Sonet SLP 2512 MADE IN ENGLAND (LP) . . . 35
71 Sonet SNTF 621 MAD RIVER (LP) . . . 45

MAD HATTERS

76 Epic EPC 4151 The Humphrey Song/Loving You Ain't Easy . . . 6
76 Epic EPC 4600 Love Potion No. 9/Loser . . . 8

BETTY MADIGAN

54 MGM SP 1109 Always You/That Was My Heart You Heard! . . . 5
55 MGM SP 1119 And So I Walked Home/Be A Little Darlin' . . . 5
55 MGM SP 1131 Salute/The Wheels Of Love . . . 5
55 MGM SP 1137 I Had A Heart/Wonderful Words . . . 5
55 MGM SP 1138 Teddy Bear/Strangers . . . 5
69 MGM MGM 1482 I'm Gonna Make You Love Me/Goodnight . . . 5

MAD JOCKS & ENGLISHMEN

80 Wild Dog DOGLP 18 TONGUE IN CHEEK (LP) . . . 18
80s Wild Dog DOGLP 50 THUD & BLUNDER (LP) . . . 18

MAD LADS (Jamaica)

69 Coxsone CS 7099 Losing You/WINSTON JARRETT: Peck Up A Pagan . . . 30

MAD LADS (U.S.)

65 Atlantic AT 4051 Don't Have To Shop Around/Tear Maker . . . 15
66 Atlantic AT 4083 I Want Someone/Nothing Can Break Through . . . 15
66 Atlantic 584 038 Sugar Sugar/Get Out Of My Life Woman . . . 15

MADNESS

(see also Argonauts, Fink Brothers)

SINGLES

79 2-Tone TT 3 The Prince/Madness (paper label, company sleeve) . . . 15
79 2-Tone TT 3 The Prince/Madness (later blue plastic label, company sleeve) . . . 35
79 Stiff BUY IT 56 One Step Beyond/Mistakes/Nutty Theme (12", p/s) . . . 15
79 Stiff MAD 1 Don't Quote Me On That/Swan Lake (12", promo only) . . . 20
80 Stiff BUY IT 62 My Girl/In The Rain/Stepping Into Line (12" p/s) . . . 8
80 Stiff BUY 71 WORK, REST & PLAY EP (P/s, mispress, white 'Madness' lettering instead of blue)
8
80 Stiff BUY 84 Baggy Trousers/The Business (p/s, blue labels instead of green, Mike Barson not credited as songwriter) . . . 75
81 Stiff BUY IT 108 The Return Of The Los Palmas 7/My Girl (Demo)/That's The Way To Do It/ Swan Lake (live) (12", p/s, with M.I.S. Nutty Boys comic) . . . 8
81 Stiff BUY IT 112 Grey Day/Baggy Trousers/Take It Or Leave It/Un Paso Adelante (12", p/s, white or yellow labels) . . . 20
81 Stiff BUY 112 Grey Day/Memories (p/s, rare edition with legs instead of feet on label) . . . 15
82 Stiff BUY IT 134 It Must Be Love/Mrs. Hutchinson/Shadow On The House (12", p/s credits Limited Edition Special 12 Dance Mix", record plays standard mix) . 8
82 Stiff PBUY 146 House Of Fun/Don't Look Back (picture disc) . . . 5
82 Stiff BUY 153 Driving In My Car/Animal Farm (poster p/s) . . . 5
82 Stiff PBUY 153 Driving In My Car/Animal Farm (picture disc) . . . 5
82 Stiff GRAB 1 THE MADNESS PACK (6 x 7" in clear plastic folder) . . . 20
83 Stiff PBUY 169 Tomorrow's (Just Another Day)/Madness (Is All In The Mind) (picture disc) . . . 5
83 Stiff BUY IT 169 Tomorrow's (Just Another Day) (Warped Mix)/Blue Skinned Beast (warped mix)/ Tomorrow's (Just Another Day) (Elvis Costello vocal) (12", p/s) . . . 8
84 Stiff BUY IT 196 Michael Caine (extended version)/Michael Caine/ If You Think There's Something (12", p/s) . . . 8
84 Stiff PBUY 196 Michael Caine/If You Think There's Something (picture disc) . . . 12
84 Stiff BUY 201 One Better Day/Guns (poster p/s) . . . 5
84 Stiff PBUY 201 One Better Day/Guns (picture disc) . . . 7
85 Zarjazz JAZZ SD5 Yesterday's Men/All I Knew (square picture disc)//Yesterday's Men (Harmonica Mix)/It Must Be Love (live) (double pack, gold PVC wallet) . . . 12

			MINT VALUE £
85	Zarjazz JAZZF 7	Uncle Sam/Please Don't Go ('flag bag' edition)	20
85	Zarjazz JAZZY 7	Uncle Sam/Please Don't Go/Insanity Over Christmas (picture disc)	18
86	Zarjazz JAZZ B9-12	(Waiting For) The Ghost-Train/Maybe In Another Life/ Seven Year Scratch (12", p/s with 8-page booklet)	10
86	Zarjazz JAZZS 9	(Waiting For) The Ghost Train/Maybe In Another Life (square picture disc)	45
86	Strange Fruit SFPS 0007	THE PEEL SESSIONS (12" p/s, brown label)	10
86	80s	Sweetest Girl/Jenny (A Portrait Of) (picture disc, stickered PVC sleeve)	18
87	Virgin VS 876	Our House/Walking With Mr. Wheeze	15
88	Virgin VSX 1054	I Pronounce You/4BF/Patience/11th Hour (as The Madness, box with badge, 2 cards & sticker)	8
88	Virgin VSCD 1054	I Pronounce You/4BF/Patience/11th Hour (CD, as The Madness)	8
88	Virgin VS 1078	What's That/Be Good Boy (p/s)	8
88	Virgin VSJ 1078	What's That/Flashings ('Jig' disc, 1st of 2 interlocking shaped picture discs)	30
88	Virgin VSS 1078	What's That/Be Good Boy ('Saw' disc, 2nd of 2 interlocking shaped picture discs)	30
88	Virgin VST 1078	What's That/Be Good Boy/Flashings (12", p/s)	10
92	Go! Discs GOD 93	The Harder They Come/Tomorrow's Just Another Day/ Take It Or Leave It (p/s, blue labels)	8
99	Virgin VSLH 1737	Love Struck/We Are Love (Jukebox issue)	10
99	Virgin VSLH 1740	Johnny The Horse/I Was The One (Jukebox issue)	12
05	V2 VVR55033247	Shame And Scandal/Shame And Scandal (Dub Mix) p/s, 2500 only)	6

LPs

79	Stiff SEEZ 17	ONE STEP BEYOND (LP, first pressing, sleeve lists 'Bed & Breakfast' not 'Bed & Breakfast Man')	12
80	Stiff SEEZ 29	ABSOLUTELY (LP, first pressing with slightly different front cover image)	12
82	M.I.S. (no cat. no)	THIRTY MINUTES OF CULTURE (fan club cassette)	25
84	Stiff PSEEZ 53	KEEP MOVING (LP, picture disc, U.S. running order)	15
85	Zarjazz JZLP1	MAD NOT MAD (LP, withdrawn edition, alternative sleeve omitting gold on front)	75
86	M.I.S. (no cat. no)	SONGS FROM AROUND THE PLONET (fan club cassette, live compilation)	35
90	Virgin VVIP 107	IT'S MADNESS (LP, 1000 copies)	70
90	Virgin TPAK 8	ONE STEP BEYOND/ABSOLUTELEY/RISE & FALL (3-CD box set, picture discs)	50
92	Virgin 463 166	DIVINE (Digital compact cassette)	20
92	Virgin MDV 2692	DIVINE (Mini disc)	20
92	Go! Discs 828 367-1	MADSTOCK (LP, with picture inner sleeve)	20
94	Simply Vinyl SVLP 309	DIVINE (LP, Simply Vinyl reissue)	15
99	Virgin MADBOX 2	THE LOT (6-CD box set of first 6 studio albums)	50
09	Lucky 7 003SE	THE LIBERTY OF NORTON FOLGATE (LP + 3CD box set including poster, membership card, rule book, letter & badge)	40

FLEXIDISCS

80	Stiff/Lyntone LYN 8680	Patches Brings You A Few Minutes Of Madness (with Patches mag)	6
81	Lyntone LYN 10208	Take It or Leave It (free with Take It Or Leave It magazine)	10
81	Lyntone LYN 10208	Take It or Leave It (without Take It Or Leave It magazine)	6
81	Lyn. LYN 10353/EVENT 2	Event - The Madness (with Event magazine)	10
82	Lyntone LYN 11546	My Girl (Ballad) (green or white vinyl, with Flexipop mag issue 19)	8
82	Lyntone LYN 11546	My Girl (Ballad) (green or white vinyl, without Flexipop mag issue 19)	5
82	Lyntone LYN 11546	My Girl (Ballad) (hard vinyl test pressing of Flexipop free flexi)	200
82	Lyntone LYN 10719	Carols On 45 (fan club disc)	10
84	Lyntone LYN 15280/1	Insanity Over Christmas/Visit To Castle Dracstein (fan club disc)	10
85	Lyntone LYN 16676	From Us ... To You (Mad Not Mad tour disc, with tour programme)	18
85	Lyntone LYN 16676	From Us ... To You (Mad Not Mad tour disc)	8
85	Lyntone LYN 16981	Merry Christmas: Samantha (live)/Mad Not Mad (live)	10
86	Lyntone LYN 18251	Last Christmas With Madness:Ghost Train (The Demo)/ The Final Goodbye (fan club disc)	20

RUTH MADOC

86	Sain 1375	Our Song Of Love/The Colours Of Christmas (with Bill Tarmey) (p/s)	5

MADONNA

(see also Jellybean)

SIRE SINGLES

82	Sire W 9899	Everybody/Everybody (Dub Version) (WEA sleeve, no p/s)	150
82	Sire W 9899T	Everybody/Everybody (Dub Version) (12", WEA sleeve, no p/s)	125
83	Sire W 9522	Lucky Star (Edit)/I Know It ('sunglasses' p/s with no Jellybean credit on label)	1000
83	Sire W 9522T	Lucky Star (Full Length Version)/I Know It (12", 'sunglasses' p/s;	50
83	Sire W 9522TV	Lucky Star (U.S Remix)/I Know It (12", stickered plain white die-cut sleeve)	35
83	Sire W 9405	Holiday (Edit)/Think Of Me ('train' p/s)	6
83	Sire W 9405T	Holiday (Full Length Version 6.08)/Think Of Me (12", 'train' p/s)	8
84	Sire W 9522	Lucky Star (Edit)/I Know It (reissue, 'bangles & stars' Jellybean credit on label, p/s)	5
84	Sire W 9522T	Lucky Star (Full Length Version)/I Know It (12" reissue, stickered 'TV screen' p/s)	10
84	Sire W 9522T	Lucky Star (Full Length Version)/I Know It (12" reissue, stickered 'TV screen' p/s, with poster)	30
84	Sire W 9260	Borderline (Edit)/Physical Attraction (p/s, large 'A' on paper A-side label)	5
84	Sire W 9260F	Borderline (Edit)/Physical Attraction//Holiday (Edit)/Think Of Me ('map' p/s, double pack with European p/s, copies of "Holiday", shrinkwrapped & stickered: beware of counterfeits with less than Mint picture sleeves)	100
84	Sire W 9260P	Borderline (edit)/Physical Attraction (uncut picture disc)	1000
84	Sire W 9210T	Like A Virgin (U.S. Dance Remix)/Stay (12", p/s, with poster & sticker)	35
85	Sire W 9083	Material Girl/Pretender (p/s)	5
85	Sire W 9083T	Material Girl (Jellybean Dance Mix)/Pretender (12", with poster p/s)	35
85	Sire WA6323	Crazy For You/Sammy Hagar "I'll Fall In Love Again" (7" Madonna shaped picture Disc in stickered PVC sleeve. No p/s.)	50
85	Sire WA6323	Crazy For You/Sammy Hagar "I'll Fall In Love Again" (Uncut 7" Picture disc on 10" vinyl in PVC sleeve. No p/s)	800
85	Sire W 8934P	Into The Groove/Shoo-Be-Doo (heart-shaped picture disc with 2 stickers)	40
85	Sire W 8934P	Into The Groove/Shoo-Be-Doo (12" uncut heart-shaped picture disc, very few copies)	1000

			MINT VALUE £
85	Sire W 8934T	Into The Groove/Everybody/Shoo-Be-Doo (12", p/s, with poster)	25
85	Sire W 9405T	Holiday (Full Length Version 6.08)/Think Of Me (12", 'cross earring' p/s reissue)	15
85	Sire W 9405P	Holiday (Full Length Version 6.08)/Think Of Me (12", picture disc)	30
85	Sire W 8881P	Angel (Edit)/Burning Up (shaped pic disc, with cardboard plinth)	45
85	Sire W 8881P	Angel (Edit)/Burning Up (shaped pic disc)	35
85	SireW8881P	Angel (Edit)/Burning Up (Uncut 7" pic disc on 12" vinyl in PVC sleeve, no p/s)	1000
85	Sire A6585	Gambler/Black 'n' Blue:Nature Of The Beach (7" p/s)	7
85	Sire QA6585	Gambler/Black 'n' Blue:Nature Of The Beach (7" foldout poster p/s)	30
85	Sire TA6585	Gambler (Extended Dance Mix)/(Instrumental Remix) Black 'n' Blue: Nature Of The Beach (12" p/s)	20
85	Sire W 8848T	Dress You Up (12" Formal Mix)/(Casual Instrumental)/I Know It (12", p/s)	8
85	Sire W 8848TF	Dress You Up (12" Formal Mix)/(Casual Instrumental)/I Know It (12", foldout p/s with Virgin Tour Video Advert on back)	35
85	Sire W 8848TF	Dress You Up (12" Formal Mix)/(Casual Instrumental) /I Know It (12", p/s, '4 Track Studio' or 'Live Like A Virgin Tour' rear video advert)	7
85	Sire W 8848P	Dress You Up/I Know It ('Xmas tree star'-shaped picture disc)	35
85	Sire W 8848P	Dress You Up (Uncut 7" picture disc on 12" vinyl, no p/s)	750
86	Sire W 9560P	Borderline/Physical Attraction (Madonna-shaped picture disc in PVC sleeve no p/s)	50
86	Sire W 9560P	Borderline/Physical Attraction (Uncut 7" picture disc on 12" vinyl,pvc sleeve no p/s)	750
86	Sire W 8717T(W)	Live To Tell (LP Version)/(Edit)/(Instrumental) (12", p/s, with poster)	20
86	Sire W 8717T(W)	Live To Tell (LP Version)/(Edit)/(Instrumental) (12", p/s)	5
86	Sire W8636T	Papa Don't Preach(Extended Version)/(LP Version) Ain't No Big Deal (12" with poster in stickered p/s)	20
86	Sire W 8636T(W)	Papa Don't Preach (Extended Version)/Papa Don't Preach (LP Version)/ Ain't No Big Deal (12", p/s, initially with free poster)	15
86	Sire W 8636T(W)	Papa Don't Preach (Extended Version)/Papa Don't Preach (LP Version)/ Ain't No Big Deal (12", p/s, initially with free poster)	8
86	Sire W 8636TP	Papa Don't Preach (Extended Remix)/Ain't No Big Deal (LP Version)/ Papa Don't Preach (LP version) (12", picture disc	20
86	Sire W 8550TP	True Blue (Extended Dance Version)/Holiday (Full Length Version) (12" picture disc)	20
86	Sire W 8480TP	Open Your Heart (Extended Version)/Open Your Heart (Dub Mix)/ Lucky Star (Full Length Version) (12", picture disc)	10
87	Sire W 8378TP	La Isla Bonita (Extended Remix)/(Extended Instrumental) (12", picture disc)	20
87	Sire W 8341TX	Who's That Girl (Extended Version)/Who's That Girl (Dub Mix)/ White Heat (12" Remix) (12", p/s)	20
87	Sire W 8341TP	Who's That Girl (Extended Version)/White Heat (12", picture disc; beware of original decaying PVC sleeves)	40
87	Sire W 8224	Causing A Commotion (Silver Screen Single Mix)/Jimmy Jimmy (p/s, with badge shrinkwrapped to p/s)	50
87	Sire W 8224TP	Causing A Commotion (Silver Screen Mix)/Causing A Commotion (Movie House Mix)/Jimmy Jimmy (Fade) (12", picture disc)	15
87	Sire W 8224C	Causing A Commotion (Silver Screen Mix)/Causing A Commotion (Movie House Mix)/Jimmy Jimmy (Fade) (Cassette Single p/s)	6
87	Sire W 8115TW	The Look Of Love/Love Don't Live Here Anymore/I Know It (12", p/s & poster)	15
87	Sire W 8115TP	The Look Of Love/Love Don't Live Here Anymore/I Know It (12", picture disc)	20
89	Sire 925 681-2	Papa Don't Preach (7" Version)/(12" Version)/Pretender (Video)(5" CD-Video p/s)	40
89	Sire W 7539TX	Like A Prayer (12" Dance Mix)/(Churchapella Mix)/(7"Remix Edit) (12", p/s)	10
89	Sire W 7539TP	Like A Prayer (12" Extended Remix)/(12" Club Version)/ Act Of Contrition (12", picture disc)	15
89	Sire W 7539C	Like A Prayer (12" Extended Remix)/(12" Club Version)/ Act Of Contrition (Cassette Single p/s)	6
89	Sire W 7539CD	Like A Prayer/(12" Extended Remix)/(12" Club Version)/Act Of Contrition (3" Gatefold CD)	12
89	Sire W 2948X	Express Yourself (7" Remix)/The Look Of Love (LP) (poster p/s)	25
89	Sire W 2948W	Express Yourself (7" Remix)/The Look Of Love (LP) (Cassette Single p/s)	6
89	Sire W 2948C	Express Yourself (7" Remix)/The Look Of Love (LP) ('jeans zipper' p/s)	30
89	Sire W 2948CX	Express Yourself (Non-Stop Express Mix)/(Stop + Go Dubs) (cassette)	20
89	Sire W 2948TP	Express Yourself/(Non-Stop Express Mix)/(Stop + Go Dubs) (12", 'nude' picture disc)	15
89	Sire W 2948 CD	Express Yourself/(Non-Stop Express Mix)/(Stop + Go Dubs) (3" CD)	15
89	Sire W 2883TP	Cherish (Extended Version)/(7" Version)/Supernatural (12")	10
89	Sire W 2883 CD	Cherish (extended)/Cherish/Supernatural (3" CD)	15
89	Sire W 2668P	Dear Jessie/Till Death Do Us Part (picture disc)	12
89	Sire W 2668TW	Dear Jessie/Till Death Do Us Part/Holiday (12" Version) (12", poster p/s)	12
89	Sire W 2268CDX	Dear Jessie/Till Death Do Us Part/Holiday (12" Version) (CD, picture disc)	125
89	Sire 925 681-2	Papa Don't Preach (7" Version)/(12" Version)/Pretender (LP Version)/ Papa Don't Preach (CD Video)	35
90	Sire W 9851P	Vogue/Keep It Together (Single Remix) (picture disc)	12
90	Sire W 9851TW	Vogue (12" Version)/Keep It Together (12" Remix) (12", p/s, with 'Face of the 80s' poster)	15
90	Sire W 9851TX	Vogue (12" Version)/Vogue (Strike-A-Pose Dub) (12", p/s, with 'X-rated' 30" x 20" poster)	20
90	Sire W 9851TP	Vogue (12" Version)/Keep It Together (12" Remix) (12", picture disc)	20
90	Sire W 9789TP	Hanky Panky (Bare Bottom 12" Mix)/(Bare Bones Single Mix)/More (LP Version) (12", picture disc with gatefold insert & foldout poster)	15
90	Sire W 9000TP	Justify My Love (William Orbit Remix)/Justify My Love/Express Yourself (Shep's 'Spressin' Himself Remix) (12", picture disc with insert)	10
90	Sire 7599382253	Justify My Love/Vogue (Live at MTV Awards 1990) (video single, p/s)	8
91	Sire W 0008P	Crazy For You (Remix)/Keep It Together (Single Remix) (shaped picture disc with plinth & insert)	15
91	Sire W 0008CD	Crazy For You (Remix)/Keep It Together (Shep Pettibone Remix)/ Into The Groove (Shep Pettibone Remix) (CD, picture disc)	8
91	Sire W0024	Rescue Me/Spotlight (7" p/s)	5
91	Sire W0024TW	Rescue (Titanic Mix)/(Houseboat Mix)/(Titanic Mix) (12" with free poster, p/s)	10

			MINT VALUE £
91	Sire W 0037TP	Holiday/True Blue (12", clear vinyl picture disc with insert in PVC sleeve)	15
91	Sire W 0037CD	THE HOLIDAY COLLECTION (Holiday/True Blue/ Who's That Girl/ Causing A Commotion) (CD)	8

MAVERICK SINGLES

92	Maverick W 0138TP	Erotica (Album Version 5.12)/Erotica (Instrumental 5.12)/Erotica (Radio Edit 4.31) (12", picture disc with gold insert, withdrawn, 138 only)	2500
92	Maverick W 0138TW	Erotica (Album Version 5.12)/Erotica (Instrumental 5.12)/Erotica (Radio Edit 4.31) (12", Free Poster, p/s)	10
92	Maverick W 0146TP	Deeper And Deeper (Shep's Classic 12")/(Shep's Deep Makeover Mix)/ (Shep's Deep Beats)/(David's Klub Mix)/(David's Deep Mix)/(Shep's Deeper Dub) (12", picture disc)	15
93	Maverick W0154TW	Bad Girl (Edit)/Erotica (William Orbit 12")/Erotica (William Orbit Dub)/ Erotica (Madonna's In My Jeep Mix) (12", Free Poster, p/s)	10
93	Maverick W 0168P	Fever (Edit)/Fever (Radio Edit Remix) (picture disc with numbered insert)	10
93	Maverick W0168T	Fever (Hot Sweat 12")/(Extended 12")/(Shep's Remedy Dub)/ (Murk Boys Miami Mix)/(Murk Boys Deep South Mix)/(Oscar G's Dope Dub) (12" stickered, p/s)	10
94	Maverick W 0268P	Secret (Edit)/Let Down Your Guard (Rough Mix Edit) (picture disc w/insert)	12
95	Maverick W 0278P	Take A Bow (Edit)/Take A Bow (picture disc with insert)	8
95	Maverick W 0285CDX	Bedtime Story (Junior's Single Mix)/Secret (Allstar Mix)/Secret (Some Bizarre Mix)/Secret (Some Bizarre Single Mix) (CD, booklet sleeve)	10

OTHER SINGLES

92	Receiver RRSP 1007	Shine A Light/On The Ground (picture disc, withdrawn)	12
92	Reciever RRSPT 1007	Shine A Light/On The Ground/Little Boy (12", picture disc)	15
95	Warner Bros W0285TX	Bedtime Story (Junior's Sound Factory Mix)/(Junior's Sound Factory Dub/ (Orbital Mix)/Junior's Wet Dream Mix) (12" Glitter Holographic Sleeve)	15
95	Warner Bros W0285CDX	Bedtime Story (Junior's Single Mix)/Secret (Allstar Mix)/Secret (Some Bizarre Mix)/ Secret/(Some Bizarre Single Mix) (CD, 'Bedtime Storybook' Digipack, p/s)	15
03	Warner Bros W634T	Love Profusion (Passengerz Club Mix)/Nobody Knows Me (Above & Beyond 12" Mix) (12" stickered, p/s)	8

PROMOS

85	Sire SAM 251	Into The Groove (Edit) Holiday (Edit) (12" white label, die-cut sleeve, stickered	100
87	Sire SAM 412	Spotlight (Dub)/Holiday (Dub)/Over And Over (Dub)/Into The Groove (Dub) 12" white label, die-cut WEA sleeve, no p/s)	50
89	Sire SAM 641	Keep It Together (12" Remix)/(Dub)/(Extended Remix)/(12" Mix)/ (Bonus Beats)/(Instrumental) (12")	15
90	Sire SAM 659	Vogue (12" Version)/Vogue (Strike A Pose Dub) (12")	15
90	Sire SAM 738	Justify My Love (Remix) (One-sided 12" die-cut sleeve, p/s)	15
91	Sire SAM 800	Holiday (Edit) (CD)	50
92	Sire SAM 1103	Erotica (Album Version) (12")	25
92	Sire SAM 1118	Deeper And Deeper (Edit)/Shep's Deep Makeover Mix)/Shep's Classic 12") David's Klub Mix)/David's Love Dub)/David's Deeper Dub) 12" white label no p/s	25
93	Sire SAM 1131	Fever (Hot Sweat 12" Mix)/(Shep's Remedy Dub)/(Dub One)/(Dub Two)/ (Bugged Out Bonzai Mix)/(Peggy's Nightclub Mix)/(Radio Edit)/ (Murk Boys Miami Mix)/(Murk Boys Deep South Mix)/(Album Version)/ (Oscar G's Dope Dub)/(Back To The Dub One)/(Back To The Dub T.	50
94	Warner Bros W 0278 CDDJ	Take A Bow (Edit) (CD with insert, no p/s)	12
94	Warner Bros SAM 1526	Bedtime Story (Junior's Sound Factory Mix)/(Mixes) (12")	15
94	Warner Bros SAM 1653	Human Nature: The Remixes/(Mixes) (12", stickered title sleeve)	15
94	Warner Bros W0300CDDJ	Human Nature (4'30" Radio Edit) (CD)	12
95	Warner Bros SAM 1526	Bedtime Story (Junior's Sound Factory Mix)/(Junior's Sound Factory Dub)/ (Orbital Mix)/Junior's Wet Dream Mix)/(Junior's Wet Dream Dub) (12")	15
95	Warner Bros W 0285 CDDJ2	Bedtime Story (Junior's Singles Mix) (CD in standard p/s)	25
95	Warner Bros W 0326 CDDJ	Oh Father (Edit) (CD)	20
96	Sire SAM 1880	Love Don't Live Here Anymore (Mark!s It's A Girl Dub)/(Mark!s It's A Boy Dub)/ (Mark!s Full On Vocal) (12")	25
96	Warner Bros SAM 1982	Don't Cry For Me Argentina (Miami Mix)/(Mixes) (12", title sleeve)	10
96	Warner Bros W0384CDDJ2	Don't Cry For Me Argentina (Miami Mix Edit)/Miami Mix) (CD)	15
96	Warner Bros W0388CDDJ	Another Suitcase In Another Hall (CD, title inlay)	10
96	Warner Bros W0337CDDJ	One More Chance (Album Version) (CD)	10
98	Warner Bros 3331000037	Drowned World/Substitute For Love (BT & Sasha's Bucklodge Ashram Remix)/ Sky Fits Heaven (Sasha Remix)/Substitute For Love (Victor Calderone Remix Edit) (12")	20
98	Sire SAM 3173	Frozen (Extended Club Mix)/(Stereo MC's Mix)/(Meltdown Mix - Long Version) (12" no p/s)	10
98	Warner Bros SAM 3247	Ray Of Light (Sasha's Ultra Violet Mix)/(William Orbit's Liquid Mix) (12")	15
98	Warner Bros SAM 3248	Ray Of Light (Calderone Club Mix)/(Album Version) (12" no p/s)	15
98	Warner Bros SAM 3268	Ray Of Light (Sasha's Twilo Mix)/(Victor Calderone Drum Mix) (12")	15
98	Warner Bros SAM 3269	Ray Of Light (Sasha's Strip Down Mix)/(Orbit's Ultra Violet Mix) (12")	15
98	Warner Bros 0444 CDDJ	Ray Of Light (Album Version) (CD, stickered p/s)	15
98	Warner Bros W 459 CDDJ	Little Star (CD)	15
99	Warner Bros W 471CDDJ	Nothing Really Matters (Album Version)/Nothing Really Matters (Club 69 Radio Mix) (CD, slimline jewel case)	10
00	Warner Bros PR01802	American Pie (Album Version)/(Richard 'Humpty' Vission Radio Mix) (CD)	15
00	Warner Bros PRO 6584	Music (mixes) (12" doublepack, title-stickered sleeve)	15
00	Warner Bros PR02054	Music (Album Version) (CD)	10
01	Warner Bros PR02296	Don't Tell Me (Thunderpuss Radio Mix)/(mixes) (CD)	15
01	Warner Bros MADZ 01	What It Feels Like For A Girl (Perfecto Mix)/(Above & Beyond Remix) (12" stickered white label, A4 press release, die-cut sleeve no p/s)	25
01	Warner Bros	GHV2 (CD, slimline jewel case, 'collage' insert)	25
01	Warner Bros SAM 00586	GHV2 (CD, 10" x 10" gatefold p/s)	50
02	Warner Bros SAM 00721	Die Another Day (Dirty Vegas Main Mix)/(mixes) (12" double pack, stickered title sleeve)	15
03	Warner Bros SAM 00824	Hollywood (Oakenfold 12" Full Remix)/Jacques Lu Cont Thin White Duck Mix) / Album Version/(Deepsky Home Sweet Home Vocal Remix) (12")	10

ALBUMS

			MINT VALUE £
85	Sire WX 20P	LIKE A VIRGIN (LP, picture disc in die-cut sleeve)	50
86	Sire WX 54	TRUE BLUE (LP, with tour poster)	15
87	Sire WX 76	YOU CAN DANCE (LP, with poster & gold 'obi')	15
90	Sire 7599 264932	ROYAL BOX (box set with "Immaculate Collection" CD in satin digipak, video, poster & postcards)	75
92	Sire WX49	EROTICA (Dirty Version) (2xLP, gatefold, stickered)	15
92	Sire WX49	EROTICA (Clean Version) (2xLP, gatefold, stickered)	15
94	Sire 9362 45767 1	BEDTIME STORIES (LP)	35
95	Sire 9362 46100-1	SOMETHING TO REMEMBER (LP)	35
98	Sire 9362 46847-1	RAY OF LIGHT (2xLP with inner sleeve, stickered)	15
00	Sire 9362 47865-1	MUSIC (2xLP with gold die-cut inners, stickered)	15
03	Sire 9362 48454-1	AMERICAN LIFE (2xLP, inner sleeve gatefold)	15
04	Sire 9362 46847-1	RAY OF LIGHT (Reissue, 2xLP with inner sleeve 180gm deluxe vinyl, stickered)	20
06	Sire 9362 494601	CONFESSIONS ON A DANCE FLOOR (2-LP, gatefold, pink vinyl)	30

ALBUM PROMO

89	Sire MER 0120	LIKE A PRAYER (Box set in 10" x 7" x 1" box, includes CD, sealed cassette, press Release, badge, slides Rolling Stone re-print, 2 photos)	200

MADONNA & MISSY (ELLIOTT)

03	Maverick RRCG 0301	Into The Hollywood Groove/Hollywood (Jack Lu Cont's Thin White Dick Mix) (GAP in-store promo)	25

MAD PROFESSOR

82	Ariwa ARILP 001	DUB ME CRAZY (LP)	25
83	Ariwa ARILP 005LP	THE AFRICAN CONNECTION - DUB ME CRAZY PART 3 (LP)	18
83	Ariwa ARILP 011	ESCAPE TO THE ASYLUM OF DUB (LP)	20
94	Ariwa ARILP 057	PSYCHEDELIC DUB DUB - DUB ME CRAZY PART 10 (LP)	12

MADRIGAL

72	Sovereign SOV 1071	Time Of The Season/Tapestry	20
73	Madrigal MAD 100	BENEATH THE GREENWOOD TREE (LP, private pressing)	60

MAD RIVER

69	Capitol (S)T 2985	MAD RIVER (LP)	70

JOHNNY MAESTRO

(see also Crests, Brooklyn Bridge)

61	HMV POP 875	What A Surprise/The Warning Voice	30
61	HMV POP 909	Mr. Happiness/Test Of Love	30
64	United Artists UP 1004	Before I Love Her/Fifty Million Heartbeats	30
71	Buddah 2011 061	Rain Came/Never Knew This Kind Of Hurt Before	10

MAGAZINE

(see also Buzzcocks)

78	Virgin VS 200	Shot By Both Sides/My Mind Ain't So Open (card p/s)	6
78	Virgin VS 200	Shot By Both Sides/My Mind Ain't So Open (paper p/s)	5
78	Virgin VS 207	Touch And Go/Goldfinger (p/s)	5

MAGENTA

78	Cottage COT 821	CANTERBURY MOON (LP, with insert)	40
80	Little Stan LSP 811	RECOLLECTIONS (2-LP, gatefold sleeve with insert)	35
81	Little Stan LSP 831	WOT'S NEXT THEN (LP, with insert)	25

MAGGIE

68	Columbia DB 8389	L. David Sloane/Too Young To Get Married	6

MAGIC CARPET

(see also Clem Alford)

72	Mushroom 200 MR 20	MAGIC CARPET (LP, white/brown labels)	150

MAGIC CHRISTIANS

(see also Trevor Burton, Gary Wright, Denny Laine, Steve Gibbons)

69	Major Minor MM 673	If You Want It/Nuts	7
69	Major Minor MM 673	Come And Get It/Nuts (2nd pressing with correct title)	20
70	Major Minor SMLP 71	THE MAGIC CHRISTIANS (LP)	35

MAGICIAN

79	Hobo	MAGICIAN (LP)	40

MAGICIANS

66	Decca F 12361	Wet Your Whistle/Take The A Train	5
66	Decca F 12374	The Liars/Poggy Goes Pop	6
67	Decca F 12602	The Tarzan March/What A Day For A Metamorphosis	10
68	MCA MU 1046	Painting On Wood/Slow Motion	40

MAGIC LANTERNS

66	CBS 202094	Excuse Me Baby/Greedy Girl	7
66	CBS 202250	Rumplestiltskin/I Stumbled	55
67	CBS 202459	Knight In Rusty Armour/Simple Things	10
67	CBS 202637	Auntie Grizelda/Time Will Tell (If I'm A Loser)	10
67	CBS 2750	We'll Meet Again/What Else Can It Be But Love?	10
68	Camp 602 007	Shame Shame/Baby I Gotta Go Now	10
69	Camp 602 009	Melt All Your Troubles Away/Bossa Nova 1940 - Hello You Lovers	10
70	Polydor 2038 058	One Night Stand/Frisco Annie	6
73	Polydor 2058 322	Stand For Our Rights/Pa Bradley	5
67	CBS (S)BPG 62935	LIT UP WITH THE MAGIC LANTERNS (LP)	30

MAGIC MICHAEL

(see also Damned, Captain Sensible)

80	Atomic MAGIC 1	Millionaire/My Friend And I (p/s)	5

MAGIC MIXTURE

68	Saga FID 2125	THIS IS MAGIC MIXTURE (LP, black/silver labels)	120

MINT VALUE £

MAGIC MUSCLE
(see also Keith Christmas, Hawkwind, High Tide, Twink)

88	Five Hours Back TOCK 009	THE PIPE, THE ROAR, THE GRID (LP, with booklet)	15
90	Pilgrim (no cat. no.)	LIVING WEEDS FROM ANCIENT SEEDS (cassette, box set, autographed with booklet, posters & postcard)	15
89	One Big Guitar OBGLP 9005	100 MILES BELOW (LP)	15
91	Woronzow WOO 17	GULP! (LP)	20

MAGIC MUSHROOM BAND

85	Magick Eye MUSH 001	THE MAGIC MUSHROOM BAND (cassette EP)	12
85	Magick Eye MUSH 002	FEED YOUR HEAD (cassette)	12
86	Pagan PM 003	THE POLITICS OF ECSTASY (LP, 100 with A1 poster)	50
86	Pagan PM 003	THE POLITICS OF ECSTASY (LP, 500 with A3 insert)	25
87	Aftermath AFT 3	BOMSHAMKAR (LP)	15
90	Fungus FUN 003	PROCESS OF ILLUMINATION (LP, signed with insert & foldaround sleeve & comic in printed PVC sleeve)	12
91	Fungus FUN 005	SPACED OUT (LP, foldout sleeve with A4 booklet)	15

MAGIC NIGHT

75	Pye 7N 25698	If You And I Had Never Met/(version)	10

MAGIC NOTES

60	Blue Beat BB 9	Album Of Memory/Why Did You Leave Me	8
61	Blue Beat BB 51	Rosabel/I'm Not Worthy2	8

THE MAGIC NUMBERS

04	Heavenly HVN 143	Hymn For Her/Oh Sister (500 only, with 2 stickers of different band members p/s)	10
05	Heavenly HVN 147	Anima Sola/HAL: Keep Love As Your Golden Rule (Tour single - 500 only p/s)	7
05	Heavenly HVN 155P	Cold Fingers/THE WEBB BROTHERS : Try (Tour 7", 1000 only)	15

MAGIC SAM

69	Python PEN 701	Twenty One Days In Jail/Easy Baby (99 copies only)	50
69	Rooster 707	MEAN MISTREATER (EP)	20
70	Blue Horizon 7-63223	MAGIC SAM: 1937-1969 (LP)	90
70	Delmark DS 615	WEST SIDE SOUL (LP, blue label)	30
71	Delmark DS 620	BLACK MAGIC (LP, blue label)	35

MAGIC SHOP

87	Sha La La Ba Ba 8	It's Time/VISITORS: Goldmining (flexidisc with various fanzines)	7
87	Sha La La Ba Ba 8	It's Time/VISITORS: Goldmining (flexidisc without various fanzines)	5

MAGIC SLIM & TEARDROPS

81	Rooster R 707	THREE THUNDERIN' TRACKS (EP)	7

MAGIC VALLEY
(see also Pete Dello, Honeybus)

69	Penny Farthing PEN 701	Taking The Heart Out Of Love/Uptight Basil	10

MAGISTRATES
(see also Jane Hillery)

68	MGM MGM 1425	Here Comes The Judge/Girl	15
68	MGM MGM 1437	After The Fox/Tear Down The Walls (with Jean Hillary)	10

MAGITS
(see also Rudimentary Peni)

79	Outer H. SRTS/79/CUS/401	Fragmented/Disconnected/Disjointed/Detached (p/s)	60

MAGMA

74	A&M AMS 7119	Mekanik Machine/Mekanik Machine (Version)	20
70	Philips 6359 051/2	MAGMA (2-LP)	40
71	Philips 6397 031	1001 CENTIGRADE (LP)	25
74	A&M AMLH 64397	MEKANIK DESTRUCTIW KOMMANDOH (LP)	20
74	A&M AMLH 68260	KOHN TARKOSZ (LP)	15

MAGNA CARTA

69	Fontana TF 1060	Romeo Jack/7 O'Clock Hymn	20
69	Mercury MF 1096	Mid-Winter/Spinning Wheels Of Time	20
70	Vertigo 6059 013	Airport Song/Elizabethan	10
71	Vertigo 6059 043	Time For The Leaving/Wayfarin'	8
72	Vertigo 6059 073	All My Life/Falkland Green	12
73	Vertigo 6059 092	Give Me Luv/Song Of Evening	10
70s	London Borough of Camden	When You're Young (charity issue for RoSPA)	5
69	Mercury SMCL 20166	MAGNA CARTA (LP, laminated sleeve, black/silver labels)	80
70	Vertigo 6360 003	SEASONS (LP, gatefold sleeve, large swirl label)	35
71	Vertigo 6360 040	SONGS FROM WASTIES ORCHARD (LP, gatefold sleeve, large swirl label)	45
72	Vertigo 6360 068	IN CONCERT (LP, gatefold sleeve, small swirl label)	18
73	Vertigo 6360 093	LORD OF THE AGES (LP, gatefold sleeve, lyric insert, spaceship label)	15
76	GTO GTLP 012	PUTTING IT BACK TOGETHER (LP)	12
77	GTO GTLP 112	TOOK A LONG TIME (LP)	12

MAGNA JAZZ BAND
(see also Brian White & Magna Jazz Band)

57	Parlophone R 4387	Buddy's Habits/Flat Foot	7

MAGNET

69	CBS 4472	Let Me Stay/Mr Guy Fawkes	40
70	CBS 4844	Something To Remember Me By/Everything	6

MAGNETS

86	Hurricane FIRE 1	Who's The Fool (Me Or You)/Best	22

MAGNIFICENT MEN

66	Capitol CL 15462	Peace Of Mind/All Your Lovin's Gone To My Head	30
68	Capitol CL 15530	Sweet Soul Medley Parts 1 & 2	10
68	Capitol CL 15570	Save The Country/So Much Love Waiting	6

MINT VALUE £

MAGNIFICENT MERCURY BROTHERS
(see also Decameron)

74	Transatlantic BIG 532	New Girl In School/What About Us	8
74	Transatlantic BIG 536	Why Do Fools Fall In Love/(I'm Not A) Juvenile Delinquent	8

MAGNOG

90s	Enraptured RAPT 4508	Mist Waves Riding The Hills/Moving Ahead Again/Ghost States (p/s)	6

MAGNUM

75	CBS S CBS 2959	Sweets For My Sweet/Movin' On (no p/s)	45
78	Jet SJET 116	Kingdom Of Madness/In The Beginning	6
78	Jet SJET 128	Invasion/Universe	6
79	Jet JET 155	Changes/Lonesome Star (silver p/s, with sew-on patch)	10
79	Jet JET 155	Changes/Lonesome Star (silver p/s)	8
79	Jet JET 163	Foolish Heart/Baby Rock Me (p/s)	6
80	Jet JET 175	Magnum Live [All Of My Life (live)/Great Adventure (live)//Invasion (live)/ Kingdom Of Madness (live)] (double pack, stickered p/s)	6
80	Jet JET 188	Changes (live Remix)/Everybody Needs/Changes (live) (black p/s)	7
81	Jet JET 7007	Black Nights (possibly promo only)	12
82	Jet JET 7020	The Lights Burned Out/Long Days Black Nights (p/s)	6
82	Jet JET 7027	Back To Earth (live)/Hold Back Your Love (live)//Soldier Of The Line (live)/ Sacred Hour (live) (double pack)	8
86	Polydor POSP 798	Lonely Night/Les Morts Dansant (live) (p/s)	5
86	Polydor POSPG 798	Lonely Night/Les Morts Dansant (live)//All England's Eyes (live)/ Hit And Run (live) (double pack)	7
86	Polydor POSPP 833	Midnight (Remix)/Back Street Kid/Kingdom Of Madness (live) (12", picture disc)	10
87	Polydor POSP 850	When The World Comes Down (Edit)/Vigilante (live) (p/s)	5
88	Polydor POSPG 910	Days Of No Trust/Maybe Tonight ('oct-o-pack', gatefold p/s)	8
88	Polydor POSPP 910	Days Of No Trust/Maybe Tonight (p/s, with sew-on patch)	7
88	Polydor POSPG 920	Start Talking Love/C'est La Vie (gatefold pop-up p/s)	5
88	Polydor POSPG 930	It Must Have Been Love/Crying Time ('prismatic' pack)	5
78	Jet JETLP 210	KINGDOM OF MADNESS (LP, original 'king' sleeve)	18
83	FM WKFMPD 111	THE ELEVENTH HOUR (LP, picture disc)	15
85	FM WKFM LP 34	ON A STORYTELLER'S NIGHT (LP, with bonus single)	15
85	FM WKFM G/C LP 34	ON A STORYTELLER'S NIGHT (LP, gold or clear vinyl, with poster)	15
85	FM WKFM PD 34	ON A STORYTELLER'S NIGHT (LP, picture disc, with poster)	18
86	Polydor POLD 5198	VIGILANTE (LP, with inner)	12
87	FM Revolver WKFMHP 106	MIRADOR (LP, blue vinyl, gatefold sleeve, poster and Blue vinyl 12" (12HP106)	15
88	Polydor POLDP 5221	WINGS OF HEAVEN (LP, picture disc with extra track, die-cut sleeve)	12
88	FM Revolver WKFMPD 110	MAGNUM II (LP, reissue, picture disc)	15
90	FM Revolver WKFMBX 145	FOUNDATION (6-LP box set)	45

TEDDY MAGNUS

71	Green Door GD 4008	Flying Machine/VERSION BOYS: Machine Version	5

MAGOO

95	Noisebox NBX 013	MUDSHARK EP: Tom, Lou And Me/Elsie's Skinny Arms/Hop Your Mouth (orange vinyl, numbered p/s, 500 only)	10
95	Noisebox NBX 016	ROBOT CARNIVAL EP: Robot Carnival/Sampa Calmida (Land Of Joy)/ Candle Buddah/Rocket To Spector City (blue vinyl, p/s)	6
96	Noisebox NBX 020	EYESPY EP: Eye Spy/Motel Mining/Soaterama/Polka Party No.2/ Silver Screen/Word Is Out/Diving Bell (lemon yellow vinyl, p/s, 500 only)	5
98	Fierce Panda NING 47	Black Sabbath/MOGWAI: Sweet Leaf (p/s)	7

MAGPIES

68	Doctor Bird DB 1129	Lulu/Must I Be Lonely	12
68	Doctor Bird DB 1132	Blue Boy/I Guess I'm Crazy	12

MAG SPIES/MAGAZINE SPIES/MAGSPIES
(see also The Cure)

79	Dance Fools Dance GLITCH 1	LIFEBLOOD (12" EP, 2 tracks by Mag Spies/2 by Obtainers)	400

ALEX MAGUIRE

87	Incus INCUS 52	LIVE AT OSCARS (LP)	35

LEO MAGUIRE

62	Parlophone R 4917	Small World /Crying For The Moon	8

MAGUS
(see also Blue Epitaph)

80	Northern Sound NSR 200	BREEZIN' AWAY (LP, private pressing)	50

TAJ MAHAL

68	Direction 58-3547	Everybody's Got To Change Sometime/Statesboro Blues	10
69	Direction 58-4044	Ee Zee Rider/You Don't Miss Your Water	10
70	Direction 58-4586	Give Your Woman What She Wants/Further On Down The Road	8
71	CBS 7413	Diving Duck Blues/Fishin' Blues	10
67	Direction 8-63279	TAJ MAHAL (LP)	30
69	Direction 8-63397	THE NATCH'L BLUES (LP)	30
69	Direction 8-66226	GIANT STEP/DE OLE FOLKS AT HOME (2-LP)	20
71	CBS 66288	THE REAL THING (2-LP)	18
72	CBS 64447	HAPPY JUST TO BE LIKE I AM (LP)	12
73	CBS 65090	RECYCLING THE BLUES AND OTHER RELATED STUFF (LP)	12
73	CBS 65814	OOOH SO GOOD 'N BLUES (LP)	12
73	CBS 70123	SOUNDER (LP, soundtrack)	12

MAHAVISHNU ORCHESTRA
(see also John McLaughlin)

75	CBS 3007	Can't Stand Your Funk/Eternity's Breath Part 1	6
72	CBS 64717	THE INNER MOUNTING FLAME (LP, with insert)	15
74	CBS CQ 31996	BIRDS OF FIRE (LP, quadrophonic)	20

MINT VALUE £

MITCH MAHON & EDITIONS
69 Pye 7N 17844 You've Got What I Need/I've Thrown Our Love Away 5

SKIP MAHONEY & CASUALS
76 Contempo CLP 539 LAND OF LOVE (LP) 20

MAIL
71 Parlophone R 5916 Omnibus/Life Goes On 20

MAINFRAME
84 YYY INTO TROUBLE WITH THE NOISE OF ART (12", 7-track EP) 10

MAINHORSE
71 Polydor 2383 049 MAINHORSE (LP) 45

MAIN INGREDIENT
74 RCA PB 0305 Happiness Is Just Around The Bend/Why Can't We All Unite 8
71 RCA LSA 3020 TASTEFUL SOUL (LP) 15
72 RCA APL0335 EUPHRATES RIVER (LP) 20

MIKE MAINIERI
69 Solid State USS 7006 INSIGHT (LP) 20

MAINLAND
79 Christy ACML 0200 EXPOSURE (LP) 15

MAINLINER
(see also Acid Mothers Temple)
03 Reopse LP 01 MELLOW OUT (LP, red vinyl) 15

JULIE MAIRS & CHRIS STOWELL
77 Cottage COT 211 SOFT SEA BLUE (LP) 25

MAISON ROUGE
85 Red Barn RBR 0001 Questions (p/s) 5

MAJAMOOD
66 Doc. Bird/W.I.R.L. DB 1052 Two Hundred Million Red Ants/Faces Amassed 30

MAJESTERIANS
81 Daddy Kool DKR 125 So Many Times/Flute On Fire (12") 20

MAJESTICS
73 Cube BUG 54 Living It All Again/She Troubles My Mind 25

MAJOR ACCIDENT
(see also Accident)
82 M. Melodies MAME 1001 Warboots/Terrorist Gang (unissued, test pressings only) 40
83 Step Forward SF 23 Mr. Nobody/That's You (p/s) 12
83 Flicknife FLS 216 Fight To Win/Free Man (p/s) 12
83 Flicknife FLS 023 Leaders Of Tomorrow/Dayo/Breakaway (p/s) 12
84 Flicknife FLS 026 Respectable/Man On The Wall (p/s) 12
83 Step Forward SFLP 9 MASSACRED MELODIES (LP) 30
84 Syndicate SYNLP 9 TORTURED TUNES LIVE (LP) 25
85 Flicknife SHARP 027 PNEUMATIC PNEUROSIS (LP) 25

MAJORETTES
63 Lyntone LYN 982 White Levi's (flexidisc) 15

MAJOR FORCE
(see also Major Force West)
94 Mo' Wax MW 082LP Return Of The Original Artform/(Mixes) (5 x 12" box set) 25

MAJOR FORCE WEST
(see also Major Force)
94 Mo' Wax MWMFWCD 001 HEADTURNER (CD) 20

MAJORINE
69 Pyramid 6069 Loving Shrine/I Live 20

MAJORITY
65 Decca F 12186 Pretty Little Girl/I Don't Wanna Be Hurt No More 20
65 Decca F 12271 A Little Bit Of Sunlight/Shut 'Em Down In London Town 25
66 Decca F 12313 We Kiss In A Shadow/Ring The Bells 15
66 Decca F 12453 Simplified/One Third 100
66 Decca F 12504 To Make Me A Man/Tears Won't Help 15
67 Decca F 12573 I Hear A Rhapsody/Wait By The Fire 20
67 Decca F 12638 Running Away With My Baby/Let The Joybells Ring 20
68 Decca F 12727 All Our Christmases/People 25

MAJORS
62 London HLP 9602 A Wonderful Dream/Time Will Tell 25
62 London HLP 9627 She's A Troublemaker/A Little Bit Now 25
63 London HLP 9693 What In The World/Tra La La 22
64 Liberty LBF 66009 Ooh Wee Baby/I'll Be There 22
63 London RE-P 1358 MEET THE MAJORS (EP) 100
63 London HA-P 8068 MEET THE MAJORS (LP) 150

MAJOR SURGERY
77 Next 104 NEXT CUT (LP) 15

MAJOR TOM
76 Satril SAT 113 Spaceman Boy/Spaceman Boy (Instrumental) 25

MAKADOPOLOUS
60 Palette PG 9005 Never On Sunday/Yasou (p/s) 10
60 Palette PG 9005 Never On Sunday/Yasou 6

MINT VALUE £

PETER MAKANA & HIS RHYTHM BOYS
58 Oriole CB 1445 Baboon Shepherd (with Black Duke)/Black John ... 5
58 Oriole CB 1446 Cool Mood/Sweet Baby ... 5

MIRIAM MAKEBA
63 London HL 9747 The Click Song/Mbube ... 8
60 London HA 2332 MIRIAM MAKEBA (LP) ... 15

CARMEN MAKI
69 CBS 4298 (Sometime I Feel Like) A Lonely Baby/Anata Ga Hoshii ... 7

MAKIN' TIME
(see also Charlatans)
85 Countdown VAIN 1 Here Is My Number/Nothing Else (p/s) ... 8
86 Countdown TVAIN 1 Here Is My Number/Nothing Else (picture disc) ... 8
86 Countdown VAIN 5 Pump It Up/Walk A Thin Line (p/s) ... 8
86 Countdown 12 VAIN 5 PUMP IT UP EP: Once Again/Walk A Thin Line/Eating Up The Cold ... 8
85 Countdown DOWN 1 RHYTHM 'N' SOUL (LP) ... 15
86 Ready To Eat READY 1 NO LUMPS OF FAT OR GRISTLE GUARANTEED (LP) ... 18
87 Re-Elect/President ELECT 1 TIME, TROUBLE AND MONEY (LP) ... 18

MAKKA BEES
77 Congo CO 1 Nation Fiddler/Fire ... 20

MAL & PRIMITIVES
(see also Primitives, Mal Ryder & Spirits)
65 Pye 7N 15915 Every Minute Of Every Day/Pretty Little Face ... 80

MALAGON SISTERS & CHA CHA RHYTHM BOYS
59 Pye International 7N 25008 In A Little Spanish Town/Lessons In Cha-Cha-Cha ... 5

MALARIA!
82 Jungle JUNG 3 NEW YORK PASSAGE (12" EP) ... 8

CARL MALCOLM
75 Black Wax WAX 7 Miss Wire Waist/SKIN, FLESH & BONES: Wire Dub ... 10
77 Grove Music GMDM 1 Repatriation (feat. Ranking Trevor)/Take A Tip From Me (feat. Ranking Trevor) (12") ... 40

CARLOS MALCOLM & AFRO CARIBS
65 Island WI 173 Bonanza Ska/Papa Luiga ... 20

GEORGE MALCOLM
53 Parlophone MSP 6058 Bach Goes To Town/Bach Before The Mast ... 6

HUGH MALCOLM
68 Amalgamated AMG 827 Good Time Rock/LYNN TAITT & JETS: Sleepy Ludy ... 35
68 Amalgamated AMG 829 Mortgage/CANNONBALL BRYAN TRIO: Man About Town ... 45

MALCOLM & ALWYN
73 Pye NSPL 18404 FOOL'S WISDOM (LP, with poster) ... 15
74 Key KL 022 WILDWALL (LP) ... 15

MALLARD
(see also Captain Beefheart & His Magic Band)
77 Virgin VS 168 Harvest/Green Coyote ... 7
76 Virgin V 2045 MALLARD (LP) ... 15
77 Virgin V 2077 IN A DIFFERENT CLIMATE (LP) ... 15

MALLET
80 Rox ROX 014 C C Rider/Route 66 ... 25

STEPHEN MALLINDER
(see also Cabaret Voltaire)
82 Fetish FM 2010 POW-WOW (LP) ... 12

SIW MALMKVIST
59 Oriole CB 1486 Sermonette/The Preacher ... 5
61 Parlophone R 4765 Wedding Cake/Red Roses And Little White Lies ... 5
64 Columbia DB 7411 Sole Sole Sole/Sabato Sera (as Siw Malmkvist & Umberto Marcato) ... 5
68 Atlantic 584 229 The Man Who Took The Valise Off The Floor Of Grand Central Station/ Sadie The Cleaning Lady ... 5

CINDY MALONE
61 RCA RCA 1254 Weird Beard/Young Marriage ... 8

WIL MALONE
(see also Barnaby Rudge, Motherlight, Wilson Malone Voiceband)
70 Fontana STL 5541 WIL MALONE (LP) ... 1500
10 Morgan Bluetown BT 5005 WIL MALONE (LP, reissue, 750 signed numbered copies) ... 25

WILSON MALONE VOICEBAND
(see also Motherlight, Wil Malone)
68 Morgan MR 112P FUNNY SAD MUSIC (LP) ... 25

RICHARD MALTBY
56 HMV 7M 393 Man With The Golden Arm Theme/Heart Of Paris ... 8
61 Columbia DB 4606 The Rat Race/Walkie Talkie ... 15

MAMA LAPATO
82 Bead Records BEAD 20 MAMA LAPATO (LP) ... 20

MAMA LION
72 Philips 6078002 Ain't Too Proud To Beg/Mr. Invitation ... 6

MAMAS & PAPAS
(see also Mama Cass [Elliot], John Phillips, Michelle Phillips, Scott McKenzie, Barry McGuire, Mugwumps, Big Three [U.S], Spanky & Our Gang)
66 RCA Victor RCA 1503 California Dreamin'/Somebody Groovy ... 10

MAMAS & PAPAS

MINT VALUE £

66	RCA Victor RCA 1516	Monday, Monday/Got A Feelin'	5
66	RCA Victor RCA 1533	I Saw Her Again/Even If I Could	6
66	RCA Victor RCA 1551	Look Through My Window/Once There Was I Time I Thought	5
67	RCA Victor RCA 1564	Words Of Love/I Can't Wait	7
67	RCA Victor RCA 1576	Dedicated To The One I Love/Free Advice	5
67	RCA Victor RCA 1613	Creeque Alley/No Salt On Her Tail	6
67	RCA Victor RCA 1630	12.30/Straight Shooter	6
67	RCA Victor RCA 1649	Glad To Be Unhappy/Hey Girl	6
68	RCA Victor RCA 1710	Safe In My Garden/Too Late	5
68	RCA Victor RCA 1726	Dream A Little Dream Of Me/Midnight Voyage (as Mama Cass and the Mamas & Papas)	5
68	RCA Victor RCA 1744	For The Love Of Ivy/Strange Young Girls	8
66	RCA Victor RD 7803	IF YOU CAN BELIEVE YOUR EYES AND EARS (LP)	20
66	RCA Victor RD/SF 7834	CASS, JOHN, MICHELLE, DENNY (LP)	20
67	RCA Victor RD/SF 7880	DELIVER (LP)	20
68	RCA Victor RD/SF 7960	THE PAPAS AND THE MAMAS (LP)	20
68	Stateside (S)SL 5002	THE MAMAS AND THE PAPAS GOLDEN ERA VOL. 2 (LP)	15
70	Probe SPB 1013/14	A GATHERING OF FLOWERS (2-LP)	20
71	Probe SPB 1048	PEOPLE LIKE US (LP)	15
78	St. Michael MO 101225	CALIFORNIA DREAMIN' (LP, exclusive to Marks & Spencer)	15

MAMA'S BOYS

83	Spartan 12SP 6	Too Little Of You To Love/Freedom Fighters (12", p/s, with free "Official Bootleg" LP)	10
84	Spartan SP 11	Midnight Promises (p/s)	5
84	Spartan 12SP 11	MIDNIGHT PROMISES (12" EP)	8
85	Jive JIVEP 96	Needle In The Groove/Don't Tell Mama (shaped picture disc)	8
82	Ultra Noise ULTRA 1	PLUG IT IN (LP)	12
85	Jive HIP 24	POWER AND PASSION (LP, with 12" interview picture disc)	12

MAMMATH

84	Neat NEAT 42	Rock Me/Rough 'N' Ready (p/s)	7

MAMMOTH

(see also John McCoy, Gillan, Samson, Tiger, Nicky Moore Band, Hackensack)

87	Jive MOTHCD 1	Fatman (Admiral Amour Mix)/Political Animal/Bad Times/Fatman(7" Version) (CD)	8
89	Jive MOTHX 4	All The Days/Fatman/Bet You Wish (12", picture disc, PVC sleeve, withdrawn)	20

MAN

(see also Bystanders, Eyes Of Blue, Ancient Grease, Big Sleep, Clive John, Alkatraz, Help Yourself, Deke Leonard, Neutrons, Gary Pickford-Hopkins & Friends, Wild Turkey)

69	Pye 7N 17684	Sudden Life/Love	25
71	Liberty LBF 15448	Daughter Of The Fireplace/Country Girl	18
74	United Artists UP 35643	Don't Go Away (possibly unissued)	15
74	United Artists UP 35703	Taking The Easy Way Out Again/California Silks And Satins	6
74	United Artists UP 35739	Day And Night/A Hard Way To Live	5
76	MCA MCA 236	Out Of Your Head/I'm A Love Taker	5
76	United Artists REM 408	BANANAS (EP)	8
69	Pye NPL 18275	REVELATION (LP, mono, original pressing with sky blue label with black at top)	70
69	Pye NSPL 18275	REVELATION (LP, stereo, original pressing with sky blue label with black at top)	40
69	Pye N(S)PL 18275	REVELATION (LP, mono/stereo, reissues with blue label but black on the side)	12
69	Dawn DNLS 3003	2 OZ'S OF PLASTIC WITH A HOLE IN THE MIDDLE (LP, orange label, g/f sleeve)	45
69	Dawn DNLS 3003	2 OZ'S OF PLASTIC WITH A HOLE IN THE MIDDLE (LP, later pressings with lilac then pink 'sun' labels, gatefold sleeve)	20
70	Liberty LBG 83464	MAN (LP, gatefold textured sleeve)	40
72	United Artists UAS 29236	DO YOU LIKE IT HERE NOW, ARE YOU SETTLING IN? (LP)	30
72	United Artists USP 100	LIVE AT THE PADGET ROOMS, PENARTH (LP)	30
72	United Artists UAG 29417	BE GOOD TO YOURSELF AT LEAST ONCE A DAY (LP, fold out 'map' in gatefold sleeve with 'family tree' inner)	30
73	United Artists UDX 205/6	CHRISTMAS AT THE PATTI (LP, 2 x 10", with other artists)	22
73	Utd Artists UAD 60053/4	BACK INTO THE FUTURE (2-LP, gatefold sleeve, some stickered)	20
74	United Artists UAG 29631	RHINOS WINOS AND LUNATICS (LP, laminated gatefold)	15
74	United Artists UAG 29675	SLOW MOTION (LP, lyric inner sleeve)	15
75	United Artists UAG 29872	MAXIMUM DARKNESS (LP, gatefold sleeve, with poster)	15
77	MCA MCF 2815	ALL'S WELL THAT ENDS WELL (LP, initial batch with History Of Man booklet)	20
77	MCA MCF 2815	ALL'S WELL THAT ENDS WELL (LP)	12

T. MAN & T. BONES

72	Sioux SI 007	True Born African (actually by Winston Jarrett & Righteous Flames)/ Tropical Chief	5

(STEPHEN STILLS') MANASSAS

(see also Stephen Stills, Crosby Stills & Nash, Flying Burrito Brothers)

72	Atlantic K 60021	MANASSAS (2-LP, with 2 inner sleeves & lyric poster)	22
73	Atlantic K 40440	DOWN THE ROAD (LP, with inner sleeve)	15

MANASSEH

77	Genesis 12	MANASSEH (LP, with insert)	20

JUNIOR MANCE

60	HMV CLP 1342	JUNIOR (LP)	25
71	Atlantic 2400 028	WITH A LOTTA HELP FROM MY FRIENDS (LP)	20

STEVE MANCHA/J.J. BARNES

(see also J.J. Barnes)

69	Stax SXATS 1012	RARE STAMPS (LP)	50

MINT VALUE £

MANCHESTER CITY F.C.

72	RCA 2200	Boys In Blue/Funky City	6

MANCHESTER MEKON

79	Newmarket NEW 102	No Forgetting/Have A Go-Go/Jonathan Livingstone Seafood (hand-painted p/s with insert, 1,000 only)	25

MICKY MANCHESTER

75	Rainbow RBW 2001	Have You Seen Your Daughter, Mrs Jones?/Chamberlain Said	10

MANCHESTER MOB

(see also Graham Gouldman, High Society, 10cc, Friday Browne)

67	Parlophone R 5552	Bony Maronie At The Hop/Afro Asian	40

MANCHESTER UNITED F.C.

78	Jet 775	Just One Of Those Teams/Na Na Hey Hey Kiss Him Goodbye (As Manchester United Supporters Club)	6
81	Goldspinners GOLD 1	Manchester United/Tribute To The Fans (as Manchester United)	6
86	Columbia DB 9107	We All Follow Man. United/They're The Best/Southbound Glory Glory Man. United (as Manchester United Football Team)	6

MANCHESTER UNITED FOOTBALL SQUAD

76	Decca F 13633	Manchester United/MARTIN BUCHAN: Old Trafford Blues	8
79	RCA MAN 1	Onward Sexton's Soldiers/Come On You Reds (red vinyl)	8
94	PolyGram TV MANUP 12	Come On You Reds/(Instrumental) (12" picture disc, with insert)	15

MANCHESTERS

66	Ember	TRIBUTE TO THE BEATLES (LP)	20

MANCHESTER'S PLAYBOYS

66	Fontana TF 745	I Feel So Good/I Close My Eyes	175

MANCINI & FOX

72	Polydor 2066 170	Light Song/The Colours Are Still There	8

HENRY MANCINI & HIS ORCHESTRA

59	RCA RCA 1134	Peter Gunn Theme/The Brothers Go To Mother's	8
61	RCA RCA 1256	Moon River/Breakfast At Tiffanys	5
62	RCA RCA 1285	Experiment In Terror/Tooty Twist	10
62	RCA RCA 1312	Man Of The World Theme/Fluter's Ball	6
64	RCA RCA 1431	Dear Heart/A Shot In The Dark	5
70	RCA RCA 1934	Z-Theme/Midnight Cowboy	5
61	RCA RCX 205	BREAKFAST AT TIFFANY'S (EP)	15
62	RCA RCX 7107	HATARI! (EP)	8
64	RCA RCX 7136	THE PINK PANTHER (EP)	15
57	Brunswick LAT 8162	ROCK, PRETTY BABY (LP, soundtrack, with Rod McKuen)	90
59	RCA RD 27123/SF 5033	PETER GUNN (LP, soundtrack)	15
63	RCA SF 7620	CHARADE (LP, soundtrack)	20
64	RCA RD 7667	THE BEST OF MANCINI (LP)	12
65	RCA RD 7759	THE GREAT RACE (LP, soundtrack)	15
66	RCA SF 7818	WHAT DID YOU DO IN THE WAR, DADDY? (LP, soundtrack)	15
66	RCA RD 7817	ARABESQUE (LP, soundtrack)	15
67	RCA RD/SF 7891	TWO FOR THE ROAD (LP, soundtrack)	15
67	RCA RD/SF 7899	GUNN (LP, soundtrack)	18
70	CBS 70061	ME, NATALIE (LP, soundtrack, with Rod McKuen)	12
70	Avco Embassy 6466 002	SUNFLOWER (LP, soundtrack)	12
70	United Artists UAS 29122	MASTER OF THE ISLANDS (LP, soundtrack)	15
70	RCA SF 8138	DARLIN' LILI (LP, soundtrack, gatefold sleeve)	12
72	RCA Victor SF 8127	FILM THEMES A TO Z (LP)	15
73	Elektra K 46239	THE THIEF WHO CAME TO DINNER (LP, soundtrack)	15
75	RCA Red Seal RS 1010	THE RETURN OF THE PINK PANTHER (LP, soundtrack)	15
75	MCA MCF 2707	THE GREAT WALDO PEPPER (LP, soundtrack)	15

MANDALABAND

75	Chrysalis CHR 1095	MANDALABAND (LP)	15
78	Chrysalis CHR 1181	THE EYE OF WENDOR: PROPHECIES (LP, with booklet)	15

HARVEY MANDEL

(see also Canned Heat, Dewey Terry)

74	Janus 6146 024	Uno Ino/Shangrenade	6
68	Philips SBL 7873	CRISTO REDENTOR (LP)	25
69	Philips SBL 7904	RIGHTEOUS (LP)	20
70	Philips SBL 7915	GAMES GUITARS PLAY (LP)	15
71	Dawn DNLS 3015	BABY BATTER (LP)	20
71	Philips 6336 009	CRISTO REDENTOR (LP, reissue)	12
72	London SH-O 8426	GET OFF IN CHICAGO (LP)	12
72	Janus 6310 210	THE SNAKE (LP)	15
73	Janus 6499 831	SHANGRENADE (LP)	12

RICHARD MANDEL

69	London HL 10256	Loneliness/Young And Warm And Wonderful	20

NELSON MANDELA

64	Ember CEL 905	WHY I'M READY TO DIE (LP, spoken word, narrated by Peter Finch)	20

MANDINGO

(see also Geoff Love, Manuel & Music Of The Mountains)

73	EMI EMI 2014	Medicine Man/Black Rite	15
73	EMI EMC 3010	MANDINGO 1: SACRIFICE (LP)	15
73	Studio Two TWO 400	MANDINGO 2: PRIMEVAL RHYTHM OF LIFE (LP)	40
73	Studio Two Q4TWO 400	MANDINGO 2: PRIMEVAL RHYTHM OF LIFE (LP, quadrophonic)	40
75	EMI EMC 3038	MANDINGO 3: STORY OF SURVIVAL (LP)	30
77	EMI EMC 3217	MANDINGO 4: SAVAGE RITE (LP)	25

MINT VALUE £

MANDRAGORA

86	SAB 01	OVER THE MOON (LP)	50
91	Resonance 33-9133	HEAD FIRST (LP)	20

MANDRAKE

60	Philips PB 1093	Mandrake/The Witch's Twist	12
61	Philips BF 1153	Thank Goodness It's Friday/Queen Of Sheba	7

MANDRAKE MEMORIAL

69	RCA SF 8028	MEDIUM (LP)	60
70	RCA/Poppy PYS 11003	PUZZLE (LP)	50

MANDRAKE PADDLE STEAMERS

(see also Liverpool Echo)

69	Parlophone R 5780	Strange Walking Man/Steam	130
88	Bam Caruso NRIC 033	Strange Walking Man/Steam (reissue, gatefold p/s)	12

MANDRILL

73	Polydor 2066 320	Mandrill/Hang Loose	5
73	Polydor 2066 357	Fencewalk/Polk Street Carnival	5
72	Polydor 2391 030	MANDRILL IS (LP, gatefold)	20
73	Polydor 2391 061	COMPOSITE TRUTH (LP)	15
73	Polydor 2391 092	JUST OUTSIDE OF TOWN (LP)	18
73	United Artists UAS 29923	SOLID (LP)	12

MANDY (SMITH)

87	PWL PWLP 1	I Just Can't Wait/Instrumental/You're Never Alone (12" picture disc)	10
88	PWL PWCD 11	Boys & Girls/Mandy's Theme (I Just Can't Wait) (The Cool & Breezy Jazz Mix)/ He's My Boy (3" CD)	15
88	PWL PWCD 18	Victim Of Pleasure (Red Rooster Mix)/Say It's Love/Victim Of Pleasure (Instrumental) (3" CD)	15
88	PWL HFCD 2	MANDY (CD)	30

MANEATERS

(see also Adam & The Ants)

82	Editions EG EGO 8	Nine To Five/SUZI PINNS: Jerusalem (withdrawn 'Adam & Toyah' p/s)	100
82	Editions EG EGO 8	Nine To Five/SUZI PINNS: Jerusalem (title p/s)	5

MAN FRIDAY & JIVE JUNIOR

(see also Queen)

83	Malaco MAL 011	Picking Up Sounds/Picking Up Sounds (Radio Mix) (p/s, features John Deacon)	30
83	Malaco MAL 1211	Picking Up Sounds (Extended)/Picking Up Sounds (Radio Mix) (12", p/s, features John Deacon)	50

MAN FROM DELMONTE

87	Ugly Man UGLY 3	Drive Drive Drive/Twenty Two And Still In Love With You/Sun Serious (p/s)	6
87	Ugly Man UGLY 5T	Water In My Eyes/Bred By You (12", p/s)	18
88	Ugly Man UGLY 7T	Will Nobody Save Louise/Good Things In Life/Like A Millionaire (12", p/s)	30
89	Bop Cassettes BIP 502	WAITING FOR ANN (12" EP)	15

MANGO GREEN

70	Ackee ACK 109	Birds Of A Feather/Run Down	15

MANHATTANS

65	Sue WI 384	I Wanna Be (Your Everything)/Searchin' For My Baby	50
66	Carnival CAR 100	Baby I Need You/Teach Me (The Philly Dog)	20
66	Carnival CAR 101	That New Girl/Can I	20
74	CBS 2117	Soul Train/I'm Not A Run Around	6
73	London SHB 8449	A MILLION TO ONE (LP)	30
76	CBS 81513	THE MANHATTANS (LP)	12
78	CBS 81828	IT FEELS GOOD (LP)	12

MANIAC

85	Rentaracket Recordings RKT 1	KILLING FOR PLEASURE EP (p/s, with booklet)	6

MANIACS

(see also Rings, Physicals)

77	United Artists UP 36327	Chelsea 1977/Ain't No Legend (p/s)	20

MANIAX

66	White Label WLR 101/102	Out Of Reach/The Devil's Home	20

MANIC JABS

81	Waldo's MS 009	Autophagus/The Injuns Are Comin'/Thing Wild (p/s)	10

MANIC STREET PREACHERS

SINGLES

88	SBS SBS 002	Suicide Alley/Tennessee (I Get Low) (hand-made p/s with press-cuttings glued to plain card cover)	750
88	SBS SBS 002	Suicide Alley/Tennessee (I Get Low) (blue p/s, 200 only)	400
88	SBS SBS 002	Suicide Alley/Tennessee (I Get Low) (no p/s, 100 only)	200
90	Hopelessly Devoted 1	UK Channel Boredom/LAURENS: I Don't Know What The Trouble Is (p/s flexidisc, free with Hopelessly Devoted fanzine; later repressed)	60
90	Hopelessly Devoted 1	UK Channel Boredom/LAURENS: I Don't Know What The Trouble Is (p/s flexidisc, without Hopelessly Devoted fanzine; later repressed)	45
90	Damaged Goods YUBB 4	NEW ART RIOT EP: New Art Riot/Strip It Down/ Last Exit On Yesterday/ Teenage 20/20 (12", white label, 100 copies, plain sleeves rubber stamped with "Made In Wales")	35
90	Damaged Goods YUBB 4	NEW ART RIOT EP: New Art Riot/Strip It Down/Last Exit On Yesterday/ Teenage 20/20 (12" EP, p/s, 1st 1,000 black & white label)	20
90	Damaged Goods YUBB 4	NEW ART RIOT EP: New Art Riot/Strip It Down/Last Exit On Yesterday/ Teenage 20/20 (12" EP, p/s, 2nd 1,000 on black-on-yellow labels)	15
90	Damaged Goods YUBB 4	NEW ART RIOT EP: New Art Riot/Strip It Down/Last Exit On Yesterday/ Teenage 20/20 (12" EP, p/s, later pressing on red, orange & silver & green labels)	10

			MINT VALUE £
91	Damaged Goods YUBB 004P	NEW ART RIOT EP: New Art Riot/Strip It Down/Last Exit On Yesterday/ Teenage 20/20 (12" EP, p/s, reissue on pink vinyl)	25
91	Heavenly HVN 812	Motown Junk/Sorrow 16/We Her Majesty's Prisoners (12", withdrawn p/s)	35
91	Heavenly HVN 8CD	Motown Junk/Sorrow 16/We Her Majesty's Prisoners (CD, withdrawn sleeve)	80
91	Heavenly HVN 10	You Love Us/Spectators Of Suicide (p/s)	15
91	Heavenly HVN 1012	You Love Us/Spectators Of Suicide/Starlover/Strip It Down (live) (12", p/s)	20
91	Heavenly HVN 10CD	You Love Us/Spectators Of Suicide/Starlover/Strip It Down (live) (CD)	25
91	Columbia 657337 6	Stay Beautiful/R.P. McMurphy/Soul Contamination (12", p/s)	10
91	Columbia 657337 8	Stay Beautiful/R.P. McMurphy/Soul Contamination (12", stickered poster p/s)	10
91	Columbia 657582 6	Repeat (U.K.)/Love's Sweet Exile/Democracy Coma (12", p/s)	12
91	Columbia 657582 8	Repeat/Democracy Coma/Love's Sweet Exile/Stay Beautiful (live) (12", gatefold, stickered p/s)	12
91	Caff CAFF 15	FEMININE IS BEAUTIFUL: Repeat After Me/New Art Riot (p/s, 500 only)	150
92	Columbia 657724 6	You Love Us/A Vision Of Dead Desire/It's So Easy (live) (12" gatefold p/s)	10
92	Columbia 657873 7	Slash'N'Burn/Motown Junk (p/s)	6
92	Columbia 657873 6	Slash'N'Burn/Motown Junk/Ain't Goin' Down (12", with print, stickered p/s)	12
92	Columbia 657873 2	Slash'N'Burn/Motown Junk/Ain't Goin' Down (gold CD, digipak)	15
92	Columbia 658083 6	Motorcycle Emptiness/Bored Out Of My Mind/Under My Wheels (12", picture disc, stickered PVC sleeve)	18
92	Damaged Goods YUBB 4CD	New Art Riot/Strip It Down/Last Exit On Yesterday/Teenage 20/20 (CD, picture disc, reissue, 3,000 only)	10
92	Columbia 658382 7	Theme From MASH EP (Suicide Is Painless)/FATIMA MANSIONS: Everything I Do (I Do It For You) (p/s)	6
92	Columbia 658382 6	Theme From MASH EP (Suicide Is Painless)/FATIMA MANSIONS/ Everything I Do (I Do It For You)/Sleeping With The NME (12", p/s)	8
93	Columbia 6597277	Roses In The Hospital/Us Against You/Donkeys (red vinyl, p/s)	8
93	Columbia 6597272	Roses In The Hospital/Us Against You/Donkeys/Wrote For Luck (CD)	10
93	Columbia 6597337 6	From Despair To Where/Hibernation/Spectators Of Suicide (Heavenly Version) (12", p/s)	8
93	Columbia 659477 6	La Tristesse Durera/Patrick Bateman/Repeat (live)/Tennessee (12", poster p/s)	8
07	Columbia 8697075597	Underdogs (1-sided, p/s)	20

PROMOS

91	Heavenly HVN 10P	You Love Us (Radio Edit) (promo-only, some with stickered p/s, 1-sided white label, 500 only)	30
92	Columbia XPCD 171	GENERATION TERRORISTS (CD, 5-track sampler, digipak)	15
92	Columbia XPCD 185	Motorcycle Emptiness/Motorcycle Emptiness (Radio Edit) (CD)	18
93	Columbia XPCD 285	GOLD AGAINST THE SOUL (CD, 4-track sampler, digipak)	20
93	Columbia/Damont XPS 272	Symphony Of Tourette (1-sided, white label, no p/s)	70
94	Columbia	DONE AND DUSTED (12", Chemical Brothers remixes)	20
96	Columbia XPR 3043	A Design For Life (Stealth Sonic Orchestra Remix)/(Instrumental) (12")	20
96	Columbia XPR 3049	Kevin Carter (Stealth Sonic Orchestra Remix) (12", white label, 1-sided, stickered card sleeve, 30 only)	30
96	Columbia XPR 3094	Australia (Lionrock Remix) (12", white label, 1-sided, stickered card sleeve, 20 only)	60
97	Columbia MANIC 1-6CD	SIX SINGLES FROM GENERATION TERRORISTS (6-CD box set)	90
99	Epic XPR 3320	Tsunami (Cornelius Remix)/(Electron Ray Tube Mix by Stereolab) (12", p/s, sealed with sticker, promo only)	10

ALBUMS

92	Columbia 471060 0	GENERATION TERRORISTS (2-LP, picture discs, inner sleeves, 5,000 only)	40
92	Columbia 471060 9	GENERATION TERRORISTS (CD, picture disc, 5,000 only)	40
93	Columbia 474064 1	GOLD AGAINST THE SOUL (LP, inner sleeve, in custom carrier-bag)	15
93	Columbia 4740649	GOLD AGAINST THE SOUL (gold CD)	20
94	Epic 477421 0	THE HOLY BIBLE (LP, picture disc)	30
94	Epic 4774219	THE HOLY BIBLE (CD, picture disc)	20
98	Epic 4917031	THIS IS MY TRUTH TELL ME YOURS (LP)	15
03	Sony 5123861	LIPSTICK TRACES (3 x LP, 1,000 only with tactile sleeve)	45

MANICURED NOISE

(see also Weatherman & Friends)

80	Pre PRE 003	Metronome/Moscow (die-cut p/s with postcard)	5
80	Pre PRE 006	Faith/Free Time (p/s)	5

MANIFESTO

80s	Fire BLAZE 66055	Pattern 26 (1-sided white/label in bag with biography)	5

MANISH BOYS

(see also David Bowie)

65	Parlophone R 5250	I Pity The Fool/Take My Tip	800
65	Parlophone R 5250	I Pity The Fool/Take My Tip (Demo copy)	450

MANISH BOYS/DAVY JONES & LOWER THIRD

(see also David Bowie, Davy Jones, Davie Jones & King Bees)

79	EMI EMI 2925	I Pity The Fool/Take My Tip/DAVY JONES & LOWER THIRD: You've Got A Habit Of Leaving/Baby Loves That Way (p/s)	10
82	Charly CYM 1	I Pity The Fool/Take My Tip/DAVY JONES & LOWER THIRD: You've Got A Habit Of Leaving/Baby Loves That Way (10", p/s, reissue)	7

MANITOBA

70	RCA 2016	You'll Never Get Back/Something In You	10

MANIX

91	Reinforced RIVET 1209	Manic Minds (12", die-cut p/s)	8
91	Reinforced RIVET 1209R	Manic Minds EP (Remixes) (12")	8
94	Reinforced RIVET 1275	Intelligent Hoodlums EP (2x12")	12

EARLE MANKEY

78	Bronze BRO 53	Mau Mau/Crazy	15

MANKIND

78	Pinnacle PIN 71-12	Dr. Who/Time Traveller (12", p/s, blue vinyl)	10

ABEL MANN

70	Trend TNY 51	The Sun In The Morning/It's So Easy	7

MINT VALUE £

BARRY MANN

61	HMV POP 911	Who Put The Bomp/Love True Love	30
61	HMV POP 949	Little Miss U.S.A./Find Another Fool	22
62	HMV POP 1084	Hey Baby I'm Dancin'/Like I Don't Love You	15
63	HMV POP 1108	Bless You/Teenage Has Been	18
64	Colpix PX 776	Talk To Me Baby/Amy	15
66	Capitol CL 15463	Angelica/Looking At Tomorrow	15
68	Capitol CL 15538	The Young Electric Psychedelic Hippy Flippy Folk And Funky Philosophic Turned On Groovy 12 String Band/Take Your Love	10
63	HMV CLP 1559	WHO PUT THE BOMP IN THE BOMP BOMP BOMP? (LP)	150
72	CBS 64805	LAY IT ALL OUT (LP, gatefold)	20

CARL MANN

59	London HLS 8935	Mona Lisa/Foolish One	40
59	London HLS 8935	Mona Lisa/Foolish One (78)	60
59	London HLS 9006	Pretend/Rockin' Love	30
59	London HLS 9006	Pretend/Rockin' Love (78)	100
60	London HLS 9170	South Of The Border/I'm Comin' Home	25
60	London HA-S 2277	LIKE MANN - CARL MANN SINGS (LP)	300

GARY MANN ORCHESTRA

73	Penny Farthing PEN 820	The Original 'Big Match' Theme/Newscoop (The Original 'Grandstand' Theme)	12

GEOFF MANN

84	Food For Thought GRUB 4	I MAY SING GRACE (LP)	12
85	Wobbly WOB 1	PSALM ENCHANTED EVENING (LP)	12

GLORIA MANN

56	Brunswick 05569	Why Do Fools Fall In Love/Partners For Life	20
56	Brunswick 05610	It Happened Again/My Secret Sin	10

HERBIE MANN

66	Atlantic 584 052	Philly Dog/DAVE PIKE: Sunny	10
68	A&M AMS 719	Unchain My Heart/Glory Of Love	10
67	Atlantic 584112	The Beat Goes On/Free For All	10
69	Atlantic 584 297	Memphis Underground/New Orleans	10
72	Atlantic K 10179	Philly Dog/Memphis Underground/It's A Funky Thing	6
75	Atlantic K 10580	Hijack/Orient Express	15
75	Atlantic SAM 26	Hijack (Disco Cut)/Bertha Boogie Part 1 (12")	50
58	Fontana TFL 5013	SALUTE TO THE FLUTE (LP)	15
60	Top Rank 25/015	FLUTE FOR ETERNITY (10" LP, with Buddy Collette)	15
63	London HA-K/SH-K 8043	RIGHT NOW (LP)	15
64	Atlantic ATL 5008	HERBIE MANN AT NEWPORT (LP)	15
65	Atlantic ATL/SAL 5035	THE ROAR OF THE GREASE PAINT (LP)	20
66	CBS (S)BPG 62585	LATIN MANN (LP)	18
66	Atlantic ATL/SAL 5038	STANDING OVATION AT NEWPORT (LP)	15
66	Atlantic 587/588 003	MONDAY NIGHT AT THE VILLAGE GATE (LP)	15
66	Atlantic 587/588 028	NIRVANA (LP, with Bill Evans)	15

JOHNNY MANN SINGERS

67	Liberty LIB 55972	Up Up And Away/Joey Is The Name	5

LORIE MANN

59	Top Rank JAR 116	A Penny A Kiss, A Penny A Hug/Dream Lover	7
59	Top Rank JAR 148	Just Keep It Up/You Made Me Care	10
59	Top Rank JAR 237	So Many Ways/I Wonder	7

MANFRED MANN

(see also Paul Jones, Blues Band, Mike Hugg, Henry Lowther, Mike D'Abo, McGuinness Flint, Jack Bruce, Coulson & Dean, Lyn Dobson, Paddy Klaus & Gibson)

63	HMV POP 1189	Why Should We Not/Brother Jack	35
63	HMV POP 1225	Cock-A-Hoop/Now You're Needing Me	22
64	HMV POP 1252	5-4-3-2-1/Without You	8
64	HMV POP 1282	Hubble Bubble (Toil And Trouble)/I'm Your Kingpin	8
64	HMV POP 1320	Do Wah Diddy Diddy/What You Gonna Do?	5
64	HMV POP 1346	Sha La La/John Hardy	5
65	HMV POP 1381	Come Tomorrow/What Did I Do Wrong?	5
65	HMV POP 1413	Oh No Not My Baby/What Am I Doing Wrong	6
65	HMV POP 1466	If You Gotta Go, Go Now/Stay Around	6
66	HMV POP 1541	You Gave Me Somebody To Love/Poison Ivy	10
65	HMV 7TEA 2124	There's No Living Without Your Loving/Tired Of Trying, Bored With Lying, Scared Of Dying (demo-only EP sampler)	30
66	Fontana TF 730	Just Like A Woman/I Wanna Be Rich	5
66	Fontana TF 757	Semi-Detached, Suburban Mr. James/Morning After The Party	5
67	Fontana TF 812	Ha! Ha! Said The Clown/Feeling So Good (in p/s)	8
67	Fontana TF 828	Sweet Pea/One Way	10
67	Fontana TF 862	So Long, Dad/Funniest Gig	7
68	Fontana TF 908	Up The Junction/Sleepy Hollow (in p/s)	15
68	Fontana TF 908	Up The Junction/Sleepy Hollow	5
68	Fontana TF 943	My Name Is Jack/There Is A Man	5
68	Fontana TF 985	Fox On The Run/Too Many People	5
69	Fontana TF 1013	Ragamuffin Man/A 'B' Side	5
64	HMV 7EG 8848	MANFRED MANN'S COCK-A-HOOP WITH 54321 (EP)	25
65	HMV 7EG 8876	GROOVIN' WITH MANFRED MANN (EP)	20
65	HMV 7EG 8908	THE ONE IN THE MIDDLE (EP)	15
65	HMV 7EG 8922	NO LIVING WITHOUT LOVING (EP)	18
66	HMV 7EG 8942	MACHINES (EP)	25
66	HMV 7EG 8949	INSTRUMENTAL ASYLUM (EP, with Jack Bruce)	25
66	HMV 7EG 8962	AS WAS (EP)	25
66	Fontana TE 17483	INSTRUMENTAL ASSASSINATION (EP)	10
64	HMV CLP 1731	THE FIVE FACES OF MANFRED MANN (LP)	80
65	HMV CLP 1911	MANN MADE (LP, mono)	30

			MINT VALUE £
65	HMV CSD 1628	MANN MADE (LP, stereo)	40
66	HMV CLP 3559	MANN MADE HITS (LP)	35
66	Fontana TL 5377	AS IS (LP, 'alcove' cover, mono)	20
66	Fontana STL 5377	AS IS (LP, 'alcove' cover, stereo)	30
66	Fontana (S)TL 5377	AS IS (LP, 'locomotive' cover, mono/stereo)	70
67	HMV CLP 3594	SOUL OF MANN (LP, mono)	50
67	HMV CSD 3594	SOUL OF MANN (LP, stereo)	70
68	Fontana (S)TL 5460	UP THE JUNCTION - ORIGINAL SOUNDTRACK RECORDING (LP)	60
68	Fontana SFL 13003	WHAT A MANN (LP)	18
68	Fontana TL 5470	MIGHTY GARVEY! (LP, mono)	25
68	Fontana STL 5470	MIGHTY GARVEY! (LP, stereo)	15
70	Fontana 6852 005	UP THE JUNCTION - ORIGINAL SOUNDTRACK RECORDING (LP, reissue)	25

MANFRED MANN & MIKE HUG(G)

71	Ski SKI 1	Ski 'Full-Of-Fitness' Theme/Baby Jane (in p/s)	15
71	Ski SKI 1	Ski 'Full-Of-Fitness' Theme/Baby Jane	7
71	Michelin MIC+01	The Michelin Theme (Go Radial, Go Michelin) (1-sided, gatefold p/s)	15

MANFRED MANN'S CHAPTER III

70	Vertigo 6059 012	Happy Being Me/Devil Woman	10
69	Vertigo VO 3	MANFRED MANN CHAPTER III (LP, gatefold sleeve, large swirl label)	80
70	Vertigo 6360 012	MANFRED MANN CHAPTER III VOL. 2 (LP, gatefold sleeve, large swirl label)	80

MANFRED MANN'S EARTH BAND

(see also Australian Playboys, Trifle, AC/DC, Thin Lizzy, Alan Parsons Project, Skeleton Crew, Jeff Wayne)

70	Lyntone LYN 1981	The Maxwell House Shake (1-sided flexidisc)	8
71	Philips 6006 122	Living Without You/Tribute (as Manfred Mann)	6
71	Philips 6006 159	Mrs Henry/Prayer (as Manfred Mann)	6
72	Philips 6006 251	Meat/Glorified Magnified (as Earth Band)	6
73	Vertigo 6059 078	Get Your Rocks Off/Sadjoy (as Earth Band)	7
79	Bronze BPO 77	Don't Kill It Carol/Blinded By The Light (picture disc)	7
71	Philips 6308 062	STEPPING SIDEWAYS (LP, unissued)	0
72	Philips 6308 086	MANFRED MANN'S EARTH BAND (LP, black/silver labels)	40
72	Philips 6308 125	GLORIFIED MAGNIFIED (LP, gatefold sleeve, 1st pressing, black/silver labels)	50
72	Philips 6308 086	GLORIFIED MAGNIFIED (LP, gatefold sleeve, 2nd pressing, blue/silver labels)	20
73	Vertigo 6360 087	MESSIN' (LP, die cut gatefold sleeve, 'spaceship' label)	25
73	Bronze ILPS 9265	SOLAR FIRE (LP, gatefold sleeve, lyric inner sleeve, Island label credit)	20
74	Bronze ILPS 9306	THE GOOD EARTH (LP, lyric inner sleeve with cut corner, Island label credit)	20

ROBERTO MANN ORCHESTRA

68	Decca F13904	Love Theme From Witchfinder General/Both Sides Now	30

SHADOW MANN

69	Roulette RO 504	Come Live With Me/One By One	12

SHELLY MANNE

(see also Gerry Mulligan & Shelly Manne, Shorty Rogers & His Orchestra)

68	Atlantic 584 180	Daktari/Out On A Limb	8
54	Vogue LDE 072	SHELLY MANNE AND HIS MEN VOL. 1 (10" LP)	15
55	Contemporary LDC 143	SHELLY MANNE VOL. 2 (10" LP, with Andre Previn & Leroy Vinegar)	15
56	Contemporary LDC 190	SHELLY MANNE, SHORTY ROGERS AND JIMMY GIUFFRE - THE THREE (10" LP)	15
56	Contemporary LDC 192	SHELLY MANNE AND RUSS FREEMAN (10" LP)	15
56	Contemporary LAC 12075	SHELLY MANNE AND HIS FRIENDS (LP, with Andre Previn & Leroy Vinegar)	15
61	Contemporary LAC 12305/6	AT THE MANNE HOLE (2-LP)	15
65	Stateside SL 10125	SHELLY MANNE AND CO. (LP)	12
62	Contemporary LAC12315	CHECKMATE (LP)	15

MANNIN FOLK

76	Kelly MAN 2	KING OF THE SEA (LP)	35
70s	Kelly KEP 1	MANNIN FOLK SING (LP)	20

BERNARD MANNING

72	Decca SKL 5030	SINGS 16 FAVOUORITE SONGS (LP)	12

BOB MANNING

54	Capitol CL 14190	I'm A Fool For You/It's All Right With Me	6
55	Capitol CL 14220	The Very Thought Of You/Just For Laughs	6
55	Capitol CL 14256	Majorca (Isle Of Love)/It's My Life	6
55	Capitol CL 14234	My Love Song To You/After My Laughter Came Tears	6
55	Capitol CL 14288	The Mission San Michel/You Are There	6
55	Capitol CL 14318	What A Wonderful Way To Die/Why Didn't You Tell Me?	6

LINDA MANNING

66	King KG 1039	Buy Me Something Pretty, Joey/Downtown Lonely Girl Blues	7

MARTY MANNING & CHEETAHS

67	CBS 2721	Tarzan March/Sunny	10

MICHAEL MANNING

03	Ai AI 007	THE LOST ABERRANT DRAGONFLY EP (12", p/s)	8

EDDIE MANNION

60	HMV POP 804	Just Driftin'/Quiet Girl	50

MAN ON THE MOON

69	Philips 88457 DE	MAN ON THE MOON (EP, spoken word, 2-part tri-foldout p/s with insert, 'historic souvenir' available via News Of The World newspaper)	10

WINGY MANONE ORCHESTRA

57	Brunswick 05655	Party Doll/Real Gone	20

MAN...OR ASTROMAN

94	One Louder LOUDER 4	YOUR WEIGHT ON THE MOON (10", pink vinyl)	12
94	One Louder LOUDER 4	YOUR WEIGHT ON THE MOON (10" LP, silver vinyl)	12

MINT VALUE £

95	One Louder LOUD 5	RETURN TO CHAOS EP (string-sealed 'folder' p/s)	8
95	Clawfist XPIG 28	WELCOME TO THE SONIC SPACE AGE EP (p/s)	10
96	One Louder LOUDER 12	EXPERIMENTAL ZERO (LP, yellow vinyl, with poster)	15

MANOWAR

(see also Orson Welles)

83	M. F. Nations 12 KUT 102	Defender (featuring Orson Welles)/Gloves Of Metal (12", p/s)	15
84	10 TEN 3012	All Men Play On 10/Mountains (12", p/s, gatefold)	18
84	10 TEN 3012	All Men Play On 10/Mountains (12", p/s)	12
87	Atlantic B 9463	Blow Your Speakers/Violence And Bloodshed (p/s)	7
87	Atlantic BT 9463	Blow Your Speakers/Violence And Bloodshed (12", embossed p/s, with poster)	12
87	Atlantic BT 9463	Blow Your Speakers/Violence And Bloodshed (12", embossed p/s, without poster)	8

JOE MANSANO

(see also Joe The Boss, Joe's Allstars, Dice The Boss)

69	Blue Cat BS 150	Life On Reggae Planet/RECO & RHYTHM ACES: Z.Z. Beat	40
72	Sioux SI 022	The Trial Of Pama Dice/JACKIE ROWLAND: Lonely Man	15
70	Trojan TBL 106	BRIXTON CAT (LP)	35

TONY MANSELL

(see also Johnny Dankworth)

54	Parlophone MSP 6130	The High And The Mighty/Hold My Hand (with Johnny Dankworth Orchestra)	8
56	Parlophone MSP 6222	Zambesi (Sweet African)/11th Hour Melody (with Johnny Dankworth Orchestra)	8
58	Parlophone R 4471	Impossible/Who Are They To Say	5

JAYNE MANSFIELD

(see also Jimi Hendrix)

67	London HL 10147	As The Clouds Drift By/Suey (with Jimi Hendrix, demos more common, £35)	50
62	World Record Club TP 262	JAYNE MANSFIELD IN LAS VEGAS (LP)	80

KEITH MANSFIELD ORCHESTRA

68	CBS 3895	Beautiful/Soul Thing	20
72	2066 170	Beautiful/The Colours Are Still There	8
68	CBS 63426	ALL YOU NEED IS KEITH MANSFIELD (LP)	35
69	CBS 64666	RACE ON THE WIND (LP)	12
70	CBS 70073	LOOT (LP, soundtrack, with Steve Ellis)	60

MANSFIELD ORGANISATION

67	President PT131	Daddy Russian Stoned/Ol' Nick	20

CHARLES MANSON

86	Fierce FRIGHT 006	Rise/Sick City (p/s, 1 side etched, handwritten labels)	20
88	Fierce FRIGHT 012	It's Comin' Down Fast (Helter Skelter) (p/s, 1 side etched, hand-made labels)	20
86	Fierce FRIGHT 001	LOVE AND TERROR CULT (LP)	30

EDDY MANSON

55	HMV 7M 325	Oh! No!/The Lovers	8

JEANE MANSON

79	CBS S CBS 7222	I've Already Seen It In Your Eyes/J'ai Deja Vu Ca Dans Tes Yeux	15

MARILYN MANSON

97	Interscope INVP 95541	The Horrible People/The Not So Beautiful People (10" picture disc)	12
97	Interscope INVP 95552	Tourniquet/(remix) (10" picture disc)	12
97	Interscope INDX 95552	Tourniquet/Lunchbox/Next MF (CD)	8
98	Nothing INVP 95610	The Dope Show/The Dope Show (10" picture disc, same track on both sides)	12
99	Interscope SAM 175 CD	I Don't Like Drugs (But The Drugs Like Me) (radio edit)/(album version) (CD, card sleeve, promo only)	10
00	Nothing/Universe 4974581	Disposable Teens/Five To One/Diamonds & Pollen (12" picture disc, PVC sleeve.)	10
01	Universal 4974911	The Fight Song/(Slipknot Remix)/(Love Song Remix) (12" picture disc, stickered sleeve)	10
03	Universal 9807728	Mobscene/Paranoiac (poster p/s)	5
03	Universal 9810794	This Is The New Shit/(Goldfrapp Version) (10" picture disc)	10
95	Simply Vinyl SVLP 208	SMELLS LIKE CHILDREN (LP, 180 gm vinyl)	18
96	Interscope IND 90086	ANTICHRIST SUPERSTAR (CD, in slipcase)	18
98	Simply Vinyl SVLP 195	MECHANICAL ANIMALS (2-LP, 180 gm vinyl)	20
98	Interscope IND 90273	MECHANICAL ANIMALS (CD, in slipcase)	18
99	Interscope ADV 490 394-2	MECHANICAL ANIMALS (CD, promo, numbered, card sleeve, with comic, PVC slipcase)	45
02	Simply Vinyl SVLP 055	ANTICHRIST SUPERSTAR (2-LP, 180 gm vinyl, gatefold sleeve)	25

MANSUN

95	Polygram no cat. no.	Take It Easy Chicken (Demo)/Naked Twister/Drastic Sturgeon (cassette, promo only, with title inlay)	30
95	Sci Fi Hi Fi MANSON 1	Take It Easy Chicken/Take It Easy Chicken (as Manson, same track both sides, die-cut sleeve, 500 only; promos with "Manson Promo" on label £30)	20
95	Regal REG 3	Skin Up Pin Up/Flourella (white vinyl)	12
95	Regal REG 3CD	Skin Up Pin Up/Flourella (CD, PVC sleeve with barcode sticker)	15
96	Parlophone CDRS 6453	Wide Open Space/The Gods Of Not Very Much/Moronica (Acoustic Version)/ Lemonade Secret Drinker (Acoustic Version) (CD, fold-out card p/s)	15
97	Parlophone 12 RDJ 6501	Wide Open Space (Perfecto Mix)/Wide Open Space (Trouser Enthusiasts Mix) (12")	15
99	fan club MANSUN 001	Taxloss/Everyone Must Win (live) (fanclub-only release)	30
96	Parlophone R 6430	ONE EP (p/s)	12
96	Parlophone R 6437	TWO EP (p/s)	8
97	Parlophone CPCS 7387	ATTACK OF THE GREY LANTERN (2-LP, gatefold sleeve, with inners and poster)	30

JOHN MANTELL

65	CBS 201783	Remember Child/I'll See You Around	10

MIKE MANTLER

(see also Carla Bley, Jazz Composers Orchestra)

75	Watt WATT 3	133/4 (LP, with Carla Bley; with insert)	20

MINT VALUE £

BOB MANTON
(see also Purple Hearts)

81	Mainstreet MS 101	No Trees In Brixton Prison/Brixton Walkabout (p/s)	8
57	Decca F 10888	Around The World/The Heart Of Budapest	8

MANTOVANI

53	Decca F 10168	Swedish Rhapsody/Jamaican Rumba	10
55	Decca F 10395	Lonely Ballerinia/Lazy Gondolier	10

MANUELLA

65	Decca F 22275	The Nitty Gritty/Two Shadows	150

MANUFACTURED ROMANCE

81	Fresh FRESH 16	The Time Of My Life/Room To Breathe (various colours of p/s)	5

MANYANA

80	Modello	LIVE CARROTS (LP)	15

PHIL MANZANERA (& 801)
(see also Roxy Music, Quiet Sun)

76	Island ILPS 9444	801 LIVE (LP)	12

RAY MANZAREK
(see also Doors, Philip Glass)

74	Mercury SRM 1703	THE WHOLE THING STARTED WITH ROCK'N'ROLL (LP)	15
83	A&M AMLX 64945	CARMINA BURANA (LP, with Philip Glass)	12

MAP OF AFRICA

05	Whatever We Want WEWW 004	Black Skin Blue Eyed Boys (12")	30

MAPLEOAK

70	Decca F 13008	Son Of A Gun/Hurt Me So Much	20
71	Decca SKL 5085	MAPLEOAK (LP, blue/silver label, boxed logo)	160

LUCILLE MAPP

57	Columbia DB 3916	Mangos/On Treasure Island	10
57	Columbia DB 3949	Jamie Boy/Moonlight In Vermont	7
57	Columbia DB 4040	I'm Available/Lovin' Ya, Lovin' Ya, Lovin' Ya	8
58	Columbia DB 4071	Love Is/The Early Birdie	7
58	Columbia DB 4168	Remember When/I'm A Dreamer, Aren't We All?	7
59	Columbia DB 4261	Chinchilla/Follow Me	15
57	Columbia SEG 7726	STREET OF DREAMS (EP)	18
57	Columbia SEG 7773	LUCILLE MAPP (EP)	20

TOMMY MARA

55	MGM SP 1128	Pledging My Love/Honey Bunch	10
58	Felsted AF 109	Where The Blues Of The Night/What Makes You So Lonely	10
59	Felsted AF 116	You Don't Know/Marie	7
59	Felsted AF 123	Until I Hear From You/Now Is The Hour	7
58	Felsted GEP 1003	PRESENTING TOMMY MARA (EP)	20

MARABAR CAVES

85	Tiki MBAR 1	Sally's Place Crew/Seeds That Never Grew	10

(JOSEPH) MARAIS & MIRANDA

53	Columbia SCM 5025	Old Johnnie Goggabie/The Zulu Warrior	5
59	Fontana H 225	I-Ha-She/The Queen Bee (as Marais & Miranda))	5

MARATHONS

61	Pye International 7N 25088	Peanut Butter/Down In New Orleans	20
61	Vogue V 9185	Peanut Butter/Talkin' Trash	20

MARAUDERS
(see also Danny Davis)

63	Decca F 11695	That's What I Want/Hey What'd You Say	15
63	Decca F 11748	Always On My Mind/Heart Full Of Tears	12
64	Decca F 11836	Lucille/Little Egypt	15
65	Fontana TF 609	Baby I Wanna Be Loved/Somebody Told My Girl	12

MARBLE STAIRCASE

83	Whaam! WHAAM 11	Still Dreaming/Dark Ages (p/s)	12

MARBLES
(see also Graham Bonnet, Fut)

69	Polydor 56310	The Walls Fell Down/Love You	12
70	Polydor 56378	Breaking Up Is Hard To Do/I Can't See Nobody	6
68	Polydor 56272	Only One Woman/The Light Of a Burning Candle	5

MARC & MAMBAS
(see also Soft Cell, Marc Almond)

82	Some Bizzare BZS 512	Fun City/Sleaze (Take It, Shake It)/Taking It And Shaking It (12", p/s, fan club issue, mail-order only)	20
82	Some Bizzare BZS 15	Big Louise/Empty Eyes (unreleased, artwork only)	0
82	Some Bizzare BZS 1512	Big Louise/Empty Eyes/The Dirt Behind The Neon (Sleaze Revisited) (12", unreleased, artwork only)	0
83	Some Bizzare BZS 19	Black Heart/Your Aura (p/s, with postcard insert)	7
83	Some Bizzare BZS 1912	Black Heart/Your Aura/Mamba (12", p/s)	8
83	Some Bizzare BZSDJ 21	Torment/You'll Never See On Sunday (promo)	15
83	Some Bizzare BZS 2112	Torment/First Time/You'll Never See Me On A Sunday/ Megamillionmania - Multimaniamix (12", p/s)	10
82	Some Bizzare B2A 4	UNTITLED (2-LP, gatefold sleeve)	15
83	Some Bizzare BZA 13	TORMENTS & TOREROS (2-LP)	15
84	Gutterhearts GH 1	BITE BLACK AND BLUES - RAOUL & THE RUINED LIVE (LP, fan club issue)	30
92	Some Bizarre 510 298-2	UNTITLED (CD)	18
92	Some Bizarre 812 872-2	TORMENT AND TOREROS (2 x CD)	30

MINT VALUE £

LYDIA MARCELLE

66	Sue WI 4025	Another Kind Of Fellow/I've Never Been Hurt Like This Before	80

MUZZY MARCELLINO

56	London HLU 8355	Mary Lou/MR. FORD & MR. GOON-BONES: Ain't She Sweet	25

MARCELS

(see also Tommy Regan)

61	Pye International 7N 25073	Blue Moon/Goodbye To Love	10
61	Pye International 7N 25083	Summertime/Teeter Totter Love	12
61	Pye International 7N 25105	You Are My Sunshine/Find Another Fool	18
61	Pye International 7N 25114	Heartaches/My Love For You	18
62	Pye International 7N 25124	My Melancholy Baby/Really Need Your Love	15
63	Pye International 7N 25201	I Wanna Be The Leader/Give Me Back Your Love	40
61	Pye Intl. NPL 28016	BLUE MOON (LP)	80

GLORIA MARCH

58	London HLB 8568	Baby Of Mine/Nippon Wishing Well	25

HAL MARCH

58	London HLD 8534	Hear Me Good/One Dozen Roses	25

JO MARCH

58	London HLR 8696	Dormi, Dormi, Dormi (Sleep, Sleep, Sleep)/Fare Thee Well, Oh Honey	12
58	London HLR 8696	Dormi, Dormi, Dormi (Sleep, Sleep, Sleep)/Fare Thee Well, Oh Honey (78)	12
58	London HLR 8763	The Virgin Mary Had One Son/I, Said The Donkey	5

(LITTLE) PEGGY MARCH

63	RCA RCA 1338	I Will Follow Him/Wind Up Doll (as Little Peggy March)	10
63	RCA RCA 1350	My Teenage Castle/I Wish I Were A Princess (as Little Peggy March)	10
63	RCA RCA 1362	Hello Heartache, Goodbye Love/Boy Crazy (as Little Peggy March)	10
64	RCA RCA 1426	Watch What You Do With My Baby/Can't Stop (Peggy March)	10
65	RCA RCA 1472	Let Her Go/Your Girl	10
68	RCA RCA 1687	If You Loved Me/Thinking Through My Tears	30
68	RCA RCA 1687	If You Loved Me/Thinking Through My Tears (DJ copy)	60
68	RCA RCA 1752	I've Been Here Before/Time And Time Again	7
69	RCA RCA 1809	What Am I Going To Do Without You/Lilac Skies	7

BOBBY MARCHAN

(see also Huey 'Piano' Smith & Clowns)

68	Atlantic 584 155	Get Down With It/Half A Mind	10
69	Action ACT 4533	Ain't No Reason For Girls To Be Lonely Parts 1 & 2	20

VICTOR MARCHESE

53	MGM SP 1018	Fandango/Flamingo	5

MARCH HARE

(see also Gary & Stu, Koobas)

68	Chapter One CH 101	Cry My Heart/With My Eyes Closed	20
69	Deram DM 258	I Could Make It There With You/Have We Got News For You	30

MARCHING GIRLS

81	Pop:Aural POP 011	True Love/First In Line (p/s)	5

MARCH VIOLETS

82	Merciful Release MR 013	Religious As Hell/Fodder/Children On Stun/Bon Bon Babies (p/s)	20
83	Merciful Release MR 017	Grooving In Green/Stream (p/s)	8

MARCIA & JEFF

68	Studio One SO 2047	Words/SHARKS: How Could I Live	40

MARCO

74	Torpedo 31	Do Me Bump/Bump On	12
75	Torpedo 33	I'm Coming Home/Instrumental Version	20

MARCUS

76	United Artists UAS 30000	MARCUS (LP)	15

MARCY JO

(see also Eddie Rambeau)

63	Stateside SS 235	Lover's Medley : The More I See You/When I Fall In Love/When You Wore A Tulip	8

GUY MARDEL

65	Vogue VRS 7000	V'Avoue Jamais (actually "N'Avoue Jamais")/Si Tu N'y Crois Pas	5

JANIE MARDEN

55	Decca F 10600	Soldier Boy/Hard To Get	10
55	Decca F 10605	I'll Come When You Call/Thank You For The Waltz (with Frank Weir & His Saxophone)	10
55	Decca F 10673	You Are My Love/A Teen Age Prayer	10
56	Decca F 10765	Allegheny Moon/Magic Melody	10
63	Piccadilly 7N 35128	Make The Night A Little Longer/Walk Alone	10
65	Decca F 12101	They Long To Be Close To You/This Empty Place	15
65	Decca F 12155	You Really Didn't Mean It/Only The One You Love	10

MARDEN HILL

86	él GPO 18	Curtain/Let's Make Shane & MacKenzie (p/s)	10
87	él GPO 30	Robe/Hangman (p/s)	8
88	él GPOT 36	Oh Constance/The Execution Of Emperor Maximillian/Bar Roof Fly (10", p/s)	8

ARIF MARDIN

69	Atlantic 584 295	Glass Onion/How Can I Be Sure	7
73	Atlantic K10309	Theme From Brother Sun, Sister Moon/Yester Year	10

ERNIE MARESCA

62	London HLU 9531	Shout Shout Knock Yourself (Out) /Crying Like A Baby Over You	15

MINT VALUE £

62 London HLU 9579 Mary Jane/Down On The Beach 30
63 London HLU 9720 Love Express/Lorelei 22
64 London HLU 9834 Rovin' Kind/Please Be Fair 15
65 London HLU 10008 It's Their World/I Can't Dance 10
66 Stateside SS 560 Rockin' Boulevard Street/Am I Better Off Than Them 25

MARGO
69 Deram DM 274 The Spark That Lights The Flame/Left Over Love 20

MARGO & MARVETTES
(see also Liza Dulittle)
64 Parlophone R 5154 Say You Will/Cherry Pie 18
64 Parlophone R 5227 Copper Kettle/So Fine 15
67 Piccadilly 7N 35387 Seven Letters/That's How Love Goes 12
67 Pye 7N 17423 When Love Slips Away/I'll Be Home (When You Call) 50
67 Pye 7N 17423 When Love Slips Away/I'll Be Home (When You Call) (DJ copy) 75

MARGUERITA
64 Black Swan WI 431 Woman Come/ERIC MORRIS: Number One 40

CHARLES MARGULIS
59 London HLL 8774 Gigi/Malaguena 6

MARIANNE
68 Columbia DB 8420 As For Marionettes/You Know My Name 18
68 Columbia DB 8456 You Had Better Change Your Evil Ways/Like A See Saw 40

MARIANNE & MIKE
(see also Friday Brown. These records do not feature Mick Jagger or Marianne Faithfull)
64 Vocalion V 9218 As He Once Was Mine/MARIANNE: Go On 8
64 Vocalion V 9225 You're The Only One/One Good Turn Deserves Another 8

CHARLIE MARIANO
56 London LTZN15031 CHARLIE MARIANO QUARTET (LP) 70

ANNE MARIE
65 Fontana TF 523 Runaround/There Must Be A Reason 10

MARIE CELESTE
71 private pressing AND THEN PERHAPS (LP) 400

MARIETTA
(see also Status Quo)
82 Polydor POSP 305 You're Only Lonely/Making Up My Mind (p/s, with Rick Parfitt & Andy Bown) 6
82 Polydor POSP 483 Do You Wanna Dance/Only In Your Eyes (p/s, with Rick Parfitt & Andy Bown) 6

MARILLION
(see also Fish, Chemical Alice)
82 EMI EMI 5351 Market Square Heroes/Three Boats Down From The Candy (p/s) 5
82 EMI 12 EMI 5351 Market Square Heroes/Three Boats Down From The Candy/Grendel (12", p/s) ... 8
82 EMI 12 EMIP 5351 Market Square Heroes/Three Boats Down From The Candy/Grendel (12", picture disc, 3,000 only) 25
83 EMI EMI 5362 He Knows, You Know/Charting The Single (p/s, originally with blue plastic label & paper sleeve) 5
83 EMI 12 EMI 5362 He Knows, You Know/Charting The Single/He Knows, You Know (Full Length Version) (12", p/s) 8
83 EMI 12 EMIP 5362 He Knows, You Know/Charting The Single/He Knows, You Know (Full Length Version) (12", picture disc, unreleased) 0
83 EMI EMI 5393 Garden Party/Margaret (live) (p/s) 5
83 EMI EMIP 5393 Garden Party/Margaret (live) ('jester'-shaped picture disc) 15
83 EMI 12 EMIS 5393 Garden Party (Extended Version)/Charting The Single (live)/ Margaret (Extended Live Version) (12", p/s with poster) 10
84 EMI 12 MARILP 1 Punch And Judy/Market Square Heroes (New Version)/ Three Boats Down From The Candy (New Version) (12", picture disc) 10
84 EMI MARIL 2 Assassing/Cinderella Search (p/s) 5
84 EMI 12 MARIL 2 Assassing (Full Length Version)/Cinderella Search (Full Length Version) (12", p/s) 15
84 EMI 12 MARILP 2 Assassing (Full Length Version)/Cinderella Search (Full Length Version) (12", picture disc) 10
85 EMI MARILP 3 Kayleigh/Lady Nina (picture disc) 8
85 EMI 12 MARILP 3 Kayleigh (Alternative Mix)/Kayleigh (Extended Version)/ Lady Nina (Extended Version) (12", picture disc) 12
85 EMI 12 MARILP 4 Lavender (Remix)/Freaks/Lavender (12", picture disc) 10
85 EMI 12 MARILP 5 Heart Of Lothian (Full Length Version)/Chelsea Monday (live)/ Heart Of Lothian (7" Version) (12", picture disc) 12
87 EMI 12MARILP 6 Incommunicado (LP Version)/(Alternative Mix)/Going Under (12", picture disc) ... 8
87 EMI MARILP 7 Sugar Mice (Radio Edit)/Tux On (picture disc with poster) 8
87 EMI 12MARILP 7 Sugar Mice (Extended Version)/(Album Version)/Tux On (12", picture disc) 10
87 EMI CD MARIL 7 Sugar Mice (Radio Edit)/Tux On/Sugar Mice (Radio Edit)/ (CD, card p/s, 3,000 only, withdrawn) 15
88 EMI MARILP 9 Freaks (live)/Kayleigh (live) ('jester'-shaped picture disc) 8
99 Raw Power RAWP 2144 MARILLION.COM (CD, 3-track sampler, card p/s, promo only) 10
84 EMI EMCP 3429 SCRIPT FOR A JESTER'S TEAR (LP, picture disc) 20
84 EMI MRLP 1 FUGAZI (LP, picture disc) 18
85 EMI JESTP 1 REAL TO REEL (LP, picture disc) 18
85 EMI MRLP 2 MISPLACED CHILDHOOD (LP, picture disc) 15

MARINE GIRLS
(see also Tracey Thorn, Everything But The Girl, Jane, Grab Grab The Haddock)
82 In Phaze COD 2 On My Mind/The Lure Of The Rockpools (p/s, with insert) 15
82 Cherry Red CHERRY 40 On My Mind/The Lure Of The Rockpools (reissue, different p/s) 5
80 private release A DAY BY THE SEA (cassette, 50 copies only) 30
81 In Phaze Tapes 002 BEACH PARTY (cassette, with photocopied drawings, game & handmade sl.) .. 25
81 Whaam!/In Phaze COD 1 BEACH PARTY (LP, black & white sleeve & labels, with 2 inserts) 12

MINT VALUE £

MARINERS

55	London HLA 8201	I Love You Fair Dinkum/(At The) Steamboat River Ball	15
56	London HA-A 2007	SPIRITUALS (LP)	12

MARINO MARINI QUARTET

58	Durium DC 16632	Volare (Nel Blu Dip Into Di Blu)/Come Prima	6
59	Durium DC 16636	Ciao Ciao Bambina (Piove)/Alevamo La Stessa Eta'	7
60	Durium DC 16648	Mustapha/Abbracciami	6
59	Durium DLU 96034	COME PRIMA (10" LP)	12

MARION (Finland)

73	Columbia DB 8987	Tom Tom Tom/My Son John	15

MARIONETTES

(see also Rag Dolls [U.K.], Katie Kissoon, Mac Kissoon)

65	Decca F 12056	Whirlpool Of Love/Nobody But You	10
65	Parlophone R 5300	Was It Me?/Under The Boardwalk	10
65	Parlophone R 5356	Raining It's Pouring/Pick Up Your Feet (withdrawn)	12
65	Parlophone R 5374	At The End Of The Day/Pick Up Your Feet	7
66	Parlophone R 5416	Like A Man/Tonight It's Going To Storm	15

MARIONETTES

90	Maze Music DSMBC	AVE DEMENTIA (LP)	20

MARK B

95	Jazz Fudge JFR003	ANY MORE QUESTIONS (EP)	15
98	K'Boro KBR 1002	New School Dean/It's Impossible (12")	12

MARK B/BLADE

(see also Blade)

98	Jazz Fudge JFR011	HITMEN FOR HIRE (EP)	15
98	Jazz Fudge JFR013	Nobody Relates/We'll Survive (12")	12

JON MARK

(see also Johnny Almond Music Machine, John Mayall, Mark-Almond)

69	Philips BF 1772	All Neat In Black Stockings/Run To Me	10

LOUISA MARK

78	Bushays BFM 100	Even Though You're Gone/Gone Clear (12")	10
79	Bushays BFM 107	Six Street Six/Instrumental (12")	12
79	Safari SF1105	Caught You In A Lie/Caught Dubbing	25
79	Robot RRS 2	Six Street Six/Version	8
81	Bushays BFM LP 101	BREAKOUT (LP)	25

MARK-ALMOND

(see also Johnny Almond Music Machine, Jon Mark, John Mayall)

71	Harvest HAR 5044	The City/The Ghetto	12
71	Harvest SHSP 4011	MARK-ALMOND (LP, no EMI logo on label)	25
73	Harvest SHVL 809	RISING (LP, EMI logo on label)	20

MARK & JOHN

64	Decca F 12044	Walk Right Back/Karen	6

MARKETTS

62	Liberty LIB 55401	Surfer's Stomp/Start (as Mar-kets)	15
62	Liberty LIB 55443	Balboa Blue/Stompede	15
64	Warner Bros WB 120	Out Of Limits/Bella Delana	30
64	Warner Bros WB 130	Vanishing Point/Borealis	15
66	Warner Bros WB 5696	The Batman Theme/Richie's Theme (with p/s)	40
66	Warner Bros WB 5696	The Batman Theme/Richie's Theme	20
67	Warner Bros WB 5847	Tarzan's March/Stirrin' Up Some Soul	50
67	Warner Bros WB 5847	Tarzan's March/Stirrin' Up Some Soul (DJ copy)	75
63	Warner Bros WM 8140	THE MARKETTS TAKE TO WHEELS (LP)	45
64	Warner Bros WM 8147	OUT OF LIMITS (LP)	40
66	Warner Bros W 1642	BATMAN (LP)	50

MAR-KEYS

(see also Booker T. & M.G.'s)

61	London HLK 9399	Last Night/Night Before	25
61	London HLK 9449	Morning After/Diana	20
62	London HLK 9510	Foxy/One Degree North	20
66	Atlantic AT 4079	Philly Dog/Honey Pot	20
67	Atlantic 584 074	Last Night/Night Before	10
69	Stax STAX 132	Black/Jive Man	7
62	London HA-K 8011	DO THE POP-EYE (LP)	70
66	Atlantic 587/588 024	THE GREAT MEMPHIS SOUND (LP)	30
68	Atlantic 587/588 135	MELLOW JELLY (LP)	25
69	Stax SXATS 1021	DAMNIFIKNOW! (LP)	20
69	Stax 2363 008	DAMNIFIKNOW! (LP, reissue)	12

MARK FIVE

(see also Nazareth)

64	Fontana TF 513	Baby What's Wrong/Tango	50

MARK IV

59	Mercury AMT 1025	Aah-Oo-Gah/I Got A Wife	10
59	Mercury AMT 1025	Aah-Oo-Gah/I Got A Wife (78)	12
59	Mercury AMT 1045	Move Over Rover/Dante's Inferno	10
59	Mercury AMT 1060	Ring, Ring, Ring Those Bells/Mairzy Doats	5

MARK FOUR

(see also Creation)

64	Mercury MF 815	Rock Around The Clock/Slow Down	30
64	Mercury MF 825	Try It Baby/Crazy Country Hop	65

			MINT VALUE £
65	Decca F 12204	Hurt Me If You Will/I'm Leaving	70
66	Fontana TF 664	Work All Day (Sleep All Night)/Going Down Fast	120
85	Bam-Caruso OPRA 037	LIVE AT THE BEAT SCENE CLUB (EP, promo, 500 only)	12

PIGMEAT MARKHAM

68	Chess CRS 8077	Here Comes The Judge/The Trial	12
68	Chess CRS 8085	Sock It To 'Em Judge/The Hip Judge	15

ALFRED MARKS

68	RCA 1777	My Young Visitors And Me/When I Wed Miss Ethel Montigue	7

GUY MARKS

68	Stateside SS 2107	Loving you Has Made Me Bananas/Forgive Me My Love	6

MARKSMEN

(see also Mark Rogers & Marksmen, Houston Wells & Marksmen)

63	Parlophone R 5075	Smersh/Orbit Three	20

MARK II

60	Columbia DB 4549	Night Theme/Confusion	10

MIKE MARLAN

73	Bronze ILPS 9221	FAIR WARNING (LP, gatefold sleeve, label with Island credit)	20

BOB MARLEY/WAILERS

(see also Peter Tosh, Rita Marley, Ernest Ranglin, Interns, Skatalites, Rass Dawkins & Wailers, Family Man, Norma Frazer)

SINGLES

63	Island WI 088	Judge Not/Do You Still Love Me (as Robert Marley)	300
63	Island WI 128	ERNEST RANGLIN: Exodus/R. MARLEY: One Cup Of Coffee	300
65	Island WI 188	It Hurts To Be Alone/Mr. Talkative	90
65	Island WI 206	Play Boy/Your Love	90
65	Island WI 211	Hoot Nanny Hoot (actually by Peter Tosh & Wailers)/ BOB MARLEY: Do You Remember (actually with Wailers)	100
65	Island WI 212	Hooligan/Maga Dog (B-side actually by Peter Tosh & Wailers)	70
65	Island WI 215	Shame And Scandal (as Peter Touch [Tosh] & Wailers)/The Jerk	60
65	Island WI 216	Donna/Don't Ever Leave Me	60
65	Island WI 254	What's New Pussycat/Where Will I Find	80
65	Ska Beat JB 186	Simmer Down/I Don't Need Your Love	75
65	Ska Beat JB 211	Lonesome Feelings/There She Goes	70
65	Ska Beat JB 226	I Made A Mistake/SOUL BROTHERS: Train To Skaville	45
66	Ska Beat JB 228	Love And Affection/Teenager In Love	70
66	Ska Beat JB 230	And I Love Her/Do It Right	70
66	Ska Beat JB 249	Lonesome Tracks/Zimmerman	60
66	Island WI 260	Jumbie Jamboree/SKATALITES: Independent Anniversary Ska (I Should Have Known Better)	80
66	Island WI 268	Put It On/Love Won't Be Mine	40
66	Island WI 3001	He Who Feels It Knows It/Sunday Morning	90
66	Island WI 3009	Let Him Go (Rude Boy Get Bail)/Sinner Man (B-side matrix: WI-3009B+)	70
66	Island WI 3009	Let Him Go (Rude Boy Get Bail)/The Masher (actually by Beverley's All Stars or Soul Brothers) (B-side matrix: WI-3009 B+2)	70
66	Rio R 116	Dancing Shoes/Don't Look Back	45
66	Doctor Bird DB 1013	Rude Boy/ROLANDO AL & SOUL BROTHERS: Ringo's Theme (This Boy)	90
66	Doctor Bird DB 1021	Good Good Rudie (Jailhouse)/CITY SLICKERS: Oceans II	60
66	Doctor Bird DB 1039	Rasta Put It On/ROLAND AL & SOUL BROTHERS: Ska With Ringo	100
67	Island WI 3035	Baby I Need You (credited to Ken Boothe)/KEN BOOTHE: I Don't Want To See You Cry	90
67	Island WI 3042	I Am The Toughest (by Peter Touch [Tosh] & Wailers)/ MARCIA GRIFFITHS: No Faith	70
67	Island WI 3043	Bend Down Low/Freedom Time	70
67	Coxsone CS 7021	Oh My Darling/HAMLINS: Trying To Keep A Good Man Down	90
67	Doctor Bird DB 1091	Nice Time/Hypocrite	65
67	Studio One SO 2010	Have Faith In The Lord (with Heavenly Sisters; actually by Peter Austin)/ JOE HIGGS: Dinah	40
67	Studio One SO 2024	I Stand Predominate/NORMA FRAZER: Come By Here	250
68	Fab FAB 34	Pound Get A Blow/Funeral (white label only)	100
68	Fab FAB 36	Thank You Lord/Mellow Mood (white label only)	170
68	Fab FAB 37	Nice Time/Hypocrites (white label only)	80
68	Fab FAB 41	Burial/Bus Them Shut (existence unconfirmed)	0
68	Trojan TR 617	Stir It Up/This Train	60
70	Bamboo BAM 55	Jailhouse (Good Rudy)/JOHN HOLT: A Stranger In Love	70

(All the above singles are credited to Wailers unless stated.)

70	Trojan TR 7759	Soul Shake Down Party/BEVERLY'S ALLSTARS: Version	25
70	Escort ERT 842	Run For Cover/To The Rescue	70
70	Unity UN 562	Duppy Conqueror/UPSETTERS: Duppy Conqueror (Version)	40
70	Jackpot JP 730	Mr Chatterbox (as Wailing Wailers)/DOREEN SHAEFFER: Walk Thru' This World	35
70	Upsetter US 340	My Cup (solo)/LEE PERRY & WAILERS: Son Of Thunder	35
70	Upsetter US 342	Version Of Cup (solo)/UPSETTERS: Dreamland	45
70	Upsetter US 348	Doppy Conqueror (song actually titled "Duppy Conqueror" but plays Runaway Child by Dave Barker)/UPSETTERS: Justice	20
70	Upsetter US 349	UPSETTERS: Upsetting Station (actually plays "Dig Your Grave" by Bob Marley & Wailers/UPSETTERS: Justice (Instrumental)	40
71	Upsetter US 354	Mr. Brown/UPSETTERS: Dracula	35
71	Upsetter US 356	Kaya/UPSETTERS: Version	35
71	Upsetter US 357	Small Axe/All In One	20
71	Upsetter US 368	Picture On The Wall (as Rass Dawkins & Wailers)/UPSETTERS: Version	22
71	Upsetter US 369	More Axe (as Bob Marley)/UPSETTERS: Axe Man	25
71	Upsetter US 371	Dreamland (as Wailers)/UPSETTERS: Version	25
71	Upsetter US 372	More Axe (as Bob Marley, different version)/UPSETTERS: Axe Man	25
71	Bullet BU 464	Soultown/Let The Sun Shine On Me	50
71	Bullet BU 493	Lick Samba/Samba	35

			MINT VALUE £
71	Punch PH 69	Small Axe/DAVE BARKER: What A Confusion	45
71	Punch PH 77	Down Presser (as Wailers)/JUNIOR BYLES: Got The Tip	40
71	Summit SUM 8526	Stop The Train/Caution (as Wailers)	35
71	Green Door GD 4005	Trench Town Rock/Grooving Kingston 12	25
71	Green Door GD 4022	Lively Yourself Up/TOMMY McCOOK: Lively	25
72	Green Door GD 4025	Guava Jelly/Redder Than Red	20
72	Upsetter US 392	Keep On Moving/African Herbsman	25
72	CBS 8114	Reggae On Broadway/Oh Lord, I Got To Get There (as Wailers)	25
73	Blue Mountain BM 1021	Baby Baby We've Got A Date/Stop That Train	15
73	Punch PH 101	Screw Face/Face Man	22
73	Punch PH 102	Lively Up Yourself/TOMMY McCOOK: Version	20
73	Supreme SUP 216	I Like It Like This (as Bob Marley)/(other artist)	45
73	Island WIP 6164	Concrete Jungle/Reincarnated Soul	8
73	Island WIP 6167	Get Up, Stand Up/Slave Driver (as Wailers)	8
73	Island IDJ 2	I Shot The Sheriff/Pass It On/Duppy Conqueror (promo only)	30
74	Island 12WIP 6244	No Woman No Cry/Jamming (12", p/s)	8
74	Trojan TR 7911	Soul Shake Down Party/Caution	8
74	Trojan TR 7926	Mr Brown/Version	10
75	Island WIP 6212	Natty Dread/So Jah Seh	5
76	Island WIP 6478	Stir It Up/Rat Race (withdrawn, demos only)	15
77	Island WIP 6390	Exodus/Exodus (dub)	5
77	Island WIP 6402	Waiting In Vain/Roots	5
77	Island WIP 6402 1DJ	Promotional Advert For "Exodus" (handwritten label, same track both sides, with Marley commentary)	30
77	Island WIP 6410	Jamming/Punky Reggae Party (p/s)	5
77	Island IPR 2000	Exodus (7:38) / Exodus (3:08, inst. version)(12", pre-release Island sleeve)	8
78	Island WIP 6420	Is This Love?/Crisis (Version) (p/s)	5
78	Island WIP 6440	Satisfy My Soul/Smile Jamaica (p/s)	5
78	Island IPR 2026	War/No More Trouble/Jamming (12", p/s)	8
83	Island ISP 180	Waiting In Vain/Blackman Redemption (picture disc)	8
84	Daddy Kool DK 12101	Rainbow Country (Vocal)/Rainbow Country (Dub)/ PABLO & UPSETTERS: Lama Lava (12", p/s)	15
84	Daddy Kool DK 12102	Natural Mystic/Natural Mystic Rhythm (12", p/s)	15
84	Island 12ISPX 169	One Love/One Love (Dub Version) (p/s)	7
84	Island 12ISP 169	One Love/One Love (Dub Version) (12", white label, p/s)	8
84	Island 12ISPP 169	One Love/One Love (Dub Version) (12", picture disc)	12
80s	Island 12 BMRM 1	Get Up Stand Up/Get Up Stand Up (live) ('Rasta' p/s, promo only)	8
99	Columbia XPR 2533	Turn Your Lights Down Low (with Lauryn Hill)/(original version) (die-cut p/s, promo only)	8

(Island singles with the words "DJ Copy" in the middle are worth the same as regular issues. All the above singles are credited to Bob Marley & Wailers unless stated)

LPs

71	Upsetter TBL 126	SOUL REBEL	100
71	Trojan TBL 126	SOUL REBEL (reissue)	50
71	Trojan TTL 66A/B	SOUL REVOLUTION (LP, white label, test pressing only)	125
72	Island ILPS 9241	CATCH A FIRE (original 'pink rim' label, 'zippo lighter' sleeve)	80
73	Island ILPS 9256	BURNIN' (original label, gatefold sleeve with photos on innner)	20
73	Trojan TRLS 62	AFRICAN HERBSMAN (original issue with "12 Neasden Lane" address and rough orange/white paper labels)	40
73	BBC TS 133425/6	POP SPECTACULAR IN CONCERT (LP, in buff sleeve with printed sheets)	300
74	Trojan TRLS 89	RASTA REVOLUTION (reissue of TBL 126 with 2 extra tracks)	20
75	Island ISS 3	BOB MARLEY & THE WAILERS RADIO SAMPLER (with photos & press release, promo only)	30
75	Island ISS 3	BOB MARLEY & THE WAILERS RADIO SAMPLER (promo only)	12
77	BBC	ROCK GOES TO COLLEGE IN CONCERT (LP, re-issue of BBC TS 133425/6)	80
78	Island ISLD 11	BABYLON BY BUS (2-LP, with poster)	15
83	Island PILPS 97690	CONFRONTATION (picture disc)	25
84	Island PBMW 1	LEGEND - THE BEST OF BOB MARLEY (picture disc)	12
84	Island BMSP 100	THE BOX SET (All 9 Island albums in presentation box - 10,000 only)	125

RITA MARLEY

(see also Soulettes, Soul Brothers)

65	Island WI-226	One More Chance (as Rita and Soulettes)/SKALITES: Dick Tracey	75
67	Rio R 108	Pied Piper/It's Alright	80
67	Island WI 3052	Come To Me/SOUL BOYS: Blood Pressure	70

MICKI MARLO

(see also Paul Anka)

55	Capitol CL 14271	Prize Of Gold/Foolish Notion	15
57	London HL 8481	That's Right/What You've Done To Me (B-side with Paul Anka)	25

MARLON

(see also Roger Glover, Ray Fenwick)

74	Purple PUR 120	Let's Go To The Disco/Broken Man	7

ROBERT MARLOW

(see also Vince Clarke, Erasure)

83	Reset 7REST 1	Pictures Of Dorian Grey/The Tale Of Dorian Grey (p/s)	5
83	Reset 12REST 1	Pictures Of Dorian Grey/The Tale Of Dorian Grey (12", p/s)	10
83	Reset 7REST 3	I Just Want To Dance/No Heart (p/s)	5
83	Reset 7RESTP 3	I Just Want To Dance/No Heart (picture disc)	6
83	Reset 12REST 3	I Just Want To Dance/No Heart (12", p/s)	10
84	Reset 12REST 4	Claudette/This Happy World (12", p/s)	10
85	Reset 7REST 6	Calling All Destroyers/In Retrospect (p/s)	10
85	Reset 12REST 6	Calling All Destroyers/In Retrosepct (12", p/s, existence unconfirmed)	0

MARION MARLOWE

56	London HLA 8306	The Hands Of Time/Ring, Phone, Ring (withdrawn)	100
56	London HLA 8306	The Hands Of Time/Ring, Phone, Ring (78)	50

MINT VALUE £

MARMALADE
(see also Dean Ford [& Gaylords], Gaylords, Junior Campbell, Chris McClure Section)

66	CBS 202340	It's All Leading Up To Saturday Night/Wait A Minute Baby	20
67	CBS 202643	Can't Stop Now/There Ain't No Use In Hangin' On	20
67	CBS 2948	I See The Rain/Laughing Man	20
67	CBS 3088	Man In A Shop/Cry	15
68	CBS 3412	Lovin' Things/Hey Joe	6
68	CBS 3708	Wait For Me Mary-Anne/Mess Around	12
68	CBS 3892	Ob-La-Di, Ob-La-Da/Chains	5
69	CBS 4287	Baby Make It Soon/Time Is On My Side	6
69	CBS 4615	Butterfly/I Shall Be Released	6
68	CBS 63414	THERE'S A LOT OF IT ABOUT (LP)	20
70	CBS SPR 36	THE BEST OF THE MARMALADE (LP)	15
70	Decca SKL 5047	REFLECTIONS OF THE MARMALADE (LP)	15
71	Decca SKL 5111	SONGS (LP)	15

MARQUIS DE SADE

81	Xpose XP-02	Somewhere Up In The Mountain/Black Angel (p/s with insert)	200
82	Out Of Town HOOT 8	Crystal Grieff/Vampire Affair (p/s)	5

MARQUIS OF KENSINGTON

67	Immediate IM 052	Changing Of The Guard/Reverse Thrust	30

HANK MARR

60	Blue Beat BB 26	Tonk Game/Hob-Nobbin	15

RANDY MARR

70	Warner Bros WB 6115	I Wonder Who's Kissing Her Now/1941	6

MARRAKESH

73	Bell Bell 1325	The Prodigal Son Returns/Let Me Down Easy	18

MARRATXI

79	Clubland SJP 901	Rock With Me/Swedish Lady	150

MARRIAGE

71	Decca F13178	Ever Find Yourself Running/She Follows The Band	6

A MARRIAGE OF CONVENIENCE
(see also Stranglers)

85	Stranglers Info Service SIS2	My Young Dreams/Two Sides To Every Story (no p/s, fan club issue)	5

STEVE MARRIOTT
(see also Small Faces, Humble Pie, Spectrum, Pollcats)

63	Decca F 11619	Give Her My Regards/Imaginary Love	175
76	A&M AMS 7230	Star In My Life/Midnight Rollin'	6
85	Aura AUS 145	Wha'cha Gonna Do About It/All Shook Up	6
76	A&M AMLH 64572	MARRIOTT (LP)	20
85	Aura AUL 792	PACKET OF THREE (LP)	12

M/A/R/R/S
(see also A.R. Kane, Colourbox)

87	4AD BAD 707R	Pump Up The Volume (Remix)/Anitina (The First Time I See She Dance) (Remix) (12", p/s)	8
87	4AD CAD 707R	Pump Up The Volume (Remix)/Anitina/Pump Up The Volume (12" Version)/ Anitina (The First Time I See She Dance) (Remix) (CD, gatefold p/s)	10

MARS FENWICK BAND

86	President PT 556	Fire In The City/A Lover Not A Fighter	5
86	President PTLS 1083	FIRE IN THE CITY (LP)	12

JOHNNY MARS

81	Ace NS 73	Born Under A Bad Sign/Horses And Places/Mighty Mars (p/s, withdrawn)	5
72	Polydor 2460 168	BLUES FROM MARS (LP)	15

BERNIE MARSDEN
(see also Jon Lord, Whitesnake, Cozy Powell, Jack Bruce, Babe Ruth, Bogdon)

81	Parlophone R6047	Sad Clown/You And me (p/s)	6
81	Parlophone R6050	Look At Me Now/Always Love You So (p/s)	6
81	Parlophone R6052	Shakey Ground/After All The Madness (p/s)	6
82	Parlophone R6053	Thunder And Lightning/Bylbo's Shack (p/s)	6
79	Parlophone PCS 7215	AND ABOUT TIME TOO (LP, with inner sleeve)	12
81	Parlophone PCS 7217	LOOK AT ME NOW (LP, with inner sleeve)	12

BERYL MARSDEN
(see also Shotgun Express, She Trinity)

63	Decca F 11707	I Know (You Don't Love Me No More)/I Only Care About You	15
64	Decca F 11819	When The Lovelight Starts Shining Through His Eyes/ Love Is Going To Happen To Me	20
65	Columbia DB 7718	Who You Gonna Hurt?/Gonna Make Him My Baby	30
65	Columbia DB 7797	Music Talk/Break-A-Way	30
66	Columbia DB 7888	What's She Got/Let's Go Somewhere	30

GERRY MARSDEN
(see also Gerry & Pacemakers)

67	CBS 2784	Please Let Them Be/I'm Not Blue	10
67	CBS 2946	Gilbert Green/What Makes Me Love You	15
68	CBS 3575	Liverpool/Charlie Girl (as Gerry Marsden & Derek Nimmo)	10
68	NEMS 56-3831	In The Year Of April/Every Day	10
69	NEMS 56-4229	Every Little Minute/In Days Of Old	5
71	Decca F 13172	I've Got My Ukelele/What A Day	5
72	Phoenix NIX 129	Amo Credo/Come Break Bread	5
76	DJM DJS 10708	My Home Town/Lovely Lady (p/s)	10
76	DJM DJS 10708	My Home Town/Lovely Lady	6

MINT VALUE £

LYNNE MARSDEN
84 Derelict DRL1 — Cocktails For Two/Firefly ... 10

MARSEILLE
(see also Paul Dale)
84 Ultra Noise ULTRA 3 — TOUCH THE NIGHT (LP, with inner sleeve) ... 12

BRENDA MARSH
68 Mercury MF 1044 — Cross Town Bus/Close ... 7

STEVIE MARSH
59 Decca F 11181 — If You Were The Only Boy In The World/Leave Me Alone ... 5
60 Decca F 11209 — You Don't Have To Tell Me (I Know)/Wish ... 10
60 Decca F 11244 — A Girl In Love/Over And Done With ... 10
62 Ember EMB S 139 — I Shouldn't Be Kissing You/Time And Time Again ... 8

WARNE MARSH
57 London LTZ-P 15080 — JAZZ OF TWO CITIES (LP) ... 20

CHUCK MASHALL & TWIST STARS
62 Brunswick STA 3062 — TWIST TO SONGS EVERYBODY KNOWS (LP) ... 15

GARY MARSHALL
61 Parlophone R 4758 — One Twitchy Baby/Ev'ry Chance I Get ... 12
60 Parlophone R 4636 — Oh You Beautiful Doll/Large As Life ... 6

JACK MARSHALL ORCHESTRA & CHORUS
58 Capitol CL 14888 — Thunder Road Chase/Finger Poppin' ... 10

JOY MARSHALL
64 Decca F 11863 — When You Hold Me Tight /Rain On Snow ... 8
65 Decca F12189 — Heartache Hurry On By/He's For Me ... 8
65 Decca F 12222 — My Love Come Home/When A Girl Really Loves You ... 6
66 Decca F 12422 — The More I See You/Taste Of Honey ... 10

LARRY MARSHALL
(see also Larry & Alvin, Irving Brown, Fitzroy D. Long, Kingston Pete & Buster's Allstars, Max Romeo, Jackie Mittoo)
67 Blue Beat BB 374 — Move Your Feet/Find A New Baby ... 40
67 Blue Beat BB 380 — Suspicion/Broken Heart ... 100
67 Doctor Bird DB 1008 — Snake In The Grass/ROLAND ALPHONSO: V.C. 10 ... 80
68 Caltone TONE 126 — No One To Give Me Love/PHIL PRATT: Safe Travel ... 120
70 Bamboo BAM 22 — Girl Of My Dreams/SOUND DIMENSON: Give It Away ... 20
70 Bamboo BAM 52 — Man From Galilee/Give It Away (as Larry Marshall & Enid Cumberland) ... 15
70 Bamboo BAM 61 — Let's Make It Up/BURNING SPEAR: Free ... 25
70 Banana BA 300 — Stay A Little Longer/MAYTALS: He'll Provide ... 12
71 Banana BA 364 — Maga Dog/OSSIE ROBINSON: Economical Heatwave ... 12
73 Pama PM 873 — True Believer/FLAMES: Water Your Garden ... 6
75 Ocean OC 004 — Can't You Understand/KING TUBBY : Locks Of Dub ... 18
75 Black & White CP 4326 — I Admire You/KING TUBBY: Watergate Rock ... 10
79 Yard International YI 103 — Birdsong/She's Gone (12") ... 15

LOIS MARSHALL
59 HMV ALP 1671 — BRITISH FOLK SONGS (LP) ... 12

WAYNE MARSHALL
85 Jah Tubbys JT 013 — Give Me The Mix/Mike In My Hand (12", with the Offbeat Posse) ... 25

WILLIE MARSHALL
70 Torpedo TOR 20 — Loosen Up Strong Man/Strong Man ... 5

MARSHMALLOW WAY
69 United Artists UP 35031 — C'mon Kitty Kitty/Michigan Mints ... 8

MARSHMELLOW HIGHWAY
68 London HLR 10204 — I Don't Wanna Live This Way/Loving You Makes Everything Alright ... 18

MARSUPILAMI
70 Transatlantic TRA 213 — MARSUPILAMI (LP, white/lilac label, 't' logo) ... 110
71 Transatlantic TRA 230 — ARENA (LP, white/lilac label, 't' logo) ... 120

LENA MARTELL
67 Pye 7N 17276 — The Pop Group Song/Reflections ... 10

PIERA MARTELL
74 CBS S CBS 2293 — My Ship Of Love/Mein Ruf Nach Dir ... 12

RAY MARTELL
70 Joe JRS 3 — She Caught The Train/PAMA DICE: Tea House From Emperor Rosko ... 35
70 Attack ATT 8015 — Loving Lover/Cora ... 6
70 Doctor Bird DB 1503 — This Little Light/Lover ... 6
70 Trojan TR 7787 — This Little Light/Lover ... 6
72 Sioux SI 012 — She Caught The Train/JOE'S ALLSTARS: Tony B.'s Theme ... 12
73 Rays RA 1 — Working For My Love/King Fuzz - Downtown Rock ... 12
73 Rays RA 2 — Lover/Dub ... 8
73 Rays RA 3 — I Wish You Luck/Version ... 8
73 Rays RA 4 — Angelina/Angelina Part 2 ... 8
77 Rays RA 077 — Falling In Love/Everlasting Love ... 8

MARTELLS
66 Decca F 12463 — Time To Say Goodnight/The Cherry Song ... 40

RALPH MARTERIE & HIS ORCHESTRA
57 Mercury MEP 9517 — PRESENTING RALPH MARTERIE (EP) ... 8

MARTHA & THE MUFFINS
80 DinDisc DID 5 — TRANCE & DANCE (LP, with bonus 7" [WAS E 20]) ... 12

MINT VALUE £

MARTHA (REEVES) & VANDELLAS

63	Oriole CBA 1814	I'll Have To Let Him Go/My Baby Won't Come Back	400
63	Oriole CBA 1819	Come And Get These Memories/Jealous Lover	250
63	Stateside SS 228	Heatwave/A Love Like Yours (Don't Come Knockin' Every Day)	65
63	Stateside SS 228	Heatwave/A Love Like Yours (Don't Come Knockin' Every Day) (DJ copy)	150
64	Stateside SS 250	Quicksand/Darling, I Hum Our Song	50
64	Stateside SS 250	Quicksand/Darling, I Hum Our Song (DJ copy)	100
64	Stateside SS 272	Live Wire/Old Love (Let's Try It Again)	55
64	Stateside SS 272	Live Wire/Old Love (Let's Try It Again) (DJ copy)	100
64	Stateside SS 305	In My Lonely Room/A Tear For The Girl	70
64	Stateside SS 305	In My Lonely Room/A Tear For The Girl (DJ copy)	150
64	Stateside SS 345	Dancing In The Street/There He Is (At My Door)	20
64	Stateside SS 345	Dancing In The Street/There He Is (At My Door) (DJ copy)	100
65	Stateside SS 383	Wild One/Dancing Slow	50
65	Stateside SS 383	Wild One/Dancing Slow (DJ copy)	200
65	Tamla Motown TMG 502	Nowhere To Run/Motoring	30
65	Tamla Motown TMG 502	Nowhere To Run/Motoring (DJ copy)	120
65	Tamla Motown TMG 530	You've Been In Love Too Long/Love (Makes Me Do Foolish Things)	35
65	Tamla Motown TMG 530	You've Been In Love Too Long/Love (Makes Me Do Foolish Things) (DJ copy)	100
66	Tamla Motown TMG 549	My Baby Loves Me/Never Leave Your Baby's Side	40
66	Tamla Motown TMG 549	My Baby Loves Me/Never Leave Your Baby's Side (DJ copy)	120
66	Tamla Motown TMG 567	What Am I Going To Do Without Your Love/Go Ahead And Laugh	35
66	Tamla Motown TMG 567	What Am I Going To Do Without Your Love/Go Ahead And Laugh (DJ copy)	100
66	Tamla Motown TMG 582	I'm Ready For Love/He Doesn't Love Her Anymore	20
66	Tamla Motown TMG 582	I'm Ready For Love/He Doesn't Love Her Anymore (DJ copy)	50
67	Tamla Motown TMG 599	Jimmy Mack/Third Finger, Left Hand	12
72	Tamla Motown TMG 599	Jimmy Mack/Third Finger, Left Hand (reissue)	6
67	Tamla Motown TMG 621	Love Bug Leave My Heart Alone/One Way Out	30
67	Tamla Motown TMG 621	Love Bug Leave My Heart Alone/One Way Out (DJ copy)	75
68	Tamla Motown TMG 636	Honey Chile/Show Me The Way	18
68	Tamla Motown TMG 657	I Promise To Wait, My Love/Forget Me Not	15
68	Tamla Motown TMG 669	I Can't Dance To That Music You're Playing/I Tried	20
69	Tamla Motown TMG 684	Dancing In The Street/Quicksand	7
69	Tamla Motown TMG 694	Nowhere To Run/Live Wire	7
71	Tamla Motown TMG 762	Forget Me Not/I Gotta Let You Go	7
71	Tamla Motown TMG 794	Bless You/Hope I Don't Get My Heart Broke	7
73	Tamla Motown TMG 843	No One There/(I've Given You) The Best Years Of My Life	75
73	Tamla Motown TMG 843	No One There/(I've Given You) The Best Years Of My Life (DJ Copy)	150
65	Tamla Motown TME 2009	MARTHA AND THE VANDELLAS (EP)	170
66	Tamla Motown TME 2017	HITTIN' (EP)	100
63	Oriole PS 40052	COME AND GET THESE MEMORIES (LP)	400
65	Tamla Motown TML 11005	HEATWAVE (LP)	60
65	T. Motown TML 11013	DANCE PARTY (LP)	70
67	T. Motown TML 11040	GREATEST HITS (LP, original with flipback sleeve, mono)	25
67	T. Motown STML 11040	GREATEST HITS (LP, original with flipback sleeve, stereo)	30
67	T. Motown STML 11040	GREATEST HITS (LP, re-pressing non-flipback sleeve)	15
67	T. Motown TML 11051	WATCH OUT! (LP, mono)	40
67	T. Motown STML 11051	WATCH OUT! (LP, stereo)	50
68	T. Motown TML 11078	RIDIN' HIGH (LP, mono)	25
68	T. Motown STML 11078	RIDIN' HIGH (LP, stereo)	30
69	T. Motown (S)TML 11099	DANCING IN THE STREET (LP, mono/stereo)	25
70	T .Motown (S)TML 11134	SUGAR N' SPICE (LP, mono/stereo)	25
70	T. Motown STML 11166	NATURAL RESOURCES (LP)	25
72	T. Motown STML 11204	BLACK MAGIC (LP)	30

MARTIAN SCHOOLGIRLS

79	Red Planet RPR 1	Life In The 1980's/Lonely Nights (p/s)	10

MARTIN

68	Coxsone CS 7056	I Second That Emotion (actually by Martin Riley)/ ROY TOMLINSON: I Stand For I	120

ALAN MARTIN

63	Rio R 3	The Party/Indeed	8
63	Rio R 6	You Came Late/Dreaming	8
63	Rio R 9	Secretly/Fame And Fortune	8
63	Rio R 10	Mother Brother/Tell Me	8
65	Rio R 66	Must Know I Love You/VIC BROWN'S COMBO: Rio Special	12
65	Rio R 67	Sweet Rosemarie/HONEY DUCKERS: Banjo Man	8
65	Rio R 68	Why Must I Cry/Shirley I Love You	8
65	Rio R 74	Since I Married Dorothy/You Promised Me	8
65	Venus VE 1	Cry Myself To Shame/Baby Don't Go	10
66	Rio R 94	Days Are Lonely/My Baby	8
66	Rio R 96	Rome Wasn't Built In A Day/I'm Hurt	8

BARRY MARTIN

61	RCA RCA 1234	Little Lonely One/Are You Sure	5

BENNY MARTIN

63	Realm RM 174	COUNTRY MUSIC'S SENSATIONAL ENTERTAINER (LP)	15

BOBBI MARTIN

64	Coral Q 72477	Don't Forget I Still Love You/On The Outside (Lookin' In)	5
65	Coral Q 72478	I Can't Stop Thinking About You/Million Thanks To You	6

CHRIS MARTIN

59	HMV POP 664	Lonely Street/Swing A Little Lover	10
60	HMV POP 692	Point Of No Return/I Don't Regret A Thing	6

DAVE MARTIN

64	Port-O-Jam PJ 4112	Let Them Fight/OSSIE IRVING SIX: Why I Love You	18
64	Port-O-Jam PJ 4115	All My Dreams/Take Your Belongings	18

MINT VALUE £

DEAN MARTIN

(see also Jerry Lewis, Line Renaud & Dean Martin, Frank Sinatra)

SINGLES

54	Capitol CL 14123	Hey Brother, Pour The Wine/I'd Cry Like A Baby (green label)	40
54	Capitol CL 14123	Hey Brother, Pour The Wine/I'd Cry Like A Baby (purple label)	25
54	Capitol CL 14138	Sway/Pretty As A Picture	30
54	Capitol CL 14150	How Do You Speak To An Angel?/Ev'ry Street's A Boulevard In Old New York (with Jerry Lewis)	15
54	Capitol CL 14170	The Peddlar Man (Ten I Loved)/Try Again	15
54	Capitol CL 14180	One More Time/If I Could Sing Like Bing	15
55	Capitol CL 14215	Open Up The Doghouse (Two Cats Are Trying To Get In) (with Nat 'King' Cole)/Long, Long Ago	15
55	Capitol CL 14226	Let Me Go, Lover/The Naughty Lady Of Shady Lane	15
55	Capitol CL 14227	Mambo Italiano/That's All I Want From You	15
55	Capitol CL 14253	Belle From Barcelona/Confused	10
55	Capitol CL 14255	What Could Be More Beautiful/Under The Bridges Of Paris	10
55	Capitol CL 14311	Chee Chee-Oo Chee (Sang The Little Bird)/Ridin' Into Love	10
55	Capitol CL 14356	Relax-Ay-Voo/Two Sleepy People (with Line Renaud)	10
55	Capitol CL 14367	Simpatico/Love Is All That Matters	10
55	Capitol CL 14370	In Napoli/I Like Them All	10

(The above 45s were originally issued with triangular centres; round-centre reissues are worth around half these values.)

56	Capitol CL 14505	When You Pretend/The Lucky Song	7
56	Capitol CL 14507	Inamorata/You Look So Familiar	7
56	Capitol CL 14519	Young And Foolish/Just One More Chance	6
56	Capitol CL 14523	Memories Are Made Of This/Change Of Heart	15
56	Capitol CL 14586	Watching The World Go By/The Lady With The Big Umbrella	7
56	Capitol CL 14624	The Test Of Time/I'm Gonna Steal You Away	5
56	Capitol CL 14625	Me 'N' You 'N' The Moon/The Wind, The Wind	5
56	Capitol CL 14626	Pardners (with Jerry Lewis)/Buckskin Beauty	5
59	Capitol CL 15015	Rio Bravo/My Rifle, My Pony And Me	10
64	Reprise R 20307	The Door Is Still Open/Every Minute, Every Hour	7
67	Pye DMA 1	I'm Not The Marrying Kind (Dean Martin Assoc. issue, 1-sided, promo only)	15

EPs

55	Capitol EAP 1-9123	DEAN MARTIN	20
55	Capitol EAP 1-481	SUNNY ITALY	10
56	Capitol EAP 1007	SWINGIN' DOWN YONDER NO. 1	10
56	Capitol EAP 1022	SWINGIN' DOWN YONDER NO. 2	10
56	Capitol EAP 1033	DEAN MARTIN AND JERRY LEWIS: "PARDNERS" (with Jerry Lewis)	10
56	Capitol EAP 1037	SWINGIN' DOWN YONDER NO. 3	10
57	Capitol EAP 1-806	HOLLYWOOD OR BUST - FILM SELECTION	10
57	Capitol EAP 1-840	TEN THOUSAND BEDROOMS - FILM SELECTION	15
61	Capitol EAP 1-20124	DEAN MARTIN IN MOVIELAND	10
61	Capitol EAP 1-20152	I'M YOURS	10
64	Capitol EAP 6-1702	SOMEBODY LOVES YOU	10
65	Capitol EAP 7-1702	CHA CHA D' AMOUR	10

LPs

53	Capitol LC 6590	CAPITOL PRESENTS DEAN MARTIN (10")	30
56	Britone LP 1002	DEAN MARTIN SINGS, NICOLINI LUCCHESI PLAYS (10")	30
57	Capitol T 849	PRETTY BABY	15
58	Capitol T 1047	THIS IS DEAN MARTIN!	15
59	Capitol T 1150	SLEEP WARM (orchestra conducted by Frank Sinatra, mono)	15
59	Capitol ST 1150	SLEEP WARM (orchestra conducted by Frank Sinatra, stereo)	18
61	Capitol T 1442	THIS TIME I'M SWINGIN'! (mono)	15
61	Capitol ST 1442	THIS TIME I'M SWINGIN'! (stereo)	18
62	Reprise R/R9 6021	FRENCH STYLE (mono/stereo)	15
62	Capitol (S)T 1659	DINO (stereo)	12
63	Capitol (S)T 1702	CHA CHA DE AMOR (stereo)	12
67	Stateside SL/SSL 10201	LOVE IS A CAREER	15

DEREK MARTIN

64	Sue WI 308	Daddy Rolling Stone/Don't Put Me Down Like This (credited as Derak Martin)	100
65	Columbia DB 7694	You Better Go/You Know	40
68	Stax 601 039	Soul Power/Sly Girl	30

DON MARTIN & DANDY (& SUPERBOYS)

(see also Dandy & Superboys)

67	Giant GN 6	Got A Feelin'/CONNECTIONS: At The Junction	12
68	Giant GN 24	Keep On Fighting/Rock Steady Boogie (with Superboys)	15

GEORGE MARTIN & HIS ORCHESTRA

(see also Beatles, Ray Cathode)

64	Parlophone R 5135	I Saw Her Standing There/All My Loving	12
64	Parlophone R 5166	And I Love Her/Ringo's Theme (This Boy)	12
65	Parlophone R 5222	All Quiet On The Mersey Front/Out Of The Picture	15
65	Parlophone R 5256	I Feel Fine/The Niagara Theme	10
65	Parlophone R 5375	Yesterday/Another Girl	15
66	United Artists UP 1154	By George! - It's The David Frost Theme/Double Scotch	15
66	United Artists UP 1165	Love In The Open Air/Theme From "The Family Way"	20
67	United Artists UP 1194	Theme One/Elephants And Castles	20
72	United Artists UP 35423	Pulp - Theme/Pulp - Love Theme	10
65	Parlophone GEP 8930	MUSIC FROM "A HARD DAY'S NIGHT" (EP)	35
64	Parlophone PMC 1227	OFF THE BEATLE TRACK (LP, mono)	25
64	Parlophone PCS 3057	OFF THE BEATLE TRACK (LP, stereo)	30
65	Parlophone TA-PMC 1227	OFF THE BEATLE TRACK (reel-to-reel, mono only)	12
65	Columbia SX 1775	PLAYS HELP! (LP, mono)	20
65	Studio Two TWO 102	PLAYS HELP! (LP, stereo)	20
66	United Artists (S)ULP 1157	INSTRUMENTALLY SALUTES THE BEATLES GIRLS (LP)	30

			MINT VALUE £
66	Studio Two TWO 141	AND I LOVE HER (LP)	20
67	Decca (S)KL 4847	THE FAMILY WAY (LP, soundtrack)	100
68	United Artists (S)ULP 1196	BRITISH MAID (LP)	25
70	Sunset SLS 50182	BY GEORGE! (LP)	20
73	United Artists UAS 29475	LIVE AND LET DIE (LP, soundtrack, gatefold sleeve)	25
74	Polydor Super 2383 304	BEATLES TO BOND AND BACH (LP)	15
78	St. Michael IMP 105	BEATLES TO BOND AND BACH (LP, exclusive to Marks & Spencer)	20
93	EMI RNB 1	THE BEATLES - GEORGE MARTIN INTERVIEW (CD, card sleeve, promo only)	18

GRADY MARTIN & THE SLEWFOOT FIVE
(see also Jane Turzy)

56	Brunswick 05535	Nashville/Don't Take Your Love From Me	15

HONEYBOY MARTIN
(see also Lynn Tait & Jets)

67	Caltone TONE 103	Dreader Than Dread (and the Voices)/DANDY: In The Mood	45
70	Gas GAS 123	Unchained Melody/SAMMY JONES: You're My Girl	10
72	Sioux SI 011	Unchained Melody/SAMMY JONES: You're My Girl (reissue)	8
72	Harry J HJ 6643	Have You Ever Seen The Rain/Spanish Harlem	5

IRVING MARTIN
(see under Martin's Magic Sounds)

JACKI MARTIN

64	Fontana TF 487	Will You/Till He Tells Me	12

JANIS MARTIN

60	Palette PG 9000	Here Today And Gone Tomorrow Love/Hard Times Ahead	25
80	RCA PL 43153	THE COMPLETE RCA JANIS MARTIN (2-LP)	25

JEAN MARTIN

63	Decca F 11751	Ain't Gonna Kiss Ya/Three Times Three Is Love	10
64	Decca F 11897	Save The Last Dance For Me/Will You Still Love Me Tomorrow	10

JERRY MARTIN

63	London HLU 9692	Shake-A Take-A/Exchange Student	15

KERRY MARTIN

58	Parlophone R 4449	Stroll Me/Cold Hands, Warm Heart	12

LUCIA MARTIN

62	Parlophone R 4915	Big Jim/Star From Heaven	12

MARK MARTIN

67	Page One POF 020	Extraordinary Girl/Love Could Be Like Hell	6

MARY MARTIN

64	London HLR 9938	A Spoonful Of Sugar/Feed The Birds	5

MILES MARTIN FOLK GROUP

71	Amber	MILES MARTIN FOLK GROUP (LP, private pressing)	70

MILLICENT MARTIN
(see also Ronnie Carroll, David Frost)

58	Columbia DB 4171	Our Language Of Love/Seriously	10
63	Parlophone R5033	Get Lost My Love/Gravy Waltz	8
63	Parlophone R 4998	That Was The Week That Was/Gotta Lotta Lovin' (with David Frost)	7
64	Parlophone R 5096	In The Summer Of His Years/If I Can Help Somebody	5
64	Parlophone R 5120	Suspicion/Nothing But The Best	6
59	Columbia 33SX 1145	MILLICENT (LP)	80
64	Philips BL 7591	MR & MRS (LP)	25

PATRICK D. MARTIN

79	Deram DMR 432	I Like Electric Motors/Time (p/s)	5
80	Deram DM 433	Lucy 'Lectric/I Like Electric Motors/Mutant (p/s)	10
80	IRS/MCA ILS 0023	COMPUTER DATIN' EP	8

PAUL MARTIN

67	Sue WI 4041	Snake In The Grass/I've Got A New Love	60

RAY MARTIN (& HIS) CONCERT ORCHESTRA
(see also Ray Burns)

53	Columbia SCM 5001	Blue Tango/Belle Of The Ball	10
53	Columbia SCM 5002	The Marching Strings/The Waltzing Cat	10
53	Columbia SCM 5063	Swedish Rhapsody/Hi-Lili Hi-Lo	8
56	Columbia SCM 5264	The Carousel Waltz/ort Au Prince	8

RICKY MARTIN & TYME MACHINE

68	Olga OLE 4	Something Else/Blue Suede Shoes	15

RODGE MARTIN

67	Polydor 56725	When She Touches Me/Lovin' Machine	15

RON MARTIN & JUBILEE STOMPERS

68	Doctor Bird DB 1151	Give Your Love To Me/I Cry My Heart	20

RUPIE MARTIN('S ALLSTARS)

69	Ackee ACK 101	The Arena/Naturally	60
70	Torpedo TOR 24	Last Flight/Super Lotus	40
70	Torpedo TOR 26	Musical Container (Parts 1 & 2)	40
70	Punch PH 43	Death In The Arena (actually by Rupie Martin All Stars)/ MAN COMETH: Julia Caesar (actually by Charlie Ace)	30

SETH MARTIN

68	Page One POF 073	Another Day Goes By/Look At Me	15
69	Page One POF 134	What A Lovely Way To Spend Forever/Mystery Lady	5

SHANE MARTIN

68	CBS 2894	You're So Young/I Need You	275
68	CBS 2894	You're So Young/I Need You (DJ copy)	350

MINT VALUE £

SKIP MARTIN VIDEO ALL-STARS

60	Golden Guinea GGL 0060	TV JAZZ THEMES (LP, mono)	12
60	Golden Guinea GGLS 10060	TV JAZZ THEMES (LP, stereo)	15

STEVE MARTIN

56	Columbia DB 3703	Only You/Lola	5
58	Philips PB 820	Stairway Of Love/Chanson D'Amour	5
58	Philips PB 853	The Man Inside/Blue-Eyed Sue	5

TONY MARTIN

(see also Gogi Grant)

53	HMV 7M 105	Tenement Symphony (both sides)	7
53	HMV 7M 136	The Golden Years/April In Portugal	7
54	HMV 7M 203	Here/I Could Write A Book	7
54	HMV 7M 258	I Love Paris/Boulevard Of Nightingales	5
55	HMV 7M 302	Stranger In Paradise/Vera Cruz	6
55	HMV 7M 320	Domani/What's The Time In Nicaragua	7
56	HMV 7M 414	Walk Hand In Hand/Flamenco Love	8
56	HMV 7MC 41	Walk Hand In Hand/Flamenco Love (export issue)	8
57	HMV POP 282	All Of You/Moderation	8
57	RCA RCA 1002	The Man From Idaho/One Is A Lonely Number	5
59	RCA RCA 1101	She Is Not Thinking Of Me/GOGI GRANT: Say A Prayer For Me Tonight	6
65	Stateside SS 394	Talkin' To Your Picture/Our Rhapsody	120
65	Tamla Motown TMG 537	The Bigger Your Heart Is (The Harder You'll Fall)/The Two Of Us	150
65	Tamla Motown TMG 537	The Bigger Your Heart Is (The Harder You'll Fall)/The Two Of Us (DJ copy)	300
54	HMV 7EG 8006	TONY MARTIN (EP)	8
55	HMV 7EG 8124	TENEMENT SYMPHONY (EP)	8
55	Brunswick LA 8713	TONY MARTIN SINGS VOL. 1 (10" LP)	15
56	Mercury MPT 7005	TONY MARTIN FAVOURITES (10" LP)	15
57	Mercury MPT 7516	DREAM MUSIC (10" LP)	15
57	HMV DLP 1137	SPEAK TO ME OF LOVE (10" LP)	15

TRADE MARTIN

63	London HL 9662	Hula Hula Dancin' Doll/Something In The Wind	15

VINCE MARTIN

(see also Tarriers)

56	London HL 8340	Cindy Oh Cindy/Only If You Praise The Lord	18
56	London HLN 8340	Cindy Oh Cindy/Only If You Please The Lord	15
59	HMV POP 594	Old Grey Goose (Aunt Rhodie)/Goodnight, Irene	10

MARTIN & DERRICK

(see also Derrick Morgan)

61	Blue Beat BB 48	Times Are Going/I Love You Baby (with Cavaliers Combo)	15
62	Island WI 024	Come On/MONTY & CYCLONES: Organisation	20

MARTIN & FINLEY

73	Tamla Motown TMG 867	It's Another Sunday/Best Friends (withdrawn, demo only)	250

MARTIN & THE BROWNSHIRTS

78	Lightning GIL 507	Taxi Driver/Boring	40

WINK MARTINDALE

59	London HLD 8962	Deck Of Cards/Now You Know How It Feels (tri centre)	12
59	London HLD 8962	Deck Of Cards/Now You Know How It Feels (round centre)	5
59	London HLD 8962	Deck Of Cards/Now You Know How It Feels (78)	20
60	London HLD 9042	Life Gits Tee-Jus Don't It?/I Never See Maggie Alone	7
61	London HLD 9419	Black Land Farmer/Make Him Happy	8
63	London RED 1370	DECK OF CARDS (EP)	20
65	Dot DEP 20000	DECK OF CARDS (EP)	8
60	London HA-D 2240	WINK MARTINDALE (LP)	20

TONY MARTINEZ QUINTET

54	HMV 7M 264	Cucusa Tune Mambo/Bernie's Tune Mambo	5

AL MARTINO

54	Capitol CL 14128	Wanted/There'll Be No Teardrops Tonight (Green label, tri centre)	20
54	Capitol CL 14128	Wanted/There'll Be No Teardrops Tonight (Purple label, tri centre)	15
54	Capitol CL 14148	On And On (In Love With You)/Give Me Something To Go With The Wine (Green label, tri centre)	20
54	Capitol CL 14148	On And On (In Love With You)/Give Me Something To Go With The Wine (Purple label, tri centre)	15
54	Capitol CL 14163	The Story Of Tina/Destiny (No One Can Change) (Green label, tri centre)	20
54	Capitol CL 14163	The Story Of Tina/Destiny (No One Can Change) (Purple label, tri centre)	15
54	Capitol CL 14192	I Still Believe/When?	10
54	Capitol CL 14202	Not As A Stranger/No One But You	10
55	Capitol CL 14224	Don't Go To Strangers/Say It Again	10
55	Capitol CL 14284	The Snowy, Snowy Mountains/Love Is Eternal	10
55	Capitol CL 14343	The Man From Laramie/To Please My Lady	20
55	Capitol CL 14379	Come Close To Me/Small Talk	10

(All the above 45s were originally issued with triangular centres; round-centre reissues are worth around half these values.)

56	Capitol CL 14550	Journey's End/Sound Advice	6
56	Capitol CL 14614	The Girl I Left In Rome/Some Cloud Above	6
57	Capitol CL 14680	I'm Sorry/A Love To Call My Own	6
59	Top Rank JAR 108	I Can't Get You Out Of My Heart/Two Hearts Are Better Than One	6
59	Top Rank JAR 187	Darling I Love You/The Memory Of You	6
60	Top Rank JAR 312	Summertime/I Sold My Heart	6
60	Top Rank JAR 337	Mama/Dearest (Cara)	6
61	Capitol EAP 1.20153	TO PLEASE MY LADY (EP)	10

MINT VALUE £

MARTIN'S MAGIC SOUNDS

67	Deram DM 141	Mon Amour, Mon Amour/Midem Melody	6
67	Deram DML/SML 1014	MARTIN'S MAGIC SOUNDS (LP)	12

JOHN MARTYN

71	Island WIP 6116	May You Never/Just Now	7
77	Island WIP 6385	Over The Hill/Head And Heart	6
78	Island WIP 6414	Dancing/Dealer (Version)	6
80	Island WIP 6547	Johnny Too Bad/Johnny Too Bad (Version)	6
81	Island IPR 2046	Johnny Too Bad (Extended Dub Version)/Big Muff (Extended Mix) (12", promo)	10
82	WEA K 259987-7	Gun Money (US Remix)/Hiss On the Tape (live)	6
86	Island CID 265	Classic John Martyn: Angeline/Tight Connection To My Heart (Has Anybody Seen My Love)/May You Never/Solid Air/Glistening Glyndebourne (CD, foldout sleeve)	15
92	Permanent CDPERM 6	Sweet Little Mystery (CD)	12
97	Blueprint BP 276CD	SNOOO... EP (She's A Lover/All In Your Favour/Step It Up/Little Strange) (CD)	8
67	Island ILP 952	LONDON CONVERSATION (LP, 1st pressing, with black & orange 'circle' logo)	130
69	Island ILP 952	LONDON CONVERSATION (LP, 2nd pressing, pink label, white 'i' logo)	70
69	Island ILP 952	LONDON CONVERSATION (LP, 3rd pressing, 'pink rim' label, 'palm tree' logo)	25
68	Island ILP 991	THE TUMBLER (LP, 1st pressing, with black 'circle' logo, mono)	120
68	Island ILPS 9091	THE TUMBLER (LP, 1st pressing, with black 'circle' logo, stereo)	40
70	Island ILPS 9091	THE TUMBLER (LP, 2 nd pressing, 'pink rim' label, 'palm tree' logo)	20
71	Island ILPS 9167	BLESS THE WEATHER (LP, 'pink rim' label, 'palm tree' logo)	25
73	Island ILPS 9226	SOLID AIR (LP, gatefold sleeve with lyric sheet 'pink rim' label, 'palm tree' logo)	30
73	Island ILPS 9253	INSIDE OUT (LP, gatefold sleeve with inner, 'pink rim' label, 'palm tree' logo)	15
75	Island ILPS 9296	SUNDAY'S CHILD (LP, with lyric inner sleeve, 'palm tree' label)	15
75	Island ILPS 9343	LIVE AT LEEDS (LP, mail-order, 10,000 only, numbered & signed)	30
86	Bodyswerve JMLP 001	PHILENTROPY (LP, red sleeve)	12
91	Permanent PERMLP 4	COOLTIDE (LP, with inner)	12

JOHN & BEVERLEY MARTYN

(see also Beverley)

70	Island WIP 6076	John The Baptist/The Ocean	12
70	Island ILPS 9113	STORMBRINGER (LP, 1st pressing, pink label with 'i' logo)	60
70	Island ILPS 9113	STORMBRINGER (LP, 2nd pressing, 'pink rim' label, 'palm tree' logo)	12
70	Island ILPS 9133	THE ROAD TO RUIN (LP, 'pink rim' label, 'palm tree' logo)	22

KID MARTYN

62	77 77LA 12/20	IN NEW ORLEANS WITH KID SHEIK'S BAND (LP)	15

MARVELETTES

61	Fontana H 355	Please Mr Postman/So Long Baby	50
62	Fontana H 386	Twistin' Postman/I Want A Guy	75
62	Oriole CBA 1764	Beechwood 4-5789/Someday Someway	150
63	Oriole CBA 1817	Locking Up My Heart/Forever	350
64	Stateside SS 251	As Long As I Know He's Mine/Little Girl Blue	55
64	Stateside SS 251	As Long As I Know He's Mine/Little Girl Blue (DJ copy)	90
64	Stateside SS 273	He's A Good Guy (Yes He Is)/Goddess Of Love	55
64	Stateside SS 273	He's A Good Guy (Yes He Is)/Goddess Of Love (DJ copy)	100
64	Stateside SS 334	You're My Remedy/A Little Bit Of Sympathy, A Little Bit Of Love	45
64	Stateside SS 334	You're My Remedy/A Little Bit Of Sympathy, A Little Bit Of Love (DJ copy)	100
65	Stateside SS 369	Too Many Fish In The Sea/Need For Love	50
65	Stateside SS 369	Too Many Fish In The Sea/Need For Love (DJ copy)	125
65	Tamla Motown TMG 518	I'll Keep Holding On/No Time For Tears	130
65	Tamla Motown TMG 518	I'll Keep Holding On/No Time For Tears (DJ copy)	400
65	Tamla Motown TMG 535	Danger Heartbreak Dead Ahead/Your Cheating Ways	50
65	Tamla Motown TMG 535	Danger Heartbreak Dead Ahead/Your Cheating Ways (DJ copy)	150
66	Tamla Motown TMG 546	Don't Mess With Bill/Anything You Wanna Do	45
66	Tamla Motown TMG 546	Don't Mess With Bill/Anything You Wanna Do (DJ copy)	85
66	Tamla Motown TMG 562	You're The One/Paper Boy	45
66	Tamla Motown TMG 562	You're The One/Paper Boy (DJ copy)	75
67	Tamla Motown TMG 594	The Hunter Gets Captured By The Game/I Think I Can Change You	30
67	Tamla Motown TMG 594	The Hunter Gets Captured By The Game/I Think I Can Change You (DJ copy)	60
67	Tamla Motown TMG 609	When You're Young And In Love/The Day You Take One, You Have To Take The Other	15
68	Tamla Motown TMG 639	My Baby Must Be A Magician/I Need Someone	20
68	Tamla Motown TMG 659	Here I Am Baby/Keep Off, No Trespassing	25
69	Tamla Motown TMG 701	Reachin' For Something I Can't Have/Destination Anywhere	15
73	Tamla Motown TMG 860	Reachin' For Something I Can't Have/Here I Am Baby	10
73	Tamla Motown TMG 860	Reachin' For Something I Can't Have/Here I Am Baby (DJ copy, plays "My Baby Must Be A Magician")	100
75	Tamla Motown TMG 1000	Finders Keepers, Losers Weepers/KIM WESTON: Do Like I Do	100
65	Tamla Motown TMG 2003	THE MARVELETTES (EP)	100
65	T. Motown TML 11008	THE MARVELLOUS MARVELETTES (LP)	250
67	T. Motown TML 11052	THE MARVELETTES (LP, mono)	50
67	T. Motown STML 11052	THE MARVELETTES (LP, stereo)	60
69	T. Motown (S)TML 11090	SOPHISTICATED SOUL (LP, mono/stereo)	40
70	T. Motown STML 11145	IN FULL BLOOM (LP)	35

MARVELOWS

65	HMV POP 1433	I Do/My Heart	40
65	HMV POP 1433	I Do/My Heart (DJ Copy)	60

MARVELS (Jamaica)

62	Dice CC 8	Come To The Wedding/Angelo	10
63	Blue Beat BB 191	Sonia/The More We Are Together	12
64	Blue Beat BB 221	Millie/Saturday	12
70	Pama PM 813	Love One Another/Falling Rain	5
70	Pama PM 817	Don't Let Him Take Your Love From Me/A Little Smile	5

MINT VALUE £

70	Gas GAS 138	Sail Away/Fight A Broke	12
70	Gas GAS 139	Someday We'll Be Together/MOHAWKS: The Rhythm	5
71	Pama PM 819	Oh Lord Why Lord/NEVILLE HINDS: Love Letter	5
71	Pama Supreme PS 338	Rocksteady/ Be My Baby	30
71	New Beat NB 081	Co Co/Hey Girl Don't Bother Me	5
72	Pama PM 832	Do You Know You Have To Cry/Love Power	5
72	Pama Supreme PS 348	What A Hurricane/If You Love Her	5
70s	Trojan TRLS 67	THE MARVELS (LP)	12

MARVELS (U.K.)

68	Columbia DB 8341	Keep On Searching/Heartache	100

MARVELS FIVE

65	HMV POP 1423	Bye Bye Baby Bunting/In Front Of Her House	7
65	HMV POP 1452	Don't Play That Song/(You Lied) I Forgive	15

MARVETTE

68	Amalgamated AMG 804	Tit For Tat (actually by Lyn Taitt & Jets)/You Take So Long To Know	50
68	Sacred Sound SS 001	We Are Not Divided/He Is So Real To Me	8
68	Sacred Sound SS 002	We Shall Have A Grand Time/Let The Power Fall On Me	8
68	Sacred Sound SS 003	I Was Once Lost In Sin/What A Wonderful Thing	8
68	Tabernacle TS 1001	I Want A Revival/Tell It	15
68	Tabernacle TS 1003	Sweet Jesus/When I Look Back	7
60s	Coxsone TLP 1002	IT'S REVIVAL TIME (LP)	80

BRETT MARVIN & THUNDERBOLTS

(see also Jona Lewie)

70	Sonet SNTF 616	BRETT MARVIN AND THE THUNDERBOLTS (LP)	15
71	Sonet SNTF 619	12 INCHES OF BRETT MARVIN & THE THUNDERBOLTS (LP)	15
71	Sonet SNTF 620	BEST OF FRIENDS (LP)	12
72	Sonet SNTF 630	ALIAS TERRY DACTYL AND THE DINOSAURS (LP)	12

HANK (B.) MARVIN

(see also Shadows, Marvin & Farrar, Marvin Welch & Farrar, Bruce Welch, Cliff Richard, Spaghetti Junction, Jean-Michel Jarre)

68	Columbia DB 8326	London's Not Too Far/SHADOWS: Running Out Of World	15
69	Columbia DB 8552	Goodnight Dick/Wahine	12
69	Columbia DB 8601	Sacha/Sunday For Seven Days	12
69	Columbia DB 8628	Midnight Cowboy/SHADOWS: Slaughter On Tenth Avenue	18
70	Columbia DB 8693	Break Another Dawn/Would You Believe It? (demo-only, unissued B-side)	135
70	Columbia DB 8693	Break Another Dawn/Morning Star	15
78	EMI EMI 2744	Flamingo/Syndicated (as Hank Marvin Guitar Syndicate)	5
69	Columbia SCX 6352	HANK MARVIN (LP, blue/black label, mono)	35
69	Columbia SCX 6352	HANK MARVIN (LP, blue/black label, stereo)	30
70	Columbia SCX 6352	HANK MARVIN (LP, silver/black label re-pressing)	12

JOEL MARVIN

(see also Gregory Isaacs)

70	Explosion EX 2028	Too Late/Each Day (both actually by Gregory Isaacs)	15

MARVIN & FARRAR

(see also Shadows, Hank Marvin, Marvin Welch & Farrar)

73	EMI EMI 2044	Music Makes My Day/Skin Deep (with Olivia Newton-John)	10
75	EMI EMI 2335	Small And Lonely Light/Galadriel (Spirit Of Starlight)	7
73	EMI EMA 755	HANK MARVIN AND JOHN FARRAR (LP, with Olivia Newton-John)	20

MARVIN & JOHNNY

57	Vogue V 9074	Yak Yak/Pretty Eyes	500
57	Vogue V 9074	Yak Yak/Pretty Eyes (78)	150
58	Vogue V 9099	Smack, Smack/You're In My Heart	500
58	Vogue V 9099	Smack, Smack/You're In My Heart (78)	150
65	Black Swan WI 467	Cherry Pie/Ain't That Right	40

MARVIN, WELCH & FARRAR

(see also Shadows, Marvin & Farrar, Bruce Welch [& Hank Marvin])

71	Regal Zonophone RZ 3030	Faithful/Mr. Sun	5
71	Regal Zonophone RZ 3035	Lady Of The Morning/Tiny Robin	5
72	Regal Zonophone RZ 3048	Marmaduke/Strike A Light	5
71	Regal Zono. SRZA 8502	MARVIN, WELCH AND FARRAR (LP)	15
71	Regal Zono. SRZA 8504	SECOND OPINION (LP)	15
72	Regal Zono. Q4SRZA 8504	SECOND OPINION (LP, quadrophonic)	25

GROUCHO MARX

(see also Danny Kaye, Jimmy Durante, Jerry Colonna & Groucho Marx)

72	A&M AMS 7057	Show Me A Rose/Lydia The Tattooed Lady	7

MARX BROTHERS

70	MCA MCF 2533	ORIGINAL VOICE TRACKS FROM THEIR GREATEST MOVIES (LP)	12

MARY JANE with BARRY GRAY & SPACEMAKERS

(see also Barry Gray)

63	Philips 326 587 BF	Robot Man/Just The Same As I Do (in p/s)	40
63	Philips 326 587 BF	Robot Man/Just The Same As I Do	18

MARZ

80s	Frozen Owl SRR 0023	Lady Of The Night/On The Road To Freedom/Daydreamer (p/s, with badge)	90

MARZIPAN

70	Trend 6099 007	My Kind Of Music/Sweet Water Mary	10

MASAI

74	Contempo CS 2007	Across The Track (We Better Go Back) (Parts 1 & 2)	40

MASAI

82	Turbo TURB 01	Stranger To Myself/Lightning (p/s)	8

MINT VALUE £

MASCOTS

63	Pye International 7N 25189	Hey Little Angel/Once Upon A Love	20

HUGH MASEKELA

68	Uni UN 504	Grazing In The Grass/Bajabula Bonke	10
69	Uni UN 510	I Haven't Slept/Where Has All The Grass Gone?	6
68	Uni UNL(S) 101	ALIVE AND WELL AT THE WHISKEY (LP)	20
69	Fontana SFL 13056	HUGH MASEKELA (LP)	18
71	Rare Earth SRE 3002	HUGH MASEKELA AND THE UNION OF SOUTH AFRICA (LP)	25
72	Blue Thumb ICD 3	HOME IS WHERE THE MUSIC IS (LP)	30

MASHMAKAN

70	CBS S 5170	As The Years Go By/Days When We Are Free	15
74	Youngblood YB1063	Dance A Little Step/One Night Stand	6

MASKMAN & AGENTS

69	Direction 58-4059	One Eye Open/Y'awll	10

MASON

73	Dawn DNS 1040	Fading/It's Alright	5
73	Dawn DNLS 3050	MASON (LP, export issue, do finished copies exist?)	20
74	Antic K 11505	Follow Me/Peacefully	8

BARBARA MASON

65	London HL 9977	Yes, I'm Ready/Keep Him	40
65	London HL 9977	Yes, I'm Ready/Keep Him (DJ copy)	75
68	Direction 58-3382	Oh How It Hurts/Ain't Got Nobody	40
69	Action ACT 4542	Slipping Away/Half A Love	20
72	Buddah 2011 133	Bed And Board/Yes It's You	10
73	Buddah 2011 154	Give Me Your Love/You Can Be With The One You Don't Love	7
75	Buddah BDS 425	From His Woman To You/When You Wake Up In Georgia	6
69	Action ACLP 6002	OH HOW IT HURTS (LP)	75
75	Buddah BDLP 4027	TRANSITION (LP)	20
75	Buddah BDLP 4032	LOVE'S THE THING (LP)	20

BARRY MASON

(see also Sounds Of Les & Barry)

66	Decca F 12401	Misty Morning Eyes/Take Your Time	10
66	Deram DM 104	Over The Hills And Far Away/A Collection Of Recollections	45
67	MGM MGM 1356	Rowbottom Square/American Girl	12
69	Decca F 12895	I'm In Love With You, Pom Pom/Mister D.J. Play Me A Sad Song	7
76	Magnet MAG 5012	THE SONGWRITER (LP)	12

BILL MASON BAND

79	Kingsway KMS 903	Out On The Streets/Mr. G (p/s)	15

DAVE MASON

(see also Hellions, Revolution, Traffic, Fox, Jaguars)

68	Island WIP 6032	Just For You/Little Woman	15
70	Harvest HAR 5017	World In Changes/Can't Stop Worrying, Can't Stop Lovin'	5
70	Harvest HAR 5024	Only You Know And I Know/Sad And Deep As You	5
70	Harvest SHTC 251	ALONE TOGETHER (LP, gatefold sleeve, no EMI logo)	25
72	Blue Thumb ILPS 9203	HEAD KEEPER (LP)	15
72	Island ICD 5	SCRAPBOOK (2-LP)	15
73	CBS 65258	IT'S LIKE YOU NEVER LEFT (LP, gatefold sleeve)	12

DAVE MASON & CASS ELLIOT

(see also Dave Mason, Mama Cass [Elliot])

71	Probe PRO 513	Something To Make You Happy/Next To You (as Mason & Cass, special sleeve)	6
71	Probe SPBA 6259	DAVE MASON AND CASS ELLIOT (LP, gatefold sleeve, pink label)	15

GLEN MASON

56	Parlophone MSP 6240	Hot Diggity (Dog Ziggity Boom)/Baby Girl Of Mine	12
56	Parlophone R 4203	Love, Love, Love/Glendora	12
56	Parlophone R 4244	The Green Door/Why Must You Go, Go, Go	12
57	Parlophone R 4271	Don't Forbid Me/Amore	10
57	Parlophone R 4291	Round And Round/Walking And Whistling	5
57	Parlophone R 4334	Crying My Heart Out For You/Why Don't They Understand	5
57	Parlophone R 4357	By My Side/By The Fireside	5
58	Parlophone R 4390	What A Beautiful Combination/I'm Alone Because I Love You	5
58	Parlophone R 4415	I May Never Pass This Way Again/A Moment Ago	5
58	Parlophone R 4451	I Know Where I'm Going/Autumn Souvenir	5
58	Parlophone R 4485	The End/Fall In Love	5
59	Parlophone R 4562	The Battle Of New Orleans/I Don't Know	5
60	Parlophone R 4626	You Got What It Takes/If There's Someone	6
60	Parlophone R 4723	That's What I Want!/I Like It When It Rains	5
61	Parlophone R 4834	Don't Move/Shadrack	5
62	Parlophone R 4900	St. Louis Blues/That's Life	5

HARVEY MASON

77	Arista ARIST 12188	Till You Take My Love/What's Going On (12")	10
77	Arista SPART 1049	FUNK IN A MASON JAR (LP)	12

MARLIN MASON

56	Vogue Coral Q 72168	Don't Throw My Love Away/The Mystery Of Love	10

NICK MASON (& RICK FENN)

(see also Pink Floyd, 10cc)

85	Harvest HAR 5238	Lie For A Lie/And The Address (with Rick Fenn, p/s)	5
85	Harvest 12 HAR 5238	Lie For A Lie (Extended 12" Version)/And The Address/ Mumbo Jumbo (with Rick Fenn) (12", p/s)	8
85	EMI MAF 1	PROFILES (LP, with Rick Fenn)	12
81	Harvest SHSP 4116	FICTITIOUS SPORTS (LP, solo, with inner sleeve)	12

MINT VALUE £

SPENCER MASON
67 Parlophone R 5555 — Flugel In Carnaby Street/Albuferia ... 10

MASQUERADERS
(see also Lester Tipton)
68 Bell BLL 1023 — I Ain't Got To Love Nobody Else/I Got It ... 15
70 Now! NOW 1001 — Love Peace And Understanding/Tell Me You Love Me ... 10

MASS
(see also Models, Rema-Rema, Wolfgang Press)
80 4AD AD 14 — You And I/Cabbage (with poster insert in die-cut sleeve) ... 12
80 4AD AD 14 — You And I/Cabbage (in die-cut sleeve) ... 8
81 4AD CAD 107 — LABOUR OF LOVE (LP, with inner sleeve) ... 15

MASSIEL
68 Philips BF 1667 — La La La/He Gives Me Love (La La La) ... 7

MASSIVE ATTACK
91 Wild Bunch WBRT 2 — Unfinished Sympathy/Instrumental (12", p/s, as MASSIVE) ... 10
91 Wild Bunch WBRR 2 — Unfinished Sympathy (Nellee Hooper 12" Mix)/(Nellee Hooper Instrumental Mix)/(Original) (12", p/s) ... 15
98 Circa MASBOX 2 — SINGLES 90/98 (11 x 12" singles in numbered heat sensitive box) ... 80
88 Massive Attack MASS 001 — Any Love/Any Love (Bonus) Any Love (Instrumental)/Any Love (Acapella) (12", stickered plain black die-cut sleeve) ... 12
09 Vinyl Factory VF 006 — SPLITTING THE ATOM EP (12", numbered p/s. 180 gram vinyl, 1000 only) ... 20
91 Wild Bunch WBRLP1 — BLUE LINES (LP, as Massive) ... 20
03 Virgin V2967 — 100th WINDOW (3-LP, gatefold) ... 18

MASSIVE DREAD
79 His Majesty HM 1001 — MASSIVE DREAD (LP) ... 30

MASTER SINGERS
66 Parlophone R 5428 — The Highway Code/Rumbletum Song ... 5
66 Parlophone R 5523 — Weather Forecast/Roadilore ... 5

MASTERFLEET
73 Sussex LPSX 5 — HIGH ON THE SEA (LP) ... 25

MASTERMINDS
(see also Badfinger)
65 Immediate IM 005 — She Belongs To Me/Taken My Love ... 40

MASTERPLAN
78 Satril SAT 136 — Love Crazy (Theme From 'Carry On Emmanuel')/Since I've Been Away From My Love (p/s) ... 10

CARL MASTERS
(see also Max Romeo, Dennis Alcapone)
72 Big Shot BI 604 — Va Va Voom/GOD SONS: Rebel ... 15

SAMMY MASTERS
60 Warner Bros WB 10 — Rockin' Red Wing/Lonely Weekend ... 25
60 Warner Bros WB 10 — Rockin' Red Wing/Lonely Weekend (78) ... 150
65 London HLR 9949 — I Fought The Law (And The Law Won)/Big Man Cried ... 15

VALERIE MASTERS
58 Fontana H 132 — Sharing/The Secret Of Happiness ... 8
58 Fontana H 145 — (Well-a, Well-a) Ding-Dong/Merci Beaucoup ... 8
59 Fontana H 175 — Dreams End At Dawn/Wonder ... 8
59 Fontana H 195 — Jack O' Diamonds/Say When ... 8
59 Fontana H 224 — If There Are Stars In My Eyes/Just Squeeze Me ... 8
60 Fontana H 238 — Oh, Gee/No One Understands ... 8
60 Fontana H 253 — Banjo Boy/Cow Cow Boogie ... 8
60 Fontana H 268 — Sweeter As The Day Goes By/Fools Fall In Love ... 8
61 Fontana H 293 — Too Late For Tears/I Got Rhythm ... 8
62 Fontana H 367 — African Waltz/All Night Long ... 7
63 HMV POP 1125 — The End Of The World/Sometime Kind Of Love ... 10
64 Columbia DB 7426 — Christmas Calling/He Didn't Fool Me ... 75
66 Polydor 56135 — Don't Ever Go/Say Hello ... 20

MASTER'S APPRENTICES
71 Regal Zonophone RZ 3031 — I'm Your Satisfier/Because I Love Her ... 35
71 Regal Zono. SLRZ 1016 — MASTER'S APPRENTICES (LP, red/silver labels with no EMI logo) ... 300
71 Regal Zono. SLRZ 1022 — A TOAST TO PANAMA RED (LP, red/silver label with EMI logo) ... 250

MASTERS AT WORK
96 Talkin' Loud 578795-1 — NUYORICAN (6-LP box set) ... 40

MASTERS OF REALITY
88 Def American DEFA 1 — The Candy Song/The Blue Garden ... 10
88 Def American 838 474-1 — THE MASTERS OF REALITY (LP) ... 20
88 Def American 838 474-2 — THE MASTERS OF REALITY (CD) ... 20

MASTERSTROKE
80s DTS DTS 043 — Prisoner Of Love/Burning Heart (no p/s) ... 75

MATADOR
71 Big Shot BI 594 — Nyah Festival (actually "What Am I Living For" by Derrick Morgan)/ Brixton Serenade ... 8

MATADORS
(see also Emotions, Little Roys, Ethiopians)
69 Crab CRAB 27 — Death A Come (actually by Lloyd Robinson)/The Sword (actually "Zylon" by Lloyd Tyrell [Charmers]) ... 20
70 Camel CA 45 — Dark Of The Sun (actually by Jackie Mittoo)/Dreader Than Dread ... 30
71 Green Door GD 4017 — I'm Sorry(actually by Tony Brevett)/JOE WHITE: I'm Sorry Version ... 10

MINT VALUE £

MATATA (AIR-FIESTA)
72 President PT 380 — I Wanna Do My Thing/Wild River … 10
73 President PT 406 — I Feel Funky/I Want You … 15
74 President PT 417 — Return To You/Something On My Mind … 10
75 President PT 438 — Good Good Understanding/Gimme Some Lovin' … 10
72 President PTLS 1052 — MATATA: AIR FIESTA (LP) … 40
75 President PTLS 1057 — INDEPENDENCE (LP) … 80

MATAYO
75 RAK RAK 222 — Matayo/I Like Rock 'N' Roll … 20

MATCHBOX
71 Rak 113 — Don't Shut Me Out/Rod … 8
78 Raw — Rock Rollin' Boogie/Troublesome Bay (p/s) … 15
81 Dawn DNS 1104 — Rock 'N' Roll Bank/Born To R 'N' R … 12

MATCHBOX
69 Polydor 56327 — Run Much Faster/Every Little Thing She Does … 150

MATCHING MOLE
(see also Robert Wyatt, Soft Machine, Caravan, Hatfield & The North)
72 CBS 8101 — O Caroline/Signed Curtain … 20
72 CBS 64850 — MATCHING MOLE (LP) … 30
72 CBS 65260 — MATCHING MOLE'S LITTLE RED RECORD (LP, with inner sleeve) … 30

MATCHMAKERS
(see also Mark Wirtz, Philwit & Pegasus, Fickle Finger)
71 Chapter One — BUBBLEGUM A GO GO (LP) … 20

KAREN MATHESON
(see also Capercaillie)
96 Survival SURCD 020B — THE DREAMING SEA (CD, limited edition in box, with 6 postcards) … 20

MATHETAI
77 Cavs CAV 017 — KNOWING (LP) … 50

MIREILLE MATHIEU
67 Columbia DB 8323 — La Dernier Valse/Seuls Au Monde … 6
68 Columbia DB 8513 — Les Bicyclettes De Belsize/Sometimes … 6
66 Fontana TL 5363 — MIREILLE MATHIEU (LP) … 12

COUNTRY JOHNNY MATHIS
60 Top Rank JKP 2064 — COUNTRY AND WESTERN EXPRESS NO. 5 (EP) … 10

JODI MATHIS
75 Capitol CL 15827 — Mama/Don't You Care Anymore … 10

JOHNNY MATHIS
57 Philips JK 1029 — The Twelfth Of Never/Chances Are (jukebox issue) … 15
60 Fontana H 267 — My Love For You/Oh That Feeling (in p/s) … 8
63 HMV POP 1217 — Your Teenage Dreams/Come Back (in export p/s) … 6
57 Fontana TFL 5003 — WONDERFUL, WONDERFUL (LP) … 12
66 HMV CLP 1926/CSD 1638 — AWAY FROM HOME (LP) … 20

MATIC 16
82 Music Hive (No cat. No) — Jahovah/Ten Man (12") … 50

MATRIX RISE
92 Mutant 12 MUTATE 6 — D.O.Y.L.E. Factor/Reality (12") … 25
92 Mutant 12 MUTATE 8 — Moments Of Pleasure/The Preacher (12") … 40

BRIAN MATTHEW
61 Pye 7N 15403 — Trad Mad/Sing With Me, Mates … 7

BRIAN MATTHEW & PETE MURRAY
60 Decca F 11305 — What's It All About Eh?/Gee Ma, I Wanna Go Home … 7

IAN MATTHEWS
(see also Pyramid, Fairport Convention, Matthews Southern Comfort, Plainsong, Hi-Fi)
71 Vertigo 6059041 — Hearts/Little Knows … 12
71 Vertigo 6360 034 — IF YOU SAW THRO' MY EYES (LP, textured gatefold sleeve, large swirl label) … 50
72 Vertigo 6360 056 — TIGERS WILL SURVIVE (LP, textured gatefold sleeve, small swirl label) … 50
73 Elektra K 42144 — VALLEY HI (LP, textured gatefold sleeve, 'butterfly' label) … 30
74 Elektra K 42160 — SOME DAYS YOU EAT THE BEAR, SOME DAYS THE BEAR EATS YOU (LP) … 20
74 Mooncrest CREST 18 — JOURNEYS FROM GOSPEL OAK (LP) … 20
76 CBS 81316 — GO FOR BROKE (LP) … 18

JESSIE MATTHEWS
66 Music For Pleasure MFP 1127 — ORIGINAL RECORDINGS (LP) … 12
66 Woman's Own AZ 9 — THE KING AND I (LP) … 12

JOE MATTHEWS
68 Sue WI 4046 — Sorry Ain't Good Enough/You Better Mend Your Ways … 80

MILT MATTHEWS
75 London HLF 10479 — All These Changes/When Kids Rule The World … 8

RANDY MATTHEWS
70s Myrrh MXX 1035 — NOW DO YOU UNDERSTAND (LP, gatefold sleeve) … 40

TOBIN MATTHEWS
63 Warner Brothers WB 117 — Can't Stop Talking About You/When You Came Along … 6

WINSTON MATTHEWS
71 Banana BA 329 — Sun Is Shining/INN KEEPERS: My Friend
(B-side actually "The Pressure Is On" by Purpleites) … 18

MINT VALUE £

MATTHEWS SOUTHERN COMFORT
(see also Ian Matthews, Marc Ellington, Southern Comfort)

70	Uni UNS 513	Colorado Springs Eternal/The Struggle	12
70	Uni UNS 521	Ballad Of Obray Ramsey/Parting	7
70	Uni UNS 526	Woodstock/Scion	5
70	Uni UNLS 108	MATTHEWS SOUTHERN COMFORT (LP, gatefold, lyric insert, yellow swirl label)	40
70	Uni UNLS 112	SECOND SPRING (LP, textured sleeve, lyric insert, yellow swirl label)	30
70	Uni MKPS 2015	LATER THAT SAME YEAR... (LP, red/pink 'dogbone' label)	20

MATUMBI

73	G.G. GG 4540	Brother Louie Parts 1 & 2	10
77	Matumbi Music MA004	Music In The Air/Guide Us (12")	30
78	Matumbi Music MR 86	After Tonight/Take It From Me (12")	30
79	EMI 12RIC 101	This View/Another View (12" 'Matumbi' die cut sleeve)	8
78	EMI SHSP 4090	SEVEN SEALS (LP)	15
80	Extinguish MR 007	DUB PLANET ORBIT 1 (LP)	200

HARVEY MATUSOW'S JEWS HARP BAND

69	Head HDS 4004	Afghan Red/Wet Socks	8
69	Head HDLS 6001	WAR BETWEEN THE FATS & THE THINS (LP)	40

MAUDS

67	Mercury MF 1000	Hold On/C'mon And Move	10
68	Mercury MF 1062	Soul Drippin'/Forever Gone	10
68	Philips PF 1679	I Remember Loving You/Why Don't You say You Love Me	6
67	Philips BL 7791	HEY, LOOK ME OVER (LP)	25

SUSAN MAUGHAN

61	Philips BF 1216	Mama Do The Twist/Blue Night In Yokohama	20
62	Philips BF 1236	Baby Doll Twist/Some Of These Days	20
62	Philips 326 533BF	I've Got To Learn To Forget/I Didn't Mean What I Said	10
62	Philips 326 544BF	Bobby's Girl/Come A Little Closer	10
63	Philips 326 562BF	Hand A Handkerchief To Helen/I'm A Lonely One Too	10
63	Philips 326 586BF	She's New To You/Don't Get Carried Away	10
63	Philips BF 1266	The Verdict Is Guilty/Bachelor Girl	10
64	Philips BF 1301	Hey Lover/Stop Your Foolin'	10
64	Philips BF 1336	Kiss Me Sailor/Call On Me	5
64	Philips BF 1363	Little Things Mean A Lot/That Other Place	15
64	Philips BF 1382	Make Him Mine/South American Joe	5
65	Philips BF 1399	You Can Never Get Away From You/Don't Be Afraid	5
65	Philips BF 1417	When She Walks Away/Come Along Down And See	5
65	Philips BF 1445	Poor Boy/Your Girl	5
66	Philips BF 1495	Come And Get Me/Don't Love Him Too Much	5
66	Philips BF 1518	Where The Bullets Fly/I'll Never Stop Loving You	5
67	Philips BF 1564	Don't Go Home (My Little Darlin')/Somebody To Love	6
68	Philips BF 1713	Cable Car For Two/Off My Mind	5
69	Philips BF 1824	We Really Go Together/I'll Never Forget You	5
62	Philips BBE 12525	HI, I'M SUSAN MAUGHAN AND I SING (EP)	15
63	Philips BBE 12549	FOUR BEAUX AND A BELLE (EP)	15
62	Philips 433 621 BE	EFFERVESCENT MISS MAUGHAN (EP)	15
63	Philips 433 641 BE	MORE OF MAUGHAN (EP)	15
63	Philips 632 300 BL	I WANNA BE BOBBY'S GIRL BUT ... (LP)	40
64	Philips BL 7577	SWINGIN' SUSAN (LP)	20
65	Philips BL 7637	SENTIMENTAL SUSAN (LP)	20

MAU-MAUS

82	Pax PAX 6	SOCIETY'S REJECTS (EP, black or blue sleeve)	18
82	Pax PAX 8	No Concern/Clampdown/Why Do We Suffer (p/s)	15
83	Pax/Paragon PAX 12	FACTS OF WAR (EP)	15
85	Rebellion REBEL 01	TEAR DOWN THE WALLS (EP)	15
85	Rebellion REBEL 1202	SCARRED FOR LIFE (12" EP)	15
83	Pax PAX 16	LIVE AT THE MARPLES (LP)	18
84	Pax PAX 20	RUNNING WITH THE PACK (LP)	30
85	Rebellion	FEAR NO EVIL (LP)	12

MAUREENY WISHFULL
(see also Jimmy Page, Big Jim Sullivan, John Williams)

68	Moonshine WO 2388	THE MAUREENY WISHFULL ALBUM (LP, 300 copies, beware of counterfeits)	85

PAUL MAURIAT ORCHESTRA

67	Philips BF 1637	Love Is Blue (L'Amour Est Bleu)/Une Petite Cantate	6

MAURICE & MAC
(see also Radiants)

68	Chess CRS 8074	You Left The Water Running/You're The One	12
68	Chess CRS 8081	Why Don't You Try Me/Lean On Me	12

MAWAMBA DUB
(see also Dennis Bovell, Alton Ellis)

78	Warrior DRLP 1001	MAWANDA DUB (LP)	60

MAX

74	Caroline C1506	MAX (LP, black Virgin inner, black/red 'Twin' label)	20

MAX & ELAINE
(see also Max Romeo)

73	Ackee ACK 516	I'm Leaving/Version	5

MAX & GREGORY
(see also Max Romeo)

73	Ackee ACK 525	My Jamaican Collie/Push It Down, Rub It Up	5

MAX GROUP

69	Fab FAB 110	Abraham Vision/My Heart Was Breaking	5

MINT VALUE £

MAX HEADROOM & CARPARKS
80 Parlophone R 6034 Don't Panic/Rhythm And Bluebeat (p/s) 6
82 Bandwagon B001 Soldier (no p/s) 20

PAT MAX AND THE SPECIALISTS
68 Pye 7N 17470 Too Much/Girl From New Orleans 12

SMILEY MAXEDON & HIS OKAW VALLEY BOYS
54 Columbia SCMC 3 Crazy To Care/In The Window Of My Heart (export issue) 15

JOE S. MAXEY
73 Action ACT 4607 Sign Of The Crab/May The Best Man Win
(actually plays Packers' "Hole In The Wall"/"Go Ahead On") 15

MAXI
73 Decca F 13394 Do I Dream/Here Today And Gone Tomorrow 6

MAXIE (Romeo) & GLEN
(see also Max Romeo, Ethiopians)
71 G.G. GG 4520 Jordan River (actually by Max Romeo & Glen Adams)/
GLEN ADAMS:Version Two 10

MAXIMILIAN
61 London HLX 9356 The Snake/The Wanderer 35

MAXIMO PARK
03 Billingham Records Graffiti/Going Missing (red vinyl, 500 only, p/s) 50
04 Warp 7WAP183 The Coast Is Always Changing/The Night I Lost My Head (500 only, p/s) 25

MAXIM'S TRASH
(see also Sunset Boys, Captain Sensible, Johnny Moped)
79 Gimp GIMP 1 Disco Girls/Blu Shoes (plastic p/s & inner, hand-stamped white labels,
tracks actually recorded in 1975) 40

MAXIMUM BAND
68 Fab FAB 51 Cupid/Hold Me Tight 5

MAXIMUM BREED
69 Revolution REV 1 Sitting In The Park/You've Got It 5

MAXIMUM JOY
81 Y 11 Stretch/Silent Street (p/s) 5
81 Y Y 11 Stretch/Silent Street (12", p/s) 10
82 Y Y 15 White And Green Place/Building Bridges (12", p/s) 8

ERNEST MAXIN
59 Top Rank JAR 267 On The Beach/Take A Giant Step 6
60 Top Rank JAR 335 Conspiracy Of Hearts/No Orchids For My Lady 6

MAXINE
70 Smash SMA 2301 My Boy Lollipop/Everybody Needs Love 6

BRIAN MAXINE
(see also Fairport Convention)
72 EMI Starline SRS 5140 BRIAN MAXINE SINGS (LP) 40

HOLLY MAXWELL
69 Buddah 201 056 Suffer/No-One Else 8

MAXWELL PLUMM
75 Raven KS1007 WE CAN WORK IT OUT (LP) 12

BRIAN MAY
(see also Queen, MC Spy-D & 'Friends', Eddie Howell, Holly Johnson, Bad News, D-Rok, Ian & Belinda, Rock Aid Armenia, Cozy Powell, Black Sabbath)
83 EMI EMI 5436 Starfleet (Single Version)/Son Of Starfleet (p/s) 15
91 Parlophone RDJ 6304 Driven By You (Edited Version)/(Pollarded Version)/(Special Version)/
(Proper Version) (promo only, no stars on p/s) 70
91 Parlophone CDR 6304 Driven By You (Single Version)/Driven By You (Ford Advert Version)/
Just One Life (Album Version)/Just One Life (Guitar Version) (CD) 8
91 Parlophone CDRDJ 6304 Driven By You (Edited Version)/(Pollarded Version)/(Special Version)/
(Proper Version) (CD, promo only, no stars on p/s) 100
92 Parlophone CDRS 6320 Too Much Love Will Kill You (Album Version)/I'm Scared (Single Version)/
Too Much Love Will Kill You (Guitar Version)/Driven By You (New Version)
(CD, red circular gatefold card p/s) 8
92 Parlophone MAYDJ 1 Too Much Love Will Kill You/Resurrection/Last Horizon/Driven By You
(CD, promo only "Back To The Light" sampler, blue circular g/fold card p/s) 15
92 Parlophone RDJ 6329 Back To The Light (Radio Version)/Nothin' But Blue (Guitar Version)
(promo only, p/s) 50
93 Parlophone 12RPF 6351 Resurrection/Love Token/Too Much Love Will Kill You (live)
(12", picture disc with insert) 8
93 Parlophone CDRS 6371 Last Horizon (Radio Edit)/Last Horizon (live)/Last Horizon (LP version)/
We Will Rock You (live) (CD, fold-out card sleeve) 8
98 Parlophone R 6504 Why Don't We Try Again/Only Make Believe/F.B.I. (picture disc with poster) 6
83 EMI SFLT 1078061 STARFLEET PROJECT (mini-LP) 12
93 Parlophone 0 7777 80400 19 BACK TO THE LIGHT (LP, textured sleeve) 15
93 Parlophone CDPCSD X123 BACK TO THE LIGHT (Commemorative Issue)
(gold CD, 10,000 only, stickered jewel case) 30
98 EMI 4949731 ANOTHER WORLD (LP, picture disc, with inner sleeve) 15

DERRICK MAY
90s R&S TMT 2 INNOVATOR (2xCD) 25

MARY MAY
64 Fontana TF 440 Anyone Who Had A Heart/They Say It's Wonderful 15

MINT VALUE £

JOHN MAYALL (& BLUESBREAKERS)

(see also Paul Butterfield, Eric Clapton, Jack Bruce, Peter Green, McGuinness Flint, Johnny Almond Music Machine, Alan Skidmore, Mick Taylor, Dick Heckstall-Smith, Keef Hartley, Paul Williams, Ray Warleigh, Colosseum, Henry Lowther, Jon Mark, Aynsley Dunbar, Fleetwood Mac)

SINGLES

64	Decca F 11900	Crawling Up A Hill/Mr. James (as John Mayall & Blues Breakers)	50
65	Decca F 12120	Crocodile Walk/Blues City Shakedown	40
65	Immediate IM 012	I'm Your Witchdoctor/Telephone Blues	50
66	Purdah 45-3502	Lonely Years/Bernard Jenkins (as John Mayall & Eric Clapton, 500 copies only)	300
66	Decca F 12490	Parchman Farm (solo)/Key To Love (B-side with Bluesbreakers)	25
66	Decca F 12506	Looking Back/So Many Roads (as John Mayall's Bluesbreakers & Peter Green)	15
67	Decca F 12545	Sitting In The Rain/Out Of Reach (as John Mayall's Bluesbreakers)	15
67	Decca F 12588	Curly/Rubber Duck (as Bluesbreakers)	12
67	Decca F 12621	Double Trouble/It Hurts Me Too (as John Mayall's Bluesbreakers)	20
67	Immediate IM 051	I'm Your Witchdoctor/Telephone Blues (reissue, as John Mayall with Eric Clapton)	25
67	Decca F 12684	Suspicions (Parts 1 & 2) (as John Mayall's Bluesbreakers)	12
68	Decca F 12732	Picture On The Wall/Jenny (as John Mayall)	12
68	Decca F 12792	No Reply/She's Too Young (as John Mayall's Bluesbreakers)	12
68	Decca F 12846	The Bear/2401	10
69	Polydor 56544	Don't Waste My Time/Don't Pick A Flower	12
70	Polydor 2066 021	Thinking Of My Woman/Plan Your Revolution	12

EPs

67	Decca DFE-R 8673	THE BLUESBREAKERS WITH PAUL BUTTERFIELD (EP)	50

LPs

65	Decca LK 4680	PLAYS JOHN MAYALL - LIVE AT KLOOKS KLEEK!	90
66	Decca LK 4804	BLUES BREAKERS WITH ERIC CLAPTON (original label, mono, "Beano" cover)	100
67	Decca LK/SKL 4853	A HARD ROAD (as John Mayall & Bluesbreakers)	40
67	Decca LK/SKL 4890	CRUSADE (as John Mayall & Bluesbreakers)	30
67	Ace of Clubs ACL/SCL 1243	THE BLUES ALONE	20
68	Decca LK/SKL 4918	THE DIARY OF A BAND VOL. 1	25
68	Decca LK/SKL 4919	THE DIARY OF A BAND VOL. 2	25
68	Decca LK/SKL 4945	BARE WIRES (gatefold sleeve, as John Mayall & Blues Breakers)	35
68	Decca LK/SKL 4972	BLUES FROM LAUREL CANYON (gatefold sleeve)	40

(The above LPs were originally issued with unboxed Decca label logos. 1970s boxed-logo repressing are worth half to two-thirds of these values)

69	Polydor 583 571	THE TURNING POINT	18
69	Decca LK/SKL 5010	LOOKING BACK	25
69	Decca SKL 4804	BLUES BREAKERS WITH ERIC CLAPTON (reissue, original label, stereo)	40
70s	Decca LK 4804	BLUES BREAKERS WITH ERIC CLAPTON (reissue, boxed logo, mono)	18
70s	Decca SKL 4804	BLUES BREAKERS WITH ERIC CLAPTON (reissue, boxed logo, stereo)	15
70	Decca (S)PA 47	THE WORLD OF JOHN MAYALL	12
70	Polydor 583 580	EMPTY ROOMS (with lyric insert)	15
70	Polydor 2425 020	U.S.A. UNION	12
71	Decca SPA 138	THE WORLD OF JOHN MAYALL VOL. 2	12
71	Polydor 2657 005	BACK TO THE ROOTS (2-LP)	30
71	Polydor 2483 016	BEYOND THE TURNING POINT	15
71	Decca SKL 5086	THRU THE YEARS	25
71	Polydor 2425 085	MEMORIES	15
72	Polydor 2425 103	JAZZ-BLUES FUSION	15
73	Polydor 2391 047	MOVING ON	12
75	ABC ABCL 5115	NEW YEAR, NEW BAND, NEW COMPANY (gatefold sleeve)	12
76	Polydor 2482 272	JOHN MAYALL	12

MAY BLITZ

(see also Jeff Beck,Boxer, Sounds Inc.)

70	Vertigo 6360 007	MAY BLITZ (LP, gatefold sleeve, large swirl label)	100
71	Vertigo 6360 037	THE 2ND OF MAY (LP, gatefold sleeve, swirl label)	200

MAYDAY

80	Reddingtons R.R. DAN 2	Day After Day/Love In The Spaceage (p/s)	20

MAYDAY

88	Kool Kat KOOL T14	NUDE PHOTO '88 EP (12")	30

JOHN MAYER (GROUP)

(see also Joe Harriott & John Mayer, Radha Krishna)

66	Columbia DB 8037	Acka Raga (as John Mayer's I-J-7)/Gana (as John Mayer & Joe Harriott)	8
60s	National Petrol W 1	Music For People Who Go Your Own Way Themes 1 & 2 (p/s, with Frank Cordell)	10
67	Columbia SX 6122	INDO-JAZZ FUSIONS (LP)	35
69	Sonet SNTF 603	ETUDES (LP, as John Mayer Indo-Jazz Fusions)	15

NATHANIEL MAYER & FABULOUS TWILIGHTS

62	HMV POP 1041	Village Of Love/I Want A Woman	55

CURTIS MAYFIELD

(see also Impressions)

70	Buddah 2011 055	(Don't Worry) If There's A Hell Below We're All Going To Go (Edit)/ The Makings Of You	8
71	Buddah 2011 080	Move On Up/Give It Up/Beautiful Brother Of Mine (maxi-single)	10
71	Buddah 2011 101	We Got To Have Peace/People Get Ready	6
72	Buddah 2011 119	Keep On Keepin' On/Stone Junkie	6
72	Buddah 2011 141	Freddie's Dead (Theme From "Superfly")/Underground	6
72	Buddah 2011 156	Superfly/Give Me Your Love (Love Song)	6
73	Buddah 2011 187	Back To The World (edit)/The Other Side Of Town	6
74	Buddah BDS 402	Kung Fu/Right On For The Darkness	6
74	Buddah BDS 410	Move On Up/Give It Up	8
75	Buddah BDS 426	Mother's Son/Love Me Right In The Pocket	6
71	Buddah 2318 015	CURTIS (LP, gatefold sleeve)	25
71	Buddah 2659 004	CURTIS/LIVE (2-LP)	20

MINT VALUE £

72 Buddah 2318 045 ROOTS (LP, gatefold sleeve) 15
72 Buddah 2318 065 SUPERFLY (LP, soundtrack, gatefold sleeve) 15
73 Buddah 2318 085 BACK TO THE WORLD (LP, gatefold sleeve). 12
73 Buddah 2318 091 CURTIS IN CHICAGO (LP, TV soundtrack, gatefold sleeve, with Impressions, Jerry Butler, Gene Chandler & Leroy Hutson). 15
74 Buddah BDLP 2001 CURTIS/LIVE (2-LP, reissue) 18
74 Buddah BDLP 4010 CLAUDINE (LP, soundtrack, with Gladys Knight) 15
74 Buddah BDLP 4015 MOVE ON UP (THE BEST OF CURTIS MAYFIELD) (LP) 12

PERCY MAYFIELD

63 HMV POP 1185 The River's Invitation/Baby Please. 10
76 Speciality SPE 5007 Please Send Me Someone To Love/The River's Invitation. 6
67 HMV CLP/CSD 3572 MY JUG AND I (LP). 40

MAYFIELD'S MULE

(see also Elastic Band, Sweet, Amen Corner, Andy Scott)

69 Parlophone R 5817 Double Dealing Woman/(Drinking My) Moonshine (in p/s). 30
69 Parlophone R 5817 Double Dealing Woman/(Drinking My) Moonshine 15
70 Parlophone R 5843 I See A River/"Queen" Of Rock'n'Roll 15
70 Parlophone R 5858 We Go Rollin'/My Way Of Living. 10

JUDY MAYHAN

71 Atlantic 2466006 MOMENTS (LP) 15

MAYHEM

85 Vigilante VIG 1 Bloodrush/Addictive Risk (p/s) 6
85 Vigilante VIG 1T Bloodrush/Addictive Risk (12", p/s) 10

MAYHEM

97 Misanthropy Amazon 012 WOLF'S LAIR ABYSS (LP). 30

JENNY MAYNARD

68 Inter-zel DR 001 He Gives Me Love/Something Here In My Heart 5

(TOOTS &) THE MAYTALS

(see also Vikings, Flames, Philip James & Blues Busters, Don Drummond, Stranger, Lord Creator, Larry Marshall, Derrick Morgan, Brentwood Road Allstars, Roland Alphonso, Charmers)

63 Blue Beat BB 176 Hallelujah/Helping Ages Past 20
64 Blue Beat BB 215 He Is Real/Domino 20
64 Blue Beat BB 220 Pain In My Belly/BUSTER'S ALL STARS: City Riot. 100
64 Blue Beat BB 231 Dog War/RECO & CREATORS: I'll Be Home 70
64 Blue Beat BB 245 Little Slea (song actually "Little Flea")/Don't Talk (song actually Pain In My Belly) (both sides miscredited as V. Maytals). 25
64 Blue Beat BB 254 Sweet Love/PRINCE BUSTER: Wings Of A Dove 30
64 Blue Beat BB 255 Judgement Day/Goodbye Jane 20
64 Blue Beat BB 270 You've Got Me Spinning/Lovely Walking 40
64 R&B JB 130 Hurry Up/Love Divide 20
64 R&B JB 141 Another Chance/FRANKIE ANDERSON: Always On A Sunday 20
64 R&B JB 153 Give Me Your Love/He Will Provide 20
64 R&B JB 164 Hello Honey/ROLAND ALPHONSO: Crime Wave 50
64 R&B JB 174 Christmas Feelings/Let's Kiss. 25
65 Blue Beat BB 281 Looking Down The Street/PRINCE BUSTER: Blues Market. 35
65 Blue Beat BB 299 Light Of The World/Lovely Walking 30
65 Blue Beat BB 306 Ska War (song actually "Treating Me Bad")/SKATALITES: Perhaps. 70
65 Ska Beat JB 202 Let's Jump/Joy And Jean. 20
65 Island WI 200 Never You Change/What's On Your Mind. 25
65 Island WI 213 My New Name/It's No Use 25
65 Black Swan WI 464 John James/THEO BECKFORD: Sailing On 25
66 Doctor Bird DB 1019 If You Act This Way/SIR LORD COMIC & HIS COWBOYS: Ska-ing West. 40
66 Doctor Bird DB 1038 Bam Bam/So Mad In Love (with Byron Lee and the Dragoniares) 35
68 Pyramid PYR 6030 54-46, That's My Number/ROLAND ALPHONSO: Dreamland. 30
68 Pyramid PYR 6043 Struggle/ROLAND ALPHONSO: Stream Of Life. 60
68 Pyramid PYR 6048 Just Tell Me/Reborn 20
68 Pyramid PYR 6050 Bim Today, Bam Tomorrow/Hold On. 25
68 Pyramid PYR 6052 We Shall Overcome/DESMOND DEKKER & ACES: Fu Manchu. 70
68 Pyramid PYR 6055 Schooldays/Big Man. 15
68 Pyramid PYR 6057 Do The Reggay/BEVERLEY'S ALLSTARS: Motoring 35
68 Pyramid PYR 6064 Scare Him/In My Heart 20
69 Pyramid PYR 6066 Don't Trouble Trouble/BEVERLEY'S ALLSTARS: Double Action 20
69 Pyramid PYR 6070 Aldina/Hold On 20
69 Pyramid PYR 6073 Pressure Drop/BEVERLEY'S ALLSTARS: Express. 15
69 Pyramid PYR 6074 Sweet And Dandy/Oh Yeah 15
69 Trojan TR 7709 Pressure Drop/BEVERLEY'S ALLSTARS: Smoke Screen 18
69 Nu Beat NB 031 My Testimony/JOHNSON BOYS: One Dollar Of Soul (actually by Ethiopians) . . . 12
69 Trojan TR 7711 Monkey Man/Night And Day 15
70 Trojan TR 7726 Sweet And Dandy/54-46, That's My Number 8
70 Trojan TR 7741 Bla Bla Bla/Reborn 6
70 Trojan TR 7757 Water Melon/She's My Scorcher 10
70 Trojan TR 7786 Doctor Lester/Sun, Moon And Star. 6
70 Summit SUM 8510 Peeping Tom/BEVERLEY'S ALLSTARS: Version. 8
71 Trojan TR 7808 54-46 Was My Number/BEVERLEY'S ALLSTARS: 54-46 Instrumental 8
71 Trojan TR 7849 Johnny Cool Man/BEVERLEY's ALLSTARS: Version. 8
71 Summit SUM 8513 Monkey Girl/BEVERLEY'S ALLSTARS: Version 8
71 Summit SUM 8520 One Eye Enos/BEVERLEY'S ALLSTARS: Enos Version. 6
71 Summit SUM 8527 It's You/BEVERLEY'S ALLSTARS: Version 6
71 Summit SUM 8529 Walk With Love/BEVERLEY'S ALLSTARS: Version 6
71 Summit SUM 8533 Never You Change/BEVERLEY'S ALLSTARS: Version. 6
72 Attack ATT 8042 It Was Written Down/Sweet And Dandy 5
72 Summit SUM 8536 Thy Kingdom Come/BEVERLEY'S ALLSTARS: Version. 6
72 Summit SUM 8537 It Must Be True Love/BEVERLEY'S ALLSTARS: Version 6

			MINT VALUE £
72	Blue Mountain BM 1020	Christmas Song/I Can't Believe	6
72	Dynamic DYN 438	Redemption Song	6
72	Trojan TR 7865	Louie Louie/Pressure Drop '72	5
73	Dragon DRA 1007	Sit Right Down/Screwface Underground/Pomps & Pride (as Toots & Maytals)	5
73	Dragon DRA 1013	Country Road/Funky Kingston (as Toots & Maytals)	12
73	Dragon DRA 1016	In The Dark/Sailing On (as Toots & Maytals)	5
74	Dragon DRA 1021	Fever/It Was Written Down	5
74	Dragon DRA 1024	Time Tough/Time Tough Version	5
74	Dragon DRA 1026	Sailing On/If You Act This Way (as Toots & Maytals)	5
64	Ska Beat JBL 1113	PRESENTING THE MAYTALS (NEVER GROW OLD) (LP)	225
66	Doctor Bird DLM 5003	THE SENSATIONAL MAYTALS (LP)	200
70	Trojan TBL 107	MONKEY MAN (LP, laminated front cover)	50
73	Trojan TRLS 65	FROM THE ROOTS (LP)	35
73	Dragon DRLS 5002	FUNKY KINGSTON (LP)	20
74	Dragon DRLS 5004	IN THE DARK (LP)	25
74	Prince Buster PB 11	ORIGINAL GOLDEN OLDIES VOLUME 3 (LP)	20
77	State ETAT16	TOOTS PRESENTS THE MAYTALS (LP)	15

MAYTONES

(see also Vern & Alvin, Vern & Son, Roland Alphonso, G.G. Rhythm Section, Cynthia Richards, Max Romeo, Charlie Ace, Dennis Alcapone)

68	Blue Cat BS 149	Billy Goat/Call You Up	40
69	Blue Cat BS 152	Loving Reggae/Musical Beat	40
69	Blue Cat BS 166	Copper Girl/Love	40
69	Blue Cat BS 173	We Nah Tek You Lick/Dig Away De Money	30
69	Camel CA 27	Sentimental Reason/Lover Girl	10
69	Songbird SB 1009	I've Been Loving You/Memphis Reggae	10
70	Punch PH 35	Serious Love/CHARLIE ACE: Musical Combination	10
70	Explosion EX 2012	Funny Man/G.G. ALLSTARS: Champion	10
70	Explosion EX 2013	Sentimental Reason/Lover Girl	7
70	Explosion EX 2014	Barrabus/G.G. ALLSTARS: Barrabus Part 2 (B-side actually "This Kind Of Life")	8
70	Explosion EX 2027	Cecelia (actually by Keeling Beckford)/Chariot Without Horse (B-side actually "Willie My Darling")	6
70	Explosion EX 2033	Another Festival/Happy Time	6
70	Bullet BU 446	I Don't Like To Interfere/Preaching Love	5
70	Camel CA 47	Black And White/GLORIA'S ALLSTARS: Jumbo Jet	10
70	Camel CA 49	Since You Left/GLORIA'S ALL STARS: Bird Wing	15
71	Duke DU 116	Babylon A Fall/TONY KING: Version Buggy	10
71	Camel CA 61	Judas (actually by Gladstone Anderson & Followers)/Mi Nah Tek	7
71	Camel CA 63	Cleanliness/Sister Hold On	20
71	G.G. GG 4508	Cleanliness/G.G. ALL STARS: Cleanliness Version 2	10
71	G.G. GG 4511	Let The Version Play/Lonely Nights	10
71	G.G. GG 4522	Black And White/TREVOR BROWN: Mr. Brown	6
71	G.G. GG 4525	Bongo Man Rise/ROY & BIM: Remember	6
72	G.G. GG 4530	Donkey Face/G.G. ALL STARS: Donkey Face - Version	8
72	G.G. GG 4531	As Long As You Love Me (Side One)/As Long As You Love Me (Side Two)	6
72	Attack ATT 8029	Hands And Feet/LLOYD & CAREY: Scorpion	6
72	Grape GR 3028	If Loving You Was Wrong/FLOWERS & ALVIN: In De Pum Pum	6
72	Pama PM 846	I'm Feeling Lonely/G.G. ALLSTARS: Version	6
72	Explosion EX 2076	Brown Girl/SHORTY PERRY: Half-Way-Tree Rock	6
73	Pama PM 871	All Over The World People Are Changing/Changing World (Dubwise)	5
73	Bread BR 1114	All Over The World People Are Changing/Changing World (Dubwise)	5
73	Bullet BU 528	People Get Funny/G.G. ALL STARS: Version	6
77	GG's GG 021	Money Trouble (with I Roy)/GG'S ALL STARS: Dub Part Two (12")	20

MAZE (U.K.)

(see also M.I. Five, Deep Purple)

66	Reaction 591 009	Hello Stranger/Telephone	75
67	MGM MGM 1368	Catari Catari/Easy Street	40

MAZZY STAR

93	R. T. Singles Club 45 rev 19	Five String Serenade/Under My Car (p/s)	20
94	Capitol 10CL720	Fade Into You/Five String Serenade/Under My Car/ Bells Ring (Acoustic) (10" p/s)	20
96	Capitol CL 781	FLOWERS IN DECEMBER (EP, blue vinyl)	20
90	Rough Trade ROUGH 158	SHE HANGS BRIGHTLY (LP)	60
93	Capitol EST2206	SO TONIGHT THAT I MIGHT SEE (LP)	60
96	Capitol 8272241	AMONG MY SWAN (LP)	40

M.B.P. MIX

69	Major Minor MM66	Light My Fire/There's A Baby	25

WINSTON McANUFF

79	Third World	I Love Jah/FREDDIE McGREGOR : Massachusetts (12")	30

JACKIE McAULEY

(see also Them, Belfast Gypsies, Trader Horne, Freaks Of Nature)

71	Dawn DNS 1011	Turning Green/It's Alright	8
72	Dawn DNS 1020	Rocking Shoes/One Fine Day	7
71	Dawn DNLS 3023	JACKIE McAULEY (LP, gatefold sleeve)	120

McAULEY SCHENKER GROUP

(see also Michael Schenker, Michael Schenker Group)

90	EMI EMPD 127	Anytime/What We Need/Anytime (Edit) (12", picture disc)	8

GERRY McAVOY

79	Bridgehouse BHS 004	Street Talk/Many Rivers To Cross (p/s)	10

JIMMY McBEATH

60	Collector JPSP	THY BALLADS (EP)	8
67	Topic 12T 173	WILD ROVER NO MORE (LP, blue label with booklet)	12

MINT VALUE £

CECIL McBEE

79	Inner City IC3023	MUSIC FROM THE SOURCE (LP)	15

NICKO McBRAIN

(see also Iron Maiden, Streetwalkers, Pat Travers)

91	EMI NICKO 1	Rhythm Of The Beast/Beehive Boogie (p/s)	6
91	EMI NICKOPD 1	Rhythm Of The Beast/McBrain Damage Interview (shaped picture disc with insert & plinth)	10

FRANKIE McBRIDE

67	Emerald MD 1081	Five Little Fingers/Do You Mind If You Leave Me Sleeping	6

DAN McCAFFERTY

(see also Nazareth, Sensational Alex Harvey Band, Mitchell/Coe Mysteries, Roger Glover)

75	Mountain TOP 5	Watcha Gonna Do About It/Nightingale	5
75	Mountain DAN 1	Stay With Me Baby/Out Of Time/Watcha Gonna Do About It (p/s)	7
79	Mountain TOP 47 DJ	Watcha Gonna Do About It/(7.30 maxi version)/ Boots Of Spanish Leather (12" promo)	10
75	Mountain TOPS 102	DAN McCAFFERTY (LP, with inner sleeve)	12

JERRY McCAIN

69	Python 02	Homogenised Love/728 Texas (99 copies only)	50

CASH McCALL

63	Ember EMB S 173	Anytime/From The Very First Rose	10
65	Ember EMB S 204	Many Are The Words (I've Left Unspoken)/Buenos Noches	12
67	Chess CRS 8056	It's Wonderful (To Be In Love)/Let's Try It Over	20

DARRELL McCALL

61	Capitol CL 15196	My Kind Of Lovin'/Beyond Imagination	8
63	Philips 304 002 BF	Dear One/I've Been Known	10
63	Philips BF 1259	Hud/No Place To Hide	7

TOUSSAINT McCALL

67	Pye International 7N 25420	Nothing Takes The Place Of You/Shimmy	20
72	Mojo 2092 035	Nothing Takes The Place Of You/Shimmy (reissue)	5

DAVID McCALLUM

66	Capitol CL 15439	Communication/My Carousel	12
66	Capitol CL 15474	In The Garden/The House On Breckenridge Lane	5
66	Capitol (S)T 2432	MUSIC ... A PART OF ME (LP)	25
66	Capitol (S)T 2498	MUSIC ... A BIT MORE OF ME (LP)	15

McCALMANS

68	One Up OU 2161	McCALMANS' FOLK (LP)	15
70	CBS 564145	TURN AGAIN (LP)	35

JIM McCANN

(see also Ludlows)

72	Polydor 2489 053	McCANNED! (LP)	40

LES McCANN (LTD)

60	Vogue V 2417	Fish This Week/Vakushna (as Les McCann Ltd)	5
67	Mercury MF 973	All/Bucket O'Grease	15
69	Atlantic 584 284	With These Hands/Burnin' Coal	15
60	Vogue LAE 12238	THE TRUTH (LP)	12
66	Mercury LML 4026	PLAYS THE HITS (LP, mono)	12
69	Atlantic 588 176	MUCH LES (LP)	12
60s	Fontana 688 150ZL	THE WAILERS! (with Gerald Wilson Orchestra)	12

DON McCARLOS

80	Negus Roots NERT 003	I Don't Care/I Love Jah (12")	45

McCARTHY

(see also Stereolab)

86	Wall Of Salmon MAC 001	In Purgatory/The Comrade Era/Something Wrong Somewhere (foldover p/s in poly bag, white labels)	20
86	Pink PINKY 12	Red Sleeping Beauty/From The Damned (stickered p/s)	8
86	Pink PINKY 12T	Red Sleeping Beauty/The Comrade Era/From The Damned/ For The Fat Lady (12", p/s with foldover insert)	8
87	Pink PINKY 17	Frans Hals/The Fall (p/s)	5
87	Pink PINKY 17T	Frans Hals/The Fall (Remix)/Kill Kill Kill Kill/Frans Hals (Version) (12", p/s)	8
87	September SEPT 1	The Well Of Loneliness/Antiamericancretin/Unfortunately (p/s)	6
87	September SEPT 1T	The Well Of Loneliness/Bad Dreams/Someone Worse Off/ Antiamericancretin/Unfortunately (12", p/s)	8
88	September SEPTT 4	This Nelson Rockefeller (p/s)	10

KEITH McCARTHY

67	Coxsone CS 7014	Everybody Rude Now/BASES: Beware	30

LYN & GRAHAM McCARTHY

65	Columbia DB 7584	Seven Doves/Out After Ale	6
66	Columbia DB 7921	I Can't Help But Wonder/There's Got To Be Love	6
66	Columbia DB 8087	The Turkey's Trial/Bitter Withy	6
68	Columbia DB 8422	I Think It's Going To Rain/Once I Was	7
68	RCA RCA 1759	Scarborough Fair - Canticle/Wild Berries	5

MARY McCARTHY

67	CBS 2832	The Folk I Love/You Know He Did	100
67	CBS 2987	Happy Days And Lonely Night/Easy Kind Of Love	70

CECIL McCARTNEY

68	Columbia DB 8474	Hey Aleuthia I Want You/Liquid Blue	25
69	Columbia DB 8595	Orange And Green/Cloudy	15
68	Columbia S(C)X 6283	OM (LP, first pressing with blue/black label with "Sold in UK..." text)	150
60s	Columbia S(C)X 6283	OM (LP, second pressing with black/silver label, boxed logo)	40

MINT VALUE £

LINDA McCARTNEY

(see under Suzy & The Red Stripes)

PAUL McCARTNEY/WINGS

(see also Beatles, Country Hams, Percy 'Thrills' Thrillington, Fireman, Mike McGear, Suzy & The Red Stripes, George Martin, Spirit Of Play, Ferry Aid, Michael Jackson)

SINGLES

71	Apple R 5889	Another Day/Oh Woman, Oh Why	8
71	Apple R 5914	The Back Seat Of My Car/Heart Of The Country (as Paul & Linda McCartney)	10
72	Apple R 5932	Love Is Strange/I Am Your Singer (unreleased)	1500
72	Apple R 5936	Give Ireland Back To The Irish/(Version) (as Wings, yellow 'Wings' die-cut sl.)	10
72	Apple R 5949	Mary Had A Little Lamb/Little Woman Love (p/s)	10
72	Apple R 5949	Hi Hi Hi/C Moon	6
73	Apple R 5985	My Love/The Mess (as McCartney's Wings)	20
73	Apple R 5985	My Love/The Mess (as McCartney's Wings, later pressing as Paul McCartney/Wings)	5
73	Apple R 5987	Live And Let Die/I Lie Around	6
73	Apple R 5993	Helen Wheels/Country Dreamer	6
74	Apple R 5996	Jet/Let Me Roll It	6
74	EMI R 5997	Band On The Run/Zoo Gang	10
74	Apple R 5999	Juniors Farm/Sally G	8
75	Capitol R 6006	Listen To What The Man Said/Love In Song (p/s)	6
75	Capitol R 6008	Letting Go/You Gave Me The Answer	8
75	Capitol R 6010	Venus And Mars; Rock Show/Magneto And Titanium Man	8
76	Parlophone R 6015	Let 'Em In/Beware My Love	5
78	Parlophone R 6018	Mull Of Kintyre/Girls School (yellow juke box 'Best selling British single ever' p/s)	60
78	Parlophone R 6020	I've Had Enough/Deliver Your Children (p/s, as Wings)	10
79	Parlophone R6026	Old Siam Sir/Spin It On (die-cut p/s)	5
80	Parlophone 12R 6039	Temporary Secretary/Secret Friend (12", p/s)	30
82	Parlophone R 6054	Ebony And Ivory/Rainclouds (unreleased sepia-toned 'studio photo' p/s; beware of clever counterfeits)	50
82	Epic A 11-2729	The Girl Is Mine (with Michael Jackson)/MICHAEL JACKSON: Can't Get Outta The Rain (picture disc)	15
82	Parlophone R 6057	Tug Of War/Get It (p/s)	5
84	Parlophone 12RP 6080	No More Lonely Nights (Extended Version)/Silly Love Songs/ No More Lonely Nights (Ballad) (12", picture disc)	20
84	Parlophone RP 6086	We All Stand Together/We All Stand Together (Humming Version) (with Frog Chorus, shaped picture disc, in printed PVC sleeve)	15
85	Parlophone RP 6118	Spies Like Us/My Carnival (shaped picture disc)	15
85	Parlophone 12RP 6118	Spies Like Us (Party Mix)/Spies Like Us (Alternative Mix)/Spies Like Us (DJ Version)/My Carnival (Party Mix) (12", picture disc)	20
86	Parlophone 10R 6133	Press/It's Not True/Press (Video Edit) (10", circular foldout p/s)	12
86	Parlophone R 6133	Press (video edit)/It's Not True (P/s)	10
86	Parlophone R 6145	Pretty Little Head/Write Away (p/s)	5
86	Parlophone R 6148/ R 6018	Only Love Remains/Tough On A Tightrope//Mull Of Kintyre/Girls' School (p/s, stickered double pack in PVC sleeve, no p/s on R 6018)	8
87	Parlophone CDR 6170	Once Upon A Long Ago/Back On My Feet/Don't Get Around Much Anymore/ Kansas City (CD, card sleeve with anti-static inner)	15
87	A&M FREE 21	Long Tall Sally (live)/I Saw Her Standing There (live) (p/s, free with "The Prince's Trust 10th Anniversary Birthday Party" LP [AMA 3906])	6
89	Parlophone RX 6223	This One/The Long And Winding Road (p/s, envelope pack with 6 postcards)	12
89	Parlophone R 6238	Party Party (1 side etched, p/s)	10
92	Parlophone R 6330	Hope Of Deliverance/Long Leather Coat (p/s)	5
97	Parlophone RP 6472	The World Tonight/Used To Be Bad (Picture disc)	6
97	Parlophone RP 6489	Beautiful Night/Love Come Tumbling Down (picture disc)	10
99	Parlophone R 6257	No Other Baby/Brown Eyed Handsome Man	5
01	Parlophone R 6567	From A Lover To A Friend/Riding Into Jaipur (p/s)	5
04	Parlophone R6649	Tropic Island Hum/We All Stang Together (p/s, yellow vinyl)	5
05	Parlophone R 6673	Fine Line/Growing Up Falling Down (p/s, plus art print)	5
05	Parlophone R 6678	Jenny Wren/Summer Of '59 (red vinyl, p/s)	5
05	GRA2010	Really Love You/Lalula (1-side etched, McCartney remixes by TWIN FREAKS 2,500 only)	20
07	Hear Music 88072306219	Ever Present Past/House Of Wax (live) (p/s)	5

PROMO SINGLES

74	EMI R 5997	Band On The Run (Edited Version)/(Full Version) (demo)	150
74	Apple R 5999	Junior's Farm (Edited Version)/Junior's Farm (Full Version) (demo)	100
75	Apple R 5999	Sally G/Junior's Farm (reversed sides, demo)	120
76	Parlophone R 6014	Silly Love Songs (Edited Version)/Silly Love Songs (Full Version) (demo)	50
76	Parlophone R 6015	Let 'Em In (Edited Version)/Let 'Em In (Full Version) (demo)	50
77	Capitol R 6018	Mull Of Kintyre (Edited Version)/Girls' School (Edited Version) (demo)	50
77	MPL Publishing MPL 1	We've Moved! (music publishing sampler with excerpts by Wings, Peggy Lee, Gene Vincent, Frank Sinatra, etc.; with press pack and insert)	350
77	MPL Publishing MPL 1	We've Moved! (music publishing sampler with excerpts by Wings, Peggy Lee, Gene Vincent, Frank Sinatra, etc.; without press pack and insert)	250
78	Parlophone R 6019	With A Little Luck (Edited Version)/Backwards Traveller-Cuff Link (demo)	40
80	Parlophone R 6037DJ	Waterfalls (3.22) (edit)/Check My Machine (demo)	40
80	Parlophone R 6039A	Temporary Secretary (1-sided demo, no p/s)	75
84	Parlophone 12RDJ 6080T	No More Lonely Nights (Mole Mix) (12", 1-sided, plain white numbered sleeve with plain white inner sleeve & insert, 250 only; beware of counterfeits with scratched [not stamped] matrix)	250
84	Parlophone 12R(DJ) 6080	No More Lonely Nights (Extended Version)/Silly Love Songs/ No More Lonely Nights (Ballad) (12", promo, blue 'Give My Regards To Broad Street' label, black die-cut sleeve)	50
85	Parlophone RDJ 6118	Spies Like Us (DJ Version 3.46)/My Carnival (demo, white printed die-cut sleeve)	30
88	Parlophone PMBOX 11-19	ALL THE BEST! ('Special Edition') (9 x 7" box set, in black die-cut sleeves, with signed 7" print; with genuine signatures)	200

			MINT VALUE £
88	Parlophone PMBOX 11-19	ALL THE BEST! ('Special Edition') (9 x 7" box set, in black die-cut sleeves, with signed 7" print)	75
89	Parl. 12R LOVE 6223	This One (Lovejoy's Remix) (12", 1-sided, plain label, black die-cut sleeve)	35
89	Parlophone GOOD 1	Good Sign (6.51)/Good Sign (Groove Mix) (7.22) (12", black die-cut sleeve)	45
89	Parlophone RDJ 6235	Figure Of Eight (Edited Version 3.59)/Ou Est Le Soleil? (Edited Version 3.57) (demo, standard p/s)	30
89	Parlophone RDJ 6238	Party (Remix By Bruce Forest)/Party (different remix) (12", some listed as 'Party Party', with insert)	40
89	Parlophone RDJ 6238	Party (Remix By Bruce Forest)/Party (different remix) (12")	30
90	Parlophone 12 SOL 1	Où Est Le Soleil? (Tub Dub Mix)/Où Est Le Soleil? (Instrumental Mix) (12", black die-cut stickered sleeve, with insert)	40
90	Parlophone 12 SOL 1	Où Est Le Soleil? (Tub Dub Mix)/Où Est Le Soleil? (Instrumental Mix) (12", black die-cut stickered sleeve, some without insert)	20
93	Parlophone 12 DELIVDJ 1	Deliverance/Deliverance (Dub Mix) (12", green label, plain black die-cut sleeve)	20
93	Parlophone CDRDJ 6338	C'mon People (Radio Edit)/C'mon People (CD)	30
93	Parlophone CDRS 6347	Biker Like An Icon/Things We Said Today/Mean Woman Blues/ Midnight Special (CD, unissued)	0
93	Parlophone CDRDJ 6347	Biker Like An Icon/Things We Said Today/Mean Woman Blues/ Midnight Special (CD, no inlay, jewel case with large sticker; beware of counterfeits with thicker blurred label print & smaller sticker on case)	70
99	Parlophone RDR03	Run Devil Run/Blue Jean Bop (mock 50's Parlophone label/sleeve)	30
01	WINDJ 002	Silly Love Songs (Loop Da Loop Mix)/Coming Up (Linus Loves Mix) (12" 50 copies)	150
03	Parlophone TEMPSEC 01	Temporary Secretary (Re-edited by Audioslave) (12", 1-sided)	20

LPs

70	Apple PCS 7102	McCARTNEY (LP, gatefold sleeve)	25
70	Apple TA 7102	McCARTNEY (reel-to-reel tape, jewel case, mono)	100
70	Apple TD-PCS 7102	McCARTNEY (reel-to-reel tape, jewel case, stereo)	50
71	Apple PAS 10003	RAM (LP, gatefold sleeve)	20
71	Apple PCS 7142	WILDLIFE (LP, sleeve with 'sniped' spine edges, flipbacks, yellow inner)	25
73	Apple PCTC 251	RED ROSE SPEEDWAY (LP, gatefold sleeve, with booklet and poster)	70
73	Apple PCTS 251	RED ROSE SPEEDWAY (LP, gatefold sleeve, without booklet and poster)	25
73	Apple PAS 10007	BAND ON THE RUN (LP, with lyric inner sleeve & poster)	20
75	Capitol PCTC 254	VENUS AND MARS (LP, gatefold sleeve, inner sleeve, 2 posters & stickers)	30
75	Capitol PCTC 254	VENUS AND MARS (LP, gatefold sleeve, inner sleeve)	12
84	Fame FA 413100-1	McCARTNEY (LP, gatefold sleeve)	15
84	Fame FA 416101-1	WINGS - WILD LIFE (LP, yellow inner)	12
84	Nimbus PAS 10007	BAND ON THE RUN (LP, with 'Nimbus' sticker)	60
87	Fame FA 3191	RED ROSE SPEEDWAY (LP, gatefold sleeve)	12
89	Parlophone PCSDX 106	FLOWERS IN THE DIRT (LP, World Tour pack with outer folder, 'Part' 7" single, poster, familty tree, sticker, postcards & tour itinary)	40
91	EMI PAUL 1	LIVERPOOL ORATORIO (2-LP, in box with booklet with Carl Davis and others)	20
93	Parlophone PCSD 125	OFF THE GROUND (LP, gatefold)	20
93	Parlophone PCSD 147	PAUL IS LIVE (2 x LP)	30
97	Parlophone PCSD 171	FLAMING PIE (LP, gatefold)	30
99	Parlophone 4991761	BAND ON THE RUN (2 x LP, gatefold, 25th Anniversary)	25
99	Parlophone 5223511	RUN DEVIL RUN (LP, gatefold)	30
99	Parlophone 5232291	RUN DEVIL RUN (8 x 7", box set with booklet)	40
99	EMI Classics 5568971	WORKING CLASSICAL (2 x LP, gatefold)	25
01	Parlophone 5328501	WINGSPAN (3 x LP, gatefold)	20
01	Parlophone 5355101	DRIVING RAIN (2 x LP)	20
05	Parlophone 3383452	CHAOS AND CREATION IN THE BACKYARD (LP, gatefold with 4 art prints)	20

PROMO ALBUMS

79	Parlophone PCTCP 257	BACK TO THE EGG (LP, as Wings, MPL in-house picture disc; die-cut sleeve, matrix numbers YEX 987-2 & YEX 988-4 or -1; beware counterfeits)	900
79	Parlophone PCTC 257	BACK TO THE EGG (LP, box set with badge, booklet, sticker, postcard & 5 cigarette cards; with or without T-shirt; beware of counterfeits with blurred printing)	300
79	Capitol (no cat. no.)	MPL PRESENTS (6-LP, box set, hand-numbered, 25 only)	700
93	Parlophone CDPMCOLDJ 1	PAUL McCARTNEY COLLECTION (CD, 18-track sampler)	25

CAROLINE McCAUSLAND

60s	Happy Face MMLP 1022	SONGS FOR GALA (LP)	40

DAVE McCLAREN

71	Big BG 323	Love Is What I Bring (actually by Dave Barker & Uniques)/ RUPIE EDWARDS ALL STARS: Love Version (with U Roy Junior)	18

TOMMY McCLENNAN

75	Flyright LP 112	TRAVELIN' HIGHWAY MAN (LP)	15

DELBERT McCLINTON

62	Decca F 11541	Hully Gully/Baby Heartbreak	12

BOBBY McCLURE

(se under Bobby Mclure)

CHRIS McCLURE (SECTION)

(see also Marmalade)

66	Decca F 12346	The Dying Swan/The Land Of The Golden Tree	10
68	Polydor 56227	Hazy People/I'm Just A Country Boy	15
68	Polydor 56259	Answer To Everything/Meditation	7
69	RCA RCA 1849	Our Song Of Love/Weather Vane	7
69	CBS 7646	You're Only Passing Time/Sing Our Song (as Chris McClure Section)	8

BRIAN McCOLLOM FOLK GROUP

66	Pye 7N 17198	This Dusty Road/Henry Joy McCraken	6

MINT VALUE £

TOMMY McCOOK (& SUPERSONICS)

(see also Denis Alcapone, Dave Barker, Dennis Brown, Chuck & Joe White, Shenley Duffas, Dennis & Lizzy, Dobby Dobson, Dynamics, Alton Ellis, Ethiopians, Eagles, Emotions, Herman, Heptones, Jamaicans, Hopeton Lewis, Lloyd & Glen, Lloyd & Groovers, Bob Marley, Maytals, Melodians, Mellodites, Millions, Paragons, Hugh Roy, Karl Walker Allstars)

63	Island WI 102	Adam's Apple/MAYTALS: Every Time (B-side actually by Tonettes)	25
63	Island WI 118	Below Zero/LEE PERRY: Never Get Weary	40
63	Island WI 124	Junior Jive/HORACE SEATON: Power	25
64	R&B JB 139	Sampson/ROY & ANNETTE: My Arms Are Waiting	50
64	R&B JB 163	Bridge View/NAOMI & CO: What Can I Do (B-side actually by Naomi & Clive)	45
64	Port-O-Jam PJ 4001	Exodus (& His Group)/LEE PERRY: Help The Weak	40
64	Port-O-Jam PJ 4003	Jam Rock/LEE PERRY: Band Minded People	40
64	Port-O-Jam PJ 4010	Road Bloack/LEE PERRY: Chatty Chatty Woman	70
64	Black Swan WI 422	Two For One/LASCELLES PERKINS: I Don't Know	25
65	Island WI 232	Rocket Ship/JUSTIN HINDS & DOMINOES: Turn Them Back	50
66	Rio R 100	Jerk Time (with Supersonics)/UNIQUES: The Journey	70
66	Rio R 101	Out Of Space (with Supersonics)/UNIQUES: Do Me Good	40
66	Rio R 103	Ska Jam/Smooth Sailing (with Supersonics)	80
66	Rio R 104	Riverton City/HEPTONES: Gunmen Coming To Town	70
66	Doctor Bird DB 1028	More Love/SILVERTONES: True Confession	35
66	Doctor Bird DB 1032	Naked City (with Supersonics)/NORMA FRASER: Heartaches	30
66	Doctor Bird DB 1047	Spanish Eyes (with Lynn Taitt)/STRANGER & HORTENSE: Loving Wine	20
66	Doctor Bird DB 1051	A Little Bit Of Heaven (& His Band)/LLOYD WILLIAMS: Sad World	25
66	Doctor Bird DB 1053	Indian Love Call (with Supersonics)/OWEN & LEON: How Would You Feel	25
66	Doctor Bird DB 1056	Danger Man (with Supersonics)/ERIC MORRIS: If I Didn't Love You	40
66	Doctor Bird DB 1061	What Now/Don't Stay Away	60
67	Doctor Bird DB 1058	Jam Session (with Supersonics)/LLOYD & GLEN: Jezebel	45
67	Island WI 3047	One Two Three Kick/TREASURE ISLE BOYS: What A Fool (B-side actually by Silvertones)	50
67	Island WI 3049	Saboo (with Supersonics)/MOVING BROTHERS: Darling I Love You	40
67	Treasure Isle TI 7017	Persian Cat/JUSTIN HINDS: Once A Man	20
67	Treasure Isle TI 7018	Saboo (with Supersonics)/MOVING BROTHERS: Darling I Love You (reissue)	25
67	Treasure Isle TI 7020	Shadow Of Your Smile/SILVERTONES: Cool Down	25
68	Treasure Isle TI 7027	Soul For Sale/SILVERTONES: In The Midnight Hour	20
68	Treasure Isle TI 7032	Venus/Music Is My Occupation (with Supersonics)	20
68	Treasure Isle TI 7039	Our Man Flint (with Supersonics)/SILVERTONES: Old Man River	50
68	Treasure Isle TI 7042	Moving (with Supersonics)/SILVERTONES: Slow And Easy	20
68	Doctor Bird DB 1135	Mad Mad World/Wonderful World (with Lloyd Williams)	30
68	Unity UN 501	Last Flight To Reggie (Reggae) City (with Stranger Cole)/Watch Dem Go	20
69	Trojan TR 642	Breaking Up/Party Time (with Supersonics) (both actually by Alton Ellis)	10
69	Trojan TR 652	Third Figure/You Should've Known Better	15
69	Trojan TR 657	When The Saints Go Marching In/SOUL OFROUS: Ease Me Up Officer (B-side actually by Righteous Flames)	15
69	Trojan TR 671	Moonshot/PHYLLIS DILLON: The Right Shot	15
69	Trojan TR 686	Tribute To Rameses/PHYLLIS DILLION: Lipstick On Your Collar	12
69	Trojan TR 7706	Black Coffee (with Supersonics)/VIC TAYLOR: Heartaches	12
69	Unity UN 506	The Avengers/LAUREL AITKEN: Donkey Man	20
69	Unity UN 534	Dream Boat/Tommy's Dream	20
69	Unity UN 535	Peanut Vendor/100,000 Tons Of Rock	20
70	Duke DU 76	The Rooster (with Supersonics) (actually by Jeff Barnes)/ PHYLLIS DILLON: Walk Through This World	10
70	Duke DU 77	Open Jaw (with Supersonics)/JOHN HOLT: The Working Kind	10
70	Duke DU 78	Key To The City (with Supersonics)/DOROTHY REID: Give It To Me	10
71	Treasure Isle TI 7058	My Best Dress/PHYLISS DILLON: One Life To Live	15
71	Treasure Isle TI 7061	Testify Version/JOHN HOLT: Let's Build Our Dreams	18
71	Treasure Isle TI 7065	Black River/JOHN HOLT: Sister Big Stuff	20
71	Treasure Isle TI 7066	Paragon's Medley Version/JOHN HOLT: Paragon's Medley	18
71	Treasure Isle TI 7070	Midnight Confession Version/PHYLLIS DILLON: Midnight Confession	15
71	Big Shot BI 585	Psalm Nine To Keep In Mind (with Observers)/Psalm Nine (Version)	10
71	Spinning Wheel SW 109	Crying Everynight (with Supersonics) (actually by Stranger Cole)/ HERMAN MARQUIS: Tom's Version	40
71	Spinning Wheel SW 110	Stupid Doctor (with Supersonics)/ROB WALKER: Grooving In Style (B-side actually by Ken Parker)	60
73	Technique TE 927	Rub It Down/Rub It Down (Version) (as Tommy McCook Stars)	6
73	G.G. GG 4539	Bad Cow Skank (with Bobby Ellis)/ GLADSTONE ANDERSON: Drummer Roach	5
75	Vulcan VUL 1002	Kojak/Cannon (with Aggrovators)	5
79	Grove Music GMDM 26	Sensimena/TONY TUFF: You Wrong (12")	20
70	Trojan TBL 111	GREATER JAMAICA (MOONWALK REGGAE) (LP, actually by various artists)	30
74	Attack ATLP 1007	TOMMY McCOOK (LP)	30
77	Third World TWS 920	HOT LAVA (LP)	25
77	Justice JUS LP 07	INSTRUMENTAL (LP)	45

TOMMY McCOOK & GLEN BROWN

76	Groundation GROL 10	HORNY DUB (LP, white label)	300

TOMMY McCOOK & BOBBY ELLIS

75	Grove Music GMLP 002	BLAZING HORNS (LP)	40

JASON McCORD

65	Pye 7N 15925	It Was A Very Good Year/Song Of The Pine Tree	35

McCORMICK BROTHERS

63	Polydor NH 66986	Red Hen Boogie/Blue Grass Express	50
66	Hickory LPE 1509	AUTHENTIC BLUEGRASS HITS (EP)	22

GEORGE McCORMICK

55	MGM SPC 6	Don't Fix Up The Doghouse/Gold Wedding Band (export issue)	18

BUDD McCOY

58	RCA RCA 1106	Hiawatha/The Midnight Ride Of Paul Revere	5

MINT VALUE £

CLYDE McCOY
57 Mercury MEP 9513 — DANCING TO THE BLUES (EP) — 15

JOE McCOY
(see also Gillan, Samson, Mammoth, Zzebra, Split Knee Loons)
59 Collector JDL 81 — One In A Hundred/One More Greasing — 30

(JOHN) McCOY
83 Legacy LGY 9 — Oh Well! (Edit)/Because You Lied (p/s) — 5
84 Mausoleum SKULL 8373 — THINK HARD (LP, with inner sleeve) — 12

VIOLA McCOY
50s Ristic LP 27 — VIOLA McCOY 1923-1927 (10" LP) — 60

McCOYS
(see also Rick Derringer)
65 Immediate IM 001 — Hang On Sloopy/I Can't Explain It — 8
65 Immediate IM 021 — Fever/Sorrow — 12
66 Immediate IM 028 — Don't Worry Mother, Your Son's Heart Is Pure/Ko-Ko — 10
66 Immediate IM 029 — Up And Down/If You Tell A Lie — 10
66 Immediate IM 034 — Runaway/Come On Let's Go — 10
66 Immediate IM 037 — (You Make Me Feel) So Good/Every Day I Have To Cry — 8
67 Immediate IM 046 — I Got To Go Back/Dynamite — 15
67 London HLZ 10154 — Say Those Magic Words/I Wonder If She Remembers Me — 25
68 Mercury MF 1067 — Jesse Brady/Resurrection — 8
69 Immediate IM 076 — Hang On Sloopy/This Is Where We Came In — 5
66 Immediate IMEP 002 — HITS VOL. 1 (EP) — 40
66 Immediate IMEP 003 — HITS VOL. 2 (EP) — 40
65 Immediate IMLP 001 — HANG ON SLOOPY (LP) — 55
68 Mercury (S)MCL 20128 — THE INFINITE McCOYS (LP) — 40
71 Joy JOYS 196 — HANG ON SLOOPY (LP, reissue) — 15

JIMMY McCRACKLIN
58 London HLM 8598 — The Walk/I'm To Blame (as Jimmy McCracklin & His Band) — 50
58 London HLM 8598 — The Walk/I'm To Blame (as Jimmy McCracklin & His Band) (78) — 20
58 London HL 7035 — The Walk/I'm To Blame (export issue, as Jimmy McCracklin & His Band) — 40
62 Top Rank JAR 617 — Just Got To Know/The Drag — 25
65 R&B MRB 5001 — I Got Eyes For You/I'm Gonna Tell Your Mother — 25
66 Outasite 45 120 — Christmas Time (Parts 1 & 2) (99 copies only) — 60
65 Liberty LIB 66094 — Every Night, Every Day/Can't Raise Me — 12
66 Liberty LIB 66129 — Think/Steppin' Up In Class — 12
68 Minit MLF 11003 — How Do You Like Your Love/Get Together — 10
68 Minit MLF 11009 — Pretty Little Sweet Thing/A And I — 10
65 Vocalion VEP 170160 — JIMMY McCRACKLIN (EP) — 100
68 Minit MLL/MLS 40003 — A PIECE OF JIMMY McCRACKLIN (LP) — 40

GWEN McCRAE
74 President PT 416 — It's Worth The Hurt/90% Of Me Is You — 20
82 Atlantic FLAM 1 — Keep The Fire Burning/Funky Sensation — 10
82 Atlantic FLAM 1T — Keep The Fire Burning/Funky Sensation (12") — 25
75 President — GWEN McCRAE (LP) — 20

DANNY McCULLOCH
(see also Animals)
69 Capitol CL 15607 — Blackbird/Time Of Man — 6
70 Pye Intl./Festival 7N 25514 — Colour Of The Sunset/Smokeless Zone — 6
69 Capitol E-(S)T 174 — WINGS OF A MAN (LP, black/silver label with boxed logo) — 40

IAN McCULLOCH
64 Decca F11855 — Come On Home/Down By The River — 40

HENRY McCULLOUGH
(see also Grease Band, Eire Apparent, Paul McCartney & Wings)
75 Dark Horse AMLH 22005 — MIND YOUR OWN BUSINESS! (LP, some with inner sleeve) — 12

ED MCCURDY
60s Elektra ELK 110 — WHEN DALLIANCE WAS IN FLOWER AND MAIDENS LOST THEIR HEADS (LP, with insert) — 40
60s Elektra ELK 140 — WHEN DALLIANCE WAS IN FLOWER VOL 2 (LP) — 40

GEORGE McCURN
63 London HLH 9705 — I'm Just A Country Boy/In My Little Corner Of The World — 10

LUKE McDANIEL
55 Parlophone CMSP 29 — The Automobile Song/I Can't Steal Another's Bride (export issue) — 40
55 Parlophone DP 407 — The Automobile Song/I Can't Steal Another's Bride (78) — 12

MAISIE McDANIEL
(see also Hunters)
61 Beltona BE 2744 — Christmastime In Ireland/The Old Pigsty — 5
63 Fontana TF 400 — Something Special/This Song Is Just For You — 5
63 Fontana TE 17397 — MEET MAISIE McDANIEL! (EP, with The Hunters) — 15
63 Fontana TE 17398 — COUNTRY STYLE (EP, with The Hunters) — 15
65 Fontana TL 5215 — ARE YOU LONESOME TONIGHT (LP) — 15

EUGENE McDANIELS
71 Atlantic 2465 022 — OUTLAW (LP) — 30

GENE McDANIELS
61 London HLG 9319 — A Hundred Pounds Of Clay/Take A Chance On Love — 12
61 London HLG 9396 — A Tear/She's Come Back — 20
61 London HLG 9448 — Tower Of Strength/Secret — 12
62 Liberty LIB 55405 — Chip Chip/Another Tear Falls — 10
62 Liberty LIB 55480 — Point Of No Return/Warmer Than A Whisper — 15

MINT VALUE £

63	Liberty LIB 55510	Spanish Lace/Somebody's Waiting	7
63	Liberty LIB 55541	The Puzzle/Cry Baby Cry	7
63	Liberty LIB 55597	It's A Lonely Town/False Friends	30
63	Liberty LIB 10130	Anyone Else/New Love In Old Mexico	8
64	Liberty LIB 55723	In Times Like These/Make Me A Present Of You	15
65	Liberty LIB 55752	(There Goes The) Forgotten Man	40
65	Liberty LIB 55805	Walk With A Winner/A Miracle	100
65	Liberty LIB 55805	Walk With A Winner/A Miracle (DJ copy)	250
61	London REG 1298	GENE McDANIELS (EP)	60
62	Liberty LEP 2054	A CHANGE OF MOOD (EP)	40
61	London HA-G 2384	A HUNDRED POUNDS OF CLAY (LP, mono)	80
61	London SAH-G 6184	A HUNDRED POUNDS OF CLAY (LP, stereo)	100
62	Liberty LBY 1003	... SOMETIMES I'M HAPPY (LP)	40
62	Liberty LBY 1021	TOWER OF STRENGTH (LP)	40
63	Liberty (S)LBY 1128	SPANISH LACE (LP)	40
63	Liberty LBY 1179	THE WONDERFUL WORLD OF GENE McDANIELS (LP)	40
68	Sunset SLS 50017E	FACTS OF LIFE (LP)	15

BILL McDAVID

61	Starlite ST45 63	Kiss Me For Christmas/Little Shepherd Boy	8

McDERMOTTS

89	Hag HAGLP 2	THE ENEMY WITHIN (LP)	12

CHAS McDEVITT (SKIFFLE GROUP)

(see also Nancy Whiskey, Cranes Skiffle Group, Coffee Bar Skifflers)

57	Oriole CB 1352	Freight Train (with Nancy Whiskey)/The Cotton Song	20
57	Oriole CB 1357	It Takes A Worried Man/The House Of The Rising Sun	15
57	Oriole CB 1371	Green Back Dollar (with Nancy Whiskey)/I'm Satisfied	12
57	Oriole CB 1386	Face In The Rain (with Nancy Whiskey)/Sporting Life (with Tony Kohn)	15
57	Oriole CB 1395	Sing, Sing, Sing/My Old Man	15
58	Oriole CB 1403	Johnny-O (with Nancy Whiskey)/Bad Man Stack-O-Lee	15
58	Oriole CB 1405	Across The Bridge (with Shirley Douglas)/Deep Down	15
58	Oriole CB 1457	Real Love (with Shirley Douglas)/Juke-Box Jumble	25
59	Oriole CB 1511	Teenage Letter (with Shirley Douglas)/SHIRLEY DOUGLAS: Sad Little Girl	12
59	Oriole CB 1511	Teenage Letter (with Shirley Douglas)/SHIRLEY DOUGLAS: Sad Little Girl (78)	15
60	Top Rank JAR 338	Dream Talk/Forever (with Shirley Douglas)	10
61	HMV POP 845	One Love/Can It Be Love (with Shirley Douglas)	5
61	HMV POP 928	Mommy Out De Light/I've Got A Thing About You (with Shirley Douglas)	5
62	HMV POP 999	Happy Family/Throwing Pebbles In A Pool (with Shirley Douglas)	5
65	Columbia DB 7595	The Most Of What Is Least/Don't Blame Me (with Shirley Douglas)	5
68	Fontana TF 957	City Smoke/One Man Band	5
57	Oriole EP 7002	CHAS AND NANCY (EP, with Nancy Whiskey)	20
57	Oriole MG 10018	THE INTOXICATING MISS WHISKEY (10" LP, with Nancy Whiskey)	45
65	Columbia 33SX 1738	SIXTEEN BIG FOLK HITS (LP, with Shirley Douglas)	15

ALISTAIR McDONALD

69	Major Minor MMLP 51	BATTLE BALLADS (LP)	15

(COUNTRY) JOE McDONALD

71	Vanguard 6076 252	Hold On It's Coming Parts 1 & 2	6
70	Vanguard (S)VRL 19057	THINKING OF WOODY GUTHRIE (LP)	12
71	Vanguard 6359 004	TONIGHT I'M SINGING JUST FOR YOU (LP)	15
71	Sonet SNTF 622	QUIET DAYS IN CLICHY (LP, soundtrack)	15
71	Vanguard VSD 79314	HOLD ON - IT'S COMING (LP)	15
71	Vanguard VSD 79315	WAR WAR WAR (LP)	15
72	Vanguard VSD 79316	INCREDIBLE! LIVE! (LP)	12
73	Vanguard VSD 79328	PARIS SESSIONS (LP)	12

LARRY McDONALD & DENZIL LAING

71	Clandisc CLA 228	Name Of The Game/FABULOUS FLAMES: Holly Version	6

RITCHIE McDONALD & GLEN BROWN

72	Duke DU 141	Boat To Progress/Boat To Progress - Version	10

SHELAGH McDONALD

(see also Keith Christmas)

70	B&C CAS 1019	THE SHELAGH McDONALD ALBUM (LP)	100
71	B&C CAS 1043	STAR GAZER (LP, with inner sleeve)	100

SKEETS McDONALD

56	Capitol CL 14566	Fallen Angel/It'll Take Me A Long, Long Time	15
56	Capitol CL 14566	Fallen Angel/It'll Take Me A Long, Long Time (78)	18
59	Capitol EAP1 1040	GOING STEADY WITH THE BLUES (EP)	80

TESFA McDONALD

72	Dynamic DYN 455	Life Is The Highest/Recarnate (Re-Incarnate) (actually by Bobby Ellis and Tommy McCook)	18

McDONALD & GILES

(see also King Crimson; Giles, Giles & Fripp)

70	Island ILPS 9126	McDONALD AND GILES (LP, 1st pressing, pink label, with 'i' logo)	70
70	Island ILPS 9126	McDONALD AND GILES (LP, 2nd pressing, 'pink rim' label, 'palm tree' logo)	20
70	Polydor 2302 070	McDONALD AND GILES (LP)	12

ROSE McDOWALL

(see also Strawberry Switchblade, Ornamental, Psychic TV, Current 93, Death In June)

88	Rio Digital 7RDS 3	Don't Fear The Reaper/Crystal Days (p/s)	5
88	Rio Digital 12RDS 3	Don't Fear The Reaper/Crystal Days (12", p/s)	8

(MISSISSIPPI) FRED McDOWELL

66	Bounty BY 6022	MY HOME IS IN THE DELTA (LP)	45
66	Fontana 688 806 ZL	MISSISSIPPI DELTA BLUES (LP)	40
69	CBS 63735	LONG WAY FROM HOME (LP)	30
69	Polydor 236 278	GOING DOWN SOUTH (LP)	30

MINT VALUE £

70 Capitol E-ST 409 I DO NOT PLAY NO ROCK & ROLL (LP) 25
70 Transatlantic TRA 194 LONDON 1 (LP) 15
71 Transatlantic TRA 203 LONDON 2 (LP) 15
71 Revival RVS 1001 EIGHT YEARS RAMBLIN' (LP, with Johnny Woods) 18
74 Xtra XTRA 1136 MISSISSIPPI FRED McDOWELL 1904-1972 (LP) 15

FRED & ANNIE MAE McDOWELL

64 Polydor 236 570 GOING DOWN SOUTH (LP) 18

BROTHER JACK MCDUFF

(see also Roland Kirk, Kenny Burrell, Jimmy Witherspoon)

64 Stateside SS 275 Sanctified Samba/Whistle While You Work 10
64 Stateside SS 302 Rock Candy/Real Good 'Un 12
64 Stateside SS 328 Carpetbaggers (Main Theme)/The Pink Panther (Theme) 10
66 Atlantic 584 036 Down In The Valley/A Change Is Gonna Come 8
64 Stateside SL 10060 BROTHER JACK McDUFF LIVE! (LP) 15
64 Stateside SL 10101 THE DYNAMIC JACK McDUFF (LP, as Brother Jack McDuff Quartet) 15
65 Stateside SL 10121 BROTHER JACK McDUFF QUARTET LIVE! AT THE JAZZ WORKSHOP (LP) 20
65 Stateside SL 10142 PRELUDE (LP) 20
66 Stateside SL 10165 THE CONCERT McDUFF (LP) 18
66 Atlantic 587 030 A CHANGE IS GONNA COME (LP) 20
67 Transatlantic PR 7404 SILK AND SOUL (LP) 15
67 Transatlantic PR 7476 WALK ON BY (LP) 15
68 Transatlantic PR 7286 AT THE JAZZ WORKSHOP (LP) 15
68 Transatlantic ATRA 5056 DYNAMIC JACK McDUFF (LP) 15
72 York FYK 407 IF THE CAP FITS ... WEAR IT (LP, as Jack McDuff Band) 12
72 Prestige PR 24013 ROCK CANDY (LP) 12

MC DUKE

88 Music Of Life NOTE15 I Don't care Anymore/Free (12") 8
89 Music Of Life NOTE25 I'm Rifin' (12") 8
89 Music Of Life NOTE20 Miracles (12") 8

MC DUKE

88 Music Of Life NOTE25 I'm Rifin' (12") 8

McENROE & CASH With The FULL METAL RACKETS

(see also Iron Maiden, Roger Daltrey)

91 M. For Nations KUT 141 Rock'N'Roll (7" Version)/(Instrumental) (p/s) 5
91 M. For Nations 12KUT 141 Rock'N'Roll (Dance Mix)/(7" Version)/(Instrumental) (12", p/s) 8

JOHNNY McEVOY

(see also Rambler)

73 Hawk HALPX 112 JOHNNY McEVOY (LP) 15
74 Hawk HALPX 117 SOUNDS LIKE JOHNNY McEVOY (LP) 20

BOB McFADDEN & DOR

(see also Rod McKuen)

59 Coral Q 72378 The Mummy/The Beat Generation (tri centre) 30
59 Coral Q 72378 The Mummy/The Beat Generation (round centre) 20
59 Coral Q 72378 The Mummy/The Beat Generation (78) 10

MC5

(see also Wayne Kramer, Destroy All Monsters, Rob Tyner & Hot Rods)

69 Elektra EKSN 45056 Kick Out The Jams/Motor City Is Burning 35
69 Elektra EKSN 45067 Ramblin' Rose/Borderline 35
69 Elektra EKL 4042 KICK OUT THE JAMS (LP, orange label, gatefold sleeve, mono) 150
69 Elektra EKS 74042 KICK OUT THE JAMS (LP, orange label, gatefold sleeve, stereo) 90
70 Atlantic 2400 016 BACK IN THE U.S.A. (LP) 75
71 Atlantic 2400 135 HIGH TIME (LP) 75

MIKE McGEAR

(see also Grimms, Scaffold, McGough & McGear, Paul McCartney)

72 Island WIP 6131 Woman/Kill 15
74 Warner Bros K 16446 Leave It/Sweet Baby (p/s) 12
74 Warner Bros K 16446 Leave It/Sweet Baby 8
75 Warner Bros K 16520 Sea Breezes/Givin' Grease A Ride 8
75 Warner Bros K 16573 Dance The Do/Norton 10
75 Warner Bros K 16658 Simply Love You/What Do We Really Know (in p/s) 15
75 Warner Bros K 16658 Simply Love You/What Do We Really Know 8
76 EMI EMI 2485 Doing Nothing All Day/A To Z 6
80 Carrere CAR 144 All The Whales In The Ocean/I Juz Want What You Got - Money! (in p/s) 30
80 Carrere CAR 144 All The Whales In The Ocean/I Juz Want What You Got - Money! 15
81 Conn SRTS/81/CUS 1112 No Lardidar/God Save The Gracious Queen (in p/s) 55
81 Conn SRTS/81/CUS 1112 No Lardidar/God Save The Gracious Queen 35
72 Island ILPS 9191 WOMAN (LP, gatefold, pink rim palm tree label) 50
74 Warner Bros K 56051 McGEAR (LP, gatefold sleeve with folded lyric insert) 25
74 Warner Bros KMG 1 McGEAR'S LIMITED EDITION (7-track white label sampler & press kit) 45
80s Centre Labs McGEAR (LP, 6-track reissue, 500 only, numbered & signed) 60

BROWNIE McGHEE

51 Melodisc 1127 Secret Mojo Blues/Me And My Dog (78) 25
63 Columbia SEG 8226 BLUES ON PARADE NO. 1 (EP) 35
60s Xtra 1021 BROWNIE McGHEE (LP) 22

BROWNIE McGHEE & DAVE LEE

(see also Sonny Terry & Brownie McGhee)

57 Pye Jazz NJE 1060 THE BLUEST (EP) 22

DONNA MCGHEE

78 Anchor ANCT 1061 Do As I Do/Mr Blindman (12") 20
78 Anchor ANCL 2027 MAKE IT LAST FOREVER (LP) 25

MINT VALUE £

HOWARD McGHEE
(see also Scaffold, Adrian Henri, Mike McGear, Jimi Hendrix, Grimms)

61	Fontana FJL906	THE SHARP EDGE (LP)	30

(Roger) McGOUGH & (Mike) McGEAR

68	Parlophone PMC/PCS 7047	McGOUGH AND McGEAR (LP, with phasing on "So Much"; black/yellow label with "Sold in U.K..." text)	250
89	Parlophone PCS 7332	McGOUGH AND McGEAR (LP, stereo reissue with inner sleeve, without phasing on "So Much")	15
89	Parlophone CDP 7 91877-2	McGOUGH AND McGEAR (CD, without phasing on "So Much")	40

ROGER McGOUGH & BRIAN PATTEN

75	Argo ZPL 1190	READ THEIR OWN VERSE - BRITISH POETS OF OUR TIME (LP)	25

MAUREEN McGOVERN

73	Pye Intl. 7N 25603	The Morning After/Midnight Storm (p/s)	8

CHRIS McGREGOR('S BROTHERHOOD OF BREATH)
(see also Brotherhood Of Breath, Tunji)

68	Polydor 184 137	VERY URGENT (LP, as Chris McGregor Group)	75
68	Polydor 583 072	UP TO EARTH (LP, unreleased, test pressings only)	150
70	RCA Neon NE 2	CHRIS McGREGOR'S BROTHERHOOD OF BREATH (LP, gatefold sleeve)	50
72	RCA SF 8260	BROTHERHOOD (LP, gatefold sleeve, as Chris McGregor's Brotherhood Of Breath)	65
74	Ogun OG 100	LIVE, WILLISAU (LP)	15
77	Ogun OG 521	IN HIS OWN TIME (LP)	15
78	Ogun OG 524	PROCESSION (LP)	15

FREDDIE McGREGOR
(see also Soul Brothers,Young Freddie)

73	Fab FAB 261	Wise Words/NEW ESTABLISHMENT: Version	20
79	Observer OBS 903	Run Come Rally (12")	40
81	Yashemabeth YM01	Wine Of Violence/Once A man (12")	15
81	JB JBD 030	Leave Yah/20 Miles Blackstar Liner/U BROWN: Step It Up (12", blue/yellow vinyl)	40
83	Intense INT 007	Jumping Jack/Pretty Woman (12")	12
84	Real Authentic RAS 7008	Across The Border/Version (12")	30
96	Blacker Dread BDTL 05	Mr. Pressure Man/CLIVE HYLTON: Babylon Keep On Knocking (12")	35
79	Jackal JALP 7000	FREDDIE McGREGOR (LP)	15

JIMMY McGRIFF

64	Sue WI 303	All About My Girl/M.G. Blues	40
64	Sue WI 310	Last Minute (Parts 1 & 2)	40
64	Sue WI 317	I've Got A Woman (Parts 1 & 2)	40
64	Sue WI 333	'Round Midnight/Lonely Avenue	40
66	United Artists UP 1170	See See Rider/Hallelujah	15
70	United Artists UP 35025	The Worm/What's That	30
64	Sue ILP 907	I'VE GOT A WOMAN (LP)	110
64	Sue ILP 908	GOSPEL TIME (LP)	100
65	London HA-C 8247	BLUES FOR MISTER JIMMY (LP)	60
66	London HA-C 8242	AT THE APOLLO (LP)	75
66	United Artists (S)ULP 1158	A BAG FULL OF SOUL (LP)	30
68	United Artists (S)ULP 1170	THE BIG BAND (LP)	25
69	Solid State USS 7012	I'VE GOT A NEW WOMAN (LP)	12
72	Groove Merchant GM 503	GROOVE GREASE (LP)	15
73	Groove Merchant GM 2205	GOOD THINGS DON'T HAPPEN EVERY DAY (LP, with Junior Parker)	12
74	People PLEO 14	FLY DUDE (LP)	15
74	People PLEO 19	LET'S STAY TOGETHER (LP)	15
74	People PLEO 23	IF YOU'RE READY COME GO WITH ME (LP)	15

BILL McGUFFIE (TRIO)

53	Parlophone MSP 6040	Concerto For Boogie/Begin The Beguine (as Bill McGuffie Trio)	7
67	Philips BF 1550	Fugue For Thought (from the film 'Dalek Invasion Earth 2150AD')/ Fair's Fair	25
55	Philips BBR 8054	JAZZ WITH McGUFFIE (LP)	15
56	Philips BBR 8087	McGUFFIE MAGIC (LP)	20
56	Philips BBL 7072	MORE JAZZ WITH McGUFFIE (LP)	20
58	Philips BBL 7261	CONTINENTAL TOUR (LP)	20
61	Philips BBL 7450	PLAYING FOR PLEASURE (LP)	12
68	Philips LPS 16001	LATIN OVERTONES (LP)	12

ROGER McGUINN
(see also Byrds)

74	CBS 2649	Peace On You/Without You	6
77	CBS 5231	American Girl/Russian Hill	6
73	CBS 65274	ROGER McGUINN (LP)	12
74	CBS 81071	PEACE ON YOU (LP)	12
75	CBS 80877	ROGER McGUINN AND BAND (LP)	12
76	CBS 81369	CARDIFF ROSE (LP)	12

McGUINNESS FLINT
(see also Manfred Mann, Blues Band, John Mayall, Coulson Dean McGuinness Flint, Gallagher & Lyle, Paladin)

70	Capitol EA-ST 22625	McGUINNESS FLINT (LP, gatefold sleeve)	20
71	Capitol ST 22794	HAPPY BIRTHDAY, RUTHY BABY (LP)	15
73	Bronze ILPS 9244	RAINBOW (LP, gatefold sleeve with inner, Island credit on label)	12

BARRY McGUIRE
(see also Mamas & Papas, New Christy Minstrels)

65	Ember EMB S 208	So Long Stay Well/Far Side Of The Hill	6
65	Ember EMB S 224	Greenback Dollar/One By One	6
65	RCA Victor RCA 1493	Child Of Our Times/Upon A Painted Ocean	6
66	RCA Victor RCA 1497	This Precious Time/Don't You Wonder Where It's At	6
66	RCA Victor RCA 1508	Walking My Cat Named Dog/I'd Have To Be Outta My Mind	5

			MINT VALUE £
66	RCA Victor RCA 1525	Cloudy Summer Afternoon/You've Got To Hide Your Love Away (B-side with Mamas & Papas)	15
67	RCA Victor RCA 1638	Masters Of War/Why Not Stop And Dig It While You Can	7
65	RCA Victor RD 7751	SINGS EVE OF DESTRUCTION (LP)	30
66	Ember EMB 3362	THE EVE OF DESTRUCTION MAN (LP, with New Christy Minstrels)	15
71	A&M AMLS 2008	BARRY McGUIRE AND THE DOCTOR (LP, with Eric Hord)	15
70s	Sparrow BIRD 105	C'MON ALONG (LP)	25
70s	Sparrow BIRD 111	HAVE YOU HEARD? (LP)	25

McGUIRE SISTERS

54	Vogue Coral Q 2028	Lonesome Polecat/Muskrat Ramble	15
55	Vogue Coral Q 72050	Sincerely/No More	20
55	Vogue Coral Q 72052	Melody Of Love/Open Up Your Heart	10
55	Vogue Coral Q 72082	Something's Gotta Give/It May Sound Silly	15
55	Vogue Coral Q 72108	Christmas Alphabet/He	15
56	Vogue Coral Q 72117	Young And Foolish/Doesn't Anybody Love Me?	10
56	Vogue Coral Q 72145	Missing/Be Good To Me (Baby, Baby)	10
56	Vogue Coral Q 72161	Delilah Jones/Picnic	15
56	Vogue Coral Q 72188	Weary Blues/In The Alps	10
56	Vogue Coral Q 72201	My Baby's Got Such Lovin' Ways/Endless	10
56	Vogue Coral Q 72209	Tip Toe Through The Tulips With Me/Do You Remember When?	10
56	Vogue Coral Q 72216	Goodnight My Love, Pleasant Dreams/Mommy	10
57	Vogue Coral Q 72238	Heart/Sometimes I'm Happy	10
57	Vogue Coral Q 72249	Kid Stuff/Without Him	10
57	Vogue Coral Q 72265	Rock Bottom/Beginning To Miss You	10
57	Vogue Coral Q 72272	He's Got Time/Interlude	10
57	Vogue Coral Q 72296	Forgive Me/Kiss Them For Me	10
58	Coral Q 72305	Sugartime/Banana Split	7
58	Coral Q 72327	Ding Dong/Since You Went Away To School	5
58	Coral Q 72334	Volare/Do You Love Me Like You Kiss Me?	5
59	Coral Q 72356	May You Always/Achoo-Cha-Cha	6
59	Coral Q 72379	Red River Valley/Compromise	5
60	Coral Q 72387	Lovers' Lullaby/Livin' Dangerously	5
60	Coral Q 72399	The Unforgiven Theme (The Need For Love)/I Give Thanks	5
60	Coral Q 72406	Nine O'Clock/The Last Dance	5
60	Coral Q 72415	I Don't Know Why/To Be Loved	5
61	Coral Q 72427	Really Neat/Just For Old Time's Sake	5
61	Coral Q 72435	Will There Be Space In The Spaceship/Tears On My Pillow	10
61	Coral Q 72446	I Can Dream Can't I/Old Devil Moon	5
62	Coral Q 72452	Sugartime Twist/More Hearts Are Broken That Way	6
58	Coral FEP 2001	THE McGUIRE SISTERS (EP)	20
58	Coral FEP 2006	VOLARE (EP)	20
59	Coral FEP 2033	MAY YOU ALWAYS (EP)	20
56	Vogue Coral LVA 9024	DO YOU REMEMBER WHEN? (LP)	30
57	Vogue Coral LVA 9072	CHILDREN'S HOLIDAY (LP)	20
58	Coral LVA 9073	TEENAGE PARTY (LP)	20
58	Coral LVA 9082	WHILE THE LIGHTS ARE LOW (LP)	20
59	Coral LVA 9115	MAY YOU ALWAYS (LP)	20
60	Coral LVA 9133	OUR GOLDEN FAVORITES (LP)	20
61	Coral LVA 9140	HIS AND HERS (LP)	20
61	Coral LVA 9146	JUST FOR OLD TIME'S SAKE (LP)	20

KEN McINTIRE

60	Esquire 32-133	LOOKING AHEAD (LP, with Eric Dolphy)	60

DAVID McIVOR

69	Warner Bros WB8002	Closing My Eyes/Love That Burns	20

FREDDIE McKAY

(see also Lizzy)

71	Banana BA 348	Picture On The Wall/SOUND DIMENSION: Version	25
71	Banana BA 353	Sweet You, Sour You/High School Dance	18
71	Banana BA 358	High School Dance/SOUND DIMENSION: High School Version	12
71	Moodisc HM 110	Old Joe/Too Much Fire	10
72	Banana BA 370	Drunken Sailor/SOUND DIMENSION: Version	18
73	Bullet BU 525	Go On This Way/SANTIC ALL STARS: Santic Dub	10
73	Dragon DRA 1012	Our Rendezvous/Black Beauty	15
73	Atra ATRA 003	I'm A Freeman/SWEET HARMONY: Santic Special	10
73	Grape GR 3060	Our Rendezvous/SOUL DYMAMITES: Version	10
74	Dragon DRA 1022	Dream My Life Over/YOUTH STARS: Version	5
78	Art & Craft ACD 004	A Love Like Mine/Version (12")	12
81	Greensleeves GRED 46	Another Weekend/EARL SIXTEEN: Live Together (12")	30
82	Greensleeves GRED 84	Roots Man Skanking/TOYAN: Version (12")	12
82	Live & Love LLDIS 2014	In Times Of Trouble/Version (12")	20
71	Banana BALPS 01	PICTURE ON THE WALL (LP)	45
73	Attack ATLP 1013	PICTURE ON THE WALL (LP, reissue)	15
74	Dragon DRLS 5005	LONELY MAN (LP)	12

SCOTT McKAY

67	Columbia DB 8147	I Can't Make Your Way/Take A Giant Step	30

SCOTTY McKAY

64	London HLU 9885	Cold Cold Heart/What You Wanna	10

TONY McKAY

66	Polydor BM 56513	Nobody's Perfect/Detroit	8

LONETTE McKEE

75	Sussex SXX 4	Save It/Do It To Me	15

McKENDREE SPRING

69	MCA MUPS 277	McKENDREE SPRING (LP)	12
71	MCA MUPS 433	SECOND THOUGHTS (LP)	12
72	MCA MUPS 454	THREE (LP)	12

MINT VALUE £

MAE McKENNA
(see also Contraband)

75 Transatlantic TRA 297 MAE McKENNA (LP) 12

VAL McKENNA

65 Piccadilly 7N 35237 Baby Do It/I Believe In Love 15
65 Piccadilly 7N 35256 Mixed Up Shook Up Girl/Now That You've Made Up Your Mind 25
66 Piccadilly 7N 35286 I Can't Believe What You Say/Don't Hesitate 15
69 Spark SRL 1005 House For Sale/I'll Be Satisfied 10
69 Spark SRL 1023 It's All In My Imagination/Sweet Sweet Lovin' 7
70 Spark SRL 1038 Love Feeling/It's All In My Imagination 15

McKENNA MENDELSON MAINLINE

69 Liberty LBF 15235 You Better Watch Out/She's Alright 8
69 Liberty LBF 15276 Don't Give Me No Goose For Christmas/Beltmaker 7
69 Liberty LBS 83251 STINK (LP) 40

MERLENE MCKENZIE

68 Double D DD 106 Left Me For Another/BOBBY AITKEN & CARIBBEATS: Cell Block Eleven 20

SCOTT McKENZIE
(see also Mamas & Papas)

67 CBS 2816 San Francisco (Be Sure To Wear Some Flowers In Your Hair)/ What's The Difference 5
67 Capitol CL 15509 Look In Your Eyes/All I Want Is You 20
67 CBS 3009 Like An Old-Time Movie/What's The Difference Chapter II 7
68 CBS 3393 Holy Man/What's The Difference (Chapter 3) 6
73 CBS 1168 San Francisco (Be Sure To Wear Some Flowers In Your Hair)/ Reason To Believe ("Hall Of Fame Hits" series, p/s) 5
67 CBS (S)BPG 63157 THE VOICE OF SCOTT McKENZIE (LP) 22
70 A&M AMLS 999 STAINED GLASS MORNING (LP) 18

TOMMY McKENZIE

68 Pama PM 720 Fiddlesticks/Please Stay 15
71 Pama Supreme PS 327 Eastern Promise/Fiddlesticks (as Tommy McKenzie Orchestra) 7

McKENZIE, DOUG & BOB
(see also Rush)

82 Mercury HOSER 1 Take Off/Elron McKenzie (p/s) 20

MCKENZIE & GARDINER

83 Sound Of London TSOLL 501 From Time/From TIme (Version) (12") 80

LESLIE MCKEOWN

79 Ego Trip EGOS 7 Shall I Do It (One More Number One)/Do It All Again (p/s) 7
79 Ego Trip EGO 001 ALL WASHED UP (LP, gatefold with poster) 20

McKINLEYS

64 Columbia DB 7230 Someone Cares For Me/Million Miles Away 20
64 Columbia DB 7310 When He Comes Along/Then I'll Know It's Love 12
64 Parlophone R 5211 Sweet And Tender Romance/That Lonely Feeling 10
65 Columbia DB 7583 Give Him My Love/Once More 15

ROD McKUEN
(see also Bob McFadden & Dor, Mike Redway, Mike Sarne, Henri Mancini)

57 London HLU 8390 Happy Is A Boy Named Me/Jaydee 40
60 Brunswick 05828 Two Brothers/Time After Time 15
64 Capitol CL 15348 The World I Used To Know/Someplace Green 5
66 Ember EMB 223 Soldiers Who Want To Be Heroes/Wayfarin' Stranger 5
68 RCA Victor RCA 1734 Cat Named Sloopy/Where Are We Now 5
71 Buena Vista DF 482 Pastures Green/Theme From Scandalous John/Train To Quivira (p/s) 5

HAL McKUSICK SEXTET/QUINTET

57 Vogue Coral Q 72258 Kelly And Me (as Sextet)/When I Fall In Love (as Quintet) 6

IAN McLAGAN
(see also Faces)

79 Mercury MER1 La De Da/Hold On (p/s) 5
80 Mercury 9100 072 TROUBLEMAKER (LP) (with poster) 12

ALTON McLAIN & DESTINY

78 Polydor 2391 370 IT MUST BE LOVE (LP) 15

TOMMY McLAIN

66 London HL 10065 Sweet Dreams/I Need You So 10
66 London HL 10091 Think It Over/I Can't Take No More 10

(MAHAVISHNU) JOHN McLAUGHLIN

69 Marmalade 608 007 EXTRAPOLATION (LP) 75
70 Polydor 012 EXTRAPOLATION (LP, reissue) 15
71 Douglas DGL 65075 DEVOTION (LP, gatefold sleeve) 15
71 Douglas DGL 69014 MY GOAL'S BEYOND (LP, as Mahavishnu John McLaughlin, gatefold sleeve) 15
74 CBS Q 69037 LOVE, DEVOTION, SURRENDER (LP, quadrophonic issue) 12

JACKIE McLEAN QUINTET
(see also Lifetime, Tony Williams [Lifetime], Mahavishnu Orchestra, John Surman, Santana)

55 Esquire 32-041 LIGHTS OUT (LP) 30
56 Esquire 32-111 JACKIE'S PAL (LP) 30

NANA McLEAN

71 Banana BA 355 A Little Love/SOUND DIMENSION: Heavy Beat 30

PHIL McLEAN

61 Top Rank JAR 597 Small Sad Sam/Chicken 12
62 Top Rank JAR 613 Big Mouth Bill/Come With Us 7

MINT VALUE £

GERALD McLEASH
71 G.G. GG 4516 — False Reaper/G.G. ALL STARS: Reaping Version — 10

LARIS McLENNON
67 CBM 04 — Confusion/Turn Me Loose — 6

ENOS McLEOD
(see also Enos & Sheila)
68 Blue Cat BS 135 — You Can Never Get Away/ENOS & SHEILA: La La La Bamba — 25

SEAN McLEOD
69 Aurora 4594 — Living Without You/Love Songs From Another Planet — 12

VINCENT McLEOD
69 Jackpot JP 711 — Too Late/SIR COLLINS: Late Night — 12

OSCAR McLOLLIE & HIS HONEYJUMPERS
55 London HL 8130 — Take Your Shoes Off, Pop/Love Me Tonight — 250
55 London HL 8130 — Take Your Shoes Off, Pop/Love Me Tonight (78) — 40

EDDIE McLOYD
75 Brunswick BR 27 — Once You Fall In Love/Baby Get Down — 20

BOBBY McLURE
(see also Fontella Bass)
66 Chess CRS 8048 — Peak Of Love/You Got Me Baby — 40
66 Chess CRS 8048 — Peak Of Love/You Got Me Baby (DJ copy) — 75
75 Island USA 006 — You Bring Out The Love In Me/SURVIVAL KIT: Daybreak — 20

McLYNNS
70 CBS 63836 — OLD MARKET ST. (LP) — 50

ROSS McMANUS
(see also Day Costello)
64 HMV POP 1279 — Patsy Girl/I'm The Greatest — 10
66 HMV POP 1543 — Stop Your Playing Around/Girlie Girlie — 8
67 Decca F 12618 — Can't Take My Eyes Off Of You/If I Were A Rich Man — 6

MC MELLO
90 Republic LICT033 — Open Up Your Mind/Words Spoken (12") — 8
90 Republic LICT033R — Open Up Your Mind (Remixes) (12") — 8
92 Funki Dreds PA6640 — Gone Crazy/Talk Dem Way/Firm Stance (EP) — 40
89 Republic LICT007 — Bizzie Rhymin'/Comin' Correct/Wize (EP) — 20
94 Natural Response 74321208511 — THE FIRST CHRONICLES OF DETT (EP) — 10
90 Republic 4353ILE — THOUGHTS RELEASED (LP) — 12

MARGARET McMILLEN
65 Decca F 12272 — You Can't Be True Dear/The Love Of My Man — 6

IAN MCNABB
91 Way Cool WAY 147 — Great Dreams Of Heaven/That's Why I Believe — 8

BARBARA McNAIR
(see also Billy Williams & Barbara McNair)
66 Tamla Motown TMG 544 — You're Gonna Love My Baby/The Touch Of Time — 350
66 Tamla Motown TMG 544 — You're Gonna Love My Baby/The Touch Of Time (DJ copy) — 400
59 Coral FEP 2021 — FRONT ROW CENTRE VOL. 1 (EP) — 40
64 Warner Bros WEP 6129 — I ENJOY BEING A GIRL (EP) — 40

CHARLIE McNAIR'S JAZZ BAND
60 Waverly SLP 504 — Big House Blues/Fish Man — 6

HAROLD McNAIR
(see also Ginger Baker's Airforce)
68 RCA Victor RCA 1742 — The Hipster/Indecision — 100
65 Island ILP 926 — AFFECTIONATE FINK (LP, with Ornette Coleman's Sidemen) — 400
68 RCA SF 7969 — HAROLD McNAIR (LP) — 100
70 RCA Intl. INTS 1096 — FLUTE AND NUT (LP) — 60
70 B&C CAS 1016 — THE FENCE (LP, gatefold with pink envelope containing balloon) — 80
70 B&C CAS 1016 — THE FENCE (LP, gatefold with pink envelope without balloon) — 40
72 B&C CAS 1045 — HAROLD McNAIR (LP) — 70

JOHN McNALLY
69 CBS 4517 — Mary In The Morning/My Love Forgive Me — 5
(this is NOT John McNally of the Searchers)

TREVOR McNAUGHTON
(see also The Melodians)
72 Hillcrest HCT 5 — No Sins At All/No Sins At All Version — 5

BIG JAY McNEELY
59 Top Rank JAR 169 — There Is Something On Your Mind/...Back...Shac...Track ('vocal: Little Sonny') — 40
59 Top Rank JAR 169 — There Is Something On Your Mind/...Back...Shac...Track ('vocal: Little Sonny') (78) — 20
65 Sue WI 373 — There Is Something On Your Mind/...Back...Shac...Track ('vocal: Little Sonny') (reissue) — 30
64 Warner Bros WM 8143 — BIG JAY'S PARTY (LP) — 40

AARON McNEIL
73 Action ACT 4619 — Soul Of A Black Man/Reap What You Sow — 12

DAVID McNEIL
68 President PT 212 — Don't Let Your Chance Go By/Space Plane — 40

PAUL McNEILL
66 Decca LK 4803 — TRADITIONALLY AT THE TROUBADOUR (LP) — 50

MINT VALUE £

PAUL McNEILL & LINDA PETERS
(see also Linda Peters, Richard & Linda Thompson)

68	MGM MGM 1408	You Ain't Goin' Nowhere/I'll Show You How To Sing	6

RONNIE McNEIR

75	London HLA 10494	Wendy Is Gone/Give Me A Sign	10

McPEAKE FAMILY/FOLK GROUP

60s	Topic TOP 92	WILD MOUNTAIN THYME (EP)	12
60s	Topic	IRISH TRADITIONAL FOLK SONGS AND MUSIC (LP, blue label)	30
60s	Topic 12T 87	THE McPEAKE FAMILY (LP)	20
64	Fontana TL 5214	IRISH FOLK! (LP, as McPeake Family)	35
65	Fontana TL 5358	AT HOME WITH THE McPEAKES (LP)	20
67	Fontana TL 5433	PLEASANT AND DELIGHTFUL (LP, as McPeake Family)	20
69	Evolution Z 1002	WELCOME HOME (LP, as McPeake Folk Group)	40
72	Windmill WMD 151	IRISH TO BE SURE (LP, as McPeake Family)	25

CLYDE McPHATTER
(see also Drifters, Jackie Wilson, Dominoes, Billy Ward & Dominoes, Jackie Wilson/Clyde McPhatter)

SINGLES

56	London HLE 8250	Seven Days/I'm Not Worthy Of You	400
56	London HLE 8250	Seven Days/I'm Not Worthy Of You (78)	30
56	London HL 7006	Seven Days/I'm Not Worthy Of You (export issue)	125
56	London HLE 8293	Treasure Of Love/When You're Sincere (gold label lettering)	150
56	London HLE 8293	Treasure Of Love/When You're Sincere (silver label lettering)	60
56	London HLE 8293	Treasure Of Love/When You're Sincere (78)	10
57	London HLE 8462	Just To Hold My Hand/No Matter What (triangular centre)	150
57	London HLE 8462	Just To Hold My Hand/No Matter What (78)	20
57	London HLE 8476	Long Lonely Nights/Heartaches (triangular centre)	100
57	London HLE 8476	Long Lonely Nights/Heartaches (78)	20
57	London HLE 8525	Rock And Cry/You'll Be There (triangular centre)	90
57	London HLE 8525	Rock And Cry/You'll Be There (later round centre)	35
57	London HLE 8525	Rock And Cry/You'll Be There (78)	25
58	London HLE 8707	Come What May/Let Me Know (triangular centre)	60
58	London HLE 8707	Come What May/Let Me Know (78)	35
58	London HLE 8755	A Lover's Question/I Can't Stand Up Alone (triangular centre)	30
58	London HLE 8755	A Lover's Question/I Can't Stand Up Alone (78)	30
59	MGM MGM 1014	I Told Myself A Lie/(I'm Afraid) The Masquerade Is Over	20
59	London HLE 8878	Lovey Dovey/My Island Of Dreams (triangular centre)	35
59	London HLE 8878	Lovey Dovey/My Island Of Dreams (78)	25
59	London HLE 8906	Since You've Been Gone/Try Try Baby (triangular centre)	40
59	London HLE 8906	Since You've Been Gone/Try Try Baby (78)	30
59	MGM MGM 1040	Twice As Nice/Where Did I Make My Mistake	18
59	London HLE 9000	You Went Back On Your Word/There You Go	40
59	London HLE 9000	You Went Back On Your Word/There You Go (78)	70
59	MGM MGM 1048	Bless You/Let's Try Again	18
60	London HLE 9079	Just Give Me A Ring/Don't Dog Me	50
60	MGM MGM 1061	Think Me A Kiss/When The Right Time Comes Along	18
60	Mercury AMT 1108	I Ain't Givin' Up Nothin' (If I Can't Get Something)/Ta Ta	15
60	Mercury AMT 1120	You're For Me/I Just Want To Love You	15
61	Mercury AMT 1136	Tomorrow Is A-Comin'/I'll Love You Till The Cows Come Home	40
62	Mercury AMT 1174	Lover Please/Let's Forget About The Past	20
62	Mercury AMT 1181	Little Bitty Pretty One/Next To Me	20
66	Stateside SS 487	Everybody's Somebody's Fool/I Belong To You	18
66	Stateside SS 567	A Shot Of Rhythm And Blues/I'm Not Going To Work Today	20
67	Stateside SS 592	Lavender Lace/Sweet And Innocent	20
68	Deram DM 202	Only A Fool/Thank You Love	20
69	Deram DM 223	Baby I Could Be So Good At Loving You/Baby You've Got It	25
69	Pama PM 775	A Shot Of Rhythm And Blues/I'm Not Going To Work Today (reissue)	8
69	B&C CB 106	Denver/Tell Me	12

EPs

59	London RE-E 1202	CLYDE McPHATTER	300
60	London RE-E 1240	CLYDE MCPHATTER NO. 2 (unissued)	0
59	MGM MGM-EP 705	TWICE AS NICE	100
60	MGM MGM-EP 739	THIS IS NOT GOODBYE	100

LPs

63	Mercury MMC 14120	LOVER PLEASE	125
64	Atlantic ATL 5001	THE BEST OF CLYDE McPHATTER	90
71	MCA MUPS 418	WELCOME HOME	20
73	Atlantic K 30033	A TRIBUTE TO CLYDE McPHATTER	20

TONY (T.S.) McPHEE
(see also Groundhogs, Champion Jack Dupree, Jo-Ann Kelly, John Dummer Blues Band, Hapshash & Coloured Coat, Herbal Mixture)

66	Purdah 45-3501	Someone To Love Me/Ain't Gonna Cry No Mo' (as T.S. McPhee)	240
83	TS 001	Time Of Action/Born To Be With You (sold at gigs)	10
68	Liberty LBL/LBS 83190	ME AND THE DEVIL (LP)	60
71	Sunset SLS 50209	THE SAME THING ON THEIR MINDS (LP, with Jo-Ann Kelly)	30
73	World Wide Artists WWA 1	THE TWO SIDES OF TONY (T.S.) McPHEE (LP, with insert)	25

CHARLES McPHERSON

65	Stateside SL 10151	BEBOP REVISITED (LP)	15
73	Mainstream MSL 1004	SIKU YA BIBI (LP)	12

GILLIAN McPHERSON

71	RCA Victor RCA 2089	It's My Own Way/Is Somebody In Tune With My Song	5
71	RCA Victor SF 8220	POETS AND PAINTERS AND PERFORMERS OF THE BLUES (LP)	60

KEVIN McQUINN

62	Top Rank JAR 598	Every Step Of The Way/Keep Me On Your Mind	10

MINT VALUE £

RON MCQUINN

77	Decca F13693	Look At Love Bleed/Banshee	20

CARMEN McRAE

(see also Sammy Davis Jnr.)

55	Brunswick 05502	Love Is Here To Stay/This Will Make You Laugh	8
56	Brunswick 05588	You Don't Know Me/Never Loved Him Anyhow	7
56	Brunswick 05632	Star Eyes/I'm A Dreamer (Aren't We All)	7
57	Brunswick 05652	Whatever Lola Wants (Lola Gets)/Ooh (What 'Cha Doin' To Me) (with Dave Lambert Quartet)	10
57	Brunswick 05723	It's Like Getting A Donkey To Gallop/The Party's Over	7
59	London HLR 8837	Play For Keeps/Which Way Is Love	15
57	London RE-N 1094	LONDON'S GIRL FRIENDS (EP)	20
56	Brunswick LAT 8104	BY SPECIAL REQUEST (LP)	18
56	Brunswick LAT 8133	TORCHY (LP)	20
56	Brunswick LAT 8147	BLUE MOON (LP)	15
58	Brunswick LAT 8257	AFTER GLOW (LP)	15
59	London HA-R 2185	BOOK OF BALLADS (LP)	15

CARMEN McRAE & DAVE BRUBECK FIVE

(see also Dave Brubeck)

62	Fontana H 379	Take Five/It's A Raggy Waltz	6

IAN MCSHANE

62	Columbia DB 4932	Harry Brown/The Tinker	6

JAY McSHANN

55	Brunswick LA 8735	KANSAS CITY MEMORIES (10" LP)	15

MC SPY-D & 'FRIENDS'

(see also Brian May)

95	Parlophone 12RDJ 6404	The Amazing Spider-Man (Solution Mix)/(Solution Chilled Mix)/(B&J White Trouser Mix) (12", no p/s, promo only)	25

BLIND WILLIE McTELL

66	Transatlantic PR 1040	LAST SESSION (LP)	35
67	Storyville 670 816	BLIND WILLIE McTELL 1940 (LP)	22
60s	Roots RL 324	BLIND WILLIE McTELL 1929-1935 (LP)	20
73	Atlantic K 40400	ATLANTA TWELVE STRING GUITAR (LP)	18

RALPH McTELL

69	Big T BIG 125	Summer Comes Along	8
70	Big T BIG 131	Kew Gardens/Father Forgive Them	8
70	Big T BIG 134	Spiral Staircase/Terminus	8
68	Transatlantic TRA 165	8 FRAMES A SECOND (LP, white/lilac label with 't' logo)	35
69	Transatlantic TRA 177	SPIRAL STAIRCASE (LP, with insert)	35
69	Transatlantic TRA 209	MY SIDE OF YOUR WINDOW (LP)	25
70	Transatlantic TRA 227	REVISITED (LP)	20

McTELLS

87	Frank TRUFFAUT 303	Jesse Man Rae/If Only/Rotten/M.T.B. (p/s in bag)	10

RAY McVAY SOUND

65	Pye 7N 15777	Raunchy/Revenge (Promo copies have "Macvay" spelling)	45
65	Pye 7N 15816	Kinda Kinky/Kinkdom Come	45
66	Parlophone R 5460	Genesis/House Of Clowns (as Ray MacVay Band)	10
69	Mercury MF 1121	Destination Moon/Mexican Scavenger	10
71	Philips 6006 083	They Call Me Mr. Tibbs (as Ray McVay & Orchestra)	25

CHRISTINE McVIE

(see also Christine Perfect, Fleetwood Mac, Chicken Shack)

84	Warner Bros W 9372T	Got A Hold On Me/Who's Dreaming This Dream (12", p/s)	8
84	Warner Bros W 9372PT	Got A Hold On Me/Who's Dreaming This Dream (12", picture disc)	10

CARL McVOY

58	London HLU 8617	Tootsie/You Are My Sunshine	275
58	London HLU 8617	Tootsie/You Are My Sunshine (78)	70

DAVID McWILLIAMS

66	CBS 202348	God And My Country/Blue Eyes	10
67	Major Minor MM 533	The Days Of Pearly Spencer/Harlem Lady	15
68	Major Minor MM 561	This Side Of Heaven/Mister Satisfied	8
69	Major Minor MM 592	The Stranger/Follow Me	10
69	Major Minor MM 616	Oh Mama Are You My Friend?/I Love Susie In The Summer	8
67	Major Minor MMLP 2	SINGING SONGS BY DAVID McWILLIAMS (LP, also stereo SMLP 2)	15
67	Major Minor MMLP 10	DAVID McWILLIAMS VOL. 2 (LP, also stereo SMLP 10)	15
68	Major Minor MMLP 11	VOLUME III (LP, also stereo SMLP 11)	15
69	Major Minor MCP 5026	THE DAYS OF DAVID McWILLIAMS (LP)	15
72	Dawn DNLS 3039	LORD OFFALY (LP, textured gatefold sleeve)	20
73	Dawn DNLS 3047	THE BEGGAR AND THE PRIEST (LP)	20
74	Dawn DNLS 3059	LIVING'S JUST A STATE OF MIND (LP)	18

M.D.C.

(see also Millions Of Dead Children)

83	Crass 121984/5	MULTI DEATH CORPORATION (EP)	10

VAUGHN MEADER

63	MGM MGM 1239	No Hiding Place/The Elephant Song	6

MEADOW MIST

81	Lorraines LRN 001	Christmas Isn't Christmas When You're Not There/Lover Your Neighbour	10

ME & THEM

64	Pye 7N 15596	Feels So Good/I Think I'm Gonna Kill Myself	18

MINT VALUE £

64	Pye 7N 15631	Everything I Do Is Wrong/Show You Mean It Too	15
64	Pye 7N 15683	Get Away/Tell Me Why	15

MEANIES

79	Vendetta VD 002	Waiting For You/It's True (p/s)	80

MEAN STREET DEALERS

(see also Tea & Sympathy)

79	Graduate GRAD 5	Japanese Motorbikes/Tight Skirts (p/s)	20
79	Mean St. Dealers MSD 001	BENT NEEDLES (LP)	25
79	Graduate GRADLP 1	BENT NEEDLES (LP, reissue)	18

MEANWHILE BACK IN COMMUNIST RUSSIA...

00	Jitter JTR 1SP	No Cigar/Morning After Pill (p/s, 300 only)	7

MEASLES

65	Columbia DB 7531	Casting My Spell/Bye Birdie Fly	40
65	Columbia DB 7673	Night People/Dog Rough Dan	25
66	Columbia DB 7875	Kicks/No Baby At All	35
66	Columbia DB 8029	Walkin' In/Looking For Love	25

MEAT LOAF

(see also Stoney & Meat Loaf, Jim Steinman, Rocky Horror Show)

75	Ode ODS 66304	Clap Your Hands, Stamp Your Feet/Stand By Me (withdrawn)	25
79	Epic S EPC 12-7018	Bat Out Of Hell/Heaven Can Wait (12", p/s, red vinyl)	8
81	Epic EPCA 11-1697	Dead Ringer For Love/More Than You Deserve (picture disc)	5
82	Epic EPCA 12-2251	MEAT LOAF IN EUROPE '82 (12" EP, clear vinyl, p/s, Irish issue)	10
83	Epic EPCA WA 3748	Midnight At The Lost And Found (Remix)/Fallen Angel/Bat Out Of Hell (live)/ Dead Ringer For Love (Long Version) (picture disc)	5
84	Arista ARISDP 585	Modern Girl/Take A Number (bike-shaped picture disc, with poster & plinth)	5
84	Arista ARIST 12585D/	Modern Girl (Freeway Mix)/Take A Number (Extended)//Modern Girl (Freeway Mix)/ Take A Number (Extended) (12", double pack, 2nd 12" is picture disc)	10
85	Arista ARISD 600	Nowhere Fast/Clap Your Hands (bike-shaped picture disc)	5
85	Arista ARISD 603	Piece Of The Action/Sailor To A Siren (jaw-shaped picture disc)	5
82	Epic EPC 11 82419	BAT OUT OF HELL (LP, picture disc)	15

MEAT WHIPLASH

(see also Jesus & Mary Chain)

85	Creation CRE 020	Don't Slip Up/Here It Comes (foldaround p/s in poly bag; 1st pressing has photo of band by fence)	20
85	Creation CRE 020	Don't Slip Up/Here It Comes (foldaround p/s in poly bag; 2nd pressing has photo of band in field)	8

MECHANICAL HORSETROUGH

70s	Kap KAPS 96	Dogshit On Your Shoes/Jeremy Germoline/Horsetrough Hoedown (p/s)	5
75	Sonet SON 2068	When Santa Lost His Trousers/The Ballad Of Big Bruce	5

MECKENBURG ZINC

70	Orange OAS 205	Hard Working Woman/I'd Like To Help You	5

MEDALLION STRINGS

60	London HLR 9218	Green Leaves Of Summer/Spellbound	5
60	London HLR 9242	Gloria's Theme (From "Butterfield 8")/Suzie Wong	5

Meddy EVILS

(see also Stu James and the Mojos, the Quik)

65	Pye 7N 15941	Find Somebody To Love/A Place Called Love	90
66	Pye 7N 17091	It's All For You/Ma's Place	120

MEDIA

79	Takeaway TA 001	TV Kids/Don't Sit Back/Just For You/Rose And Crown (500 only, p/s)	50

MEDIA

80	Brain Booster Music 4	Back On The Beach Again/South Coast City Rockers (p/s)	5

MEDIATORS

(see also Meditators)

69	Success RE901	Look Whoa Bust Style/RUPIE EDWARDS : Same	15
70	Supreme SUP 210	When You Go To A Party (actually by Meditators)/ RUPIE EDWARDS ALLSTARS: Stop The Party	10

MEDICINE HEAD

(see also Ashton Gardner & Dyke, British Lions)

69	Dandelion S 4661	His Guiding Hand/This Love Of Old	20
70	Dandelion S 5075	Coast To Coast/All For Tomorrow	12
71	Dandelion DAN 7003	(And The) Pictures In The Sky/Natural Sight (also listed as K 19002) (in p/s)	10
72	Dandelion 2001 276	Kum On/On The Land	6
72	Dandelion 2001 325	Only To Do What Is True/Sittin' In The Sun	6
72	Dandelion 2001 383	How Does It Feel/Morning Light	6
69	Dandelion 63757	NEW BOTTLES, OLD MEDICINE (LP)	50
71	Dandelion DAN 8005	HEAVY ON THE DRUM (LP, gatefold sleeve, 1st pressing with lyric insert with DAN 8005 on sleeve, label and matrix)	100
71	Dandelion DAN 8005	HEAVY ON THE DRUM (LP, gatefold sleeve, later pressing listed as K 49005; without lyric insert)	40
71	Dandelion 2310 166	DARK SIDE OF THE MOON (LP, with insert)	30
73	Polydor 2310 248	ONE & ONE IS ONE (LP, gatefold sleeve)	15

MEDITATIONS

68	Liberty LBF 15045	Transcendental Meditation/Beautiful Experience	7

MEDITATIONS

78	Island IPR 2022	Life Is Not Easy/Much Smarter (12")	10
77	United Artists UAS30178	MESSAGE FROM THE MEDITATIONS (LP)	20
78	Third World TWS 929	WAKE UP! (LP)	25
79	Tad's TRDLP 101579	GUIDANCE (LP)	20

MINT VALUE £

MEDITATORS
(see also Busty Brown, Pat Satchmo)
69 Bullet BU 403 Duba Duba/CECIL NICKY THOMAS: Running Alone . . . 12
69 Success RE 901 Look Who Bust A Style/RUPIE EDWARDS ALL STARS: Look Who Bust A Style . . . 15
70 Big BG 302 When You Go To A Party/Good Morning Mother Cuba. . . . 10
71 Big BG 305 Music Alone Shall Live/RUPIE EDWARDS AND ALL STARS: Music Alone - Version . 10
73 Pyramid PYR 7010 Great Messiah/Nana Nana . . . 8
73 Smash SMA 2331 Things Not Easy/BONGO HERMAN & BINGY BUNNY: Ration . . . 10

MEDIUM
68 CBS 3404 Edward Never Lies/Colours Of The Rainbow . . . 40

MEDIUM MEDIUM
80 APT SAP-01 Them Or Me/Freeze (p/s) . . . 7
81 Cherry Red CHEER 18 Hungry, So Angry/Nadsat Dream (p/s) . . . 7
81 Cherry Red BRED 19 THE GLITTERHOUSE (LP) . . . 15

MEDIUM WAVE
69 Ember EMB 5265 Walk In The Sunshine/Looking Towards The Sky (p/s) . . . 15

BILL MEDLEY
(see also Righteous Brothers, Garnet Mimms)
67 Verve VS 564 That Lucky Old Sun/My Darling Clementine . . . 5
68 MGM MGM 1418 I Can't Make It Alone/One Day Girl . . . 6
68 MGM MGM 1432 Brown Eyed Woman/Let The Good Times Roll . . . 6
68 MGM MGM 1456 Peace Brother Peace/Winter Won't Come This Year. . . . 5
69 MGM MGM 1475 This Is A Love Song/Something's So Wrong. . . . 5
69 MGM MGM 1491 Someone Is Standing Outside/Reaching Back . . . 5
71 A&M AMS 898 You've Lost That Lovin' Feelin'/We've Only Just Begun . . . 5
69 MGM MGM-C(S) 8091 BILL MEDLEY 100% (LP) . . . 20

JOE MEDLIN
59 Mercury AMT 1032 I Kneel At Your Throne/Out Of Sight, Out Of Mind . . . 25
59 Mercury AMT 1032 I Kneel At Your Throne/Out Of Sight, Out Of Mind (78) . . . 10

MICHAEL MEDWIN
58 HMV POP 490 The Army Game/What Do We Do In The Army?
(with Bernard Bresslaw, Alfie Bass & Leslie Fyson). . . . 5
59 HMV POP 645 Blankety-Blankety-Blank/Do It Yourself (with Norman Rossington). . . . 5

KEITH MEEHAN
69 Marmalade 598 016 Darkness Of My Life/TONY MEEHAN: Hooker Street . . . 30

TONY MEEHAN
(see also Shadows, Jet Harris & Tony Meehan, Keith Meehan, John Paul Jones)
64 Decca F 11801 Song Of Mexico/Kings Go Fifth. . . . 6

JOE MEEK ORCHESTRA
(see also Blue Men)
63 Decca F 11796 The Kennedy March/The Theme Of Freedom . . . 30

MEGADETH
(see also Marty Friedman, Cacophony)
87 Capitol CL 476 Wake Up Dead/Black Friday (live) (p/s). . . . 8
87 Capitol CLP 476 Wake Up Dead/Black Friday (live) (skull-shaped picture disc with insert) . . . 15
87 Capitol 12CL 476 Wake Up Dead/Black Friday (live)/Devil's Island (live)/Wake Up Dead/
Black Friday (live) (12", p/s, allegedly shrink-wrapped with 7" picture disc) . . . 25
87 Capitol 12CL 476 Wake Up Dead/Black Friday (live)/Devil's Island (live)/Wake Up Dead/
Black Friday (live) (12", p/s) . . . 12
87 Capitol 12CL 476 Wake Up Dead/Black Friday (Tommy Vance Show)/Devil's Island
(Tommy Vance Show) (12", stickered p/s, with 'Deth' certificate) . . . 15
88 Capitol CL 480 Anarchy In The U.K./Liar (p/s). . . . 8
88 Capitol CLP 480 Anarchy In The U.K./Liar (U.K.-shaped picture disc) . . . 15
88 Capitol CLP 489 Mary Jane/Hook In Mouth (picture disc). . . . 10
90 SBK SBKPD 4 No More Mr. Nice Guy/DEAD ON: "Different Breed" (chair-shaped pic disc). . . . 10
90 SBK 12 SBKP 4 No More Mr. Nice Guy/DEAD ON: "Different Breed"/DANGEROUS TOYS:
Demon Bell [The Ballad Of Horace Pinker] (12", poster p/s). . . . 8
90 SBK CDSBK 4 No More Mr. Nice Guy/(DEAD ON: "Different Breed")/(DANGEROUS TOYS:
Demon Bell [The Ballad Of Horace Pinker]) (CD) . . . 8
91 Capitol CLS 604 Hangar 18 (MJ 12 Edit)/The Conjuring (live) (p/s, shrinkwrapped with patch) . . . 10
91 Capitol CLPD 604 Hangar 18 (MJ 12 Edit)/The Conjuring (live) (Vic-shaped picture disc). . . . 12
91 Capitol CDCL 604 Hangar 18/Conjuring/Hangar 18 (version)/Hangar 18 (Live)/Hook In Mouth (CD) . . . 15
92 Capitol 12CLS 662 Symphony Of Destruction/Breakpoint/Go To Hell
(12", p/s, clear vinyl with giant autographed poster) . . . 15
92 Capitol CLP 669 Skin O' My Teeth (LP Version)/Holy Wars... The Punishment Due
(The General Schwarzkopf Mix)/High Speed Dirt (live)/The Passes (Mustaine
Remarks On Game) (10" bronze Megadeth box with passes & game rules) . . . 18
92 Capitol CL 669 Symphony Of Destruction/Skin O' My Teeth (yellow vinyl, p/s) . . . 8
92 Capitol CLP 669 Symphony Of Destruction/Skin O' My Teeth (picture disc and card in PVC sleeve). . . 7
88 M. For Nations MFN 46P KILLING IS MY BUSINESS ... AND BUSINESS IS GOOD
(LP, picture disc with insert) . . . 15
88 Capitol ESTP 2022 PEACE SELLS ... BUT WHO'S BUYING? (LP, picture disc with insert) . . . 15
88 Capitol ESTP 2053 SO FAR, SO GOOD ... SO WHAT (LP, picture disc with insert). . . . 25
90 Capitol ESTPD 2132 RUST IN PEACE (LP, picture disc, die cut sleeve) . . . 25
94 Capitol ESTPD 2244 YOUTHANASIA (LP, picture disc). . . . 22
94 Capitol ESTPD 2244 YOUTHANASIA (LP, blue vinyl). . . . 25
95 Capitol CDESTS 2244 YOUTHANASIA/HIDDEN TREASURES (2-CD, card sleeve, 2,000 only). . . . 25
07 EMI 50995 13187 28 WARCHEST ('ammo' box set with 4 CD's, DVD and booklet) . . . 30

MEGATON
71 Deram DM-R 331 Out Of Your Own Little World/Niagara . . . 30
71 Deram SML-R 1086 MEGATON (LP, white/red label with small logo) . . . 600

MINT VALUE £

MEGATON

81	Hot Metal HMM 69	Aluminium Lady/Diehard (p/s)	40

MEGATONS (Jamaica)
(see also Revelation)

70	Downtown DT 464	Take It Easy/Funk The Beat	10
70	Downtown DT 469	Militant Man/MUSIC DOCTORS: Reggae Jeggae Version	10

MEGATONS (U.S.)
(see also Billy Lee Riley)

65	Sue WI 325	Shimmy Shimmy Walk (Parts 1 & 2)	40

GEORGE MEGGIE

72	Bullet BU 504	Hard To Believe/MAX ROMEO: Softie	7
72	Punch PH 112	People Like People/MAX ROMEO: Softie	7

JOHN MEHEGAN TRIO

56	London EZC 19005	THE FIRST MEHEGAN VOLUME ONE (EP)	8
56	London EZC 19015	THE FIRST MEHEGAN VOLUME TWO (EP)	8

MEKONS
(see also Batfish Boys, Sally Timms & Drifting Cowgirls, Ut)

78	Fast Products FAST 1	Never Been In A Riot/32 Weeks/Heart And Soul (p/s)	12
78	Fast Products FAST 7	Where Were You?/I'll Have To Dance Then (On My Own) (p/s)	6
80	Virgin SV 101	Teeth/Guardian//Kill/Stay Cool (double pack, gatefold p/s)	5
80s	Catalogue CAT 075/3	Amnesia (square flexidisc with The Catalogue magazine)	5
82	CNT CNT 1	This Sporting Life (6.12)/Frustration (6.21)/(mystery live track) (12", p/s)	8
82	CNT CNT 008	This Sporting Life/Fight The Cuts (p/s)	5
82	CNT CNT 014	THE ENGLISH DANCING MASTER (12" EP)	8
82	CNT CNT 009	THE MEKONS STORY (LP)	18
87	Sin 006	HONKY TONKIN' (LP)	12
85	Sin 001	FEAR AND WHISKEY (LP)	12
90s	Virgin	THE QUALITY OF MERCY IS NOT STRNEN (CD)	25

MEL & DAVE

70	Upsetter US 330	Spinning Wheel/Version	15

MEL & TIM

70	Concord CON 004	Backfield In Motion/Do Right Baby (pink label design)	6
70	Concord CON 004	Backfield In Motion/Do Right Baby (multi design)	6
70	Concord CON 004	Backfield In Motion/Do Right Baby (egg design)	6
73	Stax 2025 125	Starting All Over Again/It Hurts To Want You So Bad	8
73	Stax 2025 171	What's Your Name/Free For All	8
73	Stax 2325 090	STARTING ALL OVER AGAIN (LP)	25

MELANIE

68	Buddah 2011 033	Alexander Beetle/Christopher Robin/Animal Crackers (p/s)	10
69	Buddah 201 063	Tuning My Guitar/Beautiful People (withdrawn, demos may exist)	10
69	Buddah 203 019	BORN TO BE (LP, gatefold sleeve)	15
69	Buddah 203 028	AFFECTIONATELY MELANIE (LP, with inner lyric sheet)	15
70	Buddah 2318 009	CANDLES IN THE RAIN (LP, gatefold sleeve)	15
70	Buddah 2318 011	LEFTOVER WINE (LP, gatefold sleeve)	15
71	Buddah 2322 001	THE GOOD BOOK (LP, gatefold sleeve, with booklet)	12
71	Buddah 2322 002	GATHER ME (LP, gatefold sleeve)	12
72	Buddah 2318 054	GARDEN IN THE CITY (LP, scratch 'n' sniff sleeve)	15
72	Buddah 2659 013	THE FOUR SIDES OF MELANIE (2-LP)	18

TERRY MELCHER
(see also Terry Day, The Rip Chords, Freeway)

68	Rex R 11039	Indian Lake/Be My Girl	8
74	Reprise K 54016	TERRY MELCHER (LP)	20

GIL MELLE (QUINTET)

55	Vogue LDE 141	GIL MELLE QUINTET (10" LP)	15

SUSAN MELLEN

75	MAM MAMAS 1014	THE MELLEN BIRD (LP, with insert)	30

JOHN COUGAR MELLENCAMP
(see also John Cougar)

MELLODITIES

64	R&B JB 179	Vacation/TOMMY McCOOK: Music Is My Occupation	45

MELLO & MELLOTONES
(see also Mellotones)

72	Summit SUM 8538	Haile Selasie/Old Man River	10

MELL(O)TONES
(see also Sexy Girls)

68	Amalgamated AMG 812	Fat Girl In Red/VERSATILES: Trust The Book	20
68	Amalgamated AMG 817	Feel Good (actually maybe by Bleechers)/Soulful Mood (actually by Tommy McCook & Supersonics)	25
68	Doctor Bird DB 1136	None Such/VAL BENNETT: Popeye On The Shore	20
68	Trojan TR 612	Uncle Charlie/What A Botheration	12
68	Pyramid PYR 6060	Let's Join Together/BEVERLEY'S ALLSTARS: I Don't Know	12
69	Camel CA 18	Facts Of Life/TERMITES: I'll Be Waiting	20
70	Escort ERT 844	Work It/SOUL MAN: Good Lover	10

MELLOW CANDLE

68	SNB 55-3645	Feeling High/Tea With The Sun	100
72	Deram DM 357	Dan The Wing/Silversong	80
72	Deram SDL 7	SWADDLING SONGS (LP)	1500

MELLOW CATS with Count Ossie & Warrickas
(see also Melo Cats)

61	Blue Beat BB 68	Rock A Man Soul/MONTO & CYCLONES: Lazy Lou (B-side actually by Monty [Alexander] & Cyclones)	12

MINT VALUE £

MELLOW FRUITFULNESS

67	Columbia S(C)X 6242	MEDITATION (LP, mono/stereo)	15

MELLOW LARKS

(see also Basil Gabbidon)

60	Blue Beat BB 16	Time To Pray (Alleluia)/Love You Baby	8
61	Blue Beat BB 38	No More Wedding/Lite Of My Life	8

MELLOW ROSE

80	Studio 16 WE 348	Imitation Love/SGT. PEPPER: Dub A Rub Ina Imitation Way (12")	25

GEORGE MELLY (& MICK MULLIGAN BAND)

(see also Mick Mulligan Band)

51	Tempo A 96	Rock Island Line/Send Me To The 'Lectric Chair (78, as The George Melly Trio)	15
55	Decca F 10457	Frankie And Johnny/I'm Down In The Dumps	8
56	Tempo A 144	Jenny's Ball/Muddy Water	8
56	Tempo A 147	Death Letter/Cemetery Blues	8
56	Tempo EXA 41	GEORGE MELLY WITH MICK MULLIGAN'S JAZZ BAND (EP)	10
56	Tempo EXA 47	GEORGE MELLY SINGS DOOM (EP, with Mick Mulligan's Jazz Band)	10
58	Decca DFE 6552	MICHIGAN WATER BLUES (EP)	10
58	Decca DFE 6557	ABDUL ABULBUL AMIR (EP)	10
61	Columbia SEG 8093	THE PSYCHOLOGICAL SIGNIFICANCE OF ANIMAL SYMBOLISM IN AMERICAN NEGRO FOLK MUSIC AND ALL THAT JAZZ (EP)	10

MELO CATS

(see also Mellow Cats)

61	Blue Beat BB 54	Another Moses/ROLAND ALPHONSO & ALLEY CATS: Hully Gully Rock	10

MELODIANS

(see also Gentiles, Tony Brevett, Brent Dowe, Jaylads, Trevor McNaughton, Gaylads, Joe Grinne)

66	Island WI 3014	Lay It On/Meet Me	30
67	Coxsone CS 7004	I Should Have Made It Up/JOE HIGGS: Neighbour Neighbour	80
67	Treasure Isle TI 7006	You Don't Need Me/I Will Get Along	30
67	Treasure Isle TI 7022	You Have Caught Me/I Know Just How She Feels	50
67	Treasure Isle TI 7023	Last Train To Expo. '67/TOMMY McCOOK & SUPERSONICS: Expo	30
68	Treasure Isle TI 7028	Come On, Little Girl/TOMMY McCOOK & SUPERSONICS: Got Your Soul	30
68	Doctor Bird DB 1125	Little Nut Tree/You Are My Only Love	25
68	Doctor Bird DB 1139	Swing And Dine/I Could Be King	25
68	Fab FAB 61	Sweet Rose/It Comes And Goes	30
69	Gas GAS 108	Ring Of Gold/You've Got It	12
69	Gas GAS 116	Personally Speaking/LLOYD ROBINSON: Trouble Trouble	8
69	Crab CRAB 15	When There Is You/UNIQUES: My Woman's Love	30
69	Trojan TR 660	Everybody Bawlin'/TOMMY McCOOK: Kilowatt	8
69	Trojan TR 695	Sweet Sensation/It's My Delight	5
70	Trojan TR 7720	A Day Seems So Long/BEVERLEY'S ALLSTARS: Project	6
70	Trojan TR 7764	Say Darling Say/Come Rock It To Me	8
70	High Note HS 044	Love Is A Good Thing/No Nola	6
70	Summit SUM 8505	Walking In The Rain/Rivers Of Babylon	7
70	Summit SUM 8508	Rivers Of Babylon/BEVERLEY'S ALL STARS: Babylon Version	6
71	Duke DU 128	The Sensational Melodians (Parts 1 & 2)	5
71	Summit SUM 8512	It Took A Miracle/BEVERLEY'S ALLSTARS: Miraculous Version	5
71	Summit SUM 8522	Come Ethiopians, Come/BEVERLEY'S ALL STARS: Version Two	8
71	Summit SUM 8532	My Love, My Life/My Love, My Life - Version	6
72	Summit SUM 8534	The Time Has Come/BEVERLEY'S ALL STARS: McIntosh (B-side actually "No Sins At All" by Melodians)	6
72	Bullet BU 496	Tropical Land/HUGH ROY & SLIM SMITH: Love I Bring	6
72	Duke DU 130	The Mighty Melodians (Adapted) (Parts 1 & 2)	6
72	Attack ATT 8025	This Beautiful Land/MELODIOUS RHYTHMS: Version	6
72	Attack ATT 8031	Without You (What Would I Do)/DYNAMITES: Instrumental	6
72	Punch PH 111	Round And Round/UPSETTERS: Round Version	8
73	Randy's RAN 530	Passion Love/Love Makes The World Go Round	6

BOBBY MELODY

79	Hit Run HIT DD5	Anger & Strife (ft. Jah Lion)/JAH LION: Johnnie Walker (12")	30

JOHNNY MELODY

(see also Lloyd & Johnny Melody under 'L', Lloyd Terrell)

67	Pyramid PYR 6023	Govern Your Mouth (actually by George Dekker)/ROLAND ALPHONSO: Peace And Love	20

MELODY ENCHANTERS

63	Island WI 049	Enchanter's Ball/I'll Be True	20
63	R&B JB 117	Gone Gone/Blueberry Hill	18

MELODY FAIR

68	Decca F 12801	Something Happened To Me/Sittin', Watchin', Waitin'	6

MELO'S MARITIME

67	Philips BF 1602	Blow The Man Up/Maneater	5

KANSAS CITY MELROSE/CASINO SIMPSON

72	Chicago Piano 12-001	KANSAS CITY MELROSE/CASINO SIMPSON (LP)	15

MONIQUE MELSEN

71	Decca F 23170	The Love Beat/Pomme Pomme Pomme	12

JOE MELSON

61	Polydor NH 66959	Oh Yeah!/What's The Use I Still Love You	50
61	Polydor NH 66961	Hey Mister Cupid/No One Really Cares	40
64	Hickory 45-1229	Stay Away From Her/His Girl	5

MELTING BEAR

(see also Icicle Works)

85	Beggars Banquet BEG 144	It Makes No Difference/Nature's Way/Sea Song (unreleased, white label test pressings only)	6

MINT VALUE £

MELTON CONSTABLE

70s	SIS private pressing	MELTON CONSTABLE (LP)	150

HAROLD MELVIN & BLUE NOTES

72	CBS 8496	If You Don't Know Me By Now/Let Me Into Your World	5
75	Route RT 06	Get Out/You May Not Love Me	8
73	CBS 65350	HAROLD MELVIN & THE BLUES NOTES (LP)	12
73	CBS Q 65859	BLACK AND BLUE (LP, quadrophonic)	12

MELVINS

90	Tupelo TUPEP 10	Sweet Young Thing Ain't Sweet No More/STEEL POLE BATH TUB: I Dreamed I Dream (12", p/s, green vinyl, 600 only)	18

MEMBERS

78	Stiff/One Off OFF 3	Solitary Confinement/Rat Up A Drainpipe (p/s)	15
79	Virgin VS 242	The Sound Of The Suburbs/Handling The Big Jets (clear vinyl, window p/s)	5
80	Virgin VS 352	Flying Again/Disco Oui Oui//Live In A Lift/Rat Up A Drainpipe (double pack, gatefold p/s)	5

MEMO

74	Decca F13539	Kick A Tin Can/Attilah	8

MEMO

05	Not Apple NA 001	I Play My Ipod (You Gave Me For Christmas)/A Juno 8 is Never Out Of Date (12" no p/s)	8

MEMORIES

74	Rex 11091	Lay It On Me/Did Ya Get It	20

MEMOS

59	Parlophone R 4616	The Biddy Leg/My Type Of Girl	60

MEMPHIS BEND

76	United Artists UP 36132	Ubangi Stomp/Tennessee	8
77	United Artists UAS 30036	GOOD ROCKIN' TONITE (LP)	12
73	United Artists UP 35571	Louisiana Hoedown/Right String Baby But The Wrong Yo Yo	10

MEMPHIS HORNS

71	Atlantic 2091 080	Woolly Bully/I Can't Turn You Loose	10
77	RCA PB 0836	Get Up And Dance/Don't Abuse It	6
71	Mojo 2466 010	THE MEMPHIS HORNS (LP)	25

MEMPHIS JUG BAND

55	HMV 7EG 8073	MEMPHIS JUG BAND (EP, withdrawn)	60
70s	Saydisc Matchbox RL 33	MEMPHIS JUG BAND (LP)	20
71	Saydisc Matchbox RL 337	MEMPHIS JUG BAND VOLUME 2 (LP)	20

MEMPHIS MINNIE

64	Heritage H 103	MEMPHIS MINNIE (EP)	75
69	Limited Edition (no cat. no.)	MEMPHIS MINNIE 1934-1936 (LP)	40
69	Limited Edition (no cat. no.)	MEMPHIS MINNIE 1934-1941 (LP)	40
69	Sunflower ET 1400	MEMPHIS MINNIE 1941-1949 (LP, 99 copies only)	50
74	Flyright LP 108	MEMPHIS MINNIE 1934-1941 (LP, reissue)	12
74	Flyright LP 109	MEMPHIS MINNIE 1941-1949 (LP, reissue)	12

MEMPHIS SLIM

(see also Washboard Sam, Ivory Joe Hunter, Otis Spann)

53	Esquire 10-319	Harlem Bound/ST. LOUIS JIMMY R&B BAND: Holiday For Boogie (78)	30
60	Collector JDN 102	Pinetop's Blues/How Long	25
62	Storyville A 45055	Big City Girl/El Capitan	15
61	Collector JEN 5	GOING TO KANSAS CITY (EP)	30
62	Storyville SEP 385	STORYVILLE BLUES ANTHOLOGY VOL. 5 - BOOGIE WOOGIE AND THE BLUES (EP)	22
63	Vocalion VEP 170155	MEMPHIS SLIM AND LITTLE RICHARD (EP)	80
63	Summit LSE 2041	WORLD'S FOREMOST BLUES SINGERS (EP)	12
61	Collector JGN 1004	MEMPHIS SLIM U.S.A. (LP)	45
61	Collector JGN 1005	MEMPHIS SLIM U.S.A. (VOL. 2) (LP)	45
62	Bluesville BV 1018	JUST BLUES (LP)	30
62	Storyville SLP 118	MEMPHIS SLIM (LP)	22
62	Storyville SLP 138	THIS IS A GOOD TIME TO WRITE A SONG (LP)	22
62	Fontana 688 302 ZL	NO STRAIN (LP)	20
63	United Artists ULP 1042	BROKEN SOUL BLUES (LP)	30
64	Storyville SLP 118	TRAVELLIN' WITH THE BLUES (LP)	22
64	Xtra XTRA 1008	MEMPHIS SLIM (LP)	18
64	Fontana 688 701	ALONE WITH MY FRIENDS (LP)	30
65	Fontana TL 5254	CLAP YOUR HANDS (LP)	25
65	Melodisc MLPS 12-149	FATTENIN' FROGS FOR SNAKES (LP)	25
66	Fontana 688 315 ZL	FRISCO BAY BLUES (LP)	30
67	Polydor 623 211	PINETOP'S BLUES (LP)	18
68	Polydor 623 263	BLUESINGLY YOURS (LP, with Mickey Baker)	18
68	Xtra XTRA 5060	ALL KINDS OF BLUES (LP)	15
69	Xtra XTRA 1085	CHICAGO BLUES (LP)	15
72	Barclay 920 214	BLUE MEMPHIS (LP, with Peter Green)	75
72	Barclay 920 332-3	OLD TIMES, NEW TIMES (2-LP)	18
70s	Xtra XTRA 5063	ALL KINDS OF BLUES (LP)	15

MEMPHIS THREE

68	Page One POF 070	Wild Thing/She's A Yum Yum	7

MEN

(see also Human League)

79	Virgin VS 269	I Don't Depend On You/Cruel (p/s)	6
79	Virgin VS 269-12	I Don't Depend On You/Cruel (12", p/s)	8

MINT VALUE £

MENACE
(see also Aces, Vermilion & Aces)

77	Illegal IL 004	Screwed Up/Insane Society (p/s)	15
77	Illegal IL 004	Screwed Up/Insane Society (12", p/s)	20
77	Small Wonder SMALL 5	G.L.C./I'm Civilized (p/s)	15
78	Illegal IL 008	I Need Nothing/Electrocutioner (p/s)	15
82	Fresh FRESH 14	The Young Ones/Tomorrow's World/Live For Today (p/s)	15
79	Small Wonder SMALL 16	Final Vinyl: Last Year's Youth/Carry No Banners (p/s)	8
86	Razor RAZ 18	GLC - RIP (LP)	25

MENACE

01	Plastica DPFT 004	Reap What You Sow (12")	15

MENACE MAKES 3

92	Danse City DC 1203	Pure Hysteria (Give Me A Mother Mix)/Do You Feel What I'm Feeling? (Matrix Rise Remix)(12")	50

CARLOS MENDES

72	Pye International 7N 25581	Shadows/Glow-Worm	8

MENDES PREY

83	MP AM 076	On To The Borderline/Runnin' For You (p/s)	20
86	Wag WAG 2	Wonderland/Can You Believe It (p/s)	25
86	Wag 12 WAG 2	Wonderland/Can You Believe It (12", p/s)	25

ENOCH & CHRISTY MENSAH

60	Melodisc M 1569	Rebecca/Dakuku Dum	5

E.T. MENSAH & HIS TEMPO'S BAND

55	Decca WAL 1001	DECCA PRESENTS (10" LP)	22

MENTAL

79	Kamikaze Pig RAM 1	God For A Day/18/Kill The Bill/Off The Rails (600 only, p/s)	80

MENTATZ

81	Naff N 001	Never Trust A Russian/Dead To The World (p/s)	5

IAN MENZIES
(see also Clyde Valley Stompers)

58	Pye Jazz 7NJ 2027	Polly Wolly Doodle/In A Persian Market (with His New Stompers)	5
58	Pye Jazz 7NJ 2028	Bill Bailey Won't You Please Come Home/Hot Time In The Old Town Tonight (as Ian Menzies & Clyde Valley Stompers)	5
61	Pye Jazz 7NJ 2046	Auf Wiedersehn/Taboo	8
58	Pye Jazz NJE 1049	MELODY MAKER ALL STARS (EP)	8
60	Pye Nixa NJE 1071	SWINGIN' SEAMUS (EP)	8
60	Pye Nixa NJL 23	HAVE TARTAN...WILL TRAD (LP)	15
60	Pye Jazz NJL 26	IAN MENZIES AND THE CLYDE VALLEY STOMPERS (LP)	12

MARY MAE MERCER

65	Decca DFE 8599	MARY MAE MERCER (EP)	50

MICKEY MERCIAN

84	Unity Sound UN 029	Ride The Rhythm/Go Anywhere (12")	25

FREDDIE MERCURY
(see also Queen, Larry Lurex, Eddie Howell, Billy Squier)

84	CBS WA 4735	Love Kills/GEORGIO MORODER: Rotwang's Party (picture disc)	30
84	CBS TA 4735	Love Kills (Extended)/GEORGIO MORODER: Rotwang's Party (12", p/s)	10
85	CBS DA 6019	I Was Born To Love You/Stop All The Fighting//Love Kills (Extended)/ Stop All The Fighting (Extended) (double pack)	15
85	CBS TA 6019	I Was Born To Love You (7.03)/Stop All The Fighting (12", p/s)	8
85	CBS A 6413	Made In Heaven (Remix 3.59)/She Blows Hot And Cold (p/s)	5
85	CBS WA 6413	Made In Heaven (Remix)/She Blows Hot And Cold (shaped picture disc)	35
85	CBS WA 6413	Made In Heaven (Remix)/She Blows Hot And Cold (uncut shaped picture disc)	500
85	CBS TA 6413	Made In Heaven (Extended Remix 4.43)/Made In Heaven (Remix 3.59)/ She Blows Hot And Cold (Extended Version) (12", p/s)	10
85	CBS TA 6555	Living On My Own (Extended 6.38)/My Love Is Dangerous (Extended 6.25) (12", p/s)	8
85	CBS GTA 6555	Living On My Own (Extended 6.38)/My Love Is Dangerous (Extended 6.25) (12", gatefold p/s)	15
85	CBS A 6725	Love Me Like There's No Tomorrow/Let's Turn It On (p/s)	20
85	CBS TA 6725	Love Me Like There's No Tomorrow (Extended Version)/Let's Turn It On (Extended Version) (12", p/s)	40
85	CBS DTA 6725	Love Me Like There's No Tomorrow (Extended Version)/Let's Turn It On (Extended Version)//Living On My Own (Extended 6.38)/My Love Is Dangerous (Extended 6.25) (12" double pack, shrinkwrapped with sticker)	50
85	CBS TA 6725	Love Me Like There's No Tomorrow (Extended Version)/Let's Turn It On (Extended Version) (12", promo, white card sleeve, with sticker)	50
86	EMI EMI 5559	Time (From The Musical)/Time (Instrumental) (p/s, with inner sleeve)	5
87	Parlophone RP 6151	The Great Pretender/Exercises In Free Love (Mercury Vocal) (shaped picture disc)	30
87	Parlophone RP 6151	The Great Pretender/Exercises In Free Love (Mercury Vocal) (shaped picture disc, with unfolded or folded plinth)	60
87	Parlophone RP 6151	The Great Pretender/Exercises In Free Love (Mercury Vocal) (shaped picture disc, with unfolded or folded plinth)	40
87	Parlophone RP 6151	The Great Pretender/Exercises In Free Love (Mercury Vocal) (uncut shaped picture disc)	350
87	Parlophone 10R 6151	The Great Pretender (Extended Version)/(7" Version)/Exercises In Free Love (7" Version) (10", 1-sided, printed white label, plain black die-cut sleeve, promo only)	25
87	Polydor POSP 887	Barcelona/Exercises In Free Love (Caballé Vocal) (with Montserrat Caballé, with gatefold p/s)	5
87	Polydor POSPX 887	Barcelona (Single Version)/Exercises In Free Love (Caballé Vocal) (12" Version)/Barcelona (Extended) (12", some with gatefold p/s)	8
87	Polydor POSPX 887	Barcelona (Single Version)/Exercises In Free Love (Caballé Vocal) (12" Version)/Barcelona (Extended) (12", some with gatefold p/s)	6

			MINT VALUE £
87	Polydor POSPP 887	Barcelona (7" Version)/Exercises In Free Love (Caballé Vocal) (7" Version)/ Barcelona (Extended Version) (12", picture disc)	40
87	Polydor POCD 887	Barcelona (7" Version)/Exercises In Free Love (Caballé Vocal) (7" Version)/ Barcelona (Extended Version) (CD, card p/s)	15
87	Polydor POCD 887	Barcelona/Exercises In Free Love (Version 2) (Caballé Vocal)/ Barcelona (Extended) (CD, autographed card p/s, promo only)	300
87	Polydor PO 23 DJ	The Golden Boy (with Montserrat Caballé) (radio edit) (1-sided DJ sampler, p/s, with sticker)	100
88	Polydor POSPX 23	The Golden Boy/The Fallen Priest/The Golden Boy (Instrumental) (12", p/s)	20
88	Polydor PZCD234	The Golden Boy/The Fallen Priest/The Golden Boy (Instrumental) (CD)	35
88	Polydor PO 29	How Can I Go On/Overture Piccante (with Montserrat Caballe) (p/s)	15
88	Polydor POSX 29	How Can I Go On/Overture Piccante (with Montserrat Caballe) (picture disc)	45
89	Polydor PZ 29	How Can I Go On/Guide Me Home/Overture Piccante (12", p/s)	25
89	Polydor PZCD 29	How Can I Go On/Guide Me Home/Overture Piccante (CD, picture disc)	35
88	Polydor CD 3 125 211	The Golden Boy/La Japanese/Barcelona (CD promo, unreleased p/s, jewel case)	100
89	Polydor 0805 548-2	Ensueno/Barcelona (Edit 4.24)/Exercises In Free Love/Barcelona (Extended Version 7.02)/Barcelona (Video) (CD Video)	40
89	Polydor 0805 580-2	The Fallen Priest/The Golden Boy (Album Version)/The Golden Boy (Instrumental Version)/The Golden Boy (Video) (CD Video)	40
92	Polydor PO 234	How Can I Go On/The Golden Boy (yellow p/s)	6
92	Polydor PZCD 234	How Can I Go On/The Golden Boy/The Fallen Priest (CD, yellow p/s)	10
92	Parlophone R 6331	In My Defence/Love Kills (Wolf Euro Mix) (p/s)	6
06	Parlophone KILLS 001	Love Kills (Glimmer Mix)/(Pixel 82 Mix)/I Was Born To Love You (George Demure Mix) (12" promo)	15
06	Parlophone KILLS 003	Living On My Own (mixes) (12" promo)	15
85	CBS 40-86312	MR. BAD GUY (cassette, with extra remix)	15
85	CBS CD 86312	MR. BAD GUY (CD, with 3 extended mixes; beware of counterfeits)	25
94	Parlophone 7234 8 2814 10	FREDDIE MERCURY REMIXES (LP, unreleased)	150
00	Parlophone FMRARE001	THE SOLO COLLECTION (10 CD & 2 DVD box set)	80

MERCURY REV
(see also Shady)

91	Mint Film MINT 5	Car Wash Hair/Coney Island Cyclone (4 track demo) (200 copies only, p/s)	10
91	Mint Film MINT 5 T	Car Wash Hair/Chasing A Bee (4 track demo)/Coney Island Cyclone (12", p/s)	10
92	Rough Trade 45REV 6	If You Want Me To Stay/Left Handed Raygun of Paul Sharits (Retirement Just Like That) (p/s, with insert)	12
93	Beggars Banquet BBQ 5 T	The Hum Is Coming From Her (as Mercury Theremin Sextet)/ So There (as Mercury Rev Orchestra with Robert Creely) (10", p/s)	8
93	Beggars Banquet BBQ 14	Something For Joey/There's Spiders Eggs In Bubbla Yhum (blue vinyl, two different p/s)	6
91	Mint Film MINTLP 4	YERSELF IS STEAM (LP, with bonus LP 'Lego My Ego')	25
93	Beggars Banquet BBQLP 140	BOCES (LP, clear red vinyl)	20
95	B. Banquet BBQLP 176 P	SEE YOU ON THE OTHER SIDE (LP, picture disc)	12
98	V2 VVR 1002772	DESERTER'S SONGS (CD, with cardboard sleeve and stamps)	20
98	V2 VVR 1002771	DESERTERS SONGS (LP)	25

MERCY

69	London HLZ 10273	Love (Can Make You Happy)/Fireball	30

BURGESS MEREDITH

63	Colpix PX 690	Home In The Meadow/No Goodbye	6

LOTTIE MERLE

72	Flyright 001	Howling In The Moonlight/Catfish	10

MERLIN

88	Rhythm King LEFTR22T	Born Free (Wizard Mix) (12")	10

MERLIN Q

69	Pye 7N 17828	The Secret/Love's Beautiful	25
69	Pye 7917828	The Secret/Loves Beautiful	15

RAY MERRELL

60	Ember EMB S 113	Why Did You Leave Me?/Teenage Love (p/s)	10
60s	Aral PS 115	Battle Of Waterloo/Not Any More (p/s)	10
70	Jay Boy BOY 22	Tears Of Joy/Searchin' (withdrawn) (Beware of bootlegs!)	200
70	Jay Boy BOY 22	Tears Of Joy/Searchin' (withdrawn) (Beware of bootlegs!) (DJ copy)	300

TONY MERRICK

66	Columbia DB 7913	Lady Jane/Michelle	10
66	Columbia DB 7995	Wake Up/It's For You	6

BOB MERRILL

58	Columbia DB 4086	Nairobi/Jump When I Say Frog	15

BUDDY MERRILL

66	Vocalion VN 9261	Sweet September/Sherk	12

HELEN MERRILL

58	Mercury ZEP 10064	SOFTLY AS IN A MORNING SUNRISE (EP)	8

MERRITTS

70	Hot Rod HR 113	I Don't Want To (Part 1)/HOT ROD ALL STARS: Version	12

MERRY MAKER

76	Western Kingston WK 505	Untouchable Special/Straight To Music City Head	10

MERRYMEN
(see also Soul Brothers)

66	Doctor Bird DB 1004	Big Bamboo/Island Woman	8
69	Trojan TR 7707	Little Drummer Boy/Mary's Boy Child	5
71	Duke DU 113	Big Bamboo/King Ja-Ja (both sides actually with Emille Straker)	5
68	Island ILP 984	CARIBBEAN TREASURE CHEST (LP)	30

MINT VALUE £

JASON MERRYWEATHER
(see also Ricky Valance)

69	Crystal CR 001	My Summer Love/Abigail	10

MERSEYBEATS
(see also Merseys, Rockin' Horse, Tony Crane, Kirkbys, Quotations, Johnny Gustavson)

63	Fontana TF 412	It's Love That Really Counts/The Fortune Teller	12
64	Fontana TF 431	I Think Of You/Mister Moonlight	5
64	Fontana TF 459	Don't Turn Around/Really Mystified	5
64	Fontana TF 482	Wishin' And Hopin'/Milkman	5
64	Fontana TF 504	Last Night/See Me Back	10
65	Fontana TF 568	Don't Let It Happen To Us/It Would Take A Long Long Time	10
65	Fontana TF 607	I Love You, Yes I Do/Good Good Lovin'	8
65	Fontana TF 645	I Stand Accused/All My Life	10
69	Fontana TF 1025	I Think Of You/Wishin' And Hopin' (p/s)	10
81	Tudor CHEM 001	This Is Merseybeat (both sides) (p/s)	6
64	Fontana TE 17422	ON STAGE (EP)	40
64	Fontana TE 17423	I THINK OF YOU (EP)	30
64	Fontana TE 17432	THE MERSEYBEATS (EP)	30
64	Fontana TL 5210	THE MERSEYBEATS (LP)	70
69	Wing WL 1163	THE MERSEYBEATS (LP)	15
77	Look LKLP 6160	GREATEST HITS (LP)	12

MERSEYBOYS

64	Ace Of Clubs ACL 1169	15 GREAT SONGS BY JOHN, PAUL AND GEORGE (LP)	20

MERSEYS
(see also Merseybeats, Crackers)

66	Fontana TF 694	Sorrow/Some Other Day	6
66	Fontana TF 732	So Sad About Us/Love Will Continue	10
66	Fontana TF 776	Rhythm Of Love/Is It Love?	10
67	Fontana TF 845	The Cat/Change Of Heart	25
68	Fontana TF 916	Penny In My Pocket/I Hope You're Happy	10
68	Fontana TF 955	Lovely Loretta/Dreaming	10
73	Philips 6006 258	Sorrow/MERSEYBEATS: I Think Of You	5

MERSEYSIPPI JAZZ BAND

54	Esquire 20-063	WEST COAST SHOUT (LP)	12
55	Esquire 20-083	ALL THE GIRLS (LP)	12
55	Esquire 20-088	MERSEY TUNNEL JAZZ (LP)	12
56	Esquire 20-093	ANY OLD RAGS (LP)	12

MERTON PARKAS
(see also Style Council)

79	Beggars Banquet BEG 22	You Need Wheels/I Don't Want To Know You (coloured p/s with patch)	10
79	Beggars Banquet BEG 22	You Need Wheels/I Don't Want To Know You (coloured p/s)	5
79	Beggars Banquet BEG 25	Plastic Smile/The Man With The Disguise (p/s)	5
79	Beggars Banquet BEG 30	Give It To Me Now/Gi's It (p/s)	5
80	Beggars Banquet BEG 43	Put Me In The Picture/In The Midnight Hour (p/s)	5
83	Well Suspect BLAM 002	Flat 19/Band Of Gold (p/s)	8
80s	Beggars Banquet BEG 22	You Need Wheels/I Don't Want To Know You (reissue, with silver moulded label, black & white p/s)	7
79	Beggars Banquet BEGA 11	FACE IN THE CROWD (LP)	18

MESCALINE UNITED

92	R&S RS 92019	We Have Arrived (Aphex Twin QQT Reconstruction Mix)/We Have Arrived (Aphex Twin TTQ Reconstruction Mix) (limited issue 12", also known as "PCP Remixed" plain paper sleeve)	70

MESSAGE
(see also Boris Gardner)

70	Doctor Bird DB 1503	Rum-Bum-A-Loo/Drummer Boy	70
72	Reggae REG 3004	Wrestling/Tricia	60

MESSAGE

75	Decca SKL-R 5213	MESSAGE (LP, blue/silver label)	25

RICKY MESSENGER & SEMI PROFESSIONALS

80s	Kim 019	Now Is The Time For Jah/Mr. Richman (12")	20

MESSENGERS

64	Columbia DB 7344	I'm Stealin' Back/This Little Light Of Mine	10
65	Columbia DB 7495	When Did You Leave Heaven/More Pretty Girls Than One	8

MESSENGERS (Jamaica)

73	Attack ATT 8057	Crowded City/Thula Thula	5
73	Bread BR 1116	Cherry Baby/B.B. SEATON: Summertime	5

METABOLIST

79	Drömm DRO 1	Drömm/Slaves/Eulam's Beat (p/s, rough screen-printed & folded p/s)	12
79	Drömm DRO 1	Drömm/Slaves/Eulam's Beat (p/s, smooth printed & stapled p/s)	10
79	Drömm DRO 3	Identity/Tiz Hoz Nam (p/s)	8
79	Drömm NCN	GOATMANAUT (cassette)	20
70s	Metabolists	GOATMANAUT (cassette)	12
70s	Drömm D 1	GOATMANAUT (LP)	15
70s	Drömm DRO 2	HANSTEN KLORD (LP)	12

METAL BOYS
(see also Metal Urbain)

79	Rough Trade RT 016	Sweet Marilyn/Fugue For A Darkening Island (p/s)	5

METALLICA
SINGLES

84	Music For Nations 12 KUT 105	Jump In The Fire/Seek And Destroy (live)/Phantom Lord (live) (12", p/s, initial pressing with beige labels)	25

			MINT VALUE £
84	Music For Nations 12 KUT 105	Jump In The Fire/Seek And Destroy (live)/Phantom Lord (live) (12", p/s, later pressing with red/yellow labels)	20
84	Music For Nations CV12 KUT 105	Jump In The Fire/Seek And Destroy (live)/Phantom Lord (live) (12", red vinyl, p/s)	35
84	Music For Nations 12 KUT 105XP	Jump In The Fire/Seek And Destroy (live)/Phantom Lord (live) (12", stickered sleeve with sew-on patch)	30
84	Music For Nations T 12 KUT 105	Jump In The Fire/Seek And Destroy (live)/Phantom Lord (live) (cassette)	5
84	Music For Nations T 12 KUT 112	Creeping Death/Am I Evil?/Blitzkrieg (cassette)	8
84	Music For Nations 12 KUT 112	Creeping Death/Am I Evil?/Blitzkrieg (12", p/s, initial pressing with beige label)	18
84	Music For Nations 12 KUT 112	Creeping Death/Am I Evil?/Blitzkrieg (12", p/s, later pressing with red/yellow labels)	15
84	Music For Nations CV12 KUT 112	Creeping Death/Am I Evil?/Blitzkrieg (12", p/s, blue vinyl, red/yellow or 'Special Anniversary Edition' labels)	35
84	Music For Nations GV12 KUT 112	Creeping Death/Am I Evil?/Blitzkrieg (12", no p/s, 'Anniversary Gold Edition', gold vinyl, 3000 only; mispressing with 1 side gold, 1 side black vinyl)	70
84	Music For Nations GV12 KUT 112	Creeping Death/Am I Evil?/Blitzkrieg (12", no p/s, 'Anniversary Gold Edition', gold vinyl, 3000 only)	60
84	Music For Nations P12 KUT 112	Creeping Death/Am I Evil?/Blitzkrieg (12", picture disc, initially without barcode)	30
84	Music For Nations CD12 KUT 112	Creeping Death/Am I Evil?/Blitzkrieg Jump In The Fire/ Seek And Destroy (live)/Phantom Lord (live) (CD)	60
86	Music For Nations PKUT 105	Jump In The Fire/Phantom Lord (live) (shaped picture disc, initial pressing without barcode)	20
86	Music For Nations PKUT 105	Jump In The Fire/Phantom Lord (live) (shaped picture disc, later pressing with barcode)	18
86	Music For Nations PKUT 105	Jump In The Fire/Phantom Lord (live) (uncut picture disc)	150
87	Vertigo METAL 112	$5.98 EP - GARAGE DAYS RE-REVISITED: Helpless/Crash Course In Brain Surgery/The Small Hours/Last Caress - Green Hell (medley) (12" p/s, later copies add "The Wait")	35
88	Vertigo METAL 212	Harvester Of Sorrow/Breadfan/The Prince (12", p/s, with 'skull' label)	15
88	Vertigo METAL CD 2	Harvester Of Sorrow/Breadfan/The Prince (CD, card sleeve)	20
89	Vertigo METAL 312	Jump In The Fire/Seek And Destroy (live)/Phantom Lord (live) (12", p/s, reissue)	8
89	Vertigo METAL 412	Creeping Death/Am I Evil?/Blitzkrieg (12", p/s, reissue)	8
89	Vertigo 842-219-2	Creeping Death/Am I Evil?/Blitzkrieg/Jump In The Fire/ Seek And Destroy (live)/ Phantom Lord (live) (CD)	50
89	Vertigo METAL 5	One/Seek And Destroy (live) (silver/black labels, paper p/s)	8
89	Vertigo METAP 5	One/Seek And Destroy (live) (card p/s, some stickered, with rolled poster)	15
89	Vertigo METPD 510	One/Seek And Destroy (live) (10", picture disc with card)	30
89	Vertigo METAL 512	One (Demo Version)/For Whom The Bell Tolls (live)/Welcome Home (Sanitarium) (live) (12", p/s initial pressing with white labels)	12
89	Vertigo METAL 512	One (Demo Version)/For Whom The Bell Tolls (live)/Welcome Home (Sanitarium) (live) (12", p/s later pressing with yellow labels)	8
89	Vertigo METAL 512	One (Demo Version)/For Whom The Bell Tolls (live)/Welcome Home (Sanitarium) (live) (12", p/s mis-labelled as "Seek and Destroy" [live])	10
89	Vertigo METG 512	One (Demo Version)/For Whom The Bell Tolls (live)/Welcome Home (Sanitarium) (live) (12", gatefold p/s, with booklet, mispressed with B-side label on both sides)	18
89	Vertigo METCD 5	One/For Whom The Bell Tolls (live)/Welcome Home (Sanitarium) (live) (CD)	18
90	Vertigo 875 487 1	THE GOOD, THE BAD AND THE LIVE - THE 61/2 YEARS ANNIVERSARY COLLECTION (6 x 12", with live 4-track EP [METAL 612])	70
91	Vertigo METAL 7	Enter Sandman/Stone Cold Crazy (p/s)	8
91	Vertigo METAL 7	Enter Sandman/Stone Cold Crazy (picture disc in p/s, stickered)	12
91	Vertigo METAL 712	Enter Sandman/Stone Cold Crazy/Holier Than Thou (Demo)/ Enter Sandman (Demo) (12", p/s, with stickered sleeve)	8
91	Vertigo METBX 712	Enter Sandman/Stone Cold Crazy/Enter Sandman (Demo) (12", box with 4 photo prints)	30
91	Vertigo METCD 7	Enter Sandman/Stone Cold Crazy/Enter Sandman (Demo) (CD, picture disc in box with room for 3 more CDs)	30
91	Vertigo METAP 812	The Unforgiven/Killing Time /The Unforgiven (Demo) (picture disc, card insert)	8
91	Vertigo METAL 812	The Unforgiven/Killing Time/So What/The Unforgiven (Demo) (12", p/s, some stickered)	8
91	Vertigo METCD 8	The Unforgiven/Killing Time/The Unforgiven (Demo) (CD)	8
92	Vertigo METCB 9	Wherever I May Roam/Last Caress-Am I Evil?-Battery (Live Medley) (digipak CD)	8
92	Vertigo METAL 10	Nothing Else Matters/Enter Sandman (live) (p/s, black & white label)	8
92	Vertigo METCD 10	Nothing Else Matters/Enter Sandman (live)/Harvester Of Sorrow (live)/ Nothing Else Matters (Demo) (picture CD)	8
92	Vertigo METCL 10	Nothing Else Matters - Live At Wembley 20/4/92: Enter Sandman/ Sad But True/Nothing Else Matters (CD)	25
93	Vertigo METAL 11	Sad But True/Nothing Else Matters (p/s, stickered, no labels)	5
93	Vertigo METAL 1112	Sad But True/Nothing Else Matters (Elevator Version)/Creeping Death (live)/ Sad But True (Demo) (12" picture disc with insert)	20
93	Vertigo METCH 11	Sad But True/Nothing Else Matters (live)/Sad But True (Live) (CD, picture disc)	8
96	Vertigo METJB 12	Until It Sleeps/Until It Sleeps (jukebox issue, no p/s)	10
96	Vertigo METAL 12	Until It Sleeps/2x4 (live)/Until It Sleeps (Moby Remix) (10" red vinyl, stickered)	8
96	Vertigo METCX 12	Until It Sleeps/Kill-Ride (Medley)/Until It Sleeps (Moby Remix) (digipak CD)	8
97	Vertigo METJB 13	Hero Of The Day/Hero Of The Day (jukebox issue, no p/s)	8
96	Vertigo METCY 13	Hero Of The Day/Overkill/Damage Case/Stone Dead Forever/Too Late Too Late (CD, with poster in card cover)	8
96	Vertigo METAL 14	Mama Said/Ain't My Bitch (live) (picture disc with insert)	8
97	Vertigo METJB 15	The Memory Remains/For Whem The Bell Tolls (Haven't Heard It Yet Remix) (Jukebox issue no p/s)	15
90s	Vertigo METJB 19	Whiskey In The Jar/Turn The Page (Jukebox issue no p/s)	15
03	Columbia GABBA 1	53rd & 3rd/Outsider (by GREEN DAY)/I Wanna Be Sedated (by OFFSPRING) (blue vinyl, stickered p/s withdrawn single)	300

MINT VALUE £

LPs

83	Music For Nations MFN 7	KILL 'EM ALL (LP, 1st issue with beige labels)	35
83	M. For Nations MFN 7	KILL 'EM ALL (LP, later pressing with red/yellow])	30
84	M. For Nations MFN 27	RIDE THE LIGHTNING (LP, with inner sleeve, initial pressing with beige labels & without barcode)	25
86	M. For Nations MFN 27P	RIDE THE LIGHTNING (LP, picture disc, initial pressing with no barcode)	30
86	M. For Nations MFN 27P	RIDE THE LIGHTNING (LP, picture disc, with barcode)	20
86	M. For Nations MFN 7P	KILL 'EM ALL (LP reissue, picture disc, lacking picture on 1 side, initially lacking barcode)	25
86	M. For Nations MFN 7P	KILL 'EM ALL (LP reissue, picture disc, with picture on 1 side and barcode)	22
86	M. For Nations MFN 60	MASTER OF PUPPETS (LP, with inner sleeve & insert)	18
86	M. For Nations MFN 60	MASTER OF PUPPETS (LP, mispressing, Side 1 label on both sides)	30
86	M. For Nations MFN 60P	MASTER OF PUPPETS (LP, picture disc, initially without barcode)	22
86	M. For Nations MFN 60P	MASTER OF PUPPETS (LP, picture disc, with barcode)	18
87	M. For Nations MFN 7DM	KILL 'EM ALL (2-LP, 'direct metal mastered' reissue, gatefold sleeve)	35
87	M. For Nations MFN 60DM	MASTER OF PUPPETS (2-LP, 'direct metal mastered' reissue, gatefold sleeve with poster)	25
87	M. For Nations MFN 27DM	RIDE THE LIGHTNING (2-LP, 'direct metal mastered' reissue, gatefold sleeve with insert)	30
89	Vertigo 838-140-1	RIDE THE LIGHTNING (LP, reissue, mispressing, Side 1 lists Master Of Puppets tracks)	15
84	M. For Nations MFNCD 7	KILL 'EM ALL (CD)	25
84	M. For Nations MFN 27P	RIDE THE LIGHTNING (CD)	25
86	M. For Nations MFNCD 60	MASTER OF PUPPETS (CD)	25
91	Vertigo MECAN 1/510-022-0	THE METALLICAN (CD, gold disc in metal 'paint can' with video & T-shirt; 35,000 only)	90
93	Vertigo 518-725-0	LIVE SHIT, BINGE & PURGE (3-CD box set with 3 videos & 72-page book)	70
08	Universal 0600753101162	MASTER OF PUPPETS (2-LP, reissue, gatefold with obi)	18
08	Universal 0600753085240	RIDE THE LIGHTNING (2-LP, reissue, gatefold with obi)	18
08	Universal 0600753085271	KILL 'EM ALL (2-LP, reissue, gatefold with obi)	18

PROMOS

88	Vertigo MET CD 100	THE WHIPLASH SAMPLER (CD)	60
88	Vertigo METDJ 2	Harvester Of Sorrow/Harvester Of Sorrow (unique p/s)	40
89	Vertigo METDJ 5	One/One (Edit) (unique blue cover, plus insert)	70
89	Vertigo METDJ 512	One (Demo Version)/For Whom The Bell Tolls (live)/Welcome Home (Sanitarium) (live) (12", unissued, promo-only p/s)	65
91	Vertigo METDJ 7	Enter Sandman (Radio Edit)/Stone Cold Crazy (p/s B-side actually silent)	15
93	Vertigo PRCD 8879-2	15 PIECES OF LIVE SH*T BINGE & PURGE (Promo CD, stickered card sleeve)	30
90s	Vertigo METDJ8	The Unforgiven (edit)/Killing Time (p/s)	20
96	Vertigo MET INT 1	LOAD - THE INTERVIEW (CD, with cue booklet)	65
96	Mercury MM CJ-1	MANDATORY METALLICA (CD, 7-track sampler)	30
97	Vertigo MMCJ-2	MANDATORY METALLICA 2 (2-CD, 17-track sampler)	40
03	Vertigo FRANTICDJ 1	Frantic (12" promo)	15
03	Vertigo SACDP 1	SAINT ANGER (2-CD promo)	20

METAL MIRROR

80	M&M MM 001	Rock 'N Roll Ain't Never Gonna Leave Us/English Booze (in p/s)	150
80	M&M MM 001	Rock 'N Roll Ain't Never Gonna Leave Us/English Booze	50

METAL URBAIN

78	Radar ADA 20	Hysterie Connective/Pas Poubelle	10
79	Rough Trade RT 001	Paris Maquis/Cle De Contact (p/s)	6

METAPHORCE

95	Ill Gotten Gains FDN004	Recipes For Disaster/Behind Enemy Lines (12")	15

METEORS

64	Polydor NH 52263	Get A Load Of This/Ruby Ann	8

METEORS

79	EMI EMI 2987	It's Only You/Blitzkreig (p/s)	8
79	EMI EMI 5000	My Balls Ache/Action (p/s)	5

METEORS

(see also Tall Boys, Clapham South Escalators, [Screamin'] Lord Sutch, Deadbeats)

81	Ace SW 65	METEOR MADNESS (EP, on blue vinyl)	15
81	Ace SW 65	METEOR MADNESS (EP)	10
81	Ace SWT 65	METEOR MADNESS (10" EP, white label test pressings only, custom p/s)	80
81	Chiswick CHIS 147	Radioactive Kid/Graveyard Stomp (p/s)	12
81	Lost Soul LOST 101	The Crazed/Attack Of The Zorch Men (p/s)	12
81	Ace NS 74	Radioactive Kid/Graveyard Stomp (p/s, reissue, black vinyl)	8
81	Ace NS 74	Radioactive Kid/Graveyard Stomp (p/s, reissue, clear or blue vinyl)	10
82	WXYZ ABCD 5	Mutant Rock/The Hills Have Eyes (p/s)	10
82	I.D. EYE 1	Johnny Remember Me/Fear Of The Dark/Wreckin' Crew (p/s)	8
82	I.D. EYE 1P	Johnny Remember Me/Fear Of The Dark/Wreckin' Crew (picture disc)	7
82	Lyntone LYN 12647	METEORS: Mutant Rock (Instrumental)/ANTI NOWHERE LEAGUE: World War Three/DEFECTS: Dance (red flexidisc with Flexipop magazine, issue 26)	7
84	Mad Pig PORK 1	I'm Just A Dog/Electro Rock (p/s)	6
85	Mad Pig PORK 1T	I'm Just A Dog (Wild Hog Mix Down)/Hoover Rock/Electro (12", p/s)	8
85	Mad Pig PORK 2	Fire, Fire/Little Red Riding Hood (p/s)	5
85	Mad Pig PORK 2T	Fire, Fire/Little Red Riding Hood/Stampede (King Ray Bat Scalator In The Dark Mix) (12", p/s)	8
85	Mad Pig PORK 3	Bad Moon Rising/Rhythm Of The Bell (p/s)	5
85	Mad Pig PORK 3T	Hogs And Cuties /Bad Moon Rising/Rhythm Of The Bell (What? Another Cover Mix) (12", p/s)	8
86	I.D. EYE 10	MUTANT ROCK (EP, green vinyl)	8
86	I.D. EYET 10	MUTANT ROCK (12" EP, green or blue vinyl)	12
86	Anagram 12ANA 31	Surf City (Has Beens From Outer Space Mix)/The Edge/Johnny's Here (12", p/s)	15
86	Anagram ANA 31	Surf City/The Edge (p/s)	10

			MINT VALUE £
87	Anagram 12ANA 35	Go Buddy Go (The Wonkey Donkey Mix)/Wildkat Ways/You Crack Me Up (12", p/s)	8
87	Anagram ANA 35	Go Buddy Go/Wildkat Ways (p/s)	7
81	Ace MAD 1	THE METEORS MEET SCREAMIN' LORD SUTCH (mini-LP, 1 side each, 1,000 only, stickered cartoon print on plain card sleeve)	100
81	Lost Soul LOSTLP 3001	IN HEAVEN (LP)	20
86	Big Beat WIKA 47CD	TEENAGERS FROM OUTER SPACE (CD)	18
86	Big Beat WIKA 47	TEENAGERS FROM OUTER SPACE (LP)	18
86	Anagram GRAM 27	SEWERTIME BLUES (LP)	15
87	Dojo LP56P	NIGHT OF THE WEREWOLF (LP, picture disc)	12

METERS

69	Stateside SS 2140	Sophisticated Cissy/Sehorn's Farm	10
70	Direction 58-4751	Look-Ka-Py-Py/This Is My Last Affair	10
74	Reprise K 14367	People Say/Africa	6
75	Reprise K 14405	Fire On The Bayou/They All Ask'd For You	6
72	Reprise K 44242	CABBAGE ALLEY (LP)	20
74	Reprise K 54027	REJUVENATION (LP)	20
74	Island ILPS 9250	CISSY STRUT (LP)	30
75	Reprise K 54044	FIRE ON THE BAYOU (LP)	15
76	Reprise K 54076	BEST OF THE METERS (LP)	15
76	Reprise K 54078	TRICK BAG (LP)	18
77	Reprise K 56378	NEW DIRECTIONS (LP)	12
79	Pye PKL 5578	GOOD OLD FUNKY MUSIC (LP)	12

METGUMBNERBONE

83	Private Pressing	DREUN (cassette)	30
83	Aeon (No Cat. No.)	DREUN (cassette)	20
83	Aeon (No Cat. No.)	COPS OF MATTER (cassette)	35
83	Amission REV 13:15	LIGELIAHORN (LP, 500 only, with insert)	50
84	Private cassette	FOR THE RAVEN (cassette)	40

METHOD ACTORS

80	Armageddon AS 6	The Method/Can't Act (p/s)	7
81	Armageddon AS 11	Round World/Eye (p/s)	7

METHODS

70	DJM DJS 225	Chasing The Sun/And That Is Life	15

PETER METRO

82	Greensleeves GRED 97	Warn Them Teach Them (with Squiddly Ranking)/Carribean Connection (12")	10

METRONOME ALL STARS

51	Capitol CL 13545	Local 802 Blues/Early Spring (78, with Stan Getz & Miles Davis)	10

METROPAK

80	Metropak PAK 001	You're A Rebel/OK Let's Go/Run Run Run (numbered p/s)	6
80	Metropak PAK 002	Here's Looking At You/Walking (foldout card p/s)	5

METROPHASE

(see also Swell Maps)

79	Neo London MS 01	In Black/Neo Beauty/Cold Rebellion (photocopied p/s with lyric insert)	8
79	Neo London MS 02	New Age/Frames Of Life (foldout p/s, stamped white labels)	8
81	Fresh FRESH 6	In Black/Neo Beauty/Cold Rebellion (reissue, better quality p/s with insert)	6

METROPOLITAN POLICE BAND

66	Columbia DB 8095	Thunderbirds March/P.C. ALEXANDER MORGAN: Sussex By The Sea	8

METROTONE

97	Wurlitzer Jukebox WJ 40	Kiss Me Awake/Byddant Fel Y Ser/Four Continuous Tones (p/s, 1,000 only)	5
98	Earworm WORM 21	THE LESS YOU HAVE THE MORE YOU ARE (LP, 4 copies only on black vinyl)	25

PAUL METSERS

81	Highway SHY 7014	CAUTION TO THE WIND (LP)	18

M.E.V.

69	Polydor 583 769	MUSICA ELETTRONICA VIVA (LP)	15

MEXICANO

75	Angen ANG 111	Cut Throat/Gorilla In Manilla	5

MEXICANS

68	Pye 7N 17613	Alexander Higginbottom/Julie	12
68	Pye 7N 17657	Without Your Love	12

AUGIE MEYERS

(see also Sir Douglas Quintet, Doug Sahm)

70s	Sonet SNTF 883	STILL GROWIN' (LP, with Doug Sahm)	12

ANTHONY MEYNELL

(see also Squire)

82	Hi-Lo LO 01	HITS FROM 3000 YEARS AGO (LP, purple sleeve)	15

LEE MEZA

67	Stateside SS 589	If It Happens/One Good Thing Leads To Another	30

MEZZ MEZZROW

(see also Mezzrow-Bechet Quartet)

62	Storyville SEP 394	KING JAZZ STORY (EP)	8
55	Vogue LAE 12007	PLEYEL CONCERT (LP)	12

MEZZROW-BECHET QUINTET

(see also Sidney Bechet)

56	Vogue LAE 12017	THE MEZZROW-BECHET QUINTET (LP)	12

M.F.Q.

(see under Modern Folk Quartet)

MINT VALUE £

M-G-M SINGING STRINGS

66	MGM 1307	Lara's Theme From "Dr Zhivago"/The Old And The New	6

M-G-M STUDIO ORCHESTRA

55	MGM SP 1144	Rock Around The Clock/"Blackboard Jungle" Love Theme	25

MIAMI

74	Jay Boy BOY 81	Party Freaks/(Part 2)	5
75	Jay Boy BOY 86	Hey Y'all We're Miami/Chicken Yellow	5
75	Jay Boy BOY 96	Funk It Up/Freak On Down My Way	5
76	Jay Boy BOY 111	Kill That Roach/Mr Notorious	5

MIAOW

85	Venus VENUS 1	Belle Vue/Fate (p/s)	6
86	Venus VENUST 1	Belle Vue/Fate/Grocer's Devil Daughter (12", p/s)	10
87	Factory FAC 189	Break The Code/Stolen Ears (p/s)	10

MICHA

65	Pye 7N 15982	Protest Singer/Serpent	8

GEORGE MICHAEL

(see also Wham!, Deon Estus, High, Elton John, Queen)

84	Epic A 4603	Careless Whisper/Careless Whisper (Instrumental) (poster p/s)	20
84	Epic QTA 4603	Careless Whisper (Extended Mix)/Careless Whisper (Special Version Wexler)/Careless Whisper (Instrumental) (12", title p/s)	25
84	Epic WA 4603	Careless Whisper (Extended Mix)/Careless Whisper (Instrumental) (12", picture disc, clear or black rim)	20
87	Epic CDLUST 1	I Want Your Sex (Monogamy Mix: Rhythm 1 Lust, Rhythm 2 Brass In Love, Rhythm 3 A Last Request) (CD, gatefold gard p/s)	8
87	Epic EMUP 3	Faith/Faith (Instrumental)/Hand To Mouth (12", picture disc)	20
87	Epic EMU 4	Father Figure/Love's In Need Of Love Today (with calendar & stickered p/s)	8
87	Epic EMUT 4	Father Figure/Love's In Need Of Love Today/Father Figure (Instrumental) (12", stickered p/s with poster)	8
88	Epic EMUP 4	Father Figure/Love's In Need Of Love Today (oblong shaped picture disc)	10
88	Epic CD EMU 3	Faith/Hand To Mouth/Hard Day (Remix) (CD)	8
88	Epic EMU B5	One More Try/Look At Your Hands (p/s, shrinkwrapped with badge)	8
88	Epic EPC 651 5322	One More Try/Look At Your Hands (3" CD, 5" case with adaptor)	8
88	Epic EMU G6	Monkey/Monkey (A Capella) (gatefold p/s, with photo insert)	5
88	Epic CD EMU 6	Monkey (Extended Version)/(A'Capella)/(Extra Bits)/(7" Edit) (CD)	12
88	Epic CD EMU 7	Kissing A Fool/(Instr.)/A Last Request (I Want Your Sex Part 3) (CD, card p/s)	8
89	Epic Solid Gold 654 601-3	I Want Your Sex (Parts 1 & 2)/A Different Corner/Careless Whisper (3" CD)	8
90	Epic XPCD 140	Cowboys And Angels (Radio Edit 4.34)/(7.14) (CD single promo only)	30
87	Epic 460000 9	FAITH (CD, extra tracks, picture disc, PVC box)	40
90	Epic 467295 2	LISTEN WITHOUT PREJUDICE VOLUME 1 (CD, picture disc, stickered case)	20

RAS MICHAEL & THE SONS OF NEGUS

75	Groundnation GRD 2037	None A Jah Children/Glory Dawn	10
75	Trojan	DADAWAH (PEACE & LOVE) (LP)	40
75	Vulcan VUL 005	RASTAFARI (LP)	25
75	Grounation GROL 505	RASTAFARI (LP)	25

MICHAEL SCHENKER GROUP

(see also McAuley Schenker Group, Michael Schenker, Scorpions, UFO, Cozy Powell, Graham Bonnet, Alex Harvey Band)

82	Chrysalis CHS 2636	Dancer/Girl From Uptown (picture disc)	5
82	Chysalis PCHR 1393	ASSAULT ATTACK (LP, picture disc)	15
83	Chysalis CHRP 1441	BUILT TO DESTROY (LP, picture disc, U.S. remixes)	15

CODY MICHAELS

79	Grapevine GRP 121	7 Days - 52 Weeks/VIRTUE ORCHESTRA: Don't Look Back (Instrumental)	8

MARILYN MICHAELS

60	RCA RCA 1208	Tell Tommy I Miss Him/Everyone Was There But You	8

MICHEL

74	EMI EMI 2210	In My Mind/Just A Part Of The Sky	8

MICHIGAN RAG

72	Blue Horizon 2096 009	Don't Run Away/She's Looking Good	20

MICHIGANS

63	Vogue V 9207	Intermission Riff/Tea For Two	15

MICKEY (Baker) & KITTY (Noble)

60	London HLE 9054	Buttercup/My Reverie	35

MICKEY (Baker) & SYLVIA

(see also Sylvia [Robbins])

57	HMV POP 331	Love Is Strange/I'm Going Home	225
57	HMV POP 331	Love Is Strange/I'm Going Home (78)	50
58	RCA RCA 1064	Rock And Stroll Room/Bewildered	40
58	RCA RCA 1064	Rock And Stroll Room/Bewildered (78)	40
60	RCA RCA 1206	Sweeter As The Day Goes By/Mommy Out De Light	15
65	RCA Victor RCA 1487	Love Is Strange/Dearest	25
65	RCA Camden CDN 5133	LOVE IS STRANGE (LP)	200

MICKEY FINN

64	Blue Beat BB 203	Tom Hark/Please Love Me (as 'Mickey Finn & the Blue Men')	25
64	Oriole CB 1927	Pills/Hush Your Mouth (as 'Mickey Finn & the Blue Men')	80
64	Oriole CB 1940	Reelin' & A'Rockin'/I Still Want You (as 'Mickey Finn')	50
65	Columbia DB 7510	The Sporting Life/Night Comes Down (as 'The Mickey Finn')	100
66	Polydor 56719	I Do Love You/If I Had You Baby (as 'The Mickey Finn')	100
67	Direction 58-3086	Garden Of My Mind/Time To Start Loving You (as 'The Mickey Finn')	200
95	Noiseburger 3	Ain't Necessarily So/God Bless The Child (foldaround p/s in poly bag, 1,000 only, 1st 500 signed)	8

MINT VALUE £

95	Noiseburger 3	Ain't Necessarily So/God Bless The Child (foldaround p/s in poly bag, 1,000 only, unsigned)	5

BOBBY "BOBCATS" MICKLEBURGH

55	Esquire EP 40	MICKLEBURGH'S BOBCATS (EP)	10
56	Esquire EP 73	MICKLEBURGH'S BOBCATS (EP)	10

MICROBE

69	CBS 4158	Groovy Baby/MICROBOP ENSEMBLE: Your Turn Now	5

MICRODISNEY

82	Kabuki KAMD 2	Hello Rascals/The Helicopter Of The Holy Ghost (p/s)	6
83	Kabuki KAMD 4	Pink Skinned Man/Fiction Land (p/s)	5
80s	Virgin V2505	39 MINUTES (LP)	18
80s	Rough Trade ROUGH 75	EVERYBODY IS FANTASTIC (LP)	15
80s	Rough Trade ROUGH 85	THE CLOCK COMES DOWN THE STAIRS (LP)	12
88	Rough Trade RTM 155	WE HATE YOU SOUTH AFRICAN BASTARDS (LP)	20

MICRON

88	White SG045	Eastenders Rap (12")	20

MIDAS

70	Solar SL003	I've Seen A New Life/Visit The Sun	40

MIDAS

83	Small Run SRR 0008	Can't Stop Loving You/Power In The Sky (p/s with insert)	200

RAS MIDAS

77	Black Swan WIP 6371	Kude A Bamba/Congo Dub	10
79	Tribesman TM 24	Natty Dread Surprise/Good Old Days Original (with I-Roy) (12")	80
79	Warrior WAR 138	Can't Stop Rasta Now/Rain And Fire (12")	20

MIDDLE OF THE ROAD

72	RCA 2264	Bottoms Up/See The Sky	5
73	RCA Camden CDS 1131	THE MIDDLE OF THE ROAD (LP)	12
74	RCA Camden CDS 1141	MIDDLE OF THE ROAD (LP)	12

TONY MIDDLETON

(see also Willows, Burt Bacharach)

65	London HLR 9983	My Little Red Book (as Burt Bacharach Orchestra with Tony Middleton)/ BURT BACHARACH ORCHESTRA: What's New Pussycat	30
66	Polydor BM 56704	To The Ends Of The Earth/Don't Ever Leave Me	400
66	Polydor BM 56704	To The Ends Of The Earth/Don't Ever Leave Me (DJ copy)	650
78	Grapevine GRP 115	Paris Blues/Out Of This World	10

MIDNIGHT

78	Ariola ATTA 514	Don't Bother To Knock/Keep Walking By	40

MIDNIGHT CRUISER

77	It IT 2	Rich Bitch/Striker (p/s)	10

MIDNIGHTERS

(see also Hank Ballard)

55	Parlophone DP 399	Work With Me Annie/Sexy Ways (78, export issue)	70
55	Parlophone DP 422	Annie Had A Baby/THUNDERBIRDS: Pledging My Love (78, export issue)	70

MIDNIGHT RAGS

(see also Paul Roland, Weird Strings)

80	Ace ACE 005	Public Enemy/Alcatraz/Mamma Said (p/s)	8
80	Velvet Moon VM 1	The Cars That Ate New York/Oscar Automobile (p/s, withdrawn)	8

MIDNIGHT SHIFT

66	Decca F 12487	Saturday Jump/Living Fast	30

MIDNIGHT SUN

71	MCA MKPS 2019	MIDNIGHT SUN (LP, red/pink 'dogbone' label)	60
72	MCA MKPS 2024	WALKING CIRCLES (LP, black/blue hexagon label)	60

MIDNIGHTS

66	Ember EMB S 220	(Won'tcha) Show Me Around/Only Two Can Play	18
63	MEP 101/MN 1/EAG-EP-134	MIDNIGHTS (EP, private pressing)	130

MI5

80	Public PUB 002	Alright On The Night/Television Screen Heroes/Don't Make Waves (p/s)	7

M.I. FIVE

(see also Maze, Deep Purple)

66	Parlophone R 5486	You'll Never Stop Me Loving You/Only Time Will Tell	100

MIGHT OF COINCIDENCE

72	Entropia BM 0001	WHY COULDN'T PEOPLE WAIT (LP)	100

MIGHTY AVENGERS (Jamaica)

66	Rymska RA 101	Scatter Shot (actually by Byron Lee & Dragonaires)/BYRON LEE: Like You Do (B-side actually "No One" by Techniques)	20

MIGHTY AVENGERS (U.K.)

(see also Andrew Oldham)

64	Decca F 11891	Hide Your Pride/Hey Senorita	18
64	Decca F 11962	So Much In Love/Sometime They Say	25
65	Decca F 12085	Blue Turns To Grey/I'm Lost Without You	25
65	Decca F 12198	(Walkin' Thru The) Sleepy City/Sir Edward And Lady Jane	35

MIGHTY BABY

(see also Action, Robin Scott, Habibiyya, Keith Christmas, Gary Farr, Stone's Masonry, Andy Roberts)

71	Blue Horizon 2096 003	Devil's Whisper/Virgin Spring	40
69	Head HDLS 6002	MIGHTY BABY (LP, gatefold sleeve, yellow label)	225
71	Blue Horizon 2931 001	A JUG OF LOVE (LP, with lyric insert)	400

MINT VALUE £

71	Blue Horizon 2931 001	A JUG OF LOVE (LP)	300
84	Psycho PSYCHO 31	EGYPTIAN TOMB (LP, reissue of "Mighty Baby" in different sleeve)	30

THEE MIGHTY CAESARS

(see also Milkshakes, Prisoners, Billy Childish, Thee Headcoats)

86	Empire LWC 604	Ten Bears Of The Comanches/Baby What's Wrong (p/s)	6
86	Media Burn MB 5	Little By Little/The Swag/What You've Got/Cyclonic (12", p/s)	7
88	Swag SWG 001	She's Just Fifteen Years Old/The Swag (flexi with Pandora's Box fanzine)	10
88	Swag SWG 001	She's Just Fifteen Years Old/The Swag (flexi without Pandora's Box fanzine)	7
85	Milkshakes NER - 0	S.T. (LP)	20
86	Mikshakes APOLL - 0	THEE CAESARS OF TRASH (LP)	15
86	Milkshakes PLAT - 0	ACROPOLIS NOW (LP)	20
86	Big Beat WIK45	BEWARE OF THE IDES OF MARCH (LP)	25
87	Hangman HANG 3 UP	DON'T GIVE ANY DINNER TO HENRY CHINASKI (LP)	25
87	Hangmen HANG 7 UP	PUNK ROCK SERENADE (LP)	25
87	Big Beat WIK 60	LIVE IN ROME (LP)	20
92	Hangman HANG 46 UP	CAESARS REMAINS (LP)	18

MIGHTY DIAMONDS

75	Black Wax WAX13	I Need A Roof/Joe Joe Dub	8
75	Locks LOX 10	Back Weh (You No Mafia)/Mafia Dub	8
79	Virgin Frontline FLS 122 12	Bodyguard/One Brother Short (12", p/s)	10
80	Greensleeves GRED 45	Gates Of Zion/SLY AND ROBBIE - Zion In Dub (12", green vinyl)	40
76	Virgin V2052	RIGHT TIME (LP)	18
79	Virgin Frontline FLD 6001	DEEPER ROOTS (LP, with bonus dub LP)	12
80	Mobiliser SRE 31	LEADER OF THE BLACK COUNTRY (LP)	20

MIGHTY DOUGLAS

60s	Jump Up JU 501	Laziest Man/Dance Me Lover	8
60s	Jump Up JU 508	Teacher Teacher/Split Me In Two	8
60s	Jump Up JU 509	Ugliness/My Wicked Boy Child	8

MIGHTY 'EM

73	Decca FR 13446	Jekyll And Hyde/What A Way To Go	20

MIGHTY ETHNICZ

88	Good Times EB20	Freestyle/B Style (12")	30
89	Damage efa75-17701	Any R'ddim (12")	8
90	Laylow LAY101	Harmony Hall/Murder/From Da Mind (12")	10
93	Lowdown LOWT01	Can I Get A Deal?/Bedrock (12")	15

MIGHTY FLEA & MICKEY BAKER

72	Polydor 2058 328	Bloodshot Eyes/Charley Stone	6
73	Polydor 2460 185	LET THE GOOD TIMES ROLL (LP)	22

MIGHTY FLYERS

(see also Mick Abrahams)

74	Myrrh MYR 1016	LOW FLYING ANGELS (LP, with insert)	20

MIGHTY HARD

70	Pye 7N 17878	Save The Life Of My Child/House Of The Rising Sun	30

MIGHTY MAYTONES

(see also Maytones)

76	Mango MAN 1010	Madness/Madness Version	6
78	GG's GG 029	Searching In Disco (with Trinity)/Madness In Disco (with U Brown) (12")	20
76	Burning Sounds BS 1002	MADNESS (LP)	18
78	Burning Sounds BS 1022	BOAT TO ZION (LP)	18

MIGHTY MEN

62	Salvo SLO 1804	No Way Out/You Too Much (99 copies only)	30

MIGHTY MO

72	Columbia DB 8851	Ape Call/Heavy Bear	10

MIGHTY POWER

67	Jump Up JU 513	You're Wasting Your Time/Smart Barbarian	8

MIGHTY SAM

66	Stateside SS 534	Sweet Dreams/Good Humor Man	22
66	Stateside SS 544	Fannie Mae/Badmouthin'	22
68	Stateside SS 2076	When She Touches Me/Just Like Old Times	22
70	Soul City SC 115	Papa True Love/I Need A Lot Of Lovin'	25
70	Soul City SCM 004	MIGHTY SOUL (LP)	85

MIGHTY SPARROW

(see also Sparrow, King Sparrow, Lord Melody)

59	Melodisc 1491	Goaty/LORD MELODY: I Confess (78)	10
60	Kalypso XX 22	Mr. Herbert/Simpson	6
68	NEMS 56-3558	Mr. Walker/Carnival In '68	6
60s	Jump Up JU 523	Village Ram/Pull Pistle Gang	6
69	Fab FAB 116	Mr. Walker/Jane	6
70	Fab FAB 147	I Don't Wanna Lose You/The Truth	6
60	Kalypso XXEP 1	THIS IS SPARROW (EP)	10
60	Kalypso XXEP 2	MAN, DIG THIS SPARROW (EP)	10
60	Kalypso XXEP 3	A PARTY WITH SPARROW (EP)	10
61	Kalypso XXEP 4	THIS IS THE SPARROW AGAIN (EP)	10
61	Kalypso XXEP 5	GREETINGS FROM SPARROW (EP)	10
62	Kalypso XXEP 6	SPARROW THE CONQUEROR (EP)	10
63	Island ILP 902	THE SLAVE (LP)	30
66	RCA RD 7516	SPARROW COME BACK (LP)	15
68	Melodisc MLPWI 12-146	CALYPSO CARNIVAL (LP)	25
68	Melodisc MLPWI 12-148	MR WALKER (LP)	30

MINT VALUE £

MIGHTY TERROR & HIS CALYPSONIANS

50	Melodisc 1033	The Queen Is In/Chinese Children (78)	10
59	Pye N 15177	Women Police In England/Patricia Gone With Millicent (78)	10
59	Pye N 15178	Brown Skin Gal/Kitch Cavalcade (78)	10

MIGHTY VIKINGS

67	Island WI 3060	Do Re Mi/The Sound Of Music	15
67	Island WI 3074	Rockitty Fockitty/Give Me Back My Gal (both actually with Sammy Ismay)	15

MIGHTY WAH

00	Essental	THE HANDY WAH! WHOLE (2 x CD)	20

MIGIL FIVE

(see also Migil Four, Mike Felix)

64	Pye 7N 15597	Mockingbird Hill/Long Ago And Far Away	5
64	Pye 7N 15645	Near You/Don't Wanna Go On Shaking	6
64	Pye 7N 15677	Boys And Girls/I Saw Your Picture	6
65	Pye 7N 15757	Just Behind The Rainbow/Seven Lonely Days	7
65	Pye 7N 15874	One Hundred Years/I'm In Love Again	7
66	Pye 7N 17023	Pencil And Paper/Nevertheless (I'm In Love With You)	7
67	Columbia DB 8196	Together/Superstition	20
68	Jay Boy BOY 4	If I Had My Way/Somebody's Stolen The Moon	6
64	Pye NEP 24191	MEET THE MIGIL FIVE (EP)	22
64	Pye NPL 18093	MOCKING BIRD HILL (LP)	45

MIGIL FOUR

(see also Migil Five)

63	Pye 7N 15572	Maybe/Can't I?	7

MIKA

06	Casablanca MIKA 7001	Relax (Take It Easy)/Billy Brown (die-cut p/s with printed inner sleeve, 500 only)	30

MIKE & MECHANICS

(see also Mike Rutherford, Genesis, Paul Carrack)

85	WEA U 8908P	Silent Running/I Get The Feeling (engine-shaped picture disc)	5
91	Virgin VSCDG 1359	Get Up/I Think I Got The Message/Before The Next Heartache Falls (CD, withdrawn)	8

MIKE & MODIFIERS

62	Oriole CB 1775	I Found Myself A Brand New Baby/It's Too Bad	800

MIKE STUART SPAN

(see also Leviathan, High Defenders, Tony's Defenders, High Broom)

66	Columbia DB 8066	Come On Over To Our Place/Still Nights	70
67	Columbia DB 8206	Dear/Invitation	60
68	Jewel JL 01	Children Of Tomorrow/Concerto Of Thoughts	400
68	Fontana TF 959	You Can Understand Me/Baubles And Bangles	25
93	117 CPAT 1171	EXSPANSIONS: Second Production/Rescue Me/Remember The Times/World In My Head (EP)	15
95	Tenth Planet TP 014	TIMESPAN (LP, gatefold sleeve, numbered, 1,000 copies only)	25

MIKI & GRIFF

59	Pye Nixa 7N 15213	Hold Back Tomorrow/Deedle-Dem-Doo-Die-Day	6
59	Pye 7N 15296	Rockin' Alone (In An Old Rocking Chair)/I'm Here To Get My Baby Out Of Jail	6
62	Pye 7N 15412	Litty Bitty Tear/I Missed Me	6
63	Pye 7N 15555	I Want To Stay Here/My Heart Will Make A Fool Out Of Me	6

BOBBY MILANO

55	Capitol CL 14252	A King Or A Slave/If You Cared	10
55	Capitol CL 14309	If Tears Could Bring You Back/Make Me A Present Of You	10

MILBURN

03	Private Pressing	Along Comes Mary (Disc only, no p/s)	5

AMOS MILBURN

57	Vogue V 9064	Every Day Of The Week/Girl Of My Dreams (triangular centre)	150
57	Vogue V 9064	Every Day Of The Week/Girl Of My Dreams (round centre)	75
57	Vogue V 9064	Every Day Of The Week/Girl Of My Dreams (78)	40
57	Vogue V 9069	Rum And Coca Cola/Soft Pillow (triangular centre)	250
57	Vogue V 9069	Rum And Coca Cola/Soft Pillow (78)	85
57	Vogue V 9080	Thinking Of You Baby/If I Could Be With You (One Hour Tonight) (tri centre)	200
57	Vogue V 9080	Thinking Of You Baby/If I Could Be With You (One Hour Tonight) (78)	70
60	Vogue V 9163	One Scotch, One Bourbon, One Beer/Bad, Bad Whiskey	150
57	Vogue VE 1-70102	ROCK AND ROLL (EP)	250
78	United Artists UAS 30203	CHICKEN SHACK BOOGIE (LP)	12

AMOS MILBURN JNR

63	London HLU 9795	Gloria/Look At Me Fool	20

PERCY MILEM

66	Stateside SS 566	Crying Baby, Baby, Baby/Call On Me	100
66	Stateside SS 566	Crying Baby, Baby, Baby/Call On Me (DJ copy)	150

BERNARD MILES

56	HMV 7EG 8176	OVER THE GATE (EP)	8

BUDDY MILES (EXPRESS)

(see also Electric Flag, Jimi Hendrix, Carlos Santana & Buddy Miles)

68	Mercury MF 1065	Train (Parts 1 & 2)	10
69	Mercury MF 1098	Miss Lady/'69 Freedom Special	8
71	Mercury 6052 036	Them Changes/Your Feeling Is Mine (solo)	6
69	Mercury 20137 SMCL	EXPRESSWAY TO YOUR SKULL (LP)	18
69	Mercury 20163 SMCL	ELECTRIC CHURCH (LP)	18
70	Mercury 6338 016	THEM CHANGES (LP)	15
71	Mercury 6338 028	WE GOT TO LIVE TOGETHER (LP)	15

MINT VALUE £

71	Mercury 6338 048	A MESSAGE TO THE PEOPLE (LP)	12
72	Mercury 6641 033	LIVE (2-LP)	12

DICK & SUE MILES

79	Sweet Folk & Country SFA 106	THE DUNMOW FLITCH (LP)	18

GARRY MILES

60	London HLG 9155	Look For A Star/Afraid Of Love	12
60	London REG 1264	LOOK FOR A STAR (EP)	40

JOHN MILES

(see also Influence)

70	Orange OAS 508	Why Don't You Love Me?/If I Could See Through	20
71	Decca F 13196	Jose/You Make It So Hard	5
72	Orange OAS 207	Come Away Melinda/Walking With My Head Held High	5
72	Orange OAS 208	Yesterday (Was Just The Beginning)/Road To Freedom	5
73	Orange OAS 209	Hard Road/You're Telling Me Lies	5
73	Orange OAS 211	Jacqueline/Keep On Tryin'	5
73	Orange OAS 213	One Minute Every Hour/Hollywood Queen	5
74	Orange OAS 220	Fright Of My Life/Good Time Woman	5
74	Orange OAS 223	What's On Your Mind/Rock'n'Roll Band	5
74	Orange OAS 224	What's On Your Mind/To Be Grateful	5
79	Decca FR 13827	I Can't Keep A Man Down/Sweet Lorraine	6

LENNY MILES

61	Top Rank JAR 546	Don't Believe Him Donna/Invisible	30

LIZZIE MILES

56	HMV 7EG 8178	THE BLUES THEY SANG (EP, 1 side by Billy Young, both with Jelly Roll Morton)	20
59	Columbia Clef SEB 10088	SCINTILLATING LIZZIE (EP, with Bob Scobey's Band)	10
50s	Melodisc EPM7 55	NEW ORLEANS BOYS (EP, with New Orleans Boys)	20
57	Capitol T 792	A NIGHT IN NEW ORLEANS (LP)	25

SARAH MILES

65	Fontana TF 552	Where Am I/Here Of All Places	5

MILITANT BARRY

77	Conflict COND 2000	Idi Amin Blood Up/Free Black People (12", die-cut p/s)	15
78	Conflict COND 2003	Ambition/Can't Stop Me (12")	15
79	Vista Sounds STLP 1012	GREEN VALLEY (LP)	20

MILK & COOKIES

75	Island WIP.6222	Little Lost And Innocent/Good Friends	12

MILKSHAKES

(see also Thee Mighty Caesars, Prisoners/Milkshakes, Pop Rivits, Len Bright Combo, Billy Childish, Thee Headcoats)

82	Bilko BILK-O	Please Don't Tell My Baby/It's You (p/s)	8
83	Upright UP 6	Soldiers Of Love/Shimmy Shimmy (p/s)	6
84	Big Beat NS 94	Brand New Cadillac/Commanche/Jezebel/Jaguar And Thunderbird (p/s)	5
84	Big Beat SW 105	The Ambassadors Of Love/No More/Gringles And Groyles Again/ Remarkable (p/s)	5
86	Empire UXF 228	Let Me Love You/She Tells Me She Loves Me (p/s)	5
83	Big Beat NED 4	14 RHYTHM AND BEAT GREATS (LP)	18
83	Upright UPLP 1	AFTER SCHOOL SESSIONS (LP, laminated sleeve)	18
84	Milkshake GARB-O	THEE KNIGHTS OF TRASH (LP)	30
84	Milkshake HARP-O	NOTHING CAN STOP THESE MEN (LP)	18
84	Big Beat WIKM 20	ROCK 'N' ROLL HITS OF THE 50's AND 60's (LP)	18
84	Big Beat WIK22	SHOWCASE (LP)	20
85	Big Beat WIK 30	THEY CAME, THEY SAW, THEY CONQUERED (LP)	15
86	Milkshake MILK-O	TALKING 'BOUT MILKSHAKES (LP)	15
87	Hangman HANG 1 UP	REVENGE - TRASH FROM THE VAULT (THE LEGENDARY MISSING 9th ALBUM) (LP)	18

MILK TEETH

74	Bead Records BEAD 1	A TOUCH OF THE SUN (LP)	150

MILLENIUM

84	Guardian GRC 2163	MILLENIUM (LP)	20

MILLER

(see also Big Boy Pete, Peter Jay & Jaywalkers, Pete Miller, News)

65	Oak RGJ 190	Baby I've Got News For You/The Girl With The Castle	275
65	Columbia DB 7735	Baby I Got News For You/The Girl With The Castle	300

ANN MILLER & KATHRYN GRAYSON

(see also Kathryn Grayson & Howard Keel)

54	MGM SP 1078	Always True To You In My Fashion/I Hate Men	6

BETTY MILLER

59	Top Rank JAR 115	Pearly Gates/Old Time Religion	6
59	Top Rank JAR 127	Jack O' Diamonds/(It Took) One Kiss	8

BOB MILLER & MILLERMEN

57	Columbia DB 4017	The Scamp/The Sack Line (as Bob Miller Music)	5
58	Columbia DB 4140	Square Bash/Muchacha (as Bob Miller Music)	5
59	Fontana H 181	Dig This!/The Poacher	10
59	Fontana H 192	Little Dipper/The Keel Row	5
59	Fontana H 228	In The Mood/Joey's Song	5
60	Fontana H 236	The Busker's Tune/My Guy's Come Back	5
60	Fontana H 245	77 Sunset Strip/Manhunt	5
60	Fontana H 284	Night Theme/Last Date	10
61	Parlophone R 4779	Trouble Shooter/Hootin'	8
61	Parlophone R 4854	The "Oliver" Twist/That's It	7

			MINT VALUE £
65	Mercury MF 947	Uptown And Downtown/Carnaby Street Parade	10
65	Polydor 56005	6-5 Special/Dick Van Dyke Theme	10
66	Columbia DB 7877	Get Smart/Bony's Blues (as Bob Miller & His Millermen)	8
72	Spiral DIT 3	Doin' The Slosh/Sloshing Around	8

BOBBIE MILLER
(see also Mongrels, Rolling Stones)

65	Decca F 12064	What A Guy/You Went Away	40
65	Decca F 12252	Every Beat Of My Heart/Tomorrow	15
66	Decca F 12354	Everywhere I Go/IAN STEWART & RAILROADERS: Stu-Ball	80

CHUCK MILLER

56	Capitol CL 14543	Rogue River Valley/No Baby Like You	15
57	Mercury 7MT 153	The Auctioneer/Me Head's In De Barrel	20
58	Mercury 7MT 215	Down The Road A-Piece/Mad About Her Blues	100
58	Mercury MT 215	Down The Road A-Piece/Mad About Her Blues (78)	12
59	Mercury AMT 1026	The Auctioneer/Baby Doll	8
59	Mercury AMT 1026	The Auctioneer/Baby Doll (78)	18
60	Mercury ZEP 10058	GOING GOING GONE (EP)	50

COUNT PRINCE (MILLER)
(see also Jimmy James & The Vagabonds)

70	Downtown DT 460	I'm Gonna Keep On Trying/Girl I Need You (as Count Prince)	5
70	MCA MK 5042	Mule Train/Lucille (p/s)	5

FRANKIE MILLER

59	Melodisc MEL 1519	True Blue/Black Land Farmer	15
59	Melodisc MEL 1519	True Blue/Black Land Farmer (78)	30
59	Melodisc MEL 1529	Poppin' Johnnie/Family Man	15
59	Melodisc MEL 1529	Poppin' Johnnie/Family Man (78)	30
60	Melodisc MEL 1552	Rain, Rain/Baby Rocked Her Dolly	15
62	Top Rank JKP 3013	COUNTRY MUSIC (EP)	30
64	Ember CW 107	THE TRUE COUNTRY STYLE OF FRANKIE MILLER (LP)	25

GARY MILLER
(see also Kenny Ball)

58	Pye 7N 15120	The Story Of My Life/Put A Light In The Window	5
58	Pye 7N 15136	Lollipop/Dancing With My Shadow	5
61	Pye 7N 15404	There Goes That Song Again/The Night Is Young	5
64	Pye 7N 15698	Aqua Marina/Stingray	12
56	Pye NEP 24013	YELLOW ROSE OF TEXAS (EP, 2 different sleeves)	10
57	Pye NEP 24047	HIT PARADE VOL. 1 (EP)	10
57	Nixa NPL 18008	MEET MISTER MILLER (LP)	20

GLEN MILLER

67	Doctor Bird DB 1089	Where Is The Love/Funky Broadway	350
68	Doctor Bird DB 1128	Rocksteady Party/Book Of Memories	25

GLENN MILLER & HIS ORCHESTRA

54	Columbia SCM 5086	I Got Rhythm/Sleepy Time Gal	5
54	HMV 7M 195	Little Brown Jug/Don't Sit Under The Apple Tree	5
59	Top Rank JAR 114	Boom Shot/You Say The Sweetest Things, Baby	6
54	HMV RLS 599	GLENN MILLER LIMITED EDITION (5-LP, presentation set, 'snakeskin' cover)	20
56	HMV CLPC 6-10/RLS 598	GLENN MILLER LIMITED EDITION VOL. 2 (5-LP, in presentation album)	20
56	HMV RLS 637	GLENN MILLER & THE ARMY AIRFORCE BAND (5-LP, presentation box, [CLP 1077-CLP 1081])	20

JACOB MILLER

78	Hawkeye HD 009	Each One Teach One/Matthews Lane Dub/ TETRACK: Let's Get It Together/Black ArtsDub (12")	60

JAMES MILLER

70	Trojan TR 7804	You Got To Me/2001	12

JIMMY MILLER & (NEW) BARBECUES
(see also Station Skiffle Group)

57	Columbia DB 4006	Sizzlin' Hot/Free Wheelin' Baby (as Jimmy Miller & Barbecues)	80
57	Columbia DB 4006	Sizzlin' Hot/Free Wheelin' Baby (as Jimmy Miller & Barbecues) (78)	15
58	Columbia DB 4081	Jelly Baby/Cry, Baby, Cry (as Jimmy Miller & New Barbecues)	70
58	Columbia DB 4081	Jelly Baby/Cry, Baby, Cry (as Jimmy Miller & New Barbecues) (78)	30

JODY MILLER

64	Capitol CL 15335	He Walks Like A Man/Looking At The World Through A Tear	5
64	Capitol CL 15356	The Fever/In My Room	15
65	Capitol CL 15393	Queen Of The House/The Greatest Actor	5
65	Capitol CL 15404	Silver Threads And Golden Needles/Melody For Robin	6
65	Capitol CL 15415	Home Of The Brave/This Is The Life	15
66	Capitol CL 15482	If You Were A Carpenter/Let Me Walk With You	5
65	Capitol T 2416	HOME OF THE BRAVE (LP, mono)	20
65	Capitol (S) T 2416	HOME OF THE BRAVE (LP, stereo)	25
66	Capitol T 2446	JODY MILLER SINGS THE GREAT HITS OF BUCK OWENS (LP, mono)	20
66	Capitol (S) T 2446	JODY MILLER SINGS THE GREAT HITS OF BUCK OWENS (LP, stereo)	25

KENNY MILLER

65	Stateside SS 405	Restless/Take My Tip (B-side is first David Bowie song ever released)	100

MITCH MILLER

60	Philips PB 1146	The Guns Of Navarone/Alouette March	6
62	CBS AAG 118	The Longest Day (Vocal Version)/The Longest Day (Instrumental Version)	6
63	CBS AAG 158	The Great Escape March/It's A Darn Good Thing	7

MRS MILLER

66	Capitol CL 15444	Downtown/A Lover's Concerto	10
66	Capitol T 2494	MRS. MILLER'S GREATEST HITS (LP)	25
66	Capitol T 2579	WILL SUCCESS SPOIL MRS. MILLER (LP)	25

MINT VALUE £

MRS MILLER
(see also Lloyd Terrell)

69	Jackpot JP 707	Feel It/LYN BECKFORD: Kiss Me Quick (actually by Keeling Beckford)	7

NED MILLER

63	Capitol CL 15301	Go On Back You Fool/Dark Moon	7
63	London HL 9658	From A Jack To A King/Parade Of Broken Hearts	5
63	London HL 9728	Just Before Dawn/Mona Lisa	5
63	London HL 9766	Another Fool Like Me/Magic Moon	5
64	London HL 9838	Sunday Morning Tears/Big Love	6
64	London HL 9873	Invisible Tears/Old Restless Ocean	6
64	London HL 9937	Do What You Do Do Well/Dusty Guitar	5
63	Capitol EAP1 20492	NED MILLER (EP)	20
63	London RE 1382	NED MILLER (EP)	20
63	London HA 8072	FROM A JACK TO A KING (LP)	20
66	Capitol T 2414	THE BEST OF NED MILLER (LP)	20
69	Capitol ST 2914	IIN THE NAME OF LOVE (LP)	15

PAULETTE MILLER

79	Rocerks PR 157	Woman In Love/In Love Dub (12")	20

PETE MILLER
(see also Miller, Big Boy Pete)

97	Tenth Planet TP 030	SUMMERLAND (LP, numbered, 1000 only)	15

ROGER MILLER

64	Philips BF 1354	Dang Me/Got 2 Again	6
64	Philips BF 1365	Chug-A-Lug/Reincarnation	7
65	Philips BF 1390	Do-Wacka-Do/Love Is Not For Me	6
65	Stateside SS 445	Can't Stop Loving You/You're Forgetting Me	5
65	Philips BE 12578	ROGER MILLER (EP)	10

RUSS MILLER

57	HMV POP 391	I Sit In My Window/Wait For Me, My Love	50
57	HMV POP 391	I Sit In My Window/Wait For Me, My Love (78)	15

STEPHEN MILLER & LOL COXHILL
(see also Lol Coxhill)

73	Caroline C 1503	COXHILL MILLER (LP, black/white/red 'Twin' label)	30
74	Caroline C 1507	THE STORY SO FAR ... OH REALLY? (LP)	30

STEVE MILLER BAND
(see also Boz Scaggs)

68	Capitol CL 15539	Sittin' In Circles/Roll With It	15
68	Capitol CL 15564	Living In The U.S.A./Quicksilver Girl	15
69	Capitol CL 15604	My Dark Hour/Song For Our Ancestors	15
69	Capitol CL 15618	Little Girl/Don't Let Nobody Turn You Around	7
70	Capitol CL 15656	Going To The Country/Never Kill Another Man	6
72	Capitol CL 15712	My Dark Hour/The Gangster Is Back/Song For Our Ancestors (33rpm)	5
73	Capitol CL 15765	The Joker/Something To Believe In	5
74	Capitol CL 15786	Living In The U.S.A./Kow Kow Calqulator	5
68	Capitol (S)T 2920	CHILDREN OF THE FUTURE (LP, 'rainbow rim' label)	35
69	Capitol (S)T 2984	SAILOR (LP, 'rainbow rim' label)	20
70	Capitol E-(S)T 184	BRAVE NEW WORLD (LP)	18
70	Capitol E-ST 331	YOUR SAVING GRACE (LP)	12

SUZI MILLER
(see also Johnston Brothers)

54	Decca F 10389	Happy Days And Lonely Nights/Tell Me, Tell Me (with Johnston Brothers)	20
54	Decca F 10423	Two Step, Side Step (with Johnston Brothers)/ Hang My Heart On A Christmas Tree (with Keynotes)	10
55	Decca F 10475	Tweedlee-Dee (with Johnston Brothers)/That's All I Want From You	15
55	Decca F 10512	Dance With Me Henry (Wallflower) (with Johnston Brothers)/ Butterfingers (with Marilyn Sisters)	15
55	Decca F 10593	The Banjo's Back In Town/Go On By	10
56	Decca F 10677	Ay-Ay-Senores/Reckless	10
56	Decca F 10722	Get Up! Get Up! (You Sleepy Head)/The Key To My Heart	7
57	Decca F 10848	I Love My Baby/The Money Tree	5

MILLER'S THUMB

76	Tradition TSC 3	SITTING ON THE RIGHT SIDE (LP, 100 copies only)	20

MILLIE (SMALL)
(see also Jackie & Millie, Roy & Millie, Owen & Millie)

63	Fontana TF 425	Don't You Know/Until You're Mine	10
64	Fontana TF 449	My Boy Lollipop/Something's Gotta Be Done	6
64	Fontana TF 479	Sweet William/Oh Henry	10
64	Fontana TF 502	I Love The Way You Love/Bring It On Home To Me	8
64	Cadbury's BNVT 01F	The Bournvita Song/Three Nights A Week (p/s)	20
65	Fontana TF 515	I've Fallen In Love With A Snowman/What Am I Living For	10
65	Fontana TF 529	See You Later Alligator/Chilly Kisses	10
65	Fontana TF 591	My Street/It's Too Late	10
65	Fontana TF 617	Bloodshot Eyes/Tongue Tied	15
65	Brit WI 1002	My Street/A Mixed Up, Fickle, Moody, Self-Centred, Spoiled Kind Of Boy	15
66	Fontana TF 740	Killer Joe/Carry Go Bring Come (as Millie Small)	8
67	Fontana TF 796	Chicken Feed/Wings Of A Dove (as Millie Small)	8
67	Island WIP 6021	You Better Forget/I Am In Love	10
68	Fontana TF 948	When I Dance With You/Hey Mr. Love	10
69	Decca F 12948	Readin' Writin' Arithmetic/I Want You Never To Stop	12
70	Pyramid PYR 6080	My Love And I/Tell Me About Yourself	10
70	Trojan TR 7744	Enoch Power/Mayfair	10

MINT VALUE £

70	President PT 306	We're All In A Zoo/Piccaninny Man	10
70	Trojan TR 7801	Honey Hush/Sunday Morning	10
61	Blue Beat BBEP 302	MILLIE (EP, with Little Roy & Owen Gray; with sleeve)	140
61	Blue Beat BBEP 302	MILLIE (EP, with Little Roy & Owen Gray; without sleeve)	20
64	Fontana TE 17425	MY BOY LOLLIPOP (EP)	50
66	Island IEP 705	MILLIE AND HER BOYFRIENDS (EP)	60
64	Fontana TL 5220	MORE MILLIE (LP, mono)	50
64	Fontana STL 5220	MORE MILLIE (LP, stereo)	60
65	Fontana TL 5276	MILLIE SINGS FATS DOMINO (LP)	90
67	Island ILP 953	THE BEST OF MILLIE SMALL (LP)	70
69	Trojan TTL 17	MILLIE AND HER BOYFRIENDS (LP)	20
69	Trojan TTL 49	THE BEST OF MILLIE SMALL (LP, reissue)	15
70	Trojan TBL 108	TIME WILL TELL (LP)	20

SPIKE MILLIGAN

(see also Goons, Famous Eccles, Peter Sellers)

58	Parlophone R 4406	Wish I Knew/Will I Find My Love Today?	10
61	Parlophone R 4839	I'm Walking Out With A Mountain/The Sewers Of The Strand	10
62	Parlophone R 4891	Wormwood Scrubs Tango/Postman's Knock	10
64	Pye 7N 15720	The Olympic Team/Epilogue (with John Bluthal)	8
66	Parlophone R 5513	Purple Aeroplane/Nothing At All	10
66	Parlophone R 5543	Tower Bridge/Silent Night	10
69	Parlophone R 5771	The Q.5 Piano Tune/Ning, Nang, Nong	10
73	Warner Bros. K 16240	Girl On A Pony/Old Man's Protest Song	5
76	RCA 2752	Goose Walk/Theme From Paul Galligo's 'The Snow Goose'	6
79	United Artists UP 36489	One Sunny Day/Woe Is Me (with Ed Welch)	6
61	Parlophone PMC 1148	MILLIGAN PRESERVED (LP, mono)	15
61	Parlophone PCS 18	MILLIGAN PRESERVED (LP, stereo)	25
65	Decca LK 4701	MUSES WITH MILLIGAN (LP)	15
68	Pye NPL 18271	THE WORLD OF THE BEACHCOMBER (LP)	15
71	BBC RED 98M	A RECORD LOAD OF RUBBISH (LP)	12

MARY MILLINGTON

99	Trunk/Bonk B 01	COME PLAY ME (EP)	60

SIR EUGENE MILLINGTON-DRAKE

65	Decca LK 4659	MIXED GRILL (LP)	60

JEB MILLION

86	WEA YZ 82	Speed Up My Heartbeat/Who Sent You (p/s)	6
86	WEA YZ 82T	Speed Up My Heartbeat (Extended Mix)/Speed Up My Heartbeat/ Who Sent You (12", p/s)	12

MILLIONAIRES (Ireland)

66	Decca F 12468	Wishing Well/Chatterbox	100

MILLIONAIRES (U.S.)

67	Mercury 6052301	Never For Me/If I Had You Babe (paper labels)	30
67	Mercury 6052301	Never For Me/If I Had You Babe (plastic labels)	15

MILLIONS

73	Duke DU 154	Murmuring/TOMMY McCOOK & BOBBY ELLIS: Murmuring - Version	6
73	Downtown DT 516	Love Of Jah Jah Children/Jah Jah Version	7

MILLIONS OF DEAD CHILDREN

(see also M.D.C.)

85	Radical MDC 3	CHICKENSQUAWK EP (poster p/s)	6

BARBARA MILLS

65	Hickory 45-1323	Queen Of Fools/Make It Last, Take Your Time	400
65	Hickory 45-1323	Queen Of Fools/Make It Last, Take Your Time (DJ copy)	450
65	Hickory 45-1392	Try/Let's Make A Memory	15
75	London HLE 10491	Queen Of Fools/Make It Last, Take Your Time (reissue)	15

BETTY LOU MILLS

60s	Shal SHAL 1	Where Is My Star/Rock Him	30
60	Pilgrim JLPS 101	EVERYWHERE I LOOK (LP)	25

FREDDIE MILLS

57	Parlophone R 4374	One For The Road/One For The Band	10

GARRY MILLS

(see also Gary & Ariels)

59	Top Rank JAR 119	Hey Baby (You're Pretty)/You Alone	25
59	Top Rank JAR 219	Seven Little Girls Sitting In The Back Seat/The Night You Became 17	10
59	Oriole CB 1529	Living Lord/Big Story Breaking	10
59	Oriole CB 1530	I Am The Great I Am/Rhythm In Religion	10
60	Top Rank JAR 301	Running Bear/Teen Angel	7
60	Top Rank JAR 336	Look For A Star/Footsteps	7
60	Top Rank JAR 393	Comin' Down With Love/I'm Gonna Find Out	10
60	Top Rank JAR 500	Top Teen Baby/Don't Cheat Me Again (in p/s)	12
60	Top Rank JAR 500	Top Teen Baby/Don't Cheat Me Again	8
61	Top Rank JAR 542	Who's Gonna Take You Home Tonight?/Christina	10
61	Decca F 11358	I'll Step Down/Your Way Is My Way	10
61	Decca F 11383	Bless You/Footprints In The Sand	10
61	Decca F 11415	Treasure Island/Sad Little Girl	10
62	Decca F 11471	Never Believed In Love/Save A Dream For Me	10
61	Top Rank JKP 3001	LOOK FOR A STAR (EP)	40

HAYLEY MILLS

61	Decca F 21396	Let's Get Together/Cobbler Cobbler	6
62	Decca F 21442	Jeepers Creepers/Johnny Jingo	5
62	Decca LK 4426	LET'S GET TOGETHER (LP)	15

MINT VALUE £

HAYLEY MILLS & EDDIE HODGES
(see also Eddie Hodges)

63	HMV POP 1179	Flitterin'/Beautiful Beulah	7

JEFF MILLS

61	Ember EMB S 133	Daddy's Home/TIMMY REYNOLDS: Lullaby Of Love	70

MAUDE MILLS

60s	Vintage Jazz VEP 34	MAUDE MILLS (EP)	8

RUDY MILLS

67	Island WI 3092	A Long Story/BOBBY ELLIS: Now We Know (actually. with Desmond Miles Seven)	40
68	Island WI 3136	I'm Trapped/BOBBY ELLIS & CRYSTALLITES: Dollar A Head	22
69	Big Shot BI 509	John Jones/A Place Called Happiness	35
69	Explosion EX 2007	Lemi Li/Goody Goody	10
69	Crab CRAB 20	Tears On My Pillow/I'm Trapped	10
69	Crab CRAB 24	A Heavy Load/Wholesale Love	12
69	Pama SECO 12	REGGAE HITS (LP)	100

STEPHANIE MILLS

74	Paramount PARA 3050	I Knew It Was Love/The Passion And The Pain	6
76	Tamla Motown TMG 1020	This Empty Place/I See You For The First Time (unissued)	70
76	T. Motown STML 12017	FOR THE FIRST TIME (LP)	20

MILLS BROTHERS
(see also Louis Armstrong)

54	Brunswick 05325	How Blue?/Why Do I Keep Lovin' You?	7
55	Brunswick 05439	Smack Dab In The Middle/Opus One	7
55	Brunswick 05488	That's All I Ask Of You/Suddenly There's A Valley	7
55	Brunswick 05487	Mi Muchacha (Little Girl)/Gum Drop	10
56	Brunswick 05606	That's Right/Don't Get Caught	8
58	London HLD 8553	Get A Job/I Found A Million Dollar Baby	15
60	London HLD 9169	I Got You/Highways Are Happy Ways	8
54	Brunswick LA 8664	MEET THE MILLS BROTHERS (10" LP)	10
58	London HAD 2192	GREATEST HITS (LP)	12

MILLWALL F.C.

72	Decca F1 3350	Millwall/The Ballad Of Harry Cripps	8

RONNIE MILSAP

66	Pye International 7N 25392	Ain't No Soul (Left In These Old Shoes)/ Another Branch From The Same Old Tree	50
66	Pye International 7N 25392	Ain't No Soul (Left In These Old Shoes)/ Another Branch From The Same Old Tree (DJ copy)	100
69	Pye International 7N 25490	Denver/Nothing Is As Good As It Used To Be	6
72	Wand WN 26	Ain't No Soul (Left In These Old Shoes)/ Another Branch From The Same Old Tree (reissue)	10

RONNIE MILSAP/ROSCOE ROBINSON

66	Pye Intl. NEP 44078	SOUL SENSATIONS (EP)	50

JOHNNY MILTON & CONDORS
(see also Symbols)

61	Oriole CB 1588	Charleston Cocktail (medley) (as Johnny Milton Band)	5
64	Decca F 11862	A Girl Named Sue/Somethin' Else (as Johnny Milton & Condors)	8
64	Fontana TF 488	Cry Baby/Hurt	6

MILVA

63	Oriole CB 1899	I Can't Believe You're Leaving Me/Loneliness Of Autumn	8
64	Oriole CB 1952	I'll Set My Love To Music/Come Sempre	8
67	Major Minor MM 510	Love Is A Feeling/Seasons Of Love	6

MILWAUKEE COASTERS

68	Pama PM 733	Treat Me Nice/Sick And Tired (Oh Babe)	5
68	Pama PMLP 2	WEST COAST ROCK'N'ROLL 1968 (LP)	15
69	Pama PSP 10	BEST PARTY ALBUM (LP, reissue of PMLP 2)	12

GARNET MIMMS (& ENCHANTERS)

63	United Artists UP 1033	Cry Baby/Don't Change Your Heart (with Enchanters)	25
63	United Artists UP 1038	Baby Don't You Weep/For Your Precious Love (with Enchanters)	20
64	United Artists UP 1048	Tell Me Baby/Anytime You Want Me (with Enchanters)	20
65	United Artists UP 1090	It Was Easier To Hurt Her/So Close	30
66	United Artists UP 1130	I'll Take Good Care Of You/Looking For You	100
66	United Artists UP 1130	I'll Take Good Care Of You/Looking For You (DJ copy)	200
66	United Artists UP 1147	It's Been Such A Long Way Home/Thinkin'	20
66	United Artists UP 1153	My Baby/It Won't Hurt Half As Much	20
66	United Artists UP 1172	All About Love/The Truth Hurts	20
67	United Artists UP 1181	Roll With The Punches/Only Your Love	20
67	United Artists UP 1186	As Long As I Have You/Yesterday	25
68	Verve VS 569	I Can Hear My Baby Crying/Stop And Think It Over	20
68	Verve VS 569	I Can Hear My Baby Crying/BILL MEDLEY: That Lucky Old Sun (mispress)	10
68	Verve VS 574	We Can Find That Love/Can You Top This	25
76	United Artists REM 403	REMEMBER GARNET MIMMS (EP)	10
63	United Artists ULP 1067	CRY BABY AND 11 OTHER HITS (LP, with Enchanters)	120
66	United Artists (S)ULP 1145	WARM AND SOULFUL (LP)	100
67	United Artists (S)ULP 1174	LIVE (LP, as Garnet Mimms & Senate)	50

MINA

78	EMI EMC 3243	MINA (LP)	12

MINT VALUE £

MINDBENDERS

(see also Wayne Fontana & Mindbenders, Hotlegs, Lulu)

66	Fontana TF 644	A Groovy Kind Of Love/Love Is Good	6
66	Fontana TF 697	Can't Live With You, Can't Live Without You/One Fine Day	8
66	Fontana TF 731	Ashes To Ashes/You Don't Know About Love	7
66	Fontana TF 780	I Want Her, She Wants Me/The Morning After	18
67	Fontana TF 806	We'll Talk About It Tomorrow/Far Across Town	8
67	Fontana TF 869	The Letter/My New Day And Age	10
67	Fontana TF 877	Schoolgirl/Coming Back	25
68	Fontana TF 910	Blessed Are The Lonely/Yellow Brick Road	15
68	Fontana TF 961	Uncle Joe, The Ice Cream Man/The Man Who Loved Trees	15
69	Fontana H 1026	A Groovy Kind Of Love/Ashes To Ashes (p/s)	10
66	Fontana TL 5324	THE MINDBENDERS (LP, mono)	45
66	Fontana STL 5324	THE MINDBENDERS (LP, stereo)	55
67	Fontana (S)TL 5403	WITH WOMAN IN MIND (LP)	60
68	Fontana SFL 13045	THE MINDBENDERS (LP, reissue)	12

SAL MINEO

57	Philips JK 1024	Start Movin' (In My Direction)/Love Affair (jukebox issue)	40
58	Fontana H 118	Little Pigeon/Cuttin' In	50
58	Fontana H 135	Seven Steps To Love/A Couple Of Crazy Kids	30
58	Fontana TFL 5004	SAL (LP)	70

CORINA MINETTE

60	HMV POP 752	He'll Have To Stay/TOMMY THOMAS ORCHESTRA: Young At Cha Cha	5

SEXTON MING

(see also Billy Childish)

88	Hangman HANG-1-UP	OLD HORSE OF THE NATION (LP)	18
98	Hangman HANG 018UP	6 MORE MILES TO THE GRAVEYARD (LP)	15

SEXTON MING (& HIS DIAMOND GUSSETS)

96	D. Goods DAMGOOD 71	I'm In Love With Danny Edwards/Break His Spirit/Son Of Tractor Nits (p/s)	6

CHARLES/CHARLIE MINGUS

63	Parlophone GEP 8786	SCENES IN THE CITY (EP)	10
65	Mercury 10021 MCE	JAZZ MAKERS (EP, as Charlie Mingus Orchestra)	8
56	Vogue LDE 178	CHARLIE MINGUS PRESENTS JAZZ WORKSHOP VOL. 2 (10" LP)	15
59	Parlophone PMC 1092	EAST COASTING (LP)	25
59	Philips BBL 7352	MINGUS AH HUM (LP)	25
60	London Jazz LTZ-K 15194	BLUES AND ROOTS (LP, also stereo SAH-K 6087)	20
62	Atlantic SD 8005	CHARLES MINGUS PRESENTS CHARLES MINGUS (LP, U.K. issue of U.S. LP)	20
62	United Artists ULP 1004	JAZZ PORTRAITS (LP)	15
62	London HA-K/SH-K 8007	OH YEAH (LP, by Charlie Mingus & Jazz Group)	20
63	RCA RD/SF 7514	TIJUANA MOODS (LP)	18
63	Vocalion LAE 543	CHAZZ (LP)	15
64	HMV CLP 1694	THE BLACK SAINT AND THE SINNER LADY (LP)	20
65	United Artists ULP 1068	TOWN HALL CONCERT (LP)	15
65	Vocalion LAEF/SEAF 591	CHARLIE MINGUS QUINTET WITH MAX ROACH (LP)	15
65	HMV CLP 1742	MINGUS, MINGUS, MINGUS (LP, also stereo CSD 1545)	15
65	HMV CLP 1796	MINGUS PLAYS PIANO (LP)	15
65	Atlantic ATL/SAL 5019	CHARLIE MINGUS (LP)	15
66	Realm RM 211	JAZZ COMPOSERS WORKSHOP (NO. 1) (LP)	12
66	CBS (S)BPG 62261	MINGUS DYNASTY (LP)	15

MINIM

67	Polydor 582 011	WRAPPED IN A UNION JACK (LP)	22

MINISTRY

92	Sire W 0096	Jesus Built My Hotrod/T.V. Song (p/s)	10

MINISTRY OF SOUND

66	Decca F 12449	White Collar Worker/Back Seat Driver	40

LIZA MINNELLI

66	Capitol CL 15483	The Middle Of The Street/I (Who Have Nothing)	8
63	Capitol CL 15311	One Summr Love/How Much Will I Love You	6

MINNY POPS

81	Factory FAC 31	MINNY POPS EP: Dolphin Spurt/Goddess	8
82	Factory FAC 57	Secret Story/Island	15

KYLIE MINOGUE

SINGLES

87	PWL PWLT 8R	I Should Be So Lucky (Bicentennial Mix)/(Instrumental) (12", stickered p/s)	12
88	PWL PWLT 12R	Got To Be Certain (Extra Beat Boys Mix)/Got To Be Certain (7" Mix)/ Got To Be Certain (Out For A Duck Bill Platter Plus Dub Mix) (12", stickered p/s)	15
88	PWL PWCD 12	Got To Be Certain (Extended Mix)/Got To Be Certain (Instrumental)/ I Should Be So Lucky (Extended Mix 6.03) (CD)	30
88	PWL PWLT 14R	The Loco-Motion (Sankie Mix)/I'll Still Be Loving You (12", stickered p/s)	18
88	PWL PWLT 21R	Je Ne Sais Pas Pourquoi (Revolutionary Mix)/Made In Heaven (Maid In England Mix) (12", stickered p/s)	15
88	PWL PWCD 21	Je Ne Sais Pas Pourquoi (Moi Non Plus Mix)/Made In Heaven (Maid In England Mix)/The Loco-Motion (Sankie Mix) (CD)	20
88	PWL PWCD 24	Especially For You (7" Mix)/Especially For You (Extended)/ All I Wanna Do Is Make You Mine (Extended) (with Jason Donovan) (CD)	15
89	PWL PWLT 35R	Hand On Your Heart (Heartache Mix)/Hand On Your Heart (Dub mix) Just Wanna Love You (12", with stickered p/s)	40
89	PWL PWCD 35	Hand On Your Heart (Great Aorta Mix)/Just Wanna Love You It's No Secret (Extended Mix) (CD)	15
89	PWL PWLT 42R	Wouldn't Change A Thing (Espagna Mix)/Wouldn't Change A Thing (7" Mix)/ It's No Secret (Extended) (12", stickered p/s)	25

			MINT VALUE £
89	PWL PWCD 42	Wouldn't Change A Thing (7" Mix)/Wouldn't Change A Thing (Your Thang Mix)/ Je Ne Sais Pas Pourquoi (Revolutionary Mix) (CD)	15
89	PWL PWCD 45	Never Too Late (7" Mix)/(Extended)/(Kylie Smiley Extended Mix) (6.17) (CD)	12
90	PWL PWCD47	Tears On My Pillow (7" Mix)/Tears On My Pillow (Extended Mix)/ We Know The Meaning Of Love (Extended Mix) (CD)	12
90	PWL PWCD 56	Better The Devil You Know (Mad March Hare Mix)/ I'm Over Dreaming Over You (7" Remix) (CD)	12
90	PWL PWCD 64	Step Back In Time (7" Mix)/Step Back In Time (Walkin' Rhythm Mix)/ Step Back In Time (Extended instrumental) (CD)	15
91	PWL PWLP 72	What Do I Have To Do (New Mix)/What Do I Have To Do (Instrumental) (stickered p/s, with postcards)	15
91	PWL PWLT 72R	What Do I Have To Do (Between The Sheets Mix) (12", withdrawn, no p/s)	100
91	PWL PWCD 72	What Do I Have To Do (New Mix)/What Do I Have To Do (Pumpin Polly Mix)/ What Do I Have To Do (Extended Instrumental) (CD)	15
91	PWL PWL P81	Shocked (DNA 7" Mix)/Shocked (Harding & Curnow 7" Mix) (picture disc)	15
91	PWL PWCD 81	Shocked (DNA 7" Mix)/Shocked (DNA Extended Mix)/Shocked (Harding & Curnow Extended Mix) (CD)	15
91	PWL PWLT204R	Word Is Out (Summer Breeze Remix) (1-sided 12" Limited Edition with etched Kylie autograph on other side, p/s)	0
91	PWL PWCD 204	Word Is Out (Extended Mix)/Word Is Out (Instrumental)/ Say The Word - I'll Be There (CD)	12
91	PWL PWL 207	Keep On Pumpin' It (Angelic Remix Edit)/(Astral Flight Mix Edit) (with Vision Masters) (p/s)	5
91	PWL PWLT 207	Keep On Pumpin' It (Angelic Remix)/(Astral Flight Mix) (with Vision Masters) (12", p/s)	10
91	PWL PWCD 207	Keep On Pumpin' It (Angelic Remix Edit)/(Angelic Remix)/ (Astral Flight Mix) (with Vision Masters) (CD)	20
91	PWL PWCD 508	If You Were With Me Now (with Keith Washington) (7" Mix)/(Extended)/ I Guess I Like It Like That (Full Length Version) (CD)	8
92	PWL PWCD 212	Give Me Just A Little More Time (7" Mix)/(Extended)/ Do You Dare (NRG Mix)/(New Rave Mix) (CD)	8
94	Polygram PSPMC 344	Hand On Your Heart/Give Me Just A Little More Time (Woolworths giveaway cassette)	10
94	DeConstruction 278482-0	Confide In Me (Master Mix)/Nothing Can Stop Us/ If You Don't Love Me (CD)	8
95	MUTE MUTE185	Where The Wild Roses Grow (with Nick Cave)/The Ballad of Robert Moore & Betty Coltrane (non-Kylie track) (limited 7", p/s)	6
97	DeCon. 7432 1517257	Some Kind Of Bliss/Love Takes Over Me (numbered limited edition 7", die-cut p/s)	25
98	Arthrob ART021 CD1	GBI/(The Sharp Boys Deee-Liteful Dub)/Boldline (with Towa Tei) (CD)	8
98	Arthrob ART021 CD2	GBI/(Rekut)/(Ebony Boogie Down Mix) (with Towa Tei) (CD)	8
00	Parlophone 12R 6542 A/B	Spinning Around (Sharp Vocal Mix)/(Sharp Double Dub)/ (7th Spinnin' Dizzy Dub)/(7th District Club Mix) (12" double-pack)	12
03	Parlophone 12R6625	Slow (Extended Mix)/Slow (Radio Slave Remix)/Slow (Medicine 8 Remix) (12" picture disc, PVC title sleeve, sealed with sticker)	8
03	BMG BMGSM94	Breathe/Where Is The Feeling? (Little Chef 'Music Collection' giveaway 2-track CD, Includes enhanced CD-Rom section, unique Kylie card p/s)	12
01	Parlophone 12RDJZ6562	Can't Get You Out Of My Head (Extended)/(Extended Instrumental)	8
04	Parlophone 12R6633	Red Blooded Woman (Whitey Mix)/Slow (Chemical Brothers Remix)/ Red Blooded Woman (Narcotic Thrust Mix)	8
04	Parlophone 12R6639	Chocolate (Tom Middleton Cosmos Mix)/(Radio Edit)/(Emo Mix) (12" picture disc, PVC title sleeve, sealed with sticker)	8
04	Parlophone 12R6656	I Believe In You/(Mylo Dub)/(Skylark Dub) (12" picture disc, PVC title sleeve, sealed with sticker)	8
05	Parlophone 12R6661	Giving You Up (Riton Re-Rub Dub)/(Single Version)/(Alter Ego Remix) (12" picture disc, PVC title sleeve, sealed with sticker)	8

LPs

88	PWL HFD 4	KYLIE (DAT)	150
90	PWL HF 18	RHYTHM OF LOVE (LP, with free poster)	12
90	PWL HFL 18	RHYTHM OF LOVE (LP, gold leaf sleeve, 100 only)	200
91	PWL HFCL 18	RHYTHM OF LOVE (cassette, with 3 bonus tracks, gold case)	12
91	PWL HFCDL 18	RHYTHM OF LOVE (CD, with 3 bonus tracks, gold case)	18
98	30DeCon. 74321 58715 1	MIXES (3xLP, inner sleeves, pink silhouette Kylie outer p/s)	30
98	20DeCon. 74321 58715 2	MIXES (2xCD, pink silhouette Kylie p/s)	20
07	Parlophone (Lc0299)	X (Very limited USB format in shape of Kylie robotic, house in a long pull-out box includes full album plus 'White Diamond' trailer and '2 Hearts' video etc)	30

PROMOS & TEST PRESSINGS

88	PWL (no cat. no.)	Made In Heaven (3:26) PWL 1-track in-house promo cassette, custom PWL logo inlay typled/stickered, 1 only)	60
90	PWL PWLT 56R	Better The Devil You Know (KC Cohen 'US' Remix) (1-sided 12" promo, withdrawn, die-cut sleeve, 50 only)	100
91	PWL PWLT 72R	What Do I Have To Do (Between The Sheets Mix) (1-sided 12" promo, withdrawn die-cut sleeve)	50
91	PWL ZR-A1	Keep On Pumpin' It (12" white label issued under pseudonym of 'Angel K', includes Angelic Remix' & 'Astral Flight Mix', handwritten/stamped labels, Some with 'I Guess I Like It' titles. Die-cut sleeve)	50
91	PWL (no cat. no.)	I Guess I Like It Like That (12" 1-sided white label issued under pseudonym of 'Angel K', includes 'Extended/Album Version', 200 only)	40
91	PWL ANGEL-2	Do You Dare (12" white label issued under pseudonym of 'Angel K', includes NRG Mix' & 'New Rave Mix', handwritten labels, die-cut sleeve, 100 only)	40
92	PWL PWLT 227	Finer Feelings (Brothers In Rhythm 12" Mix)/Closer (Pleasure Mix) ('Black Diamond' limited promo 12", black diamond label, die cut sleeve)	10
92	PWL PWLT 257	Celebration (Have A Party Mix)/Let's Get To It (Album Version) ('Black Diamond' limited promo 12", Christmas "leaving PWL" promo p/s, black Diamond label)	25
94	DeCon. 21 227477 JB	Confide In Me (Radio Mix)/(Truth Mix) (7" jukebox issue, no p/s)	10
94	DeCon. 21 246577 JB	Put Yourself In My Place (Radio Mix)/(All Star Mix) (7" jukebox issue, no p/s)	15

			MINT VALUE £
94	DeCon. 21 293617 JB	Where Is The Feeling? (BIR Bish Bosh Mix Edit)/(BIR Dolphin Mix) (7" jukebox issue, no p/s)	10
95	DeConstruction FEEL2	Where Is The Feeling? (BIR Dolphin Mix)/(Morales Club Mix) (12", die-cut sleeve, limited quantities)	35
95	DeConstruction FEEL3	Where Is The Feeling? (Da Klubb Feelin' Mix)/(Aphroheadz Powerlite Mix)/ (Three Rad Vid Clash Mix) (12", promo, no p/s, 200 only)	70
95	DeConstruction FEELING1	Where Is The Feeling? (UK 7" Edit) (UK export to Japan promo 1-track CD, unique Custom p/s)	70
95	DeConstruction TIME1	Time Will Pass You By (Paul Masterson's 'Wand Silver Screen Remix') (1-sided 12" White Label, handwritten labels, unreleased mix, withdrawn, 20 only)	100
97	DeConstruction DID2	Did It Again (Trouser Enthusiasts' Goddess of Contortion Mix)/ (Razor N Go Mix) (12" promo, custom Deconstruction die-cut sleeve, limited to 500 only)	35
97	DeCon. 21 535707 JB	Did It Again (Radio Edit)/Tears (7" jukebox issue, no p/s)	20
98	DeCon. 21 570137 JB	Breathe (Radio Edit)/(Tee's Radio Edit) (7" jukebox issue, no p/s)	20
98	DeConstruction BREATHE02	Breathe (3-track 'edits' promo CD, custom Deconstruction sleeve)	12
98	DeConstruction TOOFAR 1	Too Far (Brothers In Rhythm Mix)/(Junior Vasquez Remix) (12", promo, no p/s)	25
98	Arthrob ART021TJ	GBI (Sharp Boys Deee-Liteful Dub)/(Album Version)/(Kylie-Pella) (with Towa Tei) (UK promo 12" part 1, custom Arthrob sleeve)	15
98	Arthrob ART021TJX	GBI (Rekut/DJ Krust Mix)/(Ebony Boogie Down Mix)/Bold Line (not Kylie) (with Towa Tei) (UK promo 12" part 2, custom Arthrob sleeve)	15
98	Arthrob ART021CDJ	GBI (Radio Edit)/(Album Mix)/(Sharp Boys Deee-Liteful Dub) (with Towa Tei) (UK promo CD, custom Arthrob card slip case)	15
00	Parlophone BUTTERFLO1A	Butterfly (Sandstorm Dub) (12" 1-sided DJ white label, butterfly logo stamped die cut paper sleeve)	60
00	Parlophone 12MIND 1	Spinning Around (Messy Boyz Remix) (12" 1-sided promo featuring unreleased mix, die cut sleeve, Handwritten label, withdrawn, 10 only)	125
00	Parlophone SHARP DJ 1	Spinning Around (Sharp Vocal Mix)/Spinning Around (Sharp Double Dub) (12" Pink Promo DJ Vinyl, die-cut sleeve, 100 only)	60
00	Parlophone 12MIND JY 001	Spinning Around (7th District Dub Like This Mix)/Spinning Around (7th District Club-Mental Mix) (12" promo, p/s)	15
00	Parlophone 12MIND JX 001	Spinning Around (Sharp Vocal Mix)/Spinning Around (Sharp Double Dub Mix) (12" promo, p/s)	15
00	Parlophone CDMIND J 001	Spinning Around (CD promo, card insert)	15
00	Parlophone RLH6542	Spinning Around/Paper Dolls (7" jukebox issue, no p/s)	5
00	Parlophone RLH6546	On A Night Like This/Ocean Blue (7" jukebox issue, no p/s)	10
00	Parlophone 12MINDJ 002	On A Night Like This (Motiv8 Nocturnal Vocal Mix)/On A Night Like This (Bini & Martini Vocal Mix)/On A Night Like This (Rob Searle Mix)/ Your Disco Needs You (Almighty Mix) (12" promo doublepack p/s)	25
00	Chrysalis CHSLH5119	Kids (with Robbie Williams)/United (not including Kylie) (7" jukebox issue, no p/s)	5
00	Parlophone RLH6551	Please Stay/Santa Baby (7" jukebox issue, no p/s)	5
00	Parlophone 12RDJ 6551	Please Stay (Metro Mix)/Please Stay (7th District Club Flava Mix)/ Please Stay (7th District Club Dub) (12" promo, p/s, with inner sleeve)	20
00	Parlophone 12MINWL 004	Please Stay (7th District Club Dub)/Please Stay (Hatiras Dreamy Dub)/ Please Stay (7th District Club Flava Mix) (12" promo, title-stickered sleeve)	15
00	Parlophone 12MINWL005	Please Stay (Hatiras Dreamy Dub Mix) (1-sided 12" promo, die-cut sleeve)	20
00	Parlophone CDRDJX6551	Santa Baby/Please Stay (Christmas 2000 promo CD, custom violet metallic slip case With large pink Kylie logo)	20
01	Parlophone RLH6562	Can't Get You Out Of My Head/Boy (7" jukebox issue, no p/s) NOTE: Clear 7" jukebox pressings carrying this 'RLH6562' catalogue number with 'Can't Get Blue Monday out Of my Head' as the B-side are unofficial bootlegs)	20
01	Parlophone 12RDJ 6562	Can't Get Into My Head (Plastika Mix)/Can't Get Into My Head (Tim Deluxe Inst.)/Can't Get Into My Head (Time Deluxe Dub) (12" promo, no p/s)	20
01	Parlophone 12RDJY 6562	Can't Get Out Of My Head (Superchumbo Todo Mamado Mix)/ Can't Get You Out Of My Head (Superchumbo Leadhead Dub)/(Superchumbo Voltapella Mix (12" promo issued under the pseudonym of 'Special K', die-cut sleeve)	20
01	Parlophone 12RDJX 6562	Can't Get You Out Of My Head (K&M Mindprint Mix)/Can't Get You Out Of My Head (Nick Faber Mix) (12" promo, p/s, frosted PVC outer title sleeve)	20
01	Parlophone 12RDJ6562	"Get Into My Head" - Can't Get You Out Of My Head (Plastika Mix)/(Deluxe's Dirty Dub Instrumental)/(Deluxe's Dirty Dub) (12" promo issued under pseudonym of 'Special K', Die-cut sleeve)	10
01	Parlophone 12RDJ6562	"Get Into My Head" - Can't Get You Out Of My Head (Plastika Mix)/ (Deluxe's Dirty Dub Instrumental)/(Deluxe's Dirty Dub) (12" 'Limited Tastemaker' white label issued under pseudonym of 'Special K', limited to 100 copies, die-cut sleeve)	30
01	Parlophone 12RDJY6562	"Get Out Of My Head" - Can't Get You Out Of My Head (Superchumbo Todo Mamado Mix)/(Superchumbo Leadhead Dub)/ (Superchumbo Voltapella Mix) (12" promo issued under pseudonym of 'Special K', die-cut sleeve)	10
01	Parlophone KYLIE-6TRACKS	Can't Get You Out Of My Head 'Remixes' (UK export 6-track remix promo CD housed In custom card p/s)	30
01	Parlophone KBLUE1	Can't Get Blue Monday Out Of My Head (1-sided 12" promo, pink die-cut sleeve)	15
02	Parlophone 12RDJ 6569	In Your Eyes (Powder's Spaced Dub)/In Your Eyes (Powder's 12" Dub)/ In Your Eyes (Saeed & Palash Mix)/In Your Eyes (Saeed & Palash Nightmare Dub) (12" test pressing, white label, titled-stickered sleeve)	20
02	Parlophone 12RDJX 6569	In Your Eyes (The S Man's Release Mix)/In Your Eyes (Roger Sanchez Release The Dub Mix)/In Your Eyes (Jean Jacques Smoothie Dub) (12" promo, white sleeve, with title sticker)	12
02	Tripoli Trax 12RDJY 6569	In Your Eyes (Knuckleheadz Mix)/In Your Eyes (Mr. Bishi Mix) (12" promo, stickered title sleeve)	15
02	Parlophone RLH6569	In Your Eyes/Tightrope (7" jukebox issue, no p/s)	15
02	Parlophone RLH6577	Love At First Sight/Can't Get Blue Monday Out Of My Head (7" jukebox issue, No p/s)	10

			MINT VALUE £
02	Parlophone 12RDJX 6577	Love At First Sight (Twin Master Plan Mix)/(Ruff & Jam Vocal 7")/(Ruff & Jam Club Mix) (12" promo, p/s)	12
02	Parlophone 12RDJY 6577	Love At First Sight (Kid Crème Vocal Dub)/(Kid Crème Vocal-less Dub) (promo 12", custom label, die-cut sleeve, limited to 300 copies only)	12
02	Parlophone 12RDJY 6577	Love At First Sight (Kid Crème Vocal Dub)/(Kid Crème Vocal-less Dub) (promo white label 12", stamped label, die-cut sleeve, 50 only)	40
02	Parlophone RLH6590	Come Into My World (Single Version)/(Fischerspooner Mix) (7" jukebox issue, No p/s)	20
02	Parlophone RDJ 6590	Come Into My World (Fischerspooner Mix)/Come Into My World (Ashtrax Mix) (promo 7", die-cut title sleeve)	25
02	Parlophone 12RDJ 6590	Come Into My World (Robbie Rivera's Hard & Sexy Mix)/(Robbie Rivera's NYC Dub) (12" promo, title sleeve, 400 only)	15
03	Parlophone 12MINDJ 006	Slow (Radio Slave Mix)/(Medicine 8 Remix)/(Synth City Mix) (12" promo part 1)	12
03	Parlophone 12MINDJX 006	Slow (Extended Mix)/Slow (Extended Instrumental)/Slow (Acapella) (12" promo, part 2)	12
03	Parlophone 12MINDJY 006	Slow (Chemical Brothers Remix) (1-sided 12", yellow vinyl promo, 200 only)	40
03	Parlophone (no cat. no.)	Slow (CD promo, in black card fold-out sleeve)	15
03	Parlophone RLH6625	Slow/Sweet Music (7" jukebox issue, no p/s)	15
04	Parlophone RLH6633	Red Blooded Woman/Almost A Lover) (7" jukebox issue, no p/s)	20
04	Parlophone RDJ6633	Red Blooded Woman (Promo 1-sided clear 7" vinyl featuring otherwise unreleased 'Play Paul Radio Edit', 50 only)	100
04	Parlophone 12RDJ6633	Red Blooded Woman (Narcotic Thrust Mix) (1-sided white label 12", stamped title, die cut sleeve)	12
04	Parlophone 12RDJZ6633	Red Blooded Woman (Whitey Mix) (1-sided white label 'DJ friendly' 180gm heavyweight black vinyl, stamped title)	15
04	Parlophone 12RDJY6633	Red Blooded Woman (Promo 1-sided 12" featuring otherwise unreleased 'Play Paul Extended Dub', die-cut sleeve, 100 only)	30
04	Parlophone 12RDJ6639	Chocolate (Tom Middleton Cosmos Mix)/(Emo Mix)/(Emo Dub) (white label 12" promo, stamped label, die-cut sleeve)	8
04	Parlophone (no cat. no)	Chocolate (Violanti's Remix) (1-sided 12" white label, unreleased remix, Withdrawn, hand-written label)	100
04	Parlophone 12RDJ6656	I Believe In You (Skylark Mix)/(Mylo Vocal)/(Mylo Dub)(12" promo pressed on 180gm heavy-weight vinyl, promo sleeve with stripes sticker in corner)	8
05	Parlophone 12RDJ6661	Giving You Up (Riton Re-Rub Vox)/(Riton Re-Rub Dub)/(Alter Ego Remix) (12" promo pressed on 180gm heavy-weight vinyl, promo sleeve with blue stripes in corner)	12
06	Parlophone IRC14000600010	DARLING - The Exclusive CD (promo 5-track CD given away with every purchase of Kylie's 'Darling' perfume in 2006)	8
07	Parlophone (HEARTS001)	2 Hearts (Promo 1-track mini-max cd with 3" cd and 5" clear outer rim featuring red and black graphics on the disc. Housed in a picture card slip disc)	8
07	Parlophone (HEARTS002)	2 Hearts (Alan Braxe Remix)/(Studio Version)/(Mark Brown's Pacha Ibiza Upper Terrace Mix)/(Acapella) (Very limited heavyweight RED 12" promo, rubber-stamped)	15
94	DeConstruction KYLP1	KYLIE MINOGUE (10 track promo cassette, black p/s with titles)	20
94	DeConstruction KM 100	KYLIE MINOGUE (CD, promo, gatefold sl. in lilac slipcase with silver lettering)	80
97	DeConstruction KM001	KYLIE MINOGUE ('Impossible Princess' 6-track 'Interact' sampler cassette issued to People on the Kylie mailing list with a 'feedback' form to be completed. Snippets of 6 of the album tracks with a femail introducing each one, custom title inlay)	15
97	DeConstruction KYLIE 1	IMPOSSIBLE PRINCESS (CD, promo, with insert, withdrawn, some with Press Release from 'Hall Or Nothing' explaining about the withdrawal of the CD and title due to Princess Diana's death)	50
97	DeConstruction KM 002	AN INTERVIEW WITH KYLIE MINOGUE (Promo interview CD for 'Impossible Princess' album, unique p/s)	100
00	Parlophone LIGHT 001	LIGHT YEARS (CD promo, foldout 22" x 8" pack, does not include 'Kids')	40
00	Parlophone LIGHT 002	LIGHT YEARS (CD promo, foldout 22" x 8" pack, includes 'Kids')	50
00	Parlophone LIGHTX 001	LIGHT YEARS (LP Promo, unique blue outer 'Kylie' logo sleeve, inner picture sleeve, does not include 'Kids' or 'Password', 100 only)	100
00	Parlophone LIGHTX 002	LIGHT YEARS (LP Promo, unique blue outer 'Kylie' logo sleeve, inner picture sleeve, includes 'Kids' but not 'Password', 100 only)	75
00	BMG HITS1	HITS+ (CD promo, original withdrawn artwork, card slip case, withdrawn at Kylie's request when she disliked the picture used, most copies incinerated, less than 5 copies exist)	175
01	Parlophone FEVER 01	FEVER (CD-Rom promo, DVD-style picture case)	30
01	Parlophone FEVER 02	FEVER (CD promo, card sleeve, frosted PVC outer title sleeve)	20
02	PWL9224680P	GREATEST HITS - THE REMIXES (12" Promo) Hand On Your Heart (WIP 2002 Mix)/ What Do I Have To Do? (Movers & Shakers 12" Mix)/ Better The Devil You Know (Movers & Shakers Alternative 12" Mix)/' Greatest Hits 87-92 album, custom labels , die cut sleeve)	15
03	Parlophone BODYLANG01	BODY LANGUAGE (promo CD housed in picture card slip case with inner slip-case, Copy-control CD)	15
03	Parlophone MININT 02	BODY LANGUAGE INTERVIEW (CD interview promo)	20
04	Parlophone ULTIMATE01	ULTIMATE KYLIE (2xCD promo housed in glossy card slip case with 2 inner slip cases, copy-control CD)	20
04	Parlophone MININT003	ULTIMATE KYLIE - INTERVIEW DISC (promo 40-track interview CD with custom cover, Cues and questions, jewel case)	20
07	Parlophone (XINTER 001)	X 'The Interview' (promo 42-track interview CD with custom over etc)	20

MINORBOPS

58	Vogue V 9110	Need You Tonight/Want You For My Own	800
58	Vogue V 9110	Need You Tonight/Want You For My Own (78)	250

MINOR THREAT

85	Discord DISCORD 15	Salad Days/Stumped/Good Guys (p/s)	15

MINSTRELS

67	Studio One SO 2036	People Get Ready/HAMLINS: Everyone's Got To Be There	140
68	Studio One SO 2050	Miss Highty Tighty/WESTMORELITES: Let Me Be Yours Until Tomorrow	70

MINT VALUE £

MINT

69	Tangerine 014	Luv/Simone	20
73	Pye 7N.45299	I'll Meet You Halfway/Three Score And Ten	6

DEREK MINTER

60	Sound Stpries EP 304	STARS OF SPEED (EP)	10

MINTS

57	London HLP 8423	Night Air/KEN COPELAND: Pledge Of Love	300
57	London HLP 8423	Night Air/KEN COPELAND: Pledge Of Love (78)	60

MINUCCI

56	Vogue Coral LUA 9015	GINA LOLLO BRIGIDA PRESENTS MUSIC OF GINO BY MINUCCI (LP, photo of Gina on cover)	15

MINUTE MEN

61	Capitol CL 15206	Yankee Diddle/Blue Pearl	6

MINUTEMEN

83	SST SST 002	PARANOID TIME (8-track EP)	18
84	SST SST 016	BUZZ OR HOWL UNDER THE INFLUENCE OF THE HEAT (12" EP)	20
85	Homestead REFLEX-L	TOUR SPIEL (EP, live 4-track)	10

(SMOKEY ROBINSON &) MIRACLES

61	London HL 9276	Shop Around/Who's Lovin' You	50
61	London HL 9366	Ain't It Baby/The Only One I Love	100
62	Fontana H 384	What's So Good About Goodbye/I've Been So Good To You	200
63	Oriole CBA 1795	You've Really Got A Hold On Me/Happy Landing	120
63	Oriole CBA 1863	Mickey's Monkey/Whatever Makes You Happy	90
64	Stateside SS 263	I Gotta Dance To Keep From Crying/Such Is Love, Such Is Life	55
64	Stateside SS 282	The Man In You/Heartbreak Road	40
64	Stateside SS 324	I Like It Like That/You're So Fine And Sweet	45
64	Stateside SS 353	That's What Love Is Made Of/Would I Love You	35
65	Stateside SS 377	Come On Do The Jerk/Baby Don't You Go	45
65	Tamla Motown TMG 503	Ooo Baby Baby/All That's Good	40
65	Tamla Motown TMG 522	The Tracks Of My Tears/A Fork In The Road	40
65	Tamla Motown TMG 540	My Girl Has Gone/Since You Won My Heart	40
66	Tamla Motown TMG 547	Going To A Go-Go/Choosey Beggar	25
66	Tamla Motown TMG 569	Whole Lotta Shakin' In My Heart/Oh Be My Love	45
66	Tamla Motown TMG 584	(Come 'Round Here) I'm The One You Need/Save Me	25
(The above singles are credited to The Miracles.)			
67	Tamla Motown TMG 598	The Love I Saw In You Was Just A Mirage/Swept For You Baby	25
67	Tamla Motown TMG 614	More Love/Swept For You Baby	25
67	Tamla Motown TMG 614	More Love/Come Spy With Me (withdrawn B-side)	100
67	Tamla Motown TMG 631	I Second That Emotion/You Must Be Love	12
68	Tamla Motown TMG 648	If You Can Want/When The Words From Your Heart Get Caught Up In Your Throat	15
68	Tamla Motown TMG 661	Yester-Love/Much Better Off	15
68	Tamla Motown TMG 673	Special Occasion/Give Her Up	15
69	Tamla Motown TMG 687	Baby, Baby Don't Cry/Your Mother's Only Daughter	15
69	Tamla Motown TMG 696	The Tracks Of My Tears/Come On Do The Jerk	7
70	Tamla Motown TMG 745	The Tears Of A Clown/You Must Be Love (with withdrawn B-side)	40
70	Tamla Motown TMG 745	The Tears Of A Clown/Who's Gonna Take The Blame	6
71	Tamla Motown TMG 761	(Come Round Here) I'm The One You Need/We Can Make It, We Can	6
71	Tamla Motown TMG 774	I Don't Blame You At All/That Girl	6
72	Tamla Motown TMG 811	My Girl Has Gone/Crazy 'Bout The La-La-La	6
73	Tamla Motown TMG 853	Going To A Go-Go/Whole Lotta Shakin' In My Heart/Yester-Love	6
76	Tamla Motown TMG 1023	Nightlife/The Miracle Workers: Overture (as The Miracles)	6
87	Motown ZB 41147 D	Just To See Her/Te Queiro Como Si No Hubiera Um Manana//Being With You/What's In Your Life For Me? (solo, double pack)	6
61	London RE 1295	SHOP AROUND (EP, as The Miracles)	200
83	Tamla Motown CTME 2028	TEARS OF A CLOWN (cassette EP, as Smokey Robinson & The Miracles)	7
63	Oriole PS 40044	HI! WE'RE THE MIRACLES (LP)	250
64	Stateside SL 10099	THE FABULOUS MIRACLES (LP)	150
65	Tamla Motown TML 11003	I LIKE IT LIKE THAT (LP)	70
66	T. Motown TML 11024	GOIN' TO A GO-GO (LP, as Smokey Robinson & The Miracles, mono)	45
66	T. Motown STML 11024	GOIN' TO A GO-GO (LP, as Smokey Robinson & The Miracles, stereo)	55
66	T. Motown TML 11031	THE MIRACLES FROM THE BEGINNING (LP, mono)	50
66	T. Motown STML 11031	THE MIRACLES FROM THE BEGINNING (LP, stereo)	50
67	T. Motown TML 11044	AWAY WE A-GO-GO (LP, mono)	50
67	T. Motown STML 11044	AWAY WE A-GO-GO (LP, stereo)	60
68	T. Motown TML 11067	MAKE IT HAPPEN (LP, mono)	35
68	T. Motown STML 11067	MAKE IT HAPPEN (LP, stereo)	40
68	T. Motown (S)TML 11072	GREATEST HITS (LP, mono/stereo)	20
69	T. Motown (S)TML 11089	SPECIAL OCCASION (LP, mono/stereo)	25
69	T. Motown (S)TML 11107	SMOKEY ROBINSON & THE MIRACLES LIVE! (LP, mono/stereo)	40
70	T. Motown (S)TML 11129	TIME OUT FOR SMOKEY ROBINSON & THE MIRACLES (LP)	20
70	T. Motown STML 11151	FOUR IN BLUE (LP)	25
71	T. Motown STML 11172	POCKETFUL OF MIRACLES (LP)	20
73	T. Motown STMA 8008	1957-1972 (LP, gatefold sleeve)	12
73	Motown STMA 8012	SMOKEY (LP, solo)	12

MIRAGE

(see also Yellow Payges, Caleb, Jawbone, Spencer Davis Group, Portobello Explosion)

65	CBS 201772	It's In Her Kiss/What Ye Gonna Do 'Bout It	20
65	CBS 202007	Go Away/Just A Face	20
66	Philips BF 1534	Tomorrow Never Knows/You Can't Be Serious	35
67	Philips BF 1554	Hold On/Can You Hear Me	40
67	Philips BF 1571	The Wedding Of Ramona Blair/Lazy Man	90
68	Page One POF 078	Mystery Lady/Chicago Cottage	12
68	Page One POF 111	Carolyn/World Goes On Around You	12

MINT VALUE £

MIRETTES
(see also Ikettes)

68	Uni UN 501	In The Midnight Hour/To Love Somebody	10
68	Uni UN 505	The Real Thing/Take Me For A Little While	5
69	MCA Soul Bag BAG 8	Whirlpool/Ain't You Trying To Cross Over	8
72	Jay Boy BOY 65	Now That I've Found You Baby/He's Alright With Me	8
69	MCA MUP(S) 344	IN THE MIDNIGHT HOUR (LP)	20

MIRK

79	Mother Earth MUM 1205	MODDANS BOWER (LP)	175
82	Spring Thyme SPR 1009	TAK A DRAM AFOR YE GO (LP)	25

MIRKWOOD

71	Flams Ltd PR 1067	MIRKWOOD (LP)	750
93	Tenth Planet TP 003	MIRKWOOD (LP, reissue, numbered with insert, 500 only)	30

STEVE MIRO & EYES
(see also Eyes, Noyes Bros)

78	Object Music OM 03	Up And About/Smiling In Reverse (p/s)	6
79	Object Music OM 10	Dreams Of Desire/Queens Of The Sea (p/s)	5
80	Object Music OBF 008	RUDE INTRUSIONS (LP)	15
81	Object Music OBJ 015	SECOND SENTENCE (LP)	15

MIRROR

68	Philips BF 1666	Gingerbread Man/Faster Than Light	80

MIRRORS

78	Lightning GIL 503	Cure For Cancer/Nice Vice (p/s)	15
79	Lightning GIL 540	Dark Glasses/999 (p/s)	15

MISFITS (U.K.)
(see also Complex)

66	A.S.C.C. PRI 101	You Won't See Me/Hanging Around (Aberdeen Students Charities Campaign)	10

MISFITS (U.S.)

81	Plan 9/Cherry Red PLP 9	BEWARE (12" EP)	120

MISSING PRESUMED DEAD

79	Sequel PART 2	Say It With Flowers/Double Life/Driving Home/Family Tree (p/s)	5
80s	Sequel PART 4	MISSING PRESUMED DEAD (LP)	12
80s	Sequel PART 5	REVENGE (LP)	12

MISSING SCIENTISTS
(see also Television Personalities, Slaughter)

80	Rough Trade RT 057	Big City, Bright Lights/Discotheque X (p/s)	20

MISSION
(see also Sisters Of Mercy, Dead Or Alive, Pauline Murray, Artery, Red Lorry Yellow Lorry, Expelaires, Knopov's Political Package, TV Product)

86	Chapter 22 L12 CHAP 7	Like A Hurricane/Garden Of Delight/Dancing Barefoot/ The Crystal Ocean (12", autographed p/s)	8
86	Mercury MYSG 1	Stay With Me/Blood Brother (autographed, gatefold p/s)	5
87	Phonogram MYTHB 2	IV: Wasteland/Shelter From The Storm (Live)/Serpent's Kiss (Live)/1969 (Live) (doublepack, in box, with insert and photo's)	12
88	Mercury MYTHCD 6	Beyond The Pale/Tower Of Strength/Tadeusz (CD, card sleeve, numbered)	12
89	Mercury MYCDB 8	Butterfly On A Wheel (CD, in 12" x 12" collectors box)	10
80s	Mercury MYCDB 8	Butterfly On A Wheel (Complete 4 x CD set in box)	20
80s	Flexi FLEX 1	Crazy (1-track flexidisc)	12
90	Mercury MYTH 11	Hands Across The Ocean/Amelia/Love (p/s)	5
90	Phonogram MYTH 910	Deliverance/METAL GURUS: Virginia Plain (10", p/s)	7
90	Phonogram MYTHB 912	Deliverance/(Sorceror's Mix)/METAL GURUS: Virginia Plain (12", in box with poster)	8
90	Mercury MTHCD 9	Deliverance (CD)	8
92	Vertigo MYTH 1310	Like A Child Again/All Tangled Up In You (1-sided 10", etched, numbered p/s)	7
01	Playground PGND 001	Evangeline/Anyone But You//Melt/Swoon (Reprise) (doublepack, pink & blue vinyl, gatefold p/s)	8
02	Playground PGND003	Shine Like The Stars/Never Let Me Down/Spider And The Fly (In The Ointment)/ Never (2 x 7" on green and white vinyl, gatefold p/s)	8

MISSION BELLES

65	Decca F 12154	Sincerely/When A Girl Really Loves You	10

MISSISSIPPI

70	Fox FOX 1	Mr. Union Railway Man/Main Street	100

MISS JANE

68	Pama PM 704	Bad Mind People/My Heart Is Aching (B-side act. "Witch Doctor" by Coolers)	12

MISSPENT YOUTH

79	Big Bear BB20	Betcha Won't Dance/Birmingham Boys (p/s)	20

MISS X (Joyce Blair)

63	Ember EMB S 175	Christine/S-E-X	15

MISTA CHARGE

76	Target TGT 112	Show Me What You're Made Of/Down On Arcturas	5

MISTAKEN IDENTITY

85	RAM 17CHP 7010	The Answer/The Answer (Club Version) (12")	25

MR. MOST

69	Downtown DT 408	Push Wood/Reggae Train	12

MISTER VERSATILE
(see also Lester Sterling)

69	Jackpot JP 701	Apple Blossom/LITTLE BOY BLUE: Dark End Of The Street (act. by Pat Kelly)	10
69	Jackpot JP 702	Devil's Disciples/ERROL DUNKLEY: Having A Party	8

MINT VALUE £

MISTURA feat. LLOYD MICHAELS

76	Route RT 30	The Flasher/Life Is A Song Worth Singing	5

MISTY

77	Cottage COT 511	MISTY (LP)	18

MISTY IN ROOTS

79	People Unite PU 001	See Them A Come/How Long Jah (12", p/s)	10
80	People Unite PU 002	Rich Man/Salvation (12", p/s)	10
81	People Unite PU 003	Peace And Love/BallOut (12")	8
83	People Unite PU 102	Follow Fashion/Earth/Own Them Control Them/New Day (12")	8
79	People Unite PU 003	LIVE AT THE COUNTER EUROVISION '79 (LP)	20
82	People Unite PU 101 ALB	WISE AND FOOLISH (LP)	20

MISTY MEADOWS

70	Rhone RH 002	Visions/We See The Sun	45

MISUNDERSTOOD

66	Fontana TF 777	I Can Take You To The Sun/Who Do You Love	55
69	Fontana TF 998	Children Of The Sun/I Unseen (small centre hole)	70
69	Fontana TF 998	Children Of The Sun/I Unseen (large centre hole)	50
69	Fontana TF 1028	You're Tuff Enough/Little Red Rooster (as Misunderstood featuring Glenn "Fernando" Campbell, in p/s)	60
69	Fontana TF 1028	You're Tuff Enough/Little Red Rooster (as Misunderstood featuring Glenn "Fernando" Campbell)	35
69	Fontana TF 1041	Never Had A Girl (Like You Before)/Golden Glass (as Misunderstood featuring Glenn "Fernando" Campbell)	45
81	Cherry Red CHERRY 22	Children Of The Sun/Who Do You Love/I'll Take You To The Sun (p/s)	7
80s	Bucketfull Of Brains BOB 2	You're My Girl (flexidisc with Bucketfull Of Brains magazine)	8

ADRIAN MITCHELL

68	Transatlantic TRA 171	POW! A LAUGH, A SONG AND A HAND GRENADE (LP, with Leon Rosselson)	15

BLUE MITCHELL

69	Blue Note BST 84300	COLLISION IN BLACK (LP)	15
73	Mainstream MSL 1002	BLUE'S BLUES (LP)	12

CHAD MITCHELL

62	London HLR 9509	Lizzie Borden/Super Skier	7

DENNY MITCHELL SOUNDSATIONS

(see also Preachers, Moon's Train)

64	Decca F 11848	I've Been Crying/For Your Love	25

GROVER MITCHELL

68	London HLU 10221	Turned On/Blue Over You	18
76	Vanguard VS 5003	What Hurts/Super Hero	40

GUY MITCHELL

53	Columbia SCM 5018	Feet Up (Pat Him On The Po-Po)/Jenny Kissed Me	30
53	Columbia SCM 5022	Cause I Love Ya, That's A-Why/Train Of Love (both with Mindy Carson)	30
53	Columbia SCM 5032	She Wears Red Feathers/Why Should I Go Home?	30
53	Columbia SCM 5037	Pretty Little Black-Eyed Susie/MITCH MILLER HORNS: Horn Belt Boogie	30
56	Philips JK 1001	Singing The Blues/Crazy With Love (jukebox issue)	15
57	Philips JK 1005	Knee Deep In The Blues/Take Me Back Baby (jukebox issue)	15
57	Philips JK 1015	Rock-A-Billy/Got A Feeling (jukebox issue)	15
57	Philips JK 1023	Sweet Stuff/In The Middle Of A Dark, Dark Night (jukebox issue)	15
57	Philips JK 1027	Call Rosie On The Phone/Cure For The Blues (jukebox issue)	15
58	Philips PB 766	C'mon Let's Go/The Unbeliever	8
58	Philips PB 798	Wond'rin' And Worryin'/If Ya Don't Like It, Don't Knock It	6
58	Philips PB 830	Hangin' Around/Honey Brown Eyes	10
58	Philips PB 858	Let It Shine, Let It Shine/Butterfly Doll	10
58	Philips PB 885	My Heart Cries For You (2nd Version)/Till We're Engaged	7
59	Philips PB 915	Alias Jesse James/Pride O' Dixie	7
59	Philips PB 964	Heartaches By The Number/Two (with triangular centre)	12
63	Pye International 7N 25179	Go, Tiger, Go/If You Ever Go Away (unreleased)	0
63	Pye International 7N 25185	Have I Told You Lately That I Love You/Blue Violet	7
66	CBS 202238	Singing The Blues/Rock-A-Billy	8
54	Columbia SEG 7513	PRETTY LITTLE BLACK EYED SUSIE (EP, plain sleeve)	10
55	Columbia SEG 7581	MY TRULY TRULY FAIR (EP, plain sleeve)	10
55	Columbia SEG 7598	JENNY KISSED ME (EP, plain sleeve)	10
55	Philips BBE 12008	GUY MITCHELL (EP)	10
56	Philips BBE 12093	GUY MITCHELL NO. 2 (EP)	10
57	Philips BBE 12112	SINGING THE BLUES WITH GUY MITCHELL (EP)	10
58	Philips BBE 12215	GUY MITCHELL PHILIPS TV SERIES (EP)	10
54	Columbia 33S 1028	GUY MITCHELL SINGS 10" LP)	20
55	Philips BBR 8031	THE VOICE OF YOUR CHOICE (10"LP)	20
58	Philips BBL 7246	A GUY IN LOVE (LP)	20
58	Philips BBL 7265	SHOWCASE OF HITS (LP)	15
61	Philips BBL 7465	SUNSHINE GUITAR (LP)	25
68	London HA-B 8364	TRAVELING SHOES (LP, mono)	12
68	London SH-B 8364	TRAVELING SHOES (LP, stereo)	15

JONI MITCHELL

68	Reprise RS 20694	Night In The City/I Had A King	15
69	Reprise RS 23402	Chelsea Morning/Both Sides Now	12
70	Reprise RS 20906	Big Yellow Taxi/Woodstock	5
72	Asylum AYM 511	You Turn Me On, I'm A Radio/Urge For Going	8
83	Geffen DA 3122	Chinese Cafe/Ladies Man (double pack, with bonus interview 7")	8
68	Reprise RSLP 6293	JONI MITCHELL (LP, gatefold sleeve, 'steamboat' label)	50
69	Reprise RSLP 6341	CLOUDS (LP, textured single sleeve, 'steamboat' label)	45
69	Reprise RSLP 6341	CLOUDS (LP, 2nd pressing, stickered U.S. gatefold sleeve, 'steamboat' label)	15

			MINT VALUE £
70	Reprise RSLP 6376	LADIES OF THE CANYON (LP, gatefold sleeve, 'steamboat' label)	30
71	Reprise K 44128	BLUE (LP, gatefold sleeve, with blue inner sleeve)	35
71	Reprise K 44128	BLUE (LP, gatefold sleeve)	15
73	Asylum SYLA 8753	FOR THE ROSES (LP, gatefold sleeve)	15
74	Asylum SYLA 8756	COURT AND SPARK (LP, gatefold sleeve)	20
75	Asylum SYLA 8763	THE HISSING OF SUMMER LAWNS (LP)	18
75	Asylum SYSP 902	MILES OF AISLES (2-LP, gatefold sleeve with inner flap)	20
79	Asylum K 53091	MINGUS (LP, gatefold sleeve)	15
70s	Asylum K 53053	HEJIRA (LP, gatefold sleeve)	15
80	Asylum K 62030	SHADOWS AND LIGHT (2-LP, gatefold sleeve with inners)	12
82	Asylum/Nimbus K 53018	THE HISSING OF SUMMER LAWNS (LP, audiophile pressing, mail order issue)	50

McKINLEY 'SOUL' MITCHELL

68	President PT 125	The Town I Live In/No Love Like Your Love	10
68	President PTL 1005	McKINLEY 'SOUL' MITCHELL (LP)	40

PHILIP MITCHELL

71	Jay Boy BOY 37	I'm Gonna Build California From All Over The World/ The World Needs More People Like You	25
71	Jay Boy BOY 37	I'm Gonna Build California From All Over The World/ The World Needs More People Like You (DJ copy)	50
72	Jay Boy BOY 57	Free For All/Flower Child	10
72	Jay Boy BOY 57	Free For All/Flower Child (DJ copy)	10
74	London HLU 10444	Ain't No Love In My Life/Turning Over The Ground	40

RED MITCHELL

62	London LZ-N1 4017	HAPPY MINORS (10" LP)	15
63	London SH-K 8027	HEAR YE!! HEAR YE!! (LP)	12

RONNIE MITCHELL

60	London HLU 9220	How Many Times/The Only Love	8

SINX MITCHELL

(see also Crickets, Earl Sinks)

64	Hickory 45-1248	This Weird Sensation/Love Is All I'm Asking For	20

VALERIE MITCHELL

65	Oak RGJ 160	There Goes My Heart Again/If I Didn't Love You (p/s)	60
65	HMV POP 1422	Bitter Tears/Forbidden	6
65	HMV POP 1462	There Goes My Heart Again/If I Didn't Love You	6
65	HMV POP 1490	Go My Way/Green Eyes	6
66	HMV POP 1509	Play With Me/Never Let It Be Said	10
66	HMV POP 1529	You Can Go/The Windmill Girls	6
67	Columbia DB 8186	Love Can Be The Sweetest Thing/I'm Sorry	6
67	Columbia DB 8265	Sunshine/You Belong To Me	6

WARREN MITCHELL

67	CBS 2824	The Writing On The Wall/Her Heart's In the Right Place (p/s)	8
67	CBS 2824	The Writing On The Wall/Her Heart's In the Right Place (no p/s)	6

WILLIE MITCHELL

64	London HLU 9926	20-75/Secret Home	20
64	London HLU 9926	20-75/Secret Home (DJ Copy)	40
65	London HLU 10004	Everything Is Gonna Be Alright/That Driving Beat (Boxed logo)	15
65	London HLU 10004	Everything Is Gonna Be Alright/That Driving Beat	30
65	London HLU 10004	Everything Is Gonna Be Alright/That Driving Beat (DJ copy)	50
66	London HLU 10039	Bad Eye/Sugar T.	10
66	London HLU 10085	Mercy/Sticks And Stones	10
68	London HLU 10186	Soul Serenade/Buster Browne	20
68	London HLU 10215	Prayer Meetin'/Rum Daddy	8
68	London HLU 10224	Up Hard/Beale Street Mood	10
70	London HLU 10313	Robbin's Nest/Six To Go	8
73	London HLU 10407	Last Tango In Paris/Six To Go	6
74	London HLU 10545	The Champion (2 parts)	8
74	London HLU 10545	The Champion (2 parts) (DJ copy)	25
67	London HA-U 8319	THE HIT SOUND OF WILLIE MITCHELL (LP)	30
68	London HA-U/SH-U 8365	SOUL SERENADE (LP)	20
68	London HA-U/SH-U 8368	LIVE (LP)	20
69	London HA-U/SH-U 8372	SOLID SOUL (LP)	20
70	London HA-U/SH-U 8388	ON TOP (LP)	20
70	London HA-U/SH-U 8408	SOUL BAG (LP)	20

MITCHELL/COE MYSTERIES

(see also Colin Blunstone, Lesley Duncan, Dan McCafferty, Francis Rossi & Berni Frost, Ray Russell, Joe Jammer, Complex, Monsoon)

80	RCA PL 25297	EXILED (LP, with inner sleeve, with gatefold sleeve)	15
80	RCA PL 25297	EXILED (LP, with inner sleeve)	12

ROBERT MITCHUM

57	Capitol CL 14701	What Is This Generation Coming To?/Mama Looka Boo Boo	10
57	Capitol CL 14701	What Is This Generation Coming To?/Mama Looka Boo Boo (78)	15
62	Capitol CL 15251	The Ballad Of Thunder Road/My Honey's Lovin' Arms	6
67	Monument MON 1007	Little Ole Wine Drinker Me/Walker's Woods	7
55	Brunswick OE 9197	RACHEL AND THE STRANGER (EP)	15
67	Monument LMO 5011	THAT MAN (LP)	20

MITHRANDIR

82	New Leaf SVC 01	MAGICK EP (p/s)	75
82	New Leaf SVC 570	Dreamers Of Fortune/After Tomorrow (p/s)	50

MINT VALUE £

JACKIE MITTO(O)

(see also Lord Tanamo, Jamaican Actions, Matadors, Jackie Opel, Soul Vendors, Winston Francis, Donna & Freedom Singers, Skatalites)

66	Island WI 293	Killer Diller (as Jackie Mitto & Soul Brothers)/PATRICK HYTTON: Oh Lady	100
67	Rio R 114	Home Made/ETHIOPIANS: I'm Gonna Take Over Now	35
67	Rio R 123	Got My Buglaoo/ETHIOPIANS: What To Do	100
67	Coxsone CS 7002	Somebody Help Me/GAYLADS & SOUL VENDORS: The Sound Of Silence	25
67	Coxsone CS 7009	Ba Ba Boom/SLIM SMITH & FREEDOM SINGERS: Mercy Mercy	35
67	Coxsone CS 7019	Ram Jam/SUMMERTAIRES: You're Gonna Leave	20
67	Coxsone CS 7026	Something Stupid/LYRICS: Money Lover	25
68	Coxsone CS 7040	Norwegian Wood/GAYLADS: Most Peculiar Man	25
68	Coxsone CS 7042	Sure Shot/OCTAVES: The Bottle	35
68	Coxsone CS 7046	Man Pon Shot/BOP & BELTONES: Not For A Moment	25
68	Coxsone CS 7050	Napoleon Solo/CANNON BALL BRYAN: You're My Everything	60
68	Coxsone CS 7075	Mission Impossible/HEPTONES: Giddy Up (B-side actually by Actions)	50
68	Studio One SO 2043	Put It One/SOUL VENDORS: Chinese Chicken	25
68	Studio One SO 2056	Race Track/BASES: I Don't Mind	40
69	Studio One SO 2082	Hi-Jack/TREVOR CLARKE: Sufferer	40
69	Doctor Bird DB 1177	Dark Of The Sun/MATADOR ALL STARS: Bridge View	50
69	Bamboo BAM 6	Our Thing (with Sound Dimension)/C. MARSHALL: Tra La La Sweet '69	18
69	Bamboo BAM 15	Clean Up/Spring Time (as Jackie Mittoo & Sound Dimension)	18
70	Bamboo BAM 17	Dark Of The Moon/Moon Walk (as Jackie Mittoo & Sound Dimension)	30
70	Bamboo BAM 20	Gold Dust/SUPERTONES: Real Gone Loser	18
70	Bamboo BAM 31	Can I Change My Mind/BRENTFORD ALLSTARS: Early Duckling	18
70	Bamboo BAM 38	Baby Why/ETHIOPIANS: You'll Want To Come Back	25
70	Bamboo BAM 51	Dancing Groove/BLACK & GEORGE: Peanut Butter	22
70	Banana BA 315	Holly Holy/LARRY MARSHALL: I've Got To Make It	15
71	Banana BA 320	Peenie Wallie/ROY RICHARDS: Can't Go On	12
72	London HLU 10357	Wishbone/Soul Bird (as Jackie Mittoo - The Reggae Beat)	7
79	Justice DIS 001	Disco Jack/Disco Dub Version (12")	20
80	Rite Sound RTA 06	Mystic World/Version (12")	20
81	Black Roots BR20	These Eyes/Wall Street/Thriller The Killer (12", p/s)	30
67	Coxsone CSL 8009	IN LONDON (LP)	150
68	Coxsone CSL 8014	EVENING TIME (LP, with Soul Vendors)	150
69	Coxsone CSL 8020	KEEP ON DANCING (LP)	150
70	Bamboo BDLP 209	NOW (LP)	70
72	London SHU 8436	WISHBONE (LP)	25
79	Third World TWS 501	KEYBOARD KING (LP)	20

MIX BLOOD

80	Creole CR 201	Last Train To Skaville/Move And Move (p/s)	10

MIXED BAG

69	Decca F 12880	Potiphar (with Ramases III Orchestra)/Million Dollar Bash	10
69	Decca F 12907	Round And Round/Have You Ever Been In Love	10

MIXMAN

90	Citizen Kane 12KANE 2	Bright Child (Manmix)/Bright Child (Dancemix) (12", p/s)	15

MIXRACE & PRO-TON-ISOSPACE

94	Stronghold STRONG 3	The Endless Skies (Hyper-On-Experience Remix)/True Jungle (Brown & Dangerman Remix)/The Endless Skies/True Jungle (12")	20

MIXTURE

65	Fontana TF 640	One By One/Monkey Jazz	10
69	Parlophone R 5755	Sad Old Song/Never Trust In Tomorrow	7

BILLY MIZE

60	Top rank JAR 391	Little Coco Palm/The Winward Isle	6

HANK MIZELL

76	Charly CEP 115	HANK MIZELL (EP)	8
76	Charly CRL 5000	JUNGLE ROCK (LP)	12

VIC MIZZY, HIS ORCHESTRA & CHORUS

65	RCA RCA 1440	Addams Family Main Theme/Kentucky James Main Theme	20

M.J.6

60	Decca F 11212	Tracy's Theme/Private Eye	6

M.J.Q.

(see under Modern Jazz Quartet)

MO & STEVE

66	Pye 7N 17175	Oh What A Day It's Going To Be/Reach Out For Your Lovin' Touch	5

MO2VATION & APEX

92	Hypno Genesis HG 002	ANIMATION EP (12")	40

MOB

68	Mercury MF 1026	Disappear/I Wish You Would Leave Me Alone	15
71	Polydor 2001 127	I Dig Everything About You/Love's Got A Hold On Me	15
71	Polydor 2001 169	Give It To Me/I'd Like To See More Of You	10
71	Polydor 2001 200	Money/Once A Man Twice A Child	5
73	MGM 2006 278	Tear The House Down/One Way Ticket To Nowhere	5
74	UK USA 4	Give It To Me/I'd Like To See More Of You	8
75	Private Stock PVT 32	I Can't Stop This Love Song/Hot Music	8
71	Polydor 2344 001	MOB (LP)	15

MOB

80	Kalida AKB 1/2	Send Me To Coventry/Mobbed (p/s)	8

MOB

80	All The Madmen MAD 1	Youth/Crying Again (p/s)	40
80	All The Madmen MAD 002	Witch Hunt/Shuffling Souls/What's Going On (EP, handwritten white	

MINT VALUE £

		labels with sticker & foldout, stapled, gatefold p/s)	10
82	Crass 321984/7	No Doves Fly Here/I Hear You Laughing (foldout p/s)	10
83	All The Madmen MAD 6	The Mirror Breaks/Stay (screen-printed p/s, with lyric insert)	10
86	All The Madmen MAD 13	CRYING AGAIN (EP)	30
80s	All/Madmen MADPACK 1	MAD PACK 1 (3 x 7" in 12" pack)	25
83	All The Madmen MAD 4	LET THE TRIBE INCREASE (LP, with lyric poster)	20
83	Cause For Concern CFC 2	LIVE AT THE LMC (LP, with the APOSTLES)	30
84	All The Madmen MAD 4	LET THE TRIBE INCREASE (LP, second pressing, blue cover)	12

JOHN MOBLEY

62	Stateside SS 136	Tunnel Of Love/Work Out	12

MOBSTER

80	Ensign ENY 41	The Mobster Shuffle/Simmer Down (p/s)	6
81	Ensign ENY 209	Perfect Man/Trinidad (p/s)	5

MOBY DICK

82	Ebony EBON 5	Nothing To Fear/Can't Have My Body Tonight	6

MOBY GRAPE

67	CBS 2953	Omaha/Hey Grandma	25
68	CBS 3555	Can't Be So Bad/Murder In My Heart For The Judge	8
69	CBS 3945	Trucking Man/Ooh Mama Ooh	8
67	CBS (S)BPG 63090	MOBY GRAPE (LP)	50
68	CBS 63271	WOW (LP, mono & stereo)	30
69	CBS 63430	69 (LP, mono & stereo)	30
69	CBS 63698	TRULY FINE CITIZEN (LP, mono & stereo)	30
72	Reprise K 44152	20 GRANITE CREEK (LP)	15
74	CBS 64743	GREAT GRAPE (LP)	15

MOCCA-SIN & THE TP'S

78	Alaska ALA 2013	Cherokee Dance/The Raindance	10

MOCEDADES

73	Bell BELL 1303	Touch The Wind/Eres Tu	6

MOCKINGBIRDS

(see also 10cc, Graham Gouldman, Whirlwinds, Doctor Father, Hotlegs, Godley & Greme)

65	Columbia DB 7480	That's How It's Gonna Stay/I Never Should Have Kissed You	55
65	Columbia DB 7565	I Can Feel We're Parting/The Flight Of The Mockingbird	55
65	Immediate IM 015	You Stole My Love/Skit Skat	150
66	Decca F 12434	One By One/Lovingly Yours	60
66	Decca F 12510	How To Find A Lover/My Story	50

M.O.D.

(see also David Essex)

79	Vertigo 6059 233	M.O.D./M.O.D. (2) (p/s, allegedly mispressed on 2-Tone label)	30
79	Vertigo 6059 233	M.O.D./M.O.D. (2) (p/s)	7

MOD '79

79	Casino Classics CC 13	Green Onions/High On Your Love	6

MODE

66	private pressing	THE MODE (EP, white labels, no p/s)	400

MODEL MANIA

79	Boob MM1 A/MM 1AA	No Pride Slow Suicide/Epic Cowboy (250 with handmade stamped label)	100
79	Boob MM1 A/MM 1AA	No Pride Slow Suicide/Epic Cowboy (750 with black labels)	75

MODELS

(see also Adam & The Ants, Mass, Rema Rema, Wolfgang Press)

77	Step Forward SF 3	Freeze/Man Of The Year (p/s)	20

MODERATES

80	Open Eye OEEP 1001	FETISHES (12" EP)	8

MODERNAIRES (U.K.)

80	Illuminated ILL 2	Life In Our Times/Barbed Up (p/s)	5
81	Illuminated ILL 4	We Did It Again/And Again (p/s, red vinyl)	5

MODERNAIRES (U.S.)

(see also Four Guys, Bing Crosby)

54	Vogue Coral Q 2024	Teach Me Tonight/Mood Indigo (with Georgie Auld)	7
54	Vogue Coral Q 2035	New Juke Box Saturday Night/Bugle Call Rag	8
55	Vogue Coral Q 72069	Birds And Puppies And Tropical Fish/Mine! Mine! Mine!	7
55	Vogue Coral Q 72084	Wine, Women And Gold/Sluefoot (with Bob Crosby Bob Cats)	7
55	Vogue Coral Q 72112	At My Front Door/Alright, Okay, You Win	7
55	Vogue Coral LVC 10012	STOP, LOOK AND LISTEN (10" LP)	20
58	Coral LVA 9080	HERE COME THE MODERNAIRES (LP)	15

MODERN ART

84	Color Disc COLORS 1	Dreams To Live/Beautiful Truth (p/s)	25
86	Color Disc COLORS 5	Penny Valentine/One Way Ticket (1-sided, clear vinyl flexidisc, 1,000 only)	12
87	Color Disc COLOR 3	STEREOLAND (LP, hand-stencilled with insert, 300 only)	60

MODERN ENGLISH

(see also This Mortal Coil)

79	Limp LMP 2	Drowning Man/Silent World (p/s)	15
80	4AD AD 6	Swans On Glass/Incident (p/s)	6
80	4AD AD 15	Gathering Dust/Tranquility Of A Summer Moment (p/s)	6
81	4AD AD 110	Smiles And Laughter/Mesh And Lace (p/s)	5
81	4AD CAD 105	MESH AND LACE (LP)	12

MODERN EON

80	Modern Eon EON 001	PIECES (EP)	20
80	Inevitable INEV 3	Euthenics/Waiting For The Cavalry (p/s)	5
81	Dinsales 2	Euthenics/Choreography/Waiting For The Cavalry/The Real Hymn (12", white label LP sampler)	20

MINT VALUE £

MODERN FOLK QUARTET (M.F.Q.)

64	Warner Bros WB 147	The Love Of A Clown/If You All Think	25
66	RCA RCA 1514	Night Time Girl/Lifetime (as M.F.Q.)	30
63	Warner Bros WM/WS 8135	THE MODERN FOLK QUARTET (LP)	20
85	Off Beat WIK 55	MOONLIGHT SERENADE (LP)	15

MODERN JAZZ QUARTET (M.J.Q.)

(see also John Lewis, Milt Jackson, Sonny Rollins)

60	Decca F11212	Tracey's Theme/Private Eye	6
55	Esquire 20-069	MODERN JAZZ QUARTET (10" LP)	15
55	Esquire 20-038	MODERN JAZZ QUARTET VOL. 2 (10" LP)	15
55	Esquire 20-090	THE CLASSICAL PERFORMANCES OF... (10" LP)	15
57	London Jazz LTZK 15022	FONTESSA (LP, also stereo SAH-K 6031)	15
58	London Jazz LTZK 15085	AT THE MUSIC INN (LP)	12
58	London Jazz LTZ 15136	MODERN JAZZ QUARTET (LP)	12
59	London Jazz LTZ-K 15140	PLAYS ONE NEVER KNOWS (LP, also stereo SAH-K 6029)	15
59	London Jazz LTZK 15181	ODDS AGAINST TOMORROW (LP)	15
59	Columbia Clef 33CX 11028	MODERN JAZZ QUARTET & OSCAR PETERSON AT THE OPERA HOUSE (LP)	12
60	London Jazz LTZ-K 15193	PYRAMID (LP, also stereo SAH-K 6086)	15
61	London Jazz LTZ-K 15207	THIRD STREAM MUSIC (LP, with Beaux Arts String Quartet& Jimmy Giuffre Three)	15
61	London Jazz LTZK 15222	EUROPEAN CONCERT (LP)	12
61	Esquire 32-124	LOOKING BACK AT THE MODERN JAZZ QUARTET (LP)	12
63	London HA-K/SH-K 8016	LONELY WOMAN (LP)	15
63	London HA-K/SH-K 8046	THE COMEDY SUITE (LP)	12
64	London HA-K/SH-K 8161	THE SHERIFF (LP)	12
65	Stateside SL 10141	THE BEST OF THE MODERN JAZZ QUARTET (LP)	12
68	Apple APCOR 4	UNDER THE JASMINE TREE (LP, mono)	45
68	Apple SAPCOR 4	UNDER THE JASMINE TREE (LP, stereo)	35
69	Apple SAPCOR 10	SPACE (LP, gatefold sleeve, dark green label, black inner)	45
70s	Apple SAPCOR 10	SPACE (LP, later pressing, light green label, single sl., white 'Apple' inner)	75
93	Apple SAPCOR 4	UNDER THE JASMINE TREE (LP, reissue, gatefold sleeve with inner)	20
93	Apple SAPCOR 10	SPACE (LP, reissue)	15

MODERN JAZZ SEXTET

56	Columbia Clef 33CX 10048	MODERN JAZZ SEXTET (LP)	15

MODERN JAZZ SOCIETY

56	Columbia Clef 33CX 10038	A CONCERT OF CONTEMPORARY MUSIC (LP)	12

MODERN LOVERS

76	Berkeley BSERK 1	MODERN LOVERS (LP)	15

MODERN TALKING

86	RCA PD 71133	READY FOR ROMANCE (CD)	30

MO-DETTES

79	Mode/Rough Trade MODE 1	White Mice/Masochistic Opposite (pink [card or paper] or white p/s)	6
80	S.F.I. SFI 550/MODE 11/2	Twist And Shout (gig freebie flexidisc, different label design to later issue)	5
80	Deram DET-R-1/MODE 11/2	Paint It Black/Bitta Truth (with free flexidisc "Twist And Shout" & insert, black & white or blue & white p/s)	6
81	Deram DET 3	Tonight/Waltz In Blue Minor (p/s)	5
81	Human HUM 10	White Mice/Kray Twins (live) (p/s)	5
80	Deram SML 1120	THE STORY SO FAR (LP, with insert & free colour sticker)	15

MODIFIES

70	Punch PH 45	Bye Bye Happyness/Sufferation We Must Bear	6

MODS

64	RCA RCA 1399	Something On My Mind/You're Making Me Blue	25

MODS

80	Bootlegged Records 007	LOST TOUCH (LP; sold only in Portobello Market, London)	25

MODULATIONS

74	Buddah BDS 406	I Can't Fight Your Love/Your Love Has Locked Me Up	8
70s	Buddah	THE MODULATIONS (LP)	40

MOE

88	Times Five T5 01	There Were Four Other Guys/One Man Went To Moe (12", p/s)	8

PETER MOESSER'S MUSIC

70	Stateside SS 2182	Hello/Bye Bye (withdrawn)	7

MOFFAT ALL STARS

70	Jackpot JP 719	Riot/IMPERSONATORS: Girls And Boys	75

MOGUL THRASH

(see also Colosseum, Eclection, Family, King Crimson)

70	RCA RCA 2030	Sleeping In The Kitchen/St. Peter	22
71	RCA SF 8156	MOGUL THRASH (LP)	60

MOGWAI

(see also Magoo)

96	Rock Action RAR 01	Tuner/Lower (p/s, 500 only)	40
96	Che CHE 59	4 TRACK 3 BAND TOUR EP (with Urusei Yatsura & Backwater, p/s, 50 only)	45
96	Che CHE 61	Angels Vs Aliens/DWEEB: Buzzsong (p/s, 1st 500 on green vinyl)	12
96	Che CHE 61	Angels Vs Aliens/DWEEB: Buzzsong (p/s)	6
96	Love Train PUBE 014	Summer/Ithica 279 (p/s, 1,500 only)	30
97	Wurlitzer Jukebox WJ 22	New Paths To Helicon (Parts 1 & 2) (foldover p/s in polythene bag, 1,000 only)	30
97	Flotsam/Jetsam SHAG13.04	Stereo Dee/PH FAMILY: Club Beatroot Part 4 (p/s, 400 only)	45
98	Eye EYEUK 032	FEAR SATAN REMIXES: My Bloody Valentine Remix /u-ziq Remix/Surgeon Remix (12", p/s)	12
01	Chrysalis 9460013221	FIVE TRACK TOUR SINGLE: Close Encounters/Drum Machine/D To E/ You Don't Know Jesus/Helicon (tour CD, card sleeve)	45

MINT VALUE £

97	Chemikal U'gnd CHEM 015	4 SATIN EP	8
98	Chemikal CHEM 026	NO EDUCATION = NO FUTURE (FUCK THE CURFEW) EP (12")	15
99	Chemikal CHEM 036	EP (12")	12
08	Rock Action ROCKACT 43	Colours Move (Remix)/FUCK BUTTONS : Mogwai Fear Satan (tour CD single)	8
97	Chemikal CHEM 818LP	YOUNG TEAM (2-LP)	30
98	Eye Q EYEUKLP 019	KICKING A DEAD PIG (2-LP)	18
99	Chemikal CMEM 033	COME ON DIE YOUNG (2-LP)	35
01	Southpaw PAWLP1	ROCK ACTION (LP)	20
03	Pias PIASX 035LP	HAPPY SONGS FOR HAPPY PEOPLE (LP, silvered sleeve)	20
05	Pias PIAS051LP	GOVERNMENT COMMISSIONS : BBC SESSIONS 1996-2003 (2-LP)	20
07	Pias PIASX062DLP	MR BEAST (2-LP)	20

ESSRA MOHAWK

75	Mooncrest CREST 24	ESSRA MOHAWK (LP, with insert)	15
77	Private Stock PVLP 1016	ESSRA (LP)	15

MOHAWKS

(see also Sid & Joe & Mohawks)

68	Pama PM 309	The Clock/Version	35
68	Pama PM 719	The Champ/Sound Of The Witchdoctors (blue label)	30
68	Pama PM 719	The Champ/Sound Of The Witchdoctors (purple label)	20
68	Pama PM 739	Baby Hold On (Parts 1 & 2)	20
68	Pama PM 751	Sweet Soul Music/Hip Jigger	20
68	Pama PM 757	Mony Mony/Pepsi	70
69	Pama PM 758	Ride Your Pony/Western Promise	25
69	Pama PM 798	Skinhead Shuffle/RICO: Red Cow	50
70	Supreme SUP 205	Wicked Lady/For Our Liberty	15
70	Pama PM 796	Landscape/Number 1	25
70	Supreme SUP 204	Let It Be/Looking Back	15
70	Supreme SUP 205	For Our Liberty/Wicked Lady	10
70	Supreme SUP 207	Give Me Some/(Instrumental)	50
72	Supreme PS 362	Storm/And I Love Her	40
73	Supreme PS 376	The Champ/Cherry Pink	40
70s	Star PTP 1011	Whiter Shade Of Pale/My One Desire	15
86	Pama PM (T) 1	The Champ/Landscape (12", p/s)	8
68	Pama PMLP 5	THE CHAMP (LP)	200

LOUIS MOHOLO

78	Ogun OG 520	SPIRITS REJOICE (LP)	20

MOIST

86	Debris DEB 9/LYN 19589	The Cut Up 1/KING OF THE SLUMS: Haemophiliacs On Tacks (33rpm flexidisc free with Debris magazine)	8
95	Chrysalis 12CHSS 5019	SILVER (12" EP, clear vinyl)	10

MOJO HANNAH

72	Kingdom KV 8004	St. Jeremy/You'll Be Alright	25
73	Kingdom KV 8008	Six Days On The Road/Moon Dog's Gonna Howl Tonight	5
73	Kingdom KVL 9001	SIX DAYS ON THE ROAD (LP, orange label)	35

MOJO MEN

65	Pye International 7N 25336	Dance With Me/The Loneliest Boy In Town	30
66	Reprise RS 20486	Hanky Panky/She's My Baby	30
67	Reprise RS 20539	Sit Down I Think I Love You/Don't Leave Me Crying Like Before	18
67	Reprise RS 20580	Me About You/When You're In Love	15

MOJOS

(see also Stu James & Mojos, Faron's Flamingos)

63	Decca F 11732	They Say/Forever	15
64	Decca F 11853	Everything's Alright/Give Your Lovin' To Me	8
64	Decca F 11918	Why Not Tonight/Don/t Do It Any More	8
64	Decca F 11959	Seven Daffodils/Nothin' At All	10
65	Decca F 12127	Comin' On To Cry/That's The Way It Goes	15
67	Decca F 12557	Goodbye Dolly Gray/I Just Can't Let Her Go	20
68	Liberty LBF 15097	Until My Baby Comes Home/Seven Park Avenue	60
64	Decca DFE 8591	THE MOJOS (EP)	70

MOLES

68	Parlophone R 5743	We Are The Moles (Parts 1 & 2)	40

MOLESTERS

79	Small Wonder SMALL 14	Disco Love/Commuter Man (p/s)	5
79	Small Wonder SMALL 18	End Of Civilisation/Girl Behind The Curtain (p/s)	5

MOMENT

85	Diamond DIA 004	In This Town/Just Once	6
85	Diamond DIA 008	One, Two, They Fly/Karl's New Haircut	5
80s	Tenth Floor	Poor Mr. Diamond (Parts 1 & 2)	10
89	Big Stuff	Ready To Fall (promo only)	8
86	Rave RAVE UP 1	THE WORK GETS DONE (LP, coloured vinyl)	12

MOMENTS

63	London HLN 9656	Walk Right In/Walk Right In (Instrumental)	12

MOMENTS

72	London HLU 10378	Love On A Two Way Street/I Won't Do Anything	8
74	London HL 10449	Sexy Mama/Where Can I Find Her	5
74	All Platinum 6146 322	Next Time I See You/It Don't Rain In My Backyard	8
75	All Platinum 6146 309	Look At Me/French Version	6
76	All Platinum 6146313	Nine Times	10
75	All Platinum 9109 302	SHARP (LP)	20

MOMENTUM

89	Fierce FI 001	Bitter Herb Taste Sweet/Trojan Warrior (12")	8

MINT VALUE £

MOMUS
(see also Happy Family)

86	él GPO 9T	Nicky/Don't Leave/See A Friend In Tears (12")	20
87	Creation CRE 037 T	Murderers, The Hope Of Women (12", p/s)	12
88	Creation CRELP 036	TENDER PERVERT (LP, with free 7")	15
90	Creation CRELP 052	DON'T STOP THE NIGHT (LP)	15
91	Creation CRELP 059	MONSTERS OF LOVE (LP)	12
91	Creation CRELP 097	HIPPOPOTAMOMUS (LP, with "Michelin Man" track & Michelin Man style inlay, withdrawn)	15
91	Creation CRECD 097	HIPPOPOTAMOMUS (CD, with "Michelin Man" track & Michelin Man style inlay, withdrawn)	20
92	Creation	SPACEWALK EP (CD)	20
93	Creation CRECD 151	TIMELORD (CD)	18
94	Creation CRECD 052	DON'T STOP THE NIGHT (CD)	18
94	Creation CRECD 059	MONSTERS OF LOVE (CD)	18

STEPHEN MONAHAN

67	London HLR 10145	City Of Windsor/Lost People	12

MONARCHS

64	London HLU 9862	Look Homeward Angel/What's Made You Change Your Mind	30

JULIE MONDAY

66	London HLU 10080	Come Share The Good Times With Me/Time Is Running Out For Me	8

MONDO KANE
(see also Georgie Fame)

86	Lisson DOLEQ 2	New York Afternoon (Mixes)/Manhattan Morning (12", p/s)	10

MONEY

69	Major Minor MM 571	Welcome Me Love/Breaking Her Heart	8
69	Major Minor MM 620	Come Laughing Home/Power Of The Rainbow	8

MONEY
(see also Iron Maiden)

79	Gull GULL 64	Aren't We All Searching/Where Have All The Dancers Gone	8
80	Hobo HOS 011	FAST WORLD (EP, p/s)	80
79	Gull GULP 1031	FIRST INVESTMENT (LP)	18

MONEY JANGLE

72	President PT 362	Home/Away Away	20

MONEY MARK
(see also Beastie Boys)

95	Mo' Wax MW 044	LEGITIMATE POP SONGS?: Untitled Instrumental/Sometimes You Gotta Make It Alone/Untitled Instrumental (EP, die-cut sleeve)	6

MONEY PIT

97	Bluepose	Smile It's Sugar/Strange And Silent Staircase (P/S)	10

ZOOT MONEY('S BIG ROLL BAND)
(see also Paul Williams & Big Roll Band, Dantalian's Chariot, Eric Burdon & Animals, Grimms, Centipede, Ellis, Johnny Almond Music Machine)

64	Decca F 11954	The Uncle Willie/Zoot's Suit (solo)	50
65	Columbia DB 7518	Good/Bring It Home To Me	40
65	Columbia DB 7600	Please Stay/You Know You'll Cry	35
65	Columbia DB 7697	Something Is Worrying Me/Stubborn Kind Of Fellow	30
65	Columbia DB 7768	The Many Faces Of Love/Jump Back (as Paul Williams & Zoot Money Band)	30
66	Columbia DB 7876	Let's Run For Cover/Self-Discipline	30
66	Columbia DB 7975	Big Time Operator/Zoot's Sermon	20
66	Columbia DB 8090	The Star Of The Show (The La La Song)/The Mound Moves	35
67	Columbia DB 8172	Nick Knack/I Really Learnt How To Cry	15
70	Polydor 2058 020	No One But You/Prisoner	8
80	Magic Moon/MPL MACH 3	Your Feet's Too Big/Ain't Nothin' Shakin' But The Bacon (solo)	12
80	Magic Moon/MPL MACH 6	The Two Of Us/Ain't Nothin' Shakin' But The Bacon (solo)	30
66	Columbia SEG 8519	BIG TIME OPERATOR (EP)	250
66	Columbia SX 6075	ZOOT! - LIVE AT KLOOK'S KLEEK (LP, mono)	65
66	Columbia SCX 6075	ZOOT! - LIVE AT KLOOK'S KLEEK (LP, stereo)	75
65	Columbia 33SX 1734	IT SHOULD'VE BEEN ME (LP)	120
68	Direction 8-63231	TRANSITION (LP)	70
70	Polydor 2482 019	ZOOT MONEY (LP)	50
80	Magic Moon/MPL LUNE 1	MR. MONEY (LP, solo)	12

MONGREL
(see also Wizzard)

73	Polydor 2058 318	Lonely Street/Sing A Little Song	5
73	Polydor 2058 347	Last Night/Twist Her Hand	5
73	Polydor 2383 182	GET YOUR TEETH INTO THIS (LP)	25

MONGRELS
(see also Bobbie Miller)

64	Decca F 12003	I Long To Hear/Everywhere	30
65	Decca F 12086	My Love For You/Stewball	30

MONITORS

69	T. Motown (S)TML 11108	GREETINGS WE'RE THE MONITORS (LP, mono/stereo)	100

THELONIOUS MONK
(see also John Coltrane, Sonny Rollins, Art Blakey, Miles Davis)

56	Vogue EPV 1115	THELONIOUS MONK (EP)	10
55	Esquire 20-039	THELONIOUS MONK QUINTET (10" LP)	20
55	Esquire 20-049	THELONIOUS MONK (10" LP)	25
56	Esquire 20-075	THELONIOUS MONK PLAYS (10" LP)	25

			MINT VALUE £
57	London LTZU 15097	BRILLIANT CORNERS (LP)	20
60	Esquire 32-109	THELONIOUS MONK QUINTETS (LP)	20
61	Esquire 32-115	WORK! (LP, with Art Blakey & Sonny Rollins)	20
61	Esquire 32-119	MONK'S MOODS (LP)	20
61	Riverside RLP 12-201	MONK PLAYS ELLINGTON (LP)	20
61	Philips BBL 1510	THELONIOUS MONK VOL. 1 (LP)	20
61	Riverside RLP 12-226	BRILLIANT CORNERS (LP)	15
61	Riverside RLP 12-262	MONK IN ACTION (LP)	15
62	Riverside RLP 12-300	AT THE TOWN HALL (LP, also stereo RLP 1138)	20
62	Riverside RLP 12-323	AT THE BLACK HAWK (LP, also stereo RLP 1171)	15
62	Philips BBL 1511	THELONIOUS MONK VOL. 2 (LP)	20
62	Riverside RLP 12-242	MONK'S MUSIC (LP)	15
63	CBS (S)BPG 62135	MONK'S DREAM (LP)	15
63	Riverside RLP 12-235	THELONIOUS HIMSELF (LP)	20
63	Riverside JLP (9)46	THELONIOUS MONK AND JOHN COLTRANE (LP)	20
64	Riverside RLP 002	IN EUROPE (VOL. 1)	15
64	CBS (S)BPG 62173	CRISS-CROSS (LP)	20
64	Blue Note (B)BLP 1510	THE GENIUS OF MODERN MUSIC (VOL. 1) (LP)	20
64	Blue Note (B)BLP 1511	THE GENIUS OF MODERN MUSIC (VOL. 2) (LP)	20
64	Riverside RLP 279	MISTERIOSO (LP)	15
64	CBS (S)BPG 62248	BIG BAND AND QUARTET IN CONCERT (LP)	15
65	CBS (S)BPG 62391	IT'S MONK'S TIME (LP)	15
65	Riverside RLP 305	FIVE BY MONK BY FIVE (LP)	15
65	Riverside RLP 003	IN EUROPE (VOL. 2) (LP)	15
65	CBS (S)BPG 62497	MONK (LP)	15
65	Riverside RLP 312	ALONE IN SAN FRANCISCO (LP)	15
65	Fontana FJL 113	WAY OUT! (LP)	15
65	Realm RM 52223	NICA'S TEMPO (LP, with Gigi Gryce)	18
65	CBS (S)BPG 62549	SOLO (LP)	15
65	Stateside SL 10152	THE GOLDEN MONK (LP)	20
67	Transatlantic PR7169	WORK (LP)	20

MONKEES

(see also Micky Dolenz, Davy Jones, Michael Nesmith, Tommy Boyce & Bobby Hart)

66	RCA Victor RCA 1560	I'm A Believer/(I'm Not Your) Stepping Stone	6
67	RCA Victor RCA 1580	A Little Bit Me, A Little Bit You/The Girl I Knew Somewhere	6
67	RCA Victor RCA 1604	Alternate Title/Forget That Girl	6
67	RCA Victor RCA 1620	Pleasant Valley Sunday/Words	7
67	RCA Victor RCA 1645	Daydream Believer/Goin' Down	7
68	RCA Victor RCA 1673	Valleri/Tapioca Tundra	6
68	RCA Victor RCA 1706	D.W. Washburn/It's Nice To Be With You	6
69	RCA RCA 1802	Teardrop City/Man Without A Dream	10
69	RCA RCA 1824	Someday Man/Listen To The Band	10
69	RCA RCA 1862	Daddy's Song/The Porpoise Song	10
69	RCA RCA 1887	Mommy And Daddy/Good Clean Fun	10
70	RCA RCA 1958	Oh My My/Love You Better	12
74	Bell BLL 1354	Monkees Theme/I'm A Believer	6
89	Arista 112 157	THE MONKEES (EP, box set, with booklet & sew-on patch)	10
67	RCA Victor RD 7868	MORE OF THE MONKEES (LP, mono)	18
67	RCA Victor SF 7868	MORE OF THE MONKEES (LP, stereo)	20
67	RCA Victor RD 7886	HEADQUARTERS (LP, mono	20
67	RCA Victor SF 7886	HEADQUARTERS (LP, stereo)	22
67	RCA Victor RD 7886	HEADQUARTERS (LP, with different 'beard' photo on back, mono)	25
67	RCA Victor SF 7886	HEADQUARTERS (LP, with different 'beard' photo on back, stereo)	30
67	RCA Victor RD/SF 7912	PISCES, AQUARIUS, CAPRICORN AND JONES LTD. (LP)	22
68	RCA Victor RD/SF 7948	THE BIRDS, THE BEES & THE MONKEES (LP)	22

(The above albums were originally issued with black labels; later orange label copies are worth the same value.)

69	RCA RD 8016	INSTANT REPLAY (LP, mono)	30
69	RCA SF 8016	INSTANT REPLAY (LP, stereo)	25
69	RCA RD 8051	HEAD (LP, soundtrack, mono)	90
69	RCA SF 8051	HEAD (LP, soundtrack, stereo)	60
73	M.F. Pleasure SPR 90032	THE MONKEES (LP, 'Sounds Superb' series, black 'circus' sleeve)	12
79	Arista MONK-1 1/2	MONKEEMANIA (LP)	20
89	Circus BOY 1	IDOLISED, PLASTICISED, PSYCHOANYLYSED, STERILISED (LP, spoken-word convention issue, white vinyl)	15
89	Circus BOY 1	IDOLISED, PLASTICISED, PSYCHOANYLYSED, STERILISED (LP, spoken-word convention issue, picture disc)	18

BOB MONKHOUSE

68	CBS 3958	I Remember Natalie/In My Dream World	6
69	CBS 4607	Another Time, Another Place, Another World/When I Found You	7

MONKS

74	Rex R11 095	Roller Coaster Rock N Roll/It's A Crying Shame	10

MONOCHROME SET

(see also Art Attacks)

79	Rough Trade RT 005	Alphaville/He's Frank (p/s)	8
79	Rough Trade RT 019	Eine Symphonie Des Grauens/Lester Leaps In (1st 1,000 with labels on wrong side with explanatory insert, p/s)	7
79	Rough Trade RT 019	Eine Symphonie Des Grauens/Lester Leaps In (p/s)	5
79	Disquo Bleu BL 1	He's Frank (Slight Return)/Silicon Carne/Fallout (all cuts live) (no p/s)	6
80	DinDisc DID 8	LOVE ZOMBIES (LP, with lithograph)	12

MONOGRAMS

59	Parlophone R 4515	Juke Box Cha Cha/The Greatest Mistake Of My Life	8
59	Parlophone R 4545	Crystal/Teach Me	5

MONOPOLY

(see also Raymond Froggatt)

67	Polydor 56164	House Of Lords/Magic Carpet	20

MINT VALUE £

67	Polydor 56188	We're All Going To The Seaside/It Isn't Easy	6
70	Pye 7N 17940	We Belong Together/Gone Tomorrow	6

MONOTONES (U.K.)

64	Pye 7N 15608	What Would I Do/Is It Right	10
64	Pye 7N 15640	It's Great/Anymore	10
65	Pye 7N 15761	No Waiting/Like A Lover Should	10
65	Pye 7N 15814	Something's Hurting Me/A Girl Like That	10

MONOTONES (U.S.)

58	London HLM 8625	Book Of Love/You Never Loved Me	50
58	London HLM 8625	Book Of Love/You Never Loved Me (78)	50

MATT MONRO

(see also John Barry)

56	Decca F 10816	Ev'rybody Falls In Love With Someone/Out Of Sight, Out Of Mind	15
57	Decca F 10845	The Garden Of Eden/Love Me Do	15
57	Decca F 10870	My House Is Your House/The Bean Song	15
58	Fontana H 122	The Story Of Ireland/Another Time Another Place	8
58	Fontana H 167	Prisoner Of Love/Have Guitar, Will Travel	8
64	Parlophone R 5103	I Love The Little Things/It's Funny How You Know	5
66	Capitol CL 15436	Born Free/Other People	5
66	Capotol CL 15448	Honey On The Vine/My Best Girl	10
70	Capitol CL 15643	We"re Gonna Change The World/You're Closer To Me	7
63	Parlophone GEP 8889	SINGS THE THEME FROM THE FILM 'FROM RUSSIA FROM LOVE' (EP)	10
57	Decca LF 1276	BLUE AND SENTIMENTAL (10" LP)	50
61	Parlophone PMC 1151	LOVE IS THE SAME ANYWHERE (LP, gold/black label, stereo)	12

BARRY MONROE

66	Polydor 56088	World Of Broken Hearts/Never Again	6

BILL MONROE (& HIS BLUE GRASS BOYS)

(see also Monroe Brothers)

56	Brunswick 05567	New John Henry Blues/Put My Little Shoes Away	15
56	Brunswick 05567	New John Henry Blues/Put My Little Shoes Away (78)	15
57	Brunswick 05681	Four Walls/A Fallen Star	12
57	Brunswick 05681	Four Walls/A Fallen Star (78)	12
59	Brunswick 05776	Gotta Travel On/No One But My Darlin'	10
59	Brunswick 05776	Gotta Travel On/No One But My Darlin' (78)	10
66	Brunswick 05960	Blue Ridge Mountain Blues/John Hardy (solo)	6
55	Brunswick OE 9160	COUNTRY DATE (EP)	10
55	Brunswick OE 9195	COUNTRY WALTZ (EP)	10
63	RCA RCX 7105	COUNTRY GUITAR VOL. 16 (EP, 2 tracks by Monroe Brothers)	10
61	Brunswick LAT 8338	I SAW THE LIGHT (LP)	15
63	Brunswick LAT 8511	BLUEGRASS RAMBLE (LP, mono)	15
63	Brunswick STA 8511	BLUEGRASS RAMBLE (LP, stereo)	18

GERRY MONROE

70	Chapter 1 CH 122	Sally/You Always Hurt The One You Love	5
72	Chapter 1 CH 159	Girl Of My Dreams/When There's No You	7
70	Chapter 1 CHS 806	SALLY - PRIDE OF OUR ALLEY (LP)	12
71	Chapter 1 CHS 809	GERRY MONROE (LP)	12
72	Chapter 1 LRS 5011	BRING BACK THE GOOD TIMES (LP)	12

MARILYN MONROE

(see also Frankie Vaughan)

53	MGM MGM 663	Diamonds Are A Girl's Best Friend/Bye Bye Baby (78)	28
54	HMV 7M 232	The River Of No Return/I'm Gonna File My Claim	60
54	HMV B 10723	The River Of No Return/I'm Gonna File My Claim (78)	30
55	HMV B 10847	After You Get What You Want/Heat Wave (78)	40
59	London HLT 8862	I Wanna Be Loved By You/I'm Thru' With Love	40
59	London HLT 8862	I Wanna Be Loved By You/I'm Thru' With Love (78)	45
78	United Artists UP 36484	I Wanna Be Loved By You/Running Wild/I'm Thru With Love (gatefold p/s)	6
87	Zuma ZOOMP 6	When I Fall In Love/Heat Wave (picture disc)	5
55	HMV 7EG 8090	THERE'S NO BUSINESS LIKE SHOW BUSINESS - SOUNDTRACK EXCERPTS (EP, company sleeve)	40
59	London RET 1231	SOME LIKE IT HOT (EP, soundtrack; first pressing with triangular centre)	80
59	London RET 1231	SOME LIKE IT HOT (EP, soundtrack; later round centre)	50
60	Philips BBE 12414	LET'S MAKE LOVE - FILM SOUNDTRACK (EP, with Yves Montand & Frankie Vaughan; mono)	30
60	Philips SBBE 9031	LET'S MAKE LOVE - FILM SOUNDTRACK (EP, with Yves Montand & Frankie Vaughan; stereo)	40
53	MGM MGM-D 116	GENTLEMEN PREFER BLONDES (10" LP, soundtrack with other artists)	100
59	London HA-T 2176	SOME LIKE IT HOT (LP, soundtrack with other artists, mono)	60
59	London SAH-T 6040	SOME LIKE IT HOT (LP, soundtrack with other artists, stereo)	80
60	Philips BBL 7414	LET'S MAKE LOVE (LP, soundtrack, with Yves Montand & Frankie Vaughan; mono)	40
60	Philips SBBL 592	LET'S MAKE LOVE (LP, soundtrack, with Yves Montand & Frankie Vaughan; stereo)	40
63	Stateside S(S)L 10048	MARILYN (LP, soundtrack, mono)	40
63	Stateside S(S)L 10048	MARILYN (LP, soundtrack, stereo)	50
83	Liberty UASP 30226	SOME LIKE IT HOT (LP, picture disc)	12

VAUGHN MONROE (& HIS ORCHESTRA)

53	HMV 7M 144	Less Than Tomorrow (But More Than Yesterday)/Ruby	10
54	HMV 7M 247	They Were Doin' The Mambo/Mister Sandman	10
56	HMV 7M 332	Black Denim Trousers And Motorcycle Boots/All By Myself	20
57	HMV POP 354	Wringle Wrangle/Westward Ho The Wagons!	7
59	RCA RCA 1124	The Battle Of New Orleans/Hercules	8
60	London HLT 9123	Ballerina/Love Me Forever	5

MINT VALUE £

MONROE BROTHERS
(see also Bill Monroe)

63	RCA RCX 7103	COUNTRY GUITAR VOL. 14 (EP)	10
63	RCA RCX 7104	COUNTRY GUITAR VOL. 15 (EP)	10
63	RCA RCX 7105	COUNTRY GUITAR VOL. 16 (EP, 2 tracks by Bill Monroe & Bluegrass Boys)	10

MONSOON

71	Trojan TR 7831	Hot Honolulu Night/Come Back Jane	6
72	Blue Mountain BM 1006	Night Of The Fly/Caroline The Wine Was Good	40

MONSOON
(see also Complex)

81	Indipop IND 1	Ever So Lonely/Sunset Over The Ganges/The Mirror Of Your Mind/ Shout! (Till You're Heard) (in plastic sleeve with insert)	8
83	Mobile Suit Dist. MOBIL 1	THIRD EYE (LP)	12

MONSTER MAGNET

98	A&M 582822-7	Powertrip (1-sided picture disc)	5
98	A&M 563 274-7	Space Lord/The Game (picture disc)	5

MONTAG

03	Ai AI 006	OBJETS PERDUS EP (12", p/s)	8

MONTANAS
(see also Trapeze)

65	Piccadilly 7N 35262	All That Is Mine Can Be Yours/How Can I Tell	12
66	Pye 7N 17183	That's When Happiness Began/Goodbye Little Girl	50
67	Pye 7N 17282	Ciao Baby/Anyone There	10
67	Pye 7N 17338	Take My Hand/Top Hat	10
67	Pye 7N 17394	You've Got To Be Loved/Difference Of Opinion	20
68	Pye 7N 17499	A Step In The Right Direction/Someday (You'll Be Breaking My Heart Again)	12
68	Pye 7N 17597	You're Making A Big Mistake/Run To Me	10
69	Pye 7N 17697	Roundabout/Mystery	15
69	Pye 7N 17729	Ciao Baby/Someday (You'll Be Breaking My Heart Again)	6
70	MCA MK 5036	Let's Get A Little Sentimental/Hey Diddle Diddle	8
71	MAM R45	No Smoke Without Fire/Seaport	15
71	MAM MAMR62	Suzanne/Your Love Is Growing	15

MONTANA SEXTET

83	Virgin VS 600	Who Needs Enemies With A Friend Like You/Friendly Vibes (12")	15
87	10 TENT 204	Heavy Vibes pts. 1 & 2 (12")	8

MONTCLAIRS

74	Contempo CS 2008	Make Up For Lost Time/How Can One Man Live	8
75	Contempo CS 2036	Hung Up On Your Love/I Need You More Than Ever	20
74	Contempo CLP 503	DREAMING OF A SEASON (LP)	15

LOU MONTE

54	HMV 7M 176	A Baby Cried/One Moment More	10
54	HMV 7M 190	Darktown Strutters' Ball/I Know How You Feel	10
54	HMV 7M 249	Chain Reaction/Vera's Veranda	10

VINNIE MONTE

59	London HL 8947	Summer Spree/I'll Walk You Home	10
59	London HL 8947	Summer Spree/I'll Walk You Home (78)	10
63	Stateside SS 156	Joanie Don't Be Angry/Take Good Care Of Her	18

MONTEGO JOE

72	London HLP 10374	Stand Up And Be Counted/Glooey (with Seeds Of Life)	5
66	Stateside SL 10159	JARRIBA! CON MONTEGO JOE (LP)	12

MONTEGO MELON

68	Sioux SI 004	Swan Lake/HONG GANG: Reggae Mento	5

HUGO MONTENEGRO ORCHESTRA

62	Oriole CB 1765	Palm Canyon Drive/Dark Eyes	7
63	Oriole CB 1792	Get Off The Moon/Sherry	20
68	RCA Victor RCA 1727	The Good, The Bad And The Ugly/Fistful Of Dollars	5
68	RCA Victor RCA 1771	Hang 'Em High/Tomorrow's Love	8
69	RCA RCA 1807	Tony's Theme/Good Vibrations	5
65	RCA Victor RD 7758	THE MAN FROM U.N.C.L.E. (LP, soundtrack)	50
66	RCA Victor RD 7832	MORE MUSIC FROM THE MAN FROM U.N.C.L.E. (LP, soundtrack)	45
67	RCA Victor RD/SF 7877	HURRY SUNDOWN (LP, soundtrack)	25
69	RCA SF 8053	MOOG POWER (LP)	20
69	Stateside S(S)L 10267	LADY IN CEMENT (LP, soundtrack)	40
70	Pye Intl. NSPL 28136	DAWN OF DYLAN (LP)	12

BOBBY MONTEZ

60	Vogue V 9165	Holiday In Havana/Jungle Stars	8

CHRIS MONTEZ

63	London HLU 9764	My Baby Loves To Dance/In An English Towne	7
66	Pye International 7N 25348	Call Me/Go 'Head On	8
66	Pye International 7N 25369	The More I See You/You, I Love You	6
66	Pye International 7N 25381	There Will Never Be Another You/You Can Hurt The One You Love	6
66	Pye International 7N 23599	Time After Time/Keep Talkin'	5
67	Pye International 7N 25415	Because Of You/Elena	5
73	CBS S CBS 1291	Come On, Let's Go/Somebody Loves You	5
79	Old Gold OG 9011	Let's Dance/LONNIE MACK: Memphis (picture disc)	5
63	London REU 1392	LET'S DANCE (EP)	50
66	Pye Intl. NEP 44071	THE MORE I SEE YOU (EP)	20
66	Pye Intl. NEP 44080	CHRIS MONTEZ (EP)	20
63	London HA-U 8079	LET'S DANCE AND HAVE SOME KINDA FUN!!! (LP)	50

			MINT VALUE £
66	Pye Intl. NPL 28080	THE MORE I SEE YOU (LP)	20
67	Pye Intl. N(S)PL 28087	TIME AFTER TIME (LP)	20
68	A&M AML 906	FOOLIN' AROUND (LP)	15

JACK MONTGOMERY

85	Kent TOWN 102	Dearly Beloved/MARIE KNIGHT: That's No Way To Treat A Girl	10
80s	Soul City 124	My Dear Beloved/Do You Believe It	10

LITTLE BROTHER MONTGOMERY

50	Jazz Collector L 44	No Special Rider Blues/Vicksburg Blues (78)	15
61	Columbia DB 4595	Pinetop's Boogie Woogie/Cow Cow Blues	25
61	Columbia 33SX 1289	LITTLE BROTHER MONTGOMERY (LP, with Alexis Korner)	70
62	77' 77LA 12/21	LITTLE BROTHER MONTGOMERY/SUNNYLAND SLIM (LP)	30
65	Decca LK 4664	LITTLE BROTHER MONTGOMERY (LP)	30
66	Xtra XTRA 1018	LITTLE BROTHER MONTGOMERY (LP)	20
71	Xtra XTRA 1115	FARRO ST. JIVE (LP)	20
71	Saydisc SDR 213	LITTLE BROTHER MONTGOMERY 1930-1969 (LP)	20
72	Saydisc SDM 223	HOME AGAIN (LP)	20

MARIAN MONTGOMERY

65	Capitol CL 15375	When Sunny Gets Blue/Teach Me Tonight	5
67	Reaction 591 018	Love Makes Two People Sing/Monday Thru Saturday	25
68	Pye 7N 17533	Why Say Goodbye/Love Today - Cry Tomorrow	5
72	Polydor 2383 159	MARIAN IN THE MORNING (LP)	15

ROY MONTGOMERY

97	Enraptured RAPT 4510	Trajectory One/Trajectory Two (p/s, 27 in handmade p/s)	15
97	Enraptured RAPT 4510	Trajectory One/Trajectory Two (p/s, 280 clear vinyl)	8

STUART MONTGOMERY

69	private pressing	CERTAIN SEA WORDS (LP, with insert)	15

WES MONTGOMERY

60	Fontana FJL 109	GO! (LP)	12
60	Riverside RLP 12-320	THE INCREDIBLE JAZZ GUITAR OF WES MONTGOMERY (LP, mono)	15
60	Riverside RLP 12-320	THE INCREDIBLE JAZZ GUITAR OF WES MONTGOMERY (LP, stereo)	20

MONTROSE

(see also Sammy Hagar)

74	Warner Brothers K 16382	Bad Motor Scooter/One Thing On My Mind	5
74	Warner Brothers K 16428	Rock The Nation/One Thing On My Mind	5

MONTY, DERRICK & PATSY

(see also Monty Morris, Derrick Morgan)

65	Blue Beat BB 280	Stir The Pot/Mercy	20

MONTY (Morris) & ROY

(see also Monty Morris)

61	Blue Beat BB 61	In And Out The Window/Tra La La Boogie (with Dumbago's Orchestra)	8
61	Blue Beat BB 63	Sweetie Pie/ROLAND ALPHONSO'S GROUP: Green Door	18

MONTY PYTHON('S FLYING CIRCUS)

(see also John Cleese, Rutles, Barry Booth)

72	Charisma CB 192	Spam Song/The Concert (as Monty Python's Flying Circus, p/s)	6
72	Charisma CB 200	Eric The Half A Bee/The Yangtse Song (Extended) (as Monty Python with Niel [sic] Innes)	5
72	Python Productions	Teach Yourself Heath (flexidisc free with Zig Zag magazine)	12
74	Charisma CB 268	Lumberjack Song/Spam Song (p/s)	5
74	NME/Charisma SFI 1259	Monty Python's Tiny Black Round Thing (D.P. Gumby Presents "Election '74"/ The Lumberjack Song) (live flexidisc free with NME)	10
75	Charisma MP PROMO 1	In Store Commercial (promo only, jukebox single)	5
79	Warner Bros K 17495	Always Look On The Bright Side Of Life/Brian (p/s)	15
80	Charisma CB 374	I Like Chinese/I Bet You They Won't Play This Song On The Radio/Finland (p/s)	15
83	CBS WA 3495	Galaxy Song/Every Sperm Is Sacred (goldfish bowl-shaped picture disc)	8
88	Warner Bros W 7653	Always Look On The Bright Side Of Life/Brian (p/s, reissue)	10
91	Virgin PYTH 2	Galaxy Song/Every Sperm Is Sacred (p/s, reissue)	5
76	Charisma MP 001	PYTHON ON SONG (EP, double pack [CBS 268/PY 2])	10
70	BBC REB 73M	MONTY PYTHON'S FLYING CIRCUS (LP, mono, pink label)	18
70	Charisma CAS 1049	ANOTHER MONTY PYTHON RECORD (LP, inner sleeve, 3 inserts, 'scroll' label)	20
73	Charisma CAS 1063	MONTY PYTHON'S PREVIOUS RECORD (LP, with free flexidisc in p/s, Teach Yourself Heath & inner sleeve)	15
73	Charisma CAS 1080	MATCHING TIE AND HANDKERCHIEF (LP, parallel grooves on side 2, die-cut sleeve, 2 inserts)	15
74	Charisma CLASS 4	LIVE AT THE THEATRE ROYAL DRURY LANE (LP)	12
77	Charisma CAS 1134	THE MONTY PYTHON INSTANT RECORD COLLECTION (LP, foldout sleeve)	12
79	Warner Bros K 56751	LIFE OF BRIAN (LP, soundtrack, with inner sleeve)	12

MONUMENT

(see also Zior)

71	Beacon BEAS 15	THE FIRST MONUMENT (LP)	60

MONUMENTUM

95	Misanthropy AMAZON 007	IN ABSENTIA CHRISTI (LP)	20

MOOCHE

69	Pye 7N 17735	Hot Smoke And Sasafrass/Seen Through A Light	25

AMEIL MOODIE

69	Blue Cat BS 143	Mello Reggae/Lifeline	20
69	Blue Cat BS 164	Ratchet Knife/Bend The Tree	20

MOOD MOSAIC

(see also Mark Wirtz Orchestra & Chorus, Keith West)

66	Columbia DB 7801	A Touch Of Velvet, A Sting Of Brass/Bond Street P.M.	35

			MINT VALUE £
66	Columbia DB 7801	A Touch Of Velvet, A Sting Of Brass/Bond Street P.M.(DJ Copy)	35
67	Columbia DB 8149	Chinese Chequers/The Real Mr. Smith	25
68	Parlophone R 5716	The Yellow Spotted Capricorn/ELMER HOCKETT'S HURDY GURDY: Fantastic Fair	12
69	Columbia DB 8618	A Touch Of Velvet, A Sting Of Brass/Bond Street P.M. (reissue)	15
67	Columbia SX 6153	MOOD MOSAIC (LP, mono)	35
67	Studio Two TWO 160	MOOD MOSAIC (LP, stereo)	25

MOOD OF HAMILTON

67	Columbia DB 8304	Why Can't There Be More Love?/King's Message	25

MOOD REACTION

70	Pama PSP 1007	LIVE AT THE CUMBERLAND (LP)	20
69	Gas 136	Too Much Loving/Roaring Twenties	8

MOOD SIX

82	EMI EMI 5300	Hanging Around/Mood Music (p/s)	5
82	EMI EMI 5336	She's Too Far/Venus (unreleased; white label copies exist with p/s)	30
85	Psycho PSYCHO 2001	Plastic Flowers/It's Your Life (p/s)	5
85	Psycho PSYCHO 4001	PLASTIC FLOWERS (12" EP)	10
85	Psycho PSYCHO 33	THE DIFFERENCE IS... (LP)	12

MOODS

63	Starlite ST45 098	Duckwalk/Easy Going	22

GEORGE MOODY

65	Fontana TF 631	Bring A Little Sunshine (To My Heart)/Santa The Swagman	6

JAMES MOODY

55	Esquire 20-071	MOODY HI FI (10" LP)	20

RON MOODY

61	Decca F 11371	You've Gotta Pick A Pocket Or Two/Reviewing The Situation	5
64	Parlophone R 5205	Rinkety Tink/Bringing Home My Darling	7

MOODY BLUES

(see also Justin Hayward, Denny Laine, Gerry Levene & Avengers, Ray Thomas)

64	Decca F 12022	Go Now!/It's Easy Child	6
65	Decca F 12095	I Don't Want To Go On Without You/Time Is On My Side	7
65	Decca F 12166	From The Bottom Of My Heart (I Love You)/And My Baby's Gone	7
65	Decca F 12266	Everyday/You Don't (All The Time)	10
66	Decca F 12498	Boulevard De La Madelaine/This Is My House (But Nobody Calls)	12
67	Decca F 12543	Life's Not Life/He Can't Win (withdrawn)	60
67	Decca F 12607	Fly Me High/Really Haven't Got The Time	25
67	Decca F 12670	Love And Beauty/Leave This Man Alone	18
67	Deram DM 161	Nights In White Satin/Cities (1st issue, darker labels than later copies)	5
68	Deram DM 196	Voices In The Sky/Doctor Livingstone, I Presume	7
68	Deram DM 213	Ride My See-Saw/A Simple Game	8
69	Deram DM 247	Never Comes The Day/So Deep Within You	7
69	Threshold TH 1	Watching And Waiting/Out And In	8
81	Threshold THPD 29	Talking Out Of Turn/Veteran Cosmic Rocker (picture disc)	7
83	Threshold TH 30	Blue World/Going Nowhere (p/s, with free T-shirt)	6
65	Decca DFE 8622	THE MOODY BLUES (EP, original label)	30
65	Decca DFE 8622	THE MOODY BLUES (EP, reissue with boxed Decca logo)	10
65	Decca LK 4711	THE MAGNIFICENT MOODIES (LP, unboxed red/silver Decca label logo)	50
65	Decca LK 4711	THE MAGNIFICENT MOODIES (LP, boxed red/silver Decca label logo)	20
67	Deram DML 707	DAYS OF FUTURE PASSED (LP, originally with white band on sleeve & 'DSS' labels, mono)	30
67	Deram SML 707	DAYS OF FUTURE PASSED (LP, originally with white band on sleeve & 'DSS' labels, stereo)	15
68	Deram DML 711	IN SEARCH OF THE LOST CHORD (LP, gatefold sleeve, mono, 'DSS' label)	30
68	Deram SML 711	IN SEARCH OF THE LOST CHORD (LP, gatefold sleeve, stereo, 'DSS' label)	12
69	Deram DML 1035	ON THE THRESHOLD OF A DREAM (LP, gatefold sleeve with stapled booklet, mono. Label is white/brown with large logo)	30
69	Deram SML 1035	ON THE THRESHOLD OF A DREAM (LP, gatefold sleeve with stapled booklet, stereo)	20
69	Threshold THM 1	TO OUR CHILDREN'S CHILDREN'S CHILDREN (LP, gatefold, with insert, white/pink label, mono)	40
69	Threshold THS 1	TO OUR CHILDREN'S CHILDREN'S CHILDREN (LP, gatefold, with insert, white/lilac label, stereo)	20
70	Threshold THS 3	A QUESTION OF BALANCE ('flap' gatefold sleeve with lyric sheet)	15
71	Threshold THS 5	EVERY GOOD BOY DESERVES A FAVOUR (LP, gatefold, lyric insert, white/blue label)	18
72	Threshold THS 7	SEVENTH SOJOURN (LP, gatefold sleeve, lyric insert, white/blue label)	18

MOOG MACHINE

69	CBS 63807	SWITCHED ON ROCK (LP)	20

(THE) MOOG

92	Delirious DELIS 2	Rush Hour/Jungle Muffin/Live Forever/Hopelessly Volatile/Subtone (12")	30
92	Delirious DELIS 4	THE MOOG REMIX EP: Jungle Muffin (Micky Finn Remix)/Rush Hour (Rotor Remix)/LiveForever (Mercy Remix)/Going Crazy (Justice Remix) (12")	12

MOON

(see also Beach Boys)

68	Liberty LBF 15076	Someday Girl/Mothers And Fathers	25
70	Liberty LBF 15333	Pirate/Not To Know	10
68	Liberty LBL/LBS 83146	WITHOUT EARTH (LP)	45

KEITH MOON

75	Polydor 2058 584	Don't Worry Baby/Together	20
75	Polydor 2442 134	TWO SIDES OF THE MOON (LP)	30

MINT VALUE £

LARRY MOON

63	Ember EMB 171	Tia Juana Ball/Bouquet Of Roses	20

PERRY MOON

63	Sway SW 002	Nine Five Baby/PLANTES: Water Front	10

TERRY MOON

63	Planetone RC 11	Moon Man/MIKE ELLIOT: This Love Of Mine	10

MOON BOYS

(see also Hippy Boys)

69	Amalgamated AMG 846	Apollo 11/PIONEERS: Love Love Everyday	15

MOONCHILD

75	Look LKSP 5010	Hourglass/War Orphan (Brother Of The Day)	20

MOONDANCE

70	A&M AMS 792	Lazy River/Anna St Claire	5

MOONDOG

54	London REP 1010	ON THE STREETS OF NEW YORK (EP)	30
59	Esquire 32-055	MOONDOG (LP)	65
69	CBS 63906	MOONDOG (LP, gatefold sleeve)	60

MOONDOGS

78	Lyntone LT 002	Heads I Win/Two's A Crowd (p/s)	5
79	Good Vibrations GOT 10	She's Nineteen/Ya Don't Do Ya (foldout p/s)	15

MOONDOGS

80	Real ARE 13	Who's Gonna Tell Mary/Overcaring Parents (p/s)	10
81	Real ARE 14	Talking In The Canteen/Make Her Love Me (p/s, with neckerchief)	35
81	Real ARE 14	Talking In The Canteen/Make Her Love Me (p/s)	10
81	Real ARE 16	Imposter/Baby Snatcher (p/s)	15

ART MOONEY (& HIS ORCHESTRA)

(see also Ocie Smith, Shorty Long, Cloverleafs, Cathy Ryan)

53	MGM SP 1037	I Played The Fool/I Just Couldn't Take It, Baby (with Cathy Ryan)	10
53	MGM SP 1045	Baby Don't Do It/Believe In Me (with Cathy Ryan)	10
54	MGM SP 1088	Oh Boy What Joy We Had/Silhouette D'Amour	8
55	MGM SP 1134	No Regrets/Honey Babe	8
55	MGM SP 1145	Give Me A Band And My Baby/The Girl I Left Behind Me	8
56	MGM SP 1166	Memories Of You/I'm Looking Over	8
56	MGM MGM 899	Tutti Frutti/OCIE SMITH & CLOVERLEAFS: Our Melody (78)	15
57	MGM MGM 923	Rebel Without A Cause Theme/"East Of Eden" Theme	15
57	MGM MGM 943	Giant/There's Never Been Anyone Else But You	15
57	MGM MGM 951	Rock And Roll Tumbleweed/Is There A Teenager In The House (with Ocie Smith)	22
57	MGM MGM 951	Rock And Roll Tumbleweed/Is There A Teenager In The House (with Ocie Smith) (78)	15

MOONGLOWS

(see also Harvey & Moonglows, Etta & Harvey)

57	London HLN 8374	I Knew From The Start/Over And Over Again	700
57	London HLN 8374	I Knew From The Start/Over And Over Again (78)	70

MOONKYTE

71	Mother SMOT 1	COUNT ME OUT (LP, with insert, cover has a die-cut spire)	300

MOONLIGHTERS

63	Island WI 043	Going Out/Hold My Hands	20

MOONLIGHTERS

65	Columbia DB 7602	Come On Home/It's Too Late	10
66	Columbia DB 7910	We'll See It Through/Too Late To Come Home	10

MOONQUAKE

73	London HL 10446	Remember/This Winter	8

MOON ROCKS & PRINCE JAZZBO

78	Bushay's BFM 101	Unite Jah People/Have No Fear (12")	40

MOONSHINE

70	KJ Roberts ZDR56312	Susannah/Garden Of Men	60

MICKY MOONSHINE

74	Decca F 13555	Baby Blue/Name It You Got It	20
74	Decca F 13555	Baby Blue/Name It You Got It (DJ copy)	40

MOONSHINERS

65	Stateside SL 10137	THE MOONSHINERS BREAKOUT! (LP)	18
67	Page One POLS 004	HOLD UP (LP)	22

MOONSTONES

65	Parlophone R 5331	Heaven Fell Last Night/Little Roses	6
66	Parlophone R 5497	Violets Of Dawn/Power Of Decision	6
67	Mercury MF 1011	How Many Times/Louisville	6

MOON'S TRAIN

(see also Peter Frampton, Denny Mitchell, Preachers)

67	MGM MGM 1333	Deed I Do/It's In My Mind	35

MOONTREKKERS

61	Parlophone R 4814	Night Of The Vampire/Melodie D'Amour	25
62	Parlophone R 4888	There's Something At The Bottom Of The Well/Hatashiai	30
63	Decca F 11714	Moondust/The Bogey Man	20

MICHAEL MOORCOCK('S DEEP FIX)

(see also Hawkwind)

80	Flicknife FLS 200	Dodgem Dude/Star Cruiser (p/s)	5

			MINT VALUE £
82	Flicknife EJS P9831	Brothel In Rosenstrasse/Time Centre (numbered, 500 only, with autographed lyric sheet)	30
92	Cyborg (no cat. no.)	The Brothel In Rosenstrasse (cassette only)	20
75	United Artists UAG 29732	NEW WORLD'S FAIR (LP, with inner sleeve)	40

ALEXANDER MOORE

(see also Whistling Alexander Moore)

60	77 77LA 12-7	WHISTLING ALEX MOORE (LP)	20

ALICE MOORE

50s	Poydras MC 66	Prison Blues/My Man Blues	22

ANTHONY MOORE

76	Virgin VS 144	Catch A Falling Star/Back To The Top	5
71	Polydor 2310 062	PIECES FROM THE CLOUDLAND BALLROOM (LP)	60
72	Polydor 2310 079	SECRETS OF THE BLUE BAG (LP)	40
79	Quango HMS 98	FLYING DOESN'T HELP (LP)	12
81	Do It RIDE 7	WORLD SERVICE (LP, with inner)	12

BARBARA MOORE

67	CBS (S) BPG 62839	A LITTLE MOORE BARBARA (LP)	50

BOB MOORE & ORCHESTRA

61	London HLU 9409	Mexico/Hot Spot	5
62	London HLU 9538	Ooh La La/Aufwiedersehn Marlene	5
63	London HLU 9736	Kentucky/Flowers Of Florence	5

BOBBY MOORE (& RHYTHM ACES)

66	Chess CRS 8033	Searching For My Love/Hey Mr D.J.	25
75	Pye International 7N 25691	Call Me Your Anything Man/Call Me Your Anything Man (Disco Version) (solo)	6
66	Chess CRL 4521	SEARCHIN' FOR MY LOVE (LP)	75

BUTCH MOORE

64	Piccadilly 7N 35170	Foolin Time/Too Soon To Know	10
64	Piccadilly 7N 35182	I Misssed You/Touch Me	12
65	Pye 7N 15832	Walking The Streets In The Rain/I Stand Still	8
65	Pye 7N 15910	Our Love Will Go On/Words	8

CHRISTY MOORE

69	Mercury 20170 SMCL	PADDY ON THE ROAD (LP)	400
75	Polydor 2383 344	WHATEVER TICKLES YOUR FANCY (LP)	25
76	Polydor 2383 426	CHRISTY MOORE (LP)	25
70s	WEA WX 286	VOYAGE (LP)	15

CURLEY MOORE & THE COOL ONES

71	Pye 7N 25570	Shelly's Rubber Band/Funky Years	30

DOROTHY MOORE

75	Contempo CS 2087	Misty Blue/Here It Is	7
76	Contempo CS 2292	Funny How Time Slips Away/It's So Good	7

DUDLEY MOORE (TRIO)

(see also Peter Cook & Dudley Moore)

61	Parlophone R 4772	Strictly For The Birds (solo)/Duddly Dell (B-side as Dudley Moore Trio)	10
68	Decca F 12850	30 Is A Dangerous Age, Cynthia/The Real Stuff (solo)	10
69	Decca F 12882	Keep It Up/Gently (as Dudley Moore Trio)	10
65	Decca LK 4732	THE OTHER SIDE OF DUDLEY MOORE (LP)	12
66	Decca LK 4788	GENUINE DUD (LP, as Dudley Moore Trio)	20
68	Decca SKL 4923	BEDAZZLED (LP, stereo, soundtrack)	90
69	Decca LK/SKL 4976	THE DUDLEY MOORE TRIO (LP)	30
72	Atlantic K 40397	TODAY (LP)	12

G T MOORE

74	B&C CB 236	I'm Still Waiting/Judgement Day	8

GARY MOORE

(see also Granny's Intentions, Dr. Strangely Strange, Skid Row, Thin Lizzy, Gary Moore & Phil Lynott, Greg Lake, Eddie Howell, G-Force, Cozy Powell)

78	MCA MCA 386	Back On The Streets/Track Nine (in p/s)	30
78	MCA MCA 386	Back On The Streets/Track Nine	5
79	MCA MCA 419	Parisienne Walkways/Fanatical Fascists (p/s)	12
79	MCA MCA 534	Spanish Guitar/Spanish Guitar (instrumental) (p/s)	12
81	Jet JET 12016	Nuclear Attack/Don't Let Me Be Misunderstood/Run To Your Mama (12", company sleeve, as Gary Moore & Friends)	10
82	Virgin VS 528	Always Gonna Love You/Cold Hearted (p/s)	7
82	Virgin VSY 528	Always Gonna Love You/Cold Hearted (picture disc)	8
83	Virgin VSY 564	Falling In Love With You/Falling In Love With You (Instrumental) (picture disc)	12
83	Virgin VS 564	Falling In Love With You/(Instrumental) (p/s, with comic)	10
83	Virgin VS 56412	Falling In Love With You/(Instrumental) (12", p/s)	15
84	10 TEN 13	Hold On To Love/Devil In Her Heart (poster p/s)	7
84	10 TENS 13	Hold On To Love/Devil In Her Heart (plectrum-shaped picture disc)	18
84	10 TEN 1312	Hold On To Love/Devil In Her Heart/Law Of The Jungle (12", p/s)	10
84	10 TEN 19	Shapes Of Things/Blinder (p/s, with patch)	12
84	10 TENS 19	Shapes Of Things/Blinder (explosion-shaped picture disc)	15
84	10 TEN 1912	Shapes Of Things/Blinder/(Interview) (12", p/s)	8
84	10 TEN 25	Empty Rooms/Nuclear Attack (live) (in poster p/s)	8
84	10 TEN 25-12	Empty Rooms (Ext. Mix)/Empty Rooms//Nuclear Attack (live)/ Empty Rooms (live)/Rockin' Every Night (live) (12", double pack, gatefold p/s with poster)	8
85	10 TEN 58	Empty Rooms (Summer 85 Version)/Out Of My System (p/s)	5
86	10 TENS 134	Over The Hills And Far Away/Crying In The Shadows (guitar-shaped pic disc)	15
86	10 TENG 134	Over The Hills And Far Away (Extended Mix)/Over The Hills And Far Away/ The Loner/Johnny Boy/The Loner (Extended Version)/The Loner (Live at Hammersmith Odeon) (12", p/s)	10

MINT VALUE £

87	10 TENT 178	The Loner/Johnny Boy/The Loner (Extended Version)/The Loner (Live At Hammersmith Odeon (12", p/s)	10
88	Virgin GMSY 1	After The War/This Thing Called Love (picture disc, stickered PVC sleeve)	8
73	CBS 65527	GRINDING STONE (LP, as Gary Moore Band)	20
78	MCA MCF 2853	BACK ON THE STREETS (LP, with inner sleeve)	12
81	Jet JETLP 245	LIVE AT THE MARQUEE (LP, withdrawn test pressing, white sleeve with Jet Info sticker)	100
82	Virgin V 2245	CORRIDORS OF POWER (LP, with free live EP [VDJ 34])	15
84	EMI OVED 206	VICTIMS OF THE FUTURE (LP, with inner & poster)	20
84	Jet JETLP 241	DIRTY FINGERS (LP)	12
86	10 DIXP 16	RUN FOR COVER (LP, picture disc, die-cut sleeve)	30
87	10 DIXG 56	WILD FRONTIER (2-LP, gatefold sleeve)	18

GARY MOORE & PHIL LYNOTT

85	10 TENS 49	Out In The Fields/Military Man (2 1-sided interlocking shaped picture-disc set, stickered gatefold PVC sleeve)	25
85	10 TEND 49	Out In The Fields/Military Man//Still In Love With You/Stop Messin' Around (live) (double pack)	7
85	10 TEN 49-12	Out In The Fields/Military Man/Still In Love With You (12", gatefold p/s, with poster)	10
85	10 TENC 49-12	Military Man (12", 1-sided, B-side etched with signatures, promo only)	12

JACKIE MOORE

71	Jay Boy BOY 35	Dear John/Here Am I	6
71	Atlantic 2091 054	Precious Precious/Will Power	6
71	Atlantic 2091 095	Sometimes It's Got To Rain (In Your Love Life)/Wonderful, Marvellous (with Dixie Flyers)	6
74	Atlantic K 10481	Both Ends Against The Middle/Willpower	8
74	Atlantic K40544	SWEET CHARLIE BABE (LP)	18
79	CBS CBS 12-7722	This Time Baby/Let's Go Somewhere And Make Love (12")	10

JACQUELINE MOORE

65	Decca F 12165	Queen Of The House/What's Going On Here	7

JOHNNY MOORE

(see also Cannonball & Johnny Melody, Alton Ellis)

67	Caltone TONE 101	Sound And Soul/ROY SHIRLEY: Get On The Ball	40
69	Doctor Bird DB 1180	Big Big Boss/CARL CANNONBALL BRYON: Reggae This Reggae	40

MATTHEW MOORE

66	Capitol CL 15467	A Face In The Crowd/St. James Infirmary	6

MERRILL E. MOORE

54	Capitol CL 14057	Bell Bottom Boogie/The House Of Blue Lights (78)	15
54	Capitol CL 14130	Nola/Fly Right Boogie (78)	15
55	Capitol CL 14369	Five Foot Two, Eyes Of Blue/Hard Top Race (as Merrill Moore)	220
55	Capitol CL 14369	Five Foot Two, Eyes Of Blue/Hard Top Race (as Merrill Moore) (78)	220
56	Capitol F 3397	King Porter Stomp/Rock Island Line (export only)	150
68	Ember EMB S 253	Down The Road A-Piece/Buttermilk Baby	15
69	B&C CB 100	Sweet Mama Tree Top Tall/Little Green Apples	8
70	Bulldog BD 20	House Of Blue Lights/Red Light	8
67	Ember EMB 3392	BELLYFUL OF BLUE-THUNDER (LP)	40
68	Ember EMB 3394	ROUGH-HOUSE 88 (LP; repressed 1973)	20
69	B&C CAS 1001	TREE TOP TALL (LP)	20

NICKY MOORE BAND

(see also Tiger, Samson, Hackensack, Mammoth)

81	Street Tunes STS 006	Year Of The Lie	10
81	Street Tunes	7 YEARS OF THE LIE (LP)	12

OSCAR MOORE TRIO

55	London H-APB 1035	KENYA (10" LP)	15

PETE MOORE'S SOLID ROCKIN' BRASS

74	Gold Star 1500 009	PETE MOORE'S SOLID ROCKIN' BRASS (LP)	15

ROGER MOORE

65	CBS 202014	Where Does Love Go/Tomorrow After Tomorrow (in p/s)	20
65	CBS 202014	Where Does Love Go/Tomorrow After Tomorrow	10

SCOTTY MOORE

(see also Elvis Presley)

64	Columbia 33SX 1680	THE GUITAR THAT CHANGED THE WORLD! (LP)	70

SHELLEY MOORE (& MOORE SESSIONEERS)

55	Columbia SCM 5197	In The Wee Small Hours Of The Morning/When You Lose The One You Love (solo)	5
58	Starlite ST45 002	You've Tied Me Up/Gone On The Guy	7
58	Starlite ST45 003	Where Is The Bluebird?/Everything Is Gonna Be All Right	7
57	Starlite ST EP 1	PORTRAIT OF SHELLEY (EP)	8
58	Starlite ST EP 7	KOOOL KANARY (EP)	8

THURSTON MOORE & DON FLEMING

97	Via Satellite V.SAT 6	Telstar/E.A.R.: Sputnik	20

TIM MOORE

75	Mooncrest Moon 41	A Fool Like You/Aviation Man	12

ALAN MOORHOUSE ORCHESTRA

66	Pye 7N 17073	(The Ballad Of) The Green Berets/London Bridge	6
68	Page One POF 104	Stop Press/Chloe	7
70	Columbia DB 8674	Haunting Me/Soul Bossa	6

MOOSE

70	Escort ERT 840	Engine No. 9/KURASS: Do It	7

MINT VALUE £

BIG MOOSE (Walker)
68 Python PKM 1 — Puppy Howl Blues/Rambling Woman (pressed with reversed labels) — 35

MOPEDS
(see also Cindy Starr & Mopeds)
68 Col. Blue Beat DB 108 — Whiskey And Soda/Do It — 5

MOQUETTES
64 Columbia DB 7315 — Right String, But The Wrong Yo-Yo/You Came Along — 50

SANTOS MORADOS
68 Island WIP 6034 — Tonopah/Anytime — 6

NONO MORALES & HIS ORCHESTRA
54 HMV 7MC 5 — Istanbul (Not Constantinople)/Am I Blue (export single) — 6

MIKE MORAN
70s Alba TAR 053 — PENNY WHISTLES OF ROBERT LOUIS STEVENSON (LP) — 20

MIKE MORAN BAND
76 Power Exchange PXL 002 — AUTUMN LEAVES (LP) — 20

MOYA MORAY
62 Piccadilly 7N 35023 — My Heart Will Make A Fool Of Me/You're Running Out Of Kisses — 12

MORBID ANGEL
94 Earache MOSH 112 — LAIBACH REMIXES EP (God Of Emptiness/Sworn To The Black/Sworn To The Black [Laibach Remix]/God Of Emptiness [Laibach Remix]) (12", p/s) — 15
89 Earache MOSH 11 — ALTARS OF MADNESS (LP, pink splattered vinyl, stickered sleeve) — 25
89 Earache MOSH 11P — ALTARS OF MADNESS (LP, picture disc) — 30
91 Earache MOSH 31 — BLESSED ARE THE SICK (LP) — 18
91 Earache MOSH 31 — BLESSED ARE THE SICK (LP on 6 x 7" in box with 4 page insert) — 40
91 Earache MOSH 48 — ABOMINATIONS OF DESOLATION (LP) — 18
95 Earache MOSH 134 LP — DOMINATION (LP) — 20

MORE
80 Atlantic K 11561 — We Are The Band/Atomic Rock (with p/s) — 6
80 Atlantic K 11561T — We Are The Band/Atomic Rock (12", p/s, with patch) — 8
82 Atlantic K 11744 — Trickster/Hey Joe (p/s) — 15
81 Atlantic K 50775 — WARHEAD (LP) — 12
81 Atlantic K 50875 — BLOOD & THUNDER (LP) — 12

A. MORE
(see also Anthony Moore)
80 Quango HMGS 10 — Judy/Lucia (p/s) — 5

MANDY MORE
72 Philips 6308109 — BUT THAT IS ME (LP) — 250

MORECAMBE & WISE
61 HMV POP 957 — We're The Guys/Me And My Shadow — 5
63 HMV POP 1240 — Boom Oo Yatta Ta Ta/Why Did I Let You Go — 5
64 HMV POP 1373 — A-Wassailing/The Happiest Christmas Of All — 5
66 HMV POP 1518 — Now That You're Here/That Riviera Touch — 5
69 Columbia DB 8646 — Bring Me Sunshine/Just Around The Corner — 5

JOE MORELLO
62 RCA LSP 2486 — IT'S ABOUT TIME (LP, also stereo [SF 7502]) — 12

MORGAN
(see also Mott The Hoople, Love Affair, Humpy Bong)
73 RCA SF 8321 — NOVA SOLIS (LP, with insert) — 40
78 Cherry Red ARED 1 — THE SLEEPER WAKES (LP) — 12

AL MORGAN
58 London HLU 8741 — Jealous Heart/Foolish Tears — 12
50s London BEP 6043 — AL MORGAN (EP, export issue) — 8
51 London H-APB 1001 — JEALOUS HEART (10" LP) — 12
51 London H-APB 1003 — LITTLE RED BOOK (10" LP) — 12

MORGAN AND THE MARK 7
66 Polydor BM 56083 — I'm Gonna Turn My Life Around/Undercover Man — 35

DAVID/DAVY MORGAN
(see also Wishful Thinking)
65 Columbia DB 7624 — Tomorrow I'll Be Gone/Ain't Got Much More To See (as Davy Morgan) — 45
68 Parlophone R 5692 — True To Life/Dawning (as David Morgan) — 25

DERRICK MORGAN
(see also Roland Alphonso; Frank Cosmo; Copy Cats, Derrick & Lloyd; Derrick, Morris & Patsy; Derrick & Patsy; Derrick & Naomi;Derrick & Paulette; Derrick & Pauline; Morgan's All Stars; Martin & Derrick; Larry Lawrence; Matador, Jackie Robinson)
60 Blue Beat BB 7 — Fat Man/I'm Gonna Leave You — 35
60 Blue Beat BB 12 — Don't Cry/I Pray For You (as Derrick Morgan & Ebonies) — 30
60 Blue Beat BB 18 — Lover Boy/Oh My! — 30
61 Blue Beat BB 31 — Now We Know/Nights Are Lonely (with Trenton Spence Orchestra) — 30
61 Blue Beat BB 35 — Leave Earth/Wigger Wee Shuffle (with Clue J. & His Blues Busters) — 30
61 Blue Beat BB 62 — Shake A Leg/Golden Rule (as Derrick & Drumbago All Stars) — 30
62 Blue Beat BB 76 — Sunday, Monday/Be Still — 30
62 Blue Beat BB 82 — Don't You Know Little Girl (actually by Derrick & Basil)/ B. GABBIDON: Hully Gully Miss Molly — 30
62 Blue Beat BB 85 — Come On Over/Come Back My Darling (with Buster's Group) — 30
62 Blue Beat BB 91 — Headache/OWEN GRAY: Millie Girl — 25
62 Blue Beat BB 94 — Meekly Wait/Day In And Day Out (both sides with Yvonne [Sterling]) — 20
62 Blue Beat BB 100 — In My Heart/BELL'S GROUP: Kingston 13 — 30
62 Blue Beat BB 110 — Are You Going To Marry Me?/Troubles (as Derrick Morgan & Patsy) — 20

			MINT VALUE £
62	Blue Beat BB 130	Should Be Ashamed/Marjorie (with Buster's Group)	20
62	Blue Beat BB 141	Joybells (with Duke Reid Group)/Going Down To Canaan (with Denzil Dennis)	20
62	Island WI 004	Travel On/Teach Me Baby	35
62	Island WI 006	The Hop/Tell It To Me	35
62	Island WI 011	Forward March/Please Don't Talk About Me (B-side actually with Eric Morris)	35
62	Island WI 013	Cherry Home/See And Blind	35
63	Blue Beat BB 148	Jezebell/Burnette	25
63	Blue Beat BB 177	Patricia My Dear/The Girl I Left Behind	25
63	Blue Beat BB 187	Tears On My Pillow/You Should Have Known	25
63	Blue Beat BB 196	Telephone/Life Is Tough (B-side actually "Tough Man Tough")	25
63	Island WI 037	Dorothy/Leave Her Alone	25
63	Island WI 051	Blazing Fire/DERRICK & PATSY: I'm In A Jam	20
63	Island WI 053	No Raise, No Praise/Loving Baby	25
63	Island WI 080	Angel With Blue Eyes/Corner Stone	25
63	Rio R 1	Blazing Fire/Edmarine	15
64	Black Swan WI 402	Street Girl/Edmarine	15
64	Black Swan WI 425	Cherry Pie (actually by Frederick Hibbert)/BOB WALLS: Beware	20
64	Blue Beat BB 233	Let Them Talk/Sleeping	20
64	Blue Beat BB 239	Miss Lulu/DERRICK & PALOY: She's So Young (B-side act. by Derrick & Patsy)	20
64	Blue Beat BB 261	The Soldier Man/BUSTER'S ALL STARS: Jet 707	100
64	Blue Beat BB 268	Katy Katy/Call On Me	18
65	Blue Beat BB 276	Weep No More/I Want A Girl	18
65	Blue Beat BB 283	Johnny Grave/BUSTER'S ALL STARS: Yeah Yeah	30
65	Blue Beat BB 311	Throw Them Away/Baby Face	25
65	Blue Beat BB 329	Sweeter Than Honey/You Never Know (with Prince Buster)	25
65	Ska Beat JB 185	Heart Of Stone/Let Me Go (with Baba Brooks Group)	25
65	Ska Beat JB 218	Don't Call Me Daddy/BABA BROOK'S BAND: Girl's Town Ska	30
65	Island WI 193	Two Of A Kind/I Want A Lover (both actually with Naomi)	30
65	Island WI 225	Starvation/I Am A Blackhead Again	30
66	Island WI 277	It's Alright/I Need Someone (both sides actually with Blenders)	25
66	Island WI 289	Ameletia (actually by Frank Cosmo)/Don't You Worry (B-side with Patsy Todd)	20
66	Island WI 3010	Gather Together Now (Jamaican Independence Song)/Soft Hand (actually "So Hard") (both sides actually with Blenders)	30
66	Rio R 122	Cool Off Rudies/Take It Easy	25
67	Island WI 3079	Someone (actually Derrick & Pauline Morgan)/ Do You Love Me (with Pauline)	18
67	Pyramid PYR 6010	Tougher Than Tough/ROLAND ALPHONSO: Song For My Father	30
67	Pyramid PYR 6013	Greedy Gal/SOUL BROTHERS: Marcus Junior	35
67	Pyramid PYR 6014	Court Dismiss/FREDERICK McCLEAN: Fine Fine Fine	25
67	Pyramid PYR 6019	Judge Dread In Court/Last Chance	30
67	Pyramid PYR 6021	Kill Me Dead/Don't Be A Fool	20
67	Pyramid PYR 6024	No Dice/I Mean It	20
67	Pyramid PYR 6025	Do The Bang Bang/Revenge	15
68	Island WI 3094	Conquering Ruler/LLOYD & DEVON: Red Rum Ball	100
68	Island WI 3101	Gimme Back/VICEROYS: Send Requests	45
68	Island WI 3159	Hold You Jack/One Morning In May	40
68	Pyramid PYR 6029	I Am The Ruler/I Mean It	25
68	Pyramid PYR 6039	Woman A Grumble/Don't Be A Fool	25
68	Pyramid PYR 6040	Want More/ROLAND ALPHONSO: Goodnight My Love	25
68	Pyramid PYR 6045	Try Me/I'm Leaving (B-side with Pauline)	25
68	Pyramid PYR 6046	King For Tonight (with Pauline)/Last Chance	25
68	Pyramid PYR 6053	Me Naw Give Up/BEVERLEY'S ALLSTARS: Dreadnaught	30
68	Pyramid PYR 6056	Ben Johnson Day/MAYTALS: Ain't Got No Tip	30
68	Pyramid PYR 6061	What's Your Grouse/BEVERLEY'S ALLSTARS: I Don't Know	25
68	Pyramid PYR 6063	Johnny Pram Pram/Don't Say (B-side with Pauline Morgan	40
68	Amalgamated AMG 824	I Want To Go Home/JACKIE ROBINSON: Let The Little Girl Dance	20
68	Crab CRAB 3	River To The Bank/PETER KING: Reggae Limbo	6
68	Trojan TR 626	Fat Man/VAL BENNETT: South Parkway Rock	15
68	Nu Beat NB 016	I Love You/JUNIOR SMITH: Searching	25
68	Big Shot BI 506	Shower Of Rain/VAL BENNETT: It Might As Well Be Spring	12
69	Crab CRAB 8	Seven Letters/TARTANS: Lonely Heartaches (B-side act. by Clarendonians)	15
69	Crab CRAB 11	My First Taste Of Love/TARTANS: Dance All Night	12
69	Crab CRAB 18	Don't Play That Song/How Can I Forget You?	12
69	Crab CRAB 23	Send Me Some Loving/Come What May	12
69	Crab CRAB 22	Mek It Tan Deah/Gimme Back	12
69	Crab CRAB 28	Hard Time/ROY RICHARDS: Death Rides A Horse	30
69	Crab CRAB 30	Man Pon Spot/What A Thing	25
69	Crab CRAB 32	Moon Hop/Harris Wheel	5
69	Jackpot JP 700	Seven Letters/Too Bad	5
69	Unity UN 507	Belly Woman/PAULETT & LOVERS: Please Stay	5
69	Unity UN 540	Derrick - Top The Pop/GLEN ADAMS: Capone's Revenge	20
70	Unity UN 546	Return Of Jack Slade/Fat Man	10
70	Unity UN 569	The Conquering Ruler/Bedweight	40
70	Crab CRAB 44	A Night At The Hop/Telephone	30
70	Crab CRAB 51	I Wish I Was An Apple/The Story	5
70	Crab CRAB 52	Take A Letter Maria/OWEN GRAY: Just A Little Loving	5
70	Crab CRAB 57	My Dickie/Brixton Hop	5
70	Crab CRAB 58	I Can't Stand It No Longer/Beyond The Wall	5
70	Crab CRAB 59	Endlessly/Who's Making Love	5
70	Crab CRAB 62	Hurt/Julia	5
70	Pama PM 822	Love Bug/My Dickie	5
71	Bullet BU 467	Nobody's Business/Standing By	5
71	Camel CA 84	I Am Just A Sufferer/We Want To Know	5
71	Crab CRAB 67	Searching So Long/MORGAN'S ALL STARS: Drums Of Passion	5
72	Grape GR 3032	Send A Little Rain/DERRICK MORGAN ALL STARS: A Little Rain (Version)	5

			MINT VALUE £
72	Jackpot JP 793	Let Them Talk/Bringing In the Guns	5
72	Jackpot JP 794	Won't Be This Way/Ain't No Love	5
72	Jackpot JP 797	Me Naw Run/All Night Long	5
72	Jackpot JP 802	Festival 10/Festival 10 - Version	5
72	Punch PH 107	Forward March/Plenty Of One	5
72	Buster PB 60	Tears On My Pillow/KEITH REID: Worried Over You (actually by Keith & Enid)	5
73	Attack ATT 8048	Derrick's Big Eleven/My Ding A Ling	5
73	Big Shot BI 617	Housewives Choice/Don't You Worry (both sides with Hortense Ellis)	5
73	Bread BR 1119	I Who Have Nothing/I'm Not Home	5
73	Downtown DT 520	Hey Little Girl/Don't Blame The Man	5
73	Pama Supreme PS 387	I'll Never Give Up/I Who Have Nothing	5
75	Klik KL 603	Wet Dreams Part 1/Wet Dreams Part 2	5
63	Island ILP 903	FORWARD MARCH (LP)	300
69	Doctor Bird DLMB 5014	BEST OF DERRICK MORGAN (LP)	100
69	Island ILP 990	DERRICK MORGAN AND HIS FRIENDS (LP)	150
69	Pama ECO 10	DERRICK MORGAN IN LONDON (LP)	70
69	Pama PSP 1006	MOON HOP (LP)	70
69	Trojan TTL 5	SEVEN LETTERS (LP)	30
70	Trojan TTL 38	FORWARD MARCH (LP, reissue)	20
70s	Magnet MGT 004	IN THE MOOD (LP)	12

FREDDY MORGAN

59	London HL 7077	Side Saddle/64 Rue Blondell (export issue)	12

GEORGE MORGAN

68	London HLB 10197	Barbara/Sad Bird	5
57	Philips BBE 12149	COUNTRY AND WESTERN SPECTACULAR (EP)	20
68	London HAB 8353	COUNTRY HITS BY CANDLELIGHT (LP)	22

MORGAN JAMES DUO

64	Philips BF 1462	Sweet Pussycat/Bye Bye Brown Eyes	7
68	Philips BF 1707	Let's Ride/After The Storm	25
66	Fontana SFL 13071	AT THE BAR OF MUSIC (LP)	50
66	Philips BL 7702	SHHHH...TALENT STRIKES AGAIN (LP)	30

JANE MORGAN (& TROUBADORS)

(see also Troubadors, Roger Williams)

55	London HL 8148	Why - Oh Why/The Heart You Break (May Be Your Own)	40
57	London HLR 8395	From The First Hello To The Last Goodbye/ Come Home, Come Home, Come Home	30
57	London HLR 8436	Around The World/It's Not For Me To Say	20
57	London HLR 8468	Fascination (with Troubadors)/Why Don't They Leave Us Alone	20
58	London HLR 8539	I'm New At The Game Of Romance/It's Been A Long Long Time (with Troubadors)	15
58	London HLR 8611	I've Got Bells On My Heart/Only One Love	15
58	London HLR 8649	Enchanted Island/Once More, My Love, Once More	12
58	London HLR 8751	The Day The Rains Came/Le Jour Ou La Pluie Viendra	5
58	London HL 7064	The Day The Rains Came/I May Never Pass This Way Again (export issue)	10
59	London HLR 8810	If I Could Only Live My Life Again/To Love And Be Loved	5
59	London HLR 8925	With Open Arms/I Can't Begin To Tell You	5
59	London HLR 8999	Happy Anniversary/C'est La Vie, C'est L'Amour	5
59	London HLR 8999	Happy Anniversary/C'est La Vie, C'est L'Amour (78)	15
63	Colpix PX 700	Red Sails In The Sunset/My Special Dream	6
67	Columbia DB 7645	Maybe/Walking The Streets In The Rain	10
67	Columbia DB 8177	The Three Bells (Jimmy Brown Song)/I Want To Be With You	6
67	HMV POP 1608	This Is My World Without You/Somebody, Someplace	10
68	Stateside SS 2082	Masquerade/Smile	6
58	London RE-R 1161	ALL THE WAY PART 1 (EP, with Troubadours)	15
58	London RE-R 1162	ALL THE WAY PART 2 (EP, with Troubadours)	15
59	London RE-R 1204	THE DAY THAT THE RAINS CAME (EP, triangular centre)	15
59	London RE-R 1204	THE DAY THAT THE RAINS CAME (EP, round centre)	10
61	London RE-R 1331	JANE MORGAN (EP)	15
57	London HA-R 2086	FASCINATION (LP)	30
58	London HA-R 2110	ALL THE WAY (LP, with Troubadors)	20
58	London HA-R 2133	SOMETHING OLD, SOMETHING NEW, SOMETHING BORROWED, SOMETHING BLUE (LP)	20
59	London HA-R 2158	THE DAY THE RAINS CAME (LP)	20
60	London HA-R 2244	JANE IN SPAIN (LP)	20
60	London HA-R 2316	THE BALLADS OF LADY JANE (LP)	20
61	London HA-R 2371	JANE MORGAN TIME (LP)	20
61	London HA-R 2377	THE SECOND TIME AROUND (LP, mono)	15
61	London SAH-R 6177	THE SECOND TIME AROUND (LP, stereo)	20
62	London HA-R 2430	AT THE COCONUT GROVE (LP, mono)	15
62	London SAH-R 6226	AT THE COCONUT GROVE (LP, stereo)	20
62	London HA-R/SH-R 8042	WHAT NOW MY LOVE (LP, mono)	15
62	London HA-R/SH-R 8042	WHAT NOW MY LOVE (LP, stereo)	20
63	London HA-R/SH-R 8069	LOVE MAKES THE WORLD GO ROUND (LP, mono)	15

JAYE P. MORGAN

55	HMV 7M 327	The Longest Walk/Swanee	15
56	HMV 7M 348	If You Don't Want My Love/Pepper Hot Baby	25
56	HMV POP 144	If You Don't Want My Love/Pepper Hot Baby (78)	25
56	HMV 7M 365	Not One Goodbye/My Bewildered Heart	10
56	Brunswick 05519	Have You Ever Been Lonely?/Baby Don't Do It	10
57	RCA RCA 1014	You, You Romeo/Graduation Ring	8
59	MGM MGM 1005	Are You Lonesome Tonight?/Miss You	6
59	MGM MGM 1005	Are You Lonesome Tonight?/Miss You (78)	15
59	MGM MGM 1021	(It Took) One Kiss/My Reputation	5
59	MGM MGM 1039	Somebody Loses, Somebody Wins/Somebody Else Is Taking My Place	5

MINT VALUE £

60	MGM MGM 1093	I Walk The Line/Wondering Where You Are	5
62	MGM MGM 1182	Heartache Named Johnny/He Thinks I Still Ache	5
62	MGM MGM 1190	Brotherhood Of Man/Nobody's Sweetheart	5
54	London RE-P 1013	JAYE P. SINGS (EP)	15
59	MGM MGM-C 793	SLOW AND EASY (LP)	20

JOHN MORGAN
(see also Spirit Of John Morgan)

72	Carnaby 6302 010	KALEIDOSCOPE (LP, white label with red 'crab' logo)	100
70s	SWP 1007	LIVE AT DURRANT HOUSE (LP, private pressing)	100

LEE MORGAN

61	Columbia 33SX 1399	THE BIRDLAND STORY VOL. 1 (LP)	15
62	Stateside SL 10016	EXPOOBIDENT (LP)	25

MACE MORGAN THUNDERBIRDS

63	Starlite STEP 36	SHAKE AND SWING (EP)	60

MARY MORGAN

56	Parlophone MSP 6204	Jimmy Unknown/You Are My Love	10
56	Parlophone R 4227	From The Candy Store On The Corner/No-One Was There But You	10
57	Parlophone R 4348	A Call To Arms/One For Sorrow, Two For Joy	6

P.C. ALEXANDER MORGAN

66	Columbia DB 8095	Sussex By The Sea/METROPOLITAN POLICE BAND: Thunderbirds March	8

RAY MORGAN

70	B&C CB 128	Long And Winding Road/The Sweetest Wine	5

RUSS MORGAN ORCHESTRA

55	Brunswick 05464	Alabamy Bound/SCRANTON 7: The Popcorn Song	5
55	Brunswick 05493	Dog Face Soldier/Don't Cry Sweetheart	5
56	Brunswick 05537	The Poor People Of Paris (Poor John)/Silver Moon	5
56	Brunswick 05602	Lay Down Your Arms/My Best You You	5
55	Brunswick DE 9068	MOONLIGHT MUSIC (EP)	8

SAMMY MORGAN

70	Bullet BU 455	Get Out Of This Land/SYDNEY ALL STARS: Landmark	5
70	Punch PH 57	Get Out Of This Land/SYDNEY ALL STARS: Landmark	5

TONY MORGAN

69	Beacon BEA 115	Racial Segregation/Racial Segregation (instrumental)	15
72	Beacon BEA 188	Black Skin Blue Eyed Boys/Why Build A Mountain	15

MORGAN BROTHERS

59	MGM MGM 1007	Nola/Guiding Star	5
59	MGM MGM 1026	Kissin' On The Red Light/Milk From The Coconut	6

MORGAN TWINS

58	RCA RCA 1083	T.V. Hop/Let's Get Going	80
58	RCA RCA 1083	T.V. Hop/Let's Get Going (78)	50

MORGAN'S ALL STARS
(see also B. Leggs, Derrick Morgan, Marvels)

71	Camel CA 76	I Love You The Most (actually by Lloyd Clarke)/I Love You The Most - Version	5

(Ron Paul) MORIN & (Luke P.) WILSON

72	Sovereign SVNA 7252	PEACEFUL COMPANY (LP)	20

JOHNNY MORISETTE

62	Stateside SS 107	Meet Me At The Twistin' Place/Any Time Any Day Any Where	15

MORNIN

69	CBS 4863	Cheatin' On You/Let Me Love You	20

MORNING

70	Liberty LBS 83463	MORNING (LP)	40
72	United Artists UAS 29337	STRUCK LIKE SILVER (LP)	20

MORNING AFTER

71	Sky SKYLP 71014	BLUE BLOOD (LP)	80

MORNING GLORY
(see also John Surman)

73	Island ILPS 9237	MORNING GLORY (LP, gatefold, pink rim palm tree label)	30

GIORGIO MORODER

66	Page One POF 003	Full Stop/Believe Me	15
67	Page One POF 028	How Much Longer Must I Wait/Bla Bla Diddley	15
90s	Cause-N-Effect	I Wanna Rock You (Thee Maddcat Mix)/(Thee DrumDrum Mix) (12", no p/s)	15

ENNIO MORRICONE ORCHESTRA

67	RCA Victor RCA 1596	A Fistful Of Dollars/The Man With No Name	6
67	RCA Victor RCA 1634	For A Few Dollars More/La Resi Dei Conti	6
69	RCA RCA 1892	Once Upon A Time In The West (Jill's Theme)/Finale	6
69	United Artists UP 35004	A Professional Gun/Paco	6
67	RCA Victor RD/SF 7875	A FISTFUL OF DOLLARS (LP, soundtrack)	20
68	RCA Victor RD 7994	A FISTFUL OF DOLLARS/FOR A FEW DOLLARS MORE/ THE GOOD, THE BAD AND THE UGLY (LP, soundtrack)	15
68	United Artists (S)ULP 1197	THE GOOD, THE BAD AND THE UGLY (LP, soundtrack)	15
69	United Artists UAS 29005	A PROFESSIONAL GUN (LP, soundtrack)	25
70	CBS 70067	LOVE CIRCLE (LP, soundtrack)	50
70	MCA MKPS 2013	TWO MULES FOR SISTER SARA (LP, soundtrack)	30
72	United Artists UAS 29345	A FISTFUL OF DYNAMITE (LP, soundtrack)	40

CHRIS MORRIS

91	Flexi FLOP 1	THE SELECT FLOPPY DISC (EP, 33rpm, poly sleeve, with magazine)	10

MINT VALUE £

DESMOND MORRIS

63	Oriole EP 7083	A DAY AT THE ZOO (EP)	10

ERIC MORRIS

(see also Monty Morris, Byron Lee & Dragonaires, Cool Sticky, Tommy McCook, Zoot Simms, Marguerita, Cool Cats)

61	Starlite ST45 052	Search The World/Buster's Shack	40
61	Blue Beat BB 53	Humpty Dumpty/Corn Bread And Butter (as Eric 'Humpty Dumpty' Morris & Drumbago All Stars; [B-side actually by Drumbago All Stars])	20
62	Blue Beat BB 74	My Forty-Five/I've Tried Everybody (as Eric 'Humpty Dumpty' Morris & Drumbago All Stars)	20
62	Blue Beat BB 81	Sinners Repent And Pray/Now And Forever More (B-side act. by Alton Ellis)	20
62	Blue Beat BB 83	Money Can't Buy Life (with Buster's Group)/A. ELLIS: True Love	20
62	Blue Beat BB 105	Pack Up Your Troubles/Oh What A Smile Can Do (with D. Cosmo & Drumbago's All Stars)	20
62	Blue Beat BB 115	G.I. Lady/Going To The River	20
62	Blue Beat BB 128	Over The Hills/Lazy Woman (with Buster's Group)	20
62	Blue Beat BB 137	Miss Peggy's Grandmother/BUSTER'S GROUP: Megaton	10
62	Blue Beat BB 140	Seven Long Years/For Your Love	20
63	Blue Beat BB 153	Lonely Blue Boy/PRINCE BUSTER: Oh We	22
63	Blue Beat BB 184	Sweet Love/BUSTER, DEREK, ERIC: Country Girl	15
64	Blue Beat BB 218	Love Can Break A Man/Worried People	20
64	Blue Beat BB 273	Stitch In Time/For Ever	20
64	Black Swan WI 412	Sampson/BABA BROOKS: Jelly Beans	30
64	Black Swan WI 414	Solomon Grundie/BABA BROOKS: Key To The City	40
64	Black Swan WI 433	Supper In The Gutter/Words Of My Mouth	20
64	Black Swan WI 439	River Come Down/Seek And You'll Find	20
64	Black Swan WI 445	Home Sweet Home/LESTER STERLING: '64 Special	25
64	Island WI 142	Penny-Reel/DUKE REID'S GROUP: Darling When (B-side act. Dotty & Bonnie)	35
64	Island WI 147	Mama No Fret/FRANKIE ANDERSON: Santa Lucia (B-side w/Roland Alphonso)	20
64	Island WI 150	Drop Your Sword/Catch A Fire (B-side actually by Roland Alphonso)	25
64	Island WI 151	What A Man Doeth/DUKE REID'S GROUP: Rude Boy (B-side actually by Baba Brooks)	22
64	Port-O-Jam PJ 4006	Oh My Dear/Lena Belle	25
64	Rio R 39	Little District/True And Just	25
64	Rio R 48	Live As A Man/Man Will Rule	25
65	Rio R 72	By The Sea/I Wasn't Around	25
65	Island WI 177	Drop Your Sword/Catch A Fire	25
65	Island WI 183	Love Can Make A Mansion (actually "Love Can Break A Man")/ Ungodly People	15
65	Island WI 185	Suddenly/Many Long Years	25
65	Island WI 199	Fast Mouth/The Harder They Come	18
65	Island WI 234	Children Of Today/BABA BROOKS: Greenfield Ska	25
65	Blue Beat BB 298	Those Teardrops/DON DRUMMOND: Ska Town	35
66	Blue Beat BB 349	I'm The Greatest/BUSTER'S ALL STARS: Picket Line	60
60s	Fab BB 30	Humpty Dumpty (as Eric 'Humpty Dumpty' Morris & Buster All Stars)/ FOLKS BROTHERS: Carolina	7

GERRY MORRIS

73	York FYK 415	ONLY THE BEGINNING (LP)	150

HELMSLEY MORRIS

67	Caltone TONE 104	Love Is Strange/DON D. JUNIOR: Sir Pratt Special	100
68	Pama PM 720	Stay Loose Mama/You Think I'm A Fool (as Hainsley Morris)	7

JOE MORRIS & ORCHESTRA

54	London HL 8088	I Had A Notion/Just Your Way Baby (78)	25
54	London HL 8098	Travelin' Man/No, It Can't Be Done (78)	15

JOHNNY MORRIS

60s	Say Disc SAY 321	ANIMAL MAGIC (EP)	20
72	Decca PA 273	THE RAILWAY STORIES VOL 4 (LP)	15
72	BBC Roundabout 15	BEDTIME STORIES (LP)	15

LIBBY MORRIS

56	Parlophone R 4225	When Liberace Winked At Me/None Of That Now	5
65	RCA RCA 1499	One Of Those Songs/The Phoenix Love Theme (Senza Fine)	5
67	Polydor 56206	Bye, Yum, Pum, Pum/Ballad Of yesterday's Idol	5
72	Carnaby 6151 004	Build The Ladder Higher/Last Night	6

MILTON MORRIS

69	Upsetter US 318	No Bread And Butter/UPSETTERS: Soulful I	12

MONTY MORRIS

(see also Eric Morris, Monty, Derrick & Patsy, Monty & Roy, Alton Ellis)

67	Doctor Bird DB 1067	Play It Cool/BABA BROOKS' BAND: Open The Door	50
67	Doctor Bird DB 1081	Put On Your Red Dress/BABA BROOKS' BAND: Faberge	35
68	Doctor Bird DB 1162	Last Laugh/You Really Got A Hold On Me	30
68	Pama PM 721	Say What You're Saying/Tears In Your Eyes	20
68	Nu Beat NB 007	True Romance/BUNNY & RUDDY: Rhythm And Soul	15
68	Nu Beat NB 011	Simple Simon/BUNNY & RUDDY: On The Town	15
69	Doctor Bird DB 1176	Same Face/A Little Bit Of This	18
69	Big Shot BI 513	Deportation/Say I'm Back	80
69	Camel CA 12	Can't Get No Peace/UPSETTERS: For A Few Dollars More	70
69	Camel CA 28	No More Teardrops/Love Me Or Leave Me (as Monty Morris & Maples)	20
70	Unity UN 557	Do It My Way/Where In The World (Are You Going)	12
70	Explosion EX 2016	Higher Than The Highest Mountain/G.G. ALL STARS: Musical Shot	12
73	Ackee ACK 527	I'm Ready To Go/TOMMY McCOOK: Flower Pot	7

NAGGO MORRIS

79	Hit Run DD 111	Jah Will Explain/DOCTOR PABLO: Wicked Feel It (12")	25
82	S & G SG 12	A true You Na No/Going Places (12")	50
82	S & G SG 23	False Rasta/Two Time Girl (12")	70
82	Black Roots BR0036A	A True Them No Know/Version/Africa/Version (12")	30

MINT VALUE £

RICHIE MORRIS
73 Satril SAT 11 — Zimbabwa/Seasons Change . . . 8

ROGER MORRIS
72 Regal Zono. SRZA 8509 — FIRST ALBUM (LP, textured gatefold sleeve, red/silver label) . . . 400

RUSSELL MORRIS
69 Decca F 22964 — The Real Thing (Parts I & II)/It's Only A Matter Of Time . . . 80
70 Decca F 23066 — Rachel/Slow Joey . . . 5

VICTOR MORRIS
68 Amalgamated AMG 813 — Now I'm Alone/Rise And Fall . . . 10

MORRIS & MINORS
80 Round MOR 1 — STATE THE OBVIOUS (EP, p/s in poly bag) . . . 10

MORRIS & MITCH
57 Decca F 10900 — Cumberland Gap/I'm Not A Juvenile Delinquent . . . 12
57 Decca F 10929 — What Is A Skiffler?/The Tommy Rot Story . . . 8
58 Decca F 11086 — Highway Patrol/Bird Dog . . . 10
68 Trend TRE 1010 — The Magical Musherishi Tourists/Mister D.J. Man . . . 15
58 Decca DFE 6486 — SIX FIVE NOTHING SPECIAL (EP) . . . 20

MORRIS FAMILY & GOSPEL JUBILEERS
60 Top Rank JAR 322 — Wake Up Jonah/He Never Complained . . . 7

CURLEY JIM MORRISON
61 Starlite ST45 065 — Air Force Blues/Didn't I Tell You . . . 125

DOROTHY MORRISON
69 Elektra EKSN 45070 — All God's Children Got Soul/Put A Little Love In Your Heart . . . 12

HAROLD MORRISON
65 Brunswick LAT 8639 — HOSS HE'S THE BOSS (LP) . . . 12

JAMES MORRISON & TOM ENNIS
80 Topic 12T 390 — JAMES MORRISON & TOM ENNIS (LP) . . . 12

PROFESSOR MORRISON'S LOLLIPOP
68 London HLU 10228 — You Got The Love/Gypsy Lady . . . 6
69 London HLU 10254 — Oo-Poo-Pah Susie/You Take It . . . 6

TOM MORRISON
60 MGM MGM-EP 709 — THE ADVENTURES OF MIGHTY MOUSE AND HIS PALS (EP) . . . 8

VAN MORRISON
(see also Them)

67 London HLZ 10150 — Brown-Eyed Girl/Goodbye Baby (Baby Goodbye) . . . 45
70 Warner Brothers WB 7383 — Come Running/Crazy Love . . . 6
70 Warner Brothers WB 7434 — Domino/Sweet Jannie . . . 15
70 Warner Brothers WB 7434 — Domino/Sweet Jannie (DJ Copy) . . . 30
70 President PT 328 — Brown-Eyed Girl/Goodbye Baby (Baby Goodbye) (reissue) . . . 15
72 Warner Brothers K 16210 — Jackie Wilson Said/You've Got The Power . . . 10
74 London HLM 10453 — Brown-Eyed Girl/Goodbye Baby (Baby Goodbye) (2nd reissue) . . . 10
74 Warner Brothers K 16392 — Caldonia/What's Up, Crazy Pup . . . 10
77 Warner Brothers K 16939 — The Eternal Kansas City/Joyous Sound . . . 5
77 Warner Brothers K 16986 — Joyous Sound/Mechanical Bliss . . . 6
79 Mercury 6001 121 — Bright Side Of The Road/Rolling Hills (p/s) . . . 5
89 Polydor VANX 2 — Whenever God Shines His Light (Album Version) (with Cliff Richard)/ Cry For Home/I'd Love To Write Another Song (12", p/s) . . . 8
89 Polydor VANCD 2 — Whenever God Shines His Light (7" Version) (with Cliff Richard)/ I'd Love To Write Another Song/Cry For Home/Whenever God Shines His Light (Album Version) (CD) . . . 8
68 London HA-Z 8346 — BLOWIN' YOUR MIND (LP) . . . 100
69 Warner Brothers WS 1768 — ASTRAL WEEKS (LP, laminated front sleeve, flipbacks, orange label) . . . 150
69 Warner Brothers WS 1768 — ASTRAL WEEKS (LP, green label) . . . 25
70 Warner Brothers WS 1835 — MOONDANCE (LP, orange label) . . . 90
70 Warner Brothers WS 1835 — MOONDANCE (LP, green label) . . . 20
71 Warner Brothers WS 1884 — HIS BAND AND STREET CHOIR (LP, green label) . . . 25
71 President PTLS 1045 — THE BEST OF VAN MORRISON (LP) . . . 15
71 Warner Brothers K 46114 — TUPELO HONEY (LP, gatefold sleeve, green label) . . . 15
72 Warner Brothers K 46172 — SAINT DOMINIC'S PREVIEW (LP, with folded insert, green label) . . . 15
73 Warner Brothers K 46024 — ASTRAL WEEKS (LP, reissue, 'Burbank' label) . . . 15
73 Warner Brothers K 46040 — MOONDANCE (LP, reissue, 'Burbank' label) . . . 12
73 Warner Brothers K 46066 — HIS BAND AND STREET CHOIR (LP, reissue, 'Burbank' label) . . . 12
73 Warner Brothers K 46242 — HARD NOSE THE HIGHWAY (LP, gatefold sleeve, 'Burbank' label) . . . 12
74 London HSM 5008 — T.B. SHEETS (LP) . . . 15
74 Warner Brothers K 86007 — IT'S TOO LATE TO STOP NOW (2-LP, gatefold sleeve, 'Burbank' label) . . . 15
74 Warner Brothers K 56068 — VEEDON FLEECE (LP, 'Burbank' label) . . . 20
77 Bang 6467 625 — THIS IS WHERE I CAME IN (LP) . . . 12
84 Mercury MERH 54 — A SENSE OF WONDER (LP, white label test pressings with "Crazy Jane On God") . . . 25
84 Mercury MERH 54 — A SENSE OF WONDER (LP, credits but doesn't play "Crazy Jane On God") . . . 12

MORRISSEY
(see also Smiths, Durutti Column)

SINGLES
88 HMV TCPOP 1618 — Suedehead/I Know Very Well How I Got My Name . . . 20
88 HMV TCPOP 1618 — Suedehead/I Know Very Well How I Got My Name/ Hairdresser On Fire/Oh Well, I'll Never Learn (cassette) . . . 15
88 HMV TCPOP 1618 — Suedehead/I Know Very Well How I Got My Name/Oh Well, I'll Never Learn (mispressed cassette, plays "Ordinary Boys" instead of I Know Very Well... withdrawn) . . . 20

			MINT VALUE £
88	HMV 12 POP 1618	Suedehead/I Know Very Well How I Got My Name/Hairdresser On Fire (12", 1st pressings in brown p/s)	20
88	HMV CDPOP 1618	Suedehead/I Know Very Well How I Got My Name/Hairdresser On Fire/ Oh Well, I'll Never Learn (CD)	25
88	HMV POP 1619	Everyday Is Like Sunday/Disappointed (p/s)	5
88	HMV 12 POP 1619	Everyday Is Like Sunday/Sister I'm A Poet/Disappointed/ Will Never Marry (12", p/s)	8
88	HMV CDPOP 1619	Everyday Is Like Sunday/Sister I'm A Poet/Disappointed/ Will Never Marry (CD)	12
89	HMV CDPOP 1620	The Last Of The Famous International Playboys/Lucky Lisp/ Michaels Bones (CD)	15
89	HMV 12 POP 1620	The Last Of The Famous International Playboys/Lucky Lisp/ Michaels Bones (12")	10
89	HMV POP 1621	Interesting Drug/Such A Little Thing Makes Such A Big Difference (p/s)	5
89	HMV 12 POP 1621	Interesting Drug/Such A Little Thing Makes Such A Big Difference/ Sweet And Tender Hooligan (live) (12", p/s)	10
89	HMV 12 POPS 1621	Interesting Drug/Such A Little Thing Makes Such A Big Difference (12", p/s, 1 side etched)	10
89	HMV CDPOP 1621	Interesting Drug/Such A Little Thing Makes Such A Big Difference/ Sweet And Tender Hooligan (live) (CD)	10
90	HMV POP 1622	Ouija Board, Ouija Board/Yes, I Am Blind (p/s)	6
90	HMV CDPOP 1622	Ouija Board, Ouija Board/Yes, I Am Blind/East West (CD)	10
90	HMV POP 1623	November Spawned A Monster/He Knows I'd Love To See Him (p/s)	5
90	HMV 12 POP 1623	November Spawned A Monster/Girl Least Likely To/ He Knows I'd Love To See Him (12", p/s)	10
90	HMV CDPOP 1623	November Spawned A Monster/He Knows I'd Love To See Him/ Girl Least Likely To (CD)	8
90	HMV POP 1624	Piccadilly Palare/Get Off The Stage (p/s)	6
90	HMV 12 POP 1624	Piccadilly Palare/At Amber/Get Off The Stage (12, p/s)	10
90	HMV CDPOP 1624	Piccadilly Palare/At Amber/Get Off The Stage (CD)	12
91	HMV POP 1625	Our Frank/Journalists Who Lie (p/s)	5
91	HMV 12 POP 1625	Our Frank/Journalists Who Lie/Tony The Pony (12", p/s)	10
91	HMV CDPOP 1625	Our Frank/Journalists Who Lie/Tony The Pony (CD)	8
91	HMV POP 1626	Sing Your Life/That's Entertainment (p/s)	5
91	HMV CDPOP 1626	Sing Your Life/That's Entertainment/The Loop (CD)	8
91	HMV POP 1627	Pregnant For The Last Time/Skin Storm (p/s)	5
91	HMV 12 POP 1627	Pregnant For The Last Time/Skin Storm/Cosmic Dancer (live)/ Disappointed (live) (12", p/s)	10
91	HMV CDPOP 1627	Pregnant For The Last Time/Skin Storm/Cosmic Dancer (live)/ Disappointed (live) (CD)	12
91	HMV CDPOP 1628	My Love Life/I've Changed My Plea To Guilty/There's A Place In Hell For Me And My Friends (live) (CD)	8
92	HMV 12POP 1629	We Hate It When Our Friends Become Successful/Suedehead/ I've Changed My Plea To Guilty/Pregnant For The Last Time (12", p/s)	10
92	HMV CDPOP 1629	We Hate It When Our Friends Become Successful/Suedehead/ I've Changed My Plea To Guilty/Alsatian Cousin (12", p/s)	10
92	HMV CDPOP 1629	Certain People I Know/You've Had Her/Jack The Ripper (CD)	15
92	EMI CDMOZBX 1	THE SINGLES COLLECTION 1986-1992 (13 x CD singles set hinged black/purple box with numbered insert)	90
94	Parlophone R 6372	The More You Ignore Me, The Closer I Get/Used To Be A Sweet Boy/ I'd Love To (numbered p/s)	5
94	Parlophone RDJ 6372	The More You Ignore, Me The Closer I Get/Used To Be A Sweet Boy (yellow p/s)	12
94	Parlophone CDR 6383	Hold On To Your Friends/Moon River (CD)	8
94	Parlophone 12 R6383	Hold Onto Your Friends/Moonriver (12", gatefold sleeve)	12
95	Parlophone R 6400	Boxers/Have-A-Go Merchant (p/s)	6
95	RCA 74321332947	Boy Racer/London (Live Version) (p/s)	6
95	RCA 74321332952	Boy Racer/Spring Heeled Jim/Why Don't You Find Out For Yourself (CD)	10
95	RCA Victor LC 0316	Dagenham Dave/Nobody Loves Us (p/s)	6
97	Island IS 667	Alma Matters/Heir Apparent (p/s)	20
97	Island IS 671	Roy's Keen/Lost (p/s)	20
97	Island 12 IS 671	Roy's Keen/Lost (12")	40
97	Island IS 686	Satan Rejected My Soul/Now I Am A Was (p/s)	25
01	EMI EMI 8872932	SINGLES 88-91 (10 x CDs, card sleeves)	40
01	EMI EMI 8797452	SINGLES 91-95 (9 X CDs, card sleeves, in box)	40
06	Attack ATKTW 019	Irish Blood, English Heart (12" 4-track EP)	8
06	Attack ATKTW 020	First Of The Gang To Die (12" 4-track EP)	8
06	Attack ATKTW025	I Just Want To See The Boy Happy/Sweetie-Pie/I Want The One I Can't Have/ Speedway/Late Night, Maudlin Street (12" picture disc, 1,000 only)	8

LPs

90	HMV CLP 3788	BONA DRAG (LP)	15
91	EMI CSD 3789	KILL UNCLE (LP, gatefold)	18
92	HMV CSD 3790	YOUR ARSENAL (LP)	20
93	HMV CSD 3791	BEETHOVEN WAS DEAF (LP)	25
94	Parlophone/EMI PCSD 148	VAUXHALL AND I (LP, gatefold)	45
95	RCA 29953 1	SOUTHPAW GRAMMAR (LP)	30
95	Parlophone PCS 7374	BONA DRAG (LP, reissue)	20
95	Parlophone PCS 7375	KILL UNCLE (LP, reissue)	20
95	Parlophone PCS 7376	VIVA HATE (LP, reissue)	20
97	EMI EMC 2771	SUEDEHEAD: THE BEST OF MORRISSEY (2-LP, gatefold)	50
97	Island ILPS 8059	MALADJUSTED (LP)	30
97	Parlophone PCSD 163	WORLD OF MORRISSEY (LP, classic yellow/black Parlophone label)	50
04	Sanctuary ATKLP 001	YOU ARE THE QUARRY (LP, 5,000 only)	18

PROMOS

88	HMV 12POP DJ 1618	Suedehead/I Know Very Well How I Got My Name/ Hairdresser On Fire (12" promo)	20
88	HMV 12 POP DJ 1619	Everyday Is Like A Sunday (12", promo, 1-sided)	20

			MINT VALUE £
88	Factory FA 244+	I Know Very Well How I Got My Note Wrong (7" promo, as Vincent Gerrard and Stephen Patrick, 1,000 only)	40
88	Factory FACD 244+	I Know Very Well How I Got My Note Wrong (CD promo, as Vincent Gerrard and Stephen Patrick, 1,000 only)	40
89	HMV 12POP DJ 1620	The Last Of The Famous International Playboys/Lucky Lisp/ Michaels Bones (12" promo)	15
89	EMI SPM 29	Interesting Drug/Such A Little Thing Makes Such A Big Difference (12" die cut red sleeve, promo)	15
89	EMI SPM 29	Interesting Drug/etched B side (12", die cut black sleeve, promo)	60
90	HMV (No Cat. No)	November The Second (12" promo, white label 'Dance Mix' destroyed on order of Morrissey, i known copy)	2000
90	HMV POPDJ 1624	Piccadilly Palare/Get Off The Stage (promo, in die-cut HMV sleeve)	30
91	HMV POP DJ 1626	Sing Your Life/That's Entertainment (promo, die-cut HMV sleeve)	30
91	HMV POP DJ1627	Pregnant For The Last TIme/Skin Storm (promo)	30
92	HMV POP DJ 1629	We Hate It When Our Friends Become Successful/ We Hate It When Our Friends Become Sucessful (10", A-side plays at 45rpm, B-side at 78rpm, die-cut sleeve)	30
92	HMV POP DJ 1630	You're The One For Me, Fatty/You're The One For Me, Fatty (10", A-side plays at 45rpm, B-side at 78rpm, die-cut sleeve)	30
93	HMV POPDJ 1631	Certain People I Know/Jack The Ripper (die-cut 'Moz' p/s, 300 only)	75
93	HMV POPDJ 1632	Jack The Ripper/Sister I'm A Poet (p/s)	12
94	Parlophone CDRDJ 6243	Sunny/Black-Eyed Susan/A Swallow On My Neck (CD)	18
94	Parlophone CDRDJ 6372	The More You Ignore, Me The Closer I Get/Used To Be A Sweet Boy/ I'd Love To (CD, yellow card p/s)	12
94	Parlophone CDRDJ 6372	The More You Ignore, Me The Closer I Get (CD, with "45rpm" logo on disc, withdrawn)	45
94	Parlophone CDRDJ 6383	Hold On To Your Friends/Moonriver (CD, card p/s)	10
94	Parlophone R 6383	Hold Onto Your Friends/Moonriver (promo in different p/s, 150 only)	100
95	Parlophone CDRDJX 6400	Boxers/Have-A-Go Merchant/Whatever Happens I Love You (CD)	10
95	Parlophone RDJ 6400	Have-A-Go Merchant/Whatever Happens, I Love You (p/s)	25
95	Parlophone CDRDJ 6400	Have-A-Go Merchant/Whatever Happens, I Love You (CD, 'skinhead' card p/s)	25
95	Parlophone/EMI RDJ 6400	Have-A-Go Merchant/Whatever Happens, I Love You (p/s, promo for unreleased single)	50
95	RCA SOLO 1	OUTSIDE TOUR SAMPLER (CD promo features Boy Racer)	60
04	Sanctuary (No Cat. No)	YOU ARE THE QUARRY (CD-R interview promo)	35

DICK MORRISSEY

(see also If, Morrissey-Mullen)

61	77' LEU 12/8	HAVE YOU HEARD? (LP)	300
61	Fontana TFL 5149	IT'S MORRISSEY MAN! (LP)	300
67	Mercury 20093	HERE AND NOW AND SOUNDING GOOD (LP)	275
67	Mercury 20077MCL	STORM WARNING (LP)	300

MORRISSEY-MULLEN

(see also Dick Morrissey)

79	Harvest SHSP 4098	CAPE WRATH (LP)	12

BUDDY MORROW & HIS ORCHESTRA

53	HMV 7M 145	Heap Big Beat/I Can't Get Started	6
53	HMV 7M 151	I Can't Get Started/Heap Big Beat (reissue)	6
53	HMV 7M 162	Dragnet/Your Mouth's Got A Hole In It	8
54	HMV 7M 216	Knock On Wood (with Shaye Cogan)/All Night Long	10
60	RCA RCA 1167	Staccato's Theme/Scraunchy	6
60	RCA RCX 174	IMPACT (EP)	10

ELLA MAE MORSE

(see also 'Tennessee' Ernie Ford)

53	Capitol CL 13960	Forty Cups Of Coffee/Oh! You Crazy Moon (78)	10
55	Capitol CL 14223	Bring Back My Baby To Me/Lovey Dovey	50
55	Capitol CL 14223	Bring Back My Baby To Me/Lovey Dovey (78)	50
55	Capitol CL 14303	Smack Dab In The Middle/Yes, Yes I Do	50
55	Capitol CL 14303	Smack Dab In The Middle/Yes, Yes I Do (78)	50
55	Capitol CL 14332	Livin', Livin', Livin'/Heart Full Of Hope	40
55	Capitol CL 14332	Livin', Livin', Livin'/Heart Full Of Hope (78)	40
55	Capitol CL 14341	Razzle-Dazzle/Ain't That A Shame (with Big Dave & His Music)	100
55	Capitol CL 14341	Razzle-Dazzle/Ain't That A Shame (with Big Dave & His Music) (78)	100
55	Capitol CL 14362	Seventeen/Piddily Patter Song (with Big Dave & His Music)	100
55	Capitol CL 14362	Seventeen/Piddily Patter Song (with Big Dave & His Music) (78)	100
55	Capitol CL 14376	Birmin'ham/An Occasional Man	40

(The above 45s were originally issued with triangular centres; later round-centres are worth around two-thirds these values.)

55	Capitol CL 14376	Birmin'ham/An Occasional Man (78)	40
56	Capitol CL 14508	When Boy Kiss Girl (It's Love)/Sing-Ing-Ing-Ing	30
56	Capitol CL 14508	When Boy Kiss Girl (It's Love)/Sing-Ing-Ing-Ing (78)	30
56	Capitol CL 14572	Rock And Roll Wedding/Down In Mexico	40
56	Capitol CL 14572	Rock And Roll Wedding/Down In Mexico (78)	40
57	Capitol CL 14726	What Good'll It Do Me/Mister Money Maker	20
57	Capitol CL 14726	What Good'll It Do Me/Mister Money Maker (78)	20
57	Capitol CL 14760	I'm Gone/Sway Me	20
57	Capitol CL 14760	I'm Gone/Sway Me (78)	20
55	Capitol EAP1 513	BARRELHOUSE BOOGIE AND THE BLUES (EP)	20
54	Capitol LC 6687	BARRELHOUSE BOOGIE AND THE BLUES (10" LP)	40

ELLA MAE MORSE & FREDDIE SLACK

67	Ember SPE 6605	ROCKIN' BREW (LP)	25

AZIE MORTIMER

60	London HLX 9237	Lips/Wrapped Up In A Dream	100

MIKE MORTON CONGREGATION

70	Plexium PXM 19	Burning Bridges/You Gotta Be Mine	7

MINT VALUE £

JELLY ROLL MORTON('S RED HOT PEPPERS)

53	HMV 7M 132	The Chant/Tank Town Bump	5
54	HMV 7M 178	Fat Frances/Pep (solo)	5
54	HMV 7M 187	Wild Man Blues/Smoke-House Blues	5
54	HMV 7M 207	Harmony Blues/Jungle Blues	5
54	HMV 7M 256	Fussy Mabel/Burnin' The Iceberg	5

LIONEL MORTON

(see also Four Pennies)

67	Philips BF 1578	What To Do With Laurie/I'll Just	7
67	Philips BF 1607	First Love Never Dies/Try Not To Cry	7
69	RCA RCA 1875	Waterloo Road/Floral Street	7

MANDY MORTON (BAND)

79	Banshee BANS 791	Song For Me (Music Prince)/Little Inbetween (with Spriguns)	15
80	Polydor 2382 101	Ghost Of Christmas Past/Black Nights (p/s)	6
78	Banshee BAN 1011	MAGIC LADY (LP, with lyric insert, 1,000 only)	300
78	Banshee BAN 1011	MAGIC LADY (LP, with lyric insert, blue vinyl, 20 only)	500
80	Polydor 2382 101	SEA OF STORMS (LP, solo, with insert)	60
83	Banshee	VALLEY OF LIGHT (LP, private pressing)	100

MORWELLS

79	Attack TACK 5	Kingston Twelve Tuffie/PRINCE JAMMY: Jammin' For Survival (12")	12
79	Greensleeves GRED 17	Thief A Dub (12")	40
77	Burning Sounds BS 1006	CRAB RACE (LP)	35
79	Bushays BFMLP 100	COOL RUNNING (LP)	35
80	Trojan TRLS 193	A1 DUB (LP)	35

MOSAIC

71	Parlophone R5928	Blue Bird/Bird Of Fire	20

MOSAICS

66	Columbia DB 7990	Let's Go Drag Racing/Now That You're Here	35

ADRIAN MOSELY

68	Redcar RC001	Silent Night/Ellusive Face	60

JOSHUA MOSES

78	More Cut MCT 6001	Africa Is Our Land/Home (12", die-cut p/s)	50

MOSES & JOSHUA

(see under Moses & Joshua Dillard)

PABLO MOSES

75	Treble C CCC 01	I Man A Grasshopper/Grasshopper (part 2)	8
75	Treble C CCC 09	Blood Money/Version	8
76	Lizzard 001	We Should Be In Angola/Dubbing In Angola	25
80	Island 12WIP	Dubbing Is A Must/Revolutionary Step (12")	25
77	Klik KLP 9026	REVOLUTIONARY DREAM (LP)	20
78	Different GETL 104	REVOLUTIONARY DREAM (LP)	20
80	Island ILPS 9541	A SONG (LP)	12

MOSKOW

78	Moskow SRS 2103	Man From U.N.C.L.E./White Black (p/s)	8
79	Rialto TREB 107	Man From U.N.C.L.E./Too Much Commotion (reissue in different p/s)	5

BILL MOSS

69	Pama PM 765	Sock It To 'Em Soul Brother (Parts 1 & 2)	15
70	Pama PM 796	Number One/MOHAWKS: Lanscape	25

BUDDY MOSS

60s	Kokomo K 1003	GEORGIA BLUES VOLUME 2 (LP)	60

JENNY MOSS

63	Columbia DB 7061	Hobbies/Big Boys	40

STIRLING MOSS

60	HMV 7EG 8583	MOTOR RACING WITH STERLING MOSS (EP)	10
61	Redemption RLP 5004	THE STIRLING MOSS STORY (LP)	12

MOST

79	SRT SRTS/CUS/570	Carefree/In And Out (1,000 only stamped lyric insert)	60

ABE MOST OCTET

55	London RE-P 1028	PRESENTING THE ABE MOST OCTET (EP)	15

MOST DOMINANT

93	Kold Sweat KSEP210	PUSHED TO DA LIMIT (EP)	12

MICKIE MOST (& GEAR)

(see also Most Brothers)

63	Decca F 11664	Mr. Porter/Yes Indeed I Do	40
63	Columbia DB 7117	The Feminine Look/Shame On You Boy	15
63	Columbia DB 7180	Sea Cruise/It's A Little Bit Hot	15
64	Columbia DB 7245	Money Honey/That's Alright (as Mickey Most & Gear)	20

MOST BROTHERS

(see also Mickie Most, Alex Murray)

57	Decca F 10968	Whistle Bait/I'm Comin' Home	20
57	Decca F 10968	Whistle Bait/I'm Comin' Home (78)	15
58	Decca F 10998	Whole Lotta Woman/Teen Angel	20
58	Decca F 10998	Whole Lotta Woman/Teen Angel (78)	25
58	Decca F 11040	Don't Go Home/Dottie	20

MOTHER EARTH

69	Mercury MF 1081	Goodnight Melda Grebe The Telephone Company Has Cut Us Off/ I Did My Part	8

MINT VALUE £

71	Reprise K 14089	Temptation Took Control Of Me/I'll Be Long Gone	5
68	Mercury SMCL 20143	LIVING WITH THE ANIMALS (LP)	12
69	Mercury SMCL 20173	MAKE A JOYFUL NOISE (LP)	12
69	Mercury SMCL 20179	TRACY NELSON COUNTRY (LP)	12
71	Mercury 6338 023	SATISFIED (LP)	12
71	Reprise K 44133	BRING ME HOME (LP)	12

MOTHER EARTH

94	Acid Jazz JAZID 100	Jesse (Live) (company sleeve)	25
94	Acid Jazz JAZID LP 48	STONED WOMAN (LP)	18
95	Focus FOCUS 18	THE DESIRED EFFECT (2 x LP, gatefold)	15

MOTHER GONG

(see also Gong)

81	Butt BUTT 003	ROBOT WOMEN (LP)	12
82	Shanghai HAI 100	ROBOT WOMEN 2 (LP)	12
83	Shanghai HAI 109	ROBOT WOMEN 3 (LP)	12

MOTHER NATURE

71	B & C CB 166	Orange Days And Purple Nights/Where Did She Go	12

MOTHER NATURE

72	Kingdom KV8003	Once There Was A Time/Clear Blue Sky	10

MOTHER NATURES CHILDREN

77	President PT468	Money Back Ride/Rollin Down	10

MOTHER YOD

97	Prescription DRUG 1	MOTHER YOD (LP, 99 copies only)	25

MOTHERLIGHT

(see also Will Malone [Voice Band], Orange Bicycle)

69	Morgan Bluetown BT 5003	BOBAK, JONS, MALONE (LP)	300

MOTHERLODE

69	Buddah 201 064	When I Die/Hard Life	6
69	Buddah 2318 043	WHEN I DIE (LP)	15

MOTHERS OF INVENTION

(see under Frank Zappa/Mothers of Invention)

MOTHER'S RUIN

81	Spectra SPC 1	Streetfighters/Leaving You (in p/s)	55
81	Spectra SPC 1	Streetfighters/Leaving You	40
82	Spectra SPC 6	Street Lights/Turn A Corner (p/s)	20
82	Spectra SPC 7	Say It's Not True/It's Illogical (p/s)	35
81	Off Course G33303	WANT MORE (LP)	12
82	Spectra SPA 1	ROAD TO RUIN (LP)	12

MOTHER'S SONS

70	J-Dan JDN 4415	I Want To Tell The World/Underground Man	6

MOTHMEN

(see also Alberto Y Lost Trios Paranoias)

79	Absurd ABSURD 6	Does It Matter Irene?/Please Let Go (p/s)	5
81	Do It DUN 12	Show Me Your House And Car/People People (p/s, deleted after 1 day)	8
81	Do It DUNIT 12	Show Me Your House And Car/People People (12", p/s, deleted after 1 day)	10
81	Do It DUN 14	Temptation/People People (p/s)	5
82	Do It DUN 19	Wadada/As They Are (p/s)	5
82	Do It RIDE 9	ONE BLACK DOT (LP)	12
80s	On-U-Sound LP 2	PAY ATTENTION (LP)	12

MOTHS

69	Deroy	MOTHS (LP, private pressing in plain white sleeve)	400

MOTIFFE

72	Deroy 777	MOTIFFE (LP, private pressing in hand-illustrated white sleeve)	300

MOTION

(see also Aswad)

79	DD Records DDLP04	MOTION (LP)	40

MOTIONS

66	Pye International 7N 25390	Stop Your Crying/Every Step I Take	25

MOTIVATION

68	Direction 58-3248	Come On Down/Little Man	35

MOTLEY CREW

68	MJB BEV 429	MOTLEY CREW (EP, hand made sleeve)	25

MÖTLEY CRÜE

84	Elektra E 9756T	Looks That Kill/Piece Of The Action/Live Wire (12", p/s with free tattoo)	15
84	Elektra E 9756TP	Looks That Kill/Piece Of The Action/Live Wire (12", picture disc)	20
84	Elektra E 9732T (12", p/s, some with poster)	Too Young To Fall In Love/Take Me To The Top	15
86	Elektra EKR 16TP	Smokin' In The Boys' Room/Use It Or Lose It (mask-shaped pic disc & sticker)	12
86	Elektra EKR 33P	Smokin' In The Boys' Room/Home Sweet Home (2 different interlocking mask-shaped picture disc set)	20
86	Elektra EKR 33T	Smokin' In The Boys' Room/Home Sweet Home/ Shout At The Devil (12", p/s with poster)	8
87	Elektra EKR 59V	Girls, Girls, Girls/Sumthin' For Nuthin' ('X-rated' stickered p/s, 3,000 only)	8
87	Elektra EKR 59B	Girls, Girls, Girls/Sumthin' For Nuthin'/Smokin' In The Boys' Room (12", box set with patch)	8
87	Elektra EKR 59TP	Girls, Girls, Girls/Sumthin' For Nuthin'/Smokin' In The Boys' Room (12", picture disc)	8

			MINT VALUE £
88	Elektra EKR 65TB	You're All I Need/Wild Side/Home Sweet Home/Looks That Kill (12", box set with poster, tour pass & patch)	10
83	Elektra 9602 89-1	SHOUT AT THE DEVIL (LP, with bonus 12" picture disc & poster)	18
83	Elektra 9602 89-1	SHOUT AT THE DEVIL (LP, gatefold 'pentagram' black sleeve & inner)	12

MOTÖRHEAD

(see also Lemmy & Upsetters, Sam Gopal, Hawkwind, Girlschool, Wild Horses, Filthy Phil & Fast Eddie, Young & Moody, Rocking Vickers, Blue Goose)

77	Chiswick S 13	Motörhead/City Kids (p/s)	10
77	Chiswick NS 13	Motörhead/City Kids (12", p/s)	12
78	Bronze BRO 60	Louie Louie/Tear Ya Down (p/s)	6
79	Bronze BRO 67	Overkill/Too Late, Too Late (p/s, iwith 'Overkill' badge)	10
79	Bronze BRO 67	Overkill/Too Late, Too Late (p/s)	5
79	Bronze 12 BRO 67	Overkill/Too Late, Too Late (12", p/s)	10
79	Bronze BRO 78	No Class/Like A Nightmare (3 different sleeves)	50
79	Bronze BRO 85	Bomber/Over The Top (p/s, on blue vinyl)	8
79	Big Beat NS 13	Motörhead/City Kids (p/s, black, pink, blue, orange or white vinyl)	5
80	Big Beat NSP 13	Motörhead/City Kids (p/s, black & white picture disc)	8
80	Big Beat NSP 13	Motörhead/City Kids (p/s, blue & white picture disc)	12
80	Bronze BRO 92 DJ	Leaving Here (live)/Stone Dead Forever (live) (2-track promo for Golden Years EP, no p/s)	40
80	Bronze BROX 106	Ace Of Spades/Dirty Love (12", 'Xmas' sleeve)	10
81	Lyntone LYN 9661	The Train Kept-A Rollin' (live) (blue flexi free with Flexipop mag, issue 7)	8
81	Bronze BROP 124	Motörhead (live)/Over The Top (live) (picture disc)	6
82	Bronze BRO 146	Iron Fist/Remember Me I'm Gone (p/s, blue vinyl)	12
82	Bronze BRO 146	Iron Fist/Remember Me I'm Gone (p/s, red vinyl)	5
82	Bronze BRO 151	Stand By Your Man/No Class/Masterplan (p/s, as Lemmy & Wendy O. Williams)	8
83	Bronze BRO 165	I Got Mine/Turn You Round Again (p/s)	5
83	Bronze BROX 165	I Got Mine/Turn You Round Again (12", p/s)	8
83	Bronze BRO 167	Shine/Hoochie Coochie Man (live) (p/s)	5
83	Bronze BROX 167	Shine/Hoochie Coochie Man (live)/Don't Need Religion (live) (12", p/s)	8
83	Bronze BROX 167/BROX 92	Shine/Hoochie Coochie Man (live)/Don't Need Religion (live)/ THE GOLDEN YEARS (12", p/s, stickered, shrinkwrapped double pack)	18
83	Lyntone LYN 4383	In Their Own Words/BRONZ: Taken By Storm (flexi free with Kerrang! mag)	10
83	Lyntone LYN 4383	In Their Own Words/BRONZ: Taken By Storm (flexi without Kerrang! mag)	5
84	Bronze BRO 185	Killed By Death/Under The Knife (p/s)	5
84	Bronze BROP 185	Killed By Death/Under The Knife (logo skull-shaped picture disc)	12
84	Bronze BROX 185	Killed By Death (Full Length Version)/Under The Knife/Under The Knife (12", stickered p/s, with poster)	10
88	GWR GWR 15	Ace Of Spades/Dogs/Traitor (sold at concerts & through fan club, no p/s)	15
90	Epic 656578 0	The One To Sing The Blues/Dead Man's Hand (shaped picture disc)	8
80	Big Beat SWT 61	BEER DRINKERS EP (12", p/s, scarce pink or orange vinyl)	8
80	Big Beat SWT 61	BEER DRINKERS EP (12", p/s, brown vinyl)	15
81	Bronze BROX 116	ST. VALENTINES DAY MASSACRE (10" EP, with Girlschool)	12
81	Bronze BROX 116	ST. VALENTINES DAY MASSACRE (7" EP, with Girlschool)	5
77	Chiswick WIK 2	MOTÖRHEAD (LP, black & white laminated sleeve with inner)	15
77	Chiswick WIK 2	MOTÖRHEAD (LP, black and silver sleeve with inner, 600 only)	100
77	Chiswick CWK 3008	MOTÖRHEAD (LP, white vinyl)	18
79	Bronze BRON 515	OVERKILL (LP, green vinyl)	30
79	Bronze BRON 523	BOMBER (LP, 3 different shades of blue vinyl)	15
80	Bronze BRONG 531	ACE OF SPADES (LP, gold vinyl, stickered sleeve)	15
80	Big Beat WIK 2	MOTÖRHEAD (LP, reissue, red or clear vinyl with inner sleeve)	15
81	Bronze BRONG 535	NO SLEEP 'TIL HAMMERSMITH (LP, gold vinyl, stickered sleeve)	20
84	Bronze/Pro MOTOR 1	NO REMORSE (2-LP, leather sleeve with inners)	18
86	GWR GWRLP 1	ORGASMATRON (LP, picture disc)	15
91	Epic 467481-0	1916 (LP, picture disc, stickered PVC sleeve)	15
91	Epic 467481 9	1916 (CD, 'tour' picture disc shrinkwrapped with booklet, stickered case)	18
93	Castle/Bronze CTVCD 125	ALL THE ACES (CD, numbered promo, in box with metal skull, 10 only)	200
93	Castle CTVLP 125	ALL THE ACES (2xLP, gatefold)	20
04	SPV 22325	INFERNO (2xLP)	18

MOTORS

(see also Ducks Deluxe, Heroes, Snakes)

78	Virgin V 2089	APPROVED BY THE MOTORS (LP, withdrawn group photo sleeve & inner sleeve)	12

MOTORWAY

79	Neat NEAT 01	All I Wanna Be Is Your Romeo/It's Easy When You're Alone	10

MOTOWN SPINNERS

(see under Detroit Spinners)

TONY MOTTOLA

61	London HAZ 2442	STRING BAND STRUM-ALONG (LP, also stereo SAHZ 6231)	12

MOTT THE HOOPLE

(see also Ian Hunter, At Last The 1958 Rock & Roll Show, Morgan, Mick Ronson, British Lions, Luther Grosvenor, Charlie Woolfe)

69	Island WIP 6072	Rock And Roll Queen/Road To Birmingham	25
71	Island WIP 6105	Midnight Lady/The Debt (in p/s)	18
71	Island WIP 6105	Midnight Lady/The Debt	6
71	Island WIP 6112	Downtown/Home	15
74	CBS 2439	Foxy Foxy/Trudi's Song (cherry vinyl)	5
76	CBS 3963	All The Young Dudes/Roll Away The Stone (p/s)	5
89	CBS 654853 3	All The Young Dudes/Roll Away The Stone/All The Way From Memphis/ The Golden Age Of Rock'n'Roll (3" CD, gatefold card sleeve)	8
69	Island ILPS 9108	MOTT THE HOOPLE (LP, pink label; mispress with 5 alternate mixes & Road To Birmingham in place of "Backsliding Fearlessly" or one alternative mix with "Road To Birmingham", and "Rock And Roll Queen" correctly credited. This price for each copy)	60

			MINT VALUE £
69	Island ILPS 9108	MOTT THE HOOPLE (LP, gatefold sleeve, pink label with white 'i' logo; with "Backsliding Fearlessly" in correct order)	60
70	Island ILPS 9119	MAD SHADOWS (LP, pink label with pink 'i' logo, gatefold sleeve)	40
71	Island ILPS 9144	WILD LIFE (LP, gatefold, pink rim palm tree label)	20
71	Island ILPS 9178	BRAIN CAPERS (LP, pink rim palm tree label & inner sleeve, with mask)	80
71	Island ILPS 9178	BRAIN CAPERS (LP, pink rim palm tree label & inner sleeve, without mask)	20
72	CBS 65184	ALL THE YOUNG DUDES (LP, with inner sleeve)	15
72	Island ILPS 9215	ROCK AND ROLL QUEEN (LP, 'pink rim palm tree' label)	15
73	CBS 69038	MOTT (LP, die-cut gatefold sleeve with plastic flap, inner sleeve, orange label, stickered)	25
80	Island IRSP 8	TWO MILES FROM HEAVEN (LP, early copies listing "Moving On" on rear sleeve)	20
80	Island IRSP 8	TWO MILES FROM HEAVEN (LP)	12

KEN MOULE'S LONDON JAZZ CHAMBER GROUP

(see also London Jazz Chamber Group, Ken Moule Seven)

70	Ember EMB S 275	Mae West/Zsa Zsa Gabor (in p/s)	15
70	Ember EMB S 275	Mae West/Zsa Zsa Gabor	5
69	Ember CJS 823	ADAM'S RIB SUITE (LP)	70

KEN MOULE SEVEN

(see also London Jazz Chamber Group)

55	Decca DFE 6261	ARRANGED BY KEN MOULE (EP)	8
57	Decca LK 4192	KEN MOULE ARRANGES FOR (LP)	25
58	Decca LK 4261	JAZZ AT TOAD HALL (LP)	30

MATTIE MOULTRIE

67	CBS 202547	That's How Strong My Love Is/The Saddest Story Ever Told	20
67	CBS 202547	That's How Strong My Love Is/The Saddest Story Ever Told (DJ Copy)	20

MOUND CITY BLUE BLOWERS

55	HMV 7EG 8096	MOUND CITY BLUE BLOWERS (EP)	8
60	Collector JEL 1	BLUES BLOWING JAZZ VOL. 1 (EP)	10

MOUNT RUSHMORE

68	Dot DOT 115	Stonefree/She's No Good To Me	10

MOUNTAIN

(see also West Bruce & Laing, Leslie West, Jolliver Arkansas)

70	Bell BLL 1112	Mississippi Queen/The Laird	15
70	Bell BLL 1125	Sittin' On A Rainbow/To My Friend	20
71	Island WIP 6119	Roll Over Beethoven/Crossroader	8
70	Bell SBLL 133	MOUNTAIN CLIMBING! (LP)	25
71	Island ILPS 9148	NANTUCKET SLEIGHRIDE (LP, 'pink rim palm tree' label)	20
71	Island ILPS 9179	FLOWERS OF EVIL (LP, 'pink rim palm tree' label)	12
72	Island ILPS 9199	LIVE - THE ROAD GOES ON FOREVER (LP, 'pink rim' label, 'palm tree' logo)	12

MOUNTAIN ASH

75	Witches Bane LKLP 6036	THE HERMIT (LP, private pressing with insert)	200

MOUNTAIN GOATS

02	4AD AD 2208	See America Right/New Chevrolet In Flames (p/s)	5
03	4AD AD 2306	Palmcorder Yajna/Butter Teeth (p/s)	5

MOUNTAIN LINE

74	Xtra XTRA 1140	MOUNTAIN LINE (LP)	12
75	Xtra XTRA 1147	HORSEPOWER (LP)	12

VALERIE MOUNTAIN

(see also Eagles)

61	Columbia DB 4660	Go It Alone/Gentle Christ	5
62	Pye 7N 15450	Some People/Yes You Did	7
62	Pye NEP 24158	SOME PEOPLE - SOUNDTRACK (EP, some tracks by Eagles)	12

MOURNING AFTER

94	Detour DR 017	Doin' Me In/Out For The Count (p/s, 100 blue vinyl)	6

MOURNING PHASE

71	Eden	MOURNING PHASE (LP, private pressing)	200
91	Eden EDEN 1	EDEN (LP, reissue of "Mourning Phase")	20

MOUSE

(see also Ginhouse, Ray Russell Quartet, Running Man)

73	Sovereign SOV 122	We Can Make It/It's Happening To Me And You	20
74	Sovereign SOV 127	All The Fallen Teen Angels/Just Came Back	12
73	Sovereign SVNA 7262	LADY KILLER (LP, gatefold sleeve)	300

MOUSE & TRAPS

68	President PT 174	L.O.V.E. Love/Beg Borrow And Steal	40
68	President PT 210	Sometimes You Just Can't Win/Crying Inside	20

MOUSEFOLK

88	Tea Time Surf's Up 01	Don't Let It Slip Away/Spinning Round (flexidisc, with p/s)	7
88	Tea Time Surf's Up 02	HAZY TAMBOURINE DAYS EP (p/s)	7
80s	Tea Time SURFS UP 03	Grannie's Cake Crisis/Mrs Marr's Daughter (foldaround p/s, with badge)	5
89	Flowerpot 001	Motorcycle Boy/RISK: This Year's Model (p/s flexi, foldaround p/s)	5

MOUSEHOUSE

79	Fort FORT 001	Where Young Cats Fear To Tread/When Dave Says He Has He Hasn't	5

MOUSETRAP

71	Aurora AU 4324	Susie/Greenfields	35

ALPHONSE MOUZON

76	United Artists UAG 20005	THE MAN INCOGNITO (LP)	12

MINT VALUE £

ALPHONSE MOUZON & LARRY CORYELL
(see also Larry Coryell)

77	Atlantic K 50382	BACK TOGETHER AGAIN (LP)	12

MOVE
(see also Roy Wood, Jeff Lynne, ELO, Idle Race, Trevor Burton, Nicky James Movement, Ace Kefford Stand, Grunt Futtock, Rick Price, Uglys, Charlie Wayne)

66	Deram DM 109	Night Of Fear/Disturbance	8
67	Deram DM 117	I Can Hear The Grass Grow/Wave The Flag And Stop The Train	10
67	Regal Zonophone RZ 3001	Flowers In The Rain/(Here We Go Round) The Lemon Tree	7
67	Regal Zonophone	Cherry Blossom Clinic/Vote For Me (unissued)	0
68	Regal Zonophone RZ 3005	Fire Brigade/Walk Upon The Water	7
68	Regal Zonophone RZ 3012	Wild Tiger Woman/Omnibus	12
69	Regal Zonophone RZ 3015	Blackberry Way/Something	6
69	Regal Zonophone RZ 3021	Curly/This Time Tomorrow	6
70	Regal Zonophone RZ 3026	Brontosaurus/Lightnin' Never Strikes Twice	6
70	Fly BUG 2	When Alice Comes Back To The Farm/What?	5
71	Harvest HAR 5036	Ella James/No Time (unissued)	0
71	Harvest HAR 5038	Tonight/Don't Mess Me Up	5
71	Harvest HAR 5043	Chinatown/Down On The Bay	5
72	MagniFly ECHO 104	Fire Brigade/I Can Hear The Grass Grow/Night Of Fear	5
72	Harvest HAR 5050	California Man/Do Ya/Ella James	5
74	Harvest HAR 5086	Do Ya/No Time	5
68	Regal Zono. TRZ 2001	SOMETHING ELSE FROM THE MOVE (EP, 33rpm)	50
68	Regal Zono. LRZ 1002	THE MOVE (LP, mono, red/silver labels with "Sold in the U.K..." text)	90
68	Regal Zono. SLRZ 1002	THE MOVE (LP, stereo, red/silver labels with "Sold in the U.K..." text)	70
68	Regal Zono. TA-LRZ 1002	THE MOVE (reel-to-reel, mono only)	12
70	Regal Zono. SLRZ 1012	SHAZAM (LP, many with pressing flaw on track "Don't Make My Baby Blue" that makes record skip on this track, red/silver label)	120
70	Fly HIFLY 1	LOOKING ON (LP, white label, 'Fly' logo)	40
71	Harvest SHSP 4013	MESSAGE FROM THE COUNTRY (LP, with EMI logo on label)	25
72	Fly TOOFA 5/6	THE MOVE/SHAZAM (2-LP reissue)	18
74	Harvest SHSP 4035	CALIFORNIA MAN (LP)	12

MOVEMENT

68	Pye 7N 17443	Something You've Got/Tell Her	120
68	Target 7N 17443	Something You've Got/Tell Her (Irish issue)	120
68	Big T BIG 112	Head For The Sun/Mister Mann	180

MOVEMENT

80	Ballistic TRIF 2	No Man Is An Island/JAMDOWN PLAYERS: Levi's Choice (dubwise)/ Togetherness/Deviate/Consolidate/Progression (12")	40

MOVERS

65	Ska Beat JB 191	Jo-Anne/DON DRUMMOND: Don De Lion	45

MOVIES
(see also Ora, Public Foot The Roman)

75	A&M AMLH 33002	THE MOVIES (LP)	12

MOVIES

80	Gem GEMS 20	Love Is A Sacrifice/Fat Girl	6

MOVIETONE

94	Planet PUNK 003	She Smiled Mandarine Like/Orange Zero (p/s)	6
94	Planet PUNK 009	Mono Valley/Under The 3000 Foot Red Ceiling (p/s, 1,000 only)	5

MOVING BROTHERS

67	Island WI 3049	Darling I Love You/TOMMY McCOOK & SUPERSONICS: Saboo	40
67	Treasure Isle TI 7018	Darling I Love You/TOMMY McCOOK & SUPERSONICS: Saboo (reissue)	25

MOVING FINGER
(see also Anglians)

68	Mercury MF 1051	Jeremy The Lamp/Pain Of My Misfortune	40
69	Mercury MF 1077	Higher And Higher/Shake And Fingerpop	30
73	Decca F 13406	So Many People/We're Just As Happy As We Are	8

MOVING IN THE RIGHT DIRECTION

92	Kold Sweat KSEP203	TALES FROM THE SOUTHSIDE (EP)	12

JUDY MOWATT
(see also Jean & Gaytones)

73	Gayfeet GS 207	Emergency Call/Emergency Call - Version	8
80	Grove Muzik IPR 2041	Black Woman (feat. Joy Tulloch)/My My People (12")	25

MOWREY JNR. & WATSON

76	Riverdale RRL 1000	BUSKER (LP, with insert)	30

MP's

80	Moving Plastic WSP 006	Housewives' Choice/Life On The Dole	5

MR. BLOE
(see also Harry Pitch)

70	DJM DJS 216	Groovin' With Mr. Bloe/Sinful	5
70	DJM DJLPS 409	GROOVIN' WITH MR. BLOE (LP)	18

MR. BUNGLE

91	London 828 276-1	MR BUNGLE (LP, picture disc)	40

MR. CALYPSON

71	Jump Up JU 40	Mohammed Ali/SAMSON DE LARK: Undemocratic Rhodesia	6

MR CHIPPS

77	Spiral SPF 7014	The Way I Am/Lady Elaine (no p/s)	30

MINT VALUE £

MR. DYNAMITE
67 Sue WI 4027 Sh'mon/DYNAMITE ORCHESTRA: Sh'mon (Part Two) 300

Mr. FINGERS
88 Jack Trax 12 J TRAX 10 SLAM DANCE EP (12") 50
94 Black Market BMI 022 LP BACK TO LOVE (LP) 35
95 Black Market BMI 024 LP CLASSIC FINGERS (2xLP) 20

MR. FLOOD'S PARTY
(see also Mike Corbett & Jay Hirsch)
71 Ember EMB S 312 Compared To What/Unbreakable Toy 20
71 Ember EMB S 312 Compared To What/Unbreakable Toy (DJ copy) 40
75 Bulldog BD 6 Compared To What/Unbreakable Toy (reissue) 5

MR. FORD & MR. GOON-BONES
(see also Mr. Goon-Bones & Cavaliers)
56 London HLU 8355 Ain't She Sweet/MUZZY MARCELLINO: Mary Lou 25

MR FOUNDATION
(see also Sound Dimension)
67 Studio One SO 2001 See Them A Come/ KEN PARKER: Have A Good Time 35
67 Studio One SO 2003 All Rudies In Jail (actually by Zoot Sims/HORTENSE & ALTON Easy Squeeze . 100
68 Studio One SO 2061 Time Oh/DUDLEY SIBLEY & PETER AUSTIN: Hole In Your Soul 40
68 Studio One SO 2069 Reggae Rumble/MARCIA GRIFFITHS : You Keep Me On The Move 40
69 Supreme SUP 201 Time To Pray (actually by Lloyd Robinson)/Young Budd (by Leonard Dillon) 12

MR. FOX
(see also Bob Pegg, Bob & Carol Pegg)
70 Big T BIG 135 Little Woman/Join Us In Our Game 8
70 Transatlantic TRA 226 MR FOX (LP) 75
71 Transatlantic TRA 236 THE GIPSY (LP, gatefold sleeve, plastic inner with foam opening) 100
75 Transatlantic TRA 303 THE COMPLETE MR FOX (2-LP, reissue of "Mr Fox" & "The Gypsy") 20

MR. MO'S MESSENGERS
67 Columbia DB 8133 Feelin' Good/The Handyman 15

MISTER MOST
69 Downtown DT 409 Reggae Train/Pushwood 8

MR. PINK/MR. BLONDE
96 Resevoir BP1 Payin' The Price/Death Before Dishonour (12") 20
97 Resevoir BP2 Jamaica Crime Wave (12") 15

MR. REJECT
71 private pressing MR. REJECT (LP) 40

Mr. SCRUFF
99 Ninja Tune ZEN12 080 Get A Move On! (12") 20
01 Ninja Tune ZEN12 104 Get A Move On/Ug (12") 25
97 Pleasure Music JOY13 MR. SCRUFF (2xLP) 15
99 Ninja Tune ZEN 42 KEEP IT UNREAL (2xLP) 30
99 Ninja Tune ZEN 42 KEEP IT UNREAL (2xLP, purple sleeve) 20

MR. TWISTER & TORNADOS
63 Starlite ST45 099 Big Twist (Parts 1 & 2) 15

MU
74 United Artists UAG 29709 LEMURIAN MUSIC (LP) 35

MUCKRAM WAKES
76 Trailer LER 2093 MUCKRAM WAKES (LP) 20

MUCKY DUCK
70 Deram DM314 Jefferson/Psycho's On The Run 12

MUD
(see also Dum)
67 CBS 203002 Flower Power/You're My Mother (in p/s) 50
67 CBS 203002 Flower Power/You're My Mother 35
68 CBS 3355 Up The Airy Mountain/Latter Days 30
69 Philips BF 1775 Shangri-La/House On The Hill 20
70 Philips 6006 022 Jumping Jehosaphat/Won't Let It Go 20
74 Rak RAK 187 Lonely This Christmas/I Can't Stand It (p/s) 5
75 Rak RAK 194 The Secrets That You Keep/Still Watching The Clock (p/s) 5
76 Rak RR 6 Tiger Feet/Oh Boy/Dynamite (p/s) 5
76 Private Stock PVT 65 Shake It Down/Laugh, Live, Love (p/s) 5
79 Carrere CAR 117 Drop Everything And Run/Taking The Easy Way Out (picture disc) 5

MUDHONEY
(see also Sonic Youth)
89 Blast First BFFP 46 Halloween/SONIC YOUTH: Touch Me I'm Sick (12", with tour/gig flyer) 12
89 Blast First BFFP 46 Halloween/SONIC YOUTH: Touch Me I'm Sick (12") 8
92 Reprise WO 137 Suck You Dry/Version/Over The Top/Underide (12") 10
92 Reprise WO 137T Suck You Dry (LP Version)/Deception Pass (12") 10
95 Reprise 9362 458401 MY BROTHER THE COW (LP, with 6-track EP, [PRO S 7492]) 25

MUDIE'S ALL STARS
(see also I Roy, Eternals, King Cannon, John Holt, Niney, Jolly Boys, Jo Jo Bennett)
70 Moodisc HM 3503 Wha Who Wha - Version/G.G. RUSSELL: Wha Who Wha 12

MUDLARKS
58 Columbia DB 4064 Mutual Admiration Society/A New Love 10
58 Columbia DB 4099 Lollipop/Young Dove's Calling 5
58 Columbia DB 4133 Book Of Love/Yea, Yea 5
59 Columbia DB 4250 Abdul The Bulbul Amer Cha Cha/The Love Game 5

Year	Label / Cat. No.	Title	MINT VALUE £
59	Columbia DB 4331	Waterloo/Mary (78)	15
60	Columbia DB 4513	(You've Got To) Move Two Mountains/You're Free To Go	7
62	Columbia DB 4788	Them Twistin' Bones/Coney Island Washboard	7
62	Columbia DB 4861	Mañana Pasado Mañana/March Of The Broken Hearts	5
62	Decca F 11537	I've Been Everywhere/Just The Snap Of Your Fingers	7
63	Decca F 11601	The Little Cracked Bell Of San Raquel/La De Da	6
64	Fontana TF 495	Walk Around/Here's Another Day	8
58	Columbia SEG 7854	THE MUDLARKS! (EP)	30

DOMENICO MODUGNO

58	Oriole ICB 5000	Volare (Nel Blu Difinto Di Blu)/Nisciuno Po' Sape	10

MUFF

71	Mother MOT 7	Hurdy Gurdy/Why Did You Leave Me	15
74	Bell Bell 1380	Sexy Sexy Lady/Burnin'	5
75	UA UP 3595	Do The Hand Jive/Discotheque King	5

MU5

72	Crystal CR 7015	Mrs Watson/Rain Dance	70

MUGWUMPS

(see also Mamas & Papas, Mama Cass Elliot, Lovin' Spoonful, Zalman Yanovsky)

64	Warner Bros WB 144	I'll Remember Tonight/I Don't Wanna Know	12
67	Warner Bros W 1697	THE MUGWUMPS - AN HISTORICAL RECORDING (LP)	30
70	Valiant VS 134	THE MUGWUMPS - AN HISTORICAL RECORDING (LP, reissue)	18

BOBBY MUIR & BLUEBEATS

60	Blue Beat BB 20	Baby What You Done Me Wrong/Go Pretty Baby Go (as Blue Beats)	12
61	Blue Beat BB 44	Honey Please/That's My Girl (as Bobby Kingdom & Blue Beats)	12
62	Blue Beat BB 77	Brand New Automobile/Spanish Town Twist (as Bobby Kingdom & Blue Beats)	12

JAMIE MUIR & DEREK BAILEY

(see also Derek Bailey)

81	Incus INCUS 41	DART DRUG (LP)	50

LINDSAY MUIR'S UNTAMED

(see also Untamed)

66	Planet PLF 113	Daddy Long Legs/Trust Yourself A Little Bit (initial release with plain white white sleeve)	250
66	Planet PLF 113	Daddy Long Legs/Trust Yourself A Little Bit (with Planet company sleeve)	240

MULCAYS

55	London HLF 8188	Harbour Lights/Dipsy Doodle	30
54	London REP 1016	MERRY CHRISTMAS (EP)	8
56	London REF 1046	HARMONICS BY THE MULCAYS (EP)	8

MULDOONS

65	Decca F 12164	I'm Lost Without You/Come Back Now Baby	30

MULESKINNERS

(see also Small Faces, Faces)

65	Fontana TF 527	Back Door Man/Need Your Lovin'	200
65	Keepoint KEE-EP-7104	MULESKINNERS (EP, private pressing, no p/s)	750

BARBARA MULLANEY

73	Philips 6382 878	ON THE STREET WHERE I LIVE (LP)	12

ARTHUR MULLARD

74	BASF BA 1012	Not Now Arthur/If I Had My Time Again	7
67	Masquerade MA 5001	I Love You, You Love Me/Was It Something I said? (with Bill Shepherd Flock)	7

BRANKO MULLER

68	CBS 3955	Candy/Today Is Better Than Yesterday	12

MOON MULLICAN

(see also Boyd Bennett & His Rockets)

51	Vogue V 9013	Cherokee Boogie/Love Is The Light That Leads Me Home (78)	35
56	Parlophone DP 503	Yearning (Just For You)/Put Your Arms Around Me, Honey (export 78)	30
56	Parlophone DP 512	San Antonio Rose/Cedarwood Blues (export 78)	30
56	Parlophone MSP 6254	Seven Nights To Rock/Honolulu Rock-A Roll-A (with Boyd Bennett & His Rockets)	400
56	Parlophone R 4195	Seven Nights To Rock/Honolulu Rock-A Roll-A (with Boyd Bennett & His Rockets) (78)	50
59	Parlophone GEP 8794	COUNTRY ROUND UP (EP)	60
50s	Parlophone CGEP 13	MOON MULLICAN (EP, export issue)	40
50s	Parlophone CGEP 15	PIANO BREAKDOWN (EP, export issue, company sleeve)	40

GERRY MULLIGAN

(see also Gerry Mulligan, Chet Baker, Shelly Manne, Annie Ross)

53	Capitol LC 6621	THE GERRY MULLIGAN TENTETTE - ROCKER (10" LP)	15
53	Vogue LDE 029	THE GERRY MULLIGAN QUARTET VOL. 1 (10" LP)	15
53	Vogue LDE 030	THE GERRY MULLIGAN QUARTET VOL. 2 (10" LP)	15
53	Vogue LDE 031	THE GERRY MULLIGAN QUARTET VOL. 3 (10" LP)	15
54	Vogue LDE 075	THE GERRY MULLIGAN QUARTET (10" LP)	15
54	Vogue LDE 083	THE GERRY MULLIGAN QUARTET VOL. 4 (10" LP)	15
54	Esquire 20-032	GERRY MULLIGAN ALLSTARS - MULLIGAN'S TOO (10" LP)	15
55	Vogue LDE 156	GERRY MULLIGAN QUARTET WITH LEE KONITZ (10" LP)	15
56	Esquire 32-014	GERY MULLIGAN ALLSTARS (LP)	15
56	Vogue LAE 12006	THE GERRY MULLIGAN QUARTET (LP)	15
56	Vogue LAE 12015	THE GERRY MULLIGAN QUARTET (LP)	15
56	Emarcy EJL 101	PRESENTING THE GERRY MULLIGAN SEXTET (LP)	15
57	Emarcy EJL 1259	MAINSTREAM OF JAZZ (LP, by Gerry Mulligan Sextet)	15
58	Columbia Clef 33CX 10113	GERRY MULLIGAN AND PAUL DESMOND QUARTET (LP)	15
58	HMV CLP 1204	PHIL SUNKEL'S "JAZZ CONCERTO GROSSO" (LP, with Bob Brookmeyer)	15

			MINT VALUE £
59	Philips SBBL 552	WHAT IS THERE TO SAY? (LP, stereo)	15
59	Vogue SEA 5006	GERRY MULLIGAN SONGBOOK (LP, stereo)	15
59	Vogue SEA 5007	REUNION WITH CHET BAKER (LP, stereo, as Gerry Mulligan Quartet)	15
59	London Jazz LTZT 15161	I WANT TO LIVE (LP, with Shelly Manne)	12
60	HMV CLP 1373	GERRY MULLIGAN MEETS BEN WEBSTER (LP)	12
61	HMV CLP 1432	THE CONCERT JAZZ BAND (LP, also stereo CSD 1351)	12
61	Vocalion LAE 12268	THE GENIUS OF GERRY MULLIGAN (LP)	12
62	HMV CLP 1465	GERRY MULLIGAN MEETS JOHNNY HODGES (LP, also stereo CSD 1372)	12
62	HMV CLP 1488	AT THE VILLAGE VANGUARD (LP, also stereo CSD 1396)	12
62	Riverside RLP 12-247	MULLIGAN MEETS MONK (LP, with Thelonious Monk)	15
62	HMV CLP 1549	A CONCERT IN JAZZ (LP, also stereo CSD 1432)	12
62	HMV CLP 1585	ON TOUR (LP, with Zoot Sims)	12

MICK MULLIGAN'S JAZZ BAND

(see also George Melly)

50s	Saga STP 7020	YOUNG AND HEALTHY (EP)	10
55	Tempo EXA 25	MICK MULLIGAN'S JAZZ BAND (EP)	10
56	Tempo EXA 37	MICK MULLIGAN'S JAZZ BAND (EP)	10
56	Tempo EXA 41	GEORGE MELLY WITH MICK MULLIGAN'S JAZZ BAND (EP)	10
57	Tempo EXA 54	MICK MULLIGAN'S JAZZ BAND (EP)	10
58	Parlophone GEP 8750	MICK BLOWS (EP)	10
57	Tempo TAP 14	JAZZ AT THE RAILWAY ARMS (LP, with George Melly)	50
59	Pye Jazz NJL 21	MEET MICK MULLIGAN (LP)	20
59	Parlophone PMC 1103	THE SAINTS MEET THE SINNERS (LP, with George Melly & Saints Jazz Band)	15

MUM

01	TMT TMT04CD	MUM REMIXED (CD)	20
02	Fatcat FATLP 18	FINALLY WE ARE NO ONE (2 x 10")	35
07	Fat Cat FATLP46	GO GO SMEAR THE POISON IVY (LP, with bonus 7")	18

MUM & DAD

99	Twisted Nerve TN 006	Donington/13th Chime/Monster Truck (p/s)	8

GENE MUMFORD

58	Philips PB 862	More Than You Know/Please Give Me One More Chance	8

MUMFORD & SONS

08	Chess Club CC 006	LEND ME YOUR EYES EP (10", p/s)	30
08	Chess Club CC 009	LOVE YOUR GROUND EP (10", p/s)	30
09	Chess Club CC 015	The Cave/My Heart Told My Head (Winter Winds) (1-sided 10", gatefold p/s, 300 only)	40
09	Island 2720975	Little Lion Man/To Darkness (p/s)	5
09	V2 VVR 723601	SIGH NO MORE (LP)	20

MUMMY CALLS

83	MC 12	Mary i Swear/Unicorn Jones (P/S)	10

HUGH MUNDELL

(see also Ray Dorset, Good Earth, King Earl Boogie Band, Horizon, Made In England, Jigilo Jug Band, P. King, Paul King, P. Rufus King, Russian Roulette, First Impression, Good Earth)

78	Greensleeves GRE9	Let's All Unite/Unity Dub	15
79	Warrior WAR 131	Stop Them Jah/Push Dawta Push (12")	30
80	J&F 002	Jah Fire Will Be Burning/King Of Israel (12")	30
81	Greensleeves GRED 54	Can't Pop No Style/JUNIOR REID: Know Myself (12")	40
80	Live And Love LAP 13	JAH FIRE (LP, with Lacksley Castell and Augustus Pablo)	40
86	Message GREL 94	AFRICA MUST BE FREE BY 1983 (LP, reissue)	15

MUNGO JERRY

70	Dawn DNX 2502	In The Summertime/Mighty Man/Dust Pneumonia Blues (p/s)	5
70	Pye 7N 2502	In The Summertime/Mighty Man/Dust Pneumonia Blues (jukebox issue)	8
71	Dawn DNX 2505	Baby Jump/The Man Behind The Piano/Live From Hollywood: Maggie/ Midnight Special/Mighty Man (p/s)	5
71	Dawn DNX 2510	Lady Rose/Have A Whiff On Me/Milk Cow Blues/Little Louis (p/s, withdrawn)	5
71	Dawn DNX 2510	Lady Rose/She Rowed/Milk Cow Blues/Little Louis (re-pressing with different track, p/s)	5
83	Mach 1 MAGIC 008	There Goes My Heart Again/Thinking Of You (featuring Ray Dorset & Tarts)	5
85	Orbit TRIP 4	Sunshine Reggae/Nightlife (reissue of Horizon 45; as Mungo Jerry & Horizon)	6
87	Illegal MUNG 1	In The Summertime '87/Got A Job (as Mungo Jerry & Brothers Grimm, p/s)	5
96	Fan Club 12/1	Sugar In The Bowl/In The Summertime (fan club only, white label, autographed)	5
70	Dawn DNLS 3008	MUNGO JERRY (LP, gatefold sleeve, with 3-D glasses)	25
71	Dawn DNLS 3020	ELECTRONICALLY TESTED (LP, gatefold sleeve)	20
71	Dawn DNLS 3028	YOU DON'T HAVE TO BE IN THE ARMY (LP, gatefold sleeve, with lyric insert)	15
72	Dawn DNLS 3041	BOOT POWER (LP, with 'Dennis The Menace' or 'gun' gatefold sleeve)	15

RAY MUNNINGS

79	Tammi TAM 102	It Could Happen To You/Let's Boogie	30
79	Tammi TAM 103	Funky Nassau/Jump In The Water (12"0	60

CAROLINE MUNRO

(see also Gary Numan)

85	Numa NU 5	Pump Me Up/The Picture (p/s)	6
85	Numa NUM 5	Pump Me Up (Ext. 6.09)/The Picture/Pump Me Up (4.00 7" Version) (12", p/s)	10

CAROLINE MUNRO

67	Columbia DB 8189	Tar And Cement/The Sporting Life	10

HAL MUNRO

(see also Neville Taylor)

58	Embassy WB 284	Breathless/Wear My Ring Around Your Neck	6
59	Embassy WB 336	C'mon Everybody/It's Late	6
59	Embassy WB 340	Dream Lover/Where Were You	5
59	Embassy WB 386	You Got What It Takes/California Here I Come	5
60	Embassy WB 401	Good Timin'/I Wanna Go Home	5
60	Embassy WB 401	Good Timin'/I Wanna Go Home (78)	10

MINT VALUE £

JANET MUNRO & SEAN CONNERY

59	Top Rank JAR 163	Pretty Irish Girl/Ballamaquilty's Band	10
59	Top Rank JAR 163	Pretty Irish Girl/Ballamaquilty's Band (78)	10

ADRIAN MUNSEY

(see also Sparks)

79	Virgin VS 266	C'Est Sheep (Part 1)/C'Est Sheep (Part 2) (p/s)	6
79	Virgin VS 266-12	C'Est Sheep (Part 1)/C'Est Sheep (Part 2) (12", p/s)	8

STEPHAN MUNSON & FRIENDS

82	Rhythmic RMNS 2	And David Cried/And Dem Bahnhoff (fold-out photocopied p/s)	8

JERRY MURADS HARMONICATS

60	Philips PB 1105	Cherry Pink And Apple Blossom White/Lonely Love	6

MURDER INC.

(see also Business)

80	MIL MIL 1	SOUNDS SO FALSE (EP)	8

MURDER THE DISTURBED

79	Small Wonder	Walking Corpses The Ultimate System/Small Seventeen (P/S)	8

BILLY MURE (ORCHESTRA)

(see also Supersonics)

59	RCA RCX 158	SUPERSONICS IN FLIGHT (EP, mono)	8
59	RCA SRC 7032	SUPERSONICS IN FLIGHT (EP, stereo)	15
61	London HAR 2400	TOUGH STRINGS (LP)	15
64	MGM C976	FASCINATING SOUND OF THE AZTEC GUITARS (LP)	12

MURGATROYD BAND

(see also Spencer Davis Group, Ray Fenwick)

71	Decca F 12809	Magpie (Theme From The TV Series)/Twice A Week (p/s)	40
71	Decca F 13256	Magpie (Theme From The TV Series)/Twice A Week (with p/s)	25
71	Decca F 13256	Magpie (Theme From The TV Series)/Twice A Week (without p/s)	15

MURMAIDS

63	Stateside SS 247	Popsicles And Icicles/Comedy And Tragedy	20

MURMURS OF URMA

99	Dolly 002	Banoffe Boy Writing To A Friend/Super Vacillation Day Snails Into Fast Food (p/s)	8
97	Dolly 001	Coloured Rice/Magic Shop/Vacuum Cleaner/Cloudwatch HQ (P/S)	12

MICHAEL MURPHEY

72	Regal Zonophone RZ 3062	Boy From The Country/Geronimo's Cadillac	5
75	Epic EPC 3242	Wildfire/Night Thunder	6
73	EMI EMA 754	COSMIC COWBOY SOUVENIR (LP)	12

ARTHUR MURPHY

59	Parlophone R 4523	Sixteen Candles/Molly Malone	10

DELIA MURPHY

57	HMV 7EG 8295	DELIGHTFUL DELIA (EP)	8

ELLIOT MURPHY

74	Polydor 2391 100	AQUASHOW (LP)	12

KEITH MURPHY & THE DAZE

68	Polydor 56542	Slightly Reminiscent Of Her/Dirty Old Sam	35

LYLE MURPHY

58	Contemporary LAC 12135	GONE WITH THE WOODWINDS (LP)	12

MARK MURPHY

57	Brunswick 05701	Goodbye Baby Blues/The Right Kind Of Woman	6
58	Capitol CL 14962	Belong To Me/Don't Cry My Love	5
60	Capitol CL 15117	Send For Me/Come To Me	5
63	Riverside RIF 106905	Like Love/Fly Away My Sadness	5
63	Riverside RIF 106908	Fly Me To The Moon/Why Don't You Do Right	40
65	Fontana TF 572	High On Windy Hill/Broken Heart	5
67	Fontana TF 803	(Ain't That) Just Like A Woman/Do You Wonder If I Love You	5
69	Pye 7N 17661	Come Back To Me/Dear Heart	5
57	Brunswick LAT 8172	MEET MARK MURPHY (LP)	12
60	Capitol (S)T 5011	HIT PARADE (LP)	12
64	Fontana (S)TL 5217	MARK TIME! (LP)	12
66	Immediate IMLP/IMSP 004	WHO CAN I TURN TO (LP)	30

NOEL MURPHY

67	Fontana TL 5450	NYA-A-A-H! (LP)	15
73	Village Thing VTS 25	MURF (LP)	15
78	RCA PE 5090	THE BRICKLAYERS SONG (EP)	8

ROSE MURPHY

52	Oriole/Mercury MG 10004	SONGS BY ROSE MURPHY (10" LP)	20

ALEX MURRAY

(see also Most Brothers)

60	Decca F 11203	Teen Angel/Paper Doll	10
60	Decca F 11225	All On My Own/String Along	7
61	Decca F 11345	When You Walked Out/Send For Me	7

LADY MURRAY

(see also Grazina, Mr & Mrs Murray)

66	Clan 597 002	Mister Abercrombie Taught Me/In My Imagination	10

MARTIN MURRAY

66	Pye 7N 17070	I Know What I Want/Goodbye Baby	10

MINT VALUE £

MICKEY MURRAY

67	Polydor 56738	Shout Bama Lama/Lonely Room	10

MISTER MURRAY

(see also Mitch Murray Clan, Mr & Mrs Murray)

65	Fontana TF 623	Down Came The Rain/Whatever Happened To Music?	8
66	Fontana TF 674	I Drink To Your Memory/I Was A Good Song	6

MITCH MURRAY CLAN

66	Clan 597 001	Skyliner/Cherokee	15

MR & MRS MURRAY

(see also Mitch Murray Clan, Lady Murray, Grazina, Mister Murray)

68	CBS 3633	You're Outa Your Mind/A Little Bit Of You	6

RUBY MURRAY

(see also Norman Wisdom & Ruby Murray, Ray Burns, Ronnie Harris, Diana Decker)

55	Columbia SCM 5162	Softly, Softly/What Could Be More Beautiful	20
55	Columbia SCM 5165	Spring, Spring, Spring/Goin' Co'tin (with Ray Burns, Diana Decker & Ronnie Harris)	8
55	Columbia SCM 5169	If Anyone Finds This, I Love You (with Anne Warren)/Before We Know It	10
56	Columbia SEG 7620	EVERYBODY'S SWEETHEART NO 1 (EP)	10
56	Columbia SEG 7631	EVEFYBODY'S SWEETHEART NO 2 (EP)	10
56	Columbia SEG 7636	EVERYBODY'S SWEETHEART NO 3 (EP)	10
58	Columbia SEG 7952	MACUSHLA MINE (EP)	10
60	Columbia ESG 7330/SEG 8502	LOVES OLD SWEET SONG (EP)	12
58	Columbia 33S 1135	ENDEARING YOUNG CHARMS (10" LP)	12
60	Columbia 33SX 1201	RUBY (LP, mono)	22
60	Columbia SCX 3289	RUBY (LP, stereo)	25
62	Columbia 33SX 1402	IRISH AND PROUD OF IT (LP)	12

JOHN MURTAUGH

70	Polydor 2482 015	BLUES CURRENT (LP)	20

JUNIOR MURVIN

(see under Junio Murvin)

MUSE

99	Mushroom MUSH 50S	Uno/Agitated (p/s, clear vinyl)	50
99	Mushroom MUSE 1	Uno/Jimmy Kane/Forced In/Agitated (minimax CD, with slipcase)	10
99	Mushroom MUSH 50CDS	Uno/Jimmy Kane/Forced In (CD)	6
99	Mushroom MUSH 58 CDS	Cave/Twin/Cave (Remix) (CD, part 1 of 2-CD set)	8
99	Mushroom MUSH 58 CDX	Cave/Host/Coma (CD, part 2 of 2-CD set)	8
99	Mushroom MUSH 58S	Cave/Cave (Instrumental Remix) (clear vinyl, p/s)	35
99	Mushroom MUSH 66S	Muscle Museum/Escape (p/s)	20
99	Mushroom MUSH 66S	Muscle Museum/Minimum (clear vinyl, autographed p/s, 1000 only)	50
99	Mushroom MUSH 68S	Sunburn/(Live Acoustic Version) (stickered p/s, clear vinyl)	15
00	Mushroom MUSH 72S	Unintended/Sober (p/s, clear vinyl)	20
00	Mushroom MUSH 84S	Muscle Museum/Sober (The Saint Remix) (p/s)	12
01	Mushroom MUSH 89S	Plug In Baby/Nature 1 (p/s)	30
01	Mushroom MUSH 92S	New Born/Shrinking Universe (p/s, limited issue)	20
01	Mushroom MUSH 92T	New Born/Sunburn (Timo Maas Sunstroke Remix)/(Breakz Again Mix (12", p/s)	8
01	Mushroom MUSH 96S	Bliss/Hyper Chondriac Music (p/s)	15
01	Mushroom MUSH 96S	Bliss/The Gallery (p/s)	15
01	Mushroom MUSH 97S	Hyper Music/Feeling Good (p/s)	30
01	Mushroom MUSH 104S	Dead Star/In Your World (p/s)	15
03	East West EW 272	Time is Running Out/The Groove (clear vinyl, p/s)	15
03	East West EW 278	Hysteria/Eternally missed (p/s)	10
04	East West EW 285	Sing For Absolution/Fury (p/s, clear vinyl)	8
04	Atlantic ATUK 003	Butterflies And Hurricanes/Butterflies And Hurricanes (Glastonbury 2004) (p/s, clear vinyl)	8
06	Warner Brothers HEL 3001	Supermassive Black Hole/Crying Shame (picture disc, stickered PVC sleeve)	6
06	Warner Brothers HEL 3003	Starlight/Supermassive Black Hole (Remix) (picture disc, stickered)	10
06	A & E HEL 3004	Knights of Cydonia/Assassion (picture disc, stickered)	20
07	Warner Brothers HEL3005	Invincible/Glorious (picture disc, stickered)	10
98	Dangerous DREX CDEP 103	MUSE EP (CD, 999 copies, numbered sticker)	175
98	Dangerous DREX CDEP 104	MUSCLE MUSEUM EP: Sober/Uno/Unintended/Instant Messenger/Muscle Museum # 2/Muscle Museum (CD, 999 copies, numbered sticker)	175
00	Mushroom MUSH 59LP	SHOWBIZ (2-LP, clear vinyl, gatefold sleeve, with inners, numbered)	150
01	Mushroom MUSH 93LP	ORIGIN OF SYMMETRY (2-LP, gatefold sleeve, with lyric inner sleeves, 1500 only)	70
01	Mushroom MUSE 14	ORIGIN OF SYMMETRY (CD promo, clear Perspex bolted case)	20
03	East West 5046 68587-1	ABSOLUTION (double LP, gatefold sleeve)	30

MUSHROOM

(see also Joe O'Donnell)

73	Hawk HASP 320	Devil Among The Tailors/Sun Ni Dhuibir/King Of Ireland's Daughter	25
74	Hawk HASP 340	Kings And Queens/Met A Friend	25
73	Hawk HALPX 116	EARLY ONE MORNING (LP, with poster inner)	600
73	Hawk HALPX 116	EARLY ONE MORNING (LP, without poster inner)	350

(THE) MUSIC

01	Fierce Panda NING 107	Take The Long Road And Walk It/The Walls Get Smaller (p/s, 1,000 only)	10
01	Fierce Panda NINGT 107	Take The Long Road And Walk It/The Walls Get Smaller (12", p/s, 250 only)	25
01	Hut HUTT 145	THE MUSIC EP: You Might As Well Try To Fuck Me/Karma/Treat Me Right On/Too High (12", p/s, with inner)	8

MUSIC BOX

72	Westwood MRS 013	SONGS OF SUNSHINE (LP)	110

MINT VALUE £

MUSIC DOCTORS

(see also Dennis Lowe, Audrey, Desmond Riley, Megatons, Prince Of Darkness, Gene Rondo)

69	Downtown DT 447	Music Doctor (Parts 1 & 2)	20
70	J-Dan JDN 4402	Electric Shock/KING DENNIS: Black Robin	8
70	J-Dan JDN 4403	Bush Doctor/Lick Your Stick	15
70	J-Dan JDN 4411	The Wild Bunch/ISRAELITES: Born To Be Strong	12
70	J-Dan JDN 4414	In The Summertime/Foundation Track	10
70	J-Dan JDN 4417	Discretion Version/Doctor Dan, Boy Friday And Friend	10
70	Trojan TBL 117	REGGAE IN THE SUMMERTIME (LP)	25

MUSIC EMPORIUM

83	Psycho PSYCHO 11	MUSIC EMPORIUM (LP)	15

MUSIC EXPLOSION

67	Stateside SS 2028	A Little Bit O' Soul/I See The Light	25
67	Stateside SS 2054	Sunshine Games/Can't Stop Now	20
67	Philips BF 1547	Little Black Egg/Stay By My Side	7
69	London HLP 10272	A Little Bit O' Soul/Everybody	8
67	London HA-P/SH-P 8352	A LITTLE BIT O' SOUL (LP)	45

MUSIC MACHINE

67	Pye International 7N 25407	Talk Talk/Come On In	50
67	Pye International 7N 25414	The People In Me/Masculine Intuition	60

MUSIC MOTOR

70	Deram DM 282	Happy/Where Am I Going?	20

MUSIC SPECIALISTS

70	London HLJ 10309	Dynamic Pressure/Flip	7

MUSIC TAPES

98	Earworm WORM 32	The Television Tells Us/Freeing Song By Reindeer (p/s, pop-up sleeve with 2 inserts, 1,500 copies only)	5

MUSIC THROUGH SIX

(see also Jason Sims & Music Through Six)

68	Domain D3	Riff Raff/ROY DOCKER: Mellow Moonlight	20

MUSICAL THEATRE

70	Pye Intl. NSPL 28128	A REVOLUTIONARY REVELATION (LP)	12

MUSICIANS

66	King KG 1055	Jaunty Joe/The Chelsea Set	7

MUSICOLOGY

91	B12 B1201	Musicology (12")	40
91	B12 B1201	Musicology (12", clear vinyl)	100
92	B12 B1204	Outlook (12")	40
92	B12 B1206	Hall Of Mirrors (12")	15
92	B12 B1206	Hall Of Mirrors (12" Ltd, yellow vinyl)	40

MUSIQUE CONCRET

81	United Dairies UD 010	BRINGING UP BABY (LP, blue vinyl, 100 only)	100
81	United Dairies UD 010	BRINGING UP BABY (LP, black vinyl, 400 only)	70
87	United Dairies UDT 10	BRINGING UP BABY (cassette)	35

MUSKETEER GRIPWEED & THIRD TROOP

(see also John Lennon)

66	United Artists UP 1196	How I Won The War/Aftermath	150
66	United Artists UP 1196	How I Won The War/Aftermath (demo copy)	100

MUSKETEERS

69	Philips BF 1773	Fight/Magnifico	6

MUSKYTEERS

69	Upsetter US 309	Endlessly/Kidd-O	35

CHARLIE MUSSELWHITE BLUES BAND

69	Vanguard SVRL 19012	STONE BLUES (LP)	22

MUSTANG

67	Parlophone R 5579	Why/Here, There And Everywhere	25

MUSTARD

74	EMI EMI 2165	Good Time Comin'/I Saw I Heard	25

MUS-TWANGS

61	Mercury AMT 1140	Roch Lomond/Marie	12

MUTANT ROCKERS/CITY LIMITS

84	Survival SUR12 028	Keep It On (12")	15

MUTANTS

77	Rox ROX 002	Boss Man/Back Yard Boys (p/s)	6
78	Rox ROX 005	School Teacher/Hard Time/Lady (p/s, red vinyl)	6

MUTE DRIVERS

(see also Anonymes)

80s	Mute Drivers MD 001	MUTE DRIVERS (LP, with insert in handmade painted sleeve, 300 only)	15

MUTT 'N' JEFF

66	Decca F 12335	Don't Nag Me Ma/Strolling The Blues	12

Mμ-ZIQ

(see also Rude Ass Tinker)

93	Rephlex CAT 018	Bluff Limbo (Remixes) (2 x 12", 800 only)	40

MVP'S

71	Buddah BDS 469	Turnin' My Heartbeat Up/Every Man For Herself	20

MINT VALUE £

MY BLOODY VALENTINE

(see also Primal Scream, Collapsed Lung, Snowpony, Dinosaur Jr.)

86	Fever FEV 5X	No Place To Go/Moonlight (p/s)	100
86	Fever FEV 5	GEEK! (12" EP)	40
86	Kaleid. Sound KS 101	THE NEW RECORD BY MY BLOODY VALENTINE (12" EP)	60
87	Lazy LAZY 04	Sunny Sundae Smile/Paint A Rainbow (p/s)	30
87	Lazy LAZY 04T	Sunny Sundae Smile/Paint A Rainbow/Kiss The Eclipse/ Sylvie's Head (12", p/s)	50
87	Lazy LAZY 07	Strawberry Wine/Never Say Goodbye/Can I Touch You (12", p/s)	60
88	Creation CRE 055	You Made Me Realise/Slow (die-cut company sleeve)	8
88	Creation CRE 055T	You Made Me Realise/Slow/Thorn/Cigarette/Drive It All Over Me (12", p/s)	25
88	Creation CRE 061	Feed Me With Your Kiss/Emptiness Inside (plays "I Believe") (die-cut company sleeve)	20
88	Creation CRE 061T	Feed Me With Your Kiss/I Believe/Emptiness Inside/I Need No Trust (12", p/s)	25
98	Creation CRESCD061	Feed Me With Your Kisses/I Believe/Emptiness Inside/ I Need No Trust (CD single)	12
89	Creation CRE 085	Tremolo/To Hear Knows When (p/s)	10
89	Creation CRE 085T	Tremolo/To Hear Knows When (12", p/s)	20
89	Creation CRECD 085	Tremolo/To Hear Knows When (CD)	10
89	Lyntone CAT 067	Sugar/PACIFIC: December, With The Day (square flexidisc free with The Catalogue magazine, issue 67)	10
90	Creation CRE 073	Soon/Glider (p/s)	12
90	Creation CRE 073T	GLIDER EP (12", p/s)	20
90	Creation CRE 073T	GLIDER EP (12", remixed by Andy Weatherall, stickered die-cut sleeve)	25
87	Lazy LAZY 08	ECSTACY (mini-LP, 3,000 only)	70
88	Creation CRELP 040	ISN'T ANYTHING (LP, initial 3,000 copies with bonus 7", "Instrumental"/ Instrumental [CRE FRE 4, no p/s] & stickered sleeve)	45
88	Creation CRELP 040	ISN'T ANYTHING (LP, without bonus 7")	20
89	Lazy LAZY 12	ECSTACY & WINE (LP, compilation of LAZY 07 & LAZY 08)	50
89	Lazy LAZY 12CD	ECSTACY & WINE (CD)	40
91	Creation CRELP 060	LOVELESS (LP)	30

MY CAPTAINS

81	4AD AD 103	Fall/Converse/History/Nothing (EP)	8

MY CHEMICAL ROMANCE

03	20:20 TWENTY 7S 003	Honey, This Mirror Isn't Big Enough For The Two Of Us/ This Is The Best Day Ever (p/s)	50
04	20:20 TWENTY 7S 004	Headfirst For Halos/Our Lady Of Sorrows (Live) (p/s)	40
04	20:20 TWENTY CDS 004	Headfirst For Halos/Our Lady Of Sorrows (Live) (CD)	15
04	Reprise W 661	Thank You For The Venom/Jack The Ripper (Live) (red vinyl, p/s)	40
05	Reprise W 666	I'm Not Okay (I Promise)/Bury Me In Black (Demo) (red vinyl, p/s)	5
05	Reprise W 671	Helena/I'm Not Okay (I Promise) (Live AOL Session) (picture disc)	5
05	Reprise W 683	The Ghost In You/Helena (live) (picture disc)	5

TIM MYCROFT

71	Parlophone R5919	Shadra/Bournemouth Rock	15

MY DEAR WATSON

(see also Johnny & Copycats)

68	Parlophone R 5687	Elusive Face/The Shame Just Drained	30
68	Parlophone R 5737	Make This Day Last/Stop, Stop, I'll Be There	30
70	DJM DJS 224	Have You Seen Your Saviour/White Line Road	10

MY DYING BRIDE

90	private pressing	Towards The Sinister EP (4 track demo cassette)	40
92	Peaceville VILE 27	Symphonaire Infernus Et Spera Empyrium Act 1/ Symphonaire Infernus Et Spera Empyrium Act 2 (12", p/s)	25
92	Peaceville VILE 27	Symphonaire Infernus Et Spera Empyrium/God Is Alone/ De Sade Soliloquay (CD)	15
93	Peaceville VILE 37T	The Thrash Of Naked Limbs/Le Cerf Malade/Gather Me Up Forever (12", p/s)	25
93	Unbridled Voyage (no cat no)	Unreleased Bitterness: The Bitterness And The Bereavement (1-sided flexidisc, fold-out p/s in poly sleeve, 1150 only)	20
93	Peaceville VILE 44T	I Am The Bloody Earth/Transcending (Into The Exquisite) (12", p/s)	20
93	Peaceville VILE 44	I Am The Bloody Earth/Transcending (Into The Exquisite)/ Crown Of Sympathy (Remix) (CD)	12
94	Peaceville CC5	Sexuality Of Bereavement/Crown Of Sympathy (Remix) (p/s)	25
92	Peaceville	AS THE FLOWER WITHERS (LP, gatefold sleeve)	15
93	Peaceville VILE 39	TURN LOOSE THE SWANS (LP, double)	35
94	Peaceville VILE 45	THE STORIES EP (box set, 1000 only)	75
95	Peaceville VILE 50	THE ANGEL AND THE DARK RIVER (LP, picture disc)	15

AMINA CLAUDINE MYERS

80	Leo LR 100	SONG FOR MOTHER E (LP)	20
80	Leo LR 103	AMINA CLAUDINE MYERS SALUTES BESSIE SMITH (LP)	45

ROWLAND MYERS

75	MSE MSE 2SSP/P	Give Them A Hand/Pandemonium	30

MY FRIENDS AND I

69	Marroo MR 001	Susan/Wake The Dead	40

MY KIND OF PEOPLE

70	CBS 555133	Somebodys Coming/Nobody Knows Why The Butterfly Died	25

BILLY MYLES

57	HMV POP 423	The Joker (That's What They Call Me)/Honey Bee	60
57	HMV POP 423	The Joker (That's What They Call Me)/Honey Bee (78)	15

MINT VALUE £

MEG MYLES
56 Capitol CL 14555 — Sing On, Baby/Will You Shed A Tear For Me? 7

MY LIFE STORY
86 Think Tank CHAPTER 1 — HOME SWEET ZOO EP (gatefold p/s, 500 only) 40

MY LORDE SHERIFFE'S COMPLAINTE
79 Frog FROG 1 — MY LORDE SHERIFFE'S COMPLAINTE (LP, private pressing) 15

MYND MUZIC
94 Poor Person Prod. — IMAGINE THIS (LP, handmade sleeve, 500 only) 20

ROWLAND MYRES
75 MSE MSE 2SSP/P — Give Them A Hand/Pandemonium 30
74 Deroy DER 1063 — JUST FOR THE RECORD (LP, private pressing, also listed as Music Sound Enterprise MSE 1) 120

MYRTELLES
(see also Sue & Sunshine, Sue & Sunny, Stockingtops)
63 Oriole CB 1805 — Don't Wanna Cry Again/Just Let Me Cry 40

MYSTERE FIVE'S
(see also Wayne County & Electric Chairs)
80 Flicknife FLS 001 — No Message/Shake Some Action (p/s) 5
81 Flicknife FLS 202 — Never Say Thank You/Heart Rules The Head (p/s) 5

MYSTERIES
64 Decca F 11919 — Give Me Rhythm And Blues/Teardrops 30

WILLIAM MYSTERIOUS
(see also Rezillos, Revillos)
82 Mezzanine MEZ 1 — Security Of Noise/Alright (p/s, with Fay Fife & Revettes) 6

MYSTERY GIRLS
81 Strange HAM 002 — I'm A Believer/Modern Mystery Pop/Walking Backwards (p/s) 6

MYSTERY GUESTS
80 Boys Own/Heater Volume BO 1 — Wurlitzer Junction/The Merry Shark You Are (hand-made stickered white labels) 6
81 Boys Own BO 3 — The Sparrow That Ate New York/The Nude (p/s) 5

MYSTERY MAKER
77 Caves UHC 3 — MYSTERY MAKER (LP, private pressing with booklet) 120

MYSTIC EMP
80 His Majesty HMD 006 — Reality/JAH THOMAS: Throw Away Vanity/ MYSTIC EMP & JAH THOMAS: Reality Dub (12") 20

MYSTIC EYES
79 Greensleeves GRED 11 — Perilous Times (with Trinity)/REVOLUTIONARIES: Roots Man Version (12") 30
79 Warrior WAR 135 — Elaine/MIKEY DREAD: Schoolgirls (12") 25
78 Burning Sounds BS 1033 — MYSTERIOUS (LP) 45

MYSTIC INSTITUTE
(see also Global Communications, Reload, Link)
92 Evolution EVO 06 — CYBERDON EP (12") 18

MYSTIC MATT & THE ANTHILL MOB
(see also Anthill Mob)
99 Love Peace & Unity LOVE 05 — A SHOCK 2 DA SYSTEM EP (12", p/s) 25

MYSTIC MOODS
73 Warner Bros K 16265 — Cosmic Sea/Awakening 7
74 Warner Bros K 46250 — AWAKENING (LP) 15

MYSTIC NUMBER NATIONAL BANK
69 Probe SPB 1001 — THE MYSTIC NUMBER NATIONAL BANK (LP) 25

MYSTICS
59 HMV POP 646 — Hushabye/Adam And Eve 30
59 Top Rank JAR 243 — Don't Take The Stars/So Tenderly 40

MYSTICS (Jamaica)
75 Grounation GRO 2049 — God Bless The Youths/Dub 5

MYSTREATED
97 Detour DR 054 — (What's In) Your Mind Today/I'll Be There (P/S) 12

MYSTRO
00 Deal Real DR001 — Kiss That Arse Goodnight/The Word's Out (12") 10
01 Camshot CSR002 — Open Mic/Keep Smiling/The Burial 99 (EP) 10

MYTHRA
79 Guardian GRMA 16 — DEATH & DESTINY: Death And Destiny/Killer/Overload/UFO (EP, no p/s) 12
80 Streetbeat LAMP 2 — Death Or Destiny/Killer/U.F.O. (with p/s) 90
80 Streetbeat LAMP 2 — Death Or Destiny/Killer/U.F.O. 10
80 Streetbeat 12 LAMP 2 — Death Or Destiny/Killer/Overlord/U.F.O. (12", with p/s) 125
80 Streetbeat 12 LAMP 2 — Death Or Destiny/Killer/Overlord/U.F.O. (12") 20

M ZONE & DJ GOLLUM
(see also DJ Gollum)
97 UK44 UK44 EP3 — Harmony (Get Me)/Harmony (12") 12

MINT VALUE £

NABAY

Year	Label/Cat No.	Title	Value £
80	Grapevine GRP 143	Believe It Or Not/Believe It Or Not (Instrumental)	25

RICKY NADIR

(see also Peter Hammill)

Year	Label/Cat No.	Title	Value £
75	Charisma CB 345	Birthday Special/Shingle Song	8
79	Charisma CB 339	The Polaroid/PETER HAMMILL: The Old School Tie	10

NA FILI

Year	Label/Cat No.	Title	Value £
74	Dolphin DOL 1008	CHANTER'S TUNE (LP)	12

NA H-ORGANAICH

Year	Label/Cat No.	Title	Value £
73	Beltona SBE 145	THE GREAT GAELIC SOUND OF (LP)	15
74	Beltona SBE 160	GAEL FORCE 3 (LP)	15

NAKED LUNCH

Year	Label/Cat No.	Title	Value £
81	Ramkup CAC 003	Rabies/Slipping Again (p/s)	7

NAKED TRUTH

Year	Label/Cat No.	Title	Value £
70	Deram DM 287	Two Little Rooms/Rag Doll Boy	7

NAME

Year	Label/Cat No.	Title	Value £
80	Din Disc DIN 14	Forget Art, Let's Dance/Misfits (p/s)	10
87	China WOK 15	Jesus And The Devil/The Great Depression (P/S)	8

NAMES

Year	Label/Cat No.	Title	Value £
80	Factory FAC 29	Nightshift/I Wish I Could Speak Your Language (p/s)	5

ZBIGNIEW NAMYSLOWSKI MODERN JAZZ QUARTET

Year	Label/Cat No.	Title	Value £
64	Decca LK/SKL 4644	LOLA (LP)	150

NANETTE

Year	Label/Cat No.	Title	Value £
70	Columbia DB 8659	Flying Machine/You're Wasting Your Time	35
70	Columbia DB 8673	Every Night When I Cry Myself To Sleep/Jamie	10
70	Columbia DB 8733	Let Me Be The One/To Be Loved	10
71	Columbia DB 8751	Everybody's Singing Right Now/Could I Forget	10
70	Columbia SCX 6398	NANETTE (LP)	30

ED NANGLE

Year	Label/Cat No.	Title	Value £
68	Blue Cat BS 120	Good Girl/ENFORCERS: Musical Fever	30
68	Coxsone CS 7038	Whipping The Prince (actually by Ed Nangle & Alton Ellis & Soul Vendors)/ HEPTONES: If You Knew	30

NICK NANTOS & HIS FIREBALLERS

(see also Bill Haley & Comets)

Year	Label/Cat No.	Title	Value £
63	Summit LSE 2042	GUITARS ON FIRE (EP)	15
64	Summit ATL 4114	GUITARS ON FIRE (LP)	15

NAOMI

(see also Derrick Morgan, Tommy McCook)

Year	Label/Cat No.	Title	Value £
70	Gayfeet GS 207	You're Not My Kind/GAYTONES: You're Not My Kind (Version II)	10
70	High Note HS 047	Natural Woman/GAYTONES: Natural Woman - Version	10

NAPALM DEATH

Year	Label/Cat No.	Title	Value £
89	Rise Above RISE 001	NAPALM DEATH EP (poster p/s, sold at gigs)	10
89	Earache 7MOSH 14	Mentally Murdered/Cause And Effect (stickered p/s)	5
89	Earache MOSH 014	MENTALLY MURDERED EP (Rise Above/The Missing Link/Mentally Murdered Walls Of Confinement/Cause And Effect/No Mental Effort) (12", p/s)	12
90	Earache 7MOSH 24L	Suffer The Children/The Kill/Scum/Extremity Retained/Life? (stickered p/s, sticker sheet)	8
90	Earache MOSH 024	Suffer The Children/Siege Of Power/Harmony Corruption (12", p/s)	10
91	Earache 7MOSH 46	Mass Appeal Madness/Pride Assassin (p/s)	6
91	Earache MOSH 046	Mass Appeal Madness/Pride Assassin/Unchallenged Hate/ Social Sterility (12", p/s)	10
92	Earache MOSH 65	THE WORLD KEEPS TURNING EP (12", p/s)	12
92	Earache MOSH 065CD	The World Keeps Turning/A Means To An End/Insanity Excursion (CD)	10
93	Earache 7MOSH 92	Nazi Punks Fuck Off/Aryanisms/Nazi Punks Fuck Off (Live)/Contemptuous (Xtreem Mix) (p/s)	8
95	Earache MOSH 146	GREED KILLING EP (Greed Kiling/My Own Worst Enemy/Self Betrayal/ Finer Truths White Lies/Antibody/All Links Severed/Plague Rages [Live]) (10", p/s)	10
97	Strange Fruit SFPS 049	THE PEEL SESSIONS (12", p/s)	10
87	Earache MOSH 3	SCUM (LP, lyric insert, black/orange, black/green, black red orblack/yellow cover)	15
88	Earache MOSH 8	FROM ENSLAVEMENT TO OBLITERATION (LP, gatefold sleeve, free 7" EP [7MOSH 8])	30
90	Earache MOSH 19/19L	HARMONY CORRUPTION (2-LP, with inserts)	25
90	Earache MOSH 19P	HARMONY CORRUPTION (LP, picture disc)	20
91	Earache MOSH 3	SCUM (LP, reissue, white and black swirl vinyl, black and gold sleeve, 2000 only)	15
91	Earache MOSH 51	DEATH BY MANIPULATION (LP, with insert)	12
92	Earache MOSH 53	UTOPIA BANISHED (LP, free 7" EP [MOSH 53L])	25
92	Earache MOSH8/19/51/67L	BOX SET (4-CD)	25
06	Earache MOSH 003PD	SCUM (LP, 2nd reissue, picture disc, stickered PVC sleeve, 1500 only)	15

MINT VALUE £

NAPOLEON XIV
(see also Jerry Samuels, Kim Fowley)
66 Warner Bros WB 5831 They're Coming To Take Me Away Ha-Haa!/
!Aah-Ah Yawa Em Ekat Ot Gnimoc Er'Yeht 5
66 Warner Bros WB 5853 I'm In Love With My Little Red Tricycle/Doin' The Napoleon 12
66 Warner Bros W 1661 THEY'RE COMING TO TAKE ME AWAY HA-HA-A! (LP) 60

RAYMOND NAPTALI AND ROY RANKING
81 KG Imperial KG 006 New Cross Fire/Brixton Incident (12", blue vinyl) 15

PETER NARDINI
80s Kettle KS 701 I Think You're Great/Ma Maw's A Mod (in p/s) 15
80s Kettle KS 701 I Think You're Great/Ma Maw's A Mod 8

NARNIA
(see also After The Fire, Pauline Filby)
74 Myrrh MYR 1007 NARNIA - ASLAN IS NOT A TAME LION (LP) 80

BILLY NASH
61 Philips PB 1181 Sunset/Nobody Loves Me Like You (as Billy Nash Combo) 7
63 Philips 370 406 BF The Madison Step/Madison Rhythm (as Billy Nash Rock Band) 7

GENE NASH
59 Capitol CL 15042 I'm An Eskimo Too/Ja, Ja, Ja (Deutsche Rock 'N Roll) 25

GRAHAM NASH
(see also Hollies, Crosby Stills Nash & Young)
71 Atlantic 2091 096 Chicago/Simple Man 6
71 Atlantic 2091 135 Military Madness/I Used To Be A King 6
71 Atlantic 2401 011 SONGS FOR BEGINNERS (LP) 18

JOHNNY NASH
57 HMV POP 402 Ladder Of Love/I'll Walk Alone 10
57 HMV POP 402 Ladder Of Love/I'll Walk Alone (78) 12
58 HMV POP 435 Won't You Let Me Share My Love With You?/A Very Special Love 10
58 HMV POP 435 Won't You Let Me Share My Love With You?/A Very Special Love (78) 10
58 HMV POP 475 It's Easy To Say/My Pledge To You 10
58 HMV POP 475 It's Easy To Say/My Pledge To You (78) 10
58 HMV POP 553 Almost In Your Arms/Midnight Moonlight 7
58 HMV POP 553 Almost In Your Arms/Midnight Moonlight (78) 12
59 HMV POP 597 Walk With Faith In Your Heart/Roots Of Heaven 7
59 HMV POP 597 Walk With Faith In Your Heart/Roots Of Heaven (78) 15
59 HMV POP 620 As Time Goes By/Voice Of Love 7
59 HMV POP 651 And The Angels Sing/Baby, Baby, Baby 7
59 HMV POP 673 Take A Giant Step/Imagination 6
60 HMV POP 746 A Place In The Sun/Goodbye 6
60 HMV POP 822 Somebody/Kisses 6
62 Warner Bros WB 65 Don't Take Away Your Love/Moment Of Weakness 20
62 Warner Bros WB 76 Ol' Man River/My Dear Little Sweetheart 30
63 Warner Bros WB 93 Cigareets, Whuskey And Wild, Wild Women/I'm Moving On 15
64 Pye International 7N 25250 Love Ain't Nothin'/Talk To Me 60
65 Chess CRS 8005 Strange Feelin'/Rainin' In My Heart 25
66 Pye International 7N 25353 Let's Move And Groove (Together)/Understanding 20
66 Pye International 7N 25363 One More Time/Tryin' To Find Her 20
68 Regal Zono. RZ 3010 Hold Me Tight/Let's Move And Groove Together 10
68 Major Minor MM 586 You've Got Soul/Don't Cry 7
68 Major Minor MM 603 Cupid/People In Love 7
69 MGM MGM 1480 (I'm So) Glad You're My Baby/Stormy 30
71 MAM MAM R 9 Falling In And Out Of Love/People In Love 7
64 RCA Victor RCX 7163 PRESENTING JOHNNY NASH (EP) 150
59 HMV CLP 1251 JOHNNY NASH (LP) 40
59 HMV CLP 1299 QUIET HOUR WITH JOHNNY NASH (LP) 25
60 HMV CLP 1325 I GOT RHYTHM (LP, mono) 35
60 HMV CSD 1288 I GOT RHYTHM (LP, stereo) 45
62 Encore ENC 2005 LET'S GET LOST (LP) 15
69 Major Minor MML/SMLP 47 YOU GOT SOUL (LP) 15
69 Major Minor MML/SMLP 56 SOUL FOLK (LP) 15
69 Major Minor MML/SMLP 63 PRINCE OF PEACE (LP) 15

JOHNNY NASH & KIM WESTON
(see also Kim Weston)
69 Major Minor SMLP 54 JOHNNY NASH AND KIM WESTON (LP) 20

KATE NASH
07 Moshi Moshi MOMO 4 Caroline's A Victim/Birds 12

NASH THE SLASH
81 Dindisc DIN 28 Dead Man's Curve/Reactor No. 2 (p/s) 10

TONY NASH
70 Hot Rod HR 110 Keep On Trying/WINSTON JAMES: Just Can't Do Without Your Love 12

NASHVILLE FIVE
62 Decca F 11427 Stand Up And Say That/Like Nashville 7
62 Decca F 11484 Some Other Love/Brainwave 7
62 Decca DFE 6706 LIKE NASHVILLE (EP) 40

NASHVILLE TEENS
(see also Arizona Swamp Company, Jerry Lee Lewis, Carl Perkins)
64 Decca F 11930 Tobacco Road/I Like It Like That 10
64 Decca F 12000 Google Eye (some misspelled "Goggle Eye" on label)/T.N.T. 8
65 Decca F 12089 Find My Way Back Home/Devil-In-Law 8
65 Decca F 12143 This Little Bird/Whatcha Gonna Do? 8

MINT VALUE £

65	Decca F 12255	I Know How It Feels To Be Loved/Soon Forgotten	8
66	Decca F 12316	The Hard Way/Upside Down	15
66	Decca F 12458	Forbidden Fruit/Revived 45 Time	20
66	Decca F 12542	That's My Woman/Words	18
67	Decca F 12580	I'm Coming Home/Searching	10
67	Decca F 12657	The Biggest Night Of Her Life/Last Minute	10
68	Decca F 12754	All Along The Watchtower/Sun-Dog	10
69	Major Minor MM 599	The Lament Of The Cherokee Reservation Indian/Looking For You	18
69	Decca F 12929	Tobacco Road/All Along The Watchtower	6
71	Parlophone R 5925	Ella James/Tennessee Woman	15
72	Parlophone R 5961	You Shouldn't Have Been So Nice/Tell The People (unissued)	0
73	Enterprise ENT S101	Lawdy Miss Clawdy/Rocking On The Railroad/Let It Rock	7
77	Sky 1007	Tobacco Road/Chips And Peas	5
65	Decca DFE 8600	THE NASHVILLE TEENS (EP)	60
75	New World NW 6002	THE NASHVILLE TEENS (LP)	40

NASTY HABIT

92	Reinforced RIVET 1233	As Nasty As I Wanna Be (12")	25
92	Reinforced RIVET 1233R	As Nasty As I Wanna Be (Remixes) (12")	25

NASTY MEDIA

78	Lightning GIL 542	Spiked Copy/Winter (p/s)	20

NATCHBAND

78	Far In FARS 01	Cadillac (Made In USA)/Being From The Sky (p/s)	6

BARRY NATHAN TRIO

80	EMAL BNT 1	MORNING SONGRISE (LP)	50

NATIONAL-ELLS

67	Parlophone R 5609	Mr. Moon/Dance, Dance	7

NATIONAL HEAD BAND

(see also Caravan, Gary Moore, Toe-Fat, Uriah Heep)

71	Warner Bros K 46094	ALBERT 1 (LP)	25

NATIONAL HEALTH

(see also Hatfield & The North)

78	Affinity AFF 6	NATIONAL HEALTH (LP)	12
78	Charly CRL 5010	OF QUEUES AND CURES (LP)	12

NATIONAL LAMPOON

78	Island HELP 8	RADIO DINNER (LP)	12

NATIONAL PINION POLE

66	Planet PLF 111	Make Your Mark Little Man/I Was The One You Came In With (in Planet sleeve)	18
66	Planet PLF 111	Make Your Mark Little Man/I Was The One You Came In With	12

NATIONWIDE ENGLAND SUPPORTERS CLUB

86	Peak PRIDE 1	Oh Sweet England/England Supporter (picture disc, with rosette & beermat)	5

NATURAL ACOUSTIC BAND

(see also Krysia)

73	RCA RCA 2324	Echoes/Is It True Blue	5
72	RCA SF 8272	LEARNING TO LIVE (LP, textured gatefold sleeve)	35
72	RCA SF 8314	BRANCHING IN (LP)	25

NATURAL BRIDGE BUNCH

69	Atlantic 584 231	Pig Snoots (Parts 1 & 2)	10

NATURAL FOUR

75	Atlantic K 56142	HEAVEN RIGHT HERE ON EARTH (LP)	30

NATURAL GAS

(see also Badfinger, Blue Goose, Humble Pie, Uriah Heep, Quiver)

76	Private Stock PVLP 1007	NATURAL GAS (LP, gatefold sleeve with inner sleeve)	15

THE NATURAL ITES AND THE REALISTICS

83	CSA 12CSA 501	Picture On My Wall/Jah Works Mama (12")	12

NATURAL MAGIC

(see also Roger Glover, Eddie Hardin)

75	Oyster OYR 102	Strawberry Fields Forever/Isolated Lady	10

NATURAL ROOTS

82	Fasim FS106	Know Yourself/Ain't Got No Money (12")	20

NATURAL VIBES

82	Starlight Records SDLP 907	LIFE HARD IN A YARD (LP)	35

NATURALITY

69	Ackee ACK 101	The Arena/Natural	50

NATURALLY

79	Bushays BFM 111	I'll Get By/All I Have Is Written In Your Eyes (12")	15

NATURALS (U.K.)

(see also Living Daylights, Greatest Show On Earth)

64	Parlophone R 5116	Daisy Chain/That Girl	12
64	Parlophone R 5165	I Should Have Known Better/Didn' I?	15
64	Parlophone R 5202	It Was You/Look At Me Now	15
65	Parlophone R 5257	Blue Roses/Shame On You	15

NATURALS (U.K.)

81	Just For The Records	Six Girls & Alice (fold-out cover)	12

NATURALS (U.S.)

(see also Debbie Reynolds)

55	MGM SP 1123	The Finger Of Suspicion Points At You/You Forgot To Remember	12
57	MGM MGM 939	The Buccaneers/The Ballad Of Sir Lancelot	8

MINT VALUE £

FATS NAVARRO
56 London LZ-C 14015 — MEMORIAL (LP) ... 15

NAVY BLUE
82 AP 572 — THE PUSSERS (EP) ... 15

JERRY NAYLOR
61 Top Rank JAR 591 — Stop Your Crying/You're Thirteen ... 25
67 Stateside SS 2029 — Sweet Violets/Temptation Leads Me ... 6
70 CBS 4882 — But For Love/Angeline ... 5

SHEL NAYLOR
(see also Lieutenant Pigeon, Stavely Makepeace)
63 Decca F 11776 — How Deep Is The Ocean/La Bamba ... 20
64 Decca F 11856 — One Fine Day/It's Gonna Happen Soon ... 150

NAZARETH
(see also Dan McCafferty, Mark Five, Sensational Alex Harvey Band, Tandoori Cassette, Billy Rankin)
72 Pegasus PGS 2 — Dear John/Friends ... 20
72 Pegasus PGS 2 — Dear John/Friends (2nd issue, PEG label, B-side lists 'Occasional Failure') ... 25
72 Pegasus BCP 3 — Dear John/Witchdoctor Woman/Morning Dew (unreleased, promo only, stamped white labels and insert) ... 50
72 Pegasus PGS 4 — Morning Dew/Spinning Top (PEG label) ... 20
72 Pegasus BCP 8 — Fool About You/Woke Up This Morning/Morning Dew (unreleased, promo only, handwritten white labels) ... 50
72 Pegasus PGS 5 — If You See My Baby/Hard Living (PEG label) ... 20
73 Mooncrest MOON 9 — Bad Bad Boy/Hard Living/Spinning Top (in p/s) ... 5
74 Mooncrest MOON 22 — Shanghai'd In Shanghai/Love, Now You're Gone ... 5
74 Mooncrest MOON 37 — Love Hurts/Down ... 5
75 Mooncrest MOON 44 — Hair Of The Dog/Too Bad, Too Sad ... 5
75 Mooncrest MOON 47 — My White Bicycle/My White Bicycle (A label promo only) ... 12
75 Mooncrest MOON 47 — My White Bicycle/Miss Misery ... 5
76 Mountain PSLP191 — I Don't Want To Go On Without You/Waiting For The Man (12" promo) ... 15
92 Mausoleum 3670010.7 — Every Time It Rains/This Flight Tonight (p/s) ... 5
78 Mountain TOP 37 — Place In Your Heart/Kentucky Fried Blues (mispressing, B-side plays Bee Gees track, company sleeve) ... 15
79 Mountain NAZ 4 — Whatever You Want Babe/Telegram Parts 1, 2 & 3 (p/s, purple vinyl) ... 10
71 Pegasus PEG 10 — NAZARETH (LP, 1st issue, Pegasus picture label, textured matt sleeve) ... 60
72 Pegasus PEG 10 — NAZARETH (LP, 2nd issue, PEG label/glossy sleeve) ... 40
72 Pegasus PEG 14 — EXERCISES (LP, gatefold sleeve) ... 50
73 Mooncrest CREST 1 — RAZAMANAZ (LP) ... 40
73 Mooncrest CREST 4 — LOUD 'N' PROUD (LP) ... 40
74 Mooncrest CREST 15 — RAMPANT (LP) ... 50
75 Mooncrest CREST 27 — HAIR OF THE DOG (LP, with inner) ... 50
76 Mountain TOPS 109 — CLOSE ENOUGH FOR ROCK 'N' ROLL (LP) ... 18
76 Mountain TOPS 113 — PLAY 'N' THE GAME (LP, with inner sleeve) ... 18
77 Mountain TOPS 115 — EXPECT NO MERCY (LP, with inner sleeve) ... 20
79 Mountain TOPS 123 — NO MEAN CITY (LP, with inner sleeve) ... 15
80 NEMS BSD 1 — NAZARETH LIVE (2 x 7", gatefold) ... 6
85 Sahara SAH 130 — SOUND ELIXIR (LP, Marimba label, withdrawn) ... 12

NAZIS AGAINST FASCISM
(see also Vibrators)
79 Truth TRUTH 1 — Sid Did It (Intelligible)/Sid Did It (Radio Version) (p/s, 2 different issues) ... 6

NAZZ
(see also Todd Rundgren)
68 Screen Gems SGC 219001 — Open My Eyes/Hello It's Me ... 20
69 Screen Gems SGC 219002 — Hello It's Me/Crowded ... 10
69 Screen Gems SGC 219003 — Not Wrong Long/Under The Ice ... 10
69 Screen Gems SGC 221001 — NAZZ (LP) ... 50

'N BETWEENS
(see also Slade, Vendors)
66 Columbia DB 8080 — You Better Run/Evil Witchman (demos credit In-Be-Tweens) ... 420

YOUSSOU N'DOUR & PETER GABRIEL
(see also Peter Gabriel)
89 Virgin VSCD 1207 — The Lion (Gaiende)/Macoy/The Lion (Gaiende) (African Mix) (3" CD, card p/s) ... 8

CHRIS NEAL
71 Fly BUG 15 — Blame It All On Eve/All The Time In The World (p/s) ... 6

JOHNNY NEAL & STARLINERS
(see also Storyteller)
65 Pye 7N 15388 — And I Will Love You/Walk Baby Walk ... 80
70 Parlophone R 5870 — Put Your Hand In The Hand/Now ... 7

TOMMY NEAL
68 Vocalion VL 9290 — Goin' To A Happening/Tee Ta ... 50
68 Vocalion VL 9290 — Goin' To A Happening/Tee Ta (DJ copy) ... 125

NEAT
80s Neatbeat LYN 6269 — Hormones In Action/Take Your Chances (p/s) ... 50

NEAT CHANGE
(see also Peter Banks, English Rose)
68 Decca F 12809 — I Lied To Auntie May/Sandman (in foldout p/s) ... 120
68 Decca F 12809 — I Lied To Auntie May/Sandman ... 60

NEBULA II
91 Reinforced RIVET 1211 — Seance/Atheama (12") ... 8
92 Reinforced RIVET 1232 — Peace Maker/X-Plore H-Core (12") ... 8
92 Reinforced RIVET 1232R — X-Plore H-Core/Peace Maker (Remixes) (12") ... 15
93 Reinforced RIVET 1247 — Eye Memory (12") ... 8

MINT VALUE £

NECROMANDUS

90	Reflection MM 09	QUICKSAND DREAM (LP, 500 only)	18

BERNIE NEE
(see also Bernie Knee)

58	Philips PB 794	Lend Me Your Comb/Medal Of Honour	20
58	Philips PB 794	Lend Me Your Comb/Medal Of Honour (78)	15

NEEDLES

80	Ellie Jay EJSP 9340	Gotta Know You/Jayneski (no p/s)	150

LOUIS NEEFS

69	Columbia DB 8561	Jennifer Jennings/I Love You	25

ELGIN NEELY

65	Vogue V 9240	Four Walls/I Could Be	12

NEGATIVE FX

84	Fundamental HOLY 7	NEGATIVE FX (LP)	25

NEGATIVES

78	Look LK/SP 6478	Stakeout (50 copies with p/s)	200
78	Look LK/SP 6478	Stakeout (no p/s)	40

NEGATIVES

80	Aardvark STEAL 1	Electric Waltz/Money Talks (p/s)	5
81	Aardvark STEAL 3	Scene Of The Crime (p/s)	8

NEGATIVES IN COLOUR

90s	own label NEG 1	Caught In Possession	15

NEGRIL

75	Klik KLP 9005	NEGRIL (LP)	30

NEGUS ROOTS MEETS THE MAD PROFESSOR
(see also Lackley Castell)

83	Negus Roots NERLP 009	DUB ROCKERS VOLUME 2 (LP)	80

FRED NEIL

69	Elektra EKSN 45036	Candy Man/The Water Is Wide	8
69	Capitol CL 15616	Everybody's Talkin'/Badi-Da	12
67	Elektra EKS 7293	BLEECKER & MACDOUGAL (LP)	60
70	Capitol E-ST 657	OTHER SIDE OF THIS LIFE (LP)	35

DON NEILSON

60	Philips BF 1058	The House Is Haunted/For All We Know	6
63	Piccadilly 7N 35103	I Will Live My Life For You/How Do You Keep From Crying	6
62	Piccadilly 7N 35044	Forgotten Dreams/These Things Remain	6

NEKTAR
(see also Robert Calvert)

73	United Artists NEK 1	What Ya Gonna Do?/Day In The Life Of A Preacher Pt. One (Edit) (p/s)	15
74	United Artists UP 35706	Fidgety Queen/Little Boy	10
75	United Artists UP 35853	Astral Man/Nelly The Elephant	10
73	United Artists UAD 60041/2	SOUNDS LIKE THIS (2-LP)	35
74	United Artists UAS 29499	A TAB IN THE OCEAN (LP, gatefold sleeve)	20
74	United Artists UAS 29545	REMEMBER THE FUTURE (LP)	20
74	United Artists UAG 29680	DOWN TO EARTH (LP)	15
76	Decca SKL-R 5250	RECYCLED (LP)	12

NELLIE

69	Gas GAS 126	I Who Have Nothing/You Send Me	7

BILL NELSON('S RED NOISE)
(see also A - Austr, Astral Navigations, Gagalactyca, Be-Bop Deluxe)

85	Cocteau JEAN 1	PERMANENT FLAME SINGLES BOX (box set of 5 singles)	10
71	Smile LAF 2182/ HG 116	NORTHERN DREAM (LP, 250 only, numbered, in foldover gatefold sleeve with booklet; second pressings £20; reissues on the Butt label, £15)	35
71	Smile LAF 2182/ HG 116	NORTHERN DREAM (LP, 250 second pressing unnumbered, (reissues on the Butt label, £15)	20
85	Cocteau JEAN 2	TRIAL BY INTIMACY (THE BOOK OF SPLENDOURS) (4-LP, box set, with book & postcards, initial copies misspelt as "The Book Splendours")	20
86	KPM/Themes TIM	CHAMELEON - THE MUSIC OF BILL NELSON (LP, library issue)	12

CLARE NELSON

59	MGM MGM 1025	The Valley Of Love/You Are My Sunshine	8

EARL NELSON

59	London HLW 8950	No Time To Cry/Come On	40
59	London HLW 8950	No Time To Cry/Come On (78)	20

OLIVER NELSON

63	Verve VLP 9053	FULL NELSON (LP)	15
68	HMV CLP 1868	MORE BLUES AND THE ABSTRACT TRUTH (LP)	18

OZZIE & HARRIET NELSON

59	London HA-P 2145	OZZIE AND HARRIET NELSON (LP)	50

PETER NELSON

66	Piccadilly 7N 35314	Don't Make Promises (You Can't Keep)/No Need To Cry	7
72	Peacock PEA502	Good Scotch Whiskey/I Am A Ship	20

RICK(Y) NELSON

78s

57	HMV POP 355	I'm Walkin'/A Teenager's Romance	40
57	HMV POP 390	You're My One And Only Love/BARNEY KESSEL: Honey Rock	45
57	London HLP 8499	Be-Bop Baby/Have I Told You Lately That I Love You	20

			MINT VALUE £
58	London HLP 8542	Stood Up/Waitin' In School	20
58	London HLP 8594	Believe What You Say/My Bucket's Got A Hole In It	20
58	London HLP 8732	Someday/I Got A Feeling	20
58	London HLP 8738	Lonesome Town/My Babe	30
59	London HLP 8817	It's Late/Never Be Anyone Else But You	20
59	London HLP 8927	Just A Little Too Much/Sweeter Than You	40
60	London HLP 9021	I Wanna Be Loved/Mighty Good	60
60	London HLP 9121	Young Emotions/Right By My Side	60
60	London HLP 9188	Yes, Sir, That's My Baby/I'm Not Afraid	100

(All the above 78s were credited to Ricky Nelson.)

SINGLES

57	HMV POP 355	I'm Walkin'/A Teenager's Romance (gold label lettering)	150
57	HMV POP 355	I'm Walkin'/A Teenager's Romance (silver label lettering)	80
57	HMV POP 390	You're My One And Only Love/BARNEY KESSEL: Honey Rock	100
57	London HLP 8499	Be-Bop Baby/Have I Told You Lately That I Love You	30
58	London HLP 8542	Stood Up/Waitin' In School	25
58	London HLP 8594	Believe What You Say/My Bucket's Got A Hole In It	25
58	London HLP 8670	Poor Little Fool/Don't Leave Me This Way	8
58	London HLP 8732	Someday/I Got A Feeling	10
58	London HLP 8738	Lonesome Town/My Babe	10
59	London HLP 8817	It's Late/Never Be Anyone Else But You (all black or silver-top label)	8
59	London HLP 8894	Just A Little Too Much/Sweeter Than You (unreleased)	0
59	London HLP 8927	Just A Little Too Much/Sweeter Than You (triangular centre)	10

(The above 45s were credited to Ricky Nelson. Originally issued with triangular centres; later round-centre copies are worth half to two-thirds these values.)

59	London HL 7081	Just A Little Too Much/Sweeter Than You (export issue)	10
60	London HLP 9021	I Wanna Be Loved/Mighty Good	15
60	London HLP 9121	Young Emotions/Right By My Side	5
60	London HLP 9188	Yes, Sir, That's My Baby/I'm Not Afraid	5
61	London HLP 9260	You Are The Only One/Milk Cow Blues	20
61	London HLP 9260	You Are The One And Only/Milk Cow Blues (with different label credit)	15
61	London HLP 9347	Hello Mary Lou Goodbye Heart/Travelin' Man (later copies as "Hello Marylou Goodbye Heart")	5
61	London HLP 9440	Everlovin'/A Wonder Like You	6

(The above singles were credited to Ricky Nelson, all subsequent singles were credited to Rick Nelson unless stated.)

62	London HLP 9524	Young World/Summertime	10
62	London HLP 9583	Teen Age Idol/I've Got My Eyes On You (And I Like What I See)	10
63	Brunswick 05885	I Got A Woman/You Don't Love Me Anymore	5
63	Brunswick 05889	String Along/Gypsy Woman	5
63	Brunswick 05895	Fools Rush In/Down Home	5
64	Brunswick 05900	For You/That's All She Wrote	5
64	Liberty LIB 66004	Today's Teardrops/Thank You Darling	5
64	Brunswick 05908	The Very Thought Of You/I Wonder	5
64	Brunswick 05918	Lonely Corner/There's Nothing I Can Say	5
64	Brunswick 05924	A Happy Guy/Don't Breathe A Word	5
65	Brunswick 05939	Come Out Dancin'/Yesterday's Love	15
66	Brunswick 05964	Louisiana Man/You Just Can't Quit (as Ricky Nelson)	15
66	Liberty LIB 12033	I Need You/Wonder Like You	10
69	MCA MU 1106	She Belongs To Me/Promises	5
70	MCA MU 1124	Red Balloon/I Shall Be Released	5
71	MCA MU 1135	Life/California (with Stone Canyon Band)	5
72	MCA MU 1147	Love Minus Zero: No Limit/Gypsy Pilot (with Stone Canyon Band)	5
72	MCA MU 1165	Garden Party/So Long Mama	5
73	MCA MUS 1181	Palace Guard/A Flower Opens Gently By Itself	5
73	MCA MUS 1225	Lifestream/Evil Woman Child	5
74	MCA MCA 126	Windfall/Legacy (with Stone Canyon Band)	5
74	MCA MCA 144	One Night Stand/Lifestream (with Stone Canyon Band)	5
75	MCA MCA 198	Try (Try To Fall In Love)/Louisiana Belle (with Stone Canyon Band)	5
77	Epic S EPC 5821	You Can't Dance/It's Another Day	5

EPs

58	London RE-P 1141	RICKY PART 1	25
58	London RE-P 1142	RICKY PART 2	25
58	London RE-P 1143	RICKY PART 3	25
58	London RE-P 1144	RICKY PART 4	25
59	London RE-P 1168	RICKY NELSON PART 1	25
59	London RE-P 1169	RICKY NELSON PART 2	25
59	London RE-P 1170	RICKY NELSON PART 3	25
59	London RE-P 1200	RICKY SINGS AGAIN PART 1	25
59	London RE-P 1201	RICKY SINGS AGAIN PART 2	25
60	London RE-P 1238	I GOT A FEELING	25
60	London RE-P 1249	RICKY SINGS SPIRITUALS	25
61	London RE-P 1300	RICKY NELSON PART 4	25

(The above EPs were credited to Ricky Nelson; all subsequent EPs were credited to Rick Nelson)

62	London RE-P 1339	IT'S A YOUNG WORLD	30
63	London RE-P 1362	IT'S UP TO YOU	30
63	Brunswick OE 9502	ONE BOY TOO LATE	35
64	Liberty LEP 4001	SINGS FOR YOU	50
64	Liberty LEP 4019	THAT'S ALL	50
65	Liberty LEP 4028	I'M IN LOVE AGAIN	50
65	Brunswick OE 9512	HAPPY GUY	35

LPs

57	London HA-P 2080	RICKY	50
58	London HA-P 2119	RICKY NELSON	50
59	London HA-P2159	RICKY SINGS AGAIN	40
59	London HA-P 2206	SONGS BY RICKY	40
60	London HA-P 2290	MORE SONGS BY RICKY (gatefold sleeve, mono)	40

			MINT VALUE £
60	London SAH-P 6102	MORE SONGS BY RICKY (gatefold sleeve, also stereo SAH-P 6102)	45
61	London HA-P 2379	RICK IS 21 (mono)	35
61	London SAH-P 6179	RICK IS 21 (stereo)	40
(The above Lps were credited to Ricky Nelson; all subsequent LPs were credited to Rick Nelson)			
62	London HA-P 2445	ALBUM SEVEN (mono)	35
62	London SAH-P 6236	ALBUM SEVEN (stereo)	40
63	London HA-P 8066	IT'S UP TO YOU	35
63	Brunswick LAT 8545	FOR YOUR SWEET LOVE (mono)	35
63	Brunswick STA 8545	FOR YOUR SWEET LOVE (stereo)	40
64	Brunswick LAT 8562	RICKY SINGS "FOR YOU" (mono)	45
64	Brunswick STA 8562	RICKY SINGS "FOR YOU" (stereo)	50
64	Liberty LBY 3027	MILLION SELLERS	40
64	Brunswick LAT/STA 8581	THE VERY THOUGHT OF YOU	40
64	Brunswick LAT/STA 8596	SPOTLIGHT ON RICK	40
65	Brunswick LAT/STA 8615	BEST ALWAYS	40
65	Brunswick LAT/STA 8630	LOVE AND KISSES	40
66	Brunswick LAT/STA 8657	BRIGHT LIGHTS, COUNTRY MUSIC	40
67	Brunswick LAT/STA 8680	COUNTRY FEVER	40
68	Liberty LBL 83020	MILLION SELLERS (reissue)	15
68	MCA MUP(S) 302	ANOTHER SIDE OF RICK	20
70	MCA MUPS 409	IN CONCERT (with Stone Canyon Band)	12
71	MCA MUPS 422	RICK SINGS NELSON (with Stone Canyon Band)	12
72	MCA MUPS 440	RUDY THE FIFTH (with Stone Canyon Band)	12
73	MCA MDKS 8009	GARDEN PARTY (gatefold sleeve, with Stone Canyon Band)	12

SANDY NELSON

(see also Preston Epps)

59	Top Rank JAR 197	Teen Beat/Big Jump	5
59	London HLP 9015	Drum Party/The Big Noise From Winnetka	10
59	London HLP 9015	Drum Party/The Big Noise From Winnetka (78)	50
60	London HLP 9214	I'm Walkin'/Bouncy (as Sandy Nelson & His Combo)	10
61	London HLP 9377	Get With It/Big Noise From The Jungle	10
61	London HLP 9466	Let There Be Drums/Quite A Beat (as Sandy Nelson On The Drums)	5
62	London HLP 9521	Drums Are My Beat/My Girl Josephine	7
62	London HLP 9558	Drummin' Up A Storm/Drum Stomp	8
62	London HLP 9612	?And Then There Were Drums/Live It Up	8
63	London HLP 9717	Ooh Poo Pah Doo/Feel So Good	8
64	Liberty LIB 66060	Teen Beat '65/Kitty's Theme	8
66	Liberty LIB 12062	Hey Joe/Come On Let's Go	5
70	President PT 294	Teen Beat/PRESTON EPPS: Bongo Rock	8
60	Top Rank JKP 2060	RUSHING FOR PERCUSSION (EP, 2 tracks by Preston Epps)	25
62	London REP 1337	LET THERE BE DRUMS (EP)	20
63	London REP 1371	IN THE MOOD (EP)	20
65	Liberty LEP 4033	SANDY NELSON PLAYS (EP)	20
60	London HA-P 2260	TEEN BEAT (LP, mono)	30
60	London SAH-P 6082	TEEN BEAT (LP, stereo)	35
61	London HA-P 2425	LET THERE BE DRUMS (LP, mono)	30
61	London SAH-P 6221	LET THERE BE DRUMS (LP, stereo)	35
62	London HA-P 2446	DRUMS ARE MY BEAT! (LP, mono)	30
62	London SAH-P 6237	DRUMS ARE MY BEAT! (LP, stereo)	35
62	London HA-P 8009	DRUMMIN' UP A STORM (LP, mono)	30
62	London SH-P 8009	DRUMMIN' UP A STORM (LP, stereo)	35
63	London HA-P/SH-P 8029	COMPELLING PERCUSSION (LP)	25
63	London HA-P/SH-P 8051	TEENAGE HOUSE PARTY (LP)	25
65	Liberty LBY 3007	SANDY NELSON PLAYS (LP)	20
65	Liberty LBY 3035	LIVE IN LAS VEGAS (LP)	20
66	Liberty LBY 3061	DRUMS A GO-GO (LP)	20
66	Liberty (S)LBY 3080	SUPERDRUMS (LP)	20
67	Liberty LBL/LBS 83043E	THE BEAT GOES ON (LP)	15
68	Liberty LBL/LBS 83094E	SOUL DRUMS (LP)	18
68	Liberty LBL/LBS 83110E	BOOGALOO BEAT (LP)	18
68	Liberty LBL/LBS 83131E	SUPERDRUMS (LP, reissue, different sleeve)	15
69	Liberty LBL/LBS 83165E	ROCK'N'ROLL REVIVAL (LP)	15
70	Liberty LBS 83302E	GROOVY (LP)	15

TERRY NELSON (& FIREBALLS)

65	Dice CC 22	I'll Stand By You/Love On A Saturday Night	10
65	Dice CC 23	Run Run Baby/Bonita (as Terry Nelson & Fireballs)	12
65	Dice CC 25	Bulldog Push/Pretty Little Girl (as Terry Nelson & Fireballs)	12
65	Dice CC 27	Tomorrow Will Soon Be Here/My Blue Eyed Baby	8
65	Blue Beat BB 326	Help/PRINCE BUSTER: Johnny Dollar	25
66	Halagala HG 11	Take These Chains From My Heart/Let-Kiss	6
67	Halagala HG 19	That True Love Must Be Me/Bulldog Walk	5

WILLIE NELSON

63	Liberty LIB 55532	Half A Man/The Last Letter	10
64	Liberty LIB 55697	River Boy/Opportunity To Cry	10
69	RCA RCA 1867	My Own Peculiar Way/Natural To Be Gone	7
66	RCA Victor RD 7749	COUNTRY WILLIE (LP)	25
66	Liberty (S)LBY 1240	AND THEN I WROTE (LP)	20
69	RCA RD 7997	TEXAS IN MY SOUL (LP)	25

NELSON TRIO (U.K.)

57	Oriole CB 1360	Tear It Up/Roll The Carpet Up	8
57	Oriole CB 1360	Tear It Up/Roll The Carpet Up (78)	10

NELSON TRIO (U.S.)

60	London HLL 9019	All In Good Time/The Town Crier	15
60	London HLL 9019	All In Good Time/The Town Crier (78)	30

MINT VALUE £

NEMO
71 Parlophone R 5927 — The Sun Has Got His Hat On/Bernie's Song — 6

NEO MAYA
(see also Episode Six)
67 Pye 7N 17371 — I Won't Hurt You/U.F.O. — 65

CHIITRA NEOGY
68 Gemini GMX 5030 — THE PERFUMED GARDEN (LP) — 22

NEON
78 Sensible FAB 3 — Anytime Anyplace Anywhere/Bottles/I'm Only Little — 5
78 Radar ADA 27 — Don't Eat Bricks/Hanging Off An O (p/s) — 5

NEON BOYS
(see also Richard Hell, Television)
90 Overground OVER 11 — TIME (EP, purple vinyl, 2,000 only) — 6
90 Overground OVER 11 — TIME (12" EP, 20 test pressings only) — 20
91 Overground OVER 19 — That's All I Know (Right Now)/Love Comes In Spurts/High Heeled Wheels/Don't Die/Time (last 2 tracks credited to Richard Hell & Voidoids [Part III]) (12" p/s, 2,000 only, clear vinyl) — 8

NEON HEARTS
77 Neon Hearts NEON 1 — Venus Eccentric/Regulations (8" p/s) — 30
78 Satril SAT 133 — Answers/Armchair Thriller (p/s) — 8
79 Satril SAT 139 — Popular Music/Pretty As A Picture (p/s) — 8
79 Satril SATL 4012 — POPULAR MUSIC (LP) — 15

NEON NEON
07 Lex LEX 047 — Trick For Treat/Instrumental (12" picture disc, 500 only) — 8

NEPTUNE'S EMPIRE
71 Polymax PXX 01 — NEPTUNE'S EMPIRE (LP) — 100

NERO & GLADIATORS
(see also Laurie Jay, Gladiators, Screaming Lord Sutch & Savages, State Of Mickey & Tommy)
61 Decca F 11329 — Entry Of The Gladiators/Boots — 15
61 Decca F 11367 — In The Hall Of The Mountain King/The Trek To Rome — 15
61 Decca F 11413 — Czardas/That's A Long Time Ago — 20

PAUL NERO (SOUNDS)
68 Liberty LBL 83100 — NERO'S SOUL PARTY (LP) — 25

NERVE
(see also Lovin')
67 Page One POF 019 — No. 10 Downing Street/Georgie's March — 12
68 Page One POF 055 — Magic Spectacles/Come The Day — 20
68 Page One POF 081 — It Is/Mystery Lady — 18
68 Page One POF 097 — Piece By Piece/Satisfying Kind — 15

NERVE SENTA
81 Supermusic SUPLP 2002 — NERVE SENTA (LP) — 12

NERVES
78 Lightning GIL 520 — TV Adverts/Sex Education (p/s) — 35

NERVES
81 Good Vibrations BIG 3 — NOTRE DEMO (LP, official bootleg, foldover sleeve with booklet) — 20

NERVES
94 Inflammable Material BURN 2 — Bits/SUBSTANDARD: Rostock (p/s) — 7

NERVOUS CHOIR
89 Cathexis CRN 5407 — O'David/Tonight We Start On Witches/Alsatians/Introducing (p/s, with inserts) — 5

NERVOUS NORVUS
56 London HLD 8338 — Ape Call/Wild Dog Of Kentucky (gold label print) — 80
56 London HLD 8338 — Ape Call/Wild Dog Of Kentucky (silver label print) — 30
57 London HLD 8383 — Dig/Bullfrog Hop (gold label print) — 120
57 London HLD 8383 — Dig/Bullfrog Hop (silver label print) — 50
62 Salvo SLO 1812 — Does A Chinese Chicken Have A Pigtail/ROD BARTON: Dear Old San Francisco — 60
85 Big Beat NED 12 — NERVOUS NORVUS (mini-LP) — 12

JIM NESBIT
65 Vocalion V 9241 — Tiger In My Tank/I Can't Stand This Living Alone — 25

MICHAEL NESMITH (& FIRST/SECOND NATIONAL BAND)
(see also Monkees, Wichita Train Whistle)
70 RCA RCA 2001 — Joanne/The Crippled Lion (with First National Band) — 5
71 RCA RCA 2053 — Silver Moon/Lady Of The Valley (with First National Band) — 5
71 RCA RCA 2086 — Nevada Fighter/Here I Am (with First National Band) — 5
70 RCA SF 8136 — MAGNETIC SOUTH (LP, with First National Band) — 25
71 RCA SF 8209 — NEVADA FIGHTER (LP, with First National Band) — 25
72 RCA SF 8276 — TANTAMOUNT TO TREASON VOLUME ONE (LP, with Second National Band) — 20
73 RCA APL1 0164 — PRETTY MUCH YOUR STANDARD RANCH STASH (LP, solo) — 15
76 RCA RS 1064 — THE BEST OF MICHAEL NESMITH (LP) — 15

NEU!
(see also Kraftwerk, La Dusseldorf)
73 United Artists UP 35485 — Super/Neuschnee — 15
75 United Artists UP 35874 — Isi/After Eight — 12
72 United Artists UAS 29396 — NEU (LP) — 60
73 United Artists UAS 29500 — NEU II (LP, gatefold sleeve) — 60
75 United Artists UAS 29782 — NEU '75 (LP, gatefold sleeve) — 50

MINT VALUE £

NEUTRAL MILK HOTEL
98 Blue Rose BRRC 10237 Holland, 1945/Engine (numbered fold-out poster in polythene bag) 30

NEUTRONS
(see also Clive John, Gentle Giant, Man)
74 United Artists UP 35704 Dance Of The Psychedelic Lounge Lizard/Suzy And The Wonder Boy 5
74 United Artists UAG 29652 BLACK HOLE STAR (LP, with inner sleeve)........ 15
75 United Artists UAG 29726 TALES FROM THE BLUE COCOONS (LP) 15

NEVILLE (Willoughby)
(see also Whistling Willie)
72 Explosion EX 2057 I Love Jamaica/Marry Me Marie........ 5

AARON NEVILLE
67 Stateside SS 584 Tell It Like It Is/Why Worry........ 20
67 Stateside SS 584 Tell It Like It Is/Why Worry (DJ Copy)........ 40
69 B&C CB 107 Tell It Like It Is/Why Worry (reissue)........ 5
67 Liberty LBY 3089 LIKE IT 'TIS (LP) 50

ART NEVILLE
76 Specialty SON 5008 Cha-Dooky-Doo/Zing Zing 5

NEW AGE STEPPERS
80 On-U Sound ONU 1 Fade Away/LONDON UNDERGROUND: Learn A Language (p/s)........ 7
81 Statik 612 My Love/Love Forever (12")........ 20
80 On-U Sound ONULP 1 NEW AGE STEPPERS (LP) 15
81 Statik/On U Sound STATLP 2 ACTION BATTLEFIELD (LP)........ 20
82 On U Sound ONULP 21 FOUNDATION STEPPERS (LP) 20

NEWBEATS
(see also Dean & Mark, Larry Henley)
64 Hickory 45-1269 Bread And Butter/Tough Little Buggy (pink or black/blue label)........ 6
64 Hickory 45-1282 Everything's Alright/Pink Dally Rue 10
65 Hickory 45-1290 Break Away/Hey O Daddy O 10
65 Hickory 45-1305 The Birds Are For The Bees/Better Watch Your Step........ 8
65 Hickory 45-1320 I Can't Hear You No More/Little Child........ 10
65 Hickory 45-1332 Run Baby Run/Mean Woolly Willie 30
65 Hickory 45-1332 Run Baby Run/Mean Woolly Willie (DJ copy) 70
66 Hickory 45-1366 Shake Hands (And Come Out Crying)/Too Sweet To Be Forgotten 20
66 Hickory 45-1387 Crying My Heart Out/Short Of Love 40
66 Hickory 45-1387 Crying My Heart Out/Short Of Love (DJ copy) 70
66 Hickory 45-1422 My Yesterday Love/Patent On Love 10
71 London HLE 10341 Run Baby Run (Back Into My Arms)/Am I Not My Brother's Keeper 6
65 Hickory LPE 1503 NEWBEATS (EP) 30
65 Hickory LPE 1506 AIN'T THAT LOVIN' YOU BABY (EP)........ 30
66 Hickory LPE 1510 OH! GIRLS GIRLS (EP)........ 25
65 Hickory LPM 120 BREAD AND BUTTER (LP)........ 30

PHINEAS NEWBORN
(see also Roy Haines)
61 Columbia 33SX 1311 I LOVE A PIANO (LP, also stereo SCX 3370) 12

NEWBOY
73 Count Shelly CS007 Sweet Talk/J ENGLISH: One And Only........ 20

NEW BREED
65 Decca F 12295 Friends And Lovers Forever/Unto Us........ 75

MICKEY NEWBURY
72 Elektra K 12047 An American Trilogy/San Francisco Mabel Joy........ 6

NEWBY
65 Pye 7N 15986 I Can't Grow Peaches On A Cherry Tree/The Children Sleep 7

NEWCASTLE BIG BAND
(see also Last Exit, Police, Sting, Radio Actors)
72 Impulse ISS NBB 106 NEWCASTLE BIG BAND (LP, white labels, 2,000 only) 150

NEW CENSATION
75 DJM DJS 10371 First Round Knockout/Everybody's Got A Story........ 8

NEW CHRISTY MINSTRELS
(see also Barry McGuire)
62 CBS BPG 62175 NEW CHRISTY MINSTRELS (LP)........ 15
63 CBS BPG 62269 RAMBLIN' (LP)........ 12
65 CBS BPG 62492 SING AND PLAY COWBOYS AND INDIANS (LP) 12
65 CBS BPG 62586 THE WANDERING MINSTRELS (LP) 12

NEW COLONY SIX
66 London HLZ 10033 I Confess/Dawn Is Breaking........ 75
66 Stateside SS 522 At The River's Edge/I Lie Awake........ 50
68 Mercury MF 1030 I Will Always Think About You/Hold Me With Your Eyes 12
69 Mercury MF 1086 Things I'd Like To Say/Come And Give Your Love To Me 10

NEWCOMERS
72 Stax 2025 063 Pin The Tail On The Donkey/Mannish Boy........ 8
75 Stax STXS 2023 Keep An Eye On Your Close Friends/(Instrumental Version)........ 10

NEW CUOREY
73 Taurus TR 101 Vietnam/The Girl I Had 25

NEW DAWN
69 private pressing MAINLINE (LP)........ 80

NEW DEAL STRING BAND
69 Argo ZDA 104 DOWN IN THE WILLOW (LP, with insert) 40

MINT VALUE £

NEW DECADE
92 Out Of Romford ROCC 002 Get The Message/ABC Remix (12", stamped white labels) 10

NEW DEPARTURES QUARTET
(see also Stan Tracey)
60s Transatlantic TRA 134 THE NEW DEPARTURES QUARTET (LP, with Stan Tracey) 40

MARTIN NEWELL
(see also Gypp, Cleaners From Venus)
80 Off Street OSR 001 Young Jobless/Sylvie In Toytown (p/s) 15
80 Liberty BP 392 Young Jobless/Sylvie In Toytown (p/s reissue) 8

NEW ENGLAND
79 Infinity INF 110 P.U.N.K./Shoot (green vinyl, 'lightning' PVC sleeve) 5

DENNIS NEWEY
61 Philips PB 1134 Checkpoint/Title Unknown 10
61 Philips PB 1198 Border Patrol/Yes Yes 10
62 Philips 326 588 BF The Nightriders/The Pied Piper 10

NEW FACES
65 Pye 7N 15842 So Small/Blue Mist 8
65 Pye 7N 15931 Never Gonna Love Again/You'll Be Too Late 8
66 Pye 7N 17029 Like A Man/Shake Up The Party (Myra) 15
67 Pye 7N 17335 Lace Covered Window/The Life That I Lead 8
68 Decca F 12746 We Can Get There By Candlelight/The Yellow Road 7
68 Decca F 12862 Someday/Biscuit Coloured Overcoat 7
69 Decca F 12933 Carnival Day/Grandfather Dugan 7
69 Decca F 12968 There Is An Island In The Sun/Happy The Heart That I Own 7
74 Ember MBS 334 Where Would I Find Another You/Lullaby 6

NEW FORESTERS
65 Lyntone LYN 932/933 Travel/LIZARDS: My Love Goes On (Sheffield Students Rag record) 30

NEW FORMULA
67 Piccadilly 7N 35381 Do It Again A Little Bit Slower/I'm On The Outside Looking In 15
67 Piccadilly 7N 35401 I Want To Go Back There Again/Can't You See That She Loves Me 15
68 Pye 7N 17552 My Baby's Coming Home/Burning In The Background Of My Mind 20
69 Pye 7N 17818 Stay Indoors/Hare Krishna 25

NEW GENERATION
69 Spark SRL 1000 Sadie And Her Magic Mister Garland/Digger 15
69 Spark SRL 1007 Smokey Blues Away/She's A Soldier Boy 10
70 Spark SRL 1019 Police Is Here/Mister C. 25

BOB NEWHART
60 WARNER BROS WEP 6031 THE BUTTON DOWN MIND OF BOB NEWHART (EP) 8
60 Warner Bros. WEP 6113 THE BUTTON DOWN MIND ON T.V (EP) 8

NEW HEARTS
(see also Secret Affair)
77 CBS 5800 Just Another Teenage Anthem/Blood On The Knife (p/s) 10
78 CBS 6381 Plain Jane/My Young Teacher (p/s) 10

NEW HERITAGE
73 Westwood WRS 028 ALL MANNER OF THINGS (LP) 50

NEW HOPE
(see also Kit Kats)
69 London HL 10296 Won't Find Better Than Me/They Call It Love 18

NEW HORIZON
73 Decca F13463 Hullabaloo/Believe In Yourself 10

NEW INSPIRATION
70 Penny Farthing PEN 719 Thinking About The Good Times/There You Go My friend 6

NEW INSPIRATION
67 Major Minor MM 539 You Made A Fool of Me/M.T. 25
73 Penny Farthing PEN 803 Medicine Man/Is It Really That Hard To Understand 10

NEW JAZZ GROUP
56 Tempo EXA 39 MODERN JAZZ SCENE (EP) 25

NEW JAZZ ORCHESTRA
(see also Neil Ardley, Nucleus)
65 Decca LK 4690 WESTERN REUNION (LONDON 1965) (LP) 80
69 Verve SVLP 9236 DEJEUNER SUR L'HERBE (LP) 175

NEW JERSEY CONNECTION
82 Nitelife LIFE 1 Love Don't Come Easy/Love Don't Come Easy (Instrumental) (12") 12

NEW JERSEY KINGS
(see also James Taylor Quartet)
92 Acid Jazz JAZIDLP 33 PARTY TO THE BUS STOP (LP) 15

NEW JUMP BAND
68 Domain D 1 The Only Kind Of Girl/Seven Kinds Of Sweet Lovin' 25

ANTHONY NEWLEY
59 Decca F 11127 I've Waited So Long/Sat'day Night Rock-A-Boogie 5
59 Decca F 11137 Idle On Parade/Idle Rock-A-Boogie 5
59 Decca F 11142 Personality/My Blue Angel 5
59 Decca F 11163 Someone To Love/It's All Over 5
60 Decca F 11220 Do You Mind/Girls Were Made To Love And Kiss (78) 20
61 Decca F 11376 What Kind Of Fool Am I/Once In A Lifetime 5
62 Decca F 11419 D-Darling/I'll Walk Beside You 5

			MINT VALUE £
62	Decca F 11486	That Noise/The Little Golden Clown	6
64	Decca F 11818	Tribute/Lament To A Hero	10
59	Decca DFE 6566	IDLE ON PARADE (EP)	10
60	Decca DFE 6629	TONY'S HITS (EP)	8
60	Decca DFE 6655	MORE HITS FROM TONY (EP)	8
60	Decca LK 4343	LOVE IS A NOW AND THEN THING (LP)	12

ANDY NEWMAN

(see also Thunderclap Newman)

72	Track 2406 103	RAINBOW (LP, gatefold sleeve, black/silver label)	25

BRAD NEWMAN

62	Fontana H 357	Somebody To Love/This Time It's Love	15
62	Fontana H 369	Get A Move On/Here And Now And Evermore	10
62	Fontana 267 220TF	Stay By Me/Candy Lips	10
62	Fontana 267 243TF	Point Of No Return/Now I've Lost You	10
63	Fontana 267 273TF	I'll Find You Another Baby/No Man Should Ever Be Alone	10
64	Piccadilly 7N 35174	Please Don't Cry/Every Hour Of Living	8

COLIN NEWMAN

(see also Wire)

80	Beggars Banquet BEG 48	B/Classic Remains/Alone On Piano (p/s)	5
81	Beggars Banquet BEG 52	Inventory/This Picture (p/s)	5

DEL NEWMAN SOUND

67	Columbia SCX 6181	FLOWER GARDEN (LP)	20

JIMMY(C.) NEWMAN

57	London HLD 8460	A Fallen Star/I Can't Go On This Way	30
59	MGM MGM 1009	What'cha Gonna Do/So Soon	15
59	MGM MGM 1037	Grin And Bear It/The Ballad Of Baby Doe	10
60	MGM MGM 1085	A Lovely Work Of Art/What About Me	8
61	MGM MGM 1112	Now That You're Gone/Wanting You With Me Tonight	8
59	MGM MGM-EP 706	GRIN AND BEAR IT - COUNTRY AND WESTERN STYLE (EP)	30

JOE NEWMAN (SEXTET)

57	Vogue Coral Q 72244	Cocktails For Two/Later For The Happenings	5
57	Vogue Coral LVA 9052	HAPPY CATS (LP)	12
57	Pye/Vanguard PPT 12001	JOE NEWMAN (LP)	12

NANETTE NEWMAN

77	BAC BCS 0004	Fun Food Factory/Morris (The Studio Mouse)	6

PAUL NEWMAN

66	Mercury MF 969	Ain't You Got A Heart/Tears On My Pillow	50

RANDY NEWMAN

(see also Harry Nilsson, Tom Petty & Heartbreakers)

68	Reprise RS 20692	Love Story/I Think It's Going To Rain Today	5
70	Reprise RS 20945	Gone Dead Train/JACK NITZSCHE: Harry Flowers	5
68	Reprise R(S)LP 6286	RANDY NEWMAN CREATES SOMETHING NEW UNDER THE SUN (LP)	15
70	Reprise RSLP 6373	12 SONGS (LP)	15

TOM NEWMAN

(see also Jade Warrior, July, Mike Oldfield)

75	Virgin VS120	Sad Sing/Ali's Got A Broken Bone	8
75	Virgin VS130	Don't Treat Your Woman Bad/Why Does Love Hurt So Bad	5
75	Virgin VS133	Sleep/Darling Corey	6
75	Virgin V 2022	FINE OLD TOM (LP, features Mike Oldfield)	20
75	Virgin V 2042	LIVE AT THE ARGONAUT (LP, unreleased, test pressings only)	80
77	Decca TXS 123	FAERIE SYMPHONY (LP, gatefold sleeve)	30
88	Oceandisc	OZYMANDIAS (LP, unissued, 20 test pressings only in proof sleeve)	30

TONY NEWMAN

(see also Sounds Incorporated, Flying Machine, Pinkerton['s Assorted Colours], May Blitz, Three Man Army)

68	Decca F 12795	Soul Thing/Let The Good Times Roll	25
70	Decca F 13041	Soul Thing/Let The Good Times Roll (reissue)	10

THE NEW MASTERSOUNDS

00	Blow It Hard BIH 017	One Note Brown/Burnt Black	20

NEWMENS

72	Parlophone R5941	Start My Life Again/A Million Tears	15

NEW MODEL

83	Mr. Clean MERC 001	Chilean Warning/The World Thru Our Eyes/Totalitarian Terror (p/s, in 7" x 10" folder)	10
83	Mr. Clean MERC 001	Chilean Warning/The World Thru Our Eyes/Totalitarian Terror (p/s)	6

NEW MODEL ARMY

83	Shout QS 002/QF 001	Bittersweet/Betcha/Tension (p/s, with flexi "Fashion"/"The Cause")	5

NEW MONITORS

72	Buddah 2011 118	Fence Around Your Heart/Have You Seen Her	30

PETER NEWNHAM

77	B & C BCS 011	Rudi/Outside My Window (100 only)	200

NEW ORDER

(see also Joy Division, Electronic)

81	Factory FAC 33	Ceremony/In A Lonely Place (p/s)	12
81	Factory FAC 33T	Ceremony/In A Lonely Place (12")	8
81	Factory FAC 3312	Ceremony (Re-recording)/In A Lonely Place (Extended) (12", cream & blue p/s)	12
81	Factory FAC 53	Procession/Everything's Gone Green (9 different coloured sleeves : black, brown, red, orange, yellow, green, aquamarine, blue and purple)	10
81	Factory Benelux FBNL 8	Everything's Gone Green/Mesh/Cries & Whispers (12", yellow sleeve)	12

MINT VALUE £

82	Factory FAC 51B	Rocking Carol/Ode To Joy (flexidisc, given away at Hacienda, 4,000 only)	25
82	Factory FAC 63	Temptation/Hurt	5
83	Factory FAC 7312	Blue Monday/The Beach (12", die-cut sleeve, silver insert)	15
83	Factory FAC 93	Confusion (Edit)/(same) (p/s, DJ promo only)	15
84	Factory FAC 103	Thieves Like Us (Edit)/Lonesome Tonight (Edit) (p/s, DJ promo only)	15
87	Factory FACD 193	Touched By The Hand Of God (Twelve Inch Mix)/Confusion Dub 1987/ Temptation (Original Mix))CD, gatefold card sleeve)	15
88	Factory FAC 73RD	Blue Monday 1988/Blue Monday (DJ-only mix) (12", p/s, DJ promo only)	10
88	Factory FACD 73R	Blue Monday 1988 (12 Inch)/Beach Buggy (12 Inch)/ Blue Monday 1988 (7 Inch) (CD)	10
88	Factory FACDV 73R	Blue Monday 1988 (12 Inch)/Blue Monday 1988 (7 Inch)/Beach Buggy/ Blue Monday 1988 (Video) (CD Video)	50
88	Factory FACDV 183	True Faith (Remix 12 Inch)/Evil Dust/True Faith (7 Inch) (CD Video)/ True Faith (CD Video)	30
89	Factory FAC 263DJ	Round & Round (Ben Grosse Mix)/(12" Mix)/(Detroit Mix) (12", p/s, DJ only)	12
89	Factory FACD 263R	Round & Round (Seven Inch)/Vanishing Point (Instrumental Making Out Mix)/ Round & Round (Twelve Inch)/Best & Marsh (Seven Inch) (3" CD, gatefold card p/s)	8
89	Factory FAC 273/7	Run 2 (Edit)/MTO (Edit) (DJ promo only, 500 pressed)	10
81	Factory FACT 50	MOVEMENT (LP)	15
86	Factory FACT 150SP	BROTHERHOOD (LP, limited metallic sleeve)	15
86	Factory FACD 150SP	BROTHERHOOD (CD with 'State Of The Nation' & metallic booklet)	25
87	Factory FACT 200	THE GATEFOLD SUBSTANCE (LP, numbered gatefold sleeve, 1,000 only)	30
87	Factory FACT 200C	SUBSTANCE (cassette, 200 only in box set with insert)	20
93	London 8284131	REPUBLIC (LP)	18
94	London 8285801	BEST OF (2-LP, with inner sleeve)	20

NEW ORDER

(see also Come)

81	Come Org. CARA12	BRADFORD RED LIGHT DISTRICT (LP)	110

NEW ORLEANS BOOTBLACKS

54	Columbia SCM 5090	Flat Foot/Mad Dog	10

NEW OVERLANDERS

69	RCA 1861	Thought Back/These Are Not My People	6
70	RCA 1953	Unchained Melody/Memories	6

NEW PENNIES

72	Chapter One SCH 166	Marianna/B-Boom	5

NEWPORT JAZZ FESTIVAL ALL STARS

61	London Jazz LTZ-K 15202	NEWPORT JAZZ FESTIVAL ALL STARS (LP, mono)	12
61	London Jazz SAH-K 6116	NEWPORT JAZZ FESTIVAL ALL STARS (LP, stereo)	15

NEW RELIGION

72	Bamboo BAM 70	In The Black Caribbean/Black Is Black	35
73	Ackee ACK 526	Walk Away Renee/What's It All About	5

NEWS

(see also Patto, Glenn Hughes, Finders Keepers, Miller, Big Boy Pete)

66	Decca F 12356	The Entertainer/I Count The Tears	15
66	Decca F 12477	This Is The Moment (from the TV series "Adam Adamant")/Ya Ya Da Da	12

NEWS FROM BABEL

86	Recommended RE 6116	NEWS FROM BABEL (LP, hand-screened sleeve)	12
89	ReR 6116 RE 6116	WORK RESUMED ON THE TOWER (LP)	18

NEW SEEKERS

71	Coca-Cola CPZ 2593	Buy The World/Ivor Raymand's Orchestra - It's The Real Thing	10

NEW SETTLERS

74	York YR 218	She Didn't Forget Her Shoes/Lifelight	12

BOBBY NEWSOME

72	Mojo 2093 018	Jody Come And Get Your Shoes/Post Office	10

OLIVIA NEWTON-JOHN

(see also Toomorrow, Marvin & Farrar)

66	Decca F 12396	Till You Say You'll Be Mine/For Ever	150
71	Pye International 7N 25543	If Not For You/The Biggest Clown	6
80	Jet JET 10-185	Xanadu/Fool Country (10" pink vinyl, die-cut p/s, with ELO)	8
78	EMI EMAP 789	TOTALLY HOT (LP, picture disc)	20

NEWTOWN NEUROTICS

79	No Wonder A 45	Hypocrite/You Said No (no p/s, with insert & sticker)	80
79	No Wonder A 45	Hypocrite/You Said No	20
80	No Wonder NOW 4	When The Oil Runs Out/Oh No (p/s)	40
82	CNT 4/No Wonder NOW 56	Kick Out The Tories!/Mindless Violence! (p/s)	15
82	CNT CNT 010	Licensing Hours/No Sanctuary (p/s)	18
83	Razor RZS 107	Blitzkrieg Bop/Hypocrite (New Version)/I Remember You (p/s)	10
84	No Wonder NOW 6T	Suzi/Fools (p/s)	10
83	Razor RAZ 6	BEGGARS CAN BE CHOOSERS (LP)	20

NEWTRAMENT

83	Jive 19094	London Bridge Is Falling Down/(Dub Mix)/(Special Vocoder Mix) (12")	8

NEW TRENDS

67	Columbia SX 6245	THE NEW TRENDS (LP)	15

NEW VICTORY BAND

78	Topic 12TS 382	ONE MORE DANCE AND THEN (LP)	15

NEW WALK

83	Web WEB 22	Pressure Point/Shape Of Things To Come (p/s)	12

MINT VALUE £

NEW WANDERERS

79	Grapevine GRP 144	This Man In Love/Adam And Eve	10
79	Grapevine GRP 144	This Man In Love/Adam And Eve (DJ Copy)	20

NEW WORLD

68	Saga FID 2114	TRUMPET A GO-GO (LP)	12

NEW YORK DOLLS

(see also Johnny Thunders, Heartbreakers, Sylvain Sylvain, Idols)

73	Mercury 6052 402	Jet Boy/Vietnamese Baby	15
74	Mercury 6052 615	Stranded In The Jungle/Who Are The Mystery Girls	8
77	Mercury 6160 008	Jet Boy/Babylon/Who Are The Mystery Girls	6
85	Antler DOLLS 1	Personality Crisis/Subway Train (picture disc)	8
85	Antler DOLLS 2	Looking For A Kiss/Bad Girl (picture disc)	8
73	Mercury 6338 270	NEW YORK DOLLS (LP, laminated front and black sleeve)	40
74	Mercury 6338 498	TOO MUCH TOO SOON (LP)	30
77	Mercury 9286.996/7	NEW YORK DOLLS (LP)	20

NEW YORK PUBLIC LIBRARY

66	Columbia DB 7948	I Ain't Gonna Eat Out My Heart Anymore/Rejected	25
68	MCA MU 1025	Gotta Get Away/Time Wastin'	15
68	MCA MU 1045	Love Me Two Times/Which Way To Go	10
72	B & C CB 176	Whei Ling Ty Luu/Boozy Queen	8

NEW YORK ROCK ENSEMBLE

71	CBS 5292	Running Down The Highway/Law And Order	5
69	Atco 228 932	FAITHFUL FRIENDS (LP)	12
71	CBS 64126	ROLL OVER (LP)	12
72	CBS 64324	FREEDOMBURGER (LP)	12

NEXT BAND

78	Gannet SRTS/79/CUS 159	FOUR BY THREE EP (p/s)	50

NEXUS 21

89	Blue Chip BLUE C34R	(Still) Life Keeps Moving Remix (12")	15
89	Blue Chip BLUE C34T	(Still) Life Keeps Moving (12")	15
91	Network NWKT 35	I Know We Can Make It (12", white label)	12
89	Blue Chip BLUE TEC. 2	THE RHYTHM OF LIFE (LP)	20

NIADEM'S GHOST

(see also IQ)

87	Hibination HIDE 002	THIRST (EP, cassette)	15
86	Hibination HIDE 001	IN SHELTERED WINDS (LP)	25

NICE

(see also Keith Emerson, Emerson Lake & Palmer, Jackson Heights, Habits, Brian Davison, Refugee, Attack, Jet, P.P. Arnold)

67	Immediate IM 059	The Thoughts Of Emerlist Davjack/Angel Of Death	12
68	Immediate IM 068	America/The Diamond Hard Blue Apples Of The Moon (pink label, in p/s)	18
68	Immediate IM 068	America/The Diamond Hard Blue Apples Of The Moon (pink label)	10
68	Immediate IM 072	Brandenburger/Happy Freuds	10
70	Charisma CB 132	Country Pie/One Of Those People	6
70s	Immediate IM 068	America/The Diamond Hard Blue Apples Of The Moon (white label, reissue in p/s)	6
67	Immediate IMLP 016	THE THOUGHTS OF EMERLIST DAVJACK (LP, mono)	50
67	Immediate IMSP 016	THE THOUGHTS OF EMERLIST DAVJACK (LP, stereo)	40
67	Immediate AS 2	ALBUM SAMPLER - THE THOUGHTS OF EMERLIST DAVJACK (1-sided LP, promo only)	30
68	Immediate IMSP 020	ARS LONGA VITA BREVIS (LP, laminated front, flipbacks, pink label, "Sold in U.K..." text)	40
69	Immediate IMSP 026	THE NICE (LP, gatefold sleeve)	30
70	Charisma CAS 1014	FIVE BRIDGES (LP, pink label, gatefold sleeve)	15
71	Charisma CAS 1030	ELEGY (LP, gatefold sleeve pink 'scroll' label)	20

NICK NICELY

80	Voxette VOX 1001	D.C.T. Dreams/Treeline (p/s, reissue copies £4)	20
81	EMI EMI 5256	Hillyfields (1892)/49 Cigars (p/s)	15
04	Tenth Planet TP 059	PSYCHOTROPIA (LP, 1000 copies only)	20

ALBERT NICHOLAS

(see also Al Fairweather)

56	Tempo A 129	How Long Blues (with Al Fairweather)/Rose Room (with Lise West)	10

PAUL NICHOLAS

(see also Oscar, Paul Dean)

68	Polydor 56285	Where Do I Go/Here Comes The Clown	5
69	Polydor 56322	Who Can I Turn To/Sing A Sad Song For Sammy	5
70	Polydor 56374	Freedom City/Run Shaker Life (with p/s)	100
70	Polydor 56374	Freedom City/Run Shaker Life	70
71	Polydor 2058 086	The World Is Beautiful/Lamplighter	45

BILLY NICHOLLS

68	Immediate IM 063	Would You Believe/Daytime Girl (features Small Faces)	50
73	Track 2094 109	Forever's No Time At All/This Song Is Green (with Pete Townshend)	12
68	Immediate IMCP 009	WOULD YOU BELIEVE (LP, withdrawn)	3000
90s	Tenth planet	WOULD YOU BELIEVE (LP, reissue, with insert)	40

SUE NICHOLLS

68	Pye 7N.17565	Where Will You Be/Every Day	5

MIKE NICHOLS & ELAINE MAY

62	Mercury AMT 1192	A Little More Gauze/Merry Christmas Doctor	6
59	Mercury MMC 14005	IMPROVISATIONS TO MUSIC (LP)	15
65	Mercury 20031 MCL	THE BEST OF MIKE NICHOLS & ELAINE MAY (LP)	18

MINT VALUE £

PENNY NICHOLS
68 Pye int. 7N 2451 — Look Around Rock/Farina — 35

ROSEMARY NICHOLS
70 Gemini GM5013 — Once Upon A Time/Jaby — 10

LEA NICHOLSON
72 Trailer LER 3010 — HORSEMUSIC (LP) — 20

ROGER NICHOLSON
72 Trailer LER 3034 — NONSUCH FOR DULCIMER (LP, red label) — 20

STEVIE NICKS
(see also Fleetwood Mac, Buckingham-Nicks, Tom Petty & Heartbreakers)

89 EMI EMD 1008 — THE OTHER SIDE OF THE MIRROR (LP, with hologram) — 12

NiCKY AND THE DOTS
78 Small Wonder SMALL 12 — Never Been So Stuck/Linoleum Walk (p/s) — 6

NICO
(see also John Cale, Velvet Underground, Ayers Cale Nico & Eno)

65 Immediate IM 003 — I'm Not Sayin'/The Last Mile — 75
81 Flicknife FLS 206 — Vegas/Saeta (p/s) — 8
82 Immediate IMS 003 — I'm Not Saying/The Last Mile (p/s, reissue) — 5
82 Half 1?2 1 — Procession/All Tomorrow's Parties (p/s) — 5
83 Aura AUS 137 — Heroes/One More Chance (p/s) — 5
85 Beggars Banquet BEG 139 — My Funny Valentine/My Heart Is Empty (p/s, as Nico and the Faction) — 5
68 Elektra EKL 4029 — THE MARBLE INDEX (LP, orange label, mono) — 45
68 Elektra EKS 74029 — THE MARBLE INDEX (LP, orange label, stereo) — 40
71 Reprise RSLP 6424 — DESERTSHORE (LP, with John Cale) — 35
71 MGM Select 2353 025 — CHELSEA GIRL (LP) — 35
74 Island ILPS 9311 — THE END (LP) — 15
81 Aura AUL 715 — DRAMA OF EXILE (LP, colour cover) — 18

NICODEMUS
81 Cha Cha CHAD 44 — Gunman Connection/It Have To Ram (12") — 20
81 Greensleeves GRED 75 — BONE CONNECTION/LEROY SMART: All My Love (12") — 15
82 Cha Cha CHALP 011 — GUNMAN CONNECTION (LP) — 40
82 Black Joy DHLP 2003 — DANCE HALL STYLE (LP) — 50

JIMMY NICOL (& SHUBDUBS)
(see also Sound Of Jimmy Nicol, Georgie Fame)

64 Pye 7N 15623 — Humpty Dumpty/Night Train — 20
64 Pye 7N 15666 — Husky/Don't Come Back (solo) — 18
64 Pye 7N 15699 — Baby Please Don't Go/Shub Dubbery (possibly unissued) — 20

NICOLETTE
89 Shut Up & Dance SUAD 14 — Waking Up (12") — 12

WATT NICOLL
71 Xtra XTRA 1122 — NICE TO BE NICE (LP) — 15

NICRA
(see also Keith Tippett)

77 Ogun OG 010 — LISTEN/HEAR (LP) — 18

NIDDY GRIDDY BAND
68 Pye 7N 17461 — Dinny Girgy/Summertime — 6

NIE ELECTRIKK
80 Synesthesia SYN 1 — Cover Girl/Practically Isolate (p/s) — 8

NIEMEN
72 CBS 564896 — STRANGE IS THIS WORLD (LP, orange/black label) — 25

STEVE NIEVE
80 Comb 1 — OUTLINE ON A HAIRDO (EP) — 20

NIGGY HOI!
80s Deli K1Z — Theme From Niggy Hoi!/Titanium Kedi (p/s) — 8

NIGHT DOCTOR
81 Race Records RB DIS 001 — Romancin'/Menelik (12") — 35

NIGHT MOVES
83 GC GCT 2 — Transdance (New York Disco Mix)/Transdance (UK Disco Mix)/Nightdrive (12") — 30
84 GC/MCA GCT 1001 — Transdance (Robot Rock) (UK Club Mix)/You Can Take My Love/ Beat This/ Nightdrive (12", p/s) — 20

NIGHTBIRDS
59 Oriole CB 1490 — Cat On A Hot Tin Roof/The Square — 12

NIGHTBLOOMS
90 Fierce FRIGHT 041 — Crystal Eyes/Never Dream At All (p/s) — 10

NIGHTCRAWLERS
67 London HLR 10109 — The Little Black Egg/You're Running Wild — 50

NIGHT-HAWKS
58 Fontana H 120 — Cool For Cats/Time Will Tell (78) — 10

NIGHTIME FLYER
69 Pye 7N 17739 — Talk To Me/Spinning Wheel — 6
69 Pye 7N 17798 — Don't Push Me Baby/Thru' Loving You — 7
71 Pye 7N 45046 — Love On Borrowed Time/It's A Hurtin' Thing — 6

NIGHTIME FLYER
81 Red Eye EYE 2 — Out With A Vengeance/Heavy Metal Rules (p/s) — 20
03 Phoenix NWOBHM 7007 — Out With A Vengeance/Heavy Metal Rules (yellow vinyl reissue, numbered, 250 copies, 7.5 inch sleeve) — 10

MINT VALUE £

TUNDE NIGHTINGALE & HIS HIGHLIFE BOYS

68	Melodisc MLPAS 12-142	THE BIRDS THAT SINGS ALL THE NIGHT (LP)	15

NIGHTMARE

84	Ebony EBON 22	WAITING FOR THE TWILIGHT (LP)	12
83	PVK PV 119	I Wanna Be Shot/Ruth Ellis (p/s)	6

NIGHTMARES IN WAX

(see also Dead Or Alive)

79	Inevitable INEV 0002	BIRTH OF A NATION (EP, with wraparound p/s)	20
84	KY KY 9	Black Leather/Shangri-La (12", 'horror' p/s)	18
85	KY KY 9 1/2	Black Leather/Shangri-La/Girls Song (12", different p/s, 3,000 only)	20

NIGHTRIDERS

(see also Mike Sheridan & Nightriders, Mike Sheridan's Lot, Idle Race, Jeff Lynne)

66	Polydor BM 56066	Love Me Right Now/Your Friend (withdrawn)	120
66	Polydor BM 56066	Love Me Right Now/Your Friend (promo copy)	85
66	Polydor BM 56116	It's Only The Dog/Your Friend	60

NIGHTRIDERS

79	Stardust STR 1001	I Saw Her With Another Guy/London Town (picture insert)	15

NIGHTSHIFT

65	Piccadilly 7N 35243	Corrine Corrina/Lavender Tree	15
65	Piccadilly 7N 35264	That's My Story/Stormy Monday Blues	18

NIGHTSHIFT

79	Zum 9	Jetset	6

NIGHT-TIMERS

(see also Herbie Goins & Night-Timers, Ronnie Jones)

65	Parlophone R 5355	The Music Played On/Yield Not To Temptation (featuring Herbie Goins)	50

NIGHTWING

(see also Alec Johnson Band, Nutz)

80	Ovation OVS 1209	Barrel Of Pain/Nightwing (p/s)	10
84	Gull GULS 75	Treading Water/Call Your Name (p/s)	6
84	Gull GULS 7512	Treading Water/Call Your Name/Barrel Of Pain (12", red vinyl, p/s)	10
84	Gull GULS 77	Night Of Mystery/Dressed To Kill (p/s)	10
84	Gull GULS 7712	Night Of Mystery/Dressed To Kill (12", p/s)	12
85	Gull GULS 80	Strangers Are Welcome/Games To Play//The Devil Walks Behind You/ Cell 151 (double pack, gatefold p/s)	5
79	Ovation OV 1757	SOMETHING IN THE AIR (LP)	12
83	Gull PGULP 1038	STAND UP AND BE COUNTED (LP, picture disc)	15

NIGHTWISH

04	Back On Black BOBV 003 DPD	ANGELS FALL FIRST (2-LP picture discs, stickered bag)	20
04	Back On Black BOBV 004 DPD	OCEANBORN (2-LP picture discs, stickered bag)	20
04	Back On Black BOBV 007 DPD	OVER THE HILLS AND FAR AWAY (2-LP picture discs, stickered bag)	20
04	Back On Black BOBV 006 DPD	WISHMASTER 92-LP picture discs, stickered bag)	
04	Back On Black BOBV 008 DPD	CENTURY CHILD (2-LP picture discs, stickered bag)	20
05	Back On Black BOBV 035 DPD	ONCE (2-LP picture discs, stickered bag)	20

NIHILIST SPASM BAND

85	United Dairies UD 016	1X - X = X (LP)	15

BILL NILES

67	Decca F 12661	Pashionella Grundy/Bric-A-Bric Man	15

WILLY NILLY

(see also Randy Newman, Ringo Starr, Cher)

84	Ad Hoc AH 1	On The Spur Of The Moment/Half A Job (p/s, with 'time-table' insert)	45

(HARRY) NILSSON

67	RCA Victor RCA 1632	You Can't Do That/Ten Little Indians	6
68	RCA Victor RCA 1675	One/Sister Marie	6
68	RCA RCA 1707	Everybody's Talkin'/Don't Leave Me	5
68	RCA RCA 1764	Mourning Glory/Rainmaker	6
69	RCA RCA 1864	Maybe/The Puppy Song	6
69	RCA RCA 1876	Everybody's Talkin'/One	5
72	RCA RCA 2266	You're Breaking My Heart/Spaceman (possibly withdrawn, Demo stamped copy)	12
68	RCA Victor RD/SF 7928	PANDEMONIUM SHADOW SHOW (LP, mono)	18
68	RCA Victor RD/SF 7928	PANDEMONIUM SHADOW SHOW (LP, stereo)	15
68	RCA RD/SF 7973	AERIAL BALLET (LP, mono)	18
68	RCA RD/SF 7973	AERIAL BALLET (LP, stereo)	15
69	RCA SF 8010	SKIDOO (LP, soundtrack)	25
69	RCA SF 8046	HARRY (LP)	15
73	RCA SF 8326	AERIAL PANDEMONIUM BALLET (LP)	12
74	Rapple/RCA APL1-0220	SON OF DRACULA (LP, soundtrack, with Ringo Starr, fold-out sleeve)	15

NILSSON TWINS

57	Capitol CL 14698	Rain On My Window/I Dance When I Walk	5

NIMBO

71	Pye 7N 450097	Maisie Jones/Forget Her	8
72	Pye 7N 45174	When The Swallows Fly/Noticeingly By	12

DEREK NIMMO

67	CBS 3022	Toast And Honey/Tiptoe Thru The Tulips	5

MINT VALUE £

LEONARD NIMOY

68	Dot (S)LPD 511	MR. SPOCK PRESENTS MUSIC FROM OUTER SPACE (LP)	25
72	Rediffusion ZS 156	MUSIC FROM OUTER SPACE (LP, reissue of DOT (S) LPD 511)	15

NINA

69	CBS 4681	Do You Know How Christmas Trees Are Grown?/The More Things Change	12

NINE BELOW ZERO

81	A&M AMS 8127	Ain't Comin' Back/Liquor Lover (p/s)	5
81	A&M AMS 8110	Three Times Enough/Doghouse (p/s, yellow vinyl)	5
82	A&M AMSX 8210	Wipe Away Your Kiss/True Life Is A Crime (12")	8

NINE DAYS WONDER

(see also Gnidralog)

71	Harvest SHSP 4014	NINE DAYS WONDER (LP, textured sleeve, EMI logo on label)	80

NINE INCH NAILS

90	Island 12IS 482	Down In It (skin)/Terrible Lie (mix)/Down In Tt (shred - demo) (12", p/s)	10
91	Island IS 484	Head Like A Hole/Head like a hole (copper mix) (p/s)	5
91	Island 10ISP 484	Head Like A Hole (slate)/Head Like A Hole (copper) (10", poster p/s)	8
91	Island 12IS 484	Head Like A Hole (slate)/Head Like A Hole (copper) / Head Like A Hole (opal) (12", ps)	10
91	Island ISDJ 484	Head Like A Hole (radio edit) (promo, stickered p/s, same track both sides)	20
91	Island ISDJ 508	Sin (Radio Edit)/(same) (promo only, stickered p/s)	12
91	Island 9IS 508	Sin (Long)/Sin (Dub)/Get Down Make Love (9", p/s)	10
92	Island IS 552DJ	Wish (Radio Edit) (1-sided, stickered plain sleeve, promo only)	12
94	Island IS 592	March Of The Pigs/A Violent Fluid (p/s, etched disc)	5
94	Island 9IS 592	March Of The Pigs/A Violent Fluid/All the pigs, all lined up/ Underneath the skin (9", numbered p/s)	10
94	Island 12IS 596	Closer (deviation)/Closer (further away)/Closer (6.26)/Closer (precursor)/ Closer (internal) (12", p/s)	10
94	Island 12ISX 596	Closer to God/March Of The Fuckheads/Heresy (blind)/Memorabilia (12", p/s)	10
90	Island CID 482	DOWN IN IT (mixes) (CD EP, numbered case)	20
90	Island CID 484	HEAD LIKE A HOLE (CD EP)	10
92	Interscope IMCD 8004	BROKEN (CD EP, foldout digipak)	8
91	Island ILPS 9973	PRETTY HATE MACHINE (LP)	12
92	Interscope ILPM 8004	BROKEN (1-sided 6 track mini LP with free 7" 'Physical [your'e so]' / 'Suck')	30
92	Island ILPM 8005	FIXED (remix mini LP)	18
94	Island ILPSD 8012	THE DOWNWARD SPIRAL (double LP, gatefold sleeve)	18
99	Island ILPST 8091	THE FRAGILE (triple LP, inners, booklet)	30

NINE INCH WORMS

97	Martian BEER 05	A NIGHT ON THE TOWN WITH THE NINE INCH WORMS (9" LP)	12

999

(see also Kilburn & High Roads)

77	Labritain LAB 999	I'm Alive/Quite Disappointing (p/s)	10
77	United Artists UP 36299	Nasty Nasty/No Pity (p/s, green vinyl)	10
77	United Artists UP 36299	Nasty Nasty/No Pity (p/s, black vinyl)	5
77	United Artists FREE 7	Nasty Nasty/No Pity (78rpm promo, 50 copies only)	250
78	Labritain 12 FREE 10	Waiting/Action (12", mail-order freebie)	8
78	United Artists UP 36399	Emergency/My Street Stinks (p/s)	5
78	United Artists UP 36376	Me And My Desire/Crazy (p/s)	5
78	United Artists UP 36435	Feelin' Alright With The Crew/Titanic (My Over) Reaction (p/s)	5
78	United Artists UP 36467	Homicide/Soldier (p/s, green vinyl)	5
79	Radar ADA 46	Found Out Too Late/Lie, Lie, Lie	5
81	Albion ION 1011	Obsessed/Change/Lie, Lie, Lie (live) (p/s, with laminated sleeve, shrinkwrapped with patch)	6
81	Albion ION 1017	Li'l Red Riding Hood/Waiting For Your Number To Be Called/I Ain't Gonna Tell Ya (live) (p/s, with stencil; shrinkwrapped)	6
81	Albion ION 1023	Indian Reservation/So Greedy (Remixed)/Taboo (Remix) (p/s, clear vinyl, with sticker)	5
78	United Artists UAG 30199	999 (LP, with inner sleeve)	12
78	United Artists UAG 30209	SEPARATES (LP, with inner sleeve)	15

9.30 FLY

72	Ember NR 5062	9.30 FLY (LP, textured gatefold sleeve)	200

NINESENSE

(see also Elton Dean, Julie Tippetts, Keith Tippett, Mark Charig, Harold Beckett, Alan Skidmore)

76	Ogun OG 900	OH! FOR THE EDGE (LP)	20
77	Ogun OG 910	HAPPY DAZE (LP)	20

1984

69	Big T BIG 117	This Little Boy/Rosalyn	12
69	Big T BIG 120	Got To Have Your Love/Here We Are	8

1984

71	Decca F23159	Little Girl/Laramee	12

1919

82	Red Rhino RED 22	Repulsion/Tear Down These Walls (white hand-written labels, 500 only)	25

1910 FRUITGUM CO.

68	Pye International 7N 25447	Simon Says/Reflections From The Looking Glass	5
68	Pye International 7N 25458	May I Take A Giant Step (Into Your Heart)/(Poor Old) Mr. Jensen	5
68	Pye Intl. 7N 25468	1,2,3, Red Light/Sticky Sticky	6
68	Pye Int. 7N.25478	Pop Goes The Weasel/The Year 2001	6
68	Pye Intl. N(S)PL 28115	SIMON SAYS (LP)	18
69	Buddah 203 014	GOODY GOODY GUMDROPS (LP)	15
70	Buddah 2359 006	HARD RIDE (LP)	12

1910 FRUITGUM CO./LEMON PIPERS

68	Pye Intl. NEP 44091	PRESENTING (EP, 1 side each)	10

MINT VALUE £

NINEY (& DESTROYERS/OBSERVERS)
(see also Niney's All Stars, Observers)

70	Amalgamated AMG 856	Niney Special/Danger Zone	15
70	Pressure Beat PR 5501	Honey No Money/INSPIRATIONS: This Message To You	8
71	Big BG 317	You Must Believe/You Must Believe Version	12
71	Big Shot BI 568	Blood And Fire/Mud And Water	8
71	Big Shot BI 586	Message To The Ungodly/Message To The Ungodly - Version	8
71	Supreme SUP 214	You Must Believe Me/RUPIE EDWARDS ALLSTARS: Funk The Funk	12
71	Gas GAS 167	Blood And Fire/ROLAND ALPHONSO: 33 66	20
71	Moodisc HME 111	People Let Love Shine/MUDIES ALL STARS: Too Much	6
72	Big Shot BI 607	Hiding By The Riverside/The Red Sea	5
72	Big Shot BI 609	Beg In The Gutter/Beg In The Gutter Version	5
72	Big Shot BI 610	Everyday Music (by The Observers)/Observing The Avenue	6
72	Bullet BU 503	Aily And Ailaloo (& Max)/Version	5
72	Downtown DT 494	Get Out My Life/Get Out My Life - Version (with the Observers)	5
72	Downtown DT 495	Hi Diddle/Hi Diddle - Version	5

NINEY'S ALL STARS
(see also Niney, Observers)

70	Unity UN 563	Skankee/Skankee - Version	10

NING

71	Decca F 23114	Machine/More Ning	18

NINJAMAN & FLOURGON

90	Sure Delight 23 SDT	ZIG IT UP - MAIN ATTRACTION: Zig It Up (Radio/Freestyle/ Funke-Club/Funke- Instrumental Mixes) (12", p/s)	10

NINO & EBBTIDES

61	Top Rank JAR 572	Those Oldies But Goodies/Don't Run Away	40

9TH CREATION

76	Pye 7N 45622	Sexy Girl/Falling In Love	20

NIPPLE ERECTORS
(see also Nips, Pogues)

78	Soho SH 1/2	King Of The Bop/Nervous Wreck (with glossy p/s)	40
78	Soho SH 1/2	King Of The Bop/Nervous Wreck (later matt p/s)	20

NIPS
(see also Nipple Erectors, Pogues)

78	Soho SH 4	All The Time In The World/Private Eyes (foldover p/s)	30
80	Soho SH 9	Gabrielle/Vengeance	18
80	Soho SH 9	Gabrielle/Vengeance (tour copy with 'licensed to cool' stamp)	30
80	Chiswick CHIS 119	Gabrielle/Vengeance (reissue, p/s)	15
81	Test Pressing TP 5	Happy Song/Nobody To Love (p/s)	30
80	Soho HOHO 1	ONLY AT THE END OF THE BEGINNING (LP, with insert, white labels)	35

NIRVANA (U.K.)
(see also Patrick Campbell-Lyons, Ray Singer, Pica, Hat & Tie)

67	Island WIP 6016	Tiny Goddess/I Believe In Magic	25
67	Island WIP 6020	Pentecost Hotel/Feelin' Shattered	20
68	Island WIP 6029	Rainbow Chaser/Flashbulb	25
68	Island WIP 6038	Girl In The Park/C Side In Ocho Rios	20
68	Island WIP 6045	All Of Us (The Touchables)/Trapeze	12
69	Island WIP 6052	Wings Of Love/Requiem To John Coltrane	25
69	Island WIP 6057	Oh! What A Performance/Darling Darlene	20
70	Pye International 7N 25525	The World Is Cold Without You/Christopher Lucifer	20
71	Vertigo 6059 035	The Saddest Day Of My Life/(I Wanna Go) Home	25
71	Philips 6006 127	Pentecost Hotel/Lazy Day Drift	12
72	Philips 6006 166	Stadium/Please Believe Me	12
76	Bradleys BRAD 7602	Two Of A Kind/Before Midnight	6
76	Island WIP 6180	Rainbow Chaser/Tiny Goddess (p/s)	7
78	Pepper UP 36461	Love Is/Pascale	5
79	Pepper UP 36538	Restless Wind/Thank You And Goodnight	5
81	Zilch ZILCH 8	The Picture Of Dorian Gray/No It Isn't	5
82	Zilch ZILCH 15	Black And White Or Colour/Tall Trees	5
88	Bam Caruso OPRA 45	Black Flower/WIMPLE WINCH: Save My Soul (jukebox issue, die-cut sleeve)	5
68	Island ILP 959	THE STORY OF SIMON SIMOPATH (LP, mono, pink label, black/orange circle logo)	150
68	Island ILPS 9059	THE STORY OF SIMON SIMOPATH (LP, stereo, pink label, black/orange circle logo)	250
68	Island ILPS 9087	ALL OF US (LP, pink label, black/orange circle logo)	150
70	Pye Intl. NSPL 28132	DEDICATED TO MARKOS III (LP)	175
71	Vertigo 6360 031	LOCAL ANAESTHETIC (LP, gatefold sleeve, swirl label)	130
72	Philips 6308 089	SONGS OF LOVE AND PRAISE (LP)	80
87	Bam-Caruso KIRI 061	BLACK FLOWER (LP)	12

NIRVANA (U.S.)
(see also Foo Fighters)

89	Tupelo TUP EP8	Blew/Love Buzz/Been A Son/Stain (12", p/s)	40
89	Tupelo TUP CD8	Blew/Love Buzz/Been A Son/Stain (CD)	35
90	Tupelo TUP 25	Sliver/Dive (gatefold p/s, green vinyl only, 2,000 pressed)	30
91	Tupelo TUP EP25	Sliver/Dive/About A Girl (live)/Dive (12", p/s)	25
91	Tupelo TUP EP25	Sliver/Dive/About A Girl (live)/Dive (12", repressing, blue vinyl, p/s)	45
91	Tupelo TUP CDEP25	Sliver/Dive/About A Girl (live)/Spank Thru (live) (CD)	20
91	Geffen DGCT 5	Smells Like Teen Spirit (Edit)/Even In His Youth/Aneurysm (12", p/s)	20
91	Geffen DGCS 5	Smells Like Teen Spirit/Drain You (p/s)	8
91	Geffen DGCTP 5	Smells Like Teen Spirit (Edit)/Drain You (LP Version)/Aneurysm (12", picture disc, die-cut p/s)	35
91	Geffen DGCCD 5	Smells Like Teen Spirit (Edit)/Drain You/Even In His Youth/Aneurysm (CD, digipak with tour dates)	12

			MINT VALUE £
92	Geffen DGCTP 7	Come As You Are/Endless, Nameless/School (live) (12", picture disc, die-cut p/s)	35
92	Geffen DGCTP 9	Lithium/Been A Son (live)/Curmudgeon (12", picture disc, die-cut p/s)	20
92	Geffen DGCTD 9	Lithium/Been A Son (live)/Curmudgeon (CD, digipak)	10
92	Geffen GFS 34	In Bloom/Sliver (live)/Polly (live) (p/s)	10
92	Geffen DGCTP 34	In Bloom/Sliver (live)/Polly (live) (12", picture disc, die-cut p/s)	18
93	Touch & Go TG 83	Oh, The Guilt/JESUS LIZARD: Puss (p/s, blue vinyl, with poster)	25
93	Touch & Go TG 83	Oh, The Guilt/JESUS LIZARD: Puss (p/s, blue vinyl, without poster)	10
93	Touch & Go TG 83	Oh, The Guilt/JESUS LIZARD: Puss (p/s, black vinyl)	28
93	Touch & Go TGCD 83	Oh, The Guilt/JESUS LIZARD: Puss (CD)	10
93	Geffen GFST 54	Heart Shaped Box/Milk It/Marigold (12" p/s)	10
93	Geffen GFST 66	All Apologies/Rape Me (12", p/s with 2 art prints)	12
93	Geffen GFSTD 66	All Apologies/Rape Me (CD)	8
94	Geffen (no cat. no.)	Penny Royal Tea (Scott Litt Mix)/Where Did You Sleep Last Night (live) (unreleased, 10 test pressings only)	600
94	Geffen NIRPRO (no cat. no.)	Penny Royal Tea (Scott Litt Mix) (CD, 1-track, no inlay, promo only)	600
95	Geffen GED 24901	SINGLES (6 x CD box set)	20
89	Tupelo TUP LP 6	BLEACH (LP, 300 on white vinyl)	200
89	Tupelo TUP LP 6	BLEACH (LP, 2,000 on green vinyl)	60
89	Tupelo TUP LP 6	BLEACH (LP, black vinyl)	20
89	Tupelo TUP CD 6	BLEACH (CD, original issue with extra tracks "Love Buzz" & "Downer")	20
91	Geffen DGC 24425	NEVERMIND (LP, with inner sleeve)	15
91	Geffen DGCCD 24425	NEVERMIND (CD, without uncredited bonus track "Endless, Nameless")	15
94	Geffen GED 24727	UNPLUGGED IN NEW YORK (LP, white vinyl with inner sleeve)	35
02	Sub Pop 9878700341	BLEACH (LP, white vinyl, with inner)	15
04	Geffen NIRVBOXCDP1	SELECTIONS FROM WITH THE LIGHTS OUT (CD card wallet, promo)	40

NITE-LITERS

72	RCA 2214	K-Jee/Tanga Boo Gonk	8
72	RCA SF 8282	INSTRUMENTAL DIRECTIONS (LP)	20

NITE PEOPLE

(see also Banana Bunch)

66	Fontana TF 747	Sweet Tasting Wine/Nobody But You	25
67	Fontana TF 808	Trying To Find Another Man/Stay As Sweet As You Are	20
67	Fontana TF 885	Summertime Blues/In The Springtime	70
68	Fontana TF 919	Morning Sun/Where You There	35
69	Page One POF 149	Love, Love, Love/Hot Smoke And Sassafras (with insert)	25
69	Page One POF 149	Love, Love, Love/Hot Smoke And Sassafras	15
69	Page One POF 159	Is This A Dream/Cream Tea	25
70	Page One POF 174	Season Of The Rain/P.M.	15
69	Page One POLS 025	P.M. (LP)	230

NITE ROCKERS

58	RCA RCA 1079	Nite Rock (Lonely Train)/Oh! Baby	50
58	RCA RCA 1079	Nite Rock (Lonely Train)/Oh! Baby (78)	30

NITESHADES

65	CBS 201763	Be My Guest/I Must Reveal	18
65	CBS 201817	Fell So Fast/I'm Not Gonna Worry	12

NITRO FUNCTION

(see under Billy Cox)

NITS

79	CBS 8049	Tutti Raqazzi/Harrow Accident	8

NITTY GRITTY DIRT BAND

(see also Kaleidescope, Chris Darlow)

67	Liberty LIB 55948	Buy Me For The Rain/Candy Man	10
68	Liberty LBF 15099	Collegiana/End Of Your Line	8
69	Liberty LBF 15275	Some of Shelly's Blues/Yukon Railway	6
70	Liberty LBF 15358	Rave On/The Cure	6
68	Liberty LBL/LBS 83122	PURE DIRT (LP)	30
69	Liberty LBL/LBS 83286	DEAD AND ALIVE (LP)	25
71	Liberty LBG 83345	UNCLE CHARLIE AND HIS DOG TEDDY (LP, gatefold sleeve)	20
72	United Artists UAS 29284	ALL THE GOOD TIMES (LP)	15
74	United Artists USD 307/8	STARS AND STRIPES FOREVER (2-LP)	18

NITZER EBB

85	own label	BASIC PAIN PROCEDURE (EP, cassette, given away at gig)	20

JACK NITZSCHE

(see also Date With Soul, Mick Jagger, Captain Beefheart, Randy Newman, Crazy Horse)

63	Reprise R 20202	The Lonely Surfer/Song For A Summer Night	30
63	Reprise R 20237	Night Walker/Green Grass Of Texas	18
78	MCA MCA 366	Hard Workin' Man (featuring Captain Beefheart)/Coke Machine	15
74	Warner Bros K 41211	ST GILES CRIPPLEGATE (LP)	30

NIVENS

89	Woosh WOOSH 5	Yesterday/I Hope You'll Always Be My Friend (p/s)	5

WILLIE NIX

(see under Willie Love, Joe Hill Louis)

NIX-NOMADS

64	HMV POP 1354	You're Nobody (Till Somebody Loves You)/She'll Be Sweeter Than You (demos miscredited to Nix-Nomands)	100

MEL NIXON

75	Alaska ALA 26	Every Beat Of Your Heart/ASTRA NOVA ORCHESTRA: Soul Sleeper	6
72	Parlophone R5958	Pillars Of Straw/Ev'ry Little Beat Of Your Heart	6

MINT VALUE £

NMONIC

00	YNR YNR002	VOICEMAIL (EP)	12

RAB NOAKES

78	Ring O' 2017 115	Waiting Here For You/Restless (in p/s)	18
78	Ring O' 2017 115	Waiting Here For You/Restless	12
78	Ring O' 2017 117	I Won't Let You Down/Long After Dark (unreleased)	0
70	Decca SKL 5061	DO YOU SEE THE LIGHTS (LP)	40
72	A&M AMLS 68119	RAB NOAKES (LP, with Stealers Wheel)	20
78	Ring O' 2339 201	RESTLESS (LP)	12

NOBELMEN

59	Top Rank JAR 155	Thunder Wagon/Dragon Walk	20
59	Top Rank JAR 155	Thunder Wagon/Dragon Walk (78)	15

BARRY NOBLE

68	Columbia DB 8438	I've Got My Eyes On You/I've Always Wanted You	5

KEITH NOBLE & RADO KLOSE

70	Eden EDEN LP 14	MR COMPROMISE (LP,, private pressing, handmade sleeve)	500

LISA NOBLE

58	Decca F 11006	Maggie! Yes Ma!/Who's Sorry Now	10

NICK NOBLE

(see also Dick Noel)

60	Coral Q 72403	The Tip Of My Fingers/Sweet Love	6
60	Coral Q 72413	Island Farewell/Excuse Me (I Think I've Got A Heartache)	6

PATSY ANN NOBLE

(see also Trisha Noble)

61	HMV POP 980	Good Looking Boy/The Guy Who Can Mend A Broken Heart	25
63	Columbia DB 4956	Don't You Ever Change Your Mind/Sour Grapes	15
63	Columbia DB 7008	Heartbreak Avenue/I'm Nobody's Baby	12
63	Columbia DB 7060	I Was Only Foolin' Myself/Ordinary Love	10
63	Columbia DB 7088	Accidents Will Happen/He Tells Me With His Eyes	20
63	Columbia DB 7148	It's Better To Cry Today/Don't Tell Him I Told You	10
64	Columbia DB 7258	I Did Nothing Wrong/Better Late Than Never	10
64	Columbia DB 7318	Private Property/Crack In The Door	10
65	Columbia DB 7472	Then You Can Tell Me Goodbye/If You Wanna Be More Than Friends	10
65	Polydor BM 56054	He Who Rides A Tiger/City Of Night	30

TRISHA NOBLE

(see also Patsy Ann Noble)

67	MGM MGM 1371	Live For Life/The New Is Rarely Patchka	20

WOODROW NOBLE

79	Baby Mother HIT DD10	Reggae A The Best (Feat. Prince Hammer)/Strike The Hammer Wild (12")	30

CLIFF NOBLES (& CO.)

68	Direction 58-3518	The Horse/Love Is Alright	12
68	Direction 58-3738	Judge Baby, I'm Back/Horse Fever (solo)	10
69	Direction 58-4205	Switch It On/Burning Desire	10
68	Direction 8-63477	THE HORSE (LP)	40

NO CHOICE

83	Riot City RIOT 20	SADIST DREAM (EP)	8

NO COVER

82	Guardian GRC 136	200 Voices/Seen Too Much	50

NOCTURNAL EMISSIONS

(see also Caroline K)

81	Sterile ION 2	FRUITING BODY (LP)	50
84	Sterile SR 6	NO SACRIFICE (12", p/s, 2,000 only)	12
84	CFC LP 2	CHAOS - LIVE AT THE RITZY (LP)	20
84	Illuminated JAMS LP 33	VIRAL SHEDDING (LP)	20
84	Sterile EMISS 001	TISSUE OF LIES (LP, 1st batch numbered)	50
84	Sterile EMISS 001	TISSUE OF LIES (LP, later pressing in blue sleeve)	25
84	Sterile SR 4	DROWNING IN A SEA OF BLISS (LP)	50
84	Sterile SR 5	BEFEHLSNOTSTAND (LP)	25
85	Sterile SRC 003	DEATHDAY (cassette)	15
85	Sterile SR 7	SONGS OF LOVE AND REVOLUTION (LP)	15
86	Sterile SR 9	SHAKE THOSE CHAINS, RATTLE THOSE CAGES (LP)	15
87	Earthly Delights EARTH 02	THE WORLD IS MY WOMB (LP)	20
88	Earthly Delights EARTH 04	SPIRITFLESH (LP)	20
89	Earthly Delights EARTH 03	STONEFACE (LP)	12
89	Earthly Delights EARTH 05	BEYOND LOGIC (LP, 250 signed)	25
89	Earthly Delights EARTH 05	BEYOND LOGIC (LP)	18
90	Earthly Delights EARTH 06	MOUTH OF THE BABES (LP)	30
93	Earthly Delights EARTH 08	THE QUICKENING (LP, 250 signed)	25
93	Earthly Delights EARTH 08	THE QUICKENING (LP)	18

NOCTURNES

55	MGM SP 1120	Whodat? (Buck Dance)/Hey Punchinello	10
55	MGM SP 1148	Birmin'ham/Toodle-oo Igaloo	10

NOCTURNES

64	Solar SRP 102	Trioka/Rawhide	15

NOCTURNES

(see also Lyn Paul)

67	Columbia DB 8158	Wish You Would Show Me Your Mind/I Do, I Do	10
67	Columbia DB 8219	Why (Am I Treated So Bad?)/Save The Last Dance For Me	10
68	Columbia DB 8332	A New Man/Suddenly Free	10
68	Columbia DB 8453	Carpet Man/Look At Me	15

MINT VALUE £

68 Columbia DB 8493 — Montage/Fairground Man — 40
68 Columbia S(C)X 6223 — THE NOCTURNES (LP) — 20
68 Columbia S(C)X 6315 — WANTED ALIVE (LP) — 25

NOCTURNS
64 Decca F 12002 — Carryin' On/Three Cool Cats — 10

PROFESSOR ERNEST NODE & HIS MUG & JUG BAND
67 Columbia DB 8100 — The Egg Plant That Ate Chicago/I'm In The Doghouse — 7

NODENS ICTUS
(see also Ozric Tentacles)
87 (No cat no) — THE GROVE OF SELVES (Cassette LP) — 50

DICK NOEL
(see also Nick Nobel)
56 London HLH 8295 — (The Same Thing Happens With) The Birds And The Bees/Birth Of The Blues — 20

NOEL & THE FIREBALLS
70 Pama PM 807 — Confussion (sic)/We Got To Have Loving — 10
70 Pama PM 808 — Can't Turn You Loose/Skinny Legs — 10

NO FAITH
81 No Faith NF 001 — Double Trouble/Only The Good Die Young (p/s, private pressing) — 120

JACKY NOGUEZ
60 Pye Int. 7N.25063 — Hover On Sunday/Chanson Du Jan Gadeiro — 6

NOIR
71 Dawn DNLS 3029 — WE HAD TO LET YOU HAVE IT (LP, with insert) — 35

NOISE FACTORY
92 3rd Party 3RD#01 — MY MIND EP (12") — 20
92 3rd Party 3RD#02 — THE FIRE EP (12") — 50
92 3rd Party 3RD#03 — ALIENATION EP (12") — 25
92 3rd Party 3RD#04 — THE CAPSULE EP (12") — 20
93 3rd Party 3RD#07 — A NEW SOMETHING EP (12") — 20

NOIZ BOIZ
81 Caveman CMR 03 — Noiz Boiz/Flashback (p/s) — 10

NO KIDDING
74 Wave — NO KIDDING (LP) — 15

JOE NOLAN & HIS BAND
(see also Bonnie Frankson)
69 Jolly JY 013 — Cool It With Reggae/Reggae With Me — 150
69 Jolly JY 016 — Confidential/Poison Reggae — 40

NOLAN SISTERS/NOLANS
77 Hanover Grand HG 19751 — THE NOLAN SISTERS (LP, sold only at London Room Club, Drury Lane) — 12

TERRY NOLAND
58 Coral Q 72311 — Oh Baby! Look At Me/Puppy Love — 125
58 Coral Q 72311 — Oh Baby! Look At Me/Puppy Love (78) — 50

PIERRE NOLES
63 Oriole CB 1791 — Jacqueline/Marilyn — 7

NAZ NOMAD & NIGHTMARES
(see also Damned)
84 Big Beat NS 93 — I Had Too Much To Dream (Last Night)/Cold Turkey (p/s) — 5
84 Big Beat WIK 21 — GIVE DADDY THE KNIFE CINDY (LP, purple vinyl) — 20

NOMADS
65 Grampian NAN 1008 — I'm Coming Home/Hey Little Girl — 70

NOMADS
70 Pye 7N 17906 — The Singer Sang His Song/Lovin' Him — 6

NO-MAN
(see also Porcupine Tree, Japan)
90 Probe Plus PP27T — COLOURS (EP) (12") — 35
90s Hidden Art HA4 — Colours/Colours Remodelled (7", promo, fold-out cover, 8 page press sheet) — 20
91 One Little Indian 57TP12 — DAYS IN THE TREES EP (12") — 20
92 One Little Indian 63TP12 — OCEAN SONG EP (12") — 20
93 One Little Indian 73TPCD — SWEETHEART RAW EP (CD) — 20
93 One Little Indian 83TP12 — ONLY BABY EP (12") — 20
93 One Little Indian TPLP57 — LOVEBLOWS AND LOVECRIES (CD) — 25

NO MAN IS AN ISLAND
(see also No-Man, Porcupine Tree, Japan)
89 Plastic Head — The Girl From Missouri/Forest Almost Burning/Night Sky Sweet Earth/The Ballet Beast (uncedited) (12") — 60

NON
(see also Boyd Rice)
80 Mute MUTE 7 — I Can't Look Straight/SMEGMA: Flash Cards (p/s, with 2 centre holes) — 10
81 Mute MUTE 015 — NON EP (Rise/Out Out Out/Romance Fatal Dentro Deun Auto) (12", p/s) — 12
00 Mute MUTE 250 — Solitude/Receive The Flame (p/s, two centre holes, A-side plays at 45 rpm, B-side has closed grooves and plays at any speed, 700 copies only) — 8

NO NAMES
65 Polydor NH 59080 — All Because Of You/She Is Mine — 40

NOOKIE
92 Absolute 2 ABS 005DJ — THE LOVE IS EP (12", p/s) — 10
92 Absolute 2 ABS 005 DJR — THE LOVE IS EP (REMIX) (12") — 8

MINT VALUE £

92	Reflective REFLECT 003	ACCOUSTIC ASSAULT SQUAD EP (12")	40
94	Reinforced RIVET 1255	Give A Little Love/Give A Little Love (Manix Mix)/ Livin' Inside A Dream/T-Three (12")	15
94	Reinforced RIVET 1268	Only You/Celebrate Life (12")	10
93	Reinforced RIVET 1239	RETURN OF NOOKIE EP (12", p/s)	20
95	Reinforced RIVET LP 05	THE SOUND OF MUSIC (2xLP)	40

PETER NOONE

70	RAK 106	Lady Barbara/Don't Just Stand There	5
71	RAK 114	Oh You Pretty Things/Together Forever	5
71	RAK 121	Walnut Whirl/Right On Mother	6
72	RAK 129	Shoo Be Doo Ah/Because You're There	6
72	RAK 136	Should I/Each And Every Minute	6
76	Bus Stop BUS 1034	We Don't Need The Money/Love Don't Change	7
77	Bus Stop BUS 1057	Goodbye Sam Hello Samantha/Can I Put My Song In Your Heart	7

NO OTHER NAME

79	Daylight LD 500	DEATH INTO LIFE (LP, with insert)	25

NO QUARTER

83	Reel REEL 1	Survivors/Time And Space/Racing For Home (12", foldout p/s)	40
83	Bonzo Bear	BIRDS OF PREY EP (12")	30

NORA/BUNNY

72	Tropical AL 0015	Butterfly/TROPICAL ALL STARS: Fly Version	6

KEN NORDINE

(see also Billy Vaughn & His Orchestra)

57	London RE-D 1091	KEN NORDINE READS (EP, with Billy Vaughn Orchestra)	10
59	London Jazz EZ-D 19040	WORD JAZZ (EP)	10
67	Philips BL 7785	COLOURS (LP)	25

NORFOLK & JOY

79	Dara MPA 031	SCOTSOUNDS (LP)	30

NO RIGHT TURN

83	Chelful CHL 001	NO (LP)	25

NORMA & TONY

69	(No Cat. No.)	YOU ARE ALWAYS WELCOME AT OUR HOUSE (LP, private pressing, 100 only)	80

NORMAL

(see also Robert Rental)

78	Mute MUTE 001	Warm Leatherette/T.V.O.D (p/s)	10

NORMAL

03	Ai AI 005	GREEN FUELS EP (12", p/s)	8

NORMAN CONQUEST

(see also Factory, Peter & Wolves, John Pantry)

67	MGM MGM 1376	Two People/Upside Down	80

GENE NORMAN (JUST JAZZ)

51	Vogue V 2022	Hot House (Parts 1 & 2)	7
51	Vogue V 2047	Blue Lou (Parts 1 & 2)	6
50s	Vogue V 2272	Four O'Clock Jump/Three O'Clock Jump	5

NORMAN & INVADERS

64	United Artists UP 1031	Stacey/Our Wedding Day	12
64	United Artists UP 1058	Our Wedding Day/Stacey (reissue)	6
65	United Artists UP 1077	Night Train To Surbiton/Likely Lads	12

LARRY NORMAN

69	Key KL 010/Dove DOVE 64	UPON THIS ROCK (LP)	12
81	Solid Rock CS 103A	I Feel Like Dying/Alwyn Wall - Hold On	12
73	MGM 2315 135	I'M ONLY VISITING THIS PLANET (LP, with lyric sheet)	12
76	Solid Rock ROCKY 1	IN ANOTHER LAND (LP, gatefold sleeve)	15

MONTY NORMAN

55	HMV 7M 349	The Shifting, Whispering Sands/Bonnie Blue Gal	10
57	HMV POP 281	The Garden Of Eden/Priscilla	12
63	United Artists UEP 1010	DOCTOR NO SOUNDTRACK (EP)	25
63	United Artists ULP 1097	DOCTOR NO (LP, soundtrack, mono)	35
63	United Artists (S)ULP 1097	DOCTOR NO (LP, soundtrack, stereo)	40

OLIVER NORMAN

67	Polydor 56176	Down In The Basement/Drowning In My Own Despair	60
68	Polydor 56247	People People/You'll Find It Will Come	6

NORMAN & HOOLIGANS

77	President PT 461	I'm A Punk/Re-Entry	15

ROY NORTH

63	Oak RGJ 107	Blues In Three/Blues In Five	50

NORTH BANK

72	Polydor 2058225	Arsenal We're On Your Side/Half Time	5

NORTH STARS

65	Fontana TF 581	For My True Love/Nothing But The Best	10
66	Fontana TF 726	She's So Far Out She's In/Eeenie Meenie Minee Mo	30

TOM NORTHCOTT

68	Warner Bros WB 7160	1941/Other Times	12

NORTHERN LIGHT

75	CBS 3370	Minnesota/Minnesota (DJ Version)	25

MINT VALUE £

NORTHERN LIGHTS

(see also Hooten[anny] Singers, Abba)

66 United Artists UP 1123 — No Time/Time To Move Along — 50
66 United Artists UP 1161 — Through Darkness, Light/Baby Those Are The Rules — 50

NORTHWIND

(see also Elastic Band)

71 Regal Zono. SLRZ 1020 — SISTER, BROTHER, LOVER (LP) — 200

NORWICH CITY FOOTBALL CLUB

82 NCP NCFC 1 — Something To Shout About/Supporters - Canary Celebration — 7

NOSEBLEEDS

(see also Durutti Column, Ed Banger, Blue Orchids)

77 Rabid TOSH 12 — Ain't Bin To No Music School/Fascist Pigs (p/s) — 20

NO SECURITY

89 Peaceville VILE 11 — BURY THE DEBT NOT THE DEAD (split LP with DOOM) — 18

NOSMO KING

74 Pye 7N 45382 — Teenage Love/Goodbye (Nothing To Say) — 8

NO SWEAT

79 Rip Off RIP 4 — Start All Over Again/You Should Be So Lucky (p/s) — 20

NOTATIONS (U.K.)

72 Chapter One SCH 174 — Need Your Love/Just Nothing Left To Give — 20

NOTATIONS (U.S.)

76 Curtom K 16696 — Think Before You Stop/I'm Losing — 8
76 Curtom K 56212 — NOTATIONS (LP) — 30

FREDDIE NOTES & RUDIES

69 Downtown DT 427 — I Don't Wanna Lose That Girl/Train From Vietnam — 12
69 Grape GR 3010 — Guns Of Navarone/Yester-Me, Yester-You — 40
69 Grape GR 3011 — Babylon Girl/Girl I've Got A Date — 8
69 Trojan TR 7713 — Shanghai/Rome Wasn't Built In A Day — 12
70 Bullet BU 421 — The Feeling Is Fine/Girl You're Killing Me — 7
70 Trojan TR 7724 — Rocco/Don't Tell Your Mama — 8
70 Trojan TR 7734 — Down On The Farm/Easy Street — 30
70 Trojan TR 7791 — Montego Bay/RUDIES: Blue Mountain — 6
70 Trojan TR 7810 — Walk A Mile In My Shoes/JOHNNY ARTHEY ORCHESTRA: Reggae Rouser — 6
70 Duke DU 63 — The Bull/River Ben Come Up — 12
70 Duke DU 68 — Chicken Inn/Chicken Scratch — 12
70 B&C CB 125 — It Came Out The Sky/Well Oh Well (p/s) — 6
70 Trojan TBL 109 — UNITY (LP) — 25
70 Trojan TBL 152 — MONTEGO BAY (LP) — 20

NOTHINGS

65 CBS 201779 — At Times Like This/Love So Sweet — 15

NO TREND/LYDIA LUNCH

(see also Lydia Lunch)

85 Widowspeak WSP 3 — HEART OF DARKNESS (12" EP) — 8

NOTSENSIBLES

79 Redball RR 02 — (I'm In Love With) Margaret Thatcher/Little Boxes/ Gary Bushell's Band Of The Week (p/s) — 15
80 Bent SMALL BENT 5 — Death To Disco/Coronation Street Hustle/Lying On The Sofa (p/s) — 18
80 Snotty Snail NELCOL 1 — (I'm In Love With) Margaret Thatcher/Little Boxes/ Gary Bushell's Band Of The Week (p/s, reissue) — 10
80 Snotty Snail NELCOL 3 — I Thought You Were Dead/I Make A Balls Of Everything I Do/ Teenage Revolution (p/s) — 10
81 Snotty Snail NELCOL 6 — I Am The Bishop/The Telephone Rings Again (p/s) — 8
80 Bent — INSTANT CLASSICS (LP) — 50
80 Snotty Snail SSLP 1 — INSTANT CLASSICS (LP, reissue) — 30

NOTTINGHAM FOREST & PAPER LACE

73 Warner Bros. K 17110 — We Got The Whole World In Our Hands/The Forest March — 6

NOTTS ALLIANCE

72 Tradition TSR 011 — THE CHEERFUL 'ORN (LP, with Roy Harris) — 15

NOVA LOCAL

69 MCA MUPS 377 — NOVA 1 (LP) — 35

NOVAK

97 Enraptured WORM 2 — Silver Seas/Schmaltz (p/s in outer hand-sewn cloth sleeve with embroidered "Hand-knitted by Novak" label, 200 only, each different) — 15
97 Enraptured WORM 2 — Silver Seas/Schmaltz (p/s, 800 only) — 8
97 Kitty Kitty CHOOSY 007 — Rapunzel/Almost Chinook (hand crayoned p/s, 1,000 only) — 8

NOVAS

63 RCA RCA 1360 — Push A Little Harder/Oh, Gee Baby! — 35

NOVAS

65 London HLU 9940 — The Crusher/Take 7 — 45

NOW

77 Ultimate ULT 401 — Development Corporations/Why (p/s, blue vinyl) — 35
77 Ultimate ULT 401 — Development Corporations/Why (p/s) — 20
79 Raw RAW 31 — Into The 1980s/Nine O'Clock (p/s, 800 only) — 40

NOW

69 NEMS 56-4125 — Marcia/The Hands On My Clock Stand Still — 40
73 President PT 401 — I Wanna Be Free/People Are Standing — 12

MINT VALUE £

NOW GENERATION
(see also I Roy, B.B. Seaton, Audley Rollins)

73 Green Door GD 4055 — Alone Again, Naturally/MIND-BODY-SOUL: My Part (Version) — 5
73 Pyramid PYR 7007 — Baby Don't Do It/You'll Never Know — 5
74 Trojan TRLS 78 — FOR THE GOOD TIMES (LP) — 25

NO WAY
78 Our Own IS/NW/1035 — Breaking Point/TV Pox/30 Seconds (p/s) — 100

NOYES BROTHERS
(see also Steve Miro & Eyes, Spherical Objects)

80 Object Music OBJ 009/010 — SHEEP FROM GOATS (2-LP) — 25

NOY'S BAND
(see also Jan Dukes De Grey)

74 Dawn 1075 — Love Potion Number 9/Eldorado — 10

NOYS OF US
60s KPS KPS 502 — He's Alright Jill/What Can I Do — 30

NQB
72 Epic S EPC 2151 — Long Long Weekend/Free The People — 6

N.R.B.Q. (New Rhythm & Blues Quintet)
(see also Carl Perkins)

69 CBS 4290 — Stomp/I Didn't Know Myself — 5
69 CBS 4501 — C'mon Everybody/Rocket Number 9 — 5
69 CBS 63653 — N.R.B.Q. (LP) — 20
72 Buddah 2319 018 — SCRAPS (LP) — 12

NSO FORCE
88 Tickin' Time TIC TOC3 — Chains/In Too Deep (12") — 8
89 Vinyl Solution STORM10 — Give It Up (12") — 10

N.S.U.
69 Stable SLE 8002 — TURN ON OR TURN ME DOWN (LP) — 180

GUITAR NUBBIT
64 Bootleg 501 — Georgia Chain Gang/Hard Road (99 copies only) — 45
60s XX MIN 705 — GUITAR NUBBIT (EP) — 20

NUCHA
90 CBS 655885 7 — Together/Ha Sempre Alguem — 5

NUCLEAR ASSAULT
88 Under One Flag FLAG 21 — SURVIVE (LP) — 12

NUCLEAR SOCKETTS
81 Subversive SUB 002 — Play Loud/Shadow On The Map — 25
81 Subversive SUB 001 — HONOUR BEFORE GLORY (EP, folded p/s, 33rpm) — 25
82 None — Riot Squad (magazine flexi-disc with fold out picture insert) — 20

(IAN CARR'S) NUCLEUS
(see also Don Rendell & Ian Carr Quintet, Neil Ardley, Centipede, Michael Garrick, New Jazz Orchestra, Linda Hoyle)

70 Vertigo 6360 008 — ELASTIC ROCK (LP, die cut gatefold sleeve, large swirl label) — 80
70 Vertigo 6360 008 — ELASTIC ROCK (LP, die cut gatefold sleeve, later 'spaceship' label) — 15
71 Vertigo 6360 027 — WE'LL TALK ABOUT IT LATER (LP, die cut gatefold sleeve, large swirl label) — 80
71 Vertigo 6360 027 — WE'LL TALK ABOUT IT LATER (LP, die cut gatefold sleeve, 'spaceship' label) — 15
71 Vertigo 6360 039 — SOLAR PLEXUS (LP, as Ian Carr's Nucleus, gatefold sleeve, large swirl label) — 80
71 Vertigo 6360 039 — SOLAR PLEXUS (LP, as Ian Carr's Nucleus, gatefold sleeve, 'spaceship' label) — 12
72 Vertigo 6360 076 — BELLADONNA (LP, as Ian Carr, gatefold sleeve, swirl label) — 150
72 Vertigo 6360 076 — BELLADONNA (LP, as Ian Carr, gatefold sleeve, 'spaceship' label) — 30
73 Vertigo 6360 091 — LABYRINTH (LP, 'spaceship' label, any with swirl are Italian pressings!) — 25
73 Vertigo 6360 100 — ROOTS (LP, 'spaceship' label) — 35
74 Vertigo 6360 110 — UNDER THE SUN (LP, 'spaceship' label) — 18
75 Vertigo 6360 119 — SNAKE HIPS ETCETERA (LP, 'spaceship' label) — 18
75 Vertigo 6360 124 — ALLEY CAT (LP, 'spaceship' label) — 18
76 Vertigo 9286 019 — DIRECT HITS (LP, 'spaceship' label) — 12
77 Capitol EST 11771 — IN FLAGRANTI DELICTO (LP) — 12
80 Mood 24000 — AWAKENING (LP) — 12

TED NUGENT (& AMBOY DUKES)
(see also [American] Amboy Dukes)

74 Discreet K 19200 — Sweet Revenge/Ain't It The Truth (as Ted Nugent & Amboy Dukes) — 8
75 Epic S EPC 3900 — Stormtroopin'/Hey Baby (some in p/s, orange label) — 5
76 Epic S EPC 4796 — Dog Eat Dog/Love You So I Told You A Lie — 5
77 Epic S EPC 5482 — Cat Scratch Fever/A Thousand Nights — 5
78 Epic S EPC 9545 — Homebound/Death By Misadventure (p/s) — 5
75 Discreet K 59203 — CALL OF THE WILD (LP) — 15

NUGGETS
55 Capitol CL 14216 — Quirl Up In My Arms/So Help Me, I Love You — 20
55 Capitol CL 14267 — Shtiggy Boom/Anxious Heart — 20

GARY NUMAN
(see also Tubeway Army, Paul Gardiner, Dramatis, Claire Hamill, Radio Heart, Nicky Robson, Paper Toys, Caroline Munro, Generator, Bauhaus, Bill Sharpe, Sharpe & Numan)

SINGLES
79 Beggars Banquet BEG 23 — Cars/Asylum (p/s,orange plastic labels) — 6
79 Beggars Banquet BEG 23 — Cars/Asylum (p/s, 'mispressed' on dark red vinyl) — 10
79 Beggars Banquet BEG 29 — Complex/Bombers (live) (p/s, 'mispressed' on dark red vinyl) — 18
80 Beggars Banquet SPC 7 — Cars/We Are Glass (cassette, cigarette-pack style box) — 8
80 Beggars Banquet BEG 35 — We Are Glass/Trois Gymnopedies (1st Movement) (p/s, 'mispressed' on dark red vinyl) — 12

			MINT VALUE £
80	Beggars Banquet BEG 35	We Are Glass/Trois Gymnopedies (First Movement) (p/s, custom factory pressings on green and yellow vinyl)	500
80	Beggars Banquet BEG 46	I Die, You Die/Down In The Park (Piano Version) (p/s, dark red vinyl 'mispress')	8
80	Beggars Banquet BEG 46	I Die, You Die/Down In The Park (Piano Version) (p/s, mispressing, plays Remember I Was Vapour & "On Broadway" [SAM 126])	22
81	Beggars Banquet BEG 62	She's Got Claws/I Sing Rain (p/s, mispressing, plays Dollar's Hand Held In Black And White)	60
82	Beggars Banquet BEG 77	We Take Mystery (To Bed)/The Image Is (mispressed sleeve, no writing)	35
83	Beggars Banquet BEG 95P	Warriors/My Car Slides (aeroplane-shaped picture disc)	12
84	Beggars Banquet TUB 1	This Is My Life (unissued promo for "THE PLAN LP", 300 white label test pressings only)	100
84	Numa NUP 4	Berserker/Empty Bed, Empty Heart (head shaped picture disc)	5
85	Numa NU PROMO 1002	WHITE NOISE (12" 4-track sampler Beserker/ We Are Glass/Cars/Are "Friends" Electric?)	30
85	Numa NUM 7	THE LIVE EP (12", p/s, blue, white vinyl or black vinyl)	8
85	Numa NUM 7	THE LIVE EP (12", p/s, custom factory pressing on multicoloured vinyl)	200
85	Numa NUP 9	Your Fascination/We Need It (mispressed picture disc with pictures on the wrong side)	18
85	Numa NUM 13	Miracles (Extended)/The Fear (Extended) (12" mispressed sleeve: no red writing)	30
86	Numa NUMX 16	This Is Love/Survival//Call Out The Dogs (Extended)/No Shelter/This Ship Comes Apart (12", p/s, stickered double pack, shrinkwrapped)	10
86	Numa NUM 17 DJ	I Can't Stop (Special Club Mix) (12" 1-sided DJ promo)	10
86	Numa NUP 17	I Can't Stop/Faces (aeroplane-shaped picture disc)	8
87	B. Banquet BEG 199P	Cars ('E' Reg Model)/Are 'Friends' Electric? (picture disc)	6
88	Polydor POSPP 894	No More Lies (picture disc)	5
88	I.R.S. ILSP 1003	New Anger/I Don't Believe (poster p/s)	5
88	I.R.S. ILSCD 1003	New Anger/I Don't Believe/Creatures (live)/I Can't Stop (live) (CD)	15
88	I.R.S. ILSPD 1004	America/Respect (live) (Picture disc)	5
88	I.R.S. ILSPD 1004	America/Respect (live) (mispressed picture disc, 'Gary' picture both sides)	45
88	I.R.S. ILSCD 1004	America (Remix)/Respect (live)/New Anger (live)/Call Out The Dogs (live) (CD)	8
89	B. Banquet BBP 5CD	SELECTION (CD EP, picture disc)	8
91	I.R.S. NUMAN 1	Heart/Icehouse (p/s, black vinyl)	6
91	I.R.S. NUMANCD 1	Heart/Icehouse/Tread Careful (CD)	8
91	Numa NU 22	Emotion/In A Glasshouse (p/s)	5
91	Numa NUCD 22	Emotion/In A Glass House/Hanoi/Emotion (CD mix) (CD, 'mispressed' disc)	12
92	Numa NU 23	The Skin Game/Dark Mountain (p/s)	5
92	Numa NU 24DJ	Machine & Soul/Machine & Soul (fan club issue, white label, mail-order only)	8
92	NUCD 124/NUCD224	Machine & Soul (2 x CD single set)	15
93	Beggars Banquet BEG 264T	Cars (Multivalve)/Cars (Endurance Model)/Cars (Top Gear Model) (12", black vinyl, promo only)	12
93	Beggars Banquet BEG 264	Cars ('93 Sprint)/Cars (Top Gear) (poster p/s)	6
93	Beggars Banquet BEG 264L	Cars ('93 Sprint)/Cars (Endurance) (McLaren F1-shaped picture disc)	8
93	Beggars Banquet	Cars ('93 Sprint)/(Multivalve)/(Classic)/(Endurance)/(Top Gear)/(Motorway Mix)/ ('E' Reg Version) (CD, withdrawn, Extended 'E' Reg Model replaces Motorway Mix)	30
93	Beggars Banquet BEG 264CD	Cars '93 Sprint)/(Multivalve)/(Classic)/(Endurance)/(Top Gear)/(Motorway Mix)/ 'E' Reg Model) (CD, Autosports Awards issue, 300 only)	40
94	Salvation SACD 1	THE RADIAL PAIR (CD EP, fan club issue, mail order only)	25
94	Numa NUM 26	A Question Of Faith (12", withdrawn, black labels with blue print)	25
94	Numa NU 26	A Question Of Faith/Whisper Of Truth (fan club issue, white label, mail-order only)	25
95	Salvation Records SACD 2/1	BABYLON 1 (CD EP, fan club only, initial copies mailed out with withdrawn additional insert)	18
95	Salvation Records SACD 2/2	BABYLON 2 (CD EP, fan club only, initial copies mailed out with withdrawn additional insert)	18
96	The Record Label SPIND 6	Radio (with N.R.G.)/Radio (extended mix) (CD, withdrawn)	150
06	Mortal MORTAL VS 001	In A Dark Place (7" Edit)/Fold (Alternate Version) (picture disc in stickered sleeve, 1800 only)	6

ALBUMS

80	Beggars Banquet BEGA 19	TELEKON (LP, dark red vinyl 'mispressing', with stickered sleeve.; with bonus single SAM 126 "Remember I Was Vapour [live]"/"On Broadway" [Live])	20
80	Beggars Banquet BEGA 19	TELEKON (LP, dark red vinyl 'mispressing', with stickered sleeve)	15
81	Beggars Banquet BEGA 28	DANCE (LP, gatefold sleeve with poster)	12
82	Beggars Banquet BEGA 40	I, ASSASSIN (LP, initial copies at Woolworths with colour poster and merchandise sheet)	20
84	B. Banquet BEGA 55P	THE PLAN (LP, picture disc)	15
	B. Banquet BEGC 78/79	NUMAN/TUBEWAY ARMY 1978-79 (Cassette only, compiling NUMAN/ TUBEWAY ARMY 1978 [BEG 92E], NUMAN/TUBEWAY ARMY 1978-79 [BEGA 123E] & NUMAN/TUBEWAY ARMY 1978-79 [BEGA 124E])	12
86	Numa NUMAP 1003	THE FURY (LP, mispress picture disc, "Your Fascination" 12" photo on A-side with lyric insert)	25
86	Numa GNFCDA 1	IMAGES 1 & 2 (2-LP, fan club issue with photo inserts, mail-order only, initial signed copies)	20
86	Numa CDNUMA 1003	THE FURY (CD, with original mixes and artwork)	18
86	Numa CDNUMA 1005	STRANGE CHARM (CD, with original artwork and mixes)	18
87	Numa GNFCDA 2	IMAGES 3 & 4 (2-LP, fan club issue with photo inserts, mail-order only, initial signed copies)	20
87	Numa GNFCDA 3	IMAGES 5 & 6 (2-LP, fan club issue with photo inserts, mail-order only, initial signed copies)	20
87	Numa GNF CDA 4	IMAGES 7 & 8 (2-LP, fan club issue with photo inserts, mail-order only, i nitial signed copies)	20
87	Numa GNFCDA 4	IMAGES 7 & 8 (2-LP, fan club issue with photo inserts, mail-order only)	15
88	I.R.S. ILPPD 035	METAL RHYTHM (LP, picture disc)	12
88	IRS ILPCD 035	METAL RHYTHM (CD)	30
89	IRS EIRSACD 1021	METAL RHYTHM (CD, reissue)	30
89	IRS EIRSACD 1019	THE SKIN MECHANIC - LIVE (CD)	20

			MINT VALUE £
89	Numa GNF CDA 5	IMAGES 9 & 10 (2-LP, fan club issue with photo inserts, mail-order only, initial signed copies)	20
89	Numa GNFCDA 5	IMAGES 9 & 10 (2-LP, fan club issue with photo inserts, mail-order only)	15
91	Numa NUMACD 1001	BERSERKER (CD, fan club issue, mail order only, blue text on CD & inlay)	25
91	Numa GNFCCD 11	IMAGES 11 (CD, fan club issue, mail order only)	20
92	Receiver RRLP 170	THE OTHER SIDE OF GARY NUMAN (LP, withdrawn)	12
92	Numa NUMA 1009	MACHINE & SOUL (LP)	12
92	Numa NUMACD 1009	MACHINE & SOUL (CD, mispressed plays 9 tracks instead of 13)	18
93	Numa NUMACDX 1009	MACHINE & SOUL (CD, mispressed with 9 tracks instead of 13)	20
94	Numa NUMA 1010	DREAM CORROSION (3-LP, autographed gatefold sleeve; copies bought at HMV with signed 10" x 8" photo)	20
94	Numa NUMA 1011	SACRIFICE (LP, with lyric sheet, stickered sleeve & bonus single: The Seed Of A Lie [5.26]/"The Seed Of A Lie [7.07]")	30
98	Eagle EAGBX025	THE NUMA YEARS (5-CD set of Beserker, The Fury, Strange Charm, Machine and Soul Sacrifice.)	30
03	Jagged Halo JHLP 5	HYBRID (2-LP, numbered gatefold sleeve)	18
06	Mortal Records LP001	JAGGED (1,000 only, white vinyl, first 250 copies hand signed, numbered and sold via official Gary Numan website)	35
06	Mortal Records LP001	JAGGED (LP, 1,000 only, white vinyl)	20
08	OTB LP1	PURE (LP, 300 pressed in purple/red/clear vinyl (100 of each). Final 2 tracks pressed on separate yellow vinyl 7	20
08	OTB LP2	EXILE (LP, 300 copies, turquoise/white/orange vinyl (100 of each))	20
08	Beggars Banquet BBQCD 2057	REPLICAS REDUX (2-CD with additional 6 track of mixes and versions CD in card sleeve (GNCD 2008	25
08	VIN 180 LP 001	THE PLEASURE PRINCIPLE (LP, reissue, 180 gm vinyl, numbered with 6" x 8" print)	15

NUMBER NINE BREAD STREET

67	Holy Ground HG 112/1109	NUMBER NINE BREAD STREET (LP, 250 copies only)	400

NUMBERS

80s	Homegrown HG 701	Here Today/Put 'Em All To Shame/Another Day/Tear You Down (photocopied or green & white sleeve; with poster)	6
80s	Homegrown HG 701	Here Today/Put 'Em All To Shame/Another Day/Tear You Down (photocopied or green & white sleeve; without poster)	5

NUMBERS

79	Blasto SRTS 79/CUS/358	ROCK STARS (EP, with insert)	30

NUMSKULLZ

96	High Noon NUM003	Enough Of That (12")	12
98	Hombre MEX003	Signs Of The End/The Difference (12")	12
98	Hombre MEX005	THE UNEXPECTED (EP)	10
99	Hombre MEX008	VOLCANICS (EP)	8

NU NOTES

(see also Russ Sainty & Nu Notes)

63	HMV POP 1232	Hall Of Mirrors/Fury	20
64	HMV POP 1311	Kathy/Sunset	20

NUNS

81	Butt FUN 2	Wild/Suicide Child (p/s)	10

NURSE WITH WOUND

(see also Current 93, Organum/New Blockaders, Diana Rogerson, Sol Invictus, Steven Stapleton & David Tibet, Tibet & Stapleton, Whitehouse)

83	L.A.Y.L.A.H. LAY 3	GYLLENSKÖLD, GEIJERSTAM AND I AT RYDBERG'S (12" EP)	40
84	L.A.Y.L.A.H. LAY 7	BRAINED BY FALLING MASONRY (12" EP)	12
86	Torso 33016	SPIRAL INSANA (12" EP)	12
87	Crystal/Wisewound WW 01	Crank/TERMITE QUEEN: Wisecrack (numbered plain black sleeve with printed band, 500 only)	20
88	Yangki 002	FAITH'S FAVOURITES EP: Swamp Rat (with Current 93)/Ballad Of The Pale Girl (12", laminated p/s)	30
88	Idle Hole MIRROR 003	Cooloorta Moon/Great Empty Space (12", p/s)	20
90	Harbinger 001	The Burial Of The Stoned Sardine/CURRENT 93: No Hiding From The Blackbird	15
90	United Dairies UD 031	SORESUCKER EP: I Am The Poison/Journey Through Cheese (12", p/s, 2,000 only)	20
90	United Dairies UD 031CD	SORESUCKER EP: I Am The Poison/Journey Through Cheese (CD EP)	8
90	Shock SX 004	Sinister Senile: Human Human Human/Psychedelic Underground (45/33rpm, 1,000 only)	25
92	Clawfist 12	Steel Dream March Of The Metal Men/The Dadda's Intoxication ('singles club' release, 33rpm, foldover p/s in poly bag, 1,400 only)	15
93	Clawfist 20	CRUMB DUCK (10" EP, shared with Stereolab, 37 with handmade p/s (Gain/Sadier only)	100
93	Clawfist 20	CRUMB DUCK (10" EP, shared with Stereolab, 1450 regular without handmade p/s)	20
93	World Serpent WS 7003	Alien (1-sided, company sleeve 1,000 only)	25
95	WN 001	ALICE THE GOON (1-sided 12", p/s, 500 only)	75
79	United Dairies UD 01	CHANCE MEETING ON A DISSECTING TABLE OF A SEWING MACHINE AND AN UMBRELLA (LP, 500 only, originals have hand-painted numbers; beware of bootlegs with printed numbers)	150
80	United Dairies UD 03	TO THE QUIET MEN FROM A TINY GIRL (LP, numbered, 500 only, originals have hand-painted numbers; beware of bootlegs with printed numbers)	125
80	United Dairies UD 04	MERZBILD SCHWET (LP, numbered, 500 only, originals have hand-painted numbers; beware of bootlegs with printed numbers)	125
81	United Dairies UD 08	INSECT AND INDIVIDUAL SILENCED (LP, 1,000 only)	60
83	Mi Mort MI MORT iii	GYLLENSKÖLD, GEIJERSTAM & FRIENDS, LIVE AT BAR MALDOROR (LP, some with insert)	50
83	Third Mind TMR 03	OSTRANENIE 1913 (LP, 3,000 only)	45
85	L.A.Y.L.A.H. LAY 15	THE SYLVIE AND BABS HI-FI COMPANION (LP, gatefold sleeve)	25
85	United Dairies UD 110	DRUNK WITH THE OLD MAN OF THE MOUNTAINS (LP)	25
85	United Dairies UD 012	HOMOTOPY TO MARIE (LP, 5,000 only)	35

			MINT VALUE £
86	United Dairies UD 019	AUTOMATING VOL. 1 (LP, 3,000 only)	30
86	United Dairies UD 020	A MISSING SENSE (LP, 1 side only; other side by Organum; 2,000 only)	30
87	United Dairies UD 025	DRUNK WITH THE OLD MAN OF THE MOUNTAINS (LP, reissue, handmade custom sleeve, with insert, signed, 100 only)	150
88	United Dairies UD 027	ALAS THE MADONNA DOES NOT FUNCTION (mini-LP, 45/33rpm, 3,000 only)	25
88	Idle Hole MIRROR ONE	SOLILOQUY FOR LILITH (3-LP box set, 1,000 only)	80
88	Idle Hole MIRROR 1C	SOLILOQUY FOR LILITH PTS 5/6 (LP, with insert)	25
89	Idle Hole MIRROR TWO	PRESENTS THE SISTERS OF PATAPHYSICS (LP, 1,000 only)	25
89	United Dairies UD 030	AUTOMATING VOL. II (LP)	20
89	United Dairies UD 032	A SUCKED ORANGE (LP, with full colour insert)	35
89	United Dairies UD 032	A SUCKED ORANGE (LP)	30
89	Yangki 003	LUMBS SISTER (LP)	30
90	United Dairies UD 134	PSILOTRIPITAKA (3-LP [UD 01, 03 & 04], with bonus LP "Registered Nurse" [UD 00], 1,000 only, in leather bag)	400
90	United Dairies UD 134	PSILOTRIPITAKA (3-LP [UD 01, 03 & 04], with bonus LP "Registered Nurse" [UD 00], 1,000 only)	125
90	United Dairies UD 134CD	PSILOTRIPITAKA (3-CD [UD 01, 03 & 04], with bonus CD "Registered Nurse" [UD 00CD], 1,000 only, 30 in 'leather bondage bag')	400
90	United Dairies UD 134CD	PSILOTRIPITAKA (3-CD [UD 01, 03 & 04], with bonus CD "Registered Nurse" [UD 00CD], 1,000 only))	60
90	L.A.Y.L.A.H. LAY 30	BRAINED/GYLLENSKÖLD (LP, withdrawn)	35
91	United Dairies UD 038	CREAKINESS (LP, with Spasm)	20
91	United Dairies UD 09	THE 150 MURDEROUS PASSIONS (LP)	30
91	United Dairies UD 09CD	THE 150 MURDEROUS PASSIONS (CD, sealed in black plastic, 500 only)	30
93	United Dairies UD 059	CRUMB DUCK (LP, shared with Stereolab, reissue of Clawfist EP, 50 copies on pink vinyl)	50
93	United Dairies UD 059	CRUMB DUCK (LP, shared with Stereolab, reissue of Clawfist EP, 500 on fluorescent yellow vinyl)	25
94	United Dairies UD 043	SECOND PIRATE SESSION - ROCK'N'ROLL STATION - SPECIAL EDITION (LP, red vinyl, 500 only)	20
99	United Dairies UD 056	AN AWKWARD PAUSE (2-LP, translucent grey vinyl, 500 only, 1 side not available on CD)	40
00	United Dairies UD 081	ALICE THE GOON (1-sided reissue, 800 copies)	50
01	United Durtro UDOR 8	BRIGHT YELLOW MOON (CD, with Current 93, first 1,000 with bonus CD)	30
02	United Durtro UD 102	MAN WITH THE WOMAN FACE (LP, ltd. edition clear vinyl, poly sleeve, 2 inserts)	15
00s	United Dairies UDX 092	SOLILOQUY FOR LILITH (3-CD box set)	30
07	United Dairies UD 08.C	INSECT AND INDIVIDUAL SILENCED (CD, 120 copies numbered with "insect")	90
09	United Dirter DPROMOCD 72	THE SURVEILLANCE LOUNGE/THE MEMORY SURFACE (3-CD)	30

NU-SOUND EXPRESS LTD.

72	Pye Int'l 7N 25580	One More Time Y'all/A Rose For A Lady	20

NUTHIN' FANCY

(see also Terraplane, Thunder)

80s	Dynamic Cat DC 1001	Looking For A Good Time/Too Much Rock'n'Roll (p/s)	250

NU TORNADOS

58	London HLU 8756	Philadelphia U .S.A./Magic Record	20
58	London HLU 8756	Philadelphia U .S.A./Magic Record (78)	10

NUTRONS

60s	Melodisc M 1593	The Very Best Things/Stop For The Music	15

NUTSHELL

70s	Myrrh MYR 1056	FLYAWAY (LP)	18
75	Myrrh MYR 1029	IN YOUR EYES (LP, lyric inner sleeve)	20

MAY'F NUTTER

66	Vocalion VL 1282	Head Shrinker/Don't Know What To Do	15
73	London HLL 10414	I Don't Care/Hitch Hike Nightmare	6

NUTTY SQUIRRELS

59	Pye Int. 7N.25044	Uh! Oh! (Pts. 1 & 2)	7

NUTZ

(see also Rage, Nightwing)

74	A&M AMLS 68256	NUTZ (LP)	12
75	A&M AMLS 68306	NUTZ TOO (LP)	15

NYAH FEARTIES

86	Nya DOPLP 001	A TASTY HEIDFUL (LP)	25

NYAH SHUFFLE

70	Grape GR 3021	Sting Ray/Paradise	10
70	Grape GR 3019	Boot Lace/Honey Won't You Stay?	20

JUDY NYLON

(see also John Cale, Snatch)

82	On-U-Sound LP 16	PAL JUDY (LP)	12

NYLONS

82	Attic NYLON 1	A Million Ways/Up On The Roof (p/s)	8

NYMONIC

00	Y N R YNR02	REQIEM (EP)	18

LAURA NYRO

67	Verve Forecast VS 1502	Wedding Bell Blues/Stoney End	15
68	CBS 3604	Eli's Coming/Sweet Blindness	8
68	CBS 4031	Once It Was Alright Now (Farmer Joe)/Woman's Blues	6
69	CBS 4719	Time And Love/The Man Who Sends Me Home	6
68	CBS 63346	ELI AND THE THIRTEENTH CONFESSION (LP, gatefold sleeve, orange label)	35
69	CBS 63510	NEW YORK TENDABERRY (LP, orange label)	20
69	Verve Forecast SVLP 6022	THE FIRST SONGS (LP)	20
70	CBS 64157	CHRISTMAS AND THE BEADS OF SWEAT (LP, orange label)	15

MINT VALUE £

OAK

(see also Peta Webb)

71	Topic 12TS 212	WELCOME TO OUR FAIR (LP)	55

OAK TREE

70	President PT 316	The Sun It Always Shone/My Baby Don't Cry	6

OAKENSHIELD

82	Acorn OAK 001	ACROSS THE NARROW SEAS (LP)	18
85	Acorn OAK 002	AGAINST THE GRAIN (LP, with insert)	18

OASIS

*(see also Oas*s)*

SINGLES

94	Creation CRE 176	Supersonic/Take Me Away (p/s)	15
94	Creation CRE 182	Shakermaker/D'Yer Wanna Be A Spaceman? (p/s)	15
94	Creation CRE 185	Live Forever/Up In The Sky (Acoustic) (numbered foldover p/s in stickered poly bag)	15
94	Creation CRE 190	Cigarettes & Alcohol/I Am The Walrus (live at Glasgow Cathouse June '94) (numbered foldover p/s in poly bag)	15
94	Creation CRECS 190	Cigarettes & Alcohol/I Am The Walrus (live at Glasgow Cathouse June '94) (cassette, flip-top 'cigarette' pack)	20
94	Creation CRE 195	Whatever/(It's Good) To Be Free (no'd foldover p/s in stickered poly bag)	15
96	Creation CRE 221	Don't Look Back In Anger/Step Out (p/s, with poly outer)	10
97	Creation CRE 278	Stand By Me/I Got The Fever (p/s)	5
98	Creation CRELX 241	THE MASTERPLAN (mail-order 7 x 10" single box set)	60
02	Big Brother RKID 23	The Hindu Times/Just Getting Older (p/s, limited edition)	6
06	Big Brother RKID37	Stop The Clocks EP (2 x 7", stickers, numbered)	15

ALBUMS

94	Creation CRELP 169	DEFINITELY MAYBE (2-LP, gatefold sleeve)	30
95	Creation CRELP 189	(WHAT'S THE STORY) MORNING GLORY? (2-LP, gatefold sleeve)	30
97	Creation CRELP 219	BE HERE NOW	20
98	Creation CRELP 241	THE MASTERPLAN (3-LP)	60
00	Big Brother RKID LP002	STANDING ON THE SHOULDER OF GIANTS	20
00	Big Brother RKID LP005	FAMILIAR TO MILLIONS (3-LP)	70
02	Big Brother RKID LP25	HEATHEN CHEMISTRY (2-LP)	20
05	Big Brother RKID LP30X	DON'T BELIEVE THE TRUTH (LP, numbered art print)	30
06	Big Brother RKID LP36	STOP THE CLOCKS (3-LP box-set)	50
09	Big Brother RKIDBOX 58	LP BOX SET (8-LP, numbered, 1,500 only)	300

PROMO SINGLES

93	Creation CTP 8	Columbia (Demo) (12", 1-sided, white label, 510 pressed)	200
94	Creation CRE 176TP	Supersonic/Take Me Away/I Will Believe (Live) (12", company sleeve)	40
94	Creation CRESCD 176P	Supersonic/Take Me Away/I Will Believe (Live)/Columbia (White Label Demo) (CD)	15
94	Creation CRE 182TP	Shakermaker/D'Yer Wanna Be A Spaceman?/Alive (8 Track Demo) (12")	60
94	Creation CRESCD 182P	Shakermaker/D'Yer Wanna Be A Spaceman?/Alive (8 Track Demo)/ Bring It On Down (Live) (CD)	10
94	Creation CRE 185TP	Live Forever/Up In The Sky (Acoustic)/Cloudburst (12")	70
94	Creation CRESCD 185P	Live Forever/Up In The Sky (Acoustic)/Cloudburst/ Supersonic (Live April '94) (CD)	10
94	Creation CTP 190TP	I Am The Walrus (Live At Glasgow Cathouse June '94) (12", 250 only, co. sl.)	250
94	Creation CTP 190CL	Cigarettes & Alcohol (12", 1-sided)	75
94	Creation CTP 190CL	Cigarettes & Alcohol/I Am The Walrus (live Glasgow Cathouse June '94)/ Fade Away (12", 300 only)	75
94	Creation CRESCD 190P	Cigarettes & Alcohol/I Am The Walrus (live Glasgow Cathouse June '94)/ Listen Up/Fade Away (CD)	10
94	Creation CRE 195TP	Whatever (12", 1-sided, 560 only)	75
94	Creation CRESCD 195P	Whatever/(It's Good) To Be Free/Half The World Away/Slide Away (CD)	10
94	Creation CTP 195	(It's Good) To Be Free (12", 1-sided, 360 only)	50
94	Creation CREDM 001	DEFINITELY MAYBE (4 x 7" box set, in silver cigarette-pack-shaped plastic box, with booklet & interview CD)	25
95	Creation CREMG 001	(WHAT'S THE STORY) MORNING GLORY? (4 x 7" box set, in gold cigarette-pack-shaped plastic box,with booklet & interview CD)	25
95	Creation CCD 169	Slide Away (CD, 1-track Brits Awards issue, 1,000 only; beware of counterfeits)	30
95	Creation CCD 204	Some Might Say (CD, 1-track, 350 only)	60
95	Creation CRESCD 204P	Some Might Say/Talk Tonight/Acquiesce/Headshrinker (CD)	10
95	Creation CTP 204	Acquiesce (12", 1-sided, 570 only)	100
95	Creation CCD 204P	Acquiesce (CD, 1-track, 300 only)	60
95	Creation CTP 212	Roll With It (12", 1-sided)	40
95	Creation CRESCD 212P	Roll With It/Better People/Rockin' Chair/ Live Forever (Live at Glastonbury '95) (CD, 3,078 only)	10
95	Creation CRESCD 215P	Wonderwall/Round Are Way/The Swamp Song/The Masterplan (CD, 2,320 only)	10
95	Creation CTP 215	Round Are Way (12", 1-sided, 843 only)	60
96	Creation CTP 221X	Cum On Feel The Noize/Champagne Supernova (Lynchmob Beats Mix) (12", 1,203 pressed, plain die-cut sleeve; beware of counterfeits)	40
96	Creation CCD 221	Cum On Feel The Noize (CD, pic. disc, 1-track, with football motif, no inlay, 500 only)	60

MINT VALUE £

96	Creation CRESCD 221P	Don't Look Back In Anger/Step Out/ Underneath The Sky/ Cum On Feel The Noize (CD)	10
96	Creation P 96/1	OASIS (Fade Away/Half The World Away/Acquiesce/ The Masterplan) (CD sampler for singles box set)	15
97	Creation CTP 256	D'You Know What I Mean?/Heroes (12")	30
97	Creation CRESCD 256P	D'You Know What I Mean/Stay Young/Angel Child/Heroes (CD, digipak)	10
97	Creation CCD 256	D'You Know What I Mean (CD, 1-track, black card p/s)	15
97	Creation CCD 256X	D'You Know What I Mean?/Heroes (CD, 2-track, white card title p/s)	15
97	Creation CCD 219PL	Be Here Now (live)/Be Here Now (live with DJ intro) (CD)	15
97	Creation CTP 278	Stand By Me/I Got The Fever (12")	35
97	Creation CCD 278	Stand By Me (CD, 1-track, black card p/s)	15
97	Creation CCD 278X	Stand By Me (CD, 2-track, white card p/s)	15
97	Creation CRESCD 278P	Stand By Me/(I Got) The Fever/My Sister Lover/Going Nowhere (CD, digipak)	10
97	Creation CTP 282	All Around The World/Street Fighting Man (12", black die-cut sleeve)	25
97	Creation CCD 282	All Around The World (Edit) (CD, 1-track, black card sleeve)	15
97	Creation CCD 282X	All Around The World/Street Fighting Man (CD, blue card sleeve)	15
97	Creation CRESCD 282	All Around The World/The Fame/Flashbax/Street Fighting Man (CD)	10
97	Creation (no cat. no.)	VOX BOX (9-CD, wooden guitar-amp-shaped box set in outer box, with booklets from "Silver" & "Gold" CD box sets; contains commerical issues of "Supersonic" through to "Don't Look Back In Anger"; in house giveaway only)	500
98	Creation CRELP 241P	THE MASTERPLAN SAMPLER (Acquiesce/Underneath The Sky/ I Am The Walrus/ The Masterplan) (12" sampler)	25
98	Creation CCD 241	Acquiesce/Talk Tonight/Rockin' Chair/The Masterplan (CD sampler)	25
00	Creation CTP 327	Go Let It Out (12", 1-track, 1-sided, p/s)	25
00	Big Brother FITB 001	Fuckin' In The Bushes (12", 1-sided, white label)	40
00	Big Brother RKID 03TP	Who Feels Love? (12", 1-sided, laminated p/s)	25
00	Big Brother RKID 004TP	Sunday Morning Call (12", 1-sided, flipback laminated p/s)	25
00	SINE 002CD	Who Feels Love (Acoustic)/Sunday Morning Call (Acoustic) (CD, white card p/s)	20
00	Big Brother RKIDSCD 005P	FAMILIAR TO MILLIONS (Gas Panic/Supersonic/Helter Skelter) (live CD, promo-only)	12
01	own label OASIS 10	10 YEARS OF NOISE & CONFUSION (Columbia/Rock & Roll Star (Live)/ Acquiesce/Fuckin' In The Bushes) (10", promo-only, custom labels, die-cut sleeve, 200 only, with press release)	35
01	own label OASIS 10	10 YEARS OF NOISE & CONFUSION (Columbia/Rock & Roll Star (Live)/ Acquiesce/Fuckin' In The Bushes) (10", promo-only, custom labels, die-cut sleeve, 200 only, without press release)	30
02	Big Brother RKID 23TP	The Hindu Times (Spike Mix) (12", promo-only, custom logo sleeve, 250 only)	25
02	Big Brother RKID 24TP	Stop Crying Your Heart Out (Spike Mix) (12", custom sleeve, 250 only)	20
02	Big Brother RKIDSCD 24PX	Stop Crying Your Heart Out (Spike Mix) (CD, custom sleeve, 250 only)	12
02	Big Brother RKID 25TPX	Hung In A Bad Place (12", 1-track, 1-sided, custom mauve/pink or brown sleeve)	30
02	Big Brother RKID26TPX	My Generation (12" 1-sided promo with Union Jack Sleeve. 800 only)	35
02	Big Brother RKID27TP	Columbia (Live)/(You've Got) The Heart Of A Star (12", custom sleeve)	30
02	Big Brother (No cat. no)	Songbird (Demo) (CD-R promo, 25 only)	200
05	Big Brother RKID28TPX	Can You See It Now? I Can See It Now (12" 1-sided white label promo 50 only)	200
05	Big Brother RKID29TP	Lyla (12" 1-sided promo. 770 only)	25
05	Big Brother RKID31TP	Turn Up The Sun (12" 1-sided promo in card sleeve and inner sleeve. 1,120 only)	35
05	Big Brother RKID32TP	Mucky Fingers (12" 1-sided promo in double p/s. 950 copies)	30
05	Big Brother RKID1 NIL	Meaning Of Soul (CD-R promo)	150
05	Big Brother (No cat. no)	Cast No Shadow (UNKLE Beachhead Mix) (CD-R promo)	30
06	Big Brother RKIDSCD35TP	Champagne Supernova (Lynchmob Beats Mix) (12", promo-only)	20
06	Big Brother RKIDSCD35P	Champagne Supernova (Lynchmob Beats Mix) (CD-R, promo-only)	200
06	Big Brother RKIDSCD37P1	Acquiesce	10
06	Big Brother RKIDSCD37P2	The Masterplan	10
07	Big Brother RKID39TP	Lord Don't Slow Me Down (12", promo-only)	40
07	Big Brother RKIDSCD39P	Lord Don't Slow Me Down (CD-R, promo)	40

PROMO ALBUMS

94	Creation CRECD 169P	DEFINITELY MAYBE (CD)	50
95	Creation C-CRE 189PX	(WHAT'S THE STORY) MORNING GLORY? (cassette, 4-track sampler with "Hello"/"[What's The Story] Morning Glory"/ "Wonderwall"/"Don't Look Back In Anger")	15
95	Creation CRECD 189P	(WHAT'S THE STORY) MORNING GLORY? (CD, with "Step Out", black card p/s, withdrawn, beware of counterfeits)	45
95	Creation CRECD 189P	(WHAT'S THE STORY) MORNING GLORY? (CD, without "Step Out", black card p/s)	30
95	Creation C-CRE 189P	(WHAT'S THE STORY) MORNING GLORY? (cassette, with "Step Out", card p/s, withdrawn)	25
95	Creation C-CRE 189P	(WHAT'S THE STORY) MORNING GLORY? (cassette, without "Step Out", card p/s)	15
97	Creation (no cat. no.)	BE HERE NOW (LP, mail-order 12" box set, with The Making Of Be Here Now booklet, 1,000 only)	50
97	Creation (no cat. no.)	BE HERE NOW (CD, mail-order 12" box set, with The Making Of BE HERE NOW booklet, 1,000 only)	50
97	Creation C-CRE 219P	BE HERE NOW (cassette)	12
97	Creation C-CRE 219PX	BE HERE NOW (cassette, 4-track sampler with "D'You Know What I Mean?"/ All Around The World/"Stand By Me"/"It's Gettin' Better [Man!!]")	18
97	Creation CCD 219	BE HERE NOW (CD, black card sleeve, in custom picture sleeve)	30
97	Creation CCD 219	BE HERE NOW (CD, black card sleeve, not in custom picture sleeve)	25
98		THE MASTERPLAN (CD, slimline case, p/s)	35
00	Big Brother RKIDCD 002P	STANDING ON THE SHOULDER OF GIANTS (CD, g/fold card sl. with insert)	15
02	Big Brother RKIDCD 25P	HEATHEN CHEMISTRY (CD, in promo-only hardback photobook, features hidden track)	20
06	Big Brother RKIDCD 36P	STOP THE CLOCKS (2-CD promo in gatefold custom sleeve)	20

OAS*S

(see also Oasis)

95	Fierce Panda NING 12	WIBBLING RIVALRY (interview disc, stickered p/s, without barcode, 1000 only)	10

MINT VALUE £

OBENKIRCHEN CHILDREN'S CHOIR
56 Parlophone GEP 8529 ANGELS IN PIGTAILS (EP) 10

OBERON
71 Acorn (no cat. no.) A MIDSUMMER NIGHT'S DREAM (LP, private pressing) 600

OBITUARY
89 Roadracer RO 9489 SLOWLY WE ROT (LP) 12
90 Roadracer RO 9370 CAUSE OF DEATH (LP) 12

HUGH O'BRIAN
58 HMV DLP 1189 TV'S WYATT EARP SINGS (10" LP) 15

DERMOT O'BRIEN
66 Envoy ENV 016 The Merry Plough Boy/Off To Dublin/In The Green/Come Down the Mountain Katie Daly 8

IAIN O'BRIEN
96 Ferox FERLP 3 DESERT SCORES (2-LP) 12

JIMMY O'BRYANT
60 Heritage RE-101 FAMOUS ORIGINAL WASHBOARD BAND, VOL. 1 (99 copies only) (EP) 30
60 Heritage RE-106 FAMOUS ORIGINAL WASHBOARD BAND, VOL. 2 (99 copies only) (EP) 30

OBSERVERS
(see also Niney)
71 Big Shot BI 575 Brimstone And Fire/Lightning And Thunder 6
71 Big Shot BI 588 Keep Pushing/Hot Tip 8
72 Big Shot BI 610 Everyday Music/NINEY: Observing The Av 6
72 Songbird SB 1083 International Pum/Reggaematic 5

OBSERVERS ALL STARS & KING TUBBY
75 Attack ATLP 017 DUBBING WITH THE OBSERVER (LP) 40

OBTAINERS
(see also Cure)
79 Dance Fools Dance (No cat. no.) Yeh Yeh Yeh/Pussy Wussy/MAG-SPYS: Lifeblood/Bombs (stickered plain sleeve, 100 only) 100

OCCASIONALLY DAVID
79 Oven Ready OD 77901 TWIST AND SHOUT (EP) 10
80 Oven Ready OD 1/98002 I Can't Get Used To Losing You (So I'm Coming Back)/ Will You Miss Me Tonight? (foldout p/s) 10

OCCASIONAL WORD ENSEMBLE
69 Dandelion 63753 THE YEAR OF THE GREAT LEAP SIDEWAYS (LP) 30

OCCULT CHEMISTRY
(see also Twilight Zonerz)
80 Bikini Girl (no. cat. no.) Water Earth Fire Air (Rough Version) (5" clear flexidisc in stamped envelope with Bikini Girl magazine) 15
81 Dining Out TUX 4 Water Earth Fire Air/Fire Air Water Earth (handmade p/s) 8

OCEAN COLOUR SCENE
(see also Boys, Fanatics, Echo Base)
90 !Phffft WAVE 1P One Of These Days/Talk On (p/s, promo only) 20
90 !Phffft WAVE 1 One Of These Days/Talk On (12", p/s, promo only) 20
90 !Phffft FIT 001 Sway/Talk On (p/s) 10
90 !Phffft FITX 001 Sway (Extended)/Lullaby/Sway (7" Version)/One Of These Days (12", p/s) 10
96 MCA OCS 2 You've Got It Bad (Full Length Demo Version)/Mona Lisa Eyes (featuring Jimmy Miller) (p/s, mail-order only) 8
97 MCA MCD 60034 B-SIDES, SEASIDES AND FREE RIDES (2-LP, with lyric booklet) 18
97 MCA MCA 60048 MARCHIN' ALREADY (2-LP, with booklet) 18

OCEANS
82 Record Shack SHACK 129 Pacific Dreams/Pacific Dreams (Instrumental) (12", white label, stickered or stamped label) 150

PHIL OCHS
66 Elektra EKSN 45002 I Ain't Marching Any More/That Was The President 15
68 A&M AMS 716 Outside Of A Small Circle Of Friends/Miranda 8
65 Elektra EKL 269 ALL THE NEWS THAT'S FIT TO SING (LP) 35
65 Elektra EKL 287 I AIN'T MARCHIN' ANYMORE (LP) 35
66 Elektra EKL 310 PHIL OCHS IN CONCERT (LP, gold label) 30
67 A&M AML(S) 913 PLEASURES OF THE HARBOR (LP) 25
68 A&M AMLS 919 TAPE FROM CALIFORNIA (LP) 25
69 A&M AMLS 934 REHEARSALS FOR RETIREMENT (LP) 25
70 A&M AMLS 973 GREATEST HITS (LP) 18

DES O'CONNOR
62 Piccadilly 7N 35023 Thin Chow Min/Twist Drive 6

GENE OCTOBER
(see also Chelsea)
83 Illegal ILS 0034 Suffering In The Land/Suffering Love (p/s) 5

JOHNNY OCTOBER
59 Capitol CL 15070 Growin' Prettier/Young And In Love 15
60 Capitol CL 15121 So Mean/There'll Always Be A Feeling 15

OCTODRED
95 Acid Fever MDMA 9501 BIG FOOT EP (12") 40
95 Acid Fever MDMA 9502 DOUBLE DIPPED EP (12") 15
96 Acid Fever MDMA 9601 TECHNOLOGICAL ILLUSION VOL. 1 EP (12") 30
96 Acid Fever MDMA 9603 TECHNOLOGICAL ILLUSIONS VOL. 2 EP (12") 25
96 Acid Fever MDMA 9606 UNTITLED EP (12") 40
96 Acid Fever MDMA 9608 PSYCHIK MONK EP (12") 30

MINT VALUE £

OCTOPUS
(see also Cortinas)
69 Penny Farthing PEN 705 — Laugh At The Poor Man/Girl Friend — 18
70 Penny Farthing PEN 716 — The River/Thief — 18
73 Mooncrest MOON 7 — Hey Na Na/Future Feelings — 6
70 Penny Farthing PELS 508 — RESTLESS NIGHT (LP, gatefold sleeve, red/black label) — 300
96 Essex ESSEX 1013LP — RESTLESS NIGHT (LP, reissue, gatefold sleeve) — 15

RAY O'DANIEL
62 Longhorn BLH 0001 — What Goes Up Always Comes Down/You're The Only Love For Me — 8

ANITA O'DAY
56 HMV POP 245 — You're The Top/Honeysuckle Rose — 10
60 HMV POP 821 — Tea For Two/Sweet Georgia Brown — 10
55 Columbia Clef SEB 10042 — ANITA O'DAY (EP) — 8
56 HMV CLP 1085 — ANITA (LP) — 20
56 Columbia Clef 33C 9020 — ANITA O'DAY COLLATES (10" LP) — 20
57 Columbia Clef 33CX 10068 — AN EVENING WITH ANITA O'DAY (LP) — 20
58 Columbia Clef 33CX 10125 — ANITA SINGS THE MOST (LP) — 20
58 HMV DLP 1169 — PICK YOURSELF UP (10" LP) — 20
59 HMV DLP 1203 — ANITA AT MISTER KELLY'S (10" LP) — 20
60 HMV CLP 1332 — ANITA O'DAY SWINGS COLE PORTER WITH BILLY MAY (LP) — 12
63 Verve VLP 9125 — THE JAZZ STYLINGS OF (LP) — 12

PAT O'DAY
55 MGM SP 1129 — Earth Angel (Will You Be Mine?)/A Rusty Old Halo — 25
55 MGM SP 1142 — Soldier Boy/Annie Oakley — 15
60 Pye International 7N 25048 — I'll Build A Stairway To Your Paradise/No One Understands — 6

ODD
84 OK OK 007 — Last Time I Saw You/Look Into My Eyes (p/s) — 15

BILL ODDIE
(see also Ricky Livid)
64 Parlophone R 5153 — Nothing Better To Do/Traffic Island — 5
65 Parlophone R 5346 — Knitting Song/Ain't Got Rhythm — 5
66 Parlophone R 5433 — I Can't Get Through/Because She Is My Love — 5
69 Decca F 12903 — We Love Jimmy Young/Irish Get Out (as Bill Oddie & Average Mothers) — 5
70 Dandelion S 4786 — On Ilkla Moor Baht'at/Harry Krishna — 10

ODD NUMBERS
95 Detour DR 032 — The Easy Life/Clubbin' (A Jazz Odyssey) (p/s, coloured vinyl) — 5

ODDS
80 Double R RED 001 — Saturday Night/Not Another Love Song (p/s) — 6
81 JSO EAT 1 — Yesterday Man/So You Think (p/s) — 20
81 JSO EAT 7 — Dread In My Bed/Spare Rib (with press release) — 10

ODDSOCKS
(see also Bevis Frond)
75 Sweet Folk & C. SFA 030 — MEN OF THE MOMENT (LP) — 20

ANN ODELL
(see also Chopyn, Blue Mink, CMU)
73 DJM DJS 10280 — Swing Song/Everything's Fine Sunshine — 6
73 DJM DJLPS 434 — A LITTLE TASTE (LP, gatefold) — 30

DOYE O'DELL
57 London HAP-B 1073 — DOYE (10" LP) — 12

MAC ODELL
54 Parlophone CMSP 25 — The Stone Was Rolled Away/Heaven-Bound Gospel Train (export issue) — 8

RONNIE O'DELL & HIS ORCHESTRA
57 London HLD 8439 — Melody Of Napoli/Struttin' Down Jane Street — 10

ODETTA
62 RCA RD 7509 — SOMETIMES I FEEL LIKE CRYIN' (LP) — 12
65 RCA RD 7703 — SINGS DYLAN (LP) — 12

ODIN'S PEOPLE
67 Major Minor MM 501 — From A Distance/I Need You — 7
67 Major Minor MM 505 — Tommy Jones/I Need Your Hand In Mine — 7

JOE ODOM
69 Capitol CL 15600 — Big Love/It's In Your Power — 15

AL O'DONNELL
72 Trailer LER 2073 — AL O'DONNELL (LP, red label) — 20
78 Transatlantic LTRA 501 — AL O'DONNELL 2 (LP) — 12

JOE O'DONNELL
(see also East of Eden, Mushroom, Rory Gallagher, Jade Warrior)
77 Polydor 2383 465 — GAODHAL'S VISION (LP) — 22

ROCK O'DOODLE
(see also Patrick Campbell-Lyons)
73 Decca F 13450 — Queen Of Rock & Roll/Woman — 10

ODYSSEY (U.K.)
(see also Sons Of Fred)
66 Strike JH 312 — How Long Is Time/Beware — 22

ODYSSEY (U.S.)
73 Mowest MWS 7002 — ODYSSEY (LP) — 75

OEDIPUS COMPLEX
69 Phillips BF 1771 — Up Down Round & Round/Empty Highways — 25

MINT VALUE £

OFFSIDE
70 Pye Intl. 25534 — Match Of The Day/Small Deal (p/s) 20

OFO THE BLACK COMPANY
72 London FL12261 — Allah Wakbarr/Beautiful Daddy 50

JAMES O'GWYNN
59 Mercury AMT 1052 — How Can I Think Of Tomorrow/Were You Ever A Stranger 10

JOHN O'HARA
72 Spark SRL 1075 — Hand Me Down Man/I Am The Candidate For Love 12
77 President PT 465 — Starsky And Hutch/Sister Rae 5

O'HARA'S PLAYBOYS
66 Fontana TF 763 — Start All Over/I've Been Wondering 6
67 Fontana TF 872 — Ballad Of The Soon Departed/Tell Me Why 50
67 Fontana TF 893 — Island In The Sun/Harry 6
68 Fontana TF 924 — In The Shelter Of My Heart/Goodnight Mr. Nightfall 6
68 Fontana TF 974 — I Started A Joke/Show Me 15
68 Fontana (S)TL 5461 — GET READY (LP) 40

OHIO EXPRESS
(see also Joey Vine)
68 Pye Intl. TH25439 — Yummy Yummy Yummy/Zigzag 5
68 Pye Intl. 7N 25469 — Down At Lulu's/She's Not Coming Home 6
69 Pye Intl. NSPL 28117 — OHIO EXPRESS (LP) 20
69 Buddah 203 015 — CHEWY CHEWY (LP) 15

OHIO KNOX
(see also Fifth Avenue Band)
71 Reprise RSLP 6435 — OHIO KNOX (LP) 20

OHIO PLAYERS
69 Capitol CL 15587 — Here Today And Gone Tomorrow/Bad Bargain 10
72 Janus 6146 009 — Pain (Parts 1 & 2) 5
72 Janus 6146 017 — Got Pleasure/I Wanna Hear From You 5
73 Westbound 6146 100 — Funky Worm/Paint Me 5
74 Mercury 6167 012 — Skin Tight/Heaven Must Be Like This 5
75 Mercury 6167 058 — Fire/Together 5
73 Westbound CDSEWM026 — ECSTACY (LP) 12
74 Mercury 6338 497 — SKIN TIGHT (LP) 12

OHR MUSIK
(see also Spiral Sky)
97 Prescription DRUG 2 — OHR MUSIK (LP, 99 copies only) 20

OIL CITY SHEIKS
(see also Dr. Feelgood, Lew Lewis)
79 United Artists UP 36514 — Don't Take But A Few Minutes/Blues Jam (p/s) 7

OI POLLOI
86 EDR 5 — RESIST THE ATOMIC MESSAGE (EP) 10
88 Words Of Warning WOW 5 — OUTRAGE (EP) 10
89 Words Of Warning WOW 17 — OMNICIDE (EP) 12
93 Ruptured Ambition — GUILTY (EP) 8
87 Oi! OIR 011 — UNITE AND WIN (LP, with lyric sheet) 12
88 Words Of Warning WOW 13 — OUTRAGED BY THE ATOMIC MESSAGE (LP, with lyric sheet) 12

OISIN
80 Tara 2012 — OVER THE MOOR TO MAGGIE (LP) 12
82 Tara 2013 — THE JEANNIE C (LP) 12

O'JAYS
65 Liberty LIB 66102 — Lipstick Traces/Think It Over Baby 40
65 Liberty LIB 66102 — Lipstick Traces/Think It Over Baby (DJ copy) 75
66 Liberty LIB 66197 — Stand In For Love/Friday Night 20
67 Stateside SS 2073 — I'll Be Sweeter Tomorrow/I Dig Your Act 75
67 Stateside SS 2073 — I'll Be Sweeter Tomorrow/I Dig Your Act (DJ copy) 130
68 Bell BLL 1020 — Look Over Your Shoulder/I'm So Glad I Found You 30
68 Bell BLL 1020 — Look Over Your Shoulder/I'm So Glad I Found You (DJ copy) 70
68 Bell BLL 1033 — The Choice/Going Going Gone 15
70 Now! NOW 1002 — Don't You Know A True Love/That's Alright 8
72 United Artists UP 35337 — Working On Your Case/Hold On 15
73 CBS 1181 — Love Train/Who Am I? 6
73 Mojo 2092 052 — I Dig Your Act/I'll Be Sweeter Tomorrow (reissue) 8
73 CBS 1546 — Time To Get Down/Shifty Shadey Jealous Kind Of People 5
74 Power Exchange PX 101 — Peace/Little Brother 5
74 Philadelphia PIR 2186 — For The Love Of Money/People Keep Telling Me 6
75 Philadelphia PIR 3297 — Give The People What They Want/What Am I Waiting For 6
77 Philadelphia PIR 4834 — Darlin' Darlin Baby/Prayer 6
73 EPIC EPC 65469 — IN PHILADELPHIA (LP) 15

O'KAYSIONS
68 Stateside SS 2126 — Girl Watcher/Deal Me In 40
68 Stateside SS 2126 — Girl Watcher/Deal Me In (DJ copy) 75

JOHNNY O'KEEFE (& DEE JAYS)
58 Coral Q 72330 — Shake Baby Shake/Real Wild Child (as Johnny O'Keefe & Dee Jays) 150
58 Coral Q 72330 — Shake Baby Shake/Real Wild Child (as Johnny O'Keefe & Dee Jays) (78) 60
60s Zodiac ZR 0016 — Sing/Tell The Blues So Long 10

(ROGER) EARL OKIN
67 Parlophone R 5644 — Yellow Petals/I Can't Face The Animals (as Roger Earl Okin) 6
69 CBS 4495 — Stop And You'll Become Aware/You're Not There At All (as Earl Okin) 25

MINT VALUE £

OLA (& JANGLERS)

67	Decca F 12646	I Can Wait/Eeny Meeny Miney Moe	15
68	Big T BIG 108	What A Way To Die/That's Why I Cry (solo)	15
69	Sonet SON 2004	Let's Dance/Bird, Bird	10

BABATUNDE OLATUNJI

73	Paramount PARA 3038	Soul Makossa (Parts 1 & 2)	5
73	Paramount SPFL 289	SOUL MAKOSSA (LP)	15

OLD AND IN THE WAY

(see also Jerry Garcia, Seatrain, Rowan Brothers)

75	Round RX 103	OLD AND IN THE WAY (LP)	12

OLDEST PROFESSION

72	Midas Private Pressing	THE OLDEST PROFESSION (LP)	150

MIKE OLDFIELD

(see also Sallyangie, David Bedford, Kevin Ayers & Whole World, Pekka, Lea Nicholson, Tom Newman)

SINGLES

74	Virgin VS 101	Mike Oldfield's Single ("Tubular Bells" Theme)/ Froggy Went A-Courtin' (in p/s)	8
75	Virgin VS 117	Don Alfonso (with David Bedford)/In Dulci Jubilo (For Maureen)	5
76	Virgin VS 163	Portsmouth/Speak (Tho' You Only Say Farewell) (Roger Dean or blue/red label; reissued in brown wraparound p/s)	5
78	Virgin VS 238-12	Take 4 (12", white vinyl, stickered p/s)	8
79	Virgin VS 245	Guilty/Excerpt From Incantations (p/s, red/green or white/blue label)	5
79	Virgin VS 317	Blue Peter/Woodhenge (p/s, sudden or 'refined' ending (A7 matrix))	5
82	Virgin VSY 464	Five Miles Out/Live Punkadiddle (picture disc)	8
82	Virgin VSY 489	Family Man/Mount Teidi (picture disc)	8
82	Virgin VSY 541	Mistake/Waldberg (The Peak) (picture disc)	5
83	Virgin VSY 586	Moonlight Shadow/Rite Of Man (picture disc)	5
85	Virgin VSD 836	Pictures In The Dark/Legend/Moonlight Shadow/Rite Of Man (double pack in PVC gatefold stickered p/s)	8
86	Virgin VSS 863	Shine (with Jon Anderson)/The Path (uncut picture disc)	30
86	Virgin VSS 863	Shine (with Jon Anderson)/The Path (shaped picture disc)	10
88	Virgin CDT 7	Moonlight Shadow (Extended Version)/Rite Of Man/To France/ Jungle Gardenia (3" CD, card p/s)	8
89	Virgin VSCD 1189	Earth Moving (7" Version)/(Disco Mix)/Bridge To Paradise (3" CD, card p/s)	12
89	Virgin VST 1214	Innocent (7" Version)/(12" Mix)/(Club Version) (12", p/s)	8
89	Virgin VSCD 1214	Innocent (7" Version)/(12" Mix)/(Club Version) (3" CD, card p/s)	10
90	Virgin VS 1328	Etude (The Theme Music For The "Nurofen" TV Commercial)/ ONO GAGAKU KAÏ SOCIETY ORCHESTRA: Gakkain (p/s)	6
90	Virgin AMACD 1	AMAROK X-TRAX 3 extracts from the Amarok album (3" CD EP, 'discount voucher CD' free with W.H. Smith's Insight magazine)	20

ALBUMS

73	Virgin V 2001	TUBULAR BELLS (LP, White/black 'Twin' label)	20
74	Virgin QV 2001	TUBULAR BELLS (LP, quadrophonic, with model plane noise at the end of side 2, stickered sleeve)	15
75	Virgin QVQS 2043	OMMADAWN (LP, quadrophonic, stickered sleeve)	18
75	Virgin VD 2502	V (2-LP, compilation, includes long version of 'Don Alfonso')	20
76	Virgin 2043	OMMADAWN (LP, blue Virgin label)	12
76	Virgin QV 2043	OMMADAWN (LP, different quadrophonic mix, stickered sleeve)	18
76	Virgin VBOX 1	BOXED (4-LP box set, with booklet)	20
78	Virgin VDT 101	INCANTATIONS (2-LP, some with 7" red vinyl of Julie Covington, & poster)	30
78	Virgin VDT 101	INCANTATIONS (2-LP)	15
78	Virgin VP 2001	TUBULAR BELLS (LP, picture disc, die-cut sleeve, stereo remix of 1976 Boxed quadrophonic mix; with or without model plane noise)	12
78	Virgin VD 2511	EXPOSED (2-LP live, with '100,000 Limited Edition' sticker, and black inners)	12
79	Virgin V 2141	PLATINUM (LP, with inner sleeve & "Sally"; matrix reads "V 2141 B1" or B2, 30,000 copies, withdrawn)	20
79	Tellydisc TELLY 4	IMPRESSIONS (LP, mail-order only)	20
83	Virgin V 2262	CRISES (LP, with bonus 7" 'Moonlight Shadow')	12
83	Virgin V 2001	TUBULAR BELLS (LP, reissue at 1973 price, with sticker)	12
84	Virgin V 2328	THE KILLING FIELDS (LP, with 20 page film booklet)	15
93	Virgin CD BOX 2	ELEMENTS (4-CD, remastered best of in special plastic box with 64pp booklet)	30
97	Virgin LPCENT 18	TUBULAR BELLS (LP, coloured Dean label, audiophile pressing)	20
01	Simply Vinyl SVLP 322	OMMADAWN (LP, Audiophile pressing on 180g vinyl, with 2 stickers)	15
01	Virgin CD BOXY 2	ELEMENTS (4-CD remastered best of, revised "book" sleeve, 64pp booklet)	25

PROMOS

74	Virgin VS 112	Hergest Ridge (1-sided white label)	100
75	Virgin VDJ 1	Extract from The Orchestral Tubular Bells/Extract from The Orchestral Tubular Bells	25
75	Virgin VS 117	Don Alfonso ('A' label)	15
75	Virgin VDJ 9	An Extract From Ommadawn Part 1/An Extract From Ommadawn Part 2 (On Horseback) (12")	50
75	Virgin VS 131	In Dulci Jubilo/On Horseback ('A' label)	5
76	Virgin VS 163	Portsmouth/Speak (Tho' You Only Say Farewell) (Roger Dean label)	5
77	Virgin VS 167	The William Tell Overture/Argiers (blue Virgin 'A' label)	8
79	Virgin VSDJ 317	Blue Peter (1-sided)	20
85	Virgin SWALLOW 1	Etude/Moonlight Shadow/Portsmouth/In Dulci Jubilo (p/s, promo-only for "The Complete Mike Oldfield")	30
87	Virgin CDEP 6	Islands/When The Night's On Fire/The Wind Chimes(Part One)/ Islands (Extended Version) (white gatefold stickered card p/s)	20
94	WEA YZ 880 T	Let There Be Light: BT's Pure Luminescence Remix/Hardfloor Remix/ Hardfloor Dub (12" p/s with 'promo not for sale' sticker)	8
90	Virgin AMACD 1DJ	Mike Oldfield Album Sampler (CD, 5 Extracts From Amarok)	20
92	WEA SAM 1085	Sentinel (Single Restructure) (CD, stickered p/s)	10
92	WEA SAM 1094	OLDFIELD V THE ORB: Sentinel (Total Overhaul/Sentinel Nobel Prize Mix/ Sentinel Orbular Bells/Sentinel 7" Mix (12")	15

MINT VALUE £

92	WEA SAM 1150	SENTINEL RESTRUCTURE MIXES: Satoshi Tomii Interpretation/ Global Lust Mix/TranceMix/Tubular Beats (12", title stickered red sleeve)	15
92	WEA SAM 1470	A SHOT OF MOONSHINE: Jungle Mix (Featuring Rankin' Sean & Peter Lee)/ A Shot Of Moonshine (Jungle Instrumental)/A Shot of Moonshine (Solution Hoedown Mix) (12", lists artist as MOT2)	12
92	WEA YZ 708CDDJ	Tattoo (stickered p/s)	12
76	Virgin QVQS 2043	OMMADAWN (LP, unreleased different quadrophonic mix, promo stickered sleeve)	30
76	Virgin V BOX 1	COLLABORATIONS (LP, green/yellow label in stamped white sleeve)	20
79	(no cat. no.)	THE SPACE MOVIE (4 x 1-sided acetates of unreleased LP containing music from soundtrack to the 'Space Movie' video; includes Orchestral Hergest Ridge, Orchestral Tubular Bells, Incantations, Ommadawn and Portsmouth, some extracts otherwise released)	400
92	WEA 4509-90618-2	TUBULAR BELLS 2 (CD, with unique back sleeve)	18
92	WEA WX 2002	TUBULAR BELLS 2 (LP, stickered sleeve)	15
94	WEA SAM 1477	THE SONGS OF DISTANT EARTH (CD in film can, with 2 inserts)	100
98	WEA 3331000043	TUBULAR BELLS III (CD, in special 'Waterside Inn' card sleeve)	20
98	WEA 3331000043	TUBULAR BELLS III (CD, in card sleeve, with bag, TB III tag, press releases and premiere concert details)	30
98	WEA 3331000043	TUBULAR BELLS III (CD, in card sleeve)	20
99	WEA (no cat. no.)	MILLENNIUM BELL (CD-R, some tracks with different samples to released album)	40
99	WEA (no cat. no.)	MILLENNIUM BELL (CD-R)	30

OLD GOLD

70	Trend TNT 56	It's Goodbye/Teachers Of Electricity	25

ANDREW OLDHAM (ORCHESTRA)

(see also Aranbee Pop Symphony, Rolling Stones, Cleo, Bo & Peep, Jeannie & Her Redheads, Gulliver's Travels, Mighty Avengers, John Paul Jones)

64	Decca F 11878	365 Rolling Stones/Oh I Do Like To See Me On The 'B' Side	30
64	Decca F 11987	We Don't All Wear D'Same Size Boots/Right Of Way	25
64	Ace Of Clubs ACL 1180	16 HIP HITS (LP)	40
64	Decca LK 4636	LIONEL BART'S MAGGIE MAY (LP)	40
66	Decca LK/SKL 4796	THE ROLLING STONES SONGBOOK (LP)	100
82	Decca 820 186-1	THE ROLLING STONES SONGBOOK (LP, reissue)	12

OLDHAM TINKERS

74	Topic 12TS 237	BEST O' T' BUNCH (LP, blue label)	18
75	Topic 12TS 276	FOR OLD TIMES SAKE (LP, blue label)	18
77	Topic 12TS 323	SIT THEE DOWN (LP)	15
79	Topic 12TS 399	THAT LANCASHIRE BAND (LP)	15

OLD SWAN BAND

71	Dingles DIN 322	GAMESTERS, PICKPOCKETS AND HARLOTS (LP)	15
80	Free Reed 028	OLD SWAN BAND (LP)	15
81	Free Reed FRR 011	NO REELS (LP)	15

OLD TIMERS SKIFFLE GROUP

58	Fontana H 105	The Woman Who Loved A Swine/The Lynching Of Jeff Buckner (78)	12

TONY O'LEARY AND THE CAPITOL

71	Dolphin DOS61	She Meant Everything/Whole World Shaking	6

JOHNNY OLENN & HIS BAND

57	London HLU 8388	I Ain't Gonna Cry No More/My Idea Of Love	275
57	London HLU 8388	I Ain't Gonna Cry No More/My Idea Of Love (78)	60
59	Mercury AMT 1050	Born Reckless/You Lovable You (as Johnny Olenn & Blockbusters)	150

O-LEVEL

(see also Teenage Filmstars, Times, Television Personalities)

78	Psycho PSYCHO 2	East Sheen/Pseudo Punk ('map' p/s)	30
78	Psycho PSYCHO 2	East Sheen/Pseudo Punk ('schoolboy' p/s)	35
78	Kings Road KR 002	THE MALCOLM EP (photocopied wraparound p/s)	25
78	Kings Road KR 002	THE MALCOLM EP (printed p/s)	15

OLIVER

69	CBS 4435	Good Morning Starshine/Can't You See	5
70	Crewe CRW 1	Jean/Good Morning Starshine (Arrangement) (p/s)	5
70	Crewe CRWS 201	OLIVER (LP)	12
70	Crewe CRWS 202	AGAIN (LP)	12

OLIVER

74	Oliv OL 1	STANDING STONE (LP, private pressing, withdrawn blue sleeve)	250
74	Oliv OL 1	STANDING STONE (LP, private pressing, withdrawn, later green sleeve)	200
92	Tenth Planet TP 001	STANDING STONE (LP, reissue, numbered, 500 only)	20

JOHNNY OLIVER

56	MGM SP 1165	Chain Gang/These Hands	25
60	Mercury AMT 1095	What A Kiss Won't Do/That's All I'm Living For	12

OLIVER & TWISTERS

64	Pye Intl. NPL 28018	LOOK WHO'S TWISTIN' (LP)	15

OLLIE & NIGHTINGALES

69	Stax STAX 109	You're Leaving Me/Showered With Love	12

NIGEL OLSSONS DRUM ORCHESTRA & CHORUS

(see also Elton John, Hookfoot, Plastic Penny)

71	DJM DJS 239	Natures Way/Natures Way	10
72	DJM DJS 266	Alabama/Sunshine Looks Like Rain	10
71	DJM DJLP 5	NIGEL OLSSON'S DRUM ORCHESTRA AND CHORUS (LP, with poster)	20

MINT VALUE £

OLYMPICS

(see also Cappy Lewis)

58	HMV POP 528	Western Movies/Well!	15
58	HMV POP 528	Western Movies/Well! (78)	15
58	HMV POP 564	(I Wanna) Dance With The Teacher/Everybody Needs Love	20
58	HMV POP 564	(I Wanna) Dance With The Teacher/Everybody Needs Love (78)	10
59	Columbia DB 4346	Private Eye/(Baby) Hully Gully	25
60	Vogue Pop V 9174	I Wish I Could Shimmy Like My Sister Kate/Workin' Hard	20
61	Vogue Pop V 9181	Dance With A Dolly/Dodge City	25
61	Vogue Pop V 9184	Little Pedro/CAPPY LEWIS: Bullfight	20
62	Vogue Pop V 9196	The Twist/Everybody Likes To Cha Cha Cha	15
62	Vogue Pop V 9198	The Stomp/Mash Them 'Taters	20
62	Vogue Pop V 9204	Baby It's Hot/The Scotch	25
64	Sue WI 348	The Bounce/Fireworks	40
65	Warner Bros WB 157	Good Lovin'/Olympic Shuffle	15
66	Fontana TF 678	We Go Together (Pretty Baby)/Secret Agents	30
66	Fontana TF 778	Baby, Do The Philly Dog/Western Movies	30
69	Action ACT 4539	Baby, Do The Philly Dog/Mine Exclusively	20
70	Action ACT 4556	I'll Do A Little Bit More/Same Old Thing	20
71	Jay Boy BOY 27	Hully Gully/Big Boy Pete	8
72	Jay Boy BOY 56	Baby, Do The Philly Dog/Secret Agents	8
72	Jay Boy BOY 74	I'll Do A Little Bit More/Same Old Thing (reissue)	15
61	Vocalion VAH 8059	DANCE BY THE LIGHT OF THE MOON (LP)	90
67	Fontana TL 5407	SOMETHING OLD, SOMETHING NEW (LP)	70
72	Jay Boy JSX 2008	THE OLYMPICS (LP)	30

PATRICK O'MAGICK

(see also Patrick Campbell-Lyons)

74	Chrysalis CHS 2041	You're A Winner/The Proposal	5

MICHAEL O'MARTIAN

76	Myrrh MYRA 1048	WHITE HORSE (LP, gatefold sleeve, with Larry Carlton)	12
77	Myrrh MYR 1073	SEASONS OF THE SOUL (LP, with Stormie)	12
78	Sparrow BIRD 141	MAINSTREAM (LP)	12

O.M.D.

(see under Orchestral Manoeuvres In The Dark)

OMEGA

75	Decca SKL-R 5219	HALL OF FLOATERS IN THE SKY (LP)	20
76	Decca SKL-R 5243	TIME ROBBER (LP)	20

OMEGA

85	Rock Machine MACH 1	THE PROPHET (LP)	35

OMEGA RED STAR

69	Decca LK/SKL 4974	OMEGA RED STAR (LP, unboxed Decca on label)	150

OMEGA TRIBE

(see also Pete Fender)

82	Crass 221984/10	ANGRY SONGS (EP)	12
83	Corpus Christi CHRIST O5	NO LOVE LOST (LP)	12

OMEN

69	Ackee ACK 102	Don't Leave Me Never/No More	15

OMEN SEARCHER

82	OCS 001	Too Much/Teacher Of Sin (p/s)	75
82	OCS 002	Teacher Of Sin/Too Much (p/s)	75

OMENKA BROTHERS

77	Ashiko	MR CROOKED CHIAUOTU (LP)	35

ONDIOLINE BAND

66	London HL 10022	Last Bicycle To Brussels/Lovers Of Cologne	6

ONE

69	Fontana STL 5539	ONE (LP, gatefold sleeve, black/silver label)	150

ONE & ONE

(see also Ivy League, Flowerpot Men)

64	Decca F 11948	I'll Give You Lovin'/It's Me	15

ONE EYED JACKS

65	Ember EMBS 206	For Us There'll Be No Tomorrow/Soul Chart	8

ONE EYED JACKS

78	Pennine PSS 154	TAKE AWAY (LP, in "One Eyed Jacks" brown paper carrier bag)	25
78	Pennine PSS 154	TAKE AWAY (LP)	20

ONE HIT WONDERS

72	CBS 7760	Hey Hey Jump Now/Goodbye	25

101'ERS

(see also Clash, Alvaro)

76	Chiswick (N)S 3	Keys To Your Heart/5 Star Rock & Rock Petrol (with p/s)	30
76	Chiswick (N)S 3	Keys To Your Heart/5 Star Rock & Rock Petrol	10
79	Big Beat NS 3	Keys To Your Heart/5 Star Rock & Rock Petrol (reissue, with p/s)	10
79	Big Beat NS 3	Keys To Your Heart/5 Star Rock & Rock Petrol	8
80	Big Beat NS 63	Sweet Revenge/Rabies (From The Dogs Of Love) (p/s)	5
81	Andalucia AND 101	ELGIN AVENUE BREAKDOWN (LP, with booklet)	35
81	Andalucia AND 101	ELGIN AVENUE BREAKDOWN (LP, without booklet)	25

100% PROOF

80	Smile SR 929	NEW WAY OF LIVIN' (EP)	25
81	Myrrh MYR 1107	100% PROOF (LP, with insert)	50

MINT VALUE £

100% PROOF AGED IN SOUL

71	Hot Wax HWX 102	Somebody's Been Sleeping/I've Come To Save You	5
71	Hot Wax HWX 108	Somebody's Been Sleeping/I've Come To Save You (reissue)	5
72	Hot Wax HWX 113	Everything Good Is Bad/I'd Rather Fight Than Switch	5
72	Hot Wax HWX 120	Never My Love/Since You've Been Gone	5
71	Hot Wax SHW 5003	SOMEBODY'S BEEN SLEEPING IN MY BED (LP)	15

100% PURE POISON

74	EMI Untl. 501	You Keep Coming Back/(And When I Said) I Love You	30
77	EMI Intl. INS 3001	COMING RIGHT AT YOU (LP)	200

ONE IN A MILLION

(see also Thunderclap Newman)

67	CBS 202513	Use Your Imagination/Hold On	200
67	MGM MGM 1370	Fredereek Hernando/Double Sight	700

ONE MILLION FUZZTONE GUITARS

82	Monsters In Orbit TVEYE 3	Heaven/Annuese (foldover p/s, at least 2 different designs)	6
83	Monsters In Orbit TVEYE 10	26 (LP)	12

MATTY O'NEIL

54	London L 1037	Don't Sell Daddy Any More Whiskey/Little Rusty (gold label, tri-centre)	40
54	London L 1037	Don't Sell Daddy Any More Whiskey/Little Rusty (silver label, tri-centre)	25
54	London L 1037	Don't Sell Daddy Any More Whiskey/Little Rusty (silver top, round centre)	10

JOHNNY O'NEILL

59	RCA RCA 1114	Wagon Train/Somebody, Just Like You	10

1,000 MEXICANS

83	Whaam! WHAAM 12	The Art Of Love/News For You (p/s, 1,500 only)	6

1,000 VIOLINS

(see also Page Boys)

85	Dreamworld DREAM 2	Halcyon Days/I Remember When Everybody Used To Ride Bikes? Now We All Drive Cars (12", p/s, 1,000 only)	20
86	Dreamworld DREAM 8	Please Don't Sandblast My House/Time I Broke Down (p/s, 2,000 only)	12
86	Dreamworld DREAM 8T	Please Don't Sandblast My House/You Ungrateful Bastard/Though It Poured The Next Day, I Never Noticed The Rain (12", p/s)	12
87	Dreamworld DREAM 14	Locked Out Of The Love-In (p/s)	15
87	Report REPX 1	If I Were A Bullet (Then For Sure I'd Find A Way To Your Heart)/Poet (p/s)	8
88	Immaculate IMMACLP 1	HEY MAN, THAT'S BEAUTIFUL (LP)	40

ONE TWO & THREE

65	Decca F 12093	Black Pearl/Bahama Lullaby	15
65	Decca LK 4682	BLACK PEARLS AND GREEN DIAMONDS (LP)	200

ONE WAY SYSTEM

82	Lightbeat WAY 1	Stab The Judge/Riot Torn City/Me And You (p/s)	12
82	Anagram ANA 1	Give Us A Future/Just Another Hero (p/s)	5
83	Anagram ANA 5	Jerusalem/Jackie Was A Jackie (p/s)	10
83	Anagram ANA 9	Cum On Feel The Noise/Breakin' In (p/s)	6
83	Anagram ANA 14	This Is The Age/Into Fires (p/s)	5
84	Anagram ANA 19	Visions Of Angels/Shine Again (p/s)	5
93	Anagram	ALL SYSTEMS GO (LP, with lyric inner)	12
83	Anagram GRAM 008	WRITING ON THE WALL (LP, with lyric inner)	15

ONE WAY TICKET

(see also Five Day Rain)

78	President PTLS 1069	TIME IS RIGHT (LP, featuring tracks from "Five Day Rain" LP)	90

ONLOOKERS

82	Demon D 1012	You And I/Understand/Julia (p/s)	15

ONLY ONES

(see also England's Glory)

77	Vengeance VEN 001	Lovers Of Today/Peter And The Pets (p/s)	12
77	Vengeance VEN 001	Lovers Of Today/Peter And The Pets (12", with 7" x 7" sticker)	12
78	CBS S CBS 6228	Another Girl, Another Planet/Special View (p/s)	10
78	CBS S CBS 6576	Another Girl, Another Planet/As My Wife Says	10
78	CBS S CBS 12-6576	Another Girl, Another Planet/As My Wife Says (12", p/s)	10
79	CBS S CBS 7086	You've Got To Pay/This Ain't All (It's Made Out To Be) (p/s)	6
79	CBS S CBS 7285	Out There In The Night/Lovers Of Today	5
79	CBS S CBS 12-7285	Out There In The Night/Lovers Of Today/Peter And The Pets (12", p/s, blue vinyl, 2 slight sleeve variations)	10
79	CBS S CBS 7963	Trouble In The World/Your Chosen Life (withdrawn 'group' black & red p/s)	350
79	CBS S CBS 7963	Trouble In The World/Your Chosen Life (standard p/s)	5
80	CBS S CBS 8535	Fools/Castle Built On Sand (p/s, with Pauline Murray)	5
83	Vengeance VEN 002	Baby's Got A Gun/PETER PERRETT: Silent Night	5
78	CBS 82830	THE ONLY ONES (LP, orange label, with insert)	20
79	CBS 83451	EVEN SERPENTS SHINE (LP, embossed sleeve, orange label)	20
80	CBS 84089	BABY'S GOT A GUN (LP, with insert, orange label)	12
89	Strange Fruit SFRLP 102	PEEL SESSIONS ALBUM (LP)	15

YOKO ONO

(see also John Lennon, Bill Elliott & Elastic Oz Band)

71	Apple APPLE 38	Mrs. Lennon/Midsummer New York	18
72	Apple APPLE 41	Mind Train/Listen, The Snow Is Falling (p/s)	22
73	Apple APPLE 47	Death Of Samantha/Yang Yang	20
73	Apple APPLE 48	Run Run Run/Men Men Men	25
70	Apple SAPCOR 17	YOKO ONO/PLASTIC ONO BAND (LP, with inner sleeve)	50
71	Apple SAPTU 101/2	FLY (2-LP, laminated gatefold, inner sleeves, poster & postcard)	60
73	Apple SAPDO 1001	APPROXIMATELY INFINITE UNIVERSE (2-LP, with lyric inner sleeves)	25
73	Apple SAPCOR 26	FEELING THE SPACE (LP)	35

MINT VALUE £

ONSLAUGHT

83	Complete Control TROL 1	First Strike/State Control/No More (p/s)	8
85	Children/Revolution GURT 2	POWER FROM HELL (LP, with inner)	15

ONYX

(see also Salamander)

68	Pye 7N 17477	You've Gotta Be With Me/It's All Put On	30
68	Pye 7N 17622	My Son John/Step By Step	30
69	Pye 7N 17768	Tamaris Khan/So Sad Inside	60
69	CBS 4635	Time Off/Movin' In	20
71	Parlophone R 5888	Air/Our House	10
71	Parlophone R 5906	The Next Stop Is Mine/What's That You Say	10

OO BANG JIGGLY JANG

71	President PT 356	Hanging Tree/1000 Leagues	15

OPAL

(see also Mazzy Star)

85	One Big Guitar OBG 002T	Northern Line/Empty Bottles/Soul Giver (12")	15
87	Rough Trade RTT 129	Fell From The Sun/Freight Train/Grains Of Sand (12")	15
87	Rough Trade ROUGH 116	HAPPY NIGHTMARE BABY (LP)	15
89	Rough Trade ROUGH 128	EARLY RECORDINGS (LP)	18

OPAL BUTTERFLY

(see also Hawkwind, Motorhead, Mott The Hoople)

68	CBS 3576	Beautiful Beige/Speak Up	35
69	CBS 3921	Mary Anne With The Shakey Hand/My Gration Or?	60
70	Polydor 2058 041	You're A Groupie Girl/Gigging Song	60

JACKIE OPEL

(see also Jackie & Doreen, Doreen & Jackie, Hortense & Jackie)

63	Jump Up JU 512	TV In Jamaica/Worrell's Captaincy	25
64	Black Swan WI 421	You're No Good/King Liges	40
64	R&B JB 138	Stand By Me (as Jackie Opel & Hortense Ellis)/Solid Rock	35
64	R&B JB 160	Pity The Fool/The Day Will Come	40
65	King KG 1011	Cry Me A River/Eternal Love	30
65	Island WI 203	Wipe Those Tears/Don't Take Your Love	30
65	Island WI 209	Go Whey/Shelter The Storm	100
65	Island WI 227	Old Rockin' Chair/SKATALITES: Song Of Love (B-side is actually "Ska In Vienna Woods")	200
65	Ska Beat JB 190	Done With A Friend/More Wood In The Fire	40
65	Ska Beat JB 227	The Lord Is With Thee/A Little More	150
66	Island WI 264	A Love To Share/ROLAND ALPHONSO: Devoted To You	25
66	Rio R 117	I Am What I Am/JACKIE MITTOO & SKATALITES: Devil's Bug	50
66	Rio R120	I Don't Want Her/SOUL BOYS: Rudie Get Wise	60

OPEN

03	Loog 9813076	NEVER ENOUGH EP (1,000 only, p/s)	12
04	Loog 9817238	Close My Eyes/The View (mail order only 12" p/s)	12

OPEN MIND

(see also Drag Set)

69	Philips BF 1790	Horses And Chariots/Before My Time	100
69	Philips BF 1805	Magic Potion/Cast A Spell	450
69	Philips SBL 7893	OPEN MIND (LP, laminated sleeve, black/silver label)	750
86	Antar ANTAR 2	OPEN MIND (LP, reissue)	20

OPEN ROAD

(see also Warm Sounds, Denny Gerrard, Donovan)

72	Greenwich GSS 102	Swamp Fever/Lost And Found	6
71	Greenwich GSLP 1001	WINDY HAZE (LP, gatefold sleeve)	50

OPERA

79	Bead records BEAD 13	OPERA (LP)	25

OPETH

01	M. For Nations MFSN 264	BLACKWATER PARK (2xLP)	35
03	M. For Nations MFSN 297	DAMNATION (LP)	45

OPPO

76	EMI 2541	Miracles (A Mini Epic)/The Flame	5

OPPRESSED

83	Oppressed OPPO 1	Work Together/Victims (p/s)	20
83	Firm NICK 1	NEVER SAY DIE (EP)	18
84	Oppressed OPLP 1	OI! OI! MUSIC (LP)	20
85	Skinhead CREW 1	FATAL BLOW (LP)	20
88	OIR 12	DEAD AND BURIED (LP)	15

OPTIMISTS

81	Armageddon AS 018	Mull Of Kintyre/The Plumbers Song (p/s)	18

OPUS

70	Columbia DB 8675	Baby, Come On/Angela Grey	15

ORA

(see also Byzantium, Movies)

69	Tangerine OPLOP 0025	ORA (LP)	350

ORAL SEX

82	Conquest Quest 6	ORAL SEX (LP)	15

DAPHNE ORAM

62	HMV 7EG8762	LISTEN, MOVE AND DANCE 3 - ELECTRONIC SOUND PATTERNS (EP)	20

MINT VALUE £

ORANGE ALABASTER MUSHROOM

98	Earworm WORM 36	The Slug/Ethel Tripped A Mean Gloss (p/s, with sticker)	8

ORANGE BICYCLE

(see also Motherlight)

67	Columbia DB 8259	Hyacinth Threads/Amy Peate	35
67	Columbia DB 8311	Laura's Garden/Lavender Girl	25
68	Columbia DB 8352	Early Pearly Morning/Go With Goldie	20
68	Columbia DB 8413	Jenskadajka/Nicely	15
68	Columbia DB 8483	Sing This All Together/Trip On An Orange Bicycle	25
69	Parlophone R 5789	Tonight I'll Be Staying Here With You/Last Cloud Home	15
69	Parlophone R 5811	Carry That Weight/You Never Give Me Your Money/Want To B Side	12
70	Parlophone R 5827	Take Me To The Pilot/It's Not My World	18
70	Parlophone R 5854	Jelly On The Bread/Make It Rain	12
71	Regal Zonophone RZ 3029	Goodbye Stranger/Country Comforts	15
70	Parlophone PCS 7108	ORANGE BICYCLE (LP, laminated ront sleeve, black/silver label)	120
88	M'n Blue Town MBT 5003	LET'S TAKE A TRIP ON AN ORANGE BICYCLE (LP)	15

ORANGE BLOSSOM

74	Westwood WRS 038	KEEP ON PUSHING (LP)	30

ORANGE DISASTER

(see also Varicose Veins)

80s	Neuter OD 1	Something's Got To Give/Out Of The Room/Hiding From Frank	20

ORANGE GOBLIN

04	Rise Above RISE7/051	Some You Win, Some You Lose/White Night Cyanide (p/s)	6
00	The Music Cartel TMC 036LP	THE BIG BLACK (LP)	20
04	Rise Above RISELP 46	THIEVING FROM THE HOUSE OF GOD (LP, orange vinyl, 1000 only)	25
07	Mayan MYNLP 058	HEALING THROUGH FIRE (LP)	18

ORANGE JUICE

(see also Edwyn Collins, Paul Quinn & Edwyn Collins, Fun Four, Josef K)

80	Postcard 80-1	Falling And Laughing/Moscow Olympics/Moscow (foldover p/s in poly bag, with postcard; and with flexidisc "Felicity (live)" [I Wish I Was A Postcard 1], 963 only)	70
80	Postcard 80-1	Falling And Laughing/Moscow Olympics/Moscow (foldover p/s in poly bag, without postcard and without flexidisc, 963 only)	50
80	I Wish I Was A Postcard 1	Felicity (live) (freebie flexidisc, also given away with fanzines)	15
80	Postcard 80-2	Blue Boy/Lovesick (hand-coloured p/s in poly bag, blue labels)	18
80	Postcard 80-2	Blue Boy/Lovesick (yellow labels/cream cover sleeve)	8
80	Postcard 80-6	Simply Thrilled Honey/Breakfast Time (p/s, with picture insert in poly bag)	12
81	Postcard 81-2	Poor Old Soul/Poor Old Soul Pt. 2 (die-cut co. sleeve, with postcard)	8
81	Postcard 81-2	Poor Old Soul/Poor Old Soul Pt. 2 (die-cut co. sleeve, without postcard)	5
81	Postcard 81-6	Wan Light/You Old Eccentric (unreleased)	0
83	Polydor POSP 547	Rip It Up/Snake Charmer (p/s, with free live 21/4/79 cassette)	6
84	Polydor OJ 5/JUICE 1	Bridge/Out For The Count (stickered p/s, with free flexidisc Poor Old Soul [live])	6
84	Polydor OJ 6/OJC 6	What Presence?!/A Place In My Heart (Dub) (p/s, with free cassette The Felicity Flexi Session: The Formative Years)	6
92	Postcard DUBH 922	OSTRICH CHURCHYARD (LP, 1,000 with bonus 10" "Irritation Disc" [922TEN])	20

ORANGE MACHINE

(see also Danny Hughes)

68	Pye 7N 17559	Three Jolly Little Dwarfs/Real Life Permanent Dream	100
69	Pye 7N 17680	You Can All Join In/Dr. Crippen's Waiting Room	150

ORANGE PEEL

71	Reflection HRS 5	I Got No Time/Searching For A Place To Hide	25

ORANGE SEAWEED

(see also Fadin' Colours)

68	Pye 7N 17515	Stay Awhile/Pictures In The Sky	50

ORB

(see also System 7, KLF, J.A.M.s, Jah Wobble, Apollo XI, Space)

90	Wau! Mr Modo MWS 017T	A Huge Ever-Growing Pulsating Remix/From One Ear To Another/ Why Is 6 Scared Of 7? (12", white label, 100 only)	20
90	Wau! Mr Modo MWS 017R	A Huge Ever-Growing Pulsating Brain That Rules From The Centre Of The Ultraworld (Orbital Dance Mix)/(Orbital Radio Mix)/(Aubrey Mix Mk II) (12", stamped white label, 1,000 only)	15
90	Big Life ORB PROMO 1	A Huge Ever-Growing Pulsating Remix (Orbital Dance Mix)/ (9am Radio Mix)/(Aubrey Mix Mk 1) (12")	8
90	Big Life ORB PROMO 2	Little Fluffy Clouds (Dance Mk 1)/Into The Fourth Dimension/ Little Fluffy Clouds (Ambient Mk 1) (12")	10
91	Big Life ORB PICTURE 3	Perpetual Dawn: Ultrabass II (12", 1-sided picture disc, 400 only)	8
91	Big Life ORB PICTURE 3	Perpetual Dawn: Ultrabass II (12", 1-sided picture disc, mispressing, plays "Towers Of Dub (Ambient)", 400 pressed but 300 allegedly destroyed)	15
89	Wau! Mr Modo MWS 010T	KISS (12" EP, 949 only, die-cut company sleeve)	15
90	Wau! Mr Modo MWS 017T	A Huge Ever Growing Pulsating Brain That Rules From The Centre Of The Ultraworld: Loving You (Orbital Mix)/(Bucket And Spade Mix)/ Why Is 6 Scared of 7? (12" p/s, B-side matrix states 'MWS 016T')	15
90	Big Life BLR 270T	A Huge Ever-Growing Pulsating Brain That Rules From The Centre Of The Ultraworld : Loving You (edited)/(Bucket And Spade Mix)/ (Why Is 6 Scared of 7?) (12" p/s, 8,000 only, B-side matrix 'MWS 016T')	10
90	Big Life BLR 270CD	A Huge Ever-Growing Pulsating Brain That Rules From The Centre Of The Ultraworld : Loving You (Original Ambient House Mix) (CD)	12
90	Big Life BLR 27T	A Huge Ever-Growing Pulsating Remix (Orbital Dance Mix)/ (9am Radio Mix)/(Aubrey Mix I) (12", p/s, 8,000 only)	8
90	Big Life BLR 27CD	A Huge Ever-Growing Pulsating Remix (Orbital Dance Mix)/ (9am Radio Mix)/(Aubrey Mix I) (CD)	12

			MINT VALUE £
91	Big Life BLRDLP 5	THE ORB'S ADVENTURES BEYOND THE UNDERWORLD (2-LP, with inner sleeve, 'classical pressing' sticker on sleeve)	20
91	Big Life BLRLP 14	THE ORB AUBREY MIXES: THE ULTRAWORLD EXCURSIONS (LP, with inner sleeve, deleted on day of release)	15
92	Big Life BLRLA 18	U.F.ORB (2xLP, 12" and 2 art prints in unopened blue plastic cover)	30
92	Big Life BLRLA 18	U.F.ORB (2xLP, 12" and 2 art prints in opened blue plastic cover)	15

ORBIDÖIG

(see also Billy MacKenzie, Sensational Creed)

81	Situation 2 SIT 15	Nocturnal Operation/Down Periscope (p/s)	25

ROY ORBISON

(see also Traveling Wilburys)

SINGLES

60	London HLU 9149	Only The Lonely (Know How I Feel)/Here Comes That Song Again	6
60	London HLU 9149	Only The Lonely (Know How I Feel)/Here Comes That Song Again (78)	400
60	London HLU 9207	Blue Angel/Today's Teardrops	10
61	London HLU 9307	I'm Hurtin'/I Can't Stop Loving You	10
61	London HLU 7108	I'm Hurtin'/I Can't Stop Loving You (export issue)	20
61	London HLU 9342	Runnin' Scared/Love Hurts	5
61	London HLU 9405	Cryin'/Candy Man	5
62	London HLU 9511	Dream Baby/The Actress	8
62	London HLU 9561	The Crowd/Mama	5
62	London HLU 9607	Workin' For The Man/Leah	5
63	London HLU 9676	In Dreams/Shahdaroba	5
63	London HLU 9727	Falling/Distant Drums	5
63	London HLU 9777	Blue Bayou/Mean Woman Blues	5
64	London HLU 9845	Borne On The Wind/What'd I Say	5
64	London HLU 9882	It's Over/Indian Wedding	5
64	Ember EMB S 197	Rock House/You're My Baby	25
64	Ember EMB S 200	This Kind Of Love/I Never Knew (in p/s)	25
64	Ember EMB S 200	This Kind Of Love/I Never Knew	10
64	London HLU 9919	Oh, Pretty Woman/Yo Te Amo Maria	5
64	London HLU 9930	Pretty Paper/Summersong	5
65	London HLU 9951	Goodnight/Only With You	6
65	Ember EMB S 209	Sweet And Easy To Love/You're Gonna Cry (in p/s)	20
65	Ember EMB S 209	Sweet And Easy To Love/You're Gonna Cry	10
65	London HLU 9978	(Say) You're My Girl/Sleepy Hollow	5
65	London HLU 9986	Ride Away/Wondering	5
65	London HLU 10000	Crawling Back/If You Can't Say Something Nice	5
66	London HLU 10015	Breakin' Up Is Breakin' My Heart/Wait	6
66	London HLU 10034	Twinkle Toes/Where Is Tomorrow	6
66	London HLU 10051	Lana/House Without Windows	5

(London 45s from HLU 9676 to HLU 9978, and HLU 1051 were originally issued on the London Monument label, as were later pressings of HLU 9149, 9405, 9511 and 9607)

66	London HLU 10067	Too Soon To Know/You'll Never Be Sixteen Again	5
66	London HLU 10096	There Won't Be Many Coming Home/Going Back To Gloria	5
67	London HLU 10113	So Good/Memories	5
67	London HLU 10143	Cry Softly Lonely One/Pistolero	5
67	London HLU 10159	She/Here Comes The Rain Baby	5
68	London HLU 10176	Born To Be Loved By You/Shy Away	5
68	London HLU 10206	Walk On/Flowers	6
68	London HLU 10222	Heartache/Sugar Man	6
69	London HLU 10261	My Friend/Southbound Jerico Parkway	5
69	London HLU 10285	Penny Arcade/Tennessee Owns My Soul	6
69	London HLU 10294	Break My Mind (by Roy Orbison & Art Movement)/How Do You Start Over	8
70	London HLU 10310	So Young/If I Had A Woman Like You	8
71	London HLU 10339	(Love Me Like You Did It) Last Night/Close Again	8
72	Sun 6094 001	Ooby Dooby/Devil Doll	5
72	London HLU 10358	God Love You/Changes	8
72	London HLU 10388	Memphis Tennessee/I Can Read Between The Lines	6
72	London HLU 10388	Memphis Tennessee/I Can Read Between The Lines (export issue with alternate take of A-side: matrix no. MSC-8474-T2-IL)	8
74	Mercury 6167 014	Sweet Mama Blue/Heartache	7
85	ZTT DZTAS 9	Wild Hearts (...Time)/Wild Hearts (Voiceless)// Ooby Dooby/ Crying (double pack, p/s)	12

EPs

57	London RE-S 1089	HILLBILLY ROCK (orange p/s, mauve/silver label, triangular centre)	150
57	London RE-S 1089	HILLBILLY ROCK (orange p/s, mauve/silver label, round centre)	100
60	London RE-U 1274	ONLY THE LONELY	25
63	London RE-S 1089	HILLBILLY ROCK (re-pressing, yellow p/s, silver-top, round centre)	80
63	London RE-U 1354	ROY ORBISON	20

(The London EPs listed below were issued on London Monument, as were later pressings of RE-U 1274 and RE-U 1354)

63	London RE-U 1373	IN DREAMS	10
64	Ember EP 4546	SWEET AND EASY TO LOVE	70
64	Ember EP 4563	TRYIN' TO GET TO YOU	70
64	London RE-U 1435	IT'S OVER	15
64	London RE-U 1437	OH PRETTY WOMAN	15
65	London RE-U 1439	ROY ORBISON'S STAGE SHOW HITS	20
65	Ember EP 4570	DEVIL DOLL	70
65	London RE-U 1440	LOVE HURTS	25

LONDON LPs

61	London HA-U 2342	LONELY AND BLUE	40
62	London HA-U 2437	CRYIN' (mono)	30
62	London SAH-U 6229	CRYIN' (stereo)	40
63	London HA-U 8108	IN DREAMS (mono)	25
63	London SH-U 8108	IN DREAMS (stereo)	30

			MINT VALUE £
64	London HA-U 8207	OH, PRETTY WOMAN	20
65	London HA-U 8252	THERE IS ONLY ONE ROY ORBISON (mono)	30
65	London SH-U 8252	THERE IS ONLY ONE ROY ORBISON (stereo)	40
66	London HA-U 8279	THE ORBISON WAY (mono)	30
66	London SH-U 8279	THE ORBISON WAY (stereo)	40
66	London HA-U 8297	THE CLASSIC ROY ORBISON (mono)	25
66	London HA-U 8297	THE CLASSIC ROY ORBISON (black label mono)	30
66	London SH-U 8297	THE CLASSIC ROY ORBISON (blue label stereo)	40
67	London HA-U 8318	SINGS DON GIBSON (black label mono)	30
67	London SH-U 8318	SINGS DON GIBSON (blue label stereo)	40

(Unless stated, the above London LPs were originally issued with plum labels [mono] or blue labels [stereo]. Later copies were re-pressed with black labels [mono] or plum labels [stereo] with a boxed London logo)

68	London HA-U/SH-U 8357	CRY SOFTLY, LONELY ONE	30
68	London HA-U/SH-U 8358	SONGS FROM "THE FASTEST GUITAR ALIVE" FILM SOUNDTRACK	35
70	London HA-U 8406	THE BIG "O" (mono)	25
70	London SH-U 8406	THE BIG "O" (stereo)	20
72	London SH-U 8435	ROY ORBISON SINGS	30
73	London SH-U 8445	MEMPHIS	30

OTHER ALBUMS

64	Ember NR 5013	THE EXCITING SOUNDS OF ROY ORBISON (original copies list 'Great Newport Street' address on cover; reissued 1972)	25
64	Ember NR 5013	THE EXCITING SOUNDS OF ROY ORBISON (reissued 1972)	18
65	Ember FA 2005	ROY ORBISON AND OTHERS (with 4 tracks by Orbison)	15

(Copies of this above LP are rumoured to exist with all tracks solely by Orbison)

ORBIT FIVE

68	Decca F 12799	I Wanna Go To Heaven/Walking (in p/s)	25
68	Decca F 12799	I Wanna Go To Heaven/Walking	15

WILLIAM ORBIT

93	Virgin VSCDT 1465	WATER FROM A VINE LEAF (CD)	20

ORBITAL

89	Oh Zone ZONE 1	Chime/Deeper (12", p/s)	20
90	ffrr FRRFX 135	Chime/Deeper (12", reissue, die-cut p/s)	8
90	ffrr FRRXDJ 145	Omen (7")/Omen (12")/2 Deep/Open Mind (12" promo)	8
91	ffrr FRRXDJ 149	Satan (2 mixes)/LC1/Belfast (12" promo)	8
91	ffrr FRRDJ 163	Midnight (Radio Edit)/Choice (Radio Edit, promo)	5
91	ffrr FRRXDJ 163	Midnight/Midnight (Sasha Mix)/Choice/Choice Remix (12", promo)	12
96	Internal ORB CD3	EVIL SANTA (3-CD set, including LIECD 37, LICDP 37 & LICDD 37, silver box, promo)	20
91	FFRR 828248-1	ORBITAL (2-LP)	25
93	Internal TRULP 2	ORBITAL 2 (2-LP)	25
94	Internal TRULP 5	SNIVILISATION (2-LP, gatefold sleeve)	18
96	Internal TRULP 10	IN SIDES (3-LP)	30

ORBITONES

73	Explosion EX 207	Memories Of Love/SONNY EARLE: In Peace	5

ORCA

92	Micro Genetic 001	9 Lives/Shining Bright (12")	20
92	Lucky Spin LSR-ORC 1	DANCES WITH DOLPHINS EP NO. 1 (12", stickered, black die-cut sleeve)	30
92	Lucky Spin LSR 002	My Brothers/The Power (12")	30
93	Lucky Spin LRS 006	DANCES WITH DOLPHINS EP NO. 2 (12")	25
93	Lucky Spin LSR 011	4AM/Pure Bliss/Jungle Vibes/Pure Bliss (Remix) (100 on red vinyl)	50
93	Lucky Spin LSR 011	4AM/Pure Bliss/Jungle Vibes/Pure Bliss (Remix) (black vinyl)	30
93	Lucky Spin ORCA 6	BACK TO THE JUNGLE EP (12")	12
94	Lucky Spin STU 06	4AM (Remix 1)/4AM (Remix 2) (12")	12
94	Lucky Spin LSR 016	Intalect/Tranquility To Earth (12")	12

ORCHESTRA DEL ORO

62	Pye Int 7N.25143	Main theme From Lolita/Lolita Ya Ya (in PS)	8

ORCHESTRAL MANOEUVRES IN THE DARK (O.M.D.)

79	Factory FAC 6	Electricity/Almost (black 'braille' p/s)	50
79	Din Disc DIN 2	Electricity (Re-Recorded Version)/Almost (p/s, reissue)	5
80	Din Disc DIN 6	Red Frame-White Light/I Betray My Friends (p/s)	5
80	Din Disc DIN 15-10	Messages (Extended)/Waiting For The Man/Taking Sides Again (10", p/s)	6
80	Din Disc DIN 22-12	Enola Gay (Extended)/Annex (p/s)	6
80	Din Disc DIN 24-10	Souvenir (Extended)/Motion And Heart (Amazon Version)/Sacred Heart (10", p/s)	8
82	Din Disc DIN 40-12	Maid Of Orleans (The Waltz Joan Of Arc)/Navigation/Of All The Things We've Made (12", 'coin' cover; incorrectly lists "Experiments In Vertical Take-Off")	12
82	Virgin VSY 527	Genetic Engineering/4-Neu (picture disc)	5
83	Virgin VSY 580	Telegraph/66 And Fading (picture disc)	5
84	Virgin VSS 660	Locomotion/Her Body In My Soul (train-shaped picture disc)	10
84	Virgin VSY 685	Talking Loud And Clear/Julia's Song (picture disc)	5
84	Virgin VSY 727	Never Turn Away/Wrappup (picture disc)	5
85	Virgin VS 766	So In Love/Concrete Hands//Maria Gallante/White Trash (live) (double pack, stickered gatefold p/s)	6
85	Virgin VS 796	Secret/Drift (poster p/s)	6
85	Virgin VSS 811	La Femme Accident/Firegun (shaped picture disc)	6
86	Virgin VSD 911	We Love You/(Dub)//If You Leave/88 Seconds In Greensboro' (double pack)	6
80	Din Disc DID 2	ORCHESTRAL MANOEUVRES IN THE DARK (LP, 12" x 12" grid sleeve, black, blue or grey outer sleeves with orange, pink or red inner)	12
80	Din Disc DID 6	ORGANISATION (LP, stickered sleeve, with insert & 7": "Introducing Radios"/ Distance Fades Between Us/"Progress"/"Once When I Was Six" [DEP 2])	15
84	Virgin V 2310	JUNK CULTURE (LP, stickered sleeve, with free 7": "[Angels Keep Turning] The Wheels Of The Universe" [JUNK 1])	15
91	Virgin V 2648	SUGAR TAX (LP, mispressing with extra track "All She Wants Is Everything" instead of "Neon Lights")	15

MINT VALUE £

ORCHIDS
(see also Exceptions)

63	Decca F 11743	Gonna Make Him Mine/Stay At Home	25
63	Decca F 11785	Love Hit Me/Don't Make Me Mad	20
64	Decca F 11861	I've Got That Feeling/Larry	25

ORCHIDS

88	Sarah SARAH 002	I've Got A Habit/Give Me Some Peppermint Freedom/Apologies (foldover p/s with poster, 1,000 only)	20
88	Sarah SARAH 011	UNDERNEATH THE WINDOW, UNDERNEATH THE SINK EP (p/s)	10
89	Sarah SARAH 023	WHAT WILL WE DO NEXT? EP (p/s)	12
88	Sha La La BaBaBaBaBa 5	From This Day/SEA URCHINS: Summertime (flexi, 2,500 only, 1,000 in p/s)	10
88	Sha La La BaBaBaBaBa 5	From This Day/SEA URCHINS: Summertime (flexi, 2,500 only, no p/s)	8
90	Sarah SARAH 029	Something For The Longing/Farewell Dear Bonnie/On A Sunday (p/s, with inserts)	10
90	Caff CAFF 11	An Ill Wind That Blows/All Those Things (p/s, with insert)	20
91	Sarah SARAH 042	PENETRATION EP (12", p/s with insert)	12
95	Sarah SARAH 401	LYCEUM (10" mini-LP)	12
95	Sarah SARAH 611LP	EPICUREAN: A SOUNDTRACK (2-LP)	25

ORE

82	Bandit BR 003	Your Time Will Come/Yellow River (p/s)	250

CHARLES ORGANAIRE

64	Blue Beat BB 241	How Did Moses Cross The Red Sea/You May Not Believe (as Big Charlie)	18
64	R&B JB 149	Little Village/It Happens On A Holiday	35
64	Rio R 28	Little Village/It Happens On A Holiday (reissue)	15

ORGANISATION
(see also Kraftwerk)

70	RCA SF 8111	TONE FLOAT (LP)	250

ORGANISERS

66	Pye 7N 17022	Lonesome Road/The Organiser	80

ORGANUM/NEW BLOCKADERS
(see also Current 93, Nurse With Wound, Eddie Prevost Band)

80s	Aeroplane AR 7	Pulp Parts 1 & 2 (gatefold p/s)	30
85	Laylah/Antirecords LAY 19	IN EXTREMIS (LP)	20
88	Laylah LAY 012	TOWER OF SILENCE (LP)	20

ORIGINAL BARNSTORMERS SPASM BAND
(see also Barnstormers Spasm Band)

59	Tempo A 168	That's All There Is/Stormin' The Barn	8
59	Tempo A 168	That's All There Is/Stormin' The Barn (78)	15
59	Tempo EXA 95	ORIGINAL BARNSTORMERS SPASM BAND (EP)	15

ORIGINAL CHECKMATES
(see also Checkmates)

62	Pye 7N 15428	Hot Toddy/Tuxedo Junction	10
62	Pye 7N 15442	Checkmate Stomp/Begin The Beguine	15
63	Decca F 11688	Union Pacific/The Spy	30

ORIGINAL DOWNTOWN SYNCOPATORS
(see also Ron Geesin)

62	VJM VEP 14	ORIGINAL DOWNTOWN SYNCOPATORS (EP)	10
64	Columbia SEG 8293	IT'S JASS (EP)	10
63	J.R.T. Davies DAVLP 301/2	THE ORIGINAL DOWNTOWN SYNCOPATORS (10" LP, white labels only)	25

ORIGINAL DYAKS

67	Columbia DB 8184	Got To Get A Good Thing Going/Would You Love Me Too	10

ORIGINAL NEW ORLEANS RHYTHM KINGS

54	Columbia SCM 5113	Golden Leaf Strut/She's Crying For Me	10

ORIGINALS

62	Top Rank JAR 600	Gimme A Little Kiss, Will Ya, Huh/At Times Like This	35

ORIGINALS

67	Tamla Motown TMG 592	Goodnight Irene/Need Your Lovin', Want You Back	80
67	Tamla Motown TMG 592	Goodnight Irene/Need Your Lovin', Want You Back (DJ copy)	150
72	Tamla Motown TMG 822	God Bless Whoever Sent You/I Like Your Style/Baby I'm For Real	8
69	Tamla Motown TMG 702	Green Grow The Lilacs/You're The One	20
70	Tamla Motown TMG 733	Baby I'm For Real/The Moment Of Truth	15
76	T. Motown TMGT 1038	Down To Love Town/Just To Be Closer To You (12")	8
76	Tamla Motown TMG 1066	Six Million Dollar Man/Mother Nature's Best (unreleased)	0
69	T. Motown (S)TML 11116	GREEN GROW THE LILACS (LP, mono/stereo)	60

ORIGINAL SIN

84	Sin S1N	The Shadow/Salvation (12", p/s, private pressing)	25

ORIGINAL TORNADOS
(see also Tornados)

75	SRT SRTS 75350	Telstar/Red Rocket	10

ORIGINATION

92	Rudeboy RUDE 001	Break Down/Bass/R.E.S.P.E.C.T. (12")	15
92	Rudeboy RUDE 002	Breakdown (Remix)/Breakdown (Original Edit)/ Breaking Out The B-Line/ Gimme Ya Luv (12")	12
92	Rudeboy/Entity RUDE 003	NTT 12-33 Bass Remix/Sensation/Hardcore Yout/ Respect Remix/ Funky Darkness (12")	8
93	Rudeboy RUDE 005	Sunrise/Sunrise (Ruff Mix)/Make Ya Wanna Do Right/Out Of This World (12")	10
93	Rudeboy RUDE 006	Music Takes Control/Signal To Noise/Music Takes Control (Remix) (12')	10
94	Rudeboy RUDE 007	Shine on '94/Shine On (Unreleased '92 Remix)/ Shine On '94 (Dub Version)/ Shine On (Original '92 Mix) (12")	30

MINT VALUE £

ORIGINELLS 4
64 Columbia DB 7259 — My Girl/Kathy (as Origenells) — 20
64 Columbia DB 7388 — Nights/I Can Make You Mine — 18

ORIGIN UNKNOWN
92 Ram RAMM 002 — Untitled (6.03)/Untitled (5.01)/Untitled (5.22)/Untitled (6.12) (12", stamped white labels, promo only, not released) — 20
93 Ram RAMM 004 — The Touch/Valley Of The Shadows (12") — 10
93 Ram RAMM 004R — The Touch (part 2)/Valley Of The Shadows (long dark remix) (12") — 10
95 Ram RAMM 014 — Truly One/Mission Control (12") — 12
90s RAM RAMM 002 — EASTERN PROMISE EP (12", stamped white label, 4 untitled tracks, promo only) .
120
96 Ram RAMM 16 — Valley Of The Shadows (original Mix)/Valley Of The Shadows (Awake '96 Remix) (12") — 10

ORIOLES
53 London L 1180 — Hold Me, Thrill Me, Kiss Me/Teardrops On My Pillow (78) — 60
53 London L 1201 — Crying In The Chapel/Don't You Think I Ought To Know (78) — 60
54 London HL 8001 — In The Mission Of St. Augustine/Write And Tell Me Why (78) — 60

ORION
84 Lost Moment LM 02 — Insane In Another World/Storm (p/s) — 15

ORION
87 Gypsy GYP 001 — JACK ORION (LP) — 30

ORION THE HUNTER
(see also Boston)
84 Portrait PRT 25906 — ORION THE HUNTER (LP) — 12

ORLANDO
69 NEMS 56-4159 — Am I The Same Guy/Poor Little Me — 10

ORLANDO
96 Blanco Y Negro 0630-19718-2 — PASSIVE SOUL (CD) — 30

TONY ORLANDO
61 Fontana H 308 — Halfway To Paradise/Lonely Tomorrows — 20
61 Fontana H 330 — Bless You/Am I The Guy — 10
61 Fontana H 350 — Happy Times (Are Here To Stay)/Lonely Am I — 12
62 Fontana H 366 — Talkin' About You/My Baby's A Stranger — 10
62 Columbia DB 4871 — Chills/At The Edge Of Tears — 30
63 Columbia DB 4954 — Beautiful Dreamer/The Loneliest — 30
63 Columbia DB 4991 — Shirley/Joanie — 8
64 Columbia DB 7288 — Tell Me What Can I Do/She Doesn't Know It — 10
63 Columbia SEG 8238 — BLESS YOU (EP) — 70
63 Fontana TFL 5167 — BLESS YOU (LP, mono) — 60
63 Fontana STFL 582 — BLESS YOU (LP, stereo) — 70

ORLONS
(see also Rosetta Hightower)
62 Columbia DB 4865 — The Wah Watusi/Holiday Hill — 35
62 Cameo Parkway C 231 — Don't Hang Up/The Conservative — 25
63 Cameo Parkway C 243 — South Street/Them Terrible Boots — 20
63 Cameo Parkway C 257 — Not Me/My Best Friend — 15
63 Cameo Parkway C 273 — Crossfire/It's No Big Thing — 15
63 Cameo Parkway C 287 — Bon Doo Wah/Don't Throw Your Love Away — 20
63 Cameo Parkway C 295 — Shimmy Shimmy/Everything Nice — 15
64 Cameo Parkway C 319 — Rules Of Love/Heartbreak Hotel — 15
64 Cameo Parkway C 332 — Knock Knock (Who's There)/Goin' Places — 15
66 Planet PLF 117 — Spinnin' Top/Anyone Who Had A Heart — 100
72 Mojo 2092 029 — Spinnin' Top/Anyone Who Had A Heart (reissue) — 15
62 Cameo Parkway C 1033 — ALL THE HITS (LP) — 70
63 Cameo Parkway C 1061 — BIGGEST HITS (LP) — 60
78 London HA-U 8504 — CAMEO PARKWAY SESSIONS (LP) — 30

LE ORME
(see under Le Orme)

ORNAMENTAL
(see also Sugarcubes, Rose McDowall)
88 One Little Indian 18TP 7 — Crystal Nights/Yonilingaphonics (p/s) — 5

OROONIES
91 Demi Monde DMLP 1027 — OF HOOF AND HORN (LP) — 18

ORPHAN
85 Swoop RTLS 013 — Nervous/Little England (p/s) — 15

ORPHEUS
66 Red Bird RB 10-041 — My Life/Music Minus Orpheus — 40
68 MGM MGM 1413 — I've Never Seen Love Like This/Lesley's World — 12

ORPHEUS
68 MGM MGM-C(S) 8072 — ORPHEUS (LP) — 20

RIZ ORTOLANI
71 United Artists UP 35278 — The Hunting Party/CAROL CARMICHAEL: Where's Poppa? — 8

BETH ORTON
(see also Spill)
96 Heavenly HVN 56A — I Wish I Never Saw The Sunshine (p/s, 1-sided limited edition, 500 only) — 40
96 Heavenly HVN 6010 — She Cries Your Name/Tangent/Safety/It's Not The Spotlight (10", p/s) — 12
96 Heavenly HVN 6410 — Touch Me With Your Love/Galaxy Of Emptiness/Pedestal/Touch Me With Your Love (Instrumental) (10" EP, p/s with insert) — 12

MINT VALUE £

97	Heavenly HVN 6510	Someone's Daughter/I Wish I Never Saw The Sunshine/ It's This I Am I Find (10" EP, p/s)	12
96	Heavenly HVNLP 17	TRAILER PARK (LP, 100 copies only)	40
99	Heavenly HVNLP 22	CENTRAL RESERVATION (2-LP, gatefold sleeve, 1000 copies only)	25
02	Heavenly HVNLP 37	DAYBREAKER (LP)	20

EILEEN OSBORNE

75	Seagull SG1	SINGING SHORES (LP)	15

MIKE OSBORNE

(see also Stan Tracey)

71	Turtle TUR 300	OUTBACK (LP)	60
73	Cadillac SGC 1002	ORIGINAL (LP, as Mike Osborne & Stan Tracey)	20
75	Ogun OG 300	BORDER CROSSING (LP)	15
76	Ogun OG 700	ALL NIGHT LONG (LP)	20
77	Ogun OG 210	TANDEM - LIVE AT BRACKNELL FESTIVAL (LP, with Stan Tracey)	18
77	Ogun OG 810	MARCEL'S MUSE (LP)	15

OSBORNE BROTHERS

62	MGM MGM 1184	The Banjo Boys/Poor Old Cora	7
59	MGM MGM-EP 691	COUNTRY PICKING AND HILLSIDE SINGING (EP)	18
62	MGM MGM-C 914	BLUE GRASS MUSIC (LP)	15

OZZY OSBOURNE

(see also Black Sabbath, Lita Ford & Ozzy Osbourne, Billy Connolly)

80	Jet JET 197	Crazy Train/You Looking At Me Looking At You (p/s)	6
80	Jet JET 7003	Mr. Crowley (live)/You Said It All (live) (p/s)	8
80	Jet JET 12003	Mr. Crowley (live)/You Said It All (live)/Suicide Solution (live) (12", p/s)	10
80	Jet JETP 12003	Mr. Crowley (live)/You Said It All (live)/Suicide Solution (live) (12", picture disc)	15
81	Jet JET 7017	Over The Mountain/I Don't Know (p/s)	5
81	Jet JET 12017	Over The Mountain/I Don't Know (12", p/s)	8
82	Jet JET 7030	Symptom Of The Universe/N.I.B. (p/s)	6
82	Jet JETP 7030	Symptom Of The Universe/N.I.B. (picture disc)	10
82	Jet JET 12030	Symptom Of The Universe/N.I.B./Children Of The Grave (12", p/s)	8
83	Epic TA 3915	Bark At The Moon/One Up The B-Side (12", p/s, silver vinyl)	15
83	Epic WA 3915	Bark At The Moon/One Up The B-Side (12", picture disc, unreleased)	0
84	Epic DA 4452	So Tired/Bark At The Moon (live)//Waiting For Darkness/ Paranoid (live) (double pack, gatefold sleeve)	8
84	Epic TA 4452	So Tired/Bark At The Moon (live)/Waiting For Darkness/ Suicide Solution/ Paranoid (live) (12", p/s with free patch)	8
84	Epic WA 4452	So Tired/Bark At The Moon (live)/Waiting For Darkness/ Suicide Solution/ Paranoid (live) (12", p/s, gold vinyl)	12
86	Epic A 6859	Shot In The Dark/Rock'n'Roll Rebel (p/s, with signature card)	6
86	Epic QA 6859	Shot In The Dark/Rock'n'Roll Rebel (poster p/s)	8
86	Epic A 7311	The Ultimate Sin/Lightning Strikes (p/s, with free patch)	5
88	Epic 653 063-9	Miracle Man/Crazy Babies (head-shaped picture disc)	8
88	Spiral Scratch 2/Ozzy 1	An Interview With? (no p/s, free with Spiral Scratch, issue 2, 5,000 only)	5
90	Adventure ADV TS 102	The Urpney Song/Whirlypad Launch (p/s, with poster, with Frank Bruno/Billy Connolly)	6
90	Adventure ADV TS 102	The Urpney Song/Whirlypad Launch (p/s, without poster, with Frank Bruno/Billy Connolly)	5
90	Adventure ADV TS 102	The Urpney Song/Whirlypad Launch (picture disc, with Frank Bruno/ Billy Connolly)	10
91	Epic 657 4406	No More Tears (extended version)/S.I.N./Party With The Animals (12" pic. disc)	8
93	Epic 659 3406	Changes/Changes (extended version)/No More Tears (live)/ Desire (12" picture disc, with insert)	8
96	Epic 662 6391	Perry Mason/Living With The Enemy (picture disc)	6
86	Epic EPC 11-26404	THE ULTIMATE SIN (LP, picture disc)	15
89	Epic 463 0862	DIARY OF A MADMAN (CD, promo-only, with diary)	18
91	Epic 467 8592	NO MORE TEARS (CD in embossed wallet)	18
95	Epic XP CD 2007	THE BALLADS OF OZ (CD, promo-only compilation)	20

JOHNNY OSBOURNE (& SENSATIONS)

70	Big Shot BI 549	See And Blind (solo)/THE TECHNIQUES: Scar Face	12
72	Techniques TE 916	See And Blind/TECHNIQUES ALL STARS: Rema Skank	10
80	Jammys JM 002	Long Long Life/HIGH MUNDELL: Walk With Jah (12")	15
80	Cha Cha CHAD 27	Kiss Somebody/Version (12")	30
80	Black Joy DH 810	Purify Your Heart/Politician (blue vinyl)	30
80	Greensleeves GRED 34	Fally Ranking/Trench Town School (12")	30
81	Greensleeves GRED 50	Back Off (with PAPA TULLO).Dub (12")	35
81	Greensleeves GRED 60	Trying To Turn Me On/Turn On Dub (12")	15
81	Simba LION 1	13 Dead (Nothing Said)/Black Lion Band Murder (12")	25
81	Simba SIM 002	Don't Bite The Hand (with ASWAD)/Dub (10")	30
82	Oak Sounds OSD 006	Yo Yo/ECHO MINOTT : Man In Love (12")	15
86	Greensleeves GRED 208	Dub Plate Playing/COCOA TEA: Cocoa Tea Medley (12")	40
70	Trojan TTL29	COME BACK DARLING (LP)	40
73	Big Shot BILP 103	READY OR NOT (LP)	75
80	Greensleeves GREL 12	FALLY LOVER (LP, red vinyl)	30
81	Cha Cha CHALP 010	IN NAH DISCO STYLE (LP)	20
81	Black Joy DHLP 2001	WARRIOR (LP)	20
84	Selection SELP 01	REALITY (LP)	20

BOB OSBURN

64	London HLD 9869	Bound To Happen/Think Of Me	15

OSCAR

(see also Paul Dean, Paul Nicholas)

66	Reaction 591 003	Club Of Lights/Waking Up	60
66	Reaction 591 006	Join My Gang/Days Gone By	30
67	Reaction 591 012	Over The Wall We Go/Every Day Of My Life	35
67	Reaction 591 016	Holiday/Give Her All She Wants	30
68	Polydor 56257	Open Up The Skies/Wild Ones	30

MINT VALUE £

OSCAR

74	Buk BULP 2001	OSCAR (LP)	15

OSCAR BICYCLE

68	CBS 3237	On A Quiet Night/The Room Revolves Around Me	60

PETER OSGOOD

70	Penny Farthing PEN 715	Chelsea/Stamford Bridge	10

OSIBISA

(see also Del Richardson)

71	MCA MDKS 8001	OSIBISA (LP, gatefold, purple/red 'dogbone' label)	30
72	MCA MDKS 8005	WOYOYA (LP, gatefold, black/blue/white hexagon label)	25
72	MCA MDKS 8007	HEADS (LP, gatefold, black/blue/white label)	25
73	Buddah 2318 087	SUPER FLY T.N.T. (LP, soundtrack)	15

OSMOND BROTHERS

63	MGM MGM 1208	Be My Little Baby Bumble Bee/I Wouldn't Know	15
63	MGM MGM 1245	Travels Of Jamie McPheeters/Aura Lee	12
63	MGM MGM-C 1011	NEW SOUND OF THE BROTHERS (LP)	30

OSMOSIS

70	RCA VICTOR LPS 4369	OSMOSIS (LP)	20

OSSIAN

77	Spring Thyme SPR 1004	OSSIAN (LP)	12
79	Iona IR 001	ST. KILDA WEDDING (LP, with lyric insert)	12
81	Iona IR 002	SEAL SONG (LP, with lyric insert)	12

OSSIE & SWEET BOYS

67	Polydor 56167	Nothing Takes The Place Of You/Brixton Boo-Ga-Loo	10

OSSIE & UPSETTERS

(see also Upsetters, Desmond Dekkar)

66	Doctor Bird DB 1018	Turn Me On/True Love	20

AL OSTER

60s	Dominion LP 1321	ECHO OF THE YUKON (LP)	20

GILBERT O'SULLIVAN

(see also Gilbert)

71	Columbia DB 8779	I Wish I Could Cry/Mr Moody's Garden	8

PETER O'SULLIVAN

76	Charisma CAS 1160	PETER O'SULLIVAN TALKS TURF (LP)	15

RAMON OTANO

64	Jump Up/Island JU 250	Fiesta En La Joya/Mambo Trinidad	10

OTHER BROTHERS

69	Pama PM 785	Let's Get Together/Little Girl	20

OTHER TWO

(see also Storyteller, J.J. Jackson)

64	Decca F 11911	I Wanna Be With You/Grumbling Guitar	12
65	RCA RCA 1465	Don't You Wanna Love Me Baby/Hold Back The Light Of Dawn	10
66	RCA RCA 1531	I'll Never Let You Go/Hot At Night	12

OTHERS

(see also Sands, Sundragon)

64	Fontana TF 501	Oh Yeah/I'm Taking Her Home	70

JOHNNY OTIS SHOW

(see also Marie Adams)

50	Parlophone R 3291	Harlem Nocturne (solo)/SLIM GAILLARD: Jam Man (78)	20
57	Capitol CL 14794	Ma (He's Makin' Eyes At Me)/Romance In The Dark	7
58	Capitol CL 14817	Bye Bye Baby (as Johnny Otis Show with Marie Adams)/Good Golly	12
58	Capitol CL 14837	The Light Still Shines In My Window/All I Want Is Your Love (with Marie Adams)	25
58	Capitol CL 14837	The Light Still Shines In My Window/All I Want Is Your Love (78, with Marie Adams)	10
58	Capitol CL 14854	Well, Well, Well, Well!/You Just Kissed Me Goodbye (with Mel Williams)	25
58	Capitol CL 14854	Well, Well, Well, Well!/You Just Kissed Me Goodbye (with Mel Williams) (78)	10
58	Capitol CL 14875	Ring-A-Ling/The Johnny Otis Hand Jive	25
58	Capitol CL 14875	Ring-A-Ling/The Johnny Otis Hand Jive (78)	40
58	Capitol CL 14941	Crazy Country Hop/Willie Did The Cha Cha	25
59	Capitol CL 15008	You/My Dear (as Johnny Otis Show with Mel Williams)	18
59	Capitol CL 15018	Castin' My Spell/Telephone Baby (as Johnny Otis Show with Marci Lee)	25
59	Capitol CL 15057	Three Girls Named Molly Doin' The Hully Gully/I'll Do The Same Thing For You	20
60	Capitol CL 15112	Mumblin' Mosie/Hey Baby, Don't You Know?	15
64	Ember EMB S 192	Hand Jive One More Time/Baby I Got News For You	12
69	Sonet SON 608	Country Girl/Signifyin' Monkey	6
72	Epic EPC 7896	The Watts Breakaway/You Can Depend On Me	8
72	Epic EPC 8071	The Watts Breakaway/Willie And The Hand Jive	8
59	Capitol EAP1 1134	THE JOHNNY OTIS SHOW (EP)	60
65	Vocalion VEP 170162	JOHNNY OTIS (EP)	100
58	Capitol T 940	THE JOHNNY OTIS SHOW (LP)	100
69	Sonet SNTF 613	COLD SHOT (LP)	20
72	Ember SPE 6604	FORMIDABLE (LP)	20

SHUGGIE OTIS

(see also Al Kooper & Shuggie Otis)

70	CBS 63996	HERE COMES SHUGGIE OTIS (LP)	35

NOIT OTNI & PITS

79	Automotive AERS 107	A Heart Can Only Be Broken Once/Moving Target (in p/s)	35
79	Automotive AERS 107	A Heart Can Only Be Broken Once/Moving Target	25

MINT VALUE £

JOHN OTWAY

72	County COUN 215	Gypsy/Misty Mountain (private pressing, with duplicated lyric sheet)	25
76	Viking YRS CF 01	Louisa On A Horse/Beware Of The Flowers (private pressing)	15
78	Polydor 2059 001	Geneve/It's A Long Time Since I Heard Homestead On The Farm (p/s)	5
78	Polydor 2059 060	Baby's In The Club/Julie Julie Julie (p/s)	5
79	Polydor 2059 105	Frightened And Scared (instrumental)/Are You On My Side? (p/s, only 3 copies pressed!)	50
80	Stiff BUY 101	Green Green Grass Of Home/Wednesday Club (p/s)	5
82	Empire HAM 3	In Dreams/You Ain't Seen Nothing Yet (as John Otway Sweat, p/s)	5
86	'Warner Bros' OTWEAY 1	The New Jerusalem/The Tyger (private pressing)	20
82	Empire HAMLP 1	JOHN OTWAY (ALL BALLS AND NO WILLY) (LP, with Europeans)	12

JOHN OTWAY & WILD WILLY BARRETT

(see also Wild Willy Barrett)

73	Track 2094 111	Murder Man/If I Did	8
76	Track 2094 133	Louisa On A Horse/Misty Mountain	5
77	Polydor 2058 916	Racing Cars (Jet Spotter Of The Track)/Running From The Law (p/s)	10
77	Polydor 2058 951	Really Free/Beware Of The Flowers (Cos I'm Sure They're Going To Get You Yeh) (p/s)	6
77	Polydor 2058 951	Really Free/Beware Of The Flowers (Cos I'm Sure They're Going To Get You Yeh) (die-cut 'review' sleeve)	5
82	Stiff Indie STIN 1	Headbutts/Live Version Headbutts (p/s)	6
82	Empire HAM 5T	12 STITCH EP (12" EP in polythene bag with jay-card)	15
87	VM VMS 6	The Last Of The Mohicans/Fashion (brown paper bag sleeve)	5
77	Extracted EXLP 1	JOHN OTWAY AND WILD WILLY BARRETT (LP, handmade stickered sleeve)	20
77	white label OBL 1	OTWAY AND BARRETT LIVE AT THE ROUNDHOUSE (private pressing LP, freebie, handwritten labels, plain sleeve, 250 numbered copies only)	35
81	Polydor POLS 1039	GONE WITH THE BIN (THE BEST OF OTWAY-BARRETT) (LP)	12
87	VM VM 7	THE WIMP AND THE WILD (LP, 1,000 only)	12

OUR PLASTIC DREAM

67	Go AJ 11411	A Little Bit Of Shangrila/Encapsulated Marigold	90

COUSINS (Belgium)

61	Palette PG 9011	Kili Watch/Feugo	10
61	Palette PG 9017	Bouddha/Kana Kapila	10
62	Palette PG 9035	Anda/Danseuse	10

OUT

79	Rabid TOSH 113	Who Is Innocent/Linda's Just A Statue (p/s)	7

OUTCASTS

78	It IT 4	Frustration/Don't Want To Be No Adult/You're A Disease (p/s)	30
78	Good Vibrations GOT 3	Just Another Teenage Rebel/Love Is For Sops (poster p/s, various colours; 'band' p/s)	12
78	Good Vibrations GOT 3	Just Another Teenage Rebel/Love Is For Sops (poster p/s, various colours; 'type' p/s)	12
79	Good Vibrations GOT 17	Self Conscious Over You/Love You For Never (p/s)	12
81	GBH GBH 001	Magnum Force/Gangland Warfare (p/s)	20
81	Outcasts Only 0001	Programme Love/Beating And Screaming (Parts 1 & 2)/Mania (p/s)	5
79	Good Vibrations BIG 1	SELF CONSCIOUS OVER YOU (LP)	22

OUTER LIMITS

60s	Teldisc TD 154	Paradise For Two/Don't Ever Change	20

OUTER LIMITS

(see also Christie, Acid Gallery)

67	Elephant LUR 100	When The Work Is Thru'/5 MAN CARGO: What A Wonderful Feeling (Leeds Students Charity Rag record)	55
67	Deram DM 125	Just One More Chance/Help Me Please	30
68	Immediate IM 067	Great Train Robbery/Sweet Freedom (demo only)	70
68	Instant IN 001	Great Train Robbery/Sweet Freedom	50
71	Decca F 13176	The Dark Side Of The Moon/Black Boots	10

OUTER LIMITS

70s	Snow/Deroy 1049	(I'm Not) Your Stepping Stone/Great Balls Of Fire	300

OUTLAW BLUES BAND

69	Stateside SSL 10290	BREAKING IN (LP)	30

OUTLAW POSSE

90	Gee street Gee A6	My Afro's On Fire (12")	12
91	Outlaw OP1	Sonz Of The Devil (12")	12

OUTLAWS

(see also Mike Berry, Ritchie Blackmore, Bobbie Graham, Chaps, Rally Rounders, Houston Wells [& Marksmen])

61	HMV POP 844	Swingin' Low/Spring Is Near	15
61	HMV POP 877	Ambush/Indian Brave	15
61	HMV POP 927	Valley Of The Sioux/Crazy Drums	20
62	HMV POP 990	Ku-pow!/Last Stage West	20
62	HMV POP 1074	Sioux Serenade/Fort Knox	20
63	HMV POP 1124	The Return Of The Outlaws/Texan Spiritual	20
63	HMV POP 1195	That Set The Wild West Free/Hobo	20
63	HMV POP 1241	Law And Order/Do-Da-Day	20
64	HMV POP 1277	Keep-A-Knockin'/Shake With Me	35
61	HMV CLP 1489	DREAM OF THE WEST (LP, mauve label)	85
61	HMV CLP 1489	DREAM OF THE WEST (LP, later black label)	60

OUT OF DARKNESS

70	Key KL 006	OUT OF DARKNESS (LP, laminated front sleeve)	150

OUT OF ORDER

81	Daviton SPEP 120	OUT OF CONTROL (EP, export copy, 500 only)	40

MINT VALUE £

OUTRAGE

70	Kama Sutra 618 027	The Letter/The Way I See It	5

OUTSIDERS (U.K.)

(see also Second Layer, Sound)

78	Xciting Plastic	Vital Hours/Take Up (unissued)	0

OUTSIDERS (U.K.)

(see also Bunch Of Fives, Junior's Eyes, Tickle)

65	Decca F 12213	Keep On Doing It/Songs We Sang Last Summer	40
77	Raw Edge RER 002	ONE TO INFINITY (EP)	25
77	Raw Edge RER 001	CALLING ON YOUTH (LP, laminated sleeve)	40
78	Raw Edge RER 003	CLOSE UP (LP, with insert)	40

OUTSIDERS (U.S.)

66	Capitol CL 15435	Time Won't Let Me/Was It Really Real?	35
66	Capitol CL 15435	Time Won't Let Me/Was It Really Real? (DJ copy)	50
66	Capitol CL 15450	Girl In Love/What Makes You So Bad, You Weren't Brought Up That Way	15
66	Capitol CL 15468	Respectable/Lost In My World	20
66	Capitol CL 15480	Help Me Girl/You Gotta Look	10
67	Capitol CL 15495	I'll Give You Time/I'm Not Tryin' To Hurt You	20

OUTSKIRTS OF INFINITY

87	Woronzow WOO 7	LORD OF THE DARK SKIES (LP)	15
89	Infinity INF 001	SCENES FROM THE DREAMS OF ANGELS (LP)	12
89	Infinity INF 002	STONED CRAZY (LP)	12
94	Dark Skies DSKLP 2	INCIDENT AT PILATUS (2-LP)	18

OVALTINEES

83	BAA 021	BRITISH JUSTICE EP (p/s)	70

OVARY LODGE

(see also Keith Tippett)

73	RCA SF 8372	OVARY LODGE (LP)	100
76	Ogun OG 600	OVARY LODGE (LP)	25

OVATIONZ

81	Dread At The Controls DCD 005	Forever Love/Forever Dub (12")	15

OVERCOMERS

68	Bamboo BAM 64	Stop And Let Me Tell You/Take Courage Soul (unissued: white labels only)	50

OVERDRIVE

81	Boring Grantham BGR 1	ON THE RUN (EP)	80
90	Boring Grantham BGR 11	DISHONEST WORDS (LP)	12

OVERKILL

80	Killer EJSP 9357	Elemental/On My Own	75

OVERLANDERS

(see also Paul Arnold, Cuppa T)

63	Pye 7N 15544	Summer Skies And Golden Sands/Call Of The Wild	12
63	Pye 7N 15568	Movin'/Rainbow	7
66	Pye NEP 24245	MICHELLE (EP)	25
66	Pye NPL 18138	MICHELLE (LP, laminated front sleeve with flipbacks)	35

OVERLOAD

80	MCA MCA 618	Into Overload/Follow The Lines (p/s)	10
81	MCA MCA 656	Who Are You/Drift Away	10

OVERLORD

78	Airebeat ABT 3	Lucy/Guardsman/Johnny (p/s)	30

OVERLORD X

88	Hardcore HAKT12	14 Days In May (12")	10
88	Mango 1215 372	Rough In Hackney/Earth Is Moving (12")	8
89	Mango 1215 415	Radical Kickbag (12")	8
89	Mango ILPS 9924	WEAPON IS MY LYRIC (LP)	12

RUNE OVERMAN

63	Decca F 11605	Big Bass Boogie/Madison Piano	10

OVERNIGHT PLAYERS

80	Cha Cha CHALP 008	BABYLON DESTRUCTION (LP)	30

OVERTAKERS

68	Amalgamated AMG 803	That's The Way You Like It/The Big Take-Over	15
68	Amalgamated AMG 809	Girl You Ruff/KEITH BLAKE: Woo Oh Oh	25

BILL OWEN

81	Look LK/SP 6681	Compo Has Gone And Lost His Wellies/Friends (p/s)	5

OWEN (Gray) & DANDY (Livingstone)

69	Downtown DT 428	Lovey Dovey/HERBIE GRAY & RUDIES: Kitty Wait	8

OWEN (Da Silvera) & LEON

(see also Leon & Owen, Tommy McCook)

64	Island WI 146	Nextdoor Neighbour/ROLAND ALPHONSO: Feeling Fine	25
64	Island WI 163	My Love For You/How Many Times	25
64	Island WI 164	The Fits Is On Me/SKATALITES: Good News	25
64	Island WI 165	Running Around/SKATALITES: Around The World	25
65	Island WI 170	I Want My Cock/I Am Only Human (DERAK HARRIOTT) (probably withdrawn)	50
65	Ska Beat JB 189	Woman/BABA BROOKS with DON DRUMMOND: Doctor Decker	25

OWEN (Gray) & MILLIE

(see also Owen Gray, Millie, Owen & Leon, Leon & Owen)

62	Blue Beat BB 96	Sit And Cry/Do You Know (with City Slickers Orchestra)	8
62	Island WI 014	Sugar Plum/OWEN GRAY: Jezebel	15

MINT VALUE £

RAY OWEN('S MOON)

(see also Juicy Lucy)

69	Fontana TF 1045	Tonight I'll Be Staying Here With You/Down, Don't Bother Me (solo)	5
71	Polydor 2058 095	Hey Sweety/Free Man (as Ray Owen's Moon)	5
71	Polydor 2066-119	Try My Love/Talk To Me	25
71	Polydor 2325 061	RAY OWEN'S MOON (LP, textured sleeve)	60

REG OWEN & HIS ORCHESTRA

59	Pye International 7N 25009	Manhattan Spiritual/Ritual Blues	6
60	Palette PG 9004	Obsession/Sunday Morn	12
56	Parlophone PMD 1045	SWING ME HIGH (10" LP)	20
59	Pye Intl. NPL 28000	MANHATTAN SPIRITUAL (LP, mono)	15
59	Pye Intl. NSPL 93000	MANHATTAN SPIRITUAL (LP, stereo)	20
58	RCA RD 27048	DREAMING (LP)	15

BUCK OWENS (& BUCKAROOS)

59	Capitol CL 15009	Everlasting Love/Second Fiddle	10
60	Capitol CL 15123	Above And Beyond/Til These Dreams Come True	10
60	Capitol CL 15162	Excuse Me (I Think I've Got A Heartache)/I've Got A Right To Know	10
61	Capitol CL 15187	Foolin' Around/High As The Mountain	6
62	Longhorn BLH 0006	Down On The Corner Of Love/Right After The Dance	7
63	Capitol CL 15321	Love's Gonna Live Here/Getting Used To Losing You	5
64	Capitol CL 15364	Together Again/Ain't It Amazin' Gracie (as Buck Owens & Buckaroos)	5
65	Capitol CL 15379	I've Got A Tiger By The Tail/Cryin' Time	6
67	Capitol CL 15501	Sam's Place/Don't Ever Tell Me Goodbye (as Buck Owens & Buckaroos)	6
63	Capitol EAP1 1550	FOOLIN' AROUND (EP)	10
65	Capitol EAP1 20602	ACT NATURALLY (EP)	10

DONNIE OWENS

58	London HLU 8747	Need You/If I'm Wrong	25
58	London HLU 8747	Need You/If I'm Wrong (78)	15
59	London HLW 8897	Ask Me Anything/Between Midnight And Dawn (unissued)	0

JAMIE OWENS

73	Light LS 7012	LAUGHTER IN YOUR SOUL (LP)	15

OWL

68	United Artists UP 2240	Run To The Sun/Shades Of Blue And Green Water Flies	30

O.W.L.

70s	Shebazz SHE 002	Shady Tree/4TH STREET ORCHESTRA: Sun Hot	8

TONY OXLEY (QUARTET)

(see also Derek Bailey, Howard Riley)o

69	CBS 52664	THE BAPTISED TRAVELLER (LP)	110
70	CBS 64071	4 COMPOSITIONS FOR SEXTET (LP, with Derek Bailey)	110
71	RCA SF 8215	ICHNOS (LP)	80
70s	Incus INCUS 8	TONY OXLEY (LP, with Derek Bailey, et al.)	100
70s	Incus INCUS 18	FEBRUARY PAPERS (LP)	40
80s	Bead BEAD 25	THE GLIDER & THE GRINDER (LP)	30

TONY OXLEY, WOLFGANG FUCHS, PHILIPP WACHSMANN & HUGH METCALFE

87	Bead Records BEAD 25	THE GLIDER AND THE GRINDER (LP)	20

OXYM

80	Cargo CRS 003	Music Power/Mind Key (p/s)	40

OYSTER BAND

86	Cooking Vinyl FRY 001	Hal-an-Tow/Ashes To Ashes (p/s)	6
89	Cooking Vinyl FRYX 012	Love Vigilantes/Polish Plain/I Fought The Law (Live)/ Between The Wars (Live) (10", pink vinyl, poster sleeve)	10
82	Pukka YOP 01	ENGLISH ROCK 'N' ROLL, 1800-1850 (LP)	30
85	Pukka YOP 04	LIE BACK AND THINK OF ENGLAND (LP)	30
85	Pukka YOP 07	LIBERTY HALL (LP)	30

OYSTER CEILIDH BAND

80	Dingles DIN 309	JACK'S ALIVE (LP)	30

OZO

77	DJM DJT 10764	Anambra (Edited Version)/Anambra (12")	35

OZRIC TENTACLES

(see also Oroonies, Ullulators)

91	Dovetail DOVEST 3	Sploosh!/Live Throbbe (12" P/s)	10
90	Dovetail DOVE LP1	ERPLAND (2-LP)	25
91	Dovetail DOVE LP 3	STRANGETUDE (LP)	15
92	Black Adder OZT 01	MUCK KICKER (LP)	20
94	Dovetail DOVE LP7	ARBORESCENE (2-LP)	25
94	Dovetail DOVEBOX 1	VITAMIN ENHANCED (6-CD box set)	30
98	Snapper SMALP 410	CURIOUS CORN (LP)	12
00	Strechy/Pancromatic PLP 2002	THE HIDDEN STEP (LP)	12

OZZ II

83	Streamline	EXPLOITED (LP, red vinyl)	12
84	Zebra ZEB 2	THE ASSASSIN (LP)	12

MINT VALUE £

AUGUSTUS PABLO

(see also Mickey Lee, I Roy)

71	Big Shot BI 578	The Mood/HERMAN CHIN-LOY: New Love	25
71	Big Shot BI 579	East Of The River Nile/HERMAN CHIN-LOY: East Of River Nile Version (B-side actually by Aquarians)	40
71	Creole CR 1004	405 (actually "The Mood" by Tommy McCook)/Duck It Up (actually "Confidential Version" by Charmers)	18
71	Ackee ACK 134	Still Yet/AQUARIANS: Version	12
71	Ackee ACK 138	Snowball And Pudding/AQUARIANS: Version	12
71	Duke DU 122	Reggae In The Fields/TOMMY McCOOK: Love Brother	30
73	Randy's RAN 536	Bedroom Mazurka (as Augustus Pablo & Fay)/Melodica Version	20
73	Atra ATRA 011	Lover's Mood/Lover's Rock	20
74	Tropical AL 025	Too Late/Dub Organiser	10
74	Tropical AL 035	Tales Of Pablo/BOOTHE STARS: Tales Dub	10
74	Sydna DL1276	Pablo's Mercy/Version	12
75	Fay Music FM 603	Fort Augustus Rock/Augustus In Kingston	10
75	Island WIP 6226	King Tubby Meets The Rockers Uptown/Baby I Love You So	10
75	Island 12 WIP 6226	King Tubby Meets The Rockers Uptown/ JACOB MILLER: Baby I Love You So (12")	20
75	Treble C CCC06	Liberation/Dubbing Pablo	12
75	Treble C CCC014	Don Drummond/Thunderbolt Lady	10
77	Hawkeye HE 005	East Of The River Nile/East Africa	10
77	Solid Sound SS1	Doug's Love/Version	12
78	Rough Trade RT 002	Pablo Meets Mr. Bassie/Mr. Bassie Special (with Rockers All Stars) (with colour sticker)	10
77	EJI 011	No Entry/BIG YOUTH: Strictly Rockers (12")	50
79	Rockers APD 5	Power Of The Trinity/West Abyssinia Dub (12")	20
79	Rockers APD 6	Twin Seal/Dub/NORRIS REID: Entrance To Jah World (12")	25
79	Rockers AP 1023	Crucial Burial/ROCKERS ALL STARS: Pope Paul Feel It/Sound Of Redemption - Scientist In Dub (12")	30
79	Rockers AB1	Israel In Harmony/HUGH MUNDELL: Feeling Alright/Dub (12")	35
80	Rockers APD 7	Hot Milk/Dub/Robin Bay Step/Dub (12")	25
74	Tropical TROPS 101	THIS IS (LP)	30
75	Trojan TRLS 115	ITAL DUB (LP, original issue with "12 Neasden Lane" address on sleeve and rough orange/white paper labels)	30
75	Nationwide NW 03	THRILLER (LP)	20
79	Atra ATRALP 1003	LEGENDS (LP)	20

PACESETTERS

70	Big Chief BC 101	Cool Coffee/Israelites	12
70	Escort ERT 829	Bits And Pieces/Nimrod Leap	8
74	Saga SAGA 8154	REGGAE MEETS POP (LP)	25

PACIFIC DRIFT

(see also Wimple Winch, Just Four Men)

70	Deram DM 304	Water Woman/Yes You Do	20
70	Deram Nova (S)DN 13	FEELIN' FREE (LP, red/silver labels)	70

PACIFIC GAS & ELECTRIC (P.G. & E.)

70	CBS 5039	Are You Ready?/Staggolee	6
70	CBS 5204	Father Come On Home/Elvira	5
69	B&C CAS 1003	GET IT ON (LP)	40
69	CBS 63822	PACIFIC GAS & ELECTRIC (LP, orange label)	18
70	CBS 64026	ARE YOU READY (LP, orange label)	15
71	CBS 64295	HARD BURN (LP, orange label)	15

PACIFIC SOUND

(see also Theatre Of Hate, Spear Of Destiny, Senate)

71	M&M FMSS 10012	Tribute To Jimi/Thick Fog	30

PACK

65	Columbia DB 7702	Do You Believe In Magic?/Things Bring Me Down	45

PACK

79	SS PAK 1	Brave New Soldiers/Heathen (p/s, 2,500 only)	12
79	Rough Trade RT 025	King Of Kings/Number 12 (p/s)	8
80	SS SS 1N2/SS 2N1	KIRK BRANDON AND THE PACK OF LIES (EP, with printed inner sleeve)	12
82	Cyclops CYCLOPS 1	LONG LIVE THE PAST (EP)	8
82	Donut DONUT 2	THE PACK LIVE, 1979 (cassette)	15

PACKABEATS

61	Parlophone R 4729	Gypsy Beat/Big Man	20
62	Pye 7N 15480	Evening In Paris/The Traitors	25
63	Pye 7N 15549	Dream Lover/Packabeat	30

PACKERS

66	Pye International 7N 25343	Hole In The Wall/Go 'Head On	25
69	Soul City SC 111	Hole In The Wall/Go 'Head On (reissue)	18
70	Soul City SCM 003	HOLE IN THE WALL (LP)	40

MINT VALUE £

PAC-KEYS

68	Speciality SPE 1003	Stone Fox/Diggin'	15

PADDINGTONS

04	Poptones MC5093S	21/Some Old Girl (p/s)	7

PADDY, KLAUS & GIBSON

(see also Manfred Mann, Big Three, Rory Storm & Hurricanes, Kingsize Taylor)

65	Pye 7N 15906	I Wanna Know/I Tried	20
66	Pye 7N 17060	No Good Without You Baby/Rejected	40
66	Pye 7N 17112	Teresa/Quick Before They Catch Us	25

PAGAN BEAU

82	RVNIC Records AMO 24	Odd Man Out/Natures Daughter (p/s)	15

BILLY PAGE

65	London HLU 10006	It's Pop/American Girl	12

CHRIS PAGE

66	Cameo Parkway CP 751	Wait And See/Mine Mine Mine	12

PAGE FIVE

66	Parlophone R 5426	Let Sleeping Dogs Lie/I Know All About Her	35

GENE PAGE

75	Atlantic K50105	HOT CITY (LP)	12

HOT LIPS PAGE & HIS ORCHESTRA

55	Parlophone MSP 6172	Ain't Nothing Wrong With That Boy/The Cadillac Song	20

JIMMY PAGE

(see also Led Zeppelin, Page & Plant, Firm, Yardbirds, Paul, Carter-Lewis & Southerners, Neil Christian & Crusaders, Bobby Graham, Robert Plant, Honeydrippers, Brian Auger, Cartoone, Maureeny Wishfull, Coverdale-Page)

65	Fontana TF 533	She Just Satisfies/Keep Moving (promo sticker on label)	750
65	Fontana TF 533	She Just Satisfies/Keep Moving	650
88	Geffen GEF 41	Wasting My Time/Writes Of Winter (p/s, withdrawn)	8
91	Fontana TF 533	She Just Satisifies/Keep Moving (reissue as part of Fontana box set)	15
91	Fontana TFCD 533	She Just Satisfies/Keep Moving (CD, in 'Led Zeppelin, A Celebration' promo book pack)	10

LARRY PAGE (ORCHESTRA)

57	Columbia DB 3965	Cool Shake/Start Movin' (In My Direction)	25
58	Columbia DB 4012	That'll Be The Day/Please Don't Blame Me	25
58	Columbia DB 4080	Under Control/This Is My Life	20
59	Saga SAG 45-2902	Big Blon' Baby/I Vibrate	20
60	Saga SAG 45-2903	How'm I Doing, Hey Hey/Throw All Your Lovin' My Way	10
60	Saga SAG 45-2904	Little Old Fashioned You/Marylin	7
66	Decca F 12320	Waltzing To Jazz/Jo Jo (as Larry Page Orchestra)	5
66	Decca F 12368	Peyton Place Theme/Leanda's Theme (as Larry Page Orchestra)	5
68	Page One POF 068	Take Five/Michelle	5
68	Page One POF 096	Hey Jude/Those Were The Days (as Larry Page Orchestra)	5
60	Saga STP 1024	SINGS HIS PERSONAL CHOICE (EP)	8
65	Decca LK 4692	KINKY MUSIC (LP, as Larry Page Orchestra)	70
68	Page One POL(S) 002	EXECUTIVE SUITE (LP, as Larry Page Orchestra)	25
69	Page One POS 601	PRESENTING THE LARRY PAGE ORCHESTRA (LP)	15

MALLY PAGE

66	Pye 7N 17105	The Life And Soul Of The Party/You Can Be Wrong About Boys	6

PATTI PAGE

(see also Pete Rugolo)

SINGLES

58	Mercury 7MT 184	I'll Remember Today/My, How The Time Goes	5
58	Mercury 7MT 200	Bring Us Together/Belonging To Someone	5
58	Mercury 7MT 206	These Worldly Wonders/Another Time, Another Place	5
58	Mercury 7MT 223	Left Right Out Of Your Heart/Longing To Hold You Again	5
58	Mercury AMT 1000	Fibbin'/You Will Find Your Love (In Paris)	5
59	Mercury AMT 1022	Trust In Me/Under The Sun Valley Moon	5
59	Mercury AMT 1038	The Walls Have Ears/My Promise	5
59	Mercury AMT 1054	My Mother's Eyes/With My Eyes Wide Open I'm Dreaming	5
60	Mercury AMT 1089	Promise Me Thomas/Two Thousand, Two Hundred And Twenty-Three Miles	5
60	Mercury AMT 1102	One Of Us (Will Weep Tonight)/What Will My Future Be	5
60	Mercury AMT 1112	I Wish I'd Never Been Born/I Need You	5
61	Mercury AMT 1160	Broken Heart And A Pillow Full Of Tears/Dark Moon	5
63	CBS AAG 136	Just A Simple Melody/Pretty Lonely Boy	5

EPs

56	Mercury MEP 9502	PATTI PAGE	10
59	Mercury ZEP 10006	PATTI PAGE ONE	10
59	Mercury ZEP 10017	PATTI PAGE TWO	10
59	Mercury ZEP 10032	PATTI PAGE THREE	10
59	Mercury ZEP 10045	PATTI PAGE FOUR	10
60	Mercury ZEP 10073	PATTI PAGE FIVE	10
61	Mercury SEZ 19008	THIS LADY IS NO TRAMP (stereo, with Pete Rugolo All Stars)	10
61	Mercury SEZ 19020	MY KINDA LOVE (stereo)	10

LPs

54	Mercury MG 25101	FOLK SONG FAVOURITES (10")	20
55	Mercury MG 25197	PATTI'S SONGS (10")	20
56	Mercury MPT 7510	CHRISTMAS WITH PATTI PAGE (10")	20
57	Mercury MPT 7531	I'M GETTING SENTIMENTAL OVER YOU (10")	20
57	Mercury MPT 7535	PATTI'S SONGS (10", reissue)	12
61	Mercury MMC 14064	ROMANCE IN RHYTHM	12

MINT VALUE £

PAGE & PLANT

(see also Jimmy Page, Robert Plant)

94	Fontana PRCDJ 1	Gallows Pole (CD, in special brown or red sleeve, promo only)	8
94	Fontana PPCD 2	Gallows Pole/City Don't Cry/The Rain Song (CD, pic. disc, part 1 of 2-CD set)	8
94	Fontana PPDD 2	Gallows Pole/Four Sticks/What Is And What Should Never Be (CD, picture disc, part 2 of 2-CD set)	8
95	Fontana PPCDJ 3	Kashmir (CD promo, withdrawn)	30
95	Fontana PPCDJ 4	The Battle Of Evermore (CD promo)	12
98	Mercury 558 324 2	Walking Into Clarksdale (CD, limited issue digipak)	10
98	Mercury ADV 1998	Walking Into Clarksdale (CD promo, card sleeve)	40
94	Fontana PP ID 1	NO QUARTER UNLEDDED (CD, radio-promo only, with 'question' booklet)	50
94	Fontana 526 3621	NO QUARTER UNLEDDED (LP)	12
98	Mercury ADV 982	TBA (CD, advance promo for WALKING INTO CLARKSDALE)	30
98	Mercury PPTIC 1	WALKING INTO CLARKSDALE AN INTERVIEW (CD radio promo)	30
98	Mercury 558 025 1	WALKING INTO CLARKSDALE (LP)	15

PAGE BOYS (U.K.)

(see also 1,000 Violins)

83	Whaam! WHAAM 10	You're My Kind Of Girl/In Love With You (p/s, 1,000 only)	20

PAGEBOYS (U.S.)

65	London HLU 9948	When I Meet A Girl Like You/I Have Love	10

PAGE ONE & THE OBSERVERS

76	Carib Gems CGLP 004	OBSERVATION OF LIFE DUB (LP)	40

PAGE TEN

(see also Niney)

65	Decca F 12248	Boutique/Colour Talk	15

CARLOS PAIAO

81	EMI EMI 5174	Playback (English)/Playback (Portuguese)	7

PAICE, ASHTON & LORD

(see also Deep Purple, Jon Lord, Ashton & Lord, Ashton Gardner & Dyke, Elf, Bernie Marsden)

77	Polydor/Oyster 2391 269	MALICE IN WONDERLAND (LP, with inner sleeve)	15

HAL PAIGE & WHALERS

60	Melodisc MEL 1553	Going Back To My Home Town/After Hours Blues	50

JOEY PAIGE

65	Fontana TF 554	Cause I'm In Love With You/Yeah Yeah Yeah	20

ROSALIND PAIGE

55	London HL 8120	When The Saints Go Marching In/Nobody's Sweetheart Now	30
57	MGM MGM 937	Love, Oh Careless Love/That Funny Melody	10

PAINTBOX

(see also Easybeats, Haffy's Whiskey Sour)

70	Young Blood YB 1013	Get Ready For Love/Can I Get To Know You	10
71	Young Blood YB 1029	Get Ready For Love/Can I Get To Know You (reissue)	6

PAINTED SHIP

67	Mercury MF 988	Frustration/I Told Those Little White Lies	100

PAISLEYS

83	Psycho PSYCHO 7	COSMIC MIND AT PLAY (LP, reissue)	20

PALADIN

(see also Arthur Brown, Glass Menagerie, McGuinness Flint)

71	Bronze ILPS 9150	PALADIN (LP, textured sleeve, Island credit on label)	30
72	Bronze ILPS 9190	CHARGE (LP, gatefold sleeve, Island credit on label)	40

PALE FOUNTAINS

(see also Shack)

82	Operation Twilight OPT 09	(There's Always) Something On My Mind/Just A Girl (p/s)	30
82	Virgin VS 557	Thank You/Meadow Of Love (picture disc, stickered PVC sleeve)	6
82	Virgin VS 557-12	Thank You/Meadow Of Love/(There's Always) Something On My Mind (12", p/s)	15
83	Virgin VS 568	Palm Of My Hand/(Instrumental)/Love's A Beautiful Place (p/s)	8
83	Virgin VS 568-12	Palm Of My Hand/(Instrumental)/Love's A Beautiful Place (12", p/s)	15
85	Virgin VS 750	From Across The Kitchen Table/Bicycle Thieves// Thank You/ Just A Girl (double pack)	10
84	Virgin V 2274	PACIFIC STREET (LP)	15
85	Virgin V 2333	FROM ACROSS THE KITCHEN TABLE (LP, with inner sleeve)	15

PALE SAINTS

88	Panic PANIC FIRST	Children Break/SAVLONS: ?And What's More/KERRY FIDDLES: Shiver Me Timbers (33rpm flexidisc, stickered card sleeve, some with postcard)	8
90	4AD CAD 0002	COMFORTS OF MADNESS (LP, with postcards)	15
92	4AD CAD 2004	IN RIBBONS (LP, with free 7" "A Thousand Stars Burst Open"/ A Revelation [RIB 1])	12

TOM PALEY

(see also Peggy Seeger)

69	Argo ZFB 3	SUE COW (LP)	12
76	Kicking Mule SNKF 119	HARD LUCK PAPA (LP)	18

PALEY BROTHERS

(see also Ramones)

78	Sire SRE 4005	Come On Let's Go/Magic Power (p/s)	12
78	Sire 6078 613	Ecstacy/Rendezvous/Hide N' Seek/Come Out And Play (12", p/s)	12

PALI GAP

82	Sinister SYN 001	Under The Sun/The Knives Are Out (p/s, with insert)	20

MORTY PALITZ & ACES

59	London HLJ 8778	The Grocer's Cha Cha Cha/Eso Es El Amor (This Is Love)	8

MINT VALUE £

PALLAS

82	Granite Wax GWS 1	Arrive Alive/Stranger (On The Edge Of Time) (two different p/s, with insert)	50
82	Granite Wax GWS 1	Arrive Alive/Stranger (On The Edge Of Time) (two different p/s, without insert)	40
83	Cool King CK010	Paris Is Burning/The Hammer Falls (p/s)	5
83	Cool King 12CK010	Paris Is Burning/The Hammer Falls/Stranger At The Edge Of Time (12", p/s)	12
84	EMI Harvest PLSP1	Eyes In The Night (Arrive Alive)/East West (picture disc)	10
84	EMI Harvest PLSP1	Eyes In The Night (Arrive Alive)/East West/Crown Of Thorns (12", p/s)	10
84	EMI Harvest PLS2	Shock Treatment/March On Atlantis (poster p/s)	5
84	EMI Harvest 12PLS2	Shock Treatment/March On Atlantis/Heart Attack (12", p/s)	10
78	Sue-i-cide PAL/101	THE PALLAS EP (stamped plain die-cut sleeve)	50
85	Harvest 12PLS3P	THE KNIGHT MOVES EP (12" picture disc)	12
85	Harvest 12PLS3D	THE KNIGHT MOVES EP (12" + free 7" Mad Machine / Stitch In Time, sealed in plastic sleeve)	15
83	Cool King CKLP002	ARRIVE ALIVE (LP)	15
84	Harvest SHSP2400 121	THE SENTINAL (LP, gatefold sleeve, with poster and sticker)	18
84	Harvest SHSP2400 121	THE SENTINAL (LP, gatefold sleeve)	12
86	Harvest SHVL 850	THE WEDGE (LP + inner sleeve)	15

EARL PALMER & HIS TEN PIECE ROCKIN' BAND

58	Capitol CL 14859	Drum Village (Parts 1 & 2)	10
58	Capitol EAP1 1026	SWINGIN' DRUMS (EP)	12
61	Liberty LBY 1008	DRUMSVILLE (LP)	20

EDDIE PALMER

57	Decca F 10873	The Sky/The Twilight Theme	8

MICHAEL PALMER

84	Greensleeves GREL 155	Done With It/Can't Take The Fuss (12")	15
84	Simba SM 08	Me Nah Run/JACKIE PARRIS: When Your Are Young (12", with Aswad)	25

MICHAEL PALMER AND JIM BROWN

83	Greensleeves GRED 131	Ghetto Dance/JAH THOMAS & ROOTS RADICS: Ghetto Dub (12")	10

RICK PALMER

59	London HLL 8900	You Threw A Heart/My Greatest Wish (unreleased)	0

ROBERT PALMER

(see also Alan Bown [Set], Dada, Power Station, Vinegar Joe)

ROY PALMER & STATE STREET RAMBLERS

54	London AL 3518	A CHICAGO SKIFFLE SESSION (10" LP)	30

TRISTAN PALMER/PALMA

81	Greensleeves GRED 66	Entertainment/JAH THOMAS & TOYAN: Jah Guide (12")	15
82	Greensleeves GRED 93	Joker Smoker/PAPA BRUCE: Loafter Smoker (12")	25
82	Greensleeves GREL 43	JOKER SMOKER (LP)	20

PALMETTO KINGS

60	Starlite ST45 021	Ten Rum Bottles/Home Cookin' Mama	15

CHARLIE PALMIERI

68	Atlantic 588157	LATIN BUGALU (LP)	30

PAMA DICE

(see also Winston Groovy, King Horror, Ray Martell)

69	Jackpot JP 715	Bongo Man/Bear De Pussy	18
69	Jackpot JP 716	Sin, Sun And Sex/Reggae Pop-Corn	15
70	Reggae REG 3001	Brixton Fight/OPENING: Tea House	100

PAN

93	Big Cat ABB 49	HANGIN' OUT FOR JUNE (LP)	15

PANACHE

(see also Ray Dorset)

83	Mach 1 MAGIC 004	I Wanna Dance/Crazy For Your Love (with Ray Dorset)	7

PANAMA FRANCIS BLUES BAND

64	Stateside SL 10070	TOUGH TALK!! (LP)	30

PANAMA LIMITED (JUG BAND)

(see also Ian (A) Anderson)

69	Harvest HAR 5010	Lady Of Shallot/Future Blues	30
70	Harvest HAR 5022	Round And Round/Rotting Wooden In A White Collar's Grave	30
69	Harvest SHVL 753	PANAMA LIMITED JUG BAND (LP, laminated gatefold sleeve, "Sold in U.K..." text on 5 lines", no EMI on label)	150
70	Harvest SHVL 779	INDIAN SUMMER (LP, as Panama Limited, gatefold sleeve, no EMI on label)	250

ALPHONSO PANCHO

(see also Pancho Alphonso)

79	Attack TACK 3	Love Is A Pleasure/Never Give Up In A Babylon	25

GENE PANCHO

(see also Gene Rondo)

68	Giant GN 21	I Like Sweet Music/Seven Days (with Sandy & Superboys)	8

PANDEMONIUM

67	CBS 202462	Season Of The Witch/Today I'm Happy	50
67	CBS 2664	No Presents For Me/The Sun Shines From His Eyes	300
68	CBS 3451	Chocolate Buster Dam/Fly With Me Forever	55

PANDIT PRAN NATH

69	Transatlantic TRA 193	EARTH GROOVE (LP)	20

PANHANDLE

(see also Chris Spedding)

72	Decca SKL 5105	PANHANDLE (LP, blue/silver label with boxed logo	30

MINT VALUE £

PANIK

77	Rainy City SHOT 1	IT WON'T SELL (EP)	15

PAN PIPERS

69	Pye 7N 17699	Stop/Money Or Love	100

PAN'S PEOPLE

74	Epic SEPC 2606	You Can Really Rock N Roll Me/The Singer Not The Song	8

PANT

79	Redball RR019X	Mother Fo/Modern/No Possessions/Mummy Told You	25

GARY PANTER & JAY COTTON

90	Blast First FU 7	ONE HELL SOUNDWICH (LP, picture disc)	20

JAN PANTER

65	Oriole CB 1938	My Two Arms Minus You Equals Tears/Does My Heart Show	25
65	CBS 201810	Let It Be Now/Stand By And Cry	20
66	Pye 7N 17097	Scratch My Back/Put Yourself In My Place	180
69	President PT 241	Si Si Senor/Stella In Lights	10

PANTHER BURNS

(see also Tav Falco's Panther Burns, Alex Chilton)

81	Rough Trade RT 077	Train Kept A Rollin'/Red Headed Woman (p/s)	10

ROY PANTON

(see also Roy & Annette, Roy & Millie, Roy & Paulette, Roy & Yvonne, Roy & Duke Allstars, Roy & Patsy, Derrick Harriot, Leon & Owen, Charmers)

63	Blue Beat BB 182	Mighty Ruler/Run Old Man	30
64	Blue Beat BB 219	Good From The Bad/Hell Gate	30
64	Rio R 19	Cherita/Seek And You Shall Find	20
64	Rio R 33	You Don't Know Me/KING EDWARD'S ALLSTARS: Doctor No	35
64	Island WI 137	Goodbye Peggy Darling (actually "Goodbye Peggy" by Stranger Cole)/ BABA BROOKS: Portrait Of My Love	25
70	Harry J HJ 6624	The Same Old Life/JAYBOYS: Life Version	8

JOHN PANTRY

(see also Factory, Peter & Wolves, Norman Conquest, Sounds Around, Bunch)

72	Philips 6006 250	Net Of Concern/Words	10
79	Kingsway KMS 902	Nothing Is Impossible/Jesus On The Airwaves	8
72	Philips 6308 129	JOHN PANTRY (LP)	35
73	Philips 6308 138	LONG WHITE TRAIL (LP)	18
80	Kingsway KMR 323	TO STRANGERS AND FRIENDS (LP)	15
80s	Tenth Planet TP 040	THE UPSIDE DOWN WORLD OF JOHN PANTRY (LP, limited edition, 1,000 only)	50

PANZA DIVISION

82	Panza Traz PTO1	We Will Rock The World/Standing On The Outside	10

PAPA DOO RUN RUN

75	RCA RCA 2620	Be True To Your School/Disney Girls	8

PAPA MICHIGAN & GENERAL SMILEY

81	Tuff Gong IPR 2035	One Love Jame Down/FREDDIE MCGREGOR: Joggin' (12")	10

PAPA TULLO

82	Negus Roots NERLP 004	TULLO AT HOME (LP)	40
81	Negus roots NERT 006	Church And State/Righteous Rock (12")	15

NIKKI PAPAS

59	Parlophone R 4590	49 State Rock/Try Again	45
60	Parlophone R 4652	By The River/Don't Leave Me Alone	18

PAPER BLITZ TISSUE

(see also Cupid's Inspiration)

67	RCA Victor RCA 1652	Boy Meets Girl/Grey Man	275

PAPER BUBBLE

(see also Dave Cousins)

70	Deram DML/SML 1059	SCENERY (LP, white/red label)	70

PAPER DOLLS

68	Pye 7N 17456	Something Here In My Heart/All The Time In The World	5
68	Pye 7N 17547	My Life Is In Your Hands/There's Nobody I'd Sooner Love	8
68	Pye 7N 17655	Someday/Any Old Time You're Lonely And Sad	7
70	RCA RCA 1919	My Boyfriend's Back/Mister Good Time Friday	7
70	RCA RCA 2007	Remember December/Same Old Story	7
68	Pye N(S)PL 18226	PAPER DOLLS HOUSE (LP)	50

PAPER DRAGON

69	Bell BLL 1054	April Fool/Get Something Going	12

PAPERHOUSE

91	Mystic Stones RUNE LP 11	SPONGY COMESTIBLES (LP)	20

PAPERTOYS

(see also Gary Numan)

90	Armada ARMAP 003	Cold Surrender (Winston Club Mix)/Cold Surrender (D-Day 7" Radio Mix)/ Cold Surrender (Outland Mix) (12", numbered p/s, 500 only)	8

PARADE

67	A&M AMS 701	Sunshine Girl/This Old Melody	18
67	A&M AMS 720	Radio Song/I Can See Love	15

VANESSA PARADIS

87	Polydor POSPG 902	Joe Le Taxi/Varvara Pavlovna (poster p/s)	6
88	Polydor 080 466-2	Joe Le Taxi/Manolo Manolete/Joe Le Taxi (Version Espagnole)/ Joe Le Taxi (Version Longue)/Joe Le Taxi (Video) (CD Video)	15

MINT VALUE £

88 Polydor 080 468-2 Marilyn And John (Version Français) (4.40)/Soldat/Marilyn And John (Version Anglais)/Marilyn And John (Version Français) (5.44)/Marilyn And John (Version Francais) (Video) (CD video) 18
88 Polydor 081 312-2 Coup Coup (Remix)/Maxou/Marilyn And John/Coup Coup (Remix) (Video) (CD Video) 18

PARADISE
83 Priority PLP 1 LOVE IS THE ANSWER (LP) 100
80 Ebony PARADISE (LP) 125

PARADISE HAMMER
70 Polydor 2058048 She Is Love/You Got Me In 25
71 Polydor 2058084 1+1=2/To Live 15

PARADISE LOST
93 Music For Nations MFN 152 LOST (LP) 18

PARDISE SQUARE
74 White label NEVER THOUGHT I'D SEE THE DAY (LP, plain white sleeve, 5 inserts) 500

PARADONS
60 Top Rank JAR 514 Diamonds And Pearls/I Want Love 80

PARADOX
(see also David Walker)
68 Polydor 56275 The Wednesday Theme/Ring The Changes 150

PARADOX
90 Ronin RDP10 Revolutionary/Dedicated (12") 8

PARAFFIN JACK FLASH LTD
68 Pye NSPL 18252 MOVERS AND GROOVERS (LP) 18

PARAGONS
(see also Rosalyn Sweat & Paragons, John Holt, Lester Sterling)
66 Doctor Bird DB 1060 Happy-Go-Lucky Girl/Love Brings Pain 35
67 Island WI 3045 On The Beach/CAROL & TOMMY McCOOK: Sweet And Gentle (B-side actually by Tommy McCook & Supersonics) 40
67 Island WI 3067 Talking Love/If I Were You 40
67 Island WI 3093 So Depressed/We Were Meant To Be 80
67 Treasure Isle TI 7009 Only A Smile/The Tide Is High 25
67 Treasure Isle TI 7011 Mercy, Mercy, Mercy/Riding On A High And Windy Day 25
67 Treasure Isle TI 7013 The Same Song/TOMMY McCOOK & SUPERSONICS: Soul Serenade 28
67 Treasure Isle TI 7025 Wear You To The Ball/You Mean The World To Me 30
68 Treasure Isle TI 7034 Silver Bird/My Best Girl 25
68 Island WI 3138 Memories By The Score/The Number One For Me 30
69 Studio One SO 2081 Have You Ever Been In Love/Change Your Style 30
69 Duke DU 7 Left With A Broken Heart/I've Got To Get Away 80
69 Crab 13 Take Your Hand From My Neck/Equality And Justice 40
67 Doctor Bird DLM 5010 ON THE BEACH (LP) 160
77 Wildflower WF 523 Do The Best Thing/Best Thing 8

PARALEX
80 Reddingtons R.R. DAN 4 White Lightning/Travelling Man/Black Widow, (12", p/s, green vinyl) 55

PARAMEDIC SQUAD
81 Gargoyle GRGL 2 Movement In Time/For You/Thinking Psychedelia (p/s) 25

PARAMETER
70 Deroy GALACTIC RAMBLE (LP) 300

NORRIE PARAMOR & HIS ORCHESTRA
(see also Harry Gold)o
60 Columbia DB 4419 Summer Place (Theme)/Half Pint 5
62 Columbia DB 4789 Z Cars (Theme)/Ballad Of A Soldier (Theme) 5
63 Columbia DB 8430 Soul Coaxing/Autumn In London Town 7
64 Columbia DB 7114 Dream Of Tomorrow/Laramie 7
65 Columbia DB 7446 Dance Of The Warriors/Dragon Dance 6
70 Polydor 56375 Randall And Hopkirk (Deceased)/A Summer Palace 65

PARAMOUNT ALL-STARS
(see also Blind Blake, Will Ezell, Georgia Tom, Alex Hill, Papa Charlie Jackson, Blind Lemon Jefferson, Charlie Spand)
50 Tempo R 20 Hometown Skiffle (Parts 1 & 2) (78) 20

PARAMOUNTS
(see also Procol Harum)
63 Parlophone R 5093 Poison Ivy/I Feel Good All Over 12
64 Parlophone R 5107 Little Bitty Pretty One/A Certain Girl 20
64 Parlophone R 5155 I'm The One Who Loves You/It Won't Be Long 20
64 Parlophone R 5187 Bad Blood/Do I 20
65 Parlophone R 5272 Blue Ribbons/Cuttin' In 20
65 Parlophone R 5351 You Never Had It So Good/Don't Ya Like My Love 50
64 Parlophone GEP 8908 THE PARAMOUNTS (EP) 250

PARANOIA
84 Rot ASS 8 Dead Man's Dreams/Man In Black (p/s) 8
84 Rot ASS 11 SHATTERED GLASS (LP) 25

PARANOIDS
79 Hurricane FIRE 8 Stupid Guy/Road To Ruin (p/s) 10
80 Hurricane FIRE 14 The Love Job/Theme From Gravity's Rainbow (p/s) 10

PARCEL OF ROGUES
(see under Villagers)

PARCHMENT
72 Pye 7N 45178 Light Up The Fire/Let There Be Light (p/s) 5

MINT VALUE £

72	Pye NSPL 18388	LIGHT UP THE FIRE (LP, textured sleeve with poster insert)	20
73	Pye NSPL 18409	HOLLYWOOD SUNSET (LP)	12
75	Myrrh MYR 1028	SHAMBLEJAM (LP)	18
77	Pilgrim GRAPEVINE 106	REHEARSAL FOR A REUNION (LP)	12

WALTER PARDON

75	Leader LED 2063	A PROPER SORT (LP)	20

TONY PARENTI

57	London EZ V 19022	RAGTIME (EP)	10
57	London LTZU 15072	RAGTIME (LP)	12

PAULA PARFITT

69	Beacon BEA 135	I'm Gonna Give You Back Your Ring/Love Is Wonderful (Beware of bootlegs! - originals have anti-slip grips around the label)	150
70	Up Front UPF 4	Peace Of Mind/Baby You Give Me A Good Song To Sing	10

TINY PARHAM

50s	Audubon AAC	TINY PARHAM (10" LP)	25

PARIS

72	Avalanche AV 67312	I've Lost The Way/Long Time	8
76	Thunderbird THE 114	Circles/Liar	5
84	Bluebird BRT 9	I Choose You/Punkin' Funkin' (12", p/s)	8

BOBBY PARIS

68	Polydor 56747	Per So Nal Ly/Tragedy	80
69	Polydor 56762	Let The Sun Shine In/You	22
77	London HLU 10553	Night Owl/YVONNE BAKER: You Didn't Say A Word	15

MICA PARIS

91	4th & Broadway 12BRWDJ207	A STAND FOR LOVE EP (12" promo p/s. Mispress, plays Prince's vocal version of 'A Stand For Love')	100

PRISCILLA PARIS

(see also Paris Sisters)

74	Rak RAK 184	I Love How You Love Me/Over You	10

PARIS SISTERS

(see also Date With Soul, Priscilla Paris)

61	Top Rank JAR 588	I Love How You Love Me/I'll Be Crying Tomorrow	50
64	MGM MGM 1240	Dream Lover/Lonely Girl	50

JOHN PARISH & POLLY JEAN HARVEY

(see also P.J. Harvey)

96	Island IS 648	That Was My Veil/Losing Ground (p/s)	12
96	Island HEELCD1	Heela (Promo-only CD, unreleased single)	15
96	Island CIDX 8051	DANCE HALL AT LOUSE POINT (CD, 5,000 in digipak with insert)	20
96	Island ILPS 8051	DANCE HALL AT LOUSE POINT (LP)	35

PARISH HALL

70	Liberty LBS 83374	PARISH HALL (LP)	60

SIMON PARK

74	EMI EMC 3059	SOMETHING IN THE AIR (LP)	20
75	EMC 3085	VENUS FLY TRAP (LP)	12

ALAN PARKER

(see also Hungry Wolf, Ugly Custard)

70	Aristocrat AR 1022	GUITAR FANTASY (LP)	18
73	MCA MUPS 471	BAND OF ANGELS (LP)	20

BENNY PARKER & DYNAMICS

64	Decca F 11944	Boys And Girls/You'll Be On Your Way	45

BILLY PARKER

63	Decca F 11668	Thanks A Lot/Out Of Your Heart	7

BOBBY PARKER

61	London HLU 9393	Watch Your Step/Steal Your Heart Away	60
64	Sue WI 340	Watch Your Step/Steal Your Heart Away (reissue)	45
69	Blue Horizon 57-3151	It's Hard But It's Fair/I Couldn't Quit My Baby	45

CHARLIE PARKER

(see also Dizzy Gillespie & Charlie Parker, Sir Charles Thompson)

EPs

55	Vogue EPV 1011	CHARLIE PARKER PLAYS	10
56	Columbia Clef SEB 10026	NOW'S THE TIME	8
50s	Esquire EP 57	CHARLIE PARKER QUINTET	8
60	Vogue EPV 1264	ALL STARNTET/SEXTET	8
60	HMV 7EG 8626	CHARLIE PARKER BIG BAND	8

ALBUMS

52	Vogue LDE 004	CHARLIE PARKER VOLUME ONE (10")	60
53	Vogue LDE 016	CHARLIE PARKER VOLUME TWO (10")	60
	Vogue LAE 12002	CHARLIE PARKER MEMORIAL ALBUM (gatefold sleeve with 2 inserts)	20
55	Melodisc MLP 12-105	BIRD AT ST. NICK'S	30
55	Columbia Clef 33CX 10004	CHARLIE PARKER BIG BAND	40
56	Columbia Clef 33C 9026	BIRD AND DIZ (10", with Dizzy Gillespie)	40
57	Columbia Clef 33CX 10081	APRIL IN PARIS (as Charlie Parker With Strings)	35
57	Columbia Clef 33CX 10090	CHARLIE PARKER PLAYS COLE PORTER	25
58	Columbia Clef 33CX 10117	CHARLIE PARKER JAZZ PERENNIAL	15
58	London Jazz LTZ-C 15104	THE IMMORTAL CHARLIE PARKER VOL. 1	15
58	London Jazz LTZ-C 15105	THE IMMORTAL CHARLIE PARKER VOL. 2	15
58	London Jazz LTZ-C 15106	THE IMMORTAL CHARLIE PARKER VOL. 3	15

MINT VALUE £

58	London Jazz LTZ-C 15107	THE IMMORTAL CHARLIE PARKER VOL. 4	15
58	Mercury MPL 12-105	BIRD AT NICK'S	15
60	Collector JGN 1002	CHARLIE PARKER IN SWEDEN	30
61	HMV CLP 1538	THE ESSENTIAL CHARLIE PARKER	15
62	Verve VLP 9105	BIRD SYMBOLS (with insert for Egmont AJS 3)	15
62	Storyville SLP 27	IN SWEDEN 1950	15
62	Esquire 32-157	'BIRD' IS FREE	15

DAVID PARKER

(see also Andwella's Dream)

71	Polydor 2460 101	DAVID PARKER (LP)	45

DEAN PARKER & REDCAPS

62	Decca F 11555	Stormy Evening/Blue Eyes And Golden Hair	45

DYON PARKER

69	Marble Arch MAL 787	OUT ON THE HIGHWAY (LP)	20

EDDIE PARKER

55	Columbia SCM 5211	Far Away From Everybody/Bella Notte	8
56	Columbia DB 3804	Love Me As Though There Were No Tomorrow/Rich In Love	8

EULA PARKER

(see also Frank Weir)

58	Oriole CB 1411	Silhouettes/Hedgehopper	22

EVAN PARKER

75	Incus INCUS 19	SAXOPHONE SOLOS (LP)	40
78	Incus INCUS 27	MONOCEROS (LP)	30
80	Incus INCUS 39	SIX OF ONE (LP)	30
86	Incus INCUS 49	THE SNAKE DECIDES (LP)	50
89	Cadillac (no cat no)	COLLECTED SOLOS (4 x LP and cassette, hand numbered to 200)	60

EVAN PARKER, DEREK BAILEY, HAN BENNINK

70s	Incus INCUS 1	THE TOPOGRAPHY OF THE LUNGS (LP)	50

EVAN PARKER, BARRY GUY & PAUL LYTTON

83	Incus INCUS 42	TRACKS (LP)	40

EVAN PARKER & GEORGE LEWIS

80	Incus INCUS 35	FROM SAXOPHONE & TROMBONE (LP)	40

EVAN PARKER, GEORGE LEWIS, BARRY GUY & PAUL LYTTON

83	Incus INCUS 45	HOOK, DRIFT & SHUFFLE (LP)	50

EVAN PARKER & PAUL LYTTON

(see also Derek Bailey & Evan Parker, Derek Bailey Evan Parker & Han Bennink)

72	Incus INCUS 5	COLLECTIVE CALLS (URBAN) (TWO MICROPHONES) (LP)	40
75	Incus INCUS 14	AT THE UNITY THEATRE (LP)	40

FESS PARKER

57	Oriole CB 1378	Wringle Wrangle/Ballad Of John Colter	10

JIMMY PARKER

62	Top Rank JAR 608	We Gonna/No Word From Betty	10

(see also Howlin' Wolf, Bobby Bland)

(LITTLE) JUNIOR PARKER

61	Vogue V 9179	Stand By Me/I'll Forget About You (as Little Junior Parker)	30
62	Vogue V 9193	Mary Jo/Annie Get Your Yo-Yo (as Little Junior Parker)	30
66	Vocalion VP 9256	These Kind Of Blues (Parts 1 & 2)	40
66	Vocalion VP 9256	These Kind Of Blues (Parts 1 & 2) (DJ copy)	60
66	Vocalion VP 9275	Goodbye Little Girl/Walking The Floor Over You	30
67	Mercury SMCL 20097	LIKE IT IS (LP)	50
72	Groove Merchant GM 502	BLUE SHADOWS FALLING (LP)	15
73	Groove Merchant GM 2205	GOOD THINGS DON'T HAPPEN EVERY DAY (LP, with Jimmy McGriff)	15
73	Vogue LDM 30163	MEMORIAL (LP)	15
73	People PLEO 4	YOU DON'T HAVE TO BE BLACK TO LOVE THE BLUES (LP)	20

KEN PARKER

(see also Lyrics, Scotty)

67	Island WI 3082	How Could I/SONNY BURKE: Choo Choo Train	45
67	Studio One SO 2001	See Them A-Come/MR FOUNDATION: Have A Good Time	35
68	Island WI 3096	Down Low/Sad Mood	45
68	Island WI 3105	Lonely Man/ERROL DUNKLEY: I Am Going Home	100
68	Giant GN 34	Change Is Gonna Come/VAL BENNETT: Jumping With Val	50
69	Bamboo BAM 1	My Whole World Is Falling Down/The Chokin' Kind	30
69	Amalgamated AMG 847	It's Alright/COBBS: One One	40
69	Amalgamated AMG 853	Only Yesterday/COBBS: Joe Gibbs Mood	30
70	Duke DU 79	I Can't Hide/TOMMY McCOOK: Kansas City	10
70	Unity UN 553	When You Were Mine/CLAREDONIANS: The Angels (song actually "The Angels Listened In")	8
71	Duke Reid DR 2504	Sugar Pantie (as Ken Parker & Tommy McCook; actually by Andy Capp)/ TOMMY McCOOK: All Afire	10
71	Duke Reid DR 2521	Jimmy Brown/Version	6
71	Big BG 332	Ain't Misbehaving/Genuine Love	6
72	Jackpot JP 805	Guilty/AGGROVATORS: Guilty (Version)	6
72	Pama PM 844	Shake It Loose/TOMMY McCOOK: Shake It Loose - Version (actually titled "Help Me Make It Through The Night")	6
72	Treasure Isle TI 7073	Help Me Make It Through The Night/TOMMY McCOOK & ALLSTARS (Version)	8
73	Dragon DRA 1003	Will The Circle Be Unbroken/DYNAMITES: Instrumental	6
73	Dragon DRA 1015	Say Wonderful Things/It's True	6
74	Attack ATT 8063	Kiss An Angel/TOMMY McCOOK: Inez	8
74	Attack ATT 8073	Count Your Blessings/Count Your Blessings (Version)	6
74	Trojan TRLS 80	JIMMY BROWN (LP)	18

MINT VALUE £

LEWIS PARKER

96	Bite It! BITE 11	Rise/Visions Of Splendour/Sea Freestyle (12")	35
97	White LEWIS 1	Wonderwall (7")	40
98	Melankolic SADTDJ3	Shadows Of Autumn/101 Pianos (12")	25
03	Dusty Vinyl DV1JEDI	Mr Parker's Siesta/Blood (12")	18
95	White JED 1	B BOY ANTICS (EP)	75
96	Bite It! BITEDJ 10	B BOY ANTICS (EP)	25
00	M'lic LEWISTDJ1LC03098	THE OPTIONS (EP)	25
01	White SADTDJ 13	It's All Happening Now/Schemes/What The Ancients Say (remixes) (EP)	50
98	Melankolic SADT 4	MASQUERADES AND SILHOUETTES (LP)	30
02	Melankolic LPSAD 14	IT'S ALL HAPPENING NOW (LP)	18
06	Dusry Vinyl DVJED I008	MASQUERADES AND SILHOUETTES INSTRUMENTALS (LP, 200 only with unreleased track)	20

RAYMOND PARKER

66	Sue WI 4024	Ring Around The Roses/She's Coming Home	40

ROBERT PARKER

(see also Huey 'Piano' Smith & Clowns)

66	Island WI 286	Barefootin'/Let's Go Baby (Where The Action Is)	15
66	Island WI 3008	Happy Feet/The Scratch	20
74	Island USA 001	Get Ta Steppin'/Get Right On Down	8
74	Contemporaries CS 9010	Barefootin'/I Caught You In A Lie	10
66	Island ILP 942	BAREFOOTIN' (LP)	80

EDDIE PARKER (U.S.)

79	Grapevine GRP 119	Love You Baby (Parts 1 & 2) (in p/s)	10
79	Grapevine GRP 119	Love You Baby (Parts 1 & 2) (DJ copy)	20

SONNY PARKER

(see also Lionel Hampton)

56	Vogue V 2392	My Soul's On Fire/Disgusted Blues	450
56	Vogue V 2392	My Soul's On Fire/Disgusted Blues (78)	120

WILLIE PARKER

67	President PT 171	You Got Your Finger In My Eye/I Love The Life I Live	15

WINFIELD PARKER

72	Mojo 2093 019	Stop Her On Sight/I'm On My Way	8

PARKING LOT

69	Parlophone R 5779	Carpet Man/World Spinning Sadly	35

PARKINGSON'S LAW

72	RCA RCA 2291	Daughter Of Thunder And Lightning/I Need Your Loving And I Can't Let Go	8

JIMMY PARKINSON

56	Columbia SCM 5236	The Great Pretender/Hand In Hand	30
56	Columbia SCM 5267	Walk Hand In Hand/Cry Baby	10
56	Columbia DB 3808	Gina/A Lover's Quarrel	8
56	Columbia DB 3833	In The Middle Of The House/You To Me	8
57	Columbia DB 3876	But You/Together (You And I)	6
57	Columbia DB 3912	Round And Round/Whatever Lola Wants (Lola Gets)	6
57	Columbia 33S 1109	SOLO (10" LP)	20

BERNICE PARKS

55	Coral Q 72056	Lovin' Machine/Only Love Me	15

LLOYD PARKS

(see also L. Sparks)

70	Harry J. HJ 6603	Feel A Little Better/I'll Be Your Man	10
72	Randy's RAN 524	Stars/Stars - Version	12
74	Fab FAB 273	Schooldays/Version	7
75	Cactus CT 75	Mafia/Mafia Version (Dub)	8

SONNY PARKS

63	Warner Bros WB 100	New Boy In Town/Us Kids Have Got To Make Up Our Minds	10

VAN DYKE PARKS

66	MGM MGM 1301	Number Nine/Do What You Wanta	12
69	Warner Bros W(S) 1727	SONG CYCLE (LP)	35

PARLET

(see also Parliament)

79	Casablanca CAL 2052	INVASION OF THE BOOTY SNATCHERS (LP)	15

PARLIAMENT

(see also Parliaments, Funkadelic, Parlet, Bootsy's Rubber Band, P-Funk Allstars)

71	Invictus INV 513	The Silent Boatman/Livin' The Life	15
72	Invictus INV 522	Come In Out Of The Rain/Little Ole Country Boy	12
75	Casablanca CBX 505	Up On The Down Stroke/Presence Of A Brain	8
76	Casablanca CBX 518	Tear The Roof Off The Sucker (Give Up The Funk)/P. Funk	5
77	Casablanca CAN 103	Tear The Roof Off The Sucker (Give Up The Funk)/Dr. Funkenstein/P. Funk	5
78	Casablanca CAN 115	Bop Gun/I've Been Watching You	5
78	Casablanca CAN 136	Aqua Boogie/Water Sign	5
79	Casablanca CAN 154	Deep/Flashlight	5
71	Invictus SVT 1004	OSMIUM (LP)	80
74	Casablanca NBLP 7002	UP ON THE DOWN STROKE (LP)	15

PARLIAMENTS

(see also Parliament, Funkadelic)

67	Track 604 013	I Wanna Testify/I Can Feel The Ice Melting	30
69	Track 604 032	I Wanna Testify/I Can Feel The Ice Melting (reissue)	20

PARLOPHONE POPS ORCHESTRA

(see also Ron Goodwin)

56	Parlophone R 4250	Giddy Up A Ding Dong/(We're Gonna) Rock Around The Clock	15

MINT VALUE £

PARLOUR BAND

72	Deram SDL 10	IS A FRIEND? (LP, laminated gatefold sleeve, white/red label)	300

PARLOUR TALK

97	White (Acid Jazz) JAZZID152	Colouring/Super Air Conditioned (12")	22
99	Acid Jazz AJX111T	Vacation/Old, New And Blue (12")	8
00	Acid Jazz AJXLP 112	PADLOCKED TONIC (LP)	12

CHRIS PARMENTER ORCHESTRA

66	Polydor 56107	Cul De Sac/Donkey	25

JACK PARNELL (ORCHESTRA)

(see also Dennis Hale)

53	Parlophone MSP 6009	Waltzing The Blues/Catherine Wheel (as Jack Parnell Band)	10
53	Parlophone MSP 6031	Night Train/Hawk Talks (as Jack Parnell & His Music Makers)	10
53	Parlophone MSP 6046	Cotton Tail/April In Paris	10
53	Parlophone MSP 6054	Dragnet/Fuller Bounce (as Jack Parnell & His Music Makers)	10
54	Parlophone MSP 6066	Route 66/The Creep	10
54	Parlophone MSP 6078	Skin Deep/Devil's Eyes (B-side with Dennis Hale)	20
54	Parlophone MSP 6094	Knock Out/Blowin' Wild (B-side with Dennis Hale)	12
54	Parlophone MSP 6102	The Bandit (with Dennis Hale)/Annie's Blues (with Annie Ross)	15
54	Parlophone MSP 6138	Sky Blue Shirt And Rainbow Tie/Trip To Mars	10
58	Parlophone R 4500	Topsy/Cha Cha Rock	8
59	HMV POP 630	Kansas City/The Golden Striker	10
60	Philips PB 1005	77 Sunset Strip/Teen Ride	8
64	Decca F 11958	The Kiss/The Hidden Truth	7
55	Parlophone GEP 8532	JACK PARNELL AND HIS ORCHESTRA (EP)	10
55	Parlophone GEP 8564	PARNELL ON PARADE (EP)	10
58	Parlophone GEP 8707	KICK OFF! (EP)	10
66	Hanover HR 1001	MY FAIR LADY (EP)	8
52	Decca LF 1065	THE JACK PARNELL QUARTET (10" LP)	22
58	Parlophone PMD 1053	TRIP TO MARS (10" LP)	80
77	Music For Pleasure 50327	BRAZILIANA (LP)	15

CATHERINE PARR

65	Decca F 12210	You Belong To Me/He's My Guy	10

JACKIE PARRIS AND BIG YOUTH

79	Book Of Psalms BP 001	Let Him Try/Really Together (12")	15

BRIAN PARRISH

69	United Artists UP 35049	In Good Time (Love Chant)/I Wanna Go To Sleep	12

DEAN PARRISH

66	Stateside SS 531	Tell Her/Fall On Me	60
66	Stateside SS 531	Tell Her/Fall On Me (DJ copy)	100
66	Stateside SS 550	Turn On Your Lovelight/Determination	100
66	Stateside SS 550	Turn On Your Lovelight/Determination (DJ copy)	150
67	Stateside SS 580	Skate (Parts 1 & 2)	60
67	Stateside SS 580	Skate (Parts 1 & 2) (DJ copy)	100
75	UK USA 2	I'm On My Way/Watch Out	15
75	UK USA 2	I'm On My Way/Watch Out (DJ copy)	20

PARRISH & GURVITZ

(see also Baker Gurvitz Army, Three Man Army, Frampton's Camel)

71	Regal Zono. SRZA 8506	PARRISH & GURVITZ (LP, textured gatefold sleeve)	35

GAYLORD PARRY

67	CBS 2685	I'm On The Way Up/I'm Coming Home	10

SAM PARRY

73	Argo ZDA 155	IF SADNESS COULD SING (LP)	250

PARSON & SMITH

72	Polydor 2059229	The Letter/When It Rains	20

BILL PARSONS & HIS ORCHESTRA

(see also Bobby Bare)

59	London HL 8798	The All American Boy/Rubber Dolly	10
59	London HL 8798	The All American Boy/Rubber Dolly (78)	30

GENE PARSONS

(see also Byrds, Flying Burrito Brothers)

74	Warner Bros K 46257	KINDLING (LP)	18

GRAM PARSONS

(see also Byrds, Flying Burrito Brothers)

73	Reprise K 14245	The New Soft Shoe/She	6
73	Reprise K 44228	GP (LP, gatefold sleeve)	25
74	Reprise K 54018	GRIEVOUS ANGEL (LP, with Emmylou Harris)	22
76	A&M AMLH 65478	SLEEPLESS NIGHTS (LP, with Flying Burrito Brothers & Emmylou Harris)	20
82	Sundown SDLP 003	GRAM PARSONS AND THE FALLEN ANGELS (LP, featuring Emmylou Harris)	15

NICHOLAS PARSONS

70s	Orlake	The Message (1-sided p/s)	10

PARTICULAR PEOPLE

68	Big T BIG 105	Boys Cry/What's The Matter With Juliet	6

PARTISANS

82	No Future OI 2	Police Story/Killing Machine (p/s, with lyric insert)	12
82	No Future OI 12	17 Years Of Hell/The Power And The Greed/Bastards In Blue (p/s)	10
83	Cloak & Dagger PART 1	Blind Ambition/Come Clean (p/s)	15
83	No Future PUNK 4	PARTISANS (LP)	22
84	Cloak & Dagger PARTLP 1	THE TIME WAS RIGHT (LP, with inner)	35

MINT VALUE £

PARTISANS
(see also Blades)
88 Hotwire HWS 863 — Open Your Eyes/Partisan (p/s) — 8

PARTNERS IN CRIME
(see also Status Quo)
84 Epic A 4803 — Hold On/She's Got Eyes For You (p/s) — 6
84 Epic TX 4803 — Hold On (Extended)/She's Got Eyes For You (12", p/s) — 8
85 Epic A 5040 — Miracles/What You Gonna Do? (p/s) — 6
85 Epic TX 5040 — Miracles (Extended)/What You Gonna Do? (12", p/s) — 8
85 Epic A 6170 — Hollywood Dreams/She's Got Eyes For You (p/s) — 7
85 Epic TX 6170 — Hollywood Dreams (Extended)/She's Got Eyes For You (12", p/s) — 10
85 Epic EPC 26356 — ORGANISED CRIME (LP) — 12

PART ONE
82 Paraworm — FUNERAL PARADE (EP) — 12

DON PARTRIDGE
(see also Accolades)
68 Columbia DB 8484 — Top Man/We Have Ways Of Making You Laugh — 5
69 Columbia DB 8538 — Breakfast On Pluto/Stealin' — 5
69 Columbia DB 8583 — Colour My World/Homeless Bones — 6
69 Columbia DB 8617 — Going TO Germany/Ask Me Why — 6
70 Columbia DB 8723 — We're All Happy Together/Following Your Fancy — 5
60s CFP CFP 001/002 — SINGING SOHO STYLE (EP) — 15
68 Columbia S(C)X 6280 — DON PARTRIDGE (LP) — 12

MR. PARTRIDGE
(see also XTC, Three Wise Men, Dukes Of Stratosphere, Colonel)
80 Virgin V 2145 — TAKEAWAY - THE LURE OF THE SALVAGE (LP) — 12

PARTY BOYS
(see also Status Quo)
87 Epic 651230 0 — He's Gonna Step On You Again/She's A Mystery (shaped picture disc) — 12

PARVA
(see also Kaiser Chiefs)
01 Mantra MNT 66 — Heavy/Panic Attack (p/s, 500 only) — 12

PASADENA ROOF ORCHESTRA
78 CBS CBS 12-637 — Pennies From Heaven/Back In Your Own Back Yard/Pennies From Heaven (10" p/s, 2nd side plays at 78 rpm) — 15

PASHA
(see also Searchers)
69 Liberty LBF 15199 — Someone Shot The Lollipop Man/Pussy Willow Dragon — 120

JOE PASS
50s Fontana 688 137 ZL — CATCH ME (LP) — 15

PASSAGE
(see also Contact)
78 Object Music OMO 2 — Love Song/The Competition/Slit Machine/New Kind Of Love (p/s) — 10
80 Object Music OBJ 11 — PINDROP (LP) — 12

PASSENGERS
(see also U2, Brian Eno)
95 Island IS 625 — Miss Sarajevo/One (live) (7", with poster in 12" card in PVC p/s) — 10
95 Island CID 625 — Miss Sarajevo/One (live)/Bottoms (Zoo Station Remix)/Via Davidoff (CD, with shrinkwrapped poster, withdrawn) — 20
96 Island OST 3 — Your Blue Room (CD, 1-track promo, card sleeve, export issue) — 50
95 Island OST 2 — ORIGINAL SOUNDCHAT 1 (2-CD, music & interview disc, fold-out digipaks, with cue sheet, promo only) — 60
95 Island ILPS 8043 — ORIGINAL SOUNDTRACKS (LP) — 20

PASSIONS
58 Capitol CL 14874 — My Aching Heart/Jackie Brown — 80

PASSIONS
59 Top Rank JAR 224 — Just To Be With You/Oh Melancholy Me — 60
60 Top Rank JAR 313 — I Only Want You/This Is My Love — 70

THE PASSIONS
79 Soho SH5 — Needles And Pills/Body And Soul — 10
79 Fiction FICS 008 — Hunted/Oh No, It's You — 5
70 Fiction FIX 003 LP — MICHAEL & MIRANDA (LP, with gold embossed stamp "Limited Edition £2.99 Pay No More") — 12

PAST AND PRESENT
79 Rook CUS 423 — FIRST TIME OUT (LP, private pressing) — 30

PAST PRESENT ORGANISATION
90s Acid Jazz AJX 107T — Itchy Feet (12", p/s) — 10

PAST SEVEN DAYS
86 4AD AD 102 — Raindance/So Many Others/Nothing (p/s) — 10

PASTELS
(see also Buba & Shop Assistants, Jad Fair, Vaselines)
82 Whaam! WHAAM 005 — Songs For Children: Heavens Above!/Tea Time Tales (p/s) — 22
83 Rough Trade RT 137 — I Wonder Why/Supposed To Understand (p/s) — 18
83 Creation Artefact/Lyntone — I Wonder Why! (live)/THE LAUGHING APPLE: Wouldn't You? (33rpm flexidisc, initially free with The Legend! 7" "'73 In '83" [CRE 001]) — 6
84 Creation CRE 005 — Something Going On/Stay With Me Till Morning (foldaround p/s in poly bag) — 18
84 Creation CRE 011T — A Million Tears/Baby Honey/Surprise Me (12", p/s) — 8

Year	Label / Cat. No.	Title	MINT VALUE £
85	Villa 21 VILLA 3	Heavens Above!/Tea Time Tales/I Wonder Why (live)/Tea Time Tales (live) (p/s)	25
87	Glass PASTEL 001	Truck Train Tractor/Truck Train Tractor (2)/Breaking Lines//Crawl Babies/ Empty House/The Day I Got Certified (12", double pack)	8
90	Overground OVER 06	Heavens Above!/Tea Time Tales/Something Going On (demo)/ Until Morning Comes (demo) (p/s; 200 clear vinyl)	5
90	Overground OVER 06	Heavens Above!/Tea Time Tales/Something Going On (demo)/ Until Morning Comes (demo) (p/s; 157 green vinyl)	6
93	Glass 12053	Comin' Through/Sit On It Mother/Lonely Planet Boy/Not Unloved (12")	10
87	Glass GLAL P021	UP FOR A BIT WITH THE PASTELS (LP, with inner)	12

PASTEL SIX

63	London HLU 9651	The Cinnamon Cinder/Bandido	20

PASTORAL SYMPHONY

68	President PT 202	Love Machine/Spread A Little Love Around	20

PAT

71	Gas GAS 158	Teach Me (actually "Words Of Temptation" by Earl Lawrence)/ RHYTHM RULERS: Sea Breeze (actually by Im & David)	8

PAT & MARIE

(see also Pat Rhoden)

66	Ska Beat JB 234	I Try Not To Tell You/PAT RHODEN: Don't Blame It On Me	15
66	Ska Beat JB 235	You're Really Leaving/PAT RHODEN: Broken Heart	15

PAT & ROXIE

65	Caribou CRC 2	Sing To Me/Things I Used To Do	7

PATCHES

72	Warner Bros K 16201	Living In America/Quicksand	8
75	Bradley BRAD 7516	Telltale/Chug-A-Lug	5

JOHNNY PATE ORCHESTRA

59	Parlophone PMD 1057	JAZZ GOES IVY LEAGUE (10" LP)	12
59	Parlophone PMD 1072	SWINGIN' FLUTE (10" LP)	12
60s	MGM	OUTRAGEOUS (LP)	18
73	Probe SPB 1077	SHAFT IN AFRICA (LP, soundtrack, with Four Tops)	20
74	ABC ABCL 5035	SHAFT IN AFRICA (LP, soundtrack, reissue)	12

PAMELA PATERSON

72	Polydor 2001 278	Finally (Theme From 'Gumshoe')/OLYMPIC STUDIO CONCERT ORCHESTRA: Music From 'Gumshoe' (p/s)	20

PATHETIX

78	No Records NO 001	Aleister Crowley/Don't Touch My Machine/Snuffed It (p/s, with insert)	30
79	TJM TJM 12	THE PATHETIX EP (no p/s)	25

PATHFINDERS

64	Hayton Manor SP 138/139	What Do You Do/What'd I Say (private pressing)	20

PATHFINDERS

(see also [White] Trash, Poets)

65	Parlophone R 5372	Don't You Believe It/Castle Of Love	20

PATHFINDERS

64	Decca F 12038	I Love You Caroline/Something I Can Always Do	18

PATHWAY TO YOUR MIND

68	Major Minor SMLP 19	PREPARING THE MIND AND BODY FOR MEDITATION (LP, spoken word)	25

PATIENCE & PRUDENCE

56	London HLU 8321	Tonight You Belong To Me/A Smile And A Ribbon (Gold label))	40
56	London HLU 8321	Tonight You Belong To Me/A Smile And A Ribbon (Silver label)	20
57	London HLU 8369	Gonna Get Along Without Ya Now/The Money Tree (Gold label)	40
57	London HLU 8369	Gonna Get Along Without Ya Now/The Money Tree (Silver label)	20
57	London HL 7017	Gonna Get Along Without Ya Now/The Money Tree (export issue)	30
57	London HLU 8425	Dreamer's Bay/We Can't Sing Rhythm And Blues	20
57	London HLU 8493	You Tattletale/Very Nice Is Bali Bali	20
58	London HLU 8773	Tom Thumb's Tune/Golly Oh Gee	20
58	London HLU 8773	Tom Thumb's Tune/Golly Oh Gee (78)	10
57	London REU 1087	A SMILE AND A SONG (EP)	50

LEON PATILLO

70s	Maranatha MM 0049	DANCE CHILDREN, DANCE (LP)	18
70s	Myrrh MYR 1136	LIVE EXPERIENCE (LP)	18

SANDY & CAROLINE PATON

(see also Beat Brothers, Tony Sheridan & Beat Brothers)

60	Topic TOP 57	HUSH LITTLE BABY (EP)	10

BOBBY PATRICK BIG SIX

64	Decca F 11898	Shake It Easy Baby/Wildwood Days	35
64	Decca F 12030	Monkey Time/Sweet Talk Me Baby	30
64	Decca DFE 8570	TEENBEAT 3 (FROM STAR CLUB, HAMBURG) (EP)	120

DAN PATRICK

67	Stateside SS 2004	Tiger Lee/Call Of The Wild	10

KENTRICK PATRICK

(see also Lord Creator)

63	Island WI 066	Man To Man/ROLAND ALFONSO: Blockade (B-side actually "Hit And Run")	40
63	Island WI 079	Don't Stay Out Late/Forever And Ever	30
63	Island WI 104	The End Of The World/Little Princess	25
63	Island WI 119	Golden Love/Beyond	40
64	Island WI 132	Take Me To The Party/I'm Sorry	25
64	Island WI 140	I Am Wasting Time/RANDY'S GROUP: Royal Charley	120

MINT VALUE £

PATRICK & LLOYD
(see also Lloyd & Prophets)

70	Big Shot BI 550	Return Of The Pollock/PROPHETS: Concorde	15

PATRIOTS

66	Fontana TF 650	Prophet/I'll Be There	20

PATRON OF THE ARTS

66	Page One POF 012	The True Patron Of The Arts/Eleanor Rigby (USA release credits band as Queen City Show Band)	100

PATSY
(see also Patsy Todd, Derrick & Patsy, Stranger & Patsy, Emotions)

68	Doctor Bird DB 1113	A Man Is Two Faced/LENNIE HIBBERT & COUNT OSSIE: Pure Soul	120
68	Doctor Bird DB 1122	Little Flea/The Retreat Song	45
68	High Note HS012	We Were Lovers/DELANO STEWART : Give Me A Chance	35

PATSY & PEGGY

70	Hot Rod HR 107	Dog Your Woman/HOT ROD ALLSTARS: Strictly Invitation	10

BRIAN PATTEN
(see also Liverpool Scene, Roger McGough & Brian Patten)

70	Caedmon TC 1300	BRIAN PATTEN (LP)	20
76	Tangent TGS 116	VANISHING TRICK (LP)	20
77	Argo ZSW 607	SLY CORMORANT (LP)	12

PATTERN PEOPLE

68	MGM MGM 1429	Love Is A Lover/Loving To Be Loved	8

PATTERNS IN PERU

86	Vernon Bros/WEA	This Is The Night/Playing Games	60

BOBBY PATTERSON (& MUSTANGS)

68	Pama PM 735	Broadway Ain't Funky No More/I Met My Match (with Mustangs)	20
68	Pama PM 743	The Good Ol' Days/Don't Be So Mean	15
68	Pama PM 754	Busy Busy Bee/Sweet Taste Of Love (with Mustangs)	20
69	Pama PM 763	T.C.B. Or T.Y.A./What A Wonderful Night For Love (with Mustangs)	22
69	Pama PM 773	My Thing Is Your Thing/Keep It In The Family	20
72	Action ACT 4604	I'm In Love With You/Married Lady	100
72	Mojo 2092 037	How Do You Spell Love/She Don't Have To See You	15

DON PATTERSON

64	Transatlantic PR 733	THE EXCITING NEW ORGAN SOUND OF (LP)	12
67	Transatlantic PR 7349	HIP CAKE WALK (LP)	18
67	Transatlantic PR 7430	SATISFACTION! (LP)	12

MANLEY PATTERSON

72	Pama Supreme PS 337	I Stayed Away Too Long/Country Boy	5

MARY-ANNE PATTERSON

70	Joy JOYS 162	ME (LP)	300

OTTILIE PATTERSON
(see also Chris Barber)

55	Decca F 10472	I Hate A Man Like You/Reckless Blues (with Chris Barber's Jazz Band)	10
55	Decca F 10621	Weeping Willow Blues/Nobody Knows You When You're Down And Out	10
57	Pye 7N 15109	Kay-Cee Rider/I Love You Baby	10
58	Pye Jazz 7NJ 2015	Jailhouse Blues/Beale Street Blues	10
58	Pye Jazz 7NJ 2025	Trombone Cholly/Lawdy, Lawdy Blues	10
61	Columbia DB 4760	Blueberry Hill/I'm Crazy 'Bout My Baby	10
62	Columbia DB 4834	I Hate Myself/Come On Baby	12
63	Columbia DB 7140	Jealous Heart/Won't Be Long	10
63	Columbia DB 7208	Baby Please Don't Go/I Feel So Good (with Sonny Boy Williamson)	30
65	Columbia DB 7332	Tell Me Where Is Fancy/Oh Me What Eyes	10
69	Marmalade 598 016	Spring Song/Sound Of The Door As It Closes	10
69	Marmalade 598 020	Bitterness Of Death/Spring Song	10
55	Jazz Today JTE 102	THAT PATTERSON GIRL (EP)	10
56	Decca DFE 6303	BLUES (EP)	15
56	Pye Jazz Today NJE 1023	THAT PATTERSON GIRL VOL. 2 (EP)	12
59	Columbia SEG 7915	OTTILIE (EP)	8
60	Columbia SEG 7998	SWINGS THE IRISH (EP)	10
59	Pye NPL 18028	OTTILIE'S IRISH NIGHT (LP)	15
69	Marmalade 608 011	3000 YEARS WITH OTTILIE (LP)	100
69	Polydor 2384 031	SPRING SONG (LP)	35

ROBERT PATTERSON SINGERS

60s	United Artists UAS 29003	THE SOUL OF GOSPEL (LP)	25
65	Fontana 688 516 ZL	I'M SAVED (LP)	18

PATTERSONS

69	CBS 63522	AGAIN (LP)	15
68	CBS 63335	TRAVELLING PEOPLE (LP)	12
70	CBS 5083	I Can Fly/An Cailin Deas	15

PATTERSON'S PEOPLE

66	Mercury MF 913	Shake Hands With The Devil/Deadly Nightshade	35

PATTIE

69	Columbia DB 8542	Gravitation/Let The Music Start	12

PATTI & PATETTES

75	Dart ART 2053	Bill/It's My Party	8
76	United Artists UP 36077	Summer Heartbreak/Too Much	12

HUBERT PATTISON

66	Pye 7N 17207	Bare Back Rider/The Baby 1 & 2 Problem	5
67	Fontana TF 859	My Home's In My Pocket/Saturday Morning Bride	10

MINT VALUE £

LITTLE JOHN PATTISON
64 Giv-A-Disc LYN 510 Needles And Pins/All My Loving (flexidisc with Giv-A-Disc booklet) 10

(MIKE) PATTO
(see also Bo Street Runners, Breakaways, Boxer, News, Chicago Line, Timebox, Felder's Orioles, Steve York, Centipede, Grimms, Spooky Tooth, V.I.P.s)
66 Columbia DB 8091 Can't Stop Talking About My Baby/Love (as Mike Patto) 100
74 Goodear EAR 106 Sitting In The Park/Get Up And Dig It (as Mike Patto) 10
70 Vertigo 6360 016 PATTO (LP, textured gatefold sleeve, large swirl label) 120
71 Vertigo 6360 032 HOLD YOUR FIRE (LP, 3-flap gatefold, small swirl label) 300
72 Island ILPS 9210 ROLL 'EM SMOKE 'EM PUT ANOTHER LINE OUT (LP, pink rim/palm tree label) . 50

ALEXANDER PATTON
66 Capitol CL 15461 A Lil Lovin' Sometimes/No More Dreams 250
66 Capitol CL 15461 A Lil Lovin' Sometimes/No More Dreams (DJ copy) 350

CHARLIE PATTON
50s Heritage REU 4 CHARLIE PATTON (EP, 99 only) 60

JOHN PATTON
64 Blue Note 45-1889 I'll Never Be Free/Along Came John 8

PATTY & EMBLEMS
64 Stateside SS 322 Mixed Up Shook Up Girl/Ordinary Guy 70
64 Stateside SS 322 Mixed Up Shook Up Girl/Ordinary Guy (DJ copy) 100

PATTY FLABBIE'S COUGHED ENGINE
69 Stateside SS 2136 Billy's Got A Goat/Tin Can Eater 6

PAUL
(see also Jimmy Page)
65 Polydor BM 56045 Will You Follow Me/Head Death 70

ANDREW PAUL
85 Fashion FAD 038 Hustle Them A Hustle/Bad Boys (12") 25
85 Y&D YDD 0126 Under Me Sensima/Can't Take It No Longer (12", with the Offbeat Posse) 30

ANDY PAUL
84 Proto ENA 117 Anna Mari-Elena (Greek)/Anna Mari-Elena (English)/Bistepsememe (p/s, all copies mispressed with Greek version of A-side included twice) 12

BILLY PAUL
73 Epic EPC 65351 360 DEGREES OF BILLY PAUL (LP) 15
73 Epic EPC 65456 EBONY WOMAN (LP) 15
74 Phil. Intl. PIR 65861 WAR OF THE GODS (LP, gatefold sleeve) 15

BUNNY PAUL
54 Columbia SCM 5102 New Love/You'll Never Leave My Side 10
54 Columbia SCM 5112 Such A Night/I'm Gonna Have Some Fun 20
54 Columbia SCM 5131 Lovey Dovey/Answer The Call 20
54 Columbia SCM 5151 You Came A Long Way From St. Louis/You Are Always In My Heart 12
55 Capitol CL 14279 Please Have Mercy (On A Fool)/These Are The Things We'll Share 12
55 Capitol CL 14304 Leave My Heart Alone/Two Castanets 12
55 Capitol CL 14368 Song Of The Dreamer/For The Very First Time 10

DARLENE PAUL
64 Capitol CL 15344 Act Like Nothing Happened/Little Bit Of Heaven 30

DEREK PAUL
73 Youngblood YB 1006 Drugtaker/Riverboat 8

DON PAUL
68 RCA 1666 Wise/Ways Of The World 12

EUGENE PAUL
70 Pama Supreme PS 303 Don't Let The Tears Fall/Another Saturday Night 6
70 Pama Supreme PS 305 I Found A Man In My Bed/So Many Things 6
71 Pama Supreme PS 317 Farewell My Darling/Whole Lot Of Woman 6
71 Pama Supreme PS 329 Somebody's Changing My Sweet Baby's Mind/Hard Minded Neighbour 6
72 Pama PM 838 Beautiful Sunday/Take Care Son 6
72 Pama Supreme PS 357 I'll Take You There/Beautiful Baby 6
73 Pama Supreme PS 382 Power To All Our Friends/RANNY WILLIAMS ALLSTARS: Wicked And Dreadful . . 7

EUGENE PAUL & PILOTS
70 Torpedo TOR 17 Sugar Dumpling/I May Dwell 7

FRANKIE PAUL
85 Greensleeves GRED 189 Fools Fighting/Fighting Dub (12") 10

JASON PAUL
(see also Svensk)
69 Pye 7N 17710 Shine A Little Light Into My Room/Paradise Pudding 20

JOHN E. PAUL
67 Decca F 12685 Prince Of Players/I Wanna Know (DJ copy with curved Decca logo inverted matrix) 225
67 Decca F 12685 Prince Of Players/I Wanna Know (Boxed Decca logo, inverted matrix) 150
67 Decca F 12685 Prince Of Players/I Wanna Know (Matrix number 41387 correct way up) 25

LES PAUL (& MARY FORD)
54 Capitol CL 14185 Mandolino/Whither Thou Goest 15
55 Capitol CL 14212 Mister Sandman/That's What I Like 20
55 Capitol CL 14233 Someday Sweetheart/Song In Blue 15
55 Capitol CL 14300 No Letter Today/Genuine Love 15
55 Capitol CL 14342 Goodbye My Love/Hummingbird 15

			MINT VALUE £
56	Capitol CL 14502	Alabamy Bound/Texas Lady	8
56	Capitol CL 14521	Magic Melody/Amukiriki (The Lord Willing)	5
56	Capitol CL 14534	Theme From "The Threepenny Opera" (Moritat) (as Les Paul)/Nuevo Laredo	5
56	Capitol CL 14577	Send Me Some Money/Say The Words I Love To Hear	5
56	Capitol CL 14593	San Antonio Rose/Cimarron (Roll On)	5
56	Capitol CL 14665	Runnin' Wild/Blow The Smoke Away	5
57	Capitol CL 14710	Cinco Robles (Five Oaks)/Ro-Ro-Robinson	5
57	Capitol CL 14776	Strollin' Blues/I Don't Want You No More	5
57	Capitol CL 14809	(I'm Keeping My Heart Away From) Fire/A Pair Of Fools	5
58	Capitol CL 14839	Bewitched/The Night Of The Fourth (as Les Paul solo)	5
58	Philips PB 873	Put A Ring On My Finger/Fantasy	5
58	Philips PB 882	Jealous Heart/Big Eyed Girl	5
59	Philips PB 906	At The Sav-A-Penny Super Store/All I Need Is You	5
55	Capitol EAP1 9121	PRESENTING LES PAUL AND MARY FORD (EP)	10
55	Capitol EAP1 540	SITTING ON TOP OF THE WORLD (EP)	10
60	Capitol EAP1 20048	MR AND MRS MUSIC (EP)	10
61	Capitol EAP1 20145	NOLA (EP)	10
65	Capitol EAP1 20540	JAZZ ME BLUES (EP)	10
51	Capitol LC 6514	THE NEW SOUND (LP, 10")	20
53	Capitol LC 6581	THE NEW SOUND VOL. 2 (LP, 10")	20
54	Capitol T 416	HIT MAKERS (LP)	15
55	Capitol LC 6701	LES AND MARY (LP, 10")	20
55	Capitol LC 6704	LES AND MARY PART 2 (LP, 10")	15
56	Capitol LC 6806	BYE BYE BLUES! (LP, 10")	15

LYN PAUL

(see also Nocturnes)

74	Polydor 2058 472	Sail The Summer Winds/Lay Me Down (with John Barry)	7
75	Polydor 2383 340	GIVE ME LOVE (LP)	15

RIM D. PAUL

68	Philips BF 1737	Thousand Hours/Downstairs To Meet Her	5

SHELLEY PAUL

69	Jay Boy BOY 10	Clowns Are Coming In/Take Me To Your Heart	6

PAUL & LINDA

69	Page One POF 140	You're Taking My Bag/When I Hear Your Name	10

(this single is not by Paul & Linda McCartney)

PAUL & PAULA

63	Philips 304 012 BF	Hey Paula/Bobby Is The One	5
63	Philips 304 016 BF	Young Lovers/Ba-hey-be	5
63	Philips BF 1256	First Quarrel/School Is Thru	5
63	Philips BF 1269	Something Old, Something New/Flipped Over You	5
63	Philips BF 1281	First Day Back At School/A Perfect Pair	5
64	Philips BF 1380	No Other Baby/Too Dark To See	7
63	Philips BBE 12639	YOUNG LOVERS (EP)	25
63	Philips 652 026BL	SING FOR YOUNG LOVERS (LP)	30
63	Philips BL 7573	WE GO TOGETHER (LP)	35
63	Philips BL 7587	HOLIDAY FOR TEENS (LP)	25

PAUL AND RITCHIE & CRYING SHAMES

(see also Cryin' Shames, Gary Walker & Rain)

66	Decca F 12483	September In The Rain/Come On Back (more common demos = £130)	180

PAULA & JETLINERS

66	Rainbow RAI 102	The Great Pretender/The Legend Of The Man From U.N.C.L.E.	15
66	Rainbow RAI 105	I Know Someday/Something On My Mind (B-side with Carols)	8

PAULETTE (Williams)

(see also Paulette & Gee)

68	Major Minor MM 565	One Love In My Heart/Must We Say Goodbye	6
73	Summit SUM 8543	Every Day Is The Same Kind Of Thing/ SHORTY PERRY: The Sweat Of Your Brow	6

PAULETTE & DELROY

(see also Paulette, Paulette & Gee)

63	Island WI 120	Little Lover/Lovin' Baby	20

PAULETTE & GEE

(see also Paulette, Sister, Winston Wright)

70	G.G. GG 4506	Hold On Tight/G.G. ALL STARS: Tight Version	8

PAULETTE SISTERS

55	Capitol CL 14294	Dream Boat/Leave My Honey Be	15
55	Capitol CL 14310	Ring-A-Dang-A-Doo/Lonely One	15
55	Capitol CL 14347	You Win Again/Mama, El Baion	15

PAULINE (& BROWN SUGAR)

(see also Brown Sugar)

80	Studio WE 706	I Am So Proud/NATTY LOCKS: Studio 16 Workshop (12")	25
80	Isis 1	Lion, Me And My Dread/Revelation Side (12")	40

PAUL'S DISCIPLES

65	Decca F 12081	See That My Grave Is Kept Clean/Sixteen Tons	35

PAUL'S TROUBLES

67	Ember EMB S 233	You'll Find Out/You've Got Something	25

PAUPERS

(see also Lighthouse)

68	Verve Forecast VS 1514	Think I Care/White Song	15
69	Verve Forecast VS 1520	Southdown Road/Numbers	15
68	Verve Forecast (S)VLP 6017	ELLIS ISLAND (LP, mono/stereo)	30

MINT VALUE £

PAVEMENT

92	Ablaze 8	My First Mine/FLUFF: "Us" (flexi, free with Ablaze magazine)	8
92	Big Cat ABB 35S	Trigger Cut/Sue Me Jack/So Stark (You're A Skyscraper) (p/s)	10
94	Big Cat ABB 55S	Cut Your Hair/Camera/Stare (p/s)	5
94	Big Cat UK ABB 55T	Cut Your Hair/Camera/Stare (uncredited track) (12")	12
95	Big Cat ABB 86S	Rattled By La Rush/False Skorpion/Easily Fooled (p/s)	5
95	Big Cat ABB 91S	Father To A Sister Of Thought/Kris Kraft/Mussle Rock Is A Horse In Transition (p/s)	6
96	Big Cat ABB 110 S	Give It A Day/Gangsters & Pranksters/Saganaw/I Love Perth (p/s)	8
92	Big Cat ABB 38P	WATERY, DOMESTIC (12" EP, picture disc, stickered poly sleeve)	15
91	Big Cat ABB 34	SLANTED AND ENCHANTED (LP)	30
94	Big Cat ABB 56L	CROOKED RAIN CROOKED RAIN (LP, with inner sleeve, some with free 7": "Haunt You Down"/"Jam Kids")	30
95	Big Cat LC 5661	WOWEE ZOWEE (2-LP, 3-sided gatefold cover)	30

RITA PAVONE

63	RCA 1354	Il Ballo Del Mattone Part 1/Part 2	10
64	RCA RCA 1415	Remember Me/Just Once More	6
66	RCA RCA 1553	Heart/The Man Who Made Music	10
66	RCA RCA 1561	You Only You/Before You Go	5
73	Decca F 13462	He (Didn't Remember My Name)/(Vado Via) Last Summer	6
64	RCA RD 7657	RITA PAVONE (mono)	15
64	RCA SF 7657	RITA PAVONE (stereo)	20

PAX EXTERNAL

71	Decca F 13167	A Second Chance Mr. Jones/You See Him As Your Brother	6

GARY PAXTON

(see also Skip & Flip)

62	Liberty LIB 55485	Stop Twistin' Baby/Alley Oop Was A Two Dab Man	15

TOM PAXTON

66	Elektra EKSN 45001	The Last Thing On My Mind/Goin' To The Zoo	5
66	Elektra EKSN 45003	One Time And One Time Only/Bottle Of Wine	5
67	Elektra EKSN 45006	Leaving London/All The Way Home	5
69	Elektra EKSN 45021	Jennifer's Rabbit/The Marvellous Toy	5
69	Elektra EKSN 45049	Victoria Dines Alone/Clarissa Jones	5
67	Elektra EPK 802	TOM PAXTON (EP)	20
66	Elektra EKL 277/EKS 7277	RAMBLIN' BOY (LP, U.K. pressing in U.S. sleeve)	12
66	Elektra EKL 298/EKS 7298	AIN'T THAT NEWS (LP, U.K. pressing in U.S. sleeve)	12
66	Elektra EKL 317/EKS 7317	OUTWARD BOUND (LP)	12
68	Elek. EKL 4019/EKS 74019	MORNING AGAIN (LP, red label)	12

JOHNNY PAYCHECK

77	Epic SEPC 6171	Take This Job And Shove It/Colarado Cool-Aid	5

DAVEY PAYNE & MEDIUM WAVE

69	Ember EMB S 265	Walk In The Sunshine/Looking Towards The Sky (p/s)	50

FREDA PAYNE

62	HMV POP 1091	He Who Laughs Last (Desafinado)/Slightly Out Of Tune	25
70	Invictus INV 502	Band Of Gold/ The Easiest Way To Fall	6
70	Invictus INV 505	Deeper And Deeper/Unhooked Generation	6
71	Invictus INV 509	Cherish What Is Dear To You (While It's Near To You)/ The World Don't Owe You A Thing	6
71	Invictus INV 512	Rock Me In The Cradle (Of Your Lovin' Arms)/Now Is The Time To Say Goodbye	6
71	Invictus INV 515	Bring Home The Boys/Odds And Ends	6
71	Invictus INV 518	You've Got To Love Somebody/Mama's Gone	8
72	Invictus INV 520	You Brought Me Joy/Suddenly It's Yesterday	6
72	Invictus INV 526	Unhooked Generation/Come Back	5
73	Invictus INV 529	I Shall Not Be Moved/Thru' The Memory Of My Mind	5
73	Invictus INV 533	Band Of Gold/The Easiest Way To Fall (reissue, withdrawn)	30
75	ABC ABC 4087	You/Lost In Love	5
70	Invictus SVT 1001	BAND OF GOLD (LP)	20
71	Invictus SVT 1005	CONTACT (LP)	20
70s	MGM 2351 004	FREDA PAYNE (LP)	12

JACKIE PAYNE

77	Barak 4	I Found Myself/Instrumental	25

LEON PAYNE

64	London HA-B 8136	AMERICANA (LP)	12

PAZ

(see also Lol Coxhill)

79	Magnus 2	PAZ AT CHICHESTER (LP)	25
83	Spotlight SPJ 507	KANDEEN LOVE SONG (LP)	12

P BROTHERS

01	White (Heavy Bronx) PBHB01	HEAVY BRONX EXPERIENCE VOL. 1 (EP)	40

PC LTD

69	Fontana TF 1032	Sunny Was A Fool/Here We Come	6

PD3

91	Payday PD001	SYNCOPATED NOISE MUSIC (EP)	20
94	Payday PD004	SYMPHONY (EP)	15

DAVE PEACE QUARTET

(see also Birmingham)

69	Saga FID 2155	GOOD MORNING MR. BLUES (LP)	15

PEACEFUL COMPANY

(see under Morin & Wilson)

MINT VALUE £

DIXIE PEACH AND THE OFFBEAT POSSE

86	Jah Tubby's JT 018	Slaughter/Slaughter Mix (12")	25
87	Y&D YDD 0102	Raggamuffin And Rambo/Version (12")	10

PEACHES & HERB

67	CBS 202509	Let's Fall In Love/We're In This Thing Together	30
67	CBS 202509	Let's Fall In Love/We're In This Thing Together (DJ copy)	60
67	CBS 2711	Close Your Eyes/I Will Watch Over You	8
67	CBS 2866	For Your Love/I Need Your Love So Desperately	25
67	CBS 2866	For Your Love/I Need Your Love So Desperately (DJ copy)	50
67	Direction 58-3096	Love Is Strange/Two Little Kids	7
68	Direction 58-3415	Let It Be Me/I Need Your Love So Desperately	7
68	Direction 58-3548	United/Thank You	6
68	Direction 58-3829	Let's Make A Promise/Me And You	7
69	Direction 58-4085	When He Touches Me/Thank You	7
70	Direction 58-4909	Satisfy My Hunger/It's Just A Game, Love	7
70	Direction 58-5249	Soothe Me With Your Love/We're So Much In Love	8
71	CBS 5249	Soothe Me With Your Love/We're So Much In Love (reissue)	6
77	Epic EPC 4903	Soothe Me With Your Love/Satisy My Hunger (coloured vinyl)	6
67	CBS 62966	LET'S FALL IN LOVE (LP)	20
67	CBS 63119	FOR YOUR LOVE (LP)	20
68	Direction 8-63263	GOLDEN DUETS (LP)	20

ANNETTE PEACOCK

72	RCA SF 8255	I'M THE ONE (LP)	22
70s	Aura	LIVE IN PARIS (LP)	18

ANNETTE PEACOCK & PAUL BLEY

(see also Paul Bley, Bley-Peacock Synthesiser Show, Annette Peacock)

73	Freedom 2383 105	DUAL UNITY (LP)	15

ROGER PEACOCK

65	Columbia DB7764	Everybody's Talking About My Baby/Times Have Changed	20

TREVOR PEACOCK

61	Decca F 11414	I Didn't Figure On Him To Come Back/Can I Walk You Home	20

PEANUT

(see also Katie Kissoon, Ragdolls U.K.)

65	Pye 7N 15901	Thank Goodness For The Rain/I'm Not Sad	10
65	Pye 7N 15963	Home Of The Brave/I Wanna Hear It Again	25
66	Columbia DB 8032	I'm Waiting For The Day/Someone's Gonna Be Sorry	22
67	Columbia DB 8104	I Didn't Love Him Anyway/Come Tomorrow	20

PEANUT BUTTER CONSPIRACY

67	CBS 2981	It's A Happening Thing/Twice Is Life	15
68	CBS 3543	Turn On A Friend/Captain Sandwich	10
69	London HLH 10290	Back In L.A./Have A Little Faith	10
68	CBS 63277	THE GREAT CONSPIRACY (LP)	40
80s	Drop Out DO 2000	TURN ON A FRIEND (LP)	12

PEANUTS

71	Philips 6006087	Goldendays/Headin Straight For You	10

BOB PEARCE BLUES BAND

(see also Brother Bung)

74	Westwood WRS 040	LET'S GET DRUNK AGAIN (LP)	18
79	Forest Tracks FT 3015	COLOUR BLIND (LP)	12

PEARL JAM

(see also Temple Of The Dog)

92	Epic 657 572-7	Alive/Once (white/red vinyl p/s)	12
92	Epic 657 572-6	Alive/Once/Wash (12", poster p/s)	10
93	Epic 657 867-7	Even Flow/Oceans (p/s)	5
92	Epic 657 857-8	Even Flow/Dirty Frank/Oceans (12", white vinyl, p/s)	15
92	Epic 658 258-7	Jeremy/Alive (live) (white vinyl, p/s)	10
92	Epic 658 258-6	Jeremy/Alive (live)/Footsteps (12", picture disc, with card insert)	25
92	Epic 658 258-2	Jeremy/Yellow Ledbetter/Alive (live) (CD, picture disc)	15
93	Epic 660 020-6	Daughter/Blood (Live)/Yellow Ledbetter (Live) (12", ltd. ed. poster sleeve)	15
93	Epic 659 795-6	Go/Alone/Elderly Woman Behind The Counter In A Small Town (Acoustic) (12", with free cassette [plays 'Animal' (Live)])	12
93	Epic 660 020-7	Daughter/Blood (live) (red vinyl p/s)	5
94	Epic 660 441-7	Dissident/Rearviewmirror (live) (stickered poster p/s)	5
92	Epic 468 884-0	TEN (LP, picture disc)	20
94	Epic 477861-1	VITALOGY (LP, embossed gatefold sleeve)	20
96	Epic 484448-1	NO CODE (LP, gatefold sleeve, inners, 8 cards)	25
98	Epic 489365-1	YIELD (LP, die-cut sleeve, inner sleeve)	25
98	Epic 429859-1	LIVE ON TWO LEGS (2-LP, stickered gatefold sleeve with inner sleeves)	40
00	Sony E263665	BINAURAL (2-LP, 3-part fold out sleeve with booklet)	20
02	Epic 510000-1	RIOT ACT (2-LP, gatefold sleeve, inner sleeves)	80

PEARLS

(see also Bud Ashton)

72	Bell BELL 1217	Third Finger, Left Hand/Little Lady Love Me	5
72	Bell BELL 1254	You Came, You Saw, You Conquered/Sing Out To Me	5
74	Bell BELL 1352	Guilty/I'll Say It Over Again	5

PEARLS

75	Private Stock PVT39	The Cheater/I'm Gonna Steal Your Heart Away	8

PEARLS BEFORE SWINE

68	Fontana STL 5503	BALAKLAVA (LP)	30
68	Fontana STL 5505	ONE NATION UNDERGROUND (LP)	25
69	Reprise RSLP 6364	THESE THINGS TOO (LP)	20

MINT VALUE £

70 Reprise RSLP 6405 THE USE OF ASHES (LP) 20
71 Reprise RSLP 6442 CITY OF GOLD (LP) 20
71 Reprise RSLP 6467 BEAUTIFUL LIES YOU COULD LIVE (LP) 15

BUSTER PEARSON BAND

73 Action ACT 4612 Big Funky/Pretty Woman 10
75 K&B 5516 Take It Easy/Instrumental 6

DUKE PEARSON

60s Polydor ANGEL EYES (LP) 100

JOHNNY PEARSON

(see also John Barry Seven)

62 Oriole CB 1721 Doh La La/Johnny's Tune 7
62 Parlophone R 4977 Theme From The L-Shaped Room Part 1/Part 2 7
66 Columbia DB 7851 Rat Catcher's Theme/Weaver's Green Theme 20
73 BBC RESL 6 Spy Trap/Playgirl (with Quator) 10
70 Aristocrat AR 103 SOUNDS EXTRAVAGANZA (LP) 20

KEITH PEARSON'S RIGHT HAND BAND

76 Eron ER 014 KEITH PEARSON'S RIGHT HAND BAND (LP) 12

RONNIE PEARSON

58 HMV POP 489 Flippin' Over You/Teen-Age Fancy 700
58 HMV POP 489 Flippin' Over You/Teen-Age Fancy (78) 150

PEASANTS

65 Columbia DB 7642 Got Some Lovin' For You Baby/Let's Get Together 160

PEBBLES

78 Arawak AR 01 Positive vibration (12") 30

PEBBLES

68 Major Minor MM 574 40 Miles Inside Your Heart/Get Around 10
69 Decca F 22944 Incredible George/Playing Chess 15
70 Deram DM 305 Stand Up And Be Counted/May In The Morning 8
71 Parlophone R 5900 Goodnight Ma/Sadness Of A Summer's Afternoon 8
71 Parlophone R 5921 First Time Loving/Party 8

PEBBLES & BAMM BAMM / FLINTSTONES

65 Pye Int. 7N.25332 Daddy (mono)/The World Is Full OF Joys (For Girls And Boys) 7

PEDDLERS

64 Philips BF 1375 Let The Sunshine In/True Girl 8
65 Philips BF 1404 Whatever Happened To The Good Times/Song For The Blues 6
65 Philips BF 1455 Over The Rainbow/You Must Be Having Me On 6
66 Philips BF 1506 Adam's Apple/Anybody's Fool 6
66 Philips BF 1530 I've Got To Hold On/Gassin' 6
67 Philips BF 1557 What'll I Do/Delicious Lady 6
67 CBS 2947 Irresistable You/Murray's Mood 6
67 CBS 3055 You're The Reason I'm Living/Nine Miles High 6
68 CBS 3333 Handel With Care/Horse's Collar 6
68 CBS 3734 Comin' Home Baby/Empty Club Blues 25
68 CBS 4050 That's Life/Wasting My Time 6
69 CBS 4449 Birth/Steel Mill 6
69 CBS 4720 Girlie/P.S. I Love You 6
70 Phillips 6006034 Tell The World We're Not In/Rainy Day In London 20
73 Philips 6006 283 Sing Me An Old Song/It's So Easy 30
66 Philips BE 12954 SWINGING SCENE (EP) 15
67 Philips (S)BL 7768 LIVE AT THE PICKWICK (LP) 15
67 CBS (S)BPG 63183 FREE WHEELERS (LP) 15
68 CBS 63411 THREE IN A CELL (LP) 15
68 Fontana SFL 13016 THE FANTASTIC PEDDLERS (LP) 12
70 CBS 63682 BIRTHDAY (LP) 12
70 Philips 6308 028 THREE FOR ALL (LP) 12
71 Philips 6386 066 GEORGIA ON MY MIND (LP) 12
72 Philips 6308 102 SUITE LONDON (LP) 40

PEDESTRIANS

81 Metropolis MET 1 Commuter Fantasy/1984 8

MIKE PEDICIN QUINTET

62 HMV POP 1001 When Cats Come Twistin' In/Gotta Twist 15

BOBBY PEDRICK

58 London HLX 8740 White Bucks And Saddle Shoes/Stranded 25
58 London HLX 8740 White Bucks And Saddle Shoes/Stranded (78) 18

ANN PEEBLES

70 London HLU 10322 Part Time Love/I Still Love You 6
71 London HLU 10328 I Pity The Fool/Heartaches, Heartaches 6
71 London HLU 10346 Slipped, Tripped And Fell In Love/99 lbs 5
72 London HLU 10361 Breaking Up Somebody's Home/Troubles, Heartaches And Sadness 5
72 London HLU 10385 Somebody's On Your Case/I've Been There Before 5
73 London HLU 10405 I'm Gonna Tear Your Playhouse Down/One Way Street 6
73 London HLU 10428 I Can't Stand The Rain/I've Been There Before 6
75 London HLU 10484 Beware/You Got To Feed The Fire 5
75 London HLU 10508 Come On Mama/I'm Leaving You 5
72 London SHU 8434 STRAIGHT FROM THE HEART (LP) 15
74 London SHU 8468 I CAN'T STAND THE RAIN (LP) 15
76 London SHU 8490 TELLIN' IT (LP) 15

PAUL PEEK

(see also Gene Vincent & Blue Caps)

61 Pye International 7N 25102 Brother In Law/Through The Teenage Years 20
66 CBS 202073 Pin The Tail On The Donkey/Rockin' Pneumonia 12

MINT VALUE £

DAVID PEEL (& LOWER EAST SIDE)

68	Elektra EKL 4032	HAVE A MARIJUANA (LP, red label, mono)	40
68	Elektra EKS 74032	HAVE A MARIJUANA (LP, red label, stereo)	25
70	Elektra 2401 001	AMERICAN REVOLUTION (LP)	20

PEELERS

72	Polydor Folk Mill 2460 165	BANISHED MISFORTUNE (LP)	160

PEELS

66	Stateside SS 513	Juanita Banana/Fun	8
66	Audio Fidelity AFSP 527	Scrooey Mooey/Time Marches On	20

PEENUTS

67	Ember EMB S 242	The Theme For "The Monkees"/The World's Been Good To Me Tonight (in p/s)	20
67	Ember EMB S 242	The Theme For "The Monkees"/The World's Been Good To Me Tonight	10

PEEPERS

72	Bumble GE102	Ayeo/A Heavy Drinking Ego Shrinking	20

PEEPS

(see also Martin Cure & Peeps, Sabres, Rainbows)

65	Philips BF 1421	Now Is The Time/Got Plenty Of Love	15
65	Philips BF 1443	What Can I Say?/Don't Talk About Love	15
66	Philips BF 1478	Gotta Get A Move On/I Told You Before	60
66	Philips BF 1509	Tra La La/Loser Wins	10

PEEP SHOW

67	Polydor 56196	Your Servant, Stephen/Mazy	90
68	Polydor 52226	Esprit De Corps/Mino In A Mix Up	12

BEV PEGG (& HIS GOIN' NOWHERE BAND)

(see also David Cartwright, Brindley Brae)

78	Beaujangle DB 0007	NOSTALGIA IS A THING OF THE PAST (LP, private pressing, with booklet, 50 only; as Bev Pegg & His Goin' Nowhere Band)	150
80	Beaujangle DB 0008	THE FOUNDRY DITTY AND THE INDUSTRIAL AIR (LP, private pressing, 500 only, 150 destroyed so only 350 in circulation)	45

BEV PEGG (AND FRIENDS)

(see also Bev Pegg, Dave Cartwright, Brindley Brae)

75	Beaujangle DB 0006	AWAY FROM THE SAND (LP, 50 copies only)	200

BOB PEGG

74	Transatlantic TRA 280	THE SHIPBUILDER (LP, with Nick Strutt)	15
75	Transatlantic TRA 299	ANCIENT MAPS (LP, with lyric insert)	20

BOB & CAROL PEGG

(see also Carol Pegg, Mr. Fox)

71	Trailer LER 3016	HE CAME FROM THE MOUNTAIN (LP, red label)	35
72	Galliard GAL 4017	AND NOW IT IS SO EARLY - THE SONGS OF SYDNEY CARTER (LP)	25

BOB PEGG & NICK STRUTT

73	Transatlantic TRA 265	BOB PEGG & NICK STRUTT (LP)	25

CAROL(ANNE) PEGG

(see also Bob & Carol Pegg)

73	Transatlantic TRA 226	CAROLANNE PEGG (LP, gatefold sleeve)	80

PEGGY

70	Trojan TR 7752	All Kinds Of Everything Part 1/CARL LEVEY: Instrumental Version	6
70	Hot Rod HR 103	I Shall Follow The Star/CARL LEVEY: Gifted At The Top	8

PEGGY & JIMMY

70	Hot Rod HR 101	Pum Pum Lover/CARL LEVY: Remember Easter Monday	8

PEGGY'S LEG

(see also Skid Row, Jimi Slevin)

73	Bunch BAN 2001	GRINILLA (LP, with insert)	400

PEG LEG SAM

74	Flyright LP 507/8	THE LAST MEDICINE SHOW (2-LP)	15

PEKKA

77	Virgin V 2084	THE MATHEMATICIANS AIR DISPLAY (LP, features Mike Oldfield)	18

DAVE PELL OCTET

54	London RE-P 1008	IRVING BERLIN GALLERY VOL. 1 (EP)	12
55	London RE-P 1018	RODGERS AND HART (EP)	12
54	London H-APB 1034	RODGERS AND HEART GALLERY (10" LP)	15

LANA PELLAY

86	Sublime LIMET 101	Pistol In My Pocket/Dirty Harry Version (12", p/s)	12

JACK PENATE

06	Young Turks YT 001	Second Minute Or Hour/Got My Favourite? (die-cut p/s with colour Numbered Polaroid photo initialed by artist, PVC bag, 1,000 only)	8

TRACY PENDARVIS

60	London HLS 9059	A Thousand Guitars/Is It Too Late	35
60	London HLS 9213	Is It Me/South Bound Line	25

MIKE PENDER

(see also The Searchers)

86	Sierra FED 23	It's Over/Brothers And Sisters (p/s)	6
86	Sierra FED 23T	It's Over/Brothers And Sisters (12", p/s)	8

PENDLEFOLK

70	Folk Heritage FHR 007	PENDLEFOLK (LP)	18

MINT VALUE £

PENDRAGON
87 Awareness AWS 101 — Red Shoes/Searching/Contact (p/s) . . . 5
89 Toff PENDS 7S — Saved By You/Lady Luck (p/s) . . . 5
85 Elusive ARRLP 100 — FIRE IN HARMONY (LP) . . . 12
85 Elusive ARRLP 101 — THE JEWEL (LP) . . . 12

PENETRATION
77 Virgin VS 192 — Don't Dictate/Money Talks (p/s) . . . 8
78 Virgin VS 213 — Firing Squad/Never (p/s) . . . 5
78 Virgin VS 226 — Life's A Gamble/V.I.P. (p/s) . . . 5
79 Virgin VS 257 — Danger Signs/Stone Heroes (live) (p/s) . . . 5
79 Virgin VS 268 — Come Into The Open/Lifeline (p/s) . . . 5
78 Virgin V 2109 — MOVING TARGETS (LP, 15,000 on luminous vinyl) . . . 15
78 Virgin V 2109 — MOVING TARGETS (LP, black vinyl) . . . 20

BOB PENFOLD
78 A C Wall ACW 01 — Free/Mother Natures Child . . . 12

PENGUINS
55 London HL 8114 — Earth Angel/Hey Senorita (gold label print, triangular centre) . . . 2000
55 London HL 8114 — Earth Angel/Hey Senorita (large centre hole, export issue) . . . 900
55 London HL 8114 — Earth Angel/Hey Senorita (78) . . . 160

DAWN PENN
(see also Max Romeo, Viceroys)
66 Rio R 113 — Long Days Short Night/Are You There (label lists 'Dawn Tenn') . . . 60
67 Studio One SO 2030 — You Don't Love Me/SOUL VENDORS: Portobello Road . . . 50
68 Island WI 3097 — I'll Never Let You Go/MARK BROWN: Brown Low Special . . . 45

TONY PENN
62 Starlite ST45 083 — That's What I Like/I Won't Cry Anymore . . . 30

LEONARD PENNARIO
(see also Les Baxter)
54 Capitol CL 14173 — Midnight On The Cliffs/Dream Rhapsody (with Les Baxter Orchestra) . . . 10

BARBARA PENNINGTON
76 United Artists UP 36170 — 24 Hours A Day/I Can't Erase The Thoughts Of You (12") . . . 8

PENNSYLVANIA SIXPENCE
67 Pye 7N 17326 — Love Of The Common People/Midweek Excursion . . . 8

PENNY
61 Piccadilly 7N 35009 — Who Does He Think He Is/Sparks . . . 8
62 Piccadilly 7N 35045 — Shall I Take My Heart And Go/What'd I Do? . . . 8

GEORGE A. PENNY
68 Trojan TR 625 — Win Your Love/VAL BENNETT: All In The Game . . . 12

HANK PENNY
56 Parlophone MSP 6202 — Bloodshot Eyes/Wham! Bam! Thank You Ma'am . . . 100
56 Parlophone R 4120 — Bloodshot Eyes/Wham! Bam! Thank You Ma'am (78) . . . 18

PENNY LANE
70 CBS 4749 — Bouzouki/Make Up Or Break Up/ . . . 10
70 CBS 4903 — Heartbreak House/He's Got A Hold Of My Heart . . . 5
72 CBS 7916 — Legend In Your own Time/Driving Me Out Of My Mind . . . 8

PENNY PEEPS
68 Liberty LBF 15053 — Little Man With A Stick/Model Village . . . 300
68 Liberty LBF 15114 — I See The Morning/Curly, The Knight Of The Road . . . 40

PENNY WAGER
72 Folk Heritage FHR 0256 — LIGHT OF OTHER DAYS (LP) . . . 75

PENNY ARCADE
70 Pye 7N.17943 — The Two Of Us/Don't Need You Anymore . . . 20

PENNYWORTH
69 CBS 4573 — Malena Malena/Who Are You? . . . 12

CHARLES PENROSE
72 Columbia DB 8959 — Laughing Policeman/George Formby - Window Cleaner/ Stanley Holloway - The Lion And Albert . . . 6
57 Columbia SEG 7743 — THE ADVENTURE OF THE LAUGHING POLICEMAN (EP) . . . 10

PENTAD
65 Parlophone R 5288 — Silver Dagger/Nothing But Love . . . 25
65 Parlophone R 5368 — Don't Throw It All Away/Too Many Ways . . . 20
66 Parlophone R 5424 — Something Other People Call Love/It Better Be Me . . . 20

PENTAGONS
61 London HLU 9333 — To Be Loved Forever/Down At The Beach . . . 100

PENTAGRAM
85 own label DEVIL 4 — PENTAGRAM (LP) . . . 15
92 Peaceville — 1972-1979 (LP) . . . 15
93 Peaceville VILE 38 — RELENTLESS (LP) . . . 25

PENTANGLE
(see also Bert Jansch, John Renbourn, Duffy's Nucleus)
68 Big T BIG 109 — Travellin' Song/Mirage (in title die-cut sleeve) . . . 10
68 Big T BIG 109 — Travellin' Song/Mirage . . . 6
69 Big T BIG 124 — Once I Had A Sweetheart/I Saw An Angel . . . 20
70 Big T BIG 128 — Light Flight/Cold Mountain . . . 6
73 Big T BIG 567 — Light Flight/Market Song/The Time Has Come . . . 6
68 Transatlantic TRA 162 — THE PENTANGLE (LP) . . . 30

MINT VALUE £

68 Transatlantic TRA 178 — SWEET CHILD (2-LP) 40
69 Transatlantic TRA 205 — BASKET OF LIGHT (LP, gatefold sleeve) 30
70 Transatlantic TRA 228 — CRUEL SISTER (LP, gatefold sleeve) 25
71 Transatlantic TRA 240 — REFLECTION (LP, gatefold sleeve with inner sleeve) 20
72 Reprise K 44197 — SOLOMON'S SEAL (LP, with lyric insert) 60
72 Transatlantic TRASAM 23 — HISTORY BOOK (LP) 12
73 Transatlantic TRASAM 29 — PENTANGLING (LP) 12

PENTHOUSE
71 Penny Farthing PEN 765 — 40 Days Of Rain/I'm Nobody's Fool 8

PEOPLE
69 Capitol CL 15553 — I Love You/Somebody Tell Me My Name 22
69 Capitol CL 15599 — Ulla/Turnin' Me In 22
70 RCA RCA 2028 — I Am (The Preacher)/September's Son 10
71 Deram DM 346 — In Ancient Times/Glastonbury 35
70 Paramount SPFL 261 — THERE ARE PEOPLE AND THERE ARE PEOPLE (LP) 25

PEOPLE BAND
(see also Charlie Watts, Battered Ornaments)
70 Transatlantic TRA 214 — THE PEOPLE BAND (LP, with Charlie Watts) 75

PEPPER
68 Pye 7N 17569 — We'll Make It Together/(Look Out) I'm On The Way Down 10

ART PEPPER
(see also Chet Baker)
54 Vogue LDE 067 — ART PEPPER QUARTET (10" LP) 15
57 London HLZ V 14038 — ART PEPPER QUARTET (10" LP) 15
60 Contemporary LAC 12229 — MODERN JAZZ CLASSICS (LP, as Art Pepper Eleven) 15

JIM PEPPER
71 Atlantic 2400 149 — PEPPER'S POW WOW (LP) 25

KEN PEPPER
61 Top Rank JAR 535 — Just A Little At A Time/I Get The Blues When It Rains 7

DANNY PEPPERMINT (& JUMPING JACKS)
61 London HLL 9478 — The Peppermint Twist/Somebody Else Is Taking My Place (with Jumping Jacks) 12
62 London HLL 9516 — One More Time/La Dee Dah 10
62 London HLL 9614 — Maybe Tomorrow (But Not Today)/Passing Parade 10
62 London HA-L 2438 — TWIST WITH DANNY PEPPERMINT (LP) 75

PEPPERMINT CIRCUS
67 Olga OLE 007 — All The King's Horses/It Didn't Take Long 10
68 Polydor 56288 — I Won't Be There/Keeping My Head Above Water 6
69 Polydor 56312 — Please Be Patient/Take My Love 6

PEPPERMINT RAINBOW
68 MCA MU 1034 — Walking In Different Circles/Pink Lemonade 12
69 MCA MU 1076 — Will You Be Staying After Sunday/And I'll Be There 18
69 MCA MU 1091 — Don't Wake Up In The Morning Michael/Rosemary 10

PEPPERMINT TROLLEY COMPANY
68 Dot DOT 110 — Baby You Come Rolling 'Cross My Mind/Nine O'Clock Business Man 10

PEPPI
62 Decca F 11520 — Stories/When I Think Of You 5
63 Decca F 11638 — Can You Waddle/I Never Danced Before 10
64 Decca F 11991 — Pistol Packin' Mama/Roll On Baby 5
64 Fontana TF 446 — So Used To Loving You/Don't Trust My Friend 8
65 Decca F 12055 — The Skip/Do The Skip 8

ARMANDO PERAZA
68 Fontana STL 5525 — WILD THING (LP) 20

PERCELLS
63 HMV POP 1154 — What Are Boys Made Of?/Cheek To Cheek 20

LANCE PERCIVAL
63 Parlophone R 507 — The Beetroot Song/Dancing In The Streets Tonight 5
65 Parlophone R 5335 — Shame And Scandal In The Family/There's Another One Behind 5

NORMAN PERCIVAL
67 United Artists UP 1197 — Theme From "Billion Dollar Brain"/Shades Of Green 10

PERCY PAVILION
(see also Captain Sensible)
84 Dead Good Dolly P. DMS 2 — Gower Power/You're An Extra Baby (p/s) 5

PEREGRINE
72 Westwood WRS 016 — SONGS OF MINE (LP) 100

RAY PEREIRA
70 Baf BAF 5 — Don't Mess With Cupid/CATS: Falling In Love 8
70 Baf BAF 6 — On Broadway/Hey Chick 6

PERERIN
80 Gwerin SYWM 215 — HAUL AR YR EIRA (LP, with insert) 180

CARLO PERETTI AND HIS LATIN BEAT
60 Society SOC 906 — MAMBOS AND CHA CHAS (LP) 15

PERE UBU
(see also David Thomas)
79 Chrysalis CHS 2372 — The Fabulous Sequel (Have Shoes Will Walk)/Humour Me (live)/
The Book Is On The Table (p/s) 8
80 Rough Trade RT 049 — Final Solution/My Dark Ages (p/s) 8

			MINT VALUE £
81	Rough Trade RT 066	Not Happy/Lonesome Cowboy Dave (p/s)	8
78	Radar RDR 1	DATAPANIK IN THE YEAR ZERO (12" EP)	15
78	Blank BLANK 001	THE MODERN DANCE (LP)	30
78	Rough Trade ROUGHUS 14	DUB HOUSING (LP)	20
79	Rough Trade ROUGHUS 20	NEW PICNIC TIME (LP)	15
80	Rough Trade ROUGH 14	THE ART OF WALKING (LP, original with "Miles" & "Arabia")	18
81	Rough Trade ROUGH 23	390° OF SIMULATED STEREO - UBU LIVE: VOLUME 1 (LP)	15
81	Rough Trade ROUGH 22	THE MODERN DANCE (LP, reissue)	20
85	Rough Trade ROUGH 83	TERMINAL TOWER (LP, gatefold sleeve)	12

CHRISTINE PERFECT

(see also Christine McVie, Fleetwood Mac, Illusive Dream, Chicken Shack, Rick Hayward)

69	Blue Horizon 57-3165	When You Say/No Road Is The Right Road	30
70	Blue Horizon 57-3172	I'm Too Far Gone (To Turn Around)/Close To Me	30
70	Blue Horizon 7-63860	CHRISTINE PERFECT (LP)	90

PERFECT DISASTER

87	Glass GLALP 027	PERFECT DISASTER (LP)	30

PERFECT END

81	Hellfire HELL 1	Sweet Dreams/Natural Causes/Puppets	15

PERFECT PEOPLE

69	MCA MU 1079	House In The Country/Polyanna	12

PERFECTORS

80	Active ACT 4	YT50295ID/Tiny Radios (p/s)	100

PERFORMANCE

73	Polydor 2058 324	Funny Little Things/Rejoice	6

PERFORMERS

69	Action ACT 4552	I Can't Stop You/L.A. Stomp	20

EMILIO PERICOLI

62	Warner Brothers WB 69	Al Di La/GINA PAOLI: Sassi	6
63	Warner Bros. WM 8125	THE GOLDEN HITS OF ITALY (LP)	12

PERISHERS

(see also Seftones)

68	Fontana TF 965	How Does It Feel/Bye Bye Baby	45

CARL PERKINS

(see also N.R.B.Q.)

78s

56	London HLU 8271	Blue Suede Shoes/Honey Don't	30
57	London HLS 8408	Matchbox/Your True Love	55
57	London HLS 8527	Glad All Over/Forever Yours	60
58	London HLS 8608	Lend Me Your Comb/That's Right	60
59	Philips PB 983	I Don't See Me In Your Eyes Anymore/One Ticket To Loneliness	80

SINGLES

56	London HLU 8271	Blue Suede Shoes/Honey Don't	250
57	London HLS 8408	Matchbox/Your True Love	200
57	London HLS 8527	Glad All Over/Forever Yours	100
58	London HLS 8608	Lend Me Your Comb/That's Right	100
59	Philips PB 983	I Don't See Me In Your Eyes Anymore/One Ticket To Loneliness	20
61	Philips PB 1179	Anyway The Wind Blows/The Unhappy Girls	15
64	Brunswick 05905	Help Me Find My Baby/I Wouldn't Have You	15
64	Brunswick 05909	Big Bad Blues/Lonely Heart (with Nashville Teens)	15
64	Brunswick 05923	The Monkey Shine/Let My Baby Be	15
67	Stateside SS 599	A Country Boy's Dream/If I Could Come Back	15
68	London HLP 7125	A Country Boy's Dream/Shine Shine Shine (export issue)	15
68	Spark SRL 1009	Lake County, Cotton Country/It's You	10
68	London HLS 10192	Blue Suede Shoes/Matchbox	10
69	CBS 3932	Restless/11.43	10
70	CBS 4991	All Mama's Children/Step Aside (with N.R.B.Q.)	6

LPs

59	London HA-S 2202	THE DANCE ALBUM OF CARL PERKINS (plum label, flipback sleeve)	150
59	London HA-S 2202	THE DANCE ALBUM OF CARL PERKINS (plum label, non-flipback sleeve)	60
66	Ember NR 5038	SUNSTROKE (shared with Jerry Lee Lewis)	20
66	CBS Realm 52305	WHOLE LOTTA CARL PERKINS (original pressing with boxed square logo)	50
66	CBS Realm 52305	WHOLE LOTTA CARL PERKINS	30
68	CBS 63309	KING OF ROCK	20
68	London HA-P/SH-P 8366	COUNTRY BOY'S DREAM	25
69	CBS 63676	CARL PERKINS' GREATEST HITS	15
70	CBS 63826	BOPPIN' THE BLUES (with N.R.B.Q.)	15
82	Sun BOX 101	THE SUN YEARS (3-LP, box set with booklet)	20

JOE PERKINS

63	London HLU 9794	Little Eeefin Annie/Encle Eeef	5
72	Mojo 2092 047	Wrapped Up In Your Love/Looking For A Woman	8

LASCELLES PERKINS

(see also Tommy McCook)

61	Blue Beat BB 41	Creation/Lonely Robin	12
63	Island WI 038	Tango Lips (with Yvonne)/DENNIS SINDREY: Rub Up (B-side actually plays "Jamaica's Song")	25
64	R&B JB 175	I Am So Grateful/When I Survey	20
70	Escort ES 814	Please Stay/MATADORS: Voyage From The Moon	25
71	Banana BA 317	Tell It All Brothers/SOUND DIMENSION: Polkadots	18

POLLY PERKINS

(see also Academy)

63	Decca F 11583	I Reckon You (as Polly Perkins & Bill)/The Girls Are At It Again	10

MINT VALUE £

63	Oriole CB 1869	Sweet As Honey/I've Gotta Tell You	10
63	Oriole CB 1929	Young Lover/You Too Can Be A Beatle	10
63	Oriole CB 1979	Faling In Love Again/I Went By Your House Today	10
73	Chapter One CMS 1018	LIBERATED WOMAN (LP)	25
77	Greasepaint GP3/6575/SMB	POLLY (LP)	12

TONY PERKINS

57	RCA RCA 1018	Moonlight Swim/First Romance	12

KATIE PERKS

83	Plastichead PLAS 001	Small/Cold Stone (p/s)	8

PERMANENTS

63	London HLU 9803	Oh Dear, What Can The Matter Be/Let Me Be Baby	12

JEAN-JACQUES PERREY

72	Vanguard VAN 1005	Gossipo Perpetuo/Moog Indigo	10
73	Vanguard VAN 1008	Minuet Of The Robots/Porcupine Rock	10
71	Vanguard VSD 6525	KALEIDOSCOPIC VIBRATIONS - SPOTLIGHT ON THE MOOG (LP, 'kaleidoscope' sleeve, with Gershon Kingsley)	18
72	Vanguard VSD 6549	MOOG INDIGO (LP, title sleeve)	25
73	Vanguard VSD 79222	THE IN SOUND FROM WAY OUT! (LP, green/black 'starburst' sleeve, with Gershon Kingsley)	20
73	Vanguard VSD 79286	THE AMAZING NEW ELECTRONIC POP SOUND OF? (LP)	15
74	Vanguard DPS 2051	THE BEST OF THE MOOG (2-LP)	18

PAT PERRIN

68	Island WI 3115	Over You/LLOYD TERRELL: Lost Without You	25

PERRI'S

59	Oriole CB 1481	Jerri-Lee/Ballad Of A Happy Heart	15
59	Oriole CB 1481	Jerri-Lee/Ballad Of A Happy Heart (78)	15

BARBARA PERRY

70	Pama PM 795	Say You Need Me/Unloved	25

JEFF PERRY

76	Arista ARIST 51	Love Don't Come No Stronger/I've Got To See You Right Away	20

KING PERRY

(see under Lee Perry)

LEE 'SCRATCH' PERRY (& UPSETTERS)

(see also Upsetters, Defenders, Roland Alphonso, Bob Marley/Wailers, King Scratch, Punchers, Roy Shirley, Pioneers, Desmond Dekker)

63	R&B JB 102	Prince In The Black/Don't Copy	50
63	R&B JB 104	Old For New/Prince And Duke	50
63	R&B JB 106	Mad Head/Man And Wife	50
63	R&B JB 135	Royalty/Can't Be Wrong	50
63	Island WI 118	Never Get Weary/TOMMY McCOOK: Below Zero	40
64	Port-O-Jam PJ 4001	Help The Weak/TOMMY McCOOK: Exodus	40
64	Port-O-Jam PJ 4003	Bad Minded People/TOMMY McCOOK & HIS GROUP: Jam Rock	40
64	Port-O-Jam PJ 4010	Chatty Chatty Woman/TOMMY McCOOK & HIS GROUP: Road Block	70
65	Island WI 210	Please Don't Go/Bye, St. Peter (both sides with Soulettes)	40
65	Island WI 223	Country Girl/Strange Country (as Upsetters; both actually by Ossie & Upsetters and so not Lee Perry or his production)	25
65	Ska Beat JB 201	Roast Duck/Hand To Hand, Man To Man	45
65	Ska Beat JB 203	Trail And Crosses/Jon Tom	50
65	Ska Beat JB 212	Wishes Of The Wicked/Hold Down	60
65	Ska Beat JB 215	Open Up/ROLAND ALPHONSO: Twin Double	50
66	Ska Beat JB 251	The Woodman/Give Me Justice	40
66	Island WI 259	Just Keep It Up/ROLAND ALPHONSO: James Bond	150
66	Island WI 292	Doctor Dick (as King Perry)/SOUL BROTHERS: Magic Star	40
66	Island WI 298	Rub And Squeeze (as King Perry & Soulettes)/SOUL BROTHERS: Here Comes The Minx	40
67	Doctor Bird DB 1073	Run For Cover/Something You've Got (as Lee 'King' Perry & Sensations)	30
67	Doctor Bird DB 1098	Whop Whop Man/Wind-Up Doll (with Dynamites)	50
68	Amalgamated AMG 808	The Upsetter/Thank You Baby	50
68	Doctor Bird DB 1146	People Funny Boy/BURT WALTERS: Blowing In The Wind	35
68	Trojan TR 644	Uncle Desmond/Bronco (with Upsetters)	20
69	Upsetter US 303	People Funny Fi True/UPSETTERS: Ten To Twelve	20
69	Upsetter US 324	Yakety Yak/Tackio (with Upsetters)	20
70	Upsetter US 325	Kill Them All/Soul Walk (with Upsetters)	20
71	Bullet BU 461	All Combine Pts 1& 2 (as Lee Perry & Upsetters)	12
72	Upsetter US 385	French Connection (with Upsetters)/UPSETTERS: Version	15
72	Upsetter US 389	Back Biter (with Dennis Alcapone)/UPSETTERS: Version	15
73	Upsetter US 397	Jungle Lion/Freakout Skank	22
73	Upsetter US 398	Cow Thief Skank (actually by Lee Perry & Charlie Ace)/ Seven And Three Quarters Skank	18
73	Bread BR 1111	Station Underground/CARLTON & SHOES: Better Days	25
73	Downtown DT 513	Bucky Skank/Mid East Rock	25
73	Jackpot JP 812	Justice To The People/UPSETTERS: Version	20
74	Dip DL 5037	Dub A Pum Pum (with Silvertones)/Version	8
74	Dip DL 5060	Dreader Locks (& Junior Byles)/Militant Rock	8
76	Island WIP 6370	Dreadlocks In Moonlight/Cut Throat	6
79	Black Art BH 001	Reggae Music (actually by Hugo Blackwood)/DOC ALIMANTADO: Rastaman Train (12")	35
73	Rhino SNRO 8002	CLOAK & DAGGER (LP, as Scratch The Upsetter)	70
75	Cactus CTLP 112	REVOLUTION DUB (LP)	50
75	DIP DLPD 6002	KUNG FU MEETS THE DRAGON (LP, as The Mighty Upsetter)	50
70s	Jet Star PTLP 1023	THE BEST OF (LP)	30
85	Trojan PERRY 1	UPSETTER BOX SET (3-LP)	30

MINT VALUE £

MAL PERRY

58	Fontana H 133	That's When Your Heartaches Begin/Make Me A Miracle	8
58	Fontana H 149	Too Young To Love/Who Are They To Say	8
58	Fontana H 157	Things I Didn't Say/The Girl Next Door	8
59	Fontana H 172	Richer Than I/Willingly	8

MARK PERRY

(see also Alternative TV)

80	NB NB 7	You Cry Your Tears/Music Death? (with Dennis Burns, p/s in poly bag)	5
80	Deptford Fun City DFC 12	Whole World's Down On Me/I Live - He Dies (p/s)	5
80	Deptford Fun City DLP 06	SNAPPY TURNS (LP)	12

SHORT(L)Y PERRY

(see also Shorty, Cornell Campbell, Maytones, Paulette Williams)

72	Attack ATT 8043	Musical Goat/WINSTON GRENNON & J. JACKSON: Stinging Dub	8
72	Explosion EX 2067	Sprinkle Some Water/FLOWERS & ALVIN: Howdy And Tenky	7
72	Bullet BU 512	Sprinkle Some Water/FLOWERS & ALVIN: Howdy And Tenky	7
73	Bullet BU 529	Yama Skank/U ROY JUNIOR: Doctor Run Come Quick	10
73	Downtown DT 517	Dedicated To Illiteracy/G.G. ALL STARS: Illiteracy Dub	7
73	Grape GR 3052	Abusing And Assaulting (by Flowers & Alvin)/Food Control	7
73	Green Door GD 4043	President Mash Up The Resident/President Mash Up The Resident Part Two	7

STEVE PERRY

60	HMV POP 745	Step By Step/Because They're Young	20
62	Decca F 11462	Ginny Come Lately/Two Of A Kind	10
62	Decca F 11526	Young And In Love/Let It Come True	7
63	Decca F 11656	Find Me A Girl/My Dad	7
64	Decca F 11895	Crooked Little Man/Day Dreams	7

PERRY SISTERS

59	Brunswick 05802	Fabian/Willie Boy	25

PERSIAN RISK

81	SRT SRTS/81/CUS/1146	Calling For You/Chasing The Dragon (p/s)	140
83	Neat NEAT 24	Ridin' High/Hurt You (p/s)	18
86	Metal Masters METALLP 2	RISE UP (LP)	12

PERSIANS

69	Pama PM 772	I Only Have Eyes For You/The Sun Gotta Shine In Your Heart	12
72	Capitol CL 15726	Baby Come Back Home/I Want To Go Home	8

PERSIMMON'S PECULIAR SHADES

68	Major Minor MM 554	Watchmaker/Coplington	30

PERSONALITIES

65	Dice CC 30	I Remember/Suffering	15
65	Ska Beat JB 222	Hey Little Girl/Teardrops	20
66	Blue Beat BB 354	Push It Down/BUSTER'S ALL STARS: Blues Market	50

PERSONS UNKNOWN

81	Po 1	Addiction (p/s)	25

PERSUADERS!

93	Detour DR 001	Finished Forever/In The Night (p/s, 300 only)	20
94	Detour DR 011	Waiting For The Nowhere Express/Girl/The Paperchase (p/s, 100 on red vinyl)	8
94	Detour DR 011	Waiting For The Nowhere Express/Girl/The Paperchase (p/s)	5

PERSUADERS (U.S.)

72	Atlantic K 40370	THE THIN LINE BETWEEN LOVE AND HATE (LP)	20
73	Atlantic K 40476	THE PERSUADERS (LP)	15

PERSUASIONS

65	Columbia DB 7560	I'll Go Crazy/Try Me	30
65	Columbia DB 7700	Big Brother/Deep Down Love	30
66	Columbia DB 7859	La, La, La, La, La/Opportunity	30

PERSUASIONS (U.S.)

69	Minit MLF 11017	Party In The Woods/It's Better To Have Loved And Lost	20
73	MCA MUS 1222	Good Old Acappella/You Must Believe Me	7
70	Straight STS 1062	A CAPPELLA (LP)	40
72	Island ILPS 9201	STREET CORNER SYMPHONY (LP)	20

MORRIS PERT

75	Chantry ABM 21	LUMINOS/CHROMOSPHERE/4 JAPANESE VERSES (LP)	40
80	Chantry CHT 001	LUMINOS/CHROMOSPHERE/4 JAPANESE VERSES (LP, reissue)	30
82	Chantry CHT 007	BOOK OF LOVE/FRAGMENTI I/ULTIMATE DECAY (LP)	30

JON PERTWEE

(see also Rupert Hine, Derek Roy, BBC Radiophonic Workshop)o

72	Purple PUR 111	Who Is The Doctor/Pure Mystery	20
85	Safari DOCTOR 1	Who Is The Doctor/Doctor Blood Donor (p/s)	6
62	Phillips BBL 7558	SONGS FOR VULGAR BOATMEN (LP)	20
80	Decca CROW 1	WORZEL GUMMIDGE SINGS (LP)	12

PESKY GEE!

(see also Black Widow, Agony Bag)

69	Pye 7N 17708	Where Is My Mind/A Place Of Heart Break	40
69	Pye N(S)PL 18293	EXCLAMATION MARK (LP, textured sleeve)	100

PETALS

63	Decca F 11650	Let's Do The Tamoure/Look At Me	8

PETER

70	Sonet SON 2012	Peace/Values	15

PETER & ALEX

70	Carnaby 4018	Big Beat/On The Loose	7

MINT VALUE £

PETER & GORDON
(see also Gordon Waller)

65	Columbia DB 7729	Baby I'm Yours/When The Black Of Yout Eyes Turns To Grey	6
66	Columbia DB 7834	Woman/Wrong From The Start	7
66	Columbia DB 7951	Don't Pity Me/To Show I Love You	5
66	Columbia DB 8003	Lady Godiva/Morning's Calling	6
66	Columbia DB 8075	Knight In Rusty Armour/The Flower Lady	7
67	Columbia DB 8159	Sunday For Tea/Start Trying Someone Else	6
67	Columbia DB 8198	The Jokers/Red, Cream And Velvet	6
68	Columbia DB 8398	I Feel Like Going Out/The Quest For The Holy Grail	20
68	Columbia DB 8451	You've Had Better Times/Sipping My Wine	6
69	Columbia DB 8585	I Can Remember (Not Too Long Ago)/Hard Time, Rainy Day	10
64	Columbia SEG 8337	JUST FOR YOU (EP)	15
64	Columbia SEG 8348	NOBODY I KNOW (EP)	20
64	Columbia 33SX 1630	PETER AND GORDON (LP, mono)	20
64	Columbia SCX 3518	PETER AND GORDON (LP, stereo)	25
64	Columbia 33SX 1660	IN TOUCH WITH PETER AND GORDON (LP, mono)	20
64	Columbia SCN 3532	IN TOUCH WITH PETER AND GORDON (LP, stereo)	25
65	Columbia 33SX 1761	HURTIN 'N' LOVIN' (LP, mono)	20
65	Columbia SCX 3565	HURTIN 'N' LOVIN' (LP, stereo)	25
66	Columbia SX 6045	PETER AND GORDON (LP, mono)	20
66	Columbia SCX 6045	PETER AND GORDON (LP, stereo)	25
66	Columbia SX 6097	SOMEWHERE? (LP, mono)	20
66	Columbia SCX 6097	SOMEWHERE? (LP, stereo)	25
65	Columbia SCXC 25	I GO TO PIECES (LP, export issue)	30
66	Columbia SCXC 29	WOMAN (LP, export issue)	30
66	Columbia SCXC 33	LADY GODIVA (LP, export issue)	35

PETER & HEADLINES
(see also Count Downe & Zeros)

64	Decca F 11980	Don't Cry Little Girl/It Was Love	20
64	Decca F 12035	Tears And Kisses/I've Got My Reasons	20

PETER & MARY
(see also Peter Lind Hayes)

54	Columbia SCMC 6	Crazy Mix Up Song/What Shall We Do With The Lonesome Lover (export issue)	6

PETER & PAUL

66	Blue Beat BB 364	Hosana/Schoolgirl	18

PETER & PERSUADERS

65	Oak RGJ 197	The Wanderer/Wine Glass Rock/Oh My Soul/Cross My Heart (EP)	50

(see Legendary Lonnie)

PETER & TEST TUBE BABIES

81	No Future OI 4	Banned From The Pubs/Moped Lads/Peacehaven Wild Lads (p/s)	8
82	No Future OI 15	Run Like Hell/Up Yer Bum (p/s)	8
83	Trapper EARS 1	Zombie Creeping Flesh/No Invitation/Smash And Grab (p/s)	6
83	Trapper EARS 2	The Jinx/Trapper Ain't Got A Bird (p/s)	5
82	No Future Punk 3	PISSED AND PROUD (LP)	15
83	Trapper THIN 1	MATING SOUNDS OF SOUTH AMERICAN FROGS (LP, with lyric inner)	15

PETER & WOLVES
(see also Factory, Norman Conquest, John Pantry, Sounds Around, Bunch)

67	MGM MGM 1352	Little Girl Lost And Found/Is Me	35
68	MGM MGM 1374	Lanternlight/Break Up-Break Down	30
68	MGM MGM 1397	Julie/Birthday	20
68	MGM MGM 1452	Woman On My Mind/Old & The New	35
70	UPC UPC 104	Something In The Way She Moves/The Lady And Me	10

PETER B's
(see also Tony Colton, Peter Bardens, Peter Green, Cheynes, Shotgun Express)

66	Columbia DB 7862	If You Wanna Be Happy/Jodrell Blues	70

PETER, PAUL & MARY
see also Mary Travers

63	Warner Bros WB 95	Puff/Pretty Mary	6
63	Warner Bros WB 104	Blowing In The Wind/Flora	5
64	Warner Bros WB 142	The Times They Are A-Changin'/Blue	5

PETER'S FACES
(see also Flowerpot Men, White Plains)

64	Piccadilly 7N 35178	Why Did You Bring Him To The Dance/She's In Love	10
64	Piccadilly 7N 35196	Try A Little Love My Friend/I Don't Care	10
64	Piccadilly 7N 35205	Just Like Romeo And Juliet/Wait	25
65	Piccadilly 7N 35225	De-Boom-Lay-Boom/Suzie Q	10

JANICE PETERS & PLAYBOYS

58	Columbia DB 4222	This Little Girl's Gone Rockin'/Kiss Cha Cha	40
58	Columbia DB 4222	This Little Girl's Gone Rockin'/Kiss Cha Cha (78)	20
59	Columbia DB 4276	A Girl Likes/You're The One	35
59	Columbia DB 4276	A Girl Likes/You're The One (78)	25

JO PETERS

61	Pye 7N 15350	I Love The Long Light Evenings/I May Be Wrong	6
62	Pye 7N 15413	When Opportunity Knocks/Never Cheat Your Sweetheart	7

JOHNNY PETERS

65	Decca F 12172	When You Ask About Love/People Say	25

LENNIE PETERS

63	Oriole CB 1887	And My Heart Cried/For A Lifetime	7
64	Oriole CB 1956	Let The Tears Begin/Love Me, Love Me (Love Me, Love Me)	7

MINT VALUE £

LINDA PETERS

(see also Paul McNeill & Linda Peters, Richard & Linda Thompson)

70 Warlock Music WMM 101/2 WARLOCK MUSIC SAMPLER (LP, sampler, 7 tracks by Elton John) 1000

MARK PETERS & SILHOUETTES

(see also Rats)

63 Oriole CB 1836 Fragile (Handle With Care)/Janie 40
64 Oriole CB 1909 Cindy's Gonna Cry/Show Her 40
64 Piccadilly 7N 35207 Don't Cry For Me/I Told You So 15

PETER'S PRIVATE ARMY

83 Spartan SP 9 The Gaol Song (Hip For The Day)/Bounce Back 6

SCOTT PETERS

61 Pye 7N 15343 Kookie Talk/Game Of Love 7
61 Pye 7N 15363 Bobbie Allen/It's The Natural Thing To Do 6
61 Columbia DB 8244 Go Tell The World/More And More 6

WENDY PETERS

68 Saga OPP 1 Morning Dew/I Don't Understand 18

CLIVE PETERSEN

61 Columbia DB 4687 For Every Boy/If No One Tells You 15

PAUL PETERSEN

62 Pye International 7N 25153 Keep Your Love Locked/Be Everything To Anyone You Love 7
62 Pye International 7N 25163 Lollipops And Roses/Please Mr Sun 10
63 Pye International 7N 25173 My Dad/Little Boy Sad 10
63 Pye International 7N 25196 Amy/Goody Goody 8
68 Tamla Motown TMG 670 A Little Bit For Sandy/Your Love's Got Me Burnin' Alive 30

PAUL PETERSEN & SHELLEY FABARES

(see also Shelley Fabares)

62 Pye International 7N 25133 She Can't Find Her Keys/Very Unlikely 10

BOBBY PETERSON (QUINTET)

59 Top Rank JAR 232 The Hunch/Love You Pretty Baby (as Bobby Peterson Quintet) 15
64 Sue WI 342 Rockin' Charlie (Parts 1 & 2) (solo) 30
65 Sue WI 346 Piano Rock/One Day (solo) 30

OSCAR PETERSON

(see also Louis Armstrong, Lester Young, Ella Fitzgerald, Sonny Stitt)

55 Columbia 33C 1037 PLAYS PRETTY (10" LP) 20
55 Columbia Clef 33C 9012 PLAYS PRETTY (10" LP, reissue) 15
55 Columbia 33C 1038 THE OSCAR PETERSON QUARTET (10" LP) 15
55 Columbia 33C 1039 OSCAR PETERSON SINGS (10") 15
55 Columbia Clef 33CX 10012 PLAYS DUKE ELLINGTON (LP) 15
55 Columbia Clef 33CX 10016 PLAYS COLE PORTER (LP) 12
55 Columbia Clef 33CX 10028 PLAYS RICHARD RODGERS (LP) 12
55 Columbia Clef 33CX 10039 PLAYS COUNT BASIE (LP) 12
56 Columbia Clef 33C 9025 OH LADY BE GOOD (10" LP) 15
56 HMV CLP 1086 IN ROMANTIC MOOD (LP) 12

RAY PETERSON

59 RCA RCA 1131 The Wonder Of You/I'm Gone 12
59 RCA RCA 1131 The Wonder Of You/I'm Gone (78) 20
59 RCA RCA 1154 Shirley Purley/Come And Get It 20
59 RCA RCA 1154 Shirley Purley/Come And Get It (78) 20
60 RCA RCA 1175 Answer Me/Goodnight My Love, Pleasant Dreams 15
60 RCA RCA 1195 Tell Laura I Love Her/Wedding Day 10
60 London HLX 9246 Corrine, Corrina/Be My Girl 10
61 London HLX 9332 Sweet Little Kathy/You Didn't Care 10
61 London HLX 9379 Missing You/You Thrill Me 10
62 London HLX 9489 I Could Have Loved You So Well/Why Don't You Write Me 15
62 London HLX 9569 You Didn't Care/You Know Me Much Too Well 10
63 London HLX 9746 Without Love/Give Us Your Blessing 10
64 MGM MGM 1249 Oh No/If You Were Here 5
64 MGM MGM 1258 Across The Street/When I Stop Dreaming 5
65 MGM MGM 1273 House Without Windows/Wish I Could Say No To You 5
65 MGM MGM 1288 I'm Only Human/One Lonesome Rose 7
66 MGM MGM 1303 Everybody/Love Hurts 5
61 London REX 1293 CORRINE CORRINA (EP) 40

PETER, SUE & MARC & PFURI, GORPS & KNIRL

79 EMI EMI 2940 Second Hand Company/Troedler & Co. 6

PETEY, PATTY, PEGGY & BRUCE

59 Top Rank JAR 250 The Happy Penguins/IRVING KRASE ORCHESTRA: The Happy Penguin Waltz 5

PET HATE

(see also Silverwing)

83 FM 12VHF 2 Roll Away The Stone/Caught/Playing With My Heart (12", p/s) 12
84 Heavy Metal HMRLP 23W BAD PUBLICITY (LP, white vinyl) 12

PETITES

60 Philips PB 1035 Get Your Daddy's Car Tonight/Sun Showers 10

PETR & PAVEL

68 Page One POF 112 Laska/Wencelas Square 6

PETS

(see also Seph Acre & Pets)

58 London HL 8652 Cha-Hua-Hua/Cha-Kow-Ski 25
58 London HL 8652 Cha-Hua-Hua/Cha-Kow-Ski (78) 20
59 Pye International 7N 25004 (You Wandered) Beyond The Sea/Wow-ee!!! 10
59 Pye International 7N 25004 (You Wandered) Beyond The Sea/Wow-ee!!! (78) 10

MINT VALUE £

PET SHOP BOYS

(see also Eighth Wonder, Dusty Springfield, Absolutely Fabulous, Electronic, Liza Minnelli, Ian Wright)

SINGLES

84	Epic A 4292	West End Girls/Pet Shop Boys (p/s)	20
84	Epic TA 4292	West End Girls (Extended)/Pet Shop Boys (12", p/s)	30
85	Parlophone R 6097	Opportunities (Let's Make Lots of Money)/In The Night (matrix: A-3-1-2) (1st mix, white p/s)	12
85	Parlophone 12R 6097	Opportunities (Let's Make Lots of Money) (Dance Mix)/In The Night (Extended) (12", white p/s)	20
85	Parlophone 12RA 6097	Opportunities (Let's Make Lots of Money) (Version Latina)/(Dub For Money Remix)/In The Night (Extended Mix) (12", large picture labels, die-cut p/s)	40
85	Parlophone 12R 6097	Opportunities (Let's Make Lots of Money) (Dance Mix)/ In The Night (Extended) (12", p/s, mispressing, B-side plays "Opportunities [Dub For Money] Remix")	30
85	Parlophone 12R 6097	Opportunities (Let's Make Lots of Money) (Dance Mix)/ In The Night (Extended) (12", p/s, 2nd mispressing, A-side plays "Opportunities [Version Latina]")	30
85	Parlophone 10R 6115	West End Girls (Untitled Mix)/A Man Could Get Arrested (4.09 Mix)/ West End Girls (7" Mix) (10", round foldout p/s; sealed with sticker)	60
85	Parlophone 12R 6115	West End Girls (Dance Mix)/A Man Could Get Arrested (4.09 Mix)/ West End Girls (7" Mix) (12", with 6" die-cut holes in p/s, 6" picture labels)	8
86	Parlophone 12RA 6115	West End Girls (Shep Pettibone Mastermix)/West End Dub/ A Man Could Get Arrested (4.09 Mix) (12", black/blue/red p/s, standard labels)	10
86	Parlophone 12RA 6115	West End Girls (Shep Pettibone Mastermix)/West End Dub/ A Man Could Get Arrested (4.09 Mix) (12", same as above with 6" yellow circle on sleeve)	10
86	Parlophone 12RA 6115	West End Girls (Shep Pettibone Mastermix)/West End Dub/A Man Could Get Arrested (4.09 Mix) (12", stickered black/blue/red p/s with 6" die-cut hole & 6" yellow picture labels)	10
86	Parlophone 10R 6116	Love Comes Quickly (Dance Mix)/That's My Impression (Disco Mix) (10", PVC sleeve with poster)	60
86	Parlophone 12R 6116	Love Comes Quickly (Dance Mix)/That's My Impression (Disco Mix) (12", large picture labels, die-cut white sleeve)	10
86	Parlophone RD 6140	Suburbia/Paninaro/Love Comes Quickly (Shep Pettibone Remix)/ Jack The Lad/Suburbia Part Two (double pack, gatefold p/s)	6
87	Parlophone 12RX 6158	It's A Sin (Ian Levine Remix)/You Know Where You Went Wrong (Rough Mix) (12", 'video still' p/s)	8
87	Parlophone 12RX 6171	Always On My Mind (Phil Harding Remix)/Do I Have To?/ Always On My Mind (Dub) (12", title sleeve)	8
88	Parlophone CDR 6177	Heart (Disco Mix)/I Get Excited (You Get Excited Too)/Heart (Dance Mix)	8
88	Parlophone 12RX 6190	Domino Dancing (Remix)/Don Juan (Demo)/Domino Dancing (Demo) (12", 'hotel' p/s)	8
89	Parlophone 10R 6220	It's Alright (Alternative Mix)/It's Alright (Extended Dance Mix) (10", black title sleeve with poster)	8
89	Parlophone 12RS 6220	It's Alright (Extended)/One Of The Crowd/Your Funny Uncle (12", p/s, with obi)	8
93	Parlophone R 6348	Can You Forgive Her? (7" Version)/Hey Headmaster (red or blue vinyl, factory custom pressing, p/s)	600
96	Parlophone 12RX 6431	Before (Underground Mix)/(Bonus Dub)/(Underground Instrumental)/ (Bonus Beats)/(Classic Paradise Mix)/(Afrodisiac Mix)/(Hedboys Mix)/ (Hedboys Dub)/(Joey Negro Extended Mix) (3 x 12", each in p/s, boxed set)	8
96	Parlophone 12RD 6443	Se A Vida É (That's The Way Life Is) (Mark's Deep And Dark Vocal)/ (Mark's Deep And Dark Instrumental)/(Mark's Shelter Dub)/ (Deep Dish Liquid Remix)/(Pink Noise Mix)/(Deep Dish Dub)/(7" Version) (12" double pack, yellow & green vinyl, p/s 2 inner sleeves)	8
97	Parlophone Fan Club	It Doesn't Often Snow At Christmas (CD, fan club issue, in sealed silver bubble wrap)	125
06	Parlophone R6690	I'm With Stupid/Girls Don't Cry (picture disc, p/s)	5
06	Parlophone R6708	Minimal/In Private (clear vinyl, p/s)	5
06	Parlophone R6723	Numb/Party Song (p/s)	5
10	Parlophone R 6810	Love Life/A Powerful Friend (jukebox centre, blue Parlophone sleeve, 1000 only)	15

ALBUMS

87	Parlophone PCSDX 104	ACTUALLY (LP, with U.S. import "Always On My Mind" 12", stickered sleeve)	12
87	Parlophone CDPCSDX 104	ACTUALLY (CD, with U.S. import "Always On My Mind" CD single)	25
88	Parlophone PCSX 7325	INTROSPECTIVE (LP, 3 x clear vinyl 12" factory custom pressing, with wraparound paper strip, 10 copies only)	800
88	Parlophone PCSX 7325	INTROSPECTIVE (LP, 3 x black vinyl 12", with picture labels & wraparound paper obi strip)	15
93	Parlophone CDPSDX 143	VERY (CD, with 6-track bonus CD "Relentless" in foldout 'bubble' wallet)	25
96	ParlophonePCSD 170	BILINGUAL (LP)	15
00	Parlophone 724352185719	NIGHTLIFE (LP)	15
02	Parlophone 538150-1	RELEASE (LP, white vinyl)	12
09	Vinyl Factory	YES (11 x 12" in smoked perspex box with gold-plated 'tick' on cover, with art print, signed and numbered by both band members, 300 only)	500
02	Parlophone 0 724358146	DISCO 3 (3-LP)	25

PROMOS

85	Parlophone R 12R 6097	Opportunities (Let's Make Lots of Money)/In The Night (12", "photocopy" sl.)	30
86	Parlophone R 6116	Love Comes Quickly (1-sided, p/s)	40
86	Parlophone 12R 6129	Opportunities (Let's Make Lots of Money) (7.18 Shep Pettibone Mastermix)/ Opportunities (4.27 Reprise)/Opportunities (6.44 Original Dance Mix)/ Was That What It Was (12", autographed black die-cut sleeve, with press release)	35
86	Parlophone 12R 6129	Opportunities (Let's Make Lots of Money) (7.18 Shep Pettibone Mastermix)/ Opportunities (4.27 Reprise)/Opportunities (6.44 Original Dance Mix)/ Was That What It Was (12", autographed black die-cut sleeve, without press release)	35
86	Parlophone 12R 6140	Suburbia (The Full Horror)/Paninaro/Jack The Lad (12", blank red labels)	8
88	Parlophone 12RDJ 6198	Left To My Own Devices (The Disco Mix)/Left To My Own Devices/ The Sound Of The Atom Splitting (12", unique title sleeve)	12
90	Parlophone 12RXDJ 6275	Being Boring (Remix)/We All Feel Better In The Dark (After Hours Climax)/ We All Feel Better In The Dark (Ambient) (12", black die-cut sleeve)	8

			MINT VALUE £
91	Parlophone 12R 6283A	Lose My Mind (Disco Version) (12", 1-sided)	8
91	Parlophone 12RDJ 6301A	D.J. Culture (12", 1-sided)	8
91	Parlophone MFB 1	Music For Boys (12", 3 untitled mixes, hand-stamped white label)	25
91	Parlophone 12MFBX 1	Music For Boys (12", 2 untitled mixes, white label)	12
92	Parlophone CDRX 6332	Go West (7" Version)/West End Girls (Sacha Mix)/Forever/Go West (Extended Dance Mix) (cassette, title sleeve)	150
93	Parlophone 12RXDJ 6348	Can You Forgive Her? (MK Remix)/(MK Bicycle Dub)/I Want To Wake Up (Johnny Marr 1993 Remix)/(Johnny Marr Groove Mix) (12")	10
93	Abbey Road	COMPILED EP (CD-R, Abbey Road title sleeve; autographed by The Boys, 20 only)	800
94	Parlophone 12RDJ 6386	Yesterday When I Was Mad (Jam & Spoon Mix)/ (Junior Vasquez Factory Dub)/ (Junior Vasquez Fabulous Dub)/ (Junior Vasquez Body Dub)/(Coconut 12" Mix)/(RAF Zone Mix)/ (RAF Dub Zone)/Euroboy/Some Speculation (12", double pack unique p/s)	15
96	Parlophone 12RDJD 6431	Before (Classic Paradise Mix)/(Afrodisiac Mix)/(Hedboys Mix)/ (Dub)/(Extended Mix) (2 x 12", blue 'penis' p/s)	25
96	Parlophone 12RJD 6431	Before (Underground Mix)/(Bonus Dub)/(Underground Instrumental)/ (Bonus Beats) (12", red 'penis' p/s)	25
96	Parlophone CDIN 103	BILINGUAL THE INTERVIEW (CD)	20
97	Parlophone 12 BARDJ 2	The Truck Driver & His Mate/Before (Love To Infinity Classic Paradise Mix) (12", 'two knobs' p/s, 150 copies)	150
97	Parlophone 12RDJ 6460	A Red Letter Day (Trouser Enthusiasts Autoerotic Decapitation Mix)/ (Trouser Enthusiasts Congo Dongo Dubstramental) (12")	10
97	Parlophone 12BOYDJ 101	The Boy Who Couldn't Keep His Clothes On (Main Vocal)/ (INT... Club Mix)/(Banji Girlfriend Beats)/(On Stage At Twilo)/ (Radio Edit) (12", die-cut sleeve)	60
97	Parlophone 12RDJD 6470	Somewhere (Forthright Club Mix)/(Trouser Enthusiasts Mix)/ To Step Aside (Brutal Bill Mix)/Somewhere (Forthright Dub)/ To Step Aside (Ralphi's Old School Dub)/To Step Aside (Davidson Ospina Dub) (12" double pack, title p/s)	8
97	PSB 97	PET SHOP BOYS TALK (interview CD, promo-only)	15
99	Parlophone (no cat. no.)	NIGHTLIFE (10" x 10" box in PVC slip case, contains interview CD, music CD, book, EPK & 3 photographs)	50
01	10th Planet/PSBP/RUG	FIVE TITLES FROM CLOSER TO HEAVEN: Positive Role Model/ Friendly Fire/ Shameless/K-Hole/For All Of Us (CD-R, title sleeve, all sung by Neil Tennant)	150
03	Parlophone 12RDJ 6620	Miracles (Extended Version) (12", 1-sided white label test pressing)	8
03	Parlophone 12RDJX 6620	Miracles (Lemon Jelly Remix) (12", 1-sided white label test pressing)	8
03	Parlophone CDRDJ 6020	Miracles (CD 1- track in "lavender scented" p/s	8
03	Parlophone LONDON 001	London/(Remix) (12", white label)	8
06	Parlophone FUNDA001	Fundamentalism Part 1 (12", promo)	15
06	Parlophone FUNDA002	Fundamentalism Part 2 (12", promo)	15
06	Parlophone PSB002	Psychological (1-sided 12" promo, no Pet Shop Boys credit on label)	25
06	Parlophone REMIXES01	Psychological (Ewan Pearson Mixes) (12" promo)	25
06	Parlophone 0094636497921	I'm With Stupid Remixes (CD, 6-track promo, card p/s)	25
06	Parlophone STUPID002	I'm With Stupid Remixes 1 (12" promo)	15
06	Parlophone STUPID001	I'm With Stupid Remixes 2 (12" promo)	15
06	Parlophone STUPID003	I'm With Stupid Remixes 3 (12" promo)	15
06	Parlophone 0094637114421	Minimal Remixes (CD, 10-track, promo card p/s)	25
06	Parlophone NUMB01	Numb (CD, 2-track, promo p/s)	10
06	Parlophone PRIVATE001	In Private (Tomcraft Mixes (12" promo)	20
07	Parlophone INTEGRAL001	(CD, 2-track promo, card p/s)	15
88	Parlophone (no cat. no.)	INTROSPECTIVE (cassette, video-style case, with lyric booklet)	60
89	Parlophone CDPCSD 113	BEHAVIOUR (CD, commercial issue, different inlay, in white monogrammed pouch, with full-album cassette & chronology)	50
91	Parlophone CDPSBDJ 1	DISCOGRAPHY (CD, with Mark Goodyear spoken-word introductions)	12
93	Parlophone DF 118	RELENTLESS (3 x 12", on pink/yellow/blue vinyl)	30
96	Parlophone BILING 1	BILINGUAL (A4 yellow box set, including "A Taste Of Bilingual" CD: (Discoteca/Electricity/A Red Letter Day/It Always Comes As A Surprise/ Se A Vida E) (with 2 photos & inset in transparent PVC box)	50
96	Parlophone PSBCDDJ 1	BILINGUAL (A4 pale blue launch party promo box set including "A Taste Of Bilingual" CD [Before/Se A Vida É], & album cassette, unique inlay)	200
99	Parlophone CDIN 126	INTERVIEW (CD, slipcase, for NIGHTLIFE album)	15
01	Parlophone PSB 001	SAMPLER (CD, 13-track sampler, includes six unreleased versions, part-laminated card sleeve)	15
01	Really Useful Group	CLOSER TO HEAVEN (CD-R, title sleeve; 19 tracks, all sung by Neil Tennant)	250
02	Parlophone RELEASE 01	RELEASE (CD, white card sleeve sealed with title sticker)	15
02	Parlophone RELEASE02	RE: RELEASE (CD, interview, sitkcered card sleeve)	15
03	Parlophone POPART 02	THE INTERVIEW (interview CD for 'PopArt', with cue sheet)	15
06	Parlophone 009463661421	FUNDAMENTAL INTERVIEW (CD, p/s with cues)	15
07	Parlophone DISCO004	DISCO 4 ALBUM SAMPLER (12" 4-tracks)	20
07	Parlophone (no cat. No.)	DISCO FOUR (promo CD-R, 5-track album sampler and press sheet, 30 copies)	40

MARY PETTI

61	RCA RCA 1239	Hey! Lawdy Lawdy/Gee, But It Hurts	50

FRANK PETTY TRIO

53	MGM SP 1010	St. Louis Blues (Boogie Woogie)/Somebody Stole My Girl	20
53	MGM SP 1033	Side By Side/Who's Sorry Now	7
53	MGM SP 1038	Sugar/Sioux City Sue	7
53	MGM SP 1053	Sweet Jenny Lee/Yes Sir That's My Baby	6
54	MGM SP 1092	Loch Lomond/Pino Pantaloni	6
54	MGM SP 1112	Mr Pogo/Sunday	6

MINT VALUE £

NORMAN PETTY TRIO

54	HMV 7M 274	Mood Indigo/Petty's Little Polka	10

TOM PETTY (& HEARTBREAKERS)

(see also Stevie Nicks, Randy Newman, Traveling Wilburys, k.d. lang & Roy Orbison)

77	Shelter WIP 6377	American Girl/Wild One Forever (some in p/s)	5
77	Shleter WIP 12-6396	Anything That's Rock'n'Roll/Fooled Again (I Don't Like It) (live) (12")	8
77	Shelter WIP 12-6403	American Girl/Luna (live) (12")	8
76	Shelter 1DJ 24A	OFFICIAL LIVE BOOTLEG (LP, with Heartbreakers, 1-sided 5-track, promo only)	20

P.F.M.

73	Manticore ANTI 2003	PHOTOS OF GHOSTS (LP, gatefold sleeve)	25
74	Manticore K 53502	THE WORLD BECAME THE WORLD (LP)	20
74	Manticore K 53506	COOK (LP)	15
76	Manticore K 53508	CHOCOLATE KINGS (LP, gatefold sleeve with lyric sheet)	12

PHANTOM

(see also Tom Robinson, Blazing Sons)

78	Cool Ghoul COOL 1	Lazy Fascist/Power Dub	6

PHANTOM BAND

71	Polydor 2058-176	Loop-Di-Love/Funkin' About	30
72	Polydor 2058-290	Silhouettes/Drummitt	15

PHANTOM CHORDS

(see also Damned)

92	Camden Town GNAR 003	Town Without Pity/She's A Bad Motorcycle (p/s, 2,000 only)	5

PHANTOMS

61	Palette PG 9014	Phantom Guitar/Cachina	20
60s	Arc ARC	GREAT GUITAR HITS (LP)	30

PHARAOHS

58	Decca DFE 6522	THE PHARAOHS (EP)	1000
86	Ace SW 116	THE PHARAOHS (EP, reissue)	8

RORY PHARE

(see also Roy Harper)

88	Parlophone RP 1	Laughing Inside/Laughing Inside (actually by Roy Harper; p/s, promo only)	7

PHASE 4

66	Decca F 12327	What Do You Say About That/Think I'll Sit Down And Cry (1st issue)	25
66	Fab FAB 1	What Do You Say About That/I'm Gonna Sit Down And Cry (2nd issue)	20
67	Fab FAB 6	Man Am I Worried?/Listen To The Blues	50

PHASE 5

70	Polydor 2058 063	Star Trek/Enterprise	40

JAMES PHELPS

72	Paramount PARA 3019	Check Yourself/My Lover's Prayer	12

PHENOMENA

(see also Trapeze, Whitesnake, Cozy Powell, Black Sabbath, Thin Lizzy, Budgie, A-Ha)

85	Bronze BRO 193	Dance With The Devil/Hell On Wings (p/s)	7
85	Bronze BROX 193	Dance With The Devil (MIdnight Mix)/Hell On Wings (12", p/s with poster)	10

PHEON BEAR

73	Pye 7N 45232	War Against War/87th Precinct	25

PHIL & FLINTSTONES

64	Bedrock PR 5371	Love Potion No. 9/Honey Don't (private pressing)	80

PHI LIFE CYPHER

98	Compressed Knowledge CK001	Baddest Man/Da Shinn/Rap 'N' Bullshit/Forever (12")	15
00	Jazz Fudge JFR020	Earth Rulers/Drop Bombs/Phi-Life Is Here/Instrumentals (12")	8

PHILIP & HIS FOETUS VIBRATIONS

(see also You've Got Foetus On Your Breath, Foetus Art Terrorism, Foetus Ã?ber Frisco, Foetus Under Glass, Scraping Foetus Off The Wheel)

82	Self Immol. WOMB KX 07	Tell Me, What Is The Bane Of Your Life/Mother I've Killed The Cat (p/s)	25

LOUIS PHILIPPE

86	él GPO 15	Like Nobody Do/Twangy Twangy (p/s)	6
88	él ACME 15	IVORY TOWER (LP)	20
89	el ACME 23	AN APPOINTMENT WITH VENUS (LP)	30
89	él ACME 36	YURI GAGARIN (LP)	20

NOEL PHILIPS

71	CBS 7036	Eternal Loner/Snowman	10

ANTHONY PHILLIPS

(see also Genesis)

79	Arista SPART 1085/AFLP 1	SIDES (LP, 1st 500 copies sealed with free LP "Private Parts & Pieces")	20

CONFREY PHILLIPS (TRIO)

56	Columbia SCM 5223	Love And Marriage/The Others I Like	5
57	Decca F 10835	Am I Going Out Of My Mind?/Afterglow	5
57	Decca F 10866	Shotgun Rock 'n' Roll/Hokey-Kokey Rock 'n' Roll (as Confrey Phillips Trio)	20
57	Decca F 10866	Shotgun Rock 'n' Roll/Hokey-Kokey Rock 'n' Roll (as Confrey Phillips Trio) (78)	10

EDDY/EDWIN PHILLIPS

(see also Creation, Mark Four, Spectrum)

76	Charisma CB 283	Limbo Jimbo/Change My Ways (as Eddy Phillips)	5
85	T-Mac UEZT 003	Life On Earth/(Radio Mix)/(Instrumental) (12", as Edwin Phillips)	7

MINT VALUE £

(LITTLE) ESTHER (PHILLIPS)

62	Stateside SS 140	Release Me/Don't Feel Rained On	25
63	Ember EMB S 174	Am I That Easy To Forget/I Really Don't Want To Know (as Little Esther Phillips)	15
65	Sue WI 395	The Chains/Feel Like I Wanna Cry (as Esther Philips)	40
65	Atlantic AT 4028	And I Love Him/Shangri-La	15
65	Atlantic AT 4048	Let Me Know When It's Over/I Saw Me	15
66	Atlantic AT 4077	I Could Have Told You/Just Say Goodbye	100
66	Atlantic AT 4077	I Could Have Told You/Just Say Goodbye (DJ Copy)	25
66	Ember EMBS 221	Release Me/Be Honest With Me (as Little Esther Phillips)	15
66	Atlantic 584 013	When A Woman Loves A Man/Ups And Downs	15
67	Atlantic 584 062	Someone Else Is Taking My Place/When Love Comes To The Human Race	8
67	Atlantic 584 103	And I Love Him/Shangri-La (reissue)	6
67	Atlantic 584 126	I'm Sorry/Cheater Man	15
69	Roulette RO 505	Too Late To Worry, Too Blue To Cry/I'm In The Mood For Love (Moody's Mood For Love)	8
69	Roulette RO 508	Tonight I'll Be Staying Here With You/Sweet Dreams	6
72	Atlantic K 10168	Catch Me I'm Falling/Release Me	15
72	Kudu KUS 4000	Home Is Where The Hatred Is/Til My Back Ain't Got No Bone	20
73	Kudu KUS 4002	I've Never Found A Man/Cherry Red	15
75	Kudu 925	What A Difference A Day Made/Turn Around , Look At Me	5
63	Ember CW 103	REFLECTIONS OF GREAT COUNTRY AND WESTERN STANDARDS (LP)	60
65	Atlantic ATL 5030	AND I LOVE HIM (LP)	70
67	Atlantic 587/588 010	ESTHER PHILLIPS SINGS (LP)	40
72	Kudu KUL 2	FROM A WHISPER TO A SCREAM (LP)	30
73	Kudu KUL 6	ALONE AGAIN, NATURALLY (LP)	15
75	Kudu KU 18	PERFORMANCE (LP)	15
76	Atlantic K 50521	CONFESSIN' THE BLUES (LP, gatefold sleeve)	15

FLIP PHILLIPS

56	Columbia/Clef 33C 9003	FLIP PHILLIPS QUARTET (10" LP)	12

GLENN PHILLIPS

75	Caroline C 1519	LOST AT SEA (LP)	12

GREGORY PHILLIPS

(see also Remo Four)

63	Pye 7N 15546	Angie/Please Believe Me	12
64	Pye 7N 15593	Everybody Knows/Closer To Me (with Remo Four)	8
64	Pye 7N 15633	Don't Bother Me/Make Sure That You're Mine	8
65	Immediate IM 004	Down In The Boondocks/That's The One	30

JOHN PHILLIPS

(see also Mamas & Papas)

70	Stateside SS 8046	Mississippi/April Anne	6
70	Stateside-Dunhill SSL 5027	JOHN PHILLIPS: THE WOLFKING OF L.A. (LP)	35

LESLIE PHILLIPS

59	Parlophone R 4610	The Navy Lark/The Disc	7
62	Parlophone R 4912	Jolly Old Spring/ I Must Resist Temptation	6
69	Columbia DB 8562	The Man Most Likely To/Marigold	6

MICHELLE PHILLIPS

(see also Mamas & Papas)

76	A&M AMS 7250	No Love Today/Aloha Louie	7
77	A&M AMS 7340	Victim Of Romance/Lady Of Fantasy	15
77	A&M AMLS 64651	VICTIM OF ROMANCE (LP)	30

NOEL PHILLIPS

80	Jammys JM001	Youth Man/Living In The Ghetto (12")	25

PHIL PHILLIPS & TWILIGHTS

59	Mercury AMT 1059	Sea Of Love/Juella	35
60	Mercury AMT 1072	Take This Heart/Verdi Mae	30
60	Mercury AMT 1093	Your True Love Once More/What Will I Tell My Heart	30
61	Mercury AMT 1139	I Love To Love You/No One Else But You	30

SHAWN PHILLIPS

65	Columbia DB 7611	Hey Nelly Nelly/Solitude	12
65	Columbia DB 7699	Doesn't Anybody Know My Name?/Nobody Listens	12
65	Columbia DB 7789	Little Tin Soldier/London Town	8
66	Columbia DB 7956	Summer Came/Storms	8
67	Parlophone R 5606	Stargazer/Woman Mine	80
70	A&M AMS 819	Christmas Song/Lovely Lady	6
65	Columbia 33SX 1748	I'M A LONER (LP)	140
66	Columbia S(C)X 6006	SHAWN (LP)	250
70	A&M AMLS 978	CONTRIBUTION (LP)	18
71	A&M AMLS 2006	SECOND CONTRIBUTION (LP, with insert)	18
72	A&M AMLS 64324	COLLABORATION (LP)	18
73	A&M AMLS 64363	FACES (LP)	12
74	A&M AMLH 68278	FURTHERMORE (LP)	12
77	A&M AMLH 64650	SPACED (LP, with inner sleeve)	12

SID PHILLIPS BAND

56	HMV POP 269	Farewell Blues (Rock 'N' Roll Style)/It Goes Like This	6
55	HMV DLP 1102	HORS D'OEUVRES (10" LP)	15

STU PHILLIPS

58	London HL 8673	The Champlain And St. Lawrence Line/The Priest Who Slept 100 Years	15
60	Pye International 7N 25062	Strangers When We Meet/BOB MERSEY ORCHESTRA: Song Of India	6
67	RCA RCA 1601	Angel Of Love/The Great El Tigre	5
59	Pye Intl. NEP 44001	STU PHILLIPS (EP)	12

MINT VALUE £

TEDDY PHILLIPS & HIS ORCHESTRA

54	Parlophone CMSP 4	Down Boy/Meet "Miss Pippin" (export issue)	15
54	Parlophone CMSP 12	The Old Red Barn/JIMMY BLUE CREW: The Old Shoe Cobbler (export issue)	8
54	Parlophone CMSP 28	Life Is Like A Slice Of Cake/One-Sided Love Affair (export issue)	15

WARREN PHILLIPS & THE ROCKETS

(see also Savoy Brown, Foghat)

69	Decca (S)PA 43	THE WORLD OF ROCK 'N' ROLL (LP)	15

WOOLF PHILLIPS & HIS ORCHESTRA

54	Decca F 10416	Count Your Blessings Instead Of Sheep/Your Heart, My Heart (B-side with Dennis Morley - Vocal)	6

PHILOSOPHERS

69	Pye 7N 17740	The Lovedene Girls/I Believe Forever	25

VINCE PHILPOTT & DRAGS

64	Decca F 11997	The Cramp/Eenie Meenie Miny Mo	15

PHILWIT & PEGASUS

(see also Mark Wirtz)

70	Chapter One CHR 130	And She Came - Final Thought/Pauper's Son	8
70	Chapter One CHR 131	And I Try/Pauper's Son	8
70	Chapter One CHR 137	The Elephant Song/Pseudo Phoney Mixed Up Croney	8
70	Chapter One CHSR 805	PHILWIT AND PEGASUS (LP)	40

PHOENIX

69	President PT 246	Tour De France/Time To Go	5

PHOENIX

81	Rising PR 433032	PHOENIX RISING EP (Lonely Attack/The Minstrel/Understanding/ Phoenix Rising 'Av An 'Am) (12" EP)	35

PAT PHOENIX

62	HMV POP 1030	The Rovers Chorus/Coronation Street Monologue	12

PHONES SPORTSMAN BAND

(see also Swell Maps)

81	Rather GEAR 9	I REALLY LIKE YOU (EP)	8

PHOTOGRAPHED BY LIGHTNING

86	Fierce FRIGHT 008	Sleep's Terminator/Winter Trees (foldaround p/s, hand-coloured labels)	30

PHUTURE PHANTASY

88	Low Fat Vinyl LFV 1	SLAM (12")	15

PHUTURE PRIMITIVE

93	Knifeforce KF 006	Full Metal Jacket/Twinkle (12")	30
94	Knifeforce KF 026	Lift Me Up/Infect Me (12")	15

PHYSICALS

(see also Maniacs)

78	Physical PR 001	ALL SEXED UP (EP)	6
79	Big Beat NS 58	Be Like Me/Pain In Love (p/s)	6

PIANO MAGIC

96	i IRE 1071	Wrong French/Non-Fiction/General Electric With Fairylights (12", p/s)	10
97	i IRE 2031	Wintersport/Cross Country/Angel Pie/Magic Tree/Magnetic North (12", p/s)	10
97	Wurlitzer Jukebox WJ 26	For Engineers A/For Engineers AA (p/s)	7
98	Lissy's LISS 32	Music For Rolex/MATMOS: The Soldering Social (p/s)	6
98	Debut DEBT 001SP	French Mittens/Icebreaker: Melody For Nato (p/s)	8
98	Bad Jazz BEBOP 9	Music For Annahbird/Music For Wasps/Me At 19 (p/s)	8
98	Piao! PIAO! 12	The Fun Of The Century/The Sharpest Knife In The Drawer/Industrial Cutie/ I Am The Sub-Librarian (12", p/s)	12
99	Rocket Girl RGIRL 12	There's No Need For Us To Be Alone/The Canadian Brought Us Snow (p/s)	5
00	Morr MUSIC 008	Panic Amigo - Piano Magic Remixed (12" EP)	10

PIANO RED

(see also Dr. Feelgood [U.S.])

52	HMV B 10244	Rockin' With Red/Red's Boogie (78)	18
52	HMV B 10246	Just Right Bounce/Hey, Good Lookin' (78)	18
52	HMV B 10316	Count The Days I'm Gone/Bouncin' With Red (78)	18
52	HMV JO 244	Rockin' With Red/Red's Boogie (78, export issue)	18
52	HMV JO 276	Layin' The Boogie/Baby What's Wrong (78, export issue)	18
52	HMV JO 296	My Gal Jo/Let's Have A Good Time (78, export issue)	18
53	HMV JO 334	Voo Doopee Doo/Everybody's Boogie (78, export issue)	18
53	HMV 7M 108	Rockin' With Red/Red's Boogie	150
64	RCA RCX 7138	RHYTHM AND BLUES VOL. 2 (EP)	15

PIBLOKTO

(see under Pete Brown & Piblokto)

PICA

(see also Nirvana [UK])

70	Polydor 2058 056	Take The Barriers Down/Insurance Man	10
71	Philips 6006 129	Rainbow Chaser/Ad Lib	50

PICADILLY LINE

(see also Edwards Hand)

67	CBS 2785	At The Third Stroke/How Could You Say You're Leaving Me	25
67	CBS 2958	Emily Small (The Huge World Thereof)/Gone Gone Gone	25
68	CBS 3595	Yellow Rainbow/Evenings With Corrina	30
68	CBS 3595	Yellow Rainbow/I Know, She Believes (reissue with different B-side)	25
68	CBS 3743	Evenings With Corrina/My Best Friend	20
67	CBS (S)BPG 63129	THE HUGE WORLD OF EMILY SMALL (LP, laminated front sleeve)	300
67	CBS (S)BPG 63129	THE HUGE WORLD OF EMILY SMALL (LP, laminated front sleeve, promo insert)	350

MINT VALUE £

PIC & BILL

67	Page One POF 024	All I Want Is You/It's Not You	15
67	Page One POF 037	This Is It/Nobody But My Baby	15
68	Page One POF 052	Sad World Without You/Just A Tear	15

PICARDY

68	Statside SIDE 8004	Montage/How Sweet It Is	5

PIERO PICCIONI

67	Fontana TF 898	Main Theme From 'The Tenth Victim'/Part 2 (mono)	12

BUSTER PICKENS

60s	Heritage HLP 1008	TEXAS PIANO (LP, 99 only)	60

J.B. PICKERS

71	London HLU 10334	Super Soul Sounds/KIM & DAVE: Nobody Knows	15

BOBBY (BORIS) PICKETT & CRYPT-KICKERS

62	London HLU 9597	Monster Mash/Monsters' Mash Party	10
73	London ZGU 133	MONSTER MASH (LP)	30

DAN PICKETT

60s	XX MIN 710	DAN PICKETT (EP)	15

KENNY PICKETT

(see also The Creation)

80	F Beat PRO 2	Got A Gun/Same	15

NICK PICKETT

(see also John Dummer Blues Band)

72	Warner Bros K 14156	America/Lady Luck	6
72	Warner Bros K 44172	SILVERSLEEVES (LP)	30

WILSON PICKETT

(see also Falcons)

63	Liberty LIB 10115	It's Too Late/I'm Gonna Love You	25
65	Atlantic AT 4036	In The Midnight Hour/I'm Not Tired	15
65	MGM MGM 1286	Let Me Be Your Boy/My Heart Belongs To You	50
65	MGM MGM 1286	Let Me Be Your Boy/My Heart Belongs To You (DJ copy)	100
65	Atlantic AT 4052	Don't Fight It/It's All Over	10
66	Atlantic AT 4072	634-5789/That's A Man's Way	10
66	Atlantic 584 023	99 And A Half (Won't Do)/Danger Zone	10
66	Atlantic 584 039	Land Of 1000 Dances/You're So Fine	10
66	Atlantic 584 066	Mustang Sally/Three Time Loser	10
67	Atlantic 584 101	Everybody Needs Somebody To Love/Nothing You Can Do	10
67	Atlantic 584 107	New Orleans/Soul Dance III	10
67	London HLU 10146	Billy The Kid/I Don't Want No Part-Time Love (with Falcons)	18
67	Atlantic 584 130	Funky Broadway/I'm Sorry About That	8
67	Atlantic 584 142	Stag-O-Lee/I'm In Love	8
68	Atlantic 584 150	In The Midnight Hour/Danger Zone	6
68	Atlantic 584 173	That Kind Of Love/I've Come A Long Way	8
68	Atlantic 584 183	She's Looking Good/We've Got To Have Love	8
68	Atlantic 584 203	I'm A Midnight Mover/Deborah	6
68	Atlantic 584 221	I Found A True Love/For Better Or Worse	6
69	Atlantic 584 236	Hey Jude/Night Owl	6
69	Atlantic 584 261	Mini-Skirt Minnie/Back In Your Arms	10
69	Atlantic 584 281	Hey Joe/Born To Be Wild	6
70	Atlantic 584 313	You Keep Me Hangin' On/Now You See Me, Now You Don't	6
70	Atlantic 2091 005	Sugar, Sugar/Cole, Cooke And Redding	6
70	Atlantic 2091 032	(Get Me Back On Time) Engine No. 9/International Playboy	7
71	Atlantic 2091 086	Fire And Water/Don't Let The Green Grass Fool You	6
71	Atlantic 2091 124	Don't Knock My Love (Parts 1 & 2)	6
72	Atlantic K 10166	Don't Let The Green Grass Fool You/Covering The Same Old Ground	6
72	President PT 319	If You Need Me/I'm Gonna Love You	8
73	President PT 322	I Can't Stop/Down To My Last Heartbreak	8
65	Atlantic ATL 5037	IN THE MIDNIGHT HOUR (LP)	70
66	Atlantic 587/588 029	THE EXCITING WILSON PICKETT (LP)	40
66	Atlantic 587 032	IN THE MIDNIGHT HOUR (LP, reissue)	20
67	Atlantic 587/588 057	THE WICKED PICKETT (LP)	25
67	Atlantic 587/588 080	THE SOUND OF WILSON PICKETT (LP)	25
68	Atlantic 587/588 092	THE BEST OF WILSON PICKETT (LP)	20
68	Atlantic 587/588 107	I'M IN LOVE (LP)	25
68	Atlantic 587/588 111	MIDNIGHT MOVER (LP)	22
69	Atlantic 588 170	HEY JUDE (LP)	20
70	Atlantic 2465 002	RIGHT ON (LP)	15
70	Joy JOYS 181	IF YOU NEED ME (LP)	15
71	Atlantic 2400 026	ENGINE NO. 9 - IN PHILADELPHIA (LP)	15

GARY PICKFORD-HOPKINS & FRIENDS

(see also Deke Leonard, Man, Andy Fairweather-Low, Alan Ross, Big Sleep, Eyes Of Blue, Wild Turkey)

83	Spartan SP 143	Why? (The Song)/Why? (The Story) (p/s)	8
83	Spartan SP 143T	Why? (The Song)/Why? (The Story) (12", p/s)	10

PICKWICKS

64	Decca F 11901	Apple Blossom Time/I Don't Wanna Tell You Again	18
64	Decca F 11957	You're Old Enough/Hello Lady	15
65	Warner Bros WB 151	Little By Little/I Took My Baby Home	100

PICTURE FRAME SEDUCTION

84	SOSO 33	I'm Good Enough For Me/Sabotage The Classes/Fur Queue	40
87	PFS	Try With A Little Help From My Friends/And Entertainment USA	15

PIED PIPERS

54	Parlophone CMSP 21	Kissin' Drive Rock/Please Understand (export issue)	15

MINT VALUE £

PIED PIPERS

66	Columbia DB 7883	Ragamuffin/Fat Marie	30

BILLY & DEDE PIERCE/JIM ROBINSON

64	London HA-K/SH-K 8163	JAZZ AT PRESERVATION HALL VOL. 2 (LP)	12

WEBB PIERCE

(see also Red Sovine & Webb Pierce)

50s	Decca BM 311368	We'll Find A Way/Any Old Time (export issue)	30
56	Brunswick 05630	Teenage Boogie/Any Old Time	200
56	Brunswick 05630	Teenage Boogie/Any Old Time (78)	30
57	Brunswick 05682	Bye, Bye Love/Honky Tonk Song	40
57	Brunswick 05682	Bye, Bye Love/Honky Tonk Song (78)	20
59	Brunswick 05809	I Ain't Never/Shanghaied	20
59	Brunswick 05809	I Ain't Never/Shanghaied (78)	20
60	Brunswick 05820	No Love Have I/Whirlpool Of Love	10
60	Brunswick 05842	Drifting Texas Sand/All I Need Is You	10
56	Brunswick OE 9253	WEBB PIERCE PT. 1 (EP)	20
56	Brunswick OE 9254	WEBB PIERCE PT. 2 (EP)	20
56	Brunswick OE 9255	WEBB PIERCE PT. 3 (EP)	20
62	Ember EMB 4520	COUNTRY AND WESTERN FAVOURITES VOL. 1 (EP)	15
59	Parlophone GEP 8792	COUNTRY ROUND UP (EP)	40
55	Brunswick LA 8716	THE WONDERING BOY (10" LP)	50
60	Brunswick LAT 8324	WEBB! (LP)	25
65	Brunswick LAT 8540	HIDEAWAY HEART (LP)	25
65	Brunswick LAT 8551	CROSS COUNTRY (LP)	15

CLIVE PIG & THE HOPEFUL CHINAMEN

(see also Trixie's Big Red Motorbike)

79	Pinnacle PIN 21	Happy Birthday Sweet Sixteen/Our Movement (p/s)	10

PIGEON DETECTIVES

06	Dance To The Radio DTTR 08	I'm Not Sorry/I'm Always Right (p/s)	20

PIGEON FLYERS

68	Columbia DB 8449	The Heaven We Shared Together/Keep On Sayin'	8

BILLY PIGG

71	Leader LEA 4006	THE BORDER MINSTREL (LP, gatefold sleeve with booklet)	12

PIGGLESWICK FOLK

77	Acorn CF 256	PIG IN THE MIDDLE (LP)	12

PIGS

77	Bristol Recorder NBR 01	Youthenasia/They Say/Psychopath/National Front (p/s)	10

PIGSTY HILL LIGHT ORCHESTRA

70	Village Thing VTS 1	PHLOP! (LP)	15
72	Village Thing VTS 8	PIGGERY JOKERY (LP)	15

DAVE PIKE

63	Starlite ST45 094	Melvalita/Ginha - Bossa Nova	5
66	Atlantic 584 052	Sunny/HERBIE MANN: Philly Dog	15
66	Atlantic 588 005	JAZZ FOR THE JET SET (LP)	25
62	Esquire32-150	BOSA NOVA CARNIVAL (LP)	15

PiL

(see under Public Image Ltd)

RAY PILGRIM (& BEATMEN)

(see also Bud Ashton, Jaybirds, Typhoons)

60	Oriole CB 1557	Baby Doll/Gambler's Guitar (solo)	15
61	Oriole CB 1616	Little Miss Makebelieve/Granada (solo)	8
64	Embassy WB 645	Kissin' Cousins (with Beatmen)/JAYBIRDS: Some Day We're Gonna Love Again	5

PILGRIM FATHERS

69	Tangerine 009	Love And The World Will Love/Come A Day	7

PILOT

74	EMI 2217	Magic/Just Let Me Be	5
74	EMI 2250	January/Never Give Up	5

PILTDOWN MEN

60	Capitol CL 15149	McDonald's Cave/Brontosaurus Stomp	8
61	Capitol CL 15175	Piltdown Rides Again/Bubbles In The Tar	8
61	Capitol CL 15186	Goodnight Mrs Flintstone/The Great Imposter	8
61	Capitol CL 15211	Gargantua/Fossil Rock	10
62	Capitol CL 15245	A Pretty Girl Is Like A Melody/Big Lizard	25
61	Capitol EAP1 20155	GOODNIGHT MRS. FLINTSTONE (EP)	40

SIR HUBERT PIMM

(see also Duke & Duchess)

55	London HL 8155	Goodnight And Cheerio/Honky Tonk Train Blues	50
55	London RE-U 1032	PIMM'S PARTY (EP, with Ellen Sutton)	20

COURTNEY PINE

88	Island 10ISB 301	CHILDREN OF THE GHETTO (LP, 2 x 10", with 4 prints)	20

PINEAPPLE CHUNKS

65	Mercury MF 922	Drive My Car/Dream About	15

PINEWOOD STUDIO ORCHESTRA

59	Top Rank JAR 112	Sapphire/Tiger Bay	6
62	Parlophone R 4906	The Waltz Of The Toreadors/Picture Parade	6

PINEWOOD TOM/TOM TALL

59	Jazz Collector JEL 5	THE MALE BLUES VOLUME 4 (EP)	18

MINT VALUE £

'PING PING' & AL VERLANE

60	Oriole CB 1589	Sucu Sucu/Maria Della Montagna	8

PINK ELEPHANT

72	Pye 7N 45143	Down In The Valley/I'm Living In This World Just For You	15

PINK FAIRIES

(see also Twink, Larry Wallis, Deviants, Lightning Raiders, Shagrat)

71	Polydor 2058 089	The Snake/Do It	25
72	Polydor 2059 302	Well Well Well/Hold On	25
76	Stiff BUY 2	Between The Lines/Spoiling For A Fight (p/s)	7
71	Polydor 2383 045	NEVERNEVERLAND (LP, printed PVC outer & gatefold card inner, in yellow bag with photos & notes)	150
71	Polydor 2383 045	NEVERNEVERLAND (LP, printed PVC outer & gatefold card inner, pink vinyl & "pink plastic" in text on rear sleeve, around 100 pressed)	500
71	Polydor 2383 045	NEVERNEVERLAND (LP, black vinyl, standard sleeve)	30
72	Polydor 2383 132	WHAT A BUNCH OF SWEETIES (LP)	22
73	Polydor 2383 212	KINGS OF OBLIVION (LP, with poster)	35
75	Polydor 2384 071	FLASHBACK (LP)	18

PINK FLOYD

(see also Syd Barrett, Roger Waters, David Gilmour, Rick Wright, Nick Mason, Joker's Wild, Ron Geesin)

SINGLES

67	Columbia DB 8156	Arnold Layne/Candy And A Currant Bun	80
67	Columbia DB 8214	See Emily Play/Scarecrow	60
67	Columbia DB 8310	Apples And Oranges/Paintbox	110
68	Columbia DB 8401	It Would Be So Nice/Julia Dream	80
68	Columbia DB 8511	Point Me At The Sky/Careful With That Axe, Eugene	90
79	Harvest HAR 5194	Another Brick In The Wall (Part 2)/One Of My Turns (initial pressing, plain B-side label without 'window' picture)	5
81	Harvest HAR 5217	Money (Edit)/Let There Be More Light (unreleased)	0
81	Harvest 12HAR 5217	Money (Full Length)/Let There Be More Light (12", unreleased)	0
82	Harvest HAR 5222	When The Tigers Broke Free/Bring The Boys Back Home (gatefold p/s)	7
82	Harvest HAR 5222	When The Tigers Broke Free/Bring The Boys Back Home (standard p/s)	8
87	EMI EMDJ 26	Learning To Fly (Edited Version)/One Slip (Edited Version)/Terminal Frost (no p/s, mispressing without "One Slip", 50 on black vinyl)	20
87	EMI EMDJ 26	Learning To Fly (Edited Version)/One Slip (Edited Version)/Terminal Frost (no p/s, mispressing without "One Slip", 1,000 only on pink vinyl)	12
87	EMI CDEM 26	Learning To Fly (Edited Version)/One Slip (Edited Version)/Terminal Frost (Album Version)/Terminal Frost (DYOL Version) (CD, card sleeve & inner)	15
87	EMI EM 34	On The Turning Away (Album)/Run Like Hell (Live Version) (p/s)	5
87	EMI EMP 34	On The Turning Away (Album)/Run Like Hell (Live Version) (p/s, pink vinyl, 1000 only)	8
87	EMI 12EMP 34	On The Turning Away (Album)/Run Like Hell (Live Version)/ On The Turning Away (Live Version) (12", poster p/s)	12
87	EMI CDEM 34	On The Turning Away/Run Like Hell (Live Version)/ On The Turning Away (Live Version) (CD)	15
88	EMI EMG 52	One Slip/Terminal Frost (pink vinyl, gatefold p/s with ticket application)	8
88	EMI 12EMP 52	One Slip/Terminal Frost/The Dogs Of War (live) (12", poster p/s)	8
88	EMI CDEM 52	One Slip/Terminal Frost/The Dogs Of War (live) (CD)	12
94	EMI EM 309	Take It Back (Edit)/Astronomy Domine (live) (jukebox issue, black vinyl)	8
94	EMI EM 309	Take It Back (Edit)/Astronomy Domine (live) (red vinyl, p/s)	7
94	EMI EM 342	High Hopes (Radio Edit)/Keep Talking (Radio Edit) (clear vinyl, poster p/s)	8
94	EMI 12EM 342	High Hopes (Album Version)/Keep Talking (Album Version)/One Of These Days (live) (12", 1-sided, laser-etched blue vinyl, p/s in outer gatefold p/s with 7 postcards)	12
94	EMI CDEM 342	High Hopes (Radio Edit)/Keep Talking (Radio Edit)/One Of These Days (live) (CD, with 7 postcards)	8

ALBUMS

67	Columbia SX 6157	THE PIPER AT THE GATES OF DAWN (LP, mono, blue/black label, with "Sold in U.K..." text)	500
67	Columbia SCX 6157	THE PIPER AT THE GATES OF DAWN (LP, stereo, blue/black label, with "Sold in the U.K..." text)	250

(Second pressings have "File Under Pop" on the right of the flipback; first pressings do not have this. Second pressing worth half to a third less)

68	Columbia SX 6258	A SAUCERFUL OF SECRETS (LP, mono, blue/black label, "Sold in U.K..." text)	400
68	Columbia SCX 6258	A SAUCERFUL OF SECRETS (LP, stereo, blue/black label, "Sold in U.K..." text)	300
69	Columbia SCX 6346	SOUNDTRACK FROM THE FILM 'MORE' (LP, laminated flipback sleeve, 'couple facing west' photo on green-tinted rear sleeve. 1st pressing with black/silver label, boxed logo and "Sold in UK..." text)	70
69	Harvest SHDW 1/2	UMMAGUMMA (2-LP, without EMI logo, laminated gatefold sleeve)	100
69	Harvest SHDW 1/2	UMMAGUMMA (2-LP, with EMI logo, laminated gatefold sleeve)	40
70	Columbia SCX 6157	THE PIPER AT THE GATES OF DAWN (LP, re-pressing, silver & black label)	25
70	Columbia SCX 6258	A SAUCERFUL OF SECRETS (LP, re-pressing, silver & black label)	25
70s	Columbia SCX 6346	SOUNDTRACK FROM THE FILM 'MORE' (LP, laminated non-flipback sleeve, 'couple facing west' photo on black-tinted rear sleeve)	45
70s	Columbia SCX 6346	SOUNDTRACK FROM THE FILM 'MORE' (LP, laminated non-flipback sleeve, 'couple facing east' photo on black-tinted rear sleeve)	50
70	MGM 2315 002	ZABRISKIE POINT (LP, soundtrack, with Jerry Garcia/Kaleidoscope, et al.)	30
70	Harvest SHVL 781	ATOM HEART MOTHER (LP, gatefold sleeve, no EMI logo)	90

(First pressing of the above Harvest LPs have "The Gramophone..." text on label rim and "Harvest" on the left side of the label; second pressings have "The Gramophone..." text with a boxed EMI logo above "Harvest")

71	Harvest SHVL 795	MEDDLE (LP, textured inside/outside gatefold sleeve)	40
71	Harvest SHVL 795	MEDDLE (LP, textured outside gatefold sleeve)	20
71	Starline SRS 5071	RELICS (LP, white textured sleeve)	15
72	Harvest SHSP 4020	OBSCURED BY CLOUDS (LP, rounded sleeve, EMI logo on label)	25

			MINT VALUE £
73	Harvest SHVL 804	THE DARK SIDE OF THE MOON (LP, first pressing, solid light blue triangle label, black inner, 2 posters & 2 stickers, gatefold sleeve, only one side opening)	500
73	Harvest SHVL 804	THE DARK SIDE OF THE MOON (LP, blue & black label, gatefold sleeve with black inner, 2 posters & 2 stickers, with stickered sleeve)	20
73	Harvest SHVL 804	THE DARK SIDE OF THE MOON (LP, blue & black label, gatefold sleeve with black inner, 2 posters & 2 stickers, without stickered sleeve)	15
70s	Harvest SHVL 804	THE DARK SIDE OF THE MOON (LP, repressing, blue & silver label, gatefold sleeve with black inner, 2 posters & 2 stickers)	20
73	Harvest Q4 SHVL 781	ATOM HEART MOTHER (LP, quadrophonic, gatefold sleeve, with 'quadrophonic' logo on front sleeve)	30
73	Harvest Q4 SHVL 781	ATOM HEART MOTHER (LP, quadrophonic, gatefold sleeve, without 'quadrophonic' logo on front sleeve, logo is inside)	25
73	Harvest Q4 SHVL 804	THE DARK SIDE OF THE MOON (LP, quadrophonic, gatefold sleeve, no inserts)	40
73	Harvest SHDW 403	A NICE PAIR (2-LP, gatefold sleeve, with 2 inner sleeves; early copies with 'Mr Phang' dentist cover)	35
73	Harvest SHDW 403	A NICE PAIR (2-LP, gatefold sleeve, with 2 inner sleeves)	15
75	Harvest SHVL 814	WISH YOU WERE HERE (LP, with inner sleeve, postcard & black cellophane wraparound with sticker, sealed)	200
75	Harvest SHVL 814	WISH YOU WERE HERE (LP, with inner sleeve, postcard & black cellophane wraparound with sticker, unsealed)	50
76	Harvest Q4 SHVL 814	WISH YOU WERE HERE (LP, quadrophonic, with inner sleeve)	75
70s	Harvest SHVL 814	WISH YOU WERE HERE (LP, audiophile edition, Nimbus supercut sold through Hi-FI Today magazine	100
77	Harvest SHVL 815	ANIMALS (LP, picture labels, non-barcode gatefold sleeve with inner)	12
78	Harvest SHDW 411	THE WALL (2-LP, plastic stickered gatefold sleeve, with inners)	12
79	Harvest PF 11	THE FIRST XI (11-LP set, original sleeves, plus exclusive "The Dark Side Of The Moon" & "Wish You Were Here" picture discs, 1,000 only)	200
83	Harvest SHPF 1983	THE FINAL CUT (LP, gatefold sleeve with title sticker)	15
87	EMI EMD 1003	A MOMENTARY LAPSE OF REASON (LP, gatefold sleeve with inner)	15
92	EMI CDS 7805572	SHINE ON (9-CD box set, with book and postcards)	90
93	EMI CDDSOM 20	THE DARK SIDE OF THE MOON (CD, 20th anniversary box set with booklet & 5 art cards)	18
94	EMI EMD 1055	THE DIVISION BELL (LP, gatefold sleeve, with inner)	12
95	EMI EMD 578	PULSE (4-LP box set in slipcase with hardback book)	100
97	EMI 859 857-1	THE PIPER AT THE GATES OF DAWN (LP, reissue, gatefold sleeve with inner, mono)	12
97	EMI CDEMD 1110	THE PIPER AT THE GATES OF DAWN (CD, mono, 30th anniversary box set with prints)	18
97	EMI SIGMA 630	'97 VINYL COLLECTION (7-LP set, die-cut box, includes "The Piper At The Gates Of Dawn" [EMD 1110], "The Wall" [EMD 1111], "Atom Heart Mother" [EMD 1112], "Relics" [EMD 1113], "The Dark Side Of The Moon" [EMD 1114], "Wish You Were Here" [EMD 1115], each in card gatefold sleeve)	80
97	EMI CDEMD 1118	THE FIRST THREE SINGLES (CD, mono, mini album in card gatefold sleeve)	20
97	EMI EMD 1133	RELICS (LP, gatefold with poster)	30

PROMOS

67	Columbia DB 8156	Arnold Layne/Candy And A Currant Bun (demo copy in promo-only p/s)	1500
67	Columbia DB 8214	See Emily Play/Scarecrow (demo copy in promo-only p/s)	1500
67	Columbia DB 8310	Apples And Oranges/Paintbox (demo copy in promo-only p/s)	1500
68	Columbia DB 8401	It Would Be So Nice (1-sided demo)	800
68	Columbia DB 8511	Point Me At The Sky/Careful With That Axe, Eugene (demo, with newsletter)	800
68	Columbia DB 8511	Point Me At The Sky/Careful With That Axe, Eugene (demo, with postcard)	750
69	Emidisc no cat. no.	The Narrow Way (acetate, different version, 1 copy only)	300
81	Harvest HAR 5217	Money (Edited Version) (1-sided, pink vinyl, 200 only)	35
81	Harvest HAR 5217	Money (1-sided pink vinyl promo in p/s, 200 only)	100
81	Harvest HAR 5217	Money (Edited Version) (1-sided, pink vinyl, mispressing with "Let There Be More Light" label on B-side)	50
87	EMI EMDJ 34	On The Turning Away (edit)/On The Turning Away (album) (stickered p/s)	8
88	EMI 12PF 1	Delicate Sound Of Thunder Sampler: Another Brick In The Wall Part 2/ One Of These Days/Run Like Hell (12", black & pink sleeve)	20
88	EMI PSLP 1026	Pink Floyd In Europe '88: Money/Shine On/Another Brick In The Wall Part 2/ One Slip/On The Turning Away/Learning To Fly (12", with "Another Brick...Part 1" miscredit on rear p/s)	20
88	EMI CDPINK 1	Wish You Were Here/Learning To Fly/Run Like Hell (CD)	20
92	EMI SHINE 1	SELECTED TRACKS FROM "SHINE ON" (CD, card sleeve)	18

PINK INDUSTRY

(see also Pink Military, Big In Japan)

82	Zulu ZULU 1	Is This The End?/47/Don't Let Go/Final Cry (12", p/s)	8
85	Zulu ZULU RA 8	What I Wouldn't Give	6
83	Zulu ZULU 2	LOW TECHNOLOGY (LP)	12
83	Zulu ZULU 4	WHO TOLD YOU - YOU WERE NAKED (LP)	12

PINK MILITARY

(see also Pink Industry, Big In Japan, Ambrose Reynolds)

79	Last Trumpet LT 001	BUDDHA WALKING DISNEY SLEEPING (EP, foldout sleeve)	8
79	Eric's ERIC'S 002	BLOOD AND LIPSTICK (12" EP, die-cut p/s)	8
80	Eric's ERIC'S 005	Did You See Her/Everyday (p/s)	5
80	Virgin/Eric's ERIC'S 004	DO ANIMALS BELIEVE IN GOD? (LP)	15

PINK PEOPLE

(see also Four Squares)

64	Philips BF 1355	Psychologically Unsound/Cow Catcher	40
64	Philips BF 1356	Indian Hate Call/I Dreamt I Dwelt In Marble Halls	20

PINK RHYTHM

85	Beggars Banquet BEG 136T	Can't Get Enough Of Your Love/Can't Get Enough Of Your Dub (12", p/s)	15
85	Beggars Banquet BEG 149T	India/Trust Me/More And More/India (Instrumental) (12", p/s)	15

PINKERTON'S ('ASSORTED' COLOURS)

(see also Flying Machine, Liberators, Tony Newman)

65	Decca F 12307	Mirror Mirror/She Don't Care (as Pinkerton's 'Assorted' Colours)	8

			MINT VALUE £
66	Decca F 12377	Don't Stop Loving Me Baby/Will Ya? (as Pinkerton's 'Assorted' Colours)	15
66	Decca F 12493	Magic Rocking Horse/It Ain't Right (as Pinkerton's Colours)	35
67	Pye 7N 17327	Mum And Dad/On A Street Car (as Pinkerton's Colours)	18
67	Pye 7N 17414	There's Nobody I'd Sooner Love/Look At Me (as Pinkerton's)	40
68	Pye 7N 17574	Kentucky Woman/Behind The Mirror (as Pinkerton's)	18

PINKOES

79	Popular POP1	INTO THE RED (EP)	12

PINKY (& FELLAS)

65	Polydor BM 56009	All Cried Out/Back Where I Belong	6
68	Decca F 12748	Manchester And Liverpool/Come Back Again (as Pinky & Fellas)	5
69	Polydor BM 56338	Let The Music Start/Oh, A Beautiful Day (as Pinky & Fellas)	5

PINKY & PERKY

58	Decca F 11095	Tom Dooley/The Velvet Glove (Pinky & Perky Theme) (in p/s)	10
59	Decca F 11116	The Little Mountaineer/Does Your Chewing Gum Lose Its Flavour (some in p/s)	15
63	Columbia 33SX 1550	PINKY & PERKY'S MELODYMASTER (LP)	25

PINNACLE

74	Stag HP 125	ASSASSIN (LP, laminated sleeve, black/silver label)	150

DELROY PINNOCK

81	SG 5	Babylon Walls/MIKEY RANKS: I Want To Be	70

PINPOINT

79	Albion CEL 8	Richmond/Love Substiture (p/s)	25
80	Albion ALB103	THIRD STATE (LP, with free 12")	20

PIONEERS

(see also Sir Gibbs, Rebels [Jamaica], Jackey Robinson, Moonboys, Sidney George & Jackie)

66	Rio R 102	Good Nannie/Doreen Girl	40
66	Rio R 106	Too Late/Give Up	40
68	Blue Cat BS 100	Shake It Up/Rudies Are The Greatest	45
68	Blue Cat BS 103	Give It To Me/LEADERS: Someday Someway	40
68	Blue Cat BS 105	Whip Them/Having A Bawl	40
68	Blue Cat BS 139	Reggae Beat/Miss Eva	60
68	Caltone TONE 119	I Love No Other Girl/MILTON BOOTHE: I Used To Be A Fool	60
68	Amalgamated AMG 811	Give Me A Little Loving/This Is Soul (B-side actually by Lyn Tait & Jets)	18
68	Amalgamated AMG 814	Long Shot/Dip And Fall Back	30
68	Amalgamated AMG 821	Jackpot/CREATORS: Kimble (B-side actually by Lee Perry)	25
68	Amalgamated AMG 823	No Dope Me Pony/LORD SALMONS: Great - Great In '68	35
68	Amalgamated AMG 826	Tickle Me For Days/VERSATILES: The Time Has Come	15
68	Amalgamated AMG 828	Catch The Beat/SIR GIBB'S ALLSTARS: Jana (B-side actually Immortals' "Jane Anne")	20
68	Amalgamated AMG 830	Sweet Dreams/DON DRUMMOND JUNIOR: Caterpillar Rock	20
68	Pyramid PYR 6062	Easy Come, Easy Go/BEVERLEY'S ALLSTARS: Only A Smile (B-side actually by Lyn Tait & Jets)	55
69	Pyramid PYR 6065	Pee Pee Cluck Cluck/BEVERLEY'S ALLSTARS: Exclusively	15
69	Amalgamated AMG 833	Don't You Know/Me Naw Go A Believe	40
69	Amalgamated AMG 835	Mama Look Deh/BLENDERS: Decimal Currency	35
69	Amalgamated AMG 840	Who The Cap Fits/I'm Moving On	60
69	Amalgamated AMG 850	Alli Button/HIPPY BOYS: Death Rides	60
69	Trojan TR 672	Long Shot Kick The Bucket/RICO: Jumping The Gun	15
69	Trojan TR 685	Black Bud/Too Late	10
69	Trojan TR 698	Poor Rameses/BEVERLEY'S ALLSTARS: In Orbit	5
70	Trojan TR 7781	Money Day/BEVERLEY ALL STARS: Ska Ba Do	8
71	Summit SUM 8511	Starvation/BEVERLEY'S ALLSTARS: Version	7
72	Summit SUM 8535	Story Book Children/SIDNEY, GEORGE AND JACKIE: Gorgeous, Marvellous	5
76	Mercury 6198061	Feel The Rhythm Of You and I/Version	8
77	Mercury 6007147	My Good Friend James/Secrets Of You	100
78	Ice GUY 14	My Good Friend James/Secrets Of You (reissue)	150
68	Amalgam. AMGLP 2003	GREETINGS FROM THE PIONEERS (LP)	70
70	Trojan TBL 103	LONGSHOT (LP)	25
70	Trojan TBL 139	BATTLE OF THE GIANTS (LP)	25
71	Trojan TRL 24	YEAH! (LP)	15

PIPE DREAM

70	Penny Farthing PEN 710	If You Do What You Gotta Do/Here We Go Again	5

PIPES OF PAN

67	Page One POF 038	Monday Morning Rain/Monday Morning Rain (Instrumental Mix)	20

PIPES OF PAN

(see also Rolling Stones)

71	Rolling Stones COC 49100	BRIAN JONES PLAYS WITH THE PIPES OF PAN AT JOUJOUKA (LP, gatefold sleeve with foldout insert; front cover with misprinted title)	90
71	Rolling Stones COC 49100	BRIAN JONES PRESENTS THE PIPES OF PAN AT JOUJOUKA (LP, gatefold sleeve with foldout insert; "Presents" sticker on misprinted cover)	70
71	Rolling Stones COC 49100	BRIAN JONES PRESENTS THE PIPES OF PAN AT JOUJOUKA (LP, gatefold sleeve with foldout insert; corrected title on front cover)	65

PIPETTES

04	No label or cat no	In The Bleak Midwinter (CD, gig freebie, 200 only)	40
05	Unpopular UNPOP 6	I Like A Boy In Uniform/It Hurts To See You Dance So Well (hand-numbered p/s, insert, 500 only)	30
05	Transgressive TRANS 005	ABC/Judy/Simon Says (white vinyl, p/s, 500 only)	20
05	Memphis Industries MI 053S	Dirty Mind/Because It's Not Love (But It's Still A Feeling) (die-cut p/s)	5
06	Memphis Ind. MI 062S1	Your Kisses Are Wasted On Me/Your Guitars Are Wasted On Me (white vinyl, die-cut p/s)	5
06	Memphis Ind. MI 062S2	Your Kisses Are Wasted On Me/Judy (Acoustic Version) (green vinyl, die-cut p/s)	5

MINT VALUE £

06 Memphis Ind. MI 071S1 Pull Shapes/Guess Who Ran Off With The Milkman (white vinyl, p/s) . . . 5
06 Memphis Ind. MI 071S2 Pull Shapes/Magician Man (yellow vinyl, p/s) . . . 5
06 Memphis Ind. MI 077S1 Judy (Single Mix)/Feminist Complaints (white vinyl, die-cut p/s) . . . 5
06 Memphis Ind. MI 077S2 Judy (Single Mix)/The Burning Ambition Of The Early Diuretics (blue vinyl, die-cut p/s) . . . 5

PIPKINS
(see under Sweet)

PIPP
70 Decca F 23030 Otaki/Which Way Did She Go . . . 12

PIPS
(see also Gladys Knight & Pips)
61 Top Rank JAR 574 Every Beat Of My Heart/Room In Your Heart . . . 50

PIRATES
(see also Johnny Kidd & Pirates, [Billy J. Kramer &] Dakotas)
64 HMV POP 1250 My Babe/Casting My Spell . . . 40
66 Polydor BM 56712 Shades Of Blue/Can't Understand . . . 30
77 Warner Bros K 17002 Sweet Love On My Mind/You Don't Own Me (p/s) . . . 15
78 Warner Bros K 17113 All In It Together/Dr. Feelgood (p/s) . . . 10
78 Warner Bros K 17231 Shakin' All Over/Saturday Night Shoot Out . . . 5
79 Sound For Industry SFI 431 All By Myself/Cat Clothes (1-sided fan club flexidisc, gold vinyl) . . . 5
79 Cube Hi Fly 33 HAPPY BIRTHDAY ROCK N' ROLL (LP, with flexidisc [PIR 2]) . . . 12
99 Diamond OUT OF THEIR SKULLS...PLUS (CD) . . . 20

PISCES
71 Trailer LER 2025 PISCES (LP) . . . 30

HARRY PITCH
(see also Mr. Bloe)
68 MOR MR 101P HARMONICA JEWEL BOX (LP) . . . 20

PITCH SHIFTER
92 Earache MOSH 66 SUBMIT EP (12") . . . 8

PITMAN
02 Son/White Witness The Pitness (12" EP) . . . 10
02 Son HM001 Phone Pitman/pitman Sez . . . 15

GENE PITNEY
(see also Marc Almond & Gene Pitney, George Jones)

SINGLES
61 London HL 9270 (I Wanna) Love My Life Away/I Laughed So Hard I Cried . . . 15
61 HMV POP 933 Every Breath I Take/Mr Moon, Mr Cupid & I . . . 30
61 United Artists POP 952 Town Without Pity/Air Mail Special . . . 10
62 United Artists POP 1018 The Man Who Shot Liberty Valance/Take It Like A Man . . . 10
62 United Artists UP 1005 If I Didn't Have A Dime/Only Love Can Break A Heart . . . 6
63 United Artists UP 1012 Half Heaven, Half Heartache/Tower Tall . . . 5
63 United Artists UP 1021 Mecca/Teardrop By Teardrop . . . 8
63 United Artists UP 1030 True Love Never Runs Smooth/Donna Means Heartbreak . . . 5
63 United Artists UP 1035 24 Hours From Tulsa/Lonely Night Dreams (blue or black label) . . . 5
64 United Artists UP 1045 That Girl Belongs To Yesterday/Who Needs It? . . . 7
64 United Artists UP 1055 I'm Gonna Find Myself A Girl/Lips Are Redder On You . . . 10
64 United Artists UP 1063 It Hurts To Be In Love/Hawaii . . . 7
64 Stateside SS 358 I'm Gonna Be Strong/Aladdin's Lamp . . . 5
64 Stateside SS 365 It Hurts To Be In Love/Hawaii (reissue) . . . 5
65 Stateside SS 390 I Must Be Seeing Things/Save Your Love . . . 5
65 Stateside SS 420 Lookin' Thru The Eyes Of Love/Last Chance To Turn Around . . . 5
65 Stateside SS 471 Princess In Rags/Amore Mio . . . 5
66 Stateside SS 490 Backstage/In Love Again . . . 5
66 Stateside SS 518 Nobody Needs Your Love/Dream World . . . 5
66 Stateside SS 558 Just One Smile/The Boss's Daughter . . . 6
67 Stateside SS 597 (In The) Cold Light Of Day/Flower Girl . . . 8
67 Stateside SS 2060 Something's Gotten Hold Of My Heart/Building Up My Dream World (withdrawn) . . . 20
67 Stateside SS 2060 Something's Gotten Hold Of My Heart/Where Did The Magic Go . . . 5
68 Stateside SS 2103 Somewhere In The Country/Lonely Drifter . . . 5
68 Stateside SS 2118 Love Grows/Conquistador . . . 5
68 Stateside SS 2131 Yours Until Tomorrow/She's A Heartbreaker . . . 15
68 Stateside SS 2131 Yours Until Tomorrow/She's A Heartbreaker (DJ copy) . . . 30
69 Stateside SS 2142 Maria Elena/The French Horn . . . 6
70 Stateside SS 2177 Shady Lady/Billy, You're My Friend . . . 5
71 Pye International 7N 25564 Run Run Road Runner/Rain Maker . . . 10
72 Pye International 7N 25579 I Just Can't Help Myself/Beautiful Sounds . . . 5

EPs
63 HMV 7EG 8832 TOWN WITHOUT PITY . . . 30
64 United Artists UEP 1001 TWENTY FOUR HOURS FROM TULSA . . . 10
64 United Artists UEP 1002 THAT GIRL BELONGS TO YESTERDAY . . . 10
65 Stateside SE 1030 I MUST BE SEEING THINGS . . . 8
65 Stateside SE 1032 GENE ITALIANO . . . 10
66 Stateside SE 1036 GENE PITNEY SINGS JUST FOR YOU . . . 10

LPs
62 HMV CLP 1566 THE MANY SIDES OF GENE PITNEY . . . 30
63 United Artists ULP 1028 ONLY LOVE CAN BREAK A HEART (mono) . . . 20
63 United Artists SULP 1028 ONLY LOVE CAN BREAK A HEART (stereo) . . . 30
63 United Artists ULP 1043 GENE PITNEY SINGS JUST FOR YOU . . . 20
64 United Artists ULP 1061 BLUE GENE . . . 20
64 United Artists ULP 1064 GENE PITNEY MEETS THE FAIR YOUNG LADIES OF FOLKLAND . . . 20
64 United Artists ULP 1073 GENE PITNEY'S BIG SIXTEEN . . . 15
65 Stateside SL 10120 I'M GONNA BE STRONG . . . 15

			MINT VALUE £
65	Stateside SL 10132	GENE PITNEY'S MORE BIG SIXTEEN (VOL. 2)	18
65	Stateside SL 10147	GEORGE JONES AND GENE PITNEY (with George Jones)	18
65	Stateside SL 10148	LOOKING THRU THE EYES OF LOVE	15
65	Stateside SL 10156	SINGS THE GREAT SONGS OF OUR TIME	18
66	Stateside SL 10173	IT'S COUNTRY TIME AGAIN (with George Jones)	15

TERRY PITTS JAZZ BAND

61	Oriole CB 1621	A Drop Of The Hard Stuff/Show Me The Way To Go Home	6

PIXIES

(see also Breeders, Frank Black)

88	4AD BAD 805	GIGANTIC EP (12", p/s)	10
89	4AD BAD 904	THIS MONKEY'S GONE TO HEAVEN EP (12")	8
89	4AD BAD 909	HERE COMES YOUR MAN EP (12", p/s)	10
90	4AD BAD 0014	DIG FOR FIRE EP (12", p/s)	8
88	4AD BAD 805CD	Gigantic/River Euphrates/Vamos (live)/In Heaven (Lady In The Radiator Song) (live) (CD)	12
89	4AD PIX ONE	DOOLITTLE SAMPLER: Debaser/Wave Of Mutilation/I Bleed/Gouge Away (12", 1-sided, title sleeve, promo only)	20
89	4AD PIX 2	Into The White/Wave Of Mutilation (U.K. Surf) (12", 1-sided, promo only)	10
90	4AD PIX 3	EXTRACTS FROM BOSSANOVA: Allison/Rock Music/Down To The Well/ The Happening (12", 1-sided, promo only)	15
90	4AD AD 0014	Dig For Fire (p/s)	6
91	4AD PIX 4	EXTRACTS FROM TROMPE LE MONDE: U-Mass/Letter To Memphis/ Subbacultcha (10", same track both sides, promo only)	15
04	4AD PIX 2004CD	BEST OF PIXIES (CD, 5-track sampler, promo only)	20
87	4AD MAD 709	COME ON PILGRIM (mini-LP)	18
88	4AD CAD 803	SURFER ROSA (LP, with inner)	20
89	4AD CAD 905	DOOLITTLE (LP, with lyric booklet & postcard, in carrier bag)	40
89	4AD CAD 905	DOOLITTLE (LP, with lyric booklet & postcard)	30
90	4AD CAD 0010	BOSSANOVA (LP, with booklet)	25
90	4AD CAD 1014	TROMPE LE MONDE (LP)	15
97	4AD DADD 7011	DEATH TO THE PIXIES (4x10" LP, box set)	60

PIXIES THREE

63	Mercury AMT 1214	Birthday Party/Our Love	25

P.J. HARVEY

(see under 'H')

PLACEBO

95	Fierce Panda NING 13	Bruise Pristine/SOUP: M.E.L.T.D.O.W.N. (foldover p/s, 1500 only)	60
96	Deceptive BLUFF 024	Come Home/Drowning By Numbers (p/s)	10
96	Deceptive BLUFF 024	Come Home/Drowning By Numbers (CD)	25
96	Elevator FLOOR 001	36 degrees/Dark globe (p/s)	10
96	Hut FLOOR 3	Teenage Angst/Hug Bubble/Been Smoking Too Long (part 1 of 2, p/s)	8
96	Hut FLOORCD 3	Teenage Angst/Hug Bubble/Been Smoking Too Long (CD, card sleeve)	12
96	Hut FLOOR 4	Nancy Boy (Sex Mix)/Slackerbitch (p/s)	6
97	Hut FLOOR 5	Bruise Pristine/(One Punch Remix) (p/s)	12
98	Hut SILVER 1	THE ORIGINAL DEMOS: Nancy Boy/Teenage Angst/36 Degrees/ Bruise Pristine (CD, fan club issue, card sleeve)	18
99	Hut FLOOR TP 10	Without You I'm Nothing (with David Bowie) (UNKLE Remix)/ (Flexirol Mix)/(Brothers In Rhythm Club Mix) (12" promo, 500 only, stickered die-cut sleeve)	20
99	Hut FLOOR CD 10	Without You I'm Nothing (Single Mix)/(UNKLE Remix)/(Flexirol Mix)/ (Brothers In Rhythm Club Mix) (multimedia CD, gatefold card sleeve)	15
99	Elevator SILVER 2	I Feel You (1-track cassette, fan club issue)	50
03	Virgin 7432547480743	Special Needs/English Summer Rain (p/s)	8
04	Virgin 724381618776	Twenty Years/Detox 5	8
96	Hut LPFLOORY 2	PLACEBO (LP)	35
96	Hut CD FLOOR 2	PLACEBO (CD, digipak, 5000 only)	30
98	Elevator FLOORLP 8	WITHOUT YOU I'M NOTHING (LP)	30

PLAGUE

68	Decca F 12730	Looking For The Sun/Here Today, Gone Tomorrow	200

PLAGUE

79	Psycho P2615	In Love/Wimpey Bar Song (some in p/s)	50

PLAID

(see also Black Dog)

92	GPR GENP(X) 7	Scoobs In Columbia (remixes) (12", custom sleeve)	30
94	Clear CLR 409	ANDROID (12" EP, p/s, clear vinyl)	20
94	Clear CLR 409	ANDROID (12" EP, p/s, black vinyl)	15
95	Rumble RUMBLE 01	MIND OVER RHYTHM MEET THE MEN FROM PLAID (3 x 10" in p/s)	15
92	Black Dog Prods. LP 1	MBUKI MVUKI (LP)	80

PLAIN CHARACTERS

(see under Gadgets)

PLAINSONG

(see also Andy Roberts, Ian Matthews)

72	Elektra K 12976	Even The Guiding Light/Yoko Man/Call The Tune	7
72	Elektra K 42120	IN SEARCH OF AMELIA EARHART (LP, gatefold sleeve with lyric insert)	25
73	Elektra K 42136	PLAINSONG II (LP, white label, promo only)	120

PLANET EARTH

78	Pye NSPL 18556	PLANET EARTH (LP)	25

PLANET GONG

(see also Daevid Allen, Gong)

77	Affinity AF 5101	Opium For The People/Poet For Sale (p/s)	8
78	Charly CYX 202	Opium For The People/Stoned Innocent Frankenstein (10", p/s)	18
78	Charly	FLOATING ANARCHY - LIVE 1977 (LP)	18

MINT VALUE £

PLANET P PROJECT

(see also Tony Carey, Rainbow)

83	Geffen A3205	Why Me/Only You And Me (p/s)	6
83	Geffen GEF25367	PLANET P PROJECT (LP + inner sleeve)	12
85	MCA MCSP311	PINK WORLD (2LP, gatefold sleeve)	18

PLANETS

60	Palette PG 9008	Like Party/Ippy Yippy Beatnik (only this value if in p/s)	25

PLANETS

73	Bullet BU 528	People Get Funny/DOCBIRD ALL STARS: Funny Version	10

PLANETS

60	HMV POP 818	Chunky/Screwball	20
61	HMV POP 832	Jam Roll/Delaney's Theme	25
61	HMV POP 895	Jungle Street/The Grasshopper	25

ROBERT PLANT

(see also Led Zeppelin, Listen, Jimmy Page, Robert Plant & The Strange Sensation, Page & Plant, Honeydrippers)

67	CBS 202656	Our Song/Laughin', Cryin', Laughin'	300
67	CBS 202656	Our Song/Laughin' Cryin' Laughin' ('A' label demo)	250
67	CBS 202858	Long Time Coming/I've Got A Secret	300
67	CBS 202858	Long Time Coming/I've Got A Secret ('A' label demo)	250
82	Swan Song SSK 19429T	Burning Down One Side/Far Post (12", p/s)	10
82	Swan Song SAM154	PICTURES AT ELEVEN (LP, promo interview disc with cue sheet)	18
82	Es Paranza SAM 169	THE PRINCIPLE OF MOVEMENTS (LP, promo interview disc with cue sheet)	18
88	Es Paranza PR 2244	NON STOP GO! (LP, two disc set interview promo for NOW AND ZEN album)	15
90	Es Paranza WX 339X	MANIC NIRVANA (LP, gatefold)	12
02	Mercury 063094-1	DREAMLAND (2 x LP, numbered)	20

PLASTIC BERTRAND

78	Sire 9103258	AN 1 (LP, gatefold)	20

PLASTIC GANGSTERS

(see also 4 Skins)

83	Secret SHH 144	Plastic Gangsters/Sretsgnag Citsalp (7", 12", no p/s on 12" stamped p/s on 7", unissued, DJ copies only)	250

PLASTIC ONO BAND

(see under John Lennon, Yoko Ono)

PLASTIC PENNY

(see also Universals, Circles, Brian Keith, Mick Grabham)

67	Page One POF 051	Everything I Am/No Pleasure Without Pain My Love	5
68	Page One POF 062	Nobody Knows It/Just Happy To Be With You	10
68	Page One POF 079	Your Way To Tell Me Go/Baby You're Not To Blame	15
69	Page One POF 107	Hound Dog/Currency	20
69	Page One POF 146	She Does/Genevieve	10
68	Page One POL(S) 005	TWO SIDES OF THE PENNY (LP, laminated front sleeve, flipbacks)	100
69	Page One POLS 014	CURRENCY (LP, laminated front sleeve, flipbacks)	140
70	Page One POLS 611	HEADS YOU WIN, TAILS I LOSE (LP)	65

PLASTICS

81	Island ILPS 9627	WELCOME BACK (LP)	12

PLASTIKMAN

94	NovaMute L NO MU 37	MUSIK (2-LP, with bonus 1-sided etched 12")	15

PLATFORM SIX

65	Piccadilly 7N 35255	Money Will Not Mean A Thing/Girl Down Town	15

EDDIE PLATT

58	Columbia DB 4101	Tequila/Pop Corn	25

PLATTERS

(see also Buck Ram's Ramrocks, Linda Hayes)

78s

55	Parlophone DP 433	Voo-Vee-Ah-Bee/STRANGERS: Just Don't Care (export issue)	30
56	Parlophone DP 506	Beer Barrel Boogie/Roses Of Picardy (export issue)	30
56	Mercury MT 107	(You've Got) The Magic Touch/Winner Takes All	15
58	Mercury MT 197	Helpless/Indiff'rent	15
58	Mercury MT 205	Don't Let Go/Are You Sincere?	10
58	Mercury MT 227	You're Making A Mistake/My Old Flame (sung by Zola Taylor)	15
58	Mercury AMT 1001	I Wish/It's Raining Outside	12
58	Mercury AMT 1016	Smoke Gets In Your Eyes/No Matter What You Are	15
59	Mercury AMT 1039	Enchanted/The Sound And The Fury	20
59	Mercury AMT 1053	Remember When/Love Of A Lifetime (featuring Tony Williams)	30
60	Mercury AMT 1081	Harbour Lights/(By The) Sleepy Lagoon	40

SINGLES

56	Mercury MT 117	The Great Pretender/Only You (And You Alone) (export issue)	40
58	Mercury 7MT 197	Helpless/Indiff'rent	40
58	Mercury 7MT 205	Don't Let Go/Are You Sincere?	30
58	Mercury 7MT 214	Twilight Time/Out Of My Mind	10
58	Mercury 7MT 227	You're Making A Mistake (featuring Tony Williams)/My Old Flame	20
58	Mercury AMT 1001	I Wish/It's Raining Outside	18
58	Mercury AMT 1016	Smoke Gets In Your Eyes/No Matter What You Are	5
59	Mercury AMT 1039	Enchanted/The Sound And The Fury	6
59	Mercury AMT 1053	Remember When/Love Of A Lifetime (featuring Tony Williams)	10
59	Mercury AMT 1066	My Blue Heaven/Wish It Were Me	6
60	Mercury AMT 1076	My Secret/What Does It Matter	5
60	Mercury AMT 1081	Harbour Lights/(By The) Sleepy Lagoon	5
60	Mercury AMT 1098	Ebb Tide/(I'll Be With You In) Apple Blossom Time (featuring Tony Williams)	5
60	Mercury AMT 1106	Red Sails In The Sunset/Sad River (featuring Tony Williams)	5

MINT VALUE £

60	Mercury AMT 1118	To Each His Own/Down The River Of Golden Dreams	5
61	Mercury AMT 1128	If I Didn't Care/True Lover	5
61	Mercury AMT 1154	I'll Never Smile Again/You Don't Say	5
62	Ember JBS 701	Only You/Tell The World	150
66	Stateside SS 511	I Love You 1000 Times/Hear No Evil, Speak No Evil, See No Evil	25
66	Stateside SS 568	I'll Be Home/(You've Got) The Magic Touch	12
67	Stateside SS 2007	With This Ring/If I Had A Love	25
67	Stateside SS 2042	Washed Ashore (On A Lonely Island In The Sea)/ What Name Shall I Give You My Love	25
67	Stateside SS 2042	Washed Ashore (On A Lonely Island In The Sea)/ What Name Shall I Give You My Love (DJ copy)	60
67	Stateside SS 2067	Sweet Sweet Lovin'/Sonata	20
67	Stateside SS 2067	Sweet Sweet Lovin'/Sonata (DJ copy)	60
69	Stateside SS 2150	With This Ring/If I Had A Love (reissue)	8
71	Pye Intl. 7N 25559	Sweet Sweet Lovin'/Going Back To Detroit	15
71	Pye Intl. 7N 25569	With This Ring/I Washed Ashore (On A Lonely Island In The Sea)	8

EPs

56	Mercury MEP 9504	THE FABULOUS PLATTERS	10
57	Mercury MEP 9514	THE FABULOUS PLATTERS VOL. II	10
57	Mercury MEP 9524	THE FABULOUS PLATTERS VOL. III	12
58	Mercury MEP 9526	THE FLYING PLATTERS VOL. I	15
58	Mercury MEP 9528	THE FLYING PLATTERS VOL. II	15
58	Mercury MEP 9537	THE PLATTERS	15
59	Mercury ZEP 10000	PICK OF THE PLATTERS NO. 1	12
59	Mercury ZEP 10008	PICK OF THE PLATTERS NO. 2	12
59	Mercury ZEP 10025	PICK OF THE PLATTERS NO. 3	12
59	Mercury ZEP 10031	PICK OF THE PLATTERS NO. 4	15
59	Mercury ZEP 10042	PICK OF THE PLATTERS NO. 5	12
60	Mercury ZEP 10056	PICK OF THE PLATTERS NO. 6	12
60	Mercury ZEP 10070	PICK OF THE PLATTERS NO. 7	12
61	Mercury ZEP 10112	HARBOUR LIGHTS	15
62	Mercury ZEP 10126	THE PLATTERS ON A PLATTER	25

LPs

57	Mercury MPL 6504	THE PLATTERS	35
57	Mercury MPL 6511	THE PLATTERS VOL. 2	30
58	Mercury MPL 6528	THE FLYING PLATTERS	30
58	Parlophone PMD 1058	THE PLATTERS (10")	250
59	Mercury MMC 14009	AROUND THE WORLD WITH THE FLYING PLATTERS	30
59	Mercury MMC 14010	THE PLATTERS ON PARADE	30
59	Mercury MMC 14014	REMEMBER WHEN?	30
60	Mercury MMC 14045	REFLECTIONS	25
61	Mercury MMC 14072	LIFE IS JUST A BOWL OF CHERRIES	25
64	Mercury MCL 20000	THE PLATTERS SING LATINO	12
67	Stateside S(S)L 10208	GOING BACK TO DETROIT	20

(BUNNIES OF THE) PLAYBOY CLUB

69	Decca LK 4951	CAUGHT LIVE AT THE PLAYBOY CLUB (LP)	20

PLAYBOYS (Jamaica)

71	Tropical AL 007	Change Change/TROPICAL ALL STARS: Version 2	5

PLAYBOYS (U.S.)

58	London HLU 8681	Over The Weekend/Double Talk	50
58	London HLU 8681	Over The Weekend/Double Talk (78)	15

PLAYBOYS (U.S.)

(see also Rad Bryan)

69	Capitol CL 15621	Let's Get Back To Rock And Roll/Homemade Cookin'	6

PLAY DEAD

81	Fresh FRESH 29	Poison Takes A Hold/Introduction (p/s)	7
81	Fresh FRESH 38	T.V. Eye/Final Epitaph (p/s)	7

PLAYERS

63	Oriole CB 1861	Mockingbird/Bizet As It May	25

PLAYERS ASSOCIATION

80	Vanguard VSL 5017	The Get down Mellow Mellow Sound/Version	15

PLAYGIRLS (Jamaica)

65	Black Swan WI 456	Looks Are Deceiving/BABA BROOKS: Dreadnaught	30

PLAYGIRLS (U.S.)

59	RCA RCA 1133	Hey Sport/Young Love Swings The World	20
59	RCA RCA 1133	Hey Sport/Young Love Swings The World (78)	20

PLAYGROUND

67	MGM MGM 1351	At The Zoo/Yellow Balloon	20
69	NEMS 56-4019	I Could Be So Good/The Girl Behind The Smile	10
69	NEMS 56-4442	Things I Do For You/Lazy Days	10

PLAYING AT TRAINS

(see also Waving At Trains)

87	Idea	A World Without Love/Just Around The Mountain/Playing At Trains/ A Japanese Intervention (12" p/s)	70

PLAYMATES

53	London L 1198	My Love Was Wasted On You/You Never Get Too Old To Fall In Love (78)	10
57	Columbia DB 3941	Pretty Woman/Barefoot Girl	15
57	Columbia DB 4033	Island Girl/Darling, It's Wonderful	15
58	Columbia DB 4084	Jo-Ann/You Can't Stop Me From Dreaming	12
58	Columbia DB 4127	Let's Be Lovers/Give Me Another Chance	10

MINT VALUE £

58	Columbia DB 4224	Beep Beep/Your Love	8
59	Columbia DB 4288	Star Love/The Thing-A-Ma-Jig	5
58	Columbia SEG 7864	AT PLAY WITH THE PLAYMATES (EP)	10
59	Columbia SEG 7949	PARTY PLAYMATES NO. 1 (EP)	10
59	Columbia SEG 7966	PARTY PLAYMATES NO. 2 (EP)	10

PLAYMATES (Ireland)

70	Emerald MD 1150	Don't Fight It/Jodi	10

PLAYTHINGS

70	Pye 7N 45212	Stop What You're Doing To Me/Sad (light blue label)	6
70	Pye 7N 45212	Stop What You're Doing To Me/Sad	10
73	Pye 7N 45399	Surrounded By A Ray Of Sunshine/Dance The Night Away	5

BOBBY PLEASE

57	London HLB 8507	Your Driver's Licence, Please/Heartache Street (unissued, 2x1-sided demos - price is for both demos together)	300
57	London HLB 8507	Your Driver's Licence, Please/Heartache Street (78)	40

PLEASERS

77	Solid Gold SGR 104	You Know What I'm Thinking/Hello Little Girl	8
77	Arista ARIST 21	Girl I Know/Don't Go Breaking My Heart (p/s)	5
77	Arista ARIST 152	You Keep Tellin' Lies/I'm In Love/Who Are You (p/s, silver label)	5
77	Arista ARIST 152	You Keep Tellin' Lies/I'm In Love/Who Are You (p/s, blue label)	10
78	Arista ARIST 180	The Kids Are Alright/Stay With Me (p/s)	12
96	Lost Moment LMCD 032	THAMESBEAT (CD)	25

PLEASURE

76	Fantasy FTC 138	Ghettos Of The Mind/I'm Mad (12")	10

PLEASURE BEACH

90s	Acid Jazz AJX 124S	Rollercoaster/Smells Like Teen Spirit (p/s)	20

PLEASURE FAIR

(see also Bread)

68	Uni UN 500	Morning Glory Blues/Fade Out Fade In	12
67	Uni UNL(S) 100	PLEASURE FAIR (LP)	25

PLEASURE GARDEN

(see also Iveys)

68	Sound For Industry SFI 31H/32H	Permissive Paradise/EMPEROR ROSKO & JONATHAN KING: Young London (flexidisc, art sleeve)	100

PLEASURES

65	Sue WI 357	Music City/If I Had A Little Money	45

PLEBS

64	Decca F 12006	Bad Blood/Babe I'm Gonna Leave You	80
60s	Oak	THE PLEBS (LP, 1-sided, private pressing)	1000

PLEXUS

78	Look LKLP 6175	PLEXUS (LP)	65
79	Hill & Dale HD004	LIFE UP THE CREEK (LP)	55

PLUGS

79	Cathedral CATH 1	Too Late/UFO/Sally (gatefold p/s)	20
80	Pop 1	CRACKIN' UP EP	12

JEAN PLUM

76	London HLU 10514	Look At The Boy/Back At You	15

JON PLUM

69	SNB 55-3971	Alice/Sunshine	20
69	SNB 55-4317	You Keep Changing Your Mind/An Apple Falls	15

PLUM & YOUTH

(see also Cozy Powell, Rainbow, Bernie Marsden, Big Bertha)

80s	Checkmount CHK 1	I Got You Babe/Got To Be Moving On (p/s, withdrawn)	15

PLUMMERS

64	Blue Beat BB 260	Johnny/Little Stars (actually by Plamers)	22

PLUS

70	Probe SPB 1009	SEVEN DEADLY SINS (LP, laminated front sleeve, flipbacks)	120

PLUTO

(see also Dry Ice, Foundations)

71	Dawn DNS 1017	Rag A Bone Joe/Stealing My Thunder	20
72	Dawn DNS 1026	I Really Want It/Something That You Loved	30
71	Dawn DNLS 3030	PLUTO (LP, laminated sleeve, lilac label)	160

PNEUMONIA

68	Oak RGJ 625	I Can See Your Face	400

PNEUMONIA

(see also U.K. Decay)

79	Plastic PLAS 001	Exhibition/Coming Attack/U.K. DECAY: U.K. Decay/Carcrash (folded p/s)	25

POACHER

79	RK 1022	Star Love/Question Of Trust	5

POCKETS

77	CBS 5780	Come Go With Me/Pt. 2	8

POCO

(see also Buffalo Springfield, Au Go-Go Singers)

71	Epic EQ 30209	DELIVERIN' (LP, quadrophonic)	12

MINT VALUE £

POEMS
(see also Strawberry Switchblade)
81 Polka DOT 1 ACHIEVING UNITY (EP, initially with booklet) ... 10

POET & ONE MAN BAND
(see also Tony Colton, Nicky Hopkins, Heads Hands & Feet)
69 Verve Forecast SVLP 6012 THE POET AND THE ONE MAN BAND (LP, laminated front sleeve, flipbacks) .. 100

POETS
(see also Pathfinders, [White] Trash, Blue)
64 Decca F 11995 Now We're Thru/There Are Some ... 20
65 Decca F 12074 That's The Way It's Got To Be/I'll Cry With The Moon ... 60
65 Decca F 12195 I Am So Blue/I Love Her Still ... 70
65 Immediate IM 006 Call Again/Some Things I Can't Forget ... 120
66 Immediate IM 024 Baby Don't You Do It/I'll Come Home ... 120
67 Decca F 12569 Wooden Spoon/In Your Tower ... 500
71 Strike Cola SC 1 Heyla Hola/Fun Buggy ... 60
88 Bam Caruso OPRA 088 I Love Her Still/GHOST: Time Is My Enemy (company sleeve, promo only) ... 12

POETS (Ireland)
68 Pye 7N 17668 Locked In A Room/Alone Am I ... 240
68 Target 7N 17668 Locked In A Room/Alone Am I (Irish issue, different label) ... 240

POETS (U.S.)
(see under American Poets)

POGUE MAHONE
(see also Pogues)
84 Pogue Mahone PM 1 Dark Streets Of London/The Band Played Waltzing Mathilda ... 10
84 Pogue Mahone PM 1 Dark Streets Of London/The Band Played Waltzing Mathilda (white label tour copy with 'harp' stamp, 237 only) ... 50

POGUES
(see also Pogue Mahone, Nips, Nipple Erectors, Radiators From Space)
84 Stiff BUY 207 Dark Streets Of London/The Band Played Waltzing Mathilda (reissue of Pogue Mahone) ... 10
84 Stiff BUY 212 Boys From The County Hell/Repealing Of The Licensing Laws (green-tinted p/s) .. 10
84 Stiff BUY 212 Boys From The County Hell/Repealing Of The Licensing Laws (A-label promos in blue-tinted p/s) ... 12
84 Stiff BUY 207/BUY 212 Dark Streets Of London/The Band Played Waltzing Mathilda//Boys From The County Hell/Repealing Of The Licensing Laws (shrinkwrapped double pack) ... 20
85 Stiff DBUY 220 A Pair Of Brown Eyes/Whiskey You're The Devil (picture disc) ... 15
85 Stiff BUYIT 220 A Pair Of Brown Eyes/Whiskey You're The Devil/Muirshin Durkin (12", p/s) ... 15
85 Stiff BUY 212/BUY 220 Boys From The County Hell/Repealing Of The Licensing Laws//A Pair Of Brown Eyes/Whiskey You're The Devil (shrinkwrapped double pack) ... 15
85 Stiff BUY 224 Sally MacLennane/Wild Rover (wraparound poster p/s, green vinyl) ... 10
85 Stiff BUY 224 Sally MacLennane/Wild Rover (wraparound poster p/s) ... 7
85 Stiff BUY 224 Sally MacLennane/Wild Rover (standard p/s) ... 6
85 Stiff PBUY 229 Dirty Old Town/A Pistol For Paddy Garcia (picture disc) ... 10
85 Stiff BUYIT 229 Dirty Old Town/A Pistol For Paddy Garcia/The Parting Glass (12", with poster & stickered p/s) ... 20
85 Stiff BUYIT 229 Dirty Old Town/A Pistol For Paddy Garcia/The Parting Glass (12", without poster & stickered p/s) ... 15
85 Stiff MAIL 3 Dirty Old Town (live)/Sally MacLennane (live)/(interview) (12", mail-order) ... 12
86 Stiff PBUY 243 POGUETRY IN MOTION (EP, picture disc) ... 5
86 MCA MCAT 1084 Haunted/Junk Theme/Hot Dogs With Everything (12", p/s, with poster) ... 7
87 Stiff/Hell BLOOD 1 The Good, The Bad & The Ugly/Rake At The Gates Of Hell (unreleased) ... 0
87 Stiff/Hell BLOODY 1 The Good, The Bad & The Ugly/Rake At The Gates Of Hell (12", unreleased) ... 0
88 Pogue Mahone SGG 1-12 ST. PATRICK'S NIGHT EP (12" EP) ... 7
89 WEA SAM 553 Misty Morning Albert Bridge/(same track) (12" promo, green vinyl) ... 8

POGUES featuring KIRSTY MacCOLL
87 Pogue Mahone CDNY 7 A Fairytale Of New York/The Battle March Medley/Shane Bradley (CD) ... 12

POINDEXTER BROTHERS
66 Verve VS 550 (Git Your) Backfield In Motion/(Grandma) Give That Girl Some Slack ... 20

POINT BLANK MCS
92 Kold Sweat KS120 Planting Semtex/Revenge Of The Ghetto Child (12") ... 15

POINTED STICKS
79 Stiff BUY 59 Out Of Luck/What Do You Want Me To Do/Somebody's Mom (p/s) ... 8
79 Stiff BUY 59 Out Of Luck/What Do You Want Me To Do/Somebody's Mom (12", p/s) ... 10

BONNIE POINTER
78 Motown TMG 1125 Free Me From My Freedom/Tie Me To A Tree ... 8
78 Motown TMG 1134 I Wanna Make It In Your World/Heaven Must Have Sent You ... 15

POINTS PROVEN
92 Payday PD002 Pass The Mic/Noisy Music Pt2/Funky Rhymes, Funky Style (EP) ... 22
93 Payday PD003 ONLY FOOLS AND HORSES (EP) ... 18

POISON GIRLS
(see also Crass, Fatal Microbes/Poison Girls)
79 Small Wonder WEENY 4 HEX (12" EP, with lyric insert) ... 15
80 Crass/Xntrix 421984/1 Persons Unknown/CRASS: Bloody Revolutions (folded 21" x 14" poster p/s) ... 5
81 Crass 421984/10 Pretty Polly/Bully Boys (live) (square red or clear flexidisc free with In The City fanzine, with magazine) ... 10
81 Crass 421984/8 All Systems Go/Promenade Immortelle/Dirty Work (p/s with lyrics) ... 5
83 Illuminat ed ILL 23 One Good Reason/Cinnamon Gardens (p/s) ... 5
83 Illuminated ILL 25 Are You Happy Now?/Cream Dream (p/s) ... 5
80 Crass 421984/2 CHAPPAQUIDICK (LP, with free flexidisc "Statement" [421984/7]) ... 12
81 Xentrix XN 2003 WHERE'S THE PLEASURE? (LP) ... 12
84 Xentirx RM 101 7 YEAR SCRATCH (2-LP) ... 15

MINT VALUE £

POISON IDEA

89	In Your Face FACE 06	IAN MACKAYE (EP)	15
91	Vinyl Solution VS 29	Plastic Bomb/We Got The Beat/Harder They Come/Lawdy Miss Clawdy (double pack, p/s)	8
91	Vinyl Solution VS325	Punish Me/Mario The Cop (p/s, purple vinyl)	8

POISON IVY

64	Granta GR 7EP 1011	CLINGING MEMORIES (EP)	110

POISONED ELECTRIC HEAD

89	Dead Fly ACAD 002	Cap Of Flies/Trickeroo (p/s)	10

POLARBEAR

(see also Snow Patrol)

97	Electric Honey EHRCD007	Starfighter Pilot/Holy Cow/Safety (CD single)	20

POLECAT

76	DJM DJF 20475	MONEY TALKIN' (LP)	12

POLECATS

81	Nervous NER 001	Rockabilly Guy/Chicken Shack (p/s)	6
81	Mercury POLE 1	John I'm Only Dancing/Big Green Car (P/S)	5
81	Nervous NERD 001	CULT HEROES (LP, with Robin Scott aka Boorer)	12

ROLO POLEY

69	Jackpot JP 704	Zapatoo The Tiger/Music House (both sides actually by Lester Sterling)	40

POLICE

(see also Sting, Radio Actors, Zoot Money's Big Roll Band, Last Exit, Newcastle Big Band, Eberhard Schoener, Andy Summers & Robert Fripp)

77	Illegal IL 001	Fall Out/Nothing Achieving (black & white p/s, red & black label, various designs)	10
78	A&M AMS 7348	Roxanne/Peanuts (2.52) ('telephone' p/s, typed matrix no., 'All Rights...' on top half of label)	5
78	A&M AMS 7348	Roxanne/Peanuts (12", 'telephone' p/s)	15
78	A&M AMS 7381	Can't Stand Losing You/Dead End Job (glossy p/s, original issue, label credited to 'Police', rarer black vinyl)	10
78	A&M AMS 7381	Can't Stand Losing You/Dead End Job (glossy p/s, original issue, label credited to 'Police', mid-blue vinyl)	7
78	A&M AMS 7402	So Lonely/Time This Time (p/s, miscredited flip, label credited to 'Police')	5
79	A&M AMS 7348	Roxanne/Peanuts (3.54) reissue, 'group' p/s, handwritten matrix number, blue vinyl)	6
79	A&M AMS 7348	Roxanne/Peanuts (2.52) (reissue, 'group' p/s, typed matrix number, blue)	6
79	A&M AMSP 7348	Roxanne/Peanuts (12", reissue, 'group' p/s)	10
79	A&M AMS 7381	Can't Stand Losing You/Dead End Job (reissue, label credited to 'The Police'; dark blue or light blue vinyl)	10
79	A&M AMS 7381	Can't Stand Losing You/Dead End Job (p/s, reissue, red, yellow, green or white vinyl)	10
79	A&M AMS 7381	Can't Stand Losing You/Dead End Job (p/s, mispressed B-side, plays "No Time This Time")	20
79	Illegal IL 001	Fall Out/Nothing Achieving (reissue, various label designs, green/black p/s)	5
79	Illegal IL 001	Fall Out/Nothing Achieving (reissue, various label designs, purple/blue p/s)	15
79	Illegal IL 001	Fall Out/Nothing Achieving (reissue, various label designs, black & orange p/s)	30
80	A&M AMPP 6001	POLICE PACK (6 x 7" printed foldout PVC pack [AMS 7348, 7381, 7402, 7474 & 7494] & "The Bed's Too Big Without You"/"Truth Hits Everybody" [AMPP 6001/E]; on blue vinyl with 6 inserts)	25
80	A&M SAMP 5	SIX-TRACK RADIO SAMPLER (custom p/s, promo radio sampler)	15
80	A&M AMS 7564	Don't Stand So Close To Me/Friends (poster p/s)	7
81	A&M AMS 8194	Spirits (In The Material World)/Low Life (poster p/s, with badge)	8
83	A&M AM 117	Every Breath You Take/Murder By Numbers (p/s, with free badge)	5
83	A&M AM 117/AM 01	Every Breath You Take/Murder By Numbers//Truth Hits Everybody/ Man In A Suitcase (double pack, gatefold p/s)	10
83	A&M AMSP 117	Every Breath You Take/Murder By Numbers (picture disc)	10
83	A&M AMP 127	Wrapped Around Your Finger/Someone To Talk To (Sting picture disc)	8
83	A&M AMP 127	Wrapped Around Your Finger/Someone To Talk To (Andy Summers or Stewart Copeland picture disc, 1,000 each)	10
78	A&M AMLN 68502	OUTLANDOS D'AMOUR (LP, blue vinyl)	15

POLIPHONY

73	Zella JHLPS 136	POLIPHONY (LP, private pressing)	150

POLITICIANS

72	Hot Wax HWX 114	Love Machine/Free Your Mind	15
72	Hot Wax SHW 5007	THE POLITICIANS (LP)	25

FRANK POLK

65	Capitol CL 15389	Trying To Keep Up With The Joneses/Welcome Home, Baby	60
65	Capitol CL 15389	Trying To Keep Up With The Joneses/Welcome Home, Baby (DJ copy)	125

POLKA DOTS

(see also Teddy Johnson, Laurie Johnson)

63	Philips BL 7576	NICE WORK AND YOU CAN BUY IT (LP)	12

RAY POLLARD

(see also Wanderers)

65	United Artists UP 1111	The Drifter/Let Him Go (And Let Me Love You)	200
65	United Artists UP 1111	The Drifter/Let Him Go (And Let Me Love You) (DJ Copy)	300
66	United Artists UP 1133	It's A Sad Thing/All The Things You Are	100
66	United Artists UP 1133	It's A Sad Thing/All The Things You Are (DJ Copy)	200

POLLCATS

(see also Steve Marriott)

90	Community Charge AXT 1	Poll Tax Blues/Poll Tax Blues (same track both sides, p/s)	10

MINT VALUE £

POLYGON WINDOW
(see also Aphex Twin)

92	Warp WARP LP 7	SURFING ON SINE WAVES (2-LP)	30
93	Warp WARP 33	QUOTH (12" EP, clear vinyl)	25
92	Warp WARP LP 7LTD	SURFING ON SINE WAVES (LP, clear vinyl)	50

POLYPHEMUS

92	Placebo PILL 001	GREAT VILLAGE TRIP EP (10")	8
93	Beggars Banquet BB 212	Masses Of Tiny Dots/Fire Breathing Annabella (p/s)	10
95	B. Banquet BBQ 57CD	Stonecutter (p/s)	8
95	Acme AC 8010LP	SCRAPBOOK OF MADNESS (LP, reissue with insert, 500 only)	18
95	Acme AC 8016LP	STONEHOUSE (LP, gatefold sleeve, 700 only)	18

POLYPHONIC SPREE

02	679 679LO14	ORCHESTRAL: Light And Day/Soldier Girl (p/s, 500 only)	15
02	Good 679L011TLP	BEGINNING STAGES OF (LP)	12

HERB POMEROY BIG BAND

57	Columbia SX 1091	LIFE IS A MANY SPLENDOURED GIG (LP)	12

POMPHEY

72	Green Door GD 4029	Jamaica Skank/JOHNNY MOORE: Bing Comes To Town	10

PONI-TAILS

58	HMV POP 516	Born Too Late/Come On Joey, Dance With Me (as Pony-Tails)	10
58	HMV POP 558	Close Friends/Seven Minutes In Heaven	15
58	HMV POP 558	Close Friends/Seven Minutes In Heaven (78)	12
59	HMV POP 596	Early To Bed/Father Time	15
59	HMV POP 596	Early To Bed/Father Time (78)	12
59	HMV POP 644	Moody/Oom Pah Polka	20
59	HMV POP 663	I'll Be Seeing You/I'll Keep Tryin'	25
58	HMV 7EG 8427	THE PONI-TAILS (EP)	150

JEAN-LUC PONTY
(see also Frank Zappa)

69	Liberty LBL/LBS 83262	ELECTRIC CONNECTION (LP)	20
70	Liberty LBL/LBS 83375	KING KONG (LP)	20

POOGY

74	EMI EMI 2136	She Looked Me In The Eye (I Gave Her My Life)/Morris And His Turtle	8

POOH

72	CBS 7930	I'll Close The Door Behind Me/The Suitcase	20

POOH STICKS
(see also Dumb Angels)

88	Fierce FRIGHT 011	On Tape (p/s, 1-sided, etched)	40
88	Fierce FRIGHT 011	On Tape (p/s, 1-sided, with unetched B-side)	35
88	Fierce FRIGHT 021	1-2-3 Red Light (p/s, 1-sided)	20
88	Fierce FRIGHT 023	Heartbreak (1-sided, etched B-side, hand-coloured promo p/s, with insert)	40
88	Fierce FRIGHT 021-025	FIERCE BOX SET (5 x 1-sided etched discs, hand-coloured labels, with insert)	50
88	Fierce FRIGHT 026	ALAN McGEE (CD EP, with FRIGHT 021-025 tracks plus "On Tape"/ Please Hue, Please, in 7" box with booklet)	20
88	Fierce FRIGHT 026	ALAN McGEE (CD EP, with FRIGHT 021-025 tracks plus "On Tape"/ Please Hue, Please)	10
88	Fierce FRIGHT 028	HEROES AND VILLAINS (LP, with inner)	18
89	Fierce FRIGHT 034	Dying For It (p/s, sold at U.L.U. gig, 300 only, signed)	25
89	Fierce FRIGHT 034	Dying For It (p/s, sold at U.L.U. gig, 300 only, unsigned)	15
89	Fierce FRIGHT 034	Dying For It (1-sided, different p/s to above)	15
89	Cheree CHEREE 3	Go Go Girl/Simon E (flexidisc with foldout Cheree fanzine/sleeve)	8
89	Woosh WOOSH 007/WOOSH 6	Hard On Love (yellow flexi with Pooh Sticks fanzine)//GROOVE FARM: Heaven Is Blue/ESMERALDA'S KITE: Vampire girl (red flexi) (with Woosh fanzine 3)	12
89	Anonymous ANON 2	ENCORES (EP, numbered box set, multi-coloured 1-sided 7" with sweet watch, badge, sticker & booklet)	8
92	Fierce/BMG FRIGHT 42	Million Seller (1-sided)	6
89	53rd & 3rd AGAMC 5	ORGASM (LP, pink vinyl with insert for export)	12
89	Fierce FRIGHT 025	THE POOH STICKS (mini-LP, with inner, black & white sleeve, 1-sided, side 2 etched)	12
89	Fierce FRIGHT 035	TRADE MARK OF QUALITY (LP, mail-order only, plain stickered sleeve with insert, numbered)	18
91	Cheree 18LP	GREAT WHITE WONDER (LP)	12
93	Zoo 11043	MILLION SELLERS (LP)	12

BRIAN POOLE
(see also Brian Poole & Tremeloes)

66	Decca F 12402	Hey Girl/Please Be Mine	10
66	CBS 202349	Everything I Touch Turns To Tears/I Need Her Tonight	22
67	CBS 202661	That Reminds Me Baby/Tomorrow Never Comes	6
67	CBS 3005	Just How Loud/The Other Side Of The Sky	20
69	President PT 239	Send Her To Me/Pretty In The City (as Brian Poole & Seychelles)	5
69	President PT 264	What Do Women Most Desire/Treat Her Like A Woman (with Seychelles)	5

BRIAN POOLE & TREMELOES
(see also Brian Poole, Tremeloes)

62	Decca F 11455	Twist Little Sister/Lost Love	15
62	Decca F 11515	That Ain't Right/Blue	12
63	Decca F 11567	A Very Good Year For Girls/Meet Me Where We Used Meet	10
63	Decca F 11616	Keep On Dancing/Run Back Home	10
63	Decca F 11694	Twist And Shout/We Know	6
63	Decca F 11739	Do You Love Me/Why Can't You Lover Me	5
63	Decca F 11771	I Can Dance/Are You Loving Me At All	8

MINT VALUE £

64	Decca F 11823	Candy Man/I Wish I Could Dance	6
64	Decca F 11893	Someone Someone/Till The End Of Time	5
64	Decca F 11951	Twelve Steps To Love/Don't Cry	8
64	Decca F12037	Three Bells/Tell Me How You Care	6
65	Decca F 12124	After A While/You Know	6
65	Decca F 12197	I Want Candy/Love Me Baby	10
65	Decca F 12274	Good Lovin'/Could It Be You	6
64	Decca DFE 8566	BRIAN POOLE AND THE TREMELOES (EP)	30
65	Decca DFE 8610	BRIAN POOLE AND THE TREMELOES (EP)	30
63	Ace of Clubs ACL 1146	BIG BIG HITS OF '62 (LP)	25
63	Decca LK 4550	TWIST AND SHOUT WITH BRIAN POOLE AND THE TREMELOES (LP)	50
65	Decca LK 4685	IT'S ABOUT TIME (LP)	50

GLYN POOLE

73	York SYK 565	Milly Molly Mandy/Beautiful City	5

LOU & LAURA POOLE

72	Jay Boy BOY 63	Only You And I Know/Look At Me	15

POOR SOULS

65	Decca F 12183	When My Baby Cries/My Baby She's Not There	25
66	Alp ALP 595 004	Love Me/Please Don't Change Your Mind	50

POOR THINGS

66	CBS 202431	We Trust In A Better Way Of Life/Danny Boy	50

GROOVY JOE POOVEY

70	Injun 100	Ten Long Fingers/Thrill Of Love	15
70	Injun 101	Move Around/BILL REEDER: Till I Waltz Again With You	10
81	President PR 497	Lightning From The Sky/You Are My Sunshine	10

IGGY POP

(see also Stooges)

77	RCA PB 9093	China Girl/Baby	5
77	RCA PB 9160	Success/The Passenger	5
77	RCA PB 9160	Some Weird Sin/The Passenger	5
78	RCA PB 9213	I Got A Right/Sixteen (some in b/w picture sleeve)	10
78	Radar ADA 4	Kill City (with James Williamson)/I Got Nothin' (p/s)	5
79	Arista ARISP 274	Five Foot One/Pretty Flamingo (picture disc)	5
79	Arista ARIST 255	I'm Bored/African Man	5
79	Arista ARIST 274	Five Foot One/Pretty Flamingo	5
80	Arista ARIST 327	Loco Mosquito/Take Care Of Me (p/s)	5
81	Arista ARIST 407	Bang Bang /Sea Of Love	5
88	A&M AMCD 909	COMPACT HITS (EP)	8
73	CBS 65586	RAW POWER (LP, with inner, orange label, as Iggy & Stooges)	20
78	Radar RAD 2	KILL CITY (LP, as Iggy Pop & James Williamson)	12
77	RCA PL12275	THE IDIOT (LP)	12
77	RCA PL12488	LUST FOR LIFE (LP)	15
84	RCA NL82488	LUST FOR LIFE (LP, reissue)	12

POPCORNS

63	Columbia DB 4968	Zero Zero/Chinese Twist	15

DAVE POPE

70s	Myrrh MYR 1003	TIME TO TAKE ACCOUNT (LP)	12

TIM POPE

(see also Cure)

84	Fiction FICS 21	I Want To Be A Tree/The Double Crossing Of Two Faced Fred (p/s)	15
84	Fiction FICSX 21	I Want To Be A Tree/(Elephant) Song/ The Double Crossing Of Two Faced Fred (12", p/s)	25

POP GROUP

(see also Slits)

79	Radar ADA 29	She Is Beyond Good And Evil/3.38 (p/s)	10
79	Radar ADA 1229	She Is Beyond Good And Evil/3.38 (12", p/s)	15
79	Rough Trade RT 023	We Are All Prostitutes/Amnesty International Report On British Army Torture Of Irish Prisoners (p/s)	10
80	Rough Trade RT 039/Y Y1	Where There's A Will There's A Way/SLITS: In The Beginning There Was Rhythm (p/s)	8
79	Radar RAD 20	Y (LP, with foldout colour poster)	30
80	Rough Trade ROUGH 9	FOR HOW MUCH LONGER DO WE TOLERATE MASS MURDER? (LP, with 4 black-and-white posters)	20
80	Y/Rough Trade ROUGH 12	WE ARE TIME (LP, plain black sleeve)	15

FRANK POPP ENSEMBLE

01	Blow Up BU026	Hip Teens Don't Wear Blue Jeans/The Catwalk	5

POPPIES

66	Columbia DB 7879	Lullaby Of Love/I Wonder Why	30

KEITH POPPIN

73	Randy's RAN 531	Kick The Bucket/I'm A Man Of My Word	6
75	Sunshot SS001	Envious/Fed Up	10
76	Sunshot SS004	Who Are You/Dub Heavier Than Lead	8
76	Sunshot SS006	It's Too Late/Part 2	8
76	Sunshot SS012	Someday Girl/Version	8
76	Mango 1002	Time Slipping Away/King Tubby's Time	12
79	JB Music JBD 006	Hold Not Thy Peace/Birdie (12")	80

POPPY FAMILY

69	Decca F 22976	Which Way You Going Billy/Endless Sleep	8
71	Decca F 13132	I Was Wondering/Where Evil Grows	6

MINT VALUE £

70	Decca KL-R 5022	WHICH WAY YOU GOING BILLY? (LP, mono)	15
70	Decca SKL-R 5022	WHICH WAY YOU GOING BILLY? (LP, stereo)	12
72	Decca SKL 5114	POPPY SEEDS (LP)	12

POPPYHEADS

88	Sha La La Ba Ba Ba Ba 4	POSTCARD FOR FLOSSY (EP, 1-sided flexidisc, p/s in poly bag)	8
88	Sarah SARAH 006	Cremation Town/Pictures You Weave/Dreamboat (foldaround p/s with large poster in poly bag)	10

POP RIVETS

(see also Milkshakes)

79	Hypocrite HEP 001	POP RIVITS (EP, no p/s)	12
79	Hypocrite HEP 002	Pop Rivits/Sulphate	15
79	Hypocrite JIM 1	FUN IN THE U.K. (EP, no p/s, double pack)	30
79	Hypocrite HIP-O	EMPTY SOUNDS FROM ANARCHY RANCH (LP, coloured back, stamped labels)	30
80	Hypocrite HIP 007	THE POP RIVETS GREATEST HITS (LP, screen-printed sleeve)	15
90s	Damaged Goods DAMGOOD 142	CHATHAM'S BURNING (LP, brown vinyl)	12

POPSICLES

(see also Ellie Greenwich, Raindrops)

65	Vocalion VH 9243	I Don't Want To Be Your Baby Anymore/Baby I Miss You	50

POP TOPS

72	A&M AMS7001	Susan Susan/Oh Lord Why Lord	15
69	Major MInor MM 594	That Woman/The Man I m Today (Adagio Cardinal)	10

POPULAR 5

68	Minit MLF 11011	I'm A Lovemaker/Little Bitty Pretty One	15

POP WORKSHOP

68	Page One POF 091	Fairyland/When My Little Girl Is Happy	30
69	Page One POF 129	Punch And Judy Man/Love Is A One Way Highway	10

PORCUPINE TREE

94	Delerium DELEC EP 032	Stars Die/Moonloop (12", p/s)	15
99	K-Scope/Snapper SMAS 103	Piano Lessons/Oceans Have No Memory (p/s, 1,000 copies)	15
99	K-Scope/Snapper SMAS 107	Stranger By The Minute/Hallogallo (p/s, 1,000 only)	15
99	K-Scope/Snapper SMAS 110	Pure Narcotic/Nine Cats - Acoustic (p/s)	15
00	K-Scope/Snapper SMAS 120	Shesmovedon/Novak (P/s, 1000 only)	10
00	K-Scope/Snapper SMAS 7111	4 Chords That Made A Million/Orchidia (p/s, 1,000 only)	12
90	Private (No Cat. No.)	LOVE, DEATH AND MUSSOLINI (EP, 10 copies, plain black cassette with 3 page booklet)	400
92	Delerium DELEC EP 007	VOYAGE 34 (Astralasia Remix) (12" EP)	15
92	Delerium DELEC EP 010	VOYAGE 34 (12" EP)	45
92	Delerium DELECD EP 010	VOYAGE 34 (CD EP, first 100 with blue not green artwork)	60
98	Chromatic CHR 003	METANOIA (EP, 2 x 10", 1,000 only)	60
01	Delerium (No Cat. No.)	TRANSMISSION IV - MOONLOOP EP (Free to Transmission Subscribers, 500 only)	80
89	Delerium DELC 0002	TARQUIN'S SEAWEED FARM (cassette, 1st issue, around 50 only)	300
91	Delerium DELC 0002	TARQUIN'S SEAWEED FARM (cassette, 2nd issue, silver print, with A4 booklet, red/black text, 300 only)	100
91	Delerium DELC 0002	TARQUIN'S SEAWEED FARM (cassette, silver print, with photocopied A5 booklet, label on Side 1, 200 only)	40
91	Delerium DELC 0003	THE NOSTALGIA FACTORY (cassette, silver print, with A4 booklet, red/black text, 200 only)	200
91	Delerium DELC 0003	THE NOSTALGIA FACTORY (cassette, with photocopied A5 booklet, label on Side 1, 200 only)	50
92	Delerium DELEC 008	ON THE SUNDAY OF LIFE (2-LP, gatefold sleeve, 1,000 only)	80
92	Delerium DELEC CD 008	ON THE SUNDAY OF LIFE (CD)	25
93	Delerium DELEC 020	UP THE DOWN STAIR (LP)	60
94	Delerium DELEC PROMO CASS 5	SPIRAL CIRCUS (cassette give away free with Transmission newsletter)	150
94	Magic Gnome MG 4299325	YELLOW HEADGROW DREAMSCAPE (CD, 2,500 only)	100
95	Delerium DELEC LP 028	THE SKY MOVES SIDEWAYS (LP, 2,000 on blue vinyl with poster)	40
96	Delerium DELECLP 045	SIGNIFY (double LP, gatefold sleeve)	30
97	Chromatic CHR 002	SPIRAL CIRCUS (LP, 500 only)	130
01	K-Scope/Snapper SMACD840	23 RECORDINGS (CD, numbered slipcase)	50
06	Delerium DELECLP999	MOONLOOP (LP, in screen printed blue vinyl bag)	25
06	Gates Of Dawn GOD 011	STUPID DREAM (2-LP, silver vinyl)	60

PORK DUKES

77	Wood WOOD 9	Bend And Flush/Throbbing Gristle (p/s)	10
77	Wood BRANCH 9	Making Bacon/Tight Pussy (12", p/s, yellow vinyl)	12
78	Wood Standard WOOD 56	Telephone Masturbator/Melody Makers (p/s)	10
78	Wood PORK 001	THE PORK DUKES (LP, pink vinyl with warning sticker & postcard)	25
80	Wood PORK 2	PIG OUT OF HELL (LP)	25

DAVID PORTER

70	Stax STAX 150	One Part - Two Parts/Can't I See You When I Want To	8
70	Stax SXATS 1034	GRITTY, GROOVY AND GETTIN' IT (LP)	15
71	Stax STX 1030	VICTIM OF THE JOKE (LP)	20
71	Stax 2362 006	INTO A REAL THING (LP)	15

NOLAN PORTER

72	Probe PRO 580	If I Could Only Be Sure/Work It Out In The Morning	75
72	Probe PRO 580	If I Could Only Be Sure/Work It Out In The Morning (DJ copy)	100
72	Probe SPB 1067	NOLAN (LP)	25

ROBIE PORTER

66	MGM 1313	Either Way I Lose/That's The Way Love Goes	20
66	MGM 1306	Here In My Arms/I've Often Wondered	6

PORTER CUNNINGHAM

72	Folk Heritage FHR 027	OBSERVATIONS (LP)	130

MINT VALUE £

PORTION CONTROL

82	In Phaze POR CON 006	Surface And Be Seen/Spinola (Blotch)/Terror Leads To Better Days/Simple As ABC/Monstrous Bulk/He Is A Barbarian (12" p/s, with plastic outer sleeve)	60
83	Illuminated ILL 2612	Raise The Pulse/Collapse/Bite My Head	8
83	Illuminated ILL 2612	Raise The Pulse/Collapse/Bite My Head (12", p/s)	10
84	Illuminated ILL 3212	Rough Justice/The Man Who Did Backwards Somersaults (12", p/s with inner)	8
85	Illuminated ILL 4312	Go-Talk/Upside Down/Drag Down (12", p/s)	8
85	Rhythmic/Havoc 7RMIC 7	The Great Divide/Totall Recall (p/s)	5
85	Rhythmic/Havoc 12RMIC 7	The Great Divide/Divided/Bolt It Down (12", p/s)	8
85	Rhythmic/Havoc 12RMICX 7	The Great Divide (Julian Mendelsohn Remix)/Divided/Bolt It Down (12", p/s)	12
86	Dead Man's Curve DMC 1	PRESENT PURGE (12" EP)	8
81	In Phaze PORCON 002	DINING ON THE FLESH (cassette box set with free flexi 7")	70
81	In Phaze PORCON 002	GAINING MOMENTUM (cassette)	45
82	In Phaze CP 007	I STAGGERED MENTALLY (LP)	25
82	In Phase NCN	WITH MIXED EMOTION (cassette)	40
82	Third Mind TMT 07	SHOT IN THE BELLY (cassette)	40
83	In Phaze EZ 2	HIT THE PULSE (mini-LP, 45/33rpm)	18
84	Illuminated JAMS 44	STEP FORWARD (LP)	12
85	In Phaze PHA 5	SIMULATE SENSUAL (LP, clear vinyl, PVC sleeve with insert)	25
86	Dead Man's Curve DMC 8	PSYCHO-BOD SAVES THE WORLD (LP, with inner sleeve)	12

PORTISHEAD
(see also Jimi Entley Sound)

94	Go Beat GODX 120	Glory Box/Toy Box/Scorn/Sheared Box (12", p/s)	12
97	Go Beat 571 597-1	All Mine/Cowboys/Cowboys (Instrumental) (12", p/s)	10
94	Go Beat 828 522	DUMMY (LP)	30
97	Go Beat 539189-1	PORTISHEAD (LP, gloss sleeve)	20
08	Island 1766390	THIRD (2-LP, etched 12", print, with USB stick, numbered)	45

PORTOBELLO EXPLOSION
(see also Mirage, Jawbone, Spencer Davis Group)

69	Carnaby CNS 4001	We Can Fly/Hot Smoke And Sasafrass (label credits Portebello Explosion)	30

PORTRAIT

71	Pye 7N 45043	Tokaido Lines/Cuddle Me Closer	6

PORTRAIT OF DAN TRACY

94	Direct Lite 726	Silly Girl/I Know Where Syd Barrett Lives/Remember Bridget Riley A Picture Of Dorian Grey (p/s)	10

PORTSMOUTH FOOTBALL PLAYERS

70s	Solent SS 046	Sing Along With Pompey/Pompey Cirty With A Heart	8

PORTWAY PEDLARS

84	Greenwich Village GVR 229	IN GREENWOOD SHADES (LP)	15

SANDY POSEY

66	MGM MGM 1321	Born A Woman/Caution To The Wind	5
66	MGM MGM 1330	Single Girl/Blue Is My Best Colour	6
67	MGM MGM 1335	What A Woman In Love Won't Do/Shattered	8
67	MGM MGM 1342	I Take It Back/The Boy I Love	8
67	MGM MGM 1364	Are You Never Coming Home/I Can Show You How To Live	8
67	MGM MGM-C(S) 8035	BORN A WOMAN (LP)	25
67	MGM MGM-C(S) 8042	SINGLE GIRL (LP)	20
68	MGM MGM-C(S) 8051	SANDY POSEY (LP)	20
68	MGM MGM-C 8060	THE BEST OF SANDY POSEY (LP, original with blue label)	20
68	MGM MGM-C(S) 8073	LOOKING AT YOU (LP)	20

POSH

81	Marathon RUN 1	Letter To Linda/Racey Tracey (p/s)	10

POSITIVE FORCE

79	Sugarhill SH 102	We Got The Funk/Tell Me What You See (12")	8

HOWIE POST & SWIFTIES

63	Fontana TF 421	Tom Swift/The Elephant	10

ADRIENNE POSTER/POSTA

63	Oriole CB 1890	Only Fifteen/There's Nothing You Can Do About That	30
63	Decca F 11797	Only Fifteen/There's Nothing You Can Do About That (reissue)	20
64	Decca F 11864	Shang A Doo Lang/When A Girl Really Loves You	25
65	Decca F 12079	He Doesn't Love Me/The Way You Do The Things You Do	25
65	Decca F 12181	The Winds That Blow/Back Street Girl	25
66	Decca F 12329	Something Beautiful/So Glad You're Mine	35
66	Decca F 12455	They Long To Be Close To You/How Can I Hurt You (as Adrienne Posta)	20
73	DJM DJS 286	Dog Song/Express Yourself	12

POST MORTEM

83	Regime FM 006	BETER OFF DEAD (EP)	25

POTATOES

66	Fontana TF 756	The Bend/Bend Ahead	7

POTENTIAL BAD BOY

06	Sublogic/Ninety-Two Retro SLVR 001/9T2RX	Everyday Child (1-sided 12", 100 only, stamped and hand-numbered labels)	40

POTENTIAL THREAT

82	Out Of Town HOOT 7	WHAT'S SO GREAT BRITAIN! (EP)	30
80s	Mortarhate MORT 24	DEMAND AN ALTERNATIVE (LP)	30

KEITH POTGER
(see also Seekers, Judith Durham)

69	Mercury MF 1073	The World Would Never Turn Again/Santa Marie (in p/s)	8
69	Mercury MF 1073	The World Would Never Turn Again/Santa Marie	6

MINT VALUE £

POTLIQUOR

72	Janus 6146 011	Cheer/Chatanooga	8
70	Dawn DNLS 3016	FIRST TASTE (LP, withdrawn)	90
72	Janus 6310 202	LEVEE BLUES (LP)	30
72	Janus 6310 203	FIRST TASTE (LP, reissue)	12

PHIL POTTER

76	Genesis GEN 10	MY SONG IS LOVE UNKNOWN (LP)	20
79	Dove DOVE 61	THE RESTORER (LP)	15
70s	Kingsway KMR 321	LEAD ME ON (LP)	12

POTTERS

72	Trent JT 100	We'll Be With You/Theme For A Team	20

POUND HOUNDS

(see also Peggy Lee)

55	Brunswick 05484	Home Sweet Home/MELLOMEN: Lady	5

ALLEN POUND'S GET RICH

66	Parlophone R 5532	Searchin' In The Wilderness/Hey You (rare stock copy)	900
66	Parlophone R 5532	Searchin' In The Wilderness/Hey You (more common demo)	500

FRANCK POURCEL

59	HMV POP 622	Only You/Rainy Night In Paris	8

FRANK POURCEL

73	Paramount PAS 6064	JAMES BOND'S GREATEST HITS (LP)	20

BUD POWELL (TRIO)

55	Vogue EPV 1030	BUD POWELL TRIO (EP)	15
55	Vogue EPV 1033	BUD POWELL'S MODERNISTS (EP)	15
55	Vogue EPV 1036	BUD POWELL TRIO (EP)	15
55	Columbia Clef SEB 10013	BUD POWELL (EP)	15
57	Columbia Clef SEB 10074	GENIUS OF BUD POWELL (EP)	15
58	Columbia Clef SEB 10094	GENIUS OF BUD POWELL NO. 2 (EP)	15
52	Vogue LDE 010	THE BUD POWELL TRIO (10" LP)	20
54	Vogue LDE 053	JAZZ AT THE MASSEY HALL VOL. 2 (10" LP)	20
56	Columbia Clef 33C 9016	BUD POWELL TRIO (10" LP)	25
57	Columbia Clef 33CX 10069	JAZZ ORIGINAL (LP)	30
58	Columbia Clef 33CX 10123	BLUES FOR BUD (LP)	30
59	HMV CLP 1294	THE LONELY ONE (LP)	30
63	Vogue LAE 558	THE BUD POWELL TRIO (LP)	15
63	Columbia 33SX 1575	THE BUD POWELL TRIO FEATURING MAX ROACH (LP)	25
64	Fontana FJL 903	HOT HOUSE (LP)	25
68	Fontana SFJL 901	BLUES FOR BOUFFEMONT (LP)	25
73	Mainstream MSL 1007	UPS 'N' DOWNS (LP, gatefold)	12

COZY POWELL

(see also Rainbow, Young Blood, Big Bertha, Ace Kefford Stand, Bedlam, Bernie Marsden, Phenomena, Black Sabbath, Jeff Beck, Whitesnake, Michael Schenker Group, Donovan, Gary Moore, Young & Moody, Brian May, Chick Churchill, Graham Bonnet, Forcefield, Emerson Lake & Powell, Jack Bruce, Plum & Youth, Suzi Quatro)

73	Rak RAK 164	Dance With The Devil/And Then There Was Skin (export copy, European diff p/s)	10
73	Rak 4C 006 94962	Dance With The Devil/And Then There Was Skin (export issue, p/s, RAK 164 in run-out groove, blue or yellow vinyl)	20
73	Rak 4C 006 94962	Dance With The Devil/And Then There Was Skin (export issue, p/s, RAK 164 in run out groove)	12
74	Rak RAK 4C006-95491	The Man In Black/After Dark (export issue, p/s)	10
74	Rak RAK 4C006-95491	The Man In Black/After Dark (export issue, p/s)	10
79	Ariola ARO 189	Theme One/Over The Top pt. 1 (p/s, red vinyl)	5
79	Ariola ARPD 189	Theme One/Over The Top (full version) (12")	10
79	Ariola ARO 205	The Loner/El Sid (p/s, blue vinyl)	5
80	Ariolo ARO 222	Heidi Goes To Town/Over The Top Part 2 (p/s, clear vinyl)	5
92	Old Gold OG 6177	Dance With The Devil/Na Na Na/The Man In Black (CD, single)	10

DICK POWELL

63	Ace Of Hearts AH 50	DICK POWELL SONG BOOK (LP)	12

JANE POWELL

(see also Marilyn Monroe)

53	MGM SP 1061	Something Wonderful/I Whistle A Happy Tune	5
53	MGM SP 1062	Hello, Young Lovers/We Kiss In A Shadow	5
56	HMV POP 267	True Love/Mind If I Make Love To You	6
59	MGM MGM-EP 701	JANE POWELL SINGS (EP)	8
54	Capitol LC 6665	THREE SAILORS AND A GIRL (10" LP)	15
57	HMV CLP 1131	JANE POWELL (LP)	15

JIMMY POWELL (& DIMENSIONS)

62	Decca F 11447	Sugar Babe (Parts 1 & 2) (solo)	15
62	Decca F 11544	Tom Hark/Dance Her By Me (solo)	10
63	Decca F 11570	Remember Them/Everyone But You (solo)	8
64	Pye 7N 15663	That's Alright/I'm Looking For A Woman	60
64	Pye 7N 15735	Sugar Babe/I've Been Watching You (as Jimmy Powell & 5 Dimensions)	20
66	Strike JH 309	I Can Go Down/Love Me Right	15
67	Decca F 12664	Unexpected Mirrors/Time Mends Broken Hearts (with Dimensions)	10
68	Decca F 12751	I Just Can't Get Over You/Real Cool (with Dimensions)	8
68	Decca F 12793	Sugar Babe (Parts 1 & 2)	10

JUDITH POWELL

67	RCA RCA 1569	Greener Days/No Goodbyes	6

KEITH POWELL (& VALETS)

(see also Move, Carl Wayne & Vikings)

63	Columbia DB 7116	The Answer Is No!/Come On And Join The Party (with Valets)	15

			MINT VALUE £
64	Columbia DB 7229	Tore Up/You Better Let Him Go (with Valets)	25
64	Columbia DB 7366	I Should Know Better (But I Don't)/Too Much Monkey Business (with Valets)	35
65	Piccadilly 7N 35235	People Get Ready/Paradise	15
65	Piccadilly 7N 35249	Come Home Baby/Beyond The Hill	15
66	Piccadilly 7N 35275	Goodbye Girl/It Was Easier To Hurt Her	15
66	Piccadilly 7N 35300	Victory/Some People Only	15
66	Piccadilly 7N 35353	It Keeps Rainin'/Song of The Moon	20

KEITH (POWELL) & BILLIE (DAVIES)

(see also Keith Powell, Billie Davis)

66	Piccadilly 7N 35288	When You Move, You Lose/Tastes Sour, Don't It? (as Keith & Billie)	15
66	Piccadilly 7N 35321	You Don't Know Like I Know/Two Little People	15
66	Piccadilly 7N 35340	Swingin' Tight/That's Really Some Good	15

MARILYN POWELL

64	Fontana TF 448	All My Loving/After The Party	7
65	Fontana TF 526	Please Go Away/Where Did I Go Wrong	5
65	Fontana TF 557	As Long As You Come Back To Me/Go Away	5
65	Fontana TF 687	Showdown/Came The Day	5
68	CBS 2331	Something To Hold On To/Kiss Me Again	5

RAY POWELL

74	RCA 2490	King Kong/Rock Ness Monster	5

POWER

82	Malaco MAL1	Groovin'/Instrumental	8

DUFFY POWER

(see also Alexis Korner, John McLaughlin, Jack Bruce, Graham Bond, Duffy's Nucleus)

59	Fontana H 194	Dream Lover/That's My Little Suzie	15
59	Fontana H 194	Dream Lover/That's My Little Suzie (78)	20
59	Fontana H 214	Kissin' Time/Ain't She Sweet	15
59	Fontana H 214	Kissin' Time/Ain't She Sweet (78)	20
59	Fontana H 230	Starry-Eyed/Prettier Than You	15
59	Fontana H 230	Starry-Eyed/Prettier Than You (78)	20
60	Fontana H 279	Whole Lotta Shakin' Goin' On/If I Can Dream	30
61	Fontana H 302	I've Got Nobody/When We're Walking Close	15
61	Fontana H 344	No Other Love/What Now	12
63	Parlophone R 4992	It Ain't Necessarily So/If I Get Lucky Someday	12
63	Parlophone R 5024	I Saw Her Standing There (with Graham Bond Quartet)/Farewell Baby	40
63	Parlophone R 5059	Hey Girl/Woman Made Trouble	15
64	Parlophone R 5111	Parchman Farm/Tired, Broke And Busted (with Paramounts)	40
64	Parlophone R 5169	Where Am I?/I Don't Care	40
67	Parlophone R 5631	Davy O'Brien (Leave That Baby Alone)/July Tree	30
70	CBS 5176	Hell Hound/Hummingbird	15
71	Epic EPC 7139	Hummingbird/Hell Hound (reissue)	6
73	GSF GSZ 6	River/Little Soldiers	5
73	GSF GSZ 8	Liberation/Song About Jesus	5
71	Transatlantic TRA 229	INNOVATIONS (LP)	50
73	GSF GS 502	DUFFY POWER (LP)	20
73	Spark SRLM 2005	DUFFY POWER (LP)	20
76	Buk BULP 2010	POWERHOUSE (LP, revised reissue of GSF GS 502)	15

JIMMY POWER

76	Topic 12TS 306	IRISH FIDDLE PLAYER (LP)	12

POWERCUT CREW

88	PowerCut PC001	Powercut 1/African Beats (12")	30
88	Vinyl Lab VL003	Powercut 1/African Beats (12")	8
89	Vinyl Lab VL007T	You Get Down (12")	8

POWERHOUSE

66	Decca F 12471	Chain Gang/Can You Hear Me?	20
66	Decca F 12507	Raindrops/La Bamba	10

POWERLINE

81	Elite DAZZ 7	Journey (6.54)/Double Journey (13.05) (12", stickered die cut sleeve)	25

POWERLORDS

89	Pow DOT 001T	British Mic Control (12")	10
90	Commercial DOT005T	The Posse's Ready (12")	10

POWERPACK

(see also Procol Harum, Emperor Rosko & Power Pack)

66	CBS 202335	It Hurts Me So/What You Gonna Do	40
67	CBS 202551	I'll Be Anything For You/The Lost Summer	20
69	Polydor 56319	Hannibal Brooks/Juliet Simkins	8
70	Polydor 2001 077	Oh Calcutta/Soul Searchin'	20
69	Polydor 583 057	SOUL CURE (LP)	60

POWERPILL

(see also Aphex Twin)

92	ffrreedom TABX 110	PAC MAN EP: Powerpill Mix/Ghost Mix/Choci's Hi Score Mix/ Mickey Finn's Yum Yum Mix (12", limited edition yellow vinyl)	30
92	ffrreedom TABX 110	PAC MAN EP: Powerpill Mix/Ghost Mix/Choci's Hi Score Mix/ Mickey Finn's Yum Yum Mix (12")	20
92	ffrreedom TABX 110	PAC MAN EP: Powerpill Mix/Ghost Mix/Choci's Hi Score Mix/ Mickey Finn's Yum Yum Mix (CD)	30

JETT POWERS

(see also P.J. Proby)

70	Liberty LBS 83320	CALIFORNIA LICENCE (LP)	40

JOEY POWERS

63	Stateside SS 236	Midnight Mary/Where Do You Want The World Delivered	12

MINT VALUE £

KID CONGO POWERS
(see also Gun Club)
89 Night Shift NISHI 208T — In The Heat Of The Night/Cat Tabu/La Historia Des Un Amour (12", p/s) . . . 8

POWERS OF BLUE
67 CBS 62953 — FLIP OUT! (LP) . . . 20

POWER STATION
(see also Duran Duran, Robert Palmer)
85 Parlophone 12 RP 6091 — Some Like It Hot (Full Length Version)/The Heat Is On/ Some Like It Hot (12", picture disc) . . . 8

P.P. & PRIMES
(see also Primal Scream, P.P. Arnold)
96 Nice (no cat. no.) — Understanding/STEVIE'S BUZZ (i.e. Buzzcocks): Autumn Stone (promo only) . . 10

PEREZ 'PREZ' PRADO & HIS ORCHESTRA
54 HMV 7M 255 — Skokiaan - Mambo/The High And The Mighty . . . 8
55 HMV 7M 295 — Cherry Pink And Apple Blossom White/Maria Elena . . . 15
55 HMV 7MC 29 — Mambo De La Telefonista/En Las Calles De La Habana (export issue) . . . 8
58 RCA RCA 1067 — Patricia/Why Wait . . . 7
58 RCA RCA 1082 — Guaglione/Paris . . . 10
59 RCA RCA 1129 — Tic Toc Polly Woc/My Roberta . . . 5
58 RCA RD 27102 — DILO (LP) . . . 20
60 RCA RD 27046 — LATIN SATIN (LP) . . . 20
64 Parlophone PMC 1226 — A CAT IN LATIN (LP) . . . 20
74 Contour 2870 385 — NOW (LP) . . . 20

PRAG VEC
(see also Foetus etc.)
78 Spec SP 001 — Wolf/Cigarettes/Existential/Bits! (p/s) . . . 10
79 Spec SP 002 — Expert/The Follower! (p/s) . . . 10
81 Spec RESPECT 1 — NO COWBOYS (LP, with insert) . . . 18

PRAISE
76 No Seven 001 — BLESSED QUIETNESS (LP) . . . 40

PRAM
93 Too Pure PURE 17 — IRON LUNG EP (12") . . . 10
01 Too Pure PURE 41 — HELIUM (LP) . . . 20

PRAMS
81 Product/Ltd. Edition TAKE 3 — Nowhere's Safe/TV PRODUCT: Jumping Off Walls (foldout p/s) . . . 15
86 Classic Quotes CLASS 1 — Black Sheep/Classic Quotes (p/s) . . . 5
80s Wabbit — WHAT'S THE TIME, MR WOLF? (LP) . . . 20

PRATS
80 Rough Trade RT 042 — 1990's POP EP (p/s) . . . 8

ANDY PRATT
69 Polydor 2489 003 — RECORDS ARE LIKE LIFE (LP) . . . 12

GRAHAM & EILEEN PRATT
78 Cottage — CLEAR AIR OF THE DAY (LP) . . . 20
80 Dingle's DIN 308 — TO FRIEND & FOE (LP) . . . 20
81 Dingle's DIN — BANDSTAND (LP) . . . 18
85 Plant Life PLR 068 — HEIROGLYPHICS (LP) . . . 15

PRATT & MCCLAIN
76 Reprise K 14435 — Happy Days/Cruisin' With The Fonz (PS) . . . 6

PHIL PRATT
(see also Charlie Ace, Larry Marshall, Don Drummond)
69 Jolly JY 008 — Sweet Song For My Baby/THRILLERS: I'm Restless . . . 95

PHIL PRATT ALL STARS
(see also Dennis Alcapone, Horace Andy, Dennis Brown, Ken Boothe, Erroll Dunkley, John Holt, Delroy Wilson)
70 Jackpot JP 748 — Cut Throat/KEN BOOTHE: You Left The Water Running . . . 20
71 Punch PH 94 — Winey Winey (actually "Kingstonians Medley" by Kingstonians)/ There Is A Place (actually by Barrington Spence) . . . 20

PRAYING MANTIS
(see also Stratus, Grand Prix, Uriah Heep)
79 Ripper/Harvest HAR 5201 — THE SOUNDHOUSE TAPES PART 2: Captured City/Johnny Cool (p/s) . . . 50
79 Ripper/Harvest 12HAR 5201 — THE SOUNDHOUSE TAPES PART 2 (12") . . . 15
80 Gem GEMS 36 — Praying Mantis/High Roller (p/s, with transfer) . . . 20
80 Gem GEMS 36 — Praying Mantis/High Roller (p/s) . . . 18
81 Arista ARIST 397 — All Day And All Of The Night/Beads Of Ebony (p/s) . . . 12
81 Arista ARIST 478 — Cheated/Thirty Pieces Of Silver/Flirting With Suicide/ Panic In The Streets (2x7", gatefold sleeve) . . . 8
82 Jet JET 7026 — Tell Me The Nightmare's Wrong/A Question Of Time/Turn The Tables (p/s) . . . 20
81 Arista SPART 1153 — TIME TELLS NO LIES (LP, with inner sleeve) . . . 20

PREACHERS
(see also Herd, Peter Frampton, Denny Mitchel & Soundsations, Moon's Train)
65 Columbia DB 7680 — Hole In My Soul/Too Old In The Head . . . 80

PRECISIONS
67 Track 604 014 — If This Is Love (I'd Rather Be Lonely)/You'll Soon Be Gone . . . 40
79 Grapevine GRP 129 — Such Misery/A Lovers Plea . . . 10

PREDATOR
78 Bust! SOL 2 — Punk Man/Paperboy Song (with insert) . . . 60

PREDATOR
85 CTM C 001 — Don't Stop/Shotdown (in p/s) . . . 80
85 CTM C 001 — Don't Stop/Shotdown . . . 30

MINT VALUE £

PREDATORS
83 Ears And Eyes EER 012 — SOCIAL DECAY (LP) — 40

PREDATUR
82 Quicksilver QUICK 5 — Take A Walk/Seen You Here (p/s) — 125

PREFAB SPROUT
82 Candle CANDLE 1 — Lions In My Own Garden (Exit Someone)/Radio Love — 20

PREFECTS
87 Strange Fruit SFPS 025 — PEEL SESSIONS (12") — 8
79 Rough Trade TR 040 — Going Through The Motions/Things In General — 10

PREGNANT INSOMNIA
67 Direction 58-3132 — Wallpaper/You Intrigue Me — 50

PRELUDE
72 Crotchet CME 18A/B — PRELUDE (LP, private pressing) — 70
73 Dawn DNLS 3052 — HOW LONG IS FOREVER (LP, gatefold sleeve) — 20

PRELUDE
72 Decca F13292 — Edge Of The Sea/Looking For Indians — 10
74 Dawn DNLS 3061 — DUTCH COURAGE (LP) — 12

PRELUDE (3)
83 Black Crow CROS 1 — Freedom/Prelude — 10

PREMIERS (U.K.)
64 Silver Phoenix 1002 — Tears, Tears/Bye Bye Johnny — 45

PREMIERS (U.S.)
64 Warner Bros WB 134 — Farmer John/Duffy's Blues — 15
64 Warner Bros W 1565 — FARMER JOHN "LIVE" (LP) — 60

YVONNE PRENOSILOVA
65 Pye 7N 15775 — When My Baby Cries/Come On Home — 50

PRESENCE
76 NC SLCW 1031 — PRESENCE (LP) — 35

PRESENCE
(see also Cure)
91 Reality LOL 1 — In Wonder/Soft (p/s, withdrawn) — 5
91 Reality LOLX 1 — In Wonder/Soft/In Wonder (Didgeribdub Mix) (12", p/s, withdrawn) — 8

PRESIDENT REAGAN IS CLEVER
86 Hyena HAHA 001 — FROM THIS TO THAT EP (12") — 8

PRESIDENTS
72 A&M AMS 856 — 5-10-15-20 Years Of Love/Triangle Of Love — 6
72 Sussex AMLS 65001 — 5-10-15-20-25-30 (LP) — 20

PRESIDENTS
64 Decca F 11826 — Candy Man/Let The Sunshine In — 50

ELVIS PRESLEY
(see also Jordanaires, Scotty Moore, Bill Black's Combo)

HMV 78s
56 HMV POP 182 — Heartbreak Hotel/I Was The One — 20
56 HMV POP 213 — Blue Suede Shoes/Tutti Frutti — 25
56 HMV POP 235 — I Want You, I Need You, I Love You/My Baby Left Me — 25
56 HMV POP 249 — Hound Dog/Don't Be Cruel — 15
56 HMV POP 253 — Love Me Tender/Anyway You Want Me (That's How I Will Be) — 20
56 HMV POP 272 — Blue Moon/I Don't Care If The Sun Don't Shine — 30
57 HMV POP 295 — Mystery Train/Love Me — 45
57 HMV POP 305 — Rip It Up/Baby, Let's Play House — 40
57 HMV POP 330 — Too Much/Playing For Keeps — 30
57 HMV POP 359 — All Shook Up/That's When Your Heartaches Begin — 15
57 HMV POP 378 — Paralyzed/When My Blue Moon Turns To Gold Again — 30
57 HMV POP 408 — Tryin' To Get To You/Lawdy, Miss Clawdy — 40
58 HMV POP 428 — I'm Left, You're Right, She's Gone/How Do You Think I Feel? — 40

HMV 45s: PURPLE LABEL/GOLD PRINT
56 HMV 7M 385 — Heartbreak Hotel/I Was The One ('removable/replaceable' centre) — 350
56 HMV 7M 385 — Heartbreak Hotel/I Was The One (solid centre) — 200
56 HMV 7M 405 — Blue Suede Shoes/Tutti Frutti — 300
56 HMV 7M 424 — I Want You, I Need You, I Love You/My Baby Left Me ('removable/replaceable centre) — 300
56 HMV 7M 424 — I Want You, I Need You, I Love You/My Baby Left Me ('solid centre) — 200
56 HMV POP 249 — Hound Dog/Don't Be Cruel — 120
56 HMV POP 253 — Love Me Tender/Anyway You Want Me (That's How I Will Be) — 150
56 HMV POP 272 — Blue Moon/I Don't Care If The Sun Don't Shine ('removable/replaceable' centre) — 200
56 HMV POP 272 — Blue Moon/I Don't Care If The Sun Don't Shine (solid centre) — 150
57 HMV POP 295 — Mystery Train/Love Me ('removable/replaceable' centre) — 350
57 HMV POP 295 — Mystery Train/Love Me (solid centre) — 200
57 HMV 7MC 42 — Mystery Train/I Forgot To Remember To Forget (U.K. issue of export single, gold label print only, smooth edge to labels) — 300
57 HMV POP 305 — Rip It Up/Baby, Let's Play House ('removable/replaceable' centre) — 250
57 HMV POP 305 — Rip It Up/Baby, Let's Play House (solid centre) — 200
57 HMV POP 330 — Too Much/Playing For Keeps — 120
57 HMV POP 359 — All Shook Up/That's When Your Heartaches Begin (push-out centre) — 150
57 HMV POP 359 — All Shook Up/That's When Your Heartaches Begin (solid centre) — 100
57 HMV POP 378 — Paralyzed/When My Blue Moon Turns To Gold Again — 100

HMV 45s: PURPLE LABEL/SILVER PRINT
56 HMV 7M 385 — Heartbreak Hotel/I Was The One — 200

			MINT VALUE £
56	HMV 7M 405	Blue Suede Shoes/Tutti Frutti	250
56	HMV 7M 424	I Want You, I Need You, I Love You/My Baby Left Me	150
56	HMV POP 249	Hound Dog/Don't Be Cruel	100
56	HMV POP 253	Love Me Tender/Anyway You Want Me (That's How I Will Be)	100
56	HMV POP 272	Blue Moon/I Don't Care If The Sun Don't Shine	130
57	HMV POP 295	Mystery Train/Love Me	250
57	HMV POP 305	Rip It Up/Baby, Let's Play House	200
57	HMV POP 330	Too Much/Playing For Keeps	150
57	HMV POP 359	All Shook Up/That's When Your Heartaches Begin ('removable/replaceable' centre)	150
57	HMV POP 359	All Shook Up/That's When Your Heartaches Begin (solid centre)	50
57	HMV POP 378	Paralyzed/When My Blue Moon Turns To Gold Again	90
57	HMV POP 408	Tryin' To Get To You/Lawdy, Miss Clawdy	70
58	HMV POP 428	I'm Left, You're Right, She's Gone/How Do You Think I Feel?	70

HMV EXPORT 45s

57	HMV 7MC 42	Mystery Train/I Forgot To Remember To Forget (gold label print, serrated edge to labels)	300
57	HMV 7MC 45	I Want You, I Need You, I Love You/My Baby Left Me (gold label print)	300
57	HMV 7MC 50	Hound Dog/Don't Be Cruel (gold label print)	300
57	HMV JO 465	Love Me Tender/Anyway You Want Me (That's How I'll Be) (gold label print)	300
57	HMV JO 466	Too Much/Playing For Keeps (gold label print)	250
57	HMV JO 473	All Shook Up/That's When Your Heartaches Begin (gold label print)	250

RCA 78s

57	RCA RCA 1013	(Let Me Be Your) Teddy Bear/Loving You	12
57	RCA RCA 1020	Party/Got A Lot O' Livin' To Do	12
57	RCA RCA 1025	Santa Bring My Baby Back (To Me)/Santa Claus Is Back In Town	25
58	RCA RCA 1028	Jailhouse Rock/Treat Me Nice	15
58	RCA RCA 1043	Don't/I Beg Of You	25
58	RCA RCA 1058	Wear My Ring Around Your Neck/Doncha' Think It's Time	30
58	RCA RCA 1070	Hard Headed Woman/Don't Ask Me Why	30
58	RCA RCA 1081	King Creole/Dixieland Rock	40
58	RCA RCA 1088	All Shook Up/Heartbreak Hotel	150
58	RCA RCA 1095	Hound Dog/Blue Suede Shoes	150
59	RCA RCA 1100	One Night/I Got Stung	60
59	RCA RCA 1113	(Now And Then There's) A Fool Such As I/I Need Your Love Tonight	60
59	RCA RCA 1136	A Big Hunk O' Love/My Wish Came True	100
60	RCA RCA 1187	Stuck On You/Fame And Fortune	750
60	RCA RCA 1194	A Mess Of Blues/The Girl Of My Best Friend	1000

ORIGINAL RCA 45s: BLACK LABELS

57	RCA RCA 1013	(Let Me Be Your) Teddy Bear/Loving You	20
57	RCA RCA 1020	Party/Got A Lot O' Livin' To Do	20
57	RCA RCA 1025	Santa Bring My Baby Back (To Me)/Santa Claus Is Back In Town	20
58	RCA RCA 1028	Jailhouse Rock/Treat Me Nice	15
58	RCA RCA 1043	Don't/I Beg Of You	15
58	RCA RCA 1058	Wear My Ring Around Your Neck/Doncha' Think It's Time	15
58	RCA RCA 1070	Hard Headed Woman/Don't Ask Me Why	15
58	RCA RCA 1081	King Creole/Dixieland Rock	15
58	RCA RCA 1088	All Shook Up/Heartbreak Hotel	50
58	RCA RCA 1095	Hound Dog/Blue Suede Shoes	50
59	RCA RCA 1100	One Night/I Got Stung	15
59	RCA RCA 1113	(Now And Then There's) A Fool Such As I/I Need Your Love Tonight	15
59	RCA RCA 1136	A Big Hunk O' Love/My Wish Came True	15

(The above RCA 45s were issued with a triangular centre, round-centre re-pressings are worth half to two-thirds these values. RCA Victor re-pressings are on a par with Triangular centre prices)

60	RCA RCA 1187	Stuck On You/Fame And Fortune	5
60	RCA RCA 1194	A Mess Of Blues/The Girl Of My Best Friend	5
60	RCA RCA 1207	It's Now Or Never (O Sole Mio)/Make Me Know It	5
61	RCA RCA 1216	Are You Lonesome Tonight?/I Gotta Know	5
61	RCA RCA 1226	Wooden Heart/Tonight Is So Right For Love	5
61	RCA RCA 1227	Surrender (Torna A Surriento)/Lonely Man	5
61	RCA RCA 1244	Wild In The Country/I Feel So Bad	5
61	RCA RCA 1258	(Marie's The Name) His Latest Flame/Little Sister	5
62	RCA RCA 1270	Rock-A-Hula Baby/Can't Help Falling In Love	5
62	RCA RCA 1280	Good Luck Charm/Anything That's Part Of You	5
62	RCA RCA 1303	She's Not You/Just Tell Her Jim Said Hello	5
62	RCA RCA 1320	Return To Sender/Where Do You Come From	5

ORIGINAL RCA VICTOR 45s: BLACK LABELS

62	RCA Victor RCA 1280	Good Luck Charm/Anything That's Part Of You	6
62	RCA Victor RCA 1303	She's Not You/Just Tell Her Jim Said Hello	6
62	RCA Victor RCA 1320	Return To Sender/Where Do You Come From	6
63	RCA Victor RCA 1337	One Broken Heart For Sale/They Remind Me Too Much Of You	8
63	RCA Victor RCA 1355	(You're The) Devil In Disguise/Please Don't Drag That String Around	5
63	RCA Victor RCA 1374	Bossa Nova Baby/Witchcraft	6
63	RCA Victor RCA 1375	Kiss Me Quick/Something Blue	6
64	RCA Victor RCA 1390	Viva Las Vegas/What'd I Say	8
64	RCA Victor RCA 1404	Kissin' Cousins/It Hurts Me	6
64	RCA Victor RCA 1411	Such A Night/Never Ending	7
64	RCA Victor RCA 1422	Ain't That Loving You Baby/Ask Me	6
64	RCA Victor RCA 1430	Blue Christmas/White Christmas	8
65	RCA Victor RCA 1443	Do The Clam/You'll Be Gone	7
66	RCA Victor RCA 1509	Frankie And Johnny/Please Don't Stop Loving Me	15
66	RCA Victor RCA 1526	Love Letters/Come What May	7
66	RCA Victor RCA 1545	All That I Am/Spinout	10
66	RCA Victor RCA 1557	If Every Day Was Like Christmas/How Would You Like To Be?	8
67	RCA Victor RCA 1565	Indescribably Blue/Fools Fall In Love	20
67	RCA Victor RCA 1593	The Love Machine/You Gotta Stop	20

			MINT VALUE £
67	RCA Victor RCA 1616	Long-Legged Girl (With The Short Dress On)/That's Someone You Never Forget	20
67	RCA Victor RCA 1628	Judy/There's Always Me	40
67	RCA Victor RCA 1642	Big Boss Man/You Don't Know Me	20
68	RCA Victor RCA 1663	Guitar Man/Hi-Heel Sneakers	10
68	RCA Victor RCA 1688	U.S. Male/Stay Away	15
68	RCA Victor RCA 1714	Your Time Hasn't Come Yet Baby/Let Yourself Go	15
68	RCA Victor RCA 1747	You'll Never Walk Alone/We Call On Him	30
68	RCA Victor RCA 1768	A Little Less Conversation/Almost In Love	25

RCA VICTOR 45s: BLACK LABEL REISSUES

64	RCA Victor RCA 1020	Party/Got A Lot O' Livin' To Do	20
64	RCA Victor RCA 1025	Santa Bring My Baby Back (To Me)/Santa Claus Is Back In Town	30
64	RCA Victor RCA 1028	Jailhouse Rock/Treat Me Nice	25
64	RCA Victor RCA 1043	Don't/I Beg Of You	25
64	RCA Victor RCA 1058	Wear My Ring Around Your Neck/Doncha' Think It's Time	20
64	RCA Victor RCA 1070	Hard Headed Woman/Don't Ask Me Why	30
64	RCA Victor RCA 1081	King Creole/Dixieland Rock	30
64	RCA Victor RCA 1088	All Shook Up/Heartbreak Hotel	30
64	RCA Victor RCA 1095	Hound Dog/Blue Suede Shoes	30
64	RCA Victor RCA 1100	One Night/I Got Stung	20
64	RCA Victor RCA 1113	(Now And Then There's) A Fool Such As I/I Need Your Love Tonight	20
64	RCA Victor RCA 1136	A Big Hunk O' Love/My Wish Came True	20
64	RCA Victor RCA 1187	Stuck On You/Fame And Fortune	15
64	RCA Victor RCA 1194	A Mess Of Blues/The Girl Of My Best Friend	12
64	RCA Victor RCA 1207	It's Now Or Never (O Sole Mio)/Make Me Know It	25
64	RCA Victor RCA 1216	Are You Lonesome Tonight?/I Gotta Know	25
64	RCA Victor RCA 1226	Wooden Heart/Tonight Is So Right For Love	8
64	RCA Victor RCA 1227	Surrender (Torna A Surriento)/Lonely Man	8
64	RCA Victor RCA 1244	Wild In The Country/I Feel So Bad	8
64	RCA Victor RCA 1258	(Marie's The Name) His Latest Flame/Little Sister	6
64	RCA Victor RCA 1270	Rock-A-Hula Baby/Can't Help Falling In Love	7

RCA VICTOR 45s: ORANGE LABEL REISSUES

69	RCA Victor RCA 1088	All Shook Up/Heartbreak Hotel	30
69	RCA Victor RCA 1095	Hound Dog/Blue Suede Shoes	30
69	RCA Victor RCA 1207	It's Now Or Never (O Sole Mio)/Make Me Know It	30
69	RCA Victor RCA 1216	Are You Lonesome Tonight?/I Gotta Know	30
69	RCA Victor RCA 1226	Wooden Heart/Tonight Is So Right For Love	50
69	RCA Victor RCA 1688	U.S. Male/Stay Away	100
71	RCA MAXI 2104	Heartbreak Hotel/Hound Dog/Don't Be Cruel ('Maximillion' sleeve)	10
71	RCA MAXI 2153	Jailhouse Rock/Are You Lonesome Tonight?/(Let Me Be Your) Teddy Bear/Steadfast, Loyal And True ('Maximillion' sleeve)	10
75	RCA MAXI 2601	Blue Moon/You're A Heartbreaker/I'm Left, You're Right, She's Gone ('Maximillion' sleeve)	20

ORIGINAL RCA VICTOR ORANGE LABEL 45s

69	RCA Victor RCA 1795	If I Can Dream/Memories	10
69	RCA Victor RCA 1831	In The Ghetto/Any Day Now	6
69	RCA Victor RCA 1869	Clean Up Your Own Backyard/The Fair's Moving On	6
69	RCA Victor RCA 1900	Suspicious Minds/You'll Think Of Me (p/s)	10
70	RCA Victor RCA 1916	Don't Cry Daddy/Rubberneckin' (p/s)	15
70	RCA Victor RCA 1949	Kentucky Rain/My Little Friend (p/s)	10
70	RCA Victor RCA 1999	I've Lost You/The Next Step Is Love	6
71	RCA Victor RCA 2060	There Goes My Everything/I Really Don't Want To Know (p/s)	10
71	RCA Victor RCA 2084	Rags To Riches/Where Did They Go, Lord (p/s)	10
71	RCA Victor RCA 2125	I'm Leavin'/Heart Of Rome	6
71	RCA Victor RCA 2158	I Just Can't Help Believin'/How The Web Was Woven	6
72	RCA Victor RCA 2188	Until It's Time For You To Go/We Can Make The Morning (p/s)	10
72	RCA Victor RCA 2229	American Trilogy/The First Time Ever I Saw Your Face	10
72	RCA Victor RCA 2267	Burning Love/It's A Matter Of Time	8
72	RCA Victor RCA 2304	Always On My Mind/Separate Ways	7
73	RCA Victor RCA 2359	Polk Salad Annie/See See Rider	7
73	RCA Victor RCA 2393	Fool/Steamroller Blues	7
73	RCA Victor RCA 2435	Raised On Rock/For Ol' Times Sake	7
74	RCA Victor APBO 0196	Take Good Care Of Her/I've Got A Thing About You Baby (solid centre, no p/s)	250
74	RCA Victor APBO 0196	Take Good Care Of Her/I've Got A Thing About You Baby (U.S. import with large centre hole)	15
74	RCA Victor APBO 0280	If You Talk In Your Sleep/Help Me	10
74	RCA Victor RCA 2458	My Boy/Loving Arms	5
74	RCA Victor PB 10074	Promised Land/It's Midnight (1st pressing)	5
74	RCA Victor PB 10074	Promised Land/It's Midnight And I Miss You (2nd pressing with correct B-side title)	15
75	RCA Victor RCA 2562	T-R-O-U-B-L-E/Mr. Songman	5
75	RCA Victor RCA 2635	Green Green Grass Of Home/Thinking About You	5
76	RCA Victor RCA 2674	Hurt/For The Heart	10

RETROSPECTIVE RCA BLUE LABEL 45s

78	RCA PB 9265	Don't Be Cruel/Hound Dog (p/s)	5
78	RCA PB 9334	Old Shep/Paralysed (p/s)	5
80	RCA RCA 4	It's Only Love/Beyond The Reef (p/s)	5
80	RCA RCA 16	Santa Claus Is Back In Town/I Believe (p/s)	5
81	RCA RCA 43	Guitar Man/Faded Love (with matt U.K. p/s [cat. no. RCA 43])	50
81	RCA RCA 43	Guitar Man/Faded Love (with glossy U.S. p/s [cat. no. PB 12158])	5
82	RCA RCA 196	Are You Lonesome Tonight? (Laughing Version)/From A Jack To A King (p/s)	6

OTHER RCA 45s

82	RCA RCAP 232	The Sound Of Your Cry/I'll Never Know (picture disc)	5
83	RCA RCAP 1028	Jailhouse Rock/The Elvis Medley (without "Hound Dog" credit on B-side) (reissue, picture disc)	5

			MINT VALUE £
83	RCA RCAP 1028	Jailhouse Rock/The Elvis Medley (with "Hound Dog" credit on B-side) (reissue, picture disc)	25
83	RCA RCAP 332	Baby, I Don't Care/One-Sided Love Affair/Tutti Frutti (picture disc)	5
83	RCA RCA 369	I Can Help/The Lady Loves Me (p/s)	5
83	RCA RCAP 369	I Can Help/If Every Day Was Like Christmas/The Lady Loves Me (10", picture disc in clear plastic sleeve)	20
84	RCA RCA 405	Green Green Grass Of Home/Release Me (And Let Me Love Again)/ Solitaire (p/s, with poster)	25
84	RCA RCA 405	Green Green Grass Of Home/Release Me (And Let Me Love Again)/Solitaire (p/s)	5
84	RCA RCA 459	The Last Farewell/It's Easy for You (p/s)	5
84	RCA RCAT 459	The Last Farewell/It's Easy for You (10", p/s)	10
85	RCA RCA 476	The Elvis Medley/Blue Suede Shoes (p/s)	5
85	RCA PB 49943	Always On My Mind (Alternate Version)/Tomorrow Night (p/s)	5
87	RCA ARON 1	Bossa Nova Baby/Ain't That Loving You Baby (p/s)	5
87	RCA ARONT 1	Bossa Nova Baby/Ain't That Loving You Baby (12", p/s)	15
87	RCA ARON 2	Love Me Tender/If I Can Dream (p/s)	5
87	RCA ARONT 2	Love Me Tender/If I Can Dream (p/s) (12", p/s)	10
88	RCA PB 49177	Are You Lonesome Tonight/Reconsider Baby (p/s)	5
88	RCA PB 49177	Are You Lonesome Tonight/Reconsider Baby (12", p/s)	10
88	RCA PB 49473	Mean Woman Blues/I Beg Of Of You (p/s)	10
88	RCA PT 49474	Mean Woman Blues/I Beg Of Of You (12", p/s)	20
88	RCA PB 49545	Stuck On You/Any Way You Want Me (p/s)	5
88	RCA PT 49546	Stuck On You/Any Way You Want Me (12", p/s)	10
88	RCA PB 49943	Always On My Mind/Tomorrow Night (p/s)	10
88	RCA PT 49944	Always On My Mind/Tomorrow Night (12", p/s)	20
89	RCA PD 49467	Heartbreak Hotel/I Was The One/Don't Be Cruel (To A Heart That's True)/ Hound Dog (3" CD, gatefold card sleeve)	8
90	RCA TCB 1	(Now And Then There's) A Fool Such As I (Take 3)/Danny (promo only)	12
04	BMG 82876 619211	That's All Right/Blue Moon Of Kentucky (10", brown die-cut sleeve, with 'Sun' labels)	40

SINGLES BOX SET

77	RCA (no cat. no.)	PRESLEY GOLD - 16 NUMBER ONES (16 x 7", each in p/s, black box set)	40

OTHER SINGLES AND FLEXIDISCS

57	Weekend Mail (no cat. no.)	THE TRUTH ABOUT ME (1-sided 6" 78 rpm, mail-order only, in mailer)	70
57	Weekend Mail (no cat. no.)	THE TRUTH ABOUT ME (1-sided 6" 78 rpm, mail-order only, not in mailer)	50
75	Reader's Digest/RCA	Brian Matthew Introduces Excerpts From Elvis Presley's Greatest Hits (6" flexidisc, with newsletter & advertising leaflet)	7
75	Reader's Digest/RCA RD ELV 785/65	Brian Matthew Introduces Excerpts From Elvis Presley's Greatest Hits (6" flexidisc, without newsletter & advertising leaflet)	5
77	RCA Victor 2694-2709	GOLD 16 SERIES (16 x p/s 7" in foldout cardboard carrier)	30
79	RCA LB 1	The Wonder Of You/Noel Edmonds Introduces Record Year (Lever Brothers premium)	20
81	Chiswick NS 71	Press Conference 1957/DEKE RIVERS: Elvis Presley Medley (picture disc)	6
83	Buttons BUT 3	A.F.N. RADIO INTERVIEW (p/s, fan club interview flexidisc)	5
83	Buttons BUT 4	NEW YORK PRESS CONFERENCE (orange vinyl fan club flexidisc, free with Elvis Monthly Collector's Special, issue 2)	5
83	Buttons BUT 5	INTERVIEW BETWEEN ELVIS, PETER NOONE AND TOM MOFFETT (fan club flexidisc free with Elvis Monthly Collector's Special, issue 4)	5
84	Buttons BUT 6	GERMAN RADIO INTERVIEW (fan club flexidisc free with Elvis Monthly Collector's Special, issue 6)	5
84	Buttons BUT 7	ELVIS' 1964 GREETING TO HIS BRITISH FANS/THE TRUTH ABOUT ME (fan club flexi with Elvis Monthly Collector's Special, issue 8)	5
85	Buttons BUT 8	1956 NEW ORLEANS INTERVIEW (fan club flexidisc free with Elvis Monthly Collector's Special, issue 10)	5
85	Buttons BUT 9	JACKSON, FLORIDA 1955 INTERVIEW/MEMPHIS 1957 INTERVIEW (fan club flexidisc free with Elvis Monthly Collector's Special, issue 10)	5

HMV EPs

57	HMV 7EG 8199	LOVE ME TENDER (soundtrack, round centre)	150
57	HMV 7EG 8199	LOVE ME TENDER (soundtrack, removeable/replaceable centre)	175
57	HMV 7EG 8256	GOOD ROCKIN' TONIGHT (round centre only)	200

RCA EPs: ROUND CENTRE RE-PRESSINGS

57	RCA RCX 101	PEACE IN THE VALLEY	40
57	RCA RCX 104	ELVIS PRESLEY	40
58	RCA RCX 106	JAILHOUSE ROCK (soundtrack)	40
58	RCA RCX 117	KING CREOLE VOL. 1 (soundtrack, black label, cream or white rear p/s)	30
58	RCA RCX 118	KING CREOLE VOL. 2 (soundtrack, cream or white rear sleeve)	30
58	RCA RCX 121	ELVIS SINGS CHRISTMAS SONGS (1st issue, single sleeve)	60
58	RCA RCX 131	ELVIS SAILS (interview record, sleeve laminated front & back)	50
59	RCA RCX 135	ELVIS IN TENDER MOOD (with red print on rear sleeve)	65

(The above RCA EPs were originally issued with laminated front and back sleeves; later copies with front-only laminate are worth three quarters of these values.)

59	RCA RCX 1045	A TOUCH OF GOLD (laminated front sleeve only)	70
59	RCA RCX 175	STRICTLY ELVIS	40
60	RCA RCX 1048	A TOUCH OF GOLD VOL. 2	120

RCA EPs: TRIANGULAR CENTRES

60s	RCA RCX 101	PEACE IN THE VALLEY	20
60s	RCA RCX 104	ELVIS PRESLEY	15
60s	RCA RCX 106	JAILHOUSE ROCK (soundtrack)	15
60s	RCA RCX 117	KING CREOLE VOL. 1 (soundtrack)	15
60s	RCA RCX 118	KING CREOLE VOL. 2 (soundtrack)	15
60s	RCA RCX 121	ELVIS SINGS CHRISTMAS SONGS (gatefold p/s)	100
60s	RCA RCX 131	ELVIS SAILS (interview record)	25
60s	RCA RCX 135	ELVIS IN TENDER MOOD	20

MINT VALUE £

60s	RCA RCX 1045	A TOUCH OF GOLD	25
60s	RCA RCX 175	STRICTLY ELVIS	20
60s	RCA RCX 1048	A TOUCH OF GOLD VOL. 2	50

ORIGINAL RCA EPs: ROUND CENTRES

60	RCA RCX 190	SUCH A NIGHT	25
62	RCA RCX 211	FOLLOW THAT DREAM (soundtrack)	10
62	RCA RCX 211	FOLLOW THAT DREAM (mispressing, 2nd side features Jim Reeves)	100
62	RCA RCX 7109	KID GALAHAD (soundtrack)	10
64	RCA Victor RCX 7141	LOVE IN LAS VEGAS (soundtrack)	20
64	RCA Victor RCX 7142	ELVIS FOR YOU VOL. 1	75
64	RCA Victor RCX 7143	ELVIS FOR YOU VOL. 2	75
65	RCA Victor RCX 7173	TICKLE ME (soundtrack)	45
65	RCA Victor RCX 7174	TICKLE ME VOL. 2 (soundtrack)	45
67	RCA Victor RCX 7187	EASY COME, EASY GO (soundtrack)	50

RCA VICTOR EPs: BLACK LABEL RE-PRESSINGS

64	RCA Victor RCX 101	PEACE IN THE VALLEY	20
64	RCA Victor RCX 104	ELVIS PRESLEY	15
64	RCA Victor RCX 106	JAILHOUSE ROCK (soundtrack)	25
64	RCA Victor RCX 117	KING CREOLE VOL. 1 (soundtrack)	15
64	RCA Victor RCX 118	KING CREOLE VOL. 2 (soundtrack)	15
64	RCA Victor RCX 121	ELVIS SINGS CHRISTMAS SONGS (single p/s)	45
64	RCA Victor RCX 131	ELVIS SAILS (interview record)	40
64	RCA Victor RCX 135	ELVIS IN TENDER MOOD	30
64	RCA Victor RCX 1045	A TOUCH OF GOLD	25
64	RCA Victor RCX 175	STRICTLY ELVIS	15
64	RCA Victor RCX 1048	A TOUCH OF GOLD VOL. 2	40
64	RCA Victor RCX 190	SUCH A NIGHT	10
64	RCA Victor RCX 211	FOLLOW THAT DREAM (soundtrack)	10
64	RCA Victor RCX 7106	KID GALAHAD (soundtrack)	10

RCA VICTOR EPs: ORANGE LABEL RE-PRESSINGS

69	RCA Victor RCX 101	PEACE IN THE VALLEY (push-out centre)	15
69	RCA Victor RCX 101	PEACE IN THE VALLEY (solid centre)	15
69	RCA Victor RCX 104	ELVIS PRESLEY (push-out centre)	15
69	RCA Victor RCX 104	ELVIS PRESLEY (solid centre)	12
69	RCA Victor RCX 106	JAILHOUSE ROCK (soundtrack, push-out centre)	8
69	RCA Victor RCX 106	JAILHOUSE ROCK (soundtrack, solid centre)	12
69	RCA Victor RCX 117	KING CREOLE VOL. 1 (soundtrack, push-out centre)	15
69	RCA Victor RCX 117	KING CREOLE VOL. 1 (soundtrack, solid centre)	12
69	RCA Victor RCX 118	KING CREOLE VOL. 2 (soundtrack, push-out centre)	15
69	RCA Victor RCX 118	KING CREOLE VOL. 2 (soundtrack, solid centre)	12
69	RCA Victor RCX 131	ELVIS SAILS (interview record, push-out or solid centre)	15
69	RCA Victor RCX 135	ELVIS IN TENDER MOOD (push-out or solid centre, with different take of "Lover Doll")	15
69	RCA Victor RCX 1045	A TOUCH OF GOLD (push-out centre)	22
69	RCA Victor RCX 1045	A TOUCH OF GOLD (solid centre)	18
69	RCA Victor RCX 175	STRICTLY ELVIS (push-out or solid centre)	18
69	RCA Victor RCX 1048	A TOUCH OF GOLD VOL. 2 (push-out centre)	22
69	RCA Victor RCX 1048	A TOUCH OF GOLD VOL. 2 (solid centre)	18
69	RCA Victor RCX 190	SUCH A NIGHT (push-out centre)	18
69	RCA Victor RCX 190	SUCH A NIGHT (solid centre)	12

EP BOXED SETS

82	RCA EP 1	THE EP COLLECTION (11-EP box set, reissues, with booklet)	60
83	RCA EP 2	THE EP COLLECTION VOL. 2 (11-EP box set, reissues, with booklet)	60

LPs: HMV ISSUES

56	HMV CLP 1093	ROCK 'N' ROLL	500
57	HMV CLP 1105	ROCK 'N' ROLL NO. 2	700
57	HMV DLP 1159	THE BEST OF ELVIS (10")	300

LPs: ORIGINAL BLACK/SILVER SPOT RCA ISSUES

57	RCA RC 24001	LOVING YOU (10", soundtrack)	90
57	RCA RD 27052	ELVIS' CHRISTMAS ALBUM (laminated front & back covers with 4 pictures on back cover)	100
58	RCA RD 27088	KING CREOLE (soundtrack)	35
59	RCA RD 27120	ELVIS	75
59	RCA RD 27128	A DATE WITH ELVIS	50
60	RCA RD 27159	ELVIS' GOLDEN RECORDS VOL. 2	30
60	RCA RD 27171	ELVIS IS BACK! (gatefold sleeve, mono)	40
60	RCA SF 5060	ELVIS IS BACK! (gatefold sleeve, stereo)	60
60	RCA RD 27192	G.I. BLUES (soundtrack, mono)	18
60	RCA SF 5078	G.I. BLUES (soundtrack, stereo)	25
61	RCA RD 27211	HIS HAND IN MINE (mono)	25
61	RCA SF 5094	HIS HAND IN MINE (stereo)	45
61	RCA RD 27224	SOMETHING FOR EVERYBODY (mono)	22
61	RCA SF 5106	SOMETHING FOR EVERYBODY (stereo)	45
61	RCA RD 27238	BLUE HAWAII (soundtrack, mono)	15
61	RCA SF 5115	BLUE HAWAII (soundtrack, stereo)	30
62	RCA RD 27265	POT LUCK (mono)	20
62	RCA SF 5135	POT LUCK (stereo)	40

LPs: SILVER SPOT/'RED SEAL' RCA ISSUES

58	RCA RB 16069	ELVIS' GOLDEN RECORDS (maroon 'silver spot' label, gatefold sleeve with stapled-in 4-page photo booklet)	80
60	RCA RB 16069	ELVIS' GOLDEN RECORDS ('Red Seal'/'silver spot' label, gatefold sleeve with stapled-in 2-page photo booklet)	35
63	RCA RB 16069	ELVIS' GOLDEN RECORDS ('Red Seal'/'black spot' label, no booklet, gatefold sleeve)	25

			MINT VALUE £
67	RCA RB 16069	ELVIS' GOLDEN RECORDS ('Red Seal'/'black spot' label, no booklet, single sleeve)	18

LPs: ORIGINAL BLACK/SILVER SPOT RCA VICTOR ISSUES

63	RCA Victor RD 7534	GIRLS! GIRLS! GIRLS! (soundtrack, mono)	15
63	RCA Victor SF 7534	GIRLS! GIRLS! GIRLS! (soundtrack, stereo)	35
63	RCA Victor RD 7565	IT HAPPENED AT THE WORLD'S FAIR (soundtrack, mono)	18
63	RCA Victor SF 7565	IT HAPPENED AT THE WORLD'S FAIR (soundtrack, stereo)	35
63	RCA Victor RD 7609	FUN IN ACAPULCO (soundtrack, mono)	20
63	RCA Victor SF 7609	FUN IN ACAPULCO (soundtrack, stereo)	35

LPs: ORIGINAL BLACK/RED SPOT RCA VICTOR ISSUES

64	RCA Victor RD 7630	ELVIS' GOLDEN RECORDS VOL. 3 (mono)	20
64	RCA Victor SF 7630	ELVIS' GOLDEN RECORDS VOL. 3 (stereo)	30
64	RCA Victor RD 7645	KISSIN' COUSINS (soundtrack, mono)	18
64	RCA Victor SF 7645	KISSIN' COUSINS (soundtrack, stereo)	30
64	RCA Victor RD 7678	ROUSTABOUT (soundtrack, mono)	15
64	RCA Victor SF 7678	ROUSTABOUT (soundtrack, stereo)	25
65	RCA Victor RD 7714	GIRL HAPPY (soundtrack, mono)	20
65	RCA Victor SF 7714	GIRL HAPPY (soundtrack, stereo)	30
65	RCA Victor RD 7723	FLAMING STAR AND SUMMER KISSES (soundtrack, mono only, black label)	75
65	RCA Victor RD/SF 7752	ELVIS FOR EVERYONE (mono, 'orange shirt' sleeve)	35
65	RCA Victor SF 7752	ELVIS FOR EVERYONE (stereo, 'orange shirt' sleeve)	45
65	RCA Victor RD 7767	HAREM HOLIDAY (soundtrack, mono)	18
65	RCA Victor SF 7767	HAREM HOLIDAY (soundtrack, stereo)	25
66	RCA Victor RD 7793	FRANKIE AND JOHNNY (soundtrack, mono)	20
66	RCA Victor SF 7793	FRANKIE AND JOHNNY (soundtrack, stereo)	30
66	RCA Victor RD 7810	PARADISE, HAWAIIAN STYLE (soundtrack, mono)	20
66	RCA Victor SF 7810	PARADISE, HAWAIIAN STYLE (soundtrack, stereo)	30
66	RCA Victor RD 7820	CALIFORNIA HOLIDAY (soundtrack, mono)	20
66	RCA Victor SF 7820	CALIFORNIA HOLIDAY (soundtrack, stereo)	30
67	RCA Victor RD 7867	HOW GREAT THOU ART (mono)	25
67	RCA Victor SF 7867	HOW GREAT THOU ART (stereo)	35
67	RCA Victor RD 7892	DOUBLE TROUBLE (soundtrack, mono)	18
67	RCA Victor SF 7892	DOUBLE TROUBLE (soundtrack, stereo)	25
68	RCA Victor RD 7917	CLAMBAKE (soundtrack, black/red dot labels, mono)	20
68	RCA Victor SF 7917	CLAMBAKE (soundtrack, black/red dot labels, stereo)	30
68	RCA Victor RD 7924	ELVIS' GOLD RECORDS VOLUME 4 (with "Never Ending" listed on sleeve instead of "Love Letters"; mono)	40
68	RCA Victor SF 7924	ELVIS' GOLD RECORDS VOLUME 4 (with "Never Ending" listed on sleeve instead of "Love Letters"; stereo)	55
68	RCA Victor RD 7924	ELVIS' GOLD RECORDS VOLUME 4 (corrected sleeve, mono)	25
68	RCA Victor SF 7924	ELVIS' GOLD RECORDS VOLUME 4 (corrected sleeve, stereo)	30
68	RCA Victor RD 7957	SPEEDWAY (soundtrack, with Nancy Sinatra, mono)	50
68	RCA Victor SF 7957	SPEEDWAY (soundtrack, with Nancy Sinatra, stereo)	30

LPs: ORIGINAL ORANGE RCA VICTOR ISSUES

69	RCA Victor RD 8011	ELVIS ("TV Special" Soundtrack)	15
69	RCA Victor RD 8029	FROM ELVIS IN MEMPHIS (mono)	15
69	RCA Victor SF 8029	FROM ELVIS IN MEMPHIS (stereo)	12
70	RCA Victor SF 8080/1	FROM MEMPHIS TO VEGAS - FROM VEGAS TO MEMPHIS (2-LP, with 2 x 10" x 8" photos, glossy cover)	30
70	RCA Victor SF 8080/1	FROM MEMPHIS TO VEGAS - FROM VEGAS TO MEMPHIS (2-LP, with 2 x 10" x 8" photos, matt cover)	25
70	RCA SF 8128	ON STAGE, FEBRUARY 1970 (with 30" x 20" colour poster; glossy cover)	15
70	RCA SF 8128	ON STAGE, FEBRUARY 1970 (with 30" x 20" colour poster; matt cover)	12
70	RCA LPM 6401	WORLDWIDE 50 GOLD AWARD HITS VOL. 1 - A TOUCH OF GOLD (4-LP, box set with 20-page photo book)	30
71	RCA LPM 6402	THE OTHER SIDES - WORLDWIDE 50 GOLD AWARD HITS VOL. 2 (4-LP, box with material patch & colour portrait)	30
71	RCA Victor SF 8162	THAT'S THE WAY IT IS (glossy cover)	15
71	RCA Victor SF 8162	THAT'S THE WAY IT IS (matt cover)	12
71	RCA Victor SF 8172	I'M 10,000 YEARS OLD - ELVIS COUNTRY (with colour print, glossy cover)	15
71	RCA Victor SF 8202	LOVE LETTERS FROM ELVIS	18
71	RCA Victor SF 8221	ELVIS SINGS THE WONDERFUL WORLD OF CHRISTMAS	25
72	RCA Victor SF 8266	ELVIS NOW	22
72	RCA Victor SF 8275	HE TOUCHED ME	22
72	RCA Victor SF 8296	ELVIS AS RECORDED AT MADISON SQUARE GARDEN	15
73	RCA Victor SF 8378	ELVIS (with "Fool" sticker, must be UK disc and UK cover!)	50
73	RCA DPS 2040	ALOHA FROM HAWAII VIA SATELLITE (2-LP)	20
73	RCA APL1 0388	RAISED ON ROCK/FOR OL' TIMES SAKE (U.K. disc in U.K. sleeve)	220
74	RCA CPL1 0341	ELVIS - A LEGENDARY PERFORMER VOL. 1	15
74	RCA APL1 0475	GOOD TIMES (back cover credits "Loving Arms" or "Lovin' Arms")	18
74	RCA APL1 0606	ELVIS AS RECORDED ON STAGE IN MEMPHIS	15
74	RCA LPL1 7527	HITS OF THE 70s	15
75	RCA APL1 0873	PROMISED LAND	15
75	RCA APM1 0818	HAVING FUN WITH ELVIS ON STAGE	40
75	RCA RS 1011	TODAY	18
76	RCA CPL1 1349	ELVIS - A LEGENDARY PERFORMER VOL. 2	25
76	RCA RS 1060	FROM ELVIS PRESLEY BOULEVARD, MEMPHIS, TENNESSEE	15
77	RCA LP 3021	MOODY BLUE	12
77	RCA PL 02587	ELVIS IN CONCERT	18
77	RCA PL 12274	WELCOME TO MY WORLD	15
77	RCA PL 12772	HE WALKS BESIDE ME	15
77	RCA PL 42003	ELVIS IN DEMAND	15
80	RCA CPL8 3699	ELVIS ARON PRESLEY (8-LP, box set)	60
83	RCA RCALPP 9020	JAILHOUSE ROCK/LOVE IN LAS VEGAS (picture disc)	12
84	RCA PLP 89287	I CAN HELP (picture disc)	12
84	RCA PL 85172	A GOLDEN CELEBRATION (6-LP box set with inserts)	40

MINT VALUE £

LPs: BLACK/SILVER SPOT RCA VICTOR RE-PRESSINGS

64	RCA Victor RC 24001	LOVING YOU (10" LP, mono only)	110
64	RCA Victor RD 27052	ELVIS' CHRISTMAS ALBUM (laminated front & back covers, no pictures on back cover, mono only)	60
64	RCA Victor RD 7528	ROCK 'N' ROLL NO. 2 (reissue of HMV LP, mono)	18
64	RCA Victor SF 7528	ROCK 'N' ROLL NO. 2 (reissue of HMV LP, stereo)	25
64	RCA Victor RD 27088	KING CREOLE (soundtrack, mono only)	35
64	RCA Victor RD 27120	ELVIS (mono only)	35
64	RCA Victor RD 27128	A DATE WITH ELVIS (mono only)	20
64	RCA Victor RD 27159	ELVIS' GOLDEN RECORDS VOL. 2 (mono only)	15
64	RCA Victor RD 27171	ELVIS IS BACK! (gatefold sleeve, mono)	30
64	RCA Victor SF 5060	ELVIS IS BACK! (gatefold sleeve, stereo)	40
64	RCA Victor RD 27192	G.I. BLUES (soundtrack, mono)	15
64	RCA Victor SF 5078	G.I. BLUES (soundtrack, stereo)	30
64	RCA Victor RD 27211	HIS HAND IN MINE (mono)	25
64	RCA Victor SF 5094	HIS HAND IN MINE (stereo)	30
64	RCA Victor RD 27224	SOMETHING FOR EVERYBODY (mono)	18
64	RCA Victor SF 5106	SOMETHING FOR EVERYBODY (stereo)	30
64	RCA Victor RD 27238	BLUE HAWAII (soundtrack, mono)	18
64	RCA Victor SF 5115	BLUE HAWAII (soundtrack, stereo)	25
64	RCA Victor RD 27265	POT LUCK (mono)	15
64	RCA Victor SF 5135	POT LUCK (stereo)	30

LPs: BLACK/RED SPOT RCA VICTOR RE-PRESSINGS

64	RCA Victor RD 7528	ROCK 'N' ROLL NO. 2 (reissue of HMV LP, mono)	18
64	RCA Victor SF 7528	ROCK 'N' ROLL NO. 2 (reissue of HMV LP, stereo)	25

LPs: 'SMALL' ORANGE RCA VICTOR MONO RE-PRESSINGS

69	RCA Victor RD 27052	ELVIS' CHRISTMAS ALBUM	40
69	RCA Victor RD 27088	KING CREOLE (soundtrack)	30
69	RCA Victor RD 27120	ELVIS	30
69	RCA Victor RD 27128	A DATE WITH ELVIS	30
69	RCA Victor RD 27159	ELVIS' GOLDEN RECORDS VOL. 2	30
69	RCA Victor RD 27171	ELVIS IS BACK! (gatefold sleeve)	30
69	RCA Victor RD 27192	G.I. BLUES (soundtrack)	30
69	RCA Victor RD 27211	HIS HAND IN MINE	30
69	RCA Victor RD 27224	SOMETHING FOR EVERYBODY	30
69	RCA Victor RD 27238	BLUE HAWAII (soundtrack)	30
69	RCA Victor RD 7528	ROCK 'N' ROLL NO. 2	30
69	RCA Victor RD 7630	ELVIS' GOLDEN RECORDS VOL. 3	30
69	RCA Victor RD 7723	FLAMING STAR AND SUMMER KISSES (soundtrack, orange label)	500
69	RCA Victor RD 7810	PARADISE, HAWAIIAN STYLE (soundtrack)	30
69	RCA Victor RD 7867	HOW GREAT THOU ART	30
69	RCA Victor RD 7917	CLAMBAKE (soundtrack)	40
69	RCA Victor RD 7924	ELVIS' GOLD RECORDS VOLUME 4	30
69	RCA Victor RD 7957	SPEEDWAY (soundtrack, with Nancy Sinatra)	30

LPs: 'LARGE' ORANGE RCA VICTOR STEREO RE-PRESSINGS

72	RCA Victor SF 8232	ELVIS FOR EVERYONE ('blue shirt'/'TV Special' sleeve)	40

LPs: GREEN RCA INTERNATIONAL ISSUES

70	RCA Intl. INTS 1103	LET'S BE FRIENDS	15
72	RCA Intl. INTS 1414	BURNING LOVE AND HITS FROM HIS MOVIES (U.K. disc in U.K. sleeve)	40

OTHER LPs

71	Camden CDS 1088	YOU'LL NEVER WALK ALONE (LP, withdrawn)	400
78	St. Michael IMP 113	ELVIS (exclusive to Marks & Spencer)	60
78	St. Michael IMPD 204	THE WONDERFUL WORLD OF ELVIS PRESLEY (2-LP, via Marks & Spencer)	80
79	Hammer HMR 6002	THE KING SPEAKS (green sleeve)	30
84	Imperial Records DR 1124	AMERICAN TRILOGY (3-LP, box set)	25
85	Sunday 1	ELVIS: THE GOLDEN ALBUM (LP, available via Sunday Times magazine)	20
86	RCA AREP 1	ACUFF-ROSE PRESENTS ELVIS (promo-only, 300 copies)	150
00	Castle EL BOX	THAT'S THE WAY IT IS (5-LP)	35

CDs

84	RCA PD 89061/2/3	THE LEGEND (3-CD, gold box set, with booklet, numbered, 5,000 only)	300
84	RCA PD 89061/2/3	THE LEGEND (3-CD, silver box set, 5,000 only, with booklet, numbered)	350

REG PRESLEY

(see also Troggs, Suzi Quatro)

69	Page One POF 131	Lucinda Lee/Wichita Lineman	8
73	CBS 1478	'S Down To You Marianne/Hey Little Girl	5

PRESSGANG

89	Vox Pop VOX 022	ROGUES (LP)	15

RAY PRESSLEY

62	Longhorn BLH 0002	Living, Learning, Trying To Forget/Half A Love	8

PRESSURE 28

82	Helen Of Oi! HOO 01	Get Ready/Up Yours	8

PRESSURE CO.

(see also Eric Random, Cabaret Voltaire)

82	Paradox SOLID 1	LIVE IN SHEFFIELD 19 JAN '82 (LP)	12

PRESTIGE BLUES SWINGERS

59	Esquire 32-082	BLUES GROOVE (Tiny Grimes & Coleman Hawkins as Prestige Blues Swingers (LP)	20
60	Esquire 32-110	OUTSKIRTS OF TOWN (LP)	20

BILLY PRESTON

(see also Beatles)

66	Sue WI 4012	Billy's Bag/Don't Let The Sun Catch You Cryin'	25
66	Capitol CL 15458	In The Midnight Hour/Advice	25

			MINT VALUE £
66	Capitol CL 15458	In The Midnight Hour/Advice (DJ copy)	50
66	Capitol CL 15471	Sunny/Let The Music Play	15
69	President PT 263	Billy's Bag/Don't Let The Sun Catch You Crying (reissue)	10
69	President PT 263	Billy's Bag/Goldfinger (different B-side)	15
69	Apple APPLE 12	That's The Way God Planned It/What About You (p/s)	10
69	Apple APPLE 19	Everything's Alright/I Want To Thank You	20
70	Apple APPLE 21	All That I've Got/As I Get Older (some in p/s)	25
70	Apple APPLE 21	All That I've Got/As I Get Older (some in p/s)	8
70	President PT 298	If I Had A Hammer/Ferry 'Cross The Mersey	5
70	Soul City SC 107	Greazee (Parts 1 & 2)	20
70	Soul City SC 107	Greazee (Parts 1 & 2) (DJ Copy)	100
67	Capitol (S)T 2532	THE WILDEST ORGAN IN TOWN (LP)	35
67	Sue ILP 935	THE MOST EXCITING ORGAN EVER (LP)	60
69	President PTLS 1034	APPLE OF MY EYE (LP)	18
69	Apple SAPCOR 9	THAT'S THE WAY GOD PLANNED IT (LP)	30
70	Apple SAPCOR 14	ENCOURAGING WORDS (LP)	60
70	Soul City SCM 002	GREAZEE SOUL (LP)	30
70	Joy JOYS 174	GOSPEL IN MY SOUL (LP)	20
91	Apple SAPCOR 9	THAT'S THE WAY GOD PLANNED IT (LP, gatefold sleeve, with bonus 12" [SAPCOR 92])	15
93	Apple SAPCOR 14	ENCOURAGING WORDS (LP, gatefold sleeve with bonus 12" [SAPCOR 142])	15

EARL PRESTON

(see also Realm)

63	Fontana TF 406	I Know Something/Watch Your Step (as Earl Preston & T.T.'s)	20
64	Fontana TF 481	Raindrops/That's For Sure (as Earl Preston & Realms)	20

JOHNNY PRESTON

60	Mercury AMT 1079	Running Bear/My Heart Knows	8
60	Mercury AMT 1079	Running Bear/My Heart Knows (78)	60
60	Mercury AMT 1092	Cradle Of Love/City Of Tears (some in p/s)	20
60	Mercury AMT 1092	Cradle Of Love/City Of Tears (some in p/s)	8
60	Mercury AMT 1104	Feel So Fine/I'm Starting To Go Steady	10
60	Mercury AMT 1114	Charming Billy/Up In The Air	12
61	Mercury AMT 1129	Leave My Kitten Alone/Do What You Did	20
61	Mercury AMT 1145	Big Chief Heartbreak/Madre De Dios (Mother Of God)	20
61	Mercury AMT 1164	New Baby For Christmas/Rock And Roll Guitar	25
61	Mercury AMT 1167	Free Me/Kissing Tree	25
60	Mercury ZEP 10078	RUNNING BEAR (EP)	80
60	Mercury ZEP 10098	RING TAIL TOOTER (EP)	90
61	Mercury ZEP 10116	TOKEN OF LOVE (EP)	100
60	Mercury MMC 14051	JOHNNY PRESTON - RUNNING BEAR (LP)	100

MIKE PRESTON

58	Decca F 11053	A House, A Car And A Wedding Ring/My Lucky Love	8
58	Decca F 11087	Why, Why, Why/Whispering Grass	8
59	Decca F 11120	Dirty Old Town/In Surabaya	8
59	Decca F 11167	Mr. Blue/Just Ask Your Heart	5
60	Decca F 11222	A Girl Like You/Too Old	5
60	Decca F 11255	I'd Do Anything/Where Is Love?	5
60	Decca F 11287	Togetherness/Farewell My Love	5
61	Decca F 11335	Marry Me/Girl Without A Heart	5
64	Decca F 11810	No Strings/Nobody Told Me	5
66	Emerald MD1028	Our Love Will Go On/Forgive Me	10
60	Decca DFE 6635	FOUR SONGS BY RAY NOBLE (EP)	15
61	Decca DFE 6679	MARRY ME (EP)	15

PRETTY BOY FLOYD & GEMS

79	Rip Off RIP OFF 1	Spread The Word Around/Hold Tight (p/s)	15
79	Rip Off RIP 10	Sharon/The Instigator (p/s)	20

PRETTY THINGS

(see also Electric Banana, Twink, Viv Prince, Sunshine, Fenmen, Kate, Zac Zolar & Electric Banana)

64	Fontana TF 469	Rosalyn/Big Boss Man	15
64	Fontana TF 503	Don't Bring Me Down/We'll Be Together	12
65	Fontana TF 537	Honey I Need/I Can Never Say	12
65	Fontana TF 585	Cry To Me/Get A Buzz	20
65	Fontana TF 647	Midnight To Six Man/Can't Stand The Pain	20
66	Fontana TF 688	Come See Me/£.s.d.	25
66	Fontana TF 722	A House In The Country/Me Needing You	25
66	Fontana TF 773	Progress/Buzz The Jerk	30
67	Fontana TF 829	Children/My Time	20
67	Columbia DB 8300	Defecting Grey/Mr. Evasion	80
68	Columbia DB 8353	Talkin' About The Good Times/Walking Through My Dreams	80
68	Columbia DB 8494	Private Sorrow/Balloon Burning	40
69	Fontana TF 1024	Rosalyn/Don't Bring Me Down (p/s)	12
70	Harvest HAR 5016	The Good Mr. Square/Blue Serge Blues	8
70	Harvest HAR 5031	October 26/Cold Stone	8
71	Harvest HAR 5037	Stone-Hearted Mama/Summertime/Circus Mind	8
72	Warner Bros K 16225	Over The Moon/Havana Bound	5
64	Fontana TE 17434	THE PRETTY THINGS (EP)	60
65	Fontana TE 17442	RAININ' IN MY HEART (EP)	60
66	Fontana TE 17472	ON FILM (EP)	150
65	Fontana TL 5239	THE PRETTY THINGS (LP)	120
65	Fontana TL 5280	GET THE PICTURE (LP)	150
67	Wing WL 1164	BEST OF THE PRETTY THINGS (LP)	25
67	Fontana (S)TL 5425	EMOTIONS (LP, mono/stereo)	100
67	Wing WL 1167	THE PRETTY THINGS (LP, reissue)	40
68	Columbia SX 6306	S.F. SORROW (LP, gatefold sleeve, blue/black label, mono)	350

			MINT VALUE £
68	Columbia SCX 6306	S.F. SORROW (LP, gatefold sleeve, blue/black label, stereo)	200
70	Columbia SCX 6306	S.F. SORROW (LP, gatefold sleeve; silver/black label re-pressing, stereo)	35
70	Harvest SHVL 774	PARACHUTE (LP, gatefold sleeve)	80
72	Fontana Special SFL 13140	EMOTIONS (LP, reissue)	20
72	Warner Bros K 46190	FREEWAY MADNESS (LP, gatefold sleeve)	18
74	Swan Song SSK 59400	SILK TORPEDO (LP, gatefold sleeve with insert)	12
75	Harvest SHDW 406	S.F. SORROW/PARACHUTE (2-LP)	20
75	Swan Song SSL 59401	SAVAGE EYE (LP, gatefold sleeve with inner)	12
78	Butt Nott DO1	ELECTRIC BANANA THE SEVEN TIES (LP)	15
77	Harvest SHSM 2022	SINGLES A'S & B'S (LP)	15

ANDRE PREVIN

74	EMI 2222	Theme From Jennie Churchill/Stanley Myers - Cavatina	5

DORY PREVIN

70	United Artists UAG 29176	ON MY WAY TO WHERE (LP)	12
71	United Artists UAG 29186	MYTHICAL KINGS & IGUNAS (LP, gatefold sleeve)	12

EDDIE PREVOST BAND

(see also Amm, Organum)

78	Matchless MR 1	LIVE VOLUME 1 (LP, private pressing)	15

JOEL PREVOST

78	CBS SCBS 6300	Somewhere Sometime/Il Y Aura Toujours Des Violins	10

ALAN PRICE (SET)

(see also Animals, Paul Williams Set, Johnny Almond Music Machine, Dave Greenslade)

65	Decca F 12217	Any Day Now (My Wild Beautiful Baby)/Never Be Sick On Sunday	12
66	Decca F 12367	I Put A Spell On You/Iechyd-Da	7
66	Decca F 12518	Willow Weep For Me/Yours Until Tomorrow	6
67	Decca F 12691	Shame/Don't Do That Again	8
68	Decca F 12774	When I Was A Cowboy/Tappy Turquoise (export issue)	20
68	Decca F 12808	Love Story/My Old Kentucky Home	6
69	Deram DM 263	Trimdon Grange Explosion/Falling In Love Again	6
70	Decca F 13017	Sunshine And Rain (The Name Of The Game)/ Is There Anybody Out There? (solo)	6
67	Decca DFE 8677	THE AMAZING ALAN PRICE (EP)	30
66	Decca LK 4839	THE PRICE TO PLAY (LP, laminate front cover, flipbacks)	35
67	Decca LK/SKL 4907	A PRICE ON HIS HEAD (LP, laminated front cover)	25
73	Warner Bros K 46227	O LUCKY MAN! (LP, soundtrack)	15

BILL PRICE

72	Folk Heritage FHR 038	THE FINE OLD YORKSHIRE GENTLEMAN (LP)	22

KENNY PRICE

66	Stateside SS 554	Walking On New Grass/Wasting My Time	6

LLOYD PRICE

57	London HL 8438	Just Because/Why (triangular centre)	150
57	London HL 8438	Just Because/Why (round centre)	80
57	London HL 8438	Just Because/Why (78)	20
59	HMV POP 580	Stagger Lee/You Need Love	12
59	HMV POP 580	Stagger Lee/You Need Love (78)	50
59	HMV POP 598	Where Were You (On Our Wedding Day)?/Is It Really Love?	12
59	HMV POP 598	Where Were You (On Our Wedding Day)?/Is It Really Love? (78)	30
59	HMV POP 626	Personality/Have You Ever Had The Blues?	10
59	HMV POP 626	Personality/Have You Ever Had The Blues? (78)	30
59	HMV POP 650	I'm Gonna Get Married/Three Little Pigs	12
59	HMV POP 650	I'm Gonna Get Married/Three Little Pigs (78)	50
59	HMV POP 672	Won't 'Cha Come Home/Come Into My Heart	10
60	HMV POP 712	Lady Luck/Never Let Me Go	15
60	HMV POP 712	Lady Luck/Never Let Me Go (78)	70
60	HMV POP 741	For Love/No If's - No And's	10
60	HMV POP 772	Question/If I Look A Little Blue (as Lloyd Price Orchestra)	10
60	HMV POP 772	Question/If I Look A Little Blue (as Lloyd Price Orchestra) (78)	80
60	HMV POP 799	Just Call Me (And I'll Understand)/Who Coulda' Told You (They Lied)	10
61	HMV POP 826	Know What You're Doin'/That's Why Tears Come And Go (as Lloyd Price Orchestra)	10
61	HMV POP 926	Boo Hoo/I Made You Cry	10
62	HMV POP 983	Be A Leader/'Nother Fairy Tale	10
62	HMV POP 1100	Under Your Spell, Again/Happy Birthday Mama	10
63	Liberty LIB 10127	Misty/Cry On	12
72	President PT 321	Ready For Betty/Beat In Trinidad	10
73	GSF GSZ 5	Love Music/Just For Baby	10
73	GSF GSZ 11	Trying To Slip Away/They Get Down	10
59	HMV 7EG 8538	THE EXCITING LLOYD PRICE (EP, mono)	80
59	HMV GES 5784	THE EXCITING LLOYD PRICE (EP, stereo)	100
59	HMV CLP 1285	THE EXCITING LLOYD PRICE (LP)	80
59	HMV CLP 1314	MR. PERSONALITY (LP)	65
60	London HA-U 2213	LLOYD PRICE (LP)	80
60	HMV CLP 1361	MR. PERSONALITY SINGS THE BLUES (LP)	55
60	HMV CLP 1393	THE FANTASTIC LLOYD PRICE (LP, mono)	50
60	HMV CSD 1323	THE FANTASTIC LLOYD PRICE (LP, stereo)	70
62	HMV CLP 1519	COOKIN' (LP, mono)	50
62	HMV CSD 1413	COOKIN' (LP, stereo)	70
63	Encore ENC 2004	PRICE SINGS THE MILLION DOLLAR SELLERS (LP)	25
69	Major Minor SMLP 57	LLOYD PRICE NOW (LP)	25

MALCOLM PRICE (TRIO)

61	Oak RGJ 106	PICKIN' ON THE COUNTRY STRINGS! (EP)	18
64	Decca LK 4627	COUNTRY SESSION (LP, as Malcolm Price Trio)	15

MINT VALUE £

65 Decca LK 4665 WAY DOWN TOWN (LP) 15
69 Saga FID 2156 HIS SONGS, HIS GUITARS (LP) 12
75 Sweet Folk & C. SFA 017 THEN WE ALL GOT UP AND WALKED AWAY (LP) 12

RAY PRICE
(see also Cherry Wainer)
57 Philips BBE 12137 RAY PRICE (EP) 25

RED PRICE & BLUE BEATS
64 Blue Beat BB 209 Blue Beats Over (The White Cliffs Of Dover)/Kiss The Baby (When You Grow Too Old To Dream) 10

(ROCKIN') RED PRICE
56 Decca F 10822 Rocky Mountain Gal/Rock O' The North (as Red Price & His Rockin' Rhythm) . . 15
56 Decca F 10822 Rocky Mountain Gal/Rock O' The North (78) 10
57 Woodbine Woodbine Rock (78, with picture on label, promo only) 40
57 Woodbine Woodbine Rock (78, without picture on label, promo only) 15
58 Pye 7N 15169 Weekend/The Sneeze 20
58 Pye 7N 15169 Weekend/The Sneeze (78) 25
60 Pye 7N 15262 Wow!/My Baby's Door 10
61 Parlophone R 4789 Theme From "Danger Man"/Blackjack (as Red Price Combo) 30

RICK PRICE
(see also Move, Sheridan-Price, Sight & Sound)
70 Gemini GMS 012 Davey Has No Dad/Bitter Sweet 10
71 Gemini GMS 017 Top Ten Record/Beautiful Sally 10
71 Gemini GME 1017 TALKING TO THE FLOWERS (LP, laminated front sleeve) 40

RIKKI PRICE
(see also Sheridan-Price)
58 Fontana H 162 Tom Dooley/(It Looks Like Rain In) Cherry Blossom Lane 6
59 Fontana H 171 Honey, Honey/The Very Thought Of You 8
59 Fontana H 217 Mr. Blue/Man On My Trail 6
62 Fontana H 371 You're For Real/When You Pass By 6
58 Fontana TFE 17100 RIKKI PRICE (EP) 25

SAMMY PRICE
(see also SIster Rosetta Tharpe)
63 Storyville A 45 068 Boogieing With Big Sid/133 Street Boogie (with p/s) 30
63 Storyville A 45 068 Boogieing With Big Sid/133 Street Boogie 20
57 Columbia SEG 7679 ORIGINAL SAMMY BLUES (EP) 20
58 Vogue EPV 1146 SAMMY PRICE (EP) 60
58 Vogue EPV 1151 SAMMY PRICE'S BLUESICIANS (EP) 60
58 Vogue LAE 12027 SWINGIN' PARIS STYLE (LP) 40
62 London Jazz LTZ-R 15240 THE BLUES AIN'T NOTHIN' (LP, mono) 30
62 London Jazz SAH-R 6234 THE BLUES AIN'T NOTHIN' (LP, stereo) 40

VINCENT PRICE
77 EMI EMI 2659 The Monster Mash/The Bard's Own Recipe 10
59 Columbia 33SX 1141 VINCENT PRICE (LP) 45

DICKIE PRIDE
(see also Guvners)
59 Columbia DB 4283 Slippin' 'N' Slidin'/Don't Make Me Love You 45
59 Columbia DB 4296 Fabulous Cure/Midnight Oil 40
59 Columbia DB 4340 Frantic/Primrose Lane 25
60 Columbia DB 4403 Betty, Betty (Go Steady With Me)/No John 25
60 Columbia DB 4451 You're Singin' Our Love Song To Somebody Else/Bye Bye Blackbird 10
59 Columbia SEG 7937 SHEIK OF SHAKE (EP) 300
61 Columbia 33SX 1307 PRIDE WITHOUT PREJUDICE (LP, mono) 80
61 Columbia SCX 3369 PRIDE WITHOUT PREJUDICE (LP, stereo) 100

LOUIS PRIMA (& HIS ORCHESTRA)
(see also Sam Butera's Witnesses)
56 Capitol CL 14669 5 Months, 2 Weeks, 2 Days/Banana Split For My Baby 20
58 Capitol CL 14821 Buona Sera/Beep! Beep! 15
60 London HLD 9230 Ol' Man Moses (with Sam Butera's Witnesses)/Wonderland By Night 10
58 Capitol T 908 THE WILDEST SHOW AT TAHOE (LP) 20
59 Capitol EAP1 1132 STRICTLY PRIMA (EP) 12
57 Capitol T 755 THE WILDEST (LP) 30
58 Capitol T 836 THE CALL OF THE WILDEST (LP) 20
58 Capitol T 1010 LAS VEGAS PRIMA STYLE (LP) 15
62 Ember EMB 3348 LOUIS PRIMA SWINGS (LP) 15

LOUIS PRIMA & KEELY SMITH
(see also Keely Smith)
54 Columbia SCM 5092 Take A Little Walk Around The Block/LOUIS PRIMA: Oh! Cumari 15
58 Capitol CL 14862 The Lip/KEELY SMITH: Foggy Day 8
58 Capitol CL 14948 That Old Black Magic/KEELY SMITH: You Are My Love 8
59 Capitol CL 14994 I've Got You Under My Skin/KEELY SMITH: Don't Take Your Love From Me 5
59 London HLD 8923 Bei Mir Bist Du Schon/I Don't Know Why 10
60 London HLD 9084 I'm Confessin' (That I Love You)/Night And Day 8
59 Capitol T 1160 HEY BOY! HEY GIRL! (LP) 25
60 London HA-D 2243 LOUIS AND KEELY (LP) 15
61 London HA-D 2350 ON STAGE (LP, also stereo SAH-G 6149) 15

PRIMAL SCREAM
(see also Jesus & Mary Chain, Revolving Paint Dream, P.P. & Primes, Death In Vegas)
85 Creation CRE 017 All Fall Down/It Happens (foldaround p/s in poly bag) 25
86 Creation CRE 026 Crystal Crescent/Velocity Girl (p/s) 8
86 Creation CRE 026T Crystal Crescent/Velocity Girl/Spirea X (12", p/s) 10
87 Elevation ACID 3 Gentle Tuesday/Black Star Carnival (p/s) 5

			MINT VALUE £
87	Elevation ACID 3T	Gentle Tuesday/Black Star Carnival/I'm Gonna Make You Mine (12", p/s)	10
87	Elevation ACID 5	Imperial/Star Fruit Surf Rider (p/s)	5
87	Elevation ACID 5T	Imperial/Star Fruit Surf Rider/So Sad About Us/Imperial (demo) (12", in poster p/s with 'special price' sticker)	10
87	Elevation ACID 5T	Imperial/Star Fruit Surf Rider/So Sad About Us/Imperial (demo) (12")	8
91	Creation DOCKERS 001	Come Together (Original Recording) (12" promo)	15
89	Creation CRELP 054	PRIMAL SCREAM (LP, with bonus 45 "Split Wide Open 1"/ Lone Star Girl 1 [CREFRE 6, no p/s])	20
91	Creation CRELP 076	SCREAMADELICA (2-LP)	20
97	Creation CREL 7224	ECHO DEK (5x7", box set)	15
98	Creation CRELP 178	VANISHING POINT (2-LP)	30
02	Columbia 508923	EVIL HEAT (2-LP)	18

PRIME-MATES

69	Action ACT 4530	Hot Tamales (Versions 1 & 2)	20

PRIMETTES

(see also Supremes, Eddie Floyd)

68	Ember EMBS 3398	LOOKING BACK WITH THE PRIMETTES AND EDDIE FLOYD (LP, 1 side each)	50
73	Windmill WMD 192	THE ROOTS OF DIANA ROSS AND EDDIE FLOYD (LP, reissue)	20

PRIME MOVERS

89	Cyanide CND 001	SINS OF THE FOURFATHERS (LP)	20

PRIME RHYME MASTERS

91	Kold Sweat KS115	You Need Discipline/To Kill A Mockingbird (12")	15

PRIMITIVE MAN

71	Decca F13188	Animal Love/Major Barmy From The Army	30

PRIMITIVES

(see also Mal & Primitives)

64	Pye 7N 15721	Help Me/Let Them Tell	220
65	Pye 7N 15755	You Said/How Do You Feel	250

PRIMITIVES

86	Head HEAD 010	Thru The Flowers/Across My Shoulder/Lazy/She Don't Need You (12", unreleased, white label test pressings only)	30
86	Lazy LAZY 01	Thru The Flowers/Across My Shoulder/She Don't Need You/Lazy (12", p/s)	10
86	Lazy LAZY 02	Really Stupid/We Found A Way To The Sun (p/s)	5
86	Lazy LAZY 02T	Really Stupid/We Found A Way To The Sun/Where The Wind Blows (12", p/s)	8
86	Lazy LAZY 03	Stop Killing Me/Buzz Buzz Buzz (p/s, with postcard, sleeves printed back-to-front; with badge)	5
87	Lazy LAZY 05	Ocean Blue/Shadow (2,000 only, given away free at London Astoria gig)	6
88	RCA PB 41761X	Crash/I'll Stick With You/Crash (Live In Studio) (10", 1,500 signed, gatefold p/s)	5

PRIMO & HOPETON

67	Rio R 139	Your Safekeep/Loving And Kind	10
68	Pama PM 753	Peace On Earth/SCHOOL BOYS: Love Is A Message	12

PRIMROSE

69	NEMS 56-4129	Just For You/Nine Till Five	25

PRIMROSE CIRCUS

70	President PT 314	P.S. Call Me Lulu/In My Mind	10

PRINCE

SINGLES

79	Warner Bros K 17537	I Wanna Be Your Lover/Just As Long As We're Together	5
79	Warner Bros K 17537T	I Wanna Be Your Lover/Just As Long As We're Together (12", company sleeve)	15
80	Warner Bros K 17590	Sexy Dancer/Bambi (die-cut company sleeve)	25
80	Warner Bros K 17590T	Sexy Dancer (Remix)/Bambi (12", die-cut company sleeve)	50
81	Warner Bros K 17768	Do It All Night/Head (die-cut company sleeve)	25
81	Warner Bros K 17768T	Do It All Night/Head (12", die-cut company sleeve)	60
81	Warner Bros K 17819	Gotta Stop (Messin' About)/Uptown (p/s)	60
81	Warner Bros K 17819	Gotta Stop (Messin' About)/I Wanna Be Your Lover (p/s)	60
81	Warner Bros LV 47	Gotta Stop (Messin' About)/Uptown/Head (12", stickered p/s)	60
81	Warner Bros LV 47	Gotta Stop (Messin' About)/I Wanna Be Your Lover/Head (12", stickered, colour p/s)	60
81	Warner Bros K 17866	Controversy/When You Were Mine (p/s)	20
81	Warner Bros K 17866T	Controversy/When You Were Mine (12", p/s)	30
82	Warner Bros K 17922	Let's Work/Ronnie, Talk To Russia (p/s)	40
82	Warner Bros K 17922T	Let's Work (Extended)/Ronnie, Talk To Russia (12", p/s)	40
83	Warner Bros W 9896	1999/How Come U Don't Call Me Anymore (paper labels, p/s, with free cassette mini-album in card p/s: "1999 (Edit)"/"Uptown"/ "Controvesy"/"Dirty Minds"/"Sexuality")	40
83	Warner Bros W 9896	1999/How Come U Don't Call Me Anymore (paper labels, p/s)	8
83	Warner Bros W 9688	Little Red Corvette/Lady Cab Driver (p/s)	10
83	Warner Bros W 9688T	Little Red Corvette (Full Length Version)/Automatic/International Lover (12", stickered p/s, with poster insert)	40
83	Warner Bros W 9688T	Little Red Corvette (Full Length Version)/Automatic/International Lover (12", stickered p/s)	12
83	Warner Bros W 9688T	Little Red Corvette (Full Length Version)/Automatic/International Lover (12", 'negative image' p/s)	20
83	Warner Bros W 9436	Little Red Corvette/Horny Toad (poster calendar p/s)	55
83	Warner Bros W 9436	Little Red Corvette/Horny Toad (standard p/s)	40
83	Warner Bros W 9436T	Little Red Corvette (Full Length Version)/Horny Toad/D.M.S.R. (12", p/s)	15
83	Warner Bros W 9436T	Little Red Corvette (Full Length Version)/Horny Toad/D.M.S.R. (12", p/s, with spiral-bound calendar)	85
83	Warner Bros W 9436T	Little Red Corvette (Full Length Version)/Horny Toad/D.M.S.R. (12", p/s, with poster)	75
84	Warner Bros W 9286T	When Doves Cry/17 Days//1999/D.M.S.R. (12", stickered shrinkwrapped double pack)	20

			MINT VALUE £
84	Warner Bros W 9174P	Purple Rain/God (motorbike-shaped picture disc)	20
84	Warner Bros W 9174T	Purple Rain/God (instrumental)/God (12", p/s, initial pressing with poster)	15
84	Warner Bros W 9174T	Purple Rain/God (instrumental)/God (12", p/s)	8
84	Warner Bros W 9121TE	I Would Die 4 U (U.S. Remix)/Another Lonely Christmas (U.S. Remix) (12", p/s)	20
85	Paisley Park W 9052P	Paisley Park/She's Always In My Hair (shaped picture disc)	25
85	Paisley Park W 9052T	Paisley Park/She's Always In My Hair/Paisley Park (Remix) (12", p/s)	8
85	Paisley Park W 9052T	Paisley Park/She's Always In My Hair/Paisley Park (Remix) (12", mispressing with repeated 2nd track "She's Always In My Hair")	25
85	Paisley Park W 8929T	Raspberry Beret (Extended Remix)/Hello (Extended Remix) (12", p/s)	8
85	Paisley Park W 8858T	Pop Life (Extended)/Girl (12", p/s)	8
86	Paisley Park W 8751P	Kiss/Love Or Money (shaped picture disc with plinth)	30
86	Paisley Park W 8751T	Kiss (Extended)/Love Or Money (12", p/s, with poster)	15
86	Paisley Park W 8711TE	Mountains (Ext.)/Alexa De Paris (Extended) (10", white vinyl in PVC sleeve)	20
86	Paisley Park W 8711T	Mountains (Extended 9.56)/Alexa De Paris (12", p/s, with poster)	20
86	Paisley Park W 8586F	Girls And Boys (Edit)/Under The Cherry Moon//She's Always In My Hair/ 17 Days (double pack, gatefold p/s)	15
86	Paisley Park W 8586P	Girls And Boys (Edit)/Under The Cherry Moon (shaped picture disc)	40
86	Paisley Park W 8586T	Girls And Boys/Under The Cherry Moon/Erotic City (12", p/s, with poster advertising London gigs)	18
86	Paisley Park W 8521W	Anotherloverholenyohead/I Wanna Be Your Lover (paper or plastic labels, poster p/s)	12
86	Paisley Park W 8521T	Anotherloverholenyohead (Extended)/I Wanna Be Your Lover (12", p/s)	10
87	Paisley Park W 8399TP	Sign O' The Times (Extended)/La La La He He Hee (Extended) (12", picture disc)	10
87	Paisley Park W 8334W	If I Was Your Girlfriend/Shockadelica (poster p/s)	8
87	Paisley Park W 8334E	If I Was Your Girlfriend/Shockadelica (peach vinyl, PVC cover, with postcards & stickers)	15
87	Paisley Park W 8334TP	If I Was Your Girlfriend/Shockadelica (Extended) (12", picture disc)	12
87	Paisley Park W 8289TP	U Got The Look (Long Look)/Housequake (7 min MoQuake)/ U Got The Look (Single Cut) (12", picture disc)	8
87	Paisley Park W 8288TP	I Could Never Take The Place Of Your Man/Hot Thing (Remixed Edit)/ Hot Thing (Extended) (12", picture disc)	15
88	Paisley Park W 7900CD	Alphabet Street (Album Version)/This Is Not Music, This Is A Trip (Alphabet Street) (Extended) (3" CD, with adaptor, 5" case)	10
88	Paisley Park W 7806CD	Glam Slam (Edit)/Escape (Free Yo Mind) (Edit)/Glam Slam (Remix) (3" CD, with adaptor, 5" case)	10
88	Paisley Park W 7745	I Wish U Heaven (Edit)/Scarlet Pussy (Edit) (poster p/s)	5
88	Paisley Park W 7745TW	I Wish U Heaven (Parts 1/2/3)/CAMILLE: Scarlet Pussy (Edit) (12", p/s with poster)	8
88	Paisley Park W 7745CD	I Wish U Heaven (Parts 1/2/3)/CAMILLE: Scarlet Pussy (Edit) (3" CD, with adaptor, 5" case)	10
89	Paisley Park W 2814TP	Partyman (Video Mix)/Feel U Up (Long Stroke) (12", picture disc, PVC sleeve)	8
89	Paisley Park W 2814CDX	Partyman (Video Mix)/Feel U Up (Long Stroke) (3" CD, octagonal foldout sleeve with film stills)	15
89	Paisley Park W 2814CDT	Partyman (The Purple Party Mix)/(Partyman Music Mix)/(The Video Mix)/ Feel U Up (Short Stroke) (3" CD, card sleeve)	8
88	Paisley Park W 8751TP	Kiss/Love Or Money (shaped picture disc, 're-promoted' edition with longer, extended version of B-side & without plinth)	10

ALBUMS

83	Warner Bros 923 809-1	1999 (LP, original issue, single disc)	18
84	Warner Bros 925 110-1	PURPLE RAIN - MUSIC FROM THE MOTION PICTURE (LP, purple vinyl with poster)	25
86	Paisley Park WX 39P	PARADE - MUSIC FROM "UNDER THE CHERRY MOON" (LP, pic. disc, die-cut sleeve)	35
89	Paisley Park 925 978-2	BATMAN (CD, picture disc in 'Bat' tin with booklet)	15
94	Warners 936245793-1	BLACK ALBUM (LP, title sticker)	15
95	NPG 6103-1	EXODUS (LP, as NPG)	15
96	NPG EMI CDEMO 1102	EMANCIPATION (3-CD, as ß)	25
98	NPG BCT 9871	CRYSTAL BALL (4-CD, import only, as ß)	40

PROMOS

84	Warner Bros	Purple Rain (promo only p/s, purple vinyl)	60
84	Warner Bros SAM 230	I Would Die 4 U/I would Die 4 U	30
91	Warner Brothers SAM 888	Gett Off (Urge Single Edit) (1-sided promo)	15
92	Paisley Park W 0113	Thunder (DJ Edit) (1-sided promo only white label, stickered company sleeve)	15
95	NPG 61225	Get Wild (Money Maker Radio Mix) (CD, as NPG, radio programmer's picture disc)	45
95	NPG 61047	Get Wild/Beautiful Girl (no p/s, as NPG)	6
96	NPG 60667	Lovesign/MARGIE COX: Standing At The altar (no p/s, as ß)	10
96	NPG 60600	Lovesign (Radio Edit Mix)/(1-800 New Funk Version)/ (The Storyboard Video Mix) (12", as ß, most with title sticker)	35
96	NPG 60605	Lovesign (Radio Edit Mix)/(1-800 New Funk Version)/ (The Storyboard Video Mix) (CD, as ß)	30
01	Warners PRO 2721	THE VERY BEST OF PRINCE: (When Doves Cry/Purple Rain/Kiss/ Cream/1999/Money Don't Matter) (CD, radio sampler)	20

PRINCE ALLAH

78	Freedom Sounds FSD 020	Bucket Bottom/FULL WOOD: Stop And Think Me Over (12")	25

PRINCE BROTHERS

77	Carib Gems CG 010	Ram Jam/REVOLUTIONARIES: Version To Jam	6

PRINCE BUSTER (& ALL STARS)

(see also Buster's Allstars, Buster's Group, Dennis Alcapone, Jim Dakota, Hortense Ellis, Heptones, Eric Morris, Terry Nelson, Schoolboys, Protegue, Vietnam All Stars)

61	Starlite ST45 052	Buster's Shack (as Buster's Group)/ERIC MORRIS: Search The World	30
62	Blue Beat BB 101	My Sound That Goes Around/They Got To Go (with Torchlighters)	20
62	Blue Beat BB 116	Independence Song (with Bluebeats)/RICO & BLUEBEATS: August 1962	20
62	Blue Beat BB 133	Time Longer Than Rope/Fake King (with Voice Of The People)	30
62	Blue Beat BB 138	One Hand Washes The Other/Cowboy Comes To Town	30

			MINT VALUE £
63	Blue Beat BB 150	Run Man Run/Danny, Dane And Lorraine	25
63	Blue Beat BB 158	Open Up, Bartender/Enjoy It (B-side actually "Enjoy Yourself")	25
63	Blue Beat BB 162	Money/SCHOOL BOYS: Little Boy Blue	40
63	Blue Beat BB 163	King, Duke, Sir/I See Them In My Sight	30
63	Blue Beat BB 167	The Ten Commandments (with All Stars)/Buster's Welcome	20
63	Blue Beat BB 170	Madness/PRINCE BUSTER ALL STARS: Toothache	20
63	Blue Beat BB 173	Burning Creation/PRINCE BUSTER ALL STARS: Boop	30
63	Blue Beat BB 180	Three More Rivers To Cross/RAYMOND HARPER & PRINCE BUSTER ALL STARS: African Blood	30
63	Blue Beat BB 186	Fowl Thief/Remember Me	60
63	Blue Beat BB 189	Watch It Blackhead/Hello My Dear	30
63	Blue Beat BB 192	Rollin' Stone (with Charmers)/RICO & HIS BLUES BAND: This Day	30
63	Blue Beat BB 197	Window Shopping/Sodom And Gomorrah	35
63	Blue Beat BB 199	Spider And Fly/Three Blind Mice	30
63	Blue Beat BB 200	Wash All Your Troubles Away/RICO & BLUE BEATS: Soul Of Africa	18
63	Dice CC 6	They Got To Come/These Are The Times (with Voice Of The People)	15
63	Dice CC 11	Blackhead Chinaman/You Ask (I Had A Girl)	18
63	Dice CC 18	World Peace/The Lion Roars (as Prince Buster & Hazel)	15
64	Stateside SS 335	30 Pieces Of Silver/Everybody Ska	12
64	Blue Beat BB 210	Wash All Your Troubles Away/RICO & BLUE BEATS: Soul Of Africa (p/s reissue)	50
64	Blue Beat BB 211	Bluebeat Spirit/Beggars Are No Choosers	35
64	Blue Beat BB 216	You're Mine/Tongue Will Tell	35
64	Blue Beat BB 225	Three Blind Mice/I Know	35
64	Blue Beat BB 232	Sheep On Top (song actually titled "She Pon Top")/Midnight	35
64	Blue Beat BB 234	She Loves You/Healing	60
64	Blue Beat BB 243	Jealous/Buster's Ska	35
64	Blue Beat BB 248	Thirty Pieces Of Silver/The National Dance	35
64	Blue Beat BB 254	Wings Of A Dove/MAYTALLS: Sweet Love	30
64	Blue Beat BB 262	Old Lady/Dayo Ska	35
64	Blue Beat BB 271	No Knowledge In College/In The Middle Of The Night	45
64	Blue Beat BB 274	I May Never Love You Again/Hey Little Girl	35
65	Blue Beat BB 278	Blood Pressure/Islam	120
65	Blue Beat BB 281	Blues Market/MAYTALS: Looking Down The Street	35
65	Blue Beat BB 282	Big Fight/Red Dress	35
65	Blue Beat BB 293	Agua Fumar/Long Winter (with Charmers)	40
65	Blue Beat BB 302	Ling Ting Tong/Walk Along	100
65	Blue Beat BB 307	Bonanza/Wonderful Life	30
65	Blue Beat BB 309	Here Comes The Bride (with Patsy Todd, as Jamaica's Greatest)/BUSTER'S ALLSTARS: Burkes' Law	40
65	Blue Beat BB 313	Everybody Yeah Yeah (as Jamaica's Greatest)/BUSTER'S ALLSTARS: Gun The Man Down	50
65	Blue Beat BB 314	Float Like A Butterfly/Haunted Room	50
65	Blue Beat BB 316	Sugar Pop/Feel Up (as Prince & Jamaica's Greatest)	40
65	Blue Beat BB 317	Come Home/I Thank You (as Jamaica's Greatest)	45
65	Blue Beat BB 321	My Girl/BUSTER'S ALL STARS: The Fugitive	50
65	Blue Beat BB 324	Al Capone/One Step Beyond (as Prince Buster's Allstars) (blue label)	12
65	Blue Beat BB 324	Al Capone/One Step Beyond (as Prince Buster's Allstars) (other label colours)	15
65	Blue Beat BB 328	Ambition/BUSTER'S ALL STARS: Ryging	30
65	Blue Beat BB 330	Rum And Coca Cola/I Love Her	25
65	Blue Beat BB 334	The Ten Commandments/BUSTER'S ALL STARS: Sting Like A Bee (reissue)	15
65	Blue Beat BB 335	Respect/BUSTER'S ALL STARS: Virginia (B-side actually Dance Jamaica by Val Bennett & Prince Buster's All Stars)	45
66	Blue Beat BB 338	Big Fight (Prince Buster Versus Duke Reid)/Adios, Senorita	40
66	Blue Beat BB 339	Under Arrest (But Officer)/PRINCE BUSTER'S ALLSTARS: Say Boss Man	40
66	Blue Beat BB 343	Prince Of Peace/Don't Throw Stones	110
66	Blue Beat BB 352	Day Of Light (song actually "Dayo")/It's Too Late	25
66	Blue Beat BB 355	Sunshine With My Girl/Girl Answer Your Name	120
66	Blue Beat BB 357	I Won't Let You Cry/Hard Man Fe Dead	80
66	Blue Beat BB 359	The Prophet (actually "Feel The Spirit" with Slim Smith)/BUSTER'S ALL STARS: Lion Of Judah	90
66	Blue Beat BB 362	To Be Loved/BUSTER'S ALLSTARS: Set Me Free	30
66	Rainbow RAI 107	Your Turn (Sad Song)/If You Leave Me (with Allstars)	25
67	Blue Beat BB 370	Shanty Town (Get Scanty)/BUSTER'S ALL STARS: Duppy	30
67	Blue Beat BB 373	Knock On Wood/And I Love Her	45
67	Blue Beat BB 377	Dark End Of The Street/Love Oh Love	45
67	Blue Beat BB 378	Drunkard's Psalm (Wise Man)/7 Wonders Of The World (as Prince Buster All Stars)	150
67	Blue Beat BB 382	Sit And Wonder (with His All Stars)/ROLAND ALFONSO: Sunrise In Kingston	60
67	Blue Beat BB 383	Sharing You/You'll Be Lonely On The Blue Train (as Prince Buster's Allstars; A-side actually by Prince Buster, B-side actually by Rico's Band)	30
67	Blue Beat BB 384	Take It Easy/Why Must I Cry (2nd issue, B-side actually by Hopeton Lewis)	20
67	Blue Beat BB 387	Judge Dread (Judge Four Hundred Years)/FITZROY CAMPBELL & PRINCE BUSTER ALL STARS: Waiting For My Rude Girl	25
67	Blue Beat BB 388	Dance Cleopatra/All In My Mind	100
67	Blue Beat BB 390	Soul Serenade/Too Hot	30
67	Blue Beat BB 391	Land Of Imagination/The Appeal (B-side actually "The Barrister Appeal")	30
67	Blue Beat BB 393	Johnny Dollar/Rude Boys Rude	45
67	Blue Beat BB 395	This Gun's For Hire/Yes, Daddy	30
67	Blue Beat BB 397	Quit Place/Rude Boys Rude	40
67	Blue Beat BB 400	All In My Mind/Judge Dread Dance (The Pardon)	30
67	Blue Beat BB 402	Vagabond/PRINCE BUSTER ALL STARS: Come Get Me	30
67	Philips BF 1552	The Ten Commandments/Don't Make Me Cry	15
67	Fab FAB 10	Shakin' Up Orange Street/Black Girl (with Allstars)	30
67	Fab FAB 11	Johnny Cool (Parts 1 & 2) (with Allstars)	30
67	Fab FAB 16	Bye Bye Baby/Human (with Allstars)	30
67	Fab FAB 25	Train To Girls Town/Give Love A Try (with Allstars)	20

			MINT VALUE £
67	Fab FAB 26	Going To The River (as Prince Buster & Allstars)/ PRINCE BUSTER'S ALLSTARS: Julie On My Mind	20
68	Fab FAB 31	Kings Of Old (My Ancestors)/Sweet Inspiration (with Allstars)	45
68	Fab FAB 35	Try A Little Tenderness/All My Loving (with Allstars)	200
68	Fab FAB 36	The Glory Of Love/Another Sad Nite	30
68	Fab FAB 37	This Is A Hold Up/Julie On My Mind (with Allstars)	30
68	Fab FAB 38	Free Love (with Allstars)/DALTONS: All Over The World	18
68	Fab FAB 40	Rough Rider (with Allstars)/PRINCE BUSTER: 127 Orange Street (B-side actually by Prince Buster Allstars)	20
68	Fab FAB 41	Shepherd Beng Beng (with Teddy King)/TENNORS: Ride Your Donkey	20
68	Fab FAB 47	Going To Ethiopia (as Prince Buster & Allstars)/ PRINCE BUSTER ALLSTARS: Shakin' Up Orange Street	20
68	Fab FAB 49	Glory Of Love/WAILERS: Mellow Mood (possibly white labels only)	100
68	Fab FAB 56	Intensified Dirt/Don't You Know I Love You (with Allstars)	35
68	Fab FAB 57	Green Green Grass Of Home (as Prince Buster's Allstars; actually by Prince Buster & Allstars)/SOUL MAKERS: Girls Like You	15
68	Fab FAB 58	We Shall Overcome/Keep The Faith (as Prince Buster's Allstars; actually by Prince Buster & Allstars)	15
68	Fab FAB 64	Cool Stroker/It's You I Love (B-side actually by Little Roy)	20
68	Fab FAB 80	Hypocrite/New Dance (B-side actually by Little Roy)	20
68	Fab FAB 81	Wine And Grind/The Scorcher (with Allstars)	20
69	Unity UN 522	30 Pieces Of Silver/Everybody Ska (reissue)	20
69	Fab FAB 82	Dr. Rodney (Black Power)/Taxation	35
69	Fab FAB 92	Pharaoh House Crash/Ob-La-Di, Ob-La-Da	20
69	Fab FAB 93	Ob-La-Di, Ob-La-Da/Wreck A Pum Pum	10
69	Fab FAB 94	Hey Jude/Django Fever	35
69	Fab FAB 102	Black Soul/CALEDONIANS: Oh Baby (B-side actually by Claredonians)	15
69	Fab FAB 108	Wine And Grind/The Scorcher (with Allstars) (reissue)	20
69	Fab FAB 118	Bull Buck/ROLAND ALPHONSO: One Heart	15
69	Fab FAB 119	Let Her Go/Tie The Donkey's Tail	15
69	Fab FAB 122	Stand Up/Happy Reggae (with Allstars)	10
70	Fab FAB 127	Young Gifted And Black/PRINCE BUSTER'S ALLSTARS: The Rebel	10
70	Fab FAB 131	That's All/The Preaching (B-side actually titled "The Preacher")	10
70	Fab FAB 132	Ganja Plant/Creation	10
70	Fab FAB 140	Hit Me Back/Give Peace A Chance	10
70	Fab FAB 150	Big Five/Musical College	10
70	Prince Buster PB 1	Big Five/Musical College (reissue)	8
70	Prince Buster PB 2	Rat Trap/Black Organ (B-side with Allstars but actually by Ansell Collins & Prince Buster's Allstars)	8
71	Fab FAB 162	Baby Version (with Jan Fender)/Holly	8
71	Fab FAB 176	Police Trim Rasta (with Allstars)/Smooth (B-side actually by Ansell Collins & Prince Buster Allstars)	10
71	Prince Buster PB 4	Fishey/More Fishey	7
71	Prince Buster PB 7	I Wish Your Picture Was You/PRINCE BUSTER ALLSTARS: It Mash Up - Version (B-side actually by Dennis Alcapone)	8
71	Prince Buster PB 8	Sons Of Zion (actually by Dennis Alcapone)/ANSELL COLLINS: Short Circuit	8
71	Prince Buster PB 9	My Happiness/Human (with Allstars)	7
72	Prince Buster PB 14	Big Sister Stuff/Satta Massagana (with Allstars)	12
72	Prince Buster PB 15	Protection/Cool Operator (with Allstars)	8
72	Prince Buster PB 16	I Stand Accused/My Heart is Gone (with Allstars)	7
72	Prince Buster PB 19	Four In One Medley/Drums Drums (as Prince Buster & Allstars, B-side actually by Prince Buster Allstars)	7
72	Prince Buster PB 32	Still/Sister Big Stuff (with Allstars)	7
72	Prince Buster PB 36	South Of The Border/South Of The Border (Version) (with Allstars)	7
72	Fab FAB 36	South Of The Border/South Of The Border (Version) (with Allstars)	7
72	Prince Buster PB 47	Baldhead Pum Pum/Giver Her (with Allstars)	7
79	Blue Beat DDBB 324	Al Capone/One Step Beyond (12", p/s)	12
79	Blue Beat DDBB 334	THREE OF THE BEST (12" EP, p/s)	10
79	Blue Beat DDPB 1	Big Five/FOLK BROTHERS: Carolina/PRINCE BUSTER: Shaking Up Orange Street (12", p/s)	8
79	Blue Beat DDPB 2	PICK OF THE PUNCH (12" EP, p/s, 2 tracks each by Tennors & Prince Buster)	8
79	Blue Beat DDPB 3	NAUGHTY BUT NICE (12" EP, p/s)	8
79	Blue Beat DDPB 4	BEHIND BARS (12" EP, p/s)	8
63	Blue Beat BBLP 802	I FEEL THE SPIRIT (LP)	120
65	Blue Beat BBLP 805	SKA-LIP-SOUL (LP, with His All Stars)	150
65	Blue Beat BBLP 806	IT'S BURKE'S LAW - JAMAICA SKA EXPLOSION! (LP, as Prince Buster All Stars; 2 different sleeves, laminated plain and unlaminated 'explosion')	250
67	Blue Beat BBLP 807	WHAT A HARD MAN FE DEAD - PRINCE BUSTER SINGS FOR THE PEOPLE (LP, with Baba Brooks)	300
67	Blue Beat BBLP 808	ON TOUR (LP)	120
67	Blue Beat BBLP 809	JUDGE DREAD (LP)	100
67	Blue Beat BBLP 820	SHE WAS A ROUGH RIDER (LP)	70
68	Fab BBLP 820	SHE WAS A ROUGH RIDER (LP, reissue on Fab label)	40
68	Fab BBLP 821	WRECK A PUM PUM (LP)	40
69	Fab BBLP 822	THE OUTLAW (LP, title listed as "Queen Of The Outlaws" on disc)	75
70	Fab MS 1	FABULOUS GREATEST HITS (LP, original issue with 'West Brothers Printers' credit on rear of sleeve)	18
70	Fab MS 2	I FEEL THE SPIRIT (LP)	60
70	Fab MS 6	TUTTI FRUTTI (LP)	45
72	Melodisc MLP 12-156	SISTER BIG STUFF (LP)	45
72	Melodisc MLP 12-157	BIG FIVE (LP)	30
73	Prince Buster PB 9	ORIGINAL GOLDEN OLDIES VOLUME 1 (LP)	20
70s	Fab MS 7	THE MESSAGE DUBWISE (LP)	70

PRINCE CHARLIE

69	Coxsone CS 7101	Hit And Run/Darling, There I Stand	35

PRINCE FAR I

(see also Arabs)

78	Virgin Front Line FLS 112	No More War/Version	10

MINT VALUE £

82	On-U Sound DP 1	Virgin/Danger (10")	15
83	Pre PRE 11-12	83 Struggle (with ASHANTIE ROY)/KONGO ASHANTIE ROY/ Weeping Waiing (12")	20
77	Virgin Front Line FL 1013	MESSAGE FROM THE KING (LP)	15
79	Virgin Frontline FLX 4002	CRY TUFF DUB ENCOUNTER PART 2 (LP)	35
79	Hit Run APLP 9006	DUB TO AFRICA (LP, as Prince Far I & The Arabs)	20
79	TRLS 205	CRY TUFF DUB ENCOUNTER CHAPTER IV (LP)	20
80	Daddy Kool DKLP 15	CRY TUFF DUB ENCOUNTER CHAPTER III (LP, as Prince Far I & the Arabs)	25
80	Pre PRE XF 3	SHOWCASE IN A SUITCASE (LP)	35
81	Pre PRE X 7	LIVITY (LP)	25

PRINCE HAMMER

77	Baby Mother HIT DD 11	Them Must Fall/Ball Of Fire (12")	30
78	Hit Run HIT DD 15	Ten Thousand Lions/North London Thing (Carry The Swing) (12")	50
79	Hit Run APLP 9007	WORLD WAR DUB PART 1 (LP)	80
83	Saab (No cat. no.)	Warika Hill/Africa Dance Hall (12")	45

PRINCE HAROLD

66	Mercury MF 952	Forget About Me/Baby You've Got Me	20

PRINCE JAMMY

79	TRLS 174	KAMIKAZI DUB (LP)	18

PRINCE JAZZBO

(see also Earl George)

73	Count Shelley CS 025	Wise Shepherd (with Linval Carthy)/ EARL GEORGE: Gonna Give Her All The Love I've Got	10
74	Cactus CT 31	Concubine Donkey/Part 2	8
74	Count Shelley CS 057	Step Forward Youth/Black Is Power	8
73	Grape GR 3047	Free From Chains/LLOYD & PATSY: Papa Do It Sweet	8
73	Techniques TE 921	Mr. Harry Skank/GLEN BROWN: Telavid Drums	8
74	Ackee ACK 532	Kick Boy Face/Version	8
74	Dip DL 5036	Penny Reel/Good Things	8
75	ABI AB 001	Bag A Wolf/Version	8
76	Attack ATT 8122	The Wormer/The Great Pablo	10
76	Third World TWLP 109	KICK BOY FACE (LP)	30
76	Black Wax WAXLP 1	NATTY PASSING THRU' (LP)	90

PRINCE JAZZBO & I ROY

78	Live & Love LAP 003	STEP FORWARD YOUTH (LP)	25

PRINCE LASHA ENSEMBLE

66	CBS SBPG 62409	INSIGHT (LP)	30

PRINCE OF DARKNESS

69	Downtown DT 441	Burial Of Long Shot/MUSIC DOCTORS: Burial Of Long Shot	15
69	Downtown DT 448	Meeting Over Yonder/MUSIC DOCTORS: Ghost Rider	12
71	Downtown DT 467	Sound Of Today/MUSIC DOCTORS: Red Red Wine Version	12

PRINCE PATO EXPEDITION

70s	Beacon BEAS 18	FIREBIRD (LP)	30

PRINCE & PRINCESS

65	Aladdin WI 609	Ready Steady Go/Take Me Serious	25

PRINCE TALLIS & THE CHALLIS

72	Upsetter US 383	Who Feels It/THE UPSETTERS: He Who Feels It (Chapter 2)	20

VIV PRINCE

(see also Pretty Things, Bunch Of Fives, Kate, Vamp, Chicago Line)

66	Columbia DB 7960	Light Of The Charge Brigade/Minuet For Ringo	40

PRINCE WILLIAMS

73	Atra ATRA 004	Action Wood Part 1/Action Wood Part 2	8

PRINCESS

86	Supreme SU 1	PRINCESS (LP)	12
86	Supreme CDSU 1	PRINCESS (CD)	60

PRINCESS BALOU

81	PB YYS 11	Making Love To You/Making Love To You (Part II) (p/s)	10

PRINCESS & SWINEHERD

68	Oak RGJ 633	PRINCESS AND THE SWINEHERD (LP, plain black sleeve)	100

PRINCIPAL EDWARDS MAGIC THEATRE

69	Dandelion S 4405	Ballad Of The Big Girl Now/Lament For The Earth	10
73	Deram DM 391	Captain Lifeboy/Nothing	5
73	Deram DM 398	Weekdaze/Whizzmore Kid	15
69	Dandelion 63752	SOUNDTRACK (LP, gatefold sleeve)	50
71	Dandelion DAN 8002	THE ASOMOTO RUNNING BAND (LP, gatefold sleeve)	35
74	Deram SML 1108	ROUND ONE (LP, white/red label with small logo)	30

MADDY PRIOR

(see also Steelye Span, Tim Hart & Maddy Prior)

78	Chrysalis CHS 2232	Baggy Pants/Woman In The Wings	6
80	EMI EMI 5903	Wake Up England/Paradise (p/s, as Maddy Prior Band)	6
82	Plant Life PLRS 001	Face To Face/Half Listening (p/s, as Maddy Prior Band)	6
83	RCA/Spindrift RCA 379	Deep In The Darkest Night/Western Movies (p/s)	6
85	Making Waves SURF 108	Stookie/Incidental Music From Stookie (p/s)	6
85	Making Waves SURF 109	Deep In The Darkest Night/Western Movies (p/s, reissue)	6
78	Chrysalis CHR 1185	WOMAN IN THE WINGS (LP, with insert)	12
87	Saydisc SDL 366	A TAPESTRY OF CAROLS (LP)	20

PRISONERS

(see also James Taylor Quartet)

83	Big Beat NS 90	Hurricane/Tomorrow (She Said) (p/s)	12

			MINT VALUE £
84	Big Beat SW 98	ELECTRIC FIT (EP)	12
82	Own Up OWN UP U2	A TASTE OF PINK (LP)	30
83	Big Beat WIK 19	THE WISERMISERDEMELZA (LP)	15
85	Own Up OWN UP U2	A TASTE OF PINK (LP, reissue in pink sleeve on pink vinyl)	30
85	Own Up OWN UP U3	THE LAST FOURFATHERS (LP)	20
86	Countdown DOWN 2	IN FROM THE COLD (LP)	20
89	Hangman HANG 23 UP	RARE AND UNISSUED (LP)	20

PRISONERS/MILKSHAKES

(see also Milkshakes, Thee Mighty Caesars)

86	Empire MIC 001	THE LAST NIGHT AT THE MIC CLUB (LP, live, 1 side each)	18
86	Media Burn MB 17	THEE MILKSHAKES VS. THE PRISONERS (LP, live, 1 side each)	18

PRIVATE DICKS

79	Heartbeat PULSE 6	She Said So/Private Dicks (p/s)	20

PRIVATE LIFE

72	Realm RM 3	Put her Down/Chasing Dragons	400

PRIVATE PARTY

87	IMW 1201	Puppet Capers/Tennants Super Mix (12")	10

PRIVATE SECTOR

78	TJM TJM 8	Just Just (Wanna) Stay Free/Things Get Worse (p/s)	20

P.J. PROBY

(see also Jett Powers, Marc Almond)

62	Liberty LIB 55367	Try To Forget Her/There Stands The One	10
64	Decca F 11904	Hold Me/The Tips Of My Fingers	7
64	Decca F 11967	Together/Sweet And Tender Romance	7
64	Liberty LIB 10182	Somewhere/Just Like Him	6
65	Liberty LIB 10188	I Apologise/What's On Your Mind	7
65	Liberty LIB 10206	Let The Water Run Down/I Don't Want To Hear It Anymore	10
65	Liberty LIB 10215	That Means A Lot/My Prayer	12
65	Liberty LIB 10218	Maria/She Cried	6
66	Liberty LIB 10223	You've Come Back/It Ain't Necessarily So	8
66	Liberty LIB 10236	To Make A Big Man Cry/Wicked Woman	10
66	Fab FAB 2	You've Got Me Cryin'/I Need Love (in die-cut p/s)	20
66	Fab FAB 2	You've Got Me Cryin'/I Need Love	7
66	Liberty LIB 10250	I Can't Make It Alone/Sweet Summer Wine	12
67	Liberty LIB 55936	Nicki Hoeky/Good Things Are Coming My Way	15
67	Liberty LIB 55974	You Can't Come Home Again/Work With Me Annie	15
67	Liberty LIB 55974	You Can't Come Home Again/Work With Me Annie (DJ Copy)	30
68	Liberty LBF 15046	It's Your Day Today/I Apologise Baby	10
68	Liberty LBF 15046	It's Your Day Today/I Apologise Baby (DJ Copy)	30
68	Liberty LBF 15085	What's Wrong With My World/Why Baby Why	7
68	Liberty LBF 15152	The Day That Lorraine Came Down/Mery Hoppkins Never Had Days Like These (B-side features Led Zeppelin)	15
69	Liberty LBF 15245	Hanging From Your Loving Tree/Empty Bottles	15
70	Liberty LBF 15280	Today I Killed A Man/It's Too Good To Last	10
70	Liberty LBF 15386	It's Goodbye/Gift Of Love	10
70s	Rooster ROO 101	You've Got It All (with Polly Brown)/Starting All Over Again	20
72	Columbia DB 8874	We'll Meet Again/Clown Shoes	10
73	Ember EMB S 328	Put Your Head On My Shoulder/Momma Married A Preacher	7
74	Seven Sun SSUN 13	The Champ (Parts 1 & 2)	8
81	Rooster RONS 101	You've Got It All/Starting All Over Again (with Polly Brown)	5
64	Liberty LEP 2192	P. J. PROBY (EP)	15
65	Liberty LEP 2229	SOMEWHERE (EP)	15
65	Liberty LEP 2239	CHRISTMAS WITH P. J. (EP)	15
66	Liberty LEP 2251	P. J.'s HITS (EP)	20
67	Liberty LEP 2267	PROBY AGAIN (EP)	30
65	Liberty LBY 1235	I AM P. J. PROBY (LP)	15
65	Liberty LBY 1264	P. J. PROBY (LP)	15
66	Liberty LBY 1291	P. J. PROBY IN TOWN (LP)	15
67	Liberty LBY 1361	ENIGMA (LP)	18
67	Liberty LBL/LBS 83045	PHENOMENON (LP)	18
68	Liberty LBL/LBS 83087	BELIEVE IT OR NOT (LP)	15
69	Liberty LBS 83219E	THREE WEEK HERO (LP, featuring Led Zeppelin on "Jim's Blues")	60
73	Ember NR 5069	I'M YOURS (LP)	15
78	Astoria 1	ELVIS (LP; sold at theatres)	15

PROCESSION

68	Mercury MF 1053	Every American Citizen/Essentially Susan (p/s)	10
68	Mercury MF 1070	One Day In Every Week/Wigwam City	10
69	Mercury SMCL 20132	PROCESSION (LP)	30

PROCOL HARUM

(see also Paramounts, Legend, Matthew Fisher, Robin Trower, Matthew Ellis, Freedom, Mick Grabham, Power Pack)

67	Deram DM 126	A Whiter Shade Of Pale/Lime Street Blues (1st issue with darker labels)	5
67	Regal Zonophone RZ 3003	Homburg/Good Captain Clack	5
68	Regal Zonophone RZ 3007	Quite Rightly So/In The Wee Small Hours Of Sixpence	8
69	Regal Zonophone RZ 3019	A Salty Dog/Long Gone Geek	10
72	Fly Magni Fly ECHO 101	A Whiter Shade Of Pale/A Salty Dog/Homburg (p/s)	5
72	Chrysalis CHS 2003	Conquistador/Luskus Delph (p/s)	6
79	RCA LB 6	A Whiter Shade Of Pale/Noel Edmonds Introduces Record Year (Lever Brothers premium)	5
67	Regal Zono. LRZ 1001	PROCOL HARUM (LP, laminated front sleeve, flipbacks, blue/silver label)	60
68	Regal Zono. LRZ 1004	SHINE ON BRIGHTLY (LP, mono), laminated front sleeve, blue/silver label)	150
67	Regal Zono. SLRZ 1004	SHINE ON BRIGHTLY (LP, stereo), laminated front sleeve, blue/silver label)	60
69	Regal Zono. SLRZ 1009	A SALTY DOG (LP, laminated sleeve, red/silver label)	50

			MINT VALUE £
70	Regal Zono. SLRZ 1014	HOME (LP, with lyric sheet)	50
71	Chrysalis ILPS 9158	BROKEN BARRICADES (LP, gatefold sleeve, first pressing with a small white "I" at the top of the label)	15
71	Chrysalis ILPS 9158	BROKEN BARRICADES (LP, gatefold sleeve)	12
73	Chrysalis CHR 1037	GRAND HOTEL (LP, gatefold sleeve, booklet, green label)	25

JUDD PROCTOR

see also Ray Ellington

61	Parlophone R 4769	Rio Grande/Plainsman	10
61	Parlophone R 4809	Palamino/Nola	10
61	Parlophone R 4841	Speakeasy/Clearway	10
62	Parlophone R 4885	The Turk/Mad	10
62	Parlophone R 4920	Backfire/It's Bluesy	10
64	Parlophone R 5126	Better Late/Boots	10
60s	Morgan MR 103P	GUITARS GALORE (LP)	40
70s	Gemini GMX 5004	GUITARS GALORE (LP, reissue)	25

MIKE PROCTOR

67	Columbia DB 8254	Mr. Commuter/Sunday, Sunday, Sunday	160

PRODIGY

91	XL XLT 17	WHAT EVIL LURKS EP (What Evil Lurks/We Gonna Rock/Android/ Everybody In The Place) (12", company sleeve)	50
91	XL XLS 21	Charly/Charly (Original Mix)	8
91	XL XLS 26	Everybody In The Place (Fairground Edit)/G-Force (Energy Flow)	5
92	XL XLS 30	Fire (Edit)/Jericho (Original Version)	5
92	XL XLS 35	Out Of Space/Ruff In The Jungle Bizness (Uplifting Vibes Remix)	5
93	XL XLS 39	Wind It Up (Rewound)/We Are The Ruffest	5
93	XL EB 1	EARTHBOUND 1: One Love (original Mix)/Full Throttle (Original Mix) (12")	50
95	XL SC 1	SCIENIDE (12", white label, 500 hand-stamped promos only)	50
96	XL 76 XLC 76	Minefields (Radio Edit)/Minefields (Monkey Mafia Mix)/Minefields (Headrock Beats)/Minefields (Full Length) (cassette promo only 50 copies with photocopied inlay)	60
96	XL XL70CDPR	Firestarter Sampler (CD picture disc, promo only)	12
98	XL XLT90DJ	Smack My Bitch Up/(DJ Hype Remix)/No Man Army/Minefields (Headrock Dub) (12" promo)	8
04	XL XLXV1501	What Evil Lurks/We Gonna Rock/Android/Everybody In The Place (12")	8
92	XL XLLP 110	THE PRODIGY EXPERIENCE (2-LP)	18
94	XL XLLP 114	MUSIC FOR THE JILTED GENERATION (LP)	15
97	XL XLLP 121	THE FAT OF THE LAND (2-LP)	18

PROFESSIONALS

(see also Sex Pistols, Greedies, Lightning Raiders, Steve Jones)

80	Virgin VS 353	Just Another Dream/Action Man (p/s)	5
80	Virgin VS 376	1-2-3/White Light White Heat/Baby I Don't Care (p/s, with giant foldout poster in stickered PVC sleeve)	5
80	Virgin VS 376	1-2-3/White Light White Heat/Baby I Don't Care (p/s, signed by Cook & Jones)	15
81	Sounds FREEBIE No. 2	Little Boys In Blue (extract)/GILLAN: I'll Rip Your Spine Out (extract) (33rpm 1-sided flexi, printed die-cut sleeve, free with Sounds)	5
81	Virgin VS 426	Join The Professionals/Has Anybody Got An Alibi? (gatefold p/s)	7
81	Virgin V 2220	I DIDN'T SEE IT COMING (LP)	15

PROFESSOR LONGHAIR

65	Sue WI 397	Baby Let Me Hold Your Hand/Looka' No Hair	40
78	Harvest HAR 5154	Mess Around/Tipitina	15
72	Speakeasy 10-78	NEW ORLEANS 88 (10" LP)	50
72	Atlantic K 40402	NEW ORLEANS PIANO (LP)	30
78	Harvest SHSP 4086	LIVE ON THE QUEEN MARY (LP)	30
80	Sonet SNTF 830	CRAWFISH SIESTA (LP)	15
83	Stateside SSL 6004	LIVE ON THE QUEEN MARY (LP, reissue)	18
81	JSP 1025	THE LONDON CONCERT (LP)	15

PROFESSOR LUDLOW & DR. SMITH

99	Fat Cat 12FAT 029	Professor's Saying Raas (12", custom sleeve)	8

FRANK PROFFITT

66	Topic 12T 162	NORTH CAROLINA SONGS AND BALLADS (LP)	20

PROFIL

80	CBS S CBS 8574	Hey Music Man/Jour De Chance (p/s)	10

PROFILE

(see also Karl Stuart & Profiles, Voice)

65	Mercury MF 875	Haven't They Got Better Things To Do/Touch Of Your Hand	12
65	Mercury MF 981	Got To Find A Way/Don't Say Goodbye	12
69	Philips BF 1757	Politician Man/Where Is Love	8

PROLES

79	Rock Against Racism RAR 1	Stereo Love/Thought Crime/CONDEMNED: Soldier Boys/ Endless Revolution (p/s)	45
79	Small Wonder SMALL 23	Softground/SMK (p/s)	6

PROMISE

69	NEMS 56-4129	Just For You/Nine To Five	80

PROPAGANDA

(see also Act, Ralph Dorper, Claudia Brucken)

85	ZTT 12 ZTAS 2	Das Testaments Des Mabuse/Femme Fatale/The 9th Life (Of Dr. Mabuse) (12", white p/s, title sticker reads "13th Life New Mix")	15
85	ZTT P ZTAS 8	Duel/Jewel (Rough Cut) (ZTT logo-shaped picture disc)	10
85	ZTT DUAL 1	Duel/Jewel//Lied/The Lesson (double pack, gatefold sleeve)	8
85	ZTT PROP 1	Bejewelled (12", 1-sided, white label, stickered title sleeve, promo only)	12

MINT VALUE £

85	ZTT PZTAS 12	P-Machinery/Frozen Faces (clear vinyl, printed PVC sleeve)	5
85	ZTT 12X ZTAS 12	P-Machinery (Beta)/Complete Machinery/Frozen Faces (12", 'sofa' p/s)	10
85	ZTT 12P ZTAS 12	P-Machinery (Polish)/P Machinery (Passive)/Frozen Faces (12", p/s, clear vinyl, printed PVC sleeve)	8
02	ZTT ZTT 180CDX	Outside World (CD, with bonus DVD, digipak)	25

PROPERTY

70	Staple ST01	My Mind Sleeps/Calling You	60

PROPHET

74	UK UK 64	Have Love Will Travel/Blues In B Sharp	40

MICHAEL PROPHET

79	Grove GMDM 17	Turn Me Loose/Praise You Jah Jah (12")	18
79	Grove GMDM 25	Warn Them Jah/Don't Interfere (12")	18
80	Greensleeves GRED 44	Help Them Please/WAILING SOULS : See Baba Joe	15
82	Greensleeves GRED 72	Here Comes The Bride/MYSTIC EYES: Bring The Kuchie Come	20
80	Island / Grove Music 12WIP 6583	Fight To The Top (Discomix)/Love And Unity/ Mash Down Rome (12")	20
80	Lovelinch LL 002	True Born African (with Soul Syndicate)/ RANKING TOYAN: What A Bam Bam (12")	30
80s	WLN WLN 003	Rock Me Baby/Don't Throw Stone (12")	20
81	Greensleeves GRED 59	Gunman/Cassandra (12")	12
82	Greensleeves GRED 87	Boom Him Up Now/Trouble Nobody (12")	15
82	Greensleeeves GRED 104	Just Talking/Thru Me (with Papa Dimes) (12")	15
80	Island ILPS 9606	SERIOUS REASONING (LP)	18

ORVAL PROPHET

63	London HLL 9729	Run Run Run/My Lois And Me	10

REX PROPHET

55	Brunswick OE 9144	CANADIAN PLOWBOY (EP)	10

PROPHETS

78	Grove Music GMDM 12	Give Thanks And Praise/Till I Kiss You (12")	30
79	Grover Music GMDM 4	Blessed Are The Meek (feat Trinity)/TOMMY MCCOOK: Stepping High (12")	25

PROPHETS (Jamaica)

(see also Lloyd & Prophets, Claudette, Lloyd & Claudette, Patrick & Lloyd)

70	Big Shot BI 554	Crystal Blue Persuasion (Parts 1 & 2)	15
70	Big Shot BI 555	Tumble Time (Parts 1 & 2)	12
70	Big Shot BI 557	Revenge Of Eastwood Version One/Version Two	12
70	Jackpot JP 712	Let's Fall In Love/Purple Moon	30

PROPHETS (U.S.)

(see also Creation [U.S.])

69	Mercury MF 1097	I Got The Fever/Soul Control	30
69	Mercury MF 1097	I Got The Fever/Soul Control (DJ copy)	50

PROS & CONS

66	CBS 202341	Bend It/No Time	7

PROTEGUE (& PRINCE BUSTER'S ALL STARS)

67	Blue Beat BB 398	Foul Dance/PRINCE BUSTER'S ALL STARS: This Is It.	25

PROTEX

78	Good Vibrations GOT 6	Don't Ring Me Up/(Just Want) Your Attention/Listening In (wraparound p/s)	20
79	Rough Trade GOT 1	Don't Ring Me Up/(Just Want) Your Attention/Listening In (reissue, p/s)	8
79	Polydor 2059 124	I Can't Cope/Popularity (p/s)	12
79	Polydor 2059 167	I Can Only Dream/Heartache (p/s)	15
80	Polydor 2059 245	A Place In Your Heart/Jeepster (p/s)	15

BRIAN PROTHEROE

74	Chrysalis CHS 2043	Pinball/Money Love	5

PROTON

80	Ballistic 12BP 264	We're Funkin'/Make Your Move (Instrumental Version)	20

PROTOS

82	Airship AP 391	ONE DAY A NEW HORIZON (LP)	140

PROVIDENCE

73	Threshold TH 14	Fantasy Fugue/Island Of Light	5
72	Threshold THS 9	EVER SENCE THE DAWN (LP, gatefold sleeve with insert)	30

PROWLER

73	Parlophone R 5986	Pale Green (Hnmmmm) Driving Man/Jaywick Cowboy	25

PROWLER

85	SRT SRT5KS/368	Alcatraz/So Lonely (p/s)	70

PRUDES

89	Yo Yo PRU 1	P.S. I'm Leaving/Lighthouse Keeper's Daughter (p/s, white vinyl)	5

JEANNE PRUETT

73	MCA MU 1209	Satin Sheeets/Sweet Sweetheart.	6

PRUNES

(see also Eric Donaldson, West Indians)

70	Songbird SB 1023	Come A Little Closer/Come A Little Closer Version II	5

SNOOKY PRYOR

70	Flyright LP 100	SNOOKY PRYOR (LP)	15

ARTHUR PRYSOCK

65	CBS 201820	It's Too Late, Baby Too Late/My Special Prayer	10
77	Polydor 2058842	When Love Is Now/All I Need Is You Tonight.	10
66	CBS EP 6076	AGAIN (EP)	15
67	Verve SVLP 9176	MISTER PRYSOCK (LP)	15

MINT VALUE £

RED PRYSOCK

59	Mercury AMT 1028	Chop Suey/Margie	20
58	Mercury MPL 6535	THE BEAT (LP)	50
58	Mercury MPL 6550	FRUIT BOOTS (LP)	40
56	Mercury MPT 7517	JUMP RED JUMP (10" LP)	40

PSEUDO EXISTORS

80	Dead Good DEAD 2	Pseudo Existence/Coming Up For Air/New Modern Warfare (rubber-stamped folded p/s, pink/white label)	60
80	Dead Good DEAD 2	Pseudo Existence/Coming Up For Air/New Modern Warfare (rubber-stamped folded p/s, later red/black label & stamped white sleeve)	35

PSYCHEDELIC FURS

(see also Unwanted)

79	Epic EPC 8005	We Love You/Pulse (green, pink or orange p/s)	5
81	CBS A 1166	Dumb Waiters/Dash (1st 5,000 with playable p/s)	5
81	CBS A 13 1327	Pretty In Pink/Mack The Knife/Soap Commercial (12", shrinkwrapped with free T-shirt)	8

PSYCHEOUT

00	Discord DISCORD 002	BOOM EP (12")	15
00	Discord DISCORD 003	WARP EP (12") (12")	60
00	Discord DISCORD 004	TRAIN TRAX EP (12")	15
00	Discord DISCORD 005	SURGE EP (12")	10

PSYCHIC PHENOMENA

97	Lowlife LOW05	THE WHOLE CIRCUMFERENCE (12", EP)	25

PSYCHIC TV

82	Some Bizzare PTV 1	Just Drifting/Breakthrough (p/s)	10
82	Some Bizzare PTV 1T	Just Drifting/Just Drifting (Midnight) (12", p/s)	15
84	Temple TOPY 001	Unclean/Mirrors (12", p/s)	10
86	Temple TOPYS 009	Godstar/Godstar (BJ Mix)/Discopravity/Yes It's The B Side (double pack, gatefold p/s)	8
86	Temple TOPIC 009	Godstar/Godstar (California Mix) (12", picture disc)	15
86	Temple TOPYD 023	Good Vibrations/Interzone/Roman P/Hex-Sex/Godstar (Ugly Mix)/Je T'Aime (double pack, gatefold p/s)	6
86	Temple TOPYT 023	Roman P (Fireball Mix)/Interzone/Good Vibrations (Kundalini Mix)/ Hex-Sex (Voodoo Mix) (12", p/s)	10
88	Temple TOPY 037	Tune In (Turn On To Thee Acide House) (12", p/s, as (Psychic TV/Jack The Tab)	10
88	DC DC 23	Superman/Jack The Tab (12", p/s, no artist credit on label)	15
89	Temple TOPY 048	Love, War, Riot/Eve Of Destruction (Vocoder Mixes) (12", p/s, including sticker)	10
82	Some Bizzare PSY 1	FORCE THE HAND OF CHANCE (LP, with bonus LP & double-sided poster, featuring Marc Almond)	40
83	CBS 25737	DREAMS LESS SWEET (LP, with inner sleeve, some with free 12" EP [XPR 1251])	30
83	CBS 25737	DREAMS LESS SWEET (LP, with inner sleeve)	25
84	Temple TOPY 003	PAGAN DAY (LP, picture disc, 999 copies)	40
84	Gramm GRAMM 23	THOSE WHO DO NOT (2-LP, 5000 copies)	30
85	Temple TOPY 004	THEMES 2 (LP)	15
85	Temple TOPY 008	THEMES 3 (LP)	15
85	Temple TOPIC 010	MOUTH OF THE NIGHT (LP, picture disc)	18
86	Temple TOPIC 009	GODSTAR (LP, with picture disc)	15
88	Temple TOPY 031	PSYCHIC TV (LP, picture disc)	15
88	Temple TOPY 032	ALBUM 10 (LP, picture disc)	15
88	Temple TOPY 038	ALLEGORY AND SELF (LP, blue vinyl)	15
89	Temple TOPY 047	LIVE AT THE PYRAMID NYC (LP, picture disc)	12

PSYCHOPATHS

91	Elicit 12 ELIC 2	NIGHTMARES (12", no p/s)	8

PSYCHO'S MUM

89	Woronzow W 011	A SIBILANT SIN (LP, with insert)	15

PSYCOMETRIC

97	Acid Fever MDMA 9701	Piano Dreams/Funk Bits/The Kaison Ogle/DJ CYCLONE: Spare Parts/Meltdown/Chaos (12")	12

PSYKYK VOLTS

79	Ellie Jay EJPS 9262	Totally Useless/Horror Story No. 5 (p/s)	20
79	MHG GHM 109	Totally Useless/Horror Story No. 5	35

PSYLONS

86	E Type ETYPE 1	The Mockery Of Decline/Clear Sky	10
87	Iron Lung IL 001	All The Things We Need (12", p/s)	15
90	Unsigned UN 001	No Choice (p/s)	8
91	Unsigned UN 002	SAND MAN EP	8

PTOLOMY PSYCON

71	Hollick and Taylor HT/IPS 1306	LOOSE CAPACITOR (10" LP, 50 only, silkscreened front, printed back sleeve)	1200

PUBLIC ENEMY

87	Def Jam 651 245-0	Rebel Without A Pause (Vocal Mix)/(Instrumental) (picture disc)	8
88	Def Jam 652 833-0	Don't Believe The Hype/Prophets Of Rage (p/s, with patch)	5
88	Def Jam 653 089-7	Night Of The Living Baseheads/Terminator X To The Edge Of Panic (p/s, badge pack)	5
87	Def Jam 450482-1	YO BUM RUSH THE SHOW (LP)	12

PUBLIC FOOT THE ROMAN

(see also Movies)

73	Sovereign SVNA 7259	PUBLIC FOOT THE ROMAN (LP, gatefold sleeve)	50

MINT VALUE £

PUBLIC IMAGE LTD (PiL)

(see also Sex Pistols, Jah Wobble, Don Letts & Jah Wobble, Vivien Goldman, Time Zone, Cowboys International)

78	Virgin VS 228	Public Image/The Cowboy Song (foldout 'newspaper' p/s)	15
79	Virgin VS 274-12	Death Disco/And No Bird Do Sing (1/2 Mix)/Death Disco Megamix (12", p/s, 5,000 only)	8
86	Virgin VSD 855	Home/Round//Rise/Rise (Instrumental) (double pack)	5
87	Virgin VS 988	Seattle/Selfish Rubbish (box set with 7", badge, postcard & sew-on patch)	6
89	Virgin VSCD 1195	Warrior (Edit)/U.S.L.S.I. (Extended Mix) (3" CD, card sleeve)	8
78	Virgin V2114	FIRST ISSUE (with colour inner sleeve and PiL on both labels)	15
79	Virgin METAL 1	METAL BOX (LP, 3 x 12" with circular paper dividers & inner sheet in round tin)	50
90	Virgin TPAK 5	METAL BOX (CD, in round tin with insert)	20

GARY PUCKETT (& UNION GAP)

68	CBS 3365	Young Girl/I'm Losing You (as Union Gap featuring Gary Puckett)	5
68	CBS 3551	Lady Willpower/Daylight Stranger	5
68	CBS 3714	Over You/If The Day Would Come	7
69	CBS 4122	Don't Give In To Him/Could I	7
69	CBS 4505	This Girl Is A Woman Now/His Other Woman	8
68	CBS (S) 63342	YOUNG GIRL (LP)	25
68	CBS (S) 63429	INCREDIBLE (LP)	25
70	CBS 63794	THE NEW GARY PUCKETT AND THE UNION GAP ALBUM (LP)	25

PUDDING

67	Decca F 12603	The Magic Bus/It's Too Late	50

TITO PUENTE

57	RCA RD 27002	LET'S CHA-CHA WITH PUENTE (LP)	12
58	RCA SF 5008	MUCHO PUENTE (LP)	12

DUDU PUKWANA

83	Jika ZL 2	LIFE IN BRACKNELL & WILLISAU (LP, featuring Dinise Saul)	25

VERNE PULLENS

70	Injun 107	Mama Don't Allow No Boppin'/Bop Crazy Baby	10
70	Injun 111	Bop Crazy Baby/Would You Be Happy	12

LEROY PULLINS

66	London HLR 10056	I'm A Nut/Knee Deep	18
79	Pulp Music PB 1	Low Flying Aircraft/Something Just Behind My Back/So Lo (blank labels, some numbered up to 2,000 & signed, with handmade sleeve)	25
79	Pulp Music PB 1	Low Flying Aircraft/Something Just Behind My Back/So Lo (blank labels, some numbered up to 2,000 & signed)	20
77	MCA 315	I'm A Nut/Knee Deep (Reissue)	7

PULP

83	Red Rhino RED 32	My Lighthouse (Remix)/Looking For Life (p/s)	50
83	Red Rhino RED 37	Everybody's Problem/There Was (p/s)	50
85	Fire BLAZE 5	Little Girl (With Blue Eyes)/Simultaneous/Blue Glow/ The Will To Power (12", p/s)	15
85	Fire BLAZE 5	Little Girl (With Blue Eyes)/Simultaneous/Blue Glow/ The Will To Power, 12" promo)	40
86	Fire BLAZE 10	Dogs Are Everywhere/The Mark Of The Devil/97 Lovers/Aborigine/ Goodnight (12", p/s)	12
87	Fire BLAZE 17	They Suffocate At Night (Edited Version)/Tunnel (Cut Up Version) (p/s)	10
87	Fire BLAZE 17T	They Suffocate At Night (Uncut Version)/Tunnel (Full Length Version) (12", p/s)	12
87	Fore BLAZE 21T	Masters Of The Universe (Sanitised Vresion)/Manon/Silence (12", promo)	40
87	Fire BLAZE 21T	Masters Of The Universe (Sanitised Version)/Manon/Silence (12", p/s)	12
90	Fire BLAZE 44T	Is This House?/This House Is Condemned (12" promo, 1-sided)	50
90	Fire BLAZE 44T	My Legendary Girlfriend/Is This House?/This House Is Condemned (12", p/s)	10
91	Fire BLAZE 51T	Countdown/Death Goes To The Disco/Countdown (Radio Edit) (12", p/s)	10
92	Gift GIF 1	O.U. (Gone Gone)/Space/O.U. (Gone Gone) (Radio Edit) 12" promo & press sheet)	40
92	Gift GIF 1	O.U. (Gone Gone)/Space/O.U. (Gone Gone) (Radio Edit) (12", p/s)	8
92	Gift GIF 1CD	O.U. (Gone Gone) (Radio Edit)/Space/O.U. (Gone Gone) (CD)	15
92	Caff CAFF 17	My Legendary Girlfriend/Sickly Grin/Back In L.A. (foldover p/s with insert in poly bag, 500 only)	50
92	Fire BLAZE 44CD	My Legendary Girlfriend/Is This House?/This House Is Condemned (CD)	20
92	GIF 3	Babies/Styloroc (Nites Of Suburbia)/Sheffield: Sex City (12" promo with press sheet)	40
92	Gift GIF 3	Babies/Styloroc (Nites Of Suburbia)/Sheffield: Sex City (12", p/s)	10
92	Gift GIF 3CD	Babies/Styloroc (Nites Of Suburbia)/Sheffield: Sex City/ Sheffield: Sex City (Instrumental) (CD, card sleeve)	20
93	Gidt GIF 6	Razzmatazz/Inside Susan: A Story In 3 Songs (Stacks/Inside Susan/59 Lyndhurst Grove) (12" promo with press sheet)	40
93	Gift GIF 6CD	Razzmatazz/Inside Susan: A Story In 3 Songs (Stacks/Inside Susan/ 59 Lyndhurst Grove) (CD)	15
94	Island 12IS 595	THE SISTERS EP (12", p/s with print)	10
93	Island IS 567	Lipgloss/You're A Nightmare (p/s)	8
95	Island CIDX 613	Common People/Razzmatazz/Dogs Are Everywhere/Joyriders (CD, with sticker)	8
96	Island ISC 567	Lipgloss/You're A Nightmare (p/s, reissue, red vinyl)	10
96	Island ISC 574	Do You Remember The First Time/Street Lites (reissue, brown vinyl, p/s)	10
96	Island ISC 595	THE SISTERS EP (p/s, reissue, white vinyl)	10
96	Island ISC623	Disco 2000/Ansaphone (orange vinyl)	15
98	Evil (no cat no)	That Boy's Evil (12", white label, 500 only as "The Chocolate Layers")	20
84	Red Rhino REDLP 29	IT (mini-LP)	25
84	Red Rhino REDLP 29	IT (mini-LP)	25
94	Island ILPS 8025	HIS 'N' HERS (LP)	40
94	Cherry Red CDMRED 112	IT (CD, with extra tracks, withdrawn, 1,000 only)	20

MINT VALUE £

94	Cherry Red CDMRED 112	IT (CD, with extra tracks; withdrawn, 1,000 only)	20
95	Island ILPS 8041	DIFFERENT CLASS (LP, die-cut sleeve with 12 inserts)	60
95	Island ILPS 8041	DIFFERENT CLASS (LP, with 1 insert)	30
98	Island ILPSD 8066	THIS IS HARDCORE (2-LP with insert)	40

PULSAR

76	Decca SKL-R 5228	POLLEN (LP)	20
77	Decca TXS 119	STRANDS OF THE FUTURE (LP, gatefold sleeve)	25

PULSE

70	Major Minor SMLP 64	PULSE (LP)	50

PUMPHOUSE GANG

(see also Slush)

77	Kitsch FAD 1	Motorcity Fantasy/Cocaine (p/s)	7

PUNCHERS

70	Punch PH 46	Sons Of Thunder (actually by Lee Perry & The Upsetters)/ Only If You Understand	22

PUNCHIN' JUDY

(see also Downliner Sect)

73	Transatlantic TRA 272	PUNCHIN' JUDY (LP, laminated front sleeve)	20

PUNCTURE

77	Small Wonder SMALL 1	Mucky Pup/Can't Rock'n'Roll (p/s)	20

PUNISHMENT OF LUXURY

79	United Artists UP 36537	Secrets/Brainbomb (p/s)	6
79	United Artists UAG 30258	LAUGHING ACADEMY (LP, with inner sleeve)	12

PUNKETTES

77	Response SR 511	Going Out Wiv A Punk/Polythene	25

PUPILS

(see also Eyes)

66	Wing WL 1150	A TRIBUTE TO THE ROLLING STONES (LP)	50
69	Fontana SFL 13087	A TRIBUTE TO THE ROLLING STONES (LP, reissue)	20

PUPPETS

63	Pye 7N 15556	Poison Ivy/Everybody's Talking	60
64	Pye 7N 15625	Shake With Me/Three Boys Looking For Love (existence unconfirmed)	0
64	Pye 7N 15634	Baby Don't Cry/Shake With Me	60

DANNY PURCHES

55	Columbia SCM 5183	Mama/Just One More Time	10
58	Columbia DB 4129	The Shrine On The Second Floor/He	10
58	Columbia DB 4129	The Shrine On The Second Floor/He (78)	10

(BERNARD) PRETTY PURDEY

68	Direction 58-3301	Funky Donkey/Caravan	15
68	Direction 58-3628	Soul Clappin'/Blow Your Lid	12
71	Philips 6073 708	Good Livin' Good Lovin'/Day Dreaming	6
68	Direction 8-63290	SOUL DRUMS (LP)	40
71	Philips 6369 421	SOUL IS ? (LP)	20

PURE GOLD

69	President PT 250	Fairground/You've Gotta Give It Time	10

PURE HELL

78	Golden Sphinx GSX 002	These Boots Are Made For Walking/No Rules (p/s)	20

PURE LOVE & PLEASURE

70	Stateside SSL 5026	A RECORD OF PURE LOVE AND PLEASURE (LP)	30

PURE REASON REVOLUTION

04	Poptones MC50896	Apprentice Of The Universe/Nimos & Tambos (p/s)	5

PURESSENCE

92	Damn Loud 2DM01	PETROL SKIN (EP, 1,000 only)	30
93	Damn Loud 2DM02	OFFSHORE (EP, 1,000 only)	30

PURGE

69	Corn CP 101	The Mayor Of Simpleton Hall/The Knave (p/s)	200
69	Corn CP 101	The Mayor Of Simpleton Hall/The Knave (without p/s)	90

JAMES & BOBBY PURIFY

66	Stateside SS 547	I'm Your Puppet/So Many Reasons	20
67	Stateside SS 595	Wish You Didn't Have To Go/You Can't Keep A Good Man Down	15
67	Stateside SS 2016	Shake A Tail Feather/Goodness Gracious	25
67	Stateside SS 2039	I Take What I Want/Sixteen Tons	12
67	Stateside SS 2049	Let Love Come Between Us/I Don't Want To Have To Wait	25
68	Stateside SS 2093	Do Unto Me/Everybody Needs Somebody	20
68	Bell BLL 1008	I Can't Remember/I Was Born To Lose Out	10
68	Bell BLL 1024	Help Yourself To All My Lovin'/Last Piece Of Love	10
69	Bell BLL 1043	Untie Me/We're Finally Gonna Make It	8
69	Bell BLL 1056	Let Love Come Between Us/Shake A Tail Feather	10
69	Bell BLL 1067	Do Unto Me/Wish You Didn't Have To Go	8
72	Mojo 2092 056	I'm Your Puppet/Wish You Didn't Have To Go	8
67	Stateside SL 10206	JAMES AND BOBBY PURIFY (LP)	60
67	Bell MBLL/SBLL 101	THE PURE SOUND OF THE PURIFYS (LP)	40

ALTON PURNELL

(see also Bonnie Raitt)

70	Dixie DIX 4	TRAVELLING LIGHT (LP)	30

PURPLE ALGAE

95	Poor Person Prod. PPPR 7	ADRIFT ON A SEA OF SOUND (LP, handmade sleeve & insert, no'd, 500 only)	15

MINT VALUE £

PURPLE GANG

67	Big T BIG 101	Granny Takes A Trip/Bootleg Whisky	15
68	Big T BIG 111	Kiss Me Goodnight Sally Green/Auntie Monica	7
68	Transatlantic	THE PURPLE GANG STRIKES (LP)	60

PURPLE HAZE

85	S.R.S. SRS 6	Hear It On The Radio (p/s)	55

PURPLE HEARTS

(see also Bob Manton, Rage)

79	Fiction FICS 003	Millions Like Us/Beat That! (p/s)	10
79	Fiction FICS 007	Frustration/Extraordinary Sensations (p/s)	10
80	Fiction FICS 9	Jimmy/What Am I Gonna Do (p/s)	10
80	Safari SAFE 30	My Life's A Jigsaw/The Guy Who Made Her A Star/Just To Please You (in foldout jigsaw p/s)	12
80	Safari SAFE 30	My Life's A Jigsaw/The Guy Who Made Her A Star/Just To Please You	8
82	Road Runner RR 1	Plane Crash/Scooby Doo/Gun Of Life (p/s)	12
86	UNICORN PHZ3	Friends Again/Head On Collision Time (p/s)	8
80	Fiction FIX 002/2383 568	BEAT THAT! (LP)	20
85	Razor RAZS 13	HEAD ON COLLISION TIME (LP)	12
85	Razor RAZS 19	POPISH FRENZY (LP)	12

PURPLE WINE

71	The Mental Health Council	It's My Mind/I'm Lonely/Friends (p/s)	80

GEOFF PURVIS

77	Fellside FE 003	THE BORDER FIDDLER (LP)	12

PUSSY

(see also Angel Pavement, Fortes Mentum)

69	Morgan Bluetown BT 5002	PUSSY PLAYS (LP)	900
09	Morgan Bluetown BT 5002	PUSSY PLAYS (LP, reissue by Secret Records/Record Collector, 350 only with signed and numbered laminated insert)	30

PUSSY

(see also Jerusalem)

72	Deram DM 368	Feline Woman/Ska Child	25

PUSSYFOOT

(see also Rare Breed)

66	Decca F 12474	Freeloader/Things That Still Remind Me	25
67	Decca F 12561	Mr Hyde/Hasty Words	30
67	Pye 7N 17395	Dee Dee Do Your Dance/Big Brown Eyes	30
68	Pye 7N 17520	Good Times/Till You Don't Want Me Anymore	25

PUSSY GALORE

(see also Jon Spencer Blues Explosion)

87	Vinyl Drip SUK 001	GROOVY HATE FUCK (LP)	18
87	Product Inc. 33PROD 19	RIGHT NOW (LP)	15
89	Product INCLP 1	DIAL M FOR MOTHERFUCKER (LP)	18

ASHA PUTHLI

76	CBS 4623	The Devil Is Loose/Space Talk	10
73	CBS 65804	ASHA PUTHLI (LP)	20
75	CBS 80978	SHE LOVES TO HEAR THE MUSIC (LP)	15
76	CBS 81443	THE DEVIL IS LOOSE (LP)	30

PUTNEY BRIDGE

71	Chapter One CH 145	Take A Ride/Road To Purity	5

PUZZLE

69	Stateside SS 2146	Hey Medusa/Make The Children Happy	18
69	Stateside SSL 10285	PUZZLE (LP)	30

PUZZLE

72	Jam JAM 1	Houla/Do You Feel The Pain	25

PVC 2

(see also Midge Ure, Zones)o

77	Zoom ZUM 2	Put You In The Picture/Pain/Deranged, Demented and Free (p/s)	8

PYEWACKET

81	Dingles DIN 312	PYEWACKET (LP)	12
83	Familiar FAM 43	THE MAN IN THE MOON DRINKS CLARET (LP)	12

PYLONS

80	Hi Voltage HVVS 701	Marvel World/Spoof (p/s)	30

NATASHA PYNE

66	Polydor 56713	It's All In Your Head/I'm A Dreamer	15

PYRAMID

(see also Fairport Convention, Ian Matthews)

67	Deram DM 111	Summer Of Last Year/Summer Evening	55

PYRAMIDS (Jamaica)

(see also Symarip, Equals, Little Grants & Eddie, Seven Letters, Bruce Ruffin)

67	President PT 161	Train Tour To Rainbow City/John Chewey	20
68	President PT 177	Wedding In Peyton Place/Girls Girls Girls	10
68	President PT 195	All Change On The Bakerloo Line/Playing Games	10
68	President PT 206	Mexican Moonlight/Mule	10
68	President PT 225	Tisko My Darling/Movement All Around	10
69	President PT 243	Do-Re-Mi/I'm Outnumbered	10
69	President PT 274	I'm A Man/Dragon Fly	10
69	Doctor Bird DB 1307	Stay With Him/Chicken Mary	20

MINT VALUE £

70	Duke DU 80	Geronimo/Feel Alright	10
70	Trojan TR 7755	Feel Alright/Telstar	8
70	Trojan TR 7770	To Sir With Love/Reggae Shuffle	8
71	Trojan TR 7803	All For You/All For You Version	8
71	Creole CR 1003	Mosquito Bite/Mother's Bath	8
68	President PTL 1021	THE PYRAMIDS (LP)	40

PYRAMIDS (U.S.)

64	London HLU 9847	Penetration/Here Comes Marsha	50

PYTHAGORAS THEOREM

70	Pye 7N 17924	Give A Damn/London Bridge	12
70	Pye 7N 17990	Our House/Free Like Me	7

PYTHON LEE JACKSON

(see also Rod Stewart)

70	Young Blood YB 1017	In A Broken Dream/Doing Fine	6
76	Young Blood YB 1077	The Blues/Cloud Nine	10
80	Young Blood YB 0089	In A Broken Dream/The Blues	6
80	Young Blood YEP 89	In A Broken Dream (mono)/In A Broken Dream (stereo)/The Blues/ Cloud Nine (EP, "Kelly Girl" Employment Agency advert on p/s)	10

Q

Q-CHASTIC

(see also Aphex Twin)

92	Rephlex 002EP	Q-CHASTIC EP (double pack)	200

Q-PROJECT

92	QTIP 001	FREESTYLE FANATIC EP (12", stamped white label, 4 untitled tracks)	40

QUAD

(see also Sun Dial)

97	Acme AC 8020LP	QUAD (LP, clear vinyl in printed clear PVC cover)	15
97	Prescription DRUG 3	QUAD (LP, 99 copies only, handmade sleeve, mail-order only)	25

QUADS

80s	Big Bear BB29	UFO/Astronaut's Journey (p/s)	10

CHRISTINE QUAITE

62	Oriole CB 1739	Guilty Eyes/Oh My!	20
62	Oriole CB 1772	Your Nose Is Gonna Grow/Our Last Chance	20
63	Oriole CB 1845	Mister Heartache/Whisper Wonderful Words	20
63	Oriole CB 1876	In The Middle Of The Floor/Tell Me Mama	60
63	Oriole CB 1921	I Believe In Love/Here She Comes	20
64	Oriole CB 1945	Mister Stuck Up/Will You Be The Same Tomorrow	20
65	Stateside SS 435	If You've Got A Heart/So Near So Far	20
66	Stateside SS 482	Long After Tonight Is All Over/I'm Hoping	50
66	Stateside SS 482	Long After Tonight Is All Over/I'm Hoping (DJ copy)	100

QUAKER CITY BOYS

59	London HLU 8796	Teasin'/Won't Y' Come Out, Mary Ann	15
59	London HLU 8796	Teasin'/Won't Y' Come Out, Mary Ann (78)	12

QUAKERS

65	Oriole CB 1992	I'm Ready/Down The Road A Piece	200
65	Studio 36 KSP 109/110	She's Alright/Talk To Me (only 50 pressed)	600

QUALITY DRIVEL

81	No Cure WHOOP 1	SUBLIMINAL CUTS EP (p/s)	30

QUANDO QUANGO

84	Factory FAC 102	Atom Rock (p/s)	6
85	Factory FAC 137	Genius/This Feeling (p/s)	6
85	Factory FAC 137	Genius/This Feeling (12", p/s)	6
85	Factory FACT 110	PIGS & BATTLESHIPS (LP)	18
85	Factory FACT 110C	PIGS & BATTLESHIPS (cassette, with postcards)	18

QUANTIC

01	Tru Thoughts TRU 014	Life In The Rain/Common Knowledge/Time Is The Enemy (12")	15
01	Tru Thoughts TRU LP 016	THE 5TH EXOTIC (2-LP)	40
02	Tru Thoughts TRU LP 034	APRICOT MORNING (2xLP)	30
04	Tru Thoughts TRU LP 062	MISHAPS HAPPENING (2xLP)	15
00	Breakin' Bread BNB 002	We Got Soul/Fresh Rhythm	25

QUANTIC SOUL ORCHESTRA

01	Tru Thoughts TRU7 018	Super 8 (Part 1)/Super 8 (Part 2)	12
02	Tru Thoughts TRU7 023	Assassin (Part 1)/Assassin (Part 2)	5
03	Tru Thoughts TRU7 051	Pushin' On/Pushin' On My Thing	8
03	Tru Thoughts TRU7 055	Babarabatiri/The Conspirator	10
03	Tru Thoughts TRU LP 029	STAMPEDE (LP)	15
05	Tru Thoughts TRU LP 074	PUSHIN' ON (LP)	12

QUARRY MEN

(see also Beatles, Trad Grads)

58	'P.F. Phillips Kensington'	That'll Be The Day/In Spite Of All The Danger (78 shellac acetate, handwritten labels, 1 copy owned by Paul McCartney, worth at least £150,000)	
81	'Percy Philips, Kensington'	That'll Be The Day/In Spite Of All The Danger (78rpm, private pressing reproduction of 1958 demo disc, repro Parlophone co. sleeve, 25 only)	10,000

MINT VALUE £

81 'Percy Philips, Kensington' That'll Be The Day/In Spite Of All The Danger (45rpm, private pressing reproduction of 1958 demo disc, repro Parlophone co. sleeve, 25 only). 10,000

JOE QUARTERMAN & FREE SOUL
73 GSF GSZ 3 So Much Trouble In My Mind (Parts 1 & 2). 8
74 GSF GSZ 12 Thanks Dad Parts 1 & 2 5
73 GSF GS 504 JOE QUARTERMAN & FREE SOUL (LP) 50

QUARTER NOTES
57 Parlophone R 4365 My Fantasy/Ten Minutes To Midnight 15

QUARTET
69 Decca F12974 Now/Will My Lady Come 8
70 Decca F13072 Mama Where Did You Fail/Joseph 10

QUARTZ
(see also Black Sabbath, Copperfield, Bandy Legs)
77 Jet UP 36290 Sugar Rain/Street Fighting Lady/Mainline Riders 15
77 Jet UP 36317 Street Fighting Lady/Mainline Riders 12
80 Reddingtons R.R. DAN 1 Nantucket Sleighride/Wildfire (p/s, white or blue vinyl) 10
80 Reddingtons R.R. DAN 1 Nantucket Sleighride/Wildfire (p/s, black vinyl). 5
80 Jet SJET 189 Street Fighting Lady/Mainline Riders (p/s, reissue, demos £15). 10
80 Logo GO 387 Satan's Serenade/Bloody Fool (p/s) 5
80 Logo GOT 387 Satan's Serenade/Bloody Fool/Roll Over Beethoven (live) (12", p/s, blue vinyl). . 25
80 Logo GOT 387 Satan's Serenade/Bloody Fool/Roll Over Beethoven (live) (12", p/s, red vinyl). . . 18
80 Sound For Industry SFI 549 Satan's Serenade (flexidisc) 7
80 MCA MCA 642 Stoking The Fires Of Hell/Circles (p/s). 10
80 Logo MOGO 4007 LIVE QUARTZ (12" EP). 18
81 MCA MCA 661 Stand Up And Fight/Charlie Snow (p/s) 18
83 Heavy Metal HEAVY 17 Tell Me Why/Streetwalker (p/s) 7
77 Jet UAG 30081 QUARTZ (LP, with inner sleeve) 50
79 Jet JETLP 233 DELETED (LP, in sealed brown paper bag with insert. Reissue of 1st LP) 18
80 Reddingtons R.R. REDD 001 QUARTZ LIVE - COUNT DRACULA (LP, in b&w 'live' sleeve) 15
80 Reddingtons R.R. REDD 001 QUARTZ LIVE - COUNT DRACULA (LP). 12
80 Logo MOGO 4007 LIVE QUARTZ (LP) 12
80 MCA MCF 3080 STAND UP AND FIGHT (LP, with lyric insert). 25
83 Heavy Metal HMRLP 9 AGAINST ALL ODDS (LP, with inner sleeve) 12
83 Heavy Metal HMRPD 9 AGAINST ALL ODDS (LP, picture disc) 25

QUASAR
(see also Solstice)
82 Q QUA 1 FIRE IN THE SKY (LP, with insert). 20

QUATERMASS
(see also Ian Gillan Band, Episode Six, Hard Stuff)
70 Harvest SVHL 775 QUATERMASS (LP, gatefold sleeve, no EMI logo on label) 120
75 Harvest SHSM 2002 QUATERMASS (LP, reissue, different sleeve) 20

QUATERMASS
97 Metropolitan MM 027 The Judgement (12", no p/s). 15

QUATRAIN
69 Polydor 583 743 QUATRAIN (LP). 50

SUZI QUATRO
72 Rak RAK 134 Rolling Stone/Brain Confusion (For All The Lonely People) 30
75 Rak RAK 200 I Bit Off More Than I Could Chew/Red Hot Rosie 5
75 Rak RAK 215 I May Be Too Young/Don't Mess Around 5
75 Rak RAK 256 Roxy Roller/I'll Grow On You. 5
73 Rak PSR 355 Primitive Love/Shakin' All Over (promo only) 30
78 Rak RAK 285 Stumblin' In/Stranger With You (with Chris Norman) (2 different p/s) 5
79 Rak RAK 299 She's In Love With You/Space Cadets (p/s). 5
87 Hackenbacker HACK 101 Am I Dreaming/Who Needs Chairs/Will You Take This Woman (only available at pantomime show). 10

QUBISM
94 em:t 2294 QUBISM (CD, digipak) 50

QUEEN
(see also Freddie Mercury, Brian May, Roger Taylor, Larry Lurex, Cross, Immortals, Hilary Hilary, Eddie Howell, Man Friday & Jive Junior)

SINGLES
73 EMI EMI 2036 Keep Yourself Alive/Son And Daughter 40
74 EMI EMI 2121 Seven Seas Of Rhye/See What A Fool I've Been 5
74 EMI EMI 2229 Killer Queen/Flick Of The Wrist. 5
75 EMI EMI 2256 Now I'm Here/Lily Of The Valley 5
75 EMI EMI 2375 Bohemian Rhapsody/I'm In Love With My Car (p/s; beware counterfeits with 'computer-scanned' logo). 30
76 EMI EMI 2565 Somebody To Love/White Man (p/s, beware of counterfeit sleeves) 10
77 EMI EMI 2593 Tie Your Mother Down/You And I 8
77 EMI EMI 2623 QUEEN'S FIRST EP: Good Old Fashioned Lover Boy/Death On Two Legs/ Tenement Funster/White Queen (As It Began) (p/s) 10
77 EMI EMI 2708 We Are The Champions/We Will Rock You (p/s) 8
78 EMI EMI 2575 Spread Your Wings/Sheer Heart Attack (p/s). 6
78 EMI EMI 2870 Bicycle Race/Fat Bottomed Girls (p/s) 6
78 EMI EMI 2870 Bicycle Race/Fat Bottomed Girls (different p/s for export to Belgium) 200
79 EMI EMI 2910 Don't Stop Me Now/In Only Seven Days (p/s) 6
79 EMI EMI 2959 Love Of My Life (live)/Now I'm Here (live) 18
79 EMI EMI 5001 Crazy Little Thing Called Love/We Will Rock You (live) (p/s). 5
80 EMI EMI 5022 Save Me/Let Me Entertain You (live) (p/s). 5
80 EMI EMI 5076 Play The Game/A Human Body (p/s, beige label with red 'EMI' logo or white label with large black 'Queen' logo). 6

			MINT VALUE £
80	EMI EMI 5102	Another One Bites The Dust/Dragon Attack (p/s)	8
82	EMI EMI 5293	Body Language/Life Is Real (Song For Lennon) (p/s)	6
82	EMI EMI 5316	Las Palabras De Amor (The Words Of Love)/Cool Cat (p/s)	6
82	EMI EMI 5325	Backchat/Staying Power (p/s)	10
82	EMI 12EMI 5325	Backchat (Extended)/Staying Power (12", p/s)	20
84	EMI 12QUEEN 1	Radio Ga Ga (Ext. Version)/Radio Ga Ga (Instrumental)/I Go Crazy (12", p/s)	10
84	EMI QUEEN 2	I Want To Break Free (Remix)/Machines (Back To Humans) ('Freddie' p/s, gold lettering)	12
84	EMI QUEEN 2	I Want To Break Free (Remix)/Machines (Back To Humans) ('Freddie' p/s, white lettering)	8
84	EMI QUEEN 2	I Want To Break Free (Remix)/Machines (Back To Humans) ('Brian', p/s, with gold lettering)	12
84	EMI QUEEN 2	I Want To Break Free (Remix)/Machines (Back To Humans) ('Roger' p/s, with gold lettering)	15
84	EMI QUEEN 2	I Want To Break Free (Remix)/Machines (Back To Humans) ('John' p/s, with gold lettering)	18
84	EMI 12QUEEN 2	I Want To Break Free (Extended Remix)/Machines (Back To Humans) (12", p/s, with red background with gold lettering)	20
84	EMI 12QUEEN 2	I Want To Break Free (Extended Remix)/Machines (Back To Humans) (12", p/s, with red background with black lettering)	12
84	EMI 12QUEEN 2	I Want To Break Free (Extended Remix)/Machines (Back To Humans) (12", p/s, with white background)	10
84	EMI QUEEN 3	It's A Hard Life/Is This The World We Created...? (p/s)	6
84	EMI QUEEN 3	It's A Hard Life/Is This The World We Created...? ('Roger Taylor' overprinted photo p/s)	20
84	EMI 12QUEEN 3	It's A Hard Life (Extended)/It's A Hard Life/ Is This The World We Created...? (12")	25
84	EMI 12QUEENP 3	It's A Hard Life/Is This The World We Created...? (12", picture disc)	20
84	EMI QUEEN 4	Hammer To Fall (Edit)/Tear It Up ('live' p/s, withdrawn)	100
84	EMI QUEEN 4	Hammer To Fall (Edit)/Tear It Up (red p/s)	6
84	EMI 12 QUEEN 4	Hammer To Fall (The Headbangers Mix)/Tear It Up (12", 'live' p/s, withdrawn)	100
84	EMI 12 QUEEN 4	Hammer To Fall (The Headbangers Mix)/Tear It Up (12", red p/s)	12
84	EMI QUEEN 5	Man On The Prowl/Keep Passing The Open Windows (unreleased, white label test pressings only)	150
84	EMI QUEEN 5	Thank God It's Christmas/Man On The Prowl/ Keep Passing The Open Windows (p/s)	8
84	EMI 12QUEEN 5	Thank God It's Christmas/Man On The Prowl (Extended Version)/ Keep Passing The Open Windows (Extended Version) (12", p/s)	10
84	EMI G 45 1	You're My Best Friend/Killer Queen (re-issue, Golden 45's series)	20
85	EMI QUEEN 6	One Vision (7" Mix)/Blurred Vision (p/s, with red lyric inner sleeve)	7
85	EMI QUEEN 6	One Vision (7" Mix)/Blurred Vision (p/s)	5
85	EMI 12QUEEN 6	One Vision (Extended Vision)/Blurred Vision (12", p/s, with red lyric inner sleeve)	12
85	EMI 12QUEEN 6	One Vision (Extended Vision)/Blurred Vision (12", p/s)	10
85	EMI 12QUEEN 6	One Vision (Extended Vision)/Blurred Vision (12", printed PVC sleeve & red inner)	20
86	EMI 12QUEEN 7	A Kind Of Magic (Ext. Version)/A Dozen Red Roses For My Darling (12", p/s)	12
86	EMI 12QUEENP7	A Kind Of Magic (Extended Version)/Don't Lose Your Head (Instrumental Version) (12", picture disc)	35
86	EMI QUEEN 8	Friends Will Be Friends/Seven Seas Of Rhye (p/s)	6
86	EMI QUEEN P8	Friends Will Be Friends/Seven Seas Of Rhye (picture disc)	40
86	EMI 12QUEEN 8	Friends Will Be Friends (Extended Version)/Friends Will Be Friends (7" Version)/Seven Seas Of Rhye (12", p/s)	10
86	EMI QUEEN 9	Who Wants To Live Forever/Killer Queen (p/s)	8
86	EMI 12QUEEN 9	Who Wants To Live Forever (7" Version)/(Album Version)/Killer Queen/ Who Wants To Live Forever (Piano Version) (12", p/s)	15
89	Parlophone 12QUEEN 10	I Want It All (Single Version)/Hang On In There/ I Want It All (Album Version) (12", p/s)	12
89	Parlophone CDQUEEN 10	I Want It All (Album Version)/Hang On In There/I Want It All (Single Version) (CD, picture disc)	20
89	Parlophone QUEEN PD 11	Breakthru' (7" Mix)/Stealin' (shaped picture disc, 12" PVC sleeve with insert)	20
89	Parlophone QUEEN PD 11	Breakthru' (7" Mix)/Stealin' (uncut picture disc, 12" PVC sleeve with insert)	90
89	Parlophone QUEEN C11	Breakthru' (7" Mix)/Stealin' (cassette)	6
89	Parlophone 12QUEEN 11	Breakthru' (12" Version)/Breakthru' (Single Version)/Stealin' (12", p/s)	8
89	Parlophone CD QUEEN 11	Breakthru' (12" Version)/Stealin'/Breakthru' (7" Mix) (CD)	25
89	Parlophone QUEEN 12	The Invisible Man/Hijack My Heart (black vinyl, p/s)	5
89	Parlophone QUEEN X12	The Invisible Man/Hijack My Heart (clear vinyl, p/s)	12
89	Parlophone 12QUEEN 12	The Invisible Man (12" Version)/(7" Version)/Hijack My Heart (12", p/s)	12
89	Parlophone 12QUEENX12	The Invisible Man (12" Version)/The Invisible Man (7" Version)/ Hijack My Heart (12", clear vinyl, PVC sleeve with insert)	20
89	Parlophone CD QUEEN 12	The Invisible Man (12" Version)/Hijack My Heart/ The Invisible Man (Single Version) (CD)	30
89	Parlophone QUEEN 14	Scandal/My Life Has Been Saved (p/s)	8
89	Parlophone QUEEN P14	Scandal/My Life Has Been Saved (poster p/s)	20
89	Parlophone 12QUEEN 14	Scandal (12" Version)/Scandal (7" Version)/My Life Has Been Saved (12", p/s)	10
89	Parlophone 12QUEENS 14	Scandal (12" Version)/My Life Has Been Saved/Scandal (7" Version)/ (12", p/s, 1-sided, B-side etched with group's signatures)	20
89	Parlophone CD QUEEN 14	Scandal (12" Version)/My Life Has Been Saved/Scandal (7" Version) (CD)	25
89	Parlophone QUEEN 15	The Miracle/Stone Cold Crazy (live) (p/s)	8
89	Parlophone QUEEN H15	The Miracle/Stone Cold Crazy (live) (orange hologram p/s)	15
89	Parlophone QUEEN H15	The Miracle/Stone Cold Crazy (live) (proof sleeve with negative hologram p/s)	300
89	Parlophone 12QUEEN 15	The Miracle/Stone Cold Crazy (live)/My Melancholy Blues (live) (12", yellow p/s)	15
89	Parlophone 12QUEENP 15	The Miracle/Stone Cold Crazy (live)/My Melancholy Blues (live) (12", turquoise p/s with insert print)	18
89	Parlophone QUEENCD 15	The Miracle/Stone Cold Crazy (live)/My Melancholy Blues (live) (CD)	30
91	Parlophone QUEEN 16	Innuendo/Bijou (p/s)	6

			MINT VALUE £
91	Parlophone 12QUEEN 16	Innuendo (Explosive Version)/Under Pressure/Bijou (12", p/s)	8
91	Parl. 12QUEEN PD16	Innuendo (Explosive Version)/Under Pressure/Bijou (12", picture disc, PVC sleeve with insert)	20
91	Parlophone QUEEN 17	I'm Going Slightly Mad/The Hitman (p/s)	5
91	Parlophone QUEEN PD 17	I'm Going Slightly Mad/The Hitman (shaped picture disc with insert)	20
91	Parlophone QUEEN PD 17	I'm Going Slightly Mad/The Hitman (uncut picture disc with insert)	125
91	Parlophone 12QUEENG 17	I'm Going Slightly Mad/The Hitman/Lost Opportunity (12", gatefold p/s)	15
91	Parlophone CDQUEEN 17	I'm Going Slightly Mad/The Hitman/Lost Opportunity (CD)	10
91	Parlophone 12QUEEN PD18	Headlong/All God's People/Mad The Swine (12", clear vinyl picture disc, with insert in PVC sleeve)	15
91	Parlophone CD QUEEN 18	Headlong/All God's People/Mad The Swine (CD)	10
91	Parlophone QUEEN 19	The Show Must Go On/Keep Yourself Alive (p/s)	5
91	Parlophone QUEEN C19	The Show Must Go On/Keep Yourself Alive (cassette)	15
91	Parlophone 12QUEENSG 19	The Show Must Go On/Keep Yourself Alive/Queen Talks (12", 1-sided, B-side etched with group's signatures, gatefold p/s)	18
91	Parlophone CDQUEEN 19	The Show Must Go On/Keep Yourself Alive/Queen Talks/Body Language (CD)	10
91	Parlophone CDQUEENS 19	The Show Must Go On/Now I'm Here/Fat Bottomed Girls/Las Palabras De Amor (The Words Of Love) (CD, in box with foldout poster, 10,000 only)	20
91	Parlophone QUEEN 19/20	The Show Must Go On/Bohemian Rhapsody (unissued, no p/s)	500
93	Parlophone CDR 6340	FIVE LIVE EP: Killer/Papa Was A Rolling Stone (PM Dawn Remix)/ Somebody To Love/These Are The Days Of Our Lives (as Queen featuring George Michael & Lisa Stansfield) (CD, picture disc, silver inlay)	8
95	Parlophone QUEENLH 24	Let Me Live/Fat Bottomed Girls (jukebox 45, black vinyl no p/s)	15
95	Parlophone CDQUEENS 22	A Winter's Tale/Thank God It's Christmas/Rock In Rio Blues (CD, 'Merry Christmas' box)	8
96	Parlophone QUEEN 23	Too Much Love Will Kill You/We Will Rock You/We Are The Champions (p/s, pink vinyl)	6
96	Parlophone QUEENPD 24	Let Me Live/Fat Bottomed Girls/Bicycle Race (picture disc with poster)	6
97	parlophone QUEENLH 26	No-One But You/We Will Rock You (Original 1977 version) (unreleased)	20
97	Parlophone QUEEN 26	No-One But You (Only The Good Die Young)/Princes Of The Universe/ We Will Rock You (Rick Rubin 'Ruined' Remix)/Gimme The Prize (Instrumental 'Eye' Remix) (Unissued 7")	150
97	Parlophone QUEENPD 27	No-One But You (Only The Good Die Young)/We Will Rock You (Rick Rubin 'Ruined' Remix)/Tie Your Mother Down/Gimme The Prize (Instrumental 'Eye' Remix) (picture disc)	6
96	Parlophone 12QUEEN25	You Don't Fool Me - Remixes (12", silver vinyl, p/s, numbered)	8
98	Parlophone QUEENPD28	Under Pressure - Rah Mix/Bohemian Rhapsody (picture disc)	8

3" CD SINGLES

88	Parlophone QUECD 1	Seven Seas Of Rhye/See What A Fool I've Been/Funny How Love Is	12
88	Parlophone QUECD 2	Killer Queen/Flick Of The Wrist/Brighton Rock	12
88	Parlophone QUECD 3	Bohemian Rhapsody/I'm In Love With My Car/You're My Best Friend	12
88	Parlophone QUECD 4	Somebody To Love/White Man/Tie Your Mother Down	12
88	Parlophone QUECD 5	QUEEN'S FIRST EP: Good Old Fashioned Lover Boy/Death On Two Legs/ Tenement Funster/White Queen (As It Began)	12
88	Parlophone QUECD 6	We Are The Champions/We Will Rock You /Fat Bottomed Girls	12
88	Parlophone QUECD 7	Crazy Little Thing Called Love/Spread Your Wings/Flash	12
88	Parlophone QUECD 8	Another One Bites The Dust/Dragon Attack/Las Palabras De Amor	12
88	Parlophone QUECD 9	Under Pressure/Soul Brother/Body Language	12
88	Parlophone QUECD 10	Radio Ga Ga/I Go Crazy/Hammer To Fall	12
88	Parlophone QUECD 11	I Want To Break Free/Machines (Back To Humans)/It's A Hard Life	12
88	Parlophone QUECD 12	A Kind Of Magic/A Dozen Red Roses For My Darling/One Vision	12
80s	Parlophone	QUEEN : THE 3" SINGLES (gatefold wallet, card insert)	150

(The above 3" CDs were Issued in card sleeves with generic plastic EMI outer packages.)

ALBUMS

73	EMI EMC 3006	QUEEN (LP)	30
74	EMI EMA 767	QUEEN II (LP, laminated gatefold sleeve, lyric inner sleeve)	35
74	EMI EMC 3061	SHEER HEART ATTACK (LP, laminated sleeve, inner lyric sleeve)	25
75	EMI EMTC 103	A NIGHT AT THE OPERA (LP, gatefold sleeve)	25
76	EMI EMTC 104	A DAY AT THE RACES (LP, gatefold, inner sleeve)	20
77	EMI EMA 784	NEWS OF THE WORLD (LP, gatefold with lyric inner sleeve)	20
78	EMI EMA 788	JAZZ (LP, gatefold sleeve with attached poster)	30
81	EMI EMTV 30	GREATEST HITS (LP, mispress, side 2 plays "Anne Murray's Greatest Hits")	15
85	EMI QB 1	THE COMPLETE WORKS (14-LP box set including "Complete Vision" LP of non-LP tracks, 2 booklets & map, numbered; 600 autographed)	1000
85	EMI QB 1	THE COMPLETE WORKS (14-LP box set including "Complete Vision" LP of non-LP tracks, 2 booklets & map, numbered)	100
86	EMI EU 3509	A KIND OF MAGIC ('Princes Of The Universe' proof sleeve; unreleased)	400
89	Band Of Joy BOJLP 001	QUEEN AT THE BEEB (LP)	15
91	Parlophone PMTV 2	GREATEST HITS 2 (2-LP, embossed gatefold sleeve)	25
91	Parlophone PCSD 115	INNUENDO (LP)	20
92	Parlophone PCSP 725	LIVE AT WEMBLEY (2-LP, gatefold sleeve)	25
92	Parlophone CDQTEL 0001	BOX OF TRIX (CD, box set, with video, book, poster, T-shirt, patch & badge)	60
92	Parlophone CQTEL 0001	BOX OF TRIX (cassette, box set, with video, book, poster, T-shirt, patch & badge)	50
95	Parlophone 724383608812	MADE IN HEAVEN (LP, gatefold with inserts)	40
95	Parlophone QUEEN BOX 20	ULTIMATE QUEEN (20 x CD set, in numbered glazed box and numbered cardboard outer box, with Freddie hologram and 2 booklets)	450

PROMOS

77	EMI SP SLP 241 A1U	We Will Rock You/We Are The Champions/Spread Your Wings (12", 1-sided)	400
78	EMI EMI 2375	Bohemian Rhapsody/I'm In Love With My Car (EMI 'Queen's Award For Export' in-house edition, blue vinyl, Queen crest label, hand-numbered, purple p/s)	3500
78	EMI EMI 2375	Bohemian Rhapsody/I'm In Love With My Car (EMI 'Queen's Award For Export' in-house edition, blue vinyl, Queen crest label, hand-numbered, purple p/s., with outer 'EMI International' carrying envelope)	3800
78	EMI EMI 2375	Bohemian Rhapsody/I'm In Love With My Car (EMI 'Queen's Award For Export' in-house edition, blue vinyl, Queen crest label, hand-numbered, purple p/s., with invites, matches, pen, ticket, menu, outer card sleeve, scarf & EMI goblets in card box)	5000

			MINT VALUE £
		(The blue vinyl 'Bohemian Rhapsody' was limited to 200 numbered copies)	
84	EMI QUEEN 1	Radio Ga Ga (Edit)/I Go Crazy ('video shoot' p/s, unreleased, proofs only)	450
84	EMI QUEENDJ 5	Man On The Prowl/Thank God It's Christmas	150
84	Flexi Ltd. (no cat. no.)	Excerpts From Their New Album 'The Works' (flexidisc sampler, p/s)	15
86	Parlophone EMCDV 2	THE HIGHLANDER SELECTION (CD Video, 50 only)	400
86	EMI/Channel 4 QUEEN 7	NETWORK QUEEN ('A Kind Of Magic' 7" housed in promotional fold-out sleeve that opens up to depict illustrated band playing to audience. 50 made to promote TV advertising for July 1986 Wembley Stadium concerts)	2000
86	(no label or cat. no.)	A Message From Queen (cassette, 1st Fan Club Convention issue)	20
89	Flexi Ltd. (no cat. no.)	A Message From Queen (flexidisc, 4th Fan Club Convention issue)	25
89	Parlophone QUEEN 10	I Want It All/Hang On In There (p/s in promo gatefold p/s, press release, B&W photo)	20
89	Parlophone TEASER 1	THE TEASER TAPE (cassette, edits sampler for "The Miracle")	15
95	EMI QUEEN DJ95	Bohemian Rhapsody/I'm In Love With My Car (purple vinyl, hand numbered, p/s, 10th anniversary Fan Club Convention issue, 2,000 only)	150
95	Parlophone CDD JUKE	Heaven For Everyone (single version)	10
95	Parlophone QUEENLHDJ 21	Heaven For Everyone (Album Version)/Heaven For Everyone (Single Version) (jukebox issue, plain white sleeve, with poster, fold-out card & jukebox strip)	20
95	Parlophone QUEENDJ 22	A Winter's Tale/Thank God It's Christmas (jukebox issue, plain white sleeve, with jukebox strip)	10
96	Parlophone QUEENDJ 23	Too Much Love Will Kill You/We Are The Champions (jukebox issue, plain white sleeve, with jukebox strip)	10
96	Parlophone VIRGIN 1	Heaven For Everyone/Heaven For Everyone (12", white label, Virgin Radio 'Queen Day' competition prize, black 'Queen crest' p/s with handwritten details; mispressing with same tracks both sides, unreleased)	0
96	Parlophone VIRGIN 2	Heaven For Everyone (12", 1-sided, white labels, Virgin Radio 'Queen Day' competition prize, 'Queen crest' p/s w/ handwritten details, 15 copies only)	750
96	Parlophone VIRGIN 3	A Winter's Tale (12", 1-sided, white labels, Virgin Radio 'Queen Day' competition prize, 'Queen crest' p/s with handwritten details, 15 only)	750
96	Parlophone VIRGIN 4	Mother Love (12", 1-sided, white labels, Virgin Radio 'Queen Day' competition prize, 'Queen crest' p/s with handwritten details, 15 only)	750
96	Parlophone VIRGIN 5	Let Me Live (12", 1-sided, white labels, Virgin Radio 'Queen Day' competition prize, 'Queen crest' p/s with handwritten details, 15 only)	750
96	Parlophone VIRGIN 6	You Don't Fool Me (12", 1-sided, white labels, Virgin Radio 'Queen Day' competition prize, 'Queen crest' p/s with handwritten details, 15 only)	750
96	Parlophone VIRGIN 7	It's A Beautiful Day (12", 1-sided, white labels, Virgin Radio 'Queen Day' competition prize, 'Queen crest' p/s with handwritten details, 15 only)	750
96	Parlophone VIRGIN 8	I Was Born To Love You (12", 1-sided, white labels, Virgin Radio 'Queen Day' competition prize, 'Queen crest' p/s with handwritten details, 15 only)	750
99	EMI QUEENWL 28	Under Pressure (Remixes) (with David Bowie) (12", white label, unreleased mix, promo only)	30
99	EMI QUEEN DJ 28	Under Pressure (Rah Mix)/(Mike Spencer Mix)/The Show Must Go On (CD, card p/s, promo only)	15
73	EMI (no cat. no.)	QUEEN (LP, white label, EMI conference custom issue, die-cut sleeve, with/without outer envelope)	450
73	EMI (no cat. no.)	QUEEN (LP, white label, EMI conference custom issue, die-cut sleeve, with/without outer envelope)	250
77	EMI (no cat. no.)	NEWS OF THE WORLD (LP, box set, with factory sample sticker, 5 photos, bio, badge & demo copy of "We Are The Champions"/ "We Will Rock You", 50 only)	500
91	Parlophone (no cat. no.)	HINTS OF INNUENDO (cassette, edits/out-takes sampler for "Innuendo")	30
91	EMI	INNUENDO (promo boxed set with CD, cassette, calendar, folder, bio & photos)	45
91	Parlophone (no cat. no.)	EIGHT GOOD REASONS TO BUY GREATEST HITS 2 (cassette, segued excerpts)	30
91	Parlophone (no cat. no.)	A SAMPLE OF MAGIC (CD, segued excerpts from "Greatest Hits 2")	60
94	EMI CD DIG 1	DIGITAL MASTER SAMPLER (CD, picture disc)	45
97	Parlophone CDQT 1	QUEEN ROCKS (CD, Brian May interview)	75

MISPRESSINGS

75	EMI EMI 2378	Bohemian Rhapsody/I'm In Love With My Car (2nd issue, with incorrect cat. no.)	12
78	EMI EMI 2870	Bicycle Race/Fat Bottomed Girls (p/s, B-side plays Crystal Gayle's 3 O'Clock In The Morning or Dollar track)	10
79	EMI EMI 2975	CLIFF RICHARD: We Don't Talk Anymore/Count Me Out (A-side plays "Bohemian Rhapsody")	12
79	EMI EMI 5001	Crazy Little Thing Called Love/We Will Rock You (live) (p/s, both sides play "We Will Rock You")	15
80	EMI EMI 5076	Play The Game/A Human Body (p/s, both sides play "A Human Body")	12
86	Parlophone RP 5452	BEATLES: Paperback Writer/Rain (picture disc, A-side plays Friends Will Be Friends)	75

QUEENS OF THE STONE AGE

02	Interscope 497 812-7	No One Knows/Tension Head (Live From The Mean Fiddler) (p/s, grey vinyl)	12
98	Roadrunner RR 8674-2	QUEENS OF THE STONE AGE (LP)	20
00	Interscope 490 683-1	RATED R (LP, gatefold sleeve)	25
02	Interscope 493435-2	SONGS FOR THE DEAF (2-LP, gatefold, red vinyl)	35

QUEENSRYCHE

83	EMI America 12EA 162	Queens Of The Reich/Nightrider/Blinded/Lady Wore Black (12", p/s)	8
84	EMI America EA 183	Take Hold Of The Flame/Nightrider (p/s)	6
86	EMI America EA 22	Gonna Get Close To You/Prophecy (p/s)	6
86	EMI America EAD 22	Gonna Get Close To You/Prophecy//Queen Of The Reich (live)/ Deliverance (live) (double pack)	10
89	EMI USA 12MTG 65	Eyes Of A Stranger/Queen Of The Reich/Walk In The Shadows/ Take Hold Of The Flame (12", gatefold p/s)	8
88	EMI Manhattan 10QR 1	OVERSEEING THE OPERATION (10" EP)	8

QUEERS

90	Shakin Street YEAH HUP 010	GROW UP (LP)	30

MINT VALUE £

? & THE MYSTERIANS
66 Cameo Parkway C 428 96 Tears/Midnight Hour . . . 35
66 Cameo Parkway C 441 I Need Somebody/'8' Teen . . . 40
67 Cameo Parkway C 467 Can't Get Enough Of You, Baby/Smokes . . . 30
67 Cameo Parkway C 479 Girl (You Captivate Me)/Got To . . . 25
67 Cameo Parkway C 496 Do Something To Me/Love Me Baby . . . 25
76 London HLU 10534 96 Tears/'8' Teen . . . 10

QUESTIONS
68 Decca F 22740 We Got Love/Something Wonderful . . . 25

TOMMY QUICKLY (& REMO FOUR)
(see also Remo Four)
63 Piccadilly 7N 35137 Tip Of My Tongue/Heaven Only Knows (solo) . . . 30
63 Piccadilly 7N 35151 Kiss Me Now/No Other Love . . . 8
64 Piccadilly 7N 35167 Prove It/Haven't You Noticed . . . 6
64 Piccadilly 7N 35183 You Might As Well Forget Him/It's As Simple As That . . . 6
64 Pye 7N 15708 The Wild Side Of Life/Forget The Other Guy . . . 6
64 Pye 7N 15748 Humpty Dumpty/I'll Go Crazy . . . 8

QUICKSAND
(see also Man)
70 Carnaby CNS 4015 Passing By/Cobblestones . . . 15
73 Dawn DNS 1046 Time To Live/Empty Street, Empty Heart . . . 10
74 Dawn DNLS 3056 HOME IS WHERE I BELONG (LP, gatefold sleeve, pink 'sun' label) . . . 60

QUICKSILVER MESSENGER SERVICE
(see also Dino Valenti, Nicky Hopkins)
76 Capitol CL 15859 Gypsy Lights/Witches' Moon . . . 5
68 Capitol (S)T 2904 QUICKSILVER MESSENGER SERVICE (LP, black label with rainbow rim) . . . 40
69 Capitol E-(S)T 120 HAPPY TRAILS (LP) . . . 20
70 Capitol E-ST 391 SHADY GROVE (LP) . . . 18
70 Capitol EA-ST 498 JUST FOR LOVE (LP) . . . 15
71 Capitol EA-ST 630 WHAT ABOUT ME? (LP) . . . 15
72 Capitol E-SW 819 QUICKSILVER (LP) . . . 12
72 Capitol EA-ST 11002 COMIN' THRU (LP) . . . 12
75 Capitol E-ST 11462 SOLID SILVER (LP) . . . 12
83 Psycho PSYCHO 10 MAIDEN OF THE CANCER MOON (2-LP) . . . 40

QUICKSPACE (SUPERSPORT)
94 Love Train PUBE 04 Found A Way/Do It My Own Way (12", p/s, 1,500 only) . . . 15
97 Kitty Kitty Corp. CHOOSY 8 QUICKSPACE (LP, die-cut spray-painted sleeve, 1000 only) . . . 12

QUIET FIVE
(see also Kris Ife, Patrick Dane, Richard Barnes)
65 Parlophone R 5273 When The Morning Sun Dries The Dew/Tomorrow I'll Be Gone (in p/s) . . . 20
65 Parlophone R 5273 When The Morning Sun Dries The Dew/Tomorrow I'll Be Gone . . . 10
65 Parlophone R 5302 Honeysuckle Rose/Let's Talk It Over . . . 8
66 Parlophone R 5421 Homeward Bound/Ain't It Funny What Some Lovin' Can Do . . . 18
66 Parlophone R 5470 I Am Waiting/What About The Time For Me . . . 10
67 CBS 202586 Goodnight Sleep Tight/Just For Tonight . . . 6

QUIET SUN
(see also Phil Manzanera, Roxy Music)
75 Island HELP 19 MAINSTREAM (LP, black label with pink 'i' label) . . . 20

QUIET WORLD
(see also Steve Hackett, Genesis)
69 Dawn DNS 1001 Miss Whittington/There Is A Mountain (as Quiet World Of Lea & John) . . . 40
70 Dawn DNS 1005 Children Of The World/Love Is Walking . . . 40
70 Pye 7N 45005 Rest Comfortably/Gemima . . . 12
71 Pye 7N 45074 Visitor/Sam . . . 10
70 Dawn DNLS 3007 THE ROAD (LP) . . . 150

QUIK
(see also Meddy Evils)
67 Deram DM 121 Love Is A Beautiful Thing/Bert's Apple Crumble . . . 150
67 Deram DM 139 King Of The World/My Girl . . . 50
67 Deram DM 155 I Can't Sleep/Soul Full Of Sorrow . . . 70
98 Klooks Kleek 60 Bert's Apple Crumble/THE SONICS: The Witch (re-issue) . . . 10

QUILL
79 Kite KR 10 LIVE (LP) . . . 15

QUILLER
75 BBC RESL 25 Quiller/General Direction . . . 7

QUINCEHARMON
71 Columbia DB 8772 Suddenly The Whole World Is Mine/Strange Feeling . . . 12
71 Columbia DB 8798 On The Buses/Don't Tell Me It's Over . . . 7

PAUL QUINCHETTE
57 Esquire 32-057 ON THE SUNNY SIDE (LP) . . . 40

QUINCICASM
73 Saydisc SDL 249 QUINCICASM (LP) . . . 20

ANTHONY QUINN
70 Capitol CL 15649 I Love You And You Love Me/Sometimes (I Just Can't Stand You) . . . 6
67 Capitol CL 15520 I Love You And You Love Me/Sometimes (I Just Can't Stand You) (Re-issue) . . . 10

MIKE QUINN
66 Fontana TF 761 Someone's Slipping Into My Mind/I Know What You Know . . . 7
69 CBS 4506 Apple Pie/There's A Time . . . 6
69 Jay Boy BOY 7 Toothbrush Nell/Fairy Cakes . . . 5

MINT VALUE £

PAUL QUINN & EDWYN COLLINS
(see also Edwyn Collins, Orange Juice)

84	Swamplands SWP 1	Pale Blue Eyes (Edited Version)/Burro (p/s)	5
84	Swamplands SWX 1	Pale Blue Eyes/Pale Blues Eyes (Western)/Burro (12", original pressing with 'film' p/s, inner sleeve & yellow obi)	10
84	Swamplands SWX 1	Pale Blue Eyes/Pale Blues Eyes (Western)/Burro (12")	7

QUINTESSENCE
(see also Kala)

70	Island WIP 6075	Notting Hill Gate/Move Into The Light	7
71	Neon NE 1003	Sweet Jesus/You Never Stay The Same (in p/s)	15
71	Neon NE 1003	Sweet Jesus/You Never Stay The Same	6
69	Island ILPS 9110	IN BLISSFUL COMPANY (LP, gatefold,pink label with white 'i' logo)	60
70	Island ILPS 9128	QUINTESSENCE (LP, pink label with white 'i' logo)	40
70	Island ILPS 9143	DIVE DEEP (LP, inner sleeve, pink rim palm tree label)	40
72	RCA SF 8273	SELF (LP)	20
72	RCA SF 8317	INDWELLER (LP)	15

QUINTET MODERNE

87	Bead Records BEAD 26	IKKUNAN TAKANA (LP)	20

QUINTET OF HOT CLUB OF FRANCE
(see also Django Reinhardt)

53	Decca LF 1139	SWING FROM PARIS (10" LP)	15

QUINTET OF THE YEAR

54	Vogue L.D.E. 087	JAZZ AT THE MASSAY HALL VOL. 3 (10" LP)	18

QUIREBOYS
(see also Wildhearts)

90	Parlophone RPD 6248	I Don't Love You Anymore/Mayfair (Original Version) (uncut shaped picture disc)	10

DARYL QUIST

63	Pye 7N 15538	Thanks To You/Keep Moving (in p/s)	10
63	Pye 7N 15538	Thanks To You/Keep Moving	5
63	Pye 7N 15563	Goodbye To Love/All Through The Night	5
64	Pye 7N 15605	True To You/Above And Beyond	5
64	Pye 7N 15656	See The Funny Little Clown/When She Comes To You	5
65	Decca F 12058	Put Away Your Teardrops/Across The Street	5

QUIVER
(see also Bridget St. John, Natural Gas, Sutherland Brothers, Village)

72	Warner Bros K 16165	Green Tree/I Might Stumble	6
71	Warner Bros K 46089	QUIVER (LP)	20
72	Warner Bros K 46153	GONE IN THE MORNING (LP, gatefold sleeve)	12

QUODLING'S DELIGHT

76	Fanfare FR 2179	AMONG THE LEAVES SO GREEN (LP)	25

QUOTATIONS (U.K.)
(see also Fleur De Lys, Johnny B. Great, Johnny Gustafson, Merseybeats, Johnny Goodison)

64	Decca F 11907	Alright Baby/Love You All Over Again	25
68	CBS 3716	Cool It/Mark Of Her Head	30
69	CBS 4378	Hello Memories/Pretend	10

QUOTATIONS (U.S.)

61	HMV POP 975	Imagination/Ala-Men-Sy	130

QUOTING MARX

77	Full Stop PUNC 28	Opening And Closing/66 And 99	12

QUO VARDIS
(see under Vardis)

R

RABBI JOSEPH GORDAN
(see also Julian Cope)

85	Bam Caruso Intl. NRICO 30	Competition/Belief In Him (large centre hole, plain beige sleeve)	10

RABBIT
(see also Free; Kossoff, Kirke, Tetsu & Rabbit)

73	Island WIP6161	Broken Arrows/Blues My Guitar	5
73	Island ILPS 9238	BROKEN ARROWS (LP, gatefold sleeve, pink rim palm tree label)	18
74	Island ILPS 9289	DARK SALOON (LP)	15

RABBITS

79	Stortbeat BEAT 4	Kitchen Parties/Tonight (numbered p/s, 1000 only)	12

RABID

82	Fallout FALL 007	BLOODY ROAD TO GLORY (EP)	5

MIKE RABIN (& DEMONS)

64	Columbia DB 7350	Head Over Heels/Leaving You (as Mike Rabin & Demons)	85
65	Polydor BM 56007	If I Were You/What Do You Do	25

OSCAR RABIN & HIS BAND
(see also David Ede Band)

MINT VALUE £

JOSEPH RACAILLE

80s	Recommended RRA 16.5	6 PETITES CHANSONS (EP, clear vinyl, foldaround p/s)	6

STEVE RACE

61	Parlophone R 4808	Crosstrap/Stop Look Listen	10

RACE FANS

68	Trojan TR 610	Bookie Man/UNIQUES: More Love	30
68	Trojan TR 637	Time Marches On/SILVERTONES: Party Night	40

YANK RACHELL TENNESSEE JUG BUSTERS

64	'77' LA 12-23	MANDOLIN BLUES (LP)	22

RACING CARS

	Chrysalis CHS 2129	They Shoot Horses Don't They/Four Wheel Drive	5

RACONTEURS

(see also White Stripes)

08	XL XLS 227	Steady As She Goes/Store Bought Bones (1st issue, 1,000 only, p/s Jack White to right of cover)	15

RADAR

83	House Of Wax WAX 1	Leave Her Alone/Reach For The Sky (p/s)	10

JIMMY RADCLIFFE

(see also Steve Karmen Big Band)

65	Stateside SS 374	Long After Tonight Is Over/What I Want I Can Never Have	50
65	Stateside SS 374	Long After Tonight Is Over/What I Want I Can Never Have (DJ copy)	170
73	Pye International 7N 25614	Long After Tonight Is Over/What I Want I Can Never Have (reissue)	8
77	DJM DJS 10772	Long After Tonight Is Over/What I Want I Can Never Have (2nd reissue) (p/s) (Promo)	7

RADHA KRISHNA

(see also John Mayer)

71	Columbia SCX 6462	RADHA KRISHNA (LP, composed & directed by John Mayer)	45

RADHA KRISHNA TEMPLE (LONDON)

69	Apple APPLE 15	Hare Krishna Mantra/Prayer To The Spiritual Masters (p/s, as Radha Krishna Temple [London], with insert)	30
69	Apple APPLE 15	Hare Krishna Mantra/Prayer To The Spiritual Masters (p/s, as Radha Krishna Temple [London], without insert)	20
69	Apple APPLE 15	Hare Krishna Mantra/Prayer To The Spiritual Masters (no p/s, as Radha Krishna Temple [London])	6
70	Apple APPLE 25	Govinda/Govinda Jai Jai (p/s)	40
70	Apple APPLE 25	Govinda/Govinda Jai Jai (in company sleeve)	12
70	Apple APPLE 25	Govinda/Govinda Jai Jai	5
71	Apple SAPCOR 18	THE RADHA KRISHNA TEMPLE (LP, gatefold sleeve, with insert)	50
71	Apple SAPCOR 18	THE RADHA KRISHNA TEMPLE (LP, gatefold sleeve, without insert)	40
93	Apple SAPCOR 18	THE RADHA KRISHNA TEMPLE (LP, reissue, gatefold sleeve with inner)	15
93	Apple SAPCOR 18	THE RADHA KRISHNA TEMPLE (CD)	18

RADIANTS

(see also Maurice & Mac, Caston & Majors)

64	Chess CRS 8002	Voice Your Choice/If I Only Had You	40
64	Chess CRS 8002	Voice Your Choice/If I Only Had You (DJ copy)	60
68	Chess CRS 8073	Hold On/I'm Glad I'm The Loser	20
68	Chess CRS 8073	Hold On/I'm Glad I'm The Loser (DJ copy)	50

RADIATORS (FROM SPACE)

(see also Pogues)

77	Chiswick S 10	Television Screen/Love Detective (p/s, original issue)	5
77	Chiswick NS 19	Enemies/Psychotic Reaction (p/s)	5
78	Chiswick NS 24	Prison Bars/(Why Can't I Be A) Teenager In Love (unreleased, promo only white label in stamped white sleeve & loose printed labels)	40
79	Chiswick NS 45	Walkin' Home Alone Again/Try And Stop Me/The Hucklebuck (unreleased; white label test pressings exist with loose labels; as Radiators)	40
79	Chiswick CHIS 115	Kitty Ricketts/Ballad Of The Faithful Departed (company sleeve)	8
77	Chiswick WIK 4	TV TUBE HEART (LP)	12
79	Chiswick CWK 3003	GHOSTOWN (LP)	12

RADICAL DANCE FACTION

80	Earth Zone EZ 001	BORDERLAND CASES (LP)	15
81	Earth Zone EZ 003	WATERLAND (LP)	15

MARK RADICE

72	Paramount PARA 3024	Hey My Love/Your Love Is Like Fire	8
72	Paramount PARA 3025	New Day/Take Me To The Park	6
72	Paramount SPFA 7004	MARK RADICE (LP)	12

RADIOACTIVE

77	Beeb BEEB 021	Ten Years After/All Time Needletime Loser (no p/s)	80

RADIO ACTORS

(see also Fast Breeder & Radio Actors, Sting, Newcastle Big Band, Police, Gilli Smyth, Inner City Unit, Steve Hillage, Sphynx)

79	Charly CYS 1058	Nuclear Waste/Digital Love (p/s, reissue of Fast Breeder & Radio Actors single, 2 slightly different label designs)	20
79	DB DBS 5	Nuclear Waste/Digital Love (different p/s, 2nd reissue)	5

RADIO BIRDMAN

78	Sire 6078 617	What Gives/Anglo Girl Desire	10
78	Sire 9103 332	RADIOS APPEAR (LP, with inner sleeve)	25
78	Sire SRK 6050	RADIOS APPEAR (LP, reissue)	12

RADIO CITY

80	Media Wave MW 001	Love And A Picture/She's A Radio (p/s)	200

MINT VALUE £

RADIOHEAD

(see also Headless Chickens, Thom Yorke)

SINGLES

92	Parlophone TCR 6312	DRILL EP (Prove Yourself/Stupid Car/You/Thinking About You) (cassette, 3,000 only)	40
92	Parlophone 12R 6312	DRILL EP (Prove Yourself/Stupid Car/You/Thinking About You) (12", p/s, 3,000 only)	100
92	Parlophone CDR 6312	DRILL EP (Prove Yourself/Stupid Car/You/Thinking About You) (CD, 3,000 only)	100
92	Parlophone TCR 6078	Creep/Lurgee/Inside My Head/Million $ Question (cassette, 6,000 only)	8
92	Parlophone 12R 6078	Creep/Lurgee/Inside My Head/Million $ Question (12", p/s, 6,000 only)	20
92	Parlophone CDR 6078	Creep/Lurgee/Inside My Head/Million $ Question (CD, 6,000 only)	40
93	Parlophone 12R 6333	Anyone Can Play Guitar/Faithless, The Wonder Boy/Coke Babies (12", p/s)	20
93	Parlophone CDR 6333	Anyone Can Play Guitar/Faithless, The Wonder Boy/Coke Babies (CD)	30
93	Parlophone 12R 6345	Pop Is Dead/Banana Co. (Acoustic)/Creep (live)/Ripcord (live) (12", g/fold p/s)	20
93	Parlophone CDR 6345	Pop Is Dead/Banana Co. (Acoustic)/Creep (live)/Ripcord (live) (CD)	30
93	Parlophone RS 6359	Creep/Yes I Am/Blow Out (Remix)/Inside My Head (live) (p/s, clear vinyl)	25
93	Parlophone 12RG 6359	U.S. LIVE EP (Creep [Acoustic KROQ]/You [live]/Vegetable [live]/ Killer Cars [live]) (12", numbered gatefold p/s)	20
93	Parlophone CDR 6359	Creep/Yes I Am/Blow Out (Remix)/Inside My Head (live) (CD, digipak)	12
94	Parlophone 12R 6394	My Iron Lung/Punchdrunk Lovesick Singalong/The Trickster/ Lewis (Mistreated) (12", numbered p/s)	15
94	Parlophone CDRS 6394	My Iron Lung/Punchdrunk Lovesick Singalong/Lozenge Of Love (card sleeve, CD)	10
94	Parlophone CDR 6394	My Iron Lung/The Trickster/Lewis (Mistreated)/Permanent Daylight/ You Never Wash Up After Yourself (CD)	10
95	Parlophone 12R 6405	Planet Telex/(remixes)/High & Dry (12", limited edition, numbered p/s)	15
95	Parlophone CDR 6405	Planet Telex/High & Dry/Killer Cars/Planet Telex (LFO JD Mix) (CD 2 of 2-CD set)	12
95	Parlophone CDRS 6405	High & Dry/Planet Telex/Maquiladora/Planet Telex (Hexidecimal Mix) (CD)	8
95	Parlophone CDRS 6411	Fake Plastic Trees/India Rubber/How Can I Be Sure? (1 of 2 CD set)	12
95	Parlophone CDR 6411	Fake Plastic Trees/Fake Plastic Trees (Acoustic)/Bulletproof (...I Wish I Was) (Acoustic)/Street Spirit (Fade Out) (Acoustic) (CD, 2 of 2-CD set)	10
95	Parlophone CDR 6411	Fake Plastic Trees/Fake Plastic Trees (Acoustic)/Bulletproof (...I Wish I Was) (Acoustic)/Street Spirit (Fade Out) (Acoustic) (CD, with poster)	10
95	Parlophone CDR 6415	Just/Bones (live)/Planet Telex (live)/Anyone Can Play Guitar (live) (CD, box set with 2 prints)	12
95	Parlophone 8 83115 2	The Bends/My Iron Lung (Live At Forum)/Bones (Live At Forum) (CD, for export to Ireland, slimline jewel case)	40
95	Parlophone 8 83115 2	The Bends/My Iron Lung (Live At Forum)/Bones (Live At Forum) (CD, for export to Ireland, mispressed with "Planet Telex" instead of "The Bends" slimline jewel case)	40
96	Parlophone R 6419	Street Spirit (Fade Out)/Bishop's Robes (die-cut p/s, white vinyl)	20
96	Parlophone R 6419LH	Street Spirit (Fade Out)/Bishop's Robes (jukebox issue, black vinyl)	12
96	Parlophone CDRS 6419	Street Spirit (Fade Out)/Talk Show Host/Bishop's Robes (CD, with poster)	15
97	Parlophone NODATA 01	Paranoid Android/Polyethelene (Parts 1 & 2) (blue vinyl, die-cut p/s)	15
97	Parlophone NODATALH 03	Karma Police (Album Version)/Lull (jukebox issue, black vinyl)	12
97	Parlophone 12NODATA 03	Karma Police/Meeting Up The Aisle/Climbing Up The Walls (Zero 7 Mix) (12", p/s)	12
97	Parlophone NODATALH 04	No Surprises/Palo Alto (jukebox issue, black vinyl)	10
98	Parlophone 12NODATA 04	No Surprises/Palo Alto (12", p/s)	30

LPs

93	Parlophone PCS 7360	PABLO HONEY (LP)	30
95	Parlophone PCS 7372	THE BENDS (2-LP)	20
97	Parlophone NODATA 02	OK COMPUTER (2-LP)	35
00	Parlophone LPKIDA	KID A (2-LP 10")	15
01	Parlophone LPFHEIT 45101	AMNESIAC (2-LP, 10")	15
01	Parlophone CDKIDA 4	KID A (CD, in 6"x 6" hardback book)	25
01	Parlophone 12FHEIT 45104	I MIGHT BE WRONG (mini-LP)	15
03	Parlophone 5848052	HAIL TO THE THIEF (CD, limited issue, with foldout map)	18
03	Parlophone 724358454314	HAIL TO THE THIEF (2-LP)	18
07	Parlophone 5.09995E+12	RADIOHEAD (Mail-order 4GB shaped USB stick, bespoke box, 7 albums as WAV files)	50
07	Xurbia Xendless Ltd X X001	IN RAINBOWS (box set, 2-CD, 2-LP, 2 booklets in presentation case)	70

PROMOS

92	Parlophone 12 R 6312	DRILL EP (white label promo in die cut sleeve)	100
92	Parlophone 12RDJ 6078	Creep/Lurgee/Inside My Head/Million Dollar Question (12", die-cut sleeve)	60
92	Parlophone CDRDJ 6078	Creep (Radio Version)/Lurgee/Inside My Head/Million Dollar Question (CD)	60
93	Parlophone 12RDJ 6369	Ripcord/Prove Yourself/Faithless, The Wonderboy/ Stop Whispering (Album Version) (12", p/s)	80
93	Parlophone CDRDJ 6345	Pop Is Dead/Banana Co. (live)/Creep (live)/Ripcord (live) (CD)	75
93	Parlophone CDRDJ 6359	Creep (CD, picture disc)	40
93	Parlophone CDRDJ 6369	Stop Whispering (U.S. Version)/Prove Yourself/Lurgee (CD, promo only, card p/s & inner sleeve)	15
93	Parlophone (no cat. No.)	Stop Whispering (U.S. Version - Chris Sheldon Remix)/Creep (Acoustic)/ Pop Is Dead/Inside My Head (Live) (CD)	20
93	Parlophone 12RDJ 6333	Anyone Can Play Guitar/Faithless, The Wonder Boy/Coke Babies (12", die-cut sleeve)	80
94	Parlophone (no cat. no.)	PLANET TELEX: LFO & Hexidecimal mixes (12")	25
94	Parlophone 12RSDJ 6394	My Iron Lung/Lozenge Of Love/The Trickster/ Punchdrunk Lovesick Singalong (12", die-cut red sleeve)	25
94	Parlophone 12RSDJ 6394	My Iron Lung/Lozenge Of Love/The Trickster/ Punchdrunk Lovesick Singalong (12", die-cut blue sleeve)	20
94	Parlophone 12RSDJ 6394	My Iron Lung/Lewis (Mistreated)/Permanent Daylight/ You Never Wash Up After Yourself (12" die-cut red sleeve)	25
94	Parlophone 12RSDJ 6394	My Iron Lung/Lewis (Mistreated)/Permanent Daylight/ You Never Wash Up After Yourself (12" die-cut blue sleeve)	20
95	Parlophone 12RDJ 6405	CLUB MIX DJ: PLANET TELEX (Album version)/Hexadecimal Mix) /L.F.O DJ Mix)/Trashed Mix) (12")	18

MINT VALUE £

95 Parlophone 12RDJ 6411 Fake Plastic Trees/India Rubber/How Can You Be Sure? (12", die-cut sleeve) 30
95 Parlophone 12RDJ 6411 Fake Plastic Trees (Edit) (Album Version) (CD) 10
95 Parlophone 12RDJ 6145 Just/Planet Telex/Killer Cars (12", die-cut sleeve) 20
95 Parlophone 12RDJ 6145 Just/Planet Telex (Karma Sun Ra Mix)Killer Cars (Mogadon Version) (12") 25
95 Parlophone CDRDJ 6415 Just (Album Version)/(Edit Version) (CD, custom sleeve) 8
95 Parlophone HIGH-1 High & Dry (1-track CD, custom sleeve) 15
95 Parlophone RHEAD US 1 JUST FOR COLLEGE: India Rubber/Maquiladora/How Can I Be Sure?/Just (CD) . . . 90
96 Parlophone 12RDJ 6419 Street Spirit (Fade Out)/Talk Show Host/Bishop's Robes (12", promo-only) 20
96 Parlophone CDRDJ 6419 Street Spirit (Fade Out)/Talk Show Host/Bishop's Robes (CD) 20
97 EMI (no cat. no.) Airbag (1-track Abbey Road CD-R with mini bio and title sleeve) 20
98 Parlophone 12DATADJO3 Climbing Up The Walls (Zero 7 Mix)/(Fila Brazilia Mix) (1-sided 12", 200 only) 70
00 Parlophone 12KIDA 6 Idioteque (12", white label test pressing, p/s) 30
05 Parlophone 7PRO 7087 There There/Paperbag Writer (p/s) 6
01 Parlophone AMNESIAC 01 4 SONGS FROM AMNESIAC: Pyramid Song/I Might Be Wrong/
Packt Like Sardines In A Crushd Tin Box/Dollars & Cents (CD, card sleeve) 12
03 Parlophone 12RDJWL 6623 SKTTERBRAIN (Four Tet Mix)/REMYXOMOTOSIS (Super Collider Mix)
(12", 100 only) 40
97 Parlophone 724385522925 OK COMPUTER (Stickered jewel case, printed disc,
mispressing plays Deep Purple's 'The Collection') 40
97 Parlophone (no cat. no.) OK COMPUTER (cassette, in customized jiffy bag) 40
97 Parlophone (no cat. no.) OK COMPUTER (promo Aiwa personal stereo, glued-in cassette, two stickers) 120
97 Parlophone CDPP 005 OK COMPUTER (CD, numbered title sleeve) 70
97 Parlophone NODATA 02 OK COMPUTER (EPK, with CD & video in polystyrene case in jiffy bag) 60
00 Parlophone CDKIDA 3 KID A (CD, card title sleeve) 18
01 Parlophone AMNESIAC 02 AMNESIAC (CD, in facsmile library book, with press release & inserts) 30
03 Parlophone LC 0299 INTERVIEW CD (p/s 22 track promo for HAIL TO THE THIEF) 20

RADIO HEART
(see also Gary Numan)
87 NBR NBRCD 1 All Across The Nation (Extended Remix)/All Across The nation
(Radio Mix)/River/All Across The Nation (Instrumental) 8
(CD single in card sleeve)
87 NBR NBRL 1 RADIO HEART (LP, withdrawn) 12

RADIO MOSCOW
87 Status RM 100 Hand Of Freedom (p/s) 8
91 Status RMLP 103 WORLD SERVICE (LP) 15
92 Status RMLP 104 GET A NEW LIFE (LP) 15

RADIO 9
90s Enraptured RAPT 1031 Motorik/Fluid/Moving In Two Directions/Pianosong (10", 9 only) 15

RADIOPHONIC WORKSHOP
(see also BBC Radiophonic Workshop)
73 BBC RESL 13 Moonbase 3/World Of Dr. Who 20

RADIO RADIO
83 Radio RAD 101 Calling/Signed With A Star 20

RADIO STARS
(see also John's Children, Andy Ellison, Trevor White)
78 Chiswick CWK 3001 HOLIDAY ALBUM (LP, with inner sleeve) 15

RADIUM
81 Isotope THROUGH THE SMOKE (EP) 50

JACKIE RAE
60 Fontana H 242 Summer Place/The Moon Got In My Eyes 6

RAELET(T)S
(see also Ray Charles, Clydie King, Merry Clayton)
67 HMV POP 1591 One Hurt Deserves Another/One Room Paradise (as Raelets) 30
71 Tangerine 6121 002 Bad Water/That Goes To Show You 5
71 Tangerine 6121 003 Here I Go Again/Leave My Man (Woman) Alone 5

GERRY RAFFERTY
(see also Humblebums, Fifth Column)
71 Transatlantic TRA 241 CAN I HAVE MY MONEY BACK? (LP) 12

RAG DOLLS (U.K.)
(see also Marionettes, Peanut, Katie Kissoon, Mac Kissoon)
67 Columbia DB 8289 Never Had So Much Loving/Any Little Bit 10
68 Columbia DB 8378 My Old Man's A Groovy Old Man/They Didn't Believe Me 10

RAG DOLLS (U.S.)
64 Cameo Parkway P 921 Society Girl/Ragen (with Caliente Combo) 30
65 Stateside SS 398 Dusty/Hey Hoagy 45

RAGE
(see also Nutz)
80 Carrere CAR 159 Money/Thank That Woman (p/s) 8
80 Carrere CAR 159CT Money/Thank That Woman (10", red vinyl, stickered clear sleeve) 12
81 Carrere CAR 182 Out Of Control/Double Dealer (p/s) 5
81 Carrere CAR 182CT Out Of Control (Extended Version)/Double Dealer (12", yellow vinyl, PVC sleeve) . 15
83 Carrere CAR 304 Cry From A Hill (p/s) 10
81 Carrere CAL 124 OUT OF CONTROL (LP) 12
82 Carrere CAL 138 NICE N' DIRTY (LP) 12
83 Carrere CAL 149 RUN FOR THE NIGHT (LP) 12

RAGE
(see also Case, Long Tall Shorty, Purple Hearts, Chords)
86 Diamond RAGE 1 Looking For You/Come On Now (p/s) 20
86 Diamond RAGE 112 Looking For You/Come On Now/Great Balls Of Fire/Hallelujah I Love Her
So (12", unissued, test pressings only) 25

MINT VALUE £

RAGE AGAINST THE MACHINE

93 Epic 658 492-6 Killing In The Name/Clear The Lane/Darkness Of Greed (12" white vinyl, p/s) . . . 15
93 Epic 659 258-6 Bullet In The Head (Remix)/Bullet In The Head (Album Version)
Settle For Nothing (live) (12" picture disc, p/s) . . . 8
93 Epic 658 492-7 Killing In The Name/Clear The Lane/Darkness Of Greed (white vinyl, p/s) . . . 6
93 Epic 659 258-7 Bullet In The Head/Bullet In The Head (Remix) (picture disc, p/s) . . . 6
96 Epic 663 152-7 Bulls On Parade/Hadda Be Playing On The Jukebox (red vinyl) . . . 8
96 Epic 481026 EVIL EMPIRE (LP) . . . 20

RAGGAMUFFINS

67 London HLU 10134 Four Days Of Rain/It Wasn't Happening At All . . . 15
72 Decca F 13312 Can I have My Money Back/Fresh As A Daisy . . . 12

RAGGED HEROES

83 Celtic CM 013 ANNUAL (LP) . . . 25

RAGING STORMS

62 London HLU 9556 The Dribble/Hound Dog . . . 30

LOU RAGLAND

73 Warner Bros K 16312 Since You Said You'd Be Mine/I Didn't Mean To Love You . . . 60

RAGPICKERS

(see also Bert Weedon)
59 Saga SAG 45-2906 Fifi/Cat On A Cool Tin Roof (p/s) . . . 5

RAH BAND

83 TMT RAH-1 GOING UP (LP) . . . 20

RAIDER OF THE LOST DUB

81 Island ILPS 9705 RAIDERS OF THE LOST DUB (LP) (withdrawn due to legal action) . . . 40

RAIDERS

(see also Paul Revere)
70 CBS 4801 Just Seventeen/Sorceress With Blue Eyes . . . 10
70 CBS 5015 Gone Movin' On/Interlude (To Be Forgotten) . . . 10
71 CBS 7474 Birds Of A Feather/The Turkey . . . 6
72 CBS 7808 Country Wing/It's Hard Getting Up Today . . . 6
72 CBS 8428 Song Seller/A Simple Song . . . 10

RAINBEAUS

(see also Ritchie Blackmore,Deep Purple, Elf, Dio, Graham Bonnet, Cozy Powell, Roger Glover, Wild Horses, Tony Carey)
60 Vogue V 9161 That's All I'm Asking Of You/Maybe It's Wrong . . . 170

(RITCHIE BLACKMORE'S) RAINBOW

74 Oyster OYR 103 Man On The Silver Mountain/Snake Charmer (as Ritchie Blackmore's Rainbow) . . 8
77 Polydor 2066 845 Kill The King (live)/Man On The Silver Mountain (live)/Mistreated (live) (p/s) . . . 7
78 Polydor 2066 913 Long Live Rock'n'Roll/Sensitive To Light (p/s) . . . 5
78 Polydor 2066 968 L.A. Connection/Lady Of The Lake (p/s, initial pressing on red vinyl) . . . 10
78 Polydor 2066 968 L.A. Connection/Lady Of The Lake (p/s) . . . 5
82 Polydor POSPX 421 Stone Cold/Rock Fever (12", on blue vinyl) . . . 10
82 Polydor POSPX 421 Stone Cold/Rock Fever (12") . . . 8
83 Polydor POSP 631 Street Of Dreams/Anybody There? (p/s) . . . 5
83 Polydor POSPP 631 Street Of Dreams/Anybody There? (picture disc, 2000 only) . . . 20
83 Polydor POSPX 631 Street Of Dreams/Anybody There?/Power (live) (12", p/s) . . . 10
83 Polydor POSP 654 Can't Let You Go/All Night Long (live) (p/s) . . . 5
83 Polydor POSPP 654 Can't Let You Go/All Night Long (live) (guitar-shaped picture disc) . . . 15
83 Polydor POSPX 654 Can't Let You Go/All Night Long (live)/Stranded (live) (12", p/s) . . . 10
75 Oyster OYA 2001 RITCHIE BLACKMORE'S RAINBOW (LP, gatefold sleeve) . . . 15
77 Polydor 2808 010 010 RAINBOW ON STAGE (LP, music & interview disc, with insert, promo only) . . . 75
79 Polydor POLD 5023 DOWN TO EARTH (LP, clear vinyl, with inner sleeve) . . . 15

CHRIS RAINBOW

81 EMI 12EMI 5215 Body Music/Girl In Collision (12", p/s) . . . 15
81 EMI 5215-6 Body Music/Girl In Collision (p/s) . . . 8

RAINBOW FAMILY

72 President PT 375 Travellin' Lady/My Father . . . 80

RAINBOW FFOLLY

(see also Love Affair)
68 Parlophone R 5701 Go Girl/Drive My Car . . . 60
67 Parlophone PMC/PCS 7050 SALLIES FFORTH (LP, laminated front, flipbacks,
black/yellow label, "Sold in U.K..." text) . . . 400

RAINBOW PEOPLE

68 Pye 7N 17582 Walk'll Do You Good/Dream Time . . . 15
68 Pye 7N 17624 The Sailing Song/Rainbows . . . 15
69 Pye 7N 17759 Living In A Dream World/Happy To See You Again . . . 30

RAINBOWS

(see also Peeps, Martin Cure & Peeps)
69 CBS 3995 Rainbows/Nobody But You . . . 20
69 CBS 4568 New Day Dawning/Days And Nights . . . 40

RAINCHECKS

64 Solar SRP 104 Something About You/You're My Angel . . . 20
65 R&B MRB 5002 How Are You Boy/Bye Bye Baby . . . 40

RAINCOATS

(see also Slits)
82 Rough Trade Running Away/No Ones Little Girl . . . 10
79 Rough Trade RT 013 Adventures Close to Home/In Love/Fairytale In The Supermarket . . . 12
81 Rough Trade ROUGH 13 ODYSHAPE (LP) . . . 30
79 Rough Trade ROUGH 3 THE RAINCOATS (LP, with lyric booklet) . . . 25

MINT VALUE £

RAINDANCE

87	Raindance X1S 121	RAINDANCE (LP)	40

RAINDROPS (U.K.)

(see also Jackie & Raindrops, Jackie Lee, Jacky, Emma Rede, Vince Hill)

59	Parlophone R 4559	Italian Style/Along Came Jones	10
60	Oriole CB 1544	Let's Make A Foursome/If I Had My Life To Live Over	6
60	Oriole CB 1555	Banjo Boy/Crazy Rhythm	6
61	Oriole CB 1595	Will You Love Me Tomorrow/Raindrops	10
62	Oriole CB 1707	Paintin' The Town With Teardrops/A Letter From Anne	6
67	CBS 202669	Foolman/Got To Find A Reason (credited to Raindrops '67)	6

RAINDROPS (U.S.)

(see also Ellie Greenwich, Popsicles)

63	London HL 9718	What A Guy/It's So Wonderful	22
63	London HL 9769	The Kind Of Boy You Can't Forget/Even Though You Can't Dance	30
64	London HL 9825	That Boy John/Hanky Panky	20
64	Fontana TF 463	The Book Of Love/I Won't Cry	25
64	London RE 1415	WHAT A GUY (EP)	120
64	London HA 8140	THE RAINDROPS (LP)	110

LORRY RAINE

54	London HL 8043	You Broke My Broken Heart/I'm In Love With A Guy	25
55	London HL 8132	Love Me Tonight/What Would I Do	40

MA RAINEY

53	London AL 3502	MA RAINEY VOLUME 1 (10" LP)	25
55	London AL 3538	MA RAINEY VOLUME 2 (10" LP)	25
56	London AL 3558	MA RAINEY VOLUME 3 (10" LP)	25
50s	Ristic LP 13	MA RAINEY (10" LP)	30
50s	Ristic LP 19	MA RAINEY (10" LP)	30
62	Riverside RL 12-108	MA RAINEY SINGS THE BLUES (LP)	20
64	Riverside RLP 8807	MOTHER OF THE BLUES (LP, gatefold sleeve with booklet)	20
70	CBS 52798	MA RAINEY AND THE CLASSIC BLUES SINGERS (LP)	15

MA RAINEY & IDA COX

(see also Ida Cox, Tommy Ladnier)

60	Jazz Collector JEL 12	THE FEMALE BLUES VOL. 1 (EP)	10
64	Jazz Collector JEL 22	THE FEMALE BLUES VOL. 3 (EP, with Trixie Smith)	10

MA RAINEY & PAPA CHARLIE JACKSON

50s	Poydras 11	Ma And Papa Poorhouse Blues/Big Feeling Blues	15

RAIN PARADE

83	Enigma BOB 4/LYN 15263	Sad Eyes Kill (3.16) (1-sided flexi with Bucketfull Of Brains mag, issue 10)	6
83	Enigma BOB 4/LYN 15263	Sad Eyes Kill (3.16) (hard vinyl white label test pressing)	12

MARVIN RAINWATER

(see also Connie Francis & Marvin Rainwater)

55	MGM SP 1150	Tennessee Houn' Dog Yodel/Albino (Pink-Eyed) Stallion	60
55	MGM 876	Tennessee Houn' Dog Yodel/Albino (Pink-Eyed) Stallion (78)	18
56	MGM MGM 929	What Am I Supposed To Do/Why Did You Have To Go And Leave Me	30
57	MGM MGM 961	Gonna Find Me A Bluebird/So You Think You've Got	30
58	MGM MGM 974	Whole Lotta Woman/Baby, Don't Go	7
58	MGM MGM 980	I Dig You Baby/Two Fools In Love (B-side with Sister Patty)	10
58	MGM MGM 988	Dance Me Daddy/Because I'm A Dreamer (B-side with Sister Patty)	12
59	MGM MGM 1030	Half-Breed/A Song Of New Love	8
59	MGM MGM 1030	Half-Breed/A Song Of New Love (78)	20
60	MGM MGM 1052	Nothin' Needs Nothin' (Like I Need You)/The Valley Of The Moon	20
61	London HLU 9447	Boo Hoo/I Can't Forget	100
58	MGM MGM-EP 647	MEET MARVIN RAINWATER (EP)	60
58	MGM MGM-EP 662	WHOLE LOTTA MARVIN (EP)	75
59	MGM MGM-EP 685	MARVIN RAINWATER (EP)	70
63	Ember EMB 4521	COUNTRY AND WESTERN FAVOURITES VOL. 2 (EP)	30
58	MGM MGM-D 152	SONGS BY MARVIN RAINWATER (10" LP)	100
72	Philips 6414 110	MARVIN RAINWATER GETS COUNTRY FEVER (LP)	15

RAINY DAY

84	EMI EMI 5472	Painting Pictures/Welche Farbe Hat Der Sonnenschein (p/s)	12

RAINY DAZE

67	CBS 3200	What Do You Think/Autumn Leaves	18
67	Polydor 56731	That Acapulco Gold/In My Mind Lives A Forest	20
68	Polydor 56737	Blood Of Oblivion/Stop Sign	20

RAISINS

(see also Coloured Raisins)

68	Major Major MM 540	Ain't That Lovin' You Baby/Stranger Things Have Happened	15
69	Major Minor MM 602	I Thank You/Don't Leave Me Like This	8
68	Major Minor MMLP 20	THE RAISINS (LP, also stereo SMLP 20)	30

BONNIE RAITT

(see also Roy Orbison, Alton Purnell)

75	Warner Bros. K 56160	HOME PLATE (LP)	12

RAKES

04	Trash Aesthetics TA 702	22 Grand Job/Something Clicked And I Fell Off The Edge (pink vinyl, insert and fold-out sleeve. 480 only)	10
04	City Rockers ROCKERS28CD	Strasbourg/Just Got Paid/Ausland Mission -Demo (CD)	8
04	City Rockers ROCKERS28	Strasbourg/Just Got Paid/Ausland Mission - Demo (p/s)	5

RALFI

75	Island USA 005	The Gambler/Wonderful Things	15

MINT VALUE £

DON RALKE ORCHESTRA

59	Vogue V 9152	Maverick/Travellin' West	5
60	Warner Brothers WB 2	77 Sunset Strip (as Big Sound Of Don Ralke)/ PETE CANDOLI & HIS ORCHESTRA: 77 Sunset Strip Cha-Cha	5
60	Warner Bros. WM 4007/WS8007	BUT YOU NEVER HEARD GERSHWIN WITH BONGOS (LP)	20
60	Warner Brothers WM 8014	DANCE CAPER IN HI-FI (LP) (& WS 8014)	20
60	Warner Brothers WS 8031	SAVAGE AND THE SENSUOUS BONGOS (LP)	20

RALLY ROUNDERS

(see also Outlaws, Ritchie Blackmore)

64	Lyntone LYN 573/574	Bike Beat Part 1/Bike Beat Part 2 (actually by The Outlaws) (p/s, flexidisc)	50

RALPH & PONYTAILS

80	Pony Tunes RATP 1	James Bond/James Bond (Different Version) (p/s)	5

BUCK RAM'S RAMROCKS

(see also Little Richard, Platters)

63	London HLU 9677	Benfica/Odd Man Theme	15

RAMA

69	Polydor 56328	God Created Love/Memory Of Love	6

RAMA (4th STREET ORCHESTRA)

(see also Dennis Bowell, Matumbi)

77	Rama RM 001	AH WHO SHE? GO-DEH! (LP)	60
77	Rama RM 004	(SCIENTIFIC) HIGHER RANKING DUB (LP)	80

RAMASES

(see also 10cc, Ramases & Seleka, Ramases & Selket)

71	Philips 6113 001	Ballroom/Muddy Water	20
71	Philips 6113 003	Jesus Come Back/Hello Mister	10
71	Vertigo 6360 046	SPACE HYMNS (LP, foldout poster sleeve, small swirl label)	90
71	Vertigo 6360 046	SPACE HYMNS (LP, foldout sleeve, later 'spaceship' label)	20
75	Vertigo 6360 115	GLASS TOP COFFIN (LP, gatefold sleeve, 'spaceship' label)	30

RAMASES & SELEKA

(see also Ramases)

70	Major Minor MM 704	Love You/Gold Is The Ring	50

RAMASES & SELKET

(see also Ramases)

68	CBS 3717	Crazy One/Mind's Eye	80

RAMATAM

(see also Iron Butterfly)

72	Atlantic K 40415	RAMATAM (LP)	15

EDDIE RAMBEAU

(see also Marcy Jo & Eddie Rambeau)

62	Stateside SS 116	Summertime Guy/Last Night Was My Last Night	10
64	Stateside SS 301	Come Closer/She's Smilin' At Me	8
65	Stateside SS 448	My Name Is Mud/I Just Need Your Love	8
66	Stateside SS 486	The Train/Yesterday's Newspapers	8
66	Stateside SS 501	I'm The Sky/I Just Need Your Love	7
66	Stateside SS 561	The Clock/If I Were You	7

RAMBLER

(see also Johnny McEvoy)

66	Pye 7N 17164	Love Minus Zero No Limit/An Bonnan Bui	7

RAMBLERS

63	Decca F 11775	Dodge City/Just For Chicks	40

RAMBLERS TWO

65	Pye 7N 15989	Today Is The Highway/The Mountains And The Sea	5

RAMBLETTES

65	Brunswick 05932	Thinking Of You/On Back Street	20

RAMBLIN' JIMMY DOLAN

51	Capitol CL 13600	Wine, Women And Pink Elephants/GENE O'QUIN: Boogie Woogie Fever (78)	18
53	Capitol CL 13982	Playin' Dominoes And Shootin' Dice/The Wheel That Does The Squeekin' (78)	10

RAMBLING SYD RUMPO

(see also Kenneth Williams)

67	Parlophone R 5638	The Ballad Of The Wogglers Moulie/Green Grow My Nadgers Oh!	6
70	Starline SRS 5034	THE BEST OF RAMBLING SYD RUMPO (LP)	12

SID RAMIN

70	CBS 4813	Stiletto/Sugar In The Rain	12
69	CBS 70062	STILETTO (LP, soundtrack)	30

LOUIE RAMIREZ

67	Mercury 20113	IN THE HEART OF SPANISH HARLEM (LP)	20

RAM JAM BAND

(see also Geno Washington & Ram Jam Band, Ram John Holder, Ram Holder Brothers)

65	Columbia DB 7621	Shake Shake Senora/Akinla	25

RAMLEH

(see also Skullflower)

83	Broken Flag BF V4	THE HAND OF GLORY (EP, p/s)	30
87	Broken Flag BF 57	Redcap/AIN-TOW: Intolerant (cassette)	10
87	Broken Flag BF 70	Bite The Bolster/Fistfuck 2 (cassette)	10
91	Shock SX 013	Slammers/Black Moby Dick (p/s, numbered, 500 only)	8

			MINT VALUE £
92	Dying Earth DE 003	Loser Patrol/Tracers (p/s, numbered, 500 only, 1st 30 in red sleeve)	15
92	Dying Earth DE 003	Loser Patrol/Tracers (p/s, numbered, 500 only)	8
93	Dying Earth DE 007	Say Fuck/Slackjaw (wraparound p/s, numbered, 500 only)	8
94	Format Supremacy 1 Of EACH	Welcome/Pristine Womankind (cardboard p/s, 500 only)	8
94	Freek FRR 006	HOMELESS (CD-only EP)	15
95	Broken Flag BS 78	ADIEU ALL YOU JUDGES (CD-only live EP, features Skullflower, 500 only)	15
82	Broken Flag BF 01	31/5/1962 - 1982 (cassette)	70
83	Broken Flag BF V2	A RETURN TO SLAVERY (LP, with Libertarian Recordings)	30
83	Broken Flag BF 07	LIVE McCARTHY (cassette)	50
83	Broken Flag BF 20	LIVE NEW FORCE (cassette)	50
83	Broken Flag BF 24	LIVE PHENOL (cassette)	50
83	Broken Flag BF 25	LIVE PROSSNECK (cassette)	50
83	Broken Flag BF 28	LIVE AT MORDEN TOWER (cassette)	50
84	Broken Flag BF 37	104 WEEKS (cassette)	40
84	Broken Flag BF 38	AS I HAVE WON (cassette)	40
85	Broken Flag BF 40	AWAKE! (6 cassettes in lockable steel box with booklet)	400
87	Broken Flag BF 59	HOLE IN THE HEART (cassette)	40
94	Broken Flag BF 75	SOUNDCHECK CHANGLING (cassette)	20
95	Broken Flag BF 77	AIRBORNE BABEL (cassette)	20
95	Broken Flag BF 80	ELITE GYMNASTICS/LIVE 1983 (cassette)	20

RAMON & CRYSTALITES

71	Songbird SB 1053	Golden Chickens/Stranger Version	18

DEE DEE RAMONE

97	Blackout BLK 5000-7	I Am Seeing UFOs (featuring Joey Ramone)/Bad Horoscope (2,500 copies only)	8

DEE DEE RAMONE & ICLC

(see also Ramones)

94	Rough Trade/World Service RDT 157.1757.2	Chinese Bitch/I Don't Want To Get Involved With You/ That's What Everybody Else Does/We're A Creepy Family (CD)	10
94	World Service/Rough Trade RTD 157.1757.1	I HATE FREAKS LIKE YOU (LP, with inner)	15

RAMONES

(see also Paley Brothers & Ramones, Holly & Joey, Dee Dee Ramone)

76	Sire 6078 601	Blitzkrieg Bop/Havana Affair (in p/s)	170
76	Sire 6078 601	Blitzkrieg Bop/Havana Affair	12
77	Sire 6078 603	I Remember You/California Sun (live)/I Don't Wanna Walk Around With You (live) (p/s)	40
77	Sire RAM 001 (6078 606)	Sheena Is A Punk Rocker/Commando/I Don't Care (12", with T-shirt offer on perforated centre of numbered p/s, 12,000 only)	15
77	Sire RAM 001 (6078 606)	Sheena Is A Punk Rocker/Commando/I Don't Care (12", without T-shirt offer on perforated centre of numbered p/s, 12,000 only)	10
77	Sire 6078 607	Swallow My Pride/Pinhead/Let's Dance (live) (p/s)	10
77	Sire 6078 611	Rockaway Beach/Teenage Lobotomy/Beat On The Brat (p/s)	10
77	Sire 6078 611	Rockaway Beach/Teenage Lobotomy/Beat On The Brat (12", p/s, with poster)	30
77	Sire 6078 611	Rockaway Beach/Teenage Lobotomy/Beat On The Brat (12", p/s, without poster)	12
78	Sire 6078 615	Do You Wanna Dance?/It's A Long Way Back To Germany/Cretin Hop (p/s)	10
78	Sire (no cat. no.)	Questioningly/Don't Come Close/Sedated/I Just Want To Have Something To Do (with p/s, promo only, with spoken intros by Joey Ramone)	45
78	Sire (no cat. no.)	Questioningly/Don't Come Close/Sedated/I Just Want To Have Something To Do (without p/s, promo only, with spoken intros by Joey Ramone)	15
78	Sire SRE 1031	Don't Come Close/I Don't Want You (p/s, yellow vinyl)	10
78	Sire SRE 1031	Don't Come Close/I Don't Want You (p/s)	5
78	Sire SRE 1031	Don't Come Close/I Don't Want You (12", p/s, yellow or red vinyl, red vinyl lacks p/s)	10
79	Sire SIR 4009	She's The One/I Wanna Be Sedated (p/s)	8
79	Sire SIR 4021	Rock'n'Roll High School/Rockaway Beach (live)/Sheena Is A Punk Rocker (live) (p/s)	7
80	Sire SIR 4037	Do You Remember Rock'n'Roll Radio/I Want You Around (p/s)	5
80	RSO RSO 70 (2090 512)	I Wanna Be Sedated/The Return Of Jackie And Judy (p/s)	15
80	Sire SREP 1	MELTDOWN WITH THE RAMONES: I Just Want To Have Something To Do/ Here Today Gone Tomorrow/I Wanna Be Your Boyfriend/Questioningly (EP)	15
81	Sire SIR 4051	We Want The Airwaves/You Sound LIke You're Sick (p/s)	6
81	Sire SIR 4052	She's A Sensation/All Quiet On The Eastern Front (no p/s)	8
83	Sire W 9606	Time Has Come Today/Psycho Therapy (p/s)	15
83	Sire W 9606T	Time Has Come Today/Sheena Is A Punk Rocker/Teenage Lobotomy/ Rock'n'Roll Radio (12", p/s)	20
85	Beggars Banquet BEG 128	Howling At The Moon/Chasing The Night (p/s)	5
85	Beggars Banquet BEG 128D	Howling At The Moon//Smash You/ Chasing The Night/Street Fighting Man (double pack, gatefold sleeve)	8
85	Beggars Banquet	Howling At The Moon/Chasing The Night/ Smash You/Street Fighting Man (12", p/s)	8
85	Beggars Banquet BEG 140	Bonzo Goes To Bitburg/Go Home Ann (p/s)	7
85	Beggars Banquet BEG 140T	Bonzo Goes To Bitburg/Go Home Ann/Daytime Dilemma (12", p/s)	8
86	Beggars Banquet BEG 157	Somebody Put Something In My Drink/Something To Believe In (p/s)	5
86	Beggars Banquet BEG 157T	Somebody Put Something In My Drink/(You) Can't Say Anything Nice/ Something To Believe In (12", p/s, with promo poster)	15
86	Beggars Banquet BEG 157T	Somebody Put Something In My Drink/(You) Can't Say Anything Nice/ Something To Believe In (12", p/s, without promo poster)	8
86	Beggars Banquet BEG 167	Crummy Stuff/She Belongs To Me (p/s)	7
86	Beggars Banquet BEG 167T	Crummy Stuff/Something To Believe In/I Don't Want To Live This Life (12", p/s)	12
87	Beggars Banquet BEG 198	Real Cool Time/Life Goes On (p/s)	5
87	Beggars Banquet BEG 198T	Real Cool Time/Life Goes On/Indian Giver (12", p/s)	8
87	Beggars Banquet BEG 201	I Wanna Live/Merry Christmas (I Don't Want To Fight Tonight) (p/s)	5
87	Beggars Banquet BEG 201T	I Wanna Live/Merry Christmas (I Don't Want To Fight Tonight) (12", p/s)	8
89	Chrysalis CHS 3423	Pet Semetary/All Screwed Up (p/s)	5
92	Chrysalis CHS 3917	Poison Heart/Censorshit (p/s)	5

			MINT VALUE £
92	Chrysalis 0946 3 23917 66	Poison Heart/Chinese Rocks/Sheena Is A Punk Rocker (live)/ Rockaway Beach (live) (12", yellow vinyl, p/s)	8
76	Sire 9103 253	RAMONES (LP, with insert)	20
77	Sire 9103 254	RAMONES LEAVE HOME (LP, with "Carbona Not Glue" with inner sleeve)	15
77	Sire 9103 255	ROCKET TO RUSSIA (LP, with inner sleeve)	12
78	Sire SRK 6063	ROAD TO RUIN (LP, yellow vinyl)	20
79	Sire SRK 6077	END OF THE CENTURY (LP)	12
81	Sire SRK 3571	PLEASANT DREAMS (LP)	12
85	Beggars Banquet BEGA 59	TOO TOUGH TO DIE (LP)	12
86	Beggars Banquet BEGA 70	ANIMAL BOY (LP, picture inner sleeve and poster)	15
90	Beggar's Banquet	END OF THE DECADE (6 x 12" singles, box set with T-shirt, postcards & poster, 2,500 copies only)	50
91	Chysalis CHR 1901	LOCO LIVE (LP)	15
92	Chrysalis 094632196019	MONDO BIZARRO (LP)	15
93	Chrysalis CHR 6052	ACID EATERS (LP)	15
95	Chrysalis 724383413614	ADIOS AMIGOS (LP)	15

MICHEL RAMOS

60s	London DEP 95013	PLAYING THE CLASSICS (EP, export)	30

RAMP

77	ABC/Blue Thumb BT 6028	COME INTO KNOWLEDGE (LP)	40

RAM RAM GO GO SOUND

69	Halagala HG 26	Pep 77/USA Outcry	15

RAM RAM KINO

(see also Crispy Ambulance)

85	Temple TOPY 006	Advantage - Tantric Routines 1-4 (3.23)/(Basket Mix) (4.00)/Into The Bush (3.26)/Special (3.56) (12", p/s)	8

RAMRODS (U.S.)

61	London HLU 9282	Riders In The Sky/Zig Zag	6
61	London HLU 9355	Loch Lomond Rock/Take Me Back To My Boots And Saddle	20
61	London RE-U 1292	RIDERS IN THE SKY (EP)	80

RAMRODS

65	United Artists UP 1113	Overdrive/Stalker	15

BILL RAMSEY

62	Polydor NH 66812	Go Man Go/Rocking Mountain	12

LEE RAMSEY

96	Real Deal RD 001	RISE TO SHINE (EP)	10
96	Real Deal RD002	RD STYLE (EP)	15

RANCHERS

(see also Phil Brady & Ranchers)

65	Cavern Sound IMSTL 2	An American Sailor At The Cavern/Sidetracked	25

RANCID

95	Out Of Step WOOS 8 S	Time Bomb/The War's End/Blast 'Em (p/s)	6
96	Epitaph 86464-7	Ruby Soho/That's Entertainment/Disorder and disarray (p/s)	6
98	Epitaph 1005-7	Bloodclot/Endrine/Stop (p/s)	6
98	Epitaph 1009-7	Hooligans/Cash, Culture and Violence (Bass Drop Mix)/Things to Come (Dance Hall Mix) (p/s)	6
00	Epitaph 1040-7	Let Me Go/Ben Zanotto/Dead And Fone (p/s)	6
03	Warner Brothers W 618	Fall Back Down/Killing zone (p/s)	5
94	Epitaph 86434-1	LET'S GO (LP, 2 x 10", gatefold sleeve, white vinyl)	12

ALAN RANDALL (& SHEP'S BANJO BOYS)

70	Domino 110	The Coventry City Song/Football Football	6

RANDALL AND ANDY C.

(see also Andy C)

94	Ram RAMM 11	Sound Control/Feel It (12")	15

ELLIOTT RANDALL

71	Polydor 2489 004	RANDALL'S ISLAND (LP)	12

FREDDY RANDALL & HIS BAND

58	Parlophone GEP 8715	CHICAGO JAZZ (EP)	10
58	Parlophone PMD 1046	DR JAZZ (LP)	20

TONY RANDALL & JACK KLUGMAN

73	Decca F 13439	You're So Vain/When Banana Skins Are Falling (I'll Come Sliding Back To You)	7
72	Decca Phase Four PFS 4277	THE ODD COUPLE SINGS (LP)	15

TEDDY RANDAZZO (& DAZZLERS)

(see also Three Chuckles)

59	HMV POP 578	It's Magic/Richer Than I	10
60	HMV POP 806	Journey To Love/Misery	10
61	HMV POP 866	Happy Ending/But You Broke My Heart	10
61	HMV POP 925	Let The Sunshine In/Broken Bell	10
62	HMV POP 1067	Dance To The Locomotion/Cottonfields (as Teddy Randazzo & Dazzlers)	15
63	HMV POP 1119	Echoes/It Wasn't A Dream	5
63	Pye International 7N 25181	Big Wide World/Be Sure, My Love	10
62	HMV CLP 1527	JOURNEY TO LOVE (LP, mono)	60
62	HMV CSD 1421	JOURNEY TO LOVE (LP, stereo)	65
63	HMV CLP 1601	TEDDY RANDAZZO TWISTS (LP, with Dazzlers)	100

LYNNE RANDELL

67	CBS 2847	Ciao Baby/Stranger In My Arms	250
67	CBS 2927	That's A Hoe Down/I Need You Boy	22

RAN-DELLS

63	London HLU 9760	The Martian Hop/Forgive Me Darling (I Have Lied)	25

MINT VALUE £

BARBARA RANDOLPH

67	Tamla Motown TMG 628	I Got A Feelin'/You Got Me Hurtin' All Over	40
67	Tamla Motown TMG 628	I Got A Feelin'/You Got Me Hurtin' All Over (DJ copy)	75
71	Tamla Motown TMG 788	I Got A Feelin'/You Got Me Hurtin' All Over (reissue)	10
79	Tamla Motown TMG 1133	Can I Get A Witness/You Got Me Hurtin' All Over/I Got A Feeling	10

BOOTS RANDOLPH

62	London HLU 9567	Bluebird Of Happiness/Keep A Light In Your Window Tonight	6
63	London HLU 9685	Yakety Sax/I Really Don't Want To Know	10
63	London HLU 9798	Windy And Warm/Lonely Street	5
64	London HLU 9891	Hey, Mr. Sax Man/Baby Go To Sleep	7
66	London HLU 10017	Theme From A Dream/King Of The Road	5
66	London HLU 10028	These Boots Are Made For Walking/Honey In Your Heart	5
66	Monument MON 1001	The Shadow Of Youtr Smile/I'll Just Walk Away	5
63	London RE-U 1365	THE YAKETY SAX OF BOOTS RANDOLPH (EP)	30
63	London HA-U 8106	YAKETY SAX (LP)	35
66	London HA-U 8280	MORE YAKETY SAX (LP, as Boots Randolph & His Combo)	20
67	Monument LMO/SMO 5002	HIP BOOTS (LP)	15

CHARLES RANDOLPH GREEN SOUND

69	London HLD 10283	Quintin's Theme/Number One At The Blue Whale	6

ERIC RANDOM

(see also Tiller Boys, Cabaret Voltaire, Free Agents, Pressure & Co.)

80	New Hormones CAT 4	LIVE IN EUROPE (cassette)	10

RANDOM HARVEST

82	Random Harvest RH 501	RANDOM HARVEST (LP)	12

RANDY & RAINBOWS

63	Stateside SS 214	Denise/Come Back	70

RANDY'S ALLSTARS

(see also Impact Allstars, Lyrics, Dave Barker, Ethiopians, Jimmy London)

70	Randy's RAN 500	I'm The One, You're The One/End Us	12
70	Randy's RAN 501	Pepper Pot (act. with Count Machuki)/Same Thing (B-side actually by Gaylads)	80
70	Randy's RAN 502	Dixie/Five Cents (B-side actually "A Lover's Question" by Winston Samuels)	7
70	Randy's RAN 505	Emperor Waltz/War	10
70	Randy's RAN 506	Blue Danube Waltz/Together (B-side actually by Delroy Wilson)	8
70	Randy's RAN 507	Bridge Over Troubled Water (actually by Lyrics)/Waterfall	5
71	Explosion EX 2052	Hold On Girl (actually by Lyrics)/Hold On Girl (Version)	5

RANEE & RAJ

68	Fontana TF 920	Feel Like A Clown/Rainbow Land	20
68	Fontana TF 941	Don't Tell Me I Must Go/Razor Edge	10

SUE RANEY

57	Capitol CL 14757	The Careless Years/What's The Good Word, Mr. Bluebird	6
57	Capitol CL 14792	Please Hurry Home/Don't Take My Happiness	6
58	Capitol T 964	WHEN YOUR LOVER HAS GONE (LP)	15

WAYNE RANEY (STRING BAND)

53	Parlophone DP 333	If You Never Slip Around/The Child's Side Of Life (78, export issue)	10
54	Parlophone CSMP 20	Adam/The Roosters Are Crowing (export issue)	25
58	Parlophone GEP 8746	COUNTRY AND WESTERN (EP)	45

RANGLERS

68	Trend TRE 1007	You Never Said Goodbye/Step Down	50

ERNEST RANGLIN

(see also Owen Gray, Graham Bond)

62	Island WI 015	Harmonica Twist/Mitty Gritty (as Ernest Ranglin Orchestra)	35
63	Island WI 128	Exodus/ROBERT MARLEY: One Cup Of Coffee	300
66	Black Swan IEP 704	ERNEST RANGLIN & THE G.B.'s (EP, with p/s)	180
66	Black Swan IEP 704	ERNEST RANGLIN & THE G.B.'s (EP)	50
64	Island ILP 909	WRANGLIN' (LP)	125
64	Island ILP 915	REFLECTIONS (LP)	120
60s	Vista Sounds	FROM KINGSTON J.A. TO MIAMI U.S.A. (LP)	25

MASSIMO RANIERI

71	CBS 7207	Goodbye My Love/The Sun Shining Down On Me	12

BILLY RANKIN

(see also Nazareth)

83	A&M AM 172	Baby Come Back/Part Of The Scenery (p/s)	6

KENNY RANKIN

60	Brunswick 05845	As Sure As You're Born/Teasin' Heart	8
70	Mercury MF1128	Peaceful/The Dolphin	15
73	Atlantic K 10275	Comin' Down/Stringman	5
74	Little David	Carfish/Silver Morning	8

ROY RANKIN AND RAYMOND NAPTALI

81	KG Imperial KG 004	Go Deh In A Late Night Blues/Late Night Session/ Babylon Policy/ Peaceful Something (12", green vinyl)	20

RANKING ANN

82	Ariwa ARIL 002	A SLICE OF ENGLISH TOAST (LP)	20
82	Ariwa ARILP 010	SOMETHING FISHY GOING ON (LP)	15

RANKING DREAD

80	Art & Craft AC006	DISCO EP SHOWCASE: My Liza/Same Thing/Hard Times Leave My Life/ Jah Walk Through Galilee (12" green vinyl)	20
81	Greensleeves GRED 65	Fattie Boom Boom/SLY & ROBBIE : Dub Boom (12")	12
82	Greensleeves GRED 82	Shut Me Mouth/Shut Up Shut Up (dub version)	25

MINT VALUE £

76	Burning Sounds BS 1025	GIRLS FIESTA (LP)	25
79	Burning Sounds BS 1037	KUNTA KINTE ROOTS (LP)	25
80	Freedom Sounds FSLP 001	LOTS OF LOVING (LP)	25

RANKING JOE

78	Greensleeves GRE10	Dub Sister Dub It/Nine Months Belly	10
80	Art And Craft ACD 005	DISCO EP SHOWCASE: Honda Accord/ Joe Grine Girl/Baby Mother/ Nice Up The Lawn (12")	15
78	Greensleeves GREL 2	WEAKHEART FADEAWAY (LP)	30
81	Copasetic COPLPS 003	DISCO SKATE (LP, blue vinyl)	25

PETER RANKING AND GENERAL LUCKY

82	Greensleeves GRED 98	Beverly Black/Walk And Talk (12")	15

RANKING TREVOR AND TRINITY

78	Cha Cha CHALP 001	THREE PIECE CHICKEN AND CHIPS (LP)	25

RANSOME HEAD

71	York SYK 506	Sing/Wide Wide River	25

FELA RANSOME KUTI

(see under 'K')

PETER RANSOME

72	York FYK 402	PETER RANSOME (LP, blue/silver label)	25

RAOUL & RUINED

(see also Marc Almond)

84	Gutter Hearts GH 1	BITE BACK + BLUES (LP, fan-club only issue)	50

RAPED

(see also Cuddly Toys)

78	Parole KNIT 1	PRETTY PAEDOPHILES (EP)	25
78	Parole PURL 1	Cheap Night Out/Foreplay Playground (p/s, with ad sheet)	12
84	Iguana PILLAGED 1	PHILES AND SMILES (LP, official bootleg, with booklet)	50

RAPEMAN

(see also Big Black)

88	Fierce FRIGHT 031	Hated Chinee/Marmoset (p/s)	35

RAPHAEL

67	Hispa Vox HXS 303	Please Speak To Me Of Love/While I Live	8

JOHNNY RAPHAEL

58	Vogue V 9104	We're Only Young Once/The Lonely Road To Nowhere	90
58	Vogue V 9104	We're Only Young Once/The Lonely Road To Nowhere (78)	40

RAPIERS

60s	Ilford Sound ILF 272	The Phantom Stage/Valencia	20
91	Fury FEP 3018	THE RETURN OF THE RAPIERS (EP)	10

RAPIERS

86	Off Beat NS 112A	The Closing Theme/Still I Cry	10
83	Red Door RA 001	THE RAPIERS VOL. 1 (EP)	18
84	Twang RA 002	THE RAPIERS VOL. 2 (EP)	12
85	Twang RA 003	THE RAPIERS VOL. 3 (EP)	12
86	Twang RA 004	THE RAPIERS VOL. 4 (EP)	12
85	Off Beat WIK 40	STRAIGHT TO THE POINT (LP)	18
87	Off Beat WIK 67	1961 (LP)	18

BRIAN RAPKIN & KELVIN JONES

70s	MSR	DREAMS OF THE BEAST (LP)	20

RAPOLOGISTS

84	Billy Boy Whiz1	Kid's Rap/Party Rap (12")	8

MARIE RAPP

53	London L 1207	When A Man Loves A Woman/When I'm With You (78)	12

RARE AMBER

69	Polydor BM 56309	Malfunction Of The Engine/Blind Love	30
69	Polydor 583 046	RARE AMBER (LP)	100

HERMAN RAREBELL

81	Harvest HAR 5125	I'll Say Goodbye/Junk Funk	10

RARE BIRD

(see also Fields, Fruit Machine)

70	Charisma CB 120	Sympathy/Devil's High Concern (in p/s)	10
70	Charisma CB 138	What You Want To Know/Hammerhead	7
72	Charisma CB 179	Sympathy/Devil's High Concern/What Do You Want To Know/Hammerhead (p/s)	8
73	Polydor 2058 402	Virgina/Lonely Street	5
74	Polydor 2058 471	Body And Soul/Redman	5
74	Polydor SH 1041/2	Diamonds/BARCLAY JAMES HARVEST: Negative Earth (flexi, with Sounds)	10
69	Charisma CAS 1005	RARE BIRD (LP, laminated front sleeve, pink 'scroll label)	70
70	Charisma CAS 1011	AS YOUR MIND FLIES BY (LP, textured gatefold, pink 'scroll' label)	50
72	Polydor 2442 101	EPIC FOREST (LP & poster, with bonus EP "Roadside Welcome"/ Four Grey Walls/"You're Lost" [2814 011], p/s)	80
72	Polydor 2442 101	EPIC FOREST (LP, gatefold with free EP but no poster)	40
72	Polydor 2442 101	EPIC FOREST (LP with no poster or free EP)	20
73	Polydor 2383 211	SOMEBODY'S WATCHING (LP, gatefold sleeve)	20

RARE BREED

(see also Ohio Express)

66	Strike JH 316	Beg, Borrow And Steal/Jeri's Theme	40

MINT VALUE £

RARE EARTH

71	Rare Earth RES 104	Hey Big Brother/Under God's Light	8
71	Rare Earth RES 102	I Just Want To Celebrate/The Seed	6
70	Tamla Motown TMG 742	Get Ready/Magic Key	20
70	Tamla Motown STML 11165	GET READY (LP)	25
71	Tamla Motown STML 11180	ECOLOGY (LP)	25
71	Rare Earth SREA 4001	ONE WORLD (LP)	18
72	Rare Earth SRESP 301	IN CONCERT (2-LP satchel sleeve)	15
73	Rare Earth SRE 3008	WILLIE REMEMBERS (LP, gatefold sleeve)	12

RARE PLEASURE

76	DJM DJS 10738	Let Me Down Easy/Let Me Down Easy (Long Version) (Promo p/s)	10
76	DJM DJS 10738	Let Me Down Easy/Let Me Down Easy (Long Version)	7

RASCALS

(see also Young Rascals)

68	Atlantic 584 182	A Beautiful Morning/Rainy Day	7
68	Atlantic 584 210	People Got To Be Free/My World	7
69	Atlantic 584 255	Heaven/Baby I'm Blue	7
69	Atlantic 584 274	See/Away Away	7
69	Atlantic 584 292	Carry Me Back/Real Thing	6
70	Atlantic 584 307	Hold On/I Believe	8
70	Atlantic 2091 029	Glory, Glory/You Don't Know	6
71	CBS 7363	Love Me/Happy Song	6
71	CBS 7672	Lucky Day/Love Letter	6
68	Atlantic 587/588 098	ONCE UPON A DREAM (LP)	18
68	Atlantic 587/588 120	TIME PEACE - RASCALS' GREATEST HITS (LP)	12
69	Atlantic 588 183	FREEDOM SUITE (LP)	12
70	Atlantic 588 210	SEE (LP)	12
71	Atlantic 2400 113	SEARCH AND NEARNESS (LP)	12
71	CBS S 64406	PEACEFUL WORLD (2-LP)	18

RENATO RASCEL

(see also Royal Rasses)

60	RCA RCA 1177	Romantica/Dimmelo Con Un Fiore	5

(EMPRESS) RASHEDA

95	Roots Music RRLP 011	HAIL H.I.M (LP)	25

RAS IMRU

80	Jah Shaka KMD001	Marshall/SHAKA RYDIM SECTION : Warrior Style (12")	60

RAS MIDAS

78	Tribesman TM24	Good Old Days/Natty Dread Surprise (12")	70

RASTA TWINS

(see under Aggrovators)

RASTAFARI

73	Satril SAT8	Funky City/In The Garden	30

THE RAT & THE WHALE

(see also Alternative TV, Rat Scabies)

80	Rewind REWIND 5	Wheels On Fire/Wheels On Fire (Long Version) (p/s)	5

BASIL RATHBONE

60s	Caedmon TC 1028	EDGAR ALLAN POE (LP)	15

RATIO

70	Big Chief BC 102	Let There Be Peace In The World/Pharaoh's Walk	7

RATIONAL ANTHEM

86	Radio Humberside/HLS 001	THE NORTHERN TRAWL (LP)	50

ARMAN RATIP

70	Columbia SCX 6532	INTRODUCING THE ARMAN RATIP TRIO (LP)	100
73	Regal Zono. SLRZ 1038	THE SPY FROM ISTANBUL (LP, gatefold sleeve)	100

RATS

(see also Beat Boys, Mark Peters)

64	Oak RGJ 145	Spoonful (1-sided, with foldout p/s)	400
64	Oak RGJ 145	Spoonful (1-sided)	250
65	Columbia DB 7483	Spoonful/I've Got My Eyes On You Baby	120
65	Columbia DB 7607	I Gotta See My Baby Everyday/Headin' Back (To New Orleans)	90
95	Tenth Planet TP	THE RISE AND FALL OF BERNIE GRIPPLESTONE & THE SPIDERS FROM HULL (LP, gatefold sleeve, 1,000 only)	15

RATS

64	Oriole CB 1967	Parchman Farm/Every Day I Have The Blues	100
65	CBS 201740	Sack Of Woe/Gimme That Wine	85

RATS

74	MAM MAM 113	Don't Let Go/Dragon Child	10

RATS

(see also World of Oz)

74	Goodear EAR. 101	Turtle Dove/Oxford Donna (in p/s)	25
74	Goodear EAR. 101	Turtle Dove/Oxford Donna	15
74	Goodear EARLH 5003	FIRST (LP)	18

RATT

85	Atlantic A 9546P	Lay It Down/Got Me On The Line (shaped picture disc)	6
86	Atlantic A 9502P	You're In Love/Between The Eyes (shaped picture disc)	8

RATTLES

(see also Wonderland)

63	Philips BF 1277	The Stomp/Zip A Dee Doo Dah	20

MINT VALUE £

64	Decca F 11873	Bye Bye Johnny/Roll Over Beethoven	25
64	Decca F 11936	Tell Me What I Can Do/Sunbeam At The Sky	25
65	Fontana TF 618	Come On And Sing/Candy To Me	25
66	Fontana TF 724	Say All Right/Love Of My Life	25
70	Decca F 23058	The Witch/Geraldine	6
71	Decca F 23119	You Can't Have Sunshine Everyday/Where Is The Friend	10
64	Decca DFE 8568	TEENBEAT FROM THE STAR CLUB HAMBURG (EP)	125
64	Philips BL 7614	TWIST AT THE STAR CLUB HAMBURG (LP)	100
67	Mercury MG 1127	GREATEST HITS (LP)	30
71	Decca SKL-R 5088	THE RATTLES (LP)	30

CARL RAVAZZA

51	HMV B 10202	Rock, Rock, Rock/Like A Dream (78)	10

CHRIS RAVEL & RAVERS

(see also Chris Andrews)

63	Decca F 11696	I Do/Don't You Dig This Kind Of Beat	20

RAVEN

80	Neat NEAT 06	Don't Need Your Money/Wiped Out (p/s)	8
81	Neat NEAT 11	Hard Ride/Crazy World (p/s)	6
82	Neat NEAT 1512	CRASH BANG WALLOP (Crash Bang Wallop/Firepower/ Run Them Down/ Rock Hard) (12" EP, mauve splattered vinyl)	15
86	WEA A 9453	Gimme Some Lovin' (no p/s)	8
81	Neat NEAT1001	ROCK UNTIL YOU DROP (LP + lyric insert)	12
81	Neat NEAT1004	WIPED OUT (LP + poster)	12
83	Neat NEATP1001	ROCK UNTIL YOU DROP (reissue picture disc LP)	15

JON RAVEN

(see also Halliard, Black Country Three, John Kirkpatrick)

70s	Broadside	HARVEST (LP, with book)	15
71	Argo ZFB 29	KATE OF COALBROOKDALE (LP, as Jon & Mike Raven with Jean Ward)	100
73	Trailer LER 2083	SONGS OF A CHANGING WORLD (LP, with Nic Jones & Tony Rose, red label with insert)	25
75	Tradition TSR 019	THE BOLD NAVIGATORS: THE STORY OF ENGLAND'S CANALS IN SONG (LP, with John Kirkpatrick, Sue Harris, & Gary & Vera Aspey)	20
76	Broadside BRO 117	HARVEST (LP)	50
76	Broadside BRO 118	THE ENGLISH CANALS (LP, with John Kirkpatrick & Sue Harris)	15
81	Dingles DIN 319	REGAL SLIP (LP)	30

PAUL RAVEN

61	Parlophone R 4812	Walk On Boy/All Grown Up	15
61	Parlophone R 4842	Tower Of Strength/Livin' The Blues	12
68	MCA MU1035	Soul Thing/We'll Go Where The World Can't	12
77	EMI NUT 2855	PAUL RAVEN (EP)	10

SIMON RAVEN

66	Piccadilly 7N 35301	I Wonder If She Remembers Me/Sea Of Love	80

RAVENS

53	Oriole CB 1148	Rock Me All Night Long/Write Me One Sweet Letter (78)	30
53	Oriole CB 1149	Begin The Beguine/Looking For My Baby (78)	30
53	Oriole CB 1258	Who'll Be The Fool?/Rough Ridin' (78)	30

RAVENS

63	Oriole CB 1910	I Just Wanna Hear You Say/Send Me A Letter	30

RAVENS ROCK GROUP

61	Pye International 7N 25077	The Ghoul Friend/Career Girl	20

RAVE ONS

60s	Sounds Good MT 103	She's A Spoon/Keep Wrong	120

RAVERS

69	Upsetter US 312	Badam Bam/UPSETTERS: Medical Operation	50

RAW DEAL

81	White Witch WIT 701	Out Of My Head/In The Mood (no p/s)	125
81	Neat NEAT 12	Lonewolf/Take The Sky (p/s)	10

RAW DEAL

95	Mental Disorder MAD 666	THE LEGENDARY RAW DEAL (10" LP)	12

PETER RAWES

(see also Jet Harris)

87	Official OFFA 5	Why Should I Ask Her To Stay?/Theme From Shark/Theme From Forever (with Jet Harris) (p/s)	6

LOU RAWLS

65	Capitol CL 15398	Three O'Clock In The Morning/Nothing Really Feels The Same	10
66	Capitol CL 15465	Love Is A Hurtin' Thing/Memory Lane	10
67	Capitol CL 15488	You Can Bring Me All Your Heartaches/A Woman Who's A Woman	15
67	Capitol CL 15499	Dead End Street/Yes It Hurts Doesn't It	20
67	Capitol CL 15507	Show Business/When Loves Goes Wrong	25
67	Capitol CL 15515	Hard To Get Thing Called Love/(How Do You Say) I Don't Love You Anymore	10
67	Capitol CL 15522	Little Drummer Boy/Child With A Toy	8
68	Capitol CL 15533	My Ancestors/Evil Woman	8
68	Capitol CL 15548	You're Good For Me/Soul Serenade	10
68	Capitol CL 15560	Down Here On The Ground/I'm Satisfied	8
69	Capitol CL 15583	It's You/Sweet Charity	8
69	Capitol CL 15611	Your Good Thing (Is About To End)/Season Of The Witch	8
70	Capitol CL 15630	You've Made Me So Very Happy/Let's Burn Down The Cornfield	5
74	Bell BLL 1390	She's Gone/Hourglass	5
63	Capitol EAP-1 20646	LOST AND LOOKIN' (EP)	50

			MINT VALUE £
65	Capitol T 1824	BLACK AND BLUE (LP)	25
66	Capitol (S)T 2459	LIVE (LP)	20
67	Capitol (S)T 2566	SOULIN' (LP)	22
67	Capitol (S)T 2632	CARRYIN' ON! (LP)	20
68	Capitol (S)T 2864	FEELIN' GOOD (LP)	30
69	Capitol ST 2927	YOU'RE GOOD FOR ME (LP)	20
69	Capitol E-ST 215	THE WAY IT WAS THE WAY IT IS (LP)	20

RAW MATERIAL
(see also Deep Feelings, Shoot)

69	Evolution E 2441	Time And Illusion/Bobo's Party	50
70	Evolution E 2445	Hi There Hallelujah/Days Of The Fighting Cock	35
70	Evolution E 24495	Travelling Man (Part 1)/Part 2	30
71	RCA Neon NE 1002	Ride On Pony/Religion	22
70	Evolution Z 1006	RAW MATERIAL (LP)	400
71	RCA Neon NE 8	TIME IS (LP, gatefold sleeve)	350

ANNITA RAY

62	MGM 1177	Wouldn't It Be Lovely/I'm In Love With Jim	6

CLYDE RAY

57	Columbia DB 3875	Follow Me/Steady As A Rock	10
58	Columbia DB 4106	Locked In The Arms Of Love/I'm Not Afraid Anymore	10

CONGO ASHANTI RAY

83	On U Sound DP5	Africa Blood/Hands And Hearts	15

DANNY RAY

76	Doctor DR 01	REVOLUTION ROCK (LP)	30

DANNY RAY & FALCONS

70	MCA MK 5037	Scorpion/I Love You Girl	10

DIANE RAY

63	Mercury AMT 1209	Please Don't Talk To The Lifeguard/That's All I Want From You	22

FROGGIE RAY

71	Big BG 313	Uncle Charlie/Party Version	8
71	Big BG 314	Half Moon/RUPIE EDWARDS ALL STARS: Full Moon	7

JAMES RAY

62	Pye International 7N 25126	If You Gotta Make A Fool Of Somebody/It's Been A Drag	22
62	Pye International 7N 25147	Itty Bitty Pieces/You Remember The Face	20

JOHNNIE RAY
(see also Four Lads, Frankie Laine & Johnnie Ray, Timi Yuro)

53	Columbia SCM 5015	Walkin' My Baby Back Home/The Lady Drinks Champagne (B-side with the Four Lads)	30
53	Columbia SCM 5033	Ma Says, Pa Says/A Full Time Job (with Doris Day)	30
53	Columbia SCM 5041	Whiskey And Gin/Tell The Lady I Said Goodbye	30
53	Columbia SCM 5074	Please Don't Talk About Me When I'm Gone/Coffee And Cigarettes (B-side with the Four Lads)	30
54	Columbia SCM 5111	Nobody's Sweetheart/I Can't Escape From You	20
54	Columbia SCM 5122	She Didn't Say Nothin' At All/I'm Just A Shadow Of Myself	20
57	Philips JK 1004	You Don't Owe Me A Thing/Look Homeward, Angel (jukebox issue)	30
57	Philips JK 1011	So Long/I Miss You So (jukebox issue)	30
57	Philips JK 1016	Yes, Tonight, Josephine/No Wedding Today (jukebox issue)	30
57	Philips JK 1025	Build Your Love (On A Strong Foundation)/Street Of Memories (jukebox issue)	30
57	Philips JK 1026	Up Above My Head, I Hear Music On The Air/Good Evening Friends/ Memories (with Frankie Laine, jukebox issue only)	30
57	Philips JK 1033	Pink Sweater Angel/Texas Tambourine (jukebox issue)	30
58	Philips PB 785	Miss Me Just A Little/Soliloquy Of A Fool	7
58	Philips PB 808	Strollin' Girl/Plant A Little Seed	7
58	Philips PB 829	Lonely For A Letter/Endlessly	7
58	Philips PB 849	No Regrets/Up Until Now	7
58	Philips PB 884	What More Can I Say/You're The One Who Knows	7
59	Philips PB 901	When's Your Birthday, Baby/One Man's Love Song Is Another Man's Blues	7
59	Philips PB 918	Call Me Yours/Here And Now	6
59	Philips PB 918	Call Me Yours/Here And Now (78)	20
59	Philips PB 952	You're All That I Live For/I'll Never Fall In Love Again	6
59	Philips PB 952	You're All That I Live For/I'll Never Fall In Love Again (78)	20
60	Philips PB 990	When It's Springtime In The Rockies/Wagon Wheels	6
60	Philips PB 1025	Before You/I'll Make You Mine	6
60	Philips PB 1047	Tell Me/Don't Leave Me Now	6
60	London HLA 9216	In The Heart Of A Fool/Let's Forget It Now	7
61	Philips PB 1126	An Ordinary Couple/Cool Water	5
61	United Artists POP 902	How Many Nights How Many Days/I'll Bring Along My Banjo	5
62	London HLG 9484	I Believe (with Timi Yuro)/TIMI YURO: Smile	10
63	Brunswick 05884	Lookout Chatanooga/After My Laughter Came Tears	8
69	Pye 7N 17691	Wise To The Ways Of The World/Since I Lost You Baby	7
69	Pye 7N 17760	Long And Lonely Nights/Brokenhearted Me, Evilhearted You	7
76	EPIC MEPC 4533	Cry/The Little White Cloud That Cried	8
54	Columbia SEG 7511	JOHNNIE RAY (EP, company sleeve)	20
55	Philips BBE 12006	JOHNNIE RAY (EP)	15
57	Philips BBE 12115	WALKING AND CRYING (EP)	15
58	Philips BBE 12192	YES, TONIGHT, JOSEPHINE (EP)	8
58	Philips BBE 12217	T.V. SERIES (EP)	8
61	Philips BBE 12460	ON THE TRAIL (EP)	8
54	Philips BBR 8001	AT THE LONDON PALLADIUM (10" LP, red sleeve)	20
54	Philips BBR 8001	AT THE LONDON PALLADIUM (10" LP, blue sleeve)	18
55	Philips BBR 8062	THE VOICE OF YOUR CHOICE (10" LP)	20
57	Philips BBL 7148	THE BIG BEAT (LP)	25
58	Philips BBL 7254	AT THE DESERT INN - LAS VEGAS (LP)	20
58	Philips BBL 7264	SHOWCASE OF HITS (LP)	20

MINT VALUE £

59 Philips BBL 7285 'TIL MORNING (LP, also stereo SBBL 555) 15
59 Philips BBL 7348 A SINNER AM I (LP) 15
60 Philips BBL 7363 ON THE TRAIL (LP) 15

RICARDO RAY
68 Roulette RO 501 Nitty Gritty/Mony Mony 10

WADE RAY
63 London HL 9700 Burning Desire/Two Red Red Lips 12

RAY & COLLUNEY
71 Westwood WRS 001 TYRANTS OF ENGLAND (LP) 40

RAY & HIS COURT
00 Jazzman JM 014 Soul Freedom/RAY & HIS FAMILY: Cookie Crumbs 5

CHRIS(TINE) RAYBURN
63 Parlophone R 5098 Slow Loving Woman/Same Old Places 10
64 Parlophone R 5144 I've Cried My Last Tear/You Forgot To Say When 10
66 Parlophone R 5422 I Wanna Be In Love Again/Another Night Alone 10
68 Music Factory CUB 2 One Way Ticket/Photograph Of Love 10
69 Pye 7N 17679 Skip A Rope/Starlight (as Christine Rayburn) 10
66 Parlophone PCS7001 CHRIS RAYBURN (LP) 25

MARGIE RAYBURN
56 Capitol CL 14532 The Wedding Song/That's The Chance I've Got To Take 10
57 London HLU 8515 I'm Available/If You Were 25
58 London HLU 8648 I Would/Alright, But It Won't Be Easy 18

ANTHONY RAYE
80 Grapevine GRP 147 Give Me One More Chance/Hold On To What You've Got 8

SOL RAYE
63 Oriole CB 1855 Dear Michelle/I Love You Because 10
67 Deram DM 154 While I'm Here/To Be With You 10

BILLY RAYMOND
58 HMV POP 503 Making Love/I Would 5
58 HMV POP 526 One In Particular/Seven Daughters 5
59 HMV POP 614 Charlie Is Their Darling/Loch Lomond 5

DANNY RAYMOND
71 Big Shot BI 587 Sister Big Stuff/BOY FRIDAY: Free Man 7

LEE RAYMOND with COSTELLO SISTERS
55 Brunswick 05438 Foolishly Yours/Baby Darling 12

MARK RAYMOND & CROWD
64 Columbia DB 7308 Girls/Remember Me To Julie 15

TONY RAYMOND
59 Fontana H 213 Broken-Hearted Melody/This Earth Is Mine 8
59 Fontana H 213 Broken-Hearted Melody/This Earth Is Mine (78) 10
62 Oriole CB 1708 Handful Of Songs/She'll Have To Go 6
62 Oriole CB 1777 The Infant King/Because Of You 6

IVOR RAYMONDE & HIS ORCHESTRA
65 Mercury MF 866 Feelin' Fruggy/Grotty 12

JULIE RAYNE
59 HMV POP 665 Waltz Me Around/Love Where Can You Be? 15
60 HMV POP 785 Bim Bam Bom/One More Time 15
61 HMV POP 868 Green With Envy Purple With Passion/My First Romance 15
63 Windsor WPS 123 Faithfully/Free To Love 12
64 Windsor WPS 128 You Can't Come Back/Straight To Your Arms 12

LISA RAYNE
65 Fontana TF 563 Don't Ever Change/It Had To Be You 10

MARTIN RAYNOR & SECRETS
(see also Secrets, Simon's Secrets, Clifford T. Ward)
65 Columbia DB 7563 Candy To Me/You're A Wonderful One 60

RAYS
57 London HLU 8505 Silhouettes/Daddy Cool 40
57 London HLU 8505 Silhouettes/Daddy Cool (78) 20

RAZAR
(see also Third World War, Soho Jets)
78 Polydor 2058 983 Ascension Day/Ain't No Mystery 30

RAZBERRY HOLIDAY BAND
89 Caleche LIS 001 Hangover Square/Promise 20

RAZORCUTS
(see also Cinematics, Red Chair Fadeaway)
86 Subway Org. SUBWAY 5 Big Pink Cake/I'll Still Be There (foldover p/s with insert, poly bag, 2,000 only) 18
86 Subway Org. SUBWAY 8 Sorry To Embarrass You/Summer In Your Heart (p/s, with insert, 2,000 only) 15
87 Sha La La BaBaBaBaBa 02 Sad Kaleidoscope/TALULAH GOSH: I Told You So (flexidisc p/s, 2,500 only) 10
80s Caff CAFF 10 Sometimes I Worry About You/For Always/Sorry To Embarrass You/ Music From The Big Pink (foldaround p/s with insert, 500 only) 20
88 Creation CRELP 026 STORYTELLER (LP) 25
89 Creation CRELP 045 THE WORLD KEEPS TURNING (LP) 20
91 Creation CRECD 119 PATTERNS ON THE WATER (CD, compilation) 20
02 Matinee MATCD 12 R IS FOR RAZORCUTS (CD) 20

RAZORLIGHT
03 Mercury 9814044 Rip It Up/Here It Comes (numbered p/s) 8
03 Mercury 9800413 Rock 'n' Roll Lies/Action/Yeah Yeah Yeah (CD, card sleeve) 8

MINT VALUE £

03	Mercury 9800414	Rock 'n' Roll Lies/In The City (numbered p/s)	10
03	Mercury 9800414	Rock 'n' Roll Lies/In The City (p/s)	5

RAZOR'S EDGE

66	Stateside SS 532	Let's Call It A Day, Girl/April	15

CHRIS REA

74	Magnet MAG 10	So Much Love/Born To Lose (no p/s)	25
79	Magnet MAGL 5028	DELTICS (LP, blue vinyl, stickered sleeve)	12

REACTA

(see also Television Personalities)

79	Battery Operated WAC 1	Stop The World/SUS (p/s)	100

REACTION

68	President PT 208	That Man/Falling In Love With You	12

REACTION

(see also Ezz Reco, Joe Higgs)

70	Columbia Blue Beat DB 119	Oh Me, Oh My/RECO: It's Love	12
70	Attack ATT 8022	You Yes You/CIMARONS: Be There	10

REACTION

(see also Talk Talk)

78	Island WIP 6437	I Can't Resist/I Am A Case (p/s)	15

AL READ

56	HMV POP 278	We Haven't Any Money/What Is A Home	6
59	HMV POP 575	That's Life/Our Maggie's Going To Get Married	6
59	HMV 7EG 8440	SUCH IS LIFE (EP)	15

PAT READER

60	Triumph RGM 1024	Ricky/Dear Daddy	60
62	Piccadilly 7N 35077	Cha Cha On The Moon/May Your Heart Stay Young Forever	60
63	Oriole CB 1903	Helpless/Lover's Lane	40

BERTICE READING

57	Decca F 10965	No Flowers By Request/September In The Rain	15
58	Parlophone R 4462	Rock Baby Rock/It's A Boy	60
58	Parlophone R 4462	Rock Baby Rock/It's A Boy (78)	20
58	Parlophone R 4487	My Big Best Shoes/No More In Life	15

WILMA READING

74	Pye 7N 45380	Play It Again/Two Can Have A Party	5

REALISTICS

77	Epic SEPC 5723	So Sad/The Magic That You Do	7

REALITY

82	Subversive SUB	BLIND TO THE TRUTH (EP, foldout sleeve and insert)	8
84	Fight Back FIGHT 3	WHO KILLED THE GOLDEN GOOSE? (EP)	8

REALITY FROM DREAM

75	(no label) CP 109	REALITY FROM DREAM (LP, private pressing)	140

REAL KIDS

78	Bronze BRO 54	All Kindsa Girls/Common At Noon (p/s)	8
78	Bronze BRON 509	REAL KIDS (LP)	20

REALM

(see also Earl Preston & Realms)

66	CBS 202044	Hard Time Loving You/Certain Kind Of Girl	35

REALMS

70s	Summertime BUSS 11	Happiness Is Your Name/Happiest Dread	10

REAL McCOY

(see also Tony Colton)

67	Fontana TF 794	Show Me How You Milk A Cow/I Paid For My Laughs	8
68	Target 7N 17669	Quick Joey Small/Happiness Is Love	20
68	Pye 7N 17618	I Get So Excited/Somebody's Taken Maria Away	8
69	Pye 7N 17669	Quick Joey Small/Happiness Is Love	8
69	Pye 7N 17704	Round The Gum Tree/I Will	8
69	Pye 7N 17772	Gitarzan/Anytime You Need Me	8
69	Pye 7N 17850	Many The Memories/She's Different, She's Beautiful	8
70	Marble Arch MAL 1251	THIS IS THE REAL McCOY (LP)	20
71	CBS 7065	I'll Give You Things/Baby, Go Home	8

REAL THING

(see also Chants)

72	Bell BLL 1232	Vicious Circles Parts 1 & 2	5

REASONS

78	Island WIP 6467	Hard Day At The Office/Baby Bright Eyes (p/s)	30

REBEL

81	Bridge House BHS 2	Rocka Shocka/Drift Away (p/s)	12
86	Flying Pig REBS 1	Valentino/Lonely Traveller (p/s, with free single)	12

REBEL ROUSERS

(see also Cliff Bennett & Rebel Rousers, Soul Sounds)

68	Fontana TF 973	Should I?/As I Look	150

REBELS (Jamaica)

(see also The Pioneers)

70	Bullet BU 440	Nice Grind/SIDNEY ALL STARS: Nice Grind - Version	10
70	Trojan TR 7779	It's All In The Game/Easy Come	12

MINT VALUE £

REBELS (U.K.)
67 Page One POF 017 Hard To Love You/Call Me 40

REBELS
78 Rigid IS REB 1029 Suicide/The Leader Of The Rebellion 250

REBOUNDS
64 Fontana TF 461 Help Me/The World Is Mine 40

REBS
58 Capitol CL 14932 Bunky/Renegade 15

RECKLESS
92 Pulse-8 12LOSE 24 Time To Make The Floor Burn (The Reckless Hypermix)/Take Me (Ruff Mix)/ Take Me (Uplifting Piano Mix) (12", p/s) 25

RECO
(see also Reaction, Don Reco, Rico Rodriguez, Father Sketto, Joe Monsano, Slim Smith, Laurel Aitken)
69 Downtown DT 417 Quando Quando/Reg 'A' Jeg (as Reco & Rudies) 12
69 Jackpot JP 710 Memory Of Don Drummond/THE TOBIES: Resting 15
69 Treasure Isle TI 7052 The Lion Speaks/ANDY CAPP: Pop A Top 10
69 Pama ECO 14 RECO IN REGGAE LAND (LP) 120

DON RECO
(see also Reco)
71 Big Shot BI 597 Waterloo Rock/LLOYD'S ALL STARS: Walls Soul 15

EZZ RECO & LAUNCHERS
(see also Reaction)
64 Columbia DB 7217 King Of Kings/Blue Beat Dance 10
64 Columbia DB 7222 Little Girl/The Bluest Beat 5
64 Columbia DB 7290 Please Come Back/At A Party 5
64 Columbia SEG 8326 JAMAICAN BLUE BEAT (EP) 20

RECORD PLAYERS
78 Wreckord WRECK 001 DOUBLE C SIDE (EP, label also listed as Aerco AERO 1104) 8
80 Wreckord WRECK 002 Give An Inch/Squirming In The Vermin By The Bonny Banks Of Clyde/ 67/Parasite (p/s) 6

RECTIFY
88 Taffcore TAFF 001 20TH CENTURY EP (foldout p/s) 10

RED
83 Jigsaw SAW 2 RED (LP, private pressing) 25

RED ALERT
69 Total TL3 Witch Woman/Sabra 35

RED ALERT
82 No Future OI 5 In Britain/Screaming At The Nation/Murder Missile (p/s) 10
82 No Future OI 13 Take No Prisoners/Empire Of Crime/Sell Out (p/s) 10
83 No Future OI 20 City Invasion/Negative Reaction (p/s) 8
80 Guardian GM-RA/B 61 BORDER GUARDS (EP) 250
83 No Future OI 27 THERE'S A GUITAR BURNING (12" EP) 15
83 No Future PUNK 5 WE'VE GOT THE POWER (LP) 15

RED ALERT
82 Steel City AJS7R Run To Ground/Wild You (no p/s) 10

RED ALLIGATOR
(see Jimmy Powell)
69 Youngblood YB1004 Real Cool/Slow Down 25

RED BALUNE
78 MCCB 001 Capitalist Kid/Spider In Love (p/s) 12

REDBEAT
80 Malicious Damage MD 440 Machines In Motion/More Or Less Cut (12", p/s) 8

REDBONE
70 CBS 5061 Crazy Cajun Cakewalk Band/Night Come Down 5
70 CBS 5326 Maggie/New Blue Sermonette 6
70 CBS 64069 REDBONE (LP) 15
70 CBS 64198 POTLATCH (LP) 15
71 Epic EPC 64709 WITCH QUEEN OF NEW ORLEANS (LP) 12
72 Epic EQ 30815 MESSAGE FROM A DRUM (LP, quadraphonic) 15

REDCAPS
63 Decca F 11716 Shout/Little Things You Do 20
63 Decca F 11789 Talkin' 'Bout You/Come On Girl 20
64 Decca F 11903 Mighty Fine Girl/Funny Things 15

REDCELL
92 B12 B1205 REDCELL EP (12") 25
92 B12 B1205 REDCELL EP (12", purple vinyl) 80
92 B12 B1207 RETREAT FROM UNPLEASANT REALITIES EP (12") 40
92 B12 B1207 RETREAT FROM UNPLEASANT REALITIES EP (12", blue vinyl) 60
92 B12 B1207 RETREAT FROM UNPLEASANT REALITIES EP (12", red vinyl) 60
93 B12 B1208 INTERIM OUTERIM EP (12") 15
93 B12 B1208 INTERIM OUTERIM EP (12", white vinyl) 60
96 B12 B1215 Untitled (12", white label promo) 60

RED CHAIR FADEAWAY
(see also Razorcuts)
89 Cosmic Eng. M. CTA 103 Let It Happen/Myra/Dragonfly/Grasshopper (12", p/s, 500 only) 15
90 Cosmic Eng. M. CTA 105 Mr Jones/Chimney Pots/Faraway Lights/Out Of The Grey (12", p/s, 450 only) 15

			MINT VALUE £
91	Waterbomb SPLAT 002	Never Remember/FUDGE: Girlwish (flexi, p/s)	12
91	Tangerine MM 10	CURIOUSER AND CURIOUSER (LP, foldaround sleeve with booklet, no'd)	20
93	Aural AUR 102	MESMERISED (LP, 500 only)	12

RED CRAYOLA

78	Radar ADA 22	Wives In Orbit/Yik Yak (p/s, red vinyl)	7
78	Radar/Sound For Industry	Hurricane Fighter Plane/13TH FLOOR ELEVATORS: Reverberation (flexidisc free with Zig Zag magazine, issue 88)	6

FREDDIE REDD

58	Nixa NJL 19	GET HAPPY (LP)	50

GENE REDD & GLOBETROTTERS

59	Parlophone R 4584	Red River Valley Rock/Kentucky Home Rock	15

NOEL REDDING BAND

(see also Loving Kind, Jimi Hendrix, Fat Mattress, Lord Sutch, Road)

75	RCA RS 1030	CLONAKILTY COWBOYS (LP)	12

OTIS REDDING

SINGLES

64	London HLK 9833	Pain In My Heart/Something Is Worrying Me	25
64	London HLK 9876	Come To Me/Don't Leave Me This Way	25
65	Atlantic AT 4024	Mr Pitiful/That's How Strong My Love Is	15
65	Sue WI 362	Shout Bamalama/Fat Girl	30
65	Atlantic AT 4029	I've Been Loving You Too Long/Winter Wonderland (unissued, demos only)	70
65	Atlantic AT 4039	Respect/I've Been Loving You Too Long	15
65	Atlantic AT 4050	My Girl/Down In The Valley	15
66	Atlantic AT 4080	(I Can't Get No) Satisfaction/Any Ole Way	10
66	Atlantic 584 019	My Lover's Prayer/Don't Mess With Cupid	10
66	Atlantic 584 030	I Can't Turn You Loose/Just One More Day	10
66	Atlantic 584 049	Fa-Fa-Fa-Fa-Fa (Sad Song)/Good To Me	10
67	Atlantic 584 070	Try A Little Tenderness/I'm Sick Y'all	8
67	Atlantic 584 091	Respect/These Arms Of Mine	8
67	Atlantic 584 092	My Girl/Mr Pitiful	8
67	Stax 601 005	Day Tripper/Shake (dark blue labels)	10
67	Stax 601 007	Let Me Come On Home/I Love You More Than Words Can Say (dark blue labels)	10
67	Stax 601 011	Shake (live)/634-5789 (live)	10
67	Stax 601 017	The Glory Of Love/I'm Coming Home	8
67	Stax 601 027	(I Can't Get No) Satisfaction/I've Been Loving You Too Long	8
68	Stax 601 031	(Sittin' On) The Dock Of The Bay/My Sweet Lorene	8
68	Stax 601 040	The Happy Song/Open The Door	8
68	Pye International 7N 25463	She's All Right/Gama Lama	10
68	Atlantic 584 199	Hard To Handle/Amen	8
68	Atlantic 584 220	Champagne And Wine/I've Got Dreams To Remember	8
68	Atlantic 584 234	Papa's Got A Brand New Bag/Direct Me	8
69	Atlantic 584 249	A Lover's Question/You Made A Man Out Of Me	8
69	Atco 226 001	Love Man/That's How Strong My Love Is	10
69	Atco 226 002	Free Me/Higher And Higher	8
69	Evolution E 2442	She's All Right/Tuff Enuff	15
70	Atco 226 012	Look At That Girl/That's A Good Idea	8
70	Atco 2091 020	Wonderful World/Security	8
71	Atlantic 2091 062	I've Been Loving You Too Long/Try A Little Tenderness	5
71	Atlantic 2091 112	(Sittin' On) The Dock Of The Bay/Respect/Mr Pitiful (reissue)	5
72	Atlantic K 10206	White Christmas/Merry Christmas, Baby	5
66	Sue IEP 710	EARLY OTIS REDDING (EP)	100
65	Atlantic ATL 5029	THE GREAT OTIS REDDING SINGS SOUL BALLADS (LP)	50
66	Atlantic ATL 5041	OTIS BLUE: OTIS REDDING SINGS SOUL (LP)	45
66	Atlantic 587 011	THE SOUL ALBUM (LP)	30
66	Atlantic 587 035	THE GREAT OTIS REDDING SINGS SOUL BALLADS (LP, reissue)	20
66	Atlantic 587/588 036	OTIS BLUE: OTIS REDDING SINGS SOUL (LP, reissue, mono/stereo)	20
67	Atlantic 587/588 050	COMPLETE AND UNBELIEVABLE: THE OTIS REDDING DICTIONARY OF SOUL (LP)	30
67	Atlantic 587 042	PAIN IN MY HEART (LP)	30
67	Stax VOLT 418	THE HISTORY OF OTIS REDDING (LP)	25
68	Stax 589 016	OTIS REDDING IN EUROPE (LP)	25
68	Stax 230 001/231 001	THE DOCK OF THE BAY (LP)	25
68	Atlantic 587/588 113	THE IMMORTAL OTIS REDDING (LP)	25
68	Atlantic 587/588 148	OTIS REDDING AT THE WHISKEY A GO GO, LOS ANGELES (LP)	20
69	Atco 228 001	THE HISTORY OF OTIS REDDING (LP, reissue)	12
69	Atco 228 022	THE DOCK OF THE BAY (LP, reissue)	12
69	Atco 228 025	LOVE MAN (LP)	25
70	Atlantic 2464 003	REMEMBERING (LP)	18
71	Atco 2400 018	TELL THE TRUTH (LP)	18
71	Reprise K 40430	LIVE AT THE MONTEREY INTERNATIONAL POP FESTIVAL (LP, shared with Jimi Hendrix)	30

OTIS REDDING & CARLA THOMAS

(see also Carla Thomas)

67	Stax 601 012	Tramp/Oooh Carla, Oooh Otis (with Carla Thomas)	8
67	Stax 601 021	Knock On Wood/Let Me Be Good To You	8
68	Stax 601 033	Lovey Dovey/OTIS REDDING: New Year's Resolution	8
67	Stax 589 007	THE KING AND QUEEN OF SOUL	30

RED DIRT

70	Fontana STL 5540	RED DIRT (LP)	900
10	Morgan Bluetown BT 5004	RED DIRT (LP, reissue, 500 only, signed insert)	25

EMMA REDE

(see also Jacky, Jackie Lee, Jackie & Raindrops, Raindrops)

67	Columbia DB 8136	Just Like A Man/I Gotta Be With You	20

MINT VALUE £

TEDDY REDELL
60 London HLK 9140 — Judy/Can't You See — 60

REDGEE SEEBOE
74 Bug 38 — Please Don't Bring Your Sister/Daphnies Brains — 15

VANESSA REDGRAVE
64 Topic STOP 111 — Hanging On A Tree/Where Have All The Flowers Gone (in title sleeve) — 6

REDHEAD
73 UK UK R 38 — We Ran And We Ran/Lookin' For You — 8

RED HERRING
87 Crystal 717 — Albert Road/Harbour Lights — 30

RED HOT & BLUE
85 Northwood NOR 1 — RED HOT & BLUE (LP) — 25

RED HOT CHILI PEPPERS
85 EMI America EA 205 — Hollywood (Africa)/Never Mind (p/s) — 10
85 EMI America 12EA 205 — Hollywood (Africa) (Remix)/Hollywood (Africa) (Dub Mix)/Never Mind (12", p/s) — 12
88 EMI CDP 790 869-2 — ABBEY ROAD EP (CD) — 8
89 EMI 12MT 70 — KNOCK ME DOWN EP (12", p/s) — 15
89 EMI 12MT 75 — Higher Ground/Catholic Schoolgirls Rule (p/s) — 10
90 EMI 12MTX 85 — TASTE THE PAIN EP (12", push-out sleeve with inner) — 12
90 EMI 10MTX 85 — TASTE THE PAIN EP (square disc, numbered) — 12
90 EMI 12MTG 88 — Higher Ground/Catholic Schoolgirls Rule/None As Weird As Me (12", gatefold sleeve) — 15
90 EMI 12MTPD 88 — Higher Ground/Catholic Schoolgirls Rule/None As Weird As Me (12", picture disc, card insert) — 12
06 Warner Bros 9362499961 — STADIUM ARCADIUM (4-LP box set with foil outer & 2 booklets) — 60
06 Warner Bros 9362443911 — STADIUM ARCADIUM (4-LP, standard edition) — 20

RED HOUSE PAINTERS
94 4AD BAD 4004 — Shock Me/Sundays And Holidays/Three-Leged Cat/Shock Me (12", p/s) — 12
92 4AD CAD 2014 — DOWN COLOURFUL HILL (LP) — 40
93 4AD DAD 3008 — RED HOUSE PAINTERS (2-LP, inner sleeves) — 60
93 4AD CAD 3016 — RED HOUSE PAINTERS (LP, different release from DAD 3008) — 40
95 4A DADD 5005 — OCEAN BEACH (LP, 2 x 10" with inner sleeves) — 40

RED LETTERS
70s Burning Bing CPS 025 — SACRED VOICES EP (p/s) — 50

RED LIGHTS
78 Free Range PF 5 — Never Wanna Leave/Seventeen (p/s) — 60

RED LONDON
83 Razor RZS 105 — Sten Guns In Sunderland/This Is England/Soul Train/Revolution Times (p/s) — 12
84 Razor RAZ 10 — THIS IS ENGLAND (LP) — 30

RED LORRY, YELLOW LORRY
82 Red Rhino RED 20 — Beating My Head/I'm Still Waiting (p/s) — 10
83 Red Rhino RED 28 — Take It All/Happy (p/s) — 5

RED MEAT
72 Worsley WR 1 — She/My Mind Sleeps On (P/S) — 50

ROY REDMOND
67 Warner Bros WB 2075 — Good Day Sunshine/That Old Time Feeling — 15

RED ONION JAZZ BABIES
(see also Louis Armstrong)
60 Collector JE 19 — RED ONION JAZZ BABIES (EP) — 10

JEAN REDPATH
66 Bounty BY 6004 — LOVE LILT AND LAUGHTER (LP) — 20

RED RAGE
80 Flicknife FLS 203 — Total Control/I Give You This (p/s) — 40

RED RIVER BAND
70 Banana BA 35 — I'm Gonna Use What I've Got/Shame Shame — 8

REDS
79 A&M AMS 7454 — Whatcha' Doin' To Me/Not You (p/s, green vinyl) — 5

REDSKINS
82 CNT CNT 007 — Lev Bronstein/The Peasant Army (p/s) — 25
83 CNT CNT 016 — Lean On Me!/Unionize! (p/s) — 7
94 Dojo DOJOCD 188 — REDSKINS LIVE (CD) — 20

RED SQUARES
67 Columbia DB 8160 — Mountain's High/Pity Me — 20
67 Columbia DB 8257 — True Love Story/Lollipop — 12

RED TELEVISION
71 Brecht Times — RED TELEVISION (LP, private pressing with insert) — 120

REDUCERS
78 Vibes XP 1/VR 001 — Things Go Wrong/We Are Normal (p/s) — 50
79 Vibes VR 003 — Man With A Gun/Vengeance/Can't Stop Now (p/s) — 50

MIKE REDWAY
(see also Rod McKuen, Typhoons, Bud Ashton)
64 Oriole CB 1948 — Many People/It's So Funny I Could Cry — 8
65 CBS 201755 — Darling Take Me Back/That's The Way Love Goes — 5
65 CBS 202017 — Magic Rocking Chair/When You Go — 8
66 CBS 202092 — One Day/Let Me Be The Someone — 5

Mike REDWAY

			MINT VALUE £
67	Deram DM 124	Have No Fear, Bond Is Here (Casino Royale)/My Poem For You	10
67	Deram DM 157	Don't Speak Of Me/Sometimes I Remember	5
69	RCA 1873	Through The Eyes Of Love/Love Me	6

REDWOODS

62	Columbia DB 4859	Please Mr Scientist/Where You Used To Be	25

DIZZY REECE QUINTET

(see also Victor Feldman, Ronnie Scott)

56	Tempo A 140	Chorus/Basie Line	6
58	Tempo EXA 84	A VARIATION ON MONK (EP)	150
59	Tempo EXA 86	NOWHERE TO GO (EP, featuring Tubby Hayes)	150
59	Tempo EXA 89	ON THE SCENE (EP)	50
55	Tempo LAP 3	A NEW STAR? (10" LP)	200
57	Tempo TAP 9	PROGRESS REPORT (LP)	450
58	Esquire 32 185	ASIA MINOR (LP)	100
80s	Jasmine JASM 2013	PROGRESS REPORT (LP, reissue)	18

CHUCK REED

57	Brunswick 05646	Whispering Heart/Another Love Has Ended	15
58	Columbia DB 4113	No School Tomorrow/Let's Put Our Hearts Together	30
62	Stateside SS 108	Just Plain Hurt/Talking No Trash	15

DEAN REED

59	Capitol CL 14986	The Search/Annabelle	10
59	Capitol CL 15030	I Kissed A Queen/A Pair Of Scissors (And A Pot Of Glue)	10

DENNY REED

61	London HLK 9274	A Teenager Feels It Too/Hot Water	18

JERRY REED

58	Capitol CL 14851	Bessie Baby/Too Young To Be Blue	275
58	Capitol CL 14851	Bessie Baby/Too Young To Be Blue (78)	65
69	RCA RCA 1798	Oh What A Woman/Claw	7
70	RCA RCA 2025	Georgia Sunshine/Singing '69	5
71	RCA RCA 2063	Amos Moses/The Preacher And The Bear	5
69	RCA SF 8006	ALABAMA WILD MAN (LP)	18

JIMMY REED

60	Top Rank JAR 333	Baby What You Want Me To Do/Caress Me Baby	22
60	Top Rank JAR 394	Found Love/Where Can You Be	20
60	Top Rank JAR 533	Hush-Hush/Going By The River	20
63	Stateside SS 205	Shame Shame Shame/Let's Get Together	20
64	Stateside SS 330	Shame Shame Shame/Let's Get Together (reissue)	12
66	Sue WI 4004	Odds And Ends/Going By The River Pt. II (B-side actually Pt. I)	40
67	HMV POP 1579	Two Ways To Skin A Cat/Got Nowhere To Go	20
64	Stateside SE 1016	BLUES OF JIMMY REED (EP)	40
64	Stateside SE 1026	I'M JIMMY REED (EP)	40
62	Stateside SL 10012	JIMMY REED AT CARNEGIE HALL (LP)	30
64	Stateside SL 10055	JUST JIMMY REED (LP)	40
64	Stateside SL 10069	SINGS THE BEST OF THE BLUES (LP)	30
64	Stateside SL 10086	PLAYS 12-STRING GUITAR BLUES (LP)	30
64	Stateside SL 10091	THE BOSS MAN OF THE BLUES (LP)	40
65	Fontana 688 514 ZL	THINGS AIN'T WHAT THEY USED TO BE (LP)	30
67	HMV CLP/CSD 3611	THE NEW JIMMY REED (LP)	30
68	Stateside S(S)L 10221	SOULIN' (LP)	30
69	Action ACLP 6011	DOWN IN VIRGINIA (LP)	60

JOE REED

71	Dawn DNS 1012	Ain't That A Shame/Follow Me	6

LES REED

(see also Sounds of Les & Barry)

67	Deram DM 128	Imogene/Pay Off	10

LOU REED

(see also Velvet Underground)

72	RCA RCA 2240	Walk And Talk It/Wild Child	8
72	RCA RCA 2303	Walk On The Wild Side/Perfect Day	5
73	RCA RCA 2318	Vicious/Satellite Of Love	5
73	MGM 2006 283	I'm Waiting For The Man/Run Run Run/Candy Says (with Velvet Underground)	8
74	RCA APBO 0221	Caroline Says (Parts 1 & 2)	5
74	RCA APBO 0238	Sweet Jane/Lady Day	5
74	RCA RCA 2467	Sally Can't Dance/Ennui	5
76	RCA RCA 2666	Charley's Girl/Nowhere At All	5
72	RCA SF 8281	LOU REED (LP, orange label)	15
72	RCA LSP 4807	TRANSFORMER (LP)	12
73	RCA RS 1002	BERLIN (LP, orange label with insert)	12
75	RCA CPL 2 1101	METAL MACHINE MUSIC (2-LP, U.S. import with U.K. sticker)	35

LULA REED

55	Parlophone CMSP 34	Troubles On Your Mind/Bump On A Log (export issue)	60
55	Parlophone DP 408	Troubles On Your Mind/Bump On A Log (78, export issue)	15

LULA REED & SYL JOHNSON

63	Ember EMB EP 4535	RHYTHM & BLUES BLUE BEAT STYLE (EP)	70

LULA REED & FREDDIE KING

(see also Freddie King)

63	Ember EMB 4536	LULA REED AND FREDDIE KING (EP)	50

OLIVER REED

61	Decca F 11390	The Wild One/Lonely For A Girl	30
62	Piccadilly 7N 35037	Sometimes/Ecstasy	20

MINT VALUE £

TAWNY REED

65	Pye 7N 15935	Needle In A Haystack/I've Got A Feeling	50
66	Pye 7N 17078	You Can't Take It Away/My Heart Cries	30

VIVIEN REED

68	Direction 58-3574	I Wanna Be Free/Yours Until Tomorrow	8

WINSTON REED

72	Pama Supreme PS 365	Breakfast In Bed/RANNY WILLIAMS: Guitar Shuffle	7
73	Pama PM 863	Big Eight/RANNY WILLIAMS & CLASSICS: Big Eight - Version	7

WINSTON REEDY

83	Carousel 12CAR 48	Dim The Light/Shower Of Rain (12")	20
82	SG SG 17	Daughter Of Zion/Zion Dub (12")	30

VALA REEGAN & VALARONS

66	Atlantic 584 009	Fireman/Living In The Past	200
66	Atlantic 584 009	Fireman/Living In The Past (DJ copy)	300

TONY REES & COTTAGERS

75	Sonet SON 2059	Viva El Fulham/Rainbow	7

DELLA REESE

57	London HL 7024	I Cried For You (Now It's Your Turn To Cry Over Me)/ And That Reminds Me (export issue)	15
58	London HLJ 8687	You Gotta Love Everybody/I Wish	15
59	London HLJ 8814	Sermonette/Dreams End At Dawn	15
59	RCA RCA 1160	Not One Minute More/Soldier Won't You Marry Me	7
66	HMV POP 1553	It Was A Very Good Year/Solitary Woman	30
66	HMV POP 1553	It Was A Very Good Year/Solitary Woman (DJ Copy)	35
68	Stateside SS 2128	It Was A Very Good Year/I Had To Know My Way Around	20
68	Stateside SS 2128	It Was A Very Good Year/I Had To Know My Way Around (DJ Copy)	25
72	Avco Embassy 6105 010	If It Feels Good, Do It/Good Lovin' (Makes It Right) (paper label)	10
74	People PEO 106	Who Is She And What Is She To You/If Loving You Is Wrong	6
59	London LTZ-J 15163	THE HISTORY OF THE BLUES (LP)	30
60	RCA RD 27167/SF 5057	DELLA (LP)	15
61	RCA RD 27208/SF 5091	DELLA DELLA CHA-CHA-CHA (LP)	18
62	RCA RD 27234/SF 5112	SPECIAL DELIVERY (LP)	20
63	RCA Victor RD/SF 7508	ON STAGE (LP)	15
74	People PLEO 7	LET ME IN YOUR LIFE (LP)	30

TONY REESE

59	London HLJ 8987	Just About This Time Tomorrow/Lesson In Love	25
59	London HLJ 8987	Just About This Time Tomorrow/Lesson In Love (78)	12

DEL REEVES

65	United Artists UP 1092	Girl On The Billboard/Eyes Don't Come Crying To Me	7
66	United Artists UP 1122	Women Do Funny Things To Me/My Half Of Our Past	7
66	United Artists UP 1145	Gettin' Any Feed For Your Chickens/Plain As The Tears On My Face	7

EDDIE REEVES

62	London HL 9548	Cry Baby/Talk Talk	20

JIM REEVES

78s

54	London HL 8014	Bimbo/Gipsy Heart	20
54	London HL 8030	Mexican Joe/I Could Cry (with Circle O Ranch Boys)	25
54	London HL 8055	Butterfly Love/It's Hard To Love Just One (with String Band)	30
54	London HL 8064	Echo Bonita/Then I'll Stop Loving You (with Louisiana Hayride Band)	30
54	London HL 8105	Padre Of Old San Antone/Mother Went A-Walkin'	30
55	London HL 8118	Penny Candy/I'll Follow You (with Louisiana Hayride Band)	30
55	London HL 8159	Drinking Tequila/Red-Eyed And Rowdy	35
55	London HLU 8185	Tahiti/Give Me One More Kiss	30
56	London HLU 8351	The Wilder Your Heart Beats, The Sweeter You Love/ Where Does A Broken Heart Go	30
57	RCA RCA 1005	Four Walls/I Know And You Know	20
58	RCA RCA 1074	Blue Boy/Theme Of Love	25
59	RCA RCA 1144	Partners/I'm Beginning To Forget You	45
60	RCA RCA 1168	He'll Have To Go/In A Mansion Stands My Love	60

SINGLES

54	London HL 8014	Bimbo/Gipsy Heart	200
54	London HL 8030	Mexican Joe/I Could Cry (with Circle O Ranch Boys)	200
54	London HL 8055	Butterfly Love/It's Hard To Love Just One (with String Band)	200
54	London HL 8064	Echo Bonita/Then I'll Stop Loving You (with Louisiana Hayride Band)	200
54	London HL 8105	Padre Of Old San Antone/Mother Went A-Walkin'	150
55	London HL 8118	Penny Candy/I'll Follow You (with Louisiana Hayride Band)	150
55	London HLU 8185	Tahiti/Give Me One More Kiss	150
55	London HL 8159	Drinking Tequila/Red-Eyed And Rowdy	250

(All of the above 45s were Issued with gold label print)

56	London HLU 8351	The Wilder Your Heart Beats, The Sweeter You Love/ Where Does A Broken Heart Go	180
57	RCA RCA 1005	Four Walls/I Know And You Know	30
58	RCA RCA 1074	Blue Boy/Theme Of Love	20
59	RCA RCA 1144	Partners/I'm Beginning To Forget You (triangular or round centre)	20

EPs/LPs

54	London RE-P 1015	THE BIMBO BOY (EP)	100
55	London RE-P 1033	THE BIMBO VOL. 2 (EP)	100
60	RCA RD 27176	HE'LL HAVE TO GO (LP)	15
61	RCA RD 27193	THE INTIMATE JIM REEVES (LP, also stereo SF 5079)	15
62	London HA-U 8015	BIMBO (LP)	20

(All the above LPs were originally issued with black labels, later orange label reissues are worth around £3 each.)

MINT VALUE £

MARTHA REEVES & VANDELLAS
(see under Martha & Vandellas)

REFLECTION
(see also Sounds Of Salvation)

68	Reflection RL 3015	THE PRESENT TENSE: SONGS OF SYDNEY CARTER (LP)	18

REFLECTIONS (U.K.)

74	Purple PUR 124	Love And Affection/No More	7
75	Purple PUR 127	Moon Power/Little Star	7

REFLECTIONS (U.S.)
(see also The High and Mighty)

64	Stateside SS 294	(Just Like) Romeo & Juliet/Can't You Tell By The Look In My Eyes	60
64	Stateside SS 294	(Just Like) Romeo & Juliet/Can't You Tell By The Look In My Eyes (DJ copy)	100
65	Stateside SS 406	Poor Man's Son/Comin' At You	30
74	Tamla Motown TMG 907	(Just Like) Romeo & Juliet/Can't You Tell By The Look In My Eyes (reissue)	15
77	ABC ABC 4181	Like Adam And Eve/AUGUST & DENEEN: We Go Together	15
65	Stateside SE 1034	POOR MAN'S SON (EP)	100

REFLECTIONS A.O.B.

86	Keep KEEP 1 12	ONLY IN MY DREAMS EP (12")	40

REFUGEE
(see also Nice, Yes)

74	Charisma CAS 1087	REFUGEE (LP, with lyric inner sleeve, large 'Mad Hatter' label)	20

REGAL DEWY

78	RCA XB 1032	Love Music/Where Would I Be Without Me	8

JOAN REGAN
(see also Edmund Hockridge)

54	Decca F 10362	Wait For Me, Darling (with Johnston Brothers)/Two Kinds Of Tears (gold lettering)	30
54	Decca F 10362	Wait For Me, Darling (with Johnston Brothers)/Two Kinds Of Tears (silver lettering)	20
54	Decca F 10373	If I Give My Heart To You/Faded Flowers	15
54	Decca F 10397	This Ole House/Can This Be Love?	15
55	Decca F 10432	Prize Of Gold/When You're In Love	12
55	Decca F 10474	Open Up Your Heart And Let The Love In (with Rusty Regan)/ If You Learn To Love Each Other	12
55	Decca F 10505	Danger! Heartbreak Ahead/Don't Be Afraid Of Love	12
55	Decca F 10521	Just Say You Love Her/Nobody Danced With Me	12
55	Decca F 10598	The Shepherd Boy/The Rose And The Flame	10
56	Decca F 10659	Love And Marriage/Cross Of Gold (Croce Di Oro)	10
59	HMV POP 593	May You Always/Have You Ever Been Lonely	7
60	Pye Nixa 7n 15238	Happy Anniversary/So Close To My Heart	7
60	Pye 7N 15278	Papa Loves Mama/When You Know Somebody Loves You	7
60	Pye 7N 15303	Must Be Santa/Will Santa Come To Shanty Town	7
60	Pye 7N 15310	One Of The Lucky Ones/My Thanks to You	15
61	Pye 7N 15367	We Who Are In Love/My Foolish Heart	5
61	Pye 7N 15400	Surprisin'/In The Arms Of My Love (some with p/s)	8
66	CBS 202100	Don't Talk To Me About Love/I'm No Toy	20
66	CBS 202100	Don't Talk To Me About Love/I'm No Toy (DJ copy)	35
67	CBS 2657	No-One Beside Me/A Love So Fine	20
55	Decca DFE 6235	JOAN REGAN SUCCESSES (EP)	10
56	Decca DFE 6278	JOAN REGAN SUCCESSES VOL. 2 (EP)	10
54	Decca LF 1182	THE GIRL NEXT DOOR (10" LP)	40
56	Decca LK 4153	JUST JOAN (LP)	60
60	Pye NPL 18048	JOAN AND TED (LP, with Edmund Hockridge)	20

RUSS REGAN

59	Capitol CL 15084	Adults Only/Just The Two Of Us	10

TOMMY REGAN
(see also Marcels)

64	Colpix PX 725	I'll Never Stop Loving You/This Time I'm Losing You	100

REGENTS (U.K.)
(see also Buddy Britten)

63	Oriole CB 1912	Bye Bye Johnny/Come Along	40

REGENTS (U.K.)

66	CBS 202247	Words/Worryin' Kind	45

REGENTS (U.K.)

79	Rialto TREB 111	7 Teen (Uncensored Version)/Hole In The Heart (p/s)	6

REGENTS (U.S.)

61	Columbia DB 4666	Barbara Ann/I'm So Lonely	30
61	Columbia DB 4694	Runaround/Laura My Darling	28

REGGAE BOYS
(see also Glen Adams, Alva Lewis, Upsetters)

69	Amalgamated AMG 841	Me No Born Ya/The Wicked Must Survive	30
69	Amalgamated AMG 843	The Reggae Train/Dolly House On Fire	30
69	Gas GAS 135	Ba Ba/GLEN ADAMS: Power Cut	20
69	Unity UN 530	What You Gonna Do/HEDLEY BENNETT: Hot Coffee	70
70	Bullet BU 431	Pupa Live On Eye Top/Give Me Faith	35
70	Gas GAS 122	Phrases/Give Me Faith	45
70	Upsetter US 339	Hurry Up/Thanks We Get	20
70	Pressure Beat PR 5503	Walk By Day, Fly By Night/JOE GIBBS & DESTROYERS: Unknown Tongue	20

REGGAE GEORGE

83	Greensleeves GRED 114	You'll Never Know/We Still Survive (12")	15

MINT VALUE £

REGGAE GIRLS

69 Nu Beat NB 024 — Rescue Me/SOULMATES: Unity Is Strength 18

REGGAE REGULAR

77 Greensleeves GRE 001 — Where Is Jah?/Jah Is Here 6
78 Greensleeves GRE 004 — The Black Star Liner/It's Coming 6
78 Greensleeves GRED 2 — The Black Star Liner/Where Is Jah? (12") 10
82 Greensleeves GRED 83 — House Party (with Clint Eastwood)/Dub Party (12") 8

REGGAE STRINGS

(see also Horace Faith)
73 Trojan TRLS 54 — REGGAE STRINGS (LP) 15

LOU REICHNER BAND

80 ESR S/80/CUS 733 — Photograph/I Sit And Stare/The End Of The World/Out On The Streets (also listed as ESR 4, 300 only, with insert) 50
80 ESR S/80/CUS 733 — Photograph/I Sit And Stare/The End Of The World/Out On The Streets (also listed as ESR 4, 300 only, without insert) 20

AL REID

69 Blue Cat BS 161 — Vietcong/MAX ROMEO: Me Want Man 40
69 Blue Cat BS 163 — Darling/MAX ROMEO: It's Not The Way 50

ALTYMAN REID

(see also Roy Shirley)
72 Green Door GD 4026 — A Sugar/A Sugar Part Two (with Roy Shirley) 7

CARLTON REID

66 Ska Beat JB 254 — Funny/Turn On The Lights 18
69 Blue Cat BS 162 — Leave Me To Cry/Warning 100

DENNIS REID

77 Greensleeves GRE 6 — Land Of The Rising Sun/DENNIS REID & REVOLUTIONARIES: Rising Sun Version 8

DUKE REID (& HIS GROUP)

(see also Chuck & Darby, Derrick Morris, Stranger)
60 Blue Beat BB 24 — Duke's Cookies (with His Group)/JIVING JUNIORS: I Wanna Love 20
62 Blue Beat BB 119 — Twelve Minutes To Go (actually by Don Drummond)/HORTENSE ELLIS: Midnight Train 30
63 Duke DK 1002 — Pink Lane Shuffle (with His Group)/LAUREL AITKEN: Low Down Dirty Girl 20
67 Master's Time MT 003 — Religious Service At Bond Street Gospel Hall/Religious Service At Bond Street Gospel Hall (Continued) 15
67 Trojan TR 001 — Judge Sympathy (actually by Freedom Singers & Duke Reid All Stars)/ROLAND ALPHONSO: Never To Be Mine 45
60s Doctor Bird DB 1028 — True Confessions/TOMMY McCCOOK: More Love 35
72 Duke Reid DR 2522 — Hurt Parts 1 & 2 (actually by Eagles [Jamaica]) 15

LEYROY REID

(see also Nehemiah Reed)
68 Blue Cat BS 125 — The Fiddler/LOVELETTES: Shook 30
68 Blue Cat BS 127 — Great Surprise/TEN(N)ORS: Khaki 30

MARC REID

66 CBS 202244 — For No One/Lonely City Blues 15
67 CBS 202581 — Magic Book/My World Turns Around 15
67 CBS 2950 — We Should Live Together/Sale By Auction 15

NEHEMIAH REID

(see also Leyroy Reid, Cynthia Richards)
68 Island WI 3102 — Family War/Give Me That Love 18
70 Hot Shot HS 03 — Hot Pepper/Seawave (as Nehemiah Reid's All Stars) 20
70s Torpedo TOR 23 — Mafia/H.E.L.L. 5 (as Nehemiah Reid's All Stars) 12

NORVELLE REID

57 Brunswick 05725 — All The Way/The World Won't End (export issue) 5

P. REID

65 Ska Beat JB 197 — Redeemed/Goodbye World 18

PATTI REID

87 Fellside FE 061 — PATTI REID (LP) 12

TERRY REID (& JAYWALKERS)

(see also Peter Jay & Jaywalkers)
67 Columbia DB 8166 — The Hand Don't Fit The Glove/This Time (as Terry Reid & Jaywalkers) 12
68 Columbia DB 8409 — Better By Far/Fires Alive 18
69 Columbia PSRS 323 — Superlungs (promo only, as "Terry Reid Is Superlungs") 25
76 ABC 4137 — Oooh Baby/Brave Awakening 5
79 Capitol CL 16071 — Ain't No Shadow/Bowangi 5
69 Columbia SCX 6370 — TERRY REID (LP, laminated front, flipbacks) 50
71 M. For Pleasure MFP 5220 — THE MOST OF TERRY REID (LP) 12
73 Atlantic K 40340 — RIVER (LP, gatefold sleeve) 20
76 ABC ABCL 5162 — SEED OF MEMORY (LP) 12

REIGN

(see also Yardbirds, Keith Relf, Renaissance, Armageddon, Illusion)
70 Regal Zonophone RZ 3028 — Line Of Least Resistance/Natural Lovin' Man 60

JOHN REILLY

78 Topic 12T 359 — THE BONNY GREEN TREE (LP, with booklet) 12

TOMMY REILLY

60 Philips PB 1094 — Theme From "The Sundowners"/Down Under 7
63 Philips PB 1248 — So Little Time/Moon Fire 6

MINT VALUE £

REINCARNATE
82 Zipp REIN 001 Take It Or Leave It/Metal In Disguise ... 70

DJANGO REINHARDT
(see also Quintet Of Hot Club Of France)
54 Oriole/Mercury MG 10019 DJANGO (10" LP) ... 12
54 Vogue LDE 049 DJANGO REINHARDT VOL. 1 (10" LP) ... 12
54 Vogue LDE 084 DJANGO REINHARDT VOL. 2 (10" LP) ... 12
54 Vogue LDE 106 DJANGO REINHARDT VOL. 3 (10" LP, as Django Reinhardt Quintet) ... 12
54 HMV DLP 1045 DJANGO REINHARDT (10" LP) ... 12
54 Felsted EDL 87005 NUAGES (10" LP, as Django Reinhardt & His Rhythm) ... 12
59 HMV CLP 1249 DJANGO (LP) ... 12

JOE REISMAN ORCHESTRA
56 HMV 7M 364 Robin Hood/His Name Was Judas ... 5
60 Columbia DB 4553 The World Of Suzi Wong (Theme)/Melodie D'Amour ... 5
61 Pye International 7N 25087 The Guns Of Navarone/Yassu ... 5

LOU REIZNER
69 Phillips On Days Like This/Get A Bloomin' Move On ... 15

REJOICE!
69 Stateside SS 8010 November Snow/Quick Draw Man ... 5
69 Stateside S(S)L 5009 REJOICE! (LP) ... 20

BOB RELF
(see also Bob & Earl)
75 Black Magic BM 101 Blowin' My Mind To Pieces/PAULA RUSSELL: Blowin' My Mind To Pieces ... 5

JANE RELF
(see also Stairway, Renaissance, Gordon Jackson)
71 Decca F 13231 Without A Song From You/Make My Time Pass By ... 30
Findus Frozen Foods SD/DS/7001 Gone Fishing/Gordon Jackson - Hints From The Findus Kitchen (p/s) ... 10

KEITH RELF
(see also Yardbirds, Jim McCarty, Renaissance, Reign, Together, Armageddon)
66 Columbia DB 7920 Mr. Zero/Knowing ... 50
66 Columbia DB 8084 Shapes In My Mind/Blue Sands ... 55

RELIGIOUS OVERDOSE
80 Glass GLASS 004 Control Addicts/25 Minutes (p/s with green label) ... 5

RELOAD
(see also Global Communications, Link, Mystic Institute)
92 Evolution EVO 01 RELOAD EP (12", plain sleeve) ... 20
92 Evolution EVO 02 AUTO RELOAD EP (12", with E 621) ... 30
92 Evolution EVO 03 RELOAD EP (12", 1-side credited to E 621) ... 40
93 Infonet INF 13 AUTO RELOAD EP VOLUME 2 (12", p/s) ... 10
93 Infonet INF 04LP A COLLECTION OF SHORT STORIES (2-LP, with colour booklet) ... 50
93 Infonet INF 04LP A COLLECTION OF SHORT STORIES (2-LP) ... 40
93 Infonet INF 04CD A COLLECTION OF SHORT STORIES (CD, with colour booklet) ... 18
95 Surreal Sound TAPE 2 THE BIOSPHERE (cassette, free with initial copies of 'Surreal Sound' magazine) ... 15

R.E.M.
(see also Full Time Men, Syd Straw)

I.R.S. SINGLES
83 I.R.S. PFP 1017 Radio Free Europe/There She Goes Again (p/s) ... 50
83 I.R.S. PFSX 1026 Talk About The Passion/Shaking Through/Carnival Of Sorts (Box Cars)/ 1,000,000 (12", p/s) ... 15
84 I.R.S. IRS 105 S. Central Rain (I'm Sorry)/King Of The Road (p/s) ... 8
84 I.R.S. IRSX 105 S. Central Rain (I'm Sorry)/Voice Of Harold/Pale Blue Eyes (12", p/s) ... 12
84 I.R.S. IRS 107 (Don't Go Back To) Rockville/Wolves (Lower) (p/s) ... 8
84 I.R.S. IRSX 107 (Don't Go Back To) Rockville/Wolves/9 - 9 (Live Version)/ Gardening At Night (live) (12", p/s) ... 12
85 I.R.S. IRM 102 Can't Get There From Here/Bandwagon (p/s) ... 8
85 I.R.S. IRT 102 Can't Get There From Here (sleeve states 'Extended Mix', label states 'LP Version', but actually 3.39 edit)/Bandwagon/Burning Hell (12", p/s, with printed banner crediting unissued tracks) ... 15
85 I.R.S. IRT 102 Can't Get There From Here (sleeve states 'Extended Mix', label states 'LP Version', but actually 3.39 edit)/Bandwagon/Burning Hell (12", p/s) .. 8
85 I.R.S. IRM 105 Wendell Gee/Crazy (p/s) ... 10
85 I.R.S. IRMD 105 Wendell Gee/Crazy//Ages Of You/Burning Down (double pack) ... 12
85 I.R.S. IRT 105 Wendell Gee/Crazy/Driver 8 (live) (12", p/s) ... 10
86 I.R.S. IRM 121 Fall On Me/Rotary Ten (p/s, blue, gold or silver label) ... 8
86 I.R.S. IRMT 121 Fall On Me/Rotary Ten/Toys In The Attic (12", p/s) ... 10
86 I.R.S. IRM 128 Superman/White Tornado (p/s, gold or silver label) ... 10
86 I.R.S. IRMT 128 Superman/White Tornado/Femme Fatale (12", p/s) ... 10
86 I.R.S. DIRM 128 Superman/White Tornado/Femme Fatale (CD, unissued) ... 0
87 I.R.S. IRM 145 It's The End Of The World As We Know It (And I Feel Fine) (2.59 edit)/ This One Goes Out (live) (p/s, gold or metallic blue label) ... 8
87 I.R.S. IRMT 145 It's The End Of The World As We Know It (And I Feel Fine)/ This One Goes Out (live)/Maps And Legends (live) (12", p/s) ... 8
87 I.R.S. IRM 146 The One I Love/Last Date (bronze label, glossy p/s; silver label, matt p/s) ... 8
87 I.R.S. IRMT 146 The One I Love/Last Date/Disturbance At The Heron House (live) (12", p/s) ... 8
87 I.R.S. DIRM 146 The One I Love/Last Date/Disturbance At The Heron House (live) (CD) ... 8
88 I.R.S. DIRM 161 Finest Worksong (LP Version)/Time After Time, Etc. (live)/ It's The End Of The World As We Know It (And I Feel Fine) (CD, numbered stencilled 7" box, 5,000 only) ... 15
88 I.R.S. IRM161 Finest Worksong/Time After Time Etc live (p/s) ... 8
88 I.R.S. IRMT161 Finest Worksong Lengthy Club Mix/Other Mix/Time After Time Etc medley (12", p/s) . 10

			MINT VALUE £
88	I.R.S. IRM173	The One I Love /Fall On Me (p/s)	8
88	I.R.S. IRMT173	The One I Love/Fall On Me/So. Central Rain (12", p/s)	10
88	I.R.S. DIRM173	The One I Love/Fall On Me/So. Central Rain (CD)	15
91	I.R.S. DIRMX178	The One I Love/Driver Eight (Live)/Disturbance At The Heron House (Live)/Crazy (CD)	10
91	I.R.S. DIRMT 178	The One I Love/This One Goes Out (live)/Maps And Legends (CD, with 10-page insert)	10
91	I.R.S. DIRMX 180	It's The End Of The World As We Know It (And I Feel Fine)/ Radio Free Europe (Hib-Tone Version)/Last Date/White Tornado (CD, withdrawn)	8
92	I.R.S. DIRM 180	It's The End Of The World As We Know It (And I Feel Fine)/ Radio Free Europe (Hib-Tone Version) (gold or silver labels, p/s, with Album version of 'Radio Free Europe')	8
92	I.R.S. DIRM 180	It's The End Of The World As We Know It (And I Feel Fine)/ Radio Free Europe (Hib-Tone Version) (gold or silver labels, p/s)	5

WARNER BROTHERS SINGLES

89	Warner Bros W 7577X	Stand/Memphis Train Blues (recycled paper p/s)	5
89	Warner Bros W 7577CD	Stand/Memphis Train Blues/(The Eleventh Untitled Song) (3" CD, card sleeve)	10
89	Warner Bros W 7577CDX	Stand/Memphis Train Blues/(The Eleventh Untitled Song) (3" CD, 'maple-leaf' pack)	15
89	Warner Bros W 2960X	Orange Crush/Ghost Riders (recycled paper p/s)	5
89	Warner Bros W 2960B	Orange Crush/Ghost Riders ('The Green Package' box set with poster)	8
89	Warner Bros W 2960CD	Orange Crush/Ghost Riders/Dark Globe (3" CD, gatefold card sleeve)	15
89	Warner Bros W 2833W	Stand/Pop Song '89 (Acoustic) (stencil die-cut p/s)	15
89	Warner Bros W 2833CD	Stand/Pop Song '89 (Acoustic)/Skin Tight (live) (3" CD, gatefold card sleeve)	15
89	Warner Bros W 2833CDX	Stand/Pop Song '89 (Acoustic)/Skin Tight (live) (3" CD, black die-cut sleeve in Velcro seal envelope)	15
91	Warner Bros W0015CDX	Losing My Religion/Stand (live)/Turn You Inside-Out (live)/ World Leader Pretend (live) (CD, with fold-out poster)	10
91	Warner Bros W0072CDX	Radio Song (CD in 'Out Of Time' collectors box set)	10
91	Warner Bros W 0143 CDX	Man On The Moon/Fruity Organ/New Orleans Instrumental #2/ Arms Of Love (Collectors Edition)	8
93	Warner Bros W0184TP	Nightswimming (12" picture disc)	8
95	Warner Bros W0281X	Crush With Eyeliner (p/s, orange vinyl + calendar)	8
95	Warner Bros W0290X	Strange Currencies/Strange Currencies Instrumental (p/s, Dayglo yellow/green vinyl + pin badge)	8
95	Warner Bros W0308X	Tongue/Instrumental (numbered tour booklet p/s)	8

FLEXIDISCS & OTHER RELEASES

85	Bucketfull Of Brains BOB 5	Tighten Up (flexidisc [LYN 15742] with Bucketfull Of Brains magazine)	15
85	Bucketfull Of Brains BOB 5	Tighten Up (hard vinyl test pressing, 50 only)	50
92	Lyntone BOB 32	Academy Fight Song (live)/COAL PORTERS: Watching Blue Grass Burn (p/s, free with Bucketfull Of Brains magazine, double issue 39/40)	8
92	Lyntone BOB 32	Academy Fight Song (live)/COAL PORTERS: Watching Blue Grass Burn (white label test pressing)	10

PROMOS

83	I.R.S. PFP 1026	Talk About The Passion/Talk About The Passion (plain sleeve, promo only)	30
88	I.R.S. WIRM(T) 161 DL	Finest Worksong (Lengthy Club Mix)/Finest Worksong (Other Mix)/ Time After Time Etc. (12" in 'media' p/s)	20
92	I.R.S. CDREM 92	THE ALTERNATIVE RADIO SAMPLER (CD, 7-track promo, includes unreleased version of 'Gardening At Night')	60
92	Warner Bros REM 1	SAMPLER FROM THE BEST OF REM (CD, Brit Awards nomination issue)	25
03	Warners PR 04359	THE BEST OF REM - IN TIME 1980-2003 (promo box set containing 18 1-track CDs each housed in individual card sleeve in flip top box)	60

REMA-REMA

(see also Adam & The Ants, Mass, Models, Wolfgang Press)

80	4AD BAD 5	WHEEL IN THE ROSES: Feedback Song/Rema-Ream/Instrumental/ Fond Affections (12" EP, original pressing with blue labels)	20
80	4AD BAD 5	WHEEL IN THE ROSES: Feedback Song/Rema-Ream/Instrumental/ Fond Affections (12" EP)	15

REMAYNS

85	Bam Caruso NRIC 029	FIRST (EP, coloured vinyl)	5

HERBIE REMINGTON

66	Fontana FJL 313	REMINGTON RIDES AGAIN (LP)	15

REMO FOUR

(see also Tommy Quickly, Johnny Sandon, Gregory Phillips, Ashton Gardner & Dyke, Mike Hurst, George Harrison)

64	Piccadilly 7N 35175	I Wish I Could Shimmy Like My Sister Kate/Peter Gunn	25
64	Piccadilly 7N 35186	Sally Go Round The Roses/I Know A Girl	25
67	Fontana TF 787	Live Like A Lady/Sing Hallelujah	70

RENAISSANCE (U.K.)

(see also Jim McCarty, Keith Relf, Jane Relf, Yardbirds, Rupert's People, Reign, Stairway)

70	Island WIP 6079	Island/The Sea	15
75	Warner Bros. K 17177	Northern Lights/Opening Out	5
78	Sire SRE 1022	Northern Lights/Opening Out (picture disc, export issue)	15
79	Sire SIR 4019	Jekyll And Hyde/Forever Changing (withdrawn)	15
69	Island ILPS 9114	RENAISSANCE (LP, gatefold, pink label with white 'i' logo)	30
71	Island HELP 27	ILLUSION (LP, withdrawn, export only, black labeil with pink 'i' logo)	40
72	Sovereign SVNA 7253	PROLOGUE (LP, gatefold sleeve)	12
73	Sovereign SVNA 7261	ASHES ARE BURNING (LP)	12

RENAISSANCE (U.S.)

68	Polydor BM 56736	Mary Jane (Get Off The Devil's Merry-Go-Round)/Daytime Lovers	35

RENAULTS

60	Warner Bros WB 11	Meloncolie/Stella	7

DIANE RENAY

(see also Laura Greene)

64	Stateside SS 270	Navy Blue/Unbelievable Guy	15
64	Stateside SS 290	Kiss Me Sailor/Soft Spoken Guy	15

MINT VALUE £

64 MGM MGM 1262 — Watch Out Sally/Billy Blue Eyes ... 25
65 MGM MGM 1274 — Troublemaker/I Had A Dream ... 25

JOHN RENBOURN

(see also Pentangle, Bert Jansch & John Renbourn, Steve Tilston, Dorris Henderson)

65 Transatlantic TRA 135 — JOHN RENBOURN (LP) ... 30
66 Transatlantic TRA 149 — ANOTHER MONDAY (LP) ... 25
68 Transatlantic TRA 167 — SIR JOHN ALOT OF MERRIE ENGLANDE'S MUSICK THYNGE AND YE GREENE KNIGHT (LP) ... 20
70 Transatlantic TRA 224 — THE LADY AND THE UNICORN (LP) ... 18
72 Transatlantic TRA 247 — FARO ANNIE (LP) ... 20
73 Transatlantic TRA 336 — THE HERMIT (LP) ... 15
73 Transatlantic TRASAM 20 — THE JOHN RENBOURN SAMPLER (LP) ... 12
73 Transatlantic TRASAM 28 — SO CLEAR - THE JOHN RENBOURN SAMPLER VOL. 2 (LP) ... 15

JOHN RENBOURN & STEFAN GROSSMAN

(see also Stefan Grossman)

70s Kicking Mule SNKF 139 — JOHN RENBOURN & STEFAN GROSSMAN (LP) ... 12
70s Kicking Mule SNKF 161 — UNDER THE VOLCANO (LP) ... 12

JOHN RENBOURN'S SHIP OF FOOLS

88 Run River 009 — SHIP OF FOOLS (LP) ... 20

DON RENDELL

55 Tempo A 108 — Muskrat Ramble/Thames Walk ... 25
55 Tempo A 108 — Muskrat Ramble/Thames Walk (78, as Don Rendell Sextet) ... 10
55 Tempo A 110 — You Stepped Out Of A Dream/Slow Boat To China (78, as Don Rendell Quartet) . 10
55 Tempo A 112 — Didn't We/Dance Of The Ooblies (78, as Don Rendell Sextet) ... 10
55 Tempo A 114 — From This Moment On/Blow Mr. Dexter (78, as Don Rendell Quartet) ... 10
55 Tempo EXA 11 — DON RENDELL QUARTET (EP) ... 50
55 Tempo EXA 12 — DON RENDELL SEXTET (EP) ... 30
55 Tempo EXA 16 — DON RENDELL SEXTET/DAMIAN ROBINSON TRIO (EP, 2 tracks each) ... 50
55 Tempo EXA 20 — DON RENDELL QUINTET (EP) ... 55
57 Pye Jazz NJE 1044 — DON RENDELL JAZZ SIX (EP) ... 30
58 Decca DFE 6501 — PACKET OF BLUES (EP, as Don Rendell Jazz Six) ... 20
54 Decca LK 4087 — JAZZ AT THE FESTIVAL HALL (LP) ... 70
54 Vogue LDE 050 — MUSIC IN THE MAKING (10" LP) ... 100
55 Vogue LDE 144 — DON RENDELL IN PARIS (10" LP, with Bobby Jaspar) ... 100
55 Tempo LAP 1 — MEET DON RENDELL (10" LP) ... 800
56 Nixa NJL 4 — TENORAMA (LP) ... 200
57 Nixa Jazz Today NJL 7 — DON RENDELL PRESENTS THE JAZZ SIX (LP) ... 200
58 Decca LK 4265 — PLAYTIME (LP, as Don Rendell Jazz 6) ... 100
62 Jazzland JLP 51 — ROARIN' (LP, as Don Rendell New Jazz Quintet [with Graham Bond]) ... 150
72 Columbia SCX 6491 — SPACEWALK (LP, as Don Rendell Quintet) ... 150

DON RENDELL & IAN CARR QUINTET

(see also Neil Ardley, Ian Carr, Nucleus)

65 Columbia 33SX 1733 — SHADES OF BLUE (LP) ... 1000
66 Columbia S(C)X 6064 — DUSK FIRE (LP, first pressing with blue label) ... 600
66 Columbia S(C)X 6064 — DUSK FIRE (LP) ... 250
68 Columbia S(C)X 6214 — PHASE III (LP) ... 200
69 Columbia S(C)X 6316 — LIVE (LP) ... 150
69 Columbia SCX 6368 — CHANGE IS (LP) ... 200

DON RENDELL QUARTET/JOE HARRIOT QUARTET

(see also Joe Harriott)

57 MGM MGM-EP 615 — JAZZ BRITANNIA (EP, 2 tracks each) ... 40

DON RENDES

76 Neville King NK 3 — Beware/Dun Beware ... 8

RENDEZVOUS

71 Philron ADR — It Shouldn't Have Happened/I'll Give You Love ... 20

RENE & HIS ALLIGATORS

66 Decca F 22324 — She Broke My Heart/I Can Wait ... 18

GOOGIE RENE COMBO

60 London HLY 9056 — Forever/Ez-zee ... 20
66 Atlantic AT 4076 — Smokey Joe's La La/Needing You ... 30
66 Atlantic 584 015 — Chica-Boo/Mercy Mercy (Too Much For The Soul) ... 10

HENRI RENE

55 HMV 7M 308 — Enchantment/Crystal Chandelier (with Hugo Winterhalter Orchestra) ... 7
59 London HLP 8960 — La Shabla (The Shovel)/Destiny (with His Orchestra & Chorus) ... 7

RENE & RENE

65 HMV POP 1468 — Chantilly Lace/I'm Not The Only One ... 10
67 Island WIP 6001 — Loving You Could Hurt Me So Much/Little Diamonds ... 8

RENEGADE

74 Dawn DNS 1067 — A Little Rock 'N' Roll/My Revolution ... 15
73 Parlophone R 5981 — Loving And Forgiving/Never Let Me Go ... 20

RENEGADE

80 White Witch WIT 1 — LONELY ROAD (12" EP, with insert) ... 100

RENEGADES

66 Polydor BM 56508 — Cadillac/Every Minute Of The Day ... 30
66 President PT 106 — Thirteen Women/Walking Down The Street ... 200
67 Parlophone R 5592 — Take A Message/Second Thoughts ... 25
68 Columbia DB 8383 — No Man's Land/Sugar Loaf Mountain ... 25

RENIA

73 Transatlantic TRA 261 — FIRST OFFENDERS (LP) ... 30

MINT VALUE £

TONY RENIS

62 HMV POP 1036 Quando, Quando, Quando/Blu ... 6

JON RENNARD

70 Tradition TSR 003 BRIMBLEDON FAIR (LP) ... 12
71 Tradition TSR 010 THE PARTING GLASS (LP) ... 12

DON RENNIE

56 Parlophone MSP 6218 To Love, To Love Is Wonderful/One Girl - One Boy ... 7
56 Parlophone MSP 6237 Who Are We?/Can You Find It In Your Heart? ... 7

DON RENO & RED SMILEY

58 Parlophone GEP 8777 COUNTRY AND WESTERN (EP) ... 30
61 Melodisc MLP 12-123 HYMNS SACRED GOSPEL SONGS (LP) ... 15
64 Ember CW 104 SING SWEET BALLADS OF THE WEST (LP) ... 18

GERRY RENO

62 Decca F 11477 Don't Ever Change/What Would You Do ... 8
62 Decca F 11516 Who's Fooling You/Three Deadly Sins ... 8
63 Decca F 11774 It Only Happens In The Movies/One Lonely Guy ... 15

GINETTE RENO

69 Decca F 22972 Don't Let Me Be Misunderstood/Everything That I Am ... 8

PAUL RENO

63 Oriole CB 1872 Lonely Little Girl/Angela ... 10

CHRIS RENSHAW & THE KEEPERS

73 Pye 7N 45285 Banksie (A Tribute To Gordon Banks)/National (Health) Anthem (p/s) ... 6

ROBERT RENTAL

(see also Thomas Leer, Normal)

78 Regular ER 102 Paralysis/A.C.C. (photocopied black & white foldover p/s) ... 30
78 Company/Regular RECO 2 Paralysis/A.C.C. (reissue, card gatefold p/s) ... 20
80 Mute MUTE 010 On Location/Double Heart (p/s) ... 15
79 Industrial IR 0007 THE BRIDGE (LP, with Thomas Leer) ... 30
80 Rough Trade ROUGH 17 ROBERT RENTAL AND THE NORMAL (LP, 1-sided, plain red sleeve) ... 25

REPARATA & DELRONS

65 Stateside SS 382 Whenever A Teenager Cries/He's My Guy ... 30
65 Stateside SS 414 Tommy/Momma Don't Allow ... 25
68 Bell BLL 1002 Captain Of Your Ship/Toom Toom Is A Little Boy ... 12
68 RCA Victor RCA 1691 I Can Hear The Rain/Always Waitin' ... 30
68 Bell BLL 1014 Saturday Night Didn't Happen/Panic ... 40
68 Bell BLL 1014 Saturday Night Didn't Happen/Panic (DJ copy) ... 60
68 Bell BLL 1021 Weather Forecast/You Can't Change A Young Boy's Mind ... 20
72 Dart ART 2057 Your Life Is Gone/Octopus Garden ... 10
74 Polydor 2066 562 Shoes/A Song For All ... 5
76 Polydor 2058 688 Jesabee Lancer (The Belly Dancer)/We Need You ... 7
72 Avco 6467 250 ROCK AND ROLL REVOLUTION (LP) ... 40

THE REPLACEMENTS

86 Sire W 8727 Swingin' Party/Left Of The Dial ... 5
86 Sire W 8679 Kiss Me On The Bus/Little Mascara (p/s) ... 5
87 Sire W 8297 Alex Chilton/Election day (p/s) ... 5
85 Sire 925330 TIM (LP) ... 15
89 What Goes On GOES ON 17 SORRY MA, FORGOT TO TAKE OUT THE TRASH (LP) ... 12

REQUIEM

80 Sacrificial SAC 001 Angel Of Sin/Sacrificial Wanderer (no p/s) ... 220

RESCUE COMPANY NO 1

72 Jam JAM 14 I Want To Save You/Amanda ... 15
72 Jam JAM 27 I Stand Alone/You Shouldn't Have Been So Nice ... 15
73 Jam JAM 45 It's Only Words/Look Out ... 20

RESERVE

88 Sha La La Ba Ba Ba-Ba Ba 006 Wherever You Go/SIDDELEYS: The Sun Slid Down/Behind The Tower (flexidisc, foldover p/s) ... 10

RESIDENTS

80 Pre PRE 009 THE COMMERCIAL SINGLE (p/s) ... 5
84 Korova KOW 36 It's A Man's Man's Man's World/I'll Go Crazy (p/s, 5,000 only) ... 5
83 London RALPH 1 INTERMISSION (12" EP) ... 8
79 Virgin VR 3 NIBBLES (LP, stickered sleeve, 5,000 only) ... 12
80 Pre PRE X2 THE COMMERCIAL ALBUM (LP, 5,000 only, with incorrect song order) ... 12

RESISTANCE

81 Fontana KIT 1 Survival Kit/Big Flame (p/s) ... 6

RESISTANCE 77

84 Resistance RESIST 1 You Reds/Young And Wrong (p/s) ... 5
84 Rot ASS 6 Vive The Resistance ... 20
82 Riot City RIOT 18 NOWHERE TO PLAY (EP) ... 15
84 Rot ASS 14 THOROUGHBRED MEN (LP) ... 80

RESISTORS

80 Break SMASH 1 For Jeanie/Takeaway Love/End Of The Line (p/s) ... 10

JOHNNY RESTIVO

59 RCA RCA 1143 The Shape I'm In/Ya Ya (with triangular centre) ... 40
59 RCA RCA 1143 The Shape I'm In/Ya Ya (later round centre pressing) ... 20
59 RCA RCA 1143 The Shape I'm In/Ya Ya (78) ... 40
59 RCA RCA 1159 I Like Girls/Dear Someone ... 20
59 RCA RCA 1159 I Like Girls/Dear Someone (78) ... 60
60 Ember EMB S 135 Look Here Now/Sweet Sweet Lovin' ... 15

MINT VALUE £

RESTRICTED HOURS
(see also Astronauts)
79 Stevenage (no cat. no.) Getting Things Done/Still Living Out The Car Crash/SYNDICATE: One Way Or Another/I Want To Be Somebody (white label, foldover p/s) . . . 10

RETREADS
81 Eddi Osmo EO 101 Would You Listen Girl/One After 909/You Said You Knew (p/s, with mini-poster insert) . . . 55

RETURN TO FOREVER
(see also Chick Corea)
74 Polydor 2310 283 HYMN OF THE SEVENTH GALAXY (LP) . . . 12

MARTIN REV
(see also Suicide)
85 New Rose ROSE 52 CLOUDS OF GLORY (LP, red vinyl) . . . 12

REVELATION
78 Write Sounds WTS 1003 With You Boy/Dub You . . . 8
78 Write Sounds WTS 1003 Jah Feelings/With You Boy (12") . . . 15
78 Write Sounds WTS 1004 Jah Feelings/Dub Feelings . . . 8
81 Kingdom KV 8013 Tonight/Fussin' And Fightin' . . . 6
81 Kingdom KV 8013-12 Tonight/Fussin' And Fightin' (12") . . . 10
78 Burning Sounds BS 1030 BOOK OF REVELATION (LP) . . . 25
79 Burning Vibrations BV 1007 VARIATION ON A THEM (LP) . . . 20

REVELATION
80 Handshake HANDS 1 Feel It/When I Fall In Love . . . 8

REVELATION
91 Rise Above RISE 6 SALVATIONS ANSWER (LP, stickered sleeve) . . . 25

REVELATION (Jamaica)
70 Trojan TR 7727 Suffering/MEGATONS: Crazy Elephant . . . 7

REVELLERS
66 Columbia DB 8093 Believe, Believe/Love Is The Greatest Thing . . . 7
67 Spin SP2002 Yasmin/When I Needed A Neighbour . . . 12
67 Spin LP 1703 REVELLERS AGAIN (LP) . . . 35

REVELLS
71 CBS 7050 Mind Party/Indian Ropeman . . . 80

DIGGER REVELL'S DENVERMEN
63 Decca F 11657 Surfside/Lisa Marie . . . 20

REVELS
59 Top Rank JAR 235 Midnight Stroll/Talking To My Heart . . . 70

REVENGE
76 Normal QS 000 Go Away/Game . . . 12
70s Blood CUS 614 Don't Tell Me Lies/Gimme The Good Times . . . 10

REVENGE
78 Loony LOO 1 Our Generation/I Love Her Way (counterfeits lack ridge around label) . . . 300
78 Loony LOO 2 We're Not Gonna Take It/Pornography (glossy p/s, counterfeits have matt sleeve, and lack ridge around label) . . . 200

REVERB
94 Ochre OCH 001 Pedal/Swift (foldover p/s in poly bag) . . . 10

PAUL REVERE & THE RAIDERS (featuring Mark Lindsay)
(see also Mark Lindsay, Raiders)
61 Top Rank JAR 557 Like Long Hair/Sharon . . . 20
65 Sue WI 344 Like Long Hair/Sharon (reissue) . . . 30
65 CBS 202003 Steppin' Out/Blue Fox . . . 10
66 CBS 202027 Just Like Me/B F D R F Blues . . . 20
66 CBS 202205 Kicks/Shake It Up . . . 15
66 CBS 202253 Hungry/There She Goes . . . 10
66 CBS 202411 The Great Airplane Strike/In My Community . . . 12
67 CBS 202502 Good Thing/Undecided Man . . . 12
67 CBS 202610 Ups And Downs/Leslie . . . 10
67 CBS 2737 Him Or Me - What's It Gonna Be?/The Legend Of Paul Revere . . . 10
67 CBS 2919 I Had A Dream/Upon Your Leaving . . . 6
67 CBS 3186 Mo'reen/Oh! To Be A Man . . . 10
68 CBS 3310 Too Much Talk/Happening '68 (featuring Mark Lindsay) . . . 20
68 CBS 3586 Don't Take It So Hard/Observation From Flight 285 (featuring Mark Lindsay) . . . 8
68 CBS 3757 Cinderella Sunshine/Theme From It's Happening (featuring Mark Lindsay) . . . 6
69 CBS 4025 Mr. Sun, Mr. Moon/With You (featuring Mark Lindsay) . . . 6
69 CBS 4260 Let Me/I Don't Know (featuring Mark Lindsay) . . . 7
69 CBS 4504 We Gotta All Get Up Together/Frankfurt Side Street (featuring Mark Lindsay) . . . 6
76 Jay Boy BOY 108 Ain't Nothin' Wrong/ou're Really Sayin' Something . . . 7
66 CBS (S)BPG 62406 JUST LIKE US (LP) . . . 25
66 CBS (S)BPG 62797 MIDNIGHT RIDE (LP) . . . 25
67 CBS (S)BPG 62963 GOOD THING (LP) . . . 20
68 CBS (S)BPG 63095 REVOLUTION (LP) . . . 20
69 CBS 63265 GOIN' TO MEMPHIS (LP, mono/stereo) . . . 20
69 CBS 63649 HARD 'N' HEAVY (LP) . . . 20

REVIEW
80s All The Madmen England's Glory . . . 8

REVILLOS
(see also Rezillos)
79 Snatzo/Dindisc DIN 1 Where's The Boy For Me/The Fiend (p/s) . . . 5

MINT VALUE £

79	Snatzo/Dindisc DIN 5	Motor Bike Beat/No Such Luck (p/s)	5
80	Snatzo/Dindisc DINZ 16	Scuba Scuba/Scuba Boy Bop (p/s)	5
80	Snatzo/Dindisc DINZ 20	Hungry For Love/Voodoo 2 (p/s, label also lists SP 703)	5
82	Superville SV 1001	She's Fallen In Love With A Monster Man/Mind Bending Cutie Doll (p/s)	10
82	Superville SV 2001	Bongo Brain/Hip City - You Were Meant For Me (p/s)	6
82	Aura AUS 135	Tell Him/Graveyard Groove (p/s)	6
83	EMI RVL 1	Bitten By A Love Bug/Cat Call	5
83	EMI 12 RVL 1	Bitten By A Love Bug (Extended Version)/Cat Call (12", p/s)	8
84	EMI RVL 2	Midnight/Z-X-7 (p/s)	5
84	EMI 12 RVL 2	Midnight (Extended Version)/Midnight (7" Version)/Z-X-7 (12", p/s)	8
80	Snatzo/Dindisc DID X 3	REV UP (LP, green or pink titles)	20
82	Superville SV 4001	ATTACK! (LP, withdrawn)	60

REVOLUTION

(see also Hellions, Luther Grosvenor, Family, Traffic, Dave Mason & Cass Elliot, Spirit)

66	Piccadilly 7N 35289	Hallelujah/Shades Of Blue	65

(THE) REVOLUTIONARIES

77	Sky Note SKY DD 002	Afro Rock Part 1/Afro Rock Part 2 (12")	40
77	Sky Note SKY 1002	El Bamba	20
78	Island IPR 2024	Headache/Bellyache/Toothache/Headache (12")	30
78	Ballistic FORCE 2003	FATAL DUB (12" EP)	20
75	Love LOV 01	GUN COURT DUB (LP)	40
76	Trenchtown TRELP 001	REVOLUTIONARY DUB (LP, with We The People Band)	40
78	Hawkeye HALP 001	DREAD AT THE CONTROLS (LP)	40
78	Cha Cha CHALP 002	REACTION IN DUB (LP)	35
78	Cha Cha CHALP 005	JONKANOO DUB (LP)	30
79	Burning Vibrations BV 1002	DUTCH MAN DUB (LP)	30
79	Burning Vibrations BV 1004	GREEN BAY DUB (LP)	40
79	Burning Vibrations BV 1010	BURNING DUB (LP)	30
79	Trojan TRLS 169	OUTLAW DUB (LP)	25
80	Manzie DRS LP 002	KING'S DUB (LP)	25
82	Cha Cha CHALP 014	REVIVAL (LP)	30

REVOLUTIONARY ARMY OF INFANT JESUS

87	Probe Plus PROBE 12	THE GIFT OF TEARS (LP)	40

REVOLUTIONARY BLUES BAND

70	MCA MUP(S) 402	REVOLUTIONARY BLUES BAND (LP)	20

REVOLUTIONARY CORPS OF TEENAGE JESUS VS SUICIDE

(see also Suicide, Future Pilot A.KA.)

96	Creeping Bent BENT 005	FRANKIE TEARDROP EP (Frankie Teardrop [126 b.p.m.]/U.S.A. '95/ Frankie Teardrop [114 b.p.m.]/Womb 17) (12", p/s, 1,000 only)	10

REVOLVER

69	Young BLood YB 1006	Frisco Annie/Imaginations	20

REVOLVING PAINT DREAM

(see also Laughing Apple, Primal Scream)

84	Creation CRE 002	Flowers In The Sky/In The Afternoon (foldaround p/s in poly bag)	25

REVS

91	Vinyl Japan TASK 9	Just Ask Why/We're So Modern/Stay With Me/Julie Got A Raise (12", p/s)	8

REVULSION

85	Radical Change RC 7	Ever Get The Feeling Of Utter? (12")	20

KIMBERLEY REW

(see also Soft Boys, Waves)

80	Armageddon AS 004	Stomping All Over The World/Nothing's Going To Change In Your Life/ Fighting Someone's War (p/s)	5
81	Armageddon AS 012	My Baby Does Her Hairdo Long/Fishing (p/s, with dB's)	5

REX

77	CBS 82186	WHERE DO WE GO FROM HERE (LP)	12

REX (Morris) & MINORS

60	Triumph RGM 1023	Chicken Sax/Snake Eyes	50

ROBERTA REX

68	Fontana TF 967	Joey/I Can Feel It	6

ALVINO REY

61	London HLD 9431	Original Mama Blues/Steel Guitar Rag	10
62	London HA-D 2414	ALVINO REY'S GREATEST HITS (LP)	20

LITTLE BOBBY REY & HIS BAND

60	Top Rank JAR 525	Rockin' "J" Bells/Dance Of The New Year	8

REYNARD

76	Pilgrim/Grapevine GRA 102	FRESH FROM THE EARTH (LP)	40

AMBROSE REYNOLDS

(see also Pink Military)

83	Zulu ZULU 3	GREATEST HITS (LP)	12

DEBBIE REYNOLDS

(see also Naturals [U.S.])

55	MGM SP 1127	Carolina In The Morning/Never Mind The Noise In The Market (B-side as Debbie Reynolds' Naturals)	10
56	MGM SP 1155	(Love Is) The Tender Trap/Canoodlin' Rag	8
57	Vogue Coral Q 72274	Tammy/French Heels	5
60	London HLD 9028	Am I That Easy To Forget?/Ask Me To Go Steady	5
60	London HLD 9128	City Lights/Just For A Touch Of Your Love	5
61	London HLD 9351	Lonely People/Just A Little Girl	5

MINT VALUE £

69	Pye Int 7N 25507	With A Little Love (Just A Little Love)/I Think You're Gonna Be Alright	6
58	MGM MGM-EP 670	DEBBIE REYNOLDS (EP)	20
58	MGM MGM-EP 671	SINGING IN THE RAIN (EP, with Gene Kelly & Donald O'Connor)	10
59	MGM MGM-EP 694	DELIGHTFUL DEBBIE REYNOLDS (EP)	15
60	MGM MGM-EP 725	FROM DEBBIE WITH LOVE (EP)	15
59	London HA-D 2200	DEBBIE (LP, mono)	40
59	London SAH-D 6051	DEBBIE (LP, stereo)	45
60	London HA-D 2294	AM I THAT EASY TO FORGET? (LP, mono)	20
60	London SAH-D 6106	AM I THAT EASY TO FORGET? (LP, stereo)	25
61	London HA-D 2326	FINE AND DANDY (LP)	20
63	London HA-D 8075	GREAT FOLK HITS (LP, mono)	20
63	London HA-D/SH-D 8075	GREAT FOLK HITS (LP, stereo)	25

DONN REYNOLDS

58	MGM MGM 996	Blue Eyes Crying In The Rain/Bella Belinda	6
58	Pye 7N 15122	Swing Low Sweet Chariot/Ramona	6
59	Pye NEP 24098	THE DONN REYNOLDS SONGBAG (EP)	10

ELI REYNOLDS

70	Punch PH 37	Mr Car Man/Chiney Man	10

JODY REYNOLDS

58	London HL 8651	Endless Sleep/Tight Capris	25
58	London HL 8651	Endless Sleep/Tight Capris (78)	15

TIMMY REYNOLDS

62	Ember EMB S 133	Lullaby Of Love/JEFF MILLS: Daddy's Home	70

REZILLOS

(see also Revillos, Shake, Jo Callis, William Mysterious)

77	Sensible FAB 1	Can't Stand My Baby/I Wanna Be Your Man (p/s, 15,000, 5,000 numbered)	15
77	Sensible FAB 1	Can't Stand My Baby/I Wanna Be Your Man (p/s, 15,000, 10,000 unnumbered)	10
77	Sensible FAB 2	Flying Saucer Attack/(My Baby Does) Good Sculptures (p/s, unissued)	0
77	Sire 6078 612	Flying Saucer Attack/(My Baby Does) Good Sculptures (p/s)	12
78	Sire 6198 215	Cold Wars/William Mysterious Overture (unissued)	0
78	Sire SIR 4001	Top Of The Pops/20,000 Rezillos Under The Sea (p/s)	8
78	Sire SIR 4008	Destination Venus/Mystery Action (p/s)	6
79	Sire SIR 4014	Cold Wars (live)/Flying Saucer Attack (live)/Twist & Shout (live) (p/s)	12
79	Sensible FAB 1 (Mark 2)	Can't Stand My Baby/I Wanna Be Your Man (reissue, new p/s, run-out groove reads "Come Back John Lennon")	7
79	Sensible FAB 1 (Mark 2)	Can't Stand My Baby/I Wanna Be Your Man (reissue, p/s, mispressing, B-side plays "(My Baby Does) Good Sculptures (live)", run-off groove reads "De-sire-able product?", 4,000 only)	6
81	Sire SPC 3	Top Of The Pops/Destination Venus (cassette, flip-up box)	7
78	Sire K 56530	CAN'T STAND THE REZILLOS (LP, with inner sleeve & postcard insert)	20
78	Sire SRK 6069	MISSION ACCOMPLISHED ? BUT THE BEAT GOES ON (LP, live)	18

RHABSTALLION

81	Rhab RHAB 001	Day To Day/Breadline (p/s, with badge)	30
81	Rhab RHAB 001	Day To Day/Breadline (p/s)	20

RHINOCEROS

69	Elektra EKSN 45051	I Don't Want To Discuss It/Apricot Brandy	10
69	Elektra EKSN 45058	I Will Serenade You/Belbuekul	7
70	Elektra EKSN 45080	Back Door/In A Little Room	6
70	Elektra 2101 009	Old Age/Let's Party	6
69	Elektra EKL 4030	RHINOCEROS (LP, orange label, also stereo EKS 74030)	20
69	Elektra EKL 4056	SATIN CHICKENS (LP, also stereo EKS 74056)	20
70	Elektra 2469 006	BETTER TIMES ARE COMING (LP)	15

RHODA with The SPECIAL A.K.A.

(see also Special A.K.A.)

82	2-Tone CHS TT 18	The Boiler/Theme From The Boiler	5
82	2-Tone CHS TT 1218	The Boiler/Theme From The Boiler (12", p/s existence unconfirmed)	20

JAN RHODE & HIS COOL CATS

60	Qualiton Offbeat PSP 7128	Come Back Baby/So Shy	8

PAT RHODEN

(see also Pat Riden, Pat & Marie, Denzil & Pat)

65	Ska Beat JB 195	Jezebel/You Can Hold My Hand	20
66	Blue Beat BB 360	Send Your Love/Make Believe	15
68	Trojan TR 606	Woman Is Greedy/Endlessly	8
70	Pama PM 811	Maybe The Next Time/Got To See You	8
70	Pama Supreme PS 298	Do What You Gotta Do/Crying Won't Help You	8
70	Mary Lyn ML 101	Time Is Tight/MILTON & DENZIL: I Like It Like That	8
73	Pama Supreme PS 378	Out Of Time/Put A Little Rain Into My Life	8

EMITT RHODES

71	Probe PRO 520	Fresh As A Daisy/You Take The Dark Out Of The Night	7
71	Probe PRO 529	With My Face On The Floor/Somebody Made For Me	7
71	A&M AMS 865	You're A Very Lovely Woman/Till The Day After	6
72	Probe PRO 565	Tame The Lion/Golden Child Of God	7
71	Probe SPBA 6256	EMITT RHODES (LP, gatefold sleeve)	22
71	A&M AMLS 64254	AMERICAN DREAM (LP)	22
71	Probe SPBA 6262	MIRROR (LP)	15
72	Probe SPBA 6266	FAREWELL TO PARADISE (LP)	15
90s	Edsel	DAISY FRESH FROM HAWTHORNE CALIFORNIA - THE BEST OF THE DUNHILL YEARS (2-CD)	25

TODD RHODES ORCHESTRA

55	Parlophone MSP 6171	Specks/Silver Sunset	30

MINT VALUE £

RHODESIANS
80	Period PER 001	Clock!!!/Postmortem (p/s)	15

RHUBARB RHUBARB
68	President PT 229	Rainmaker/Moneylender	140

RHYME AND REASON
77	Decca F 13711	Good Morning England/Night Life	6

RHYTHM ACES
61	Starlite ST45 061	A Thousand Teardrops/Wherever You May Go	20
61	Starlite ST45 066	Please Don't Go Away/Oh My Darling	20
62	Blue Beat BB 134	I'll Be There/DON DRUMMOND: Dewdrops	20
62	Island WI 032	C-H-R-I-S-T-M-A-S/TOP GRANT: A Christmas Drink	18

RHYTHM & BLUES INC.
65	Fontana TF 524	Louie Louie/Honey Don't	75

RHYTHMETTES
59	Coral Q 72358	Page From The Future/I'll Be With You In Apple Blossom Time	10

RHYTHM FORCE
72	Tropical AL 0013	Satta Call/Satta Version	6

RHYTHM KINGS
63	Vocalion POP V 9212	Blue Soul/Exotic	30

RHYTHM OF LIFE
(see also Josef K, Paul Haig)

81	Rational RATE 6	Soon/Summertime (p/s; label also lists Rhythm RHYTHM 1)	6
82	Rational RATE 7	Uncle Sam/Portrait Of The Heart (p/s; label also lists Rhythm RHYTHM 2)	5

RHYTHM RULERS
(see also Lloyd Jones, U Roy Junior, Matadors, Winston Groovy, Pat, Winston Wright)

70	Bullet BU 447	Second Pressure/Sammy Dead	10

RIBS
78	Aerco AERS 101	Man With No Brain/Long Time Coming (p/s)	25

BOYD RICE & FRIENDS
(see also Non, Death In June, Current 93)

90	New European BADVC 1969	MUSIC, MARTINIS AND MISANTHROPY (LP, with inner sleeve)	25

MACK RICE
69	Atlantic 584 250	Love's A Mother Brother/Coal Man	10

TIM RICE & WEBBER GROUP
(see also Tales Of Justine, Nightshift)

69	RCA RCA 1895	Come Back Richard (Your Country Needs You)/Roll On Over The Atlantic	8

MANDY RICE-DAVIES
64	Ember EMB 4537	MANDY (EP)	40

BOB RICH
70	Mother MOT 1	Christas In My Pants/My Woman	8
73	Mother MOT 5	Filthy Rich/Navy Blue Blues	10

BUDDY RICH
56	HMV CLP 1092	BUDDY RICH SINGS JOHNNY MERCER (LP)	12
56	Columbia Clef 33CX 10052	THE WAILING BUDDY RICH (LP)	12
57	Columbia Clef 33CX 10071	THIS ONE'S FOR BASIE (LP)	12
57	Columbia Clef 33CX 10080	BUDDY AND SWEETS (LP, with Harry 'Sweets' Edison)	12

CHARLIE RICH
60	London HLU 9107	Lonely Weekends/Everything I Do Is Wrong	50
62	London HLS 9482	Just A Little Bit Sweet/It's Too Late	40
65	RCA RCA 1433	Too Many Teardrops/It's All Over Now	10
65	Philips BF 1432	Mohair Sam/I Washed My Hands In Muddy Water	20
67	London HLU 10104	Love Is After Me/Pass On By (silver-top label)	30
67	London HLU 10104	Love Is After Me/Pass On By (later boxed logo label)	15
67	London HLU 10104	Love Is After Me/Pass On By ((DJ copy)	70
69	Mercury MF 1109	Mohair Sam/I Washed My Hands In Muddy Water (reissue)	10
65	RCA RD 7719	THAT'S RICH (LP)	50
66	Philips BL 7695	THE MANY NEW SIDES OF CHARLIE RICH (LP)	20

DAVE RICH
58	RCA RCA 1092	Burn On Love Fire/City Lights	20
58	RCA RCA 1092	Burn On Love Fire/City Lights (78)	12
66	Polydor BM 56113	Last Two People On Earth/I Just Wanna Dance	6

JOHNNY RICH
64	Mercury MF 836	Dream On/Together	6

LEWIS RICH
66	Parlophone R 5434	I Don't Want To Hear It Anymore/Shedding Tears	15

RICHIE RICH
89	ffrr FX 113	Salsa House (Silver On Black Mix)/(Original Mix)/(Orbital Mix) (12")	12
89	ffrr FXR 156	You Used To Salsa/You Used To Hold Me (12", remix)	20

SKETTO RICH
(see Buddy & Sketto, Ruddy & Sketto, Father Sketto, Owen Gray)

70	Pama PM 806	Hound Dog/Black Girl	7
71	Big Shot BI 596	Know Your Friend/Know Your Friend - Version	5

TONY RICH
(see also Tony Sheveton)

66	Piccadilly 7N 35291	Save Your Love/Don't Mention Your Name	10
66	Piccadilly 7N 35323	It's All Up To You Now/See Saw	15

MINT VALUE £

RICHARD

69	Parlophone R 5754	A Little Bit/Take Me	15

CLIFF RICHARD (& DRIFTERS/SHADOWS)

(see also Drifters [U.K.], Shadows, Olivia Newton-John, Sheila Walsh, Janet Jackson, Elton John, Phil Everly, Grazina)

78s

58	Columbia DB 4178	Move It!/Schoolboy Crush	35
58	Columbia DB 4203	High Class Baby/My Feet Hit The Ground	30
59	Columbia DB 4249	Livin' Lovin' Doll/Steady With You	80
59	Columbia DB 4290	Mean Streak/Never Mind	80
59	Columbia DB 4306	Living Doll/Apron Strings	40
(The above 78s were credited to Cliff Richard & Drifters)			
59	Columbia DB 4351	Travellin' Light/Dynamite	45
60	Columbia DB 4398	A Voice In The Wilderness/Don't Be Mad At Me	100
(The above 78s were credited to Cliff Richard & Shadows)			

COLUMBIA 45s

58	Columbia DB 4178	Move It!/Schoolboy Crush (green label)	25
58	Columbia DB 4178	Move It!/Schoolboy Crush (later pressing with black label)	40
58	Columbia DB 4203	High Class Baby/My Feet Hit The Ground (green label)	25
58	Columbia DB 4203	High Class Baby/My Feet Hit The Ground (later pressing with black label)	35
59	Columbia DB 4249	Livin' Lovin' Doll/Steady With You (green label)	10
59	Columbia DB 4249	Livin' Lovin' Doll/Steady With You (later pressing with black label)	40
59	Columbia DB 4290	Mean Streak/Never Mind (green label)	25
59	Columbia DB 4290	Mean Streak/Never Mind (later pressing with black label)	35
59	Columbia DB 4306	Living Doll/Apron Strings (green label)	10
59	Columbia DB 4306	Living Doll/Apron Strings (later pressing with black label)	35
(The above singles were credited to Cliff Richard & Drifters, black label pressings are ultra rare)			
59	Columbia DB 4351	Travellin' Light/Dynamite	7
60	Columbia DB 4398	A Voice In The Wilderness/Don't Be Mad At Me	5
60	Columbia DB 4431	Fall In Love With You/Willie And The Hand Jive	5
60	Columbia DB 4479	Please Don't Tease/Where Is My Heart	5
60	Columbia DB 4506	Nine Times Out Of Ten/Thinking Of Our Love	6
60	Columbia DB 4547	I Love You/"D" In Love	5
61	Columbia DB 4593	Theme For A Dream/Mumblin' Mosie	5
61	Columbia DB 4667	A Girl Like You/Now's The Time To Fall In Love	5
61	Columbia DB 4716	When The Girl In Your Arms Is The Girl In Your Heart/ Got A Funny Feeling (solo)	5
62	Columbia DB 4761	The Young Ones/We Say Yeah (green label)	5
62	Columbia DB 4761	The Young Ones/We Say Yeah (later black label)	7
62	Columbia DB 4828	I'm Lookin' Out The Window/Do You Want To Dance?	5
62	Columbia DB 4886	It'll Be Me/Since I Lost You	6
(The above 45s were originally green labels; later black label copies are worth at least twice the listed values)			
62	Columbia DB 4950	The Next Time/Bachelor Boy	5
63	Columbia DB 4977	Summer Holiday/Dancing Shoes	5
63	Columbia DB 7034	Lucky Lips/I Wonder	5
63	Columbia DB 7089	It's All In The Game/Your Eyes Tell On You (solo)	5
63	Columbia DB 7150	Don't Talk To Him/Say You're Mine	5
64	Columbia DB 7203	I'm The Lonely One/Watch What You Do With My Baby	5
64	Columbia DB 7272	Constantly (solo)/True True Lovin'	5
64	Columbia DB 7305	On The Beach/A Matter Of Moments	5
64	Columbia DB 7372	The Twelfth Of Never/I'm Afraid To Go Home (solo)	5
64	Columbia DB 7420	I Could Easily Fall (In Love With You)/I'm In Love With You	5
(The above singles were credited to Cliff Richard & Shadows unless stated: the singles listed below were solo unless stated.)			
64	Columbia DB 7435	This Was My Special Day/I'm Feeling Oh So Lovely (withdrawn, credited to Cliff Richard, Audrey Bayley, Joan Palethorpe & Faye Fisher)	20
65	Columbia DB 7496	The Minute You're Gone/Just Another Guy	5
65	Columbia DB 7596	On My Word/Just A Little Bit Too Late	6
65	Columbia DB 7660	The Time In Between/Look Before You Love (as Cliff Richard & Shadows)	6
65	Columbia DB 7745	Wind Me Up (Let Me Go)/The Night	5
66	Columbia DB 7866	Blue Turns To Grey/Somebody Loses (as Cliff Richard & Shadows)	6
66	Columbia DB 7968	Visions/What Would I Do (For The Love Of A Girl?)	6
66	Columbia DB 8017	Time Drags By/La La La Song (as Cliff Richard & Shadows)	7
66	Columbia DB 8094	In The Country/Finders Keepers (as Cliff Richard & Shadows)	5
66	Columbia PSRS 304	Finders Keepers (promo only, 1-sided, with spoken intro by Simon Dee)	30
67	Columbia DB 8150	It's All Over/Why Wasn't I Born Rich?	5
67	Columbia DB 8210	I'll Come Runnin'/I Get The Feelin'	7
67	Columbia DB 8245	The Day I Met Marie/Our Story Book	5
67	Columbia DB 8293	All My Love/Sweet Little Jesus Boy	5
68	Columbia DB 8376	Congratulations/High 'N' Dry	5
68	Columbia DB 8437	I'll Love You Forever Today/Girl, You'll Be A Woman Soon	10
68	Columbia DB 8476	Marianne/Mr Nice	6
68	Columbia DB 8503	Don't Forget To Catch Me/What's More (I Don't Need Her)	8
69	Columbia DB 8548	Good Times (Better Times)/Occasional Rain	7
69	Columbia DB 8581	Big Ship/She's Leaving You	7
69	Columbia DB 8615	Throw Down A Line (as Cliff & Hank)/Reflections	5
69	Columbia DB 8641	With The Eyes Of A Child/So Long	7
70	Columbia DB 8657	Joy Of Living (as Cliff & Hank)/CLIFF RICHARD: Leave My Woman Alone/ HANK MARVIN: Boogatoo	8
70	Columbia DB 8685	Goodbye Sam, Hello Samantha/You Never Can Tell	5
70	Columbia DB 8708	I Ain't Got Time Anymore/Monday Comes Too Soon	7
71	Columbia DB 8747	Sunny Honey Girl/Don't Move Away (with Olivia Newton-John)/ I Was Only Fooling Myself	7
71	Columbia DB 8774	Silvery Rain/Annabella Umbrella/Time Flies	8
71	Columbia DB 8797	Flying Machine/Pigeon	10
71	Columbia DB 8836	Sing A Song Of Freedom/A Thousand Conversations	6
72	Columbia DB 8864	Jesus/Mister Cloud	10
72	Columbia DB 8917	Living In Harmony/Empty Chairs	5
72	Columbia DB 8957	Brand New Song/The Old Accordion	6

			MINT VALUE £
EXPORT SINGLES			
61	Columbia DC 756	Gee Whiz It's You/I Cannot Find A True Love	5
63	Columbia DC 758	What'd I Say/Blue Moon	150
65	Columbia DC 762	Angel/Razzle Dazzle	60
EMI SINGLES			
73	EMI EMI 2012	Power To All Our Friends/Come Back Billie Joe	5
73	EMI EMI 2022	Help It Along/Tomorrow Rising/The Days Of Love/Ashes To Ashes (in p/s)	10
73	EMI EMI 2022	Help It Along/Tomorrow Rising/The Days Of Love/Ashes To Ashes	5
73	EMI EMI 2088	Take Me High/Celestial Houses	5
74	EMI PSR 368	Nothing To Remind Me/The Learning (promo only)	40
74	EMI EMI 2150	(You Keep Me) Hangin' On/Love Is Here	5
75	EMI EMI 2279	It's Only Me You've Left Behind/You're The One	5
75	EMI EMI 2344	Honky Tonk Angel/(Wouldn't You Know It) Got Myself A Girl	15
76	EMI EMI 2376	Miss You Nights/Love Enough	6
76	EMI EMI 2376	Miss You Nights/Love Enough (p/s in box set)	5
77	EMI EMI 2633	When Two Worlds Drift Apart/That's Why I Love You	6
78	EMI EMI 2730	Yes! He Lives/Good On The Sally Army	15
78	EMI EMI 2832	Please Remember Me/Please Don't Tease	5
78	EMI EMI 2885	Can't Take The Hurt Anymore/Needing A Friend (p/s)	10
79	EMI EMI 2920	Green Light/Imagine Love (in p/s)	15
79	EMI EMI 2920	Green Light/Imagine Love	5
79	EMI EMI 2975	We Don't Talk Anymore/Count Me Out (p/s, mispress, A-side plays Queen's "Bohemian Rhapsody")	12
FLEXIDISCS & OTHER RELEASES			
60	Serenade Magazine/	Serenade Presents Cliff Richard's Personal Message To You (turquoise flexidisc with magazine)	20
60s	Serenade Magazine	Cliff's Rock Party (flexidisc with magazine)	20
60s	Boyfriend Magazine	untitled flexidisc with magazine	20
60s	Rainbow Magazine	Music From America (flexidisc with magazine)	20
90	EMI CRTBX 31	Miss You Nights (Acapella version) (1-sided 7" etched message and autograph on reverse)	10
60s	New Spotlight	Star Souvenir Greetings (208 Radio Luxembourg flexidisc)	20
73	Spree (no cat. no.)	Good News (plain black flexidisc with spoken/sung introduction from Cliff, other side by Johnny Cash)	20
98	Cruisin' The 50's CASB 007	Breathless/Lawdy Miss Clawdy (10" 78, p/s, with 6 inserts)	50
EPs			
59	Columbia SEG 7895	SERIOUS CHARGE (soundtrack)	30
59	Columbia SEG 7903	CLIFF NO. 1 (mono)	25
59	Columbia ESG 7754	CLIFF NO. 1 (stereo)	35
59	Columbia SEG 7910	CLIFF NO. 2 (mono)	20
59	Columbia ESG 7769	CLIFF NO. 2 (stereo)	25
59	Columbia SEG 7971	EXPRESSO BONGO (soundtrack, mono)	20
59	Columbia ESG 7783	EXPRESSO BONGO (soundtrack, stereo)	30
60	Columbia SEG 7979	CLIFF SINGS NO. 1 (mono)	25
60	Columbia ESG 7788	CLIFF SINGS NO. 1 (stereo)	35
60	Columbia SEG 7987	CLIFF SINGS NO. 2 (mono)	25
60	Columbia ESG 7794	CLIFF SINGS NO. 2 (stereo)	35
60	Columbia SEG 8005	CLIFF SINGS NO. 3 (mono)	25
60	Columbia ESG 7808	CLIFF SINGS NO. 3 (stereo)	35
60	Columbia SEG 8021	CLIFF SINGS NO. 4 (mono)	25
60	Columbia ESG 7816	CLIFF SINGS NO. 4 (stereo)	35
60	Columbia SEG 8050	CLIFF'S SILVER DISCS	20
60	Columbia SEG 8065	ME AND MY SHADOWS NO. 1 (mono)	25
60	Columbia ESG 7837	ME AND MY SHADOWS NO. 1 (stereo)	35
61	Columbia SEG 8071	ME AND MY SHADOWS NO. 2 (mono)	25
61	Columbia ESG 7481	ME AND MY SHADOWS NO. 2 (stereo)	35
61	Columbia SEG 8078	ME AND MY SHADOWS NO. 3 (mono)	25
61	Columbia ESG 7843	ME AND MY SHADOWS NO. 3 (stereo)	35
61	Columbia SEG 8105	LISTEN TO CLIFF NO. 1 (mono)	25
61	Columbia ESG 7858	LISTEN TO CLIFF NO. 1 (stereo)	35
61	Columbia SEG 8119	DREAM (mono)	20
61	Columbia ESG 7867	DREAM (stereo)	25
61	Columbia SEG 8126	LISTEN TO CLIFF NO. 2 (mono)	25
61	Columbia ESG 7870	LISTEN TO CLIFF NO. 2 (stereo)	35
62	Columbia SEG 8133	CLIFF'S HIT PARADE	20
62	Columbia SEG 8151	CLIFF RICHARD	30
62	Columbia SEG 8159	HITS FROM 'THE YOUNG ONES'	20
62	Columbia SEG 8168	CLIFF RICHARD NO. 2	30
(The above EPs were originally issued with turquoise labels, later blue/black label copies are worth half to two-thirds these values.)			
62	Columbia SEG 8203	CLIFF'S HITS	20
63	Columbia SEG 8228	TIME FOR CLIFF AND THE SHADOWS (mono)	20
63	Columbia ESG 7887	TIME FOR CLIFF AND THE SHADOWS (stereo, turquoise label)	20
63	Columbia ESG 7887	TIME FOR CLIFF AND THE SHADOWS (stereo, turquoise blue/black label)	25
63	Columbia SEG 8246	HOLIDAY CARNIVAL (mono)	20
63	Columbia ESG 7892	HOLIDAY CARNIVAL (stereo)	25
63	Columbia SEG 8250	HITS FROM 'SUMMER HOLIDAY' (mono)	20
63	Columbia ESG 7896	HITS FROM 'SUMMER HOLIDAY' (stereo)	25
63	Columbia SEG 8263	MORE HITS FROM 'SUMMER HOLIDAY' (mono)	25
63	Columbia ESG 7898	MORE HITS FROM 'SUMMER HOLIDAY' (stereo)	35
63	Columbia SEG 8269	CLIFF'S LUCKY LIPS	20
63	Columbia SEG 8272	LOVE SONGS (mono)	20
63	Columbia ESG 7900	LOVE SONGS (stereo)	25
64	Columbia SEG 8290	WHEN IN FRANCE	20
64	Columbia SEG 8299	CLIFF SINGS 'DON'T TALK TO HIM'	20
64	Columbia SEG 8320	CLIFF'S PALLADIUM SUCCESSES	30

			MINT VALUE £
64	Columbia SEG 8338	WONDERFUL LIFE (mono)	20
64	Columbia ESG 7902	WONDERFUL LIFE (stereo)	25
64	Columbia SEG 8347	A FOREVER KIND OF LOVE	20
64	Columbia SEG 8354	WONDERFUL LIFE NO. 2 (mono)	20
64	Columbia ESG 7903	WONDERFUL LIFE NO. 2 (stereo)	25
64	Columbia SEG 8376	HITS FROM 'WONDERFUL LIFE' (mono)	20
64	Columbia ESG 7906	HITS FROM 'WONDERFUL LIFE' (stereo)	25
65	Columbia SEG 8384	WHY DON'T THEY UNDERSTAND?	20
65	Columbia SEG 8395	CLIFF'S HITS FROM 'ALADDIN AND HIS WONDERFUL LAMP'	20
65	Columbia SEG 8405	LOOK IN MY EYES, MARIA	20
65	Columbia SEG 8444	ANGEL	20
65	Columbia SEG 8450	TAKE FOUR	25
66	Columbia SEG 8474	WIND ME UP	25
66	Columbia SEG 8478	HITS FROM 'WHEN IN ROME'	25
66	Columbia SEG 8488	LOVE IS FOREVER	25
66	Columbia SEG 8510	THUNDERBIRDS ARE GO! (3 tracks by Cliff & Shadows, 1 solo)	50
66	Columbia SEG 8517	LA LA LA LA LA (1 track by Bruce Welch & Hank Marvin)	35
67	Columbia SEG 8527	CINDERELLA	50
67	Columbia SEG 8533	CAROL SINGERS	30
68	Columbia SEG 8540	CONGRATULATIONS	20
77	EMI PSR 410	EVERY FACE TELLS A STORY (promo, issued to shops only)	15
77	EMI PSR 414/415	40 GOLDEN GREATS (double pack promo, issued to shops only)	15

COLUMBIA LPs

59	Columbia 33SX 1147	CLIFF (green labels)	50
59	Columbia 33SX 1147	CLIFF (later blue/black labels)	30
59	Columbia 33SX 1192	CLIFF SINGS (green labels)	50
59	Columbia 33SX 1192	CLIFF SINGS (later blue/black labels)	30
60	Columbia 33SX 1261	ME AND MY SHADOWS (mono)	35
60	Columbia SCX 3330	ME AND MY SHADOWS (stereo)	55
61	Columbia 33SX 1320	LISTEN TO CLIFF! (mono)	30
61	Columbia SCX 3375	LISTEN TO CLIFF! (stereo)	65
61	Columbia 33SX 1368	21 TODAY (mono)	30
61	Columbia SCX 3409	21 TODAY (stereo)	65
61	Columbia 33SX 1384	THE YOUNG ONES (soundtrack with inner, mono)	15
61	Columbia SCX 3397	THE YOUNG ONES (soundtrack with inner, stereo)	30
62	Columbia 33SX 1431	32 MINUTES AND 17 SECONDS WITH? (mono)	30
62	Columbia SCX 3436	32 MINUTES AND 17 SECONDS WITH?	65

(The above LPs were originally issued with green labels, later blue/black copies are worth half to two-thirds these values unless stated.)

63	Columbia 33SX 1472	SUMMER HOLIDAY (soundtrack with inner sleeve, mono)	12
63	Columbia SCX 3462	SUMMER HOLIDAY (first pressing, stereo, with green labels)	25
63	Columbia SCX 3462	SUMMER HOLIDAY (second pressing, stereo, with blue/black labels)	18
63	Columbia SX 1512	CLIFF'S HIT ALBUM	12
63	Columbia SX 1541	WHEN IN SPAIN (mono)	20
63	Columbia SCX 3488	WHEN IN SPAIN (stereo)	30
64	Columbia SX 1628	WONDERFUL LIFE (soundtrack, mono, gatefold sleeve with inner sleeve)	12
64	Columbia SCX 3515	WONDERFUL LIFE (soundtrack, stereo, gatefold sleeve with inner sleeve)	20
64	Columbia SX 1676	ALADDIN AND HIS WONDERFUL LAMP (with stage cast, gatefold sleeve, mono)	18
64	Columbia SCX 3522	ALADDIN AND HIS WONDERFUL LAMP (with stage cast, gatefold sleeve, stereo)	25
65	Columbia SX 1709	CLIFF RICHARD (mono)	35
65	Columbia SCX 3546	CLIFF RICHARD (stereo)	40
65	Columbia SX 1737	MORE HITS BY CLIFF (mono)	15
65	Columbia SCX 3555	MORE HITS BY CLIFF (stereo)	18
65	Columbia SX 1762	WHEN IN ROME	30
65	Columbia SX 1769	LOVE IS FOREVER (also stereo SCX 3569)	25
66	Columbia SX 6039	KINDA LATIN (mono)	30
66	Columbia SCX 6039	KINDA LATIN (stereo)	35
66	Columbia SX 6079	FINDERS KEEPERS (soundtrack, with inner sleeve, mono)	15
66	Columbia SCX 6079	FINDERS KEEPERS (soundtrack, with inner sleeve, stereo)	20
67	Columbia S(C)X 6103	CINDERELLA (with stage cast)	20
67	Columbia S(C)X 6133	DON'T STOP ME NOW	30
67	Columbia S(C)X 6167	GOOD NEWS	15
67	Columbia JSX 6167	GOOD NEWS (export issue)	35
68	Columbia S(C)X 6244	CLIFF IN JAPAN (blue/black labels)	30
68	Columbia S(C)X 6244	CLIFF IN JAPAN (later pressing with white/black labels)	20
68	Columbia S(C)X 6262	TWO A PENNY (blue/black labels)	20
68	Columbia S(C)X 6262	TWO A PENNY (later pressing with white/black labels)	15
68	Columbia SX 6282	ESTABLISHED 1958 (gatefold sleeve, half tracks by Shadows, mono)	15
68	Columbia SCX 6282	ESTABLISHED 1958 (gatefold sleeve, half tracks by Shadows, stereo)	12

(The above Columbia LPs were originally issued with blue/black labels; white/black copies are worth half these values.)

69	Columbia SX 6357	SINCERELY CLIFF RICHARD (mono)	15
69	Columbia SCX 6357	SINCERELY CLIFF RICHARD (stereo)	12
70	Columbia SCX 6408	ABOUT THAT MAN (4 songs plus narration)	40
70	Columbia SCX 6435	TRACKS 'N' GROOVES	15
70	Columbia SCX 6443	HIS LAND (documentary soundtrack, with Cliff Barrows)	20

EMI LPs

73	EMI EMC 3016	TAKE ME HIGH (soundtrack, with poster)	20
73	EMI EMC 3016	TAKE ME HIGH (soundtrack)	12
74	EMI EMA 768	HELP IT ALONG (gatefold sleeve)	20
74	EMI EMC 3048	THE 31ST OF FEBRUARY STREET	15
74	EMI TC EXSP 1601	THE MUSIC AND LIFE OF CLIFF RICHARD (6-cassette box set, music & intervews, with Brian Bennett, Olivia Newton-John, Cilla Black etc.)	15
82	EMI PSLP 350	CLIFF (promo-only sampler)	20
87	EMI EMDB 1004	ALWAYS GUARANTEED (box set, some in embossed sleeve with free 7" "Another Christmas Day")	15
89	EMI CR 1	THE 30TH ANNIVERSARY PICTURE RECORD COLLECTION (2-LP, picture discs, gatefold sleeve, mail-order only)	15

MINT VALUE £

OTHER LPs

63 Elstree Extra Range SUMMER HOLIDAY (2-LP, full soundtrack recording, 80 copies only) 700
64 Elstree Extra Range WONDERFUL LIFE (2-LP, full soundtrack recording, 150 copies only) 700
64 World Record Club T 643 HOW WONDERFUL TO KNOW (mono) 15
64 World Record Club (S)T 643 HOW WONDERFUL TO KNOW (stereo) 20
64 EMI Regal SREG 1120 ME AND MY SHADOWS (export issue) 70
69 World R. Club STP 1051 CLIFF RICHARD 30

WENDY RICHARD & DIANA BERRY

(see also Mike Sarne)

63 Decca F 11680 We Had A Dream/Keep 'Em Looking Around 15

RICHARD & GLEN

72 Duke DU 141 Boat To Progress (Parts 1 & 2) 15

RICHARD & YOUNG LIONS

66 Philips BF 1520 Open Up Your Door/Once Upon Your Smile 50

RICHARD BROTHERS

(see also Joe White)

63 Island WI 060 I Need A Girl/Desperate Lover 12
63 Island WI 109 I Shall Wear A Crown/BABA BROOKS: Robin Hood 20

CYNTHIA RICHARDS

(see also Bobby Aitken, Lord Comic, Sir Lord Comic)

69 Clandisc CLA 203 Foolish Fool/KING STITT: On The Street 15
70 Clandisc CLA 210 Conversation/DYNAMITES: Conversation Version II 12
70 Clandisc CLA 216 Can't Wait/Promises 7
70 Clandisc CLA 220 Foolish Fool/CLANCY & STITT: Dance Beat 12
71 Clandisc CLA 229 Stand By Your Man (actually by Merlene Webber)/DYNAMITES: Version 2 6
71 Big Shot BI 581 I'm Moving On/HIPPY BOYS: I'm Moving On - Version 7
71 Escort ERT 861 Love & Unity/MAYTONES: Wah Noh Dead 7
71 G.G. GG 4528 Place In My Heart/You've Got A Friend (act. Irving [Brown] & Cynthia Richards).. 8
72 Pama Supreme PS 366 Mr Postman/SKIN, FLESH AND BONES: Version 10
73 Attack ATT 8047 Aily I/REID'S ALL STARS: Aily I - Version 6
70 Trojan TBL 123 FOOLISH FOOL (LP, actually Clancy Eccles productions compilation) 30

JOHNNY RICHARDS

59 Esquire 32-076 THE RITES OF DIABLO (LP) 25

KEITH RICHARDS

(see also Rolling Stones, Aranbee Pop Symphony Orchestra, Dirty Strangers, Screamin' Jay Hawkins)

79 Rolling Stones RSR 102 Run Rudolph Run/The Harder They Come (p/s) 18
86 Arista ARIST 678P Jumping Jack Flash/Integrity (with Aretha Franklin) (shaped pic disc & plinth).. 12
88 Virgn VS 1125 Take It So Hard/I Could Have Stood You Up (p/s) 5
88 Virign VST 1125 Take It So Hard/I Could Have Stood You Up/It Means A Lot (12", p/s) 8
89 Virgin VS 1179 Make No Mistake (Edit)/It Means A Lot (p/s) 6
89 Virgin VST 1179 Make No Mistake (Extended Version)/(LP Version)/It Means A Lot (12", p/s)...... 8
88 Virgin KEITH 1234 Make No Mistake/Locked Away/Struggle/Big Enough (4 x 1-sided 7", "Talk Is Cheap" sampler box set, promo only) 90
88 Virgin 2-91047 A/B/C TALK IS CHEAP (3 x 3" CDs in tin) 40

LISA RICHARDS

65 Vocalion VP 9244 Mean Old World/Take A Chance 70
65 Vocalion VP 9244 Mean Old World/Take A Chance (DJ copy) 70

LLOYD RICHARDS

64 Port-O-Jam PJ 4004 Be Good/I Need You 25

ROY RICHARDS

(see also Roland Alphonso, Lord Comic, Soul Vendors, Jackie Mittoo, Derrick Morgan, Righteous Flames)

66 Doctor Bird DB 1012 Contact/Maureen 20
66 Island WI 297 Green Collie/MARCIA GRIFFITHS: You No Good 25
66 Island WI 283 Double Trouble/FITSY & FREDDY: Why Did You Do It 30
66 Island WI 299 Western Standard Time/(JA) EAGLES: What An Agony 35
66 Island WI 3000 South Viet Nam/You Must Be Sorry (Vocal) 20
67 Island WI 3027 Rub-A-Dub/SHARKS: Baby Come Home 25
67 Island WI 3037 Hopeful Village Ska/DELROY WILSON: Ungrateful Baby 35
67 Island WI 3050 Port-O-Jam/DELROY WILSON: Get Ready 45
67 Studio One SO 2020 Hanky Panky/ALTON ELLIS: I Am Still In Love 50

RUSTY RICHARDS

60 Top Rank JAR 297 Middle Hand Road/Golden Moon (China Night) 7

TRUDY RICHARDS

57 Capitol CL 14728 Wishbone/Hangin' Around 10
57 Capitol CL 14744 Weaker Than Wise/I Want A Big Butter And Egg Man 6
58 Capitol CL 14857 Somebody Just Like You/The Night When Love Was Born 6
57 Capitol T 838 CRAZY IN LOVE (LP) 15

VIC RICHARDS

67 Polydor 56163 Jonathan Whatsit/Goodbye 70

WINSTON RICHARDS

67 Rio R 124 Studio Blitz/Don't Up 20

DEL RICHARDSON

(see also Osibisa, Sundae Times)

73 MCA MUPS 491 PIECES OF A JIGSAW (LP, black/silver label) 100

JOE 'GROUNDHOG' RICHARDSON

69 Major Minor MM 632 Take It Off/Blues To Take It Off 15

MARK RICHARDSON

65 Stateside SS 440 Baby, I'm Sorry/Blanket Fair 7
65 Stateside SS 467 See It My Way/Think 7

MINT VALUE £

RICH FEVER
70 Parlophone R5869 — Everything's Moving/King Of All The Kingdoms . . . 25
71 Parlophone R 5894 — Song Of A Sad Man/Island Dreams . . . 12

RICH GYPSY
80 Splash SP 016 — What Hit Me (no p/s) . . . 25

RICH KIDS
(see also Sex Pistols, Ultravox, Spectres, Swingers, Visage)
78 EMI EMI 2738 — Rich Kids/Empty Words (red vinyl, p/s) . . . 5
78 EMI EMI 2803 — Marching Men/Here Comes The Nice (p/s) . . . 6
78 EMI EMC 3263 — GHOSTS OF PRINCES IN TOWERS (LP) . . . 15

JONATHAN RICHMAN & MODERN LOVERS
75 United Artists UP 36006 — Road Runner/It Will Stand . . . 7
77 Beserkley BZZ 1 — Road Runner (Once)/Road Runner (Twice) (p/s) . . . 5
77 Beserkley BSERK 9 — ROCK 'N' ROLL WITH THE MODERN LOVERS (LP) . . . 20
77 Beserkley BSERK 2 — JONATHAN RICHMAN AND THE MODERN LOVERS (LP) . . . 25
77 Beserkley BSERK 12 — MODERN LOVERS LIVE (LP) . . . 12
77 Beserkley BSERK 17 — BACK IN YOUR LIFE (LP) . . . 18
84 Rough Trade ROUGH 52 — JONATHAN SINGS (LP) . . . 15
85 Rough Trade ROUGH 72 — ROCKIN' & ROMANCE (LP) . . . 15

RICH MIX
83 Satril 12 SAT 509 — I Got The Love/Version (12") . . . 15

RICHMOND
73 Dart ART 2008 — Candy Dora/Willow Farm . . . 12
73 Dart ART 2025 — Frightened/Breakfast . . . 8
73 Dart ART 2031 — Raise Your Heads To The Wind/All I Really Need . . . 5
74 Dart ART 2044 — Peaches/Work For My Baby . . . 6
73 Dart ARTS 65371 — FRIGHTENED (LP, textured sleeve, lyric insert) . . . 30

BEN RICHMOND
63 Piccadilly 7N 35092 — Blue Bird/Bells All Started Ringing . . . 6
63 Piccadilly 7N 35132 — You Gotta Have Love/I Don't Care . . . 6

FIONA RICHMOND
73 Raymond PR 112 — FRANKLY FIONA (LP) . . . 50

JANET RICHMOND
60 Top Rank JAR 288 — You Got What It Takes/Not One Minute More . . . 10
60 Top Rank JAR 378 — June Bride/My One And Only Love . . . 7
61 Top Rank JAR 536 — Senora/I Need You . . . 10

RICHUS FLAMES
(see also Righteous Flames)
67 Fab FAB 17 — Need To Be Loved/I Am Going Home . . . 15

RICK & KEENS
61 Mercury AMT 1150 — Peanuts/I'll Be Home . . . 75

RICK & SANDY
65 Decca F 12196 — Lost My Girl/I Can't Help It . . . 35
65 Decca F 12311 — Creation/In A 100 Years From Now . . . 25

RICK AND SANDY
65 Decca F 12311 — Creation/In A Hundred years Form Now . . . 6
65 Mercury MF 843 — Half As Much/Cotton Fields . . . 6

BERESFORD RICKETTS
60 Starlite ST45 025 — Cherry Baby/I Want To Know . . . 30
60 Starlite ST45 029 — Baby Baby/When I Woke Up . . . 30
61 Starlite ST45 048 — Hold Me Tight/Dream Girl (as Ricketts & Rowe) . . . 30
62 Starlite ST45 079 — I'm Going To Cry/Waiting For Me . . . 30
62 Blue Beat BB 107 — You Better Be Going/I've Been Walking (as Beresford Ricketts & Blue Beats) . . . 22
63 Dice CC 12 — Oh Jean/Rivers Of Tears (as Lauren Aitken's Group) . . . 20
66 Blue Beat BB 350 — Jailer Bring Me Water/Careless Love . . . 22

RICO (RODRIGUEZ)
(see also Special A.K.A., Reco, Andy Capp, Don Reco, Prince Buster, Pioneers, Stranger)
61 Blue Beat BB 56 — Luke Lane Shuffle (as Rico Rodrigues & Buster's All Stars)/ BUSTER'S GROUP: Little Honey . . . 20
62 Island WI 022 — Rico Special (as Emanuel Rodrigues Orchestra; some copies may credit Reco & His Happy Orchestra)/BUNNY & SKITTER: A Little Mashin' . . . 35
62 Planetone RC 1 — London Here I Come/Midnight In Ethiopia . . . 25
62 Planetone RC 4 — Planet Rock/You Win . . . 20
62 Planetone RC 5 — Youth Boogie/Western Serenade (as Rico's Combo) . . . 20
67 Fab FAB 12 — Jingle Bells/Silent Night (with His Boys) . . . 10
68 Pama PM 706 — Soul Man/It's Not Unusual (as Reco Rodriguez) . . . 12
68 Pama PM 715 — Tender Foot Ska/Memories (as Reco Rodriguez) . . . 15
69 Blue Cat BS 160 — The Bullet/Rhythm In (as Reco Rodriguez & His Rhythm Aces) . . . 25
69 Doctor Bird DB 1302 — Baby Face (as Reco & Rudies)/RUDIES: News . . . 25
69 Bullet BU 407 — Tribute To Don Drummond/Japanese Invasion (as Rico Rodriquez) . . . 40
71 Duke DU 96 — Surprise Package (as Rico & Satch)/PETE JOHNSON: I'm Sorry . . . 20
70s Island IPR 2006 — Ska-Wars/Ramble (12") . . . 25
78 Island IPR 2002 — Dial Africa/Dub (12") . . . 25
79 Island IPR 2016 — Take 5/Sound Check (12") . . . 20
80 Island IPR 2030 — Children Of Sanchez/You Really Got Me/Midnight In Ethiopia (12") . . . 30
80 2-Tone CHS TT 15 — Sea Cruise/Carolina . . . 20
82 2-Tone CHS TT 19 — Jungle Music/Rasta Call You (paper label, 2-Tone sleeve, with Special A.K.A.) . . . 25
82 2-Tone CHS TT 1219 — Jungle Music/Rasta Call You/Easter Island (12", p/s, with Special A.K.A.) . . . 20
69 Trojan TTL 12 — BLOW YOUR HORN (LP, as Rico & Rudies) . . . 35

MINT VALUE £

78	Island ILPS 9485	MAN FROM WARREIKA (LP)	12
78	Ghetto Rockers PRE 1	WARREIKA DUB (LP, white label, white sleeve, beware of bootlegs)	80
81	2 Tone CHR TT 5005	THAT MAN IS FORWARD (LP)	25
82	2 Tone CHR TT5006	JAMA RICO (LP)	50

RICOCHET

80	Heavy Rock HER 1	Midas Light/Off The Rails (p/s)	400

RICOCHET KLASHNEKOFF

02	Y n R YNR09	Daggo Mentality/Jankrowville (12")	12
03	Kemet KERRK002	Murder/Parrowdice (12")	8

RICOTTI & ALBUQUERQUE

(see also Frank Ricotti, Henry Lowther)

71	Pegasus PEG 2	FIRST WIND (LP)	30

FRANK RICOTTI QUARTET

(see also Ricotti & Albuquerque, Chris Spedding)

69	CBS 52668	OUR POINT OF VIEW (LP)	40

NELSON RIDDLE ORCHESTRA

(see also Shirley Bassey)

63	Capitol CL 15253	Route 66 Theme/Lolita Ya Ya	5
66	Stateside SS 517	Batman Theme (from the T.V. series)/Nelson's Riddler	8
62	Capitol (S)T 1771	ROUTE 66 AND OTHER GREAT T.V. THEMES (LP)	12
62	MGM MGM-C 896	LOLITA (LP, soundtrack)	25
64	Stateside SL 10090	WHAT A WAY TO GO! (LP, soundtrack)	12
64	Reprise R 2021	ROBIN AND THE SEVEN HOODS (LP, soundtrack)	20
66	Stateside S(S)L 10179	BATMAN (LP, TV soundtrack)	60
67	Columbia S(C)X 6155	EL DORADO (LP, soundtrack)	25

RIDDLERS

66	Polydor BM 56716	Batman Theme/Weegie Walk	30

RIDE

89	Creation CRE 072T	Chelsea Girl EP (12")	10
90	Creation CRE 075T	Play EP (12")	10
90	Creation CRE 087T	FALL EP (12")	10
94	Creation CRE 189T	I Don't Know Where It Comes From/Drive Blind/From Time To Time/ How Does It Feel To Feel (p/s)	5
90	Creation CRELP 074	NOWHERE (LP)	30
92	Creation CRELP 124	GOING BLANK AGAIN (LP)	20
94	Creation CRELP 147	CARNIVAL OF LIGHT (LP)	15
96	Creation CRELP 180	TARANTULA (LP)	20

PAT RIDEN & BROTHER LLOYD'S ALL STARS

(see also Pat Rhoden)

69	Mercury MF 1072	I Need Help/Let The Red Wine Flow (actually by Pat Rhoden)	6

JACKIE RIDING & IMESON SOUND

66	Fab FAB 4	Don't Wanna Leave/The Wave	8

RIFF

64	Blue Beat BB 242	Oh What A Feeling/Primitive Man	70

RIFF-RAFF

73	RCA RCA 2396	Copper Kettle/You Must Be Joking	5
73	RCA SF 8351	RIFF-RAFF (LP, with booklet)	45

RIFF RAFF

78	Chiswick SW 34	I WANNA BE A COSMONAUT (EP)	10
73	RCA SF 8351	RIFF-RAFF (LP, without booklet)	25
74	RCA LPL1 5023	ORIGINAL MAN (LP)	25

RIFKIN

68	Page One POF 071	Continental Hesitation/We're Not Those People Any More	70

THE RIFLES

05	Blow Up BU 029	Peace And Quiet/Breakdown (die-cut Blow Up sleeve)	10
05	Xtra Mile XMR 007	When I'm Alone/Holiday In The Sun (p/s)	5

BRAM RIGG SET

67	Stateside SS 2020	Take The Time Be Yourself/I Can Only Give You Everything	70

DIANA RIGG

72	RCA RCA 2178	Forget Yesterday/Sentimental Journey	20
02	Harkit HRKLP	DIANA RIGG SINGS (LP, test pressings only)	40

JACKIE RIGGS

56	London HLF 8244	The Great Pretender/His Gold Will Melt	40

RIGHTEOUS BROTHERS

(see also Bill Medley, Bobby Hatfield)

63	London HL 9743	Little Latin Lupe Lu/I'm So Lonely	10
63	London HL 9814	My Babe/Fee-Fi-Fidily-I-Oh	10
65	Pye International 7N 25297	Bring Your Love To Me/Try To Find Another Man	8
65	Pye International 7N 25304	Something's Got A Hold On Me/Night Owl	5
65	London HL 9962	Just Once In My Life/The Blues (withdrawn)	25
65	London HL 10011	Ebb Tide/(I Love You) For Sentimental Reasons	12
66	Pye International 7N 25358	Georgia On My Mind/My Tears Will Go Away	7
66	Verve VS 535	(You're My) Soul And Inspiration/B Side-Blues	7
66	Verve VS 537	He/He Will Break Your Heart	7
66	Sue WI 4018	You Can Have Her/Justine	20
66	London HL 10086	The White Cliffs Of Dover/Baby She's Mine	7
66	Verve VS 547	Island In The Sun/What Now My Love	8
77	Phil Spector Int'l 2010 022	You've Lost That Lovin' Feelin'/RIGHTEOUS BROTHERS BAND: Rat Race (ins't)	5

			MINT VALUE £
65	Pye Intl. NEP 44043	THE RIGHTEOUS BROTHERS (EP)	15
66	Verve VEP 5024	SOUL AND INSPIRATION (EP)	15
66	Verve VEP 5025	THE RIGHTEOUS BROTHERS (EP, reissue)	10
65	Pye Intl. NPL 28056	SOME BLUE-EYED SOUL (LP)	20
65	London HA-U 8226	YOU'VE LOST THAT LOVIN' FEELIN' (LP)	20
65	Pye Intl. NPL 28059	RIGHT NOW! (LP)	15
65	London HA 8245	JUST ONCE IN MY LIFE (LP)	15
66	London HA 8278	BACK TO BACK (LP)	15
66	Verve (S)VLP 9131	SOUL AND INSPIRATION (LP)	15
66	Sue ILP 937	IN ACTION! (LP)	40
68	Verve (S)VLP 9190	SOULED OUT (LP)	15
67	Verve VS 560	Standing In The Middle Of No Place/Been So Nice	12

RIGHTEOUS FLAMES
(see also Richus Flames, Alton Ellis, Flames, Soul Vendors)

67	Fab FAB 18	Gimme Some Sign Girl/Let's Go To The Dance (B-side act. by Prince Buster)	60
67	Fab FAB 30	When A Girl Loves A Boy	40
68	Coxsone CS 7061	You Don't Know/ROY RICHARDS & SOUL VENDORS: Summertime	200
71	High Note HS 052	Run To The Rock/GAYTONES: Run To The Rock Version	10
71	Nu Beat NB 083	Love And Emotion/Version	10

RIGHTEOUS HOMES (FLAMES)

68	Coxsone CS 7049	I Was Born To Be Loved/NORMA FRAZER: Heartaches	40
68	Blue Cat BS 112	Seven Letters (actually by Winston Jarrett)/SOUL VENDORS: To Sir With Love	40

RIGHTEOUS SOULS

71	Supreme SUP 217	Mount Zion/ECCLE & NEVILL: All Over	10

RIGHTEOUS TWINS

69	Blue Cat BS 174	If I Could Hear My Master/Satan Can't Prevail	40

RIGOR MORTIS
(see John Entwistle, Who)

73	Track 2094 107	Made In Japan/Hound Dog	8
73	Track 2406 106	RIGOR MORTIS SETS IN (LP, gatefold, inner sleeve)	20

RIKKI & CUFFLINKS

79	Different HAVE 17	Nervous Breakdown/Steamin' On	5

RIKKI & THE LAST DAYS OF EARTH

77	(own label)	Oundle 29/5/77 (1-sided)	60
77	DJM DJS 10814	City Of The Damned/Victimized (p/s)	10
77	DJM DJF 20526	FOUR MINUTE WARNING (LP)	12

RILEY ALL STARS

76	Concrete Jungle CJDPLP	CONCRETE JUNGLE DUB (LP, 300 pressed)	400

BILLY LEE RILEY
(see also Megatons)

65	King KG 1015	I've Been Searchin'/Everybody's Twistin'	8
69	Stax STAX 120	Going Back To Memphis/Family Portrait	10
72	CBS 8182	I Got A Thing About You Baby/You Don't Love Me A.K.A Shimmy Shimmy Walk	7

BOB RILEY

58	MGM MGM 977	The Midnight Line/Wanda Jean	65
58	MGM MGM 977	The Midnight Line/Wanda Jean (78)	25

DESMOND RILEY

69	Downtown DT 432	Tear Them/GEORGE LEE & RUDIES: Chaka Ground	15
69	Downtown DT 435	Tears On My Pillow/RUDIES: Man Pon Spot	10
69	Downtown DT 436	If I Had Wings/AUDREY: You'll Lose A Good Thing	10
69	Downtown DT 438	Out Your Fire/No Return	12
69	Downtown DT 450	Skinhead, A Message To You/MUSIC DOCTORS: Going Strong	45
69	Downtown DT 454	If I Had Wings/AUDREY: You'll Lose A Good Thing (reissue)	6

HOWARD RILEY (TRIO)
(see also Colosseum, Karyobin)

68	Opportunity CP 2499	DISCUSSIONS (LP with insert, as Howard Riley Trio)	800
69	CBS 52669	ANGLE (LP)	40
70	CBS 64077	THE DAY WILL COME (LP)	60
71	Turtle TUR 301	FLIGHT (LP, gatefold sleeve)	140
76	Incus INCUS 13	SYNOPSIS (LP, as Howard Riley Trio with Tony Oxley & Barry Guy)	100
79	Spotlite	THE OTHER SIDE (LP)	15

JEANNIE C. RILEY

68	Polydor 56748	Harper Valley P.T.A/Yesterday All Day Long Today	6
68	Polydor 56856	The Girl Most Likely/Scrapbook	6
69	Polydor 583 716	HARPER VALLEY P.T.A. (LP)	12
69	Polydor 583 733	YEARBOOKS AND YESTERDAYS (LP)	12

JIMI/JIMMY RILEY
(see also Martin Riley, Sensations, Uniques)

71	Supreme SUP 217	Mount Zion (actually by Jimi Riley & Stranger Cole)/ECCLE & NEVIL: All Over	7
75	Dip DL 5067	Ram Goat Liver/OMAR & MARSHA PERRY: Ram Goat Dub	5
79	Attack TACK 1	Give Thanks And Praise/Feeling Is Believing (12")	20
78	Burning Sounds BS 1011	SHOWCASE (LP)	25
78	Burning Sounds BS 1029	MAJORITY RULE (LP)	25
79	Trojan TRLS 167	TELL THE YOUTHS THE TRUTH (LP)	20

MARTIN RILEY
(see also Slim Smith, Slickers)

69	Gas GAS 114	Walking Proud/LLOYD CHARMERS: Why Baby	35
69	Punch PH 7	Trying To Be Free/I've Got It Bad	10
70	Camel CA 53	Catch This Sound/Suspense	10

MINT VALUE £

70	Escort ES 823	It Grows (actually "It's Growing")/We Had A Good Thing Going	20
71	Camel CA 77	When Will We Be Paid/WILLIE FRANCIS: He's Got The Whole World In His Hands	8

TERRY RILEY
(see also John Cale)

71	CBS 64259	CHURCH OF ANTHRAX (LP, with John Cale)	20
71	CBS 64564	A RAINBOW IN CURVED AIR (LP)	15
71	CBS 64565	IN "C" (LP)	18
72	Shandar 83501/2	PERSIAN SURGERY DERVISHES (2-LP)	30

WINSTON RILEY
(see also Techniques)

73	Techniques TE 922	Woman Don't You Go Astray/Travelling Man	8

RILEY'S ALLSTARS
(see also Bobby Davis, Techniques)

71	Banana BA 343	Glory Of Love (actually "Mystic Blue" by Hugh Hendricks & Buccaneers)/ We'll Cry Together - Version	10

RIMBARA

85	Cordelia	ON DRY LAND (LP, with free 7", 400 copies only)	30

RIMINGTON

73	Man MAM 95	In The Grip Of The Mullah/Dragon Child	20

SHANE RIMMER

59	Columbia DB 4293	(Roll Along) Wagon Train/A Touch Of Pink	10
59	Columbia DB 4343	The Three Bells (Jimmy Brown Song) (as Shane Rimmer & Spinners)/ I Want To Take You Home	10

RIMSHOTS

82	Respond RESP 3	Sweet Talk/What's The Matter Baby (p/s)	6

RINGS
(see also Maniacs, Twink)

77	Chiswick S 14	I Wanna Be Free/Automobile (p/s)	10

RINGS & THINGS

68	Fontana TF 987	Strange Things Are Happening/To Me: To Me: To Me	140

RINKY DINKS
(see also Bobby Darin)

58	London HLE 8679	Early In The Morning/Now We're One (as Rinky-Dinks featuring Bobby Darin)	40
58	London HLE 8679	Early In The Morning/Now We're One (78)	30
59	London HLE 8793	Mighty Mighty Man/You're Mine (as Bobby Darin with Rinky Dinks)	30
59	London HLE 8793	Mighty Mighty Man/You're Mine (78)	30

BOBBY RIO (U.S.)

63	Stateside SS 211	Don Diddley/I Got You	25

BOBBY RIO (& REVELLES)

65	Pye 7N 15790	Boy Meets Girl/Don't Break My Heart And Run Away	60
65	Pye 7N 15897	Everything In The Garden/When Love Was Young	50
65	Pye 7N 15958	Value For Love/I'm Not Made Of Clay	50
66	Piccadilly 7N 35303	Ask The Lonely/Be Lonely Little Girl (solo)	25
66	Piccadilly 7N 35337	Angelica/Lovin' You (solo)	12

RIO GRANDE

71	RCA SF 8208	RIO GRANDE (LP)	15

RIO GRANDES

66	Pyramid PYR 6001	Soldiers Take Over/Moses	15

RIOT

77	Ariola ARL 5007	ROCK CITY (LP)	12
78	Capitol E-ST 12081	NARITA (LP)	12

RIOT CLONE

82	Riot Clone RC 001	THERE'S NO GOVERNMENT LIKE NO GOVERNMENT (EP)	15
82	Riot Clone RC 002	DESTROY THE MYTH OF MUSICAL DESTRUCTION (EP)	12
84	Riot Clone RCR 004	BLOOD ON YOUR HANDS (EP)	8

RIOTS
(see also Techniques)

65	Island WI 176	Telling Lies/Don't Leave Me (actually by Techniques)	40
65	Island WI 195	You Don't Know (actually by Techniques)/ DON DRUMMOND & DRUMBAGO: Treasure Island	40
65	Island WI 197	I Am In Love/When You're Wrong (actually by Techniques)	40
65	Island WI 247	Yeah Yeah/BABA BROOKS: Virginia Ska	40

RIOT SQUAD
(see also Graham Bonney, Jimi Hendrix Experience, Blue Aces)

65	Pye 7N 15752	Any Time/Jump	40
65	Pye 7N 15817	I Wanna Talk About My Baby/Gonna Make You Mine	45
65	Pye 7N 15869	Nevertheless/Not A Great Talker	45
66	Pye 7N 17041	Cry Cry Cry/How Is It Done	45
66	Pye 7N 17092	I Take It We're Through/Working Man	100
66	Pye 7N 17130	It's Never Too Late To Forgive/Try To Realise	45
67	Pye 7N 17237	Gotta Be A First Time/Bitter Sweet Love	50

RIOT SQUAD

82	Final Hour FHE001	TOTAL ONSLAUGHT EP (p/s)	7

RIOT SQUAD

82	Rondelet ROUND 23	Fuck The Tories/Civil Destruction (p/s)	8
82	Rondelet ROUND 25	Riot In The City/Religion (p/s)	8
83	Rot ASS 1	DON'T BE DENIED (EP)	20

			MINT VALUE £
83	Rot ASS 2	I'm OK Fuck You/In The Future/Friday Night (p/s)	15
84	Rot ASS 3	THERE AIN'T NO SOLUTION (EP)	6
84	Rot ASS 13	NO POTENTIAL THREAT (LP, with free single [ASS3], stickered sleeve)	12

RIOT SQUAD & MATUMBI

82	Extinguish EXT 004	Why Do You Make Me Wait/Paraphrase (12")	20

RIP CHORDS

78	Cells SELL 1	Ringing In The Streets/Music's Peace Artist/Television Television (p/s)	18

RIP CHORDS (U.S.)

(see also Terry Day, Terry Melcher, Bruce Johnston)

63	CBS AAG 143	Here I Stand/Karen	20
63	CBS AAG 162	Gone/She Thinks I Still Care	20
64	CBS AAG 181	Hey Little Cobra/The Queen	30
64	CBS AAG 202	Three Window Coupe/Hot Rod USA	35
64	CBS BPG 62228	HEY LITTLE COBRA (LP)	80

RIPCORD

89	private pressing	HARVEST HARDCORE (EP, foldout sleeve)	15
86	Raging RAGE 1	DAMAGE IS DONE (flexi)	10
88	Raging RAGE 001	POETIC JUSTICE (LP, with inner)	15

RIPLEY WAYFARERS

71	Tradition TSR 006	CHIPS AND BROWN SAUCE (LP, 500 only with front-laminated dark green and white flipback sleeve, title in blue)	30
72	Tradition TSR 013	FIVE WELLS (LP)	15
74	Tradition TSR 018	GENTLEMEN OF HIGH RENOWN (LP)	15
78	MWM MWM 1017	SONG AND DANCE TUNES (LP, as The Wayfarers)	12
73	Tradition TSR 006	CHIPS AND BROWN SAUCE (LP, reissue, plain green sleeve, title in black)	15

RIP 'N' LAW

71	Crab CRAB 64	In The Ghetto/Something Sweet	6

RIPPERS

68	Saga	HONESTLY (LP)	30

MINNIE RIPPERTON

74	Epic KE32561	PERFECT ANGEL (LP)	20

RIP RIG & PANIC

81	Virgin VZZ13	GOD (2x12")	15

RISAN

82	Saffron	Eastern Palace/Part 2	15
82	Saffron	Eastern Palace/Part 2	30

RISING MOON

74	Theatre Projects	RISING MOON (LP)	30

RISING SONS (U.K.)

68	Pye 7N 17554	Hold Me Just A Little While Longer/Fountain Of Love	10

RISING SONS (U.S.)

65	Stateside SS 426	You're My Girl/Try To Be A Man	35

RITA

69	Major Minor MM 653	Erotica/Sexologie	15

RITA (Alston)

(see also Rita Alston)

69	Jackpot JP 718	Love Making/NAT COLE: My Love	5

RITA & TIARAS

79	Destiny DS 1002	Gone With The Wind Is My Love/Wild Times (with p/s)	8
79	Destiny DS 1002	Gone With The Wind Is My Love/Wild Times	10
79	Destiny DS 1002	Gone With The Wind Is My Love/Wild Times (DJ copy with p/s)	25

JEAN RITCHIE

53	Argo ARL 1012	SONGS FROM KENTUCKY VOL. 1 (10" LP)	30
53	Argo ARL 1013	SONGS FROM KENTUCKY VOL.2 (10" LP)	30
53	Argo TM.17	SONGS FROM KENTUCKY VOL. 1 (10" LP, reissue)	35
53	Argo TM.18	SONGS FROM KENTUCKY VOL. 2 (10" LP, reissue)	35
60s	Transatlantic XTRA 1030	JEAN RITCHIE (LP)	15

TEX RITTER

54	Capitol CL 14175	Is There A Santa Claus?/Old Tex Kringle	5
55	Capitol CL 14277	A Whale Of A Tale/High On A Mountain Top	5
55	Capitol CL 14335	Marshal Of Wichita/September Song	5
56	Capitol CL 14581	The Wayward Wind/Gunsmoke	5
56	Capitol CL 14605	The Searchers/Remember The Alamo	5
56	Capitol CL 14660	The Last Wagon/Paul Bunyan Love	5
57	Capitol CL 14684	Green Grow The Lilacs/The Touch Of The Masters Hand	5
52	Capitol LC 6552	COWBOY FAVOURITES (10" LP)	20
60	Capitol (S)T 1292	BLOOD ON THE SADDLE (LP)	15

BOB RITTERBUSH

59	Top Rank JAR 118	I Wish That You Were Mine/Darling Corey	7

RITZ

(see also Paul Ryder & The Time Machine)

74	Dawn DNS 1070	Jenny Gentle/Why Love	15

RIVALS

74	Decca F 13509	Speedway/Hoskins Still Rides	10

RIVALS

78	Sound On Sound SOS 100	Skateboarding In The UK/Top Of The Pops	35

MINT VALUE £

RIVALS
80 Ace ACE 007 — Future Rights/Flowers (p/s) — 100
80 Oakwood/Ace ACE 011 — Here Comes The Night/Both Sides (p/s) — 40

RIVAL SAVAGES
80 Savage VC 1968 — Get Some (gatefold p/s) — 25

HECTOR RIVERA
67 Polydor 65728 — At The Party/Do It To Me — 60

BLUE RIVERS & MAROONS
67 Columbia Blue Beat DB 103 — Witchcraft Man/Searching For You Baby — 25
68 Spectrum SP 105 — Take It Or Leave It/I've Been Pushed Around — 10
68 Columbia S(C)X 6192 — BLUE BEAT IN MY SOUL (LP) — 50

CLIFF RIVERS
63 London HLU 9739 — True Lips/Marsha — 40
(pseudonym for Joey Castle)

DANNY RIVERS
60 Top Rank JAR 408 — Hawk/I Got — 40
60 Decca F 11294 — Can't You Hear My Heart/I'm Waiting For Tomorrow — 25
61 Decca F 11357 — Once Upon A Time/My Baby's Gone Away (with Alexander Combo) — 40
64 Decca F 11865 — There Will Never Be Anyone Else/I Don't Think You Know How I Feel — 20
62 HMV POP 1000 — We're Gonna Dance/Movin' In (as Danny Rivers & River Men) — 50

DEEK RIVERS
62 Oriole CB 1735 — One Kiss/Outsider — 25
81 Chiswick NS 71 — Elvis Presley Medley/ELVIS PRESLEY: Press Conference Vancouver 1957 (picture disc) — 5

JOHNNY RIVERS
61 Pye Intl. 7n 25118 — Blue Skies/That Someone Should Be Me — 10
64 Liberty LIB 66032 — Memphis/It Won't Happen With Me — 10
64 Liberty LIB 66056 — Maybellene/Walk Myself n Home — 10
65 Liberty LIB 66087 — Midnight Special/Cupid — 10
65 Liberty LIB 66112 — The Seventh Son/Un-Square Dance — 8
65 Liberty LIB 12021 — He Don't Love You Like I Love You/Where Have All The Flowers Gone — 7
66 Liberty LIB 12023 — Secret Agent Man/Tom Dooley — 15
66 Liberty LIB 66144 — Under Your Spell Again/Long Time Man — 7
66 Liberty LIB 66175 — I Washed My Hands In Muddy Water/Roogalator — 15
66 Liberty LIB 66205 — Poor Side Of Town/A Man Can Cry — 12
67 Liberty LIB 66227 — Baby I Need Your Loving/Getting Ready For Tommorrow — 10
68 Liberty LIB 15078 — Look To Your Soul/Something Strange — 7
69 Liberty LBF 15241 — Muddy River/Resurrection — 7
66 Liberty LEP 4049 — MORE JOHNNY RIVERS (EP) — 15
64 Liberty LBY 3031 — AT THE WHISKY A GO-GO (LP) — 15
65 Liberty LBY 3036 — HERE WE A GO-GO AGAIN (LP) — 15

MAVIS RIVERS
60 Capitol CL 15120 — So Rare/Longing, Longing, Longing — 5
63 Reprise RS 20115 — Slightly Out Of Tune/Footsteps Of A Fool — 8
60 Capitol ST 1408 — THE SIMPLE LIFE (LP) — 12

ROYD RIVERS & CLIFF AUNGIER
(see also Cliff Aungier)
65 Decca LK 4696 — WANDERIN' (LP) — 35

TONY RIVERS & THE CASTAWAYS
(see also Capability Brown, Grapefruit, Harmony Grass, Senators, Sugarbeats)
63 Columbia DB 7135 — Shake Shake Shake/Row Row Row — 20
64 Columbia DB 7224 — I Love The Way You Walk/I Love You — 15
64 Columbia DB 7336 — Life's Too Short/Tell On Me — 15
65 Columbia DB 7448 — She/Till We Get Home — 15
65 Columbia DB 7536 — Come Back/What To Do — 15
66 Columbia DB 7971 — God Only Knows/Charade — 20
66 Parlophone R 5400 — Nowhere Man/The Girl From New York City — 25
66 Immediate IM 027 — Girl Don't Tell Me/The Girl From Salt Lake City — 40
68 Polydor 56245 — I Can Guarantee Your Love/Pantomime — 12

RIVIERA
69 Pye 7N 17712 — Baby Won't Leave Me Alone/The Love Story — 5

RIVIERAS
60 HMV POP 773 — Blessing Of Love/Moonlight Cocktails — 120

RIVIERAS (U.S.)
64 Pye International 7N 25237 — California Sun/H B Goose Step — 45

RIVINGTONS
62 Liberty LIB 55427 — Papa Oom Mow Mow/Deep Water — 50
63 Liberty LIB 55553 — The Bird's The Word/I'm Losing My Grip — 60
66 CBS 202088 — Rose Growing In The Ruins/Tend To Business — 40

RIVVITS
79 Alien AUX 1 — Saturday Night At The Dance/Girl Next Door (p/s, with flexi) — 10

FREDDIE ROACH
67 Transatlantic PR 7490 — THE SOUL BOOK (LP) — 15

MAX ROACH
62 HMV CLP 1522 — PERC 'N' BITTER SUITE (LP) — 15

MAX ROACH (& CLIFFORD BROWN GROUP)
(see also Clifford Brown)
58 Emarcy ERE 1572 — MAX ROACH AND CLIFFORD BROWN (EP, withdrawn) — 12

MINT VALUE £

55	Vogue LDE 117	MAX ROACH & CLIFFORD BROWN IN CONCERT VOL. 1 (10" LP)	12
55	Vogue LDE 128	MAX ROACH & CLIFFORD BROWN IN CONCERT VOL. 2 (10" LP)	12
58	Emarcy EJL 1282	JAZZ IN THREE-QUARTER TIME (LP)	12
59	Emarcy MMB 12005	MAX ROACH, NEWPORT (LP, by Max Roach)	12
59	Emarcy MMB 12009	THE MAX ROACH FOUR PLUS FOUR (LP, by Max Roach)	12

ROAD

(see also Noel Redding)

73	Rare Earth SRE 3006	ROAD (LP)	50

ROADHOUSE

92	Vertigo VERP 57	Hell Can Wait/Loving You/Jackson High/More Than I Want (12", picture disc)	8

ROADRUNNERS

65	Cavern Sound 2BSNL 7	PANTOMANIA (EP, with tracks by Chris Edwards & Clive Wood)	35

ROADSTER

81	Mayhem SRTS 81	Fantasy/45 MPH (p/s)	100

ROADSTERS

64	Stateside SS 293	Joy Ride/Drag	40

ROARING SIXTIES

(see also Family)

66	Marmalade 598 001	We Love The Pirates/I'm Leaving Town	50

ROBAN'S SKIFFLE GROUP

61	Storyville A45 062	Careless Love/Frankie And Johnny (with p/s)	35
61	Storyville A45 062	Careless Love/Frankie And Johnny	18

E.G. ROBB

63	Columbia DB 7100	Stage To Cimarron/Jezebel	15

MARTY ROBBINS

(see also Jordanaires)

SINGLES

56	Philips PB 590	Long Tall Sally/Mr. Teardrop (78)	20
57	Philips PB 696	A White Sport Coat (And A Pink Carnation)/Grown-Up Tears (78)	25
57	Philips JK 1019	A White Sport Coat (And A Pink Carnation)/Grown-Up Tears (jukebox issue)	40
57	Philips PB 741	Please Don't Blame Me/Teen-Age Dream (78)	10
57	Philips PB 741	Please Don't Blame Me/Teen-Age Dream	10
58	Fontana H 102	The Story Of My Life/Once-A-Week Date (78)	10
58	Fontana H 128	Stairway Of Love/Just Married	20
58	Fontana H 128	Stairway Of Love/Just Married (78)	15
58	Fontana H 150	Sittin' In A Tree House/She Was Only Seventeen	15
58	Fontana H 150	Sittin' In A Tree House/She Was Only Seventeen (78)	10
59	Fontana H 184	The Hanging Tree (from film)/The Blues Country Style	10
59	Fontana H 184	The Hanging Tree (from film)/The Blues Country Style (78)	20
59	Fontana H 212	Cap And Gown/Last Night About This Time	10
59	Fontana H 212	Cap And Gown/Last Night About This Time (78)	25
59	Fontana H 229	Big Iron/Cool Water	8
59	Fontana H 229	Big Iron/Cool Water (78)	30
59	Fontana H 233	El Paso/Running Gun	8
59	Fontana H 233	El Paso/Running Gun (78)	30
60	Fontana H 263	I Told My Heart/Is There Any Chance	5
60	Fontana H 270	Ballad Of The Alamo/Five Brothers (in p/s)	10
61	Fontana H 301	Don't Worry/Like All Other Times	5
61	Fontana H 324	Ghost Train/Jimmy Martinez	5
61	Fontana H 342	It's Your World/You Told Me So	6
62	CBS AAG 114	Devil Woman/April Fool's Day	5
63	CBS AAG 128	Ruby Ann/Won't You Forgive	5
63	CBS AAG 141	Cigarette And Coffee Blues/Teenager's Dad	6
65	CBS 201789	Ribbon Of Darkness/Little Robin	5

EPs

59	Fontana TFE 17161	MARTY'S BIG HITS	15
59	Fontana TFE 17168	WEDDING BELLS	10
60	Fontana TFE 17167	SONG OF THE ISLANDS	10
61	Fontana TFE 17224	GUNFIGHTER	10

LPs

59	Fontana TFL 5063	GUNFIGHTER BALLADS AND TRAIL SONGS	20
60	Fontana TFL 5086	MARTY'S GREATEST HITS	15
61	Fontana TFL 5113	MORE GUNFIGHTER BALLADS AND TRAIL SONGS (stereo STFL 541)	20
61	Fontana TFL 5145	MORE GREATEST HITS (also stereo STFL 565)	15
61	Fontana TFL 5162	JUST A LITTLE SENTIMENTAL (with Jordanaires, also stereo STFL 579)	15
62	CBS (S)BPG 62041	MARTY AFTER MIDNIGHT	15
63	CBS (S)BPG 62113	DEVIL WOMAN (mono/stereo)	15
63	CBS BPG 62131	PORTRAIT OF MARTY (mono/stereo)	15
66	CBS (S)BPG 62689	WHAT GOD HAS DONE (LP)	12
63	CBS BPG/SBPG 62169	HAWAII'S CALLING ME (LP)	15
63	CBS 62190	THE RETURN OF THE GUNFIGHTER (LP)	15
66	CBS (S)BPG 62782	THE DRIFTER	18
65	CBS BPG 62499	TURN THE LIGHTS DOWN LOW (LP)	15

MEL ROBBINS

59	London HLM 8966	Save It/To Know You (initially pressing with triangular centre)	600
59	London HLM 8966	Save It/To Know You (later round centre)	320
59	London HLM 8966	Save It/To Know You (78)	150

SYLVIA ROBBINS

(see also Mickey & Sylvia)

60	London HLJ 9118	Frankie And Johnny/Come Home	35

MINT VALUE £

ROBERT & REMOULDS
79 Black & White BW 1 — X No. 1/Do Eyes Ever Meet? (p/s) — 60

ALAN ROBERTS
(see also Dougie MacLean)
70s Plant Life PLR 012 — CALEDONIA (LP, with Dougie Maclean) — 12

ANDY ROBERTS
(see also Clayton Squares, Liverpool Scene, Everyone, Plainsong, Mighty Baby)
73 Elektra K 12109 — Baby Baby/All Around My Grandmother's Floor — 5
70 RCA SF 8086 — HOME GROWN (LP, laminated front sleeve, lyric insert) — 80
71 Charisma CAS 1034 — HOME GROWN (LP, reissue, different sleeve) — 15
71 B&C — HOME GROWN (LP, reissue) — 18
71 Pegasus PEG 5 — NINA AND THE DREAM TREE (LP) — 40
73 Elektra K 42139 — URBAN COWBOY (LP, with insert, 'butterfly' label) — 20
73 Elektra K 42151 — ANDY ROBERTS AND THE GREAT STAMPEDE (LP, gatefold sleeve) — 15

BOB ROBERTS
70 Explosion EX 2021 — Stick By Me/TOMMY McCOOK: The Designer — 7

BOB ROBERTS (U.K.)
81 Solent SS 054 — BREEZE FOR A BARGEMAN (LP) — 15

HUGH ROBERTS
70 Explosion EX 2041 — California Dreaming/One Woman (both sides actually by Lloyd Charmers) — 8

J. ROBERTS
70 Bamboo BAM 30 — Someday We'll Be Together/SOUND DIMENSION: Everyday People — 20

JOHN ROBERTS
68 Sue WI 4042 — Sockin' 1, 2, 3, 4/Sophisticated Funk — 35
68 Action ACT 4511 — I'll Forget You/Be My Baby — 30

KEITH ROBERTS
72 Trailer LER 3031 — PIER OF THE REALM (LP, red label) — 15

KENNY ROBERTS
57 Brunswick 05638 — I'm Looking For The Bully Of The Town/Broken Teenage Heart — 12

KENNY ROBERTS
(see also Kenny Damon)
65 Pye 7N 15882 — Say, Do You Mean It/Since My Love Has Gone — 15
66 Pye 7N 17054 — Run Like The Devil/Where Goes My Heart — 40

KIM ROBERTS
64 Decca F 11813 — I'll Prove It/For Loving Me This Way — 90

MALCOLM ROBERTS
69 Major Minor MMLP 49 — MALCOLM (LP) — 12

PADDY ROBERTS
62 Decca F 11552 — Merry Christmas You Suckers/Got 'n' Idea — 6

RENEE ROBERTS
62 Oriole CB 1731 — I Want To Love You/Aching Heart — 10

RICK ROBERTS
(see also Flying Burrito Brothers)
72 A&M AMLH 64372 — WINDMILLS (LP) — 12

ROCKY ROBERTS
67 Durium DRL 50026 — SABATO SERA (LP) — 40

STEVE ROBERTS
(see also U.K.Subs)
80s EXPLP 2002 — DO YOU KNOW WHO I AM (LP) — 15

DALE ROBERTSON
60 RCA SF 5064 — PRESENTS HIS ALBUM OF WESTERN CLASSICS (LP) — 20

DON ROBERTSON
56 Capitol CL 14575 — The Happy Whistler/You're Free To Go (B-side with Lou Dinning) — 12
56 Capitol CL 14629 — Every Day That I Live (with Lou Dinning)/You — 5
59 Capitol CL 15088 — Fine Day/The Merry Men — 5

JEANNIE ROBERTSON
59 Topic 10T 52 — I KEN WHERE I'M GOING (10" LP) — 15
59 Topic 12T 96 — JEANNIE ROBERTSON (LP, blue label, with card insert) — 15
60 Collector JFS 4001 — LORD DONALD (LP) — 15

JIM ROBERTSON
55 MGM SPC 7 — Pride Of My Heart/Walkin' And Talkin' With The Lord (export issue) — 15

IVO ROBIC
59 Polydor NH 23923 — Morgen (One More Sunrise)/Ay Ay Ay Paloma (Currurrucucu Paloma) — 10

DAVE ROBIN
65 Eyemark EMS 1003 — You I Don't Want To Share/Life's Too Short — 6

EDE ROBIN
75 Crystal CR 7023 — There Must Be A Love Somewhere/Soul Over Easy — 8

RICHIE ROBIN
60 Top Rank JAR 262 — Strange Dream/GERRY GRANAHAN: It Hurts — 15

TINA ROBIN
57 Vogue Coral Q 72284 — Over Somebody Else's Shoulder/Lady Fair — 10
57 Vogue Coral Q 72294 — Never In A Million Years/Ça C'est L'Amour — 10
58 Coral Q 72309 — Everyday/Believe Me — 20
58 Coral Q 72323 — No School Tomorrow/Sugar Blues — 20
62 Mercury AMT 1199 — Get Out Of My Life/Why Did You Go — 5

MINT VALUE £

ROBIN HOODS
65 Mercury MF 865 — Wait For The Dawn/Love You So — 15

ROBINS
(see also H.B. Barnum)
60 Vogue V 9168 — Cherry Lips/Out Of The Picture — 100
60 Vogue V 9173 — Just Like That/Whole Lot Imagination — 100

JIMMY ROBINS
68 President PT 118 — I Can't Please You/I Made It Over — 150

ALVIN ROBINSON
64 Pye International 7N 25248 — Something You Got/Searchin' — 25
64 Red Bird RB 10010 — Down Home Girl/Fever — 30
66 Strike JH 307 — You Brought My Heart Right Down To My Knees/Whatever You Had — 20

ANDY ROBINSON
68 Philips SBL 7887 — PATTERNS OF REALITY (LP, laminated sleeve, black/silver label) — 30

BROTHER CLEOPHUS ROBINSON
57 Vogue EPV 1196 — BROTHER CLEOPHUS ROBINSON (EP) — 25

ROBINSON CREW
(see also Lord Rockingham's XI)
63 Decca F 11706 — Taxi (Theme From TV Series)/Stormalong — 7

DAVE ROBINSON
79 Bushays BFM 124 — Ruby & Diamond (feat. Jah Thomas/Dub (12") — 20

EDDIE ROBINSON
71 Ember EMB S 301 — Hey Blackman Parts 1 & 2 — 5
74 Myrrh MYR 1013 — REFLECTIONS OF THE MAN INSIDE (LP) — 15

ELZADIE ROBINSON
(see also Will Ezell)
50 Tempo R 33 — The Santa Claus Crave/St. Louis Cyclone Blues (78) — 10
50 Tempo R 36 — Arkansas Mill Blues/Gold Mansion Blues (78, with Will Ezell) — 10
50 Tempo R 37 — Rowdy Man Blues/Going South Blues (78) — 10

FLOYD ROBINSON
59 RCA RCA 1146 — Makin' Love/My Girl (initially with triangular centre) — 10
59 RCA RCA 1146 — Makin' Love/My Girl (later round centre) — 5
59 RCA RCA 1146 — Makin' Love/My Girl (78) — 12
60 RCA RCA 1179 — I Believe In Love/Tattletale — 8
60 RCA RD 27166 — FLOYD ROBINSON (LP) — 40

FREDDY ROBINSON
72 Stax 2325 085 — AT THE DRIVE-IN (LP) — 18

HARRY ROBINSON
(see also Lord Rockingham's XI)
60 Top Rank JAR 325 — The Skirl/Wimoweh (as Harry Robinson "String Sound") — 5
61 Decca F 11319 — Heavy Date/Sentimental Journey (as Harry Robinson's XV) — 5

JACKEY ROBINSON
(see also Jackie Robinson, Pioneers)
70 Punch PH 50 — Heart Made Of Stone (actually by Jackie Bernard)/BOB TAYLOR: I May Never See My Baby Anymore — 20

JACKIE ROBINSON
68 Amalgamated AMG 819 — Over And Over/Woman Of Samaria — 20
68 Amalgamated AMG 824 — Let The Little Girl Dance/DERRICK MORGAN: I Want To Go Home — 20
74 Harry J. HJ 6695 — My Love For You/R.D. Livingstone: Smokey Mountains — 5

JIM ROBINSON NEW ORLEANS BAND
61 Riverside RLP 369 — NEW ORLEANS: THE LIVING LEGENDS (LP) — 15
64 Riverside RLP 393 — PLAYS SPIRITUAL AND BLUES (LP) — 15

J.P. ROBINSON
72 Atlantic K 10149 — George Jackson/Wall To Wall Love — 10
72 Atlantic K 10209 — What Can I Tell Her/Please Accept My Call — 15

JUNE ROBINSON
56 Oriole CB 1319 — 45 Men In A Telephone Box/Oo-Shoo-Be-Doo-Be (78) — 10

LLOYD ROBINSON
(see also Lloyd Clarke, Lloyd Charmers, Harry J. Allstars, Matadors, Melodians)
62 Blue Beat BB 122 — Give Me A Chance/When You Walk — 20
63 Blue Beat BB 159 — I Need Your Love/You Told Me — 20
69 Duke DU 5 — Cuss Cuss/Lavender Blue — 30
70 Camel CA 41 — The Worm/NEVILLE HYNES: Afro (actually by Neville Hinds) — 12
72 Green Door GD 4028 — I Can't Forget/LLOYD AND THE NOW GENERATION: I Can't Forget - Version — 5
77 Cactus CT 109 — Rocky Road/Version — 20

M. ROBINSON
64 Port-O-Jam PJ 4114 — Who Are You/Follow You — 20

MARTEL ROBINSON
75 Arrow AR 006 — Sunny Soil/Sunny — 8

PAUL ROBINSON
83 King City KCD 006 — Come On Sister (12") — 100

ROSCO ROBINSON
66 Pye International 7N 25385 — That's Enough/One More Time — 50
66 Pye International 7N 25385 — That's Enough/One More Time (DJ copy) — 100
72 Wand WN 27 — That's Enough/One More Time (reissue) — 10
73 Contempo C 16 — We're Losing It Baby/We Got A Good Thing Going — 8

MINT VALUE £

SANDRA ROBINSON

85	Trojan TROT 9079	Sensi For Sale (part 1)/TUFF TONES: Boogie Mix (Part 2)/ SANDRA ROBINSON & TUFF TONES: Depression/DAN AMBRASSA: Life's Riddle/TUFF TONES: Boogie Mix (12")	20

SUGAR CHILE ROBINSON

53	Capitol LC 6586	CAPITOL PRESENTS SUGAR CHILE ROBINSON (10" LP)	40

TOM ROBINSON (BAND)

(see also Cafe Society, Phantom, Billy Karloff [& Extremes])

75	Chebel SRT/CUS 015	GOOD TO BE GAY (EP, as Bradford Gay Liberation Front)	15
79	EMI EMI 2946	All Right All Night/Black Angel (withdrawn, demo-only)	8

CARSON ROBISON (& HIS PLEASANT VALLEY BOYS)

53	MGM SP 1004	Lady Round The Lady/Pokeberry Promenade	10
53	MGM SP 1024	Square Dance Jitterbug/Keep On Circlin' 'Round	18
58	MGM MGM-EP 669	LIFE GETS TEEJUS (EP)	15
61	MGM MGM-EP 755	SQUARE DANCE - WITH CALLS (EP)	10
52	MGM MGM-D 101	EIGHT SQUARE DANCES (10" LP)	15

RALPH ROBLES

69	London HA/SH 8385	TAKING OVER (LP)	20

NICKY ROBSON

(see also Gary Numan)

80	Scratch SCR 006	Stars/Eye To Eye (p/s)	20
80	Scratch SCRT 006	Stars (Extended)/Eye To Eye (12")	45

ROCAMARS

65	King KG 1031	All In Black Woman/Give Me Time	20

TONY ROCCO

62	Parlophone R 4886	Stalemate/Keep A Walking	15
62	Parlophone R 4946	Competition/Torture	15

HARRY ROCHE CONSTELLATION

67	CBS 202653	Casino Royale/In The Pad Of The Mountain King	10
67	CBS SBPG 63013	CASINO ROYALE (LP)	35
71	Studio Two TWO 340	SPINDRIFT (LP)	20
73	Pye Intl. NSPL 41024	SPIRAL (LP)	40
73	Pye QUAD 1022	SOMETIMES (LP, quadrophonic)	20

ROCHEE & SARNOS

85	Nervous NERD 018	UNDERSTANDING SARNO (LP)	12

JACKIE ROCHELLE

68	Olga OLE 011	Till The End/Grown Up Games	5

DICKIE ROCK & MIAMI SHOWBAND

63	Piccadilly 7N 35154	Boys/There's Always Me	5
64	Piccadilly 7N 35202	From The Candy Store/Twenty Flight Rock	5
64	Pye 7N 15729	Just For Old Times Sake/Me Not You	5
65	Pye 7N 15750	Round And Around/Little Baby	5
65	Pye 7N 15855	Every Step Of The Way/Rock And Roll Music	5
65	Pye 7N 17063	Come Back To Stay/Can't Make Up My Mind (p/s)	5
65	Pye NEP 24251	COME BACK TO STAY (EP)	8

JOHNNY ROCK

55	Vogue VE170112	JOHNNY ROCK (EP)	40

ROCKABILLY PSYCHOSIS

84	Big Beat WIK 18	ROCKABILLY PSYCHOSIS AND THE GARAGE DISEASE (LP)	12

ROCKABILLY REBS

79	SRTS 79 CUS 524	ROCKABILLY REBS (EP, no p/s)	100

ROCK AID ARMENIA

(see also Brian May, Roger Taylor, Ritchie Blackmore, Dave Gilmour, Black Sabbath, Rush, Bruce Dickinson,

89	Life Aid Armenia ARMEN 01	Smoke On The Water/BLACK SABBATH: Paranoid (1970) (p/s)	5
89	L. A. Armenia ARMEN T01	Smoke On The Water/BLACK SABBATH: Paranoid (1970) (12", blue or white p/s)	8
89	Life Aid Armenia ARMENCD 01	Smoke On The Water (Radio Mix)/Smoke On The Water (Extended Mix)/BLACK SABBATH: Paranoid (1970) (CD)	10
90	L. A. Armenia ARMEN 002	Smoke On The Water '90 (Radio Edit)/BLACK SABBATH: Paranoid ('90) (p/s)	5

ROCK-A-TEENS

59	Columbia DB 4361	Woo-Hoo/Untrue	40

ROCK BROTHERS

56	Parlophone MSP 6201	Dungaree Doll/Livin' It Up	90
56	Parlophone R 4119	Dungaree Doll/Livin' It Up (78)	30

ROCK CANDY

71	MCA MK 5069	Remember/Don't Put Me Down	6

ROCKERS

59	Oriole CB 1501	Get Cracking/Counter Melody	10

ROCKERS

(see also Phil Lynott, Roy Wood, Status Quo)

83	CBS A 3929	We Are The Boys (Who Make All The Noise)/Rockin' On Stage (p/s)	8
83	CBS TA 3929	We Are The Boys (Who Make All The Noise) (Extended Version)/ Rockin' On Stage (12", p/s)	12

ROCKET 88

(see also Charlie Watts, Alexis Korner, Jack Bruce, Dick Heckstall-Smith)

81	Atlantic K 50776	ROCKET 88 (LP)	20

MINT VALUE £

ROCKET FROM THE CRYPT

93 Southern Studios PUS 007 Glazed/Pressures/Cut It Loose (white label test pressing, 5-10 copies only) 30
95 Elemental ELM 32S Born in 69/Ciao Patsy (p/s) 8
96 Elemental ELM 33S Young Livers/Burning Army Men (p/s) 8
96 Dinked 1 Used/Lose Your Clown (in-store giveaway) 25
98 Elemental ELM 47PIC When In Rome/Tarzan/Tiger Feet Tonight (picture disc) 8
98 Elemental ELM 48S Lipstick/Hot Heart (p/s) 10
98 Elemental ELM 49S Break It Up/Turkish Revenge (p/s) 10
95 Elemental ELM 27LP HOT CHARITY (LP) 15
08 One Little Indian ELM 50DMM ROCKET FROM THE CRYPT (LP, 1000 only) 18

ROCKETS

60 Philips PB 982 Gibraltar Rock/Walkin' Home 22
60 Philips PB 982 Gibraltar Rock/Walkin' Home (78) 40
61 Zodiac ZR 0010 Warrior/Countdown 22

ROCKIN' BERRIES

(see also Jefferson)

63 Decca F 11698 Wah Wah Wah Woo/Rockin' Berry Stomp 25
63 Decca F 11760 Itty Bitty Pieces/The Twitch 20
64 Piccadilly 7N 35197 I Didn't Mean To Hurt You/You'd Better Come Home 10
64 Piccadilly 7N 35203 He's In Town/Flashback 6
65 Piccadilly 7N 35217 What The World's Come Over You/You Don't Know What To Do 6
65 Piccadilly 7N 35236 Poor Man's Son/Follow Me 6
65 Piccadilly 7N 35254 You're My Girl/Brother Bill 10
65 Piccadilly 7N 35270 The Water Is Over My Head/Doesn't Time Fly 10
66 Piccadilly 7N 35304 I Could Make You Fall In Love/Land Of Love 6
66 Piccadilly 7N 35327 Midnight Mary/Money Grows On Trees 6
67 Piccadilly 7N 35373 Sometimes/Needs To Be 6
67 Piccadilly 7N 35400 Smile/Breakfast At Sam's 6
67 Pye 7N 17411 Dawn (Go Away)/She's Not Like Any Girl 6
68 Pye 7N 17519 When I Reach The Top/Pain 10
68 Pye 7N 17589 Mr. Blue/Land Of Love 10
73 Satril SAT 9 Day To Day/Big Louis' Birthday 10
74 Pye 7N 45394 Rock-A-Bye Nursery Rhyme/Long Time Ago 10
75 Pye 7N 45439 Black Gold/Eve 5
75 Satril SAT 101 Lonely Summertime/Send Me No Letters 6
65 Piccadilly NEP 34039 I DIDN'T MEAN TO HURT YOU (EP) 35
65 Piccadilly NEP 34043 NEW FROM THE BERRIES (EP) 35
65 Piccadilly NEP 34045 HAPPY TO BE BLUE (EP) 50
64 Piccadilly NPL 38013 IN TOWN (LP) 50
65 Piccadilly NPL 38022 LIFE IS JUST A BOWL OF BERRIES (LP) 50

ROCKIN' DUPSEE

76 Sonet SNTF718 DOIN' THE ZYDECO (LP) 20
82 Flyright FLY 592 ROCKIN' WITH DUPSEE (LP) 12

ROCKIN' FOO

70 Stateside SS 2168 Rochester River/Stranger In The Attic 6
70 Stateside SSL 10303 ROCKIN' FOO (LP) 22

ROCKIN' HENRI & HAYSEEDS

63 Decca F 11700 Sally/Sweet Adeline 5

ROCKIN' HORSE

(see also Jimmy Campbell, 23rd Turnoff, Kirkbys, Merseys)

71 Philips 6006 156 The Biggest Gossip In Town/You Say 12
72 Philips 6006 200 Julian The Hooligan/Stayed Out Late Last Night 12
70 Philips 6308 075 YES IT IS (LP, laminated sleve, black/silver label) 100

ROCKIN' RAMRODS

66 Polydor BM 56512 Don't Fool With Fu Manchu/Tears Melt The Stone 25

ROCKIN' REBELS

(see also Hot-Toddys)

63 Stateside SS 162 Wild Weekend/Wild Weekend Cha Cha 25
63 Stateside SS 187 Rockin' Crickets/Hully Gully Rock (both sides actually by Hot-Toddys) 20

ROCKIN' R's

59 London HL 8872 The Beat/Crazy Baby 50
59 London HL 8872 The Beat/Crazy Baby (78) 30

ROCKIN' SAINTS

60 Brunswick 05843 Cheat On Me, Baby/Half And Half 100

ROCKIN' STRINGS

59 Columbia DB 4349 Red Sail In The Sunset/Autumn Leaves 7

ROCKIN' VICKERS

(see also Sam Gopal, Motorhead)

64 Decca F 11993 I Go Ape/Someone Like You (as Rocking Vickers) 40
66 CBS 202051 It's Alright/Stay By Me 55
66 CBS 202241 Dandy/I Don't Need Your Kind 40

ROCKING DEVILS

75 Hot Stuff HSL 002 THAT OLD ROCK MUSIC'S HERE TO STAY (LP, most copies signed on front cover) 25
79 Hot Stuff HS 007 GOT THEM BLUES (EP, red vinyl) 20

ROCKING HORSE

71 Camel CA 75 Running Back Home/SOUL SYNDICATE BAND: Running Back - Version 6
72 Randy's RAN 522 Hard Time/Change Your Ways 8

MINT VALUE £

73	Randy's RAN 535	I'm So Fed Up/I'm So Fed Up - Version	5
74	Pyramid PYR 7009	New Situation/New Version	5
74	Sydna SYD 5026	Be Thankful/Thankful Dub	8

ROCKITS

73	Mowest MW 3012	Livin' Without You/Love My Love	6
74	Mowest MW 3016	Gimme True Love/I'm Losing You	8

ROCK MACHINE

(see also Ugly Custard)

73	T.I.M.	THEMES (LP)	60

ROCK 'N' ROLL ALLSTARS

72	B&C BCM 104	RED CHINA ROCKS (LP)	12

ROCK'N'ROLL REVIVAL SHOW

(see also Tommy Bishop's Ricochets)

68	Decca F 12752	Midnight Train/Oh Boy (both sides featuring Tommy Bishop)	5

ROCK-OLGA

60	Ember EMB S 105	Red Sails In The Sunset/My Dixieland Doll (in p/s)	10
60	Ember EMB S 105	Red Sails In The Sunset/My Dixieland Doll	5

ROCKSTAR

76	MCA MCA 265	Mummy/Over The Hill	15

ROCKSTEADYS

67	Giant GN 2	Squeeze And Freeze/JUNIOR SMITH: I'm A Good Boy	12

ROCKSTONES

(see also Gaylads)

70	Trojan TR 7762	A.B.C. Reggae/BEVERLEY'S ALLSTARS: Be Yours	6
70	Summit SUM 8501	Everything Is Beautiful/BEVERLEY'S ALLSTARS: Give Up	6

ROCK WORKSHOP

(see also Bob Downes, Alex Harvey)

70	CBS 5046	You To Lose/Born In The City	6
71	CBS 7252	Very Last Time/Light Is Light	5
70	CBS 64075	ROCK WORKSHOP (LP, orange label)	35
71	CBS 64394	THE VERY LAST TIME (LP, gatefold sleeve, orange label)	35

ROCKY FELLERS

63	Stateside SS 175	Killer Joe/Lonely Teardrops	20
63	Stateside SS 212	Like The Big Guys Do/Great Big World	18
63	Pye International 7N 25225	Ching A Ling Baby/Hey Little Donkey	22

ROCKY HORROR SHOW

(see also Tim Curry, Meat Loaf, Original Soundtracks)

75	Ode ODS 66305	Science Fiction Double Feature/Time Warp	8
87	Ode RHVX 1	ROCKY HORROR BOX SET (4-LP box, with inserts, numbered)	20
87	Ode RHBXLP 1	ROCKY HORROR BOX SET (4-LP box, with different inserts to above)	20
90	Ode RHBXCD 1	THE ROCKY HORROR PICTURE ALBUMS (15th ANNIVERSARY) (4-CD, with booklet)	40

ROCOCO

76	Mountain TOP 9	Follow That Car/Lucinda	6
73	Deram DM 375	Ultrastar/Wildfire	6

ROD & CAROLYN

63	Pye 7N 15519	How Can You Tell/What About The Teardrops	8
63	Pye 7N 15565	Bye-Bye My Lover/To Be Alone	8
64	Pye 7N 15629	Young Love/Talk To Me	8
64	Pye 7N 15706	Love Is Where You Are/I've Got You On My Mind	8

GENE RODDENBERRY

76	CBS 4692	Star Trek Theme/Star Trek Philosophy	12

RODD-KEN & CAVALIERS

(see also Blue Men)

60	Triumph RGM 1001	Magic Wheel/Happy Valley	40

CLODA(GH) RODGERS

62	Decca F 11534	Believe Me I'm No Fool/End Of The Line	10
63	Decca F 11607	Sometime Kind Of Love/I See More Of Him	10
63	Decca F 11667	To Give My Love To You/I Only Live To Love You	10
64	Decca F 11812	Mister Heartache/Time	10
65	Columbia DB 7468	Wanting You/Johnny Come Home	8
66	Columbia DB 7926	Every Day Is Just The Same/You'll Come A Running	7
66	Columbia DB 8038	Stormy Weather/Lonely Room	8
68	RCA 1684	Room Full Of Roses/Play The Drame To The End	8
68	RCA 1748	Rhythm Of Love/River Of Tears	8
69	RCA 1891	Biljo/Spider	6
69	RCA SF 8033 / RD 8033	CLODAGH RODGERS (LP)	20
69	RCA SF 8071	MIDNIGHT CLODAGH (LP)	20
71	RCA SF 8180	RODGERS AND HEART (LP)	20
72	RCA SF 8271	IT'S DIFFERENT NOW (LP, gatefold)	20
73	RCA SF 8394	YOU ARE MY MUSIC (LP)	20
77	Polydor 2383473	SAVE ME (LP)	20

EILEEN RODGERS

58	Fontana H 136	Careful, Careful/I'm Alone Because I Love You	12
58	Fontana H 156	Treasure Of Your Love/Little Bit Bluer	12
61	London HLR 9271	Sailor (Your Home Is The Sea)/Wait Till Tomorrow	15

IKE RODGERS

(see under Henry Brown)

MINT VALUE £

JEAN RODGERS

65	Columbia DB 7637	Take What I Have/Baby What You Gonna Do?	6

JIMMIE RODGERS (The Blue Yodeller)

56	HMV MH 192	Blue Yodel No. 4/Waiting For A Train (78, export issue)	15
56	HMV MH 193	In The Jailhouse Now No. 2/ Peach Picking Time Down In Georgia (78, export)	12
56	HMV MH 194	Blue Yodel No. 9/Jimmie The Kid (78, export issue)	12
58	HMV 7EG 8163	JIMMIE RODGERS (EP)	15
60	RCA RCX 1058	LEGENDARY JIMMIE RODGERS (EP)	15
59	RCA RD 27110	TRAIN WHISTLE BLUES (LP)	20
59	RCA RD 27138	NEVER NO MO' BLUES (JIMMIE RODGERS MEMORIAL ALBUM) (LP)	20
61	RCA RD 27203	MY ROUGH AND ROWDY WAYS (LP)	20
61	RCA RD 27241	JIMMIE THE KID (LP)	20
62	RCA RD 7505	COUNTRY MUSIC HALL OF FAME (LP)	20
63	RCA RD 7562	THE SHORT BUT BRILLIANT LIFE OF JIMMIE RODGERS (LP)	20
64	RCA RD 7644	MY TIME AIN'T LONG (LP)	20

JIMMIE RODGERS

58	Columbia DB 4130	Secretly/Make Me A Miracle	10
57	Columbia DB 3986	Honeycomb/Their Hearts Were Full Of Spring (as Jimmy Rodgers)	25
57	Columbia DB 4052	Kisses Sweeter Than Wine/Better Loved You'll Never Be	10
58	Columbia DB 4078	Oh-Oh, I'm Falling In Love Again/The Long Hot Summer	10
58	Columbia DB 4175	Are You Really Mine/The Wizard	5
58	Columbia DB 4206	Woman From Liberia/Girl In The Wood	5
59	Columbia DB 4235	Bimbombey/You Understand Me	5
59	Columbia DB 4281	Because You're Young/I'm Never Gonna Tell	5
59	Columbia DB 4327	Soldier, Won't You Marry Me?/Ring-A-Ling-A-Lario	5
59	Columbia DB 4327	Soldier, Won't You Marry Me?/Ring-A-Ling-A-Lario (78)	12
59	Columbia DB 4362	Tucumcari/The Night You Became Seventeen	6
59	Columbia DB 4401	Waltzing Matilda/T.L.C Tender Love And Care	6
62	Columbia DB 4904	The Fox And The Goose/Soldier, Won't You Marry Me	6
62	London HLD 9582	No One Will Ever Know/Because	6
63	London HLD 9654	Rhumba Boogie/Rainbow At Midnight	7
63	London HLD 9697	Face In A Crowd/Lonely Tears	6
58	Columbia SEG 7770	JIMMIE RODGERS (EP)	10
58	Columbia SEG 7811	JIMMIE RODGERS SINGS (EP)	10
59	Columbia SEG 7911	JIMMIE RODGERS NO. 2 (EP)	10

RODNEY & BRUNETTES

(see also Blondie, Debbie Harry)

79	London/Bomp HLZ 10574	NEW YORK BLONDES featuring MADAME X: Little GTO/ Holocaust On Sunset Boulevard (no p/s)	12

RODNEY P

97	Pussyfoot PUSSY018	TINGS IN TIME (EP)	15
01	Riddim Killah RK001	Murderer Style/Friction (12")	10
04	Riddim Killah RKP04LP	THE FUTURE (LP- limited white vinyl)	20

RODS

79	Rods ROD 1	Like A Mirror/Hear I Am	10

TOMMY ROE (& ROEMANS)

62	HMV POP 1060	Sheila/Save Your Kisses	7
62	HMV POP 1092	Susie Darlin'/Piddle De Pat	8
63	HMV POP 1117	Gonna Take A Chance.Don't Cry Donna	5
63	HMV POP 1138	The Folk Singer/Count On Me	5
63	HMV POP 1174	Kiss And Run/What Makes The Blues (Want To Pick On Me)	6
63	HMV POP 1207	Everybody/There's A Great Day A-Coming	5
63	HMV POP 1259	Come On/There Will Be Better Years	6
64	HMV POP 1290	Be A Good Little Girl/Carol	6
64	HMV POP 1364	Little Miss Heartache/You Might As Well Forget Him	10
65	HMV POP 1368	Diane From Manchester Square/Part Girl	8
65	HMV POP 1469	Doesn't Anybody Know My Name/I'm A Rambler, I'm A Gambler	10
66	HMV POP 1539	Sweet Pea/Much More Love	10
69	Stateside SS 2143	Dizzy/The You I Need	5
69	Stateside SS 2152	Heather Honey/Money Is My Pay	8
63	HMV 7EG 8806	THE FOLK SINGER (EP)	20
63	HMV CLP 1614	SHEILA (LP)	40
64	HMV CLP 1704	EVERYBODY LIKES TOMMY ROE (LP)	30
65	HMV CLP 1860	BALLADS AND BEAT (LP)	40
69	Stateside S(S)L 10282	DIZZY (LP)	20

BOB ROGERS

71	Chapter One LRS 5005	SOUNDS (LP)	12

CE CE ROGERS

89	WEA A 8852T	Forever (12" Extended MIx)/Forever (Club MIx)/Someday (12" Extended Mix) (12",no p/s)	10

DANE ROGERS & NU BEATS

64	Pye 7N 15621	Mary Jane/Jeanette	10

DEAN ROGERS

(see also Sydney James)

60	Parlophone R 4732	End Of Time (as Dean Rogers & Hi-Fi's)/Keep The Miracle Going	10
61	Parlophone R 4835	Timber/High In A Misty Sky	10

ERIC ROGERS

63	Decca F 11585	The Iron Maiden/Fly-Wheel	7

MINT VALUE £

JULIE ROGERS

64	Mercury MF 809	It's Magic/Without Your Love	5
64	Mercury MF 838	Like A Child/Our Day Will Come	5
65	Mercury MF 849	Hawaiian Wedding Song/Turn Around Look At Me	6
68	Philips BF 1727	Tar And Cement/The Muffin Man	7
64	Mercury 10023 MCE	JULIE ROGERS (EP)	10
65	Mercury 10028 MCE	THE SOUND OF JULIE (EP)	10
65	Mercury 20048 (S)MCL	THE SOUND OF JULIE (LP, mono/stereo)	12
66	Mercury 20086 (S)MCL	CONTRASTS (LP, mono/stereo)	12
67	Mercury 20100 (S)MCL	SONGS OF INSPIRATION (LP, mono/stereo)	12

KENNY ROGERS (& FIRST EDITION)

(see also First Edition)

69	Reprise RSLP 6352	RUBY DON'T TAKE YOUR LOVE TO TOWN (LP)	12

LINCOLN ROGERS

73	Phoenix NIX 137	Let Love Come Between Us/She Looked At Me With Love	15

LYNNE ROGERS

65	RCA RCA 1479	Sometimes/I Shouldn't Care	7

MARK ROGERS & MARKSMEN

(see also Marksmen, Mark Wirtz)

63	Parlophone R 5045	Bubble Pop/Hold It!	25

PAUL ROGERS

61	HMV POP 872	Four An' Twenty Thousand Kisses/Free To Love	10
63	HMV POP 1121	Always/Joanie Don't Be Angry	10

PAULINE ROGERS

54	Columbia SCM 5106	Spinnin' The Blues/But Good	20

PIERCE ROGERS & OVERLANDERS

61	Parlophone R 4838	Do You Still Love Me?/That Someone	12

ROY ROGERS

55	HMV 7EG 8145	KING OF THE COWBOYS (EP)	10
55	HMV 7EG 8182	HAPPY TRAILS (EP)	10

ROY ROGERS & DALE EVANS

54	HMV 7MC6	Old Rugged Cross/In The Garden (export issue)	8

SHORTY ROGERS & HIS ORCHESTRA

(see also Boots Brown, Bud Shank, Shelly Manne, Jimmy Giuffre)

54	HMV 7EG 8044	THE WILD ONE (EP)	15
52	Capitol LC 6549	MODERN SOUNDS (10" LP, as Shorty Rogers & His Giants)	15
54	HMV DLP 1030	COOL AND CRAZY (10" LP, featuring Giants)	15
54	HMV DLP 1058	EIGHT SHORTY ROGERS' NUMBERS (10" LP)	15
56	Contemporary LDC 190	SHELLY MANNE, SHORTY ROGERS AND JIMMY GIUFFRE – THE THREE (10" LP, with Shelly Manne & Jimmy Giuffre)	18

SIDNEY ROGERS

73	Techniques TE 923	Don't Throw Stones/Toughness	8
75	Ethnic EF 2222S	TIPPIN' IN (LP)	30

TIMMIE ROGERS

57	London HLU 8510	Back To School Again/I've Got A Dog Who Loves Me	80
57	London HLU 8510	Back To School Again/I've Got A Dog Who Loves Me (78)	25
58	London HLU 8601	Take Me To Your Leader/Fla-Ga-La-Pa	100
58	London HLU 8601	Take Me To Your Leader/Fla-Ga-La-Pa (78)	30

TRACY ROGERS

65	Polydor 56029	How Love Used To Be/When I Realise	7
65	Polydor 56037	Love Story/I Remember When I Loved You (p/s)	10
66	Polydor 56077	Baby/Through Thick And Thin	25
67	Polydor 56197	Back With You Baby/In The Morning	12

VERN ROGERS & HI-FI'S

62	Oriole CB 1785	That Ain't Right/Be Everything To Anyone You Love	20
63	Oriole CB 1826	He's New To You/Can't Complain	15
63	Oriole CB 1885	I Will/One Way Love Affair	20
63	Oriole CB 1923	Anna/Pride	15

DIANA ROGERSON

(see also Nurse With Wound)

85	United Dairies UD 017	THE INEVITABLE CHRYSTAL BELLE SCRODD RECORD (LP)	25
86	United Dairies UD 021	CHRYSTAL BELLE SCRODD: BELLE DE JOUR (LP)	25

ROGUES (U.K.)

67	Decca F 12718	Memories Of Missy/And You Let Her Pass By	30

ROGUES (U.S.)

(see also Terry Day, Terry Melcher, Bruce Johnston)

65	CBS 201731	Everyday/Rogers Reef	20

CHRIS ROHMANN

73	RCA Victor SF 8364	THE MAN I AM TODAY (LP)	22
77	Old Fangled OLDF 1	TECHNICOLOUR DREAM (LP)	12

ROKES

67	RCA RCA 1587	Let's Live For Today/Ride On	30
67	RCA RCA 1646	Hold My Hand/Regency Sue	50
68	RCA RCA 1694	When The Wind Arises/The Works Of Bartholemew	70

ROKKA

80	Rock Trax RT 01	Come Back	10

MINT VALUE £

CHERRY ROLAND

(see also Cherry Rowland)

63	Decca F 11579	Handy Sandy/Stay As I Am	12
63	Decca F 11648	What A Guy/Just For Fun	12

PAUL ROLAND

(see also Weird Strings, Midnight Rags)

82	Aristocrat ARC 1389	Doctor Strange/Madelaine (p/s)	8
83	Aftermath AEP 12011	Blades Of Battenburg (Remix)/Captain Blood/Puppet Master/Cavalier (12", p/s)	10
85	Aftermath AEP 12012	Death Or Glory (Revamped Version)/The Great Edwardian Air Raid/ Beau Brummel/The Curious Case Of Richard Fielding (12", p/s)	8
86	Aftermath AEP 12013	Gabrielle/Berlin/Sword & Sorcery (p/s)	8
86	Imaginary MIRAGE 002	Demon In A Glass Case/In The Opium Den (oversized p/s)	7
87	Bam Caruso PABL 094	Alice's House/Go Down You Murderers/Happy Families/Jumbee (demo) (p/s)	8
85	Aftermath SCOOP 2	BURNT ORCHIDS (mini LP)	12
80	Ace ACE 013	THE WEREWOLF OF LONDON (LP)	18
81	Armageddon ARM 9	THE WEREWOLF OF LONDON (Revamped Version) (LP, different sleeve)	12

WALTER ROLAND/GEORGIA SLIM

59	Jazz Collector JEL 2	THE MALE BLUES VOL. 1 (EP)	22

BARRY ROLFE

73	Philips 6006 331	Look The Business/Molly Molly	25
73	Philips 6006 348	Beam Me Aboard, Mr. Spock/Boadecia	8
74	Philips 6006 381	Going Up/Johnny Bo Jangle	6

ROLFE, GIFFORD & ANDREW MULLINS

72	Look REM 104	Tutankamun/Sad Eyes	10

ROLLERS

61	London HLG 9340	Continental Walk/I Want You So	18

ROLLING STONES

(see also Mick Jagger, Keith Richards, Pipes Of Pan, Bill Wyman, Charlie Watts, Mick Taylor, Andrew Oldham, Bobbie Miller)

DECCA SINGLES

63	Decca F 11675	Come On/I Want To Be Loved	40
63	Decca F 11675	Come On/I Want To Be Loved (demo copy)	300
63	Decca F 11742	Fortune Teller/Poison Ivy (solid centre, withdrawn)	1500
63	Decca F 11764	I Wanna Be Your Man/Stones (B-side mis-spelled)	35
63	Decca F 11764	I Wanna Be Your Man/Stoned	20
64		We Were Falling In Love (EMI disc acetate, unreleased single)	1000
64	Decca F 11845	Not Fade Away/Little By Little	12
64	Decca F 11934	It's All Over Now/Good Times, Bad Times	12
64	Decca F 12014	Little Red Rooster/Off The Hook	12
65	Decca F 12104	The Last Time/Play With Fire	12
		(The above singles were originally issued with "Recording First Published..." text & 'wide' label lettering)	
65	Decca F 12220	(I Can't Get No) Satisfaction/The Spider And The Fly	12
65	Decca F 12263	Get Off Of My Cloud/The Singer Not The Song	12
66	Decca F 12331	19th Nervous Breakdown/As Tears Go By	10
66	Decca F 12395	Paint It, Black/Long Long While	12
		(The above singles were originally issued with a round Decca logo; later boxed-logo pressings are worth £4 each.)	
66	Decca F 12497	Have You Seen Your Mother, Baby, Standing In The Shadow?/ Who's Driving Your Plane	15
67	Decca F 12546	Let's Spend The Night Together/Ruby Tuesday	12
67	Decca F 12654	We Love You/Dandelion	15
68	Decca F 12782	Jumping Jack Flash/Child Of The Moon	12
69	Decca F 12952	Honky Tonk Women/You Can't Always Get What You Want (in demo-only p/s)	70
69	Decca F 12952	Honky Tonk Women/You Can't Always Get What You Want	10
71	Decca F 13195	Street Fighting Man/Surprise Surprise/Everybody Needs Somebody To Love (33rpm maxi-single)	10
71	Decca F 13203	Street Fighting Man/Surprise Surprise (jukebox edition)	25
73	Decca F 13404	Sad Day/You Can't Always Get What You Want	20
74	Decca F 13517	Paint It Black/It's All Over Now (release cancelled, demo-only)	220
75	Decca F 13584	I Don't Know Why I Love You (credited to either 'Jagger/Richard/ Taylor'/Try A Little Harder	20
75	Decca F 13584	I Don't Know Why I Love You (credited Stevie Wonder')/Try A Little Harder	15
75	Decca F 13597	Out Of Time/Jiving Sister Fanny	8
76	Decca F 13635	Honky Tonk Women/Sympathy For The Devil	8
70s	Decca F 11934	It's All Over Now/Good Times, Bad Times (re-pressing, with stereo mix on A-side, [ZXDR instead of XDR matrix no.] boxed Decca logo)	8
87	Decca F 102	Jumping Jack Flash/Child Of The Moon (p/s, reissue)	8
87	Decca FX 102	Jumping Jack Flash/Child Of The Moon/Sympathy For The Devil (12", p/s, reissue)	15

EXPORT SINGLES

63	Decca AT 15005	I Wanna Be Your Man/Stoned	110
64	Decca AT 15006	Not Fade Away/Little By Little	110
64	Decca AT 15032	Come On/Tell Me (You're Coming Back)	150
64	Decca AT 15035	Empty Heart/Around And Around	150
65	Decca AT 15039	Time Is On My Side/Congratulations	150
65	Decca AT 15040	Little Red Rooster/Off The Hook	110
65	Decca AT 15043	(I Can't Get No) Satisfaction/The Under Assistant West Coast Promotional Man (p/s)	150
65	Decca F 12104	The Last Time/Play With Fire (with Dutch or Scandinavian p/s)	85
65	Decca F 22180	Heart Of Stone/What A Shame (in p/s)	140
65	Decca F 22180	Heart Of Stone/What A Shame	100
65	Decca F 12220	(I Can't Get No) Satisfaction/The Under Assistant West Coast Promotional Man (with p/s)	75
65	Decca F 12220	(I Can't Get No) Satisfaction/The Under Assistant West Coast Promotional Man	30

			MINT VALUE £
65	Decca F 22265	Get Off My Cloud/I'm Free (in p/s)	75
65	Decca F 22265	Get Off My Cloud/I'm Free	30
66	Decca F 12331	19th Nervous Breakdown/As Tears Go By (with Dutch p/s)	50
66	Decca F 12395	Paint It, Black/Long Long While (p/s)	50
67	Decca F 12546	Let's Spend The Night Together/Ruby Tuesday (p/s)	50
67	Decca F 12654	We Love You/Dandelion (p/s)	50
67	Decca F 22706	2,000 Light Years From Home/She's A Rainbow	50
68	Decca F 22825	Street Fighting Man (remix)/No Expectations (in p/s)	50
68	Decca F 22825	Street Fighting Man (remix)/No Expectations	30
69	Decca F 12952	Honky Tonk Women/You Can't Always Get What You Want (p/s)	50
71	Decca F 13126	Little Queenie/Love In Vain (in p/s)	55
71	Decca F 13126	Little Queenie/Love In Vain	20
71	Decca F 13195	Street Fighting Man/Surprise Surprise/Everybody Needs Somebody To Love (33rpm maxi-single, p/s)	40
71	Decca F 13204	Street Fighting Man/Everybody Needs Somebody To Love (in p/s)	40
71	Decca F 13204	Street Fighting Man/Everybody Needs Somebody To Love	20

SINGLES BOX SETS

80	Decca STONE 1-12	SINGLE STONES (12x7" single box set)	60
80	Decca BROWSE 1	SINGLE STONES (in-store, 7" single box set [STONE 1-12], with poster & badge, also available via mail-order)	150

ROLLING STONES LABEL SINGLES

71	Rolling Stones RS 19100	Brown Sugar/Bitch/Let It Rock (in p/s)	50
71	Rolling Stones RS 19100	Brown Sugar/Bitch/Let It Rock	7
74	Rolling Stones RS 19114	It's Only Rock 'N' Roll/Through The Lonely Nights	6
78	R. Stones 12EMI 2802	Miss You (8.26)/Faraway Eyes (12", p/s, pink vinyl)	12
81	Rolling Stones	Beast Of Burden/Everything Is Turning Gold (unreleased)	0
82	Rolling Stones RSR 111	Time Is On My Side (live)/Twenty Flight Rock (live) (p/s)	5
82	Rolling Stones 12RSR 111	Time Is On My Side (live)/Twenty Flight Rock (live)/ Under My Thumb (live) (12", p/s)	10
84	Rolling Stones RSR 114	She Was Hot/I Think I'm Going Mad (p/s)	5
84	Rolling Stones RSRP 114	She Was Hot/I Think I'm Going Mad (shaped picture disc)	25
84	Rolling Stones SUGAR 1	Brown Sugar/Bitch (p/s, reissue)	5
84	Rolling Stones SUGARP 1	Brown Sugar/Bitch (shaped picture disc)	20
93	Rolling Stone RS LH 1	Brown Sugar/Start Me Up (jukebox issue, no p/s)	15
93	Rolling Stone ORDER LH 1	Gimme Shelter/TOM JONES: Gimme Shelter (jukebox issue, no p/s)	15

OTHER SINGLES

74	Atlantic K 19107	Brown Sugar/Happy/Rocks Off (unissued)	100
72	Sound For Industry 107	Mick Jagger Introduces 'Exile On Main Street' (flexidisc free with NME)	15
72	Sound For Industry 107	Mick Jagger Introduces 'Exile On Main Street' (flexidisc free without NME)	6
10	Universal 273 547-7	Plundered My Soul/All Down The Line (p/s)	6

CBS SINGLES

86	CBS QA 6864	Harlem Shuffle/Had It With You (poster p/s)	6
86	CBS TA 6864	Harlem Shuffle (N.Y. Mix)/(London Mix)/Had It With You (12", p/s)	8
86	CBS QTA 6864	Harlem Shuffle (N.Y. Mix)/(London Mix)/Had It With You (12", p/s)	12
86	CBS A 7160	One Hit (To The Body)/Fight (p/s)	5
86	CBS TA 7160	One Hit (To The Body) (London Mix)/Fight (12", p/s)	8
89	CBS 655 193-2	Mixed Emotions (7" Version)/Mixed Emotions (Chris Kimsey's 12")/ Fancyman Blues (CD, picture disc, card sleeve)	12
89	CBS 655 193-5	Mixed Emotions (7" Version)/Fancyman Blues/Tumbling Dice/Miss You (CD, picture disc, in circular tin with 'tongue' logo sticker)	35
89	CBS 655 193-6	Mixed Emotions (Chris Kimsey's 12")/Fancyman Blues (12", p/s)	8
89	CBS 655 193-6	Mixed Emotions (Chris Kimsey's 12")/Fancyman Blues/ Mixed Emotions (7" Version) (12", p/s)	8
89	CBS 655 214-2	Mixed Emotions (7" Version)/Fancyman Blues/Shattered/Waiting On A Friend (CD, picture disc, in circular tin with 'tongue' logo sticker)	35
89	CBS 655 422-7	Rock And A Hard Place/Cook Cook Blues (p/s)	5
89	CBS 655 422-6	Rock And A Hard Place (Dance Mix)/Emotional Rescue/Some Girls/ Rock And A Hard Place (Hard Dub Mix)/Cook Cook Blues (12", p/s)	8
89	CBS 655 422-5	Rock And A Hard Place (Michael Brauer Mix)/Rock And A Hard Place (Bonus Beats Mix)/Rock And A Hard Place (Edited 7" Version) (2nd 12", p/s)	8
89	CBS 655 422-8	Rock And A Hard Place (Dance Mix)/(Hard Dub Mix)/Cook Cook Blues (3rd 12", p/s)	8
89	CBS 655 422-2	Rock And A Hard Place (7" Version)/(Dance Mix)/(Bonus Beats Mix)/ Cook Cook Blues (CD, picture disc, card sleeve)	15
89	CBS 655 422-3	Rock And A Hard Place (Dance Mix)/Cook Cook Blues/ Rock And A Hard Place (Hard Dub Mix) (2nd CD)	8
89	CBS 655 448-2	Rock And A Hard Place (7" Version)/Cook Cook Blues/It's Only Rock'n'Roll (But I Like It)/Rocks Off (3rd CD, picture disc, 7" box set with poster)	25
89	CBS 655 448-5	Rock And A Hard Place (7" Version)/Cook Cook Blues/Emotional Rescue/ Some Girls (CD, tongue-shaped card sleeve)	25
90	CBS 656 065-6	Almost Hear You Sigh/Beast Of Burden/Angie/Fool To Cry (12", gatefold p/s)	8
90	CBS 656 065-2	Almost Hear You Sigh/Beast Of Burden/Angie/Fool To Cry (CD, gold disc)	20
90	CBS 656 065-5	Almost Hear You Sigh/Miss You/Waiting On A Friend/Wish I'd Never Met You (CD, in tin with 'Urban Jungle' sticker)	30
90	CBS 656 122-6	Terrifying (12" Dance Remix)/Rock And A Hard Place (Dance Mix)/ Harlem Shuffle (London Mix) (12", p/s)	8
90	CBS 656 122-2	Terrifying (7" Remix Edit)/(12" Remix)/Rock And A Hard Place (7" Version)/ Harlem Shuffle (LP Version) (CD)	8
90	CBS 656 122-5	Terrifying (7" Remix Edit)/Start Me Up/Shattered/If You Can't Rock Me (2nd CD, card p/s)	8
91	CBS 656 756-6	Highwire/2,000 Light Years From Home (live)/Sympathy For The Devil (live)/ I Just Wanna Make Love To You (live) (12", gatefold p/s)	8
91	CBS 656 756-2	Highwire/2,000 Light Years From Home (live)/Sympathy For The Devil (live)/ I Just Wanna Make Love To You (live) (CD)	8

			MINT VALUE £
91	CBS 656 756-5	Highwire/Play With Fire (live)/Factory Girl (live) (CD)	10
91	CBS 656 892-6	Ruby Tuesday/Play With Fire (live)/You Can't Always Get What You Want (live)/ Rock And A Hard Place (live) (12", p/s)	10
91	CBS 656 892-2	Ruby Tuesday/Play With Fire (live)/You Can't Always Get What You Want (live)/ Undercover Of The Night (live) (CD)	10
91	CBS 656 892-5	Ruby Tuesday/Harlem Shuffle (live)/Winning Ugly (CD)	10
91	CBS 657 334-2	Sex Drive (single edit)/(Dirty Hands Mix)/(Club Version) (CD)	10
VIRGIN SINGLES			
94	Virgin VS 1503	Love Is Strong/The Storm (numbered p/s, 7,000 only)	10
94	Virgin VS 1518	You Got Me Rocking/Jump On Top Of Me (numbered p/s, 7,000 only)	10
94	Virgin VST 1518	You Got Me Rocking (Perfecto Mix)/(Sexy Disco Dub Mix)/(Trance Mix) (12", p/s)	10
94	Virgin VS 1524	Out Of Tears/I'm Gonna Drive (numbered p/s, 7,000 only)	10
94	Virgin VSCDX 1524	Out Of Tears (Don Was Edit)/I'm Gonna Drive/Sparks Will Fly (Radio Clean)/ Out Of Tears (Bob Clearmountain Remix Edit) (CD, tear-shaped card p/s)	15
94	Virgin VSCDG 1524	Out Of Tears (Don Was Edit)/I'm Gonna Drive/So Young/The Storm/ Jump On Top Of Me (CD, digipak, numbered, 4,000 only, withdrawn)	250
94	Virgin VSP 1539	I Go Wild/I Go Wild (live) (picture disc)	20
96	Virgin VS 1578	Wild Horses/Tumbling Dice/Gimme Shelter (unreleased)	0
96	Virgin VSCDT 1578	Wild Horses/Tumbling Dice/Gimme Shelter (CD, unreleased)	0
97	Virgin VS 1653	Anybody Seen My Baby? (LP Edit)/(Soul Solution Remix Edit) (numbered picture disc, p/s, 7,500 only)	15
97	Virgin VST 1653	Anybody Seen My Baby? (Armand's Rolling Steelo Mix)/(Soul Solution Remix)/ (Bonus Roll) (12", p/s)	15
97	Virgin VS 1653	Anyone Seen My Baby?/Anyone Seen My Baby (Soul Solution Remix) (7" picture disc)	5
98	Virgin VSY 1667	Saint Of Me (Radio Edit)/Anyway You Look At It (picture disc)	10
98	Virgin VSTX 1667	Saint Of Me (remixes)/Anybody Seen My Baby? (remixes) (12", double pack, stickered p/s)	15
98	Virgin VS 1667	Saint Of Me/Anyway You Look At It (7" picture disc)	5
98	Virgin VSTTDT 1667	Saint Of Me (remixes)/Anybody Seen My Baby? (remixes) (12", double pack, stickered p/s)	15
98	Virgin VSY 1700	Out Of Control (Album Radio Edit)/(In Hand With Fluke Radio Edit)	10
98	Virgin VS 1700	Out Of Control/Out Of Control (In Hand With Fluke Mix) (7" picture disc)	5
PROMO SINGLES			
83	R. Stones RSR 112 (DJ)	Let's Spend The Night Together (live)/Start Me Up (live)	20
91	CBS A 026/B 027	Highwire/Sympathy For The Devil (live) (12")	15
93	EMI ORDERLH 1	Gimme Shelter (live) (1-sided jukebox issue)	20
93	Virgin STONES 1	JUMP BACK (EP)	25
94	Virgin VSCDJ 1518	You Got Me Rocking (Original Version)/(Perfecto Mix) (CD)	15
95	Virgin VSCDJ 1539	I Go Wild (CD, 1-track)	15
95	Virgin VSCDJ 1562	Like A Rolling Stone (Edit)/(Album Version) (CD)	12
96	Virgin VSCDJ 1578	Wild Horses (Edit) (CD, 1-track)	10
97	Virgin VSCDJ 1653	Anybody Seen My Baby? (LP Edit)/(Don Was Radio Remix) (CD)	10
97	Virgin VSCDXJ 1653	Anybody Seen My Baby? (Armand's Rolling Steelo Mix)/(Soul Solution Remix)/ (Bonus Roll) (CD)	10
98	Virgin VSCDJ 1667	Saint Of Me (Radio Edit)/(Album Version) (CD)	8
98	Virgin VSTDJ 1667	Saint Of Me (Deep Dish Grunge Garage Remix) (Part 1)/(Part 2)/ (Grunge Garage Dub)/(Rolling Dub)/Anyone Seen My Baby? (Armand's Rolling Steelo Mix)/Anyone Seen My Baby? (Bonus Roll) (12" double pack, stickered sleeve)	20
98	Virgin VSP 1700	Out Of Control (Bi-Polar At The Controls)/(Bi-Polar Outer Version) (withdrawn brown label)	30
98	Virgin VSP 1700	Out Of Control (Bi-Polar At The Controls)/(Bi-Polar Outer Version) (withdrawn silver label)	15
98	Virgin VSTDJ 1700	Out Of Control (In Hand With Fluke)/(In Hand Full Version)/ (Bi-Polar's Fat Controller Mix)/(Bi-Polar At The Controls) (12")	10
98	Virgin VSTDDJ 1700	Out Of Control (In Hand With Fluke Instrumental)/(In Hand Full Version)/ (Bi-Polar's Fat Controller Mix)/(Bi-Polar At The Controls) (12")	10
98	Virgin VSCDJ 1700	Out Of Control (Album Radio Edit)/(Album Version) (CD)	8
98	Virgin VSCDXJ 1700	Out Of Control (In Hand With Fluke Edit)/(In Hand With Fluke Instrumental)/ (Bi-Polar At The Controls)/(Bi-Polar's Fat Controller Mix) (CD)	8
98	Virgin VSCDF 1700	Out Of Control (Album Radio Edit)/(In Hand With Fluke)/ (In Hand With Fluke Instrumental)/(Bi-Polar At The Controls) (CD)	8
98	Virgin VSCDJ 1700	Out Of Control (Album Radio Edit)/(Saber Master With Fade)/ (In Hand With Fluke Radio Edit) (CD)	8
90s	Virgin VSCDY 1838	Don't Stop (1-track CD)	10
02	Virgin VS1838	Don't Stop (Limited edition red vinyl, numbered)	10
00s	Virgin DEVIL 666	Sympathy For The Devil (Fatboy Slim Remix)/(Neptunes Remix)// (Full Phat Remix)/(Original Version) (2x12", with press sheet)	20
02	Virgin VS1838	Don't Stop (limited edition red vinyl, numbered)	12
EPs			
64	Decca DFE 8560	THE ROLLING STONES (with unboxed Decca logo)	40
64	Decca DFE 8560	THE ROLLING STONES (later boxed Decca logo)	12
64	Decca DFE 8590	FIVE BY FIVE (with unboxed Decca logo)	40
64	Decca DFE 8590	FIVE BY FIVE (later boxed Decca logo)	12
65	Decca DFE 8620	GOT LIVE IF YOU WANT IT! (with unboxed Decca logo)	40
65	Decca DFE 8620	GOT LIVE IF YOU WANT IT! (later boxed Decca logo)	12
83	Decca DFEX 8560	THE ROLLING STONES (12", reissue)	12
83	Decca DFEX 8590	FIVE BY FIVE (12", reissue)	12
83	Decca DFEX 8620	GOT LIVE IF YOU WANT IT (12", reissue)	12
EXPORT EPS			
64	Decca SDE 7260	ROLLING STONES	120
64	Decca SDE 7501	THE ROLLING STONES VOLUME 2	110
65	Decca SDE 7502	GOT LIVE IF YOU WANT IT!	120
65	Decca DFE 8620	GOT LIVE IF YOU WANT IT! (red label, some with yellow titles on p/s)	110
65	Decca SDE 7503	ROLLING STONES (with "Out Of Our Heads [U.K. version]" sleeve)	110

MINT VALUE £

DECCA ALBUMS

Year	Cat. No.	Title	Mint Value £
64	Decca LK 4605	ROLLING STONES (1st pressing, plays 2.52 version of "Tell Me"; Side 2 matrix: XARL 6272-1A)	1000
64	Decca LK 4605	ROLLING STONES (2nd pressing, plays 4.06 version of "Tell Me"; sleeves list "Mona")	250
64	Decca LK 4605	ROLLING STONES (2nd pressing, plays 4.06 version of "Tell Me"; more common, with sleeves that list "I Need You, Baby")	130
65	Decca LK 4661	ROLLING STONES NO. 2	130
65	Decca LK 4661	ROLLING STONES NO. 2 (with 'blind man' text pasted over on rear sleeve)	180
65	Decca LK 4733	OUT OF OUR HEADS (mono)	110

(The above LPs were simultaneously pressed with both flipback and non-flipback sleeves. Values are the same)

Year	Cat. No.	Title	Mint Value £
65	Decca SKL 4733	OUT OF OUR HEADS (stereo)	110
66	Decca LK 4786	AFTERMATH (mono)	110
66	Decca SKL 4786	AFTERMATH (stereo)	110
66	Decca LK 4786	AFTERMATH (mono, front cover title is shadowed)	125
66	Decca SKL 4786	AFTERMATH (stereo, front cover title is shadowed)	125
66	Decca LK 4786	AFTERMATH (mono, front cover title has purple shadow)	150
66	Decca TXL 101	BIG HITS (HIGH TIDE AND GREEN GRASS) (1st pressing, gatefold sleeve, with stapled 12" x 12" picture booklet, mono)	80
66	Decca TXS 101	BIG HITS (HIGH TIDE AND GREEN GRASS) (1st pressing, gatefold sleeve, with stapled 12" x 12" picture booklet, stereo)	80
67	Decca TXL 101	BIG HITS (HIGH TIDE AND GREEN GRASS) (2nd pressing, gatefold sleeve, without booklet, mono)	30
67	Decca TXS 101	BIG HITS (HIGH TIDE AND GREEN GRASS) (2nd pressing, gatefold sleeve, without booklet, stereo)	50
67	Decca LK 4852	BETWEEN THE BUTTONS (mono)	150
67	Decca SKL 4852	BETWEEN THE BUTTONS (stereo)	120
67	Decca TXL 103	THEIR SATANIC MAJESTIES REQUEST (3-D gatefold sleeve with red inner, mono)	200
67	Decca TXS 103	THEIR SATANIC MAJESTIES REQUEST (3-D gatefold sleeve with red inner, stereo)	150
68	Decca LK 4955	BEGGARS BANQUET (gatefold sleeve, with Stones Decca label insert, mono)	200
68	Decca SKL 4955	BEGGARS BANQUET (gatefold sleeve, with Stones Decca label insert, stereo)	150
69	Decca LK 5019	THROUGH THE PAST, DARKLY (BIG HITS VOL. 2) (octagonal gatefold sleeve, mono)	80
69	Decca SKL 5019	THROUGH THE PAST, DARKLY (BIG HITS VOL. 2) (octagonal gatefold sleeve, stereo)	65
69	Decca LK 5025	LET IT BLEED (mono, red inner, with poster, with stickered sleeve)	400
69	Decca LK 5025	LET IT BLEED (mono, red inner, with poster, without stickered sleeve)	100
69	Decca SKL 5025	LET IT BLEED (stereo, blue inner, with poster, with stickered sleeve)	150
69	Decca SKL 5025	LET IT BLEED (stereo, blue inner, with poster, without stickered sleeve)	60
69	Decca TXL/TXS 103	THEIR SATANIC MAJESTIES REQUEST (2nd pressing, gatefold sleeve with red inner, mono)	50
69	Decca TXL/TXS 103	THEIR SATANIC MAJESTIES REQUEST (2nd pressing, gatefold sleeve with red inner, stereo, stereo disc in stickered mono sleeve)	50

(The above LPs were originally issued with Decca labels with large-print logo without a box surrounding it; later pressings with smaller print & boxed logo are worth between half the value for earlier LPs to two-thirds the value for later LPs and three-quarters for "Let It Bleed".)

Year	Cat. No.	Title	Mint Value £
70	Decca SKL 5065	GET YER YA-YA'S OUT!	25
71	Decca SKL 5084	STONE AGE	15
71	Decca SKL 5101	GIMME SHELTER	12
71	Decca NPS2	THEIR SATANIC MAJESTIES REQUEST (LP, gatefold, stereo reissue, boxed Decca logo)	25
72	Decca SKL 5098	MILESTONES	12
72	Decca SKL 5149	ROCK 'N' ROLLING STONES	12
73	Decca SKL 5165	GOLDEN B-SIDES (unreleased, test pressings only)	600
73	Decca SKL 5173	NO STONE UNTURNED	15

(Except where noted, the above Decca LPs were originally issued with dark blue labels & laminated sleeves; later copies are worth two-thirds the value.)

Year	Cat. No.	Title	Mint Value £
75	Decca SKL 5212	METAMORPHOSIS (dark blue label, matt sleeve)	15
70s	Decca TXS 101	BIG HITS (HIGH TIDE AND GREEN GRASS) (2nd pressing, gatefold sleeve, later issue with foldout insert & later Decca logo, stereo only)	15
75	Decca TXS 103	THEIR SATANIC MAJESTIES REQUEST (3rd pressing, 3-D matt gatefold sleeve, stereo only)	25
70s	Decca SKL 4733	OUT OF OUR HEADS (2nd pressing, light green sleeve, box Decca logo)	30
75	Decca (no cat. no.)	THE HISTORY OF THE ROLLING STONES (3-LP box set; 3x12" pink label test pressings exist, no sleeves, matrices read: ZAL 12996/7, ZAL 12998/9 & ZAL 13000/1; release cancelled in favour of "Rolled Gold" 2-LP)	800
75	Decca ROST 3/4	LIVE STONES (2-LP, compilation, pink label test pressings only, follow-up to "Rolled Gold", unreleased)	500
83	Decca ROLL 1	THE FIRST EIGHT STUDIO ALBUMS (8-LP set, with 192-page book; wraparound card box, each LP has star printed on rear sleeve)	250

EXPORT LPS

Year	Cat. No.	Title	Mint Value £
65	Decca LK 4725	OUT OF OUR HEADS (export, LP, with U.S. track listing & cover design, unboxed Decca label logo, mono, withdrawn)	170
65	Decca SKL 4725	OUT OF OUR HEADS (with U.S. track listing & cover design, unboxed Decca label logo, stereo, withdrawn)	200
66	Decca LK 4838	HAVE YOU SEEN YOUR MOTHER, LIVE (export LP, laminated sleeve & unboxed Decca label logo, mono)	125
66	Decca SKL 4838	HAVE YOU SEEN YOUR MOTHER, LIVE (export LP, laminated sleeve & unboxed Decca label logo, stereo)	150

amazon.co.uk

Thank you for shopping at Amazon.co.uk!

[illegible]517 C2

Invoice for
Your order of [illegible] April, 2011
Order ID [illegible]
Invoice number [illegible]
Invoice date [illegible] 2011

Billing Address
Mrs Lesley Blosse
[illegible]

Shipping Address
Mrs Lesley Blosse
Catshorough Cottage
Catshorough Cross
[illegible], Bideford, Devon EX39 5LE
United Kingdom

Qty	Item	Price (excl. VAT)	VAT Rate	Total Price
1	Record Collector Rare Record Price Guide (Record Collector Magazine) [illegible]	[illegible] 45	0%	£17.45
	[illegible]	[illegible] 00	0%	£0.00
				£17.45
				£0.00
				£17.45

[illegible] at the top of each page on our site.

Thinking of returning an item? PLEASE USE OUR ON-LINE RETURNS SUPPORT CENTRE.

[illegible] and provide you with a printable personalised return label. [illegible] Returns Policy does not affect your statutory rights.

Please note - this is not a returns address - for returns - please see above for details of our **online returns centre**

[illegible]

			MINT VALUE £
67	Decca SKL 4888	FLOWERS (export LP, stereo, laminated sleeve, unboxed Decca label logo)	250
67	Decca LK 4888	FLOWERS (export LP, mono, laminated sleeve, unboxed Decca label logo)	400
70	Decca SKL 4786	AFTERMATH (export LP, white label, black print, supposedly for export)	25
70	Decca TXS 103	THEIR SATANIC MAJESTIES REQUEST (export LP, gatefold sleeve, white label, black print, supposedly for export)	25
70	Decca SKL 5065	GET YER YA-YA'S OUT! (export LP, white label, black print, supposedly for export)	20
72	Decca LK/SKL 4838	HAVE YOU SEEN YOUR MOTHER, LIVE (export LP, later pressing, boxed logo, laminated sleeve)	80
72	Decca LK/SKL 4888	FLOWERS (export LP, later pressing, laminated sleeve, boxed Decca label logo)	100

ROLLING STONES LABEL LPS

71	Rolling Stones COC 59100	STICKY FINGERS ('big' zip sleeve with insert)	50
71	Rolling Stones COC 59100	STICKY FINGERS (zip sleeve with insert)	40
72	Rolling Stones COC 69100	EXILE ON MAIN STREET (2-LP, gatefold, with inners, postcard inserts)	100
72	Rolling Stones COC 69100	EXILE ON MAIN STREET (2-LP, with inners, without postcard inserts)	40
73	Rolling Stones COC 59101	GOAT'S HEAD SOUP (gatefold sleeve, with 2 inserts)	30
78	Rolling Stones CUN 39108	SOME GIRLS (LP, die cut sleeve with uncensored inner sleeve)	30
80	Rolling Stones CUN 39111	EMOTIONAL RESCUE (LP with poster)	12
82	R. Stones CUNP 39115	STILL LIFE (AMERICAN CONCERT 1981) (LP, picture disc, mispressed with wrong tracks)	140
82	R. Stones CUNP 39115	STILL LIFE (AMERICAN CONCERT 1981) (LP, picture disc)	25
84	Rolling Stones 450196	EXILE ON MAIN STREET (2-LP, reissue in single sleeve)	20

OTHER ALBUMS

83	R. Digest GROLA 119	THE GREAT YEARS (4-LP, box set)	25
89	ABKCO 820900-1	ROLLING STONES SINGLES COLLECTION/LONDON YEARS (4-LP set)	45
89	CBS 466 918 2	COLLECTION 1971-1989 (15-CD box set, with bonus CD, 'Collector's Edition')	130
91	Sony 468 135-9/468 135-2	FLASHPOINT/INTERVIEW 1990 (2-CD pack, shrinkwrapped with tongue logo sticker, numbered)	40
94	Virgin V2750	VOODOO LOUNGE (2-LP)	30
95	Virgin V 2801	STRIPPED (2-LP with inner sleeves)	20
97	Virgin V2840	BRIDGES TO BABYLON (2-LP, with inner sleeves)	20
02	Virgin CDVDXX2964	FORTY LICKS (ltd edition CD box set)	35

PROMO LPS

67	Decca TXL/TXS 103	THEIR SATANIC MAJESTIES REQUEST (LP, padded silk sleeve)	2000
69	Decca RSM. 1	PROMOTIONAL ALBUM (LP, U.K. disc in U.S. sleeve [lists RSD-1], 200 copies pressed [100 each for U.K. & U.S.], U.K. issues include a letter from Decca)	2000
86	CBS SAMP 1103	STONES ON CD - A RADIO SAMPLER (CD, poly sleeve)	200
89	CBS SAMPC 1347	SAY AHHH! (LP, promo-only compilation)	175
89	CBS (no catalogue no.)	STEEL WHEELS - THE ALBUM OF THE TOUR (box set, with LP, CD, cassette and "Terrifying" 12", European tour dates & sticker)	150
95	Virgin IVDG 2801	STRIPPED (2-CD, interview disc & album, fold-out digipak)	40
97	Virgin CDVDJ 2840	BRIDGES TO BABYLON (CD, with spoken-word intros, 200 only)	70
97	Virgin IVDG 2840	BRIDGES TO BABYLON INTERVIEW (2-CD, interview disc & album, fold-out digipak)	30
97	Virgin (no catalogue no.)	BRIDGES TO BABYLON (CD in promo press box, with "Anybody Seen My Baby?" promo CD, press release, bottle opener, notebook and sheet of stamps, 200 only)	150
99	Virgin CDVDJ 2880	NO SECURITY ALBUM SAMPLER (CD, card p/s)	15
99	Virgin CDIDJ 2880	NO SECURITY (3-CD [2 interview discs], foldout digipak)	45
90s	Virgin CDVDY 2964	FORTY LICKS (CD)	45

AUDLEY ROLLINS

(see also A. Boyne)

72	Explosion EX 2062	Repatriation/HUGH ROY JUNIOR: Repatriation - Version	10
73	Attack ATT 8060	Without You In My World/It's Flowing (actually "It's Growing")	6
73	Harry J HJ 6654	What's Your Name/NOW GENERATION: What's Your Name - Version	6

(HENRY) ROLLINS BAND

91	Vinyl Solution VS 30	Let There Be Rock/Carry Me Down (12", p/s, as Henry Rollins & Hard-Ons)	18
91	Vinyl Solution VS 30CD	Let There Be Rock/Carry Me Down (CD, as Henry Rollins & Hard-Ons)	18
92	Imago 72787250181	TEARIN' (12" EP, poster p/s)	8
92	Imago 72787250187	TEARIN' (CD EP, poster p/s)	10
94	Imago 7432323057	LIAR (EP, poster p/s)	10
92	Quarter Stick QS 13CD	DEEP THROAT (4-CD box set, spoken-word)	45

BIRD ROLLINS

72	Mojo 2092 049	Love Man From Carolina/She Needs Loving All The Time	10

SONNY ROLLINS

(see also Modern Jazz Quartet, Thelonious Monk, Clifford Brown, Coleman Hawkins, Kenny Durham)

58	Esquire EP 198	WAILING MISTER ROLLINS (EP)	12
56	Esquire 20-050	SONNY ROLLINS QUARTET (10" LP)	40
57	Esquire 20-080	SONNY ROLLINS QUINTET (10" LP)	25
57	Esquire 32-025	SONNY ROLLINS PLUS FOUR (LP)	35
57	Esquire 32-035	PERSPECTIVES (LP, with Modern Jazz Quartet)	40
58	Esquire 32-038	SONNY ROLLINS QUARTET (LP)	45
58	Esquire 32-045	SAXOPHONE COLOSSUS (LP, as Sonny Rollins Four)	50
58	Contemporary LAC 12118	WAY OUT WEST (LP)	20
58	Esquire 32-058	TENOR MADNESS (LP)	45
59	Esquire 32-075	SONNY ROLLINS QUINTET (LP)	30
59	Esquire 32-085	TOUR-DE-FORCE (LP)	22
59	MGM MGM-C 776	SONNY ROLLINS AND THE BIG BRASS (LP)	15
60	Contemporary SCA 5013	SONNY ROLLINS AND THE CONTEMPORARY LEADERS (LP, stereo only)	20
61	Riverside RLP 12-241	THE SOUND OF SONNY (LP)	15
62	Riverside RLP 12-258	FREEDOM SUITE (LP)	15
62	Esquire 32-155	MOVIN' OUT (LP)	35
62	RCA RD/SF 7504	THE BRIDGE (LP)	15
63	Esquire 32-175	SONNY BOY (LP)	30

			MINT VALUE £
63	RCA RD/SF 7524	WHAT'S NEW (LP)	15
63	RCA RD/SF 7546	OUR MAN IN JAZZ (LP)	15
64	RCA RD/SF 7593	SONNY MEETS HAWK (LP, with Coleman Hawkins)	15
64	RCA RD/SF 7626	SONNY ROLLINS & CO. (LP)	15
65	RCA RD 7670	NOW'S THE TIME (LP)	15
65	Fontana FJL 124	BLOW! (LP)	25
66	HMV CLP 1915	ROLLINS ON IMPULSE (LP)	15
66	Stateside SL 10164	SAXOPHONE COLOSSUS (LP, reissue)	12
67	RCA RD/SF 7736	STANDARD SONNY ROLLINS (LP)	15
67	HMV CLP/CSD 3529	SONNY PLAYS ALFIE (LP)	15
67	HMV CLP/CSD 3610	EAST BROADWAY RUNDOWN (LP)	15

ROLL MOVEMENT

67	Go AJ 11410	I'm Out On My Own/Just One Thing	35

ROLL-UPS

80	Bridgehouse BHS 6	Blackmail/Hold On (p/s)	15
79	Bridgehouse BHLP 004	LOW DIVES FOR HIGHBALLS (LP)	25

GLORIA ROMA

64	Decca F 12001	It Hurts Me So/I Didn't Know What Time It Was	8

DICK ROMAN

59	MGM MGM 1004	Party Girl/My Greatest Mistake	5
65	London HLU 10007	The Truth Hurts/What Good Does It Do Me	5
63	Stateside SL 10023	TOUCH OF LOVE (LP)	8

MIMI ROMAN

61	Warner Bros WB 55	Johnny Will/Let It Be Me	8

MURRAY ROMAN

69	Track 613 007	YOU CAN'T BEAT PEOPLE UP AND HAVE THEM SAY I LOVE YOU (LP)	25
69	Track 613 015	A BLIND MAN'S MOVIE (LP)	30

SANDY ROMAN

66	Columbia DB 7931	Dale Anne/Home Is Where The Heart Is	5

TONY ROMAN

67	Stateside SS 2022	Shadows On A Foggy Day/Maggie	7

MAX ROMEO

(see also Max & Elaine, Maxie & Glen, Al Read, Henry & Lisa, Dennis Alcapone, George Meggie, David Isaacs)

68	Island WI 3104	Put Me In The Mood/My One Girl	25
68	Island WI 3111	Walk Into The Room/DAWN PENN: I'll Get You	40
68	Island WI 3124	Twelfth Of Never (actually by Pat Kelly)/VAL BENNETT: Caledonia	40
68	Unity UN 503	Wet Dream/She's But A Little Girl	10
69	Blue Cat BS 161	We Want Man/AL REID: Vietcong	40
69	Blue Cat BS 163	It's Not The Way/AL REID: Darling	50
69	Nu Beat NB 022	Blowing In The Wind/LARRY MARSHALL: Money Girl	12
69	Trojan TR 656	Sweet Chariot/Far Far Away (with Hippy Boys)	20
69	Unity UN 507	Belly Woman (actually by Derrick Morgan)/PAULETT & LOVERS: Please Stay	7
69	Unity UN 511	Twelfth Of Never (actually by Pat Kelly)/TARTONS: Solid As A Rock (actually by Tartans)	15
69	Unity UN 516	Wine Her Goosie/KING CANNON: Fire Ball	10
69	Unity UN 532	Mini-Skirt Vision/Far Far Away	20
70	Unity UN 544	Melting Pot/HIPPY BOYS: Death Rides A Horse	30
70	Unity UN 545	Clap Clap (with Hippy Boys)/Death Rides A Horse	30
70	Unity UN 547	What A Cute Man/Buy You A Rainbow	30
70	Unity UN 560	Fish In The Pot/Feel It	10
71	Bullet BU 478	Mother Oh Mother/Dreams Of Passion (actually "Judgement Rock" by Charlie Ace)	10
71	Pama Supreme PS 328	Ginal Ship/UPSETTERS: Version 2	10
71	Pama Supreme PS 306	Let The Power Fall On I/The Raid	7
71	Pama Supreme PS 318	Don't You Weep/Weeping (Version)	7
71	Punch PH 73	Chie Chie Bud/Version	7
71	Unity UN 571	Macabee (Version)/SOUL SYNDICATE: Music Book	6
71	Camel CA 66	Black Equality/Suffering	20
71	Camel CA 82	The Coming Of Jah/Watch And Pray	6
72	Camel CA 85	Rasta Bandwagon/When Jah Speaks	6
72	Camel CA 86	Public Enemy Number One/How Long Must We Wait	6
72	Big BG 334	Are You Sure/RUPIE EDWARDS ALL STARS: Are You Sure - Version	6
72	Dynamic DYN 444	We Love America/SOUL RHYTHM: We Love Jamaica Version	6
72	G.G. GG 4535	Is It Really Over?/MAYTONES: Born To Be Loved	6
72	High Note Hs 058	Pray For Me (with Gaytones)/GAYTONES: Pray For Me - Version	8
72	Pama PM 836	Wet Dream/("Bang Bang Lulu" by Lloyd Tyrell)/("Birth Control" by Lloyd Tyrell)/ Sex Education by Classics) (Maxi-Single)	5
72	Pama Supreme PS 345	Pray For Me/Version	5
72	Pama Supreme PS 359	Are You Sure/CARL MASTERS: Va-Va-Voom	8
72	Prince Buster PB 11	River Jordan/Words Sound And Power	8
73	Dragon DRA 1028	No Joshua No/JOSHUA'S ALL STARS: No Joshua No (Version)	5
73	Magnet MA 032	Murder In The Place/Version	7
73	Magnet MA 032	I Woke Up In Love/Version	5
73	Pama PM 875	Pussy Watchman/You Are My Sunshine	5
73	Pama Supreme PS 383	Hide Away/SOUL SYNDICATE: Sweet And Gentle	5
73	Pama Supreme PS 385	Everyman Aught To Know/Version	6
73	Unity UN 572	Rent Crisis/Version	7
74	Ackee ACK 529	Sixpence/Eating Competition	5
75	Tropical Sound Tracs TST 107	Big Jack/Cross Over The Bridge/Please Help Me, I'm Falling	5
76	Island WIP 6305	One Step Forward/One Step Dub	10
76	Island WIP 6330	Chase The Devil/UPSETTERS FEAT. PRINCE JAZZBO: Croaking Lizard	15

			MINT VALUE £
69	Pama PMLP 11	A DREAM (LP)	50
71	Pama PMP 2010	LET THE POWER FALL (LP)	50
76	Island ILPS 9392	WAR INA BABYLON (LP)	20
76	Sound Trac TSL 1000	REVELATION TIME (LP)	30
92	Jah Shaka SHAKA 921	FAR I - CAPTAIN OF MY SHIP (LP)	12
95	Jah Shaka SHAKA 951	OUR RIGHTS (LP)	15
78	Mango MLPS 9503	RECONSTRUCTION (LP)	15

ROMEO Z

66	CBS 202645	Come Back Baby/Since My Baby Said Goodbye	30

ROMEO & EMOTIONS

67	Caltone TONE 106	Don't Want To Let You Go/I Can't Do No More	80

CHAN ROMERO

59	Columbia DB 4341	The Hippy Hippy Shake/If I Had A Way	100
60	Columbia DB 4405	My Little Ruby/I Don't Care Now	200

ROMI & JAZZ

90	Chrysalis CHSR 123545	One Love One World (Feel The Rhythm Mix)/One Love One World (Unity '90 Mix)/Love Crime (Sunrise Mix) (12", p/s)	12

RON AND MEL

65	Columbia DB 7469	In A Shabby Little Hut/I See Your Face	6

RONALD & LLOYD

74	Magnet MG 042	Back In My Arms/HEPTONES: Drifting Away	8

RONALD & RUBY

58	RCA RCA 1053	Lollipop/Fickle Baby	30
58	RCA RCA 1053	Lollipop/Fickle Baby (78)	15

RONDELLS

58	London HLU 8716	Good Good/Dreamy (with Ned Jr.)	100
58	London HLU 8716	Good Good/Dreamy (with Ned Jr.) (78)	60

RONDELS

61	London HLU 9404	Back Beat No. 1/Shades Of Green	20

DON RONDO

57	London HLJ 8466	White Silver Sands/Stars Fell On Alabama	10
58	London HLJ 8567	What A Shame/Made For Each Other	10
58	London HLJ 8610	I've Got Bells On My Heart/School Dance	8
58	London HLJ 8641	Blonde Bombshell/Her Hair Was Yellow	6
59	London RE-J 1154	RONDO PT. 1 (EP)	8
59	London RE-J 1155	RONDO PT. 2 (EP)	8

GENE RONDO

(see also Gene Pancho)

68	Giant GN 39	Ben Nevis/Grey Lies	15
68	Jolly JY 004	Mary, Mary/Baby, Baby	10
69	Downtown DT 422	A Lover's Question/HERBIE GRAY & RUDIES: Blue Moon	12
69	Downtown DT 431	Sentimental Reasons/Then You Can Tell Me Goodbye	7
70	Downtown DT 459	Spreading Peace/MUSIC DOCTORS: Guitar Riff	7
72	Downtown DT 490	Wanna Be Like Daddy/STUDIO SOUND: A Little More	5
72	Count Shelly CS 005	Happy Birthday Sweet Sixteen/Meditation	5
73	Magnet MA 001	Prisoner Of Love/How Many Times Girl	5
73	Magnet MA 006	Each Moments/If You Do Want Me	5
73	Magnet MA 028	Oh Sweet Africa/This Is Love	8
73	Magnet MA 035	Valley Of Tears/He'll Break Your Heart	5

RONDO VENEZIANO

88	Fanfare CDRON 1	VENICE IN PERIL (CD)	20

RONETTES

(see also Ronnie Spector, Joey Dee & Starlighters)

63	London HLU 9793	Be My Baby/Tedesco And Pitman	10
64	London HLU 9826	Baby I Love You/Miss Joan And Mr Sam	10
64	London HLU 9905	(The Best Part Of) Breakin' Up/Big Red	20
64	London HLU 9922	Do I Love You?/When I Saw You	20
64	London HLU 9931	(Walking) In The Rain/How Does It Feel?	15
65	London HLU 9952	Born To Be Together/Blues For Baby	20
65	London HLU 9976	Is This What I Get For Loving You?/You Baby	30
66	London HLU 10087	I Can Hear Music/When I Saw You (withdrawn)	100
69	London HLU 10240	Be My Baby/Baby I Love You	7
69	A&M AMS 748	You Came, You Saw, You Conquered/I Can Hear Music	8
75	Phil Spector Intl. 2010 009	I'm A Woman In Love/When I Saw You	18
77	Phil Spector Intl. 2010 017	I Wonder/Walking In The Rain	20
64	London HA-U 8212	PRESENTING THE FABULOUS RONETTES FEATURING VERONICA (LP, original pressing on plum label)	100
64	London HA-U 8212	PRESENTING THE FABULOUS RONETTES FEATURING VERONICA (LP, later pressing on black label)	50
65	Colpix PXL 486	THE RONETTES (LP)	150
75	Phil Spector Intl. 2307 003	SING THEIR GREATEST HITS (LP)	15

RONNIE & DEL AIRES

64	Coral Q 72473	Drag/Wigglin' 'N' Wobblin'	35

RONNIE & HI-LITES

62	Pye International 7N 25140	I Wish That We Were Married/Twistin' And Kissin'	30

RONNIE & RAINBOWS

61	London HL 9345	Loose Ends/Sombrero	25

RONNIE & ROBYN

80	Grapevine GRP 137	As Long As You Love Me/Sidra's Theme (unissued)	0

MINT VALUE £

RONNIE & ROY
59 Capitol CL 15028 Big Fat Sally/Here I Am 150

RONNO
(see also Mick Ronson, Rats)
71 Vertigo 6059 029 Fourth Hour Of My Sleep/Powers Of Darkness 65

RONNY
64 Decca F 21908 Oh! My Darling Caroline/Lu La Lu 10

RONNY & THE DAYTONAS
(see also Buzz & Bucky)
64 Stateside SS 333 G.T.O./Hot Rod Baby 25
64 Stateside SS 367 California Bound/Hey Little Girl 25
65 Stateside SS 391 Bucket T/Little Rail Job 30
65 Stateside SS 432 Beach Boy/No Wheels 30
66 Stateside SS 484 Sandy/Sandy (Instrumental) 20

MARK RONSON
05 Exit (No cat. no.) EXIT EP (12", 200 only, promo) 20

MICK RONSON
(see also Ronno, David Bowie, Mott The Hoople, Slaughter & The Dogs, Ian Hunter)
74 RCA APBO 0212 Love Me Tender/Only After Dark 6
74 RCA 11474 XSP Love Me Tender/Slaughter On 10th Avenue (1-sided red or black interview flexidisc, included in press kits) 15
74 RCA LPBO 5022 Slaughter On 10th Avenue/Leave My Heart Alone 6
75 RCA RCA 2482 Billy Porter/Seven Days 6
74 RCA Victor APL1-0353 SLAUGHTER ON 10th AVENUE (LP) 15
74 RCA APL1-0681 PLAY DON'T WORRY (LP, laminated gatefold sleeve) 15
94 Epic EPC 474742 1 HEAVEN AND HULL (LP, picture disc) 15

LINDA RONSTADT
(see also Stone Poneys)
69 Capitol E-ST 208 HOME SOWN, HOME GROWN (LP) 20
70 Capitol E-ST 407 SILK PURSE (LP) 15
72 Capitol EA-ST 635 LINDA RONSTADT (LP) 12

RONYSAN
88 2 Man MAN 1 I Take Pictures Of You/In The Valley Of The Larne 5

ROOFTOP SINGERS
(see also Tarriers)
63 Fontana 680 999 TL WALK RIGHT IN (LP) 15
66 Fontana TFL 6065 RAINY RIVER (LP) 15

ROOM
70 Deram SML 1073 PRE-FLIGHT (LP, non-laminated sleeve, white/red label) 700

ROOM
80 Box BOX 001 Motion/Waiting Room (p/s) 6
81 Box BOX 003 In Sickness And Health/Bated Breath (p/s) 5

ROOM 10
65 Decca F 12249 I Love My Love/Going Back 5

ROOM 13
(see also Bevis Frond)
82 Woronzow W 002 Murder Mystery/Need Some Dub (12", p/s) 25

MARY ROOS
72 CBS 7959 Wake Me Early In The Morning/When You're Singing (Don't Forget) 6

ROOSEVELT SINGERS
73 Sioux SI 025 Heavy Reggae/HONG GANG: Smoking Wild 5

ROOT BOYS
70 Columbia Blue Beat DB 115 Please Don't Stop The Wedding/Your Love, Your Love 10

ROOTS
78 Greensleeves GRE 7 Mash Down/Solja Man Skank 20

ROOTS & JENNY JACKSON
(see also (Root and) Jenny Jackson)

ROOTS MANUVA
95 Sound Of Money SNM006 Next Typa Motion/Raw Uncut (12") 50
99 Big Dada BD009 Juggle Tings Proper/Strange Behaviour (12") 18
99 Big Dada BD011 Motion 5000/Skiver's Guide (12") 12
01 Big Dada BD022/7 Witness (1 Hope)/(Walworth Rockers Dub) 20
01 Big Dada BD022 Witness/Son Of The Soil (12") 10
01 Big Dada BD033 Dreamy Days/Fly Turd Fly (12") 10
02 Ultimate Dilema UDR050 Yellow Submarine (12" 1-sided p/s) 20
05 Big Dada BD073 Colossal Insight (12") 8
05 Big Dada BD073P Colossal Insight (Royskopp remix) 10
05 Big Dada BD078 Too Cold (12") 8
05 Big Dada BDS078 Too Cold (7" Yellow Vinyl Dub Mix) 15
05 Big Dada BD085 Awfully Deep (remixes) (12") 8
05 Banana Klan TBR002 Let's Get Live (AS LORD GOSH MANUZA) 12
99 Big Dada BD010 BRAND NEW SECOND HAND (LP) 12
01 Big Dada BDLP032 RUN COME SAVE ME (LP) 12
02 Big Dada BDLP040 DUB COME SAVE ME (LP) 12

ROOTS MANUVA/MC SKEME
96 Wayward AHP01 Fever/Herbman Hustling/Life's Funny (12") 50

MINT VALUE £

ROOTS MANUVA/SKITZ

96	Ronin RDP5	Where My Mind Is At/Blessed Be The Manner/Fuck Being Polite (12")	18

ROOTS RADICS

84	Kingdom KV 8032	Earsay/I'm Not A King	10
79	Form BB1004	OUTERNATIONAL RIDDIM (LP, with Revolutionaries)	30
82	Cha Cha CHALP 012	RADICFATION (LP)	25

ROOTS TRUNK & BRANCES

(see also WJW & Roots Trunk & Branches)

GEORGE ROPER & PIPEDREAM

70s	Goldspinners GOLD 1	Manchester United/Tribute To The Fans	5

RO RO

(see also Ross)

70	Parlophone R 5920	Here I Go Again/What You Gonna Do	15
72	Regal Zonophone RZ 3056	Goin' Round My Head/Down On The Road	10
73	Regal Zonophone RZ 3076	Blackbird/Feel It Coming	10
72	Regal Zono. SRZA 8510	MEET AT THE WATER (LP, textured gatefold sleeve, red/silver label)	200

ANDY ROSE

58	London HLU 8761	Lov-A Lov-A Love/Just Young	25

DAVID ROSE ORCHESTRA

(see also Woody Herman, Rush Adams)

53	MGM SP 1009	Harlem Nocturne (with Woody Herman)/Vanessa	5
56	MGM SP 1181	Forbidden Planet/The Portuguese Washerwomen	8
60	MGM MGM 1110	Bonanza/Gloria's Theme From Butterfield 8	5
62	MGM MGM 1158	The Stripper/Ebb Tide	5

DUSTY ROSE

55	London HLU 8162	The Birds And The Bees/It Makes Me So Mad	50
57	London RE-U 1078	COUNTRY SONGS (EP)	50

JOHNNY ROSE

60	Capitol CL 15166	Linda Lee/The Last One To Know	18

TIM ROSE

67	CBS 202631	Morning Dew/You're Slipping Away From Me	6
68	CBS 3277	I Got A Loneliness/Long Time Man	30
68	CBS 3478	I Guess It's Over/Hello Sunshine	6
68	CBS 3598	Long-Haired Boy/Looking At A Baby	6
69	CBS 4209	Roanoke/Baby You Turn Me On	6
70	CBS 2631	Morning Dew/You're Slipping Away From Me (reissue)	6
70	Capitol CL 15664	I've Gotta Get A Message To You/Ode To An Old Ball	5
74	Dawn DN51085	You've Got To Hide Your Love Away/If I Were A Carpenter	8
67	CBS (S)BPG 63168	TIM ROSE (LP)	25
69	CBS 63636	THROUGH ROSE COLOURED GLASSES (LP)	25
71	Capitol ST 22673	LOVE - A KIND OF HATE STORY (LP)	20
74	Dawn DNLS 3062	TIM ROSE (LP)	18

TONY ROSE

70	Trailer LER 2013	YOUNG HUNTING (LP)	15
72	Trailer LER 2024	UNDER THE GREENWOOD TREE (LP)	15

ROSE GARDEN

68	Atlantic 584 163	Next Plane To London/Flower Town	10

ROSEHIPS

87	Subway Organisation SUBWAY 10	Room In Your Heart/Thrilled To Bits/Dead End (foldaround p/s with insert in poly bag)	10
87	Subway Organisation SUBWAY 10T	Room In Your Heart/Middle Of Next Week/Thrilled To Bits/So Naive/ Just Another Girl/Dead End (12", p/s)	12
87	Subway Organisation SUBWAY 16	I Shouldn't Have To Say/Loophole/Wastin' My Time/All Mine/ Sad As Sunday (p/s, with insert)	8
87	Subway Organisation SUBWAY 16T	I Shouldn't Have To Say/Loophole/Wastin' My Time/All Mine/ Sad As Sunday (12", p/s with insert)	12
88	Sweet William BILLY 001	Ask Johnny Dee/FAT TULIPS: You Opened My Eyes (33rpm flexi, p/s w/insert)	12

ROSEMARY'S CHILDREN

86	él GPO 012	Southern Fields/Whatever Happened To Alice	12
87	Cherry Red MRED 077	KINGS AND PRINCES EP (12", p/s)	12

LEONARD ROSENMAN ORCHESTRA

57	London HA-P 2040	A TRIBUTE TO JAMES DEAN (LP)	20

ROSE OF AVALANCHE

89	Avalanche AVE4T	A PEACE INSIDE (LP)	20
86	Fire BLAZE 14	Velveteen/Who Cares (p/s)	6

ROSE OF VICTORY

(see also Blitz)

83	No Future OI 24	Suffragette City/Overdrive (p/s)	12

ROSES ARE RED

79	Posthumous Petal PET 1	Can't Understand/Your Love Is Like A Ballistic Missile (p/s)	40

ROSE TATTOO

78	Carrere CAL 125	Bad Boy For Love/Tramp (p/s)	6
78	Carrere CAL 125	Bad Boy For Love/Tramp (12", p/s)	8
78	Epic EPC 9411	Rock 'N' Roll Outlaw/One Of The Boys (p/s)	5
80	Repeal PRS 2724	Release Legalise/COL PATERSON: Bong On Aussie (500 only)	40
81	Mirage PR 405	Rock 'N' Roll Is King/Sidewalk Sally (12", promo only)	10
81	Carrere CAR 200P	Rock 'N' Roll Outlaw/Remedy (picture disc)	5

MINT VALUE £

81	Carrere CAR 220	Assault And Battery/Astra Wally//One Of The Boys/Manzil Madness (double pack, gatefold p/s)	5
83	Carrere CARP 263	It's Gonna Work Itself Out/Fightin' Sons (picture disc)	5
82	Albert Productions AP 854	We Can't Be Beaten/Fightin' Sons	5
82	Albert Productions AP 898	Branded/Dead Set	5
82	Albert Productions AP 1007	It's Gonna Work Itself Out/Sydney Girls	5

ROSETTA STONE

95	Whatever Got.H 000000 Ru 12	GENDER CONFUSION (CD, 500 only first pressing)	20

ROSIE (& ORIGINALS)

61	London HLU 9266	Angel Baby/Give Me Love (as Rosie & Originals)	30
61	Coral Q 72426	Lonely Blue Nights/We'll Have A Chance	40

ROSKO

(see also Emperor Rosko & Power Pack)

70	Trojan TR 7758	Al Capone/Kaiser Bill	7
70	Philips 6009 070	Grab The Rabbit/Mohammed Ben Ali	15

EMPEROR ROSKO & POWER PACK

(see also Rosko, Power Pack, Pleasure Garden)

69	Polydor 56316	Opposite Lock Parts 1 & 2	10
71	B&C CB 148	The Customs Man/Take It In Your Stride	12

FRANK ROSOLINO SEXTET

54	Capitol KC 65001	That Old Black Magic/Yo Yo	5

ROSS

(see also Indian Summer, Gary Pickford-Hopkins, Ro Ro)

74	RSO 2394 127	ROSS (LP)	12
75	RSO 2394 144	THE PIT AND THE PENDULUM (LP)	12

ANNIE ROSS

(see also Tony Crombie, Dave Lambert, Gerry Mulligan, Zoot Sims, Jack Parnell, Teacho Wiltshire, Art Blakey, Quincy Jones)

54	Esquire 10-344	Jackie/The Song Is You (78, with Quincy Jones)	10
55	Decca F 10514	Mama (He Treats Your Daughter Mean)/The Fish	12
55	Decca F 10637	I Want You To Be My Baby (with Tony Crombie)/ TONY CROMBIE & HIS ORCHESTRA: Three Little Words	6
56	Decca F 10680	Cry Me A River/Only You	10
63	Ember EMB S 182	Bye Bye Blues/A Lot Of Livin' To Do	10
72	Columbia DB 8912	Straight On Till Morning/God Bless The Child	10
57	Pye Jazz NJE 1035	NOCTURNE FOR VOCALIST (EP)	60
50s	Esquire EP 1	WITH THE TEACHO WILTSHIRE GROUP (EP)	25
50s	Pieces Of Eight PEP 604	WITH THE TONY CROMBIE FOURTET (EP)	12
64	Transatlantic TRAEP 112	GO TO THE WALL (EP)	15
57	Nixa Jazz NJT 504	ANNIE BY CANDLELIGHT (10" LP)	125
59	Vogue LAE 12203	ANNIE ROSS (LP, with Gerry Mulligan Quintet)	60
60	Vogue LAE 12233	A GASSER (LP, with Zoot Sims)	60
63	Ember NR 5008	A HANDFULL OF SONGS (LP)	75
63	Transatlantic TRA 107	LOGUERRHYTHMS (LP)	60
65	Golden Guinea GGL 0316	ANNIE BY CANDLELIGHT (LP, reissue)	60
66	Xtra XTRA 1049	ANNIE ROSS WITH THE TONY KINSEY QUINTET (LP)	60
71	Decca SKL 5099	YOU AND ME BABY (LP)	20

DAVID ROSS

58	Oriole CB 1416	Pit-A-Patter Boom Boom/Everybody's Got A Girl But Tino (as Dave Ross)	6

DIANA ROSS

(see also Supremes)

70	Tamla Motown TMG 743	Reach Out And Touch (Somebody's Hand)/Dark Side Of The World	6
70	Tamla Motown TMG 751	Ain't No Mountain High Enough/Can't It Wait Until Tomorrow	6
71	Tamla Motown TMG 768	Remember Me/How About You	6
71	Tamla Motown TMG 781	I'm Still Waiting/Reach Out I'll Be There	6
71	Tamla Motown TMG 792	Surrender/I'm A Winner (mono)	6

DIANA ROSS & MICHAEL JACKSON

(see also [Diana Ross &] Supremes, Michael Jackson, Quincy Jones)

78	MCA MCA 396	Ease On Down The Road/QUINCY JONES: Poppy Girls (p/s)	5
78	MCA MCAT 12-396	Ease On Down The Road (U.S. Version)/THE WIZ: Poppy Girls (12", p/s)	8

DOCTOR (Isaiah) ROSS

66	Blue Horizon LP 1	THE FLYING EAGLE (LP, 99 copies only)	1500
66	Xtra XTRA 1038	DOCTOR ROSS (LP, reissue of "The Flying Eagle")	40
66	Bounty BY 6020	CALL THE DOCTOR (LP)	60
72	Polydor 2460 169	LIVE AT MONTREUX (LP)	30
75	Big Bear BEAR 2	THE HARMONICA BOSS (LP)	25

ERROL ROSS

80	Carrere CAR 149	Round And Round In Circles/Reggae Music Of Today (p/s)	6

GENE ROSS

58	Parlophone R 4434	Endless Sleep/The Only One	25
58	Parlophone R 4434	Endless Sleep/The Only One (78)	10

JACK ROSS

62	London HLD 9534	Cinderella/Margarita	6

JACKIE ROSS

64	Pye International 7N 25259	Selfish One/Everything But Love	60
64	Pye International 7N 25259	Selfish One/Everything But Love (DJ copy)	100
64	Chess CRS 8003	Jerk And Twine/New Lover	40
64	Chess CRS 8003	Jerk And Twine/New Lover (DJ copy)	70

JOAN ROSS

70	Crab CRAB 61	Band Of Gold/HAMMERS: Midnight Sunshine	10

MINT VALUE £

JOE E. ROSS
64 Columbia 335X1710 LOVE SONGS FROM A COP (LP) . . . 18

RONNIE ROSS
(see also Bill Le Sage)
58 Parlophone PMC 1079 DOUBLE EVENT (LP) . . . 75
61 Ember EMB 3323 STOMPIN' WITH (LP) . . . 80
65 Ember FA 2023 THE SWINGIN' SOUNDS OF THE JAZZ MAKERS (LP, with Allan Ganley) . . . 60
69 Fontana SFJL 915 CLEOPATRA'S NEEDLE (LP) . . . 200

SONNY ROSS
71 Mojo 2093 001 Alakazam/The Piper Must Be Paid . . . 10

SPENCER ROSS
60 Philips PB 992 Tracy's Theme/Thanksgiving Day Parade . . . 6
60 London HLX 9141 Theme Of A Lonely Evening/Bobby's Blues . . . 7

T.T. ROSS
75 Dip DL 5079 Single Girl/Funny What Love Can Do . . . 5
76 Dip DL 5104 Last Date/I Am Sorry . . . 5
76 Lucky LY 6000 No Charge/When I Was A Little Girl . . . 5
76 Lucky LY 6014 Baby Why/TOUGH GANG: Part 2 . . . 5
76 Lucky LY 6017 Misty Blue/Version . . . 5
76 House Of Eve 001 Let The World Go Away/Part 2 . . . 5
76 House Of Eve 002 Piece Of My Heart/Part 2 . . . 5
77 Lovers Rock CJ 622 I Will/I Will Dub . . . 5

LEON ROSSELSON
(see also Three City Four, Roy Bailey)
70 Acorn CF 206 SONGS FOR SCEPTICAL CIRCLES . . . 20
71 Trailer LER 3015 THE WORD IS HUGGA MUGGA CHUGGA HUMBUGGA BOOM CHIT (LP, with Roy Bailey & Martin Carthy) . . . 20
75 Acorn CF 249 PALACES OF GOLD (LP) . . . 18
75 Acorn CF 251 THAT'S NOT THE WAY IT'S GOT TO BE (LP, with Roy Bailey) . . . 18
62 Topic TOP 77 SONGS FOR CITY SQUARES (EP) . . . 15

NITA ROSSI
(see also Status Quo, Bernie Frost, Boz Frost, Mickey Jupp, Mitchell/Coe Mysteries, Demis Roussos, Tokyo Olympics)
65 Piccadilly 7N 35258 Every Little Day Now/Untrue Unfaithful . . . 30
66 Piccadilly 7N 35307 Here I Go Again/Something To Give . . . 40
66 Piccadilly 7N 35307 Here I Go Again/Something To Give (DJ copy) . . . 70
66 Piccadilly 7N 35354 The Daddy Christmas Song/Our Love Was Meant To Be . . . 8
67 Piccadilly 7N 35384 Misty Blue/Come Around . . . 12

(Francis) ROSSI & (Bernard) FROST
85 Vertigo VER 17/FROS 1 Modern Romance (I Want To Fall In Love Again)/I Wonder Why (p/s) . . . 5
85 Vertigo VERX 17/FROSX 1 Modern Romance (I Want To Fall In Love Again) (Extended Remix)/ I Wonder Why (Extended Remix) (12", p/s) . . . 10
85 Vertigo VER 24 Jealousy/Where Are You Now? (p/s) . . . 6
85 Vertigo VERX 24 Jealousy/Where Are You Now?/That's Alright (12", p/s) . . . 12

JOHN HENRY ROSTILL
(see also Shadows)
71 Columbia DB 8794 Funny Old World/Green Apples . . . 40

STEVE ROSTRON
74 Sweet Folk & Country SFA 009 NO STRANGER'S FACE (LP) . . . 30

NINO ROTA
72 Paramount PARA 3023 Love Theme Form "The Godfather"/The Godfather Waltz . . . 6

ROTARY CONNECTION
68 Chess CRS 8072 Soul Man/Ruby Tuesday . . . 6
69 Chess CRS 8103 The Weight/Respect . . . 6
70 Chess CRS 8106 Want You To Know/Memory Band . . . 10
68 Chess CRL 4538 ROTARY CONNECTION (LP) . . . 25
69 Chess CRL(S) 4547 ALADDIN (LP) . . . 25
69 Chess CRLS 4551 SONGS (LP) . . . 25

ROTATION
70 Polydor 2041-037 Ra-Ta-Ta/Rotation . . . 15

ROTEN ROSEN
87 Virgin VS 1031 Itsy Bitsy Teenie Weenie Honolulu-Strand Bikini (German Version) Itsy Bitsy Teenie Weenie Honolulu-Strand Bikini (English Version) (p/s) . . . 100
87 Virgin VST 1031 Itsy Bitsy Teenie Weenie Honolulu-Strand Bikini (German Version) Itsy Bitsy Teenie Weenie Honolulu-Strand Bikini (English Version)/ Agent X (12", p/s . . . 150

DAVID LEE ROTH
(see also Van Halen)
86 Warner Bros W 8656P Yankee Rose/Shy Boy (pin-up shaped picture disc) . . . 10

ROTHCHILDS
66 Decca F 12411 You've Made Your Choice/It's Love . . . 10
66 Decca F 12488 Artificial City/I Let Her Go . . . 15

LINDA ROTHWELL
73 Chapter One SCH 180 Write Me A Letter/Tell Me . . . 8

ROOTS TRUNKS AND BRANCHES
79 Splendor Heights Just The Way You Are/Chicken Disco (12") . . . 20

MINT VALUE £

ROUGE
78 SRT SRTSCUS 78104 Have You Seen Gene (no p/s) ... 75

ROUGH DIAMOND
90 Bedrock BR 1 Woman's Touch (p/s) ... 12

ROUGH ELEMENT
92 UAR UAR120020 The Elements/Breaking The Silence/Unbound Rage (remix) (EP) ... 60
94 UAR 003 Reflex Reaction/Criminal Behaviour (12") ... 30

ROUGH JUSTICE
80s Rough Justice RJ 001 MILLION TO ONE (EP, p/s) ... 200

ROUGH RIDERS
74 Rare Earth RES 118 Hot California Beach/Do You See Me ... 20

ROULETTES
(see also Adam Faith, Unit 4 + 2, Argent)
62 Pye 7N 15467 Hully Gully Slip 'N' Slide/La Bamba ... 15
63 Parlophone R 5072 Soon You'll Be Leaving Me/Tell Tale Tit ... 15
64 Parlophone R 5110 Bad Time/Can You Go ... 20
64 Parlophone R 5148 I'll Remember Tonight/You Don't Love Me ... 15
64 Parlophone R 5218 Stubborn Kind Of Fellow/Melody ... 20
65 Parlophone R 5278 I Hope He Breaks Your Heart/Find Out The Truth ... 15
65 Parlophone R 5382 The Long Cigarette/Junk ... 25
66 Parlophone R 5419 The Tracks Of My Tears/Jackpot ... 20
66 Oak RGJ 205 I Can't Stop (1-sided, with p/s) ... 250
66 Oak RGJ 206 I Can't Stop (1-sided) ... 150
66 Parlophone R 5461 I Can't Stop/Yesterday, Today And Tomorrow ... 20
67 Fontana TF 822 Rhyme Boy, Rhyme/Airport People ... 40
67 Fontana TF 876 Help Me To Help Myself/To A Taxi Driver ... 20
65 Parlophone PMC 1257 STAKES AND CHIPS (LP, laminated front cover, flipbacks, black/yellow label with "Sold in the U.K..." text) ... 500

ROUND ROBIN
64 London HLU 9908 Kick That Little Foot Sally Ann/Slauson Party ... 30
64 London HLU 9908 Kick That Little Foot Sally Ann/Slauson Party (DJ copy) ... 70

ROUNDTABLE
69 Jay Boy BOY 18 Saturday Gigue/Scarborough Fair ... 20
69 Jay Boy JSL 2 SPINNING WHEEL (LP) ... 40

CHARLIE ROUSE QUINTET
60 Riverside/Jazzland JLP19 TAKIN' CARE OF BUSINESS (LP) ... 15

DEMIS ROUSSOS
(see also Aphrodite's Child, Forminx, Rossi & Frost)
80 Mercury MER 25 Sorry/Love Is The Answer (p/s, A-side written by & featuring Francis Rossi/ Bernie Frost) ... 5

ROUTERS
(see also Scott Walker)
62 Warner Bros WB 77 Let's Go (Pony)/Mashy ... 10
63 Warner Bros WB 91 Make It Snappy/Half Time ... 10
63 Warner Bros WB 97 Stingray/Snap Happy ... 10
63 Warner Bros WB 108 Big Band/A Ooga ... 10
64 Warner Bros WB 139 Stamp And Shake/Ah Ya ... 10
73 Warner Bros K 16156 Let's Go/Mashy (reissue) ... 5
63 Warner Bros WM/WS 8126 LET'S GO! WITH THE ROUTERS (LP, features Scott Walker) ... 40
64 Warner Bros WM/WS 8144 PLAY 1963'S GREAT INSTRUMENTALS (LP) ... 20
65 Warner Bros WM/WS 8162 CHARGE! (LP) ... 20

JONATHAN ROUTH
57 Nixa NPT 19016 CANDID MIKE (10" LP) ... 12
62 Pye NPL 18077 CANDID CAMERA (LP) ... 12

ROVERS
55 Capitol CL 14283 Ichi-Bon Tami, Dachi/Why Oh-h (Why Do You Lie To Me?) ... 500
55 Capitol CL 14283 Ichi-Bon Tami, Dachi/Why Oh-h (Why Do You Lie To Me?) (78) ... 90

ROVING KIND
65 Decca F 12264 Ain't It True/Don't Tell Me The Time ... 8
66 Decca F 12381 Lies A Million/How Many Times ... 7

ROWAN BROTHERS
72 CBS 1125 All Together/Lady Of Laughter ... 20

ROWAN & MARTIN
69 CBS 63490 ROWAN AND MARTIN'S LAUGH-IN (LP) ... 12
69 Atlantic 588 151 ROWAN AND MARTIN AT WORK (LP) ... 15

ROWDIES
(see also Boys, Lurkers, Steve Sharp & Cleancuts)
78 Birds Nest BN 109 A.C.A.B. (All Coppers Are Bastards)/Negative Malfunction/Freeze Out ... 50
79 Teenage Depression TD 1/2 She's No Angel/Had Me A Real Good Time (p/s) ... 20

KEITH ROWE
77 Black Swan WIP 6405 Groovy Situation/Groovy Dub ... 15
77 Black Swan BS 6 Groovy Situation/Groovy Dub ... 20
81 Seven Leaves SLD 02 Groovy Situation/Groovy Dub ... 15

NORMIE ROWE
66 Polydor 56132 It's Not Easy/Mary Mary ... 6
66 Polydor 56144 Ain't Nobody Home/Ooh La La ... 6
67 Polydor 56159 Going Home/I Don't Care (Just Take Me There) (in p/s) ... 10
67 Polydor 56159 Going Home/I Don't Care (Just Take Me There) ... 5
67 Polydor 56169 But I Know/Sunshine Secret ... 10

MINT VALUE £

MAJOR ROWELY

65 Stateside SS 438 There's A Riot Going On/Do It The Right Way 15

JEFF ROWENA FIVE

63 Oriole CB 1797 Dance Baby Dance/Love Me once Again 10

CHERRY ROWLAND

(see also Cherry Roland)

63 Fontana TF 420 Nobody But Me/Boys 12
74 Decca F 13491 Here Is Where The Love Is/I Can Give You Back Yourself 6

JACKIE ROWLAND

(see also Joe Higgs)

72 Sioux SI 015 Indian Reservation/JUNIOR SMITH: I'm In A Dancing Mood 5
72 Sioux SI 022 Lonely Man/JOE MANSANO: The Trial Of Pama Dice 15

KEVIN ROWLAND

(see also Dexys Midnight Runners)

88 Mercury DEXYB 1412 Young Man/The Way You Look Tonight/Even When I Hold You/ Walk Away (12", gatefold p/s) 8

STEVE ROWLAND

(see also Family Dogg)

67 Fontana TF 844 So Sad/I See Red 40

JOHN ROWLES

69 MCA MKPS 2001 THAT LOVIN' FEELING (LP) 12
68 MCA HUP 335 JOHN ROWLES (LP) 15

ROX

82 Teenteeze ROX 100 HOT LOVE IN THE CITY (Hot Love In The City/Do Ya Feel Like Lovin'/Love Ya Like A Diamond (EP) 25
83 MFN 12KUT 103 KRAZY KUTZ (12" EP) 8
83 Music For Nations MFN 11 VIOLENT BREED (LP, with innersleeve) 15

ROXY MUSIC

(see also Brian Eno, Bryan Ferry, Andy Mackay, Phil Manzanera, Dumbelles, 801, Fripp & Eno)

72 Island WIP 6144 Virginia Plain/The Numberer (initially pink labels, later orange) 5
73 Island WIP 6159 Pyjamarama/The Pride And The Pain 5
74 Island WIP 6173 Street Life/Hula Kula 5
74 Island WIP 6208 All I Want Is You/Your Application's Failed 5
78 Polydor/EG 2001 756 Do The Strand/Editions Of You (12", p/s) 8
86 E.G. EGOX 26 Love Is The Drug/Let's Stick Together (12", p/s, promo only) 15
72 Island ILPS 9200 ROXY MUSIC (LP, laminated gatefold sleeve, pink rim palm tree label) 20
73 Island ILPS 9232 FOR YOUR PLEASURE (LP, laminated gatefold, pink rim/palm tree label) 15
79 Polydor/E.G. EGPD 001 MANIFESTO (LP, picture disc, mispress, 1 side plays Gordon Giltrap's Fear Of The Dark LP) 12
81 Polydor/E.G. EGBS 001 THE FIRST SEVEN ALBUMS (7-LP box set plus insert) 50

ALVIN ROY & THE SARATOGA JAZZ BAND

61 Interdisc INT 45001 Yogi/Broken Promises 5

D ROY BAND

70s D Roy MFLP 1001 ORTHODOX DUB (white label LP in stamped, plain white sleeve) 150

DEREK ROY

(see also Jon Pertwee, Bob Monkhouse)

57 Oriole CB 1415 Derek Roy's All-Star Party (with Bob Monkhouse, Richard Murdoch, Jon Pertwee, Ted Ray & others) 8

HUGH ROY JUNIOR

71 Big BG 329 Papacito/RUPIE EDWARDS: I'm Gonna Live Some Life 12
71 Supreme SUP 211 Double Attack/MURPHY'S ALL STARS: Puzzle 12
72 Ashanti ASH 405 King Of The Road/ROOSEVELT ALL STARS: Version 8
72 Jackpot JP 806 Two Ton Guletto/Version 8

HUGH ROY/U ROY

(see also Jeff Barnes, Melodians, Delroy Wilson)

70 Supreme SUP 211 Double Attack/Puzzle 15
70 Explosion EX 2040 Whisper A Little Prayer (actually by Audley Rollins)/ Rain A Fall (actually by Melanie) 15
70 Punch PH 34 Scandal/Son Of The Wise 12
70 Duke Reid DR 2509 Wake The Town/Big Boy And Teacher 18
70 Duke Reid DR 2510 Rule The Nation/NORA DEAN: Ay Ay Ay Ay 20
70 Duke Reid DR 2513 Wear You To The Ball (with John Holt)/EARL LINDO: The Ball 20
70 Duke Reid DR 2514 You'll Never Get Away/TOMMY McCOOK QUINTET: Rock Away 12
70 Duke Reid DR 2515 Version Galore/TOMMY McCOOK: Nehru 25
71 Duke Reid DR 2516 Testify/TOMMY McCOOK: Super Soul 12
71 Duke Reid DR 2517 Tom Drunk (with Hopeton Lewis)/TOMMY McCOOK: Wailing 12
71 Duke Reid DR 2518 True True/On The Beach 12
71 Duke Reid DR 2519 Flashing My Whip/Do It Right 18
71 Treasure Isle TI 7059 Drive Her Home (Parts 1 & 2) (with Hopeton Lewis) 15
71 Treasure Isle TI 7062 Behold/Way Back Home (with Tommy McCook) 12
71 Treasure Isle TI 7064 Everybody Bawlin'/Ain't That Loving You 15
71 Upsetter US 375 Earthquake/Suspicious Minds 20
71 Duke DU 105 Love I Tender/JOYA LANDIS: When The Lights Are Low 12
71 Duke Reid DR 2517 Tom Drunk/Wailing (as U Roy, B-side actually by Tommy McCook) 12
72 G.G. GG 4532 Way Down South/BILLY DYCE: Be My Guest 12
72 Duke DU 137 Live It Up/DENNIS BROWN: Baby Don't Do It 12
72 Jackpot JP 806 Two Ton Gulleto/Version 10
72 Dynamic DYN 448 Festival Wise/Festival Wise Part 2 8
72 Banana BA 367 Keep On Running/LARRY'S ALL STARS: Version 12
72 Grape GR 3026 On Top The Peak/TYPHOON ALLSTARS: Race Attack 8

			MINT VALUE £
72	Pama PM 835	Way Down South/BILLY DYCE: Be My Guest	12
72	Punch PH 104	Nannyscrank (title actually "Nanny Skank")/ PITTSBURG ALLSTARS: Scank Version	12
72	Green Door GD 4034	Hudson Affair/KEITH HUDSON: Hot Stick - Version	18
72	Trojan TR 7884	Hat Trick/Wet Version	8
73	Green Door GD 4052	King Tubby's Special/Here Come The Heartaches	12
73	Gayfeet GS 210	Hard Feeling/Regular Style	12
73	Duke DU 157	Higher The Mountain/OLD BOYS INC.: Version	8
73	Harry J. HJ 6651	Treasure Isle Skank/Words Of Wisdom	12
73	Lord Koos KOO 25	Call On I (with D. Wilson)/DJ Special	8
75	Virgin VS 138	Runaway Girl/Chalice In The Palace	6
76	Soulfood SF 001	High Priest/London City Rock	15
71	Trojan TBL 161	VERSION GALORE (LP, as U Roy)	35
73	Attack ATLP 1006	U ROY (LP, as U Roy)	25
75	Virgin V2048	DREAD IN A BABYLON (LP)	20
79	Virgin Frontline FLX 4004	WITH WORDS OF WISDOM (LP)	20

I ROY

(see also Keith Hudson & I Roy)

71	Moodisc MU 3509	Musical Pleasure/JO JO BENNETT: Hot Pop	15
71	Moodisc MU 3510	Heart Don't Leap (as I. Roy & Dennis Walks)/ DENNIS WALKS & MUDIE'S ALLSTARS: Snow Bird	15
71	Moodisc MU 3512	Let Me Tell You Boy (with Ebony Sisters)/MUDIE'S ALLSTARS: Version	15
71	Moodisc HM 104	The Drifter (with Dennis Walks)/JO JO BENNETT: Snowbird	18
72	Green Door GD 4030	Hot Bomb (with Jumpers)/JUMPERS: The Bomb	12
72	Green Door GD 4044	Make Love/STAGE: Tic Toc Bill	10
73	Pyramid PYR 7001	Tip From The Prince/Fat Beef Skank	15
73	Attack ATT 8050	Space Flight/JERRY LEWIS: Burning Wire	15
73	Downtown DT 503	Blackman's Time/High Jacking	18
73	Downtown DT 519	Clapper's Tail/Live And Learn	18
73	Duke DU 156	Buck And The Preacher/PETE WESTON ALLSTARS: Preacher - Version	12
73	Smash SMA 2337	The Magnificent Seven/Leggo Beast	12
73	Smash SMA 2338	Rose Of Sheron/Slip Out	15
73	Techniques TE 926	Pauper And The King/GREGORY ISAACS: Loving Pauper	12
73	Techniques TE 930	Monkey Fashion/Medley Mood	10
73	Ackee ACK 503	Great Great Great (with Ken Parker)/RUPIE EDWARDS ALLSTARS: Version	22
73	Ackee ACK 510	Sound Education/AUGUSTUS PABLO: Cinderella In Black	18
73	Harry J HJ-6655	Musical Drum Sound/NOW GENERATION: Musical Drum - Version	12
73	Pama PM 854	Cowtown Skank/AUGUSTUS PABLO: Cowtown Skank Version	12
74	Atra ATRA 017	Yah Ma Ride/SWEET HARMONY: Mexican Rockin'	12
74	Ashanti ASH 412	Mood For Love (Parts 1 & 2)	12
75	Bullet BU 551	Step Right Up/ANDY'S ALLSTARS: Banjo Serenade	8
75	Lucky DL 5098	I Man Time/Version	12
75	Third World TW 015	Mr Benwood Dick/Mad Mad Hatter	8
75	Third World TW 85	New York City/CORNELL CAMPBELL: Blessed Are They	8
76	Dip DL 5107	Padlock/Lock And Key (copies also exist with Lucky label)	10
77	Observer OB 002	Jamaican Girl/River Jordan/OBSERVER IN FINE STYLE: First Cut/Second Cut (12", p/s)	25
78	GG's GG 011	Natty Get Ready/Version	6
79	Virgin Front Line FLS 124 12	Fire In A Wire/Hill And Gully (12")	12
70s	Nationwide NW 005	Tea Pot/Tea Cup	12
73	Trojan TRLS 63	PRESENTING I ROY (LP, original issue with "12 Neasden Lane" address and rough orange/white paper labels)	35
74	Trojan TRLS 71	HELL AND SORROW (LP, original issue with "12 Neasden Lane" address and rough orange/white paper labels)	30
74	Trojan TRLS 91	THE MANY MOODS OF I ROY (LP, original issue with "12 Neasden Lane" address and rough orange/white paper labels)	30
75	Grounation GROL 504	TRUTH & RIGHTS (LP)	25
76	Klik 9020	DREAD BALDHEAD (LP)	45
77	Justice JUS LP 08	CAN'T CONQUER RASTA (LP)	30
77	ATA ATA 1005	Roots Man/Observer Mix	10
78	Third World TWS 930	THE GODFATHER (LP)	20
70s	Virgin VDJ 19	MUSICAL SHARK ATTACK (LP)	20
77	Virgin Frontline VF 1001	HEART OF A LION (LP)	15

LEE ROY

65	Island WI 251	Oh Ee Baby/My Loving Baby Come Back	10

LITTLE ROY

(see also Roy & Joy, Little Roys)

69	Crab CRAB 39	Without My Love (actually by Roy & Joy)/WINSTON SAMUELS: Here I Come Again	10
70	Bullet BU 445	Keep Trying/THE MATADORS: Version II	10
70	Camel CA 43	Scrooge/In The Days Of Old	12
70	Camel CA 46	You Run Come/THE LITTLE ROYS: Skank King (actually "Skank Me" by Little Roy)	12
70	Camel CA 52	Fight Them/Dreadlock	12
71	Escort ERT 850	Yester-Me Yester-You Yesterday/MATADOR ALL-STARS: Yes Sir	10
71	Punch PH 75	Hard Fighter/COUNT OSSIE: Back To Africa Version	12

MAD ROY

(pseudonym for Leroy Wallace)

70	Banana BA 324	Nanny Version (actually by Dennis Alcapone)/BIGGER D: Freedom Version	20
71	Banana BA 326	Home Version (actually by Dennis Alcapone)/SOUND DIMENSION: One Time	15
71	Banana BA 327	Universal Love/ROLAND ALPHONSO: Shelly Belly	15
71	Banana BA 328	Duppy Serenade/Sunshine Version (both sides actually by Dennis Alcapone)	12

U ROY JUNIOR

(see also Hugh Roy, Dennis Alcapone, Sir Harry, Shorty Perry, Heptones, Herman Chin-Loy)

72	Duke Reid DR 2520	Rock To The Beat/Love Is Not A Gamble (both actually by Dennis Alcapone)	12
72	Attack ATT 8030	This Is A Pepper (as U Roy Junior)/JOHN HOLT: Justice	12

MINT VALUE £

72	Sioux SI 024	The Wedding (as U Roy Junior)/LLOYD'S ALL STARS: Buttercup	8
73	Randy's RAN 532	Froggie (as U Roy Junior)/RHYTHM RULERS: Version	10
73	Techniques TE 928	Aunt Kereba (as U Roy Junior)/DON RECO: Waterloo Rock (B-side actually by Reco Rodriquez)	12

ROY & ANNETTE
(see also Tommy McCook, Lester Sterling)

63	R&B JB 107	My Baby/Go Your Ways	20

ROY & DUKE ALL STARS
(see also Roy Panton)

68	Blue Cat BS 113	Pretty Blue Eyes Parts 1 & 2	40
68	Blue Cat BS 117	The Train Parts 1 & 2	40

ROY & ENID
(see also Little Roys)

68	Coxsone CS 7063	Rocking Time/RALPH BLAKE: High Blood Pressure	100
68	Coxsone CS 7069	He'll Have To Go/CARLTON & SHOES: Love Is A Treasure	50
69	Coxsone CS 7088	Reggae For Days/SOUND DIMENSION: Holy Moses	30

(Little) ROY & JOY

73	Camel CA 107	Rainy Weather/THE DEN BROTHERS: Version	8

ROY (Panton) & MILLIE
(see also Roy Panton, Millie [Small])

62	Island WI 005	We'll Meet/ROLAND ALPHONSO: Back Beat (B-side act. with City Slickers)	25
63	Island WI 050	This World/Never Say Goodbye	25
63	Island WI 090	There'll Come A Day/I Don't Want You	25
63	Blue Beat BB 154	Over And Over/I'll Go (with Prince Buster All Stars)	20
64	Black Swan WI 409	Cherry I Love You/You're The Only One	30
64	Black Swan WI 410	Oh Merna/DON DRUMMOND: Dog War Bossa Nova	30
64	Black Swan WI 427	Oh Shirley/Marie	25

ROY (Richards) & PAULETTE

63	Island WI 067	Have You Seen My Baby/Since You're Gone	25

ROY (Panton) & YVONNE (Harrison)
(see also Roy Panton)

64	Blue Beat BB 258	Little Girl/No More	20
64	Black Swan WI 436	Two Roads/Join Together	20

ROY (Panton) & PATSY
(see also Roy Panton)

62	Blue Beat BB 118	My Happy Home/In Your Arms Dear (with Hersang & His Combo)	20

BILLY JOE ROYAL

62	Oriole CB 1751	Never In A Hundred Years/We Haven't A Moment To Lose	20
65	CBS 201802	Down In The Boondocks/Oh! What A Night	15
65	CBS 201983	You Make Me Feel Like A Man/I've Got To Be Somebody	6
65	CBS 202009	I Knew You When/Steal Away	6
66	CBS 202052	It's A Good Time/Don't Wait Up For Me Mama	6
66	CBS 202087	Heart's Desire/Everbody's Gotta Cry	40
66	CBS 202087	Heart's Desire/Everbody's Gotta Cry (DJ copy)	75
66	CBS 202400	High On A Hilltop/I'm Gonna Get Right Tonight	6
66	Atlantic 584 002	Never In A Hundred Years/We Haven't A Moment To Lose (reissue)	8
67	CBS 202548	Yo Yo/We Tried	10
67	CBS 3044	Hush/Watching From The Bandstand	8
68	CBS 3644	Storybook Children/Just Between Me And You	8
68	CBS 3859	Gabriel/Movies In My Mind	7
69	CBS 4470	Cherry Hill Park/Helping Hand	7
71	CBS 7302	Tulsa/Pick Up The Pieces	7
72	CBS 7727	We Go Back/Colorado Rain	7
66	CBS BPG 62590	INTRODUCING BILLY JOE ROYAL (LP)	25

BOBBY ROYAL

63	HMV POP 1253	Big Big Star/Little Word Of Love	12
65	Decca F 12097	Within My Lonely Heart/When I Found You	10

ROYAL HOLIDAYS

58	London HLU 8722	Margaret/I'm Sorry (I Did You Wrong)	140
58	London HLU 8722	Margaret/I'm Sorry (I Did You Wrong) (78)	50

ROBBIE ROYAL

65	Mercury MF 923	Only Me/I Don't Need You	8
65	Decca F 12097	Within My Lonely Heart/When I Found You	6

ROYAL BLUES

69	Pye 7N 17670	Mountain Of Love/Wishful Thinking	6
69	Pye 7N 17732	Mendocino/Hi-Lili Hi-Lo	5
69	Pye 7N 17769	Proud Mary/Sunny Girl Friend	6
69	Pye 7N 17847	High As A Mountain/Wildwood Flower	5

ROYALETTES

65	MGM MGM 1272	Poor Boy/Watch What Happens	15
65	MGM MGM 1279	It's Gonna Take A Miracle/Out Of Sight Out Of Mind	30
65	MGM MGM 1279	It's Gonna Take A Miracle/Out Of Sight Out Of Mind (DJ copy)	60
65	MGM MGM 1292	I Want To Meet Him/Never Again	20
66	MGM MGM 1302	You Bring Me Down/Only When You're Lonely	20
66	MGM MGM 1324	It's A Big Mistake/I Want To Meet Him	15
68	Big T BIG 106	River Of Tears/Something Wonderful	15
66	MGM MGM-C 8028	THE ELEGANT SOUND OF THE ROYALETTES (LP)	100

ROYAL GUARDSMEN

67	Stateside SS 2010	The Return Of The Red Baron/Sweetmeats Slide	7
67	Stateside S(S)L 10202	SNOOPY VS THE RED BARON (LP)	20
68	London HA-P/SH-P 8351	THE RETURN OF THE RED BARON (LP)	20

MINT VALUE £

JAMES ROYAL (& HAWKS)

65	Parlophone R 5290	She's About A Mover/Black Cloud (as James Royal & Hawks)	25
65	Parlophone R 5383	Work Song/I Can't Stand It	35
67	CBS 202525	Call My Name/When It Comes To My Baby	20
67	CBS 2739	It's All In The Game/Green Days	7
68	CBS 2959	Take Me Like I Am/Sitting In The Station	5
68	CBS 3232	I Can't Stand It/Little Bit Of Rain	30
68	CBS 3450	Hey Little Boy/Thru' The Love	25
68	CBS 3624	A Woman Called Sorrow/Fire	20
69	CBS 3797	Time Hangs On My Mind/Anna-Lee	6
69	CBS 3915	House Of Jack/Which Way To Nowhere	30
69	CBS 4139	I've Something Bad On My Mind/She's Independent	6
69	CBS 4181	That Kind Of Girl/Will You Be Staying After Sunday	6
69	CBS 4463	Send Out Love/I've Lost You	30
70	CBS 5032	And Soon The Darkness/I'm Going Home	6
70	Carnaby CNS 4021	Carolina/Big Heat On The Loose	6
71	Carnaby 6151 002	Carolina/A Woman Called Sorrow	8
72	Carnaby 6151 006	Two Of Us/Who Are We (with Liz Christian)	5
69	CBS 63780	CALL MY NAME (LP)	30
70	Carnaby CNLS 6008	ONE WAY (LP)	50
72	Carnaby 6302 011	THE LIGHT AND SHADE OF JAMES ROYAL (LP)	40

ROYAL RASSES

79	12 Bakistuc 315	You Gotta Have Love (Jah Love)/Humanity (Love The Way It Should Be)/ They Know Not Jah (12", clear vinyl)	12
79	Warrior BP 327	Royal Rasses - Aint' Nobody Here But Me/Kingston 11 (Ghetto Rock) (12")	15
79	Ballistic 12UP36496	Old Time Friend (Disco Style)/San Salvador (Disco Style) (12", clear vinyl, p/s)	8
78	Ballistic UAG 30259	EXPERIENCE (LP)	12
79	Ballistic PRE 1	GOD SENT DUB (white label/plain sleeve) (LP)	40
79	Warrior WARLP 2002	HARDER NA RASS! (LP)	40
80	Ballistic LBR 1031	HARDER NA RASS (LP)	20
76	Neville King NK 01	Love The Way It Should Be/Bud The Way It Should Be	10
77	Neville King NK 4	Kingston 11/Dub Up Kingston	10

ROYAL ROCKERS

60	Top Rank JAR 326	Jet II/Swinging Mambo	20

ROYALS

64	Blue Beat BB 259	Save Mama/Out De Fire	30
68	Amalgamated AMG 831	Never See Come See/CANNONBALL BRYAN TRIO: Jumping Jack	45
69	Trojan TR 662	Pick Out Me Eye/Think You Too Bad	60
69	Duke DU 29	Never Gonna Give You Up/Don't Mix Me Up	20
73	Dip DL 5016	Promised Land/Every Jamaican Is A Rebel	6
81	Kingdom KVLP 9006	MOVING ON (LP)	20
79	Warrior WAR 143	Rising Sun/It's Real (Gone Sweet)	15

ROYAL SHOWBAND WATERFORD

62	HMV POP 1011	Come Down The Mountain Katie Daly/I Heard The Bluebirds Sing	6
63	HMV POP 1238	No More/Fountain Of Love	6
64	HMV POP 1377	Hucklebuck/Sorry (I Ran All The Way Home, as Royal Showband)	7
65	HMV POP 1444	Count Me In/She Was You Again (as Royal Showband)	6
65	HMV POP 1460	Hucklebuck Shoes/The Hawaiian Wedding Song (as Royal Showband)	6

ROYAL TEENS

58	HMV POP 454	Short Shorts/Planet Rock	35
58	HMV POP 454	Short Shorts/Planet Rock (78)	20
59	Capitol CL 15068	Little Cricket/Believe Me	30

ROYALTONES

58	London HLJ 8744	Poor Boy/Wail!	20
58	London HLJ 8744	Poor Boy/Wail! (78)	20
61	London HLU 9296	Flamingo Express/Tacos	20
64	Stateside SS 309	Our Faded Love/Holy Smokes	12

ROYAL TRUX

93	Domino WIGLP 6	CATS & DOGS (LP)	20

ROYALTY

69	CBS 4181	That Kind Of Girl/Will You Be Staying After Sunday	30

EARL ROYCE & OLYMPICS

64	Columbia DB 7433	Que Sera Sera/I Really Do	25
65	Parlophone R 5261	Guess Things Happen That Way/Sure To Fall (In Love With You)	25

ROY'S BOYS

64	Columbia DB 7425	Do Wah Diddy Diddy-I'm Into Something Good-I Want To Hold Your Hand/ Oh! Pretty Woman-Have I The Right?-It's All Over Now	7

LITA ROZA

(see also Stargazers, Johnston Brothers)

53	Decca F 10070	(How Much Is) That Doggie In The Window/Tell Me We'll Meet Again (78)	20
53	Decca F 75082	(How Much Is) That Doggie In The Window/Tell Me We'll Meet Again (export issue)	70
54	Decca F 10240	Changing Partners/Just A Dream Or Two Ago (B-side with Stargazers)	15
54	Decca F 10269	Bell Bottom Blues (with Johnston Brothers)/Make Love To Me (both with Ted Heath Orchestra)	15
54	Decca F 10277	Young At Heart/Secret Love	15
54	Decca F 10393	Call Off The Wedding/The "Mama-Doll" Song	15
55	Decca F 10427	Heartbeat/Leave Me Alone	15
55	Decca F 10431	Let Me Go, Lover!/Make Yourself Comfortable	15
55	Decca F 10479	Tomorrow/Foolishly	15
55	Decca F 10536	Two Hearts, Two Kisses (Make One Love)/Keep Me In Mind	15

MINT VALUE £

55	Decca F 10541	The Man In The Raincoat/Today And Ev'ry Day	12
55	Decca F 10611	Hey There/Hernando's Hideaway	15
56	Decca F 10679	Jimmy Unknown/The Rose Tattoo	15
56	Decca F 10728	Too Young To Go Steady/You're Not Alone	5
56	Decca F 10761	No Time For Tears/But Love Me (Love But Me)	5
56	Decca F 10792	Innismore/The Last Waltz	5
56	Decca F 10830	Hey! Jealous Lover/Julie	5
57	Decca F 10861	Lucky Lips/Tears Don't Care Who Cries Them	5
57	Decca F 10884	Tonight My Heart She Is Crying/Five Oranges, Four Apples	5
58	Pye Nixa 7N 15149	Hillside In Scotland/Sorry, Sorry, Sorry	5
58	Pye Nixa 7N 15155	Nel Blu Dipinto Di Blu (Volare)/It's A Boy	5
59	Pye Nixa 7N 15204	Allentown Jail/Once In A While	5
63	Ember EMB S 168	Mama (He Treats Your Daughter Mean)/(He's My) Dreamboat (as Lisa Rosa)	30
65	Columbia DB 7689	Keep Watch Over Him/Stranger Things Have Happened	8
57	Decca DFE 6386	LITA ROZA SELECTION (EP)	40
57	Decca DFE 6399	LITA ROZA (EP)	35
58	Decca DFE 6443	BETWEEN THE DEVIL AND THE DEEP BLUE SEA NO. 1 (EP)	30
54	Decca LF 1187	PRESENTING LITA ROZA (10" LP)	100
56	Decca LF 1243	LISTENING IN THE AFTER HOURS (10" LP, features Tony Kinsey Quartet)	120
57	Decca LK 4171	LOVE IS THE ANSWER (LP)	80
57	Decca LK 4218	BETWEEN THE DEVIL AND THE DEEP BLUE SEA (LP)	75
58	Pye Nixa NPL 18020	ME ON A CAROUSEL (LP, mono)	40
58	Pye Nixa NSPL 83003	ME ON A CAROUSEL (LP, stereo)	50
60	Pye NPL 18047	DRINKA LITA ROZA DAY (LP)	50
64	Ember NR 5009	LOVE SONGS FOR NIGHT PEOPLE (LP)	35
83	President PLE 509	YOU'RE DRIVING ME CRAZY (LP)	15

RT & B

79	Splendor Heights SH 1	Forward/Join Them (12")	20

MISTER JACK RUANE ESQUIRE

68	Pye 7N 17529	Everybody Wants To Go To Heaven/Just For Fun	7

RUB-A-DUBS WITH DANDY

(see also Dandy)

65	Blue Beat BB 304	Without Love/I Know	25

RUBAIYATS

68	Action ACT 4516	Omar Khayam/Tomorrow	40

GIDEON JAH RUBBAAL

77	Greensleeves GRE 003	Love Rasta/GIDEON JAH RUBBAAL ALL STARS: Rasta Version	8

RUBBER BAND

73	Youngblood YB 1052	Moonwalker/Wichita	6
69	Major Minor SMCP 5045	CREAM SONGBOOK (LP)	20
69	Major Minor SMCP 5048	HENDRIX SONGBOOK (LP)	20

RUBBER BOOTZ

67	Deram DM 134	Joy Ride/Chicano	30

RUBBER BUCKET

(see also Paul Raven)

69	MCA MK 5006	We're All Living In One Place/Take Me Away	10

JOHNNY RUBBISH

78	United Artists UP 36405	Living In NW3 4JR/Other Side (p/s)	10

RUBIN

75	MCA MU 196	You've Been Away/Baby, You're My Everything	10
75	MCA MU 196	You've Been Away/Baby, You're My Everything (DJ copy)	20

RUBY

(see also Procol Harum)

74	Chrysalis CHR 1061	RED CRYSTAL FANTASIES (LP, textured sleeve, green label)	20

RUBY & GLORIA

71	Big Shot BI 583	Worried Over You/Worried Over You - Version	8
71	Black Swan BW 1409	Talk To Me Baby/LLOYD'S ALL STARS: Talk To Me Baby - Version	8

RUBY & ROMANTICS

(see also Danny Davis Orchestra)

63	London HLR 9679	Our Day Will Come/Moonlight And Music	15
63	London HLR 9734	My Summer Love/Sweet Love And Sweet Forgiveness	15
63	London HLR 9771	Hey There Lonely Boy/Not A Moment Too Soon	15
63	London HLR 9801	Young Wings Can Fly/Day Dreaming	15
64	London HLR 9881	Our Everlasting Love/Much Better Off Than I've Ever Been	30
64	London HLR 9916	Baby Come Home/Every Day's A Holiday	30
64	London HLR 9935	When You're Young And In Love/I Cry Alone	15
65	London HLR 9972	Your Baby Doesn't Love Me Anymore/We'll Meet Again	15
69	A&M AMS 750	Hurting Each Other/Baby I Could Be So Good At Loving You	15
63	London RE-R 1389	OUR DAY WILL COME (EP)	75
64	London RE-R 1427	HEY THERE LONELY BOY (EP)	70
63	London HA-R 8078	OUR DAY WILL COME (LP)	70
66	London HA-R 8282	GREATEST HITS (LP)	65

RUD(D)Y (Grant) & SKETTO (Rich)

(see also Ruddy & Sketto)

62	Dice CC 5	Summer Is Just Around The Corner/Nothing Like Time (as Ruddy & Sketto & Reco's All Stars)	25
62	Dice CC 7	Little Schoolgirl/Hush Baby (as Ruddy & Sketto & Baron Twist & His Knights)	25
62	Dice CC 10	Mr Postman/Christmas Blues (as Rudy & Sketto with Laurel's Group)	25
63	Dice CC 16	Hold The Fire/Good Morning Mr Jones	25
63	Dice CC 19	Never Set You Free/Brothers And Sisters	20

MINT VALUE £

63	Blue Beat BB 198	Was It Me/Minna Don't Deceive Me	20
64	Blue Beat BB 208	Show Me The Way To Go Home/Let Me Dream	20
64	Blue Beat BB 230	Ten Thousand Miles From Home/I Need Someone (as Ruddy & Sketto)	25
64	Blue Beat BB 252	I Love You/If Only Tomorrow	25
65	Blue Beat BB 297	See What You Done/Heart's Desire (as Ruddy & Sketto)	20
65	Blue Beat BB 310	Oh Dolly/You're Mine (as Ruddy & Sketto)	20

RUDDY & SKETTO

(see also Sketto Rich)

62	Dice CC 7	Little Schoolgirl/Hush Baby	10
63	Dice CC16	Hold The Fire/Good Morning Mr Jones	15
71	Supreme SUP 218	Every Night/Ethiopia	8

RUDE AND DEADLY

95	Unity UNITY 002	Lightnin' and Tundra/Mash Dem Down (12")	40
95	No Smoking SMOKE 7	Give Me A Dub/Murder De boy (12", as Rude And Deadly Vs. The Dogz)	15
97	Smokers Inc. SINC 1200	Give Me A Dubplate (97 Remix) (12", 1-sided, stamped white labels)	15
97	Smokers Inc SINC 1200	Give Me A Dubplate (97 Remix)/Give Me A Dubplate (Original Mix) (12")	15

RUDE ASS TINKER

(see also Mu-Ziq, Tusken Raiders, U-Ziq)

90s	Deathchant DEATH 30	Imperial Break/Silk Ties (12", limited issue)	18

RUDE BOY BUSINESS

90	Rude Boy Biz RBB001	I Play For Keeps (12")	12
90	Kold Sweat KS103	Chasing Competition/Cool Sailing (12")	12

RUDE BOYS

67	Island WI 3088	Rock Steady Massachusetts/Going Home	20

RUDI

78	Good Vibrations GOT 1	Big Time/Number 1 (folded p/s, 3,000 only)	30
79	Good Vibrations GOT 1	Big Time/No. 1 (reissue, p/s)	10
79	Good Vibrations GOT 12	I Spy/Genuine Reply/Sometimes/Ripped In Two (p/s)	30
81	Jamming! CREATE 1	When I Was Dead/The Pressure's On (p/s)	5
82	Jamming! CREATE 3	Crimson/14 Steps (p/s)	5

RUDIES (FANATICS)

(see also Freddie Notes, Sonny, Binns & Rudies, Rico, Dandy, Owen & Dandy, Downtown All Stars, Desmond Riley)

68	Blue Cat BS 107	The 7-11 Go To The Go Go Club (Parts 1 & 2)	120
68	Blue Cat BS 109	Cupid/RECO'S ALLSTARS: Wise Message	35
68	Nu Beat NB 001	Train To Vietnam/Skaville To Rainbow City	25
68	Nu Beat NB 005	Engine 59/My Girl	25
68	Fab FAB 46	I Wanna Go Home/La Mer	18
68	Fab FAB 70	Give Me The Rights/I Do Love You (as Rudies Fanatics)	18
68	Fab FAB 71	Mighty Meaty/Go (as Rudies Fanatics)	18
69	Doctor Bird DB 1301	Sin Thing/What's Your Name	15
69	Doctor Bird DB 1302	Boss Sound/RECO & RUDIES: Peace	25
69	Fab FAB 104	Brixton Rocket/Rudie's Joy	200
70	Pama PM 789	Give Peace A Chance/She	8
70	Trojan TR 7798	Patches/Split	10
70	Grape GA 3016	Henry The Great/Black Scorcher	45
71	Spinning Wheel SW 106	My Sweet Lord/Devil's Lead Soup	45

RUDIMENTARY PENI

(see also Magits)

81	Outer Himalayan OH 003	RUDIMENTARY PENI (EP, A4 foldout p/s with booklet)	20
81	Outer Himalayan OH 003	RUDIMENTARY PENI (EP, later 14" x 7" sleeve)	15
82	Crass 211984/2	FARCE (EP, initial pressing in 21" x 14" foldout black & white p/s)	20
82	Crass 211984/2	FARCE (EP, p/s)	15
83	Corpus Christi CHRISTITS 6	DEATH CHURCH (LP)	20
80s	Corpus Christi	CACOPHONY (LP, with booklet)	15
97	Outer Himalayan BOOB 006	ECHOES OF ANGUISH (12", EP)	12

RUEFREX

80	Good Vibrations GOT 8	One By One/Cross The Line/Don't Panic (foldover p/s, 2 different designs)	12
83	Kabuki KAR 7	Capital Letters/April Fool (p/s)	5

RUF

93	Ruf BOOM01	THE NORTHERN CONQUEST (EP)	8

RAY RUFF & CHECKMATES

64	London HLU 9889	I Took A Liking To You/A Fool Again	15

RUFF WITH THE SMOOTH

(see also Jack Smooth)

93	Basement BRSS 023	Art Of Intelligence/Sounds Superior (12")	15
94	Basement BRSS 037	Twisted Girl/Who's Loving Me (12")	10

RUFFIANS

(see Al Brown, Sensations)

71	Banana BA 359	Room Full Of Tears (actually by Sensations)/Black Soul (actually "Black And White - Version" by Riley's Allstars)	12

BRUCE RUFFIN

(see also Bruce Downer)

69	Songbird SB 1002	Long About Now/Come See About Me (as Bruce Ruffin & Temptations)	20
69	Trojan TR 7704	Dry Up Your Tears/BEVERLEY'S ALLSTARS: One Way Street	10
70	Trojan TR 7737	I'm The One/Who's Gonna Be Your Man?	8
70	Trojan TR 7776	Cecelia/BEVERLEY ALL STARS: Stand Up	5
70	Summit SUM 8509	O-o-h Child/Bitterness Of Life	12
71	Summit SUM 8516	Candida/Are You Ready	10
71	Trojan TR 7814	Rain/THE PYRAMIDS: Geronimo (B-side actually by Pyramids)	8

MINT VALUE £

71	Trojan TR 7814	Rain/THE PYRAMIDS: Off Limits (B-side actually by Aquarians)	8
71	Trojan TR 7832	One Big Happy Family (Parts 1 & 2)	5
72	Trojan TRM 9000	Songs Of Peace/You Are The Best/We Can Make It	12
72	Rhino RNO 101	Mad About You/Save The People	6
73	Rhino RNO 114	Tickle Me/I Like Everything About You	6
71	Trojan TRL 23	RAIN (LP)	12

DAVID RUFFIN

(see also Temptations)

69	Tamla Motown TMG 689	My Whole World Ended (The Moment You Left Me)/ I've Got To Find Myself A Brand New Baby	18
69	Tamla Motown TMG 711	I've Lost Everything I've Ever Loved/We'll Have A Good Thing Going On	15
76	Tamla Motown TMG 1022	Heavy Love/Me And Rock And Roll Are Here To Stay	6
69	T. Motown (S)TML 11118	MY WHOLE WORLD ENDED (LP, mono/stereo)	35
70	T. Motown (S)TML 11139	FEELIN' GOOD (LP)	40
73	Tamla Motown STML 11228	DAVID RUFFIN (LP)	20

JIMMY RUFFIN

(see also Council Collective)

66	Tamla Motown TMG 577	What Becomes Of The Broken-Hearted?/Baby I've Got It	18
66	Tamla Motown TMG 577	What Becomes Of The Broken-Hearted?/Baby I've Got It (DJ copy)	85
67	Tamla Motown TMG 593	I've Passed This Way Before/Tomorrow's Tears	20
67	Tamla Motown TMG 593	I've Passed This Way Before/Tomorrow's Tears (DJ copy)	60
67	Tamla Motown TMG 603	Gonna Give Her All The Love I Got/World So Wide, Nowhere To Hide (DJ copy)	15
67	Tamla Motown TMG 603	Gonna Give Her All The Love I Got/World So Wide, Nowhere To Hide	50
67	Tamla Motown TMG 617	Don't You Miss Me A Little Bit Baby/I Want Her Love	15
67	Tamla Motown TMG 617	Don't You Miss Me A Little Bit Baby/I Want Her Love (DJ copy)	40
68	Tamla Motown TMG 649	I'll Say Forever My Love/Everybody Needs Love	15
68	Tamla Motown TMG 649	I'll Say Forever My Love/Everybody Needs Love (DJ copy)	45
68	Tamla Motown TMG 664	Don't Let Him Take Your Love From Me/Lonely Lonely Man Am I	15
68	Tamla Motown TMG 664	Don't Let Him Take Your Love From Me/Lonely Lonely Man Am I (DJ copy)	30
69	Tamla Motown TMG 703	I've Passed This Way Before/Tomorrow's Tears	7
70	Tamla Motown TMG 726	Farewell Is A Lonely Sound/If You Let Me, I Know I Can	6
70	Tamla Motown TMG 740	I'll Say Forever My Love/Everybody Needs Love	6
70	Tamla Motown TMG 753	It's Wonderful (To Be Loved By You)/Maria (You Were The Only One)	6
71	Tamla Motown TMG 767	Let's Say Goodbye Tomorrow/Living In A World I Created For Myself	7
71	Tamla Motown TMG 784	On The Way Out (On The Way In)/Honey Come Back	10
67	T. Motown TML 11048	THE JIMMY RUFFIN WAY (LP, mono)	40
67	T. Motown STML 11048	THE JIMMY RUFFIN WAY (LP, stereo)	40
69	T. Motown (S)TML 11106	RUFF 'N' READY (LP, mono/stereo)	40
70	T. Motown STML 11161	JIMMY RUFFIN... FOREVER (LP)	18
73	Polydor 2383 240	JIMMY RUFFIN (LP)	15
70s	Sounds Superb SPR 90041	I'VE PASSED THIS WAY BEFORE (LP)	12

JIMMY & DAVID RUFFIN

(see also David Ruffin, Temptations)

71	Tamla Motown STML 11176	I AM NOT MY BROTHER'S KEEPER (LP)	25

RUFFNECK

93	Represent REPREC 1	Radford(You Get Me)/You And Me (12")	18

RUFIGE CRU

92	Reinforced RIVET 1220	Krisp Biscuit (Power)/Killa Muffin (The Band Dog Mix) (12", die-cut title sleeve with tracks and artist mispelt)	15
92	Reinforced RIVET 1224	Darkrider/Believe/Menace/Jim Skreech (12", p/s)	30
93	Reinforced RIVET 1244	Terminator II Remix/Fabio's Ghost (The Edit)/ Ghosts Of My Life/ High Rollerz Ghostin' Out (12", promo only)	25
07	Exit EXIT 010	Is This Real/Is This Real (I'm Not Sure Remix) (12", p/s, yellow vinyl, poster)	25

RUFUS

74	ABC ABC 4022	You Got The Love/Rags To Rufus/Chaka Khan	5
75	ABC ABC 4038	Stop On By/Rufusized	5
75	ABC ABC 4055	Once You Get Started/Right Is Right (p/s)	5
84	Warner Bros RCKT 1	Ain't Got You/Stop On By/Don't Go To Strangers (12", with Chaka Khan)	12
75	ABC ABCL 5151	RUFUS WITH CHAKA KHAN (LP)	12

RUGBYS

69	Polydor 56781	You And I/Stay With Me	45
70	Polydor 56789	Wendegahl The Warlock/Light	20

PETE RUGOLO (& DIAMONDS)

(see also Diamonds, Patti Page)

60	Warner Bros WM 4001	BEHIND BRIGITTE BARDOT - COOL SOUNDS FROM HER HOT SCENES (LP, gatefold, also stereo WS 8001)	25
58	Mercury MPL 6512	BRASS IN HI-FI (LP)	12

RULERS

66	Rio R 105	Don't Be A Rude Boy/Be Good	15
66	Rio R 107	Copasetic/Too Late	20
67	Rio R 132	Wrong 'em Boyo/Why Don't You Change	25
67	Rio R 135	Well Covered/CARL DAWKINS: Help Time	15
67	Rio R 138	Be Mine/CARL DAWKINS: Hot And Sticky	15
69	Trojan TR 696	Got To Be Free/Situation	25

RUMBLE

70	Warner Bros WB 8011	Rich Man, Poor Man/Let Me Down	30

RUMBLERS

63	London HLD 9684	Boss/I Don't Need You No More	40
65	King KG 1021	Soulful Jerk/Hey Did A Da Da	60
63	London RE-D 1396	BOSSOUNDS (EP)	150
63	London HA-D 8081	BOSSOUNDS (LP, mono)	90
63	London SH-D 8081	BOSSOUNDS (LP, stereo)	100

MINT VALUE £

RUMPLESTILTSKIN
(see also Clem Cattini)

70	Bell BLL 1101	Squadron Leader Johnson/Rumplestiltskin	20
71	Bell BLL 1157	Wimoweh/Through My Looking Glass	6
70	Bell SBLL 130	RUMPLESTILTSKIN (LP, gatefold sleeve)	50

RUNAWAYS
(see also Joan Jett, Lita Ford & Ozzy Osbourne)o

76	Mercury 6167 392	Cherry Bomb/Blackmail	10
77	Mercury 6167 493	Queens Of Noise/Born To Be Bad	6
77	Mercury 6167 587	School Days/Wasted (p/s)	8
79	Cherry Red CHERRY 8	Right Now/Black Leather (p/s)	12
76	Mercury 9100 029	THE RUNAWAYS (LP, with gatefold sleeve & lyric sheet; U.S. pressing, with cat. no. SRM 1 1090, in U.K. sleeve)	18
77	Mercury 9100 032	QUEENS OF NOISE (LP, with lyric sheet)	15
77	Mercury 9100 046	LIVE IN JAPAN (LP)	15
77	Mercury 9100 047	WAITIN' FOR THE NIGHT (LP)	15
79	Cherry Red ARED 38	AND NOW... THE RUNAWAYS (LP, 1,000 copies each in yellow, red, blue & orange vinyl, numbered)	25
80	Cherry Red BRED 9	FLAMING SCHOOLGIRLS (LP)	12

TODD RUNDGREN

72	Bearsville K 15502	I Saw The Light/Marlene	6

RUN DMC

86	Profile LOXPD 104	Walk This Way/Walk This Way (instrumental)/My Adidas (12" picture disc)	10

RUNESTAFF

85	FM VHF 5	Road To Ruin/Last Chances (p/s)	7
85	FM VHF 17	Do It!/Runestaff (no p/s)	6
85	Heavy Metal HMRLP 26	RUNESTAFF (LP)	15

RUNNER

79	Acrobat BAT 2	Run For Your Life/Gone Too Long	8
79	Acrobat ACRO1	RUNNER (LP, with inner)	15

RUNNING MAN
(see also Ray Russell Quartet, Mouse, Rock Workshop)

72	RCA Neon NE 11	THE RUNNING MAN (LP)	400

RUNNING RIOT

00	Rejected 001	RECLAIM THE STREETS (LP)	12

RUNRIG

83	Ridge RRS 003	Loch Lomond/Tuireadh Iain Ruaida (p/s)	15
84	Simple SIM 4	Dance Called America/Na H Uain A's T-Earrach (p/s)	30
84	Simple 12 SIM 4	Dance Called America/Na H Uain A's T-Earrach/Ribhinn (12", p/s)	20
84	Simple SIM 8	Skye/Hey Mandu (p/s)	15
86	Ridge RRS 006	The Work Song/This Time Of Year (p/s)	10
86	Ridge RRS 007	Alba/Worker For The Wind (p/s)	12
88	Chrysalis CHS 3284	Protect And Survive/Hearts Of Olden Glory (live) (p/s)	6
88	Chrysalis CHS 12 3284	Protect And Survive/Hearts Of Olden Glory (live)/ Protect And Survive (live) (12", p/s)	10
88	Chrysalis CHSCD 3284	Protect And Survive/Hearts Of Olden Glory (live)/Protect And Survive (live) (CD)	15
89	Chrysalis CHS 3404	News From Heaven/Chi Mi'n Tir (p/s)	5
89	Chrysalis CHS 12 3404	News From Heaven/Chi Mi'n Tir/The Times They Are A'Changing (12", p/s)	8
89	Chrysalis CHS 12T 3404	News From Heaven/Chi Mi'n Tir/The Times They Are A'Changing (12", picture disc)	20
89	Chrysalis CHSCD 3404	News From Heaven/Chi Mi'n Tir/The Times They Are A'Changing (CD)	20
89	Chrysalis CHS 3451	Every River/This Time Of Year (p/s)	6
89	Chrysalis CHS 12 3451	Every River/This Time Of Year/Our Earth Was Once Green (12", p/s)	8
89	Chrysalis CHSCD 3451	Every River/This Time Of Year/Our Earth Was Once Green (CD)	15
90	Chrysalis CHSCD 3594	CAPTURE THE HEART EP: Stepping Down The Glory Road/ Satellite Flood/ Harvest Moon/The Apple Came Down (10", p/s)	8
90	Chrysalis CHSCD 1235941	CAPTURE THE HEART EP: Stepping Down The Glory Road/ Satellite Flood/ Harvest Moon/The Apple Came Down (12", p/s)	15
90	Chrysalis CHSCD 3594	CAPTURE THE HEART EP: Stepping Down The Glory Road/ Satellite Flood/ Harvest Moon/The Apple Came Down (CD)	15
90	Chrysalis CHS 38051	Flower Of The West/Ravenscraig/Ch Mi'n Greamhradh (p/s)	5
90	Chrysalis CHSCD 3805	Flower Of The West/Ravenscraig/Ch Mi'n Greamhradh/ Harvest Moon (CD, digipak)	12
91	Chrysalis CHSG 123754	HEARTHAMMER EP (12", gatefold p/s, with booklet)	8
91	Chrysalis CHS 123805	FLOWER OF THE WEST EP (12", numbered box set, with poster, discography & sticker)	10
93	Chrysalis CHSS 3952	Wonderful/April Come She Will (limited edition blue vinyl)	5
93	Chrysalis CHS 3975	THE GREATEST FLAME (EP, numbered postcard pack)	5
78	Neptune NA 105	RUNRIG PLAY GAELIC (LP)	20
79	Ridge RR 001	THE HIGHLAND CONNECTION (LP)	15
81	Ridge RR 002	RECOVERY (LP, with inner)	20

RUNS

80	Carrere CAR 139	Bun In The Oven (no p/s)	20

RUNT
(see also Todd Rundgren, Utopia, Nazz)

71	Bearsville K 44505	RUNT (LP)	15
71	Bearsville K 44506	RUNT - THE BALLAD OF TODD RUNDGREN (LP)	15

R.U.1.2.

78	SRTS/78/CUS 131	She's Gone/Purely Physical/Teenage Girl (p/s)	20

RUN 229

80	MM JR 7040S	Soho/Dance/In This Day And Age	40

MINT VALUE £

RUPERT'S PEOPLE

(see also Renaissance, Fleur-De-Lys, Gun, Sweet Feeling)

67	Columbia DB 8226	Reflections Of Charles Brown/Hold On	60
	(this is the Fleur-De-Lys, they do not appear on the other 2 singles)		
67	Columbia DB 8278	A Prologue To A Magic World/Dream In My Mind	100
68	Columbia DB 8362	I Can Show You/I've Got The Love	120

RUPIE AND SIDY

70	Success RE 910	Return Of Herbert Spliffington/RUPIE EDWARDS ALL STARS: Young, Gifted And Black	15

RUSH (Australia)

67	Decca F 12614	Happy/Once Again	20
67	Decca F 12635	Make Mine Music/Enjoy It	20

RUSH (Canada)

(see also McKenzie Doug & Bob, Max Webster Band)

77	Mercury RUSH 7	Closer To The Heart/Bastille Day/Temples Of Syrinx (metallic blue label)	18
77	Mercury RUSH 7	Closer To The Heart/Bastille Day/Temples Of Syrinx (beige label)	8
78	Mercury RUSH 12	Closer To The Heart/Anthem/Bastille Day/Temples Of Syrinx (12", p/s)	10
80	Mercury RADIO 7	Spirit Of Radio/The Trees (p/s)	10
80	Mercury RADIO 12	Spirit Of Radio/The Trees/Working Man (12", p/s)	10
81	Mercury VITAL 7	Vital Signs/In The Mood (p/s)	8
81	Mercury VITAL 12	Vital Signs/In The Mood/A Passage To Bangkok/Circumstances (12", p/s)	8
81	Mercury EXIT 7	Tom Sawyer (live)/A Passage To Bangkok (live) (p/s)	6
81	Mercury EXIT 12	Tom Sawyer (live)/A Passage To Bangkok (live)/Red Barchetta (live) (12", p/s)	8
81	Mercury RUSH 1	Closer To The Heart (live)/The Trees (live) (p/s)	5
82	Mercury RUSH 8	New World Man/Vital Signs (live) (p/s)	5
82	Mercury RUSH 812	New World Man/Vital Signs (live)/Freewill (live) (12", p/s)	15
82	Mercury RUSH P9	Subdivisions/Red Barchetta (live) (picture disc)	10
82	Mercury RUSH 10 PD	Countdown/New World Man (shaped picture disc)	12
82	Mercury RUSH 1012	Countdown/New World Man/Spirit Of Radio (live)/Interview Excerpts (12", p/s)	10
84	Vertigo RUSH 11	The Body Electric/The Analog Kid (p/s)	5
84	Vertigo RUSH 1110	The Body Electric/The Analog Kid/Distant Early Warning (10", p/s, red vinyl)	12
84	Vertigo RUSH 1112	The Body Electric/The Analog Kid/Distant Early Warning (12", p/s)	50
78	Mercury 9100 059	HEMISPHERES (LP, mispressing, both sides play Side 1)	50
80	Mercury 9100 071	PERMANENT WAVES (LP, with newspaper)	12
85	Vertigo VERHP 31	POWER WINDOWS (LP, picture disc, with discography on sleeve)	20

ED RUSH

92	Primavera PRIM 001	Edrush/Fat Girl (12", as Edrush)	20
92	ER 007	I Wanna Stay In The Jungle/5AM/Touch Me/Keep On (12")	20
92	PSY 001	Look What They've Done/What If My Heart Stops?/ Look What They've Done (Dub Mix) (12")	20
93	No U-Turn NUT 002	Bludclot Artattack/Bludclot Artattack (Dark Mix) (12")	20
94	No U-Turn NUT 007	BLUDCLOT ARTATTACK REMIXES (12")	8
94	Jet Star XCT 001	Selecta/Selecta (Remix) (12")	30
95	No U-Turn NUT 011	Gangsta Hardstep/The Force Is Electric (12")	8
95	No U-Turn NUT 012	Guncheck/The Force Is Electric (Remix) (12")	8

MERRILEE RUSH & TURNABOUTS

68	Bell BLL 1013	Angel Of The Morning/Reap What You Sow	6
68	Bell BLL 1026	That Kind Of Woman/Sunshine And Roses	6
69	Bell BLL 1041	Reach Out I'll Be There/Love Street	10
68	Bell MBLL/SBLL 109	MERRILEE RUSH (LP)	25

OTIS RUSH

66	Vocalion V-P 9260	Homework/I Have To Laugh	85
66	Vocalion V-P 9260	Homework/I Have To Laugh (DJ copy)	125
69	Blue Horizon 57-3159	All Your Love/Double Trouble	25
68	Blue Horizon 7-63222	THIS ONE'S A GOOD UN (LP)	85
69	Atlantic 588 188	MOURNING IN THE MORNING (LP)	40
70s	Atlantic K 40495	MOURNING IN THE MORNING (LP, reissue)	15
70	Python KM 3	GROANING THE BLUES (LP)	50
76	Delmark DS 63?	COLD DAY IN HELL (LP)	25
78	Sonet SNTF756	TROUBLES, TROUBLES (LP)	12

TOM RUSH

67	Elektra EKSN 45004	Who Do You Love/On The Road Again	8
67	Elektra EKSN 45015	On The Road Again/Love's Made A Fool Of You	8
68	Elektra EKSN 45025	No Regrets/Shadow Dream Song	7
68	Elektra EKSN 45032	Something In The Way She Moves/Rockport Sunday	8
66	Xtra XTRA 5024	BLUES, SONGS & BALLADS (LP)	30
66	Xtra XTRA 5053	I GOT A MIND TO RAMBLE (LP)	30
67	Elektra EKL 308	TAKE A LITTLE WALK WITH ME (LP, also stereo EKS 7308)	35
68	Elektra EKL 4018	THE CIRCLE GAME (also stereo EKS 74018) (LP, 1st issue black 'Elektra' on red label)	25
68	Elektra EKL 4018	THE CIRCLE GAME (also stereo EKS 74018) (LP, 2nd issue white 'Elektra' on redder label.)	15
69	Elektra EKL 4062	CLASSIC RUSH (LP, red label, also stereo EKS 74062)	22
70	CBS 63940	TOM RUSH (LP)	15
70	CBS 64268	WRONG END OF A RAINBOW (LP)	15

JIMMY RUSHING (with ADA MOORE & BUCK CLAYTON)

(see also Count Basie, Dave Brubeck, Buck Clayton)

57	Philips BBE 12150	CAT MEETS CHICK (EP, as Jimmy Rushing, Buck Clayton & Ada Moore)	20
57	Vanguard EPP 14003	LITTLE JIMMY ALL STAR BAND (EP)	15
57	Parlophone GEP 8597	JIMMY RUSHING (EP)	15
58	Parlophone GEP 8695	THE WAY I FEEL (EP)	15
63	Ember EMB 4523	JIMMY RUSHING (EP)	15

MINT VALUE £

55	Vanguard PPT 12002	SINGS THE BLUES (10" LP)	50
57	Vanguard PPT 12016	SHOWCASE (10" LP)	45
57	Philips BBL 7105	CAT MEETS CHICK (LP, with Ada Moore & Buck Clayton)	20
57	Philips BBL 7166	THE JAZZ ODYSSEY OF JAMES RUSHING ESQ (LP, with Buck Clayton)	20
58	Vanguard PPL 11008	IF THIS AIN'T THE BLUES (LP)	20
58	Philips BBL 7252	LITTLE JIMMY RUSHING AND THE BIG BRASS (LP, also stereo SBBL 524)	20
60	Philips BBL 7360	RUSHING LULLABIES (LP)	18
61	Philips BBL 7484	THE SMITH GIRLS - BESSIE, CLARA (LP, mono)	20
61	Philips SBBL 631	THE SMITH GIRLS - BESSIE, CLARA (LP, stereo)	25
66	Ace Of Hearts AH 119	BLUES I LOVE TO SING (LP)	15
67	Golden Guinea GGL 0384	FIVE FEET OF SOUL (LP)	12

JIMMY RUSHING/CHAMPION JACK DUPREE

(see also Champion Jack Dupree)

64	Ember CJS 800	TWO SHADES OF BLUE (LP, 1 side each)	30

BARBARA RUSKIN

65	Piccadilly 7N 35224	Halfway To Paradise/I Can't Believe In Miracles	10
65	Piccadilly 7N 35246	You Can't Blame A Girl For Trying/No More To Fall	12
66	Piccadilly 7N 35274	Well How Does It Feel/Wishing Your Life Away	10
66	Piccadilly 7N 35296	Song Without End/Love Came Too Late	10
66	Piccadilly 7N 35328	Light Of Love/At Times Like These Mama	10
67	Parlophone R 5571	Take It Easy/Sunshowers	10
67	Parlophone R 5593	Euston Station/Hear That Telephone	10
67	Parlophone R 5642	Come Into My Arms Again/Just A Little While Longer	10
68	Parlophone R 5685	Is This Another Way/The Night Of The Spanish Tightrope Walker	5
68	President PT 217	Pawnbroker Pawnbroker/Almost	25
69	President PT 238	Gentlemen Please/24th Of July	6
69	President PT 261	Hail Love/Lady Of Leisure	6
70	President PT 280	A Little Bit Of This (And A Little Bit Of That)/Where Are We	6
70	President PT 315	For The First Time In My Life/Merry-Go-Round	6
71	President PT 350	(I Wanna Be) Your Teddy Bear/It Really Doesn't Matter	6

EDDIE RUSS

76	Impact IMP 5	Zauis/See The Light/Tea Leaves (12")	150

LONNIE RUSS

62	Fontana 267263 TF	Something Old Something New/My Wife Can't Cook	7

THANE RUSSAL (& THREE)

66	CBS 202049	Security/Your Love Is Burning Me (in p/s)	300
66	CBS 202049	Security/Your Love Is Burning Me	150
66	CBS 202403	Drop Everything And Run/I Need You (solo)	150

CHARLOTTE RUSSE

68	Fontana BF1683	Anyway The Wind Blows/High On A Roof Top	25

ROLAND RUSSEL

68	Nu Beat NB 019	Rhythm Hips/RHYTHM FLAMES: Deltone Special	50

ANDY RUSSELL

58	RCA RCA 1076	Seven Daughters/A Certain Smile	6

ARTHUR RUSSELL

87	Rough Trade ROUGH 114	WORLD OF ECHO (LP)	20
04	Soul Jazz SJRLP 083	THE WORLD OF ARTHUR RUSSELL (3-LP, original 2004 pressing)	20

BOBBY RUSSELL

68	Bell BLL 1019	Dusty/I Made You This Way	6
68	Bell BLL 1034	1432 Franklin Pike Circle Hero/Let's Talk About It	6
69	Bell BLL 1050	Carlie/Ain't Society Great?	6
71	United Artists UP 35283	Saturday Morning Confusion/Little Ole Song About Love	5

BRENDA RUSSELL

79	A&M AMSP 7515	In The Thick Of It/So Good So Right (12", p/s)	10
79	A&M AMLJ 739	BRENDA RUSSELL (LP)	12

CONNIE RUSSELL

54	Capitol CL 14171	No One But You/One Arabian Night	10
54	Capitol CL 14197	Love Me/Papa's Puttin' The Pressure On	10
55	Capitol CL 14214	Foggy Night In San Francisco/This Is My Love	10
55	Capitol CL 14236	Ayuh, Ayuh/I'm Making Believe	15
55	Capitol CL 14246	Snow Dreams/Green Fire	6
55	Capitol CL 14268	Farewell, Farewell/The Magnificent Matador	6
57	Capitol CL 14676	All Of You/This Is My Love	6

DAVE RUSSELL

(see also Dave & Diamonds)

66	Columbia DB 7828	When I Grow Too Old To Dream/All The Tears In The World	5

DOROTHY RUSSELL

71	Duke Reid DR 2524	You're The One I Love/Version	6

GEORGE RUSSELL

71	Flying Dutchman FD10124	ELECTRONIC SONATA FOR SOULS (LP)	20

JANE RUSSELL

51	London L 956	Dear Dear Dear/I Can't Get Started With You (78)	10
51	London L 969	Five Little Miles From San Berdoo/You'll Know (78)	10
53	Columbia SCM 5043	Please Do It Again/Two Sleepy People (B-side with Bob Lowery)	25
53	Columbia SCM 5043	Please Do It Again/Two Sleepy People (B-side with Bob Lowery) (78)	19
53	MGM MGM 662	A Little Girl From Little Rock/When Love Goes Wrong (78)	10
53	MGM MGM 664	Bye Bye Baby/Ain't There Anyone Here For Love? (78)	10
56	Capitol CL 14590	If You Wanna See Mamie Tonight/Keep Your Eyes On The Hands	10
59	MGM MGM-EP 702	JANE RUSSELL (EP)	50

MINT VALUE £

JANET RUSSELL
88 Harbourtown HAR 003 GATHERING THE FRAGMENTS (LP) ... 20

JOHN RUSSELL/RICHARD COLDMAN
79 Incus INCUS 31 HOME COOKING/GUITAR SOLOS (LP, 1 side each) ... 35

JOHNNY RUSSELL
60 MGM MGM 1074 Lonesome Boy/Baby Won't You Tell Me So ... 10

KEITH RUSSELL
65 Piccadilly 7N 35235 People Get Ready/Paradise ... 10

KIT RUSSELL
73 Deram DM 399 Peppers Last Stand/Shuffle Back ... 15

LEON RUSSELL
(see also Asylum Choir)
65 Dot DS 16771 Everybody's Talkin' 'Bout The Young/It's Alright With Me ... 8

RAY RUSSELL QUARTET
(see also Running Man, Mouse, Chopyn)
68 CBS Realm 52586 TURN CIRCLE (LP) ... 40
69 CBS Realm 52663 DRAGON HILL (LP) ... 40
71 RCA SF 8214 JUNE 11TH 1971 (LP) ... 40
71 CBS 64271 RITES AND RITUALS (LP) ... 45
73 Black Lion BLP 12100 SECRET ASYLUM (LP, gatefold) ... 30

ROSALIND RUSSELL & EDITH ADAMS
55 Brunswick 05406 Ohio/Little Bit Of Love ... 5

RUSSELL FAMILY
75 Topic 12TS 251 OF DOOLIN COUNTY CLARE (LP, with insert) ... 12

RUSSIAN ROULETTE
(see also Paul King, Mungo Jerry)
84 Red Bus RBUS 86 Come Into My Room/Lyin' Again (p/s) ... 5

CHARLIE RUSSO
63 Stateside SS 165 Preacherman/Teresa ... 10

WILLIAM RUSSO
63 Columbia 33SX 1508 RUSSO IN LONDON (LP) ... 20
66 Columbia 33SX 1758 STONEHENGE (LP, with the London Jazz Orchestra) ... 35

RUSTIKS
64 Decca F 11960 What A Memory Can Do/Hello Anne ... 10
65 Decca F 12059 I'm Not The Loving Kind/Can't You See ... 10

RUSTLERS
61 Pye 7N 15398 High Strung/Matter Of Who ... 12

RUSTY & DOUG (Kershaw)
(see also Doug Kershaw)
59 Oriole CB 1510 Hey Mae!/Why Don't You Love Me ... 150
59 Oriole CB 1510 Hey Mae!/Why Don't You Love Me (78) ... 50
59 London HL 8972 I Like You (Like This)/Dancing Shoes ... 30
59 London HL 8972 I Like You (Like This)/Dancing Shoes (78) ... 30
62 Polydor NH 66970 Hey Mae!/Sweet Thing ... 40
62 Fontana 267 238 TF Cajun Joe (The Ballad Of The Bayou)/Sweet Sweet Girl To Me ... 15

RUSTY HARNESS
70 Ember EMB S 283 Ain't Gonna Get Married/Goodbye (in p/s) ... 10
70 Ember EMB S 283 Ain't Gonna Get Married/Goodbye ... 5
73 Ember SE 8024 DISCOTHEQUE EXPLOSION (LP) ... 12

RUSTY NAIL
60s Hi-Fi MEP 3093 RUSTY NAIL (EP, in p/s) ... 100
60s Hi-Fi MEP 3093 RUSTY NAIL (EP, no p/s) ... 40

RUTH
67 Columbia DB 8218 Leaf In The Wind/Society's Child ... 10
68 Columbia DB 8386 Cherish/Until It's Time For You To Go ... 10

RUTH & BEAUTY
72 Montagu MONT 3000 29 Days To Doomsday/Cutting The Traces ... 18

MIKE RUTHERFORD
(see also Genesis, Mike & Mechanics)
80 Charisma CB 364 Time And Time Again/At The End Of The Day (p/s, correct B-side & label) ... 5
80 Charisma CB 364 Time And Time Again/Overnight Job
(p/s, with new label on B-side, credits & plays "Overnight Job") ... 5

RUTHLESS RAP ASSASINS
87 White (Murdertone) AMC001 We Don't Care/Kiss AMC (12", 500 pressed) ... 20

RUTLES
(see also Dirk & Stig, Neil Innes, Monty Python, Beach Boys, Patto)
78 Warner Bros K 17125 I Must Be In Love/Cheese And Onions/With A Girl Like You (p/s) ... 5
78 Warner Bros K 17180 Let's Be Natural/Piggy In The Middle ... 6
78 Warner Bros. WB K56459 THE RUTLES (LP, gatefold, booklet and inner sleeve) ... 20

RUTS (D.C.)
(see also Laurel Aitken, Typhoons, Pete Zear)
79 People Unite SJP 795 In A Rut/H-Eyes (1,000 only, black-ringed label) ... 35
79 People Unite RUT 1 In A Rut/H-Eyes (repressing) ... 8
79 Virgin VS 271 Babylon's Burning/Society (p/s) ... 8
79 Virgin VS 298 Jah War/I Ain't Sofisticated (p/s) ... 5

			MINT VALUE £
79	Virgin VS 285	Something That I Said/Give Youth A Chance (p/s)	5
80	RSO RSO 71	Babylon's Burning/XTC: Take This Town (p/s)	5
81	Virgin VS 396	Different View/Formula Eyes (p/s, as Ruts D.C.)	5
82	Bohemian BO 2	Whatever We Do/Push Yourself - Make It Work (p/s,as Ruts D.C.)	5
83	Bohemian BO 3	Weak Heart/Militant (white label, with paper insert; as Ruts D.C., promo only)	15
83	Bohemian BO 4	Stepping Bondage/Lobotomy/Rich Bitch (p/s)	15
79	Virgin V 2132	THE CRACK (LP, stickered sleeve with "Pay no more than £3.99")	15
82	Bohemian BOLP 4	RHYTHM COLLISION (LP)	20
87	Link LP 013	LIVE AND LOUD (LP)	12
86	Strange Fruit SFPS 011	PEEL SESSIONS (12" EP)	12

BARRY RYAN (& MAJORITY)

(see also Paul & Barry Ryan)

68	MGM MGM 1423	Goodbye/I'm So Sad	10
68	MGM MGM 1442	Eloise/Love I Almost Found You (as Barry Ryan & Majority)	7
68	MGM MGM 1464	Love Is Love/I'll Be On My Way Dear	5
69	Polydor 56348	The Hunt/No Living Without Her	8
70	Polydor 56370	Magical Spiel/Caroline	8
70	Polydor 2001 035	Kitsch/Give Me A Sign	8
71	Polydor 2001 154	It Is Written/Annabella	8
71	Poyldor 2001 256	Can't Let You Go/When I Was A Child	7
72	Polydor 2001 335	From My Head To My Toes/Alimony Money Blues	7
72	Polydor 2001 362	I'm Sorry Susan/L.A. Woman	7
75	Dawn DNS 1109	Do That/The Summers Over	7
76	Private Stock PVT 70	Where Were You/Making A Do	7
77	Private Stock PVT 87	Brother/Life's So Easy	7
69	MGM MGM-C(S) 8106	SINGS PAUL RYAN (LP)	40
69	Polydor 583 067	BARRY RYAN (LP)	25

CATHY RYAN

(see also Art Mooney)

53	MGM SP 1051	Show Me The Way To Go Home/If I Had You	7

KRIS RYAN (& QUESTIONS)

64	Mercury MF 818	Miss Ann/She Told Me Lies (as Kris Ryan & Questions)	10
64	Mercury MF 832	Don't Play That Song/If You Don't Come Back	10
64	Mercury MF 852	Marie Marie/I've Had Enough Of You Baby	10
65	Mercury MF 877	Tell Me How/She Belongs To Me	10
65	Mercury 10024 MCE	ON THE RIGHT TRACK (EP, as Kris Ryan & Questions)	40

MARION RYAN

(see also Ray Ellington, Gary Miller)

58	Pye NIXA 7N 15121	Love Me Forever/Make The Man Love Me	7
58	Pye NIXA 7N 15130	Always And Forever/Oh Oh I'm Falling In Love Again	7
58	Pye NIXA 7N 15138	Stairway Of Love/I Need You	7
58	Pye 7NSR 15157	The World Goes Around And Around/Please Don't Say Goodnight (stereo)	10
59	Pye NIXA 7N 15184	Wait For Me (Ti Piro)/Jeepers Creepers	7
59	Pye 7N 15200	Jo-Jo The Dog Faced Boy/Doin' What Comes Naturally	6
60	Columbia DB 4448	Sixteen Reasons/Mangos	7
60	Columbia DB 4550	Somebody/It's You That I Love	6
68	Philips BF 1721	Better Use Your Head/The Seasons Change	40
57	Pye Nixa NEP 24041	THAT RYAN GIRL! (EP)	20
58	Pye NEP 24079	MARION RYAN HIT PARADE (EP)	30
59	Pye NPL 18030	A LADY LOVES! (LP, mono)	30
59	Pye NSPL 18030	A LADY LOVES! (LP, stereo)	40

PAT RYAN

77	Folk Heritage FHR 094	LEA BOY'S LASSIE (LP)	15

PAUL RYAN

72	Maple Annie MA 104	Born On A Beautiful Day/Come With Me	6
72	Maple Annie MA 107	Natural Gas/Hellow Hellow	6

PAUL & BARRY RYAN

(see also Barry Ryan)

65	Decca F 12260	Don't Bring Me Your Heartaches/To Remind You Of My Love	8
66	Decca F 12319	Have Pity On The Boy/There You Go	8
66	Decca F 12391	I Love Her/gotta Go Out To Work	8
66	Decca F 12445	I Love How You Love Me/Baby I'm Sorry	8
66	Decca F 12494	Have You Ever Loved Somebody?/I'll Tell You Later	12
66	Decca F 12520	Missy, Missy/Rainbow Weather	12
67	Decca F 12567	Keep It Out Of Sight/Who Told You?	10
67	Decca F 12633	Claire/I'll Make It Worth Your While	12
67	MGM 1354	Heartbreaker/Night Time	8
68	MGM 1385	Pictures Of Today/Madrigal	8
74	Polydor 2001511	Carry The Blues/Reincarnation Games	6
67	Decca LK 4878	THE RYANS - TWO OF A KIND (LP)	50
68	MGM MGM-C(S) 8081	PAUL AND BARRY RYAN (LP)	30

PHIL RYAN & CRESCENTS

64	Columbia DB 7406	Mary Don't You Weep/Yes I Will	8
65	Columbia DB 7574	Gypsy Woman/Be Honest With Yourself	20

BOBBY RYDELL

(see also Chubby Checker & Bobby Rydell)

59	Top Rank JAR 181	Kissin' Time/You'll Never Tame Me	15
59	Top Rank JAR 181	Kissin' Time/You'll Never Tame Me (78)	85
59	Top Rank JAR 227	We Got Love/I Dig Girls	15
60	Columbia DB 4429	Wild One/Little Bitty Girl	8
60	Columbia DB 4471	Swingin' School/Ding-A-Ling	12
60	Columbia DB 4495	Volare/I'd Do It Again	10
60	Columbia DB 4545	Sway/Groovy Tonight	8
61	Columbia DB 4600	Good Time Baby/Cherie	12
61	Columbia DB 4651	Don't Be Afraid/That Old Black Magic	6

			MINT VALUE £
61	Columbia DB 4690	The Fish/The Third House	6
61	Columbia DB 4731	I Wanna Thank You/The Door To Paradise	6
62	Columbia DB 4785	I've Got Bonnie/Lose Her	6
62	Columbia DB 4858	I'll Never Dance Again/Gee, It's Wonderful	6
63	Cameo Parkway C 108	Forget Him/Hey Ev'rybody (in p/s)	10
63	Cameo Parkway C 108	Forget Him/Hey Ev'rybody	7
63	Cameo Parkway C 129	It's Time We Parted/Too Much too Soon	6
63	Cameo Parkway C 228	The Cha Cha Cha/The Best Man Cried	6
63	Cameo Parkway C 242	Butterfly Baby/Love Is Blind	6
64	Cameo Parkway C 309	Make Me Forget/Darling Jenny	6
65	Capitol CL 1537	I Can't Say Goodbye/Two Is The Loneliest Number	8
60	Top Rank JKP 2059	LOVINGEST (EP)	40
63	Cameo Parkway CPE 551	SWAY WITH BOBBY RYDELL (EP)	30
63	Cameo Parkway CPE 553	BOBBY RYDELL (EP)	25
63	Summit LSE 2036	BEST OF BOBBY RYDELL (EP)	10
60	Columbia 33SX 1243	WILD ONE (LP)	60
61	Columbia 33SX 1308	SINGS AND SWINGS (LP)	20
61	Columbia 33SX 1352	SALUTES "THE GREAT ONES" (LP)	25
62	Columbia 33SX 1425	RYDELL AT THE COPA (LP)	30
62	Cameo Parkway C 1019	ALL THE HITS (LP)	15
63	Cameo Parkway C 1040	ALL THE HITS VOL. 2 (LP)	15
63	Cameo Parkway C 1055	WILD (WOOD) DAYS (LP)	15
65	Capitol T 2281	SOMEBODY LOVES YOU (LP)	15

RYDER

74	BUG 39	Ain't That Nice/Sugar Mama	10

FREDDIE RYDER

(see also Freddie Self, Trends)

65	Mercury MF 864	To Get Your Love Back/A Little Thing Called Love	6
65	Mercury MF 879	Some Kind Of Wonderful/Slow Down	12
65	Mercury MF 935	Man Of The Moment/My Block	10
68	Columbia DB 8335	Shadows (I Can't See You)/Airport	6
68	Columbia DB 8427	Worst That Could Happen/World Of My Own	6

MAL RYDER (& SPIRITS)

(see also Mal & Primitives)

63	Decca F 11669	Cry Baby/Take Over (as Mal Ryder & Spirits)	20
64	Vocalion V 9219	See The Funny Little Clown/Slow Down	70
64	Piccadilly 7N 35209	Your Friend/Forget It (as Mal Ryder & Spirits)	40
65	Piccadilly 7N 35234	Lonely Room/Tell Your Friend	22

MITCH RYDER (& DETROIT WHEELS)

(see also Detroit)

66	Stateside SS 481	Jenny Take A Ride/Baby Jane	20
66	Stateside SS 498	Little Latin Lupe Lu/I Hope	20
66	Stateside SS 521	Breakout/I Need Help	50
66	Stateside SS 521	Breakout/I Need Help (DJ copy)	100
66	Stateside SS 549	Devil With A Blue Dress On (Medley)/I Had It Made	20
67	Stateside SS 596	Sock It To Me Baby/I Never Had It Better	20
67	Stateside SS 2023	Too Many Fish In The Sea/Three Little Fishes/One Grain Of Sand	20
67	Stateside SS 2037	Joy/I'd Rather Go To Jail (solo)	10
67	Stateside SS 2063	What Now My Love/Blessing In Disguise (solo)	25
68	Stateside SS 2075	You Are My Sunshine/Wild Child (solo)	7
68	Stateside SS 2096	Personality/Chantilly Lace/I Make A Fool Of Myself (solo)	7
69	Dot DOT 129	Sugar Bee/I Believe (There Must Be Someone)	6
66	Stateside SE 1039	RIDIN' (EP)	60
66	Stateside S(S)L 10178	TAKE A RIDE... (LP)	30
67	Stateside S(S)L 10189	BREAKOUT. . . !! (LP)	30
67	Stateside S(S)L 10204	SOCK IT TO ME (LP)	25
68	Stateside S(S)L 10229	WHAT NOW MY LOVE (LP, solo)	30
69	Bell MBLL/SBLL 114	ALL MITCH RYDER HITS (LP)	20

PAUL RYDER & TIME MACHINE

74	Penny Farthing PEN 834	Are You Ready/If You Ever Get To Heaven	8

TONY RYMOND

62	Oriole 1708	Handful Of Songs/She'll Have To Go	12

S

SABICAS

70	Polyor 2482 023	ROCK ENCOUNTER (LP, with Joe Beck)	30

PARK SABLE & JUNGLE 'N' BEATS

64	Fontana TF 457	Never Be Blue/Rave On	40

SABOTAGE

80	Optimistic OPT 001	WHEN THE WAR IS OVER (EP)	10
80	Optimistic OPT 004	SUBTERFUGE (EP)	12

SABRE

83	Neat NEAT 23	Miracle Man/On The Loose (p/s)	8

SABRES

(see also Peeps)

66	Decca F 12528	Roly Poly/Will You Always Love Me?	30

MINT VALUE £

SABRES OF PARADISE

93	Sabres Of Paradise PT 001	United (Andrew Weatherall Mix) (12", p/s, actually remix of Throbbing Gristle's "United", 800 only)	25
94	Sabres Of Paradise PT 009	Smokebelch II (Entry)/(Exit) (12", red p/s)	20
94	Sabres Of Paradise PT 009R	Smokebelch II (David Holmes Mix)/(Flute Mix) (12", yellow p/s)	20
94	Sabres Of Paradise PT 014	Theme/Return Of Carter & Edge 6 (Original Mix) (12")	10
94	Sabres Of Paradise PT 014R	Theme (Underdog Vs Sabres)/(Version) (10" remix)	10
94	Warp WAP 50	Wilmot/Rumble Summons (12")	15
94	Warp 10WAP 50	WILMOT II: Wilmot Meets Lord Scruffage/Wilmot's Last Skank (10", p/s)	8
95	Warp WARP 62	Tow Truck/(mixes) (12")	10
96	Emissions SEO 11	Ysaebud (PVC sleeve, 1-sided, etched B-side, 1,000 only)	10
90s	Sabres Of Paradise 002	Internal/Internment/Internalized/The Creator Speaks (12", blue vinyl)	8
93	Warp LP 16	SABRESONIC (2-LP, with unreleased 7", 5,000 only)	20

SACRED

93	Twilight 7R5010A	You're The Only One/Lost In Time	15

SACRED ALIEN

81	Greenwood GW 001	Spiritual Planet/Energy (stickered labels, in p/s)	30
81	Greenwood GW 001	Spiritual Planet/Energy (stickered labels)	10
83	Heighway Robbery SAD 001	Legends/VIRGIN: Sittin' In Front Row (gatefold p/s)	30

SACRILEGE

85	C.O.T.R. GURT 4	BEHIND THE REALMS OF MADNESS (12" EP)	8

SAD

72	Phoenix NIX 124	It Ain't Easy/Box	10

SAD AFFAIR

71	Lifelong LF 1	Coloured Rice/Strange Sky	30

SADDAR BAZAAR

98	Earworm WORM 13/WJ37	Crystalline/ELECTROSCOPE: Circus Heights/TRANSPARENT THING: Ahh (p/s, 1,500 in hand painted sleeve, 1st 176 embossed)	10
98	Earworm WORM 13/WJ37	Crystalline/ELECTROSCOPE: Circus Heights/TRANSPARENT THING: Ahh (p/s, 1,500 in hand painted sleeve)	5

SADIE'S EXPRESSION

69	Plexium PXM 4	Deep In My Heart/My Way Of Living	7

BARRINGTON SADLER

69	Clandisc CLA 204	Soul Power/Rub It Down	12

S/SGT. BARRY SADLER

66	RCA RCA 1506	Ballad Of The Green Berets/I'm A Lucky One	7
66	RCA RCA 1520	The A Team/An Empty Glass	5

SAD LOVERS & GIANTS

81	Last Movement LM 003	CLE (EP)	15
83	Last Movement LM 005	COLOURLESS DREAM (EP)	12
83	Midnight CHIME 03	FEEDING THE FLAME (LP)	12
84	Midnight CHIME 07	IN THE BREEZE (LP)	12
86	Midnight CHIME 022	TOTAL SOUND (LP)	12

JERRY SADOWITZ

88	Gobshite GOBSHITE 01	GOBSHITE (LP)	12

SAD PEOPLE

69	Chapter One CH113	Lonely Man/Turn Around	15

SAD SOCIETY

87	X Cert	Contaminate/Nothing ever Changes	12

SAFARI PARTY

85	Pure & Vain 1 PAV	Hope In Hell/Not There (p/s)	5

SAFARIS (& PHANTOM BAND)

60	Top Rank JAR 424	Image Of A Girl/Four Steps To Love	50
60	Top Rank JAR 528	The Girl With The Story In Her Eyes/Summer Nights (with Phantom Band)	40

SAFFIRE

76	Safari SFR 4	Lay You Boogie Down (Part One)/Lay Your Boogie Down (Part Two)	10

SAFFRON SUMMERFIELD

74	Mother Earth MUM 1001	SALISBURY PLAIN (LP)	60
76	Mother Earth MUM 1202	FANCY MEETING YOU HERE (LP)	50
76	Spectator	FANCY MEETING YOU HERE (LP, reissue)	20

SA 55

82	1966 EISP 9868	Compromise/Love Love Love Here I Come	80

SAGA

72	Westwood WRS 017	SAGA (LP)	50
73	Westwood WRS 036	SWEET PEG O'DERBY (LP)	100

MIKE SAGAR (& CRESTERS)

(see also Cresters, Richard Harding)

60	HMV POP 819	Deep Feeling/You Know (as Mike Sagar & Cresters)	20
61	HMV POP 988	The Brothers Three/Set Me Free	10

SAGE

80	Redball RR 032	GOING STRONG (LP)	45

SAGITTARIUS

(see also Bruce Johnston, Glen Campbell)

67	CBS 2867	My World Fell Down/Libra	20
68	CBS 3276	Another Time/Virgo	25

MINT VALUE £

SALLY SAGOE
75 Dart ART 2055 — A Little Bit Of Soap/Stop 8

SAGRAM
(see also Clem Alford, Magic Carpet)
72 Windmill WMD 118 — POP EXPLOSION SITAR STYLE (LP) 20

SAHARA
75 Dawn DNLS 3068 — SUNRISE (LP) 35

DOUG SAHM
(see also Sir Douglas Quintet, Augie Meyers)
73 Atlantic K 10293 — Is Anybody Going To San Antoine/Don't Turn Around 5
73 Atlantic K 40466 — DOUG SAHM AND BAND (LP) (inc Dylan and Dr. John in his band) 18
74 Warner Bros K 56067 — GROOVERS PARADISE (LP) 12
70s Chrysalis CHR 1249 — HELL OF A SPELL (LP) 12

OLIVER SAIN (& SHIRLEY BROWN)
(see also Shirley Brown, Fontella Bass)
72 Mojo 2092 031 — St. Louis Breakdown/I Ain't Gonna Tell (with Shirley Brown) 5

ST. CHRISTOPHER
84 Bluegrass GM 001 — Crystal Clear/My Fond Farewell (p/s) 10
86 Bluegrass GM 003 — Go Ahead Cry/Charmelle (p/s) 8
87 Veston VOD 001 — Forevermore Stars Here/Remember Me To Her/Sinking Ships (flexidisc, p/s) 6
89 Sarah SARAH 015 — You Deserve More Than A Maybe/The Kind Of Girl/The Summer Of Love (foldaround p/s with poster in poly bag) 10
89 Sarah SARAH 020 — All Of A Tremble/My Fortune/The Hummingbird 7

CHERYL ST. CLAIR
(see also Alison Wonder)
66 CBS 202041 — My Heart Is Not In It/We Want Love 15
66 Columbia DB 8077 — What About Me/I'll Forget You Tonight 12

ISLA ST. CLAIR
81 Clare ISLA 1 — THE SONG AND THE STORY (LP) 20
85 Topic 12TS 436 — SCOTCH MEASURE (LP) 15

JERRY ST. CLAIR
69 Philips BF 1796 — Summer Exodus/Mrs. Jensen Sits Alone 15

SAINT DAVIDS ROAD
69 Tangerine DP003 — Let The Sun Come In/Mama Ain't Gonna Like What She Sees 15

SAINT ETIENNE
(see also 50 Year Void, Sarah Cracknell, Lovecut D.B., Mike Vickers)
90 Heavenly HVN 2 — Only Love Can Break Your Heart/Only Love Can Break Your Heart (Version) (p/s) 6
90 Heavenly HVN 212 — Only Love Can Break Your Heart/Only Love Can Break Your Heart (Original Version) (12", p/s) 10
90 Heavenly HVN 212R — Only Love Can Break Your Heart (A Mix Of Two Halves)/The Official Saint Etienne World Cup Theme (12", die-cut p/s) 12
90 The Catalogue CAT 084 — Only Love Can Break Your Heart (remixed by Flowered Up)/FLOWERED UP: It's On (The Posh Facker Mix) (square flexidisc with The Catalogue mag) 5
90 Heavenly HVN 4 — Kiss And Make Up/Sky's Dead (p/s) 5
90 Heavenly HVN 412 — Kiss And Make Up/Sky's Dead (12", p/s) 10
90 Heavenly HVN 412R — Kiss And Make Up (Midsummer Madness Remix)/Kiss And Make Up (Midsummer Dubness Mix) (12", p/s) 10
90 Heavenly HVN 4CD — Kiss And Make Up (7")/Kiss And Make Up (12")/Sky's Dead (CD) 12
91 Heavenly HVN 912R — Speedwell (Flying Mix)/Speedwell (Project Mix)/Nothing Can Stop Us (Instrumental)/3D Tiger (12", p/s) 10
91 Heavenly HVN 9CD — Nothing Can Stop Us/Speedwell/Nothing Can Stop Us (Instrumental) (CD) 10
92 Heavenly HVN 12CD — Only Love Can Break Your Heart/Only Love Can Break Your Heart (A Mix Of Two Halves)/Filthy (CD) 8
92 Heavenly HVN 22 — Live - Paris '92 (clear flexidisc, gig freebie, 1,000 only) 20
93 Heavenly HVN 2912 — Hobart Paving/Who Do You Think You Are (12", p/s, mispressed with Hobart Paving & "Your Head My Voice" on both sides) 18
93 Heavenly HVN 36CD — I Was Born On Christmas Day/My Christmas Prayer/Snowplough/Peterloo (CD, picture disc) 8
95 Heavenly HVN 41 — XMAS '95: A Christmas Gift To You/Driving Home For Christmas/A Message In A Bottle (CD, signed fan club edition) 90
98 Creation CRECS 279 — Sylvie/(Trouser Enthusiast's Tintinnabulation Edit) (cassette) 6
03 Mantra MNT 78 — Soft Like Me/Gimp Crisis (p/s, limited edition) 8
93 Heavenly HVNCDX 6 — SO TOUGH/YOU NEED A MESS OF HELP TO STAND ALONE (2-CD) 25
95 Heavenly HVNLP 9CD — I LOVE TO PAINT (CD, fan club edition, 600 only) 140
95 Heavenly HVNCD 10 — TOO YOUNG TO DIE (CD, with bonus CD "Too Young To Die - The Remix Album" [HVN LP 10CDR]) 30
97 Heavenly HVN41-2 — VALENTINES DAY (CD, EP fan club edition) 100
98 Fan Club SPCD 463 — XMAS '98: I Don't Intend To Spend Christmas Without You/Kofi Annan (CD, fan club edition, in card sleeve) 80
00 Mantra MNSTET 1 — BUILT ON SAND: RARITIES 1994-1999 (CD, fan club edition) 120
03 Heavenly HVN136CD — XMAS 2003 (CD, EP fan club issue) 60
08 Foreign Office FOREIGN OFFICE 004 — BOXETTE (4-CD, 3000 only) 80

BARRY ST. JOHN
64 Decca F 11933 — A Little Bit Of Soap/Thing Of The Past 20
64 Decca F 11975 — Bread And Butter/Cry To Me 20
65 Decca F 12111 — Mind How You Go/Don't You Feel Proud 20
65 Decca F 12145 — Hey Boy/I've Been Crying 20
65 Columbia DB 7783 — Come Away Melinda/Gotta Brand New Man 15
66 Columbia DB 7868 — Everything I Touch Turns To Tears/Sounds Like My Baby 65
66 Columbia DB 7868 — Everything I Touch Turns To Tears/Sounds Like My Baby (DJ copy) 65

MINT VALUE £

68	Major Minor MM 587	Cry Like A Baby/Long And Lonely Night	15
69	Major Minor MM 604	By The Time I Get To Phoenix/Turn On Your Light	15
75	Bradleys BRAD 7507	I Won't Be A Party/Do Me Good	7
69	M. Minor MMLP/SMLP 43	ACCORDING TO ST. JOHN (LP)	50

BERNIE ST. JOHN & BARTHOLEMEW

70	Beacon BEA 167	Believe In Your Love/Run Run	5

BRIDGET ST. JOHN

(see also Kevin Ayers, Ron Geesin, Mike Oldfield, Quiver)

69	Dandelion K 4404	To B Without A Hitch/Autumn Lullaby	12
70	Warner Bros WB 8019	If You've Got Money/Yep	12
72	Polydor 2001 280	Fly High/There's A Place I Know/Suzanne (p/s)	12
72	Polydor 2001 361	Nice/Goodbye Baby Goodbye	8
73	MCA MUS 1203	Passing Thru'/The Road Was Lonely On My Own	10
69	Dandelion 63750	ASK ME NO QUESTIONS (LP, gatefold sleeve)	70
71	Dandelion DAN 8007	SONGS FOR THE GENTLE MAN (LP, gatefold sleeve)	80
71	Dandelion K 49007	SONGS FOR THE GENTLE MAN (LP, g/f sleeve, with cat no K 49007)	30
72	Dandelion 2310 193	THANK YOU FOR? (LP, gatefold sleeve)	50
74	Chrysalis CHR 1062	JUMBLE QUEEN (LP)	18

PAUL ST. JOHN

70	Pye 7N 45190	Flying Saucers Have Landed/Spaceship Love	90

TAMMY ST. JOHN

(see also Trends)

64	Pye 7N 15682	Boys/Hey Hey Hey Hey	15
65	Pye 7N 15762	He's The One For Me/I'm Tired Of Just Looking At You	15
65	Pye 7N 15948	Dark Shadows And Empty Hallways/I Mustn't Cry	15
66	Pye 7N 17042	Nobody Knows What's Goin' On (In My Mind But Me)/ Stay Together Young Lovers	50
66	Pye 7N 17042	Nobody Knows What's Goin' On (In My Mind But Me)/ Stay Together Young Lovers (DJ copy)	85
69	Tangerine DP 0007	Concerning Love/Sound Of Love	300

ST. LOUIS JIMMY

53	Esquire 10-319	Holiday For Boogie/MEMPHIS SLIM: Harlem Bound (78)	20

ST. LOUIS UNION

(see also Medicine Head)

66	Decca F 12318	Girl/Respect	15
66	Decca F 12386	Behind The Door/English Tea	50
66	Decca F 12508	East Side Story/Think About Me	150

SAINT ORCHESTRA

78	Pye 7N 46127	Return Of The Saint/Funko (p/s)	12

OLIVER ST. PATRICK & DIAMONDS

67	Trojan TR 005	I Want To Be Loved By You/Tulips	12

CRISPIAN ST. PETERS

65	Decca F 12080	At This Moment/Goodbye, You'll Forget Me	15
65	Decca F 12207	No No No/Three Goodbyes	15
66	Decca F 12287	You Were On My Mind/What I'm Gonna Be	5
66	Decca F 12359	The Pied Piper/Sweet Dawn My True Love	6
66	Decca F 12480	Changes/My Little Brown Eyes	15
66	Decca F 12525	But She's Untrue/Your Ever Changin' Mind	8
67	Decca F 12596	Almost Persuaded/You Have Gone	8
67	Decca F 12677	Free Spirit/I'm Always Crying	8
70	Decca F 13055	So Long/My Little Brown Eyes	10
74	Santa Ponsa PNS 17	Do Daddy Do/Every Time You Sinned	7
75	Route RT 18	Carolina/Samantha	7
67	Decca DFE 8678	ALMOST PERSUADED (EP)	55
66	Decca LK 4805	FOLLOW ME? (LP)	50
70	Square SQA 102	SIMPLY? CRISPIAN ST. PETERS (LP)	40

KIRBY ST. ROMAIN

63	Stateside SS 199	Summer's Comin'/Miss You So	10

SAINT STEVEN

69	Probe SPB 1005	OVER THE HILLS/THE BASTICH (LP)	75

ST. VALENTINE'S DAY MASSACRE

(see also Artwoods)

67	Fontana TF 883	Brother Can You Spare A Dime/Al's Party (with p/s)	180
67	Fontana TF 883	Brother Can You Spare A Dime/Al's Party	80

BUFFY SAINTE-MARIE

65	Fontana TF 574	Until It's Time For You To Go/The Flower And The Apple Tree	5
65	Fontana TF 614	The Universal Soldier/Cripple Creek	5
66	Fontana TF 695	Timeless Love/Lady Margret	5
71	RCA 2081	Soldier Blue/Moratorium (Bring Our Brothers Home)	5
72	Vanguard VRS 35143	I'm Gonna Be A Country Girl Again/The Piney Wood Hills	6
65	Fontana TFL 6040	IT'S MY WAY! (LP)	15
65	Fontana TFL 6047	MANY A MILE (LP)	15
66	Fontana (S)TFL 6071	LITTLE WHEEL SPIN AND SPIN (LP)	15
71	Vanguard VSD 79250	FIRE AND FLEET AND CANDLELIGHT (LP)	12
71	Vanguard VSD 79300	ILLUMINATIONS (LP)	12
71	Vanguard VSD 79311	SHE USED TO WANNA BE A BALLERINA (LP)	12

SAINTS (Australia)

76	Power Exchange PX 242	I'm Stranded/No Time (p/s)	15
77	Power Exchange PXE 101	I'm Stranded/(STANLEY FRANK: 2 tracks) (p/s)	8
77	Harvest HAR 5123	Erotic Neurotic/One Way Street (with p/s)	150

			MINT VALUE £
77	Harvest HAR 5123	Erotic Neurotic/One Way Street	10
77	Harvest HAR 5130	This Perfect Day/L-I-E-S	6
77	Harvest 12 HAR 5130	This Perfect Day/L-I-E-S/Do The Robot (12", with 'disclaimer' stickered p/s)	10
77	Harvest HAR 5137	1, 2, 3, 4 (River Deep, Mountain High/Lipstick On Your Collar/One Way Street/ Demolition Girl) (EP, double pack, gatefold p/s)	15
77	Harvest HAR 5137	1, 2, 3, 4 (River Deep, Mountain High/Lipstick On Your Collar/One Way Street/ Demolition Girl) (EP, p/s)	6
78	Harvest HAR 5148	Know Your Product/Run Down (no p/s)	10
78	Harvest HAR 5166	Security/All Times Through Paradise (p/s)	12
89	Bucketfull Of Brains BOB 26	I Dreamed Of Marie Antoinette/MOCK TURTLES: Croppies Lie Down with Bucketfull Of Brains magazine, issue 32)	6
77	Harvest SHSP 4065	I'M STRANDED (LP)	25
78	Harvest SHSP 4078	ETERNALLY YOURS (LP, with inner sleeve)	25
78	Harvest SHSP 4094	PREHISTORIC SOUNDS (LP)	22
86	Razor RAZ 21	BEST OF (LP)	12

SAINTS (Jamaica)

66	Doctor Bird DB 1009	Brown Eyes/BABA BROOKS & HIS BAND: King Size	40
69	Big Shot BI 522	Windy Part One/Windy Part Two	12

SAINTS (Jamaica)

73	Count Shelley CS 043	How Long/Feeling Good	6

SAINTS (U.K.)

64	MJB BEV 73/4	SAINTS (10" LP, private pressing)	300
64	MJB BEVLP 127/8	SAINTS ALIVE! (LP, private pressing)	300

SAINTS (U.K.)

(see also Tornados, Heinz)

63	Pye 7N 15548	Wipe Out/Midgets	25
63	Pye 7N 15582	Husky Team/Pigtails	25

RUSS SAINTY (& NU NOTES)

(see also Nu Notes)

60	Top Rank JAR 381	Happy-Go-Lucky-Me/Standing Around	15
60	Decca F 11270	Race With The Devil/Too Shy (solo)	18
61	Decca F 11325	Don't Believe Him, Donna/Your Other Love (solo)	10
62	HMV POP 1055	Keep Your Love Locked/I've Got A Girl (as Russ Sainty & Nu Notes)	10
62	HMV POP 1069	Send Me The Pillow That You Dream On/What Do You Know About That (solo)	10
63	HMV POP 1181	Unforgettable Love/The Twinkle In Your Eye (solo)	10
64	Parlophone R 5168	That's How I'm Gonna Love You/Lonesome Town (as Russ Sainty & Nu-Notes)	7
64	Columbia DB 7394	This Is My Lovely Day/Bless You, Girl (as Russ Sainty & Nu-Notes)	7
65	Columbia DB 7521	It Ain't That Easy/And Then (solo)	6
65	Columbia DB 7708	Saving My Tears (For A Rainy Day)/She (solo)	6
65	Society SOC 1035	THE GENIUS OF LENNON AND McCARTNEY (LP)	15

KYU SAKAMOTO

63	HMV POP 1171	Sukiyaki/Anoko No Namae Wa Nantenkana	8
63	HMV POP 1211	China Nights/Benkyo No Cha Cha Cha	8
64	HMV POP 1342	Rose Rose I Love You/Sayonara Tokyo	10
62	HMV CLP 1674	SUKIYAKI (LP)	30

RYUICHI SAKAMOTO

(see also David Sylvian, Yellow Magic Orchestra)

80	Island IPR 2048	Riot In Lagos/Iconic Storage (12", company sleeve)	10
80	Island ILPS 9656	B-2 UNIT (LP)	12
90	Virgin VUSLP 14	BEAUTY (LP, with inner)	12

(BOB) SAKER

68	Polydor BM 56231	Still Got You/Imagination (as Bob Saker)	30
68	Parlophone R 5740	Foggy Tuesday/Ooh Nana Na (as Bob Saker)	40
69	Parlophone R 5752	Hey Joe!/Christianity	15
71	CBS 7010	What A Beautiful World/City Of The Angels	6
71	CBS 7399	Even Though We Ain't Got Money/Wild Winds Are Blowing	6

SAL SALVADOR

55	KPL 105	SAL SALVADOR QUARTET (10" LP)	12

SALAMANDER

(see also Onyx)

70	CBS 5102	Crystal Ball/Billy	15

SALAMANDER

71	Youngblood SSYB 14	THE TEN COMMANDMENTS (LP, gatefold poster sleeve)	200

SALEM

82	Hilton FMR 056	Cold As Steel/Reach To Eternity	45

SALFORD JETS

78	WEA K 18008	Lookin' At The Squares/Dancing School (no p/s)	5
79	EMI INT 590	Manchester Boys/Last Bus (p/s)	20

SALLY & ALLEY CATS

64	Parlophone R 5183	Is It Something I Said/You Forgot To Remember	15

SALLYANGIE

(see also Mike Oldfield, Sally Oldfield)

69	Big T BIG 126	Two Ships/Colours Of The World	100
72	Philips 6006 259	Child Of Allah/Lady Go Lightly	100
68	Transatlantic TRA 176	CHILDREN OF THE SUN (LP, gatefold sleeve, purple/white textured label)	60
78	Transatlantic TRA 176	CHILDREN OF THE SUN (LP, reissue, different single sleeve)	20

DOUG SALMA & HIGHLANDERS

63	Philips BF 1279	Highland Fling/The Scavenger	15

MINT VALUE £

SALMONTAILS

80 Oblivion OBL 001 SALMONTAILS (LP, with Dave Pegg) 18

SALOME

69 Page One POF 137 Vivo Cantando/Amigos Amigos 7

SALSOUL STRUT

96 Records Inc. no cat. no. Better Days/(Mixes) 12

SALT

78 Grapevine GRA 111 BEYOND A SONG (LP, with insert) 18

SALT & PEPPER

61 London HLU 9338 High Noon/Come Softly To Me 15

SALVATION

69 United Artists UP 35048 Cinderella/The Village Shuck 15
69 United Artists UAS 29062 SALVATION (LP) 30

SALVATION

83 Merciful Release MR 025 Girlsoul/Evelyn (p/s) 12
83 Merciful Release MRX 025 Girlsoul/Evelyn/Dust Up (12", p/s) 15
86 Batfish Inc. BF 103 Jessica's Crime/The Shining (p/s) 12
86 Batfish Inc. USS 104 Jessica's Crime (Extended Mix)/The Shining/Shattered Sky (12", p/s) 8

SAMMY SALVO

58 RCA RCA 1032 Oh Julie/Say Yeah 30
58 RCA RCA 1032 Oh Julie/Say Yeah (78) 20
59 London HLP 8997 Afraid/Marble Heart 15
59 London HLP 8997 Afraid/Marble Heart (78) 20
62 Polydor NH 66974 Billy Blue/French Poodle 8

SAM

72 Pye 7N 45175 Johnny Rebel/He Loves Me, He Loves Me Not 6

SAM APPLE PIE

69 Decca F 22932 Tiger Man (King Of The Jungle)/Sometime Girl 15
72 DJM DJS 274 Call Me Boss/Old Tom 8
69 Decca LK-R 5005 SAM APPLE PIE (LP, mono, laminated front sleeve, unboxed logo label) 200
69 Decca SKL-R 5005 SAM APPLE PIE (LP, stereo, laminated sleeve, unboxed logo label) 150
73 DJM DJLPS 429 EAST 17 (LP) 30

SAM, ERV & TOM

(see also Diplomats)
68 Direction 58-3339 Soul Teacher/Hard To Get 12

SAM GOPAL

(see under 'G')

SAM & BILL

66 Pye International 7N 25355 Fly Me To The Moon/Treat Me Right 15
67 Brunswick 05973 I Feel Like Cryin'/I'll Try 40
67 Brunswick 05973 I Feel Like Cryin'/I'll Try (DJ copy) 75

SAM & DAVE

66 King KG 1041 No More Pain/You Ain't No Big Thing Baby 50
66 Atlantic AT 4066 You Don't Know Like I Know/Blame Me, Don't Blame My Heart 20
66 Atlantic 584 003 Hold On I'm A Comin'/I Got Everything I Need 10
66 Atlantic 584 047 If You Got The Loving (I Got The Time)/Said I Wasn't Gonna Tell Nobody 10
67 Atlantic 584 064 You Got Me Hummin'/Sleep Good Tonight 10
67 Atlantic 584 086 You Don't Know Like I Know/Blame Me, Don't Blame My Heart (reissue) 7
67 Stax 601 004 Soothe Me/Sweet Pains (initial dark blue label) 25
67 Stax 601 004 Soothe Me/Sweet Pains (later light blue label) 20
67 Stax 601 006 When Something Is Wrong With My Baby/A Small Portion Of Your Love (initial dark blue label) 10
67 Stax 601 006 When Something Is Wrong With My Baby/A Small Portion Of Your Love (later light blue label) 8
67 Stax 601 023 Soul Man/May I Baby 8
68 Stax 601 030 I Thank You/Wrap It Up 8
68 Atlantic 584 192 You Don't Know What You Mean To Me/This Is Your World 7
68 Atlantic 584 211 Can't You Find Another Way/Still Is The Night 7
68 Atlantic 584 228 Everybody's Got To Believe In Somebody/If I Didn't Have A Girl Like You 6
69 Atlantic 584 237 Soul Sister, Brown Sugar/Come On In 8
69 Atlantic 584 247 You Don't Know Like I Know/Hold On I'm A Comin' 6
69 Atlantic 584 303 Ooh, Ooh, Ooh/Holdin' On 6
70 Atlantic 584 324 Baby, Baby, Don't Stop Now/I'm Not An Indian Giver 6
66 King KGL 4001 SAM AND DAVE (LP) 75
66 Atlantic 587/588 045 HOLD ON, I'M A COMIN' (LP) 50
67 Stax 589 003 DOUBLE DYNAMITE (LP) 50
68 Stax 589 015 SOUL MEN (LP) 40
68 Major Minor MCP 5000 SAM AND DAVE (LP) 22
69 Atlantic 588 154 I THANK YOU (LP) 25
69 Atlantic 588 155 THE BEST OF SAM AND DAVE (LP) 18
69 Atlantic 587/588 181 DOUBLE TROUBLE (LP) 22
69 Atlantic 588 185 SOUL MEN (LP, reissue) 15

SAM & KITTY

80 Grapevine GRP 132 I've Got Something Good/Love Is The Greatest 10

SAME

79 Wessex WEX 267 Wild About You/Movements (p/s) 70
80 Blue Print BLU 2008 Movements/Wild About You (reissue with reversed sides & blue print on p/s) 30
80 Blue Print BLU 2008 Movements/Wild About You (reissue with reversed sides no p/s) 20

MINT VALUE £

MIKE SAMMES SINGERS

68	Davjon DJ 1006	HYMNS A SWINGING (LP, with Ted Taylor Organisation)	35
06	Trunk JBH 109 LP	MUSIC FOR BISCUITS (LP)	25

MICHAEL SAMMES SINGERS

59	Top Rank JAR 166	Upstairs And Downstairs/Ivor Raymonde - Mylene	6

SAMMY

(see also Ian Gillan, Audience, Episode Six, Quatermass, Roy YOung Band, Stackridge, Ginhouse)

72	Philips 6006 227	Goo Ger Woogie/Big Lovin' Woman	5
72	Philips 6308 136	SAMMY (LP, laminated sleeve, black/silver label)	35

SAMPLES

80	Sample	VENDETTA (Vendetta/ (EP)	20
84	No Future OI 14	Dead Hero/Fire Around Round/Suspicion (p/s)	15

DAVE SAMPSON & HUNTERS

(see also Hunters [U.K.])

60	Columbia DB 4449	Sweet Dreams/It's Lonesome	20
60	Columbia DB 4502	If You Need Me/See You Around	20
61	Columbia DB 4597	Why The Chicken?/1999	15
61	Columbia DB 4625	Easy To Dream/That's All	15
62	Fontana H 361	Wide, Wide World/Since Sandy Moved Away (solo)	15
61	Columbia SEG 8095	DAVE (EP, mono)	60
61	Columbia ESG 7853	DAVE (EP, stereo)	80

TOMMY SAMPSON

58	Melodisc MEL 1411	Rockin'/Rock'n'Roll Those Big Brown Eyes (with His Strongmen)	22
58	Parlophone R 4458	Lazy Train/Smooth Mood (as Tommy Sampson Orchestra)	7

SAM'S FRIENDS

66	Decca F12519	If I Gave You My Love/I Feel	5

SAMSON

(see also Strider)

69	Instant INSP 004	ARE YOU SAMSON (LP)	70

SAMSON

70	Parlophone R5867	Venus/Wool & Water	8

SAMSON

(see also Bruce Dickinson, Iron Maiden, John McCoy, Tiger, Colin Towns, Thunderstick, Nicky Moore, Mammoth, Egypt)

78	Lightning GIL 547	Telephone/Leavin' You (p/s)	35
79	Lightning GIL 553	Mr. Rock'n'Roll/Drivin' Music (p/s)	35
79	Laser LAS 6	Mr. Rock'n'Roll (remix)/Primrose Shuffle	10
80	EMI EMI 5061	Vice Versa (Edit)/Hammerhead (p/s, withdrawn, 1,000 demos only)	40
80	Gem GEMS 34	Vice Versa (Edit)/Hammerhead (reissue, p/s, with sticker)	8
80	Gem GEMS 34	Vice Versa (Edit)/Hammerhead (reissue, p/s)	5
80	Gem GEMS 38	Hard Times (Remix)/Angel With A Machine Gun (p/s)	5
81	RCA RCA 67	Riding With The Angels (Edit)/Little Big Man (no p/s)	10
81	RCA RCA 67	Riding With The Angels (Edit)/Little Big Man (picture disc)	10
82	Polydor POSPP 471	Losing My Grip/Pyramid To The Stars (picture disc)	6
82	Polydor POSPX 471	Losing My Grip/Pyramid To The Stars/Mr. Rock'n'Roll (live)/ Tomorrow Or Yesterday (live) (12" EP)	10
82	Polydor POSPG 519/	Life On The Run/Drivin' With ZZ!//Walking Out On You (live)/ Bright Lights (live) (double pack, gatefold p/s)	7
82	Polydor SAM 2	Red Skies/Young Idea (unissued, promo only)	18
83	Polydor PODJ 554	Red Skies (DJ Edit) (1-sided promo)	12
83	Polydor POSPP 554	Red Skies/Livin', Lovin', Lyin' (picture disc)	6
83	Polydor POSPX 554	Red Skies/Livin', Lovin', Lyin'/Running Out Of Time (12", p/s)	10
84	Polydor POSP 670	Are You Ready?/Front Page News (p/s)	7
84	Polydor POSPP 670	Are You Ready?/Front Page News (picture disc)	8
84	Polydor POSPX 670	Are You Ready?/Front Page News/La Grange (12", p/s)	8
84	Polydor POSP 680	The Fight Goes On/Riding With The Angels (re-recording) (p/s)	5
84	Polydor POSPX 680	The Fight Goes On (Long Version)/Riding With The Angels (re-recording)/ Vice Versa (live) (12", p/s)	8
84	Thunderbolt THBE 1.003	Mr Rock'n'Roll/Primrose Shuffle/Telephone/Leavin' You (12", p/s)	8
86	Capitol CL 395	Vice Versa (Remix)/Losing My Grip (Remix) (p/s)	8
86	Capitol 12CLP 395	Vice Versa (Remix)/Losing My Grip (Remix) (12", picture disc)	15
87	Metal Hammer METAL 1	One Day's Heroes (as Paul Samson's Empire)/CHARIOT: Life On The Line/ HEAVY PETTIN': Heaven Sent/STRANGEWAYS: Never Gonna Lose It (EP with Metal Hammer magazine)	6
79	Laser LAP 1	SURVIVORS (LP)	15
80	Gem GEMLP 108	HEAD ON (LP, 2 different mixes, A1/B1 or A2/B2 in matrix; each with insert, with free patch, stickered sleeve)	25
80	Gem GEMLP 108	HEAD ON (LP, 2 different mixes, A1/B1 or A2/B2 in matrix; each, with insert but no patch)	12
81	RCA LP 5031	SHOCK TACTICS (LP, with insert)	18
82	Polydor POLS 1077	BEFORE THE STORM (LP, with poster, stickered sleeve)	20
82	Polydor POLS 1077	BEFORE THE STORM (LP, without poster, stickered sleeve)	12
84	Polydor POLD 5132	DON'T GET MAD, GET EVEN (LP, with insert)	15
84	Polydor POLD 5132	DON'T GET MAD, GET EVEN (2-LP, white labels, 2 different mixes of same album, promo only)	35

SAM THE SHAM & THE PHARAOHS

65	MGM MGM 1269	Woolly Bully/Ain't Gonna Move	12
65	MGM MGM 1269	Woolly Bully/Ain't Gonna Move (DJ Copy)	50
65	MGM MGM 1278	Ju Ju Hand/Big City Lights	10
65	MGM MGM 1285	Ring Dang Doo/Don't Try It	10
66	MGM MGM 1298	Red Hot/Long Long Way	15
66	MGM MGM 1315	Li'l Red Riding Hood/Love Me Like Before	10

			MINT VALUE £
66	MGM MGM 1326	The Hair On My Chinny Chin Chin/The Out Crowd	8
66	MGM MGM 1331	How Do You Catch A Girl/The Love You Left Behind	10
67	MGM MGM 1337	Oh That's Bad No That's Good/Take What You Can Get	10
67	MGM MGM 1343	Black Sheep/My Day's Gonna Come	15
68	MGM MGM 1379	Yakety Yak/Let Our Lovelight Shine	10
69	MGM MGM 1473	Woolly Bully/Ring Dang Doo	6
66	MGM MGM-EP 794	RED HOT (EP)	70
65	MGM MGM-C 1007	WOOLY BULLY (LP)	40
66	MGM MGM-C(S) 8032	LI'L RED RIDING HOOD (LP)	30

LEROY SAMUEL (actually Leroy Smart)

72	Punch PH 113	Trying To Wreck My Life/JOHN HOLT: Pride And Joy	12

(Phillip) SAMUEL THE FIRST

71	Summit SUM 8515	Sounds Of Babylon/BEVERLEY'S ALL STARS: Second Babylon Version	10

JERRY SAMUELS

(see also Napoleon XIV)

56	HMV 7M 411	Puppy Love/The Chosen Few	15
56	HMV 7M 411	Puppy Love/The Chosen Few (78)	10

WINSTON SAMUELS

64	Columbia DB 7405	You Are The One/Angela	12
64	Rio R 26	Follow/I'm So Glad	12
64	Black Swan WI 419	Luck Will Come My Way/LLOYD BREVITT: One More Time	25
64	Black Swan WI 426	You Are The One/Gloria Love (B-side actually by Beltones)	15
65	Ska Beat JB 196	Be Prepared/Jericho Wall	20
65	Ska Beat JB 213	My Bride To Be/LLOYD PREVITT: Wayward Ska	25
65	Ska Beat JB 214	Never Again/My Angel	18
66	Ska Beat JB 238	What Have I Done/Broken Hearted	25
66	Ska Beat JB 241	Ups And Downs/Come What May	18
66	Ska Beat JB 244	Time Will Tell/I'm Sorry	18
67	Island WI 3051	The Greatest/FREDDIE & FITZY: Truth Hurts	40
67	Island WI 3053	I Won't Be Discouraged/FREDDIE & FITZIE: Why Did My Little Girl Cry	40
67	Fab FAB 21	Peace Of Mind/Shepherd Ben (by Prince Buster & Teddy King)	25
67	Fab FAB 14	Holding Out/To The Other Man	20
67	Fab FAB 28	Peace Of Mind/I'm Still Here	20

SAMURAI

68	United Artists UP 2242	Good Morning Starshine/Temple Of Gold	35

SAMURAI

(see also Greenslade, Web)

71	Greenwich GSLP 1003	SAMURAI (LP, gatefold sleeve, white/brown label)	200

SAMURAI

85	Ebony EBON 25	Fires Of Hell/Dreams Of The World (no p/s)	12
84	Ebony EBON 24	SACRED BLADE (LP)	15

SAND

71	Philips 6006157	Soft Lady/Babylon	20

SANDALS

90s	Acid Jazz JAZID 47	A Profound Gas (p/s)	10

SANDEENO

03	Wizkidz WK 011	Ah Mankind/Preaching the Board	12

ALEX SANDERS

70	A&M AMLS 984	A WITCH IS BORN (LP, foldout sleeve with warning sticker, withdrawn)	125

GARY SANDERS

66	Warner Bros WB 5676	Ain't No Beatle/Ain't I Good To You	12

GEORGE SANDERS

58	HMV 7EG 8395	THE GEORGE SANDERS TOUCH (EP)	8

PHARAOH SANDERS

66	ESP Disk/Fontana SFJL 931	PHARAOH SANDERS QUINTET (LP)	35
71	Probe SPB 1019	DEAF, DUMB AND BLIND (LP)	25
70s	Impulse AS 9138	TAUHID (LP)	20
70s	Impulse AS 9199	SUMMUN BUKMUN UMYUN (LP)	25
70s	Impulse AS 9219	BLACK UNITY (LP)	25
70s	Impulse AS 9227	LIVE AT THE EAST (LP)	25
70s	Impulse AS 9229	THE BEST OF PHARAOH SANDERS (2-LP)	20
70s	Impulse 9233	WISDOM THROUGH MUSIC (LP)	20
70s	Impulse 9254	VILLAGE OF PHARAOHS (LP)	20
70s	Impulse 9261	ELEVATION (LP)	20
70s	Impulse 9280	LOVE IN US ALL (LP)	20
82	Jasmine JAS 53	THEMBI (LP)	18

RAY SANDERS

60	London HLG 7106	A World So Full Of Love/A Little Bitty Tear (export issue)	12

TOMMY SANDERSON & SANDMEN

61	Ember EMB 131	Deadline/Candelglow	10
62	Ember EMB 152	Ding Dong Rag/Piano A-Go Go	10

CHRIS SANDFORD (& CORONETS)

63	Decca F 11778	Not Too Little - Not Too Much/I'm Lookin'	5
64	Decca F 11842	You're Gonna Be My Girl/Don't Leave Me Now (with Coronets)	6
65	Fontana TF 633	I Wish They Wouldn't Always Say I Sound Like The Guy From The U.S.A. Blues/Little Man, Nobody Cares	7

SANDGATE

75	Dawn DWS 1114	A Thousand Years/Such A Sad Song	6

MINT VALUE £

GERRY SANDON
96 Twangsville TW 001 — JUST GERRY (EP) — 10

JOHNNY SANDON (& REMO FOUR)
(see also Remo Four)
63 Pye 7N 15542 — Lies/On The Horizon (as Johnny Sandon & Remo Four) — 15
63 Pye 7N 15559 — Magic Potion/Yes (as Johnny Sandon & Remo Four) — 15
64 Pye 7N 15602 — Sixteen Tons/The Blizzard — 10
64 Pye 7N 15665 — Donna Means Heartbreak/Some Kinda Wonderful — 10
64 Pye 7N 15717 — The Blizzard/(I'd Be A) Legend In My Time — 10

SAND PEBBLES
67 Track 604 015 — Love Power/Because Of Love — 20
68 Toast TT 505 — If You Didn't Hear Me The First Time/Flower Power — 8
69 Track 604 028 — Love Power/Because Of Love (reissue) — 15

SANDPIPERS
66 Pye Intl. 7N 25380 — Guantanamera/What Makes You Dream, Pretty Girl — 5
66 Pye International 7N 25396 — Louie Louie/Things We Said Today — 8
68 A & M AMS 723 — Quando M'Immamoro (A Man Without Love)/I'll Remember You — 8
76 Satril SAT 111 — For The Last Time/Down By The River — 8
76 Satril SAT 114 — Hango On Sloopy/Skid Row Joe — 7

SANDRA
86 10 TENY 78-12 — (I'll Never Be) Maria Magdalena/Party Games/Little Girl (12", picture disc) — 15
86 10 TEN 113-12/TENY 78-12 — In The Heat Of The Night/Heatwave (Instrumental)//(I'll Never Be) Maria Magdalena/Party Games/Little Girl (12", double pack, including picture disc, gatefold PVC sleeve) — 20
89 Siren SRNCD 85 — Everlasting Love/Stop For A Minute/Everlasting Love (Remix)/(I'll Never Be) Maria Magdalena (CD) — 50
89 Siren SRNCD 104 — Heaven Can Wait (Single Version 4.05)/(Dub Mix)/Heaven's Theme (Instrumental)/Heaven Can Wait (Extended Version) (3" CD, card sleeve) — 20

SANDROSE
73 Polydor 2480 137 — SANDROSE (LP) — 250

SANDS (Ireland)
(see also Tony Kenny & Sands)
69 Tribune TRS 122 — Dance Dance Dance/The Cheater — 20
69 Tribune TRS 129 — Bubble Gum Music/Sherry — 15
70 Major Minor MM 681 — Venus/Cara Mia — 10
69 Tribune — SAND DOIN'S (LP) — 50
70s Plough PLX 501 — TIME OUT WITH THE SANDS (LP) — 15

SANDS (U.K.)
(see also Others, Sundragon)
67 Reaction 591 017 — Mrs. Gillespie's Refrigerator/Listen To The Sky — 350

CLIVE SANDS
(see also Brothers Kane, Sarstedt Brothers, Wes Sands)
69 S.N.B. 55-3955 — Lo Mucho Que Te Quiro/Picture On The Wall — 7
69 S.N.B. 55-4058 — Hooked On A Feeling/Marie — 7
69 S.N.B. 55-4431 — Whitchi Tai Yo/In A Dream — 12
69 CBS 4672 — A Very Lonely Man/You Made Me What I Am — 7

DAVEY SANDS & ESSEX
65 Decca F 12170 — Please Me Mine/All The Time — 20
67 CBS 202620 — Advertising Girl/Without You I'm Nothing — 25
71 Parlophone R5899 — The Puppet Man/Oh What A Naughty Man — 15

EVIE SANDS
65 Red Bird BC 118 — Take Me For A Little While/Run Home To Mama — 50
65 Red Bird BC 118 — Take Me For A Little While/Run Home To Mama (DJ copy) — 85
66 Cameo Parkway C 413 — Picture Me Gone/It Makes Me Laugh — 125
66 Cameo Parkway C 413 — Picture Me Gone/It Makes Me Laugh (DJ copy) — 200
68 A&M AMS 736 — Shadow Of The Evening/Until It's Time For You To Go — 10
69 A&M AMS 748 — I'll Hold Out Of My Hand/One Fine Summer Morning — 10
69 A&M AMS 760 — Anyway That You Want Me/I'll Never Be Alone — 10
75 Capitol CL 15818 — You Brought The Woman Out In Me/Early Morning Sunshine — 7

JODI(E) SANDS
57 London HL 8456 — With All My Heart/More Than Only Friends (as Jodi Sands) — 20
57 London HL 8530 — Please Don't Tell Me (Sayonara)/If You're Not Completely Satisfied — 20
57 London HL 8530 — Please Don't Tell Me (Sayonara)/If You're Not Completely Satisfied (78) — 15
58 Starlite ST45 005 — All I Ask Of You/The Way I Love You — 12
58 HMV POP 533 — Someday (You'll Want Me To Want You)/Always In My Heart — 10

SYLVIA SANDS
61 Columbia DB 4579 — Autumn Tears/Steppin' Out With My Baby — 8

TOMMY SANDS
57 Capitol CL 14695 — Teen-Age Crush/Hep Dee Hootie (Cutie Wootie) — 25
57 Capitol CL 14724 — Ring-A-Ding-A-Ding/My Love Song — 25
57 Capitol CL 14724 — Ring-A-Ding-A-Ding/My Love Song (78) — 10
57 Capitol CL 14745 — Goin' Steady/Ring My 'Phone — 25
57 Capitol CL 14745 — Goin' Steady/Ring My 'Phone (78) — 10
57 Capitol CL 14781 — Let Me Be Loved/Fantastically Foolish — 15
57 Capitol CL 14811 — Man, Like Wow!/A Swingin' Romance — 20
57 Capitol CL 14811 — Man, Like Wow!/A Swingin' Romance (78) — 12
58 Capitol CL 14834 — Sing, Boy, Sing/Crazy 'Cause I Love You — 20
58 Capitol CL 14872 — Hawaiian Rock/Teen-Age Doll — 25
58 Capitol CL 14889 — After The Senior Prom/Big Date — 20
58 Capitol CL 14925 — Blue Ribbon Baby/I Love You Because (as Tommy Sands & Raiders) — 30

MINT VALUE £

59 Capitol CL 14971 The Worryin' Kind/Bigger Than Texas 35
59 Capitol CL 15013 Is It Ever Gonna Happen/I Ain't Gittin' Rid Of You 30
59 Capitol CL 15047 Sinner Man/Bring Me Your Love 10
59 Capitol CL 15071 That's The Way I Am/I'll Be Seeing You 10
60 Capitol CL 15109 I Gotta Have You/You Hold The Future. 10
60 Capitol CL 15143 The Old Oaken Bucket/These Are The Things You Are 8
61 Capitol CL 15219 Love In A Goldfish Bowl/I Love My Baby. 7
63 HMV POP 1193 Connie/Young Man's Fancy 8
63 HMV POP 1247 Only 'Cause I'm Lonely/Cinderella 8
66 Liberty LIB 55842 The Statue/Lolita. 45
66 Liberty LIB 55842 The Statue/Lolita (DJ Copy). 85
57 Capitol EAP1 848 STEADY DATE WITH TOMMY SANDS PT. 1 (EP). 40
57 Capitol EAP2 848 STEADY DATE WITH TOMMY SANDS PT. 2 (EP). 30
57 Capitol EAP3 848 STEADY DATE WITH TOMMY SANDS PT. 3 (EP). 30
57 Capitol EAP1 851 TEENAGE CRUSH (EP) 30
59 Capitol EAP1 1081 SANDS STORM PART 1 (EP) 25
59 Capitol EAP2 1081 SANDS STORM PART 2 (EP) 25
59 Capitol EAP3 1081 SANDS STORM PART 3 (EP) 25
59 Capitol EAP1 1123 THIS THING CALLED LOVE (EP). 25
57 Capitol T 848 STEADY DATE WITH TOMMY SANDS (LP) 60
58 Capitol T 929 SING, BOY, SING (soundtrack) (LP) 50
59 Capitol T 1081 SANDS STORM! (LP) 80
59 Capitol T 1123 THIS THING CALLED LOVE (LP). 35
60 Capitol T 1239 WHEN I'M THINKING OF YOU (LP, mono) 15
60 Capitol ST 1239 WHEN I'M THINKING OF YOU (LP, (stereo) 20
61 Capitol T 1426 A DREAM WITH TOMMY SANDS (LP). 15

TONY SANDS & DRUMBEATS

60s Studio 36 NSRS EP 1/22 Shame Shame Shame/I Got A Feeling 250

WES SANDS

(see also Brothers Kane, Sarstedt Brothers, Clive Sands)

63 Columbia DB 4996 There's Lots More Where This Came From/Three Cups 45

SANDS OF TIME

66 Pye 7N 17140 Where Did We Go Wrong/When I Look Back. 10
67 Pye 7N 17236 One Day/Ev'ry Time We Say Goodbye 8

PAT SANDY

69 Attack ATT 8000 Gentle On My Mind/BIG L: Soulful 6

SANDY & TEACHERS

(see also Sandy Brown)

64 Columbia DB 7244 Listen With Mammy/Real Sweet 5

SANDY COAST

71 Polydor 2121 046 True Love/That's A Wonder 7
73 Polydor 2001 457 Blackboard Jungle Lady/Don't Get Me Wrong 7
69 Page One POLS 020 FROM THE STEREO WORKSHOP (LP). 200
69 Page One MORS 201 SHIPWRECK (LP) 200
73 Polydor 2310 277 STONEWALL (LP) 20

SAN FRANCISCO EARTHQUAKE

68 Mercury MF 1036 Fairy Tales Can Come True (Have You Heard About Lucy)/Su Su. 10

CLAUDE SANG

70 Sugar SU 105 I'm In Love Again/You'll Never Fool Me Again. 6
70 Sugar SUM 1 THE WORLD OF REGGAE VOL. 1 (LP). 15

SAN REMO STRINGS

71 Tamla Motown TMG 795 Festival Time/All Turned On 12
71 Tamla Motown TMG 795 Festival Time/All Turned On (DJ copy). 30
72 Tamla Motown TMG 807 Reach Out, I'll Be There/Hungry For Love 10
72 Tamla Motown TMG 807 Reach Out, I'll Be There/Hungry For Love (DJ copy) 30
73 Tamla Motown STML 11216 SAN REMO STRINGS SWING (LP) 20

SANS NOMS

71 Decca Eclipse ECs2095 LARGELY LATIN (LP) 12

BOBBY SANSOM (& GIANTS)

63 Oriole CB 1837 There's A Place/Lucille (as Bobby Sansom & Giants) 20
63 Oriole CB 1888 Where Have You Been/Do You Promise (as Bobby Sansom & Giants) 18
70 Decca F 13104 Lady One And Only/Handbags And Gladrags 8
71 Decca F 13151 I Believe In Music/The Valley Of The Shadows Of Tears 8

MONGO SANTAMARIA

63 Riverside RIF 106909 Watermelon Man/Don't Bother Me No More. 20
65 CBS 201766 El Pussycat/Black Eyed Peas And Rice 20
69 Direction 58-4086 Cloud Nine/Son Of A Preacher Man 18
69 Direction 58-4430 Twenty Five Miles/El Tres. 15
66 CBS SS 62123 HEY! LET'S PARTY (LP). 20
69 CBS S 233811 ALL STRUNG OUT (LP) 20
71 CBS 63904 WORKING ON A GROOVY THING (LP). 20
71 Atlantic 2400 140 MONGO'S WAY (LP) 20

SANTANA

69 CBS 4593 Persuasion/Savor 5
70 CBS 4940 Evil Ways/Jin-Go-Lo-Ba 5
70 CBS 5325 Black Magic Woman/Hope You're Feeling Better 5
69 CBS 63015 SANTANA (LP, laminated sleeve original, orange label). 20
70 CBS 63815 SANTANA (LP, non-laminated sleeve reissue, orange label). 12
70 CBS 64087 ABRAXAS (LP, orange label). 15
71 CBS 69015 SANTANA (III) (LP, gatefold sleeve, some stickered, orange label). 12

			MINT VALUE £
72	CBS CQ 30595	SANTANA (III) (LP, gatefold sleeve, quadrophonic)	18
72	CBS 65299	CARAVANSERAI (LP, gatefold sleeve, orange label)	12
73	CBS CQ 31610	CARAVANSERAI (LP, gatefold sleeve, quadrophonic)	15
74	CBS CQ 32445	WELCOME (LP, embossed gatefold sleeve, quadrophonic)	15
75	CBS CQ 30130	ABRAXAS (LP, gatefold sleeve, quadrophonic)	15
75	CBS Q 69081	GREATEST HITS (LP, quadrophonic)	15
75	CBS Q 69084	BORBOLETTA (LP, quadrophonic)	15
76	CBS Q 86005	AMIGOS (LP, quadrophonic)	15

CARLOS SANTANA & BUDDY MILES

(see also Santana, Buddy Miles, Mahavishnu Orchestra, John McLaughlin, John Lee Hooker)

72	CBS 8338	Evil Ways/Them Changes	5
83	CBS A 3359	They All Went To Mexico (with Willie Nelson)/BUDDY MILES: Mudbone (p/s)	5
72	CBS 65142	CARLOS SANTANA & BUDDY MILES LIVE (LP, gatefold sleeve)	12
73	CBS CQ 31308	CARLOS SANTANA & BUDDY MILES LIVE (LP, quadrophonic)	15

SANTELLS

66	Sue WI 4020	So Fine/These Are Love	40

DAVID SANTO

68	London HLK 10219	Jingle Down A Hill/Rising Of Scorpio	8

SANTO & JOHNNY

59	Pye International 7N 25037	Sleep Walk/All Night Diner	20
59	Pye International N 25037	Sleep Walk/All Night Diner (78 rpm)	15
60	Parlophone R 4619	Tear Drop/The Long Walk Home	20
60	Parlophone R 4644	Caravan/Summertime	10
61	Pye International 7N 25111	Theme From Come September/Hopscotch	10
61	Parlophone R 4844	Bullseye!/Twistin' Bells	10
62	Parlophone R 4865	Birmingham/The Mouse	10
62	Stateside SS 110	Spanish Harlem/Stage To Cimarron	10
64	Stateside SS 253	Three Cabelleros/Manhattan Spiritual	10
64	Stateside SS 292	In The Still Of The Night/Song For Rosemary	10
60	Parlophone GEP 8806	SANTO AND JOHNNY NO. 1 (EP)	30
60	Parlophone GEP 8813	SANTO AND JOHNNY NO. 2 (EP)	20
64	Stateside S(S)L 1008	HAWAII (LP)	20

SAPODILLA PUNCH

69	Mercury MF 1112	Hold On I'm Coming/Bach To Minor	8

SAPPHIRE

72	SRT SRT 72226	SAPPHIRE (LP)	180

SAPPHIRE

82	Sapphire Rocks SRR 001	Jealousy (p/s)	150

SAPPHIRES

63	Stateside SS 223	Where Is Johnny Now/Your True Love	60
64	Stateside SS 267	Who Do You Love/Oh So Soon	70
65	HMV POP 1441	Gotta Have Your Love/Gee Baby I'm Sorry	180
65	HMV POP 1441	Gotta Have Your Love/Gee Baby I'm Sorry (DJ copy)	350
65	HMV POP 1461	Evil One/How Could I Say Goodbye	180
65	HMV POP 1461	Evil One/How Could I Say Goodbye (DJ copy)	300
72	Probe PRO 556	Gotta Have Your Love/Gee Baby I'm Sorry (reissue)	15
74	Probe PRO 609	Slow Fizz/Our Love Is Everywhere	12
78	ABC 4221	Gonna Be A Big Thing/EDDIE REGAN: Playin' Hide And Seek	8

SARABAND

73	Folk Heritage FHR 050	CLOSE TO IT ALL (LP)	22

SARACEN

82	Nucleus SAR 1	No More Lonely Nights/Rock Of Ages (p/s, with patch)	8
82	Nucleus SAR 1	No More Lonely Nights/Rock Of Ages (p/s	6
83	Neat NEAT 30	We Have Arrived/Face In The Crowd (p/s)	7
82	Nucleus MPGR 492	HEROES, SAINTS AND FOOLS (LP)	15
84	Neat NEAT 1016	CHANGE OF HEART (LP)	12

SARAH JANE

66	Pye 7N 17114	Listen People/The World Is Round	7

SARASOTA

96	BIT Productions MIKE 004	We're Gettin' Hot (1-sided 12")	40
97	BIT Productions MIKE 009	Pleasure/We're Gettin' Hot (the Maximum Project Pumped Up Remix) (stickered white label 12")	40

SARDONICUS

73	Country Recording Service COUN 240	Nympth/Evaporated Brain	300

DON SARGENT

60	Vogue Pop V 9160	St. James' Infirmary/Gypsy Boots (triangular centre)	500

SARI & SHALIMARS

68	United Artists UP 2235	It's So Lonely (Being Together)/You Walked Out On Me Before	30

DEREK SARJEANT

61	Oak RGJ 101	FOLK SONGS SUNG BY DEREK SARJEANT (EP)	20
61	Oak RGJ 103	SONGS WE LIKE TO SING (EP, with tracks by Lisa Turner & Mick Wells)	15
61	Oak RGJ 105	FOLK SONGS SUNG BY DEREK SARJEANT VOL. 2 (EP)	15
63	Oak RGJ 117	MAN OF KENT (EP)	18

MIKE SARNE

(see also Wendy Richards, Le Roys, Billie Davis, Rod McKuen)

63	Parlophone R 5010	Code Of Love/Are You Satisfied	5
63	Parlophone R 5060	Please Don't Say/Now You've Moved	5

			MINT VALUE £
63	Parlophone R 5090	Hello Lover Boy/Baby I'm On My Way	10
64	Parlophone R 5129	Out And About/A Place To Go	10
64	Parlophone R 5170	Love Me Please/You've Got Something (as Mike Sarne & Le Roys)	10
63	Parlophone DP 558	Just Like Eddie/Slow Twistin' Round The Totem Pole (export issue)	80
63	Parlophone GEP 8879	MIKE SARNE HIT PARADE (EP)	30
62	Parlophone PMC 1187	COME OUTSIDE (LP)	20

SAROFEEN & SMOKE

71	Pye International 7N 25556	Susan Jane/Tomorrow	15
71	Pye Intl. NSPL 28153	DO IT (LP)	25

SAROLTA

68	Island WIP 6035	Open Your Hands/L.O.V.E.	15
69	President PT248	I Am A Woman/Change Of Heart	10

SARR BAND

78	Calendar LDAY 115	Magic Mandrake/Double Action (12")	25

PETER SARSTEDT

(see also Sarstedt Brothers, Brothers Kane, Peter Lincoln)

68	Island WIP 6028	I Must Go On/Mary Jane	30
68	United Artists UP 2228	I Am A Cathedral/Blagged	10
69	United Artists UP 2262	Morning Mountain/Step Into The Candlelight	10
69	United Artists UP 35021	Frozen Orange Sea/Arethusa Loser	15
69	United Artists UP 35041	As Though It Were A Movie/Take Off Your Clothes	8
69	United Artists UP 35075	Without Darkness (There's No Light)/Step Into The Candlelight	8
69	United Artists (S)ULP 1219	PETER SARSTEDT (LP)	12
69	United Artists UAL 29037	AS THOUGH IT WERE A MOVIE (LP)	12
71	United Artists UAS 29247	EVERY WORD YOU SAY (LP, with inner sleeve)	12

SARSTEDT BROTHERS

(see also Brothers Kane, Peter Sarstedt, Eden Kane, Clive Sands, Wes Sands)

73	Regal Zonophone RZ 3081	Chinese Restaurant/Beloved Illusions	7
73	Regal Zono. SRZA 8516	WORLDS APART TOGETHER (LP, gatefold sleeve with booklet)	20

SASPARELLA

69	Decca F 12892	Spooky/Come Inside	30

SASSAFRAS

73	Polydor 2383 245	EXPECTING COMPANY (LP)	15

SASSENACHS

64	Fontana TF 518	That Don't Worry Me/All Over You	30

SATAN

82	Guardian GRC 145	Kiss Of Death/Heads Will Roll (with p/s)	200
82	Guardian GRC 145	Kiss Of Death/Heads Will Roll	50
85	Neat NEAT 1012	COURT IN THE ACT (LP)	30

SATANIC RITES

81	Heavy Metal HEAVY 8	Live To Ride/Hit And Run (p/s)	12
85	Chub CHUBLP 001	WHICH WAY THE WIND BLOWS (LP)	25
87	Chub CHUBLP 002	NO USE CRYING (LP)	30

SATAN'S RATS

77	DJM DJS 10819	In My Love For You/Façade (p/s)	30
77	DJM DJS 10821	Year Of The Rats/Louise (p/s)	25
78	DJM DJS 10840	You Make Me Sick/Façade (p/s)	25
89	Overground OVER 01	Year Of The Rats/Louise (p/s, 600 yellow vinyl)	6
89	Overground OVER 01	Year Of The Rats/Louise (p/s, 400 white vinyl)	7
89	Overground OVER 01	Year Of The Rats/Louise (p/s, 25 gold vinyl, numbered test pressings)	15
89	Overground OVER 02	In My Love For You/Facade (p/s, 600 yellow vinyl)	12
89	Overground OVER 02	In My Love For You/Facade (p/s, 400 white vinyl)	12
89	Overground OVER 02	In My Love For You/Facade (p/s, 25 gold vinyl, numbered test pressings)	15
91	Overground OVER 14	You Make Me Sick/Louise (p/s, clear vinyl, 567 copies only)	7

YOUNG SATCH

70	Black Swan BW 1401	Bongo Bongo/BOYS: Ramba	12

GIRL SATCHMO

(see also Pat Satchmo, Sugar & Dandy)

61	Blue Beat BB 45	Satchmo's Mash Potato/Darling	25
62	Blue Beat BB 79	Twist Around Town/My New Honey (with Karl Rowe & Bluebeats)	25
63	Blue Beat BB 156	Don't Be Sad/Brother Joe (with Les Dawson Combo)	25
64	Blue Beat BB 227	Rhythm Of The New Beat/Blue Beat Chariot	25
69	Fab FAB 111	Take You For A Ride/I'm Coming Home	20
69	Trojan TR 676	Taken For A Ride/I'm Coming Home	15

PAT SATCHMO

69	Punch PH 9	Hello Dolly/ERIC DONALSON: Never Get Away	20
69	Upsetter US 316	Hello Dolly/King Of The Trombone	15
70	Punch PH 24	Wonderful World/MEDITATORS: Purple Mast	15
70	Songbird SB 1039	A Handful Of Friends/CRYSTALITES: Handful - Version	10
72	Attack ATT 8024	What's Going On/LLOYD & CAREY: Tubby's In Full Swing	30

SATELLITES

(see also Girl Satchmo, Hortense Ellis)

84	Brickyard	HERE IS TODAY'S NEWS (LP)	15

SATIN BELLS

(see also Three Bells)

68	Pye 7N 17531	Baby You're So Right For Me/When You're Ready	10
68	Pye 7N 17608	Da-Di-Da-Da/Oh No Oh Yes	6
69	Decca F 22937	I Stand Accused (Of Loving You)/Sweet Darlin'	20
70	Decca F 23044	The Power Of Love/Baby Come Back	6

MINT VALUE £

SATIN STORM

91	Satin Storm SSP 201	Satin Storm 1999/Pleasurezone (inst)/Buzz/Feel The Spirit (12")	30
91	Satin Storm SSHC 1	See The Light/Call In The Hardcore/Kick Up A Sound Boy/Chill Out (12". As Satin Storm Dancers)	15
92	Satin Storm DJT DAPSS 1	Let's Get Together/Free Your Mind (12". Artist not credited on labels)	40
92	Satin Storm ST 01	Sweat/Can't Wait/Can't Take No More/Tekno/Satin Storm/EBGB (12")	20
92	Satin Storm SSHC 2	What About What I Need /Drop That Bass/House Of My Dreams/Ram it (12", artist not credited on labels)	15
92	Satin Storm SSHC 3	Think I'm Going Out Of My Head/Unknown/What Do You Do? (12")	15
93	Satin Storm SSHC 4	Return Of The Blopblingers/Rough And Smooth & The Driven) (12")	10
93	Satin Storm SSHC 5	Come On, Get Together/I'm A Technician/He's On It, All Night Long (12")	10

SATISFACTION

(see also Mike Cotton Sound)

71	Decca F 13129	Love It Is/Cold Summer	10
71	Decca F 13207	Don't Rag The Lady/Gregory Shan't	10
71	Decca SKL 5075	SATISFACTION (LP, laminated front sleeve, blue/silver boxed label)	50

SATISFACTION

79	Live & Love LAP 005	SATISFACTION IN DUB (LP)	40

SATISFIERS

57	Vogue Coral Q 72247	Where'll I Be Tomorrow Night?/Come Away, Love	12
57	Vogue Coral LVA 9068	THE SATISFIERS (LP)	20

LIZZARD SATTAI

76	Trojan TRLS 138	LIZZARD (LP)	30

LONNIE SATTIN

56	Capitol CL 14552	Trapped (In The Web Of Love)/Your Home Can Be A Castle	6
56	Capitol CL 14638	High Steel/What Time Does The Sun Go Down?	5
57	Capitol CL 14771	I'll Never Stop Loving You/Whoo-Pie Shoo-Pie	5
58	Capitol CL 14831	Ring Around The Moon/My Heart's Your Home	5
60	Warner Bros WB 15	I'll Fly Away/Any More Than I	5

SATURNALIA

(see also Horse)

71	Matrix TRIX 1	MAGICAL LOVE (LP, picture disc with 3D labels, with booklet & ticket)	80
71	Matrix TRIX 1	MAGICAL LOVE (LP, allegedly copies in laminated sleeve, picture disc with 3D labels, with booklet & ticket)	500
73	Matrix TRIX 1	MAGICAL LOVE (LP, picture disc, reissue)	25

SATYR

79	Stardust STAR 001	Love Slide Boogie/Problem In The City	10

SAUCERMAN

(see also Kray Cherubs)

88	Fierce FRIGHT 029	Scatterbrain/Beyond Repair (12", p/s with inner, 1 side etched, 1,000 only)	8
89	Fierce FRIGHT 035	I Will Be King/Sid James Rules (withdrawn)	25
80s	Fierce	WRESTLING (12", sampler, withdrawn)	12

LARRY SAUNDERS

74	London HLU 10469	On The Real Side/Let Me Be The Special One	20
74	London HLU 10469	On The Real Side/Let Me Be The Special One (DJ copy)	40

MAHALIA SAUNDERS

71	Moodisc HME 112	Down The Aisle/IAN ROBINSON: Three For One	8
71	Upsetter US 374	Pieces Of My Heart/UPSETTERS: Version	10

TUPPER SAUSSY

63	London HAU 8127	DISCOVER TUPPER SAUSSY (LP)	15

LES SAUTERELLES

68	Decca F 22824	Heavenly Club/Dream Machine	45

SAVAGE

82	Ebony EBON 10	Ain't No Fit Place/China Run	8
83	Ebony EBON 12	LOOSE 'N' LETHAL (LP)	25
85	Zebra ZEB 4	HYPERACTIVE (LP)	12

EDNA SAVAGE

(see also Michael Holliday)

55	Parlophone MSP 6175	Stars Shine In Your Eyes/A Star Is Born	6
55	Parlophone MSP 6181	Candlelight/In The Wee Small Hours Of The Morning	6
55	Parlophone MSP 6189	Arrivederci Darling/Bella Notte	6
56	Parlophone MSP 6217	Tell Me, Tell Me, Tell Me That You Love Me/Please Hurry Home	6
56	Parlophone R 4226	My Prayer/Me 'n' You 'n' The Moon	6
56	Parlophone R 4253	Never Leave Me/Don't Ever Go (I Need You)	5
57	Parlophone R 4301	Me Head's In De Barrel/Five Iranges Four Apples	5
57	Parlophone R 4360	Let Me Love/Diano Marina	5

JOAN SAVAGE

57	Columbia DB 3929	Five Oranges, Four Apples/Bamboozled	5
57	Columbia DB 3968	With All My Heart/Love Letters In The Sand	5
57	Columbia DB 4039	Shake Me, I Rattle/Lula Rock-A-Hula	20
58	Columbia DB 4159	Hello Happiness, Goodbye Blues/Left Right Out Of My Heart	5

SAVAGE PENCIL

(see also Art Attacks, Kray Cherubs)

88	Blast First FU 3LP	PRESENTS ANGEL DUST: MUSIC FOR MOVIE BIKERS (LP, picture disc, 1,000 only)	12

SAVAGE RESURRECTION

68	Mercury MF 1027	Thing In E/Fox Is Sick	50
68	Mercury SMCL 20123	SAVAGE RESURRECTION (LP)	160

MINT VALUE £

SAVAGE ROSE

68	Polydor 184206	IN THE PLAIN (LP, red label)	40
69	Polydor 184316	TRAVELLIN' (LP, red label)	40
72	RCA Victor SF 8250	REFUGEE (LP, laminated front sleeve, orange label)	30
71	RCA Victor SF 8169	YOUR DAILY GIFT (LP, laminated front sleeve, orange label)	30

SAVAGES

(see also Soul Sounds, Screaming Lord Sutch, Circles, Tony Dangerfield & Thrills)

63	Decca DFE 8546	EVERYBODY SURF! WITH THE SURFIN' SAVAGES (EP)	200

TELLY SAVALAS

74	MCA 174	If/You And Me Against The World	5

JULIAN JAY SAVARIN

(see also Julian's Treatment)

73	Lyntone LYN 3426	I Am You/Kizeesh (Corgi Books sampler)	30
73	Birth RAB 2	WAITERS ON THE DANCE (LP, textured sleeve with insert)	250
73	Birth RAB 2	WAITERS ON THE DANCE (LP, textured sleeve without insert)	150
87	Five Hours Back TOCK 002	WAITERS ON THE DANCE (LP, reissue)	20

JIMMY SAVILE

(see also Vernons Girls)

62	Decca F 11493	Ahab The Arab/Very Unlikely	10
63	Decca F 11576	The Bosa Nova/Don't Do Anything I'd Like	10

RONNIE SAVOY

61	MGM MGM 1122	And The Heavens Cried/Big Chain	15
61	MGM MGM 1131	Bewitched/It's Gotta Be love	10

SAVOY BROWN (BLUES BAND)

(see also Warren Philips & The Rockets, Chris Youlden, Stone's Masonry, Jackie Lynton, Foghat)

66	Purdah 45-3503	I Tried/Can't Quit You Baby (as Savoy Brown's Blues Band)	250
67	Decca F 12702	Taste And Try, Before You Buy/Someday People (as Savoy Brown Blues Band)	20
68	Decca F 12797	Walking By Myself/Vicksburg Blues	12
69	Decca F 12843	Train To Nowhere/Tolling Bells	20
69	Decca F 12978	I'm Tired/Stay With Me Baby	30
70	Decca F 13019	A Hard Way To Go/Waiting In The Bamboo Grove	15
70	Decca F 13098	Poor Girl/Master Hare	12
71	Decca F 13247	Tell Mama/Let It Rock	12
73	Decca F 13372	So Tired/The Saddest Feeling	7
73	Decca F 13431	Coming Down Your Way/I Can't Find You	7
67	Decca LK 4883	SHAKE DOWN (LP, mono, unboxed logo label)	100
67	Decca SKL 4883	SHAKE DOWN (LP, stereo, unboxed logo label)	90
68	Decca LK 4925	GETTING TO THE POINT (LP, mono, unboxed logo label)	100
68	Decca SKL 4925	GETTING TO THE POINT (LP, stereo, unboxed logo label)	75
69	Decca LK 4994	BLUE MATTER (LP, mono, unboxed logo label)	60
69	Decca SKL 4994	BLUE MATTER (LP, stereo, unboxed logo label)	45
69	Decca LK 5013	A STEP FURTHER (LP, mono, unboxed logo label)	50
69	Decca SKL 5013	A STEP FURTHER (LP, stereo, unboxed logo label)	40
70	Decca LK 5043	RAW SIENNA (LP, mono, laminated gatefold sleeve, boxed logo label)	50
70	Decca SKL 5043	RAW SIENNA (LP, stereo, laminated gatefold sleeve, boxed logo label)	30
70	Decca SKL 5066	LOOKING IN (LP, 1st pressing, dull laminated gatefold sleeve)	50
70	Decca SKL 5066	LOOKING IN (LP, 2nd pressing, glossy laminated gatefold sleeve)	25
71	Decca TXS 104	STREET CORNER TALKING (LP, gatefold sleeve)	20
72	Decca TXS 107	HELLBOUND TRAIN (LP, gatefold sleeve)	15
73	Decca SKL 5152	LION'S SHARE (LP)	15
73	Decca TXS 112	JACK THE TOAD (LP)	18
74	Decca SKL 5186	BOOGIE BROTHERS (LP)	12

SAVWINKLE AND TURNERHOPPER

70	Pye 7N 17913	Your Mother Thinks I'm A Hoodlum/Dirtyin' My Thing	22

TOM SAWYER

(see also Unit 4 + 2)

69	CBS 4243	Cookbook/Gates	10

'ACE' DINNING SAX

59	Top Rank JAR 184	Mulholland Drive/My Love	15
59	Top Rank JAR 184	Mulholland Drive/My Love (78)	10

MIKE SAX & IDOLS

(see also Idols)

65	Mercury MF 886	My Little One/Come Back To Me	10

SAXON

63	Ace Of Clubs ACL 1173	MEET THE SAXONS (LP)	80

SAXON

(see also Son Of A Bitch)

79	Carrere SAM 109	Big Teaser/Stallions Of The Highway (12", promo only)	10
79	Carrere CAR 118	Big Teaser/Stallions Of The Highway (p/s)	7
79	Carrere CAR 129	Backs To The Wall/Militia Guard (p/s)	7
80	Carrere CAR 165	Suzy Hold On/Judgement Day (live)	6
81	Carrere CAR 180	And The Bands Played On/Hungry Years/Heavy Metal Thunder (7" picture disc)	6
83	Carrere CARP 284	Nightmare/Midas Touch (7" picture disc)	6
83	Carrere SAXON P1	Power And The Glory/See The Light Shining (live) (7" picture disc)	5
85	Parlophone RP 6103	Back On The Streets/Live Fast Die Young (7" shaped picture disc)	6
86	EMI EMIP 5587	Rock The Nations/747 (Strangers In The Night)/And The Bands Played On (7" shaped picture disc)	6
86	EMI 12EM15587	Rock The Nations/747 (Strangers In The Night)/And The Band Played On (12", clear vinyl)	8
88	EMI EMP 41	Ride Like The Wind/Red Alert (shaped 7" picture disc)	6

MINT VALUE £

91	Virgin DINSY 105	We Will Remember/Altar Of The Gods (shaped 7" picture disc, insert)	6
82	Carrere CAL 137	THE EAGLE HAS LANDED (LP, picture disc)	15
83	Carrere CAL 147	THE POWER AND THE GLORY (LP, picture disc)	15
84	Carrere CALP 200	CRUSADER (LP, picture disc)	15
85	Parlophone SAXONP 2	INNOCENCE IS NO EXCUSE (LP, picture disc)	15
87	EMI EMS 1163	DENIM AND LEATHER (LP, blue vinyl reissue)	15

AL SAXON

(see also Lana Sisters, Ella Stone & Moss)

58	Fontana H 138	Where The Black Eyed Susans Grow/She Screamed	6
58	Fontana H 164	The Day The Rains Came (Le Jour Ou La Pluie Viendra)/You're The Top-Cha	8
59	Fontana H 188	Chattanooga Choo-Choo/Chip Off The Old Block	5
59	Fontana H 205	Only Sixteen/I'm All Right, Jack	8
59	Fontana H 222	Linda Lu/Heart Of Stone	6
59	Fontana H 231	Marina/Me Without You	5
60	Fontana H 278	Blue-Eyed Boy/Don't Push Your Luck	10
61	Piccadilly 7N 35011	There I've Said It Again/You Came A Long Way From St. Louis	10
61	Piccadilly 7N 35021	Don't Get Around Much Anymore/Saturday Night	6
62	Parlophone R 4966	I Got A Girl/But I Do	5
63	Parlophone R 5016	The Man Who Broke The Bank At Monte Carlo/If You Want To Go To Dreamland	5
64	Mercury MF 801	Who Was That Girl?/All Night Long	5
64	Mercury MF 811	Another You/Hot And Bothered	5
72	Phoenix NIX 125	Beautiful/Count To Ten	10

SKY 'SUNLIGHT' SAXON

(see also Seeds)

87	Fierce FRIGHT 009	Dog=God (p/s, with badge, piece of shirt, sugar 'skycubes' & inserts)	20
84	Psycho PSYCHO 29	STARRY EYED (LP, clear vinyl)	20
84	Psycho PSYCHO 29	STARRY EYED (LP)	12
90s	Water NOXAS 39	DRAGON SLAYER (LP, multicoloured vinyl)	12

SKY SAXON & THE NEW SEEDS

90s	Expression EXP 777-3	In Love With Life/Starry Ride/Queen/Tired Of Being Poor	6

LINDA SAXONE

64	Pye 7N 15624	Love Is A Many Splendoured Thing/The Other Side Of The Street	10
65	Polydor BM 56015	I've Got To Say No/Another Day Another Night	6
65	Polydor BM 56032	Only Last Night/Lucky Girl	6

SAXONS

(see also Tornados)

65	Decca F 12179	Saxon War Cry/Click-Ete-Clack	60

JOHNNY SAYLES

66	Liberty LIB 12042	Deep Down In Your Heart/Anything For You	30

RAT SCABIES

(see also Damned, The Rat & The Whale, Pete Zear)

84	Paradiddle Music HIT 1	Let There Be Rats/Wiped Out/Drums Drums Drums (mail-order only, no p/s)	8

SCABS

79	Clubland Records SJP 799	Amory Building/Leave Me Alone/Don't Just Sit There/ U.R.E. (blue/black or red/black fold out 'envelope' p/s, 2 inserts)	40

SCAFFOLD

(see also McGough-McGear, Roger McGough, Mike McGear, Liverpool Scene, Grimms, John Gorman)

66	Parlophone R 5443	2 Day's Monday/3 Blind Jellyfish	10
66	Parlophone R 5548	Goodbat Nightman/A Long Strong Black Pudding	10
67	Parlophone R 5643	Thank U Very Much/Ide B The First	5
68	Parlophone R 5734	Lily The Pink/Buttons On Your Mind	5
68	Parlophone R 5679	Do You Remember?/Carry On Krow	8
68	Parlophone R 5703	1-2-3/Today	6
69	Parlophone R 5784	Charity Bubbles/Goose	6
69	Parlophone R 5812	Gin Gan Goolie/Liver Birds	8
70	Parlophone R 5847	All The Way Up/Please - Sorry	8
70	Parlophone R 5866	Busdreams/If I Could Start All Over Again	8
71	Parlophone R 5922	Do The Albert/Commercial Break	8
74	Warner Bros K 16400	Liverpool Lou/Ten Years On After Strawberry Jam	6
68	Parlophone PMC/PCS 7051	SCAFFOLD - LIVE AT QUEEN ELIZABETH HALL (LP, black/yellow label with "Sold in U.K..." text)	30
69	Parlophone PMC/PCS 7077	L THE P (LP, black/yellow label with "Sold in U.K..." text)	30
73	Island ILPS 9234	FRESH LIVER (LP, gatefold sleeve, pink rim palm tree label)	20

BOZ SCAGGS

(see also Steve Miller Band, Steve York's Camelo Pardalis)

69	Atlantic 588 205	BOZ SCAGGS (LP)	12
71	CBS 64248	MOMENTS (LP, plain orange label)	12

HARVEY SCALES & 7 SOUND

67	Atlantic 584 146	Get Down/Love It Is	15

SCAMPS

59	London HLW 8827	Petite Fleur/Naomi	12
62	Ace Of Clubs ACL 1116	TEEN DANCE AND SING ALONG PARTY (LP)	15

JOHNNY SCAR

85	Solomonic SM12 025	United Africa/Dub It In Africa (12")	50

SCARAB

80	Inferno HEADBANGER 1	Rock Night/Wicked Woman	30
84	Pharaoh PR-001	Poltergeist/Hell On Wheels (p/s)	50
03	Phoenix NWOBHM 7013	Rock Night/Wicked Woman (reissue, p/s, red vinyl 250 only, numbered)	10

SCARECROW

78	Spilt Milk SMFM 11278	SCARECROW LIVE (LP, numbered foldout sleeve with insert; beware of watermarked unnumbered copies)	30

MINT VALUE £

SCARLET ALIVE

82	Jive Alive JA001	THE TERMINAL JIVE AND SCARLET ALIVE EP (2 tracks on one side, p/s, insert)	15
82	S.R.R. SRR011	On Earth And In Heaven/Always	15

SCARLETS

64	Philips BF 1376	Let's Go/Tambourine Shake	6

CHARLES FRANCIS SCARRATT III

59	Felsted AF 113	Two Innocent Lovers/Lovemobile	6

SCARS

79	Fast Product FAST 8	Horrorshow/Adult-ery (p/s)	5
80	Pre PRE 005	Love Song/psychomodo (p/s)	12
81	Pre PRE 014	All About You/Author Author (p/s)	7
81	I.D. ID-1	Your Attention Please (gold vinyl flexidisc with ID magazine, issue 3)	8
81	Pre PREX 5	AUTHOR! AUTHOR! (LP)	12

SCENE

80	Inferno BEAT 2	I've Had Enough/Show 'Em Now (p/s)	12

SCENE

80	Hole In The Wall HS 1	Hey Girl/Reach The Top (p/s)	50

SCENE

(see also Diplomats)

83	Diamond DIA 001	Looking For A Love/Let Me Know (p/s)	8
85	Diamond DIA 003	Something That You Said/Stop-Go (p/s)	7
85	Diamond DIA 007	Good Lovin'/2 Plus 2 (with p/s)	15
85	Diamond DIA 007	Good Lovin'/2 Plus 2	5

SCEPTRES

69	Spark SRL 1006	What's The Matter With Juliet/Something's Coming Along	30

SCHADEL

66	Parlophone R5899	The Puppet Man/Oh What A Naughty Man	8
68	Pye 7N 17528	With The Sun In My Eyes/Goodbye Thimble Mill Lane	30
70	United Artists UAS 29114	SCHADEL NO.1 (LP) (gatefold)	12

JANNE SCHAFFER

74	Vertigo 6360 107	THE CHINESE (LP, 'spaceship' label)	15
75	Vertigo 6360 118	SECOND LP (LP, 'spaceship' label)	15

SCHEER

93	Son BUACD 293	Wish You Were Dead/Green Room Sex Kitten/Don't Know Why (p/s)	20

SCHEME

86	Scheme LP1	BLACK & WHITES (LP)	25
82	No Label SS001	SCHEME SONGS (EP, 500 only, 2 inserts)	30

MICHAEL SCHENKER

(see also McAuley Schenker Group, Michael Schenker Group, Scorpions, UFO)

94	EMI 724382861 1423	THE STORY OF MICHAEL SCHENKER (2-CD)	20

HANK SCHIFNER

69	Liberty LBF15244	Long John/How Or When	15

LALO SCHIFRIN

68	Dot DOT 103	Mission: Impossible/Jim On The Move	22
74	20th Century BTC 2150	Ape Shuffle (Theme From 'Planet Of The Apes')/Escape From Tomorrow	25
74	Warner Bros K16333	Theme From Enter The Dragon/The Big Battle	10
76	CTI CTSP 5	Jaws Theme/Quiet Village	5
77	CTI CTSP008	Theme From 'Most Wanted'/Roller Coaster	6
68	Dot (S)LPD 503	'MISSION: IMPOSSIBLE' - MUSIC FROM THE TV SERIES (LP, TV soundtrack)	40
69	Paramount SPFL 252	MORE 'MISSION: IMPOSSIBLE' (LP, TV soundtrack)	40
70s	Verve 2304 051	ROCK REQUIEM (LP)	12

SCHMETTERLINGE

77	Pye International 7N 25743	Boom Boom Boomerang/Mr Moneymaker's Music Show	10

TOBIAS SCHMIDT

96	Mosquito MSQ 06	THE FINGERPRINT EP (12", p/s)	15

ZAPPATTA SCHMIDT

(see also Equals, Eddy Grant)

70	President PT 318	You Got The Love/Someone In The Crowd	40
70	Torpedo TOR 28	Let's Do It Together/Hey Man. Why	25
71	President PTLS 1041	IT'S GONNA GET YOU (LP)	90

OLIVER LINDSEY SCHMITT

72	private pressing	GRAFFENSTADDEN (LP)	30

WOLFGANG SCHMITT

69	RCA 1301	The Girl From the Monmouth County/Country Girl	6

EBERHARD SCHOENER

(see also Police)

79	Harvest HAR 5196	Video Magic/Code Word Elvis (p/s)	8

SCHOLARS

64	Stagesound SDE 29370/1	THE SCHOLARS (EP, no p/s)	15

SCHOOL TIES

81	School Ties SCF 01	No Future	45

SCHOOL BOYS

(see also Bill Gentles)

63	Blue Beat BB 162	Little Boy Blue/PRINCE BUSTER: Money	40
63	Blue Beat BB 174	Little Dilly/The Joker (B-side actually by Prince Buster's Allstars)	40
64	Port-O-Jam PJ 4000	Dream Lover/I Want To Know	40

MINT VALUE £

SCHOOLERS

69	Doctor Bird DB 1170	Ugly Man (actually by Scorchers)/Whip Cracker (actually by Vincent Gordon)	40

SCHOOLGIRL BITCH

78	Garage!/Aerco AERS 102	Abusing The Rules/Thinking For Yourself (no p/s)	40
78	Garage!/Aerco AERS 102	Abusing The Rules/Thinking For Yourself (spray-painted p/s)	150
78	Garage!/Aerco AERS 102	Abusing The Rules/Thinking For Yourself ('gasmask' p/s)	100
78	Garage!/Aerco AERS 102	Abusing The Rules/Thinking For Yourself ('queen' p/s)	45

SCHOOL GIRLS

63	Blue Beat BB 168	Love Another Love/Little Keithie	20
63	Blue Beat BB 185	Live Up To Justice/Give Up	20
64	Blue Beat BB 214	Sing And Shout/Last Time	20
64	Blue Beat BB 263	Never Let You Go/BUSTER'S ALL STARS: Supercharge	80

SCHOOL MEALS

80s	Edible EAT 001	Headmaster (with insert, re-labelled Defendents)	20

SCHOOL OF CULTURE

91	White CS12 01	Detonate To Activate/Come On 33	70

DON SCHROEDER

62	Philips BF 3040033	Quicksand/My Kind Of Woman	10

JOHN SCHROEDER ORCHESTRA

65	Piccadilly 7N 35240	The Fugitive Theme/Don't Break The Heart Of Kimble (in p/s)	10
65	Piccadilly 7N 35240	The Fugitive Theme/Don't Break The Heart Of Kimble	6
65	Piccadilly 7N 35253	You've Lost That Lovin' Feeling/Funny How Love Can Be	6
66	Piccadilly 7N 35280	Ave Maria No Morro/Peter Popgunn	5
66	Piccadilly 7N 35285	Hungry For Love/Soul Destroyer	30
65	Piccadilly 7N 35271	Agent 00 Soul/Night Rider	30
66	Piccadilly 7N 35319	On The Ball (Theme For The World)/The Britannia March	15
67	Piccadilly 7N 35362	Soul For Sale/Loving You Girl	30
69	Pye 7N 17862	The Virgin Soldiers' March/Sweet Soul Talk	8
66	Piccadilly N(S)PL 38025	JOHN SCHROEDER'S WORKING IN THE SOULMINE (LP)	50
67	Piccadilly N(S)PL 38036	THE DOLLY CATCHER! (LP)	40
68	Marble Arch MAL 839	WORKING IN THE SOULMINE (LP, reissue)	25
71	Pye NSPL 18362	WITCHI-TAI-TO (LP, textured gatefold sleeve)	30
72	Polydor 2460 149	TV VIBRATIONS (LP)	20
71	Polydor 2460 134	DYLAN VIBRATIONS (LP)	20
73	Polydor 2460 188	WAR AND PEACE & OTHER TELEVISION THEMES (LP)	12

IVY SCHULMAN & BOWTIES

57	London HLN 8372	Rock, Pretty Baby/BOWTIES: Ever Since I Can Remember	50
57	London HLN 8372	Rock, Pretty Baby/BOWTIES: Ever Since I Can Remember (78)	35

KLAUS SCHULZE

(see also Tangerine Dream) (Voices Of)

74	Caroline CA 2003	BLACK DANCE (LP, gatefold, black/white/red 'twin' label)	15

(Voices Of) WALTER SCHUMANN

54	HMV 7M 229	Haunted House/I Only Have Eyes For You	8
55	HMV 7M 323	The Man From Laramie/Let Me Hear You Whisper	8

SCHUNGE

72	Regal Zonophone RZ 3066	Misty/Joseph Demanio	7
73	Regal Zonophone RZ 3077	Ballad Of A Simple Love/Enter The Violins	7
72	Regal Zono. SLRZ 1033	BALLAD OF A SIMPLE LOVE (LP, unlaminated front sleeve)	30
72	Regal Zono. SLRZ 1033	BALLAD OF A SIMPLE LOVE (LP, laminated front sleeve)	25

SCHWARTZENEGGER

94	Rugger Bugger SEEP 009	THE WAY THINGS ARE AND OTHER STORIES (LP)	20

SCIENCE POPTION

67	Columbia DB 8106	You've Got Me High/Back In Town	60

SCIENTIST

69	Amalgamated AMG 848	Professor In Action/SUPERSONICS: Reflections Of Don D	28

SCIENTIST

80	Greensleeves GREL 13	HEAVYWEIGHT DUB CHAMPION (LP)	25
80	JB JBLP 004	INTRODUCING (LP)	60
81	Jah Guidance VPRLP 1007	IN DUB (LP)	20
81	Starlight SLD 901	DUB LANDING (LP)	60
81	Greensleeves GREL 25	RIDS THE WORLD OF THE EVIL CURSE OF THE VAMPIRE (LP)	25
82	Greensleeves GREL 46	ENCOUNTERS PAC MAN (LP)	15
89	Tamoki Wambesi TWP 1022	INTERNATIONAL HEROES DUB (LP, with The Forces Of Music)	25

SCIENTIST & PRINCE JAMMY

82	Starlight SLDLP 903	DUB LANDING VOL 2 (LP)	20

SCIENTIST VERSUS PRINCE JAMMY

80	Greensleeves GRED 10	THE BIG SHOWDOWN 1980 (LP)	25

SCIENTIST V THE PROFESSOR

(see also Scientist)

83	Kingdom KVL 9015	DUB DUEL AT KING TUBBY'S (LP)	25

SCIENTISTS

85	Karbon KAR 007	You Only Live Twice/If It's The Last Thing I Do (p/s)	25
85	Karbon KAR 101 L	YOU GET WHAT YOU DESERVE (LP)	20
86	Karbon KAR 103 L	WEIRD LOVE (LP)	20
87	Karbon KAR 105 L	THE HUMAN JUKEBOX (LP)	20

SCIENTISTS OF SOUND

92	Bite It! BITE5	LIKE A SCIENTIST (EP, p/s)	8
96	Downlow DL3	Landmine Situation (12")	10

MINT VALUE £

SCISSOR FITS
79	Dubious DUB 1/SJP 793	TAUT? TENSE? ANGULAR? AND OTHER BRITISH RAIL SANDWICHES (EP, gatefold sleeve)	8

SCONEHEADS
81	Linden Soun LS 01	GO BUCKSKIN (EP, 700 pressed)	30

SCOOP
80	Sharp POINT 1	You Can Do It/Disco/My Friend Tony/Anonymity (p/s)	50

SCORCHED EARTH
85	Carrere CAR 342	Tomorrow Never Comes/Questions (promo only)	35
85	Carrere CART 342	Tomorrow Never Comes/Questions/So Long/Where Do We Go From Here (12", initial black sleeve)	70
85	Carrere CART 342	Tomorrow Never Comes/Questions/So Long/Where Do We Go From Here (12", later red sleeve with insert)	60

ERROL SCORCHER
78	Ballistic UAS 30198	RASTAFIRE (LP, with the Revolutionaries)	25

SCORCHERS
(see also Neville Hinds)

69	Camel CA 17	Hold On Tight/THE ROYALS: 100 Lbs Of Clay	35
69	Duke DU 26	Hear Ya/VIBRATORS: Live Life	15

SCORE
66	Decca F 12527	Please Please Me/Beg Me	150

SCORN
95	Earache SCORN 001	ELLIPSIS (5 x 12" box set)	18

SCORPION & BORIS GARDINER HAPPENING
73	Dragon DRA 1002	Deadly Sting/BORIS GARDINER HAPPENING: Boing Boing	5

SCORPIONS (Germany)
(see also Michael Schenker, Michael Schenker Group, UFO)

77	RCA PB 5556	He's A Woman, She's A Man/Suspender Love	8
79	Harvest HAR 5185	Is Anybody There?/Another Piece Of Meat (12", p/s)	10
79	Harvest 12HAR 5188	Love Drive/Coast To Coast (12", p/s)	8
79	RCA PC 9402	All Night Long/Fly To The Rainbow/Speedy's Coming/In Trance (12", p/s)	8
84	Harvest 12HARP 5231	Big City Nights/Bad Boys Running Wild (12" picture disc, die-cut sleeve)	12
85	Harvest 12HAR 5232	Still Loving You/Holiday/Big City Night (12", p/s)	8
85	Harvest 12HAR 5232	Still Loving You/Holiday/Big City Night (12", picture disc)	8
91	Vertigo VERXP 54	Wind Of Change (12", etched red vinyl)	8
91	Vertigo VERXP 54	Wind Of Change/Restless Nights/Hit Between The Nights/ Blackout (live) (12", picture disc)	8
91	Vertigo VERX 58	Wind Of Change (12", white vinyl, 3-D sleeve)	12
93	Mercury MERX 395	Under The Same Sun/Ship Of Fools/Partners In Crime (12", yellow vinyl)	8
79	Harvest LP SHSP 4097	LOVE DRIVE (LP)	18
80	Harvest SHSP 4113	ANIMAL MAGNETISM (LP)	15
82	H.M. worldwide HMILP 2	LONESOME CROW (LP, "castle" cover, clear vinyl)	20
82	H.M. Worldwide HMILP 2	LONESOME CROW (LP, "castle" cover, black vinyl)	15
82	H.M. Worldwide HMIPD 2	LONESOME CROW (LP, picture disc, re-issue)	15
82	Harvest SHVL 823	BLACKOUT (LP, black or green print on label)	15
88	Harvest SHSPP 4125	SAVAGE AMUSEMENT (LP, picture disc, with lyric sheet)	15

SCORPIONS (Jamaica)
(see also Bill Gentles, Lloyd Jackson)

72	Green Door GD 4019	Breaking Your Heart/IN CROWD BAND: Breaking Your Heart Version	6

SCORPIONS (U.K.)
61	Parlophone R 4740	(Ghost) Riders In The Sky/Torquay	20
61	Parlophone R 4768	Rockin' At The Phil/Scorpio	20

COLIN SCOT
(see also Peter Hammill, Peter Gabriel)

71	United Artists UP 35216	Hey! Sandy/Nite People	5
73	Warner Bros K 16330	Call Me Mr Blue/It's Gonna Be Alright	7
71	United Artists UAG 29154	COLIN SCOT WITH FRIENDS (LP, laminated gatefold sleeve, with Peter Hammill & Peter Gabriel)	25
73	Warner Bros. KY6236	JUST ANOTHER CLOWN (LP, gatefold sleeve)	12

WINSTON SCOTLAND
(see also Bunny Flip, Big Youth, Bongo Les, Lennox Brown, Dennis Alcapone)

72	Green Door GD 4027	My (Girl) Little Filly/BUNNY BROWN: My Girl	7
72	Punch PH 100	Butter Cup/RONALD WILSON: I Care	7

SCOTS OF ST. JAMES
(see also Hopscotch, Forever More, Five Day Rain)

66	Go AJ 111404	Gypsy/Tic Toc	200
67	Spot JW 1	Timothy/Eiderdown Clown	300

ANDY SCOTT
(see also Sweet, Elastic Band, Mayfield's Mule)

75	RCA RCA 2629	Lady Starlight/Where D'Ya Go (p/s)	12
83	Static TAK 10	Krugerrands/Face (p/s)	8
84	Static TAK 24	Let Her Dance/Suck It And See (p/s)	10
84	Static TAK 24-12	Let Her Dance (Full Version)/(Instrumental)/Suck It And See (12", p/s)	10
84	Static TAK 31	Invisible/Never Too Young (clear vinyl, stickered PVC sleeve)	12
84	Statik TAK 31-12	Invisible (Single Version)/(Instrumental)/Invisible (Extended Version)/ Never Too Young (12", clear vinyl, stickered PVC sleeve)	12

ANITA SCOTT
61	Columbia DB 4623	A Million And One Tears/Come On And Dance With Me	15

MINT VALUE £

ARTIE SCOTT ORCHESTRA

70 Major Minor MM 670 March Of The Skinheads/Love At First Sight. . . . 7

BILLY SCOTT

58 London HLU 8565 You're The Greatest/That's Why I Was Born 20
60 Top Rank JAR 270 Carole/Stairway To The Stairs 5

BOBBY SCOTT

70 Reflection RS2 Witness To A War/I Wish I Could Walk Away 6

BOBBY SCOTT

56 London HL 8254 Chain Gang/Shadrack 40
55 London Jazz LZ-N 14001 BOBBY SCOTT TRIO (10" LP) 15

BRUCE SCOTT

65 Mercury MF 857 I Made An Angel Cry/Don't Say Goodbye To Me 25
65 MGM MGM 1291 Once A Thief Twice A Thief/So Much To Live For 7

BUNNY SCOTT

75 KLIK KLP 9004 TO LOVE SOMEBODY (LP) 15

DEREK SCOTT ORCHESTRA

63 Pye 7N 15500 Hancock's Tune/Spying Tonight 5
67 Philips BF 1568 Honey Lane/Song Without Words 5

FREDDIE SCOTT

63 Colpix PX 692 Hey Girl/The Slide 35
63 Colpix PX 709 I Got A Woman/Brand New World 35
67 London HLZ 10103 Are You Lonely For Me/Where Were You 15
67 London HLZ 10123 Cry To Me/No One Could Ever Love You 15
67 London HLZ 10139 Am I Grooving You?/Never You Mind 10
67 London HLZ 10172 He Ain't Give You None/Run Joe 10
69 Roulette RO 509 Sugar Sunday/Johnny's Hill 6
71 Jay Boy BOY 34 Just Like A Flower/Spanish Harlem 10
72 Jay Boy BOY 59 Are You Lonely For Me Baby/The Woman Of My Love 10
70s Upfront UP 1 The Great If/Deep In The Night 10
71 Joy JOYS 215 ARE YOU LONELY FOR ME (LP) 25

HAZEL SCOTT

53 Capitol LC 6607 LATE SHOW (10" LP) 20

JACK SCOTT (& CHANTONES)

58 London HLU 8626 My True Love/Leroy 12
58 London HLU 8626 My True Love/Leroy (78) 15
58 London HLL 8765 With Your Love/Geraldine (as Jack Scott with Chantones) 20
58 London HLL 8765 With Your Love/Geraldine (as Jack Scott with Chantones) (78) 15
59 London HLL 8804 Goodbye Baby/Save My Soul (as Jack Scott with Chantones) 20
59 London HLL 8804 Goodbye Baby/Save My Soul (as Jack Scott with Chantones) (78) 20
59 London HL 7069 Goodbye Baby/Save My Soul (export issue) 20
59 London HLL 8851 I Never Felt Like This/Bella 20
59 London HLL 8851 I Never Felt Like This/Bella (78) 40
59 London HLL 8912 The Way I Walk/Midgie (triangular or round centre) 25
59 London HLL 8912 The Way I Walk/Midgie (78) 30
59 London HLL 8970 There Comes A Time/Baby Marie (triangular or round centre) 25
59 London HLL 8970 There Comes A Time/Baby Marie (78) 40
60 Top Rank JAR 280 What In The World's Come Over You/Baby, Baby 7
60 Top Rank JAR 375 Burning Bridges/Oh, Little One 10
60 Top Rank JAR 419 Cool Water/It Only Happened Yesterday 10
60 Top Rank JAR 524 Patsy/Old Time Religion 10
61 Top Rank JAR 547 Is There Something On Your Mind/Found A Woman 10
61 Capitol CL 15200 A Little Feeling/Now That I 10
61 Capitol CL 15216 My Dream Come True/Strange Desire 15
62 Capitol CL 15236 Steps 1 And 2/One Of These Days 15
62 Capitol CL 15261 I Can't Hold Your Letters In My Arms/Sad Story 15
63 Capitol CL 15302 All I See Is Blue/Meo Myo 15
59 London RE-I 1205 MY TRUE LOVE (EP, initial triangular centre) 90
59 London RE-I 1205 MY TRUE LOVE (EP, later round centre) 60
61 Top Rank JKP 3002 WHAT IN THE WORLD'S COME OVER YOU (EP) 40
61 Top Rank JKP 3011 I REMEMBER HANK WILLIAMS (EP) 50
58 London HA-L 2156 JACK SCOTT (LP) 100
60 Top Rank BUY 034 I REMEMBER HANK WILLIAMS (LP) 40
60 Top Rank 25-024 WHAT IN THE WORLD'S COME OVER YOU (LP) 50
61 Top Rank 35-109 THE SPIRIT MOVES ME (LP) 60
64 Capitol T 2035 BURNING BRIDGES (LP, mono) 60
64 Capitol ST 2035 BURNING BRIDGES (LP, stereo) 70

JANET SCOTT & JACKIE RAE

(see also Jackie Rae)

60 Fontana STFE 8009 SWEET TALK (EP, also mono TFE 17203) 12
60 Fontana STFL 533 WE LOVE LIFE! (LP, also mono TFL 5102) 15

JIMMY SCOTT

69 Revolution REV 002 Ob-La-Di, Ob-La-Da/Story Part 2 - Allulo & Doh 8

JOHN SCOTT

73 JSD JSD 100 JOHN SCOTT DEMONSTRATION RECORD (LP, beware, many warped) 80

JOHN SCOTT

60 Parlophone R 4697 Hi-Flutin' Boogie/Peace Pipe 6
65 Parlophone R 5333 Sailing By/The Song Of The Cuckoo (as Johnny Scott) 7
65 Parlophone R 5380 A Study In Terror/Punjab 8
67 Polydor 56184 Rocket To The Moon Theme/The Long Duel Theme 10
68 Spark SRL 1008 Amsterdam Affair Theme/Kathleen 8
66 Columbia SX 6026 LONDON SWINGS (LP) 15
67 Columbia S(C)X 6149 COMMUNICATION (LP) 30

MINT VALUE £

JUDI SCOTT

68	Page One POF 066	Billy Sunshine/Happy Song	25

JUDY SCOTT

57	Brunswick 05687	The Game Of Love (A-One And A-Two)/With All My Heart	10
57	Brunswick 05704	Parlour Piano Theme/A Tender Word	8

JULIAN SCOTT

61	Columbia DB 4571	My Steady Date/So Tired	7

LINDA SCOTT

60	Columbia DB 4638	I've Told Every Little Star/Three Guesses	8
61	Columbia DB 4692	Don't Bet Money, Honey/Starlight Starbright	15
61	Columbia DB 4748	I Don't Know Why/It's All Because	10
61	Columbia DB 4829	Count Every Star/Land Of Stars	10
62	Pye International 7N 25146	Never In A Million Years/Through The Summer	15
63	London HLR 9802	Let's Fall In Love/I Know It, You Know It	15
61	Columbia 33SX 1386	STARLIGHT, STARBRIGHT (LP)	85

LINDA SCOTT

69	CBS 4528	The Composer/You Made A Fool Out Of Me	15
69	CBS 4246	First Of All/The Answer's In My Eyes	5

MAUREEN SCOTT

63	HMV POP 1184	He's So Near/Ugly Bug Ball	6

McBEAN SCOTT & CHAMPIONS

70	Jackpot JP 744	Top Of The World/LARRY LAWRENCE & CHAMPIONS: Everybody Reggae	8

MIKE SCOTT

65	Mercury MF 906	I Am A Rock/I'm Gonna Be Somebody Someday	6

MIKE SCOTT

(see also Waterboys)

95	Chrysalis CHR 6108	BRING'EM ALL IN (LP, gatefold with inner)	15

NEIL SCOTT

61	Pye International 7N 25096	Bobby/I Haven't Found It With Another	8

NICKY SCOTT

(see also Diane Ferraz & Nicky Scott)

67	Immediate IM 044	Big City/Everything's Gonna Be Alright	50
67	Immediate IM 045	Backstreet Girl/Chain Reaction	50
69	Pye 7N 17688	Honey Pie/No More Tomorrow	7

PEGGY SCOTT

(see also Peggy Scott & Jo Jo Benson)

69	Polydor 56722	Every Little Bit Hurts/You Can Never Get Something For Nothing	8
79	Pinnacle PIN 73	You've Got It All/Let Me Unite You (p/s)	5

PEGGY SCOTT & JO JO BENSON

(see also Peggy Scott)

68	Polydor 56745	Lover's Holiday/Here With Me	10
69	Polydor 56750	Pickin' Wild Mountain Berries/Pure Love And Pleasure	8
69	Polydor 56761	Soulshake/We Were Made For Each Other	10
69	Polydor 56773	We Got Our Own Bag/I Want To Love You Babe	8
71	Atlantic 2091 066	I Thank You/Spreadin' Love	5
69	Polydor 583 731	SOULSHAKE (LP)	25
70	Polydor 583 756	LOVER'S HEAVEN (LP)	25

ROBIN SCOTT

(see also Mighty Baby, M)

69	Head HDS 4003	The Sailor/Sound Of The Rain	60
69	Head HDLS 6003	WOMAN FROM THE WARM GRASS (LP, textured sleeve with insert, yellow/black label)	350
07	Sunbeam SBBLP 5009	WOMAN FROM THE WARM GRASS (LP, reissue)	15

RONNIE SCOTT

(see also Jazz Couriers, Tubby Hayes, Dizzy Reece)

54	Esquire 10-335	Night And Day	10
56	Decca FJ 10712	Basie Talks/Flying Home (as Ronnie Scott Orchestra)	8
57	Tempo A 153	I'll Take Romance/Speak Low (as Ronnie Scott New Quintet)	35
55	Esquire EP 31	RONNIE SCOTT ORCHESTRA (EP)	20
55	Esquire EP 51	RONNIE SCOTT QUARTET (EP)	20
55	Esquire EP 61	RONNIE SCOTT ORCHESTRA (EP)	20
55	Esquire EP 65	RONNIE SCOTT QUINTET (EP)	10
56	Esquire EP 81	RONNIE SCOTT ORCHESTRA (EP)	20
56	Esquire EP 85	RONNIE SCOTT ORCHESTRA (EP)	25
56	Esquire EP 95	RONNIE SCOTT ORCHESTRA (EP)	20
56	Tempo EXA 45	RONNIE SCOTT BLOWS WITH THE DIZZY REECE QUARTET (EP)	80
52	Esquire 20-006	RONNIE SCOTT QUINTET (10" LP)	80
54	Esquire 32-001	THE RONNIE SCOTT JAZZ CLUB VOLUME 1 (LP)	50
54	Esquire 32-002	THE RONNIE SCOTT JAZZ CLUB VOLUME 2 (LP)	50
54	Esquire 32-003	THE RONNIE SCOTT JAZZ CLUB VOLUME 3 (LP)	50
54	Esquire 32-006	THE RONNIE SCOTT JAZZ CLUB VOLUME 4 (LP)	50
56	Decca LF 1261	AT THE ROYAL FESTIVAL HALL (10" LP)	45
57	Philips BBL 7153	PRESENTING THE RONNIE SCOTT SEXTET (LP)	80
66	Fontana TL 5332	THE NIGHT IS SCOTT AND YOU'RE SO SWINGABLE (LP)	40
69	CBS Realm Jazz 523661	LIVE AT RONNIE SCOTT'S (LP)	25
74	RCA Victor LPL1	SCOTT AT RONNIE'S (LP)	20
77	Pye NSPL 18542	SERIOUS GOLD (LP)	15

SHIRLEY SCOTT

66	Transatlantic PR 7205	HIP SOUL (LP)	18
69	Atlantic 588 175	SOUL SONG (LP)	15
71	Chess 6310 109	MYSTICAL LADY (LP)	15

MINT VALUE £

SIMON SCOTT (& LE ROYS)
(see also Le Roys)

64 Parlophone R 5164 — Move It Baby/What Kind Of Woman (with Le Roys) 15
64 Parlophone R 5207 — My Baby's Got Soul/MIdnight (with Le Roys) 12
65 Parlophone R 5298 — Tell Him I'm Not Home (as Simon Scott & All Nite Workers)/Heart Cry 18
69 Polydor 56355 — Brave New World/I'm The Universe 40

TERRY SCOTT
62 Parlophone R 4967 — My Brother/Don't Light The Fire 'Til After Santa's Gone 10
66 Pye 7N 17093 — Juanita Banana/I Like Birds 5
76 DJM DJS 665 — A Bed Full Of Foreigners/Nicholas The Circus Clown (with June Whitfield) 5

TOM SCOTT
77 Epic EPC 5589 — Gotcha (Theme From 'Starsky & Hutch')/Smoothin' On Down 12

RAMBLIN' TOMMY SCOTT
54 Parlophone CMSP 15 — Ain't Love Grand/What Do You Know - I Love Her (export issue) 20

TOMMY SCOTT
62 Decca F 11474 — Angela/Did You (as Jay & Tommy Scott) 6
64 Decca F 11839 — Who Will It Be?/If It's Me That You Want 5
64 Decca F 11942 — Wrap Your Troubles In Dreams/Blueberry Hill 5

TONY SCOTT
69 Escort ES 805 — What Am I To Do/Bring Back That Smile 10

GIL SCOTT-HERON (& BRIAN JACKSON)
73 Philips 6073 705 — Lady Day And John Coltrane/When You Are Who You Are (with Pretty Purdie & The Playboys) 20
78 Arista ARIST 169 — The Bottle (live)/Hello Sunday, Hello Road 8
78 Arista ARIST 169 — The Bottle (live)/Hello Sunday, Hello Road (12") 20
79 Inferno HEAT 23 — The Bottle (Drunken Mix)/The Bottle (Sober Mix) (with Brian Jackson) 10
79 Inferno HEAT 23-12 — The Bottle (Drunken Mix)/The Bottle (Sober Mix) (12", with Brian Jackson) 15
73 Philips 6369 415 — PIECES OF A MAN (LP) 35
74 RCA SF 8428 — THE REVOLUTION WILL NOT BE TELEVISED (LP) 25
75 Arista ARTY 106 — FIRST MINUTES OF A NEW DAY (LP) 15
76 Arista DARTY 1 — IT'S YOUR WORLD (LP, with Brian Jackson) 30

MICHELLE SCOTTI
64 Philips BF 1384 — Little Drummer Boy/Lonely Lonely Lonely 6

SCOTTY (David Scott)
(see also Lloyd Charmers, Joe White)

70 Songbird SB 1044 — Sesame Street/CRYSTALITES: Version 20
71 Duke DU 106 — Donkey Skank (with Tennors)/MURPHY'S ALLSTARS: Version 15
71 Songbird SB 1049 — Riddle I This/Musical Chariot 12
71 Songbird SB 1051 — Jam Rock Style/Jam Rock Style Version (with Crystalites) 10
71 Songbird SB 1056 — Penny For Your Song/CRYSTALITES: Version 10
72 Songbird SB 1080 — Clean Race/CRYSTALITES: Version Train 10
72 Harry J. HJ 6642 — Skank In Bed/BONGO HERMAN: African Breakfast 8
73 Count Shelley CS 036 — Salvation Train/KEN PARKER: Message To Mary 8
71 Trojan TRL 33 — SCHOOLDAYS (LP) 45

SCRAPING FOETUS OFF THE WHEEL
(see also Foetus, You've Got Foetus On Your Breath, Philip & His Foetus Vibrations, Foetus Corruptus, Foetus Inc, Foetus Uber Frisco)

80s Womb 12 — Ramrod/Boxhead/Smut 5
81 Womb WOMB-OYBL-2 — HOLE (LP, gatefold sleeve with lyrics, also listed as FDL 3) 25

SCRAPYARD
58 Abbey APR 168 — RECIPRICAL RHUMBAS (LP, private press, 250 copies, with insert) 200

SCRATCH ACID
87 Fundamental HOLY 2 — BESERKER (LP) 20

SCREAMING DEAD
82 Skull DEAD 1 — Valley Of The Dead/Schoolgirl Junkie (p/s) 8
83 Skull DEAD 2 — Paint It Black 10
83 No Future OI 25 — NIGHT CREATURES EP (12") 10

DELTON SCREECHIE
80 Kim KIM 18 — My Black Girl/Diamond & Pearl/B DONALDSON & U BLACK : You Are Mine (12") 15
80 Moa Anbessa MA004 — She Is My Woman/Woman Version (12") 15
81 Moa Anbessa Intl MALP 001 — LIVING IN THE GHETTO (LP) 25
81 Moa Anbessa Intl MALP 002 — SUFFERING IN THE GHETTO (LP) 30

SCREECHING WEASEL
88 Wet Spots WETLP 005 — BOOGADA BOOGADA BOOGADA (LP) 25
88 What Goes On GOES ON 18 — SCREECHING WEASEL (LP, with insert) 20

SCREEMER
76 Bell Bell 1483 — Interplanetary Twist/Billy 10

SCREEN
95 Muzic W'out Control MWC 021 — I Wait For You (Sweep Sweep Mix)/I Wait For You (Radio Sweep Mix)/ I Wait For You (Pink Noize Mix)/ I Wait For You (T Rex Mix) (12', p/s) 60

SCREEN IDOLS
79 Cobra COB 2 — Blindman/Hit Me Where It Hurts (P/S) 10

SCRITTI POLITTI
78 St. Pancras SCRIT 1 — Skank Bloc Bologna/Is And Ought Of The Western World/ 28.8.78 (photocopied stapled foldout p/s, hand-stamped white labels) 10
79 Rough Trade RT 027T — 4 A SIDES: Doubt Beat/Confidences/Bibbly O'Tek/P.A.s (12" EP) 10
79 Rough Trade — Songs To Remember/The Cassette Interview (cassette, with 12-page booklet & 2 photos, promo only) 10

MINT VALUE £

SCROTUM POLES

79	Scrotum Poles ERECT 1	Revelation: Why Don't You Come Out Tonight?/Night Train/ Pick The Cat's Eyes Out/Helicopter Honeymoon/Radio Tay (handwritten labels, 2 p/s designs, with insert)	120
79	Scrotum Poles ERECT 1	Revelation: Why Don't You Come Out Tonight?/Night Train/ Pick The Cat's Eyes Out/Helicopter Honeymoon/Radio Tay (handwritten labels, 2 p/s designs, without insert)	100
80s	One-Tone ERECT 1	AUCHMITHY CALLING (cassette)	12

SCRUBS

86	Anubis ANU 003	Battle (p/s)	15
87	Flicknife FLS 035	Time For You (p/s)	10

SCRUGG

(see also Floribunda Rose, John T. Kongos)

68	Pye 7N 17451	I Wish I Was Five/Everyone Can See	70
68	Pye 7N 17551	Lavender Popcorn/Sandwichboard Man	50
69	Pye 7N 17656	Will The Real Geraldine Please Stand Up/Only George	80

EARL SCRUGGS

(see also Flatt & Scruggs, Byrds)

72	CBS 64777	EARL SCRUGGS: HIS FAMILY AND FRIENDS (LP, with Byrds, Joan Baez, Bob Dylan, etc.)	15

IRENE SCRUGGS

50s	Poydras 80	You've Got What I Want/My Back To The Wall	8

MR. JOHNNY SEA

60s	Fontana FJL 315	EVERYBODY'S FAVOURITE (LP)	15

SEA & CAKE

(see also Tortoise)

94	Rough Trade THRILL 021	SEA & CAKE (LP)	20

SEA-DERS

(see also Cedars)

67	Decca F 22576	Thanks A Lot/Undecidedly	80
67	Decca DFE-R 8674	THE SEA-DERS (EP, export issue)	250

DAVE SEALEY

69	DJM DJS 210	Picking Up The Pieces/I Can't Go On Living Without You	6

MILT SEALEY TRIO

60s	Duc. Thompson DEP 95017	MILTON SEALEY AND KANSAS FIELDS (EP)	8

PHIL SEAMAN

68	Verve (S)VLP 9220	PHIL SEAMAN NOW... LIVE (LP)	150
60s	Decibel BSN 103	PHIL SEAMAN STORY (LP)	50
60s	Saga OPP 102	MEETS EDDIE GOMEZ (LP)	100
74	77 Records 77 SEU 12/53	PHIL ON DRUMS (LP)	45

SEARCHERS

(see also Tony Jackson & Vibrations, Chris Curtis, Pasha)

SINGLES

63	Pye 7N 15533	Sweets For My Sweet/It's All Been A Dream	6
63	Philips BF 1274	Sweet Nuthins/What'd I Say	12
63	Pye 7N 15566	Sugar And Spice/Saints And Searchers (dark maroon label)	12
63	Pye 7N 15566	Sugar And Spice/Saints And Searchers (lighter pink label)	6
64	Pye 7N 15594	Needles And Pins/Saturday Night Out	5
64	Pye 7N 15630	Don't Throw Your Love Away/I Pretend I'm With You	5
64	Pye 7N 15670	Someday We're Gonna Love Again/No One Else Could Love You	5
64	Pye 7N 15694	When You Walk In The Room/I'll Be Missing You	7
64	Pye 7N 15739	What Have They Done To The Rain/This Feeling Inside (maroon label)	7
64	Pye 7N 15739	What Have They Done To The Rain/This Feeling Inside (lighter pink label)	5
65	Pye 7N 15794	Goodbye My Love/Till I Met You	6
65	Pye 7N 15878	He's Got No Love/So Far Away	8
65	Pye 7N 15950	When I Get Home/I'm Never Coming Back	10
65	Pye 7N 15992	Take Me For What I'm Worth/Too Many Miles (in export p/s)	25
65	Pye 7N 15992	Take Me For What I'm Worth/Too Many Miles	8
66	Pye 7N 17094	Take It Or Leave It/Don't Hide It Away	10
66	Pye 7N 17170	Have You Ever Loved Somebody/It's Just The Way	12
67	Pye 7N 17225	Popcorn, Double Feature/Lovers	20
67	Pye 7N 17308	Western Union/I'll Cry Tomorrow	15
67	Pye 7N 17424	Secondhand Dealer/Crazy Dreams	65
68	Liberty LBF 15159	Umbrella Man/Over The Weekend	50
69	Liberty LBF 15340	Kinky Kathy Abernathy/Suzanna	70
71	RCA RCA 2057	Desdemona/The World Is Waiting For Tomorrow	15
71	RCA RCA 2139	Love Is Everywhere/And A Button	10
72	RCA RCA 2231	Sing Singer Sing/Come On Back To Me	10
72	RCA RCA 2248	Needles And Pins/When You Walk In The Room/Come On Back To Me	10
72	RCA RCA 2288	Vahevala/Madman	15
73	RCA RCA 2330	Solitaire/Spicks And Specks	6
79	Sire SIR 4029	Hearts In Her Eyes/Don't Hang On (p/s)	10
80	Sire SIR 4036	It's Too Late/This Kind Of Love Affair (p/s)	7
81	Sire SIR 4046	Love's Melody/Changing (p/s)	12
81	Sire SIR 4049	Another Night/Back To The War (p/s)	10
80s	private pressing	Don't Make Promises	10
80s	private pressing	Four Strong Winds	10

EPs

63	Pye NEP 24177	AIN'T GONNA KISS YA	12
63	Pye NEP 24183	SWEETS FOR MY SWEET (some copies with white & maroon label)	15
64	Pye NEP 24184	HUNGRY FOR LOVE	20
64	Pye NEP 24201	THE SEARCHERS PLAY THE SYSTEM	15

MINT VALUE £

64 Pye NEP 24204 WHEN YOU WALK IN THE ROOM 20
65 Pye NEP 24218 BUMBLE BEE 20
65 Pye NEP 24222 SEARCHERS '65 30
65 Pye NEP 24228 FOUR BY FOUR 35
66 Pye NEP 24263 TAKE ME FOR WHAT I'M WORTH 100

LPs

63 Pye NPL 18086 MEET THE SEARCHERS 30
63 Pye NPL 18089 SUGAR AND SPICE 20
64 Pye NPL 18092 IT'S THE SEARCHERS 25
65 Pye NPL 18111 SOUNDS LIKE SEARCHERS 25
65 Pye NPL 18120 TAKE ME FOR WHAT I'M WORTH 40
67 Marble Arch MAL 640 SMASH HITS VOL. 1 12
67 Marble Arch MAL(S) 673 SMASH HITS VOL. 2 (mono/stereo) 12
72 RCA SF 8289 SECOND TAKE 18
79 Sire SRK 6082 SEARCHERS 15
80 Sire SRK 6086 THE SEARCHERS 12
81 Sire SRK 3523 PLAY FOR TODAY 12
83 PRT DOW 11 LOVE LIES BLEEDING (10") 12

SEARGENT SMILEY RAGS

70 Decca F13088 Smoke Smoke/Hey Na I Think I Love You 12

SEARS

84 Bluurg FISH 9 IF ONLY? (LP) 15

SEA STONE

82 Plankton 02 AGAINST THE TIDE (EP, foldout sleeve) 40
78 Plankton PKN 101 MIRRORED DREAMS (LP, with insert) 80

SEATHROUGH

73 private pressing LALA LAPLA (LP) 40

B.B. SEATON (HORACE SEATON)

(see also Bibby, Winston & Bibby, Gaylads, Messengers)

63 Island WI 123 I'm So Glad/Tell Me 30
64 R&B JB 143 Hold On/LESTER STERLING: Peace And Love 30
72 Big BG 336 I Want Justice/RUPIE EDWARD'S ALL STARS: Justice (Version) 8
72 Bullet BU 514 I Miss My Schooldays/CONSCIOUS MINDS: School Days - Version 5
72 Camel CA 100 Lean On Me/NOW GENERATION: Samba Pati 8
72 Pama PM 864 I Want Justice/RUPIE EDWARD'S ALL STARS: Justice - Version 8
72 Pama Supreme PS 374 Sweet Caroline/Eleanor Rigby 5
73 Trojan TRLS 59 THE THIN LINE BETWEEN LOVE AND HATE (LP) 20

SEA TRAIN

(see also Blues Project, Old & In The Way)

68 A&M AMS 737 Let The Duchess Know/As I Lay Losing 5
69 A&M AMLS 941 SEA TRAIN (LP) 25
71 Capitol EA-ST 659 SEA TRAIN (LP) 18
72 Capitol EA-ST 829 MARBLEHEAD MESSENGER (LP, gatefold sleeve) 15
73 Warner Bros K 46222 WATCH (LP) 15

SEA URCHINS

87 Kvatch KVATCH 001/ Clingfilm/GROOVE FARM: Baby Blue Marine (flexidisc, 1,000 only, 500 in p/s) 6
87 Sha La La Ba Ba Ba Ba 5 Summershine/ORCHIDS: From This Day (flexidisc, 2,500 only, 1,000 with p/s) 15
87 Sha La La Ba Ba Ba Ba 5 Summershine/ORCHIDS: From This Day (flexidisc, 2,500 only, no p/s) 6
87 Sarah SARAH 001 Pristine Christine/Sullen Eyes/Everglades (foldaround p/s with 14" x 10" poster in poly bag, 1,600 only) 70
88 Sarah SARAH 008 Solace/Please Rain Fall (foldaround p/s in poly bag) 20
89 Fierce FRIGHT 032 30.10.88 (live) (1-sided, p/s) 10
91 Cheree CHEREE 15 Please Don't Cry/Time Is All I've Seen (die-cut company sleeve) 7

JOHN SEBASTIAN

54 London HL 8029 Inca Dance/Foolish Waltz 20
55 London HL 8131 Stranger In Paradise/Autumn Leaves 15

JOHN (B.) SEBASTIAN

(see also Lovin' Spoonful, Even Dozen Jug Band)

69 Kama Sutra 618 026 She's A Lady/The Room Nobody Lives In 6
70 Reprise RS 20902 Magical Connection/Fa-Fana-Fa 5
70 Reprise RSLP 6379 JOHN B. SEBASTIAN (LP, gatefold sleeve) 18
70 Buddah 2361 003 JOHN SEBASTIAN SONGBOOK VOLUME ONE (LP, with Lovin' Spoonful) 12
71 Reprise K 44127 REAL LIVE JOHN SEBASTIAN (LP) 15
71 Reprise K 44149 THE FOUR OF US (LP, gatefold sleeve) 12
74 Reprise K 54028 TARZANA KID (LP) 12

SECESSION

80s Siren SRN12 23 Michael (12", p/s) 12
88 Siren SRNLP 11 A DARK ENCHANTMENT (LP, with inner) 40

SECOND CITY SOUND

65 Decca F 12310 Tchaikovsky One/Shadows 6
66 Decca F 12366 Greig One/In A Mist 6
66 Decca F 12406 Love's Funny/Tell Me Where I'm Going 6
69 Major Minor MM 600 The Dream Of Olwyn/A Touch Of Velvet, A Sting of Brass 10

SECOND COMING

71 Mercury 6338 030 SECOND COMING (LP) 30

SECOND HAND

(see also Andreas Thomopoulos, Fungus, Chillum, Vulcans, Seventh Wave)

68 Polydor 583 045 REALITY (LP, early copies crediting band as Moving Finger) 300
68 Polydor 583 045 REALITY (LP, later copies not crediting band as Moving Finger) 200
72 Mushroom MR 2006 DEATH MAY BE YOUR SANTA CLAUS (LP, some copies omit "Funeral") 250

MINT VALUE £

SECOND LAYER
(see also Outsiders, Sound)

79	Tortch-r TOR 001	FLESH AS PROPERTY (EP, white p/s, black printed labels)	25
80	Tortch TOR 006	State Of Emergency/I Need Noise/The Cutting Motion (p/s)	30
81	Tortch/Fresh FRESH 5	FLESH AS PROPERTY (EP, reissue, yellow p/s & white labels)	20
81	Cherry Red CHERRY 21	FLESH AS PROPERTY (EP, 2nd reissue, unreleased)	0
82	Cherry Red BRED 14	WORLD OF RUBBER (LP, with inner)	50

SECRET

77	Arista ARIST 142	The Young Ones/Handel A Vandel	10
78	Arista ARIST 173	Do You Really Care?/I Wanna Car Like That	15

SECRET AFFAIR
(see also New Hearts, Advertising, Innocents [U.K.])

79	I-Spy SEE 1	Time For Action/Soho Strut (brown p/s, black print/paper labels)	10
79	I-Spy SEE 1	Time For Action/Soho Strut (black p/s, white print with plastic labels)	5
79	I-Spy SEE 3	Let Your Heart Dance/Sorry Wrong Number (p/s, paper label)	6
80	I-Spy SEE 5	My World/So Cool (paper labels)	6
80	I-Spy SEE 8	Sound Of Confusion/Take It Or Leave It (p/s, paper labels)	6
81	I-Spy SEE 10	Do You Know?/Dance Master (keyhole company sleeve, paper labels)	6
82	I-Spy SEE 11	Lost In The Night (Mack The Knife)/The Big Beat (p/s)	8
79	I-Spy I SPY 1	GLORY BOYS (LP, with 2 inserts)	15
80	I-Spy I SPY 2	BEHIND CLOSED DOORS (LP, with inner sleeve)	12
82	I-Spy I SPY 3	BUSINESS AS USUAL (LP, stickered sleeve)	15
90s	own label	CITY OF DREAMS (LP, handmade sleeve - this is a bootleg)	25

SECRET KNOWLEDGE

90s	Sabres Of Paradise	Sugar Daddy (mixes) (12")	10

SECRET OYSTER

74	CBS 80489	SEA SON (LP)	15

SECRET SERVICE

79	Sonet SON 2193	Oh Susie/Give Me Your Love	6

SECRET SQUIRREL
(See also Undercover Elephant and DJ Secret Squirrel)

92	Bogwoppa BOGWOPPA 05	E Drop/Come Rudeboy (12", handwritten white label, with AJ Flex)	60
92	Dance Bass 01	Mu-Venom/DDT (12", stamped white label)	50
92	Dance Bass 02	VOLUME 2 EP (12")	30
92	Dance Bass 06	THE MAGIC FLUTE EP (12")	30

SECRETS (U.K.)
(see also Simon's Secrets, Clifford T. Ward, Martin Raynor & Secrets)

66	CBS 202466	I Suppose/Such A Pity	35
67	CBS 202585	Infatuation/She's Dangerous	35
67	CBS 2818	I Intend To Please/I Think I Need The Cash	35

SECRETS (U.S)

64	Philips BF 1298	The Boy Next Door/Learnin' To Forget	25
64	Philips BF 1318	Hey Big Boy/Other Side Of Town	25

SECT

81	Shoestring SHOE 1	This is Your Life/Private Eye (p/s)	5

SECT

80s		PLAYING WITH FIRE EP (12")	20
80s	Damaged Goods YUBB 2	SUMMER GIRL EP, blue vinyl)	20
86	Insect NASTY 1	A Free England	20

SECTION A

82	Subversive SUB	TIME STANDS STILL EP	15

SECTION 5

85	Oi OIR 002	WE WON'T CHANGE (LP)	20
80s	OI	STREET ROCK 'N' ROLL (LP)	15
87	Link LP 08	FOR THE LOVE OF OI! (LP)	15

SECTION 25

80	Factory FAC 18	Girls Don't Count/New Noise/Up To You (tracing paper p/s)	12
80	Factory FAC 18	Girls Don't Count/New Noise Up To You (12")	10
81	Factory FACT 45	ALWAYS NOW (LP, in envelope/folder)	20
84	Factory FACT 90	FROM THE HIP (LP, with inner)	25
88	Factory FACT 160	LOVE & HATE (LP)	12

NEIL SEDAKA
(see also Sam Cooke, Paul Anka, 10cc)

59	RCA RCA 1099	The Diary/No Vacancy	25
59	RCA RCA 1099	The Diary/No Vacancy (78)	15
59	RCA RCA 1115	I Go Ape/Moon Of Gold	20
59	RCA RCA 1115	I Go Ape/Moon Of Gold (78)	15
59	RCA RCA 1130	You've Got To Learn Your Rhythm And Blues/Crying My Heart Out For You	25
59	RCA RCA 1130	You've Got To Learn Your Rhythm And Blues/Crying My Heart Out For You (78)	20
59	London HLW 8961	Ring A Rockin'/Fly Don't Fly On Me	40

(The above RCA 45s were originally issued with triangular centres; later round-centres are worth two-thirds these values.)

59	London HLW 8961	Ring A Rockin'/Fly Don't Fly On Me (78)	40
59	RCA RCA 1152	Oh! Carol/One Way Ticket (triangular centre)	20
59	RCA RCA 1152	Oh! Carol/One Way Ticket (round centre)	5
59	RCA RCA 1152	Oh! Carol/One Way Ticket (78)	70
60	RCA RCA 1178	Stairway To Heaven/Forty Winks Away	5
60	RCA RCA 1178	Stairway To Heaven/Forty Winks Away (78)	70
60	RCA RCA 1198	Run Samson Run/You Mean Everything To Me	10
60	RCA RCA 1198	Run Samson Run/You Mean Everything To Me (78)	70

MINT VALUE £

62	Stateside SS 105	Oh Delilah/MARVELS: Neil's Twist	10
63	RCA RCA 1368	Bad Girl/Wait 'Til You See My Baby	18
65	RCA RCA 1475	World Through A Tear/High On A Mountain	6
59	RCA RCX 166	NEIL SEDAKA (EP)	40
60	RCA RCX 186	NEIL SEDAKA VOL. 2 (EP)	30
62	RCA RCX 212	NEIL SEDAKA VOL. 3 (EP)	30
59	RCA RD 27140	NEIL SEDAKA (LP)	60
60	RCA RD 27207	CIRCULATE (LP, mono)	50
60	RCA SF 5090	CIRCULATE (LP, stereo)	60

MIKE SEDGEWICK
(see also Adam Mike & Tim)

68	Parlophone R 5694	The Good Guys In The White Hats Never Lose/ Woman (She's Got To Be Treated Right)	5

SEDUCER

83	Sticky SSR 0017	Call Your Name/Survivor (p/s)	60
84	Thunderbolt THBE 1007	Indecent Exposure/Down Down/No No Baby/DTs/Wild Joker (12", p/s)	10
85	Thunderbolt THBL 016	CAUGHT IN THE ACT (LP)	15
86	Stud STUDLP 2	'EADS DOWN - SEE YOU AT THE END (LP)	15

REDGIE SEEBOE

74	BUG 38	Please Don't Bring Your Sister/Daphne's Brains	10

RUDY SEEDORF

65	Island WI 189	One Million Stars/Mr. Blue	18

SEEDS
(see also Sky Saxon, Ya Ho Wa 13)

66	Vocalion VN 9277	Pushin' Too Hard/Try To Understand	55
66	Vocalion VN 9277	Pushin' Too Hard/Try To Understand (DJ copy)	85
67	Vocalion VN 9287	Can't Seem To Make You Mine/Daisy Mae	40
88	Bam Caruso OPRA 091	Pushin' Too Hard/Greener Day	15
67	Vocalion VAN 8062	A WEB OF SOUND (LP)	80
67	Vocalion VAN 8070	FUTURE (LP, mono)	50
67	Vocalion SAVN 8070	FUTURE (LP, stereo)	60
78	Sonet SNTF 746	THE SEEDS (LEGENDARY MASTER RECORDINGS) (LP)	15
88	Strange Things STRANGEP 1	`EVIL HOODOO (LP, picture disc)	15

SEEDS OF THE EARTH

75	Contempo CS 2052	Planting Seeds/Brother Bad	20
75	Contempo CS 2073	Zion Plus/Phire	20

BOB SEEGER SYSTEM

68	Capitol CL15574	Tales Of Lucy Blue/Ramblin Gamblin Man	15
70	Capitol CL 15642	Lucifer/Big RIver	12

MIKE SEEGER
(see also Peggy & Mike Seeger)

65	Fontana TFL 6039	MIKE SEEGER (LP)	15

PEGGY SEEGER
(see also Al Lloyd)

57	Topic TRC 107	Freight Train/Cumberland Gap (78)	20
58	Topic TRC 108	Pretty Little Baby/Child Of God (78)	10
65	Decca F 12282	Pretty Little Baby/My Love And I Are One	6
57	Pye Jazz NJE 1043	ORIGINS OF SKIFFLE (EP)	20
57	Topic 7T 18	COME ALONG JOHN (EP, 33 rpm with insert)	20
58	Topic TOP 18	COME ALONG JOHN (EP, 45 rpm reissue, with insert)	15
60	Topic TOP 38	SHINE LIKE A STAR (EP)	10
61	Topic TOP 72	TROUBLED LOVE (EP)	10
61	Topic TOP 73	EARLY IN THE SPRING (EP)	10
50s	Topic 10T 9	PEGGY SEEGER (10" LP)	15
61	PRE 13005	THE BEST OF PEGGY SEEGER (LP)	15
64	Topic 12T 113	WHO'S GOING TO SHOE? (LP, with Tom Paley)	15
69	Argo (Z)DA 81	PEGGY ALONE (LP)	15

PEGGY SEEGER & GUY CARAWAN
(see also Guy Carawan)

58	Nixa NPT 19029	WE SING AMERICA (10" LP)	30
58	HMV CLP 1174	AMERICA AT PLAY (LP)	20

PEGGY & MIKE SEEGER
(see also Ewan MacColl & Peggy Seeger, Mike Seeger)

68	Argo (Z)DA 80	PEGGY 'N' MIKE (LP)	20

PETE SEEGER
(see also Big Bill Broonzy, Sonny Terry [& Brownie McGhee], Weavers)

60	Top Rank TR 5020	Careless Love/LEON BIBB: Times Are Getting Hard (p/s)	10
63	CBS AAG 187	Little Boxes/Mail Myself To You	5
58	Melodisc EPM7 78	TRIBUTE TO LEADBELLY (EP)	8
58	Topic TOP 33	PETE AND FIVE STRINGS (EP)	8
59	Topic TOP 37	HOOTENANNY NEW YORK CITY (EP, with Sonny Terry)	15

PETE SEEGER & BIG BILL BROONZY
(see also Big Bill Broonzy)

64	Xtra XTRA 1006	IN CONCERT - PETE SEEGER & BIG BILL BROONZY (LP)	20

SEEKERS

65	Oriole CB 1935	With A Swag On My Shoulder/Myra	8
65	Decca F 22167	Chilly Winds/Kumbaya	5
67	Columbia DB 8313	Emerald City/Music Of The World A Turnin'	12

MINT VALUE £

SEEMON & MARIJKE
71 A&M AMLS 64309 SON OF AMERICA (LP) ... 30

SEFTONS
(see also Perishers)
66 CBS 202491 I Can See Through You/Here Today ... 25

VIVIENNE SEGAL & HAROLD LANG
54 Columbia SCM 5114 Den Of Iniquity/BARBARA ASHLEY: That Terrific Rainbow ... 7

BOB SEGER (SYSTEM)
68 Capitol CL 15574 Ramblin' Gamblin' Man/Tales Of Lucy Blue (as Bob Seger System) ... 15
70 Capitol CL 15642 Lucifer/Big River (as Bob Seger System) ... 8
72 Reprise K 14208 If I Were A Carpenter/Jesse James ... 5
73 Reprise K 14243 Rosalie/Back In '72 ... 5
74 Reprise K 14364 Get Out Of Denver/Long Song Comin' ... 5
72 Reprise K 44214 SMOKIN' O.P.'s (LP) ... 15

LLOYD SEIVRIGHT
70 Creole CR 1001 Mary's Boy Child/And Glory Walked Among Men ... 5

SEIZE
81 Why Not? NOT 001 Grovelands Road/Why? (p/s) ... 15
82 Why Not? NOT 002 EVERYBODY DIES EP (p/s) ... 15

RICHARD SELANO
69 Jolly JY 019 All Of The Time/Broken Romance ... 7

SELECTED FOUR
71 Banana BA 351 Selection Train/SOUND DIMENSION: Version Train ... 12

SELECTER
(see also Special A.K.A.)
79 2-Tone CHS TT 4 On My Radio/Too Much Pressure (paper label, company sleeve) ... 10
80 2-Tone CHS TT4 On My Radio/Too Much Pressure (sliver plastic labels, colour p/s) ... 6
80 2-Tone CHS TT 8 Three Minute Hero/James Bond (silver plastic label, company sleeve) ... 10
80 2-Tone CHS TT 8 Three Minute Hero/James Bond (paper labels, company sleeve) ... 10
80 2-Tone CHS TT 10 Missing Words/Carry Go Bring Home (paper label, company sleeve) ... 6
80 2-Tone CMS TT10 Missing Words/Carry Go Bring Home (sliver plastic labels, colour p/s) ... 5
82 Flexipop 001/SFI 566 Ready Mix Radio (1-sided clear flexidisc with Flexipop mag, issue 1) ... 8
80 2-Tone CDLTT 5002 TOO MUCH PRESSURE (LP) ... 15

FREDDIE SELF
(see also Freddie Ryder, Trends)
64 Mercury MF 839 Don't Cry/Why Should I? ... 7

RONNIE SELF
58 Philips PB 810 Bop-A-Lena/Ain't I A Dog (78) ... 250

SELF ABUSE
83 Radical Change RC 5 SOLDIERS (EP) ... 15

SELF DESTRUCT
91 Retch RR 12004 AFFRAY (12" EP) ... 8

BROTHER JOHN SELLERS
56 Vanguard EPP 14002 BLUES AND SPIRITUALS (EP) ... 15
57 Columbia SEG 7740 BLUES AND SPIRITUALS (EP) ... 15
57 Decca DFE 6457 BROTHER JOHN SELLERS IN LONDON (EP) ... 15
56 Vanguard PPT 12008 BROTHER JOHN SELLERS SINGS BLUES AND FOLK SONGS (10" LP) ... 25
57 Vanguard PPT 12017 JACK OF DIAMONDS AND OTHER FOLK SONGS AND BLUES (10" LP) ... 25

PETER SELLERS (& SOPHIA LOREN)
57 Parlophone R 4337 Any Old Iron/Boiled Bananas And Carrots ... 8
58 Parlophone R 4491 I'm So Ashamed/A Drop Of The Hard Stuff ... 5
59 Parlophone R 4605 Puttin' On The Smile/My Old Dutch ... 5
60 Parlophone R 4702 Goodness Gracious Me! (with Sophia Loren)/Grandpa's Grave ... 5
61 Parlophone R 4724 Bangers And Mash (with Sophia Loren)/SOPHIA LOREN: Zoo Be Zoo Be Zoo ... 5
65 Parlophone R 5393 A Hard Day's Night/Help! ... 5
66 United Artists UP 1152 After The Fox (as Peter Sellers & Hollies)/BURT BACHARACH: The Fox-Trot ... 35
79 United Artists BP 335 There Are Camels Where The Taxis Used To Be/Night And Day ... 5
59 Parlophone PMC 1111 SONGS FOR SWINGIN' SELLERS (LP, mono) ... 15
59 Parlophone PCS 3003 SONGS FOR SWINGIN' SELLERS (LP, stereo) ... 20
60 Parlophone PMC 1131 PETER AND SOPHIA (LP, with Sophia Loren, mono) ... 20
60 Parlophone PCS 3012 PETER AND SOPHIA (LP, with Sophia Loren, stereo) ... 25
(Prices for Parlophone albums are for gold on black labels. Yellow and black labels are half of these prices)
74 Decca SKL 5194 HE'S INNOCENT OF WATERGATE (LP, with Spike Milligan) ... 15
79 United Artists UAG 30266 SELLERS' MARKET (LP) ... 12

PETER SELLERS, SPIKE MILLIGAN & HARRY SECOMBE
(see also Goons, Spike Milligan, Sophia Loren, Hollies, Harry Secombe, Peter Ustinov)
64 Philips AL 3464 HOW TO WIN AN ELECTION (LP) ... 15

SELOFANE
68 CBS 3413 Girl Called Fantasy/Happiness Is Love ... 15
68 CBS 3700 Shingle I.A.O./Chase The Face ... 30

SELWYN & JOHN
67 CBS 2708 Bogey Man/When God Gave Us Names ... 50

SEMA
82 Le Rey LR 06 THEME FROM HUNGER (EP) ... 40
82 Le Rey LR 04 NOTES FROM UNDERGROUND (LP) ... 90
83 Le Rey LR 101 EXTRACTS FROM ROSA SILBER (LP) ... 40
84 Le Rey LR 102 THREE SEASONS ONLY (LP) ... 35

MINT VALUE £

SEMA 4

79	Pollen PBM 022	4 FROM SEMA 4 (EP, 2 different coloured sleeves, 500 only, numbered)	100
79	Pollen PBM 024	UP DOWN AROUND (EP, 1,000 only)	75

ARCHIE SEMPLE

60	Columbia 33SX 1240	JAZZ FOR YOUNG LOVERS (LP)	25
62	Columbia 33SX 1450	EASY LIVING (LP)	20
63	Columbia 33SX 1580	THE TWILIGHT COMETH (LP)	20
64	77 LEU 12/6	THE CLARINET OF ARCHIE SEMPLE (LP)	20

SEMPRINI

61	HMV POP 842	Exodus - Main Title Theme/Lark In The Clear Air	6

SENATE

(see also Garnet Mimms)

67	Columbia DB 8110	I Can't Stop/Ain't As Sweet As You	20
68	United Artists (S)ULP 1180	THE SENATE SOCK IT TO YOU ONE MORE TIME (LP)	40

SENATOR BOBBY

62	Cameo Parkway P 127	Wild Thing/SENATOR EVERETT McKINLAY: Wild Thing	8

SENATORS

(see also Tony Rivers & Castaways)

64	Dial DSP 7001	She's A Mod/Lot About You	55
64	Oriole CB 1957	When Day Is Done/Breakdown	50
65	CBS 201768	The Tables Are Turning/Stop Wasting Time	30

RAY SENDIT & HIS ROCKEY TEAM

57	Felsted SD 80052	Rocket 0869/Spike's Rock	8

LOS SENORS

63	Cameo Parkway C 290	Amapola/Acapulco	5

SENSATION

73	Sticky STY 5	Black Eyed Woman/Baby	10

SENSATIONAL CREED

(see also Orbidoig)

84	Beggars Banquet BEG 125	Nocturnal Operation/Down Periscope (p/s, reissue of Orbidöig single)	15
84	Beggars Banquet BEG 125T	Nocturnal Operation/Down Periscope/Voyage Of The Titanic (12", p/s, reissue of Orbidöig single)	25

SENSATIONS (Jamaica)

(see also Roy Shirley, Baba Dise, Winston Wright)

67	Doctor Bird DB 1074	A Thing Called Soul/BOBBY LEE & SENSATIONS: I Was Born A Loser	35
67	Doctor Bird DB 1100	Right On Time/Lonely Lover	35
67	Doctor Bird DB 1102	Born To Love You/Your Sweet Love	60
68	Duke DU 2	Those Guys/I'll Never Fall In Love	80
68	Island WI 3110	Long Time Me No See You Girl/ROY SHIRLEY: Million Dollar Baby	25
69	Camel CA 31	The Warrior (actually by Johnny Osbourne & Sensations)/ JOHNNY ORGAN: Don Juan	10
70	Techniques TI 902	War Boat/Mr Blue	8
71	Duke DU 120	Remember/LARRY'S ALLSTARS: Madhouse	6
71	Duke DU 121	What Are You Doing Sunday/RUFFIANS: Sweet Dream	6

SENSATIONS (U.K.)

66	Decca F 12392	Look At My Baby/What A Wonderful Feeling	20
71	MCA MK 5078	Oh My Eli/Let's Get A Little Sentimental	5

SENSATIONS (featuring Yvonne) (U.S.)

(see also Yvonne Baker)

61	Pye International 7N 25110	Music, Music, Music/A Part Of Me (as Sensations featuring Yvonne)	25
62	Pye International 7N 25128	Let Me In/Oh Yes I'll Be True	30

SEONA DANCING

83	London LON 22	More To Lose (p/s)	18
83	London LONX 22	More To Lose (12", p/s)	10
83	London LON 32	Bitter Heart/Tell Her (p/s)	18
83	London LONX 32	Bitter Heart/Tell Her (12", p/s)	12

SEPTIC DEATH

85	Pusmort 0012-01D	NOW THAT I HAVE THE ATTENTION? (LP, with inner sleeve, 18 tracks)	15
88	Pusmort PUS 00703	Kichigai (p/s)	5

SEPULTURA

94	Roadrunner RR2377-8	Refuse/Resist (12", die cut sleeve)	8
96	Roadrunner RR 23145	Ratamahatta/War/Slave New World (Live)/Amen/Inner Self (Live) (CD, digipak)	15
91	Roadracer RO 9328-8	ARISE (LP, picture disc)	25
94	Roadrunner RR 90000 0	CHAOS A.D. (CD, limited edition tin box; CD has embossed cover & different sleeve, Brazilian flag & 2 bonus tracks, "Policia" & "Inhuman Nature")	50
91	Roadracer RO 93281	ARISE (LP)	12

SERENADERS

59	Top Rank JAR 111	Sudden Holiday/Tango Madeira	5

SERENDIPITY

68	CBS 3733	Through With You/I'm Flying	130
69	CBS 4428	If I Could/Castles	50

SERENDIPITY SINGERS

64	Philips BF 1333	Don't Let The Rain Come Down (Crooked Little Man)/Freedom's Star	6
64	Philips BL 7620	THE SERENDIPITY SINGERS (LP)	12
64	Philips BL 7651	TAKE YOUR SHOES OFF (LP)	12
65	Philips BL 7685	SING OF LOVE, LIES AND FLYING FESTOONS (LP)	12

MINT VALUE £

SERFS
69 Capitol E-ST 207 THE SERFS (LP) 15

SERGEANT PEPPER
83 Ariwa ARILP 006 JUDGEMENT DAY (LP) 25

WILL SERGEANT
(see also Echo & Bunnymen)
82 WEA K 19238 Favourite Branches/RAVI SHANKAR & BILL LOVEDAY: Himalaya (p/s) 8
95 Ochre OCH 003 Cosmos/Venus In Flares (as GLIDE, p/s, orange vinyl) 7
78 No label or cat. no. WEIRD AS FISH (cassette, 7 copies only, each with a different cover) 30
83 92 Happy Cust. HAPLP 1 THEMES FOR "GRIND" (LP) 12

SERGIO & ESTIBALIZ
75 Epic S EPC 3187 Love Come Home/Tu Volveras 12

SERIOUS DRINKING
82 Upright YOURS 4 Love On The Terraces/Hypocrite/Bobby Moore Was Innocent (p/s) 10
84 Vistacope UP 8 Country Grild Became Drugs & Sex Punk/Other 10

SERPENTINE
70 Decca F23001 Powerful Jim/I've Only Got Myself 20

JUAN MANUEL SERRAT
68 Philips BF 1654 She Gives Me Love (La La La)/La La La 6

NANCY SESAY & MELODAIRES
(see also Homosexuals)
81 It's War Boys S 1 C'est Fab/The Ballad Of Hong Kong/National Honk (gatefold p/s) 5

SESSION MEN
(see also Michael Smith)
80 LKJ 001 THE SESSION MEN: Solitude/ABU BAKE : Introducing Abu Baka/ MICHAEL SMITH : Mi Cyaan Believe It/Roots (12") 25

CAMILO SESTO
72 Pye Intl. 7N 25589 To Be A Man/Now Is My Time (Yo Soy Asi) 40

BOLA SETE
76 Sonet SNTF 695 OCEAN (LP) 15

SETTERS
70 Duke DU 65 Paint Your Wagon/Organ Man (both sides actually by Hot Rod All Stars) 70
70 Trojan TR 7738 Virgin Soldier/Brixton Reggae Festival (both actually by Hot Rod All Stars) 8

SETTLERS
66 Pye 7N 17065 Nowhere Man/Call Again 7
65 Pye 7N 159645 Woman Called Freedom/I Know I'm Right 6
67 Pye 7N 17375 Major Minor/I Love 'Oo Kazoo ('Cos 'Oo Love Me) 6
70 Columbia DB 8695 Nessie The Monster/Jesus Met the Woman (At The Well) 6
71 York SYK 505 The Lightning Tree/Just This Side Of Nowhere 7
74 York YR 215 On Top Of The World/Let's Tell The World 6

SEVEN AGES OF MAN
(see also Madeline Bell, Gordon Beck)
72 Rediffusion ZS 115 SEVEN AGES OF MAN (LP, yellow/black label) 40

SEVEN LETTERS/SYMARIP
(see also Pyramids, Equals, Laurel Aitken)
69 Doctor Bird DB 1189 People Get Ready/The Fit (as Seven Letters) 40
69 Doctor Bird DB 1194 Please Stay/Special Beat (as Seven Letters) 40
69 Doctor Bird DB 1195 Flour Dumpling/Equality (as Seven Letters [Symarip]) 35
69 Doctor Bird DB 1206 Mama Me Want Girl/Sentry (as Seven Letters) 25
69 Doctor Bird DB 1207 Soul Crash/Throw Me Things (as Seven Letters) 40
69 Doctor Bird DB 1208 There Goes My Heart/Wish (as Seven Letters) 30
69 Doctor Bird DB 1209 Bam Bam Baji/Hold Him Joe (as Seven Letters [Symarip]) 100
69 Doctor Bird DB 1306 Fung Sure/Tomorrow At Sundown (as Symarip) 40
69 Treasure Isle TI 7050 Skinhead Moonstomp/Must Catch A Train (as Symarip) 30
70 Treasure Isle TI 7054 Parson's Corner/Redeem (as Symarip) 30
70 Treasure Isle TI 7055 La Bella Jig/Holidays By The Sea (as Symarip) 10
70 Attack ATT 8013 I'm A Puppet/Vindication (as Symarip) 15
70 Trojan TBL 102 SKINHEAD MOONSTOMP (LP, as Symarip) 30
80 Trojan TRO 9062 Skinhead Moonstomp/Skinhead Jamboree (p/s) 8

7 SECONDS
82 Alt. Tentacles VIRUS 15 SKIN, BRAINS AND GUTS (EP, with insert) 12
84 BYO BY008 CREW (LP) 12

SEVEN YEAR ITCH
81 Cargo CRS 007 I wanna Make Ya/Oo Ya Ha 10

SEVENTEEN
(see also Alarm)
80 Vendetta VD 001 Don't Let Go/Bank Holiday Weekend (p/s) 100

SEVENTH ANGEL
90 Under One Flag FLAG 51 THE TORMENT (LP) 15

SEVENTH SEAL
90 Mystic Red Corp MRC 8004 Sound Iration/Dub Seal (12") 50

SEVENTH SEAL
97 Acme ACLP 8018LP THE SEVENTH SEAL (LP) 12

SEVENTH SON
82 Rising Son FMR 067 Man In The Street/Immortal Hours (in p/s) 75
82 Rising Son FMR 067 Man In The Street/Immortal Hours 20

			MINT VALUE £
84	Rising Son SRT4KS 282	Metal To The Moon/Sound And Fury (in gatefold p/s)	60
84	Rising Son SRT4KS 282	Metal To The Moon/Sound And Fury	30
87	Music Factory MF 0043	Northern Boots/The Harder You Rock (p/s)	18
89	Rising Son SRT9KLS	What More Do You Want/Sister Strange/Bitter Ashes (12", p/s)	12

SEVENTH WAVE

(see also Second Hand, Fungus)

75	Gull GULS 14	Manifestations/Only The Beginning (Part 1)	5
74	Gull GULP 1001	THINGS TO COME (LP)	15
75	Gull GULP 1010	PSI-FI (LP)	18

SEVENTH WAVE

89	SRT SRT9KS 2018	Tonight (p/s)	20

SEVENTH WONDER

80	Grapevine GRP 130	Captain Of My Ship/Pharaoh	8

SEVERED HEAD

83	Plastic Canvas PC 002	Heavy Metal/Killin' The Kidz (p/s)	40

SEVERINE

71	CBS 7230	Chance In Time/Nothing Bad Can Be This Good	8
71	Philips 6009 135	Un Banc, Un Arbre, Une Rue/Viens	5
71	Philips 6009 152	La La Melodie/Je Ferme Les Yeux, Je Compte Dix	5

DAVID SEVILLE & HIS ORCHESTRA (& THE CHIPMUNKS)

(see also Alfi & Harry)

57	London HLU 8359	Armen's Theme/Carousel In Rome (initially gold label print)	18
57	London HLU 8359	Armen's Theme/Carousel In Rome (later silver label print)	10
58	London HLU 8619	Witch Doctor/Don't Whistle At Me Baby	5
59	London HLU 8916	Ragtime Cowboy Joe/Flip Side	5
57	London RE-U 1085	DAVID SEVILLE & HIS ORCHESTRA (EP)	20
59	London RE-U 1219	WITCH DOCTOR AND FRIENDS (EP)	20
59	London HA-U 2153	THE WITCH DOCTOR PRESENTS DAVID SEVILLE AND HIS FRIENDS (LP)	20
60	London HAG 2268	SING AGAIN WITH THE CHIPMUNKS (LP)	20
64	Liberty LBY 1218	THE CHIPMUNKS SING THE BEATLES (LP)	15

ALEC SEWARD

56	Vogue LDE 165	CITY BLUES (10" LP)	40

SEX AIDS

(see also Vice Squad)

83	Riot City RIOT 23	BACK ON THE PISS AGAIN (EP)	15

SEX BEATLES

79	Charly CYS 1061	Well You Never/Fatal Fascination (p/s)	8

SEX GANG CHILDREN

82	Illuminated ILL 1112	Beasts (12", EP)	30

SEXHURT

98	Dobbstown BOB 23	A ROMANTIC EVENING WITH BIG RED STRAPS (LP, with free straps)	12

SEX PISTOLS

(see also Public Image Ltd, Professionals, Rich Kids, Steve Jones, Cash Pussies, Spectres (UK), Swingers)

76	EMI 401	Anarchy In The U.K (4.01 longer version)/No Fun (Abbey Road 2-sided acetate, only 3 known to exist)	6000
76	EMI	Anarchy In The U.K. (3.36 version) (1-sided Abbey Road Acetate)	4000
76	EMI EMI 2566	Anarchy In The U.K./I Wanna Be Me (black p/s, with Chris Thomas production credit on B-side)	90
76	EMI EMI 2566	Anarchy In The U.K./I Wanna Be Me ('Demo, not for sale'. Black p/s, Chris Thomas credit on both sides and with information slip)	225
76	EMI EMI 2566	Anarchy In The U.K./I Wanna Be Me (Dave Goodman production credit on B-side)	40
	(no label or cat. no.)	God Save The Queen/No Feelings (double sided 7" acetate on LTS - few copies pressed and used by Malcolm McLaren to get gigs and record deal)	6000
77	A&M AMS 7284	God Save The Queen/No Feelings (withdrawn, in brown envelope with press release)	8000
77	A&M AMS 7284	God Save The Queen/No Feelings (withdrawn, without brown envelope and press release)	7500
77	Virgin VS 181	God Save The Queen/Did You No Wrong (1st issue, with silver on blue sleeve and labels)	10
77	Virgin VS 181	God Save The Queen/Did You No Wrong (Plain blue no Queen's head sample sleeve, Jamie Reid autograph added later to one)	1500
77	Virgin VS 181	God Save The Queen/Did You No Wrong (2nd issue, white on blue sleeve and labels)	8
77	Virgin VS 184	Pretty Vacant/No Fun (p/s)	10
77	Virgin VS 184	Pretty Vacant/No Fun (p/s with push-out centre)	30
77	Virgin VS 191	Holidays In The Sun/Satellite (withdrawn p/s)	18
77	Virgin/Lyntone LYN 3261	Lentilmas - A Seasonal Offering To You From Virgin Records (flexidisc, Xmas freebie to journalists; with Xmas card)	1500
77	Virgin/Lyntone LYN 3261	Lentilmas - A Seasonal Offering To You From Virgin Records (flexidisc, Xmas freebie to journalists; without Xmas card)	450
78		SID VICIOUS: My Way (1-sided Pye Studios Acetate)	700
78	Virgin VS 220	No-One Is Innocent (mispress, plays Motors track)/SID VICIOUS: My Way (p/s)	35
78	Virgin VS 22012	The Biggest Blow (A Punk Prayer By Ronald Biggs)/(Interview)/SID VICIOUS: My Way (12", p/s [matrix: VS 22012A3], without interview [VS 22012 A1])	20
78	Virgin VS 22012	The Biggest Blow (A Punk Prayer By Ronald Biggs)/(Interview)/SID VICIOUS: My Way (12", p/s [matrix: VS 22012A3], with interview [VS 22012 A1])	10
79	Virgin VS 240	Something Else/Friggin' In The Riggin' (p/s, black & white labels)	7
79	Virgin VS 290	The Great Rock 'n' Roll Swindle/Rock Around The Clock (vocals by Tenpole Tudor) ('American Express' p/s)	6

			MINT VALUE £
79	Virgin VS 290	The Great Rock 'n' Roll Swindle (mispressing with 'lawyers' telephone conversation' track)/Rock Around The Clock ('American Express' p/s)	30
79	Virgin VS 272	C'mon Everybody/The God Save The Queen Symphony/ Watcha Gonna Do About It (p/s)	5
80	Virgin VS 339	(I'm Not Your) Stepping Stone/Pistols Propaganda (p/s, mispressing, B-side plays "Substitute")	25
80	Virgin VS 339	(I'm Not Your) Stepping Stone/Pistols Propaganda (p/s, mispressing, B-side plays Gillan track "No Laughing In Heaven")	30
80	Virgin SEX 1	PISTOLS PACK (6 x 7" in p/s; all in plastic wallet)	50
81	Virgin VS 443	Who Killed Bambi?/Rock Around The Clock (by Tenpole Tudor & Pistols, p/s)	10
85	Chaos DICK1	Submission/No Feelings (p/s, 5,000 only, blue vinyl)	7
85	Chaos DICK1	Submission/No Feelings (p/s, 5,000 only, pink vinyl)	15
85	Chaos DICK1	Submission/No Feelings (p/s, 5,000 only, yellow vinyl)	5
85	Chaos SUB 1	Submission (12", 1-sided test pressing, die-cut sleeve, label has big red 'A')	20
85	Chaos	Pretty Vacant (unreleased, 20 copies only)	50
85	Chaos CARTEL 1	Submission (12" 1-track promo)	25
86	Archive 4 TOF 104	THE ORIGINAL SEX PISTOLS LIVE (4-track 12", p/s, 5,000 only)	6
86	Archive 4 TOF 104	THE ORIGINAL SEX PISTOLS LIVE (4-track 12", p/s, blue vinyl)	12
88	Virgin CDT 3	Anarchy In The U.K./No Fun/EMI (3" CD, card sleeve)	10
88	Virgin CDT 37	God Save The Queen/Did You No Wrong/Don't Give Me No Lip Child (3" CD, gatefold card sleeve)	10
88	Spiral Scratch SCRATCH 4	Pretty Vacant (Demo)/I Wanna Be Me (Demo) (with Spiral Scratch magazine, issue 4, B-side actually plays "Seventeen")	10
77	Virgin V 2086/SPOTS 001	NEVER MIND THE BOLLOCKS, HERE'S THE SEX PISTOLS (LP, pink rear sleeve, with no track listing, with poster & 1-sided single, "Submission" [VDJ 24], shrinkwrapped, with orange or green-stickered versions extremely rare)	600
77	Virgin V 2086/SPOTS 001	NEVER MIND THE BOLLOCKS, HERE'S THE SEX PISTOLS (LP, pink rear sleeve, with no track listing, with poster & 1-sided single, "Submission" [VDJ 24], shrinkwrapped, with orange or green-stickered versions extremely rare)	125
77	Virgin V 2086	NEVER MIND THE BOLLOCKS, HERE'S THE SEX PISTOLS (LP, with track listing, no shrinkwrap)	25
77	Virgin V 2086	NEVER MIND THE BOLLOCKS, HERE'S THE SEX PISTOLS (LP, pink rear sleeve with no track listing)	25
78	Virgin VP 2086	NEVER MIND THE BOLLOCKS, HERE'S THE SEX PISTOLS (LP, picture disc)	40
79	Virgin VD 2510	THE GREAT ROCK 'N' ROLL SWINDLE (2-LP, including "Watcha Gonna Do About It", with paper insert)	30
79	Virgin VD 2510	THE GREAT ROCK 'N' ROLL SWINDLE (2-LP, "I Wanna Be Me" and "Who Killed Bambi?" replace "Watcha Gonna Do About It", with spoken overdubs on "God Save The Queen Symphony")	20
80	Factory FACT 30	THE HEYDAY (gold interview cassette in satin pouch with Xmas card)	50
80	Factory FACT 30	THE HEYDAY (cassette, in vinyl pouch without Xmas card)	20
86	Virgin CDV 2086	NEVER MIND THE BOLLOCKS, HERE'S THE SEX PISTOLS (CD, mispressing, plays country music titles)	20
89	Link LINKLP 063	LIVE AND LOUD (LP)	12
98	Virgin VP 2087	NEVER MIND THE BOLLOCKS, HERE'S THE SEX PISTOLS (LP, pink vinyl reissue, numbered on rear sleeve)	15

TONY SEXTON

78	Burning Sounds BSD 005	Desire (with Jah Son)/BOB DAVIS: World In My Arms (12")	15

SEXY GIRLS

69	Fab FAB 100	Pom-Pom Song/LITTLE JOE & BUSTER'S ALLSTARS: Hy There (B-side actually by Melltones)	15
69	Dice CC 100	Pom-Pom Song/LITTLE JOE & BUSTER'S ALLSTARS: Hy There (B-side actually by Melltones) (reissue)	15

DENNY SEYTON & SABRES

64	Mercury MF 800	Tricky Dicky/Baby What You Want Me To Do	20
64	Mercury MF 814	Short Fat Fanny/Give Me Back My Heart	20
64	Mercury MF 824	The Way You Look Tonight/Hands Off	25
65	Parlophone R 5363	Just A Kiss/In The Flowers By The Trees (as Denny Seyton Group)	35
65	Wing WL 1032	IT'S THE GEAR (14 HITS) (LP)	45

TONY SHABAZZ

79	Ethnic Fight FT DD 4436	Mr Fitzy/RUDDIE MOWATT: Public Enemy (12")	60

SHABBY TIGER

76	RCA Victor RS 1065	SHABBY TIGER (LP)	15

SHACK

(see also Pale Fountains)

88	Ghetto GTG B 1	Emergency/Liberation (p/s)	6
88	Ghetto GTG T 1	Emergency/Liberation/Faith (12", p/s)	12
88	Ghetto GTG CD 1	Emergency/Liberation/Faith/What's It Like (CD)	8
89	Ghetto GTG B 2	High Rise Low Life/Who Killed Clayton Square? (p/s)	5
89	Ghetto GTG T 2	High Rise Low Life/Who Killed Clayton Square?/High Rise Low Life (Bert Hardy Mix) (12", p/s)	10
90	Ghetto GTG B 11	I Know You Well/I Feel No Way (p/s)	5
90	Ghetto GTG 11T	I Know You Well (Extended Mix)/I Feel No Way/(If You Want It Mix) (12", p/s)	8
06	Sour Mash JDNC 007	Cup Of Tea/Lizzie Mallaly (p/s numbered)	5
88	Ghetto GHETT 1	ZILCH (LP, distributed by Epic)	15
88	Ghetto GHETT 1	ZILCH (LP, later independent issue)	25
88	Ghetto GHETT D 1	ZILCH (CD)	18
90s	Marina MA 16	WATERPISTOL (LP)	12

SHADE JOEY & NIGHTOWLS

64	Parlophone R 5180	Bluebirds Over The Mountain/That's When I Need You Baby	90

MINT VALUE £

SHADER
81 Piston Broke REDASH 1 Bad News Blues (no p/s) . . . 100

SHADES
62 Starlite ST45 074 Weird Walk/Joe's Shuffle . . . 22

SHADES (Jamaica)
(see also Techniques)
69 Gas GAS 119 Never Gonna Give You Up/Let Me Remind You (both actually by Techniques) . . . 12

SHADES (U.S.)
58 London HLX 8713 Sun Glasses (with Knott Sisters)/KNOTT SISTERS: Undivided Attention . . . 40
58 London HLX 8713 Sun Glasses (with Knott Sisters)/KNOTT SISTERS: Undivided Attention (78) . . . 10

SHADES OF BLUE (U.K.)
65 Parlophone R 5270 Voodoo Blues/Luceanne . . . 50
65 Pye 7N 15988 Where Did All The Good Times Go/I Ain't No Use . . . 15

SHADES OF BLUE (U.S.)
66 Sue WI 4022 Oh! How Happy/Little Orphan Boy . . . 35

SHADES OF JOY
69 Fontana STL 5498 SHADES OF JOY (LP) . . . 20

SHADES OF MACMURROUGH
73 Polydor 2908 007 CRAIG RIVER (LP, red label, Irish pressing) . . . 150

SHADES OF MORLEY BROWN
68 Mercury MF1054 Silly Girl/Pretty Bluebird . . . 35

JOHNNY SHADOW (& DANNY GAVAN)
(see also Ivy League)
63 Pye 7N 15506 Golli Golli/I'm Coming Home To You (with Danny Gavan) (in p/s) . . . 15
63 Pye 7N 15506 Golli Golli/I'm Coming Home To You (with Danny Gavan) . . . 7
63 Pye 7N 15529 Golli Guitar/Week (with Danny Gavan) . . . 7
65 Parlophone R 5286 Kiss Me Now/What Colour Is The Wind . . . 7
65 Parlophone R 5308 Atom Bomb Song Part 3/Talented Man . . . 7

SHADOWFAX
79 BFD SFX 100 Really Into You (p/s) . . . 50
80 Risky Discs RISK 1 The Russians Are Coming/Calling The Shots . . . 8

SHADOWS (U.K.)
(see also Cliff Richard, Drifters, Five Chesternuts, Hank Marvin, Marvin Welch & Farrar, Bruce Welch, John Henry Rostill, Brian Bennett, Jet Harris, Tony Meehan, Vipers Skiffle Group, Marty Wilde, Krew Kats, Interns, Strangers, Wasp, MacArthur Park, Thunder Company, Alan Hawkshaw)

SINGLES
59 Columbia DB 4387 Saturday Dance/Lonesome Fella . . . 50
59 Columbia DB 4387 Saturday Dance/Lonesome Fella (78) . . . 200
60 Columbia DB 4484 Apache/Quartermaster's Stores (green label) . . . 8
60 Columbia DB 4484 Apache/Quartermaster's Stores (later black label) . . . 18
60 Columbia DB 4530 Man Of Mystery/The Stranger . . . 5
61 Columbia DB 4580 F.B.I./Midnight . . . 5
61 Columbia DB 4637 The Frightened City/Back Home . . . 5
61 Columbia DB 4698 Kon-Tiki/36-24-36 . . . 5
61 Columbia DB 4726 The Savage/Peace Pipe . . . 5
62 Columbia DB 4790 Wonderful Land/Stars Fell On Stockton . . . 5
62 Columbia DB 4870 Guitar Tango/What A Lovely Tune . . . 5
(The above singles were originally issued with green labels; later black label copies are worth £10.)
62 Columbia DB 4948 Dance On!/All Day . . . 5
63 Columbia DB 4984 Foot Tapper/The Breeze And I . . . 5
63 Columbia DB 7047 Atlantis/I Want You To Want Me . . . 5
63 Columbia DB 7106 Shindig/It's Been A Blue Day . . . 5
63 Columbia DB 7163 Geronimo/Shazam . . . 5
64 Columbia DB 7231 Theme For Young Lovers/This Hammer . . . 5
64 Columbia DB 7261 The Rise And Fall Of Flingel Bunt/It's A Man's World . . . 5
64 Columbia DB 7261 The Rise And Fall Of Flingel Bunt/It's A Man's World (mispressing with A-side on both sides) . . . 10
64 Columbia DB 7342 Rhythm 'n' Greens/The Miracle . . . 6
64 Columbia DB 7416 Genie With The Light Brown Lamp/Little Princess . . . 10
65 Columbia DB 7476 Mary Anne/Chu-Chi . . . 6
65 Columbia DB 7588 Stingray/Alice In Sunderland (in export p/s) . . . 20
65 Columbia DB 7650 Don't Make My Baby Blue/My Grandfather's Clock (in export p/s) . . . 20
65 Columbia DB 7769 The War Lord/I Wish I Could Shimmy Like My Sister Arthur . . . 10
66 Columbia DB 7853 I Met A Girl/Late Night Set . . . 10
66 Columbia DB 7952 A Place In The Sun/Will You Be There . . . 10
66 Columbia DB 8034 The Dreams I Dream/Scotch On The Socks ('B' label demos worth £50) . . . 30
67 Columbia PSR 305 Thunderbirds Are Go (1-sided advance promo) . . . 60
67 Columbia DB 8170 Maroc 7/Bombay Duck . . . 10
67 Columbia PSR 308 Maroc 7 (1-sided demo with spoken-word intro) . . . 60
67 Columbia PSR 310 Chelsea Boot/Jigsaw (demo only) . . . 80
67 Columbia DB 8264 Tomorrow's Cancelled/Somewhere . . . 15
68 Columbia DB 8326 Running Out Of World/HANK MARVIN: London's Not Too Far . . . 15
68 Columbia DB 8372 Dear Old Mrs. Bell/Trying To Forget The One You Love . . . 15
69 Columbia DB 8628 Slaughter On Tenth Avenue/HANK MARVIN: Midnight Cowboy . . . 15

EPs
61 Columbia SEG 8061 THE SHADOWS (mono) . . . 10
61 Columbia ESG 7834 THE SHADOWS (stereo) . . . 20
61 Columbia SEG 8094 THE SHADOWS TO THE FORE . . . 10
(The above EPs were originally issued with turquoise labels; later blue/black label copies are worth two-thirds the values listed.)
62 Columbia SEG 8193 THE BOYS (mono) . . . 10
62 Columbia ESG 7881 THE BOYS (stereo, turquoise labels) . . . 30
62 Columbia ESG 7881 THE BOYS (stereo, later black/blue labels) . . . 25

			MINT VALUE £
63	Columbia SEG 8218	OUT OF THE SHADOWS (mono)	10
63	Columbia ESG 7883	OUT OF THE SHADOWS (stereo, turquoise labels)	30
63	Columbia ESG 7883	OUT OF THE SHADOWS (stereo, black/blue labels)	25
63	Columbia SEG 8233	DANCE ON WITH THE SHADOWS	10
63	Columbia SEG 8249	OUT OF THE SHADOWS NO. 2 (mono)	10
63	Columbia ESG 7895	OUT OF THE SHADOWS NO. 2 (stereo ESG 7895)	25
63	Columbia SEG 8268	FOOT TAPPING WITH THE SHADOWS	10
63	Columbia SEG 8278	LOS SHADOWS (2 different sleeves)	10
63	Columbia SEG 8286	SHINDIG WITH THE SHADOWS	20
64	Columbia SEG 8321	THOSE BRILLIANT SHADOWS	20
64	Columbia SEG 8342	DANCE WITH THE SHADOWS	20
64	Columbia SEG 8362	RHYTHM AND GREENS (mono))	18
64	Columbia ESG 7904	RHYTHM AND GREENS (stereo)	30
64	Columbia SEG 8375	DANCE WITH THE SHADOWS NO. 2	20
65	Columbia SEG 8396	THEMES FROM "ALADDIN AND HIS WONDERFUL LAMP"	20
65	Columbia SEG 8408	DANCE WITH THE SHADOWS NO. 3	20
65	Columbia SEG 8445	ALICE IN SUNDERLAND	20
65	Columbia SEG 8459	THE SOUND OF THE SHADOWS	25
66	Columbia SEG 8473	THE SOUND OF THE SHADOWS NO. 2	25
66	Columbia SEG 8494	THE SOUND OF THE SHADOWS NO. 3	25
66	Columbia SEG 8500	THOSE TALENTED SHADOWS	22
66	Columbia SEG 8510	THUNDERBIRDS ARE GO! (with Cliff Richard)	60
67	Columbia SEG 8528	THE SHADOWS ON STAGE AND SCREEN	40
ALBUMS			
61	Columbia 33SX 1374	THE SHADOWS (mono)	20
61	Columbia SCX 3414	THE SHADOWS (stereo)	40
62	Columbia 33SX 1458	OUT OF THE SHADOWS (mono)	20
62	Columbia SCX 3449	OUT OF THE SHADOWS (stereo)	30
(The above LPs were originally issued with green labels; later blue/black label copies are worth two-thirds the values listed.)			
63	Columbia 33SX 1522	GREATEST HITS (stereo SCX 1522)	15
64	Columbia 33SX 1619	DANCE WITH THE SHADOWS (mono)	20
64	Columbia SCX 3511	DANCE WITH THE SHADOWS (stereo)	22
65	Columbia 33SX 1736	THE SOUND OF THE SHADOWS (mono)	20
65	Columbia SCX 3554	THE SOUND OF THE SHADOWS (stereo)	22
65	Columbia 33SX 1791	MORE HITS! (stereo SCX 3578)	15
66	Columbia 33SX/SCX 6041	SHADOW MUSIC	15
67	Columbia S(C)X 6148	JIGSAW	18
67	Columbia S(C)X 6199	FROM HANK, BRUCE, BRIAN AND JOHN	18
68	Columbia SX 6282	ESTABLISHED 1958 (half by Cliff Richard, mono)	18
68	Columbia SCX 6282	ESTABLISHED 1958 (half by Cliff Richard, stereo)	15
(The above LPs were originally issued with blue/black labels; later silver/black label copies are worth half the values listed.)			
70	Columbia SCX 6420	SHADES OF ROCK	18
72	World Records ALBUM 72	THE SHADOWS (6-LP box set)	30
73	EMI EMA 762	ROCKIN' WITH CURLY LEADS	15
75	EMI EMC 3066	SPECS APPEAL	12
77	EMI EMTV 3	TWENTY GOLDEN GREATS (mispressing, side 2 plays Pink Floyd's "Animals")	30

SHADOWS (U.S.)

58	HMV POP 563	Jungle Fever/Under Stars Of Love	110
58	HMV POP 563	Jungle Fever/Under Stars Of Love (78)	110

SHADOWS OF KNIGHT

66	Atlantic AT 4085	Gloria/Dark Side	35
66	Atlantic 584 021	Oh Yeah/Light Bulb Blues	25
66	Atlantic 584 045	Bad Little Woman/Gospel Zone	25
67	Atlantic 584 136	Someone Like Me/Three For Love	25
69	Buddah 201 024	Shake/From Way Out To Way Under	30
79	Radar ADA 11	GLORIA (LP)	15

SHADROCKS

67	Island WI 3061	Go Go Special/Count Down	12
68	Jay Boy BOY 2	There Is/Jigsaw	6

SHADY

(see also Mercury Rev)

98	Narcotic Candy BBQ 41 TT	Narcotic Candy/Micro Bodi Dot Con (10", p/s)	8
98	Narcotic Candy BBQ 41 CD	Narcotic Candy/Micro Bodi Dot Con (CD)	8

SHADY BARD

06	Static Caravan Van 108	TREEOLOGY EP (CD, hand wrapped in brown paper and string, 100 only)	15

DOREEN SHAFFER

(see also Bob Marley/Wailers, Lloyd Clarke, Doreen & Jackie)

69	Unity UN 536	No Matter What/Walk Through This World	8
69	Unity UN 538	How Much Is That Doggy In The Window/As Long As He Needs Me	6
70	Pama SECO 31	FIRST LADY OF REGGAE (LP)	80

JOHN SHAFT

72	Downtown DT 488	Forever Music/BLOSSOM JOHNSON: The Boy I Love	6

SHAFTESBURY

80	O.K. SRT CUS 025	Hit Man	5
80	O.K. OKA 001	THE LULL BEFORE THE STORM (LP, with insert)	15
81	O.K. OKA 002	WE ARE THE BOYS (LP)	12

BOBBY SHAFTO

62	Parlophone R 4870	Over And Over/I Want My Bed	5
62	Parlophone R 4958	Feel So Blue/I Haven't Got A Girl	5
64	Parlophone R 5130	She's My Girl/Wonderful You	5
64	Parlophone R 5167	Love, Love, Love (Don't Let Me Down)/I Don't Love You Anymore	5
64	Parlophone R 5184	Who Wouldn't Love A Girl Like That/I Remember	5

MINT VALUE £

65 Parlophone R 5252 How Could You Do A Thing Like That To Me/Baby Then ... 5
66 Parlophone R 5403 Lonely Is As Lonely Does/The Same Old Room ... 15
66 Parlophone R 5481 A Little Like You/See Me Cry ... 5

SHAG 'N' SKOOB
92 WINTER 3 SKOOBY CHEWNZ VOL. 1 EP (12") ... 40

SHAG NASTY
79 Shag Nasty SN 1 No Bullshit Just Rock 'n' Roll/Looking For A Love? (p/s) ... 30

SHAGRAT
90 Shagrat ORC 001 Amanda/Peppermint Flickstick (p/s, 500 only, autographed) ... 10
90 Shagrat ORC 001 Amanda/Peppermint Flickstick (p/s, 500 only, some autographed) ... 6
91 Shagrat ENT 001 NOTHING EXCEEDS LIKE EXCESS
(mini LP, as Steve Took's Shagrat, numbered, 400 only) ... 12

SHAKA FATMAN
80 Live And Love LAP 12 CONFRONTATION DUB - SHAKA (WARRIOR) VS. FATMAN (KILLER) (LP) ... 30

SHAKANE
76 United Artists UP 36087 Jenny/Gang Man ... 12

SHAKE
(see also Rezillos, Jo Callis, TV 21)
79 Sire SIR 4016 Culture Shock/Dream On ... 10
79 Sire SIR 4016-10 Culture Shock/Glass House/Dream On/(But) Not Mine (10", p/s) ... 12

SHAKEOUTS
65 Columbia DB 7613 Every Little Once In A While/Well Who's That ... 60

SHAKERS (U.K.)
(see also Kingsize Taylor & Dominoes)
63 Polydor NH 52158 Money/Memphis Tennessee ... 25
63 Polydor NH 52213 Hippy Hippy Shake/Dr. Feelgood ... 25
63 Polydor NH 66991 Hippy Hippy Shake/Dr. Feelgood ... 25
63 Polydor NH 52258 Money/Hippy Hippy Shake ... 25
63 Polydor NH 52272 Whole Lotta Lovin'/I Can Tell ... 25
63 Polydor 237 139 LET'S DO THE SLOP, TWIST, MADISON,
HULLY GULLY WITH THE SHAKERS (LP) ... 70

SHAKERS (U.S.)
73 Probe PRO 582 One Wonderful Moment/Love, Love, Love ... 8
74 ABC ABC 4018 One Wonderful Moment/Love, Love, Love (reissue) ... 6

CHRIS SHAKESPEARE GLOBE SHOW
(see also Globe Show)
69 Page One POF 113 Ob-La-Di, Ob-La-Da/Tin Soldier ... 25

JOHN SHAKESPEARE
69 Decca F 12896 Number One Theme/Fade Out (with p/s) ... 30
69 Decca F 12896 Number One Theme/Fade Out ... 10

SHAKESPEARES
(see also Fynn McCool)
68 RCA Victor RCA 1695 Something To Believe In/Burning My Fingers ... 50

SHAKEY JAKE
69 Liberty LBL 83217E FURTHER ON UP THE ROAD (LP) ... 40

SHAKEY VICK
69 Pye NPL 18276 LITTLE WOMAN, YOU'RE SO SWEET (LP mono) ... 50
69 Pye NSPL 18276 LITTLE WOMAN, YOU'RE SO SWEET (LP stereo, in mono sleeve
with 'STEREO NSPL' sticker on rear) ... 35

SAM SHAM
69 Blue Cat BS 157 Drumbago's Dead/SPARTERS: Song Of The Year ... 15

SHAMBLES
(see also Mandrake Paddle Steramers, Prowler)
75 RCA RCA 2533 Hello Baby/Held Me Spellbound ... 40

SHAME
(see also Shy Limbs, King Crimson, Gods, Emerson Lake & Palmer)
67 MGM MGM 1349 Don't Go Away Little Girl/Dreams Don't Bother Me (125 with picture insert) ... 150
67 MGM MGM 1349 Don't Go Away Little Girl/Dreams Don't Bother Me (125 without picture insert) .. 90

SHAMEN
(see also Alone Again Or, Stretchheads)
86 One Big Guitar OBG 003T THEY MAY BE RIGHT... BUT THEY'RE CERTAINLY WRONG (12" EP) ... 12

SHAMES
(see also Isaac Guillory)
66 CBS 202344 Sugar And Spice/Ben Franklin's Almanac ... 25
66 CBS 202450 I Wanna Meet You/We Could Be Happy ... 18
67 CBS 2704 Mr Unreliable/Georgia ... 12
67 CBS 2929 It Could Be We're In Love/I Was Lonely When ... 22
68 CBS 3820 Greenburg, Glickstein, Charles, David, Smith And Jones/Warm ... 15

SHAMPOO
93 Icerink DAV 06 Blisters & Bruises/Paydirt/I Love Little Pussy (p/s, pink vinyl) ... 20

SHAMROCKS
65 Polydor BM 56503 La La La La La/And I Need You ... 20

SHAM 69
(see also Jimmy Edwards)
77 Step Forward SF 4 I Don't Wanna/Ulster/Red London (black & white photo p/s) ... 15
77 Step Forward SF 412 I Don't Wanna/Ulster/Red London (12", black & white photo p/s) ... 10

			MINT VALUE £
77	Polydor (no cat. no.)	Song Of The Streets/Fanx (1-sided concert freebie, red brick-wall label; white label copies are counterfeits)	20
78	Polydor 2058 966	Borstal Breakout/Hey Little Rich Boy (p/s)	15
78	Polydor 2059 023	Angels With Dirty Faces/The Cockney Kids Are Innocent (p/s)	8
78	Polydor 2059 050	If The Kids Are United/Sunday Morning Nightmare (p/s)	6
78		What Have We Got? (1-sided gig only 45, 500 only)	25
79	Step Forward SF 412	I Don't Wanna/Red London/Ulster (12" reissue, yellow p/s)	8
79	Step Forward SF 4	I Don't Wanna/Red London (reissue, p/s)	5
79		Hersham Boys/Day Tripper (Original "Pye Studios" acetate for 'Hersham' single, release withdrawn as unable to clear copyright)	250
79	Polydor POSP 64	Hersham Boys/I Don't Wanna (live)/Tell Us The Truth (live) (p/s)	5
79	Polydor POSPX 64	Hersham Boys/I Don't Wanna (live)/Rip Off (live)/I'm A Man, I'm A Boy (live)/ Tell Us The Truth (live) (12", p/s)	8
79	Polydor POSP 82	You're A Better Man Than I/Give A Dog A Bone (p/s)	5
87	Legacy LGY 70	Ban The Gun/Ban The Gun	15
79	Polydor POLD 5025	THE ADVENTURES OF THE HERSHAM BOYS (LP, with 12" EP [2812 045], stickered sleeve)	12
80	Polydor 2383 596	THE FIRST, THE BEST AND THE LAST (LP, with live EP [RIOT 1/2816 028])	15

VALERIE SHAND

58	Philips PB 833	When The Boys Talk About Girls/Careful, Careful	10
58	Philips PB 879	Meet Me Tonight In Dreamland.One Billion Seven Million Thirty-Three	8
59	Philips PB 929	Make Love To Me/Baisez Moi	8

WINSTON SHAN(D)

69	Bullet BU 399	Throw Me Corn/Darling Remember (B-side actually by Pat Edwards)	25
69	Bullet BU 411	Matilda (as Wilston Shan)/HARMONIANS: Come To Me	25
70	Moodisc MU 3505	I'll Run Away/Time Is The Master	100
72	Camel CA 88	Audrey (as Winston Shan)/So Nice (as Winston Shan)	6

TRISTRAM SHANDY

74	Tiffany 6121 505	Saccharine Sandie, Fingers 'N Thumbs/Mr. Blue	6

LISA SHANE

66	Pye 7N 17124	Come And Get Me/Big Wide World	6

SHANE & SHANE GANG

64	Pye 7N 15662	Whistle Stop/Who Wrote That Song	35

SHANES

65	Columbia DB 7601	I Don't Want Your Love/New Orleans	70

SHANE SISTERS

60	Ember EMB S 115	My Mommy Told Me/Presents On The Christmas Tree	7

SHANGAANS

65	Columbia DB 7551	Genzene (What Have I Done)/Yeh Girl	12
65	Columbia Studio 2 TWO 109	JUNGLE DRUMS (LP)	20

SHANGO

69	A&M AMS 754	Mama Lion/Ljuba Ljuba	6

SHANGRI-LAS

64	Red Bird RB 10008	Remember (Walking In The Sand)/It's Easier To Cry	10
64	Red Bird RB 10014	Leader Of The Pack/What Is Love?	10
65	Red Bird RB 10018	Give Him A Great Big Kiss/Twist And Shout	15
65	Red Bird RB 10025	Out In The Streets/The Boy	15
65	Red Bird RB 10030	Give Us Your Blessings/Heaven Only Knows	15
65	Red Bird RB 10036	Right Now And Not Later/Train From Kansas City	30
66	Red Bird RB 10043	I Can Never Go Home Anymore/Bulldog	15
66	Red Bird RB 10048	Long Live Our Love/Sophisticated Boom Boom	15
66	Red Bird RB 10053	He Cried/Dressed In Black	15
66	Red Bird RB 10068	Past, Present, And Future/Paradise	20
66	Philips 6051027	Train From Kansas City/Past Present And Future	10
67	Mercury MF 962	The Sweet Sound Of Summer/I'll Never Learn	15
67	Mercury MF 979	Take The Time/Footsteps On The Roof	15
65	Red Bird RB 40 002	THE SHANGRI-LAS (EP)	50
66	Red Bird RB 40 004	I CAN NEVER GO HOME ANYMORE (EP, unreleased)	0
65	Red Bird RB 20 101	THE SHANGRI-LAS - LEADER OF THE PACK (LP)	80
66	Mercury MCL 20096	GOLDEN HITS OF THE SHANGRI-LAS (LP)	15

BUD SHANK

(see also Shorty Rogers)

56	Vogue V 2376	Royal Garden Blues/It Had To Be You (with Bill Perkins Quintet)	5
56	Vogue V 2383	When Your Lover Has Gone/There's A Small Hotel (with Bob Brookmeyer)	5
56	Vogue V 2385	Shank's Pranks/Left Bank (with Shorty Rogers Quintet)	7
59	Vogue LAE 12248	LATIN CONTRASTS (LP)	20

ANANDA SHANKAR

69	Reprise RSLP 6398	ANANDA SHANKAR (JUMPING JACK FLASH) (LP)	80
70	EMI	ANANDA SHANKAR AND HIS MUSIC (LP)	60
71	Reprise K 44092	ANANDA SHANKAR (LP, reissue)	30

RAVI SHANKAR

(see also Ali Akbar Khan, Will Sergeant)

72	Apple APPLE 37	Joi Bangla/Oh Bhaugowan/Raga Mishri-Jhinjhoti (p/s)	40
71	Mushroom 300 MR 8	FOUR RAGA MOODS (2-LP)	20
72	United Artists UAG 29379	AT THE WOODSTOCK FESTIVAL (LP, gatefold)	15
73	Apple SAPDO 1002	IN CONCERT - 1972 (2-LP, with Ali Akbar Khan, gatefold sleeve)	90

BILL SHANKLY

70s	Technical TECLP 001A	SHANKS ON SOCCER (2-LP)	20

JOHNNY SHANLY

60	Columbia DB 4526	I Wonder/It Happens That Way	6

MINT VALUE £

SHANNON
(See also Marty Wilde)

75	Magnet MAG 38	Come Back And Love Me/She's A High Flyer	10

DEAN SHANNON

60	HMV POP 820	Blinded With Love/Jezebel	25
62	HMV POP 1103	Ubangi Stomp/Blowing Wild	35

DEL SHANNON
(see also Maximilian)

SINGLES

61	London HLX 9317	Runaway/Jody	5
61	London HLX 9317	Runaway/Jody (mispressed B-side, plays "The Snake" by Maximilian)	30
61	London HLX 9402	Hats Off To Larry/Don't Gild The Lily, Lily	5
61	London HLX 9462	So Long Baby/The Answer To Everything	5
62	London HLX 9515	Hey! Little Girl/You Never Talked About Me	5
62	London HLX 9587	Cry Myself To Sleep/I'm Gonna Move On	10
62	London HLX 9609	The Swiss Maid/Ginny In The Mirror	5
63	London HLX 9653	Little Town Flirt/The Wamboo	5
63	London HLX 9710	Two Kinds Of Teardrops/Kelly	5
63	London HLX 9761	Two Silhouettes/My Wild One	10
63	London HLU 9800	Sue's Gonna Be Mine/Since She's Gone	10
64	London HLU 9858	That's The Way Love Is/Time Of The Day	10
64	Stateside SS 269	Mary Jane/Stains On My Letter	10
64	Stateside SS 317	Handy Man/Give Her Lots Of Lovin'	10
64	Stateside SS 349	Do You Want To Dance/This Is All I Have To Give	10
64	Stateside SS 368	Keep Searching (We'll Follow The Sun)/Broken Promises	5
65	Stateside SS 395	Stranger In Town/Over You	15
65	Stateside SS 430	Break Up/Why Don't You Tell Him	10
65	Stateside SS 452	Move It On Over/She Still Remembers Tony	15
66	Stateside SS 494	I Can't Believe My Ears/I Wish I Wasn't Me Tonight	15
66	Liberty LIB 55866	The Big Hurt/I Got It Bad	10
66	Liberty LIB 55889	For A Little While/Hey Little Star	15
67	Liberty LIB 55939	She/What Makes You Run	15
67	Liberty LIB 10277	Mind Over Matter/Led Along	10
67	Liberty LBF 15020	Runaway/Show Me	10
68	Liberty LBF 15061	Thinkin' It Over/Runnin' On Back	15
68	Liberty LBF 15079	Gemini/Magical Musical Box	40
69	Stateside SS 8025	Comin' Back To Me/Sweet Mary Lou	10
70	Stateside SS 8040	Sister Isabelle/Colorado Rain	10
74	United Artists UP 35740	And The Music Plays On/In My Arms Again	8

EPS

62	London RE-X 1332	RUNAWAY WITH DEL SHANNON	20
63	London RE-X 1346	DEL SHANNON NO. 2	20
63	London RE-X 1383	DEL'S OWN FAVOURITES	20
63	London RE-X 1387	FROM DEL TO YOU	20
67	Liberty LEP 2272	THE NEW DEL SHANNON	40

ALBUMS

61	London HA-X 2402	RUNAWAY WITH DEL SHANNON	35
63	London HA-X 8071	HATS OFF TO DEL SHANNON	35
63	London HA-X 8091	LITTLE TOWN FLIRT	35
65	Stateside SL 10115	HANDY MAN	35
65	Stateside SE 1029	DEL SHANNON HITS	35
65	Stateside SL 10130	DEL SHANNON SINGS HANK WILLIAMS	40
65	Stateside SL 10140	ONE THOUSAND SIX HUNDRED AND SIXTY-ONE SECONDS WITH DEL SHANNON	40
66	Liberty LBY 1320	THIS IS MY BAG (mono)	25
66	Liberty SLBY 1320	THIS IS MY BAG (stereo)	30
66	Liberty LBY 1335	TOTAL COMMITMENT (mono)	25
66	Liberty SLBY 1335	TOTAL COMMITMENT (stereo)	30
68	Liberty LBL/LBS 83114E	THE FURTHER ADVENTURES OF CHARLES WESTOVER	80
73	United Artists UAS 29474	LIVE IN ENGLAND	15

LINDA SHANNON

59	Parlophone R 4603	Goodbye Charlie/If You Only Knew	6

MIKE SHANNON & STRANGERS
(see under Strangers)

SHAPE OF THE RAIN

71	RCA Neon NE 1001	Woman/Wasting My Time	10
71	RCA RCA 2129	My Friend John/Yes	5
71	RCA Neon NE 7	RILEY, RILEY, WOOD & WAGGETT (LP, gatefold sleeve)	90

SHAPE & SIZES

66	Decca F 12441	A Little Lovin' Somethin'/Rain On My Face	10

SHAPES

79	Sofa SEAT 1/FRR 004	THE SHAPES (WOT'S FOR LUNCH, MUM?) (EP, no p/s, with insert)	12
79	Good Vibrations GOT 13	Blast Off/Airline Disasters (p/s)	15

HELEN SHAPIRO
(see also Ella Stone & Moss)

SINGLES

61	Columbia DB 4589	Don't Treat Me Like A Child/When I'm With you	5
61	Columbia DB 4670	You Don't Know/Marvellous Lie	5
61	Columbia DB 4715	Walkin' Back To Happiness/Kiss 'N' Run	5
61	Columbia DB 4782	Tell Me What He Said/I Apologise	5
62	Columbia DB 4824	Let's Talk About Love/Sometime Yesterday	5

			MINT VALUE £
62	Columbia DB 4869	Little Miss Lonely/I Don't Care	5
62	Columbia DB 4908	Keep Away From Other Girls/Cry My Heart Out	10
63	Columbia DB 4966	Queen For Tonight/Daddy Couldn't Get Me One Of Those	20
63	Columbia DB 7026	Woe Is Me/I Walked Right In	5
63	Columbia DB 7072	Not Responsible/No Trespassing	5
63	Columbia DB 7130	Look Who It Is/Walking In My Dreams	10
64	Columbia DB 7190	Fever/Ole Father Time	25
64	Columbia DB 7266	Look Over Your Shoulder/You Won't Come Home	10
64	Columbia DB 7340	Shop Around/He Knows How To Love Me	100
64	Columbia DB 7395	I Wish I'd Never Loved You/I Was Only Kidding	10
65	Columbia DB 7517	Tomorrow Is Another Day/It's So Funny I Could Cry	10
65	Columbia DB 7587	Here In Your Arms/Only Once	10
65	Columbia DB 7690	Something Wonderful/Just A Line	10
66	Columbia DB 7810	Forget About The Bad Things/Wait A Little Longer	10
66	Columbia DB 8073	In My Calendar/Empty House	10
67	Columbia DB 8148	Make Me Belong To You/The Way Of The World	10
67	Columbia DB 8256	She Needs Company/Stop And You Will Become Aware	125
67	Columbia DB 8256	She Needs Company/Stop And You Will Become Aware (DJ copy)	125
68	Pye 7N 17600	You'll Get Me Loving You/Silly Boy (I Love You)	12
69	Pye 7N 17714	Today Has Been Cancelled/Face The Music	12
69	Pye 7N 17785	You've Guessed/Take Me For A While	20
70	Pye 7N 17893	Take Down A Note Miss Smith/Couldn't You See	12
70	Pye 7N 17975	Waiting On The Shores Of Nowhere/A Glass Of Wine	12
75	DJM DJS 363	You're A Love Child/That's The Reason I Love You	10
77	Arista 131	Can't Break The Habit/For All The Wrong Reasons	10
78	Arista 178	Every Little Bit Hurts/Touchin' Wood	10

EPs

61	Columbia SEG 8128	HELEN (mono, 'smiling' or 'cross-armed' sleeve)	15
61	Columbia ESG 7872	HELEN (stereo, 'smiling' or 'cross-armed' sleeve)	20
61	Columbia SEG 8136	HELEN'S HIT PARADE	15
62	Columbia SEG 8170	A TEENAGER SINGS THE BLUES (mono)	20
62	Columbia ESG 7880	A TEENAGER SINGS THE BLUES (stereo)	25
62	Columbia SEG 8174	MORE HITS FROM HELEN	15
62	Columbia SEG 8209	EVEN MORE HITS FROM HELEN	15
63	Columbia SEG 8229	TOPS' WITH ME NO. 1 (mono)	20
63	Columbia ESG 7888	TOPS' WITH ME NO. 1 (stereo)	25
63	Columbia SEG 8243	TOPS' WITH ME NO. 2 (mono)	20
63	Columbia ESG 7891	TOPS' WITH ME NO. 2 (stereo)	25

LPs

62	Columbia 33SX 1397	TOPS' WITH ME (mono)	15
62	Columbia SCX 3438	TOPS' WITH ME (stereo)	40
63	Columbia 33SX 1494	HELEN'S SIXTEEN (mono)	35
63	Columbia SCX 3470	HELEN'S SIXTEEN (stereo)	60
63	Columbia 33SX 1561	HELEN IN NASHVILLE	30
64	Columbia 33SX 1661	HELEN HITS OUT (mono)	35
64	Columbia SCX 3533	HELEN HITS OUT (stereo SCX 3533)	60
65	EMI Encore! ENC 209	12 HITS AND A MISS HELEN SHAPIRO	20
74	Columbia SCX 6565	THE VERY BEST OF HELEN SHAPIRO	12

SHARADES

(see also Ladybirds, Breakaways)

64	Decca F 11811	Dumb Head/Boy Trouble	85

BILLY SHA RAE

71	Action ACT 4602	Do It/Crying Clown	15

BILLY SHARI

58	Decca F 11069	Going Home For Christmas/Count Every Star (as Shari)	5
68	United Artists UP 2235	It's So Lonely Being Together/You Walked Out On Me Before	5

SHARKS

(see also Marcisa & Jeff, Roy Richards)

68	RCA RCA 1776	Goodbye Lorene/Funkology	20

SHARKS

(see also Baker-Gurvitz Army, Chris Spedding, Andy Fraser Band, Free)

73	Island ILPS 9233	FIRST WATER (LP, 'pink rim palm tree' label with inner sleeve)	12
74	Island ILPS 9271	JAB IT IN YORE EYE (LP, 'palm tree' label with inner sleeve)	12

RALPH SHARON

(see also Tony Bennett)

53	Decca LF 1107	SPRING FEVER (10" LP)	12
53	Decca LF 1138	AUTUMN LEAVES (10" LP)	20
53	Lyragon AF 1	COCKTAIL TIME (10" LP)	15

SHARONETTES

75	Black Magic BM 102	Papa Ooh Mow Mow/Instrumental	6
75	Black Magic BM 104	Going To A Go Go/Instrumental	7

BOBBY SHARP & OTHERS

65	Stateside SS 404	Blues For Mr. Charlie (Parts 1 & 2) (with Paul Sindap, Joe Lee Wilson & Little Butler)	20

DEE DEE SHARP

(see also Chubby Checker & Dee Dee Sharp)

62	Columbia DB 4818	Mashed Potato Time/Set My Heart At Ease	25
62	Columbia DB 4874	Gravy (For My Mashed Potatoes)/Baby Cakes	25
62	Cameo Parkway C 230	Ride/Night	40
63	Cameo Parkway C 244	Do The Bird/Lover Boy	25
63	Cameo Parkway C 260	Rock Me In The Cradle Of Love/You'll Never Be Mine	20
63	Cameo Parkway C 274	Wild/Why Doncha Ask Me	20

			MINT VALUE £
65	Cameo Parkway C 375	I Really Love You/Standing In The Need Of Love	80
65	Cameo Parkway C 375	I Really Love You/Standing In The Need Of Love (DJ copy)	125
65	Cameo Parkway C 382	It's A Funny Situation/There Ain't Nothing I Wouldn't Do (demo-only)	150
66	Atlantic 584 056	My Best Friend's Man/Bye Bye Baby	20
69	Action ACT 4522	What Kind Of Lady/You're Gonna Miss Me	70
79	London HA-U 8514	CAMEO PARKWAY SESSIONS (LP)	25

STEVE SHARP & THE CLEANCUTS
(see also Rowdies)

80	Happy Face MM 122	We Are The Mods/He Wants To Be A Mod	125

BERNARD SHARPE

66	Parlophone R 5519	Lost In Space/Jorrocks	7

RAY SHARPE

59	London HLW 8932	Linda Lu/Red Sails In The Sunset (triangular centre)	50
59	London HLW 8932	Linda Lu/Red Sails In The Sunset (round centre)	40
59	London HLW 8932	Linda Lu/Red Sails In The Sunset (78)	40
63	United Artists UP 1032	Hey Little Girl/Day You Left Me	15

ROCKY SHARPE & THE REPLAYS

82	Chiswick DICE 9	Heart/Mary (Won't You Marry Me) (withdrawn, approx. 100 only)	10

SHARPE & NUMAN
(see also Gary Numan)

85	Polydor PODJ 722	Change Your Mind (p/s, 1-sided DJ promo)	10
88	Polydor POSPCD894	No More Liex (Extended Version)/Voices/Change Your Mind/ No More Lies (7" Version)	8
88	Polydor POSPCD894	No More Lies (Extended Version)/Voices/Change Your Mind/ No More Lies (7" Version)) (CD, some signed by Gary Numan)	12
89	Polydor POPB 43	I'm On Automatic/No More Lies (New Version, stickered poster sleeve)	6
89	Polydor 839-5201	AUTOMATIC	30

SHARPEES

66	Stateside SS 495	Tired Of Being Lonely/Just To Please You	75
66	Stateside SS 495	Tired Of Being Lonely/Just To Please You (DJ copy)	150
73	President PT 389	Do The 45/Make Up Your Mind	15
73	President PT 399	Tired Of Being Lonely/Just To Please You (reissue)	15

SHARPS
(see also Thurston Harris)

57	Vogue V 9086	Lock My Heart/Love Is Here To Stay	750
57	Vogue V 9086	Lock My Heart/Love Is Here To Stay (78)	120
58	Vogue V 9096	Shufflin'/What Will I Gain	750
58	Vogue V 9096	Shufflin'/What Will I Gain (78)	120

S-HATERS

81	Outer Himmilayan OHR 02	Death Of A Vampire/Research (p/s)	12

SHATTERED DOLLS

80	Rox ROX 1	Lipstick Killer/Talk To Me/Valley Of The Dolls 1 & 2	20

MIKE SHAUN

63	Decca F 11733	So Lonely/Let's Fall In Love	15

ADRIAN SHAW
(see also Hawkwind, Bevis Frond)

96	Woronzow W0027	TEA FOR THE HYDRA (LP, 299 copies only, in hand-finished sleeves)	15

ARTIE SHAW

54	MGM EPC 3	ARTIE SHAW (EP, export issue)	7

MARLENA SHAW

67	Chess CRS 8054	Mercy Mercy Mercy/Go Away Little Boy	10
76	United Artists UP 36125	It's Better Than Walking Out/Be For Real	8

NINA SHAW

68	CBS 3239	Woven In My Soul/Love So Fine	7
68	CBS 3556	From Now Till Then/Window Of My Mind	8
69	CBS 4227	One Fine Day/Somewhere In The World	10

RICKY SHAW

62	London HLU 9606	No Love But Your Love/Be Still, Be Still, My Own	8

ROLAND SHAW ORCHESTRA

65	Decca LK 4730	JAMES BOND IN ACTION (LP)	12
67	Phase 4 Stereo PFS 4125	MORE JAMES BOND IN ACTION (LP)	12
60s	London BSP	DIAMONDS ARE FOREVER (LP, gatefold sleeve, export issue)	12

SANDIE SHAW
SINGLES

64	Pye 7N 15671	As Long As You're Happy Baby/Ya-Ya-Da-Da	40
65	Pye 7N 15783	I'll Stop At Nothing/You Can't Blame Him	6
65	Pye 7N 15841	Long Live Love/I've Heard About Him	5
66	Pye 7N 17163	Run/Long Walk Home	8
66	Pye 7N 17212	Think Sometimes About Me/Hide All Emotion	10
67	Pye 7N 17239	I Don't Need Anything/Keep In Touch	10
67	Pye 7N 17346	Tonight In Tokyo/You've Been Seeing Her Again	6
68	Pye 7N 17441	Today/London (pink label, later blue)	6
68	Pye 7N 17504	Don't Run Away/Stop	10
68	Pye 7N 17564	Show Me/One More Lie	10
68	Pye 7N 17587	Together/Turn On The Sunshine	10
68	Pye 7N 17611	Those Were The Days/Make It Go	8
69	Pye 7N 17726	Think It All Over/Send Me A Letter	12

MINT VALUE £

70 Pye 7N 17954 Wight Is Wight/That's The Way He's Made. 10
70 Pye 7N 45040 Rose Garden/Maybe I'm Amazed 10
84 Rough Trade RTT 130 Hand In Glove/I Don't Owe You Anything/Jeanne (12", p/s, with The Smiths). . . . 10

EPS

64 Pye NEP 24208 (THERE'S) ALWAYS SOMETHING THERE TO REMIND ME 15
65 Pye NEP 24220 LONG LIVE LOVE 15
65 Pye NEP 24232 TALK ABOUT LOVE 15
65 Pye NEP 24234 SANDIE 15
66 Pye NEP 24236 MESSAGE UNDERSTOOD 15
66 Pye NEP 24247 TOMORROW 20
66 Pye NEP 24254 NOTHING COMES EASY 20
66 Pye NEP 24264 RUN WITH SANDIE SHAW 20
67 Pye NEP 24271 SANDIE SHAW IN FRENCH 30
67 Pye NEP 24273 SANDIE SHAW IN ITALIAN. 30
67 Pye NEP 24281 TELL THE BOYS 20

LPs

65 Pye NPL 18110 SANDIE SHAW. 15
65 Pye NPL 18122 ME. 15
69 Pye N(S)PL 18323 REVIEWING THE SITUATION. 50

THOMAS SHAW

72 Xtra XTRA 1132 THOMAS SHAW (LP) 15

TIMMY SHAW & STERNPHONES

64 Pye International 7N 25239 Gonna Send You Back To Georgia/I'm A Lonely Guy 30

TREVOR SHAW

81 CMS PR 26 WHEELS IN MOTION (LP) 20

DOROTHY SHAY

53 Capitol LC 6618 THE PARK AVENUE HILLBILLIE (10" LP). 12

SHE

85 Neat NEAT 50 Never Surrender/Breaking Away (p/s) 5
85 Neat NEAT 5012 Never Surrender/Breaking Away/On My Way (12", p/s) 8

GEORGE SHEARING (QUINTET)

(see also Peggy Lee)

61 Capitol CL 15269 Baubles, Bangles And Beads/Cocktails For Two 10
51 Decca LF 1036 THE NEARNESS OF YOU (10" LP, as George Shearing Trio) 12
52 MGM MGM-D 103 YOU'RE HEARING GEORGE SHEARING (10" LP). 12
53 MGM MGM-D 118 I HEAR MUSIC (10" LP) 12
54 MGM MGM-D 129 TOUCH OF GENIUS (10" LP) 12
56 Vogue LDE 188 THE VERY FIRST SESSION (10" LP). 12
56 Capitol LC 6803 THE SHEARING SPELL (10" LP) 12
59 Capitol T/ST 1275 LATIN AFFAIR (LP) 12
62 MGM 6912 SOFT AND SILKY (LP) 12

GARY SHEARSTON

74 Charisma CB241 Without A Song/Aborigini 10

SHEDS

(see also Super 8)

85 John Wayne's S/bags 1 BIMBO EP (cassette, shrinkwrapped with free packet of tomato seeds) 7

BOBBY SHEEN

(see also Bob B. Soxx & Blue Jeans)

66 Capitol CL 15455 Dr. Love/Sweet, Sweet Love 125
66 Capitol CL 15455 Dr. Love/Sweet, Sweet Love (DJ copies) 175
72 Capitol CL 15713 Dr. Love/Sweet, Sweet Love (reissue) 20

SHEEP (U.K.)

(see also Lonesome Stone)

73 Myrrh MYR 1000 SHEEP (LP, with insert) 20

SHEEP (U.S.)

66 Stateside SS 493 Hide And Seek/Twelve Months Later 25
69 Stateside SS 2147 Hide And Seek/HAWKS: The Grissle 12

SHEEPHOUSE

71 Decca Ladder/Part 2. 60

SHEEPS HEAD BAY

71 Parlophone R5897 My Name Is In The Wind/The River Song. 8

IREEN SHEER

70 Bell BLL 1129 Hey Pleasure Man/You Walked Away 5
71 Parlophone R 5930 Many Rivers/Is It Me 5
74 Polydor 2041 533 Bye Bye I Love You/Roseberry Avenue 6

SHEER KHAN

84 SRT 4KS 140 Last Generation/Lady's Dance (p/s) 70
85 Mill QUIET ENOUGH FOR LOVE (LP) 30

SHEFFIELDS

64 Pye 7N 15600 It Must Be Love/Say Girl 50
64 Pye 7N 15627 I Got My Mojo Working/Hey Hey Lover Boy. 70
65 Pye 7N 15767 Bag's Groove (Skat Walking)/Plenty Of Love 75

SHEIKS (Portugal)

66 Parlophone R 5500 Missing You/Tell Me Bird 15

SHEIKS (U.S.)

59 London HLW 9012 Très Chic/Little French Doll. 15
59 London HLW 9012 Très Chic/Little French Doll (78) 15

MINT VALUE £

SHEILA & JENNY

64	Ember EMB S 3202	When The Boy's Happy/Please Don't Break Her Heart (in p/s)	10
64	Ember EMB S 3202	When The Boy's Happy/Please Don't Break Her Heart	6

SHELBY

74	Santa Ponsa PNS 21	Dance With The Guitar Man/Jump Into The Fire	6
75	Route RT 02	Motorbike Girl/Cirrus	8

ERNIE SHELBY

73	Mojo 2093 026	Bend Over Backwards/Punish Me	5

ALLEN SHELDON

70	Plexium PXM 14	Mirror Of My Mind/Old Windmill Tree	30

DOUG SHELDON

61	Decca F 11368	The Book Of Love/Play Me The Blues	10
61	Decca F 11398	Runaround Sue/Come With Me	10
61	Decca F 11416	Your Ma Said You Cried In Your Sleep/You're Only Fooling Yourself	12
62	Decca F 11433	My Kingdom For A Girl/You Never Had It So Good	10
62	Decca F 11463	A Big Big Baby/If You'd Be Mine	10
62	Decca F 11514	Lollipops And Roses/One Way To Say Goodbye	10
62	Decca F 11529	Live Now Pay Later/Me	7
63	Decca F 11564	I Saw Linda Yesterday/My Billy	8
63	Decca F 11654	Let's Make A Habit Of This/I Was Alone	10
63	Decca F 11790	Mickey's Monkey/Falling In Love With Love	10
65	Sue WI 332	Take It Like A Man/Lonely Boy	40
65	Pye 7N 17011	It's Because Of You/How Can I Tell Her?	7
63	Decca DFE 8527	HERE I STAND (EP)	70

SANDI SHELDON

76	Epic EPC 4186	You're Gonna Make Me Love You/Baby You're Mine	15

SHELL

66	Columbia DB 8082	Goodbye Little Girl/Little Bit Of Lovin'	15

SHELLEY

64	Pye 7N 15711	I Will Be Wishing/Why Won't You Say (That You Love Me)	15
65	Pye 7N 15773	Stairway To A Star/I Heard A Whisper	10
65	Pye 7N 15913	Where Has Your Smile Gone/Paradise	10

LIZ SHELLEY

65	Brunswick 05940	Make Me Your Baby/You Made Me Hurt	10
66	Brunswick 05953	No More Love/I Can't Find You	10

PETE SHELLEY

(see also Buzzcocks, Free Agents, Tiller Boys)

82	Lyntone 10952/53	Qu'est-Ce Que C'est, Qu'est Que Ça (Dub)/ANIMAL MAGNET: More (hard vinyl test pressing, numbered, with info sheet/letter)	15
82	Lyntone 10952/53	Qu'est-Ce Que C'est, Qu'est Que Ça (Dub)/ANIMAL MAGNET: More (hard vinyl test pressing, numbered)	12
80	Groovy STP 2	SKY YEN (mini-LP)	12

SHELLS

61	London HLU 9288	Baby, Oh Baby/Angel Eyes	55
62	London HLU 9644	It's A Happy Holiday/Deep In My Heart	45

ALAN SHELLY & MANU DIBANGO'S BROTHERS

69	Philips BF 1709	Lady Black Wife/Give Me Time	12

ANNE SHELTON

53	HMV 7M 164	Answer Me/The Bridge Of Sighs	20
54	HMV 7M 186	The Book/Why Does It Have To Be Me	20
54	HMV 7M 197	Cross Over The Bridge/(Oh Baby Mine) I Get So Lonely	20
54	HMV 7M 240	Goodnight, Well It's Time To Go/If I Give My Heart To You	20
54	HMV 7M 279	My Gypsy Heart/Teach Me Tonight	20
57	Philips JK 1012	Absent Friends/Seven Ages Of Man (Jukebox issue)	20
59	Philips PB 969	The Village Of St. Bernadette/You're Not Living in Vain	8
61	Philips PB 1095	Sailor/A Souvenir Of Ireland (p/s)	10
61	Philips PB 1095	Sailor/A Souvenir Of Ireland	6
56	Decca DFE 6321	FOUR STANDARSS (EP)	15
56	Philips BBE 12090	ANNE SHELTON (EP)	12
58	Philips BBE 12169	THE SHELTON SOUND (EP)	12
58	Philips BBE 12205	ITALIAN TOUCH (EP)	12
58	Philips BBE 12218	ANNE SHELTON (EP)	12
59	Philips BBE 12292	JUST LOVE ME (EP)	12
60	Philips BBE 12344	SONGS OF FAITH (EP)	10
60	Philips BBE 12347	MY YIDDISHE MOMMA (EP)	8
61	Philips BBE 12430	FAVOURITES (EP)	10
62	Philips BBE 12526	SPRING FEVER (EP)	10
52	Decca LF 1023	FAVOURITES (10" LP)	40
53	Decca LF 1106	FAVOURITES VOL 2 (LP)	40
57	Philips BBL 7188	THE SHELTON SOUND (LP)	25
59	Philips BBL 7291	SONGS FROM THE HEART (LP)	25
60	Philips BBL 7393	SHOWCASE (LP)	25
62	Philips BBL 7541	SOUVENIR OF IRELAND (LP)	20

JO SHELTON

59	Top Rank JAR 124	Tread Softly (You're Stepping On My Heart)/More More More Romancing	6
59	Top Rank JAR 245	If There Are Stars In My Eyes/I Need Your Arms Around Me	6

ROSCOE SHELTON

65	Sue WI 354	Strain On My Heart/Question (A- & B-side labels reversed)	40

CAROL SHELYNE

65	Liberty LIB 55794	The Girl With The Horn Rim Glasses/ Boys Do Make Passes At Girls Who Wear Glasses	5

MINT VALUE £

DEANNA SHENDEREY
65 Decca F 12090 Comin' Home Baby/I've Got That Feeling 15

SHENLEY (Duffas) & ANNETTE
61 Blue Beat BB 72 Million Dollar Baby/The First Time I Met You..... 20

SHENLEY (Duffas) & HYACINTH (Brown)
(see also Baba Brooks)
66 Rio R 80 The World Is On A Wheel/ROY & CORNELL: Salvation 15

SHENLEY (Duffas) & (Little) LUNAN
(see also Shenley Duffas)
65 Rio R 52 Something On Your Mind/The Rain Came Tumbling Down 12

SHEP & LIMELITES
61 Pye International 7N 25090 Daddy's Home/This I Know 75
61 Pye International 7N 25112 Ready For Your Love/You'll Be Sorry..... 100

JEAN SHEPARD
56 Capitol EAP 1030 SONGS OF A LOVE AFFAIR NO. 1 (EP) 10
56 Capitol EAP2 728 SONGS OF A LOVE AFFAIR NO. 2 (EP) 10
60 Capitol T 1253 THIS IS JEAN SHEPARD (LP) 12

BILLY SHEPHARD
59 Felstad AF 117 You Call Everybody Darling/Somebody Stole My Gal 5

PAULINE SHEPHERD
57 Columbia DB 4010 Love Me To Pieces/Just Between You And Me 12

SHEPHERD BOYS (& GIRLS)
56 Columbia SCM 5282 Little Girls And Little Boys/Teenage Love (as Shepherd Boys & Girls) 8
56 Columbia DB 3816 Summer Sweetheart/Song For A Summer Night..... 6

TOM SHEPLEY'S BAND
78 Tradition TSR 031 HOW DO YOU DO? (LP)..... 15

ARCHIE SHEPP
(see also John Coltrane)
66 HMV CLP/CSD 3524 FOUR FOR TRANE (LP)..... 25
66 HMV CLP/CSD 3561 ON THIS NIGHT (LP)..... 20
67 HMV CLP/CSD 3600 LIVE IN SAN FRANCISCO (LP) 20
67 Polydor 623 235 ARCHIE SHEPP AND THE NEW YORK CONTEMPORARY FIVE (LP) 20
67 Fontana 681 014 ZL RUFUS (LP, with John Tchicai) 20
68 Impulse MIPL/SIPL 508 MAMA TOO TIGHT (LP) 20
68 Polydor 623 267 NEW YORK CONTEMPORARY FIVE VOL. 2 (LP) 20
69 Impulse MILP/SIPL 512 THE MAGIC OF JU-JU (LP) 20
69 Impulse MIPL/SIPL 516 THE WAY AHEAD (LP) 20

SHEPPARDS
71 Jay Boy BOY 30 How Do You Like It/Stubborn Heart 40

SHEPHERD/SHEPPARD SISTERS
57 HMV POP 411 Alone (Why Must I Be Alone)/Congratulations To Someone 12
58 Mercury 7MT 196 Gettin' Ready For Freddy/Best Thing There Is (Is Love)(Sheppard Sisters 15
58 Mercury 7MT 218 Eating Pizza/A Boy And A Girl (as Sheppard Sisters)..... 10
58 Mercury AMT 1005 Dancing Baby/Is It A Crime? 10
63 London HLK 9681 Don't Mention My Name/What Makes Little Girls Cry..... 20
63 London HLK 9758 Talk Is Cheap/Greatest Lover 15

SHEPPERTON FLAMES
(see also Mike Berry)
69 Deram DM 257 Take Me For What I Am/Goodbye 20

SHERE KHAN
69 Tepee TPR 1007 Little Louise/No Reason..... 200
71 UPC 110 Rhone/Find The Lady..... 60

SHERIDAN
(see also Sheridan-Price, Mike Sheridan & Night Riders, Mike Sheridan's Lot)
70 Gemini GMS 001 Follow Me Follow/When Love Breaks Your Heart..... 15

DANI SHERIDAN
66 Planet PLF 106 Guess I'm Dumb/Songs Of Love..... 60

LEE SHERIDAN
73 Deram DM 373 Sweet Tasting Candy Sugar/Big Louis' Gun 8

MIKE SHERIDAN & NIGHT RIDERS
(see also Roy Wood, Idle Race, Mike Sheridan's Lot, Nightriders, Sheridan-Price, Sight & Sound)
63 Columbia DB 7141 Tell Me What'cha Gonna Do/No Other Guy 30
63 Columbia DB 7183 Please Mr. Postman/In Love 30
64 Columbia DB 7302 What A Sweet Thing That Was/Fabulous 25
65 Columbia DB 7462 Here I Stand/Lonely Weekends 25

MIKE SHERIDAN'S LOT
(see also Roy Wood, Idle Race, Mike Sheridan & Night Riders, Nightriders, Sheridan-Price, Sight & Sound)
65 Columbia DB 7677 Take My Hand/Make Them Understand 40
66 Columbia DB 7798 Don't Turn Your Back On Me, Babe/Stop, Look, Listen 40

TONY SHERIDAN & THE BEAT BROTHERS
(see also Bobby Patrick Big Six, Beat Brothers, Pete Best Four)
64 Polydor NH 52315 Jambalaya/Will You Still Love Me Tomorrow (with The Beat Brothers) 12
64 Polydor NH 52927 Skinny Minny/You'd Better Move On (with The Beat Brothers)..... 12

TONY SHERIDAN & THE BEATLES
(see under The Beatles)

MINT VALUE £

SHERIDAN-PRICE
(see also Rick Price, Mike Sheridan & Nightriders, Mike Sheridan's Lot, Idle Race, Sight & Sound, Sheridan)

70	Gemini GMS 009	Sometimes I Wonder (as Sheridan & Rick Price)/SHERIDAN: Lightning Never Strikes Twice	25
70	Gemini GME 1002	THIS IS TO CERTIFY THAT? (LP, gatefold sleeve)	30

ROGER SHERLOCK

78	Inchecronin INC 7419	MEMORIES OF SLIGO (LP)	12

ALLAN SHERMAN

63	Warner Bros WB 106	Hello Muddah Hello Faddah/Rat Fink	6

BIM SHERMAN

77	Hawkeye HE 003	Ever Firm/GUSSIE ALLSTARS: Rigid	8
78	Yard International YI 1001	What Sweet You So/U BLACK: Pot A Bubble (12")	15
79	Hit Run DD6/7	Down In Jamtown (with Jah Lion)/TEEM ALL STARS: Version (12")	40
79	Hit Run HIT DD 11	Love Jah Only (with Jah Buzz)/CRYTUFF ALL STARS : Version (12")	45
79	Attack TACK 9	Lightning And Thunder/Why Don't You Come On? (12")	25
83	On-U Sound DP 10	Keep You Dancing (with Dub Syndicate)/Can't Stop Jumping (with Dub Syndicate and Augustus Pablo) (10", p/s)	15
77	Tribesman TM 007	LOVE FOREVER (LP)	80
88	On U Sound 17	ACROSS THE RED SEA (LP)	15
84	Century 200 C200	DANGER (LP)	15

BOBBY SHERMAN

69	Pye Intl. 7N 25508	La La La (If I Had You)/Time	15
70	CBS 5118	Hey, Mister Sun/Two Blind Minds	5
71	CBS 57468	Waiting At The Bust Stop/Runaway	12
71	CBS 7468	Waiting At The Bus Stop/Run Away	6

JOE SHERMAN

58	Fontana H 129	Miraculous Music Box/Make Me Laugh	6
58	Fontana H 147	Buttermilk/Please Don't Say Goodnight	6

BILLY SHERRILL

61	Mercury AMT 1131	Like Making Love/Rules Of The Game	8

SHERRYS

62	London HLW 9625	Pop Pop Pop-Pie/Your Hand In Mine	20
63	London HL 9686	Let's Stomp Again/Slop Time	25
63	London RE 1363	DO THE POPEYE (EP)	70

SHERWOOD

86	Sherwood SRT6KL 901	RIDING THE RAINBOW (12" EP)	50

BOBBY SHERWOOD

55	Vogue Coral Q 72097	The Kentuckian Song/Far Away Places	6

HOLLY SHERWOOD

71	Bell BLL 1183	Day By Day/Great Golden Day	6

ROBERTA SHERWOOD

56	Brunswick 05572	Lazy River/This Train	10
57	Brunswick 05654	Tears Don't Care Who Cries Them/ You're Nobody Till Somebody Loves You	7
57	Brunswick 05670	Mary Lou/What Does It Matter	7
63	Stateside SS 154	You Always Hurt The One You Love/In San Francisco	6
63	Stateside SL 10039	ON STAGE (LP)	20

TONY SHERWOOD TRIO

60s	Zodiac ZR 010	Piano Boogie Twist/Tom Dooley	15

SHERWOODS

64	Solar SRP 105	Memories/Some Other Time	8

SHERWOODS

61	Pye International 7N 25097	Nanette/El Scorpion	12

SHE TRINITY
(see also Shotgun Express, Beryl Marsden, Gilded Cage)

66	Columbia DB 7874	He Fought The Law/The Union Station Blues	20
66	Columbia DB 7943	Have I Sinned/Wild Flower	10
66	Columbia DB 7959	Wild Flower/The Man Who Took The Valise Off The Floor Of Grand Central Station At Noon	7
66	Columbia DB 7992	Yellow Submarine/Promise Me You'll Never Cry	20
67	CBS 2819	Across The Street/Over And Over Again	8
70	President PT 283	Hair/Climb That Tree	40

SHEVELLES

63	Oriole CB 1915	Ooh Poo Pa Doo/Like I Love You	25

SHEVELLS
(see also Mike Stevens & Shevells)

64	United Artists UP 1059	I Could Conquer The World/How Would You Like Me To Love You	30
65	United Artists UP 1076	Walking On The Edge Of The World/Not So Close	20
65	United Artists UP 1081	Watermelon Man/Taking Over Your Life	20
66	United Artists UP 1125	Come On Home/I Gotta Travel All Over	45
68	Polydor 56239	Big City Lights/Coffee Song	15

TONY SHEVETON
(see also Tony Rich)

62	Oriole CB 1705	Lullaby Of Love/I Have A Feeling	20
62	Oriole CB 1726	Lonely Heart/Foolish Doubts	20
62	Oriole CB 1766	Hey Little Girl/Kissing Date	25
63	Oriole CB 1788	Runaround Sue Is Getting Married/I Love The Girl Next Door	25

MINT VALUE £

63 Oriole CB 1895 A Million Drums/Dance With Me . . . 20
64 Oriole CB 1975 Excuses/Is It Me, Is It You? . . . 18

SHIDE & ACORN
(see also Jeremy Cahill)
73 private pressing UNDER THE TREE (LP) . . . 180
94 Acme AC 8006LP UNDER THE TREE (LP, reissue, 500 only, numbered) . . . 15

SHIELA
71 Nu Beat NB 079 Only Heaven Knows/GRANT & RICHARDS: Freedom Psalm . . . 7

TREVOR SHIELD
(see also Beltones, Trevor)
69 Harry J TR 664 The Moon Is Playing Tricks On Me/KING CANNON: Soul Special. . . . 35
69 Trojan TR 665 Please/JAY BOYS: Splendour Splash. . . . 40
72 Ashanti ASH 407 Rough Road/JAY BOYS: Rough The Road . . . 12

SHIELDS
58 London HLD 8706 You Cheated/That's The Way It's Gonna Be . . . 30

KEITH SHIELDS
(see also Marty Wilde [& Wildcats])
67 Decca F 12572 Hey Gyp (Dig The Slowness)/Deep Inside Your Mind. . . . 70
67 Decca F 12609 The Wonder Of You/Run, Run, Run . . . 30
67 Decca F 12666 So Hard Livin' Without You/Baby Do You Love Me. . . . 30

ALLAN SHIERS
74 Profle GMOR 003 THE MAN IN ME (LP) . . . 40

SU SHIFRIN
76 EMI 2442 Over The Rainbow/When You Wish Upon A Star/Secrets . . . 6
78 United Artists UP 36438 We Must Believe In Magic/All I Wanna Do In Life . . . 6

SUSAN SHIFRIN
71 Decca F13145 To Love/25 Miles . . . 30

SAHIB SHIHAB QUARTET
70 Youngblood SSYB 12 SEEDS (LP) . . . 100

SHILLINGFORD MILL
71 Mam Frightened/Again . . . 12
71 Mam MAM 15 It's A Thing Called Love/Walking Along . . . 6

PETER SHILTON & JON SAMMELS
73 Sports Talk ST 102 SIMON SMITH INTERVIEWS?. 1973 (LP) . . . 12

YASUKI SHIMIZU
88 Benelux Crammed MTM 12 MUSIC FOR COMMERCIALS (LP) . . . 12

SHINDIGS
65 Parlophone R 5316 One Little Letter/What You Gonna Do . . . 40
65 Parlophone R 5377 A Little While Back/Why Say Goodbye. . . . 40

SHINDOGS
(see also Delaney & Bonnie, James Burton)
67 Fontana TF 790 Who Do You Think You Are/Yes, I'm Going Home . . . 18

JOHNNY SHINES
69 Blue Horizon 7-63212 LAST NIGHT'S DREAM (LP, with Otis Spann, mono or stereo). . . . 80
74 Xtra XTRA 1142 COUNTRY BLUES (LP). . . . 25

DON SHINN (& THE SOUL AGENTS)
(see also The Soul Agents)
66 Polydor BM 56075 A Minor Explosion/Pits Of Darkness (with The Soul Agents) . . . 70
69 Columbia S(C)X 6319 TEMPLES WITH PROPHETS (LP) . . . 100
69 Columbia SCX 6355 DEPARTURES (LP). . . . 150

SHINS
04 Sub Pop SP644 So Says I/When I Goose Step (1,000 only, picture disc). . . . 7
07 Sub Pop Sea Legs/Strange Powers (p/s) . . . 20
07 Transgressive TRANS 057 Turn On Me/Little Boxes/Breathe (Peter, Bjorn & John Remix) (p/s, 1000 only) . . 10
07 Transgressive TRANS 046 Phantom Limbs/Wincing The Night Away/Split Needles (p/s, double grooved b-side, 1000 only). . . . 10
02 Sub Pop SP550 OH INVERTED WORLD (LP). . . . 12

SHINY TWO SHINY
83 Red Flame RFB 29 Waiting For Us/Ritual Hate (p/s) . . . 8

SHIP
72 Elektra K 42122 THE SHIP - A CONTEMPORARY FOLK JOURNEY (LP, gatefold sleeve). . . . 30

SHIRALEE
67 Fontana TF 855 I'll Stay By Your Side/Penny Wren . . . 20

SHIRELLES
(see also Shirley & Shirelles, Shirley Alston)
58 Brunswick 05746 I Met Him On A Sunday/I Want You To Be My Boyfriend . . . 70
58 Brunswick 05746 I Met Him On A Sunday/I Want You To Be My Boyfriend (78) . . . 30
60 London HL 9233 Tonight's The Night/The Dance Is Over . . . 20
60 Top Rank JAR 540 Will You Love Me Tomorrow/Boys . . . 8
61 Top Rank JAR 549 Dedicated To The One I Love/Look-A-Here Baby . . . 18
61 Top Rank JAR 567 Mama Said/Blue Holiday . . . 15
61 Top Rank JAR 578 What A Sweet Thing That Was/A Thing Of The Past. . . . 12
61 Top Rank JAR 590 Big John/Twenty One . . . 12
62 Top Rank JAR 601 Baby It's You/The Things I Want To Hear. . . . 20
62 HMV POP 1019 Soldier Boy/Love Is A Swingin' Thing . . . 12
62 Stateside SS 119 Welcome Home Baby/Mama Here Comes The Bride . . . 15

			MINT VALUE £
62	Stateside SS 129	Stop The Music/It's Love That Really Counts	15
63	Stateside SS 152	Everybody Loves A Lover/I Don't Think So	12
63	Stateside SS 181	Foolish Little Girl/Not For All The Money In The World	18
63	Stateside SS 213	Don't Say Goodnight And Mean Goodbye/I Didn't Mean To Hurt You	15
63	Stateside SS 232	What Does A Girl Do/Don't Let It Happen To Us	15
63	Pye International 7N 25229	It's A Mad, Mad, Mad, Mad World/31 Flavours	20
64	Pye International 7N 25233	Tonight You're Gonna Fall In Love With Me/20th Century Rock And Roll	20
64	Pye International 7N 25240	Sha La La/His Lips Get In The Way	15
64	Pye International 7N 25279	Maybe Tonight/Lost Love	15
65	Pye International 7N 25288	Are You Still My Baby/I Saw A Tear	12
66	Pye International 7N 25386	Shades Of Blue/When The Boys Talk About The Girls	12
67	Pye International 7N 25425	Too Much Of A Good Thing/Bright Shiny Colours	20
69	Mercury MF 1093	There's A Storm Going On In My Heart/Call Me (If You Want Me)	22
71	United Artists UP 35192	Take Me/Dedicated To The One I Love	10
75	Pye Disco Demand DDs 115	Last Minute Miracle/March	15
61	Top Rank JKP 3012	THE SHIRELLES SOUND FEATURING "WILL YOU LOVE ME TOMORROW" (EP)	100
61	Top Rank 35-115	THE SHIRELLES SING - TO TRUMPET AND STRINGS (LP)	90
62	Stateside SL 10006	BABY IT'S YOU (LP)	80
63	Stateside SL 10041	THE SHIRELLES' HITS (LP)	50
70	Wand WNS 4	ETERNALLY SOUL (LP, with King Curtis)	25
71	Wand WCS 1001	TONIGHT'S THE NIGHT (LP)	18
72	RCA Victor SF 8237	HAPPY AND IN LOVE (LP)	15
72	RCA Victor SF 8279	THE SHIRELLES (LP)	15
72	Wand WCS 1009	REMEMBER WHEN VOL. 1 (LP)	15
72	Wand WCS 1010	REMEMBER WHEN VOL. 2 (LP)	15

SHIRLEY

74	London HLA 10477	I Hear Those Church Bells Ringing/Chapel Of Love/I Do Love You	7

DON SHIRLEY

56	London HA-A 2003	PIANO PERSPECTIVES (LP)	12
56	London HA-A 2004	TONAL EXPRESSIONS (LP)	12
62	London HAA 2448	DROWN IN MY OWN TEARS (LP, also stereo [SAHA 6238])	12
57	London HAA 2046	IMPROVISATIONS (LP)	12

ROY SHIRLEY

(see also Val Bennett, Glen Adams, Shirley & Charmers, Sensations, Denzil, Errol & His Group, Ronsig, Stranger & Glady, Untouchables)

66	Ska Beat JB 253	Paradise/Calling	20
66	Doctor Bird DB 1068	Hold Them/Be Good	25
67	Doctor Bird DB 1079	I'm A Winner/Sleeping Beauty	20
67	Doctor Bird DB 1088	Prophet/What To Do	20
67	Doctor Bird DB 1093	Musical Field/LEE PERRY & DYNAMITES: Trial And Crosses	35
67	Doctor Bird DB 1108	Thank You/Touch Them	18
67	Caltone CAL 101	Get On The Ball/JOHNNY MOORE: Sound And Soul	40
67	Island WI 3070	People Rock Steady/I'm Trying To Find A Home (actually by Uniques)	60
67	Island WI 3071	Musical War/Soul Voice	100
67	Island WI 3120	Girlie/GLEN ADAMS: She's So Fine	45
68	Doctor Bird DB 1165	Hush A Bye/Musical Dinner	15
68	Doctor Bird DB 1168	Dance The Reggae/The Agreement	20
68	Giant GN 32	Dance Hall Arena/The Musical Train	12
68	Giant GN 33	Warming Up The Scene/GLEN ADAMS: Lonely Girl	50
68	Island WI 3098	Thank You/Touch Them	25
68	Island WI 3108	Move All Day/Rollin' Rollin'	25
68	Island WI 3110	Million Dollar Baby/SENSATIONS: Long Time No See You Girl	25
68	Island WI 3118	Good Is Better Than Bad/Fantastic Lover	25
68	Island WI 3119	Facts Of Life/Lead Us Not Into Temptation (as Roy Shirley & Uniques; B-side actually by Roy Shirley & Slim Smith)	25
68	Island WI 3125	If I Did Know/Good Ambition	25
68	Amalgamated AMG 815	The World Needs Love/Dance The A	12
68	Fab FAB 54	Think About The Future/Golden Festival	10
69	Duke DU 18	Life/I Like Your Smile	8
71	Nu Beat NB 090	Hold Them One/Two Three Four	5
72	Punch PH 103	Don't Be A Loser/Jamaican Girl	6
72	Punch PH 108	A Sugar/ALTYMAN REID: A Sugar - Version	6
75	R&JJ 001	Heart Breaking Jepsey/Version	5
80s	Shirley SHIRLEY 1	For Everyone/Version (p/s)	5
74	Arrow AR 001	Welcome HOme/What Am I Loving For	10

SUSAN SHIRLEY

68	Mercury MF 1038	Sun Shines Out Of Your Shoes/Tomorrow Today	5
69	Mercury MF 1087	Too Many Tears/Boy From Boston Massachusetts USA	5
70	Philips 6006 037	Really Into Somethin'/My Friend The Clown	40
71	Columbia DB 8787	True Love And Apple Pie/To Find Out (p/s)	15
71	Columbia DB 8835	Jealous Guy/Oh Yoko	6
72	Columbia DB 8937	The Other Side Of Me/Imagine	5

SHIRLEY AND JOHNNY

64	Parlophone R 5149	I Don't Want To Know/It Must Be Love	7
69	Mercury MF 1074	Don't Make Me Over/Baby, Baby, Baby	7

SHIRLEY & CHARMERS

(see also Roy Shirley)

72	Bullet BU 502	Rum Rhythm/LLOYD CHARMERS: Rhythm (Version)	6

SHIRLEY & LEE

56	Vogue V 9059	Let The Good Times Roll/Do You Mean To Hurt Me So	150
56	Vogue V 9059	Let The Good Times Roll/Do You Mean To Hurt Me So (78)	30
57	Vogue V 9063	I Feel Good/Now That It's Over	100
57	Vogue V 9063	I Feel Good/Now That It's Over (78)	30

			MINT VALUE £
57	Vogue V 9067	That's What I Wanna Do/When I Saw You	95
57	Vogue V 9067	That's What I Wanna Do/When I Saw You (78)	30
57	Vogue V 9072	Rock All Nite/Don't You Know I Love You	120
57	Vogue V 9072	Rock All Nite/Don't You Know I Love You (78)	30
57	Vogue V 9084	Rockin' With The Clock/The Flirt	130
57	Vogue V 9084	Rockin' With The Clock/The Flirt (78)	30
57	Vogue V 9088	I Want To Dance/Marry Me	80
57	Vogue V 9088	I Want To Dance/Marry Me (78)	30
57	Vogue V 9094	Feel So Good/You'd Be Thinking Of Me	80
57	Vogue V 9094	Feel So Good/You'd Be Thinking Of Me (78)	30
58	Vogue V 9103	I'll Thrill You/Love No One But You	85
58	Vogue V 9103	I'll Thrill You/Love No One But You (78)	30
58	Vogue V 9118	Everybody's Rockin'/Don't Leave Me Here To Cry	120
58	Vogue V 9118	Everybody's Rockin'/Don't Leave Me Here To Cry (78)	40
59	Vogue V 9129	All I Want To Do Is Cry/Come On And Have Your Fun	80
59	Vogue V 9129	All I Want To Do Is Cry/Come On And Have Your Fun (78)	30
59	Vogue V 9135	A Little Word/That's What I'll Do	80
59	Vogue V 9135	A Little Word/That's What I'll Do (78)	30
59	Vogue V 9137	I'll Do It/Lee's Dream	80

(The above 45s were originally issued with triangular centres; later round-centre issues are worth two-thirds of these values.)

59	Vogue V 9137	I'll Do It/Lee's Dream (78)	45
59	Vogue V 9156	True Love/When Day Is Done	80

(Later Vocalion pressings of the above singles are worth two-thirds of the values listed.)

59	Vogue V 9156	True Love/When Day Is Done (78)	60
60	London HLI 9186	I've Been Loved Before/Like You Used To Do	25
60	London HLI 9209	Let The Good Times Roll/Keep Loving Me	20
65	Island WI 257	Let The Good Times Roll/I'm Gone	20
57	Vogue VE 1-70101	ROCK 'N' ROLL (EP, triangular centre)	300
57	Vogue VE 1-70101	ROCK 'N' ROLL (EP, later round centre)	220
60	Vogue VE 1-70145	SHIRLEY AND LEE (EP)	250
71	Jay Boy JSX 2005	LET THE GOOD TIMES ROLL (LP)	20

SHIRLEY & RUDE BOYS

67	Blue Beat BB 375	Gently Set Me Free/BUSTER'S ALL STARS: Rock Steady	150

SHIRLEY & SHIRELLES

(see also Shirelles)

69	Bell BLL 1049	Look What You've Done To My Heart/A Most Unusual Boy	15
69	Bell BLL 1065	Plaything/Looking Glass	6
72	Bell BLL 1251	Look What You've Done To My Heart/A Most Unusual Boy (reissue)	8

SHIRTS

78	Harvest HAR 5165	Tell Me Your Plans/Cyrinda	6
78	Harvest HAR 5170	Lonely Android/Running Through The Night (p/s)	5
78	Harvest SHSP 4089	THE SHIRTS (LP)	12
79	Harvest SHSP 4104	STREET LIGHT SHINE (LP)	12

SHITMAT

03	Planet Mu ZIQ 072	Shopliftin' Gabba/Witness	8
04	Planet Mu ZIQ 089	KILLABABYLONKUTZ (2-LP)	20

SHIVA

82	Heavy Metal HEAVY 13	Rock Lives On/Sympathy For The Devil (p/s)	20
82	Heavy Metal HEAVY 16	Angel Of Mons/Stranger Lands (p/s)	10
82	Heavy Metal HMRLP 6	FIREDANCE (LP)	20

BUNNY SHIVEL

67	Capitol CL 15487	You'll Never Find A Love Like Mine/The Slide	20

SHOCK

81	RCA RCAT 133	Dynamo Beat/Dream Games (12")	12

JOYCE SHOCK

58	Philips PB 824	Take Your Foot From The Door!/I've Got Bells On My Heart	6
58	Philips PB 872	Hoopa Hoola/You're Not Losing A Daughter, Mama	6
59	Philips PB 934	Personality/I Can't Love You Anymore	6
59	Philips PB 957	Cry, Baby, Cry/Dear Diary	6

SHOCK ABSORBERS

69	Major Minor SMCP 5028	GUITAR PARTY (LP)	20

SHOCK HEADED PETERS

(see also Lemon Kittens, Underneath, Karl Blake, Sol Invictus)

84	él EL 1	I, Blood Brother Be/Truth Has Come (p/s)	7

SHOCKING BLUE

69	Olga OLE 015	Send Me A Postcard/Harley Davidson (demo only)	60
69	Penny Farthing PEN 702	Venus/Hot Sand	5
70	Penny Farthing PEN 713	Mighty Joe/Wild Wind	5
70	Penny Farthing PEN 721	Never Marry A Railroad Man/Roll Engine Roll	5
70	Penny Farthing PEN 744	Sally Was A Good Old Girl/Long And Lonesome Road	6
70	Penny Farthing PELS 500	SHOCKING BLUE AT HOME (LP)	50
70	Penny Farthing PELS 510	SCORPIO'S DANCE (LP)	40
71	Penny Farthing PEN 748	Hello Darkness/Pickin' Tomatoes	5

SHOCK TREATEMENT

80s	Skull SKR 2001	The Mugger/Nuclear Warfare (p/s)	125

SHOES

67	Polydor 56739	Farewell In The Rain/What In The World Is Love	7

SHOES FOR INDUSTRY

80	Fried Egg FRY 1	TALK LIKE A WHELK (LP)	20

MINT VALUE £

SHOESTRING BAND

73	CBS SCBS 1284	Thingumajig/Don't It Make You Feel Good	6
86	Attack ATA 913	High In The Sky/When The Lights Go Down (p/s)	30
87	Jet JET 12049	Cloak And Dagger/Too Late For The Hunter/Tokyo Girl (12", p/s, red vinyl)	8
86	Attack ATA 006	SHOGUN (LP)	40

TROY SHONDELL

61	London HLG 9432	This Time/Girl After Girl	10
62	Liberty LIB 55398	Island In The Sky/Tears From An Angel	15
63	London HL 9668	I Got A Woman/Some People Never Learn	12
64	London HAY 8128	MANY SIDES OF TROY SHONDELL (LP)	90

SHONDELLS

64	Ember EMB S 191	My Love/Don't Cry My Soldier Boy	50

SHOOT

(see also Manfred Mann Chapter 3, Yardbirds, Raw Material)

73	EMI EMI 2026	On The Frontier/Ships And Sails	5
72	EMI EMA 73	ON THE FRONTIER (LP)	20
78	EMI Intl. INS 3020	SHOOTER (LP)	12

SHOOTING PARTY

88	Lisson DOLER 9	Safe In The Arms Of Love (Phil's Extra Beat Update)/Safe In The Arms Of Love	12

SHOP ASSISTANTS

(see also Buba & Shop assistants)

85	Subway Organisation SUBWAY 1	All Day Long/All That Ever Mattered/It's Up To You/Switzerland (red foldaround hand-coloured p/s in poly bag)	12
85	Subway Organisation SUBWAY 1	All Day Long/All That Ever Mattered/It's Up To You/Switzerland (later blue foldaround hand-coloured p/s in poly bag)	6
90	Avalanche AGAP 001C	Here It Comes/I'd Rather Be With You//You Trip Me Up/The Other One (with 33rpm Flexi Records flexidisc)	5
90	Avalanche AGAP 001B	Here It Comes/Look Out/I'd Rather Be With You/Adrenalin (12", box set with flexidisc, badge, postcard & lyric sheet, 1st 200 numbered)	8
90	Avalanche AGAP 001B	Here It Comes/Look Out/I'd Rather Be With You/Adrenalin (12", box set with flexidisc, badge, postcard & lyric sheet)	5
86	Blue Guitar AZLP 2	SHOP ASSISTANTS (LP)	15

DINAH SHORE

(see also Doris Day)

53	HMV 7M 119	Keep It A Secret/Bella Musica	10
53	HMV 7M 139	Sweet Thing/Three-Cornered Tune	10
54	HMV 7M 183	Changing Partners/Think	10
54	HMV 7M 221	This Must Be The Place/Come Back To My Arms	10
54	HMV 7M 236	Three Coins In The Fountain/Pakistan	10
54	HMV 7M 250	If I Give My Heart To You/Let Me Know	10
56	HMV 7M 352	Love And Marriage/Compare	10
57	RCA RCA 1003	The Cattle Call/Promises, Promises (Skip Redwine)	7
58	RCA RCA 1054	Thirteen Men/I'll Never Say "Never Again" Again	5
56	HMV 7EG 8217	THE DELECTABLE DINAH (EP)	15
58	RCA RD 27072	HOLDING HANDS AT MIDNIGHT (LP)	20
59	Capitol (S)T 1247	DINAH, YES INDEED! (LP)	15
60	Fontana Fortune Z 4026	BUTTONS AND BOWS (LP)	15
60	Capitol (S)T 1296	SOMEBODY LOVES ME (LP)	15
60	Capitol (S)T 1354	DINAH SINGS SOME BLUES WITH RED (LP, with Red Norvo)	15

BRIAN SHORT

(see also Black Cat Bones)

71	Transatlantic TRA 245	ANYTHING FOR A LAUGH (LP, textured gatefold sleeve)	30

J.D. SHORT

73	Sonet SNTF 648	THE LEGACY OF THE BLUES VOL. 8 (LP)	12

KEVIN SHORT

79	EMI INT 574	Punk Strut/Short Cut (no p/s, demos only)	30

SHORT KUTS with Eddie Harrison

68	United Artists UP 2233	Your Eyes May Shine/Letting The Tears Tumbling Down	25

SHORTCAKES

71	Decca F13185	I Can Try/Save Me	10

ERROL SHORTER

81	Greensleeves GRED 58	Wild Inna Eighty-One Style/EEK A MOUSE: Wa Do Dem (12")	10

WAYNE SHORTER

79	Blue Note LBR 1021	THE SOOTHSAYER (LP)	15

SHORTWAVE (BAND)

75	RCA Victor SF 8400	SHORTWAVE BAND (LP, with lyric sheet)	12
77	Crescent/Avada ARS 111	GREATEST HATS (LP)	20
79	Pye 2CN 111	SHORTWAVE (LP)	12

SHORTY (THE PRESIDENT)

(see also Shorty Perry)

73	Ackee ACK 509	Aquarius Pressure/Halfway Tree Pressure (as Shorty The President)	10
73	Ackee ACK 517	Jelly-Belly-Nelly/Message Of Love (as Shorty)	6
75	Treble C CCC 03	Beast From The East/Version	8
76	Cactus CTLP	PRESENTING (LP)	25
79	Freedom Sounds FSLP 002	DUB CONFERENCE IN LONDON (LP)	25

SHORTY & THEM

64	Fontana TF 460	Pills Or Love's Labours Lost/Live Laugh And Love	40

MINT VALUE £

SHOTGUN EXPRESS

(see also Rod Stewart, Peter Bardens, Spencer Davis, Brian Auger, She Trinity, Beryl Marsden, Fleetwood Mac)

66 Columbia DB 8025 I Could Feel The Whole World Turn Round/Curtains . . . 65
67 Columbia DB 8178 Funny 'Cos Neither Could I/Indian Thing . . . 70
83 See For Miles CYM 2 I Could Feel The Whole World Turn Round/Curtains/Funny 'Cos Neither Could I/Indian Thing (10", p/s) . . . 15

SHOTS

(see also Smoke)

65 Columbia DB 7713 Keep A Hold Of What You've Got/She's A Liar . . . 40

SHOUT

72 Explosion 2058 Life Is Rough/Life Is Rough - Version . . . 5

SHOUT

92 Entity SHOUT Is It Ever Going To End (Remix 1)/ Is It Ever Going To End (Remix 2)/Is It Ever Going To End(Remix 3)/ Is It Ever Going To End (Radio Edit)/Is It Ever Going To End (Stiff Organ Mix)(12") . . . 60

SHOUTS

(see also Gene Vincent)

64 React EA 001 She Was My Baby/That's The Way It's Gonna Be . . . 50

SHOVE

81 Shove Off PBM033/S/81 Raise The Roof Tonite/Violence/Pigs/Nutters Of York (foldover p/s, 500 only) . . . 40
81 Shove Off ROUGH AND READY EP (with p/s) . . . 25

SHOWBIZ KIDS

(see also Toy Dolls)

80s Top Secret CON 1 She Goes To Finos/I Don't Want To Discuss That (p/s) . . . 35

SHOW BOYS

69 Gas GAS 129 People Are Wondering/Long Time . . . 10

SHOWMEN

(see also Norman Johnson, General Johnson, Chairmen Of The Board)

62 London HLP 9481 It Will Stand/Country Fool . . . 70
62 London HLP 9571 The Wrong Girl/I Love You Can't You See . . . 175
69 Pama PM 767 Action/What Would It Take . . . 15

SHOWSTOPPERS

68 Beacon 3-100 Ain't Nothing But A House Party/What Can A Man Do (red swirly label) . . . 15
68 Beacon 3-106 Shake Your Mini/Heartbreaker . . . 40
68 MGM MGM 1436 Eeny Meeny/How Easy Your Heart Forgets Me . . . 15
69 Beacon BEA 110 Don't Leave Me Standing In The Rain/Do You Need My Love . . . 10
69 Beacon BEA 130 Just A Little Bit Of Lovin'/School Prom . . . 15
69 Beacon BEA 100 Ain't Nothing But A House Party/What Can A Man Do (reissue, yellow label) . . . 10
70 Beacon BEA 100 Ain't Nothing But A House Party/What Can A Man Do (reissue, green label) . . . 8
71 Beacon BEA 177 Reach In The Goody Bag/How Do You Feel . . . 10
71 Beacon BEA 3-182 Actions Speak Louder Than Words/ Pick Up Your Smile . . . 30

SHOWTIMERS

64 HMV POP 1328 You Must Be Joking/Don't Say Goodbye . . . 15

SHOX

80 Axis AXIS 4 No Turning Back/Lying Here (p/s) . . . 15
80 Beggars Banquet BEG 33 No Turning Back/Lying Here (p/s, reissue) . . . 8

MARK SHREEVE

83 Uniton U 021 ASSASSIN (LP) . . . 15

SHRIEKBACK

81 Y T104 Working On The Ground/Nightwork (12", p/s) . . . 12

SHRINK

79 Oval AMS 7409 Valid Or Void/You Chauffeur Me (p/s) . . . 6

SHRUG

(see also Snow Patrol)

95 Private Pressing THE YOGURTS VS YOGURT DEBATE (demo cassette, glued sleeve) . . . 80

SHUBERT

68 Fontana TF 942 Until The Rains Come/Let Your Love Go . . . 20

SHUDDER TO THINK

90s Dischord Vacation Brain (p/s, with insert) . . . 12

MORT SHUMAN

59 Decca F 11184 Turn Me Loose/I'm A Man . . . 50
59 Decca F 11184 Turn Me Loose/I'm A Man (78) . . . 25
66 Fontana TF 685 Cry A Little/She Ain't Nothing But A Little Child . . . 10
67 Immediate IM 048 Monday Monday/Little Children . . . 20

SHUTDOWNS

63 Colpix PX 11016 Four In The Floor/Beach Buggy . . . 45

SHY

74 Deram DM417 Disney Girls (1957)/The Time That I Love You The Most . . . 7

SHY

87 RCA PT 41180 Break Down The Walls/Under Fire/Young Heart (12", gatefold p/s) . . . 8
83 Ebony EBON 15 ONCE BITTEN TWICE SHY (LP) . . . 20

SHY LIMBS

(see also Shame)

69 CBS 4190 Reputation/Love . . . 70
69 CBS 4624 Lady In Black/Trick Or Two . . . 150

MINT VALUE £

SHY ONES
(see also Spotnicks)

63	Oriole CB 1848	Nightcap/Carry Me Back	20
64	Oriole CB 1924	La Route/Susanna	18

SHYSTER
(see also Fleur-De-Lys)

68	Polydor 56202	Tick Tock/That's A Hoe Down	220

SHYWOLF

82	MRS SW 001	Lucretia/California Jam (p/s)	40

LEROY SIBBLES & ROCKY ELLIS
(see also John Holt, King Rocky)

68	Studio One SO 2042	Love Me Girl/WRIGGLERS: Reel Up	30
79	Warrior Records WAR 133	Ras-Tafari/MYSTIC EYES: Forward With Love/Dub (12")	30

DON E SIBLEY & DIXIE PHOENIX

79	Hot Rock HR35-002	Punk Bashing Boogie/Rock With The Devil	7

DUDLEY SIBLEY
(see also Delroy & Sporty, King Sporty, Mr. Foundation)

67	Coxsone CS 7010	Run Boy Run/Message Of Old (B-side actually by Joe Higgs & Ken Boothe)	45
67	Island WI 3034	Gun Man/Monkey Speaks His Mind (B-side actually by Dinsdell Thorpe)	50

SICK THINGS

83	Chaos CHS 3	ANTI SOCIAL (EP)	25

SIDAN

75	Sain 1017	TEULU YNCL SAM (LP)	40

SID & JOE & MOHAWKS
(see also Mohawks)

70	Pama PM 800	Down On The Corner/Who Is That Stranger	20

SIDDELEYS

86	Sha La La Ba Ba Ba 006	Wherever You Go/RESERVE: The Sun Slid Down (flexidisc with fanzines, p/s)	10
87	Medium Cool MC 005	What Went Wrong This Time? (p/s)	18
88	Sombrero THREE	Sunshine Thuggery/Are You Still Evil When You're Sleeping/ Falling Off My Feet Again (12", p/s)	18

SIDEKICKS

66	RCA RCA 1538	Suspicions/Up On The Roof	20

ANN SIDNEY

65	HMV POP 1411	The Boy In The Woolly Sweater/Lonely Doll	6

SIDNEY, GEORGE & JACKIE
(see also Pioneers)

71	Summit SUM 8528	Lady Of My Complexion/No Sad Song	5
72	Summit SUM 8535	Story Book Children/Gorgeous Marvellous	5
74	Attack ATT 8064	At The Club/Reggae Fever	30

PAUL SIEBEL

70	Elektra EKSN 45085	Bride 1945/Miss Cherry Lane	5
70	Elektra EKS 74064	WOODSMOKE AND ORANGES (LP)	18
71	Elektra EKS 74081	JACK-KNIFE GYPSY (LP)	20

SIEGE

85	Siege THM 1	Goddess Of Fire (no p/s)	18
90	Revolution	Infest/Drop Dead (p/s)	20

SIEGEL-SCHWALL BAND

68	Vanguard SVRL 19044	SHAKE (LP)	20

CHRIS SIEVEY
(see also Freshies, Going Red?)

79	Rabid TOSH 109	Baiser/Last (p/s)	10
79	Razz RAZZXEP 1	BAISER (33rpm EP, 2 tracks each by Sievey & Freshies, handwritten labels)	35
80	Razz RAZZ 4	My Tape's Gone/Moon Midsummer (with True Life Revealing Confessions Of Romance And Love fanzine)	10
80	Razz RAZZ 4	My Tape's Gone/Moon Midsummer (without True Life Revealing Confessions Of Romance And Love fanzine)	5
81	Razz RAZZ 5	Hey/FRESHIES: We're Like You (p/s)	6
82	Razz RAZZ 8	RED INDIAN MUSIC (EP)	8
82	Razz RAZZ 9	Skip The Flight/Jim Baiser ("Baiser"/"Last" with new labels & sleeve)	8

LABI SIFFRE

71	Pye Intl. 7N 25572	It Must Be Love/To Find Love	6
70	Pye Intl. NSPL 28135	LABI SIFFRE (LP)	15
71	Pye Intl. NSPL 28147	THE SINGER AND THE SONG (LP, gatefold sleeve)	15
72	Pye Intl. NSPL 28163	CRYING, LAUGHING, LOVING, LYING (LP, gatefold sleeve with lyric insert)	12
73	Pye Intl. NSPL 28132	FOR THE CHILDREN (LP)	12
75	EMI EMC 3065	REMEMBER MY SONG (LP)	90
98	EMI/Mr. Bongo MRBLP 011	REMEMBER MY SONG (LP, reissue)	12
06	EMI EMC 3065	REMEMBER MY SONG (LP, reissue)	15

RON SIG

71	Camel CA 58	1970's/Version	6
71	Camel CA 59	You Girl/ROY SHIRLEY & SLIM SMITH: Facts Of Life	8

SIGHT & SOUND
(see also Jefferson, Sheridan & Price, Mike Sheridan)

68	Fontana TF 927	Ebenezer/Our Love (Is In The Pocket)	40
68	Fontana TF 982	Alley Alley/Little Jack Monday	20

MINT VALUE £

BUNNY SIGLER
67 Cameo Parkway P 153 — Let The Good Times Roll - Feel So Good/There's No Love Left — 40
67 Cameo Parkway P 153 — Let The Good Times Roll - Feel So Good/There's No Love Left (DJ copy) — 80
76 Philadelphia SPIR 4935 — Can't Believe That You Love Me/Woman, Woman — 6
76 London HLU 10518 — Let The Good Times Roll/Girl Don't Make Me Wait — 10

SIGNS
66 Decca F 12522 — Ain't You Got A Heart/My Baby Comes To Me — 10

SIGUE SIGUE SPUTNIK
(see also Generation X, Sisters Of Mercy)
86 Parlophone PCSS 7305 — FLAUNT IT (LP, box set with insert) — 12

SIGUR RóS
99 Fat Cat 12FAT 036 — Svefn-G-Englar (12" EP, custom sleeve 2,000 only) — 25
99 Fat Cat CD FAT 036 — Svefn-G-Englar (CD, 2000 only) — 20
00 Fat Cat 12FAT 039 — NY BATTERY (mini-LP, 2,000 only) — 40
00 Fat Cat CATCD FAT 039 — NY BATTERY (CD, mini-LP, 2,000 only) — 20
03 FAT KAT FATPK 01 A — Ineractive press kit for () album (2-CD in DVD-style case) — 20
05 EMI 17571 — Hoppipolla/Meo Bloonasir/Hafsol (12") — 8
00 Fat Cat FATLP 11 — AGAETIS BYRJUN (2-LP) — 50
03 Fat Cat FATLP 22 — () (LP) — 40
05 EMI 3384632 — TAKK (LP, special book edition) — 25
05 EMI 337252 — SIGUR RóS (2-LP, gatefold with inner sleeves and free 10") — 30
09 Fat Cat FATLP 11X — AGAETIS BYRJUN (2-LP, reissue, 180 gm vinyl) — 15
09 Fat Cat FATLP 22X — () (2-LP, reissue, 180 gm vinyl) — 15

SILENT ECLIPSE
(see also Two Times Def)
92 White (Mendoza) MEN018 — How Many Miles Back To London/MCs (12") — 40
92 Mendoza MEN018 — How Many Miles Back To London/Mcs (12") — 15
93 Monroe RLP001 — THE DAMNED (12", EP as The Principle featuring Silent Eclipse) — 10
92 Dope Jams DJAM1 — Take The Stage (3 Mixes, promo 12" only) — 10

SILENT MAJORITY
71 Hot Wax HWX 110 — Frightened Girl/Colours Of My Love — 15

SILENT MOVIES
79 ESR Records ESR 1 — Ain't No Van Gough/What Did Ya Say? (p/s) — 40

SILENT NOISE
79 Silent Noise/Easy ER 02 — I've Been Hurt (Too Many Times Before)/Heart To Heart — 75

SILENT ONES
70 Pulse P1 — When It Rains/Lost Dreams (p/s) — 50

SILHOUETTES (Jamaica)
69 Sound System SSR 103 — In Times Like These (act. by Lloyd Jackson & Groovers)/In Times Like These — 6

SILHOUETTES (U.S.)
58 Parlophone R 4407 — Get A Job/I Am Lonely — 100
58 Parlophone R 4407 — Get A Job/I Am Lonely (78) — 85
58 Parlophone R 4425 — Headin' For The Poorhouse/Miss Thing — 150
58 Parlophone R 4425 — Headin' For The Poorhouse/Miss Thing (78) — 150

SILICON TEENS
79 Mute MUTE 003 — Memphis Tennessee/Let's Dance (p/s, with poster) — 10
79 Mute MUTE 003 — Memphis Tennessee/Let's Dance (p/s) — 5
80 Mute CC 8AX — Sunflight/Just Like Eddie (p/s) — 6
80 Mute STUMM 2 — MUSIC FOR PARTIES (LP) — 18

ERIC SILK (& His Southern Jazz Band)
57 Esquire 20-065 — SOUTHERN JAZZ (LP) — 12
58 Esquire 20-095 — THE SILKEN TOUCH (LP) — 12
67 Polydor 582 002 — OFF THE CUFF (LP) — 12

SILKIE
65 Fontana TF 556 — Blood Red River/Close The Door Gently — 5
65 Fontana TF 603 — You've Got To Hide Your Love Away/City Winds — 7
66 Fontana TF 659 — Keys To My Soul/Leave Me To Cry — 5
66 Fontana TF 709 — Born To Be With You/So Sorry Now — 5
65 Fontana TL 5256 — THE SILKIE SING THE SONGS OF BOB DYLAN (LP) — 20

JUDEE SILL
71 Asylum AYM 502 — Jesus Was A Cross Maker/The Phantom Cowboy — 7
72 Asylum AYM 509 — Enchanted Sky Machines/My Man On Love — 6
72 Asylum SYLA 8751 — JUDEE SILL (LP, gatefold sleeve) — 40
73 Asylum SYL 9006 — HEART FOOD (LP) — 25

SILLY SISTERS
(see also Steeleye Span, Maddy Prior, June Tabor)
76 Chrysalis CHR 1101 — SILLY SISTERS (LP, with lyric insert) — 12

SILVER EAGLE
67 MGM MGM 1345 — Theodore/True As A Brand New Lie — 30

SILVER (Jamaica)
68 Jolly JY 006 — Baby Oh Yeah/Rock Steady Is Here To Stay (as Silver & Magnets) — 20
68 Jolly JY 012 — Things/Sweet Lovin' — 15
68 Jolly JY 017 — I Need A Girl/Lost And Found — 12
70 Columbia Blue Beat DB 117 — Love Me Forever/Sugar, Sugar (B-side as Silver & Noreen) — 5
71 Fab FAB 163 — Change Has Got To Come/Magnet Stomp (as Silver & Magnets) — 6

MINT VALUE £

SILVER (U.S.)
(see also Grateful Dead)

76	Arista ARIST 79	Musician (It's Not An Easy Life)/Right On Time	6
76	Arista ARTY 144	SILVER (LP, U.S. disc & inner [AL 4076] in U.K. sleeve)	12

ANDEE SILVER

64	HMV POP 1297	Too Young To Go Steady/Sleeping Beauty	10
64	HMV POP 1344	The Boy I Used To Know/What Do You Do	10
66	Fontana TF 666	Only Your Love Can Save Me/Window Shopping	25
69	Decca F 22872	Go Now/You're Just What I Was Looking For Today	20
69	Decca F 22953	With A Little Love/Te Quiero (unreleased)	0
70	Decca F 23071	Love Me/You're Breaking My Heart (export issue)	10
70	Decca SKL-R 5059	A HANDFUL OF SILVER (LP)	50

EDDIE SILVER

58	Parlophone R 4439	Seven Steps To Love/Put A Ring On Her Finger	15
58	Parlophone R 4439	Seven Steps To Love/Put A Ring On Her Finger (78)	15
58	Parlophone R 4483	Rockin' Robin/The Ways Of A Woman In Love	20
58	Parlophone R 4483	Rockin' Robin/The Ways Of A Woman In Love (78)	20

HORACE SILVER QUINTET/TRIO

54	Vogue LDE 065	THE HORACE SILVER TRIO (10" LP)	15
69	Blue Note BST 84277	SERENADE TO A SOUL SISTER (LP)	15

LORRAINE SILVER

65	Pye 7N 15922	Lost Summer Love/I'll Know You'll Be There	75
65	Pye 7N 15922	Lost Summer Love/I'll Know You'll Be There (DJ copy)	75
66	Pye 7N 17055	The Happy Faces/When The Love Light Starts Shining Thru His Eyes	40

MIKE SILVER & MIKE BEASON

69	Fontana STL 5506	THE APPLICANT (LP)	150

SILVER APPLES

90s	Enraptured RAPT 4507	Fractal Flow/Love Fingers (p/s)	12
97	Rocket Girl RGIRL 1	I Havek Known Love/WINDY & CARL: Crazy In The Sun (p/s, green vinyl)	8

SILVER BIRCH

73	Brayford BRO 2	SILVER BIRCH (LP, private pressing)	150

SILVERBIRD

72	CBS 51279	I See The Writing On The Wall/The Summer's Gone (And I'm Alone)	8
73	CBS 51800	That's Why You Remember/You And Me	8

SILVER BULLET

89	Tam Tam TTT008	Bring Forth The Guillotine (12")	10
89	Tam Tam TTT013	Bring Forth The Guillotine remixes (12")	10
89	Tam Tam TTT019	20 Seconds To Comply (12")	8
91	Parlophone R 6290	Ruff Karnage/Never Authorise Apocalypse (p/s)	12

SILVER BYKE

68	London HLZ 10200	Who Needs Tomorrow/I've Got Time	20

SILVERCHAIR

95	Sony 480430	FROGSTOMP (LP, green vinyl, inner, sleeve in PVC outer sleeve)	20

SILVERGINGER 5
(see also Ginger, Super$hit666, Wildhearts)

01	Infernal INFERNAL 13CD/X	BLACK LEATHER MOJO (2-CD, in stickered leather-effect slipcase, 5000 only)	25

SILVERHEAD
(see also Michael Des Barres, Blondie)

72	Purple PUR 104	Ace Supreme/Oh No No No	7
72	Purple PUR 110	Rolling With My Baby/In Your Eyes	7
73	Purple TPSA 7506	SILVERHEAD (LP, gatefold)	30
73	Purple TPSA 7511	SIXTEEN AND SAVAGED (LP, gatefold sleeve)	25

SILVER JEWS

98	Domino WIGLP 56	AMERICAN WATER (LP)	18

SILVER METRIC

71	Department Of Health MET1	Inch By Inch/Centimetre By Centimetre	5

SILVER MOUNTAIN

83	Road Runner RR 9884	SHAKIN' BRAINS (LP)	15

SILVERS

66	Polydor BM 56094	What A Way To Start A Day/Blue Blue Eyes	7

PHIL SILVERS

57	Fontana Fortune Z 4040	BUGLE CALLS FOR BIG BAND (LP)	15

SILVER SISTERS

60	Parlophone R 4669	Waiting For The Stars To Shine/When A Boy Meets A Girl	10

DOOLEY SILVERSPOON

76	Seville SEV 1022	Game Players/Believe In Me	8

SILVERSTARS

69	Trojan TR 646	Old Man Say/Promises	12
70	Bamboo BAM 23	Love At first Sight/MAYTALS : Life Could Be A Dream	35

SILVER STARS STEEL BAND
(see also Clancy Eccles)

63	Island ILP 904	THE SILVER STARS STEEL BAND (LP)	20

SHEL SILVERSTEIN
(see also Dr. Hook)

73	CBS 65452	FREAKIN' AT THE FREAKER'S BALL (LP, with Dr. Hook)	12

MINT VALUE £

SILVERTONES

(see also Valentines, Tommy McCook, Vincent Gordon, Alton Ellis, Carl Bryon, Charmers)

66	Doctor Bird DB 1028	True Confession (with Duke Reid)/TOMMY McCOOK & SUPERSONICS: More Love	35
66	Doctor Bird DB 1041	It's Real (with Lynn Tait & Boys)/LYNN TAIT & BOYS: Storm Warning	35
67	Treasure Isle TI 7020	Cool Down/TOMMY McCOOK & SUPERSONICS: Shadow Of Your Smile	25
68	Treasure Isle TI 7027	In The Midnight Hour/TOMMY McCOOK & SUPERSONICS: Soul For Sale	20
68	Treasure Isle TI 7039	Old Man River/TOMMY McCOOK & SUPERSONICS: Our Man Flint	50
68	Treasure Isle TI 7042	Slow And Easy/TOMMY McCOOK & SUPERSONICS: Moving	20
69	Trojan TR 7705	Intensified Change/Marie	12
71	Clandisc CLA 234	Tear Drops Will Fall/DYNAMITES: Tear Drops - Version	6
73	Techniques TE 924	That's When It Hurts/I'll Take You Home	6
77	Trojan TRO 9013	African Dub/Version	25
71	Trojan TRLS 69	SILVER BULLETS (LP)	35
66	RYMSKA RA 105	True Confession/Honky Tonky Ska (with Granville Williams)	30

SILVERWING

(see also Pet Hate, Big Amongst Sheep)

80	Mayhem SILVER 1	Rock'n'Roll Are Four-Letter Words/High Class Woman/Hot City Streets	7
82	Mayhem SILV 02	Sittin' Pretty/Teenage Love Affair (p/s)	8
82	Mayhem SILV 212	Sittin' Pretty/Teenage Love/Flashbomb Fever/Rock'n'Roll Mayhem (12")	10
82	Mayhem SILV 3	That's Entertainment/Flashbomb Fever (poster p/s)	8
83	Bullet BULP 1	ALIVE AND KICKING (LP)	15

VICTOR SILVESTER & HIS ROCK 'N' ROLL RHYTHM

57	Columbia DB 3888	Rockin' Rhythm Roll/Society Rock	12
57	Columbia DB 3907	Alligator Roll/Off Beat Rock	12

VICTOR SILVESTER ORCHESTRA

62	Columbia	World Cup Cha Cha Santiago	5
66	Columbia DB 7900	The World Cup Waltz/The World Cup Cha Cha Cha	8

SIMBA

71	Fire FIR 100	Louie Louie/Movin'	5

TYRONE SIMEON

79	Burning Rockers BRD 010	Do Good In This Time/Do Good Dub (12")	15

SIMEONS

78	Freedom Sounds FSLP 002	DUB CONFERENCE IN LONDON (LP)	25

LEO SIMMO

66	Big Beat BB351	I Love Her So/It's Good To Be seen	25

BEVERLEY SIMMON(D)S

(see also Little Beverly)

68	Pama PM 716	Mr. Pitiful/That's How Strong My Love Is	15
73	Pama Supreme PS 380	You're Mine/What A Guy (as Beverley Simmonds)	8
69	Pama PMLP 1	PAYS TRIBUTE TO OTIS REDDING (LP)	50
69	Pama PMLP/PMSP 9	REMEMBER OTIS (LP)	30

CHRIS SIMMONS

69	MCA MK 5009	Soraya/Gone Gone Gone	6

(JUMPIN') GENE SIMMONS

64	London HLU 9913	Haunted House/Hey, Hey Little Girl	20
64	London HLU 9933	The Jump/The Dodo	20

GENE SIMMONS

(see also Kiss)

79	Casablanca CAN 134	Radioactive/When You Wish Upon A Star (p/s, red vinyl with mask, picture label, mispressed with black/red vinyl)	50
79	Casablanca CAN 134	Radioactive/When You Wish Upon A Star (p/s, red vinyl with mask, picture label)	20
79	Casablanca CAN 134	Radioactive/When You Wish Upon A Star (p/s, black vinyl)	8

JEFF SIMMONS

(see also Frank Zappa)

69	Straight STS 1057	LUCILLE HAS MESSED UP MY MIND (LP)	70

LITTLE MAC SIMMONS

66	Outasite OSEP 1	BLUES FROM CHICAGO (EP, 99 copies only)	200

JASON SIMMS & MUSIC THROUGH SIX

(see also Music Through Six)

68	Domain D 5	It's Got To Be Mellow/MUSIC THROUGH SIX: Floppy Ears	20

(Zoot) SIMMS & (Lloyd) ROBINSON

62	Blue Beat BB 143	White Christmas/Searching	10

ZOOT SIMMS (Jamaica)

63	Blue Beat BB 183	Press Along/PRINCE BUSTER ALLSTARS: 100 Ton Megaton (B-side actually "Mighty As A Rose" by Raymond Harper)	25
63	Blue Beat BB 193	Golden Pen/ERIC MORRIS: So You Shot Reds	35
64	Port-O-Jam PJ 4007	Please Don't Do It/Don't Do It (as Simms & [Lloyd] Robinson)	40
68	Blue Cat BS 118	Bye Bye Baby/AL & THRILLERS: Heart For Sale	70
69	Coxsone CS 7095	Tit For Tat/We Can Talk It Over (as Simms & Elmond)	40

SEIJA SIMOLA

78	Sonet SON 2145	Give Love A Chance/Little Smile (p/s)	12

SIMON

67	RCA Victor RCA 1609	I Like The Way/Little Tin Soldier	10
68	RCA Victor RCA 1668	Dream Seller/Sweet Reflections Of You	15
69	Plum PLS 002	Mrs Lillyco/There's No More You	30

MINT VALUE £

JOE SIMON

66	London HLU 10057	Teenager's Prayer/Long Hot Summer	30
67	Monument MON 1004	My Special Prayer/Travelin' Man	10
68	Monument MON 1010	Nine Pound Steel/The Girl's Alright With Me	20
68	Monument MON 1014	No Sad Songs/Come On And Get It	10
68	Monument MON 1019	You Keep Me Hangin' On/What Makes A Man Feel Good	7
68	Monument MON 1025	Message From Maria/I Worry About You	7
69	Monument MON 1029	Looking Back/Standing In The Safety Zone	7
69	Monument MON 1032	The Chokin' Kind/Come On And Get It	7
70	Monument MON 1042	Moon Walk (Parts 1 & 2)	5
70	Monument MON 1049	Yours Love/I Gotta Whole Lot Of Lovin'	25
70	Monument MON 1051	That's The Way I Want Our Love/When	15
71	Polydor 2066 066	Your Time To Cry/I Love You More (Than Anything)	8
74	Mojo 2093 030	Step By Step/Talk Don't Bother Me	6
67	Monument LMO/SMO 5005	SIMON PURE SOUL (LP)	20
68	Monument LMO/SMO 5017	NO SAD SONGS (LP)	20
69	Monument LMO/SMO 5026	SIMON SINGS (LP)	20
70	Monument LMO/SMO 5030	THE CHOKIN' KIND (LP)	20
70	Monument LMO/SMO 5033	BETTER THAN EVER (LP)	20
71	Mojo 2918 001	THE SOUNDS OF SIMON (LP)	20
72	Mojo 2918 003	DROWNING IN THE SEA OF LOVE (LP)	20

PAUL SIMON

(see also Simon & Garfunkel, Jerry Landis, Tom & Jerry)

65	CBS 201797	I Am A Rock/Leaves That Are Green	25
73	CBS 1545	Kodachrome (withdrawn, any pressed?)	15
65	CBS (S) 62579	THE PAUL SIMON SONGBOOK (LP, mono, flipback sleeve)	25
65	CBS (S) 62579	THE PAUL SIMON SONGBOOK (LP, stereo, flipback sleeve)	30
72	CBS CQ 30750/Q 69007	PAUL SIMON (LP, quadrophonic)	20
74	CBS CQ 32280/Q 69035	THERE GOES RHYMIN' SIMON (LP, quadrophonic)	18
75	CBS Q 86001	STILL CRAZY AFTER ALL THESE YEARS (LP, quadrophonic)	18

TONY SIMON

67	Track 604 012	Gimme A Little Sign/Never Too Much To Love	40

SIMON & GARFUNKEL

(see also Paul Simon, Art Garfunkel, Tom & Jerry)

65	CBS 201977	The Sound Of Silence/We've Got A Groovy Thing Goin'	10
66	CBS 202045	Homeward Bound/Leaves That Are Green	10
66	CBS 202303	I Am A Rock/Flowers Never Bend With The Rainfall	10
66	CBS 202285	The Dangling Conversation/The Big Bright Green Pleasure Machine	15
66	CBS 202378	A Hazy Shade Of Winter/For Emily, Whenever I May Find Her	10
67	CBS 202608	At The Zoo/The 59th Street Bridge Song (Feelin' Groovy)	10
67	CBS 2911	Fakin' It/You Don't Know Where Your Interest Lies	20
68	CBS Special Prods. WB 73	The Sound Of Silence/GEORGIE FAME: By The Time I Get To Phoenix (p/s)	5
68	CBS Special Prods. WB 728	The 59th Street Bridge Song (Feelin' Groovy)/TREMELOES: Here Comes My Baby (p/s, mail-order only with Pepsi Cola tokens)	7
69	CBS 4162	The Boxer/Baby Driver (p/s)	7
70	CBS 4916	Cecelia/The only Living Boy In New York	6
65	CBS EP 6053	WEDNESDAY MORNING 3AM (EP)	15
66	CBS EP 6074	I AM A ROCK (EP)	15
67	CBS EP 6360	FEELING GROOVY (EP)	15
68	CBS EP 6400	MRS ROBINSON (EP)	10
66	CBS BPG 62690	THE SOUNDS OF SILENCE (LP, mono)	12
66	CBS SBPG 62690	THE SOUNDS OF SILENCE (LP, stereo)	15
66	CBS BPG 62860	PARSLEY, SAGE, ROSEMARY AND THYME (LP, mono)	12
66	CBS SBPG 62860	PARSLEY, SAGE, ROSEMARY AND THYME (LP, stereo)	15

(The above LPs were originally issued with flipback sleeves & textured orange labels)

67	Allegro ALL 836	SIMON AND GARFUNKEL (LP)	20
68	CBS (S) 70042	THE GRADUATE (LP, soundtrack, blue label, mono/stereo)	12
68	CBS (S) 63370	WEDNESDAY MORNING 3AM (LP, flipback sleeve, textured orange label, mono)	18
68	CBS (S) 63370	WEDNESDAY MORNING 3AM (LP, flipback sleeve, textured orange label, stereo)	15
72	CBS CQ 30995	BRIDGE OVER TROUBLED WATER (LP, quadrophonic)	18

NINA SIMONE

59	Parlophone R 4583	I Loves You Porgy/Love Me Or Leave Me	20
59	Pye International 7N 25029	Solitaire/Chilly Winds Don't Blow	7
63	Colpix PX 200	You Can Have Him/Return Home	8
64	Colpix PX 799	Exactly Like You/The Other Woman	8
65	Philips BF 1388	Don't Let Me Be Misunderstood/Monster	8
65	Philips BF 1415	I Put A Spell On You/Gimme Some	8
66	Philips BF 1465	Either Way I Lose/Break Down And Let It Out	15
69	RCA RCA 1903	Save Me/To Be Young Gifted And Black	15
61	Parlophone GEP 8844	MY BABY JUST CARES FOR ME (EP)	70
62	Parlophone GEP 8864	INTIMATE NINA SIMONE (EP)	25
64	Colpix PXE 303	FINE AND MELLOW (EP)	15
66	Colpix PXE 306	JUST SAY I LOVE HIM (EP)	15
66	Colpix PXE 307	I LOVE TO LOVE (EP)	15
65	Philips BE 12585	DON'T LET ME BE MISUNDERSTOOD (EP)	12
65	Philips BE 12589	STRANGE FRUIT (EP)	12
61	Pye Intl. NPL 28014	AT THE TOWN HALL (LP)	18
62	Pye Jazz NJL 36	FORBIDDEN FRUIT (LP)	18
64	Colpix PXL 419	FORBIDDEN FRUIT (LP, reissue)	15
64	Colpix PXL 421	NINA AT THE VILLAGE GATE (LP)	20
65	Colpix PXL 465	FOLKSY NINA (LP)	20
65	Fontana SFJL 954	TELL ME MORE (LP)	18

MINT VALUE £

65	Philips BL 7662	BROADWAY . . . BLUES . . . BALLADS (LP)	18
65	Philips BL 7671	I PUT A SPELL ON YOU (LP)	20
65	Philips BL 7678	IN CONCERT (LP)	18
66	Philips BL 7683	PASTEL BLUES (LP)	18
66	Philips (S)BL 7722	LET IT ALL OUT (LP)	18
66	Philips (S)BL 7726	WILD IS THE WIND (LP)	18
67	Philips (S)BL 7764	HIGH PRIESTESS OF SOUL (LP)	18
67	RCA RD/SF 7883	SINGS THE BLUES (LP)	18
68	RCA RD/SF 7967	SILK AND SOUL (LP)	18

SUGAR SIMONE

(see also Sugar & Dandy, Les Foster, Larry Foster & Soul Explosion, Lance Hannibal)

66	Rainbow RAI 103	Is It Because/I Want To Know	20
67	Rainbow RAI 115	I Love My Baby/I'll Keep You Satisfied	8
67	Sue WI 4029	Suddenly/King Without A Throne	40
67	Go AJ 11409	It's Alright/Take It Easy	28
68	CBS 3250	The Vow/Spinning Wheel	18
69	Doctor Bird DB 1192	Black Is Gold/The Invitation	20
69	Doctor Bird DB 1193	The Squeeze Is On/Tell Me	20
69	Doctor Bird DB 1201	Come And Try/Don't Listen To What They Say	12
69	Fab FAB 106	Boom Biddy Boom/RUDIES: What Can I Do	8
69	Fab FAB 107	I Need A Witness/Johnny Dollar	10
69	Upfront UPF 1	Turns On The Heatwave/Crying Blues	7
70	Beacon BEA 156	Keep On Trying/Only The Lonely	7
70	Beacon BEA 174	Why Can't I Touch You/Gotta Get It Off My Mind	7
73	Smash SAM 2333	Rock And Cry/September	10

SIMON PLUG & GRIMES

70	Deram DM 296	Is This A Dream?/I'm Going Home	12
70	President PT 310	Way In, Way Out/Long Long Summer	5
71	President PT 354	Pull Together/I'll Keep Smiling	5

SIMON'S SECRETS

(see also Secrets, Clifford T. Ward, Martin Raynor & Secrets)

68	CBS 3406	Naughty Boy/Sympathy	35
68	CBS 3856	I Know What Her Name Is/Keeping My Head Above Water	35

SIMON SISTERS

64	London HLR 9893	Winkin', Blinkin' And Nod/So Glad I'm Here	20
65	London HLR 9984	Cuddlebug/No One To Talk My Trouble To	15

NIC SIMPER'S FANDANGO

(see also Deep Purple, Warhorse)

83	Paro PAR 0S4	Just Another Day (In The Life Of A Fool)/Wish I'd Never Woke Up	6
79	Gull GULP 1033	SLIPSTREAMING (LP)	20

SIMPLE IMAGE

70	Carnaby CNS 4013	Spinning Spinning Spinning/Shy Boy	15

SIMPLE MINDS

(see also Johnny & Self Abusers)

79	Zoom ZUM 10	Life In A Day/Special View (p/s)	5
79	Zoom ZUM 11	Chelsea Girl/Garden Of Hate (p/s)	5

SIMPLICITY PEOPLE

73	Grape GR 3062	Murderer/BIG YOUTH: The Killer	12
73	Harry J HJ 6649	Time Is Getting Harder/HARRY J ALLSTARS: Time Is Getting Harder	6

SIMPLY RED

(see also Frantic Elevators)

85	Elektra EKT 27P	PICTURE BOOK (LP, picture disc, die-cut sleeve)	15

BILL SIMPSON

64	Piccadilly 7N 35179	I Love You For Sentimental Reasons/My Love Is Like A Red Red Rose (p/s)	8

DANNY SIMPSON

69	Trojan TR 653	Outa Sight/JOHN HOLT: I Want You Closer	30

DUDLEY SIMPSON & BRIAN HODGSON

(See also BBC Radiophonic Workshop)

73	Polydor 2383 210	IN A COVENT GARDEN (LP)	25

HOKE SIMPSON

58	HMV POP 442	I Finally Found You/Gi-Gi	8

JEANETTE SIMPSON

67	Giant GN 16	Rain/Whatcha Gonna Do About It	15
68	Giant GN 29	My Baby Just Cares For Me/Don't Let Me Cry No More (with Superboys)	40
68	Giant GN 35	Through Loving You/Send Me Some Lovin' (with Missions)	15

LEO SIMPSON

(see also Lionel Simpson)

65	Blue Beat BB 351	I Love Her So/Good To Be Seen (as Leo Simmo)	18
73	Pyramid PYR 7004	Waxy Doodle/Go Away	6

LIONEL SIMPSON

(see also Leo Simpson)

65	Ska Beat JB 205	Tell Me What You Want/Love Is A Game	15
65	Ska Beat JB 221	Red River Valley/Eight People	15
66	Ska Beat JB 233	Give Over/Never Before	15

MARTIN SIMPSON

76	Trailer LER 2099	GOLDEN VANITY (LP)	12
81	Waterfront WF 008	SPECIAL AGENT (LP)	12
83	Topic 12TS 430	GRINNING IN YOUR FACE (LP, tan label)	12
85	Topic 12TS 438	SAD OR HIGH KICKING (LP, tan label)	12
86	Dambuster DAM 013	NOBODY'S FAULT BUT MINE (LP)	15

MINT VALUE £

DUDLEY SIMPSON ORCHESTRA

78	BBC RESL 58	Blake's 7/The Federation March (p/s)	8

RED SIMPSON

66	Capitol ST 2468	ROLL TRUCK ROLL (LP)	12

VALERIE SIMPSON

(see also Ashford & Simpson)

72	Tamla Motown STML 11194	EXPOSED (LP)	20

CHUCK SIMS

58	London HLR 8577	Little Pigeon/Life Isn't Long Enough	350
58	London HLR 8577	Little Pigeon/Life Isn't Long Enough (78)	60

FRANKIE LEE SIMS

71	Specialty SPE 5009	Married Woman Blues/Lucy Mae Blues	5
71	Specialty SNTF 5004	LUCY MAE BLUES (LP)	15

JOAN SIMS

63	Parlophone R 5021	Oh Not Again Ken/Hurry Up Gran	5
63	Parlophone R 5089	Spring Song/Men	5
67	CBS 202635	Sweet Lovely Whatsisname/The Lass With The Delicate Hair	5

KELLY SIMS

60	Top Rank JAR 321	Betrayed By Love/A Girl In Love	6

SIMS TWINS/VALENTINOS

68	Soul City SCM 001	THE VALENTINOS/THE SIMS TWINS (LP, 1 side each)	60

ZOOT SIMS

(see also Sims-Wheeler Vintage Jazz Band)

57	Esquire EP 183	ZOOT! (EP)	20
57	Esquire EP 204	ZOOT'S CASE (EP)	20
52	Esquire 20-002	ZOOT SIMS QUARTET/QUINTET (10" LP)	40
53	Esquire 20-010	ZOOT SIMS ALLSTARS (10" LP)	20
53	Esquire 20-018	ZOOT SIMS QUARTET/QUINTET (10" LP)	20
54	Vogue LDE 056	ZOOT SIMS GOES TO TOWN (10" LP)	200
55	Esquire 20-040	ZOOT SIMS QUARTET/QUINTET (10" LP)	60
50s	Esquire 32-040	ZOOT SIMS SEPTET (LP)	30
58	HMV CLP 1165	GEORGE HANDY COMPOSITIONS (LP)	18
58	HMV CLP 1188	PLAYS FOUR ALTOS (LP)	20
61	Vogue LAE 12309	CHOICE (LP)	20
61	Fontana TFL 5176	ZOOT AT RONNIE SCOTT'S (LP)	150
62	Fontana (S)TFL 588	ZOOT AT RONNIE SCOTT'S (LP, reissue)	100
62	Fontana 886 151 TY	SOLO FOR ZOOT (LP, also mono [680 982 TL], £20)	50
65	Fontana FJL 123	COOKIN'! (LP)	150
60s	Xtra XTRA 5001	TROTTING! (LP)	15

FRANK SINATRA

(see also Nancy Sinatra, Count Basie, Tommy Dorsey, Dean Martin, Doris Day)

53	Columbia SCM 5052	Birth Of The Blues/Why Try To Change Me Now?	20
53	Columbia SCM 5060	You Do Something To Me/Lover	20
53	Columbia SCM 5076	Santa Claus Is Comin' To Town/My Girl	20
54	Capitol CL 14064	Young-At-Heart/Take A Chance	10
54	Capitol CL 14120	Three Coins In The Fountain/I Could Have Told You	20
54	Capitol CL 14174	White Christmas/The Christmas Waltz	12
54	Capitol CL 14188	When I Stop Loving You/It Worries Me	12
55	Capitol CL 14221	Someone To Watch Over Me/The Gal That Got Away	8
55	Capitol CL 14238	Melody Of Love/I'm Gonna Live Till I Die	8
55	Columbia SCM 5167	S'posin'/How Deep Is The Ocean	20
55	Capitol CL 14240	You, My Love/Just One Of Those Things	8
55	Capitol CL 14270	Don't Change Your Mind About Me/Why Should I Cry Over You	8
55	Capitol CL 14292	Two Hearts, Two Kisses (Make One Love)/From The Bottom To The Top	8
55	Capitol CL 14296	Learnin' The Blues/If I Had Three Wishes	8
55	Capitol CL 14326	Not As A Stranger/How Could You Do A Thing Like That To Me	8
55	Capitol CL 14352	My Funny Valentine/I Get A Kick Out Of You	8
55	Capitol CL 14360	It Never Entered My Mind/In The Wee Small Hours Of The Morning	8
55	Capitol CL 14373	Fairy Tale/Same Old Saturday Night	8

(The above Capitol 45s were originally issued with triangular centre; later round-centre copies are worth half these values.)

54	Capitol LC 6654	SONGS FOR YOUNG LOVERS (10")	20
54	Capitol LC 6689	SWING EASY (10") Decca Pressing/EMIo	20
55	Capitol LC 6702	IN THE WEE SMALL HOURS VOL. 1 (10")	20
55	Capitol LC 6705	IN THE WEE SMALL HOURS VOL. 2 (10")	20

(The above LPs were originally pressed by Decca. Subsequent pressings were by EMI, and are worth 40% less)

56	Capitol LCT 6106	SONGS FOR SWINGIN' LOVERS	15
56	Capitol LCT 6111	FRANK SINATRA CONDUCTS TONE POEMS OF COLOUR	15
85	Capitol SINATRA 20	FRANK SINATRA: THE CAPITOL YEARS (20-LP, box set)	40
54	Philips BBR 8003	SING AND DANCE WITH FRANK SINATRA (10")	15
55	Philips BBR 8038	FABULOUS FRANK (10")	12
55	Philips BBR 8040	YOUNG AT HEART (10", with Doris Day)	12
57	Philips BBR 8114	CHRISTMAS DREAMING (10")	15
57	Philips BBL 7137	DORIS AND FRANK (6 tracks each by Doris Day & Frank Sinatra)	12
57	Philips BBL 7168	FRANKIE	12
57	Philips BBL 7180	THAT OLD FEELING	12
58	Fontana TFL 5000	THE VOICE	12
58	Fontana TFL 5006	ADVENTURES OF THE HEART	12
58	Fontana TFL 5030	THE FRANK SINATRA STORY	12
59	Fontana TFL 5048	PUT YOUR DREAMS AWAY	12
62	Reprise R(9) 1006	SINATRA SINGS GREAT SONGS FROM GREAT BRITAIN (mono)	20
62	Reprise R(9) 1006	SINATRA SINGS GREAT SONGS FROM GREAT BRITAIN (stereo)	30
56	HMV DLP 1123	IT'S D-LOVELY (with Tommy Dorsey Orchestra)	15
83	Mobile Fidelity SC 1	THE SINATRA COLLECTION (16-LPs in silver box, with Swing Easy LP unavailable elsewhere)	100

MINT VALUE £

FRANK & NANCY SINATRA

67	Reprise REP 30082	SOMETHING STUPID (EP)	10
69	Reprise R(S)LP 1026	THE SINATRA FAMILY WISH YOU A HAPPY CHRISTMAS (LP)	15

NANCY SINATRA

(see also Elvis Presley)

61	Reprise RS 20017	Cuff Links And Tie Clips/Not Just Your Friend (with p/s)	15
61	Reprise RS 20017	Cuff Links And Tie Clips/Not Just Your Friend	10
62	Reprise RS 20045	To Know Him Is To Love Him/Like I Do	12
63	Reprise RS 20144	I See The Moon/Put Your Head On My Shoulder	10
64	Reprise RS 20335	True Love/The Answer To Everything	8
65	Reprise RS 20407	So Long Babe/If He'd Loved Me	10
66	Reprise RS 20432	These Boots Are Made For Walkin'/The City Never Sleeps At Night	6
66	Reprise R 20461	How Does That Grab You Darlin'/I Move Around	7
66	Reprise RS 20491	Friday's Child/Hutchinson Jail	7
66	Reprise RS 20514	In Our Time/Leave My Dog Alone	7
67	Reprise RS 20527	Sugar Town/Summer Wine	7
67	Reprise RS 20559	Love Eyes/Coastin'	7
67	Reprise RS 20620	Lightning's Girls/Until It's Time For You To Go	8
69	Reprise RS 20869	The Highway Song/Are You Growing Tired Of My Love	7
77	Private Stock PVT 114	It's For My Dad/A Gentle Man Like You	7
66	Reprise REP 30069	RUN FOR YOUR LIFE (EP)	20
66	Reprise REP 30072	I MOVE AROUND (EP)	15
67	Reprise REP 30080	SORRY 'BOUT THAT (EP)	15
67	Reprise REP 30086	NASHVILLE NANCY (EP)	15
66	Reprise R 6202	BOOTS (LP)	25
66	Reprise R 6207	HOW DOES THAT GRAB YOU? (LP)	25
66	Reprise R(S)LP 6221	NANCY IN LONDON (LP)	30
67	Reprise RLP 6239	SUGAR (LP)	25
67	Reprise R(S)LP 6251	COUNTRY, MY WAY (LP)	20
68	Reprise R(S)LP 6277	MOVIN' WITH NANCY (LP)	20
69	Reprise RSLP 6333	NANCY (LP)	20
73	RCA SF 8331	WOMAN (LP)	15

NANCY SINATRA & LEE HAZLEWOOD

(see also Lee Hazlewood, Frank Sinatra)

67	Reprise RS 20629	Lady Bird/Sand	7
67	Reprise RS 23215	Some Velvet Morning/Tony Rome	8
71	Reprise K 14093	Did You Ever?/Back On The Road Again	6
67	Reprise REP 30083	JACKSON (EP)	15
68	Reprise R(S)LP 6273	NANCY & LEE (LP)	20
72	RCA Victor SF 8240	DID YOU EVER? (LP)	18

BETTY SINCLAIR

70	Torpedo TOR 19	Why Why Why/HOT ROD ALL STARS: Fistful Of Dollars	15

JIMMY SINCLAIR

62	Wasp W005	To Prove My Love/Verona	12

JIMMY SINCLAIR & TRENTON SPENCE ORCHESTRA

(see also Jimmy Sinclair)

61	Blue Beat BB 47	Verona/To Prove My Love	10

PAUL SINCLAIR

76	Angen ANG 115	Jah Is My Saviour/Version	8

WINSTON SINCLAIR

(see also Harmonisers)

69	Nu Beat NB 026	Another Heartache/Come On Little Girl	8

SINDECUT

92	VST 1326DJ	Won't Change/Panic Stricken!!/Crack Business	8
87	BAAD BD666	SINDECUTS KICKIN' IT (EP)	20
88	BAAD BD 777	CAN'T GET ENOUGH (EP)	12
90	Virgin V2635	CHANGING THE SCENERY (LP)	15

SINDELFINGEN

73	Medway	ODGIPIG (LP, private pressing, with insert)	550
90	Cenotaph CEN 111	ODGIPIG/TRIANGLE (2-LP, reissue with live album, 300 only)	25

SINEWAVE

72	Chapter One SCH 172	Clochemerle/Star Trek	10

PETE SINFIELD

(see also Emerson Lake & Palmer, King Crimson, Greg Lake)

73	Manticore K 43501	STILL (LP, textured gatefold pink sleeve)	25
73	Manticore K 43501	STILL (LP, textured gatefold blue sleeve)	20

SINGAROUND

69	G. Guinea GSGL 10436	SINGAROUND (LP)	15

RAY SINGER

(see also Nirvana [U.K.])

64	Ember EMB S 187	Tell Me Now/I'm Comin' Home	10
64	Ember EMB S 199	It's Gotta Be/Hey, Who?	10
65	Ember EMB S 215	I'm The Richest Man Alive/Pretty Little Rambling Rose (in p/s)	15
65	Ember EMB S 215	I'm The Richest Man Alive/Pretty Little Rambling Rose	10
65	Fontana TF 621	You'll Come Crying To Me/Who Can I Talk To About You	10
67	Ember EMB S 231	What's Done Has Been Done/Won't It Be Fine	60
	Ember EMB 3364	RAY SINGER (LP)	40

SUSAN SINGER

(see also Susan Holiday)

62	Oriole CB 1703	Gee It's Great To Be Young/Hello First Love	20
62	Oriole CB 1741	Bobby's Loving Touch/Johnny Summertime	120

MINT VALUE £

62 Oriole CB 1778 — Love Me With All Your Heart/Autumn Leaves ... 20
63 Oriole CB 1802 — Lock Your Heart Away/Answer To A Prayer ... 20
63 Oriole CB 1882 — I Know (You Don't Love Me No More)/That Old Feeling ... 20

SINGERS AND PLAYERS

81 Silent SSH3 — Love All Over The Place/Over You (p/s) ... 15
81 On U Sound LP 5 — WAR OF WORDS (LP) ... 15
83 On U Sound LP 23 — STAGGERING HEIGHTS (LP) ... 15

SINGING BELLES

60 Top Rank JAR 350 — The Empty Mailbox/Someone Loves You, Joe ... 8

SINGING DOGS

57 Pye NEP 24029 — SINGING DOGS (EP) ... 10

SINGING POSTMAN

66 Parlophone R 5505 — The Ladies Darts Team/Roundabout ... 5
67 Parlophone R 5584 — Mind How You Go/Daddy's Trombone ... 5
67 Parlophone R 5632 — Sound Barrier/Old North Walsham Line ... 5
64 Ralph Tuck Promotions Ltd. BEV EP 153 — Come Along A Me/Moind Yer Hid Boy/ Hev Yew Gotta Loight Boy/Miss From Diss (EP) ... 10
65 Ralph Tuck BEV EP 179 — BBC SINGING POSTMAN (EP) ... 10
66 Parlophone GEP 8956 — FIRST DELIVERY (EP) ... 10
66 Parlophone GEP 8960 — FOURTH DELIVERY (EP) ... 10
67 Parlophone GEP 8964 — PLEASE MR. POSTMAN (EP) ... 10
66 Parlophone PMC 7013 — RECORDED DELIVERY (LP) ... 15

SINGING PRINCIPAL

73 Action ACT 4608 — Thank You Baby/Women's Lib ... 60

SINGLE FACTOR

84 SF Records SINFAX 001 — Fresh Upon Her Lips/I Think I'm Falling In Love (p/s, 2 inserts) ... 50

MARGIE SINGLETON

60 Melodisc 45-1544 — Angel Hands/The Eyes Of Love ... 15
62 Mercury AMT 1197 — Magic Star/Only Your Shadow Knows ... 20
68 Fontana TL 5456 — SINGS COUNTRY WITH SOUL (LP) ... 18

SINISTER DUCKS

(see also Bauhaus)

83 Situation 2 SIT 25 — Suicide: March Of The Sinister Ducks/Homicide: Old Gangsters Never (foldout p/s) ... 10

EARL SINK(S)

(see also Crickets, Sinx Mitchell)

61 Warner Bros WB 38 — Look For Me, I'll Be There/Super Market (as Earl Sink) ... 15
61 Warner Bros WB 51 — Superstitious/Little Suzie Parker ... 20
63 Capitol CL 15310 — Looking For Love/Raining On My Side Of Town (as Earl Sinks) ... 15

SINNER

79 Whitetower AMC 705 — Need Your Love/Beggar/God's In His Heaven (foldout p/s) ... 75

SINNERMAN & SARA

68 MGM 1450 — Don't Think Twice It's Allright/Buffalo Boy ... 10
68 MGM MGM-C(S) 8099 — SINNERMAN AND SARA (LP) ... 20

SINNERS

(see also Linda Laine & Sinners)

63 Columbia DB 7158 — I Can't Stand It/If You Leave Me Now ... 10
64 Columbia DB 7295 — It's So Exciting/Leave Him ... 10

SINS OF THE FLESH

90s Plastic Head 014 — In The Image Of Torture (12", p/s) ... 10

SINYX

82 Reality attack — BLACK DEATH (EP) ... 20

SIOUXSIE & BANSHEES

(see also Creatures, Cure, Glove)

78 Polydor 2059 052 — Hong Kong Garden/Voices (10,000 only in gatefold p/s; beige plastic, silver plastic, red plastic or red paper label) ... 18
78 Polydor 2059 052 — Hong Kong Garden/Voices (p/s) ... 5
79 Polydor 2059 151 — Mittageisen (Metal Postcard)/Love In A Void (p/s) ... 5
80 Polydor POSPX 205 — Israel (Extended)/Red Over White (Extended) (12", a few with Made In England' credit, most with 'Made In France' credit) ... 8
83 Fan Club FILE 1 — Head Cut/Running Town (freebie, p/s) ... 20
85 Wonderland SHEX 9 — Cities In Dust/An Execution/Quarterdrawing Of The Dog (12", p/s, banned picture label) ... 8
86 Wonderland SHEDP 10 — Candyman/Lullaby (with free 2nd single, gatefold p/s, 2,000 only) ... 8
87 Wonderland SHEPK 4 — The Passenger/Hall Of Mirrors/You're Lost Little Girl/Sea Breezes/This Town Ain't Big Enough For Both Of Us/Gun (3 X promo 7" in plain black sleeves in foldout stickered and printed PVC wallet, single cat. no's SHESP 1/2/3) ... 15
78 Polydor POLD 5009 — THE SCREAM (LP, with inner sleeve; with labels reversed) ... 12
79 Polydor POLD 5024 — JOIN HANDS (LP, gatefold, with inner sleeve) ... 12
87 Wonderland SHELP 4 — THROUGH THE LOOKING GLASS (LP, mispressing, 1 side plays Jimi Hendrix's "War Heroes") ... 25

SIR ALEC & HIS BOYS

67 Deram DM 116 — I'm A Believer/Green Green Grass Of Home ... 8

SIR ALICK & PHRASER

(see also Homosexuals)

82 Recommended/Black Noise 7 NO 5 — In Search Of The Perfect Baby/PROLIFIKURDS: Nursery Crymes (printed p/s in PVC sleeve or standard p/s) ... 10

MINT VALUE £

SIR BEANZ OBE
99 Mapache Chet002 MARS ATTACKS (EP) . . . 15
01 SFDB 005 HIEROGLYPHIC AUDIO VISUAL (EP) . . . 8

SIR CHAUNCEY
60 Warner Bros. WB 9 Beautiful Obsession/Tenderfoot . . . 7
60 Warner Bros. WB 36 Midi-Midinette/Beyond Our Love . . . 6

SIR (Clancy) COLLINS BAND
(see also Bob Stackie, Earthquakes, Collins Band, Owen Gray)
68 Collins Downbeat CR 005 Sock It Softly (with Bob Stackie)/LESTER STERLING, SIR COLLINS & BAND: Three Wise Men . . . 45
68 Collins Downbeat CR 0011 Collins And The Boys/Bob Stackie In Soho (both with Bob Stackie) . . . 40
68 Collins Downbeat CR 0017 Soul Feelings/SIR COLLINS: Hello Stella . . . 45
69 Duke DU 46 Black Panther/I Want To Be Loved . . . 150
69 Duke DU 47 Black Diamonds (with Diamonds)/DIAMONDS: I Remember . . . 40
69 Duke DU 55 Brother Moses/Funny Familiar Feeling (both with Earthquakes) . . . 40
69 Duke DU 69 Pair Of Wings/I Can't Stop Loving . . . 50

SIR COXSONE SOUND (LLOYD COXON)
75 Safari SFA 100 KING OF DUB ROCK (LP) . . . 35
76 Regal RLP 001 KING OF DUB ROCK PART 2 (LP) . . . 20

SIR D's GROUP
(see also Kent Brown & Rainbows)
61 Blue Beat BB 66 Hey Diddle Diddle (with K. Brown)/Pocket Money (with Mossman & Zeddze) . . . 25

SIR DOUGLAS QUINTET
65 London HLU 9964 She's About A Mover/We'll Take Our Last Walk Tonight . . . 10
65 London HLU 9982 The Tracker/Blue Norther . . . 10
65 London HLU 10001 The Story Of John Hardy/In Time . . . 8
66 London HLU 10019 The Rains Came/Bacon Fat . . . 8
69 Mercury MF 1079 Mendocino/I Wanna Be Your Mama Again . . . 10
69 Mercury MF 1129 Dynamite Woman/Too Many Dociled Minds . . . 8
65 London HA-U 8311 THE SIR DOUGLAS QUINTET (LP) . . . 60
69 Mercury SMCL 20160 MENDOCINO (LP) . . . 30
69 Mercury SMCL 20186 TOGETHER AFTER FIVE (LP) . . . 30
75 Oval OVLM 5001 MENDOCINO (LP, with insert) . . . 15

SIREN
71 Dandelion DAN 7002 Strange Locomotion/I'm All Aching (label also lists K 19004) . . . 6
69 Dandelion 63755 SIREN (LP, laminated front sleeve, black/red/silver labels) . . . 45
71 Dandelion DAN 8001 STRANGE LOCOMOTION (LP, gatefold sleeve) . . . 45
71 Dandelion DAN 8001 STRANGE LOCOMOTION (LP, with later label listing K 49001) . . . 25

SIREN
84 Distant Cousins DC4R Deceiving Lies/American Girl (white or black sleeve) . . . 10

SIR GIBBS
68 Amalgamated AMG 822 People Grudgeful/Pan Ya Machet (both sides actually by Pioneers) . . . 50

SIR HARRY
(see also Barbara Jones)
71 Duke DU 127 Last Call/ORGAN D: Hot Organ . . . 10
72 Duke DU 136 Apples To Apples/DRUM BEAT ALL STARS: Good Life . . . 10
72 Bullet BU 519 Mr. Parker's Daughter/U.ROY: On Top Of The Peak . . . 12
72 Downtown DT 493 Meet The Boss/Musical Fight . . . 12
73 Downtown DT 504 Apollo 17 (with Cables)/Uptown Rock . . . 12

SIR HENRY (& HIS BUTLERS)
68 Columbia DB 8351 Camp/Pretty Style (as Sir Henry & His Butlers) . . . 10
68 Columbia DB 8497 The Rolo Sensation (Camp)/Pretty Style (reissue, as Sir Henry & His Butlers) . . . 10
70 Columbia DB 8740 Annie Got A Date/Like A Rose . . . 8

SIR HORATIO
(see also A Certain Ratio)
82 Rock Steady/666 Mix 1T Abracadubra/Sommadub (12", plain sleeve) . . . 15

SIR LORD COMIC
(see also Lord Comic)
67 Doctor Bird DB 1019 Ska-ing West/MAYTALS: If You Act This Way . . . 40
67 Doctor Bird DB 1070 The Great Wuga Wuga (with Cowboys)/THREE TOPS: Feel So Lonesome . . . 45
70 Pressure Beat PR 5507 Jack Of My Trade/CYNTHIA RICHARDS: United We Stand . . . 70

SIRUS
91 White 002 THE ONE AND ONLY (EP) . . . 35
93 SBP SBPR004 Clubland/DETT (12") . . . 8

SIR WASHINGTON
69 Star ST 1 Apollo 12/When You Kiss Me . . . 12
70 Saga BC 100 Apollo 13/Space . . . 10
70 Saga BC 102 Let There Be Peace in The World/Pharoah's Walk . . . 10

SISTER
70 Camel CA 55 Feel It/MAYTONES: Serious . . . 12
73 Camel CA 106 Every Day Is The Same Kind Of Thing/Sweat Of Your Brow . . . 10

SISTERHOOD
(see also Sisters Of Mercy, James Ray & Performance)
86 Merciful Release SIS 010 Giving Ground (RSV)/Giving Ground (AV) (p/s) . . . 5

SISTERS
73 Bell BELL 1307 Kick Your Boots Off/Driving Me Home . . . 12
74 Warner Brothers K 16445 There's A Raver Coming Home/Help The Music . . . 12

MINT VALUE £

SISTERS LOVE

70 A&M AMS 772 — Forget It, I've Got It/Eye To Eye ... 5
70 A&M AMS 808 — The Bigger Your Love/Piece Of My Heart ... 5
72 Tamla Motown TMG 828 — Mr. Fix It Man/You've Got To Make Your Choice ... 8
73 Mowest MW 3009 — I'm Learning To Trust My Man/Try It You'll Like It ... 10
75 Tamla Motown TMG 1002 — I'm Learning To Trust My Man/Try It You'll Like It (reissue) ... 8

SISTERS OF MERCY

(see also Mission, Sisterhood, Ghost Dance, Dead Or Alive)

80 Merciful Release MR 7 — The Damage Done/Watch/Home Of The Hitmen (p/s, 1,000 only; beware of counterfeits without 'MR 7' matrix number) ... 200
82 CNT CNT 002 — Body Electric/Adrenochrome (p/s) ... 85
82 Merciful Release MR 015 — Alice/Floorshow (white background p/s) ... 30
84 Merciful Release/WEA — ALICE/TEMPLE OF LOVE/REPTILE HOUSE/BODY AND SOUL (4 x 12" box set, promo only) ... 100
84 Merciful Release MR 033 — Walk Away/Poison Door (p/s, with flexidisc "Long Train" [SAM 218]) ... 15
84 Merciful Release MR 033T — Walk Away/Poison Door/On The Wire (12", p/s, with flexi "Long Train") ... 15
85 Merciful Release MR 335 — No Time To Cry/Blood Money (p/s) ... 6
85 Merciful Release MR 035T — No Time To Cry/Blood Money/Bury Me Deep (12", p/s) ... 8
87 Merciful Release MR 39 — This Corrosion/Torch (box set, with 3 postcards, 5,000 only) ... 8
87 Merciful Release MR 39CD — This Corrosion (11.15)/Torch/Colours (CD, black disc, gatefold card sleeve with gauze inner, some without 'WEA' logo on back sleeve) ... 8
88 Merciful Release MR 43C — Dominion/Untitled/Sandstorm/Ozymandias (cassette in presentation box) ... 5
88 Merciful Release MR 43TB — Dominion (Extended)/Untitled/Sandstorm/Emma (12", box set with poster) ... 15
88 Merciful Release MR 43CD — Dominion (Extended)/Untitled/Sandstorm/Ozymandias (3" CD, black disc with adaptor, 5" case) ... 12
88 Merciful Release MR 44CD — Lucretia My Reflection (Extended 9.52)/Long Train (1984) (3" CD, with adaptor, 5" case) ... 12

SITUATION

66 CBS 202392 — Situation Now/Time ... 25

SIVUCA

74 Vanguard VSD 79337 — SIVUCA (LP) ... 30

SIX OF ONE

64 Mercury MF 812 — He's The One You Love/I Love My Little Girl ... 10

SIXPENCE

67 London HLJ 10124 — You're The Love/What To Do ... 10

EARL SIXTEEN

79 Sufferers Heights SUFF 007 — African Tribesman/MIKEY DREAD: Yoruba Dub (12") ... 20
79 Cha Cha CHAD 16 — The World Has Begun (with the Heptones)/Make Up Your Mind (12") ... 20
81 DATC DCD 004 — MR D.J./GILLY BUCHANAN: Ghetto Youths/DATC MUSIC STABLE : Dub (12") ... 25
81 Dread At The Controls DATC LP003 — REGGAE SOUND (LP) ... 45

SIX TEENS

56 London HLU 8345 — A Casual Look/Teen Age Promise ... 375
56 London HLU 8345 — A Casual Look/Teen Age Promise (78) ... 50

SIXTH COMM

87 Eyas Media EYAS 002 — CONTENT WITH BLOOD/TURN OF THE WHEEL (LP, embossed, textured sleeve, 2,000 only) ... 20
87 Eyas Media EYAS 005 — TASTE FOR FLESH (1st 2,000 in laminated, full-cover sleeve) ... 18
87 Eyas Media EYAS 005 — TASTE FOR FLESH (LP) ... 12
88 Eyas Media EYAS 006 — FRUITS OF YGGDRASIL (LP, limited issue, 669 copies only) ... 25
90 Eyas Media EYAS 013 — ASYLUM (LP) ... 15
90 Eyas Media EYAS 071 — COMING OF SEVEN (LP) ... 12

64 SPOONS

78 Bushbaby — LADIES DON'T HAVE WILLIES (EP) ... 10

SIZE SEVEN GROUP

65 Mercury MF 845 — Where Do We Go From Here/Till I Die ... 10
65 Mercury MF 854 — In Time/Walking Proud ... 10
65 Mercury MF 896 — It's Got To Be Love/I Met Her In The Rain ... 8

SKA CHAMPIONS

65 Blue Beat BB 305 — My Tears/Yesterday's Dreams ... 20

SKA CITY ROCKERS

80 Inferno BEAT 1 — Time Is Tight/Roadrunner/You Don't Know Like I Know (p/s) ... 6
80 Inferno BEAT 1 — Time Is Tight/Roadrunner/You Don't Know Like I Know (12", p/s) ... 10

SKA-DOWS

80 Cheapskate CHEAP 1 — Apache/The Tune That Time Forgot (p/s) ... 7
80 Cheapskate CHEAP 4 — Telstar/Yes Yes Yes (p/s) ... 8
81 Cheapskate CHEAP 25 — Yes Yes Yes/Twice (p/s) ... 8
81 Penthouse PENT 7 — Ska's On 45/Rhapsody In Buh (plain stickered sleeve) ... 6
81 Penthouse PENT 127 — Ska's On 45/The Ska-Dows Live (Let's Twist Again/Everybody Knows It's Shocking/Aye-Ho - Kinky Reggae) (12", p/s) ... 12
81 Cheapskate CHEAP 36 — Ska's On 45/Rhapsody In Buh (p/s, reissue) ... 6
81 Cheapskate CHEAPT 36 — Ska's On 45/The Ska-Dows Live (Let's Twist Again/Everybody Knows It's Shocking/Aye-Ho - Kinky Reggae) (12", p/s, reissue) ... 8
82 Cheapskate CHEAP 41 — We Gotta Get Out Of This Place/Ska'd For Life ... 5
82 Cheapskate SKATE 3 — SKA'D FOR LIFE (LP) ... 15

SKA KINGS

64 Atlantic AT 4003 — Jamaica Ska (actually by Keith Lynn & Ken Lazarus, & Byron Lee/ Dragonaires)/Oil In My Lamp (actually by Eric Morris with Byron Lee & Dragonaires) ... 20
65 Parlophone R 5338 — Bimbo/Ska'ville ... 10

MINT VALUE £

SKANNA
(see also The Joker)

92	White House WYHS 010	Intimidator/Jungle Rain/Cease Fire/Dreamin' (12")	20
93	White House WYHS 013	The Future/Nightstalker/Intimidator (Technoid Mix)/Exit The Lights (12")	50
93	Skanna 03	NIGHT STALKER EP (12")	50
93	Skanna 04	Until The Night Is Morning/Untitled (12")	50
93	Skanna 05	Heaven/Run To Me/This Way (12")	30
94	Skanna 07	The Greatest Thing (Summertime Mix)/The Greatest Thing/Heaven (Remix) (12")	12
94	Skanna 08	All You Wanted/The Greatest Thing (Criminal Minds Mix) (12")	15
96	Skanna 09	Find Me/Find Me (Classic Skanna Mix) (12")	20

SKATALITES (Jamaica)
(see also Justin Hinds, Deltas, Four Aces, Maytals, Jackie Opel, Joe White, Jackie Mittoo)

65	Island WI 161	Trip To Mars/DOTTIE & BONNIE: Bunch Of Roses	45
65	Island WI 164	Good News/OWEN & LEON: The Fits Is On Me	25
65	Island WI 168	Guns Of Navarone (actually by Roland Alphonso & Studio One Orchestra) Marcus Garvey (actually "Where's Marcus Garvey" by Bongoman Byfield)	8
65	Island WI 175	Dragon Weapon/DESMOND DEKKER & FOUR ACES: It Was Only A Dream	100
65	Island WI 191	Dr. Kildare/Sucu Sucu	75
65	Island WI 207	Ball O' Fire/LINVAL SPENCER: Can't Go On	30
65	Island WI 226	Dick Tracy/RITA & SOULETTES: One More Chance	75
65	Island WI 228	Beardman Ska/BONNIE & RITA: Bless You	20
65	Island WI 244	Lucky Seven/JUSTIN HINDS & DOMINOES: Never Too Young	25
66	Island WI 260	Independent Anniversary Ska (I Should Have Known Better)/WAILERS: Jumbie Jamboree	80
65	Ska Beat JB 177	Latin Goes Ska/LORD TANAMO: Night Food Ska	35
65	Ska Beat JB 178	Silver Dollar/My Business	20
65	Ska Beat JB 182	Street Corner/DREAMLETS: Really Now	30
65	Ska Beat JB 206	Timothy/KING SCRATCH & DYNAMITES: Gumma	40
73	Trojan Maxi TRM 9008	Guns Of Navarone/Bonanza Ska/Napolean Solo	5
75	Tropical ALO64	Jumbo Malt/747 Dub (as Original Skatalites)	10
67	Studio One SOL 9006	SKA AUTHENTIC (LP)	300

SKATALITES (U.K.)

68	Decca F 12743	Don't Knock It/I Know	10
69	Spark SRL 1034	Cos You're The One I Love/Please Let Me Hide	10

SKAVENGERS

80	Identity Discs ID 001	Party Girls/Go To Pieces/Happy	10

SK'BOO
(see also Them)

70s	Cuecumber CUE 1001	It's A Hard Road/Music Is Life/Talking Pictures/God's Peace In Mind	5

BOBBY SKEL

64	London HLU 9942	Kiss And Run/Say It Now	15

SKELETAL FAMILY
(see also Ghost Dance)

83	Luggage RRP 00724	Trees/Just A Friend (foldout p/s)	12
86	Cave CAVE IN 1	Sharp Cheekbones In Black Clothing/Blood-Stained (p/s)	12
84	Red Rhino REDL LP 44	BURNING OIL (LP, picture inner and A5 booklet)	12
85	Red Rhino REDLP 57	FUTILE COMBAT (LP)	15

SKELETON CREW
(see also King Earl Boogie Band, Manfred Mann's Earth Band)

87	B BS 1	BOOGIE-WOOGIE, SKIFFLE & BLUES (12" EP, p/s)	15
88	B BS 2	House Of The Rising Sun/Hurricane Janine (white label promo only)	15

SKELLATON

94	Viceroy GREEB028	Bangers 'n' Mash (12")	18

SKEPTIX

82	Zenon SKEP 001	Routine Machine/Curfew (p/s)	15
83	Zenon SKEP 002	Scarred For Life/Born To Lose/Peaceforce (p/s)	15
83	Zenon SKEP 003	RETURN TO HELL (EP)	15

SKERNE

81	Guardian GRC 81	BETTER LATE THAN NEVER (LP, private pressing)	15

SKETTO
(Father Sketto, Ruddy and Sketto)

71	Big Shot BI 596	Know Your Friend/Three Sevens Version	15

FATHER SKETTO
(see also Sketto Rich, Ruddy & Sketto)

73	Pama PM 877	Big Nine/RECO'S GROUP: Old Lady	5

SKIDDY & DETROIT

72	Grape GR 3030	The Exile Song/BUNNY GALE: In The Burning Sun Joh-Ho	8

ALAN SKIDMORE (QUINTET)
(see also John Mayall's Bluesbreakers, Brian Bennett, Centipede)

69	Deram Nova SDN 11	ONCE UPON A TIME (LP)	150
71	Philips 6308 041	T.C.B. (LP)	130

JIMMY SKIDMORE

72	DJM DJSL 026	SKID MARKS (LP)	50

SKID ROW (Ireland)
(see also Gary Moore, Thin Lizzy, Peggy's Leg, UFO)

70	Song SO 002	New Places Old Faces/Misdemeanour Dream Felicity (Irish pressing)	100
70	Song SO003	Saturday Morning Man (Irish pressing)	25
70	CBS 4893	Sandie's Gone (Parts 1 & 2)	15

MINT VALUE £

71	CBS 7181	Night Of The Warm Witch/Mr. Deluxe	10
70	CBS 63965	SKID (LP, orange label, red & blue sleeve)	40
71	CBS 64411	34 HOURS (LP, gatefold sleeve, orange label)	35

SKIDS
(see also Big Country)

78	No Bad NB 1	Charles/Reasons/Test Tube Babies (p/s)	10
78	Virgin VS 227	Sweet Suburbia/Open Sound (p/s, white vinyl)	5
79	Virgin VS 262	Masquerade/Out Of Town//Another Emotion/Aftermath Dub (double pack)	5
79	Virgin VS 306	Working For The Yankee Dollar/Vanguard's Crusage//All The Young Dudes/ Hymns From A Haunted Ballroom (double pack)	5
79	Smash Hits HIT 002	The Olympian/XTC: Ten Feet Tall (33rpm red flexi with Smash Hits mag)	5
79	Virgin V 2116	SCARED TO DANCE (LP, blue vinyl, withdrawn)	300
79	Virgin V 2138	DAYS IN EUROPA (LP, with insert, 1st pressing with withdrawn cover featuring German 'gothic' lettering & 1936 Olympics picture)	12
80	Virgin V 2174	THE ABSOLUTE GAME (LP, with free LP "Strength Through Joy" [VDJ 33])	12

BJORN SKIFS

78	EMI EMI 2785	When The Night Comes/Don't Stop Now	6
81	EMI EMI 5172	Haunted By A Dream/Fangad I En Drom	8

SKILLETS

70	Pantonic PAN 6303	BOTH SIDES NOW (LP)	15

SKIN

80s	Product Inc. 33 PROD 11	SHAME, HUMILITY, REVENGE (LP, with inner)	12

SKIN ALLEY

70	CBS 5045	Tell Me/Better Be Blind	20
72	Transatlantic BIG 506	You Got Me Danglin'/Skin Valley Serenade	8
72	Transatlantic BIG 511	In The Midnight Hour/Broken Eggs	8
73	Transatlantic BIG 514	If Only I Had The Time/Instrumental	10
69	CBS 63847	SKIN ALLEY (LP, laminated front sleeve, orange label)	110
70	CBS 64140	TO PAGHAM AND BEYOND (LP, gatefold sleeve, orange label)	50
72	Transatlantic TRA 260	TWO QUID DEAL (LP, laminated front with inner sleeve & poster)	45
73	Transatlantic TRA 273	SKIN TIGHT (LP)	18
75	Klik KLP 9007	BAG-O-WIRE (LP)	15

SKIN DEEP

85	Enemy ENEMY 1	FOOTBALL VIOLENCE (EP)	200
88	Skank LP 103	MORE THAN SKIN DEEP (LP)	15

SKIN, FLESH & BONES
(see also Vincent Gordon, Cynthia Richards)

74	Pyramid PYR 7014	Butter Te Fish/Bammie And Fish	5
74	Opal PAL100	Man Come, Man Go/Guitar Rhythm	15

J SCOTT SKINNER

75	Topic 12T 280	STRATHSPEY KING (LP, blue label)	15

JIMMIE SKINNER

59	Mercury AMT 1030	Walkin' My Blues Away/Dark Hollow	15
59	Mercury AMT 1062	John Wesley Hardin/Misery Loves Company	10
60	Mercury AMT 1088	Riverboat Gambler/Married To A Friend	6
60	Mercury AMT 1117	Reasons To Live/I'm A Lot More Lonesome Now	6
64	London RE-B 1421	KENTUCKY COLONEL VOL. 1 (EP)	15
64	London RE-B 1422	KENTUCKY COLONEL VOL. 2 (EP)	15
64	London RE-B 1423	KENTUCKY COLONEL VOL. 3 (EP)	15

JIMMIE SKINNER/GEORGE JONES

59	Mercury ZEP 10012	COUNTRY AND WESTERN (EP, 2 tracks each)	20

SKINNYMAN/DJ FLIP

05	Netgroove NET7003	Forever Rangers/Not Bonny And Clyde (7" - 500 pressed)	20

SKIP BIFFERTY
(see also Chosen Few, Heavy Jelly, Griffin, Graham Bell, Arc, Bell & Arc, Every Which Way, Loving Awareness)

67	RCA Victor RCA 1621	On Love/Cover Girl	30
67	RCA Victor RCA 1648	Happy Land/Reason To Live	40
68	RCA Victor RCA 1720	Man In Black/Mr. Money Man	55
68	RCA Victor RD/SF 7941	SKIP BIFFERTY (LP, black label)	200
68	RCA Victor RD/SF 7941	SKIP BIFFERTY (LP, later pressing with orange label)	150

SKIP & FLIP
(see also Gary Paxton, Skip Battin, Hollywood Argyles)

59	Top Rank JAR 156	It Was I/Lunch Hour	10
59	Top Rank JAR 248	Fancy Nancy/It Could Be	15
60	Top Rank JAR 358	Cherry Pie/(I'll Quit) Cryin' Over You	10

SKI PATROL
(see also Wall)

80	Clever Metal VIN 1	Everything Is Temporary/Silent Screams (p/s)	10
80	Malicious Damage MD 2	Agent Orange/Driving (p/s, with insert)	12
81	Malicious Damage MD 3	Cut/Faith In Transition (p/s)	10

SKITZO

86	Nervous NERD 028	SKITZO MANIA (LP)	12
88	Nervous NERD 039	TERMINAL DAMAGE (LP)	12

SAM SKLAIR

69	Pye 7N 25488	Zulu Warrior/Phata Phata	15

YANI SKORDALIDIS

75	Pinnacle P81413	Little Drummer Boy/Here Pussy Pussy	15

MINT VALUE £

SKREWDRIVER

77	Chiswick S 11	You're So Dumb/Better Off Crazy (green p/s)	50
77	Chiswick S 11	You're So Dumb/Better Off Crazy (orange p/s)	45
77	Chiswick NS 18	Anti-Social/19th Nervous Breakdown (p/s)	25
78	Chiswick NS 28	Streetfight/Unbeliever (unissued, Trident label)	300
80	TJM TJM 4	Built Up, Knocked Down/A Case Of Pride/Breakout (p/s)	25
82	Skrewdriver SKREW 1T	BACK WITH A BANG (12", p/s)	40
83	White Noise WN 1	White Power/Smash The I.R.A./Shove The Dove (p/s)	50
83	White Noise WN 2	Voice Of Britain/Sick Society (p/s)	50
77	Chiswick CH 3	ALL SKREWED UP (mini-LP, 12-track, 45rpm, 3 different colour sleeves)	50
77	Chiswick WIK 3	ALL SKREWED UP (LP, 15-track, 33rpm, unissued in U.K.; German-only)	100

SKROTEEZ

82	Skroteez SPILL 1	OVERSPILL (EP)	15

SKULLFLOWER

(see also Ramleh)

86	Broken Flag BF V9	BIRTHDEATH (12" EP)	80
89	Shock SX 001	(I Live) In The Bottomless Pit/Bo Diddley's Shitpump (foldaround p/s in poly bag, 500 only, 75 copies in 'burns victim' sleeve)	20
89	Shock SX 001	(I Live) In The Bottomless Pit/Bo Diddley's Shitpump (foldaround p/s in poly bag, 500 only)	12
90	Toe Jam FLUF 005	Rotten Sun/Spook Rise (p/s, numbered, 500 only)	12
92	Dying Artefact DE 002	Bad Alchemy/Blues For H.M. (p/s in poly bag, numbered, 500 only)	10
94	Freak Records RR 001	White Fang 2/Glassy Essence (wraparound sleeve, stamped label)	8
89	Shock SX 008	XAMAN (LP, 1000 only)	20
89	Broken Flag BFV 10	FORM DESTROYER (LP)	30
92	HEADdIRT HD 01	IIIRD GATEKEEPER (CD)	20

SKULLS

89	Snake Skin SS 001	Graveyard Signal/Idols And Dolls (p/s, 300 only)	10

SKULLSNAPS

73	GSF GSZ 7	My Hang Up Is You/It's A New Day	70

SKUNKS

(see also Craze, Hard Corps)

78	Eel Pie EPS 001	Good From The Bad/Back Street Fightin' (2,000 only, die-cut 'swirl' sleeve)	12

SKY

(see also Knack)

68	United Artists UP 2234	Air-O-Plane Ride/Weather Forecast	7
69	Decca F 12971	On Our Way/The Singer Is Singing His Song	7

SKY

71	RCA RCA 2070	Goodie Two Shoes/Make It On Time (as U.S. Sky)	5
71	RCA SF 8168	DON'T HOLD BACK (LP, as U.S. Sky)	12

PATRICK SKY

65	Vanguard VSD 79179	PATRICK SKY (LP)	20
70	Vanguard SVRL 19054	A HARVEST OF GENTLE CLANG (LP)	20

SKYBIRD

74	Holyground HGS 118	SUMMER OF '73 (LP, 250 copies only)	60

SKY BLUES

67	Centaur CPC 1003	PLAYERS AT EASE: COVENTRY CITY (LP)	12

SKYLARK

72	Capitol CL 15747	The Writings On The Wall/Wildflower	8

SKYLINERS

59	London HLB 8829	Since I Don't Have You/One Night, One Night	225
59	London HLB 8829	Since I Don't Have You/One Night, One Night (78)	70
59	London HLU 8924	This I Swear/Tomorrow	80
59	London HLU 8924	This I Swear/Tomorrow (78)	70
59	London HLU 8971	It Happened Today/Lonely Way	75
59	London HLU 8971	It Happened Today/Lonely Way (78)	80
60	Polydor NH 66951	Pennies From Heaven/I'll Be Seeing You	15
61	Pye International 7N 25091	I'll Close My Eyes/The Door Is Still Open	20

SKY PONEY

70	Decca F 23082	Jubeldown/Chubby	8

SKYSOUNDS

66	Anglo TPMA 101/102	Two Timer/No Matter Where I Wander (private pressing)	10

SLACK ALICE

(see also Sandra Alfred, Sandra Barry)

74	Fontana 6007 038	Motorcycle/Ridin' The Wind	5
74	Philips 6308 214	SLACK ALICE (LP)	15

FREDDIE SLACK (& Orchestra)

(see also Ella Mae Morse & Freddie Slack)

51	Capitol LC 6529	FREDDIE SLACK'S BOOGIE WOOGIE (10" LP)	35

SLADE

(see also Ambrose Slade, Steve Brett, 'N Betweens, Vendors, Dummies, Jimmy Lea, Gary Holton, China Dolls, Clout, Gang Of Angels, Metal Gurus)

SINGLES

69	Fontana TF 1056	Wild Winds Are Blowing/One Way Hotel (credited to The Slade)	100
70	Fontana TF 1079	Shape Of Things To Come/C'mon C'mon	50
70	Polydor 2058 054	Know Who You Are/Dapple Rose	80
71	Polydor 2058 112	Get Down With It/Do You Want Me/The Gospel According To Rasputin (with writing credit: Holder/Hill/Lea/Powell/Penniman; some copies re-pressed as "Get Down And Get With It")	5

			MINT VALUE £
74	Polydor 2058 453	Everyday/Good Time Gals (mispressed with Hollies' The Air That I Breathe on A-side)	6
75	Polydor 2058 663	In For A Penny/Can You Just Imagine (p/s)	5
76	Polydor 2058 716	Nobody's Fool/L.A. Jinx	5
77	Barn 2014 105	Gypsy Roadhog/Forest Full Of Needles	5
77	Barn 2014 106	Burning In The Heat Of Love/Ready Steady Kids	18
77	Barn 2014 114	My Baby Left Me; That's Alright/O.H.M.S. (p/s)	6
78	Barn 2014 121	Give Us A Goal/Daddio	8
78	Barn 2014 127	Rock'n'Roll Bolero/It's Alright By Me	15
79	Barn BARN 002	Ginny Ginny/Dizzy Mama (yellow vinyl only, with sticker)	10
79	Barn BARN 002	Ginny Ginny/Dizzy Mama (yellow vinyl only, without sticker)	8
79	Barn BARN 010	Sign Of The Times/Not Tonight Josephine	15
79	Barn BARN 011	Okey Cokey/My Baby's Got It	10
80	RSO RSO 051	Okey Cokey/My Baby's Got It (withdrawn reissue, existence unconfirmed)	0
80	S.O.T.B. SUPER 45 3	SIX OF THE BEST - NIGHT STARVATION (12" EP, die-cut sleeve)	15
80	Cheapskate CHEAP 5	ALIVE AT READING '80 (EP, die-cut sleeve)	7
80	Cheapskate CHEAP 11	Merry Xmas Everybody/Okey Cokey/Get Down And Get With It (as Slade & Reading Choir, some in die-cut p/s)	8
80	Cheapskate CHEAP 11	Merry Xmas Everybody/Okey Cokey/Get Down And Get With It (as Slade & Reading Choir, some in die-cut p/s)	5
80	Polydor 2058 422	Merry Xmas Everybody/Don't Blame Me (reissue, green background, holly leaf design, colour group photo p/s)	5
81	Cheapskate CHEAP 16	We'll Bring The House Down/Hold On To Your Hats (p/s)	7
81	Cheapskate CHEAP 21	Wheels Ain't Comin' Down/Not Tonight Josephine (p/s)	7
81	Cheapskate CHEAP 24	Knuckle Sandwich Nancy/I'm Mad (p/s)	10
81	RCA	Tak Me Bak 'Ome/Gudbuy T'Jane) (12" EP, p/s)	10
82	RCA RCA 191	Ruby Red/Funk Punk And Junk (p/s)	10
82	RCA RCAD 191	Ruby Red/Funk Punk And Junk//Rock And Roll Preacher (live)/Take Me Bak 'Ome (live) (double pack, gatefold p/s)	5
82	RCA RCA 291	(And Now The Waltz) C'est La Vie/Merry Xmas Everybody (p/s)	5
82	Speed SPEED 201	Okey Cokey/Get Down And Get With It (no p/s)	8
82	Speed SPEEDP 201	Okey Cokey/Get Down And Get With It (picture disc)	5
83	RCA RCA 373	My Oh My/Merry Xmas Everybody (live)/ Keep Your Hands Off My Power Supply (12", p/s)	8
84	RCA RCAT 455	All Join Hands/My Oh My/Here's To? (The New Year)/ Merry Xmas (Live & Kickin') (12", stickered p/s)	8
85	RCA PB 40027	Myzterious Mizster Jones/Mama Nature Is A Rocker (picture disc, PVC sleeve)	6
85	Polydor POSPX 780	Merry Xmas Everybody/Don't Blame Me (12", p/s)	12
85	RCA PB 40449/PB 40549	Do You Believe In Miracles/My Oh My (Swing Version)// Santa Claus Is Coming To Town/Auld Lang Syne/ You'll Never Walk Alone To Town/Auld Lang Syne/You'll Never Walk Alone	15
85	RCA PT 40450D	Do You Believe In Miracles/My Oh My (Swing Version)/Time To Rock/ Santa Claus Is Coming To Town/Auld Lang Syne/You'll Never Walk Alone (12", 'Slade Xmas' double pack, separate sleeves in gatefold PVC cover)	10
87	RCA PB 41147D	Still The Same/Gotta Go Home//The Roaring Silence/ Don't Talk To Me About Love (21st anniversary double pack, gatefold p/s)	8
88	Counterpoint CDEP 12 C	How Does It Feel/Far Far Away/(WIZZARD: 2 tracks) (CD)	10
80s	Polydor 2058 422	Merry Xmas Everybody/Don't Blame Me (export p/s from various artist box set, green background, 4 individual photos)	15
80s	SLADE 1	An Interview With Slade (picture disc, 2,000 only, PVC sleeve)	5
91	Polydor PZ 189	Universe/Red Hot/Gypsy Roadhog/Merry Xmas Everybody (12", stickered p/s)	8

FLEXIDISCS

72	Polydor/Sound For Industry SFI 122	The Whole World's Going Crazee/MIKE HUGG: Bonnie Charlie (33rpm with Music Scene magazine)	18
72	Polydor/Sound For Industry SFI 122	The Whole World's Going Crazee/MIKE HUGG: Bonnie Charlie (33rpm without Music Scene magazine)	8
73	Lyntone LYN 2645	Slade Talk To Melanie readers (with Melanie magazine)	15
73	Lyntone LYN 2645	Slade Talk To Melanie readers (without Melanie magazine)	8
74	Lyntone LYN 2797	Slade exclusive to all 19 readers (with 19 magazine)	15
74	Lyntone LYN 2797	Slade exclusive to all 19 readers (without 19 magazine)	8
75	Lyntone LYN 3156/7	Far Far Away/Thanks For The Memory (with Smith's Crisps offer)	8
75	Fan Club LYN 2645/2797	Slade Talk To Melanie readers/Slade talk to 19 readers	10

PROMOS

72	Polydor 2814 008	Hear Me Calling/Get Down With It (33rpm sampler for "Slade Alive", 500 only)	125
74	Polydor 2058 492	The Bangin' Man/She Did It To Me (export p/s)	25
75	Polydor 2058 585	Thanks For The Memory (with altered lyrics)/Raining In My Champagne	25
77	Barn 2014 105	Gypsy Roadhog/Forest Full Of Needles (mono, DJ copy)	25
80	S.O.T.B. SUPER 3	Night Starvation/When I'm Dancing I Ain't Fightin'	45

LPs

70	Polydor 2383 026	PLAY IT LOUD (LP, sleeve printed by E.J. Day)	40
70	Polydor 2383 026	PLAY IT LOUD (LP, later sleeve printed by Upton printers)	25
72	Polydor 2383 101	SLADE ALIVE (LP, gatefold sleeve)	20
72	Polydor 2283 163	SLAYED? (LP)	12
73	Polydor 2442 119	SLADEST (LP, with booklet)	20
73	Polydor 2383 261	OLD NEW BORROWED AND BLUE (LP, gatefold sleeve)	12
74	Polydor 2442 126	SLADE IN FLAME (LP, gatefold sleeve)	12
76	Polydor 2383 377	NOBODY'S FOOLS (LP, with inner sleeve)	15
77	Barn 2314 103	WHATEVER HAPPENED TO SLADE (LP, with lyric sheet)	18
78	Barn 2314 106	SLADE ALIVE VOLUME 2 (LP)	15
79	Barn NARB 003	RETURN TO BASE (LP)	30

PAUL SLADE

69	Decca F12885	Odyssey/Sound Of Love	12
68	Decca F12840	Heaven Held/Remember Daphne	6

PRENTIS SLADE

61	Parlophone R 4850	I Can Tell/Looking For A Friend	6

MINT VALUE £

SLADE BROTHERS

66	Pye 7N 17080	Peace In My Mind/Life's Great Race	80

SLAM CREEPERS

68	Olga OLE 009	Saturday/Hold It Baby	15
73	Sonet SON 2003	We Are Happy People/Yansbro Memories	5

SLANES

65	Blue Beat BB 300	It Takes Time/LIGES: Have Mercy Baby (B-side actually by Frank Cosmo)	20

IVOR SLANEY ORCHESTRA

61	HMV POP 943	The Sir Francis Drake Theme/Midsummer Madness	6
64	HMV POP 1347	High Wire/Sacramento	10
66	Columbia DB 8020	Long Weekend/Eleven Up (as Slaney Strings)	8

SLAPP HAPPY

(see also Henry Cow, Peter Blegvad, Anthony Moore, Art Bears)

74	Virgin VS 105	Casablanca Moon/Slow Moon's Rose	12
75	Virgin VS 124	Johnny's Dead/Mr. Rainbow (p/s)	12
83	Half Cat HC 001	Everybody's Slimmin' (Even Men And Women!)/Blue-Eyed Villain (p/s)	12
72	Polydor 2310 204	SORT OF (LP, with German sleeve & insert)	400
74	Virgin V 2014	SLAPP HAPPY (LP)	25
74	Virgin V 2024	DESPERATE STRAIGHTS (LP, with Henry Cow)	22
86	Recommended RRS 5	SORT OF (LP, reissue)	15

MUTTER SLATER

76	Rocket ROKN 510	Dancing On Air/Solitude	5

FELIX SLATKIN

60	London HLG 9256	Theme From "The Sundowners"/Gaythers Gone	7

SLAUGHTER (& THE DOGS)

(see also Studio Sweethearts, Ed Banger)

77	Rabid TOSH 101	Cranked Up Really High/The Bitch (p/s, blue, later cream plastic labels)	12
77	Rabid TOSH 101	Cranked Up Really High/The Bitch (p/s, re-pressings with b&w paper label)	10
77	Decca FR 13723	Where Have All The Boot Boys Gone/You're A Bore (paper label)	8
77	Decca LF 13723	Where Have All The Boot Boys Gone/You're A Bore (12", p/s, 10,000 only)	12
77	Decca FR 13743	Dame To Blame/Johnny T	12
78	Decca F 13758	Quick Joey Small/Come On Back (promo with self sealing 'spit proof' sticker on PVC sleeve)	75
78	Decca FR 13758	Quick Joey Small/Come On Back (with Mick Ronson)	6
79	TJM TJM 3	It's Alright/Edgar Allen Poe/Twist & Turn/UFO (12", p/s)	12
79	DJM DJS 10927	You're Ready Now/Runaway (p/s)	6
80	Decca FR	Where Have All The Boot Boys Gone/You're A Bore (reissue, p/s)	10
80	DJM DJS 10936	East Side Of Town/One By One (p/s, as Slaughter)	6
80	DJM DJS 10945	I'm The One/What's Wrong Boy? (live)/Hell In New York (p/s, as Slaughter)	5
82	Thrush THRUSH 1	HALF ALIVE (12" EP)	10
88	Damaged Goods FNARR 1	Where Have All The Boot Boys Gone/You're A Bore/Johnny T. (p/s, 1,000 only: 500 on green vinyl, 500 on red vinyl)	15
78	Decca SKL 5292	DO IT DOG STYLE (LP)	30
78	Rabid HAT 23	LIVE SLAUGHTER RABID DOGS (LP, plain white sleeve with large sticker)	12
80	DJM DJF 20566	BITE BACK (LP, as Slaughter)	12
89	Damaged Goods FNARR 2	DO IT DOG STYLE (LP, reissue, 1,000-only, multi-coloured vinyl, numbered, with 2 multi-coloured stickers)	12
89	Link LINK LP 092	THE SLAUGHTER TAPES (LP)	12

SLAUGHTER JOE

(see also Television Personalities, Missing Scientists)

85	Creation CRE 019	I'll Follow You Down/Napalm Girl (foldaround p/s in poly bag)	5
87	Kaleidoscope S. KLSLP 003	ALL AROUND MY HOBBY HORSE'S HEAD (LP)	12

SLAVE

84	Cotillion BT 6955	Just A Touch Of Love/Wait For Me (12")	20

MARTIN SLAVIN & HIS GANG

(see also Martinas & His Music)

60	Oriole CB 1587	Rock-A-Charleston/The Charleston's Gonna Rock The Hop	5

FRANK SLAY & HIS ORCHESTRA

61	Top Rank JAR 599	Flying Circle/Cincinnati	8

SLAYER

84	Roadrunner RR 2444 2	HAUNTING THE CHAPEL (12" EP)	20
87	London LON 133	Criminally Insane/Aggressive Perfector (Remix) ('cross' p/s, on red vinyl with patch)	30
87	London LONX 133	Criminally Insane/Postmortem/Aggressive Perfector (Remix) (12", red vinyl, no p/s)	25
89	Roadrunner RR 2444 2	Haunting The Chapel/Chemical Warfare/Captor Of Sin (CD, reissue)	15
91	DEF DEFAP 912	Seasons In The Abyss/Aggressive Perfector (7" picture disc)	10
87	Enigma 720151	LIVE UNDEAD (LP, picture disc)	25
86	London/Def Jam LONLP 34	REIGN IN BLOOD (LP, with inner)	15
87	London LONPP 34	REIGN IN BLOOD (LP, picture disc)	30
88	London/Def Jam LONLP 63	SOUTH OF HEAVEN (LP, stickered sleeve, inner)	15
90	Def American 846 871	SEASONS IN THE ABYSS (LP, with inner)	12
91	Phonogram 510605-1	DECADE OF AGGRESSION (2-LP, booklet, 6,500 copies only)	20
03	Universal B 00001519-02	SOUNDTRACK TO THE APOCALYPSE (4-CD set in 'ammo box' with Backstage laminate, flag, bonus DVD in 'blood pack' and booklet)	40
03	Universal B 00001619-02	SOUNDTRACK TO THE APOCALYPSE (3-CD/DVD set in triple gatefold sleeve)	20

F. SLEDGE

67	Blue Beat BB 386	Red Eye Girl/Try To Love Again (actually by "Go On Girl"/"Giving You A Try Girl" by Freddie McKay & Buster's Group)	40

MINT VALUE £

PERCY SLEDGE

66	Atlantic 584 001	When A Man Loves A Woman/Love Me Like You Mean It	6
66	Atlantic 584 034	Warm And Tender Love/Sugar Puddin'	6
66	Atlantic 584 055	Heart Of A Child/My Adorable One	10
67	Atlantic 584 071	It Tears Me Up/Oh, How Happy	8
67	Atlantic 584 080	Baby, Help Me/You've Lost That Something Wonderful	15
67	Atlantic 584 108	Out Of Left Field/It Can't Be Stopped	8
67	Atlantic 584 140	Pledging My Love/You Don't Miss Your Water	8
68	Atlantic 584 177	Take Time To Know Her/It's All Wrong But It's Alright	8
68	Atlantic 584 225	Come Softly To Me/You're All Around Me	8
69	Atlantic 584 264	Any Day Now/The Angels Listened In	10
69	Atlantic 584 286	Kind Woman/Woman Of The Night	6
69	Atlantic 584 300	True Love Travels On A Gravel Road/Faithful And True	6
72	Atlantic K 10144	Rainbow Road/Standing on The Mountain	8
72	Atlantic K 10165	Baby, Help Me/Warm And Tender Love/Take Time To Know Her	8
74	Capricorn 2089 009	I'll Be Your Everything/Walkin' In The Sun	6
67	Atlantic 587/588 048	WARM AND TENDER SOUL (LP)	20
67	Atlantic 587/588 081	THE PERCY SLEDGE WAY (LP)	20
68	Atlantic 587/588 105	WHEN A MAN LOVES A WOMAN (LP)	20
69	Atlantic 587/588 153	THE BEST OF PERCY SLEDGE (LP)	15

SLEDGEHAMMER

79	Slammer SRTS79CUS 395	Sledgehammer/Feel Good (with p/s)	20
79	Slammer SRTS79CUS 395	Sledgehammer/Feel Good	10
80	Slammer CELL 2	Living In Dreams/Fantasia (p/s)	10
80s	Slammer MRSB 2	In The Middle Of The Night	10
80	Valiant STRONG 1	Sledgehammer/Feel Good (p/s, reissue)	10
80	Valiant ROUND 2	Sledgehammer/Feel Good (p/s, 2nd reissue)	6
85	Illuminated ILL 33	In The Queue/Oxford City (shaped picture disc)	25
83	Illuminated JAMS 32	BLOOD ON THEIR HANDS (LP)	30
83	Illuminated JAMS 32	BLOOD ON THEIR HANDS (LP)	25
84	Mausoleum LUST 834950	SLEDGEHAMMER (LP, with free 12")	30

SLEEPING DOGS

82	Crass 221984/11	BEWARE SLEEPING DOGS (EP)	8

SLEEPWALKERS

59	Parlophone R 4580	Sleep Walk/Golden Mile	15

SLEEPY

(see also Grapefruit, Fynn McCool)

68	CBS 3592	Love's Immortal Fire/Is It Really The Same	200
68	CBS 3838	Rosie Can't Fly/Mrs. Bailey's Barbecue And Grill	60
68	No label, no cat no	You'll See Me/Time Gone (White label test pressing)	250

SLENDER LORIS

76	Reverence DM 70	I'm Only Heavy When You Get Me Down/A Week Of A Day	6

SLENDER PLENTY

67	Polydor BM 56189	Silver Tree Top School For Boys/I've Lost A Friend And Found A Lover	22

SLENDER THREAD

80	Rock MHMS 193	I See The Light/Where Is The Beat	30

JIMI SLEVIN

(see also Peggy's Leg)

82	Claddagh CCF 7	FREEFLIGHT (LP)	45

GRACE SLICK

68	CBS 63476	CONSPICUOUS ONLY IN IT'S ABSENCE (LP, as Grace Slick And The Great Society)	40

RICKY SLICK

72	Dynamic DYN 449	Family Man/Family Man - Version	5

SLICKERS

(see also G.G. Allstars, Clancy Eccles, Viceroys)

68	Blue Cat BS 133	Wala Wala/LESTER STERLING: Super Special	35
68	Blue Cat BS 134	Nana (actually by George Dekker)/MARTIN RILEY: I May Never See My Baby Anymore	35
69	Blue Cat BS 154	Frying Pan/RARFIELD WILLIAMS: Code It	45
69	Amalgamated AMG 852	Man Beware/Matty Matty	20
69	Amalgamated AMG 866	Money Reaper/Man Beware	20
70	Bullet BU 449	Coolie Girl/BIGGIE: Bawling Baby	10
70	Trojan TR 7718	Run Fattie/Hoola Bulla (song actually "Bulla Man")	8
71	G.G. GG 4524	Oh My Baby/WINSTON WRIGHT: Change Of Love Version	6
71	Punch PH 59	Johnny Too Bad/Johnny Too Bad - Version	20
71	Dynamic DYN 406	Johnny Too Bad/ROLAND ALFONSO: Saucy Horde (act. by Roland Alphonso)	8
71	Dynamic DYN 419	You Can't Win/Don't Fight The Law	6
72	Explosion EX 2061	Bounce Me Johnny/Bounce Me 'Version' (actually "Say You")	6

SLIM

97	Em:t 0097	SLIM: 0097 (CD, digipak)	30

SLIM & FREEDOM SINGERS

70	Banana BA 304	Do Dang Do (actually by Leroy Sibbles)/ JACKIE MITTOO & SOUND DIMENSION: Hot Milk	35

SLIME

(see also Johnny Moped)

78	Toadstool GOOD 1	Controversial/Loony (p/s)	8

SLIPKNOT

00	Roadrunner RR 2090-7	Spit It Out/Surfacing (Live) (p/s, red vinyl)	10
00	Roadrunner RR 8655-6	SLIPKNOT (LP, picture disc)	15

MINT VALUE £

SLITS
(see also Raincoats)

79	Island WIP 6505	Typical Girls/I Heard It Through The Grapevine (p/s)	10
79	Island 12 WIP 6505	Typical Girls/I Heard It Through The Grapevine/Typical Girls (Brink Style)/ Liebe And Romanize (12", p/s)	20
80	Rough Trade RT 039/Y Y 1	In The Beginning There Was Rhythm/POP GROUP: Where There's A Will There's A Way (p/s)	8
80	Rough Trade/Y RT044/Y4	Man Next Door/Man Next Door (Version (p/s)	8
80	Human HUM 4	Animal Space/Animal Spacier (p/s)	8
81	CBS A1498	Earthbeat/Begin Again Rhythm (7", p/s)	8
81	CBS A1498	Earthbeat/Begin Again Rhythm (p/s)	8
81	CBS A 131498	Earthbeat/Earthdub/Begin Again Rhythm (12", p/s)	12
88	Strange Fruit SFPS 021	THE PEEL SESSIONS (Mini-LP)	12
79	Island ILPS 9573	CUT (LP, with inner sleeve)	25
80	Rough Trade/Y Y 3	BOOTLEG RETROSPECTIVE (LP, plain sleeve, with SUBWAY SECT)	30
81	CBS 85269	THE RETURN OF THE GIANT SLITS (LP, some with bonus 45 American Radio Interview/"Face Dub" [XPS 125])	22
81	CBS 85269	THE RETURN OF THE GIANT SLITS (LP)	18

P.F. SLOAN
(see also Grass Roots, Fantastic Baggys, Willie & Wheels)

65	RCA Victor RCA 1482	Sins Of The Family/This Mornin'	10
67	RCA Victor RCA 1623	Sunflower Sunflower/The Man Behind The Red Balloon	10
72	Epic EPC 65179	RAISED ON RECORDS (LP)	25
80s	Big Beat WIK 73	SONGS OF OTHER TIMES (LP, some tracks as Grass Roots)	25

SAMMI SLOAN

68	Columbia DB 8480	Yes I Would/Be His Girl	20

SLOWBONE
(see also Roll Ups)

74	Rare Earth RES 119	Get What You're Given/Oh Man	6

SLOWBONE & THE WONDERBOYS

74	Rare Earth RES 116	Tales Of A Crooked Man/Happy Birthday Sweet Sixteen	8

SLOWBURNER

89	Burn BURN LP 001	AN EMOTIONAL BUSINESS (LP)	12

SLOWDIVE

90	Creation CRE 093T	Slowdive/Avalyn 1/Avalyn 2	15
91	Creation CRE 098T	Morningrise/She Calls/Losing Today (12")	12
93	Creation CRE 119T	OUTSIDE YOUR ROOM EP (12")	20
93	Creation CRESCD 119	OUTSIDE YOUR ROOM EP (CD single)	15
91	Creation CRELP 094	JUST FOR A DAY (LP)	30
93	Creation CRELP 139	SOUVLAKI (LP, picture inner sleeve)	50
95	Creation CRELP 168	PYGMALION (LP)	20

SLOW DOG

72	Parlophone R5942	Walking Through The Blue Grass/Ain't Never Going Home	25

SLOWGUNS

79	MPA SMP 088	TV Movie/American Heartbeat	15
80	Cult 45 CULT 001	Karma/The Time Is Right For Us	12

SLOWLOAD
(see also Fruit Eating Bears)

71	MAM MAM 27	On The Road Again/Big Boobs Boogie	20

SLOW MOTION

79	RK RK 1024	Maybe/Xmas Charade	75

SLOWTRAIN

80	Spirit SR 1	Ronnie/Just One Way	30

SLR CREW

88	SLR XPR1536	Bass Drum/Life's A Bitch (12")	45

SL TROOPERS

88	Global Rhythm GR001	Debut (Unarmed And Dangerous) (12", 500 pressed)	30
89	Music Of Life NOTE32	Movement (12")	15
90	Kold Sweat KS101	Knowledge/Put Your Brain In Gear (12")	12
91	Kold Sweat KSEP201	SYSTEMATIC TERROR (EP)	10

SLUSH
(See also Pumphouse Gang)

78	Ember EMB 5367	White Christmas/Rich Man (no p/s)	70

SLY & THE FAMILY STONE
(see under Sly (& Family) Stone)

SLY & THE REVOLUTIONARIES

80	Trojan TRLS 186	BLACK ASH DUB (LP)	15

SMACK

78	Asprin 001	Edward Fox/Came Again (p/s, original issue)	5

SMALL ADS

81	Bronze BRO 115	Small Ads/Motorway Madness (p/s)	5
81	Bronze BRO 125	HP Man/Radio Love (p/s)	5
81	Bronze BRO 135	Friday Nite Cowboy/I Wanna Fly Concorde (p/s)	5

JOAN SMALL

56	Parlophone MSP 6219	Change Of Heart/Come Next Spring	10
56	Parlophone R 4211	Love Is A Stranger/Autumn Concerto	10
57	Parlophone R 4269	Gonna Get Along Without You Now/ You Can't Say I Love You To A Rock & Roll Tune	15

MINT VALUE £

58	Parlophone R 4431	Afraid/How Many Times (Can I Fall In Love)	10
60	Parlophone R 4622	The Big Hurt/Ask Me To Go Steady	10

KAREN SMALL

66	Vocalion V 9281	To Get You Back Again/That's Why I Cry	30

MILLIE SMALL

(see under Millie)

SMALL FACES

(see also Faces, Steve Marriott, Humble Pie, Jimmy Winston & His Reflections, Winston's Fumbs, Billy Nicholls, Kenney Jones)

SINGLES

65	Decca F 12208	Whatcha Gonna Do About It?/What's A Matter, Baby?	20
65	Decca F 12276	I've Got Mine/It's Too Late	25
66	Decca F 12317	Sha-La-La-La-Lee/Grow Your Own	10
66	Decca F 12393	Hey Girl/Almost Grown	15
66	Decca F 12470	All Or Nothing/Understanding (curved or boxed Decca logo)	12
66	Decca F 12500	My Mind's Eye (alternate demo mix, matrix no. ends T1-1C)/ I Can't Dance With You (withdrawn)	30
66	Decca F 12500	My Mind's Eye (matrix no. ends T2-1C)/I Can't Dance With You	10
67	Decca F 12565	I Can't Make It/Just Passing	25
67	Decca F 12565	I Can't Make It/Just Passing (export p/s)	60
67	Decca F 12619	Patterns/E Too D (export p/s)	140
67	Decca F 12619	Patterns/E Too D	70
67	Immediate AS 1	Small Faces (1-sided sampler for "Small Faces", promo only)	200
67	Immediate IM 050	Here Comes The Nice/Talk To You	12
67	Immediate IM 057	Itchycoo Park/I'm Only Dreaming	12
67	Immediate IM 062	Tin Soldier/I Feel Much Better (in p/s)	80
67	Immediate IM 062	Tin Soldier/I Feel Much Better	15
68	Immediate IM 064	Lazy Sunday/Rollin' Over	12
68	Immediate IM 069	The Universal/Donkey Rides, A Penny A Glass (lilac label)	12
68	Immediate IM 069	The Universal/Donkey Rides, A Penny A Glass (later pink label)	8
69	Immediate IM 077	Afterglow (Of Your Love)/Wham Bam, Thank You Mam (demos [perhaps some copies] have demo version of B-side)	60
69	Immediate IM 077	Afterglow (Of Your Love)/Wham Bam, Thank You Mam (demos)	15
75	Immediate IM 064	Lazy Sunday/Rollin' Over (p/s, reissue with white label)	8
80	Virgin VS 367	Tin Soldier/Tin Soldier (live)/Rene	6
86	Archive 4 TOF 103	Itchycoo Park/Lazy Sunday/Sha-La-La-La-Lee/Here Comes The Nice (12", p/s)	10
88	Castle Comms. Special Edition CD 3-9	THE SMALL FACES (Itchycoo Park/Lazy Sunday/All Or Nothing (live)/ Autumn Stone) (3" CD EP, with adaptor, 5" case, 5,000 only)	10

LPs

66	Decca LK 4790	SMALL FACES (original red label)	200
67	Decca LK 4879	FROM THE BEGINNING (original red label)	230
67	Immediate IMLP 008	SMALL FACES (mono)	190
67	Immediate IMSP 008	SMALL FACES (stereo)	200
68	Immediate IMLP 012	OGDENS' NUT GONE FLAKE (lilac label, circular foldout sleeve, mono)	180
68	Immediate IMSP 012	OGDENS' NUT GONE FLAKE (lilac label, circular foldout sleeve, stereo)	150
68	Immediate IMLP 012	OGDENS' NUT GONE FLAKE (pink label, circular foldout sleeve, mono)	120
68	Immediate IMSP 012	OGDENS' NUT GONE FLAKE (pink label, circular foldout sleeve, stereo)	80
69	Decca LK 4790	SMALL FACES (boxed Decca label)	50
69	Decca LK 4879	FROM THE BEGINNING (boxed Decca label)	40
69	Immediate IMLP/IMSP 022	IN MEMORIAM (export issue [German copies more common, £60])	150
69	Immediate IMAL 01/02	THE AUTUMN STONE (2-LP, gatefold sleeve)	80
75	Immediate/NEMS IML 1001	OGDENS' NUT GONE FLAKE (reissue, round sleeve, white label)	40
76	NEMS AML 1008	MAGIC MOMENTS	15
77	Immediate/NEMS IML 2001	OGDENS' NUT GONE FLAKE (reissue, square sleeve)	15
77	Decca ROOTS 5	ROCK ROOTS - THE DECCA SINGLES	15
78	Charly CR 300005	OGDENS' NUT GONE FLAKE (export release, square sleeve)	15
78	Charly CR 300025	THE SMALL FACES - LIVE U.K. 1969 (export release)	15
80	Virgin/Immediate V 2166	SMALL FACES: BIG HITS (gatefold sleeve)	15
80	Virgin/Immediate V 2178	FOR YOUR DELIGHT, THE DARLINGS OF WAPPING WHARF LAUNDERETTE	25
97	Castle CLA 016	OGDENS' NUT GONE FLAKE (reissue, round sleeve with obi)	15
91	Castle CLACT 016	OGDENS' NUT GONE FLAKE (CD, in round tin box with beer mats & booklet)	60

SMALL FOUR

66	Pye 7N 17191	One Up On Me/I'll Find Him	20

SMALL HOURS

80	Automatic K 17708	The Kid/Business In Town/Midnight To Six/End Of The Night (p/s)	30
80	Automatic K 17708X	The Kid/Business In Town/Midnight To Six/End Of The Night (10", p/s)	20

SMALL WONDER

75	Dawn DNS 1094	Ordinary Boy/Ride A Black Sheep	18

SMALL WORLD

81	Whaam! WHAAM 003	Love Is Dead/Liberty (p/s)	100
83	Valid VC 001	First Impressions/Stupidity Street/Tomorrow Never Comes (p/s)	100

SMART

82	Complex CPX 001	This Time (p/s)	35

SMART ALEC

79	B&C BCS 20	Scooter Boys/Soho (p/s)	100

LEROY SMART

70	Attack ATT 8012	Life Is A Funny Thing/TRINITY: Psalms	12
77	Conflict COND 2001	Jahovia/Dub (12")	20
78	Andinet AT 001	Zion/Version	10
78	Andinet AT 002	Faith/Version	10
78	Aries AR 003	It's A Long Time Now/Long Time Version	6

			MINT VALUE £
78	Write Sounds WTS 1001	Children Of The Getto [sic]/Version	8
78	Write Sounds WTS 001	What I Will Do/ROY SINCLAIR: Rite Mix/LEROY SMART: Jah Almighty (12")	25
79	Burning Sounds BDS 010	Find Your Destination/Jamaica In Peace (12")	15
79	Burning Sounds BDS 011	No One Remember Me/Don't Be Late (12")	15
70s	Aries ARI 002	Peace Is What We Want (with U. Brown)/Version (12", p/s)	30
80	Black Joy DH 803	Hooligan/HaveMercy (12")	10
77	Conflict COLPD 2001	BALLISTIC AFFAIR (LP)	20
77	Dread Hot DHLP 1001	DREAD HOT IN AFRICA (LP)	30
77	Third World TWS 601	SUPER STAR (LP)	20
78	Burning Sounds BS 1004	DREAD HOT IN AFRICA (LP)	25
78	Burning Sounds BS 1005	IMPRESSIONS OF LEROY SMART (LP)	15
78	Burning Sounds BS 1008	JAH LOVES EVERYONE (LP)	25
78	Dread Hot DHLP 1004	IMPRESSIONS (LP)	20
78	Burning Sounds BS 1009	PROPAGANDA (LP, clear vinyl)	25

LEROY SMART & BIG YOUTH

79	Dub Vendor DVD 01	Pride And Ambition (original style)/'78 Style (12")	60

SMART PILLS

87	Bluurg FISH 17	NO GOOD NO EVIL (LP, with insert)	12

SMART SYSTEMS

91	Jumpin' & Pumpin' 12TOT18	Tingler (Meltram Mix)/(Mingler Mix)/(State Side Swamp Mix (12" p/s)	10

SMASHING PUMPKINS

91	Hut	I Am One (1-sided blue flexidisc)	100
91	Caroline SMASH 1	Siva/Rhinoceros (no p/s, promo only)	80
91	Hut HUTT 6	Siva/Window Paine (12", p/s, 5,000)	30
92	Hut HUTT 10	LULL EP (Rhinoceros/Blue/Slunk/Bye June [Demo]) (12", p/s)	12
92	Hut CDHUT 10	LULL EP (Rhinoceros/Blue/Slunk/Bye June [Demo]) (CD)	12
92	Hut HUTC 017	PEEL SESSIONS: Siva/A Girl Named Sandoz/Smiley (cassette EP)	5
92	Hut HUTT 017	PEEL SESSIONS: Siva/A Girl Named Sandoz/Smiley (12" EP, p/s)	12
92	Hut HUTEN 018	I Am One/Terrapin (live)/Bullet Train To Osaka (10", p/s, 6,000 only)	20
92	Hut HUTT 18	I Am One/Plume/Starla (12", p/s)	12
93	Sup Pop SP 90	Tristessa/La Dolly Vita/Honeyspider (12", 5,000 only)	35
93	Hut HUT 31	Cherub Rock/Purr Snickety (p/s, clear vinyl, numbered, 5,000 only)	20
93	Hut HUTT 31	Cherub Rock/Pissant/French Movie Theme/(Star Spangled Banner) (12", p/s, last track uncredited)	8
93	Hut HUT 37	Today/Apathy's Last Kiss (p/s, red vinyl, 5,000 only)	12
93	Hut HUTT 37	Today/Hello Kitty Kat/Obscured (12", p/s)	8
94	Hut HUT 43	Smile (Disarm/Siamese Dream) (stickered p/s, purple vinyl)	10
94	Hut HUTL 48	Rocket/Never Let Me Down (box set, salmon pink vinyl, 1,500 only)	40
93	Hut HUTTDJ 73	Zero (12", promo only)	12
94	Hut SPBOX 1	SIAMESE SINGLES (Rocket/Never Let Me Down/Cherub Rock/Purr Snickety// Today/Apathy's Last Kiss/Smile [Disarm/Siamese Dream]) (4 x 7" box set, black vinyl, 6,000 only)	50
94	Hut HUTLPX 2	GISH (LP, with inner)	12
95	Hut HUTDLP 30	MELLON COLLIE AND THE INFINITE SADNESS (3 x LP, 12 page booklet, numbered)	80
96	Hut HUTLP 41	PISCES ISCARIOT (LP, yellow vinyl)	18
96	Hut	THE AEROPLANE FLIES HIGH (5 x CD single box set with handle, lock & booklet)	50

PHILIP LLOYD SMEE & DONATO CINICOLO III

71	Deroy PLS 1	DAS LUNE/SYNTHI-A (LP, private pressing, handmade sleeve, 2 copies only)	400

SMIFFY

74	Antic K 11501	See You Later (Little Baby Love)/How Can You Be A Millionaire	5

SMILEY

(see also Creation)

72	Philips 6006 206	Penelope/I Know What I Want	5

BRETT SMILEY

74	Anchor ANC 70	Va Va Va Voom/Space Age (with p/s)	30
74	Anchor ANC 70	Va Va Va Voom/Space Age	15

K. SMILEY

72	Pressure Beat PB 5514	Tipatone/Do It To Me	8

SMILIN' JOE

54	London HL 8106	A.B.C.'s Parts 1 & 2 (78)	90

SMIRKS

78	Besmirkly BZZ17	OK UK/Streets (p/s)	8

SMITH

69	Stateside-Dunhill SS 8028	Baby It's You/I Don't Believe	6
70	Stateside-Dunhill SS 8042	Take A Look Around/Mojalesky Ridge	6
70	Stateside-Dunhill SS 8055	What Am I Gonna Do/Born In Boston	6
69	Stateside-Dunhill SSL 5016	A GROUP CALLED SMITH (LP)	25
70	Stateside-Dunhill SSL 5031	MINUS-PLUS (LP)	25

SMITH

70	Probe PRO 508	Comin/Back To Me/Minus Plus	25

SMITH (U.K.)

81	Rarn RARNS 1	Here Comes My Baby/Just Another Line/Too Late (p/s)	25

ADAM (Eric) SMITH

62	Island WI 057	I Wonder Why/My Prayer	20

A.S.A.P. (Adrian Smith & Project)

(see also Iron Maiden, Urchin)

89	EMI 12 EMPD 107	Silver And Gold/Blood Brothers (12", silver & gold vinyl)	10
90	EMI EMPD 131	Down The Wire (Crossed Line Mix)/When She's Gone (shaped picture disc)	7

MINT VALUE £

ARTHUR 'GUITAR BOOGIE' SMITH (& HIS CRACKERJACKS)

53	MGM SP 1008	Guitar Boogie/Be Bop Rag	25
53	MGM SP 1021	Five String Banjo Boogie/South	15
53	MGM SP 1039	Express Train Boogie/River Rag	15
54	MGM SP 1096	Oh, Baby Mine, I Get So Lonely/Outboard	15
54	MGM SP 1110	Redheaded Stranger/Texas Hop	20
55	MGM SP 1122	Hi Lo Boogie/Truck Stop Grill	10
54	MGM MGM-EP 510	ARTHUR 'GUITAR BOOGIE' SMITH AND HIS CRACKERJACKS (EP)	15
54	MGM MGM EPC 5	ARTHUR 'GUITAR BOOGIE' SMITH (EP, export issue)	15
59	MGM MGM-EP 695	ARTHUR 'GUITAR BOOGIE' SMITH AND HIS CRACKERJACKS (EP)	15
63	Stateside SE 1005	MISTER GUITAR (EP)	15
53	MGM MGM-D 111	FINGERS ON FIRE (10" LP)	20
54	MGM MGM-D 131	FOOLISH QUESTIONS (10" LP)	20

BEASLEY SMITH & HIS ORCHESTRA

56	London HLD 8235	Goodnight, Sweet Dreams/Parisian Rag	20
56	London HLD 8273	My Foolish Heart/Old Spinning Wheel	20

BESSIE SMITH

50s	Parlophone	Gimme A Pigfoot/Take Me For A Buggy Ride (78)	20
55	Philips BBL 7019	THE BESSIE SMITH STORY VOLUME 1 (LP, with Louis Armstrong)	12
55	Philips BBL 7020	THE BESSIE SMITH STORY VOLUME 2 (LP)	12
55	Philips BBL 7042	THE BESSIE SMITH STORY VOLUME 3 (LP)	12
55	Philips BBL 7049	THE BESSIE SMITH STORY VOLUME 4 (LP)	12
62	Philips BBL 7513	BESSIE'S BLUES 1923-1924 (LP)	18

BETTY SMITH SKIFFLE GROUP

(see also Betty Smith Quintet)

57	Tempo A 162	There's A Blue Ridge Round My Heart, Virginia/Double Shuffle	10
57	Tempo A 162	There's A Blue Ridge Round My Heart, Virginia/Double Shuffle (78)	10

BETTY SMITH QUINTET

(see also Betty Smith Skiffle Group)

57	Tempo A 163	Sweet Georgia Brown/Little White Lies	20
58	Decca F 10986	Hand Jive/Bewitched (as Betty Smith Group)	8
58	Decca F 11031	Will The Angels Play Their Harps For Me/Betty's Blues	8
58	Decca F 11071	Begin The Beguine/Song Of The Boulevards	5
59	Decca F 11124	Song Of India/Stormy Weather	10
59	Decca F 11124	Song Of India/Stormy Weather (78)	12
57	Tempo EXA 74	BETTY SMITH QUINTET (EP)	15
57	Decca DFE 6446	BETTY SMITH QUINTET (EP)	15
58	Decca DFE 6547	BETTY SMITH GROUP (EP)	15

BRODERICK SMITH

72	Spark SRL 1087	Going Down To The End Of The World/She's Gone	8

BUSTER SMITH

61	London Jazz LTZ-K 15206	THE LEGENDARY BUSTER SMITH (LP)	12

CAL SMITH

73	MCA 143	Country Bumpkin/It's Not The Miles You Travelled	5

CARL SMITH

60	Philips BBL 7437	THE CARL SMITH TOUCH (LP)	12

CLARA SMITH

69	VJM VLP 15	CLARA SMITH VOLUME 1 (LP)	15
69	VJM VLP 16	CLARA SMITH VOLUME 2 (LP)	15
69	VJM VLP 17	CLARA SMITH VOLUME 3 (LP)	15

CLARA SMITH & FLETCHER HENDERSON

(see also Fletcher Henderson)

61	Philips BBE 12491	BLUES BY CLARA SMITH 1926-1928 (EP)	10

CONNIE SMITH

66	RCA Victor RD 7785	CUTE AND COUNTRY (LP)	15
71	RCA LSA 3042	WHERE IS MY CASTLE (LP)	12
73	RCA LSA 3150	IT AIN'T LOVE (LP)	12

DAVE SMITH & ASTRONAUTS

67	C'mbia Blue Beat DB 104	A Lover Like You/Cup Of Love	15
67	Amusicon SLE 10	A Lover Like You/Cup Of Love	15

DAVE SMITH & JUDY DINNING

83	Rubber RUB 043	WAITING FOR THE CHANGE (LP)	20

DICK SMITH BAND

79	Smile SR 012	Body Heat/Motorway Madness (p/s)	75
80	Hol-O-Gram HOL 001	Way Of The World/Giving The Game Away (with p/s)	45
80	Hol-O-Gram HOL 001	Way Of The World/Giving The Game Away	25

EDDIE SMITH

55	Parlophone MSP 6186	Silver Star Stomp/Stumbling (as Eddie Smith & Chiefs)	15
60	Top Rank JAR 285	Upturn/Border Beat (as Eddie Smith & Hornets)	25

EDGEWOOD SMITH & FABULOUS TAILFEATHERS

67	Sue WI 4037	Ain't That Lovin'/Yeah	50

EFFIE SMITH

66	Sue WI 4010	Dial That Telephone Parts 1 & 2	20

ELLIOTT SMITH

98	Domino RUG 074	Ballad Of Big Nothing/Some Song (p/s)	6
98	Dreamworks DRMS 22347	Waltz No. 2/Our Thing (p/s)	10
99	Dreamworks DRMS 7	Baby Britain/Waltz No. 1 (p/s)	6

			MINT VALUE £
98	Domino REWIGLP 001	ELLIOTT SMITH (LP)	60
98	Domino REWIGLP 002	ROMAN CANDLE (LP)	60
98	Domino REWIGLP	EITHER/OR (LP)	60

ELSON SMITH

61	Fontana H 291	Flip Flop/Are You Ready For That	30

ERNIE SMITH

71	Duke DU 119	Bend Down/Heaven Help Us All	6
71	Horse HOSS 6	Sunday Morning/One Three	5
74	Attack ATT 8071	Duppy Gunman/Duppy Gunman Version	8
73	London SHS 8442	ERNIE SMITH (LP)	12

(LITTLE) GEORGE (HARMONICA) SMITH

(see also Bacon Fat)

65	Blue Horizon 45-1002	Blues In The Dark/Telephone Blues (as Little George Smith)	90
70	Blue Horizon 57-3170	Someday You're Gonna Learn/Before You Do Your Thing (as George Smith)	20
69	Liberty LBL/LBS 83218E	BLUES WITH FEELING - A TRIBUTE TO LITTLE WALTER (LP, with Chicago Blues Band)	45
70	Blue Horizon 7-63856	NO TIME TO JIVE (LP)	100
71	Deram SML 1082	ARKANSAS TRAP (LP)	60

GLORIA SMITH

59	London HLU 8903	Playmates/Don't Take Your Love From Me	18
59	London HLU 8903	Playmates/Don't Take Your Love From Me (78)	18

GORDON SMITH

(see also Kevin Coyne)

69	Blue Horizon 57-3156	Too Long/Funk Pedal	20
69	Blue Horizon 7-63211	LONG OVERDUE (LP)	80

HAROLD SMITH'S MAJESTIC CHOIR

69	Chess CRS 8100	We Can All Walk A Little Bit Prouder/Why Am I Treated So Bad	8

HARVEY SMITH

75	Hankerchief Hanky 3	True Love/ End Of The World (p/s)	7

HOBART SMITH

69	Topic 12T187	THE OLD TIMEY RAP (LP)	20

HUEY 'PIANO' SMITH & THE CLOWNS

(see also Frankie Ford, Lee Allen, Bobby Marchan, Robert Parker)

58	Columbia DB 4138	Don't You Just Know It/High Blood Pressure	85
58	Columbia DB 4138	Don't You Just Know It/High Blood Pressure (78)	50
60	Top Rank JAR 282	Don't You Just Know Kokomo/FRANKIE FORD: Cheatin' Woman	25
62	Top Rank JAR 614	Pop-Eye/Scald-Dog (as Huey Smith)	12
65	Sue WI 364	If It Ain't One Thing It's Another/Tu-Ber-Cu-Lucas And The Sinus Blues	25
65	Sue WI 380	Rockin' Pneumonia And The Boogie Woogie Flu (Parts 1 & 2)	25
78	Chiswick NS 43	Rockin' Pneumonia And The Boogie Woogie Flu (unissued)	0
65	Sue ILP 917	ROCKIN' PNEUMONIA AND THE BOOGIE WOOGIE FLU (LP, titled "Havin' A Good Time" on labels)	40

HURRICANE SMITH

71	Columbia DB 8735	Don't Let It Die/The Writer Sings His Songs	6
72	Columbia DB 8878	Oh Babe, What Would You Say/Getting To Know You	6
72	Columbia SCX 6510	DON'T LET IT DIE (LP)	15

IAN SMITH & INNER MIND

(see also Smithy All Stars)

71	Bullet BU 490	Devil Woman/Nenn Street Rub	6

JENNIE SMITH

59	Philips PB 924	Huggin' My Pillow (Sweet Side)/Huggin' My Pillow (Sweet Beat Side)	5
59	Philips PB 924	Huggin' My Pillow (Sweet Side)/Huggin' My Pillow (Sweet Beat Side) (78)	15

JIMMY SMITH

(see also Kenny Burrell)

62	HMV POP 1025	Walk On The Wild Side Parts 1 & 2 (blue label)	10
62	HMV POP 1025	Walk On The Wild Side Parts 1 & 2 (black label)	5
65	Verve VS 509	Hobo Flats Parts 1 & 2	5
65	Verve VS 521	Who's Afraid Of Virginia Woolf Parts 1 & 2	5
65	Verve VS 523	The Cat/Basin Street Blues	20
65	Verve VS 531	The Organ Grinder's Swing/I'll Close My Eyes	6
66	Verve VS 534	Slow Theme From "Where The Spies Are" Parts 1 & 2	5
66	Verve VS 536	Got My Mojo Working Parts 1 & 2	6
66	Verve VS 540	I'm Your Hoochie-Coochie Man Parts 1 & 2	6
67	Verve VS 551	Cat In A Tree Parts 1 & 2	6
67	Verve VS 562	Mickey Mouse Parts 1 & 2	6

LPs

62	Verve CLP 1596/CSD 1462	BASHIN' THE UNPREDICTABLE (Verve label with HMV number)	15
63	Verve (S)VLP 9039	HOBO FLATS	15
64	Verve VLP 9057	ANY NUMBER CAN WIN	15
64	Verve VLP 9068	WHO'S AFRAID OF VIRGINIA WOOLF	15
64	Verve (S)VLP 9079	THE CAT	20
65	Verve (S)VLP 9093	MONSTER	20
66	Verve (S)VLP 9108	ORGAN GRINDER SWING	15
66	Verve (S)VLP 9123	GOT MY MOJO WORKING	15
66	Verve (S)VLP 9142	HOOCHIE COOCHIE MAN	15
67	Verve (S)VLP 9159	PETER & THE WOLF	15
67	Verve (S)VLP 9160	THE DYNAMIC DUO (with Wes Montgomery)	15
67	Verve (S)VLP 9182	RESPECT	20
68	Verve (S)VLP 9218	STAY LOOSE	15
68	Verve (S)VLP 9227	LIVIN' IT UP	15

			MINT VALUE £
68	Verve (S)VLP 9231	CHRISTMAS COOKIN'	15
69	Verve (S)VLP 9241	FURTHER ADVENTURES OF JIMMY AND WES (with Wes Montgomery)	15
71	Verve 2304 020	I'M GON' GIT MYSELF TOGETHER	15
74	Verve 2304 167	PORTUGUESE SOUL	15

JOEY SMITH & BABA BROOKS BAND

64	R&B JB 131	Maybe Once/Tell Me You're Mine	25

JUDI SMITH

65	Decca F 12132	Leaves Come Tumbling Down/Come My Way	15

JUNIOR SMITH

(see also Stranger Cole, Derrick Morgan, Rocksteadys)

67	Giant GN 1	Cool Down Your Temper/I'm Groovin'	12
68	Giant GN 18	I'm Gonna Leave You Girl/I Love You, I Love You	10
68	Giant GN 25	Come Cure Me/I Want Your Lovin'	10
68	Gas GAS 132	Gimme Little/Trip To War Land	15
69	Crystal CR 7002	Put On The Pressure/I Don't Know	8
72	Sioux SI 019	Saturday Child/JUMBO STERLING: Hot Dog	8
72	Sioux SI 023	You Don't Know/JUMBO STERLING: My Sugar Ain't Sweet	6

KATHY SMITH

70	Polydor 2310 081	SOME SONGS I'VE SAVED (LP)	60

KEELY SMITH (& LOUIS PRIMA)

(see also Louis Prima, Frank Sinatra)

57	Capitol CL 14717	Hurt Me/High School Affair	8
57	Capitol CL 14739	Young And In Love/You Better Go Now	6
57	Capitol CL 14754	Good Behaviour/You'll Never Know	6
57	Capitol CL 14803	Autumn Leaves/I Keep Forgetting	5
58	Capitol CL 14862	Foggy Day/The Lip (B-side with Louis Prima)	6
58	Capitol CL 14948	That Old Black Magic (with Louis Prima)/You Are My Love	6
59	Capitol CL 14994	I've Got You Under My Skin (with Louis Prima)/Don't Take Your Love From Me	6
59	London HLD 8984	If I Knew I'd Find You (I'd Climb The Highest Mountain)/ Don't Let The Stars Get In Your Eyes	8
60	London HLD 9240	Here In My Heart/Close	6
64	Reprise R 20346	You're Breaking My Heart/Crazy	5
61	London RE-D 1269	YOU LOVERS (EP)	20
58	Capitol (S)T 914	I WISH YOU LOVE (LP, mono/stereo)	15
59	Capitol T 1160	HEY BOY! HEY GIRL! (LP, soundtrack, with Louis Prima)	25

LONNIE LISTON SMITH (& THE COSMIC ECHOES)

75	RCA RCA 2568	Expansions (Parts 1 & 2) (& Cosmic Echoes)	10
76	RCA RCA 2668	Chance For Peace/Sunset	5
76	RCA RCA 2727	Get Down Everybody/Inner Beauty	5
79	RCA PB 9450	Expansions/A Chance For Peace	6
79	RCA PC 9450	Expansions/A Chance For Peace (12")	35
75	RCA SF 8434	EXPANSIONS (LP, with Cosmic Echoes)	15
76	RCA SF 8461	VISIONS OF A NEW WORLD (LP)	12
76	RCA RS 1053	REFLECTIONS OF A GOLDEN DREAM (LP, with Cosmic Echoes)	12
77	RCA PL 11822	RENAISSANCE (LP, with Cosmic Echoes)	15
83	Bluebird BRT 4	Expansions/Voodoo Woman (12")	20

LONNIE SMITH

67	CBS 63146	FINGER LICKIN' GOOD (LP)	25
70s	Blue Note BST 84290	THINK (LP)	25
70s	Blue Note BST 84313	TURNING POINT (LP)	25
70s	Blue Note BST 84326	MOVE YOUR HAND (LP)	28
70s	Blue Note BST 84351	DRIVES (LP)	25

LORENZO SMITH

66	Outasite 45-503	(Too Much) Firewater/Count Down (99 copies only)	110

LOU SMITH

60	Top Rank JAR 520	Cruel Love/Close To My Heart	10

MARK E. SMITH

(see also The Fall)

98	Artful ARTFULCD 14	THE POST NEARLY MAN (CD)	18

MARTHA SMITH

65	Pye 7N 15778	As I Watch You Walk Away/It Always Seems Like Summer	20
65	Pye 7N 15860	Love Means Nothing To You/The Song Is Love	7

MARVIN SMITH

66	Coral Q 72486	Time Stopped/Have More Time	50
66	Coral Q 72486	Time Stopped/Have More Time (DJ copy)	125
74	Contempo CS 2034	Let The Good Times Roll/Ain't That A Shame	5

MEL SMITH

81	Mercury MEL 1	Mel Smith's Greatest Hits/Richard & Joey (p/s, with Roger Taylor)	15

MELODY SMITH

71	CBS CBS 7561	You Never Hear A Teardrop Fall/Rastus Ravel	10

MICHAEL SMITH

82	Island ILPS 9717	MI CYAAN BELIEVE IT (LP)	12

MICK SMITH

76	Midas MFHR 078	SOMEBODY NOBODY KNOWS (LP)	35
77	Alida Star AS 771	WORDS AND MUSIC (LP)	30
79	Repercussion RR 1000	RAINDANCE (LP, as Mike Smith)	25

MIKE SMITH

(see also Dave Clark 5, Smith & D'Abo)

85	Proto ENA 130	Medley (7" version)/Bits And Pieces (in p/s)	7
85	Proto ENAT 130	Medley (12" version)/Glad All Over (12", p/s)	12
90	Mooncrest MOON 1010	You Gotta Play Rock'N'Roll/Operator	6

MINT VALUE £

O.C. (OCIE) SMITH
(see also Art Mooney)

57	London HLA 8480	Lighthouse/Too Many (as Ocie Smith)	90
57	London HLA 8480	Lighthouse/Too Many (as Ocie Smith) (78)	90
68	CBS 3343	The Son Of Hickory Holler's Tramp/On A Clear Day You Can See Forever	8
70	CBS 5203	Baby I Need Your Loving/San Francisco Is A Lonely Town	5
68	CBS (S) 63147	THE DYNAMIC O.C. SMITH (LP)	20
68	CBS (S) 63362	HICKORY HOLLER REVISITED (LP)	15
69	CBS 63805	AT HOME (LP)	25

OTELLO SMITH & TOBAGO BAD BOYS

67	Direction 58-3082	My Home Town/Trouble	5
68	Direction 8-63242	THE BIG ONES GO SKA (LP)	40

PATTI SMITH (GROUP)

76	Arista ARIST 47	Gloria (In Excelsis Deo) (Edit)/My Generation (p/s)	5
77	Arista ARIST 12135	Gloria (In Excelsis Deo)/My Generation (live) (12", Rough Trade copies in brown paper bag with titles in felt pen)	10
78	Arista ARIST 181	Because The Night/God Speed (p/s)	5
78	Sire 6078 614	Hey Joe (Version)/Piss Factory (p/s)	15
78	Arista ARIST 197	Privilege (Set Me Free)/Ask The Angels (p/s)	5
78	Arista ARIST 12197	Privilege (Set Me Free)/Ask The Angels/25th Floor (Live Version)/ Babelfield (12", p/s)	10
79	Arista ARIST 264	Frederick/Fire Of Unknown Origin (p/s)	5
79	Arista ARIST 281	Dancing Barefoot/5-4-3-2-1 (live) (p/s)	5
79	Arista ARIST 291	So You Want To Be A Rock'n'Roll Star/Frederick (live) (p/s)	5
88	Fierce FRIGHT 017	Brian Jones/Stockinged Feet/Jesus Christ (1-sided, white label)	15
75	Arista ARTY 122	HORSES (LP, blue label)	15
76	Arista SPARTY 1001	RADIO ETHIOPIA (LP, as Patti Smith Group, with lyric insert)	15

PAUL SMITH

65	Columbia DB 7636	Piccadilly Paper Boy/Yakety Yak	10

SMITH, PERKINS & SMITH

72	Island ILPS 9198	SMITH, PERKINS & SMITH (LP)	12

PETER SMITH

70s	Pilgrim JLPS 148P	FAITH, FOLK & CLARITY (LP, with Kinfolk)	18
70s	Galliard GAL 4016P	FAITH, FOLK & FESTIVITY (LP)	12

RAY SMITH

60	London HL 9051	Rockin' Little Angel/That's All Right	80

ROY SMITH (& THE STARGAZERS) (U.K.)
(see also Stargazers)

55	Decca F 10529	Red Roses (For My Lady Fair)/The Devil's In Your Eyes	5
55	Decca F 10644	He/Glengarry (solo)	5

ROY SMITH (Jamaica)

70	Grape GR 3013	See Through Craze/TERRY CARL & DERRICK: I'm The One	12
70	Jackpot JP 723	The Wedding/Air Balloon	8

SLIM SMITH (& THE UNIQUES)
(see also Wonder Boy, Pioneers, Uniques, Roy Shirley, Ron Sig, Dakota Jim, Dennis Alcapone, David Isaacs, John Holt, Heptones, Melodians, Count Ossie, Winston Williams)

66	Island WI 3023	I've Got Your Number/The New Boss	55
67	Coxsone CS 7016	Hip Hug/FREEDOM SINGERS: I Want Money	70
67	Coxsone CS 7034	Rougher Yet/I'll Never Let Go	80
67	Coxsone CS 7009	Mercy Mercy/JACKIE MITTOO: Baba Boom	50
68	Trojan TR 619	Watch This Sound/Out Of Love (as Slim Smith & Uniques)	45
69	Unity UN 504	Everybody Needs Love/JUNIOR SMITH: Come Back Girl	10
69	Unity UN 508	For Once In My Life/Burning Desire	15
69	Unity UN 510	Zip A Dee Doo Dah/On Broadway	15
69	Unity UN 513	Let It Be Me/Love Makes Me Do Foolish Things (both with Paulette)	15
69	Unity UN 515	Somebody To Love/Confusion	15
69	Unity UN 520	Slip Away/Spanish Harlem	10
69	Unity UN 524	Sunny Side Of The Sea/A Place In The Sun	40
69	Unity UN 527	Blessed Are The Meek/Conversation	10
69	Unity UN 537	Keep That Light Shining On Me/Build My World Around You	10
69	Unity UN 539	Love Me Tender/This Feeling	10
69	Unity UN 542	Honey/There's A Light	10
69	Jackpot JP 703	If It Don't Work Out/Love Power	7
69	Gas GAS 132	The Vow (& Doreen Shaeffer)/JAMES NEPHEW: Why Don't You Say	5
70	Gas GAS 150	What Kind Of Life/MARTIN RILEY: It's All In The Game	7
70	Unity UN 570	Jenny/The Race	7
70	S&S SC 001	Strong Love/Strange World	15
71	Supreme SUP 219	Stay/You're My Everything	7
71	Pama Supreme PS 334	Send Me Some Loving/I'm Lost	7
71	Camel CA 81	Spanish Harlem/Slip Away	8
71	Escort ERT 851	My Love Come True/This Feeling	6
71	Escort ERT 852	Life Keeps Turning/My Girl	6
71	Escort ERT 859	My Girl/RECO: Plus One	10
71	Jackpot JP 779	Keep Walking/Will You Still Love Me Tomorrow	7
72	Jackpot JP 786	I Need Your Loving/You've Got What It Takes	7
72	Jackpot JP 788	Take Me Back/Where Do I Turn	6
72	Jackpot JP 789	Rain From The Skies/You're No Good	8
72	Jackpot JP 798	Closer Together/Blinded By Love	6
72	Jackpot JP 799	Turning Point/Money Lover	6
72	Dynamic DYN 428	Just A Dream/Send Me Some Loving	6
72	Pama PM 850	The Time Has Come/RECO & HIS BAND: Version	6
72	Pama Supreme PS 373	A Place In The Sun/Stranger On The Shore	6

MINT VALUE £

Year	Label / Cat. No.	Title	Value
72	Camel CA 89	Take Me Back/Where Do I Turn	6
72	Explosion EX 2074	The Time Has Come/Blessed Is The Man	6
73	Explosion EX 2078	Stand Up And Fight/The Sunny Side Of The Sea	8
73	Green Door GD 4058	Let Me Love You/If It Don't Work Out	8
73	Bullet BU 523	A Place In The Sun/Burning Fire	30
69	Pama ECO 9	EVERYBODY NEEDS LOVE (LP)	40
72	Trojan TBL 186	JUST A DREAM (LP)	25
73	Trojan TBL 198	GREATEST HITS (LP)	25
70s	Lord Koos KLP 1	SLIM SMITH (LP)	18
76	Angen ANGL 1	THE LATE AND GREAT (LP)	40
84	Pama PMLP 3240	TIME HAS COME (LP)	40

SLIM SMITH & THE FREEDOM SINGERS

Year	Label / Cat. No.	Title	Value
70	Banana BA 304	Do Dang DO/JACKIE MITTO: Hot Milk	60

SOMETHIN' SMITH & THE REDHEADS

Year	Label / Cat. No.	Title	Value
58	Fontana TFR 6005	PUT THE BLAME ON ME (10" LP)	18

STUART SMITH

Year	Label / Cat. No.	Title	Value
69	Polydor 56336	My Head Goes Around/Where Are You	6

TAB SMITH & HIS ORCHESTRA

Year	Label / Cat. No.	Title	Value
56	Vogue V 2410	Jump Time/Rock City	15
59	London HLM 8801	Smoke Gets In Your Eyes/My Happiness Cha-Cha	10
59	London HLM 8801	Smoke Gets In Your Eyes/My Happiness Cha-Cha (78)	10

TERRY SMITH

(see also If)

Year	Label / Cat. No.	Title	Value
69	Philips (S)BL 7871	FALL OUT (LP, laminated sleeve, black/silver label)	125
77	Lambert LAM 002	TERRY SMITH AND TONY LEE TRIO (LP)	20

TRIXIE SMITH

Year	Label / Cat. No.	Title	Value
51	Tempo R 42	Black Bottom Stomp/He Likes It Slow (78)	25
52	Vocalion V 1006	Freight Train Blues/Trixie's Blues (78)	30
52	Vocalion V 1017	My Daddy Rocks Me (Parts 1 & 2) (78)	30
53	Jazz Collector L 102	The World's Jazz Crazy And So Am I/Railroad Blues (78)	12
50s	Poydras 101	TRIXIE SMITH (10" EP, 45 rpm)	15
50s	Ristic 12	TRIXIE SMITH (10" EP, 45 rpm)	15
50s	Audubon AAE	TRIXIE SMITH (10" LP)	30

TRIXIE SMITH/MA RAINEY

Year	Label / Cat. No.	Title	Value
64	Jazz Collector JEL 22	FEMALE BLUES VOL. 3 (EP, 2 tracks each)	15

TRULY SMITH

Year	Label / Cat. No.	Title	Value
66	Decca F 12373	My Smile Is Just A Frown Turned Upside Down/Love Is Me, Love Is You	25
66	Decca F 12415	I Love Him/Buttermilk Hill	5
66	Decca F 12489	You Are The Love Of My Life/The Merry Go Round Is Slowing	5
67	Decca F 12554	Windows And Doors/Take A Broken Heart	5
67	Decca F 12645	I Wanna Go Back There Again/Window Cleaner	35
67	Decca F 12700	The Boy From Chelsea/Little Man With A Stick	5
68	MGM MGM 1431	This Is The First Time/Taking Time Off	20

VERDELLE SMITH

Year	Label / Cat. No.	Title	Value
66	Capitol CL 15234	In My Room/Like A Man	18
66	Capitol CL 15456	Tar And Cement/A Piece Of The Sky	12
66	Capitol CL 15481	I Don't Need Anything/If You Can't Say Anything Nice	12
67	Capitol CL 15516	There's So Much Love Around Me/Baby Baby	12

WARREN SMITH

Year	Label / Cat. No.	Title	Value
60	London HL 7101	I Don't Believe I'll Fall In Love/Cave-In (export issue)	25
61	London HLG 7110	Odds And Ends/A Whole Lot Of Nothin' (export issue)	25
64	Liberty LIB 55699	Blue Smoke/Judge And Jury	10

WAYNE SMITH

Year	Label / Cat. No.	Title	Value
81	Black Joy DH 815	Life Is A Moment In Space/Ain't No Me Without You (12")	40
84	Greensleeves GRED 162	Come Along/Change Your Style (12")	30
85	Greensleeves GRED 169	Under Me Sleng Teng/MICHAEL BUCKLEY: Dance Gate (12")	30
85	Greensleeves GRED 183	Ickie All Over/TONTO IRIE: Life Story (12")	30
80s	Unity UN 019	My Sweet Love/TONTO IRIE: Murder Commit (12")	12
85	Greensleeves GRED 177	Sleng Teng Mix Down Remix/PAD ANTHONY: Cry For Me (12")	20
81	Black Joy BHLP 2005	YOUTHMAN SKANKING (LP)	50

WHISPERING SMITH

Year	Label / Cat. No.	Title	Value
72	Blue Horizon 2431 015	OVER EASY (LP)	120

WILLIE 'THE LION' SMITH

Year	Label / Cat. No.	Title	Value
72	Polydor 2460 156	PORK AND BEANS (LP)	12

SMITH & MIGHTY

Year	Label / Cat. No.	Title	Value
00	Studio !K7 !K700lp	BASS IS MATERNAL (LP)	12

SMITH & WESTON

Year	Label / Cat. No.	Title	Value
73	Decca F 13441	A Shot Of Rhythm And Blues/Run Run Run	15

SMITH BROTHERS (U.S.)

Year	Label / Cat. No.	Title	Value
78	Grapevine GRP 109	There Can Be A Better Way/Payback's A Drag	10

SMITHFIELD MARKET

Year	Label / Cat. No.	Title	Value
73	Gloucester GLS 0435	LONDON IN 1665 (LP, private pressing, gatefold sleeve)	800
74	Globe/Gloucester GLS 0443	AFTER SHAKESPEARE (LP, private pressing, die-cut sleeve, with insert)	700

THE SMITHS

(see also Morrissey, Sandie Shaw, The The, Electronic)

SINGLES

Year	Label / Cat. No.	Title	Value
83	Rough Trade RT 131	Hand In Glove/Handsome Devil (p/s, original pressing with Manchester address on rear sleeve)	25

			MINT VALUE £
83	Rough Trade RT 131	Hand In Glove/Handsome Devil (p/s, second pressing with London address on rear label)	15
83	Rough Trade RT 131	Hand In Glove/Handsome Devil (p/s, third pressing with no address)	20
83	Rough Trade RT 131	Hand In Glove/Handsome Devil (later pressing with misprinted blue/negative p/s - beware of counterfeits!)	2000
83	Rough Trade RT 136	This Charming Man/Jeane (unreleased first pressing with Rough Trade/Capitol logo and solid centre, p/s with Manchester address on rear)	50
83	Rough Trade RT 136	This Charming Man/Jeane (Rough Trade/Capitol logo or reissued 'stamped' logo, p/s)	10
83	Rough Trade RTT 136	This Charming Man (Manchester)/This Charming Man (London)/Accept Yourself/Wonderful Woman (12", p/s; later pressing with band title on sleeve)	30
83	Rough Trade RTT 136	This Charming Man (Manchester)/This Charming Man (London)/Accept Yourself/Wonderful Woman (12", p/s)	15
83	Rough Trade RTT 136NY	This Charming Man (New York Vocal)/This Charming Man (New York Instrumental) (12", p/s)	15
83	Rough Trade RTT 136NY	This Charming Man (New York Vocal)/This Charming Man (New York Instrumental) (12", p/s; later pressing with band title on sleeve)	50
84	Rough Trade RT 146	What Difference Does It Make?/Back To The Old House (Morrissey p/s)	10
84	Rough Trade RT 146	What Difference Does It Make?/Back To The Old House (Terence Stamp p/s)	10
84	Rough Trade RTT 146	What Difference Does It Make?/Back To The Old House/These Things Take Time (12", Morrissey or Terence Stamp p/s)	10
84	Rough Trade RTT 146	What Difference Does It Make?/Back To The Old House/These Things Take Time (Terence Stamp p/s, later pressing with band title on sleeve)	20
84	Rough Trade RT 156	Heaven Knows I'm Miserable Now/Suffer Little Children (p/s)	5
84	Rough Trade RTT 156	Heaven Knows I'm Miserable Now/Girl Afraid/Suffer Little Children (12", p/s)	8
84	Rough Trade RTT 156	Heaven Knows I'm Miserable Now/Girl Afraid/Suffer Little Children (mispressed 12" with extended version)	60
84	Rough Trade RT 166	William, It Was Really Nothing/Please Please Please Let Me Get What I Want (original issue with green 'man on bed' p/s)	8
84	Rough Trade RTT 166	William, It Was Really Nothing/How Soon Is Now?/Please Please Please Let Me Get What I Want (12", original issue with green 'man on bed' p/s)	10
85	Rough Trade RT 176	How Soon Is Now?/Well I Wonder (p/s)	5
85	Rough Trade RTT 176	How Soon Is Now?/Well I Wonder/Oscillate Wildly (12", p/s)	8
85	Rough Trade RT 181	Shakespeare's Sister/What She Said (p/s)	5
85	Rough Trade RTT 181	Shakespeare's Sister/What She Said/Stretch Out And Wait (12", p/s, with yellow & blue inner)	8
85	Rough Trade RTT 181	Shakespeare's Sister/What She Said/Stretch Out And Wait (12", p/s, with misprinted red & green inner)	50
85	Rough Trade RT 186	That Joke Isn't Funny Anymore/Meat Is Murder (live) (p/s)	5
85	Rough Trade RTT 186	That Joke Isn't Funny Anymore/Nowhere Fast (live)/Stretch Out And Wait (live)/Shakespeare's Sister (live)/Meat Is Murder (live) (12", p/s)	8
85	Rough Trade RT 191	The Boy With The Thorn In His Side/Asleep (p/s)	5
85	Rough Trade RTT 191	The Boy With The Thorn In His Side/Rubber Ring/Asleep (12", p/s)	8
86	Rough Trade RT 192	Bigmouth Strikes Again/Money Changes Everything (p/s)	5
86	Rough Trade RTT 192	Bigmouth Strikes Again/Money Changes Everything/Unloveable (12", p/s)	8
86	Rough Trade RT 193	Panic/Vicar In A Tutu (p/s, with 'Hang The DJ' stickers)	10
86	Rough Trade RTT 193	Panic/Vicar In A Tutu/The Draize Train (12", p/s, with 'Hang The DJ' stickers)	15
86	Rough Trade RT 194	Ask/Cemetry Gates (p/s)	5
86	Rough Trade RTT 194	Ask/Cemetry Gates/Golden Lights (12", p/s)	8
86	Rough Trade RTT 194C	Ask/Cemetry Gates/Golden Lights (cassette with picture inlay)	10
87	Rough Trade RT 195	Shoplifters Of The World Unite/Half A Person (p/s)	5
87	Rough Trade RTT 195	Shoplifters Of The World Unite/London/Half A Person (12", p/s; in carrier bag)	30
87	Rough Trade RTT 195	Shoplifters Of The World Unite/London/Half A Person (12", p/s)	8
87	Rough Trade RTT 195	Shoplifters Of The World Unite/London/Half A Person (12", p/s, mispressing, A-side plays "You Just Haven't Earned It Yet Baby")	70
87	Rough Trade RT 196	Sheila Take A Bow/Is It Really So Strange? (p/s)	5
87	Rough Trade RTT 196	Sheila Take A Bow/Is It Really So Strange?/Sweet And Tender Hooligan (12", p/s)	8
87	Rough Trade RT 197	Girlfriend In A Coma/Work Is A Four Letter Word (grey p/s)	5
87	Rough Trade RT 197	Girlfriend In A Coma/Work Is A Four Letter Word (misprinted green p/s, incorrectly shows additional 12" track 'I Keep Mine Hidden' on reverse of sleeve)	500
87	Rough Trade RTT 197	Girlfriend In A Coma/Work Is A Four Letter Word/I Keep Mine Hidden (12", green p/s; some in grey p/s)	35
87	Rough Trade RTT 197	Girlfriend In A Coma/Work Is A Four Letter Word/I Keep Mine Hidden (12", green p/s)	8
87	Rough Trade RTT 197C	Girlfriend In A Coma/Work Is A Four Letter Word/I Keep Mine Hidden (cassette with picture inlay)	10
87	Rough Trade RT 198	I Started Something I Couldn't Finish/Pretty Girls Make Graves (Troy Tate demo) (p/s)	5
87	Rough Trade RTT 198	I Started Something I Couldn't Finish/Pretty Girls Make Graves (Troy Tate demo)/Some Girls Are Bigger Than Others (Live) (12", p/s)	8
87	Rough Trade RTT 198C	I Started Something I Couldn't Finish/Pretty Girls Make Graves/Some Girls Are Bigger Than Others/What's The World (live) (cassette)	10
87	Rough Trade RT 200	Last Night I Dreamt That Somebody Loved Me/Rusholme Ruffians (John Peel version) (p/s)	5
87	Rough Trade RTT 200	Last Night I Dreamt That Somebody Loved Me/Rusholme Ruffians (John Peel version)/Nowhere Fast (John Peel Version) (12", p/s)	8
87	Rough Trade RTT 200CD	Last Night I Dreamt That Somebody Loved Me/Rusholme Ruffians (John Peel version)/Nowhere Fast (John Peel version)/William, It Was Really Nothing (John Peel Version) (CD)	20
87	Rough Trade RT 166	William, It Was Really Nothing/How Soon Is Now? (reissue, Billie Whitelaw p/s)	20
87	Rough Trade RTT 166	William, It Was Really Nothing/How Soon Is Now?/Please Please Please Let Me Get What I Want (12", reissue, Billie Whitelaw p/s)	30
88	Rough Trade CAT 063	London (Live) (Square 1-sided black flexi, 33rpm free with The Catalogue magazine, reverse has reproduction of hand-written poem for 'Poppycocteau' by Morrissey)	10

			MINT VALUE £
92	WEA YZ0001	This Charming Man/Jeane (p/s, reissue)	5
92	WEA YZ0002	How Soon Is Now? (p/s, reissue)	15
92	WEA YZ0003	There Is A Light That Never Goes Out/Handsome Devil (live) (p/s)	15

PROMOS & TEST PRESSINGS

83	Rough Trade RT 131	Hand In Glove (white label 1983 test pressing - approx. 5 only)	1500
83	N/A	3-Pack (Rough Trade promo cassette, promoting Hand In Glove and tracks by two other bands)	100
83	Rough Trade RT 136	Reel Around The Fountain/Jeane (unissued, white label test pressings only - beware of counterfeits!)	1000
83	Rough Trade RT 136	This Charming Man (London Version) (rejected white label test pressing)	500
83	Rough Trade RT 136	This Charming Man (Manchester) (one-sided white label test pressing)	300
83	Rough Trade RTT 136NY	This Charming Man (New York vocal)/(New York Instrumental) (12" white label test pressing)	300
84	Rough Trade RT 146	What Difference Does It Make?/Back To The Old House (white label test pressing)	30
84	Rough Trade RTT 146	What Difference Does It Make?/Back To The Old House/ These Things Take Time (12" white label test pressing)	100
84	Rough Trade RT 61 DJ	Still Ill/You've Got Everything Now (promo)	25
84	Rough Trade ROUGH 61	THE SMITHS (white label test pressing)	30
84	Rough Trade RT 131	Hand In Glove (one-sided white label 1984 test pressing)	250
84	Rough Trade RT 131	Hand In Glove/Handsome Devil (white label test pressing for 1984 re-pressing)	200
84	Rough Trade RT 156	Heaven Knows I'm Miserable Now/Suffer Little Children (rejected white label test pressing with extended version)	1000
84	Rough Trade RTT 156	Heaven Knows I'm Miserable Now/Girl Afraid/Suffer Little Children (rejected 12" white label test pressing with extended version)	1000
84	Rough Trade RT 156	Heaven Knows I'm Miserable Now/Suffer Little Children (standard white label test pressing)	20
84	Rough Trade RTT 156	Heaven Knows I'm Miserable Now/Girl Afraid/Suffer Little Children (standard 12" white label test pressing)	100
84	Rough Trade RT 166	William, It Was Really Nothing/Please Please Please Let Me Get What I Want (white label test pressing)	20
84	Rough Trade RTT 166	William, It Was Really Nothing/How Soon Is Now?/Please Please Please Let Me Get What I Want (12" white label test pressing)	100
84	Rough Trade ROUGH 76	HATFUL OF HOLLOW (white label test pressing)	30
84	Copymasters	HATFUL OF HOLLOW (cassette, early version with unreleased tracks)	100
85	Rough Trade RTT 171	Barbarism Begins At Home (12", 2 different 1-sided white label test pressings)	400
85	Rough Trade RTT 171	Barbarism Begins At Home (12" one-sided, promo)	35
85	Rough Trade RTT 171	Barbarism Begins At Home (edited version)/(long version)	45
85	Rough Trade RTT 171	Barbarism Begins At Home (12", p/s, one-sided promo)	40
85	Rough Trade RT 176	How Soon Is Now?/Oscillate Wildly (white label test pressing with Oscillate Wildly instead of Well I Wonder on the B-side)	300
85	Rough Trade RTT 176	How Soon Is Now?/Well I Wonder/Oscillate Wildly (12" white label test pressing)	100
85	Rough Trade ROUGH 81	MEAT IS MURDER (white label test pressing)	300
85	Rough Trade RT 181	Shakespeare's Sister/What She Said (white label test pressing)	100
85	Rough Trade RT 186	Meat Is Murder/Nowhere Fast/Stretch Out And Wait (live EP, unissued, test pressings only)	1000
85	Rough Trade RT 186	Meat Is Murder/Nowhere Fast/Stretch Out And Wait (live EP, unissued, Mayking test pressings - beware of counterfeits!)	600
85	Rough Trade RTT 186	Meat Is Murder/William It Was Really Nothing/Nowhere Fast/ Stretch Out And Wait /Miserable Lie (live 12" EP, unissued, test pressings only-beware of counterfeits!)	1000
85	Rough Trade RT 186	That Joke Isn't Funny Anymore/Meat Is Murder (live) (white label test pressing)	100
85	RT 186	That Joke Isn't Funny Anymore/Meat Is Murder (live) (Mayking test pressing)	300
85	Rough Trade RTT 191	The Boy With The Thorn In His Side/Rubber Ring/Asleep (white label test pressing)	20
86	Rough Trade RT 192	Bigmouth Strikes Again/Money Changes Everything (white label test pressing)	100
86	Rough Trade RTT 192	Bigmouth Strikes Again/Money Changes Everything/Unloveable (12" white label test pressing)	30
86	Rough Trade ROUGH 96	THE QUEEN IS DEAD (white label test pressing)	100
86	Rough Trade ROUGH 96	THE QUEEN IS DEAD (Mayking test pressing)	300
86	Rough Trade RTT 193	Panic/Vicar In A Tutu/The Draize Train (12" white label test pressing with promo posters)	50
86	Rough Trade RT 194	Ask/Cemetry Gates (white label test pressing)	200
87	Rough Trade RTT 195	You Just Haven't Earned It Yet Baby/London/Half A Person (12", white label test pressing)	500
87	Rough Trade ROUGH 101	THE WORLD WON'T LISTEN (white label test pressing)	20
87	Rough Trade RT 196	Sheila Take A Bow/Is It Really So Strange? (white label test pressing)	200
87	Rough Trade ROUGH 255	LOUDER THAN BOMBS (2-LP, white label test pressings)	100
87	Rough Trade RT 197	Girlfriend In A Coma/Work Is A Four Letter Word (white label test pressing)	200
87	Rough Trade ROUGH 106	STRANGEWAYS, HERE WE COME (white label test pressing)	20
87	Rough Trade RT 198	I Started Something I Couldn't Finish/Pretty Girls Make Graves (Troy Tate demo) (white label test pressing)	200
87	Rough Trade RT 198	I Started Something I Couldn't Finish/Pretty Girls Make Graves (Mayking test pressing)	400
87	Rough Trade RT 166-B	How Soon Is Now? (1-sided white label test pressing for B-side of re-issued William, It Was Really Nothing 7")	250
88	Rough Trade ROUGH 126	RANK (white label test pressing; in misprinted sleeve, no cover star or title on sleeve, just states 'The Smiths')	200
88	Rough Trade ROUGH 126	RANK (white label test pressing)	20

ALBUMS

84	Rough Trade ROUGH 76	HATFUL OF HOLLOW (LP, original gatefold issue, with incorrect sleeve, no black dot appears between 'Accept Yourself' and 'Girl Afraid' on reverse of sleeve)	20
85	Rough Trade ROUGH 81	MEAT IS MURDER (LP, with lyric inner sleeve)	15
85	Rough Trade ROUGH 81	MEAT IS MURDER (LP, with lyric inner sleeve)	15

			MINT VALUE £
85	Rough Trade ROUGH CD 81	MEAT IS MURDER (CD, original issue)	18
85	Rough Trade ROUGH CD 76	HATFUL OF HOLLOW (CD, original sleeve)	50
86	Rough Trade ROUGH CD 61	THE SMITHS (CD, original issue)	18
86	Rough Trade ROUGH 96	THE QUEEN IS DEAD (LP, gatefold, inner sleeve)	15
86	Rough Trade ROUGH CD 96	THE QUEEN IS DEAD (CD, original issue)	18
87	Rough Trade ROUGH CD 101	THE WORLD WON'T LISTEN (CD, original issue)	18
87	Rough Trade ROUGH 106	STRANGEWAYS HERE WE COME (LP, embossed sleeve)	15
87	Rough Trade ROUGH CD 106	STRANGEWAYS, HERE WE COME (CD, original issue)	18
87	Rough Trade ROUGH 255	LOUDER THAN BOMBS (2-LP, gatefold sleeve)	20
87	Rough Trade ROUGH CD 255	LOUDER THAN BOMBS (CD)	20
88	Rough Trade ROUGH CD 76	HATFUL OF HOLLOW (CD, reissue sleeve)	18
88	Rough Trade ROUGH 126	RANK (LP, gatefold sleeve, with inner, ltd. edition with poster and cover sticker denoting amended catalogue number)	20
88	Rough Trade ROUGH 126D	RANK (DAT)	50
93	WEA SMITHS 1	THE SMITHS (10" LP, reissue)	12
93	WEA SMITHS 2	HATFUL OF HOLLOW (2-LP, 10" reissue)	12
93	WEA SMITHS 3	MEAT IS MURDER (10" LP reissue)	12
93	WEA SMITHS 4	THE QUEEN IS DEAD (10" LP reissue)	12
93	WEA SMITHS 5	THE WORLD WON'T LISTEN (10" LP reissue)	12
93	WEA SMITHS 6	STRANGEWAYS, HERE WE COME (10" LP reissue)	12
93	WEA SMITHS 7	RANK (10" 2-LP reissue)	12

REISSUES CD SINGLES

88	Rough Trade RTT 146CD	What Difference Does It Make?/Back To The Old House/These Things Take Time	25
88	Rough Trade RTT 156CD	Heaven Knows I'm Miserable Now/Girl Afraid/Suffer Little Children	25
88	Rough Trade RTT 166CD	William, It Was Really Nothing/How Soon Is Now?/ Please Please Please Let Me Get What I Want	30
88	Rough Trade RTT 171CD	Barbarism Begins At Home/Shakespeare's Sister/Stretch Out And Wait	35
88	Rough Trade RTT 191CD	The Boy With The Thorn In His Side/Rubber Ring/Asleep	25
88	Rough Trade RTT 193CD	Panic/Vicar In A Tutu/The Draize Train	25
88	Rough Trade RTT 194CD	Ask/Cemetry Gates/Golden Lights	15
88	Rough Trade RTT 215CD	The Headmaster Ritual/Nowhere Fast (live)/Stretch Out And Wait (live)/ Meat Is Murder (live)	40
93	WEA YZ0003 CD1	There Is A Light That Never Goes Out/Hand In Glove (live)/ Some Girls Are Bigger Than Others (live)/Money Changes Everything	10
93	WEA YZ0003 CD2	There Is A Light That Never Goes Out/Hand In Glove (Sandie Shaw)/ I Don't Owe You Anything (Sandie Shaw)/Jeane (Sandie Shaw)	10

SMITHY ALL STARS

(see also Ian Smith & Inner Mind)

71	Hillcrest HCT 3	Witchfinder General/Deserted	5

SMOG

95	City Slang EFAD 49517	A Hit/Wine Stained Lips (p/s, yellow vinyl)	10

SMOKE

(see also Shots)

67	Columbia DB 8115	My Friend Jack/We Can Take It	35
67	Columbia DB 8252	If The Weather's Sunny/I Would If I Could, But I Can't	35
67	Columbia DB 8252	If The Weather's Sunny/I Would If I Could, But I Can't (in export p/s)	80
67	Island WIP 6023	It Could Be Wonderful/Have Some More Tea	65
68	Island WIP 6031	Utterly Simple/Sydney Gill (unreleased)	0
70	Revolution Pop REVP 1002	Dreams Of Dreams/My Birth	50
71	Pageant SAM 101	Ride Ride Ride/Guy Fawkes	12
72	Regal Zonophone RZ 3071	Sugar Man/That's What I Want	25
74	Decca FR 13484	Shagalagalu/Gimme Good Loving	5
74	Decca FR 13514	My Lullaby/Looking High	15
70s	Gull 128 301	IT'S SMOKE TIME (LP, reissue of German-only LP)	20
88	M. Blue Town MBT 5001	MY FRIEND JACK (LP)	15

SMOKESTACK LIGHTNIN'

68	Bell BLL 1046	Light In My Window/Long Stemmed Eyes (John's Song)	20
69	Bell MBLL/SBLL 116	OFF THE WALL (LP)	30

SMOKEY BABE

62	77' LA 12-12	SMOKEY BABE AND HIS FRIENDS (LP)	25

SMOKEY CIRCLES

70	Carnaby CNS4011	Long Live Love/Love Me While You Can	5
70	Carnaby CNLS 6006	THE SMOKEY CIRCLES ALBUM (LP, union jack flag label)	60

SMOKEY SMOTHERS

69	Polydor 623 239	THE DRIVING BLUES (LP)	40

SMOKIE & HIS SISTER

67	CBS 202605	Creators Of Rain/In Dreams Of Silent Seas	10

THE SMOKIN' MOJO FILTERS

(See also Paul Weller, Oasis)

95	Go! Discs GOD 136	Come Together/THE BEAUTIFUL SOUTH: A Minute's Silence/DODGY: Is It Me/ BLACK GRAPE: In The Name Of The Father (Crown Of Thorns Mix) (7")	5

SMOKIN' ROADIE

83	Zone To Zone ZON 3	Midnight/Ripp Off (p/s)	30

SMOOTH BUT HAZZARDOUS

92	Basement BRSS 007	Smooth But Hazzardous/Made U Dance/Violent Headrush (12")	20
93	Sound Entity SENT 1200	We Are The Creator/Push Up The Levels (12")	40
93	Sound Entity SENT 1205	Made You Dance (Carl Cox Remix)/Push Up The Levels (SBH Remix)/ Push Up The Levels (Originla Mix) (12")	15
94	Sinister SNS 003	Help Me/DMX Override (12")	10

MINT VALUE £

JACK SMOOTH
(see also Ruff With The Smooth, DJ Chemistry Meets Jack Smooth)

91	Sound Entity SE 001	WAVEFORMS EP (12")	15
91	Sound Entity SE 03	Untitled/Untitled/Untitled/Untitled (12", white label, hand-written labels, some in stamped sleeve)	15
93	Sound Entity SENT 1201	Tell Me Something/Happy Nonsense (12", with Spencer T)	20
93	Sound Entity SENT 120220	HURTS EP (12", with Alex Reece)	40

SMYLE

71	CBS 7225	Glory Glory/Will I Get Back Tomorrow	8

DES SMYTH & COLLEGEMEN

65	Pye 7N 15867	The Pillow That Whispers/Lonely Streets	5
65	Pye 7N 15996	Wedding Bells/All For The Love Of A Girl	5

GILLI SMYTH & MOTHER GONG
(see also Gong)

78	Charly CRL 5007	MOTHER (LP, with insert)	15

DONALD SMYTHE

71	Punch PH 83	Where Love Goes/HURRICANES: You Can Run	40

GLORIA SMYTHE

60	Vogue V 9159	I'll Be Over After A While/Gee Baby Ain't I Good To You	10

SNAFU
(see also Whitesnake, Freedom)

74	WWA WWS 007	Dixie Queen/Monday Morning	5
74	WWA WWA 003	SNAFU (LP, gatefold sleeve)	18
74	WWA WWA 013	SITUATION NORMAL (LP)	12

SNAKEBITE

83	Astor ASTOR 1	Blow You Away/Thin Ice (no p/s)	25

SNAKES
(see also The Motors)

76	Dynamite DYR45006	Teenage Head/Lights Out (p/s)	8

SNAPE
(see also Alexis Korner)

73	Transatlantic TRA 269	ACCIDENTALLY BORN IN NEW ORLEANS (LP)	22

SNAPPERS

59	Top Rank JAR 167	Big Bill/If There Were	18
59	Top Rank JAR 167	Big Bill/If There Were (78)	25

SNAPPERS

67	CBS 2719	Upside Down Inside Out/Memories	20

SNATCH
(see also Johnny Thunders, Judy Nylon)

78	Lightning LIG 502	Stanley/I.R.T. (p/s)	10
78	Lightning LIG 505	All I Want/When I'm Bored ('foil' p/s)	10
80	Fetish FET 004	Shopping For Clothes/Joey/Red Army (12", die-cut p/s)	8

SNEAKY PETES

60	Decca F 11199	Savage (Parts 1 & 2)	15

SNEEKERS

64	Columbia DB 7385	I Just Can't Get To Sleep/Bald Headed Woman	150

SNEEKY FEELINS

79	Warped W102	Private Mail/Only The Rain (p/s with insert)	50

DAVID SNELL

66	Decca SKL 4745	THE SUBTLE SOUND OF DAVID SNELL (LP)	18

LEN SNIDER

63	London HLU 9790	Everyone Knows/I'll Be Coming Home Tonight	8

SNIFF 'N' THE TEARS

79	Chiswick NS 40	Driver's Seat (cancelled, test pressings only)	15

SNIFTERS

78	Lightning GIL 534	I Like Boys/Baby Punker	15

SNIPERS

81	Crass 321984/4	THREE PEACE SUITE (EP)	12

SNIVELLING SHITS
(see also Doctor Dark)

77	Ghetto Rockers PRE 2	Terminal Stupid/I Can't Come (p/s, first pressing of 500, paper labels/black print)	60
77	Ghetto Rockers PRE 2	Terminal Stupid/I Can't Come (p/s, 2nd pressing, plastic labels/juke box centre)	25
89	Damaged Goods FNARR 4	Isgodaman?/Terminal Stupid/I Can't Come (p/s)	20
89	Dam. Goods FNARR4B	Isgodaman?/Terminal Stupid/I Can't Come (box set with badge & inserts, pink vinyl in stamped plain white sleeve)	25
90	Dam. Goods FNARR LP 3	I CAN'T COME (LP, brown vinyl)	12

SNOBS

64	Decca F 11867	Buckle Shoe Stomp/Stand And Deliver	20

SNOOKY & MOODY

66	Blue Horizon 45-1003	Snooky And Moody's Blues/Telephone Blues (99 copies only)	135

HANK SNOW (& RAINBOW RANCH BOYS)
(see also Chet Atkins)

54	HMV 7MC 7	Why Do You Punish Me (For Loving You)/When Mexican Joe Meets Jole Blon (with Rainbow Ranch Boys) (export issue)	15

MINT VALUE £

54	HMV 7MC 15	Spanish Fire Ball/Between Fire And Water (with Rainbow Ranch Boys) (export issue)	15
54	HMV 7MC 24	My Arabian Baby/I Don't Hurt Anymore (with Rainbow Ranch Boys) (export issue)	15
54	HMV 7MC 25	My Religion's Not Old-Fashioned (But It's Real Genuine)/The Alphabet (with Rainbow Ranch Boys) (export issue)	15
54	HMV 7MC 31	Yellow Roses/Would You Mind (with Rainbow Ranch Boys) (export issue)	15
59	RCA RCA 1151	Old Shep/The Last Ride	10
61	RCA RCA 1248	Poor Little Jimmie/Beggar To A King	5
58	RCA RCX 116	COUNTRY GUITAR NO. 4 (EP)	8
59	RCA RCX 142	COUNTRY GUITAR NO. 7 (EP)	10
63	RCA RCX 7125	WHEN TRAGEDY STRUCK (EP)	10
64	RCA RCX 7154	THAT COUNTRY GENTLEMAN (EP)	12
59	RCA RD 27115	WHEN TRAGEDY STRUCK (LP)	15

SNOWBOY

90s	Acid Jazz JAZIDLP 146	THE MANY FACES OF SNOWBOY (2-LP)	20

SNOWBOY & NOEL McKOY

90s	Acid Jazz JAZID 42T	Lucky Fellow (12", p/s)	12

SNOW PATROL

(see also Shrug)

98	Jeepster JPR7004	Little Hide/Sticky Teenage Twin (1,000 only, p/s)	30
99	Jeepster JPRCDS 013	Starfighter Pilot/Raze The City/Riot Please (CD)	8
04	Polydor 9866356	Chocolate/One Night Is Not Enough (Live) (p/s orange vinyl)	10
04	Polydor FICTION 001	Run (Jacknife Lee Mix)/Run (Freelance Hellraiser Mix) (10" clear vinyl stickered poly bag)	12
06	Fiction 0602517043985	Chasing Cars/Play Me Like You Own Hand (p/s, with inner p/s)	10
98	Jeepster JPRLP004	SONGS FOR POLAR BEARS (LP)	30

SNUGGY

(see also Jade Warrior)

71	Philips 6006138	Creole Jive/Jungle King	6

BILL SNYDER & HIS (MAGIC PIANO &) ORCHESTRA

54	London REP 1011	BEWITCHED (EP)	8
51	London H-APB 1004	BEWITCHED (10" LP)	12

RON SNYDER

63	Parlophone R 4993	Oh My Twisted Bach/Narcissus	6

TERRY SNYDER

65	Pye Command PCLS 800	PERSUASIVE PERCUSSION (LP)	12

SO WHAT!

86	No label or Cat. No.	It Is All Over/Now I Don't Want You Around (no p/s)	50
70	CBS 5005	Flowers/Tell Me Now	10

S.O.B.

89	Rise Above RISE 002	THRASH NIGHT EP (p/s)	8

ERROL SOBERS

(see also Bobby Bridger)

70	Beacon BEA 159	Sugar Shaker/You're In Love	12

SOCIAL DISEASE

83	Carnage	TODAY (EP)	8

SOCIALITES

64	Warner Bros WB 148	Jive Jimmy/You're Losing Your Touch	45

SOCIAL SECURITY

78	Heartbeat PULSE 1	I Don't Want My Heart To Rule My Head/Stella's Got A Fella/Cider/Choc Ice (p/s)	30

SOCIETIE

67	Deram DM 162	Bird Has Flown/Breaking Down	65

SOCRATES

72	Deram DM 362	Eating Momma's Cookin'/Dearest Agnes	15

SODS

79	Tap TAP 1	Moby Grape/Negative Positive (p/s)	30
79	Stortbeat SB 5	No Pictures Of Us/Plaything (p/s)	40

SODS

79	Step Forward SFLP 3	MINYUTES TO GO (LP)	30

SOFERNO B

80	Soferno B SOLP 001	IN DUB (LP)	75

SOFT BOYS

(see also Robyn Hitchcock, Kimberley Rew)

77	Raw RAW 5	GIVE IT TO THE SOFT BOYS (EP, acetate with withdrawn track, Vyrna Knowl Is A Headbanger in place of "Ventilator")	200
77	Raw RAW 5	GIVE IT TO THE SOFT BOYS (EP)	20
78	Radar ADA 8	(I Want To Be An) Anglepoise Lamp/Fat Man's Son (p/s)	8
79	Raw RAW 37	GIVE IT TO THE SOFT BOYS (EP, unreleased reissue)	0
79	Raw RAW 41	Where Are The Prawns (unreleased)	0
80	Armageddon AEP 002	NEAR THE SOFT BOYS (EP)	8
80	Armageddon AS 005	I Wanna Destroy You/I'm An Old Pervert (Disco) (p/s)	8
81	Armageddon AS 029	Only The Stones Remain/The Asking Tree (p/s)	8
82	Bucketfull Of Brains BOB 1	Love Poisoning/When I Was A Kid (p/s, with Bucketfull Of Brains magazine)	15
82	Bucketfull Of Brains BOB 1	Love Poisoning/When I Was A Kid (p/s, without Bucketfull Of Brains magazine)	12
83	Midnight Music DING 4	He's A Reptile/Song No. 4 (p/s, 2 different designs)	8
87	Bucketfull Of Brains BOB 17	Deck Of Cards/ROBYN HITCHCOCK & PETER BUCK: Flesh No. 1 (flexidisc with Bucketfull Of Brains magazine, issue 23)	8

			MINT VALUE £
89	Overground OVER 4	The Face Of Death/The Yodelling Hoover (p/s, 600 yellow viny or 400 white vinyl)	6
89	Overground OVER 4	The Face Of Death/The Yodelling Hoover (p/s, 15 gold test pressings)	15
85	Delorean SOFT 1P	WADING THROUGH A VENTILATOR (12" EP, picture disc)	10
79	Two Crabs CLAW 1001	A CAN OF BEES (LP, original issue, black & white labels)	20
80	Aura AUL 709	A CAN OF BEES (LP, reissue)	12
80	Armageddon ARM 1	UNDERWATER MOONLIGHT (LP)	15
82	Armageddon BYE 1	TWO HALVES FOR THE PRICE OF ONE (LP)	12
83	M. Music CHIME 0002	INVISIBLE HITS (LP)	12
84	Two Crabs CLAW 1001	A CAN OF BEES (LP, 2nd reissue, black & red labels)	12

SOFT CELL

(see also Marc Almond, Marc & Mambas, Anne Hogan)

80	Big Frock ABF 1	MUTANT MOMENTS (EP, plain p/s with postcard; beware of counterfeits without postcard & in wraparound p/s)	60
81	Some Bizzare HARD 1	A Man Can Get Lost/Memorabilia (p/s, 10,000 only)	10
81	Some Bizzare HARD 12	Memorabilia (Extended)/Persuasion (Extended) (12", p/s)	10
81	Some Bizzare BZS 212	Tainted Love/Where Did Our Love Go/Tainted Dub/Memorabilia (12", p/s, limited edition with 4 tracks)	10
81	Some Bizzare No cat. no.	Metro Mr. X/B-MOVIE: Remembrance Day (white label test pressing)	60
81	Lyntone LYN 10410	Metro Mr. X/B-MOVIE: Remembrance Day (red or green flexidisc, with Flexipop magazine, issue 12)	8
82	Some Bizzare CELBX 1	THE 12" SINGLES (6 x 12" box set, with booklet)	50
83	Some Bizzare BZS 17	Numbers/Memorabilia (live) (foldout card p/s)	7
83	Some Bizzare BZS 2020	Soul Inside/You Only Live Twice/Loving You - Hating Me/ Her Imagination (double pack)	8
83	Lyntone (no cat. no.)	Say Hello, Wave Goodbye (live) (flexidisc, blue vinyl, fan club issue, 500 only)	15
84	Lyntone (no cat. no.)	Ghostrider (live '83) (flexidisc, blue, black or green vinyl, fan club issue)	15
84	Some Bizzare BZSR 2212	Down In The Subway (Remix)/Disease And Desire/Born To Lose (12", p/s)	18
91	Some Bizzare SOFCP 1	Say Hello, Wave Goodbye - '91/Numbers/Torch (Original Extended Version) (CD, picture disc)	8
91	Some Bizzare (no cat no)	Megamix '91 (12", promo only, custom p/s)	12

SOFT DRINKS

82	Outer Himalayan OH 4	Pepsi Cola/Pop Stars In Their Pyjamas (with booklet and sticker)	30

SOFTIES

(see also Captain Sensible)

77	Charly CYS 1036	Suicide Pilot/C.I. Angel (p/s)	5

MICK SOFTLEY

65	Immediate IM 014	I'm So Confused/She's My Girl	40
67	CBS 202469	Am I The Red One/That's Not My Kind Of Love	180
70	CBS 5130	Can You Hear Me Now/Time Machine	7
71	CBS 7337	Goin' Down The Road/Gypsy	7
72	CBS 8269	Lady Willow/From The Land Of The Crab	7
65	Columbia 33SX 1781	SONGS FOR SWINGIN' SURVIVORS (LP)	150
70	CBS 64098	SUNRISE (LP, gatefold sleeve)	50
71	CBS 64395	STREET SINGER (LP)	35
72	CBS 64841	ANY MOTHER DOESN'T GRUMBLE (LP)	40

SOFT MACHINE

(see also Robert Wyatt, Kevin Ayers, Hugh Hopper, Elton Dean, Daevid Allen, Matching Mole, 'Igginbottom, Lyn Dobson)

67	Polydor 56151	Love Makes Sweet Music/Reelin' Feelin' Squeelin'	150
78	Harvest HAR 5155	Soft Space (Parts 1 & 2) (p/s)	8
69	Probe SPB 1002	THE SOFT MACHINE VOLUME TWO (LP, black/silver label)	60
70	CBS 66246	THIRD (2-LP, gatefold)	40
71	CBS 64280	FOURTH (LP, embossed textured sleeve)	25
72	CBS 64806	FIFTH (LP)	25
73	CBS 68214	SIX (2-LP, gatefold sleeve)	25
73	CBS 65799	SEVEN (LP, gatefold sleeve)	20
75	Harvest SHSP 4044	BUNDLES (LP, with inner sleeve)	12
76	Harvest SHSP 4056	SOFTS (LP)	12
77	Harvest SHTW 800	TRIPLE ECHO (3-LP, box set, with colour booklet)	40
78	Harvest SHSP 4083	ALIVE & WELL (LP)	12
88	Reckless RECKLP5	LIVE AT THE PROMS (LP)	15

SOFT PEDALLING

70	Decca F 23034	It's So Nice/Rolling On Home	5

SOFT SHOE

78	Aardvark AARD 1	FOR THOSE ALONE (LP, with insert)	100

SOFT TOUCH

67	W+G WG 001	A Silent Life/Ilusive Face (private pressing)	300

SOHEP

81	Merciful Release MR 3	So Much Fun/You Could Be So Nice Dear (p/s)	10

SOHO JETS

75	Polydor 2058 525	Hi Heel Tarzan/Night Flight	20
75	Polydor 2058 598	Denim Goddess/Smile	20

SOHO SKIFFLE GROUP

57	Melodisc 1403	Give Me A Big Fat Woman/The Midnight Special (78)	20
57	Melodisc 1421	Frankie And Johnny/Streamline Train (78)	20
57	Melodisc EMP 7 72	SOHO SKIFFLE GROUP (EP)	75

SOL INVICTUS

(see also Current 93, Death In June, Nurse With Wound, Karl Blake, Shock Headed Peters)

90	Cerne 004	Abbatoirs Of Love/CURRENT 93: This Ain't The Summer Of Love (live in Japan, gig freebie, 93 with insert & gig ticket)	50
90	Cerne 004	Abbatoirs Of Love/CURRENT 93: This Ain't The Summer Of Love (live in Japan, gig freebie, [200 without insert])	25

MINT VALUE £

91	Shock SX 016	See The Dove Fall/Somewhere In Europe (numbered foldover p/s in poly bag, 1,000 only)	15
91	World Serpent WS7 002	Looking For Europe (1-sided, etched B-side, foldover sleeve in poly bag, 963 only)	15
00	Tursa 026	EVE (picture disc, 1,000 only)	20
01	Tursa 029	HILL OF CROSSES (LP, 1,000 only, signed)	20
02	Tursa 030	THRONES (LP, 1,000 only, signed)	12
02	Tursa 014	THE BLADE (LP, 1,000 only, signed)	12
89	SVL SVL 009	IN THE JAWS OF THE SERPENT (LP, with insert)	20
90	Tursa 001	TREES IN WINTER (LP)	30
90	Tursa 002	LEX TALIONIS (CD, special edit in leather wallet)	30
91	Tursa 003	KILLING TIDE (LP)	25
91	Tursa 003	KILLING TIDE (CD, special edit in felt bag)	20

MARTIAL SOLAL

63	RCA Victor RD/SF 7614	AT NEWPORT '63 (LP)	12

SOLAR PLEXUS

73	Polydor 2383 222	SOLAR PLEXUS (LP)	35

SOLDIER

82	Heavy Metal HEAVY 12	Sheralee/Force (p/s, with postcard)	35
82	Heavy Metal HEAVY 12	Sheralee/Force (p/s, without postcard)	25
04	Killer Metal KMRS 001	Murderous Night/I'm Taken In (red vinyl, 500 copies, numbered)	7

SOLDIER DOLLS

83	Scream 1	WHAT DO THEY KNOW? (EP)	8
84	Scream 2	A TASTE OF BLOOD (EP, red vinyl)	8

SOLENT

73	Decca F 13375	My World Fell Down/The Sound Of Summer's Over	10

SOLID GOLD CADILLAC

(see also Battered Ornaments, Chris Spedding, Mike Westbrook)

73	RCA SF 8311	SOLID GOLD CADILLAC (LP)	30
73	RCA SF 8365	BRAIN DAMAGE (LP)	45

SOLID N MIND

90	Liberty Grooves LIB001	An Original Break (12")	20
91	Liberty Grooves PPP001	Centre Stage/Woke With Nuthin' (promo cassette)	25

SOLID ROCK BAND

78	Chapel Lane RWA 1	FOOTPRINTS ON THE WATER (LP, gatefold sleeve)	15

SOLID SENDERS

(see under Wilko Johnson)

SOLITAIRES

58	London HLM 8745	Walking Along/Please Kiss This Letter	150
58	London HLM 8745	Walking Along/Please Kiss This Letter (78)	60

NORMAN SOLOMAN

81	Black Joy DH 816	Joy Bells Ringing/JAYS: Unity Call (12")	25

SOLSTICE

82	private pressing	MORNING LIGHT (cassette EP)	10
84	Equinox EQRLP 001	SILENT DANCE (LP, gatefold sleeve)	18

SOLSTICE

08	Iron Kodex IK 003	ONLY THE STRONG SURVIVE (2-LP with free 7")	20

SOLUTION

72	Decca SKL-R 5124	SOLUTION (LP)	25

SOME CHICKEN

77	Raw RAW 7	New Religion/Blood On The Wall (p/s)	20
78	Raw RAW 13	Arabian Daze/No. 7	15
78	Raw RAW 13	Arabian Daze/No. 7 (purple vinyl)	120
78	Raw RAWT 13	Arabian Daze/No. 7 (12")	8

SOMEONE'S BAND

70	Deram DM 313	Story/Give It To You	20
70	Deram SML 1068	SOMEONE'S BAND (LP)	200

GORDON SOMERS & HIS GROUP

64	Top Ten TPSX 101	THE SOUND OF THE BEATLES (EP)	8

SOMERVILLE GENTLEMAN'S BAND

80	Somerville PLR 026	FAR FROM HOME (LP)	25

SOMETHING HAPPENS!

86	Prophet PRS 002	TWO CHANCES (EP, p/s)	8

ELKE SOMMER

61	Columbia DB 4688	Be Not Notty/The Faithful Hussar	5

JOANIE SOMMERS

(see also Ed Byrnes)

65	Warner Bros WB 150	If You Love Him/I Think I'm Gonna Cry	15
60	Warner Bros WB 23	Be My Love/Why Don't You Do Right?	7
60	Warner Bros WB 31	Ruby-Duby-Du/Bob White	7
60	Warner Bros WB 44	One Boy/I'll Never Be Free	7
61	Warner Bros WB 71	Johnny Get Angry/Theme From A Summer Place	10
64	Warner Bros WB 78	When The Boys Get Together/Passing Strangers	7
62	Warner Bros WB 85	Goodbye Joey/Bobby Is Bobby	7
63	Warner Bros WB 105	Little Girl Bad/Wishing Well	7
60	Warner Bros WEP 6013	POSITIVELY THE MOST (EP, also stereo WSEP 2013)	20
61	Warner Bros WEP 6047	THE VOICE OF THE SIXTIES (EP, also stereo WSEP 2047)	15

MINT VALUE £

SONGSTERS

54	London HL 8100	Bahama Buggy Ride/It Isn't Right	18
54	London HL 8100	Bahama Buggy Ride/It Isn't Right (78)	18

SON HOUSE

60s	Saydisc Roots SL 504	THE VOCAL INTENSITY OF SON HOUSE (LP)	40
66	CBS (S)BPG 62604	THE LEGENDARY FATHER OF FOLK BLUES (LP)	35
70	Liberty LBS 83391	JOHN THE REVELATOR (LP)	30

SON HOUSE/J.D. SHORT

69	Xtra XTRA 1080	DELTA BLUES (LP)	20

SONIA

79	D Roy DRDD 18	Ooh Baby Baby/Back Street Dub (12")	12
79	Karn-Na KRN 002	Again (Suddenly You're Mine)/UNDIVIDED ROOTS: Version (12", purple vinyl)	12
81	S & S FERGY 001	Checking It Out/Version (12", with Creation Rebel)	20
80	Cha Cha CHAD 26	Easier To Love/That's The Way You Feel (12", with Earth & Stone)	15

SONIC ASSASSINS

(see also Hawkwind)

81	Flicknife FLEP 101	SONIC ASSASSINS (12" EP, p/s)	8

SONIC BOOM

(see also Spacemen 3, Spectrum)

90	Silvertone SONIC 1	Octaves/Tremeloes (10", orange vinyl PVC sleeve, mail-order only)	18
91	Silvertone SONIC 2	(I Love You) To The Moon And Back/Capo Waltz (live) (gig freebie in black die-cut sleeve, promo only, 33rpm)	12
91	Silvertone SONIC 2	(I Love You) To The Moon And Back/Capo Waltz (live) (gig freebie in black die-cut sleeve, promo only, 33rpm, p/s later available separately)	8
90	Silvertone ORE ZLP 506	SPECTRUM (LP, gatefold rotatable plastic disc sleeve with inner)	25

SONIC YOUTH

(see also Ciccone Youth, Mudhoney)

86	Blast First BFFP 3	Flower/Halloween (12", p/s, on yellow vinyl)	25
86	Blast First BFFP 3	Flower/Halloween (12", p/s, some on yellow vinyl)	15
86	Blast First BFFP 3	Flower/Rewolf (12", p/s, censored version)	25
86	Blast First BFFP 3(B)	(Savage Pencil etch)/Halloween II (12", p/s, A-side engraved, 1st 100 signed)	40
86	Blast First BFFP 3(B)	(Savage Pencil etch)/Halloween II (12", p/s, A-side engraved)	20
86	Blast First BFFP 3X	Flower/Halloween/Satan Supermix (12", unreleased)	0
86	Blast First BFFP 7	Starpower (edit)/Bubblegum (p/s, some with badge & poster)	12
86	Blast First BFFP 7	Starpower (edit)/Bubblegum (p/s, some with badge & poster)	25
88	Fierce FRIGHT 015/016	Stick Me Donna Magick Momma/Making The Nature Scene (live) (p/s, 2 x 1-sided 7" with etched B-sides)	5
88	Fierce FRIGHT 015/016	Stick Me Donna Magick Momma/Making The Nature Scene (live) (p/s, single disc reissue)	15
88	Catalogue CAT 064	Teenage Riot (square flexidisc sewn into 'The Catalogue' magazine)	15
88	Catalogue CAT 064	Teenage Riot (square flexidisc not sewn into 'The Catalogue' magazine)	8
89	Blast First BFFP 46	Touch Me I'm Sick/MUDHONEY: Halloween (12", p/s)	18
89	Blast First BFFP 48	Providence (stereo)/Providence (mono) (promo only)	5
87	Blast First BFFP 26 T	MASTER DIK (12" EP, with inner)	8
90	Geffen GEF 81	KOOL THING EP: Kool Thing/That's All I Know (p/s)	8
92	Geffen DGCV 11	100% (10" EP, orange vinyl, numbered p/s)	10
92	Geffen DGCV 11	100% (10" EP, black vinyl promo)	40
92	Geffen DGCT 11	100% (12" EP, promo only, white label)	50
92	Geffen DGCTD 11	100% (CD EP, digipak)	10
92	Geffen 7-19664 DJ	Personality Crisis/Dirty Boots (DJ promo only)	8
92	Geffen GFSV26	YOUTH AGAINST FASCISM (10" white vinyl EP, numbered p/s)	10
92	Geffen GFS 26	YOUTH AGAINST FASCISM (7", p/s)	5
92	Geffen GFST 26	YOUTH AGAINST FASCISM EP (12", p/s)	8
92	DGC DGCS 11	100%/Creme Brulee (p/s)	5
93	Geffen GFSV37	SUGAR KANE (10" blue vinyl EP, numbered p/s)	10
94	Geffen GFSV 72	Bull In The Heather/Razor Blade/Doctor's Orders (10", silver vinyl, numbered p/s)	10
83	Neutral NEUTRAL 9	CONFUSION IS SEX (LP)	20
85	Blast First BFFP 1	BAD MOON RISING (LP, with lyric insert)	25
85	NOT NOT 1/BUT 2	WALLS HAVE EARS (2-LP, 2,000 copies only, numbered)	50
86	Blast First BFFP 4	EVOL (LP)	20
87	Blast First CHAT 1	SISTER INTERVIEW DISC (LP)	18
87	Blast First BFFP 20	SISTER (LP)	20
88	Blast First BFFP 34	DAYDREAM NATION (2-LP, 1st 1,000 with signed poster)	30
88	Blast First BFFP 34	DAYDREAM NATION (2-LP)	20
90	WEA 7599 24297-1	GOO (LP)	15
92	Geffen GEF24485[2]	DIRTY (2-LP)	15
94	Geffen GEF 24632	EXPERIMENTAL JET SET, TRASH & NO STAR (LP, blue vinyl)	20
95	Geffen GEF24825	WASHING MACHINE (2-LP)	20

SONNY

71	Ackee ACK 127	Love And Peace/LARRY & ALVIN: Throw Me Corn	10

SONNY (& SONNY'S GROUP)

(see also Sonny & Cher)

65	Atlantic AT 4038	Laugh At Me/Tony (as Sonny & Sonny's Group)	8
65	Atlantic AT 4060	The Revolution Kind/Georgia And John Quetzal (as Sonny & Sonny's Group)	10
67	Atlantic 584 131	I Told My Love To Go Away/Misty Roses (solo)	5

SONNY & CHER

(see also Caesar & Cleo, Cher, Sonny, Date With Soul)

64	Reprise R 20309	Baby Don't Go/Walkin' The Quetzal	8
65	Atlantic AT 4035	I Got You Babe/It's Gonna Rain	5
65	Atlantic AT 4047	But You're Mine/Hello	7
65	Vocalion VL 9247	The Letter/Spring Fever (B-side by 'Sonny & Cher (Instrumental)')	15
66	Atlantic AT 4069	What Now My Love/I Look For You	7
66	Atlantic 584 018	Have I Stayed Too Long/Leave Me Be	5
66	Atlantic 584 040	Little Man/Monday	6

MINT VALUE £

66	Atlantic 584 057	Living For You/Turn Around	5
67	Atlantic 584 078	The Beat Goes On/Love Don't Come	5
67	Atlantic 584 110	Podunk/Beautiful Story	7
67	Atlantic 584 129	It's The Little Things/Plastic Man	7
68	Atlantic 584 162	Good Combination/You And Me	12
68	Atlantic 584 168	Circus/SONNY BONO: I Would Marry You Today	8
68	Atlantic 584 215	You Gotta Have A Thing Of Your Own/I Got You Babe	8
65	Reprise R 30056	CAESAR AND CLEO (EP, 2 tracks each by Sonny & Cher, Caesar & Cleo)	25
64	Atlantic ATL 5036	LOOK AT US (LP, mono)	12
64	Atlantic STL 5036	LOOK AT US (LP, stereo)	15
66	Atlantic 587 006	THE WONDROUS WORLD OF SONNY AND CHER (LP)	12
67	Atlantic 587/588 052	IN CASE YOU'RE IN LOVE (LP)	12

SONNY & DAFFODILS

63	Ember EMB EP 4538	SONNY & DAFFODILS (EP)	65

SONNY (Burke) & YVONNE

(see also Sonny Burke)

64	Island WI 134	Life Without Fun/SONNY BURKE GROUP: Mount Vesuvius	25

SON OF A BITCH

(see also Saxon)

96	Hengest SOABCDS 1	Treacherous Times/Victim You (CD, stickered jewel case)	10

SON OF A GUN

75	RCA 2526	La Maison De L'Amour/All Smoke And No Fire	7

SON OF NOISE

(see also Hardnoise)

91	Music Of Life NOTE 53	Son Of Noise/Ill Justice (12")	20
91	Kold Sweat KS 117	Master Of Menace/Milk In The Chocolate (12")	15
93	Little Rascool LR001	Crazy Mad Flow/Retrocide 93 (12")	10
92	Kold Sweat KSEP 207	NEGATIVE FORCES/THE MIGHTY SON/THE MISSION (EP)	12
92	Kold Sweat KSLP 03	THE MIGHTY SON OF NOISE (LP)	18
95	Little Rascool MZE 2711	ACCESS DENIED (LP)	12

SONS & LOVERS

67	Camp 602 002	Matters/Peaceful Is The River	6
68	Beacon 3-101	Help Me (I'm On Top Of The World)/Feel Alright	5
68	Beacon 3-107	Happiness Is Love/Things You Do	5
68	Beacon BEA116	From Now On The Sunshine/How Could We Ever Get This Way	12

SONS OF ALBATROSS

75	Decca FR 13605	Africa/Ha-ri-ah	35

SONS OF CAIN

80	Loppylugs LOPPY 1	Endo Of Something/Kennedy Waltz (p/s)	10

SONS OF DEMENTED CHILDREN

87	Hatter MAD 003	Spoof Dealer/Busking (p/s, with insert)	18

SONS OF FRED

(see also Odyssey)

65	Columbia DB 7605	Sweet Love/I'll Be There	200
65	Parlophone R 5391	I, I, I (Want Your Lovin')/She Only Wants A Friend	80
66	Parlophone R 5415	Baby What Do You Want Me To Do/You Told Me	200

SONS OF JAH

75	Bullet BU 557	Nyah Chant/Rasta Waltz	20

SONS OF JAH

(see also Aubrey Small)

79	Natty Congo PFULP 3502	BURNING BLACK (LP)	25
82	Natty Congo NCLP 001	UNIVERSAL MESSAGE (LP)	15

SONS OF MAN

67	Oak RGJ 612	SONS OF MAN (EP, no p/s)	400

SONS OF MOSES

75	MCA MCA 169	Soul Symphony/Fatback	8

SONS OF NUBIA

90	White SON1	RAPS THE LAST MEANS (EP, 10-20 copies exist due to a pressing fault)	150

SONS OF PILTDOWN MEN

63	Pye International 7N 25206	Mad Goose/Be A Party	20

SONS OF PIONEERS

54	HMV 7EG 8069	SONS OF THE PIONEERS (EP)	10
57	RCA RD 27016	FAVOURITE COWBOY SONGS (LP)	15

SONS OF SOUL

66	Doctor Bird DB 1037	Yeah Yeah Baby/So Ashamed	20

SONSONG

76	Zebra ZM 5761	SONSONG (LP)	30

SOPHISTICATES

60s	Spectrum SPEEP 701	AT THE WOODVILLE (EP)	15

SOPHOMORES

60s	Seeco CELP 451	THE SOPHOMORES (LP)	30

SORE THROAT

88	Meantime COX	UNHINDERED BY TALENT (LP)	15
89	Manic Ears ACHE	INDESTROY (LP, with lyric poster)	20
89	Earache MOSH 10	DISGRACE TO THE CORPSE OF SID (LP)	15
80s	Manic Ears ACHE	NEVER MIND THE NAPALM HERE'S SORE THROAT (LP)	20

MINT VALUE £

SORROWS
(see also Don Fardon)

65	Piccadilly 7N 35219	I Don't Wanna Be Free/Come With Me	35
65	Piccadilly 7N 35230	Baby/Teenage Letter	40
65	Piccadilly 7N 35260	Take A Heart/We Should Get Along Fine	25
66	Piccadilly 7N 35277	You've Got What I Want/No, No, No, No (export p/s)	35
66	Piccadilly 7N 35277	You've Got What I Want/No, No, No, No	20
66	Piccadilly 7N 35309	Let The Live Live/Don't Sing No Sad Songs For Me	40
66	Piccadilly 7N 35336	Let Me In/How Love Used To Be	40
67	Piccadilly 7N 35385	Pink, Purple, Yellow And Red/My Gal	100
66	Piccadilly N(S)PL 38023	TAKE A HEART (LP, mono)	160
66	Piccadilly N(S)PL 38023	TAKE A HEART (LP, stereo)	225

SORT SOL

81	4AD AD 101	Marble Station/Misguided (p/s)	8

S.O.U.L. (Sounds Of Unity & Love)

72	Pye Intl. NSPL 28162	CAN YOU FEEL IT (LP)	30

HORATIO SOUL

68	Island WI 3132	Ten White Horses/Angela (Sweet Sweet)	8
69	Crystal CR 7006	Nobody's Gonna Sleep Tonight/Turn Around Baby	6

JIMMY SOUL

62	Stateside SS 103	Twistin' Matilda/I Can't Hold Out Any Longer	10
63	Stateside SS 178	If You Wanna Be Happy/Don't Release Me	20
64	Stateside SS 274	I Hate You Baby/Change Partners	10
64	Stateside SE 1010	IF YOU WANNA BE HAPPY (EP)	50

SHARON SOUL

65	Stateside SS 411	How Can I Get To You/Don't Say Goodbye Love	100
65	Stateside SS 411	How Can I Get To You/Don't Say Goodbye Love (DJ copy)	100

SOUL AGENTS
(see also Loot, Don Shinn, Hookfoot)

64	Pye 7N 15660	I Just Wanna Make Love To You/Mean Woman Blues	45
64	Pye 7N 15707	Seventh Son/Let's Make It Pretty Baby	75
65	Pye 7N 15768	Don't Break It Up/Gospel Train	70

SOUL AGENTS (Jamaica)

67	Coxsone CS 7007	Get Ready It's Rocksteady/BOB & BELTONES: Smile Like An Angel (B-side actually by Bop & Beltones)	25
67	Coxsone CS 7018	For Your Education/SUMMERTAIRES: Tell Me	40
67	Coxsone CS 7027	Lecture/SOUL BOYS: Blood Pressure	40

SOUL BOYS
(see also Soul Agents [Jamaica])

66	Rio R120	Rudie Get Wise/JACKIE OPEL: I Don't Want Her	60
67	Island WI 3052	Blood Pressure/RITA MARLEY: Come To Me	70

SOUL BROTHERS

65	Mercury MF 916	Gotta Get A Good Thing Going/Good Lovin' Never Hurt	20
65	Decca F 12116	I Keep Ringing My Baby/I Can't Take It	18
65	Parlophone R 5321	I Can't Believe It/You Don't Want To Know	15

SOUL BROTHERS (Jamaica)
(see also Earl Van Dyke & Soul Brothers, Soul Twins, Lee Perry, Tony Gregory, Ethiopians, Itals, Hortense & Delroy, Gaylads, Jennors, Derrick Morgan, Summertaires, Delroy Wilson)

65	Ska Beat JB 226	Train To Skaville/WAILERS: I Made A Mistake	45
66	Ska Beat JB 259	Bugaloo/I'll Come Back	50
66	Rio R 118	Crawfish/RITA MARLEY: You Lied	30
66	Rio R 121	Mr T.N.T./MARCIA GRIFFITHS: Mr Everything	50
66	Island WI 282	Green Moon/E Gal OK	20
66	Island WI 294	Ska-Bostello/DON DRUMMOND: Looking Through The Window	25
66	Island WI 296	Sound One/MARTINE: Grandfather's Clock (B-side actually by Emille Straker & Merrymen or Martinis)	20
66	Island WI 3013	More & More/DELROY WILSON: Dancing Mood	30
66	Island WI 3016	Mr Flint/Too Young To Love (B-side actually by Freddie McGregor)	30
67	Island WI 3036	Sound Pressure/ETHIOPIANS: For You	30
67	Island WI 3039	Hi-Life/DELROY WILSON: Close To Me	20
67	Coxsone CS 7001	Take Ten/HUGH GODFREY: Deh Pon Dem	100
67	Coxsone CS 7020	Hey Windell/KEN BOOTHE: Home Home Home	60
67	Coxsone CS 7024	One Stop/TENNORS: Pressure And Slide	20
67	Studio One SO 2006	Hot And Cold/TERMITES: Mercy Mr. Percy	80
67	Island WI 3038	Cherry/SOUL JUNIOR : Out Of My Mind (Some list Bumps Oakley as the B-side)	60
67	Studio One SO 2016	Honeypot/VICEROYS: Lose And Gain	50
70	Pressure Beat PR 5506	Pussy Catch A Fire (actually by Soul Twins)/DESTROYERS: Follow This Beat (B-side actually "Secret Weapon" by Ansell Collins)	15
67	Coxsone CSL 8001	HOT SHOT SKA (LP)	200
67	Coxsone CSL 8002	CARIB SOUL (LP)	120

SOUL BROTHERS SIX

67	Atlantic 584 118	Some Kind Of Wonderful/I'll Be Loving You	60
69	Atlantic 584 256	Some Kind Of Wonderful/Somebody Else Is Loving My Baby	10
72	Atlantic K 10204	Some Kind Of Wonderful/Check Yourself	6

SOUL CATS

69	Camel CA 23	Keep It Moving/Your Sweet Love	10
69	Gas GAS 109	Choo Choo Train/The Load (actually "Swinging For Joy" by Count Ossie Band)	10
71	Hillcrest HCT 2	Reggay Got Soul (actually by Carl Bryan)/Land Of Love	8
70s	Junior JR 103	Reggay Got Soul (actually by Carl Bryan)/Land Of Love (reissue)	8

MINT VALUE £

SOUL CITY

62	Cameo Parkway P 103	Everybody Dance Now/Who Knows	75
62	Cameo Parkway P 103	Everybody Dance Now/Who Knows (DJ copy)	125

SOUL CITY EXECUTIVES

69	Soul City SC 109	Happy Chatter/Falling In Love	20

SOUL CLAN

(see also Solomon Burke, Arthur Conley, Don Covay, Ben E. King, Joe Tex)

68	Atlantic 584 202	Soul Meeting/That's How It Feels (in p/s)	12
68	Atlantic 584 202	Soul Meeting/That's How It Feels	8
68	Atlantic 587 127	SOUL MEETING (LP)	20

SOUL CONDOR

70	Polydor 2344002	CERTAIN LIONS & TIGERS	30

SOUL DEFENDERS

(see also Eric Donaldson, Carey Johnson)

71	Banana BA 354	Way Back Home/SOUL REBELS: Stand For Your Rights	18
72	Ackee ACK 147	Sound Almighty/COUNT OSSIE: Meditation	12

SOUL DESTROYERS

00	Stark Reality STARK008	Blow Your Top Pt. 1/Blow Your Top Pt. 2	12

SOUL DIRECTIONS

70	Attack ATT 8011	Su Su Su/Better Hearing	10

GEORGE SOULE

75	United Artists UP 35771	Get Involved/Everybody's Got A Song To Sing	8

SOULETTES

(see also Rita Marley, Ken Boothe, Roland Alphonso, Uniques)

65	Ska Beat JB 204	Opportunity/DIZZY JOHNNY & STUDIO 1 ORCHESTRA: Sudden Destruction	40
70	Upsetter US 337	Let It Be/UPSETTERS: Big Dog Bloxie	20
71	Jackpot JP 766	My Desire/Bring It Up	15
71	Jackpot JP 767	All Of Your Loving/LLOYD CLARKE: Love Me	15
73	Attack ATT 8044	This World/Same Thing	5

SOUL EXPLOSION

69	Downtown DT 455	Let's Try It Again/Gumpton Rock	6
70	J-DAN JDN 4405	My Mother's Eyes/Gum Pot	7

SOUL FLAMES

68	Nu Beat NB 020	Mini Really Fit Dem/Soul Train	9

SOULFUL STRINGS

67	Chess CRS 8068	Burning Spear/Within You, Without You	30
67	Chess CRS 8068	Burning Spear/Within You, Without You (DJ Copy)	50
69	Chess CRS 8094	I Wish It Would Rain/Listen Here	10
69	Chess CRLS 4534	GROOVIN' WITH THE SOULFUL STRINGS (LP)	20

SOUL GENERATION

79	Grapevine GRP 131	Hold On/The Lonely Sea	8
73	Sticky SBL 135	BEYOND BODY AND SOUL (LP)	25

SOUL KINGS

69	Blue Cat BS 169	The Magnificent Seven/RUPIE EDWARDS: Long Lost Love	40

SOUL LEADERS

67	Rio R 134	Pour On The Sauce/Beauty Is Only Skin Deep	25

SOULMATES (Jamaica)

69	Amalgamated AMG 836	Them A Laugh And A Ki Ki/The Hippys Are Here (B-side actually by Hippy Boys)	60
69	Amalgamated AMG 842	On The Move/Jump It Up (B-side actually by Viceroys)	70
69	Camel CA 33	Beware Of Bad Dogs/Short Cut (actually by Glen Adams)	50
70	Unity UN 555	Ten Cent/DOREEN SHAFFER: Stay With Me Forever	10

SOULMATES (U.K.)

(see also Liza Strike)

65	Parlophone R 5334	Too Late To Say You're Sorry/Your Love	90
66	Parlophone R 5407	Bring Your Love Back Home (with Jet Set)/When Love Is Gone	15
66	Parlophone R 5506	Mood Melancholy/Sayin' Something	10
67	Parlophone R 5601	Is That You?/Time's Run Out	10

SOUL MERCHANTS

67	President PT 166	Whole Lot Of Lovin'/Stormy Weather	7

SOUL ON DELIVERY

75	Decca F13601	Hustle/Crescent Boogie	8

SOUL PARTNERS

69	Pama PM 766	Walk On Judge/Lose The One You Love	20

SOUL PEOPLE

68	Island WIP 6040	Hummin'/Soul Drink	20

SOUL PROPRIETORS

65	Concord CON STD 74	All/Lonely Separation (private pressing)	300

SOUL REBELS

(see also Soul Defenders)

72	Banana BA 374	Listen And Observe/What's Love	45
72	Count Shelley CS 001	Judgement Day Is Near/Solid As A Rock	10
72	Count Shelley CS 003	I'm The One Who Loves You/I ROY: War Zone	10

SOUL RHYTHMS

(see also Hippy Boys, Max Romeo)

69	Bullet BU 404	Work Boy Work/CECIL THOMAS: Girl Lonesome Fever	15
69	High Note HS 013	National Lottery/Round Seven	12
69	Gas GAS 113	Soul Call/Musical Gate	10

MINT VALUE £

SOUL RUNNERS
67 Polydor 56732 Grits 'n' Cornbread/Spreading Honey 15

SOUL SEARCHERS
74 Sussex SXX 2 Blow Your Whistle (Parts 1 & 2) 6
74 Sussex LPSX 4 SALT OF THE EARTH (LP) 25

SOUL SISTERS (Jamaica)
(see also Dennis Brown)
69 Amalgamated AMG 839 Wreck A Buddy/VERSATILES: Push It In 25

SOUL SISTERS (U.S.)
64 Sue WI 312 I Can't Stand It/Blueberry Hill 40
64 Sue WI 336 Loop De Loop/Long Gone 50
65 London HLC 9970 Foolish Dreamer/Good Time Tonight 60
65 London HLC 9970 Foolish Dreamer/Good Time Tonight (DJ copy) 100
72 United Artists UP 35388 Good Time Tonight/Some Soul Food 10
64 Sue ILP 913 THE SOUL SISTERS (LP) 150

SOUL SOUNDS
(see also Savages, Rebel Rousers)
67 Columbia S(C)X 6158 SOUL SURVIVAL (LP) 30

SOUL STIRRERS
(see also Sam Cooke)
69 Duke DU 25 Come See About Me/LLOYD CHARMERS: 5 To 5 15

SOUL SURVIVORS
67 Stateside SS 2057 Expressway To Your Heart/Hey Gyp 28
68 Stateside SS 2094 Explosion (In Your Soul)/Dathon's Theme 18
69 Atlantic 584 275 Mama Soul/Tell Daddy 30

SOUL SYNDICATE
(see also Rockin' Horse)
72 Green Door GD 4021 Riot (actually by Johnny Moore & Soul Syndicate)/ Smoke Without Fire (actually by Keith Hudson) 25

SOUL TONES
70 Pama PM 790 Dancing Time/BUNNY BARRETT: Love Locked Out 15

SOUL TOPS
67 Fab FAB 27 Baby I Got News/TEDDY KING & BUSTER'S ALL STARS: Mexican Divorce 20
68 Nu Beat NB002 Rain And Thunder/Swing Baby 20

SOUL TWINS (Jamaica)
70 High Note HS 043 Little Suzie/Cherrie 8
72 Clandisc CLA 238 Don't Call Me Nigga/DYNAMITES: Joe Louis 6

SOUL TWINS (U.S.)
77 Grapevine GRP 101 Quick Change Artist/Give The Man A Chance 8

SOUL VENDORS
(see also Dobby Dobson)
67 Coxsone CS 7028 You Troubled Me/BOP & BELTONES: Love 25
67 Coxsone CS 7029 Fat Fish/MARCIA GRIFFITHS: Call To Me 100
67 Studio One SO 2018 Rocking Sweet Pea/JOE HIGGS: Change Of Plans 45
67 Studio One SO 2022 Cool Shade/RICHARD ACE: I Need You 100
67 Studio One SO 2028 Just A Little Bit Of Soul/ALTON ELLIS: I Am Just A Guy 40
67 Studio One SO 2031 Take Me/DELROY WILSON: I'm Not A King 50
67 Studio One SO 2032 Pe Da Pa/ERNEST WILSON: Money Worries 40
67 Studio One SO 2034 Hot Rod/GAYLADS: Africa (We Want To Go) 100
67 Studio One SO 2035 Pupa Lick/ETHIOPIANS: Leave My Business Alone 40
68 Studio One SO 2038 Psychedelic Rock/GAYLADS: I'm Free 100
68 Studio One SO 2043 Chinese Chicken/JACKIE MITTOO: Put It On 25
68 Studio One SO 2044 Happy Ogan (actually titled "Happy Organ")/INVADERS: Soulful Music 100
68 Studio One SO 2048 Evening Time/RIGHTEOUS FLAMES: Ease Up 35
68 Studio One SO 2058 Frozen Soul/ERNEST WILSON: If I Were A Carpenter 40
68 Studio One SO 2066 Soul Joint/Soul Limbo 45
68 Studio One SO 2070 Captain Cojoe/JACKIE MITTOO: Drum Song 50
68 Coxsone CS 7037 Grooving Steady/ROY RICHARDS: Warm And Tender Ska 80
68 Coxsone CS 7038 Whipping The Prince (actually by Ed Hangle & Alton Ellis)/ HEPTONES: If You Knew 30
68 Coxsone CS 7048 Last Waltz/HAMLINS: Sentimental Reasons 120
68 Coxsone CS 7057 Real Rock/AL CAMPBELL: Don't Run Away 90
68 Coxsone CS 7071 West Of The Sun/ALTON ELLIS: A Fool 50
69 Coxsone CS 7084 Sixth Figure/DENZIL LAING: Man Payaba 50
67 Coxsone CSL 8010 ON TOUR (LP) 300

SOUND
(see also Outsiders, Second Layer)
80 Korova KOW 10 Heyday/Brute Force (p/s) 5
81 Korova KOW 21 Sense Of Purpose/Point Of No Return (p/s) 5
79 Tortch TOR 003 PHYSICAL WORLD (EP) 18
80 Korova KODE 2 JEOPARDY (LP, with inner) 12
85 Statik STAB 1 SHOCK OF DAYLIGHT (mini-LP) 12

SOUND BARRIER
68 Beacon BEA 109 She Always Comes Back To Me/Groovin' Slow 60

SOUND CEREMONY
89 Celestial Sound SRT 8KF You're Breaking My Heart (p/s) 10
79 Celestial Sound RWG 001 GUITAR STAR (LP) 20
79 Celestial Sound RWG 002 RON WARREN GANDERTON & SOUND CEREMONY (LP) 40
81 Celestial Sound RWG 003 PRECIOUS AS ENGLAND (LP) 20

MINT VALUE £

SOUND DIMENSION

(see also Brentford Road Allstars, Jackie Mittoo, Bob Andy, Horace Andy, John Holt, Larry Marshall, Irving Brown, Heptones, Freedom Singers, Winston Francis, Jerry Jones, Ethiopians, Cables, Alton Ellis, Gladiators, Ken Boothe, Soul Vendors)

69	Coxsone CS 7083	Scorcia/CECIL & JACKIE: Breaking Up (B-side actually "Hold Me Baby" by Basil Daley)	30
69	Coxsone CS 7085	Soul Trombone (Suffering Stink)/LARRY & ALVIN: Your Cheating Heart	30
69	Coxsone CS 7090	Soulful Strut/Breaking Up	120
69	Coxsone CS 7093	More Scorcha/LENNIE HIBBERT: Village Soul	40
69	Coxsone CS 7097	Time Is Tight/BARRY LLEWELLYN: Sad Song	40
69	Bamboo BAM 5	Doctor Sappa Too/Soul Eruption (B-side actually by Roy Richards & Sound Dimension)	40
69	Bamboo BAM 7	Baby Face/GLADIATORS: Anywhere	30
69	Bamboo BAM 9	Jamaica Rag/C. MARSHALL: I Need Your Loving	25
69	Bamboo BAM 13	Whoopee/NORMA FRAZER: Working (B-side actually by Marcia Griffiths)	25
69	Bamboo BAM 14	Black Onion/Bitter Blood	35
70	Bamboo BAM 18	Poison Ivy/Botheration - Version	20
70	Bamboo BAM 50	Soul Food/BURNING SPEAR: Door Peeper	50
70	Banana BA 313	In The Summertime/In The Summertime - Version	35
70	Banana BA 338	My Sweet Lord (Instrumental)/DENNIS BROWN: Silky (B-side actually by Monty Alexander & Cyclones)	15
70	Supreme SUP 202	More Games/MR. FOUNDATION: Maga Dog (actually by Invaders)	30
72	Ackee ACK 149	Solas/GLADIATORS: Sonia	15

SOUNDGARDEN

90	A&M AMX 560	Hands All Over/Come Together/Heretic/Big Dumb Sex (10", foldout pack)	8
90	A&M AMY 574	Loud Love/Big Dumb Sex/Get On The Snake/Fresh Deadly Roses (12", etched, stickered p/s)	8
92	A&M AMY 102	Outshined/I Can't Give You Anything/Homicidal Suicidal (12", p/s, limited ed.)	8
92	A&M AMY 723	Rusty Cage/Touch Me/Show Me (12", poster p/s, 5000 only)	12
96	A&M 5818457	Burden In My Hand/Karaoke (p/s, white vinyl, numbered, 5000 only)	15
94	A&M 540215-1	SUPERUNKNOWN (2 x LP, clear or blue vinyl, stickered, 2 lyric sheets)	18

SOUND IRATION

90s	Mystic Red Corp MRC 8888	Seventh Seal/Dub Seal (12")	30
89	Wau Mr. Modo MOWLP 001	IN DUB (LP)	35

SOUND NETWORK

65	Mercury MF 944	Watching/How About Now	25

SOUND OF JIMMY NICOL

(see also Jimmy Nicol)

65	Decca F 12107	Clementine/Bim Bam	25

SOUND OF SHA'BASS

91	Guerilla GRRR16	Take It Or Leave It (12")	10

SOUNDPROOF

71	Look LKSP511-301	Friday Every Friday/Lonely Boy Lonely Girl	100

SOUNDS AROUND

(see also Peter & Wolves, John Pantry, Norman Conquest, Factory)

66	Piccadilly 7N 35345	What Does She Do?/Sad Subject	25
67	Piccadilly 7N 35396	Red White And You/One Of Two	25

SOUNDS COMBINE

71	Escort ERT 862	African Museum/African Museum - Version	8

SOUNDS GALACTIC

70	Phase 4 Stereo PFS 4208	AN ASTROMUSICAL ODYSSEY (LP)	12

SOUNDS INCORPORATED

(see also Jeff Beck, May Blitz, Boxer, Tony Newman)

61	Parlophone R 4815	Mogambo/Emily	15
62	Decca F 11540	Sounds Like Locomotion/Taboo	8
63	Decca F 11590	Stop/Go	10
63	Decca F 11723	Order Of The Keys/Keep Moving	25
64	Columbia DB 7239	The Spartans/Detroit	7
64	Columbia DB 7321	Spanish Harlem/Rinky Dink	10
64	Columbia DB 7404	William Tell/Bullets	7
65	Columbia DB 7545	Time For You/Hall Of The Mountain King	7
65	Columbia DB 7676	My Little Red Book/Justice Neddi	10
65	Columbia DB 7737	On The Brink/I'm Comin' Thru	40
67	Polydor 56209	How Do You Feel/Dead As You Go	15
69	Decca 22883	Warmth Of The Sun/Apollo (export)	10
64	Columbia SEG 8360	TOP GEAR (EP)	25
64	Columbia 33SX 1659	SOUNDS INCORPORATED (LP, mono)	25
64	Columbia SCX 3531	SOUNDS INCORPORATED (LP, stereo)	30
65	EMI Regal SREG 1071	RINKY DINK (LP, export issue)	20
66	Studio Two TWO 144	SOUNDS INCORPORATED (LP)	20

SOUNDS NICE

(see also Third Ear Band, Chris Spedding, Clem Cattini Ork)

69	Parlophone R 5797	Love At First Sight/Love You Too ('featuring Tim Mycroft')	8
69	Parlophone R 5821	Sleepless Night/Continental Exchange ('featuring Tim Mycroft')	6
69	Parlophone PMC/PCS 7089	LOVE AT FIRST SIGHT (LP)	25

SOUNDS OF BOB ROGERS

67	CBS 3018	Among My Souveneirs/Dream With Me	20

SOUNDS OF JOHNNY HAWKSWORTH

(see also Johnny Hawksworth)

66	Columbia DB 8059	Goal/"Goal - World Cup 1966" Theme	15

Year	Label / Cat. No.	Title	MINT VALUE £
SOUNDS OF LES AND BARRY			
65	Fontana TF 657	Looie Girl/She Who Needs Me.	6
SOUNDS OF MODIFICATION			
68	Stateside SL/SSL 10262	SOUNDS OF MODIFICATION (LP)	20
SOUNDS OF REFLECTION			
68	Reflection RS6001SM	Brave New Day/Lord Of Believe (p/s)	50
SOUNDS OF SALVATION			
(see also Reflection)			
74	Reflection RL 310	SOUNDS OF SALVATION (LP, with booklet)	90
SOUNDS ORCHESTRAL			
66	Piccadilly 7N 35284	Thunderball/Mr Kiss Kiss Bang Bang	10
65	Pye NPL 38016	THUNDERBALL - SOUNDS ORCHESTRAL MEET JAMES BOND (LP, in gatefold sleeve)	20
65	Pye NPL 38016	THUNDERBALL - SOUNDS ORCHESTRAL MEET JAMES BOND (LP)	30
SOUNDS PROGRESSIVE			
70	Eyemark EMCL 1009S	KID JENSEN INTRODUCES SOUNDS PROGRESSIVE (LP)	40
SOUNDS SENSATIONAL			
67	HMV POP 1584	Love In The Open Air/Night Cry	18
SOUND SCIENCE			
91	Sound Entity SE 0002	HERT'Z SO GOOD EP (12")	15
91	Sound Entity SE 0002	HERT'Z SO GOOD EP (12")	15
SOUND SIXTY-SIX			
66	Decca F 12323	Flight 4864/The Bouncer	12
SOUND STAGE ORCHESTRA			
76	BBC RESL 30	Grandstand/Rugby Special	8
SOUND SYSTEM			
(see also Owen Gray)			
65	Island WI 258	You Don't Know Like I Do/Take Me Serious	15
EPIC SOUNDTRACKS			
(see also Swell Maps, Thurston Moore Kim Gordon & Epic Soundtracks)			
81	Rough Trade RT 084	Popular, Classical: Jelly Babies/A 3-Acre Floor/Pop In Packets (p/s)	5
SOUND VISION			
70s	Key KL 007	IN CONCERT (LP, featuring Judy MacKenzie)	25
SOUP DRAGONS			
(see also BMX Bandits, Future PIlot A.K.A.)			
86	Popshop 001/ Lyntone LYN 16674	If You Were The Only Girl In The World/LEGEND: Talk Open (33rpm flexi with Pure Popcorn fanzine)	8
86	Popshop 001/ Lyntone LYN 16674	If You Were The Only Girl In The World/LEGEND: Talk Open (33rpm flexi with The Legend fanzine)	6
86	Subway Organisation SUBWAY 4	Whole Wide World/I Know Everything (with insert in poly bag, orange or blue foldaround p/s)	5
86	Raw TV Products RTV 1	Hang Ten!/Slow Things Down (p/s, blue or red vinyl)	5
86	Raw TV Products RTV 2	Head Gone Astray/Girl In The World/So Sad I Feel (PVC sleeve, with poster)	10
86	Subway Organisation SUBWAY 2	THE SUN IS IN THE SKY (EP, unreleased, 1,000 only, foldaround p/s in poly bag)	15
90	Raw TV SOUPLP 2	LOVEGOD (LP, with foiled sleeve & lyric sheet)	12
SOUP GREENS			
65	Stateside SS 457	That's Too Bad/Like A Rolling Stone	70
SOUPHERBS			
65	Oak RGJ 601	SOUPHERBS (LP)	350
HARRY SOUTH ORCHESTRA			
75	EMI EMI 2252	The Sweeney (TV Theme) (Parts 1 & 2)	20
67	Mercury 20081 MCL	PRESENTING HARRY SOUTH (LP)	25
JOE SOUTH			
62	Oriole CB 1752	Masquerade/I'm Sorry For You	20
63	MGM MGM 1206	Same Old Song/Standing Invitation	7
65	MGM MGM 1267	Concrete Jungle/Last One To Know	7
65	HMV POP 1474	I Want To Be Somebody/Deep Inside Me	7
68	Capitol CL 15535	Birds Of A Feather/It Got Away	6
69	Capitol CL 15568	Don't Throw Your Love To The Wind/Redneck	5
69	Capitol CL 15579	Games People Play/Mirror Of Your Mind	6
69	Capitol CL 15608	Don't It Make You Want To Go Home/Heart's Desire	15
70	Capitol CL 15666	Hush/Party People	5
69	Capitol E-(S)T 108	INTROSPECT (LP)	12
70	Capitol ST 21548	WALK A MILE IN MY SHOES (LP)	12
SOUTH COAST SKA STARS			
(see also Ray Fenwick)			
80	Safari SAFE 27	South Coast Rumble/Head On (p/s)	8
JERI SOUTHERN			
54	Brunswick 05343	Remind Me/Little Boy Grown Tall	8
55	Brunswick 05367	The Man That Got Away/Speak Softly To Me	8
55	Brunswick 05490	An Occasional Man/It's D'Lovely	8
56	Brunswick 05529	Where Walks My True Love?/Don't Explain	7
57	Brunswick 05665	Fire Down Below/Smoke Gets In Your Eyes	8
57	Brunswick 05709	Scarlet Ribbons (For Her Hair)/Would I	5
57	Brunswick 05722	Bells Are Ringing/Just In Time	5
58	Brunswick 05737	I Waited So Long/The Mystery Of Love	5

MINT VALUE £

59	Capitol CL 15054	Run/Don't Look At Me That Way	5
59	Brunswick OE 9438	CARESSES (EP)	10
59	Columbia SEG 7935	RIDIN' HIGH (EP)	10
55	Brunswick LA 8699	WARM (10" LP)	20
56	Brunswick LAT 8100	THE SOUTHERN STYLE (LP)	20
57	Brunswick LAT 8209	JERI GENTLY JUMPS (LP)	20
58	Columbia 33SX 1110	SOUTHERN BREEZE (LP)	20
58	Columbia 33SX 1134	COFFEE, CIGARETTES AND MEMORIES (LP)	20
59	Columbia 33SX 1155	JERI SOUTHERN MEETS JOHNNY SMITH (LP)	20
59	Capitol T 1278	AT THE CRESCENDO (LP)	12

JOHNNY SOUTHERN & HIS WESTERN RHYTHM KINGS

57	Melodisc MEL 1413	We Will Make Love/Crazy Heart	10
57	Melodisc MEL 1434	She's Long, She's Tall/Lonesome Whistle	10

SHEILA SOUTHERN

62	HMV POP 1089	White Wedding/LittleStar/Il Nostro Amore	5

SOUTHERN COMFORT

(see also Matthews Southern Comfort)

71	Harvest HAR 5035	Willie Urricane/Berkshire Berk	10
71	Harvest HAR 5047	Morning Has Broken/Cosmic Jig	10
71	Harvest SHSP 4012	FROG CITY (LP, no EMI logo on label)	18
72	Harvest SHSP 799	SOUTHERN COMFORT (LP, gatefold, EMI logo on label)	20
72	Harvest SHSP 4021	STIR DON'T SHAKE (LP, with EMI logo on label)	18

SOUTHERN DEATH CULT

(see also Death Cult, Cult)

83	Situation 2 SIT 19	Fatman/Moya (wraparound p/s)	20

SOUTHERN SOUND

66	Columbia DB 7982	Just The Same As You/I Don't Wanna Go	400

SOUTHERN TONES

64	Jazz Collector JEN 10	WAITING FOR THE LORD (EP)	10

SOUTHLANDERS

55	Parlophone MSP 6182	Ain't That A Shame/Have You Ever Been Lonely	10
56	Parlophone MSP 6236	Hush-A-Bye Rock/The Wedding Of The Lucky Black Cat	10
57	Decca F 10946	Alone/Swedish Polka	5
57	Decca F 10958	Peanuts/I Never Dreamed	5
58	Decca F 10982	Put A Light In The Window/Penny Loafers And Bobby Socks	10
58	Decca F 11032	I Wanna Jive Tonight/Torero	15
58	Decca F 11067	The Mole In A Hole/Choo-Choo-Choo-Choo Cha-Cha-Cha (tri-centre)	15
58	Decca F 11067	The Mole In A Hole/Choo-Choo-Choo-Choo Cha-Cha-Cha (repressing with solid centre)	7
58	Decca DFE 6508	THE SOUTHLANDERS NUMBER ONE (EP)	30

SOUTHSIDE JOHNNY & THE ASBURY DUKES

77	Epic EPC 5230	Little Girl So Fine/I Ain't Got The Fever (withdrawn)	20

SOUTH SIDE MOVEMENT

73	Pye International 7N 25615	I Been Watchin' You/Have A Little Mercy	8

SOUTHWEST F.O.B.

68	Stax STAX 107	Smell Of Incense/Green Skies	20

SOUTHWIND

70	Harvest HAR 5019	Boogie Woogie Country Girl/Honky Tonkin'	5

PHIL SOUTHWOOD

61	QRS 1-462	D's Dilemma/Sister Sadie (in p/s)	20
61	QRS 1-462	D's Dilemma/Sister Sadie	12

SOVEREIGNS

66	King KG 1050	Bring Me Home Love/That's The Way Love Is	15

RED SOVINE

(see also Webb Pierce)

56	Brunswick 05513	Why Baby Why? (with Webb Pierce)/Sixteen Tons	40
56	Brunswick 05513	Why Baby Why? (with Webb Pierce)/Sixteen Tons (78)	40
75	RCA 2738	Teddy Bear/Daddy	8
62	Top Rank JKP 3015	COUNTRY MUSIC (EP)	10

SOWELL RADICS

82	SG SG 15	Wheel O' Matlida/Rub Dis Ya One Ya (12")	40

The SOWELL RADICS

81	Attack TACK 24	Caution/Bali-Hi Special (12")	40
81	Attack TACK 27	Fight Fight Fight/Aces Rock (12")	40

SOWERS WITH EILEEN GREAVES

69	Galliard GAL 4002	SEEDS (LP)	30

BOB B. SOXX & THE BLUE JEANS

(see also Darlene Love, Bobby Sheen, Blossoms, Crystals, Phil Spector)

63	London HLU 9646	Zip-A-Dee-Doo-Dah/Flip And Nitty	20
63	London HLU 9694	Why Do Lovers Break Each Other's Heart?/Dr Kaplan's Office	25
63	London HLU 9754	Not Too Young To Get Married/Annette	20
69	London HLU 10243	Zip-A-Dee-Doo-Dah/Why Do Lovers Break Each Other's Heart?	7
63	London HA-U 8121	ZIP-A-DEE-DOO-DAH (LP)	80
75	Phil Spector Intl. 2307 004	BOB B. SOXX & THE BLUE JEANS (LP)	25

CATHERINE SPAAK

65	Fontana TL 5282	NOI SIAMO I GIOVANI (LP)	15

SPACE

(see also Madeline Bell)

79	Pye NSPH 28725	JUST BLUE (LP, picture disc)	20

MINT VALUE £

SPACE

(see also J.A.M.S., KLF, Timelords, Disco 2000)

90	Space LP 1	SPACE (LP)	50
90	Space CD 1	SPACE (CD, beware of counterfeits)	40

SPACE

93	Hug HUG 1T	If It's Real/Lookin'/I'm Free (12", p/s with free 'fortune fish')	12

SPACE ART

77	Arista AHAL 8001	SPACE ART (LP)	15

SPACEMEN

59	Top Rank JAR 228	The Clouds/The Lonely Jet Pilot	12

SPACEMEN 3

(see also Sonic Boom, Spiritualized, Darkside, Spectrum)

86	Glass GLAEP 105	Walkin' With Jesus (Sound Of Confusion)/Rollercoaster/Feel So Good (12" maxi-single, p/s, with numbered insert)	70
86	Glass GLAEP 105	Walkin' With Jesus (Sound Of Confusion)/Rollercoaster/Feel So Good (12" maxi-single, p/s, without numbered insert)	60
87	Glass GLAEP 108	Transparent Radiation/Ecstasy Symphony/Transparent Radiation (Flashback)/Things'll Never Be The Same/Starship (12" maxi-single, p/s)	50
88	Glass GLASS 12054	Take Me To The Other Side/Soul 1/That's Just Fine (12", p/s)	35
88	Cheree CHEREE 5	Extract From An Evening Of Contemporary Sitar Music (flexi, p/s, with Cheree fanzine)	8
88	Fire BLAZE 29S	Revolution/Che (die-cut company sleeve)	6
88	Fire BLAZE 29T	Revolution/Che/May The Circle Be Unbroken (12")	8
88	Fire BLAZE 29CD	Revolution/Che/May The Circle Be Unbroken (3" CD)	8
89	Fire THREEBIE 3	Revolution/Suicide/Repeater/Love Intro Theme (Xtacy) (12", mail-order only, numbered p/s)	25
89	Sniffin' Rock SR 008	When Tomorrow Hits (with Sniffin' Rock magazine)	15
89	Sniffin' Rock SR 008	When Tomorrow Hits (without Sniffin' Rock magazine)	10
89	Fire BLAZE 36S	Hypnotized/Just To See You Smile (Honey Pt 2) (die-cut company sleeve)	5
89	Fire BLAZE 36T	Hypnotized/Just To See You Smile (Honey Pt 2)/The World Is Dying (12", with poster)	10
89	Fire BLAZE 36CD	Hypnotized/Just To See You Smile (Honey Pt 2)/The World Is Dying (3" CD, with adaptor, 5" case)	12
91	Fire BLAZE 41	Big City (Edit)/Drive (p/s)	5
91	Fire BLAZE 41TR	Big City (Remix)/I Love You (Remix) (12", unissued, white label promo, 50 only)	50
91	Catalogue CAT 089	I Love You//Sometimes (2 x flexis, with The Catalogue magazine)	10
86	Glass GLALP 018	SOUND OF CONFUSION (LP)	25
87	Glass GLALP 026	THE PERFECT PRESCRIPTION (LP, gold/silver or bronze/silver sleeve)	50
88	Glass GLALP 030	PERFORMANCE (LP)	30
88	Glass GLACD 030	PERFORMANCE (CD)	25
88	Fire FIRELP 16	PLAYING WITH FIRE (LP, embossed sleeve)	30
90	Fire FIRELP 16	RECURRING (LP)	25

SPACEPIMP

95	Clear CLR 415	The Pimp/Spacechace/K9 Law (12", p/s, on clear vinyl)	25
95	Clear CLR 415	The Pimp/Spacechace/K9 Law (12", p/s)	20

SPACE TURKEYS

81	Tavern Sound	Fun With A Social Worker/Disco Not Disco (p/s)	15

SPAGHETTI HEAD

(see also Clem Cattini Ork, Tornados)

75	RCA RCA 2513	Big Noise From Winnetka/Funky Axe	30

SPAGHETTI JUNCTION

(see also Hank Marvin)

72	Columbia DB 8935	Work's Nice - If You Can Get It/Step Right Up	25

SPANIELS

60	Joy JOYS 197	THE SPANIELS (LP)	20

MUGGSY SPANIER & DIXIELAND/RAGTIME BAND

(see also Sidney Bechet)

56	Tempo A 36	Tin Roof Blues/Muskrat Rumble	7

SPANISH BOYS

65	Blue Beat BB 331	I Am Alone/BUSTER'S ALL STARS: Vera Cruz	150

SPANISHTONIANS

67	Pyramid PYR 6005	Kisses/ROLAND ALPHONSO: Women Of The World	25
67	Pyramid PYR 6009	Suffer Me Not/ROLAND ALPHONSO: Guantanamera Ska	30
67	Pyramid PYR 6018	Rudie Gets Plenty/ROLAND ALPHONSO: Sock It To Me	100

SPANISHTOWN SKABEATS

65	Blue Beat BB 315	Oh My Baby (actually by Charmers)/Stop That Train	200
65	Blue Beat BB 320	King Solomon/BUSTER'S ALLSTARS: Devil's Daffodil	60

SPANKY & OUR GANG

(see also Mama & Papas)

67	Mercury MF 982	Sunday Will Never Be The Same/Distance	20
67	Mercury MF 999	Making Every Minute Count/If You Could Only Be Me	8
67	Mercury MF 1010	Lazy Day/It Ain't Necessarily Byrd Avenue	10
68	Mercury MF 1018	Sunday Mornin'/Echoes	8
68	Mercury MF 1023	Like To Get To Know You/Three Ways From Tomorrow	12
68	Mercury MF 1052	Give A Damn/The Swingin' Gate	10
69	Mercury MF 1123	And She's Mine/Leopard Skin Phone	7
76	Epic S EPC 3850	I Won't Brand You/When I Wanna	5
67	Mercury 20114 (S)MCL	SPANKY AND OUR GANG (LP)	35
68	Mercury 20121 SCML	LIKE TO GET TO KNOW YOU (LP)	30
69	Mercury 20150 SCML	ANYTHING YOU CHOOSE/WITHOUT RHYME OR REASON (LP)	30

MINT VALUE £

OTIS SPANN

(see also Fleetwood Mac, Memphis Slim, Johnny Shines, Lonnie Johnson)

64	Decca F 11972	Stirs Me Up/Keep Your Hand Out Of My Pocket	20
68	Blue Horizon 57-3142	Bloody Murder/Can't Do Me No Good	15
69	Blue Horizon 57-3155	Walkin'/Temperature Is Rising (with Fleetwood Mac)	20
64	Decca LK 4615	THE BLUES OF OTIS SPANN (LP)	70
64	Storyville SLP 157	GOOD MORNING MR. BLUES (LP)	30
64	Storyville SLP 168	PIANO BLUES (LP, with Memphis Slim)	30
65	Decca LK 4661	BLUES NOW (LP)	65
66	Stateside SL 10169	THE BLUES NEVER DIE (LP)	35
67	HMV CLP/CSD 3609	BLUES ARE WHERE IT'S AT (LP)	35
67	Storyville 670 157	PORTRAITS IN BLUES VOL. 3 (LP, reissue of SLP 157)	15
67	Polydor 545 030	NOBODY KNOWS MY TROUBLES (LP)	35
67	Bounty BY 6037	NOBODY KNOWS MY TROUBLES (LP)	40
68	Stateside (S)SL 10255	BOTTOM OF THE BLUES (LP)	40
69	Chess CRLS 4556	FATHERS AND SONS (LP)	40
69	Blue Horizon 7-63217	BIGGEST THING SINCE COLOSSUS (LP, with Fleetwood Mac)	90
69	Deram DML/SML 1036	CRACKED SPANNER HEAD (LP)	45
69	Python KM 4	RAISED IN MISSISSIPPI (LP, 99 copies only, with Robert Jnr. Lockwood)	90
70	Vanguard VSD 6514	CRYIN' TIME (LP)	20

SPANNER THRU MA BEATBOX

87	Earthly Delights EARTH 3	SPANNER THRU MA BEATBOX (LP)	15

77 Spark SRL 1157

SPARKERS

(see also Samuel Edwards)

69	Blue Cat BS 155	Dig It Up/DELROY WILSON: This Life Makes Me Wonder	60

LOU SPARKES

69	Gayfeet GS 203	By The Time I Get To Phoenix/Lover Boy	8
70	Gayfeet GS 208	We Will Make Love/ROLAND ALPHONSO: Sticker	8

KRISTINE SPARKLE

74	Decca F 13485	Hokey Cokey/Baby I Love You	6

SPARKS

(see also Adrian Musey, Trevor White)

72	Bearsville K 15505	Wonder Girl/(No More) Mr. Nice Guy	15
74	Bearsville K 15516	Girl From Germany/Beaver O'Lindy (brown or white label)	10
74	Island WIP 6211	Never Turn Your Back On Mother Earth/Alabamy Right (p/s)	6
75	Island WIP 6221	Something For The Girl With Everything/Marry Me (title sleeve)	6
75	Island WIP 6236	Get In The Swing/Profile (title sleeve)	6
75	Island WIP 6239	Looks, Looks, Looks/Pineapple (title sleeve)	6
75	Island WIP 6249	Looks, Looks, Looks/Pineapple (DJ copy in promo p/s)	12
76	Island WIP 6282	I Want To Hold Your Hand/England (withdrawn after 1 day)	20
76	Island WIP 6357	I Like Girls/England	5
77	Island WIP 6282	I Want To Hold Your Hand/Under The Table With Her (promo only)	20
77	Island WIP 6193	This Town Ain't Big Enough For The Both Of Us/ Barbecutie (reissue, orange sunset label)	20
79	Virgin VS 244	The No. 1 Song In Heaven/The No. 1 Song In Heaven (Version) (p/s, green vinyl)	5
79	Virgin VS 244-12	The No. 1 Song In Heaven/The No. 1 Song In Heaven (Long Version) (12", p/s, blue or red vinyl)	8
79	Virgin VS 270-12	Beat The Clock/Beat The Clock (Long Version) (12", black, blue, orange, yellow or pink vinyl, picture disc label, die-cut p/s)	8
79	Virgin VS 289-12	Tryouts For The Human Race/Tryouts For The Human Race (Long Version) (12", die-cut p/s, orange, yellow, blue or green vinyl, picture disc label)	8
79	Island WIP 6532	This Town Ain't Big Enough For The Both Of Us/Looks, Looks, Looks	7
80	Virgin VS 343-12	Young Girls (Disco Version)/Young Girls (Long Version)/ Just Because You Love Me (12", p/s)	8
81	Why Fi WHYT 1	Tips For Teens/Don't Shoot Me (12", p/s)	8
83	Atlantic A 9866	Cool Places/Sports (no p/s)	5
85	London LONX 69	Change/This Town Ain't Big Enough For Both Of Us (Acoustic Version) (12", p/s)	8
85	Epic A 6671	Armies Of The Night/EVELYN KING: Give It Up (p/s)	5
85	Epic TA 6671	Armies Of The Night/EVELYN KING: Give It Up (12", p/s)	10
86	Consolidated TOON T2	Music That You Can Dance To (UK Extended Club Version)/Fingertips (Extended Club Version) (12", p/s)	8
87	Consolidated TOON T4	Rosebud (Extended Club Mix)/Theme For Rosebud (Cinematic Mix)/ Rosebud (FM Mix) (12", p/s)	8
88	Carrere CART 427	So Important (Extremely Important Mix)/(Incredibly Important Mix)/ (Single Version) (12", p/s)	8
93	Finiflex FF 1004	National Crime Awareness Week (13 Minutes In Heaven)/ National Crime Awareness Week (Perkins Playtime) (12", p/s)	20
93	Finiflex FFCD 1004	National Crime Awareness Week (Psycho Cut)/National Crime Awareness Week (Highly Strung Hoedown)/National Crime Awareness Week (Complete Psycho)/ National Crime Awareness Week (13 Minutes In Heaven) (CD)	20
94	Logic 7432 134461	When Do I Get To Sing My Way/(mixes) (12", double-pack, p/s)	12
94	Logic 74321 24302-2	Excerpts From Gratuitous Sax & Senseless Violins (CD, picture disc, gatefold card p/s, promo only)	20
97	Roadrunner RR 2262-6	The No. 1 Song In Heaven (Tin Tin Out Mix)/part 2/(Heavenly Dub) (with Jimmy Somerville) (12", die-cut sleeve)	8
99	Winney CD IFPI LAE 1	The Cute Candidate/This Town Ain't Big Enough For The Both Of Us (1920 Archival Recording)/The Winney Empire/The Cute Candidate On TV/ The Race For President (CD, fan club only issue)	8
00	Recognition CDREC 14	The Calm Before The Storm (Radio Edit)/The Calm Before The Storm/ It's Educational (CD, unreleased)	12
73	Bearsville K 45510	A WOOFER IN TWEETERS CLOTHING (LP)	18

MINT VALUE £

Year	Label/Cat. No.	Title	Value
76	Bearsville K 85505	TWO ORIGINALS OF SPARKS (2-LP, gatefold sleeve with 12-page booklet)	18
79	Virgin V 2115	NO. 1 IN HEAVEN (LP, yellow vinyl with lyric inner sleeve)	12
04	Universal LBRV001	LIL' BEETHOVEN (LP)	15

L. SPARKS

(see also Lloyd Parks, Termites)

Year	Label/Cat. No.	Title	Value
72	Big Shot BI 601	You Don't Care/TONY'S ALL STARS: Must Care (Version)	6
72	Pama PM 833	You Don't Care/TONY'S ALL STARS: Must Care (Version)	6

SPARKY

Year	Label/Cat. No.	Title	Value
72	UK UK 13	(Do You Remember) That Summertime Woman/You Gotta Have It Sometime	8

SPARKY AND THE INNER CITIZENS

Year	Label/Cat. No.	Title	Value
76	Contempo CS2102	Golden Gate Get Down (Short version)/ Golden Gate Get Down (Long Version)	10

CANDY SPARLING

Year	Label/Cat. No.	Title	Value
62	Piccadilly 7N 35046	When's He Gonna Kiss Me?/Lonely For You	15
63	Piccadilly 7N 35096	Can You Keep A Secret/Charm Bracelet	12

SPARROW (Jamaica)

(see also Mighty Sparrow, King Sparrow)

Year	Label/Cat. No.	Title	Value
60	Kalypso XX 10	Carnival Boycott/Gloria (with Lord Melody)	6
60	Kalypso XX 17	The Sack/Round And Around	5
60s	Melodisc CAL 15	Leading Calypsonians/Love Is Everywhere	6
60s	Melodisc CAL 17	Clara Honey Bunch/Family Sized Cokes	5
60s	Melodisc CAL 18	Goaty/I Confess	5

SPARROW (U.S.)

(see also Steppenwolf)

Year	Label/Cat. No.	Title	Value
66	CBS 202342	Tomorrow's Ship/Isn't It Strange	75

JACK SPARROW

Year	Label/Cat. No.	Title	Value
66	Doctor Bird DB 1005	Ice Water/ROLAND ALPHONSO: Ska-Culation	150
66	Doctor Bird DB 1027	More Ice Water/ROLAND ALPHONSO: Miss Ska-Culation	60

SPARTA

(see also Ethiopians)

Year	Label/Cat. No.	Title	Value
80	Suspect SUS 1	Fast Lane/Fighting To Be Free (in p/s)	50
80	Suspect SUS 1	Fast Lane/Fighting To Be Free	18
81	Suspect SUS 2	Angel Of Death/Tonight (wraparound p/s)	20

SPARTANS

Year	Label/Cat. No.	Title	Value
62	Stateside SS 117	Can You Waddle? (Parts 1 & 2)	12

SPARTAN WARRIOR

Year	Label/Cat. No.	Title	Value
83	Guardian GRC 2164	STEEL 'N' CHAINS (LP)	20

SPAZZTIC BLUR

Year	Label/Cat. No.	Title	Value
87	Earache MOSH 5	BEFO DA AWBUM (LP)	15

ROGER RUSKIN SPEAR

(see also Bonzo Dog Doo-Dah Band, Topo D. Bill)

Year	Label/Cat. No.	Title	Value
74	United Artists UP 35683	On Her Doorstep Last Night/Frank The Ripper	10
74	United Artists UP 35721	I Love To Bumpity Bump/ When Yuba Plays The Rhumba On The Tuba Down In Cuba	20
71	United Artists UP 35221	REBEL TROUSER: Trouser Freak/Trouser Press/Release Me/Drop Out (EP)	12
72	United Artists UAG 29381	ELECTRIC SHOCKS (LP)	25
74	United Artists UAS 29508	UNUSUAL (LP)	20

SPECIAL DUTIES

Year	Label/Cat. No.	Title	Value
81	Charnel H. SARCOPHAGI 2	Violent Society/Colchester Council (wraparound p/s)	30
82	Rondelet ROUND 15	VIOLENT SOCIETY (EP)	15
82	Rondelet ROUND 20	POLICE STATE (EP)	10
82	Rondelet ROUND 24	Bullshit Crass/You're Doing Yourself No Good (p/s)	10
83	Expulsion OUT 1	Punk Rocker/Too Much Talking (p/s)	12
82	Rondelet ABOUT 9	77 IN 82 (LP)	20

SPECIALS (THE SPECIAL A.K.A.)

(see also Colourfield, Selecter, Rhoda, Rico)o

Year	Label/Cat. No.	Title	Value
91	Two Tone CHSTT 12 30	Ghost Town/Ghost Dub '91 (12", p/s)	30
79	2-Tone TT 1/TT 2	Gangsters (as The Special A.K.A.)/THE SELECTER: The Selecter (paper label, in stamped plain white sleeve; matrix numbers TT1-3 & TT2-1)	45
79	2-Tone TT 1/TT 2	Gangsters (as The Special A.K.A.)/THE SELECTER: The Selecter (paper label)	15
79	2-Tone TT 1/TT 2	Gangsters (as The Special A.K.A.)/THE SELECTER: The Selecter (paper label, die-cut 2-Tone sleeve, 2nd issue with Chrysalis CHS TT 1/2 matrix no.)	6
79	2-Tone CHS TT 5	Message To You Rudy/Nite Klub (paper label, company sleeve, as The Specials featuring Rico)	6
80	2-Tone CHS TT 7	THE SPECIAL A.K.A. LIVE (EP, p/s, paper label)	6
80	2-Tone CHS TT 11	Rat Race/Rude Boys Outa Jail (company sleeve, paper label, as The Specials)	6
80	2-Tone CHS TT 13	Stereotype/International Jet Set (company sleeve, paper label, as The Specials)	6
80	2-Tone CHS TT 16	Do Nothing/Maggie's Farm (p/s, paper label, as The Specials)	6
81	2-Tone CHS TT 17	Ghost Town/Why/Friday Night Saturday Morning (paper labels p/s)	6
81	2-Tone CHS TT 1217	Ghost Town (6.02 Extended Version)/Why/ Friday Night, Saturday Morning (12", p/s)	10
82	2-Tone CHS TT 23	War Crimes (The Crime Is Still The Same)/War Crimes (p/s)	5
82	2-Tone CHS TT 1023	War Crimes (The Crime Is Still The Same)/War Crimes (The Crime Is Still The Same) (Version) (10", p/s, as The Special A.K.A.)	6
83	2-Tone CHS TPTT 25	Racist Friend/Bright Lights	5
83	2-Tone CHS TPTT 25	Racist Friend/Bright Lights (picture disc, as The Special A.K.A.)	6

MINT VALUE £

84	2-Tone CHS TT 26	Nelson Mandela/Break Down The Door (p/s)	5
84	2-Tone CHS TT 1226	Nelson Mandela/Break Down The Door (12", p/s)	8
84	2-Tone CHS TT 27	What I Like Most About You Is Your Girlfriend/Can't Get A Break/War Crimes (The Crime Is Still The Same)/(Version) (double pack, as The Special A.K.A.)	8
84	2-Tone CHS TPTT 27	What I Like Most About You Is Your Girlfriend/Can't Get A Break (picture disc)	6
84	2-Tone CHS TT 1227	What I Like Most About You Is Your Girlfriend/Can't Get A Break (12", poster p/s with free single)	10
91	Two Tone CHSTT 30	Ghost Town/Ghost Dub '91 (p/s)	40
86	Strange Fruit SFPS 018	THE PEEL SESSIONS (EP)	10
79	2-Tone TT 5001	SPECIALS (LP)	25
80	2-Tone CDL TT 5001	MORE SPECIALS (LP, with poster & bonus 7": Roddy Radiation & The Specials' "Braggin' And Tryin' Not To Lie"/Judge Roughneck's "Rude Buoys Outa Jail" [TT 999])	30
80	2-Tone CDL TT 5001	MORE SPECIALS (LP)	15
81	2-Tone CDL TT5001-P	SPECIALS (LP, picture disc)	12
84	2 Tone CHRTT 5008	IN THE STUDIO (LP)	12
91	2 Tone CHRTT 5010	SINGLES (LP)	12

SPECIMEN

83	London LON 24	Returning From A Journey/Kiss Kiss Bang Bang (bat-shaped disc)	10
80s	Trust TRUE T 001	Sharp Teeth (12", p/s)	8

SPECKLED RED

60s	Storyville SEP 384	STORYVILLE BLUES ANTHOLOGY VOL. 4 (EP)	15
63	Esquire 32-190	THE DIRTY DOZENS (LP)	30
66	Storyville DL 601	THE DIRTY DOZENS (LP, reissue)	12
71	VJM LC 11	OH RED (LP)	20

PHIL SPECTOR

(see also Ronettes, Crystals, Darlene Love, Bob B. Soxx & Blue Jeans, Teddy Bears)

63	London HA-U 8141	A CHRISTMAS GIFT FOR YOU (LP, various artists, Spector as producer; plum label)	100
63	London HA-U 8141	A CHRISTMAS GIFT FOR YOU (LP, various artists, Spector as producer; later black label)	50
72	Apple APCOR 24	PHIL SPECTOR'S CHRISTMAS ALBUM (LP, reissue of London HA-U 8141)	30
74	Warner Bros K 59010	PHIL SPECTOR'S CHRISTMAS ALBUM (LP, 2nd reissue, with poster)	18
76	Phil Spector Intl. 2307 008	RARE MASTERS VOL. 1 (LP, various artists, Spector as producer)	35
76	Phil Spector Intl. 2307 009	RARE MASTERS VOL. 2 (LP, various artists, Spector as producer)	35
80	Phil Spector Intl. 2307 015	PHIL SPECTOR '74/'79 (LP, various artists, Spector as producer)	25
81	Phil Spector Intl. WOS 001	WALL OF SOUND (9-LP box set, various artists, Spector as producer)	130

RONNIE SPECTOR

(see also Ronettes)

71	Apple APPLE 33	Try Some, Buy Some/Tandoori Chicken (with p/s)	30
71	Apple APPLE 33	Try Some, Buy Some/Tandoori Chicken	10
77	Epic EPC 5185	Say Goodbye To Hollywood/Baby Please Don't Go (with E Street Band, p/s)	12
81	Red Shadow LP 002	SIREN (LP)	20

SPECTRES

(see also Traffic Jam, Status Quo)

66	Piccadilly 7N 35339	I (Who Have Nothing)/Neighbour, Neighbour	300
66	Piccadilly 7N 35352	Hurdy Gurdy Man/Laticia	300
67	Piccadilly 7N 35368	We Ain't Got Nothin' Yet/I Want It (beware bootlegs)	250

(Demos are more common and worth £50 less than stock copies)

SPECTRES (Ireland)

65	Lloyd Sound UED QU 1	The Facts Of Life/Whirlpool	300

SPECTRES

(see also Rich Kids, Swingers)

80	Direct Hit DH 1	This Strange Effect/Getting Away With Murder (p/s)	7
81	Demon D 1002	Stories/Things (p/s)	5

SPECTRUM

65	Columbia DB 7742	Little Girl/Asking You	10
67	RCA RCA 1589	Samantha's Mine/Saturday's Child	10
67	RCA RCA 1619	Portobello Road/Comes The Dawn	10
67	RCA RCA 1651	Headin' For A Heatwave/I Wanna Be Happy With You	10
68	RCA RCA 1700	London Bridge Is Coming Down/Tables And Chairs	10
68	RCA RCA 1753	Little Red Boat By The River/Forget Me Not	10
68	RCA RCA 1775	Ob-La-Di, Ob-La-Da/Music Soothes The Savage Beast	10
69	RCA RCA 1853	Free/The Tale Of Wally Toft	10
69	RCA RCA 1883	Glory/Nodnol	10
70	RCA RCA 1976	Portobello Road/Comes The Dawn (reissue)	10
71	Parlophone R 5908	I'll Be Gone/Launching Place - Pt II	20
69	RCA Intl. INTS 118	THE LIGHT IS DARK ENOUGH (LP)	30

SPECTRUM

(see also Steve Marriott, Chris Farlowe, P.P. Arnold, Creation)

87	Phoenix Modernist THE 1	All Or Nothing (Contemporary Version)/All Or Nothing (Traditional Version) (12", p/s with 2 inserts & free 7", distributed by Nine Mile & Cartel)	8

SPECTRUM

(see also Spacemen 3, Sonic Boom)

92	Beechwood TT 015e	Taste The Ozone/MOONSHAKE: Night Tripper	5
94	Silvertone	Soul Kiss Glide Divine/STEREOLAB: Tone Burst (demo)/Tempter (demo) (unreleased, with colour photocopied wraparound p/s, 25 test pressings only)	150

CHRIS SPEDDING

(see also Sharks, Nucleus, Sounds Nice, Panhandle, Solid Gold Cadillac, Matthew Ellis, Vibrators, Battered Ornaments, IOFR)

70	Harvest HAR 5013	Rock'n'Roll Band/BATTERED ORNAMENTS: Goodbye We Loved You (Madly)	25
75	Island WIP 6225	My Bucket's Got A Hole In It/I Can't Boogie	8

MINT VALUE £

75 RAK RAK 210 Motor Bikin'/Working For The Union ... 5
76 RAK RAK 236 Guitar Jamboree/Sweet Disposition ... 5
76 RAK RAK 246 Pogo Dancing/Pose (p/s) ... 6
77 RAK RAK 261 Get Outa My Pagoda/Hey Miss Betty ... 5
70 Harvest SHSP 4004 BACKWOOD PROGRESSION (LP, no EMI logo on label) ... 50
72 Harvest SHSP 4017 THE ONLY LICK I KNOW (LP, with EMI logo on label) ... 40

SPEED
(see also Cobra, Tearjerkers)
78 It IT 1 Big City/All Day And All The Night (in p/s) ... 40
78 It IT 1 Big City/All Day And All The Night ... 15

SPEED
(see also Bruce Dickinson, Iron Maiden)
80 Speed GJS 001 Man In The Street/Down The Road (p/s) ... 100

SPEED (Jamaica)
71 Bullet BU 477 There's A Train/Blue Moon ... 7

SPEEDBALL(S)
80 No Pap/Dirty Dick DD 1/2 No Survivors/Is Somebody There? (miscredited as 'Speedballs' on label, in withdrawn printed die-cut sleeve) ... 60
80 No Pap/Dirty Dick DD 1/2 No Survivors/Is Somebody There? (miscredited as 'Speedballs' on label) ... 25

SPEEDOMETERS
78 Mascot NICE 1 Disgrace/Work (p/s) ... 5
78 Mascot NICE 2 Liverpool Ladies (p/s) ... 5

SPEEDY J
94 Warp WAP 46 Pepper (The Hot Mix)/Beam Me Up (The Pegasus Mix) (12") ... 8

DAVEY SPEIRS
69 Beltona LBA/LBS 61 A MAN OF CONSTANT SORROW (LP) ... 15

SPELLBINDERS
66 CBS 202453 Help Me (Get Myself Back Together)/Danny Boy ... 40
66 CBS 202453 Help Me (Get Myself Back Together)/Danny Boy (DJ copy) ... 85
67 CBS 202622 Chain Reaction/For You ... 40
67 CBS 202622 Chain Reaction/For You (DJ copy) ... 75
67 CBS 2776 Since I Don't Have You/I Believe ... 12
69 Direction 58-3970 Help Me/Chain Reaction ... 22

SPELLING MISSTEAKS
79 Stortbeat BEAT 7 POPSTAR (EP) ... 50

BENNY SPELLMAN
62 London HLP 9570 Lipstick Traces/Fortune Teller ... 80
62 London HLP 9570 Lipstick Traces/Fortune Teller (DJ Copy) ... 100

BRUCE SPELMAN
69 Beacon BEA 112 Lady/Long Time Gone ... 8
72 Montagu MONT 3000 29 Years To Doomsday/Cutting The Traces ... 12
70 Beacon BES 3 YOU DON'T KNOW WHAT YOU'RE PADDLING IN (LP) ... 70
70 Montague MONS 1 YOU DON'T KNOW WHAT YOU'RE PADDLING IN (LP, different sleeve, blue/black label) ... 40

BARRINGTON SPENCE
75 Grounation GRO 2009 For The Rest Of My Life/Version ... 5
76 Student STU 1005 Mash It Up/Straight To Radd Head ... 10

JOHNNIE SPENCE
61 Parlophone R 4736 Wheels/First Romance ... 6
68 Verve (S)VLP 9222 WHY NOT? (LP, as Johnnie Spence Big Band) ... 18
62 Parlophone R 4872 The Dr. Kildars Theme/The Midnight Theme ... 6

BRINDLEY D SPENCER
68 Domain D8 The Company Of Keep/On A Day Like Today ... 10

DON SPENCER
(see also Le Roys)
62 HMV POP 1087 Fireball/I'm All Alone Again (blue or black labels) ... 12
63 HMV POP 1186 Busy Doing Nothing/The Joker ... 7
63 HMV POP 1205 Worried Mind/Give Give Give A Little ... 6
64 HMV POP 1306 Pride Is Such A Little Word/For Love (with Le Roys) ... 6
67 Talus TP1010 Uproar In The House/On The G.P.O Tower ... 20

DON SPENCER/XL5
63 HMV 7EG 8802 FIREBALL AND OTHER TITLES (EP, 2 tracks each) ... 40

JEREMY SPENCER (Band)
(see also Fleetwood Mac)
70 Reprise RS 27002 Linda/Teenage Darling ... 10
79 Atlantic K 11363 Travelling/Cool Breeze (as Jeremy Spencer Band) ... 5
70 Reprise RSLP 9002 JEREMY SPENCER (LP) ... 40
71 Reprise K 44105 JEREMY SPENCER (LP, reissue) ... 20
73 CBS 65387 JEREMY SPENCER AND THE CHILDREN OF GOD (LP) ... 12

JO SPENCER
71 Dynamic DYN 415 Bed Of Roses/Forgive Me ... 5

JON SPENCER BLUES EXPLOSION
(see also Pussy Galore)
92 Clawfist 13 History Of Sex/Write A Song/Smoke Cigarettes (foldover p/s in poly bag) ... 12
94 Matador OLE 077 Afro/Relax Her (p/s) ... 8
91 Hut HUTLP 3 THE JON SPENCER BLUES EXPLOSION (LP) ... 15

SONNY SPENCER
59 Parlophone R 4611 Oh Boy/Gilee ... 20

MINT VALUE £

TARNEY SPENCER BAND
78 A+M AMS 7339 Takin Me Back/Set The Minstrel Free ... 6

SPENCER & THE SAINTS
68 Tabernacle TS 1005 Something Within/When You Get To Heaven ... 15

SPENCERS WASHBOARD KINGS
66 Pye 7N 17245 The Egg Plant That Ate Chicago/Somebody Stole My Gal ... 7
69 Parlophone R 5782 Pimlico/Ordinary People ... 15

SPERMICIDE
79 No Wonder NOW 3 Femme Prothèse/Belgique (p/s with lyrics) ... 30

JIMMIE SPHEERIS
72 CBS 8092 Let It Flow/The Nest ... 5

SPHERES
(see also Jimmy Winston)
78 Sphere FESTIVAL AND SUNS (LP, with insert) ... 25

SPHERICAL OBJECTS
(see also Alternomen Unlimited, Noyes Brothers)
78 Object Music OM 01 The Kill/The Knot (p/s) ... 5
78 Object Music OM 04 Seventies Romance/Sweet Tooth (p/s) ... 5
78 Object Music PBJ 001 PAST & PARCEL (LP) ... 12
79 Object Music OBJ 004 ELLIPTICAL OPTIMISM (LP) ... 12

SPHYNKTA
83 Sultanic SUL 666 In The Shade Of The Gods/Jesus Bless My Upside-Down Cross (p/s, red vinyl, with 'devil' tattoo) ... 60
83 Sultanic SUL 999 Death And Violence/Ritual Slaughter (Of Your Daughter) (p/s, red vinyl) ... 40
84 Sultanic SUL 000 Spike Up My Sphynkta/No Pain No Gain (unissued) ... 100

SPHYNX
(see also Inner City Unit, Gong, Radio Actors)
78 Charisma CDS 4011 XITINTODAY (LP, with booklet) ... 30
78 Charisma CDS 4011 XITINTODAY (LP, without booklet) ... 15

SPICE (U.K.)
(see also Uriah Heep, Godz, Toe-Fat)
68 United Artists UP 2246 What About The Music?/In Love ... 250

GEORGE SPICER
74 Topic 12T 235 BLACKBERRY FOLD (LP) ... 15

SPIDELLS
66 Sue WI 4019 Find Out What's Happening/That'll Make My Heart Break ... 40

SPIDER
66 Decca F 12430 The Comedown Song/Blow Ya Mind ... 35

SPIDER
80 Alien ALIEN 14 Children Of The Street/Down 'N' Out (in p/s) ... 35
80 Alien ALIEN 14 Children Of The Street/Down 'N' Out ... 8
80 Alien ALIEN 16 College Luv/Born To Be Wild (in p/s) ... 35
80 Alien ALIEN 16 College Luv/Born To Be Wild ... 8

SPIDER-MAN
73 Buddah 2318 075 FROM BEYOND THE GRAVE (LP) ... 12

SPIDERS
66 Philips BF 1531 Sad Sunset/Hey Boy ... 55

SPIDERS (U.S.)
54 London HL 8086 I'm Slippin' In/I'm Searching (78) ... 65

SPIDERS FROM MARS
(see also David Bowie, Kestrel, Mick Ronson)
75 Pye 7N 45549 White Man Black Man/National Poll ... 6
76 Pye NSPL 18479 SPIDERS FROM MARS (LP) ... 12

BERND SPIER
65 Oriole CB 1987 A Million And One Times/My Mistake ... 10

SPILL
(see also Beth Orton)
92 Virgin VS 1141 Don't Wanna Know About Evil (7" Wireless Road Mix)/(Saspelofiska Dub Mix) (p/s) ... 12
92 Virgin VST 1141 Don't Wanna Know About Evil (Tumble Mix)/(Rumble Mix)/(Danny's Moto Mix)/(The Groovy Beats Mix) (12", p/s) ... 15

ARTHUR SPINK BAND
68 Beltona BL 2766 Beatles Och Aye/Harry Lauder Medley ... 5

SPINNERS
(see also Liverpool Spinners, Shane Rimmer)
66 Fontana TE17468 THE SINGING CITY (EP) ... 8

SPINNERS (U.S.)
(see also Detroit Spinners)
61 Columbia DB 4693 That's What Girls Are Made For/Heebie Jeebies ... 200
61 Columbia DB 4693 That's What Girls Are Made For/Heebie Jeebies (DJ copy) ... 250
65 Tamla Motown TMG 514 Sweet Thing/How Can I? (demo with 'Spinners' credit) ... 300
65 Tamla Motown TMG 514 Sweet Thing/How Can I? (demos with 'Detroit Spinners' credit) ... 250
65 Tamla Motown TMG 514 Sweet Thing/How Can I? (stock copies credited to 'Spinners') ... 400

SPINNING JENNY
71 Midas MR004 SPINNING JENNY (LP) ... 100

MINT VALUE £

SPINNING WHEEL
(see also Dragonsfire)
79 private pressing — JACOB'S FLEECE (LP) 15

SPIRALS
58 Capitol CL 14958 — The Rockin' Cow/Everybody Knows 15

SPIRAL SKY
(see also Sun Dial, Ohr Musik)
93 Acme AC 8002LP — SPIRAL SKY (LP, numbered & sealed with insert, 500 only) 15

SPIRAL STAIRCASE
68 CBS 3507 — Baby What I Mean/Makin' Your Mind Up 25
69 CBS 4187 — More Today Than Yesterday/Broken Hearted Man 50
69 CBS 4187 — More Today Than Yesterday/Broken Hearted Man (DJ copy) 65
69 CBS 4524 — No One For Me To Turn To/Sweet Little Thing 25

SPIRAL TRIBE
92 Big Life BLRT 79 — Breach The Peace/Do ET/Seven/23 minute warning (12", p/s) 25
92 Big Life BLRT 85 — Forward The Revolution/World Traveller Adventurer/Ragga Boom/Track 13 (Criminal Drug) (12", p/s) 25
92 Big Life BLRR 85 — Forward The Revolution (the Youth Remix) (1-sided, etched 12") 15
93 Butterfly BFLT 04 — Sirius 23/Earthworm/Going All The Way/Predator (12", p/s, as Spiral Tribe Sound System) 20
93 Butterfly BFL LP 6 — TECNO TERRA (2-LP) 140

SPIRIT
(see also Kapt. Kopter & Fabulous Twirlybirds, Jo Jo Gunne)
68 CBS 3523 — Uncle Jack/Mechanical World 15
69 CBS 3880 — I Got A Line On You/She Smiles 25
69 CBS 4511 — Dark Eyed Woman/Ice 5
69 CBS 4565 — Dark Eyed Woman/New Dope In Town 10
70 CBS 4773 — 1984/Sweet Stella Baby 8
70 CBS 5149 — Animal Zoo/Red Light Roll On 6
70 Epic SEPC 7082 — Mr Skin/Nature's Way 5
70 Epic SEPC 8083 — Cadillac Cowboys/Darkness 6
78 Sound For Industry SFI 326 — Midnight Train/Potatoland Theme (flexidisc free with Dark Star magazine) 6
68 CBS 63278 — SPIRIT (LP, orange label) 35
68 CBS 63523 — THE FAMILY THAT PLAYS TOGETHER (LP, orange label) 25
69 CBS 63729 — CLEAR (LP, orange label) 30
71 Epic EPC 64191 — THE TWELVE DREAMS OF DR. SARDONICUS (LP, g/fold sleeve, yellow label) .. 15
72 Epic EPC 64507 — FEED-BACK (LP, yellow label) 12
81 Beggars Banquet BEGA 23 — POTATOLAND (LP, with cartoon book) 12

SPIRIT OF JOHN MORGAN
(see also John Morgan)
69 Carnaby CNS 4005 — Ride On/Along Came John 10
71 RCA RCA 2085 — Floating Opera Show/Never Let Go 10
69 Carnaby CNLS 6002 — THE SPIRIT OF JOHN MORGAN (LP, union jack flag label) 150
70 Carnaby CNLS 6007 — AGE MACHINE (LP, gatefold, union jack flag label) 130
71 Carnaby GOLD 6437 503 — THE SPIRIT OF JOHN MORGAN (LP, reissue, 'crab' label logo) 50

SPIRIT OF MEMPHIS QUARTET
58 Parlophone PMD 1070 — NEGRO SPIRITUALS (10" LP) 25
65 Vogue LAE 1033 — NEGRO SPIRITUALS (LP, reissue) 15

SPIRIT OF PLAY
88 Release KIDS 1988 — Children In Need/Children In Need (Instrumental) (with Paul McCartney) (in p/s) .. 50
88 Release KIDS 1988 — Children In Need/Children In Need (Instrumental) (with Paul McCartney) 10

SPIRIT OF PROGRESS
71 Philips 6006089 — Om Pa Pa/It's A Beautiful Day 40

SPIRIT OF THE SECT
(see also Subway Sect, Vic Godard)
96 Garcia POUM 003 — No Love Now/VIC GODARD: She's My Best Friend (1,000 only) 5

SPIRITBORN
84 Spearhead — Pity The Unborn Child/Sing To The Lord 20

SPIRITUALIZED
(see also Spacemen 3)
90 Dedicated ZB 43783 — Anyway That You Want Me/Step Into The Breeze (p/s) 15
90 Dedicated ZT 43784 — Anyway That You Want Me (Extended)/Step Into The Breeze 1 & 2 (12", p/s) 18
90 Dedicated ZT 43780 — Anyway That You Want Me (Remix)/Step Into The Breeze 1 & 2 (12", p/s) 25
90 Dedicated ZD 43784 — Anyway That You Want Me/Step Into The Breeze 1 & 2 (CD) 20
91 Fierce FRIGHT 053 — Feel So Sad/I Want You (gig freebie, no p/s, stamped plain white sleeve with date & venue details) 35
91 Dedicated SPIRT 001T — Feel So Sad (Rhapsodies)/(Glides And Chimes) (12", p/s) 12
91 Dedicated SPIRT 001CD — Feel So Sad (Rhapsodies)/(Glides And Chimes) (CD) 8
91 Dedicated SPIRT 002 — Run/I Want You (p/s, with luminous sleeve & clear luminous vinyl) 25
91 Dedicated SPIRT 002 — Run/I Want You (p/s) 8
91 Dedicated SPIRT 002T — Run/Luminescence (Stay With Me)/I Want You/Effervescent (Chimes) (12", with luminous sleeve) 20
91 Dedicated SPIRT 002T — Run/Luminescence (Stay With Me)/I Want You/Effervescent (Chimes) (12") 10
91 Dedicated SPIRT 002CD/ZD 44846 — Run/Luminescence (Stay With Me)/I Want You/Effervescent (Chimes) (CD) 18
91 Dedicated SPIRIT 003 — Why Don't You Smile Now? (Edit)/Sway (clear vinyl, p/s) 10
91 Dedicated SPIRT 003 CD — Why Don't You Smile Now? (Edit)/Sway/Why Don't You Smile Now? (CD, front cover has "Smile/Sway") 8
91 Dedicated SPIRT 004 — I Want You/You Know It's True (Instrumental)/100 Bars (Flashback) (p/s, mail-order with NME coupon only) 12

			MINT VALUE £
92	Dedicated SPIRT 004CD	I Want You/You Know It's True (Instrumental)/100 Bars (Flashback) (CD, no p/s, mail-order with NME coupon only)	15
92	Dedicated DEDCD 004	LAZER GUIDED MELODIES (CD EP, 4-track sampler of album)	15
92	Dedicated SPIRIT 005	Medication/Smiles (p/s, red vinyl, 3000 only)	10
92	Dedicated SPIRT 005	Medication/Angel Sigh/Feel So Sad (white label test pressing, signed and inscribed by Jason Pierce in silver, limited availability through band website)	30
92	Dedicated SPIRT 005T	Medication/Angel Sigh/Feel So Sad (12", p/s, with poster, 3000 only)	10
93	Dedicated SPIRT 006	Smiles (Live)/100 Bars (A Cappella) (7" flexidisc, fan-club only)	22
93	Greenpeace GR'NP'CE 001	Good Dope, Good Fun/MERCURY REV: 'Boys Peel Out (Live)' (gig 7", with booklet)	15
94	Dedicated SPIRT 009	Let It Flow/Don't Go/Stay With Me/Don't Go/Stay With Me (The Individual) (10", p/s)	8
95	Dedicated 7432 13 11782	Lay Back In The Sun/The Slide Song/Spread Your Wings/Lay Back In The Sun (CD)	15
96	Dedicated SPIRT 101T	Pure Phase Tones For DJs (12")	15
97	Dedicated SPIRT 011CD	Broken Heart (Instrumental) (CD, available via NME and Spiritualized Information Service, 500 only)	25
98	Dedicated SPIRT 014DJ	I Think I'm In Love/(Chemical Brothers Vocal Mix)/ (Chemical Brothers Inst.) (12", DJ promo, 200 only)	25
98	Dedicated SPIRT 015DJ	Come Together (Death In Vegas Mix)/(Two Lone Swordsmen Mix) (12" promo, p/s)	8
92	Dedicated DEDLP 004S	LAZER GUIDED MELODIES (LP, limited Edition, with bonus 7" single Anyway That You Want Me' /'Why Don't You Smile Now?' [CWNN 7001])	30
92	Dedicated DEDLP 004S	LAZER GUIDED MELODIES (LP, limited. Edition, without bonus 7" single)	20
93	Dedicated no cat. no.	SUMMER EUROPEAN 93 BOX (3-CD promo set, with ribbon and insert)	70
93	Dedicated DEDLP 008	FUCKED UP INSIDE (LP, mail-order only)	50
93	Dedicated DEDCD 008	FUCKED UP INSIDE (CD, mail-order only)	40
93	Dedicated DEDLP 017	PURE PHASE (2-LP 45rpm)	50
93	Dedicated DEDCD 017S	PURE PHASE (CD in luminous slide out sleeve)	30
97	Dedicated DEDLP 034	LADIES AND GENTLEMEN WE ARE FLOATING IN SPACE (2-LP, limited issue)	90
97	Dedicated DEDCD 034	LADIES AND GENTLEMEN WE ARE FLOATING IN SPACE (CD in sealed blister pack, card outer sleeve and 'prescription' sleeve notes)	20
97	Dedicated DEDCD 034S	LADIES AND GENTLEMEN WE ARE FLOATING IN SPACE (12 x 3" CDs, in blister packs in card box with insert, 1000 only, 200 with clear plastic backs)	120
97	Dedicated DEDCD 034S	LADIES AND GENTLEMEN WE ARE FLOATING IN SPACE (12 x 3" CDs, in blister packs in card box with insert, 1000)	70
97	Dedicated DEDCD 034P	LADIES AND GENTLEMEN WE ARE FLOATING IN SPACE (CD, 'Elvis version', given to Mercury Music Prize personnel, 50 copies only)	50
98	Deconstruction 74321 66285 1	ROYAL ALBERT HALL (2 x LP)	20
01	Dedicated OPM 001 CD	LET IT COME DOWN: RADIO INTERVIEW (CD, Jason Pierce speaks to Stuart Maconie plus 7 tracks)	20
08	Sanctuary 1768732	SONGS IN A&E (2-LP green vinyl, only available from Rough Trade)	50

SPIROGYRA

72	Pegasus PGS 3	Dangerous Dave/Captain's Log	12
73	Polydor 2001-419	I Hear You're Going Nowhere/Old Boot Wine	35
71	B&C CAS 1042	ST. RADIGUND'S (LP, with lyric inner)	130
72	Pegasus PEG 13	OLD BOOT WINE (LP, textured sleeve)	200
73	Polydor 2310 246	BELLS, BOOTS AND SHAMBLES (LP)	500

SPITFIRE (& BLACKFIRE BARMIES)

82	Carrere CAR 253	So You Want To Be A Rock'n'Roll Star/Spitfire Boogie	50

SPITFIRE BOYS

(see also Frankie Goes To Hollywood)

77	RK RK 1001	British Refugee/Mein Kampf (push-out centre)	75
77	RK RK 1001	British Refugee/Mein Kampf (reissue, solid centre, p/s)	60
79	Impeccable SRTS/79/CUS481	Funtime/Transendental Changing	35
83	RK RK 1001	British Refugee/Mein Kampf (2nd reissue, p/s, no solid centre)	75

SPITZBROOK

79	Ace SPIT 1	Stranger/Looking At You (p/s)	60

SPIV

73	Pye 7N 45293	Oh You Beautiful Child/Little Girl	75

VICTORIA SPIVEY

60	Fontana TFE 17264	TREASURES OF NORTH AMERICAN NEGRO MUSIC NO. 5 (EP)	15
56	HMV 7EG 8190	VICTORIA SPIVEY (EP)	20
65	Xtra XTRA 1022	VICTORIA SPIVEY (LP)	22

SPIZZ (OIL/ENERGI)

79	Rough Trade RTSO 1	6000 Crazy/1989/Fibre (p/s)	8
79	Rough Trade RTSO 2	Cold City/Red And Black/Solarisation (Shun)/Platform 3 (as Spizz Oil) (p/s)	5
79	Rough Trade RTSO 3	Soldier Soldier/Virginia Plain (as Spizz Energi) (p/s)	5
79	Rough Trade RTSO 4	Where's Captain Kirk?/Amnesia (as Spizz Energi) (p/s)	5

S.P.K. (SEPPUKU/SURGICAL PENIS KLINIK)

80	Industrial IR 0011	MEAT PROCESSING SECTION (Mekano/Slogun) (p/s, labels list "Slogan"/Factory, with insert, as Surgical Penis Klinik)	30
83	Side Effekts SER 003	Dekompositiones (12", p/s, as Seppuku)	20
81	Side Effekts SER 01	INFORMATION OVERLOAD UNIT (LP, 1st 1,000 with booklet)	45
81	Side Effekts SER 01	INFORMATION OVERLOAD UNIT (LP)	30
83	Walter Ulbright WULP 002	AUTO-DA-FE (LP)	15
84	WEA WX 10	MACHINE AGE VOODOO (LP)	12
80s	Side Effekts SER 002	LEICHENSCHREI (LP)	30

SPLINTER

(see also Elastic Oz Band)

74	Dark Horse AMS 7135	Costafine Town/Elly May	5
75	Dark Horse AMS 5501	Drink All Day/Haven't Got Time (withdrawn)	12

MINT VALUE £

75 Dark Horse AMS 5502 China Light/Drink All Day. 10
75 Dark Horse AMS 5503 Which Way Will I Get Home/Green Bus Line 8
76 Dark Horse AMS 5506 Half Way There/What Is It (If You Never Ever Tried It Yourself) 8
77 Dark Horse K 17009 Round And Round/I'll Bend For You 7
77 Dark Horse K 17116 New York City (Who Am I)/Baby Love 7
78 Barn BARN 4 Danger Zone/Swear To God 8
76 Dark Horse DH 2 SPLINTER (LP, promo only, plain white sleeve) 130

SPLIT BEAVER
81 Heavy Metal HEAVY 7 Savage/Hound Of Hell (with p/s) 25
81 Heavy Metal HEAVY 7 Savage/Hound Of Hell 8
82 Heavy Metal HMRLP 3 WHEN HELL WON'T HAVE YOU (LP, silver label) 18
82 Heavy Metal HMRLP 3 WHEN HELL WON'T HAVE YOU (LP, red label) 15

SPLIT ENZ
(see also Crowded House, Tim Finn)
76 Chrysalis CHS 2120 Late Last Night/Walking Down The Road (p/s) 5
77 Chrysalis CHS 2131 Another Great Divide/Stranger Than Fiction (p/s) 5
77 Chrysalis CHS 2170 My Mistake/Crosswords (p/s) 5
77 Chrysalis CHS 2170-12 My Mistake/Crosswords/The Woman Who Loves You (12", p/s) 8
79 Illegal ILS 19 I See Red/Give It A Whirl/Hermit McDermitt (p/s) 5
80 A&M AMLH 64822 TRUE COLOURS (LP, laser etched) 12

SPLIT IMAGE
82 Heroes ER 01 Now That We've Parted 25

SPLIT KNEE LOONS
(see also Gillan, Bernie Torme, John McCoy, Colin Towns)
81 Avatar AAA 111 THE SPECIAL COLLECTORS EP (p/s, brown vinyl, with badge) 10
81 Avatar AAA 111 THE SPECIAL COLLECTORS EP (p/s, brown vinyl) 8

SPLIT SCREENS
78 Rok ROK III/IV Just Don't Try/JUST FRANK: You (die-cut company sleeve) 10

SPLODGENESSABOUNDS
80 Deram ROLF 1 Two Little Boys/Horse/Sox/Butterfly (p/s, with 'Splodge' boomerang) 15
81 Deram BUM 3 COWPUNK MEDLUM (EP, p/s, with free flexi [BUMF 3]) 8

SPODE
71 Decca F 13142 Singalong Song/Cincinatti Woman 6
71 Decca F23114 Machine/More Ning 18

SPOILERS
72 London HLU 10399 Turbo Rock/Sad Man's Land 20

SPOILT BRATZ
(see also Terrorvision)
88 Spoilt Bratz SB 1 SPOILT BRATZ: (Not So) Hot/You Talk Too Much/I Could Die/ She's A Drag (cassette, private issue, 200 only) 30
88 Spoilt Bratz SB 2 GASOLINE & SUICIDE: Sex Doll, Love Cramp/Going Down Again/ Stuck In A Rut/Crawling On Broken Glass (cassette, private issue, 200 only) 30
89 Spoilt Bratz BRAT 3 BE MY GUEST: Pain Reliever/Past Times/Ignorance (cassette, private issue) 30

SPOKESMEN
65 Brunswick 05941 The Dawn Of Correction/For You Babe 12
65 Brunswick 05948 It Ain't Fair/Have Courage Be Careful 12
66 Brunswick 05950 Michelle/Better Days Are Yet To Come 8
66 Brunswick 05958 Today's The Day/Enchanté 8

SPONTANEOUS COMBUSTION
(see also Time)
71 Harvest HAR 5046 Lonely Singer/200 Lives/Leaving 15
72 Harvest HAR 5060 Gay Time Night/Spaceship 10
73 Harvest HAR 5066 Sabre Dance/Sabre Dance 10
72 Harvest SHVL 801 SPONTANEOUS COMBUSTION (LP, with EMI logo on label) 70
72 Harvest SHVL 805 TRIAD (LP, with 3 inserts, with EMI logo on label) 60

SPONTANEOUS MUSIC ENSEMBLE
(see also Howard Riley Trio)
66 Eyemark EMP L1002 CHALLENGE (LP) 350
68 Island ILP 979 KARYOBIN... ARE THE IMAGINARY BIRDS SAID TO LIVE IN PARADISE (LP, pink label) 200
69 Marmalade 608 008 SPONTANEOUS MUSIC ENSEMBLE (LP) 100
71 Tangent TNGS 107 SOURCE FROM AND TOWARDS (LP) 30
72 Marmalade 2384 009 SPONTANEOUS MUSIC ENSEMBLE (LP, reissue) 22
73 Emanem 303 FACE TO FACE (LP) 30
73 Tangent TNGS 118 SO WHAT DO YOU THINK (LP) 20
77 Incus INCUS 24 BIOSYSTEM (LP) 50

SPOOKY TOOTH
(see also Gary Wright, V.I.P.s, Art, Luther Grosvenor, Hellions, Revolution, State Of Mickey & Tommy, Mike Harrison, Foreigner)
67 Island WIP 6022 Sunshine Help Me/Weird 25
68 Island WIP 6037 Love Really Changed Me/Luger's Grove 15
68 Island WIP 6046 The Weight/Do Right People 10
69 Island WIP 6048 Nobody There At All/ART: Room With A View (unissued, white labels only) 40
69 Island WIP 6060 Son Of Your Father/I've Got Enough Heartache 7
73 Island WIP 6168 All Sewn Up/As Long As The World Keeps Turning 6
68 Island ILP 980/ILPS 9080 IT'S ALL ABOUT (LP, pink label) 70
68 Island ILP 980/ILPS 9080 IT'S ALL ABOUT (LP, palm tree label) 25
69 Island ILPS 9098 SPOOKY TWO (LP, pink label) 40
69 Island ILPS 9107 CEREMONY (LP, with Pierre Henry, pink label, gatefold sleeve) 40
70 Island ILPS 9117 THE LAST PUFF (LP, pink label) 30

MINT VALUE £

73	Island ILPS 9227	YOU BROKE MY HEART SO I BUSTED YOUR JAW (LP, pink rim label)	15
73	Island ILPS 9255	WITNESS (LP, pink rim label)	18
74	Good Ear EARL 2001	THE MIRROR (LP)	12
74	Island ILPS 9292	THE MIRROR (LP, export issue)	18

SPOONFUL

78	Bunbury DCS 340	Troubled Times/Country Blues (2 known copies, p/s)	300

SPORTS

78	Stiff LAST 5	WHO LISTENS TO THE RADIO EP: Who Listens To The Radio/Step By Step/ So Obvious/Suspicious (originals have 'koala photo' p/s)	8
79	Sire SIR 6001	Who Listens To The Radio/Hit Single ('fireplace' p/s)	5
80	Sire SRUK 6001	WHO LISTENS TO THE RADIO (LP)	15

SPOTLIGHTERS

59	Vogue Pop V 9130	Please Be My Girlfriend/Whisper (with Bob Thompson & His Band)	500
59	Vogue Pop V 9130	Please Be My Girlfriend/Whisper (with Bob Thompson & His Band) (78)	100

SPOTLIGHTS

66	Philips BF 1485	Batman And Robin/Day Flower	20

SPOTNICKS

(see also Bob Lander & Spotnicks, Shy Ones)

62	Oriole CB 1724	Orange Blossom Special/The Spotnicks Theme	10
62	Oriole CB 1755	Galloping Guitars/The Rocket Man	10
63	Oriole CB 1790	Hava Nagila/High Flyin' Scotsman	8
63	Oriole CB 1818	Just Listen To My Heart/Pony Express	10
63	Oriole CB 1844	Valentina/Save The Last Dance For Me/No Yaga Daga Blues	12
63	Oriole CB 1886	Anna/The Sailor's Hornpipe	12
64	Oriole CB 1953	Lovesick Blues/The Space Creatures	15
64	Oriole CB 1981	Donner Wetter/Shamus O'Toole	15
63	Oriole EP 7075	ON THE AIR (EP)	20
64	Oriole EP 7078	SPOTNICKS IN PARIS (EP)	25
64	Oriole EP 7079	SPOTNICKS AT THE OLYMPIA PARIS (EP)	25
63	Oriole PS 40036	OUT-A SPACE: THE SPOTNICKS IN LONDON (LP, mono)	30
63	Oriole SPS 40037	OUT-A SPACE: THE SPOTNICKS IN LONDON (LP, stereo)	40
64	Oriole PS 40054	THE SPOTNICKS IN SPAIN (LP)	30
65	Oriole PS 40064	THE SPOTNICKS IN BERLIN (LP)	30
77	Air CHM 1171	THE VERY BEST OF (LP)	12

JACK SPRATT & LEROY SIBBLES & HEPTONES

69	Coxsone CS 7100	Give Me Your Love/LARRY & ALVIN: Magic Moments	70

SPREADEAGLE

72	Charisma CB 183	How Can We Be Lost/Nightmare	5
72	Charisma CAS 1055	THE PIECE OF PAPER (LP, pink 'scroll' label)	20

SPREDTHICK

78	An Actual ACT 003	SPREDTHICK (LP, with insert)	18

SPRIGUNS (OF TOLGUS)

(see also Mandy Morton Band, Terra Cotta)

76	Decca F 13676	Nothing Else To Do/Lord Lovell	12
77	Decca F 13739	White Witch/Time Will Pass	12
74	private pressing	ROWDY DOWDY DAY (cassette, as Spriguns Of Tolgus)	50
75	Alida Star C'tage ASC7755	JACK WITH A FEATHER (LP, as Spriguns Of Tolgus)	1200
76	Decca SKL 5262	REVEL WEIRD & WILD (LP, with lyric insert)	250
77	Decca SKL 5286	TIME WILL PASS (LP, with lyric insert)	200
92	Kissing Spell KSLP 002	ROWDY DOWDY DAY (LP, reissue)	15

SPRING

71	RCA Neon NE 6	SPRING (LP, foldout sleeve, black inner sleeve)	400

SPRINGBOARD

(see also Ian Carr)

69	Polydor 545007	SPRINGBOARD (LP)	100

DUSTY SPRINGFIELD

(see also Lana Sisters, Springfields, Tom Springfield, Pet Shop Boys)

63	Philips BF 1292	I Only Want To Be With You/Once Upon A Time	5
64	Philips BF 1313	Stay Awhile/Something Special	5
64	Philips BF 1348	I Just Don't Know What To Do With Myself/My Colouring Book	5
64	Philips BF 1369	Losing You/Summer Is Over	5
64	Philips BF 1381	Oh Holy Child/SPRINGFIELDS: Jingle Bells (with p/s)	6
65	Philips BF 1396	Your Hurtin' Kinda Love/Don't Say It Baby	5
65	Philips BF 1418	In The Middle Of Nowhere/Baby Don't You Know	5
65	Philips BF 1430	Some Of Your Lovin'/I'll Love You For A While	5
66	Philips BF 1466	Little By Little/If It Hadn't Been For You	5
66	Philips BF 1482	You Don't Have To Say You Love Me/Every Ounce Of Strength	5
66	Philips BF 1502	Goin' Back/I'm Gonna Leave You	5
66	Philips BF 1510	All I See Is You/Go Ahead On (with p/s)	8
67	Philips BF 1553	I'll Try Anything/The Corrupt Ones	5
67	Philips BF 1577	Give Me Time/The Look Of Love	6
67	Philips BF 1608	What's It Gonna Be/Small Town Girl	15
68	Philips BF 1682	I Close My Eyes And Count To Ten/No Stranger Am I	5
68	Philips BF 1706	I Will Come To You/The Colour Of Your Eyes	5
68	Philips BF 1730	Son Of A Preacher Man/Just A Little Lovin'	10
69	Philips BF 1811	Am I The Same Girl/Earthbound Gypsy	15
69	Philips BF 1826	Brand New Me/Bad Case Of The Blues	7
70	Philips BF 1835	Morning Please Don't Come (with Tom Springfield)/TOM SPRINGFIELD: Charley	5
70	Philips 6006 045	How Can I Be Sure/Spooky	20
72	Philips 6006 214	Yesterday When I Was Young/I Start Counting	6

MINT VALUE £

73	Philips 6006 295	Who Gets Your Love/Of All The Things	6
74	Philips 6006 325	Learn To Say Goodbye/Easy Evil	6
74	Philips 6006 350	What's It Gonna Be/Bring Him Back	15
75	Philips 6006 446	Yesterday When I Was Young/The Look Of Love	7
78	Mercury DUSTY 1	A Love Like Yours (Don't Come Knocking Every Day)/Hollywood Movie Girls	5
78	Mercury DUSTY 002	That's The Kind Of Love I've Got For You/Sandra	5
79	Mercury DUSTY 003	I'm Coming Home Again/Save Me Save Me	5
79	Mercury DUSTY 4	Baby Blue/Get Yourself To Love (p/s)	6

EPs

64	Philips BE 12560	I ONLY WANT TO BE WITH YOU	10
64	Philips BE 12564	DUSTY	12
65	Philips BE 12572	DUSTY IN NEW YORK	20
65	Philips BE 12579	MADEMOISELLE DUSTY	20
68	Philips BE 12605	IF YOU GO AWAY	8

LPs

64	Philips BL 7594	A GIRL CALLED DUSTY (mono)	15
64	Philips SBL 7594	A GIRL CALLED DUSTY (stereo)	20
65	Philips RBL 1002	EVERYTHING'S COMING UP DUSTY (gatefold sleeve with booklet, mono)	25
65	Philips SRBL 1002	EVERYTHING'S COMING UP DUSTY (gatefold sleeve with booklet, stereo)	30
67	Philips (S)BL 7820	WHERE AM I GOING?	25
68	Philips (S)BL 7864	DUSTY... DEFINITELY	15
69	Philips SBL 7889	DUSTY IN MEMPHIS	40
70	Philips SBL 7927	FROM DUSTY... WITH LOVE	20
80	Philips PRICE 83	IN MEMPHIS PLUS (LP)	30

RICK SPRINGFIELD

72	Capitol EA-ST 80001	BEGINNINGS (LP)	12

TOM SPRINGFIELD (& HIS) ORCHESTRA

(see also Springfields, Dusty Springfield)

63	Philips BF 1294	The Moon Behind The Hill/The Londonderry Air	6
64	Philips BF 1331	Brazilian Shake/Brazilian Blues	6
69	Philips BF 1759	Theme From From The Troubleshooters/Homage To Spewdley Parsons (with p/s)	8
69	Philips BF 1759	Theme From From The Troubleshooters/Homage To Spewdley Parsons	6
69	Decca LK/SKL 5003	LOVE'S PHILOSOPHY BY... (LP, featuring Dusty Springfield)	30
68	Decca SKL 4967	SUN SONGS (LP)	80

SPRINGFIELD PARK

68	CBS 3775	Never An Everyday Thing/I Can See The Sun Shine	7

SPRINGFIELDS

(see also Dusty Springfield, Lana Sisters, Tom Springfield, Mike Hurst)

61	Philips PB 1145	Dear John/I Done What They Told Me To	6
61	Philips PB 1168	Breakaway/Good News	7
61	Philips PB 1178	Bambino/Star Of Hope (with p/s)	8
62	Philips PB 1220	Goodnight Irine/Far Away Places	6
62	Philips PB 1241	Silver Threads And Golden Needles/Aunt Rhody	5
62	Philips 326 536 BF	Swahili Papa/Gotta Travel On	6
62	Philips 326 557BF	Island Of Dreams/The Johnson Boys	5
63	Philips 326 577 BF	Say I Won't Be There/Little Boat	5
63	Philips BF 1263	Come On Home/Pit-A-Pat	7
64	Philips BF 1306	If I Was Down And Out/Maracabamba	7
61	Philips BBE 12476	THE SPRINGFIELDS (EP, mono)	12
61	Philips SBBE 9068	THE SPRINGFIELDS (EP, stereo)	15
62	Lyntone P125E	CHRISTMAS WITH THE SPRINGFIELDS (EP, mail-order via Woman's Own)	8
62	Philips 433 622 BE	KINDA FOLKSY (EP)	8
63	Philips 433 623 BE	KINDA FOLKSY No. 2 (EP)	8
63	Philips 433 624 BE	KINDA FOLKSY No. 3 (EP)	8
63	Philips BBE 12538	HIT SOUNDS (EP)	8
63	Philips 433 643 BE	FOLK SONGS FROM THE HILLS (EP)	8
62	Philips BBL 7551	KINDA FOLKSY (LP, mono)	15
62	Philips SBBL 674	KINDA FOLKSY (LP, stereo)	20
63	Philips 632 304 BL	FOLK SONGS FROM THE HILLS (LP)	15
64	Philips BET 606	THE SPRINGFIELDS STORY (2-LP)	18
69	Fontana SFL 13098	THE SPRINGFIELDS SING AGAIN (LP)	12

SPRINGFIELDS

88	Sarah SARAH 010	Sunflower/Clown/Are We Gonna Be Alright? (foldaround p/s with 14" x 10" poster in polyester bag; yellow p/s)	25
88	Sarah SARAH 010	Sunflower/Clown/Are We Gonna Be Alright? (foldaround p/s with 14" x 10" poster in polyester bag; later orange p/s)	18
91	Sarah SARAH 040	Wonder (p/s, with insert)	7

BRUCE SPRINGSTEEN

(see also Nils Lofgren, Roy Orbison)

75	CBS A 3661	Born To Run/Meeting Across The River	15
76	CBS A 3940	Tenth Avenue Freeze-Out/She's The One	20
78	CBS A 6424	Prove It All Night/Factory	15
78	CBS A 6532	Badlands/Something In The Night	15
78	CBS A 6720	Promised Land/Streets Of Fire	60
80	CBS A 9309	Hungry Heart/Held Up Without A Gun (p/s, withdrawn first issue, black and white p/s, blue lettering)	25
80	CBS A 9309	Hungry Heart/Held Up Without A Gun	6
81	CBS A 9568	Sherry Darling/Independence Day (white label promo, 100 only 2 known copies with p/s listing 'Independence Day')	2500
81	CBS A 9568	Sherry Darling/Independence Day (white label promo, 100 only)	2000
81	CBS A 9568	Sherry Darling/Be True (p/s)	15
81	CBS A 1179	The River/Independence Day (p/s)	15
81	CBS A 13-1179	The River/Born To Run/Rosalita (12", p/s, sleeves credit 'East Street Band')	15

			MINT VALUE £
81	CBS A 13-1179	The River/Born To Run/Rosalita (12", p/s)	12
81	CBS A 1557	Cadillac Ranch/Wreck On The Highway (p/s)	15
82	CBS A 2794	Atlantic City/Mansion On The Hill (p/s)	20
82	CBS A 2969	Open All Night/The Big Pay Back (p/s)	25
84	CBS WA 4436	Dancing In The Dark/Pink Cadillac (Cadillac-shaped picture disc)	20
84	CBS A 4662	Cover Me/Jersey Girl (live) (poster p/s)	5
84	CBS WA 4662	Cover Me/Jersey Girl (live) (Bruce-shaped picture disc with plinth)	25
84	CBS DA 4662/A 4436	Cover Me/Jersey Girl (live)//Dancing In The Dark/Pink Cadillac (shrinkable double pack, both 45s in p/s)	12
84	CBS DA 4662/A 7077	Cover Me/Jersey Girl (live)//Born To Run/Meeting Across The River (shrinkwrapped double pack, no p/s on 2nd 45)	12
84	CBS A 6561	I'm Going Down/Janey, Don't You Lose Heart (p/s)	7
85	CBS A 7077	Born To Run/Meeting Across The River (reissue, blue p/s, withdrawn)	25
85	CBS A 6342	I'm On Fire/Born In The U.S.A. (p/s, with competition postcard)	8
85	CBS WA 6342	I'm On Fire/Born In The U.S.A. (p/s, flag-shaped picture disc)	20
85	CBS QTA 6375	Glory Days/Stand On It/Sherry Darling/Racing In The Street (12", poster p/s)	8
85	CBS BRUCE 1	BORN IN THE U.S.A. - THE 12" COLLECTION (4 x 12" & 7", box with poster)	20
86	CBS 650 193-0	War (live)/Merry Xmas Baby (live)//My Home Town (live)/Santa Claus Is Coming To Town (live) (shrinkwrapped double pack, both 45s in p/s)	10
86	CBS 650 193-6	War/Merry Xmas Baby (live)/Incident On 57th Street (live) (12", poster p/s)	8
87	CBS 650 381-6	Fire (live)/For You (live)/Born To Run (live)/No Surrender (live)/ 10th Avenue (live) Freeze-Out (live) (12", p/s)	12
87	CBS BRUCE B2	Born To Run/Spirit In The Night//Johnny 99/Because The Night (double pack box set)	8
87	CBS BRUCE C2	Born To Run (live)/Spirit In The Night (live)/Johnny 99 (live)/Seeds (live) (CD, card sleeve with gauze inner)	10
87	CBS 651 141-0	Brilliant Disguise/Lucky Man (gatefold p/s, with discography)	6
87	CBS 651 141-6	Brilliant Disguise/Lucky Man (12", p/s, with poster)	8
87	CBS 651 295-0	Tunnel Of Love/Two For The Road (postcard-shaped picture disc)	15
87	CBS 651 295-8	Tunnel Of Love/Two For The Road/Santa Claus Is Coming To Town (12", p/s with poster)	8
87	CBS 651 295-2	Tunnel Of Love/Santa Claus Is Coming To Town (live)/Two For The Road (CD, card sleeve)	20
88	CBS BRUCE C3	Tougher Than The Rest/Roulette/Be True (Live)/Born To Run (New Live) (CD, card sleeve)	8
88	CBS BRUCE Q4	Spare Parts/Cover Me (live)/Spare Parts (live)/I'm On Fire (live) (12", different p/s)	10
88	CBS BRUCE B4	Spare Parts/Pink Cadillac/Spare Parts (live)/Chimes Of Freedom (live) (CD, BRUCE C4 disc in silver tin)	20
92	Sony 658 138-5	57 Channels (And Nothin' On)/Stand On It/Janey, Don't You Lose Heart (CD, picture disc, digipak)	12
94	Columbia 660 065-8	Streets Of Philadelphia/If I Should Fall Behind/Growing Up/Big Muddy (12", picture disc)	10

LPs

73	CBS 65480	GREETINGS FROM ASBURY PARK, N.J. (cutaway gatefold sleeve, orange label)	20
74	CBS 65780	THE WILD, THE INNOCENT AND THE E STREET SHUFFLE (orange label, yellow lettering on sleeve; with "Ashbury" mis-spelling on label)	20
75	CBS 69170	BORN TO RUN (with "John Landau" misprint on rear sleeve)	20
79	CBS 66353	BRUCE SPRINGSTEEN (3-LP, box set)	18
84	CBS 11-86304	BORN IN THE U.S.A. (picture disc)	25
87	CBS 460 270-0	TUNNEL OF LOVE (picture disc)	15
87	CBS CDCBS 460 270-9	TUNNEL OF LOVE (CD, picture disc)	20
90	CBS LSP 980636 1	COLLECTED WORKS OF BRUCE SPRINGSTEEN (7-LP box set)	200
92	Sony 471 423-0	HUMAN TOUCH (picture disc)	12
92	Sony 471 424-0	LUCKY TOWN (picture disc, with side 1 on both sides)	75
92	Sony 471 424-0	LUCKY TOWN (picture disc)	12
02	Sony 50800	THE RISING (2-LP, stickered)	30

SPRINGTIME

78 Sonet SON 2143 — Mrs Caroline Robinson/Honey Bye Bye (p/s) — 6

SPRINGWATER

80 Fabulous JC6 — Move A Little Closer/Rescue Me (p/s) — 5

70 Fabulous JC 2 — Sailing/Captain Of The Sea — 6

SPRINGWELL

71 London HLU 10345 — It's For You/Our Question — 15

SPROG & WIDGIT

72 Diddley Do DIDLP 02 — 32 ENGLISH FOLK SONGS IN THE SILLY TRADITION (2-LP, gatefold sleeve) — 18

SPRONG & NYAH SHUFFLE

69 Grape GR 3001 — Moonwalk/Think — 25

BILLY SPROUD & ROCK 'N' ROLL SIX

57 Columbia DB 3893 — Rock Mr. Piper/If You're So Smart (How Come You Ain't Rich) — 25

57 Columbia DB 3893 — Rock Mr. Piper/If You're So Smart (How Come You Ain't Rich) (78) — 20

SPROUTS

58 RCA RCA 1031 — Teen Billy Baby/Goodbye, She's Gone — 40

58 RCA RCA 1031 — Teen Billy Baby/Goodbye, She's Gone (78) — 35

SPUD

75 Philips 9108 002 — A SILK PURSE (LP) — 20

SPUD AND THE FABS

80 Whitetower AMC 706 — Your Place Or Mine (p/s) — 25

SPUNKY ONION

74 Contempo CS2006 — Cookie Man (Part 1)/Cookie Man (part 2) — 6

SPUNKY SPIDER

73 Phoenix S-NIX 143 — You Won't Come/Perchance — 60

MINT VALUE £

WILD JIMMY SPURRILL
(see also Noble 'Thin Man' Watts, Guitar Crusher)
60s XX MIN 717 NOBLE 'THIN MAN' WATTS AND WILD JIMMY SPURRILL (EP) . . . 20

SPURS
88 Outback OUT 1 Soldier (p/s) . . . 12

SPYROGYRA
79 Infinity (no cat. no.) MORNING DANCE (LP, picture disc, in-house issue, top-flap poly sleeve, 50 copies) . . . 50

SPYS
79 No Bad NB 3 The Young Ones/Heavy Scene (p/s) . . . 5

SQUAD
79 Squad SQS 1 Red Alert/£8 A Week (in die cut p/s) . . . 40
79 Squad SQS 1 Red Alert/£8 A Week . . . 20
79 Squad SQS 2 Millionaire/Brockhill Boys (p/s) . . . 40

SQUADRONAIRES
54 Decca F 10248 Coach Call Boogie/Donegal Cradle Song . . . 10
54 Decca F 10274 Wolf On The Prowl/Mudhopper . . . 10
57 Columbia DB 3882 Rock And Roll Boogie/Right Now, Right Now . . . 12
53 Decca LF 1141 CONTRASTS IN JAZZ (10" LP) . . . 12

LESTER SQUARE & THE SQUARE DEAL SURFS
(see also Monochrome Set)
84 Thin Sliced TSR 4T The Plug (12", p/s) . . . 8

SQUARE SET
71 Decca FR 13197 That's What I Want/Come On . . . 80

SQUARES
78 Sire SIR 4003 No Fear/Nobodys Fool (p/s) . . . 5

SQUEEK
72 Bronze BRO 130 Make Hay While The Sun Shines/L Amour D'un Apres Midi . . . 20

SQUEEZE
77 BTM SBT 107 Take Me I'm Yours/No, Disco Kid, No (unreleased) . . . 0
77 Deptford Fun City DFC 01 PACKET OF THREE (EP, red & blue photo p/s) . . . 10
77 Deptford Fun City DFC 01 PACKET OF THREE (12" EP, plain pink die-cut sleeve, 500 only) . . . 10
78 A&M AMSP 7335 Take Me I'm Yours/Night Nurse (12", p/s) . . . 7
78 A&M AMS 7360 Bang Bang/All Fed Up (p/s, green vinyl) . . . 5
78 A&M AMS 7398 Goodbye Girl/Saints Alive (3-D p/s) . . . 5
79 A&M AMS 7426 Cool For Cats/Model (p/s, brilliant pink vinyl, 5,000 only) . . . 6
79 A&M AMS 7426 Cool For Cats/Model (p/s, red vinyl, 1,000 only) . . . 7
79 A&M AMSP 7426 Cool For Cats/Model (12", p/s, pale pink vinyl) . . . 8
79 A&M AMS 7495 Christmas Day/Going Crazy (p/s, white vinyl) . . . 5
79 A&M AMS 7507 Another Nail In My Heart/Pretty Thing (p/s, clear vinyl) . . . 5
80 Lyntone LYN 7010/1 Wrong Way (green vinyl flexidisc, with Smash Hits) . . . 5
81 A&M AMS 8147 Tempted/Yap Yap Yap (p/s, with free U.S. 5" single "Another Nail In My Heart"/"If I Didn't Love You", p/s, shrinkwrapped) . . . 5
81 A&M AMS 8166 Labelled With Love/Squabs On Forty Five (withdrawn p/s) . . . 12

SQUIBBY & REFLECTIONS
68 Direction 58-3453 Ragamuffin/For A Little While . . . 5
68 Direction 58-3606 Loving You Has Made My Life Worthwhile/Better Off Without You . . . 5
69 Direction 58-4073 You Got It/Come Back To Me . . . 8

SQUIBS
81 Oily SLICK 1 On The Line (plain sleeve, with insert) . . . 25
81 Oily SLICK 3 Parades/Out On The Town (p/s) . . . 20

BILLY SQUIER
(see also Freddie Mercury, Roger Taylor)
82 Capitol CL 261 Emotions In Motion/Catch 22 (p/s) . . . 12
82 Capitol CL 261 Emotions In Motion/Catch 22 (picture disc) . . . 15
84 Capitol SQD 1 Rock Me Tonite/Can't Get Next To You//She's A Runner/Listen To The Heart (double pack) . . . 6
86 Capitol CL 433 Love Is The Hero/Learn How To Live (live) (p/s) . . . 7
86 Capitol 12CL 433 Love Is The Hero (extended version with Freddie Mercury intro)/Learn How To Live (live) (12", p/s) . . . 55

SQUIRE
(see also Anthony Meynell)
79 Rok ROK I/II Get Ready To Go/COMING SHORTLY: Doing The Flail (company sleeve) . . . 30
79 I-Spy SEE 2 Walking Down The King's Road/It's A Mod Mod Mod Mod World (company sleeve) . . 7
79 I-Spy SEE 4 The Face Of Youth Today/I Know A Girl (keyhole company sleeve,plastic labels) . . . 6
80 Stage One STAGE 2 My Mind Goes Round In Circles/Does Stephanie Know? (p/s) . . . 6
82 Hi-Lo HI 001 No Time Tomorrow/Don't Cry To Me (p/s) . . . 5
82 Hi-Lo HI 002 Girl On A Train/Every Trick In The Book (p/s) . . . 5
83 Hi-Lo HIT 003 Every Trick In The Book/Every Trick In The Book (Elastic Mix) (12", p/s) . . . 8
83 Hi-Lo HI 004 Jesamine/When I Try, I Lie (p/s) . . . 10
84 Hi-Lo HI 005/SFC 2 The Young Idea/It's Getting Better (Squire Fan Club issue) . . . 10
85 Hi-Lo LOX 1 Does Stephanie Know? (flexidisc) . . . 6
94 Detour DR 020 The Place I Used To Live/Make Love To You/Over You (p/s, 900 only, 50 on white vinyl) . . . 10
94 Detour DR 020 The Place I Used To Live/Make Love To You/Over You (p/s, 2nd pressing of 250 copies, white labels & purple print: 3rd pressing, 588 copies on clear splattered vinyl) . . . 5
83 Hi-Lo LO 01 HITS FROM 3,000 YEARS AGO (LP) . . . 18
83 Hi-Lo LO 02 GET SMART (LP, with poster) . . . 15
85 Hi-Lo LO 03 THE SINGLES ALBUM (LP) . . . 15

MINT VALUE £

JOHN SQUIRE
(see also Stone Roses)

02	North Country Records NC001	Joe Louis/Home Sweet Home (p/s)	5

SQUIRES

69	MCA MU 1060	Funky Bayswater/Games People Play	8

ROSEMARY SQUIRES

56	Decca F 10685	Band Of Gold/Where You Are	10
58	HMV POP 462	Happy Is The Bride/Give Me The Simple Life	8
58	HMV POP 541	There Goes My Lover/Please Be Kind	8
64	HMV POP 1288	Bluesette/Nothing's Changed	8
56	MGM MGM-EP 640	MY LOVE IS A WANDERER (EP)	40
60	HMV 7EG 8588	ROSEMARY (EP)	40
63	HMV CLP 1669	EVERYTHINGS COMING UP ROSY (LP, mono)	80
63	HMV CSD 1508	EVERYTHINGS COMING UP ROSY (LP, stereo)	150
65	HMV CLP 1832	SOMETHING TO REMEMBER ME BY (LP, mono)	80
65	HMV CSD 1586	SOMETHING TO REMEMBER ME BY (LP, stereo)	120

S.R.C.
(See also Streamliners with Joanne)

69	Capitol CL 15576	Black Sheep/Morning Mood	35
87	Bam Caruso OPRA 063	Black Sheep/BRAIN: Nightmares In Red (jukebox issue, die-cut company sleeve)	5
69	Capitol (S)T 2991	S.R.C. (LP)	60
69	Capitol E-(S)T 134	MILESTONES (LP)	50
70	Capitol E-(S)T 273	TRAVELLER'S TALE (LP)	50

ASHBURY STABBINS DUO

76	Bead Records BEAD 4	FIRE WITHOUT STICKS (LP)	50

STACCATOS

61	Parlophone R 4828	Main Line/Topaz	15
68	Fontana TF 966	Butchers And Bakers/Imitations Of Love	25

STACCATOS

68	NEMS 3003	Why Care About Today/Cry To Me	25

STACCATOS (U.S.)

66	Capitol CL 15478	Let's Run Away/Face To Face (With Love)	7
67	Capitol CL 15505	Half Past Midnight/Weatherman	7

CLARENCE STACEY

59	Pye International 7N 25025	Just Your Love/Lonely Guy	35
59	Pye International 7N 25025	Just Your Love/Lonely Guy (78)	35

GWEN STACEY

65	RCA RCX 7166	INTRODUCING GWEN STACEY (EP)	150

STACK OF HEARTS

86	SOH SOH 001	Danger Zone/Searching For A Spirit (no p/s)	25

BOB STACKIE
(see also Sir Collins [Band], Owen Gray)

68	Collins Downbeat CR 009	Grab It Hold It Feel It (with Sir Collins Band)/ DAN SIMMONDS: Way Out Sound	50

STACKRIDGE

71	MCA MKS 5065	Dora, The Female Explorer/Everyman	5
72	MCA MKS 5103	Anyone For Tennis?/Amazingly Agnes	5
71	MCA MDKS 8002	STACKRIDGE (LP, gatefold sleeve, pink/orange 'dogbone' label)	25
72	MCA MKPS 2025	FRIENDLINESS (LP, blue/black 'hexagon' label)	20
74	MCA MCG 3501	THE MAN IN THE BOWLER HAT (LP, gatefold sleeve)	12
74	Rocket PIGL 11	EXTRAVAGANZA (LP, gatefold label)	12
76	MCA MCF 2747	DO THE STANLEY (LP)	12
76	Rocket ROLL 3	MR. MICK (LP)	12

STACKWADDY

70	Dandelion S 5119	Roadrunner/Kentucky	12
72	Dandelion 2001 331	You Really Got Me/Willie The Pimp	10
71	Dandelion DAN 8003	STACKWADDY (LP, gatefold sleeve with lyric insert)	90
71	Dandelion DAN 8003	STACKWADDY (LP, gatefold sleeve with lyric insert, as K 49003)	40
72	Dandelion 2310 231	BUGGER OFF! (LP)	100

STADIUM DOGS

77	Audiogenic A 17	Easy Beat/Android Rocker/Media Withdrawal (die-cut p/s)	10

JIM STAFFORD

73	MGM 2006 374	Spiders & Snakes/Undecided	5

JO STAFFORD
(see also Jonathan & Darlene Edwards, Gordon MacRae, Tommy Dorsey)

53	Columbia SCM 5011	Star Of Hope/Somebody	10
53	Columbia SCM 5012	It Is No Secret/He Bought My Soul At Calvary	15
53	Columbia SCM 5013	You Belong To Me/Jambalaya (On The Bayou)	40
53	Columbia SCM 5026	Keep It A Secret/Once To Every Heart	15
53	Columbia SCM 5046	Something To Remember You By/Blue Moon	15
53	Columbia SCM 5064	September In The Rain/JO STAFFORD & FRANKIE LAINE: Chow, Willy	15
57	Philips JK 1003	On London Bridge/Perfect Love (jukebox issue)	25
58	Philips PB 818	With A Little Bit Of Luck/Wouldn't It Be Loverly	5
58	Philips PB 876	Hibiscus/How Can We Say Goodbye	5
59	Philips PB 898	My Heart Is From Missouri/It Won't Be Easy	5
59	Philips PB 935	Pine Top's Boogie Woogie/All Yours	8

			MINT VALUE £
59	Philips PB 935	Pine Top's Boogie Woogie/All Yours (78)	15
60	Philips PB 991	It Is No Secret/He Bought My Soul At Calvary (reissue)	5
60	Philips PB 1034	Candy/Indoor Sport	5
60	Pye Intl. 7N 25139	If My Heart Had A Window/Symphony	6
54	Columbia SEG 7516	WITH NELSON EDDY (plain sleeve)	10
54	Columbia SEG 7548	SHOW SONGS (plain sleeve)	10
55	Philips BBE 12014	JO STAFFORD No. 1	10
57	Philips BBE 12138	JO STAFFORD No. 2	10
57	Philips BBE 12141	JO STAFFORD WITH THE ART VAN DAMME QUINTET	10
58	Philips BBE 12214	T.V. SERIES	10
60	Capitol EAP 20049	THE JO STAFFORD TOUCH	10
61	Capitol EAP 20154	SIMPLE MELODY	10
61	Philips BBE 12459	JO + JAZZ	10
50	Capitol LC 6500	AMERICAN FOLK SONGS (10")	20
51	Capitol LC 6515	KISS ME KATE (10", with Gordon MacRae)	15
53	Capitol LC 6575	CAPITOL PRESENTS JO STAFFORD (10")	15
53	Capitol LC 6611	SUNDAY EVENING SONGS (10", with Gordon MacRae)	12
54	Capitol LC 6635	CAPITOL PRESENTS JO STAFFORD, VOL. 2 (10")	15
54	Columbia 33S 1024	AS YOU DESIRE ME (10")	15
54	Philips BBR 8011	MY HEART'S IN THE HIGHLANDS (10")	12
56	Philips BBR 8076	THE VOICE OF YOUR CHOICE (10")	20
56	Philips BBL 7100	HAPPY HOLIDAY (soundtrack)	15
57	Philips BBL 7169	ONCE OVER LIGHTLY	15
57	Philips BBL 7187	SKI TRAILS	15
58	Philips BBL 7243	SWINGIN' DOWN BROADWAY	15
59	Philips BBL 7290	I'LL BE SEEING YOU	15
59	Philips BBL 7327	BALLAD OF THE BLUES	15
60	Philips BBL 7395	JO STAFFORD SHOWCASE	15
61	Philips BBL 7428	JO + JAZZ (also stereo SBBL 595)	15

JO STAFFORD & FRANKIE LAINE
(see also Frankie Laine)

53	Columbia SCM 5014	Settin' The Woods On Fire/Piece A-Puddin'	25
55	Philips BBR 8075	FLOATIN' DOWN TO COTTON TOWN (10" LP)	40

TERRY STAFFORD

63	Stateside SS 225	Heartache On The Way/You Left Me Here To Cry	15
64	London HLU 9871	Suspicion/Judy	10
64	London HLU 9902	I'll Touch A Star/Playing With Fire	12
64	London HLU 9923	Follow The Rainbow/Are You A Fool Like Me	12
64	London RE-U 1436	SUSPICION (EP)	60
64	London HA-U 8200	SUSPICION (LP)	70

STAGEFRIGHT

85	STN STN 1	Strangers In The Night/Heartless/Rock City (no p/s)	150

ROSS STAGG

74	Dawn DNS 1059	I'll Never Be A Star (But I Might)/Oh Captain	6

STAIFFI ET SES MUSTAFA'S

59	Pye Intl. 7N 25057	Mustafa Cha Cha Oriental/Zoubida Cha Cha Oriental	10

STAINED GLASS

74	Sweet Folk & C. SFA 019	OPEN ROAD (LP)	90

CHRIS STAINTON & GLEN TURNER

76	Decca SKL-R 5259	TUNDRA (LP)	12

STAIRS

92	Imaginary MIRAGE 029	Weed Bus (12", unissued, test pressings only, proof p/s)	40

STAIRSTEPS
(see also Five Stairsteps)

71	Buddah 2011 092	Stay Close To Me/I Made A Mistake	8
75	Dark Horse AMS 5505	From Us To You/Time (in USA p/s)	10
75	Dark Horse AMS 5505	From Us To You/Time	8
76	Dark Horse AMS 5507	Pasado/Throwin' Stones Atcha	10
71	Buddah 2359 021	STEP BY STEP BY STEP (LP)	20
71	Buddah 2365 015	STAY CLOSE TO ME (LP)	20
72	Buddah 2365 016	THE STAIRSTEPS (LP)	20
76	Dark Horse AMLH 22004	2ND RESSURECTION (LP)	20

STAIRWAY
(see also Jane Relf, Yardbirds, Renaissance)

88	New World NWCD 168	MOONSTONE (CD)	18

STAKKA AND SKYNET

00	Underfire UDFR 016	Knight Lore/Global Report (12")	10
01	Underfire UDFRLPS 04	CLOCKWORK SAMPLER EP: Decoy/Side Effects (Kemal and Rob Data remix)/ 9000 series/Side Effects (Teebee remix) (2 x 12", stickered, die-cut sleeve)	20
01	Underfire UDRFRLP 04	CLOCKWORK (LP, 5 discs)	40

STAKKER
(see under Humanoid)

STALLION

75	Flyright FLY 45 003	Skinny Kid/Cobra	45

STAMFORD BRIDGE

70	Penny Farthing PEN 715	Chelsea/Ossie	12
71	Penny Farthing PELS 515	FIRST DAY OF YOUR LIFE (LP)	20

TERRY STAMP
(see also Third World War)

75	A&M AMLH 68329	FAT STICKS (LP, with lyric insert)	30

MINT VALUE £

STAMPEDE

82	Polydor POSP 507	Days Of Wine And Roses/Photographs (p/s)	12
82	Polydor POSP 507	Photographs/Days Of Wine And Roses (A-side switched, no p/s)	30
82	Polydor POSPX 507	Days Of Wine And Roses/Movin' On/Photographs/Missing You (12", p/s)	20
83	Polydor POSP 592	The Other Side/The Runner (p/s)	10
82	Polydor ROCK 1	OFFICIAL BOOTLEG (LP)	15
83	Polydor POLS 1083	HURRICANE TOWN (LP)	15
70	United Artists UP 35111	Que Sera Sera/Harpsichord	8

STAMPEDERS

71	Stateside SS2197	Devil You/Giant In The Streets	8
72	Stateside SS 2202	Monday Morning Choo Choo/Then Came The White Man	5
73	Regal Zonophone RZ 3083	Minstrel Gypsy/Mumbo Jumbo	5
72	Regal Zonophone RZ 3069	Johnny Lightning/Today's The Beginning Of The Rest Of Your Life	6
73	Regal Zonophone RZ 3079	Oh My Lady/No Destination	6
73	Regal Zonophone RZ 3085	Ride In The Wind/Running Wild	20
72	Regal Zono. SLRZ 1032	THE STAMPEDERS (LP)	30
74	Regal Zono. SLRZ 1039	FROM THE FIRE (LP)	30

JOE STAMPLEY

73	Dot DOT 145	Soul Song/Not Too Long Ago	10

JEAN STANBACK

69	Deep Soul DS 9101	I Still Love You/If I Ever Needed Love	50

STANDELLS

64	Liberty LIB 55722	I'll Go Crazy/Help Yourself	35
66	Capitol CL 15446	Dirty Water/Rari	50
65	Liberty LBY 1243	THE STANDELLS IN PERSON AT P.J.'s (LP)	60

STANDING OVATION

92	Kold Sweat KS126	Shadows Of Mayhem (12")	12

JOHNNY STANDLEY

56	Capitol EAP 1020	IT'S IN THE BOX (EP)	12

STANDS

00s	Echo ECS 142	When This River Rolls Over You/She Speaks Of These Things (autographed p/s, 1000 only)	8

ARNOLD STANG

59	Fontana H 226	Ivy Will Cling/Where Ya' Calling From, Charlie	8

PAUL STANLEY

79	Casablanca CAN 140	Hold Me Touch Me/Goodbye (p/s, purple vinyl with mask & picture label, most with mispressed B-side: "Love In Chains")	20

PETE STANLEY & ROGER KNOWLES

70s	Xtra TRANS 1146	PICKING AND SINGING (LP)	25

PETE STANLEY & WIZZ JONES

(see also Wizz Jones)

65	Columbia DB 7776	The Ballad Of Hollis Brown/Riff Minor	20
66	Columbia SX 6083	SIXTEEN TONS OF BLUEGRASS (LP)	60

STANLEY BROTHERS

61	Melodisc MLP 12-118	MOUNTAIN SONG FAVOURITES (LP)	12
61	Melodisc MLP 12-122	SACRED SONGS FROM THE HILLS (LP)	12

ROY STANNARD AND HIS MUSIC

87	SS SS 100	The Peanut Vendor/'Swingin' ' The Blues	5

LISA STANSFIELD

81	Devil DEV 2	Your Alibis/Thought Police (p/s)	5

VIV(IAN) STANSHALL

(see also Bonzo Dog [Doo Dah] Band, Grimms)

70	Liberty LBF 15309	Labio-Dental Fricative/Paper Round (with Sean Head Show Band featuring Eric Clapton)	30
71	Fly BUG 4	Suspicion (with Gargantuan Chums)/Blind Date (with Big Grunt)	12
74	Warner Bros K 16424	Lakonga/Baba Tunde	7
76	Harvest HAR 5114	Young Ones/Are You Havin' Any Fun/Question	20
80	Charisma CB 373	Terry Keeps His Clips On/King Cripple (p/s)	6
81	Charisma CB 382	Calypso To Colapso/Smoke Signals At Night (p/s)	5
74	Warner Bros K 56052	MEN OPENING UMBRELLAS AHEAD (LP, with inner)	60
78	Charisma CAS 1139	SIR HENRY AT RAWLINSON END (LP, soundtrack, with insert)	20
81	Charisma CAS 1153	TEDDY BOYS DON'T KNIT (LP)	22
84	Demon Verbals VERB 1	SIR HENRY AT NDIDDI'S KRAAL (LP)	20

STAPLE SINGERS

64	Riverside 106902 RIF	Hammer And Nails/Glory Land	10
67	Columbia DB 8292	For What It's Worth/Are You Sure?	30
69	Soul City SC 117	For What It's Worth/Are You Sure? (reissue)	20
69	Stax STAX 118	I See It/The Ghetto	6
71	Stax 2025 019	Heavy Makes You Happy/Love Is Plentiful	6
72	Stax 2025 068	Respect Yourself/You're Gonna Make Me Cry	6
72	Stax 2025 110	I'll Take You There/Just Another Soldier	6
62	Riverside REP 3220	THE SAVIOUR IS BORN (EP)	15
63	Stateside SL 10015	SWING LOW (LP)	30
63	Riverside RLP 3501	HAMMER AND NAILS (LP)	25
65	Fontana 688 515 ZL	UNCLOUDY DAY (LP)	20
66	Columbia SX 6023	FREEDOM HIGHWAY (LP)	20
69	Stax (S)XATS 1004	SOUL FOLK IN ACTION (LP)	18
69	Stax SXATS 1018	WE'LL GET OVER (LP)	18

MINT VALUE £

71	Stax 2362 005	THE STAPLE SINGERS (LP)	18
71	Stax 2362 011	SOUL FOLK IN ACTION (LP, reissue)	12
72	Stax STX 1001	CITY IN THE SKY (LP)	15
72	Stax 2325 069	BEALTITUDE/RESPECT YOURSELF (LP)	15

CYRIL STAPLETON & HIS ORCHESTRA

(see also Gordon Langhorn, Desmond Lane)

54	Decca F 10293	Long Distance Love/There'll Be No Teardrops Tonight	5
55	Decca F 10456	Tango Mambo/Mexican Madness	6
55	Decca F 10470	Fanfare Boogie/Time After Time	7
55	Decca F 10488	Elephant Tango/Gabrielle	7
55	Decca F 10559	Blue Star (The "Medic" Theme) (with Julie Dawn)/Honey Babe (with Gordon Langhorn)	7
56	Decca F 10703	The Italian Theme/Come Next Spring	7
56	Decca F 10735	The Happy Whistler (with Desmond Lane)/Tiger Tango	7
56	Decca F 10793	Highway Patrol/Maids Of Madrid	6
57	Decca F 10883	Rock, Fiddle, Rock/Chantez, Chantez	5
57	Decca F 10912	Forgotten Dreams/It's Not For Me To Say	7
58	Decca F 10979	Monday Blues (Parts 1 & 2)	5
62	Decca F 11443	Afrikaan Beat/My Sad Girl	6
69	Pye 7N 17807	Department S (Theme)/W. Somerset Maugham TV Theme (in p/s)	20
69	Pye 7N 17807	Department S (Theme)/W. Somerset Maugham TV Theme	10
62	Ace Of Clubs ACL 1114	COME TWISTIN' (LP)	20

STEVEN STAPLETON & DAVID TIBET

(see also Current 93, Nurse With Wound, Tibet & Stapleton)

91	United Dairies UD 037	THE SADNESS OF THINGS/THE GRAVE AND BEAUTIFUL NAME OF SADNESS (LP, one side each)	35

STA-PREST

80	Avatar AAA 103	Schooldays/Tomorrow (p/s)	75

STAR

73	Bradley BRAD 315	Children Of the Sun/Your Day Will Come	12

STAR SPANGLES

02	Capitol R 6593	Which Of The Two Of Us Is Gonna Burn This House Down/ Stain Glass Shoes (p/s)	10

STAR WITH PETER COLLINS

60s	SRT/Custom 10	Give It Up/Wake Up	10

STARBUCK

(see also Mandrake Paddle Steamer, Shambles)

73	RCA RCA 2350	Wouldn't You Like It/Manana	8
73	Bradleys BRAD 312	Do You Like Boys?/You Never Wanna Rock 'N' Roll	20
74	Bradleys BRAD 7411	Heart Throb/Ricochet	8

BUDDY STARCHER

64	London RE-B 1424	BUDDY STARCHER AND HIS MOUNTAIN GUITAR VOL. 1 (EP)	10
64	London RE-B 1425	BUDDY STARCHER AND HIS MOUNTAIN GUITAR VOL. 2 (EP)	10
64	London RE-B 1426	BUDDY STARCHER AND HIS MOUNTAIN GUITAR VOL. 3 (EP)	10

STARFIGHTERS

80	Motor City MCR 105	I'm Falling/Heaven And Hell (in p/s)	40
80	Motor City MCR 105	I'm Falling/Heaven And Hell	7
81	Jive JIV 003	Alley Cat Blues/Don't Touch Me (p/s)	7
81	Jive JIVET 003	Alley Cat Blues/Don't Touch Me (12", p/s)	15
81	Jive JIVET 6	Power Crazy/I Want You (p/s)	6
81	Jive JIVET 6	Power Crazy/I Want You/Get Out While You Can (12", p/s)	8
81	Jive HOP 200	STARFIGHTERS (LP, with inner)	22
82	Jive HOP 205	IN FLIGHT MOVIE (LP)	12

STARGAZERS

(see also Roy Smith & Stargazers, Lita Roza, Dickie Valentine)

54	Decca F 10213	I See The Moon/Eh Cumpari	25
54	Decca F 10259	The Happy Wanderer/Till We Two Are One	15
54	Decca F 10379	365 Kisses/I Need You Now	6
54	Decca F 10412	Rose Of The Wildwood/Come The Morning	6
55	Decca F 10437	Somebody/(My Baby Don't Love Me) No More (& Sonny Farrar Banjo Band)	10
55	Decca F 10523	The Crazy Otto Rag/Hey, Mr. Banjo	10
55	Decca F 10569	At The Steamboat River Ball/I Love You A Mountain (with Sonny Farrar Banjo Band)	5
55	Decca F 10594	Close The Door/I've Got Four Big Brothers	10
55	Decca F 10626	Twenty Tiny Fingers/An Old Beer Bottle	10
55	Decca F 10668	(Love Is) The Tender Trap/When The Swallows Say Goodbye	5
56	Decca F 10696	Zambesi/When The Swallows Say Goodbye	10
56	Decca F 10731	Hot Diggity (Dog Ziggity Boom)/Rockin' And Rollin'	10
56	Decca F 10775	She Loves To Rock/John Jacob Jingleheimer Smith	10
57	Decca F 10867	You Won't Be Around/Mangos	5
57	Decca F 10898	Honky Tonk Song/Golly!	5
60	Palette PG 9003	Three Beautiful Words/Manhattan Spiritual	6
56	Decca DFE 6341	THE STARGAZERS (EP)	25
56	Decca DFE 6362	ROCKIN' AND ROLLIN' (EP)	25
54	Decca LF 1186	PRESENTING THE STARGAZERS (10" LP)	30
59	Decca LK 4309	SOUTH OF THE BORDER (LP)	30

STARJETS

78	Epic S EPC 6902	Here She Comes Again/Watch Out	8
79	Epic S EPC 6968	It Really Doesn't Matter/Schooldays	5
79	Epic S EPC 7123	Run With The Pack/Watch Out	5

MINT VALUE £

79 Epic S EPC 6968/7123 It Really Doesn't Matter/Schooldays//Run With The Pack/ Watch Out (double pack, die-cut sleeves, promo only) 15
79 Epic S EPC 7417 Ten Years/One More Word (p/s) 5
79 Epic S EPC 7417 Ten Years/One More Word (Manchester gig issue, stamped white labels) 12
79 Epic S EPC 7770 War Stories/Do The Push (p/s) 5
79 Epic S EPC 7986 Schooldays/What A Life (p/s) 6
80 Epic S EPC 8276 Shiraleo/Standby 19 (p/s) 5
79 Epic EPC 83534 GOD BLESS STARJETS (LP) 15

STARLAND VOCAL GROUP

76 RCA RCA 2726 Afternoon Delight/Starland 6

STARLINGS

80s Ruffin A-M 029 NEW BLOOD (EP) 8

STARLITES

(see also Bellfield)

73 Downtown DT 502 You're A Wanted Man/G.G. ALL STARS: Back To Dubwise 7
74 Big Shot BI 629 Mama Dee Part One/Mama Dee Part Two 8
75 Bullet BU 554 Healing In The Barnyard/G.G. ALL STARS: Version 6
68 Philips BF 1725 Good Morning Mr Milkman/Don't Break My Heart Again 12

CINDY STARR

(see also Mopeds, Teardrops)

68 Columbia Blue Beat DB 107 Pain Of Love/Hippy Ska (as Cindy Starr & Rude Boys) 20
68 Columbia Blue Beat DB 110 The Way I Do/Sad Movies (Make Me Cry) (as Cindy Starr & Mopeds) 15

EDWIN STARR

(see also Blinky & Edwin Starr, Holidays)

66 Polydor BM 56702 Stop Her On Sight (S.O.S.)/I Have Faith In You (demo) 500
66 Polydor BM 56702 Stop Her On Sight (S.O.S.)/I Have Faith In You 25
66 Polydor BM 56717 Headline News/Harlem 20
67 Polydor BM 56726 It's My Turn Now/Girls Are Getting Prettier 25
68 Polydor BM 56753 Stop Her On Sight (S.O.S.)/Headline News (reissue) 10
67 Tamla Motown TMG 630 I Want My Baby Back/Gonna Keep On Tryin' Till I Win 30
67 Tamla Motown TMG 630 I Want My Baby Back/Gonna Keep On Tryin' Till I Win (DJ copy) 50
68 Tamla Motown TMG 646 I Am The Man For You Baby/My Weakness Is You 30
68 Tamla Motown TMG 646 I Am The Man For You Baby/My Weakness Is You (DJ copy) 90
68 Tamla Motown TMG 672 25 Miles/Mighty Good Lovin' 10
68 Tamla Motown TMG 672 25 Miles/Mighty Good Lovin' (DJ copy) 45
69 Tamla Motown TMG 692 Way Over There/If My Heart Could Tell The Story 20
69 Tamla Motown TMG 692 Way Over There/If My Heart Could Tell The Story (DJ copy) 50
69 Tamla Motown TMG 720 Oh How Happy/O, O, O, Baby (demos only, unissued, with Blinky) 300
70 Tamla Motown TMG 725 Time/Running Back And Forth 20
70 Tamla Motown TMG 754 War/He Who Picks A Rose 6
71 Tamla Motown TMG 764 Stop The War Now!/Gonna Keep On Tryin' Till I Win 8
71 Tamla Motown TMG 790 Agent Double 0 Soul/Back Street 12
71 Tamla Motown TMG 790 Agent Double 0 Soul/Back Street (DJ copy) 40
72 Tamla Motown TMG 810 Funky Music Sho' Nuff Turns Me On/Cloud Nine 8
73 Tamla Motown TMG 875 Love The Lonely People's Prayer/You've Got My Soul On Fire 20
73 Tamla Motown TMG 930 Ain't It Hell Up In Harlem/Who's Right Or Wrong 8
75 Bradleys BRAD 7520 Stay With Me/I'll Never Forget You 15
75 Bradleys BRAD 7531 Pain/Party 10
76 GTO GT 65 Accident/Eavesdropper 8
70s Tamla Motown TMG 905 Stop Her On Sight/Headline News (reissue) 6
70s Tamla Motown TMG 1028 Time/Running Back And Forth (reissue) 10
69 T. Motown STML 11094 SOUL MASTER (LP, mono) 35
69 T. Motown STML 11094 SOUL MASTER (LP, stereo) 40
69 T. Motown (S)TML 11115 25 MILES (LP, mono/stereo) 30
70 T. Motown (S)TML 11131 JUST WE TWO (LP, as Edwin Starr & Blinky) 25
70 Tamla Motown STML 11171 WAR AND PEACE (LP) 20
72 Tamla Motown STML 11199 INVOLVED (LP) 20
72 Tamla Motown STML 11209 THE HITS OF EDWIN STARR (LP) 15
74 Tamla Motown STML 11260 HELL UP IN HARLEM (LP, soundtrack) 15

FRANK STARR

62 London HLU 9545 Little Bitty Feeling/Lost In A Dream 12

FREDDIE STARR & MIDNIGHTERS

(see also Howie Casey & Seniors)

63 Decca F 11663 Who Told You?/Peter Gunn Locomotion 30
63 Decca F 11786 It's Shaking Time/Baby Blue 30
64 Decca F 12009 Never Cry On Someone's Shoulder/Just Keep On Dreaming 40
71 A&M AMS 838 Naomi/Free To Carry On (solo) 5
78 PVK PVK 004 FREDDIE STARR (LP) 12

JIMMY STARR

58 London HL 8731 It's Only Make Believe/Ooh Crazy 30
58 London HL 8731 It's Only Make Believe/Ooh Crazy (78) 15

KAY STARR

54 Capitol CL 14151 Am I A Toy Or A Treasure?/Fortune In Dreams 20
54 Capitol CL 14167 Fool, Fool, Fool/Allez-Vous En 20
55 HMV 7M 300 If Anyone Finds This, I Love You/Turn Right 15
55 HMV 7M 307 Foolishly Yours/For Better Or Worse 10
55 HMV 7M 315 Where, What Or When?/Good And Lonesome 10
56 HMV 7M 371 Rock And Roll Waltz/I've Changed My Mind 1,000 Times 20
56 HMV 7M 420 Second Fiddle/Love Ain't Right 10
57 HMV POP 345 A Little Loneliness/Touch And Go 8
57 HMV POP 357 Jamie Boy/The Things I Never Had 8
58 RCA RCA 1065 Stroll Me/Rockin' Chair 6

			MINT VALUE £
60	Capitol CL 15105	Riders In The Sky/Night Train	7
60	Capitol CL 15137	Wheel Of Fortune/If You Love Me (Really Love Me)	12

EPs/LPs

55	Vogue EPV 1014	KAY STARR (EP)	15
56	HMV 7EG 8165	WHAT A STAR IS KAY (EP)	10
56	HMV 7EG 8184	KAY STARR'S AGAIN (EP)	10
60	Top Rank JKP 2042	HEAVENLY KAY STARR (EP)	10
60	Capitol EAP1 1254	MOVING (EP)	10
60	Capitol EAP2 1254	MOVING PT. 2 (EP)	10
60	Capitol EAP3 1254	MOVING PT. 3 (EP)	10
61	Capitol EAP 1-20063	WHEEL OF FORTUNE (EP)	10
62	Capitol EAP 1-20210	WELL I ASK YOU (EP)	10
53	Capitol LC 6574	CAPITOL PRESENTS KAY STARR (10"LP)	20
54	Capitol LC 6630	THE KAY STARR STYLE (10" LP)	20
56	Capitol LC 6835	THE HITS OF KAY STARR (10" LP)	20
57	Capitol T 580	IN A BLUE MOOD (LP)	20
57	London HA-U 2039	SWINGING WITH THE STARR (LP)	20
58	RCA RD 27056	BLUE STARR (LP)	20
60	Capitol (S)T 1254	MOVIN'! (LP)	12
60	Capitol (S)T 1303	LOSERS, WEEPERS (LP)	12
60	Capitol (S)T 1374	MOVIN' ON BROADWAY (LP)	12
61	Capitol T 1358	ONE MORE TIME (LP)	12
61	Capitol (S)T 1438	JAZZ SINGER (LP)	12

LUCILLE STARR

64	London HL 9900	The French Song/Sit Down And Write A Letter To Me	12

LUCKY STARR

62	Parlophone R 4963	I've Been Everywhere/Wrong	7

MAXINE STARR

63	London HLU 9712	The Wishing Star/Sailor Boy	8

RANDY STARR

57	London HL 8443	After School/Heaven High (Man So Low)	45
57	London HL 8443	After School/Heaven High (Man So Low) (78)	18
58	Felsted AF 106	Pink Lemonade/Count On Me	15
58	Felsted AF 106	Pink Lemonade/Count On Me (78)	10
60	Top Rank JAR 264	Workin' On The Santa Fe/You're Growing Up	7

RINGO STARR

(see also Beatles, Harry Nilsson, Billy Connolly & Chris Tummings, Traveling Wilburys)

71	Apple R 5898	It Don't Come Easy/Early 1970 (p/s, B-side with Ringo or George Harrison production credit)	6
71	Apple R 5898	It Don't Come Easy/Early 1970 (p/s, B-side with Ringo or George Harrison production credit)	5
72	Apple R 5944	Back Off Boogaloo/Blindman (p/s, blue label)	6
73	Apple R 5992	Photograph/Down And Out (p/s)	6
74	Apple R 5995	You're Sixteen/Devil Woman (p/s)	5
74	Apple R 6000	Only You/Call Me (p/s)	5
75	Apple R 6004	Snookeroo/Oo-wee	12
76	Apple R 6011	Oh My My/No No Song	20
76	Polydor 2001 694	A Dose Of Rock 'N' Roll/Cryin'	15
76	Polydor 2001 695	You Don't Know Me At All/Cryin' (unissued in U.K., Europe only)	0
76	Polydor 2001 699	Hey Baby/Lady Gaye	15
77	Polydor 2001 734	Drowning In The Sea Of Love/Just A Dream	100
78	Polydor 2001 782	Lipstick Traces/Old Time Relovin' (unissued in U.K., Europe only)	0
78	Polydor 2001 795	Tonight/Heart On My Sleeve	100
72	R.O.R. ROR 2001	Steel (1-sided promo-only interview disc for 'Ringo Or Robin' reception at Liberty's department store; available for 1 week only, p/s)	2000
74	Parlophone PSR 374	Interview By Bob Mercer With Ringo For The Salesmen and Uxbridge Road/ Only You (promo only)	1000
70s	Apple R 5944	Back Off Boogaloo/Blindman (green apple label)	250
84	Apple G45 13	It Don't Come Easy/Back Off Boogaloo (P/s EMI Golden 45s series)	20
99	Mercury 546 668-2	I Wanna Be Santa Claus (CD)	25
70	Apple PCS 7101	SENTIMENTAL JOURNEY (LP)	25
70	Apple TD-PCS 7101	SENTIMENTAL JOURNEY (reel-to-reel tape)	18
70	Apple PAS 10002	BEAUCOUPS OF BLUES (LP, gatefold sleeve)	25
78	Polydor 2480 429	SCOUSE THE MOUSE (LP, with Adam Faith, Donald Pleasance etc.; with stickered sleeve & printed [not photocopied] competition insert)	130
78	Polydor 2480 429	SCOUSE THE MOUSE (LP, with Adam Faith, Donald Pleasance etc.; without stickered sleeve & printed [not photocopied] competition insert)	50
78	Polydor 3194 429	SCOUSE THE MOUSE (cassette)	30
90	EMI EMS 1375	RINGO STARR AND HIS ALL STARR BAND (LP)	35
00	Eagle EEECDO11	THE ANTHOLOGY...SO FAR (3-CD in slipcase)	30

STELLA STARR

67	Piccadilly 7N 35366	Bring Him Back/Say It	50
67	Piccadilly 7N 35366	Bring Him Back/Say It (DJ copy)	80

TONY STARR

64	Decca F 11847	I'll Take A Rocket To The Moon/Next Train Leaving	60

STARR BOUNDS

75	Horse HOSS 95	Heavenly (parts 1 & 2)	8

STARRY EYED

76	CBS 4805	Saturday/Believe	6

STARSHIP

77	Scratch SCH 01	Vampire For Your Love/You Can Dance/Hey Girl/Never Thought I'd See the day	15

MINT VALUE £

STARS OF HEAVEN
85 Hotwire HWS 853 Clothes Of Pride/All About You (beige or black label, with p/s) ... 8
85 Hotwire HWS 853 Clothes Of Pride/All About You (beige or black label) ... 6

STARTLED INSECTS
87 Antilles ANCD 8708 CURSE OF THE PHEREMONES (CD, plastic covered booklet) ... 18

STATEN ISLAND FERRY
69 Major Minor MM 643 Candy Bar/Charlie Chan ... 20

STATE OF GRACE
83 PRT 12P266 Touching The Times/Instrumental Mix (12") ... 60

STATE OF MICKEY & TOMMY
(see also Spooky Tooth, Nero & Gladiators, Foreigner)
67 Mercury MF 996 With Love From One To Five/I Know What I Will Do ... 150
67 Mercury MF 1009 Frisco Bay/Nobody Knows Where You've Been ... 150

STATESMEN
63 Fontana TF 432 I've Just Fallen In Love/It's All Happening ... 8
63 Decca F11687 Look Around/I'm Wondering ... 8
63 Studio Republic FIVE PLUS ONE (LP, private pressing) ... 100

STATE STREET SWINGERS/CHICAGO BLACK SWANS
73 Collectors Items 003 STATE STREET SWINGERS (LP) ... 12

STATE TROOPER
85 Neat 5212 SHE GOT THE LOOK (12" EP) ... 10

STATIC
67 Page One POF 039 When You Went Away/Let Me Tell You ... 7

STATIC
(see also White Lightning)
81 Eeyo EEYO 1 Voice On The Line/Stealin' (no p/s, 1,000 only) ... 15

STATION SKIFFLE GROUP
(see also Jimmy Miller)
57 Esquire 10-503 Don't You Rock Me Daddy-O/Hugged My Honey (78) ... 15
57 Esquire 10-516 Steamboat Bill/Titanic (78) ... 22
58 Esquire EP 161 STATION SKIFFLE GROUP (EP) ... 50

STATION 360
84 SRT STA 360 Optimist ... 30

STATLER BROTHERS
(see also Johnny Cash)
65 CBS 201796 Flowers On The Wall/Billy Christian ... 8
66 CBS BPG 62713 FLOWERS ON THE WALL (LP) ... 15

CANDI STATON
69 Capitol CL 15601 I'd Rather Be An Old Man's Sweetheart/For You ... 8
69 Capitol CL 15620 Heart On A String/I'm Just A Prisoner ... 10
70 Capitol CL 15646 Sweet Feeling/Evidence ... 8
70 Capitol CL 15658 Stand By Your Man/How Can I Put Out The Flame (When You Keep The Fire Burning) ... 8
75 United Artists UP 35823 Love Chain/I'm Gonna Hold On ... 6
70 Capitol ST 21631 I'M JUST A PRISONER (LP) ... 30

DAKOTA STATON
55 Capitol CL 14314 Don't Leave Me Now/A Little You ... 12
55 Capitol CL 14339 I Never Dreamt/Abracadabra ... 12
58 Capitol CL 14931 A Foggy Day/My Funny Valentine ... 7

STATUES
60 London HLG 9192 Blue Velvet/Keep The Hall Burning ... 45

STATUS QUO
(see also Spectres, Traffic Jam, Rossi & Frost, Bob Young, Andy Bown, Alan Lancaster's Bombers, Partners In Crime, Party Boys, Rockers, John Du Cann, Manchester United Football Squad, Marietta, Stretch, Jimmy Sweep)

PYE SINGLES
68 Pye 7N 17449 Pictures Of Matchstick Men/Gentleman Joe's Sidewalk Café (some with '75c Minimum' on B-side label credit) ... 12
68 Pye 7N 17497 Black Veils Of Melancholy/To Be Free ... 20
68 Pye 7N 17581 Ice In The Sun/When My Mind Is Not Live ... 8
68 Pye 7N 17650 Technicolor Dreams/Paradise Flat ... 600
69 Pye 7N 17665 Make Me Stay A Bit Longer/Aunt Nellie ... 22
69 Pye 7N 17728 Are You Growing Tired Of My Love/So Ends Another Life ... 20
69 Pye 7N 17825 The Price Of Love/Little Miss Nothing ... 25
70 Pye 7N 17907 Down The Dustpipe/Face Without A Soul (black, blue or reissue Precision labels) ... 5
70 Pye 7N 17998 In My Chair/Gerdundula (with p/s) ... 45
70 Pye 7N 17998 In My Chair/Gerdundula ... 8
71 Pye 7N 45077 Tune To The Music/Good Thinking ... 20
73 Pye 7N 45229 Mean Girl/Everything (blue labels) ... 5
73 Pye 7N 45253 Gerdundula/Lakky Lady (red label) ... 5
77 Pye BD 103 Down The Dustpipe/Mean Girl/In My Chair/Gerdundula (12", generic sleeve, reissued on PRT) ... 8
78 Pye 7N 46103 Pictures of Matchstick Men/Ice In The Sun (red labels, reissued on PRT) ... 5
79 Pye Flashbacks FBS 2 Pictures Of Matchstick Men/Down The Dustpipe (yellow vinyl, p/s) ... 6
79 Pye Flashbacks FBS 2 Pictures Of Matchstick Men/Down The Dustpipe (black vinyl, no p/s, reissued on PRT) ... 5
79 Pye 7P 103 In My Chair/Gerdundula (p/s) ... 5
79 Pye QUO 1/SFI 434 In My Chair (flexi, concert freebie, with Record Mirror Quo special) ... 10

MINT VALUE £

VERTIGO SINGLES

72	Vertigo 6059 071	Paper Plane/Softer Ride (swirl label, solid centre)	6
73	Vertigo 6059 085	Caroline/Joanne (with B-side miscredited to Lancaster)	5
74	Vertigo 6059 101	Break The Rules/Lonely Night (mispressed, B-side labels on both sides)	7
76	Vertigo 6059 153	Wild Side Of Life/All Through The Night (brown plastic labels)	6
77	Vertigo 6059 184	Rockin' All Over The World/Ring Of A Change (p/s, with small poster)	15
77	Vertigo 6059 184	Rockin' All Over The World/Ring Of A Change (p/s)	5
78	Vertigo QUO 2	Accident Prone/Let Me Fly (p/s)	5
82	Vertigo QUO 9	Jealousy/Calling The Shots (unreleased in U.K.; Irish promos only)	150
82	Vertigo QUOP 10	Caroline (Live At The NEC)/Dirty Water (live) (picture disc)	5
83	Vertigo QUOP 14	Marguerita Time/Resurrection (picture disc)	8
83	Vertigo QUO 1414	Marguerita Time/Resurrection//Caroline/Joanne (double pack, stickered gatefold p/s)	10
84	Vertigo QUO 15	Too Close To The Ground/I Wonder Why (release cancelled)	0
85	Vertigo QUO 17	Naughty Girl (actually "Dreamin' ") (unreleased)	0
86	Vertigo QUOPD 18	Rollin' Home/Lonely ('Q'-shaped picture disc)	8
86	Vertigo QUOPD 18	Rollin' Home/Lonely (uncut picture disc)	150
86	Vertigo QUODP 19	Red Sky/Don't Give It Up//Rockin' All Over The World/Whatever You Want (double pack, gatefold p/s)	6
86	Vertigo QUOPB 191	Red Sky/Don't Give It Up/The Milton Keynes Medley (12", 'Wembley Souvenir Pack', poster p/s)	15
86	Vertigo QUO 20	In The Army Now/Heartburn (stickered p/s, with sew-on patch, shrinkwrapped)	10
86	Vertigo QUOPD 20	In The Army Now/Heartburn (picture disc)	15
86	Vertigo QUODP 20	In The Army Now/Heartburn//Marguerita Time/What You're Proposing (double pack, gatefold p/s)	6
86	Vertigo QUO 2012	In The Army Now (Military Mix)/Heartburn/Late Last Night (12", stickered p/s, with poster)	8
86	Vertigo QUOP 21	Dreamin'/Long-Legged Girls (p/s, with foldout poster/calendar)	6
88	Vertigo QUOCD 22	Ain't Complaining (Extended)/That's Alright/Lean Machine/ In The Army Now (Remix) (CD, card sleeve)	15
88	Vertigo QUOCD 23	Who Gets The Love? (Extended)/Hallowe'en/The Reason For Goodbye/ The Wanderer (Sharon The Nag Mix) (CD, card sleeve)	25
88	Vertigo QUACD 1	Running All Over The World (Extended)/Magic/Whatever You Want (CD, card sleeve)	20
88	Vertigo QUO 2512	Burning Bridges (On And Off And On Again) (Extended Version)/ Whatever You Want/Marguerita Time (12", mispressing also including 7" edit)	10
88	Vertigo QUOCD 25	Burning Bridges (On And Off And On Again) (Extended Version)/ Whatever You Want/Marguerita Time (CD)	15
89	Vertigo 080 322-2	Ain't Complaining (Extended)/That's Alright/Lean Machine/ In The Army Now (Remix)/Ain't Complaining (Video) (CD Video)	20
89	Vertigo 080 630-2	Burning Bridges (On And Off And On Again) (Extended Version)/ Whatever You Want (Extended Version)/Marguerita Time/Who Gets The Love?/ Burning Bridges (Video) (CD Video)	0
89	Vertigo QUOCD 26	Not At All/Everytime I Think Of You/Gone Thru The Slips (CD)	10
89	Vertigo QUOCD 27	Little Dreamer/Rotten To The Bone/Doing It All For You (CD)	10
90	Vertigo QUO 2812	The Anniversary Waltz/The Power Of Rock/Perfect Remedy (12", p/s, mispress, B-side plays "Little Lady" (live) & exclusive "Paper Plane" re-recording)	45
90	Vertigo QUO 2812	The Anniversary Waltz/The Power Of Rock/Perfect Remedy (12", p/s, mispress, A-side plays "The Power Of Rock [Full Version]")	45
91	Vertigo QUO 31	Fakin' The Blues (Edit)/Heavy Daze (p/s, swirl label, release cancelled, approximately 25 copies only)	450
91	Vertigo QUO 3112	Fakin' The Blues (Edit)/Fakin' The Blues (Album Version)/Heavy Daze/ Better Times (12", swirl label, p/s, cancelled, approx. 25 copies only)	250
91	Vertigo QUOCD 31	Fakin' The Blues (Edit)/Fakin' The Blues (Album Version)/Heavy Daze/ Better Times (CD, unissued, 2,000 later sent out by fan club, no inlay)	40
92	Vertigo QUO 3212	Rock 'Til You Drop/Medley/Forty-Five Hundred Times (12", p/s, mispressing, omits "Forty-Five Hundred Times")	15
92	Vertigo QUOCD 32	Rock 'Til You Drop/Medley/Forty-Five Hundred Times (CD in no'd guitar-shaped case)	12

OTHER SINGLES

75	Lyntone LYN 3154/5	Down Down/Break The Rules (Smiths Crisps flexidisc, with 'Smiths' p/s)	15
75	Lyntone LYN 3154/5	Down Down/Break The Rules (Smiths Crisps flexidisc)	6
80s	Lyntone QUO 1-4	Interview picture discs (4-single pack)	20
92	Polydor QUODD 33	Roadhouse Medley (Anniversary Waltz Part 25) (Radio Edit)/(Extended)/ Don't Drive My Car (Live) (CD, numbered 4-fold digipak, 2nd CD card template)	10
94	Polydor QUO 34	I Didn't Mean It/Whatever You Want (p/s, blue vinyl)	5
94	Polydor QUODD 34	I Didn't Mean It (Acoustic Version)/(Hooligan Version)/Survival/ She Knew Too Much (CD, numbered digipak, 2nd CD card template)	10
94	Polydor QUODD 35	Sherri Don't Fail Me Now (Extended)/Tossin' And Turnin'/Down To You (CD, numbered digipak, 2nd CD card template)	8
94	Polydor QUODD 36	Restless (LP Version)/And I Do/Democracy (CD, no'd digipak, 2nd CD card template)	8
95	PolyGram TV 576262 7	Fun Fun Fun (with The Beach Boys)/Mortified (numbered picture disc)	5
96	PolyGram TV 5759447	All Around My Hat (with Maddy Prior)/I'll Never Get Over You (numbered picture disc)	6
99	From The Makers Of? FTMOCD1	FAKIN' THE BLUES (MILLENNIUM EDITION) (CD, fanclub mail order-only edition, hand-no'd exclusive p/s, contains unreleased Vertigo CD [QUOCD 31])	50
00	PolyGram PSPCD464	NIGHT & DAY (CD EP, 4-track sampler, mail order-only via tokens from The Mail On Sunday, insufficient pressed to meet demand)	25

PROMO ONLY SINGLES

68	Pye 7N 17449	Pictures Of Matchstick Men/Gentleman Joe's Sidewalk Café (75c Minimum) ('A' label)	60
68	Pye 7N 17497	Black Veils Of Melancholy/To Be Free ('A' label)	70
68	Pye 7N 17581	Ice In The Sun/When My Mind Is Not Live ('A' label)	60

			MINT VALUE £
68	Pye 7N 17650	Technicolor Dreams/Paradise Flat('A' label)	400
69	Pye 7N 17665	Make Me Stay A Bit Longer/Aunt Nellie ('A' label)	70
69	Pye 7N 17728	Are You Growing Tired Of My Love/So Ends Another Life ('A' label)	70
69	Pye 7N 17825	The Price Of Love/Little Miss Nothing ('A' label)	70
70	Pye 7N 17907	Down The Dustpipe/Face Without A Soul ('A' label)	60
70	Pye 7N 17998	In My Chair/Gerdundula ('A' label)	60
71	Pye 7N 45077	Tune To The Music/Good Thinking ('A' label)	60
72	Phonogram DJ 005	Roadhouse Blues/BLACK SABBATH: Children Of The Grave (DJ Copy, 100 only)	400
72	Vertigo 6059 071	Paper Plane/Softer Ride ('A' label)	45
73	Pye 7N 45229	Mean Girl/Everything ('A' label)	50
73	Pye 7N 45253	Gerdundula/Lakky Lady ('A' label)	40
75	Lyntone LYN 3154	Down Down (Smiths Crisps 1-sided gold flexidisc test pressing, plays Bye Bye Baby by Bay City Rollers)	25
75	Lyntone LYN 3155	Break The Rules (Smiths Crisps 1-sided gold flexidisc test pressing, plays Bye Bye Baby by Bay City Rollers)	25
79	Pye 7P 103	In My Chair/Gerdundula ('A' label)	20
81	Vertigo QUO JB 6	Rock 'N' Roll/Hold You Back (jukebox issue, B-side at 33rpm)	10
86	Vertigo QUODJ 2112	Dreamin' (Wet Mix)/Long-Legged Girls/The Quo Xmas Cake Mix (12")	15
88	Vertigo QUOLP 99	Ain't Complaining (12" promo, 1-sided)	30
88	Vertigo QUODJ 2212	Ain't Complaining (Extended)/That's Alright/Lean Machine (12")	10
88	Vertigo QUODJ 25	Burning Bridges (On & Off & On Again)/Burning Bridges (On & Off & On Again)	12
90	Vertigo (no cat. no.)	The Power Of Rock (Album Version)/(Single Edit)/Perfect Remedy (12" white label)	50

LPs

68	Pye NPL 18220	PICTURESQUE MATCHSTICKABLE MESSAGES (mono)	100
68	Pye NSPL 18220	PICTURESQUE MATCHSTICKABLE MESSAGES (stereo)	70
69	Pye NPL 18301	SPARE PARTS (blue label, mono/stereo)	90
69	Pye NSPL 18301	SPARE PARTS (blue label, mono/stereo)	70
69	Marble Arch MAL 1193	STATUS QUO-TATIONS (mono)	30
69	Marble Arch MAL(S) 1193	STATUS QUO-TATIONS (stereo, most copies exported)	50
70	Pye NSPL 18344	MA KELLY'S GREASY SPOON (very early copies with poster)	120
70	Pye NSPL 18344	MA KELLY'S GREASY SPOON	15
71	Pye NSPL 18371	DOG OF TWO HEAD (gatefold sleeve, blue labels, later reissued with red, black or PRT "Piccadilly Circus" labels)	25
72	Vertigo 6360 082	PILEDRIVER (swirl label, gatefold sleeve)	30
73	Vertigo 6360 098	HELLO! (spaceship label, with inner sleeve & poster)	20
74	Vertigo 9102 001	QUO (with poster/lyric sheet)	15
74	Record Club ACB 00217	QUO	25
77	Pye FILD 005	THE FILE SERIES (2-LP, single sleeve with inner sleeves; repressed on Precision)	15
79	Pye NPSL 18607	JUST FOR THE RECORD (red vinyl)	15
79	Pye FILD 005	THE FILE SERIES (2-LP, reissue with different sleeve, inners; repressed on PRT)	15
82	Phonogram PRO BX 1	FROM THE MAKERS OF... (3-LP, with inserts in round metal tin, some numbered)	20
82	Phonogram PRO LP 1	FROM THE MAKERS OF... (3-LP, with inserts in cardboard box)	15
83	Vertigo VERH 10	BACK TO BACK (in-store promo copies with poster insert)	18
85	PRT Flashbacks FBLP 8082	NANANA	12
88	PRT PYX 4007	FROM THE BEGINNING (picture disc)	18
90	Essential! ESBLP 136	THE EARLY WORKS (5-LP box set with book)	30
91	Baktabak LINT 5003	INTROSPECTIVE (clear vinyl, 6 Pye-era tracks & interview)	20
92	Polydor 517 367-1	LIVE ALIVE QUO (with inner sleeve)	12
94	Polydor 523 607-1	THIRSTY WORK (with inner sleeve)	12

CDs

83	Vertigo 800 035-2	1+9+8+2	18
83	Vertigo 800 053-2	NEVER TOO LATE	18
83	Vertigo 814 66-2	BACK TO BACK	18
85	PRT CDNSP 773	THE BEST OF STATUS QUO (THE EARLY YEARS)	18
86	PRT CDMP 8834	MA KELLY'S GREASY SPOON	18
89	Vertigo 842 098-2	PERFECT REMEDY (two different inlay designs)	30
98	Readers Digest RDCD1831-4	THE COMPLETE STATUS QUO (4-CD, mail-order only)	60
01	From The Makers Of FTMOCD2	FTMO LIVE! NO.1 (fanclub mail-order only, soundchecks & interviews)	50
02	Time Life TL SQC 069 827-2	THE ULTIMATE COLLECTION (4-CD, mail-order only)	45
03	From The Makers Of FTMO LIVE 2-1/2 [matrix]	FTMO LIVE! NO.2 (2-CD, fan club mail-order only)	25

PROMO ONLY ALBUMS & ALBUM SAMPLERS

82	Phonogram PRO BX 1	FROM THE MAKERS OF... (3-LP, 20 copies in bronze tin for in-house use)	300
86	Vertigo MADDOX 18	IN THE ARMY NOW (LP, 4-track sampler, includes unreleased version of Dreamin')	50
88	Vertigo QUOLP 99	AIN'T COMPLAINING (LP, 4-track one-sided sampler)	25
88	Vertigo	AIN'T COMPLAINING (box set containing LP sampler [QUOLP 99], cassette, 1-track video, photo & press sheet)	70
88	Music & Media MM 1221	INTERVIEW (LP, uncut test pressing for unreleased saw-shaped picture disc)	50
89	Vertigo 842 077-9	LITTLE DREAMER (CD, card p/s, 4-track sampler for PERFECT REMEDY album)	50
90	Phonogram (no cat. no.)	ROCKING ALL OVER THE YEARS SNIPPETS (cassette, titles inlay)	20
90	Vertigo 846 797-2	ROCKING ALL OVER THE YEARS (CD, in Butlin's party pack containing Kiss Me Quo baseball cap, stick of Status Quo rock, and selection of party poppers, streamers, whistle, trumpet, silver Quo balloons & pack of condoms, all with "Anniversary Waltz" stickers	75
97	PolyGram TV QUO 5-2	WHATEVER YOU WANT - THE VERY BEST OF STATUS QUO (CD, 5-track sampler different to above, no p/s, withdrawn)	18
02	Sanctuary CMRCD 490	SWEDISH RADIO SESSIONS (CD-R, titles insert, commercial release cancelled)	50

STAVELY MAKEPEACE

(see also Lieutenant Pigeon, Shel Naylor)

69	Pyramid PYR 6072	(I Want To Love You Like A) Mad Dog/Greasy Haired Woman	5
70	Pyramid PYR 6082	Tarzan Harvey/Reggae Denny (unissued, test pressings exist)	6
77	Unigram U6312	Baby Blue Eyes/Big Bad Baby Blonde	8

MINT VALUE £

STAVERTON BRIDGE
70s Saydisc SDL 266 STAVERTON BRIDGE (LP, with lyrics) . . . 30

MARY STAVIN & GEORGE BEST
70s Lifestyle LEG 22 IT TAKES TWO TO SHAPE UP (LP) . . . 12

STEAK CATS
93 April 10 TEN 1 The Steak Song/Dead Real Soon/Fluffy's Lament/My Name Is Miguel (12") . . . 10
94 April 10 TEN 2 Intergalactic Competition/Foxy Roxy (200 only, hand-written labels) . . . 5
95 April 10 TEN 3 Ladyboy/Not Supposed To Love (200 only, hand-written labels) . . . 5
96 April 10 TEN 4 Last Night In A Porn Stars Bed I Became A Man/From Behind (12" 200 only) . . . 15
97 April 10 TEN 5 If I Can't Have You, Then Nobody Can/Ben's Men/
(Easy) You Make It So/Sutler's Cabin (12") . . . 12

STEAM
69 Fontana TF 1058 Na Na Hey Hey Kiss Him Goodbye/It's The Magic In You Girl . . . 5

STEAMHAMMER
(see also Armageddon, Rod Stewart)
69 CBS 4141 Junior's Wailing/Windmill . . . 25
69 CBS 4496 Autumn Song/Blues For Passing People . . . 18
71 Reflection HRS 9 Junior's Wailing/You'll Never Know . . . 12
68 CBS (S) 63611 STEAMHAMMER (LP) . . . 70
70 CBS (S) 63694 STEAMHAMMER MK. II (LP) . . . 55
70 B&C CAS 1024 MOUNTAINS (LP, stickered gatefold sleeve) . . . 40
70 Reflection REFL 1 STEAMHAMMER (LP, reissue, different sleeve) . . . 40
71 Reflection REFL 12 STEAMHAMMER MK. II (LP, reissue) . . . 40

STEAM-SHOVEL
(see also Locomotive)
68 Trojan/Big Bear TR 635 Rudi, The Red Nosed Reindeer/White Christmas . . . 7
68 Decca F 22863 Rudi, The Red Nosed Reindeer/White Christmas (export issue) . . . 12

STEEL
81 Neat NEAT 14 Rock Out/All Systems Go (p/s) . . . 10

STEEL AN' SKIN
85 Cougar (no cat. no.) STEEL AN' SKIN (LP) . . . 20

BETTE ANNE STEELE
55 Capitol CL 14315 Barricade/Give Me A Little Kiss Will Ya, Huh? . . . 8

DAVY STEELE
83 Bracken BKN 1001 LONG TIME GETTING THERE (LP) . . . 12

DORIS STEELE
59 Oriole CB 1468 Why Must I?/Never Again (78 rpm = £8) . . . 10

JAN STEELE & JOHN CAGE
76 Obscure OBS 5 VOICES AND INSTRUMENTS (LP) . . . 12

SONDRA & JON STEELE
55 Parlophone MSP 6166 I'm Crazy With Love/Fill My Heart With Happiness . . . 8

TOMMY STEELE (& THE STEELMEN)
58 Weekend Mail (no cat. no.) THE TRUTH ABOUT ME (6" in envelope, mail-order only) (78) . . . 15
56 Decca F 10795 Rock With The Caveman/Rock Around The Town (with The Steelmen) . . . 25
56 Decca F 10795 Rock With The Caveman/Rock Around The Town (with The Steelmen) (78) . . . 15
56 Decca F 10808 Doomsday Rock/Elevator Rock . . . 30
56 Decca F 10819 Singing The Blues/Rebel Rock (with The Steelmen) . . . 20
57 Decca F 10849 Knee Deep In The Blues/Teenage Party (with The Steelmen) . . . 10
57 Decca F 10877 Butterfingers/Cannibal Pot . . . 5
57 Decca F 10896 Shiralee/Grandad's Rock . . . 5
57 Decca F 10923 Water Water/A Handful Of Songs . . . 7
57 Decca F 10941 Hey You!/Plant A Kiss . . . 5
58 Decca F 11072 Come On Let's Go/Put A Ring On Her Finger . . . 10
59 Decca F 11152 Tallahassee Lassie/Give! Give! Give! . . . 10
(The above 45s were originally issued with triangular centres; later round-centre copies are worth two-thirds the values listed)
59 Decca F 11177 Little White Bull/Singing Time (in p/s) (78) . . . 10

EPs
56 Decca DFE 6388 YOUNG LOVE . . . 15
56 Decca DFE 6389 SINGING THE BLUES . . . 15
57 Decca DFE 6398 THE TOMMY STEELE STORY NO. 1 . . . 8
57 Decca DFE 6424 THE TOMMY STEELE STORY NO. 2 . . . 8
57 Decca F 10915 ALL STAR HIT PARADE NO. 2 (with other artists) . . . 10
(The above EPs were originally issued with triangular centres; later round-centre reissues are worth two-thirds the values listed)
58 Decca DFE 6472 THE DUKE WORE JEANS . . . 10
58 Decca DFE 6551 C'MON LET'S GO . . . 15

LPs
57 Decca LF 1287 THE TOMMY STEELE STAGE SHOW (10") . . . 15
57 Decca LF 1288 THE TOMMY STEELE STORY (10") . . . 15
58 Decca LF 1308 THE DUKE WORE JEANS (10", soundtrack) . . . 15

STEELERS
70 Direction 58-4675 Get It From The Bottom/I'm Sorry . . . 10

STEELEYE SPAN
(see also Maddy Prior, Tim Hart & Maddy Prior, Gay & Terry Woods, Ashley Hutchings, Fairport Convention, Martin Carthy, Silly Sisters, Bob Johnson & Pete Knight)
71 B&C CB 164 Rave On/Reels/Female Drummer (p/s) . . . 7
72 Pegasus PGS 6 JIGS AND REELS (maxi-single, with p/s) . . . 10
72 Pegasus PGS 6 JIGS AND REELS (maxi-single) . . . 6

			MINT VALUE £
72	Chrysalis CHS 2005	John Barleycorn/Bride's Favourite/Tansey's Fancy	5
70	RCA SF 8113	HARK! THE VILLAGE WAIT (LP, with lyric insert)	30
71	United Artists UAG 29160	HARK! THE VILLAGE WAIT (LP, reissue)	12
71	B&C CAS 1029	PLEASE TO SEE THE KING (LP, in 'hessian' textured sleeve, insert)	35
71	B&C CAS 1029	PLEASE TO SEE THE KING (LP)	12
72	Charisma CS 5	INDIVIDUALLY AND COLLECTIVELY (LP)	12
72	Pegasus PEG 9	TEN MAN MOP, OR MR. RESERVOIR BUTLER RIDES AGAIN (LP, gatefold sleeve, initially with 8-page booklet)	30
72	Pegasus PEG 9	TEN MAN MOP, OR MR. RESERVOIR BUTLER RIDES AGAIN (LP)	12
72	Chrysalis CHR 1008	BELOW THE SALT (LP, gatefold, green label)	18

STEEL MILL

71	Penny Farthing PEN 770	Green Eyed God/Zang Will	8
72	Penny Farthing PEN 783	Get On The Line/Summer's Child	20
75	Penny Farthing PEN 894	Green Eyed God/Zang Will (reissue)	8
71	Penny Farthing PELS 549	GREEN EYED GOD (LP)	350

STEEL PULSE

76	Concrete Jungle CJ 602	Kibudu Mansatta Abuku/Version	35
77	Anchor ANC 1046	Nyah Luv/Luv Nyah (p/s)	5

STEELY DAN

(see also Donald Fagen)

72	Probe PRO 562	Dallas/Sail The Waterway	5
73	Probe PRO 577	Do It Again/Fire In The Hole	5
73	Probe PRO 587	Reelin' In The Years/Only A Fool	7
73	Probe PRO 602	Show Biz Kids/Razor Boy	5
73	Probe PRO 606	My Old School/Pearl Of The Quarter	5
74	Probe PRO 622	Rikki Don't Lose That Number/Any Major Dude Will Tell You (gatefold sleeve, 1974 'Spacemen' tour logo)	50
82	MCA MCAT 786	FM EP	25
85	MCA MCAT 852	Reelin' In The Years/Rikki Don't Lose That Number/Do It Again/ Haitian Divorce (12", p/s)	20
73	Probe SPB 1062	CAN'T BUY A THRILL (LP, original, with 'pink' label)	25
73	Probe SPD 1079	COUNTDOWN TO ECSTASY (LP, original)	12
80s	MCA 203 16009	GAUCHO (LP, audiophile pressing)	12
82	MCA MCF 3165	GOLD (LP, with free EP [MSAMT 21])	20

WOUT STEENHUIS

65	Columbia DB 7722	Desert Island/Teran Boelan	6
66	Columbia DB 8027	Nivram/Bay Of Paradise	6
63	Columbia DB 7021	Kassian/Minehaha	6

STEEPLECHASE

(see also Dean Parrish)

71	Polydor 2489 001	LADY BRIGHT (LP)	15

STEERPIKE

68	(no label credit) ADM 417	STEERPIKE (LP, private pressing)	550

BILL STEGMEYER & HIS ORCHESTRA

54	London HL 8078	On The Waterfront (From The Film)/We Just Couldn't Say Good-Bye	35

LOU STEIN

57	London HLZ 8419	Almost Paradise/Soft Sands	20
58	Mercury 7MT 226	Who Slammed The Door/Got A Match?	8

JIM STEINMAN

(see also Meat Loaf)

81	Epic EPCA 13-1236	Rock And Roll Dreams Come Through/ Love And Death And An American Guitar/The Storm (12", p/s, blue vinyl)	8
81	Epic EPCA 1561	Lost Boys And Golden Girls/Left In The Dark (p/s)	5
81	Epic EPCA 1707	Dance In My Pants/Dance In My Pants (unissued, promo only)	5
84	MCA MCA 889	Tonight Is What It Means To Be Young/Hold That Snake (p/s)	5
81	Epic EPC 11-84361	BAD FOR GOOD (LP, picture disc)	12

STEINWAYS

85	Kent TOWN 106	You've Been Leading Me On/JOHNNY CASWELL: You Don't Love Me No More	20

TENA STELIN

(see also Iration Steppas and Tena Stelin)

89	Wau! MR Modo MWS 011T	Jah Equity/Jah Equity (Version) (12")	50
89	Wau! Mr Modo MWS 015T	King Of Kings/Give Thanks And Praise (12")	50
00	Jah Tubbys JT 7005	Look After Yourself/DISCIPLES RHYTHM SECTION: Dub Yourself	20
89	Wai! Mr Modo MOWLP 002	WICKED INVENTION (LP)	40
92	Conscious Sounds DNC 001	SUN AND MOON (LP, as Tena Stelin meets Century)	25

STELLA

82	President PT 504	Si Tu Aimes Ma Musique/If You Do Like My Music (p/s)	7

STELLASTARR

00s	2220 TWENTY-7 S001	Somewhere Across Forever/No Weather (p/s, 1000 only)	8
00s	2220 TWENTY-CDS 001	Somewhere Across Forever/No Weather/School Ya (CD, 1000 only)	8

STAN STENNETT

60s	Audio JDT 1	STYLE (EP)	8

MALCOLM STENT

70s	Starline SWL 2002	GO AND PLAY UP YOUR OWN END (LP)	15

STEP

80	Epic/Direction S DIR 8733	Love Letter/Land Of 1,000 Dances (p/s)	5
80	Epic/Direction S DIR 8944	Let Me Be The One/634 5789 (p/s)	5
80	Epic/Direction S DIR 9311	Tears That I Cry/Shake (p/s)	5
81	Epic EPC A 1291	Chain Gang/In The House (p/s)	5
81	Epic EPC A 1412	Model Soldiers/Hightime Havana (p/s)	5

MINT VALUE £

STEPASIDE

80	Gale GALELP 01	SIT DOWN AND RELAPSE (LP)	20

ANN STEPHENS

56	HMV 7EG 8187	CHILDREN'S CHOICE (EP)	8

EWAN STEPHENS

(see also Turquoise)

71	Decca F 13219	Queen Of The Good Times/We Can Give It A Try	5
72	Decca F 13299	Brother, Surely We Can Work It Out/Long, Long Summer	5

LEIGH STEPHENS

(see also Blue Cheer)

69	Philips SBL 7897	RED WEATHER (LP)	60
71	Charisma CAS 1040	AND A CAST OF THOUSANDS (LP)	20

STEPPENWOLF

(see also Sparrow, John Kay)

68	RCA RCA 1679	Sookie Sookie/Take What You Need	10
68	RCA RCA 1735	Born To Be Wild/Everybody's Next One	10
68	Stateside-Dunhill SS 8003	Magic Carpet Ride/Sookie Sookie	10
69	Stateside-Dunhill SS 8013	Rock Me/Jupiter Child	7
69	Stateside-Dunhill SS 8017	Born To Be Wild/Everybody's Next One (reissue)	8
69	Stateside-Dunhill SS 8027	Magic Carpet Ride/Sookie Sookie (reissue)	6
70	Stateside-Dunhill SS 8035	Monster/Move Over	6
70	Stateside-Dunhill SS 8038	The Pusher/Your Wall's Too High	6
70	Stateside-Dunhill SS 8049	Hey Lawdy Mama/Twisted	6
70	Stateside-Dunhill SS 8056	Screaming Night Hog/Spiritual Fantasy	5
70	Probe PRO 510	Who Needs Ya/Earschplittenloudenboomer	5
71	Probe PRO 525	Snowblind Friend/Hippo Stomp	5
71	Probe PRO 534	Ride With Me/For Madmen Only	6
71	Probe PRO 544	For Ladies Only/Sparkle Eyes	6
68	RCA RD/SF 7974	STEPPENWOLF (LP, initial white sleeve)	35
68	RCA RD/SF 7974	STEPPENWOLF (LP, later silver sleeve)	25
68	Stateside (S)SL 5003	STEPPENWOLF THE SECOND (LP)	18
69	Stateside (S)SL 5011	AT YOUR BIRTHDAY PARTY (LP)	18
69	Stateside (S)SL 5015	EARLY STEPPENWOLF (LP)	15
69	Stateside (S)SL 10276	CANDY (LP, soundtrack, 2 tracks by Steppenwolf, 1 track by Byrds)	30
70	Stateside-Dunhill SSL 5020	STEPPENWOLF (reissue)	15
70	Stateside-Dunhill SSL 5021	MONSTER (LP, gatefold sleeve)	20
70	Stateside-Dunhill SSL 5029	STEPPENWOLF 'LIVE' (2-LP, gatefold sleeve)	15
70	Probe SPBA 6254	STEPPENWOLF 7 (LP)	15
71	Probe SPBA 6260	FOR LADIES ONLY (LP)	12
71	Probe SPBA 1033	GOLD (LP)	12
72	Probe SPBA 1059	REST IN PEACE (LP)	12

STEPPES

87	Help HELPF 101	History Hates No Man/BEVIS FROND: African Violets (flexi)	8

STEPPES

(see also Fifty Fantastics, Disco Zombies)

79	South Circular SGS 108	The Beat Drill/FIFTY FANTASTICS: God's Got Religion (p/s, white label)	10

STEPPING TALK

79	Eustone/Rough Trade TO1	Alice In Sunderland/Health And Safety/Common Problems/John Turtles (p/s, with stamped inner)	15

STEPTOE & SON

(see under Wilfred Brambell & Harry H. Corbett)

STEREOLAB

(see also McCarthy, Spectrum, Mouse On Mars, Clear Spot)

SINGLES

91	Duophonic DS 45-01	SUPER 45: The Light That Will Cease To Fail/Au Grand Jour/Brittle/Au Grand Jour! (10" EP, with insert, mail-order, sold at gigs and some record shops 40 with hand-painted p/s, in poly bag)	150
91	Duophonic DS 45-01	SUPER 45: The Light That Will Cease To Fail/Au Grand Jour/Brittle/Au Grand Jour! (10" EP, with insert, mail-order, sold at gigs and some record shops)	100
91	Duophonic DS 45-01	SUPER 45: The Light That Will Cease To Fail/Au Grand Jour/Brittle/Au Grand Jour! (25 test pressings, 10" cut into 12" discs)	175
91	Too Pure PURE 4	SUPER ELECTRIC: Super-Electric/High Expectation/The Way Will Be Opening/Contact (10" EP, with red and yellow sleeve, w/insert)	5
91	Duophonic DS 45-02	STUNNING DEBUT ALBUM: Doubt/Clanger (20 black test pressings withdrawn due to pressing fault/warping, different cut of both tracks)	100
91	Duophonic DS 45-02	STUNNING DEBUT ALBUM: Doubt/Clanger (p/s, mail-order, sold at gigs and some record shops gatefold p/s with insert in poly bag; mulit coloured vinyl, unknown quantity but probably over 200)	175
91	Duophonic DS 45-02	STUNNING DEBUT ALBUM: Doubt/Clanger (p/s, mail-order, gigs and some record Shops, gatefold p/s with insert in poly bag; 985 copies on clear vinyl)	55
92	Duophonic DS 45-04	Harmonium/Farfisa (p/s, mail-order, gigs and some record shops 1,306 copies on transparent amber vinyl, with insert & fluorescent sticker)	35
93	Duophonic DS45-05/06	SHIMMIES IN SUPER 8 (2 x 7", green and white vinyl, foldout sleeve with inserts)	25
92	Too Pure PURE 14	Low Fi/Varoom!/Laissez-Faire/Elektro (He Held The World In His Iron Grip) (10", p/s, clear vinyl, 2,000 only, numbered)	25
93	Sub Pop SP107/283	Lo Boob Oscillator/Tempter (clear vinyl, p/s with US address on rear sleeve)	20
93	Sub Pop SP107/283	Lo Boob Oscillator/Tempter (clear vinyl, p/s with German address on rear sleeve)	15
93	Spacewatch FLX 2107	Ronco Symphony (demo)/Seeming And The Meaning (demo)/SUBMARINER: Lyricist Downer (clear vinyl flexi comes with Spacewatch fanzine in sleeve)	18
93	Duophonic D-UHF-D 01	Jenny Ondioline/Fruition/Golden Ball/French Disko (10", p/s)	10
93	Duophonic D-UHF-D 01	Jenny Ondioline (Part 1)/Golden Ball (Studio) (10", factory custom pressings; 3 on 'thick' clear vinyl, later endorsed & signed by band; no p/s)	220

			MINT VALUE £
93	Duophonic D-UHF-D 01	Jenny Ondioline (Part 1)/Golden Ball (Studio) (10", factory custom pressings; 5 copies on multicoloured vinyl; 25 on 'thin' clear vinyl, no p/s)	80
93	Duophonic D-UHF-CD 01	Jenny Ondioline/Fruition/Golden Ball/French Disko (CD)	12
93	Clawfist 20	CRUMB DUCK (10" EP, shared with Nurse With Wound; 37 with hand-drawn p/s (Gain/Sadier only)	120
93	Clawfist 20	CRUMB DUCK (10" EP, shared with Nurse With Wound; 1,450 regular p/s)	20
93	Duophonic D-UHF-D 03	French Disko/Jenny Ondioline ('teaser' single, p/s, 1,500 only, with hand printed sleeves)	25
93	Duophonic D-UHF-D 03	French Disko/Jenny Ondioline ('teaser' single, p/s, 1,500 only, regular printed sleeves)	15
93	Duophonic D-UHF-D 01P	French Disko/Jenny Ondioline (CD, 1,000 only, hand-made p/s)	15
94	Duophonic D-UHF-D 04S	Ping Pong/Moogie Wonderland (p/s, 2,150 on pink vinyl)	10
94	Duophonic D-UHF-D 04S	Ping Pong/Moogie Wonderland (p/s, 3,322 on green vinyl)	10
94	Duophonic D-UHF-D 04T	Ping Pong/Moogie Wonderland (10", p/s)	7
94	Silvertone	Tone Burst (demo)/Tempter (demo)/SPECTRUM: Soul Kiss Glide Divine (unreleased, with colour photocopied wraparound p/s, 25 test pressings only)	150
94	Duophonic D-UHF-07	Wow And Flutter/Heavy Denim (3,000 only with hand-painted p/s)	12
95	Wurlitzer Jukebox WJ 3	The Eclipse/Yes Sir! I Can Moogie/CAT'S MIAOW: Shoot The Moon (flexidisc, 1,000 only with insert and info sheet)	18
95	Duophonic Super 45s DS 45-10	Long Hair Of Death/YO LA TENGO: Evanescent Psychic Pez Drop (gig single, fluorescent yellow vinyl, plain white stickered card sleeve, 3,000 only)	12
95	Independent Project IP 060	Blue Milk/One Thousand Miles An Hour/Aluminum Tune (set of 4 singles all With same tracks in different coloured vinyl and different sets of gatefold sleeve. American Import. Singles worth £10 each)	50
95	Flying Nun STEREO 1	French Disko/Super Electric (CD, also listed as B 8595, promo only)	15
95	Duophonic STEREO 2	John Cage Bubblegum/Revox (CD, also listed as B 8895, promo only)	10
96	Duophonic D-UHF-D 10S	Cybele's Reverie/Brigitte (p/s, with insert)	5
96	Duophonic D-UHF-D 10	Cybele's Reverie/Les Yper Yper Sound/Brigitte/Young Lungs (25 black vinyl test pressing and 102 cut into 12" disc)	25
96	Duophonic D-UHF-D 10	Cybele's Reverie/Les Yper Yper Sound/Brigitte/Young Lungs(10", p/s, 2,000 only)	10
96	Lissy's LISS 15	You Used To Call Me Sadness/FUXA: Skyhigh (p/s, 400 on white vinyl)	20
96	Lissy's LISS 15	You Used To Call Me Sadness/FUXA: Skyhigh (p/s, 1,500 on black vinyl)	8
96	Duophonic D-UHF-D 12	Speedy Car/TORTOISE: Yaus (gig freebie, blue vinyl, p/s, 3,000 only)	10
96	Duophonic D-UHF-D 12	Speedy Car/TORTOISE: Yaus (orange vinyl export issue, p/s, 3,000 only)	15
96	Duophonic D-UHF-D 14S	Fluorescences/Pinball (p/s)	5
96	Duophonic D-UHF-D 14	Fluorescences/Pinball/You Used To Call Me Sadness/Soop Groove (12", p/s)	8
96	Duophonic D-UHF-D 15	Metronomic Underground (Wagon Christ Mix)/Percolations (12", plain red sleeve, 2,500 only)	12
97	Duophonic DS 4517	Splitting The Atom (Parts 1 & 2) (with Sonic Boom)/Monkey Brain (p/s, 2,500 only)	10
97	Duophonic D-UHF-D 18	Iron Man/The Incredible He Woman (red vinyl, p/s, gig single, 2,000 only)	5
97	Duophonic Super 45s DS 3311	Simple Headphone Mind/NURSE WITH WOUND: Trippin' With The Birds (12", 5,000 copies)	12
97	Duophonic Super 45s DS 3311	Simple Headphone Mind/NURSE WITH WOUND: Trippin' With The Birds (12", 1,000 copies on yellow vinyl, in sealed foil sleeve)	25
97	Duophonic Super 45s CD 3311	Simple Headphone Mind/NURSE WITH WOUND: Trippin' With The Birds (CD, sealed foil sleeve, 1,000 only)	35
98	Duophonic D-UHF-D 19	Refractions In The Plastic Pulse/Contronatura (12", die-cut stickered sleeve, yellow vinyl)	6
98	Duophonic D-UHF-D 19	Refractions In The Plastic Pulse/Contronatura (12", die-cut stickered sleeve, black vinyl)	10
99	Duophonic D-UHF-D24	THE UNDERGROUND IS COMING: The Super-It/Monkey Jelly/ Fried Monkey Eggs (Instrumental)/Fried Monkey Eggs (Vocal) (p/s)	10
01	Duophonic D-UHF 026	Captain Easychord (12")	10

ALBUMS

90	Too Pure PURE 19	SPACE AGE BACHELOR PAD MUSIC (LP)	12
92	Too Pure PURELP 11	PENG! (LP)	12
93	Duophonic D-UHF-D 02	TRANSIENT RANDOM NOISE-BURSTS WITH ANNOUNCEMENTS (2-LP, with inner sleeves, poor playing-quality gold vinyl, with stickered sleeve, 1,500 only, numbered)	55
95	Duophonic D-UHF-D 05X	MARS AUDIAC QUINTET (2-LP, gatefold sleeve, 1st 1,000 copies with bonus coloured vinyl single "Klang Tone"/"Ulan Bator" [D-UHF-06])	55
95	Duophonic D-UHF-D 08	MUSIC FOR THE AMORPHOUS BODY STUDY CENTRE (40 black vinyl test pressings 10" sides cut into 12" discs)	90
95	Duophonic D-UHF-D 08	MUSIC FOR THE AMORPHOUS BODY STUDY CENTRE (10" LP, 3,000 only, insert)	30
95	Duophonic D-UHF-CD 08	MUSIC FOR THE AMORPHOUS BODY STUDY CENTRE (CD, first issue with white cover & "1st edition" printed on disc available at Charles Long art exhibition; reissue has yellow sleeve and is worth £20)	30
95	Duophonic D-UHF LP 09	REFRIED ECTOPLASM - SWITCHED ON VOL 2 LP, orange vinyl, card insert)	25
96	United Dairies UD 059	CRUMB DUCK (LP, shared with Nurse With Wound (2 extra tracks, reissue of Clawfist EP, 50 copies on pink vinyl)	70
96	United Dairies UD 059	CRUMB DUCK (LP, shared with Nurse With Wound (2 extra tracks, reissue of Clawfist EP, 500 on fluorescent green vinyl)	40
96	Duophonic UHF D-UHF-D11	EMPEROR TOMATO KETCHUP (2-LP, yellow glitter vinyl, gatefold sleeve)	60
98	Drag City CD 159	ALUMINIUM TUNES - SWITCHED ON VOL. 3 (3 x LP)	25
06	No cat. no.	FAB FOUR SUTURE (LP as 6 x 7" hand-stamped box)	20

STEREOLAB & BRIGITTE FONTAINE

90s	Duophonic Super 45s DS 45-25	Calimèro/MONADE: Cache Cache (white vinyl, p/s)	8

STEREOPHONICS

96	V2 SPH 1	Looks Like Chaplin/More Life In A Tramp's Vest (p/s, 500 only)	60
96	V2 SPHD 1	Looks Like Chaplin/More Life In A Tramp's Vest/Raymond's Shops (CD)	30
96	V2 SPH 2	Local Boy In The Photograph/Too Many Sandwiches (p/s, 2,000 only)	12
97	V2 SPH 4	More Life In A Tramp's Vest/Raymond's Shop (p/s)	8
97	V2 VVR 500 0448	A Thousand Trees/Home To Me/Looks Like Chaplin/Summertime (CD, digipak)	12
99	V2 VVR 500 6777	Pick A Part That's New/Nice To Be Out (Demo) (p/s)	6

			MINT VALUE £
99	V2 no catalogue number	PERFORMANCE AND COCKTAILS (7 x 10" box set, with booklet and CD, promo mail order only)	40
97	Banana VVR 1000431	WORD GETS AROUND (LP, with bonus 12")	25
99	V2 VVR1004499	PERFORMANCE AND COCKTAILS (LP, gatefold)	25

STEREOS

61	MGM MGM 1143	I Really Love You/Please Come Back To Me	50
61	MGM MGM 1149	The Big Knock/Sweet Water	30
66	MGM MGM 1328	Sweet Water/The Big Knock (reissue)	5

STEREOTYPES

79	Hinterland/SRT no cat. no.	THE STEREOTYPES EP (no p/s)	250

STEREOTYPES

80	Art Theft AT 001	Calling All The Shots/Lovers Of The Future (p/s)	8

DEAN STERLING & TEENBEATS

61	Pye 7N 15345	Send Me A Girl/Lost Love	12

FITZROY STERLING

68	Gas GAS 102	Got To Play It Cool/Jezebel	12
70	Bullet BU 422	That's My Life/Queen Of Hearts	8
70	Bullet BU 438	Freedom Street/FITZROY ALL STARS: Freedom Street Version	8
71	Escort ERT 858	Girl Tell Me What To Do/Be Careful	8
71	Pama PM 820	My Sweet Lord/Darling That's Right	5

LESTER STERLING (& HIS GROUP)

(see also Mister Versatile, Bobby Aitken, Eric Morris, Sir Collins Band, Slickers, Uniques)

63	Island WI 121	Clean The City/Long Walk Home (B-side actually by Charmers)	20
63	R&B JB 111	Air Raid Shelter/ROY & ANNETTE: I Mean It	25
63	R&B JB 115	Gravy Cool/WINSTON & BIBBY: Lover Lover Man	35
64	R&B JB 143	Peace And Love/HORACE SEATON: Hold On	30
64	R&B JB 150	Hot Cargo/MAYTALS: Marching On	30
64	R&B JB 155	Baskin' Hop (as Lester Sterling & His Group)/MAYTALS: Shining Light	20
64	R&B JB 172	Indian Summer (as Lester Sterling & His Group)/STRANGER & PATSY: I'll Forgive You	20
66	Doctor Bird DB 1057	Inez (with Tommy McCook & Supersonics)/GLORIA CRAWFORD: Sad Movies	40
67	Doctor Bird DB 1107	Soul Voyage/ALVA LEWIS: Revelation	40
67	Collins Downbeat CR 001	Sir Collins Special/Lester Sterling '67	50
68	Coxsone CS 7080	Africkaan Beat/PARAGONS: My Satisfaction	60
68	Blue Cat BS 116	Zigaloo/Wiser Than Solomon	40
68	Unity UN 502	Bangarang (with Stranger Cole)/STRANGER COLE: If We Should Ever Meet	8
69	Unity UN 505	Reggae On Broadway/CLIQUE: Love Can Be Wonderful	6
69	Unity UN 509	Spoogy/TOMMY McCOOK: Monkey Fiddle	8
69	Unity UN 512	Regina/Bright As A Rose	7
69	Unity UN 517	1,000 Tons Of Megaton/KING CANNON: Five Card Stud	10
69	Unity UN 518	Man About Town/Man At The Door	8
69	Unity UN 531	Lonesome Feeling/Bright As A Rose	6
69	Big Shot BI 507	Forest Gate Rock/RAVING RAVERS: Rock Rock And Cry	8
69	Gas GAS 103	Reggae In The Wind/SOUL SET: Try Me One More Time (B-side actually by Stranger & Gladdy)	6
70	Unity UN 562	Slip Up/DAVE BARKER: On Broadway	10
71	Nu Beat NB 095	Iron Side Part 1/COXSON'S ALL STARS: Iron Side Part 2	8
71	Nu Beat 96	War Is Not The Answer Part 2/Iron Side Part 2	15
71	Smash SMA 2321	Sir Collins Special/Version (actually "Heart Of The Knight" by Gaytones)	8
72	Ashanti ASH 409	Iron Side Part 1/COXSON'S ALL STARS: Iron Side Part 2	6
72	Ashanti ASH 410	War Is Not The Answer/COXSON'S ALL STARS: Version	6
69	Pama SECO 15	BANGARANG (LP)	55

NINA STERN

65	Pye 7N 15823	Take It From Me/Please Come Back To Me	8

STEROID KIDDIES

70s	Steroid/Grundinga SK 001	THE KIDDIES EP	55

STEROID MAXIMUS

90s	Big Cat ABB 28	QUILOMBO (LP)	20

STEROIDS

78	Radar ADA 11	In The Colonies/Sha La La Loo Ley (p/s)	6

STEVE 'N' BONNIE

72	Young Blood YB 1033	Brief Encounter/Don't/Lady	6
73	Sovereign SOV123	Me 'N' My Soul/A Screw Called Kirk	8
72	Young Blood SSYB 16	BRIEF ENCOUNTER (LP)	18

STEVE & STEVIE

(see also Tin Tin, Fut)

68	Toast TT510	Merry-Go-Round/Remains To Be Seen	12
68	Toast TLP 2	STEVE AND STEVIE (LP)	30

APRIL STEVENS

(see also Nino Tempo & April Stevens)

53	Parlophone MSP 6060	C'est Si Bon/Soft Warm Lips	12
54	Parlophone MSP 6088	How Could Red Riding Hood (Have Been?)/You Said You'd Do It	12
67	MGM MGM 1366	Falling In Love Again/Wanting You	100
67	MGM MGM 1366	Falling In Love Again/Wanting You (DJ copy)	200
76	MGM 2006 586	Wanting You/Falling In Love Again (reissue)	5

CAT STEVENS

66	Deram DM 102	I Love My Dog/Portobello Road	5
66	Deram DM 110	Matthew And Son/Granny	7
67	Deram DM 118	I'm Gonna Get Me A Gun/School Is Out	5

			MINT VALUE £
67	Deram DM 140	Bad Night/Laughing Apple	5
67	Deram DM 156	Kitty/Blackness Of The Night	10
68	Deram DM 178	Lovely City/Image Of Hell	7
68	Deram DM 211	Here Comes My Wife/It's A Supa (Dupa) Life	7
69	Deram DM 260	Where Are You/The View From The Top	7
70	Island WIP 6086	Lady D'Arbanville/Time/Fill My Eyes (in p/s)	8
67	Deram DML/SML 1004	MATTHEW AND SON (LP)	25
67	Deram DML/SML 1018	NEW MASTERS (LP)	25
67	Deram	CATS AND DOGS (LP, unreleased, test pressings only)	30
70	Island ILPS 9118	MONA BONE JAKON (LP, pink label with white 'i' logo)	80
70	Island ILPS 9135	TEA FOR THE TILLERMAN (LP, gatefold, pink label, with white 'i' logo)	60
71	Island ILPS 9154	TEASER AND THE FIRECAT (LP, pink label)	12

CHUCK STEVENS

57	Columbia DB 3883	Take A Walk/The Way I Do	7
57	Columbia DB 3938	My London/Couldn't Care More	7

CONNIE STEVENS

(see also Edward Byrnes)

60	Warner Bros WB 3	Sixteen Reasons (with Don Ralke)/Little Sister (with Buddy Cole Trio)	10
60	Warner Bros WB 17	Too Young To Go Steady/A Little Kiss Is A Kiss, Is A Kiss	10
60	Warner Bros WB 25	Apollo/Why Do I Cry For Joey	10
61	Warner Bros WB 41	And This Is Mine/Make-Believe Lover	10
61	Warner Bros WB 47	The Greenwood Tree/If You Don't, Somebody Else Will	10
62	Warner Bros WB 63	Why'd You Wanna Make Me Cry/Just One Kiss	15
62	Warner Bros WB 73	Mr. Songwriter/I Couldn't Say No	10
64	Warner Bros WB 128	They're Jealous Of Me/A Girl Never Knows	10
60	Warner Bros WEP 6007	CONNIE STEVENS AS CRICKET (EP, mono)	15
60	Warner Bros WSEP 2007	CONNIE STEVENS AS CRICKET (EP, stereo)	20
63	Warners WEP 6105	CONNIE STEVENS AS CRICKET NO. 2 (EP, mono)	15
63	Warners WSE 6105	CONNIE STEVENS AS CRICKET NO. 2 (EP, stereo)	20
63	Warners WEP 6112	CONNIE STEVENS AS CRICKET NO. 3 (EP, mono)	15
63	Warners WSE 6112	CONNIE STEVENS AS CRICKET NO. 3 (EP, stereo)	20
62	Warner Bros WM 4061	CONNIE (LP, mono)	20
62	Warner Bros WS 8061	CONNIE (LP, stereo)	25
63	Warner Bros WM/WS 8111	THE HANK WILLIAMS SONG BOOK (LP)	15

DEAN STEVENS

62	Philips 326540 BF	Sad And Lonely/I've Just Heard	10
64	Philips BF 1300	Only 'Cause I'm Lonely/Love Me Like I Love You	8
63	Philips 326580	Let Me Show You How/High On The Hill Of Hope	8

DODIE STEVENS

59	London HLD 8834	Pink Shoe Laces/Coming Of Age	20
60	London HLD 9174	No/A-Tisket A-Tasket	10
61	London HLD 9280	Yes, I'm Lonesome Tonight/Too Young	10
63	London HLP 9672	Don't Send Me Roses/Daddy Couldn't Get Me One Of Those	10
64	Liberty LIB 83	I Wore Out Our Record/You Don't Have To Prove A Thing	8

JERRY STEVENS

66	CBS 2831	You Make My Life Worthwhile/So This Is Love	6

JIMMY STEVENS

66	Fontana TF 721	I Love You/Wharf 130	7

JOHN STEVENS AWAY

76	Vertigo 6059154	Can't Explain (Part 1)/Can't Explain (Part 2)	5

JOHNNY STEVENS & BLUE BEATS

64	Blue Beat BB 229	Shame/Ball And Chain	20

JOHNNY STEVENS & LES DAWSON SYNDICATE

62	Melodisc M 1586	Last Chicken In The Shop/Oh Yeah (some in p/s)	10

KIRK STEVENS

57	Decca F 10863	Once/This Silver Madonna	8

MEIC STEVENS (MIKE STEVENS)

(see also Gary Farr)

65	Decca F 12174	Did I Dream/I Saw A Field (as Mike Stevens)	40
70	Warner Bros WB 8007	Ballad Of Old Joe Blind/Blue Sleep	15
70	Wren WSP 2005	Nid Oes Un Gwydr Ffenestr/Rhywbeth Gwell I Ddod	40
68	Wren WRE 1048	MIKE STEVENS (EP, p/s)	50
68	Wren WRE 1053	RHIF 2 (EP, p/s)	50
69	Wren WRE 1073	MWG (EP, p/s)	50
70	Newyddion Da ND1	MEIC STEVENS (EP, p/s)	100
70	Sain SAIN 004	Y BRAWD HOUDINI (EP, p/s)	50
71	Wren WRE 1107	BYW YN Y WLAD (EP, p/s)	50
71	Sain SAIN 13	DIOLCH YN FAWR (EP, p/s)	50
70	Warner Brothers WS 3005	OUTLANDER (LP, with insert)	300
72	Wren WRL 536	GWYMON (LP)	300
77	Sain SAIN 1065	GOG (LP)	120
79	Tic Toc no cat. no.	CANAEON CYNNAR (LP, private pressing)	220
82	Sain SAIN 1239	NOS DU NOS DA (LP)	50
83	Sain SAIN 1312	LAPIS LAZULI (LP)	50
97	Tenth Planet TP 028	GHOST TOWN (LP, gatefold sleeve, numbered, 1000 only)	12

MICK STEVENS

71	Deroy (no cat. no.)	SEE THE MORNING (LP, private pressing)	400
75	Deroy (no cat. no.)	NO SAVAGE WORD (LP, private pressing)	300

MIKE STEVENS

(see also Shevells)

66	Pye 7N 17243	Cathy's Clown/Go-Go Train	60
68	Polydor 56269	Guaranteed To Drive You Wild/Hog-Tied	10

MINT VALUE £

MORT STEVENS & HIS ORCHESTRA

70	Capitol CL 15655	Hawaii Five-O Theme/McGarrett's Theme	8

RAY STEVENS

58	Capitol CL 14881	Chickie-Chickie Wah Wah/Crying Goodbye	10
61	Mercury AMT 1158	Jeremiah Peabody's Polyunsaturated Quick Dissolving Fast Acting Pleasant Tasting Green And Purple Pills/Teen Years	7
62	Mercury AMT 1184	Ahab The Arab/It's Been So Long	8
63	Mercury AMT 1207	Harry The Hairy Ape/Little Stone Statue	7
68	Monument MON 1022	Mr Businessman/Face The Music	8

RICKY STEVENS

61	Columbia DB 4739	I Cried For You/I Am	10
62	Columbia DB 4778	Forever/Now, It's All Over	7
63	Columbia DB 4981	My Mother's Eyes/I'll Get By	7
62	Columbia SEG 8172	I CRIED FOR YOU (EP)	50

ROY STEVENS

66	London HLU 10016	Party People/ABC	10

SHAKIN' STEVENS (& SUNSETS)

70	Parlophone R 5860	Spirit Of Woodstock/Down On The Farm	60
72	Polydor 2058 213	Sweet Little Rock'n'Roller/White Lightning	50
74	Emerald MD 1176	Honey Honey/Holey Moley 2001	35
76	Mooncrest MOON 51	Jungle Rock/Girl In Red	18
77	Track 2094 134	Never/You Always Hurt The One You Love	15
77	Track 2094 136	Somebody Touched Me/Way Down Yonder In New Orleans (in p/s)	20
77	Track 2094 136	Somebody Touched Me/Way Down Yonder In New Orleans	8
78	Track 2094 141	Justine/Wait And See	20
78	Epic SEPC 6567	Treat Her Right/I Don't Want No Other Baby	15
79	Epic SEPC 6845	Endless Sleep/Fire	15
79	Epic SEPC 7235	Spooky/I Don't Want No Other Baby	30
80	Epic SEPC 8090	Hot Dog/Apron Strings	10
80	Epic SEPC 8573	Hey Mae/I Guess I Was A Fool (in p/s)	60
80	Epic SEPC 8573	Hey Mae/I Guess I Was A Fool	5
80	Epic SEPC 9064	Shooting Gallery/Make It Right Tonight (p/s)	10
81	Battle Of The Bands BOB 2	Jungle Rock/Girl In Red (p/s, reissue, as Shakin' Stevens & Sunsets)	5
81	Mint CHEW 51	No Other Baby/Manhattan Melodrama (p/s)	5
81	Epic A 1643	It's Raining/You And I Were Meant To Be (picture disc)	5
81	Solid Gold SGR 107	Shaky Sings Elvis (Parts 1 & 2) (medley) (p/s)	5
82	Epic EPCA 1742	Oh Julie/I'm Knocking (poster p/s)	5
82	Epic EPCA 2656	Give Me Your Heart Tonight/Thinkin' Of You (p/s, with poster)	5
82	Epic EPCA 2656	Give Me Your Heart Tonight/Thinkin' Of You (picture disc)	5
82	Everest/Premier EV 1000	Tiger/Sweet Little Sixteen/Give Me A Break (picture disc)	5
82	Everest/Premier EV 1000	Tiger/Sweet Little Sixteen/Give Me A Break	10
83	Epic WA 3565	It's Late/It's Good For You Baby (feet-shaped picture disc)	8
83	Epic WA 3774	Cry Just A Little Bit/Love Me Tonight (picture disc)	5
83	Kelloggs KELL 1	Oh Julie/ABBA: I Have A Dream (free with Kelloggs' 'Rice Krispies')	5
84	Epic A 4291	A Love Waiting For You/As Long As I Have You (live) (poster p/s)	5
84	Epic QA 4677	A Letter To You/Come Back And Love Me (p/s, with free post bag game)	5
84	Epic DA 4882	Teardrops/You Shake Me Up//Shakin' Stevens Party Mix (Parts 1 & 2) (double pack)	8
85	Epic GA 6072	Breakin' Up My Heart/I'll Give You My Heart (gatefold pop-up p/s)	5
86	Epic SHAKY 2	Because I Love You/Tell Me One More Time (2 picture sleeves, sealed together on edge with sticker, with autograph)	8
87	Epic SHAKY P5	What Do You Want To Make Those Eyes At Me For/You're Evil (picture disc)	5
89	Epic SHAKY C10	Love Attack/Love Attack (Extended Version)/As Long As I Have You (live) (CD, card sleeve)	8
81	Magnum Force MFEP 001	Memphis Earthquake/You Mostest Girl/Evil Hearted Ada/ My Bucket's Got A Hole In It (EP, p/s)	8
82	Magnum Force MFEP 007	Frantic/Ready Teddy/Tear It Up/Monkey's Uncle (EP, p/s)	8
83	Epic 40-2620	GREATEST ORIGINAL HITS (EP, cassette)	12
70	Parlophone PCS 7112	A LEGEND (LP)	55
71	CBS 52901	I'M NO J.D. (LP)	70
72	Contour 2870 152	ROCKIN' AND SHAKIN' (LP)	15
73	Emerald GES 1121	SHAKIN' STEVENS AND THE SUNSETS (LP)	18
78	Track 2406 011	SHAKIN' STEVENS (LP, with insert)	15
80	Epic EPC 84547	MARIE MARIE (LP, withdrawn)	18
83	Epic BX 86301	THE BOP WON'T STOP (LP & cassette, box set, with Shaky autograph book)	18

TERRI STEVENS

59	Felsted AF 112	My Wish Tonight/All Alone	5
59	Felsted AF 126	Adonis/Vieni, Vieni	6

VIRGINIA STEVENS

77	Mulligan LUN A 332	TIOCFAIDH AN SAMHRADH - TRADITIONAL SONGS FROM THE WEST OF IRELAND (LP, with booklet)	15

RICHARD STEVENSEN

70	Pye 7N 45004	The Day That You Came Back/The Gates Of Me	8
70	Pye NSPL 18358	GATES OF ME (LP, textured sleeve)	25

MICKEY STEVENSON

72	Ember EMBS 320	Here I Am/Joe Poor Loves Daphne Elizabeth Richard	6
72	Ember NR 5063	HERE I AM (LP)	30

N A STEVENSON AND THE 4 ACES

70	Injun 103	Boogie Woogie Country Girl/Pins & Needles	10

STEVIE'S BUZZ

(see also P.P. Arnold, Buzzcocks, Primal Scream)

96	Nice no cat. no.	Autumn Stone/P.P. & THE PRIMES: Understanding (promo only, large centre)	8

MINT VALUE £

AL STEWART
(see also Jimmy Page)

66	Decca F 12467	The Elf/Turn To Earth	60
67	CBS 3034	Bedsitter Images/Swiss Cottage Manoeuvres	10
70	CBS 4843	Electric Los Angeles Sunset/My Enemies Have Sweet Voices	8
70	CBS 5351	The News From Spain/Elvaston Place	7
72	CBS 7763	You Don't Even Know Me/I'm Falling	6
72	CBS 7992	Amsterdam/Songs Out Of Clay	6
73	CBS SCBS 1971	Terminal Eyes/Last Day Of June 1934	10
67	CBS (S)BPG 63087	BEDSITTER IMAGES (LP)	85
69	CBS (S) 63460	LOVE CHRONICLES (LP, gatefold sleeve)	25
70	CBS 63848	ZERO SHE FLIES (LP, gatefold sleeve)	22
70	CBS 64023	FIRST ALBUM (BEDSITTER IMAGES) (LP, remixed reissue, different track listing)	18
72	CBS 64739	ORANGE (LP)	12

ANDY STEWART

60	Top Rank JAR 427	Donald, Where's Your Troosers?/Dancing In Kyle	7
65	HMV POP 1454	Dr. Finlay/Oh! What A Ceildh	7

BILLY STEWART

62	Pye International 7N 25164	Reap What You Sow/Fat Boy	15
63	Pye International 7N 25222	Strange Feeling/Sugar And Spice	15
65	Chess CRS 8009	I Do Love You/Keep Loving	10
65	Chess CRS 8017	Sitting In The Park/Once Again	10
66	Chess CRS 8028	Because I Love You/Mountains Of Love	10
66	Chess CRS 8038	Love Me/Why Am I Lonely	10
66	Chess CRS 8040	Summertime/To Love To Love	10
66	Chess CRS 8045	Secret Love/Look Back And Smile	10
66	Chess CRS 8050	Ole Man River/Every Day I Have The Blues	10
67	Chess CRS 8067	Cross My Heart/Why (Do I Love You So)	10
69	Chess CRS 8092	Summertime/I Do Love You	15
72	Chess 6145 017	Sitting In The Park/Summertime	8
65	Chess CRE 6010	IN CROWD (EP, with Ramsey Lewis Trio, et al)	30
67	Chess CRE 6024	I DO LOVE YOU (EP)	30
66	Chess CRL 4523	UNBELIEVABLE (LP)	30
72	Chess 6310 125	GOLDEN DECADE (LP)	12

BOB STEWART

55	MGM SP 1114	It's A Woman's World/I Went Out Of My Way	6

DAVID A. STEWART
(see also Eurythmics, Longdancer, Stewart & Harrison)

92	Anxious ZT 43046	LILY WAS HERE (12", with 2 Orb mixes, featuring Candy Dulfer, p/s)	8

DAVIE STEWART

78	Topic 12T 293	DAVIE STEWART (LP, with insert)	12

DELANO STEWART
(see also Winston Stewart, Gaylads, Patsy Todd)

68	Doctor Bird DB 1138	That's Life/Tell Me Baby	30
68	High Note HS 004	Let's Have Some Fun/Dance With Me	20
69	High Note HS 014	Rocking Sensation/GAYTONES: One Look	60
70	High Note HS 027	Got To Come Back/Don't Believe In Him	15
70	High Note HS 034	Hallelujah/I Wish It Could Last	10
70	High Hote HS 039	Wherever I Lay My Hat/Don't Believe Him (B-side actually by Gladstone Anderson & Gaytones)	12
70	High Note HS 041	Stay A Little Bit Longer/Stay A Little Bit Longer (Version II) (B-side actually by Gladstone Anderson & Gaytones)	12
70	Trojan TBL 138	STAY A LITTLE BIT LONGER (LP)	30

GRAHAM STEWART SEVEN

59	Tempo EXA 91	GRAHAM STEWART SEVEN (EP)	10

(Dave) STEWART & HARRISON
(see also Longdancer, Eurythmics, David A. Stewart)

70	Multicord MULT SH 1	GIRL (EP)	15

JAMES STEWART

65	Brunswick 05938	The Legend Of Shenandoah/ CHARLES 'BUD' DANT CHORUS: We're Ridin' Out Tonight	5

JAMES STEWART & HENRY FONDA

70	Stateside SS 2179	Rolling Stone/Theme From Cheyenne Social Club	8

JOHN STEWART
(see also Kingston Trio, Cumberland Three, Scott Engel)

60	Capitol CL 15589	July, You're A Woman/Shackles And Chains	6
69	Capitol E-(S)T 203	CALIFORNIA BLOODLINES (LP)	12

JOHNNY STEWART

58	HMV POP 480	Wishing For Your Love/Promise Me	7

PAUL STEWART (MOVEMENT)
(see also Hamilton & [Hamilton] Movement)

66	Philips BF 1513	Queen Boadicea/Talkin'	7
67	Decca F 12577	Saturday Morning Man/Too Too Good (as Paul Stewart Movement)	12

RAPHAEL STEWART & HOT TOPS

71	Punch PH 71	Put Your Sweet Lips/JUSTINS: Stand By Me	10

REX STEWART'S LONDON FIVE

55	Tempo EXA 8	REX STEWART'S LONDON FIVE (EP)	15

MINT VALUE £

ROD STEWART
(see also Jeff Beck, Shotgun Express, Faces, Python Lee Jackson, Long John Baldry, Steamhammer, Ted Wood)

SINGLES

64	Decca F 11996	Good Morning Little Schoolgirl/I'm Gonna Move To The Outskirts Of Town	160
65	Columbia DB 7766	The Day Will Come/Why Does It Go On?	150
66	Columbia DB 7892	Shake/I Just Got Some	200
68	Immediate IM 060	Little Miss Understood/So Much To Say	100
70	Vertigo 6086 002	It's All Over Now/Jo's Lament	15
72	Phonogram DJ004	Twisting the Night Away (EP 1-track on 4 track promo 7" also featuring Chuck Berry, Diane Davidson and the Stylistics)	20
73	Mercury 6052 371	Oh No Not My Baby/Jodie (tartan sleeve)	6
76	Mercury 6160 006	Maggie May/You Wear It Well/Twistin' The Night Away (p/s)	5
77	Mercury 6160 007	Mandolin Wind/Girl From The North Country/Sweet Little Rock'N'Roller	5
76	Mercury 6167 327	It's All Over Now/Handbags And Gladrags	7
77	Riva RIVA 1	You're Insane/You're Insane (DJ copy, 500 only)	25
77	Riva RIVA 3	Tonight's The Night/The First Cut Is The Deepest (withdrawn B-side)	10
78	Riva RIVA 9	Sailing/Stone Cold Sober (p/s)	5
78	Riva RIVA 9	Sailing/Stone Cold Sober(HMS Ark Royal Commemorative issue, blue vinyl, p/s)	150
78	Riva RIVA 15	Ole Ola/Que Sera Sera - I'd Walk A Million Miles For One Of Your Goals (p/s)	5
80	Riva RIVA 23	If Lovin' You Is Wrong/Last Summer (p/s)	5
80	Virgin VS 366	Little Miss Understood/So Much To Say (p/s, reissue)	5
80	Riva W 7929TP	Excerpts From "Foolish Behaviour" (flexidisc with London Evening News)	10
80	Riva W 7929TP	Excerpts From "Foolish Behaviour" (flexidisc without London Evening News)	6
82	Riva RIVA 35	How Long/Jealous (p/s, with free sticker)	5
82	Decca F 11996	Good Morning Little Schoolgirl/I'm Gonna Move To The Outskirts Of Town (reissue)	8
82	Immediate IM 060	Little Miss Understood/So Much To Say (reissue, p/s)	5
83	Warner Bros W 9440P	Sweet Surrender/Ghetto Blaster (picture disc)	5
84	Warner Bros SAM 194	Infatuation (1-sided picture disc in wallet with interview cassette)	12
86	Warner Bros W 8668TP	Love Touch/Heart Is On The Line/Hard Lesson To Learn (12", picture disc)	8
88	Warner Bros WX 152TP	Lost In You (Extended Remix)/Lost In You (Fade)/Almost Illegal (12", pic disc)	8
89	Warner Bros W 2686P	This Old Heart Of Mine/Ain't Love A Bitch/Tonight I'm Yours (Don't Hurt Me) (with Ronald Isley, shaped picture disc)	8

LPs

70	Vertigo VO 4	AN OLD RAINCOAT WON'T EVER LET YOU DOWN (gatefold sleeve, large swirl label, original pressing with 'Philips' credit on label)	100
70	Vertigo VO 4	AN OLD RAINCOAT WON'T EVER LET YOU DOWN (gatefold sleeve, large swirl label, later pressing without 'Philips' credit on label)	20
70	Vertigo 6360 500	GASOLINE ALLEY (gatefold sleeve, swirl label)	70
71	Mercury 6338 063	EVERY PICTURE TELLS A STORY (black label, with poster)	30
72	Mercury 6499 153	NEVER A DULL MOMENT (gatefold sleeve)	15
73	Mercury 6499 484	SING IT AGAIN, ROD	12
75	Riva RVLP 4	ATLANTIC CROSSING (gatefold sleeve, blue vinyl/orange vinyl)	25
76	Mercury 6672 013	THE VINTAGE YEARS	12
76	Philips SON 001	RECORDED HIGHLIGHTS & ACTION REPLAYS	12
78	St. Michael 21020 102	REASON TO BELIEVE (only available in Marks & Spencer)	20
84	Warner Bros 9250 951	CAMOUFLAGE (with bonus 1-sided picture disc "Infatuation" in wallet with interview tape [SAM 194])	20

ROMAN STEWART

72	Songbird SB 1075	Changing Times (with Dave)/CRYSTALITES: Changing Times Version	12
73	Downtown DT 518	Try Me/BIG YOUTH: Rhythm Style	12
73	Techniques TE 932	Tonight I'm Staying Here (& Tennors)/Lady Love (& Tennors)	8
75	Camel CA 2002	Wolverton Mountain/PITTERSON ALL STARS: Version	5
79	GGS 049	Don't Get Jumpy/GG ALL STARS: Dub Cut (12")	25
78	Pirate PIR 002	Herbalist/Version (12", various coloured vinyl)	35

SANDY STEWART

58	London HLE 8683	A Certain Smile/Kiss Me Richard	10
63	Pye International 7N 25176	My Colouring Book/I Heard You Cried Last Night	5

SONNY STEWART & HIS SKIFFLE KINGS

57	Philips PB 719	The Northern Line/Black Jack (78)	20
57	Philips PB 773	Let Me Lie/Mama Don't Allow It (78)	20

TINGA STEWART

71	Songbird SB 1048	Hear That Train/CRYSTALITES: Hear That Train - Version	7
72	Tropical AL 0018	A Brand New Me/BROWNS ALL STARS: Nice Version	6
74	Dragon DRA 1025	The Message/Dub	12

WINSTON STEWART
(see also Andy & Clyde, Gaylads, Delano Stewart, Winston & Tonettes)

64	R&B JB 147	But I Do/MAYTALS: Four Seasons	35
64	Port-O-Jam PJ 4002	All Of My Life/How Many Times	30
65	Ska Beat JB 225	You Made Me Cry/CHECKMATES: Invisible Ska	40

WYNN STEWART

60	London HL 7087	Wishful Thinking/Uncle Tom Got Caught (export issue)	30

STEWPOT & SAVE THE CHILDREN FUND CHOIR

68	MGM 1448	I Like My Toys/Myrtles Birthday	20

J.E. STICK & DRUMBAGO

61	Blue Beat BB 64	Boss Gill/COUNT OSSIE : Cassavuba	20

STICKERS
(see also Jackie Brown)

71	Bullet BU 492	One Night Of Sin/Sin (Version) (both sides actually by Jackie Brown)	5

STICK SHIFTS

80	Chiswick CHIS 118	Automobile/Parramatta Road (3 different p/s)	12

MINT VALUE £

ARBEE STIDHAM

70s	Mainstream MSL 1011	A TIME FOR BLUES (LP)	12

STIFF LITTLE FINGERS

(see also Billy Karloff & Extremes)

78	Rigid Digits SRD-1	Suspect Device/Wasted Life (hand-made p/s, 500 only, red label with catalogue number on right-hand side)	100
78	Rigid Digits SRD-1	Suspect Device/Wasted Life (re-pressing, different machine-cut p/s, various colour labels/yellow labels)	18
78	Rough Trade RT 004	78 R.P.M./Alternative Ulster (p/s, A & B-sides reversed)	10
78	Rough Trade RT 004	Alternative Ulster/78 R.P.M. (p/s)	5
78	Rough Trade RT 006	Suspect Device/Wasted Life (reissue)	8
79	Rough Trade RT 015	Gotta Getaway/Bloody Sunday (p/s)	5
79	Chrysalis CHS 2368	Straw Dogs/You Can't Say Crap On The Radio (p/s)	7
81	SLFDJ1	Just Fade Away/Go For It (DJ promo)	10
82	Chrysalis CHSDJ 2580	Listen/Two Guitars Clash (p/s, jukebox issue)	12
82	Chrysalis/Melody Maker (no cat no)	Excerpts From "Now Then"/IGGY POP: Excerpts From "Zombie Birdhouse" (flexidisc, free with Melody Maker)	6
89	Virgin SLFDJ1	St. Patrix, The Wild Rover/Johnny Was (DJ promo, unreleased as 7")	12
91	Essential ESSX 2007	Beirut Moon/Stand Up And Shout/Interview With Jake Burns (CD, limited edition)	30
89	Link 1203	THE LAST TIME (EP)	10
02	EMI Gold 7243 5 38560 21	LIVE IN ABERDEEN (CD)	35
86	Strange Fruit SFPS 004	PEEL SESSIONS (12")	12

STIFFS

79	Dork UR 1	Standard English/S.C. Rip/Brookside Riot Squad (die-cut sleeve)	25
79	Dork UR 2	Inside Out/Kids On the Street (die cut sleeve or later Zonophone Z3 p/s)	20
80	Zonophone Z 14	Volume Control/Nothing To Lose (p/s)	10
80	Stiff BUT 86	Goodbye My Love/Magic Roundabout (p/s)	10
85	Dork UR 7(12)	The Young Guitars/Yer Under Attack (12", red p/s)	10
85	Dork UR 7(12)	The Young Guitars/Yer Under Attack (12", blue p/s)	8

STILETTOS

80	Ariola ARO 200	This Is The Way/Who Can It Be (p/s)	20

STILL COOL

79	Hit Run HITDD 22	Insane Love/Stereo Version '79 (12")	25

STILL LIFE

(see also Jon, Titus Groan)

68	Columbia DB 8345	What Did We Miss/My Kingdom Cannot Lose	70
71	Vertigo 6360 026	STILL LIFE (LP, gatefold sleeve, large swirl label)	250

STEPHEN STILLS

(see also Buffalo Springfield, Al Kooper Mike Bloomfield & Stephen Stills, Crosby Stills Nash & Young, Manassas, Stills-Young Band)

71	Atlantic 2091 046	Love The One You're With/To A Flame	5
71	Atlantic 2091 069	Sit Yourself Down/We Are Not Helpless	5
71	Atlantic 2091 117	Change Partners/Relaxing Town	5
71	Atlantic 2091 141	Marianne/Nothing To Do But Today	5
70	Atlantic 2401 004	STEPHEN STILLS (LP)	18
71	Atlantic 2401 013	STEPHEN STILLS 2 (LP, gatefold sleeve)	15
73	Atlantic K 40440	DOWN THE ROAD (LP)	15

STILLS-YOUNG BAND

(see also Stephen Stills, Manassas, Neil Young, Buffalo Springfield, Crosby Stills Nash & Young)

76	Reprise K 14446	Long May You Run/12-8 Blues	5
76	Reprise K 14482	Like A Hurricane (edit)/Hold Back The Tears	5
76	Reprise K 54081	LONG MAY YOU RUN (LP)	15

STILLWATER TRIO

70s	Sharon 330	LIFE'S RAILROAD (LP)	18

STING

(see also Police, Last Exit, [Fast Breeder &] Radio Actors, Newcastle Big Band)

82	A&M PARTY 1	Need Your Love So Bad/PAULINE BLACK: No Woman, No Cry (Promo)	10
85	A&M DREAMP 1	THE DREAM OF THE BLUE TURTLES (LP, picture disc, die-cut sl., with insert)	15
91	A&M 397 171-2	ACOUSTIC LIVE IN NEWCASTLE (CD, box set with book)	18

STINGERS

72	Upsetter US 395	Preacher Man/UPSETTERS: Version	12
72	Explosion EX 2075	Forward Up/UPSETTERS: Forward	25

STINGRAY (TV series)

(see under Century 21)

STING-RAYS

82	Rocket XPRES 78	Radiator Rock/Slap Bass Boogie (die-cut sleeve)	8
82	Big Beat SW 82	Dinosaurs/Math Of Trend/Another Cup Of Coffee/You're Gonna Miss Me (white label test pressing, 100 Club gig freebie, 80 only)	20
83	Big Beat SW 82	Dinosaurs/Math Of Trend/Another Cup Of Coffee/You're Gonna Miss Me (p/s)	5
84	Big Beat NS 95	Escalator/Loose Lip Synch Ship/Escalator (Instrumental) (p/s)	5
85	Big Beat NS 109	Don't Break Down/Don't Break Down (Version) (p/s)	5
85	Media Burn MB 2/ Lyntone LYN 16436	Bonus Track/I Want My Woman/Flash On You (33 rpm, red vinyl flexidisc with The Sting-Rays Story magazine)	5
86	Kaleidoscope Sound 102	BEHIND THE BEYOND (12" EP)	8
83	Big beat WIKM 16	DINOSAURS (LP)	12
84	Media Burn MB 1	LIVE RETALIATION (LP, white or black vinyl)	12
87	K'scope Sound KSLP 1	CRYPTIC AND COFFEE TIME (LP)	12
88	Media Burn MB 18	GOODBYE TO ALL THAT - LIVE VOL. 2 (LP, red or black vinyl)	12

STINKY TOYS

77	Polydor 2056 630	Boozy Creed/Driver Blues (p/s)	15
77	Polydor 2393 174	STINKY TOYS (LP)	25

MINT VALUE £

(PETER) LEE STIRLING (& BRUISERS)

(see also Bruisers, Hungry Wolf)

63	Columbia DB 4992	My Heart Commands Me/Welcome Stranger (as Lee Stirling & Bruisers)	5
63	Parlophone R 5063	I Could If I Wanted To/Right From The Start (as Lee Stirling & Bruisers)	5
64	Parlophone R 5112	Now That I've Found You/I Believe (as Peter Lee Stirling & Bruisers)	5
64	Parlophone R 5158	Sad, Lonely And Blue/I'm Looking For Someone To Love (as Peter Lee Stirling & Bruisers)	5
64	Parlophone R 5198	Everything Will Be Alright/You'll Be Mine (as Peter Lee Stirling & Bruisers)	5
66	Decca F 12433	The Sweet And Tender Hold Of Your Love/Everybody Needs A Someone	5
66	Decca F 12535	Oh What A Fool/I'm Sportin' A New Baby	5
67	Decca F 12628	You Don't Live Twice/8.35 On The Dot	25
67	Decca F 12674	Goodbye Thimblemill Lane/Hey Conductor	120
69	MCA MU 1093	Big Sam/Mr. Average Man	5
70	MCA MK 5027	Goodbye Summer Girl/Judas In Blue	5

STITCH

76	RCA 2526	La Maison De L'Amour/All Smoke & No Fire	8

GARY STITES

59	London HLL 8881	Lonely For You/Shine That Ring	25
59	London HLL 8881	Lonely For You/Shine That Ring (78)	15
59	London HLL 9003	Starry Eyed/Without Your Love	20
59	London HLL 9003	Starry Eyed/Without Your Love (78)	15
60	London HLL 9082	Lawdy, Miss Clawdy/Don't Wanna Say Goodbye	25

SONNY STITT

(see also Oscar Peterson, J.J. Johnson)

59	HMV 7EG 8532	SONNY STITT PLAYS JIMMY GIUFFRE (EP)	8
53	Esquire 20-013	SONNY STITT-BUD POWELL QUARTET (10" LP)	20
58	Esquire 32-049	S.P.J. JAZZ (LP, with Bud Powell & J.J. Johnson)	18
58	Columbia Clef 33CX 10114	NEW YORK JAZZ (LP)	18
59	Esquire 32-078	STITT'S BITS (LP)	18
59	HMV CLP 1280	ONLY THE BLUES (LP)	15
60	HMV CLP 1363	PERSONAL APPEARANCE (LP)	12
60	HMV CLP 1384	SONNY STITT WITH THE OSCAR PETERSON TRIO (LP)	12
61	HMV CLP 1420	BLOWS THE BLUES (LP, mono)	12
61	HMV CSD 1341	BLOWS THE BLUES (LP, stereo)	15
64	Chess CRL 4503	MY MAIN MAN (LP)	15
67	Marble Arch MAL 753	SONNY STITT (LP)	15

ALAN STIVELL

71	Philips 6009208	The Wind Of Ketta/Pop Plinn	8

STOCKER, GREENWOOD & FRIENDS

(see also Slack Alice)

79	Changes CR1400	BILLY + NINE (LP)	25

STOCK, HAUSEN & WALKMAN

(see also Dummy Run)

96	Hot Air QRM SP 101	ORGAN TRANSPLANTS (EP)	10
97	Hot Air SPME 2	Buy Me/Sue Me (500 only on pink vinyl)	10
97	Hot Air SPME 2	Buy Me/Sue Me (300 on clear vinyl)	12
97	Hot Air SPME 2	Buy Me/Sue Me (200 on light blue vinyl)	15
99	Hot Air ALERT 01	Alert/Crash (500 only)	10
91	Hot Air SHWCASS 001	WHAT'S UP? (Cassette in small cereal box, various inserts)	20
95	Hot Air QRM CD 011	HAIRBALLS (CD, hairy sleeve)	18
96	Hot Air QRM LP 101	ORGAN TRANSPLANTS VOL 1 (LP)	15
00	Hot Air QRM LP 0000	ORGAN TRANSPLANTS VOL 2 (LP)	12

STOCKHOLM MONSTERS

81	Factory FAC 41	Fairytales/Death Is Slowly (p/s)	15
82	Factory FAC 58	Happy Ever After/Soft Babies (p/s)	15
84	Factory FAC 107	All At Once (p/s)	15

STOCKINGTOPS

(see also Sue & Sunny, Sue & Sunshine, Myrtelles)

68	Toast TT 500	You're Never Gonna Get My Lovin'/You Don't Know What Love Is All About	18
68	CBS 3407	I Don't Ever Wanna Be Kicked By You/The World We Live In Is A Lonely Place	15

STOCKTON'S WING

78	Tara 2004	STOCKTON'S WING (LP)	12

STOICS

68	RCA RCA 1745	Earth, Fire, Air And Water/Search Of The Sea	25

STOKES

65	London HLU 9955	Whipped Cream/Pie Crust	15

SIMON STOKES & NIGHTHAWKS

70	Elektra EKSN 45082	Voodoo Woman/Can't Stop Now	20

RHET STOLLER (& HIS ECHOES)

60	Decca F 11271	Walk Don't Run/All Rhet	10
60	Decca F 11302	Chariot/Night Theme	10
63	Decca F 11738	Countdown/Over The Steppes (as Rhet Stoller & His Echoes)	10
64	Melodisc MEL 1595	Beat That/Treble Gold + One	15
64	Windsor PS 119	Caravan/Short Cut	20
64	Windsor PS 130	Ricochet/Knockout	20
66	Columbia DB 8013	Uncrowned King/Surf Ride (unissued, demos only)	20
69	Mosaic MOSAIC 1	SUNSHINE ANYTIME (EP, as Rhet Stoller & Music)	10
67	Coronet EC 101	THE INCREDIBLE RHET STOLLER (LP)	25

MINT VALUE £

JACKIE STOLLINGS (& NASHVILLE BOYS)
(See also Jess Conrad)
62 Starlite ST45 092 Footsteps Of A Fool/And Then I Knew (B-side with Nashville Boys) . . . 6

MORRIS STOLOFF (& COLUMBIA PICTURES ORCHESTRA)
56 Brunswick 05553 Moonglow/Theme From "Picnic" . . . 7
56 Brunswick 05597 Theme From "The Solid Gold Cadillac"/Sweet Sue Just You . . . 5
57 Brunswick 05666 Theme From "Fire Down Below"/Theme From "Full Of Life" . . . 5
61 Warner Bros WB 48 Fanny/Panisse And Son . . . 6

STOMPERS
62 Fontana H 385 Quarter To Four Stomp (Surf Stompin')/Foolish One . . . 60

ALEXANDER STONE
70 Gemini GMS 003 I Try To Make You Good/Man In A Suitcase . . . 10

CLIFFIE STONE & HIS ORCHESTRA
(see also Jeanne Gayle, Billy Strange)
55 Capitol CL 14330 Barracuda/The Popcorn Song (with Billy Strange & Speedy West) . . . 100
55 Capitol CL 14330 Barracuda/The Popcorn Song (with Billy Strange & Speedy West) (78) . . . 20
56 Capitol CL 14666 Jingle Bells/Rudolph The Red Nosed Reindeer . . . 5
58 Capitol CL 14928 Near You/Nobody's Darlin' But Mine . . . 5
59 Capitol CL 14996 Blood On The Saddle/Cool Water . . . 5
59 Capitol T 1080 THE PARTY'S ON ME (LP) . . . 15

ELLA STONE & MOSS
(see also Helen Shapiro, Al Saxon)
70s Phoenix SNIX 128 The Prophet/Now Or Never . . . 6

GEORGE STONE
65 Stateside SS 479 Hole In The Wall/My Beat . . . 20

KIRBY STONE QUARTET/FOUR
56 Vogue Coral Q 72129 Honey Hush/Lassus Trombone . . . 15
56 Vogue Coral Q 72129 Honey Hush/Lassus Trombone (78) . . . 10
59 Philips PB 903 That "I Had A Dream, Dear" Rock/Sweet Nothings . . . 5
63 Warner Bros WB 102 The Great Escape (March)/Fancy Dan . . . 5
63 Warner Bros WB 118 Washington Square/Blue Guitar . . . 7
59 London HA-A 2164 MAN, I FLIPPED WHEN I HEARD THE KIRBY STONE FOUR (LP) . . . 15

MARK STONE
58 London HLR 8543 Ever Since I Met Lucy/The Stroll . . . 85
58 London HLR 8543 Ever Since I Met Lucy/The Stroll (78) . . . 30

SLY (& FAMILY) STONE
68 Columbia DB 8369 Dance To The Music/Let Me Hear It From You . . . 100
68 Columbia DB 8369 Dance To The Music/Let Me Hear It From You (DJ copy) . . . 150
68 Direction 58-3568 Dance To The Music/Let Me Hear It From You (reissue) . . . 8
68 Direction 58-3707 M'Lady/Life . . . 8
69 Direction 58-3938 Everyday People/Sing A Simple Song . . . 8
69 Direction 58-4279 Stand!/I Want To Take You Higher . . . 8
69 Direction 58-4471 Hot Fun In The Summertime/Fun . . . 10
70 Direction 58-4782 Thank You (Falettinme Be Mice Elf Agin)/Everybody Is A Star . . . 8
70 CBS 5054 I Want To Take You Higher/You Can Make It If You Try . . . 6
71 Epic EPC 7632 Family Affair/Luv n' Haight . . . 5
68 Direction 8-63412 DANCE TO THE MUSIC (LP) . . . 20
68 Direction 8-63461 M'LADY (LP) . . . 20
69 Direction 8-63655 STAND! (LP, CBS sleeve with Direction label) . . . 20

STONE ANGEL
(see also Ken Saul)
75 SSLP 04 STONE ANGEL (LP, private pressing, blue/silver label) . . . 220
94 Acme AC 8008 LP STONE ANGEL (LP, reissue, 500 only) . . . 15

STONEFIELD TRAMP
(see also Terry Friend, Rob Van Spyk)
74 Acorn/Tramp CF 247 DREAMING (LP) . . . 130

STONE GRAPHICS
68 Parlophone R 5735 A Tale Of Long Ago/Travelling Man . . . 12

STONEGROUND
71 Warner Bros K 16126 You Must Be One Of Us/It Takes A Lot To Laugh . . . 5
71 Warner Bros K 46087 STONEGROUND (LP) . . . 15
71 Warner Bros K 53999 FAMILY ALBUM (LP) . . . 15

STONEGROUND BAND
70s Nut SUNSTRUCK!! (LP, stickered sleeve) . . . 30

HARRY STONEHAM
76 One UP OU 2127 I FEEL GOOD, I FEEL FUNKY (LP) . . . 15

HARRY STONEHAM & JOHNNY EYDEN
67 Tepee TPRLP 100 TWO GUYS TO FOLLOW (LP, mono [70s reissues credited to Harry Stoneham £15]) . . . 25

STONEHENGE MEN
62 HMV POP 981 Big Feet/Pinto . . . 45

STONEHOUSE
71 RCA SF 8197 STONEHOUSE CREEK (LP, laminated front sleeve, orange label) . . . 125

E.V. STONEMAN
63 London HA-B/SH-B 8089 E.V. STONEMAN AND THE STONEMAN FAMILY (LP) . . . 12

STONE PONEYS
(see also Linda Ronstadt)
67 Capitol CL 15523 A Different Drum/I've Got To Know . . . 10

MINT VALUE £

STONE RISK

94	Stone Risk SR001	This Is Stone Risk (12")	8

STONE ROSES

(see also Ian Brown, John Squire)

SINGLES

85	Thin Line THIN 001	So Young/Tell Me (12", p/s, 1,200 only; beware of counterfeits!)	80
87	Black/Revolver 12 REV 36	Sally Cinnamon/Here It Comes/All Across The Sand (12", 'Printed In England' on rear p/s & no barcode, "All Across The Sands" listed on label; different mixes of 2 tracks to later reissue - increasingly difficult to find original)	30
88	Silvertone ORE 1	Elephant Stone/The Hardest Thing In The World (catalogue number in black print on rear of p/s)	8
88	Silvertone ORET1	Elephant Stone (4.48)/Elephant Stone (7" Version) (3.00)/Full Fathom Five/ The Hardest Thing In The World (12", p/s, cat. no. in black print on rear of p/s) (unique recording of Full Fathom Five on original pressing)	18
89	Silvertone ORE 2	Made Of Stone/Going Down (p/s, cat. no. in black print on rear of p/s)	7
89	Silvertone ORET 2	Made Of Stone/Going Down/Guernica (12", p/s, catalogue number in black print on rear of p/s)	20
89	Silvertone ORET 6	She Bangs The Drums/Mersey Paradise/Standing Here (12" p/s)	8
89	Silvertone OREX 6	She Bangs The Drums/Standing Here (p/s, with postcard, 3,000 only)	8
89	Silvertone OREZ 6	She Bangs The Drums/Mersey Paradise/Standing Here (12", p/s with colour print (I Wanna Be Adored cover), 5,000 only)	15
89	Silvertone ORE 13	What The World Is Waiting For/Fools Gold 4.15 (paper label, with postcard stickered p/s credits "What The World Is Waiting For")	8
89	Silvertone ORET 13	What The World Is Waiting For/Fools Gold 9.23 (12", stickered p/s credits What The World Is Waiting For, with print)	12
89	Silvertone ORECD 13	Fools Gold 9.23/What The World Is Waiting For/Fools Gold 4.15 (CD, inlay credits "What The World Is Waiting For")	8
89	Black/Revolver 12 REV 36	Sally Cinnamon/Here It Comes/All Across The Sand (12", 'Printed in W Germany' on rear p/s, barcode)	8
89	Black/Revolver REV 36	Sally Cinnamon/Here It Comes (p/s)	5
90	Silvertone ORE 1	Elephant Stone (7" Version)/The Hardest Thing In The World (catalogue number in red print on rear of p/s)	5
90	Silvertone ORE 2	Made Of Stone/Going Down (p/s, cat. no. in blue print on rear of p/s)	5
90	Fierce FRIGHT 044	SPIKE ISLAND EP (fan interviews, P.A. announcements & fireworks, with cigarette, badge, bag of grass & banana sweet)	20
90	Silvertone OREZ 13	Fools Gold (The Top Won Mix!)/(The Bottom Won Mix!) (12")	15
90	Silvertone OREZCD 13	Fools Gold (The Top Won Mix!)/(The Bottom Won Mix!) (Gold CD)	10
90	Silvertone ORE 17	One Love/Something's Burning (p/s, with postcard)	5
90	Silvertone OREZ 17	One Love/Something's Burning (12", p/s, with print)	8
91	Silvertone ORE 31	I Wanna Be Adored (3.28)/Where Angels Play (p/s)	5
91	Silvertone ORET 31	I Wanna Be Adored (4.52)/Where Angels Play/Sally Cinnamon (live at the Hacienda) (12" p/s)	8
91	Silvertone OREZ 31	I Wanna Be Adored (4.52)/Where Angels Play/Sally Cinnamon (live at the Hacienda) (12", stickered p/s with print)	20
92	Silvertone ORE 35	Waterfall (7" Version 3.31)/One Love (7" Version 3.40) (p/s)	8
92	Silvertone OREZT 35	Waterfall (12" Version 5.23)/One Love (Adrian Sherwood 12" Version 7.10) (12", p/s with print)	18
92	Silvertone ORE 40	I Am The Resurrection (Pan And Scan Radio Version)/ I Am The Resurrection (Highly Resurrected Dub) (p/s)	5
92	Silvertone ORET 40	I Am The Resurrection (Extended 19:9 Ratio Club Mix)/(Original LP Version)/ Fools Gold (Bottom Won Mix) (12", with print)	40
92	Silvertone ORET 40	I Am The Resurrection (Extended 19:9 Ratio Club Mix)/(Original LP Version)/ Fools Gold (Bottom Won Mix) (12", without print)	10
93	Silvertone ORECD 37	So Young/Tell Me (CD, from "CD Singles Collection")	15
92	Silvertone SRBX 2	12" SINGLES COLLECTION (10 x 12" singles box set, numbered 1,000 only)	170
92	Silvertone SRBX 1	COMPACT DISC SINGLES COLLECTION (8 x CD singles box set, 1,000 only)	70
95	Geffen GFST 87	Ten Storey Love Song/Moses/Ride On (12", stickered/numbered p/s)	20
95	Geffen GFST 22060	Begging You (Album Version)/(Chic Mix)/(Cox's Ultimatum Mix)/ (Stone Corporation Vox) (12" p/s with art print)	20

PROMOS

85	Thin Line THIN 001	So Young/Tell Me (12" promo (pale) pink label test press) 100 pressed (in Cartel sleeve with press pack)	400
85	Thin Line THIN 001	So Young/Tell Me (12" promo (pale) pink label test pressing, 100 pressed, this price without press pack)	250
89	Silvertone ORE DJ 6	She Bangs The Drums (7" promo)	15
89	Silvertone ORE DJ T 13	Fools Gold 9.53/ What The World Is Waiting For (12" promo, B-side white label)	20
89	Silvertone ORE DJ 13	Fools Gold 4.15/ What The World Is Waiting For (7" promo)	10
90	Silvertone ORE DJ T 17	One Love/Something's Burning (12" promo, B-side white label)	10
90	Silvertone ORE DJ 17	One Love (7" edit) /Something's Burning (7" edit) (7" promo)	10
92	Silvertone ORE T DJ 34	Waterfall (12" Version 5.23)/One Love (Adrian Sherwood 12" Version 7.10) (12" promo)	15
94	Geffen STONEPRO1	Love Spreads (Radio Edit, Album version) (CD promo, no p/s)	20
95	Silvertone OREDJ 71	Fools Gold (The Tall Paul Remix)/Fools Gold 9.23/Fools Gold (Cricklewood Ballroom Mix) (12")	8
95	Geffen WGFSX 22060	Begging You (Album Version)/(Chic Mix)/(Stone Corporation Vox)/ (Young American Primitive Remix) (12", no p/s, with press sheet)	10
95	Geffen WGFSX 22060	Begging You (Album Version)/(Chic Mix)/(Stone Corporation Vox)/ (Young American Primitive Remix) (12", no p/s)	8

ALBUMS

89	Silvertone ORE LP 502	THE STONE ROSES (LP, original pressing, embossed sleeve with gold lettering)	30
89	Silvertone ORE LP 502	THE STONE ROSES (LP, original pressing, not embossed gold lettering)	20
91	Silvertone OREZ LP 502	THE STONE ROSES (2-LP, reissue, numbered gatefold sleeve with silver lettering)	20
91	Silvertone OREZ CD 502	THE STONE ROSES (CD, reissue, numbered with silver lettering)	18

			MINT VALUE £
92	Silvertone ORE LP 521	TURNS INTO STONE (LP, original pressing)	20
94	Geffen GEF 24503	SECOND COMING (2-LP, original pressing, gatefold)	20
95	Silvertone ORE LP 535	THE COMPLETE STONE ROSES (2-LP)	20
95	Silvertone OREZ CD 535	THE COMPLETE STONE ROSES (2-CD includes two rare tracks on bonus disc)	18
96	Garage Flower GARAGE LP 1	GARAGE FLOWER (LP, with print)	40
96	Garage Flower GARAGE LP 1	GARAGE FLOWER (LP, without print)	20
99	Geffen/Simply Vinyl SVLP 111	SECOND COMING (2-LP, limited edition, gatefold, 180gm vinyl)	18
99	Silvertone 0591242	THE STONE ROSES - 10th Anniversary Edition (2-CD ltd edition in slipcase, enhanced with videos, booklet & sleevenotes)	20

STONE'S MASONRY
(see also Action, Mighty Baby, Savoy Brown)

66	Purdah 45-3504	Flapjacks/Hot Rock (99 copies only)	200

STONE THE CROWS
(see also White Trash, Maggie Bell)

70	Polydor 2066 060	Mad Dogs & Englishmen/Sad Mary	5
72	Polydor 2058 301	Good Time Girl/On The Highway	5
70	Polydor 2425 017	STONE THE CROWS (LP)	30
70	Polydor 2425 042	ODE TO JOHN LAW (LP, gatefold sleeve)	30
71	Polydor 2425 701	TEENAGE LICKS (LP, gatefold sleeve)	25
72	Polydor 2391 043	ONTINUOUS PERFORMANCE (LP)	18

STONEY BROOK PEOPLE

69	CBS 4538	Easy To Be Hard/There's Tomorrow	30

STONEY & MEAT LOAF
(see also Meat Loaf)

71	Rare Earth RES 103	What You See Is What You Get/The Way You Do The Things You Do	12
79	Prodigal PROD 10	What You See Is What You Get/The Way You Do The Things You Do (reissue)	8
72	Rare Earth SRE 3005	STONEY AND MEAT LOAF (LP)	25
79	Prodigal PDL 2010	MEAT LOAF (FEATURING STONEY & MEAT LOAF) (LP, revised reissue of "Stoney And Meat Loaf" with different tracks)	15
86	Motown ZL 72217	MEAT LOAF (FEATURING STONEY & MEAT LOAF) (LP, 2nd reissue)	12

STOOGES
(see also Iggy Pop)

69	Elektra EKS 74051	THE STOOGES (LP, red label)	120
70	Elektra 2410 009	FUN HOUSE (LP, red label)	150
73	CBS 65586	RAW POWER (LP, as Iggy & Stooges, no name on front cover, plain orange label, with inner sleeve)	30
77	Elektra K 42032	THE STOOGES (LP, reissue, 'butterfly' label)	12
77	Elektra K 42051	FUN HOUSE (LP, reissue, 'butterfly' label)	12

STOP

80	Elite CAB 101	I Can Feel It/Iauwata (12")	8

STOPOUTS

78	Skeleton LYN 5912	Strange Thoughts/Just For You And Me (p/s)	15

STOREY SISTERS

58	London HLU 8571	Bad Motorcycle/Sweet Daddy	100
58	London HLU 8571	Bad Motorcycle/Sweet Daddy (78)	40

STORM/CUTMASTER SWIFT

91	White SOLID001	Playing The Field/Live In Spain (12")	50

STORM/MIGHTY ETHNICZ

91	Bite It! BITE 3	You're Out There (12")	12

BILLY STORM

59	Philips PB 916	I've Come Of Age/This Is Always	15
59	Philips PB 916	I've Come Of Age/This Is Always (78)	15
60	London HLK 9236	Sure As You're Born/In The Chapel In The Moonlight	12

DANNY STORM (& STROLLERS)

62	Piccadilly 7N 35025	Honest I Do/Sad But True (in p/s)	15
62	Piccadilly 7N 35025	Honest I Do/Sad But True	10
62	Piccadilly 7N 35053	Just You/I Told You So	10
62	Piccadilly 7N 35091	I Just Can't Fool My Heart/Thinking Of You	12
63	Piccadilly 7N 35143	Say You Do/Let The Sunshine In (as Danny Storm & Strollers)	15

GALE STORM

56	London HLD 8222	I Hear You Knocking/Never Leave Me	50
56	London HLD 8232	Memories Are Made Of This/A Teen-Age Prayer	35
56	London HLD 8283	Ivory Tower/I Ain't Gonna Worry	35
56	London HLD 8286	Why Do Fools Fall In Love/I Walk Alone	30
56	London HL 7008	Why Do Fools Fall In Love/I Walk Alone (export issue)	20
56	London HLD 8311	Don't Be That Way (Please Listen To Me)/Tell Me Why	25
56	London HLD 8329	A Heart Without A Sweetheart/Now Is The Hour	15
57	London HLD 8393	Lucky Lips/On Treasure Island	30
57	London HLD 8413	Orange Blossoms/My Heart Belongs To You	15
57	London HLD 8424	Dark Moon/A Little Too Late	15
58	London HLD 8570	Love Theme From "Farewell To Arms"/I Get That Feeling	10
58	London HLD 8632	You/Angry	10
56	London HB-D 1056	PRESENTING GALE STORM (10" LP)	60
58	London HA-D 2104	SENTIMENTAL ME (LP)	50

RORY STORM & HURRICANES
(see also Keef Hartley, Paddy Klaus & Gibson)

63	Oriole CB 1858	Dr. Feelgood/I Can Tell	45
64	Parlophone R 5197	America/Since You Broke My Heart	25

STORM BUGS

80	Storm Bugs	STORM BUGS (EP, white label, foldout insert, plain white sleeve)	5

MINT VALUE £

ROBB STORME (& WHISPERS)

60 Decca F 11282 1000, 900 And When/I Don't Need Your Love Anymore . . . 7
61 Decca F 11313 Music/Five Minutes More (as Robb Storme & Whispers) . . . 6
61 Decca F 11364 Near You/Lonely Town (as Robb Storme & Whispers) . . . 6
61 Decca F 11388 Transistor Sister/Earth Angel . . . 10
62 Decca F 11432 Pretty Hair And Angel Eyes/A Mile Of Broken Hearts . . . 7
63 Pye 7N 15515 Sixteen Years Ago Tonight/Surprise Surprise . . . 7
63 Piccadilly 7N 35133 Happens Ev'ryday/Surprise Surprise . . . 5
63 Piccadilly 7N 35160 To Know Her Is To Love Her/Bu Bop A Lu Bop A Lie . . . 5
65 Pye 7N 15819 Love Is Strange/Shy Guy . . . 10
65 Columbia DB 7756 Where Is My Girl?/Double Oh Seven (as Robb Storme & Whispers) . . . 10
66 Columbia DB 7993 Here Today/Don't Cry (as Robb Storme Group) . . . 20
62 Decca DFE 6700 WHEELS (EP) . . . 110

STORMER

78 Ring O' 2017 113 My Home Town/Shake It Baby (in promo p/s) . . . 70
78 Ring O' 2017 113 My Home Town/Shake It Baby . . . 40

STORMQUEEN

82 Real Fire RF 001 Come Silent To The World/Raising The Roof (no p/s, 500 only) . . . 400

STORMTROOPER

78 Solent SS 047 I'm A Mess/It's Not Me (in stamped plain sleeve with insert) . . . 30
78 Solent SS 047 I'm A Mess/It's Not Me . . . 12

STORMTROOPER

80 Heartbeat BEAT 1 Pride Before A Fall/Still Comin' Home (p/s) . . . 25

STORMY PETREL

71 CBS 7271 Hello Hello Hello/The Light Of Day . . . 10

STORYTELLER

(see also Johnny Neal & Starliners, Terry Durham, Other Two, Andy Bown)

71 CBS 7182 Remarkable/Laugh That Came Too Soon . . . 5
70 Transatlantic TRA 220 STORYTELLER (LP, gatefold sleeve, white/lilav label, 't' logo) . . . 40
71 Transatlantic TRA 232 MORE PAGES (LP, textured sleeve) . . . 35

STORYTELLER

79 Alladin MDS 1002 Just Another Cloud In The Sky/Weatherman . . . 20

STORYTELLER

85 Storyteller ZELSP 438 Mystery Girl (p/s) . . . 50

LALLY STOTT

71 Philips 6025029 Jakaranda/Love Is Free Love Is Blind . . . 8
71 Philips 6323 006 CHIRPY CHIRPY CHEEP CHEEP (LP) . . . 12

WALLY STOTT

60 Pye 7N 15271 The Unforgiven/Mr. Lucky . . . 6

BABE STOVALL

76 Southern Sound SD 203 THE BABE STOVALL STORY (LP) . . . 12

STOWAWAYS

79 Supermusic SUP 27 I Wanna Be Me/My Friends/You'll Tie Me Down (p/s) . . . 25

STP 23

89 Wau! Mr. Modo WMS 001R Let Jimi Take Over/Let Jimi Take Over (Remix By Youth) (12", p/s) . . . 10

STRAFE FÜR REBELLION

80s Touch TO 6 SANTA MARIA (LP, with inner) . . . 15

STRAIGHT EIGHT

78 Eel Pie EPS 003 Modern Times/Tell Me If You Wanna Bleed (p/s) . . . 10
79 Warner Bros K 18049 Spread It Around/It Ain't Easy/Oh No (p/s) . . . 5
80 Logo DEAL 1 I'm Sorry/Satisfied (p/s) . . . 6
80 Logo DEAL 2 Tombstone/On The Rebound (p/s) . . . 5
82 Logo GO 416 Tomorrow/Faded Stars/You Are What You Are (with p/s) . . . 10
82 Logo GO 416 Tomorrow/Faded Stars/You Are What You Are . . . 8
79 Eel Pie EPRP 001 NO NOISE FROM HERE (LP) . . . 15
80 Logo LOGO 1032 STRAIGHT TO THE HEART (LP) . . . 12
80 Logo FLUSH 1 SHUFFLE'N'CUT (LP) . . . 12

STRAIGHT UP

80 Rok XX/XIX One Out All Out/JUSTIN CASE: T.V. (die-cut company sleeve) . . . 10

STRAIGHTSHOOTER

79 Strolling Bone S 79 CUS 398 Straightshooter/She's So Fine (no p/s) . . . 120

EMILLE STRAKER & HIS MERRYMEN

(see under Merrymen)

NIK STRAKER

83 Pinnacle PIN 100T Turn Me Down/We Can Still Be Friends (12") . . . 15

PETER STRAKER

69 Polydor 56345 Breakfast In Bed/The Right To Cry . . . 5
69 Polydor 56362 I Never Thought I'd Fall In Love/Birdie Told Me . . . 5
70 Polydor 2058 039 Carousel/It's A New Day . . . 5
77 EMI EMI 2700 Ragtime Piano Joe/Saddest Clown . . . 10
78 EMI EMI 2758 Jackie/I've Been To Hell And Back . . . 12
77 EMI EMC 3204 THIS ONE'S ON ME (LP) . . . 12
74 RCA LPBO 5011 From The Underworld/Love Motion . . . 8

BILLY STRANGE (& CHALLENGERS)

(see also Cliffie Stone)

61 London HLG 9321 Where Your Arms Used To Be/Sadness Done Come . . . 10

MINT VALUE £

64	Vocalion V-N 9228	The James Bond Theme/007 Theme	15
64	Vocalion V-N 9231	Goldfinger/"Munsters" Theme	15
66	Vocalion V-N 9257	Thunderball/"Ninth Man" Theme	12
66	Vocalion V-N 9259	Get Smart/Run Spy, Run	15
67	Vocalion V-N 9289	A Few Dollars More Theme/You Only Live Twice	10
63	Vocalion VA/SVN 8022	12-STRING GUITAR (LP)	15
64	Vocalion VAN 8026	MR GUITAR (LP)	15
64	Vocalion VAN/SAVN 8032	THE JAMES BOND THEME (LP)	20
65	Vocalion VAN/SAVN 8038	GOLDFINGER (LP)	20
65	Vocalion VAN/SAVN 8042	ENGLISH HITS OF '65 (LP)	15
65	Vocalion VAN/SAVN 8045	STRANGE PLAYS THE HITS (LP)	15
66	Vocalion VAN/SAVN 8050	FOLK-ROCK HITS (LP)	12
67	Vocalion VAN/SAVN 8052	SECRET AGENT FILE (LP)	18
66	London HA-F/SH-F 8274	THE FUNKY 12 STRING GUITAR (LP, as Billy Strange & Transients)	12
66	Vocalion VAN/SAVN 8065	BILLY STRANGE & THE CHALLENGERS (LP)	12
70	London 2GL 104	GREAT WESTERN THEMES (LP)	12

STRANGE BROTHERS SHOW

70	Polydor 2001-116	Right On/Shakey Jakes	15

GILES STRANGE

66	Stateside SS 570	Watch The People Dance/You're Goin' Up To The Bottom	70

STEVE STRANGE

(see also Visage)

82	Palace PALACE 1	In The Year 2525/Strange Connexions (white label, unreleased)	30
82	Palace PALACE 1	In The Year 2525/Strange Connexions (p/s, available separately)	20

STRANGE CRUISE

86	EMI 12EMI 5549	Rebel Blue Rocker/Love Addiction (12", p/s)	10
86	EMI EMC 3513	STRANGE CRUISE (LP)	18

STRANGE DAYS

75	Retreat RTS 263	Monday Morning/Joe Soap	5
75	Retreat RTL 6005	NINE PARTS TO THE WIND (LP, lyric inner sleeve, blue label)	25

STRANGE DAYS

83	Powerstation OHM 1	Within These Walls/Swimming Into The Doctor	6

STRANGE FOX

73	Parlophone R5978	Rock 'N' Roll Band/Tamarin Girl	15
70	Parlophone R5876	Bring It On HOme/Time And Tide	30

STRANGE FRUIT

71	Village Thing VTSX 1001	Cut Across Shorty/Shake That Thing	25

STRANGELOVE

92	Sermon SERT 001	Visionary/Front/Chances/Snakes (12", p/s, 1,000 only)	10
93	Sermon SERT 002	Hysteria/Unknown/My Dark Walls/Sea (12", p/s)	15
93	Sermon SERT 002CD	Hysteria/My Dark/Walls/Sea (CD)	12
93	R. T. Singles Club 45REV 18	Zoo'd Out/Circles (p/s)	8
96	Food FOODLP 15	LOVE AND OTHER DEMONS (LP, with 12-page booklet)	15

STRANGELOVES

(see also Beach-Nuts)

65	Stateside SS 446	I Want Candy/It's About My Baby	25
65	Immediate IM 007	Cara-Lin/Roll On Mississippi	30
66	London HLZ 10020	Night Time/Rhythm Of Love	35
66	London HLZ 10063	Hand Jive/I Gotta Dance	12
69	London HLZ 10238	Honey Do/I Wanna Do It	15

STRANGE MOVEMENTS

79	Good Vibrations GOT 5	Dancing In The Ghetto/Amuse Yourself (foldout p/s)	25

STRANGER (Cole)

(see also Stranger Cole)

63	Blue Beat BB 165	Rough And Tough (with Duke Reid Band)/DUKE REID BAND: The Mood I Am In	20
63	Blue Beat BB 195	Miss Reamer/RICO & HIS BLUES BAND: Blues From The Hills	20

STRANGER (Cole) & GLADY (Anderson)

(see also Stranger Cole, Gladdy & Followers, Gladstone Anderson, Gladdy & Stranger, Charlie Kelly)

67	Island WI 3128	Love Me Today/Over Again	60
68	Amalgamated AMG 806	Seeing Is Knowing/ROY SHIRLEY: Music Is The Key	25
71	Clandisc CLA 230	Tomorrow (as Stranger & Gladdy)/DYNAMITES: Tomorrow Version	7
71	Supreme SUP 227	My Application (as Stranger & Gladdy)/TADDY & DIAMONDS: Oh No, My Baby	7
73	Count Shelley CS 015	Don't Give Up The Fight (as Stranger & Gladdy)/TIDALS: Stand Firm	5
73	Dragon DRA 1014	Conqueror/Conqueror (Instrumental Version)	5

STRANGER (Cole) & HORTENSE (Ellis)

74	Count Shelley CS 049	Mocking Bird/Corra Bella Baby	6

STRANGER (Cole) & KEN (Boothe)

(see also Stranger Cole, Ken Boothe)

63	R&B JB 120	Thick In Love/All Your Friends	30

STRANGER (Cole) & PATSY (Todd)

(see also Stranger Cole, Patsy)

63	Blue Beat BB 171	When I Call Your Name/Take My Heart (with Duke Reid All Stars)	20
63	Island WI 113	Senor And Senorita/DON DRUMMOND: Snowboy	30
64	Island WI 141	Oh Oh I Need You/DON DRUMMOND: J.F.K.'s Memory	35
64	Island WI 144	Tom, Dick And Harry/We Two, Happy People	20
64	Island WI 152	Yeah Yeah Baby/BABA BROOKS: Boat Ride	25
64	Island WI 160	Miss B/Thing Come To Those Who Wait	20
65	Black Swan WI 462	Hey Little Girl/CORNELL CAMBELL: Make Hay	30
66	Rio R 81	Give Me One More Chance/Fire In Cornfield	18

			MINT VALUE £
66	Doctor Bird DB 1050	Give Me The Right/Tonight	30
67	Doctor Bird DB 1084	Tell It To Me/Your Photograph	40
67	Doctor Bird DB 1087	Down The Trainlines/Sing And Pray	40
69	Escort ES 807	My Love/SWEET CONFUSION: Windsor Castle	15
69	Escort ES 811	Why Did You/Do You Remember	8

STRANGERS (with Mike Shannon)

(see also Shadows)

64	Philips BF 1335	One And One Is Two/Time And The River (as Strangers with Mike Shannon)	40
64	Philips BF 1378	Do You Or Don't You/What Can I Do	8

STRANGERS

67	Pye 7N 17240	Look Out (Here Comes Tomorrow)/Mary Mary	40
67	Pye 7N 17351	You Didn't Have To Be So Nice/Daytime Turns To Night	15
68	Pye 7N 17585	I'm On An Island/Step Inside	20

STRANGER THAN FICTION

80s	Ellie Jay EJSP 9301	Into The Void/Darkness (p/s)	25

STRANGE STONE

77	own label DER 1399	STRANGE STONE (LP, private pressing, numbered sleeve with insert, 255 only)	500

STRANGLERS

SINGLES

79	Real ARE 7	All The Sounds Of Fear/Wasting Time (p/s)	55
77	United Artists UP 36211	(Get A) Grip (On Yourself)/London Lady (card p/s)	5
77	United Artists UP 36248	Peaches/Go Buddy Go ('group' p/s with 'blackmail' lettering, withdrawn)	750
77	United Artists UP 36248	Peaches/Go Buddy Go ('peach' p/s)	7
77	United Artists UP 36277	Something Better Change/Straighten Out (p/s)	5
77	United Artists UP 36300	No More Heroes/In The Shadows (p/s, 'wreath' label)	6
80	United Artists 12-BP 344	Bear Cage (Extended)/Shah Shah A Go Go (Extended) (12", p/s)	10
82	Epic EPCA A-2893	The European Female/Savage Breast (p/s)	5
82	Epic EPCA 11-2893	The European Female/Savage Breast (picture disc)	5
84	Epic A 4738	Skin Deep/Here And There ('skin-feel' p/s, with 'Skin Deep' tattoo, 10,000 only)	6
84	Epic EPC GA 4921	No Mercy/In One Door/Hot Club (Riot Mix)/Head On The Line (gatefold)	6
84	Epic WA 4921	No Mercy/In One Door (ear-shaped picture disc)	7
86	Epic 650 055-0	Nice In Nice/Since You Went Away (shaped picture disc)	6
86	Epic SOLAR P1	Always The Sun/Norman Normal (shaped picture disc)	7
86	Epic SOLAR D1	Always The Sun/Norman Normal//Nice In Nice/Since You Went Away (double pack, shrinker & stickered)	8
86	Epic HUGE P1	Big In America/Dry Day (shaped picture disc)	7
86	Epic HUGE D1	Big In America/Dry Day//Always The Sun/Norman Normal (double pack, shrinkwrapped & stickered)	8
87	Epic SHEIK P1	Shakin' Like A Leaf/Hit Man (shaped picture disc)	7
88	Epic VICE 1	All Day And All Of The Night/¡Viva Vlad! ('Monica Coughlan' p/s, withdrawn, sold via fan club)	7
88	Epic VICE P1	All Day And All Of The Night/¡Viva Vlad! (shaped picture disc)	5
89	Liberty EMR 84	Grip '89 - (Get A) Grip (On Yourself)/Waltzinblack (p/s, red vinyl with poster in gatefold PVC wallet, 5,000 only)	5

ALBUMS

77	United Artists UAG 30045	STRANGLERS IV - RATTUS NORVEGICUS (LP, 10,000 with 7" Choosey Susie/ "Peasant In The Big Shitty" (Live At The Nashville, 12/76) [FREE 3, orange p/s, "What Do You Expect?" in run-off groove], some with sticker)	20
77	United Artists UAG 30045	STRANGLERS IV - RATTUS NORVEGICUS (LP)	12
78	United Artists UAK 30222	BLACK AND WHITE (LP, 75,000 with white vinyl 7" "Walk On By"/"Tits"/ Mean To Me [FREE 9, black die-cut sleeve & card insert], mispressed on blue or beige vinyl)	65
78	United Artists UAK 30222	BLACK AND WHITE (LP, 75,000 with white vinyl 7" "Walk On By"/"Tits"/ Mean To Me [FREE 9, black die-cut sleeve & card insert])	12
79	United Artists UAG 30262	THE RAVEN (LP, 20,000 with 3-D cover, cartoon on inner sleeve)	20
82	Liberty LBG 30353	THE COLLECTION '77-82 (LP, withdrawn plastic logo sleeve)	25
83	Epic EPC 25237	FELINE (LP, with bonus 1-sided 7" "Aural Sculpture" [XPS 167])	12
86	Epic EPC 26648	DREAMTIME (LP, picture disc)	12

FREEBIES, PROMOS & MISCELLANEA

75	(no cat no)	My Young Dreams/Wasted (existence unconfirmed)	150
77	United Artists FREE 4	Peaches (radio version)/Go Buddy Go (promo only, p/s)	750
77	United Artists FREE 4	Peaches (radio version)/Go Buddy Go (promo only, no p/s)	150
77	United Artists UP 36262	Mony Mony/Mean To Me (p/s, as Celia And The Mutations)	7
77	United Artists UP 36277	Something Better Change/Straighten Out	25
77	United Artists FREE 8	No More Heroes (1-sided radio edit, promo only)	70
77	United Artists UP 36300	No More Heroes (1-sided, misprinted "No More Stheroes")	25
77	United Artists UP 36300	No More Heroes/In The Shadows (p/s, stamped, misprinted "No More Stheroes")	25
78	United Artists UP 36429	Walk On By (Promo Edit)/Old Codger/Tank	25
79	United Artists UA STR 1 DJ	Don't Bring Harry/HUGH CORNWELL: Wired (45rpm, promo only)	20
79	United Artists (no cat. no.)	Two Sunspots (unreleased)	30
80	Stranglers Info Service SIS 001	Tomorrow Was The Hereafter/Bring On The Nubiles (Cocktail Version) (numbered p/s, label has "Nublies")	8
82	SIS/Liberty FREE 3	Peasant In The Big Shitty (Live At The Nashville, 12/76)/Choosey Susie (fan club reissue, black p/s, with "Ello 'Elen" in run-off groove)	5
82	Epic EPC A2893	The European Female (In Celebration Of)/(Promo Edit)	10
82	Liberty BP 410	La Folie (Promo Edit)/Waltzinblack	10
82	SIS/Liberty UP 36350	5 Minutes/Rok It To The Moon (reissue)	5
82	SIS/Liberty UP 36429	Walk On By/Old Codger/Tank (reissue, 33rpm)	5
82	SIS/Liberty FREE 18	Mony Mony/Mean To Me (reissue, as Celia & the Mutations)	5
83	Epic/S.I.S. XPS 167	Aural Sculpture (reissue, 1-sided)	5
91	Stranglers Info S. SIS 004	New Day Today (flexidisc with Strangled fan magazine, issue 32)	5
78	United Artists UP 36248	Peaches/Go Buddy Go (p/s, mispressing, B-side plays Buzzcocks' "Oh Shit")	60
78	United Artists FREE 9	Walk On By/Mean To Me/Tits (EP [free with LP U.A. UAK 30222], mispressing, black die-cut sleeve & card insert, blue/clear vinyl)	30

		MINT VALUE £
78 United Artists FREE 9	Walk On By/Mean To Me/Tits (EP [free with LP U.A. UAK 30222], mispressing, black die-cut sleeve & card insert, pink/clear vinyl)	15
78 United Artists UP 36379	Nice 'N' Sleazy/Shut Up (p/s, mispressing, B-side plays tracks by other artist)	30
81 Liberty BP 393	Just Like Nothing On Earth/Maninwhite (p/s, mispressing, plays A-side both sides)	20
82 United Artists BP 407	Golden Brown/Love 30 (B-side plays "Everybody Salsa")	20
79 United Artists UAG 30262	THE RAVEN (LP, mispressing, 2nd side plays country & western [B-side matrix: UAK 30263])	25

STRAPS
(see also Public Image Ltd.)

80 Donut DONUT 1	Just Can't Take Anymore/New Age (p/s)	6
82 Donut DONUT 3	Brixton/No Liquor (p/s)	8
83 Cyclops CYC 2	THE STRAPS ALBUM (LP)	15

STRATEGY

82 Ebony EBON 7	Technical Overflow/Astral Planes (in p/s)	60
82 Ebony EBON 7	Technical Overflow/Astral Planes	50

STRATE JACKET

70s Wessex	You're A Hit (stamped plain sleeve)	12

STRATUS
(see also Grand Prix, Uriah Heep, Iron Maiden, Praying Mantis)

85 Steel Trax STEEL 31001	THROWING SHAPES (LP)	18

STRAWBERRY ALARM CLOCK

67 Pye International 7N 25436	Incense And Peppermints/The Birdman Of Alkatrash	25
68 Pye International 7N 25446	Tomorrow/Birds In My Tree	20
68 Pye International 7N 25456	Sit With The Guru/Pretty Song From Psych-Out	20
69 MCA MU 1080	Good Morning Starshine/Me And The Township	10
68 NPL 28106	INCENSE AND PEPPERMINTS (LP, mono)	80
68 Pye Intl. NSPL 28106	INCENSE AND PEPPERMINTS (LP, stereo)	60

STRAWBERRY CHILDREN
(see also Jim Webb)

67 Liberty LBF 15012	Love Years Coming/One Stands Here	35

STRAWBERRY JAM

69 Pye 7N 17711	Per-Son-Al-Ly/This Is To A Girl	15

STRAWBERRY PARK

82 Sonet 2245	Summer Is A Coming/Beach Party (in p/s)	8
82 Sonet 2245	Summer Is A Coming/Beach Party	7

STRAWBERRY SMELL

97 Detour DR 053	Penelope Bloomington/Kangeroo In My Garden (p/s, blue vinyl, 100 only)	6

STRAWBERRY SWITCHBLADE
(see also Poems, Rose McDowall)

85 Korova KODE 11	STRAWBERRY SWITCHBLADE (LP, with bonus 7" "Trees And Flowers", mispressed with some tracks playing twice & others out of order)	15
85 Korova KODE 11	STRAWBERRY SWITCHBLADE (LP, with bonus 7" "Trees And Flowers")	12

STRAWBS
(see also Dave Cousins, Sandy Denny, Fire, Foggy, Monks, Davey & Morris, Hudson-Ford)

68 A&M AMS 725	Oh How She Changed/Or Am I Dreaming	7
68 A&M AMS 738	The Man Who Called Himself Jesus/Poor Jimmy Wilson	8
70 A&M AMS 791	Forever/Another Day	8
71 A&M AMS 837	Witchwood/Keep The Devil Outside/We'll Meet Again Sometime (live) (withdrawn)	20
71 A&M AMS 874	Benedictus/Keep The Devil Outside	6
73 A&M AMS 7047	Part Of The Union/Will You Go (p/s)	5
69 private pressing	STRAWBERRY MUSIC SAMPLER NO. 1 (LP, publisher's sampler, 100 only)	500
69 A&M AMLS 936	STRAWBS (LP; disc inserted in middle of sleeve)	35
69 A&M AMLS 936	STRAWBS (LP; disc inserted at edge of sleeve)	20
70 A&M AMLS 970	DRAGONFLY (LP, textured sleeve, lyric insert, mustard label)	25
70 A&M AMLS 994	JUST A COLLECTION OF ANTIQUES AND CURIOS (LP, gatefold sleeve, mustard label; 2 different rear sleeves)	15
71 A&M AMLH 64304	FROM THE WITCHWOOD (LP, gatefold sleeve)	15
72 A&M AMLH 68078	GRAVE NEW WORLD (LP, triple gatefold sleeve, with 12-page booklet)	15
73 A&M AMLH 68144	BURSTING AT THE SEAMS (LP, with inner sleeve)	12
73 Hallmark SHM 813	ALL OUR OWN WORK (LP, with Sandy Denny)	15

STRAY

72 Big T BIG 141	Our Song/Mama's Coming Home	5
70 Transatlantic TRA 216	STRAY (LP, die-cut gatefold sleeve, white/lilac 't' logo label)	45
71 Transatlantic TRA 233	SUICIDE (LP, textured sleeve, white/lilac 't' logo label)	30
72 Transatlantic TRA 248	SATURDAY MORNING PICTURES (LP, gatefold sleeve)	20
73 Transatlantic TRA 268	MUDANZAS (LP, gatefold sleeve)	18
74 Transatlantic TRA 281	MOVE IT (LP, die-cut sleeve with inner)	12
75 Transatlantic TRA 3066	TRACKS (LP)	12
75 Dawn DNLS 3066	STAND UP AND BE COUNTED (LP, lyric insert, pink 'sun' label)	15
76 Pye NSPL 18482	HOUDINI (LP)	12
76 Pye NSPL 18512	HEARTS OF FIRE (LP)	12

STRAY DOG
(see also Emerson Lake & Palmer)

73 Manticore K13502	Speak Of The Devil/A Letter	5
74 Manticore K 13508	Junkyard Angel/World Winds	6
74 Manticore K 43506	STRAY DOG (LP, textured sleeve)	20
74 Manticore K 53504	WHILE YOU'RE DOWN THERE (LP)	20

MINT VALUE £

STREAK
72	A&M AME 602	Gonna Have A Good Time/Be Your Ryder/Hard Times (In New York City) (promo, B-side plays at 33 rpm)	40
72	A&M AMS 7012	Gonna Have A Good Time/Be Your Ryder	15
73	Deram DM 376	Bang Bang Bullet/Black Jack Man	15

STREAKERS
74	Dawn DNS 1066	Turn Me Down/Wake Up Sunshine	6

STREAMLINERS (WITH JOANNE)
(See also Rosemary Squires)

61	Columbia DB 4689	Frankfurter Sandwiches/Pachalata	7

STREET
69	London HLU 10275	Apollo? Amen/Why Concern Yourself	5

DANNY STREET
63	Phillips BF 1250	Only Love Can Break A Heart/ Cold Cold Winter	5
64	Philips BF 1309	The Eyes Of The Young Ones/Someone As Wonderful As You	5
65	Philips BF 1387	Don't Go To Him/As It's Meant To Be	5
60s	Domino DO 114	Melanie/Birds An' Bees An' Things	5
71	London HLU 10342	My Little Guy/You Blew It	5

GARY STREET & FAIRWAYS
(see also Fairways)

68	Domain D 2	Flipperty Flop/Hold Me Closer	20

JOHN STREET & INMATES OF NO. 12
67	Deram DM 147	Keep A Little Love/My Kind Of Luck	7

JUDY STREET
78	Grapevine GRP 106	What/You Turn Me On	8
78	Grapevine GRP 106	What/You Turn Me On (DJ Copy)	10

STREET LEGAL
84	Weird Brothers SLW 1	Rollin' On/Mississippi Moonshine (p/s, initially with sticker over typo error in sleeve)	150
84	Weird Brothers SLW 1	Rollin' On/Mississippi Moonshine (p/s, without sticker)	150

STREETFIGHTER
82	J.R. JR 7049S	CRAZY DREAM (EP)	40

STREETFIGHTER (U.K.)
81	Streetfighter 749	STREETFIGHTER (12" EP)	25

STREET PEOPLE
79	Ellie Jay Special Pressing EJSP 9276	PERSONAL VALUES EP (500 only, p/s)	75

STREET PEOPLE
70	Stateside SS 2163	Jennifer Tomkins/All Night Long	10

STREETS
04	679 071	Fit But You Know It/FUTUREHEADS: Fit But You Know It (10", die-cut p/s, 150 only)	8

STREET SERVICE
90	I Like It ILIT 01	JUST FOR YOU (LP)	18

STREETWALKERS
(see also Family, Hummingbird, Nicko McBrain)

75	Vertigo 6360 123	DOWNTOWN FLIER (LP, gatefold sleeve, 'spaceship' label)	12
76	Vertigo 9102 010	RED CARD (LP, red vinyl with inner sleeve, numbered, 'spaceship' label)	15
77	Vertigo 9102 012	VICIOUS BUT FAIR (LP, lyric inner sleeve)	12
77	Vertigo 6641 703	LIVE (2-LP, gatefold sleeve)	15

BARBRA STREISAND
62	CBS AAG 130	My Colouring Book/Lover Come Back To Me	7
63	CBS AAG 179	Happy Days Are Here Again/Down With Love	6
64	CBS AAG 223	People/Draw Me A Circle	6
64	CBS 201543	People/I Am A Woman You Are Man (p/s)	6
84	CBS TA 4754	Left In The Dark/Here We Are At LastWoman In Love/ Guilty Memory (12", p/s, withdrawn)	15

TEXAS' BILL STRENGTH
55	Capitol CL 14357	Cry, Cry, Cry/The Yellow Rose Of Texas	15

STRESS
85	Adventures In Reality ARR 14	THE BIG WHEEL (LP, with insert)	40

STRETCH
(see also Elmer Gantry, Kirby, Status Quo, Clifford Davis, Legs, Curved Air)

75	Anchor ANCL 2014	ELASTIQUE (LP)	15
76	Anchor ANCL 2016	YOU CAN'T BEAT YOUR BRAIN FOR ENTERTAINMENT (LP)	15
77	Anchor ANCL 2023	LIFE BLOOD (LP)	15
78	Hot Wax HW 1	FORGET THE PAST (LP)	30

WILLIAM R. STRICKLAND
69	Deram DML/SML 1041	WILLIAM R. STRICKLAND IS ONLY THE NAME (LP)	25

PETE STRIDE & JOHN PLAIN
(see also Lurkers)

80	Beggars Banquet BEGA 17	NEW GUITARS IN TOWN (LP, with inner sleeve)	12

STRIDER
(see also Samson)

73	GM GMS 002	Higher And Higher/Ain't Got No Love	5
74	GM GMS 023	Seems So Easy/Arthur Hydrogen	5

MINT VALUE £

73	GM GML 1002	EXPOSED (LP, gatefold sleeve)	15
74	GM GML 1012	MISUNDERSTANDING (LP)	15

STRIFE

77	Outlaw OUT 1	School/Go/Feel So Good (p/s)	10
75	Chrysalis 1063	RUSH (LP)	15
78	Gull GULP 1029	BACK TO THUNDER (LP, on green vinyl with poster)	18
78	Gull 1029	BACK TO THUNDER (LP)	12

LIZA STRIKE

(see also Liza & Jet Set, Soulmates, Vice Versa)

68	Parlophone R 5725	All's Quiet On West 23rd/Mr Daddy-Man	10

STRIKERS & CHILDREN OF SELSTON BAGTHORPE PRIMARY SCHOOL CHOIR

78	Eagle EGL 003	Good Old Charlie/Forest Fire	8

STRING-A-LONGS

61	London HLU 9278	Wheels/Am I Asking Too Much	5
61	London HLU 9354	Panic Button/Brass Buttons	7
61	London HLU 9394	Should I/Take A Minute	6
61	London HLU 9452	Scottie/Ming Bird	10
62	London HLD 9535	Sunday/Twistwatch	10
62	London HLD 9588	Spinning My Wheels/My Blue Heaven	10
63	London HLD 9652	Mathilda/Replica	10
61	London RE-U 1322	THE STRING-A-LONGS (EP)	50
63	London RE-D 1350	THE STRING-A-LONGS (EP)	50
63	London RE-D 1398	STRINGALONG WITH THE STRING-A-LONGS (EP)	40
63	London HA-D 8054	THE STRING-A-LONGS (LP, mono)	50
63	London SH-D 8054	THE STRING-A-LONGS (LP, stereo)	60
69	London HAU/SHU 8371	WIDE WORLD HITS (LP)	40

STRING CHEESE

72	RCA SF 8222	STRING CHEESE (LP)	20

STRING DRIVEN THING

70	Concord CON 7	Another Night/Say What You Like	15
72	Charisma CB 195	Eddie/Hooked On The Road	5
70	Concord CON 1001	STRING DRIVEN THING (LP)	220
72	Charisma CAS 1062	STRING DRIVEN THING (LP, gatefold, insert,large 'Mad Hatter' label)	30
73	Charisma CAS 1070	THE MACHINE THAT CRIED (LP, gatefold sleeve, large 'Mad Hatter' label)	30
74	Charisma CAS 1097	PLEASE MIND YOUR HEAD (LP, lyric sheet, small 'Mad Hatter' label)	15
76	Charisma CAS 1112	KEEP YOUR 'AND ON IT (LP)	12

STRIPES

82	Ellie Jay EJSP 9808/PINK01	One Step Ahead	20

STRIPES OF GLORY

62	Vogue V 9194	The Denial/O' Send The Fire	18

SYLVIA STRIPLIN

86	Music Of Love MOLS 8	Give Me Your Love/Will You Ever Pass This Way Again/ Look Towards The Sky (12")	20

(THE) STROKES

01	Rough Trade RTRADES 010	The Modern Age/Last Night (p/s, 2000 only)	30
01	R. Trade RTRADESCD 010	The Modern Age/Last Night/Barely Legal (CD, card sleeve)	8
01	R. Trade RTRADES 023	Hard To Explain/New York City Cops (p/s, 2000 only)	8
01	R. Trade RTRADESCD 0041	Last Nite/When It Started (CD, withdrawn)	8
01	R. Trade RTRADES 041	Last Nite/When It Started (p/s)	10
02	R. Trade RTRADES 063	Someday/Alone Together/Is This It (p/s, yellow vinyl)	10
01	R. Trade RTRADELP050	IS THIS IT? (LP)	20

STROLLERS

61	London HLL 9336	Come On Over/There's No One But You	50

STROLLERS

58	Vogue V 9113	Jumping With Symphony Sid/Swinging Yellow Rose Of Texas	30
58	Vogue V 9113	Jumping With Symphony Sid/Swinging Yellow Rose Of Texas (78)	10
58	Vogue V 9124	Little Bitty Pretty One/Flute Cha-Lypso	30
58	Vogue V 9124	Little Bitty Pretty One/Flute Cha-Lypso (78)	15

BARRETT STRONG

60	London HLU 9088	Money (That's What I Want)/Oh I Apologise	120
73	Epic S EPC 1778	Stand Up And Cheer For The Preacher/Instrumental	10
76	Capitol CL 15864	Man Up In The Sky/Gonna Make It Right	40

JOE STRUMMER

(see also The Clash)

88	Epic TRASHP 1	Trash City/Theme From Permanent Record (picture disc)	8
89	Island STRUM T2	Island Hopping (12")	8
03	Hellcat 1137-7	Coma Girl/Yalla Yalla (Live) (with The Mescaleros, picture disc, stickered polythene sleeve)	10
03	Hellcat 1149-7	Redemption Song/Arms Aloft/Junco Partner (Live) (with the Mescaleros, picture disc, stickered polythene sleeve)	10
89	EPIC 465347	EARTHQUAKE WEATHER (LP, with inner)	15

STRYDER

80	Quartz QS 010	Forcin' Thru'/Settle Down	20

CHAD STUART & JEREMY CLYDE

(see under Chad & Jerry)

GLEN STUART

60s	Honey Hit TB 126	Make Me An Angel/Walking To Heaven (with p/s)	10
60s	Honey Hit TB 126	Make Me An Angel/Walking To Heaven	6

MINT VALUE £

GLEN STUART & CLANSMEN

59	Pye 7N 15232	Weepy Willow/Della Darling	10

KARL STUART & PROFILES

(see also Profile, Voice)

65	Mercury MF 870	Love Of My Eyes/Not A Girl In A Million	5
65	Mercury MF 875	Haven't They Got Better Things To Do/The Touch Of Your Hand	5

SHAWN STUART

74	Epic SEPC 2496	It's All Because Of YOu/Wise Old Man	8

MIKE STUART SPAN

(see under 'M')

FRANKIE STUBBS

(see also Leatherface)

90s	Sounds Of Subterrania S09	SECOND HAND SUIT (10" EP)	20
95	Rugger Bugger DUMP 025	UNHINGED (EP)	15

NAT STUCKEY

67	Pye International 7N 25403	Sweet Thang/Paralyze My Mind	6
69	RCA RCA 1833	Loving You/Joe And Mabel's 12th Street Bar And Grill	5
69	RCA RCA 1890	Cut Across Shorty/Understand, Little Man	7

STUD

(see also Taste, Family, Blossom Toes, Eric Burdon & Animals)

70	Deram SML-R 1084	STUD (LP, laminated front sleeve, white/red label with small logo)	70

STUDD PUMP

71	Penny Farthing PEN 757	Spare The Children/Floatin'	8

STUDIO G's

70	LPSG 100	BETA GROUP (LP, library edition)	150
96	Tenth Planet TP 023	BEAT GROUP (LP, 600 only)	20

STUDIO ONE ALLSTARS

67	Island WI 3038	Sherry (actually by Bumps Oakley)/Out Of My Mind (actually by Soul Junior)	35

STUDIO SIX

66	Polydor 56131	When I See My Baby/Don't Tell Lies	10
67	Polydor 56162	Bless My Soul (I've Been And Gone And Done It)/People Say	10
67	Polydor 56174	Times Were When/I Can't Sleep	10
67	Polydor 56219	Strawberry Window/Falling Leaves	40
69	Polydor 56361	Bless My Soul/People Say	10

STUDIO SWEETHEARTS

(see also Cult, Slaughter & Dogs)

79	DJM DJS 10915	I Believe/It Isn't Me (p/s)	20

STUD LEATHER

73	Dart ART 2024	Cut Loose/Emma Louise	40

STUKAS

77	Sonet SON 2134	I Like Sport/I'll Send You A Postcard/Dead Lazy (p/s)	8
77	Chiswick NS 21	Klean Living Kids/Oh Little Girl (p/s)	10

STUMPY

74	Dawn DNS 1080	Make Me A Superman/Keep It Coming	6

STUPIDS

85	Children Of Rev. COR 3	VIOLENT NUN (EP, some mispressed)	20
88	C.O.R. GURT 9	PERUVIAN VACATION (LP, blue cover, lyric sheet)	12

STYLE COUNCIL

(see also Council Collective, Paul Weller, Jam, Merton Parkas, King Truman)

84	Lyntone LYN 15344/45	It Just Came To Pieces In My Hands (Coventry)/Speak Like A Child (London) (live flexidisc)	8
85	Polydor TSCX 8	Walls Come Tumbling Down!/Spin' Drifting/The Whole Point II/Blood Sports (12", limited edition with poster)	8
85	Polydor TSCDP 10/DP 1	The Lodgers (re-recorded)/You're The Best Thing/The Big Boss Groove// You're The Best Thing/Long Hot Summer (shrinkwrapped double pack)	5
86	Polydor CINE 1/ CINEC1	Have You Ever Had It Blue/Mr. Cool's Dream//Have You Ever Had It Blue (Uncut Version)/With Everything To Lose (Recorded Live In London Dec. '85) (7" with cassette single, printed PVC sleeve)	6
87	Polydor TSCCD 14	Wanted (Or Waiter, There's Some Soup In My Flies)/The Cost/ The Cost Of Loving (CD, card sleeve)	8
88	Polydor TSCCD 15	Spank! (Live At A Top People's Health Club)/Life At A Top People's Health Farm (7" Version)/Life At A Top People's Health Farm (Um & Argh Mix)/ Sweet Loving Ways (CD)	8
88	Polydor TSCCD 16	1-2-3-4 - A SUMMER QUARTET EP (CD)	8
89	Polydor TSCB 17	Promised Land (Juan Atkins Mix)/Can You Still Love Me? (7", stickered box set with numbered 7" in p/s & poster)	5
89	Polydor TSCCD 17	Promised Land (Longer Version)/Promised Land (Pianopella Version)/ Can You Still Love Me? (Dub)/Can You Still Love Me? (Vocal) (CD)	8
89	Polydor LHSCD 1	Long Hot Summer 89 Mix (Extended Version)/Everybody's On The Run/ (Version One)/(Version Two) (CD)	8
89	Polydor TSC 18	Sure Is Sure/Love Of The World (unissued, acetates may exist)	0
87	Polydor TSCCD 1	CAFÉ BLEU (CD, card sleeve)	8
87	Polydor TSCCD 2	THE BIRD'S AND THE B'S (CD, card sleeve)	8
87	Polydor TSCCD 3	MICK TALBOT IS AGENT 88 (CD)	8
88	Polydor	CONFESSIONS OF A POP GROUP (box set, VHS & cassette; some with promo CD [CPGCD 1])	55
88	Polydor	CONFESSIONS OF A POP GROUP (box set, VHS & cassette;some without promo CD [CPGCD 1])	40

MINT VALUE £

98 Polydor TSCLP 6 MODERNISM: A NEW DECADE (LP, promo only) ... 40
98 Polydor TSCLP 6 MODERNISM: A NEW DECADE (LP, 2 x 12" set, promo only) ... 60

STYLOS
64 Liberty LBS 10173 Head Over Heels/Bye Bye, Baby, Bye Bye ... 120

POLY STYRENE
(see also X-Ray Spex, Mari Elliott)
80 United Artists BP 370 Talk In Toytown/Sub Tropical (p/s) ... 5
80 United Artists UAG 30320 TRANSLUCENCE (LP, with lyric inner) ... 12

STYVAR MANOR
70 Polydor 2058034 Just Dropped In/That's What I Need Most Of All ... 15

LAURIE STYVERS
72 Chrysalis CHR 1007 SPILT MILK (LP, green label, lyric inner sleeve) ... 12

STYX
75 RCA RCA 2518 Lady/Children Of The Land ... 5

SUBCULTURE
83 Essential LOUD AND CLEAR (EP) ... 20

SUBHUMANS
81 Spiderleg SDL 3 Religious Wars/Love Is?/Work Experience/It's Gonna Get Worse (p/s) ... 8
82 Spiderleg SPIDL 5 Big City/Reason For Existence/Cancer/Peroxide (p/s) ... 7
81 Spider Leg SDL 3 DEMOLITION WAR (EP, gatefold p/s with "Pay no more than 85p" rubber stamped on front cover) ... 6
83 Bluurg FISH 2 EVOLUTION (EP, fold-out p/s) ... 6
84 Bluurg FISH 10 RATS (EP, fold-out p/s) ... 6
82 Spiderleg SDL9 THE DAY THE COUNTRY DIED (LP, gatefold, original pressing with "Pay no more than £3.25" on front cover) ... 15
83 Bluurg Fish 8 FROM THE CRADLE TO THE GRAVE (LP, gatefold, original pressing with "Pay no more than £3.50" on front cover) ... 15

SUBMARINER
93 Spacewatch FLX 2107 Lyricist Downer/Seeming And The Meaning (demo)/ STEREOLAB:Ronco Symphony (demo) (clear vinyl flexi with paper strip insert) ... 25

SUBMARINES
87 Head HEAD 4 Grey Skies Blue/I Saw The Children (p/s) ... 6

SUBS
(see also Larry Wallis)
78 Stiff OFF 1 Gimme Your Heart/Party Clothes (p/s) ... 5

SUBSTITUTE
(see also Vibrators)
79 Ignition IR 2 The One/Look Sharp (in p/s) ... 35
79 Ignition IR 2 The One/Look Sharp ... 20

SUB SUB
(see also Doves)
90s Ten Records Ltd. TENX 373 Space Face/Ecto-Jam-Sub (12", die-cut sleeve) ... 35
90s Robs 12 ROB 07 Coast/Inside Of This/Past/Inside Out (12", p/s) ... 10
90s Robs 7 ROB 9 Ain't No Love/Parkside Mix (p/s) ... 8
90s Robs 12 ROB 9 Ain't No Love (Original Mix)/(Parkside Mix)/(Parkside Raw Dub) (12", die-cut p/s) 8
90s Robs 12 ROB 09R Ain't No Love (On The Floor)/(On The House)/(On Yer Face) (12", die-cut p/s) ... 8
90s Robs CD ROB 9 Ain't No Love (Radio Edit)/(Original Mix)/(Parkside Mix)/(On The House Mix) (CD) 8
90s Robs 7 ROB 19 Respect (Radio Edit)/(Dasliva-McCready Mix) ... 8
90s Robs 12 ROB 19 Respect (Original Mix)/(Dasliva-McCready Mix)/(Dasliva's Acid Dub) (12", p/s) ... 8
90s Robs 12 ROB 29 Angel (Original Mix)/(Primetime Mix)/Senna/Southern Trees (Instrumental)(12", p/s) ... 8
90s Robs Records 12ROB 29X Angel (Primetime Dub)/(Deep Love Mix)/(Deep Love Instrumental)/ (Pegasus (12", p/s) ... 8
90s Robs Records 12ROB 39 Southern Trees/Jaggernath/Northern Trees (12", p/s) ... 8
90s Robs Records 12ROB 51 Smoking Beagles/Crunch/(Instrumental Version) (12", custom stickered p/s) ... 5
90s Robs Records 12ROB 53 This Time I'm Not Wrong/Heads Will Roll (Instrumental Demo)/ Firesuite (12", p/s) ... 8

SUBTERRANEANS
87 Mother MUM 6 Slum/Maxi Joy (p/s) ... 5
87 Mother 12MUM 6 Slum/Maxi Joy/Head For The Light (12", p/s) ... 8

SUBURBAN STUDS
77 Pogo POG 001/LYN 44845 No Faith/Questions (no p/s, 'with horns' version) ... 15
77 Pogo POG 001/LYN 44845 No Faith/Questions (p/s) ... 6
78 Pogo POG 002 I Hate School/Young Power (p/s) ... 15
78 Pogo POW 001 SLAM (LP) ... 25

SUBWAYS
03 Bus Stop BS0502 No Heart, No Soul/We Get Around/Young For Eternity (live) (CD) ... 20
04 Private pressing DEMO (CD, sold at gigs, p/s) ... 30
04 Transgressive 58241H1 I Am/I Want To Hear What You Gotta Say/You Got Me (500 only, p/s) ... 12

SUBWAY SECT
(see also Vic Godard [& Subway Sect], Spirit Of The Sect)
78 Braik BRS 01 Nobody's Scared/Don't Split It (p/s) ... 15
79 Rough Trade RT 007 Ambition/A Different Story (initially in yellow text p/s) ... 10
79 Rough Trade RT 007 Ambition/A Different Story (later orange text p/s) ... 8

NIKKI SUDDEN
(see also Swell Maps, Last Bandits, Jeremy Gluck)
81 Rather GEAR 11 Back To The Start/Ringing On My Train (p/s) ... 5
82 Abstract ABS 009 Channel Steamer/Chelsea Embankment (p/s) ... 5

MINT VALUE £

80s	Rather RATHER 10	BEAU GESTE (cassette, with insert)	12
85	Hotwire HWLP 8504	THE LAST BANDITS IN THE WORLD (LP)	12

(A) SUDDEN SWAY

80	Chant CHANT 1	Jane's Third Party/Don't Go (p/s, as A Sudden Sway)	15
80	own label	Jane's Third Party/Don't Go (cassette, as A Sudden Sway)	8
81	Chant CHANT 2/EJSP 9692	TO YOU, WITH REGARD (12" EP, with insert)	20
84	Chant CHANT 3	The Traffic Tax Scheme (12" with badge & inserts in folder)	12
86	WEA BYN 8B	Spacemate (2 x 12" box set with stickers, info sheets, 2 booklets & poster)	12
87	Strange Fruit SFPSC 005	PEEL SESSION 16.11.83 (EP, cassette)	5

SUE & MARY

62	Decca F 11517	Traitor In Disguise/I Love You (Oh Yes I Do)	8

SUE & SUNNY

(see also Sue & Sunshine, Myrtelles, Stockingtops, Brotherhood Of Man)

65	Columbia DB 7748	Every Ounce Of Strength/So Remember	15
67	Columbia DB 8099	You Can't By-Pass Love/I Like Your Style	25
68	CBS 3874	Little Black Book/The Show Must Go On	20
68	Island WIP 6043	Set Me Free/NIRVANA ORCHESTRA: City Of The South	20
69	CBS 4567	Let Us Break Bread/Stop Messing About With My Heart	10
70	CBS 4757	You Devil, Cotton-Eyed Joe/Night In The City	10
70	Deram DM 318	Ain't That Telling You People/Didn't I Blow Your Mind	10
71	Deram DM 328	Freedom/Break Up	10
71	Reflection HRS 10	Let Us Break Bread Together/Michael From Mountains	6
72	Deram DM 355	I'm Gonna Make You Love Me/High On The Thought Of You	8
70	CBS 63740	SUE AND SUNNY (LP)	20
70	Reflection REFL 4	SUE AND SUNNY (LP)	20

SUE & SUNSHINE

(see also Sue & Sunny, Myrtelles, Stockingtops)

64	Columbia DB 7409	A Little Love/If You See Me Crying	10
65	Columbia DB 7533	We're In Love/Don't Look Behind	7

SUEDE

(see also Elastica)

91	RML RML 001	Be My God/Art (12", unissued, 250+ white label copies only, MPO pressings,no p/s; counterfeits have off-white labels and no MPO etchings)	100
92	Nude NUD 1 S	The Drowners (Radio Edit)/To The Birds (p/s, 1,000 copies only)	18
92	Nude NUD 1 CD	The Drowners (Radio Edit)/To The Birds/My Insatiable One (CD, promo only)	8
92	Nude NUD 3 T	Metal Mickey/Where Pigs Don't Fly/He's Dead (12", test pressing, plain sleeve)	30
93	Nude SUEDE 1	My Insatiable One (clear flexidisc, fan club/gig freebie)	10
94	Nude NUD 9T	Stay Together/The Living Dead/My Dark Star (12" numbered gatefold p/s)	10
94	Nude NUD 10 S	We Are The Pigs/Killing Of A Flash Boy (numbered gatefold p/s)	5
94	Nude NUD 11 T	The Wild Ones/Eno's Introducing The Band/Asda Town (12", photo insert, p/s)	10
94	Nude NUD 11 CD 2	The Wild Ones/Eno's Introducing The Band/Asda Town (CD)	8
95	Nude NUD 12 CD 2	New Generation/Animal Nitrate (live)/The Wild Ones (live)/Pantomime Horse (live) (CD, digipak)	5
96	Nude NUD 21S	Trash/Europe Is Our Playground (p/s, mail order only)	15
97	Nude SIS 1 CD	LIVE (CD EP, 6-track fan club-only issue)	20
97	Nude NUD 24 S	Saturday Night/Beautiful Ones (double pack, p/s, mail-order only)	10
	Nude NUD SIS 1 CD	Film Star (live)/Rent (live)/Saturday Night (live) (CD, featuring Neil Tennant)	10
98	Nude SIS 2 CD	IMPLEMENT YEAH! (CD fan club-only issue)	10
99	Nude NUD 667043	ELECTRICITY EP (minidisc, withdrawn)	10
98	Nude SUEDE 1 CDF	ON FILM EP (CD EP 6-track, promo only)	15
99	Nude NUD 667043	ELECTRICITY EP (minidisc – withdrawn)	10
99	Nude INT 1 CD	Head Musing (2-CD with DVD in numbered box)	15
03	Fan Club (no cat. no.)	Attitude (2-CD with DVD in numbered box)	20
02	Fan Club (no cat. no.)	Positivity (2-CD with DVD in numbered box)	20
02	Fan Club (no cat. no.)	Obsessions (2-CD with DVD in numbered box)	20
93	Nude NUDE 1LP	SUEDE (LP, with inner sleeve; with carrier bag from Chain With No Name stores)	20
93	Nude NUDE 1LP	SUEDE (LP, with inner sleeve)	12
94	Nude NUDE 3	DOG MAN STAR (LP, with poster)	35
96	Nude 4851212	COMING UP (LP, with inner sleeve)	18

SUFFERER SOUND

78	Tempus TEMD 2	I A Sufferer/National Front (12")	12

SUGAR

69	CBS 4226	It Was Yesterday Today/11AM Tuesday Morning Taxi	28

SUGAR

92	Creation CRELP 129	COPPER BLUE (LP, lyric insert)	20

SUGAR MINOTT

79	Warrior WAR 124	Never Too Young/DON CARLOS: Hey Little Girl (12")	10
70s	Uptempo UT 1	SHOWCASE (10" mini-LP, no ps)	15
83	PCJ PCJ 001	Can't Stop Jah Music/PCJ: Nah Stop Jah Music (12")	50
79	United Artists UAG 30310	GIVE THE PEOPLE (LP)	20
79	Island ILPS 9591	BLACK ROOTS (LP)	20
79	Trojan TRLS 173	GHETTO-OLOGY (LP)	15
82	black roots BRLP 001	MEET THE PEOPLE IN A LOVER DUBBER STYLE (LP)	15

SUGAR (Simone) & DANDY (Livingstone)

(see also Sugar Simone)

63	Carnival CV 7006	One Man Went To Mow/Cryin'	8
64	Carnival CV 7009	Oh Dear What Can The Matter Be/Tra La La	8
64	Carnival CV 7015	What A Life/Time And Tide	8
64	Carnival CV 7016	I'm Not Crying Now/Blues Got A Hold On Me	8
65	Carnival CV 7023	Let's Ska/Only Heaven Knows	8
65	Carnival CV 7024	I'm Into Something Good/Crazy For You	8

SUGAR (Simone) & DANDY (Livingstone)

MINT VALUE £

65	Carnival CV 7027	Think Of The Good Times/Girl Come See	8
65	Carnival CV 7029	I Want To Be Your Lover/I Don't Know What I'm Going To Do Now	7
66	Blue Beat BB 367	Meditation (as Jetliners)/GIRL SATCHMO & JET LINERS: Nature Of Love	15
67	Page One POF 044	Let's Ska/Only Heaven Knows	8
64	Carnival CX 1000	THE SKA'S THE LIMIT (LP)	40
67	Page One FOR 006	THE SKA'S THE LIMIT (LP, reissue)	20

SUGAR & PEE WEE

58	Vogue Pop V 9112	One, Two, Let's Rock/Just A Few Little Words	750
58	Vogue Pop V 9112	One, Two, Let's Rock/Just A Few Little Words (78)	150

SUGAR & SPICE

69	London HLU 10259	Cruel War/Not To Return	8

SUGAR BEARS

72	Philips 6073 812	You Are The One/Someone Like You	5

SUGARBEATS

(see also Tony Rivers & Castaways)

66	Polydor BM 56069	I Just Stand Here/The Ballad Of Ole Betsy	20
66	Polydor BM 56120	Alice Designs/Sunny Day Girl	20

SUGARCUBES

(see also Bjork, Kukl, Ornamental)

87	One Little Indian 7z TP 7	Birthday/Birthday (Icelandic) (p/s)	6
87	One Little Indian 12 TP 7	Birthday/Birthday (Icelandic)/Cat (Icelandic) (12", p/s)	8
87	One Little Indian 7TP 7CD	Birthday/Motorcrash/Cat (Icelandic)/Birthday (Icelandic) (CD)	10
87	One Little Indian L12 TP 9	Cold Sweat (Remix)/Birthday (Original Demo Version)/Dragon (Icelandic)/Traitor (Icelandic) (12", p/s, 5,000 only)	8
87	One Little Indian 7TP 9CD	Cold Sweat/Dragon (Icelandic)/Traitor (Icelandic)/Revolution (CD)	8
88	One Little Indian 10 TP 10	Deus (Remix)/Luftgitar (Icelandic) (with Johnny Triumph)/ Organic Prankster (10", p/s)	7
88	One Little Indian 12TP 11L	BIRTHDAY CHRISTMAS MIX (12" EP, double groove, with Jesus & Mary Chain)	12
89	House Of Dolls HOD 010	Dark Disco/HOST: Homelands/MURRUMBRIDGE WHALERS: Giving Away To Trains/SHARK TABOO: Tinsel Town (live) (no p/s, with House Of Dolls mag)	6
89	One Little Indian OLI26TP7	Regina/Hot Meat/Hey/Regina (Propellor vs Jet) (with poster)	6
89	One Little Indian OLI26TP12	Regina/Hot Meat/Regina (Icelandic) (12")	8
91	One Little Indian OLI62TP12	Hit/Theft/Hit (Instrumental)/Leash Called Love (12")	8
92	One Little Indian OLI104TP12	Birthday (Justin Robertson 12" mix)/Tommy D Dub Mix/ Christmas Eve Mix/ Original 7" Mix/Tommy D 12" Mix/Justin Robertson Dub/Christmas Day Mix/ Demo (12")	10
90	One Little Indian TP BOX 2	7.8 (8 x 7" box set)	25
90	One Little Indian TP BOX 1	12.11 (11 x 12" box set)	40
90	One Little Indian TP BOX 3	CD.6 (6 x CD box set)	45
88	One Little Indian TPLP 5	LIFE'S TO GOOD (LP, green/blue/yellow/orange/pink sleeve)	15
88	One Little Indian DTPLP 5	LIFE'S TOO GOOD (DAT)	20
89	One Little Indian TPLP 15SP	HERE TODAY, TOMORROW NEXT WEEK! (LP, silver vinyl, gatefold sleeve with sticker & inner)	20
89	One Little Indian TPLP 15L	SYKURMOLARNIR ILLUR ARFUR! (LP, as Sykurmolarnir, gatefold sleeve)	15
92	One Little Indian TPLP40	IT'S IT (2 x LP)	20

SUGAR DEE & THE OFFBEAT POSSE

89	YND YDD 0137	Danger/Having A Party (12")	25

SUGAR LOAF

70	RCA INTS 1113	SOUL STRUTTING (LP)	40

SUGARLOAF

70	Liberty LBF 15401	Green-Eyed Lady/West Of Tomorrow	18
71	Liberty LBS 83415	SUGARLOAF (LP)	15
74	United Artists UAS 29165	SPACESHIP EARTH (LP)	12
75	Polydor 2310 394	DON'T CALL US, WE'LL CALL YOU (LP, with Jerry Corbetto)	15

SUGAR LUMPS

69	Jay Boy BOY 16	Sugar Sugar/Can't We Be Friends	20

SUGARPLUMS

70	Fab FAB 160	Red River Reggae/Too Much	7

SUGAR SHOPPE

68	Capitol CL 15555	Skip-A-Long Sam/Let The Truth Come Out	20

SUICIDAL TENDENCIES

87	Virgin VS 967-12	Possessed To Skate/Human Guinea Pig/Two Wrongs Don't Make A Right (12", picture disc)	15
88	Virgin VST 1039	Institutionalised/War Inside My Head/Cyco (12", p/s)	15
87	Virgin V 2495	SUICIDAL TENDENCIES (LP, with poster)	12
88	Virgin V 2551	HOW WILL I LAUGH TOMORROW WHEN I CAN'T EVEN SMILE TODAY? (LP)	15

SUICIDE

(see also Alan Vega, Martin Rev)

77	Sound For Industry SFI 323	Johnny/(Real Kids track) (flexidisc via Circuit magazine)	8
78	Red Star/Bronze BRO 57	Cheree/I Remember (p/s)	10
78	Red Star/Bronze 12 BRO 57	Cheree/I Remember (12", 'limited edition', p/s)	12
79	Island WIP 6543	Dream Baby Dream/Radiation (p/s)	6
79	Island 12 WIP 6543	Dream Baby Dream (Long Version)/Radiation (12", p/s)	20
86	Demon D 1046	Cheree/I Remember (promo only)	5
89	Chapter 22 12CHAP 36	Rain Of Ruin/Surrender (12")	10
89	Chapter 22 12CHAP 42	SUICIDE (12", unissued)	0
77	Red Star/Bronze BRON 508	SUICIDE (LP)	18
78	Red Star FRANKIE 1	24 MINUTES OVER BRUSSELS (LP, official bootleg, 1,000 only, no p/s)	30
80	Ze/Island ILPS 7007	SUICIDE: ALAN VEGA/MARTIN REV (LP, with printed inner sleeve)	18

MINT VALUE £

89	Contempo CONTE 148	HALF ALIVE (LP, clear vinyl, 1,000 only)	12
98	Blast First BFFP 133 1/2	SUICIDE (2-LP)	18
99	Blast First BFFP 162	FIRST REHEARSAL TAPES (2-LP)	15

SUICIDE TWINS
(see also Hanoi Rocks)

86	Lick LICLP 9	SILVER MISSILES AND NIGHTINGALES (LP)	15

BIG JIM SULLIVAN
(see also Maureeny Wishfull, Brian Bennett, Tiger)

61	Decca F 11387	You Don't Know What You've Got/Hot Hiss Of Steam (as Big Jim Sullivan Combo)	10
65	Mercury MF 928	She Walks Through The Fair/Don't Know What I'm Doing (as Jim Sullivan Sound)	25
73	MAM MAM 100	Out Of The Question/Alone Again	6
67	Mercury SML 30001	SITAR BEAT (LP)	40
74	Retreat RTA 4001	BIG JIM'S BACK (LP, gatefold sleeve, blue/green label)	15

MAXINE SULLIVAN

54	Parlophone MSP 6086	Boogie Woogie Maxine/Piper In The Glen (with Vic Ash)	15

PHIL SULLIVAN with LONZO & OSCAR'S PEAPICKERS

59	Melodisc MEL 1512	Love Never Dies/Luckiest Man In Town	5

PETER SULLY

70	Pye 7N 17935	Row Row Row/Everybodys Talkin' About The War	8
68	Polydor 56291	My Idea/Evil Woman (as Pete Sully And The Orchard)	35

YMA SUMAC

55	Capitol EAP1 564	YMA SUMAC MAMBO (EP)	8
55	Capitol EAP2 564	YMA SUMAC MAMBO (EP)	8
57	Capitol EAP1 770	LEGEND OF JIVARO PT. 1 (EP)	8
57	Capitol EAP2 770	LEGEND OF JIVARO PT. 2 (EP)	8
57	Capitol EAP3 770	LEGEND OF JIVARO PT. 3 (EP)	8
53	Capitol LC 6522	VOICE OF THE XTABAY (10" LP)	20
54	Capitol LC 6609	LEGEND OF THE SUN VIRGIN (10" LP)	20
59	Capitol T 1169	FUEGO DEL ANDE (LP)	20
64	Regal REG 2007	VOICE OF THE XTABAY (LP, export issue)	15
72	London HLU/SHU 8431	MIRACLES (LP)	15

HUBERT SUMLIN
(see also Howlin' Wolf)

65	Blue Horizon 45-1000	Across The Board/Sumlin Boogie (99 copies only)	110

DONNA SUMMER
(see also Donna Gaines, John Barry)

74	People PEO 115	The Hostage/Let's Work Together Now	10
79	Casablanca SANL 151	Hot Stuff/Journey To The Centre Of Your Heart (12", red vinyl)	10
89	WEA U 7780P	This Time I Know It's For Real/Whatever Your Heart Desires (shaped pic disc)	5

SUMMERHILL

69	Polydor 583 746	SUMMERHILL (LP)	35

ANDY SUMMERS & ROBERT FRIPP
(see also Police, King Crimson)

82	A&M (no cat. no.)	Hardy Country/Stultified/Yellow Leader/I Advance Masked (clear flexidisc)	6

BOB(BY) SUMMERS

59	Capitol CL 15063	Rattle Rhythm/Excitement (as Bob Summers)	15
60	Capitol CL 15130	Little Brown Jug/Twelfth Street Rag (as Bobby Summers)	8

JOHN SUMMERS

65	Pye 15918	Don't Fool Yourself/Looking In Windows	30
66	Pye 7N 17081	That's A Magic Moment/One A Day	10

SUMMER SET
(see also Candy Choir)

66	Columbia DB 8004	Farmer's Daughter/Papa-Oom-Mow-Mow	40
66	Columbia DB 8004	Farmer's Daughter/What Are You Gonna Do (2nd issue with different B-side)	40
67	Columbia DB 8215	Overnight Changes/It's A Dream	90

SUMMERTAIR GIRLS
(see also Jackie Mittoo, Soul Agents)

66	Ska Beat JB 258	My Heart Cries Out/SOUL BROTHERS: James Bond Girl	50

SUMMER WINE
(see also Tony Rivers, John Perry)

72	Philips 6006 217	Why Do Fools Fall In Love/Ode To Steel Guitar	5
72	Philips 6006 238	Take A Load Off Your Feet/ Sound Of Summer's Over	5
73	Philips 6006 288	Living Right Next Door To An Angel/Sound Of Summer's Over	7
77	EMI EMI 2634	Why Do Fools Fall In Love/Sound Of Summer's Over	5

SUN ALSO RISES

70	Village Thing VTS 2	THE SUN ALSO RISES (LP, with insert)	80

SUN DIAL
(see also Modern Art, Spiral Sky, Quad)

90	UFO 45 001T	Exploding In Your Mind/Otherside/Slow Motion (12", 1-sided, p/s)	10
91	Tangerine TANGERINE 111	Exploding In Your Mind (Colour Mix)/Otherside/Slow Motion (12", unreleased, 80 white label test pressings only)	30
91	UFO PF 2	Fireball/Only A Northern Song ('Pre-Flight' 7", promo only)	20
91	UFO UFO 45002 T	OVERSPILL EP (12", orange vinyl)	10
92	UFO UFO 45008 T	FAZER EP (12")	10
90	Tangerine MM 07	OTHER WAY OUT (LP, with insert, signed in silver ink)	30
90	Tangerine MM 07	OTHER WAY OUT (LP, with insert)	20

MINT VALUE £

91	UFO UFO 1LP	OTHER WAY OUT (LP, reissue in gatefold sleeve)	12
92	UFO UFO 8	REFLECTER (LP, clear vinyl)	15
94	Acme AC 8001	RETURN JOURNEY (LP, official bootleg; 200 promos with inserts)	20
94	Acme AC 8001	RETURN JOURNEY (LP, official bootleg; 500 numbered commercial copies)	12
95	Acme AC 8011LP	ACID YANTRA (LP, gatefold sleeve)	12

SUN & MOON
(see also Chameleons)

88	Geffen GEF 39	The Speed Of Life/Death Of Imagination (p/s)	5
88	Geffen GEF 39T	The Speed Of Life/Death Of Imagination/The Boy Who Sees Everything/ I Love You, You Bastard (12", p/s)	8

SUNBIRD
(see also Nirvana)

70	Phillips 6011070	Brother Bird/Love Of The Free	18

SUNCHARIOT

73	Decca F13407	Firewater/The Only Girl I Knew	10

SUNDAE TIMES
(see also Osiba, Crosyby Stills Nash & Young, One)

68	President PT 203	Baby Don't Cry/Aba-Aba	5
68	President PT 219	Jack Boy/I Don't Want Nobody	5
70	President PT 285	Live Today/Take Me Higher Baby	5
70	Joy JOYS 159	US COLOURED KIDS (LP, laminated front sleeve, flipbacks)	40

SUNDANCE

73	Decca F 13423	Coming Down/Eagles	5
73	Decca F 13461	Stand By/Willie The Gambler	5
74	Decca F 13494	Loving You/Can You Feel It	5
73	Decca TXS 111	RAIN STEAM SPEED (LP, with insert)	18
74	Decca SKL 5183	CHUFFER (LP)	18

SUNDAY AFTERNOONS

70s	Longman	SUNDAY AFTERNOONS (LP)	90

SUNDAYS

89	Rough Trade RTX 218	Can't Be Sure/I Kicked A Boy (export issue, brown p/s)	6
89	Rough Trade RTTX 218	Can't Be Sure/I Kicked A Boy/Don't Tell Your Mother (12", export issue, brown p/s)	10
89	Rough Trade RTT 218CD	Can't Be Sure/I Kicked A Boy/Don't Tell Your Mother (3" CD, card sleeve)	8
90	Catalogue CAT 076	I Won (square flexidisc with The Catalogue magazine)	10
97	Parlophone CDR 6475	Summertime/Nothing Sweet/Gone (CD)	8
90	Rough Trade ROUGH 148P	READING, WRITING AND ARITHMETIC (LP, picture disc, stickered sleeve)	15

SUNDAY SING TRIO

70s	Sharon SHLP 1221	ONE OF THESE DAYS (LP)	15

SUNDERLAND FIRST TEAM SQUAD

73	RCA 2362	Sunderland All The Way/Bobby Knoxall - I'm Feeling Happy	7

SUNDOWNERS

63	Piccadilly 7N 35142	Baby Baby/House Of The Rising Sun	8
64	Piccadilly 7N 35162	Come On In/Shot Of Rhythm And Blues	8
65	Parlophone R 5243	Where Am I/Gonna Make The Future Bright	8
68	Columbia DB 8339	Dr. J. Wallace-Brown/Love Is In The Air	10
68	Spark SRL 1016	Gloria The Bosom Show/Don't Look Back	8

SUNDOWN PLAYBOYS

72	Apple APPLE 44	Saturday Nite Special/Valse De Soleil Couche (in p/s)	35
72	Apple APPLE 44	Saturday Nite Special/Valse De Soleil Couche	10
72	Apple APPLE 44	Saturday Nite Special/Valse De Soleil Couche (10", 78rpm, pink-patterned die-cut sleeve)	250

SUNDRAGON

03	Y n R YNR014	The Path/Watching (12")	12

SUNDRAGON
(see also Sands, Others)

68	MGM MGM 1380	Green Tambourine/I Need All The Friends I Can Get	12
68	MGM MGM 1391	Blueberry Blue/Far Away Mountain	12
68	MGM MGM 1458	Five White Horses/Look At The Sun	30
68	MGM MGM-C(S) 8090	GREEN TAMBOURINE (LP, yellow/black 'lion' label)	110

SUNFIGHTER
(see also Chris Rainbow)

77	EMI EMI 2612	Café A Go-Go/Café A Go-Go (instrumental)	5
76	EMI EMI 2493	Drag Race Queen/Riding On Your Star	15
76	EMI EMI 2553	Such A Lovely Night/Don't Get Me Wrong	10

SUNFIRE

82	Warner Bros.	Step In The Light/Lady (12")	15

SUNFLAYRE

70	Realm RM 1	The Passing Dream/RIch Woman (private pressing)	300

SUNFOREST

70	Deram Nova DN 7	SOUND OF SUNFOREST (LP, mono, laminated front sleeve)	200
70	Deram Nova SDN 7	SOUND OF SUNFOREST (LP, stereo, laminated front sleeve)	175

SUNN 0)))

04	Anti-Mosh 444	Candlewolff Ov Thee Golden Chalice (12")	40

SUNNY & HI-JUMPERS

65	Carnival CV 7022	Tarry Till You're Better/Dance Til You're Better	6
65	Carnival CV 7025	Going To Damascus/Sweet Potatoes	6

MINT VALUE £

SUNNY & THE SUNGLOWS/SUNLINERS
63 London HL 9792 Talk To Me (as Sunny & the Sunglows)/Every Week, Every Month, Every Year (as Sunny & the Sunliners) . . . 25

SUNNYLAND SLIM
65 77' LA 12-23 CHICAGO BLUES SESSION (LP, with Little Brother Montgomery) . . . 30
65 Storyville SLP 169 I DONE YOU WRONG (LP) . . . 20
68 Storyville 670 169 PORTRAITS IN BLUES (LP, reissue of SLP 169) . . . 12
69 Liberty LBS 83237 SLIM'S GOT THIS THING GOIN' ON (LP) . . . 30
69 Blue Horizon 7-63213 MIDNIGHT JUMP (LP) . . . 90
74 Sonet SNTF 671 THE LEGACY OF THE BLUES VOL. II (LP) . . . 12

SUNNYSIDERS
55 London HL 8135 Hey! Mr. Banjo/Zoom, Zoom, Zoom . . . 50
55 London HL 8160 Oh Me Oh My Oh/(Let's Gather Round) The Parlour Piano . . . 30
55 London HLU 8180 Banjo Woogie/She Didn't Even Say Goodbye . . . 30
55 London HLU 8202 I Love You Fair Dinkum/Stay On The Sunny Side . . . 25
56 London HLU 8246 Doesn't He Love Me/Humdinger . . . 30

SUN RA ARKESTRA
74 Decca F 13542 Don't Go/Can We Change . . . 20
82 Y 1 RA NUCLEAR WAR (12" EP) . . . 30
69 Fontana STL 5514 HELIOCENTRIC WORLDS VOL. 1 (LP) . . . 40
69 Fontana STL 5499 HELIOCENTRIC WORLDS VOL. 2 (LP) . . . 40
60s Sonet 23 SPL JAZZ BY SUN RA (LP) . . . 30
71 Black Lion BLP 30103 PICTURES OF INFINITY - IN CONCERT (LP) . . . 20
71 Byg 529 341 THE SOLAR MYTH APPROACH VOL. 2 (LP) . . . 25
71 Polydor 2460 106 PICTURES OF INFINITY (LP) . . . 25
78 Affinity AFF 10 S-M APPROACH (LP, with Solar-Myth Ark) . . . 15
79 Cobra COB 37001 FATE IN A PLEASANT MOOD (LP) . . . 15
80 Y Y 19 STRANGE CELESTIAL ROAD (LP) . . . 15
90 Blast First BFFP 60 SUN RA & MYTH SCIENCE ARKESTRA (3 x 10", box set, with insert) . . . 35

SUNRAYS
65 Capitol CL 15416 I Live For The Sun/Bye, Baby, Bye . . . 12
66 Capitol CL 15433 Andrea/You Don't Phase Me . . . 15

SUNRISE
76 Grapevine GRA 105 BEFORE MY EYES (LP) . . . 30

SUN SET
67 Polydor BM 56193 East Baby/You Can Ride My Rainbow . . . 15

SUNSET BOYS
(see also Maxim's Trash)
79 Gimp GIM 1234 Wreck My Bed/Tutti Frutti/Copy Cat (Blues)/Wreck My Bed (Hippy Version) (p/s) . . . 5

SUNSETS
61 Ember EMB S 125 Cry Of The Wild Goose/Manhunt . . . 15

SUNSHINE
(see also Pretty Things)
72 Warner Brothers K 46169 SUNSHINE (LP, gatefold sleeve) . . . 15

SUNSHINE COMPANY
67 Liberty LBF 15008 Happy/Blue May . . . 12
67 Liberty LBF 15034 Back On The Street Again/A Year Of Janie's Time . . . 10
68 Liberty LBF 15060 Look Here Comes The Sun/It's Sunday . . . 8
68 Liberty LBF 15149 On A Beautiful Day/To Put Up With You . . . 10
68 Liberty LBL/LBS 83120 THE SUNSHINE COMPANY (LP) . . . 30
69 Liberty LBL/LBS 83159 SUNSHINE AND SHADOWS (LP) . . . 35

SUNSHINE KID
73 RCA RCA 2413 My Linda/Get Your Rocks Off Baby . . . 40

MONTY SUNSHINE
(see also Lonnie Donegan)
63 London HLR 9822 Carnival/Charmaine E. . . . 5
61 Columbia SEG 8059 MONTY (EP) . . . 8
63 London HAR 8037 MONTY SUNSHINE AND HIS BAND (LP, also stereo [SHR 8037]) . . . 12
64 London HAR 8158 BLACK MOONLIGHT & SUNSHINE (LP, also stereo [SHR 8158]) . . . 12

MR. SUNSHINE
56 MGM SP 1160 Along The China Coast/MRS. SUNSHINE: Two Car Garage . . . 7

SUNSPOTS
63 Decca F 11672 Paella/Vancouver . . . 5

SUNTREADER
73 Island HELP 13 ZIN ZIN (LP, innser sleeve, black label, pink 'i' logo) . . . 15

SUPER 8
(see also Sheds)
95 García POUM 001 Billy The Kid/It Doesn't Matter/How Can I Understand The Flies? ('hairloss' p/s, 500 only, 37 sold, 35 returned for refund, the rest believed burned) . . 25

SUPERBOYS
(see also Dandy & Superboys, Little Sal)
68 Giant GN 22 Ain't That A Shame/Do It Right Now . . . 8
68 Giant GN 31 You're Hurtin' Me/Funky Soul . . . 8

SUPER CAT
88 Blue Trac BTRD 020 Nuff Man Dead Ya/ABC (12") . . . 30

SUPERCHARGE
76 Virgin VS 145 Lonely And In Love/Give It The Nasty . . . 6
78 Virgin VS 20212 I Think I'm Gonna Fall In Love/Long Version (12") . . . 10

MINT VALUE £

SUPER FURRY ANIMALS

95	SFAP1	Frisbee (12" promo, 1-sided, unreleased intended debut single. Not on a label)	40
96	Creation CRE 222	Hometown Unicorn/Don't Be A Fool Billy (p/s)	12
96	Creation CRESCD 231	God! Show Me Magic/Death By Melody/Dim Bendith (CD, picture disc)	10
96	Creation CRE 235	Something 4 The Weekend/Waiting To Happen (p/s)	8
96	Creation CRE 243	If You Don't Want Me To Destroy You/Guacamole (poster p/s)	8
96	Creation CRE 243	If You Don't Want Me To Destroy You (picture disc)	10
96	Creation CRE 247	The Man Don't Give A Fuck (p/s, 1-sided, blue vinyl)	20
96	Creation CRE 247 T	The Man Don't Give A Fuck/(Howard Marks Mix)/(Wishmountain Mix)/ (Darren Price Mix) (12", p/s)	15
96	Creation CRESCD 247	The Man Don't Give A Fuck/(Howard Marks Mix)/(Wishmountain Mix) (CD, picture disc)	15
96	Creation CTP 229	The Man Don't Give A Fuck/Dim Brys Dim Chwys (12" 1-sided promo)	15
96	Debiel SS 01	(Nid) Hon Yw'r Gan Sy'n Mynd I Achub Yr Laith (1-sided gig freebie)	15
97	Creation CRE 275	Play It Cool/Pass The Time (fold out poster sleeve)	5
97	Creation CRE 283	Demons/Hit And Run (fold out poster sleeve)	5
98	Creation CRE 288	Ice Hockey Hair/Smokin' (stickered p/s, limited edition)	10
99	Creation CTP 323X	Wherever I Lay My Phone (That's My Home) (12" 1-sided promo p/s)	10
00	Placid Casual PLC02	Ysbediau Heulog/Charge (white vinyl in PVC sleeve, 3000 only)	10
03	Epic 6739067	Golden Retriever/Summer Snow/Blue Fruit (picture disc, limited edition, numbered, stickered poly sleeve)	10
04	Placid Casual PLC08EP	Slow Life/Motherfokker/Lost Control (CD promo, 'floppy disc' sleeve)	8
95	Ankst ANKST 057	LLANFAIRPWLLGWYNGYLLGOGERYCHWYRNDROBWLLANTYSILIOGOGO-GOCHYNYGOFOD (IN SPACE) (EP) (1st issue)	15
95	Ankst ANKST 057	LLANFAIRPWLLGWYNGYLLGOGERYCHWYRNDROBWLLANTYSILIOGOGO-GOCHYNYGOFOD (IN SPACE) (EP) (2nd issue, same cat no)	10
95	Ankst ANKST 057	LLANFAIRPWLLGWYNGYLLGOGERYCHWYRNDROBWLLANTYSILIOGOGO-GOCHYNYGOFOD (IN SPACE) (EP) (CD, 1st issue)	20
95	Ankst ANKST 057	LLANFAIRPWLLGWYNGYLLGOGERYCHWYRNDROBWLLANTYSILIOGOGO-GOCHYNYGOFOD (IN SPACE) (EP) (CD, 2nd issue, same cat no)	18
95	Ankst ANKST 62	MOOG DROOG EP (EP, 1st issue, p/s)	15
95	Ankst ANKST 62	MOOG DROOG EP (EP, 2nd issue, same cat no, p/s)	10
95	Ankst ANKST 62	MOOG DROOG EP (CD, 1st issue)	20
95	Ankst ANKST 62	MOOG DROOG EP (CD, 2nd issue, same cat no)	18
96	Creation CRELP 190	FUZZY LOGIC (LP, with insert)	20
97	Creation CRELP 214	RADIATOR (2-LP)	35
98	Creation CRECD 229 L	OUT SPACED (CD, rubber pack [black, yellow or blue])	30
99	Creation CRELP 242	GUERRILLA (2-LP, gatefold, pop up sleeve)	25
00	Placid Casual PLC03LP	MWNG (LP, ltd white vinyl, p/s PVC sleeve. 2000 copies)	25
01	Sony/Epic 5024131	RINGS AROUND THE WORLD (2-LP, side 3 plays from inside out, with free 7" white label 7")	30
03	Epic 5123751	PHANTOM POWER (2-LP etched vinyl with insert, 3000 copies)	15
04	Placid Casual PL07CD	PHANTON PHORCE (2-LP ltd version with bonus 'Slow Life' EP disc, fold-out packaging. 3000 copies)	25
05	Epic 5176711	SONGBOOK - THE SINGLES VOLUME ONE (2x12" pop up gatefold sleeve)	25
05	Sony 5205011	LOVE KRAFT (2-LP, gatefold)	15

SUPERGRASS

(see also Jennifers, Hot Rats)

94	Backbeat BEAT 4	Caught By The Fuzz/Strange Ones (hand-stamped labels, 1,000 only, later re-pressed)	20
94	Backbeat BEAT 6	Mansize Rooster/Sitting Up Straight (luminous green vinyl, printed green cardboard sleeve, 500 only)	25
94	Backbeat BEAT 6	Mansize Rooster/Sitting Up Straight (luminous green vinyl, plain die-cut sleeve, 500 only)	15
94	Backbeat BEAT 6	Mansize Rooster/Sitting Up Straight (marbled green vinyl, plain sleeve)	15
94	Parlophone R 6396	Caught By The Fuzz/Strange Ones (p/s, reissue)	8
94	Parlophone 12R 6396DJ	Caught By The Fuzz/Strange Ones (12", p/s, promo only)	10
94	Parlophone CDR 6396	Caught By The Fuzz/Strange Ones/Caught By The Fuzz (Acoustic) (CD)	8
95	Parlophone 12RDJ6402	Mansize Rooster (12" promo)	12
95	Parlophone R 6402	Mansize Rooster/Sitting Up Straight (p/s, red vinyl)	8
95	Parlophone CDR 6402	Mansize Rooster/Sitting Up Straight/Odd (CD)	8
95	Parlophone RS 6410	Lenny/Wait For The Sun (p/s, light blue vinyl)	6
96	Parlophone R 6428	Going Out/Melanie Davis (p/s, burgundy vinyl)	5
97	Parlophone R 6461	Richard III/Nothing More's Gonna Get In My Way (p/s, yellow vinyl)	6
97	Parlophone R 6469	Sun Hits The Sky/Some Girls Are Bigger Than Others (numbered p/s, white vinyl)	6
97	Parlophone 12RDJ 6469	Sun Hits The Sky (Bentley Rhythm Ace Sun Hits The Sky Mix) (12", no p/s, promo only)	10
99	EMI CDIN 125	INTERVIEW (CD, tri-fold digipak, promo only)	15
99	Parlophone R6518	Pumping On Your Stereo/You'll Never Walk Again (green vinyl), p/s)	7
99	Parlophone R6524	Moving/Believer (blue vinyl, p/s)	6
99	Parlophone R 6531	Mary/(Live Version) (p/s, silver vinyl)	5
02	Parlophone R 6583	Never Done Nothing Like That Before (1-sided, stamped white label, die-cut black sleeve with barcode sticker, numbered, 1,500 only)	8
02	Parlophone R 6586	Grace/Velvetine (pink vinyl, p/s)	6
97	Parlophone GRASS 9497	THE SINGLES 1994-1997 (8 x 7" black vinyl, 'grass'-covered box set, with signed & numbered insert, promo only)	50
95	Parlophone PCSX 7373	I SHOULD COCO (LP, with inner & bonus single "Stone Free"/"Odd?" [PCSS 7373])	35
99	Parlophone 5220561	SUPERGRASS (LP, with poster)	20
04	EMI 5789941	SUPERGRASS IS 10 : BEST OF 94-04 (2 x 10" LP, clear vinyl, gatefold)	15

SUPERMAN AND SPIDERMAN

85	Kingdom KVL 9025	SUPERMAN AND SPIDERMAN (LP)	12

SUPERMATIX

81	MC 4	BAD TIMING EP (p/s)	20

SUPER$HIT666

(see also Backyard Babies, Hellacopters, Wildhearts)

00	Infernal INFERNAL003LP	SUPER$HIT666 (10" LP, with inner sleeve, purple or black vinyl)	10

MINT VALUE £

SUPERSISTER

72 Polydor 2001 379 No Tree Will Grow/She Was Naked ... 12
71 Dandelion 2310 146 TO THE HIGHEST BIDDER (LP, gatefold sleeve) ... 70
71 Polydor 2419 030 SUPER STARSHINE 3 (LP) ... 30
72 Polydor 2419 061 PRESENT FROM NANCY (LP) ... 35
73 Polydor 2480 153 PUDDING & YESTERDAY (LP) ... 50
73 Polydor 2925 021 ISKANDER (LP, gatefold sleeve with lyric sheet) ... 25
53 London L 1197 New Guitar Boogie Shuffle/The Sheik Of Araby (78) ... 15
54 London HL 8022 Cherokee/Linger Awhile (B-side with Arlene James) (78) ... 15
70 Banana BA 312 Freedom Blues/First Time I Met You ... 40

SUPERTRAMP

70 A&M AMLS 981 SUPERTRAMP (LP, laminated sleeve, brown label) ... 20
71 A&M AMLH 64306 INDELIBLY STAMPED (LP, gatefold sleeve, brown label) ... 20

SUPPORTERS

70 RCA 1972 Sing Your Own Team/On The Ball ... 30

(DIANA ROSS &) SUPREMES

(see also Primettes, Diana Ross, Temptations, Four Tops, Florence Ballard)

64 Stateside SS 257 When The Lovelight Starts Shining Thru' His Eyes/ Standing At The Crossroads Of Love ... 50
64 Stateside SS 257 When The Lovelight Starts Shining Thru' His Eyes/ Standing At The Crossroads Of Love (DJ copy) ... 100
64 Stateside SS 327 Where Did Our Love Go/He Means The World To Me ... 10
64 Stateside SS 327 Where Did Our Love Go/He Means The World To Me (DJ copy) ... 100
64 Stateside SS 350 Baby Love/Ask Any Girl ... 12
64 Stateside SS 350 Baby Love/Ask Any Girl (DJ copy) ... 100
65 Stateside SS 376 Come See About Me/(You're Gone But) Always In My Heart ... 12
65 Stateside SS 376 Come See About Me/(You're Gone But) Always In My Heart (DJ copy) ... 100
65 Tamla Motown TMG 501 Stop! In The Name Of Love/I'm In Love Again ... 12
65 Tamla Motown TMG 501 Stop! In The Name Of Love/I'm In Love Again (DJ copy) ... 100
65 Tamla Motown TMG 516 Back In My Arms Again/Whisper You Love Me Boy ... 25
65 Tamla Motown TMG 516 Back In My Arms Again/Whisper You Love Me Boy (DJ copy) ... 85
65 Tamla Motown TMG 527 Nothing But Heartaches/He Holds His Own ... 20
65 Tamla Motown TMG 527 Nothing But Heartaches/He Holds His Own (DJ copy) ... 85
65 Tamla Motown TMG 543 I Hear A Symphony/Who Could Ever Doubt My Love ... 20
65 Tamla Motown TMG 543 I Hear A Symphony/Who Could Ever Doubt My Love (DJ copy) ... 75
66 Tamla Motown TMG 548 My World Is Empty Without You/Everything Is Good About You ... 20
66 Tamla Motown TMG 548 My World Is Empty Without You/Everything Is Good About You (DJ copy) ... 75
66 Tamla Motown TMG 560 Love Is Like An Itching In My Heart/He's All I Got ... 50
66 Tamla Motown TMG 560 Love Is Like An Itching In My Heart/He's All I Got (DJ copy) ... 150
66 Tamla Motown TMG 575 You Can't Hurry Love/Put Yourself In My Place ... 15
66 Tamla Motown TMG 575 You Can't Hurry Love/Put Yourself In My Place (DJ copy) ... 70
66 Tamla Motown TMG 585 You Keep Me Hangin' On/Remove This Doubt ... 15
66 Tamla Motown TMG 585 You Keep Me Hangin' On/Remove This Doubt (DJ copy) ... 60
67 Tamla Motown TMG 597 Love Is Here And Now You're Gone/There's No Stopping Us Now ... 12
67 Tamla Motown TMG 597 Love Is Here And Now You're Gone/There's No Stopping Us Now (DJ copy) ... 70
67 Tamla Motown TMG 607 The Happening/All I Know About You ... 12
67 Tamla Motown TMG 607 The Happening/All I Know About You (DJ copy) ... 75

(The singles listed above are credited to Supremes.)

67 Tamla Motown TMG 616 Reflections/Going Down For The Third Time ... 12
67 Tamla Motown TMG 616 Reflections/Going Down For The Third Time (DJ copy) ... 60
67 Tamla Motown TMG 632 In And Out Of Love/I Guess I'll Always Love You ... 12
67 Tamla Motown TMG 632 In And Out Of Love/I Guess I'll Always Love You (DJ copy) ... 40
68 Tamla Motown TMG 650 Forever Came Today/Time Changes Things ... 10
68 Tamla Motown TMG 650 Forever Came Today/Time Changes Things (DJ copy) ... 40
68 Tamla Motown TMG 662 Some Things You Never Get Used To/You've Been So Wonderful To Me ... 10
68 Tamla Motown TMG 662 Some Things You Never Get Used To/You've Been So Wonderful To Me (DJ copy) ... 40
68 Tamla Motown TMG 677 Love Child/Will This Be The Day? ... 8
68 Tamla Motown TMG 677 Love Child/Will This Be The Day? (DJ copy) ... 40
68 Tamla Motown PSRS 317 Love Child (special Royal Command Performance promo sent to journalists with Ken East "talking invite" and Love Child playing in the background) ... 70
69 Tamla Motown TMG 695 I'm Living In Shame/I'm So Glad I Got Somebody (Like You Around) ... 10
69 Tamla Motown TMG 695 I'm Living In Shame/I'm So Glad I Got Somebody (Like You Around) (DJ copy) . 40
69 Tamla Motown TMG 704 No Matter What Sign You Are/The Young Folks ... 8
69 Tamla Motown TMG 704 No Matter What Sign You Are/The Young Folks (DJ copy) ... 35
69 Tamla Motown TMG 721 Someday We'll Be Together/He's My Sunny Boy ... 7
69 Tamla Motown TMG 721 Someday We'll Be Together/He's My Sunny Boy (DJ copy) ... 35

(The singles listed above are credited to Diana Ross & Supremes)

70 Tamla Motown TMG 735 Up The Ladder To The Roof/Bill, When Are You Coming Back ... 7
70 Tamla Motown TMG 735 Up The Ladder To The Roof/Bill, When Are You Coming Back (DJ copy) ... 30
70 Tamla Motown TMG 747 Everybody's Got The Right To Love/But I Love You More ... 8
70 Tamla Motown TMG 747 Everybody's Got The Right To Love/But I Love You More (DJ copy) ... 25
71 Tamla Motown TMG 760 Stoned Love/Shine On Me ... 7
71 Tamla Motown TMG 760 Stoned Love/Shine On Me (DJ copy) ... 30
71 Tamla Motown TMG 782 Nathan Jones/Happy (Is A Bumpy Road) ... 7
71 Tamla Motown TMG 782 Nathan Jones/Happy (Is A Bumpy Road) (DJ copy) ... 30

(The singles listed above are credited to Supremes and do not feature Diana Ross.)

EPs

65 Tamla Motown TME 2008 THE SUPREMES HITS (with flipback sleeve & push-out centre) ... 30
65 Tamla Motown TME 2008 THE SUPREMES HITS ... 35
66 Tamla Motown TME 2011 SHAKE (EP) ... 70

LPs

64 Stateside SL 10109 MEET THE SUPREMES ... 40
65 Tamla Motown TML 11002 WITH LOVE - FROM US TO YOU ... 50

MINT VALUE £

65	Tamla Motown TML 11012	WE REMEMBER SAM COOKE	50
65	Tamla Motown TML 11018	THE SUPREMES SING COUNTRY, WESTERN AND POP	50
65	Tamla Motown TML 11020	MORE HITS BY THE SUPREMES	30
66	T. Motown STML 11026	THE SUPREMES AT THE COPA (stereo)	25
66	T. Motown (S)TML 11028	I HEAR A SYMPHONY	25
66	T. Motown (S)TML 11039	SUPREMES A-GO GO (mono)	25
67	T. Motown STML 11047	THE SUPREMES SING MOTOWN (stereo)	25
67	T. Motown STML 11054	THE SUPREMES SING RODGERS AND HART (stereo)	25

(The LPs listed above are credited to Supremes, flipback sleeves.)

68	T. Motown (S)TML 11063	GREATEST HITS (stereo/mono, original pressing with flipback laminated sleeve)	15
68	T. Motown (S)TML 11070	'LIVE' AT LONDON'S TALK OF THE TOWN (mono/stereo)	18
68	T. Motown (S)TML 11073	REFLECTIONS (mono/stereo)	25
69	T. Motown TML 11088	SING & PERFORM FUNNY GIRL (mono)	20
69	T. Motown STML 11088	SING & PERFORM FUNNY GIRL (stereo)	20
69	T. Motown TML 11095	LOVE CHILD (mono)	25
69	T. Motown STML 11095	LOVE CHILD (stereo)	20
69	T. Motown TML 11114	LET THE SUNSHINE IN (mono)	25
69	T. Motown STML 11114	LET THE SUNSHINE IN (stereo)	25
70	T. Motown TML 11137	CREAM OF THE CROP (mono)	20
70	T. Motown STML 11137	CREAM OF THE CROP (stereo)	20

(The LPs listed above are credited to Diana Ross & Supremes. All the albums listed above were originally issued with flipback sleeves; later pressings are worth two-third of this value)

70	Tamla Motown STML 11157	RIGHT ON (as Supremes)	15
71	Tamla Motown STML 11189	TOUCH (LP, as Supremes)	15
73	T. Motown STML 11222	PRODUCED AND ARRANGED BY JIMMY WEBB (LP, as Supremes)	15

SUPREMES & FOUR TOPS

71	Tamla Motown TMG 777	River Deep, Mountain High/It's Gotta Be A Miracle (This Thing Called Love)	7
71	Tamla Motown TMG 793	You Gotta Have Love In Your Heart/I'm Glad About It	7
71	T. Motown STML 11179	THE SUPREMES AND THE FOUR TOPS - MAGNIFICENT 7 (LP)	18

DIANA ROSS & THE SUPREMES & THE TEMPTATIONS

69	Tamla Motown TMG 685	I'm Gonna Make You Love Me/A Place In The Sun	7
69	Tamla Motown TMG 709	I Second That Emotion/The Way You Do The Things You Do	7
70	Tamla Motown TMG 730	Why (Must We Fall In Love)/Uptight (Everything Is Alright)	8
69	T. Motown TML 11096	DIANA ROSS & THE SUPREMES JOIN THE TEMPTATIONS (LP, mono)	20
69	T. Motown STML 11096	DIANA ROSS & THE SUPREMES JOIN THE TEMPTATIONS (LP, stereo)	18
69	T. Motown (S)TML 11110	THE ORIGINAL SOUNDTRACK FROM TCB (LP, gatefold laminated sleeve)	20
70	T. Motown STML 11122	TOGETHER (LP, flipback sleeve)	15

SUPREME WARRIOR

83	Supreme Warrior SW001	Treading The Tightrope/Mad & Cynical	50

ADAM SURF & PEBBLE BEACH BAND

76	Paladin PAL 3	Fun Fun Fun/Blue Surf	10

SURFARIS

63	London HLD 9751	Wipe Out/Surfer Joe	15
63	Brunswick 05894	Waikiki Run/Point Panic	15
64	Brunswick 05902	Scatter Shield/Bat Man	15
66	Dot DS 26756	Wipe Out/Surfer Joe (reissue)	10
63	London RE-D 1405	WIPE OUT (EP)	70
63	London HA-D 8110	WIPE OUT (LP)	65
63	Brunswick LAT 8561	THE SURFARIS PLAY (LP, mono)	50
63	Brunswick STA 8561	THE SURFARIS PLAY (LP, stereo)	60
64	Brunswick LAT 8567	HIT CITY '64 (LP, mono)	50
64	Brunswick STA 8567	HIT CITY '64 (LP, stereo)	60
64	Brunswick LAT 8582	FUN CITY (LP)	60
65	Brunswick LAT 8605	HIT CITY '65 (LP)	60
65	Brunswick LAT 8631	IT AIN'T ME BABE (LP, mono)	50
65	Brunswick STA 8631	IT AIN'T ME BABE (LP, stereo)	60
66	Dot DLP 3535	WIPE OUT (LP, reissue)	25
76	MCA MCF 2761	SURFERS RULE (LP)	15
77	MCA Coral CDL 8050	GONE WITH THE WAVE (LP)	15
87	MCA MCL 1842	WIPE OUT - THE SINGLES ALBUM 1963-1967 (LP, withdrawn)	35

SURFERS

59	Vogue V 9147	Mambo Jambo/ALAN KALANI: A Touch Of Pink	10

LES SURFS

64	RCA RCA 1432	Just For The Boy/Stop	10
65	RCA RCA 1461	Go Your Way/Chained To A Memory	7
67	Fontana TF 832	When I Tell You (That I Love You)/I Want To Be Free	6

SURGEONS

79	Surgery S-100	Sid Never Did It/Breaking Rocks On Ricker's Island	50

SURGICAL SUPPORTS

81	Industrious Youth CONSTRUCT 2	WITHDRAWN FOR DISPOSAL EP	30

JOHN SURMAN (Trio)

(see also Morning Glory, Trio, Mike Westbook, John McLaughlin, Alan Skidmore/Mike Osborne/John Surman)

69	Deram DM 224	Obeah Wedding/Can't Stop The Carnival	40
68	Deram DML/SML 1030	JOHN SURMAN (LP)	80
69	Deram DML-R/SML-R 1045	HOW MANY CLOUDS CAN YOU SEE? (LP)	100
70	Futura GER 12	ALORS! (LP)	45
71	Dawn DNLS 3006	THE TRIO (LP, with Stu Martin, poster)	70
71	Dawn DNLS 3018	WHERE FORTUNE SMILES (LP, with insert, with John McLaughlin, Karl Berger, Stu Martin & Dave Holland)	40
71	Dawn DNLS 3022	CONFLAGRATION (LP)	60

MINT VALUE £

71 Deram SML 1094 TALES OF THE ALGONQUIN (LP, with John Warren) . . . 90
72 Island HELP 10 WESTERING HOME (LP) . . . 20
73 Island ILPS 9237 MORNING GLORY (LP) . . . 20

SURPLUS STOCK
79 Outatune OUT 7911 Spiv/Vips (p/s) . . . 7

SURPRISE SISTERS
76 Good Earth GD1 Seashore/La Booga Rooga . . . 8

SURPRISES
79 Dead Dog DEAD 01 Jeremy Thorpe Is Innocent/Flying Attack/Little Sir Echo (p/s) . . . 35

SURVIVORS
(see also The Beach Boys)
79 Capitol PSR 436 Pamela Jean/After The Game (Credits the Beach Boys on p/s, Survivors on disc) . . 10

SURVIVORS
65 Rio R 55 Take Charge/Ska-Ology . . . 10
65 Rio R 70 Rawhide Ska/OWEN GRAY: Girl I Want You . . . 10

SUSIE
71 Decca F 13217 I Feel The Earth Move/We Are All The Same . . . 8

SUSPECT
71 Decca FR 13218 Mariooka/Belinda . . . 20

SUSPECT
93 Union Hall UH002 Under Suspicion (12") . . . 12
94 Union Hall UH004 BURY THE BULLSHIT (EP) . . . 12
96 Move MV 7021-1 THE UNDERGROUND STRIKES BACK (LP) . . . 12

SUSSED
79 Shoestring LACE 002 I Like You/Tango/The Perv (p/s) . . . 15
80 Graduate GRAD 7 I've Got Me A Parka/Myself, Myself And I Repeated (p/s, paper labels; later reissued [1986] with silver labels) . . . 6

SUSSED
(see also Savages, Meteors, Led Zeppelin, Cliff Bennett & Rebel Rousers, Circles, Nero & Gladiators, Neil Christian & Crusaders)

(SCREAMING) LORD SUTCH (& THE SAVAGES)
(see also Savages, Meteors, Led Zeppelin, Cliff Bennett & Rebel Rousers, Circles, Nero & Gladiators, Neil Christian & Crusaders)
61 HMV POP 953 Till The Following Night/Good Golly Miss Molly . . . 30
63 Decca F 11598 Jack The Ripper/Don't You Just Know It . . . 20
63 Decca F 11747 I'm A Hog For You/Monster In Black Tights . . . 20
64 Oriole CB 1944 She's Fallen In Love With A Monster Man/Bye Bye Baby . . . 50
64 Oriole CB 1962 Dracula's Daughter/Come Back Baby . . . 50
65 CBS 201767 The Train Kept A-Rollin'/Honey Hush (as Lord Sutch) . . . 50
66 CBS 202080 The Cheat/Black And Hairy . . . 50
70 Atlantic 584 321 Cause I Love You/Thumping Beat . . . 12
70 Atlantic 2091 006 Cause I Love You/Thumping Beat (reissue) . . . 6
70 Atlantic 2091 017 Election Fever/Rock The Election . . . 10
72 Atlantic K 10221 Gotta Keep A-Rockin'/Flashing Lights/Hands Of Jack The Ripper . . . 10
76 SRT SRTS 76361 Monster Ball/Rang-Tang-A-Lang . . . 8
76 SRT SRTS 76375 I Drink To Your Health Marie (Parts 1 & 2) . . . 8
77 Decca F 13697 Jack The Ripper/I'm A Hog For You . . . 5
80 Ace SW 70 All Black A Hairy/London Rocker/Oh Well . . . 6
81 Ridgemount RMR 45 010 LOONABILLY (EP, p/s, with bonus "Loon Party" single) . . . 10
70 Atlantic 2400 008 LORD SUTCH AND HIS HEAVY FRIENDS (LP) . . . 25
72 Atlantic K 40313 HANDS OF JACK THE RIPPER (LP, as Lord Sutch & Heavy Friends) . . . 25
81 Ace MAD 1 THE METEORS MEET SCREAMING LORD SUTCH (mini-LP, 1 side each, stickered cartoon print on plain grey card sleeve, 1,000 only) . . . 100
82 Ace CHA 65 ROCK A HORROR (LP, gatefold) . . . 15

SUTHERLAND BROTHERS BAND
71 Island ILPS 9181 THE SUTHERLAND BROTHERS BAND (LP, blue inner) . . . 15

GLEN SUTTON
(see under Murray Kellum)

SUZANNE
77 Ring O' 2017 108 Born On Hallowe'en/Like No One Else (in promo p/s) . . . 25
77 Ring O' 2017 108 Born On Hallowe'en/Like No One Else . . . 12
78 Ring O' 2017 111 You Really Got A Hold On Me/You Could Be Right This Time . . . 10
78 Ring O' 2017 115 single (unreleased) . . . 0

SUZI & BIG DEE IRWIN
(see also Big Dee Irwin)
66 Polydor BM 65715 Ain't That Lovin' You Baby/I Can't Get Over You . . . 15

PAT SUZUKI
60 RCA RCA 1171 I Enjoy Being A Girl/Sunday . . . 10

SUZY & THE RED STRIPES
(see also Paul McCartney [& Wings])
77 A&M AMS 7461 Seaside Woman/B-side To The Seaside (yellow vinyl, die-cut p/s) . . . 12
79 A&M AMSP 7461 Seaside Woman/B-side To The Seaside (yellow vinyl, die-cut p/s, in box set with badge & 10 'saucy' mini-postcards) . . . 40
80 A&M AMS 7548 Seaside Woman/B-side To The Seaside (reissue, cartoon p/s, as Linda McCartney alias Suzy & Red Stripes) . . . 10
80 A&M AMSP 7548 Seaside Woman/B-side To The Seaside (12", as Linda McCartney alias Suzy & Red Stripes) . . . 12
86 EMI EMI 5572 Seaside Woman/B-side To The Seaside (p/s) . . . 6
86 EMI 12EMI 5572 Seaside Woman/B-side To The Seaside (12", p/s) . . . 10

			MINT VALUE £
SVANTE			
68	United Artists UP 2224	Baby I Need Your Lovin'/Just One Word From You	5
SVENSK			
(see also Jason Paul)			
67	Page One POF 036	Dream Magazine/Getting Old	25
67	Page One POF 050	You/All I Have To Do Is Dream	18
SWALLOWS			
56	Vogue EPV 1113	RHYTHM AND BLUES (EP, 2 tracks by Dominoes)	350
SWALLOWS with SONNY THOMPSON			
(see also Sonny Thompson & His Rhythm & Blues Band)			
52	Vogue V 2136	Roll, Roll Pretty Baby/It Ain't The Meat (78)	50
SWAMP DOGG			
(see also Jerry Williams, Brooks & Jerry)			
74	Island USA 002	Did I Come Back Too Soon/I Wouldn't Leave Here	5
72	Mojo 2916 014	TOTAL DESTRUCTION TO YOUR MIND (LP)	12
SWAMPFOXX			
72	Polydor 2058251	I've Got A Thing About You Baby/On Your Side	5
BILLY SWAN			
75	Monument MNT 80615	I CAN HELP (LP)	15
75	CBS 69162	ROCK & ROLL MOON (LP)	12
76	Monument MNT 81387	BILLY SWAN (LP)	12
SWAN ARCADE			
73	Trailer LER 2032	SWAN ARCADE (LP)	18
84	Fellside FE 037	TOGETHER FOREVER (LP)	18
SWANEE RIVER BOYS			
54	Parlophone CMSP 7	Do You Believe/Gloryland Boogie (export issue)	15
54	Parlophone DP 385	Was He Quiet Or Did He Cry/I Have Desire (78, export issue)	12
BETTYE SWANN			
(see also Sam Dees & Bettye Swann)			
67	CBS 2942	Make Me Yours/I Will Not Cry	60
67	CBS 2942	Make Me Yours/I Will Not Cry (DJ copy)	100
67	CBS 2942	Make Me Yours/I Will Not Cry (DJ copy in p/s)	150
69	Capitol CL 15586	Don't Touch Me/(My Heart Is) Closed For The Season	30
72	Atlantic K 10174	Victim Of A Foolish Heart/Cold Day In Hell	10
72	Atlantic K 10273	Today I Started Loving You Again/I'd Rather Go Blind	6
73	Mojo 2092 059	Make Me Yours/I Will Not Cry (reissue)	6
75	Atlantic K 10622	Doing It For The One I Love/All The Way In Or All The Way Out	5
75	Contempo CS 9019	Make Me Yours/I Will Not Cry (reissue)	5
76	Atlantic K 10851	Heading In The Right Direction/Be Strong Enough To Hold On	5
RUTH SWANN			
75	Spark SRL 1124	Tainted Love/Boy, You'd Better Move On	5
SWANS			
63	Stateside SS 224	He's Mine/You Better Be A Good Girl Now	40
64	Cameo Parkway C 302	The Boy With The Beatle Hair/Please Hurry Home	30
SWANS			
86	K.422/Some Bizzare KDE 312	A Screw (Holy Money)/Blackmail/A Screw (12", p/s)	8
88	Product Inc. 12PROD 23	Love Will Tear Us Apart (Red Version)/Trust Me/Love Will Tear Us Apart (black Version)/Our Love Lies (12", black vinyl, p/s)	20
88	Product Inc. PROD 23	Love Will Tear Us Apart/Trust Me (red vinyl, 750 only, p/s)	10
84	K.422/Some Bizzare KCC 1	COP (LP, with inner)	25
85	Zensor NDO 3	FILTH (LP)	30
86	K. 422/Some Bizzare KCC 2	GREED (LP, with inner)	15
86	K. 422/Some Bizzare KCC 3	HOLY MONEY (LP)	15
87	Product Inc. 33PROD 17	CHILDREN OF GOD (2-LP)	20
86	no label BURN ONE	PUBLIC CASTRATION IS A GOOD IDEA (2-LP)	20
89	MCA MCG 6047	THE BURNING WORLD (LP, with insert)	12
95	Young God YGLP 004	BODY TO BODY, JOB TO JOB (LP)	20
95	Young God YGLP 005B	LOVE OF LIFE (LP, in box)	25
BENRICE SWANSON			
65	Chess CRS 8008	Lying Awake/Baby I'm Yours	30
65	Chess CRS 8008	Lying Awake/Baby I'm Yours (DJ copy)	50
DAVE SWARBRICK			
(see also Martin Carthy & Dave Swarbrick, Fairport Convention, Young Tradition, Vashti Bunyan, Ian Campbell)			
67	Bounty BYI 6030	RAGS, REELS AND AIRS (LP, with Martin Carthy & Diz Disley)	40
67	Polydor Special 236 514	RAGS, REELS AND AIRS (LP, reissue, with Martin Carthy & Diz Disley)	25
76	Transatlantic TRA 337	SWARBRICK (LP)	12
77	Transatlantic TRA 341	SWARBRICK 2 (LP)	12
78	Sonet SNTF 763	LIFT THE LID AND LISTEN (LP)	12
78	Sonet SNTF 764	THE CEILIDH ALBUM (LP, as Dave Swarbrick & Friends)	12
81	Logo LOGO 1029	SMIDDYBURN (LP)	12
DAVE SWARBRICK & SIMON NICOL			
(see also Dave Swarbrick, Fairport Convention, Young Tradition)			
81	White Bear WBR 001	LIVE AT THE WHITE BEAR (LP)	15
83	Woodworm WR 006	CLOSE TO THE WIND (LP)	12
SWARBRIGG (PLUS TWO)			
75	MCA MCA 179	That's What Friends Are For/Love Is	6

MINT VALUE £

ROSALYN SWEAT & PARAGONS
(see also Paragons)

73	Duke DU 160	Blackbird Singing/Always	8
74	Horse HRLP 703	BLACKBIRD SINGING (LP)	15

SWE-DANES
(see also Alice Babsi)

60	Warner Bros WB 7	Scandinavian Shuffle/Hot Toddy	10
60	Warner Bros WB 22	Swe-Dane Shuffle/At A Georgia Camp Meeting	6
61	Warner Bros WEP 6017	THE SWE-DANES (EP; mono)	20
61	Warner Bros SWEP 2017	THE SWE-DANES (EP; stereo)	25

SWEDEN THROUGH THE AGES
(see also Billy MacKenzie)

86	Snappy SW 001	IT HELPS TO CRY EP (12", p/s)	12

SWEDISH MODERN JAZZ GROUP

61	Tempo TAP 31	SAX APPEAL (LP)	220

SWEENEY'S MEN
(see also Gay & Terry Woods, Dr. Strangely Strange)

67	Pye 7N 17312	Old Maid In The Garrett/Derby Ram	10
68	Pye 7N 17459	Waxies Dargle/Old Woman In Cotton	10
69	Transatlantic TRASP 19	Sullivan's John/Rattlin' Roarin' Willy	8
68	Transatlantic TRA 170	SWEENEY'S MEN (LP)	90
69	Transatlantic TRA 200	THE TRACKS OF SWEENEY (LP)	90
76	Transatlantic TRASAM 37	SWEENEY'S MEN (LP, reissue)	20
77	Transatlantic TRASAM 40	THE TRACKS OF SWEENEY (LP, reissue)	18

SWEENY BEAN

72	Sonet SON 2028	Rock 'N' Roll Wedding/Overcoat	8

JIM SWEENY

58	Philips PB 811	The Midnight Hour/Till The Right One Comes Along	20

SWEENY TODD

70s	London L2616	Shut Up/Wastin' Time	20
76	London HLU 10540	Roxy Roller/Rue De Chance	8

JIMMY SWEEP
(see also Status Quo)

81	Tamarin TAM 3	London Town/Bridgetown Girls (written, produced by & feat. Alan Lancaster)	10
82	PRT 7P 233	London Town/Bridgetown Girls (reissue)	8

SWEEPERS

73	Warner Bros K16318	Harlem Song/Something's Real	5

SWEET
(see also Brian Connolly, Mayfield's Mule, Elastic Band, Andy Scott)

SINGLES

68	Fontana TF 958	Slow Motion/It's Lonely Out There	400
69	Parlophone R 5803	The Lollipop Man/Time	100
70	Parlophone R 5826	All You'll Ever Get From Me/The Juicer	40
70	Parlophone R 5848	Get On The Line/Mr. McGallagher	70
71	RCA RCA 2051	Funny Funny/You're Not Wrong For Loving Me	12
71	RCA RCA 2087	Co Co/Done Me Wrong, All Right	5
71	Parlophone R 5902	All You'll Ever Get From Me/The Juicer (reissue)	15
71	RCA RCA 2121	Alexander Graham Bell/Spotlight	5
73	RCA RCA 2403	Ballroom Blitz/Rock & Roll Disgrace (mispressed at wrong speed, 49rpm; matrix: 2403-A-1E)	15
74	RCA RCA 2480	Turn It Down/Someone Else Will	5
75	RCA RCA 2578	Action/Sweet FA	5
76	RCA RCA 2541o	The Lies In Your Eyes/Cockroach	5
76	RCA RCA 2748	Lost Angels/Funk It Up	5
77	RCA PB 5011	Fever Of Love/A Distinct Lack Of Ancient	6
77	RCA PB 5046	Stairway To The Stars/Why Don't You Do It To Me	8
78	Polydor POSP 5	California Nights/Show Me The Way (unreleased)	0
79	Polydor POSP 36	Call Me/Why Don't You	7
79	Polydor POSP 73	Big Apple Waltz/Why Don't You	35
80	RCA PE 5226	Fox On The Run/Hellraiser/Ballroom Blitz/Blockbuster (EP, p/s)	15
80	Polydor POSP 131	Give That Lady Some Respect/Tall Girls	7
80	Polydor POSP 160	Sixties Man/Tall Girls	5
80	Polydor POSP 160	Sixties Man/Oh Yeah	15
80	Polydor POSP 160	Sixties Man/Oh Yeah (mispressing, B-side plays "Tall Girls")	20
81	RCA GOLD 524	Blockbuster/Hellraiser (pink 'Golden Groove' p/s)	8
81	RCA GOLD 551	Ballroom Blitz/Wig Wam Bam (pink 'Golden Groove' p/s)	8
84	Anagram ANA 27	The Sixteens/Action (p/s)	10
84	Anagram ANA 28	It's The Sweetest Mix/Fox On The Run (p/s)	5
84	Anagram 12 ANA 28	It's The Sweetest Mix/Fox On The Run (12" p/s; matrix no. 12 ANA 28 AI)	8
84	Anagram 12 ANA 28	It's The Sweetest Mix/Fox On The Run (12" p/s; matrix no. 12 ANA 28.A)	8
85	Anagram ANA 29	Sweet 2th - The Wig Wam-Willy Mix/The Teen Action Mix (p/s)	8
85	Anagram ANA 29	Sweet 2th - The Wig Wam-Willy Mix/The Teen Action Mix (12", p/s)	8
89	RCA PB 43337	Wig Wam Bam/Little Willy (p/s)	12

LPs

71	MFP MFP 5248	GIMME DAT DING (1 side each by Sweet & Pipkins)	12
71	RCA SF 8288	FUNNY HOW SWEET CO-CO CAN BE	25
74	RCA LPL 15039	SWEET FANNY ADAMS	12
74	RCA LPL 15080	DESOLATION BOULEVARD (LP, gatefold sleeve)	15
75	RCA SPC 0001	STRUNG UP (2xLP)	18
76	RCA RS 1036	GIVE US A WINK	12
77	RCA PL 25072	OFF THE RECORD (gatefold, with inner sleeve)	15
78	RCA Camden CDS 1168	THE SWEET	12
79	Polydor POLD 5022	CUT ABOVE THE REST (with inner sleeve)	15

MINT VALUE £

70s	RCA SF 8316	THE SWEET'S BIGGEST HITS (LP)	12
80	Polydor POLS 1021	WATER'S EDGE	18
82	Polydor 2311 1179	IDENTITY CRISIS	22
84	Anagram GRAM 16	SWEET SIXTEEN (LP)	15
84	Anagram P GRAM 16	SWEET SIXTEEN (LP, picture disc)	25

SWEET AIR

70	Chime CH 1	Pictures In A Puddle/Sally FInne	170

SWEET AROMA

73	Rhino RNO 113	Happiness/Rock Reggae (demos or stock copies)	5

SWEET CHARIOT

69	MCA MK 5010	Heavenly Road/Wish I Were A Child	8
73	Columbia DB 8999	When I'm A Kid/Mozart '73	8
70s	T.O.G. SCEP 001	Angelina/Young At Heart/America	8
72	De Wolfe DWLP 3230	SWEET CHARIOT & FRIENDS (LP, library issue only)	40

SWEET CHARLES

88	Urban URBLP 9	FOR SWEET PEOPLE FROM SWEET CHARLES (LP)	12

SWEET CONFUSION

(see also Stranger & Patsy)

69	Escort ES 809	Elizabeth Serenade/Don At Rest	8
69	Escort ES 812	Hotter Scorcher/Conquer Lion	8

SWEET CORPORALS

59	Top Rank JAR 217	The Same Old Army/Warm And Willing	5

SWEET CREAM

78	Ember EMBS 368	I Don't Know What I'd Do.Skunk Funk	8

SWEET DREAMS

(see also Polly Brown, Jimmy Thomas)

74	Bradleys BRADL 1008	WE'LL BE YOUR MUSIC (LP)	15

SWEET FEELING

(see also Rupert's People)

67	Columbia DB 8195	All So Long Ago/Charles Brown	180

SWEETHEARTS

65	Blue Beat BB 389	Sit Down And Cry (actually with Clinton & Rufus)/PRINCE BUSTER: Ghost Dance	80

HARRY SWEETING

68	Coxsone CSL 8012	FROM JAMAICA WITH LOVE (LP)	100

SWEET INSPIRATIONS

(see also Cissy Houston)

67	Atlantic 584 117	Why (Am I Treated So Bad)/I Don't Want To Go On Without You	10
67	Atlantic 584 132	Let It Be Me/When Something Is Wrong With My Baby	10
68	Atlantic 584 167	Sweet Inspiration/I'm Blue	10
68	Atlantic 584 233	What The World Needs Now Is Love/You Really Didn't Mean It	10
69	Atlantic 584 241	Sweet Inspiration/I'm Blue	5
69	Atlantic 584 279	Sweets For My Sweet/Get A Little Older	5
70	Atlantic 584 312	(Gotta Find) A Brand New Lover (Parts 1 & 2)	5
71	Atlantic 2091 073	Evidence/Change Me Not	5
68	Atlantic 587/588 090	THE SWEET INSPIRATIONS (LP)	20
69	Atlantic 587/588 137	WHAT THE WORLD NEEDS NOW IS LOVE (LP)	20
69	Atlantic 587/588 194	SWEETS FOR MY SWEET (LP)	20
70	Atlantic 2465 003	SWEET SWEET SOUL (LP)	20

SWEET JESUS

91	Chapter 22 CHAP 63	Cat Thing/Honey Loving Honey/Peach/Baby Blue (12" EP)	10

SWEET LITTLE BUNTY

75	Ackee ACK 540	I (Who Have Nothing)/Oh Me Oh My	6

SWEET PAIN

(see also Dick Heckstall-Smith)

71	United Artists UP 35268	Timber Gibbs/Chain Up The Devil	5
69	Mercury 20146 SMCL	SWEET PAIN (LP, laminated gatefold, black/silver label)	150

SWEET PLUM

69	Middle Earth MDS 103	Lazy Day/Let No Man Steal Your Thyme	30
70	Middle Earth MDS 105	Set The Wheels In Motion/Catch A Cloud	30

SWEET REACTION

72	Satril SAT 5	Come Back My Dream/Call Me Maria	10

SWEET REVENGE

80s	SRS SRS 15	Feel The Bullets Bite/Inside Your Head	125

SWEET SAVAGE

(see also Dio, Whitesnake)

81	Park PRK 1001	Take No Prisoners/Killing TIme (p/s, red and yellow label)	60
81	Park PRK 1001	Take No Prisoners/Killing TIme (p/s, black and yellow label)	40
80s	Crashed CAR 48	Straight Through The Heart/Teaser (no p/s)	150
80s	private pressing	The Raid/Prosecutors Of Greed (possibly unreleased)	50

SWEETSHOP

(see also Mark Wirtz)

68	Parlophone R 5707	Barefoot And Tiptoe/Lead The Way	25

SWEET SLAG

71	President PTLS 1042	TRACKING WITH CLOSE-UPS (LP)	100

SWEET THUNDER

78	Fantasy FTC 158	Everybody's Singin' Love Songs/Joyful Noise	5

MINT VALUE £

SWEET THURSDAY
(see also Nicky Hopkins, Mark-Almond)

69	Polydor 2310 051	SWEET THURSDAY (LP)	25

SWEET TOOTH

90	Staindrop/Earache MOSH 26	SOFT WHITE UNDERBELLY (LP)	12

SWEGAS

70	Trend 6099 001	What You Gonna Do/There Is Nothing In It	10
71	Trend 6480 002	CHILD OF LIGHT (LP, gatefold sleeve)	20

SWELL

92	Mean MEAN LP 002	...WELL? (LP, marble vinyl)	15
94	Beggars Banquet ARBLP 6	41 (LP)	12

SWELL MAPS
(see also Cult Figures, Nikki Sudden, Steve Treatment, Phones Sportsman Band, Epic Soundtracks, Metrophase, Last Bandits)

78	Rather GEAR ONE	Read About Seymour/Ripped And Torn/Black Velvet (p/s)	15
79	Rough Trade RT 010/Rather GEAR ONE MK. 2	Read About Seymour/Ripped And Torn/Black Velvet (p/s, reissue, different back sleeve)	7
79	R. Trade RT 012/GEAR 3	Dresden Style/Mystery Track/Ammunition Train/Full Moon (Dub) (p/s)	7
79	R. Trade RT 021/GEAR 6	Real Shocks/English Verse/Monlogues (p/s, 2 different colours)	8
79	R. Trade RT 036/GEAR 7	Let's Build A Car/Big Maz In The Country/?Then Poland (p/s)	7
81	Rough Trade RT 012/Rather GEAR 3	Dresden Style (new vocal)/Ammunition Train/Full Moon (Dub) (p/s, reissue, different back sleeve)	7
79	Rough Trade ROUGH 2/ Rather TROY 1	A TRIP TO MARINEVILLE (LP, with inner sleeve, with bonus EP in die-cut sleeve [Rather GEAR FIVE])	40
79	Rough Trade ROUGH 2/ Rather TROY 1	A TRIP TO MARINEVILLE (LP, with inner sleeve, without bonus EP in die-cut sleeve [Rather GEAR FIVE])	25
80	Rough Trade ROUGH 15	SWELL MAPS IN 'JANE FROM OCCUPIED EUROPE' (LP)	30
81	Rough Trade ROUGH 21	WHATEVER HAPPENS NEXT? (2-LP)	18
84	Rough Trade ROUGH 41	SWELL MAPS IN 'COLLISION TIME' (LP)	12

SWERVEDRIVER

91	Creation CRE 079T	SON OF MUSTANG FORD EP (12")	8
91	Creation CRE 088T	RAVE DOWN EP (12")	8
91	Creation CRELP 093	RAISE (LP, with free 7")	25
91	Creation CRELP 093	RAISE (LP, without free 7")	20
93	Creation CRELP 143	MEZCAL HEAD (LP)	20
95	Creation CRELP 157	EJECTOR SEAT RESERVATION (LP, with free 7")	20
95	Creation CRELP 157	EJECTOR SEAT RESERVATION (LP, without free 7")	15

ANTHONY SWETE

69	RCA RCA 1905	Backfield in Motion/Soul Deep	8

JONATHAN SWIFT

71	CBS 64412	INTROVERT (LP, side opening gatefold, nude cover)	18
72	CBS 64751	SONGS (LP, with lyric insert)	15

TUFTY SWIFT

77	Free Reed FRR 017	HOW TO MAKE A BAKEWELL TART (LP, with booklet)	25
85	Shark SHARK 04	YOU'LL NEVER DIE FOR LOVE (LP, private pressing)	15

ALAN SWIMMER & DEE DAVIDSON

70s	Fab FAB 242	Take Me Back To Jamaica/Thousands Of Children	5

STEVE SWINDELLS
(see also Hawkwind)

74	RCA LPL1 5057	MESSAGES (LP, with insert)	12

SWINDLEFOLK

68	Deroy	A-ROVIN' (LP, private pressing)	75
69	Deroy	SWINDLED (LP, private pressing)	75

SWINGERS
(see also Spectres, Rich Kids)

81	Magnet MAG 202	Be My Baby/Swinging	5

SWINGERS

60	Vogue V 9158	Love Makes The World Go Round/Jackie	20

SWINGERS

67	Blue Beat BB 379	Simpleton/FRANCIS: Warn The People	40

SWINGING BLUE JEANS
(see also Ray Ennis & Blue Jeans, Blue Jeans, Escorts, Terry Sylvester)

63	HMV POP 1170	It's Too Late Now/Think Of Me	15
63	HMV POP 1206	Do You Know/Angie	15
63	HMV POP 1242	Hippy Hippy Shake/Now I Must Go	5
64	HMV POP 1273	Good Golly Miss Molly/Shakin' Feelin'	5
64	HMV POP 1304	You're No Good/Don't You Worry About Me	5
64	HMV POP 1327	Promise You'll Tell Her/It's So Right	7
64	HMV POP 1375	It Isn't There/One Of These Days	7
65	HMV POP 1409	Make Me Know You're Mine/I've Got A Girl	10
65	HMV POP 1477	Crazy 'Bout My Baby/Good Lovin'	8
66	HMV POP 1501	Don't Make Me Over/What Can I Do Today	8
66	HMV POP 1533	Sandy/I'm Gonna Have You	15
66	HMV POP 1564	Rumours, Gossip, Words Untrue/Now The Summer's Gone	15
67	HMV POP 1596	Tremblin'/Something's Coming Along	18
67	HMV POP 1605	Don't Go Out Into The Rain/One Woman Man	18
64	HMV 7EG 8850	SHAKE WITH THE SWINGING BLUE JEANS (EP)	40
64	HMV 7EG 8868	YOU'RE NO GOOD MISS MOLLY (EP)	40
64	HMV CLP 1802	BLUE JEANS A' SWINGING (LP, mono)	60
64	HMV CSD 1570	BLUE JEANS A' SWINGING (LP, stereo)	75

MINT VALUE £

64	Regal SREG 1073	TUTTI FRUTTI (LP, export issue)	50
67	MFP MFP 1163	SWINGING BLUE JEANS (LP, reissue of HMV CLP 1802)	15
74	Dart BULL 1001	BRAND NEW AND FADED (LP)	18

SWINGING CATS

80	Two Tone CHS TT 14	Mantovani/Away (paper label, company sleeve)	7
80	Two Tone CHS TT 14	Mantovani/Away (silver plastic label, company sleeve)	15

SWINGIN' MEDALLIONS

66	Philips BF 1500	Double Shot Of My Baby's Love/Here It Comes Again	10
66	Philips BF 1515	She Drives Me Out Of My Mind/You Gotta Have Faith	10

SWINGING SOUL MACHINE

(see also Machine)

69	Polydor 56760	Spooky's Day Off/Nobody Wants You	15

SWORN LORD

90	Davy G DG003	The Vengeance Is Mine (12")	30

SWS

88	DTI MAC2	Boys From The Bec/Our Rhymes Are Fly (12")	25
90	Cue TCUE003	Overture/Empirical Expansions/Info Nation/Leaf In The Wind	18

SYD & JOE

72	Bullet BU 498	Three Combine/LES FOSTER: I'm The Nearest To Your Heart	5

SYDNEY (Crooks) ALL STARS

(see also Pioneers, Junior English, Sammy Morgan)

70	Bullet BU 436	The Return Of Batman/In Action	10
70	Bullet BU 437	Outer Space/Full Moon	30

ERIC SYKES & HATTIE JACQUES

(see also Eric & Hattie, Goons)

62	Decca F 11512	Doctor Kildare/Bedtime Story	5

JOHN SYKES

(see also Thin Lizzy, Phil Lynott, Tygers Of Pan Tang, Whitesnake)

82	MCA MCA 792	Please Don't Leave Me/(Instrumental) (with Phil Lynott, in p/s)	35
82	MCA MCA 792	Please Don't Leave Me/(Instrumental) (with Phil Lynott)	10

SYKES & MEDINA

69	CBS 4529	Everything's Fine Fine Fine/I Can Feel The Thickness	10

ROOSEVELT SYKES

(see also Robert Pete Williams)

50	Jazz Collector L 40	Three, Six And Nine/We Can Sell That Thing (78)	10
56	Vogue V 2389	Fine And Brown/Too Hot To Hold	75
56	Vogue V 2389	Fine And Brown/Too Hot To Hold (78)	30
56	Vogue V 2393	Walkin' This Boogie/Security Blues	75
56	Vogue V 2393	Walkin' This Boogie/Security Blues (78)	30
66	Delmark DJB 2	BACK TO THE BLUES (EP)	30
59	Encore ENC 183	BIG MAN OF THE BLUES (LP)	20
61	Columbia 33SX 1343	FACE TO FACE WITH THE BLUES (LP)	30
62	Columbia 33SX 1422	THE HONEYDRIPPER (LP, with Alexis Korner)	60
65	Bluesville BVLP 1006	THE RETURN OF ROOSEVELT SYKES (LP)	25
67	77' 77LEU 12-50	BLUES FROM BAR ROOMS (LP)	30
67	Riverside RLP 8819	MR SYKES' BLUES 1929-1932 (LP)	22
67	Ember EMB 3391	ROOSEVELT SYKES SINGS THE BLUES (LP)	20
71	Barclay 920 294	THE HONEYDRIPPERS' DUKE'S MIXTURE (LP)	15
70s	Delmark DL 607	HARD DRIVIN' BLUES (LP, blue label)	15

SYKO & CARIBS

64	Blue Beat BB 213	Do The Dog/Jenny	15
64	Blue Beat BB 223	Big Boy/Sugar Baby	15

SYLTE SISTERS

63	London HLU 9753	Summer Magic/Well it's Summertime	15

SYLVAIN SYLVAIN

(see also New York Dolls)

80	RCA PB 9500	Every Boy And Every Girl/Emily	5

SYLVAN

65	Columbia DB 7674	We Don't Belong/Life's Colours Have Gone	20

GOOD PAUL SYLVAN

70	Polydor 2001 090	Ophelia/Stop Making A Fool Of Me	6

C. SYLVESTER & PLANETS

64	Blue Beat BB 206	Going South/LITTLE JOYCE: Oh Daddy	12

ROLAND SYLVESTER

64	Carnival CV 7018	Grandfather's Clock/SANDRA MURRAY: Nervous	6

TERRY SYLVESTER

(see also Escorts, Swinging Blue Jeans, Hollies)

74	Polydor 2383 394	I BELIEVE (LP, with insert)	12

SYLVESTER'S JUKE BOX

73	CBS 8419	Juke Box/It's Because	45

SYLVIA

67	Fontana TF 884	Make Me A Woman/Without Your Love	10
68	Fontana TF 932	Down Hill/A Few Sweet Moments Of Love	10
73	London SHU 8453	PILLOW TALK	12

SYLVIA (U.S.)

68	Soul City SC 103	I Can't Help It/It's A Good Life	20
75	London HLU 10415	Pillow Talk/My Thing	7

MINT VALUE £

DAVID SYLVIAN

(See also Japan, Virginia Astley)

84	Virgin VSY 633	Red Guitar/Forbidden Colours (Version) (picture disc)	5
84	Virgin VS 717	Pulling Punches (7" Mix)/Backwaters (Remix) (p/s, with 3 postcards)	5
84	Virgin VSY 717	Pulling Punches (7" Mix)/Backwaters (Remix) (picture disc)	6
86	Virgin VSS 815	Taking The Veil/Answered Prayers (rectangular picture disc, stickered PVC sleeve)	8
88	Virgin CDT 23	Words With The Shaman: Part 1 - Ancient Evening/Part 2 - Incantation/ Part 3 - Awakening (Songs From The Tree Tops) (3" CD, gatefold card p/s)	12
89	Virgin VSCD 1221	Pop Song/A Brief Conversation Ending In Divorce/ The Stigma Of Childhood (Kin) (3" CD, card sleeve)	20
89	Virgin VSCDX 1221	Pop Song/A Brief Conversation Ending In Divorce/ The Stigma Of Childhood (Kin) (CD, presentation card pack, with discography)	12
85	Virgin SYL 1	ALCHEMY (Cassette)	12
89	Virgin DSCD 1	WEATHERBOX (5-CD box set, with poster & booklet)	100
04	Samadhisound SOUNDLP 1	BLEMISH (LP, gatefold sleeve, featuring Derek Bailey, 2,000 only)	60
87	Virgin V2471	SECRETS OF THE BEEHIVE (LP)	15

DAVID SYLVIAN & ROBERT FRIPP

93	Virgin VSC 1462	Jean The Birdman/Earthbound/Endgame (cassette, in slipcase)	10
94	Virgin DAMAGE 1	DAMAGE (gold CD in silver-coloured box)	20

SYLVIN & GLENROY

70	Torpedo TOR 25	What You Gonna Do 'Bout It/KEN JONES: Sad Mood	6

SYMARIP

(see under Seven Letters/Symrip, see also Pyramids)

SYMBOL

79	Art & Craft AC 001	Motherless Children/RANKING CARETAKER: Take It Away (12")	40
79	Kebra Nagast KH 04	Black Man's Word/Mr. Oppressor (12")	15

SYMBOLICS

76	Angen ANG 119	Tell Them Jah Jah/Version	8

SYMBOLS

(see also Johnny Milton & Condors)

65	Columbia DB 7459	One Fine Girl/Don't Go	10
65	Columbia DB 7664	You're My Girl/Why Do Fools Fall In Love	10
66	President PT 104	See You In September/To Make You Smile Again	8
66	President PT 113	Canadian Sunset/The Gentle Art Of Loving	6
67	President PT 128	You'd Better Get Used To Missing Her/Hideaway	6
67	President PT 144	Bye Bye Baby/The Things You Do To Me	10
67	President PT 173	(The Best Part Of) Breaking Up/Again	10
68	President PT 190	Lovely Way To Say Goodnight/Pretty City	18
68	President PT 216	Do I Love You/Schoolgirl	20
75	Crystal CR 7021	Canadian Sunset (Instrumental)/Canadian Sunset (Vocal Recording)	6
68	President PTL 1018	THE BEST PART OF THE SYMBOLS (LP)	25
72	CBS 7725	No No No/Woman	8

SYMON & PI

68	Parlophone R 5662	Sha La La La Lee/Baby Baby	25
68	Parlophone R 5719	Got To See The Sunrise/Love Is Happening To Me	12

DAVID SYMONDS

68	Philips BF 1652	Here Is The News/Don't Worry About A Thing	10

SYMPHONICS

73	Polydor 2058 341	Heaven Must Have Sent You/Using Me	15

SYMPHONIC SLAM

76	A&M AMLH 69023	SYMPHONIC SLAM (LP)	20

PAT SYMS

64	Oriole CB 1971	It's Got To Be You Or No One/Lost	7

SYLVIA SYMS

58	Brunswick 05771	The Night They Invented Champagne/The Nature Of Things	7

SYN

(see also Syndicats, Yes, Peter Banks)

67	Deram DM 130	Created By Clive/Grounded	120
67	Deram DM 145	14-Hour Technicolour Dream/Flowerman	100

SYNANTHESIA

69	RCA SF 8058	SYNANTHESIA (LP)	250

SYNCHROJAK

95	Ferox FER 014	SYNCHROJAK (12" EP, plain sleeve)	8
95	Ferox FER 108	PHAZE 11 (12" EP, plain sleeve)	8

SYNCHROMESH

80	Rok ROK XI/XII	October Friday/E.F. BAND: Another Day Gone (company die-cut sleeve)	40

SYNCOPATORS

61	Decca F 11359	Everything Stops For Tea/If I Had A Talking Picture Of You	7

SYNDICATE

(see also Astronauts)

79	Stevenage/ Rock Against Racism	One Way Or Another/I Want To Be Somebody/RESTRICTED HOURS: Getting Things Done/Still Living Out The Car Crash (white label, foldover p/s)	12

SYNDICATE

81	EMI 12EMI 5182	Dance You To The Ground/Step On The Gas (12")	35

SYNDICATE OF SOUND

66	Stateside SS 523	Little Girl/You	35

MINT VALUE £

66 Stateside SS 538 Rumours/The Upper Hand ... 18
66 Stateside S(S)L 10185 LITTLE GIRL (LP) ... 50

SYNDICATS
(see also Peter Banks, Ray Fenwick, Syn, Tomorrow, Yes)
64 Columbia DB 7238 Maybellene/True To Me ... 150
65 Columbia DB 7441 Howlin' For My Baby/What To Do ... 250
65 Columbia DB 7686 On The Horizon/Crawdaddy Simone ... 650
65 Columbia DB 7686 On The Horizon/Crawdaddy Simone (demos) ... 420

SYREETA
(see under Syreeta Wright)

SYRUP
70 Amity OTS 501 Gentlemen Joe's Sidewalk Café/Love Is Love ... 6

SYSTEM
82 Spiderleg SDL 4 THE WARFARE (EP) ... 10
82 Spiderleg SDL 11 THE SYSTEM IS MURDER (EP) ... 10

SYSTEM
77 Tash THE OTHER SIDE OF TIME (LP, 250 copies only) ... 110

SYSTEM OF A DOWN
99 Columbia/American Sugar/War (live) ... 25

SYZYGY
(see also Blackthorn)
85 Taptag TAP 3 LADY IN GREY (mini-LP) ... 20

GABOR SZABO
66 HMV CLP 3614 JAZZ RAGA (LP) ... 50
67 Impulse MILP 506 THE SORCERER (LP, mono) ... 30

BERNARD SZAJNER
80 IRC IRC 005 SOME DEATHS TAKE FOREVER (LP) ... 12

T

ANDY T
(see also Crass)
82 221984/05 WEARY OF THE FLESH (EP) ... 8

ERROL T. & ROOSEVELT ALL STARS
72 Ashanti ASH 406 Jamaica Born And Bred/Version ... 7

JAMIE T.
05 Pacemaker PANICSDJ 001 So Lonely Was The Ballad/Back In The Game (p/s, 500 only) ... 10
07 Virgin 0094637885512 PANIC PREVENTION (LP) ... 18

T. & UNKNOWN
80 Carrere CAR 142 My Generation/Woodstock Rock (p/s) ... 12

TABLE
77 Virgin VS 176 Do The Standing Still/Magical Melon Of The Tropics (p/s) ... 8
78 Chiswick NS 28 Sex Cells/The Road Of Lyfe (p/s) ... 7

TABLE TOPPERS
62 Starlite ST45 069 Rocking Mountain Dew/My Wild Irish Rose Rock ... 20

CHARLIE TABOR
63 Island WI 061 Blue Atlantic/Red Lion Madison ... 20

JUNE TABOR
(see also Silly Sisters)
86 Strange Fruit SFPS 015 THE PEEL SESSIONS (12" EP) ... 15
76 Topic 12TS 298 AIRS AND GRACES (LP) ... 12
77 Topic 12TS 360 ASHES AND DIAMONDS (LP) ... 12

TACTICS
86 Red Flame RF 49 MY HOUDINI (LP) ... 12

TAD & SMALL FRY
62 London HLU 9542 Checkered Continental Pants/Pretty Blue Jean Baby ... 15

TADPOLES
69 High Note HS 032 Rasta/Like Dirt ... 8

TAG
75 Philips 6006 477 Off Down The Road/Guitar Love ... 15

TAGES
(see also Blond)
66 Columbia DB 8019 Crazy 'Bout My Baby/In My Dreams ... 15
66 HMV POP 1515 So Many Girls/I'm Mad ... 50
67 Parlophone R 5640 Treat Me Like A Lady/Wanting ... 15
68 Parlophone R 5702 There's A Blind Man Playin' Fiddle In The Street/Like A Woman ... 15
68 MGM MGM 1443 Halcyon Days/I Read You Like An Open Book ... 15

BLIND JOE TAGGART
52 Tempo R 55 Religion Is Something Within You/Mother's Love (78) ... 20
55 Jazz Collector L 129 Religion Is Something Within You/Mother's Love (78, reissue) ... 15

MINT VALUE £

TAGMEMICS
(see also Art Attacks)
80 Index INDEX 003 — Chimneys/(Do The) Big Baby/Take Your Brain Out For A Walk (p/s, with insert) . 12

JACQUELINE TAIEB
68 Fontana TF 952 — Tonight I'm Going Home/7 A.M.. 150

LYN(N) TAIT(T) (& THE JETS)
(see also Justin Hines, Mike Thompson Jnr, ALton Ellis, Ken Boothe, Baba Brooks)
66 Doctor Bird DB 1006 — Vilma's Jump Up (as Lyn Taitt & The Comets)/ GLEN MILLER & HONEYBOY MARTIN: Dad Is Home 25
66 Doctor Bird DB 1047 — Spanish Eyes (with Tommy McCook)/STRANGER & HORTENSE: Loving Wine . . 25
67 Island WI 3066 — Something Stupid/Blue Tuesday (as Lyn Tait & The Jets) 40
67 Island WI 3075 — I Don't Want To Make You Cry/Nice Time (as Lyn Tait & The Jets) 40
68 Island WI 3139 — Napoleon Solo/Pressure And Slide (as Lyn Taitt & The Jets) 50
68 Amalgamated AMG 810 — El Casino Royale/Dee's Special (as Lynn Taitt & The Jets) 20
68 Pama PM 723 — Soul Food/Music Flames (as Lyn Tait & The Jets) 30
68 Island ILP 969 — SOUNDS ROCK STEADY (LP, as Lyn Taitt & The Jets) 200
68 Big Shot BBTL 4002 — GLAD SOUNDS (LP, as Lynn Taitt & The Jets) 60

TAJ MAHAL
(see under 'M')

TAKE FIVE
60s D.S.C.A (no cat. no.) — MY GIRL (EP, oversized p/s; Dundee Students Charity Appeal record) 70

TAKE IT
80s Fresh Hold TRI — Man Made World/Taking Sides/How It Is (p/s) 40
80 Fresh Hold FHR 1 — Twenty Lines/Armchairs/Friends And Relations (foldout p/s with insert) 20

'TAKERS
(see also Undertakers, Jackie Lomax)
64 Pye 7N 15690 — If You Don't Come Back/Think. 25

TAKE THAT
(see also Robbie Williams)
91 Dance U.K. DUK 2 — Do What U Like/Waiting Around (p/s). 15
91 Dance U.K. 12DUK 2 — Do What U Like (Club Mix)/Do What U Like (Radio Mix)/Waiting Around (12", p/s; most with wrong tracks listed on sleeve) 25
91 RCA PB 45085 — Promises/Do What U Like (p/s) 5
91 RCA PB 45085P — Promises/Do What U Like (poster p/s) 8
91 RCA PT 45086 — Promises (12" Mix)/Do What U Like (12" Mix) (12", p/s) 10
92 RCA PB 45257 — Once You've Tasted Love/Guess Who Tasted Love (p/s) 5
92 RCA PB 45265 — Once You've Tasted Love/Guess Who Tasted Love (spined p/s with pull-out hexagonal pop-up calendar) 15
92 RCA PB 45258 — Once You've Tasted Love (Aural Mix)/Guess Who Tasted Love (Guess Who Mix)/ Once You've Tasted Love (Radio Version) (12" picture disc, with insert) 12
92 RCA 74321 10100 7 — It Only Takes A Minute/Satisfied (p/s, with Mark & Robbie prints) 15
92 RCA 74321 10101 7 — It Only Takes A Minute/It Only Takes A Minute (Royal Rave Mix) (different p/s, with Jason & Howard prints & paper frame) 8
92 RCA 74321 10814 7 — I Found Heaven (7" Radio Mix)/(Mr. F's Garage Mix) (poster p/s) 6
92 RCA 74321 10813 7B — I Found Heaven (7" Radio Mix)/I'm Out (picture disc) 6
92 RCA 74321 11600 7 — A Million Love Songs/A Million Love Songs (The Lovers Mix) (p/s, with tattoos). 10

TAKE 3
84 Elite DAZZ 32 — Music & Time/Music & Time (extended version) (12") 15

TALAN
89 Talan SRT 9KS 2208 — Spellbinder/Undreground Madness (p/s) 20

TALBOT BROTHERS
59 Melodisc MEL 1507 — Bloodshot Eyes/She's Got Freckles 15
60s Melodisc CAL 20 — Bloodshot Eyes/She's Got Freckles (reissue) 6

ZIGGY TALENT
55 Brunswick 05506 — Cheek To Cheek (Cha Cha)/Bozooki Blues 7

TALES
73 MAM 93 — Someone Like You/Rockin' Suzanna 5

TALES OF JUSTINE
(see also Tim Rice)
67 HMV POP 1614 — Albert/Monday Morning (in p/s). 180
67 HMV POP 1614 — Albert/Monday Morning 60
97 Tenth Planet TP 034 — PETALS FROM A SUNFLOWER (LP, gatefold sleeve, numbered, 1,000 only) 25

TALION
89 Major WADES 1 — KILLING THE WORLD (LP). 12

TALISKER
75 Caroline CA 1513 — DREAMING OF GLENISLA (LP). 15

TALISMAN
73 Argo AFW 110 — Stepping Stones/Dr Jazz 5
72 Argo ZFB 33 — PRIMROSE DREAMS (LP) 12
73 Argo ZDA 161 — STEPPING STONES (LP) 12

TALISMEN
65 Stateside SS 408 — Masters Of War/Casting My Spell 70

TALKING HEADS
77 Sire 6078 604 — Love Goes To Building On Fire/New Feeling (p/s) 7
77 Sire SAM 87 — Love Goes To Building On Fire/New Feeling (limited edition, in p/s) 12
77 Sire SAM 87 — Love Goes To Building On Fire/New Feeling. 10
77 Sire 6078 610 — Psycho Killer/I Wish You Wouldn't Say That (p/s). 8

			MINT VALUE £
77	Sire 6078 610	Psycho Killer/Psycho Killer (Acoustic)/I Wish You Wouldn't Say That (12", p/s)	12
78	Sire 6078 620	Pulled Up/Don't Worry About The Government (p/s)	8
79	Sire SIR 4004	Take Me To The River/Found A Job (p/s)	7
79	Sire SIR 4004/SAM 87	Take Me To The River/Found A Job//Love Goes To Building On Fire/ Psycho Killer (double pack, gatefold p/s)	15
79	Sire SIR 4027	Life During Wartime (live version)/Electric Guitar (p/s)	12
79	WEA SPC 9	Take Me To The River/Psycho Killer (cassette)	5
80	Sire SIR 4033	I Zimbra/Paper (p/s)	8
80	Sire SIR 4040	Cities/Cities (live) (p/s)	7
80	Sire SIR 4040T	Cities/Cities (live)/Artists Only (live) (12", p/s)	10
80	Sire SIR 4048	Once In A Lifetime/Seen And Not Seen (p/s)	5
80	Sire SIR 4050	Houses In Motion (Special Re-Mixed Version)/Air (p/s)	8
84	Sire W 9451T/SAM 176	This Must Be The Place (Full Version)/Moon Rocks//Slippery People (Remix)/ Making Flippy Floppy (Remix) (12", p/s, double pack)	12
84	EMI 12EMI 5509	Girlfriend Is Better/Once In A Lifetime (12", p/s)	10
85	EMI 12EMID 5520	Lady Don't Mind/Give Me Back My Name//Slippery People (live)/ This Must Be The Place (Naive Melody) (live) (12", p/s, double pack)	10
85	EMI EMIP 5530	Road To Nowhere/Television Man (picture disc)	5
85	EMI 12 EMID 5530/	Road To Nowhere/Television Man (Extended)//Slippery People (Long Live Version)/Naive Melody (live) (12", stickered double pack)	8
79	Sire K 56707	FEAR OF MUSIC (LP, with free single "Psycho Killer"/"New Feeling" [SAM 108])	15
83	EMI 9237711	SPEAKING IN TONGUES (LP, clear vinyl in special cover)	18

TALK TALK
(see also Reaction)

82	EMI EMI 5265	Mirror Man/Strike Up The Band (p/s)	5
82	EMI 12EMI 5314	Today (Extended)/It's So Serious (12", p/s)	8
82	EMI EMIP 5352	Talk Talk (Remix)/Mirror Man (picture disc)	5
82	EMI EMIP 5352	Talk Talk (Extended)/Talk Talk (BBC Version) (12", p/s)	8
84	EMI EMID 5433	THE TALK TALK DEMOS (double pack, poster p/s [EMI 5433 & PSR 467])	10
86	EMI 12EMID 5540	Life's What You Make It (Extended)/It's Getting Late In The Evening// It's My Life/ Does Caroline Know? (12", p/s, double pack)	15
86	EMI EMIP 5551	Living In Another World/For What It's Worth (shaped picture disc)	10
90	Parlophone CDR 6264	Life's What You Make it/(live)/Tomorrow Started (live) (CD)	8
91	Verve TALKD 1	After The Flood/Myrrhman (CD, picture disc in 3-CD box)	15
91	Verve TALKD 2	New Grass/Stump (CD, picture disc)	10
91	Verve TALKD 3	Ascension Day/5.09 (CD, picture disc)	10
91	Verve TALKD1/2/3	After The Flood/Myrrhman//New Grass/Stump//Ascension Day/5.09 (3-CD, in die-cut box)	40
88	Parlophone PC50105	SPIRIT OF EDEN (LP)	20
98	Voiceprint	LONDON 1986 (CD)	30

TOM TALL
(see also Ginny Wright)

55	London HL 8150	Are You Mine/Boom Boom Boomerang (as Ginny Wright & Tom Tall)	50
55	London HLU 8216	Give Me A Chance/Remembering You	50
55	London HLU 8216	Give Me A Chance/Remembering You (78)	10
56	London HLU 8231	Underway/Goldie Jo Malone	50
56	London HLU 8231	Underway/Goldie Jo Malone (78)	15
57	London HLU 8429	Don't You Know/If You Know What I Know (with Ruckus Taylor)	40
57	London HLU 8429	Don't You Know/If You Know What I Know (with Ruckus Taylor) (78)	22
55	London RE-U 1035	COUNTRY SONGS VOL. 2 (EP, as Tom Tall & Ginny Wright)	40

TALL BOYS
(see also Meteors)

82	Big Beat NS 79	Island Of Lost Souls/Another Half Hour Till Sunrise (p/s)	6
84	Big Beat NED 8	WEDNESDAY ADDAM'S BOYFRIEND (12" EP)	8
85	Big Beat NST 107	Final Kick/Interceptor/Dragster/Action Woman (12" EP)	8
86	Big Beat NST 114	Brand New Gun/Last House On The Left/Took A Long Time (12" EP)	8

TALMY/STONE BAND

62	Decca F 11543	Madison Time/Madison Time (A-side with Alan Freeman)	10
62	Ace Of Clubs ACL 1134	ROSES ARE RED & OTHER HITS OF 1962 (LP)	18

TALULAH GOSH

86	53rd & 3rd AGARR 4	Beatnik Boy/My Best Friend (p/s)	8
86	53rd & 3rd AGARR 5	Steaming Train/Just A Dream (p/s)	5
86	53rd & 3rd AGARR 4/5T	Beatnik Boy/My Best Friend/Steaming Train/Just A Dream (12", p/s)	8
86	Sha La La 002/LYN 18147	WHO NEEDS THE BLOODY CARTEL ANYWAY (EP, p/s, flexidisc)	8
87	53rd & 3rd AGARR 8	Talulah Gosh/Don't Go Away (p/s)	5
87	53rd & 3rd AGARR 8T	Talulah Gosh/Don't Go Away (12", p/s)	8
88	53rd & 3rd AGARR 14	Bringing Up Baby/The Girl With The Strawberry Hair (p/s)	6
88	53rd & 3rd AGARR 14T	Bringing Up Baby/I Can't Get No Satisfaction, Thank God/ The Girl With The Strawberry Hair/Do You Remember?/Sunny Inside (12", p/s)	8
88	53rd & 3rd AGARR 16	Testcard Girl (p/s)	5
87	53rd & 3rd AGAS 004	ROCK LEGENDS VOL. 69 (LP, clear vinyl)	15
91	Sarah 064	THEY'VE SCOFFED THE LOT (LP)	12

KO KO TAYLOR

66	Chess CRS 8035	Wang Dang Doodle/Blues Heaven	25
66	Chess CRS 8035	Wang Dang Doodle/Blues Heaven (DJ copy)	50
72	Chess 6145 018	Violent Love/The Egg Or The Hen/Wang Dang Doodle	8

TAMANGOES

79	Grapevine GRP 122	I Really Love You/You've Been Gone So Long	20

JAMES TAMLIN

65	Columbia DB 7438	Is There Time/Main Line Central Station	20
65	Columbia DB 7577	Yes I Have/Now There Are Two	10

TAMLINS

79	Deb Music DEB 007	Still Water/AUGUSTUS PABLO: Spirit Of Umoja (12")	20

MINT VALUE £

TAMPA RED

50	Jazz Collector L 58	Easy Rider Blues/Come On Mama Do That Dance (78)	15
52	HMV JO 301	Pretty Baby Blues/Since Baby's Been Gone (78, export issue)	40
50s	Square M 2	Moot It Boy/She Rocks Me (With One Steady Roll) (78)	40
64	RCA RCX 7160	R & B VOL. 3 (EP)	25
60s	Memory TR 1	TAMPA RED (LP)	35

TAMPA RED/GEORGIA TOM

59	Jazz Collector JEL 3	THE MALE BLUES VOLUME 2 (EP)	20

TAMS

63	Stateside SS 146	Untie Me/Disillusioned	30
63	HMV POP 1254	What Kind Of Fool Do You Think I Am/Laugh It Off	25
64	HMV POP 1298	It's All Right, You're Just In Love/You Lied To Your Daddy	18
64	HMV POP 1331	Hey Girl Don't Bother Me/Take Away	150
64	HMV POP 1331	Hey Girl Don't Bother Me/Take Away (DJ copy)	200
65	HMV POP 1464	Concrete Jungle/Till The End Of Time	15
69	Stateside SS 2123	Be Young, Be Foolish, Be Happy/That Same Old Song	15
70	Capitol CL 15650	Too Much Foolin' Around/How Long Love	15
75	ABC ABC 4020	Hey Girl Don't Bother Me/Be Young, Be Foolish, Be Happy	8
68	Stateside (S)SL 10258	A LITTLE MORE SOUL (LP)	40
70	Stateside SSL 10304	BE YOUNG, BE FOOLISH, BE HAPPY (LP)	35
74	Probe SPB 1044	THE BEST OF THE TAMS (LP)	15
74	ABC ABCL 5118	THE BEST OF THE TAMS (LP, reissue)	12

TANAMO

63	Island WI 108	Come Down/I Am Holding On (actually by Lord Tanamo)	30

TANDOORI CASSETTE

(see also Nazareth, Alex Harvey, Tear Gas, Stone The Crows)

83	IKA IKA 001	Angel Talk/Third World Brief Case (p/s, 5,000 only)	15

SHARON TANDY

(see also Fleur-De-Lys, Tony & Tandy)

65	Mercury MF 898	Love Makes The World Go Round/By My Side	30
65	Pye 7N 15806	Now That You've Gone/Hurtin' Me	25
65	Pye 7N 15939	I've Found Love/Perhaps Not Forever	15
67	Atlantic 584 098	Toe Hold/I Can't Get Over It	20
67	Atlantic 584 124	Stay With Me/Hold On	50
67	Atlantic 584 137	Our Day Will Come/Look And Find	20
68	Atlantic 584 166	Fool On The Hill/For No One	20
68	Atlantic 584 181	Love Is Not A Simple Affair/Hurry Hurry Choo-Choo	40
68	Atlantic 584 194	You've Gotta Believe It/Border Town	20
68	Atlantic 584 214	The Way She Looks At You/He'll Hurt Me	30
68	Atlantic 584 219	Hold On/Daughter Of The Sun	100
69	Atlantic 584 242	Gotta Get Enough Time/Somebody Speaks Your Name	80

NORMA TANEGA

66	Stateside SS 496	Walkin' My Cat Named Dog/I'm In The Sky	6
66	Stateside SS 520	A Street That Rhymes At Six A.M./Treat Me Right	12
66	Stateside SS 537	Bread/Waves	7
71	RCA 2072	Nothing Much Is Happening Today/Antarctic Rose	6
66	Stateside S(S)L 10182	WALKIN' MY CAT NAMED DOG (LP)	25

TANGERINE DREAM

(see also Edgar Froese, Klaus Schulze)

74	Virgin PR 214	Phaedra (Edit)/Mysterious Semblance At The Strand Of Nightmares (promo)	30
76	Virgin VDJ 17	Stratosfear/The Big Sleep In Search Of Hades (promo only)	25
77	MCA PSR 413	Betrayal (Sorceror Theme)/Search (promo only)	25
77	Virgin VS 199	Encore/Hobo March	5
81	Virgin VS 444	Chronozon/Network 23 (p/s)	8
84	Jive Electro P 74	Warsaw In The Sun/Polish Dance (map-shaped picture disc)	20
84	Jive Electro T 74	Warsaw In The Sun (Parts 1 & 2)/Polish Dance/Rare Bird (12", p/s)	15
85	Jive JIVE 101	Streethawk/Tear Garden (p/s)	15
85	Jive Electro T 101	STREETHAWK (12" EP)	20
87	Jive Electro 143	Tyger/21st Century Common Man II (p/s)	6
87	Jive Electro T 143	Tyger/Tyger (7" Version)/21st Century Common Man II (12", p/s)	10
89	Private 663 747	ORANGES DON'T DANCE (CD EP, promo only)	30
74	Polydor Super 2383 297	ATEM (LP)	18
75	Polydor Super 2383 314	ALPHA CENTAURI (LP)	18
79	Virgin V 2111	FORCE MAJEURE (LP, clear vinyl)	15
80	Virgin VBOX 2	TANGERINE DREAM '70-80 (4-LP box set)	20
80	Virgin TCVX 2	TANGERINE DREAM '70-80 (4-cassette box set)	25
81	Virgin V 2212	EXIT (LP, 1st 1,000 with poster)	12
84	MCA MCF 3233	FIRESTARTER (LP, soundtrack)	12
84	Jive HIP 22	POLAND - THE WARSAW CONCERT (2-LP, gatefold sleeve, with inners)	15
84	Jive Electro HIPX 22	POLAND - THE WARSAW CONCERT (2-LP, picture disc)	25
85	Heavy Metal HMI PD 29	FLASHPOINT (LP, soundtrack, picture disc)	12
85	Heavy Metal HMXD 29	FLASHPOINT (CD, soundtrack; playable CD [most copies faulty])	50
86	Jive Electro TANG 1	IN THE BEGINNING (6-LP box set, with booklet)	25
87	Jive HIP 26	LE PARC (LP)	12
90	Virgin TD AK 11	TANGERINE DREAM (3-CD, 'Collector's Edition' box set)	25
03	Virgin 724359612829	TANGENTS 1973 - 1983 (5-CD box set with booklet)	30

TANGERINE PEEL

67	United Artists UP 1193	Every Christian Lion-Hearted Man Will Show You/Trapped	30
68	CBS 3402	Solid Gold Mountain/Light Across The River	130
68	CBS 3676	Talking To No One/Wishing Tree	20
69	MGM MGM 1470	Never Say Never Again/A Thousand Miles Away	15
69	MGM MGM 1487	Play Me A Sad Song And I'll Dance/Wish You Could Be Here With Me	15

			MINT VALUE £
70	RCA RCA 1936	Move Into My World/In Between	6
70	RCA RCA 1990	Soft Delights/Thinking Of Me	6
70	RCA RCA 2036	What Am I To Do?/Don't Let Me Be Misunderstood	6
70	RCA LSA 3002	SOFT DELIGHTS (LP)	25

TANGO

92	Formation FORM 12004	THE IMPACT EP (12", p/s)	15

TANGO PROJECT

92	White 004	Untitled/Untitled (12", white label test pressing)	30

TANK

72	Bumble GE 105	Heads I Win, Tails You Lose/Burgundy, Port And Red Wine	12

TANK

(see also Damned, UK)

81	Kamaflage KAM 1	Don't Walk Away/Shellshock/Hammer On (p/s, with cover-mounted patch)	10
81	Kamaflage KAM 1	Don't Walk Away/Shellshock/Hammer On (p/s)	8
82	Kamaflage KAM 3	Turn Your Head Around/Steppin' On A Landmine (p/s)	15
82	Kamaflage KAM 7	Crazy Horses/Filth Bitch Boogie (p/s)	5
82	Kamaflage KAP 1	(He Fell In Love With A) Stormtrooper/Blood Guts And Beer (picture disc)	7
83	MFN KUT 101	ECHOES OF A DISTANT BATTLE (EP)	8
82	Kamaflage KAMLP 1	FILTH HOUNDS OF HADES (LP, 1st pressing, with black & yellow sleeve)	15
82	Kamaflage KAMLP 1	FILTH HOUNDS OF HADES (LP, 2nd pressing, with bonus p/s 7" Don't Walk Away (live)/"The Snake" [KAM F1])	15
83	Music For Nations MFN 3P	THIS MEANS WAR (LP, picture disc)	20

TANNAHILL WEAVERS

76	Plant Life PLR 001	ARE YE SLEEPING MAGGIE? (LP, with lyric insert)	20
78	Plant Life PLR 010	THE OLD WOMAN'S DANCE (LP)	12

HOLLY TANNEN & PETE COOPER

79	Plant Life PLR 015	FROSTY MORNING (LP)	15

PHIL TANNER

68	EDF SSLP 1005	PHIL TANNER (LP, with lyric book)	25

TAN TAN

81	Maccabees MPCLP TT1	MUSICAL NOSTALGIA FOR TODAY (LP)	40

TANTONES

57	Vogue V 9085	So Afraid/Tell Me	850
57	Vogue V 9085	So Afraid/Tell Me (78)	150

TANTRUM

80	Ovation OV 1247	RATHER BE ROCKIN' (LP)	12

TANZ DER YOUTH

(see also Brian James, Damned)

78	Radar ADA 19	I'm Sorry, I'm Sorry/Delay (p/s)	5

TAO JONES INDEX

(see also David Bowie)

97	RCA 512541	Pallas Athena (live)/V-2 Schneider (live) (12", p/s)	12

TAPESTRY

67	London HLZ 10138	Carnaby Street/Taming Of The Shrew	30
68	NEMS 56-3679	Like The Sun/Florence	20
69	NEMS 5639-64	Heart & Soul/Who Wants Happiness	45

DEMETRISS TAPP

64	Coral Q 72470	Lipstick Paint A Smile On Me/If You Find Love	40

TARANTULA

70	A&M AMLS 959	TARANTULA (LP)	15

JIMMY TARBUCK

65	Immediate IM 018	Someday/(We're) Wastin' Time	7
67	Philips BF 1573	Stewball/When My Little Girl Is Smiling (p/s)	5
67	Parlophone R 5641	Doctor Dolittle/Butterfly	6
68	RCA RCA 1788	You Wanted Someone To Play With/Little Green Apples	6

TARHEEL SLIM & LITTLE ANN

65	Sue WI 390	You Make Me Feel So Good/Got To Keep On Lovin' You	40

DAVE TARRIDA

99	Mosquito MSQ 013	PLAYING THE GAME (12" EP)	10

TARRIERS

(see also Vince Martin, Rooftop Singers)

56	London HLN 8340	Cindy, Oh Cindy/Only If You Praise The Lord (gold label lettering, as Vince Martin & Tarriers)	25
56	London HLN 8340	Cindy, Oh Cindy/Only If You Praise The Lord (silver label lettering, as Vince Martin & Tarriers)	15
57	Columbia DB 3891	The Banana Boat Song/No Hidin Place	10
57	Columbia DB 3961	Tom Dooley/Everybody Loves Saturday Night	6
57	Columbia DB 4025	Dunya/Quinto (My Little Pony)	5
58	Columbia DB 4148	I Know Where I'm Going/Acres Of Clams	5
58	London HLU 8600	Lonesome Traveller/East Virginia	10
57	Columbia 33S 1115	THE TARRIERS (10" LP)	20
62	London STA 8525	A LIVE PERFORMANCE AT THE BITTER END (LP)	20

TARTAN HORDE

(see also Nick Lowe, Rat Scabies, Roogalator)

75	United Artists UP 35891	Bay City Rollers, We Love You/Rollers Theme	15

MINT VALUE £

TARTANS
(see also Devon & Tartans, Kaddo Strings, Max Romeo, Derrick Morgan)

67	Island WI 3058	Dance All Night/What Can I Do	20
68	Caltone TONE 115	Awake The Town (with Lynn Taitt's Band)/LYNN TAITT & JETS: The Brush	60
68	Caltone TONE 117	Coming On Strong/It's Alright (with Tommy McCook's Band)	50
71	Escort ERT 843	A Day Will Come/ROBI'S ALL STARS: Version	8

TARTS

81	If You Can't Take A Joke JOKE1	Tie Me Kangeroo Down/Gene Queenie	80

TASAVALLAN PRESIDENTTI

73	Sonet SNTF 636	LAMBERTLAND (LP)	30
74	Sonet SNTF 658	MILKY WAY MOSES (LP, with insert)	30

TASKFORCE

00	White(Lowlife) grafpromo 1	Graf Da Bus Up (12" - 1-sided, 500 pressed)	25
00	White(Lowlife)	Wha Blow (12", 1-Sided white label, 200 only)	25
00	Lowlife LOW 10	VOICE OF THE GREAT OUTDOORS (EP, 2000 only p/s)	15
01	Rehab RHB 001	A LIFE WITHOUT INSTRUCTIONS (EP)	15
02	White	Graf Da Bus Up/Wha Blow (white label, 2 Mixes of A-side, 12")	25
03	MFTC MFT 02	Music From The Corner Vol. 2 (2-LP)	15
06	White WS 01	The Bitches (3 versions) (12")	12
99	K'Boro KBR1005	NEW MIC ORDER (LP)	60

TASSELS

59	London HL 8885	To A Soldier Boy/The Boy For Me	100
59	London HL 8885	To A Soldier Boy/The Boy For Me (78)	50
59	Top Rank JAR 229	To A Young Lover/My Guy And I	30

TASTE
(see also Rory Gallagher, Stud)

68	Major Minor MM 560	Blister On The Moon/Born On The Wrong Side Of Time	35
69	Polydor 56313	Born On The Wrong Side Of Time/Same Old Story	10
70	Major Minor MM 718	Born On The Wrong Side Of Time/Blister On The Moon	10
69	Polydor 583 042	TASTE (LP)	35
70	Polydor 583 083	ON THE BOARDS (LP)	25
71	Polydor 2310 082	LIVE TASTE (LP)	12
72	Polydor 2383 120	TASTE - LIVE AT THE ISLE OF WIGHT (LP)	12

A TASTE OF HONEY

68	Original Rim RIM 11	Goody Goody Gum Drops/Sunshine Rainbows	12

TASTE OF HONEY

69	Rim RIM 19	8.05/Charleston	5

TASTY

77	DJM DJS 10751	Just A Little Too Much/You're A Heartbreaker (Promo PS)	8

BUDDY TATE

58	Felsted FAJ 7004	SWINGING LIKE TATE (LP)	30

HOWARD TATE

66	Verve VS 541	Ain't Nobody Home/How Come My Bulldog Won't Bark	15
67	Verve VS 549	Look At Granny Run Run/Half A Man	20
67	Verve VS 552	Get It While You Can/Glad I Knew Better	15
67	Verve VS 555	Baby I Love You/How Blue Can You Get	25
67	Verve VS 556	I Learned It All The Hard Way/Part Time Love	15
68	Verve VS 565	Stop/Shoot 'Em All Down	15
68	Verve VS 571	Night Owl/Every Day I Have The Blues	20
70	Major Minor MM 696	My Soul's Got A Hole In It/It's Too Late	10
67	Verve (S)VLP 9179	GET IT WHILE YOU CAN (LP)	70

TOMMY TATE

66	Columbia DB 8046	Big Blue Diamonds/A Lover's Reward	75
66	Columbia DB 8046	Big Blue Diamonds/A Lover's Reward (DJ Copy)	125

JACQUES TATI

58	Fontana TFE 17175	MY UNCLE (EP)	15

TATTY OLLITY

70s	Tatty TR 101	Punktuation	20

ART TATUM

51	Capitol LC 6524	ART TATUM (10" LP)	12
53	Capitol LC 6625	OUT OF NOWHERE (10" LP)	15
54	Vogue LDE 081	ART TATUM "JUST JAZZ" (10" LP)	15
55	Vogue Coral LRA 10011	THE ART TATUM TRIO (10" LP)	12
55	Columbia Clef 33CX 10005	THE GENIUS OF ART TATUM (LP)	12
55	Capitol LC 6638	ART TATUM ENCORES (10" LP)	12
56	Columbia Clef 33CX 10053	THE GENIUS OF ART TATUM (NO. 2) (LP)	12
57	Columbia Clef 33C 9033	THE GENIUS OF ART TATUM (NO. 3) (10" LP)	12
57	Columbia Clef 33C 9039	PRESENTING THE ART TATUM TRIO (10" LP)	12
57	Vogue Coral LVA 9047	HERE'S ART TATUM (LP)	12
58	Columbia Clef 33CX 10115	ART TATUM (LP)	12
59	Columbia Clef 33CX 10137	ART TATUM-BEN WEBSTER QUARTET (LP)	15
60	Top Rank 35/067	ART TATUM DISCOVERIES (LP)	12

BERNIE TAUPIN

71	DJM DJLPS 415	TAUPIN (LP, textured gatefold sleeve with booklet)	50
71	DJM DJLPS 415	TAUPIN (LP, textured gatefold sleeve without booklet)	20

JOHN TAVENER

70	Apple SAPCOR 15	THE WHALE (LP, gatefold sleeve)	40
71	Apple SAPCOR 20	CELTIC REQUIEM (LP, gatefold sleeve, with insert & 'Apple' inner sleeve)	80
77	Ring O' 2320 104	THE WHALE (LP, reissue, different single sleeve)	45

Year	Label / Cat. No.	Title	MINT VALUE £
92	Apple SAPCOR 15	THE WHALE (LP, 2nd reissue, gatefold sleeve with inner sleeve)	25
92	Apple SAPCOR 15	THE WHALE (CD)	25
93	Apple SAPCOR 20	CELTIC REQUIEM (LP, reissue, gatefold sleeve with inner sleeve)	25
93	Apple SAPCOR 20	CELTIC REQUIEM (CD)	25

TAVERNERS

69	Saga EROS 8146	SELDOM SOBER (LP)	12
73	Trailer LER 2080	BLOWING SANDS (LP, red label)	15
74	Folk Heritage FHR 062	TIMES OF OLD ENGLAND (LP)	15
78	Folk Heritage FHR 101	SAME OLD FRIENDS (LP, with insert)	12

TAW FOLK

75	Sentinel SENS 1030	DEVONSHIRE CREAM AND CIDER (LP)	12

CYRIL TAWNEY

62	HMV 7EG 8738	BABY LIE EASY (EP)	15
69	Polydor 236 577	THE OUTLANDISH KNIGHT (LP)	20
70	Argo ZFB 4	SINGS CHILDREN'S SONGS FROM DEVON AND CORNWALL (LP)	20
70	Argo ZFB 9	A MAYFLOWER GARLAND (LP)	25
72	Argo ZFB 28	TAWNEY IN PORT (LP)	12
73	Argo ZFB 87	I WILL GIVE MY LOVE (LP)	12

ALLAN TAYLOR

(see also Fairport Convention)

71	Liberty LBF 15447	Sometimes/Song For Kathy	6
73	United Artists UP 35541	My Father's Room/Always You	6
71	Liberty LBS 83483	SOMETIMES (LP, gatefold sleeve)	50
72	United Artists UAS 29275	THE LADY (LP)	45
73	United Artists UAG 29468	THE AMERICAN ALBUM (LP, gatefold sleeve)	20

AUSTIN TAYLOR

60	Top Rank JAR 511	Push Push/A Heart That's True	20

BILLY TAYLOR (TRIO)

57	Esquire EP 115	MAMBO! (EP)	15
57	Esquire EP 169	BILLY TAYLOR TRIO (EP)	20
54	Felsted EDL 87009	JAZZ AT STORYVILLE (10" LP)	35
54	Esquire 20-053	AT THE TOWN HALL 1954 (LP)	30
54	Esquire 32-010	A TOUCH OF TAYLOR (LP)	30
57	HMV DLP 1181	MY FAIR LADY LOVES JAZZ (10" LP)	20
60	Vogue LAE 12192	TAYLOR MADE PIANO (LP)	20

BOBBY TAYLOR

64	Columbia DB 7282	Temptation/Mod Bod	15

BOBBY TAYLOR (& VANCOUVERS)

68	Tamla Motown TMG 654	Does Your Mama Know About Me/Fading Away (with Vancouvers)	50
73	Epic EPC 1720	I Can't Quit Your Love/Queen Of The Ghetto (solo)	8
69	T. Motown (S)TML 11093	BOBBY TAYLOR AND THE VANCOUVERS (LP, mono/stereo)	60
70	T. Motown (S)TML 11125	TAYLOR MADE SOUL (LP, solo)	150

BRYAN TAYLOR

61	Piccadilly 7N 35018	The Donkey's Tale/Let It Snow On Christmas Day	30

CECIL TAYLOR

60	Contemporary LAC12216	LOOKING AHEAD! (LP)	20
60s	Fontana SFJL 926	NEFERTITI, THE BEAUTIFUL ONE HAS COME (LP)	18
88	Leo LR 152	CHINAMPAS (LP)	15
88	Leo LR 162	TZOTZIL MUMMERS TZOTZIL (LP)	15
88	Leo LR 404/405	LIVE IN BOLOGNA (2-LP)	25
88	Leo LR 408/409	LIVE IN VIENNA (2-LP)	25

CHIP TAYLOR

(see also Wes Voigt)

62	Warner Bros WB 82	Here I Am/I Love You But I Know	6
73	Buddah 2011 151	Angel Of The Morning/Swear To God, Your Honor	5
73	Buddah 2318 074	GASOLINE (LP)	25
74	Warner Bros K 56032	CHIP TAYLOR'S LAST CHANCE (LP)	15

DEBBIE TAYLOR

76	Arista ARISTA 50	I Don't Wanna Leave You/Just Don't Pay	20

DREW TAYLOR

70s	One Up OU 2175	DREW'S BREW (LP)	12

DUFFY TAYLOR BLUES

69	Page One POF 130	You Wrecked My Life/I'll Be There	12

EDDIE TAYLOR

65	Big Bear BEAR 6	READY FOR EDDIE (LP)	12

ELIZABETH TAYLOR

(see also John Barry)

63	Colpix PXL 459	IN LONDON (LP, TV soundtrack, music by John Barry, mono)	30
63	Colpix PXL 459	IN LONDON (LP, TV soundtrack, music by John Barry, stereo)	35

FELICE TAYLOR

67	President PT 120	It May Be Winter Outside/BOB KEENE ORCHESTRA: Winter Again	8
67	President PT 133	I'm Under The Influence/BOB KEENE ORCHESTRA: Love Theme	8
67	President PT 155	I Feel Love Comin' On/BOB KEENE ORCHESTRA: Comin' On Again	8
68	President PT 193	Captured By Your Love/I Can Feel Your Love (Coming Down On Me)	10
68	President PT 220	Suree-Surrender/All I Want To Do Is Love You	8

(Original President issues have an horizontal artist credit. Re-issues have a vertical credit)

GEOFF TAYLOR

55	Esquire EP 55	GEOFF TAYLOR SEXTET (EP)	10
57	Esquire EP 105	GEOFF TAYLOR ALL STARS (EP)	10

MINT VALUE £

GLORIA TAYLOR

70	Polydor BM 56788	You Gotta Pay The Price/Loving You And Being Loved By You	15

HOUND DOG TAYLOR

66	Outasite 45-504	Christine/Alley Music (99 copies only)	100

JAMES TAYLOR

70	Apple APPLE 32	Carolina In My Mind/Something's Wrong	15
68	Apple APCOR 3	JAMES TAYLOR (LP, gatefold sleeve, black inner, orange cover lettering, mono)	45
68	Apple SAPCOR 3	JAMES TAYLOR (LP, gatefold sleeve, black inner, orange cover lettering, stereo)	35
70	Apple SAPCOR 3	JAMES TAYLOR (LP, 2nd issue, gatefold sleeve, 'Apple' inner sleeve, black cover lettering)	35
70	Warner Bros WS 1843	SWEET BABY JAMES (LP, orange label, later green label)	20
71	Warner Bros WS 2561	MUD SLIDE SLIM AND THE BLUE HORIZON (LP, g/fold sleeve, green label)	18
72	Warner Bros K 46043	SWEET BABY JAMES (LP, reissue, green label)	15
72	Warner Bros K 46085	MUD SLIDE SLIM AND THE BLUE HORIZON (LP, reissue, gatefold sleeve, green label)	12
73	Warner Bros K 46185	ONE MAN DOG (LP, green label, with insert & stickered sleeve)	12
91	Apple SAPCOR 3	JAMES TAYLOR (LP, reissue, gatefold sleeve)	18
91	Apple SAPCOR 3	JAMES TAYLOR (CD)	18

JAMES TAYLOR QUARTET

(see also Prisoners, Daggermen, New Jersey Kings)

87	Re-Elect President FORD 1	Blow Up/One Mint Julep (p/s)	8
88	Urban URB 24	Starsky And Hutch Theme/(Version)	5
88	Urban URBX 24	Starsky And Hutch Theme/(Version) (12")	8
92	Big Life JTQ 7 PROMO 1	Absolution (live) (gig freebie, plain black sleeve with postcard, 1 side etched)	5
90s	Big Life	Hope And Pray (p/s)	5
95	Acid Jazz JAZID 124S	Whole Lotta Love (white label, withdrawn)	100
95	Acid Jazz JAZID 124T	Whole Lotta Love (12" EP, company sleeve)	25
96	Acid Jazz JAZID 139	Creation (10", p/s, mispressed with Hungarian porn music on A-side)	75
96	Acid Jazz JAZID 139	Creation (10", p/s)	15
96	Acid Jazz JTQ 1	Europa (Extended)/Redneck (12", company sleeve)	40
87	Re-Elect Pres. REAGAN 2	MISSION: IMPOSSIBLE (mini-LP, 45rpm)	15
87	Re-Elect Pres. REAGAN 2D	MISSION: IMPOSSIBLE (min-LP, with film dialogue, 500 only)	70
87	Re-Elect Pres. KENNEDY 1	THE MONEY SPYDER (LP)	20
94	Acid Jazz JAZID 110	EXTENDED PLAY (12" EP)	10
95	Acid Jazz JAZIDLP 115L	IN THE HANDS OF THE INEVITABLE (LP, with bonus 2-track 12")	12
90s	Acid Jazz AJXLP 117	THE PENTHOUSE SUITE (LP)	12

JEREMY TAYLOR

66	Decca LK 4731	ALWAYS SOMETHING NEW (LP)	30
68	Fontana (S)TL 5475	HIS SONGS (LP)	20
69	Fontana (S)TL 5523	MORE OF HIS SONGS (LP)	20
72	Galliard GAL 4018	PIECE OF GROUND (LP)	15
62	Decca F 11502	Ag Pleez Daddy/Jo'burg Talking Blues	8

JOHN TAYLOR

71	Turtle TUR 301	PAUSE AND THINK AGAIN (LP)	200

JOHNNIE TAYLOR

67	Stax 601 003	Ain't That Lovin' You/Outside Love (dark blue label)	30
67	Stax 601 003	Ain't That Lovin' You/Outside Love (light blue label)	20
68	Stax STAX 106	Who's Makin' Love/I'm Trying	8
69	Stax STAX 114	Take Care Of Your Homework/Hold On This Time	8
69	Stax STAX 122	(I Wanna) Testify/I Had To Fight With Love	10
69	Stax STAX 129	I Could Never Be President/It's Amazing	8
70	Stax STAX 141	Love Bones/Separation Line	8
70	Stax STAX 150	Steal Away/Friday Night	20
70	Stax STAX 156	I Am Somebody (Parts 1 & 2)	8
71	Stax 2025 021	Jody's Got Your Girl And Gone/A Fool Like Me	8
73	Stax 2025 083	Standing In For Jody/Shackin' Up	8
73	Stax 2025 194	I Believe In Love/Love Depression	8
75	Stax STXS 2021	It's September/Just One Moment	8
75	Stax STXS 2025	Friday Night/I Ain't Particular	10
76	CBS 4886	Disco Lady/Somebody's Gettin' It (blue vinyl)	8
67	Stax 589 008	WANTED, ONE SOUL SINGER (LP)	70
69	Stax (S)XATS 1006	WHO'S MAKING LOVE (LP)	30
69	Stax 228 008	LOOKING FOR JOHNNIE TAYLOR (LP)	25
69	Stax SXATS 1024	THE J.T. PHILOSOPHY CONTINUES (LP)	25
70	Soul City SCB 2	ROOTS OF JOHNNIE TAYLOR (LP)	75

(LITTLE) JOHNNY TAYLOR

65	Vocalion V 9234	Part Time Love/Somewhere Down The Line	50
65	Vocalion V 9234	Part Time Love/Somewhere Down The Line (DJ copy)	75
66	Vocalion VP 9264	One More Chance/Looking At The Future	30
72	Mojo 2092 033	Everybody Knows About My Good Thing (Parts 1 & 2)	8
72	Mojo 2092 044	It's My Fault Darling/There's Something On Your Mind	8
65	Vocalion VA-F 8031	LITTLE JOHNNY TAYLOR (LP)	100
72	Mojo 2916 015	EVERYBODY KNOWS ABOUT MY GOOD THING (LP)	30
73	Contempo COLP 1003	OPEN HOUSE AT MY HOUSE (LP)	15
74	Contempo CLP 502	SUPER TAYLORS (LP, with Ted Taylor)	15

JOSEPH TAYLOR

72	Leader LEA 4050	UNTO BRIGG FAIR (LP, gatefold sleeve with booklet)	20

KINGSIZE TAYLOR (& DOMINOS)

(see also Shakers, Paddy Klaus & Gibson)

64	Polydor NH 66990	Memphis Tennessee/Money (reissue of Shakers single)	25
64	Polydor NH 66991	Hippy Hippy Shake/Dr. Feelgood (reissue of Shakers single)	25
64	Decca F 11874	Stupidity/Bad Boy	45

MINT VALUE £

64 Decca F 11935 Somebody's Always Trying/Looking For My Baby (solo) 150
65 Polydor BM 56152 Thinkin'/Let Me Love You 35
63 Polydor EPH21 628 TWIST AND SHAKE (EP, manufactured in Germany) 110
64 Decca DFE 8569 TEENBEAT 2 - FROM THE STAR CLUB, HAMBURG (EP) 130

KO KO TAYLOR
(see under 'K')

LINDA TAYLOR
82 Groove Production GPLP 31 TAYLOR MADE (LP) 20

LIVINGSTON TAYLOR
70 Warner Bros WS 3006 LIVINGSTONE TAYLOR (LP) 12

MICK TAYLOR
65 CBS 201770 London Town/Hoboin' 40

MICK TAYLOR
(see also Rolling Stones, Gods, Institute Of Formal Research)
79 CBS 82600 MICK TAYLOR (LP, with inner sleeve) 12
90 Maze 084 649 STRANGER IN THIS TOWN (LP) 12

MIKE TAYLOR
(see also Jack Bruce)
65 Columbia SX 6042 PENDULUM (LP) 300
66 Columbia SX 6137 TRIO (LP) 400
07 Trunk JBH 016 LP MIKE TAYLOR REMEMBERED (LP) 25

NEVILLE TAYLOR (& CUTTERS)
(see also Hal Munro, Bobbie Britton)
58 Parlophone R 4447 House Of Bamboo/Mercy, Mercy, Percy (solo) 40
58 Parlophone R 4447 House Of Bamboo/Mercy, Mercy, Percy (solo) (78) 20
58 Parlophone R 4476 Tears On My Pillow/I Don't Want To Set The World On Fire (solo) 20
58 Parlophone R 4476 Tears On My Pillow/I Don't Want To Set The World On Fire (solo) (78) 10
58 Parlophone R 4493 A Baby Lay Sleeping/The Miracle Of Christmas (solo) 10
58 Parlophone R 4493 A Baby Lay Sleeping/The Miracle Of Christmas (solo) (78) 10
59 Parlophone R 4524 Crazy Little Daisy/The First Words Of Love (solo) 30
59 Parlophone R 4524 Crazy Little Daisy/The First Words Of Love (solo) (78) 12
60 Oriole CB 1546 Dance With Dolly/Free Passes 30
60 Oriole CB 1546 Dance With Dolly/Free Passes (78) 18
60 Embassy WB 373 It Ain't Necessarily So/BOBBIE BRITTON: Woman Is A Sometime Love 6
60s Honey Hit TB 127 Joshua Fit The Battle Of Jericho/It's Me, It's Me, My Love (in p/s) 12
60s Honey Hit TB 127 Joshua Fit The Battle Of Jericho/It's Me, It's Me, My Love 6

PEGGY TAYLOR
60 Top Rank JAR 421 (Don't You Come Home) Bill Bailey/So Similar 7

R. DEAN TAYLOR
68 Tamla Motown TMG 656 Gotta See Jane/Don't Fool Around 10
71 Tamla Motown TMG 763 Indiana Wants Me/Love's Your Name 7
71 Tamla Motown TMG 786 Ain't It A Sad Thing/Backstreet (unissued) 0
71 Rare Earth RES 101 Ain't It A Sad Thing/Backstreet (has TMG 786 matrix in run-out groove) 15
74 Tamla Motown TMG 896 There's A Ghost In My House/Let's Go Somewhere 5
74 Tamla Motown TMG 896 There's A Ghost In My House/Let's Go Somewhere (DJ Copy) 25
71 Tamla Motown STML 11185 INDIANA WANTS ME (LP) 18

ROD TAYLOR
78 Little Lute HITDD 311 If Jah Should Come Now/Africa Be Free/PRINCE HAMMER: Maccabee Bible (12") 30
78 Freedom Sounds FSD 004 Ethiopian King/PHILIP FRAZER: Come Ethiopians (12") 40
78 Hit Run APLP 9031 IF JAH SHOULD COME NOW (LP) 50
79 Hit Run DD 16 No One Can Tell I About Jah/ERROL HOLT : Yes Yes Yes (12") 40
80 Greensleeves GREL 17 WHERE IS YOUR LOVE MANKIND? (LP, green vinyl) 22

ROD TAYLOR & MIKEY DREAD & KING TUBBY
79 Sufferers Heights SUFF 006 Behold Him/Parrot Jungle/His Majesty/Dread All The Way (12") 30

ROGER TAYLOR
(see also Queen, Cross, Hilary Hilary, Ian Hunter, Fox, Kansas, Camy Todorow, Mel Smith, Billy Squier)
77 EMI EMI 2679 I Wanna Testify/Turn On The TV (demo copies £80) 50
81 EMI EMI 5200 My Country (Edit)/Fun In Space (p/s) 30
84 EMI EMI 5478 Man On Fire/Killing Time (p/s) 10
84 EMI 12 EMI 5478 Man On Fire (Extended)/Killing Time (12", p/s) 25
84 EMI EMI 5490 Strange Frontier/I Cry For You (Remix) (p/s) 15
84 EMI 12 EMI 5490 Strange Frontier (Extended)/I Cry For You (Extended Remix)/
Two Sharp Pencils (Get Bad) (12", p/s) 20
94 Parlophone RR 6379 Nazis 1994/Nazis 1994 (Version) (red vinyl, numbered p/s) 5
94 Parlophone 12RC 6379 Nazis 1994 (Single Version)/(Radio Mix)/(Makita Mix - Extended)/
(Big Science Mix) (12" clear vinyl, numbered insert in PVC sleeve) 10
94 Parlophone NAZIS 1 Nazis 1994 (Radio Mix)/Nazis 1944 (Kick Mix) (12", black vinyl, p/s, promo only) 15
94 Parlophone NAZIS 3 Nazis 1994 (Radio Mix)/(Kick Mix)/(Big Science Mix)/(Makita Mix)
(12", black vinyl, p/s, promo only) 15
94 Parlophone NAZIS 4 Nazis 1994 (Schindler's Mix)/(Big Science Mix)/(Makita Mix - Extended)
(12", black vinyl, p/s, promo only) 10
94 Parlophone 12RDJ 6379 Nazis 1994 (Schindler's Mix)/(Big Science Mix)/(Makita Mix - Extended)
(12", white label DJ promo) 30
94 Parlophone R 6389 Foreign Sand (Single Version)/You Had To Be There
(as Roger Taylor & Yoshiki) (blue vinyl, numbered p/s) 5
94 Parlophone CDPCS 157 Happiness/Dear Mr. Murdoch/Everybody Hurts Sometime
(live)/Old Friends (live) (CD, numbered) 10
81 EMI EMC 3369 FUN IN SPACE (LP) 12
84 EMI RTA 1 STRANGE FRONTIER (LP) 12
93 Parlophone PCSD 157 HAPPINESS? (LP, some numbered) 20

MINT VALUE £

ROSEMARY TAYLOR
(see also Great Saturday Night Swindle)
75 JD 2009 TAYLORMAID (LP, private pressing with insert) 200

SAM ('THE MAN') TAYLOR
(see also Claude Cloud)
54 MGM SP 1106 Please Be Kind/This Can't Be Love (as Sam 'The Man' Taylor & Cat Men) 30
56 MGM MGM-EP 531 SAM TAYLOR ORCHESTRA (EP) 35

TAYLOR SHARP & TAYLOR
70 CBS 5197 The Look Of Love/Mr Snow 15

TED TAYLOR FOUR
58 Oriole CB 1464 Son Of Honky Tonk/Farrago 15
58 Oriole CB 1464 Son Of Honky Tonk/Farrago (78) 10
60 Oriole CB 1573 M.1./You Are My Sunshine 12
61 Oriole CB 1574 Fried Onions/Yellow Rock Of Texas 12
61 Oriole CB 1628 Cat's Eyes/Canyon 10
61 Oriole CB 1630 Flyover/Haunted Pad 15
62 Oriole CB 1713 Jericho/Everytime We Say Goodbye 20
62 Oriole CB 1767 Surfrider/Talent Spot 20

TYRONE TAYLOR
78 Observer OBMM 1000 Sufferation/Rock On/Christine (12") 35

VERNON TAYLOR
59 London HLS 8905 Today Is A Blue Day/Breeze (unreleased) 0
60 London HLS 9025 Mystery Train/Sweet And Easy To Love 100

VIC TAYLOR
(see also Tommy McCook)
67 Treasure Isle TI 7021 Heartaches/When It Comes To Loving You I'm Alright
(B-side actually "Loving Pauper" by Dobby Dobson) 80
71 Trojan TRLS 38 DOES IT HIS WAY (LP) 20

VINCE TAYLOR (& HIS PLAYBOYS)
58 Parlophone R 4505 Right Behind You Baby/I Like Love (solo) 60
58 Parlophone R 4505 Right Behind You Baby/I Like Love (solo) (78) 40
59 Parlophone R 4539 Brand New Cadillac/Pledging My Love 50
60 Palette PG 9001 I'll Be Your Hero/Jet Black Machine 25
61 Palette PG 9020 Move Over Tiger/What'cha Gonna Do 25
76 Chiswick (N)S 2 Brand New Cadillac/Pledging My Love (no p/s) 5
97 Cruisin' 50 CASB 006 Brand New Cadillac/Right Behind You Baby (78, 300 only) 30

VINCENT TAYLOR
80 Live & Love LLDIS 115 Can't Seem To Forget You/Living A Lie (12") 40
80 Live & Love LLDIS 117 Got To Have You/TAYLOR PLAYERS: Got You Version (12") 30

WALTER TAYLOR
50s Poydras 2 Thirty-Eight And Plus/Diamond Ring Blues 8

TAYLOR MAIDS
55 Capitol CL 14322 Po-Go Stick/Theme From "I Am A Camera" (Why Do I) 12

TAX DODGERS
93 TAX 2 Ragamuffin Bizness/Flying High (12", stamped white label) 20
94 TAX IT Hot Off D Press/Rebel Without Applause (Two Mixes)
(12", stamped white labels) 20

T-BONES
(see also Gary Farr & T-Bones, Kevin Westlake)
64 Columbia DB 7401 How Many More Times/I'm A Lover Not A Fighter 60
65 Columbia DB 7489 Won't You Give Him (One More Chance)/Hamish's Express Relief 35

JOHN TCHKAI
66 Fontana 881014/681 014ZL RUFUS (LP, with ARCHIE SHEPP) 20

TEA
74 Vertigo 6147 006 Good Times/Judy 5
75 Philips 6305 238 TEA (LP) 15
75 Philips 9118 001 THE SHIP (LP) 12

TEA & SYMPHONY
69 Harvest HAR 5005 Boredom/Armchair Theatre 20
69 Harvest SHVL 761 AN ASYLUM FOR THE MUSICALLY INSANE (LP, laminated gatefold sleeve) 200
70 Harvest SHVL 785 JO SAGO (LP, gatefold sleeve no EMI logo on label) 400

TEACH YOURSELF TURNTABLISM
04 Pedestrian TUTORITOOL - INTERACTIVE TURNTABLISM TUTORIAL
(LP, gatefold with inserts and inner sleeves, 1000 only) 25

TEACHO & HIS STUDENTS
58 Felsted AF 104 Rock-et/Stop 60
58 Felsted AF 104 Rock-et/Stop (78) 30

TEA COMPANY
68 Mercury SMCL 20127 COME AND HAVE SOME TEA WITH THE TEA COMPANY (LP) 50

ANTHONY TEAGUE
62 Decca F 11548 Like I Don't Love You/My Guardian Angel 7

TEAM DOKUS
94 Tenth Planet TP 007 TEAM DOKUS (LP, numbered, 500 only) 15

TEAM 3B
84 Elite DAZZ33 Closer To You/Machine Rap (12") 12

MINT VALUE £

TEA PARTY

94	Chrysalis CHR 6072	SPLENDOR SOILS (LP)	12
95	Chrysalis CHR 6108	THE EDGES OF TWILIGHT (LP)	12

TEARDROP EXPLODES

(see also Julian Cope, Rabbi Joseph Gordan, Lori & Chameleons)

79	Zoo CAGE 003	Sleeping Gas/Camera Camera/Kirkby Workers' Dream Fades (red p/s)	12
79	Zoo CAGE 003	Sleeping Gas/Camera Camera/Kirkby Workers' Dream Fades (blue p/s)	10
79	Zoo CAGE 005	Bouncing Babies/All I Am Is Loving You (p/s)	10
80	Zoo CAGE 008	Treason (It's Just A Story)/Read It In Books (in blue & green p/s)	10
80	Zoo CAGE 008	Treason (It's Just A Story)/Read It In Books	6
80	Mercury TEAR 1	When I Dream/Kilimanjaro (p/s)	5
80	Vertigo TEAR 2	Reward/Strange House In The Snow (p/s)	6
81	Mercury TEAR 312	Treason (It's Just A Story) (Remix)/Traison (C'est Juste Une Histoire)/ Use Me (12", p/s)	8
81	Mercury TEAR 4	Ha Ha I'm Drowning/Poppies In The Field (in withdrawn p/s)	15
81	Mercury TEAR 44	Ha Ha I'm Drowning/Poppies In The Field/Bouncing Babies/ Read It In Books (double pack, gatefold p/s)	6
81	Mercury TEAR 44	Ha Ha I'm Drowning/Poppies In The Field/Bouncing Babies/ Read It In Books (double pack, withdrawn gatefold p/s)	20
81	Mercury TEAR 5	Passionate Friend/Christ Versus Warhol (p/s)	6
81	Mercury TEAR 6	Colours Fly Away/Window Shopping For A New Crown Of Thorns (p/s & insert)	6
83	Mercury TEAR 88	You Disappear From View/Suffocate//Ouch Monkey's/Soft Enough For You/ The In-Psychlopedia (double pack, gatefold p/s)	6
89	Fontana DROP 112	Serious Danger/Sleeping Gas/Seven Views Of Jerusalem (p/s)	6
80	Mercury 6359 035	KILIMANJARO (LP, original issue, 'group photo' on cover & inner sleeve)	18
81	Mercury 6359056	WILDER (LP)	12
90	Mercury 8424391	EVERYBODY WANTS TO SHAG THE TEARDROP EXPLODES (LP, with inner)	15

TEARDROPS

78	Bent BIGB 3	IN AND OUT OF FASHION (12" EP, foldout p/s in poly bag)	18
79	TJM TJM 9	Seeing Double/Teardrops And Heartaches (p/s)	20
80s	Illuminated JAMS 2	FINAL VINYL (LP)	15

TEARDROPS (Jamaica)

71	Ackee ACK 126	Let Me Be Free/CINDY STARR: Sentimental Girl	7
71	Big Shot BI 582	Two In One/LAURIE'S ALL STARS: Rock-A-Boogie	7

TEAR GAS

(see also Alex Harvey, Tandoori Cassette)

70	Famous SFMA 5751	PIGGY GO-GETTER (LP, textured gtefold sleeve)	70
71	Regal Zono. SLRZ 1021	TEAR GAS (LP)	200

TEARJERKERS

(see also Speed)

80	Back Door DOOR 1	Murder Mystery/Heart On The Line (die cut p/s with insert)	8
81	Good Vibrations GOT 9	Love Affair/Bus Stop (p/s)	5

TEARS FOR FEARS

(see also Graduate)

81	Mercury IDEA 1	Suffer The Children/Wino (p/s, original issue with light labels)	10
81	Mercury IDEA 12	Suffer The Children (Remix)/Wino/Suffer The Children (Instrumental) (12", p/s)	12
82	Mercury IDEA 212	Pale Shelter (You Don't Give Me Love) (Extended)/Pale Shelter/ The Prisoner (12", original p/s)	8
82	Mercury IDEA 33	Mad World/Mad World (World Remix) (p/s)	5
82	Mercury IDEA 33	Mad World/Mad World (World Remix)//Suffer The Children/ Ideas As Opiates (double pack)	10
82	Mercury IDEA 4	Change/The Conflict (poster p/s)	7
82	Mercury IDEA 4	Change/The Conflict (withdrawn 'fishing net' sleeve)	75
82	Mercury IDEA 412	Change/The Conflict (12" withdrawn 'fishing net' sleeve)	150
83	Mercury IDEA R/B 5	Pale Shelter/We Are Broken (p/s, red or blue vinyl)	10
83	Mercury IDEAG 5	Pale Shelter/We Are Broken (p/s, translucent green vinyl)	7
83	Mercury IDEAP 5	Pale Shelter/We Are Broken (picture disc)	12
83	Mercury IDEA 512	Pale Shelter/We Are Broken (12", p/s)	10
83	Mercury IDEA 6	(The) Way You Are/The Marauders (rumours of poster issue remain unconfirmed)	5
83	Mercury IDEAS 6	(The) Way You Are/The Marauders//Change (Live)/Start Of The Breakdown (live) (shrinkwrapped double pack)	8
84	Mercury IDEA 7	Mother's Talk/Empire Building (clear vinyl picture disc)	5
84	Mercury IDEA 7	Mother's Talk/Empire Building (green vinyl, p/s, with window sticker)	8
84	Mercury IDEA 12	Mother's Talk (Beat Of The Drum Mix)/Empire Building (12", p/s)	8
85	fan club ANTAR 4502	Mother's Talk/Interview	18
85	Mercury IDEC 8	Shout/The Big Chair (calendar pack with 6 cards)	7
85	Mercury IDEA 99	Everybody Wants To Rule The World/Pharaohs//Everybody Wants To Rule The World (Urban Mix)/Interview (double pack)	8
85	Mercury IDEA 910	Everybody Wants To Rule The World/Pharaohs (10", p/s)	7
85	Mercury RACE 112	Everybody Wants To Run The World/(Running Version) (12", p/s)	12
85	Mercury IDEAP 10	Head Over Heels (Remix)/When In Love With A Blind Man (poster p/s)	5
85	Mercury IDEP 10	Head Over Heels (Remix)/When In Love With A Blind Man (clover-shaped picture disc)	8
85	Mercury IDEA 11	I Believe/Sea Song (p/s, sealed with set of postcards, withdrawn)	8
85	Mercury IDEA 1111	I Believe (A Soulful Re-Recording)/Sea Song//I Believe (Original Version)/ Shout (Dub Version) (double pack, gatefold p/s)	5
85	Mercury IDEP 10	Head Over Heels/When In Love With A Blind Man (poster p/s)	8
89	Fontana IDCDL 12	Sowing The Seeds Of Love (Full Version)/Tears Roll Down/Shout (U.S. Remix) (3" CD, red/yellow plastic sunflower pack)	15
89	Fontana IDSUN 13	Woman In Chains/Always In The Past/My Life In The Suicide Ranks/ Woman In Chains (Instrumental) (3" CD, gold card 'sun' pack)	15
88	Mercury 080 032-2	Everybody Wants To Rule The World/The Marauders/When In Love With A Blind Man/Pharaohs/Everybody Wants To Rule The World (Video) (CD Video)	15

			MINT VALUE £
88	Mercury 080 064-2	Shout/Everybody Wants To Rule The World (Urban Mix)/Shout (U.S.A. Mix)/ Shout (Video) (CD Video)	15
88	Mercury 080 062-2	Head Over Heels/Sea Song/The Working Hour/Mother's Talk (U.S.A.)/ Head Over Heels (Video) (CD Video)	15
88	Mercury 080 068-2	I Believe (A Soulful Re-Recording)/Start Of The Breakdown/ Ideas As Opiates/Change/I Believe (Video) (CD Video)	12
89	Fontana IDPT 12	Sowing The Seeds Of Love/Tears Roll Down/Shout (US Remix) (12" picture disc, PVC sleeve)	10
89	Fontana 081 376-2	Sowing The Seeds Of Love (Full Version)/Tears Roll Down/ Shout (U.S. Remix)/Sowing The Seeds Of Love (Video) (CD Video)	10
89	Fontana IDEAB 13	Woman In Chains/Always In The Past (p/s, with badges)	6
89	Fontana IDSUN 13	Woman In Chains/(Instrumental Version)/Always In The Past (3" CD, in sun-shaped pack)	10
90	Fontana IDCDS 14	Advice For The Young At Heart/Johnny Panic And The Bible Of Dreams/ Music For Tables (CD)	10
92	Fontana IDEAP 16	Woman In Chains/Always In The Past/Woman In Chains (Instrumental) (12" picture disc, numbered, with poster)	8

TEARS ON THE CONSOLE

75	Holyground HG 120	TEARS ON THE CONSOLE (LP, with booklet, 120 demo copies only)	150
90	Magic Mixture MM 3	TEARS ON THE CONSOLE (LP, reissue, 425 only, with insert)	20

(Band's name is actually Chick Shannon & Last Exit)

TEASER

89	LTW 9KS 2049	Here Tonight (p/s)	20

TEA SET

66	King KG 1048	Join The Tea Set/Ready Steady Go!	25
78	Waldo's Beat Series 003	CUPS AND SAUCERS (EP, with stapled lyric book sleeve)	10

TEA SET

79	Waldo's Beat PS 006	Parry Thomas/Tri-X Pan (gatefold p/s with poster 'mystery' envelope)	8
80	Demon D 1009	South Pacific/The Preacher (foldout p/s with inserts)	8

TECHNIQUES (Jamaica)

(see also Techniques All Stars, Riots, Tommy McCook, Mighty Avengers, Gaylads, Rad Bryan)

65	Island WI 231	Little Did You Know/DON DRUMMOND: Cool Smoke	25
67	Treasure Isle TI 7001	You Don't Care (with Tommy McCook & Supersonics Band)/ TOMMY McCOOK & SUPERSONICS BAND: Down On Bond Street	30
67	Treasure Isle TI 7019	Queen Majesty/Fighting For The Right	35
67	Treasure Isle TI 7026	Love Is Not A Gamble/Bad-Minded People	30
68	Treasure Isle TI 7031	My Girl/Drink Wine (with Tommy McCook & Supersonics)	25
68	Treasure Isle TI 7038	Devoted/Bless You (with Tommy McCook & Supersonics)	25
68	Treasure Isle TI 7040	It's You I Love/Travelling Man (with Tommy McCook & Supersonics)	60
68	Duke DU 1	I Wish It Would Rain/There Comes A Time	60
69	Duke DU 6	A Man Of My Word/The Time Has Come	60
69	Duke DU 22	What Am I To Do/You're My Everything	60
69	Duke DU 60	Where Were You/Just One Smile	18
69	Camel CA 10	Who You Gonna Run To/Hi There (B-side act. "Look Who's Back" by Carl Bryan)	25
69	Camel CA 19	Everywhere Everyone/Find Yourself Another Fool	25
70	Treasure Isle TI 7054	He Who Keepeth His Mouth/One Day (act. by Johnny Osborne & Sensations)	15
70	Techniques TE 904	Lonely Man/I Feel Alive	10
70	Techniques TE 906	Feel A Little Better (actually by Techniques Allstars)/You'll Get Left	10
70	Big Shot BI 536	He Who Keepeth His Mouth/One Day (act. by Johnny Osborne & Sensations)	12
71	Banana BA 350	Since I Lost You/RILEY'S ALLSTARS: Version	15

TECHNIQUES (U.S.)

58	Columbia DB 4072	Hey! Little Girl/In A Round About Way	60
58	Columbia DB 4072	Hey! Little Girl/In A Round About Way (78)	15

TECHNIQUES ALL STARS

(see also Dennis Alcapone, Ansell Collins)

70	Big Shot BI 543	Come Back Darling/Move Over (actually by Johnny Osborne & Sensations)	12
70	Big Shot BI 545	Elfrego Bacca (actually by Dave Barker)/TECHNIQUES: Iron Joe (B-side actually by Techniques All Stars)	35
70	Techniques TE 900	Something Tender/CANNONBALL: Bewitch	8
70	Trojan TR 7728	El Dora/TECHNIQUES: If It's Not True (B-side actually by Techniques All Stars)	8

TECHNOSAURUS

93	Invention TBH 1	YOU GAVE ME NOTHING EP (12", stamped white labels)	40

TED

74	Epic SPEC 3126	Gonna Make You My Angel/Can't Stop The Train	8

TEDDIE & THE TIGERS

67	Spin SP 2004	Hold On I'm Comin'/First Love Never Dies	20

TEDDY

71	Upsetter US 353	Elusion/UPSETTERS: Big John Wayne	15

TEDDY & THE CONQUERORS

71	High Note HS 053	Homebound/GAYTONES: Homebound Chapter 3	8

TEDDY & THE FRAT GIRLS

85	Alternative Tentacles VIRUS 19	I Wanna Be A Man/I Owe It All To The Girls/Clubnite/ Alophen Baby/ The Eggman Don't Cometh (p/s)	5

TEDDY & THE TWILIGHTS

63	Stateside SS 167	I'm Just Your Clown/Bikini Bimbo	25

TEDDY BEARS

(see also Phil Spector, Carol Connors)

58	London HL 8733	To Know Him Is To Love Him/Don't You Worry, My Little Pet	8

MINT VALUE £

58 London HL 8733 To Know Him Is To Love Him/Don't You Worry, My Little Pet (78) 10
59 London HLP 8836 I Don't Need You Anymore/Oh Why 25
59 London HLP 8836 I Don't Need You Anymore/Oh Why (78) 10
59 London HLP 8889 You Said Goodbye/If You Only Knew 30
59 London HLP 8889 You Said Goodbye/If You Only Knew (78) 15
59 London HA-P 2183 THE TEDDY BEARS SING! (LP) 250

WILLIE TEE

67 Atlantic 584 116 Thank You John/Walking Up A One-Way Street 30
71 Mojo 2092 025 Walking Up A One-Way Street/Thank You John/Teasin' You 8

TEEGARDEN & VAN WINKLE

69 Atco 228028 BUT ANYHOW (LP) 15
70 Pye 7N 25535 God, Love And Rock And Roll/Work Me Tomorrow 6

TEENAGE FANCLUB

(see also Boy Hairdressers, BMX Bandits, Clouds, Eugenius)

90 Paperhouse PAPER 003 Everything Flows/Primary Education/Speeeder (1,500 only, die-cut p/s) 8
90 Paperhouse PAPER 005 The Ballad Of John And Yoko (p/s, 1-sided, 5,000 only, 2nd side engraved) 8
91 Creation CRESCD 105 Star Sign/(Demo Version)/Heavy Metal 6/Like A Virgin (CD, card sleeve) 12
91 Creation CRESCD 111 The Concept/What You Do To Me (Demo) (CD, card sleeve) 10
95 Creation CRESCD 216 HAVE LOST IT EP (CD, digipak) 8
03 Creation POOLS 5 Did I Say/The Cabbage (p/s, 500 only) 5
90 Paperhouse PAPLP 004 A CATHOLIC EDUCATION (LP, gatefold sleeve) 15
91 Creation CRELP 096 THE KING (LP, available for 1 week only, sprayed plain sleeve) 25
91 Creation CRECD 096 THE KING (CD, available for 1 week only, sprayed plain sleeve) 20
91 Creation CRELP 106 BANDWAGONESQUE (LP, with inner) 12
95 Creation CRELP GRAND PRIX (LP, with free 7") 20
97 Creation CRELP 196 SONGS FROM NORTHERN BRITAIN (LP) 25

TEENAGE FILMSTARS

(see also Television Personalities, Times, O Level)

79 Clockwork COR 002 (There's A) Cloud Over Liverpool/Sometimes Good Guys Don't Follow Trends (1st 150 with foldout p/s) 100
79 Clockwork COR 002 (There's A) Cloud Over Liverpool/Sometimes Good Guys Don't Follow Trends 25
80 Wessex WEX 275 The Odd Man Out/I Apologise 25
80 Blueprint BLU 2013 The Odd Man Out/I Apologise (reissue, p/s) 20
80 Fab Listening FL 1 I Helped Patrick McGoohan Escape/We're Not Sorry (p/s) 15

TEENAGERS

57 RCA RCX 102 THE TEENAGERS (EP) 60

TEENAGERS featuring FRANKIE LYMON

(see under Frankie Lymon)

TEEN BEATS (U.S.)

60 Top Rank JAR 342 The Slop Beat/Califf Boogie (featuring Don Rivers & Califfs) 25

TEENBEATS

79 Safari SAFE 17 I Can't Control Myself/I'll Never Win (p/s) 8
79 Safari SAFE 19 Strength Of The Nation/I'm Gone Tomorrow (in p/s) 15
79 Safari SAFE 19 Strength Of The Nation/I'm Gone Tomorrow 6

TEEN QUEENS

65 R&B MRB 5000 Eddie My Love/Just Goofed 30

TEEN STARLETS

61 Top Rank JAR 583 The Children's Picnic Song/Theme From 'Spinster' 5

TEE SET

68 Pye 7N 25452 What Can I Do/Colours Of The Rainbow 15

TEE SET

70 Major Minor MM 666 Ma Belle Amie/Angels Coming 8
70 Columbia DB 8375 Mr Music Man/In My House 5
70s Waldo's 3 CUPS AND SAUCERS EP (foldout sleeve) 8
70 Columbia SCX 6419 MA BELLE AMIE (LP) 15

TEESIDE FETTLER

74 Tradition TSR 016 RING OF IRON (LP) 15
75 Tradition TSR 021 TRAVELLING THE TEES (LP) 12

TEETH

79 Soho SH 8 Say Hello To Suzy/Human Bondage (p/s) 5

JOHN TEJADA

98 Ferox 030 SONIC LIFE EP (12", plain sleeve) 8

TEK 9

91 Reinforced RIVET 1205 KINGDOM OF DUB EP(12") 10
92 Reinforced RIVET 1229 JUST A DREAM EP (12") 20
92 Reinforced RIVET 1229R JUST A DREAM EP (Remixes) (12") 10
93 Reinforced RIVET 1238 THE RETURN OF TEK 9 EP (12") 15
93 Reinforced RIVET 1238R THE RETURN OF TEK 9 (Rpt) (12") 10
93 Reinforced RIVET 1253 BREAKIN' THE SOUND BARRIERS EP (12") 15
94 Reinforced RIVET 1262 KILLING TIME EP (10") 12
94 Reinforced RIVET 1269 JUS' A LIKKLE SUMTIN' EP (2x12") 25

TELEGRAMS

(See also Steve Allan, Alan Carvell, Carvells, Five Sapphires)

78 Creole CR 163 Oh Baby Please/Hey Baby 5

TELESCOPES

87 private cassette THE TREE 'ATES EP (demo cassette) 10
88 Cheree CHEREE 1 Forever Close Your Eyes/LOOP: Soundhead (33rpm flexi, p/s, 1,000 only) 6
89 Cheree CHEREE 2 Kick The Wall/This Is The Last Of What's Coming Now (p/s, with insert, 1,000 only, light grey/blue p/s) 5

			MINT VALUE £
89	Cheree CHEREE 2	Kick The Wall/This Is The Last Of What's Coming Now (numbered re-pressing, 500 only, red wraparound p/s)	8
89	Cheree CHEREE 4	7th Disaster/Nothing/This Planet/Cold (12" p/s)	8
89	What Goes On WHAT GOES 15T	THE PERFECT NEEDLE EP (12")	8
89	What Goes On WHAT GOES ON 32	TASTE (LP)	15

TELEVISION

(see also Neon Boys)

77	Elektra K 12252	Marquee Moon Parts 1 & 2	5
78	Elektra K 12287	Foxhole/Careful (12", red vinyl)	8
79	Ork/WEA NYC 1T	Little Johnny Jewel Parts 1 & 2/Little Johnny Jewel (live) (12", p/s)	15
77	Elektra K52046	MARQUEE MOON (LP)	20
78	Elektra K52072	ADVENTURE (LP, red vinyl)	12

TELEVISION PERSONALITIES

(see also Teenage Filmstars, Times, O Level, Missing Scientists, Reacta, Dry Rib, Slaughter, Gifted Children)

78	Teen '78 SRTS/CUS/77/089	14th Floor/Oxford Street W1 (p/s, various different sleeve designs)	50
78	Teen '78 SRTS/CUS/77/089	14th Floor/Oxford Street W1 (p/s, various different sleeve designs)	35
78	Kings Road LYN 5976/7	WHERE'S BILL GRUNDY NOW? (EP, hand-stamped label, 2,000 only)	25
78	Kings Road LYN 5976/7	WHERE'S BILL GRUNDY NOW? (EP, white labels, various sleeves)	12
79	Rough Trade RT 033	WHERE'S BILL GRUNDY NOW? (EP, reissue, different p/s, printed labels)	10
80	Rough Trade RT 051	Smashing Time/King & Country (p/s)	15
81	Rough Trade RT 063	I Know Where Syd Barrett Lives/Arthur The Gardener (p/s)	12
82	Whaam! WHAAM 4	Three Wishes/Geoffrey Ingram/And Don't The Kids Just Love It (p/s, 2 different sleeve designs, 2,000 only)	15
82	Creation Artefact 002/ Lyntone LYN 13546	Biff Bang Pow!/A Picture Of Dorian Gray (1-sided flexidisc, with Communication Blur fanzine)	25
82	Creation Artefact 002/ Lyntone LYN 13546	Biff Bang Pow!/A Picture Of Dorian Gray (1-sided flexidisc, without Communication Blur fanzine)	18
83	Rough Trade RT 109	A Sense Of Belonging/Paradise Estate (p/s)	12
86	Dreamworld DREAM 4	How I Learnt To Love The Bomb/Then God Snaps His Fingers/ Now You're Just Being Ridiculous (12", p/s, 3,700 only)	15
86	Dreamworld DREAM 10	How I Learnt To Love The Bomb/Grocer's Daughter/Girl Called Charity (7", reissue, p/s, 1,000 only)	15
87	Dreamworld DREAM 13(T)	Privilege/Me And My Desires (unreleased)	0
89	Overground OVER 03	14th Floor/Oxford Street W1 (numbered p/s, 600 yellow vinyl)	6
89	Overground OVER 03	14th Floor/Oxford Street W1 (numbered p/s, 400 white vinyl)	7
89	Caff CAFF 5	I Still Believe In Magic/Respectable (p/s, in poly bag, 500 only)	35
89	Caff CAFF 5	I Still Believe In Magic/Respectable (p/s, 500 only)	25
90	Overground OVER 13	I Know Where Syd Barrett Lives/Arthur The Gardener (reissue, p/s, 2000 only)	6
90	Overground OVER 15	Silly Girl (unissued, 100 test pressings only)	18
91	Clawfist XPIG 8	Your Class/BMX BANDITS: Somebody To Share My Life With	12
92	Seminal Twang TWANG 15	We Will Be Your Gurus/Miro/An Exhibition By Jane/Love Is Better Than War (p/s)	7
81	Rough Trade ROUGH 24	AND DON'T THE KIDS JUST LOVE IT (LP, 1st 1,000 with insert)	50
81	Rough Trade ROUGH 24	AND DON'T THE KIDS JUST LOVE IT (LP)	35
81	Whaam! WHAAM 3	MUMMY YOU'RE NOT WATCHING ME (LP, 3,500 only, 1st 1,000 with insert)	50
81	Whaam! WHAAM 3	MUMMY YOU'RE NOT WATCHING ME (LP, 3,500 only, 2,500 without insert)	35
82	Whaam! BIG 5	THEY COULD HAVE BEEN BIGGER THAN THE BEATLES (LP, 2,500 only, hand-painted sleeve)	35
84	Dreamworld HWDS 001	I KNOW WHERE DAN TREACY LIVES (live at Forum 20/9/84) (cassette only, fan club issue)	35
85	Illuminated JAMS 37	THE PAINTED WORD (LP)	25
86	Dreamworld BIG DREAM 2	THEY COULD HAVE BEEN BIGGER THAN THE BEATLES (LP, reissue with insert)	20
86	Dreamworld BIG DREAM 4	MUMMY YOU'RE NOT WATCHING ME (LP, reissue with insert)	20

TELEX

78	Sire SIR 4006	Twist A Saint-Tropez/Le Fond De L'Air (p/s)	5
79	Sire SIR 4017	Moskow Diskow/Twist A Saint-Tropez (p/s)	5
79	Sire SIR 4017T	Moskow Diskow (Disco Version)/Twist A Saint-Tropez (Disco Version) (12")	8
79	Sire SIR 4020	Rock Around The Clock/Moskow Diskow	5
82	Interdisc IN 2	L'amour Toujours/Cloche Et Sifflets (p/s)	5
79	Sire SRK 6072	LOOKING FOR ST. TROPEZ (LP, with lyric inner sleeve)	12
82	Interdisc INTO 1	BIRDS AND BEES (LP)	15

TELHAM TINKERS

84	Eron ERON 031	HOT IN ALICE SPRINGS (LP, with insert)	12

TELLERS

74	Pyramid PYR 7011	No Work, No Pay/Version	6
74	Dragon DRA 1031	Ta It Deh/Hit Dib	6

TELSTARS

62	Oriole CB 1754	I Went A' Walkin'/A Rose And A Thorn	20

TEMPERANCE SEVEN

(see also Ted Wood)

63	Parlophone R 5070	From Russia With Love/P.C.Q/Please Charleston Quietly	7
61	Argo EAF 14	THE TEMPERANCE SEVEN INCH RECORD (EP)	8

TEMPEST

(see also Colosseum, Patto)

73	Bronze ILPS 9220	TEMPEST (LP, foldover cover with lyric inner sleeve)	45
74	Bronze ILPS 9267	LIVING IN FEAR (LP, die-cut cover with inner sleeve)	25

TEMPEST

85	Magnet PEST 1	Always The Same/Love In The Wintertime (p/s)	50
85	Magnet 10PEST 1	Always The Same/The Physical Act (10")	25
85	Magnet PEST 2	Bluebelle/I Want To Live (p/s)	50

MINT VALUE £

85	Magnet 10PEST 2	Bluebelle/I Want To Live (10")	25
86	Magnet LAZY 1	Lazy Sunday/You've Always Got Something To Say (p/s)	15
86	Magnet PEST 3	Didn't We Have A Nice Time?/The Physical Act	50

BOBBY TEMPEST

59	Decca F 11125	Love Or Leave/Don't Leave Me	12
59	Decca F 11125	Love Or Leave/Don't Leave Me (78)	10

BOB TEMPLE

57	Parlophone R 4264	Come Back, Come Back/Vim Vam Vamoose	100
57	Parlophone R 4264	Come Back, Come Back/Vim Vam Vamoose (78)	10

GERRY TEMPLE

61	HMV POP 823	No More Tomorrows/So Nice To Walk You Home	40
61	HMV POP 939	Seventeen Come Sunday/Tell You What I'll Do	35
63	HMV POP 1114	Angel Face/Since You Went Away	45
68	RCA Victor RCA 1670	Lovin' Up A Storm/Everything I Do is Wrong	20

RICHARD TEMPLE

70	Jay Boy BOY 31	That Beatin' Rhythm/Could It Be	15
70	Jay Boy BOY 31	That Beatin' Rhythm/Could It Be (DJ copy)	30

SHIRLEY TEMPLE

59	Top Rank JAR 139	On The Good Ship Lollipop/Animal Crackers In My Soup	5
59	Top Rank JAR 139	On The Good Ship Lollipop/Animal Crackers In My Soup (78)	10
59	Top Rank JKR 8003	I REMEMBER (EP)	20

TEMPLEAIRES

60s	Vogue V 2421	He Spoke/What Will Heaven Have In Store For Me	20

TEMPLE OF LIFE

91	T Life 001	EDP/Relax Your Soul/Slayer/Trancetone (12", stamped white labels)	50

TEMPLE OF THE DOG

(see also Pearl Jam)

92	A&M AM 0091	Hunger Strike/All Night Thing (picture disc)	15
92	A&M AMY 0091	Hunger Strike/Your Saviour/All Night Thing (12", p/s, with poster)	15
92	A&M AMCD 0091	Hunger Strike/Your Saviour/All Night Thing (CD, digipak)	20
91	A&M 395350-1	TEMPLE OF THE DOG (LP)	30

TEMPLE ROW

72	Polydor 2058254	King & Queen/One Of A Million Faces	50
73	Polydor 2058-329	Walk The World Away/Mystery Man	8

TEMPLETON TWINS

70	Liberty LBF 15379	Hey Jude/Macarthur Park	6

NINO TEMPO

(see also Nino Tempo & April Stevens, April Stevenso)

57	London HLU 8387	Tempo's Tempo/June's Blues (as Nino Tempo & His Band)	300
57	London HLU 8387	Tempo's Tempo/June's Blues (as Nino Tempo & His Band) (78)	50
75	A&M AMS 7190	Come See Me Round Midnight/High On Music (as Nino Tempo & 5th Avenue)	5
58	London HB-U 1075	ROCK 'N' ROLL BEACH PARTY (10" LP)	300

NINO TEMPO & APRIL STEVENS

(see also Nino Tempo, April Stevens)

62	London HLK 9580	Sweet And Lovely/TOP NOTES: Twist And Shout	15
63	London HLK 9782	Deep Purple/I've Been Carrying A Torch For You So Long That I Burned A Great Big Hole In My Heart	5
64	London HLK 9829	Whispering/Tweedle Dee	5
64	London HLK 9859	Stardust/1-45	5
64	London HLK 9890	Tea For Two/I'm Confessin' (That I Love You)	5
66	London HLU 10084	All Strung Out/I Can't Go On Living Baby Without You	6
67	Atlantic 584 048	Coldest Night Of The Year/Ooh La La (as April Stevens & Nino Tempo)	6
67	London HLU 10106	The Habit Of Lovin' You Baby/You'll Be Needing Me Baby	6
67	London HLU 10130	My Old Flame/Wings Of Love	5
68	Atlantic 584 151	Deep Purple/Sweet And Lovely	5
68	London HLU 10209	Ooh Poo Pah Doo/Let It Be Me	5
69	London HLU 10245	All Strung Out/My Old Flame	8
69	Bell BLL 1087	Sea Of Love/On The Dock Of The Bay/Twilight Time	5
73	A&M AMS 7075	Put It Where You Want It/I Can't Get Over You Baby	5
64	London RE-K 1412	DEEP PURPLE (EP)	10
64	London HA-K 8168	NINO TEMPO AND APRIL STEVENS - DEEP PURPLE (LP)	35
64	Atlantic AL 5006	SING THE GREAT SONGS (LP, mono)	25
64	Atlantic SAL 5006	SING THE GREAT SONGS (LP, stereo)	30
66	Atlantic	HEY BABY (LP)	20
67	London HA-U/SH-U 8314	ALL STRUNG OUT (LP)	30

TEMPOS

59	Pye International 7N 25026	See You In September/Bless You My Love	100
59	Pye International 7N 25026	See You In September/Bless You My Love (78)	40

TEMPTATIONS

(see also Dave Ruffin, Diana Ross)

SINGLES

60	Top Rank JAR 384	Barbara/Someday	40
64	Stateside SS 278	The Way You Do The Things You Do/Just Let Me Know	60
64	Stateside SS 319	I'll Be In Trouble/The Girl's Alright With Me	70
64	Stateside SS 348	Why You Wanna Make Me Blue/Baby Baby I Need You	90
65	Stateside SS 378	My Girl/(Talking 'Bout) Nobody But My Baby	45
65	Tamla Motown TMG 504	It's Growing/What Love Has Joined Together	40
65	Tamla Motown TMG 526	Since I Lost My Baby/You've Got To Earn It	40
65	Tamla Motown TMG 541	My Baby/Don't Look Back	45

			MINT VALUE £
66	Tamla Motown TMG 557	Get Ready/Fading Away	35
66	Tamla Motown TMG 565	Ain't Too Proud To Beg/You'll Lose A Precious Love (spelt "Previous")	35
66	Tamla Motown TMG 578	Beauty Is Only Skin Deep/You're Not An Ordinary Girl	30
66	Tamla Motown TMG 578	Beauty Is Only Skin Deep/You're Not An Ordinary Girl (DJ copy)	140
66	Tamla Motown TMG 587	(I Know) I'm Losing You/Little Miss Sweetness	25
67	Tamla Motown TMG 610	All I Need/Sorry Is A Sorry Word	20
67	Tamla Motown TMG 620	You're My Everything/I've Been Good To You	20
67	Tamla Motown TMG 633	(Loneliness Made Me Realise) It's You That I Need/I Want A Love I Can See	40
68	Tamla Motown TMG 641	I Wish It Would Rain/I Truly, Truly Believe	20
68	Tamla Motown TMG 658	I Could Never Love Another (After Loving You)/ Gonna Give Her All The Love I've Got	15
68	Tamla Motown TMG 671	Why Did You Leave Me Darling/How Can I Forget	15
69	Tamla Motown TMG 688	Get Ready/My Girl	7
69	Tamla Motown TMG 699	Ain't Too Proud To Beg/Fading Away	7
69	Tamla Motown TMG 707	Cloud Nine/Why Did She Have To Leave Me (Why Did She Have To Go)	7
69	Tamla Motown TMG 716	Runaway Child, Running Wild/I Need Your Lovin'	8
70	Tamla Motown TMG 722	I Can't Get Next To You/Running Away (Ain't Gonna Help You)	7
70	Tamla Motown TMG 749	Ball Of Confusion (That's What The World Is Today)/It's Summer	7
70	Tamla Motown TMG 741	Psychedelic Shack/That's The Way Love Is	6
71	Tamla Motown TMG 773	Just My Imagination (Running Away With Me)/You Make Your Own Heaven And Hell Right Here On Earth	6
71	Tamla Motown TMG 783	It's Summer/Unite The World (Ungena Za Ulimwengu)	6
71	Tamla Motown TMG 783	Unite The World (Ungena Za Ulimwengu)/It's Summer (reissue)	8
72	Tamla Motown TMG 800	Superstar/Gonna Keep Tryin' Till I Win Your Love	8
72	Tamla Motown TMG 808	Take A Look Around/Smooth Sailing (From Now On)	6
72	Tamla Motown TMG 832	Smiling Faces Sometimes/Mother Nature	8
73	Tamla Motown TMG 839	Papa Was A Rolling Stone (Parts 1 & 2)	5
83	Tamla Motown TMG 1320	Papa Was A Rolling Stone/FOUR TOPS: Medley	35
PROMOS			
64	Stateside SS 278	The Way You Do The Things You Do/Just Let Me Know (DJ copy)	120
64	Stateside SS 319	I'll Be In Trouble/The Girl's Alright With Me (DJ copy)	120
64	Stateside SS 348	Why You Wanna Make Me Blue/Baby Baby I Need You (DJ copy)	240
65	Stateside SS 378	My Girl/(Talking 'Bout) Nobody But My Baby (DJ copy)	150
65	Tamla Motown TMG 504	It's Growing/What Love Has Joined Together (DJ copy)	100
65	Tamla Motown TMG 526	Since I Lost My Baby/You've Got To Earn It (DJ copy)	200
65	Tamla Motown TMG 541	My Baby/Don't Look Back (DJ copy)	100
66	Tamla Motown TMG 557	Get Ready/Fading Away (DJ copy)	100
66	Tamla Motown TMG 565	Ain't Too Proud To Beg/You'll Lose A Precious Love (spelt "Previous") (DJ copy)	130
66	Tamla Motown TMG 587	(I Know) I'm Losing You/Little Miss Sweetness (DJ copy)	80
67	Tamla Motown TMG 610	All I Need/Sorry Is A Sorry Word (DJ copy)	60
67	Tamla Motown TMG 620	You're My Everything/I've Been Good To You (DJ copy)	50
67	Tamla Motown TMG 633	(Loneliness Made Me Realise) It's You That I Need/I Want A Love I Can See (DJ copy)	45
68	Tamla Motown TMG 641	I Wish It Would Rain/I Truly, Truly Believe (DJ copy)	30
68	Tamla Motown TMG 658	I Could Never Love Another (After Loving You)/ Gonna Give Her All The Love I've Got (DJ copy)	30
68	Tamla Motown TMG 671	Why Did You Leave Me Darling/How Can I Forget (DJ copy)	30
69	Tamla Motown TMG 688	Get Ready/My Girl (DJ copy)	30
69	Tamla Motown TMG 699	Ain't Too Proud To Beg/Fading Away (DJ copy)	25
69	Tamla Motown TMG 707	Cloud Nine/Why Did She Have To Leave Me (Why Did She Have To Go) (DJ copy)	25
EPs			
65	Tamla Motown TME 2004	THE TEMPTATIONS (EP)	45
66	Tamla Motown TME 2010	IT'S THE TEMPTATIONS	35
LPs			
65	Tamla Motown TML 11009	MEET THE TEMPTATIONS	200
65	T. Motown TML 11016	SING SMOKEY	55
66	T. Motown TML 11023	THE TEMPTIN' TEMPTATIONS (mono)	45
66	T. Motown STML 11023	THE TEMPTIN' TEMPTATIONS (stereo)	55
66	T. Motown TML 11035	GETTIN' READY (mono)	40
66	T. Motown STML 11035	GETTIN' READY (stereo)	50
67	T. Motown TML 11042	GREATEST HITS (mono)	20
67	T. Motown STML 11042	GREATEST HITS (stereo)	25
67	T. Motown STML 11053	THE TEMPTATIONS LIVE! (stereo)	30
67	T. Motown TML 11053	TEMPTATIONS LIVE! (mono)	25
67	T. Motown STML 11057	WITH A LOT O'SOUL (stereo)	40
67	T. Motown TML 11057	WITH A LOT O'SOUL (mono)	35
68	T. Motown STML 11068	IN A MELLOW MOOD (stereo)	40
68	T. Motown TML 11068	IN A MELLOW MOOD (mono)	35
68	T. Motown STML 11079	WISH IT WOULD RAIN (LP, stereo)	35
68	T. Motown TML 11079	WISH IT WOULD RAIN (LP, mono)	30
69	T. Motown STML 11104	THE TEMPTATIONS LIVE AT THE COPA (stereo)	25
69	T. Motown TML 11104	THE TEMPTATIONS LIVE AT THE COPA (mono)	30
69	T. Motown (S)TML 11109	CLOUD NINE (mono/stereo)	25
70	T. Motown (S)TML 11133	PUZZLE PEOPLE (mono/stereo)	25
70	T. Motown (S)TML 11141	'LIVE' AT LONDON'S TALK OF THE TOWN	20
70	T. Motown STML 11147	PSYCHEDELIC SHACK	25
70	T. Motown STML 11170	GREATEST HITS Vol. 2	15
71	T. Motown STML 11184	THE SKY'S THE LIMIT	20
72	T. Motown STML 11202	SOLID ROCK	15
72	T. Motown STML 11218	ALL DIRECTIONS	15
73	T. Motown STML 11229	MASTERPIECE	15

TEMPUS FUGIT

(see also Jensens)

69	Philips BF 1802	Come Alive/Emphasis On Love	60

MINT VALUE £

10cc

(see also Godley & Creme, Graham Gouldman, Mindbenders, Mockingbirds, Hotlegs, Whirlwinds, Tristar Airbus, Yellow Bellow Room Boom, Nick Mason & Rick Fenn, Frabjoy & Runcible Spoon, Manchester Mob, Ramases)

72	UK UK 22	Johnny Don't Do It/4% Of Something	6
74	UK UK 57	The Worst Band In The World/18 Carat Man Of Means	6
73	UK UKAL 1005	10cc (LP, lyric insert)	12
80s	Mercury HS 9102 500	THE ORIGINAL SOUNDTRACK (LP, half-speed master)	12
80s	Mercury HS 9102 504	GREATEST HITS (LP, half-speed master)	12
95	Avex AVEXLP	MIRROR MIRROR (LP)	12

TENDER TONES

69	Crab CRAB 38	Devil Woman/Nobody Cares	10

TEN FEET

66	RCA RCA 1544	Got Everything But Love/Factory Worker	100
67	CBS 3045	Shoot On Sight/Losing Game	100

TEN FEET FIVE

(see also Troggs)

65	Fontana TF 578	Baby's Back In Town/Send Me No More Lovin'	45

TEN FOOT BONELESS

(see also Pooh Sticks)

88	Fierce FRIGHT 027	Powerslide/Duane Peters Is God (12", yellow or white p/s, with inner)	12

TENNENT & MORRISON

(see also Joe Soap)

72	Polydor 2383 152	TENNENT & MORRISON (LP, with lyric insert)	150

TENNESSEE JAY BIRDS

51	London L 1007	Sticks And Stones/Trouble Trouble (78)	10

TENNIS SHOES

78	Bonaparte BONE 3	(Do The) Medium Wave/Rolf Is Stranger Than Richard/So Large (p/s)	8

TEN(N)ORS

(see also Jennors, Prince Buster, Soul Brothers)

68	Doctor Bird DB 1152	Massy Massa/CLIVE ALLSTARS: San Sebastian	40
68	Doctor Bird DB 1175	Sufferer (Make It)/Little Things	40
68	Island WI 3133	Ride Your Donkey/I've Got To Get You Off My Mind	15
68	Island WI 3140	Copy Me Donkey (as Tenors)/The Stage (B-side actually by Ronnie Davis)	30
68	Island WI 3156	Grampa/ROMEO STEWART: While I Was Walking	30
68	Blue Cat BS 127	Khaki/LEYROY REID: Great Surprise (Pound Get A Blow)	30
68	Big Shot BI 501	Reggae Girl/CLIVE ALLSTARS: Donkey Trot	80
68	Fab FAB 41	Ride Your Donkey/I've Got To Get You Off My Mind	25
68	Fab FAB 50	Let Go Yah Donkey/ROMEO STEWART: While I Was Walking	25
69	Big Shot BI 514	You're No Good/Do The Reggae	40
69	Big Shot BI 517	Another Scorcher/My Baby	40
69	Duke Reid DR 2502	Hopeful Village/TOMMY McCOOK: The Village	10
69	Bullet BU 406	Greatest Scorcher/Making Love	10
69	Crab CRAB 26	Baff Boom/Feel Bad	12
69	Crab CRAB 29	True Brothers/Sign Of The Time	6
69	Crab CRAB 36	I Want Everything/Cherry	8
73	Explosion EX 2079	Weather Report/Weather Report - Version	8
73	Pyramid PYR 7000	Money Never Built A Mountain/My World	5

TENOR SAW

84	SKD SKD 092	Bad Bwoy/Dub (12")	18
84	Hawkeye HLD 0012	CLASH (LP, with Coco Tea)	15

TENPOLE TUDOR

(see also Sex Pistols)

80	Korova KOW 4	Real Fun/What's In A Word (p/s)	5

10,000 MANIACS

84	Reflex RE 1	My Mother The War (Remix)/Planned Obsolescence/ National Education Week (12", p/s)	20
84	Press P 2010	HUMAN CONFLICT 5 (12" EP, gatefold p/s)	30
85	Lyntone LYN 15914	Grey Victory/SIMPLY RED: Something's Burning (33rpm 1-sided clear flexidisc free with Jamming! magazine, issue 29)	12
85	Lyntone LYN 15914	Grey Victory/SIMPLY RED: Something's Burning (33rpm 1-sided clear flexidisc without Jamming! magazine, issue 29)	8
84	Press P 3001 LP	SECRETS OF THE I-CHING (LP, with insert)	25
84	Press P 3001 LP	SECRETS OF THE I-CHING (LP, with insert; later re-pressing in different 'Chinese Chicken' sleeve, some with insert)	15

TEN WHEEL DRIVE (with GENYA RAVAN)

(see also Goldie [& Gingerbreads])

71	Polydor 2066 034	Mornin' Much Better/Stay With Me	5
69	Polydor 583 577	CONSTRUCTION NO. 1 (LP)	15
70	Polydor 2425 002	BRIEF REPLIES (LP, with Genya Ravan)	15
71	Polydor 2425 065	PECULIAR FRIENDS (LP, with Genya Ravan)	15

TEN YEARS AFTER

(see also Alvin Lee, Chick Churchill)

68	Deram DM 176	Portable People/The Sounds	20
68	Deram DM 221	Hear Me Calling/I'm Going Home	8
71	Deram XDR 48532	She Lies In The Morning/Sweet Little Sixteen (demo only)	15
72	Chrysalis/Philips 6155 006	One Of These Days/Baby Won't You Let Me Rock 'n' Roll You	5
89	Chrysalis CHS 3477	Highway Of Love/Rock 'n' Roll Music To The World (p/s)	5
67	Deram DML 1015	TEN YEARS AFTER (LP, mono)	60
67	Deram SML 1015	TEN YEARS AFTER (LP, stereo)	40
68	Deram DML 1023	UNDEAD (LP, mono)	40

MINT VALUE £

68	Deram SML 1023	UNDEAD (LP, stereo)	30
69	Deram DML 1029	STONEDHENGE (LP, gatefold sleeve, mono)	35
69	Deram SML 1029	STONEDHENGE (LP, gatefold sleeve, stereo)	30
69	Deram DML/SML 1052	SSSSH! (LP, gatefold sleeve, mono/stereo)	30
70	Deram DML 1065	CRICKLEWOOD GREEN (LP, gatefold sleeve, with 'Alvin Lee' poster, mono)	45
70	Deram SML 1065	CRICKLEWOOD GREEN (LP, gatefold sleeve, with 'Alvin Lee' poster, stereo)	35
71	Deram SML 1078	WATT (LP, gatefold sleeve)	18
71	Chrysalis CHR 1001	A SPACE IN TIME (LP)	15
72	Deram SML 1096	ALVIN LEE AND COMPANY (LP)	12
72	Chysalis CHR 1009	ROCK & ROLL MUSIC TO THE WORLD (gatefold sleeve)	12
78	Deram SML 1023	UNDEAD (LP, reissue)	12

TERMINAL

80s	Cargo CRS 0081	Hold On (in p/s)	100
80s	Cargo CRS 0081	Hold On	50

TERMINAL JIVE

82	Jive Alive JA001	THE TERMINAL JIVE AND SCARLET ALIVE EP (2 tracks on one side, p/s)	8

TERMITES

65	Oriole CB 1989	Tell Me/I Found My Place	40
65	CBS 201761	Every Day Every Day/No-One In The Whole Wide World	20

TERMITES (Jamaica)

(see also L. Sparks, Ken Boothe, Upsetters)

67	Studio One SO 2006	Mercy Mr. Percy/SOUL BROTHERS: Hot And Cold	80
67	Studio One SO 2029	It Takes Two To Make Love/Beach Boy	80
67	Coxsone CS 7008	Sign Up/DELROY WILSON: Troubled Man	25
67	Coxsone CS 7025	Do It Right Now/SUMMERTAIRES: Stay (B-side actually by Gaylads)	25
68	Studio One SO 2040	Mr D.J. (actually by Delroy Wilson)/Tripe Girl (actually by Heptones)	40
68	Coxsone CS 7039	Mama Didn't Know/I Made A Mistake	100
68	Pama PM 729	Push It Up/Two Of A Kind (B-side act. by Clancy Eccles & Cynthia Richards)	35
68	Pama PM 738	Show Me The Way/What Can I Do	20
68	Trojan TR 634	Love Up Kiss Up/TOMMY McCOOK : Regay	30
69	Nu Beat NB 017	Push Push/Girls (actually by Hi Tones)	18
67	Studio One SOL 9003	DO THE ROCK STEADY (LP)	100

PETE TERRACE

67	Pye International 7N 25427	At The Party/No! No! No!	30
67	Pye International 7N 25440	Shotgun Boo-Ga-Loo/I'm Gonna Make It	40
67	Pye Intl. NPL 28102	BOOGALOO (LP)	50

TERRA COTTA

(see also Spriguns)

78	Terra Cotta TC 001	To Be Near You (p/s, with insert)	15

TERRAIN

83	Terrain Musak TS 001	Who's To Blame?/Vacation (no p/s)	150

TERRAPLANE

(see also Thunder, Nuthin' Fancy)

85	Epic 26439	BLACK AND WHITE (LP)	15
87	Epic 460157 1	MOVING TARGET (LP)	12

LLOYD TERRELL

(see also Charmers, Lloyd Charmers, Lloyd & Johnny, Lloyd & Ken, Lloydie & Lowbites)

68	Island WI 3158	My Argument (as Lloyd & Johnny Melody)/JOHNNY MELODY: Foey Man (B-side actually by George Dekker)	60
68	Pama PM 710	Bang Bang Lulu/MRS MILLER: I Never Knew	5
68	Pama PM 740	How Come (actually by Lee Perry)/MRS MILLER: Oh My Lover	10
69	Pama PM 752	Lulu Returns/MRS MILLER: I Feel The Music	10
69	Nu Beat NB 023	Mr Rhya/After Dark	18
70	Pama PM 792	Birth Control/VAL BENNET: Return To Peace	5
70	Bullet BU 434	Exposure/Baby Huey	15
70	Bullet BU 443	Oh Me Oh My/I Did It	12
71	Escort ERT 855	One Woman/CHARMERS: What Should I Do (act. by Dave Barker & Charmers)	7
72	Bullet BU 508	Oily Sounds/Oily Version (as Lloyd Tyrell)	8
73	Pama PM 863	Big Eight/JUNIOR BYLES: Auntie Lu Lu	7

TAMMI TERRELL

(see also Marvin Gaye & Tammi Terrell)

66	Tamla Motown TMG 561	Come On And See Me/Baby Don'tcha Worry	110
66	Tamla Motown TMG 561	Come On And See Me/Baby Don'tcha Worry (DJ copy)	200
69	T. Motown (S)TML 11103	THE IRRESISTIBLE TAMMI TERRELL (LP, mono/stereo)	90

TAMMI TERRELL/CHUCK JACKSON

(see also Chuck Jackson)

69	Marble Arch MAL 1110	THE EARLY SHOW (LP)	20

TERRI & TERRORS

79	Fresh FRESH 4	Laugh At Me/Laugh At Me (Again) (folded p/s)	5

TERRORIZER

89	Earach MOSH 16	WORLD DOWNFALL (LP, with inner)	18

TERRORVISION

(see also Spoilt Bratz)

90	(own label)	TERRORVISION: Brand New Toy/Human Error/Pain Reliever/ The Pilgrims Rest (cassette, private issue)	20
91	(own label)	PUMP ACTION SUNSHINE: Urban Space Crime/My House/Jason (cassette, private issue)	20
91	(own label)	TERRORVISION: Blackbird/American TV/Pain Reliever/Human Being (cassette, private issue)	20
92	Total Vegas 12VEGAS 1	THRIVE EP (12" EP)	12

			MINT VALUE £
92	Total Vegas CDVEGAS 1	THRIVE EP (CD EP)	20
92	Total Vegas CDVEGAS 2	My House/Coming Up/Tea Dance (CD)	20
93	Total Vegas CDATVR 1	Problem Solved/Corpse Fly/We Are The Roadcrew/Sailing Home (CD)	25
93	Total Vegas CDPVEGAS 3	American TV/Psycho Killer/Hole For A Soul (CD)	15
92	Total Vegas ATVRLP 1	FORMALDEHYDE (LP, 14 tracks, green vinyl, 500 only, stickered sleeve)	40
92	Total Vegas ATVRCD 1	FORMALDEHYDE (CD, 14 tracks, 1,000 only)	20
93	Total Vegas VEGASLPS 1	FORMALDEHYDE (reissue LP, 12 tracks, 1,000 copies with 12-page booklet, stickered sleeve & lyric inner)	20
93	Total Vegas BOOT 1	LIVE AT THE DON VALLEY STADIUM (CD, picture disc, 250 promo copies only)	30

TERRY

66	Fontana TF 751	Spilt Milk/The Way That I Remember Him	10

TERRY, CARL & DERRICK

69	Grape GR 3012	True Love/ROY SMITH: Another Saturday Night	8

CLARK TERRY (& BOB BROOKMEYER)

(see also Coleman Hawkins)

61	Riverside RLP 12-246	DUKE WITH A DIFFERENCE (LP)	12
65	Fontana TL 5265	TONIGHT (LP, with Bob Brookmeyer)	12
66	Fontana TL 5290	POWER OF POSITIVE SWINGING (LP, with Bob Brookmeyer)	12
66	Fontana TL 5373	MUMBLES (LP)	12
67	Fontana (S)TL 5394	GINGERBREAD MEN (LP, with Bob Brookmeyer)	12
68	Impulse MIPL/SIPL 507	IT'S WHAT'S HAPPENIN' (LP)	12

DEWEY TERRY

(see also Don & Dewey, Don Harris, Harvey Mandel)

73	Tumbleweed TW 3502	CHIEF (LP)	18

GORDON TERRY

57	London REA 1098	COUNTRY CLAMBAKE (EP)	20

PAT TERRY (GROUP)

70s	Myrrh MYR 1031	PAT TERRY GROUP (LP)	18

SONNY TERRY (TRIO)

(see also Woody Guthrie)

53	Parlophone MSP 6017	Hootin' Blues/TOMMY REILLY: Bop! Goes The Weasel	35
56	Vogue EPV 1095	SONNY TERRY (EP)	50
55	Vogue LDE 137	FOLK BLUES (10" LP)	40
55	Vogue LDE 165	CITY BLUES (10" LP)	40
58	Melodisc MLP 516	WHOOPIN' THE BLUES (10" LP)	40
58	Topic 10T 30	HARMONICA BLUES (10" LP)	40
65	Topic 12T 30	HARMONICA BLUES (12" LP, reissue)	35
66	Xtra XTRA 5025	SONNY'S STORY (LP)	25
67	Capitol T 20906	WHOOPIN' THE BLUES (LP, reissue)	12
69	Ember CW 136	BLIND SONNY TERRY & WOODY GUTHRIE (LP)	15
69	Xtra XTRA 1064	SONNY TERRY (LP)	15
60s	Mainstream MSL 1037	GOING DOWN SLOW (LP, with BROWNIE McGHEE & PEPPERMINT HARRIS)	18
70	Xtra XTRA 1099	BLUES FROM EVERYWHERE (LP)	15
71	Xtra XTRA 1110	ON THE ROAD (LP, with J.C. Burris)	15

SONNY TERRY & BROWNIE McGHEE

(see also Brownie McGhee, Chris Barber, Pete Seeger, Big Bill Broonzy, Lightnin' Hopkins, Big Joe Turner)

60	Columbia DB 4433	Talking Harmonica Blues/Rockin' And Whoopin'	35
64	Oriole CB 1946	Dissatisfied Woman/SONNY TERRY: Goin' Down Slow	20
50s	Melodisc EPM7 83	ME AND SONNY (EP)	25
58	Pye Jazz NJE 1060	THE BLUEST (EP)	10
59	Pye Jazz NJE 1073	SONNY TERRY & BROWNIE McGHEE & CHRIS BARBER'S JAZZ BAND (EP)	10
59	Pye Jazz NJE 1074	TERRY AND McGHEE IN LONDON PT. 1 (EP)	15
59	Topic TOP 37	HOOTENANNY NEW YORK CITY (EP, with Pete Seeger)	15
61	Top Rank JKP 3007	WORK-PLAY-FAITH-FUN-SONGS (EP)	15
64	Ember EP 4562	SONNY TERRY AND BROWNIE McGHEE (EP)	20
64	Topic TOP 121	R AND B FROM S AND B (EP)	15
64	Realm REP 4002	PAWNSHOP BLUES (EP)	15
64	Vocalion EPV 1274	SONNY TERRY AND BROWNIE McGHEE (EP)	20
65	Vocalion EPV 1279	I SHALL NOT BE MOVED (EP)	20
58	Topic 12T 29	BROWNIE McGHEE AND SONNY TERRY (LP)	30
58	Pye Nixa Jazz NJT 515	SONNY, BROWNIE AND CHRIS (10" LP, with Chris Barber)	45
58	Pye Nixa Jazz NJL 18	SONNY TERRY AND BROWNIE McGHEE IN LONDON (LP)	30
58	London Jazz LTZ-C 15144	BACK COUNTRY BLUES (LP)	50
60	Columbia 33SX 1223	BLUES IS MY COMPANION (LP)	50
61	World Record Club 7379	SONNY TERRY AND BROWNIE McGHEE (LP)	20
61	Vogue LAE 12247	BLUES IS A STORY (LP, mono)	30
61	Vogue SEA 5014	BLUES IS A STORY (LP, stereo)	40
63	Vogue LAE 12266	DOWN SOUTH SUMMIT MEETIN' (LP)	25
63	CBS 52165	BACK COUNTRY BLUES (LP)	25
64	Xtra XTRA 1004	BIG BILL BROONZY/SONNY TERRY/BROWNIE McGHEE (LP)	30
64	Vogue LAE 552	BROWNIE McGHEE AND SONNY TERRY (LP)	30
64	Realm RM 165	BACK COUNTRY BLUES (LP)	18
64	Stateside SL 10076	BLUES HOOT (LP, some tracks by Lightnin' Hopkins)	40
64	Fontana 688 006ZL	LIVIN' WITH THE BLUES (LP)	30
65	Society SOC 1015	BROWNIE & SONNY SING AND PLAY (LP)	12
66	Philips BL 7675	AT THE BUNK HOUSE (LP)	30
66	Verve VLP 5010	GUITAR HIGHWAY (LP, mono)	20
66	Verve SVLP 5010	GUITAR HIGHWAY (LP, stereo)	25
66	Fontana TL 5289	HOMETOWN BLUES (LP)	30
67	Ace Of Hearts (Z)AHT 182	HOMETOWN BLUES (LP, reissue)	12
69	Capitol T 20906	WHOOPIN' THE BLUES (LP)	30
69	Stateside SSL 10291	LONG WAY FROM HOME (LP)	25

			MINT VALUE £
69	Marble Arch MAL 843	SONNY TERRY AND BROWNIE McGHEE IN LONDON (LP)	12
70	Fontana SFJL 979	WHERE THE BLUES BEGAN (LP)	20
73	Mainstream MSL 1019	HOMETOWN BLUES (LP, gatefold sleeve)	15

SUSAN TERRY

62	Piccadilly 7N 35026	Along Came Love/Looking For A Boy	15

TERRY & JERRY

65	R&B MRB 5009	People Are Doing It Every Day/Mama Julie	22

TERRY SISTERS

57	Parlophone R 4364	It's The Same Old Jazz/Broken Promises	6
58	Parlophone R 4509	Sweet Thing (Tell Me That You Love Me)/You Forgot To Remember	6

TESCO BOMBERS

(see also Homosexuals)

82	Y Y14	Hernando's Hideaway/Break The Ice At Parties/Girl From Ipanema (p/s)	5

TEST DEPARTMENT

83	Some Bizzare TEST 112	Compulsion/Pulsations (12", p/s)	10
87	Some Bizzare 12MOP 13	Victory (12", p/s)	10
80s	Media City CMC 1	Gododdin (12", p/s, Welsh gig freebie with Brith Gof)	10
90	Mop MOP 5T	Jihad/(Desert Mix)/(Oil Mix) (12", p/s)	12
93	Mop MOP 8T	Bang On It/(Tao Systems Mix)/(TC Ruff House Remix) (12", die-cut p/s)	10
82	Test TEST ONE	HISTORY (cassette, with booklet in plastic bag)	15
80s	Pleasantly Surprised PS 5	ECSTASY UNDER DURESS (cassette, in bag with inserts, 2 editions)	20
80s	Pleasantly Surprised PS 5	ECSTASY UNDER DURESS (cassette, in bag with inserts, 2 editions)	15
85	Test TEST 33	BEATING THE RETREAT (LP, box set)	12
90s	Mop MOP 3	A GOOD NIGHT OUT (LP)	12

TETRACK

77	Hawkeye HE 006	Let's Get Started/PABLO EXPERIENCE: Go it	10
78	Greensleeves GRE 8	Only Jah Knows/ROCKERS ALL STARS: Jah Jah Dub	20
78	Rockers APD 2	Love And Unity/JAH LEVE & JAH BULL: Two The Hard Way/ JUNIOR DAN: Jah Foundation (12")	30

ALAN TEW ORCHESTRA

76	Epic EPC 4676	The Sweeney/The Prowler	15
67	Decca Phase 4 PFS 4120	THIS IS MY SCENE (LP)	35
72	CBS 64665	LET'S FLY (LP)	30

JOE TEX

(see also Soul Clan)

65	Atlantic AT 4015	Hold What You've Got/Fresh Out Of Tears	20
65	Atlantic AT 4021	You Better Get It/You Got What It Takes	20
65	Sue WI 370	Yum Yum Yum/You Little Baby Face Thing	40
65	Atlantic AT 4027	A Woman Can Change A Man/Don't Let Your Left Hand Know	12
65	Atlantic AT 4045	I Want To (Do Everything For You)/Funny Bone	15
65	Atlantic AT 4058	A Sweet Woman Like You/Close Your Door	15
66	Atlantic AT 4081	The Love You Save/If Sugar Was As Sweet As You	12
66	Atlantic 584 016	S.Y.S.L.J.F.M. (Letter Song)/I'm A Man	10
66	Atlantic 584 035	You Better Believe It/I Believe I'm Gonna Make It	25
67	Atlantic 584 068	Papa Was Too/The Truest Woman In The World	8
67	Atlantic 584 096	Hold What You've Got/A Sweet Woman Like You	8
67	Atlantic 584 102	Show Me/Woman Sees A Hard Time (When Her Man Is Gone)	15
67	Atlantic 584 119	Woman Like That, Yeah/I'm Going And Get It	8
67	Atlantic 584 144	Skinny Legs And All/Watch The One (That Brings The Bad News)	8
68	Atlantic 584 171	Men Are Getting Scarce/You're Gonna Thank Me Woman	8
68	Atlantic 584 212	Go Home And Do It/Keep The One You Got	8
69	Atlantic 584 296	We Can't Sit Down Now/It Ain't Sanitary	8
70	Atlantic 584 318	You're Alright Ray Charles/Everything Happens On Time	8
71	Mercury 6052 067	I Knew Him/Bad Feet	6
72	Mercury 6052 111	Give The Baby Anything/Takin' A Chance	6
72	Mercury 6052 129	I Got 'Cha/Mother Prayer	6
72	Mercury 6052 156	You Said A Bad Word/It Ain't Gonna Work Baby	6
65	Atlantic ATL 5043	THE NEW BOSS (LP)	50
66	Atlantic ATL 587 009	THE LOVE YOU SAVE (LP)	40
67	Atlantic 587 053	I'VE GOT TO DO A LITTLE BETTER (LP)	30
67	Atlantic 587/588 059	THE NEW BOSS (LP, reissue)	20
67	London HA-U 8334	THE BEST OF JOE TEX (LP)	50
67	Atlantic 587/588 079	GREATEST HITS (LP)	20
68	Atlantic 587/588 104	LIVE AND LIVELY (LP)	30
68	Atlantic 587/588 118	SOUL COUNTRY (LP)	25
69	Atlantic 587/588 130	YOU BETTER GET IT (LP)	25
69	Atlantic 588 193	BUYING A BOOK (LP)	18
72	Atlantic K 40239	FROM THE ROOTS CAME THE RAPPER (LP)	12
72	Mercury 6338 093	I GOTCHA (LP)	12
77	EPIC EPC 81931	BUMPS AND BRUISES (LP)	15

TEXANS

64	Columbia DB 7242	Being With You/Wondrous Look Of Love	6

TEXAS BOYS' CHOIR

63	Brunswick LAT 8546	FOLKSONGS AND WESTERN BALLADS (LP)	12

TEXTONES

87	Enigma 3268-1	CEDAR CREEK (LP)	18

TEXTOR SINGERS

54	Capitol CL 14211	Sobbin' Women/Remember Me	10

RUDY THACKER & STRINGBEANS

62	Starlite ST45 087	The Ballad Of Johnny Horton/Tomorrow Is My Last Day	20

MINT VALUE £

JAKE THACKRAY

67	Columbia SCX 6178	LAST WILL AND TESTAMENT (LP)	15

THAMESIDERS/DAVY GRAHAM

(see also Davy Graham)

63	Decca DFE 8538	FROM A LONDON HOOTENANNY (EP, 2 tracks each)	50

SISTER ROSETTA THARPE

(see also Little Richard)

52	Brunswick 04989	Cain't No Grave Hold My Body Down/Ain't No Room In Church For Liars (78)	12
57	Mercury MT 185	Up Above My Head There's Music In The Air/Jericho (Joshua Fit The Battle Of Jericho) (78)	10
60	MGM MGM 1072	If I Can Help Somebody/Take My Hand, Precious Lord	6
57	Mercury MPL 6529	GOSPEL TRAIN (LP)	25
59	Brunswick LAT 8290	GOSPEL TRAIN (LP)	15
61	Mercury MMC 14057	THE GOSPEL TRUTH (LP)	20
65	Ember NR 5023	SPIRITUALS IN RHYTHM (LP)	20

SISTER ROSETTA THARPE & SISTER MARIE KNIGHT

(see also Marie Knight, Rev. Kelsey, Sammy Price)o

51	Brunswick 04851	Didn't It Rain/SISTER ROSETTA THARPE: Two Little Fishes And Five Loaves Of Bread (78, with Sam Price Trio)	15

T.H.C. ROLLER

94	Poor Person Prod. PPPR 4	CHAPTER IN THE LIFE OF T.H.C. ROLLER (LP, handmade sleeve with insert & king-size rolling papers, numbered, 500 only)	20
94	Poor Person Prod.	THIS MUST BE THE JOINT (LP, 500 only)	70

THEATRE OF HATE

(see also Pack, Spear Of Destiny, Senate, Cult, Crisis)

80	S.S. SS 3	Original Sin/Legion (p/s)	10
81	Burning Rome BRR 1	Rebel Without A Brain/My Own Invention (p/s, mispress with 2 B-side labels)	8
81	Burning Rome BRR 1	Rebel Without A Brain/My Own Invention (p/s)	6
82	Burning Rome BRRT 4	Eastworld/Assegai (12")	8
85	Bliss TOH 1EP	The Wake/Love Is A Ghost/Poppies/Legion (EP, 33rpm, with T-shirt in stickered pack, sealed)	10
85	Bliss TOH 1EP	The Wake/Love Is A Ghost/Poppies/Legion (EP, 33rpm, with T-shirt in stickered pack, unsealed)	5
81	S.S. SSSSS 1P	HE WHO DARES WINS - LIVE AT THE WAREHOUSE, LEEDS (LP, white labels, some copies autographed)	12
81	Straight Music TOH 1	LIVE AT THE LYCEUM (cassette)	12

THE BABY

69	Spark SRL 1030	Heartbreaker/Michael's Blues	20

THEE

65	Decca F 12163	Each And Every Day/There You Go!	50

THEE MIGHTY CAESARS

(see also Milkshakes, Prisoners, Billy Childish, Thee Headcoatees)

80s	Swag SWG 001	She's Just Fifteen Years Old/The Swag (1-sided flexidisc)	6
88	Crypt LP 014	ENGLISH PUNK ROCK EXPLOSION (LP)	12

HANS THEESINK

80	Kettle KOP 7	LATE LAST NIGHT (LP)	25

BOB THEIL

82	Private (no cat. no.)	SO FAR (LP, private pressing)	180
80	Ellie Jay EJSP 9459	ANOTHER FLIGHT (EP)	8

LLANS THELWELL & HIS CELESTIALS

66	Island WI 262	Choo Choo Ska/Lonely Night (B-side vocal: Busty Brown)	35

THEM

(see also Van Morrison, Trader Horne, Taste, Sk'boo, Belfast Gypsies, Moses K. & Prophets, Peter Barden, Jackie McCauley)

64	Decca F 11973	Don't Start Crying Now/One Two Brown Eyes	70
64	Decca F 12018	Baby Please Don't Go/Gloria	10
65	Decca F 12094	Here Comes The Night/All For Myself	10
65	Decca F 12175	One More Time/How Long Baby?	10
65	Decca F 12215	(It Won't Hurt) Half As Much/I'm Gonna Dress In Black	10
65	Decca F 12281	Mystic Eyes/If You And I Could Be As Two	10
66	Decca F 12355	Call My Name/Bring 'Em On In	10
66	Decca F 12403	Richard Cory/Don't You Know?	12
67	Major Minor MM 509	Gloria/Friday's Child	20
67	Major Minor MM 513	The Story Of Them (Parts 1 & 2)	25
73	Deram DM 394	Gloria/Baby Please Don't Go (reissue)	7
65	Decca DFE 8612	THEM (EP, unboxed decca logo)	130
65	Decca DFE 8612	THEM (EP, export-only 'band-on-ladder' p/s)	500
65	Decca LK 4700	(THE ANGRY YOUNG) THEM (LP, original label, with flipback sleeve)	150
65	Decca LK 4700	(THE ANGRY YOUNG) THEM (LP, original label)	120
66	Decca LK 4751	THEM AGAIN (LP, original label, with flipback sleeve)	150
66	Decca LK 4751	THEM AGAIN (LP, original label)	120
70	Decca LK 4700	(THE ANGRY YOUNG) THEM (LP, re-pressing, red label, boxed Decca logo)	40
70	Decca LK 4751	THEM AGAIN (LP, re-pressing, red label, boxed Decca logo)	40
70	Decca PA 86	THE WORLD OF THEM (LP, original issue, mono)	20
70	Decca (S) PA 86	THE WORLD OF THEM (LP, original issue, stereo)	15
73	Deram DPM 3001/2	THEM - FEATURING VAN MORRISON LEAD SINGER (2-LP)	25
78	Sonet SNTF 738	BELFAST GYPSIES (LP, features Them without Van Morrison)	25
78	Sonet SNTF 738	THEM BELFAST GYPSIES (LP)	20

THEME

82	Creed CR 001	Sacred/Conflict	6

MINT VALUE £

JOHN THEMIS
83 Coda CODS 1 — Goblins In Sherwood/Post Hypnotic Suggestions (p/s) 6

THERAPY
72 CBS 69017 — ALMANAC (LP, gatefold sleeve with inside centre opening) 25
73 Indigo IRS 5124 — ONE NIGHT STAND (LP, private pressing) 15

THERAPY?
89 demo cassette — THIRTY SECONDS OF SILENCE (cassette, 100 only) 15
90 demo cassette — MEAT ABSTRACT (cassette sold at gigs, 150 only) 15
90 Multifuckingnational MFN 1 — Meat Abstract/Punishment Kisses (p/s, labels on wrong sides, 1,000 only) 20
92 A&M (no cat. no.) — TEETHGRINDER (12", double pack, white labels in presentation pack) 30
92 A&M THX 1 — Have A Merry Fucking Christmas: Teenage Kicks/With Or Without You (Xmas gig freebie) 15
92 Wiiija WIJ 11 — PLEASURE DEATH (mini-LP, 10 white labels) 35

THERMOMETERS
80 Fokker FEP 100 — 20th Century Girl/Newtown Refugees/Stole Your Drugs (in oversized p/s) 20
80 Fokker FEP 100 — 20th Century Girl/Newtown Refugees/Stole Your Drugs (p/s) 15

THE THE
(see also Matt Johnson, Gadgets)
80 4AD AD 10 — Controversial Subject/Black And White (p/s) 30
81 Some Bizzare BZS 4 — Cold Spell Ahead/Hot Ice (p/s) 25
86 Epic PS 215 — Sweet Bird Of Truth (Radio Edit) (1-sided, promo only) 5
86 Epic TRUTH Q3 — Infected/Infected (Energy Mix)/Disturbed (12", uncensored 'wank' p/s) 15
83 Epic EPC 25525 — SOUL MINING (LP, with inner sleeve, initially with 12" single Perfect/"Soup Of Mixed Emotions"/"Fruit Of The Heart") 15
86 Epic EPC 26770 — INFECTED (LP, with poster & inner, 1st 25,000 with 'torture' sleeve) 15
86 Epic EPC 26770 — INFECTED (LP, with poster & inner) 12
02 Sony 5079022 — LONDON TOWN (5-CD box set) 30

THEY MUST BE RUSSIANS
(see also Joe 9T & Thunderbirds)
80 No label — Nagasaki's Children/Nellie The Elephant/Circus/I Want To Hold You Now (mail-order only, p/s with poster insert) 10

THICK PIGEON
80s Factory FACT 85 — TOO CRAZY COWBOYS (LP) 40

THIEVES
(see also Fairport Convention)
79 Arista ARIGV 226 — 400 Dragons/Headlights (green vinyl) 5

THIEVES LIKE US
80 Earlobe ELS 1 — Mind Made/Strike Out (p/s) 8

THIGHPAULSANDRA
(see also Coil)
01 World Serpent ESKATON 27 — Michel Publicity Window/Paralysed (p/s) 5

THIN END OF THE WEDGE
(see also Damascus)
81 Jungle JR 051S — Lights Are On Green/I'm Not Dead Yet (in p/s) 30
81 Jungle JR 051S — Lights Are On Green/I'm Not Dead Yet 6

THINGS
(see also Buzzcocks)
80 Imperial IP 4301 — Pieces Of You/Lost Love (p/s) 10
88 Epitaph E 86402 — THINGS (LP) 12

THINGS FALL APART
72 President PT378 — Bye Bye My Rose/Manna 20

THIN ICE
88 Blag It SJP 858 — Freedom Road (p/s) 40

THIN LIZZY
(see also Phil Lynott, Wild Horses, Phenomena, Eric Bell Band, Funky Junction, Greedies, John Sykes, Gary Moore)

SINGLES
70 Parlophone DIP 513 — The Farmer/I Need You (Irish only, as Thin Lizzie) 1000
71 Decca F 13208 — NEW DAY (EP, 33rpm, gatefold p/s) 300
71 Decca F 13208 — NEW DAY (EP, 33rpm, without p/s) 150
72 Decca F 13355 — Whiskey In The Jar/Black Boys On The Corner 8
72 Decca F 13355 — Whiskey In The Jar/Black Boys On The Corner (demos in p/s) 30
73 Decca F 13402 — Randolph's Tango/Broken Dreams (2 versions of A-side: matrices ZDR 53384 & ZCPDR 53312) 15
73 Decca F 13467 — The Rocker/Here I Go Again (demos £25) 5
74 Decca F 13507 — Little Darlin'/Buffalo Gal 8
74 Vertigo 6059 111 — Philomena/Sha La La 8
75 Vertigo 6059 124 — Rosalie/Half Caste 6
75 Vertigo 6059 129 — Wild One/For Those Who Love To Die 8
76 Vertigo 6059 150 — Jailbreak/Running Back (p/s) 25
77 Vertigo 6059 177 — Dancing In The Moonlight/Bad Reputation (p/s) 10
78 Decca F 13748 — Whiskey In The Jar/Vagabond Of The Western World/Sitamoia (p/s) 6
79 Vertigo LIZZY 3 — Waiting For An Alibi/With Love (p/s, with cartoon lyric sheet) 8
79 Vertigo LIZZY 3 — Waiting For An Alibi/With Love (p/s, without cartoon lyric sheet) 5
79 Decca THIN 1 — Things Ain't Working Out Down At The Farm/The Rocker (10,000 with p/s) 8
79 Vertigo LIZZY 5 — Sarah/Got To Give Up (3 different p/s designs) 5
70s Vertigo DJ 016 — It's Only Money/JANNE SCHAFFER: Dr Abraham (promo only, no p/s) 200
80 Vertigo LIZZY 7 701 — Killer On The Loose/Don't Play Around//Got To Give It Up (live)/Chinatown (live) (double pack) 8
82 Vertigo LIZZY 10 — Hollywood (Down On Your Luck) (10", p/s, 1-sided, existence unconfirmed) 0

MINT VALUE £

82	Vertigo LIZZY PD 10	Hollywood (Down On Your Luck)/Pressure Will Blow (picture disc)	6
83	Vertigo LIZZY 1111/22	Cold Sweat/Bad Habits//Angel Of Death (live)/ Don't Believe A Word (live) (double pack)	8
83	Vertigo LIZZY 1112	Cold Sweat/Bad Habits/Angel Of Death (live)/ Don't Believe A Word (live) (12", p/s)	8
83	Vertigo LIZZY 1212	Thunder And Lightning/Still In Love With You (live) (12", p/s, some with poster)	10
83	Vertigo LIZZY 13	The Sun Goes Down/Baby Please Don't Go (p/s)	5
83	Vertigo LIZZY 1312	The Sun Goes Down (Remix)/The Sun Goes Down/ Baby Please Don't Go (12", p/s)	8
ALBUMS			
71	Decca SKL 5082	THIN LIZZY (dark blue/silver label, early copies with laminated sleeve)	70
71	Decca SKL 5082	THIN LIZZY (dark blue/silver label, later pressing with matt sleeve)	35
72	Decca TXS 108	SHADES OF A BLUE ORPHANAGE (gatefold sleeve, dark blue label)	40
73	Decca SKL 5170	VAGABONDS OF THE WESTERN WORLD (dark blue/silver label, with lyric insert)	35
73	Decca SKL 5170	VAGABONDS OF THE WESTERN WORLD (dark blue/silver label, without insert)	20
74	Vertigo 6360 116	NIGHT LIFE (LP, 'spaceship' label)	15
75	Vertigo 6360 121	FIGHTING (LP, 'spaceship' label)	15
76	Vertigo 9102 008	JAIL BREAK (LP, die-cut sleeve, 'spaceship' label)	20
76	Vertigo 9102 012	JOHNNY THE FOX (LP, inner sleeve, 'spaceship' label)	15
76	Decca SKL 5249	REMEMBERING	12
83	Vertigo VERL 3	THUNDER AND LIGHTNING (with free 12")	18
83	Vertigo	LIFE - LIVE (2-LP, gatefold sleeve, with inners)	12
92	Windsong WINLP024	BBC RADIO 1 LIVE IN CONCERT (2-LP emerald green vinyl)	20

THIRD & FOURTH GENERATION

(see also Peter Tosh)

72	Punch PH 91	Rudies Medley (actually by Peter Tosh & Soulmates)/Rude Boy - Version	10

3rd ARMY

81	Elite DAZZ 10	March Of 10,000 Soldiers (All Set To Go)/Step One (12")	20

THIRD DIMENSION

70	Unity UN 566	Peace And Love/Peace And Love - Version	6

THIRD EAR BAND

(see also High Tide, Sounds Nice)

69	Harvest SHVL 756	ALCHEMY (LP, with "Sold in U.K..." label text on 4 lines)	80
69	Harvest SHVL 756	ALCHEMY (LP, later pressing without "Sold in U.K..." label text)	40
70	Harvest SHSP 773	THIRD EAR BAND: ELEMENTS (LP, no EMI logo on label)	60
72	Harvest SHSP 4019	MUSIC FROM MACBETH (LP, EMI logo on label)	30
76	Harvest SHSM 2007	EXPERIENCES (LP)	12

THIRD EYE BAND

82	Scarlet Quest 01	Pass Myself/May The Circle Remain Unbroken (p/s)	80

THIRD MEN

79	SCHOOL 1	You're So Fashionable/The Robot Age (p/s)	20

THIRD QUADRANT

82	Rock Cottage (no cat. no.)	SEEING YOURSELF AS YOU REALLY ARE (LP, private pressing, wraparound sleeve with handwritten insert, blank white label)	40
88	Own label	LAYERED (private cassette, 500 only)	12

3rd RAIL

92	Delirious DELIS 5	Look No Further/123 Break/Stand By For Fast Beats/Drop (KZ1 Remix) (12")	40

THIRD RAIL

67	Columbia DB 8274	Run, Run, Run/No Return	30

THIRD WORLD

71	CBS 7182	Miracles/Baby Boeing	6

THIRD WORLD ALL STARS

75	Third World TWLP 103	REBEL ROCK (LP)	25

THIRD WORLD WAR

(see also Terry Stamp)

71	Fly BUG 7	Ascension Day/Teddy Teeth Goes Sailing (p/s)	8
71	Fly BUG 11	A Little Bit Of Urban Rock/Working Class Man	6
71	Fly FLY 4	THIRD WORLD WAR (LP, with lyric insert)	50
71	Fly FLY 4	THIRD WORLD WAR (LP, without lyric insert)	30
72	Track 2406 108	THIRD WORLD WAR II (LP)	60

13 AMP

75	Power Exchange PX 114	Need A Woman/Can You Feel The Music	15

THIRTEEN SENSES

02	Private Pressing	NO OTHER LIFE IS ATTRACTIVE EP (CD)	35
04	Vertigo 9816335	Thru The Glass/No Other Life Is Attractive (1,500 only p/s)	8
04	Vertigo 9816335	Thru The Glass/No Other Life Is Attractive (CD, 1,500 only)	8
03	Private Pressing	NO OTHER LIFE IS ATTRACTIVE (CD)	25

13th CHIME

81	Ellie Jay Records EJSP 9700	Cuts Of Love/Coffin Maker (foldout p/s)	50
82	13th Chime THC 1	Cursed (p/s)	25
82	13th Chime THC 2	Fire/Hide And Seek/Sally Ditch (p/s, 1,000 only)	25

13TH FLOOR ELEVATORS

(see also Roky Erickson, Red Crayola)

78	Radar/Sound For Industry SFI 347	Reverberation/RED CRAYOLA: Hurricane Fighter Plane (flexidisc free with Zig Zag magazine, No. 88)	8

MINT VALUE £

78	Radar ADA 13	You're Gonna Miss Me/Tried To Hide (green vinyl)	6
78	Radar RAD 13	THE PSYCHEDELIC SOUNDS OF ? (LP)	18
79	Radar RAD 15	EASTER EVERYWHERE (LP)	15
89	Decal LIK 28	EASTER EVERYWHERE (LP, reissue)	20
88	Decal LIK 19	THE PSYCHEDELIC SOUNDS OF... (LP, reissue)	20
92	Xgarely/Decal LIKP 003	THE PSYCHEDELIC SOUNDS OF? (LP, picture disc)	12
92	Decal LIKP002	LIVE (LP, picture disc with poster)	12

31ST OF FEBRUARY

69	Vanguard (S)VRL 19045	THE 31ST OF FEBRUARY (LP)	30

35mm DREAMS

81	More Than This ASA 100	More Than This/The Bearer (foldout p/s)	5
81	More Than This ASA 200	Fasten Your Safety Belts/Corstorphine/Instamatic Dance (p/s)	5

39 LYON ST

(see under Assocates)

32ND TURN-OFF

(see also Equals)

69	Jay Boy JSL 1	32ND TURN OFF (LP, textured sleeve, brown/black label)	50

THIS DRIFTIN'S GOTTA STOP

70s	private pressing	THIS DRIFTIN'S GOTTA STOP (LP)	15

THIS HEAT

80	Piano THIS 1201	Health And Efficiency/Graphic/Varispeed (12", p/s with insert)	15
79	Piano THIS 1	THIS HEAT (LP)	45
81	Rough Trade ROUGH 26	DECEIT (LP, original)	35
98	These 12/6	REPEAT/HEALTH AND EFFICIENCY (2 x 12")	15

THIS MORTAL COIL

(see also Cocteau Twins, Modern English, Cindytalk)

83	4AD AD 310	Song To The Siren/16 Days (Reprise) (p/s)	5
83	4AD BAD 310	16 Days/Gathering Dust/Song To The Siren/16 Days (reprise) (12", p/s)	8
84	4AD AD 410	Kangaroo/It'll End In Tears (p/s, 2 different designs & label colours, 2,500 of each)	5
86	4AD BAD 608	Come Here My Love/Drugs (10", p/s with inner sleeve)	10
91	4AD TMC 1CD	Extracts From "Blood": Late Night/You And Your Sister/ I Come And Stand At Every Door/With Tomorrow (CD, card sleeve, promo only)	20
84	4AD CAD 411	IT'LL ALL END IN TEARS (LP)	12
86	4AD DAD 609	FILIGREE AND SHADOW (2-LP)	20
80s	4AD DAD 1005	BLOOD (2-LP, with inners)	20

THIS 'N' THAT

(see also Cleo)

66	Mercury MF 938	Someday/Loving You	20
67	Strike JH 310	Get Down With It/I Care About You	10

B.J. THOMAS

66	Hickory 45-1395	Never Tell/Billy & Sue	15
66	Pye International 7N 25374	Mama/Wendy	10
68	Pye International 7N 25467	The Eyes Of A New York Woman/I May Never Get To Heaven	5
69	Pye International 7N 25487	It's Only Love/You Don't Love Me Anymore (The Train Song)	5
69	Wand WN 1	Raindrops Keep Falling On My Head/Never Had It So Good	6
70	Wand WN 5	I Just Can't Help Believing/Send My Picture To Scranton, PA	5
72	Wand WN 24	Rock And Roll Lullaby/Are We Losing Touch? (feat. Duane Eddy)	5

CARLA THOMAS

(see also Otis Redding & Carla Thomas)

61	London HLK 9310	Gee Whiz/For You	20
61	London HLK 9359	A Love Of My Own/Promises	15
62	London HLK 9618	I'll Bring It On Home To You/I Can't Take It	15
64	Atlantic AT 4005	I've Got No Time To Lose/A Boy Named Tom	15
66	Atlantic AT 4074	Comfort Me/I'm For You	10
66	Atlantic 584 011	Let Me Be Good To You/Another Night Without My Man	8
66	Atlantic 584 042	B-A-B-Y/What Have You Got To Offer Me	8
67	Stax 601 002	Something Good (Is Going To Happen To You)/It's Starting To Grow	10
67	Stax 601 008	When Tomorrow Comes/Unchanging Love (dark blue label)	15
67	Stax 601 008	When Tomorrow Comes/Unchanging Love (later light blue label)	8
68	Stax 601 032	Pick Up The Pieces/Separation	10
68	Stax STAX 103	Where Do I Go/I've Fallen In Love	8
69	Stax STAX 112	I Like What You're Doing To Me/Strung Out	8
69	Stax STAX 131	Unyielding/I've Fallen In Love	6
72	Stax 2025 082	Love Means/You've Got A Cushion To Fall On	6
91	Kent 6T 7	I'll Never Stop Loving/Prophets Band/Peaches Baby	50
67	Stax 589 004	CARLA THOMAS (LP)	30
67	Stax 589 012	THE QUEEN ALONE (LP)	20
69	Stax SXATS 1019	MEMPHIS QUEEN (LP)	40

CHARLIE THOMAS (& DRIFTERS)

75	EMI International INT 506	I'm Gonna Take You Home/Run, Run, Roadrunner	8

CLAUDETTE THOMAS

68	Caltone TONE 116	Roses Are Red My Love/YVONNE HARRISON: Near To You	80

CREEPY JOHN THOMAS

(see also Paul Kossoff, Edgar Broughton Band)

69	RCA RCA 1912	Ride A Rainbow/Moon And Eyes Song	15
69	RCA SF 8061	CREEPY JOHN THOMAS (LP, laminated front sleeve)	140

DAVID THOMAS & THE PEDESTRIANS

(see also Pere Ubu)

83	Recommended REDT 7	Didn't Have A (Very) Good Time (1-sided picture disc free with label's quarterly magazine)	6

MINT VALUE £

84	Rough Trade ROUGH 30	THE SOUND OF THE SAND (LP)	12
85	Rough Trade ROUGH 80	MORE PLACES FOREVER (LP)	12

DON THOMAS

76	DJM DJS 670	Come On Train Parts 1 & 2 (promos in p/s)	20
76	DJM DJS 10670	Come On Train Parts 1 & 2 (second pressing)	10

GENE THOMAS

64	United Artists UP 1047	Baby's Gone/Stand By Love	20

HERSAL THOMAS

50	Parlophone R 3261	Suitcase Blues/Hersal Blues (78)	65

IRMA THOMAS

64	Liberty LIB 66013	Breakaway/Wish Someone Would Care	25
64	Liberty LIB 66041	Anyone Who Knows What Love Is (Will Understand)/Time Is On My Side	20
65	Liberty LIB 66080	He's My Guy/True True Love	20
65	Liberty LIB 66095	Some Things You Never Get Used To/You Don't Miss A Good Thing (Until It's Gone)	20
65	Sue WI 372	Don't Mess With My Man/Set Me Free	30
65	Liberty LIB 66106	I'm Gonna Cry Till My Tears Run Dry/ Nobody Wants To Hear Nobody's Troubles	20
66	Liberty LIB 66137	Take A Look/What Are You Trying To Do	75
66	Liberty LIB 66137	Take A Look/What Are You Trying To Do (DJ copy)	125
66	Liberty LIB 66178	It's A Man's-Woman's World	20
72	Atlantic K 10167	Full Time Woman/She's Taking My Part	6
72	United Artists UP 35402	Time Is On My Side/Anyone Who Knows What Love Is (Will Understand) (reissue)	8
65	Liberty LEP 4035	TIME IS ON MY SIDE (EP)	100
68	Minit MLL/MLS 40004E	TAKE A LOOK (LP)	75
76	Island HELP 29	LIVE (LP)	15
83	Kent 010	TIME IS ON MY SIDE (LP)	15

JAMO THOMAS & HIS PARTY BROTHERS ORCHESTRA

66	Polydor BM 56709	I Spy (For The FBI)/Snake Hip Mama	15
69	Polydor 56755	I Spy (For The FBI)/Snake Hip Mama (reissue)	8
69	Chess CRS 8098	I'll Be Your Fool/Jamo Soul	20
71	Mojo 2092 013	I Spy (For The FBI)/Snake Hip Mama (2nd reissue)	8

JIMMY THOMAS

(see also Sweet Dreams)

69	Parlophone R 5773	The Beautiful Night/Above A Whisper (withdrawn)	250
69	Parlophone R 5773	The Beautiful Night/Above A Whisper (withdrawn; DJ copy)	200
69	Spark SRL 1035	(We Ain't Looking For) No Trouble/Springtime	6
70	Spark SRL 1040	White Dove/You Don't Have To Say Goodbye	12
72	Jay Boy BOY 67	Where There's A Will/Just Tryin' To Please You	6

JOE THOMAS

72	People PLE 015	JOY OF COOKIN' (LP)	15

KID THOMAS

79	JSP 4503	Rockin' This Joint Tonight/Cozy Lounge Blues	5

KID THOMAS/EMANUEL BAND

64	77' LA 12/26	VICTORY WALK (LP, with Barry Martyn's Band)	30

LEON THOMAS

73	Philips 6369 417	BLUES & SOULFUL TRUTH (LP)	30

NICKY THOMAS

(see also Joe Gibbs)

70	Amalgamated AMG 863	Danzella/JOE GIBBS ALLSTARS: Kingstonians Reggae	25
70	Trojan TR 7750	Love Of The Common People/DESTROYERS: Compass	5
70	Trojan TR 7796	God Bless The Children/Red Eye	7
71	Trojan TR 7807	If I Had A Hammer/Lonely Feelin'	7
71	Trojan TR 7830	Tell It Like It Is/B.B.C.	5
70	Trojan TBL 143	LOVE OF THE COMMON PEOPLE (LP)	15
72	Trojan TRLS 25	TELL IT LIKE IT IS (LP)	20

PETER THOMAS SOUND ORCHESTRA

70	Polydor 2418 074	CHARIOTS OF THE GODS (LP)	35

RAMBLIN' THOMAS

(see also Blind Blake, Blind Lemon Jefferson)

52	Tempo R 51	Jug Head Blues/Hard Dallas Blues (78)	20

ROD THOMAS

72	Fly BUG 19	Timothy Jones/Arthur Smith	7

RUDDY THOMAS

78	Lightning LIG 526	Loving Pauper/TRINITY: Judgement Time	8

RUDY THOMAS

83	Mobiliser MMLP 34	VERY BEST OF (LP)	15

RUFUS THOMAS

63	London HLK 9799	Walking The Dog/Fine And Mellow	25
64	London HLK 9850	Can Your Monkey Do The Dog/I Want To Get Married	15
64	London HLK 9884	Somebody Stole My Dog/I Want To Be Loved	15
64	Atlantic AT 4009	Jump Back/All Night Worker	15
66	Atlantic 584 029	Willy Nilly/Sho' Gonna Mess Him Up	10
67	Atlantic 584 089	Jump Back/Walking The Dog	8
67	Stax 601 013	Greasy Spoon/Sophisticated Sissy	8
68	Stax 601 028	Down Ta My House/Steady Holding On	8
68	Stax 601 037	The Memphis Train/I Think I Made A Boo-Boo	15
68	Stax STAX 105	Funky Mississippi/So Hard To Get Along With	6
70	Stax STAX 144	Do The Funky Chicken/Turn Your Damper Down	8

MINT VALUE £

71	Stax 2025 060	The Breakdown (Parts 1 & 2)	6
71	Stax 2025 080	Do The Funky Penguin (Parts 1 & 2)	6
64	Atlantic AET 6001	DO THE DOG (EP)	50
65	Atlantic AET 6011	JUMP BACK WITH RUFUS (EP)	50
64	London HA-K 8183	WALKING THE DOG (LP)	95
70	Stax SXATS 1033	FUNKY CHICKEN (LP)	35
71	Stax 2363 001	FUNKY CHICKEN (LP, reissue)	15
71	Stax 2362 010	DOING THE PUSH AND PULL LIVE AT P.J.'s (LP)	25
72	Stax 2362 028	DID YOU HEAR ME? (LP)	20
74	Stax STX 1004	CROWN PRINCE OF DANCE (LP)	30

SANDRA THOMAS

76	Angen ANG 113	It Should Have Been Me/Loving Arms	5

TERRY-THOMAS ESQUIRE

56	Decca F 10804	A Sweet Old Fashioned Boy (with Rock 'N' Roll Rotters)/Lay Down Your Arms	12
61	Decca LK 4398	STRICTLY T-T (LP)	40

TIM THOMAS

66	Polydor BM 56052	Walking/Fever	8
71	Decca F13235	Silver Morning/Gravy Train	10

TIMMY THOMAS

73	Mojo 2956 002	WHY CAN'T WE LIVE TOGETHER (LP)	30

VAUGHAN THOMAS

70	Page One POF 167	Need You Girl/Come Together	12
70	Page One POF 178	Is This What I Get For Loving You/Since You've Been Mine	6
71	DJM DJS 238	I Wanna Be Famous Like My Dad/Love	15
72	Jam JAM 9	Gotta Be You, Gotta Be Me/Woman	6
72	Jam JAM 26	Giant/Good Old Sam	6
72	Jam JAL 101	VAUGHAN THOMAS (LP, textured sleeve, white/red/black label)	40

WAYNE THOMAS

67	Coral Q 72491	I've Never Known A Lady/My Life's Gonna Change	6

ANDREAS THOMOPOULOS

(see also Secondhand)

70	Mushroom 100 MR 1	SONGS OF THE STREET (LP)	80
71	Mushroom 150 MR 4	BORN OUT OF THE TEARS OF THE SUN (LP)	90

BARBARA THOMPSON

74	Explosion EX 2087	Single Girl/DANDY & COUNT PRINCE MILLER: Version	5

BOBBY THOMPSON

(see also Dandy)

69	Columbia Blue Beat DB 113	That's How Strong My Love Is/Trouble In Town	6
69	Jolly JY 001	That's How Strong My Love Is/Trouble In The Town	30

CHERYLE THOMPSON

64	Stateside SS 291	Teardrops/Black Night	15

CHRIS THOMPSON

73	Village Thing VTS 21	CHRIS THOMPSON (LP, allegedly 101 sold and 899 destroyed)	150

DONNEY THOMPSON

79	Third World TWDIS 20	Rocking Time/PAGET KING: Close Encounter (12")	60

EDDIE THOMPSON

55	Jazz Today JTE 101	THE FABULOUS EDDIE THOMPSON (EP)	50
57	Nixa NJE 1030	PIANO MOODS VOLUME 6 (EP)	50
60	Ember EMB 3303	PIANO MOODS (LP)	100
60	Tempo TAP 24	HIS MASTER'S JAZZ (LP)	250
60s	77 LEU 12/39	BY MYSELF (LP)	40

ERIC THOMPSON

68	CBS EP 6398	THE MAGIC ROUNDABOUT NO. 1 (EP)	8
68	CBS EP 6399	THE MAGIC ROUNDABOUT NO. 2 (EP)	8

HANK THOMPSON (& BRAZOS VALLEY BOYS)

56	Capitol CL 14517	Honey, Honey Bee Ball/Don't Take It Out On Me	5
56	Capitol CL 14668	I'm Not Mad, Just Hurt/The Blackboard Of My Heart	5
58	Capitol CL 14869	Li'l Liza Jane/How Do You Hold A Memory	5
58	Capitol CL 14945	Gathering Flowers/Squaws Along The Yukon	5
58	Capitol CL 14961	I've Run Out Of Tomorrows/You're Going Back To Your Old Ways Again	5
60	Capitol CL 15114	A Six Pack To Go/What Made Her Change	10
76	Capitol CL 15877	Rockin' In The Congo/I Was The First One	5

JACKIE THOMPSON

69	Direction 58-4521	Bad Women A Dime A Dozen/Games People Play	6

JOHNNY THOMPSON & ONE-EYED JACKS

65	Ember EMB S 206	For Us There'll Be No Tomorrow/Soul Chant (in p/s)	12
65	Ember EMB S 206	For Us There'll Be No Tomorrow/Soul Chant	6

KAY THOMPSON

56	London HLA 8268	Eloise/Just One Of Those Things	50
56	London HLA 8268	Eloise/Just One Of Those Things (78)	10

LEROY THOMPSON

78	Noel DN 005	Hard Times Criminal Times/Since You Left Me & Gone (12")	30

LINVAL THOMPSON

75	Ackee ACK 541	Kung Fu (Vocal)/Kung Fu (Instrumental)	6
75	Action ACT 103	Natty Dread Girl/AGGROVATORS: Natty Dread Girl (Version)	10
75	Attack ATT 8101	Don't Cut Off Your Dreadlocks/KING TUBBYS: Version	10
75	Faith FA 010	Girl You Got To Run/Run Come Feel	5

MINT VALUE £

75	Faith FA 018	Jah Redder Than Red/Version	8
78	Attack ATT 8135	I Love Marijuana/Jamaican Calley (Version)	8
78	Star PTP 1007	If I Follow My Heart/THOMPSON ALL STARS: Rocking version (12")	20
79	Burning Rockers BRD 003	Follow My Heart/THOMPSON ALL STARS: Rockers Version (12")	20
79	Burning Sounds BSD 023	Rocking Vibration/Natty Dread (12')	20
79	Burning Sounds BSD 031	Bound To Surrender/Dub Version (12")	20
79	GG's GG 056	Mad Dog (with Ranking Trevor)/REVOLUTIONARIES: Kevin At The Controls (12")	30
79	Greensleeves GRED 024	One More Chance/Long Time Me Na Rub You In A Dance (12", with Trinity)	20
80	Attack TACK 19	Here With Me/ROOTS RADICS BAND: Come On Baby Dub Style (12")	15
80	Attack TACK 22	Pop No Style/SCIENTIST: Second Hand Girl (12")	15
80	Black Joy DH 804	Brown Skin Girl/RANKING TREVOR: Brown Skin Girl Rub A Dub (12")	15
80	Strong Like Sampson SLSD 04	Mr Boss Man (with Trevor Ranking)/BARNABOUS: Stop Push Me Around (12")	20
80	Strong Like? SLSD 012	I'm Sorry/My Little Honey (12")	10
82	A1 A1 004	Poor People (with U Brown)/Reggae Dub (12")	12
78	Burning Sounds BSD 1014	LOVE IS THE QUESTION (LP)	25
78	Burning Sounds BS 1027	ROCKING VIBRATION (LP)	20
79	Burning Sounds BS 1035	I LOVE JAH (LP)	35
79	Trojan TRLS 153	NEGREA LOVE DUB (LP)	20
80	Burning Rockers BR 1006LP	FOLLOW MY HEART (LP)	30
83	Greensleeves GREL 51	BABY FATHER (LP)	15

LUCKY THOMPSON

56	Vogue V 2388	But Not For Me/East Of The Sun	10

MIKE THOMPSON Jnr.

67	Island WI 3090	Rocksteady Wedding/Flower Pot Bloomers (both with Lyn Taitt & Jets)	25

MOLLIE THOMPSON

66	Asteroid JH 101	SONG NOTES SINGS FROM WORLDS AFAR (LP, private pressing)	40

OWEN THOMPSON

72	Camel CA 103	Must I Be Blue/Version	8

PETER THOMPSON & NTH DEGREE

65	Fontana TF 656	For Me It's All Over/The Way You Used To Do	20

RICHARD THOMPSON

72	Island ILPS 9197	HENRY THE HUMAN FLY (LP, 'pink rim palm tree' label)	25

RICHARD & LINDA THOMPSON

(see also Fairport Convention, Richard Thompson, Sandy Denny, Marc Ellington, Nick Drake, Bunch, Gary Farr, Paul McNeill & Linda Peters)

74	Island WIP 6186	I Want To See The Bright Lights Tonight/When I Get To The Border	5
75	Island WIP 6220	Hokey Pokey/I'll Regret It All In The Morning	5
73	Island ILPS 9266	I WANT TO SEE THE BRIGHT LIGHTS TONIGHT (LP)	25
74	Island ILPS 9305	HOKEY POKEY (LP, blue rim palm tree label with lyric inner sleeve)	25
75	Island ILPS 9348	POUR DOWN LIKE SILVER (LP, 'palm tree' label with lyrics)	20
75	Island	OFFICIAL LIVE TOUR 1975 (LP, unreleased, test pressings may exist)	100
76	Island ICD 8	GUITAR/VOCAL (2-LP, gatefold sleeve, blue rim/palm tree label)	20
78	Chrysalis CHR 1177	FIRST LIGHT (LP)	12

ROBERT THOMPSON

75	Pinnacle P 8408	A Look At The Sun/You Can't See Me	12

ROY THOMPSON

67	Columbia DB 8108	Sookie Sookie/Love You Say	30

SIR CHARLES THOMPSON

53	Vogue LDE 032	SIR CHARLES THOMPSON'S ALL STARS WITH CHARLIE PARKER (10" LP)	20
56	Vanguard PPT 12011	AND HIS BAND FEATURING COLEMAN HAWKINS (10" LP)	15

SONNY THOMPSON & HIS RHYTHM & BLUES BAND

(see also Claude Cloud & Thunderclaps, Swallows)

52	Vogue V 2143	Real, Real Fine (Parts 1 & 2) (78)	45
53	Esquire 10-320	House Full Of Blues/Creepin' (78)	45
53	Esquire 10-339	Screamin' Boogie/The Fish (78)	45
60	Starlite ST45 008	Screamin' Boogie/The Fish	250
56	Parlophone GEP 8562	SONNY THOMPSON INSTRUMENTALS (EP, as Sonny Thompson Orchestra)	60

SUE THOMPSON

(see also Kris Jensen)

61	Polydor NH 66967	Sad Movies/Throwing Kisses	10
62	Polydor NH 66973	Norman/Never Love Again	5
62	Polydor NH 66976	Two Of A Kind/It Has To Be Me	5
62	Polydor NH 66979	Have A Good Time/If The Boy Only Knew	5
63	Polydor NH 66987	What's Wrong Bill/I Need A Harbour	5
62	Fontana 267 244TF	James (Hold The Ladder Steady)/My Hero	5
63	Fontana 267 262TF	Willie Can/Too Much In Love	5
64	Hickory 45-1240	Big Daddy/I'd Like To Know You Better	5
64	Hickory 45-1255	Bad Boy/Toys	5
65	Hickory 45-1284	Paper Tiger/Mama Don't Cry At My Wedding	6
65	Hickory 45-1328	It's Break Up Time/Afraid	8
65	Hickory 45-1340	Just Kiss Me/Sweet Hunk Of Misery	8
65	Hickory 45-1359	I'm Looking For A World/Walkin' My Baby	6
65	Hickory 45-1381	What Should I Do/After The Heartache	10
67	London HLE 10142	Ferris Wheel/Don't Forget To Cry	7
72	London HLE 1040	How I Love Them Old Songs/That's Just Too Much	7
73	London HLE 10440	Oh, Johnny, Oh Johnny, Oh/Just Pain Country	7
65	Hickory LPE 1507	INTRODUCING KRIS JENSEN AND SUE THOMPSON (EP, 2 tracks each)	10
64	Hickory LPM 102	PAPER TIGER (LP)	20

SUE THOMPSON & BOB LUMAN

(see also Bob Luman)

63	Polydor NH 66989	I Like Your Kind Of Love/Too Hot To Dance	10
63	Hickory 45-1221	I Like Your Kind Of Love/Too Hot To Dance (reissue)	5

MINT VALUE £

GUNILLA THORN
63 HMV POP 1239 Merry-Go-Round/Go On Then ... 90

TRACEY THORN
(see also Marine Girls, Everything But The Girl, Grab Grab The Haddock)
82 Cherry Red CHERRY 53 Plain Sailing/Goodbye Joe (p/s) ... 5
82 Cherry Red MRED 35 A DISTANT SHORE (LP) ... 15

DAVID THORNE
62 Stateside SS 141 The Alley Cat Song/The Moon Was Yellow ... 6
63 Stateside SS 190 One More Fool, One More Broken Heart/Don't Let It Get Away ... 6
64 Stateside SE 1020 WHAT WILL I TELL MY HEART (EP) ... 25
63 Stateside SL 10036 THE ALLEY CAT SONGSTER (LP) ... 35

KEN THORNE ORCHESTRA
63 HMV POP 1176 The Legion's Last Patrol Film Theme/Kisses In The Night ... 5
68 United Artists ULP 1201 INSPECTOR CLOUSEAU (LP, soundtrack) ... 30
69 Stateside S(S)L 10271 THE TOUCHABLES (LP, with Nirvana, Wynder K. Frog, et al.) ... 50

WOODY THORNE
62 Vogue Pop V 9202 Sadie Lou/Teenagers In Love ... 400

CLAUDE THORNHILL & HIS ORCHESTRA
54 London HL 8042 Pussy-Footin'/Adios ... 40
54 London RE-P 1009 CLAUDE THORNHILL GOES MODERN (EP) ... 20
54 London H-ABP 1019 CLAUDE THORNHILL GOES MODERN (10" LP) ... 20
54 London H-ABP 1021 DREAM MUSIC (10" LP) ... 20

WILLIE MAE 'BIG MAMA' THORNTON
54 Vogue V 2284 Hound Dog/Mischievous Boogie (78) (as Willie Mae 'Big Mama' Thornton) ... 130
65 Sue WI 345 Tom Cat/Monkey In The Barn (as Willie Mae Thornton) ... 250
69 Mercury SMCL 20176 STRONGER THAN DIRT (LP) ... 40
78 Vanguard VPC 40001 MAMA'S PRIDE (LP) ... 25

EDDIE THORNTON OUTFIT
69 Instant IN 003 Baby Be My Gal/SONNY BURKE OUTFIT: All You ... 120

GEORGE THOROGOOD & DESTROYERS
77 Sonet SON 2148 Can't Stop Lovin'/Homesick Boy ... 5
79 Sonet SON 2183 SO MUCH TROUBLE (EP) ... 7
77 Sonet SNTF 760 GEORGE THOROGOOD AND THE DESTROYERS (LP) ... 12

PETER THOROGOOD
68 Pye 7N 17597 Haunted/If No One Sang ... 100

BILLY THORPE & AZTECS
65 Parlophone R 5381 Twilight Time/Over The Rainbow ... 7

THOR'S HAMMER
66 Parlophone DP 565 Once/A Memory (export issue) ... 150
66 Parlophone DP 567 If You Knew/Love Enough (export issue) ... 185
66 Parlophone CGEP 62 THOR'S HAMMER (EP, export issue, gatefold p/s, with bonus 45 "If You Knew"/"Love Enough" [CGEP 62]) ... 1000

LINDA THORSON
68 Ember EMB S 257 Here I Am/Better Than Losing You (p/s) ... 40
68 Ember EMB S 257 Here I Am/Better Than Losing You ... 15
70 Ember EMBS 284 Wishful Thinking/You Will Want Me ... 20
70 Ember LT 1 Bad Time To Stop Loving Me/Pick Up My Heart (promo) ... 20

THOSE HELICOPTERS
80 State Of The Art STATE 1 Shark/Eskimo (p/s) ... 6
81 Lavender LAVENDER 001 Dr. Janov/Technical Smack (p/s) ... 5

THOSE INTRINSIC INTELLECTUALS
80 Fault Line CPS 040 Do The Executive/Radio Iceland (fold out p/s in printed bag, insert) ... 12

THOSE NAUGHTY LUMPS
79 Zoo CAGE 002 Iggy Pop's Jacket/Pure And Innocent (foldout p/s) ... 6
80 Open Eye OP-EP 1002 DOWN AT THE ZOO (EP) ... 6

THOUGHTS
(see also Tiffany [& Thoughts], Paul Dean & Soul Savages)
66 Planet PLF 118 All Night Stand/Memory Of Your Love ... 100

THOUGHTS & WORDS
69 Liberty LBF 15187 Morning Sky/Give Me A Reason ... 10
69 Liberty LBL 83224 THOUGHTS & WORDS (LP) ... 20

THOUGHTS OF DES COX
69 Morgan MR 4S Isn't It Nice/It's All Very Strange ... 12

THRASHPACK
87 Music Of Life NOTE010 Kinda Cool In The Place (12") ... 8

THREADBARE CONSORT
80s private pressing WEARING THIN (LP) ... 15

THREADS
86 Unicorn PHZ 2 Step Back/UNDERGROUND ARROWS: Backbeat Of Life (p/s) ... 10

THREADS OF LIFE
72 Alco ALC 530 THREADS OF LIFE (LP, actually by Alco) ... 500

THREATS
82 Rondelet ROUND 22 GO TO HELL (EP) ... 15
82 Rondelet ROUND 29 Politicians & Ministers/Writing's On The Wall/Deep End Depression (p/s) ... 20
82 Rondelet ROUND 1229 POLITICIANS & MINISTERS (12" EP) ... 18

MINT VALUE £

THREE BARRY SISTERS
(see also Barry Sisters)

59	Decca F 11099	Little Boy Blue/My Sweetie's Coming To Call	10
59	Decca F 11118	Tall Paul/Till Then	7
59	Decca F 11118	Tall Paul/Till Then (78)	10
59	Decca F 11141	Jo Jo - The Dog Faced Boy/I-Aye Ove-Lay Oo-Yay	5
60	Decca F 11201	Spoilsport/Bonnie Prince Charlie	5
60	Decca F 11201	Spoilsport/Bonnie Prince Charlie (78)	10

THREE BELLS
(see also Satin Bells)

60	Pye 7N 15252	Steady Date/In Between (Wishing I Was Sweet Sixteen)	8
64	Columbia DB 7399	Softly In The Night/He Doesn't Love Me	10
65	Columbia DB 7570	Someone To Love/Over And Over Again	7
66	Columbia DB 7980	Cry No More/He Doesn't Want You	15
61	Pye 7N 15335	You/Melody Of Love	8

THREE CAPS
(see also Capitols)

66	Atlantic 584 004	Cool Jerk/Hello Stranger	15
66	Atlantic 584 043	I Got To Handle It/Zig-Zagging	10
69	Atlantic 584 251	Cool Jerk/Hello Stranger	10
71	Atlantic 2091 105	Cool Jerk/Hello Stranger (reissue)	5

THREE CHUCKLES
(see also Teddy Randazzo)

55	HMV 7M 292	Runaround/At Last You Understand	40
55	HMV 7M 292	Runaround/At Last You Understand (78)	20
56	HMV 7M 333	Still Thinking Of You/Times Two I Love You	35
56	HMV 7M 333	Still Thinking Of You/Times Two I Love You (78)	25
57	HMV POP 292	We're Gonna Rock Tonight/Want You Give Me A Chance	80
57	HMV POP 292	We're Gonna Rock Tonight/Want You Give Me A Chance (78)	30

THREE CITY FOUR
(see also Martin Carthy, Leon Rosselson)

65	Decca LK 4705	THREE CITY FOUR (LP)	160
67	CBS 63039	SMOKE AND DUST WHERE THE HEART SHOULD HAVE BEEN (LP)	100

THREE COINS

70	Sugar SU 106	Come And Do The Right Thing/It's So Long	6

THREE DEGREES

65	Stateside SS 413	Gee Baby I'm Sorry/Do What You're Supposed To Do	60
65	Stateside SS 459	Close Your Eyes/Gotta Draw The Line	70
65	Stateside SS 459	Close Your Eyes/Gotta Draw The Line (DJ copy)	100
71	Mojo 2092 001	Maybe/There's So Much Love Around Me	6
71	Mojo 2092 002	You're The One/Rose Garden	6
71	Mojo 2092 009	There's So Much Love Around Me/Maybe (reissue)	6
71	Mojo 2092 009	There's So Much Love Around Me/Yours (different B-side)	6
75	Pye International 7N 25671	Sugar On Sunday/Maybe	6
71	Mojo 2916 002	THE THREE DEGREES (LP)	20

THREE DOG NIGHT
(see also Danny Hutton)

69	Stateside-Dunhill SS 8008	Nobody/It's For You	6
70	Stateside-Dunhill SS 8052	Mama Told Me Not To Come/Rock And Roll Widow	7
71	Probe PRO 523	Joy To The World/I Can Hear You Calling	6
69	Stateside-Dun. (S)SL 5006	THREE DOG NIGHT (LP)	15
69	Stateside-Dun. (S)SL 5013	SUITABLE FOR FRAMING (LP)	12
70	Stateside-Dunhill SSL 5023	CAPTURED LIVE AT THE FORUM (LP)	12
70	Probe SPBA 6251	IT AIN'T EASY (LP)	12

THREE DOLLS

57	MGM MGM 958	The Living End/The Octopus Song	10

THREE GOOD REASONS

65	Mercury MF 883	Build Your Love/Don't Leave Me Now	10
65	Mercury MF 899	Nowhere Man/Wire Wheels	18
65	Mercury MF 929	The Moment Of Truth/Funny Kind Of Loving	10

THREE JOHNS

82	CNT CNT 003	English White Boy Engineer/Secret Agent (p/s)	8
83	CNT CNT 011	Pink Headed Bug/Lucy In The Rain (p/s)	7
83	CNT CNT 013	Men Like Monkeys/Two Minute Ape!/Windolene/ Marx's Wife/Paris 1941 (12", p/s)	8
96	Dojo DOJOCD 255	THE BEST OF THE THREE JOHNS (CD)	20

THREE KAYES (SISTERS)
(see also Kaye Sisters, Frankie Vaughan)

56	HMV 7M 401	Ivory Tower/Mister Cuckoo (Sing Your Song)	12
56	HMV POP 251	Lay Down Your Arms/First Row Balcony (as Three Kaye Sisters)	10

THREE MAN ARMY
(see also Gun, Baker Gurvitz Army, Andy Newman, Spooky Tooth)

72	Pegasus PGS 1	What's Your Name/Travellin'	10
74	Reprise K 14292	Polecat Woman/Take Me Down From The Mountain	5
71	Pegasus PEG 3	A THIRD OF A LIFETIME (LP, gatefold)	60
74	Reprise K 54015	THREE MAN ARMY TWO (LP)	30

THREE PEOPLE
(see also John Bromley)

66	Decca F 12473	Have You Ever Been There/Good Times	10
66	Decca F 12514	Suspicions/Easy Man To Find	10
67	Decca F 12581	Got To Find A Reason/Simple Thing Would Be For You To Start Loving Me	10

MINT VALUE £

THREE PIECES
75 Fantasy FTC 116 I Need You Girl/Short'nin' Bread . . . 8

3PM
92 Busted Loop 3 Better Late Than Never (12") . . . 25

THREE QUARTERS
65 Columbia DB 7467 People Will Talk/Love Come A-Tricklin' Down . . . 15
65 Columbia DB 7576 The Pleasure Girls/Little People . . . 6

THREE SOUNDS
68 Liberty LBF 15062 Makin' Bread Again/Still I'm Sad . . . 8

3 THIEVES AND A LIAR
92 3 Thieves And A Liar 3TAL In The House/I Get A Chill/You Bring Me Joy/Tonight (12") . . . 25

THREE TOPS
(see also Dion Cameron & Three Tops, Sir Lord Comic, King Rocky)
67 Doctor Bird DB 1101 Miserable Friday/This World Has A Feeling . . . 30
67 Studio One SO 2023 Moving To Progress/Love And Inspiration . . . 80
67 Trojan TR 003 It's Raining/Sound Of Music . . . 40
67 Treasure Isle TI 7008 Do It Right/You Should Have Known . . . 30
68 Coxsone CS 7033 A Man Of Chances/HORTENSE ELLIS: A Groovy Kind Of Love . . . 120
68 Coxsone CS 7051 Great Train In '68/You Should Have Known . . . 80
73 Bullet BU 527 Take Time Out/Just Like A Log . . . 12

THREE WISE MEN
(see also XTC)
83 Virgin VS 642 Thanks For Christmas/Countdown To Christmas Partytime (p/s) . . . 10

THREE'S A CROWD
(see also Embers, Writing On The Wall)
66 Fontana TF 673 Look Around The Corner/Living In A Dream . . . 20

THRILLERS
(see also Phil Pratt)
68 Blue Cat BS 128 The Last Dance/DELTA CATS: Unworthy Baby . . . 20

PERCY 'THRILLS' THRILLINGTON
(see also Paul McCartney)
77 Regal Zono. EMI 2594 Uncle Albert - Admiral Halsey/Eat At Home . . . 100
77 Regal Zono. EMC 3175 THRILLINGTON (LP, with inner sleeve) . . . 90
77 Regal Zono. TC-EMC 3175 THRILLINGTON (cassette) . . . 40

THRILLS
66 Capitol CL 15469 No One/What Can Go Wrong . . . 100
66 Capitol CL 15469 No One/What Can Go Wrong (DJ copy) . . . 200
79 Grapevine GRP 126 Show The World Where It's At/What Can Go Wrong . . . 5

THRILLS
03 Virgin VSDJ 1855 Last Night I Dreamt That Somebody Loved Me (1-sided gig issue, p/s, 500 only) 40

THROBBING GRISTLE
(see also Psychic TV, Coil, Sabres Of Paradise)
78 Industrial IR 0003 United/Zyklon B Zombie (p/s) . . . 20
78 Industrial IR 0003/U United/Zyklon B Zombie (p/s, white or clear vinyl, 1,000 only of each) . . . 25
80 Industrial IR 0003 United/Zyklon B Zombie (longer version) (p/s, reissue, 'Memorial Issue' scratched in matrix) . . . 15
80 Industrial IR 0013 Subhuman/Something Came Over Me (in polythene camouflage bag) . . . 20
80 Industrial IR 0015 Adrenalin/Distant Dreams (Part Two) (in polythene camouflage bag) . . . 20
81 Fetish FET 006 Discipline (live, Berlin)/Discipline (live, Manchester) (12", p/s) . . . 20
76 Industrial IR 0001 BEST OF VOLUME II (private cassette, 50 copies only) . . . 40
77 Industrial IR 0002 SECOND ANNUAL REPORT (LP, 785 only, white sleeve, xerox strip & 2 stickers) . . 100
78 Industrial IR 0004 D.O.A. THE THIRD AND FINAL REPORT (LP, 1st 1,000 with calendar & postcard) . . 60
78 Industrial IR 0004 D.O.A. THE THIRD AND FINAL REPORT (LP) . . . 15
78 Fetish FET 2001 SECOND ANNUAL REPORT (LP, 2,000 only, T.G. 'lightning flash' sleeve, with questionnaire & insert, "Coom" mispelling) . . . 40
79 Fetish FET 2001 SECOND ANNUAL REPORT (LP, reissue, glossy sleeve with inserts, with correct "Coum" spelling) . . . 15
79 Industrial IR 0004 D.O.A. THE THIRD AND FINAL REPORT (LP, re-pressing, 1,000 only, banded as 16 equal length tracks) . . . 60
79 Industrial IR 0008 20 JAZZ FUNK GREATS (LP, 5,000 only, 1st 2,000 with b&w poster) . . . 70
79 Industrial IR 0008 20 JAZZ FUNK GREATS (LP, 5,000 only) . . . 15
80 Industrial IR 0009 HEATHEN EARTH (LP, gatefold sleeve, 785 on blue vinyl) . . . 90
80 Industrial IR 0009 HEATHEN EARTH (LP, gatefold sleeve) . . . 20
81 Fetish FET 2001 SECOND ANNUAL REPORT (LP, backwards version, 1st 2,000 in T.G. 'flash' sleeve) . . . 40
81 Fetish FET 2001 SECOND ANNUAL REPORT (LP, backwards version, later issue in black & white sleeve) . . . 15
81 Fetish FX 1 A BOXED SET (5-LP box set with 28-page booklet & badge, 5,000 only) . . . 140
82 Death 01 MUSIC FROM THE DEATH FACTORY, MAY '79 (LP, 50 only) . . . 350
82 Power Focus 001 ASSUME POWER FOCUS (LP, 500 only, numbered) . . . 80
82 T.G. 33033 LIVE AT THE DEATH FACTORY, MAY '79 (LP, reissue picture disc, 1,355 only) . . . 40
82 Karnage/Illuminated KILL 1 THEE PSYCHICK SACRIFICE (2-LP) . . . 30
84 Illuminated JAMS 35 IN THE SHADOW OF THE SUN (LP, soundtrack) . . . 20
84 Illuminated JAMS 39 THE INDUSTRIAL RECORDS STORY 1976-1981 (LP) . . . 35
84 Casual Abandon CAS 1J ONCE UPON A TIME (LP) . . . 15
84 Mental Decay 01-1 SPECIAL TREATMENT (LP) . . . 15
80s Sprut 001 VERY FRIENDLY - THE FIRST ANNUAL REPORT OF T.G. (LP) . . . 25
80s Industrial IRC 1-IRC 24 24 HOURS (box set of cassettes with total of 24 hours playing time; every set is unique) . . . 300

MINT VALUE £

THROWING MUSES
(see also Belly, Kristin Hersh)

89	4AD BADD 903	Dizzy/Santa Claus/Mania (live)/Downtown (live) (10", gatefold p/s)	8
93	4AD CADD 2013	RED HEAVEN (LP, with free live Kristin Hersh LP)	12

THE THRUST

80	Ellie Jay EJSP 9341	THE THRUST EP	100

THUNDER
(see also Terraplane, Nuthin' Fancy)

89	EMI EMS 11	She's So Fine/Girl's Going Out Of Her Head (p/s, with free patch)	5
90	EMI EMPD 126	Dirty Love/Fired Up (logo-shaped picture disc with insert in PVC sleeve)	10
90	EMI EMPD 126	Dirty Love/Fired Up (uncut picture disc with insert in PVC sleeve)	15
90	EMI EMS 137	Back Street Symphony/No Way Out Of The Wilderness (box set with postcards, some also with badge)	10
90	EMI 12 EMPD 137	Back Street Symphony/No Way Out Of The Wilderness/An Englishman On Holiday (live) (12", picture disc with insert in PVC sleeve)	8

JOHNNY THUNDER

63	Stateside SS 149	Loop De Loop/Don't Be Ashamed	10
63	Stateside SS 168	Rock-A-Bye My Darling/The Rosy Dance	10
63	Stateside SS 200	Jailer, Bring Me Water/Outlaw	15
63	Stateside SS 229	Hey Child/Everybody Likes To Dance With Johnny	10
64	Stateside SS 337	More, More, More Love, Love, Love/Shout It To The World	10
65	Stateside SS 370	Send Her To Me/Everybody Likes To Dance With Johnny	20
65	Stateside SS 454	Dear John I'm Going To Leave You/Suzie-Q	10
65	Stateside SS 476	Everybody Do The Sloopy/Beautiful	10
66	Stateside SS 499	My Prayer/A Broken Heart	10
63	Stateside SL 10029	LOOP DE LOOP (LP)	75

JOHNNY THUNDER & RUBY WINTERS

67	Stateside SS 2005	Make Love To Me/Teach Me Tonight	15

THUNDERBIRDS
(see also Chris Farlowe & Thunderbirds)

66	Polydor 56710	Your Ma Said You Cried (In Your Sleep Last Night)/Before It's Too Late	70

THUNDERBIRDS (Australia)

61	Oriole CB 1610	Wild Weekend/Rat Race	20
61	Oriole CB 1625	New Orleans Beat/Delilah Jones	20

THUNDERBIRDS (T.V.)
(see under Barrie Gray)

THUNDERBIRDS (U.S.)
(see also Bert Convy & Thunderbirds, Midnighters)

55	London HL 8146	Ayuh, Ayuh/Blueberries	70
55	London HL 8146	Ayuh, Ayuh/Blueberries (78)	15

THUNDERBOLTS

62	Decca F 11522	Fugitive/Feelin' In A Mood	15

THUNDERBOYS

80	Recent EJSP 9339	Fashion/Someone Like You (p/s)	40

THUNDERCLAP NEWMAN
(see also Stone The Crows, One In A Million, Paul McCartney & Wings, Speedy Keen, Andy Newman)

69	Track 604031	Something In The Air/Wilhemina	6
70	Track 2094 001	Accidents/I See It All	5
70	Track 2094 002	Wild Country/Hollywood	7
70	Track 2094 003	The Reason/Stormy Petrel	7
79	Track 2095 002	Wild Country/Hollywood (reissue, p/s)	8
70	Track 2406 003	HOLLYWOOD DREAM (LP, gatefold sleeve, lyric insert)	40
70	Track 2406 003	HOLLYWOOD DREAM (LP, gatefold sleeve, without lyric insert)	30

THUNDER COMPANY
(see also Brian Bennett, Shadows)

70	Columbia DB 8706	Ridin' On The Gravy Train (5.03)/Bubble Drum	40
70	Columbia DB 8706	Ridin' On The Gravy Train (2.35 Edit)/Bubble Drum (demo only)	50

THUNDERHEAD

93	Thunderhead TH 01	Lost In Time/Untitled (12")	20

THUNDERMUG

73	London HLZ 10411	Africa/Will They Ever	6
72	Axe AXS 502	STRIKES (LP)	15

THUNDER ROAD

73	Buddah 2011-163	Peter Gunn/Holly Golly	5

JOHNNY THUNDERS (& THE HEARTBREAKERS)
(see also New York Dolls, Heartbreakers)

78	Real ARE 1	Dead Or Alive/Downtown (p/s)	15
78	Real ARE 3	You Can't Put Your Arms Around A Memory (Edit)/Hurtin' (p/s)	12
78	Real ARE 3T	You Can't Put Your Arms Around A Memory/Hurtin' (12", p/s, blue or pink vinyl, die-cut company sleeve)	12
83	Jungle JUNG 5	VINTAGE '77 (12" EP)	12
84	Jungle JUNG 14P	Get Off The Phone/All By Myself (picture disc)	10
84	Jungle JUNG 14T	GET OFF THE PHONE EP (12")	8
85	Jungle JUNG 18T	CHINESE ROCKS (12" EP)	8
85	Jungle JUNG 23P	Crawfish/Tie Me Up (with Patti Palladin, picture disc)	8
87	Jungle JUNG 33T	QUE SERA SERA (12" EP)	8
77	Real RAL 1	SO ALONE (LP, with inner sleeve)	12
82	Jungle FREUD 1	LIVE AT THE SPEAKEASY (LP)	12

MINT VALUE £

SAM THUNDER

84 Bullet BOLT 8 — Don't Take Forever/Piece Of the Night/You Set My Heart On FIre (12", p/s) — 8

84 Bullet BULP 5 — MANOUEVRES (LP, picture disc) — 18

THUNDERSTICK

(see also Samson, Gillan)

83 Thunderbolt THBE 1002 — FEEL LIKE ROCK'N'ROLL (12" EP, p/s, with patch) — 12

83 Thunderbolt THBE 1002 — FEEL LIKE ROCK'N'ROLL (12" EP, p/s) — 8

83 Thunderbolt THBL 008 — BEAUTY AND THE BEASTS (LP) — 12

THUNDERTRAIN

77 Jelly JPLP 1 — TEENAGE SUICIDE (LP) — 12

THURSDAY'S CHILDREN

(see also Phil Cordell)

66 Piccadilly 7N 35276 — Just You/You Don't Believe Me — 25

66 Piccadilly 7N 35306 — Crawfish/Come Softly To Me — 15

THYRDS

64 Oak RGJ 133 — Hide 'N' Seek/I've Got My Mojo Working — 300

64 Decca F 12010 — Hide 'N' Seek/No Time Like The Present — 60

TIARAS

63 Warner Bros WB 92 — You Told Me/I'm Gonna Forget You — 15

TIBET & STAPLETON

(see also Current 93, Steven Stapleton & David Tibet)o

96 United Dairies UDOR 1 — MUSICALISCHE KÜRBS HÜTTE (LP, clear vinyl, with insert) — 30

TICH - TED TAYLOR FOUR WITH CORONA KIDS

(see also Ted Taylor)

65 Oriole CB 1980 — Santa Bring Me Ringo/Santa's Got Such A Terrible Cold/Tich & Quackers — 10

TICKAWINDA

75 Pennine PSS 153 — ROSEMARY LANE (LP) — 450

KATHRYN TICKELL

84 Saydisc SDL 343 — ON KIELDER SIDE (LP) — 20

TICKETS

(see also Wasted Youth)

79 Bridgehouse BHS 3 — I'll Be Your Pin Up/Guess I Have To Sit Alone (p/s) — 6

TICKLE

(see also Junior's Eyes, Outsider, Bunch Of Fives)

67 Regal Zonophone RZ 3004 — Subway (Smokey Pokey World)/Good Evening — 450

TIC TAC TOE

92 Tic Tac Toe TTT 456 — 456/Ephemerol (12", stamped white label) — 30

92 Tic Tac Toe TTT 457 — 456/(Remix)/Ephemerol (Mickey Finn Remix) (12") — 10

TIDAL WAVE

69 Decca F 22973 — With Tears In My Eyes/We Wanna Know — 10

69 Storm PD 9616 — Spider Spider/Crazy Horse — 200

70 Storm PD 9694 — Green Mamba/Colonel Mustard — 50

TIDBITS

71 Fly BUG 12 — Jean Harlow/Vietnam/Six O'Clock Blues (p/s) — 8

PETER TIERNEY & NIGHTHAWKS

65 Fontana TF 547 — Oh How I Need You/That's Too Bad (p/s) — 15

ROY TIERNEY

61 Philips BF 1159 — Cupid/The Lonely One (in p/s) — 15

61 Philips BF 1159 — Cupid/The Lonely One — 7

61 Philips BF 1194 — Just Out Of Reach (Of My Two Empty Arms)/Casanova — 10

TIERNEY'S FUGITIVES

65 Decca F 12247 — Did You Want To Run Away?/Morning Mist — 25

TIFFANIES

67 Chess CRS 8059 — It's Got To Be A Great Song/He's Good For Me — 100

67 Chess CRS 8059 — It's Got To Be A Great Song/He's Good For Me (DJ copy) — 150

TIFFANY (with THOUGHTS)

(see also Thoughts)

65 Parlophone R 5311 — I Know/Am I Dreaming — 20

66 Parlophone R 5439 — Find Out What's Happening/Baby Don't Look Down (as Tiffany with Thoughts) — 50

TIFFANY SHADE

68 Fontana (S)TL 5469 — TIFFANY SHADE (LP) — 90

JIMMY & LOUISE TIG

69 Deep Soul DS 9105 — A Love That Never Grows Cold/Who Can I Turn To — 40

TIGER

(see also Hackensack, Samson, Brinsley Schwarz, Big Jim Sullivan)

75 United Artists UP 35848 — I Am An Animal/Stop That Machine — 20

76 Retreat RTL 6006 — TIGER (LP, with lyric inner sleeve) — 15

76 EMI EMC3153 — GOIN' DOWN LAUGHING (LP) — 12

TIGER (Jamaica)

70 New Beat NB 052 — Soul Of Africa/Dallas Texas — 10

70 New Beat NB 064 — Musical Scorcher/Three Dogs Night — 10

71 Camel CA 70 — Guilty/United We Stand — 7

71 New Beat NB 075 — African Beat/Black Man Land — 7

71 New Beat NB 088 — Have You Ever Been Hurt/Our Day Will Come — 7

MINT VALUE £

TIGER LILY
(see also Ultravox)

75 Gull GULS 12 Monkey Jive/Ain't Misbehavin' ... 8
77 Gull GULS 54 Monkey Jive/Ain't Misbehavin' (reissue, p/s) ... 10
77 Gull GULS 54 Monkey Jive/Ain't Misbehavin' (reissue) ... 5
80 Dead Good DEAD 11 Monkey Jive/Ain't Misbehavin' (2nd reissue, different p/s) ... 5

TIGERMOTH
84 Rogue FMSL 2006 TIGERMOTH (LP) ... 15

TIGERS
80s Strike KIK 1 Kidding Stops/Big Expense, Small Income (p/s) ... 8

TIGERS
69 Polydor 56339 Rain Falls On The Lonely/Smile For Me ... 10

TIGHT LIKE THAT
72 Village Thing VTS 12 HOKUM (LP) ... 40

TIGHTS
78 Cherry Red CHERRY 1 Bad Hearts/It/Cracked (p/s) ... 20
78 Cherry Red CHERRY 2 Howard Hughes/China's Eternal (p/s) ... 8
78 Ch. Red CSP-CHERRY 2 Howard Hughes/China's Eternal (cassette) ... 6

TIKKI, TAKI, SUZI, LIES
70 UPC UPC 102 Welcome To My House/I Believe In Love ... 8
70 UPC UPC 109 Ba-Da-Da-Dum/Dream Stealer ... 25

TILLER BOYS
(see also Buzzcocks, Pete Shelley, Eric Random)

79 New Hormones ORG 3 Big Noise From The Jungle/Slaves And Pyramids/What Me Worry? (p/s) ... 6

TILLERMEN
(see also Greyhound)

71 Duke DU 109 Be Loving To Me/Judgement Rock ... 7

MEL TILLIS
67 London HLR 10141 Life Turned Her That Way/If I Could Only Start Over ... 5
68 London HA-R 8345 MR. MEL (LP) ... 12

BERTHA TILLMAN
62 Oriole CB 1746 Oh, My Angel/Lovin' Time ... 80

JOHNNY TILLOTSON
59 London HLA 8930 True True Happiness/Love Is Blind ... 50
59 London HLA 8930 True True Happiness/Love Is Blind (78) ... 25
60 London HLA 9048 Why Do I Love You So/Never Let Me Go ... 30
60 London HLA 9101 Earth Angel/Pledging My Love ... 30
60 London HLA 9231 Poetry In Motion/Princess, Princess ... 5
61 London HLA 9275 Jimmy's Girl/His True Love Said Goodbye ... 10
61 London HLA 9412 Without You/Cutie Pie ... 15
62 London HLA 9514 Dreamy Eyes/Much Beyond Compare ... 6
62 London HLA 9550 It Keeps Right On A-Hurtin'/She Gave Sweet Love To Me ... 8
62 London HLA 9598 Send Me The Pillow You Dream On/What'll I Do ... 7
62 London HLA 9642 I Can't Help It/I'm So Lonesome I Could Cry ... 7
63 London HLA 9695 Out Of My Mind/Judy, Judy, Judy ... 7
63 London HLA 9811 Funny How Time Slips Away/A Very Good Year For Girls ... 7
63 MGM MGM 1214 Talk Back Trembling Lips/Another You ... 7
63 MGM MGM 1225 Worried Guy/Please Don't Go Away ... 6
63 MGM MGM 1235 I'm Watching My Watch/I Rise, I Fall ... 6
64 MGM MGM 1247 Suffering From A Heartache/Worry ... 6
64 MGM MGM 1252 She Understands Me/Tomorrow ... 8
64 MGM MGM 1266 Angel/Little Boy ... 7
65 MGM MGM 1275 Then I'll Count Again/One's Yours, One's Mine ... 8
65 MGM MGM 1281 Heartaches By The Number/Your Memory Comes Along ... 8
65 MGM MGM 1290 Our World/(Wait 'Til You See) My Gidget ... 8
66 MGM MGM 1300 Hello Enemy/I Never Loved You Anyway ... 8
66 MGM MGM 1311 Me Myself And I/Country Boy, Country Boy ... 8
66 MGM MGM 1319 No Love At All/What Am I Gonna Do ... 8
68 MGM MGM 1393 Cabaret/If I Were A Rich Man ... 8
69 London HLU 10281 Tears On My Pillow/Remember When ... 5
62 London RE-A 1345 JOHNNY TILLOTSON (EP) ... 40
63 London RE-A 1388 J.T. (EP) ... 40
63 MGM MGM-EP 788 JOHNNY TILLOTSON (EP) ... 25
64 MGM MGM-EP 790 JOHNNY TILLOTSON'S HIT PARADE (EP) ... 25
61 London HA-A 2431 JOHNNY TILLOTSON'S BEST (LP) ... 60
62 London HA-A 8019 IT KEEPS RIGHT ON A-HURTIN' (LP) ... 40
64 MGM MGM-C 972 ALONE WITH YOU (LP) ... 15
65 MGM C/CS 1002 SHE UNDERSTANDS ME (LP) ... 15
65 MGM MGM-C(S) 8005 JOHNNY TILLOTSON SINGS OUR WORLD (LP) ... 15
66 MGM MGM-C(S) 8025 NO LOVE AT ALL (LP) ... 15

TILSLEY ORCHESTRA
(see also Electric Banana)

66 Fontana TF 783 Thunderbirds Theme/Theme From "The Power Game" ... 20
67 Polydor 56150 Mr. Aitch Theme/Cotton Reed ... 8
67 Fontana (S)TL 5411 TOP T.V. THEMES (LP) ... 20

STEVE TILSTON
71 Village Thing VTS 5 AN ACOUSTIC CONFUSION (LP) ... 35
72 Transatlantic TRA 252 COLLECTION (LP, gatefold sleeve) ... 18
77 Cornucopia CR 1 SONGS FROM THE DRESS REHEARSAL (LP, with Rupert Hine/John Renbourn) 25
83 TM PROP 4 IN FOR A PENNY IN FOR A POUND (LP, with Peter Bardens) ... 15

MINT VALUE £

TIMBER

71	Elektra K 12022	Bring America Home/Splinters From Timber	6
72	Elektra K 12042	Outlaw/Song For Two Signs	6
71	Elektra K 42093	BRING AMERICA HOME (LP)	12

TIME

65	Pye 7N 17019	Take A Bit Of Notice/Every Now And Then	60
66	Pye 7N 17146	The First Time I Saw The Sunshine/Annabel	30

TIME

(see also Spontaneous Combustion)

75	B.U.K. BULP 2005	TIME (LP)	60

T.I.M.E. (Trust In Men Everywhere)

69	Liberty LBF 15082	Take Me Along/Make It Alright	10
68	Liberty LBL/LBS 83144	T.I.M.E. (LP)	50
69	Liberty LBL/LBS 83232	SMOOTH BALL (LP)	70

TIME UK

(see also The Jam)

83	Red Bus TIM 123	The Cabaret/Remember Days (gatefold p/s)	10

TIMEBOX

(see also Bo Street Runners, [Mike] Patto, V.I.Ps)

67	Piccadilly 7N 35369	I'll Always Love You/Save Your Love	60
67	Piccadilly 7N 35379	Soul Sauce/I Wish I Could Jerk Like My Uncle Cyril	110
67	Deram DM 153	Walking Through The Streets Of My Mind/Don't Make Promises	25
68	Deram DM 194	Beggin'/A Woman That's Waiting	45
68	Deram DM 219	Girl Don't Make Me Wait/Gone Is The Sad Man	35
69	Deram DM 246	Baked Jam Roll In Your Eye/Poor Little Heartbreaker	25
69	Deram DM 271	Yellow Van/You've Got The Chance	25

TIME CODE

86	Jive LOUT 1	Village House Stomp/Louie Louie (12")	8

TIME CRYSTALS

91	Talisman TAL 1	The Fool/Geve Me Back What's Mine	10

TIMELORDS

(see also KLF, Disco 2000, JAMs, Bill Drummond, Orb, Space)

88	KLF 003GG	Gary In The Tardis (Radio)/(Minimal) (white label promo, 500 only)	15
88	KLF 003GG	Gary In The Tardis (Radio)/(Minimal) (12", p/s)	10
88	KLF 003P	Doctorin' The Tardis (Radio)/(Minimal) (car-shaped picture disc)	15
88	KLF 003R	Doctorin' The Tardis (Radio)/Doctorin' The Tardis (Minimal)/Gary Glitter Joins The JAMs (12", 4,000 only, this price for those in full 'Gary Glitter' p/s)	30
88	KLF 003R	Doctorin' The Tardis (Radio)/Doctorin' The Tardis (Minimal)/ Gary Glitter Joins The JAMs (12", 4,000 only, in stickered black die-cut sleeve)	8
88	KLF TCD 003	Doctorin' The Tardis (12" mix)/What Time Is Love? (KLF original) (CD)	10
88	KLF CD 003	Doctorin' The Tardis (Radio)/Doctorin' The Tardis (Minimal)/Doctorin' The Tardis (Club Mix)/Doctorin' The Tardis (Video) (CD Video)	30

TIME MACHINE

72	Play PLAY 41	Railroad/Going Down Down Down	30

TIMES

65	EMI 7ES 24	Ooh Wee/Shepherd Blues/Suzie/Running And Hiding (EP, demo only)	70
66	Columbia DB 7804	Think About The Times/Tomorrow Night	35
66	Columbia DB 7904	(She Can't Replace) The Love We Knew/Reconciled	35
68	Pye 7N 17647	What's Made Milwaukee Famous/Follw The Times	10
70	Parlophone R 5855	Looking Thru' The Eyes Of A Beautiful Girl/Flyin' High Feelin' Low	10

TIMES

(see also Television Personalities, Teenage Filmstars, O Level, Biff Bang Pow!, L'Orange Mechanik)

81	Whaam! WHAAM 2	Red With Purple Flashes/Biff! Bang! Pow! (p/s)	35
82	Art Pop POP 50	Here Come The Holidays (Voici Les Vacances)/ Three Cheers For The Sun (A-side as Joni Dee & Times, p/s, with 'Times' sticker)	15
82	Art Pop POP 50	Here Come The Holidays (Voici Les Vacances)/Three Cheers For The Sun (A-side as Joni Dee & Times, p/s)	10
83	Art Pop POP 49	I Helped Patrick McGoohan Escape/The Theme From "Danger Man" (p/s)	12
84	Art Pop POP 46	Boys Brigade/Power Is Forever (p/s)	7
84	Art Pop POP 45	Blue Fire/Where The Blue Begins (p/s)	6
85	Unicorn PHZ 1	London Boys/(Where To Go) When The Sun Goes Down (p/s)	5
89	Creation CRE 071 T	Manchester (12", p/s)	10
90	Caff CAFF 13	Extase/BIFF BANG POW!: Sleep (p/s, with insert)	20
85	Art Pop 43DOZ	BOYS ABOUT TOWN (EP)	10
81	Whaam! BIG 1	POP GOES ART (LP, hand-sprayed sleeve)	35
82	Art Pop ART 20	POP GOES ART! (LP, reissue, hand-sprayed sleeve, with magazine cuttings taped to plain white cover)	25
82	Art Pop ART 20	POP GOES ART! (LP, reissue, hand-sprayed sleeve, without magazine cuttings taped to plain white cover)	20
83	Art Pop ART 19	THIS IS LONDON (LP, white label with blue print)	18
83	Art Pop ART 19	THIS IS LONDON (LP, black label with white print)	15
83	Art Pop No. 1	I HELPED PATRICK McGOOHAN ESCAPE (mini-LP)	18
84	Art Pop ART 17	HELLO EUROPE (LP, purple or blue sleeve)	12
85	Art Pop ARTPOP 2	BLUE PERIOD (mini-LP, grey sleeve)	12
86	Art Pop ART 16	UP AGAINST IT (LP)	12
86	Art Pop ART 15	ENJOY! (LP, gatefold sleeve)	12
90	Art Pop ART 20	POP GOES ART (LP, 'hand-painted' picture disc reissue, signed)	15
93	Creation CRELP 137	ALTERNATIVE COMMERCIAL CROSSOVER (LP, with inner)	12

TIME ZONE

(see also Public Image Ltd., Sex Pistols)

88	Virgin CDT 29	World Destruction (12" A)/(12" B)/(12" Instrumental Blast) (featuring John Lydon & Afrika Bambaataa) (3" CD, gatefold card p/s)	8

MINT VALUE £

BOBBY TIMMONS
61 Riverside RLP 334 — SOUL TIME (LP, with Art Blakey, also stereo [RLP 9334]) ... 20
60 Riverside 12-317 — THIS HERE IS (LP) ... 20

SALLY TIMMS & DRIFTING COWGIRLS
(see also Marc Almond, Mekons)
87 T.I.M. 12 MOT 6 — This House Is A House Of Trouble! (Extended) (with Marc Almond)/ The Anchor Of Love/Heavenly Gates (12", p/s) ... 10

TIMON
(see also Tymon Dogg)
68 Pye 7N 17451 — Bitter Thoughts Of Little Jane/Ramblin' Boy ... 100
70 Threshold TH 3 — And Now She Says She's Young/I'm Just A Travelling Man ... 8

TIMONEERS
76 WHM WHM 1919 — ROASTED LIVE (LP) ... 20

AL TIMOTHY & HIS BAND
55 Decca F 10558 — Gruntin' Blues/You Mad Man! ... 10

TIM TAM & TURN ONS
67 Island WIP 6007 — Wait A Minute/Ophelia ... 50

TINA
61 Piccadilly 7N 35022 — What I Want For Christmas (Is Six More Years)/ My Brother Wants A Doll For Christmas ... 6

TINA & MEXICANS
68 Pye 7N 17525 — One Love Two/Longing To Hold You ... 8

TIN BISCUIT
70 Fontana TF 1077 — The Last Time You Go/I'd Give My Life To You ... 5

TINDERBOX
68 Polydor 56296 — Farewell Britannia/Rainsong ... 40

TINDERSTICKS
(see also Asphalt Ribbons)
92 Tippy Toe 1 — Patchwork/Milky Teeth (p/s, hand-coloured inner sleeve & insert; 1,000 only, numbered in positive or negative figures [from -500 to 500]) ... 60
93 Tippy Toe/Ché TIPPY-CHE 2 — Marbles/Joe Stumble/For Those?/Benn (10", p/s, stickered PVC sleeve, inner sleeve & insert, 2,000 only) ... 25
93 Rough Trade 45rev16 — A Marriage Made In Heaven/A Marriage Made In Heaven (Instrumental) ('singles club' release, p/s, 5,000 only) ... 20
93 Domino RUG 006 — UNWIRED EP: Feeling Relatively Good/Rotweilers And Mace/She/Kooks (EP, numbered p/s; 1 copy in 10 with 'Domino' stamp, 1,500 only) ... 25
93 This Way Up WAY 1811 — City Sickness/Untitled/The Bullring (p/s, 1,500 only) ... 15
93 This Way Up WAY 1899 — City Sickness/Untitled/The Bullring (CD) ... 15
93 Clawfist XPIG 21 — We Have All The Time In The World/GALLON DRUNK: Known Not Wanted ('singles club' release, p/s, 1,400 only) ... 18
93 Tippy Toe 003 — LIVE IN BERLIN: Raindrops/Tyed (in stamped brown paper bag, mail-order/tour release, 1,500 only) ... 20
94 This Way Up WAY 2899 — Kathleen/Summat Moon/Sweet, Sweet Man/E Type Joe (CD) ... 15
95 Sub Pop SP 297 — THE SMOOTH SOUND OF TINDERSTICKS: Here/Harry's Dilemma (p/s, 3,000 only) ... 15
95 This Way Up 2888 — KATHLEEN (10") ... 12
08 Lucky Dog LD 05 — What Are You Fighting For? (one-sided 7", die cut sleeve, 200 only) ... 15
93 This Way Up 518306 — TINDERSTICKS (1st album) (2-LP, first 1000 with 4 postcards) ... 80
93 This Way Up 518306 — TINDERSTICKS (1st album) (2-LP, without postcards) ... 45
95 This Way Up THIS 1.1 — TINDERSTICKS (2nd album) (LP, with free 7") ... 40
94 This Way Up WAY 3288 — LIVE IN AMSTERDAM (10" LP, brown sleeve) ... 15
94 This Way Up WAY 3299 — LIVE IN AMSTERDAM (CD, numbered brown paper sleeve) ... 25
95 This Way Up — THE BLOOMSBURY THEATRE 12/3/95 (LP, 2-10" LP) ... 35
96 This Way Up 5243002 — NENETTE ET BONI (LP) ... 20
97 This Way Up 5243441 — CURTAINS (2-LP) ... 70
98 Island ILPS 8074 — DONKEYS 92-97 (LP) ... 25
99 Simply Vinyl SVLP 112 — SIMPLE PLEASURE (LP) ... 30

TING TINGS
07 Switchflicker SWALF 11 — That's Not My Name/Great DJ (p/s) ... 15
07 No label or cat no — Fruit Machine/Impacilla Carpisung (4 x 100 7" given away at 4 live shows, customised blank sleeve) ... 50

TINGA (Stewart) & ERNIE (Wilson)
69 Explosion EX 2009 — She's Gone/Old Old Song ... 8

TINGHA & TUCKER
(see under Century 21)

TIN KAN
79 White Dove WD103A — A Thousand Miles Of White/Girl I'd Never Let You Down ... 10

TINKERBELL'S FAIRYDUST
67 Decca F 12705 — Lazy Day/In My Magic Garden ... 70
68 Decca F 12778 — Twenty Ten/Walking My Baby ... 70
69 Decca F 12865 — Sheila's Back In Town/Follow Me Follow ... 100
69 Decca LK/SKL 5028 — TINKERBELL'S FAIRYDUST (LP, unreleased; finished copies in laminated front sleeve with mono/stereo 'peephole' on rear, machine etched matrix number, blue/silver label with large unboxed Decca logo) ... 3000
69 Decca LK/SKL 5028 — TINKERBELL'S FAIRYDUST (LP, unreleased; test pressings in sleeve) ... 800
69 Decca LK/SKL 5028 — TINKERBELL'S FAIRYDUST (LP, unreleased; test pressings in finished in laminated front sleeve with mono/stereo 'peephole' on rear) ... 500

TINKERS
69 Fontana SFJL 935 — TIL THE WILD BIRDS (LP) ... 18
72 Argo ZFB 35 — SPRING RAIN (LP) ... 25

MINT VALUE £

BABS TINO
62 London HLR 9589 Forgive Me/If I Didn't Love You So Much . . . 30
63 London RE-R 1377 FORGIVE ME (EP) . . . 100

TINOPENERS
79 Logo GO 375 Set Me Free/I'm Not Your Type . . . 150

TIN PAN SKIFFLE GROUP
57 Nestles NR 06 Poor Howard (1-sided card flexi 78) . . . 12

MICK TINSLEY
(see also Hedgehoppers Anonymous)
67 Decca F 12544 Let It Be Me/How're You Gonna Tell Me . . . 6

TIN SOLDIERS
93 Detour DR 002 A New Beat/Girlfriend/Get Up And Go! (p/s, insert 1,000, only 100 on clear vinyl) 12

TINTERN ABBEY
67 Deram DM 164 Beeside/Vacuum Cleaner . . . 900

TIN TIN
(see also Steve & Stevie)
69 Polydor 56332 Only Ladies Play Croquet/He Wants To Be A Star . . . 10
70 Polydor 2058 023 Toast And Marmalade For Tea/Manhattan Woman . . . 12
70 Polydor 2058 076 Come On Over Again/Back To Winona . . . 10
71 Polydor 2001 146 Shana/Rocky Mountain . . . 10
71 Polydor 2058 114 Is That The Way/Swans On The Canal . . . 10
72 Polydor 2058 232 Toast And Marmalade For Tea/Cavalry's Coming/Ships On The Starboard . . . 10
72 Polydor 2058 238 Talking Turkey/Cavalry's Coming . . . 10
69 Polydor 2384 011 TIN TIN (LP) . . . 25
72 Polydor 2382 080 ASTRAL TAXI (LP) . . . 15

TINY ALICE
72 Kama Sutra 2013 043 Doctor Jazz/The Chocolate Dandies Of 1932/15¢ Hamburger Mama . . . 5
72 Kama Sutra 2319 015 TINY ALICE (LP) . . . 12

TINY TIM
68 Reprise RS 20760 Bring Back Those Rockabye Baby Days . . . 6
68 Reprise RS 23258 Tiptoe Through The Tulips/I Got You Babe . . . 6
68 Reprise RS 20769 Hello Hello/The Other Side . . . 10
69 Reprise RS 20802 Great Balls Of Fire/As Time Goes By . . . 6
69 Reprise RS 20845 Mickey The Monkey/Neighbourhood Children . . . 6
71 Reprise RS 27004 There Will Always Be An England/Bless 'Em All/It's A Long Way To Tipperary/ Have You Seen My Little Sue . . . 6
71 Reprise RS 27004 There Will Always Be An England/Bless 'Em All/It's A Long Way To Tipperary/ Have You Seen My Little Sue (78 rpm with union jack/plain label) . . . 10
72 Wand WN 33 Am I Just Another Pretty Face/Movies . . . 7
74 Polydor 2058 485 Happy Wanderer/My Nose Always Gets In The Way . . . 6
68 Reprise RSLP 6292 GOD BLESS TINY TIM (LP) . . . 20
69 Reprise RSLP 6323 TINY TIM'S SECOND ALBUM (LP) . . . 20
69 Reprise RSLP 6351 FOR ALL MY LITTLE FRIENDS (LP) . . . 15

TINY TOPSY (& CHARMS)
58 Parlophone R 4397 Come On, Come On, Come On/A Ring Around My Finger (with Charms) . . . 90
58 Parlophone R 4397 Come On, Come On, Come On/A Ring Around My Finger (with Charms) (78) . . . 30
58 Parlophone R 4427 You Shocked Me/Waterproof Eyes (solo) . . . 120
58 Parlophone R 4427 You Shocked Me/Waterproof Eyes (solo) (78) . . . 25
61 Pye International 7N 25104 After Marriage Blues/Working On Me Baby (solo) . . . 30

DIMITRI TIOMKIN
54 Vogue Coral Q 2016 The High And The Mighty/Dial M For Murder . . . 15

KEITH TIPPETT
(see also Centipede, King Crimson, Ovary Lodge, Nicra)
69 Polydor 2384 004 YOU ARE HERE, I AM THERE (LP) . . . 85
71 Vertigo 6360 024 DEDICATED TO YOU BUT YOU WEREN'T LISTENING (LP, gatefold sleeve, large swirl label) . . . 120
72 RCA SF 8290 BLUEPRINT (LP) . . . 75
76 Steam SJ 104 TNT (LP, with Stan Tracey) . . . 15
77 Vinyl VS 101 WARM SPIRITS, COOL SPIRITS (LP) . . . 12
78 Ogun OGD 003/4 FRAMES (2-LP) . . . 20
78 Ogun OGUN 003/004 ARK (2-LP) . . . 20

JULIE TIPPETTS
(see also Julie Driscoll, Brian Auger, Centipede, Keith Tippett, Elton Dean, Ninesense, Mark Charig)
76 Utopia UTS 601 SUNSET GLOW (LP) . . . 22

TIPPIE & THE CLOVERS
63 Stateside SS 160 My Heart Said/Bossa Nova Baby . . . 25

LESTER TIPTON
80 Grapevine GRP 138 This Won't Change/MASQUERADERS: How . . . 20

TIP TOPS
63 Cameo Parkway P 868 He's Braggin'/Oo-Kook-A-Boo . . . 35

TÍR NA NOG
72 Chrysalis CHS 2001 The Lady I Love/Heidi . . . 7
73 Chrysalis CHS 2016 Strong In The Sun/The Mountain And I . . . 6
71 Chrysalis ILPS 9153 TÍR NA NOG (LP, laminated gatefold sleeve) . . . 25
72 Chrysalis CHR 1006 A TEAR AND A SMILE (LP, gatefold sleeve) . . . 20
73 Chrysalis CHR 1047 STRONG IN THE SUN (LP) . . . 15

TITAN
80 Wild Dog DOG 26 East Wind West Wind/Losing The Fight . . . 200

MINT VALUE £

TITANIC

72	CBS 7278	Sante Fe/Half Breed	5
72	CBS 8185	Rain 2,000/Blond	20
73	CBS 1670	Richmond Express/Heia Valenga	5
71	CBS 64104	TITANIC (LP)	20
72	CBS 64791	SEA WOLF (LP, gatefold sleeve)	20
73	CBS 65661	EAGLE ROCK (LP, gatefold sleeve)	15

TITANS

58	London HLU 8609	Don't You Just Know It/Can It Be	100
58	London HLU 8609	Don't You Just Know It/Can It Be (78)	35

TITUS GROAN

70	Dawn DNX 2503	Open The Door Homer/Woman Of The World/Liverpool (p/s)	20
70	Dawn DNLS 3012	TITUS GROAN (LP, gatefold sleeve)	150

CAL TJADER

65	Verve VS 529	Soul Sauce/Naked City Theme	40
65	Verve VS 529	Soul Sauce/Naked City Theme (DJ copy)	80
58	Vocalion LAE 556	RITMO CALIENTE (LP, as Cal Tjader Quintet)	20
60	Vocalion LAE 560	THE WEST SIDE STORY (LP)	15
62	HMV/Verve CLP 1587	IN A LATIN BAG (LP, as Cal Tjader Sextet, also stereo [CSD 1454])	15
64	Verve V8585	WARM WAVE (LP)	12
65	Vocalion LAE-F 599	GREATEST HITS (LP)	15
65	Verve (S)VLP 9136	SOUL BIRD: WHIFFENPOOF (LP)	15
66	Verve (S)VLP 9155	SOUL BURST (LP)	15
68	Verve (S)VLP 9192	THE BEST OF CAL TJADER (LP)	15
68	Verve (S)VLP 9215	HIP VIBRATIONS (LP)	20
69	Fontana STL 5527	SOLAR HEAT (LP)	12
61	Vogue SEA 568	CONCERT BY THE SEA (LP)	15

TMR

92	Pirate Club PCR 001	Pirate Toon (Moose Mix)/Pirate Toon (Pirate Excursion)/Pirate Toon (Pirate Dub) (12", white stamped label)	60

T.N.T.

72	Jam JAM 4	Big Trouble (Part One)/Big Trouble (Part Two)	10

TNT

84	Neat NEAT 39	Back On The Road/Rockin' The Night (p/s)	12

TOAD

72	RCA Victor SF 8241	TOAD (LP)	150

TOAD THE WET SPROCKET

79	Sprockets BRS 004	Pete's Punk Song/Feel It (fold out p/s)	40
80	Sprockets BRS 008	Reaching For The Sky/One Glass Of Whiskey (foldout stapled p/s)	70

TOAST

70	CBS 4768	Flowers Never Bend With The Rainfall/Summer Of Miranda	10

RUTH TOBI

69	Concord CON 002	Lazy/That's When I Cry	5

AMON TOBIN

94	Ninja Tune Zen 48	SUPERMODIFIED (2 x LP)	20

TOBRUK

83	Neat NEAT 32	Wild On The Run/The Show Must Go On (p/s)	8
85	Parlophone 12R 6093	Falling/Like Lightning/Under The Gun (12", p/s)	10
85	Parlophone R 6101	On The Rebound/Poor Girl (p/s)	10
88	FM WKFMLP 105	PLEASURE AND PAIN (LP)	15

TOBY JUG

69	private pressing	GREASY QUIFF (LP, with insert)	175

TOBY TWIRL

(see also Shades Of Blue)

68	Decca F 12728	Harry Faversham/Back In Time	30
68	Decca F 12804	Toffee Apple Sunday/Romeo And Juliet 1968	200
69	Decca F 12867	Movin' In/Utopia Daydream	20

TODAY'S WITNESS

72	Emblem TDR 345	TODAY'S WITNESS (LP)	35

ART & DOTTY TODD

58	London HLB 8620	Chanson D'Amour (Song Of Love)/Along The Trail With You	18
59	London HLN 8838	Straight As An Arrow/Stand There, Mountain	18
59	London HLN 8838	Straight As An Arrow/Stand There, Mountain (78)	10

DIANE TODD

58	Decca F 10993	It's A Wonderful Thing To Be Loved/You Are My Favourite Dream	8

GARY TODD & ROGER TURNER

79	Incus INCUS 79	SUNDAY BEST (LP)	50

NICK TODD

57	London HLD 8500	Plaything/The Honey Song	50
58	London HLD 8537	At The Hop/I Do	15
59	London HLD 8902	Tiger/Twice As Nice	30

PATSY TODD

(see also Patsy, Stranger & Patsy, Derrick & Patsy)

66	Doctor Bird DB 1086	Pitta Patta Rocky Steady (with Count Ossie)/COUNT OSSIE: Nyah Bongo	20
68	High Note HS 007	Fire In Your Wire/AL & VIBRATORS: Move Up Calypso	8
69	High Note HS 012	We Were Lovers/Give Me A Chance (B-side with Delano Stewart)	35

SHARKEY TODD & MONSTERS
(see also Wally Whyton, Vipers [Skiffle Group])

59	Parlophone R 4536	Cool Gool/The Horror Show	25
59	Parlophone R 4536	Cool Gool/The Horror Show (78)	20

WILF TODD COMBO

64	Blue Beat BB 240	He Took Her Away/Have You Ever Been Lonely	12

WILF TODD & HIS MUSIC

66	Oak WT 101	WILF TODD AND HIS MUSIC (LP)	15

CAMY TODOROW
(see also Roger Taylor)

85	Virgin VS 816	Bursting At The Seams/Don't Stop It, I Like It (with Roger Taylor) (p/s)	30
85	Virgin VS 816-12	Bursting At The Seams (Backroom Version)/Bursting At The Seams (Instrumental)/Don't Stop It, I Like It (12", p/s, with Roger Taylor)	50

TOE-FAT
(see also Cliff Bennett, Uriah Heep, Glass Menagerie)

70	Parlophone R 5829	Working Nights/Bad Side Of The Moon	15
72	Chapter One SCH 175	Brand New Band/Can't Live Without You	10
70	Parlophone PCS 7097	TOE-FAT (LP, black/silver label with boxed logo)	80
70	Regal Zono. SLRZ 1015	TOE-FAT TWO (LP, red/silver label)	85

TOGETHER
(see also Keith Relf)

68	Columbia DB 8491	Henry's Coming Home/Love Mum And Dad	70

TOGETHER

69	Aurora 4278	Memories Of Melinda/Good Morning World	8

TOGETHER

90	Thumbs Up Magic GH 001	Hardcore Uproar (12", white label)	250
91	Thumbs Up Magic TUM002	The Luv Bug (12")	70
92	Thumbs Up Magic GH003	The House Sound Vol 2/Coming On Strong (12", with CYBERTEC)	60
91	Thumbs Up Magic GH 002	FFREE AT LAST EP(12")	10

TOGGERY FIVE

64	Parlophone R 5175	Bye Bye Bird/I'm Gonna Jump	45
65	Parlophone R 5249	I'd Much Rather Be With The Boys/It's So Easy	40

TOKENS
(see also U.S. Double Quartet, We Ugly Dogs, Cross Country)

61	Parlophone R 4790	Tonight I Fell In Love/I Love My Baby	30
62	RCA RCA 1313	I'll Do My Crying Tomorrow/Dream Angel Goodnight	10
62	RCA RCA 1322	Wishing/A Bird Flies Out Of Sight	6
64	Fontana TF 500	He's In Town/Oh Kathy	10
66	Fontana TF 683	I Hear Trumpets Blow/I Could See Me Dancing With You	5
67	Stateside SS 598	Green Plant/Saloogy	5
67	Warner Bros WB 5900	Portrait Of My Love/She Comes And Goes	5
67	Warner Bros WB 7056	It's A Happening World/How Nice?	5
68	Warner Bros WB 7169	Till/Poor Man	5
70	Buddah 2011 011	Don't Worry Baby/Some People Sleep	5
62	RCA RD 27256	THE LION SLEEPS TONIGHT (LP, mono)	35
62	RCA SF 5128	THE LION SLEEPS TONIGHT (LP, stereo)	45
62	RCA RD 7535	WE THE TOKENS SING FOLK (LP)	20
70	Buddah 2359 007	BOTH SIDES NOW (LP)	12

TOKYO BLADE

83	Powerstation OHM 2	Powergame/Death On Main Street (p/s)	8
85	Powerstation LEG 1T	THE CAVE SESSIONS (12" EP)	15
85	Tokyo Blade TBR 1	BLACKHEARTS AND JADED SPADES (LP, gatefold sleeve)	15

TOKYO OLYMPICS
(see also Rossi & Frost)

83	Ritz 031	Shot By Love (Part 1)/(Part 2) (p/s)	5
83	Ritz 12 031	Shot By Love (Part 1)/(Part 2) (12", p/s)	8
83	Ritz 050	Radio (Turns Her On)/(Mix Version) (p/s)	5
83	Ritz 12 050	Radio (Turns Her On)/(Mix Version) (12", p/s)	8
83	Polydor 2078 143	One Step From Paradise/Paradise Disco Mix (p/s, Ireland-only)	5
82	Polydor 2908 046	RADIO (LP, Ireland-only, produced by Francis Rossi & Bernie Frost)	12

TOKYO ROSE

83	Guardian GRC 270	Dry Your Eyes/This Is Tokyo Rose (p/s)	120

ISRAEL 'POPPER STOPPER' TOLBERT

70	Stax STAX 157	Big Leg Woman/I Got Love	7
71	Stax 2362 020	POPPER STOPPER (LP)	18

TOLL
(see also Ramleh, McCarthy)

86	Broken Flag BF V7	CHRIST KNOWS (LP, featuring Tim Gane)	20

GARY DALE TOLLETT & THE CRICKETS

01	Rollercoaster RRCT 1001	Go Boy Go/Gone (78 rpm, 250 only)	15

TOM & JERRIO

65	HMV POP 1435	Boo-Ga-Loo/Boomerang	30

TOM & JERRY
(see also Simon & Garfunkel)

59	Gala GSP 806	Baby Talk/PAUL SHELDON: Thank You Pretty Baby (picture labels)	45
63	Pye International 7N 25202	I'm Lonesome/Looking At You	95

TOM & JERRY (cartoon characters)

58	MGM MGM-EP 688	JOHANN MOUSE (EP)	15

MINT VALUE £

TOM & MICK
69 Olga OLE 014 Somebody's Taken Maria Away/Pandemonium 15

TOM CATS
61 Starlite ST45 054 Tom Tom Cat/Big Brother 25

TOMCATS
(see also July)
97 Essex ESSEX 1018LP THE TOMCATS (LP, with bonus 7": "Seventh Son"/"Walking"/"You Gotta Help"/ Looking For My Baby by Second Thoughts [10187]) 12

TOMITA
77 RCA Red Seal RL1 1919 THE TOMITA PLANETS SUITE (LP, withdrawn after 1 day) 15

LEE TOMLIN
66 CBS 202455 Sweet Sweet Lovin'/Save Me 10

ALAN TOMLINSON
81 Bead Records BEAD 17 STILL OUTSIDE (LP) 25

ALBERT TOMLINSON
68 Giant GN 28 Don't Wait For Me/LLOYD EVANS: Losing You 150

ROY TOMLINSON
68 Coxsone CS 7056 I Stand For I/MARTIN: I Second That Emotion (actually by Martin Riley) 120

TOMMI & THE SPELLBINDERS
76 Target TQT 107 I Can't Get Away From You/Love Bandit 10

TOMMY (Cowan)
(see also Jamaicans)
72 Dynamic DYN 433 Geraldine/Reverend Leroy 5

TOMMY (McCook) & UPSETTERS
(see also Tommy McCook, Upsetters)
69 Trojan TR 7717 Lock Jaw (actually by Dave Barker)/YARDBROOMS: My Desire 15

TOMORROW
(see also Keith West, Steve Howe, Twink, Four + One, In Crowd, Syndicats, Aquarian Age, Fairies, Bodast)
67 Parlophone R 5597 My White Bicycle/Claramont Lake 60
67 Parlophone R 5627 Revolution/Three Jolly Little Dwarfs 70
69 Parlophone R 5813 My White Bicycle/Claramont Lake (reissue) 50
68 Parlophone PMC TOMORROW (LP, mono, yellow/black label with "Sold in U.K..." text) 250
68 Parlophone PCS 7042 TOMORROW (LP, stereo. yellow/black label with "Sold in U.K..." text) 175
76 Harvest SHSP 2010 TOMORROW (LP, reissue) 15

TOMORROW COME SOME DAY
(see also Ithaca, Friends, Agincourt, Alice Through The Looking Glass, BBC Radiophonic Workshop/Peter Howell)
69 SNB 97 TOMORROW COME SOME DAY (LP) 400

TOMORROW'S CHILDREN
70 Plexium PXM 17 You're My Baby/Maybe Today 5
71 Plexium PXM 25 Sing A Song/Don't Believe 5
71 Plexium PXM 26 Keep A Little Love In Your Life/My Way Of Living 5
72 Plexium PXM 31 We Can Make Funtime/If It Could Be 5

TOMORROW'S CHILDREN (Jamaica)
67 Island WI 3073 Bang Bang Rock Steady/Rain Rock Steady (some w/same label on both sides) 150

TOMPALL & GLASER BROTHERS
68 MGM MGM-C 8082 THROUGH THE EYES OF LOVE (LP) 25

TONE DEAF & THE IDIOTS
(see also Idiots)
80s Lyntone BLI 1/Angel BL 12 Why Does Politics Turn Men Into Toads/Repatriate The National Front (flexi) 10

ELEANOR TONER
65 Decca F 12119 All Cried Out/A Hundred Guitars 8
65 Decca F 12192 Will You Still Love Me Tomorrow/Between The Window And The Phone 15
65 Decca F 12267 Danny Boy/It Hurts So Much (To See You Go) 6
66 Decca F 12454 Black Rose/Time To Spare Darling 6

TONES ON TAIL
(see also Bauhaus, Love & Rockets)
82 4AD BAD 203 A Bigger Splash/Means Of Escape/Copper/Instrumental (12", p/s) 10

TONETTES
(see also Marlene Webber, Lyrics, Don Drummond)
62 Island WI 064 Love That Is Real/Pretty Baby 12

OSCAR TONEY JR.
67 Stateside SS 2033 For Your Precious Love/Ain't That True Love 20
67 Stateside SS 2033 For Your Precious Love/Ain't That True Love (DJ Copy) 50
67 Stateside SS 2046 Turn On Your Love Light/Any Day Now 20
67 Stateside SS 2061 You Can Lead Your Woman To The Altar/Unlucky Guy 20
68 Bell BLL 1003 Without Love There Is Nothing/Love That Never Grows Cold 10
68 Bell BLL 1011 No Sad Songs/Never Get Enough Of Your Love 10
69 Bell BLL 1057 Down In Texas/Just For You 10
72 Capricorn K 17505 Thank You, Honey Chile/I Do What You Wish 6
73 Contempo C 6 Kentucky Bluebird/Everything I Own 6
73 Contempo CS2075 Chicken Heads/Everybody's Needed 15
74 Contempo CS 2002 Is It Because I'm Black/Make It Easy On Yourself 10
75 Contempo CS 2043 I've Been Loving You Too Long/For Your Precious Love 6
67 Stateside (S)SL 10211 FOR YOUR PRECIOUS LOVE (LP) 40

TONGUE & GROOVE
(see also Charlatans)
69 Fontana STL 5528 TONGUE & GROOVE (LP) 45

MINT VALUE £

TONIGHT
(see also Andy Arthurs, Celia & Mutations)
78 TDS 1 Drummerman/Stroll On By (p/s) . . . 8
78 TDS 2 Money, That's Your Problem/No Sympathy (p/s) . . . 5
78 TDS 4 Wheels/I Can Play Faster Than You Can (p/s) . . . 5
78 TDS 5 Jealousy Kills/Second Hand Man . . . 5

TERRY TONIK
80 Posh TOFF 1 Just A Little Mod/Smashed And Blocked (some with die-cut p/s) . . . 110
80 Posh TOFF 1 Just A Little Mod/Smashed And Blocked (with die-cut p/s, promo A4 booklet) . . 70
80 Posh TOFF 1 Just A Little Mod/Smashed And Blocked . . . 30

TONTO
(see also Tonto's Expanding Head Band)
74 Polydor 2383 308 IT'S ABOUT TIME (LP) . . . 12

TONTON (MACOUTE)
72 RCA 2190 Summer Of Our Love/Greyhound Lady (as Tonton) . . . 12
71 RCA Neon NE 4 TONTON MACOUTE (LP, gatefold sleeve, black inner) . . . 90

TONTO'S EXPANDING HEAD BAND
(see also Tonto)
71 Atlantic 2400 150 ZERO TIME (LP, gatefold sleeve) . . . 18

TONY & CHAMPIONS
(see also Errol & Champions, Domino Johnson)
70 Duke DU 90 Eye For An Eye/CHAMPIONS: Broke My Heart - Version . . . 6

TONY & DENNIS
67 Trojan TR 002 Folk Song/TOMMY McCOOK & SUPERSONICS: Starry Night . . . 35

TONY & GRADUATES
60s Hit HIT 13 The Statue . . . 50
68 Pye 7N 17578 I Wanna Live/Angel . . . 10
66 Pye 7N 17077 Just My Baby And Me/Another You . . . 10

TONY & HIPPY BOYS
69 Gas GAS 121 Janet/HARMONIANS: Believe Me . . . 20

TONY & HOWARD with DICTATORS
65 Oriole CB 307 Just In Case/Walk Right Out Of The Blues . . . 30

TONY & HOWIE
72 Banana BA 371 Fun It Up/Fun Version . . . 65

TONY & JOE
58 London HLN 8694 The Freeze/Gonna Get A Little Kissin' Tonight . . . 45
58 London HLN 8694 The Freeze/Gonna Get A Little Kissin' Tonight (78) . . . 25

TONY (Tomas) & LOUISE
(see also Tony Washington)
62 Island WI 059 Ups And Downs/TONY TOMAS: Brixton Lewisham . . . 12

TONY & TANDY
(see also Sharon Tandy, Fleur De Lys)
69 Atlantic 584 262 Two Can Make It Together/The Bitter And The Sweet (with Fleur De Lys) . . . 20
71 Atlantic 2091 075 Two Can Make It Together/Look And Find . . . 8

TONY & THE VELVETS
63 Decca F 11637 Sunday/One More Once . . . 10

TONY & TYRONE
70 Ember EMBS 290 Everyday Fun/Whip Your Loving On Me (p/s) . . . 10

TONY, CARO & JOHN
72 private pressing ALL ON THE FIRST DAY (LP, with insert) . . . 300

TONY'S ALLSTARS
72 Green Door GD 4041 Rub Up A Daughter/DENNIS ALCAPONE: Daughter Version . . . 15
72 Bullet BU 509 Dub Up A Daughter (as Prince Tony's Allstars)/
DENNIS ALCAPONE: Daughter Version . . . 8
72 Big Shot BI 601 Must Care/L. SPARKS: You Don't Care . . . 6
73 Downtown DT 508 You Don't Say/DENNIS ALCAPONE: Version . . . 12

TONY'S DEFENDERS
(see also Mike Stuart Span)
66 Columbia DB 7850 Yes I Do/It's Easy To Say Hello . . . 35
66 Columbia DB 7996 Since I Lost You Baby/Waiting For A Call From You . . . 35

TOO FUNK
95 Ferox FER 008 THE RETURN OF TOO FUNK (12" EP) . . . 15
95 Ferox FER 011 STORM THE FUNK (12" EP, plain sleeve) . . . 8
96 Ferox FER 024 HOTEL IBIS (12" EP) . . . 8

STEVE TOOK
(see under Shagrat)

TOOL
94 Zoo-RCA 74321 19432-1 Prison Sex (LP Version)/Prison Sex (Edit Version)/Opiate (Live)/
Undertow (Live) (12", grey vinyl) . . . 25

TOOLS
81 Oily SLICK 2 Gotta Make Some Money Somehow/TV Eyes (p/s) . . . 8

TOOMORROW
(see also Olivia Newton-John)
70 RCA RCA 1978 You're My Baby Now/Goin' Back (in custom RCA sleeve) . . . 60
70 Decca F 13070 I Could Never Live Without Your Love/Roll Like A River . . . 60
70 RCA LSA 3008 TOOMORROW (LP, soundtrack, with insert) . . . 80

MINT VALUE £

TOO MUCH
78 Lightning GIL 513 Who You Wanna Be/Another Time Another Place (in p/s) 35
78 Lightning GIL 513 Who You Wanna Be/Another Time Another Place........ 10
78 Lightning GIL 552 Kick Me One More TIme//Be Mine/It's Only For Me (p/s) 25

DAVID TOOP
(see also Brian Eno)
75 Obscure OBS 48 NEW AND REDISCOVERED MUSICAL INSTRUMENTS (LP, with Max Eastley & Brian Eno) 25
70s Quartz WOUNDS (LP, with Paul Burwell) 25

TOOTS & THE MAYTALS
(see under Maytals)

TOOTS (Actually LEE PERRY)
70 Upsetter US 327 Do You Like It/UPSETTERS: Touch Of Fire 12

TOP NOTES
(see under Nino Tempo & April Stevens)

TOPO D. BILL
(see also Bonzo Dog [Doo Dah] Band, Roger Ruskin Spear)
70 Charisma CB 116 Witchi Tai To/Jam (in p/s)........ 20
70 Charisma CB 116 Witchi Tai To/Jam 7

TOPO GIGIO
(see under Century 21)

TOPOL
67 CBS 202651 If I were A Rich Man/GARETH DAVIES: Bottle Dance........ 5

TOPPERS
57 Brunswick 05678 Stash Pandowski (She's Not Very Much Good For Pretty)/Pots And Pans 6

TOPPICKS
78 Basilick BVK 001 Can't Let You Go/Version........ 10

TOP SECRET
81 Cheapskate CHEAP 35 She's So Ugly/I Love Me (no p/s) 5

TINY TOPSY
(see under Tiny)

TOP TOPHAM
(see also Fox, Yardbirds)
69 Blue Horizon 57-3167 Christmas Cracker/Cracking Up Over Christmas 25
70 Blue Horizon 7-63857 ASCENSION HEIGHTS (LP)........ 90

TORA TORA
80 Mancunian Metal TT 5000 Red Sun Setting/Highway (Shooting Like A Bullet) (p/s) 15
80 Tora TT 5001 Don't Want To Let You Go/Sorry I Broke Your Heart........ 40

STEVE TORCH
(see also Gillan, Split Knee Loons, Girl)
70s Redball RR 005 Live In Fear/Smoke Your Own (p/s) 5

(BERNIE) TORMÉ (BAND)
78 Jet JET 126 I'm Not Ready/Free (p/s, as Bernie Tormé Band, orange vinyl)........ 6
78 Jet JET 126 I'm Not Ready/Free (p/s, as Bernie Tormé Band, black vinyl)........ 5
79 Jet JET 137 Weekend/Secret Service/All Night/Instant Impact (as Bernie Tormé Band, p/s) ... 5
70s Peter Collins PC 1 The Hunter/Soul Sister........ 8
80 Island WIP 6586 The Beat/I Want/Bony Maronie (p/s, pink vinyl, promos on black vinyl) 8
81 Fresh FRESH 7 All Day And All Of The Night/What's Next (p/s, also listed as Parole PURL 5) ... 12
82 Kamaflage KAMLP 2 TURN OUT THE LIGHTS (LP, white vinyl)........ 12
85 Zebra ZEB 6 BACK WITH THE BOYS (LP, red vinyl)........ 12
87 Heavy Metal HMRLP 94 DIE PRETTY DIE YOUNG (LP + bonus 12", stickered sleeve)........ 12

MEL TORME (& MEL-TONES)
SINGLES
56 Vogue Coral Q 72150 Mountain Greenery/Jeepers Creepers 15
56 Vogue Coral Q 72159 Blue Moon/That Old Black Magic 5
56 Vogue Coral Q 72185 Love Is Here To Stay/Goody Goody 5
56 London HLN 8305 Lulu's Back In Town/The Lady Is A Tramp........ 10
56 London HLN 8322 Lullaby Of Birdland/I Love To Watch The Moonlight 7
56 Vogue Coral Q 72202 All Of You/It Don't Mean A Thing........ 5
56 Decca F 10800 Walkin' Shoes/The Cuckoo In The Clock (with Ted Heath & His Music)........ 5
56 Decca F 10809 Waltz For Young Lovers/I Don't Want To Walk Without You 5
57 Vogue Coral Q 72217 My Rosemarie/How (as Mel Torme & Mel-Tones) 5
60 Philips PB 1045 The White Cliffs Of Dover/I've Got A Lovely Bunch Of Coconuts........ 5
61 HMV POP 859 Blue Moon/The Moon Song 5
61 MGM MGM 1144 The Christmas Song/Shine On Your Shoes........ 5
62 London HLK 9643 Comin' Home Baby/Right Now 40
62 London HLK 9643 Comin' Home Baby/Right Now (DJ copy)........ 60
64 Verve VS 505 Yes Indeed/Her Face........ 5

EPS
56 Decca DFE 6384 WALKIN' SHOES (EP)........ 8
56 MGM MGM-EP 562 VOICE IN VELVET (EP)........ 8
57 MGM MGM-EP 591 VOICE IN VELVET NO. 2 (EP) 8
58 Philips BBE 12181 TORME MEETS THE BRITISH (EP) 12

ALBUMS
55 Vogue Coral LVA 9004 MEL TORME AT THE CRESCENDO........ 12
56 Vogue Coral LVA 9032 MUSICAL SOUNDS ARE THE BEST SONGS 12
56 London Jazz LTZ-N 15009 MEL TORME AND THE MARTY PAICH "DEK-TETTE"........ 12
56 London HA-N 2016 IT'S A BLUE WORLD 12

MINT VALUE £

57	London Jazz LTZ-N 15076	MEL TORME SINGS FRED ASTAIRE	12
57	Philips BBL 7205	TORME MEETS THE BRITISH	20
58	HMV CLP 1238	MEL TORME	12
59	Parlophone PMC 1096	GENE NORMAN PRESENTS MEL TORME AT THE CRESCENDO	12
60	Parlophone PMC 1114	SONGS FOR ANY TASTE	12
60	HMV CLP 1315	OLÉ TORMÉ (with Billy May)	12
60	HMV CLP 1382	BACK IN TOWN (with Mel-Tones)	12
60	HMV CLP 1405/CSD 1330	SWINGS SCHUBERT ALLEY (with Marty Paich Orch., mono/stereo)	12
61	HMV CLP 1449/CSD 1349	SWINGIN' ON THE MOON (mono/stereo)	12
62	HMV CLP 1584/CSD 1442	MY KIND OF MUSIC (mono/stereo)	12
63	London HA-K/SH-K 8021	MEL TORME AT THE RED HILL (with Jimmy Wisner Trio, mono/stereo)	15
63	London HA-K 8065	COMIN' HOME BABY	25
60s	Atlantic 590008	RIGHT NOW (LP)	12
66	CBS 62809	RIGHT NOW (LP)	12

TORNADOS

(see also Heinz, Billy Fury, Clem Cattini Ork, Saints, Original Tornados, Roger LaVern & Microns, Saxons, George Bellamy, Gemini, Roger La Vern & Microns)

62	Decca F 11449	Love And Fury/Popeye Twist	15
62	Decca F 11494	Telstar/Jungle Fever	5
63	Decca F 11562	Globetrotter/Locomotion With Me (some B-sides credit "Locomotion With You")	6
63	Decca F 11606	Robot/Life On Venus	8
63	Decca F 11662	The Ice Cream Man/Theme From "The Scales Of Justice"	8
63	Decca F 11745	Dragonfly/Hymn For Teenagers	12
64	Decca F 11838	Hot Pot/Joystick	10
64	Decca F 11889	Monte Carlo/Blue Blue Beat	20
64	Decca F 11946	Exodus/Blackpool Rock	20
65	Columbia DB 7455	Granada/Ragunboneman	25
65	Columbia DB 7589	Early Bird/Stompin' Through The Rye (as Tornados '65)	25
65	Columbia DB 7687	Stingray/Aqua Marina	50
66	Columbia DB 7856	Pop-Art Goes Mozart/Too Much In Love To Hear	40
66	Columbia DB 7984	Is That A Ship I Hear/Do You Come Here Often	50
62	Decca DFE 8510	THE SOUNDS OF THE TORNADOS (EP)	20
62	Decca DFE 8511	TELSTAR (EP)	20
63	Decca DFE 8521	MORE SOUNDS FROM THE TORNADOS (EP)	30
63	Decca DFE 8533	TORNADO ROCK (EP)	40
63	Decca LK 4552	AWAY FROM IT ALL (LP)	60
72	Decca SPA 253	THE WORLD OF THE TORNADOS (LP)	12
76	Decca REM 4	REMEMBERING... THE TORNADOS (LP)	12

MITCHELL TOROK

54	London HL 8004	Caribbean/Weep Away (with Louisiana Hayride Band) (gold tri label)	40
54	London HL 8004	Caribbean/Weep Away (with Louisiana Hayride Band) (round centre)	20
54	London HL 8048	Hootchy Kootchy Henry (From Hawaii)/Gigolo	50
54	London HL 8083	The Haunting Waterfall/Dancerette (with Louisiana Hayride Band)	50
55	Brunswick 05423	The World Keeps Turning Around/A Peasant's Guitar	15
56	Brunswick 05586	When Mexico Gave Up The Rhumba/I Wish I Was A Little Bit Younger	25
56	Brunswick 05626	Red Light, Green Light (with Tulane Sisters)/Havana Huddle	25
57	Brunswick 05642	Drink Up And Go Home/Take This Heart	15
57	Brunswick 05657	Pledge Of Love/What's Behind That Strange Door	15
57	Brunswick 05718	Two Words (True Love)/You're Tempting Me (with Anita Kerr Quartet)	10
60	London HLW 9130	Pink Chiffon/What You Don't Know (Won't Hurt You)	12
54	London RE-P 1014	LOUISIANA HAYRIDE (EP, with Louisiana Hayride Band)	40
60	London HA-W 2279	CARIBBEAN (LP)	50

TORPEDO (& THE CARIBBEANS)

55	Parlophone MP 143	Montego Bay/Lazy Jane (export 78)	10
56	Parlophone MP 148	Pretty Woman/War Man Power Man (export 78)	10

MICHELLE TORR

66	Fontana TF 676	Only Tears Are Left For Me/I Love That Man	15
77	Sonet SON 2104	I'm Just A Simple Country Girl From France/Une Petite Française (p/s)	5

GEORGE TORRENCE & NATURALS

68	London HLZ 10181	Lickin' Stick/So Long Goodbye	15
71	Jay Boy BOY 48	Lickin' Stick/So Long Goodbye (reissue)	6

CLARE TORRY

67	Fontana TF 852	The Music Attracts Me/It Takes One To Make The Other Cry (as Claire Terry)	6
67	Fontana TF 878	Unsure Feelings/The End Of A Lifetime (as Claire Terry)	6
69	Decca F 12945	Love For Living/Love Tomorrow, Love Today (as Clare Torry)	6

TORTOISE

(see also Sea & Cake)

96	Duophonic D-UHF-D 12	Yaus/STEREOLAB: Speedy Car (gig freebie, blue vinyl, p/s, 3,000 only)	20
96	Duophonic D-UHF-D 12	Yaus/STEREOLAB: Speedy Car (orange vinyl export issue, p/s, 3,000 only)	20
96	City Slang EFA 04971	RHYTHMS, RESOLUTIONS & CLUSTERS (LP, clear vinyl)	20
01	Duophonic Super 45s DS 33 09	Gamera/Cliff Dweller Society (12", 1500 on red vinyl, 1500 on clear vinyl, 1500 on black vinyl)	20
01	Duophonic Super 45s DS 33 09	Gamera/Cliff Dweller Society (12", 1000 on fluorescent yellow vinyl)	25

TORTURE

81	Wildebeest WILD 1	Last Post/Lucky/Finding My Way Home	50

PETER TOSH

(see also Peter Touch, Bob Marley & Wailers, Cat & Nicky Campbell, Glen Adams)

69	Unity UN 525	The Return Of Al Capone/LENNEX BROWN: O Club (B-side actually by Lennon Brown)	25
69	Unity UN 529	Sun Valley (as Peter Touch)/HE(A)DLEY BENNETT: Drums Of Fu Manchu	25
71	Bullet BU 486	Maga Dog/THIRD & FOURTH GENERATION: Bull Dog	12

MINT VALUE £

72	Pressure Beat PR 5509	Them A Fe Get A Beatin' (as Peter Touch)/ THIRD & FOURTH GENERATION: Version	18
79	Rolling Stones RSR 103	I'm The Toughest/Toughest Version (p/s)	5
79	Rolling Stones RSR 104	Buck In Hamm Palace/The Day The Dollar Die	5
76	Virgon V2061	LEGALIZE IT (LP)	15
70	No label T 1023	No Sympathy/Boy Named Tom (actually Soulettes) (white label only)	40

TOTAL CHAOS

83	Volume VOL 1	There Are No Russians In Afghanistan/Primitive Feeling/ Revolution Part 10 (p/s)	6
83	Volume VOL 2	Factory Man/Brixton Prison/She Don't Care/Die (p/s)	7
83	Volume VOLM 6	FIELDS AND BOMBS EP(12")	15

TOTAL CONTRAST

84	Total Contrast TCR 2	Next Time I'll Know Better/Sunshine (12")	35

TOTAL FIASCO
(see also Killa Instinct)

89	White TF001	See How They Run/Method To The Madness	120

TOTAL OUTPUT AND KILLERHERTZ
(see also Killerhertz)

92	FX FXUKT 11	Acid Mind/Monolithic/Analog Xpression/Digital Kiss (12")	12

TOTALLY OUTTA HAND BAND

78	Kilgaron KIL 1	Teenage Revolution/Too Much Trouble By Far (p/s)	8

TOTNAMITES

61	Oriole CB 1615	Danny Boy/The Spurs Song	15

TOTO

78	CBS S 11-6784	Hold The Line/Takin' It Back (picture disc)	5
82	CBS A 11-2079	Rosanna/It's A Feeling (picture disc)	5
82	CBS A 11-2510	Africa/We Made It (Africa-shaped picture disc)	6
83	CBS A 11-3392	I Won't Hold You Back/Afraid Of Love (picture disc)	5
84	Polydor 422 8237-7	DUNE (LP, soundtrack, 1 track by Brian Eno)	15

TOTS

74	Philips 6006 408	Please Yourself/Time To Go Home (p/s)	7

TINA TOTT

69	Pye 7N 17823	Take Away The Emptiness Too/Burning In The Background Of My Mind	50

TOTTENHAM HOTSPUR F.C.
(see also Terry Venables)

67	Columbia SEG 8532	THE SPURS GO MARCHING ON: SINGALONG SPURS (EP)	20

DAVE TOTTERDELL

77	Cottage COT 711	WHITBY BELLS (LP)	20

TOUCH
(see also Don & Goodtimes, Kingsmen)

69	Deram DM 243	Miss Teach/We Feel Fine	18
69	Deram DML/SML 1033	THIS IS TOUCH (LP, with poster)	80
69	Deram DML/SML 1033	THIS IS TOUCH (LP, without poster)	65

TOUCH

80	Ariola ARO 209	When The Spirit Moves You/My Life Depends On You (p/s)	5
80	Ariola ARO 243	Don't You Know What Love Is/My Life Depends On You (in p/s)	20
80	Ariola ARO 243	Don't You Know What Love Is/My Life Depends On You	6
80	Ariola ARO 250	Love Don't Fail Me Now (p/s)	6
80	Ariola ARL 5036	TOUCH (LP)	12

TOUCH

88	Touch T7:45	Departing Platform 5/Touch Ritual (Radio Cut-Up) (p/s)	5

PETER TOUCH
(see also Peter Tosh, Bop & The Beltone, Glen Adams)

65	Island WI 211	Hoot Nanny Hoot (actually by Peter Tosh & Wailers)/ BOB MARLEY: Do YouRemember (actually Peter Tosh & Wailers)	100
65	Island WI 215	Shame And Scandal (with Wailers)/WAILERS: The Jerk	60
67	Island WI 3042	I Am The Toughest (actually by Peter Tosh & Wailers)/ MARCIA GRIFFITHS: No Faith	60
67	Coxsone CS 7012	Dancing Time/Treat Me Good	150
69	Jackpot JP 706	The Crimson Pirate/Moon Duck	20
69	Unity UN 525	Return Of A Capone/LENEX BROWN: Q Club	25
69	Unity 529	Sun Valley/Headley Bennett - Drums Of Fu Man Chu	20

ALI FARKA TOURE

87	World Circuit WCB 007	ALI FARKA TOURE (LP)	20

TOURS

79	Tours T 1	Language School/Foreign Girls (paper p/s)	15
79	Tours T 1	Language School/Foreign Girls (printed PVC sleeve)	12
79	Virgin VS 307	Tourist Information/You Knew (p/s)	6

AL TOUSAN
(see also Allen Toussaint)

61	London HLU 9291	Naomi/Indinna (some copies miscredited to 'Al Pousan')	8

ALLEN TOUSSAINT
(see also Al Tousan)

69	Soul City SC 119	We The People/Tequila	25
72	Reprise K 14200	Soul Sister/She Once Belonged To Me	6
72	Reprise K 44202	LIFE, LOVE AND FAITH (LP)	22
75	Reprise K 54021	SOUTHERN NIGHTS (LP)	12
85	Kent KENT 036	FROM A WHISPER TO A SCREAM (LP)	15

MINT VALUE £

CALINE & OLIVER TOUSSAINT
78 Epic S EPC 6334 The Gardens Of Monaco/Les Jardins De Monaco. . . . 12

ROBERTA TOVEY
65 Polydor BM 56021 Who's Who/Not So Old (in p/s) 45
65 Polydor BM 56021 Who's Who/Not So Old. . . . 25

TOWER OF POWER
73 Reprise K 16278 So Very Hard To Go/Clean Slate 8
73 Reprise K 16211 You're Still A Young Man/Skating On Thin Ice. . . . 8
74 Reprise K 16389 Don't Change Horses/Time Will Tell 5
75 Reprise K 16543 It's Not The Crime/Only So Much Time On The Ground. . . . 8

JOHNNY TOWERS
62 Philips 326554 BF The Lonely Man Theme/There's No Place Like Rome 8
63 Philips 326570 BF This Kind Of Love/My First Romance. . . . 7

COLIN TOWNS
(see also Gillan, Samson, Split Knee Loons)
78 Virgin VS 204 Full Circle (Main Theme)/Olivia (p/s). . . . 10
80 MCA MCA 643 Breakdown/Working Man (p/s) 15
78 Virgin V 2093 FULL CIRCLE (LP, soundtrack). . . . 15

TOWNSEL SISTERS
60 Polydor NH 66954 Will I Ever/I Know 12

DEVIN TOWNSEND
(see also Wildhearts)
98 USG/East West USG 1028-4 Christeen/Wild Colonial Boy/Night (CD, withdrawn). . . . 12

ED TOWNSEND (& TOWNSMEN)
58 Capitol CL 14867 For Your Love/Over And Over Again 10
58 Capitol CL 14927 When I Grow Too Old To Dream/You Are My Everything 10
59 Capitol CL 14976 Richer Than I/Getting By Without You 7
59 Capitol CL 15020 Don't Ever Leave Me/Lover Come Back To Me 7
59 Capitol CL 15072 This Little Love Of Mine/Hold On 7
60 Capitol CL 15141 Don't Get Around Much Anymore/Do Nothin' Till You Hear. . . . 7
60 Warner Bros WB 21 Stay With Me (A Little While Longer)/I Love Everything About You 40
59 Capitol EAP1 1091 ED TOWNSEND (EP). . . . 20
59 Capitol T 1140 NEW IN TOWN (LP). . . . 25
76 Curtom K 56180 NOW (LP). . . . 20

JOHN TOWNSEND
70s Sweet Folk All SFA 002 NO MUCKING ABOUT (LP) 18

PETE TOWNSHEND
(see also The Who, Meher Baba, Billy Nicholls, Elton John)
80 Atco K 11486 Let My Love Open The Door/Classified/Greyhound Girl (p/s, with sticker) 5
82 Atco K 11751P Uniforms/Dance It All Away (picture disc) 5
82 Atco K 11751PT Uniforms/Dance It All Away (12", picture disc) 8
82 Eva-Tone 623827XS My Generation/Pinball Wizard (U.S. square flexidisc sewn into U.K. copies of Richard Barnes' Maximum R&B book; with book) 20
82 Eva-Tone 623827XS My Generation/Pinball Wizard (U.S. square flexidisc sewn into U.K. copies of Richard Barnes' Maximum R&B book; without book) 8
89 Virgin VSCD 1198 A Friend is A Friend (3.30)/Man Machines (Extended Mix)/Real World (Can You Really Dance?)/A Friend is A Friend (Album Version 4.45) (3" CD, card p/s) 10
89 Virgin VSCD 1209 I Won't Run Anymore/A Fool Says/Dig (Original Demo Version Recorded November 1987) (3" CD, card sleeve). . . . 10
72 Track 2408 201 WHO CAME FIRST (LP, gatefold sleeve with poster) 25
72 Track 2408 201 WHO CAME FIRST (LP, gatefold sleeve without poster) 15

PETE TOWNSHEND & RONNIE LANE
(see also Who, Ronnie Lane)
77 Polydor 2058 944 Street In The City/RONNIE LANE: Annie (limited issue). . . . 20
77 Polydor 2058 944 Street In The City/RONNIE LANE: Annie (12", p/s) 12
77 Polydor 2442 147 ROUGH MIX (LP, gatefold sleeve) 12

TOXIC
92 D-Zone DANCE 26 Simple Warnin' (Ruffneck Mix)/Simple Warnin' (Riffist Mix)/Simple Warnin' (Hi Power Version)Kik The Break (12", company sleeve). . . . 60

TOXIC EPHEX
89 One Up THE ADVENTURES OF NOBBY PORTHOLE - THE COCK OF THE NORTH (LP) . . 20

TOXIC REASONS
84 T-REASON HANG 1 God Bless America/Can't Get Away/Destroyer (p/s) 6
84 Alt. Tentacles VIRUS 42 KILL BY REMOTE CONTROL (LP). . . . 15

TOYAN
81 Greensleeves GREL 20 HOW THE WEST WAS WON (LP) 25
83 Vista STLP 1023 MURDER (LP, as Toyan with Tippa Lee). . . . 45

TOY DOLLS
(see also Showbiz Kids)
81 GBH SSM 005 Tommy Kowey's Car/She Goes To Finos (500 only) 60
81 GRC GRC 104 Tommy Kowey's Car/She's A Working Ticket/Everybody Jitterbug/ Teenager In Love/I've Got Asthma (yellow paper p/s, with insert) 60
82 Zonophone Z 31 Everybody Jitterbug/(She's A) Working Ticket (p/s). . . . 30
83 Volume VOL 3 Nellie The Elephant/Dig That Groove Baby (p/s). . . . 15
83 Volume VOL 5 Cheerio And Toodle Pip/H.O. (p/s). . . . 10
83 Volume VOL 7 Alfie From The Bronx/Hanky Panky (p/s). . . . 10
84 Volume VOL 10 We're Mad/Deirdre's A Slag (p/s). . . . 6
84 Volume VOLT 10 We're Mad/Deirdre's A Slag/Rupert The Bear (12", p/s) 10

MINT VALUE £

85	Volume VOL 12	She Goes To Fino's/Spiders In The Dressing Room (p/s)	5
85	Volume VOL 17	James Bond (Lives Down Our Street)/Olga? I cannot! (p/s)	8
85	Volume VOLT 17	James Bond (Lives Down Our Street)/Olga? I cannot! / Griefsville (12", p/s)	8
86	Volume VOL 21	Geordie's Gone To Jail/Idle Gossip (p/s)	8
82	WOWLP 1	THE TOY DOLLS ALBUM (LP)	15
84	Volume VOLP 1	DIG THAT GROOVE, BABY (LP)	15
85	Volume VOLP 2	A FAR OUT DISC (LP)	12
86	Volume VOLP 3	IDLE GOSSIP (LP)	12
94	Toy Dolls NIT 2	TEN YEARS OF TOYS (LP, with inner)	12

TOY DOLLS (U.S.)

63	London HLN 9647	Little Tin Soldier/Fly Away	30

TOYS

79	SRT SRTS/79/CUS 345	My Mind Wanders/The Girl On My Wall/Toytime/I'd Do Anything For You (p/s)	10
79	Toy TOYS 2	STILL DANCING (EP, hand-stamped white label, foldaround p/s)	20

TOYS

80	Red Bus RBUS 54	Go To The Police/Breakdown	50

TOYS (U.S.)

65	Stateside SS 460	A Lover's Concerto/This Night	8
66	Stateside SS 483	Attack/See How They Run	8
66	Stateside SS 502	May My Heart Be Cast Into Stone/On Backstreet	20
66	Stateside SS 519	Silver Spoon/Can't Get Enough Of You Baby	22
66	Stateside SS 539	Baby Toys/Happy Birthday Broken Heart	10
67	Philips BF 1563	Ciao Baby/I Got Carried Away	10
67	Philips BF 1581	My Love Sonata/I Close My Eyes	10
69	Bell BLL 1053	A Lover's Concerto/Baby Toys	7
66	Stateside SL 10175	THE TOYS SING "A LOVER'S CONCERTO" AND "ATTACK" (LP, mono)	40
66	Stateside SSL 10175	THE TOYS SING "A LOVER'S CONCERTO" AND "ATTACK" (LP, stereo)	50

TOYSHOP

69	Polydor 56317	Say Goodbye To Yesterday/Send My Love To Lucy	12

T.P.I.

79	SRT SRTS 79 CUS 489	She's Too Clever For Me/You Rool Me (no p/s, 1000 only)	60

TRACE

(see also Curved Air)

74	Vertigo 6360 852	TRACE (LP)	15
75	Vertigo 6413 080	BIRDS (LP)	18

TRACER

83	Mouse Hole TRA 1	CHANNELLED AGGRESSION EP (p/s)	125

MARK TRACEY

62	Parlophone R 4944	Caravan Of Lonely Men/Never Ending (with John Barry & His Orchestra)	10

STAN TRACEY

(see also New Departures Quartet, Mike Osborne, Neil Ardley, Laurie Johnson)

58	Vogue LA 160130	STAN TRACEY SHOWCASE (LP)	70
59	Vogue LA 160155	LITTLE KLUNK (LP, as Stan Tracey Trio)	130
65	Columbia 33SX 1774	JAZZ SUITE (LP, as Stan Tracey Quartet, also stereo SCX 3589)	75
66	Columbia S(C)X 6051	ALICE IN JAZZLAND (LP, as Stan Tracey Big Band)	40
67	Columbia S(C)X 6124	STAN TRACEY... IN PERSON (LP)	40
68	Columbia S(C)X 6205	WITH LOVE FROM JAZZ (LP)	50
69	Ace Of Clubs ACL 1259	LITTLE KLUNK (LP, reissue)	30
69	Columbia S(C)X 6320	WE LOVE YOU MADLY (LP, as Stan Tracey Big Brass)	50
69	Columbia SCX 6358	THE LATIN AMERICAN CAPER (LP, with Big Brass & Woodwind)	40
70	Columbia SCX 6385	FREE AN' ONE (LP, as Stan Tracey Quartet)	70
70	Columbia SCX 6413	SEVEN AGES OF MAN (LP, as Stan Tracey Big Band)	35
72	Columbia SCX 6485	PERSPECTIVES (LP as Stan Tracey Trio)	40

ZEN TRACEY

62	Decca F 11492	Shamrocker (Phil The Fluter's Ball)/Two By Two	8

TRACK

66	Columbia DB 7987	Why Do Fools Fall In Love?/Cry To Me	18

TRACK 4

82	Track 4 TR4 001	Mr Charisma (p/s, with insert)	100

TRACTOR

(see also Way We Live)

72	Dandelion 2001 282	Stone Glory/Marie/As You Say	15
78	UK UK 93	Roll The Dice/Vicious Circle	8
81	Cargo CRS 002	No More Rock & Roll/Northern City	10
81	Roach RR 2	Average Man's Hero/Big Big Boy (p/s)	5
72	Dandelion 2310 217	TRACTOR (LP)	120

TRACY

66	Columbia DB 7802	Don't Hold It Against Me/These Four Walls	8
69	Columbia DB 8569	Life's Like That/Let Me Love You	7
69	Columbia DB 8637	Follow Me/A City Called Soul	12
71	Columbia DB 8750	Rock Me In The Cradle/Strange Love	10

ARTHUR TRACY

67	Decca F 12656	Marta/Wanderer	6

GRANT TRACY & SUNSETS

(see also Pete Dello, Honeybus)

61	Ember EMB S 126	Say When/Please Baby Please	20
61	Ember EMB S 130	Pretend/Love Me	20
62	Ember EMB S 148	The Great Matchmaker/Tears Came Rolling Down	20

MINT VALUE £

62	Ember EMB S 155	Taming Tigers/The Painted Smile	20
63	Decca F 11741	Everybody Shake/Turn The Lights Down, Jenny	20
64	Ember EMB 3352	TEENBEAT (LP)	80

WENDALL TRACY

58	London HLM 8664	Who's To Know/Corrigidor Rock	15

TRADER HORNE

(see also Them, Fairport Convention, Jackie McAuley)

69	Pye 7N 17846	Morning Way/Sheena	40
70	Dawn DNS 1003	Here Comes The Rain/Goodbye Mercy Kelly	40
70	Dawn DNLS 3004	MORNING WAY (LP, gatefold, with photo & insert)	150
70	Dawn DNLS 3004	MORNING WAY (LP, gatefold, without photo & insert)	80

TRADEWINDS

59	RCA RCA 1141	Crossroads/Furry Murray	20
59	RCA RCA 1141	Crossroads/Furry Murray (78)	25

TRADE WINDS

65	Red Bird RB 10020	New York Is A Lonely Town/Club Seventeen	22
66	Kama Sutra KAS 202	Mind Excursion/Little Susan's Dreaming	20

TRAD GRADS (WITH LEN, HERB, KIKO & RICHARD)

(see also Quarry Men)

61	Decca F 11403	Runnin' Shoes/Rag-Day Jazz-Band Ball	8

TRADITION

77	Venture VNLP 8877	MOVIN' ON (LP)	15
77	Venture CUT 6	IN DUB (LP)	45
78	RCA PL 25169	TELL YOUR FRIENDS ABOUT DUB (LP)	20
78	RAC PL 25186	ALTERNATIVE ROUTES (LP)	30

TRAFFIC

(see also Spencer Davis Group, Stevie Winwood, Revolution, Hellions, Dave Mason, Gordon Jackson)

67	Island WIP 6002	Paper Sun/Giving To You (in p/s)	12
67	Island WIP 6002	Paper Sun/Giving To You	5
67	Island WIP 6017	Hole In My Shoe/Smiling Phases (in p/s)	12
67	Island WIP 6017	Hole In My Shoe/Smiling Phases	5
67	Island WIP 6025	Here We Go Round The Mulberry Bush/Coloured Rain (1st 100,000 in p/s)	15
67	Island WIP 6025	Here We Go Round The Mulberry Bush/Coloured Rain	12
68	Island WIP 6030	No Face, No Name, No Number/Roamin' In The Gloamin' With 40,000 Headmen	12
68	Island WIP 6041	You Can All Join In/Withering Tree (unissued in U.K.)	0
68	Island WIP 6041	Feelin' Alright/Withering Tree	10
68	Island WIP 6050	Medicated Goo/Shanghai Noodle Factory	10
71	Island No Cat No	Welcome To The Canteen (promo 7" with blank labels in mini LP sleeve)	30
74	Island WIP 6207	Walking In The Wind/Walking In The Wind (Instrumental)	10
78	Island IEP 7	HOLE IN MY SHOE (EP, picture disc)	10
67	Island ILP 961	MR FANTASY (LP, gatefold sleeve internal flipbacks, 1st pressing pink label with black 'circle' logo, mono)	200
67	Island ILPS 9061	MR FANTASY (LP, gatefold sleeve internal flipbacks, 1st pressing pink label with black 'circle' logo, stereo)	150
68	Island ILPS 9081T	TRAFFIC (LP, gatefold sleeve with stapled-in booklet; pink label with black 'circle' logo)	80
68	Island ILPS 9081T	TRAFFIC (LP, gatefold sleeve with stapled-in booklet; pink rim label with 'palm tree' logo)	20
69	Island ILP(S) 9097	LAST EXIT (LP, pink label with black 'circle' logo)	80
69	Island ILP(S) 9097	LAST EXIT (LP, pink rim label with 'palm tree' logo)	20
69	Island ILP(S) 9112	THE BEST OF TRAFFIC (LP, 1st pressings with pink "I" label)	30
69	Island ILP(S) 9112	THE BEST OF TRAFFIC (LP, subsequent pressings with pink rim label with 'palm tree' logo)	12
70	Island ILPS 9081	MR. FANTASY (LP, 2nd pressing, pink rim label with 'palm tree' logo)	20
70	Island ILPS 9116	JOHN BARLEYCORN MUST DIE (LP, gatefold sleeve, 1st pressings with pink "i" label)	50
71	Island ILPS 9166	WELCOME TO THE CANTEEN (LP, 'sniped' spine edges, pink rim palm tree label)	20
71	Island ILPS 9180	THE LOW SPARK OF THE... (LP, laminated sleeve, pink rim/palm tree label)	20
73	Island ILPS 9224	SHOOT OUT AT THE FANTASY FACTORY (LP, pink rim/palm tree label)	15
73	Island ISLD 2	ON THE ROAD (2-LP, laminated gatefold sleeve)	18

TRAFFIC JAM

(see also Status Quo, Spectres)

67	Piccadilly 7N 35386	Almost But Not Quite There/Wait Just A Minute	275
67	Piccadilly 7N 35386	Almost But Not Quite There/Wait Just A Minute (demo copy)	300

JIM TRAGAS

72	Buddah 2011 157	White Buffalo/Mama Took Me From The Jungle	6

TRAGICIAN

79	Look LKSP 6411	The Wild The Scared And The Timid/Traces Of Impact (numbered gatefold p/s)	35

PHIL TRAINER

(see also Trees)

73	BASF 05 19573-5	Beautiful Jim/No No No (p/s)	5
73	BASF BAG 22 29107-3	TRAINER (LP, gatefold)	35
77	Splash CP17	Carousel/Rose Coloured Sky	8

TRAIN SET

80s	Play Hard DEC 11	She's Gone (12", p/s)	35
80s	Play Hard DEC 17	Hold On (12", p/s)	35

TRAITOR

81	Airship APP 377	That's Life/Stone Cold Sober	100

TRAITOR'S GATE

85	Bullet BOLT 12	DEVIL TAKES THE HIGH ROAD (EP)	10

MINT VALUE £

TRAITS
(see also Roy Head)
67 Pye International 7N 25404 Harlem Shuffle/Strange Lips (Start Ole Memories) 35

ALAN TRAJAN
69 MCA MK 5002 Speak To Me, Clarissa/This Might Be My Last Number 50
69 MCA MKPS 2000 FIRM ROOTS (LP, laminated front sleeve) 90

TRAMLINE
(see also Whitesnake)
68 Island ILPS 9088 SOMEWHERE DOWN THE LINE (LP, pink label black/orange circle) 90
69 Island ILPS 9095 MOVES OF VEGETABLE CENTURIES (LP, pink label) 90

BOBBY LEE TRAMMELL
64 Sue WI 326 New Dance In France/Carolyn 40

TRAMMY (Ron Wilson)
72 Techniques TE 920 Horns Of Paradise/TECHNIQUES ALL STARS: Grass Root 30

TRAMP
(see also Dave Kelly, Jo-Ann Kelly, Brunning Hall Sunflower Blues Band, Fleetwood Mac)o
69 Young Blood SBY 4 Vietnam Rose/Each Day 12
74 Spark SRL 1107 Put A Record On/You've Gotta Move 8
69 Music Man SMLS 603 TRAMP (LP, laminated front, flipbacks, white/black label) 150
73 Spark Replay SRLM 2001 TRAMP (LP, reissue) 30
74 Spark SRLP 112 PUT A RECORD ON (LP) 30

TRAMWAY
80s Sarah SRH 43 Maritime City/Boathouse/Star (p/s, with insert) 7

TRANE
71 Penny Farthing PEN 773 Still Burning Bright/Misty Lady 5
71 BBC RESL 5 Wagoner's Walk/Jenny's Song/Ragged Bird/Mansion Of Cards (p/s) 10

TRANQUILITY
72 Epic EPC 64729 TRANQUILITY (LP, yellow label) 20
72 Epic EPC 65418 SILVER (LP, lyric insert, yellow label) 15

TRANS AM
95 Thrill Jockey THRILL 024 TRANS AM (LP) 15

TRANSATLANTICS
65 Fontana TF 593 Many Things From Your Window/I Tried To Forget 35
65 Fontana TF 638 Stand Up And Fight Like A Man/But I Know 20
65 Mercury MF 948 Don't Fight It/Look Before You Leap 50
65 King KG 1033 Run For Your Life/It's All Over 15
66 King KG 1040 Louie Go Home/Find Yourself Another Guy 30

TRANSCARGO
01 Trunk TTT 003 OH BOY (12" EP) 8

TRANSCRIPT CARRIERS
93 Transcript Carriers TC998 THE HAEMORRHOID FRY UP (EP) 20
94 Transcript Carriers TC999 ALL FEAR IS BONDAGE (EP) 18

TRANSIENT WAVES
98 Fat Cat 12FAT 011 Born With A Body And Fucked In The Heads/(2 Lone Swordsmen Mix)/
`(Skye [Stasis] Mix) (12", custom embossed sleeve) 10

TRANSISTORS
81 Open Circuit RIOT SQUAD (EP) 20

TRANSIT
09 Third Man TMR 012 Come On And Ride/After Party 30

TRANSMISSION
84 PMP PMP 001 Mystery Lady/Bouncing Ball (12") 40

TRANSMITTERS
78 Ebony EYE 11 Party/0.5 Alive (p/s) 5
78 Ebony EYE 12 Nowhere Train/Uninvited Guest/Persons Unknown (die-cut p/s) 5
79 Step Forward SF 1212 The Ugly Man/The One That Won The War/Free Trade/Curious (12", p/s) 8
70s Eccentric EX 2 C50 I JAX DUB (cassette) 12
78 Ebony EBY 1002 24 HOURS (LP) 15
81 Heartbeat MB 4 AND WE CALL THIS LEISURE TIME (LP) 12

TRANSPARENT ILLUSION
81 Vortex VEX 001/002 Vortex/Nuclear Release (p/s) 20
82 Vortex VEX 5 Guilty Rich Men (p/s) 10
81 Vortex VEX 3 STILL HUMAN (LP) 35
82 Vortex VEX 4 CHAGRIN RECEIVER (LP) 20

TRANSPORTER
70s Mother Truck MT 1 Kids On The Run/Intoxicating 6

TRAPEZE
(see also Finders Keepers, Montanas, Deep Purple, Glenn Hughes, Judas Priest, Whitesnake)
69 Threshold TH 2 Send Me No More Letters/Another Day 10
72 Threshold TH 11 Coast To Coast/Your Love Is Alright 10
75 Warner Bros K 16606 Sunny Side Of The Street/Monkey 10
79 Aura AUS 114 Don't Ask Me How I Know/Take Good Care (p/s) 15
80 Aura AUS 116 Running Away/Don't Break My Heart (p/s) 15
69 Threshold THS 2 TRAPEZE (LP, gatefold sleeve) 60
70 Threshold THS 4 MEDUSA (LP) 50
73 Threshold THS 8 YOU ARE THE MUSIC... WE'RE JUST THE BAND (LP) 20
74 Warner Bros K 56064 HOT WIRE (LP) 12
81 Aura AUL 717 LIVE IN TEXAS... DEAD ARMADILLOS (LP) 12

MINT VALUE £

TRASH
(see also Poets, Pathfinders)

69	Apple APPLE 6	Road To Nowhere/Illusions (initial copies as White Trash)	200
69	Apple APPLE 6	Road To Nowhere/Illusions (later copies as Trash)	60
69	Apple APPLE 17	Golden Slumbers - Carry That Weight/Trash Can	30

TRASHCAN SINATRAS

89	Go! Discs GODX 34	Obscurity Knocks/The Best Man's Fall/Drunken Chorus/Who's He? (12", p/s)	12
89	Go! Discs GODCD 34	Obscurity Knocks/The Best Man's Fall/Drunken Chorus/Who's He? (CD)	12
90	Go! Discs GOD 41	Only Tongue/Useless Begins With You/Tonight You Belong To Me (p/s)	6
90	Go! Discs GODX 41	Only Tongue/Useless Begins With You/Tonight You Belong To Me (12", p/s)	10
90	Go! Discs GOD 46	Circling The Circumference/My Mistake (p/s)	8
90	Go! Discs GODX 46	Circling The Circumference/My Mistake/White Horses (12", p/s)	12
93	Go! Discs GODX 98	Hayfever/Say/Kangaroo Court/Skin Diving (12", p/s)	8
93	Go! Discs GODCD 98	Hayfever/Say/Kangaroo Court/Skin Diving (CD, in box)	12
93	Go! Discs GOD 100	I've Seen Everything/Houseproud/I'm The One Who Fainted (p/s)	6
96	Go! Discs GOD 151	How Can I Apply?/Save Me (p/s)	6
90	Go! Discs 828 2011	CAKE (LP)	15

TRASHMEN

64	Stateside SS 255	Surfin' Bird/King Of The Surf	35
64	Stateside SS 276	Bird Dance Beat/A-Bone	35

TRAVELING WILBURYS
(see also George Harrison, Bob Dylan, Roy Orbison, Jeff Lynne, Tom Petty)

88	Warner Bros W 7732W	Handle With Care/Margarita (gatefold p/s with sticker, sealed)	10
88	Warner Bros W 7732W	Handle With Care/Margarita (gatefold p/s with sticker, unsealed)	8
88	Warner Bros W 7732TE	Handle With Care (Extended)/Margarita (10", p/s)	10
88	Warner Bros W 7732T	Handle With Care (Extended)/Margarita (12", p/s)	10
88	Warner Bros W 7732CD	Handle With Care (LP Version)/Margarita/Handle With Care (Extended Version) (3" CD, with adaptor, 5" case)	10
89	Warner Bros W 7637TW	End Of The Line (Extended)/Congratulations (12", p/s, with sheet of stickers)	15
89	Warner Bros W 7637TW	End Of The Line (Extended)/Congratulations (12", p/s, without sheet of stickers)	10
89	Warner Bros W 7637CD	End Of The Line (Extended Version)/Congratulations (3" CD, gatefold card p/s in PVC sleeve)	12
90	Warner Bros W 9773T	Nobody's Child/DAVE STEWART: Lumière/RINGO STARR: With A Little Help From My Friends (12", p/s)	12
90	Warner Bros W 9773CD	Nobody's Child/DAVE STEWART: Lumière/RINGO STARR: With A Little Help From My Friends (CD)	10
90	Warner Bros W 9523	She's My Baby/New Blue Moon (Instrumental Version) (p/s)	6
90	Warner Bros W 9523T	She's My Baby (LP Version)/New Blue Moon (Instrumental Version)/ Runaway (12", p/s)	10
90	Warner Bros W 9523CD	She's My Baby (LP Version)/New Blue Moon (Instrumental Version)/ Runaway (CD)	10
91	Warner Bros W 0019	Wilbury Twist/New Blue Moon (Instrumental) (p/s)	6
91	Warner Bros W 0018W	Wilbury Twist/New Blue Moon (Instrumental) (card p/s with 4 postcards)	15
91	Warner Bros W 0019T	Wilbury Twist/New Blue Moon (Instrumental)/Cool Dry Place (12", p/s)	12
91	Warner Bros W 0019CD	Wilbury Twist/New Blue Moon (Instrumental)/Cool Dry Place (CD, silver or black print)	10
88	Warner Bros WX 224W	VOLUME ONE (LP, some with stickered sleeve & sticker inserts)	22
88	Warner Bros WX 224CD	VOLUME ONE (CD)	25
90	Warner Bros WX 7799-2 324-2	VOLUME THREE (CD)	25

TRAVELLERS

77	Paradise PDS 001	Jah Give Us The World (feat. U Brown)/Girl I Left Behind (12")	15

TRAVELLING FOLK

70s	Cuchulainn CCHS 1017	TRAVELLING FOLK (LP)	15

MARY TRAVERS
(See also Peter, Paul & Mary)

72	Warner Bros K 16191	Morning Glory/That's Enough For Me	7

PAT TRAVERS
(see also Nicko McBrain)

76	Polydor SFI 221/2814 040	Makes No Difference (1-sided flexidisc, promo only, black & white p/s)	10
77	Polydor Super 2383 436	MAKIN' MAGIC (LP with inner sleeve)	12
77	Polydor Super 2383 471	PUTTING IT STRAIGHT (LP)	12
79	Polydor POLS 1011	GO FOR WHAT YOU KNOW (LP, red vinyl)	12

TRAVIS

73	A&M AMS 7081	Band Of Heroes/Out In The Country	8
73	A&M AMLS 68120	SHINE ON ME (LP)	50

TRAVIS

96	Red Telephone Box PHONE 001	All I Want Do Is Rock/Line Is Fine/Funny Thing (10", numbered, stickered p/s, 750 only)	40
97	Independiente ISOM 1S	U16 Girls/Hazy Shades/Good Time Girls (p/s)	5
97	Independiente ISOM 3S	All I Want Do Is Rock/Blue On A Black Weekend (p/s)	8
97	Independiente ISOM 5S	Tied To The 90s/Me Beside You (p/s)	5
97	Independiente GOODT 1	The Line Is Fine/All I Want To Do Is Rock/More Than Us/ Tied To The 90s (12", promo only)	8
99	Independiente ISM 4946249	THE MAN WHO (CD, with bonus CD [Driftwood/Slide Show/More Than Us])	20
99	Independiente ISOM 9 LP	THE MAN WHO (LP, with bonus remix 12")	60
99	Independiente ISOM 9 LP	THE MAN WHO (LP)	40

TRAVIS
(see also Paul Travis)

01	Independiente ISOM 25	THE INVISIBLE BAND (LP)	25

MERLE TRAVIS
(see also Brown's Ferry Four)

53	Capitol CL45 13985	Gamblers Guitar/Shut Up And Drink Your Beer	40
56	Capitol EAP1 032	MERLE TRAVIS GUITAR (EP)	20

			MINT VALUE £
57	Capitol EAP2 650	MERLE TRAVIS GUITAR NO. 2 (EP)	18
59	Capitol EAP1 891	BACK HOME (EP)	15
63	Capitol EAP1 1391	WALKIN' THE STRINGS (EP)	15
57	Capitol T 891	BACK HOME (LP)	30
63	Capitol (S)T 1664	TRAVIS! (LP)	20
65	Capitol T 2102	MERLE TRAVIS & JOE MAPHIS (LP)	20

PAUL TRAVIS

(see also Travis)

75	A&M AMLS 68290	RETURN OF THE NATIVE (LP, with lyric inner)	15

TRAVIS & BOB

59	Pye International 7N 25018	Tell Him No/We're Too Young	15
59	Pye International 7N 25018	Tell Him No/We're Too Young (78)	10
61	Mercury AMT 1142	Baby Stay Close To Me/Give Your Love To Me	7

TRAX FOUR

66	Ace Of Clubs S/ACL 1216	WINGDING PARTY!!! (LP, mono/stereo)	55

JACK TRAYLOR & STEELWIND

73	Grunt FTR 0194	CHILD OF NATURE (LP)	20

TREASURE BOY

67	Trojan TR 010	Love Is A Treasure (actually by Freddie McKay)/TOMMY McCOOK: Zazuka	25

TREBLETONES

61	Butlin CP 2424	Butlin Holiday/Butlin Holiday	8
63	Oriole CB 1838	In Real Life/Dream Of A Lifetime	12

TREDEGAR

(see also Budgie)

86	Aries CEP 0001	Duma/The Jester (p/s)	75
86	Aries CEP LP 001	TREDEGAR (LP, gatefold sleeve, embossed)	15

HERBERT BEERBOHM TREE

65	OMY 69	KEEP THOSE DOGS AWAY (EP)	25

TREEBOUND STORY

86	Fon ELM 1	I REMEMBER EP (12", p/s)	8

TREES

(see also Casablanca, Juliet Lawson, Trainer)

70	CBS 5078	Nothing Special/Epitaph	25
70	CBS 63837	THE GARDEN OF JANE DELAWNEY (LP)	220
71	CBS 64168	ON THE SHORE (LP)	250
87	Decal LIK 12	ON THE SHORE (LP, reissue)	15
87	Decal LIK 15	THE GARDEN OF JANE DELAWNEY (LP, reissue)	15

TREETOPS

67	Parlophone R 5628	Don't Worry Baby/I Remember	15
68	Parlophone R 5669	California My Way/Carry On Living	12
70	Columbia DB 8727	Mississippi Valley/Man Is A Man	12
71	Columbia DB 8799	Without The One You Love/So Here I Go Again	15
73	Columbia DB 9013	Gypsey/Life Is Getting Better	15

TREKKAS

65	Planet PLF 105	Please Go/I Put A Spell On You	90

TREMBLING BLUE STARS

96	Shinkansen SHINKANSEN 1	Abba On The Jukebox/She's Always There (p/s, 1,000 only)	10

TREMELOES

(see also Brian Poole & Tremeloes, Trems, Chip Hawkes)

66	Decca F 12423	Blessed/The Right Time	20
66	CBS 202242	Good Day Sunshine/What A State I'm In	15
67	CBS 202519	Here Comes My Baby/Gentlemen Of Pleasure	6
67	CBS 2723	Silence Is Golden/Let Your Hair Hang Down (p/s)	6
67	CBS 2930	Even The Bad Times Are Good/Jenny's Alright (p/s)	6
67	CBS 3043	Be Mine/Suddenly Winter	10
68	CBS 3234	Suddenly You Love Me/As You Are	6
68	CBS 2889	Helule Helule/Girl From Nowhere	6
68	CBS 3680	My Little Lady/All The World To Me	6
68	CBS 3873	I Shall Be Released/I Miss My Baby	7
69	CBS 4065	Hello World/Up Down All Around	7
69	CBS 4582	(Call Me) Number One/Instant Whip	5
68	CBS Special Products WB 728	Here Comes My Baby/SIMON & GARFUNKEL: The 59th Street Bridge Song (p/s, mail-order only with Pepsi Cola tokens)	6
70	CBS 4815	By The Way/Breakheart Motel	8
70	CBS 5139	Me And My Life/Try Me	6
71	CBS 7294	Hello Buddy/My Woman	8
72	Epic EPC 5S 1019	Blue Suede Tie/Yodel Ay	8
73	Epic EPC 1399	Ride On/Hands Off	5
73	CBS 1139	Here Comes My Baby/Silence Is Golden (p/s, 'Hall Of Fame Hits' series)	5
84	Meteor MTS 002	Silence Is Golden (Acappella version)/The Last Word	5
75	SJM DJS 406	Be Boppin' Boogle/Asct Cowboys	7
68	CBS EP 6402	MY LITTLE LADY (EP)	18
67	CBS (S)BPG 63017	HERE COME THE TREMELOES (LP)	18
68	CBS (S)BPG 63138	THE TREMELOES: CHIP, RICK, ALAN AND DAVE (LP)	18
69	CBS 63547	THE TREMELOES 'LIVE' IN CABARET (LP)	15
70	CBS 64242	MASTER (LP)	15

TREMORS

80s	Redball RR 0002	Modern World/Smashed Reality (p/s)	15

MINT VALUE £

TREMS
(see also Tremeloes)
73 Epic EPC 1660 Make It Break It/Movin' On . . . 5

TREND
67 Page One POF 004 Boyfriends And Girlfriends/Shoot On Sight . . . 50

TREND
70 Trendy TREND 1 Teenage Crush/Cool Johnny (with press sheet) . . . 50
70 Trendy TREND 1 Teenage Crush/Cool Johnny . . . 40

TREND
80 MCA MCA 583 Polly And Wendy/Family Way (p/s) . . . 20
80 MCA MCA 629 This Dance Hall Must Have A Back Way Out/Fiction, Love & Romance (p/s) . . . 15

TRENDS
(see also Tammy St. John, Freddie Self, Freddie Ryder)
63 Piccadilly 7N 35171 All My Loving/Sweet Little Miss Love . . . 15
64 Pye 7N 15644 You're A Wonderful One/The Way You Do The Things You Do . . . 20

TRENDSETTERS
64 Silver Phoenix 1001 You Don't Care/My Heart Goes . . . 65

TRENDSETTERS
60s Oak RGJ 999 AT THE HOTEL DE FRANCE (EP) . . . 30

TRENDSETTERS LTD
(see also King Crimson, Giles Giles & Fripp, Brain)
64 Parlophone R 5118 In A Big Way/Lucky Date . . . 20
64 Parlophone R 5161 Hello Josephine/Move On Over . . . 20
64 Parlophone R 5191 Go Away/Lollipops And Roses . . . 15
65 Parlophone R 5324 You Sure Got A Funny Way Of Showing Your Love/I'm Coming Home . . . 12

CHARLES TRENET
57 Columbia SEG 7319 BOUM (EP) . . . 8
60 Columbia 33SX 1376 TRENET OF FRANCE (LP) . . . 12

TRENIERS
58 Coral Q 72319 Ooh-La-La/Pennies From Heaven . . . 25
58 Coral Q 72319 Ooh-La-La/Pennies From Heaven (78) . . . 10
58 Fontana H 137 Go! Go! Go!/Get Out Of The Car (featuring Don Hill, Alto Sax) . . . 100
58 Fontana H 137 Go! Go! Go!/Get Out Of The Car (featuring Don Hill, Alto Sax) (78) . . . 20
59 London HLD 8858 When Your Hair Has Turned To Silver/Never, Never . . . 45
59 London HLD 8858 When Your Hair Has Turned To Silver/Never, Never . . . 35

JACKIE TRENT
61 Oriole CB 1711 Pick Up The Pieces/In Your Heart . . . 15
62 Oriole CB 1749 The One Who Really Loves You/Your Conscience Or Your Heart . . . 40
63 Piccadilly 7N 35121 Melancholy Me/So Did I . . . 10
64 Piccadilly 7N 35165 If You Love Me/Only One Such As You . . . 40
64 Pye 7N 15692 Somewhere In The World/I Heard Somebody Say . . . 5
64 Pye 7N 15742 Don't Stand In My Way/How Soon . . . 5
65 Pye 7N 15776 Where Are You Now (My Love)/On The Other Side Of The Tracks . . . 5
65 Pye 7N 15865 When Summertime Is Over/To Show I Love Him . . . 7
65 Pye 7N 15949 It's All In The Way You Look At Life/Time After Time . . . 6
66 Pye 7N 17047 You Baby/Send Her Away . . . 40
66 Pye 7N 17082 Love Is Me Love Is You/This Time . . . 6
66 Pye 7N 17158 If You Ever Leave Me/There Goes My Love, There Goes My Life . . . 6
67 Pye 7N 17249 Open Your Heart/Love Can Give . . . 15
67 Pye 7N 17323 Your Love Is Everywhere/It's Not Easy Loving You . . . 6
67 Pye 7N 17415 That's You/Stop Me And Buy One . . . 6
67 Pye 7N 17437 Bye Bye Love (German Version)/Alles Okay (Send Her Away) . . . 6
69 Pye 7N 17693 I'll Be There/Close To You . . . 10
78 Casino Classics CC 4 You Baby/Send Her Away/FAMILY AFFAIR: Love Hustle . . . 6
65 Pye NEP 4225 WHERE ARE YOU NOW (EP) . . . 15
65 Pye NPL 18125 THE MAGIC OF JACKIE TRENT (LP) . . . 25
67 Pye NPL 18173 ONCE MORE WITH FEELING (LP) . . . 15
67 Pye NSPL 18201 STOP ME AND BUY ONE (LP) . . . 20
69 Pye NSPL 18315 THE LOOK OF LOVE (LP) . . . 20

JACKIE TRENT & TONY HATCH
67 Pye 7N 17300 The Two Of Us/I'll Be With You . . . 6
68 Pye 7N 17604 Our Little Boat/Play It Again . . . 5
74 Pye 7N 45392 Together/Going Our Own Sweet Way . . . 6
75 Pye 7N 45490 Mr And Mrs (Be Nice To Each Other)/Positive Thinking . . . 7
68 Pye NPL 18214 THE TWO OF US (LP) . . . 20
68 Pye NSPL 18229 LIVE FOR LOVE (LP) . . . 20
68 Pye NSPL 18304 TOGETHER AGAIN (LP) . . . 15
74 Pye NSPL 18422 OPPOSITE YOUR SMILE (LP) . . . 15

TRESPASS
79 Trial CASE 1 One Of These Days/Bloody Moon (p/s) . . . 25
80 Trial CASE 2 Jealousy/Live It Up! (p/s) . . . 18
81 Trial CASE 3 Bright Lights/The Duel/Man And Machine (p/s) . . . 20

TREVOR (Shield)
64 Blue Beat BB 228 Down In Virginia/Hey Little Schoolgirl (with Caribs) . . . 15
68 Blue Cat BS 129 Tender Arms (with Joe White & Glen Brown)/DERMOTT LYNCH: Something Is Worrying Me . . . 25
68 Blue Cat BS 130 Pretty Girl (with Joe White & Glen Brown)/DERMOTT LYNCH: You Went Away . . . 25
69 Blue Cat BS 153 Everyday Is Like A Holiday/Have You Time (by Trevor & Maytones) . . . 40

TREVOR & KEITH
(see also Carl Bryan)
70 Punch PH 41 The Ark/MINNA BOYS: False Reador (actually titled "Got To Move") . . . 7

MINT VALUE £

T. REX
(see under Marc Bolan/T. Rex; see also Tyrannosaurus Rex)

TRIARCHY
79 SRT/79/CUS 599 Save The Khan/Juliet's Tomb (in p/s, 1,000 only) . . . 80
79 SRT/79/CUS 599 Save The Khan/Juliet's Tomb (1,000 only) . . . 30
79 Direct NEON 1 Save The Khan/Juliet's Tomb (reissue, p/s) . . . 35
80 Direct NEON 2 Metal Messiah/Sweet Alcohol/Hell Hound On My Trail (in p/s) . . . 70
80 Direct NEON 2 Metal Messiah/Sweet Alcohol/Hell Hound On My Trail . . . 30

TRIBAN
69 Cambrian CSP 707 Leaving On A Jet Plane/Night In The City . . . 6
71 Decca F 13115 Black Paper Roses/One Way Mirror . . . 5
69 Cambrian MCT 592 TRIBAN (LP) . . . 15
72 Cambrian RAINMAKER (LP) . . . 15

TRIBE
73 Probe PRO 597 Koke Parts 1 & 2 . . . 5

TONY TRIBE
69 Downtown DT 419 Red Red Wine/RECO & RUDIES: Blues (some miscredited to Tony Tripe) . . . 15
69 Downtown DT 439 Gonna Give You All The Love/HERBIE GREY: Why Wait . . . 10

TRIBE (U.K.)
66 Planet PLF 108 The Gamma Goochie/I'm Leavin' . . . 75
67 RCA RCA 1592 Love Is A Beautiful Thing/Steel Guitar . . . 25

TRIBE (U.S.)
66 Polydor 56510 Dancin' To The Beat Of My Heart/Woofin' . . . 40

TRIBESMAN
79 Boa BOA 102-12 Finsbury Park/The Tribe (12") . . . 20
79 Boa BOA 001 STREET LEVEL (LP) . . . 20

TRIBUTE
73 Jam JAM 48 Bobby Charlton/City Summer . . . 12

TRICKS
70 CBS 4867 Wham! Bam! Ala Cazam!/Lucy Brown . . . 12

TRICKY DISCO
91 Warp WAP 11 HOUSEFLY EP (12") . . . 10

TRI-CORE
92 Underground UNR 001T BELFAST SAYS EP (12") . . . 80

TRIDENT
(see also Filthy Rich)
84 SRT TRI 1 Destiny/Power Of The Trident . . . 50

TRIFFIDS
63 Columbia DB 7084 Lookin Around/She's No Longer Your Girl . . . 12
65 Fontana TL 5231 THE TRIFFIDS ARE REALLY FOLK (LP) . . . 12

TRIFLE
(see also George Bean)
69 United Artists UP 2270 All Together Now/Got My Thing . . . 10
70 Dawn DNS 1008 Old-Fashioned Prayer Meeting/Dirty Old Town . . . 10
71 Dawn DNLS 3017 FIRST MEETING (LP, textured gatefold sleeve) . . . 80

PANDIT KANWAR SAIN TRIKHA
71 Mushroom 100 MR 7 THREE SITAR PIECES (LP) . . . 45

TRILOGY
71 Mercury 6338 034 I'M BEGINNING TO FEEL IT (LP) . . . 20

TOMMY TRINDER & THE GANG
59 Fontana H 204 La Plume De Ma Tante/On The Sunny Side Of The Street . . . 10

TRINIDAD ALL STARS
56 Parlophone DP 524 Trouble In Arima/Stone Cold Dead In De Market (78, export issue) . . . 12

TRINIDAD OIL COMPANY
77 Harvest SHSP 4070 THE CALENDAR SONG (LP) . . . 20

TRINIDAD STEEL BAND
52 Vogue V 9017 Mango Walk/Take Me (78) . . . 10
52 Vogue V 9018 Ramadin/Johnny (78) . . . 10

TRINITY
77 Burning Sounds BS 011 Natty Tired To Carry Load/Dubwise . . . 10
77 Caribbean CBN 314 Natty On De Banking/Banking Dub . . . 8
77 Carib Gems CG 005 Three Meals A Day/Version . . . 8
77 Conflict CON 303 Up-Town Girl/PRINCE JAMMY & AGGROVATORS: Channel One A Boy . . . 10
79 Attack TACK 2 Follow My Heart/Pope Paul Dead And Gone (12") . . . 30
70s Burning Vibrations BVD 002 Roots Man Party/Healing The Nation (12", with Mystic EMP Group) . . . 20
79 Burning Sounds BDS 012 SHOWCASE EP (12") . . . 30
77 Magnum DERD 1003 UPTOWN GIRL (LP) . . . 30
79 Trojan TRLS 170 ROCK IN THE GHETTO (LP) . . . 20
81 JB JBLP 006 FULL HOUSE (LP) . . . 20

TRINITY HOUSE
77 Profile GMOR 146 FLASHBACK THROUGH HISTORY (LP, private pressing, with insert) . . . 40

TRIO
(see also John Surnam)
71 Dawn DNLS 3022 CONFLAGRATION (LP) . . . 60
76 Dawn DNLS 3072 LIVE AT WOODSTOCK TOWN HALL (LP, with Stu Martin) . . . 25

MINT VALUE £

TRIPLE ELEMENT

88	Tam Tam TTT002	What's That Sound? (12")	8

TRIPLETS

69	President PT 245	When Lovers Say Goodbye/You Won't See Me Leaving	10

TRIPPERS

66	Pye International 7N 25388	Dance With Me/Keep A-Knockin'	20

TRISHA

65	CBS 201800	The Darkness Of My Night/Confusion	8

TRISTAR AIRBUS

(see also Wimple Winch, 10cc, Hotlegs)

72	RCA RCA 2170	Travellin' Man/Willie Morgan On The Wing	10

TRITONS

73	Bradley BAR 24	I Can't Get Not Satisfaction/Drifter	50

TRIUMVIRAT

74	Harvest SHSP 4030	ILLUSION ON A DOUBLE DIMPLE (LP)	15
75	Harvest SHSP 4048	SPARTACUS (LP)	12

TRIXIE'S BIG RED MOTORBIKE

82	Chew CH 9271	A Splash Of Red/Invisible Boyfriend (white label, stapled foldover p/s)	15
83	Lobby Ludd (no cat. no.)	TRIXIE'S BIG RED MOTORBIKE (EP, plain sleeve with stapled strip)	10
84	Lobby Ludd L 100001	Norman And Narcissus/In Timbuktu (p/s)	10
84	Lobby Ludd L 100002	A Splash Of Red/Invisible Boyfriend (reissue, different p/s)	8
84	Lobby Ludd L 100003	TRIXIE'S BIG RED MOTORBIKE (EP, reissue, stapled p/s)	8
84	Nathan NAT 001	That's The End Of That/CLIVE PIG & LEE VALLEY: As Soon As She's Gone (33rpm flexi & sweet with Wally's Dog fanzine)	5

TRIXONS

69	Major Minor MM 665	Just Another Song/Sunny Side Sam	15

MARCUS TRO

65	Ember EMB S 203	Tell Me/What's The Matter Little Girl (in p/s)	18
65	Ember EMB S 203	Tell Me/What's The Matter Little Girl	10
65	Ember EMB 3365	INTRODUCING MARCUS TRO (LP)	40

TROGGS

(see also Reg Presley, Chris Britton, Ronnie Bond, Ten Feet Five)

SINGLES

66	CBS 202038	Lost Girl/The Yella In Me	50
66	Fontana TF 689	Wild Thing/From Home	8
66	Fontana TF 717	With A Girl Like You/I Want You	7
66	Page One POF 001	I Can't Control Myself/Gonna Make You	7
66	Page One POF 010	Any Way That You Want Me/6-5-4-3-2-1	7
67	Page One POF 015	Give It To Me/You're Lyin'	7
67	Page One POF 022	My Lady/Girl In Black (withdrawn)	50
67	Page One POF 022	Night Of The Long Grass/Girl In Black	7
67	Page One POF 030	Hi Hi Hazel/As I Ride By	8
67	Page One POF 040	Love Is All Around/When Will The Rain Come	6
68	Page One POF 056	Little Girl/Maybe The Madman?	7
68	Page One POF 064	Surprise Surprise/Marbles And Some Gum?	8
68	Page One POF 082	You Can Cry If You Want To/There's Something About You	8
68	Page One POF 092	Hip Hip Hooray/Say Darlin'!	8
69	Page One POF 114	Evil Woman/Sweet Madeline	8
69	Page One POF 126	Wild Thing/I Can't Control Myself	6
70	Page One POF 164	Easy Lovin'/Give Me Something	8
70	Page One POF 171	Lover/Come Now	8
70	Page One POF 182	The Raver/You	10
71	DJM DJM 248	Lazy Weekend/Let's Pull Together	6
72	Jam JAM 25	Wild Thing/With A Girl Like You/Love Is All Around	5
72	Pye 7N 45147	Everything's Funny/Feels Like A Woman	7
73	Pye 7N 45244	Listen To The Man/Queen Of Sorrow	7
73	Pye 7N 45295	Strange Movies/I'm On Fire	8
75	Penny Farthing PEN 861	Good Vibrations/Push It Up To Me	6
75	Penny Farthing PEN 884	Wild Thing (Reggae Version)/Jenny Come Down	5
75	Penny Farthing PEN 889	Summertime/Jenny Come Down	5
75	Penny Farthing PEN 901	(I Can't Get No) Satisfaction/Memphis, Tennessee	5
76	Penny Farthing PEN 919	I'll Buy You An Island/Supergirl	5
77	Penny Farthing PEN 929	Feeling For Love/Summertime	5
78	Raw RAW 25	Just A Little Too Much/The True Troggs Tapes (p/s)	6
67	Page One POE 001	TROGGS TOPS (EP)	20
67	Page One POE 002	TROGGS TOPS VOLUME TWO (EP)	40
67	Page One	TRACK A TROGG (EP, unreleased)	0
81	DJM DJS 6	TROGGS TAPES (EP, double pack)	8

LPs

66	Fontana TL 5355	FROM NOWHERE - THE TROGGS (LP, mono)	70
66	Fontana STL 5355	FROM NOWHERE - THE TROGGS (LP, stereo)	80
66	Page One POL 001	TROGGLODYNAMITE (LP, mono)	70
66	Page One POLS 001	TROGGLODYNAMITE (LP, stereo)	90
67	Page One FOR 001	THE BEST OF THE TROGGS (LP)	30
67	Page One POL 003	CELLOPHANE (LP, mono)	60
67	Page One POLS 003	CELLOPHANE (LP, stereo)	80
68	Page One POL 1	THE TROGGS ON TOUR (LP, export issue)	150
68	Page One FOR 007	THE BEST OF THE TROGGS VOLUME TWO (LP)	35
68	Page One POL(S) 012	MIXED BAG (LP)	150
69	Page One POS 602	TROGGLOMANIA (LP)	40
70	DJM Silverline DJML 009	CONTRASTS (LP, original issue)	25
76	Pennt Farthing PELS 551	THE TROGG TAPES (LP)	20

MINT VALUE £

CHUCK TROIS & AMAZING MAZE
68 Action ACT 4517 Call On You/Woodsman 10

TROJAN
88 GI GILP 444 THE MARCH IS ON (LP) 18

TROJANS
58 Decca F 11065 Man I'm Gonna Be/Make It Up 15
58 Decca F 11065 Man I'm Gonna Be/Make It Up (78) 10

TROLL BROTHERS
73 SRT SRT 73316 You Turn Me On/Turn Out The Lights (p/s) 18

TROMBONES UNLIMITED
66 Liberty LIB 55874 Daydream/The Phoenix Love Theme (Senza Fine) 5
66 Liberty LBY 1350 YOU'RE GONNA HEAR FROM ME (LP) 12

TRONICS
61 Fontana H 348 Cantina/Pickin' & Stompin' 18

TRONICS
(see also Les Zarjaz)
78 Tronics T 001 Suzie (actually "Suzie's Vibrator")/Favourite Girls (plain sleeve with inserts) 8
79 Tronics T 002 Time Off/Goodbye (p/s) 8
81 Alien ALIEN 18 Shark Fucks/Time Off (p/s, with insert) 6
83 Red Rhino RED 3 Wild Cat Rock/Tonight (p/s) 5
82 Press PRESS 1 TRANZISTER SISTER (12" EP) 8
81 Alien BALIEN 3 LOVE BACKED BY FORCE (LP) 25

TROOPERS
57 Vogue V 9087 Get Out/My Resolution 700
57 Vogue V 9087 Get Out/My Resolution (78) 150

TROOPS OF TOMORROW
(see also Vibrators, Fallen Angels)
82 Troops TROOPS 1 TROOPS OF TOMORROW (12" EP) 8

TROPIC SHADOWS
72 Big Shot BI 603 Our Anniversary/Anniversary (Version) 6

ARCHIBALD TROTT
(see also Baba Brooks)
64 Black Swan WI 407 Get Together/Just Because 18

TROUBADORS DU ROI BAUDOUIN
69 Philips BF 1732 Sanctus (Missa Luba)/Kyrie 10

TROUBADORS/TROUBADOUR SINGERS
(see also Jane Morgan)
57 London HLR 8469 Fascination/Midnight In Athens 8
58 London HLR 8541 The Lights Of Paris/The Flaming Rose 8
58 London RE-R 1135 THE TROUBADORS (EP) 8
58 London HA-R 2095 THE TROUBADORS IN SPAIN (LP) 12

TROUBLE
88 JusticeJTT002 I Get Hype/I Guess It's Dope (12") 75

BOBBY TROUP
55 Capitol CL 14219 Julie Is Her Name/Instead Of You 12
54 Capitol LC 6660 BOBBY TROUP (10" LP) 20

BOB TROW QUARTET
54 London HL 8082 Soft Squeeze Baby/I Went Along For The Ride 40
54 London HL 8082 Soft Squeeze Baby/I Went Along For The Ride (78) 10

ROBIN TROWER
(see also Paramounts, Procol Harum)
78 Chrysalis CHS 2247 It's For You/My Love/In City Dreams (p/s, red vinyl) 5
81 Chrysalis CHS 2497 What It Is/Into Money (p/s, clear vinyl) 5
73 Chrysalis CHR 1039 TWICE REMOVED FROM YESTERDAY (LP) 12

DORIS TROY
63 London HLK 9749 Just One Look/Bossa Nova Blues 35
64 Atlantic AT 4011 What'cha Gonna Do About It/Tomorrow Is Another Day 25
65 Atlantic AT 4020 Please Little Angel/One More Chance 15
65 Atlantic AT 4032 Heartaches/You'd Better Stop 15
65 Cameo Parkway C 101 I'll Do Anything (He Wants Me To)/But I Love Him 130
65 Cameo Parkway C 101 I'll Do Anything (He Wants Me To)/But I Love Him (DJ copy) 200
68 Atlantic 584 148 Just One Look/What'cha Gonna Do About It 10
68 Toast TT 507 I'll Do Anything (Anything He Wants Me To)/Heartaches 15
70 Apple APPLE 24 Ain't That Cute/Vaya Con Dios (with p/s) 22
70 Apple APPLE 24 Ain't That Cute/Vaya Con Dios 10
70 Apple APPLE 28 Jacob's Ladder/Get Back 12
71 Mojo 2092 011 I'll Do Anything (He Wants Me To)/But I Love Him (reissue) 15
73 Mojo 2092 062 Baby I Love You/To My Father's House 6
74 People PEO 112 Stretchin' Out/Don't Tell Your Mama 6
65 Atlantic AET 6007 WATCHA GONNA DO ABOUT IT (EP) 75
70 Apple SAPCOR 13 DORIS TROY (LP) 80
73 Mojo 2956 001 THE RAINBOW TESTAMENT (LP, with Gospel Truth) 35
74 Polydor 2464 001 JUST ONE LOOK (LP) 20
74 People PLEO 12 STRETCHING OUT (LP) 20
92 Apple SAPCOR 13 DORIS TROY (LP, reissue, gatefold sleeve with bonus 12" [SAPCOR 132]) 12

TROY & THUNDERBIRDS
61 London HL 9476 Twistle/Take Ten 15

MINT VALUE £

WILLIAM TRUCKAWAY

69	Reprise RS 20842	Bluegreens On The Wing/Besides Yourself	15
71	Reprise K 44165	BREAKAWAY (LP, with lyric insert)	20

TRUE ADVENTURE

74	Decca F 13528	Where The Roxy Use To Be/Outlaw Love	15

TRUE STYLE

91	Liberty Grooves LIB002	CODES OF CONDUCT (EP)	30

TRUFFLE

81	Chesnut NUT 6	Round Tower (p/s)	150
72	JAM 8	Poco Poco/Julie's Place	6

TRUK

71	CBS 57201	Winters Coming On/You	15

JONNY TRUNK

01	Trunk TTT 001	The Snow It Melts/Scooby Don't (7", 300 only)	15
01	Trunk TTT 002	Sister Woo/Mr. Hand (300 only)	15
03	Trunk TTT 004	Dead Soon/Dead Mouse Blues (7", 400 only)	15
04	Trunk JBH 008 LP	THE INSIDE OUTSIDE (LP, 500 only)	30

TRUTH

65	Pye 7N 15923	Baby Don't You Know/Come On Home	20
65	Pye 7N 15998	Who's Wrong/She's A Roller	25
66	Pye 7N 17035	Girl/Jailer Bring Me Water	8
66	Pye 7N 17095	I Go To Sleep/Baby You've Got It	30
66	Deram DM 105	Jingle Jangle/Hey Gyp (Dig The Slowness)	110
67	Decca F 12582	Walk Away Renee/Fly Away Bird	20
68	Decca F 22764	Seuno/Old Ma Brown	60

TRUTH

83	WEA TRUTH 1F	Confusion/Me And My Girl//Love A Go Go/From The Heart (p/s, double-pack)	8
84	IRS IRS 115	Exception Of Love/If You Ever Find Love (p/s)	5

TRUTH & BEAUTY

74	Rak RAK 181	Tuff Little Surfer Boy/Touch-a Touch-a Touch Me	12

TRUTH OF TRUTHS

71	Oak OR 1001	TRUTH OF TRUTHS (LP)	25

TRUX

82	Trux TRX 01	Bad Luck (no p/s)	200

TRYDAN

80	Sain SAIN 77S	Mods A Rocers/Di-Waith, Di-'Fynedd	5

TANIA TSANAKLIDOU

78	EMI EMI 2797	Charlie Chaplin (English)/Charlie Chaplin (Greek)	12

TSD

(see also STEPS)

96	Avex AVEXCD 21	Heart & Soul (Hyper Go Go 7" Edit)/Heart & Soul (Strike 12")/Heart & Soul (Hyper Go Go 12")/Heart & Soul (Dyme Brothers 12")/Heart & Soul (Johnny Versace 12") (CD)	0

T.S.O.L.

81	Frontier FLP 1004	DANCE WITH ME (LP)	18
82	Alt. Tentacles VIRUS 10	WEATHERED STATUES (EP)	6

T2

(see also Flies, Cross & Ross)

70	Decca SKL 5050	IT'LL ALL WORK OUT IN BOOMLAND (LP, blue/silver label/boxed logo)	150
97	Essex 1019LP	T2 (LP)	12

ERNEST TUBB (& HIS TEXAS TROUBADORS)

(see also Red Foley & Ernest Tubb)

50	Decca BM 31206	The Blues/Half A Mind (Export Issue)	15
56	Brunswick 05527	Thirty Days/Answer The Phone (triangular centre)	40
56	Brunswick 05527	Thirty Days/Answer The Phone (triangular centre) (78)	10
56	Brunswick 05587	So Doggone Lonesome/If I Never Have Anything Else	20
50s	Decca BM 31214	What Am I Living For/Goodbye Sunshine, Hello Blues (export issue)	15
55	Brunswick OE 9148	COUNTRY DOUBLE DATE (EP)	10
58	Brunswick OE 9372	THE DADDY OF 'EM ALL PT. 1 (EP)	15
58	Brunswick OE 9373	THE DADDY OF 'EM ALL PT. 2 (EP)	15
58	Brunswick OE 9374	THE DADDY OF 'EM ALL PT. 3 (EP)	15
56	Brunswick LA 8736	JIMMIE RODGERS SONGS (10" LP)	30
57	Brunswick LAT 8161	FAVOURITES (LP)	15
58	Brunswick LAT 8260	THE DADDY OF 'EM ALL (LP)	15
59	Brunswick LAT 8292	THE IMPORTANCE OF BEING ERNEST (LP)	15
60	Brunswick LAT 8313	THE ERNEST TUBB STORY VOLUME ONE (LP, mono)	12
60	Brunswick STA 3022	THE ERNEST TUBB STORY VOLUME ONE (LP, stereo)	18
60	Brunswick LAT 8314	THE ERNEST TUBB STORY VOLUME TWO (LP, mono)	12
60	Brunswick STA 3023	THE ERNEST TUBB STORY VOLUME TWO (LP, stereo)	18
60	Brunswick LAT 8349	THE ERNEST TUBB RECORD SHOP (LP)	12

JUSTIN TUBB

67	RCA Victor RCA 1585	But Wait There's More/The Second Thing I'm Gonna Do	6
64	RCA RCX 7133	JUSTIN TUBB (EP)	30
63	Ember CW 100	STAR OF THE GRAND OLE OPRY (LP, pink & grey labels)	12
64	Ember CW 110	THE MODERN COUNTRY MUSIC SOUND OF JUSTIN TUBB (LP, pink & grey labels)	12

TUBES

79	A&M AMS 7423	Prime Time (promo box of 7 different coloured vinyl editions & picture disc)	30

MINT VALUE £

TUBEWAY ARMY

(see also Gary Numan, Paul Gardiner)

78	Beggars Banquet BEG 5	That's Too Bad/Oh! I Didn't Say (p/s)	10
78	Beggars Banquet BEG 8	Bombers/O.D. Receiver/Blue Eyes (p/s)	10
79	Beggars Banquet BEG 17	Down In The Park/Do You Need The Service? (p/s)	5
79	Beggars Banquet BEG 17T	Down In The Park/Do You Need The Service?/ I Nearly Married A Human 2 (12", p/s)	25
79	Beggars Banquet BEG 18	Are "Friends" Electric?/We Are So Fragile (p/s, original semi-transparent sleeve)	18
79	Banquet Banquet BEG 18P	Are "Friends" Electric?/We Are So Fragile (picture disc, with insert)	10
79	Banquet Banquet SPC 4	Are "Friends" Electric?/We Are So Fragile (cassette in cigarette-pack style box)	8
79	Beggars Banquet BACK 2	That's Too Bad/Oh! Didn't I Say/Bombers/Blue Eyes/O.D. Receiver (double pack, gatefold p/s)	5
79	Beggars Banquet BACK 2	That's Too Bad/Oh! Didn't I Say/Bombers/Blue Eyes/O.D. Receiver (double pack, gatefold p/s, mispressed 2nd disc omits "O.D. Receiver")	15
83	Beggars Banquet BEG 92E	TUBEWAY ARMY VOL. 1 (12" EP, with "That's Too Bad [Alternate Mix]", yellow vinyl)	10
81	Beggars Banquet SPC 4	Are "Friends" Electric/Down In The Park	8
85	Beggars Banquet BEG 123 E	1978-1979 VOL. 2 (12", blue vinyl, p/s)	10
85	Beggars Banquet BEG 124E	1978-1979 VOL. 3 (12", red vinyl, p/s)	10
78	Beggars Banquet BEGA 4	TUBEWAY ARMY (LP, blue vinyl, g/fold stickered sleeve, some with badge)	70
78	Beggars Banquet BEGA 4	TUBEWAY ARMY (LP, blue vinyl, g/fold stickered sleeve)	60
79	Beggars Banquet BEGA 7	REPLICAS (LP, with large black & white poster)	25
85	B. Banquet BEGC 7879	TUBEWAY ARMY 1978/1979 (cassette only)	12
08	VIN 180 LP 002	REPLICAS (LP, 180gm vinyl, numbered with 8" x 6" print)	15

TUBILAH DOG

96	S04	IN SEARCH OF PLAICE (LP, gatefold with poster)	20

TUB-THUMPER

74	Alaska ALA 18	Kick Out The Jams/Kahoutec	25

TUCHWOOD

72	Polydor 2058233	Freedom For The Stallion/Morning Light	8

BESSIE TUCKER

55	HMV 7EG 8085	BLUES BY BESSIE (EP)	20

BILLY JOE TUCKER

61	London HLD 9455	Boogie Woogie Bill/Mail Train	60

CY TUCKER

63	Fontana TF 424	My Prayer/High School Dance	8
64	Fontana TF 470	Let Me Call You Sweetheart/I Apologise	7

TERRY TUCKER'S ORANGE CLOCKWORK

70	Warner Brothers K16337	Overture To The Sun Part 1/Overture To The Sun Part II	10

TOMMY TUCKER

64	Pye International 7N 25238	Hi-Heel Sneakers/I Don't Want 'Cha	20
64	Pye International 7N 25246	Long Tall Shorty/Mo' Shorty	25
64	London HLU 9932	Oh! What A Feeling/Wine Bottles	40
69	Chess CRS 8086	Hi-Heel Sneakers/I Don't Want 'Cha (reissue)	15
64	Pye Intl. NEP 44027	HI HEEL SNEAKERS (EP)	50

WINSTON TUCKER

(see also Winston Groovy)

73	Explosion EX 2083	I'm A Believer/You'll Be Mine	5

TUCKY BUZZARD

(see also End)

71	Capitol CL 15687	She's A Striker/Heartbreaker	5
73	Purple PUR 113	Gold Medallions/Fast Bluesy Woman	7
77	Purple PUR 134	Gold Medallions/Superboy Rock 'N' Roller '73'	7
71	Capitol E-ST 864	WARM SLASH (LP, laminated front sleeve, flipbacks)	60
73	Purple TPSA 7510	ALRIGHT ON THE NIGHT (LP, laminated gatefold sleeve)	25
73	Purple TPSA 7512	BUZZARD (LP)	20

HENRY TUDOR

67	Decca F12574	How Many Times/Another Name From Nowhere	25

TUDOR LODGE

71	Vertigo 6059 044	The Lady's Changing Home/Back To The Good Times We Had	40
71	Vertigo 6360 043	TUDOR LODGE (LP, foldout textured sleeve, swirl label)	700

TUDOR MINSTRELS

66	Decca F 12536	Love In The Open Air/A Theme From "The Family Way"	22

TUDORS

83	Stiff BUY 172	Tied Up With Joe Cool/Cry Baby Cry (p/s)	7

TUESDAY

72	Pye 7N 45194	Big Mister Little Man/Sewing Machine	20

TUESDAY'S CHILDREN

(see also Warm Sounds)

66	Columbia DB 7978	When You Walk In The Sand/High And Drifting	20
66	Columbia DB 8018	High On A Hill/Summer Leaves Me With A Sigh	22
67	King KG 1051	A Strange Light From The East/That'll Be The Day	30
67	Pye 7N 17406	Baby's Gone/Guess I'm Losin' You	15
68	Pye 7N 17474	In The Valley Of The Shadow Of Love/Ain't You Got A Heart	12
68	Mercury MF 1063	She/Bright-Eyed Apples	12

T.U.F.F.

(see also Hard Corps)

80s	SONO 001	We've Got A Hot One (Speed Mix) (unreleased, white label promos only)	10

MINT VALUE £

TUFF GONG ALLSTARS
(see also Wailing Souls)

72	Punch PH 114	You Should Have Known Better (actually by The Wailing Souls)/Known Better	12

TONY TUFF

79	Niagra NIADD 101	Ease Up Oppressor/JAH THOMAS: Answer The Phone (12")	15
79	King Sounds GMDM 26	You Wrong/TOMMY McCOOK: Sensimena (12")	25
80	Art & Craft 003	Look Ya/TONY TUFF & JAH STITCH: Rumours Of War (12")	50
80	Cha Cha CHAD 11	Deliver Me/Africa We Want To Go (12")	20

TULIPS

74	Explosion EX 2091	Mocking Bird/DES ALL STARS: Version	7

LEE TULLY

57	London HL 8363	Around The World With Elwood Pretzel (Parts 1 & 2) (gold print label)	110
57	London HL 8363	Around The World With Elwood Pretzel (Parts 1 & 2) (silver print label)	60
57	London HL 8363	Around The World With Elwood Pretzel (Parts 1 & 2) (78)	25

TUMBLEWEEDS

70	Phoenix NIX 111	Making My Way Back To Louisiana/I Guess I'd Better Go	10

TUNDRA

70s	Greenwich Village GVR 208	THE KENTISH SONGSTER (LP)	15
78	Sweet Folk & C. SFA 078	A KENTISH GARLAND (LP, gatefold sleeve)	25
81	Greenwich Village GVR 218	SONGS FROM GREENWICH (LP, gatefold sleeve)	15

TUNE ROCKERS

58	London HLT 8717	The Green Mosquito/Warm Up	30
58	London HLT 8717	The Green Mosquito/Warm Up (78)	15

TUNEWEAVERS
(see also Paul Gayten)

57	London HL 8503	Happy Happy Birthday Baby/PAUL GAYTEN: Yo, Yo, Walk	200
57	London HL 8503	Happy Happy Birthday Baby/PAUL GAYTEN: Yo, Yo, Walk (78)	30

TUNJI with CHRIS McGREGOR

60s	Jika 001	Ko Gbele Oko/Lisabi Egba	8

TUNNEL RUNNERS

80	Sonic International SI 4282	Plastic Land/Drug (numbered p/s)	80

PADDY TUNNEY

65	Topic 12T 139	A WILD BEES NEST (LP, blue label)	12
66	Topic 12T 153	IRELAND HER OWN (LP, with Arthur Kearney, Frank Kelly & Joe Tunney, blue label)	12
66	Topic 12T 165	THE IRISH EDGE (LP, blue label)	12

TUNNG

04	Static Caravan VAN 72	Tales From Black/Pool Beneath The Pond (500 only)	15
05	Static Caravan VAN 73	Maypole Song/Suprize Me 44 (100 lathe cut only, p/s)	30
05	Nowhere Fast SLOW03	Magpie Bites/The Bonnie Black Hare (1000 only hand numbered poster sleeve)	5
05	Static Caravan VAN 94	Tunng Vs Dollboy Vs Dollboy Vs Tunng (1000 only, 200 with art sleeve)	5
05	Static Caravan VAN 94	Tunng Vs Dollboy Vs Dollboy Vs Tunng (1000 only)	5
05	Static Caravan VAN 88	MOTHER'S DAUGHTERS AND OTHER SONGS (LP, 300 only - withdrawn)	50

K.T. TUNSTALL

04	Outcaste OUT 56	Throw Me A Rope/Black & White (500 only)	20

TURBO

80	Cargo CRS 004	STALLION (EP, p/s)	100
82	Turbo CUS 1261	Charged For Glory/Race For The Dawn	8

TURGID TOOL

01	Stand STAND 11	Terror In A Turgid Tool!/Stand Up For England (pop-up p/s)	8

TURNBULL & ARKWRIGHT

72	Peacock PEA 501	Smuggling Man/Misty Roses	25

BRUCE TURNER

54	Columbia SCMC 9	Falling Leaves/I Wished On The Moon (export issue)	6
60	Melodisc MEL 1551	Nuages/My Guy's Come Back	6
60s	CRD 1000	Jamaica Jump/Big Noise From Winetka	6
62	Storyville SXP 2025	BRUCE TURNER AND HIS JUMP BAND (EP)	8
63	Philips 433 627 BE	JUMPING FOR JOY NO. 1 (EP)	8
63	Philips 433 627 BE	JUMPING FOR JOY NO. 2 (EP)	8
63	77 EP/EU 1	LIVING JAZZ (EP)	10
64	Philips BL 7590	GOING PLACES (LP)	12

CHUCK TURNER

87	Stereo One STO 003	Youthman Struggling/FUNNY WONDER: Jollification (12")	40
87	Live & Love LLD 44	We Rule The Dance/We Rule The Dub (12")	30
88	Live & Love LALP 21	ON THE HARDWAY (LP)	15

DENNIS TURNER

62	London HL 9537	Lover Please/How Many Times	25

GORDON TURNER

70	Charisma CAS 1009	MEDITATION (LP, 1st pressing laminated 'landscape' sleeve)	35
70	Charisma CAS 1009	MEDITATION (LP, 2nd pressing non laminated 'blue room' sleeve)	20

IKE TURNER
(see also Ike & Tina Turner)

72	United Artists UP 35411	Lawdy Miss Clawdy/Tacks In My Shoes/Soppin' Molasses (with Family Vibes)	6
84	Fleetville FV 303	New Breed Part 1/New Breed Part 2	5
60s	Ember EMB 3395	IKE TURNER ROCKS THE BLUES (LP)	45
72	United Artists UAG 29362	BLUES ROOTS (LP)	18
75	DJM DJSLM 2010	FUNKY MULE (LP)	15

MINT VALUE £

IKE & TINA TURNER

(see also Ike Turner, Tina Turner, Ikettes)

SINGLES

60	London HLU 9226	A Fool In Love/The Way You Love Me	20
61	London HLU 9451	It's Gonna Work Out Fine/Won't You Forgive Me	20
64	Sue WI 306	Gonna Work Out Fine/Won't You Forgive Me (reissue)	20
64	Sue WI 322	The Argument/Poor Fool	20
64	Sue WI 350	I Can't Believe What You Say/My Baby Now	40
65	Warner Bros WB 153	Finger Poppin'/Ooh Poo Pah Doo	30
65	Sue WI 376	Please, Please, Please/Am I A Fool In Love	40
66	London HLU 10046	River Deep - Mountain High/I'll Keep You Happy	8
66	Warner Bros WB 5753	Tell Her I'm Not Home/Finger Poppin'	20
66	HMV POP 1544	Anything You Wasn't Born With/Beauty Is Just Skin Deep	30
66	London HLU 10083	A Love Like Yours (Don't Come Knockin' Every Day)/Hold On Baby	18
66	Stateside SS 551	Goodbye, So Long/Hurt Is All You Gave Me	18
66	Warner Bros WB 5766	Somebody (Somewhere) Needs You/(I'll Do Anything) Just To Be With You	100
66	Warner Bros WB 5766	Somebody (Somewhere) Needs You/(I'll Do Anything) Just To Be With You (DJ copy)	120
67	HMV POP 1583	I'm Hooked/Dust My Broom	60
67	HMV POP 1583	I'm Hooked/Dust My Broom (DJ copy)	100
67	London HLU 10155	I'll Never Need More Than This/Save The Last Dance For Me	20
68	London HLU 10189	So Fine/So Blue Over You	10
68	London HLU 10217	We Need An Understanding/It Sho' Ain't Me	15
69	London HLU 10242	River Deep - Mountain High/Save The Last Dance For Me	5
69	Minit MLF 11016	I'm Gonna Do All I Can/You've Got Too Many Ties That Bind	15
69	London HLU 10267	I'll Never Need More Than This/A Love Like Yours	8
69	Liberty LBF 15223	Crazy 'Bout You Baby/I've Been Lovin' You Too Long	10
70	Liberty LBF 15303	Come Together/Honky Tonky Women	6
70	A&M AMS 783	Make 'Em Wait/Everyday I Have To Cry	8
70	Harvest HAR 5018	The Hunter/Bold Soul Sister	8
70	Liberty LBF 15367	I Want To Take You Higher/Contact High	5
71	Liberty LBF 15432	Proud Mary/Funkier Than A Mosquito's Tweeter	15
71	A&M AMS 829	River Deep - Mountain High/Oh Baby	6
71	United Artists UP 35245	Ooh Poo Pah Doo/I Wanna Jump	5
72	United Artists UP 35373	Feel Good/Outrageous	5

EPs

64	Sue IEP 706	THE SOUL OF IKE AND TINA TURNER	200
65	Warner Bros WEP 619	THE IKE AND TINA TURNER SHOW	50
66	Warner Bros WEP 620	SOMEBODY NEEDS YOU	70
83	Sue ENS 1	SUE SESSIONS	15

ALBUMS

65	Warner Bros WM 8170	THE IKE AND TINA TURNER SHOW	45
65	London HA-C 8248	THE GREATEST HITS OF IKE & TINA TURNER	60
66	Ember EMB 3368	THE IKE AND TINA TURNER REVUE	40
66	Warner Bros W 1579	THE IKE AND TINA TURNER SHOW	40
66	London HA-U/SH-U 8298	RIVER DEEP MOUNTAIN HIGH	50
67	Warner Bros WB 5904	THE IKE AND TINA TURNER SHOW VOL. 2	35
69	London HA-U/SH-U 8370	SO FINE (with Fontella Bass)	30
69	Liberty LBS 83241	OUTTA SEASON	22
69	Minit MLS 40014	IN PERSON	25
69	Warner Bros ES 1810	GREATEST HITS	20
70	Liberty LBS 83350	COME TOGETHER	20
70	Harvest SHSP 4001	THE HUNTER	120
71	Liberty LBS 83455	WORKIN' TOGETHER	20
71	Liberty LBS 83468/9	LIVE IN PARIS	15
71	Capitol E-ST 571	HER MAN... HIS WOMAN	15
71	United Artists UAD 60005/6	WHAT YOU HEAR IS WHAT YOU GET	15
72	United Artists UAG 29256	NUFF SAID	15
73	Mojo 2916 020	PEACHES (with tracks by Ikettes)	15

JESSE LEE TURNER

(see also Pete Johnson, Meade Lux Lewis, Pete Johnson, Albert Ammons, Sonny Terry & Brownie McGhee)

59	London HLL 8785	The Little Space Girl/Shake, Baby, Shake	60
59	London HLL 8785	The Little Space Girl/Shake, Baby, Shake (78)	30
60	London HLP 9108	I'm The Little Space Girl's Father/Valley Of Lost Soldiers	20
60	Top Rank JAR 303	That's My Girl/Teenage Misery	20
60	Top Rank JAR 516	Do I Worry (Yes I Do)/All Right, Be That Way	15
62	Vogue V 9201	The Voice Changing Song/All You Gotta Do Is Ask	15

(BIG) JOE TURNER

51	Parlophone DP 265	Roll 'Em Pete/Goin' Away Blues (with Pete Johnson) (78, export only)	60
56	London HLE 8301	Corrine Corrina/Morning, Noon And Night (triangular or centre)	400
56	London HLE 8301	Corrine Corrina/Morning, Noon And Night (round centre)	100
56	London HLE 8301	Corrine Corrina/Morning, Noon And Night (78)	40
56	London HLE 8332	Boogie Woogie Country Girl/The Chicken And The Hawk	750
56	London HLE 8332	Boogie Woogie Country Girl/The Chicken And The Hawk (78)	45
57	London HLE 8357	Lipstick, Powder And Paint/Rock A While (gold label label print)	425
57	London HLE 8357	Lipstick, Powder And Paint/Rock A While (silver label print)	290
57	London HLE 8357	Lipstick, Powder And Paint/Rock A While (78)	40
60	London HLE 9055	Honey Hush/Tomorrow Night	60
60	London HLK 9119	My Little Honey Dripper/Chains Of Love	50
65	Atlantic AT 4026	Midnight Cannonball/Baby I Still Want You	20
57	London REE 1111	PRESENTING JOE TURNER (EP, initially tri-centre)	250
57	London REE 1111	PRESENTING JOE TURNER (EP, later round centre)	150
57	London Jazz LTZ-K 15053	BOSS OF THE BLUES (LP, mono)	80
57	London Jazz SAH-K 6123	BOSS OF THE BLUES (LP, stereo)	100
59	London HA-E 2173	ROCKIN' THE BLUES (LP)	120

			MINT VALUE £
60	London Jazz LTZ-K 15205	BIG JOE RIDES AGAIN (LP, mono)	75
60	London Jazz SAH-K 6123	BIG JOE RIDES AGAIN (LP, stereo)	90
60	London HA-E 2231	BIG JOE IS HERE (LP)	80
64	Realm RM 207	JOE TURNER SINGS THE BLUES VOL. 1 (LP)	20
64	Realm RM 229	JOE TURNER SINGS THE BLUES VOL. 2 (LP)	20
65	CBS 52229	JOE TURNER SINGS THE BLUES VOL. 2 (LP, reissue)	15
65	Fontana 688 802 ZL	JUMPIN' THE BLUES (LP)	25
67	Atlantic Special 590 006	BOSS OF THE BLUES (LP)	18
68	Stateside (S)SL 10226	SINGING THE BLUES (LP)	18
70	Philips SBL 7911	THE REAL BOSS OF THE BLUES (LP)	15
74	Atlantic K 40525	HIS GREATEST RECORDINGS (LP)	12

JOE TURNER/RUTH BROWN

(see also Ruth Brown, Big Joe Turner)

56	London REE 1047	KING AND QUEEN OF R&B (EP, 2 tracks each)	200

JOE TURNER & PETE JOHNSON GROUP

(see also Pete Johnson, Big Joe Turner)

56	Emarcy ERE 1500	JOE TURNER & PETE JOHNSON GROUP (EP)	30

MEL TURNER (& BANDITS)

61	Melodisc MEL 1580	Let Me Hold Your Hand/I'll Be With You In Apple Blossom Time (with Bandits)	20
62	Columbia DB 4791	Daddy Cool/Swing Low Sweet Chariot (with Bandits)	25
63	Columbia DB 4963	Don't Cry/I Need	10
63	Columbia DB 7076	I Can't Stand Up Alone/Doing The Ton (with Mohicans)	15
63	Carnival CV 7003	Mohican Crawl/White Christmas	10
66	Island WI 276	Welcome Home Little Darlin'/C'est L'Amour	40
64	Carnival CV 1005	The Hermit And The Rosetree/What's The Matter With Me	10

NIK TURNER

(see under Inner City Unit, Sphynx, Hawkwind)

PRECIOUS CLARENCE TURNER

67	Saga SOC 1041	BOOGIE WOOGIE EXPLOSIONS (LP)	12

RUBY TURNER

86	Jive CHIP 1	WOMEN HOLD UP HALF THE SKY (CD)	25

SAMMY TURNER

59	London HLX 8918	Lavender Blue (Dilly, Dilly)/Sweet Annie Laurie	18
59	London HLX 8918	Lavender Blue (Dilly, Dilly)/Sweet Annie Laurie (78)	20
59	London HLX 8963	Always/Symphony	20
59	London HLX 8963	Always/Symphony (78)	20
60	London HLX 9062	Paradise/I'd Be A Fool Again	20
62	London HLX 9488	Raincoat In The River/Falling	25
60	London HA-X 2246	LAVENDER BLUE MOODS (LP)	90

SPYDER TURNER

67	MGM MGM 1332	Stand By Me/You're Good Enough For Me	25
74	Kwanza K 19502	Since I Don't Have You/Happy Days	10

TINA TURNER

(see also Ike & Tina Turner, Eric Clapton)

78	United Artists UP 36513	Sometimes When We Touch/Earthquakes And Hurricanes	5
82	Virgin VS 500	Ball Of Confusion/Ball Of Confusion (Instrumental) (with B.E.F.) (p/s)	8
83	Capitol 12CLP 316	Let's Stay Together/I Wrote A Letter (12", picture disc)	8
84	Capitol CLP 325	Help/Rock'n'Roll Widow (picture disc)	7
84	Capitol CLP 338	Better Be Good To Me/When I Was Young (picture disc)	5
85	Capitol CLP 364	We Don't Need Another Hero/(Instrumental) (picture disc)	5
86	Capitol CLP 338	Break Every Rule/Girls (picture disc)	5
87	Capitol CLD 439	What You Get Is What You See/Tina Turner Montage (box set)	5
91	10 FLX 2007-1	A Change Is Gonna Come (Excerpt) (with B.E.F.) (flexidisc, p/s, from Music Of Quality And Distinction Vol 2, promo only)	7
85	Capitol TINAP 1	PRIVATE DANCER (LP, picture disc)	18

TITUS TURNER

60	London HLU 9024	We Told You Not To Marry/Taking Care Of Business	25
61	Oriole CB 1611	Pony Train/Bla Bla Cha Cha Cha	20
61	Parlophone R 4746	Sound-Off/Me And My Lonely Telephone	25
61	Blue Beat BB 32	Miss Rubberneck Jones/Way Down Yonder	18

ZEB TURNER

51	Vogue V 9002	Chew Tobacco Rag/No More Nothin' (78)	20

TURNING POINT

77	Gull GULP 1022	CREATURES OF THE NIGHT (LP)	20
78	Gull GULP 1027	SILENT PROMISE (LP)	15

TURNING SHRINES

86	Temple TOPY 7	FACE OF ANOTHER (12" EP)	8

TURNSTYLE

68	Pye 7N 17653	Riding A Wave/Trot	300

TURQUOISE

(see also Ewan Stephens)

68	Decca F 12756	53 Summer Street/Tales Of Flossie Fillett	60
68	Decca F 12842	Woodstock/Saynia	90

STANLEY TURRENTINE

(see also Milt Jackson & Stanley Turrentine)

66	Fontana TL 5300	TIGER TAIL (LP)	12

HENRY TURTLE

72	Columbia DB 8859	Do You Believe/You Turned Your Back And Walked Away	30
73	Bell 1318	When Eleanor Comes Around/One Of A Million Faces	8
81	Surrey Sounds HMS 6A	Hound Dog Man/All I Ever Need Is You	5

MINT VALUE £

TURTLES
(see also Flo & Eddie, Frank Zappa)

65	Pye International 7N 25320	It Ain't Me Babe/Almost There	20
66	Pye International 7N 25341	Let Me Be/Your Ma Said You Cried (In Your Sleep Last Night)	15
66	Immediate IM 031	You Baby/Wanderin' Kind	25
66	London HLU 10095	Can I Get To Know You Better/Like The Seasons	10
67	London HLU 10115	Happy Together/We'll Meet Again	5
67	Pye International 7N 25421	Let Me Be/Almost There	8
67	London HLU 10135	She'd Rather Be With Me/The Walking Song	5
67	London HLU 10153	You Know What I Mean/Rugs Of Woods And Flowers	8
67	London HLU 10168	She's My Girl/Chicken Little Was Right	12
68	London HLU 10184	Sound Asleep/Umbassa The Dragon	10
68	London HLU 10207	The Story Of Rock And Roll/Can't You Hear The Cows	10
68	London HLU 10223	Elenore/Surfer Dan	5
69	London HLU 10251	You Showed Me/Buzz-Saw	8
69	London HLU 10279	You Don't Have To Walk In The Rain/Come Over	12
69	London HLU 10291	Love In The City/Bachelor Mother	7
67	Pye Intl. NEP 44089	IT AIN'T ME BABE (EP)	55
67	London HA-U 8330	HAPPY TOGETHER (LP)	20
68	London HA-U/SH-U 8376	THE TURTLES PRESENT THE BATTLE OF THE BANDS (LP)	20

GEOFF TURTON

68	Pye 7N 17483	Don't You believe It/I've Got To Tell Her	10

RITA TUSHINGHAM & LYNN REDGRAVE

68	Stateside SS 2081	Smashing Time/Waiting For My Friend	10

TUSKAN RAIDERS
(see also ŭ-Ziq)

95	Clear CLR 410(X)	Bantha Trax (12", p/s, on clear vinyl)	8

TUSKEN RAIDERS

99	Planet Mu ZIQ 003	BANTHA TRAX VOL. 2 EP (12", p/s)	12

TUTCH

80	Gargoyle GRGL 773	The Battle/You Don't Care/Round And Round	60

TU-TONES

51	London L 1079	Oh You Million Dollar Doll/Don't Fence Me In (78, as Lee Monti's Tu-Tones)	10
59	London HLW 8904	Still In Love WIth You/Saccharin Sally	125
59	London HLW 8904	Still In Love WIth You/Saccharin Sally (78)	30

TUTTI'S TRUMPETS
(see under Camarata)

WESLEY & MARILYN TUTTLE

55	Capitol CL 14291	Jim, Johnny And Jonas/Say You Do	10

TUXEDOMOON

80	Pre PRE 10	Dark Companion/59 To One (p/s)	5
80	PRE	DESIRE (LP, with art print insert)	15

TV ON THE RADIO

04	4AD AD 2421	Staring At The Sun/Freeway/On A Train	10
04	4AD AD 2423	New Health Rock/Modern Romance	8
06	4AD 2606	Wolf Like Me/Snakes And Martyrs	8
07	4AD 2724	Province/Dumb Animal	8
06	4AD RTCM2	Province (with David Bowie, 200 only)	40
09	Parlophone LCO 299	TV ON THE RADIO: Heroes/DAVID BOWIE: Heroes	40
04	4AD CAD 2470	DESPERATE YOUTH, BLOODTHIRSTY BABES (LP)	18
06	4AD CAD 2607	RETURN TO COOKIE MOUNTAIN (LP)	18
08	4AD CAD 2821	DEAR SCIENCE (LP)	15

T.V. PERSONALITIES
(see under Television Personalities)

T.V. PRODUCT
(see also Mission)

79	Limited Edition TAKE 3	Nowhere's Safe/Jumping Off Walls/PRAMS: Me/Modern Man (folded p/s)	12

T.V. & TRIBESMEN

66	Pye International 7N 25375	Barefootin'/Fat Man	30

TV 21
(see also DNV, Shake)

80	Powbeat AAARGH! 1	Playing With Fire/Shattered By It All (foldout p/s)	12
80	Powbeat AAARGH! 2	Ambition/Ticking Away/This Is Zero (foldout p/s)	15
81	Demon D 1004	On The Run/End Of A Dream (p/s)	8
82	Deram ATV 21	All Join Hands/A Journey Up The Zambezi (And Back) (p/s)	8

SHANIA TWAIN

95	Mercury MERCD 433	Any Man Of Mine/Raining On Our Love/ God Ain't Gonna Getcha For That/Still Under The Weather (CD)	12
99	Mercury 562 264 2	Man! I Feel Like A Woman (Original Version) (CD, digipak, with lyrics, withdrawn)	12
99	NMC PILOT 54	ON THE WAY (CD, withdrawn)	18

TWELFTH NIGHT

73	Acorn CF 239	TWELFTH NIGHT (EP)	8
82	Revolution REV 009	Eleanor Rigby/East Of Eden (p/s)	10

TWELFTH NIGHT

80	Twelfth Night TN 001	THE FIRST 7" ALBUM ("The Cunning Man"/"Für Helene") (p/s)	30
86	Virgin/Charisma CB 424	Shame/Blue Powder Monkey (p/s)	5
86	Virgin/Charisma CBY 424	Shame/Blue Powder Monkey (picture disc)	8
86	Virgin/Charisma CB 424-12	Shame (Full Mix)/Shame (7")/Blue Powder Monkey (12", p/s)	8

MINT VALUE £

86	Virgin/Charisma CBY 424-12	Shame (Full Mix)/Shame (7")/Blue Powder Monkey (12", picture disc)	10
86	Virgin/Charisma CB 425-12	Take A Look (Album Version)/Take A Look (Part 4)/ Blondon Fair (Extended) (12", p/s)	8
80	Twelfth Night TN 001	TWELFTH NIGHT (cassette)	15
81	Twelfth Night TN 002	LIVE AT THE TARGET (LP)	12

20th CENTURY FOX ORCHESTRA

(see also Ron Goodwin)

65	Stateside SS422	Those Magnificent Men In Their Flying Machines/Arizona	15

25 RIFLES

79	25 Rifles TFR 1	World War 3/Revolution Blues/Hey Little/Dance 'Bout Now (12")	15

22ND STREET

72	Polydor 2058 212	Sunny Sleeps Late/Home	8

23RD TURNOFF

(see also Kirkbys, Jimmy Campbell, Rockin' Horse)

67	Deram DM 150	Michael Angelo/Leave Me Here	70

23 JEWELS

79	Temporary TEMP 1	You Don't Know Me/Playing Bogart (white labels, plain sleeve with photocopied insert)	12
80	Temporary TEMP 2	WELTSCHMERZ A GO-GO! (EP, white label)	8

23 SKIDOO

(see also Current 93)

81	Pineapple PULP 23	Ethics/Another Baby's Face (p/s)	8
81	Fetish FE 10	Last Words/Version (promo only)	12
81	Fetish FE 11	The Gospel Comes To New Guinea/Last Words (12", p/s)	10
82	Fetish FP 20	Tearing Up The Plans/Just Like Everybody/Gregouka (12", p/s)	10
85	Illuminated ILL 2812	Coup/Version (In The Palace) (12", p/s)	10
82	Fetish FM 2008	SEVEN SONGS (mini-LP)	12
84	Illuminated JAM 40	URBAN GAMELAN (LP)	15

22:20S

90s	own label 2201	Such A Fool/Baby, You're Not In Love (1,000 only, die-cut sleeve)	8
04	Heavenly HVNLP 51	22:20S (LP, gatefold)	12

TWICE AS MUCH

66	Immediate IM 033	Sittin' On A Fence/Baby I Want You	6
66	Immediate IM 036	Step Out Of Line/Simplified	12
66	Immediate IM 039	True Story/You're So Good	18
67	Immediate IM 042	Crystal Ball/Why Don't They All Go Away And Leave Me Alone	18
66	Immediate IMLP 007	OWN UP (LP, mono)	90
66	Immediate IMSP 007	OWN UP (LP, stereo)	100
69	Immediate IMCP 013	THAT'S ALL (LP)	60

TWIGGY

67	Ember EMB S 239	Beautiful Dreams/I Need Your Hand In Mine (in p/s)	20
67	Ember EMB S 239	Beautiful Dreams/I Need Your Hand In Mine	10
67	Ember EMB S 244	When I Think Of You/Over And Over (in p/s)	20
67	Ember EMB S 244	When I Think Of You/Over And Over	10
71	Bell BLL 1158	Zoo Do Zoo Song/Little Pleasure Acre (as Twiggy & Friends)	5
72	Columbia DB 8853	A Room In Bloomsbury (with Chistopher Gable)/You Are My Lucky Star/ All I Do Is Dream	5
76	Mercury 6007 100	Here I Go Again/In Love Together (p/s)	5
78	Mercury 6007 175	Falling Angel/Virginia	5
72	Ember SE 8012	TWIGGY & THE GIRLFRIENDS (LP)	20
72	Columbia SCXA 9251	THE BOYFRIEND (LP, soundtrack, with Christopher Plummer)	15

TWIGGY & ANNE

66	Columbia DB 7799	Some Do, Some Don't/With Open Arms	6

TWILIGHT

86	Lismor Folk LIFL 7014	MODERN FOLK ARRANGEMENTS (LP)	12

TWILIGHT ZONERZ

(see also Occult Chemistry)

79	ZIP/Dining Out	ZERO ZERO ONE (EP, various silk-screened in red & hand-coloured p/s, signed & numbered)	15
80	ZIP/Dining Out ZIP 002	Brighton Rock/Diversion (p/s)	6

TWILIGHTS (Australia)

66	Columbia DB 8065	Needle In A Haystack/I Don't Know Where The Wind Will Blow Me	30
67	Columbia DB 8125	What's Wrong With The Way I Live/It's Dark	20
68	Columbia DB 8396	Cathy, Come Home/The Way They Play	30

TWILIGHTS (U.S.)

65	London HLU 9992	Take What I Got/She's There	20

TWINK (& FAIRIES)

(see also Pretty Things, Pink Fairies, Fairies, Tomorrow, Aquarian Age, Rings, Mick Farren, Magic Muscle)

78	Chiswick SWT 26	Do It '77/Psychedelic Punkeroo/Enter The Diamonds (12", p/s, with Fairies)	12
86	Twink TWK 2	SPACE LOVER (EP)	12
90	Twink 12TWK 5	PSYCHEDELIC PUNKEROO (12" EP)	8
70	Polydor 2343 032	THINK PINK (LP, with pink lyric insert)	300
70	Polydor 2343 032	THINK PINK (LP, without pink lyric insert)	150
70	Polydor 2343 032	THINK PINK (LP, red vinyl with pink lyric insert)	350
90	Twink TWKLP 1	MR RAINBOW (LP)	12
91	Twink LP 2	ODDS & BEGINNINGS (LP, with insert, numbered & signed, some on red vinyl, 1,500 only)	15
91	Twink LP 2	ODDS & BEGINNINGS (LP, with insert, numbered & signed, 1,500 only)	12

MINT VALUE £

TWINKLE (Ripley)
(see also Silkie Davis)

64	Decca F 12013	Terry/The Boy Of My Dreams	6
65	Decca F 12076	Golden Lights/Ain't Nobody Home But Me	10
65	Decca F 12139	Tommy/So Sad	12
65	Decca F 12219	Poor Old Johnny/I Need Your Hand In Mine	15
65	Decca F 12305	The End Of The World/Take Me To The Dance	15
66	Decca F 12464	What Am I Doing Here With You?/Now I Have You	15
69	Instant IN 005	Micky/Darby And Joan	15
74	Bradleys BRAD 7418	Days/Caroline (as Twinkle Ripley) (p/s)	15
74	Bradleys BRAD 7418	Days/Caroline (as Twinkle Ripley)	7
82	EMI 5278	I'm A Believer/For Sale (p/s)	15
65	Decca DFE 8621	TWINKLE - A LONELY SINGING DOLL (EP)	60

TWINKLE & HOT ROD ALL STARS

70	Torpedo TOR 3	Jook Jook/Graduate	5

TWINKLE BROTHERS
(see also Busty Brown, Sammy Jones)

70	Jackpot JP 731	Shu Be Du/All My Enemies Beware	8
70	Jackpot JP 740	Miss World/Take What You've Got	8
70	Jackpot JP 741	Sweet Young Thing/Grandma	8
71	Jackpot JP 768	Do Your Own Thing/BOY WONDER: They Talk About Love	8
71	Green Door GD 4007	Miss Labba Labba/The Best Is Yet To Come	10
71	Big Shot BI 593	You Took Me By Suprise/You Took Me By Surprise - Version (both sides actually by Tony Brevitt)	12
71	Big Shot BI 600	It's Not Who You Know/I Need Someone	8
71	Tropical AL 002	Love Sweet Love/HERON ATTAR: Poor Man's Life	5
72	Sioux SI 003	Happy Song/Little Caesar	5
73	Camel CA 105	Room Full All Full/Version	6
73	Count Shelley CS 31	Mother Whiney/JACKIE BROWN: Fight My Way	6
73	Camel CA 106	Room Full All Full/Version	7
73	Magnet MG 033	Mother And Wife/Version	5
73	Pama PM 876	Village Ram/Push It Inna	10
75	Faith FA 007	Friends/No Big Thing	5
75	Faith FA 022	Mother And Wife/GENE RONDO: Impossible Dream	6
77	Carib Gems CG 009	Jah Army/Dub The Wicked	6
79	Virgin Front Line FLS 119 12	Keep On Trying/King Pharoah (12")	10
79	Virgin Front Line FLS 123 12	Jahoviah/Free Africa (12")	25
75	Grounation GROL 506	RASTA PON TOP (LP)	35
78	Front Line FCL 5001	LOVE (10" LP)	12

TWINS

73	Downtown DT 511	Rastafari Ruler/TYRONE TAYLOR: Yesterday	8

TWINSET

67	Decca F 12629	Tremblin'/Sneakin' Up On You	25

TWIN-TONES

58	RCA RCA 1040	Jo Ann/Before You Go	60
58	RCA RCA 1040	Jo Ann/Before You Go (78)	25

TWIN TUNES QUINTET

58	RCA RCA 1046	The Love Nest/Baby Lover	12

TWIST

79	Polydor 2059 156	This Is Your Life/Life's A Commercial Break (p/s)	10
79	Polydor POSP 84	Ads/Rebound	10
79	Polydor 2383 552	THIS IS YOUR LIFE (LP)	20

TWIST

91	East West YZ 586	The Fat Lady Sings/Heavy Duty (p/s)	5

TWIST & SHOUT

79	Wessex WEX 268	Bounce Back/As It Happens (p/s)	20

TWISTED ACE

81	Heavy Metal HEAVY 9	Firebird/I Won't Surrender (in p/s)	10
81	Heavy Metal HEAVY 9	Firebird/I Won't Surrender	5

TWISTED SISTER

82	Secret SHH 137-12	RUFF CUTS (12" EP, p/s)	10
83	Atlantic A 9827P	The Kids Are Back/Shoot 'Em Down (shaped picture disc)	8
86	Atlantic A 9478D	Leader Of The Pack/I Wanna Rock (p/s, with free single)	5
86	Atlantic A 9478P	Leader Of The Pack/I Wanna Rock (shaped picture disc)	6
85	Atlantic 781 275-1P	COME OUT AND PLAY (LP, picture disc)	12

TWISTERS

60	Capitol CL 15167	Turn The Page/Dancing Little Clown	8
62	Aral/Windsor PSA 106	Peppermint Twist Time/Silly Chilli	12

CONWAY TWITTY
(see also Loretta Lynn)

78s

57	Mercury MT 173	Shake It Up/Maybe Baby	30
59	MGM MGM 1003	The Story Of My Love/Make Me Know You're Mine	10
59	MGM MGM 1016	Hey Little Lucy! (Don'tcha Put No Lipstick On)/When I'm Not With You	15
59	MGM MGM 1029	Mona Lisa/Heavenly	20
59	MGM MGM 1047	Rosaleena/Halfway To Heaven	30

SINGLES

58	MGM MGM 992	It's Only Make Believe/I'll Try	10
59	MGM MGM 1003	The Story Of My Love/Make Me Know You're Mine	10

MINT VALUE £

59	MGM MGM 1016	Hey Little Lucy! (Don'tcha Put No Lipstick On)/ When I'm Not With You	10
59	MGM MGM 1029	Mona Lisa/Heavenly	6
59	MGM MGM 1047	Rosaleena/Halfway To Heaven	6
60	MGM MGM 1056	Lonely Blue Boy/My One And Only You	10
60	MGM MGM 1066	What Am I Living For/The Hurt In My Heart	10
60	MGM MGM 1082	Is A Blue Bird Blue/She's Mine	15
60	MGM MGM 1095	What A Dream/Tell Me One More Time	6
60	MGM MGM 1108	Whole Lotta Shakin' Goin' On/The Flame	12
61	MGM MGM 1118	C'est Si Bon/Don't You Dare Let Me Down	12
61	MGM MGM 1129	The Next Kiss/Man Alone	6
61	MGM MGM 1137	It's Drivin' Me Wild/Sweet Sorry	10
62	MGM MGM 1152	Tower Of Tears/Portrait Of A Fool	12
62	MGM MGM 1170	Comfy An' Cozy/Unchained Melody	10
62	MGM MGM 1187	I Hope I Think I Wish/The Pick Up	12
63	MGM MGM 1201	Handy Man/Little Piece Of My Heart	10
63	MGM MGM 1209	She Ain't No Angel/Got My Mojo Workin'	12
63	HMV POP 1258	Go On And Cry/She Loves Me	8

EPs

58	MGM MGM-EP 684	IT'S ONLY MAKE BELIEVE	60
59	MGM MGM-EP 698	HEY LITTLE LUCY	60
60	MGM MGM-EP 719	SATURDAY NIGHT WITH CONWAY TWITTY	60
60	Mercury ZEP 10069	I NEED YOUR LOVIN'	150
60	MGM MGM-EP 738	IS A BLUEBIRD BLUE?	65
61	MGM MGM-EP 752	THE ROCK 'N' ROLL STORY	80

LPs

59	MGM MGM-C 781	CONWAY TWITTY SINGS	100
60	MGM MGM-C 801	SATURDAY NIGHT WITH CONWAY TWITTY	100
60	MGM MGM-C 829	LONELY BLUE BOY	100
63	MGM MGM-C 950	R AND B '63	70
68	MCA MUP(S) 342	HERE'S CONWAY TWITTY (AND HIS LONELY BLUE BOYS)	18
68	MGM C/CS 8100	THE ROCK AND ROLL STORY	50
69	MCA MUPS 363	NEXT IN LINE	18
69	MCA MUPS 386	DARLING, YOU KNOW I WOULDN'T LIE	15
70	MCA MUP(S) 404	I LOVE YOU MORE TODAY	15
70	MCA MUP(S) 412	TO SEE MY ANGEL CRY	15
71	MCA MUPS 426	FIFTEEN YEARS AGO	15
71	MCA MUPS 429	WE ONLY MAKE BELIEVE (with Loretta Lynn)	15
72	MCA MUPS 443	I WONDER WHAT SHE'LL THINK ABOUT ME LEAVING	15
74	MCA MCF 2547	LOUISANA WOMAN/MISSISSIPPI MAN (with Loretta Lynn)	12
74	MCA MCF 2557	YOU'VE NEVER BEEN THIS FAR BEFORE	12

TWO & A HALF

66	CBS 202248	Midnight Swim/Faith	10
66	CBS 202404	Questions/In Harmony	8
67	CBS 202526	The Walls Are High/Love You	8
67	Decca F 22672	Suburban Early Morning Station/Just Couldn't Believe My Ears	15
67	Decca F 22715	I Don't Need To Tell You/Christmas Will Be Round Again	18

TWO DARK TROOPERS

(see also Chemical, DJ Mayhem)

92	Basement BRSS 020	I Wanna Be Your Lover/Darkcore (12")	10

TWO FINGERED APPROACH

82	Virus	WORLD WAR (EP)	30

TWO FOR THE ROAD

70s	Pastiche BJ 2929	TWO FOR THE ROAD (LP)	20

TWO KINGS

65	Island WI 240	Rolling Stone/SUFFERER: Tomorrow Morning (B-side act. by Frank Cosmo)	18
65	Island WI 249	Hit You Let You Feel It/Honey I Love You (both sides actually by Fugitives)	18

TWO MAN SOUND

78	Miracle M12	Que Tal America/Brazil O Brazil (12")	12
74	Spark SRL 118	Amadeo/Somebody Is Ready To Love You	8

TWO MUCH

67	Fontana TF 858	Wonderland Of Love/Mister Money	7
68	Fontana TF 900	It's A Hip Hip Hippy World/Stay In My World	10

TWO-NINETEEN (2.19) SKIFFLE GROUP

57	Esquire 10-497	Freight Train Blues/Railroad Bill (78)	15
57	Esquire 10-502	I'm A-Lookin' For A Home/When The Saints Go Marching In (78)	15
57	Esquire 10-509	In The Valley/Tom Dooley (78)	15
57	Esquire 10-512	Where Can I Go?/Roll The Union On (78)	20
57	Esquire 10-515	This Little Light Of Mine/Union Maid (78)	20
57	Esquire EP 126	TWO-NINETEEN SKIFFLE GROUP (EP)	40
57	Esquire EP 146	TWO-NINETEEN SKIFFLE GROUP (EP)	55
58	Esquire EP 176	TWO-NINETEEN SKIFFLE GROUP (EP)	55
58	Esquire EP 196	TWO-NINETEEN SKIFFLE GROUP (EP)	60

TWO OF CLUBS

64	Columbia DB 7371	The Angels Must Have Made You/True Love Is Here	15

TWO OF EACH

67	Decca F 12626	Every Single Day/I'm Glad I Got You	8
68	Pye 7N 17555	The Summer Of Our Love/Saturday Morning	7
78	Fast Products FAST 2	Where To Now?/All Time Low (p/s)	15

TWO PEOPLE

86	Polydor	Mouth Of An Angel (p/s)	20
80s	Polydor	This Is The Shirt (p/s)	10

MINT VALUE £

2 SLICES OF JAM

92	White Label	Pressing On Ya Mind/Beat Like This (12" white label)	60

TWO SPARKS

(see also Carl Bryan, Winston Wright)

72	Moodisc HM 113	Run Away Girl/When We Were Young	8

2 THE TOP

89	Rhyme & Reason 12RNR2	The Rhythm I Give Em (12")	35
90	President PT12590	Score To Settle/The Matter At Hand (12")	20

TWO TIMES DEF

(see also Silent Eclipse)

92	White(Mendoza)MEN 016	First And Last (12")	160

TWO TONE COMMITTEE

91	Precinct PREC002	Beings From A Word Stuck Surface (12")	40

2-X-TREME

92	Empire E 001	X-TREMITY EP (12", white label stamped in red, beware of represses!)	60

TY

00	Big Dada BD023	Break The Lock/The Tale (12")	18
00	Big Dada BD025	The Nonsense (12")	15
03	Big Dada BD049	We Don't Care (12")	12
03	Big Dada BD056	Groovement/Ha Ha (12")	8
03	Big Dada BD058	Wait A Minute (12")	8
03	Big Dada BD058X	Wait A Minute Remixes (12")	8
06	Big Dada BD097	Don't Watch That (12" - Promo only 800 copies)	12
01	Big Dada BDLP026	AWKWARD (LP)	15
03	Big Dada BDLP057	UPWARDS (LP)	12

TY/ROOTS MANUVA

04	Big Dada BD066	Oh You Want More (12")	8

TY/SHORTEE BLITZ

97	Freak Street FSEP0008	Zones (EP)	15
98	Wayward W0002	I.A.A.D. (EP)	12

ARLYNE TYE

59	London HLL 8825	The Universe/Who Is The One	25
59	London HLL 8825	The Universe/Who Is The One (78)	15

TYGERS OF PAN TANG

(see also John Sykes)

79	Neat NEAT 03	Don't Touch Me There/Burning Up/Bad Times (p/s)	12
80	MCA MCA 582	Don't Touch Me There/Burning Up/Bad Times (p/s, reissue)	10
80	MCA MCA 612	Rock'n'Roll Man/All Right On The Night/Wild Man (p/s)	5
80	MCA MCA 634	Suzie Smiled/Tush (p/s)	5
80	MCA MCA 644	Euthanasia/Straight As A Die (p/s)	5
81	MCA MCA 672	Hellbound/Bad Times//Bad Times/Don't Take Nothin' ('The Audition Tapes' double pack)	6
81	MCA MCA 692	The Story So Far/Silver And Gold/All Or Nothing (p/s)	5
81	MCA MCA 723	Don't Stop By/Slave To Freedom (p/s)	5
81	MCA MCAT 723	Don't Stop By/Slave To Freedom (12", p/s)	12
81	MCA MCA 755	Love Don't Stay/Paradise Drive (p/s)	8
81	MCA MCA 759	Do It Good/Slip Away (no p/s)	30
81	MCA MCA 769	Love Potion No. 9/The Stormlands (p/s)	5
81	MCA MCAP 769	Love Potion No. 9/The Stormlands (picture disc)	5
82	MCA MCA 777	Rendezvous/Life Of Crime (white vinyl, p/s)	6
82	MCA MCA 777	Rendezvous/Life Of Crime (red or blue vinyl, p/s)	5
82	MCA MCA 777	Rendezvous/Life Of Crime (poster p/s)	5
82	MCA MCA 777	Rendezvous/Life Of Crime (p/s)	5
82	MCA MCA 790	Paris By Air/Love's A Lie (standard p/s with earring)	10
82	MCA MCA 790	Paris By Air/Love's A Lie (poster p/s)	5
82	MCA MCA 798	Making Tracks/What You Saying (p/s)	5
82	MCA MCAT 798	Making Tracks (Extended Remix)/What You Saying (12", p/s)	10
80	MCA MCF 3075	WILD CAT (LP, with lyric insert)	12
81	MCA MCF 3104	SPELLBOUND (LP, with poster)	12
81	MCA MCF 3123	CRAZY NIGHTS (LP, stickered sleeve, insert, with bonus 12")	22
81	MCA MCF 3123	CRAZY NIGHTS (LP, stickered sleeve, insert)	12
85	MFN MFN 50	THE WRECK AGE (LP, lyric sleeve)	12
86	Neat 1037	FIRST KILL (LP, with inner)	12

TYLA GANG

(see also Ducks Deluxe)

76	Stiff BUY 4	Styrofoam/Texas Chainsaw Massacre Boogie (die-cut printed sleeve)	5
78	Beserkley BSERK 16	MOONPROOF (LP, yellow vinyl, with insert)	12

BIG 'T' TYLER

57	Vogue V 9079	King Kong/Sadie Green	200
57	Vogue V 9079	King Kong/Sadie Green (78)	100

JIMMY TYLER & HIS ORCHESTRA

56	Parlophone MSP 6215	Fool 'Em Devil/Stardust	18
60	Top Rank JAR 306	Junk Village/Happy Sax	12

T. TEXAS TYLER

59	Parlophone GEP 8788	COUNTRY ROUND-UP (EP)	30
67	London HA-B 8322	MAN WITH A MILLION FRIENDS (LP)	25

TERRY TYLER

61	Pye International 7N 25119	A Thousand Feet Below/Answer Me	15

MINT VALUE £

TOBY TYLER
(see also Marc Bolan)

64	Emidisc no cat. no.	The Road I'm On (Gloria)/Blowin' In The Wind (acetate, 1 copy only)	3000
64	Emidisc no cat. no.	The Road I'm On (Gloria) (acetate, 1 copy only)	1750
89	Archive Jive TOBY 1	The Road I'm On (Gloria) (mail-order issue, numbered p/s, 1-sided, 1,500 only)	15
93	Zinc Alloy ZAR CDS 9005	Blowin' In The Wind/The Road I'm On (Gloria)/Blowin' In The Wind (Take No. 6) (CD)	10
93	Zinc Alloy ZAR CD 9006	THE MAXIMUM SOUND SESSION (CD)	22

TYMES

63	Cameo Parkway P 871	So Much In Love/Roscoe James McClain	15
63	Cameo Parkway P 884	Wonderful Wonderful/Come With Me To The Sea (in p/s)	25
63	Cameo Parkway P 884	Wonderful Wonderful/Come With Me To The Sea	15
64	Cameo Parkway P 891	Somewhere/View From My Window	15
64	Cameo Parkway P 908	To Each His Own/Wonderland Of Love	15
64	Cameo Parkway P 919	The Magic Of Our Summer Love/With All My Heart	15
64	Cameo Parkway P 924	Here She Comes/Malibu	130
64	Cameo Parkway P 924	Here She Comes/Malibu (DJ copy)	200
69	Direction 58-3903	People/The Love of Ivy	6
69	Direction 58-4450	If You Love Me Baby/Find My Way	10
71	CBS 7250	Someone To Watch Over Me/She's Gone (featuring George Williams)	6
63	Cameo Parkway P 7032	SO MUCH IN LOVE (LP)	70
69	Direction 8-63558	PEOPLE (LP, mono or stereo)	25
78	London HAU 8516	CAMEO PARKWAY SESSIONS (LP)	25

McCOY TYNER

70s	Impulse IMPL 8043	INCEPTION (LP)	12

ROB TYNER & HOT RODS
(see also MC 5, Eddie & Hot Rods)

77	Island WIP 6418	'Till The Night Is Gone (Let's Rock)/Flipside Rock (p/s)	5

TYPHOONS
(see also Bud Ashton, Ray Pilgrim, Mike Redway, Starlings)

63	Embassy WB 589	Surf City/I Want To Stay Here	7
65	Embassy WB 677	Tired Of Waiting For You/Baby Please Don't Go	7
65	Embassy WT 1115	Hard Day's Night/And I Love Her/I Should Have Known Better/Tell Me Why (EP)	10
65	Embassy WT 2006	Ticket To Ride/Here Comes The Night/I'll Be There/I Can't Explain (EP)	15

TYPHOONS
(see also Ruts)

81	Bohemian BO 1	Telstar/In Fae A Brothin' (p/s)	5

TYRANNOSAURUS REX
(see also Marc Bolan/T. Rex, John's Children, Dib Cochran & Earwigs, Shagrat)

68	Regal Zonophone RZ 3008	Debora/Child Star (with promo only p/s)	400
68	Regal Zonophone RZ 3008	Debora/Child Star (with promo only p/s, with insert)	450
68	Regal Zonophone RZ 3008	Debora/Child Star (demo copy as above, but without promo only p/s)	375
68	Regal Zonophone RZ 3008	Debora/Child Star	35
68	Regal Zonophone RZ 3011	One Inch Rock/Salamanda Palaganda (promo only p/s)	375
68	Regal Zonophone RZ 3011	One Inch Rock/Salamanda Palaganda (promo only p/s, with insert)	425
68	Regal Zonophone RZ 3011	One Inch Rock/Salamanda Palaganda	40
69	Regal Zonophone RZ 3016	Pewter Suitor/Warlord Of The Royal Crocodiles	70
69	Regal Zonophone RZ 3022	King Of The Rumbling Spires/Do You Remember (with promo only p/s)	450
69	Regal Zonophone RZ 3022	King Of The Rumbling Spires/Do You Remember (demo, without promo only p/s)	400
69	Regal Zonophone RZ 3022	King Of The Rumbling Spires/Do You Remember	40
70	Regal Zonophone RZ 3025	By The Light Of A Magical Moon/Find A Little Wood	40
72	Magni Fly ECHO 102	Debora/One Inch Rock/The Woodland Bop/The Seal Of Seasons (p/s)	5
82	Old Gold OG 9234	Debora/One Inch Rock (1,000 mispressed with "Beltane Walk" on B-side)	5
91	Tyrannosaurus Rex TYR 1	Sleepy Maurice/1968 Radio Promos (Tyrannosaurus Rex Appreciation Society release, 2,000 only, p/s with card insert)	8
68	Regal Zonophone LRZ 1003	MY PEOPLE WERE FAIR AND HAD SKY IN THEIR HAIR BUT NOW THEY'RE CONTENT TO WEAR STARS ON THEIR BROWS (LP, mono, with lyric sheet & manuscript)	80
68	Regal Zonophone LRZ 1003	MY PEOPLE WERE FAIR AND HAD SKY IN THEIR HAIR BUT NOW THEY'RE CONTENT TO WEAR STARS ON THEIR BROWS (LP, mono)	45
68	Regal Zonophone SLRZ 1003	MY PEOPLE WERE FAIR AND HAD SKY IN THEIR HAIR BUT NOW THEY'RE CONTENT TO WEAR STARS ON THEIR BROWS (LP, stereo, with lyric sheet & manuscript)	60
68	Regal Zonophone SLRZ 1003	MY PEOPLE WERE FAIR AND HAD SKY IN THEIR HAIR BUT NOW THEY'RE CONTENT TO WEAR STARS ON THEIR BROWS (LP, stereo)	20
68	Regal Zonophone TA-LRZ 1003	MY PEOPLE WERE FAIR AND HAD SKY IN THEIR HAIR BUT NOW THEY'RE CONTENT TO WEAR STARS ON THEIR BROWS (reel-to-reel tape, mono)	35
68	Regal Zonophone LRZ 1005	PROPHETS, SEERS AND SAGES, THE ANGELS OF THE AGES (LP, with lyric sheet, textured sleeve, mono)	100
68	Regal Zonophone SLRZ 1005	PROPHETS, SEERS AND SAGES, THE ANGELS OF THE AGES (LP, with lyric sheet, textured sleeve, stereo)	80
69	R. Zonophone LRZ 1007	UNICORN (LP, gatefold sleeve, original with blue/silver label, mono)	120
69	R. Zonophone LRZ 1007	UNICORN (LP, gatefold sleeve, later issue with red/silver label mono)	60
70	R. Zonophone SLRZ 1007	UNICORN (LP, gatefold sleeve, original with blue/silver label, stereo)	100
70	R. Zonophone SLRZ 1007	UNICORN (LP, gatefold sleeve, later issue with red/silver label, stereo)	30
70	R. Zonophone SLRZ 1013	A BEARD OF STARS (LP, with lyric sheet)	60
70	R. Zonophone SLRZ 1013	A BEARD OF STARS (LP, without lyric sheet)	30

TYRANT

83	SRTS 83 CUS 2046	Hold Back The Lightning/eyes Of A Stranger	150

LLOYD TYRELL
(see under Lloyd Terrell)

MINT VALUE £

TYRONE & CARR
72 Jam JAM 7 I Want To Give You My Everything/I'm Still In Love With You 8
73 Jam JAM 36 Love Me Love You/Take Me With You 6

GORDON TYRRALL
78 Hill & Dale HD 002 FAREWELL TO FOGGY HILLS (LP) 18

TYSONDOG
83 Neat NEAT 33 Eat The Rich/Dead Meat (p/s) 10
85 Neat NEAT 46 Shoot To Kill/Hammerhead (p/s) 10
85 Neat NEAT 4612 Shoot To Kill/Hammerhead/Changeling/Back To The Bullet (12", p/s) 15
86 Neat NEAT 56 School's Out/Don't Let The Bastards Grind You Down (p/s) 12
86 Neat NEAT 1031 CRIMES OF INSANITY (LP, with inner) 18
84 Neat NEAT 1017 BEWARE OF THE DOG (LP, with insert) 20

TYTAN
(see also Angel Witch)
82 Kamaflage KAM 6 Blind Men And Fools/The Ballad Of Edward Case (p/s) 18
82 Kamaflage KAMA 6 Blind Men And Fools/The Ballad Of Edward Case (12", p/s) 20
85 Metal Masters METALP 105 ROUGH JUSTICE (LP) 22

JUDIE TZUKE
(see also Tzuke & Paxo, Zookie)
78 Rocket ROKN 541 For You/Sukarita 5

TZUKE & PAXO
76 Good Earth GD 12 These Are The Laws/It's Only Fantasies 15

U

U BLACK
78 Hit Run HIT 621 Wicked Are To Blame/Dub (12") 20
77 Third World TWS 926 WESTBOUND THING A SWING (LP) 40

U BROWN
77 Klik KLP 9018 SATTA DREAD (LP) 30
77 Third World TWS 909 LONDON ROCK (LP) 30
78 Live & Love LALP 002 REVELATION TIME (LP) 30

UBX
80 Crazy Plane SP 002 Crazy Today/Mister Fix It (p/s) 150

U.F.O.
(see also Michael Schenker Group)
70 Beacon BEA 161 Shake It About/Evil 30
70 Beacon BEA 165 Come Away Melinda/Unidentified Flying Object 25
70 Beacon BEA 172 Boogie For George/Treacle People (with postcard) 30
70 Beacon BEA 172 Boogie For George/Treacle People 20
71 Beacon BEA 181 Prince Kajuku/The Coming Of Prince Kajuku 20
73 Chrysalis CHS 2024 Give Her The Gun/Sweet Little Thing (unreleased in U.K.) 0
74 Chrysalis CHS 2040 Doctor Doctor/Lipstick Traces 12
75 Chrysalis CHS 2072 Shoot Shoot/Love Lost Love (unissued) 0
77 Chrysalis CHS 2146 Alone Again Or/Electric Phase 10
77 Chrysalis CHS 2178 Gettin' Ready/Lights Out (unissued) 0
78 Chrysalis CHS 2241 Only You Can Rock Me/Cherry/Rock Bottom (p/s, red vinyl, with frisbee offer) 8
78 Chrysalis CHS 2241 Only You Can Rock Me/Cherry/Rock Bottom (p/, with frisbee offer) 6
79 Chrysalis CHS 2287 Doctor Doctor (live)/On With The Action (live)/Try Me (p/s, clear vinyl) 6
79 Chrysalis CHS 2287 Doctor Doctor (live)/On With The Action (live)/Try Me (p/s, mauve vinyl) 10
79 Chrysalis CHS 2318 Shoot Shoot (live)/Only You Can Rock Me (live)/I'm A Loser (live) (p/s, clear vinyl) 5
83 Lyntone LYN 12821 Blinded By A Lie (edit)/Diesel In The Dust (edit)/When It's Time To Rock (edit) (flexidisc with Metal Fury magazine, issue 12) 10
70 Beacon BEAS 12 U.F.O. 1 (LP) 50
72 Beacon BEAS 19 U.F.O. 2 - FLYING (ONE HOUR SPACE ROCK) (LP, with inner lyric sleeve) 70
72 Beacon BEAS 19 U.F.O. 2 - FLYING (ONE HOUR SPACE ROCK) (LP) 35
74 Chrysalis CHS 1059 PHENOMENON (LP, misprinted green label, matt sleeve) 15
77 Chrysalis CHR 1127 LIGHTS OUT (LP) 12
78 Chrysalis CDL 1182 OBSESSION (LP, with poster) 12

LESLIE UGGAME
59 Philips BBL 7370 THE EYES OF GOD (LP) 12

UGLY CUSTARD
(see also Hungry Wolf, Alan Parker, Rock Machine)
70 Kaleidoscope KAL 100 UGLY CUSTARD (LP) 120

UGLYS
(see also Steve Gibbons, Balls, Lemon Tree, Move, Trevor Burton)
65 Pye 7N 15858 Wake Up My Mind/Ugly Blues 50
65 Pye 7N 15968 It's Alright/A Friend 30
66 Pye 7N 17027 A Good Idea/A Quiet Explosion 50
66 Pye 7N 17178 End Of The Season/Can't Recall Her Name 50
67 CBS 2933 And The Squire Blew His Horn/Real Good Girl 50
69 MGM MGM 1465 I See The Light/Mary Cilento (6 demo copies only, pink/silver labels) 1500

MINT VALUE £

UK
(see also Business, Tank)

88	Chain Reaction	UK (LP)	12

U.K. BONDS

65	Polydor BM 56061	The World Is Watching Us/I Said Goodbye To The Blues	10
66	Polydor BM 56112	Anything You Do Is Alright/The Last Thing I Ever Do	20

U.K. DECAY
(see also Pneumonia)

79	Plastic PLAS 001	U.K. Decay/Car Crash/PNEUMONIA: Exhibition/Coming Attack (folded p/s)	25
80	Fresh 012	For My Country/Unwind (p/s)	8
81	Plastic PLAS 002	BLACK EP (p/s)	8
81	Plastic PLAS 002	BLACK EP (p/s, reissue with slightly different p/s)	5
81	Fresh FRESH 26	Unexpected Guest/Dresden (foldout p/s)	6
81	Fresh FRESH 33	Sexual/Twist In The Tale (poster p/s)	5
82	C. Christi CHRIST ITS 1	Rising From The Dread/Testament/Werewolf/Jerusalem Over (The White Cliffs Of Dover) (12", p/s with insert)	8
81	Fresh LP5	FOR MADMEN ONLY (LP)	18
80s	UK Decay DKLP1	FOR MADMEN ONLY (LP)	25

UK PLAYERS

82	A&M AMLH 68544	NO WAY OUT (LP)	20

U.K.s

64	HMV POP 1310	Ever Faithful, Ever True/Your Love Is All I Want	25
64	HMV POP 1357	I Will Never Let You Go/I Know	25

U.K. SUBS
(see also Urban Dogs)

78	City NIK 5	C.I.D./Live In A Car/B.I.C. (p/s, clear, red, blue, green or orange vinyl)	8
78	City NIK 5	C.I.D./Live In A Car/B.I.C. (p/s, black vinyl)	5
80	Gem GEMS 30	Teenage/Left For Dead/New York State Police (p/s, pink or orange vinyl)	5
82	Ramkup CAC 2	Party In Paris (1-sided fan club single, no p/s, 500 only)	30
83	Fall Out FALL 017	Another Typical City (p/s)	5
84	Gem FALL 12024	SPELL EP (12")	10
79	Gem GEMLP 100	ANOTHER KIND OF BLUES (LP, blue vinyl, with inner sleeve)	12
80	Gem GEMLP 106	BRAND NEW AGE (LP, clear vinyl, with insert)	12
80	Gem GEMLP 111	CRASH COURSE LIVE (LP, purple vinyl, 15,000 with export 12" [GEMEP 1])	15
80	Gem GEMLP 111	CRASH COURSE LIVE (LP)	12
80	Stidd Records MAIL 1	LIVE KICKS (LP, brown card inner sleeve, mail order only)	12
81	Gem GEMLP 112	DIMINISHED RESPONSIBILITY (LP, red vinyl with inner sleeve)	12
82	Abstract AABT 300	RECORDED '79-'81 (LP, blue vinyl with free stencil)	12
82	Abstract AABT 300	RECORDED 1979-1981 (LP, blue vinyl)	12
82	Abstract AABT 800	THE SINGLES 78-82 (LP, blue vinyl)	12
83	Scarlett FALLLP 018	FLOOD OF LIES (LP)	12

ANYAOGU UKONU & HIS AFRO-CALYPSOIANS

56	London HA-U 2019	AFRO U.S.A (LP)	30

ULLULATORS
(see also Ozric Tentacles)

89	Demi Monde DMLPP1021	FLAMING KHAOS (LP)	20

JAMES 'BLOOD' ULMER

81	Rough Trade RT 045	Are You Glad To Be In America?/T.V. Blues (p/s)	5

ULTERIOR MOTIVES

79	Motive Music MMR 1	Another Lover (p/s)	30

ULTIMATE SPINACH

68	MGM MGM-C(S) 8071	ULTIMATE SPINACH (LP)	40
68	MGM MGM-C(S) 8094	BEHOLD AND SEE (LP)	50

ULTRAFOX

71	Deram DM339	Nine By Nine/Stomping At Decca	6

ULTRAFUNK

75	Contempo CLP 509	ULTRAFUNK (LP)	15

ULTRA HIGH FREQUENCY

74	Pye International 7N 25628	We're On The Right Track/We're On The Right Track (version)	10

ULTRA VIOLENT

83	Riot City RIOT 25	CRIME FOR REVENGE (EP)	12

ULTRA VIVID SCENE

89	4AD BAD 906	Mercy Seat/Codeine/H Like In Heaven/Mercy Seat (LP Version) (12", uncut p/s [most copies die-cut])	22
89	4AD AD 908	Something To Eat/H Like In Heaven (freebie, 1,000 only)	10
90	4AD AD 0016	Special One/Kind Of Drag	7
90	4AD UVS 1	Staring At The Sun/Three Stars (12", promo only)	10
92	4AD UVS 2	Medicating Angels/Mirror To Mirror (12", promo only)	10

ULTRAVOX
(see also Tiger Lily, John Foxx, Midge Ure, Helden)

77	Island WIP 6375	Dangerous Rhythm/My Sex (initially no p/s)	5
77	Island WIP 6375	Dangerous Rhythm/My Sex (later pressing with p/s)	8
77	Island WIP 6392	Young Savage/Slip Away (p/s)	6
77	Island WIP 6404	Rockwrock/Hiroshima Mon Amour (p/s)	5
78	Island WIP 6454	Slow Motion/Dislocation (p/s)	5
78	Island 12WIP 6454	Slow Motion/Dislocation (12", p/s, translucent vinyl)	8
78	Island WIP 6459	Quiet Men/Cross Fade (p/s)	6

MINT VALUE £

78	Island 12WIP 6459	Quiet Men/Cross Fade (12", p/s, white vinyl)	8
77	Island ILPS 9449	ULTRAVOX (LP, gatefold sleeve)	15
77	Island ILPS 9505	HA! HA! HA! (LP, with 7" "Quirks"/"Modern Love" [WIP 6417] & inner sleeve)	15
78	Island ILPS 9555	SYSTEMS OF ROMANCE (LP)	15

UMPS & DUMPS

80	Topic 12TS 416	THE MOON'S IN A FIT (LP)	15

UNANIMITY

69	Clementswood CC127	Loner/All Right	40
69	Clementswood CC 12	Loner/All Right	6

UNANIMOUS DECISION

91	Reachin' REMU1204	Straight To The Point (12")	12
91	Kold Sweat KS109	Make A Living (12")	8
92	Kold Sweat KSEP211	RAP SINGS THE BLUES (EP)	15

UNAUTHORISED VERSION

69	CBS 4135	Hey Jude/Girl In A Bus Queue	20

UNCLE DOG

(see also Carol Grimes)

72	Signpost SGP 752	River Road/First Night	5
72	Signpost SG 4253	OLD HAT (LP)	200

UNCLE SAM

78	Ariola ARO 116	Oh Pretty Woman/Do It For Love	6

UNCLE 22

92	U No Dat HN 08	Wonderful Life/Love Me Once/Calling All Cars (12")	10
93	Ram RAMM 008	SPICE OF LIFE EP: 6 Million Ways To Die (DJ Hype Remix)/ 6 Million Ways To Die (Uncle 22 Mix) (12")	20
93	Pure Energy PE 003	SUPER MARIO EP: Super Mario (In Darkness)/Take You High/ Love Me Twice/Dark Forces (12")	10
93	Pure Energy PE 004	Choose One (Part 1)/Choose One (Part 2)/Crazy Kid (12", with Navigator)	15

UNCOMMUNITY

(see also McCarthy)

85	Black Dwarf BDBG 1	Brutality Of Fact/Wall Of Sleep (Soundtrack)/The Price Of Your Entry Is Sin (card sleeve, 525 only, numbered, hand-painted labels, with insert)	25

UNCOOL DANCEBAND

79	Polydor PB 30	Let Me Be Your Boyfriend/Heads I Win (no p/s)	100
81	Polydor POSP 253	Jacqueline/No. 17 (no p/s)	20

UNDEAD

82	Riot City RIOT 7	It's Corruption/Undead (p/s)	7
82	Riot City RIOT 15	VIOLENT VISIONS (EP)	10
84	City 006	KILLING OF REALITY (LP, lyric insert)	30

UNDERCOVER ELEPHANT & SECRET SQUIRREL

(see also Secret Squirrel)

92	Dance Bass DANCE BASS 03	VOLUME 3 EP (12", stamped white label)	30

UNDERDOGS

83	Riot City RIOT 26	EAST OF DACHAU (EP)	12

UNDERGROUND

(see also Madeline Bell)

69	Major Minor SMCP 5014	BEAT PARTY (LP)	30

UNDERGROUNDS

72	High Note HS 061	Skavito/Savito	12

UNDERGROUND SET

70	Pantonic PAN 6302	UNDERGROUND SET (LP, laminated front sleeve, red/black label)	70

UNDERGROUND SUNSHINE

69	Fontana TF 1049	Birthday/All I Want Is You	10

UNDERGROUND WITH STYLE

92	UAR UAR001	Lyrics Of A Gangster/Unbound Rage/Words Of Reality (EP)	35

UNDERGROUND ZERO

83	(No cat no)	GROUND ZERO (cassette EP)	10
83	(No cat no)	THE OFFICIAL BOOTLEG (cassette)	10
84	Underground UNDER 001	Seven Light Years/Canes Venatici (12")	15
84	Flicknife SHARP 023	NEVER REACH THE STARS (LP)	12

UNDERNEATH

(see also Karl Blake, Shock Headed Peters, Lemon Kittens)

86	él GPO 17T	THE IMP OF THE PERVERSE (12" EP)	8
86	él ACME 9	LUNATIC DAWN OF THE DISMANTLER (LP)	12

UNDERTAKERS

(see also 'Takers, Jackie Lomax)

63	Pye 7N 15543	Everybody Loves A Lover/Mashed Potatoes	25
63	Pye 7N 15562	What About Us/Money	25
64	Pye 7N 15607	Just A Little Bit/Stupidity	30

UNDER THE SUN

79	Redball RR 010	UNDER THE SUN (LP)	45

UNDERTONES

(see also Feargal Sharkey)

78	Good Vibrations GOT 4	TEENAGE KICKS (EP, white poster p/s)	50
78	Good Vibrations GOT 4	TEENAGE KICKS (EP, pink p/s)	70
78	Sire SIR 4007	TEENAGE KICKS (EP, reissue)	7

MINT VALUE £

79 Sire SIR 4015 Jimmy Jimmy/Mars Bars (green vinyl, printed PVC sleeve & insert) . . . 5
79 Sire SIR 4022 Here Comes The Summer/One Way Love/Top Twenty (p/s) . . . 5
79 Sire SIR 4024 You've Got My Number (Why Don't You Use It!)/Let's Talk About Girls (p/s) . . . 5
79 no label CRACKS 90 MANAGEMENT EP: Teenage Kicks/Get Over You/Jimmy Jimmy/ Here Comes The Summer (promo-only, numbered with typed insert, 250 only) . . 60
80 Sire SIR 4038 My Perfect Cousin/Hard Luck (Again) (p/s) . . . 5
81 Ardeck 12 ARDS 6 My Perfect Cousin/Hard Luck (Again)/Don't Wanna See (You Again) (12", p/s) . . . 8
81 Ardeck ARDS 9 Julie Ocean/Kiss In The Dark (p/s) . . . 5
83 Ardeck ARDS 11 The Love Parade/Like That (p/s) . . . 5
83 Ardeck 12 ARDS 11 The Love Parade/Like That/You're Welcome/Crises Of Mine/ Family Entertainment (12", p/s) . . . 10
83 Ardeck ARDS 12 Got To Have You Back/Turning Blue (p/s) . . . 8
83 Ardeck ARDS 13 Chains Of Love/Window Shopping For New Clothes (p/s) . . . 10
79 Sire SRK 6071 UNDERTONES (LP, black & white cover, without "Teenage Kicks" & "Get Over You" & different version of "Here Comes The Summer" to reissue) . 12
80 Sire SRK 6088 HYPNOTISED (LP, with cardboard mobile) . . . 12
83 Ardeck ARD 104 THE SIN OF PRIDE (LP, mispressing with different tracks: Bittersweet & "Stand So Close") . . . 40
94 Dojo DOJOLP 192 HYPNOTISED (10" LP, numbered, 500 only) . . . 12
94 Dojo DOJOLP 193 POSITIVE TOUCH (10" LP, numbered, 500 only) . . . 12
94 Dojo DOJOLP 194 THE SIN OF PRIDE (10" LP, numbered, 500 only) . . . 12

UNDERWORLD

(see also Lemon Interrupt)

92 Tomato PLUM 2001 Mother Earth/Mother Earth (FM Mix)/The Hump/ The Hump (Groove Without A Doubt Mix) (12", p/s) . . . 50
93 Boys Own BOIX 13 Mmm? Skyscraper I Love You/Mmm? Skyscraper I Love You (Telegraph 6.11.92)/Mmm? Skyscraper I Love You (Jam Scraper) (12", p/s) . . . 20
93 Boys Own BOIXCD 13 Mmm? Skyscraper I Love You/Mmm? Skyscraper I Love You (Telegraph 6.11.92)/Mmm? Skyscraper I Love You (Jam Scraper) (CD) . . . 20
93 Boys Own Collect 002 Rez/Cowgirl (12", company sleeve) . . . 10
93 Boys Own Collect 002P Rez/Cowgirl (12", glossy pink sleeve, pink vinyl, white label) . . . 20
93 Junior Boy's Own JBOLP1 DUBNOBASSWITHMYHEADMAN (2-LP) . . . 15
96 Junior Boy's Own LOC 187 SECOND TOUGHEST IN THE INFANTS (2-LP, gatefold) . . . 15

UNDISPUTED TRUTH

71 Tamla Motown TMG 776 Save My Love For A Rainy Day/Since I Lost You . . . 10
71 Parlophone TMG 776 Save My Love For A Rainy Day/Since I Lost You (mispress on Parlophone) . . . 50
71 Tamla Motown TMG 789 Smiling Faces Sometimes/You Got The Love I Need . . . 10
72 Tamla Motown TMG 818 Superstar/Ain't No Sun Since You've Been Gone . . . 10
74 Tamla Motown TMG 897 Help Yourself/What It Is . . . 8
76 Warner Bros K 16804 You + Me = Love Parts 1 & 2 . . . 8
76 Warner Bros K 16804 You + Me = Love Parts 1 & 2 (12") . . . 10
72 Tamla Motown STMA 8004 FACE TO FACE WITH THE TRUTH (LP) . . . 15
72 Tamla Motown STML 11197 THE UNDISPUTED TRUTH (LP) . . . 20
73 Tamla Motown STML 11240 THE LAW OF THE LAND (LP) . . . 15
75 Tamla Motown STML 11277 DOWN TO EARTH (LP) . . . 15
75 Tamla Motown STMA 8023 COSMIC TRUTH (LP) . . . 15
75 Tamla Motown STML 12009 HIGHER THAN HIGH (LP) . . . 12

UNDIVIDED ATTENTION

99 Hairy Parents no matrix A Change To The Scheduled Programme/Missed Treatment (12") . . . 15

UNEXPLORED BEATS

(see also Black Dog)

95 Unexplored Beats UXB 001 Skool Beats/Inner Life (12") . . . 30

UNFORGETTABLES

75 Angen ANG 108 Many A Call/Chosen Dub . . . 8

UNICORN

70 Hollick & Taylor HT 1258 Going Home/Another World . . . 250

UNICORN

71 Transatlantic BIG 138 P.F. Sloan/Going Back Home . . . 6
72 Transatlantic BIG 509 Cosmic Kid/All We Really Want To Do . . . 6
71 Transatlantic TRA 238 UPHILL ALL THE WAY (LP, gatefold, plastic inner) . . . 35
74 Charisma CAS 1092 BLUE PINE TREES (LP, small 'Mad Hatter' logo) . . . 12
76 Harvest SHSP 4054 TOO MANY CROOKS (LP, inner sleeve, EMI logo on label) . . . 15

UNIFICS

68 London HLR 10231 Court Of Love/Which One Should I Choose . . . 15

UNION EXPRESS

73 Decca F 13408 Do You Love Me/Alligator Fix . . . 12
71 Decca F 13230 Ring A Ring A Rosies/Emily Knows . . . 10

UNION GAP

(see under Gary Puckett & Union Gap)

UNIQUES

(see also Pioneers)

72 Trojan TR 7852 Mother And Child Reunion/Corner Hop . . . 5
72 Trojan TR 7866 Lonely For Your Love/LIONS DEN: Chick-A-Bow . . . 5

UNIQUES

80 Charly CTD 121 You Don't Miss Your Water/It's All Over Now/All These Things . . . 5

UNIQUES (featuring Joe Stampley) (U.S.)

65 Pye International 7N 25303 Not Too Long Ago/Fast Way Of Living . . . 40
65 Pye International 7N 25303 Not Too Long Ago/Fast Way Of Living (DJ copy) . . . 80
66 Pye Intl. NPL 28094 UNIQUELY YOURS (LP) . . . 120

UNIQUES (Jamaica)

(see also Slim Smith, Melodians, Lloyd Charmers, Tommy McCook)

67 Collins Downbeat CR 002 Dry The Water/I'm A Fool For You . . . 40

MINT VALUE £

67	Island WI 3070	People Rock Steady/I'm Trying To Find A Home (credited to Roy Shirley)	60
67	Island WI 3084	Gypsy Woman/KEN ROSS: Wall Flower	70
67	Island WI 3086	Let Me Go Girl/SOULETTES: Dum Dum	30
68	Island WI 3087	Never Let Me Go/HENRY III: Won't Go Away	25
68	Island WI 3106	Speak No Evil/GLEN ADAMS: That New Girl	25
68	Island WI 3107	Lesson Of Love/DELROY WILSON: Til I Die	25
68	Island WI 3114	Build My World Around You/LLOYD CLARKE: I'll Never Change	70
68	Island WI 3117	Give Me Some More Of Your Loving/VAL BENNETT: Lovell's Special	35
68	Island WI 3122	My Conversation/SLIM SMITH: Love One Another	25
68	Island WI 3123	The Beatitude/KEITH BLAKE: Time On The River (actually "Time & The River")	40
68	Island WI 3145	Girl Of My Dreams/LESTER STERLING: Tribute To King Scratch	75
68	Trojan TR 619	Watch This Sound/Out Of Love	25
68	Trojan TR 645	A-Yuh/Just A Mirage	25
68	Blue Cat BS 126	Girls Like Dirt/GLEN ADAMS: She Is Leaving	40
69	Gas GAS 117	Too Proud To Beg/Love And Devotion	12
69	Nu Beat NB 034	Crimson And Clover/What A Situation	10
69	Nu Beat NB 037	I'll Make You Love Me/Lover's Prayer	30
69	Unity UN 527	The Beatitude/My Conversation	12
69	Trojan TRL 15	ABSOLUTELY THE UNIQUES (LP)	150

UNIT 4 + 2

(see also Roulettes, Tom Sawyer, Capability Brown, Argent)

64	Decca F 11821	The Green Fields/Swing Down Chariot	15
64	Decca F 11994	Sorrow And Pain/The Lonely Valley	12
65	Decca F 12071	Concrete And Clay/When I Fall In Love	6
65	Decca F 12144	(You've) Never Been In Love Like This Before/Tell Somebody You Know	8
65	Decca F 12211	Hark/Stop Wasting Your Time	7
65	Decca F 12299	You've Got To Be Cruel To Be Kind/I Won't Let You Down	7
66	Decca F 12333	Baby Never Say Goodbye/Rainy Day	12
66	Decca F 12398	For A Moment/Fables	12
66	Decca F 12509	I Was Only Playing Games/I've Seen The Light	10
67	Fontana TF 834	Too Fast, Too Slow/Booby Trap	12
67	Fontana TF 840	Butterfly/A Place To Go	15
67	Fontana TF 891	Loving Takes A Little Understanding/Would You Believe What I Say? (as Unit)	120
68	Fontana TF 931	You Ain't Goin' Nowhere/So You Want To Be A Blues Player	15
69	Fontana TF 990	I Will/3.30	40
65	Decca DFE 8619	UNIT 4 + 2 (EP)	60
65	Decca LK 4697	UNIT 4 + 2 - 1st ALBUM (LP)	50
69	Fontana SFL 13123	UNIT 4 + 2 (LP)	50
76	Decca REM 6	REMEMBERING (LP)	15

UNITED SONS OF AMERICA

71	Mercury 6338 036	GREETINGS FROM THE U.S. OF A. (LP)	18

UNITED SOUNDS OF LONDON

94	USL USL 6	Making Love/Making Dub (12")	15

UNITED STATES DOUBLE QUARTET

(see also Tokens, Kirby Stone 4)

67	Stateside SS 590	Life Is Groovy/Split	20
67	BT Puppy BTS 45524	Life Is Groovy/Split (reissue)	15

UNITED STATES OF AMERICA

68	CBS 3745	Garden Of Earthly Delights/Love Song For The Dead Che	16
68	CBS (S) 63340	UNITED STATES OF AMERICA (LP, mono/stereo)	50

UNITED STATES OF EXISTENCE

87	Bam Caruso OPRA 081	Gone/PAUL ROLAND: Madam Guillotine (jukebox issue, company sleeve)	5

UNITY ALL STARS

75	Nice N 001	Africa/BIG DREAD & UNITY ALL STARS: Africa Is Our Home	35

UNIVERSAL ENERGY

77	Harvest HAR 5138	Universal Energy/Christmas For Space	6

UNIVERSAL INDICATOR

(see also Kosmik Kommando)

92	Rephlex TB-303	1-BLUE (12")	25
92	Rephlex TR-606	2-RED (12")	25
93	Rephlex MC-202	3-YELLOW (12")	20
95	Rephlex SH-101	4-GREEN (7", 10" + 12" in bag, all green vinyl)	40

UNIVERSALS

(see also Chris Lamb & Universals, Gidian, Lace, Gary Walker & Rain, Plastic Penny)

67	Page One POF 032	I Can't Find You/Hey You	140
67	Page One POF 049	Green Veined Orchid/While The Cat's Away	35

U.N.K.L.E.

(see also DJ Shadow)

97	Mo' Wax MW 069L	Berry Meditation (mixes) (12", clear etched vinyl promo, sealed poly sleeve)	30
97	Mo' Wax MW 069L	Berry Meditation (mixes) (12", clear etched vinyl promo, unsealed poly sleeve)	20
99	Mo' Wax MW 108CD 1	Be There/(Underdog Mixes) (CD, 1 of 2-CD set, card sleeve)	8
99	Mo' Wax MW 108CD 2	Be There/Knock/Rabbit In Your Headlights (CD, 2 of 2-CD set, card sleeve)	12
95	Mo' Wax MW 028	THE TIME HAS COME EP (2 x 12" EP, picture disc)	15
95	Mo' Wax MW 028	THE TIME HAS COME EP (2 x 12" EP, black vinyl)	20
94	Mo' Wax MWCD 028	THE TIME HAS COME EP (CD, picture disc, stickered card sleeve)	8
98	Mo' Wax MW 085DJ	PSYENCE FICTION SURVIVAL KIT (promo, 12" in pop-up gatefold p/s, 5" vinyl single in envelope, bag of stickers, press release, all in box mailer, 700 only)	35
98	Mo' Wax MW 035CDX	PSYENCE FICTION (CD, gatefold card sleeve)	20

UNKNOWN ARTIST

57	Woodbine Cigarettes	Big Beat (78, same track on both sides)	15
50s	Capstan Cigarettes	Capstan Go (1-sided flexi 78, promo)	15
50s	Capstan Cigarettes	Cha Cha (1-sided 78, promo)	15

		MINT VALUE £
50s Strand Cigarettes	You're Never Alone With A Strand (78, p/s, same track on both sides)	35
66 Major MAJ 1	Roarin' 'N' Scorin'/The Toast Of Merseyside (p/s)	25

UNKNOWNS

66 London HLU 10082	Melody For An Unknown Girl/Peith's Song	7

UNLEASHED

03 Century Media 77544-0	...AND WE SHALL TRIUMPH IN VICTORY (Numbered box set with 6 picture discs LPs and booklet, 2000 only)	75

UNSEEN TERROR

89 Strange Fruit SFPS 069	PEEL SESSIONS (12")	8

UNTAMED

(see also Lindsay Muir's Untamed)

64 Decca F 12045	So Long/Just Wait	60
65 Parlophone R 5258	Once Upon A Time/I'm Asking You	100
65 Stateside SS 431	I'll Go Crazy/My Baby Is Gone	60
66 Planet PLF 103	It's Not True/Gimme Gimme Some Shade	100

UNTAMED

88 Real World RWR 004	Next Please/Black Heart (p/s, with insert)	5

UNTAMED YOUTH

79 Hardcore HAR 001	Untamed Youth/Runnin' Wild (p/s, 1,000 only)	15

UNTOUCHABLES

80 Fried Egg EGG 2	Keep On Walking/Keep Your Distance (p/s)	5

UNTOUCHABLES (Jamaica)

(see also Inspirations, Dave Barker, Leroy Reid)

68 Blue Cat BS 137	Prisoner In Love/EDWARD RAPHAEL: True Love	30
68 Trojan TR 613	Tighten Up/ROY SHIRLEY: Good Ambition	30
70 Upsetter US 345	Same Thing All Over/UPSETTERS: It's Over	20
70 Upsetter US 350	Knock On Wood/UPSETTERS: Tight Spot	30
71 Bullet BU 460	Can't Reach You/CARL DAWKINS: Natural Woman	10
73 Bread BR 1113	Pay For The Wicked/Pay For The Wicked - Version (actually titled "Pray For The Wicked')	10
79 Sagittarius SUS 10	Help Us Jah/Sea Of Love (12")	20

UNWANTED

(see also Psychedelic Furs)

77 Raw RAW 6	Withdrawal/1978/Bleak Outlook (p/s)	40
77 Raw RAWT 6	Withdrawal/1978/Bleak Outlook (12", reissue)	20
78 Raw RAW 15	Secret Police/These Boots Are Made For Walking (p/s)	20
78 Raw RAW 30	Memory Man/Guns Of Love (unissued)	0
85 Delorian No One	SECRET PAST (LP)	15

UPBEATS

58 London HLU 8688	Just Like In The Movies/My Foolish Heart	25
58 London HLU 8688	Just Like In The Movies/My Foolish Heart (78)	15
59 Pye International 7N 25016	You're The One I Care For/Keep Cool Crazy Heart	15
59 Pye International 7N 25028	Teenie Weenie Bikini/Satin Shoes	15
59 Pye International 7N 25028	Teenie Weenie Bikini/Satin Shoes (78)	12

PHIL UPCHURCH COMBO

61 HMV POP 899	You Can't Sit Down Parts 1 & 2	35
66 Sue WI 4005	You Can't Sit Down Parts 1 & 2 (reissue)	25
66 Sue WI 4017	Nothing But Soul/Evad	40
72 Blue Thumb ILPS 9219	DARKNESS, DARKNESS (LP)	20

ROBERT UPCHURCH

74 Phil. Intl. PIR 2652	The Devil Made Me Do It/Glad You're Mine	15
70s Phil. Intl 82168 4ZP 2000	The Devil Made Me Do It/You're The Reason Why (12")	20

UPCOMING WILLOWS

(see also Shenley Duffas)

65 Island WI 182	Jonestown Special/SHENLEY DUFFAS: La La La	40
65 Island WI 184	Red China/SHENLEY DUFFAS: You Are Mine	40

UPFRONT RUDIES

92 Krazy Fly Recz RUDIE 9	REAL SKILLS (EP)	18

UPP

(see also Clark-Hutchinson)

75 Epic EPC 80625	UPP (LP)	15
76 CBS EPC 81322	THIS WAY (LP)	12

UPROAR

82 Beat The System RAW 1	Rebel Youth/No More War/Fallen Angel/Victims (p/s)	12
83 Lightbeat RAW 2	DIE FOR ME (EP)	12
83 Volume VOL 9	NOTHING CAN STOP YOU (EP)	8
80s Beat The System BTSLP 1	AND THE LORD SAID LET THERE BE UPROAR (LP)	30

UPSETTERS

(see also Ossie & Upsetters, Dave Barker)

65 Island WI 223	Country Girl/Strange Country (both sides actually by Ossie & Upsetters)	35
65 Rio R 70	Walk Down The Aisle/So Bad	20
66 Doctor Bird DB 1034	Wildcat/I Love You So	40

UPSETTERS

(see also Lee Perry, Ossie & Upsetters, Hippy Boys, Bob Marley/Wailers, Family Man, Tommy McCook, Max Romeo, Melodians, Lord Creator, Dennis Alcapone)

69 Duke DU 11	Eight For Eight/Stand By Me (B-side actually by Inspirations)	40
69 Camel CA 13	Taste Of Killing/My Mob	40
69 Punch PH 18	Return Of The Ugly/I've Caught You	25

MINT VALUE £

69	Punch PH 19	Dry Acid/REGGAE BOYS: Selassie	50
69	Punch PH 21	Clint Eastwood/Lennox Mood	12
69	Upsetter US 300	Eight For Eight/You Know What I Mean (B-side actually by Inspirations)	15
69	Upsetter UP 301	Return Of Django/Dollar In The Teeth	12
69	Upsetter US 303	Ten To Twelve/LEE PERRY: People Funny Fi True	30
69	Upsetter US 305	Farmers In The Den/BUSTY BROWN : To Love Somebody	30
69	Upsetter US 307	Night Doctor/TERMITES: I'll Be Waiting	20
69	Upsetter US 309	Kiddyo/Endlessly (both sides actually by Silvertones)	18
69	Upsetter US 310	A Dangerous Man From MI5/WEST INDIANS: Oh Lord	18
69	Upsetter US 313	Live Injection/BLEECHERS: Everything For Fun	10
69	Upsetter US 315	Cold Sweat/Pound Get A Blow (B-side actually by Bleechers)	30
70	Upsetter US 317	Vampire/BLEECHERS: Check Him Out	25
70	Upsetter US 318	Soulful I/MILTON HENRY: Bread And Butter	15
70	Upsetter US 321	Drugs And Poison/Stranger On The Shore	18
70	Upsetter US 325	Kill Them All/Soul Walk	18
70	Upsetter US 326	Bronco/One More	22
70	Upsetter US 332	Na Na Hey Hey/Pick Folk Kinkyest	20
70	Upsetter US 333	Granny Show/Version	20
70	Upsetter US 334	Fire Fire/Jumper	20
70	Upsetter US 335	The Pillow/Grooving	20
70	Upsetter US 336	Self Control/The Pill	22
70	Upsetter US 338	Fresh Up/Toothaches	20
70	Upsetter US 342	Dreamland/BOB MARLEY: Version Of Cup	45
70	Upsetter US 343	Sipreano/Ferry Boat	20
70	Upsetter US 346	Bigger Joke/Return Of The Vampire	15
70	Upsetter US 349	Upsetting Station (actually plays "Did Your Grave" by Bob Marley & Wailers)/ UPSETTERS: Justice (Instrumental)	40
70	Upsetter US 352	Heart And Soul/Zig Zag	18
70	Spinning Wheel SW 100	Haunted House/Double Wheel	75
70	Spinning Wheel SW 101	The Miser/CHUCK JUNIOR: Do It Madly	25
70	Spinning Wheel SW 102	The Chokin' Kind/CHUCK JUNIOR: Penny Wise	25
70	Spinning Wheel SW 103	Land Of Kinks/O'NEIL HALL: This Man	25
70	Trojan TR 7748	Family Man/Mellow Mood	12
70	Trojan TR 7749	Capo/Mama Look	15
70	Punch PH 27	The Result/Feel The Spirit	40
71	Bullet BU 461	All Combine Parts 1 & 2	10
71	Bullet BU 499	Beat Down Babylon/JUNIOR BYLES: Version	18
71	Upsetter US 353	Illusion/Big John Wayne (as Upsetters & King Teddy)	18
71	Upsetter US 361	Capasetic (actually "Copasetic" by Lord Comic)/All Africans (actually "Don't Cross The Nation" by Little Roy)	20
71	Upsetter US 365	Earthquake/JUNIOR BYLES: Palace Called Africa	20
71	Upsetter US 370	Dark Moon/DAVID ISAACS: You'll Be Sorry	15
72	Upsetter US 385	French Connection/Version	15
72	Upsetter US 387	Festival Da Da/JUNIOR BYLES: Version	18
72	Upsetter US 393	Crummy People/BIG YOUTH: Moving - Version	15
72	Upsetter US 394	Water Pump Parts 1 & 2	15
72	Randy's RAN 523	Nebuchadnezzer/JUNIOR BYLES: King Of Babylon	18
72	Punch PH 109	Hail To Power/JUNIOR BYLES: Pharaoh Hiding	18
73	Upsetter US 396	Puss Sea Hole/WINSTON GROOVY: Want To Be Loved	15
73	Upsetter US 397	Jungle Lion/Freak Out Skank	20
73	Upsetter US 398	Cow Thief Skank (with Charlie Ace)/7 3/4 Skank	20
73	Downtown DT 499	Black Ipa/Ipa Skank	18
73	Downtown DT 506	Sunshine Showdown/Sunshine Version	18
73	Downtown DT 512	Tighten Up Skank/Mid-East Rock	15
73	Downtown DT 513	Sucky Skank/Yucky Skank	18
74	Count Shelly CS 052	San-San/OSBOURNE GRAHAM: Baby Don't Go	8
74	Dip DL 5031	Enter The Dragon/JOY WHITE: Lady Lady	12
74	Dip DL 5032	Rebels Train/Rebels Dub	8
75	Dip DL 5054	Cane River Rock/Riverside Rock	12
75	Dip DL 5056	I Man Free/King Burnett: Version	12
75	Dip DL 5073	Key Card/Domino Game	8
75	Angen ANG 107	Stay Dread/Kingdom Of Dub	20
75	Attack ATT 8090	Kiss Me Neck/Da Ba Day	15
78	Island IPR 2010	Close Together/Dreadlocks In The Moonlight (12" as UPSETTERS REVIEW featuring JUNIOR MURVIN)	20
69	Pama Special PSP 1014	CLINT EASTWOOD (LP)	75
69	Trojan TRL 19	THE RETURN OF DJANGO (LP, orange/white label)	50
69	Trojan TTL 13	THE UPSETTER (LP)	30
70	Trojan TTL 28	SCRATCH THE UPSETTER AGAIN (LP)	12
70	Trojan TBL 119	THE GOOD, THE BAD AND THE UPSETTERS (LP)	30
70	Trojan TBL 125	EASTWOOD RIDES AGAIN (LP)	35
70	Pama SECO 24	THE MANY MOODS OF THE UPSETTERS (LP)	65
74	Trojan TRLS 70	DOUBLE SEVEN (LP)	35
75	DIP DLPD 6002	RETURN OF THE WAX (LP, white-label only, plain sleeve)	45
76	Island ILPS 9417	SUPER APE (LP)	30
83	Pama PTLP 1026	BEST OF THE UPSETTERS VOL. 2 (LP)	30
90	Trojan PERRY 3	BUILD THE ARK (3-LP box set)	30

UPSETTING BROTHERS

71	Supreme SUP 229	Not You Baby/DREAD LOCK ALL-STARS: Baby (Version)	12

UPTOWNERS

64	London HLU 9877	If'n/Search Is Over	15

URBAN CLEARWAY

70	Torpedo TOR 21	Open Up Wide Parts 1 & 2	6

URBAN DISTURBANCE

79	Rok ROK V/VI	Wild Boys In Cortinas/V.I.P.s: Can't Let You Go (die-cut sleeve)	25

MINT VALUE £

URBAN DOGS
(see Hanoi Rocks, U.K. Subs, Vibrators)

82	Fallout FALL 008	New Barbarians/Speed Kills/Cocaine (p/s)	5
82	Fallout FALL 011	Limo Life/Warhead (p/s)	5
88	Fallout FALL LP 12	URBAN DOGS (LP)	12

URBAN RHYME SQUAD

91	Atomic WNRX 766	History Rewritten (12")	15

URBAN SHAKEDOWN

82	Respond RESP5	Wolves/Rap The Wolf	10

URCHIN
(see also A.S.A.P., Iron Maiden)

77	DJM DJS 10776	Black Leather Fantasy/Rock & Roll Woman (promo p/s)	325
78	DJM DJS 10850	She's A Roller/Long Time No Woman (promo p/s)	325

URCHINS

66	Polydor BM 56145	I Made Her That Way/Twas On A Night Like This	10

URIAH HEEP
(see also Gods, Head Machine, Natural Gas, Spice, King Crimson, John Lawton, Grand Prix, Stratus)

71	Bronze WIP 6111	Look At Yourself/Simon The Bullet Freak	7
72	Bronze WIP 6126	The Wizard/Gypsy	6
72	Bronze WIP 6140	Easy Livin'/Why	6
73	Bronze BRO 7	Stealin'/Sunshine	6
74	Bronze BRO 10	Something Or Nothing/What Can I Do	5
75	Bronze BRO 17	Prima Donna/Shout It Out	5
76	Bronze BRO 27	One Way Or Another/Misty Eyes	5
76	Bronze BRODJ 1	One Way Or Another/Misty Eyes (promo only p/s, 750 copies)	20
77	Bronze BRO 37	Wise Man/Crime Of Passion	5
77	Bronze BRO 47	Free Me/Masquerade (p/s)	6
78	Bronze BRO 62	Come Back To Me/Cheater	5
83	Bronze BROP 166	Lonely Nights/Weekend Warriors (picture disc)	8
83	Bronze BROG 168	Stay On Top/Playing For Time//Gypsy/Easy Livin'/Sweet Lorraine/ Stealin' (double pack, gatefold p/s)	7
85	Portrait WA 6103	Rockerama/Back Stage Girl (shaped picture disc)	10
88	Legacy LGYT 65	Easy Livin' (live)/Corina (live)/Gypsy (live) (12", red vinyl)	8
88	Castle Comms. CD3-16	URIAH HEEP (CD EP, 5,000 only)	10
70	Vertigo 6360 006	VERY 'EAVY... VERY 'UMBLE (LP, gatefold sleeve, large swirl label)	150
71	Vertigo 6360 028	SALISBURY (LP, gatefold sleeve, large swirl label)	150
71	Bronze ILPS 9142	VERY 'EAVY... VERY 'UMBLE (LP, reissue)	15
71	Bronze ILPS 9152	SALISBURY (LP, reissue)	15
71	Bronze ILPS 9169	LOOK AT YOURSELF (LP, 'mirror' sleeve)	50
72	Bronze ILPS 9193	DEMONS AND WIZARDS (LP, gatefold)	20
72	Bronze ILPS 9213	THE MAGICIANS'S BIRTHDAY (LP, with inner sleeve)	20
73	Bronze ILPS 9245	SWEET FREEDON (LP, gatefold)	25
73	Bronze ISLD 1	LIVE (2-LP, gatefold sleeve with booklet)	20
89	Legacy LLP 120	RAGING SILENCE (LP, picture disc)	12
95	HTD LP 33	SEA OF LIGHT (LP, with inner)	15

URUSEI YATSURA

95	Modern Ind. MIR 001	Pampered Adolescent/BLISTERS: A Dull Thought In Itself (burgundy vinyl, p/s, 500 only)	20
95	Ché CHÉ 38	Siamese/Lo-Fi (orange & grey vinyl, p/s)	8
95	Love Train PUBE 08	Kernel/Teendream (p/s, 1,000 only)	10

US
(see also David Essex, Randells)

70s	Jeff Wayne Music SD 015	You're OK With Us/Tomorrow (p/s, promo for Johnson Wax)	10

US

67	Polydor 56179	Barefoot In The Park/Four's A Crowd	8

U.S. DOUBLE QUARTET
(see United States Double Quartet)

US FOLK

65	Eyemark EMS 1001	Funny Old World/Dives	8

U.S. SKY
(see under Sky)

U.S. T-BONES

65	Liberty LIB 55836	No Matter What Shape/Feelin' Fine	12
66	Liberty LIB 55867	Sippin'n'Chippin'/Moment Of Softness	15
66	Liberty LIB 55951	The Proper Thing To Do/Tee-Hee-Hee	15

USELESS UNICORN

74	Horny HORN 11	RUBBER HORN (LP, gatefold sleeve, with pop-up horn)	15

USERS

77	Raw RAW 1	Sick Of You/(I'm) In Love With Today (p/s, numbered on rear)	15
77	Raw RAW 1	Sick Of You/(I'm) In Love With Today (p/s)	10
77	Raw RAWT 1	Sick Of You/(I'm) In Love With Today (12", no p/s)	15
78	Warped WARP 1	Warped 45: Kicks In Style/Dead On Arrival (p/s, 5,000 only, numbered sleeve, some un-numbered)	18

PETER USTINOV
(see also Peter Sellers)

53	Parlophone MSP 6012	Mock Mozart (with Anthony Hopkins, Harpsichord)/Phoney Folk-Lore	8

UTOMICA

93	Pro-One PRONE 9T	Rok A Bye/Rok A Bye (12", stamped or hand-written white label)	50
93	Pro-One PRONE 11T	Pumpkin/Pumpkin (12", white stamped label)	15

MINT VALUE £

UTOPIA (Germany)

(see also Amon Duull)

73	United Artists UAG 29438	UTOPIA (LP)	20

UTOPIA (U.S.)

82	Epic XPS 166	Infrared And Ultra Violet/Forgotten But Not Gone/Private Heaven/Princess Of The Universe/Chapter And Verse (EP)	12
77	Bearsville K 55514	RA (LP, with lyric inner & pyramid insert)	12
82	Epic EPC 25207	UTOPIA (LP, with free 5-track EP)	20

U2

(see also Bono & Gavin Friday, The Edge, Adam Clayton & Larry Mullen, Passengers)

SINGLES: IRISH PRESSINGS

79	CBS 7951	U2: THREE (Out Of Control/Stories For The Boys/Boy-Girl) (p/s, black vinyl) (CBS 'Sunburst Label' with UK TM NoB81 809) on label (First Pressing))	150
79	CBS 7951	U2: THREE (Out Of Control/Stories For The Boys/Boy-Girl) (p/s, black vinyl)	50
80	CBS 7951	U2: THREE (Out Of Control/Stories For The Boys/Boy-Girl) (p/s, white vinyl)	300
80	CBS 7951	U2: THREE (Out Of Control/Stories For The Boys/Boy-Girl) (p/s, orange vinyl)	150
80	CBS 7951	U2: THREE (Out Of Control/Stories For The Boys/Boy-Girl) (p/s, yellow vinyl)	100
80	CBS 7951	U2: THREE (Out Of Control/Stories For The Boys/Boy-Girl) (p/s, brown vinyl mispressing, fewer than 50 copies exist)	1000
81	CBS 12-7951	U2: THREE (12" EP, with numbered sticker, orange CBS sleeve, 1,000 only)	1500
81	CBS 12-7951	U2: THREE (12" EP, reissue, die-cut CBS sleeve)	60
81	CBS 12-7951	U2: THREE (12" EP, 2nd reissue, plain black sleeve, slightly different labels)	40
85	CBS 40-7951	U2: THREE (cassette, reissue)	50
80	CBS 8306	Another Day/Twilight (Demo Version) (p/s, yellow vinyl)	80
80	CBS 8306	Another Day/Twilight (Demo Version) (p/s, orange vinyl)	150
80	CBS 8306	Another Day/Twilight (Demo Version) (p/s, white vinyl)	350
80	CBS 8306	Another Day/Twilight (Demo Version) (p/s, black vinyl, with postcard designed by Bono)	200
80	CBS 8306	Another Day/Twilight (Demo Version) (p/s, black vinyl, without postcard designed by Bono)	40
80	CBS 8687	11 O'Clock Tick Tock/Touch (p/s, yellow vinyl)	60
80	CBS 8687	11 O'Clock Tick Tock/Touch (p/s, orange vinyl)	150
80	CBS 9065	I Will Follow/Boy-Girl (live) (p/s, yellow vinyl)	50
80	CBS 9065	I Will Follow/Boy-Girl (live) (p/s, orange vinyl)	100
80	CBS 9065	I Will Follow/Boy-Girl (live) (p/s, white vinyl)	300
80	CBS 9065	I Will Follow/Boy-Girl (live) (p/s, brown vinyl, fewer than 50 copies)	1500
82	CBS PAC 1	4 U2 PLAY (4 x 7", each in p/s, black vinyl)	120
82	CBS PAC 1	4 U2 PLAY (4 x 7", each in p/s, yellow vinyl)	300
82	CBS PAC 1	4 U2 PLAY (4 x 7", each in p/s, orange vinyl)	600
82	CBS PAC 1	4 U2 PLAY (4 x 7", each in p/s, white vinyl)	1000
80s	CBS PAC 2	PAC 2 (4 x 7" with p/s in plastic wallet)	60
80s	CBS PAC 3	PAC 3 (4 x 7" with p/s in plastic wallet)	50

SINGLES: UK PRESSINGS

80	Island WIP 6601	11 O'Clock Tick Tock/Touch (p/s)	25
80	Island WIP 6630	A Day Without Me/Things To Make And Do (p/s)	20
80	Island WIP 6656	I Will Follow/Boy-Girl (live) (p/s)	15
81	Island WIP 6679	Fire/J. Swallo (p/s)	6
81	Island UWIP 6679	Fire/J. Swallo//11 O'Clock Tick Tock (live)/The Ocean (live)/Cry (live)/ The Electric Co. (live) (double pack, single p/s)	10
81	Island WIP 6733	Gloria/I Will Follow (live) (p/s)	10
82	Island WIP 6770	A Celebration/Trash, Trampoline And The Party Girl (p/s)	10
83	Island UWIP 6848	New Year's Day/Treasure (Whatever Happened To Pete The Chop)// Fire (live)/I Threw A Brick Through A Window (live)/ A Day Without Me (live) (double pack, single p/s, black inners)	10
83	Island ISD 109	Two Hearts Beat As One/Endless Deep//New Year's Day (U.S.A. Remix)/ Two Hearts Beat As One (U.S.A. Remix) (p/s, double pack)	10
84	Island ISP 202	Pride (In The Name Of Love)/Boomerang 2 (Vocal) (picture disc)	20
84	Island ISD 202	Pride (In The Name Of Love)/4th Of July//Boomerang I (Instrumental)/ Boomerang 2 (Vocal) (double pack, gatefold p/s)	6
84	Island CIS 202	Pride (In The Name Of Love)/Boomerang I/4th Of July/Boomerang 2/ A Celebration (cassette)	8
84	Island 12ISX 202	Pride (In The Name Of Love)/Boomerang I/Boomerang 2/ 11 O'Clock Tick Tock/Touch (Full Length Version) (12", blue p/s)	10
85	Island ISD 220	The Unforgettable Fire/A Sort Of Homecoming (live)/Love Comes Tumbling/ Sixty Seconds In Kingdom Come/The Three Sunrises (double pack, gatefold p/s)	6
85	Island ISP 220	The Unforgettable Fire/A Sort Of Homecoming (live) (logo-shaped pic disc)	40
87	Island CID 319	With Or Without You/Luminous Times (Hold Onto Love)/ Walk To The Water (CD, gatefold card p/s)	15
87	Island 12IS 340	Where The Streets Have No Name/Race Against Time/Silver And Gold/ The Sweetest Thing (12", p/s with "Silver And Gold" lyric insert)	15
87	Island CID 340	Where The Streets Have No Name (edit)/Race Against Time/Silver And Gold/ The Sweetest Thing (CD, gatefold p/s)	15
88	Island IS 400	Desire/Hallelujah Here She Comes (non-gatefold p/s)	5
88	Island CIDP 400	Desire/Hallelujah Here She Comes/Desire (Hollywood Remix) (CD, picture disc)	8
88	Island CIDP 402	Angel Of Harlem (Remix)/A Room At The Heartbreak Hotel/Love Rescue Me (Live At "Smile Jamaica" Concert London Oct '88) (CD, picture disc)	8
88	Island CIDX 402	Angel Of Harlem (Remix)/A Room At The Heartbreak Hotel/ Love Rescue Me (live) (3" CD, long box, U.S. import with stickered U.K. matrix number)	15
88	Island U2 PK 1	THE JOSHUA TREE SINGLES (4 x 7"s in PVC wallet with 'obi' band)	40
89	Island CIDP 411	When Love Comes To Town/Dancing Barefoot/When Love Comes To Town (Live From The Kingdom Mix) (with BB King)/God Part II (The Hard Metal Dance Mix) (CD picture disc)	15
89	Island CIDX 411	When Love Comes To Town/Dancing Barefoot/When Love Comes To Town (Live From The Kingdom Mix) (with Little Richard)/God Part II (The Hard Metal (as U2 with B.B. King) (3" CD, long box U.S. Import with stickered U.K. Matrix no)	15

			MINT VALUE £
89	Island ISB 422	All I Want Is You (Edit)/Unchained Melody (in numbered tin box)	15
89	Island 12 ISB 422	All I Want Is You (Full Version)/Unchained Melody/Everlasting Love (12", p/s, box set with 4 prints)	15
89	Island CIDP 422	All I Want Is You (4.14)/Unchained Melody/Everlasting Love/ All I Want Is You (Full Version) (CD, picture disc)	15
91	Island 12IS 509	Mysterious Ways (4.04)/(Solar Plexus Extended Club Mix 7.01)/ (Apollo 440 Magic Hour Remix)/(Tabla Motown Remix)/ (Solar Plexus Club Mix) (12" p/s, withdrawn)	15
92	Island 12IS 525	Even Better Than The Real Thing/Salomé/Where Did It All Go Wrong/ Lady With The Spinning Head (UVI) (Extended Dance Mix) (12" with giant 'Zoo TV' poster)	20
92	Island IS 550	Who's Gonna Ride Your Wild Horses (Temple Bar Edit)/Paint It Black (p/s)	5
92	Island CIDX 550	Who's Gonna Ride Your Wild Horses (Temple Bar Edit)/Paint It Black/Salomé (Zooromancer Remix)/Can't Help Falling In Love (Triple Peaks Remix) (CD, picture disc, tri-fold digipak with 4 prints)	15
95	Atlantic A 7131	Hold Me, Thrill Me, Kiss Me, Kill Me/ELLIOTT GOLDENTHAL: Themes From Batman Forever (p/s, red vinyl, black vinyl copies have correct/ incorrect B side credits)	5
95	Atlantic A 7131	Hold Me, Thrill Me, Kiss Me, Kill Me/ELLIOTT GOLDENTHAL: Themes From Batman Forever (p/s, red vinyl, B-side miscredited to U2)	8
97	Island 12IST649	Discothèque (Howie B Hairy B Mix)/Discothèque (Hexidecimal Mix)/ Discothèque (DM Deep Extended Club Mix)/Discothèque (DM Deep Beats Mix)/Discotheque (DM Tec Radio Mix)/ Discotheque (DM Deep Instrumental Mix)/Discotheque (Single Version)/Discotheque (David	12
97	Island CID 649	Discothèque/Holy Joe (Garage Mix)/Holy Joe (Guilty Mix) (CD, jewel case, withdrawn)	10
97	Island 12IS 684	Mofo (Mother's Mix)/Mofo (House Flavour Mix)/Mofo (Romin Mix)/Mofo (Phunk Force Mix)/Mofo (Black Hole Dub) (12", die-cut p/s, 2,000 only)	10

PROMOS - SINGLES

80	Island WIP 6601	11 O'Clock Tick Tock/Touch (p/s, 'A' label)	40
80	Island WIP 6630	A Day Without Me/Things To Make And Do (p/s, 'A' label)	40
80	Island WIP 6656 DJ	I Will Follow (Special Edited DJ Version) (1-sided, company sleeve)	80
81	WIP 6679	Fire (Radio Edit) (1-sided, p/s)	70
81	WIP 6733	Gloria (Radio Edit) (1-sided, p/s)	60
84	Island U2 2	Wire/Bad/The Unforgettable Fire (12", black die-cut sleeve)	70
87	Island ISJ 319	With Or Without You/Walk To The Water (jukebox issue, large centre hole)	10
87	Island ISJ 328	I Still Haven't Found What I'm Looking For/Spanish Eyes (jukebox issue, solid centre)	20
87	Island ISJ 328	I Still Haven't Found What I'm Looking For/Spanish Eyes (jukebox issue, large centre hole)	10
87	Island ISJB 340	Where The Streets Have No Name/Silver And Gold (jukebox issue, large centre hole)	10
88	Island 12ISX 400	Desire (9.23 Hollywood Remix) (12", 1-sided, custom black p/s, 800 only)	25
88	Island U2V 7	EXCERPTS FROM RATTLE AND HUM (In God's Country [live]/Hawkmoon 269/ Bad [live]/God Part II/With Or Without You [live]) (CD, card gatefold sleeve)	70
88	Island IS 319	With Or Without You/Luminous Times (Hold Onto Love)/Walk To The Water/ With Or Without You (Video) (CD Video, withdrawn, less than 100 copies)	350
89	Island 12 ISX 411	U2 3D DANCE MIXES: When Love Comes To Town (Live From The Kingdom Dance Mix)/God Part II (Hard Metal Dance Club Mix)/ Desire (Hollywood Remix 5.23) (12" EP p/s)	25
90	Island RHB 1	Night And Day (Twilight Remix)/Steel String Mix (12", p/s, numbered, 4,000 copies only)	50
91	Island U2-3	OCTOBER 1991: I Will Follow/Pride (In The Name Of Love)/God Part II/ Where The Streets Have No Name) (CD EP, 250 only)	400
92	Island 12IS 550DJ	Salomé (Zooromancer Remix 8.02)/Can't Help Falling In Love (Mystery Train Dub 8.20) (12", black die-cut sleeve, 1,000 only)	70
92	Island REAL 1	Even Better Than The Real Thing (The Perfecto Mix)/Even Better Than The Real Thing (Trance Mix)/Even Better Than The Real Thing (Sexy Dub Mix) (12" , black die-cut sleeve with title sticker)	10
92	Island REAL 2DJ	Even Better Than The Real Thing (The Perfecto Mix-Radio Edit) (2-sided radio promo, some with p/s)	40
92	Island REAL 2DJ	Even Better Than The Real Thing (The Perfecto Mix-Radio Edit) (2-sided radio promo, some with p/s)	15
93	Island NUMJB 1	Numb (2-sided jukebox issue, large centre hole)	10
93	Island NUMCD 1	Numb (CD, 1-track, with lyric inner, 250 only)	80
93	Island 12LEM DJ 1	Lemon (Bad Yard Club)/(Momo Beats)/(Version Dub)/(Serious Def Dub)/ (Perfecto Mix)/(Trance Mix) (12", double pack, p/s, 1,000 only, numbered with press sheets)	60
93	Island LEMCD 1	Lemon (Radio Edit) (CD, 1-track, with lyric inner)	30
95	Island 12 MELON 1	MELON (Salomé [Zooromancer Remix]/Lemon [Bad Yard Club Mix]/ Numb [The Soul Assassins Mix]/Numb [Gimme Some More Dignity Mix]) (12" EP, 800 only)	20
96	Island PRECD 1	U2 PREVIOUSLY: Lemon/Mysterious Ways/One/Desire/I Still Haven't Found What I'm Looking For (CD, card sleeve)	25
97	Island ISD(X) 649 D(J)	Discothèque (Howie B Hairy B Mix)/Discothèque (Hexidecimal Mix)// Discothèque (DM Deep Extended Club Mix)/Discothèque (DM Deep Beats Mix)/ Discotheque (DM Tec Radio Mix)/Discotheque (DM Deep Instrumental Mix)/Discotheque (Single Version)/ Discotheque (David	25
97	Island ISJB 649	Discotheque/Holy Joe (jukebox issue, large centre hole)	8
97	Island DISCO 1	Discotheque (CD- 1 track promo)	8
97	Island ISJB 658	Staring At The Sun/North And South Of The River (jukebox issue, large centre hole)	8
97	Island 12IS 658DJ	Staring At The Sun (Monster Truck Mix)/Staring At The Sun (Lab Rat Mix)/ Staring At The Sun (Sad Bastard's Mix) (12", p/s)	20

			MINT VALUE £
97	Island SUN CD 1	Staring At The Sun (Cd, 1-track promo)	10
97	Island ISJB 664	Last Night On Earth (Single Mix)/Last Night On Earth (First Night In Hell Remix) (jukebox issue, large centre hole)	10
97	Island 12IS 664DJ	Last Night On Earth (First Night In Hell Remix)/Happiness Is A Warm Gun (The Gun Mix)/Pop Muzik (Pop Mart Mix)/Happiness Is A Warm Gun (The Danny Sabre Mix)/ (12" p/s)	20
97	Island MUZIK 1	Pop Muzik (Pop Mart Mix - Radio Edit) (CD, 1-track, picture disc, jewel case, 250 only)	90
97	Island MART 1	Pop Muzik (Pop Mart Mix)/Last Night On Earth (First Night In Hell Mix) (12", plain black die cut sleeve)	70
97	Island ISJB 673	Please/Where The Streets Have No Name (live) (jukebox issue, large centre hole)	10
97	Island CIDDJ 673	Please/Please (Call Out Hook) (CD)	15
97	Island PLEASE CD 1	Please (Single Edit)/Please (Single Version) (CD, 2-track, yellow graphics on disc, jewel case)	10
97	Island ISJB 684	If God Will Send His Angels (Single Version)/Sunday Bloody Sunday (live from Sarajevo) (jukebox issue, large centre hole)	15
97	Island 12MOFO 1	Mofo (Phunk Force Mix)/Mofo (Black Hole Dub)/Mofo (Romin Remix) (12", orange label, orange & silver die-cut title sleeve)	15
97	Island 12MOFO 2	Mofo (Mother's Mix)/Mofo (House Flavor Mix) (12", pink label, pink & silver die-cut title sleeve, 250 only)	15
97	Island 12MOFO 3	Mofo (Explicit Mix) (12", 1-sided, stamped white label, plain black die-cut sleeve, 200 only)	50
97	Island MOFOCD 1	Mofo (Album Version) (CD, 1-track, card sleeve, export issue [to Mexico])	80
97	Island MOFOCD 2	Mofo (Phunk Force Mix) (CD, 1-track, jewel case, export issue [to Mexico])	60
98	Island SWEET CD 1	Sweetest Thing (CD, 1-track)	8
98	Island CIDDJ 727	Sweetest Thing/Twilight (Live)/An Cat Dubh (Live)/Stories For Boys Out Of Control (Live) (CD, die-cut sleeve)	50
00	Island GROUND CD 1	The Ground Beneath Her Feet/The Million Dollar Hotel Movie Trailer (CD-ROM, card sleeve, blue die-cut slipcase)	10
01	Island 12ISD 780	Beautiful Day (Quincy & Sonance Mix)/(The Perfecto Mix)/ (David Holmes Remix)/Elevation (The Vandit Club Mix)/(Influx Remix)/ (Escalation Mix)/Quincy & Sonance Remix) (2x12", p/s, inners)	15
00	Island 12 BEAUT 1	Beautiful Day (Quincey & Sonance Mix) (1-sided 12", in black die-cut title sleeve)	15
01	Island ISJB770	Stuck In A Moment You Can't Get Out Of/Big Girls Are Best (UK jukebox promo 7" with large centre)	10
01	Island 12 ELE 1	Elevation (Escalation Mix)/Elevation (Influx Mix) (12", red custom p/s, 250 only)	25
01	Island ELE CD 2	Elevation (Tomb Raider Mix) (1-track CD, Lara Croft sleeve, withdrawn)	20
01	Island 12 ELE 2	Elevation (Paul Vandyk Remix)/Elevation (The Vandit Club Mix) (12", blue custom p/s, 250 only, exclusive mixes)	10
02	Island CID 808	Electrical Storm (William Orbit Mix)/New York (Nice Mix)/New York (Nasty Mix)/ Bad (Live)/Where The Streets Have No Name (2-CD + DVD set in limited issue collectors' wallet, mail order only)	40
02	Island NEWCD U2 13	NEW SONGS AND MIXES FROM THE BEST OF 1990-2000 (CD sampler, black inner sleeve, silver outer sleeve)	25
03	Island HANDSCD 1	The Hands That Built America (promo only 1-track CD, card sleeve)	12
03	Island 12 Sun U2	Staring At The Sun (Brothers In Rhythm Club Mix)/Staring At The Sun (Brothers In Rhythm Ambient Mix) (12", black die-cut custom sleeve)	15
02	Island 12REMIX U2 13	U2 REMIXES FROM THE 1990S (2 x 12" sampler, black inner sleeves, silver outer sleeve)	20
04	Island U2PRO2	Vertigo (Jacknife Lee 7" mix) (7" vinyl promo, picture sleeve. Matt/gloss finish)	50
04	Island 10I5878DJ	Vertigo (Jacknife Lee 7" mix)/Vertigo (Jacknife Lee 10" mix) 10", p/s)	20
04	Island 12IS878DJ	Vertigo (Jacknife Lee 10" mix)/Vertigo (Jacknife Lee 12" mix) 12", p/s)	8
04	Island CID878/X878/V878	Vertigo (CD1, CD2 & DVD set in wallet issued by U2.Com)	50
05	Island CID886/X/V	Sometimes You Can't Make It On Your Own (CD1, CD2 & DVD set in wallet, issued by U2.com)	25
05	Island 12IS890DJ	City Of Blinding Lights (Phones P.D.A in N.Y.C remix/City of Blinding Lights (Paradise Soul Vocal Mix)/All Because Of You (Killahurtz Fly Mix) (12", p/s)	8
05	Island CID890/X/V	City Of Blinding Lights (CD1, CD2 & DVD set in wallet via U2.com)	20
05	Island CID906/X/V	All Because Of You (CD1, CD2 & DVD set in wallet in wallet via u2.com)	20

ALBUMS

80	Island ICT 9646	BOY ('1+1' cassette)	12
81	Island ICT 9680	OCTOBER ('1+1' cassette, in plastic case or 'cigarette pack' card box)	12
83	Island PILPS 9733	WAR (LP, picture disc, beware of counterfeits with ILPS cat. no.)	100
83	Island ICT 9733	WAR ('1+1' cassette)	12
85	Island CID 112	WAR (LP, pink cover lettering)	20
85	Island CID 110	BOY (CD, with title rear sleeve; no bar code)	20
85	Island CID 102	THE UNFORGETTABLE FIRE (CD, no bar code)	30
91	Island U2-8	ACHTUNG BABY (LP, inner sleeve, lyric insert, 10 art prints)	40
93	Island U2-9	ZOOROPA (LP, inner sleeve, lyric insert)	30
95	Island MELONCD 1	MELON (REMIXES FOR PROPAGANDA) (CD, 9-track compilation, card sleeve, fan club issue, 20,000 only; sealed with Propaganda No. 21)	50
95	Island MELONCD 1	MELON (REMIXES FOR PROPAGANDA) (CD, 9-track compilation, card sleeve, fan club issue, 20,000 only; unsealed with Propaganda No. 21)	25
97	Island U2 10	POP (2-LP, gatefold sleeve)	35
98	Island U2 11	THE BEST OF 1980-1990 (2-LP, gatefold sleeve)	50
00	Island U2 12	ALL THAT YOU CAN'T LEAVE BEHIND (LP, with booklet)	60
02	Island U2 13	THE BEST OF 1990-2000 (2xLP, gatefold)	40
04	Island U2 14	HOW TO DISMANTLE AN ATOMIC BOMB (LP, with booklet)	30
04	Island CIDXU214	HOW TO DISMANTLE AN ATOMIC BOMB (CD & DVD set in numbered slipcase)	18
06	Island U2.COM2	U2 ZOO TV LIVE (2-CD & poster in card sleeve & outer card slipcase Issued to U2.com subscribers only)	50
07	Island U2.COM3	U2 GO HOME - LIVE FROM SLANE CASTLE (2xCD issued to u2.com subscribers only)	30
08	Island	U23D (Promo CD, audio press kit, DVD box)	35
09	Island 1796038	NO LINE ON THE HORIZON (2-LP)	18
09	Island U2.COM 4	MEDIUM, RARE AND REMASTERED (2-CD, issued to u2.com subscribers only)	18

PROMOS - ALBUMS

83	Island U2 1	UNDER A BLOOD RED SKY - A DIALOGUE WITH U2 LIVE (LP, custom sleeve, with cue sheet, numbered, 1,000 only)	75
87	Island U2-6	THE JOSHUA TREE (CD, LP & cassette in black/gold 'pizza' box set)	250

			MINT VALUE £
87	Island U2 6-1 - U2 6-5	THE JOSHUA TREE COLLECTION Red Hill Mining Town/ Where The Streets Have No Name//Trip Through Your Wires/Running To Stand Still//I Still Haven't Found What I'm Looking For/One Tree Hill/Exit/ Mothers Of The Disappeared/In God's Country/Bullet The Blue Sky	500
87	Island U2 6-1 - U2 6-5	THE JOSHUA TREE COLLECTION (5 x 7" black box set, with U2 6-1 mispressed with "Red Hill Mining Town" both sides, less than 50 copies)	1000
87	Island U2CLP 1	THE U2 TALKIE: A CONVERSATION WITH LARRY, BONO, ADAM & THE EDGE (LP, music & interview with Dave Fanning for "The Joshua Tree")	30
87	Island U2CC 1	THE U2 TALKIE (cassette)	20
87	Island BOU2 1	CASSETTE SAMPLER (cassette, 17-track instore 'Best Of' compilation)	30
88	Island U2-7	RATTLE AND HUM (CD, LP & cassette in flight case with leather tag, 250 only)	1000
89	Island U2 2D1	U2 2 DATE (LP, 8-track hits compilation)	25
91	Island U2-8	ACHTUNG BABY (CD, cassette in 'User's Kit', including map/poster, torch, key ring, spanner & screwdriver in printed green nylon kit bag)	500
91	Island CIDDJ U2-8	ACHTUNG (graphics CD, in jewel case marked "promo only - not for sale")	100
97	Island CID U2 10	POP (CD, in large cube-shaped picture box set, with prismatic pen & custom notepad)	200
97	Island POP 1	U2 TALK POP (CD, interview with Dave Fanning, card sleeve)	50
97	Island POP 2	U2 TALK POP (CD, interview with Dave Fanning, card sleeve, same tracks as POP 1)	50
97	Island POP 3	U2 TALK POP (CD, interview with Dave Fanning, card sleeve, same track as POP 1)	50
98	Island CIDDU211	THE BEST OF THE 'B' SIDES 1980-1990 (2-CD, discs marked 'A' and 'B', in card sleeves with gold slipcase)	50
98	Island BXU2 11	THE 'BEST OF' COLLECTION 1980-1990 (14 x 7" singles, 2-CDs, 16-page booklet, in gold box, 2000 copies only)	250
00	Island MDH CD1	THE MILLION DOLLAR HOTEL (CD, card sleeve)	15
00	Island CID U212	ALL THAT YOU CAN'T LEAVE BEHIND (promo pack, with 1-track CD Beautiful Day [BEAUT CD 1] in blue picture slipcase, booklet, window sticker, video tape, "playback" invitation, in laminated picture bag with rope handles; with signed print)	600
00	Island CID U212	ALL THAT YOU CAN'T LEAVE BEHIND (promo pack, with 1-track CD Beautiful Day [BEAUT CD 1] in blue picture slipcase, booklet, window sticker, video tape, "playback" invitation, in laminated picture bag with rope handles; without signed print)	200
00	no cat. no.	THE DAVE FANNING INTERVIEW (CD-R, dated 4.10.00, in white card sleeve, plastic outer sleeve)	20
00	no cat. no.	ALBUM INTERVIEW (CD-R, dated 25.10.00, in white card sleeve, plastic outer sl.)	20
00	Island HASTACD 1	HASTA LA VISTA BABY! LIVE FROM MEXICO CITY (CD, fan-club only p/s)	50
02	Island CIDDJ U2 13	THE BEST OF THE B-SIDES OF 1990-2000 (2-CD set card sleeves in card wallet)	30
02	Island BX U2 13	THE BEST OF COLLECTION 1990-2000 (15 x 7", with 2 CDs & 16-page booklet in silver fliptop card box)	200
02	Island REMIXCD U2 13	REMIXES FROM THE 90S (CD, 5-track album sampler in card sleeve, in silver card wallet)	25
02	Island REMIXCD U2 13	REMIXES FROM THE 90S (2 x 12", promo p/s) card wallet)	20
05	Island UCOMV1	U2 COMMUNICATION (CD & DVD fan club issue)	30

U.V. POP

85	Flow Motion FM 007	Anyone For Me/Hands To Me	30
85	Flow motion FM 12/007	ANYONE FOR ME (12" EP)	35
85	Native NTV4	SERIOUS EP (12")	30
86	Extra EXTRA T001	MUSIC TO YEAH TO EP (12")	30
83	Flow Motion FM 004	NO SONGS TOMORROW (LP)	30
86	Extra EXTRA LP1	BENDY BABY MAN (LP)	40

UXB 80

80	Crazy Plane SP 02	Crazy Today/Mr Fixit (p/s)	100

UZI

70	Beacon BEA 152	Morning Train/Where Were You Last Night	70

U-ZIQ

95	Planet Mu FLATDLP 20	IN PINE EFFECT (2-LP)	15
97	Planet Mu PULP 5	LUNATIC HARNESS (2-LP)	20

V

DONNA V

96	Fashion FAD 153	Prophecy Revealing (Natural Mix)/Mystic Mix/GENERALY LEVY : Inna We Culture/Remember Yu Roots (12")	35

VACELS

65	Pye International 7N 25330	Can You Please Crawl Out Your Window/I'm Just A Poor Boy	30

VAGABONDS

(see also Jimmy James & Vagabonds, Jamaica's Own Vagabonds)

63	Island ILP 916	PRESENTING THE FABULOUS VAGABONDS (LP)	250

VAGINA DENTATA ORGAN

80s	WSNS 004	Cold Meat: Sex Star I/II (12", picture disc, hand-painted)	200
86	WSNS 004	Cold Meat: Sex Star I/II (12", picture disc)	35
83	WSNS 001	MUSIC FOR HASHASINS (LP, 500 copies)	70
84	WSNS 002	JIM JONES - THEE LAST SUPPER (LP, picture disc, 912 numbered)	40
84	WSNS 003	THE PAGAN DRUMS OF CALANDA (LP, picture disc, adorned with 'real' blood or hand-painted)	150

MINT VALUE £

84	WSNS 003	THE PAGAN DRUMS OF CALANDA (LP, picture disc)	40
87	Temple TOPY 012	MUSIC FOR THE HASHISHINS (LP, different cover)	30

VAGRANTS

66	Fontana TF 703	I Can't Make A Friend/Young Blues	60

VALADIERS

63	Oriole CBA 1809	I Found A Girl/You'll Be Sorry Someday	1000
63	Oriole CBA 1809	I Found A Girl/You'll Be Sorry Someday (DJ copy)	1000

RICKY VALANCE

(see also Jason Merryweather)

60	Columbia DB 4493	Tell Laura I Love Her/Once Upon A Time	5
60	Columbia DB 4543	Movin' Away/Lipstick On Your Lips	10
61	Columbia DB 4586	Jimmy's Girl/Only The Young	10
61	Columbia DB 4592	Why Can't We/Fisherboy	10
61	Columbia DB 4680	Bobby/I Want To Fall In Love	10
61	Columbia DB 4725	I Never Had A Chance/It's Not True	10
62	Columbia DB 4787	Try To Forget Her/At Times Like These	10
62	Columbia DB 4864	Don't Play No. 9/Till The Final Curtain Falls	12
65	Decca F 12129	Six Boys/Face The Crowd	12
76	Valley VLY 001	RICKY VALANCE (EP, no p/s)	25
78	Tank BBS 324	RAINBOW (LP)	40

RITCHIE VALENS

58	Pye International 7N 25000	Come On Let's Go/Dooby Dooby Wah	200
58	Pye International 7N 25000	Come On Let's Go/Dooby Dooby Wah (78)	150
59	London HL 8803	Donna/La Bamba	30
59	London HL 8803	Donna/La Bamba (78)	100
59	London HL 7068	Donna/La Bamba (export issue)	30
59	London HL 8886	That's My Little Suzie/Bluebirds Over The Mountains (tri centre)	40
59	London HL 8886	That's My Little Suzie/Bluebirds Over The Mountains (round centre)	25
59	London HL 8886	That's My Little Suzie/Bluebirds Over The Mountains (78)	150
62	London HL 9494	La Bamba/Ooh, My Head	20
79	London HLR 10751	La Bamba/Come On Let's Go/That's My Little Suzie (tri-centre)	10
59	London RE 1232	RITCHIE VALENS (EP, initial pressing with triangular centre)	200
59	London RE 1232	RITCHIE VALENS (EP, later round centre)	150
61	London HA 2390	RITCHIE (LP)	150
64	London HA 8196	HIS GREATEST HITS (LP)	60
67	President PTL 1001	I REMEMBER RITCHIE VALENS (LP)	25
79	London HA-R 8535	RITCHIE VALENS (LP)	15

DINO VALENTI

(see also Quicksilver Messenger Service)

68	CBS 65715	DINO (LP)	45

VALENTINE

72	Track 2094104	Time/Leader Of The Band	6

BILLY VALENTINE

55	Capitol CL 14320	It's A Sin/Your Love Has Got Me (Reelin' And Rockin')	10

DAVID VALENTINE

76	Warner Bros K 16311	Second Hand Ladies/Dance Lady Dance	6

DICKIE VALENTINE (& STARGAZERS)

54	Decca F 10346	Endless/I Could Have Told You	30
54	Decca F 10394	The Finger Of Suspicion (with Stargazers)/ Who's Afraid (Not I, Not I, Not I)	20
54	Decca F 10415	Mister Sandman/Runaround	40
55	Decca F 10430	A Blossom Fell/I Want You All To Myself (Just You)	15
55	Decca F 10484	Ma Cherie Amie/Lucky Waltz	10
55	Decca F 10493	I Wonder/You Too Can Be A Dreamer	10
55	Decca F 10517	Hello Mrs. Jones (Is Mary There?)/Lazy Gondolier	10
55	Decca F 10549	No Such Luck/The Engagement Waltz	10
55	Decca F 10628	Christmas Alphabet/Where Are You Tonight?	20
55	Decca F 10645	The Old Pi-Anna Rag/First Love	15
55	Decca F 10667	Dreams Can Tell A Lie/Song Of The Trees	7
56	Decca F 10714	The Voice/The Best Way To Hold A Girl	7
56	Decca F 10753	My Impossible Castle/When You Came Along	7
56	Decca F 10766	Day Dreams/Give Me A Carriage With Eight White Horses	8
56	Decca F 10798	Christmas Island/The Hand Of Friendship	15
56	Decca F 10820	Dickie Valentine's Rock 'N' Roll Party Medley (Parts 1 & 2)	10
57	Decca F 10874	Chapel Of The Roses/My Empty Arms	5
57	Decca F 10906	Puttin' On The Style/Three Sides To Every Story	5
57	Decca F 10949	Long Before I Knew You/Just In Time	5
57	Decca F 10950	Snowbound For Christmas/Convicted	5
58	Decca F 11005	Love Me Again/King Of Dixieland	6
58	Decca F 11020	In My Life/Come To My Arms	5
58	Decca F 11066	Take Me In Your Arms/An Old-Fashioned Song	5
59	Pye Nixa 7N 15192	Venus/Where? (In The Old Home Town)	7
59	Pye 7N 15202	A Teenager In Love/My Favourite Song	10
59	Pye 7N 15221	One More Sunrise (Morgen)/You Touch My Hand	5
55	Decca DFE 6236	SWING ALONG WITH DICKIE VALENTINE (EP)	15
56	Decca DFE 6279	PRESENTING DICKIE VALENTINE (EP)	15
56	Decca DFE 6363	ONLY FOR YOU (EP)	15
57	Decca DFE 6427	DICKIE GOES DIXIE (EP)	10
57	Decca DFE 6429	STANDARDS (EP)	10
58	Decca DFE 6529	WITH VOCAL REFRAIN BY DICKIE VALENTINE (EP)	10
59	Decca DFE 6549	BELONGING TO SOMEONE (EP)	10
59	Pye NPL 24120	DICKIE VALENTINE HIT PARADE (EP)	10
58	Decca LK 4269	WITH VOCAL REFRAIN BY... (LP)	20

MINT VALUE £

VALENTINE GUINNESS
80 RAK RAK 308 (Hey Hey) C.J.T./When Mandy Calls . . . 40

JACK VALENTINE
55 MGM SPC 8 Dressing Up My Heart/Song Of The Bandit (export issue) . . . 12

VALENTINES (Jamaica)
67 Doctor Bird DB 1065 Blam Blam Fever/BABA BROOKS: The Scratch . . . 50

VALENTINES (U.S.)
60 Ember EMB S 123 Hey Ruby/That's How I Feel . . . 90

VALENTINO
75 Gaiee GAE 101 I Was Born This Way/Liberation . . . 6

ANNA VALENTINO
57 London HLD 8421 Calypso Joe/You're Mine . . . 30
57 London HLD 8421 Calypso Joe/You're Mine (78) . . . 12

DANNY VALENTINO
59 MGM MGM 1049 Stampede/(You Gotta Be A) Music Man . . . 30
60 MGM MGM 1067 Biology/A Million Tears . . . 20
60 MGM MGM 1109 Pictures From The Past/'Till The End Of Forever . . . 15

MARK VALENTINO
63 Stateside SS 148 The Push And Kick/Walking Alone . . . 25
63 Stateside SS 186 Do It/Hey You're Looking Good . . . 15
63 Stateside SS 233 Jivin' At The Drive In/Part Time Job . . . 25

VALENTINOS
(see also Bobby Womack)
68 Soul City SC 106 It's All Over Now/Tired Of Livin' In The Country . . . 25
68 Stateside SS 2137 Tired Of Being Nobody/The Death Of Love . . . 18
71 Polydor 2058 090 Don't Raise Up Your Hands In Anger/Stand Up And Be Counted . . . 10
68 Soul City SCM 001 THE VALENTINOS/THE SIMS TWINS (LP, with Sims Twins) . . . 70

VALERIE (The Rock 'N' Roll Youngster)
56 Columbia DB 3832 Tonight You Belong To Me/The Man Who Owns The Sunshine . . . 20

DANA VALERY
64 Decca F 11881 This Is My Prayer/Would I Love You Again/T'en Va Pas . . . 7
64 Decca F 11977 I Wake Up Crying/Never Let Go . . . 12

VALHALLA
82 Neat NEAT 22 Coming Home/Through With You . . . 8
84 Neat NEAT 36 Still in Love With You/Jack . . . 6

JOE VALINO (& GOSPELAIRES)
57 HMV POP 283 The Garden Of Eden/Caravan . . . 25
58 London HLT 8705 God's Little Acre/I'm Happy With What I've Got (with Gospelaires) . . . 15
58 London HLT 8705 God's Little Acre/I'm Happy With What I've Got (78, with Gospelaires) . . . 10
60 Columbia DB 4406 Hidden Persuasion/Back To Your Eyes . . . 5

VALJEAN (AT THE PIANO)
62 London HLL 9593 Till There Was You/The Eighteenth Variation . . . 6

VALKYRIES
64 Parlophone R 5123 Rip It Up/What's Your Name? . . . 40

DIORIS VALLADARES ORCHESTRA
64 Island IEP 703 AUTHENTIC MERINGUE (EP) . . . 12
64 Island ILP 910 LET'S GO LATIN (LP, withdrawn) . . . 30

MARCOS VALLE
68 Verve VLP 9206 SAMBA '68 (LP) . . . 20

VALLEY OF ACHOR
(see also Achor, Wine Of Lebanon)
75 Dovetail DOVE 18 A DOOR OF HOPE (LP, gatefold sleeve) . . . 15

FRANKIE VALLI
66 Philips BF 1467 (You're Gonna) Hurt Yourself/VALLI BOYS: Night Hawk . . . 10
66 Philips BF 1512 You're Ready Now/Cry For Me . . . 10
66 Philips BF 1529 The Proud One/Ivy . . . 10
67 Philips BF 1556 Beggin'/Dody . . . 10
67 Philips BF 1580 Can't Take My Eyes Off You/The Trouble With Me . . . 7
67 Philips BF 1603 I Make A Fool Of Myself/September Rain . . . 7
68 Philips BF 1634 To Give (The Reason I Live)/Watch Where You Walk . . . 7
69 Philips BF 1795 The Girl I'll Never Know/A Face Without A Name . . . 6
70 Philips 320 226 BF You're Ready Now/Cry For Me (reissue) . . . 10
74 Private Stock PVT 1 My Eyes Adored You/Watch You Walk . . . 5
67 Philips (S)BL 7814 SOLO (LP) . . . 25
69 Philips SBL 7856 TIMELESS (LP) . . . 20
75 Mowest MWS 7007 INSIDE YOU (LP) . . . 12
77 Private Stock PVLP 1029 LADY PUT THE LIGHT OUT (LP, withdrawn) . . . 40

FRANKIE VALLI & THE FOUR SEASONS
(see also Four Seasons, Wonder Who)
71 Warner Bros K 16107 Whatever You Say/Sleeping Man (withdrawn, 300 only) . . . 45
72 Tamla Motown TMG 819 You're A Song/Sun Country . . . 10
72 Mowest MW 3002 The Night/When The Morning Comes . . . 75
73 Mowest MW 3003 Walk On, Don't Look Back/Touch The Rainchild . . . 12
75 Mowest MW 3024 The Night/When The Morning Comes (reissue) . . . 10
72 Mowest MWSA 5501 CHAMELEON (LP) . . . 20

JUNE VALLI
54 HMV 7M 245 I Understand (Just How You Feel)/Old Shoes And A Bag Of Rice . . . 7

MINT VALUE £

54 HMV 7M 259 Tell Me, Tell Me/Boy Wanted 7
55 HMV 7M 284 Wrong, Wrong, Wrong/Ole Pappy Time 7
56 HMV 7M 347 Por Favor (Please)/The Things They Say 7
59 Mercury AMT 1034 The Answer To A Maiden's Prayer/In His Arms 6
59 Mercury AMT 1048 An Anonymous Letter/Bygones 6
60 Mercury AMT 1091 Apple Green/Oh! Why 5
61 Mercury AMT 1130 I Guess Things Happen That Way/Tell Him For Me 6
62 HMV POP 1062 Hush Little Baby/Afraid 5

VALUES

66 Ember EMB S 211 Return To Me/That's The Way (in p/s) 80
66 Ember EMB S 211 Return To Me/That's The Way 50

HUBERT THOMAS VALVERDE & THE HTS

68 S n B 55 3922 Genevieve/We Don't Care 25

VALVERDE BROTHERS

69 CBS 4519 River Of My Mind/I Wanna Love You 20

VALVES

77 Zoom ZUM 1 Robot Love/For Adolfs Only (p/s) 10
77 Zoom ZUM 3 Tarzan Of The Kings Road/Ain't No Surf In Portobello (p/s) 12
79 Albion DEL 3 I Don't Mean Nothing At All/Linda Vindalco (p/s) 12

VAL & V's

67 CBS 2780 Do It Again A Little Bit Slower/For A Rainy Day 20
67 CBS 2956 I Like The Way/With This Theme 20
68 CBS 3316 This Little Girl/Dreamer 15

VAMP

(see also Sam Gopal, Viv Prince, Clark-Hutchinson)

68 Atlantic 584 213 Floatin'/Thinkin' Too Much 70
69 Atlantic 584 263 Green Pea/Wake Up And Tell Me (withdrawn) 150

VAMPIRE WEEKEND

07 Own Label A Punk/Cape Cod Kwassa Kwassa (p/s, yellow vinyl, 500 only) 25
07 Own Label A Punk/Cape Cod Kwassa Kwassa/Oxford Punk (CD, digipak, 500 only) 30

VAMPIRES

59 Parlophone R 4599 Swinging Ghosts/Clap Trap 20

VAMPIRES

68 Pye 7N 17553 Do You Wanna Dance/My Girl 20

VAN DER GRAAF GENERATOR

(see also Peter Hammill, Long Hello, Juicy Lucy, Misunderstood)

69 Polydor 56758 People You Were Going To/Firebrand 375
70 Charisma CB 122 Refugees/The Boat Of Millions Of Years 45
72 Charisma CB 175 Theme One/W (in p/s) 30
72 Charisma CB 175 Theme One/W 5
76 Charisma CB 297 Wondering/Meurglys III 8
76 Charisma PRO 002 Wondering (Song)/Wondering (Heroics) (promo only) 25
69 Mercury SMCL 20177 THE AEROSOL GREY MACHINE (LP, unreleased, finished gatefold sleeve only) 400
70 Charisma CAS 1007 THE LEAST WE CAN DO IS WAVE TO EACH OTHER (LP, pink 'scroll' label, original mix, matrices read: CAS 1007 A/B, gatefold sleeve, with poster) 200
70 Charisma CAS 1007 THE LEAST WE CAN DO IS WAVE TO EACH OTHER (LP, pink 'scroll' label, original mix, matrices read: CAS 1007 A/B, gatefold sleeve, without poster) 60
70 Charisma CAS 1007 THE LEAST WE CAN DO IS WAVE TO EACH OTHER (LP, pink 'scroll' label, remix, matrices read: CAS 1007 A+G/B+G, gatefold sleeve; with poster) 100
70 Charisma CAS 1007 THE LEAST WE CAN DO IS WAVE TO EACH OTHER (LP, pink 'scroll' label, remix, matrices read: CAS 1007 A+G/B+G, gatefold sleeve; without poster) 50
70 Charisma CAS 1027 H TO HE, WHO AM THE ONLY ONE (LP, pink label, gatefold sleeve) 50
71 Charisma CAS 1051 PAWN HEARTS (LP, gatefold sleeve, pink 'scroll' label, with insert) 90
71 Charisma CAS 1051 PAWN HEARTS (LP, gatefold sleeve, pink 'scroll' label, without insert) 35
72 Charisma CS 2 1968-71 (LP, pink label) 20
75 Charisma CAS 1109 GODBLUFF (LP, with inner sleeve) 12
76 Charisma CAS 1116 STILL LIFE (LP, small 'Mad Hatter' logo) 15
76 Charisma CAS 1120 WORLD RECORD (LP) 12
76 Charisma CAS 1007 THE LEAST WE CAN DO IS WAVE TO EACH OTHER (LP, gatefold reissue, 'Mad hatter' label) 18

HARRY VANDA

(see also Easybeats)

69 Polydor 56357 I Love Marie/Gonna Make It 10

MAMIE VAN DOREN

58 Capitol CL 14850 Something To Dream About/I Fell In Love (promos in p/s) 40
58 Capitol CL 14850 Something To Dream About/I Fell In Love 25

LINDA VAN DYCK

69 Gemini GM 004 The Seduction Song/Unlock My door 12

VANDYKE & BAMBIS

64 Piccadilly 7N 35180 Doin' The Mod/All I Want Is You 50

EARL VAN DYKE (& SOUL BROTHERS)

64 Stateside SS 357 Soul Stomp/Hot 'N' Tot 125
64 Stateside SS 357 Soul Stomp/Hot 'N' Tot (DJ copy) 200
65 Tamla Motown TMG 506 All For You/Too Many Fish In The Sea (as Earl Van Dyke & Soul Brothers) 125
65 Tamla Motown TMG 506 All For You/Too Many Fish In The Sea (as Earl Van Dyke & Soul Brothers)(DJ copy) 150
70 Tamla Motown TMG 759 Six By Six/All For You (matt black label, later shiny) 10

		MINT VALUE £
72 Tamla Motown TMG 814	I Can't Help Myself/How Sweet It Is (To Be Loved By You) (& Soul Brothers)	10
65 Tamla Motown TML 11014	THAT MOTOWN SOUND (LP)	100

LEROY VAN DYKE

61 Mercury AMT 1166	Walk On By/My World Is Caving In	5
62 Mercury AMT 1173	Big Man In A Big House/Faded Love	5
62 Mercury AMT 1183	I Sat Back And Let It Happen/A Broken Promise	5
65 Warner Bros WB 5650	It's All Over Now Baby Blue/Just A State Of Mind	8
66 Warner Bros WB 5807	You Couldn't Get My Love Back/Fool Such As I	8
67 Warner Bros WB 5777	Almost Persuaded/Less Of Me	10
62 Mercury MMC 14101	WALK ON BY (LP)	40
63 Mercury MMC 14118	MOVIN' VAN DYKE (LP)	40

VAN DYKES

66 Stateside SS 504	No Man Is An Island/I Won't Hold It Against You	30
66 Stateside SS 504	No Man Is An Island/I Won't Hold It Against You (DJ Copy)	60
66 Stateside SS 530	I've Gotta Go On Without You/What Will I Do	30

LON & DERREK VAN EATON

73 Apple APPLE 46	Warm Woman/More Than Words (in p/s)	90
73 Apple APPLE 46	Warm Woman/More Than Words	50
75 A&M AMS 7157	Wildfire/Music Lover	5
75 A&M AMS 7178	Dancing In The Dark/All You're Hungry For Is Love	5
73 Apple SAPCOR 25	BROTHER (LP, gatefold sleeve, with insert)	70
73 Apple SAPCOR 25	BROTHER (LP, gatefold sleeve, without insert)	50

NICK VAN EEDE

(see also Drivers)

78 Barn 201 4128	Rock'n'Roll Fool/Ounce Of Sense	6
79 Barn BARN 003	All Or Nothing/Hold On To Your Heart	7
79 Barn BARN 008	I Only Want To Be Number One/Dicing	60

VANGELIS

(see also Aphrodite's Child, Forminx, Cosmic Baby, Jon & Vangelis)

75 RCA RS 1025	HEAVEN AND HELL (gatefold sleeve)	12
76 Polydor 2489 113	L'APOCALYPSE DES ANIMAUX (LP, TV soundtrack)	18
83 Polydor BOX 1	CHARIOTS OF FIRE (LP, soundtrack, box set)	12
89 Polydor VGPK 1	THEMES (LP, 'display pack')	12

VAN HALEN

(see also David Lee Roth, Sammy Hagar)

78 Warner Bros K 17107	You Really Got Me/Atomic Punk	5
78 Warner Bros K 17162	Runnin' With The Devil/Eruption	5
79 Warner Bros K 17371	Dance The Night Away/Outta Love Again	7
79 Warner Bros K 17371P	Dance The Night Away/Outta Love Again (picture disc)	10
80 Warner Bros K 17645	And The Cradle Will Rock/Everybody Wants Some (p/s)	5
85 Warner Bros W 9199T	Hot For Teacher/Little Dreamer/Hear About It Later (12", p/s)	8
86 Warner Bros W 8740P	Why Can't This Be Love/Get Up (shaped picture disc with plinth, stickered PVC sleeve)	10
86 Warner Bros W 8642P	Dreams/Inside (car-shaped picture disc with stand, stickered PVC sleeve)	12
88 Warner Bros W 7816TW	When It's Love/Apolitical Blues (12", silver foldout p/s)	8
88 Warner Bros W 7816TP	When It's Love/Apolitical Blues (12", picture disc)	8

CHERRY VANILLA

77 RCA PB 5053	The Punk/Foxy Bitch (title sleeve)	8
78 RCA PL 25122	BAD GIRL (LP)	12
79 RCA PL 25217	VENUS DE VINYL (LP)	15

VANILLA FUDGE

(see also Beck Bogert & Appice, Cactus)

67 Atlantic 584 123	You Keep Me Hanging On/Take Me For A Little While	7
67 Atlantic 584 139	(Illusions Of My Childhood) Eleanor Rigby (Parts 1 & 2)	7
68 Atlantic 584 179	Where Is My Mind?/The Look Of Love	12
69 Atlantic 584 257	Shotgun/Good Good Lovin'	6
69 Atlantic 584 276	Some Velvet Morning/Thoughts	12
67 Atlantic 587/588 086	VANILLA FUDGE (LP, red & plum label)	30
68 Atlantic 587/588 100	THE BEAT GOES ON (LP)	25
68 Atlantic 587/588 110	RENAISSANCE (LP)	25
69 Atco 228 020	NEAR THE BEGINNING (LP)	20
70 Atco 228 029	ROCK 'N' ROLL (LP)	20

VANITY FARE

(see also Avengers)

68 Page One POF 075	I Live For The Sun/On The Other Side Of Life	10
68 Page One POF 100	Summer Morning/Betty Carter	7
69 Page One POF 117	Highway Of Dreams/Waiting For The Downfall	7
69 Page One POF 142	Early In The Morning/You Made Me Love You	7
69 Page One POF 158	Hitchin' A Ride/Man Child	10
70 Page One POF 170	Come Tomorrow/Megowd (Something Tells Me)	12
70 Page One PDF 180	Carolina's Coming Home/On Your Own	8
71 DJM DJS 234	Where Did All The Good Times Go/Stand	6
71 DJM DJS 250	Better By Far/Rock 'N Roll Band	7
71 DJM DJS	Our Own Way Of Living/Nowhere To Go	6
72 Philips 6006237	I'm In Love With The World/At The End Of The Pier	6
69 Page One POLS 010	THE SUN, THE WIND AND OTHER THINGS (LP)	45
70 DJM DJSL 001	COMING HOME (LP)	20

TEDDY VANN (ORCHESTRA)

60 London HLU 9097	Cindy/I'm Waiting	25
78 Capitol CL 16012	Theme From 'Coloured Man'/Intro To 'Coloured Man' (as Teddy Vann Orchestra)	5
61 Philips PB 1160	The Lonely Crowd/I Was Born to Love You	6

			MINT VALUE £
ORNELLA VANONI			
67	Decca F 22703	Only Two Can Play/Can I?	10
DAVE VAN RONK			
65	Stateside SL 10153	INSIDE (LP)	30
ROB VAN SPYK			
(see also Stonefield Tramp)			
70s	private pressing	FOLLOW THE SUN (LP)	60
TOWNES VAN ZANDT			
99	Exile EX 7013	Riding The Range/Dirty Old Town (p/s, 2000 only)	6
69	RCA SF 8040	OUR MOTHER THE MOUNTAIN (LP)	25
73	United Artists UAS 29442	THE LATE GREAT TOWNES VAN ZANDT (LP, gatefold sleeve)	30
87	Heartland HLD 003	AT MY WINDOW (LP)	15
01	Charly SNAB 903 CD	TEXAS TROUBADOUR (4-CD, book-style box set)	35
PETER VARDAS			
59	Top Rank JAR 173	He Threw A Stone/Checkerboard Love	8
VARDIS			
79	Redball RR 017	100 MPH (EP)	120
80	Castle CQUEL 2/100MPH	Out Of The Way/If I Were King	7
81	Logo VAR3	Silver Machine/Come On (7", die cut p/s)	6
81	Logo VAR4	All You'll Ever Need/If I Were King/Jumping Jack Flash (p/s)	6
80	Logo MOGO4012	100MPH (LP + poster)	12
81	Logo LOGO1026	THE WORLD'S INSANE (LP + insert)	12
81	Logo LOGO1034	QUO VARDIS (LP + free 7")	12
VARIATION			
72	Warner Bros K 16233	Snowbird/Nebula	6
VARIATIONS			
65	Immediate IM 019	The Man With All The Toys/She'll Know I'm Sorry	20
69	Major Minor MM 638	Crimson And Clover/She Couldn't Dance	20
VARIATIONS (U.S.)			
75	UK USA 10	Sayin' It And Doin' It Pts I & II	8
VARICOSE VEINS			
(see also Orange Disaster)			
78	Warped WARP 1	INCREDIBLE (EP, mail-order only, 200 only, beware of counterfeits)	60
PAUL VARNEY			
91	PWL PWLT 201	If Only I Knew (On The Buses Piano Edit)/If Only I Knew (Hurley's House Mix)/ If Only I Knew (Silk's Answer)/If Only I Knew (Maurice's Underground Mix) 12" p/s)	12
91	PWL PWCD 201	If Only I Knew (7" Version)/If Only I Knew (12" Version)/ If Only I Knew (Dub)/ If Only I Knew (On The Buses Piano Edit) (CD)	12
REG VARNEY			
72	Columbia SCX 6518	THIS IS REG VARNEY (LP)	12
SYLVIE VARTAN			
65	RCA Victor RCA 1490	One More Day/I Made My Choice	75
65	RCA Victor RCA 1495	Another Heart/Think About You	12
79	RCA PB 1578	I Don't Want The Night To End/Distant Shores (p/s, coloured vinyl)	6
65	RCA Victor RCX 7165	SYLVIE VARTAN (EP)	200
VARUKERS			
81	Tempest/Inferno HELL 1	Protest And Survive/No Scapegoat (p/s)	10
83	Riot City RIOT 27	Die For Your Government/All Systems Fail (p/s)	7
83	Riot City RIOT 29	Led To The Slaughter/The End Is Nigh (p/s)	10
82	Tempest/Inferno HELL 4	DON'T WANNA BE A VICTIM (EP)	6
83	Riot City 005	BLOODSUCKERS (LP, with inner)	18
83	Riot City RIOT 31	ANOTHER RELIGION ANOTHER WAR (12" EP)	15
84	Rot ASS 16	MASSACRED MILLIONS (12" EP)	20
84	Attack ATTACK 001	PREPARE FOR THE ATTACK (LP, 1000 only)	18
85	Liberate 1	ONE STRUGGLE ONE FIGHT (LP)	15
87	Rot DUTCH 001	LIVE IN HOLLAND (LP)	15
VASELINES			
(see also Pastels, BMX Bandits)			
87	53rd & 3rd AGARR 10	Son Of A Gun/Rory Rides Away/You Think You're A Man (12", die-cut sleeve)	20
88	53rd & 3rd AGARR 17	Dying For It/Molly's Lips (p/s)	10
88	53rd & 3rd AGARR 17T	Dying For It/Molly's Lips/Teenage Superstars/ Jesus Wants Me For A Sunbeam (12", p/s)	12
88	53rd & 3rd AGARR 17CD	Dying For It/Molly's Lips/Teenage Superstars/ Jesus Wants Me For A Sunbeam (CD)	12
90	53rd & 3rd AGAS 7	DUM DUM (LP)	15
VASHTI			
(see also Vashti Bunyan)			
65	Decca F 12157	Some Things Just Stick In Your Mind/I Want To Be Alone	60
66	Columbia DB 7917	Train Song/Love Song	40
FRANKIE VAUGHAN			
(see also Kaye Sisters, Alma Cogan & Frankie Vaughan, Marilyn Monroe)			
57	Rainbow/Weekend 14140	The Truth About Me (78, 5", mail-order only, with mailer)	15
57	Rainbow/Weekend 14140	The Truth About Me (78, 5", mail-order only)	10
53	HMV 7M 167	Istanbul (Not Constantinople)/Cloud Lucky Seven	10
54	HMV 7M 182	The Cuff Of My Shirt/Heartless	10
54	HMV 7M 252	My Son, My Son/Cinnamon Sinner (Selling Lollipop Lies)	10
54	HMV 7M 270	Happy Days And Lonely Nights/Danger Signs	10
55	HMV 7M 298	Too Many Heartaches/Unsuspecting Heart	6

			MINT VALUE £
57	Philips JK 1002	Garden Of Eden/Priscilla (jukebox issue)	10
57	Philips JK 1014	What's Behind That Strange Door/Cold, Cold Shower (jukebox issue)	10
57	Philips JK 1022	These Dangerous Years/Isn't This A Lovely Evening (jukebox issue)	10
57	Philips JK 1030	Gotta Have Something In The Bank, Frank/Single (with Kaye Sisters, jukebox issue)	10
57	Philips JK 1035	Kisses Sweeter Than Wine/Rock-A-Chicka (jukebox issue)	15
57	Philips PB 775	Kisses Sweeter Than Wine/Rock-A-Chicka	10
58	Philips PB 793	We're Not Alone/Can't Get Along Without You	5
58	Philips PB 825	Kewpie Doll/So Many Women	5
58	Philips PB 834	Wonderful Things/Judy	5
58	Philips PB 865	Am I Wasting My Time On You/So Happy In Love	5
59	Philips PB 423	Give Me The Moonlight, Give Me The Girl/Happy Go Lucky	5
59	Philips PB 865	Am I Wasting My Time On You/So Happy In Love	5
59	Philips PB 895	That's My Doll/Love Is The Sweetest Thing	6
59	Philips PB 896	Honey Bunny Baby/The Lady Is A Square	8
59	Philips PB 913	Come Softly To Me/Say Something Sweet To Your Sweetheart (& Kaye Sisters)	6
59	Philips PB 930	The Heart Of A Man/Sometime Somewhere	6
59	Philips PB 931	Walkin' Tall/I Ain't Gonna Lead This Life	6
62	Philips 326542 BF	Hercules/Madeleine (Open The Door)	10
65	Philips BF 1394	Someone Must Have Hurt You A Lot/Easter Time	10

MALCOLM VAUGHAN

56	HMV 7M 338	With Your Love/Small Talk	25
56	HMV POP 250	St. Therese Of The Roses/Love Me As Though There Were No Tomorrow	10
57	HMV POP 303	The World Is Mine/Now	10
57	HMV POP 325	Chapel Of The Roses/Guardian Angel	10
56	HMV 7M 389	Only You (And You Alone)/I'll Be Near To You	10
57	HMV POP 419	My Special Angel/The Heart Of A Child	5
58	HMV POP 459	To Be Loved/My Young Arms	5
58	HMV POP 502	Ev'ry Hour, Ev'ry Day Of My Life/Miss You	5
58	HMV POP 538	More Than Ever (Come Prima)/A Night To Remember	5
59	HMV POP 590	Wait For Me (Ti Diro)/Willingly (Melodie Perdue)	5
60	HMV POP 700	Oh So Wunderbar/For Everyone In Love	5
60	HMV POP 739	Lady Of Spain/My Love For You	6
61	HMV POP 923	The Wedding/Guardian Angel	5
61	HMV POP 846	Dolce Vita/There's No Other Love	5
59	HMV CLP 1284	HELLO MALCOLM VAUGHAN (LP)	15

NORMAN VAUGHAN

62	Pye 7N 15438	Swinging In The Rain/Put On A Happy Face (p/s)	6

SARAH VAUGHAN

SINGLES

58	Mercury 7MT 198	My Darling, My Darling/Bewitched	10
58	Mercury 7MT 212	Padre/Spin Little Bottle	10
58	Mercury 7MT 222	Too Much, Too Soon/What's So Bad About It	10
59	Mercury AMT 1010	Everything I Do/I Ain't Hurtin'	10
59	Mercury AMT 1029	Cool Baby/Are You Certain?	10
59	Mercury AMT 1029	Cool Baby/Are You Certain? (78)	10
59	Mercury AMT 1044	Careless/Separate Ways	5
59	Mercury AMT 1057	Broken-Hearted Melody/Misty	10
59	Mercury AMT 1057	Broken-Hearted Melody/Misty (78)	15
59	Mercury AMT 1080	You're My Baby/Eternally	5
59	Mercury AMT 1087	Don't Look At Me That Way/Sweet Affections	5
60	Columbia DB 4491	Ooh! What A Day/My Dear Little Sweetheart	10
60	Columbia DB 4511	If I Were A Bell/Teach Me Tonight (with Count Basie & Joe Williams)	5
60	Columbia DB 4542	Serenata/Let's	5
63	Columbia DB 4990	My Favourite Things/Great Day	5
69	Mercury AMT 1107	The Boy From Ipanema/The Fever (p/s)	5

EPs

56	London RE-U 1065	SARAH VAUGHAN SINGS (with John Kirby's Orchestra)	20
57	Emarcy YEP 9507	SARAH VAUGHAN	10
57	Mercury MEP 9511	SARAH VAUGHAN HIT PARADE	10
57	Mercury MEP 9519	SARAH VAUGHAN HIT PARADE NO. 2	10
59	Mercury ZEP 10011	SONGS FROM SARAH	10
59	Mercury ZEP 10030	AFTER HOURS AT THE LONDON HOUSE	10
59	Mercury ZEP 10041	SARAH WITH FEELING	10
59	Mercury ZEP 10101	NO COUNT SARAH	10

ALBUMS

55	Oriole/Mercury MG 26005	IMAGES (10")	20
55	Mercury MG 25188	THE DIVINE SARAH	15
56	London HB-U 1049	SARAH VAUGHAN SINGS (10", with John Kirby & His Orchestra)	20
56	Emarcy EJL 100	IN THE LAND OF HI FI (10")	20
56	Philips BBL 7082	SARAH VAUGHAN	15
56	Mercury MPT 7503	MAKE YOURSELF COMFORTABLE (10")	20
57	Mercury MPT 7518	IMAGES (10", reissue)	15
57	Emarcy EJL 1258	SASSY	15
57	Mercury MPL 6522	SINGS GREAT SONGS FROM HIT SHOWS PART 1	15
57	Philips BBL 7165	LINGER AWHILE	15
57	Mercury MPL 6523	SINGS GREAT SONGS FROM HIT SHOWS PART 2	15
57	Mercury MPL 6525	SINGS GEORGE GERSHWIN VOL. 1	15
57	Mercury MPL 6527	SINGS GEORGE GERSHWIN VOL. 2	15
58	Mercury MPL 6532	WONDERFUL SARAH	15
58	Emarcy EJL 1273	SWINGIN' EASY	15
58	Mercury MPL 6540	IN ROMANTIC MOOD	15
58	Mercury MPL 6542	AT MISTER KELLY'S	15
59	Mercury CMS 18011	SINGS GEORGE GERSHWIN VOL. 1 (stereo reissue of MPL 6525)	15

			MINT VALUE £
59	Mercury CMS 18012	SINGS GEORGE GERSHWIN VOL. 2 (stereo reissue of MPL 6527)	15
59	Mercury MMC 14001	AFTER HOURS AT THE LONDON HOUSE	15
59	Mercury MMC 14011	VAUGHAN AND VIOLINS (also stereo CMS 18003)	15
60	Mercury MMC 14021	NO COUNT SARAH	15

SARAH VAUGHAN & BILLY ECKSTINE

(see also Billy Eckstine)

59	Mercury AMT 1071	Passing Strangers/SARAH VAUGHAN: Smooth Operator	5
56	MGM MGM-EP 561	DEDICATED TO YOU (EP)	10
59	MGM MGM-EP 690	BILLY ECKSTINE AND SARAH VAUGHAN (EP)	10
59	Mercury 10025 MCE	PASSING STRANGERS (EP)	10
60	Mercury 10027 MCE	TOGETHER AGAIN (EP)	10
61	Mercury ZEP 10108	BEST OF BERLIN VOL. 1 (EP, mono)	10
61	Mercury SEZ 19016	BEST OF BERLIN VOL. 1 (EP, stereo)	10

BILLY VAUGHN (& HIS ORCHESTRA)

(see also Hilltoppers, Ken Nordine)

55	London HL 8112	Melody Of Love/Joy Ride (gold label print)	20
55	London HLD 8205	The Shifting Whispering Sands (Parts 1 & 2) (with Ken Nordine) (gold print)	20
56	London HLD 8238	Theme From 'The Threepenny Opera'/I'd Give A Million Tomorrows (gold label print)	25
56	London HLD 8238	Theme From 'The Threepenny Opera'/I'd Give A Million Tomorrows (later silver label print)	5
56	London HLD 8319	When The Lilac Blooms Again/Autumn Concerto (gold label print)	20
56	London HLD 8319	When The Lilac Blooms Again/Autumn Concerto (later silver label print)	5
56	London HLD 8342	Petticoats From Portugal/La La Colette (gold label print)	20
56	London HLD 8342	Petticoats From Portugal/La La Colette (later silver label print)	5
57	London HLD 8417	The Ship That Never Sailed/Little Boy Blue (with Ken Nordine)	10
57	London HLD 8511	Johnny Tremain/Naughty Annetta (as Billy Vaughn's Orchestra & Chorus)	10
57	London HLD 8522	Raunchy/Sail Along Silvery Moon	15
58	London HLD 8612	Tumbling Tumbleweeds/Trying	8
58	London HLD 8680	Sail Along Silvery Moon/The Singing Hills	5
58	London HLD 8703	La Paloma/Here Is My Love	5
58	London HLD 8772	Cimarron (Roll On)/You're My Baby Doll	5
59	London HLD 8797	Blue Hawaii/Tico Tico	5
59	London HLD 8859	Your Cheatin' Heart/Lights Out	5
59	London HLD 8920	All Nite Long/Blues Stay Away From Me	10
59	London HLD 8952	Morgen (One More Sunrise)/Sweet Leilani	5
59	London HLD 8996	(It's No) Sin/After Hours	5
60	London HLD 9152	Look For A Star/He'll Have To Go	5
61	London HLD 9259	Theme From The Sundowners/Old Cape Cod	5
61	London HLD 9279	Wheels/Orange Blossom Special	5
61	London HLD 9423	Berlin Melody/Theme From Come September	5
62	London HLD 9507	Everybody's Twisting In Mexico/Melody In The Night	5
62	London HLD 9541	Chapel By The Sea/A Lover's Guitar	5
62	London HLD 9568	Continental Melody/Born To Be With You	5
62	London HLD 9578	A Swingin' Safari/Summertime	5
62	London HLD 9775	Meditation/Release Me	5
63	London HLD 9735	Happy Cowboy/Sukiyaki	5
64	London HLD 9865	Blue Tango/Boss	5

MORRIS VAUGHN

69	Fontana TF 1031	My Love Keeps Growing/Make It Look Good	30

VAZZ

85	CRV 5401	Breath/Violent Silence (in folder & bag with postcards & inserts)	5

V.D.U.'s

(see also Boys Wonder)

79	Thin Sliced	Don't Cry For Me/Little White Lie/Holiday Romances (p/s)	15

VED BUENS ENDE

95	Misanthropy AMAZON 006	WRITTEN IN WATERS (2-LP, marbled purple vinyl)	60

CHUCK VEDDER

59	London HL 8951	Spanky Boy/Arriba	30
59	London HL 8951	Spanky Boy/Arriba (78)	20

BOBBY VEE

(see also Crickets, Ventures)

SINGLES

60	London HLG 9179	Devil Or Angel/Since I Met You, Baby	25
61	London HLG 9255	Rubber Ball/Everyday	5
61	London HLG 9316	More Than I Can Say/Stayin' In	5
61	London HLG 9389	How Many Tears/Baby Face	5
61	London HLG 9438	Take Good Care Of My Baby/Bashful Bob	5
61	London HLG 7111	Take Good Care Of My Baby/Bashful Bob (export issue)	10
61	London HLG 9459	Love's Made A Fool Of You/Susie-Q	15
61	London HLG 9470	Run To Him/Walkin' With My Angel	5
62	Liberty LIB 55388	Run To Him/Walkin' With My Angel (reissue)	10
62	Liberty LIB 55419	Please Don't Ask About Barbara/I Can't Say Goodbye	10
62	Liberty LIB 55451	Sharing You/At A Time Like This	5
62	Liberty LIB 10046	A Forever Kind Of Love/Remember Me, Huh?	5
63	Liberty LIB 10069	The Night Has A Thousand Eyes/Tenderly Yours	5
63	Liberty LIB 55530	Bobby Tomorrow/Charms	5
63	Liberty LIB 10124	Stranger In Your Arms/Yesterday And You	10
64	Liberty LIB 10141	She's Sorry/Buddy's Song	10
64	Liberty LIB 55700	Hickory, Dick And Doc/I Wish You Were Mine Again	10
65	Liberty LIB 10197	Keep On Trying/Cross My Heart	10
65	Liberty LIB 10213	True Love Never Runs Smooth/Hey Little Girl	10

MINT VALUE £

65 Liberty LIB 55828 Run Like The Devil/Take A Look Around Me ... 15
66 Liberty LIB 55877 Look At Me Girl/Save A Love ... 10
67 Liberty LIB 10272 Like You've Never Known Before/Growing Pains ... 10
67 Liberty LIB 15016 Come Back When You Grow Up/Let The Four Winds Blow ... 10
67 Liberty LIB 15042 Beautiful People/I May Be Gone ... 10
68 Liberty LBF 15058 Maybe Just Today/You're A Big Girl Now ... 10
68 Liberty LBF 15096 Medley, My Girl - Hey Girl/Take Good Care Of My Baby ... 10
68 Liberty LBF 15134 Do What You Gotta' Do/Thank You ... 10
69 Liberty LBF 15178 (I'm Into Looking For) Someone To Love Me/Sunrise Highway ... 15
69 Liberty LBF 15234 I'm Gonna Make It Up To You/Let's Call It A Day ... 15
69 Liberty LBF 15305 Electric Trains And You/In And Out Of Love ... 15
70 Liberty LBF 15420 Sweet Sweetheart/Rock 'N Roll Music And You ... 20

EPs

61 London RE-G 1278 BOBBY VEE NO. 1 ... 30
61 London RE-G 1299 BOBBY VEE NO. 2 ... 30
61 London RE-G 1308 BOBBY VEE NO. 3 ... 30
61 London RE-G 1323 BOBBY VEE NO. 4 ... 30
61 London RE-G 1324 HITS OF THE ROCKIN' 50's ... 35
62 Liberty LEP 2053 SINCERELY ... 20
63 Liberty LEP 2084 JUST FOR FUN (2 tracks by Bobby Vee, 2 by Crickets) ... 20
63 Liberty LEP 2089 A FOREVER KIND OF LOVE ... 20
63 Liberty LEP 2102 BOBBY VEE'S BIGGEST HITS (mono) ... 10
63 Liberty SLEP 2102 BOBBY VEE'S BIGGEST HITS (stereo) ... 15
63 Liberty LEP 2116 BOBBY VEE MEETS THE CRICKETS (mono) ... 10
63 Liberty SLEP 2116 BOBBY VEE MEETS THE CRICKETS (stereo) ... 15
64 Liberty LEP 2149 BOBBY VEE MEETS THE CRICKETS VOL. 2 ... 15
64 Liberty LEP 2181 NEW SOUNDS ... 35
65 Liberty LEP 2212 BOBBY VEE MEETS THE VENTURES (with Ventures) ... 25

ALBUMS

61 London HA-G 2320 BOBBY VEE SINGS YOUR FAVOURITES ... 60
61 London HA-G 2352 BOBBY VEE (mono) ... 30
61 London SAH-G 6152 BOBBY VEE (stereo) ... 40
61 London HA-G 2374 WITH STRINGS AND THINGS (mono) ... 30
61 London SAH-G 6174 WITH STRINGS AND THINGS (stereo) ... 40
61 London HA-G 2406 SINGS HITS OF THE ROCKIN' 50s (mono) ... 40
61 London SAH-G 6206 SINGS HITS OF THE ROCKIN' 50s (also stereo) ... 50
61 London HA-G 2428 TAKE GOOD CARE OF MY BABY (mono) ... 30
61 London SAH-G 6224 TAKE GOOD CARE OF MY BABY (stereo) ... 40
61 Liberty (S)LBY 1004 TAKE GOOD CARE OF MY BABY (reissue) ... 15
62 Liberty LBY 1084 BOBBY VEE RECORDING SESSION (mono) ... 15
62 Liberty SLBY 1084 BOBBY VEE RECORDING SESSION (stereo) ... 20
62 Liberty LBY 1086 BOBBY VEE MEETS THE CRICKETS (mono) ... 12
62 Liberty SLBY 1086 BOBBY VEE MEETS THE CRICKETS (stereo) ... 15
62 Liberty LBY 1112 BOBBY VEE'S GOLDEN GREATS (mono) ... 15
62 Liberty SLBY 1112 BOBBY VEE'S GOLDEN GREATS (stereo) ... 20
63 Liberty LBY 1139 THE NIGHT HAS A THOUSAND EYES (mono) ... 20
63 Liberty SLBY 1139 THE NIGHT HAS A THOUSAND EYES (stereo) ... 25
63 Liberty LBY 1147 BOBBY VEE MEETS THE VENTURES (with Ventures, mono) ... 25
63 Liberty SLBY 1147 BOBBY VEE MEETS THE VENTURES (with Ventures, stereo) ... 30
63 Liberty LBY 1188 I REMEMBER BUDDY HOLLY (mono) ... 20
63 Liberty SLBY 1188 I REMEMBER BUDDY HOLLY (stereo) ... 25
65 Liberty LBY 1263 BOBBY VEE LIVE! ON TOUR (mono) ... 12
65 Liberty SLBY 1263 BOBBY VEE LIVE! ON TOUR (stereo) ... 15
67 Liberty (S)LBY 1341 LOOK AT ME GIRL ... 12
68 Liberty LBL/LBS 83112E JUST TODAY ... 12
69 Liberty LBL/LBS 83130E DO WHAT YOU GOTTA DO ... 12

ALAN VEGA

(see also Suicide, Future Pilot AKA Alan Vega)

81 Celluloid WIP 6744 Jukebox Babe/Lonely (p/s) ... 6
81 Celluloid 12WIP 6744 Jukebox Babe/Lonely (12", p/s) ... 10
88 Sniffin' Rock SR 009 WACKO WARRIOR/(track by African Headcharge) (with Sniffin' Rock fanzine No. 12) ... 8
81 Ze/Island ILPS 9692 COLLISION DRIVE (LP) ... 12

VEINS

80 Redball RR 3 Complete Control Rock 'n' Roll/Champagne ... 25

(see under Intra Vein)

VEJTABLES

65 Pye International 7N 25339 I Still Love You/Anything ... 50

RUTH VELDON

66 Decca F12436 A Most Peculiar Man/Show Me The Way Back To My World ... 15

MARTHA VELEZ

69 London HLK 10266 It Takes A Lot To Laugh/Come Here Sweet Man ... 10
69 London HLK 10280 Tell Mama/Swamp Man ... 25
69 London HLK 10280 Tell Mama/Swamp Man (DJ Copy) ... 40
72 Blue Horizon 2096 010 Boogie Kitchen/Two Bridges ... 20
69 London HA-K/SH-K 8395 FIENDS AND ANGELS (LP) ... 50
70 Blue Horizon 7-63867 FIENDS AND ANGELS AGAIN (LP) ... 75
76 Sire 9103 252 ESCAPE FROM BABYLON (LP) ... 15

CAETANO VELOSO

71 Famous SFM 1002 CAETANO VELOSO (LP) ... 12

VELOURS

(see also Fantastics)

77 MGM 2006 603 I'm Gonna Change/Don't Pity Me ... 10

MINT VALUE £

VELVELETTES

64	Stateside SS 361	Needle In A Haystack/Should I Tell Them?	50
64	Stateside SS 361	Needle In A Haystack/Should I Tell Them? (DJ Copy)	100
65	Stateside SS 387	He Was Really Sayin' Something/Throw A Farewell Kiss	70
65	Stateside SS 387	He Was Really Sayin' Something/Throw A Farewell Kiss (DJ Copy)	125
65	Tamla Motown TMG 521	Lonely Lonely Girl Am I/I'm The Exception To The Rule	200
65	Tamla Motown TMG 521	Lonely Lonely Girl Am I/I'm The Exception To The Rule (DJ Copy)	300
66	Tamla Motown TMG 580	These Things Will Keep Me Loving You/Since You've Been Loving Me	50
65	Tamla Motown TMG 595	He Was Really Sayin' Something/Needle In A Haystack	20
67	Tamla Motown TMG 595	He Was Really Sayin' Something/Needle In A Haystack	25
71	Tamla Motown TMG 780	These Things Will Keep Me Loving You/Since You've Been Loving Me (reissue)	12
72	Tamla Motown TMG 806	Needle In A Haystack/I'm The Exception To The Rule	8

VELVET GLOVE

74	Fresh Air 6370 502	SWEET WAS MY ROSE (LP, laminated sleeve, lyric insert)	15

VELVET HUSH

(see also Factory [Oak label])

68	Oak RGJ 648	Broken Heart/Lover Please	300

VELVET LOVE

75	Alaska ALA 1010	Symphony Of Dreams/Ridin' High	5

VELVET OPERA

(see also Elmer Gantry's Velvet Opera, Stretch, Hudson-Ford, Johnny Joyce)

69	CBS 4189	Anna Dance Square/Don't You Realize	10
70	CBS 4802	Black Jack Davy/Statesboro' Blues	10
70	Spark SRL 1045	She Keeps Giving Me These Feelings/There's A Hole In My Pocket	7
69	CBS 63692	RIDE A HUSTLER'S DREAM (LP)	80

VEL-VETS

74	Disco Demand DDS 109	I Got To Find Me Somebody/What Now My Love	10

VELVETS

61	London HLU 9328	That Lucky Old Sun/Time And Time Again	30
61	London HLU 9372	Tonight (Could Be The Night)/Spring Fever	40
61	London HLU 9444	Laugh/Lana	50
61	London RE-U 1297	VELVETS (EP)	165

VELVETTES

64	Mercury MF 802	He's The One I Want/That Little Boy Of Mine (in p/s)	25
64	Mercury MF 802	He's The One I Want/That Little Boy Of Mine	20

VELVETT FOGG

(see also Ghost)

69	Pye 7N 17673	Telstar '69/Owed To The Dip	25
69	Pye NSPL 18272	VELVETT FOGG (LP, laminated sleeve; beware of non-laminated counterfeits)	120

VELVET UNDERGROUND

(see also Lou Reed, Nico, John Cale)

71	Atlantic 2091 008	Who Loves The Sun/Sweet Jane	30
73	MGM 2006 283	I'm Waiting For The Man/Run Run Run/Candy Says (as Lou Reed & Velvet Underground)	10
73	Atlantic K 10339	Sweet Jane/Rock And Roll (as Velvet Underground featuring Lou Reed)	10
82	Polydor POSPX 603	Heroin/Venus In Furs/I'm Waiting For The Man/Run Run Run (12", p/s)	10
88	Old Gold OG 4049	I'm Waiting For The Man/Heroin (12", no p/s)	8
88	Old Gold OG 4051	Venus In Furs/All Tomorrow's Parties (12", no p/s)	8
67	Verve VLP 9184	THE VELVET UNDERGROUND AND NICO (LP, single sleeve, 'non-banana' cover, mono)	150
67	Verve SVLP 9184	THE VELVET UNDERGROUND AND NICO (LP, single sleeve, 'non-banana' cover, stereo)	100
68	Verve 2315 056	THE VELVET UNDERGROUND AND NICO (LP, UK pressing in stickered US peelable banana gatefold censored sleeve, stereo)	130
68	Verve VLP 9201	WHITE LIGHT WHITE HEAT (LP, 'skull' sleeve, mono)	120
68	Verve SVLP 9201	WHITE LIGHT WHITE HEAT (LP, 'skull' sleeve, stereo)	85
69	MGM MGM-CS 8108	THE VELVET UNDERGROUND (LP, 'Val Valentin mix', flapped sleeve, with horizontal split of Lou Reed picture on rear sleeve)	110
71	Atlantic 2400 111	LOADED (LP)	18
71	MGM 2315 056	THE VELVET UNDERGROUND AND NICO (LP, reissue, gatefold sleeve)	18
71	MGM Select 2353 022	THE VELVET UNDERGROUND (LP, reissue, gatefold sleeve)	18
71	MGM Select 2353 024	WHITE LIGHT WHITE HEAT (LP, reissue)	18
72	MGM Select 2683 006	ANDY WARHOL'S VELVET UNDERGROUND (2-LP)	22
72	Atlantic K 30022	LIVE AT MAX'S KANSAS CITY (LP)	12
73	Polydor 2383 180	SQUEEZE (LP)	25
84	Polydor SPELP 73	WHITE LIGHT WHITE HEAT (LP, reissue, different sleeve)	12
86	Polydor VUBOX 1	THE VELVET UNDERGROUND BOX SET (5-LP box set, with booklet)	40
87	Mercury 6641 900	1969 VOL. 1 (2-LP)	15
88	HMV C88 1-15	THE VELVET UNDERGROUND AND NICO (LP or CD box set, with booklet, 1500 only)	25

VENDETTA

88	Plaza PZA 042	Don't Let The World Drag You Under/Don't Let The World Drag You Under Pt.2 (p/s)	6

VENDORS

(see also 'N Betweens, Slade)

64	Domino Studios (no cat. no.)	Don't Leave Me Now/Twilight Time/Take Your Time/Peace Pipe (acetate, private pressing, 12 copies only)	500

VENGERS

63	Oriole CB 1879	Shake And Clap/Shakedown	25

VENIGMAS

79	Graduate GRAD 2	Red Revenge/Turn The Lights Out (p/s)	10

MINT VALUE £

VENOM

81	Neat NEAT 08	In League With Satan/Live Like An Angel, Die Like An Devil (p/s)	25
82	Neat NEAT 13	Bloodlust/In Nomine Satanas (p/s)	25
82	Neat NEAT 13	Bloodlust/In Nomine Satanas (purple vinyl)	80
83	Neat NEAT 27	Die Hard/Acid Queen (p/s, with poster)	20
83	Neat NEAT 27	Die Hard/Acid Queen (p/s)	15
83	Megaforce LOM 1/NEAT 27	Die Hard/Acid Queen (picture disc, export issue, 1,000 only)	25
84	Neat NEAT 38	Warhead/Lady Lust (p/s)	10
84	Neat NEATP 38	Warhead/Lady Lust (p/s, mauve vinyl)	20
84	Neat NEAT 3812	Warhead/Lady Lust/Gates Of Hell (12", p/s)	15
85	Neat NEATP 43	Manitou/Woman (picture disc)	15
85	Neat NEATSHAPE 43	Manitou/Woman (shaped picture disc)	18
85	Neat NEATC 43	Manitou/Woman/Dead Of Night/Dutch Radio Interview (cassette)	18
85	Neat NEAT 4312	Manitou/Woman/Dead Of Night (12", p/s)	18
85	Neat NEATS 47	Nightmare/Satanarchist (shaped picture disc)	25
85	Neat NEAT 4712	Nightmare/Satanarchist/F.O.A.D./Warhead (live) (12", 'face' p/s)	20
85	Neat NEAT 4712	Nightmare/Satanarchist/F.O.A.D./Warhead (live) (12", p/s, withdrawn)	25
85	Neat NEATSP 4712	Nightmare/Satanarchist/F.O.A.D./Warhead (live) (12", picture disc, withdrawn)	40
85	Neat 5312	HELL AT HAMMERSMITH EP (Witching Hour/Teacher's Pet/Poison) (12", 10,000 only)	25
81	Neat 1002	WELCOME TO HELL (LP, 1st issue, with poster and lyric insert)	30
82	Neat 1005	BLACK METAL (LP, 1st issue, textured sleeve, with poster, on coloured vinyl)	35
82	Neat 1005	BLACK METAL (LP, 1st issue, textured sleeve, with poster)	40
82	Neat NEAT 1005	BLACK METAL (LP, green marbled vinyl)	350
83	Neat NEATP 1002	WELCOME TO HELL (LP, reissue, purple vinyl)	50
84	Neat 1015	AT WAR WITH SATAN (LP, textured sleeve, 1st 19,000 with poster)	20
84	Neat 1015	AT WAR WITH SATAN (LP, textured sleeve)	15
85	Neat NEATP 1005	BLACK METAL (LP, reissue, picture disc)	40
85	Neat NEATP 1015	AT WAR WITH SATAN (LP, picture disc)	40
85	Neat NEATP 1024	POSSESSED (LP, picture disc)	20
85	Neat NEAT 1024	POSSESSED (LP, blue vinyl)	20
86	Demon APKPD 12	OBSCENE MATERIAL (LP, picture disc)	20
86	Raw Power RAWLP 001	FROM HELL TO THE UNKNOWN (2-LP)	25
86	A.P. APK 12	OFFICIAL BOOTLEG (LP, picture disc)	15
89	Under One Flag FLAG 36P	PRIME EVIL (LP, numbered picture disc, stickered clear sleeve)	20

CAROL VENTURA

65	Stateside SS 466	Please Somebody Help Me/The Old Lady Of Threadneedle Street	20
65	Stateside SL 10146	CAROL! (LP)	20
66	Stateside S(S)L 10180	I LOVE TO SING (LP)	20

CHARLIE VENTURA

55	Vogue Coral Q 72048	I Love You/Intermezzo	7

DAVE VENTURA

64	Mercury MF 805	The Hurt Stays In The Heart/Is A Redbird Red?	8
64	Mercury MF 827	I Forgot What It Was Like/I'll Never Love Again	7

DAVE VENTURA & THE ORBITS

63	Hardy Records 001	Yo Yo Twist/Yo Yo Twist Story (Flexi)	10

TOBY VENTURA

63	Decca F 11581	If My Heart Were A Storybook/Vagabond	40

VENTURES

(see also New Ventures, Bobby Vee, Nokie Edwards)

SINGLES

60	Top Rank JAR 417	Walk Don't Run/Home	10
60	London HLG 9232	Perfidia/No Trespassing	8
61	London HLG 9292	Ram-Bunk-Shush/Lonely Heart	10
61	London HLG 9344	Lullaby Of The Leaves/Ginchy	10
61	London HLG 9411	Theme From 'Silver City'/Bluer Than Blue	10
61	London HLG 9465	Blue Moon/Wailin'	15
61	London HLG 7113	Lady Of Spain/Blue Moon (export issue)	30
62	Liberty LIB 60	Lolita Ya-Ya/Lucille	8
62	Liberty LIB 67	The 2,000 Pound Bee Parts 1 & 2	12
63	Liberty LIB 68	El Cumbanchero/Skip To M'Limbo	8
63	Liberty LIB 78	The Ninth Wave/Damaged Goods	10
64	Liberty LIB 91	Journey To The Stars/Walkin' With Pluto	10
64	Liberty LIB 96	Walk Don't Run '64/The Cruel Sea	10
64	Liberty LIB 10142	Penetration/Solar Race	10
65	Liberty LIB 300	Slaughter On Tenth Avenue/Rap City	10
65	Liberty LIB 303	Diamond Head/Lonely Girl	10
65	Liberty LIB 306	The Swingin' Creeper/Pedal Pusher	10
65	Liberty LIB 308	The Stranger/Bird Rockers	10
65	Liberty LIB 10219	Sleigh Ride/White Christmas	10
66	Liberty LIB 316	Secret Agent Man/007-11	15
67	Liberty LIB 10266	Theme From The Wild Angels/High And Dry	10
67	Liberty LIB 55967	Strawberry Fields Forever/Endless Dream	10
68	Liberty LBF 15075	Flights Of Fantasy/Pandora's Box	15
70	Liberty LBF 15221	Hawaii Five-O - Theme/Higher Than Thou	15
71	United Artists UP 36316	Theme From 'Shaft'/Tight Fit	7
72	United Artists UP 35326	Joy/Cherries Jubilee	5
73	United Artists UP 35574	Skylab/Little People	7
77	United Artists UP 36223	Starsky And Hutch/Charlie's Angels	7

EPs

61	London REG 1279	THE VENTURES	20
61	London REG 1283	THE VENTURES (export issue)	25
61	London REG 1288	RAM-BUNK-SHUSH!	25

			MINT VALUE £
62	London REG 1326	ANOTHER SMASH	25
62	London REG 1328	COLOURFUL VENTURES	25
62	Liberty LEP 2058	TWIST WITH THE VENTURES	20
62	Liberty LEP 2131	SMASH HITS	20
63	Liberty LEP 2104	THE VENTURES PLAY TELSTAR AND LONELY BULL	25
64	Liberty LEP 2174	THE VENTURES PLAY COUNTRY GREATS	25
65	Liberty LEP 2212	BOBBY VEE MEETS THE VENTURES (with Bobby Vee)	35
66	Liberty LEP 2250	SECRET AGENT MEN	35
ALBUMS			
61	London HA-G 2340	THE VENTURES (mono)	40
61	London SAH-G 6143	THE VENTURES (stereo)	50
61	London HA-G 2376	ANOTHER SMASH (mono)	30
61	London SAH-G 6209	ANOTHER SMASH (stereo)	40
61	London HA-G 2409	THE COLOURFUL VENTURES (mono)	30
61	London SAH-G 6209	THE COLOURFUL VENTURES (stereo)	40
62	Liberty LBY 1002	WALK DON'T RUN	25
62	London HA-G 2429	TWIST WITH THE VENTURES (mono)	30
62	London SAH-G 6225	TWIST WITH THE VENTURES (stereo)	45
62	Liberty LBY 1072	TWIST PARTY	25
63	Liberty LBY 1110	GOING TO THE VENTURES DANCE PARTY! (mono)	25
63	Liberty SLBY 1110	GOING TO THE VENTURES DANCE PARTY! (stereo)	35
63	Liberty LBY 1147	BOBBY VEE MEETS THE VENTURES (with Bobby Vee, mono)	25
63	Liberty SLBY 1147	BOBBY VEE MEETS THE VENTURES (with Bobby Vee, stereo)	30
63	Liberty LBY 1150	SURFING (mono)	22
63	Liberty SLBY 1150	SURFING (stereo)	30
64	Liberty LBY 1169	LET'S GO! (mono)	18
64	Liberty SLBY 1169	LET'S GO! (stereo)	25
64	Liberty LBY 1189	THE VENTURES IN SPACE (mono)	22
64	Liberty SLBY 1189	THE VENTURES IN SPACE (stereo)	30
65	Liberty LBY 1228	WALK DON'T RUN - VOL. 2 (mono)	22
65	Liberty SLBY 1228	WALK DON'T RUN - VOL. 2 (stereo)	30
65	Liberty LBY 1252	KNOCK ME OUT (mono)	20
65	Liberty SLBY 1252	KNOCK ME OUT (stereo)	20
65	Liberty LBY 1270	ON STAGE (mono)	20
65	Liberty SLBY 1270	ON STAGE (stereo)	20
66	Liberty LBY 1274	VENTURES A-GO GO (mono)	18
66	Liberty SLBY 1274	VENTURES A-GO GO (stereo)	20
66	Liberty LBY 1285	THE VENTURES' CHRISTMAS ALBUM (mono)	22
66	Liberty SLBY 1285	THE VENTURES' CHRISTMAS ALBUM (stereo)	30
66	Liberty LBY 1297	WHERE THE ACTION IS! (mono)	18
66	Liberty SLBY 1297	WHERE THE ACTION IS! (stereo)	20
66	Liberty LBY 1323	GO WITH THE VENTURES (mono)	18
66	Liberty SLBY 1323	GO WITH THE VENTURES (stereo)	20
67	Liberty LBY 1345	GUITAR FREAKOUT (mono)	18
67	Liberty SLBY 1345	GUITAR FREAKOUT (stereo)	20
67	Liberty LBY 1372	SUPER PSYCHEDELICS (mono)	18
67	Liberty SLBY 1372	SUPER PSYCHEDELICS (stereo)	20
67	Liberty LBY 1375	THE BEST OF THE VENTURES (mono)	18
67	Liberty SLBY 1375	THE BEST OF THE VENTURES (stereo)	20
68	Liberty LBL 83046E	GOLDEN GREATS (mono)	18
68	Liberty LBS 83046E	GOLDEN GREATS (stereo)	20
68	Liberty LBL/LBS 83085E	GREAT PERFORMANCES VOL. 1	18
68	Liberty LBL/LBS 83092E	$1,000,000 WEEKEND	18
68	Liberty LBL/LBS 83124E	LONELY BULL	15
68	Liberty LBX 2	VENTURES SAMPLER	15
68	Liberty LBL/LBS 83138E	FLIGHTS OF FANTASY	15
69	Liberty LBL/LBS 83164E	THE HORSE	15
69	Liberty LBL/LBS 83193E	UNDERGROUND FIRE	15
70	Liberty LBL 83279	SWAMP ROCK (mono)	15
70	Liberty LBS 83279	SWAMP ROCK (stereo)	12

VENUS & RAZORBLADES

77	Spark SRL 1153	I Wanna Be Where The Boys Are/Dogfood (numbered p/s)	8
78	Spark SRL 1159	Workin' Girl/Midnight	8

BILLY VERA

68	Atlantic 584 196	With Pen In Hand/Good Morning Blues	8

BILLY VERA & JUDY CLAY

(see also Judy Clay)

68	Atlantic 584 164	Storybook Children/Really Together	6
69	Atlantic 584 293	Reaching For The Moon/Tell It Like It Is	6
68	Atlantic 588 158	THE STORYBOOK CHILDREN (LP)	20

JOHN VERITY BAND

(see also Argent)

74	Probe SPB 1087	JOHN VERITY BAND (LP)	35

TOM VERLAINE

80	Electric EM 342	The Twilight Zone - Psychotic Reaction/ Wild Thing/Television - Poor Circulation (p/s)	10

TIM VERLANDER

72	Midas MR 007	TIM VERLANDER (LP, with booklet)	40

VERMILION

(see also Menace)

78	Illegal ILM 0010	Angry Young Women/Nymphomania/Wild Boys (p/s)	18
79	Illegal ILS 0015	I Like Motorcycles/The Letter (p/s)	10

MINT VALUE £

VERN & ALVIN
(see also Maytones)

69	Blue Cat BS 167	Everybody Reggae/Another Fool	25
69	Big Shot BI 525	Old Man Dead/G.G. RHYTHM SECTION: Reggae Me	15

VERN & SON
(see also Maytones)

71	G.G. GG 4523	Little Boy Blue/TYPHOON ALL STARS: Little Boy Blue - Version	6

LARRY VERNE

60	London HLN 9194	Mr. Custer/Okeefenokee Two Step	8
61	London HLN 9263	Mr. Livingstone/Roller Coaster	7

LYN VERNON

60	Top Rank JAR 323	Woodchoppers Ball/Caravan	7

MIKE VERNON

72	Blue Horizon 2096 007	Let's Try It Again/Little Southern Country Girl	25
71	Blue Horizon 2931 003	BRING IT BACK HOME (LP, textured sleeve with insert)	150
71	Blue Horizon 2931 003	BRING IT BACK HOME (LP, textured sleeve without insert)	100

VERNON & THE G.I.S

79	Billy Goat BILL 004	Ghost Train Boogie/(I'm A) Teddy Boy	6
80	Billy Goat BILL 006	I Wanna Be A Ted/Banjo Baby (p/s)	7

VERNONS GIRLS
(see also Krimson Kake, Wilde Three, Jimmy Saville, Lee Francis, Samantha Jones, Breakaways)

58	Parlophone R 4497	Lost And Found/White Bucks And Saddle Shoes	25
59	Parlophone R 4532	Jealous Heart/Now Is The Month Of Maying	20
59	Parlophone R 4532	Jealous Heart/Now Is The Month Of Maying (78)	10
59	Parlophone R 4596	Don't Look Now But/Who Are They To Say?	20
60	Parlophone R 4624	We Like Boys/Boy Meets Girl	15
60	Parlophone R 4654	Madison Time (with Jimmy Saville)/The Oo-We	15
61	Parlophone R 4734	Ten Little Lonely Boys/Anniversary Song	10
61	Parlophone R 4832	Let's Get Together/No Message	10
62	Decca F 11450	Lover Please/You Know What I Mean	7
62	Decca F 11495	The Loco-motion/Don't Wanna Go	10
62	Decca F 11549	Funny All Over/See For Yourself	10
63	Decca F 11629	Do The Bird/I'm Gonna Let My Hair Down	10
63	Decca F 11685	He'll Never Come Back/Stay-At-Home	5
63	Decca F 11781	Tomorrow Is Another Day/Why Why Why	10
64	Decca F 11807	We Love The Beatles/Hey Lover Boy	15
64	Decca F 11887	Only You Can Do It/Stupid Little Girl	10
64	Decca F 12021	It's A Sin To Tell A Lie/Don't Say Goodbye	10
62	Decca DFE 8506	THE VERNONS GIRLS (EP)	50
58	Parlophone PMC 1052	THE VERNONS GIRLS (LP)	85

LILI VERONA

54	HMV 7MC 13	Massa Johnny/Hoggin' In The Cocoa (export issue)	15
56	Melodisc MEL 1383	French Lesson/Pica Now (78, with Gulf Stream Calypso Boys)	10
59	HMV DLP 1202	JAMAICA SINGS (10" LP)	22

VERSATILE NEWTS
(see also Felt)

80	Shanghai No. 2	Newtrition/Blimp (p/s, stamped white label)	25

VERSATILES
(see also Pioneers, Soul Sisters)

68	Island WI 3142	Teardrops Falling/Someone To Love	28
68	Amalgamated AMG 802	Just Can't Win/LEADERS: Sometimes I Sit Down Down And Cry	25
68	Crab CRAB 1	Children Get Ready/Someone To Love	12
69	Big Shot BI 520	Worries A Yard/VAL BENNETT: Hound Dog Special	8
69	Crab CRAB 5	Spread Your Bed/Worries A Yard	50
74	Dip DL 5039	Cutting Razor/UPSETTERS: Black Belt Jones	8

VERSATILES

69	Amalgamated AMG 854	Lu Lu Bell/Long Long Time	40
70	New Beat NB 060	Pick My Pocket/FREEDOM SINGERS: Freedom	8
71	Nu Beat NB 076	Give To Me/TIGER: With Hot	7

VERSATILITY

75	President	Tequila Madness/B Side Blues	10

VERTICAL HOLD

80	Vertical Hold VH 001	Rubber Cross/Injustice (p/s)	40
84	Vertical Hold VH 002	Angel Dust/Four Years/Dub Years (p/s)	15
85	Vertical Hold VH 003	The War That TIme Won/Bio Hazard (p/s)	15

VERUKAS
(see under varukers)

VERVE

92	Hut HUT 12	All In The Mind/One Way To Go (p/s)	5
92	Hut HUTT 12	All In The Mind/Man Called Sun/One Way To Go (12" promo, white label)	25
92	Hut HUT 16	She's A Superstar (Edit)/Feel (p/s)	7
92	Hut HUTEN 21	GRAVITY GRAVE EP (Gravity Grave [Edit]/Endless Life/ She's A Superstar [Live at Clapham Grand]) (10", p/s)	12
92	Hut HUTT 16	She's A Superstar/Feel (12" promo, white label)	15
92	Strange Fruit SFPMA 214	HUT - THE PEEL SESSIONS (10", p/s)	7
92	Strange Fruit SFMCD 214	HUT - THE PEEL SESSIONS (CD)	8
93	Hut HUTUS 1/YARDCD 1	THE VERVE EP (Gravity Grave [Edit]/A Man Called Sun/She's A Superstar [Edit]/Endless Life/Feel) (CD, export issue to U.S., 3,000 issued in U.K.)	8
93	Hut HUTEN 29	Blue/Twilight/Where The Geese Go/No Come Down (10", p/s)	12

			MINT VALUE £
93	Hut HUTCD 29	Blue/Twilight/Where The Geese Go/No Come Down (CD)	8
93	Hut HUT 35	Slide Away/Make It 'Til Monday (pink vinyl, p/s)	6
93	(no label) FLEXI 1	Make It 'Til Monday (Glastonbury '93) (clear vinyl stickered flexi with magazine)	20
95	Hut HUT 54	This Is Music/Let The Damage Begin (purple vinyl, p/s)	8
95	Hut HUT 55	On Your Own/I See The Door (green vinyl, p/s)	8
95	Hut HUT 55	On Your Own/I See The Door (green vinyl, p/s, mispressing, B-side plays 'Friends' by Daryll-Ann)	12
97	Hut HUTLH 82	Bitter Sweet Symphony/So Sister (jukebox issue)	12
97	Hut HUTTR 82	Bitter Sweet Symphony (James Lavelle Remix)/(James Lavelle Instrumental Remix) (12", stickered plain die-cut sleeve, promo only)	10
97	Hut HUTTP 82	Bitter Sweet Symphony (Extended Version)/(M.S.G. Mix)/(Instrumental) (12", plain die-cut sleeve, promo only)	15
97	Hut HUTLH 88	The Drugs Don't Work/The Drugs Don't Work (Original Demo) (jukebox issue)	7
97	Hut HUTT 92	Lucky Man/Never Wanna See You Cry/MSG/The Longest Day (12", p/s)	8
98	Hut HUTTX 100	Sonnet/Stamped/So Sister/Echo Bass (12", title sleeve)	10
93	Hut HUTLP 3	A STORM IN HEAVEN (LP, gatefold)	50
95	Hut HUTLP 27	A NORTHERN SOUL (2-LP, mirrored sleeve)	50
97	Hut HUTLPX 45	URBAN HYMNS (2-LP)	35
97	Hut HUTLPX 45	URBAN HYMNS (2-LP, with inner sleeves, printed outer mailer, 5,000 only)	40
97	Hut CDPHUT 45	URBAN HYMNS (CD, ribbon-tied black gatefold sleeve, promo only)	25
93	Jolly Roger JOLLY ROGER 2	VOYAGER 1 (LP, official bootleg, blue vinyl, 1,000 only)	100

VETS

79	SRT SRTS 79	Flies/Contrix	50

V FOR VENDETTA

(see under David J)

VHF

80	Lion PAW 1	Heart Of Stone	75
81	Distill (NO Cat No)	First Impressions/In Stereo (mo p/s, most labels signed by band)	50

DANNY VIBES

00	Jah Tubbys JT 006	Want No Wickedness/Want No Dub	20

VIBRATIONS

(see also Jayhawks)

61	Pye International 7N 25107	The Watusi/Wallflower	25
64	London HLK 9875	My Girl Sloopy/Daddy Woo Woo	20
66	Columbia DB 7895	Canadian Sunset/The Story Of A Starry Night	25
67	Columbia DB 8175	Pick Me/You Better Beware	30
67	Columbia DB 8318	Talkin' 'Bout Love/One Mint Julep	25
68	Direction 58-3511	Love In Them There Hills/Remember The Rain	15
67	Columbia SX 6106	NEW VIBRATIONS (LP)	75
69	Direction 8-63644	GREATEST HITS (LP)	30
72	RCA SF 8254	THE VIBRATIONS (LP)	20

VIBRATORS

(see also Boyfriends, Chris Spedding, Nazis Against Fascism, Substitute, Troops Of Tomorrow, Urban Dogs)o

76	RAK RAK 245	We Vibrate/Whips And Furs	10
76	RAK RAK 246	Pogo Dancing/The Pose (as Vibrators with Chris Spedding)	10
77	RAK RAK 253	Bad Times/No Heart (unreleased, this price is for acetates, of which 2 copies exist)	150
77	Epic EPC 5302	Baby Baby/Into The Future (p/s)	5
77	Epic EPC 5565	London Girls/Stiff Little Fingers (live) (p/s)	5
78	Epic EPC 6393	Judy Says (Knock You On The Head)/Pure Mania (p/s)	5
80	Rat Race RAT 2	Gimme Some Lovin'/Power Cry (live) (p/s, in slightly different colours)	5
80	Rat Race RAT 4	Disco In Mosco/Take A Chance (p/s, with various coloured writing)	5
77	Epic EPC 82097	PURE MANIA (LP)	15
78	Epic EPC 82495	V2 (LP, with inner lyric sleeve)	15

VIBRATORS (Jamaica)

(see also Al & Vibrators, Wilbert Francis & Vibrators)

66	Doctor Bird DB 1036	Sloop John B/Amour	18

VIBRONICS

04	Jah Tubbys JT 10021	Terror/African Stone (10")	20

VICE CREEMS

78	Tiger GRRRR 1	Won't You Be My Girl?/01-01-212 (gatefold p/s)	30
79	Zig Zag ZZ22 001	Danger Love/Like A Tiger (p/s)	25

VICEROYS

(see also Richard Ace, Interns [Jamaica], Derrick Morgan, Vincent Gordon, Hub)

67	Island WI 3095	Lip And Tongue/DAWN PENN: When Am I Gonna Be Free	100
67	Coxsone CS 7031	Magadown/RICHARD ACE: Don't Let The Sun Catch You Crying	45
67	Studio One SO 2016	Lose And Gain (as Voiceroys)/SOUL BROTHERS: Honey Pot	50
67	Studio One SO 2025	Shake Up/NORMA FRAZER: Telling Me Lies	30
68	Studio One SO 2064	Last Night/Ya Ho	25
68	Blue Cat BS 121	Fat Fish/OCTAVES: You're Gonna Lose	150
69	Studio One SO 2077	Things A-Come To Bump/LYRICS: Old Man Say	25
69	Punch PH 3	Jump In A Fire/Give To Get (as Voiceroys)	35
69	Crab CRAB 12	Work It/You Mean So Much To Me (B-side actually by Paragons)	30
69	Crab CRAB 27	Death A-Come (actually by Lloyd Robinson)/MATADOR ALLSTARS: The Sword	20
73	Harry J. HJ 6658	Chucky (Parts 1 & 2)	5
74	Harry J. HJ 6669	Wheel & Jig (Parts 1 & 2)	5
76	Angen ANG 112	Marcus Marcus Garvey/Change Your Style	8
84	Greensleeves GRED 146	New Clothes/New Clothes Rhythm/Bubblers Version (12")	15
82	Trojan TRLS 206	WE MUST UNITE (LP)	45
83	Csa CSLP 5	BRETHEREN AND SISTREN (LP)	50

MINT VALUE £

VICEROYS (U.K.)

70	Bullet BU 441	Chariot Coming/SYDNEY ALLSTARS: Stackata	10
70	Bullet BU 444	Power Control/SLICKERS: Dip Dip	10
70	Bullet BU 450	Come On Over/SYDNEY ALLSTARS: Version	10
70	Bullet BU 453	Fancy Clothes/BIGGIE: Jack And Jill	10
71	Bullet BU 470	Rebel Nyah/Feel The Spirit	10

VICE SQUAD

(see also Sex Aids)

80	Riot City RIOT 1	Last Rockers/Living On Dreams/Latex Love (p/s, with poster)	10
81	Riot City RIOT 2	Resurrection/Young Blood/Hurricane (p/s)	6
82	Riot City RIOT 12 1/2	SINGLES (12" EP)	8
82	Zonophone Z 26	Out Of Reach/Sterile/Out Of Reach (p/s)	5
82	Zonophone Z 30	Rock 'n' Roll Massacre/Stand Strong And Proud/Tomorrow	5
80s	Vice Squad Fan Club	EVIL (EP, flexidisc)	12
82	EMI ZEM 104	STAND STRONG STAND PROUD (LP, with inner)	15

VICE VERSA

(see also Liza Strike)

80	Neutron NT 001/PX 1092	MUSIC 4 (EP, poster p/s)	10

VICIOUS PINK (PHENOMENA)

(see also Soft Cell)

82	Mobile Suit Corp. CORP 1	My Private Tokyo/Promises (p/s)	5
82	Mobile Suit Corp. CORP 12	My Private Tokyo (Long Version)/(Remix)/Promises (12", p/s)	8
83	Warehouse WARE 1T	Je T'Aime (Moi Non Plus) (12" Disco Version)/In The Swim (12", p/s)	8

VICIOUS RUMOURS

87	Link LP 022	THE SICKEST MEN IN TOWN (LP)	12

SID VICIOUS

(see also Sex Pistols)

79	Virgin V2144	SID SINGS (LP, picture inner)	12

MIKE VICKERS (ORCHESTRA)

(see also Manfred Mann, Baker Street Philharmonic)

65	Columbia DB 7657	On The Brink/The Puff Adder (as Mike Vickers & Orchestra)	50
65	Columbia DB 7657	On The Brink/The Puff Adder (as Mike Vickers & Orchestra) (DJ Copy)	110
66	Columbia DB 7825	Eleventy One/The Inkling	20
66	Columbia DB 7906	Morgan - A Suitable Case For Treatment/Gorilla Of My Dreams (as Mike Vickers Orchestra)	20
67	Columbia DB 8171	Air On A G-String/Proper Charles (as Mike Vickers Orchestra)	10
67	Columbia DB 8281	Captain Scarlet And The Mysterons/Kettle Of Fish	30
90s	Emidisc EMIDISC 101	On The Brink/SAINT ETIENNE: Emidisc Theme (promo only)	10
68	Columbia S(C)X 6180	I WISH I WERE A GROUP AGAIN (LP)	45

SUE VICKERS

72	Threshold TH 8	Loving You The Way I Do/Take Me With You	5

MACK VICKERY

60	Top Rank JAR 420	Fantasy/Hawaiian Stroll	12

VICKY

(see also Vicky Leandros)

67	Philips BF 1565	Colours Of Love (Love Is Blue)/Who Can Tell	15
67	Philips BF 1599	Sunshine Boy/Tell Me	10
68	Philips BF 1631	Dance With Me Until Tomorrow/Give Me Your Hand	10

VICKY & JERRY

60	HMV POP 715	Don't Cry/A Year Ago Tonight	20

VICTIM

78	Good Vibrations GOT 2	Strange Things By Night/Mixed Up World (wraparound p/s)	15
79	TJM TJM 13	THE VICTIM (EP, unreleased)	0
79	TJM TJM 14	Why Are Fire Engines Red/I Need You (p/s)	25
80	TJM TJM 15	The Teen Age/Junior Criminals/Hung On To Yourself (p/s)	25
80	Illuminated ILL 1	The Teen Age/Junior Criminals/Hung On To Yourself (p/s, reissue)	15

VICTIMIZE

79	I.M.E. IME 1	Baby Buyer/Hi Rising Failure (folded p/s)	70
80	I.M.E. IME 2	Wh?r? Did Th? Mon?y Go (p/s)	70

VICTIMS OF CHANCE

70	Stable SLE 8004	VICTIMS OF CHANCE (LP)	120

VICTIMS OF CIRCUMSTANCE

80s	Double Vision DV 1	Very Little Glory/OPPOSITION: Wires (p/s)	10

VICTIMS OF PLEASURE

80	P.A.M. VOP 1	When You're Young/If I Was/Sporting Pastimes (p/s)	10

VICTIMS OF VICTIMISATION

87	Death DEAD 2	Kill Or Be Killed/As A Doornail (p/s)	18

TONY VICTOR

62	Decca F 11459	Dear One/There Was A Time	25
63	Decca F 11626	Thinking Of You/Hokey Cokey	12
63	Decca F 11708	In The Still Of The Night/Money	12

VICTORIA

71	Atlantic 2091 084	Tule's Blues/Helplessly Hoping	6
71	Atlantic 2400 176	VICTORIA (LP)	30
71	Mojo 2466 008	SECRET OF THE BLOOM (LP)	45

VICTORIANS

64	Liberty LIB 55693	Oh What A Night For Love/Happy Birthday Blue	25

MINT VALUE £

VICTORS		
65 Oriole CB 1984	Take This Old Hammer/Answer's No	15
VICTORS		
69 High Note HS 019	Reggae Buddy/Easy Squeeze	12
71 Escort ERT 846	Me A Tell Yuh/LLOYD'S ALL-STARS: More Echo	8
VICTORY		
(see also Keith Howard)		
82 Rods HOT 3	TAKING THE FIGHT (LP, with lyric insert)	60
VIDELS		
60 London HLI 9153	Mister Lonely/I'll Forget You	80
VIENNA PHILHARMONIC ORCHESTRA		
71 Decca F 13259	The Onedin Line Theme/Sable Dance	5
VIETNAM ALL STARS (Actually Prince Buster with unknown vocalist)		
66 Rio R 109	The Toughest/ERROL DUNKLEY: Love Me Forever	100
VIGILANTES		
61 Pye International 7N 25082	Eclipse/Man In Space	20
VIGRASS & OSBORNE		
72 UNI UNS 544	Men Of Learning/Forever Autumn	10
(PAUL) VIGRASS		
68 RCA RCA 1755	New Man/Curly	10
69 RCA RCA 1800	Suzie/Funky Piano Joe (as Vigrass)	8
69 RCA RCA 1857	Free Lorry Ride/Flying	8
70 RCA RCA 1911	Stop/Like It Never Was	8
VIKINGS		
(see also Maytals, Flames [Jamaica], Bonnie & Skitto)		
63 Island WI 035	Maggie Don't Leave Me/Henchmen (both actually with Victor Wong)	20
63 Island WI 065	Hallelujah/Helpin' Ages (actually by Maytals)	12
63 Island WI 075	Six And Seven Books Of Moses/Zacions (actually by Maytals)	25
63 Island WI 101	Never Grow Old/Irene (actually by Maytals)	30
63 Island WI 107	Just Got To Be/You Make Me Do (actually by Maytals)	20
63 Island WI 117	Fever/Cheer Up (actually by Maytals)	20
64 Island WI 167	Daddy/It's You (actually by Maytals)	20
64 Black Swan WI 423	Down By The Riverside/This Way	25
64 Black Swan WI 428	Treat Me Bad/Sitting On Top	25
64 Black Swan WI 430	Come Into My Parlour/I Am In Love	20
VIKINGS		
66 Alp 595 011	Bad News Feeling/What Can I Do	30
VILENESS		
90 Noisome STENCH 3	March Of The Vile/Sex Is Vile (12", vile-scented p/s)	10
VILLAGE		
(see also Peter Bardens, Quiver)		
69 Head HDS 4002	Man In The Moon/Long Time Coming	55
VILLAGE IDIOTS		
66 Piccadilly 7N 35282	Laughing Policeman/I Know An Old Lady	6
VILLAGE SOUL CHOIR		
70 Direction 58-4969	Catwalk/Country Walk	8
VILLAGERS/PARCEL OF ROGUES		
73 Deroy (no cat. no.)	PARCEL OF FOLK (LP, private pressing, with insert)	90
CATERINA VILLALBA		
60 Ember EMB S 104	Quando La Luna/Amore Fantastico (p/s)	6
NICK VILLARD		
62 Pye 7N 15418	High Noon/Sail Ho	10
VILLIERS & GOLD		
68 Polydor 56235	Of All The Young Girls/This East	20
JOE VINA		
59 Top Rank JAR 251	Marina/That's Alright	5
RAE VINCE & VINCENTS		
64 Piccadilly 7N 35211	One Fine Day/Little Girl, I'm Sad	10
EDWARD J VINCENT		
69 CBS 4388	Run To The Sun/I Never Thought I'd Fall In Love	15
GENE VINCENT (& BLUE CAPS)		
78s		
56 Capitol CL 14599	Be-Bop-A-Lula/Woman Love	15
56 Capitol CL 14628	Race With The Devil/Gonna Back Up, Baby	25
56 Capitol CL 14637	Bluejean Bop/Who Slapped John?	15
57 Capitol CL 14681	Jumps, Giggles And Shouts/Wedding Bells (Are Breaking Up That Old Gang Of Mine)	30
57 Capitol CL 14693	Crazy Legs/Important Words	30
57 Capitol CL 14722	Bi-I-Bickey-Bi, Bo-Bo-Go/Five Days, Five Days	30)
57 Capitol CL 14763	Lotta Lovin'/Wear My Ring	25
57 Capitol CL 14808	Dance To The Bop/I Got It	25
58 Capitol CL 14830	Walkin' Home From School/I Got A Baby	35
59 Capitol CL 15053	Right Now/The Night Is So Lonely	150

(The above 78s are credited to Gene Vincent & Blue Caps)

MINT VALUE £

SINGLES

56	Capitol CL 14599	Be-Bop-A-Lula/Woman Love	40
56	Capitol CL 14628	Race With The Devil/Gonna Back Up, Baby	100
56	Capitol CL 14637	Bluejean Bop/Who Slapped John?	60
57	Capitol CL 14681	Jumps, Giggles And Shouts/Wedding Bells (Are Breaking Up That Old Gang Of Mine) (promo copy in p/s)	125
57	Capitol CL 14681	Jumps, Giggles And Shouts/Wedding Bells (Are Breaking Up That Old Gang Of Mine)	100
57	Capitol CL 14693	Crazy Legs/Important Words (in p/s)	75
57	Capitol CL 14693	Crazy Legs/Important Words	50
57	Capitol CL 14722	Bi-I-Bickey-Bi, Bo-Bo-Go/Five Days, Five Days (in p/s)	150
57	Capitol CL 14722	Bi-I-Bickey-Bi, Bo-Bo-Go/Five Days, Five Days	75
57	Capitol CL 14763	Lotta Lovin'/Wear My Ring	50
57	Capitol CL 14808	Dance To The Bop/I Got It	50
58	Capitol CL 14830	Walkin' Home From School/I Got A Baby (in p/s)	70
58	Capitol CL 14830	Walkin' Home From School/I Got A Baby	60
58	Capitol CL 14868	Baby Blue/True To You	40
58	Capitol CL 14908	Rocky Road Blues/Yes I Love You, Baby	40
58	Capitol CL 14935	Git It/Little Lover	40
59	Capitol CL 14974	Say Mama/Be Bop Boogie Boy	30
59	Capitol CL 15000	Who's Pushin' Your Swing/Over The Rainbow	20
59	Capitol CL 15035	Summertime/Frankie And Johnnie	25
59	Capitol CL 15053	Right Now/The Night Is So Lonely	20
59	Capitol CL 15099	Wild Cat/Right Here On Earth	15
60	Capitol CL 15115	My Heart/I've Got To Get You Yet	20

(The above singles are credited to Gene Vincent & Blue Caps. Later 45s are solo, unless otherwise stated)

60	Capitol CL 15136	Pistol Packin' Mama (as Gene Vincent & Beat Boys)/Weeping Willow	15
60	Capitol CL 15169	Anna-Annabelle/Ac-Cent-Tchu-Ate The Positive	15
61	Capitol CL 15179	Maybe/Jezebel	15
61	Capitol CL 15185	If You Want My Lovin'/Mister Loneliness	15
61	Capitol CL 15202	She She Little Sheila/Hot Dollar	15
61	Capitol CL 15215	I'm Going Home (To See My Baby)/Love Of A Man	15
61	Capitol CL 15231	Unchained Melody/Brand New Beat (with The Blue Caps)	15
62	Capitol CL 15243	Lucky Star/Baby Don't Believe Him (with Dave Burgess Band)	18
62	Capitol CL 15264	Be-Bop-A-Lula/The King Of Fools (with Charles Blackwell Orchestra)	15
63	Capitol CL 15290	Held For Questioning/You're Still In My Heart (with Charles Blackwell Orch.)	15
63	Capitol CL 15307	Rip It Up/High Blood Pressure (unissued, demo copies only)	250
63	Capitol CL 15307	Crazy Beat/High Blood Pressure	40
63	Columbia DB 7174	Temptation Baby/Where Have You Been All My Life	20
64	Columbia DB 7218	Humpity Dumpity/A Love 'Em And Leave 'Em Kinda Guy	20
64	Columbia DB 7293	La-Den-Da Den-Da-Da/The Beginning Of The End	20
64	Columbia DB 7343	Private Detective/You Are My Sunshine (as Gene Vincent & Shouts)	20
66	London HLH 10079	Bird Doggin'/Ain't That Too Much	30
66	London HLH 10099	Lonely Street/I've Got My Eyes On You	30
68	Capitol CL 15546	Be-Bop-A-Lula/Say Mama	15
69	Dandelion S 4596	Be-Bop-A-Lula '69/Ruby Baby	10
70	Dandelion S 4974	White Lightning/Scarlet Ribbons (For Her Hair)	10
71	Kama Sutra 2013 018	The Day The World Turned Blue/High On Life (some with large centre)	10
73	Spark SRL 1091	Story Of The Rockers/Pickin' Poppies (push-out or solid centre)	10
74	BBC BEEB 001	Roll Over Beethoven/Say Mama/Be-Bop-A-Lula '71 (push-out or solid centre)	5
77	Capitol CL 15906	Say Mama/Lotta Lovin'/Race With The Devil	5
81	Capitol CL 203	She She Little Sheila/Say Mama/Dance To The Bop (p/s)	5
87	Nighttracks SFNT 001	Nighttracks (Distant Drums/Be-Bop-A-Lula) (p/s, promo only with insert)	10

EPs

58	Capitol EAP 1-985	HOT ROD GANG	75
59	Capitol EAP 1-1059	A GENE VINCENT RECORD DATE	75
60	Capitol EAP 3-1059	A GENE VINCENT RECORD DATE PART 3	80
61	Capitol EAP 1-20173	IF YOU WANT MY LOVIN'	80
62	Capitol EAP 1-20354	RACE WITH THE DEVIL	80
63	Capitol EAP 1-20461	TRUE TO YOU	80
64	Capitol EAP 1-20453	THE CRAZY BEAT OF GENE VINCENT NO. 1	80
64	Capitol EAP 2-20453	THE CRAZY BEAT OF GENE VINCENT NO. 2	80
64	Capitol EAP 3-20453	THE CRAZY BEAT OF GENE VINCENT NO. 3	80
69	EMIdisc (no cat. no.)	LIVE & ROCKIN'! (fan club issue, mail-order, 99 only)	250
79	Rollin' Danny RD 1	RAINY DAY SUNSHINE (L.A. 1969 demos, 500 only)	12

LPs

56	Capitol T 764	BLUEJEAN BOP! (original pressing with turquoise labels)	130
56	Capitol T 764	BLUEJEAN BOP! (later pressing with rainbow labels)	60
57	Capitol T 811	GENE VINCENT AND THE BLUECAPS (turquoise label)	130
57	Capitol T 811	GENE VINCENT AND THE BLUECAPS (rainbow label)	60
58	Capitol T 970	GENE VINCENT ROCKS! & THE BLUECAPS ROLL (turquoise label)	130
58	Capitol T 970	GENE VINCENT ROCKS! & THE BLUECAPS ROLL (later rainbow label)	60
59	Capitol T 1059	A GENE VINCENT RECORD DATE	70
59	Capitol T 1207	SOUNDS LIKE GENE VINCENT	70
60	Capitol T 1342	CRAZY TIMES! (mono)	60
60	Capitol ST 1342	CRAZY TIMES! (stereo)	100
63	Capitol T 20453	THE CRAZY BEAT OF GENE VINCENT	65
64	Columbia 33SX 1646	SHAKIN' UP A STORM (as Gene Vincent & The Shouts)	70
65	Music F. Pleasure MFP 1053	CRAZY TIMES (reissue)	12
67	London HA-H 8333	GENE VINCENT	50

(The Capitol compilations listed above may exist with later label designs. These would be worth half the values listed)

67	Capitol T 20957	THE BEST OF GENE VINCENT ('rainbow' label; reissue with pink label = £12)	20
68	Capitol ST 21144	THE BEST OF GENE VINCENT VOL. 2 ('rainbow' label; reissue with pink label = £12)	20
70	Dandelion 63754	I'M BACK AND I'M PROUD (gatefold sleeve)	30

MINT VALUE £

71 Kama Sutra 2316 005 THE DAY THE WORLD TURNED BLUE. 20
71 Kama Sutra 2316 009 IF YOU COULD ONLY SEE ME TODAY 20
87 Charly BOX 108 GENE VINCENT: THE CAPITOL YEARS '56-'63 (10-LP box set with 36-page booklet; later remastered and reissued with slimmer box, 1989) 50
90 EMI CDGV 1 THE GENE VINCENT BOX SET (Complete Capitol & Columbia Recordings, 1956-64) (6-CD set) 40

RORY VINCENT
73 Columbia SCXA 9254 SINGS THE MUSIC OF WLODEK GULGOWSKI (LP). 20

CAROLE VINCI
78 EMI EMI 2801 Vivre/Souffire Et Sourire 12

JOEY VINE
65 Immediate IM 017 Down And Out/The Out Of Towner 30

VINEGAR JOE
(see also Dada, Robert Palmer, Elkie Brooks)
72 Island WIP 6125 Never Met A Dog/Speed Queen Of Ventura 5
72 Island WIP 6148 Rock'n'Roll Gypsies/So Long 5
73 Island WIP 6174 Black Smoke From The Calumet/Long Way Round 5
72 Island ILPS 9183 VINEGAR JOE (LP). 25
72 Island ILPS 9214 ROCK 'N ROLL GYPSIES (LP, gatefold sleeve). 18
73 Island ILPS 9262 SIX STAR GENERAL (LP, gatefold sleeve). 18

VINES
01 RexRec REKD 195 Factory/Ain't No Room/Drown The Baptists (p/s, 500 only). 8

VINEYARD
74 Decca F13518 Ghost Train/Unicorns & Minotaurs 8

EDDIE 'MR. CLEANHEAD' VINSON
(see also Wynonie Harris)
51 Vogue V 2023 Queen Bee Blues/Jump And Grunt (78) 25
64 Riverside RLP 3302 BACK DOOR BLUES (LP) 40
72 Philips 6369 406 THE ORIGINAL CLEANHEAD (LP) 18

V. VINSTRICK & J.J. ALLSTARS
68 Doctor Bird DB 1167 Love Is Not A Game/CINDERELLA: The Way I See You 30

IAN VINT
62 Columbia DB 7514 Long Lonely Nights/Satin 7
64 Columbia 33SX 1649 TELL ME WHY (LP). 25

BOBBY VINTON
61 Fontana H 307 Little Lonely One/Corrine Corrina. 10
62 London HLU 9592 I Love You The Way You Are/CHUCK & JOHNNY: You Are My Girl. 10
62 Columbia DB 4878 Roses Are Red/You And I. 5
62 Columbia DB 4900 Rain Rain Go Away/Over Over 5
63 Columbia DB 4961 Trouble Is My Middle Name/Let's Kiss And Make Up 5
63 Columbia DB 7015 Over The Mountain/Faded Pictures 5
63 Columbia DB 7052 Blue On Blue/Those Little Things. 5
63 Columbia DB 7110 Blue Velvet/Is There A Place 10
63 Columbia DB 7179 There! I've Said It Again/The Girl With The Bow In Her Hair 5
64 Columbia DB 7240 My Heart Belongs To Only You/Warm And Tender 5
64 Columbia DB 7303 Tell Me Why/Remembering 5
64 Columbia DB 7348 Clinging Vine/Imagination Is A Magic Dream. 5
64 Columbia DB 7422 Mr Lonely/The Bell That Couldn't Jingle 10
62 Columbia SEG 8212 YOUNG IN HEART (EP) 10
64 Columbia SEG 8363 SONGS OF CHRISTMAS (EP) 10
63 Columbia 33SX 1517 SINGS THE BIG ONES (LP) 15
62 Columbia 33SX1465 ROSES ARE RED (LP) 20
63 Columbia 33SX 1566 BLUE ON BLUE (LP). 20
63 Columbia 33SX 1611 MY HEART BELONGS TO ONLY YOU (LP). 20
65 Columbia 33SX1725 LAUGHING ON THE OUTSIDE (LP). 20

MATT VINYL
77 Housewife's Choice Useless Tasks (p/s). 8

VIOLATORS
82 No Future OI 9 Gangland/Fugitive (p/s, with insert) 8
82 No Future OI 19 Summer Of '81/Live Fast Die Young (p/s) 8
83 Future FS 2 Life On The Red Line/Crossing The Sangsara (p/s) 6
80s Oi 26 DIE WITH DIGNITY EP (12") 20

VIOLENT FEMMES
83 Rough Trade ROUGH 55 VIOLENT FEMMES (LP) 20
84 Slash SLAP 1 HALLOWED GROUND (LP) 15
86 Slash SLAP 10 THE BLIND LEADING THE NAKED (LP). 15

VIOLENTS
63 HMV POP 1130 Alpen Ros/Ghia. 18

VIOLENT THIMBLE
67 Polydor 56217 Gentle People Parts 1 & 2 15

VIPERS (SKIFFLE GROUP)
(see also Jet Harris & Tony Meehan, Shadows, Wally Whyton, Sharkey Todd & Monsters)
56 Parlophone R 4238 Ain't You Glad/Pick A Bale Of Cotton. 20
57 Parlophone R 4261 Don't You Rock Me Daddy-O/10,000 Years Ago. 25
57 Parlophone R 4286 Jim Dandy/Hi Liley, Liley Lo 20
57 Parlophone R 4289 The Cumberland Gap/Maggie May 25
57 Parlophone R 4308 Streamline Train/Railroad Steam Boat 25
57 Parlophone R 4351 Homing Bird/Pay Me My Money Down 20
57 Parlophone R 4371 Skiffle Party Medley Parts 1 & 2 20

MINT VALUE £

58 Parlophone R 4393 Baby Why?/No Other Baby (as Vipers) ... 25
58 Parlophone R 4393 Baby Why?/No Other Baby (as Vipers) (78) ... 10
58 Parlophone R 4435 Make Ready For Love/Nothing Will Ever Change (My Love For You)(as Vipers) ... 15
58 Parlophone R 4484 Summertime Blues/Liverpool Blues (as Vipers) ... 35
58 Parlophone R 4484 Summertime Blues/Liverpool Blues (as Vipers) (78) ... 20
57 Parlophone GEP 8615 SKIFFLE MUSIC VOL. 1 (EP) ... 20
57 Parlophone GEP 8626 SKIFFLE MUSIC VOL. 2 (EP) ... 25
57 Parlophone GEP 8655 SKIFFLING ALONG WITH THE VIPERS (EP) ... 30
57 Parlophone PMD 1050 COFFEE BAR SESSION (10" LP) ... 60

VIPERS

78 Mulligan LUNS 718 I've Got You/No Such Thing (p/s) ... 10

VIPPS

(see also VIPS)
66 CBS 202031 Wintertime/Anyone ... 65

VIPS

(see also Vipps, Art, Spooky Tooth, Felder's Orioles, Timebox, Patto, Baron & His Pounding Piano, Keith Emerson)
64 RCA RCA 1427 Don't Keep Shouting At Me/She's So Good ... 100
66 Island WI 3003 I Wanna Be Free/Don't Let It Go ... 50
67 Island WIP 6005 Straight Down To The Bottom/In A Dream ... 80

V.I.P.s

(see also Mood Six, Jed Dmochowski)
78 Bust SOL 3 MUSIC FOR FUNSTERS (EP) ... 20
79 Rok ROK V/VI Can't Let You Go/URBAN DISTURBANCE: Wild Boys In Cortinas ... 25
80 Gem GEMS 25 Causing Complications/Run Run Belinda/Love Is A Golden Word (p/s) ... 6
80 Gem GEMS 39 The Quarter Moon/Hippy Hippy Shake (p/s) ... 5
80 Gem GEMS 43 I Need Somebody To Love (Could It Be You?)/One More Chance// Stuttgart Special/Who Knows/Janine (double pack, stickered p/s) ... 8
81 Gem GEMS 47 Things Aren't What They Used To Be/I Thought You Were My Friend (p/s) ... 6
90s Tangerine BEAT CRAZY (CD) ... 18

VIRGIL BROTHERS

69 Parlophone R 5787 Temptation 'Bout To Get Me/Look Away ... 15
69 Parlophone R 5802 Good Love/When You Walk Away ... 6

VIRGIN DANCE

84 Spartan SP10 Desire/Make Love (P/S) ... 8

VIRGINIANS

63 Pye International 7N 25175 Limbo Baby/Greenback Dollar ... 10

VIRGINIA TREE

(see also Shirley Kent, Ghost)
75 Minstrel 0001 FRESH OUT (LP) ... 50

VIRGINIA WOLF

86 Atlantic A 9459 Waiting For Your Love/Take A Chance (p/s) ... 10

VIRGINIA WOLVES

66 Stateside SS 563 Stay/B.L.T. ... 50
66 Stateside SS 563 Stay/B.L.T. (DJ copy) ... 100

VIRGIN PRUNES

(see also Gavin Friday, Bono & Gavin Friday)
81 Baby BABY 001 TWENTY TENS (EP) ... 15
81 Rough Trade RT 072 Moments Of Mine (Despite Straight Lines)/In The Greylight/War/ Moments Of Mine (Despite Straight Lines) (1st issue in blue p/s with insert) ... 15
81 Rough Trade RT 072 Moments Of Mine (Despite Straight Lines)/In The Greylight/War/Moments Of Mine (Despite Straight Lines) (later issue in black p/s without insert) ... 10
81 Rough Trade RT 89 A New Form Of Beauty 1; Sandpaper Lullaby/Sleep Fantasy Dreams (p/s) ... 15
81 Rough Trade RT 090 A New Form Of Beauty Part Two: Come To Daddy/Sweet Home Under White Clouds/Sad World (10", p/s, 33rpm) ... 8
81 Rough Trade RT 091T A New Form Of Beauty Part Three: The Beast (Seven Bastard Suck)/ The Slow Children (Abbagal)/Brain Damage/No Birds To Fly (12", p/s) ... 8
82 Rough Trade TI COPY 007 A New Form Of Beauty 4:Din Glorious (cassette) ... 25
82 Rough Trade RT 106 Pagan Lovesong/Dave-id Is Dead (p/s) ... 8
82 Rough Trade 12 RT 106 Pagan Lovesong (Vibe Akimbo)/Pagan Lovesong/Dave-id Is Dead (12", p/s) ... 10
87 Baby BABY 011 HERESIE (10", double pack, gatefold p/s, 1st 1,000 on clear vinyl) ... 15
87 Baby BABY 011 HERESIE (10", double pack, gatefold p/s) ... 10

VIRGIN SLEEP

67 Deram DM 146 Love/Halliford House ... 55
68 Deram DM 173 Secret/Comes A Time ... 55

VIRGO

89 Radical VIRG01 VIRGO (LP) ... 35

VIRTUE

85 Other OTH 1 We Stand To Fight/High Treason (p/s) ... 20

VIRTUES (Jamaica)

(see also Lloyd & Devon)
65 Island WI 196 Your Wife And Mother/Amen (actually with Ambassadors) ... 35
68 Doctor Bird DB 1164 High Tide/RUPIE EDWARDS & VIRTUES: Burning Love ... 25
68 Doctor Bird DB 1166 Sweet Nanny/RUPIE EDWARDS: Falling In Love ... 30

VIRTUES (U.S.)

59 HMV POP 621 Guitar Boogie Shuffle/Guitar In Orbit ... 20
59 HMV POP 637 Flippin' In/Shufflin' Along ... 20
59 HMV POP 637 Flippin' In/Shufflin' Along (78) ... 20

FRANK VIRTUOSO ROCKETS

56 Melodisc MEL 1386 Rollin' And A-Rockin'/Rock - Good Bye Mambo (78) ... 25
56 Melodisc MEL 1393 Toodle-Oo Kangaroo/Hop-Skip-Jump Mambo (78) ... 15

			MINT VALUE £
58	Melodisc MEL 1386	Rollin' And A-Rockin'/Rock - Good Bye Mambo (red label, tri-centre, export issue)	30
58	Melodisc MEL 1386	Rollin' And Rockin'/Toodle-Oo Kangaroo (green label, round centre)	15

VISAGE

(see also Rich Kids, Steve Strange, Strange Cruise, Midge Ure, Ultravox)

79	Radar ADA 48	Tar/Frequency 7 (p/s)	10
81	Polydor POSPX 194	Fade To Grey/The Steps (12", p/s)	15
81	Polydor POSPX 236	Mind Of A Toy (Dance Mix)/We Move (Dance Mix)/Frequency 7 (Dance Mix) (12", p/s)	10
82	Polydor POSPP 441	Night Train/I'm Still Searching (picture disc)	5
82	Polydor POSPP 523	Pleasure Boys/The Anvil (picture disc)	7
82	Polydor POSPX 523	Pleasure Boys (Dance Mix)/The Anvil (Dance Mix) (12", 800 only)	10
82	Polydor POSPV 523	Der Amboss/The Anvil (Mix) (12", stickered plain black sleeve & labels, promo only)	10

TONY VISCONTI

(see also Dib Cochran & Earwigs)

79	Regal Zonophone RZ 3089	I Remember Brooklyn/Sitting In A Field Of Heather	10

VISCOUNTS

(see also Gordon Mills)

60	Pye 7N 15249	That's All Right/Rockin' Little Angel	5
60	Pye 7N 15287	Shortnin' Bread/Fee-Fi-Fo-Fum	7
61	Pye 7N 15323	Money Is The Root Of All Evil/One-Armed Bandit	5
61	Pye 7N 15344	Banned In Boston/Moonlight Promises	5
61	Pye 7N 15356	Joe Sweeney/Honey Come On And Dance With Me	5
61	Pye 7N 15379	Who Put The Bomp (In The Bomp Bomp Bomp)/What Am I saying	10
61	Pye 7N 15414	Mama's Doing The Twist/I'm Going - But I'll Be Back	5
62	Pye 7N 15431	One Of The Guys/Dear Mary Brown	5
62	Pye 7N 15445	Everybody's Got a Ya Ya/A Lot of Livin' To Do	5
63	Columbia DB 7146	I Don't Care What People Say/Roll On Little Darlin'	6
60	Pye NEP 24132	VISCOUNTS' HIT PARADE (EP)	15

VISCOUNTS (U.S.)

59	Top Rank JAR 254	Harlem Nocturne/Dig	15
60	Top Rank JAR 388	The Touch (Le Grisbi)/Chug-A-Lug	15
60	Top Rank JAR 502	Night Train/Summertime	18
64	Columbia DB 7253	Kiss Me/Where Do You Belong	8
65	Stateside SS 468	Harlem Nocturne/Dig (reissue)	10
61	Top Rank JKP 3005	VISCOUNTS ROCK (EP)	60

VISIONS

(see also King Horror)

69	Grape GR 3009	Captain Hook/The Girl	40

VISITORS

78	NRG SRTS/NRG 002	Take It Or Leave It/No Compromise	25
79	Deep Heat DEEP ONE	Electric Heat/Moth/One Line (p/s)	10

VISITORS

80	Departure RAPTURE 1	Empty Rooms/The Orcadian Visitors (foldover p/s)	7

VITAL FORCE

87	Buce BUCE 1	Roll The Dice/Poor Little Rich Boy (no p/s)	25

MIROSLAV VITOUS

79	Warner Bros. K 17448 T	New York CIty/Basic Laws (12")	40
76	Warner Bros. K56219	MAGIC SHEPHERD (LP)	15

AMOR VIVI

70	Big Shot BI 534	Dirty Dog/Round And Round The Moon	8

VIVIENNE

57	HMV 7EG 8290	VIVIENNE (EP)	8

VIXEN

88	EMI MTPD 48	Edge Of A Broken Heart/Charmed Life (shaped picture disc)	7
88	EMI MTL 1028	VIXEN (LP, early copies play extra track "Charmed Life", withdrawn)	12

VLADO & ISOLDA

84	Ariola 106 500	Ciao Amore (English)/Ciao Amore (Croatian)	10

CRISTIAN VOGEL

(see also Blue Arsed Fly)

94	Ferox FER 004	NARCO SYNTHESIS EP (12", plain sleeve)	25
94	Mosquito MSQ 01	WE EQUATE MACHINES WITH FUNKINESS EP (12", custom sleeve)	25
95	Mosquito MSQ 03	ARTISTS IN CHARGE OF EXPERT SYSTEMS EP (12", custom sleeve)	20
95	Solid SOL 002	DEFUNKT EP (12", Three untitled tracks)	20
96	Solid SOL 004	The Visit/Spoke/Small Dogs (12")	30

VOGUES (U.K.)

(see also Llan)

66	Columbia DB 7985	Younger Girl/Lies	18

VOGUES (U.S.)

65	London HLU 9996	You're The One/Some Words	20
66	London HLU 10014	Five O'Clock World/Nothing To Offer You	20
66	King KG 1035	Magic Town/Humpty Dumpty	25
68	Reprise RS 20766	My Special Angel/I Keep It Hid	6
68	Reprise RS 20686	Turn Around Look At Me/Then	6
69	Reprise RS 20788	Till/I Will	6
69	London HLG 10247	Five O'Clock World/You're The One	15
69	Reprise RS 20820	Earth Angel/P.S. I Love You	6
69	Reprise RS 23366	No, Not Much/You Were Too Good To Me	6
69	Reprise RS 20844	Green Fields/Easy To Say	5

			MINT VALUE £
66	King KGL 4003	MEET THE VOGUES (LP)	55
66	King KGL 4006	FIVE O'CLOCK WORLD (LP)	50
69	Reprise RSLP 6314	TURN AROUND, LOOK AT ME (LP)	25
69	Reprise RSLP 6326	TILL (LP)	18

VOICE
(see also Karl Stuart & Profile, Profile, Miller Anderson)

66	Mercury MF 905	Train To Disaster/Truth	250

VOICE OF PROGRESS

82	Negus Roots NERLP 003	MINI BUS DRIVER (LP)	30

STEVE VOICE

79	EMI RB 102	UFO/Radio Blue	6

VOICEROYS
(see under Viceroys)

VOICES

56	Beltona BL 2667	Rock And Roll Hit Parade Medley (Parts 1 & 2)	18
56	Beltona BL 2667	Rock And Roll Hit Parade Medley (Parts 1 & 2) (78)	12

VOICES IN LATIN

68	Morgan MR 104P	VOICE IN LATIN (LP)	60

VOIDS

66	Polydor BM 56073	Come On Out/I'm In A Fix	100

WES VOIGHT
(see also Chip Taylor)

59	Parlophone R 4586	I'm Movin' In/I'm Ready To Go Steady	80

VOIZ

77	Pilgrim/Grapevine GRA 110	BOANERGES (LP, with insert)	25

HOWARD VOKES COUNTRY BOYS

62	Starlite STEP 27	HOWARD VOKES COUNTRY BOYS (EP)	20
63	Starlite STEP 37	MOUNTAIN GUITAR (EP)	20
67	Starlite GRK 508	HOWARD VOKES COUNTRY BOYS (EP; reissue, with sleeve sticker over original catalogue number)	12

VOLCANOES

86	Hybrid HYB LP 8	INTO THE PSYCHE (LP)	12

VOLCANOS

61	Philips PB 1098	Ruby Duby Du/Redhead	20
61	Philips PB 1113	Tightrope/Great Imposter	20
62	Philips PB 1246	Polaris/Scotch Mist	20
60	Philips BBE 12432	THE VOLCANOS (EP)	100

VOLTZ

82	Airship PP 580	KNIGHT'S FALL (LP)	70

VOLUMES

62	Fontana 270 109TF	I Love You/Dreams	120
63	London HL 9733	Sandra/Teenage Paradise	75

VOLUNTEERS
(see also Karol Keyes)

63	Parlophone R 5088	Farther Along/Little David	8

VON BONDIES

03	Must Destroy DESTROYER 2	Tell Me What You See (p/s, 1-sided)	15

VON TRAP FAMILY
(see also Bevis Frond)

80	Woronzow W 001	Brand New Thrill/Dreaming/No Reflexes (p/s, 500 only)	18

VONTASTICS

66	Chess CRS 8043	Day Tripper/My Baby	35
67	Stateside SS 2002	Lady Love/When My Baby Comes Back Home	65
67	Stateside SS 2002	Lady Love/When My Baby Comes Back Home (DJ Copy)	85

VOOMINS

65	Polydor 56001	If You Don't Come Back/March Of The Voomins	35

VOXPOPPERS

58	Mercury 7MT 202	The Last Drag/Wishing For Your Love	30
58	Mercury 7MT 202	The Last Drag/Wishing For Your Love (78)	25
58	Mercury MEP 9533	VOXPOPPERS (EP)	150

VOYAGER

85	Fighting Cock	Run Away Heart/Don't Hold Back (p/s)	15

V2

78	Bent SMALL BENT 1	Speed Freak/Nothing To Do/That's It (800 only, later reissued on red vinyl)	30
79	TJM TJM 1	Man In The Box/When The World Isn't There (12", p/s)	20
79	TJM TJM 6	Is Anybody Out There? (unissued)	0
70s	Groove	Gee Whiz It's You/Face In The Crowd (p/s, stamped white labels)	30

VULCAN

73	Epic SEPC 1763	Much To Young/Action Man	6

VULCANS

72	Big Shot BI 612	Dr. Spock/Joe Kidd	5
73	Big Shot BI 615	Red Herring/Vulcanised	5
73	Trojan TRLS 53	STAR TREK (LP)	25

VULCAN'S HAMMER

73	Brown BVH 1	TRUE HEARTS AND SOUND BOTTOMS (LP, with insert)	400

MINT VALUE £

VULTURES

88	Narodnik NRK 006T	Good Thing/You're Not Scared/What I Say/Jack The Ripper (12", p/s)	7

VULTURES

79	Rubber Connection SP 522	Time Let's Go/Is This A Man (p/s, with insert & sticker)	6

W

W. GIMMICS

65	Polydor EPH 27 125	HOT RODS (EP, manufactured in Europe)	60

PHIL WACHSMANN

85	Bead Records BEAD 23	WRITING IN WATER (LP)	20

PHILIPP WACHSMANN, ROCHARD BESWICK & TONY WREN

77	Bead Records BEAD 7	SPARKS OF THE DESIRE MAGNETO (LP, with insert)	30

WACKERS

63	Oriole CB 1902	I Wonder Why/Why Can't It Happen To Me	25
64	Piccadilly 7N 35195	Love Or Money/Hooka Tooka	15
64	Piccadilly 7N 35210	The Girl Who Wanted Fame/You're Forgetting	15

WACKERS (2)

72	Elektra K12054	I Hardly Knew Her Name/Do You Know The Reason	5
72	Electra K12081	Day And Night/Last Night	5

ADAM WADE

60	HMV POP 787	Speaking Of Her/Blackout The Moon	5
60	HMV POP 807	In Pursuit Of Happiness/For The Want Of Your Love	5
60	Top Rank JAR 296	Tell Her For Me/Don't Cry My Love	5
60	Top Rank JAR 370	Ruby/Too Far	5
61	HMV POP 843	Take Good Care Of Her/Sleepy Time Gal	10
61	HMV POP 896	Point Of No Return/The Writing On The Wall	5
61	HMV POP 942	Tonight I Won't Be There/Linda	5
62	Columbia DB 4891	I'm Climbin' (The Wall)/They Don't Believe Me	5
63	Columbia DB 4891	Don't Let Me Cross Over/Rain From The Skies	70
63	Columbia DB 7045	Why Do We Have To Wait So Long/They Say	5
60	HMV 7EG 8620	AND THEN CAME ADAM (EP)	15
64	Columbia SEG 8316	FOUR FILM SONGS (EP)	15
61	HMV CLP 1451	ADAM AND EVENING (LP)	30

CLIFF WADE

69	Morgan Bluetown BT 1S	You've Never Been To My House/Sister	18

JOHNNY WADE

60	HMV POP 757	Funny Thing/Shadow Love	8

WAYNE WADE

77	Grove Music GMDM 2	Happy Go Lucky Girl/PRINCE POMPADO: Jamaican Girl/ WAYNE WADE: I Kissed A Rose (12", p/s)	10
81	Greensleeves GRED 52	Poor And Humble/BUNNY LIE LIE: Babylonian (12")	25
15	Cha Cha CHAD 34	Tell Me What Going On/WAILING COCKS: Rudeboy Say Him Bad (12")	15
78	Grove Music GMLP 3	DANCING TIME (LP)	20

WELLINGTON WADE

(see also Ian & Zodiacs)

63	Oriole CB 1857	Let's Turkey Trot/It Ain't Necessarily So	40

WADSWORTH MANSION

71	A&M AMS 842	Sweet Mary/What's On Tonight	6

WAGADU

79	Rokel ROK 12	Freetown Calypso/Easy Dancin'	25

WAGES OF SIN

70	CBS 4971	West Virginia/Hey Hey Hey (Well I'm On My Way)	10

ADRIAN WAGNER

(see also Robert Calvert)

74	Atlantic K 50082	DISTANCES BETWEEN US (LP, with Robert Calvert)	22
78	Charisma CAS 1135	THE LAST INCA (LP, with booklet)	12

ROBERT WAGNER

57	London HLU 8491	Almost Eighteen/So Young	10

CHUCK WAGON

(see also Dickies)

79	A&M AMS 7450	Rock 'n' Roll Won't Go Away/The Spy In My Face (p/s, black vinyl)	10
79	A&M AMS 7450	Rock 'n' Roll Won't Go Away/The Spy In My Face (p/s, purple vinyl)	15

PORTER WAGONER

67	RCA Victor RCA 1586	The Cold Hard Facts Of Life/You Can't Make A Heel Toe The Mark	5
64	RCA Victor RCX 7157	A LITTLE SLICE OF LIFE (EP)	10
64	RCA Victor RCX 7158	Y'ALL COME (EP)	10

WAH! (HEAT)

81	Inevitable INEV 001	Better Scream/Joe (wraparound p/s in poly bag)	5
81	Inevitable INEV 004	Seven Minutes To Midnight/Don't Step On The Cracks (p/s, different colour sleeves)	5

MINT VALUE £

WAILERS (Jamaica)
(see under Bob Marley)

WAILERS (U.S.)

59	London HL 8958	Tall Cool One/Road-Runner	25
59	London HL 8958	Tall Cool One/Road-Runner (78)	30
59	London HL 8994	Mau-Mau/Dirty Robber	150
59	London HL 8994	Mau-Mau/Dirty Robber (78)	70
64	London HL 9892	Tall Cool One/Road-Runner (reissue)	5

WAILING COCKS

78	Bird's Nest BN 116	Rockin' Youth/Stand Up For Peace	5
78	Bird's Nest BN 121	Listen To The Wailing Cocks/Listen To The Wailing Cocks	5

WAILING SOULS
(see also Denis Alcapone, Tuff Gong All Stars)

70	Banana BA 305	Row Fisherman Row/Thou Shalt Not Steal	35
70	Banana BA 307	Back Out/Pack Your Things	25
71	Banana BA 335	Walk Walk Walk/KING SPORTY: Love Me - Version (B-side actually by Denis Alcapone)	40
71	Green Door GD 4014	Harbour Shark/Harbour Shark - Version	25
76	Conflict 301	Black Out/Dub	10
81	Cha Cha CHAD 34	Rudeboy Say Him Bad/WAYNE WADE: Tell Me What Going On (12")	40
81	Cha Cha CHAD 51	Grabbing And Running/Dub	20
82	Greensleeves GRED 111	They Don't Know Jah/Sticky Stay (12")	30
82	Upfront UPF 001	Take We Back (feat Ranking Trevor)/RANKING TREVOR: Yard Oh (12")	15
82	Upfront UPF 004	Take A Taste/JOHNNY RINGO: Don't Know Much (12")	15
79	Island ILPS 9523	WILD SUSPENSE (LP)	15

WAILING WAILERS
(see under Bob Marley)

CHERRY WAINER
(see also Red Price Combo)

58	Pye 7N 15161	Itchy Twitchy Feeling/Cerveza	10
59	Top Rank JAR 253	I'll Walk The Line/Saturday Night In Tia Juana	5
60	Columbia DB 4528	Happy Like A Bell (Ding Dong)/Money (That's What I Want)	20
63	Honey Hit TB 128	Sleepwalk/Red River Rock (with Red Price Combo, with p/s)	10
63	Honey Hit TB 128	Sleepwalk/Red River Rock (with Red Price Combo)	5
59	Pye NEP 24099	CHERRY WAINER (EP)	15

PHIL WAINMAN

65	Columbia DB 7615	Hear Me A Drummer Man/Hear His Drums	30
68	Fontana TF 978	Going Going Gone/Hey Paradiddle	200

LOUDON WAINWRIGHT III

71	Atlantic 2400 103	ALBUM I (LP)	22
72	Atlantic K 40107	ALBUM I (LP, reissue)	12
72	Atlantic K 40272	ALBUM II (LP)	15

WAITING FOR THE SUN
(see also After The Fire)

78	Profile GMOR 167	WAITING FOR THE SUN (LP, private pressing)	35

TOM WAITS
(see also Roy Orbison)

79	Asylum K 12347	Somewhere/Red Shoes By The Drugstore	5
86	Island ISD 260	In The Neighbourhood/Singapore//Tango Till They're Sore/Rain Dogs (double pack, p/s)	5
73	Asylum SYM 9007	CLOSING TIME (LP, with insert)	22
74	Asylum SYM 9012	THE HEART OF SATURDAY NIGHT (LP)	18
75	Asylum SYSP 903	NIGHTHAWKS AT THE DINER (2-LP, gatefold sleeve)	20
76	Asylum K 53030	CLOSING TIME (LP, reissue)	12
76	Asylum K 53035	THE HEART OF SATURDAY NIGHT (LP, 'door' label)	12
77	Asylum K 53050	SMALL CHANGE (LP, 'sky' label)	12
77	Asylum K 53068	FOREIGN AFFAIRS (LP, with inner sleeve)	12
79	Asylum K 53088	BLUE VALENTINE (LP, gatefold sleeve)	12
80	Asylum K 52252	HEARTATTACK AND VINE (LP, with inner sleeve)	12
81	Elektra K 52316	BOUNCED CHEQUES (LP)	12
83	Island TW1	A CONVERSATION WITH TOM WAITS (LP promo interview disc)	40
85	Island ILPS 9803	RAIN DOGS (LP)	15
88	Island ITW4	BIG TIME (LP)	12
91	Island 212370	NIGHT ON EARTH (LP)	20
92	Island ILPS 9993	BONE MACHINE (LP)	60
93	Island ILPS 8021	BLACK RIDER (LP)	40

WAKE
(see also Rubettes)

69	Pye 7N 17813	Angelina/So Happy	15
70	Carnaby CNS 4010	Live Today Little Girl/Days Of Emptiness	15
70	Carnaby CNS 4014	Boys In The Band/To Make You Happy	12
70	Carnaby CNS 4016	Noah/To Make You Happy	12
71	Carnaby 6151 001	Linda/Got My Eyes On You	12
70	Carnaby CNLS 6005	23.59 (LP, union jack flag label)	160

WAKE

82	Scan SCN 01	On Our Honeymoon/Give Up (p/s in bag)	20
84	Scan 45/Factory FAC 88	Talk About The Past/Everybody Works So Hard (p/s)	7
84	Scan 45/Factory FAC 8812	Talk About The Past/Everybody Works So Hard (12", p/s)	12
87	Factory FAC12 178	Something No-one Else Can Bring/ Gruesome Castle	12
89	Sarah SARAH 21	Crush The Flowers/Carbrain (p/s)	7
90s	Sarah SARAH 48	Major John/Lousy Pop Group (p/s)	7

MINT VALUE £

83 Factory FACT 60 HARMONY (LP) 25
91 Factory FACT 130 HERE COMES EVERYBODY (LP) 20
90s Sarah SARAH 602 MAKE IT LOUD (LP) 15
90s Sarah SARAH 618 TIDAL WAVE OF HYPE (LP) 15

JIMMY WAKELY
(see also Karen Chandler, Bob Hope, Margaret Whiting)
56 Vogue Coral Q 72125 Are You Mine? (with Ruth Ross)/Yellow Roses 15
56 Brunswick 05542 Are You Satisfied? (with Gloria Wood)/Mississippi Dreamboat 15
56 Brunswick 05563 Folsom Prison Blues/That's What The Lord Can Do 20
57 Brunswick LAT 8179 SANTA FE TRAIL (LP) 25

RICK WAKEMAN (Band)
(see also Strawbs, Yes, Dib Cochran & Earwigs, Steve Howe, Jon Anderson)
73 A&M AMS 7061 Catherine/Anne 5
75 A&M AMS 7206 Love's Dream/Orpheus' Song 6
75 A&M/Lyntone LYN 3176/7 Wagner's Dream/Love's Dream/Count Your Blessings (with 2 tracks by Roger Daltrey, flexidisc with 19 magazine) 10
79 A&M AMS 7435 Birdman Of Alcatraz (Theme From 'My Son My Son')/Falcons De Neige (p/s) 5
79 A&M AMS 7436 Animal Showdown/Sea Horses (p/s) 5
79 A&M AMSP 7436 Animal Showdown/Sea Horses (picture disc, in PVC sleeve) 6
79 A&M AMS 7497 Swan Lager/Woolly Willy Tango 5
80 A&M AMS 7510 I'm So Straight I'm A Weirdo/Do You Believe In Fairies? (p/s) 5
80 WEA K 18354 The Spider/Danielle (some with p/s, 2,000 only) 8
80 WEA K 18354 The Spider/Danielle (some with p/s, 2,000 only) 5
71 Polydor 2460 135 PIANO VIBRATIONS (LP, with John Schroeder Orchestra) 100
74 A&M QU-84361 THE SIX WIVES OF HENRY VIII (LP, gatefold sleeve, quadrophonic mix) 18
73 A&M AMCH 64361 THE SIX WIVES OF HENRY VIII (LP, gatefold sleeve) 15
75 A&M AMLH 64546 LISZTOMANIA (LP, soundtrack, with Roger Daltrey) 12
89 A&M RWCD 20 RICK WAKEMAN: 20TH ANNIVERSARY (4-CD box set, 1,000 only) 80

HOWARD WALES
(see under Jerry Garcia)

WALHAM GREEN EAST WAPPING CARPET CLEANING RODENT & BOGGIT EXTERMINATING ASSOCIATION
68 Columbia DB 8426 Sorry Mr. Green/Death Of A Kind 160

ANNA WALKER & CROWNETTES
69 Pama PM 768 You Don't Know/Billy Joe 10

BILLY WALKER (U.K.)
65 Columbia DB 7724 A Certain Girl/I Don't Wanna Fall In love 5

BILLY WALKER (U.S.)
60 Philips PB 1001 Forever/Changed My Mind 6
66 London HLU 10060 Million And One/Close To Linda 7

BOOTS WALKER
69 London HLP 10265 No One Knows/Geraldine 15

CLINT WALKER
60 Warner Bros WEP 6006 INSPIRATION (EP, mono) 12
60 Warner Bros WSEP 2006 INSPIRATION (EP, stereo) 15

DAVID WALKER
(see also Paradox)
68 RCA RCA 1664 Ring The Changes/Keep A Little Love 120

GARY WALKER (& RAIN)
(see also Walker Brothers, Paul & Ritchie & Cryin' Shames, Badfinger, Universals)
66 CBS 202036 You Don't Love Me/Get It Right 20
66 CBS 202081 Twinkie-Lee/She Makes Me Feel Better 10
68 Polydor 56237 Spooky/I Can't Stand To Lose You (as Gary Walker & Rain) 20
69 Philips BF 1740 Come In You'll Get Pneumonia/Francis (as Gary Walker & Rain) 60
74 United Artists UP 35742 Hello How Are You/Fran 5
66 CBS EPS 5742 HERE'S GARY (EP) 45

GRAHAM P WALKER
72 Trojan GPW 62 Love Of The Common People/Version (white label promo only) 15

JACKIE WALKER
58 London HLP 8588 Oh Lonesome Me/Only Teenagers Allowed 250
58 London HLP 8588 Oh Lonesome Me/Only Teenagers Allowed (78) 60

JERRY JEFF WALKER
68 Atlantic 584 200 Mr Bojangles/Round And Round 7
68 Atco 228 006 MR BOJANGLES (LP) 20
71 Atlantic 2466 007 BEIN' FREE (LP) 18

JOHN WALKER
(see also Walker Brothers, John & Scott Walker, Johnny & Judy)
67 Philips BF 1593 Anabella/You Don't Understand Me 8
67 Philips BF 1612 If I Promise/I See Love In You 7
68 Philips BF 1655 I'll Be Your Baby Tonight/Open The Door Homer 7
68 Philips BF 1676 Kentucky Woman/I Cried All The Way Home 8
68 Philips BF 1724 Woman/A Dream 6
69 Philips BF 1758 Yesterday's Sunshine/Little One 6
69 Carnaby CNS 4004 Everywhere Under The Sun/Traces Of Tomorrow 6
70 Carnaby CNS 4009 True Grit/Sun Comes Up 7
70 Carnaby CNS 4012 Cottonfields/Jamie 7
70 Carnaby CNS 4017 Over And Over Again/Sun Comes Up 7
67 Philips (S)BL 7829 IF YOU GO AWAY (LP) 25
69 Carnaby CNLS 6001 THIS IS JOHN WALKER (LP) 25

MINT VALUE £

JOHN & SCOTT WALKER

(see also Walker Brothers, Scott Walker, John Walker, Scott Engel)

66	Philips BE 12597	SOLO JOHN - SOLO SCOTT (EP, 2 tracks each)	10

JUNIOR WALKER & ALL STARS

65	Tamla Motown TMG 509	Shotgun/Hot'Cha	45
65	Tamla Motown TMG 509	Shotgun/Hot'Cha (DJ copy)	100
65	Tamla Motown TMG 520	Do The Boomerang/Tune Up	75
65	Tamla Motown TMG 520	Do The Boomerang/Tune Up (DJ copy)	150
65	Tamla Motown TMG 529	Shake And Fingerpop/Cleo's Back	50
65	Tamla Motown TMG 529	Shake And Fingerpop/Cleo's Back (DJ copy)	80
66	Tamla Motown TMG 550	Cleo's Mood/Baby You Know It Ain't Right	50
66	Tamla Motown TMG 550	Cleo's Mood/Baby You Know It Ain't Right (DJ copy)	80
66	Tamla Motown TMG 559	Road Runner/Shoot Your Shot	30
66	Tamla Motown TMG 559	Road Runner/Shoot Your Shot (DJ copy)	100
66	Tamla Motown TMG 571	How Sweet It Is (To Be Loved By You)/Nothing But Soul	25
66	Tamla Motown TMG 571	How Sweet It Is (To Be Loved By You)/Nothing But Soul (DJ copy)	60
67	Tamla Motown TMG 571	How Sweet It Is (To Be Loved By You)/Nothing But Soul (later pressing)	7
66	Tamla Motown TMG 586	Money (That's What I Want) Parts 1& 2	25
66	Tamla Motown TMG 586	Money (That's What I Want) Parts 1& 2 (DJ copy)	55
67	Tamla Motown TMG 596	Pucker Up Buttercup/Any Way You Wanna	25
67	Tamla Motown TMG 596	Pucker Up Buttercup/Any Way You Wanna (DJ copy)	60
68	Tamla Motown TMG 637	Come See About Me/Sweet Soul	15
68	Tamla Motown TMG 637	Come See About Me/Sweet Soul (DJ copy)	70
68	Tamla Motown TMG 667	Hip City Parts 1 & 2	25
68	Tamla Motown TMG 667	Hip City Parts 1 & 2 (DJ copy)	40
69	Tamla Motown TMG 682	Home Cookin'/Mutiny	20
69	Tamla Motown TMG 682	Home Cookin'/Mutiny (DJ copy)	30
69	Tamla Motown TMG 691	Road Runner/Shotgun	7
69	Tamla Motown TMG 691	Road Runner/Shotgun (DJ copy)	30
69	Tamla Motown TMG 712	What Does It Take (To Win Your Love)/Brainwasher	8
70	Tamla Motown TMG 727	These Eyes/I've Got To Find A Way To Win Maria Back	10
70	Tamla Motown TMG 727	These Eyes/I've Got To Find A Way To Win Maria Back (DJ copy)	30
70	Tamla Motown TMG 750	Do You See My Love (For You Growing)/Groove And Move	8
70	Tamla Motown TMG 750	Do You See My Love (For You Growing)/Groove And Move (DJ Copy)	30
72	Tamla Motown TMG 824	Walk In The Night/Right On Brothers And Sisters/ Gotta Hold On To This Feeling (maxi-single)	8
73	Tamla Motown TMG 840	Take Me Girl, I'm Ready/I Don't Want To Do Wrong	8
73	Tamla Motown TMG 857	Way Back Home (Vocal)/Way Back Home (Instrumental)	10
73	Tamla Motown TMG 857	Way Back Home (Vocal)/Way Back Home (Instrumental)/Country Boy (reissue)	20
73	Tamla Motown TMG 872	Holly Holy/Peace And Understanding (Is Hard To Find)	6
74	Tamla Motown TMG 889	Don't Blame The Children/Soul Clappin'	6
74	Tamla Motown TMG 894	Gotta Hold On To This Feeling/I Ain't Going Nowhere	10
74	Tamla Motown TMG 894	Gotta Hold On To This Feeling/I Ain't Going Nowhere (DJ copy)	25
76	Tamla Motown TMG 1027	I'm So Glad/Dancin' Like They Do On Soul Train (as Jr. Walker)	8
66	Tamla Motown TME 2013	SHAKE AND FINGERPOP (EP)	50
65	Tamla Motown TML 11017	SHOTGUN (LP)	55
66	T. Motown TML 11029	SOUL SESSION (LP, mono)	50
66	T. Motown STML 11029	SOUL SESSION (LP, stereo)	60
66	T. Motown TML 11038	ROAD RUNNER (LP, mono)	35
66	T. Motown STML 11038	ROAD RUNNER (LP, stereo)	40
69	T. Motown TML 11097	HOME COOKIN' (LP, mono)	35
69	T. Motown STML 11097	HOME COOKIN' (LP, stereo)	35
69	T. Motown (S)TML 11120	JUNIOR WALKER'S GREATEST HITS (LP, original with flipback sleeve)	20
70	T. Motown (S)TML 11140	THESE EYES (LP)	30
70	T. Motown STML 11152	LIVE (LP)	25
70	T. Motown STML 11167	A GASSSSSSSSSS! (LP)	22
72	T. Motown STML 11198	RAINBOW FUNK (LP)	20
72	T. Motown STML 11211	MOODY JR. (LP)	20
73	T. Motown STML 11234	PEACE AND UNDERSTANDING IS HARD TO FIND (LP)	15
75	T. Motown STML 11274	JR. WALKER AND THE ALL STARS (LP)	12
76	T. Motown STML 12018	HOT SHOT (by Jr. Walker)	12
76	T. Motown STML 12033	SAX APPEAL (by Jr. Walker)	12
76	Motown STML 12048	WHOPPER BOPPER SHOW STOPPER (by Jr. Walker)	12

KARL WALKER & ALLSTARS

(see also Kent Walker, Ernel Braham)

66	Rymska RA 103	One Minute To Zero/Don't Come Back (both sides actually featuring Tommy McCook & Supersonics)	35

KENT WALKER

(see also Karl Walker, Ernel Braham)

68	Fab FAB 53	When You Going To Show Me How/Come Yah Come Yah	8

ROB WALKER

(see also Stranger Cole, Tommy McCook)

71	Upsetter US 366	Run Up Your Mouth (actually by Stranger Cole)/UPSETTERS: Mouth Version	15
71	Jackpot JP 761	Hear My Heart/Puppet On A String	15

RONNIE WALKER

69	Stateside SS 2151	It's A Good Feeling/Precious	30
69	Stateside SS 2151	It's A Good Feeling/Precious (DJ Copy)	50
75	Polydor 2006 578	Magic's In The Air/They Can't Say Hello	8

SCOTT WALKER

(see also Scott Engel, Scott Engel & John Stewart, John & Scott Walker, Walker Brothers, Routers)

67	Philips BF 1628	Jackie/The Plague	5
68	Philips BF 1662	Joanna/Always Coming Back To You	5
69	Philips BF 1793	Lights of Cincinnati/Two Weeks Since You've Gone	5

			MINT VALUE £
71	Philips 6006 168	I Still See You/My Way Home	6
73	Philips 6006 311	The Me I Never Knew/This Way Mary	6
73	CBS 1795	A Woman Left Lonely/Where Love Has Died	6
74	CBS 2521	Delta Dawn/We Had It All	6
66	Liberty LEP 2261	SCOTT ENGEL (WALKER) (EP)	40
67	Philips MCP 1006	GREAT SCOTT (cassette EP)	20
67	Philips (S)BL 7816	SCOTT (LP, mono/stereo)	18
67	Philips (S)BL 7816	SCOTT (LP, mono/stereo)	25
68	Philips BL 7840	SCOTT 2 (LP, mono, with signed portrait)	25
68	Philips BL 7840	SCOTT 2 (LP, mono, without signed portrait)	15
68	Philips SBL 7840	SCOTT 2 (LP, stereo, with signed portrait)	35
68	Philips SBL 7840	SCOTT 2 (LP, stereo, without signed portrait)	20
68	Ember EMB LP 3393	LOOKING BACK WITH SCOTT WALKER (LP, mono or stereo)	30
69	Philips SBL 7882	SCOTT 3 (LP, gatefold sleeve)	35
69	Philips SBL 7900	SCOTT WALKER SINGS SONGS FROM HIS TV SERIES (LP)	18
69	Philips SBL 7910	THE BEST OF SCOTT WALKER VOL. 1 (LP)	18
69	Philips SBL 7913	SCOTT 4 (LP)	45
70	Philips 6308 035	'TIL THE BAND COMES IN (LP)	45
72	Philips 6382 007	THIS IS? SCOTT WALKER (LP)	12
72	Philips 6308 127	THE MOVIEGOER (LP)	25
73	Philips 6308 148	ANY DAY NOW (LP)	30
73	CBS 65725	STRETCH (LP)	20
73	Philips 6850 013	THE ROMANTIC SCOTT WALKER (LP, Audio Club issue)	35
73	Philips 6856 022	TERRIFIC (LP, Audio Club issue, reissue of "Scott 2" with different tracks)	40
73	Philips 6382 052	THIS IS SCOTT WALKER VOL. 2 (LP)	12
74	CBS 80254	WE HAD IT ALL (LP)	20
76	Philips 6625 017	SPOTLIGHT ON SCOTT WALKER (2-LP)	18
81	Zoo ZOO 2	FIRE ESCAPE IN THE SKY - THE GODLIKE GENIUS OF SCOTT WALKER (LP)	18
81	Philips 6359 090	SINGS JACQUES BREL (LP)	12
95	Fontana 526859-1	TILT (LP, limited edition)	50
06	4AD DRIFT 1	THE DRIFT (2-LP, 500 promo copies with 24 page booklet)	40

STEWART WALKER

98	Mosquito MSQ 012	ARTIFICIAL MUSIC FOR ARTIFICIAL PEOPLE (12" EP)	15

SYLFORD WALKER

(see also Glen Brown)

79	Art & Craft AC 002	Book Of The Old Testament/JAH STITCH: Jah Speak Unto Moses (12")	30
80	Art & Craft ACD002	I Love You (feat. Jah Stitch)/Version (12")	20
88	Greensleeves GREL 119	LAMBS BREAD (LP)	20

T-BONE WALKER

54	London HL 8087	The Hustle Is On/Baby Broke My Heart (78)	40
65	Liberty LIB 12018	Party Girl/Here In The Dark	25
63	London REP 1404	TRAVELLIN' BLUES (EP)	70
54	Capitol LC 6681	CLASSICS IN JAZZ (10" LP)	40
63	Capitol T 1958	T-BONE WALKER (LP)	50
65	MFP MFP 1043	THE BLUES OF T-BONE WALKER (LP)	12
65	Liberty LBY 4047	SINGS THE BLUES (LP)	50
66	Liberty LBY 3057	SINGING THE BLUES (LP)	40
68	MCA MUPS 331	THE TRUTH (LP)	20
68	Stateside S(S)L 10223	STORMY MONDAY BLUES (LP)	30
69	Stateside S(S)L 10265	FUNKY TOWN (LP)	30
73	Reprise K 94001	VERY RARE (2-LP)	20
74	Atlantic K 40131	T-BONE BLUES (LP)	15

WENDY WALKER

63	Decca F 11573	Window Shopping/Ain't A Boy In The World	8
63	Decca F 11671	Boys Will Be Happy/Casanova	8

WALKER BROTHERS

(see also Scott Walker, Scott Engel, John Walker, John & Scott Walker, Gary Walker [& Rain], Routers)

65	Philips BF 1401	Pretty Girls Everywhere/Doin' The Jerk	15
65	Philips BF 1409	Love Her/The Seventh Dawn	10
65	Philips BF 1428	Make It Easy On Yourself/But I Do	6
65	Philips BF 1454	My Ship Is Coming In/You're All Around Me	6
66	Philips BF 1473	The Sun Ain't Gonna Shine Anymore/After The Lights Go Out	6
66	Philips BF 1497	(Baby) You Don't Have To Tell Me/My Love Is Growing	8
66	Philips BF 1514	Another Tear Falls/The Saddest Night In The World	8
66	Philips BF 1537	Deadlier Than The Male/Archangel	10
67	Philips BF 1548	Stay With Me Baby/Turn Out The Moon	12
67	Philips BF 1576	Walking In The Rain/Baby Make It The Last Time	12
76	GTO GT 42	No Regrets/Remember Me	5
76	GTO GT 67	Lines/First Day	6
77	GTO GT 78	We're All Alone/Have You Seen My Baby	6
66	Philips BE 12596	I NEED YOU (EP)	15
67	Philips BE 12603	THE WALKER BROTHERS (EP, probably unreleased)	0
65	Philips BL 7691	TAKE IT EASY WITH THE WALKER BROTHERS (LP)	18
66	Philips BL 7732	PORTRAIT (LP, with photo insert, mono)	20
66	Philips SBL 7732	PORTRAIT (LP, with photo insert, stereo)	30
67	Philips (S)BL 7770	IMAGES (LP)	20
67	Philips DBL 002	THE WALKER BROTHERS STORY (2-LP)	18
68	Wing WL 1188	THE FABULOUS WALKER BROTHERS (LP)	12
75	GTO GTLP 007	NO REGRETS (LP)	12
78	GTO GTLP 033	NITE FLIGHTS (LP, gatefold sleeve)	25

TREVOR WALKERS

82	Mutual Life MU 002	They'll Never Get Away/Version (12", blue vinyl)	20

WALKIE TALKIES

(see also Pauline Murray & Invisible Girls, Mission)

79	Sire SIR 4023	Rich And Nasty/Summer In Russia (p/s)	6

MINT VALUE £

WALKING FLOORS
80s My Death Telephone TEL 1 No Next Time/Removal (foldover p/s) ... 8

DENNIS WALKS
(see also I Roy)
68 Amalgamated AMG 816 Having A Party/GROOVERS: Day By Day ... 20
68 Blue Cat BS 144 Belly Lick/DRUMBAGO & BLENDERS: The Game Song ... 50
69 Bullet BU 402 Heart Don't Leap/CLARENDONIANS: I Am Sorry ... 80
69 Bullet BU 408 Love Of My Life/Under The Shady Tree ... 12
71 Moodisc HM 101 Time Will Tell/Under The Shady Tree ... 7
74 Magnet MG 062 Don't Play That Song/Version ... 6
82 greensleeves GREL 77 Roast Fish And Cornbread/Wicked She Wicked (12", with Billy Boyo) ... 20

SHELTON WALKS
73 Bullet BU 550 No Money No Friend/BOB MAC ALL STARS: Money Dub ... 6
74 Dip DL 5026 One Of Us Will Weep/KING EDWARDS ALL STARS: Version ... 6

WALL
(see also Ski Patrol)
79 Small Wonder SMALL 13 New Way/Suckers/Uniforms (p/s) ... 5
80 Fresh FRESHLP 2 PERSONAL TROUBLES AND PUBLIC ISSUES (LP) ... 15
80 Fresh FRESHLP 2 PERSONAL TROUBLES AND PUBLIC ISSUES (LP, with insert, withdrawn "Crass style" stencil lettered sleeve) ... 30

MAX WALL
73 York YR 203 The Fiddley Foodle Bird/Story Of The Fiddley Foodle Bird ... 5
75 DJM DJS 10352 Why Should I Care/Devil Bomb ... 5
77 Stiff BUY 12 England's Glory/Dream Tobacco (p/s) ... 5

REM WALL & HIS GREEN VALLEY BOYS
60 Top Rank JAR 324 Heartsick And Blue/One More Time ... 10

ERROL WALLACE
69 Escort ES 817 Bandit/ASTON BORROT: Family Man Mood (actually by Aston "Family Man" Barrett) ... 12

GIG WALLACE & HIS ORCHESTRA
60 Philips PB 981 Rockin' On The Railroad/Show Me The Way To Go Home ... 10

JERRY WALLACE
58 London HL 8719 With This Ring/How The Time Flies ... 40
58 London HL 8719 With This Ring/How The Time Flies (78) ... 15
58 London HL 7062 With This Ring/How The Time Flies (export issue) ... 30
59 London HLH 8943 Primrose Lane/By Your Side ... 10
60 London HLH 9040 Little Coco Palm/Mission Bell Blues ... 6
60 London HLH 9110 You're Singing Our Love Song To Somebody Else/King Of The Mountain ... 6
60 London HLH 9177 Swingin' Down The Lane/Teardrop In The Rain ... 5
61 London HLH 9264 There She Goes/Angel On My Shoulder ... 5
61 London HLH 9363 Life's A Holiday/I Can See An Angel ... 5
62 London HLH 9630 Shutters And Boards/Am I That Easy To Forget ... 5
64 London HLH 9914 Even The Bad Times Are Good/In The Misty Moonlight ... 5
65 Mercury MF 853 Time/Rainbow ... 5

MIKE WALLACE
70 Major Minor D570 Daffodil/Early Morning Bird ... 12
70 Polydor 2058065 Natural High/Mandrin ... 10

SIPPIE WALLACE
67 Storyville 671 198 SIPPIE WALLACE SINGS THE BLUES (LP) ... 15

WALLACE BROTHERS
64 Sue WI 334 Precious Words/You're Mine ... 40
65 Sue WI 355 Lover's Prayer/Love Me Like I Love You ... 40
67 Sue WI 4036 I'll Step Aside/Hold My Heart For A While ... 40
67 Sue ILP 950 SOUL CONNECTION (LP) ... 250

WALLACE COLLECTION
69 Parlophone R 5764 Daydream/Baby I Don't Mind ... 12
69 Parlophone R 5793 Fly Me To The Earth/Love ... 25
70 Parlophone R 5844 Serenade/Walk On Out ... 10
69 Parlophone PMC/PCS 7076 LAUGHING CAVALIER (LP) ... 12
70 Parlophone PCS 7099 WALLACE COLLECTION (LP) ... 12

GORDON (WALLER)
(see also Peter & Gordon)
68 Columbia DB 8337 Rosecrans Boulevard/Red, Cream And Velvet ... 15
68 Columbia DB 8440 Every Day/Because Of A Woman ... 10
68 Columbia DB 8518 Weeping Annaleah/The Seventh Hour ... 10
69 Bell BLL 1059 I Was A Boy When You Needed A Man/Lady In The Window ... 6
70 Bell BLL 1106 You're Gonna Hurt Yourself/Sunshine ... 6
72 Vertigo 6360 069 GORDON (LP, as Gordon, single sleeve, small swirl label) ... 400

'FATS' WALLER (& HIS RHYTHM)
(see also Louisiana Sugar Babies, Deep River Boys, James P. Johnson)
53 HMV 7M 128 My Very Good Friend The Milkman/Shortnin' Bread ... 5
53 HMV 7M 157 A Good Man Is Hard To Find/The Girl I Left Behind Me ... 5
53 HMV 7M 142 Honey Hush/You've Been Reading My Mail ... 5
54 HMV 7M 208 You've Been Taking Lessons In Love/I've Got A New Lease Of Life ... 5
54 HMV 7M 244 By The Light Of The Silvery Moon/Romance A La Mode (with Deep River Boys) ... 5
60 RCA RCA 1189 Dinah/When Somebody Thinks You're Wonderful ... 5

GEORGE WALLINGTON
50s Columbia Clef 33C9035 THE WORK SHOP OF GEORGE WALLINGTON TRIO (10" LP) ... 60
57 Esquire 32-132 NEW YORK SCENE (LP) ... 70

MINT VALUE £

BOB WALLIS & HIS STORYVILLE JAZZMEN
61 Pye Jazz 7NJ 2043 I'm Shy Mary Ellen I'm Shy/Three Live Wires . . . 5
61 Pye Jazz 7NJ 2048 Come Along Please/Bobbin' Along . . . 5
57 77' EP 10 NEW ORLEANS JAM SESSION VOLUME 1 (EP) . . . 15
59 77' Records 77LE 12/2 THE RAVING SOUNDS OF BOB WALLIS (LP) . . . 20
60 Top Rank BUY 023 EVERYBODY LOVES SATURDAY NIGHT (LP) . . . 15
61 Pye Jazz NJL 27 OLE MAN RIVER (LP) . . . 15
61 Pye Jazz NJL 30 TRAVELLIN' BLUES (LP) . . . 15

LARRY WALLIS
(see also Pink Fairies, Subs, Deviants, Shagrat, Peter Wyngarde, Motorhead)
77 Stiff BUY 22 Police Car/On Parole (with p/s) . . . 7
77 Stiff BUY 22 Police Car/On Parole (die-cut company sleeve) . . . 5

SHANI WALLIS
60 Philips PB 1019 Sixteen Reasons (Why I Love You)/Forever Forever . . . 5
60 Philips BBE 12337 SHANI! (EP) . . . 8

WALL OF SLEEP
95 Woronzow WOO 24 WALL OF SLEEP (LP, with insert) . . . 12

WALL OF VOODOO
82 Illegal ILS 31 On Interstate 15/There's Nothing On This Side . . . 5
83 Illuminated ILS 0036 Mexican Radio/Call Of The West (p/s) . . . 5

WALL STREET DIVERSION
68 Concord CON 006 She's Mine/Joey The Lipstick Collector . . . 25

WALLY
74 Atlantic K 50051 WALLY (LP, laminated sleeve) . . . 12
75 Atlantic K 50180 VALLY GARDENS (LP) . . . 12

WALLY BROTHERS
74 Explosion EX 2090 The Man Who Sold The World/Version . . . 5

WALRUS
70 Deram DM 308 Who Can I Trust?/Tomorrow Never Comes . . . 18
71 Deram DM 323 Never Let My Body Touch Ground/Why? . . . 20
71 Deram SML 1072 WALRUS (LP) . . . 70

JAMES WALSH GYPSY BAND
79 RCA PB 11403 Cuz It's You Girl/Bring Yourself Together . . . 50
79 RCA PB 11403 Cuz It's You Girl/Bring Yourself Together (DJ copy) . . . 100

SHEILA WALSH & CLIFF RICHARD
(see also Cliff Richard)
83 DJM SHEIL 100 Drifting/It's Lonely When The Lights Go Out (picture disc) . . . 6
83 DJM SHEILT 100 Drifting/It's Lonely When The Lights Go Out (12", picture disc) . . . 8
83 DJM DJF 20581 DRIFTING (LP, with inner sleeve, as Sheila Walsh) . . . 12

BURT WALTERS
(see also Lee 'Scratch' Perry)
68 Trojan TR 636 Honey Love/KING CANNONBALL BRYAN: Thunderstorm . . . 40

JULIE WALTERS
82 Deaville STL 7 Toy Boys/Bad Loser . . . 6

DAVE WALTON
(see also The First Gear)
66 CBS 202057 Love Ain't What It Used To Be/Tell Me A Lie . . . 8
66 CBS 202098 Every Window In The City/I've Left The Troubled Ground . . . 15
67 CBS 202508 After You There Can Be Nothing/Can I Get It From You . . . 30

TRAVIS WAMMACK
65 Atlantic AT 4017 Scratchy/Fire Fly . . . 45
65 Atlantic AT 4017 Scratchy/Fire Fly (DJ copy) . . . 100
72 United Artists UP 35412 Whatever Turns You On/Slip Away . . . 6
73 United Artists UP 35468 So Good/Darling, You're All That I Need . . . 6
75 Capricorn 2429 133 NOT FOR SALE (LP) . . . 12

WANDERER
59 Top Rank JAR 183 The Happy Hobo/True True Happiness . . . 6

WANDERERS
(see also Lords Of The New Church, Stiv Bators, Dead Boys)
81 Polydor POSP 239 Ready To Snap/Beyond The Law . . . 25
81 Polydor POSP 284 The Times They Are A'Changin'/Little Bit Frightening . . . 6
81 Polydor POLS 1028 ONLY LOVERS LEFT (LP) . . . 20

WANDERERS (Jamaica)
69 Trojan TR 7721 Wiggle Waggle/Jaga Jaga War . . . 8

WANDERERS (U.S.)
(see also Ray Pollard)
60 MGM MGM 1102 I Could Make You Mine/I Need You More . . . 50
61 MGM MGM 1169 As Time Goes By/There Is No Greater Love . . . 20
64 United Artists UP 1020 Run Run Senorita/After He Breaks Your Heart . . . 30

WANGLERS
79 Matchbox Classics MC 5 KICKIN' OUT FOR THE COAST (EP, white label, yellow or red stickered foldover p/s) . . . 10

WAR
(see also Eric Burdon & War)
71 Liberty LBF 15443 Sun Oh Son/Lonely Feelin' . . . 6
71 United Artists UP 35281 All Day Music/Get Down . . . 6

MINT VALUE £

72	United Artists UP 35327	Slippin' Into Darkness/Nappy Head	5
73	United Artists UP 35469	The World Is A Ghetto/Four Cornered Room	5
73	United Artists UP 35521	The Cisco Kid/Beetles In The Bag	5
73	United Artists UP 35576	Gypsy Man/Deliver The Word	5
74	United Artists UP 35623	Me And Baby Brother/In Your Eyes	8
71	Liberty LBG 83478	WAR (LP)	20
72	United Artists UAS 29269	ALL DAY MUSIC (LP)	15
73	United Artists UAS 29400	THE WORLD IS A GHETTO (LP)	15

BILL WARD

(see also Black Sabbath)

90	Chameleon 0174910	WARD ONE: ALONG THE WAY (LP, with innersleeve)	12

BILLY WARD & HIS DOMINOES

(see also Dominoes, Clyde McPhatter, Jackie Wilson)

53	Parlophone R 3789	Don't Thank Me/Rags To Riches (78)	40
54	Parlophone MSP 6112	Three Coins In The Fountain/Lonesome Road	175
54	Parlophone MSP 6112	Three Coins In The Fountain/Lonesome Road (78)	39
56	Brunswick 05599	St. Therese Of The Roses/Home Is Where You Hang Your Heart	60
57	Brunswick 05656	Evermore/Half A Love (Is Better Than None)	30
57	London HLU 8465	Stardust/Lucinda	25
57	London HLU 8502	Deep Purple/Do It Again	25
58	London HLU 8634	Jennie Lee/Music, Maestro, Please	20
58	London HLU 8634	Jennie Lee/Music, Maestro, Please (78)	10
59	London HLU 8883	Please Don't Say 'No'/Behave, Hula Girl	20
59	London HLU 8883	Please Don't Say 'No'/Behave, Hula Girl (78)	10
58	London REU 1114	BILLY WARD & HIS DOMINOES (EP)	150
58	Parlophone PMD 1061	BILLY WARD & HIS DOMINOES FEATURING CLYDE McPHATTER (10" LP)	700
58	London HA-U 2116	YOURS FOREVER (LP)	60

CHRISTIAN WARD

66	Decca F 12339	The Face Of Empty Me/Girl I Used To Know	35

CLARA WARD & HER SINGERS

65	Stateside SS 474	Gonna Build A Mountain/God Bless The Child	10

CLIFFORD T. WARD

(see also Secrets, Simon's Secrets, Martin Raynor & Secrets)

72	Dandelion 2001 327	Carrie/Sidetrack	12
72	Dandelion 2001 382	Coathanger/Rayne	10
72	Charisma CB 205	Home Thoughts From Abroad/Game	7
73	Charisma CB 212	Wherewithal/Thinking Of Something To Do	7
74	Charisma CB 233	Jayne/Maybe I'm Right	7
75	Charisma CB 248	Jigsaw Girl/Cellophane	7
75	Philips 6006 490	No More Rock'n'Roll/Gandalf	7
76	Philips 6006 542	Ocean Of Love/Tomorrow Night	7
77	Mercury 6007 132	Up In The World/Not Waving, Drowning (Revisited)	7
77	Mercury 6007 149	I Got Lost Tonight/Detriment (p/s)	7
77	Mercury LUV 1	Someone I Know/If I Had Known (gatefold p/s)	8
80	WEA K 18294	Convertible/Taking The Long Way Round	7
81	WEA K 18426	The Best Is Yet To Come/Lost Again	7
81	WEA K 18486	Contrary/Climate Of Her Favour	7
84	Philips 880 550 7	Messenger/Where Do Angels Really Come From (p/s)	8
86	Tembo TML 114	Cricket/Computer	10
86	Tembo TML 123	Sometime Next Year/Turbo (p/s)	8
72	Dandelion 2310 216	SINGER SONGWRITER (LP)	25
73	Charisma CAS 1006	HOME THOUGHTS (LP)	12
73	Charisma CAS 1077	MANTLEPEICES (LP)	12
75	Charisma CAS 1098	ESCALATOR (LP)	15
75	Philips 9109 500	NO MORE ROCK'N'ROLL (LP)	12
75	Philips 9109 216	WAVES (LP)	12

DALE WARD

64	London HLD 9835	Oh Julie/Letter From Sherry	20

DOUGLAS WARD

71	Forward FS1001	FROM AN ELEVATED PLATFORM (LP)	20

HEDLEY WARD TRIO

56	Melodisc MEL 1387	Steamboat Rock/My Baby's Got Such Lovin' Ways (78)	10

ROBIN WARD

63	London HLD 9821	Wonderful Summer/Dream Boy	25

TERRY WARD with BUMBLIES

65	Fontana TF 558	Gotta Tell/When I Come To You	10

SHEELAGH WARDE

59	Top Rank JAR 131	Let Mr. Maguire Sit Down/The Golden Jubilee	7

WARDENS

70s	SNO PEAS TIC 001	Lust Like This/Do So Well (with insert)	20

WARDS OF COURT

67	Deram DM 127	All Night Girl/How Could Say One Thing	60

WARD SINGERS

56	London Jazz EZ-C 19024	THE FAMOUS WARD SINGERS (EP)	20
56	London Jazz LZ-C 14013	THE FAMOUS WARD SINGERS (10" LP)	25

LEON WARE

77	Motown STML 12050	MUSICAL MASSAGE (LP)	20

WARFARE

83	Neat (No. cat. no.)	This Machine Kills/Burn Down The Kings Road (white label)	20
84	Neat NEAT 45-12	Two Tribes/Hell/Blown To Bits (12")	12

MINT VALUE £

84 Neat NEAT 49-12 — TOTAT DEATH (12", EP) — 15
84 Neat NEAT 1021 — PURE FILTH (LP) — 15
85 Neat NEAT 1029 — METAL ANARCH (LP) — 12

WARHORSE
(see also Deep Purple, Nic Simper's Fandango)
71 Vertigo 6059 027 — St. Louis/No Chance — 15
70 Vertigo 6360 015 — WARHORSE (LP, large swirl label, gatefold sleeve) — 100
72 Vertigo 6360 066 — RED SEA (LP, small swirl label, gatefold sleeve) — 150

FRED WARING & HIS PENNSYLVANIANS
59 Capitol CL 14981 — Dry Bones/Way Back Home — 5

RAY WARLEIGH
(see also John Mayall's Blues Breakers, Alexis Korner)
69 Philips (S)BL 7881 — RAY WARLEIGH'S FIRST ALBUM (LP) — 40

OZZIE WARLOCK & WIZARDS
(see also Tony Osbourne)
59 HMV POP 635 — Juke Box Fury/Wow! — 12

WARM
78 Warm 2001 — It's The Kooler/Teenage Space Queen (p/s) — 5
78 Warm SMS 001/2001/S — THE DEMO TAPES (EP, double pack) — 8
78 Warm WARM 2003 — Floosie/Chewing Gum Sue/Bye Bye It's Blues/Sometimes (p/s) — 5

JOHNNY WARMAN
78 Ring O' 2017 112 — Head On Collision/London's Burning/Mind Games (in p/s) — 20
78 Ring O' 2017 112 — Head On Collision/London's Burning/Mind Games — 10

WARM DUST
71 Trend 6099 002 — It's A Beautiful Day/Worm Dance — 15
70 Trend TNLS 700 — AND IT CAME TO PASS (2-LP, gatefold sleeve, grey label) — 80
71 Trend 6480 001 — PEACE FOR OUR TIME (LP, gatefold sleeve, grey label) — 50

WARM GOLD
60s Hurls 008 — A TASTE OF CORNWALL (EP) — 25

WARM JETS
78 Bridgehouse BHS 1 — Sticky Jack/Shell Shock (p/s, some with sides reversed & small extra labels) — 8
79 RSO RSO 47 — Big City Boys/Mr Natural (p/s) — 5

WARM SENSATION
(see also Ivy League)
69 Columbia DB 8568 — I'll Be Proud Of You/The Clown — 25

WARM SOUNDS
(see also Denny Gerrard, Tuesday's Children, Open Road)
67 Immediate IM 058 — Sticks And Stones/Angeline — 20
67 Deram DM 120 — The Birds And Bees/Doo-Dah — 15
68 Deram DM 174 — Nite Is A-Comin'/Smeta Mergaty — 45

FLORENCE WARNER
73 Epic EPC 1626 — For No Good Reason/Remember — 6
75 Epic EPC 3817 — Anyway I Love You/Dreamer — 6
73 Epic EPC 80077 — FLORENCE WARNER (LP) — 18

HERB & BETTY WARNER
59 Felsted AF 114 — Slowly/'BUGS' BOWER GROUP: Slowly — 7

JACK WARNER with TOMMY REILLY
58 Oriole CB 1426 — An Ordinary Copper/On The Way Up — 5

KAI WARNER'S ORIENTAL EXPRESS
77 Power Exchange PX 244 — Fly Butterfly/Funky Harem — 6

GALE WARNING
56 Pye N 15061 — Heartbreak Hotel/Met Rock (78) — 10
56 Oriole CB 1349 — Rock Those Crazy Skins/I Need Your Love (78) — 10

WARP NINE
75 Stax STXS 2030 — Theme From 'Star Trek'/Para Song One — 5

FRAN WARREN
59 MGM MGM 1008 — Shame/As Long As You Believe Me — 10

GUY WARREN OF GHANA
59 Brunswick 05791 — Monkies And Butterflies/An African's Prayer (with Rod Saunders) — 6
57 Brunswick LAJ 8237 — AFRICA SPEAKS - AMERICA ANSWERS (LP) — 35
64 Columbia 33SX 1584 — EMERGENT DRUMS (LP) — 100
69 Columbia SCX 6340 — AFRO-JAZZ (LP, as Guy Warren Of Ghana) — 75
72 Regal Zono. SLRZ 1031 — THE AFRICAN SOUNDS OF GUY WARREN OF GHANA (LP) — 100

SHORTY WARRENT & HIS WESTERN RANGE
52 London L 1125 — I Thought She Was Local/You're Breaking The Only Heart (That Truly Loves You) (78) — 10

WARRIOR
72 Eden LP 27 — INVASION! (LP, private pressing, plain white sleeve & label, some handwritten, 100 only) — 160

WARRIÖR
80 Rambert RAM ONE — Don't Let It Show/The Lord's Prayer/Silver Lady (10", p/s) — 120
80 Goodwood GM 12326 — TROUBLE MAKER (LP) — 150

WARRIOR
80 Rainbow RSL 132 — LET BATTLE COMMENCE (LP, private pressing, 500 only) — 100

WARRIOR
82 Neat NEAT 20 — Dead When It Comes To Love/Kansas City/Stab In The Back (in die-cut p/s) — 20

MINT VALUE £

84	Warrior WOO 2	Breakout/Dragon Slayer/Take Your Chance (paper sleeve)	55
83	Warrior WOO 1	FOR EUROPE ONLY (mini-LP)	20

WARRIORS

(see also Hans Christian, Jon Anderson)

64	Decca F 11926	Don't Make Me Blue/You Came Along	40

WARSAW PAKT

78	Island PAKT 1	Safe And Warm/Sick And Tired (with stamped sleeve)	30
78	Island PAKT 1	Safe And Warm/Sick And Tired	18
77	Island ILPS 9515	NEEDLE TIME (LP, numbered stamped mailer p/s, with insert)	25
79	Stuff Central	SEE YOU IN COURT (cassette only)	20

WARWICK

75	RAK RAK 211	Let's Get The Party Going/How Does It Feel	15

DEE DEE WARWICK

65	Mercury MF 860	Do It With All Your Heart/Happiness	30
65	Mercury MF 867	We're Doin' Fine/You Don't Know	35
65	Mercury MF 890	Gotta Get Hold Of Myself/Another Lonely Saturday	30
66	Mercury MF 909	A Lover's Chant/Worth Every Tear I Cry	100
65	Mercury MF 937	I Want To Be With You/Alfie	18
65	Mercury MF 953	Yours Till Tomorrow/I'm Gonna Make You Love Me	15
67	Mercury MF 974	When Love Slips Away/House Of Gold	40
68	Mercury MF 1061	I'll Be Better Off (Without You)/Monday, Monday	20
69	Mercury MF 1084	Foolish Heart/Thank God	10
69	Mercury MF 1125	That's Not Love/It's Not Fair	10
70	Atlantic 2091 011	She Didn't Know (She Kept On Talking)/Make Love To Me	8
70	Atlantic 2091 037	If This Was The Last Song/I'm Only Human	6
71	Atlantic 2091 057	Cold Night In Georgia/Searching	6
71	Atlantic 2091 092	Suspicious Minds/I'm Glad I'm A Woman	15
75	Private Stock PVT 13	Get Out Of My Life/Funny How Places Change	20
66	Mercury 10036 MCE	WE'RE DOING FINE (EP)	70
71	Atco	TURNIN' AROUND (LP)	30

DIONNE WARWICK

SINGLES

63	Stateside SS 157	Don't Make Me Over/I Smiled Yesterday	25
63	Stateside SS 157	Don't Make Me Over/I Smiled Yesterday (DJ Copy)	50
63	Stateside SS 191	This Empty Place/Wishin' And Hopin'	25
63	Pye International 7N 25223	Please Let Him Love Me/Make The Music Play (reissue)	8
64	Pye International 7N 25234	Anyone Who Had A Heart/The Love Of A Boy	10
64	Pye International 7N 25241	Walk On By/Anytime Of Day	6
64	Pye International 7N 25256	You'll Never Get To Heaven/A House Is Not A Home	8
64	Pye International 7N 25265	Reach Out For Me/How Many Days Of Sadness	8
65	Pye International 7N 25290	You Can Have Him/Don't Say I Didn't Tell You	8
65	Pye International 7N 25302	Who Can I Turn To/That's Not The Answer	6
65	Pye International 7N 25310	(Here I Go Again) Looking With My Eyes/Only The Strong, Only The Brave	6
65	Pye International 7N 25316	Here I Am/They Long To Be Close To You	6
65	Pye International 7N 25338	Are You There (With Another Girl)/If I Ever Make You Cry	6
66	Pye International 7N 25357	In Between The Heartaches/Long Day, Short Night	6
66	Pye International 7N 25368	A Message To Michael/Here Where There Is Love	6
66	Pye International 7N 25378	Trains And Boats And Planes/Don't Go Breaking My Heart	6
66	Pye International 7N 25395	Another Night/Go With Love	6
67	Pye International 7N 25424	Alfie/The Beginning Of Loneliness	6
67	Pye International 7N 25428	The Windows Of The World/Walk Little Dolly	6
67	Pye International 7N 25435	I Say A Little Prayer/Window Wishin'	7
68	Pye International 7N 25445	(Theme From) The Valley Of The Dolls/Zip-A-Dee-Doo-Dah	10
68	Pye International 7N 25457	Do You Know The Way To San Jose?/Let Me Be Lonely	7
68	Pye International 7N 25474	Who Is Gonna Love Me?/(There's) Always Something There To Remind Me	6
75	Warner Bros WB 16530	Take It From Me/Sure Thing	5
75	Warner Bros K 16595	Move Me No Mountain/We'll Burn Our Bridges Behind Us	5

EPs

64	Pye Intl. NEP 44024	IT'S LOVE THAT REALLY COUNTS	10
64	Pye Intl. NEP 44026	DON'T MAKE ME OVER	10
65	Pye Intl. NEP 44039	WISHIN' AND HOPIN'	10
65	Pye Intl. NEP 44044	DIONNE	10
65	Pye Intl. NEP 44046	FOREVER MY LOVE	10
65	Pye Intl. NEP 44049	WHO CAN I TURN TO?	10
66	Pye Intl. NEP 44051	HERE I AM	10
66	Pye Intl. NEP 44067	MESSAGE TO MICHAEL	10
66	Pye Intl. NEP 44073	WINDOW WISHIN'	10
66	Pye Intl. NEP 44077	I JUST DON'T KNOW WHAT TO DO WITH MYSELF	10
67	Pye Intl. NEP 44083	I LOVE PARIS	10
68	Pye Intl. NEP 44090	DO YOU KNOW THE WAY TO SAN JOSE?	10

ALBUMS

64	Pye Intl. NPL 28037	PRESENTING DIONNE WARWICK	20
64	Pye Intl. NPL 28046	MAKE WAY FOR DIONNE WARWICK	18
64	Pye Intl. NPL 28064	THE BEST OF DIONNE WARWICK (LP)	12
65	Pye Intl. NPL 28055	THE SENSITIVE SOUND OF DIONNE WARWICK	20
66	Pye Intl. NPL 28071	HERE I AM	20
66	Pye Intl. NPL 28076	DIONNE WARWICK IN PARIS	20
67	Pye Intl. NPL 28096	HERE WHERE THERE IS LOVE	15
67	Pye Intl. NPL 28101	ON STAGE AND IN THE MOVIES (LP)	20
67	Pye Intl. NPL 28105	THE WINDOWS OF THE WORLD (LP)	15
68	Pye Intl. N(S)PL 28114	VALLEY OF THE DOLLS (LP)	20

WASHBOARD RHYTHM KINGS

56	HMV 7EG 8101	WASHBOARD RHYTHM KINGS (EP)	15

MINT VALUE £

WASHBOARD SAM

(see also Big Bill Broonzy, Memphis Slim)

72	RCA RD 8274	FEELING LOWDOWN (LP, with Big Bill Broonzy & Memphis Slim)	15

ALBERT WASHINGTON & KINGS

67	President PT 137	Doggin' Me Around/A Woman Is A Funny Thing	10
68	President PT 182	I'm The Man/These Arms Of Mine	50
68	President PT 227	Woman Love/Bring It On Up	10
69	President PT 242	Turn On The Bright Lights/Lonely Mountain	10
73	President PT 391	Rome, GA/Telling All Your Friends	10

BABY WASHINGTON

(see also Baby Washington/Wilbert Harrison)

64	Sue WI 302	That's How Heartaches Are Made/Doodlin'	70
64	Sue WI 321	I Can't Wait Until I See My Baby/Who's Gonna Take Care Of Me	70
65	London HLC 9987	Only Those In Love/Ballad Of Bobby Dawn	25
68	United Artists UP 2247	Get A Hold Of Yourself/Hurt So Bad	70
69	Atlantic 584 299	I Don't Know/I Can't Afford To Lose Him	15
70	Atlantic 584 316	Breakfast In Bed/What Becomes Of A Broken Heart	12
73	People PEO 105	Just Can't Get You Out Of My Mind/You're Just A Dream	10
74	People PEO 107	I've Got To Break Away/Can't Get Over You	10
66	London HA-C 8260	THAT'S HOW HEARTACHES ARE MADE (LP)	75
66	London HA-C 8292	ONLY THOSE IN LOVE (LP)	70
68	United Artists SULP 1217	WITH YOU IN MIND (LP)	60

BABY WASHINGTON & DON GARDNER

(see also Don Gardner & Dee Dee Ford)

73	People PEO 101	Forever/Baby Let Me Get Close To You	5
74	People PLEO 13	LAY A LITTLE LOVIN' ON ME (LP)	20

BABY WASHINGTON/WILBERT HARRISON

71	Joy JOYS 191	BATTLE OF THE GIANTS (LP)	18

DELROY WASHINGTON

78	Burning Sounds BSD 006	Memories (with Jah Son)/ EVERARD THOMPSON & SUPERSTAR: Rasta roots (12")	15

DINAH WASHINGTON

(see also Brook Benton & Dinah Washington)

52	Oriole CB 1130	Mad About The Boy/I Can't Face The Music (78)	15
54	Oriole CB 1266	My Man's An Undertaker/Since My Man Has Gone And Went (78)	15
54	Oriole CB 1279	Fat Daddy/TV Is The Thing (78)	15
56	Mercury MT 124	Cat On A Hot Tin Roof/The First Time (78)	15
59	Mercury AMT 1051	What A Diff'rence A Day Made/Come On Home	10
59	Mercury AMT 1069	Unforgettable/Nothing In The World	5
60	Mercury AMT 1105	This Bitter Earth/I Understand	5
60	Mercury AMT 1119	Love Walked In/I'm In Heaven Tonight	5
61	Mercury AMT 1125	We Have Love/Looking Back	5
61	Mercury AMT 1162	September In The Rain/Wake The Town And Tell The People	10
62	Mercury AMT 1170	Tears And Laughter/If I Should Lose You	6
62	Mercury AMT 1176	Dream/Such A Night	8
63	Columbia DB 7049	Soulville/Let Me Be The First To Know	25
56	Emarcy EJT 501	AFTER HOURS WITH MISS D. (10" LP)	30
57	Emarcy EJL 1255	DINAH (LP)	25
57	Mercury MPL 6519	SINGS THE BEST IN BLUES (LP)	15
59	Top Rank RX 3006	THE BLUES (LP, with Betty Roche)	15
60	Mercury MMC 14030	WHAT A DIFF'RENCE A DAY MADE (LP)	15
60	Mercury MMC 14048	THE UNFORGETTABLE DINAH WASHINGTON (LP)	15
61	Mercury MMC 14063	I CONCENTRATE ON YOU (LP, mono)	18
61	Mercury CMS 18043	I CONCENTRATE ON YOU (LP, stereo)	20
61	Mercury MMC 14107	SEPTEMBER IN THE RAIN (LP)	15
62	Mercury MMC 14085	FOR LONELY LOVERS (LP)	15
62	Mercury MMC 14099	TEARS AND LAUGHTER (LP)	15

ELLA WASHINGTON

69	Monument MON 1030	He Called Me Baby/You're Gonna Cry, Cry, Cry	22

GENO WASHINGTON & RAM JAM BAND

(see also Ram Jam Band, Ram John Holder, Ram Holder Brothers, Dave Greenslade)

66	Piccadilly 7N 35312	Water/Understanding	10
66	Piccadilly 7N 35329	Hi! Hi! Hazel/Beach Bash	12
66	Piccadilly 7N 35346	Que Sera Sera/All I Need	12
66	Piccadilly 7N 35359	Michael/Hold On To My Love	12
67	Piccadilly 7N 35392	She Shot A Hole In My Soul/I've Been Hurt By Love	15
67	Piccadilly 7N 35403	Tell It Like It Is/Girl I Want To Marry	8
67	Pye 7N 17425	Different Strokes/You Got Me Hummin'	7
68	Pye 7N 17570	I Can't Quit Her/Put Out The Fire Baby	7
68	Pye 7N 17649	I Can't Let You Go/Bring It To Me Baby	10
69	Pye 7N 17745	My Little Chickadee/Seven Eleven	7
71	Pye 7N 45019	Alison Please/Each And Every Part Me	7
71	Pye 7N 45085	Feeling So Good/Would You Believe My Little Chickadee	6
66	Piccadilly NEP 34054	HI (EP)	25
68	Pye NEP 24293	DIFFERENT STROKES (EP)	20
68	Pye NEP 24302	SMALL PACKAGE OF HIPSTERS (EP)	20
66	Piccadilly NPL 38026	HAND CLAPPIN', FOOT STOMPIN', FUNKY-BUTT . . . LIVE! (LP)	20
67	Piccadilly N(S)PL 38032	HIPSTERS, FLIPSTERS, FINGER-POPPIN' DADDIES! (LP)	20
68	Piccadilly N(S)PL 38029	SHAKE A TAIL FEATHER! (LP)	15
68	Pye N(S)PL 18219	LIVE! - RUNNING WILD (LP)	15
75	DJM DJLPS 457	GENO'S BACK (LP)	12
76	DJM DJF 20486	LIVE (LP)	12

MINT VALUE £

GEORGE E. WASHINGTON
64 Fontana TF 510 Spare A Thought For Me/Words Of Love ... 5

JERRY WASHINGTON
75 Contempo CS 2040 Right Here Is Where You Belong/In My Life I Haved Loved ... 8
75 Contempo CLP 517 RIGHT HERE IS WHERE YOU BELONG (LP) ... 20

GROVER WASHINGTON JR
77 Kudu Sausalito/Mr. Magic (12") ... 35
75 Kudu KU 20 MR MAGIC (LP) ... 12
75 Kudu KU 24 FEELS SO GOOD (LP) ... 12

KENNETH WASHINGTON (& CHRIS BARBER BAND)
(see also Chris Barber)
67 CBS 202494 If I Had A Ticket/They Kicked Him Out Of Heaven (with Chris Barber & T-Bones) ... 10
67 CBS 202592 Gimme That Old Time Religion (with Chris Barber Band)/ Just A Closer Walk With Thee. ... 5

NORMAN T. WASHINGTON
68 Pama PM 730 Same Thing All Over/You've Been Cheating ... 10
68 Pama PM 741 Tip Toe/Don't Hang Around ... 20
69 Punch PH 11 Oh Happy Day/Spinning ... 7
70 Gas GAS 159 It's Christmas Time Again/If I Could See You ... 8
70 Punch PH 26 Sweeter Than Honey/1,000 Pearls ... 7
70 Punch PH 31 Last Goodbye/Mother's Pride ... 7

SHERI WASHINGTON & BAND
57 Vogue V 9070 I Got Plenty/Ain't I Talkin' To You Baby ... 500
57 Vogue V 9070 I Got Plenty/Ain't I Talkin' To You Baby (78) ... 150

SISTER ERNESTINE B. WASHINGTON
50 Melodisc MEL 1101 God's Amazing Grace/Where Could I Go But To The Lord (78) ... 10
55 Melodisc EPM 7-52 SISTER ERNESTINE WASHINGTON (EP) ... 20

TONY WASHINGTON (& HIS D.C.s)
(see also Tony & Louise)
63 React EA 002 Crying Man/Please Mr. DJ ... 20
63 Island WI 068 Something Gotta Be Done/TONY & LOUISE: I Have Said ... 20
64 Sue WI 327 Show Me How (To Milk A Cow)/Boof Ska ... 50
64 Fontana TF 478 Surely You Love Me/Man To Man ... 15
65 Black Swan WI 459 But I Do/Night Train (as Tony Washington & His D.C.s) ... 25
65 Black Swan WI 460 Dilly Dilly/Night Train (as Tony Washington & His D.C.s) ... 25

WASHINGTON D.C.s
(see also Dave Clark Five, Freedom)
64 Ember EMB S 190 Kisses Sweeter Than Wine/Where Did You Go ... 15
66 CBS 202226 32nd Floor/Whole Lot More ... 15
67 CBS 202464 Seek And Find/I Love Gerald Chevin The Great (in p/s) ... 70
67 CBS 202464 Seek and Find/I Love Gerald Chevin The Great (no p/s) ... 50
67 CBS 202464 Seek And Find/I Love Gerald Chevin The Great ... 30
69 Domain D 9 I've Done It All Wrong/Anytime ... 30

WASHINGTON FLYERS
74 Dawn DNS 1076 Another Saturday Morning/The Comets Are Coming ... 6

WASP
(see also Brian Bennett, Shadows)
75 EMI EMI 2253 Melissa/Little Miss Bristol ... 30

W.A.S.P.
84 Music For Nations PKUT 109 Animal (Fuck Like A Beast)/Show No Mercy (shaped picture disc, pig's head or codpiece designs) ... 20
84 M. For Nations 12KUT 109 Animal (Fuck Like A Beast)/Show No Mercy (12", gold vinyl, U.K. issue pressed in France) ... 35
84 M. For Nations 12KUT 109 Animal (Fuck Like A Beast)/Show No Mercy (12", white, vinyl, U.K. issue pressed in France) ... 15
84 M. For Nations 12KUT 109 Animal (Fuck Like A Beast)/Show No Mercy (12", clear vinyl, U.K. issue pressed in France) ... 20
84 M. For Nations 12KUT 109 Animal (Fuck Like A Beast)/Show No Mercy (12", red vinyl, U.K. issue pressed in France) ... 12
84 Capitol CLP 336 I Wanna Be Somebody/Tormentor (Ragewars) (p/s) ... 5
84 Capitol 12 CLP 336 I Wanna Be Somebody/Tormentor (Ragewars) (12", picture disc) ... 10
84 Capitol CL 344 Schooldaze/Paint It Black (poster p/s) ... 8
84 Capitol 12 CL 344 Schooldaze/Paint It Black (12", p/s) ... 8
85 Capitol CLP 374 Blind In Texas/Savage (shaped picture disc) ... 6
86 Capitol CLD 388 Wild Child/Mississippi Queen//On Your Knees/Hellion (double pack) ... 5
86 Capitol 12CL 388 Wild Child/Mississippi Queen (12", p/s) ... 8
86 Capitol CLP 432 9.5 N.A.S.T.Y./Easy Living (shaped picture disc) ... 5
89 Capitol CLPD 546 Forever Free (Eagle Edit)/L.O.V.E. Machine (Live '89) (die-cut pic. disc) ... 5

WASPS
77 4-Play FOUR 001 Teenage Treats/She Made More Magic (p/s) ... 25
77 NEMS NES 115 Can't Wait 'Til '78/MEAN STREET: Bunch Of Stiffs (p/s) ... 18
78 RCA PB 5137 Rubber Cars/This Time (p/s) ... 10

WASTE
86 Morterhate MORT 21 NOT JUST SOMETHING TO BE SUNG (EP, foldout p/s) ... 25

WASTED YOUTH
80 Bridge House BHS 5 Jealousy/Baby (p/s, clear vinyl) ... 5
82 Bridge House BHFNEE 1 Caveman (1-sided, limited issue) ... 8
80 Bridge House BHLP006 WILD AND WANDERING (LP) ... 12
82 Bridge House BHLP007 THE BEGINNING OF THE END (LP) ... 12

MINT VALUE £

WASTELAND
79 Ellie Jay/Disaster EJSP 9261 WANT NOT EP (p/s, 2,000 only) 30
80 Invicta INV 014 Friends, Romans, Countrymen/Leave Me Alone (p/s, 1,000 only) 30

WATCH COMMITTEE
68 Philips BF 1695 Throw Another Penny In The Well/Now I Think The Other Way 6

WATERBOYS
00 Burning Airlines THE LIVE ADVENTURES OF THE WATERBOYS (2xCD) 20

WATERFALL
76 Bob FRR 001 FLIGHT OF THE DAY (LP, private pressing) 100
79 Avada AVA 104 THREE BIRDS (LP, with insert) 22
81 Gun Dog GUN 003LP BENEATH THE STARS (LP, private pressing) 22

WATER FOR A THIRSTY LAND
74 MRA P 100 WATER FOR A THIRSTY LAND (LP, with insert) 22

WATER INTO WINE BAND
73 Myrrh MYR 1004 HILL CLIMBING FOR BEGINNERS (LP, brown cover, with insert) 150
73 Myrrh MYR 1004 HILL CLIMBING FOR BEGINNERS (LP, white cover, with insert) 100
76 CJT 002 HARVEST TIME (LP, private pressing, 500 copies) 100

WATER PISTOLS
76 State STATE 38 Gimme That Punk Junk/Soft Punk (p/s, with insert) 10

WATERPROOF CANDLE
68 RCA RCA 1717 Electrically Heated Child/Saturday Morning Repentance 15

ETHEL WATERS
(see also Ida Cox)
66 World Record Club T 949 ETHEL WATERS (LP) 12

MUDDY WATERS
(see also Little Walter, Howlin' Wolf, Bo Diddley, Luther 'Georgia Boy Snake' Johnson)
53 Vogue V 2101 Walkin' Blues/Rollin' Stone Blues (78) 80
54 Vogue V 2273 Hello Little Girl/Long Distance Call (78) 80
55 Vogue V 2372 Honey Bee/Too Young To Know (78) 80
65 Chess CRS 8001 My John The Conquer Root/Short Dress Woman 20
65 Chess CRS 8019 I Got A Rich Man's Woman/My Dog Can't Bark 15
69 Chess CRS 8083 Let's Spend The Night Together/I'm A Man 15
69 Python PKM 04 Country Boy/All Night Long (99 copies only) 85
55 Vogue EPV 1046 MUDDY WATERS WITH LITTLE WALTER (EP) 150
56 London RU-E 1060 MISSISSIPPI BLUES (EP) 175
63 Pye Intl. NEP 44010 MUDDY WATERS (EP) 38
65 Chess CRE 6006 I'M READY (EP) 55
66 Chess CRE 6022 THE REAL FOLK BLUES VOL. 4 (EP) 45
59 London Jazz LJZ-M 15152 THE BEST OF MUDDY WATERS (LP) 90
61 Pye Jazz NJL 34 AT NEWPORT (LP) 75
64 Pye Intl. NPL 28038 MUDDY WATERS - FOLK SINGER (LP) 55
64 Pye Intl. NPL 28040 THE BEST OF MUDDY WATERS (LP) 65
64 Pye Intl. NPL 28048 MUDDY SINGS BIG BILL (LP) 35
65 Chess CRL 4513 AT NEWPORT (LP, reissue) 40
66 Chess CRL 4515 THE REAL FOLK BLUES (LP) 30
67 Chess CRL 4525 MUDDY, BRASS AND THE BLUES (LP) 35
67 Chess CRL 4529 SUPER BLUES (LP, with Little Walter & Bo Diddley) 40
68 Chess CRL 4537 THE SUPER SUPER BLUES BAND (LP, with Howlin' Wolf & Bo Diddley) 45
68 Bounty BY 6031 DOWN ON STOVALL'S PLANTATION (LP) 35
69 Chess CRL 4542 ELECTRIC MUD (LP) 30
69 Chess CRL 4553 AFTER THE RAIN (LP) 25
69 Chess CRL 4556 FATHERS AND SONS (LP) 25
69 Polydor 236 574 BLUES MAN (LP) 25
69 Python PLP 12 MUDDY WATERS (LP, 99 copies only) 80
69 Python PLP 18 MUDDY WATERS VOLUME 2 (LP, 99 copies only) 80
69 Python PLP 19 MUDDY WATERS VOLUME 3 (LP, 99 copies only) 80
70 Syndicate Chapter SC 001/2 BACK IN THE EARLY DAYS (2-LP) 25
70 Syndicate Chapter SC 002 GOOD NEWS (LP) 20
70 Sunnyland KS 100 VINTAGE MUDDY WATERS (LP, gatefold sleeve with inserts, 99 copies only) 45
71 Chess 6671 001 McKINLEY MORGANFIELD AKA MUDDY WATERS (LP) 20
72 Black Bear LP 901 RARE LIVE RECORDINGS VOL. 1 (LP) 20
72 Black Bear LP 902 RARE LIVE RECORDINGS VOL. 2 (LP) 20
72 Black Bear LP 903 RARE LIVE RECORDINGS VOL. 3 (LP) 20
72 Chess 6310 121 THE LONDON SESSIONS (LP) 15
74 Chess 6310 129 CAN'T GET NO GRINDIN' (LP) 12
77 Blue Sky SKY 81853 HARD AGAIN (LP) 15

ROGER WATERS
(see also Pink Floyd, Ron Geesin)
84 Harvest HAR 5228 5.01 AM (The Pros And Cons Of Hitch-Hiking)/ 4.30 AM (Apparently They Were Travelling Abroad) (p/s) 5
84 Harvest 12HAR 5228 5.01 AM (The Pros And Cons Of Hitch-Hiking)/4.30 AM (Apparently They Were Travelling Abroad)/4.33 AM (Running Shoes) (12", p/s) 8
84 Harvest HAR 5230 5.06 AM (Every Stranger's Eyes)/4.39 AM (For The First Time Today) (p/s) 15
87 EMI EM 6 Radio Waves/Going To Live In L.A. (Demo) (p/s) 6
87 EMI CDEM 6 Radio Waves (Remix)/Going To Live In L.A. (Demo)/ Radio Waves (7" Version) (CD) 10
87 EMI EM 20 Sunset Strip/Money (live) (withdrawn) 50
87 EMI EM 37 The Tide Is Turning (After Live Aid)/Money ('live') (p/s) 5
87 EMI CDEM 37 The Tide Is Turning (After Live Aid)/Money ('live')/Get Back To Radio (Demo Recording) (CD) 10
90 Mercury 878 147-2 PIECES FROM THE WALL: Another Brick In The Wall Part 2 (Edit)/ Young Lust (Edit)/Run Like Hell/In The Flesh? (CD, promo only) 20
92 Columbia 658 139 9 What God Wants Part I (Video Edit)/What God Wants Part I (Album Version)/ What God Wants Part III (CD, box set with prints) 12

MINT VALUE £

70	Harvest SHSP 4008	MUSIC FROM THE FILM "THE BODY" (LP, with Ron Geesin, green labels, with Waters/Geesin photos)	40
70	Harvest SHSP 4008	MUSIC FROM THE FILM "THE BODY" (LP, with Ron Geesin, black labels)	12
87	EMI KAOS DJ 1	RADIO KAOS (LP, 'banded' radio promo, custom sleeve)	25

LAL & MIKE WATERSON

73	Trailer LER 2076	BRIGHT PHOEBUS (LP, yellow label)	35

LAL AND NORMA WATERSON

(see also Watersons)

77	Topic 12T5331	A TRUE HEARTED GIRL (LP)	20

MIKE WATERSON

(see also Waterson, Lal & Mike Waterson)

77	Topic 12TS 332	MIKE WATERSON (LP)	20

WATERSONS

65	Topic 12T 125	NEW VOICES (LP, blue label, with Harry Boardman & Maureen Craik)	18
65	Topic 12T 136	FROST AND FIRE (LP, blue label)	18
66	Topic 12T 142	WATERSONS (LP, blue label)	18
66	Topic 12T 167	A YORKSHIRE GARLAND (LP, blue label)	18
60s	Topic TS 346	THE WATERSONS SOUND (LP)	15

DOC WATSON

64	Fontana TFL 6045	DOC WATSON (LP)	22
65	Fontana TFL 6055	DOC WATSON & SON (LP)	20
72	Vanguard VSD 9/10	ON STAGE (2-LP)	20

EARL WATSON

61	Ember EMB S 129	Nightmare/That Old Black Magic	10

JOHN L. WATSON (& HUMMELFLUGS)

(see also Web)

64	Pye 7N 15746	Looking For Love/Dance With You	12
65	Piccadilly 7N 35233	Standing By/I'll Make It Worth Your While	10
70	Deram DM-R 285	A Mother's Love/Might As Well Be Gone (solo)	12
70	Deram SML 1061	WHITE HOT BLUE BLACK (LP)	40

JOHNNY WATSON & KAMPAI KINGS

60	Oriole CB 1532	Moshi, Moshi, Anone!/ABDULLA & HIS LITTLE BAND: Fatima's Theme	5
60	Oriole CB 1532	Moshi, Moshi, Anone!/ABDULLA & HIS LITTLE BAND: Fatima's Theme (78)	30

JOHNNY 'GUITAR' WATSON

(see also Larry Williams & Johnny 'Guitar' Watson)

76	Fantasy FTC 124	I Don't Need A Lone Ranger/You Can Stay But The Noise Must Go	8

PAULA WATSON

63	Oriole 45-CV1785	Love Me Forever/Tell All The World About You	20

ROGER WATSON

74	Tradition TSR 017	THE PICK AND THE MALT SHOVEL (LP)	15

WAH WAH WATSON

76	CBS 81582	ELEMENTARY (LP)	12

BEN WATT

(see also Everything But The Girl)

81	Cherry Red CHERRY 25	Cant/Aubade/Tower Of Silence (p/s)	8
82	Cherry Red 12CHERRY 36	SUMMER INTO WINTER (12" EP, with Robert Wyatt, p/s)	10

WATTS 103RD STREET RHYTHM BAND

(see under Charles Wright & Watts 103rd Street Rhythm Band)

CHARLIE WATTS

(see also Rolling Stones, People Band, Rocket 88)

93	Continuum CDCTUM 103	My Ship/You Got To Me Head (CD)	12
86	CBS 450 253-1	LIVE AT FULHAM TOWN HALL (LP, as Charlie Watts & His Orchestra, with insert)	15
91	UFO UFO CD	FROM ONE CHARLIE (CD box set with book & Charlie Parker photo, signed)	40
91	UFO UFO CD	FROM ONE CHARLIE (CD box set with book & Charlie Parker photo, unsigned)	20
91	UFO UFO 2 LP	FROM ONE CHARLIE (10" LP, box set with book & Charlie Parker photo, signed)	50
91	UFO UFO 2 LP	FROM ONE CHARLIE (10" LP, box set with book & Charlie Parker photo, unsigned)	20

NOBLE 'THIN MAN' WATTS (& HIS BAND)

(see also Wild Jimmy Spurrill)

57	London HLU 8627	Hard Times (The Slop)/Midnight Flight (with His Rhythm Sparks)	75
57	London HLU 8627	Hard Times (The Slop)/Midnight Flight (with His Rhythm Sparks) (78)	20
64	Sue WI 347	Noble's Theme/JUNE BATEMAN: I Don't Wanna	70
79	Flyright 547	BLAST OFF (LP, mono)	20

QUEENIE WATTS

66	Columbia SX 6047	Queen High (LP)	30

TREVOR WATTS

78	Ogun OG 526	CYNOSURE (LP)	20

WATUSI WARRIORS

59	London HL 8866	Wa-Chi-Bam-Ba/Kalahari	15

ASHANTI WAUGH

80	Attack TACK 20	Babylon Wrong/BARRY BROWN: Cool Pun Yu Corner (12")	20

WAVELENGTH

82	Ariola ARO 290	Rio/Beach Party	7

WAVING AT TRAINS

(see also Playing At Trains)

80s		WAVING AT TRAINS (EP)	30

MINT VALUE £

WAX DOCTOR
(see also Kev Bird)
92 Basement BRSS 011 A New Direction/Herbal Tekno/Protplasm (12") 15
93 Basement BRSS 018 Another Direction/The Stalker (12") 10
93 Basement BRSS 027 New Direction (93 Remix)/What's Goin' On (12", with Jack Smooth) 15
93 Basement BRSS 030 Unfriendly/Rock To The Groove (12", with Jack Smooth) 12
94 Face FACE 106 Logical Profession (Logical Mix)/Logical Progression (12") 8

WAXIES DARGLE
69 Polydor S83080 HARBOUR FOLK (LP) 20

NANCY WAYBURN
65 Warner Bros WB 5646 The World Goes On Without Me/Listen To My Heart 15

WAYGOOD ELLIS
(see also Fleur-De-Lys)
67 Polydor 56729 I Like What I'm Trying To Do/Hey Lover 50

ALVIS WAYNE
63 Starlite ST45 104 Don't Mean Maybe, Baby/I'd Rather Be With You 600
70 Injun 113 I Gottum/Lay Your Head On My Shoulder 10

ARTIE WAYNE
52 London L 1164 Rachel/Tonight Or Never (78) 12

BOBBY WAYNE
65 Pye International 7N 25315 Ballad Of A Teenage Queen/River Man 10

BOBBY WAYNE
(see also Teresa Brewer)
51 London L 924 When The Wind Was Green/Buffalo Billy (78) 10
51 London L 968 Immaculate Mother/Mother At Your Feet Is Kneeling (78) 10
51 London L 972 Runnin' Around/Always You (78) 10
51 London L 973 Wild Card/Let Me In (78) 10
51 London L 1077 I Am Free/How Long Is Forever (78) 10
51 London L 1078 If You Turn Me Down/Let's Make Up Your Mind (78) 10

CARL WAYNE (& VIKINGS)
(see also Move, Ace Kefford Stand, Cheetahs, Acid Gallery, Keith Powell [& Valets])
64 Pye 7N 15702 What's A Matter Baby/Your Loving Ways (as Carl Wayne & Vikings) 50
65 Pye 7N 15824 This Is Love/You Could Be Fun (as Carl Wayne & Vikings) 40
70 RCA RCA 2032 Maybe God's Got Something Up His Sleeve/Rosanna 6
72 RCA RCA 2177 Imagine/Sunday Kind Of Love 5
72 RCA RCA 2257 Take My Hands For A While/Sweet Seasons 5
73 Pye 7N 45290 You're A Star/Bluebird 5
75 Polydor 2058 527 Way Back In The Fifties/Candy (You Know That I'm In Love With You) 6
77 Target TGT 125 A Little Give, A Little Take/Home Lovin' Man 6
77 DJM DJS Weeken 10797 Hi Summer/My Girl And Me 6
72 RCA SF 8239 CARL WAYNE (LP) 20

CHRIS WAYNE & ECHOES
60 Decca F 11231 Lonely/Counting Girls 15

JEFF WAYNE
(see also Ran-Dells)
69 Columbia S(C)X 6330 TWO CITIES (LP, soundtrack) 35

JERRY WAYNE
60 Vogue V 9169 Half-Hearted Love/Ten Thousand Miles 25

JOHN WAYNE
73 RCA PL 13484 AMERICA, WHY I LOVE HER (LP) 15

PAT WAYNE (& BEACHCOMBERS)
63 Columbia DB 7121 Go Back To Daddy/Jambalaya 20
63 Columbia DB 7182 Roll Over Beethoven/Is It Love? 25
64 Columbia DB 7262 Bye Bye Johnny/Strictly For The Birds 25
64 Columbia DB 7417 Brand New Man/Nobody's Child 20
65 Columbia DB 7603 Come Dance With Me/I Don't Want To Cry (solo) 12
65 Columbia DB 7739 My Friend/Tomorrow Mine (solo) 10
66 Columbia DB 7944 The Night Is Over/Hombre (solo) 12

RICK WAYNE
94 Pathway To Freedom R+R 002 Almighty Father/Bad Behaviour (12") 80

RICK(Y) WAYNE (& OFF-BEATS)
(see also [Fabulous] Flee-Rekkers)
60 Triumph RGM 1009 Chick A'Roo/Don't Pick On Me (with Fabulous Flee-Rakkers) 50
60 Pye 7N 15289 Make Way Baby/Goodness Knows (as Ricky Wayne & Off-Beats) 45
65 Oriole CB 306 Say You're Gonna Be My Own/It's A Crying Shame (as Rick Wayne) 20
65 CBS 201764 In My Imagination/Don't Ever Share Your Love (as Rick Wayne) 15

TERRY WAYNE
57 Columbia DB 4002 Matchbox/Your True Love 25
57 Columbia DB 4035 Plaything/Slim Jim Tie 30
57 Columbia DB 4035 Plaything/Slim Jim Tie (78) 10
58 Columbia DB 4067 All Mama's Children/Forgive Me 25
58 Columbia DB 4067 All Mama's Children/Forgive Me (78) 10
58 Columbia DB 4112 Oh! Lonesome Me/There's Only One You 20
58 Columbia DB 4112 Oh! Lonesome Me/There's Only One You (78) 12
58 Columbia DB 4205 Little Brother/Where My Baby Goes 18
58 Columbia DB 4205 Little Brother/Where My Baby Goes (78) 15
59 Columbia DB 4312 Brooklyn Bridge/She's Mine 20
58 Columbia SEG 7758 TERRIFIC (EP) 100

MINT VALUE £

THOMAS WAYNE

59 London HLU 8846 Tragedy/Saturday Date 35
59 London HLU 8846 Tragedy/Saturday Date (78) 25
59 London HL 7075 Tragedy/Saturday Date (export issue) 20

WAYS & MEANS

66 Columbia DB 7907 Little Deuce Coupe/The Little Old Lady From Pasadena 25
66 Pye 7N 17217 Sea Of Faces/Make The Radio A Little Louder 25
68 Trend TRE 1005 Breaking Up A Dream/She 60

WAY WE LIVE

(see also Tractor, Beau)
71 Dandelion DAN 8004 A CANDLE FOR JUDITH (LP, gatefold sleeve, label and sleeve DAN 8004) 125
71 Dandelion DAN 8004 A CANDLE FOR JUDITH (LP, gatefold sleeve, as K 49004) 60

WBI RED NINJA

90 Red Ninja SRT90LS 2532 Danger Zone/This Mike's For Hire/Bad Testament (12") 25
91 Red Ninja RN002 HELLZ A PLACE I KNOW (EP) 12
91 Zoom 007 Ninja Dawn (Day Of Dread) (12") 10

WEAPON

(see also Wildfire)
80 Weapon WEAP 1 It's A Mad Mad World/Set The Stage Alight (p/s) 30
81 Virgin WEAPONE It's A Mad Mad World/Set The Stage Alight (12", p/s, reissue) 40

WEASELSNOUT

72 Weaselsnout WUS 140 UNSUNG LIES (LP, private pressing) 165

WEATHER

69 Philips BF 1734 Look In My Eyes/Running Forward 35
69 Philips BF 1819 Jamboree Special/Two Peculiar People 10

ALFIE WEATHERBY

58 Columbia DC 729 49 Juke Boxes/Why Am I Crying? (78, export issue) 20

VIVIAN WEATHERS

79 Island 12WIP6529 Just A Game/Cheat Heart Dub/Married Woman/Wounded Dub (12", p/s) 8

DENNIS WEAVER

77 DJM DJS 10758 Devil In My Arms/Flat Bed Truck (p/s, promo) 8

JANE WEAVER v DOVES

(see also Doves)
98 Manchester MANC 9 Seven Day Smile/ANDY VOTEL & JANE WEAVER: Gutter Girl (p/s) 6
98 Manchester MANCCD 9 Seven Day Smile/ANDY VOTEL & JANE WEAVER: Gutter Girl/
JANE WEAVER: You're Not The Only Person That I Used To Know (CD) 8

WEAVERS

(see also Pete Seeger)
59 Top Rank JAR 120 Wild Goose Grasses/Meet The Johnson Boys 6

WEB

96 Fat Cat 12FAT 001 EVA EP (12", plain sleeve) 20

WEB

(see also John L. Watson [& Hummelflugs], Samurai, Greenslade)
68 Deram DM 201 Hatton Mill Morning/Conscience 25
68 Deram DM 217 Baby Won't You Leave Me Alone/McVernon Street 25
69 Deram DM 253 Monday To Friday/Harold Dubbleyew 25
68 Deram SML 1025 FULLY INTERLOCKING (LP) 90
70 Deram DAL-R 1058 THERAPHOSA BLONDI (LP, mono) 120
70 Deram SML-R 1058 THERAPHOSA BLONDI (LP, stereo) 90
70 Polydor 2383 024 I SPIDER (LP, gatefold sleeve, red label) 350

BARRY WEBB (O.P.M.C.)

70 Decca F 23012 Live For Tomorrow Harry James/At The Hop 8

DEAN WEBB

59 Parlophone R 4549 Warm Your Heart/Hey Miss Fannie 50
59 Parlophone R 4587 The Rough And The Smooth/Streamline Baby 50

DON WEBB

60 Coral Q 72385 Little Ditty Baby/I'll Be Back Home 100

GEORGE WEBB DIXIELANDERS

56 Decca DFE 6351 AND HIS DIXIELANDERS (EP) 15
50s Melodisc EPM7 70 THE GEORGE WEBB DIXIELANDERS (EP) 10

JANET WEBB

71 Polydor 2058-131 I Cried For You/Mama (p/s) 10

JILLA WEBB

56 MGM SP 1180 You Gotta Love Me Now/What Do You Think It Does To Me? 10

JIM(MY) WEBB

(see also Strawberry Children, Glen Campbell)
68 CBS 3672 I Keep It Hid/I Need You (as Jim Webb) 25
71 Reprise RS 20978 P.F. Sloan/Psalm One-Five-O 10
73 Reprise K 14279 Campo De Encino/Once In The Morning 5
68 CBS (S) 63335 JIM WEBB SINGS JIM WEBB (LP, as Jim Webb) 25
71 Reprise RSLP 6421 WORDS AND MUSIC (LP, with insert) 20
71 Reprise K 44101 WORDS AND MUSIC (LP, reissue) 15
72 Reprise K 44134 AND SO ON (LP) 18
72 Reprise K 44173 LETTERS (LP) 15
74 Asylum SYL 9014 LAND'S END (LP, with inner sleeve) 15
77 Atlantic K 50370 EL MIRAGE (LP, with inner sleeve) 15

MINT VALUE £

JOHNNY WEBB
(see also June Laverick)

56	Columbia DB 3805	Dig/Glendora	10
60s	Melodisc MEL 1617	Travelin' Man/Hold Back The Town (in p/s)	8
60s	Melodisc MEL 1617	Travelin' Man/Hold Back The Town	5

PETA WEBB & PETE COOPER

86	Heart	HEART IS TRUE (LP)	15

PETA WEBB
(see also Oak)

73	Topic 12TS 223	I HAVE WANDERED IN EXILE (LP, blue label)	35

ROGER WEBB (& HIS TRIO)

67	RCA 1599	A Man And His Woman/The Spiderman	20
71	Columbia DB 8803	Strange Report/Summer Fancy	12
82	Chandos SBR 102	The Gentle Touch/Arthur's Theme	6
84	Chips CH 104	Hammer House Of Horror/Cover Theme (p/s)	12
64	Parlophone PMC 1233	JOHN, PAUL AND ALL THAT JAZZ (LP)	18

SKEETER WEBB

55	Parlophone CMSP 32	Was It A Bad Dream/Your Secret's Not A Secret Anymore (export issue)	15

SONNY WEBB & CASCADES

64	Oriole CB 1873	You've Got Everything/Border Of The Blues	45
64	Polydor NH 52158	You've Got Everything/Border Of The Blues (reissue)	15

A J WEBBER

80	Gundog GUN 002	OF THIS LAND (LP)	30

MARLENE WEBBER
(see also Webber Sisters, Tonettes)

70	Bamboo BAM 33	My Baby/BRENTFORD ALLSTARS: You Gonna Hold Me (Version)	20
71	Ackee ACK 120	Natengula/Natengula-Kera (as Merlin Webber)	8
71	Ackee ACK 122	Cumbaya/Hail-Hi Freedom (as Merlin Webber)	8
71	Smash SMA 2322	Hard Life/COLLINS ALL STARS: Version Life (as Merlene Webber)	10
71	Trojan TR 7815	Stand By Your Man/CLANCY ECCLES: Credit Squeeze	8

WEBBER SISTERS
(see also Delroy Wilson)

67	Island WI 3109	My World/ALVA LEWIS: Lonely Still	60

WEBS

68	London HLU 10188	This Thing Called Love/Tomorrow	25

WEBSPINNERS

73	Buddah 2011 150	Spider Man - Theme/Goin' 'Cross Town	6

BEN WEBSTER

55	Columbia CLEF 33CX 10014	MUSIC FOR LOVERS (LP)	20
59	HMV CLP 1336	BEN WEBSTER AND ASSOCIATES (LP)	20
65	Fontana FJL 126	INTIMATE! (LP)	20
69	Ember CJS 822	BEN WEBSTER AT EASE (LP)	12
70	Fontana FJL 316	BIG BEN TIME (LP)	18
72	Philips 6308 101	WEBSTER'S DICTIONARY (LP)	20

CHASE WEBSTER

64	Hickory 45-1283	Life Can Have Meaning/Where Is Your Heart	6

DEENA WEBSTER

68	Parlophone R 5699	You're Losing/Wish You Were Here	10
68	Parlophone R 5721	Your Heart Is Free Just Like The Wind/Queen Merka And Me	8
68	Parlophone R 5738	Scarborough Fair/The Water Is Wide	7
69	Parlophone R 5798	Joey/It's Alright With Me	6
68	Parlophone PMC/PCS 7052	TUESDAY'S CHILD (LP)	30

MAX WEBSTER (BAND)
(see also Rush)

78	Capitol EST 11776	MEETING UP MY SLEEVE (LP)	12
79	Capitol EST 11937	A MILLION VACATIONS (LP)	12
80	Mercury 6337 144	UNIVERSAL JUVENILES (LP)	12

WEDDING PRESENT

85	Reception REC 001	Go Out And Get 'Em Boy/(The Moment Before) Everything's Spoiled Again (p/s, 500 only, with poster & badge)	25
85	Reception REC 001	Go Out And Get 'Em Boy/(The Moment Before) Everything's Spoiled Again (p/s, 500 only, without poster & badge)	18
85	City Slang CSL 001	Go Out And Get 'Em Boy/(The Moment Before) Everything's Spoiled Again (reissue, different foldout p/s, 1,000 only)	10
86	Reception REC 002	Once More/At The Edge Of The Sea (p/s, 3,500 only)	8
86	Reception REC 002/12	DON'T TRY AND STOP ME MOTHER (12" EP, combines REC 001 & 002)	8
86	Reception REC 003	This Boy Can Wait/You Should Always Keep In Touch With Your Friends (p/s, matrix numbers: 003 A2 & 003 B1)	6
86	Reception REC 003	This Boy Can Wait/You Should Always Keep In Touch With Your Friends (p/s, mispress both sides play B-side, matrix numbers: 003 A1 & 003 A2)	5
86	Reception REC 003/12	This Boy Can Wait (Extended)/You Should Always Keep In Touch With Your Friends/Living And Learning (12", p/s)	8
87	Reception REC 005	My Favourite Dress/Every Mother's Son/Never Said (p/s, white vinyl, 3,000 only, 2,000 of which free with "George Best" LP)	6
87	Reception	A Million Miles/What Did Your Last Servant Die Of? (DJ promo, 200 only)	10
87	Reception REC 006/C	Anyone Can Make A Mistake/All About Eve/Getting Nowhere Fast (cassette, shrinkwrapped with badge)	5
88	Reception REC 010X	Davni Chasy/Katrusya (promo only)	6
88	House Of Dolls HOD 004	Unfaithful (Peel Session)/TRUDY: Living On A Moon/HUNTERS CLUB: Little Sister/CLAYTOWN TROUPE: Real Life (free with House Of Dolls mag)	5

MINT VALUE £

89	M'night Music DONG 39 CD	Pourquoi Es Tu Devenue Si Raisonable? (CD, unreleased)	0
89	RCA	Davni Chasy/Katrusya (promo only)	12
90	RCA PB 43403	Brassneck/Don't Talk, Just Kiss (custom hand-painted p/s, 3,000 only)	7
92	RCA PB 45185	Blue Eyes/Cattle And Cane (p/s)	7
92	RCA PB 45183	Go Go Dancer/Don't Cry No Tears (p/s)	6
92	RCA PB 45181	Three/Think That It Might (p/s)	6
92	RCA PB 45311	Silver Shorts/Falling (p/s)	6
92	RCA PB 45313	Come Play With Me/Pleasant Valley Sunday (p/s)	6
87	Reception LEEDS 1	GEORGE BEST (LP, 2,000 only with white vinyl 7": My Favourite Dress/ Every Mother's Son/Never Said [REC 005] & inner sleeve; later with bonus black vinyl 7" or 12" edition, £10)	12
88	Reception LEEDS 2	TOMMY (LP, 1,000 signed by band, with poster & inner sleeve)	18

WEDGE

69	Midas MD3904	Sleep Child/Fly Away	25

WEDGEWOODS

64	Pye 7N 15642	September In The Rain/Gone Gone Away	12
65	Pye 7N 15846	Peace/Summer Love	10

FRED WEDLOCK

70s	Trans VTS 20	FROLLICKS (LP)	15

WEE THREE

73	People PEO 104	Get On Board/Get On Board (Instrumental)	8

WEE WILLIE & WINNERS

74	Action ACT 4624	Get Some/A Plan For The Man	8
74	People PEO 116	I Don't Know What You Got But I Know What I Need (Parts 1 & 2)	8

BUDDY WEED & HIS ORCHESTRA

57	Vogue V 9075	The Kent Song/For Love	25

BERT WEEDON

(see also George Chisholm, Craig Douglas, Ragpickers)

56	Parlophone MSP 6242	The Boy With The Magic Guitar/Flannel-Foot	20
56	Parlophone MSP 6242	The Boy With The Magic Guitar/Flannel-Foot (78)	10
57	Parlophone R 4256	Theme From ITV's '$64,000 Question'/Twilight Time	20
57	Parlophone R 4315	The Jolly Gigolo/Soho Fair	20
57	Parlophone R 4381	Play That Big Guitar/Quiet, Quiet, Ssh!	10
58	Parlophone R 4446	Big Note Blues/Rippling Tango	10
59	Saga SAG 2906	Fifi/Cat On A Hot Tin Roof (as Bert Weedon & Rag Pickers)	5
59	Top Rank JAR 117	Guitar Boogie Shuffle/Bert's Boogie	5
59	Top Rank JAR 121	Sing Little Birdie/The Lady Is A Tramp	5
59	Top Rank JAR 122	Petite Fleur/My Happiness	5
59	Top Rank JAR 123	Charmaine/It's Time To Say Goodnight	5
59	Top Rank JAR 136	Teenage Guitar/Blue Guitar	5
59	Top Rank JAR 210	Jealousy/Tango, Tango	5
59	Top Rank JAR 211	Stardust/Summertime	5
59	Top Rank JAR 221	Nashville Boogie/King Size Guitar	5
60	Top Rank JAR 300	Big Beat Boogie/Theme From 'A Summer Place' (in p/s)	10
60	Top Rank JAR 300	Big Beat Boogie/Theme From 'A Summer Place'	5
60	Top Rank JAR 360	Twelfth Street Rag/Querida	7
60	Top Rank JAR 415	Apache/Lonely Guitar	12
60	Top Rank JAR 517	Sorry Robbie/Easy Beat	7
61	Top Rank JAR 537	Ginchy/Yearning	7
61	Top Rank JAR 559	Mr. Guitar/Eclipse	10
56	Esquire EP 56	WAXING THE WINNERS (EP)	25
59	Selmer Amplifiers	DEMONSTRATION RECORD WITH DAVID GELL (EP, with mailer)	20
59	Selmer Amplifiers	DEMONSTRATION RECORD WITH DAVID GELL (EP, without mailer)	10
61	Top Rank JKP 3008	WEEDON WINNERS (EP)	10
64	HMV 7EG 8856	GUITAR MAN (EP)	10
60	Top Rank BUY 026	KINGSIZE GUITAR (LP)	30
61	Top Rank 35/101	HONKY TONK GUITAR (LP)	30

WEEDS

86	In Tape IT 34	China Doll/Crazy Face (p/s)	12

WEEKENDERS

94	Blow Up (Blow UP BU 001)	All Grown Up/House Husband (mail-order only)	10

WEEZER

94	Geffen GFS 85	Undone: The Sweater Song/Mykel And Carli/Susanne/Holiday (p/s)	20
94	Geffen GFSCD 85	Undone: The Sweater Song/Mykel And Carli/Susanne/Holiday (CD)	15
95	Geffen GFS 88	Buddy Holly/Jamie (p/s)	20
95	Geffen GFSV 95	Say It Ain't So (Remix)/No One Else (Live & Acoustic)/Jamie (10", p/s)	10
95	Geffen GEF 24629	WEEZER (LP)	20
01	Geffen 497567-7	Hash Pipe/Teenage Victory Song (p/s)	10
01	Geffen 497616-7	Island In The Sun/Always (p/s, yellow vinyl)	10
02	Geffen 497771-7	Keep Fishin'/Photograph (live) (p/s)	8
05	Geffen 9881793	Beverley Hills/Butterfly (live) (picture disc, stickered PVC sleeve)	5
05	Geffen 9883498	We Are All On Drugs/Beverley Hills (Urbanix Mix) (p/s, pink vinyl)	5
96	Geffen GFS 22167	El Scorcho/You Gave Your Love To Me Softly (p/s)	15

WE FIVE

65	Pye International 7N 25314	You Were On My Mind/Small World	12
66	Pye International 7N 25346	Let's Get Together/Cast Your Fate To The Wind	20
66	Pye Intl. NEP 44056	LET'S GET TOGETHER (EP)	60
65	Pye Intl. NPL 28067	YOU WERE ON MY MIND (LP)	60

WE 4

67	HMV POP 1603	Pretty Flowers/I'll Make You A Miracle	5
69	Major Minor MM 593	Candy Floss Man/Perry Park	6

MINT VALUE £

BOB WEIR
(see also Grateful Dead, Kingfish, Bobby & Midnites)
72 Warner Bros WB 7611 One More Saturday Night/Cassidy 5
72 Warner Bros K 46165 ACE (LP) 12

FRANK WEIR & HIS ORCHESTRA
(see also Bill Darnell, Vera Lynn, Janie Marden)
54 Decca F 10271 The Happy Wanderer/From Your Lips 10
60 Oriole CB 1559 Caribbean Honeymoon/Farewell My Love 10
62 Philips 326560 BF Manhunt/Chant Of The Jungle. . . . 5

NORRIS WEIR (& JAMAICANS)
(see also Jamaicans)
70 Duke DU 85 Hard On Me (with Jamaicans)/TOMMY COWAN & JAMAICANS: Please Stop The Wedding 6
74 Dragon DRA 1030 Reggay Revolution/Version 5
75 Horse HOSS 81 Dr. Honey/Honey Dub. . . . 5

WEIRD STRINGS
(see also Paul Roland, Midnight Rags)o
80 Velvet Moon VM 1 Oscar Mobile/Ancient Square (foldover p/s) 10
80 Ace ACE 009 Criminal Cage/Mi££ionaire (p/s) 8

FRANK WEISS
71 Stax 2362 011 WEISS TO MEMPHIS (LP) 12

BRUCE WELCH
(see also Marvin, Welch & Farrar; Shadows, Cliff Richard)
74 EMI EMI 2141 Please Mr. Please/Song Of Yesterday. . . . 50

ED WELCH
71 United Artists UP35284 Clowns/The Bird Song 10
71 United Artists UAS 29248 CLOWNS (LP, with inner). . . . 15

ELIZABETH WELCH
80 Industrial IR 002 Stormy Weather/Ya're Blase (p/s) 8

HONEE WELCH
69 London HLU 10288 I'm Gonna Try/It's My Girl 7

KEN & MITZIE WELCH
62 London RE-R 1275 A PIANO, ICE BOX AND BED (EP) 15

LENNY WELCH
60 London HLA 9094 You Don't Know Me/I Need Someone. . . . 6
62 London HLA 9601 Taste Of Honey/Old Cathedral. . . . 6
63 London HLA 9810 Since I Fell For You/Are You Sincere 6
64 London HLA 9880 Ebb Tide/Congratulations Baby 6
64 London HLR 9910 If You See My Love/Father Sebastian. . . . 6
65 London HLR 9981 Darling Take Me Back/Time After Time. . . . 15
65 London HLR 9991 Two Different Worlds/I Was There. . . . 8
65 London HLR 10010 Run To My Lovin' Arms/Coronet Blue 20
66 London HLR 10031 Rags To Riches/I Want You To Worry. . . . 10
66 London HA-R/SH-R 8267 TWO DIFFERENT WORLDS (LP). . . . 20
66 London HA-R 8290 RAGS TO RICHES (LP). . . . 20

TIM WELCH
60 Columbia DB 4529 Weak In The Knees/A Boy And A Girl In Love. . . . 7

WELD OF LIQUOR
95 Weld Record WELD 05 We Are The Weld/For Manze's Sake (vinegar-scented p/s) 10

WELFARE STATE
78 Look LKLP 6347 WELFARE STATE SONGS (LP, with insert) 60

LAWRENCE WELK ORCHESTRA
56 Vogue Coral Q 72140 Chain Gang/The Poor People Of Paris. . . . 5
56 Vogue Coral Q 72141 The 'Threepenny Opera' Theme/Rock And Roll Waltz 5
57 Vogue Coral Q 72233 Pizzicato Waltz/Whispering Heart. . . . 5
57 Vogue Coral Q 72256 Around The World In 80 Days/Ten Little Trees 5
60 London HLD 9229 Last Date/Remember Lolita 5
61 London HLD 9261 Calcutta (Nicolette)/Melodie D'Amour 5
64 Dot DS 16697 The 'Addams Family' Theme/Apples And Bananas 10

PAUL WELLER
(see also Jam, Style Council, Smokin' Mojo Filters, Andy Lewis & Paul Weller, Paul Weller Movement)

SINGLES
92 Go! Discs GOD 86 Uh Huh Oh Yeh/Fly On The Wall (7"; paper or plastic labels) 6
92 Go! Discs GODX 86 Uh Huh Oh Yeh/Arrival Time/Fly On The Wall/ Always There To Fool You (12") . . . 8
92 Go! Discs GODCD 86 Uh Huh Oh Yeh/Arrival Time/Fly On The Wall/ Always There To Fool You (CD, Digipak) 8
92 Go! Discs GOD 91 Above The Clouds/Everything Has A Price To Pay (7"; paper or plastic labels) . . 6
92 Go! Discs GODX 91 Above The Clouds/Everything Has A Price To Pay/All Year Round (Live At New York City The Ritz 25.7.92)/Feeling Alright (12"). . . . 8
92 Go! Discs GODCD 91 Above The Clouds/Everything Has A Price To Pay/All Year Round (Live at New York City The Ritz 25.7.92)/Feeling Alright (CD, Digipak). . . . 8
93 Go! Discs GOD 102 Sunflower/Bull-Rush-Magic Bus (Live at RAH 10.92) (7") 6
93 Go! Discs GOD 104 Wild Wood/Ends Of The Earth (7") 6
93 Go! Discs GODT 104 Wild Wood/Ends Of The Earth (10", numbered with poster) 10
93 Go! Discs GODCD 104 Wild Wood/Ends Of The Earth (CD, digipak with 5 prints; sealed). . . . 12
93 Go! Discs GODCD 104 Wild Wood/Ends Of The Earth (CD, digipak with 5 prints; unsealed). . . . 10
93 Go! Discs GODT 107 THE WEAVER EP: The Weaver/This Is No Time/Another New Day/Ohio (Live At Royal Albert Hall 10.92) (10" EP, numbered sticker). . . . 8
93 Go! Discs GODCD 107 THE WEAVER EP: The Weaver/This Is No Time/Another New Day/Ohio (Live At RAH 10.92) (CD EP + postcards, some sealed). . . . 12

			MINT VALUE £
93	Go! Discs GODCD 107	THE WEAVER EP: The Weaver/This Is No Time/Another New Day/Ohio (Live At RAH 10.92) (CD EP + postcards, some sealed)	10
93	Matrix: WELLER+F1	The Loved (blank clear flexi with The Big Issue mag)	12
93	Matrix: WELLER+F1	The Loved (blank clear flexi without The Big Issue mag)	8
94	Go! Discs GOD 121	Out Of The Sinking/Sexy Sadie/Sunflower (Lynch Mob Dub) (7")	5
00	Island IS 760	He's The Keeper/Heliocentric/Bang-Bang (7", 3rd April 2000)	5
02	Independiente ISOM63TE	It's Written In The Stars/Horseshoe Drama/Push Button, Automatic (10")	6
05	V2 VVR 5030597	Early Morning Rain/Come Together (7", red vinyl, die-cut sleeve, 4,000 only)	6
05	V2 VVR 5033410	From The Floorboards Up/From The Floorboards Up (Lynchmob Remix - Instrumental) (7", gatefold p/s, 4,000 only)	5
05	V2 VVR 5033417	From The Floorboards Up/Oranges And Rosewater (2nd 7", green & orange vinyl, stickered PVC sleeve)	5
ALBUMS			
92	Go! Discs 828 343-1	PAUL WELLER (LP, gatefold sleeve, stapled-in lyric booklet)	25
93	Go! Discs 828 435-1	WILD WOOD (LP, gatefold sleeve with 'obi' band & poster)	22
94	Go! Discs 828 513-1	WILD WOOD (LP, gatefold sleeve with 'obi' band & poster; reissue with extra track 'Hung Up')	22
94	Go! Discs 828 561-1	LIVE WOOD (2-LP, single sleeve with picture inners)	22
95	Go! Discs 828 619-1	STANLEY ROAD (LP, gatefold sleeve with Excerpts booklet)	20
95	Go! Discs 850 070-7	STANLEY ROAD (6 x 7" singles in 7" box)	30
97	Island ILPS 8058	HEAVY SOUL (LP, gatefold sleeve with picture inner & insert)	20
97	Island CID 8058	HEAVY SOUL ("unofficial" wooden box set, 1,000 only, incl.: hinged wooden box, numbered certificate, promo CD, 5 postcards, CD booklet, promo 7", 5 guitar plectrums & polo shirt)	125
98	Island ILPSD 8080	MODERN CLASSICS - THE GREATEST HITS (2-LP, gatefold sleeve with picture inners & insert)	18
98	Island IBX 8080	MODERN CLASSICS (box set, numbered 4 x 7" + 16-page photo book & colour print)	30
00	Island ILPS 8093	HELIOCENTRIC (LP, with foldout poster)	20
01	Independiente ISOM26LP	DAYS OF SPEED (2-LP, gatefold sleeve with inners)	50
02	Independiente ISOM33LP	ILLUMINATION (LP, rounded corners, gatefold sleeve with picture inner & booklet)	20
04	V2 VVR 1026902	STUDIO 150 (CD, autographed for competition)	18
04	V2 VVR 1026901	STUDIO 150 (LP, 2,000 only, with inner sleeve)	18
FAN CLUB ITEMS			
90s	(no label)	BOOT CUT (live CD, card sleeve, fan club issue)	20
90s	(no label)	ACOUSTIC EP (live DVD, with Gem Archer, features radio interview + 5 songs including U.S. TV appearance, fan club issue)	30
PROMOS			
91	Freedom High FHP 1	Into Tomorrow/Here's A New Thing (7", white label promo, 1991)	25
91	Freedom High FHPT 1	Into Tomorrow/Here's A New Thing/That Spiritual Feeling/ Into Tomorrow (8-Track demo) (12", white label promo, 1991)	35
92	Echantillon (no cat. no.)	Uh Huh Oh Yeh/Arrival Time/Fly On The Wall/ Always There To Fool You (12", yellow label test pressing)	50
92	Go! Discs KOSX 1	Kosmos (12", 1-sided)	25
92	Go! Discs GOXDJ 102	Kosmos (12", printed label)	25
93	Go! Discs GOPRO 102	Sunflower (12")	12
93	Go! Discs GOTDJ 104	Wild Wood/Ends Of The Earth (10")	20
93	Go! Discs GOXDJ 111	Hung Up/Foot Of The Mountain (Live Royal Albert Hall 23.11.93)/ The Loved/ Kosmos (Lynch Mob Bonus Beats) (12", printed white labels)	10
94	Go! Discs PNME 1	Shadow Of The Sun (Live at Wolverhampton Civic Hall 9.3.94)/ Sunflower (Lynch Mob Dub Edit)/Wild Wood (Sheared Wood - Remixed by Portishead with A. Utley) (white label promo for NME cover mount)	35
94	Go! Discs PNPCD 2	Sexy Sadie (CD, 1-track, card sleeve, numbered, available by mail-order with 1st 500 copies of Highlights & Hang-Ups video)	12
94	Island GODJB 121	Out Of The Sinking/Sexy Sadie (7", jukebox issue)	5
95	Go! Discs LYNCH 1	Lynch Mob Beats (12", stamped 1-sided white label, 500 only)	60
95	Go! Discs STAN 1	A FEW STOPS FROM STANLEY ROAD (CD sampler, card p/s)	10
95	Go! Discs SPLINT 1	Walk On Gilded Splinters (12", white label test pressing, 1-sided, 1995)	70
95	Go! Discs (no cat. no.)	CD SAMPLER (CD, given away in queue for 100 Club gig, 200 only)	45
95	Disctronics matrix: WELLERSPEC 01	OUR PRICE PAUL WELLER SPECIAL (CD, in-store album, no inlay, PVC outer)	60
96	Go! Discs PSCD 1	Peacock Suit/Eye Of The Storm (CD, no inlay)	12
96	Go! Discs PWRT 1	PEACOCK SUIT (CD, 7-track, picture disc in cloth bag)	25
97	Island HEAVY 1	Heavy Soul (Pt 1)/Heavy Soul (Pt 2) (7", Island sleeve)	50
97	Island SOULCD 1	A PIECE OF HEAVY SOUL (CD sampler, card sleeve)	12
97	Island SOULMC 1	A PIECE OF HEAVY SOUL (cassette sampler)	8
97	Island PAUL CD 1	WILD WOOD TO HEAVY SOUL (CD, in-store sampler, no inlay)	12
97	Island PWICD 1	HEAVY SOUL (box set: interview CD, EPK, 5 cards & insert)	45
97	Southern Songs WELLER 1	LIVE... FROM THE ROOF OF THE HAYWARD GALLERY (LP, finished sleeve, white labels)	25
97	Island KINGS 1	KINGS ROAD (CD sampler, 350 only)	45
98	Island 12IS 711DJ	Brand New Start/Right Underneath It (12")	12
99	Island 12IS 734DJ	Wild Wood (The Sheared Wood Remix)/Science (Lynch Mob Remix with Psychonauts) (12", white label, only 130 copies mailed out)	18
99	Island INTCD 3	IN CONVERSATION (interview CD, gatefold card p/s)	30
00	Island HELIO-1	Heliocentric (Two Lone Swordsmen 4UR Mix)/Heliocentric (Original Version)/There's No Drinking After You're Dead (Noonday Underground Mix) (12" white label)	30
01	Independiente DOSB 1	DAYS OF SPEED SELECTIONS (3-CD set, card outer sleeve with CDs in individual card inners)	50
02	Independiente PWICD 1	ILLUMINATION: SIX TRACK SAMPLER (CD, card sleeve with inner)	20
03	Universal CUFF 1	BUTTON DOWNS (LP, promo-only vinyl edition of third disc of cover versions from Fly On The Wall))	35
05	V2 VVR 5030593P	Come Together/Early Morning Rain (CD, card sleeve)	12
05	V2 VVR 5033488P	From The Floorboards Up (7", white label test pressing, stamped white sleeve)	25

MINT VALUE £

05	V2 VVR 1033202P	SINGLES BOX (box set, mail-order only, houses all As Is Now 7"s; priced without singles)	20
05	Universal STAN 1	STANLEY ROAD - 10TH ANNIVERSARY EP (7")	10
09	Universal (No cat no)	7 & 3 Is The Striker's Name (one-sided 7", screen printed sleeve, 1000 only)	50

PAUL WELLER MOVEMENT

91	Freedom High FHP 1	Into Tomorrow/Here's A New Thing (7", with or without 'Paul Weller Movement' printed on label)	8
91	Freedom High FHPMC 1	Into Tomorrow/Here's A New Thing (cassette)	5
91	Freedom High FHPT 1	Into Tomorrow/Here's A New Thing/That Spiritual Feeling/ Into Tomorrow (8-Track Demo) (12")	12

ORSON WELLES

(see also Manowar)

59	Top Rank TR 5001	The Courtroom Scene From The Film 'Compulsion' (both sides) (in p/s)	12
84	Splash SP 29	I Know What It Is To Be Young (But You Don't Know What It Is To Be Old)/ Love Is A Lovely Word (p/s)	8

NICK WELLINGS & SECTION

77	The Label TLR 011	You Better Move On/Punk Funk	6

WELLINGTON

74	Concord CON 029	Alright I'll See You Tonight/How Would You Like To Rock With Me	8
74	Concord CON 031	Catch Us If You Can/Superstar	8

BOBBY WELLINS

78	Vortex VS1	LIVE JUBILATION (LP)	40
78	Vortex VS2	DREAMS ARE FREE (LP)	40

BOBBY WELLS

68	Beacon 3-102	Let's Copp A Groove/Recipe For Love (yellow label)	30
68	Beacon 3-102	Let's Copp A Groove/Recipe For Love (white label)	20
68	Beacon 3-102	Let's Copp A Groove/Recipe For Love (green label)	15
79	Grapevine GRP 124	Be's That Way Sometimes/Recipe For Love	10

BRIAN WELLS

72	Spark SRL 1082	Paper Party/Just A Summer High	6

HOUSTON WELLS (& MARKSMEN)

(see also Marksmen, Outlaws)

62	Parlophone R 4955	This Song Is Just For You/Paradise	10
62	Parlophone R 4980	Shutters And Boards/North Wind	10
63	Parlophone R 5031	Only The Heartaches/Can't Stop Pretending	8
63	Parlophone R 5069	Blowing Wild (The Ballad Of Black Gold)/Crazy Dreams	10
64	Parlophone R 5099	Anna Marie/Moon Watch Over My Baby	10
64	Parlophone R 5141	Galway Bay/Livin' Alone (as Houston Wells & Outlaws)	10
65	Parlophone R 5226	Blue Of The Night/Coming Home (solo)	7
68	CBS 3572	Teach Me Little Children/Does My Ring Hurt Your Finger	6
63	Parlophone GEP 8878	JUST FOR YOU (EP)	50
64	Parlophone GEP 8914	RAMONA (EP)	60
64	Parlophone PMC 1215	WESTERN STYLE (LP)	50

JEAN WELLS

71	Mojo 2092 023	After Loving You/Puttin' The Best On The Outside	10
70	Sonet SNTF 606	WORLD! HERE COMES JEAN WELLS (LP)	50

JOHNNY WELLS

59	Columbia DB 4377	Lonely Moon/The One And Only One	40

JOHNNY WELLS

67	Parlophone R 5559	Guess I'm Dumb/Wondering Why	20

JUNIOR WELLS

(see also Buddy Guy)

66	Delmark DS 9612	Hoodoo Man Blues (blue label)	30
66	Delmark DS 628	Southside Blues Jam (blue label)	20
68	Mercury MF 1056	Girl You Lit My Fire/It's A Man Down There	15
66	Delmark DJB 1	BLUES WITH A BEAT (EP)	35
68	Fontana (S)TFL 6084	IT'S MY LIFE BABY (LP)	40
68	Vanguard SVRL 19011	COMING AT YOU (LP, also stereo, VSD 79262)	30
68	Vanguard SVRL 19028	IT'S MY LIFE BABY (LP, reissue)	25
68	Mercury SMCL 20130	YOU'RE TUFF ENOUGH (LP)	45
71	Delmark DS 628	SOUTHSIDE BLUES JAM (LP)	22
75	Delmark DS 635	JUNIOR WELLS ON TAP (LP)	15

KITTY WELLS

64	Brunswick 05920	I Gave My Wedding Dress Away/I've Thought Of Leaving Too	7
55	Brunswick OE 9149	KITTY SINGS (EP)	12
61	Brunswick LAT 8361	KITTY'S CHOICE (LP)	12
64	Brunswick LAT 8575	QUEEN OF COUNTRY MUSIC (LP)	15
65	Brunswick LAT 8601	ESPECIALLY FOR YOU (LP)	15
65	Brunswick LAT 8621	LONESOME SAD AND BLUE (LP)	15
66	Brunswick STA 8646	SINGS SONGS MADE FAMOUS BY JIM REEVES (LP, stereo)	15
66	Brunswick LAT 8659	COUNTRY ALL THE WAY (LP, stereo)	15

MARY WELLS

(see also Marvin Gaye)

62	Oriole CBA 1762	You Beat Me To The Punch/Old Love	70
63	Oriole CBA 1796	Two Lovers/Operator	55
63	Oriole CBA 1829	Laughing Boy/Two Wrongs Don't Make A Right	70
63	Oriole CBA 1847	Your Old Standby/What Love Has Joined Together	65
63	Stateside SS 242	You Lost The Sweetest Boy/What's Easy For Two Is So Hard For One	25
63	Stateside SS 242	You Lost The Sweetest Boy/What's Easy For Two Is So Hard For One (DJ Copy)	100

			MINT VALUE £
64	Stateside SS 288	My Guy/Oh Little Boy	15
64	Stateside SS 288	My Guy/Oh Little Boy (DJ Copy)	100
64	Stateside SS 316	Once Upon A Time (with Marvin Gaye)/What's The Matter With You, Baby	40
64	Stateside SS 316	Once Upon A Time (with Marvin Gaye)/What's The Matter With You, Baby (DJ Copy)	85
65	Stateside SS 372	Ain't It The Truth/Stop Takin' Me For Granted	25
65	Stateside SS 372	Ain't It The Truth/Stop Takin' Me For Granted (DJ Copy)	50
65	Stateside SS 396	Use Your Head/Everlovin' Boy	25
65	Stateside SS 396	Use Your Head/Everlovin' Boy (DJ Copy)	50
65	Stateside SS 415	Never Never Leave Me/Why Don't You Let Yourself Go	20
65	Stateside SS 415	Never Never Leave Me/Why Don't You Let Yourself Go (DJ Copy)	50
65	Stateside SS 439	He's A Lover/I'm Learnin'	25
65	Stateside SS 439	He's A Lover/I'm Learnin' (DJ Copy)	50
65	Stateside SS 463	Me Without You/I'm Sorry	25
65	Stateside SS 463	Me Without You/I'm Sorry (DJ Copy)	50
68	Stateside SS 2111	The Doctor/Two Lovers' History	20
66	Atlantic AT 4067	Dear Lover/Can't You See (You're Losing Me)	45
66	Atlantic 584 054	Me And My Baby/Such A Sweet Thing	15
67	Atlantic 584 104	Hey You Set My Soul On Fire/Coming Home	15
70	Direction 58-4816	Dig The Way I Feel/Love Shooting Bandit	15
72	Atlantic K 10254	Dear Lover/Can't You See (You're Losing Me) (reissue)	10
65	Tamla Motown TME 2007	MARY WELLS (EP)	90
63	Oriole PS 40045	TWO LOVERS (LP)	100
63	Oriole PS 40051	BYE BYE BABY (LP)	100
64	Stateside SL 10095	SINGS MY GUY (LP)	70
65	Stateside SL 10133	MARY WELLS (LP)	80
65	Tamla Motown TML 11006	MY BABY JUST CARES FOR ME (LP)	60
66	Stateside S(S)L 10171	LOVE SONGS TO THE BEATLES (LP)	45
66	Tamla Motown TML 11032	GREATEST HITS (LP)	40
68	Stateside S(S)L 10266	SERVIN' UP SOME SOUL (LP)	40
68	Atlantic 587 049	THE TWO SIDES OF MARY WELLS (LP)	30

ALEX WELSH & DIXIELANDERS

55	Decca F 10538	I'll Build A Stairway To Paradise/Eccentric	5
55	Decca F 10557	Blues My Naughtie Sweetie Gives To Me/Shoe Shiner's Blues	5
55	Decca F 10652	What Can I Say After I Say I'm Sorry/Hard-Hearted Hannah	5
61	Columbia DB 4686	Tansy/Memphis March	10
55	Decca DFE 6254	DIXIELANDERS AT THE RFH (EP)	10

DANNY WELTON

60	Coral Q 72409	Boogie Woogie/To Each His Own	5

WENDY & LEMMY

(see also Motorhead)

82	Bronze BRO 151	Stand By Your Man/No Class/Masterplan (p/s)	7

WE'RE TIRED

77	Deadline DEADS 8	My Life's On The Line/Against All Odds (p/s)	20
77	Deadline DEADS 11	Guide Me Through Hell/Time Is Against Me (p/s)	25
78	Deadline DEADS 15	Over The Edge/Anal Retentive (p/s, as We're Tired & We're Proud)	8
77	Deadline DEADLP 2	FIND THE PRICE IN TIME (LP)	50

WERLWINDS

61	Columbia DB 4650	Winding It Up/Dig Deep	22

HOWARD WERTH & MOONBEAMS

(see also Audience)

74	Charisma CB 225	Lucinda/Jonah	5
75	Charisma CAS 11004	KING BRILLIANT (LP, with inner sleeve)	12

BRIAN WESKE

62	Oriole CB 1723	In The Midst Of The Crowd/All Mine Alone	15
62	Oriole CB 1776	24 Hours In A Day/Where Does The Clown Go	15

FRED WESLEY & J.B.s

(see also James Brown, J.B.s)

73	Polydor 2066 322	Doing It To Death/Everybody Got Soul (with J.B.s)	8
74	Mojo 2093 025	J.B. Shout/Back Stabbers (with J.B.s)	8
80	RSO RSO 67	Houseparty/I Make Music (solo)	8
80	RSO RSO 67	Houseparty/I Make Music (12", solo)	10
74	Polydor 2391 125	DAMN RIGHT, I AM SOMEBODY (LP, with J.B.s)	20
74	Polydor 2391 161	BREAKIN' BREAD (LP, with J.B.s)	20

WES MINSTER FIVE

(see also Maynell Wilson, Dave Greenslade)

64	Carnival CV 7017	Shakin' The Blues/Railroad Blues	15
65	Carnival CV 7019	Sticks And Stones/Mickey's Monkey	20

FRANK WESS

64	Fontana TL 5291	THE AWARD WINNER (LP)	12

ADAM 'BATMAN' WEST

76	Target TGT 111	Batman And Robin/The Story Of Batman	7

DODIE WEST

64	Decca F 12046	Goin' Out Of My Head/Is He Feeling Blue	15
65	Piccadilly 7N 35239	In The Deep Of The Night/Rovin' Boy (in p/s)	30
65	Piccadilly 7N 35239	In The Deep Of The Night/Rovin' Boy	20
65	Piccadilly 7N 35261	Thinking Of You/And Love Will Come	8
66	Piccadilly 7N 35287	Make The World Go Away/Who Does He Think He Is	8
68	Philips BF 1698	Living In Limbo/Birdie Told Me	7

HARRY & JEANIE WEST

60	Melodisc EPM 7-111	SOUTHERN MOUNTAIN FOLK SONGS (LP)	15

MINT VALUE £

HEDY WEST

65	Topic 12T 117	OLD TIMES AND HARD TIMES (LP)	20
66	Topic 12T 146	PRETTY SARO (LP)	20
67	Topic 12T 163	BALLADS (LP, with Bill Clifton)	20
67	Fontana STL 5432	SERVES'EM FINE (LP)	20

KEITH WEST

(see also Tomorrow, Four + One, In Crowd, Mark Wirtz)

67	Parlophone R 5623	Excerpt From "A Teenage Opera"/ MARK WIRTZ ORCHESTRA: Theme From "A Teenage Opera"	8
67	Parlophone R 5651	Sam (From "A Teenage Opera')/ MARK WIRTZ'S MOOD MOSAIC: Thimble Full Of Puzzles (promos in art sleeve)	30
67	Parlophone R 5651	Sam (From "A Teenage Opera')/ MARK WIRTZ'S MOOD MOSAIC: Thimble Full Of Puzzles	12
68	Parlophone R 5713	On A Saturday/The Kid Was A Killer	65
72	Parlophone R 5957	Excerpt From "A Teenage Opera"/Sam (From "A Teenage Opera")	7
73	Deram DM 402	Riding For A Fall/Days About To Rain	7
74	Deram DM 410	Havin' Someone/Know There's No Livin' Without You	7

LESLIE WEST('S MOUNTAIN)

(see also Jolliver Arkansas, Mountain, West Bruce & Laing)

69	Bell BLL 1078	Dreams Of Milk And Honey/Wheels On Fire (as Leslie West's Mountain)	20
69	Bell SBLL 126	MOUNTAIN (LP, as Leslie West's Mountain)	22
75	RCA RS 1009	THE GREAT FATSBY (LP)	12
76	Phantom PHS 701	THE LESLIE WEST BAND (LP)	12

MAE WEST

67	Stateside SS 2021	Twist And Shout/Day Tripper	20
73	MGM 2006 203	Great Balls Of Fire/Men	15
56	Brunswick LAT 8082	THE FABULOUS MAE WEST (LP)	65
67	Stateside (S)SL 10197	WAY OUT WEST (LP)	30
73	Polydor 2315 207	GREAT BALLS OF FIRE (LP)	20

SPEEDY WEST & JIMMY BRYANT

55	Capitol EAP1 520	TWO GUITARS COUNTRY STYLE PT. 1 (EP)	30
55	Capitol EAP2 520	TWO GUITARS COUNTRY STYLE PT. 2 (EP)	30
53	Capitol LC 6619	CAPITOL PRESENTS SPEEDY WEST & JIMMY BRYANT (10" LP)	30
55	Capitol LC 6694	TWO GUITARS COUNTRY STYLE (10" LP)	30

TABBY WEST

58	Capitol CL 14861	All That I Want/If You Promise Not To Tell	10

MIKE WESTBROOK (CONCERT BAND)

(see also Solid Gold Cadillac, John Surman, Norma Winstone)

69	Deram DM 234	A Life Of Its Own/Can't Get It Out Of My Mind	20
70	Deram DM 286	Requiem/Hooray	20
70	Deram DM 311	Magic Garden/Original Peter (with Norma Winstone)	30
67	Deram DML 1013	CELEBRATION (LP, as Mike Westbrook Concert Band)	100
68	Deram DML/SML 1031	RELEASE (LP)	70
69	Deram SML 1047	MARCHING SONG VOL. 1 (LP)	70
69	Deram SML 1048	MARCHING SONG VOL. 2 (LP)	70
70	Deram SML 1069	LOVE SONGS (LP, as Mike Westbrook Concert Band with Norma Winstone)	70
71	RCA SER 5612	TYGER: A CELEBRATION OF WILLIAM BLAKE (LP, with insert)	100
72	RCA Neon NE 10	MIKE WESTBROOK'S METROPOLIS (LP, gatefold sleeve)	75
72	Cadillac SGC 1001	LIVE (LP, private pressing)	25
75	RCA SF 8433	CITADEL/ROOM 315 (2-LP, with John Surman)	30
75	Transatlantic TRA 323	LOVE/DREAM & VARIATIONS (LP)	20
76	Transatlantic TRA 312	PLAYS FOR THE RECORD (LP)	18
78	Original ORA 001	GOOSE SAUCE (LP)	18
78	Original ORA 002	PIANO (LP)	18
79	RCA PL 25252	MAMA CHICAGO (LP)	18
80	Original ORA 203	WESTBROOK BLAKE (LP)	25
82	Original ORA 309	THE CORTEGE (LP)	25
83	Westbrook LWN 1	A LITTLE WESTBROOK MUSIC (LP)	25
88	Venture VEB 13	LONDON BRIDGE IS BROKEN DOWN (LP)	12

WEST, BRUCE & LAING

(see also Jack Bruce, Leslie West, Mountain)

73	RSO 2090 113	Dirty Shoes/Backfire	6
73	CBS 65314	WHY DONTCHA (LP)	12
73	RSO 2394 107	WHATEVER TURNS YOU ON (LP)	12
74	RSO 2394 128	LIVE 'N' KICKIN' (LP)	12

WEST COAST CONSORTIUM

(see also Consortium)

67	Pye 7N 17352	Some Other Someday/Looking Back	20
68	Pye 7N 17482	Colour Sergeant Lillywhite/Lady From Baltimore	45

WEST COAST DELEGATION

67	Deram DM 113	Reach The Top/Mr. Personality Man	20

WEST COAST KNACK

67	Capitol CL 15497	I'm Aware/Time Waits For No One	20

WEST COAST POP ART EXPERIMENTAL BAND

68	Reprise RSLP 6298	A CHILD'S GUIDE TO GOOD AND EVIL (LP)	150

WEST FIVE

(see also Ferris Wheel)

65	HMV POP 1396	Congratulations/She Mine	40
65	HMV POP 1428	Someone Ain't Right/Just Like Romeo And Juliet	35
66	HMV POP 1513	If It Don't Work Out/Back To Square One	20

MINT VALUE £

WEST INDIANS
(see also Eric Donaldson, Prunes, Kilowatts, Upsetters)

68	Doctor Bird DB 1121	Right On Time/Hokey Pokey	25
68	Doctor Bird DB 1127	Falling In Love/I Mean It	25
69	Camel CA 16	Strange Whisperings/CARL DAWKINS: Hard To Handle	15
71	Dynamic DYN 413	Never Gonna Give You Up/REBELLIOUS SUBJECTS: Never Give Up	10

CLIVE WESTLAKE

68	Fontana TF 940	199 Days/From The Beginning To The End	6

JILL WESTLAKE

58	Columbia DB 4132	Sharin'/Over And Over Again	12

KEVIN WESTLAKE & GARY FARR
(see also Gary Farr & T-Bones, T-Bones, Blossom Toes, B.B. Blunder)

68	Marmalade 598 007	Everyday/Green	20
70	CBS	Born Under A Bad Sign/Missouri Train	10

WESTLAND STEAMBOAT

70	CBS	Born Under A Bad Sign/Missouri Train	10

WESTMORELITES
(see also Minstrels)

70	Clandisc CLA 217	Zion/CLANCY ECCLES & DYNAMITES: Revival	8

GLEN WESTON

67	Columbia DB8253	Pattern People/In The Still Of The night	20
68	Columbia DB 8328	With This Ring/Liane	5

KIM WESTON
(see also Johnny Nash & Kim Weston, Marvin Gaye & Kim Weston)

64	Stateside SS 359	A Little More Love/Go Ahead And Laugh	110
64	Stateside SS 359	A Little More Love/Go Ahead And Laugh (DJ Copy)	150
65	Tamla Motown TMG 511	I'm Still Loving You/Just Loving You	175
65	Tamla Motown TMG 511	I'm Still Loving You/Just Loving You (DJ Copy)	300
65	Tamla Motown TMG 538	Take Me In Your Arms (Rock Me A Little While)/Don't Compare Me With Her	80
65	Tamla Motown TMG 538	Take Me In Your Arms (Rock Me A Little While)/ Don't Compare Me With Her (DJ copy)	100
66	Tamla Motown TMG 554	Helpless/A Love Like Yours	90
66	Tamla Motown TMG 554	Helpless/A Love Like Yours (DJ Copy)	400
67	MGM MGM 1338	I Got What You Need/Someone Like You (DJ Copy)	30
67	MGM MGM 1357	That's Groovy/Land Of Tomorrow	30
68	MGM MGM 1382	Nobody/You're Just The Kind Of Guy (DJ Copy)	50
69	Major Minor MM 619	From Both Sides Now/We Try Harder	6
70	Major Minor MM 683	Danger, Heartbreak Dead Ahead/I'll Be Thinking	12
75	Tamla Motown TMG 1000	Do Like I Do/MARVELETTES: Finders Keepers, Losers Weepers	100
65	Tamla Motown TME 2005	KIM WESTON (EP)	100
66	Tamla Motown TME 2015	ROCK ME A LITTLE WHILE (EP)	350
67	MGM MGM-C(S) 8055	FOR THE FIRST TIME (LP)	50
71	Stax 2362 021	KIM KIM KIM (LP)	30

MARK WESTON & THE TWO PART TARIFF

69	Tepee TPR 1006	Standing At The Bus Stop/Portrait On The Blackboard	40

PETE WESTON
(see also I Roy)

70	Gas GAS 146	Something Sweet/BIM & BAM: Love Letters	12
70	Punch PH 28	In The Mood (& His Band)/Slide Mongoose (actually "Sly Mongoose")	8
72	Ashanti ASH 402	Pup'n Temper/PETE'S ALL STARS: Version 2	8

WEST ONE

88	Que Q 9	California '69/Eurotrash (gig freebie, white label)	12

WEST POINT

70	Decca F 13050	Don't Know Why/Take What You Want	8

WEST POINT SUPERNATURAL

67	Reaction 591 013	Time Will Tell/Night Train	20

WESTSIDE

74	People PEO 111	Running In And Out Of My Life/Highway Demon	5

WESTWIND

70	Penny Farthing PEN 737	Love Is A Funny Sort Of Thing/Breakout	8
70	Penny Farthing PELS 505	LOVE IS (LP)	170

WE THE PEOPLE

66	London HLH 10089	He Doesn't Go About It Right/You Burn Me Up And Down	125

WE THREE TRIO

65	London HLA 9966	Baby The Rain Must Fall/Shine For Me	8
67	Fontana TL 5308	THE WE THREE TRIO (LP)	15

WET WILLIE

71	Atlantic 2091155	Dirty Leg/Rock And Roll Band	8

WE UGLY DOGS
(see also Tokens, U.S. Double Quartet)

67	BT Puppy BTS 45537	First Spring Rain/Poor Man	12

WHALE FEATHERS

71	Blue Horizon 2431 009	WHALE FEATHERS (LP)	130

WHALES

68	CBS 3766	Come Down Little Bird/Beachcomber	20
69	CBS 4126	Tell It To The Rain/Girl, Hey Girl	15

MINT VALUE £

WHAM!
(see also George Michael, Pepsi & Shirley)

84	Epic (no cat. no.)	Merry Xmas From Wham (fan club Christmas single, no p/s)	5
86	Epic WHAM 2	THE FINAL (2-LP box, gold vinyl picture discs, with sealed T-shirt, calendar, pencil, note-pad and no'd certificate)	50

WHAT IS OIL

83	Oof BEAT 1	HUMAN SUFFERING EP	10

WHAT THE CURTAINS

84	Rideaux WTC 0042	Crime Of Passion/Words (Can't Tell)	20

PEETIE WHEATSTRAW

69	Matchbox SDR 191	THE DEVIL'S SON IN LAW (LP)	25
69	Matchbox SDR 192	THE HIGH SHERIFF FROM HELL (LP)	25

BILLY ED WHEELER

64	London HLR 9920	On The Outside (Lookin' In)/The Right Foot In His World	8
65	London HLR 9950	Ode To The Little Brown Shack Out Back/Sister Sara	8
65	London HAR/SHR 8221	MEMORIES OF AMERICA (LP)	20

KENNY WHEELER & JOHN DANKWORTH ORCHESTRA
(see also Johnny Dankworth, Elton Dean)

68	Fontana STL 5494	WINDMILL TILTER (LP)	150
70s	Incus 10	SONG FOR SOMEONE (LP)	80

WHEELER ST JAMES & JAMES

72	RCA 2233	My Impersonal Life/Lovely To See You	20

WHEELS
(see also James Brothers, Demick & Armstrong)

65	Columbia DB 7682	Gloria/Don't You Know	120
66	Columbia DB 7827	Bad Little Woman/Road Block (mispressing, demos & a few issues play "Call My Name" on B-side)	150
66	Columbia DB 7827	Bad Little Woman/Road Block	375
66	Columbia DB 7981	Kicks/Call My Name	120

WHEELS

71	Decca F13268	Take Me Home Country Roads/She Don't Mean It	30

WHEELS OF TIME

67	Spin SP 62008	1984/So Long (not in company sleeves)	90
67	Spin SP 62008	1984/So Long (in company sleeve)	100

WHERE FORTUNE SMILES
(see under John Surman)

WHICHWHAT

69	Beacon BEA 127	Gimme Gimme Good Lovin'/Wonderland Of Love	25
69	Beacon BEA 131	Why Do Lovers Break Each Other's Heart/When I See Her Smile	6
69	Beacon BEA 133	In The Year 2525/Parting	10
69	Beacon BEA 144	I Wanna Be Free/It's All Over Again	25
70	Beacon BEA 169	Vietnam Rose/Shame And Solution	6
70	Beacon BEAS 14	WHICHWHAT'S FIRST (LP)	50

OSCAR WHIFLEY

68	Dolphin DOS6	Tommy Jones/Creeque Alley (as The Oscar Whifley Sound)	8

WHIP

71	Mother MOT 6	Julie Ivory Towers/MUFF & BANKHOUSE ASSEMBLY: Funky Shoot Out	10

WHIRL

89	Sound Of Spasm 2	Bizarre Love Triangle/CROCODILE RIDE: Shimmer (1-sided flexi-disc, foldover p/s In poly bag with fanzine)	10
89	Sound Of Spasm 2	Bizarre Love Triangle/CROCODILE RIDE: Shimmer (1-sided flexi-disc, foldover p/s In poly bag without fanzine)	5

WHIRLWIND

78	Chiswick NS 25	Hang Loose/Together Forever (p/s)	10
78	Chiswick NS 42	I Only Wish (That I'd Been Told)/Ducktails (unissued)	0
78	Chiswick CHIS 103	I Only Wish (That I'd Been Told)/Ducktails (p/s)	10
79	Chiswick CHIS 117	You Got Class/Losing To You (unissued in U.K.; France-only)	0
79	Lyntone (No Cat. No)	On Wheels (flexi, originally promo for Isle Of Man TT races, repackaged in picture sleeve with 2 inserts for 1979 Earls Court Concert)	50
80	Chiswick CHIS 122	Heaven Knows/Cruisin' Around (p/s)	10
80	Chiswick CHIS 127	Stayin' Out All Night/Running Wild (unissued; p/s only)	0
80	Chiswick PSR 447	Midnight Blue/Honey Hush/Such A Fool/Stayin' Out All Night (promo only)	8
78	Chiswick CH 4	BLOWIN' UP A STORM (10" mini-LP)	12
78	Chiswick WIK 7	BLOWIN' UP A STORM (LP, with 2 extra tracks)	15
80	Chiswick CWK 3012	MIDNIGHT BLUE (LP)	15

WHIRLWIND HEAT

03	XL XL 163	Purple/Stunning Evaseev (with poster)	20

WHIRLWINDS
(see also Mockingbirds, Graham Gouldman, 10cc)

64	HMV POP 1301	Look At Me/Baby Not Like You	75

NANCY WHISKEY (& HER SKIFFLERS)
(see also Chas McDevitt Skiffle Group)

57	Oriole CB 1394	He's Solid Gone/Ella Speed (as Nancy Whiskey & Her Skifflers)	20
57	Oriole CB 1394	He's Solid Gone/Ella Speed (as Nancy Whiskey & Her Skifflers) (78)	10
58	Oriole CB 1452	Hillside In Scotland/I Know Where I'm Goin'	10
58	Oriole CB 1452	Hillside In Scotland/I Know Where I'm Goin' (78)	10
59	Oriole CB 1485	The Old Grey Goose/Johnny Blue	12

MINT VALUE £

59 Oriole CB 1485 The Old Grey Goose/Johnny Blue (78)............ 10
65 Fontana TF 612 Bowling Green/I'm Leaving Today 5
67 CBS 3090 Freight Train/The Game 8
57 Topic 7T 10 NANCY WHISKEY SINGS (7" LP) 35
57 Oriole MG 10018 THE INTOXICATING MISS WHISKEY (10" LP, with Chas McDevitt Skiffle Group).... 45

WHISTLE
74 York YR 209 When The Lights Go Out On Broadway/Lincoln Lullabies............ 12
73 York YR 201 The Party Must Be Over/Hideaway 20

WHISTLER
71 Deram SML 1083 HO-HUM (LP)............ 250

WHISTLING JACK SMITH
67 Deram DM 112 I Was Kaiser Bill's Batman/The British Grin And Bear............ 6
68 Deram DM 179 Ja Da/Sans Fairy Anne............ 7
68 Deram DM 189 Only When I Larf/Early One Morning 7
67 Deram DML 1009 AROUND THE WORLD WHISTLING JACK (LP)............ 15

WHISTLING WILLIE
(see also Neville, Neville Willoughby)
68 Duke DU 8 Penny Reel/Soul Tonic............ 5

SHARON WHITBREAD & FRED
72 RA RALP 6011 SPICE OF LIFE (LP)............ 25
72 Ralp 6011 SPICE OF LIFE (LP)............ 25

IAN WHITCOMB
65 Capitol CL 15382 This Sporting Life/Fizz............ 6
65 Capitol CL 15395 You Turn Me On/Poor But Honest............ 12
65 Capitol CL 15418 N-N-Nervous!/The End 6
66 Capitol CL 15431 Good Hard Rock/High Blood Pressure............ 6
66 Stateside SS 573 Where Did Robinson Crusoe Go With Friday/Poor Little Bird)............ 6
72 Ember EMBS 324 You Turn Me On/This Sporting Life (mono)............ 5
73 Ember NR 5065 YOU TURN ME ON (LP, with Jimmy Page & John Paul Jones)............ 40

BARRY WHITE
67 President PT 139 All In The Run Of A Day/Don't Take Your Love From Me............ 30

BERGEN WHITE
76 Private Stock PVT 69 Duke Of Earl/She Won't Let You Down............ 7

BRIAN WHITE & MAGNA JAZZ BAND
(see also Magna Jazz Band)
62 HMV CLP 1534 BRIAN WHITE AND THE MAGNA JAZZ BAND (LP)............ 100

BUKKA WHITE
66 Fontana 688 804 ZL SKY SONGS (LP, with Big Willie)............ 40
66 CBS Realm 52629 BUKKA WHITE (LP)............ 35
69 Blue Horizon 7-63229 MEMPHIS HOT SHOTS (LP)............ 80
69 Sonet SNTF 609 THE LEGACY OF THE BLUES VOL. 1 (LP, with insert)............ 12

CHRIS WHITE
(see also Joyce's Angels)
76 Charisma CB 272 Spanish Wine/She's Only Dancing............ 8
76 Charisma CB 282 Natural Rhythm/Another Little Miracle............ 7
76 Charisma CB 294 Don't Look Down/Summertime Summertime............ 8
77 Charisma CB 303 Don't Worry Baby/Child Of The Sun............ 15
76 Charisma CAS 1118 MOUTH MUSIC (LP)............ 15

DANNY WHITE
67 Sue WI 4031 Keep My Woman Home/I'm Dedicating My Life............ 75
74 MCA MU 155 Cracked Up Over You/Taking Inventory............ 10

DUKE WHITE
63 Island WI 084 It's Over/Forever............ 15
64 Black Swan WI 442 Be Wise/BABA BROOKS: Musical Workshop............ 35
65 Black Swan WI 444 Sow Good Seeds/BABA BROOKS BAND: Bus Strike............ 35

ED WHITE (The Sounds Of)
61 Pye 7N SR15320 Coral Reef/Tropical Blue (stereo only)............ 20

GEORGIA WHITE
54 Vocalion V 1038 Was I Drunk?/Moonshine Blues (78)............ 20

IAN WHITE
70 private pressing IAN WHITE (LP)............ 20

JACK WHITE
(see also White Stripes, Raconteurs, Dead Weather)
09 Third Man TMR 013 Fly Farm Blues (luminous one-sided Halloween cover, 100-only)............ 200

JAY WHITE
56 London RE-F 1045 FAR-AWAY PLACES VOL. 1 (EP)............ 15

JEANETTE WHITE
69 A&M AMS 761 Music/No Sunshine (silver label)............ 20
69 A&M AMS 761 Music/No Sunshine (Yellow DJ copy or brown label)............ 75

JOE WHITE
(see also Chuck, Rue Lloyd)
64 R&B JB 137 Sinners (as Joe White & Maytals)/ROLAND ALPHONSO: King Solomon............ 40
64 Ska Beat JB 180 Punch You Down (with Chuck)/TOMMY McCOOK: Cotton Tree............ 45
64 Island WI 145 When Are You Young/Wanna Go Home............ 15
64 Island WI 159 Hog In A Co Co/SKATALITES: Sandy Gully............ 30
64 Island WI 166 Downtown Girl/RICHARD BROS.: You Are My Sunshine
(B-side is actually "Cool Smoke" by Don Drummond)............ 40

			MINT VALUE £
65	Island WI 201	Low-Minded People (as Chuck & Joe White)/Irene	15
66	Doctor Bird DB 1001	Every Night (with Chuck)/BABA BROOKS & HIS BAND: First Session	30
66	Doctor Bird DB 1024	My Love For You/SAMMY ISMAY & BABA BROOKS BAND: Cocktails For Two	25
66	Doctor Bird DB 1043	So Close (as Joe White & Della)/BABA BROOKS & HIS BAND: Eighth Games	25
67	Doctor Bird DB 1069	Rudies All Around/Bad Man	30
67	Doctor Bird DB 1080	Lonely Nights/I Need You	20
67	Doctor Bird DB 1090	I Need A Woman/Hot Hops	15
68	Blue Cat BS 108	Way Of Life (actually by Lyn Tait & Jets)/I'm So Proud	90
68	Blue Cat BS 119	Try A Little Tenderness/LYN TAITT & CARL BRYAN: Tender Arms	90
68	Blue Cat BS 130	Pretty Girl/DERMOTT LYNCH: You Went Away	80
69	Sugar ESS 102	My Guiding Star/If I Needed Someone	12
70	Sugar SU 103	Yesterday/I Am Free	12
70	Trojan TR 7742	So Much Love/Maybe Now	5
70	Trojan TR 7768	I'm Going To Get There/RUPIE EDWARDS ALLSTARS: Kinky Funky Reggae	10
70	Big BG 301	This Is The Time/The Other Day	8
71	Big BG 309	Baby I Care/Ain't Misbehavin'	5
72	Songbird SB 1072	Trinity/SCOTTY: Monkey Drop	12
72	Dynamic DYN 440	Kenyatta/RECORDING BAND: Version	15
73	Gayfeet GS 202	If It Don't Work Out/BABA BROOKS BAND: Ki Salaboca	12
73	Harry J. HJ 6648	Joe White (Mrs. Jones)/Joe White (Mrs. Jones) - Version (song actually titled "Me And Mrs Jones")	5
77	Ultra PFU 1002	Give And Take (On Both Sides)/Roots Dub	5
79	Splendor Heights SH 2	Forward To Zion/Only The Strong/Join Them/Are You Leavine Me (12" as Joe White Band)	20
70s	Magnet MGT 006	SINCE THE OTHER DAY (LP)	20

JOSH WHITE

(see also Teddy Moss/Josh White)

52	London L 1143	Call Me Darling/I Want You, I Need You (78)	10
52	London L 1144	Waltzing Landing/Apples, Peaches And Cherries (78)	10
52	London L 1161	Free And Equal Blues (Parts 1 & 2) (78)	10
54	London L 907	T.B. Blues/Molly Malone (78, silver label reissue)	10
54	Brunswick LA 8653	BALLADS AND BLUES VOL. 2 (10" LP)	12
54	London H-APB 1032	JOSH WHITE SINGS - VOL. 2 (10" LP)	12
54	Mercury MG 25014	SONGS BY JOSH WHITE (10" LP)	12
55	London H-APB 1038	JOSH COMES A-VISITIN' (10" LP)	12
62	Golden Guinea GGL 0160	EMPTY BED BLUES (LP)	12

JOSH & BEVERLEY WHITE

64	Realm REP 4003	BEVERLEY & JOSH WHITE JNR (EP)	12

JOY WHITE

79	Fight FDD 4438	The First Cut Is The Deepest/ITALS : Rougher Yet (12")	20
78	Hawkeye HLP 002	SENTIMENTAL REASONS (LP)	25

K.C. WHITE

72	Dynamic DYN 434	Man No Dead/Man No Dead - Version	8
73	Green Door GD 4056	First Cut Is The Deepest/No Good Girl	10
73	Technique TE 929	Anywhere But Nowhere/Bush In Session	10

KITTY WHITE

54	London HL 8102	Jesse James/Scratch My Back (B-side with Dave Howard)	90
54	London HL 8102	Jesse James/Scratch My Back (78, B-side with Dave Howard)	20

LENNY WHITE

(see also Return To Forever)

75	Atlantic K 50213	VENUSIAN SUMMER (LP)	12
78	Elektra K 12328	Lady Madonna/12 Bars From Mars	5
81	Elektra K 12500	Kid Stuff/Slipaway	5
83	Elektra ED 4921	My Turn To Love You (Special Mix)/(Dub Version) (12")	12

LOUISA JANE WHITE

69	Philips BF 1810	When The Battle Is Over/Blue Ribbons	30
70	Philips BF 1834	How Does It Feel/Truth In My Tears	100

SHEILA WHITE

66	CBS 202465	Misfit/Switch Off The Night	15

STEVE WHITE & GARY WALLACE

(see also Style Council)

90s	Acid Jazz JAZID 20T	Never Stop (12", company sleeve)	35

TAM WHITE

(see also Buzz, Boston Dexters)

67	Decca F 12711	World Without You/Someone You Should Know (unreleased)	0
68	Decca F 12723	Dancing Out Of My Heart/I'll Stay Loving You	10
68	Decca F 12849	Waiting Till The Night Comes Around/Girl Watcher	15
69	Deram DM 261	That Old Sweet Roll/Don't Make Promises	25
70	Middle Earth MDS 104	Lewis Carroll/Future Thoughts	50
70	Middle Earth MDLS 304	TAM WHITE (LP)	80

TERRY WHITE & TERRIERS

59	Decca F 11133	Rock Around The Mailbags/Blackout	70
59	Decca F 11133	Rock Around The Mailbags/Blackout (78)	20

THOMAS WHITE

79	Hit Run HD 12	Ivory Girl/KEITH FRANCIS: Prejudice Country (12")	50

TONY JOE WHITE

68	Monument MON 1024	Soul Francisco/Whompt Out On You	8
69	Monument MON 1031	Polk Salad Annie/Aspen Colorado	15
69	Monument MON 1036	Willie And Laura Mae Jones/Baby Scratch My Back	10
69	Monument MON 1040	Roosevelt And Ira Lee/The Migrant	6

MINT VALUE £

70 Monument MON 1043 Groupy Girl/High Sheriff Of Calhoun Parrish ... 7
70 Monument MON 1048 Save Your Sugar For Me/My Friend ... 6
71 Warner Bros WB 6129 A Night In The Life Of A Swamp Fox/The Daddy ... 6
68 Monument LMO/SMO 5027 BLACK AND WHITE (LP) ... 22
70 Monument LMO/SMO 5035 TONY JOE WHITE CONTINUED (LP) ... 22
70 Monument SMO 5043 TONY JOE (LP) ... 22
71 Warner Bros WS 1900 TONY JOE WHITE (LP) ... 18
71 Warner Bros K 46068 TONY JOE WHITE (LP, reissue) ... 12
72 Warner Bros K 46147 THE TRAIN I'M ON (LP) ... 15
73 Warner Bros K 46229 HOME-MADE ICE CREAM (LP) ... 18
73 Warner Bros K 56149 THE BEST OF TONY JOE WHITE (LP) ... 12

TREVOR WHITE
(see also Sparks, Radio Stars)

76 Island WIP 6291 Crazy Kids/Movin' In The Right Direction (in p/s) ... 20
76 Island WIP 6291 Crazy Kids/Movin' In The Right Direction ... 8

WHITE DOOR

84 Clay 37 Flame In My Heart/Behind The White Door (p/s) ... 6

WHITE DUCK

72 Uni UN 541 Billy Goat/Really ... 8
73 Uni UN 555 Honey, You'll Be Alright/Carry Love ... 8
72 Uni UNLS 123 WHITE DUCK (LP) ... 22
73 Uni UNLS 129 IN SEASON (LP) ... 22

WHITE ELEPHANT

70s White Elephant RIOCH 1 CITY WALLS (LP, with other artists) ... 12

RICK WHITEFIELD

71 Horse HOSS 10 Hey Mama/Ride Baby Ride ... 6

WHITEFIRE

78 Whitefire 98DB 001 SUZANNE (EP) ... 40

WHITE HART

79 Tradition TSR 033 IN SEARCH OF REWARD (LP) ... 60

WHITE HEAT

79 Valium VAL 01 Nervous Breakdown/Sammy Sez (gatefold p/s) ... 25
80 Valium VAL 02 Finished With The Fashions/Ordinary Joe (p/s, with insert) ... 20
81 Valium VAL 03 City Beat/It's No Use (Young Ones) (p/s) ... 12
82 Valium VALP 101 IN THE ZERO HOUR (LP) ... 25

WHITE HEAT

84 RSR 007 Soldier Of Fortune/Lovemaker ... 50
84 Rock Shop RSR 007 WHITE HEAT (LP) ... 20

WHITE HORN

75 Philips 6006 440 Making It Funky/Mama Said ... 8

WHITEHOUSE
(see also Come, Nurse With Wound, New Order, Skullflower, Konstruktivits)

01 SLA-003 Cruise (Force The Truth)/Instrumental Version (12") ... 20
02 SLA-004 Wriggle Like A Fucking Eel/Instrumental Version (12") ... 18
91 Sue Lawley SLS 002 Still Going Strong/Ankles And Wrists ... 15
80 Come Org. WDC 881004 BIRTHDEATH EXPERIENCE (LP, first pressing pink labels, 850 copies) ... 120
80 Come Org. WDC 881005 TOTAL SEX (LP, 400 on green vinyl) ... 100
80 Come Org. WDC 881005 TOTAL SEX (LP, 800 on black vinyl) ... 80
81 Come Org. WDC 881007 ERECTOR (LP, different coloured vinyl) ... 100
81 Come Org. WDC 881010 DEDICATED TO PETER KÜRTEN, SADIST AND MASS SLAYER (LP, some on coloured vinyl, some in custom sleeve) ... 100
81 Come Org. WDC 881013 BÜCHENWALD (LP) ... 100
82 Come Org. WDC 881017 NEW BRITAIN (LP, with insert) ... 125
(The above LPs were also issued on cassette, which are worth around £20-£25 each)
82 Come Org. WDC 881027 PSYCHOPATHIA SEXUALIS (LP, clear or black vinyl) ... 170
82 Come Org. WDC 881027 PSYCHOPATHIA SEXUALIS (LP, clear or black vinyl) ... 150
83 Come Org. WDC 883033 RIGHT TO KILL - DEDICATED TO DENNIS ANDREW NEILSEN (LP, & inserts) ... 100
85 Come Org. WDC GREAT WHITE DEATH (LP) ... 100
80s Come Org. WDC 150 MURDEROUS PASSIONS (LP, with Nurse With Wound) ... 75
80s United Dairies UD 009 150 MURDEROUS PASSIONS (LP, with Nurse With Wound, reissue) ... 40
80s United Dairies UD 009 150 MURDEROUS PASSIONS (LP, with Nurse With Wound, export issue, sealed in black vinyl) ... 125
(Many Whitehouse LP's were issued in customised white card sleeves & were later available in a generic 'Peter Kürten' sleeve, originally used for the 2nd pressing of the 'Peter Kürten' LP. This latter design was also used for counterfeits. There may also be coloured vinyl variations which are worth the same.)
90 Susan Lawley 1 CREAM OF THE SECOND COMING (2-LP) ... 45
90 Susan Lawley SL 002 THANK YOUR LUCKY STARS (LP) ... 30
92 Susan Lawley SL 003 TWICE IS NOT ENOUGH (LP) ... 30

WHITE LIES

08 Fiction 1795718 To Lose My Life (6 x 7" box set with signed print) ... 50

WHITE LIGHTNING
(see also Static)

84 Wild Party PP 1000 This Poison Fountain/Hypocrite (no p/s, 1,000 only) ... 50
90 Workshop JOB LP 2 AS MIDNIGHT APPROACHES (LP, with inner) ... 18

WHITE LINING

70 Parlophone R 5868 Back In The Sun/Mon Amour ... 20

WHITE MULE

70 UNI UNS 523 Looking Through Cat's Eyes/Hundred Franc Blues ... 15

WHITE NOISE
(see also BBC Radiophonic Workshop)

75 Virgin VDJ 2 An Extract From White Noise 2 (promo only) ... 5

			MINT VALUE £
69	Island ILPS 9099	AN ELECTRIC STORM (LP, pink label black/orange circle logo)	125
69	Island ILPS 9099	WHITE NOISE (LP, re-pressing pink label with white 'i' logo)	50
75	Virgin V 2032	WHITE NOISE 2 (LP)	12

WHITE ON BLACK

74	Saydisc SDL 251	WHITE ON BLACK (LP)	30

WHITE PLAINS

(see also Edison Lighthouse, David & Jonathan, Kestrels, Brotherhood Of Man, Peter's Faces, Carter-Lewis & Southerners, Ivy League)

70	Deram DM 280	My Baby Loves Lovin'/Show Me Your Hand	7
70	Deram DM 291	I've Got You On My Mind/Today I Killed A Man I Didn't Know	8
70	Deram DM 315	Julie Do Ya Love Me/I Need Your Everlasting Love	7
71	Deram DM 333	When You Are A King/The World Gets Better With Love	8
71	Deram DM 340	Gonna Miss Here Mississippi/I'll Go Blind	6
71	Deram DM 348	I Can't Stop/Julie Anne	6
73	Deram DM 371	Step Into A Dream/Look To See	8
73	Deram DM 388	Does Anybody Know Where My Baby Is/Just For A Change	10
70	Deram SML 1067	WHITE PLAINS (LP)	25
71	Deram SML 1092	WHEN YOU ARE A KING (LP)	20

WHITESNAKE

(see also David Coverdale, Deep Purple, Rainbow, Roger Glover, Bernie Marsden, Jon Lord, Phenomena, Cozy Powell, Young & Moody Band, Company, Snafu, Bogdon, Forcefield, Gogmagog, Tramline, National Health)

78	EMI International INEP 751	SNAKEBITE (EP, white vinyl, p/s; later black vinyl with no p/s)	12
78	EMI International INT 568	Lie Down/Don't Mess With Me	6
79	EMI International INT 578	The Time Is Right For Love/Come On (live)	6
80	United Artists BP 352	Fool For Your Loving/Mean Business/ Don't Mess With Me (luminous p/s)	8
80	United Artists BP 352	Fool For Your Loving/Mean Business/ Don't Mess With Me	5
82	Liberty BPP 416	Here I Go Again/Bloody Luxury (picture disc)	10
82	Liberty BP 418	Love An' Affection/Victim Of Love (withdrawn)	35
83	Liberty BPP 420	Guilty Of Love/Gambler (shaped picture disc)	8
84	Liberty BPP 423	Standing In The Shadows/All Or Nothing (US Mix) (picture disc)	6
87	EMI EMIW 5606	Still Of The Night/Here I Go Again (p/s, white vinyl with poster)	8
87	EMI 12 EMIP 5606	Still Of The Night/Here I Go Again/You're Gonna Break My Heart Again (12", picture disc)	8
87	EMI 10EMI 35	Here I Go Again '87 (US remix)/Guilty Of Love (10", p/s, white vinyl)	8
78	EMI Intl. INS 3022	TROUBLE (LP, grey or pink inner sleeve)	12
82	Liberty LBGP 30354	SAINTS AN' SINNERS (LP, picture disc)	15
84	Liberty LBGP 240 000 0	SLIDE IT IN (LP, picture disc, U.S. mixes)	15
87	EMI EMCP 3528	WHITESNAKE 1987 (LP, picture disc)	15
89	EMI EMCDJ 1013	SLIP OF THE TONGUE (LP, with track by track interview, promo only)	20

WHITE SOLES

76	Satril SAT 104	Beside You/Never Say Die	10

WHITE SPIRIT

(see also Gillan, Iron Maiden)

80	Neat NEAT 05	Back To The Grind/Cheetah (p/s)	10
81	MCA MCA 638	Midnight Chaser/Suffragettes (p/s)	30
81	MCA MCA 652	High Upon High/No Reprieve/Arthur Guitar	15
80	MCA MCF 3079	WHITE SPIRIT (LP, with lyric insert)	18

WHITE SS

78	White SS CIA 72	Mercy Killing/I'm Not One (live) (p/s)	25

WHITE STRIPES

(see also Raconteurs)

01	XL XLS 139	Hotel Yorba (Live At The Hotel Yorba)/Rated X (p/s, 4000 only)	10
02	XL XLS 142	Fell In Love With A Girl/I Just Don't Know What To Do With Myself (p/s, 5000 only)	10
02	XL XLS 142 CD/2	Fell In Love With A Girl/Let's Shake Hands/Lafayette Blues/Fell In Love With A Girl (Live)/Lovesick (Live At The Forum)/I Just Don't Know What To Do With Myself/Fell In Love With A Girl (Video) (2-CD)	10
02	XL XLS 148	Dead Leaves And The Dirty Ground/Stop Breaking Down (Live) (p/s, 5000 only)	5
02	XL/MOJO no cat. no.	Red Death At 6:14 (1-sided, promo only, red vinyl, numbered label, 3000 only, mail order only via Mojo magazine, with letter)	45
02	XL XLS 162	Merry Christmas From The White Stripes: Candy Cane Children/ The Reading Of The Story Of The Magi/The Singing Of Silent Night (1000 only, p/s)	20
03	XL XLS 166	I Just Don't Know What To Do With Myself/Who's To Say (p/s)	6
02	XL no cat. no.	Fell In Love With A Girl/Let's Shake Hands/Lafayette Blues (printed CD-R, promo)	10
03	XL no cat. no.	I Just Don't Know What To Do With Myself/Who's To Say/Lafayette Blues (Live On Radio 1 Evening Session)/I'm Finding It Harder To Be A Gentleman (Live On The John Peel Show) (promo CD)	20
03	XL LP 162 DJ	Seven Nation Army/In The Cold, Cold Night (p/s, ELEPHANT SAMPLER)	8
03	XL XLS 162	Seven Nation Army/Good To Me (p/s)	6
03	XL no cat. no.	Seven Nation Army (1-sided 12" promo, stamped white label, no p/s)	40
04	XL XLS 181	There's No Home For You Here/I Fought Piranhas/Let's Build A Home (die-cut sleeve)	12
05	no. cat. No.	Blue Orchid (Michel Gondry Remix)/Blue Orchid (Jim Jarmusch Remix) (2000 only remix 12" - tour only product, p/s)	15
05	XL XLS 218	My Doorbell/Same Boy You've Always Known (live) (red/white vinyl, p/s)	12
07	XL	Icky Thump/Rag And Bone Man (2 x 7" on white and red vinyl with etched B-sides of Jack and Meg's faces given away free with copies of NME)	8
03	XL XLLP 162	ELEPHANT (2-LP, promo, custom sleeve, 500 only)	60
05	XL XLLP 191 P	GET BEHIND ME SATAN (300 only worldwide. 2 x LP promo, different p/s)	120
05	XL (no. cat. no.)	DENIAL TWIST (10 x printed/stickered CD's in different artwork card wallets. One given away at each night of UK autumn tour. Each CD blank - 10 downloads were available online only, this price for complete set)	300

MINT VALUE £

WHITE TRASH
(see also Trash, Poets, Stone The Crows)

69	Apple APPLE 6	Road To Nowhere/Illusions (early copies as White Trash)	200
69	Apple APPLE 6	Road To Nowhere/Illusions (later copies as Trash)	60

WHITE ZOMBIE

89	Caroline CAROL 1457	God Of Thunder/Love Razor/Disaster Blaster 2 (12", withdrawn)	15

DAVID WHITFIELD

54	Decca F 10242	The Book/Heartless	20
54	Decca F 10327	Carla Mia/Love, Tears And Kisses	20
54	Decca F 10355	Smile/When Or Where	15
54	Decca F 10399	Santa Natale/Adeste Fideles	15
55	Decca F 10458	Beyond The Stars/Open Up Your Heart	15
55	Decca F 10515	Ev'rywhere/Mama	15
55	Decca F 10562	The Lady/Santa Rose Lea Rose	12
55	Decca F 10596	I'll Never Stop Loving You/Lady Of Madrid	12
55	Decca F 10627	When You Lose The One You Love/Angelus	12
56	Decca F 10690	My September Love/The Rudded And The Rock	15
56	Decca F 10769	My Son John/My Unfinished Symphony	10
57	Decca F 10833	The Adoration Waltz/If I Lost You	10
57	Decca F 10864	I'll Find You/I'd Give You The World	10
57	Decca F 10890	Without Him/Dream Of Paradise	8
57	Decca F 10931	Ev'rything/Martinella	8
59	Decca F 11101	Willingly/William Tell	7
60	Decca F 11289	I Believe/Hear My Song Violetta	7
54	Decca LF 1165	YOURS FROM THE HEART (10" LP)	25
58	Decca LK 4242	FAVOURITES (LP)	20
68	Decca LK 4270	FROM DAVID WITH LOVE (LP)	20
60	Decca LK 4348	MY HEART AND I (LP)	15
61	Decca LK 4384	ALONE (LP)	15

WILBUR WHITFIELD
(see also Little Wilbur & Pleasers)

57	Vogue V 9078	P.B. Baby/The One I Love	600
57	Vogue V 9078	P.B. Baby/The One I Love (78)	150

LEONARD WHITING

65	Pye 7N 15943	Piper/That's What Mama Says	40

MARGARET WHITING
(see also Jimmy Wakely, Bob Hope, Dean Martin)

55	Capitol CL 14213	My Own True Love (Tara's Theme)/Can This Be Love (triangular centre)	15
55	Capitol CL 14242	Heat Wave/Come Rain Or Shine (triangular centre)	15
55	Capitol CL 14307	Stowaway/All I Want Is All There Is And Then Some (triangular centre)	15
55	Capitol CL 14348	A Man/Mama's Pearls (triangular centre)	15
55	Capitol CL 14375	Lover, Lover/I Kiss You A Million Times (triangular centre)	15
56	Capitol CL 14527	I Love A Mystery/Bidin' My Time	10
56	Capitol CL 14591	Old Enough/Day In - Day Out	8
56	Capitol CL 14647	True Love/Haunting Love	8
57	Capitol CL 14685	The Money Tree/Maybe I Love Him	8
57	London HLD 8451	Kill Me With Kisses/Speak For Yourself, John	15
58	London HLD 8562	I Can't Help (If I'm Still In Love With You)/That's Why I Was Born	15
58	London HLD 8662	Hot Spell/I'm So Lonesome I Could Cry	15
66	London HLD 10078	Nothing Lasts Forever/The Wheel Of Hurt	10
67	London HLD 10114	Just Like A Man/The World Inside Your Arms	5
68	London HLU 10196	Faithfully/Am I Losing You	5
68	London HLU 10227	Maybe Just Once More/Can't Get You Out Of My Mind	5
53	Capitol LC 6585	CAPITOL PRESENTS MARGARET WHITING (10" LP)	20
56	Capitol LC 6811	MARGARET WHITING (10" LP)	20
58	London HA-D 2109	GOIN' PLACES (LP)	20
61	HMV CLP 1418	SINGS THE JEROME KERN SONGBOOK VOL. ONE (LP, mono)	12
61	HMV CSD 1340	SINGS THE JEROME KERN SONGBOOK VOL. TWO (LP, stereo)	12
61	London HA-D 2321	JUST A DREAM (LP)	25
67	London HA-U/SH-U 8317	THE WHEEL OF HURT (LP)	15
67	London HA-U 8332	MAGGIE ISN'T MARGARET ANYMORE (LP)	15

RAY WHITLEY

65	HMV POP 1473	I've Been Hurt/There Is One Boy	150
65	HMV POP 1473	I've Been Hurt/There Is One Boy (DJ copy)	250

BOBBY WHITLOCK
(see also Derek & Dominoes)

72	CBS 65109	BOBBY WHITLOCK (LP)	30
73	CBS 65301	RAW VELVET (LP)	20

SLIM WHITMAN
SINGLES

54	London L 1149	Indian Love Call/China Doll	20
54	London HL 1149	Indian Love Call/China Doll (re-pressing with different prefix)	15
54	London L 1214	There's A Rainbow In Every Teardrop/Danny Boy	20
54	London HL 1214	There's A Rainbow In Every Teardrop/Danny Boy (re-pressing)	20
54	London L 1226	North Wind/Darlin' Don't Cry	25
54	London HL 1226	North Wind/Darlin' Don't Cry (re-pressing with different prefix)	25
54	London HL 8018	Stairway To Heaven/Lord, Help Me To Be As Thou	30
54	London HL 8039	Secret Love/Why	25
54	London HL 8061	Rose Marie/We Stood At The Altar	15
54	London HL 8080	Beautiful Dreamer/Ride Away	20
54	London HL 8091	The Singing Hills/I Hate To See You Cry	20
55	London HL 8125	When I Grow Too Old To Dream/Cattle Call	20

			MINT VALUE £
55	London HL 8141	Haunted Hungry Heart/Roll On, Silvery Moon	20
55	London HLU 8167	I'll Never Stop Loving You/I'll Never Take You Back Again	20
55	London HLU 8196	Song Of The Wild/You Have My Heart	20
56	London HLU 8230	Tumbling Tumbleweeds/Tell Me	20
56	London HLU 8252	I'm A Fool/My Heart Is Broken In Three	20
56	London HLU 8287	Serenade/I Talk To The Waves	20
56	London HLU 8327	Dear Mary/Whiffenpoof Song	20
56	London HLU 8350	I'm Casting My Lasso Towards The Sky/There's A Love Knot In My Lariat	20
57	London HLP 8403	I'll Take You Home Again Kathleen/Careless Love	20

(The above singles were originally issued with gold label print & tri-centres; later round-centre and/or silver label print copies are worth half these values)

57	London HLP 8416	Curtain Of Tears/Smoke Signals (silver label print)	10
57	London HLP 8420	Gone/An Amateur In Love (gold label print)	25
57	London HLP 8434	Many Times/Warm, Warm Lips	10
57	London HLP 8459	Lovesick Blues/Forever	10
57	London HLP 8518	Unchain My Heart/Hush-A-Bye	10
58	London HLP 8590	A Very Precious Love/Careless Hands	10
58	London HLP 8642	Candy Kisses/Tormented	10
58	London HLP 8708	Wherever You Are/At The End Of Nowhere	10
58	London HLP 8708	Wherever You Are/At The End Of Nowhere (78)	10
59	London HLP 8835	I Never See Maggie Alone/The Letter Edged In Black	8
59	London HLP 8835	I Never See Maggie Alone/The Letter Edged In Black (78)	15
59	London HLP 8896	What Kind Of God (Do You Think You Are)/A Tree In The Meadow (unissued)	0
60	London HLP 9103	Roll, River, Roll/Twilla Lee	6
61	London HLP 9302	Vaya Con Dios/Ramona	6

EPs

54	London RE-P 1006	SLIM WHITMAN AND HIS SINGING GUITAR (at least 8 different colour sleeves, with matt finish & various label designs)	15
54	London RE-P 1006	SLIM WHITMAN AND HIS SINGING GUITAR (at least 8 different colour sleeves, gloss finish & various label designs)	10
55	London RE-P 1042	SONG OF THE WILD	15
56	London RE-P 1064	SLIM WHITMAN VOL. 2 PT. 1	15
56	London RE-P 1070	SLIM WHITMAN VOL. 2 PT. 2	15
57	London RE-P 1100	SLIM WHITMAN VOL. 2 PT. 3	15
59	London RE-P 1199	SLIM WHITMAN SINGS (triangular silver-top centre)	15
59	London RE-P 1199	SLIM WHITMAN SINGS (later round centre)	10
60	London RE-P 1258	SLIM WHITMAN SINGS No. 2	15
63	London RE-P 1360	THE WAYWARD WIND	15
64	Liberty LEP 4018	IRISH LOVE SONGS THE SLIM WHITMAN WAY	10
65	Liberty LEP 4027	SLIM WHITMAN SINGS MORE IRISH SONGS	10
66	Liberty LEP 4046	A SATISFIED MIND	12

LPs

54	London H-APB 1015	SLIM WHITMAN & HIS SINGING GUITAR (10", gold label print)	50
54	London H-APB 1015	SLIM WHITMAN & HIS SINGING GUITAR (10", silver label print)	30
56	London HA-U 2015	SLIM WHITMAN & HIS SINGING GUITAR VOL. 2	40
59	London HA-P 2139	SLIM WHITMAN SINGS	25
59	London HA-P 2199	SLIM WHITMAN SINGS VOL. 2	25
60	London HA-P 2343	SLIM WHITMAN	25
61	London HA-P 2392	JUST CALL ME LONESOME	25
62	London HA-P 2443	SLIM WHITMAN SINGS VOL. 3 (mono)	25
62	London SAH-P 6232	SLIM WHITMAN SINGS VOL. 3 (also stereo SAH-P 6232)	30
62	London HA-P 8013	SLIM WHITMAN SINGS VOL. 4	18
63	London HA-P 8059	HEART SONGS AND LOVE SONGS	18
63	London HA-P 8093	I'M A LONELY WANDERER	18

MARVA WHITNEY

(see also James Brown)

70	Polydor 2001 036	This Girl's In Love With You/He's The One	15
72	Mojo 2092 041	Daddy Don't Know About The Sugar Bear/We Need More	8
69	Polydor 583 767	IT'S MY THING (LP)	80

JAKI WHITREN

73	Epic EPC 65645	RAW BUT TENDER (LP, with insert)	45

TIM WHITSETT/STICKS HERMAN

60s	Range JRE 7002	RHYTHM & BLUES (EP)	30

TIM WHITSETT

64	Sue WI 318	Macks By The Tracks/Shine	45

PAUL WHITSUN JONES & WALLAS EATON & HOLLAND

65	Oriole CB 1991	Shake It Baby/Instant Marriage	20

WHITSUNTIDE EASTER

77	Pilgrim/Grapevine GRA 109	NEXT TIME YOU PLAY A WRONG NOTE - MAKE IT A SHORT ONE (LP, gatefold sleeve)	100

ROGER WHITTAKER (& COMPANIONS)

(see also Hank & Mellowmen)

62	Fontana H 358	The Charge Of The Light Brigade/Keep It A Secret	5
62	Fontana 267 217TF	Steel Men/After The Laughter	5

TOMMY WHITTLE (& HIS QUARTET)

55	Esquire EP 37	TOMMY WHITTLE QUINTET (EP)	40
56	Esquire EP 37	TOMMY WHITTLE QUINTET (EP)	40
58	HMV 7EG 8325	TOMMY WHITTLE QUARTET (EP)	90
54	Esquire 20-028	WAXING WITH WHITTLE (LP)	30
55	Esquire 20-048	TOMMY WHITTLE QUINTET (LP)	50
56	Esquire 20-061	SPOTLIGHTING TOMMY WHITTLE (LP)	75
56	Esquire 20-068	LULLABY & RHYTHM (LP)	125

MINT VALUE £

60	Tempo TAP 27	NEW HORIZONS (LP)	300
60s	Ember EMB 3305	EASY LISTENING (LP)	75
67	Masquerade MQ 2000	SAX FOR DREAMERS (LP)	100

WHIZZ KIDS

79	Dead Good DEAD SIX	P.A.Y.E./99% Proof/National Assistance/Cheek To Cheek (p/s, with insert)	20
80	Ovation OVS 1213	Suspect No. 1/Coma Life (p/s)	10

THE WHO

(see also High Numbers, Pete Townshend, Roger Daltrey, John Entwistle, Keith Moon, Kenney Jones, Graham Bond Organisation, Rigor Mortis, McEnroe & Cash)

SINGLES

65	Brunswick 05926	I Can't Explain/Bald Headed Woman	40
65	Brunswick 05935	Anyway Anyhow Anywhere/Daddy Rolling Stone	35
65	Brunswick 05944	My Generation/Shout And Shimmy	20
66	Brunswick 05951	Circles/Instant Party Mixture (unreleased)	0
66	Reaction 591 001	Substitute/Circles (temporarily withdrawn)	40
66	Reaction 591 001	Substitute/Instant Party (temporarily withdrawn)	30
66	Brunswick 05956	The Kids Are Alright/The Ox (existence unconfirmed)	0
66	Brunswick 05956	A Legal Matter/Instant Party	40
66	Reaction 591 001	Substitute/WHO ORCHESTRA: Waltz For A Pig (B-side actually by Graham Bond Organisation)	25
66	Brunswick 05965	The Kids Are Alright/The Ox	50
66	Brunswick 05968	La-La-La-Lies/The Good's Gone	50
66	Reaction 591 004	I'm A Boy/In The City	12
66	Reaction 591 010	Happy Jack/I've Been Away	12
67	Track 604 002	Pictures Of Lily/Doctor, Doctor	12
67	Track 604 006	The Last Time/Under My Thumb	65
67	Track 604 011	I Can See For Miles/Someone's Coming	15
68	Track 604 023	Dogs/Call Me Lightning	25
68	Track 604 024	Magic Bus/Dr. Jekyll And Mr Hyde	12
69	Track 604 027	Pinball Wizard/Dogs Part Two	10
70	Track 604 036	The Seeker/Here For More	10
70	Track 2094 002	Summertime Blues/Heaven And Hell	10
70	Track 2094 004	See Me, Feel Me/Overture From 'Tommy' (withdrawn)	40
71	Track 2094 009	Won't Get Fooled Again/Don't Know Myself (p/s, large centre)	25
71	Track 2094 009	Won't Get Fooled Again/Don't Know Myself (p/s, with middle)	35
73	Track 2094 115	5.15/Water	7
75	Polydor 2001 561	Overture/See Me Feel Me/Listening To You (from "Tommy" soundtrack, p/s)	10
76	Polydor 2058 803	Substitute/I'm A Boy/Pictures Of Lily (12", company sleeve)	8
79	Polydor WHO 2	Long Live Rock/I'm The Face/My Wife (withdrawn, blank run-off groove)	6
80	Polydor WHO 3	5.15/I'm One (p/s)	6
82	Polydor WHOP 6	Athena/A Man Is A Man (picture disc)	6
82	Polydor WHOPX 6	Athena/A Man Is A Man/Won't Get Fooled Again (12", picture disc)	8
82	Polydor WHOPX 6	Athena/A Man Is A Man/Won't Get Fooled Again (12", picture disc, mispressing, plays "Why Did I Fall For That")	15
89	Polydor POCD 907	My Generation/Substitute/Baba O'Riley/Behind Blue Eyes (CD, card sleeve)	10
89	Polydor POCD 917	Won't Get Fooled Again (Extended Version)/Bony Maronie/Dancing In The Street/Mary-Anne With The Shaky Hand (CD, card sleeve)	15

EXPORT SINGLES

66	Brunswick 05956	A Legal Matter/Instant Party (with Scandinavian p/s)	130
68	Decca AD 1001	My Generation/Shout And Shimmy (in p/s)	165
68	Decca AD 1001	My Generation/Shout And Shimmy	100
68	Decca AD 1002	A Legal Matter/Instant Party	100
72	Track 2094 102	Join Together/Baby Don't You Do It (p/s, for Spain)	25

PROMO SINGLES

69	Track PRO 1	The Acid Queen/We're Not Gonna Take It (existence unconfirmed)	0
69	Track PRO 2	Go To The Mirror!/Sally Simpson	70
69	Track PRO 3	I'm Free/1921	70
69	Track PRO 4	Christmas/Overture	70

EPs

66	Reaction 592 001	READY STEADY WHO	100
70	Track 2252 001	EXCERPTS FROM "TOMMY" (33rpm)	25
83	Reaction WHO 7	READY STEADY WHO (reissue)	20

ALBUMS

65	Brunswick LAT 8616	MY GENERATION (laminated front sleeve, black/silver label)	400
66	Reaction 593 002	A QUICK ONE (laminated sleeve, blue/silver label)	150
67	Track 612 002	THE WHO SELL OUT (mono, 500 with stickered sleeve & poster)	500
67	Track 612 002	THE WHO SELL OUT (LP, mono)	120
67	Track 613 002	THE WHO SELL OUT (stereo, 500 with stickered sleeve & poster)	500
67	Track 613 002	THE WHO SELL OUT (LP, stereo)	120
68	Track 612 006	DIRECT HITS (mono)	40
68	Track 613 006	DIRECT HITS (stereo)	50
69	Track 613 013/014	TOMMY (2-LP, fold-out glossy gatefold sleeve, with numbered 12-page booklet)	120
70	Track 2406 001	LIVE AT LEEDS (1st issue with BLACK stamp on front, foldout sleeve with 12 inserts including poster stating 'Tuesdays At The Marquee' on thick paper in glassine greaseproof bag, A1/B1 matrix)	250
70	Track 2406 001	LIVE AT LEEDS (with BLUE or RED stamp on front, foldout sleeve with 12 inserts including poster stating 'Tuesdays At The Marquee', on thinner paper A1/B1 Matrix)	80
70	Track 2406 001	LIVE AT LEEDS (with BLUE or RED stamp on front, foldout sleeve with 12 inserts including poster stating 'Live At Leeds', A1/B1 matrix)	50
70	Track 2406 001	LIVE AT LEEDS (second pressing, with BLUE or RED stamp on front, foldout sleeve with 12 inserts including poster stating 'Live At Leeds', A3/B3 matrix)	40
70	Track 2407 008	BACKTRACK 8: A QUICK ONE (mono budget reissue)	15
70	Track 2407 009	BACKTRACK 9: SELL OUT (stereo budget reissue)	15

MINT VALUE £

70	Track 2407 014	BACKTRACK 14: THE OX	22
70	Track 2856 001	WHO DID IT? (mail-order only, withdrawn)	600
71	Track 2408 102	WHO'S NEXT	20
71	Track 2406 006	MEATY, BEATY, BIG AND BOUNCY (gatefold sleeve)	20
71	Track 2406 006	MEATY, BEATY, BIG AND BOUNCY (gatefold sleeve, mispressed, plays "The Seeker" instead of "Magic Bus")	25
72	Track 2406 007	TOMMY PART ONE	12
72	Track 2406 008	TOMMY PART TWO	15
73	Track 2657 013	QUADROPHENIA (2-LP, original with 22-page photo booklet, matt labels)	25
74	Track 2406 116	ODDS AND SODS (cut-away braille sleeve, with poster & lyric sheet)	20
75	Polydor 2490 129	THE WHO BY NUMBERS	15
80	Virgin V 2179	MY GENERATION (reissue)	20
81	Polydor 2675 216	PHASES (9-LP box set, stickered cover)	100

WALLY WHYTON (& VIPERS)

(see also Vipers, Sharkey Todd & Monsters)

59	Parlophone R 4585	Don't Tell Me Your Troubles/It's All Over You	5
60	Parlophone R 4630	All Over This World/Got Me A Girl	5
60	Pye 7N 15304	It's A Rat Race/Marriage Of Convenience/95% Of Me Loves You (with Sally Miles)/You're Going To Be Caught (as Wally Whyton & Vipers)	5
61	Piccadilly 7N 35089	Little Red Pony/Christmas Land	5
68	Fontana TF 960	Gentle On My Mind/Ballad Of The Bol Weevil	5
69	Fontana TF 994	Wichita Lineman/Leave Them A Flower	5
69	Fontana TF 1030	Jig Alone/Out On The Road	5
70	Fontana STL 5535	LEAVE THEM A FLOWER (LP)	12
60	Parlophone GEP 8808	WILLUM AND ME (EP, stereo)	8

WI & HDEA

93	Hype! VEN 001	VENTURE F.M. PRESENTS SUMMER RUSH EP (12", stamped white label)	20

WICHITA FALL

69	Liberty LBS 83208	LIFE IS BUT A DREAM (LP)	25

WICHITA TRAIN WHISTLE

(see also Michael Nesmith)

68	Dot DOT 111	Don't Cry Now/Tapioca Tundra (unissued)	0
68	Dot (S)LPD 516	MICHAEL NESMITH PRESENTS THE WICHITA TRAIN WHISTLE SINGS (LP)	40

WIDERVISION

80	Widermusic 001	People/Truant (p/s)	25

WIDOWMAKER

(see also Luther Grosvenor, Steve Ellis, Huw Lloyd Langton)

76	Jet JET 766	On The Road/Pin A Rose On Me	7
76	Jet JET 767	When I Met You/Pin A Rose On Me	5
76	Jet JET 782	Pin A Rose On Me/On The Road	5
76	Jet 2310 432	WIDOWMAKER (LP)	12
77	United Artists UAG 30038	TOO LATE TO CRY (LP, gatefold sleeve)	15

DAVID WIGG

66	CBS 202233	Life Is Complicated/Turning Around	8

WIGGANS

61	Blue Beat BB 29	Rock Baby/Let's Sing The Blues	25

PERCY WIGGINS

67	Atlantic 584 113	Book Of Memories/Can't Find Nobody (To Take Your Place)	10

SPENCER WIGGINS

67	Stateside SS 2024	Uptight Good Woman/Anything You Do Is Alright	25
70	Pama PM 794	I'm A Poor Man's Son/That's How Much I Love You	25
98	Torch 1	Lets Talk It Over/Lets Talk It Over (500 copies)	10

LEO WIJNKAMP JR

75	Kicking Mule SNKF 108	RAGS TO RICHES (LP)	25
79	Kicking Mule SNKF 156	RETURN OF DR. HACKENBUSH (LP)	25

WIKKYD VIKKER

83	Boogie FUR 0235	Black Of The Night/Release (no p/s)	120

WILBURN BROTHERS

59	Brunswick 05799	That Silver-Haired Daddy Of Mine/A Boy's Faithful Friend	10
59	Brunswick LAT 8291	SIDE BY SIDE (LP)	20
61	Brunswick LAT 8501	CITY LIMITS (LP)	20
62	Brunswick LAT 8507	FOLK SONGS (LP)	15
67	Brunswick LAT 8686	COOL COUNTRY (LP)	15

JACK WILCE

69	Elektra EKSN 45068	Apple Pie, Mother & The Flag/Ballad Of Baby Browning	10

WILCO

99	Reprise 9362 47282-1	SUMMERTEETH (2-LP)	20

WILD ANGELS

68	Major Minor MM 569	Nervous Breakdown/Watch The Wheels Go Round	25
69	B&C CB 114	Buzz Buzz/Please Don't Touch	12
70	B&C CB 123	Sally-Ann/Wrong Number, Try Again	12
71	B&C CB 145	Three Nights A Week/Time To Kill	8
72	Decca F 13308	Jo-Jo Ann/My Way	7
72	Decca F 13356	Beauty School Dropout/Midnight Rider	7
73	Decca F 13374	Running Bear/Sussin'	6
73	Decca F 13412	Greased Lightning/Born To Hand-Jive/Beauty School Dropout	6
73	Decca F 13456	Clap Your Hands And Stamp Your Feet/Wild Angels Rock'n'Roll	8
70	B&C BCM 101	LIVE AT THE REVOLUTION (LP)	15
70	B&C BCM 102	RED HOT'N'ROCKIN' (LP)	15
72	Decca SKL 5134	OUT AT LAST (LP)	12

MINT VALUE £

WILD BOYS

78	Ring Piece CUS 886	Last One Of The Boys/We're Only Monsters	200

WILD BUNCH

84	Ariwa ARILP 15	THE WILD BUNCH (LP)	20

WILDCATS

80s	Wildbop WILDBOP 1	Talahassie Lassie/My Babe/Rip It UP	5

WILDCATS

59	London HLT 8787	Gazachstahagen/Billy's Cha Cha	25
59	London HLT 8787	Gazachstahagen/Billy's Cha Cha (78)	10

WILD COUNTRY

70	Trafalgar TRAF 01	Silent Village/Too Bad	65

JACK WILD(E)

69	Elektra EKSN 45068	Apple Pie Mother And The Flag/Ballad Of Baby Browning	6
70	Capitol CL 15635	Picture Of You/Some Beautiful	7
70	Capitol ST 22545	THE JACK WILD ALBUM (LP)	12
71	Buddah 2011-19	Punch & Judy/Takin It Easy	10

KIM WILDE

83	Rak 12 RAK 365	Dancing In The Dark (Extended)/Dancing In The Dark (Instrumental) (12", p/s, with poster)	8
84	MCA KIMP 1	The Second Time/Lovers On A Beach (picture disc)	10
84	MCA KIMP 2	The Touch/Shangri-La (shaped picture disc)	10
85	MCA KIMP 3	Rage To Love/Putty In Your Hands (shaped picture disc)	10

MARTY WILDE (& WILDCATS)

(see also Wilde Three, Brian Bennett, Shadows, Keith Shields, Capricorn, Deke Leonard)

78s

57	Philips PB 750	Honeycomb/Wild Cat (as Marty Wilde & Wildcats)	15
58	Philips PB 781	Love Bug Crawl/Afraid Of Love	35
58	Philips PB 804	Sing, Boy, Sing/Oh-Oh, I'm Falling In Love Again (with Wildcats)	20
58	Philips PB 835	Endless Sleep/Her Hair Was Yellow (as Marty Wilde & Wildcats)	10
58	Philips PB 850	My Lucky Love/Misery's Child (as Marty Wilde & Wildcats)	12
58	Philips PB 875	No One Knows/The Fire Of Love	15
59	Philips PB 902	Donna/Love-a, Love-a, Love-a	25
59	Philips PB 926	A Teenager In Love/Danny	30
59	Philips PB 959	Sea Of Love/Teenage Tears	40
59	Philips PB 972	It's Been Nice/Bad Boy	45
60	Philips PB 1002	Johnny Rocco/My Heart And I	70

SINGLES

57	Philips JK 1028	Honeycomb/Wild Cat (as Marty Wilde & Wildcats) (jukebox issue)	60
58	Philips PB 804	Sing, Boy, Sing/Oh-Oh, I'm Falling In Love Again (with Wildcats)	40
58	Philips PB 835	Endless Sleep/Her Hair Was Yellow (as Marty Wilde & Wildcats)	15
58	Philips PB 850	My Lucky Love/Misery's Child (as Marty Wilde & Wildcats)	12
58	Philips PB 875	No One Knows/The Fire Of Love	15
59	Philips PB 902	Donna/Love-a, Love-a, Love-a	10
59	Philips PB 926	A Teenager In Love/Danny	10
59	Philips PB 959	Sea Of Love/Teenage Tears	10
59	Philips PB 972	Bad Boy/It's Been Nice	10
60	Philips PB 1002	Johnny Rocco/My Heart And I	15
60	Philips PB 1022	The Fight/Johnny At The Crossroads	15
60	Philips PB 1037	I Wanna Be Loved By You/Angry	8
60	Philips PB 1078	Little Girl/Your Seventeenth Spring	8
61	Philips PB 1101	Rubber Ball/Like Makin' Love	8
61	Philips PB 1121	When Does It Get To Be Love/Your Loving Touch	7
61	Philips PB 1161	Hide And Seek/Crazy Dream	15
61	Philips PB 1191	Tomorrow's Clown/The Hellions	12
61	Philips PB 1206	Come Running/Ev'ryone	12
62	Philips PB 1240	Jezebel/Don't Run Away	10
62	Philips 326 546BF	Ever Since You Said Goodbye/Send Me The Pillow You Dream On	12
63	Columbia DB 4980	Lonely Avenue/Brand New Love	10
63	Philips 326 579BF	No! Dance With Me/Little Miss Happiness	7
63	Columbia DB 7145	Save Your Love For Me/Bless My Broken Heart	10
64	Columbia DB 7198	When Day Is Done/I Can't Help The Way I Feel	10
64	Columbia DB 7285	Kiss Me/My, What A Woman	10
64	Decca F 11979	The Mexican Boy/Your Kind Of Love	12
66	Philips PB 1490	I've Got So Used To Loving You/The Beginning Of The End	6
68	Philips BF 1632	By The Time I Get To Phoenix/Shutters And Boards	6
68	Philips BF 1669	Abergavenny/Alice In Blue	6
69	Philips BF 1753	All The Love I Have/Any Day	6
69	Philips BF 1783	Endless Sleep/Donna	5
69	Philips BF 1815	Shelley/Jump On The Train (with Deke Leonard)	6
70	Philips BF 1839	No Trams To Lime Street/Prelude To Old Age	7
71	Philips 6006 126	Busker/It's So Real	7
74	Magnet MAG 15	I Love You/She's A Mover	6

EPs

57	Philips BBE 12164	PRESENTING MARTY WILDE	70
58	Philips BBE 12200	MORE OF MARTY	50
59	Philips BBE 12327	SEA OF LOVE	50
60	Philips BBE 12385	VERSATILE MR. WILDE	55
60	Philips BBE 12422	MARTY WILDE FAVOURITES	50
62	Philips BBE 12517	COME RUNNING	40
63	Philips BE 433 638	MARTY	40

LPs

59	Philips BBL 7342	WILDE ABOUT MARTY	60

			MINT VALUE £
60	Philips BBL 7380	MARTY WILDE SHOWCASE	60
60	Philips BBL 7385	THE VERSATILE MR. WILDE (mono)	50
60	Philips SBBL 570	THE VERSATILE MR. WILDE (stereo)	60
69	Philips SBL 7877	DIVERSIONS	15
70	Philips 6308 010	ROCK 'N' ROLL	12
74	Philips 6382 102	GOOD ROCKIN' - THEN AND NOW (LP)	12

WILDER BROTHERS

57	HMV POP 365	I Want You/Teenage Angel	250
57	HMV POP 365	I Want You/Teenage Angel (78)	50

WILDE THREE

(see also Marty Wilde, Justin Hayward, Vernons Girls)

65	Decca F 12131	Since You've Gone/Just As Long	75
65	Decca F 12232	I Cried/Well Who's That?	75

WILDFIRE

(see also Weapon)

84	Mausoleum GUTS 8403	Nothing Lasts Forever/Blood Money	8
84	Mausoleum GUTS 8405	Jerusalem/Fight Fire With Fire (p/s)	5
83	Mausoleum SKUL 8307	BRUTE FORCE AND IGNORANCE (LP)	25
83	Mausoleum SKUL 8338	SUMMER LIGHTNING (LP, with insert)	15

WILDFIRE (2)

80	Chrysalis CHR 1288	BURNING (LP)	12

WILDHEARTS

(see also Backyard Babies, Chasers, Energetic Krusher, Ginger, Honeycrack, Jellys, Quireboys, SilverGinger 5, Super$hit666, Devin Townsend, Yo-Yo's)

SINGLES

92	East West YZ 669T	MONDO AKIMBO A-GO-GO (12" EP, with inner sleeve)	25
92	East West YZ 669TX	MONDO AKIMBO A-GO-GO (12" EP, white vinyl, with inner sleeve, advance copies with artwork postcard & press sheet)	40
92	East West YZ 669TX	MONDO AKIMBO A-GO-GO (12" EP, white vinyl, with inner sleeve)	35
92	East West YZ 669CD	MONDO AKIMBO A-GO-GO (CD EP)	40
93	East West YZ 773	Greetings From Shitsville/The Bullshit Goes On (p/s, brown vinyl, with insert)	12
93	East West YZ 784CD	TV EP: TV Tan/Show A Little Emotion/Dangerlust/Down On London (CD)	8
94	East West YZ 794	Caffeine Bomb/Girlfriend Clothes (p/s, green vinyl, with insert)	5
94	East West YZ 794CD	Caffeine Bomb/Girlfriend Clothes/Shut Your Fucking Mouth And Use Your Fucking Brain/And The Bullshit Goes On (CD, digipak)	12
94	East West YZ 828TE	Suckerpunch/Beautiful Thing You/Two-Way Idiot Mirror/29 x The Pain (10", p/s, 1-sided, etched)	12
94	East West YZ 828CD	Suckerpunch/Beautiful Thing You/Two-Way Idiot Mirror/29 x The Pain (CD)	8
94	East West YZ 874TEX	If Life Is Like A Lovebank I Want An Overdraft/Geordie In Wonderland/ Hate The World Day/Fire Up (10", gatefold sleeve with banknote)	10
94	East West YZ 874CDX	If Life Is Like A Lovebank I Want An Overdraft/Geordie In Wonderland/ Hate The World Day/Fire Up (CD, 'wallet' pack with banknote)	8
95	East West YZ 923TEX	I Wanna Go Where The People Go/Shandy Bang/Can't Do Right For Doing Wrong/Give The Girl A Gun (10", p/s)	10
95	East West YZ 976TEX	Just In Lust/Mindslide/Friend For Five Minutes/S.I.N (In Sin) (10", p/s)	10
95	Round WILD1CDX	Sick Of Drugs/Underkill/Bad Time To Be Having A Bad Time/Skychaser High (CD, with grass-growing mat, title sticker)	8
97	Mushroom MUSH 6CD	Anthem/So Good To Be Back Home/Time To Let You Go (CD, mispressing, plays country music)	12
02	Round SMALP048	Vanilla Radio/Better Than Cable (picture disc, stickered PVC sleeve, 1500 only)	8

LPs

92	East West 4509-91202-1	DON'T BE HAPPY... JUST WORRY (LP, as 2 x 12", with inner sleeves)	25
92	East West 4509-91202-2	DON'T BE HAPPY... JUST WORRY (2-CD, with bonus disc containing Anti-Dance Mixes of "Mondo Akimbo A-Go Go" tracks)	25
93	East West 4509-93287-1	EARTH VS THE WiLDHEARTS (LP, with exclusive uncredited track)	20
93	East West 4509-93201-2	EARTH VS THE WiLDHEARTS (CD, first issue with "93" rear artwork, without "Caffeine Bomb")	18
94	East West 4509-99039-2	FISHING FOR LUCKIES (CD, 6-track mini-album, fan club/mail-order only)	40
95	East West 0630-10404-1	P.H.U.Q. (LP, gatefold sleeve)	15
95	East West 0630-10437-2	P.H.U.Q. (CD, stickered felt case, unique inlay)	15
95	East West 0630-12850-1	FISHING FOR MORE LUCKIES (LP, reissue, with 3 extra tracks Underkill, "Saddened" & "I Wanna Go Where The People Go [Early Version]", unreleased, most copies destroyed)	100
95	East West 0630-12850-4	FISHING FOR MORE LUCKIES (cassette, reissue, with 3 extra tracks, unreleased, most copies destroyed)	25
96	Round 0630-14888-1	FISHING FOR LUCKIES (2-LP, reissue, gatefold, Side 3 exclusive to vinyl)	18
97	Mushroom MUSH13LP	ENDLESS, NAMELESS (LP, inner sleeve)	15
98	Kuro Neko KNEKLP3	ANARCHIC AIRWAVES - THE WiLDHEARTS AT THE BBC (2-LP, 200 mail-order copies only - 1000 copies made but 800 destroyed)	25
98	Kuro Neko KNEK3L	ANARCHIC AIRWAVES - THE WiLDHEARTS AT THE BBC (CD in square stickered metal tin, no insert, 1000 copies only)	15
99	Kuro Neko KNEK3LTD	ANARCHIC AIRWAVES - THE WiLDHEARTS AT THE BBC (2-CD, with bonus disc "THE REST OF READING")	20
98	Kuro Neko KNEK4LB	LANDMINES & PANTOMIMES - THE LAST OF THE WiLDHEARTS?? (CD in square stickered metal tin in card box with insert, 1000 copies only)	30
03	Gut GUTLP25	THE WiLDHEARTS MUST BE DESTROYED (LP, gatefold sleeve)	12
04	Gut GUTLP32	THE WILDHEARTS STRIKE BACK (2 x LP, gatefold)	15
08	Round ROUND010LP	THE WILDHEARTS (2 x LP, white vinyl, photo insert, 1,000 only)	15

WILD HONEY

(see also Tina Charles)

72	Mam MAM 154	Baby Don't You Know Anymore/He's My Sugar (featuring Tina Charles)	5

WILD HORSES

(see also Thin Lizzy, Motorhead, Rainbow, Dio)

79	EMI International INTS 599	Criminal Tendencies/The Rapist (p/s)	5

			MINT VALUE £
80	EMI EMI 5047	Face Down/Dealer (p/s)	5
80	EMI EMI 5078	Fly Away/Blackmail (p/s, white vinyl; black vinyl demos £15)	6
80	EMI 12EMI 5078	Fly Away/Blackmail (12", p/s, white vinyl)	8
81	EMI EMI 5149	I'll Give You Love/Rocky Mountain Way (p/s)	5
81	EMI EMI 5149	I'll Give You Love/Rocky Mountain Way//The Kid/On A Saturday Night (double pack, gatefold p/s)	5
81	EMI EMI 5199	Everlasting Love/The Axe (no p/s)	5
80	EMI EMC 3326	WILD HORSES (LP, with inner sleeve)	12
81	EMI EMC 3368	STAND YOUR GROUND (LP, with inner sleeve)	15

WILD MAGNOLIAS

75	Barclay BAR 30	Smoke My Peace Pipe/Handa Wanda	5
75	Barclay BAR 34	They Call Us Wild/Jumalaka Boom Boom	5
75	Barclay 80 529	THE WILD MAGNOLIAS 1 (LP, gatefold sleeve)	20
75	Barclay 90 033	THEY CALL US WILD (LP, gatefold sleeve)	20

WILD OATS

63	Oak RGJ 117	WILD OATS (EP)	750

WILD ONES (U.K.)

64	Fontana TF 468	Bowie Man/Purple Pill Eater	75

WILD ONES (U.S)

65	United Artsts ULP 1119	THE ARTHUR SOUND (LP)	40

WILD PUSSY

88	Metallion	MECHANARCH (12", EP, wih insert)	100

WILD SILK

68	Polydor 56256	Poor Man/Stop Crying	10
69	Columbia DB 8534	(Visions In A) Plaster Sky/Toymaker	30
69	Columbia DB 8611	Help Me/Crimson And Gold	20

WILD SWANS

(see also Lotus Eaters, Care)

82	Zoo CAGE 009	The Revolutionary Spirit/God Forbid (unissued, stamped white label)	12
82	Zoo CAGE 009	The Revolutionary Spirit/God Forbid (12", p/s)	10
82	Zoo CAGE 009	The Revolutionary Spirit/God Forbid (12", p/s, with 'The Lament Of Icarus' painting in top right of front sleeve, withdrawn)	15

WILD THING

69	Elektra EKSN 45076	Old Lady/Next To Me	6
70	Elektra EKS 74059	PARTYIN' (LP)	18
71	Elektra 2410 003	PARTYIN' (LP, reissue)	12

WILD TURKEY

(see also Babe Ruth, Jethro Tull, Man, Gary Pickford-Hopkins, Whitesnake)

72	Chrysalis CHS 2004	Good Old Days/Life Is A Symphony	5
72	Chrysalis CHR 1002	BATTLE HYMN (LP, gatefold sleeve)	25
73	Chrysalis CHR 1010	TURKEY (LP, gatefold sleeve)	20

WILD UNCERTAINTY

66	Planet PLF 120	Man With Money/Broken Truth	80

WILD WALLY

70	Concord CON 1003	I GO APE (LP)	12

WILD & WANDERING

(see also Pop Will Eat Itself)

86	Iguana VYK 14	2,000 LIGHT ALES FROM HOME (12" EP, with insert)	25

WILDWEEDS

67	Chess CRS 8065	It Was Fun While It Lasted/Sorrow's Anthem	20

WILD WILL'S BLUE WASHBOARD BOYS

71	Flyright LP 4701	BABY YUM YUM (LP)	12

WILDY

76	Paladin PAL 12	No Smokin'/All The Children	10

WILFRED

70	Parlophone R5836	Candle In The WInd/Between The Lines	15

WILFRED & MILLICENT

(see also Jackie [Edwards] & Millie [Small])

65	Island WI 190	The Vow/I'll Never Believe In You	12

MIKE WILHELM

(see also Charlatans, Flamin' Groovies)

76	Zigzag/United Artists ZZ 1	MIKE WILHELM (LP, sold via Zigzag magazine)	45

JOHN BUCK WILKIN

70	LBF 15375	Apartment Twenty-One/Boy Of The Country	6

ROBERT WILKINS

60s	Piedmont PLP 13162	REV ROBERT WILKINS (LP)	20
70	Spokane SPL 1002	BEFORE THE REVERENCE (LP)	40

C.T WILKINSON

76	DJM DJS 668	My Happiness/Monday Coming Up	8

WILLETT FAMILY

62	Topic 12T 84	THE ROVING JOURNEYMAN (LP, blue label with booklet)	20

E WILLIAM

67	Polydor 56181	Lazy Life/Crazy How love Slips Away	40

AL WILLIAMS

80	Grapevine GRP 136	I Am Nothing/Brand New Love	20

MINT VALUE £

ANDY WILLIAMS

56	London HLA 8284	Walk Hand In Hand/Not Any More	30
56	London HLA 8315	Canadian Sunset/High Upon A Mountain (gold label print)	40
56	London HLA 8315	Canadian Sunset/High Upon A Mountain (silver label print)	20
56	London HL 7013	Canadian Sunset/High Upon A Mountain (export issue)	20
56	London HLA 8360	Baby Doll (From The Film)/Since I've Found My Baby (gold print)	40
56	London HLA 8360	Baby Doll (From The Film)/Since I've Found My Baby (silver print)	20
57	London HLA 8399	Butterfly/It Doesn't Take Very Long	20
57	London HLA 8437	I Like Your Kind Of Love/Stop Teasin' Me	10
57	London HLA 8487	Lips Of Wine/Straight From My Heart	10
58	London HLA 8587	Are You Sincere/Be Mine Tonight	10
58	London HL 7034	Are You Sincere/Be Mine Tonight (export issue)	10
58	London HLA 8710	Promise Me, Love/Your Hand, Your Heart, Your Love	10
59	London HLA 8784	Hawaiian Wedding Song/House Of Bamboo	8
59	London HLA 8957	Lonely Street/Summer Love	7
59	London HLA 9018	The Village Of St. Bernadette/I'm So Lonesome I Could Cry	5
59	London HLA 9018	The Village Of St. Bernadette/I'm So Lonesome I Could Cry (78)	10
60	London HLA 9099	Wake Me When It's Over/We Have A Date	5
60	London HLA 9241	Don't Go To Strangers/You Don't Want My Love	5
61	London HLA 9348	The Bilbao Song/How Wonderful To Know	5
67	CBS CBS 2675	Music To Watch Girls By/The Face I Love	5
57	London RE-A 1088	ANDY WILLIAMS' BIG HITS (EP)	12
57	London RE-A 1102	ANDY WILLIAMS' BIG HITS No. 2 (EP)	12
63	London RE-A 1394	ANDY WILLIAMS' BEST (EP)	8
57	London HA-A 2054	ANDY WILLIAMS SINGS STEVE ALLEN (LP)	30
58	London HA-A 2113	ANDY WILLIAMS SINGS RODGERS AND HAMMERSTEIN (LP)	30
59	London HA-A 2203	TWO TIME WINNERS (LP)	30
60	London HA-A 2238	LONELY STREET (LP)	15
62	London HA-A 8005	ANDY WILLIAMS' BEST (LP)	12
63	London HA-A 8090	UNDER PARIS SKIES (LP)	15

AUDREY WILLIAMS

(see also Hank Williams)

56	MGM SP 1179	Ain't Nothing Gonna Be All Right No How/Livin' It Up And Havin' A Ball	25

BIG JOE WILLIAMS

(see also Poor Joe Williams)

57	Jazz Collector JEN 3	A MAN SINGS THE BLUES (EP)	10
57	Jazz Collector JEN 4	A MAN SINGS THE BLUES VOLUME 2 (EP)	10
67	Delmark DJB 4	ON THE HIGHWAY (EP)	15
63	Esquire 32-191	BLUES ON HIGHWAY 51 (LP)	40
63	77' LA 12-19	PINEY WOODS BLUES (LP)	30
64	CBS BPG 63813	CLASSIC DELTA BLUES (LP)	20
64	Storyville SLP 158	PORTRAITS IN BLUES VOLUME 4 (LP)	20
64	Storyville SLP 163	PORTRAITS IN BLUES VOLUME 7 (LP)	20
65	Fontana 688 800 ZL	TOUGH TIMES (LP)	25
66	Xtra XTRA 1033	BIG JOE WILLIAMS (LP)	30
66	Bounty BY 6018	BACK TO THE COUNTRY (LP)	40
66	Society SOC 1020	BIG JOE, SONNY, BROWNIE, LIGHTNIN' (LP, with Lightnin' Hopkins, Sonny Terry & Brownie McGhee)	15
69	Storyville 618 011	DON'T YOU LEAVE ME HERE (LP)	20
69	Liberty LBL/LBS 83207	HAND ME DOWN MY OLD WALKING STICK (LP)	20
69	Xtra XTRA 5059	LIVE AT FOLK CITY (LP)	15
70	RCA Intl. INTS 1087	CRAWLIN' KING SNAKE (LP)	18
72	Delmark DS 627	NINE STRING GUITAR (LP)	15

BILLY WILLIAMS (QUARTET)

(see also Barbara McNair)

54	Vogue Coral Q 2012	Sh'Boom/Whenever Wherever	15
54	Vogue Coral Q 2039	The Honeydripper/Love Me (as Billy Williams Quartet)	50
56	Vogue Coral Q 72149	A Crazy Little Palace/Cry Baby (as Billy Williams Quartet)	50
56	Vogue Coral Q 72180	Pray/You'll Reach Your Star	10
57	Vogue Coral Q 72222	Follow Me/Shame, Shame (as Billy Williams Quartet)	30
57	Vogue Coral Q 72241	Butterfly/The Pied Piper	20
57	Vogue Coral Q 72266	I'm Gonna Sit Right Down And Write A Letter/Date With The Blues	20
57	Vogue Coral Q 72295	Got A Date With An Angel/The Lord Will Understand	25
58	Coral Q 72303	Don't Let Go/Baby, Baby (as Billy Williams Quartet)	40
58	Coral Q 72316	Steppin' Out Tonight/There I've Said It Again (as Billy Williams Quartet)	50
58	Coral Q 72331	I'll Get By/It's Prayin' Time	20
59	Coral Q 72359	Nola/Tied To The Strings Of Your Heart	10
59	Coral Q 72369	Goodnight Irene/Red Hot Love	30
59	Coral Q 72377	Telephone Conversation/Go To Sleep, Go To Sleep, Go To Sleep (with Barbara McNair)	25
60	Coral Q 72402	I Cried For You/Lover Of All Lovers	18
60	Coral Q 72414	Begin The Beguine/For You	5
58	Coral LVA 9092	BILLY WILLIAMS	100
60	Coral LVA 9120	HALF SWEET HALF BEAT	40
61	Coral LVA 9139	THE BILLY WILLIAMS REVUE	30

BOBBY WILLIAMS

68	Action ACT 4509	Baby I Need Your Love/Try It Again	10
73	Contempo C 17	Let's Jam/You're My Baby	8

CHRIS WILLIAMS & HIS MONSTERS

59	Columbia DB 4383	The Monster/The Eton Boating Song	35
60	Triumph RGM 1003	Kicking Around/Midnight Rocker (unissued; white label demo copies only)	250

CINDY WILLIAMS

67	Parlophone R 5648	They Talk About Us/Did He Call Today Mama	8

MINT VALUE £

CLARENCE WILLIAMS (& HIS WASHBOARD BAND)

54	Columbia SCM 5134	High Society/Left All Alone With The Blues	20
58	Fontana TFE 17053	TREASURE OF NORTH AMERICAN MUSIC VOLUME 3 (EP)	15
59	Parlophone GEP 8733	CLARENCE WILLIAMS' WASHBOARD BAND (EP)	15
64	Jazz Collector JEL 18	JAZZ ORIGINATORS (EP)	10
54	London AL 3526	CLARENCE WILLIAMS AND HIS ORCHESTRA (10" LP)	20
55	Columbia 33S 1067	BACK ROOM SPECIAL (10" LP)	20
57	London AL 3561	CLARENCE WILLIAMS AND HIS ORCHESTRA VOL. 2 (10" LP)	20
60	Fontana TFL 5087	SIDNEY BECHET MEMORIAL (LP)	15
62	Philips BBL 7521	CLARENCE WILLIAMS VOL. 1: 1927-1935 (LP)	15

CLIVE WILLIAMS

69	Rock Steady Rev. REVR 6	Take Good Care Of My Baby/RICO: In Loving Memory Of Don Drummond	20

DAN WILLIAMS & HIS ORCHESTRA

55	London CAY 110	Donkey City/SHAW PARK CALYPSO BAND: Take Her To Jamaica	10

DANNY WILLIAMS

59	HMV POP 624	Tall A Tree/I Look At You	7
59	HMV POP 655	So High - So Low/My Own True Love	7
59	HMV POP 703	Youthful Years/It Doesn't Matter	7
60	HMV POP 803	A Million To One/Call Me A Dreamer	6
61	HMV POP 839	We Will Never Be As Young As This Again/Passing Breeze	5
61	HMV POP 885	The Miracle Of You/Lonely	5
64	HMV POP 1372	Forget Her, Forget Her/Lollipops And Roses	20
65	HMV POP 1388	The Roundabout Of Love/I Wanna Be Around	5
65	HMV POP 1410	Go Away/Masquerade	20
65	HMV POP 1455	Lovely Is She/Gone And Forgotten	5
65	HMV POP 1487	And So We Meet Again/Violets For Your Furs	5
66	HMV POP 1506	I've Got To Find That Girl Again/Throw A Little Lovin' My Way	30
67	Deram DM 149	Never My Love/Whose Little Girl Are You (with inverted matrix)	30
67	Deram DM 149	Never My Love/Whose Little Girl Are You (re-pressing with matrix correct way up)	10
62	HMV 7EG 8748	HITS OF DANNY WILLIAMS (EP)	15
61	HMV CLP 1458	DANNY (LP, mono)	20
61	HMV CSD 1369	DANNY (LP, stereo)	25
61	HMV CLP 1521	MOON RIVER AND OTHER TITLES (LP)	20
62	HMV CLP 1605	SWINGING FOR YOU (LP, mono)	15
62	HMV CSD 1471	SWINGING FOR YOU (LP, stereo)	20
66	HMV CLP/CSD 3523	ONLY LOVE (LP)	30
66	Woman's Privilege AZ 3	ROMANCE WITH DANNY WILLIAMS (LP, mail-order via Woman magazine)	12
67	Deram DML 1017	DANNY WILLIAMS (LP)	20

DEL WILLIAMS

72	Grape GR 3027	Searching For Your Love/G.G. ALL STARS: Searching (Version)	5

DELROY WILLIAMS

71	Trojan TR 7813	Down In The Boondocks/Baby Make It	7
76	Treble C CCC 013	Red, Green And Gold (In My Garden)/Let's Be People	8

GEORGE WILLIAMS & HIS ORCHESTRA

55	Vogue Coral Q 72053	The Rompin' Stomper/Knock-Out Choo-Choo	8
56	HMV DLP 1140	RHYTHM WAS HIS BUSINESS (10" LP)	15

GEORGE WILLIAMS

69	Bullet BU 405	No Business Of Yours/Mast It Up (actually titled "Mash It Up")	35

GRANVILLE WILLIAMS ORCHESTRA

(see also Silvertones)

67	Island WI 3062	Hi-Life/More	12
67	Island ILP 971	HI-LIFE (LP)	60

HANK WILLIAMS (& HIS DRIFTING COWBOYS)

(see also Audrey Williams)

78s

50	MGM MGM 269	Lovesick Blues/Wedding Bells	10
51	MGM MGM 381	Moanin' The Blues/The Blues Come Around	10
51	MGM MGM 405	Dear John/Fly Trouble	10
51	MGM MGM 454	Hey, Good Lookin'/Howlin' At The Moon	10
51	MGM MGM 459	Cold, Cold Heart/I'm A Long Gone Daddy	10
52	MGM MGM 471	I Can't Help It (If I'm Still In Love With You)/Baby, We're Really In Love	10
52	MGM MGM 483	Why Don't You Love Me/I'd Still Want You	10
52	MGM MGM 505	Honky-Tonk Blues/I'm Sorry For You, My Friend	10
52	MGM MGM 527	Long Gone Lonesome Blues/Half As Much	10
52	MGM MGM 553	Nobody's Lonesome For Me/Mind Your Own Business	10
52	MGM MGM 566	Jambalaya (On The Bayou)/Settin' The Woods On Fire	10
53	MGM MGM 585	I'll Never Get Out Of This World Alive/I Could Never Be Ashamed Of You (as Hank Williams & His Drifting Cowboys)	10
53	MGM MGM 609	Kaw-Liga/Take These Chains From My Heart (& His Drifting Cowboys)	10
53	MGM MGM 630	I Saw The Light/ARTHUR 'GUITAR BOOGIE' SMITH: Recitation Sonny Smith: In Memory Of Hank Williams	10
53	MGM MGM 652	Ramblin' Man/I Won't Be Home No More	10
53	MGM MGM 666	My Bucket's Got A Hole In It/Let's Turn Back The Years	10
53	MGM MGM 678	Window Shopping/You Win Again	10
54	MGM MGM 704	Weary Blues (From Waitin')/I Can't Escape From You	10
54	MGM MGM 733	There'll Be No Teardrops Tonight/Crazy Heart	10
54	MGM MGM 768	I'm Satisfied With You/I Ain't Got Nothin' But Time	10
55	MGM MGM 799	I'm Gonna Sing/California Zephyr	10
56	MGM MGM 896	Your Cheatin' Heart/A Teardrop On A Rose	10
56	MGM MGM 921	There's No Room In My Heart (For The Blues)/I Wish I Had A Nickel	10
56	MGM MGM 931	Blue Love (In My Heart)/Singing Waterfall	10

MINT VALUE £

57	MGM MGM 942	Low Down Blues/My Sweet Love Ain't Around	10
57	MGM MGM 957	Rootie Tootie/Lonesome Whistle	10
57	MGM MGM 966	Leave Me Alone With The Blues/With Tears In My Eyes	10

SINGLES

53	MGM SP 1016	I'll Never Get Out Of This World Alive/I Could Never Be Ashamed Of You (as Hank Williams & His Drifting Cowboys)	50
53	MGM SP 1034	Kaw-Liga/Take These Chains From My Heart (& His Drifting Cowboys)	50
53	MGM SP 1049	Ramblin' Man/I Won't Be Home No More	40
53	MGM SP 1048	My Bucket's Got A Hole In It/Let's Turn Back The Years	40
54	MGM SP 1067	Weary Blues (From Waitin')/I Can't Escape From You	40
54	MGM SP 1085	There'll Be No Teardrops Tonight/Crazy Heart	40
54	MGM SP 1102	I'm Satisfied With You/I Ain't Got Nothin' But Time	40
56	MGM SP 1163	The First Fall Of Snow/Someday You'll Call My Name (unreleased)	0
56	MGM MGM 921	There's No Room In My Heart (For The Blues)/I Wish I Had A Nickel	30
56	MGM MGM 931	Blue Love (In My Heart)/Singing Waterfall	30
57	MGM MGM 942	Low Down Blues/My Sweet Love Ain't Around	30
57	MGM MGM 957	Rootie Tootie/Lonesome Whistle	30
57	MGM MGM 966	Leave Me Alone With The Blues/With Tears In My Eyes	30
66	MGM MGM 1309	You Win Again/I'm So Lonesome I Could Cry	5
66	MGM MGM 1322	Kaw-Liga/Let's Turn Back The Years	5

EPs

54	MGM MGM-EP 512	HANK WILLIAMS AND HIS DRIFTING COWBOYS (company sleeve)	25
54	MGM EPC 7	HANK WILLIAMS (export issue)	30
55	MGM MGM-EP 551	JUST WAITIN' (as Luke The Drifter, company sleeve)	20
55	MGM MGM-EP 551	JUST WAITIN' (as Luke The Drifter, later issue with p/s)	30
56	MGM MGM-EP 569	I SAW THE LIGHT (No. 1) (company sleeve)	15
56	MGM MGM-EP 569	I SAW THE LIGHT (No. 1) (later issue with p/s)	20
57	MGM MGM-EP 582	HONKY TONKIN'	20
57	MGM MGM-EP 608	I SAW THE LIGHT (No. 2)	20
57	MGM MGM-EP 614	HONKY TONK BLUES	20
58	MGM MGM-EP 639	SONGS FOR A BROKEN HEART (No. 1)	20
58	MGM MGM-EP 649	SONGS FOR A BROKEN HEART (No. 2)	20
58	MGM MGM-EP 675	HANK'S LAMENTS	20
60	MGM MGM-EP 710	THE UNFORGETTABLE HANK WILLIAMS	20
60	MGM MGM-EP 726	THE UNFORGETTABLE HANK WILLIAMS (No. 2)	20
60	MGM MGM-EP 732	THE UNFORGETTABLE HANK WILLIAMS (No. 3)	20
61	MGM MGM-EP 757	HANK WILLIAMS FAVOURITES	20
63	MGM MGM-EP 770	THE AUTHENTIC SOUND OF THE COUNTRY HITS	20

ALBUMS

52	MGM MGM-D 105	HANK WILLIAMS SINGS (10" LP, company sleeve)	40
52	MGM MGM-D 105	HANK WILLIAMS SINGS (10" LP, later issue in p/s)	50
53	MGM MGM-D 119	HANK WILLIAMS AS LUKE THE DRIFTER (10" LP, company sleeve)	30
53	MGM MGM-D 119	HANK WILLIAMS AS LUKE THE DRIFTER (10" LP, later issue in p/s)	40
55	MGM MGM-D 137	HANK WILLIAMS MEMORIAL ALBUM (10")	40
56	MGM MGM-D 144	MOANIN' THE BLUES (10")	50
58	MGM MGM-D 150	SING ME A BLUE SONG (10")	40
58	MGM MGM-D 154	THE IMMORTAL HANK WILLIAMS (10")	40
59	MGM MGM-C 784	THE UNFORGETTABLE HANK WILLIAMS	20
60	MGM MGM-C 811	THE LONESOME SOUND OF HANK WILLIAMS	30
60	MGM MGM-C 834	WAIT FOR THE LIGHT TO SHINE	20
62	MGM MGM-C 893	ON STAGE	20
63	MGM MGM-C 956	THE SPIRIT OF HANK WILLIAMS	20
66	MGM MGM-C 8019	MAY YOU NEVER BE ALONE	15
66	MGM MGM-C 8020	IN MEMORY OF HANK WILLIAMS	15
66	MGM MGM-C 8021	I'M BLUE INSIDE	20
66	MGM MGM-C 8022	LUKE THE DRIFTER	15
66	MGM MGM-C 8023	THE MANY MOODS OF HANK WILLIAMS	15
67	MGM MGM-C(S) 8031	THE LEGEND LIVES ANEW	15
67	MGM MGM-C(S) 8038	MORE HANK WILLIAMS AND STRINGS	15
67	MGM MGM-C 8040	LOVE SONGS, COMEDY AND HYMNS	20
79	World Records SM 551-556	THE LEGENDARY HANK WILLIAMS (6-LP box set)	25

HANK WILLIAMS & HANK WILLIAMS Jr.

65	MGM MGM-C 1008	SINGING TOGETHER (LP)	12

HANK WILLIAMS Jr.

(see also Connie Francis)

64	MGM C978	SINGS THE SONGS OF HANK WILLIAMS (LP)	12
64	MGM MGM-C 996	YOUR CHEATIN' HEART (LP)	12
67	MGM MGM-C(S) 8049	MY OWN WAY (LP)	12
70	MGM MGM-CS 8116	LIVE AT COBO HALL, DETROIT (LP)	12

JEANETTE WILLIAMS

(see also Swamp Dogg, Brooks & Jerry)

69	Action ACT 4534	Stuff/You Gotta Come Through	8
70	Action ACT 4557	Hound Dog/I Can Feel A Heartbreak	8

(LITTLE) JERRY WILLIAMS

65	Cameo Parkway C 100	Baby You're My Everything/Just What Do You Plan To Do About It	85
65	Cameo Parkway C 100	Baby You're My Everything/Just What Do You Plan To Do About It (DJ Copy)	120
74	Pye Disco Demand DDS 102	If You Ask Me/ Yvonne (as Jerry Williams)	8

JIMMY WILLIAMS

65	Atlantic AT 4042	Walking On Air/I'm So Lost	30

JOE WILLIAMS

(see also Count Basie)

59	Columbia SCD 2116	Party Blues Parts 1 & 2	6

MINT VALUE £

60 Columbia DB 4560 Somebody/One Is A Lonesome Number 6
58 Columbia SEG 7810 JOE WILLIAMS WITH COUNT BASIE (EP) 15
59 Columbia SEG 7984 BALLADS AND BLUES COLUMBIA (EP) 10
59 Columbia/Clef SEB 10110 GROOVY JOE WILLIAMS (EP) 10
60 Columbia SEG 8001 EVERYDAY I HAVE THE BLUES (EP) 10
60 Columbia SEG 8016 JOE SINGS THE BLUES (EP) 10
56 London HB-C 1065 JOE WILLIAMS SINGS (10" LP) 25
57 HMV CLP 1109 THE GREATEST (LP) 20
58 Columbia 33SX 1087 A MAN AIN'T SUPPOSED TO CRY (LP) 25
60 Columbia 33SX 1229 JOE WILLIAMS SINGS ABOUT YOU (LP, mono) 12
60 Columbia SCX 3308 JOE WILLIAMS SINGS ABOUT YOU (LP, stereo) 15
60 Columbia 33SX 1253 THAT KIND OF WOMAN (LP, mono) 12
60 Columbia SCX 3325 THAT KIND OF WOMAN (LP, stereo) 15
61 Columbia SX 1392 TOGETHER (LP, with Harry "Sweets" Edison, also stereo SCX 3421) 15

JOHN WILLIAMS

(see also Maureeny Wishfull)

67 Columbia DB 8128 She's That Kind Of Woman/My Ways Are Set 12
67 Columbia DB 8251 Flowers In Your Hair/Can't Find Time For Anything Now 10
67 Columbia SX 6169 JOHN WILLIAMS (LP) 100

JOHN WILLIAMS

84 Island IS 155 Paul McCartney's Theme From 'The Honorary Consul'/Clara's Theme (p/s) 7

JOHN WILLIAMS ORCHESTRA (U.S.)

66 Stateside S(S)L 10187 HOW TO STEAL A MILLION (LP, soundtrack) 25
83 MCA MCA 70000 E.T. - THE EXTRA TERRESTRIAL (LP, soundtrack, box set with booklet & poster) 30
83 MCA CAC 70000 E.T. - THE EXTRA TERRESTRIAL (cassette, soundtrack box set with booklet & poster) 30

KENNETH WILLIAMS

(see also Rambling Syd Rumpo, Tony Hancock)

67 Decca LK 4856 ON PLEASURE BENT (LP) 15

LARRY WILLIAMS

57 London HLN 8472 Short Fat Fannie/High School Dance 50
58 London HLN 8532 Bony Moronie/You Bug Me Baby 30
58 London HLU 8604 Dizzy Miss Lizzy/Slow Down 40
58 London HLU 8604 Dizzy Miss Lizzy/Slow Down (78) 25
59 London HLU 8844 She Said "Yeah"/Bad Boy 30
59 London HLU 8844 She Said "Yeah"/Bad Boy (78) 30
60 London HLU 8911 I Can't Stop Loving You/Steal A Little Kiss 30
60 London HLU 8911 I Can't Stop Loving You/Steal A Little Kiss (78) 50
60 London HLM 9053 Baby, Baby/Get Ready 30
65 Sue WI 371 Strange/Call On Me 40
65 Sue WI 381 Turn On Your Lovelight/Dizzy Miss Lizzy 40
68 MGM MGM 1447 Shake Your Body Girl/Love, I Can't Seem To Find It 20
59 London RE-U 1213 LARRY WILLIAMS (EP) 125
65 Sue ILP 922 LARRY WILLIAMS ON STAGE (LP) 80
70s Speciality SNTF 5025 SLOW DOWN (LP) 20
70s Speciality SNTF 5008 ORIGINAL HITS (LP) 20

LARRY WILLIAMS & JOHNNY 'GUITAR' WATSON

(see also Johnny 'Guitar' Watson, Philip Goodhand-Tait [& Stormville Shakers])

65 Decca F 12151 Sweet Little Baby/Slow Down 20
67 Columbia DB 8140 Mercy, Mercy, Mercy/A Quitter Never Wins 75
67 Columbia DB 8140 Mercy, Mercy, Mercy/A Quitter Never Wins (DJ copy) 175
76 Epic EPC 4421 Too Late/Two For The Price Of One 20
65 Decca LK 4691 THE LARRY WILLIAMS SHOW (LP, with Stormsville Shakers) 80

LEONA WILLIAMS

74 Fountain FB 303 LEONA WILLIAMS AND HER DIXIE BAND (LP) 12

LEVI WILLIAMS

75 Locks LOX 5 Come Me Breda/MIGHTY CLOUD BAND: Call Mi Sister 5

LEW WILLIAMS

50s London (no cat. no.) Cat Talk (1-sided, orange label demo-only) 50

LLOYD WILLIAMS

66 Doctor Bird DB 1051 Sad World/TOMMY McCOOK'S BAND: A Little Bit Of Heaven 30
68 Treasure Isle TI 7029 Funky Beat/Goodbye Baby 22
68 Doctor Bird DB 1135 Wonderful World (with Tommy McCook)/TOMMY McCOOK SUPERSONICS: Mad Mad World 35
70 Bamboo BAM 41 I'm In Love With You/Little Girl 30

LORETTA WILLIAMS

66 Atlantic 584 032 Baby Cakes/I'm Missing You 45

LUCINDA WILLIAMS

89 Rough Trade 130 LUCINDA WILLIAMS (LP, with inner lyric bag) 12

LUTHER WILLIAMS ORCHESTRA

61 Limbo XL 101 Early In The Morning/Little Vilma 5
61 Melodisc MLP 12-125 TROPICAL RHYTHMS OF JAMAICA (LP) 15

MARY LOU WILLIAMS

64 Sue WI 311 Chuck-a-Lunk Jug (Parts 1 & 2) 25
55 Vogue EPV 1042 DON CARLOS MEETS MARY LOU WILLIAMS (EP) 10
56 Parlophone GEP 8567 AT THE PIANO (EP) 10
56 Columbia SEG 7608 MARY LOU WILLIAMS (EP) 10
55 Esquire EP 66 MARY LOU WILLIAMS QUARTET (EP) 10

			MINT VALUE £
53	Vogue LDE 022	PLAYS IN LONDON (10" LP)	20
54	Esquire 20-026	PIANO PANORAMA (10" LP)	20
55	Felsted EDL 87012	IN PARIS (10" LP)	20

MASON WILLIAMS

68	Warner Bros WB 7190	Classical Gas/Long Time Blues	6

MAURICE WILLIAMS (& ZODIACS)

(see also Gladiolas)

60	Top Rank JAR 526	Stay/Do You Believe (as Maurice Williams & Zodiacs)	20
61	Top Rank JAR 550	I Remember/Always	20
61	Top Rank JAR 563	Come Along/Do I	30
61	Top Rank JKP 3006	STAY WITH MAURICE WILLIAMS & THE ZODIACS (EP)	175

MIKE WILLIAMS

66	Atlantic 584 027	Lonely Soldier/If This Isn't Love	22

MOON WILLIAMS

73	DJM DJS10283	Forever Kind Of Love/All For You	250

OTIS WILLIAMS & HIS CHARMS

(see also Charms)

55	Parlophone CMSP 36	Ivory Tower/In Paradise (export issue)	300
56	Parlophone MSP 6239	Ivory Tower/In Paradise	400
56	Parlophone R 4175	Ivory Tower/In Paradise (78)	15
56	Parlophone R 4210	One Night Only/It's All Over	375
56	Parlophone R 4210	One Night Only/It's All Over (78)	25
57	Parlophone R 4293	Walkin' After Midnight/I'm Waiting Just For You	400
57	Parlophone R 4293	Walkin' After Midnight/I'm Waiting Just For You (78)	50
58	Parlophone R 4495	The Secret/Don't Wake Up The Kids	100
58	Parlophone R 4495	The Secret/Don't Wake Up The Kids (78)	70
62	Parlophone R 4860	The Secret/Two Hearts	60

PAUL WILLIAMS BIG ROLL BAND/SET

(see also Zoot Money's Big Roll Band, John Mayall's Bluesbreakers, Alan Price [Set], Juicy Lucy)

64	Columbia DB 7421	Gin House/Rockin' Chair (as Paul Williams Big Roll Band)	20
65	Columbia DB 7768	The Many Faces Of Love/Jumpback (as Paul Williams & Zoot Money Band)	30
68	Decca F 12844	My Sly Sadie/Stop The Wedding (as Paul Williams Set)	15

PAUL WILLIAMS

70s	Parry Music Library PML 168	AQUARIUS (LP)	18

PAUL WILLIAMS

73	Sonet SNTF 654	DELTA BLUES SINGER (LP)	15

PAUL WILLIAMS

74	A&M AMS 7125	That's What Friends Are For/Born To Fly	8
74	A&M AMLS 63653	PHANTOM OF THE PARADISE (LP, soundtrack)	20

PAULINE WILLIAMS

73	Explosion EX 2084	My Island/My Island (Version)	5

PIP WILLIAMS

75	RCA 2511	Hey Mr Record Man/Nightmare	6

POOR JOE WILLIAMS

(see also Big Joe Williams)

60	Collector JEN 3	A MAN SINGS THE BLUES (EP)	10
60	Collector JEN 4	A MAN SINGS THE BLUES VOL. 2 (EP)	10

PRINCE WILLIAMS

73	Atra ATRA 004	Action Wood Pt. 1/Action Wood Pt. 2	5

RANNY/RONNY WILLIAMS

(see also Winston Reed)

69	Bullet BU 426	Summer Place (with Hippy Boys)/Big Boy	10
69	Gas GAS 120	Throw Me Corn (as Ronny Williams)/HIPPY BOYS: Temptation	10
69	Unity UN 526	Ambitious Beggar/Pepper Seed	18
70	Punch PH 32	Smile/Musical I.D.	10

RITA WILLIAMS

58	Oriole CB 1417	Looking For Someone To Love/Love Me Forever	10
70	Gemini GMS 011	You're Nearer/With Love From Amsterdam	6

ROBBIE WILLIAMS

(see also Take That)

96	RCA FREELX 1	Freedom '96 (Radio Edit)/Freedom '96 (Full Length Version) (jukebox issue)	8
96	RCA PROPERDJ 1	Freedom '96 (Radio Edit)/Freedom '96 (Full Length Version) (CD, test pressing, no text on disc)	20
97	Chrysalis CHSLH 5055	Old Before I Die/Making Plans For Nigel (jukebox issue)	6
97	Chrysalis CDCHSDJ 5055	Old Before I Die (CD, withdrawn, different sleeve)	15
97	Chrysalis CHSLH 5063	Lazy Days/Teenage Millionaire (jukebox issue)	6
97	Chrysalis CHSLH 5068	South Of The Border/Cheap Love Song (jukebox issue)	6
98	Chrysalis 12CHSDJD 5080	Let Me Entertain You (remixes) (12", double-pack)	12
98	Chrysalis/HMV HMV 78	Millennium/ROYAL ALBERT HALL ORCHESTRA: Nimrod, Enigma Variations Op. 36 (78rpm, promo only, 1,000 only, numbered p/s)	25
99	Chrysalis CHSLH 5107	Strong/Antmusic (jukebox issue)	6
99	Chrysalis CDCHSLH 5112	It's Only Us/She's The One (jukebox issue)	6
00	Chrysalis CDCHSLH 5118	Rock DJ/She's The One (jukebox issue)	6
06	Chrysalis CDCHSDJX5162	Lovelight (CD, 9 remixes, promo, p/s)	12
97	Chrysalis RWEPK 01	THE EPK CD (interview and excerpts from "Life Thru A Lens")	25
98	Chrysalis CDPP 080	I'VE BEEN EXPECTING YOU (metal case with album CD, interview disc in digipak, EPK video in p/s, gold press release and photos)	150

ROBERT WILLIAMS

90	Blast First FU8	CHROME, FIRE AND SMOKE (2-LP, picture disc, 1000 only)	25

MINT VALUE £

ROBERT PETE WILLIAMS

63	77' LA 12-17	THOSE PRISON BLUES (LP)	35
70s	Blues Beacon 1932 101ST	SUGAR FARM (LP)	25
72	Saydisc AMS 2002	ROBERT PETE WILLIAMS (LP)	18
73	Sonet SNTF 649	LEGACY OF THE BLUES (LP)	12

ROBERT PETE WILLIAMS/ROOSEVELT SYKES

(see also Roosevelt Sykes)

67	77' LEU 12-50	BLUES FROM THE BOTTOM (LP)	25

ROCKMORE WILLIAMS

73	Mooncrest Moon 15	Lady Rock/Junkyard Blues	12

ROGER WILLIAMS

(see also Jane Morgan)

55	London HLU 8214	Autumn Leaves/Take Care	10
56	London HLU 8341	Two Different Worlds (with Jane Morgan)/I'll Always Walk With You	8
57	London HLU 8379	Anastasia/A Serenade For Joy	6
58	London HA-R 2089	THE BOY NEXT DOOR (LP)	12

SAM WILLIAMS

78	Grapevine GRP 116	Love Slipped Thru' My Fingers/TOWANDA BARNES: You Don't Mean It	25

SID WILLIAMS

77	ATA ATA 1001	Don't Play That Rock 'N' Roll/Time To Spare	8

SIL WILLIAMS

69	Wolf WM 04	Reggae Moon Rising/People Get Ready	10

SMITTY WILLIAMS

62	MGM MGM 1167	The Cure/Oh Seymour	7

SONNY WILLIAMS

59	London HLD 8931	Bye Bye Baby Goodbye/Lucky Linda	45
59	London HLD 8931	Bye Bye Baby Goodbye/Lucky Linda (78)	20

SPARKIE WILLIAMS

58	Parlophone R 4475	Sparkie Williams/Sparkie the Fiddle	7

SYLVIAN WILLIAMS

69	Big Shot BI 532	Sweeter Than Honey/Son Of Reggae	35
69	Big Shot BI 533	This Old Man/When Morning Comes	7

TEX WILLIAMS

(see also Roberta Lee, Rex Allen)

54	Brunswick 05327	River Of No Return/Dawn In The Meadow	10
54	Brunswick 05341	This Ole House (with Rex Allen)/They Were Doin' The Mambo	10
55	Brunswick 05393	Money/If You'd Believe Me	10
56	Brunswick 05516	Be Sure You're Right (And Then Go Ahead)/Old Betsy	5
57	Brunswick 05684	Talkin' To The Blues/Every Night (with Anita Kerr Singers)	6
60	Top Rank JAR 330	The Keeper Of Boothill/Bummin' Around	6

TOMMY WILLIAMS

76	Free Reed FRR 008	SPRINGTIME IN BATTERSEA (LP, gatefold sleeve)	18

TONY WILLIAMS

(see also Platters, Linda Hayes)

61	Reprise RS 20019	Sleepless Nights/Mandolino Mandolino	10
61	Reprise RS 20030	My Prayer/Miracle	10
63	Philips BF 1282	How Come/When I Had You	100
60	Mercury MMC 14027	A GIRL IS A GIRL IS A GIRL (LP)	40
61	Reprise R 6001	SINGS HIS GREATEST HITS (LP, mono)	20
61	Reprise ST R9 6006	SINGS HIS GREATEST HITS (LP, stereo)	30

TONY WILLIAMS' LIFETIME

(see also Lifetime, John McLaughlin)

69	Polydor 583 574	EMERGENCY! (2-LP, gatefold sleeve)	45
70	Polydor 2425 019	TURN IT OVER (LP)	25
71	Polydor 2425 065	EGO (LP, textured gatefld sleeve)	35

TREVOR WILLIAMS

75	Virgin VS 122	Lucy Brown/We Slowed Down	5

WILLIE WILLIAMS, JACKIE MITTOO & MARSHAL COUSINS

79	Ziggy FDP 001	Rocking Universally/JACKIE MITTOO & BONGO GENE: Universal Rock (12")	30

WILLY WILLIAMS

81	Black Roots BR 017	Come Mek We Rally/YABBY YOU: Thirty Pieces Of Silver (12")	45
83	WLN WLN 004	Repatriation/Come Along/Armagideon Time/Justice Tonight (12")	10

WINSTON WILLIAMS

70	Jackpot JP 733	D.J.'s Choice/SLIM SMITH: Can't Do Without It (B-side actually titled "Lesson/Story Of Love" by Uniques)	12
70	Jackpot JP 743	The People's Choice/BOBBY JAMES: Let Me Go Girl	12
71	Jackpot JP 757	Love Version/SLIM SMITH: Ball Of Confusion	12

BOBBY WILLIAMSON

54	HMV 7MC 26	Sh-Boom/Love March (export issue)	20

DUDLEY WILLIAMSON

(see also Dudley & Attractions)

67	Doctor Bird DB 1117	Coming On The Scene/Anything You Want	60

MARK WILLIAMSON

70s	Myrrh MYR 1154	MISSING IN ACTION (LP)	15

ROBIN WILLIAMSON

(see also Incredible String Band, Vashti Bunyan)

72	Island HELP 2	MYRRH (LP, textured sleeve, black label with pink 'i' logo)	35
78	Criminal STEAL 4	AMERICAN STONEHENGE (LP)	12

MINT VALUE £

SONNY BOY WILLIAMSON (I)

69	Matchbox SDR 169	SONNY BOY AND HIS PALS (LP)	30
70	RCA Intl. INTS 1088	BLUEBIRD BLUES (LP)	15

SONNY BOY WILLIAMSON (I)/BIG BILL BROONZY

65	RCA Victor RD 7685	BIG BILL BROONZY/SONNY BOY WILLIAMSON (LP)	40

SONNY BOY WILLIAMSON (II)

(see also Ottilie Patterson)

63	Pye International 7N 25191	Help Me/Bye Bye Bird	25
64	Pye International 7N 25268	Lonesome Cabin/The Goat	20
65	Sue WI 365	No Nights By Myself/Boppin' With Sonny Boy	40
66	Chess CRS 8030	Bring It On Home/Down Child	20
66	Blue Horizon 45-1008	From The Bottom/Empty Bedroom	80
64	Pye Intl. NEP 44037	SONNY BOY WILLIAMSON (EP)	25
65	Chess CRE 6001	HELP ME (EP)	35
66	Chess CRE 6013	IN MEMORIAM (EP)	35
66	Chess CRE 6018	REAL FOLK BLUES VOL. 2 (EP)	30
64	Pye Intl. NPL 28036	DOWN AND OUT BLUES (LP)	60
64	Storyville SLP 158	PORTRAITS IN BLUES, VOL. 4 (LP)	40
65	Chess CRL 4510	IN MEMORIAM (LP)	50
66	Storyville SLP 170	THE BLUES OF SONNY BOY WILLIAMSON (LP)	22
66	Fontana 670 158	PORTRAITS IN BLUES, VOL. 4 (LP, reissue)	30
67	Storyville 671 170	THE BLUES OF SONNY BOY WILLIAMSON (LP, reissue)	25
68	Marmalade 607/608 004	DON'T SEND ME NO FLOWERS (LP, with Brian Auger & Jimmy Page)	80
74	Rarity RLP 1	THE LAST SESSIONS - 1963 (LP)	25

SONNY BOY WILLIAMSON (II) & YARDBIRDS

(see also Yardbirds, Brian Auger)

65	Fontana TL 5277	SONNY BOY WILLIAMSON & THE YARDBIRDS (LP)	175
68	Fontana SFJL 960	SONNY BOY WILLIAMSON & THE YARDBIRDS (LP, reissue, different sleeve)	30
71	Philips 6435 011	SONNY BOY WILLIAMSON & THE YARDBIRDS (LP, 2nd reissue)	18

STU WILLIAMSON

56	London Jazz LZ-N 14030	SAPPHIRE (10" LP)	20

WILLIE AND THE RED RUBBER BAND

69	RCA 1842	Mary Jane/Chicky Chicky Boom Boom	12

WILLIE & ANTHONY

75	Jay Boy BOY 94	Sugar Sugar Sugar/It's Never Too Late	30

WILLIE (Francis) & LLOYD (Lindsay)

(see also Willie Francis)

71	Camel CA 80	Marcus Is Alive/GLADIATORS: Freedom Train	12

WILLIE & WHEELS

(see also P.F. Sloan,Grass Roots, Fantastic Baggys')

77	ABC ABC 4184	Skateboard Craze/Do What You Did (p/s)	10

DORIS WILLINGHAM

69	Jay Boy BOY 1	You Can't Do That/Lost Again	15

CHUCK WILLIS

57	London HLE 8444	C.C. Rider/Ease The Pain	80
57	London HLE 8444	C.C. Rider/Ease The Pain (78)	30
57	London HLE 8489	That Train Has Gone/Love Me Cherry	80
57	London HLE 8489	That Train Has Gone/Love Me Cherry (78)	20
58	London HLE 8595	Betty And Dupree/My Crying Eyes	80
58	London HLE 8595	Betty And Dupree/My Crying Eyes (78)	20
58	London HLE 8635	What Am I Living For/Hang Up My Rock And Roll Shoes	50
58	London HLE 8635	What Am I Living For/Hang Up My Rock And Roll Shoes (78)	25
58	London HL 7039	What Am I Living For/Hang Up My Rock And Roll Shoes (export issue)	30
59	London HLE 8818	My Life/Thunder And Lightning	45
59	London HLE 8818	My Life/Thunder And Lightning (78)	430
59	Fontana TFE 17138	CHUCK WILLIS WAILS (EP)	300
65	Atlantic ATL 5003	I REMEMBER CHUCK WILLIS (LP)	80
69	Atlantic 588 145	I REMEMBER CHUCK WILLIS (LP, reissue)	20

DOUG WILLIS

97	Z Records ZEDD 12029	Get Your Own (12")	10

HAL WILLIS

68	President PT 197	The Lumberjack/Klondike Mike	12

LARRY WILLIS

74	People PLEO 2	INNER CRISIS (LP)	20

LLOYD WILLIS

(see also Dynamic Gang, Urie Aldridge)

70	Pressure Beat PR 5502	Mad Rooster (Parts 1 & 2)/As Far As I Can See (actually "The Wicked Must Survive" by Reggae Boys)	15
70	Unity UN 543	Ivan Hitler The Conqueror/The Splice	30

RALPH WILLIS

54	Esquire 10-370	Lazy Woman Blues/Goodbye Blues (78)	20
54	Esquire 10-380	Old Home Blues/Salty Dog (78)	20
61	Esquire EP 241	RALPH WILLIS (EP)	40

SLIM WILLIS

65	R&B MRB 5004	Running Around/No Feeling For You	30

TIMMY WILLIS

72	United Artists UP 35352	Mr. Soul Satisfaction/I'm Wondering	8

MINT VALUE £

WILL-O-BEES
67 CBS 3263 It's Not Easy/Looking Glass ... 15

NEVILLE WILLOUGHBY
(see also Neville, Whistling Willie)
72 Duke DU 140 Wheel And Tun Me/Hey Mama ... 5

WILLOWS
(see also Tony Middleton)
56 London HLU 8290 Church Bells May Ring/Baby Tell Me ... 800
56 London HLU 8290 Church Bells May Ring/Baby Tell Me (78) ... 140

BOB WILLS & HIS TEXAS PLAYBOYS
51 MGM MGM 455 'Tater Pie/Ida Red Likes The Boogie (78) ... 10
53 MGM MGM 613 Snatchin' And Grabbin'/I Want To Be Wanted (78) ... 10

BOB WILLS with TOMMY DUNCAN
60 London HL 7102 Heart To Heart Talk/What's The Matter With The Mill (export issue) ... 20

MICK WILLS
88 Woronzow WOO 9 FERN HILL (LP) ... 15
97 Acme AC 8013LP THE MAGIC GARDEN (LP, foldover gatefold sleeve in poly bag) ... 12

VIOLA WILLS
68 President PT 108 Lost Without The Love Of My Guy/I Got Love ... 10
68 President PT 150 Together Forever/Don't Kiss Me Hello And Mean Goodbye ... 10
68 President PT 152 I've Got To Have All Of You/Night Scene ... 8
68 President PT 154 You're Out Of My Mind/Any Time ... 8
74 Goodear EAR 103 Run To The Nearest Exit/Day In The Life Of A Woman ... 5

WILMER & DUKES
68 Action ACT 4500 Give Me One More Chance/Get It ... 12

ADA WILSON
(see also Strangeways)
79 Ellie Jay EJSP 9288 In The Quiet Of My Room/I'm In Control Here (p/s) ... 12
80 Barn BARN 012 In The Quiet Of My Room/I'm In Control Here (reissue, no p/s) ... 6

AL WILSON
68 Liberty LBF 15044 Do What You Gotta Do/Now I Know What Love Is ... 20
68 Liberty LBF 15121 The Snake/Who Could Be Lovin' You ... 20
69 Liberty LBF 15236 Shake Me Wake Me/I Stand Accused ... 8
69 Liberty LBF 15257 Lodi/By The Time I Get To Phoenix ... 8
75 Bell BLL 1436 The Snake/Willoughby Brook ... 8
69 Liberty LBS 83173 SEARCHING FOR THE DOLPHINS (LP) ... 20

BRIAN WILSON
(see also Beach Boys, Date With Soul, American Spring)
66 Capitol CL 15438 Caroline, No/Summer Means New Love ... 40
88 Sire W 7814 CD Love And Mercy (LP Version)/One For The Boys (LP Version)/
He Couldn't Get His Poor Old Body To Move (3" CD) ... 15
88 Sire W 7787 CD Night Time (LP Version)/One For The Boys/Being With The One You Love (3" CD) . 15
88 Sire W 7814 B LOVE AND MERCY (7" box set, with interview and postcards, limited edition) ... 55
98 Giant/Mojo 74321 58760 2 INTERVIEW/IMAGINATION (promo CD, with Peter Buck) ... 40
04 Nonesuch 7559-79869-7 Wonderful/Wind Chimes (three different coloured vinyl - blue, yellow,green) ... 18
04 Nonesuch 7559-79885-7 Good Vibrations/Our Prayer/Good Vibrations (live)(p/s) (Ltd edition) ... 10
05 Nonesuch 7559-798957 Our Prayer (Freeform Reform) (10" one sided clear vinyl in clear plastic sleeve) ... 12

BRIAN WILSON & MIKE LOVE
67 Capitol CL 15513 Gettin' Hungry/Devoted To You (as Brian Wilson & Mike Love) ... 30

CARL WILSON
(see also Beach Boys)
81 Caribou CRB 84840 CARL WILSON (LP, with lyric insert) ... 12
82 Caribou CRB 25225 YOUNGBLOOD (LP, with lyric Insert) ... 12

CLIVE WILSON
64 R&B JB 144 Mango Tree/Midnight In Chicago ... 22

COLIN WILSON
75 Tabitha TAB 101 CLOUDBURST (LP) ... 30

DELROY WILSON
(see also Hortense & Delroy, Joe Liges, Roy Richards, Soul Brothers, Dennis Alcapone, Stranger Cole, Uniques, Soul Vendors)
63 Island WI 097 Naughty People/I Shall Not Remove ... 25
63 Island WI 103 One, Two, Three/Back Biter ... 20
63 Island WI 116 You Bend My Love/Can't You See ... 20
63 R&B JB 108 Lion Of Judah/Joe Liges ... 30
63 R&B JB 128 Prince Pharoah/Don't Believe Him ... 30
63 R&B JB 132 Squeeze Your Toe/Sugar Pie ... 30
64 Black Swan WI 405 Spit In The Sky/Voodoo Man ... 25
64 Black Swan WI 420 Goodbye/Treat Me Good ... 20
64 R&B JB 148 Lover Mouth/Every Mouth Must Be Fed ... 25
64 R&B JB 168 Sammy Dead/CYNTHIA & ARCHIE: Every Beat ... 25
65 Island WI 205 Pick Up The Pieces/Oppression ... 18
66 Doctor Bird DB 1022 Give Me A Chance/(It's) Impossible ... 25
66 Island WI 3013 Dancing Mood/SOUL BROTHERS: More And More ... 30
67 Island WI 3033 Riding For A Fall/Got To Change Your Ways ... 25
67 Island WI 3037 Ungrateful Baby/ROY RICHARDS: Hopeful Village Ska ... 35
67 Island WI 3039 Close To Me/SOUL BROTHERS: Hi-Life ... 25
67 Island WI 3050 Get Ready/ROY RICHARDS: Port-O-Jam ... 45
67 Studio One SO 2009 Won't You Come Home Baby/PETER & HORTENSE: I've Been Lonely ... 50
67 Studio One SO 2014 Mother Word/HEPTONES: Fat Girl ... 30
67 Studio One SO 2019 Never Conquer/Run For Your Life ... 80

			MINT VALUE £
67	Studio One SO 2031	I'm Not A King/HEPTONES: Take Me (B-side actually by Soul Vendors)	50
68	Island WI 3099	This Old Heart Of Mine/GLEN ADAMS: Grab A Girl	50
68	Island WI 3127	Once Upon A Time/I Want To Love You (B-side actually with Stranger Cole)	80
68	Coxsone CS 7064	True Believer/MARSHALL WILLIAMS: College Girl	25
68	Studio One SO 2040	Mr. D.J./HEPTONES: Tripe Girl	60
68	Studio One SO 2046	Rain From The Skies/How Can I Love Someone	40
68	Studio One SO 2057	Feel Good All Over/I Like The Way You Walk	40
69	Studio One SO 2074	Easy Snappin'/WEBBER SISTERS: Come On	25
69	High Note HS 011	Put Yourself In My Place/It Hurts	12
69	High Note HS 015	I'm The One Who Loves You/AFROTONES: If I'm In A Corner	20
69	High Note HS 022	Your Number One/I've Tried My Best	20
69	High Note HS 028	Good To Me/What Do You Want Me To Do	12
69	Camel CA 15	Sad Mood (actually by Ken Parker)/STRANGER COLE: Give It To Me	30
70	Trojan TR 7740	Show Me The Way/BEVERLEY'S ALLSTARS: Version	10
70	Trojan TR 7769	Gave You My Love/BEVERLEY'S ALLSTARS: Version	10
70	Summit SUM 8503	Got To Get Away/BEVERLEY'S ALLSTARS: Version	8
70	Unity UN 559	Drink Wine, Everybody/Someone To Call My Own	6
71	Smash SMA 2317	I Am Trying/COLLINS ALLSTARS: Version	6
71	Smash SMA 2318	Satisfaction/Satisfaction Version (B-side with Alton Ellis)	40
71	Smash SMA 2323	What It Was/LLOYD CLARKE: Chicken Thief	7
71	Jackpot JP 763	Better Must Come/BUNNY LEE'S ALLSTARS: Better Must Come - Version	10
71	Jackpot JP 769	Cool Operator/I'm Yours	10
71	Jackpot JP 770	Try Again/AGGROVATORS: Try Again - Version	10
71	Jackpot JP 780	Keep Your Love Strong/Nice To Be Near	10
71	Jackpot JP 781	Peace And Love/JEFF BARNES: Who's Your Brother	12
71	Banana BA 333	Just Because Of You/I Love You Madly	10
72	Banana BA 367	You Keep On Running (& U Roy)/LARRY'S ALL STARS: Running Version	15
72	Bullet BU 520	Hear Come The Heartaches (actually "Here Come The Heartaches")/ You'll Be Sorry	8
72	Jackpot JP 792	Who Cares/HUGH ROY JUNIOR: Who Cares - Version	10
72	Jackpot JP 795	The Same Old Song/Stay By Me	10
72	Jackpot JP 804	Cheer Up/Loving You	10
72	Spur SP 2	Adis Ababa/KEITH HUDSON: Rudie Hot Stuff	50
73	Downtown DT 501	Pretty Girl/JOE GIBBS & PROFESSIONALS: Face Girl	8
73	Grape GR 3038	Can I Change My Mind/Just Because	10
73	Green Door GD 4060	Ain't That Peculiar/What Is Man	8
73	Smash SMA 2336	Trying To Wreck My Life/Live And Learn	10
73	Count Shelley CS 024	Never Give Up/I ROY: Problem Of Life	8
73	Count Shelley CS 047	Dum Dum/HORACE ANDY: Rasta Saw Them Coming	8
74	Faith FA 006	Love Got Me Doing Things/PHIL PRATT ALL STARS: Version	5
74	Harry J. HJ 6667	What Will Happen To The Youth Of Today/Baby Don't Do It	5
75	Fab FAB 266	Dancing Mood/Version	12
75	Attack ATT 8111	Seven Letters/Version	8
75	Attack ATT 8120	Honey Child/Time Is Running Out	6
76	Black Wax WAX 20	Mother Nature/CHANNEL ONE: Natural Version	6
77	Tribesman TM 002	What Is Man/Version	10
78	Burning Sounds BSD 017	All In This Together/Because I Am Black (12")	25
78	Burning Sounds BSD 018	Love Got Me Doing Things/Go Away Little Girl (12")	25
79	Cha Cha CHAD 10	Money Love/I Want To Love You (12")	20
79	E & J EJD1	Sharing The Night Together/I Won't Take You Back (12")	10
88	Conqueror LD 045	I Have Been In Love/NAGG MORRIS AND THE HEPTONES: You Want To Get I Out (12")	40
64	R&B JBL 1112	I SHALL NOT REMOVE (LP)	250
68	Coxsone CSL 8016	GOOD ALL OVER (LP)	100
72	Trojan TRLS 44	BETTER MUST COME (LP)	35
73	Big Shot BILP 102	CAPTIVITY (LP)	40
78	Burning Sounds BS 1020	LOVERS ROCK (LP)	20
79	Groundnation GROL 501	FOR I AND I (LP)	25

DENNIS WILSON (& RUMBO)

(see also Beach Boys)

70	Stateside SS 2184	Sound Of Free/Lady (as Dennis Wilson & Rumbo)	70
77	Caribou CRB 5663	River Song/Farewell My Friend	15
77	Caribou CRB 81672	PACIFIC OCEAN BLUE (LP, gatefold sleeve, lyric insert, on blue vinyl)	45
77	Caribou CRB 81672	PACIFIC OCEAN BLUE (LP, gatefold sleeve, lyric insert)	40

THE DIERDRE WILSON TABAC

69	RCA RCA 1880	Get Back/Angel Baby	30

DOYLE WILSON with JIMMY LACEY & BAND

58	Vogue Pop V 9117	Hey-Hey/You're The One For Me	600
58	Vogue Pop V 9117	Hey-Hey/You're The One For Me (7)	150

EDDIE WILSON

69	Action ACT 4536	Shing-A-Ling Stroll/Don't Kick The Teenager Around	15
70	Action ACT 4555	Get Out On The Street/Must Be Love	15

EDITH WILSON

60s	Fountain FB 302	1921-1922 WITH JOHNNY DUNN'S JAZZHOUNDS (LP)	15

ERNEST WILSON

78	Cha Cha CC 001	I Know Myself/REVOLUTIONARIES: I Know Myself Dub	12

ERNEST WILSON & FREDDY (McGregor)

70	Crab CRAB 45	Sentimental Man/It's A Lie	8
70	Unity UN 564	Love Makes The World Go Round/Love (Version Instrumental)	8
71	Gas GAS 168	What You Gonna Do About It/DOBBY DOBSON: Halfway To Paradise	8
71	Jackpot JP 765	Let Them Talk/The Truth Hurts	6

ERNEST ('SOUL') WILSON

(see also Tinga & Ernest)

67	Studio One SO 2032	Money Worries/SOUL VENDORS: Pe Da Pa	40
68	Studio One SO 2058	If I Were A Carpenter/SOUL VENDORS: Frozen Soul	40

MINT VALUE £

68	Coxsone CS 7044	Storybook Children (as Ernest 'Soul' Wilson)/LITTLE FREDDIE: After Laughter (B-side actually by Freddie McGregor)	30
68	Coxsone CS 7059	Undying Love/SOUL VENDORS: Tropic Isle	30
69	Amalgamated AMG 837	Private Number/GLEN ADAMS: She's So Fine	100
69	Crab CRAB 9	Private Number/Another Chance	12
69	Crab CRAB 17	Freedom Train/STRANGER COLE: You Should Never Have To Come	12
69	Crab CRAB 21	Just Once In My Life (with Freddy)/GLEN ADAMS: Mighty Organ	30
76	Fab FAB 280	Storybook Children/SOUND DIMENSION: Version	10

FRANK WILSON & CAVALIERS

64	Fontana TF 505	Last Kiss/That's How Much I Love You	12

FRANK WILSON

79	Tamla Motown TMG 1170	Do I Love You (Indeed I Do)/Sweeter As The Days Go By	50
79	Tamla Motown TMG 1170	Do I Love You (Indeed I Do)/Sweeter As The Days Go By (DJ copy)	50

GADDY WILSON

60	Philips PB 980	Nothin'At Night/I'll Never Be Myself Again (78)	10

GARLAND WILSON

53	HMV 7M 122	Just You, Just Me/Sweet Georgia Brown	6

GARY WILSON

80	Sourgrape SG 115	Movie Queen/Movie Queen (p/s)	6

JACK WILSON QUARTET

(see also Roy Ayers)

64	London HA-K/SH-K 8170	THE JACK WILSON QUARTET (LP, featuring Roy Ayers)	20
66	Vocalion LAE-L 603	RAMBLIN' (LP)	20

JACKIE WILSON

(see also Billy Ward & Dominoes, Clyde McPhatter, Count Basie, Chi-Lites, Linda Hopkins)

78s

57	Vogue Coral Q 72290	Reet Petite/By The Light Of The Silvery Moon	10
57	Coral Q 72290	Reet Petite/By The Light Of The Silvery Moon (2nd pressing)	10
58	Coral Q 72332	I'm Wanderin'/As Long As I Live	15
58	Coral Q 72338	We Have Love/Singing A Song	15
58	Coral Q 72347	Lonely Teardrops/In The Blue Of The Evening	40
59	Coral Q 72366	That's Why/Love Is All	40
59	Coral Q 72372	I'll Be Satisfied/Ask	50
59	Coral Q 72380	You Better Know It/Never Go Away	75
59	Coral Q 72384	Talk That Talk/Only You, Only Me	80

SINGLES

57	Vogue Coral Q 72290	Reet Petite/By The Light Of The Silvery Moon	25
57	Coral Q 72290	Reet Petite/By The Light Of The Silvery Moon (2nd pressing)	15
58	Coral Q 72306	To Be Loved/Come Back To Me	25
58	Coral Q 72332	I'm Wanderin'/As Long As I Live	25
58	Coral Q 72338	We Have Love/Singing A Song	22
58	Coral Q 72347	Lonely Teardrops/In The Blue Of The Evening	25
59	Coral Q 72366	That's Why/Love Is All	20
59	Coral Q 72366	That's Why/Love Is All (mispressing, B-side plays "You Better Know It")	15
59	Coral Q 72372	I'll Be Satisfied/Ask	15
59	Coral Q 72380	You Better Know It/Never Go Away	15
59	Coral Q 72384	Talk That Talk/Only You, Only Me	15
60	Coral Q 72393	Doggin' Around/The Magic Of Love	15
60	Coral Q 72407	A Woman, A Lover, A Friend/(You Were Made For) All My Love	20
60	Coral Q 72412	Alone At Last/Am I The Man	25
61	Coral Q 72421	The Tear Of The Year/My Empty Arms (withdrawn B-side, demos only)	65
61	Coral Q 72424	The Tear Of The Year/Your One And Only Love	15
61	Coral Q 72430	Please Tell Me Why/(So Many) Cute Little Girls	15
61	Coral Q 72434	I'm Comin' On Back To You/Lonely Life	15
61	Coral Q 72439	You Don't Know What It Means/Years From Now	15
61	Coral Q 72444	The Way I Am/My Heart Belongs To Only You	15
62	Coral Q 72450	The Greatest Hurt/There'll Be No Next Time	15
62	Coral Q 72453	Sing (And Tell The Blues So Long)/I Found Love (B-side with Linda Hopkins)	15
62	Coral Q 72454	I Just Can't Help It/My Tale Of Woe	15
63	Coral Q 72460	Baby Workout/What Good Am I Without You	15
63	Coral Q 72464	Shake A Hand/Say I Do (as Jackie Wilson & Linda Hopkins)	15
63	Coral Q 72465	Shake! Shake! Shake!/He's A Fool	15
63	Coral Q 72467	Baby Get It/The New Breed	15
64	Coral Q 72474	Big Boss Line/Be My Girl	15
64	Coral Q 72476	Squeeze Her - Tease Her (But Love Her)/Give Me Back My Heart	15
65	Coral Q 72480	Yes Indeed!/When The Saints Go Marching In (with Linda Hopkins)	18
65	Coral Q 72481	No Pity (In The Naked City)/I'm So Lonely	20
65	Coral Q 72481	No Pity (In The Naked City)/I'm So Lonely (DJ copy)	45
65	Coral Q 72482	I Believe I'll Love On/Lonely Teardrops	15
66	Coral Q 72484	To Make A Big Man Cry/Be My Love	20
66	Coral Q 72484	To Make A Big Man Cry/Be My Love (DJ copy)	45
66	Coral Q 72487	Whispers/The Fairest Of Them All	40
66	Coral Q 72487	Whispers/The Fairest Of Them All (DJ copy)	85
67	Coral Q 72493	(Your Love Keeps Lifting Me) Higher And Higher/I'm The One To Do It	20
67	Coral Q 72493	(Your Love Keeps Lifting Me) Higher And Higher/I'm The One To Do It (DJ copy)	85
67	Coral Q 72496	Since You Showed Me How To Be Happy/The Who-Who Song	30
67	Coral Q 72496	Since You Showed Me How To Be Happy/The Who-Who Song (DJ copy	75
68	MCA MU 1014	For Your Precious Love/Uptight (Everything's Alright) (with Count Basie)	10
68	Decca AD 1008	For Your Precious Love/Uptight (Everything's Alright) (export issue)	25
69	MCA Soul Bag BAG 2	(Your Love Keeps Lifting Me) Higher And Higher/Whispers (Gettin' Louder)	10
69	MCA Soul Bag BAG 7	Since You Showed Me How To Be Happy/Chain Gang	10
69	MCA MU 1104	Since You Showed Me How To Be Happy/The Who-Who Song (reissue)	10
69	MCA MU 1105	Helpless/Do It The Right Way	10

MINT VALUE £

70	MCA MU 1131	(Your Love Keeps Lifting Me) Higher And Higher/Whispers (Gettin' Louder) (reissue)	6
72	MCA MU 1160	I Get The Sweetest Feeling/Soul Galore	6
73	Brunswick BR 3	Beautiful Day/What'cha Gonna Do About Love	20
75	Brunswick BR 18	I Get The Sweetest Feeling/(Your Love Keeps Lifting Me) Higher And Higher	5
75	Brunswick BR 23	Whispers (Gettin' Louder)/Reet Petite	5
75	Brunswick BR 28	Don't Burn No Bridges/Don't Burn No Bridges (Instrumental) (with Chi-Lites)	5
70s	Brunswick BR 43	It Only Happens When I Look At You/Just As Soon As The Feeling's Over	75

EPs

59	Coral FEP 2016	JACKIE WILSON (triangular centre)	100
59	Coral FEP 2016	JACKIE WILSON (round centre)	70
60	Coral FEP 2043	THE DYNAMIC JACKIE WILSON (triangular centre)	100
60	Coral FEP 2043	THE DYNAMIC JACKIE WILSON (round centre)	70

LPs

58	Coral LVA 9087	HE'S SO FINE	150
59	Coral LVA 9108	LONELY TEARDROPS	150
60	Coral LVA 9121	SO MUCH	110
60	Coral LVA 9130	JACKIE SINGS THE BLUES	125
60	Coral LVA 9135	MY GOLDEN FAVOURITES	90
61	Coral LVA 9144	A WOMAN, A LOVER, A FRIEND	115
61	Coral LVA 9148	YOU AIN'T HEARD NOTHIN' YET	85
62	Coral LVA 9151	BY SPECIAL REQUEST (mono)	75
62	Coral SVL 3018	BY SPECIAL REQUEST (stereo)	90
62	Coral LVA 9202	BODY AND SOUL	65
63	Coral LVA 9209	JACKIE (mono)	70
63	Coral SVL 9209	JACKIE (stereo)	80
63	Coral LVA 9214	THE WORLD'S GREATEST MELODIES (mono)	55
63	Coral SVL 9214	THE WORLD'S GREATEST MELODIES (stereo)	65
66	Coral LVA 9231	SPOTLIGHT ON JACKIE WILSON	70
66	Coral LVA 9232	SOUL GALORE (mono)	70
66	Coral SVL 9232	SOUL GALORE (stereo)	80
67	Coral LVA 9235	WHISPERS	75
68	MCA MUP(S) 304	HIGHER AND HIGHER	20
68	MCA MUP(S) 333	TWO MUCH (with Count Basie & His Orchestra)	20
69	MCA MUPS 361	I GET THE SWEETEST FEELING	20
70	MCA MUPS 405	DO YOUR THING	25
73	Brunswick BRLS 3001	YOU GOT ME WALKIN'	25
73	Brunswick BRLS 3004	GREATEST HITS	15
75	Brunswick BRLS 3016	THE VERY BEST OF JACKIE WILSON	15

JACKIE WILSON/CLYDE McPHATTER

(see also Clyde McPhatter)

62	Ember JBS 705	Tenderly/CLYDE McPHATTER: Harbour Lights	250
62	Ember NR 5001	MEET BILLY WARD & THE DOMINOES (LP, 1 side each)	200

JOANNE WILSON

81	Red Stripe 2222	Gotta Have You Back/Part 2	12

JOE WILSON

71	Pye International 7N 25550	Sweetness/When A Man Cries	10

MARTY WILSON & STRAT-O-LITES

58	Brunswick 05750	Hey! Eula/Hedge-Hopper	20

MAYNELL WILSON (actually Wilson Maynell) & WESTMINSTER FIVE

(see also Wes[t]minster Five)

64	Carnival CV 7014	Hey Hey Johnny/Baby	10
67	CBM CBM 001	Motown Feeling/Mean Ole World (in p/s)	20
67	CBM CBM 001	Motown Feeling/Mean Ole World	10

MURRY WILSON

(see also Beach Boys)

67	Capitol CL 15525	Plumber's Tune/Love Won't Wait	8
67	Capitol (S)T 2819	THE MANY MOODS OF MURRY WILSON (LP)	20

NANCY WILSON

64	Capitol CL 15343	The Best Is Yet To Come/Never Let Me Go	5
64	Capitol CL 15352	(You Don't Know) How Glad I Am/Never Less Than Yesterday	10
65	Capitol CL 15378	Don't Come Running Back To Me/Love Has Many Faces	10
65	Capitol CL 15412	Where Does That Leave Me/Gentle Is My Love	20
66	Capitol CL 15443	Power Of Love/Rain Sometimes	12
66	Capitol CL 15466	You've Got Your Troubles/Uptight (Everything's Alright)	20
67	Capitol CL 15508	Don't Look Over Your Shoulder/Mercy, Mercy, Mercy	15
68	Capitol CL 15536	You Don't Know Me/Ode To Billie Joe	10
68	Capitol CL 15547	Face It Girl It's Over/The End Of Our Love	40
68	Capitol CL 15547	Face It Girl It's Over/The End Of Our Love (DJ copy)	80
75	Capitol CL 15810	You're Right As Rain/There'll Always Be Forever	5
77	Capitol CL 15547	End Of Our Love/Face It Girl, It's Over (white logo, reissue)	12
62	Capitol EAP1 20604	SECOND TIME AROUND (EP)	10
64	Capitol EAP4 2082	TODAY, TOMORROW, FOREVER (EP)	10
62	Capitol (S)T 1767	HELLO YOUNG LOVERS (LP, mono/stereo)	18
63	Capitol (S)T 1828	BROADWAY - MY LOVE (LP, mono/stereo)	18
63	Capitol (S)T 1934	HOLLYWOOD - MY WAY (LP, mono/stereo)	18
63	Capitol (S)T 2012	YESTERDAY'S LOVE SONGS (LP, mono/stereo)	18
64	Capitol (S)T 2082	TODAY, TOMORROW, FOREVER (LP)	18
65	Capitol (S)T 2136	THE NANCY WILSON SHOW (LP)	18
65	Capitol (S)T 2155	HOW GLAD I AM (LP)	18
65	Capitol (S)T 2321	TODAY- MY WAY (LP)	18

MINT VALUE £

65	Capitol (S)T 2351	GENTLE IS MY LOVE (LP)	18
66	Capitol (S)T 2433	FROM BROADWAY WITH LOVE (LP)	18
66	Capitol (S)T 2495	A TOUCH OF TODAY (LP)	30
66	Capitol (S)T 2555	TENDER LOVING CARE (LP)	20
67	Capitol (S)T 2634	NANCY - NATURALLY (LP)	20

NANCY WILSON & CANNONBALL ADDERLEY

(see also Cannonball Adderley)

62	Capitol T 1657	NANCY WILSON & CANNONBALL ADDERLEY (LP, mono)	12
62	Capitol ST 1657	NANCY WILSON & CANNONBALL ADDERLEY (LP, stereo)	15

PEANUTS WILSON

58	Coral Q 72302	Cast Iron Arm/You've Got Love	500
58	Coral Q 72302	Cast Iron Arm/You've Got Love (78)	150
76	MCA MCA 240	Cast Iron Arm/DON WOODY: Barking Up The Wrong Tree	6

PHIL WILSON

(see also June Brides)

87	Creation CRE 036D	Waiting For A Change/Even Now/Down In The Valley/Love In Vain (double pack)	5
89	Caff CAFF 3	Better Days/You Won't Speak (p/s, with insert, handwritten label)	12

REUBEN WILSON

76	Chess 6078 700	Got To Get Your Own Parts 1 & 2	20

RON WILSON

(see also Winston Scotland, Douglas Brothers)

68	Island WI 3112	Dread Saras/DAVID BROWN: All My Life	40

SHARK WILSON & BASEMENT HEATERS

71	Ashanti ASH 400	Make It Reggae/Version	12

SMILEY WILSON

60	London HLG 9066	Running Bear/Long As Little Birds Fly	60

TOMY WILSON

64	Decca F12033	Yes I Do/Lost Without You	10

TONY WILSON

(see also Hot Chocolate)

67	Columbia DB 8153	Can't Waste A Good Thing/What Did I Do?	30
69	Bell BLL 1081	Baby, I Love, Love I Love You/Come Back To My Lonely World	6
76	Bearsville K 55513	I LIKE YOUR STYLE (LP)	12

TREVOR WILSON

65	Ska Beat JB 207	You Couldn't Believe/You Told Me You Care	30

GABY WILTON & CHARLIE ACE

72	Bullet BU 511	Babylon Falling/CHARLIE ACE: Make It Love	8

JOHNNY WILTSHIRE & HIS TREBLETONES

59	Oriole CB 1494	If The Shoe Fits/Cha Cha Choo Choo	10

TEACHO WILTSHIRE

(see also Annie Ross)

57	Oriole CB 1376	Coffee Break/Shut-Eye (78)	10

WIMPLE WINCH

(see also Just Four Men, Four Just Men, Pacific Drift, Tristar Airbus)o

66	Fontana TF 686	What's Been Done/I Really Love You	300
66	Fontana TF 718	Save My Soul/Everybody's Worried 'Bout Tomorrow	500
67	Fontana TF 781	Rumble On Mersey Square South/Typical British Workmanship	300
67	Fontana TF 781	Rumble On Mersey Square South/Typical British Workmanship (mispressing, B-side plays "Atmospheres")	600

WIN

87	Swamplands	UH! TEARS BABY (CD)	30

LEM WINCHESTER & BENNY GOLSON

59	Esquire 32-142	WINCHESTER SPECIAL (LP)	25
61	Esquire 32-172	ANOTHER OPUS (LP)	15

KAI WINDING

(see also Dizzy Gillespie, J.J. Johnson Quintet)

65	Verve VS 512	Comin' Home Baby/More	15
55	London LTZ-N 15003	K AND J.J. (LP, with J.J. Johnson Quintet)	15
59	Philips SBBL 515	TROMBONES (LP)	18
61	Parlophone PMC 1138	SLIDE RULE (LP, with J.J. Johnson Quintet)	20
63	Verve VLP 9049	SOUL SURFIN' (LP)	30

WIND IN THE WILLOWS

(see also Debbie Harry, Blondie)

68	Capitol CL 15561	Moments Spent/Friendly Lion	25
68	Capitol ST 2956	WIND IN THE WILLOWS (LP)	30

WINDMILL

69	MCA MU 1090	Big Bertha/Hey, Drummer Man	5
70	MCA MK 5024	Such Sweet Sorrow/I Can Fly	10
70	MCA MK 5045	Wilbur's Thing/Two's Company, Three's A Crowd	5

BARRY WINDOW

69	BAF BAF 7	I Thank You/End Of Our Road	50

WINDOWS

72	Polydor 2058 206	How Do You Do/Nobody's Baby	18

WINDOWS

(see also Mutants)

78	Skeleton SKL 008	Re-Arrange/Over Dub (p/s)	7
81	Skeleton SKULP 2	UPPERS ON DOWNERS (LP, with inserts)	12

MINT VALUE £

BARBARA WINDSOR
61 HMV POP 883 Ten Gallon Hat/Funny Face ... 5
62 HMV POP 1104 It Has Better Be A Wonderful Life/ I'm Not That Sort Of Girl (with Harry Fowler & Kenny Lynch) ... 5
63 HMV POP 1128 Sparrows Can't Sing/On Mother Kelly's Doorstep ... 5
67 Parlophone R 5629 Don't Dig Twiggy/Swinging London ... 5
70 UPC UPC 101 When I Was A Child/What A Right Carry On ... 5
72 Decca F 13323 Grin And Bare It/Cheeky Sorta' Bird ... 5

WINDY & CARL
95 Enraptured RAPT 4501 Emerald/Fragments Of Time And Space (500 in hand-painted p/s) ... 12
95 Enraptured RAPT 4501 Emerald/Fragments Of Time And Space (300 in tracing paper sleeve) ... 10
96 Enraptured RAPT 4509 Christmas Song/GRIMBLE GRUMBLE: Odyssey And Oracle (no'd p/s, coloured vinyl, 350 only) ... 20

WINDY CORNER
73 Deroy DER 977 THE HOUSE AT WINDY CORNER (LP, private pressing) ... 300

AMY WINEHOUSE
07 Island AMY 7 PRO 2 Love Is A Losing Game/(Moody Boys Dubstep Remix) promo, 300 only ... 30
03 Iniversal Island FRANK LP 3 FRANK (ALBUM SAMPLER) EP (promo 12", p/s) ... 8
05 Universal Island AMY 12PRO 1 Rehab (Hot Chip Remix)/(Hot Chip Instrumental)/(DED Instrumental)/(Original Version) (promo 12") ... 10

WINE OF LEBANON
(see also Achor)
76 Dovetail DOVE 46 WINE OF LEBANON (LP) ... 20

WINGS
(see under Paul McCartney & Wings)

PETE WINSLOW & KING SIZE BRASS
73 BBC 103S GIRL ON THE TESTCARD (LP) ... 20

WINSTON
60s Holyground WINSTON SINGS (EP) ... 10
73 Bradley BRAD 306 MOna/Rockerdile (P/S) ... 20

WINSTON (Richards) & BIBBIE (Seaton)
63 R&B JB 115 Lover Man/LESTER STIRLING: Gravy Cool ... 30

WINSTON (Francis) & CECIL (Locke)
70 Banana BA 306 United We Stand/SOUND DIMENSION: Sweet Message ... 20

WINSTON & ERROL
64 Blue Beat BB 272 Fay Is Gone/MONARCHS: Sadler ... 10
71 Punch PH 74 There Is A Land/Goodnight My Love ... 6

WINSTON & FAY
64 Blue Beat BB 272 Fay Is Gone (Winston & Errol)/MONARCHS: Sauce And Tea ... 22

WINSTON & GEORGE
66 Pyramid PYR 6002 Denham Town/Keep The Pressure On ... 20

JIMMY WINSTON (& HIS REFLECTIONS)
(see also Small Faces, Winston's Fumbs, Spheres)
66 Decca F 12410 Sorry She's Mine/It's Not What You Do (But The Way That You Do It) ... 300
76 Nems NEMS 12 Sun In The Morning/Just Wanna Smile (solo) ... 8

WINSTON (Groovy) & PAT (Rhoden)
(see also Winston Tucker)
68 Trojan TR 605 Pony Ride/Baby You Send Me ... 8
71 Bullet BU 475 The Same Thing For Breakfast/Sweeter Than Honey ... 8

WINSTON (Richards) & TONETTES
65 Ska Beat JB 225 You Make Me Cry/CHECKMATES: Invisible Ska ... 35

WINSTON & ROY
62 Blue Beat BB 80 Babylon Gone/COUNT OSSIE ON AFRICAN DRUMS: First Gone ... 25

WINSTON & RUPERT
(see also Eternals)
70 Bullet BU 425 Come By Here/Somebody ... 10
70 Moodisc HM 106 Musically Beat/Let Me Tell You Girl ... 10

ERIC WINSTONE (& HIS) ORCHESTRA
64 Pye 7N 15603 Dr. Who Theme/Pony Express ... 18
73 Avenue AVINT 1005 PLAYS 007 (LP) ... 12

NORMA WINSTONE
(see also Mike Westbrook, Michael Garrick)
72 Argo ZDA 148 EDGE OF TIME (LP) ... 120

WINSTONS
69 Pye International 7N 25493 Colour In Father/Amen, Brother ... 15
69 Pye International 7N 25500 Love Of The Common People/Wheel Of Fortune ... 7

WINSTON'S FUMBS
(see also Small Faces, Jimmy Winston & His Reflections, Yes, Spheres, Federals)
67 RCA RCA 1612 Real Crazy Apartment/Snow White ... 600

WINSTONS & M-SQUAD
71 Green Door GD 4003 Carroll Street/Carroll Street - Version (B-side act. by Ansel Collins/M-Squad) ... 6

EDGAR WINTER (GROUP)
70 CBS 64083 ENTRANCE (LP, as Edgar Winter) ... 15
71 CBS 64298 EDGAR WINTER'S WHITE TRASH (LP) ... 15
72 CBS 67244 ROAD WORK (2-LP) ... 15
73 CBS EQ 31584/Q 65074 THEY ONLY COME OUT AT NIGHT (LP, quadrophonic) ... 12

MINT VALUE £

JOHNNY WINTER
(see also Johnny & Jammers)
69 CBS 4386 I'm Yours And I'm Hers/I'll Drown In My Tears . . . 6
69 Liberty LBF 15219 Rollin' And Tumblin'/Bad Luck And Trouble . . . 7
70 CBS 4794 Johnny B. Goode/I'm Not Sure . . . 6
70 CBS 5358 Rock 'N' Roll Hoochie Koo/21st Century Man . . . 5
71 CBS 7227 Jumping Jack Flash/Good Morning Little School Girl . . . 5
69 CBS 63619 JOHNNY WINTER (LP) . . . 25
69 Liberty LBL/LBS 83240E THE PROGRESSIVE BLUES EXPERIMENT (LP) . . . 20
70 Buddah 2359 011 FIRST WINTER (LP) . . . 20
70 CBS 66231 SECOND WINTER (2-LP, 3-sided) . . . 18
70 CBS 64117 JOHNNY WINTER AND? (LP) . . . 15
71 CBS 64289 JOHNNY WINTER AND? LIVE (LP) . . . 12
73 CBS 65484 STILL ALIVE AND WELL (LP) . . . 12
74 CBS CQ 32188/Q 65484 STILL ALIVE AND WELL (LP, quadrophonic) . . . 15

DON WINTERS
60 Brunswick 05827 Someday Baby/That's All I Need . . . 15

JONATHAN WINTERS
61 HMV CLP 1482 HERE'S JONATHAN (LP) . . . 12

LIZ WINTERS & BOB CORT SKIFFLE GROUP
(see also Bob Cort Skiffle Group)
57 Decca F 10878 Freight Train/Love Is Strange . . . 20
57 Decca F 10878 Freight Train/Love Is Strange (78) . . . 10
57 Decca F 10899 Maggie May/Jessamine . . . 20
57 Decca F 10899 Maggie May/Jessamine (78) . . . 10
57 Decca DFE 6409 LIZ WINTERS AND BOB CORT (EP) . . . 25

LOIS WINTERS
56 London HLD 8266 Japanese Farewell Song/JAN GARBER & HIS ORCHESTRA: My Dear . . . 35

WINTERS REIGN
84 Scoff DTO33 Save It/Keep Trying . . . 8
87 Link LOPL 501 THE BEIGNNING (LP, with free 7") . . . 15

RON WINTERS
63 Colpix PX 11022 Snow Girl/In The Middle Of The Morning . . . 25

RUBY WINTERS
68 Stateside SS 2090 I Want Action/Better . . . 100
68 Stateside SS 2090 I Want Action/Better (DJ copy) . . . 150

WYOMA WINTERS
54 HMV 7M 222 Where Can I Go Without You?/Won't You Give A Repeat Performance . . . 7
54 HMV 7M 260 Toy Balloon/Shish Kebab . . . 7

STEVIE WINWOOD
(see also Winwood Kabaka Amoa, Anglos, Spencer Davis Group, Traffic, Blind Faith.)
77 Island WIP 6394 Time Is Running Out/Penultimate Zone (12", pre-release sleeve) . . . 10
80 Island IPR 2040 While You See A Chance/Vacant Chair (12", pre-release sleeve) . . . 8
80 Island WIP 6655 While You See A Chance/Vacant Chair (p/s) . . . 5
81 Island WIP 6747 There's A River/Two Way Stretch (p/s) . . . 5
86 Island IS 294 Freedom Overspill/Spanish Dancer (p/s, with bonus cassette of LP highlights & interview [SW 2]) . . . 6
86 Island 12 ISD 294 Freedom Overspill (Liberty Mix)/(LP Version)/Spanish Dancer (12", stickered g/fold p/s & t/p 7" "Low Spark Of High-Heeled Boys"/"Gimme Some Lovin' ") . . . 10
88 Virgin VST 1085 Roll With It (12" Mix)/The Morning Side/Roll With It (7" Version) (12", g/fold p/s) . . 8
91 Virgin VSCDX 1317 I Will Be Here/Don't You Know What The Night Can Do (live)/In The Night Of Day (CD, velvet box with family tree and print) . . . 8
86 Island SWCLP 1 A CONVERSATION WITH (LP, promo interview on "Back In The High Life" LP) . . 12
87 Island SWWLP 1 IN CONVERSATION (LP, promo interview on "Chronicles" LP) . . . 12
87 Island SW 1/2/3 BACK IN THE HIGH LIFE (3 x 7" set, each in p/s, promo only) . . . 20
87 Island CHRONICLES (5 x 7" box set, promo, 500 only) . . . 30

WINWOOD/KABAKA/AMAO
(see also Stevie WInwood)
73 Island HELP 14 AIYE-KETA THIRD WORLD (LP) . . . 15

WIPEOUT
82 M&L MNL 2/ACE 37 Baby Please Don't Go/Two-O-Five/Crawdaddy/Should A' Known Better (p/s) . . . 15
83 Out OUT 1A/B1 NO SWEAT (LP) . . . 15

WIPEOUT
90s Deluxe DELUX 002 Snowflake/Confusion Bee (12") . . . 10

WIPERS
84 Psycho PSYCHO 22 IS THIS REAL? (LP, with lyric insert) . . . 12
84 Psycho PSYCHO 23 YOUTH OF AMERICA (LP) . . . 12

WIRE
(see also Cupol, Colin Newman)
77 Harvest HAR 5144 Mannequin/Feeling Called Love/12XU (p/s) . . . 15
78 Harvest HAR 5151 I Am The Fly/Ex-Lion Tamer (p/s) . . . 15
78 Harvest HAR 5161 Dot Dash/Options R (p/s) . . . 12
79 Harvest HAR 5172 Outdoor Miner/Practice Makes Perfect (p/s, white vinyl) . . . 12
79 Harvest HAR 5172 Outdoor Miner/Practice Makes Perfect (p/s) . . . 5
79 Harvest HAR 5187 A Question Of Degree/Former Airline (p/s) . . . 10
79 Harvest HAR 5192 Map Ref 41° N 93° W/Go Ahead (p/s) . . . 10
79 Harvest SPSLP 299 154 (12", p/s, white label sampler with insert & press release; beware of counterfeits) . . . 35

			MINT VALUE £
81	Rough Trade RT 079	Our Swimmer/Midnight Bahnhof Cafe (p/s)	8
83	Rough Trade RTT 123	Crazy About Love/Second Length (Our Swimmer)/Catapult 30 (12", p/s, 2 different sleeve colours)	8
88	Mute MUTE 67	Kidney Bingos/Pieta (p/s)	5
89	Mute MUTE 87	Eardrum Buzz/The Offer (p/s, clear vinyl, withdrawn)	8
77	Harvest SHSP 4076	PINK FLAG (LP, with lyric inner)	30
78	Harvest SHSP 4093	CHAIRS MISSING (LP, 1st 10,000 with lilac lyric inner sleeve)	30
79	Harvest SHSP 4105	154 (LP, with inner lyric sleeve & bonus 7" EP: "Song 2"/ Get Down [Parts I & II]/"Let's Panic"/"Later"/"Small Electric Piece" [PSR 444])	25
84	Rough Trade ROUGH 29	DOCUMENT AND EYEWITNESS (LP, with free 12" EP [ROUGH 2912])	20
89	Harvest SHSP 4127	ON RETURNING (LP)	15
00s	Harvest SHSP 4076	PINK FLAG (LP, reissue)	15
00s	Harvest SHSP 4093	CHAIRS MISSING (LP, reissue)	15

MARK WIRTZ (ORCHESTRA & CHORUS)

(see also Mood Mosaic, Keith West, Sweet Shop, Philwit & Pegasus, Mark Rogers & Marksmen, Belle Gonzalez, Russ Loader, Zion De Gallier, Elmer Hockett's Hurdy Gurdy, Steve Flynn, Fickle Finger, Matchmaker)

68	Parlophone R 5668	(He's Our Dear Old) Weatherman (From "A Teenage Opera")/Possum's Dance	30
68	Parlophone R 5683	Mrs. Raven/Knickerbocker Glory	25
69	CBS 4306	My Daddie Is A Baddie/I Love You Because	15
69	CBS 4539	Caroline/Goody, Goody, Goody	15
64	World Record Club T 452	TEN AGAIN (LP, by Belle Gonzalez & Russ Loader, Wirtz as producer)	35

NORMAN WISDOM

(see also Ruby Murray)

56	Columbia SCM 5222	Two Rivers/Boy Meets Girl (with Ruby Murray)	10
57	Columbia DB 3864	Up In The World/Me And My Imagination	10
57	Columbia DB 3903	The Wisdom Of A Fool/Happy Ending	10
59	Top Rank JAR 246	Follow A Star/Give Me A Night In June	5
61	Columbia SCD 2160	Narcissus (The Laughing Record)/I Don't 'Arf Love You (with Joyce Grenfell)	6
61	Columbia DB 4601	If You Believe In Me/Yer Gotta Get Aht	6
64	Columbia DB 7352	The Joker/Who Can I Turn To	6
80	HMV POP 2001	The Wisdom Of A Fool/Don't Laugh At Me ('Cause I'm A Fool)	5
69	CBS 4569	Where Do I Go From Here?/Just Like The Day	5
56	Columbia SEG 7612	NORMAN WISDOM (EP)	10
57	Columbia SEG 7687	NORMAN AND RUBY (EP, with Ruby Murray)	10
58	Columbia SEG 7856	NORMAN WISDOM (EP)	10
59	Top Rank JKP 2052	FOLLOW A STAR (EP)	10
58	Columbia 33SX 1085	NORMAN WISDOM IN "WHERE'S CHARLEY?" (LP)	12
67	Wing WL 1216	I WOULD LIKE TO PUT ON RECORD (LP)	12

WISE BLOOD

(see also Foetus)

85	Wise 1-12	Motorslug/Death Rape 2000 (12", p/s)	12
86	Wise 2-12	Someone Drowned In My Pool/Stumbo (12", p/s)	12
91	Wise 003	DISHDIRT (LP, with sticker)	15
91	Big Cut 030X	PEDAL TO THE METAL (mini LP)	12

WISE BOYS

60	Parlophone R 4693	Why, Why, Why/My Fortune	10

WISE GUYS

60	Top Rank JAR 271	(Little Girl) Big Noise/As Long As I Have You	10

MAC WISEMAN

55	London HLD 8174	The Kentuckian Song/Wabash Cannon Ball	40
56	London HLD 8226	My Little Home In Tennessee/I Haven't Got The Right To Love You	40
56	London HLD 8259	Fireball Mail/When The Roses Bloom Again	40
56	London HLD 8259	Fireball Mail/When The Roses Bloom Again (78)	15
57	London HLD 8412	Step It Up And Go/Sundown	400
57	London HLD 8412	Step It Up And Go/Sundown (78)	40
59	London HL 7084	Jimmy Brown The Newsboy/I've Got No Use For Woman (export issue)	20
56	London RE-D 1056	SONGS FROM THE HILLS (EP)	20
58	London RE-D 1147	SONGS FROM THE HILLS VOL. 2 (EP)	20
60	London RE-D 1242	SONGS FROM THE HILLS VOL. 3 (EP)	20
56	London HB-D 1052	SONGS FROM THE HILLS (10" LP)	30
60	London HA-D 2217	GREAT FOLK BALLADS (LP)	20

TREVOR WISHART

78	private pressing	RED BIRD: A POLITICAL PRISONER'S DREAM (LP, with insert)	20
79	private pressing	BEACH SINGULARITY AND MENAGERIE (LP, with insert)	20

WISHBONE ASH

(see also Home, Big Daisy)

70	MCA MK 5061	Blind Eye/Queen Of Torture	8
72	MCA MKS 5097	No Easy Road/Blowin' Free	6
73	MCA MUS 1210	So Many Things To Say/Rock'n'Roll Widow	5
74	MCA MCA 165	Hometown/Persephone	5
75	MCA MCA 176	Silver Shoes/Persephone	6
76	MCA/SFI 263	Outward Bound/Runaway/Mother Of Pearl/You Rescue Me (flexidisc, with "New England" tour programme)	12
76	MCA/SFI 263	Outward Bound/Runaway/Mother Of Pearl/You Rescue Me (flexidisc, without "New England" tour programme)	5
77	MCA MCA 291	Phoenix/Blowin' Free/Jail Bait (p/s)	5
78	MCA MCA 392	You See Red/Bad Weather Blues (live) (p/s)	5
79	MCA MCA 518	Come On/Fast Johnny (p/s)	5
80	MCA MCA 549	Living Proof/Jail Bait (live) (p/s)	5
80	MCA MCA 577	Helpless (live)/Blowin' Free (live) (p/s)	5
81	MCA MCA 695	Underground/My Mind Is Made Up (p/s)	5
81	MCA MCA 726	Get Ready/Kicks On The Street (p/s, with patch)	8

			MINT VALUE £
81	MCA MCA 726	Get Ready/Kicks On The Street (p/s)	5
70	MCA MKPS 2014	WISHBONE ASH (LP, gatefold sleeve, red/pink 'dogbone' label)	75
71	MCA MDKS 8004	PILGRIMAGE (LP, gatefold sleeve, purple/red 'dogbone' label)	50
72	MCA MDKS 8006	ARGUS (LP, gatefold sleeve, black/blue 'haxagon' label)	40
73	MCA MDKS 8011	WISHBONE FOUR (LP, gatefold sleeve, black label, with poster & lyrics)	30
74	MCA MCSP 254	LIVE DATES (2-LP, gatefold sleeve, pink label)	15
78	MCA MCG 3528	NO SMOKE WITHOUT FIRE (LP, with stickered sleeve & inner, with bonus live single "Come In From The Rain"/"Lorelei" [PSR 431])	12
80	MCA MCG 4012	LIVE DATES II (LP, textured gatefold sleeve, with live bonus LP)	15
82	AVM ASH 1	TWIN BARRELS BURNING (LP)	12
85	Neat NEAT 1027	RAW TO THE BONE (LP)	18

WISHFUL THINKING

66	Decca F 12438	Turning Round/V.I.P.	20
66	Decca F 12499	Step By Step/Looking Around	7
67	Decca F 12598	Count To Ten/Hang Around Girl	8
67	Decca F 12627	Peanuts/Cherry Cherry	12
67	Decca F 22673	Meet The Sun/Easier Said Than Loving You	10
68	Decca F 22742	Alone/Vegetables (export issue)	10
68	Decca F 12760	It's So Easy/I Want You Girl	15
72	B&C CB 169	Lu La Le Lu/We're Gonna Change All This	7
72	B&C CB 184	Clear White Light/Hiroshima	10
67	Decca SKL 4900	LIVE VOL. 1 (LP)	50
71	Charisma CAS 1038	HIROSHIMA (LP)	25

WISHING STONES

(see also The Loft)

86	Head HEAD 2	Beat Girl/Two Steps Take Me Back (p/s)	6
87	Head HEAD 6	New Ways/House Is Not A Home (p/s)	5
87	Head HEAD 612	New Ways/Wildwood/Hold Up/A House Is Not A Home (12", p/s)	8

WITCHCRAFT

06	Rise Above RISE 7/089	If Crimson Was Your Colour/I Know You Killed Someone... (P/s, clear, red, green or black vinyl)	10
04	Rise Above RISELP 47	WITCHCRAFT (LP)	25
04	Rise Above RISEPD 47	WITCHCRAFT (LP, picture disc)	30
07	Rise Above RISELP 103	THE ALCHEMIST (LP, green, clear, purple or gold vinyl)	20

WITCHES BREW

80s	Pussy PU 016	Angeline (p/s)	20

WITCHFINDER GENERAL

81	Heavy Metal HEAVY 6	Burning A Sinner/Satan's Children (p/s)	40
82	Heavy Metal 12HM 17	Soviet Invasion/Rabies/R.I.P. (live) (12", p/s)	35
83	Heavy Metal HEAVY 21	Music/Last Chance (p/s)	12
83	Heavy Metal HMPD 21	Music/Last Chance (picture disc)	8
82	Heavy Metal HMRLP 8	DEATH PENALTY (LP, red, blue or clear vinyl, with inner)	30
82	Heavy Metal HMRPD 8	DEATH PENALTY (LP, picture disc)	18
83	Heavy Metal HMRLP 13	FRIENDS OF HELL (LP, red, silver or clear vinyl)	20
83	Heavy Metal HMRPD 13	FRIENDS OF HELL (LP, picture disc)	18

WITCHFYNDE

79	Rondelet ROUND 1	Give 'Em Hell/Getting' Heavy (p/s)	6
80	Rondelet ROUND 4	In The Stars/Wake Up Screaming (p/s)	5
83	Expulsion OUT 3	I'd Rather Go Wild/Cry Wolf (p/s)	20
80	Rondelet ABOUT 1	GIVE 'EM HELL (LP)	25
80	Rondelet ABOUT 2	STAGE FRIGHT (LP)	15
83	Expulsion EXIT 5	CLOAK AND DAGGER (LP)	12
83	Expulsion PEXIT 5	CLOAK AND DAGGER (LP, picture disc)	18
84	Mausoleum SKULL 8352	LORDS OF SIN (LP, gatefold sleeve, with bonus 12" [Cloak & Dagger/I'd Rather Go Wild/Moon Magic/Give 'Em Hell])	15

BILL WITHERS

71	A&M AMS 845	Everybody's Talkin'/Harlem	5
71	A&M AMS 858	Ain't No Sunshine/Harlem	5
72	A&M AMS 7004	Lean On Me/Better Off Dead	5
72	A&M AMS 7038	Use Me/Let Me In Your Life	5
73	A&M AMS 7055	Kissing My Love/I Don't Know	5
73	A&M AMS 7068	Look What I Found/The Lady Is Waiting	5
73	A&M AMS 7080	Ain't No Sunshine/Harlem/Grandma's Hands	5
72	A&M AMLH 68107	STILL BILL (LP)	20
71	A&M AMLS 65002	JUST AS I AM (LP)	15
73	A&M AMLD 3001	LIVE AT CARNEGIE HALL (2-LP)	15
74	A&M AMLH 68230	'JUSTMENTS	15

BRIAN WITHERS

66	RCA RCA 1536	For No One/Here There And Everywhere	8

JIMMY WITHERSPOON

(see also Eric Burdon & Jimmy Witherspoon, Brother Jack McDuff)

78s

54	Parlophone R 3914	It/Highway To Happiness	40
54	Parlophone R 3951	Oh Boy/I Done Told You	40
54	Vogue V 2261	Failing By Degrees/New Orleans Woman	40
54	Vogue V 2295	Who's Been Jivin' With You/Rain, Rain, Rain	40
56	Vogue V 2060	Big Fine Girl/No Rollin' Blues	40
56	Vogue V 2356	Jump, Children/Take Me Back Baby	40

SINGLES

54	Parlophone MSP 6125	It/Highway To Happiness	100
54	Parlophone MSP 6142	Oh Boy/I Done Told You	100
56	Vogue V 2060	Big Fine Girl/No Rollin' Blues	75

			MINT VALUE £
62	Vogue V 2420	When The Lights Go Out/All That's Good	75
64	Stateside SS 304	Evenin'/Money Is Getting Cheaper	15
64	Stateside SS 325	I Will Never Marry/I'm Coming Down With The Blues	15
64	Stateside SS 362	You're Next/Happy Blues	15
65	Stateside SS 429	Come Walk With Me/Oh How I Love You	15
65	Stateside SS 461	Love Me Right/Make My Heart Smile Again	15
66	Stateside SS 503	If There Wasn't Any You/I Never Thought I'd See The Day	15
66	Verve VS 538	It's All Over But The Crying/If I Could Have You Back Again	8
67	Verve VS 553	Past Forty Blues/My Baby's Quit Me	6
71	Probe PRO 526	Handbags And Gladrags/It's Time To Live	5
75	Capitol CL 15828	Fool's Paradise/Reflections	5
EPs			
61	Vogue EPV 1269	JIMMY WITHERSPOON AT MONTEREY	30
61	Vogue EPV 1270	JIMMY WITHERSPOON AT MONTEREY No. 2	30
64	Vocalion EPVH 1278	JIMMY WITHERSPOON	20
65	Vocalion EPVH 1284	OUTSKIRTS OF TOWN	20
66	Vocalion VEH 170158	FEELING THE SPIRIT VOL. 1	20
66	Vocalion VEH 170159	FEELING THE SPIRIT VOL. 2	20
LPs			
59	London Jazz LTZ-K 15150	NEW ORLEANS BLUES (with Wilbur de Paris)	40
60	Vogue LAE 12218	SINGIN' THE BLUES	40
61	Vogue LAE 12253	AT THE RENAISSANCE (with Gerry Mulligan)	35
64	Society SOC 968	SINGS THE BLUES	12
64	Stateside SL 10088	EVENIN' BLUES	35
65	Stateside SL 10105	BLUES AROUND THE CLOCK	30
65	Fontana 688 005 ZL	THERE'S GOOD ROCKIN' TONIGHT	30
65	Stateside SL 10114	SOME OF MY BEST FRIENDS ARE BLUES	25
65	Stateside SL 10139	BLUE SPOON	22
65	Vogue VRL 3005	JIMMY WITHERSPOON IN PERSON	22
66	Ember EMB 3369	JIMMY WITHERSPOON	20
67	Fontana (S)TL 5382	'SPOON SINGS AND SWINGS	20
67	Verve (S)VLP 9156	BLUE POINT OF VIEW	18
67	Transatlantic PR 7300	EVENIN' BLUES (reissue)	15
68	Transatlantic PR 7356	SOME OF MY BEST FRIENDS ARE THE BLUES (reissue)	15
68	Stateside (S)SL 10232	LIVE	20
68	Verve (S)VLP 9181	BLUES IS NOW (with Brother Jack McDuff)	15
68	Verve (S)VLP 9216	SPOONFUL OF SOUL	18
68	Transatlantic PR 7418	SPOON IN LONDON	15
68	Transatlantic PR 7475	BLUES FOR EASY LIVERS	15
69	Stateside SSL 10289	THE BLUES SINGER	18
69	Ember CJS 820	SINGS THE BLUES AT THE RENAISSANCE (reissue, with Gerry Mulligan)	12
69	Polydor Intl. 623 256	BACK DOOR BLUES	20
71	Probe SPB 1031	HANDBAGS AND GLADRAGS	15

JIMMY WITHERSPOON/HELEN HUMES

(see also Helen Humes)

60	Vogue EPV 1198	RHYTHM AND BLUES CONCERT (EP, 2 tracks each)	80

BITTER WITHY

69	Nevis NEVIS R005	SAMPLER (LP)	20

WITNESSES

60s	Herald ELR 1076	THE WITNESSES (EP)	110

D WITTER

(See also World Sound & Power Band)

78	D-Roy DRLP 1001	MAWAMBA DUB (WARRIOR) (LP)	50

WIZARD'S CONVENTION

(see also Deep Purple, Roger Glover, Jon Lord, David Coverdale, Ray Fenwick,Tony Ashton, Glenn Hughes, ELP, Hardin & York))

76	RCA RS 1085	WIZARD'S CONVENTION (LP, with insert)	15

WIZZARD

(see also Roy Wood, Balls, Idle Race, Grunt Futtock)

73	Harvest SHSP 4025	WIZZARD BREW (LP, with lyric insert)	15
74	Warner Bros. K 56029	INTRODUCING EDDY AND THE FALCONS (LP, with poster)	25

WJW & ROOTS TRUNKS & BRANCHES

79	Splendour Heights WJWX 1945	THE WEAK WILL BE STRONG (LP)	25

WKGB

79	Fetish FET 002	Non-Stop/Ultra Marine (p/s)	8

W.L.S.

77	Cancer CAND 001	Dub Punk/Simply Funky (12")	15

JEZZ WODROFFE

80	Graduate GRAD LP 1	OPPOSITE DIRECTIONS (LP)	50

CHARLES WOLCOTT

60	MGM 1115	Leatherjacket Cowboy/Ruby Duby Du	15

DARRYL WAY'S WOLF

(see also Curved Air, King Crimson, Marillion)

73	Deram DM 378	Wolf/Spring Fever	8
73	Deram DM 395	A Bunch Of Fives/Five In The Morning	8
73	Deram DM 401	Two Sisters/Go Down	8
73	Deram SDL 14	CANIS LUPUS (LP, as Darryl Way's Wolf, gatefold sleeve)	18
73	Deram SML 1104	SATURATION POINT (LP, as Darryl Way's Wolf)	15
74	Deram SML 1116	NIGHT MUSIC (LP)	18

MINT VALUE £

WOLF

81	Gremlin GREM 72	See Them Running/Creatures Of The Night (no p/s)	75
84	Mausoleum 8323	EDGE OF THE WORLD (LP)	18

WOLF

82	Chrysalis CHS 2592	Head Contact/Rock'n'Roll (p/s, clear vinyl, with sticker)	15
82	Chrysalis CHS 2592	Head Contact/Rock'n'Roll (p/s, clear vinyl, without sticker)	6

PATRICK WOLF

02	Faith & Industry FAI 001	THE PATRICK WOLF EP: Bloodbeat/ Empress/A Boy Like Me/Pumpkin Soup (12", 1000 only)	60

WOLFETONES

65	Fontana STL 5244	THE FOGGY DEW (LP)	12

WOLFGANG

70	Bell BLL 1120	Sandman/You	12

WOLFGANG PRESS

(see also Mass, Models)

83	4AD (no cat. no.)	Kings Of Soul (Crowned Mix)/(De-Throned Mix)/ (7" Mix) (12", same both sides, promo only, 50 copies pressed)	15

WOLFMAN

04	Rough Trade RTRADS177	For Lovers/Back From The Dead (with Pete Doherty p/s)	8

WOLFRILLA

71	Concord CON 015	Song For Jimi/Come Tomorrow	7

WOOLLY WOLSTENHOLME

(see also Barclay James Harvest)

80	Polydor 2374 165	MAESTOSO (LP)	12

WOLVES

64	Pye 7N 15676	Journey Into Dreams/What Do You Mean	20
64	Pye 7N 15733	Now/This Year Next Year	30
65	Pye 7N 17013	At The Club/Distant Dreams	35
66	Parlophone R 5511	Lust For Life/My Baby Loves Them	70

BOBBY WOMACK

(see also Valentinos, Ted Wood)

68	Minit MLF 11001	Broadway Walk/Somebody Special	8
68	Minit MLF 11005	What Is This?/What You Gonna Do.	15
68	Minit MLF 11010	Fly Me To The Moon/Take Me	8
69	Minit MLF 11012	California Dreamin'/Baby You Oughta Think It Over.	10
72	United Artists UP 35339	That's The Way I Feel About 'Cha/Come, L'Amore	7
72	United Artists UP 35375	Woman's Gotta Have It/If You Don't Want My Love	5
73	United Artists UP 35456	I Can Understand It/Harry Hippie (in p/s)	10
73	United Artists UP 35456	I Can Understand It/Harry Hippie	8
73	United Artists UP 35512	Across 110th Street/Hang On In There (as Bobby Womack & Peace)	10
73	United Artists UP 35565	Nobody Wants You When You're Down And Out/ I'm Through Trying To Prove My Love For You.	6
74	Jay Boy BOY 75	What Is This?/I Wonder	15
75	United Artists UP 35859	Check It Out/Interlude No. 2	6
76	United Artists UP 36042	Where There's A Will There's A Way/Everything's Gonna Be Alright	6
76	United Artists UP 36098	Daylight/Trust Me	8
79	Arista ARIST 284	How Could You Break My Heart/I Honestly Love You.	15
82	Tamla Motown TMG1267	So Many Sides of You/ Just My Imagination (7", p/s)	50
87	Arista RIS 17	How Could You Break My Heart/Give It Up (p/s)	20
87	Arista RIST 17	How Could You Break My Heart/Give It Up/ Mr. D.J. Don't Stop The Music (12", p/s).	20
72	United Artists UAS 29365	UNDERSTANDING (LP).	15
73	United Artists UAS 29451	ACROSS 110TH STREET (LP, soundtrack, with J.J. Johnson)	20
79	Arista ARTY 165	ROADS OF LIFE (LP)	20

WOMB

69	Dot DLP 25933	WOMB (LP)	25
70	Dot DLP 25959	OVERDUB (LP)	25

WOMBATS

06	Kids KIDS 005	Lost In The Post/Patricia The Stripper (in stickered mailer, 500 only)	10
07	No Label	Moving To New York/Happily Screwed/The Barman's Fault/ Ba Ba Song (EP)	20

WOMENFOLK

64	RCA RCA 1439	Turn Around/One Man's Hand	10
64	RCA LSP 2919/SF 7671	NEVER UNDERESTIMATE THE POWER OF WOMENFOLK (LP)	12
65	RCA RD 7704	AT THE HUNGRY I (LP)	12

ALISON WONDER

(see also Cheryl St. Clair)

70	Columbia DB 8667	Once More With Feeling/Black Paper Roses	6

(LITTLE) STEVIE WONDER

(See also Diana Ross, Dionne Warwick, Gary Bird.)

63	Oriole CBA 1853	Fingertips (Parts 1 & 2)	40
63	Oriole CBA 1853	Fingertips (Parts 1 & 2) (DJ copy).	85
63	Stateside SS 238	Workout, Stevie, Workout/Monkey Talk	50
63	Stateside SS 238	Workout, Stevie, Workout/Monkey Talk (DJ copy)	100
64	Stateside SS 285	Castles In The Sand/Thank You (For Loving Me All The Way).	75
64	Stateside SS 285	Castles In The Sand/Thank You (For Loving Me All The Way) (DJ copy).	100
64	Stateside SS 323	Hey, Harmonica Man/This Little Girl	50
64	Stateside SS 323	Hey, Harmonica Man/This Little Girl (DJ copy)	85

(The above singles were credited to Little Stevie Wonder.)

65	Tamla Motown TMG 505	Kiss Me Baby/Tears In Vain	60

			MINT VALUE £
65	Tamla Motown TMG 505	Kiss Me Baby/Tears In Vain (DJ copy)	100
65	Tamla Motown TMG 532	High-Heel Sneakers/Music Talk	40
65	Tamla Motown TMG 532	High-Heel Sneakers/Music Talk (DJ copy)	100
66	Tamla Motown TMG 545	Uptight (Everything's Alright)/Purple Raindrops	25
66	Tamla Motown TMG 545	Uptight (Everything's Alright)/Purple Raindrops (DJ copy)	200
66	Tamla Motown TMG 558	Nothing's Too Good For My Baby/With A Child's Heart	45
66	Tamla Motown TMG 558	Nothing's Too Good For My Baby/With A Child's Heart (DJ copy)	150
66	Tamla Motown TMG 570	Blowin' In The Wind/Ain't That Asking For Trouble	25
66	Tamla Motown TMG 570	Blowin' In The Wind/Ain't That Asking For Trouble (DJ copy)	75
66	Tamla Motown TMG 588	A Place In The Sun/Sylvia	20
66	Tamla Motown TMG 588	A Place In The Sun/Sylvia (DJ copy)	50
67	Tamla Motown TMG 602	Travelin' Man/Hey Love	18
67	Tamla Motown TMG 602	Travelin' Man/Hey Love (DJ copy)	50
67	Tamla Motown TMG 613	I Was Made To Love Her/Hold Me	10
67	Tamla Motown TMG 613	I Was Made To Love Her/Hold Me (DJ copy)	40
67	Tamla Motown TMG 626	I'm Wondering/Every Time I See You I Go Wild	12
67	Tamla Motown TMG 626	I'm Wondering/Every Time I See You I Go Wild (DJ copy)	40
68	Tamla Motown TMG 653	Shoo-Be-Doo-Be-Doo-Da-Day/Why Don't You Lead Me To Love	10
68	Tamla Motown TMG 653	Shoo-Be-Doo-Be-Doo-Da-Day/Why Don't You Lead Me To Love (DJ copy)	30
68	Tamla Motown TMG 666	You Met Your Match/My Girl	15
68	Tamla Motown TMG 666	You Met Your Match/My Girl (DJ copy)	35
68	Tamla Motown TMG 679	For Once In My Life/Angie Girl	6
68	Tamla Motown TMG 679	For Once In My Life/Angie Girl (DJ Copy)	30
69	Tamla Motown TMG 690	My Cherie Amour/I Don't Know Why I Love You	6
69	Tamla Motown TMG 690	My Cherie Amour/I Don't Know Why I Love You (DJ copy)	25
69	Tamla Motown TMG 717	Yester-Me, Yester-You, Yesterday/I'd Be A Fool Right Now	6
69	Tamla Motown TMG 717	Yester-Me, Yester-You, Yesterday/I'd Be A Fool Right Now (DJ copy)	25
70	Tamla Motown TMG 731	Never Had A Dream Come True/Somebody Knows, Somebody Cares	7
70	Tamla Motown TMG 731	Never Had A Dream Come True/Somebody Knows, Somebody Cares (DJ copy)	25
70	Tamla Motown TMG 744	Signed, Sealed, Delivered, I'm Yours/I'm More Than Happy (I'm Satisfied)	6
70	Tamla Motown TMG 744	Signed, Sealed, Delivered, I'm Yours/ I'm More Than Happy (I'm Satisfied) (DJ copy)	25
70	Tamla Motown TMG 757	Heaven Help Us All/I Gotta Have A Song	6
70	Tamla Motown TMG 757	Heaven Help Us All/I Gotta Have A Song (DJ copy)	20
71	Tamla Motown TMG 772	We Can Work It Out/Don't Wonder Why (in p/s)	30
71	Tamla Motown TMG 772	We Can Work It Out/Don't Wonder Why	6
71	Tamla Motown TMG 772	We Can Work It Out/Don't Wonder Why (DJ copy)	25
71	Tamla Motown TMG 779	Never Dreamed You'd Leave Me In Summer/If You Really Love Me	8
71	Tamla Motown TMG 779	Never Dreamed You'd Leave Me In Summer/If You Really Love Me (DJ copy)	25
72	Tamla Motown TMG 798	If You Really Love Me/Think Of Me As Your Soldier	7
64	Stateside SE 1014	I CALL IT PRETTY MUSIC BUT THE OLD PEOPLE CALL IT THE BLUES (EP)	200
65	Tamla Motown TME 2006	LITTLE STEVIE WONDER (EP)	90
63	Oriole PS 40049	TRIBUTE TO UNCLE RAY (LP)	300
63	Oriole PS 40050	THE TWELVE-YEAR-OLD GENIUS - LIVE (LP)	125
64	Stateside SL 10078	THE JAZZ SOUL OF LITTLE STEVIE WONDER (LP)	150
(The above EP's and LPs were credited to Little Stevie Wonder.)			
65	Stateside SL 10108	HEY, HARMONICA MAN (LP)	150
66	T. Motown TML 11036	UPTIGHT (EVERYTHING'S ALRIGHT) (LP, mono)	35
66	T. Motown TMG STML 11036	UPTIGHT (EVERYTHING'S ALRIGHT) (LP, stereo)	45
67	T. Motown TML 11045	DOWN TO EARTH (LP, mono)	30
67	T. Motown STML 11045	DOWN TO EARTH (LP, stereo)	40
68	T. Motown STML 11059	I WAS MADE TO LOVE HER (LP, stereo)	30
68	T. Motown TML 11059	I WAS MADE TO LOVE HER (LP, mono)	25
68	T. Motown (S)TML 11085	SOMEDAY AT CHRISTMAS (LP, mono/stereo)	40
69	T. Motown (S)TML 11098	FOR ONCE IN MY LIFE (LP, mono/stereo)	20
69	T. Motown (S)TML 11128	MY CHERIE AMOUR (LP, mono/stereo)	18
(The above albums originally came with flipback sleeves)			

WONDER BOY

(see also Slim Smith, Pat Kelly)

69	Jackpot JP 703	Sweeten My Coffee (actually by Slim Smith)/MISTER MILLER: Cherry Pink	12
69	Jackpot JP 705	Love Power (actually by Slim Smith)/PAT KELLY: Since You Are Gone	12
71	Jackpot JP 764	Just For A Day/He Ain't Heavy	8
71	Concord CON 015	Just For A Day/He Ain't Heavy	5

WONDER BOY

75	Ackee ACK 546	Pressure Parts 1 & 2	6

GIRL WONDER

66	Doctor Bird DB 1015	Mommy Out Of The Light/Cutting Wood	18

WONDERLAND

68	Polydor 56539	Poochy/Moscow	15

ALICE WONDERLAND

63	London HLU 9783	He's Mine/Cha Linde	20

WONDER STUFF

(see also Vic Reeves)

87	Far Out GONE ONE	It's Not True?/A Wonderful Day/Like A Merry-Go-Round/Down Here (EP, p/s)	25
87	Far Out GONE 002	Unbearable/Ten Trenches Deep (with p/s)	6
87	Far Out GO BIG 002	Unbearable/Ten Trenches Deep/I Am A Monster/Frank (12", p/s)	8
88	Polydor GONE 3	Give Give Give Me More More More/A Song Without An End (p/s)	6
89	House Of Dolls HOD 011	Who Wants To Be The Disco King? (King Of Disco Megamix)/PRUDES: Christmas/SANDKINGS: Colourblind/WORLD MUSIC: Stop Playing With My Heart (no p/s, free with House Of Dolls magazine)	6
87	Far Out	A HANDFUL OF SONGS (private cassette)	20
87	Polydor	A HANDFUL OF SONGS (cassette, promo only, different to above)	20
88	Polydor GONECD 1	THE EIGHT-LEGGED GROOVE MACHINE (CD, mispressed with 'Wish Away' printed on front cover)	20

MINT VALUE £

WONDERWHEEL
(see under Gary Wright)

WONDER WHO
(see also Four Seasons, Frankie Valli)

65	Philips BF 1440	Don't Think Twice, It's Alright/Sassy	20
66	Philips BF 1504	On The Good Ship Lollipop/You're Nobody Till Somebody Loves You	10
67	Philips BF 1600	Lonesome Road/FOUR SEASONS: Around And Around	20

ROYCE WONG

65	Blue Beat BB 301	Everything's Gonna Be Alright/Hang Your Head And Cry	20

WONKY ALICE

92	Pomona POM 004	SIRIUS EP (12", p/s)	12

WOOB

93	Woob	WOOB WOOB WOOB (cassette demo tape)	20
94	Em:t	WOOB 1194 (CD)	40
95	Em:t	WOOB 4495 (CD)	40

ANITA WOOD

62	London HLS 9585	I'll Wait Forever/I Can't Show You How I Feel	25
64	Sue WI 328	Dream Baby/This Happened Before	40

BOBBY WOOD

64	Pye International 7N 25264	I'm A Fool For Loving You/My Heart Went Boing! Boing! Boing!	15

BRENTON WOOD

67	Philips BF 1579	Oogum Boogum Song/I Like The Way You Love Me	8
67	Liberty LBF 15021	Gimme Little Sign/I Think You Got Your Fools Mixed Up	8
68	Liberty LBF 15065	Baby You Got It/Catch You On The Rebound	8
68	Liberty LBF 15103	Some Got It, Some Don't/Me And You	8
70	Pye International 7N 25522	Great Big Bundle Of Love/Can You Dig It	15
67	Liberty LBL/LBS 83088E	GIMME A LITTLE SIGN (LP)	20

CHUCK WOOD

67	Big T BIG 104	Seven Days Too Long/Soul Shing-A-Ling	20
67	Big T BIG 104	Seven Days Too Long/Soul Shing-A-Ling (DJ Copy)	50
68	Big T BIG 107	I've Got My Lovelight Shining/Baby You Win	10
71	Mojo 2092 010	Seven Days Too Long/Soul Shing A Ling (reissue)	5
75	Pye Disco Demand DDS 111	Seven Days Too Long (in p/s)	15
75	Pye Disco Demand DDS 111	Seven Days Too Long	10

DEL WOOD

54	London HL 8036	Ragtime Annie/Backroom Polka	50
54	London RE-P 1007	RAGTIME PIANO (EP)	15
57	RCA RD 27011	DOWN YONDER (LP)	12

RONNIE WOOD
(see also Faces, Rolling Stones, Jeff Beck, Ted Wood)

74	Warner Bros K 16463	I Can Feel The Fire/Breathe On Me (as Ron Wood)	5
75	Warner Bros K 16618	If You Don't Want Me Love/I've Got A Feeling	5
76	Warner Bros K 16679	Big Bayou/Sweet Baby Mine	5
92	Continuum 12210-2	Show Me/Breathe On Me (CD, with Ronnie Wood print, signed & numbered, in black card case tied with ribbon, 600 only)	50
74	Warner Bros K 56065	I'VE GOT MY OWN ALBUM TO DO (LP, with insert)	12
75	Warner Bros K 56145	NOW LOOK (LP)	12

ROY WOOD
(see also Wizzard, Gerry Levine & Avengers, Mike Sheridan, Danny King['s Mayfair Set], Move, ELO, Renaissance [UK], Rockers, Birds)

72	Harvest HAR 5048	When Gran'ma Plays The Banjo/Wake Up	5
75	Jet JET 754	Oh What A Shame/Bengal Jig (cartoon p/s)	5
75	Jet JET 761	Look Thru' The Eyes Of A Fool/Strider (copies miscredited as "Looking Thru' The Eyes Of A Fool")	5
76	Jet JET 785	Any Old Time Will Do/The Rain Came Down On Everything	5
77	Warner Bros K 16961	The Stroll/Jubilee (p/s, by Wizzo Band)	5
77	Warner Bros K 17028	I Never Believed In Love/Inside My Life (as Roy Wood & Annie Haslam)	5
78	Warner Bros K 17094	Dancin' At The Rainbow's End/Waiting At This Door (p/s, as Wizzo Band)	5
78	Warner Bros K 17248	Keep Your Hands On The Wheel/Giant Footsteps	5
79	Automatic K 17459P	(We're) On The Road Again/Saxmaniacs (picture disc)	5
73	Harvest SHVL 803	BOULDERS (LP, textured sleeve with EMI logo on label)	12

TED WOOD
(see also Temperance Seven)

76	Penny Farthing PEN 891	Am I Blue/Shine (B-side features Rod Stewart, Ronnie Wood, Gary Glitter & Bobby Womack)	8

WOODEN HORSE
(see also Fox)

72	York SYK 526	Pick Up The Pieces/Wake Me In The Morning	20
73	York SYK 543	Wooden Horses/Typewriter And Guitar	20
72	York FYK 403	WOODEN HORSE (LP)	250
73	York FYK 413	WOODEN HORSE II (LP, withdrawn, with sleeve, blue/silver label)	900
73	York FYK 413	WOODEN HORSE II (LP, withdrawn, without sleeve, blue/silver label)	500

WOODEN O & GUESTS
(see also 'Middle Earth Sampler' in Various Artists section)

69	Middle Earth MDLS 301	A HANDFUL OF PLEASANT DELITES (LP)	125

KEN WOODMAN & HIS PICCADILLY BRASS

66	Strike JLH 101	THAT'S NICE (LP)	35

WOODMARK

83	Ooze S83 CUS 1692	When You're Gone/Life Is Cruel	20

MINT VALUE £

WOODPECKERS

64	Decca F 11835	The Woodpecker/You Can't Sit Down	10
65	Oriole CB 311	Hey Little Girl/What's Your Name	20

STANLEY WOODRUFF & U.S. TRIO

70	Ember EMB S 288	If I Let You/Will You Still Love Me Tomorrow	7
77	Grapevine GP 102	What Took You So Long/Now Is Forever	10

CAROL WOODS

70	Ember EMB S 288	If I Let You/Will You Still Love Me Tomorrow (p/s)	10
72	Ember NR 5059	OUT OF THE WOODS (LP)	15

CORA WOODS

56	Parlophone DP 505	Rocks In Your Head/I Don't Want To Cry (export 78)	10

DONALD WOODS & EARL PALMER BAND

58	Vogue V 9107	Memories Of An Angel/That Much Of Your Love	650
58	Vogue V 9107	Memories Of An Angel/That Much Of Your Love (78)	150

GAY & TERRY WOODS

(see also Woods Band, Gay Woods, Steeleye Span, Sweeney's Men)

77	Polydor 2058 810	Save The Last Dance For Me/One More Time	10
78	Rockburgh ROCS 202	We Can Work This One Out/Piece Of Summer (p/s)	10
75	Polydor 2383 322	BACKWOODS (LP)	50
76	Polydor 2383 375	THE TIME IS RIGHT (LP, with lyric insert)	60
76	Polydor 2383 406	RENOWNED (LP, with lyric insert)	50
78	Rockburgh ROC 104	TENDER HOOKS (LP, with lyric insert)	20

NICK WOODS

62	London HLU 9621	Ballad Of Billy Budd/Don't Let Me Down	8

PHIL WOODS

55	Esquire 20-055	NEW JAZZ QUINTET (10" LP)	35

TONY WOODS

71	Spiral DIT 2	I'm Only A Man/Blues	6

WOODS BAND

(see also Gay & Terry Woods)

71	Greenwich GSLP 1004	THE WOODS BAND (LP, gatefold sleeve)	150
77	Rockburgh CREST 29	THE WOODS BAND (LP, reissue in different sleeve)	20

MAGGIE WOODWARD

59	Vogue V 9148	Ali Bama/Zulu Warrior	15
59	Vogue V 9148	Ali Bama/Zulu Warrior (78)	20

WOODY KERN

69	Pye 7N 17672	Biography/Tell You I'm Gone (demo)	110
69	Pye NSPL 18273	THE AWFUL DISCLOSURES OF MARIA MONK (LP)	140

WOOL

69	Stateside SS2153	Love Love Love Love Love/If They Left Us Alone Now	25

BRIAN WOOLEY

58	Esquire EP 170	BRIAN WOOLEY'S JAZZMEN (EP)	10
58	Esquire EP 190	WILD 'N WOOLEY (EP)	10

SHEB WOOLEY

(see also Ben Colder)

51	MGM MGM 439	Hoot Owl Boogie/Country Kisses (78)	20
54	MGM MGM 757	Panama Pete/Blue Guitar (78)	10
55	MGM SP 1130	38-24-35/I Flipped	25
55	MGM SPC 5	Hill Billy Mambo/I Go Outa My Mind (export issue)	30
58	MGM MGM 981	The Purple People Eater/I Can't Believe You're Mine	20
58	MGM MGM 981	The Purple People Eater/Recipe For Love (2nd pressing, different B-side)	6
58	MGM MGM 981	The Purple People Eater/I Can't Believe You're Mine (78)	10
58	MGM MGM 997	Santa And The Purple People Eater/Star Of Love)	5
58	MGM MGM 997	Santa And The Purple People Eater/Star Of Love) (78)	10
59	MGM MGM 1017	Sweet Chile/More	10
60	MGM MGM 1081	Luke The Spook/My Only Treasure	7
61	MGM MGM 1132	The Wayward Wind/Bars Across The Windows	6
61	MGM MGM 1147	That's My Pa/Meet Mr. Lonely	6
62	MGM MGM 1162	Laughing The Blues/Somebody Please	6
65	MGM MGM 1257	Hootenanny Hoot/Old Joe Rag	5
65	MGM MGM 1263	Blue Guitar/Natchez Landing	5
56	MGM MGM-EP 540	JEST PLAIN, WILD AND WOOLEY (EP)	40
61	MGM MGM-C 859	SONGS FROM THE DAY OF RAWHIDE (LP)	20
62	MGM MGM-C 903	THAT'S MY MA AND THAT'S MY PA (LP)	20
63	MGM MGM-C 945	SPOOFING THE BIG ONES! (LP)	15

CHARLIE WOOLFE

(see also At Last The 1958 Rock & Roll Show)

68	NEMS 56-3675	Dance Dance Dance/Home	20

WOOLIES

67	RCA RCA 1602	Who Do You Love?/Hey Girl	50

JOHN WOOLLEY & JUST BORN

71	Decca 23134	Ruby Baby/Make Love Not War	10

WOOLLY FISH

70	Plexium PXM 16	Way You Like It/Sound Of Thick	6

BRENDA WOOTTON

71	Sentinel SENS 1006	PASTIES & CREAM (LP, with John The Fish)	12
73	Sentinel SENS 1016	CROWDY CRAWN (LP, with Richard Gendall)	12
74	Sentinel SENS 1021	NO SONG TO SING? (LP, with Robert Bartlett, private pressing with lyric inner sleeve)	12
76	Sentinel SENS 1031	STARRY-GAZEY PIE (LP, with Robert Bartlett)	12

MINT VALUE £

WORD
83 Word WORD 001 Colour It!/Recurring ... 5

WORDBUG
91 Boss Tuneage BOSSTAGE6 LOSING IT ALL (LP, also listed as Home 4, with insert) ... 12

WORK
(see also Art Bears)
81 Woof WOOF 2 I Hate America/Fingers & Toes/Duty (p/s, clear vinyl) ... 5
82 Recommended SLOW CRIMES (LP, with insert) ... 12

JIMMY WORK
56 London HLD 8270 When She Said "You All"/There's Only One You ... 60
56 London HLD 8270 When She Said "You All"/There's Only One You (78) ... 20
56 London HLD 8308 You've Gotta Heart Like A Merry-Go-Round/Blind Heart ... 45
56 London HLD 8308 You've Gotta Heart Like A Merry-Go-Round/Blind Heart (78) ... 20
55 London RE-D 1039 COUNTRY SONGS - WORK STYLE (EP) ... 30

WORKFORCE
80s WF WF 1 The Right To Work/Holy Moses (p/s) ... 5

WORKS
72 London HLU 10360 Orange Medley (Music Inspired By "A Clockwork Orange")/Sweet Charity ... 5

WORLD
(see also Neil Innes, Bonzo Dog [Doo-Dah] Band)
70 Liberty LBF 15402 Angelina/Come Out Into The Open ... 10
70 Liberty LBG 83419 LUCKY PLANET (LP, textured gatefold sleeve) ... 50

WORLD COLUMN
76 Capitol CL 15852 So Is The Sun/It's Not Right ... 8

WORLD OF OZ
(see also David Kubinec)
68 Deram DM 187 The Muffin Man/Peter's Birthday (Black And White Rainbows) ... 15
68 Deram DM 205 King Croesus/Jack ... 15
69 Deram DM 233 Willow's Harp/Like A Tear ... 25
69 Deram DML/SML 1034 THE WORLD OF OZ (LP) ... 60

WORLD OF TWIST
91 Circa CIRCD 17 QUALITY STREET (CD) ... 18

WORLD SOUND & POWER BAND
(See also D Witter)
80 D Roy DRLP 1006 MAWAMBA DUB (WARRIOR) CHAPTER TWO (LP) ... 55

BIMBI WORRICK
69 Polydor 56321 Long Time Comin'/Tomorrow Is My Day ... 8

WORRYING KYNDE
67 Piccadilly 7N 35370 Call Out The Name/Got The Blame ... 80

WORTH
70 CBS 5309 Shoot 'Em Up Baby/Take The World In Your Hands ... 5

JOHNNY WORTH
57 Columbia DB 3962 Let's Go/Just Because ... 6
60 Oriole CB 1545 Nightmare/Hold Me, Thrill Me, Kiss Me ... 40

MARION WORTH
60 London HL 7089 Are You Willing, Willie/This Heart Of Mine (export issue) ... 25
60 London HL 7097 That's My Kind Of Love/I Lost Johnny (export issue) ... 25

STAN WORTH ORCHESTRA
63 London HLU 9703 Roman Holiday/Wiggle Wobble Walkers ... 8

WRANGLERS
(see also Kenny Bernard, Kenny & Wranglers)
64 Parlophone R 5163 Liza Jane/It Just Won't Work ... 70

LINK WRAY (& HIS RAY MEN)
(see also Robert Gordon with Link Wray)
58 London HLA 8623 Rumble/The Swag (as Link Wray & His Ray Men) ... 50
58 London HLA 8623 Rumble/The Swag (as Link Wray & His Ray Men) (78) ... 30
63 Stateside SS 217 Jack The Ripper/The Black Widow ... 30
64 Stateside SS 256 The Sweeper/Weekend ... 20
65 Stateside SS 397 Good Rockin' Tonight/I'll Do Anything For You ... 20
71 Polydor 2066 120 Fire And Brimstone/Jukebox Mama ... 6
73 Polydor 2066 320 Lawdy Miss Clawdy/Shine The Light ... 6
73 Virgin VS 103 I'm So Glad, I'm So Proud/Shawnee Tribe ... 6
76 Virgin VS 142 I Know You're Leaving Me Now/Quicksand ... 6
64 Stateside SE 1015 MR. GUITAR (EP, sleeve credits Link Ray) ... 100
71 Polydor 2489 029 LINK WRAY (LP) ... 30
71 Union Pacific UP 002 THERE'S GOOD ROCKIN' TONIGHT (LP) ... 25
73 Virgin V 2006 BEANS & FATBACK (LP) ... 15
74 Polydor 2391 128 THE LINK WRAY RUMBLE (LP) ... 15

RAY WRAY QUARTET
62 Salvo SLO 1808 When Your Lover Has Gone/A Song Is Born ... 25

WRECKERS
64 Granta GR 7EP 1010 THE WRECKERS' SOUND (EP) ... 120

JENNY WREN
66 Fontana TF 672 Chasing My Dreams All Over Town/A Thought Of You ... 60
66 Fontana TF 772 The Merry-Go-Round (Is Slowing You Down)/Take A Walk Bobby ... 15

MINT VALUE £

BIG JOHN WRENCHER

75	Big Bear BB 4	BIG JOHN'S BOOGIE (LP)	12

WRETCHED

81	Wretched Music GRC 102	DNR/Souls In Torment (500 only)	50

WRIGGLERS

68	Giant GN 26	The Cooler/You Cannot Know	80
68	Blue Cat BS 106	Get Right/If I Did Look	35

BETTY WRIGHT

68	Atlantic 584 216	Girls Can't Do What The Guys Do/Sweet Lovin' Daddy	6
72	Atlantic K 10143	Clean Up Woman/I'll Love You Forever	10
72	Atlantic K 10190	Is It You Girl/Cryin' In My Sleep	5
75	RCA RCA 2548	Where Is The Love/My Baby Ain't My Baby Any More	5

BILLY WRIGHT

61	Parlophone R 4852	Sing Song For Kicks Part 1/Part 2	10

CHARLES WRIGHT & WATTS 103rd STREET RHYTHM BAND

69	Warner Bros WB 7250	Do Your Thing/A Dance, A Kiss And A Song	8
69	Warner Bros WB 7298	Till You Get Enough/Light My Fire	8
70	Warner Bros WB 7365	Love Land/Sorry Charlie	8
70	Warner Bros WB 7417	Express Yourself/Living On Borrowed Time	20
72	Jay Boy BOY 71	Spreadin' Honey/Charley (as Watts 103rd Street Rhythm Band)	10
70s	Warner Bros	EXPRESS YOURSELF (LP)	20

DALE WRIGHT

58	London HLD 8573	She's Neat/Say That You Care (as Dale Wright & Rock-Its)	230
58	London HLD 8573	She's Neat/Say That You Care (as Dale Wright & Rock-Its) (78)	65
59	Pye International 7N 25022	That's Show Biz/That's My Gal (as Dale Wright & Wright Guys)	100
59	Pye International 7N 25022	That's Show Biz/That's My Gal (as Dale Wright & Wright Guys) (78)	80

EARL WRIGHT

75	Capitol CL 15825	Thumb A Ride/Like A Rolling Stone	8
75	Capitol CL 15825	Thumb A Ride/Like A Rolling Stone (DJ Copy)	20

GARY WRIGHT('S WONDERWHEEL)

(see also Spooky Tooth, Magic Christians, Thomas F. Browne)

72	A&M AMS 888	I know/Tonight It's Right	12
71	A&M AMLS 2004	EXTRACTIONS (LP, poster sleeve)	30
72	A&M AMLS 64296	FOOTPRINT (LP)	12
72	A&M AMLH 64362	RING OF CHANGES (LP, as Wright's Wonderwheel; unissued, test pressings only)	50

GEORGE WRIGHT/NEVILLE MITCHELL

82	Kingdom KV 8026	GEORGE WRIGHT - You Are The One I Love/ROOTS RADICS - I Done It Dub/ NEVILL MITCHELL - Get Out Of Hand/ROOTS RADICS - Hand Made Dub	25

GINNY WRIGHT (& TOM TALL)

(see also T. Tommy Cutrer & Ginny Wright, Tom Tall)

55	London HL 8119	Indian Moon/Your Eyes Feasted Upon Her (solo)	50
55	London HL 8119	Indian Moon/Your Eyes Feasted Upon Her (solo) (78)	12
55	London HL 8150	Are You Mine?/Boom Boom Boomerang (with Tom Tall)	40
55	London RE-U 1035	COUNTRY SONGS VOL. 2 (EP, with Tom Tall)	30

MILTON WRIGHT & TERRA SHIRMA STRINGS

77	Grapevine GRP 103	I Belong To You/The Gallop	6

NAT WRIGHT

59	HMV POP 629	Anything/For You My Love	75

OTIS WRIGHT

69	High Note HS 033	Man Of Galilee/Take Up The Cross	6
67	Doctor Bird DLM 5005	PEACE PERFECT PEACE (LP)	50
67	Doctor Bird DLM 5006	IT WILL SOON BE DONE (LP)	50
68	High Notes BSL5003	SACRED SONGS (LP)	30
60s	Coxsone TLP 1001	OVER IN GLORYLAND (LP)	40
73	Tabernacle BSLP 5021	SOUL STIRRING GOSPEL SONGS (LP)	40

O.V. WRIGHT

65	Vocalion VP 9249	You're Gonna Make Me Cry/Monkey Dog	20
66	Vocalion VP 9255	Poor Boy/I'm In Your Corner	20
66	Vocalion VP 9272	Gone For Good/How Long Baby	20
67	London HLZ 10137	8 Men 4 Women/Fed Up With The Blues	15
68	Sue WI 4043	What About You/What Did You Tell This Girl Of Mine	50
68	Action ACT 4505	Oh Baby Mine/Working Your Game	15
69	Action ACT 4527	I Want Everyone To Know/I'm Gonna Forget About You	15
65	Vocalion VEP 170165	CAN'T FIND TRUE LOVE (EP)	100
68	Island ILP 975	8 MEN, 4 WOMEN (LP)	120

OWEN WRIGHT

70	Banana BA 310	Wala Wala (actually by Burning Spear)/JERRY & FREEDOM SINGERS: Got To Be Sure (B-side actually by Horace Andy)	20

RICHARD WRIGHT

(see also Pink Floyd, Zee)

78	Harvest SHVL 818	WET DREAM (LP, gatefold stickered sleeve)	12

RITA WRIGHT

68	Tamla Motown TMG 643	I Can't Give Back The Love I Feel For You/Something On My Mind	30
68	Tamla Motown TMG 643	I Can't Give Back The Love I Feel For You/Something On My Mind (DJ copy)	40
71	Tamla Motown TMG 791	I Can't Give Back The Love I Feel For You/Something On My Mind (reissue)	10
78	Jet UP 36382	Love Is All You Need/Touch Me, Take Me	120

MINT VALUE £

RUBEN WRIGHT

66	Capitol CL 15460	Hey Girl/I'm Walking Out On You	30
66	Capitol CL 15460	Hey Girl/I'm Walking Out On You (DJ copy)	75

RUBY WRIGHT

53	Parlophone MSP 6025	Till I Waltz Again With You/When I Gave You My Love (with Charlie Gore)	20
54	Parlophone MSP 6073	Bimbo/Boy, You Got Yourself A Gal	25
54	Parlophone MSP 6133	Santa's Little Sleigh Bells/Toodle-oo To You	10
55	Parlophone MSP 6150	What Have They Told You?/I Had The Funniest Feeling	15
56	Parlophone MSP 6209	I Fall In Love With You Ev'ry Day/Do You Believe?	15
59	Parlophone R 4556	Three Stars/I Only Have One Lifetime	5
59	Parlophone R 4589	You're Just A Flower From An Old Bouquet/Sweet Night Of Love	5
59	Parlophone GEP 8785	THE THREE STARS GIRL (EP)	30

SAMUEL E. WRIGHT

73	Paramount PARA 3035	There's Something Funny Going On/300 Pounds Of Hunger	15

STEVE WRIGHT

59	London HLW 8991	Wild, Wild, Woman/Love You	250
59	London HLW 8991	Wild, Wild, Woman/Love You (78)	125

STEVEN WRIGHT

93	Reggae On Top ROT 001	Vision Of Jah/Dub Versions (12")	25

STEVIE WRIGHT

74	Polydor 2121246	Evie - Let Your Hair Down/Evie	8
74	Polydor 2480 249	HARD ROAD (LP)	20

SYREETA WRIGHT

72	Mowest MWS 7001	SYREETA (LP)	20

WINSTON WRIGHT

(see also Ethiopians, John Holt, J.J. Allstars, Slickers)

69	Doctor Bird DB 1308	Five Miles High/CARL DAWKINS: Only Girl	40
69	Camel CA 32	Power Pack/TWO SPARKS: Throwing Stones	30
69	Explosion EX 2003	Barefoot Brigade/Slippery	20
69	Trojan TR 7701	Moonlight (Lover) Groover/SENSATIONS: Everyday Is Just A Holiday	20
69	Trojan TR 7715	Moon Invader (with Tommy McCook)/RADCLIFF RUFFIN: You Got To Love Me	20
70	Trojan TR 7775	Meshwire (with Tommy McCook)/BARONS: Darling Please Return	20
70	Explosion EX 2011	Flight 404/LLOYD & ROBIN: Gawling Come Down (B-side actually Higher Than The Highest Mountain by Monty Morris)	20
70	Explosion EX 2015	Funny Girl/Funny Girl Version II	20
70	Duke DU 62	Poppy Cock (with J.J. All Stars)/CARL DAWKINS: This World And Me (B-side actually "Satisfaction")	20
70	Bamboo BAM 60	Reggae Feet/DON DRUMMOND: Royal Flush (B-side act. titled "The Rocket")	30
70	High Note HS 040	Soul Pressure/Seed You Sow (with Gaytones)	12
70	Moodisc MU 3501	Musically Red (with Maudie's Allstars; actually also with Count Sticky)/ RHYTHM RULERS: Bratah	20
70	G.G. GG 4504	It's Been A Long Time/PAULETTE & GEE: Feel It More And More	8
70	Techniques TE 907	Top Secret/Crazy Rhythm	10
71	Upsetter US 378	Example (with 3rd & 4th Generation)/UPSETTER: Version	25
71	Duke DU 111	Silhouettes/That Did It	10
71	Camel CA 71	Silhouettes/That Did It	12
71	Green Door GD 4011	Heads Or Tails/THE ROASTERS: Raunchy	6
77	Third World TWS 923	JUMP THE FENCE (LP)	20

ZACHARIAH WRIGHT

70s	Bamboo BAM 403	Lumumba Limbo/Green, Red and Gold	10

BERNARD WRIGLEY

74	Topic 12TS 241	ROUGH AND WRIGLEY (LP)	12
76	Transatlantic TRA 327	SONGS, STORIES AND ELEPHANTS (LP)	12

WRIGLEYS

69	Page One POF 118	A Little Bit/Come Down Little Bird	10

WRINKLE

01	Mook MKCDS	LA LUMINOL EP: La Luminol/Wool Box DC/The Source Of The Flood/ Canada Cool (CD single)	30

WRIT

66	Decca F 12385	Did You Ever Have To Make Up Your Mind/Solid Golden Teardrops	20

WRITING ON THE WALL

(see also 'Middle Earth Sampler' in Various Artists; Three's A Crowd)

69	Middle Earth MDS 101	Child On A Crossing/Lucifer Corpus	50
73	Pye 7N 45251	Man Of Renown/Buffalo	20
69	Middle Earth MDLS 303	THE POWER OF THE PICTS (LP, textured sleeve)	250
95	Pie & Mash PAM 003	RARITIES FROM THE MIDDLE EARTH (LP, 500 copies only)	12
95	Tenth Planet TP 017	CRACKS IN THE ILLUSION OF LIFE (LP, gatefold sleeve)	12
96	Tenth Planet TP 018	BURGHLEY ROAD (LP, 1,000 copies only)	12

W12 SPOTS

70s	Shepherds Bush SB 1	Sid Never Did/COSMIC PUNKS: 99 Years	12

WUGGERY

98	Wuggery WUG 1	Wuggery Muggery/Wugwats Weekend (p/s)	8

WURZEL

(see also Motorrhead)

87	GWR GWR 4	Bess/People Say I'm Crazy (p/s)	8
87	GWR GWT 4	Bess/People Say I'm Crazy/Midnight In London/E.S.P. (12", p/s)	15

WURZELS

77	EMI EMI 2686	One For The Bristol City/Cheddar Cheese (p/s)	6
05	Rough Trade RTRADS302	Remember Me/I Am A Cider Drinker (British Sea Power) (7" ltd ed. 1,966 copies)	10

MINT VALUE £

JOHNNY WYATT

68	President PT 109	This Thing Called Love/To Whom It May Concern (horizontal)	50
68	President PT 109	This Thing Called Love/To Whom It May Concern (vertical artist credit)	10

ROBERT WYATT

(see also Soft Machine, Matching Mole, Centipede, Ben Watt)

74	Virgin VS 114	I'm A Believer/Memories	5
77	Virgin VS 115	Yesterday Man/Sonia	6
82	Rough Trade	Shipbuilding/Memories of You (This 7" came in 4 different multi-fold art sleeves Most common are 'Blanket' and 'Rope' covers, 'Metal Rings' and 'Hot Coals' are less common)	6
97	Hannibal TRDSC 010	Free Will And Testament/The Sight Of The Wind	6
70	CBS 64189	THE END OF AN EAR (LP)	35
74	Virgin V 2017	ROCK BOTTOM (LP)	15
75	Virgin V 2034	RUTH IS STRANGER THAN RICHARD (LP)	20
82	Rough Trade ROUGH 35	NOTHING CAN STOP US (LP, early pressing without "Shipbuilding")	15
81	Virgin VGD 3505	ROCK BOTTOM/RUTH IS STRANGER THAN RICHARD (2-LP reissue)	25
87	Strange Fruit SFPS 037	PEEL SESSIONS (12")	15
85	Rough Trade ROUGH 69	OLD ROTTENHAT (LP, gatefold)	20
08	Domino REWIGLP 47	CUCKOOLAND (2-LP)	18
08	Domino REWIGLP 45	SHLEEP (2-LP)	18

RICHARD ('POPCORN') WYLIE

63	Columbia DB 7012	Brand New Man/So Much Love In My Heart (as Richard Wylie)	40
77	Grapevine GRP 100	Rosemary What Happened (Parts 1 & 2) (as Richard 'Popcorn' Wylie)	8

BILL WYMAN

(see also Rolling Stones, End)

74	Rolling Stones RS 19112	Monkey Grip Glue/What A Blow	5
74	Rolling Stones RS 19115	White Lightning/Pussy	7
76	Rolling Stones RS 19119	A Quarter To Three/Soul Satisfying	5
76	Rolling Stones RS 19120	Apache Woman/Soul Satisfying	8
81	A&M AMS 8144	(Si Si) Ju Suis Un Rock Star/Rio De Janeiro	6
81	Polydor POSP 259	Tenderness (Maria Muldaur)/Noche De Amor	7
81	Polydor POSP 291	Green Ice Theme/Cloudhoppers (p/s)	12
83	Ripple (no cat. no.)	DIGITAL DREAMS (LP, soundtrack, promo only)	50

WYNDER K. FROG

(see also Keef Hartley Band, Miller Anderson, Fair Weather, Grease Band)

66	Island WI 280	Turn On Your Lovelight/Zooming	30
66	Island WI 3011	Sunshine Superman/Blues For A Frog	30
67	Island WIP 6006	Green Door/Dancing Frog	45
67	Island WIP 6014	I Am A Man/Shook Shimmy & Shake	55
68	Island WIP 6044	Jumping Jack Flash/Baldy	35
67	Island ILPS 9044	SUNSHINE SUPERFROG (LP, white label, stereo)	125

KES WYNDHAM

71	Pye 7N 45082	Honey Call Me Home/Broken Bicycle	10

MARTYN WYNDHAM-READ

(see also A.L. Lloyd)

70	Trailer LER 2009	NED KELLY AND THAT GANG (LP, white label)	18
70	Trailer LER 2009	NED KELLY AND THAT GANG (LP, later 'highway' label)	12
71	Trailer LER 2028	MARTYN WYNDHAM-READ (LP)	12
73	Argo ZFB 82	HARRY THE HAWKER IS DEAD (LP)	15
75	Trailer LER 2092	MAYPOLES TO MISTLETOE (LP)	12
77	Broadside BRO 128	ENGLISH SPORTING BALLADS (LP, 1 side by High Level Ranters, 2000 only)	15

PETER WYNGARDE

(see also Larry Wallis, Tyrannosaurus Rex)

70	RCA Victor RCA 1967	La Ronde De L'Amour/The Way I Cry Over You	30
70	RCA Victor PW 1	Commits Rape/The Way I Cry Over You (LP sampler, promo only)	45
70	RCA Victor SF 8087	PETER WYNGARDE (LP, gatefold sleeve)	65

PETER WYNNE

59	Parlophone R 4597	Twilight Time/Chapel Of Dreams	7
60	Parlophone R 4668	Ask Anyone In Love/I Need You Close Again	6
60	Parlophone R 4705	Our Concerto/Your lover	6

SANDY WYNNS

65	Fontana TF 550	Touch Of Venus/Lovers' Quarrel	260

MARK WYNTER

(see also Joe Brown & Mark Wynter)

60	Decca F 11263	Image Of A Girl/Glory Of Love	7
60	Decca F 11279	Kickin' Up The Leaves/That's What I Thought	10
61	Decca F 11323	Dream Girl/Two Little Girls	5
61	Decca F 11354	Exclusively Yours/Warm And Willing	5
61	Decca F 11380	Girl For Ev'ry Day/The Best Time For Love	6
62	Decca F 11434	Heaven's Plan/In Your Heart	6
62	Decca F 11467	Angel Talk/I Love Her Still	8
62	Pye 7N 15466	Venus In Blue Jeans/Please Come Back To Me	6
62	Pye 7N 15492	Go Away Little Girl/That Kinda Talk	5
63	Pye 7N 15511	Aladdin's Lamp/It Can Happen Any Day	8
63	Pye 7N 15525	Shy Girl/Because Of You	8
63	Pye 7N 15554	Running To You/Don't Cry	8
63	Pye 7N 15577	It's Almost Tomorrow/Music To Midnight	6
64	Pye 7N 15595	The Boy You're Kissin'/I Learned A Lot From You	6
64	Pye 7N 15626	Only You/It's Love You Want	5
64	Pye 7N 15658	Answer Me/I Wish You Everything	5
64	Pye 7N 15686	Love Hurts/Can't Help Forgiving You	5

MINT VALUE £

Year	Label/Cat. No.	Title	Value
64	Pye 7N 15716	Forever And A Day/And I Love Her	5
65	Pye 7N 15771	Can I Get To Know You Better/Am I Living A Dream	6
65	Pye 7N 15861	Someday You'll Want Me To Want You/Here Comes Summer	5
66	Pye 7N 17051	Before Your Time/Something About You	5
66	Pye 7N 17122	We'll Sing In The Sunshine/Pencil And Paper	16
66	Pye 7N 17214	You Made Me What I Am/One Girl	5
67	Pye 7N 17438	Please Love Me Forever/The Best Thing In My Life Is You	5
69	Philips BF 1822	Where Is She/Good Money	5
60	Decca DFE 6674	MARK TIME (EP)	15
63	Pye NEP 24176	IT'S MARK TIME (EP)	10
64	Pye NEP 24185	WYNTER TIME (EP)	10
61	Decca LK 4409	THE WARMTH OF WYNTER (LP)	30
65	Ace Of Clubs ACL 1141	MARK WYNTER (LP)	20

GAIL WYNTERS

Year	Label/Cat. No.	Title	Value
67	London HLE 10144	Snap Your Fingers/Find Myself A New Love	12

WYOMING

Year	Label/Cat. No.	Title	Value
72	MAM MAMR 76	Seven Days/Two Faced Woman	12

X

X

Year	Label/Cat. No.	Title	Value
80	Slash UK SR-104	LOS ANGELES (LP, with insert)	18

JOHNNY X & THE SINGIN' SWINGIN' EIGHT

Year	Label/Cat. No.	Title	Value
63	Fontana TF 408	Lemonade/Come Closer Melinda	12

X-CALIBURS

Year	Label/Cat. No.	Title	Value
65	CBS 201805	We Will Love/Swing That Chariot	10
65	Mercury MF 941	You'll Find Out/That's What Happens (possibly as Xcalibres)	10

X-CELLS

Year	Label/Cat. No.	Title	Value
81	Snotty Snail NEL COL 4	Freedom Man/SCHIZOID: Nowhere To Go (p/s)	20

X-CERTS

Year	Label/Cat. No.	Title	Value
78	Zama	Feeling The Groove (p/s)	15
81	Recreational PLAY 1	Together/Untogether (p/s, with lyric insert)	6

X-DREAMYSTS

Year	Label/Cat. No.	Title	Value
78	Good Vibrations GOT 5	Right Way Home/Dance Away Love (p/s)	12
79	Polydor 2059 129	Bad News/Money Talks (p/s)	10
80	Polydor 2059 235	I Don't Wanna Go/Silly Games (p/s)	10
80	Polydor 2059 252	Stay The Way You Are/Race Against Time (p/s)	10
80	Polydor	XDREAMYSTS (LP)	25

X-E-CUTORS

Year	Label/Cat. No.	Title	Value
80	Rok ROK 13/14	Too Far To Look Inside My Head/X-FILMS: After My Blood (die-cut co. sleeve)	10

XENTRIX

Year	Label/Cat. No.	Title	Value
90	Roadracer RO 2435 2	Ghost Busters/Nobody's Perfect/Interrogate (CD)	10

XERO

(see also Bruce Dickinson, Iron Maiden)

Year	Label/Cat. No.	Title	Value
83	Brickyard XERO 1	Oh Baby/Hold On (2-track issue, p/s)	15
83	Brickyard XERO 1	Oh Baby/Hold On/Lone Wolf (3-track limited issue, p/s)	8
83	Brickyard XERO 1T	Oh Baby/Hold On/Lone Wolf (12", plain card sleeve with sticker, withdrawn)	15
83	Brickyard XERO 1T	Oh Baby/Hold On/Killer Frog (12", reissue)	8

XILES

Year	Label/Cat. No.	Title	Value
64	Xiles 80-XIL-1	THE XILES (EP, home-made p/s)	40
65	Xiles XIL 004	Our Love Will Never End/The Only People In This World	25

XIT

Year	Label/Cat. No.	Title	Value
72	Rare Earth RES 107	I Was Raised/End	5
73	Rare Earth RES 111	Reservation Of Education/Young Warrior	5
72	Rare Earth SREA 4002	PLIGHT OF THE RED MAN (LP)	15

XL5

Year	Label/Cat. No.	Title	Value
63	HMV POP 1148	XL5 (Zero G)/Caviare	20
63	HMV 7EG 8802	FIREBALL AND OTHER TITLES (EP, 2 tracks by Don Spencer)	50

XL5's

Year	Label/Cat. No.	Title	Value
80	Fourplay FOUR 004	Fireball/Misirlou	8

X-MAL DEUTSCHLAND

Year	Label/Cat. No.	Title	Value
83	4AD AD 311	Incubus Succubus II/Vito (12" p/s, with "Vito" listed as A-side)	10

X-MEN

Year	Label/Cat. No.	Title	Value
84	Creation CRE 006	Do The Ghost/Talk (foldaround p/s in bag, orange/blue or yellow/green p/s)	5
85	Creation CRE 013	Spiral Girl/Bad Girl (foldaround p/s in polyester bag)	5

X-O-DUS

Year	Label/Cat. No.	Title	Value
79	Factory FAC 11	English Black Boys/See Them A-Come (12", dark-grey textured p/s, later light grey p/s)	8

XPOZEZ

Year	Label/Cat. No.	Title	Value
82	Red Rhino RED 15	1,000 Marching Feet/Terminal Case (p/s)	5
83	Sexual Phonograph SPH 2	(Be My) New York Doll/It's All Been Done Before (p/s)	5

MINT VALUE £

X PRESS
75 A Rover AR 03 — Tell Me Baby/High Road — 8

X-PRESS
80 Express 1 — Junked Up Judy/Stop Start — 60

X-RAY SPEX
(see also Poly Styrene, Essential Logic)
77 Virgin VS 189 — Oh Bondage, Up Yours/I Am A Cliche (in p/s) — 30
77 Virgin VS 189 — Oh Bondage, Up Yours/I Am A Cliche — 5
77 Virgin VS 189-12 — Oh Bondage, Up Yours/I Am A Cliche (12", company sleeve) — 12
78 EMI International INT 553 — The Day The World Turned Day-Glo/Lama Poseur (p/s, 15,000 orange vinyl) — 8
78 EMI International INT 563 — Identity/Let's Submerge (p/s, on pink vinyl) — 8
78 EMI International INT 573 — Germ Free Adolescents/Age (p/s) — 5
79 EMI International INT 583 — Highly Inflammable/Warrior In Woolworths (p/s, on red vinyl) — 8
78 EMI Intl. INS 3023 — GERM FREE ADOLESCENTS (LP, with lyric inner sleeve) — 20

X-RAYS
59 London HLR 8805 — Chinchilla/Out Of Control — 35
59 London HLR 8805 — Chinchilla/Out Of Control (78) — 20

XS DISCHARGE
80 G. Marxist COMMINIQUE 3 — Across The Border/Frustration (p/s) — 15
80 Groucho Marxist WH 3 — Life's A Wank (p/s) — 20

XS ENERGY
78 World WRECK 1 — Eighteen/Jenny's Alright/Horrorscope! (numbered foldover yellow or green p/s, stamped white labels) — 18
79 Dead Good DEAD 1 — Eighteen/Jenny's Alright/Horrorscope! (reissue, 'National Souvenir Issue', different foldover p/s, stamped white labels) — 10
79 Dead Good DEAD 1 — Eighteen/Jenny's Alright/Horrorscope! (stamped white sleeve & yellow printed labels) — 10
79 Dead Good DEAD 3 — Use You/Imaginary (p/s) — 15

XTC
(see also Mr Partridge, Barry Andrews, Three Wise Men, Dukes Of Stratosphere)o Colonel, Spys)
77 Virgin VS 188 — Science Friction/She's So Square (unreleased, in picture sleeve) — 2500
77 Virgin VS 188 — Science Friction/She's So Square (unreleased, no picture sleeve) — 80
77 Virgin VS 188-12 — 3D EP (12" version of the above, p/s) — 8
78 Virgin VS 201 — Statue Of Liberty/Hang On To The Night (p/s) — 5
78 Virgin VS 209 — This Is Pop?/Heatwave (p/s) — 5
79 Virgin VS 259 — Life Begins At The Hop/Homo Safari (30,000 clear vinyl, PVC sleeve & insert) — 5
79 Virgin VS 282 — Making Plans For Nigel/Bushman President (Homo Safari Series No. 2)/ Pulsing, Pulsing (with game-board p/s with playing pieces) — 5
79 Smash Hits HIT 002 — Ten Feet Tall/SKIDS: The Olympian (33rpm red flexidisc with Smash Hits) — 8
79 Smash Hits HIT 002 — Ten Feet Tall/SKIDS: The Olympian (33rpm red flexidisc without Smash Hits) — 5
80 Virgin VS 365 — Generals And Majors/Don't Lose Your Temper//Smokeless Zone/ The Somnambulist (double pack) — 6
81 Virgin VS 372 — Towers Of London/Set Myself On Fire (live)//Battery Brides (live)/ Scissor Man (double pack) — 6
81 RSO RSO 71 — Take This Town/RUTS: Babylon's Burning (p/s) — 6
81 Virgin VS 384 — Sgt. Rock (Is Going To Help Me)/Living Through Another Cuba/ Generals And Majors (1st 20,000 in poster p/s, with stickered PVC sleeve) — 5
82 Lyntone LYN 11032 — Looking For Footprints (flexidisc free with Flexipop magazine, issue 16; on red, blue, green or yellow vinyl) — 8
82 Lyntone LYN 11032 — Looking For Footprints (flexidisc free without Flexipop magazine, issue 16; on red, blue, green or yellow vinyl) — 5
82 Virgin VS 490 — No Thugs In Our House/Chain Of Command/Limelight/ Over Rusty Water (9" die-cut gatefold p/s) — 6
87 Virgin CDEP 3 — Dear God/Homo Safari/Bushman President/Egyptian Solution/Mantis On Parole/ Frost Circus/Procession Toward Learning Land (CD, gatefold card sleeve) — 8
88 Virgin CDT 9 — Senses Working Overtime/Egyptian Solution (Homo Safari Series No. 3)/ Blame The Weather/Tissue Tigers (The Arguers) (3" CD, card sleeve) — 8
89 Virgin VSCD 1158 — Mayor Of Simpleton/Ella Guru/Living In A Haunted Heart/ The Good Things (3" CD, gatefold card sleeve) — 8
89 Virgin VSCD 1177 — King For A Day (7" Version)/King For A Day (12" Version)/ My Paint Heroes (Home Demo)/Skeletons (Home Demo) (3" CD, 'crown' pack) — 8
92 Virgin VS 1426 — Wrapped In Grey (p/s, withdrawn, 2,000 only) — 60
92 Virgin VSCDT 1426 — WRAPPED IN GREY (CD EP, withdrawn, 2,000 only) — 80
78 Virgin V 2095 — WHITE MUSIC (LP, with black inner sleeve) — 12
78 Virgin V 2108 — GO 2 (LP, with insert, 1st 15,000 with bonus 12" EP: "Go +") — 15
79 Virgin V 2129 — DRUMS AND WIRES (LP, with gatefold insert, 1st 15,000 with free 7": Chain Of Command/"Limelight" [VDJ 30]) — 12
80 Virgin V 2173 — BLACK SEA (LP, with green paper outer sleeve & lyric insert) — 12
84 Virgin V 2251 — WAXWORKS (LP, with bonus LP, "Beeswax") — 12
84 Virgin V 2325 — THE BIG EXPRESS (LP, circular sleeve & lyric inner) — 12
88 Virgin CDVT 2581 — ORANGES AND LEMONS (LP, as 3-CD single box set) — 12

XTRAVERTS
78 Spike SRTS SP 001 — Blank Generation/A-Lad-In-Sane — 90
78 Rising Sun RS 1 — Police State/PLASTIC PEOPLE: Demolition (p/s, multi-coloured vinyl) — 60
81 Xtraverts XTRA 001 — Speed/1984 (white labels, 'photo' foldout poster p/s) — 35
81 Xtraverts XTRA 001 — Speed/1984 (white labels, 'no photo' foldout poster p/s) — 50

XX
09 Young Turks YT 023 — Crystalised/Hot Like Fire (p/s) — 8

YABBY U/YABBY YOU/YABBY YOUTH

78	Prophets PHTS 2337	King Pharaoh Plague On The Land/Babylon Kingdom Fall (12")	30
78	Grove Music GMDM 6	Jah vengeance / Free Africa (12", as Vivian "Yabby U" Jackson with Trinity)	25
79	Grove Music GMDM 18	Babylon A Fall/TONY TUFF - Falling Babylon (12")	40
79	Grove Music GMDM 24	Lady Lady/Stop Your Quarelling (12", B-side with Tommy McCook)	30
79	Grove Music GMDM 6	Jah Vengeance/Free Africa (12" p/s, with Trinity)	30
76	Lucky PD LPYU	RAM-A-DAM (LP)	200
77	Grove Music GMLP 001	DELIVER ME FROM MY ENEMIES (LP, credited to The Yabby You Vibration on sleeve)	60
77	Grove Music GMLP 004	BEWARE DUB (LP)	80
78	Nationwide PRO 001	CHANT DOWN BABYLON KINGDOM (LP)	60
78	Eve PD LP	YU RAM-A-DAM (LP, reissue of Lucky PD LPYU))	35
80	Grove / Island ILPS 9615	JAH JAH WAY (LP)	40
82	WLN WNLP001	YABBY YOU MEETS SLY 'N' ROBBIE (LP, with Tommy McCook)	20

YACHTS

(see also Big In Japan)

77	Stiff BUY 19	Suffice To Say/Freedom Is A Heavy Wine (p/s)	5
78	Radar ADA 23	Look Back In Love (Not In Anger)/I Can't Stay Long (p/s, blue vinyl)	6
79	Radar RAD 19	THE YACHTS (LP, with live 7" "Suffice To Say"/"On And On" [SAM 98, p/s])	12
80	Radar RAD 27	YACHTS WITHOUT RADAR (LP)	12

YADS

92	Fairfields YAD 2	Yippee For Shtonk/It's There, You Mong (p/s)	7

YA HO WA 13

(see also Seeds)

83	Psycho PSYCHO 2	GOLDEN SUNRISE (LP, 319 copies only, different coloured vinyls, some on black vinyl without sleeve)	60

YAKS

65	Decca F 12115	Yakety Yak/Back In '57	20

YAMASUKIS

71	Dandelion DAN 7004	Yamasuki/Aieada (p/s)	15

YAMI BOLO

86	Greensleeves GREL 140	JAH JAH MADE THEM ALL (LP)	20

YANA

56	HMV POP 252	Climb Up The Wall/If You Don't Love Me	20
57	HMV POP 340	Mr. Wonderful/Too Close For Comfort	15
58	HMV POP 481	I Need You/I Miss You Mama	10
58	HMV POP 546	Papa And Mama/In The Morning	10

YANCEY

79	Octane WS 302	Standing Waiting/Woman (no p/s)	20
79	Hammer HS 302	Standing Waiting/Woman (reissue)	8

JIMMY YANCEY

54	HMV 7EG 8062	JIMMY YANCEY (EP)	20
55	HMV 7EG 8083	JIMMY YANCEY (EP)	20
58	Vogue EPV 1203	YANCEY'S PIANO (EP)	20
54	London AL 3525	JIMMY YANCEY - A LOST RECORDING DATE (10" LP)	25
56	Vogue LDE 166	JAZZ IMMORTALS VOLUME 2 (10" LP)	30
68	Atlantic 590 018	LOWDOWN DIRTY BLUES (LP)	15

MAMA YANCEY/DON EWELL

(see also Don Ewell)

57	Tempo LAP 7	MAMA YANCEY-DON EWELL (10" LP)	30

ZALMAN YANOVSKY

(see also Mugwumps, Lovin' Spoonful)

67	Kama Sutra KAS 209	As Long As You're Here/Ereh Er'uoy Sa Gnol Sa (unreleased)	0
67	Pye International 7N 25438	As Long As You're Here/Ereh Er'uoy Sa Gnol Sa	8
71	Kama Sutra 2316 003	ALIVE AND WELL IN ARGENTINA (LP)	18

YARDBIRDS

(see also Eric Clapton, Jeff Beck, Jimmy Page, Keith Relf, Reign, Stairway, Sonny Boy Williamson & Yardbirds, Shoot)

64	Columbia DB 7283	I Wish You Would/A Certain Girl	30
64	Columbia DB 7391	Good Morning Little Schoolgirl/I Ain't Got You	30
65	Columbia DB 7499	For Your Love/Got To Hurry	10
65	Columbia DB 7594	Heart Full Of Soul/Steeled Blues	10
65	Columbia DB 7706	Evil Hearted You/Still I'm Sad (some copies with A-side miscredited to Samwell-Smith & McCartney)	7
66	Columbia DB 7848	Shapes Of Things/You're A Better Man Than I	7
66	Columbia DB 7848	Shapes Of Things/Still I'm Sad (mispressing)	45
66	Columbia DB 7928	Over, Under, Sideways, Down/Jeff's Boogie	15
66	Columbia DB 8024	Happenings Ten Years Time Ago/Psycho Daisies	30
67	Columbia DB 8165	Little Games/Puzzles	30
68	Columbia DB 8368	Goodnight Sweet Josephine/Think About It (unreleased; EMIdisc acetates only)	200
64	Columbia SEG 8421	FIVE YARDBIRDS (EP)	100
67	Columbia SEG 8521	OVER UNDER SIDEWAYS DOWN (EP)	200

MINT VALUE £

64	Columbia 33SX 1677	FIVE LIVE YARDBIRDS (LP, 1st pressing, blue/black label, flipback sleeve)	150
69	Columbia 33SX 1677	FIVE LIVE YARDBIRDS (LP, 2nd pressing, black/silver label, flipback sleeve)	22
60s	Columbia TA SX 6063	FIVE LIVE YARDBIRDS (reel-to-reel tape)	20
66	Columbia SCXC 28	HAVING A RAVE UP WITH THE YARDBIRDS (LP, export issue)	180
66	Columbia SX 6063	THE YARDBIRDS (LP, 1st pressing, blue/black label, flipback sleeve, mono)	70
66	Columbia SCX 6063	THE YARDBIRDS (LP, 1st pressing, blue/black label, flipback sleeve, stereo)	60
69	Columbia S(C)X 6063	THE YARDBIRDS (LP, 2nd pressing, black/silver label, flipback sleeve)	20
70	Columbia S(C)X 6063	THE YARDBIRDS (LP, 3rd pressing, black/silver label, non-flipback sleeve; misprinted without front cover illustration)	18
70	Columbia S(C)X 6063	THE YARDBIRDS (LP, 3rd pressing, black/silver label, non-flipback sleeve)	15
84	Charly BOX 104	SHAPES OF THINGS (LP, box set)	30

PER YARROH

(see also Roy Harper)

88	HMV PY 1	Laughing Inside/Laughing Inside (p/s, promo only; actually by Roy Harper)	7

TOM YATES

67	CBS BPG 63094	SECOND CITY SPIRITUAL (LP, as Thomas Yates)	90
72	President PTLS 1053	LOVE COMES WELL ARMED (LP, with booklet)	25
77	Satril SATL 4007	SONG OF THE SHIMMERING WAY (LP, with insert)	20

Y BLEW

67	Qualiton QSP 7001	Maes 'B'/Beth Sy'n Dod Rhyngom Ni (p/s)	10

YEAH YEAH YEAHS

01	Wichita WEBB 029T	YEAH YEAH YEAHS EP: Bang/Mystery Girl/Art Star/Miles Away/Our Time (12", p/s)	10
03	Dress Up 0760611	FEVER TO TELL (LP picture disc with bonus travk 'Poor Song')	40

YEAR ONE

69	Major Minor MM 660	Eli's Comin'/Will You Be Staying After Sunday	12

YEARS

(see also Chameleons, Sun And The Moon)

79	Tuff Going TGF 123	TUFF GOING EP (p/s, 500 only)	80

YEH YEH

85	Berlin BRS 001	You Will Pay/7 Bells (1st pressing in grey p/s)	5

YELLO

(see also Associates)

81	Do It DUN 11	Bimbo/I.T. Splash (p/s)	6
82	Do It DUN 13	Bostich/She's Got A Gun (Instrumental) (p/s)	5
82	Do It DUNIT 13	Bostich/Downtown Samba/She's Got A Gun/Daily Disco (12", p/s)	10
82	Do It DUN 18	She's Got A Gun/Glue Head (p/s)	5
82	Do It DUNIT 18	She's Got A Gun/The Evening's Young/There Is No Reason (12", p/s)	8
82	Do It DUN 23	Pinball Cha Cha/Smile On You (p/s)	5
82	Do It DUNIT 23	Pinball Cha Cha/Smile On You (12", p/s)	12
83	Stiff PBUY 176	I Love You/Rubber West (3-D picture disc, with glasses)	5
83	Stiff BUY 191	Lost Again/Base For Alec (p/s)	5
83	Stiff DBUY 191	Lost Again/Base For Alec//Let Me Cry/She's Got A Gun (double pack)	6
86	Mercury MERDP 218	Goldrush/She's Got A Gun (live at Palladium N.Y.)//I Love You/ Desire (double pack, unreleased)	0
87	Mercury MERXR 253	The Rhythm Divine (Version Two)/Dr. Van Steiner (Instrumental)/ The Rhythm Divine (Original 7" Version) (12", p/s, as Yello featuring Billy MacKenzie)	15
83	Stiff SEEZ 48	YOU GOTTA SAY YES TO ANOTHER EXCESS (LP, with bonus white label 12": "I Love You"/"Lost Again"/"You Gotta Say To Another Excess [Remix]"Pumping Velvet")	15
87	Mercury MERH 100	ONE SECOND (LP, with bonus 12" in p/s: "Call It Love (Trego Snare Version 2)"/"Santiago [live At Roxy New York]")	12
88	Mercury 836 778-1	FLAG (LP, HMV competition issue, 100 only)	40

YELLOTONE

03	Ai AI 004	GREEN MAYO EP (12", p/s)	8

YELLOW

70	CBS 4869	Roll It Down The Hill/Living A Lie	40

YELLOW BALLOON

67	Stateside SS 2008	Yellow Balloon/Noollab Wolley	20
68	Stateside SS 2124	Stained Glass Window/Can't Get Enough Of Your Love	20

YELLOW BELLOW ROOM BOOM

(see also 10cc, Frabjoy & Runcible Spoon)

68	CBS 3205	Seeing Things Green/Easy Life	30

YELLOW BIRD

74	Magnet MAG 16	Attack Attack/Right On	15

YELLOW MAGIC ORCHESTRA

(see also Ruichi Sakamoto)

80	A&M JAPAN 2	Nice Age/Rydeen (p/s, yellow vinyl)	5

YELLOW PAGES

(see also Mirage)

68	Page One POF 090	Here Comes Jane/Ring-A-Ding	25

YELLOW PAYGES

70	UNI UNS 516	Follow The Bouncing Ball/Little Woman	8
71	UNI UNS 534	Birds Of A Feather/Lady Friend	5

YELLOW 6

90s	Enraptured RAPTLP 36	OVERTONE (2-LP, clear vinyl, numbered, handprinted sleeve, 300 only)	20

YELLOW TAXI

70	President PT 296	Anna Laura Lee/Mary Ann	15

MINT VALUE £

YELLOWMAN
84 Pama PMLP 3215 OPERATION RADICATION (10" LP) . . . 15
84 Greensleeves GREL 57 ZUNGGUZUNGGUGUZUNGGUNZENG!!! (LP) . . . 15

YELLOWSTONE & VOICE
72 Parlophone R5965 Philosopher/The Flying Dutchman . . . 12
72 Regal Zono. SRZA 8511 YELLOWSTONE & VOICE (LP) . . . 20

YEMM & YEMEN
66 Columbia DB 8022 Black Is The Night/Do Blondes Really Have More Fun? . . . 35

YES
(see also Jon Anderson, Hans Christian, Syn, Syndicats, Winston's Fumbs, Warriors, Federals, Peter Banks, Flash, Asia, Rick Wakeman, Steve Howe, Refugee, Chris Squire)
69 Atlantic 584 280 Sweetness/Something's Coming . . . 45
69 Atlantic 584 298 Looking Around/Everydays (unreleased; demos may exist) . . . 175
70 Atlantic 584 323 Time And A Word/The Prophet . . . 110
70 Atlantic 2091 004 Sweet Dreams/Dear Father . . . 45
71 Atlantic 2814 003 I've Seen All Good People (a) Your Move/Starship Trooper (a) Life Seeker (promo only) . . . 75
72 6-A1/-B1 Siberian Khatru/And You And I (white label promo) . . . 50
74 Atlantic K 10407 And You And I/Roundabout . . . 5
77 Atlantic K 10985 Going For The One/Parallels (unreleased, copies may exist) . . . 60
77 Atlantic K 10985T Going For The One (Extended)/Parallels (12", unreleased, copies may exist) . . . 40
70s Lyntone LYN 2535 Interview/Five Songs (vinyl or flexidisc, with 80-page Yes songbook) . . . 70
70s Lyntone LYN 2535 Interview/Five Songs (vinyl without 80-page book) . . . 35
69 Atlantic 588 190 YES (LP, gatefold, red/plum label with lyric insert) . . . 100
70 Atlantic 2400 006 TIME AND A WORD (LP, red/plum label, with lyric insert) . . . 60
71 Atlantic 2400 101 THE YES ALBUM (LP, red/plum label, gatefold sleeve) . . . 40
71 Atlantic 2401 019 FRAGILE (LP, red/plum label, gatefold sleeve with booklet) . . . 40
72 Atlantic K 50012 CLOSE TO THE EDGE (LP, textured sleeve, with lyric insert) . . . 20
77 Atlantic DSK 50379 GOING FOR THE ONE (LP, as 3 x 12" singles, promo only) . . . 100
80 Atlantic K 50842 CLASSIC YES (LP, with bonus 7" "Roundabout"/"Your Move" [SAM 141]) . . . 15
80 Atlantic K 50842 CLASSIC YES (LP, promo, with different sleeve) . . . 30

YETTIES
74 Argo AFW 113 Dorest Is Beautiful/Fling It Here! (Fling It There!) . . . 6
69 Acorn CF 203 FIFTY STONE OF LOVELINESS (LP) . . . 12
72 Argo ZBF 38 DORSET IS BEAUTIFUL (LP) . . . 18
73 Argo ZBF 86 ALL AT SEA (LP) . . . 18
74 Argo ZDA 168 OF YETMINSTER (LP) . . . 15

JOHN YLVISAKER
68 Avantgarde AV 107 COOL LIVIN' (LP) . . . 60

YOBS
(see also Boys)
77 NEMS NES 114 Run Rudolph Run/The Worm Song (p/s) . . . 10
78 Yob YOB 79 Silent Night/Stille Nacht (p/s) . . . 7
81 Safari YULE 1 Rub-A-Dum-Dum/Another Christmas (p/s) . . . 7
82 Fresh FRESH 41 Yobs On 45/The Ballad Of Warrington (p/s) . . . 7
80 Safari RUDE 1 CHRISTMAS ALBUM (LP) . . . 12

MAHARISHI MAHESH YOGI
67 Liberty LBS 83075E MAHARISHI MAHESH YOGI (LP) . . . 25

YOLANDA
(see also Kenny Graham & His Satellites)
60 Triumph RGM 1007 With This Kiss/Don't Tell Me Not To Love You . . . 40

YO LA TENGO
95 Duophonic Super 45s DS 45-10 Evanescent Psychic Pez Drop/STEREOLAB: Long Hair Of Death (gig single, fluorescent yellow vinyl, . . . 0
96 Earworm WORM 4 Blue - Green Arrow/Watching The Sun Set On Johnny Carson (2,000 only, 100 in handmade p/s) . . . 12
96 Earworm WORM 4 Blue - Green Arrow/Watching The Sun Set On Johnny Carson (2,000 only) . . . 8

STEVE YORK'S CAMELO PARDALIS
(see also Elkie Brooks, Boz Scaggs, Lol Coxhill, Graham Bond, Mike Patto)
73 Virgin V 2003 MANOR LIVE (LP) . . . 12

NOLA YORK
(see also Bow Bells)
64 HMV POP 1326 I Don't Understand/Here I Stand . . . 5
66 Philips BF 1527 A Whole Lotta Lovin'/You Just Didn't Wanna Know . . . 5
67 Philips BF 1558 I Can Hear You Calling/Clown Face . . . 6
67 Philips BF 1582 Photographs/He's Looking At Her . . . 5
67 Philips BF 1606 There's So Much Love All Around Me/Sleeping Boutique . . . 5
68 Philips BF 1714 Ciao Baby/We'll Get To Heaven . . . 6

PETE YORK PERCUSSION BAND
(see also Spencer Davis Group, Hardin & York, Deep Purple)
73 Decca TXS 109 PERCUSSION BAND (LP, with Ian Paice, gatefold sleeve) . . . 45

RUSTY YORK
(see also Bonnie Lou & Rusty York)
58 Parlophone R 4398 Peggy Sue/Shake 'Em Up Baby (unissued, demos only) . . . 1500

YORK BROTHERS
54 Parlophone CMSP 5 Why Don't You Open The Door?/You're My Every Dream Come True (export issue) . . . 20
54 Parlophone CMSP 22 Strange Town/Three O'Clock Blues (export issue) . . . 20
58 Parlophone GEP 8736 COUNTRY AND WESTERN (EP) . . . 40
58 Parlophone GEP 8753 COUNTRY AND WESTERN NO. 2 (EP) . . . 40

MINT VALUE £

THOM YORKE
(see also Radiohead)

06	XL (no cat no)	Analyse (CD-R, stickered poly sleeve)	8
06	XL XLLP 200	THE ERASER (LP, 3d effect on embossed sleeve)	15
07	XL XLT238P	Harrowdown Hill/The Drunkk Machine/Jetstream, (12" promo)	15
09	_Xurbia _Xendless XX002	Feelingpulledapartbyhorses/Thehollowearth (12", 8000 only)	10

YOU & I

73	Grape GR 3055	Morning Has Broken/Don't Take Love For A Game	5

YOU KNOW WHO GROUP

65	London HLR 9947	Roses Are Red My Love/Playboy	20

CHRIS YOULDEN
(see also Savoy Brown)

73	Deram DM 377	Nowhere Road/Standing On The Corner	12
73	Deram SML 1099	NOWHERE ROAD (LP, lyric insert)	50
74	Deram SML 1112	CITY CHILD (LP)	45

BARRY YOUNG

65	Dot DS 16756	One Has My Name (The Other Has My Heart)/Show Me The Way	10

BILLY YOUNG

72	Atlantic K 10277	The Sloopy/Same Old Thing Again	8
72	Jay Boy BOY 55	I'm Available/Sweet Woman	8

BILLY YOUNG/LIZZIE MILES

56	HMV 7EG 8178	THE BLUES THEY SANG (EP, with Jelly Roll Morton)	20

BOB YOUNG
(see also Status Quo, Young & Moody Band)

86	Making Waves SURF 115	Mean Girl/Living On An Island (p/s)	5

BRETT YOUNG (& GHOST SQUAD)

63	Pye 7N 15578	Guess What/It Just Happened	12
64	Pye 7N 15641	Never Again/You Can't Fool Me (as Brett Young & Ghost Squad)	12

COLIN YOUNG

71	Trend 6099 005	Anytime At All/You're No Good	8

DARREN YOUNG
(see also Johnny Gentle)

63	Parlophone R 4919	My Tears Will Turn To Laughter/I've Just Fallen For Someone	20

DESI YOUNG

70	Pressure Beat PB 5504	News Flash/JOE GIBBS & DESTROYERS: News Flash - Version	25

EDDY YOUNG

71	Beacon BEA 178	A Little On The Heavy Side/Give'Em A Hand	12

FARON YOUNG

55	Capitol CL 14336	Live Fast, Love Hard, Die Young/Forgive Me, Dear	40
55	Capitol CL 14336	Live Fast, Love Hard, Die Young/Forgive Me, Dear (78)	10
56	Capitol CL 14574	If You Ain't Lovin' (You Ain't Livin')/All Right	25
56	Capitol CL 14574	If You Ain't Lovin' (You Ain't Livin')/All Right (78)	10
56	Capitol CL 14655	I've Got 5 Dollars And It's Saturday Night/You're Still Mine	30
56	Capitol CL 14655	I've Got 5 Dollars And It's Saturday Night/You're Still Mine (78)	10
57	Capitol CL 14735	The Shrine Of St. Cecilia/He Was There	10 10
57	Capitol CL 14762	Love Has Finally Come My Way/Moonlight Mountain	10
57	Capitol CL 14793	Honey Stop! (And Think Of Me)/Vacation's Over	15
58	Capitol CL 14822	Snowball/The Locket	6
58	Capitol CL 14860	I Can't Dance/Rosalie (Is Gonna Get Married)	15
58	Capitol CL 14891	Every Time I'm Kissing You/Alone With You	6
58	Capitol CL 14930	I Hate Myself/That's The Way I Feel	5
59	Capitol CL 14975	Last Night At A Party/A Long Time Ago	15
59	Capitol CL 15004	That's The Way It's Gotta Be/We're Talking It Over	5
59	Capitol CL 15050	I Hear You Talkin'/Country Girl	25
57	Capitol EAP1 778	SWEETHEARTS OR STRANGERS PT. 1 (EP, with Country Deputies)	8
57	Capitol EAP2 778	SWEETHEARTS OR STRANGERS PT. 2 (EP, with Country Deputies)	8
58	Capitol EAP3 778	SWEETHEARTS OR STRANGERS PT. 3 (EP, with Country Deputies)	8
63	Capitol EAP1 1549	HELLO WALLS (EP)	8
58	Capitol T 1004	OBJECTS OF MY AFFECTION (LP)	12
59	Capitol T 1096	THIS IS FARON YOUNG (LP)	12

GEORGIE YOUNG & ROCKIN' BOCS

58	London HLU 8748	Nine More Miles/The Sneak	15
58	London HLU 8748	Nine More Miles/The Sneak (78)	15

HARRY YOUNG

65	Dot DS 16756	Show Me The Way/One Has My Name	10

YOUNG JESSIE

58	London HLE 8544	Shuffle In The Gravel/Make Believe	300
58	London HLE 8544	Shuffle In The Gravel/Make Believe (78)	50

JIMMY YOUNG

54	Decca F 10232	A Baby Cried/Remember Me	10
54	Decca F 10406	Give Me Your Word/Lonely Nightingale	10
55	Decca F 10444	These Are The Things We'll Share/Don't Go To Strangers	8
55	Decca F 10483	If Anyone Finds This, I Love You/The Sand And The Sea	8
55	Decca F 10502	Unchained Melody/Help Me Forget	15
55	Decca F 10597	The Man From Laramie/No Arms Can Ever Hold You	15
55	Decca F 10640	Someone On Your Mind/I Look At You	10
56	Decca F 10694	Chain Gang/Capri In May	10
56	Decca F 10736	Rich Man, Poor Man/The Wayward Wind	10

MINT VALUE £

56	Decca F 10774	More/I'm Gonna Steal You Away	10
57	Decca F 10842	Lovin' Baby/My Faith, My Hope, My Love	5
57	Decca F 10875	Round And Round/Walkin' After Midnight	6
57	Decca F 10925	Man On Fire/Love In The Afternoon	5
57	Decca F 10948	Deep Blue Sea/Harbour Of Desire	5
63	Columbia DB 7119	Miss You/Take Care Of Yourself	5
64	Columbia DB 7234	Unchained Melody/There's Always Me	5
55	Pye NEP 24004	JIMMY YOUNG SINGS (EP)	8
56	Decca DFE 6277	PRESENTING JIMMY YOUNG (EP)	10
57	Decca DFE 6404	JIMMY YOUNG (EP)	8
55	Decca LF 1200	PRESENTING JIMMY YOUNG (10" LP)	20
57	Decca LK 4219	THE NIGHT IS YOUNG (LP)	15
58	Columbia 33SX 1102	YOU (LP)	12

JOE E. YOUNG & TONIKS

68	Toast TT 502	Life Time Of Lovin'/Flower In My Hand	18
69	Toast TT 514	Good Day Sunshine/Life Time Of Lovin'	20
68	Toast (S)TLP 1	SOUL BUSTER! (LP)	40

JOHNNIE YOUNG

67	Polydor 56199	Every Christian/Epitath To Mr Simon Sir	20
67	Polydor 56186	Craise Finton Kirk/I Am The World	12

JOHNNY YOUNG

67	Decca F 22548	Step Back/Cara Lyn (as Johnny Young & Kompany)	15
67	Decca F 22636	Lady/Good Evening Girl	10
68	RCA RCA 1826	Always Thinking Of You/Dreaming Country (as Johnny Young Four)	10
70	Blue Horizon 7-63852	FAT MANDOLIN (LP)	90

KAREN YOUNG

65	Mercury MF 943	I'm Yours, You're Mine/Are You Kidding	8
65	Pye 7N 15956	We'll Start The Party Again/Wonderful Summer	8
68	Major Minor MM 584	Too Much Of A Good Thing/You Better Sit Down	50
69	Major Minor MM 625	Nobody's Child/Oh How I Miss You	6
70	Major Minor MM 691	One Tin Soldier/Que Sera Sera	12
69	M. Minor MMLP/SMLP 66	SINGS NOBODY'S CHILD AND 13 OTHER GREAT SONGS (LP)	20

KATHY YOUNG & INNOCENTS

(see also Innocents)

61	Top Rank JAR 534	A Thousand Stars/Eddie My Darling	40
61	Top Rank JAR 554	Happy Birthday Blues/Someone To Love	30

K.G. YOUNG

69	CBS 4302	Spider/Spider Woogie 9th Movement	20

LEON YOUNG STRINGS

64	Pye 7N 15646	This Boy/Glad All Over	50

LESTER YOUNG (QUINTET)

(see also Count Basie, Coleman Hawkins & Lester Young, Oscar Peterson)

56	Vogue V 2362	New Lester Leaps In/She's Funny That Way	6
56	Vogue V 2384	You're Driving Me Crazy/East Of The Sun	6
56	Vogue EPV 1127	LESTER YOUNG (EP)	10
53	Mercury MG 25015	KANSAS CITY 7/THE LESTER YOUNG QUARTET (LP, 1 side each)	15
55	Felsted EDL 87014	BATTLE OF THE SAXES (10" LP)	15
55	Columbia Clef 33C 9001	LESTER YOUNG WITH THE OSCAR PETERSON TRIO (10" LP)	15
56	Columbia Clef 33C 9015	LESTER YOUNG (10" LP)	15
56	Columbia Clef 33CX 10031	THE PRESIDENT, LESTER YOUNG (LP)	15
56	Columbia Clef 33CX 10054	THE JAZZ GIANTS '56 (LP)	15
57	Columbia Clef 33CX 10070	PRES (LP)	15
58	London Jazz LTZ-C 15132	BLUE LESTER (LP)	18
59	HMV CLP 1302	PRES AND TEDDY (LP, with Teddy Wilson)	12

LESTER YOUNG & CHARLIE PARKER, ET AL.

50	Melodisc 8003	JAZZ AT THE PHILHARMONIC, VOL. 2: BLUES FOR NORMAN, PARTS 1 & 2 (12" 78)	10

LLOYD YOUNG

(see also Carey & Lloyd)

72	Bullet BU 500	Bread And Butter/SHALIMAR ALLSTARS: Version	8
72	Duke DU 135	Soup/J.J. ALLSTARS: Version	12
72	Green Door GD 4037	Shalimar Special/G. MAHTANI ALLSTARS: Version	8
72	Techniques TE 917	High Explosion/ANSELL COLLINS: Version	8

YOUNG MC

88	Delicious Vinyl BRW 120	KNOW HOW (12", EP)	20

MIGHTY JOE YOUNG

72	Sonet SNTF 633	THE LEGACY OF THE BLUES VOL. 4 (LP)	12
72	Delmark DS 629	BLUES WITH A TOUCH OF SOUL (LP, blue label)	22
69	Parlophone 5794	Why Don't You Follow Me/By My Side	25

NEIL YOUNG

(see also Buffalo Springfield, Crosby Stills Nash & Young, Stills-Young Band, Crazy Horse)

69	Reprise RS 23405	The Loner/Everybody Knows This Is Nowhere	25
70	Reprise RS 20861	Oh Lonesome Me (Long Version)/Sugar Mountain	12
70	Reprise RS 23462	Down By The River (edit)/Cinnamon Girl (alternate mix)	7
70	Reprise RS 20958	Only Love Can Break Your Heart/Birds	6
71	Reprise RS 23488	When You Dance I Can Really Love/After The Goldrush	6
72	Reprise K 14167	Old Man/The Needle And The Damage Done	6
73	Reprise SAM 15	Don't Be Denied/Love In Mind/Last Dance (p/s, 1-sided, promo only sampler for "Time Fades Away" LP)	20

			MINT VALUE £
74	Reprise K 14350	Southern Man/Till The Morning Comes/After The Goldrush/ Heart Of Gold (special sleeve)	5
76	Reprise K 14431	Don't Cry No Tears/Stupid Girl	6
74	Reprise K14360	Walk On For The Turnstiles	20
93	Reprise PRO 808	The Needle And The Damage Done (from "Unplugged")/ Love Is A Rose (from "Decade") (CD, promo only)	8
93	Columbia XPCD 308	My Back Pages/All Along The Watchtower/Knocking On Heaven's Door (CD, promo only)	8
93	Geffen NYCD 1	LUCKY THIRTEEN ALBUM SAMPLER (Ain't It The Truth/Depression Blues/ This Note's For You) (CD, promo only)	15
69	Reprise RSLP 6317	NEIL YOUNG (LP, with name on front of sleeve)	40
69	Reprise RSLP 6317	NEIL YOUNG (LP, without name on front of sleeve)	60
69	Reprise RSLP 6349	EVERYBODY KNOWS THIS IS NOWHERE (LP)	35
70	Reprise RSLP 6383	AFTER THE GOLDRUSH (LP, gatefold sleeve with lyric insert)	30
71	Reprise K 44059	NEIL YOUNG (LP, reissue)	12
71	Reprise K 44073	EVERYBODY KNOWS THIS IS NOWHERE (LP, reissue)	12
71	Reprise K 44088	AFTER THE GOLDRUSH (LP, reissue, gatefold sleeve with lyric insert)	12
72	Reprise K 54005	HARVEST (LP, thick cardboard gatefold sleeve with insert)	20
72	Reprise K 64015	JOURNEY THROUGH THE PAST (2-LP, soundtrack, fold-out sleeve & inners)	35
73	Reprise K 54010	TIME FADES AWAY (LP, with lyric insert)	20
74	Reprise K 54014	ON THE BEACH (LP, with inner sleeve)	40
75	Reprise K 54040	TONIGHT'S THE NIGHT (LP, gatefold sleeve with inner sleeve & insert)	20
75	Reprise K 54057	ZUMA (LP, with inner sleeve & lyric insert)	25
77	Reprise K 54088	AMERICAN STARS AND BARS (LP, with inner sleeve)	12
77	Reprise K54088	AMERICAN STARS 'N' BARS (LP)	12
77	Resprise K64037	DECADE (3-LP)	20
79	Reprise K 54105	RUST NEVER SLEEPS (LP, with inner sleeve & lyric insert)	12
79	Reprise K 64041	LIVE RUST (2-LP, with inner sleeves)	15
80	Reprise K 54109	HAWKS & DOVES (LP, with inner sleeve)	12
85	Geffen GEF 26377	OLD WAYS (LP)	12
93	Geffen GEF24452	LUCKY THIRTEEN (LP)	30
93	Reprise 9362-4 5310-1	UNPLUGGED (LP)	15

RALPH YOUNG

(see also Jack Pleis)

55	Brunswick 05466	The Man From Laramie/The Bible Tells Me So	7
55	Brunswick 05500	Bring Me A Bluebird/A Room In Paris	5
56	Brunswick 05605	The Legend Of Wyatt Earp/Do You Know?	5

ROBERT YOUNG

71	CBS 7350	Rosemary Blue/When Time Began	7

ROGER YOUNG

66	Columbia DB 7869	Sweet, Sweet Morning/Whatcha Gonna Give Me?	60
66	Columbia DB 8092	No Address/It's Been Nice	250

ROY YOUNG (BAND)

59	Fontana H 200	Just Keep It Up/Big Fat Mama	25
59	Fontana H 200	Just Keep It Up/Big Fat Mama (78)	10
59	Fontana H 215	Hey Little Girl/Just Ask Your Heart	20
59	Fontana H 215	Hey Little Girl/Just Ask Your Heart (78)	15
60	Fontana H 237	I Hardly Know Me/Gilee	20
60	Fontana H 247	Taboo/I'm In Love	15
61	Fontana H 290	You Were Meant For Me/Plenty Of Love (as Roy Young & Hunters)	10
61	Ember EMB S 128	Four And Twenty Thousand Kisses/Late Last Evening	12

ROY YOUNG

71	MCA MKS 5071	Wild Country Wine/New Sun New Horizon (p/s)	8
73	MCA MUS 1214	Dig A Hole/I'm A Loner	12
70	RCA SF 8161	ROY YOUNG BAND (LP)	20

SUSANNAH YOUNG

67	Philips BF 1559	Lazy Afternoon/Here's That Rainy Day	5
67	Philips BL 7728	SWEETEST SOUNDS (LP)	12

TERRY YOUNG

61	Pye 7N 15321	Maverick/Partners	7
61	Pye 7N 15353	Someone New/Now Forever And A Day	12
62	Pye 7N 15416	Joe's Been A-Gittin' There/They Took John Away	6

TOMMIE YOUNG

73	Contempo C 12	Everybody's Got A Little Devil In Their Soul/Do You Still Feel The Same Way	10
73	Contempo C 23	She Don't Have To See You/That's All Part Of Loving Him	10
74	Contempo CLP 501	DO YOU STILL FEEL THE SAME WAY (LP)	75

VICKI YOUNG

(see also Joe 'Fingers' Carr)

55	Capitol CL 14228	Hearts Of Stone/Tweedlee Dee (triangular centre)	40
55	Capitol CL 14228	Hearts Of Stone/Tweedlee Dee (78)	10
55	Capitol CL 14281	Live Fast, Love Hard, Die Young/Zoom, Zoom, Zoom(triangular centre)	25
56	Capitol CL 14528	Steel Guitar/Bye Bye For Just A While	12
56	Capitol CL 14653	Spanish Main/Tell Me In Your Own Sweet Way (with Joe 'Fingers' Carr)	12
56	Capitol CL 14653	Spanish Main/Tell Me In Your Own Sweet Way (with Joe 'Fingers' Carr) (78)	10
56	Capitol EAP1 593	VICKI YOUNG (EP)	35

YOUNG AL CAPONE

71	Green Door GD 4012	Girl Called Clover/Girl Called Clover (Version)	8

YOUNG & MOODY (BAND)

(see also Bob Young, Whitesnake, Snafu, Cozy Powell, Motorhead, Nolan Sisters)

77	Magnet MAG 87	Chicago Blue/Warm Winds	5
79	Fabulous JC 1	The Devil Went Down To Georgia/You Can't Catch Me	5

MINT VALUE £

79 Fabulous JC 3 All The Good Friends/Playing Your Game (p/s) . . . 5
81 Bronze BRO 130 Don't Do That/How Can I help You Tonight . . . 6
77 Magnet MAG 5015 YOUNG AND MOODY (LP, with lyric insert, as Young & Moody) . . . 12

YOUNG BLOOD
(see also Cozy Powell, Ace Kefford Stand, Big Bertha)
68 Pye 7N 17495 Green Light/Don't Leave Me In The Dark . . . 25
68 Pye 7N 17588 Just How Loud/Masquerade . . . 20
68 Pye 7N 17627 Bang-Shang-A-Lang/I Can't Stop . . . 20
69 Pye 7N 17696 The Continuing Story Of Bungalow Bill/I Will . . . 20

YOUNG BLOOD
84 Landslide LAND 1 FIRST BLOOD (12" EP, p/s) . . . 18

YOUNGBLOODS
69 RCA RCA 1821 Darkness, Darkness/On Sir Francis Drake . . . 10
69 RCA RCA 1877 Get Together/Beautiful . . . 10
69 RCA SF 8026 ELEPHANT MOUNTAIN (LP) . . . 22
70 Warner Bros WS 1878 ROCK FESTIVAL (LP) . . . 15

YOUNG BROTHERS
68 MCA MU 1042 I've Always Wanted Love/Mirror Mirror . . . 15

YOUNG BUCKS
77 Blueport BLU 1 Get Your Feet Back On The Ground/Cold, Cold Morning (p/s) . . . 6

YOUNG DISCIPLES
90 Talkin' Loud TLKX 2 Get Yourself Together/Young Disciples Theme (12", p/s) . . . 8

COLE YOUNGER
80 Ariola AHA 555 Candy/I'd Rather Be Me . . . 6

YOUNG FOLK
72 Midas MR 001 RIBBLE VALLEY DREAM (LP) . . . 50

YOUNGFOLK
68 President PT 136 Lonely Girl/Joey . . . 20

YOUNG FREDDIE
(see also Freddie McGregor)
70 Camel CA 38 Drink And Gamble/LENNOX BROWN & HUE ROY: King Of The Road . . . 15

YOUNG GROWLER & CALYPSO RHYTHM KINGS
66 Columbia DB 7870 Amy The Sunbather/Sweet Trinidad . . . 7
66 Columbia DB 7958 V For Victory/Be Nice To Women (in 'Test Match' p/s) . . . 12
66 Columbia DB 7958 V For Victory/Be Nice To Women . . . 7
66 Columbia SEG 8502 V FOR VICTORY (EP) . . . 12

YOUNG-HOLT TRIO
67 Coral Q 72489 Wack Wack/This Little Light Of Mine . . . 15
67 Coral Q 72489 Wack Wack/This Little Light Of Mine (DJ copy) . . . 40

YOUNG-HOLT UNLIMITED
(see also Ramsey Lewis Trio)
69 MCA MU 1053 Soulful Strut/Country Slicker Joe . . . 8
72 MCA MU 1159 Just Ain't No Love/Love Makes A Woman . . . 8
73 Contempo COLP-R 1004 PLAYS SUPERFLY (LP) . . . 20
69 MCA MUP(S) 368 SOULFUL STRUT (LP) . . . 20

YOUNG IDEA
66 Columbia DB 7961 The World's Been Good To Me/It Can't Be . . . 10
66 Columbia DB 8067 Gotta Get Out Of The Mess I'm In/Games Men Play . . . 5
67 Columbia DB 8132 Peculiar Situation/Just Look At The Rain . . . 5
67 Columbia DB 8205 With A Little Help From My Friends/Colours Of Darkness . . . 12
67 Columbia DB 8284 Mister Lovin' Luggage Man/Room With A View . . . 5
68 Music For Pleasure MFP 1225 WITH A LITTLE HELP FROM MY FRIENDS (LP) . . . 20

YOUNG LIONS
78 Discovery D-DISC 001 Take Five (12", p/s) . . . 30

YOUNG MARBLE GIANTS
80 Rough Trade RT 043 Final Day/Radio Silents/Cakewalking/(uncredited 4th track) (p/s) . . . 6
81 Rough Trade RT 059 TESTCARD (EP) . . . 12
80 Rough Trade ROUGH 8 COLOSSAL YOUTH (LP) . . . 25
84 Rough Trade ROUGHL8 COLOSSAL YOUTH (LP, reissue) . . . 15
07 Domino REWIGLP 32 COLOSSAL YOUTH (LP, reissue) . . . 18

YOUNG ONES
63 Decca F 11705 How Do I Tell You/Baby That's It . . . 8

YOUNG ONES
78 Virgin VS 205 Rock 'N' Roll Radio/Little Bit Of Loving (p/s) . . . 6

YOUNG RASCALS
(see also Rascals, Joey Dee & Starlighters)
65 Atlantic AT 4059 I Ain't Gonna Eat My Heart Out Anymore/Slow Down . . . 15
66 Atlantic AT 4082 Good Lovin'/Mustang Sally . . . 12
66 Atlantic 584 024 You Better Run/Love Is A Beautiful Thing . . . 18
66 Atlantic 584 050 Come On Up/What Is The Reason . . . 18
66 Atlantic 584 067 Too Many Fish In The Sea/No Love To Give . . . 15
67 Atlantic 584 081 I've Been Lonely Too Long/If You Knew . . . 18
67 Atlantic 584 085 I Ain't Gonna Eat My Heart Out Anymore/Good Lovin' . . . 10
67 Atlantic 584 111 Groovin'/Sueno . . . 10
67 Atlantic 584 128 A Girl Like You/It's Love . . . 10
67 Atlantic 584 138 How Can I Be Sure/I Don't Love You Anymore . . . 6
68 Atlantic 584 161 It's Wonderful/Of Course . . . 10

MINT VALUE £

66	Atlantic 587/588 012	THE YOUNG RASCALS (LP)	30
67	Atlantic 587/588 060	COLLECTIONS (LP)	20
67	Atlantic 587/588 074	GROOVIN' (LP)	25

YOUNG SATCH

70	Black Swan BW 1401	Bonga Bonga Bonga/HI-TALS: Ram Buck	10

YOUNG SISTERS

62	London HLU 9610	Casanova Brown/My Guy	25

YOUNG SOULS

69	Amalgamated AMG 844	Why Did You Leave/Main A Wail	100

YOUNG TRADITION

(see also Dave Swarbrick, Peter Bellamy)

74	Argo AFW 115	The Shepherd's Hymn/The Boar's Head Carol	6
68	Transatlantic TRAEP 164	CHICKEN ON A RAFT (EP)	25
66	Transatlantic TRA 142	THE YOUNG TRADITION (LP)	22
67	Transatlantic TRA 155	SO CHEERFULLY ROUND (LP)	18
68	Transatlantic TRA 172	GALLERIES (LP, with Dave Swarbrick)	18
68	Transatlantic TRASAM 13	THE YOUNG TRADITION SAMPLER (LP)	12

YOUNG TURKS

66	CBS 202353	Duel At Diablo/Our Lady From Maxim's	12

YOUNG WORLD SINGERS

64	Brunswick 05916	Ringo For President/A Boy Like That	6

YOUR FAVOURITE HORSE

00s	Endorphin ENDORLP 010	EVERYDAY MAGIC (LP, orange vinyl)	12

YOUTH

66	Polydor 56121	As Long As There Is Your Love/Your One And Only Love	20

YOUTH

69	Deram DM 226	Meadow Of My Love/Love Me Or Leave Me	20

JOHNNY YOUTH

69	Grape GR 3002	Darling It Won't/HIP CITY BOYS: Moon Train	10

YOUTH VALLEY CHORALE

63	London HLU 9818	Do You Hear What I Hear/Little Bell	5

YOU'VE GOT FOETUS ON YOUR BREATH

(see also Foetus etc., Philip & His Foetus Vibrations, Scraping Foetus Off The Wheel)

81	Self Immolation WOMB 07	Wash It All Off/333 (p/s)	10
80s	Self Immolation	Tell Me, What Is The Bane Of Your Life?	15
81	Self Imm. WOMB OYBL-1	DEAF (LP)	30
81	Self Imm. WOMB OYBL-2	ACHE (LP)	30

LES YPER SOUND

(see also Pierre Henry)

67	Fontana TF 880	Too Fortiche/Psyche Rock	60
69	Philips TFE 8004	MASS FOR THE PRESENT TIME (LP)	80

YR HWNTWS

82	Loco LOCO 1001	YR HWNTWS (LP)	80

Y TRWYNAU COCH

70s	Record. Sqwar RSROC 1	WASTOD AR Y TU FAS (BANANAS) (EP, around 1,000 only)	50
78	Recordian Sqwar RSROC 002	Merched Dan 15 (I Often Think Of Girls Under 15)/Byw Ar Arian Fy Rhieni/ Mynd I'r Capel Mewn Levis/Ail Ddechre (around 1,000 only)	50
80s	Record. Coch OCHR 2198	RHEDEG RHAG Y TORPIDOS (LP)	30

JOHNNY YUKON

60	Top Rank JAR 347	Made To Be Loved/Magnolia	7

YUNGUN/MR THING

03	White (Janomi) JACKIT0001	STRAIGHT JACK IT (EP)	20
06	White (No Cat. No.)	JACKING FOR BREAKS (EP)	12

TIMI YURO

(see also Johnnie Ray)

61	London HLG 9403	Hurt/I Apologise	20
62	London HLG 9484	Smile/I Believe (B-side with Johnnie Ray)	1
62	Liberty LIB 55410	Let Me Call You Sweetheart/Satan Never Sleeps	10
62	Liberty LIB 55469	What's A-Matter Baby (Is It Hurting You)/Thirteenth Hour	30
63	Liberty LIB 55519	The Love Of A Boy/I Ain't Gonna Cry No More	30
63	Liberty LIB 55519	The Love Of A Boy/I Ain't Gonna Cry No More (DJ Copy)	80
63	Liberty LIB 55587	Make The World Go Away/Look Down	12
64	Liberty LIB 10177	Hurt/Be Anything (But Be Mine)	10
64	Mercury MF 826	If/I'm Afraid The Masquerade Is Over	25
65	Mercury MF 848	You Can Have Him/Could This Be Magic	12
65	Mercury MF 859	Get Out Of My Life/Can't Stop Running Away	50
65	Mercury MF 903	Once A Day/Pretend	5
65	Mercury MF 949	Turn The World Around The Other Way/Just A Ribbon	5
66	Mercury MF 978	Cuttin' In/Why Not Now	6
68	Liberty LBF 15092	Something Bad On My Mind/Wrong	30
68	Liberty LIB 15142	I Must Have Been Out Of My Mind/Interlude	25
68	Liberty LIB 15182	It'll Never Be Over For Me/As Long As There Is You	700
65	Liberty LEP 2214	TIMI YURO: SOUL! (EP)	30
66	Liberty LEP 2253	MAKE THE WORLD GO AWAY (EP)	25
62	London HA-G 2415	TIMI YURO (LP)	70
62	Liberty LBY 1042	SOUL! (LP)	35
63	Liberty LBY 1154	WHAT'S A-MATTER BABY (LP, mono)	25
63	Liberty SLBY 1154	WHAT'S A-MATTER BABY (LP, stereo)	30

			MINT VALUE £
64	Liberty LBY 1192	MAKE THE WORLD GO AWAY (LP)	25
64	Mercury 20032 MCL	THE AMAZING TIMI YURO (LP)	22
65	Liberty LBY 1247	HURT (LP)	30
66	Liberty LBY 1275	LET ME CALL YOU SWEETHEART (LP, mono)	20
66	Liberty SLBY 1275	LET ME CALL YOU SWEETHEART (LP, stereo)	30
66	Liberty (S)LBY 1290	THE BEST OF TIMI YURO (LP)	20
68	Liberty LBL/LBS 83115	GREAT PERFORMANCES (LP)	15
68	Liberty LBL/LBS 83128	TIMI IN THE BEGINNING (LP)	20
69	Liberty LBS 83198E	SOMETHING BAD ON MY MIND (LP)	50
69	Mercury SMWL 21010	TALENTED TIMI (LP)	15

Z

HELMUT ZACHARIAS

65	Polydor 236 809	PLAYS THE HITS OF THE BEATLES (LP)	12

JOHN ZACHERLE

(see also Dave Appell & Applejacks)

58	London HLU 8599	Dinner With Drac Part 1/Dinner With Drac - Conclusion	20
58	London HLU 8599	Dinner With Drac Part 1/Dinner With Drac - Conclusion (78)	25

ZAFTIG MADEL

84	Shine SHTUP 3	Dori Duz/Curvy 'N' Creamy (p/s)	6

ZAGER & EVANS

69	RCA SF 8056	2525 (LP)	20

ZAKARRIAS

71	Deram SML 1091	ZAKARRIAS (LP, white/red label, small logo)	500

ZAKATEK

73	Bell 1289	I Gotcha Now/So Good To You	7

GEORGE ZAMBETAS & THE GROUP TEN PLAYERS

66	Pye 7N 17180	Moussaka/Monlight Over The Acropolis (p/s)	6
69	RCA RCA 1860	In The Year 2525 (Exordium Terminus)/Little Kids	5

ALEX ZANETIS

71	Moodisc HM 102	Guilty/JOLLY BOYS: Do Fe Do	5

TOMMY ZANG

59	HMV POP 611	Break The Chain/I'll Put A String On Your Finger	7
62	Polydor NH 66955	I'm Gonna Slip You Offa My Mind/Every Hour, Every Day	6
62	Polydor NH 66957	Hey, Good Lookin'/With Love (For You)	10
62	Polydor NH 66960	Take These Chains From My Heart/Truly, Truly	6
62	Polydor NH 66977	I Can't Hold Your Letters (In My Arms)/She's Getting Married	6
62	Polydor NH 66980	Just Call My Name/I Love You Because	6

WILLY ZANGO

73	Jam JAM 58	Hot Rod/Goom	8
74	DJM DJS 312	Hot Rod/The Voice Of Melody	7

ZANTI MISFITZ

82	Clay 9	Kidz Songs/Alice Liddle's Bad Trip (p/s)	10

FRANK ZAPPA/MOTHERS OF INVENTION

(see also Flo & Eddie, Jeff Simmons, Wild Man Fischer, Captain Beefheart, John Lennon, Geronimo Black)

SINGLES

66	Verve VS 545	It Can't Happen Here/How Could I Be Such A Fool (as Mothers Of Invention)	45
67	Verve VS 557	Big Leg Emma/Why Don't You Do Me Right (as Mothers Of Invention)	45
71	Reprise K 14100	Tears Began To Fall/Junier Mintz Boogie (as Mothers Of Invention)	40
71	United Artists UP 35319	What Will This Evening Bring Me This Morning?/Daddy, Daddy, Daddy	35
74	Discreet K 19201	Cosmic Debris/Uncle Remus	8
74	Discreet K 19202	Don't Eat The Yellow Snow/Camarillo Brillo	8
79	CBS 7261	Dancin' Fool/Baby Snakes	5
80	CBS 7950	Joe's Garage/Catholic Girls	6
80	CBS 7950	Joe's Garage/BOB DYLAN: When You Gonna Wake Up (mispressing)	30
80	CBS 8652	I Don't Wanna Get Drafted/Ancient Armaments (p/s)	6
81	CBS A 1622	You Are What You Is/Harder Than Your Husband (p/s)	6
81	CBS A 12-1622	You Are What You Is/Pink Napkins/Harder Than Your Husband/ Soup 'N Old Clothes (12", picture disc)	15
81	CBS XPS 147	Shut Up 'N' Play Yer Guitar/Variation On The C. Santana Secret (p/s, issued free with "Ship Arriving Too Late To Save A Drowning Witch" LP)	6
82	CBS A 2412	Valley Girl/Teenage Prostitute (p/s)	6
84	EMI EMI 5499	Baby Take Your Teeth Out/Stevie's Spanking (p/s)	8

LPs: VERVE ORIGINALS

66	Verve VLP 9154	FREAK OUT! (as Mothers Of Invention, mono, single disc)	80
66	Verve SVLP 9154	FREAK OUT! (as Mothers Of Invention, stereo, single disc)	60
67	Verve VLP 9174	ABSOLUTELY FREE (as Mothers Of Invention, mono)	60
67	Verve SVLP 9174	ABSOLUTELY FREE (as Mothers Of Invention, stereo)	50
68	Verve VLP 9199	WE'RE ONLY IN IT FOR THE MONEY (as Mothers Of Invention, gatefold sleeve, mono)	60
68	Verve SVLP 9199	WE'RE ONLY IN IT FOR THE MONEY (as Mothers Of Invention, gatefold sleeve, stereo)	50

			MINT VALUE £
68	Verve VLP 9223	LUMPY GRAVY (gatefold sleeve, mono)	65
68	Verve SVLP 9223	LUMPY GRAVY (gatefold sleeve, stereo)	50
69	Verve VLP 9237	CRUISING WITH RUBEN AND THE JETS (as Mothers Of Invention, mono)	80
69	Verve SVLP 9237	CRUISING WITH RUBEN AND THE JETS (as Mothers Of Invention, stereo)	50
69	Verve VLP 9239	MOTHERMANIA - THE BEST OF THE MOTHERS (as Mothers Of Invention, mono)	40
69	Verve SVLP 9239	MOTHERMANIA - THE BEST OF THE MOTHERS (as Mothers Of Invention, stereo)	30

LPs: VERVE REISSUES

71	Verve/Polydor 2683 004	FREAK OUT (2-LP)	30
72	Verve/Polydor 2317 034	WE'RE ONLY IN IT FOR THE MONEY (gatefold sleeve)	30
72	Verve/Polydor 2317 035	ABSOLUTELY FREE (gatefold sleeve)	25
72	Verve/Polydor 2317 046	LUMPY GRAVY (gatefold sleeve)	30
72	Verve/Polydor 2317 047	MOTHERMANIA - THE BEST OF THE MOTHERS	25
73	Verve/Polydor 2352 017	MOTHERMANIA - THE BEST OF THE MOTHERS (2nd reissue)	25
73	Verve/Polydor 2317 069	CRUISIN' WITH RUBEN AND THE JETS (gatefold sleeve)	25
75	Verve/Polydor 2352 057	ROCK FLASHBACKS (LP)	15

LPs: ORIGINAL REPRISE/WARNER/DISCREET ISSUES

70	Reprise RSLP 6356	HOT RATS (1st pressing, pink, gold & green 'riverboat' label, gatefold sleeve)	40
70	Reprise RSLP 6356	HOT RATS (2nd pressing, tan 'riverboat' label, gatefold sleeve)	20
70	Reprise RSLP 6370	BURNT WEENY SANDWICH (as Mothers Of Invention, 1st pressing, pink, gold & green 'riverboat' label, gatefold sleeve)	25
70	Reprise RSLP 2028	WEASELS RIPPED MY FLESH (as Mothers Of Invention, tan 'riverboat' label)	25
70	Reprise RSLP 2030	CHUNGA'S REVENGE (tan 'riverboat' label, green or red gatefold sleeve)	25
70	Reprise RSLP 2030	CHUNGA'S REVENGE (tan 'riverboat' label, green or red gatefold sleeve)	18
71	Reprise K 44150	FILLMORE EAST, JUNE 1971 (as Mothers Of Invention)	15
72	Reprise K 44179	JUST ANOTHER BAND FROM L.A. (as Mothers Of Invention, gatefold sleeve)	18
72	Reprise K 44203	WAKA/JAWAKA (HOT RATS)	15
72	Reprise K 44209	THE GRAND WAZOO (gatefold sleeve)	15
73	DiscReet K 41000	OVER-NITE SENSATION (as Mothers Of Invention, gatefold sleeve)	15
74	DiscReet K 69201	ROXY AND ELSEWHERE (2-LP, as Mothers Of Invention, gatefold sleeve)	15
74	DiscReet K 49201	APOSTROPHE (') (no lyric insert)	12
75	DiscReet K 59207	ONE SIZE FITS ALL (as Mothers Of Invention, gatefold sleeve)	12

(First pressings of the above LPs were issued without Warner Bros logo on label or sleeve; copies with Warners logos are post-1975 pressings and worth £6-£8 each.)

76	Warner Bros K 56298	ZOOT ALLURES (LP)	12
77	DiscReet K 69204	ZAPPA IN NEW YORK (LIVE) (2-LP, with & without reference to Punky's Whips)	20
77	DiscReet K 69204	ZAPPA IN NEW YORK (LIVE) (2-LP, "Punky's Whips" listed on sleeve but not on label or LP)	20
77	DiscReet K 69204	ZAPPA IN NEW YORK (LIVE) (2-LP, plays "Punky's Whips", listed on sleeve but not on label)	60
78	DiscReet K 59210	STUDIO TAN	12
78	DiscReet K 59211	SLEEP DIRT	12
78	DiscReet K 59212	ORCHESTRAL FAVORITES	12

LPs REPRISE

71	Reprise K 44078	HOT RATS (tan 'riverboat' label, gatefold sleeve)	15
71	Reprise K 44083	BURNT WEENY SANDWICH (tan 'riverboat' label)	15
71	Reprise K 44019	WEASELS RIPPED MY FLESH (tan 'riverboat' label)	15
71	Reprise K 44020	CHUNGA'S REVENGE (tan 'riverboat' label, gatefold sleeve)	15

(The above LPs were issued without Warner Bros logo on label or sleeve; post-1975 pressings with logos are worth £6-£8)

69	Transatlantic TRA 197	UNCLE MEAT (2-LP, as Mothers Of Invention)	60
71	United Artists UDF 50003	200 MOTELS (2-LP, with booklet & poster, as Frank Zappa & Mothers Of Invention)	35
79	CBS 88339	SHEIK YERBOUTI (2-LP, gatefold sleeve printed with lyrics)	15
79	CBS 86101	JOE'S GARAGE ACT 1 (gatefold sleeve, lyric insert)	12
79	CBS 88475	JOE'S GARAGE ACTS 2 & 3 (2-LP, gatefold sleeve, lyric insert)	15
81	CBS 88560	YOU ARE WHAT YOU IS (2-LP, gatefold sleeve, lyric insert)	15
81	CBS 88516	TINSELTOWN REBELLION (2-LP, gatefold sleeve with lyrics)	15
81	CBS 66368	SHUT UP 'N' PLAY YER GUITAR (3-LP box set, with inner sleeves)	25
82	CBS 85804	SHIP ARRIVING TOO LATE TO SAVE A DROWNING WITCH (with bonus 7" Shut Up 'N' Play Yer Guitar/"Variation On The C. Santana Secret" [XPS 147])	12

LPs: EMI REISSUES

84	EMI EL 2701531	BOULEZ CONDUCTS ZAPPA: 'THE PERFECT STRANGER'	12
84	EMI no cat. no.	FRANCESCO ZAPPA (with inner sleeve)	15
84	EMI 2402943	THING-FISH (3-LP, box set, with libretto)	20
86	EMI EN 352	JAZZ FROM HELL	12
86	EMI EC 3507	FRANK ZAPPA MEETS THE MOTHERS OF PREVENTION (European version)	12
95	Simply Vinyl SLVP 0024	WEASELS RIPPED MY FLESH (180gm vinyl)	12
95	Simply Vinyl SLVP 0025	BURNT WEENY SANDWICH (gatefold sleeve, 180 gm vinyl)	12
84	EMI EMC 3500	THE MAN FROM UTOPIA	12
84	EMI EMC 3501	SHIP ARRIVING TOO LATE TO SAVE A DROWNING WITCH (with inner sleeve)	12
84	EMI FZAP1	JOE'S GARAGE ACTS 1, 2 & 3 (3-LP, box set, inner sleeves only, with libretti)	25
84	EMI E5 0021	TINSELTOWN REBELLION (2-LP, gatefold sleeve, printed with lyrics)	15
84	EMI no cat. no.	SHEIK YERBOUTI (2-LP, gatefold sleeve, printed with lyrics)	15
84	EMI no cat. no.	SHUT UP 'N' PLAY YER GUITAR (3-LP box set, with inner sleeves)	25
84	EMI EN 2402343	THEM OR US (2-LP, gatefold sleeve, printed with lyrics)	12

LPs: ZAPPA

84	Zappa Records ZAPPA 1	FREAK OUT (2-LP, gatefold sleeve, some in single sleeve £35)	18
80s	Zappa Records ZAPPA 5	LONDON SYMPHONY ORCHESTRA VOLUME II	12
88	Zappa Records ZAPPA 6	GUITAR (2-LP, gatefold sleeve)	18
88	Zappa Records ZAPPA 7	YOU CAN'T DO THAT ON STAGE ANY MORE SAMPLER (2-LP, gatefold sleeve)	15
88	Zappa Records ZAPPA 14	BROADWAY THE HARD WAY (gatefold sleeve with inner sleeve)	12
90	Zappa Records ZAPPA 30	THEM OR US (2-LP, gatefold sleeve, printed with lyrics)	15
90	Zappa Records ZAPPA 20	JOE'S GARAGE ACTS 1, 2 & 3 (3-LP, box set, original sleeves, with libretti)	22
91	Zappa Records ZAPPA 28	SHEIK YERBOUTI (2-LP, gatefold sleeve without lyrics)	15

MINT VALUE £

91 Zappa Records ZAPPA 35 BURNT WEENY SANDWICH (gatefold sleeve). . . . 12
91 Zappa Records ZAPPA 37 ZAPPA IN NEW YORK (LIVE) (2-LP, plays "Punky's Whips", listed on label, but not on sleeve). . . . 15
91 Zappa Records ZAPPA 42 SHIP ARRIVING TOO LATE TO SAVE A DROWNING WITCH 12
92 Zappa Records ZAPPA 39 ROXY AND ELSEWHERE (2-LP, as Mothers Of Invention, gatefold lyric sleeve) . 15

ZAPPO
73 Magnet MAG 2 Rock And Roll Crazy/Right On! 12

ZAP POW
72 Harry J HJ 6650 Lottery Spin/Lottery Spin - Version 8
73 Trojan TR 7741 This Is Reggae Music/Break Down The Barriers. . . . 7
73 Blue Mountain BM 1027 This Is Reggae Music/Break Down The Barriers. . . . 6
74 Island WIP 6181 This Is Reggae Music/Break Down The Barriers. . . . 6
76 Vulcan VUL 1010 Jungle Beat/Rock Your Bones. . . . 8
78 Island IPR 2028 Roots Man Reggae/Let's Fall In Love (12") 12
76 Vulcan VULP 004 NOW (LP). . . . 15

LES ZARJAZ
(see also Tronics)
85 Creation CRE 014 One Charming Nyte/My Baby Owns A Fallout Zone (foldover p/s, poly bag) 8
86 Kaleid. Sound KS 104 INTER BLOCK ROCK (12" EP). . . . 7

PETE ZEAR
(see also Ruts, Rat Scabies)
80 (no label) matrix: 22-1 Tomorrow's World/Fast Food (stamped white label, with insert, numbered). . . . 10

ZEBEDEE
71 Decca F13144 So Long Marianne/She Couldn't Make Gravy 30

ZEE
(see also Rick Wright)
84 Harvest HAR 5277 Confusion/Eyes Of A Gypsy (p/s) 5
84 Harvest HAR 125277 Confusion (Extended Mix)/Eyes Of A Gypsy (Dub) (12", p/s) 8
84 Harvest SHSP 2401 018 IDENTITY (LP, with inner sleeve). . . . 12

ZEITGEIST
80 Enchaine ENC 1 Shake-Rake/Sniper (p/s). . . . 6
82 Jamming CREATE 4 Stop (p/s) 5

ZENITH
86 ZENITH 5001 Heavy Heavy Heart (p/s). . . . 100

SI ZENTNER ORCHESTRA
64 Liberty LIB 10169 The James Bond Theme/Bond's 007 Theme 7
63 Liberty LBY 1164 RHYTHM PLUS BLUES (LP). . . . 15

ZEPHYR
(see also Tommy Bolin)
70 Probe SPB 1006 ZEPHYR (LP) 60

ZEPHYRS
63 Decca F 11647 What's All That About/Oriental Dream 40
64 Columbia DB 7199 I Can Tell/Sweet Little Baby 50
64 Columbia DB 7324 A Little Bit Of Soap/No Message. . . . 35
64 Columbia DB 7410 Wonder What I'm Gonna Do/Let Me Love You Baby. . . . 35
65 Columbia DB 7481 She's Lost You/There's Something About You 35
65 Columbia DB 7571 I Just Can't Take It/She Laughed 35

ZERO
75 BEEB 014 Angels Theme/Truckin'. . . . 5

EARL ZERO
78 Studio 16 WE 401 Rough And Tough/PRINCE JAZZBO: Suffer Must Live (12"). . . . 30
79 Sufferers Height SUF004 Please Officer/PABLO: Moonlight City (12"). . . . 50
79 Greensleeves GRED 23 City Of The Wicked/Rightous Works (12"). . . . 40

ZERO FIVE
65 Columbia DB 7751 Dusty/Just Like A Girl. . . . 6

ZERO LE CRECHE
84 Flicknife FLS 029 Last Year's Wife/Women Say (p/s) 6

ZERO 7
00 Ultimate Dilemma UDR EP VOL. 1 (12") 18
00 Ultimate Dilemma UDR 040 EP VOL. 2 (12") 18

ZERO TWENTY ONE
81 UK UK 201 Pop Song (p/s) 100

ZEROS
77 Small Wonder SMALL 2 Hungry/Radio Fun. . . . 20
79 Rok ROK XV/XVI What's Wrong With A Pop Group/ACTION REPLAY: Decisions (die-cut co. sleeve). . . . 20

MONICA ZETTERLUND
58 Columbia DB 4246 There's No You/Don't Be That Way. . . . 8
59 Columbia SEG 8015 SWEDISH SWEET (EP) 60
58 Columbia 33CSX 20 SWEDISH SENSATION (LP, export only) 100
64 Philips BL 7647 MAKE MINE SWEDISH STYLE (LP). . . . 100

Z'EV
82 Fetish FE 13 Wipeout!/Element L. (p/s). . . . 10
88 Coercion COERCIONLP 001 THE INVISIBLE MAN (LP). . . . 25

ZIMBO TRIO
68 Page One FORS 017 INTRODUCING THE ZIMBO TRIO (LP) 12

MINT VALUE £

ZIMM & DEE DEE
(see also Winston Francis)

71	Green Door GD 4006	You've Got A Friend (actually by Winston Francis & Donna Hinds)/ GROOVERS: Cheep	7

TUCKER ZIMMERMAN

69	Regal Zonophone RZ 3020	The Red Wind/Moondog	12
69	Regal Zono. (S)LRZ 1010	TEN SONGS BY TUCKER ZIMMERMAN (LP)	120
72	Village Thing VTS 13	TUCKER ZIMMERMANN (LP)	70

ZIOR
(see also Monument, Cardboard Orchestra)

71	Nepentha 6129 002	Za Za Za Zilda/She's A Bad Bad Woman	25
71	Nepentha 6129 003	Cat's Eyes/I Really Do	20
71	Nepentha 6437 005	ZIOR (LP, gatefold sleeve)	150

ZIPPER

74	Youngblood YB 170	Streak Up And Down/Funk 74	30

RB ZIPPER

76	Alaska ALA 2004	Cruisin With The Fonz/Superstream	6
77	Alaska ALA 2006	Come On Marriane/Lamplight Lady	8

ZIPPERS

64	Hickory 45-1252	My Sailor Boy/Pretend You're Still Mine	15

ZIPS

79	Black Gold ZIPS1	Take Me Down/Don't Be Pushed Around/I'm In Love Over and Over (500 only with A4 insert & 2 stickers)	150
79	Rip Off RIP 12	Friends/Don't Tell The Detectives (p/s)	60
80	Tenement Toons TEN 01	Radioactivity/I'm Not Impressed (p/s)	25

ZIPZ

80	Voyage VOY 14	As I Pass You By/Tonight (p/s)	8

ZODIAC

68	Elektra EKL 4009	COSMIC SOUNDS (LP, also stereo EKS 74009)	45

ZODIACS

57	Oriole CB 1383	Why Don't They Understand/The Game Of Love	10
58	Oriole CB 1432	The Yum-Yum Song/Secrets	6

EMIL DEAN ZOGHBY

70	Polydor 2058 032	Won't You Join Me/Misery Lane	5

ZAC ZOLAR & ELECTRIC BANANA
(see also Pretty Things, Phil May, Fenmen, Electric Banana)

84	Butt FUN 5	Take Me Home/James Marshall	5

ZOMBIES
(see also Unit Four Plus Two, Argent, Neil MacArthur, Colin Blunstone)

64	Decca F 11940	She's Not There/You Make Me Feel Good	10
64	Decca F 12004	Leave Me Be/Woman	12
65	Decca F 12072	Tell Her No/What More Can I Do	12
65	Decca F 12125	She's Coming Home/I Must Move	15
65	Decca F 12225	Whenever You're Ready/I Love You	15
65	Decca F 12296	Is This The Dream/Don't Go Away	15
66	Decca F 12322	Remember You/Just Out Of Reach	20
66	Decca F 12426	Indication/How We Were Before	25
66	Decca F 12495	Gotta Get A Hold Of Myself/The Way I Feel Inside	30
67	Decca F 12584	Goin' Out Of My Head/She Does Everything For Me	25
68	Decca F 12798	I Love You/The Way I Feel Inside	15
67	CBS 2960	Friends Of Mine/Beechwood Park	60
67	CBS 3087	Care Of Cell 44/Maybe After He's Gone	50
68	CBS 3380	Time Of The Season/I'll Call You Mine	60
65	Decca DFE 8598	THE ZOMBIES (EP)	110
65	Decca LK 4679	BEGIN HERE (LP)	350
65	RCA RD 7791	BUNNY LAKE IS MISSING (LP, soundtrack)	65
68	CBS BPG 63280	ODESSEY AND ORACLE (LP, mono)	500
68	CBS SBPG 63280	ODESSEY AND ORACLE (LP, stereo)	400
70	Decca SPA 95	THE WORLD OF THE ZOMBIES (LP)	18
73	Epic EPC 65728	TIME OF THE ZOMBIES (2-LP)	25

ZONES
(see also PVC 2)

78	Zoom ZUM 4	Stuck With You/No Angels (p/s)	5
78	Arista ARTIST 205	Sign Of The Times/Away From It All	5
79	Arista SPART 1095	UNDER INFLUENCE (LP)	12

ZOO

70	Major Minor SMLP 74	ZOO (LP)	30
71	Barclay 521172	ZOO (LP)	20

ZOO BOUTIQUE

82	Lightbeat LIGHT 006	Forgive And Forget/Happy Families (p/s, clear vinyl)	6

ZOOKIE
(see also Judie Tzuke, Tzuke & Paxo)

77	DJM DJS 10796	Judie Judie Hold On/I Couldn't Be You	8
78	DJM DJS 10866	Bubbles/Don't Rock Me	8

ZOOT ALORS

79	Decca FR 13874	Send Me A Postcard/It's A Crime	60

ZORN

01	City Centre Offices BLOCK 11	Eckerman (plain sleeve with inserts, 1000 only)	6

MINT VALUE £

ZORRO

79	Bridgehouse BHEP 1	'Arrods Don't Sell 'Em/Soldier Boy/Starflight (in p/s)	60
79	Bridgehouse BHEP 1	'Arrods Don't Sell 'Em/Soldier Boy/Starflight	25

ZORRO FIVE

70	Decca F 23042	Reggae Shhh!/Reggae Meadowlands	5

ZOSKIA

84	All The Madmen MAD 8	Rape/Thank You (p/s)	8
85	Temple TOPY 005	Be Like Me (12", p/s, transparent vinyl)	12
86	All The Madmen MADT 8	Rape/Black Action (12", p/s)	8

ZOSKIA MEETS SUGARDOG

84	Temple TOPYS 021	J.G. /'That's Heavy Baby	10

ZOUNDS

81	Crass 4219844/3	Can't Cheat Karma/War/Subvert (gatefold paper p/s, with poster)	12
81	Rough Trade RT 069	Demystification/Great White Hunter (p/s)	8
82	Rough Trade RT 094	Dancing/True Love (p/s)	8
82	Not So Brave NSB 001	LA VACHE QUI RIT (EP, with poster)	12
82	Rough Trade RT 098	More Trouble Coming Every Day/Knife (p/s)	8
80s	Recommended RR 14.15	Menáge (12.59) (1-sided, other side printed, foldout sleeve in PVC sleeve)	8
84	Rough Trade ROUGH 31	THE CURSE OF ZOUNDS (LP)	20

ZOVIET-FRANCE

82	Red Rhino RED 12	ZOVIET-FRANCE (12" EP, printed hessian sleeve)	60
83	Red Rhink RED 23	NORSCHE (LP)	35
84	Red Rhink RED 40	MOHNOMISCHE (LP)	35
84	Red Rhino REDLP 45	ELSTRE (LP)	35

ZOWLAS

67	Amusicon SLE 12	Honest I Do/Gonna Love My Baby	12

ZUIDERZEE

66	CBS 202062	(You're My) Soul And Inspiration/Please Don't Call Me	10
66	CBS 202235	Peace Of Mind/Provocative Child	10

TAPPA ZUKIE

73	Count Shelly CSLP 04	MAN A WARRIOR (LP)	50
75	Locks LOX 8	Judge I O' Lord/LLOYDIE SLIM AND KING TUBBY: State Dub	10
75	Attack ATT 8110	Natty Dread Don't Cry (as Topper Zukie)/TOMMY McCOOK : The Meducia	8
77	New Star DNEW 1	What's Yours/Make Faith (12")	25
77	Achilles ACHILLES 54	Liberation Struggle/Double Struggle	10
76	Stars (No. Cat. No.)	TAPPA ZUKIE IN DUB (LP)	100
76	KLIK 9022	M.P.L.A. (LP)	12

ZULU

77	Big Bear BB9	Red Red Libanon/Okavanga Swamp	15

ZUM ZEAUX

70s	Black Pig PUG1	WOLF AT THE DOOR (LP)	40

ZUTONS

02	Deltasonic DKTCD 007	Devil's Deal/Six Foot Man/Zutonkhamuun (CD)	20

ZYGOAT

74	Polydor 2058 124	Catching A Thief/Letitia's Song	5
74	Polydor 2383 270	ELECTROPHON (LP)	20

ZZEBRA

(see also John McCoy, Gillan)

74	Polydor 2058 446	Zardoz/Amusofi	18
75	Polydor 2058 579	Mr. J/Put The Light On Me	5
74	Polydor 2383 296	ZZEBRA (LP)	12
75	Polydor 2383 326	PANIC (LP, with insert)	15

ZZ TOP

72	London HLU 10376	Francene/Down Brownie	12
74	London HLU 10458	Beer Drinkers And Hell Raisers/La Grange	10
75	London HLU 10475	La Grange/Just Got Paid	10
75	London HLU 10495	Tush/Blue Jean Blues	10
76	London HLU 10538	It's Only Love/Asleep In The Desert	8
77	London HLU 10547	Arrested For Driving While Blind/Neighbour, Neighbour	8
77	London HLU 10547	Arrested For Driving While Blind/Neighbour, Neighbour (mispressing, B-side plays Ray Charles' "I Can See Clearly Now")	12
79	Warner Bros K 17647	Cheap Sunglasses/Esther Be The One	5
80	Warner Bros K 17576	I Thank You/A Fool For Your Stockings (p/s)	7
83	Warner Bros W 9693T	Gimme All Your Lovin'/If I Could Only Flag Her Down (car-shaped picture disc)	8
85	Warner Bros W 2001F	Sleeping Bag/Party On The Patio//Sharp Dressed Man/I Got The Fix (p/s, sealed, stickered double pack)	10
85	Warner Bros W 2001P	Sleeping Bag/Party On The Patio ('sphinx'-shaped picture disc)	8
85	Warner Bros W 2001P	Sleeping Bag/Party On The Patio (shaped pic-disc, part 1 of interlocking set)	12
86	Warner Bros W 2002BP	Stages/Hi-Fi Mama (shaped pic-disc, part 2 of interlocking set)	8
86	Warner Bros W 2003FP	Rough Boy/Delirious (shaped pic-disc, part 3 of interlocking set, shrinkwrapped with bonus 12")	30
86	Warner Bros W 2003FP	Rough Boy/Delirious (shaped pic-disc, part 3 of interlocking set)	20
71	London PS 584	ZZ TOP (LP, with inner sleeve)	30
72	London SH-U 8433	RIO GRANDE MUD (LP, original issue)	25
73	London SH-U 8459	TRES HOMBRES (LP, original issue)	25
75	London SH-U 8482	FANDANGO! (LP, original issue)	18
76	London LDU 1	TEJAS (LP, original foldout sleeve)	12
83	Warner Bros W 3774	ELIMINATOR (LP, with bonus stickered p/s 12" "Legs [Metal Mix]")	15
83	Warner Bros W3774P	ELIMINATOR (LP, picture disc)	15

MINT VALUE £

Various Artists

VARIOUS ARTISTS EPs 50s/60s (alphabetical by title)

A

62	MGM MGMEP 768	A VERY PRIVATE AFFAIR (includes Brigitte Bardot: Sidonie)	80

B

63	Concert Hall BPC 712	BEAT TIME (Timebeats/Charlie Young/Heartbeats)	15
63	Concert Hall BPC 717	THE BIG BEAT (Bob Miller & Millermen/Al Saxon/Roy Young/Duffy Power)	20
66	Fontana TF 17469	THE BIG FOUR (Dave Dee Dozy Beaky Mick & Tich/Spencer Davis Group/Mindbenders/Pretty Things)	10
66	Philips BBE 12593	THE BIG FOUR (Roger Miller/Four Seasons/Dusty Springfield/Walker Bros)	10
64	Fontana TFE 18010	BLOWIN' IN THE WIND (withdrawn; Bob Dylan/Joan Baez/Pete Seeger)	100
64	Pye Intl. NEP 44029	THE BLUES VOL. 1 PT. 1 (John Lee Hooker/Muddy Waters/Sonny Boy Williamson/Jimmy Witherspoon)	35
64	Pye Intl. NEP 44035	THE BLUES VOL. 1 PT. 2 (Howling Wolf/Buddy Guy/Little Walter/Muddy Waters)	25
66	Chess CRE 6011	THE BLUES VOL. 2 PT. 1 (Otis Rush/Chuck Berry/John Lee Hooker/ Little Walter)	25
64	Pye Intl. NEP 44038	BLUES FESTIVAL (Sugar Pie De Santo/Willie Dixon/Sonny Boy Williamson/ Howlin' Wolf)	30
63	Columbia SEG 8226	BLUES ON PARADE NO. 1 (Jimmy Cotton/Brownie McGhee/Roosevelt Sykes/Sonny Terry)	25
56	HMV 7EG 8178	THE BLUES THEY SANG (Lizzie Miles/Billy Young & Jelly Roll Morton)	20
61	RCA RCX 205	BREAKFAST AT TIFFANY'S (Henry Mancini)	18
63	Fontana TFL 6037	BLUES AT NEWPORT (LP)	20

C

63	Cameo Parkway CPE 552	CAMEO BIG FOUR (Bobby Rydell/Chubby Checker/Dovells/Orlons)	20
60s	Heritage 105	THE COUNTRY BLUES (99 only)	80

D

60s	XX MIN 706	DARK MUDDY BOTTOM (Jimmy Slim/Good Jelly Bess/Lightning Leon/Little Red Walters/Willie B.)	20
50s	Poydras 102	DEPRESSION BLUES	25
63	Decca DFE 8520	DISCS-A-GO GO (Karl Denver/Billy Fury/Jet Harris/Vernons Girls)	50
60s	Jan & Dil JR 450	DOWN HOME BLUES - SIXTIES STYLE (Lightning Leon/Jerry McCain/Little Red Walters)	30
59	Fontana TFE 17146	DRUMBEAT (Lana Sisters/Adam Faith/Bob Miller & Millermen/Sylvia Sands/Roy Young)	40

E

65	Edinburgh S.C. ESC 02	EDINBURGH STUDENTS CHARITIES APPEAL (33rpm, die-cut paper p/s; Athenians/Avengers/Ray & Archie Fisher/Lynn & Kathy)	50
66	Edinburgh S.C. ESC 03	EDINBURGH STUDENTS CHARITIES APPEAL (33rpm, Athenians/Gear System/Old Bailey's Jazz Advocates)	60
67	Philips P 160E	EXQUISITE FORM (freebie; Dave Dee, Dozy, Beaky, Mick & Tich/Herd/Walker Brothers/Dusty Springfield)	12

F

64	Pye Intl. NEP 44030	FESTIVAL OF THE BLUES NO. 1 (Willie Dixon/Buddy Guy/Muddy Waters/Sonny Boy Williamson)	20
63	Decca DFE 8538	FROM A LONDON HOOTENANNY (Davy Graham/Thamesiders)	25

G

67	Down with the Game 202	GOD DON'T LIKE IT (99 only)	40
67	Down with the Game 203	GOD DON'T LIKE IT VOLUME 2 (99 only)	40
66	Pye Intl. NEP 45054	THE GREATEST ON STAGE (Maxine Brown/Chuck Jackson/Shirelles/Dionne Warwick)	20
63	London RE-U 1393	GROUP OF GOODIES (Marcie Blane/Kokomo/Bill Black's Combo/ Ernie Maresca)	50
59	Mercury ZEP 10010	GROUPS GALORE (Del Vikings/Mark IV/Diamonds/Hi-Liters)	100

H

65	Pye NEP 24214	THE HITMAKERS NO. 2 (Honeycombs/Tony Jackson/Kinks/Shangri-La's)	18
65	Pye NEP 24215	THE HITMAKERS NO. 3 (Chuck Berry/Julie Grant/Rockin' Berries/ Sandie Shaw)	15
66	Pye NEP 24242	THE HITMAKERS VOL. 2 (Chuck Berry/Kinks/Sue Thompson/Shangri-La's)	30
66	Pye NEP 24243	THE HITMAKERS VOL. 3 (Kinks/Lancastrians/Rockin' Berries/Searchers)	12
66	Pye Intl. NEP 44065	HITMAKERS INTERNATIONAL (Fontella Bass/James Brown/Petula Clark/Lovin' Spoonful)	25
56	Mercury MEP 9003	HIT PARADE VOL. 1 (Georgia Gibbs/Platters/Crew Cuts/Patti Page)	15
56	Mercury MEP 9510	HIT PARADE VOL. 2 (Sarah Vaughan/Ralph Marterie/Patti Page/Crew Cuts)	15 10
65	Decca DFE 8648	HITS VOL. 1 (Chris Andrews/Fortunes/Hedgehoppers Anonymous/Jonathan King)	10
65	Decca DFE 8649	HITS VOL. 2 (Lulu/Chris Andrews/Marianne Faithfull/Fortunes)	10
66	Decca DFE 8663	HITS VOL. 5 (Animals/Los Bravos/Alan Price Set/Small Faces)	10
66	Decca DFE 8667	HITS VOL. 6 (Jonathan King/Lulu/Alan Price Set/Small Faces)	10
67	Decca DFE 8675	HITS VOL. 7 (Ronnie Aldrich/Val Doonican/Bachelors/Small Faces)	10
62	Mercury ZEP 10133	HITSVILLE! (Brook Benton/Crew Cuts/Phil Philips/Diamonds)	30
59	Coral FEP 2034	HITSVILLE VOL. 1 (Buddy Holly/McGuire Sisters/Betty Madigan/Billy Williams)	60
59	Coral FEP 2035	HITSVILLE VOL. 2 (Lennon Sisters/Art Lund/Teresa Brewer/Jackie Wilson)	50
65	Tamla Motown TME 2001	HITSVILLE U.S.A. NO. 1 (Marvin Gaye/Brenda Holloway/Carolyn Crawford/ Eddie Holland)	150
66	Post War Blues 100	HOBOS AND DRIFTERS	50

I

65	Chess CRE 6010	IN CROWD (Radiants/Ramsey Lewis Trio/Little Milton/Billy Stewart)	30

MINT VALUE £

K

63	Lyntone LYN 347/348	KEELE RAG RECORD (flexidisc; Rhythm Unlimited & Halettes/Keele Quintet)	18
64	Lyntone LYN 508/509	KEELE RAG RECORD NO. 2 (flexidisc; Escorts/Lance Harvey & Kingpins/ Keele Row; some in die-cut sleeve)	35
65	Lyntone LYN 765/766	KEELE RAG RECORD (flexidisc; Bob Wilson/Changing Times/ Lance Harvey & Kingpins/Incas)	40
61	RCA Victor RCX 203	KINGS OF THE BLUES VOL. 2 (Jazz Gillum/Big Maceo/Washboard Sam/ Sonny Boy Williamson)	20
61	RCA Victor RCX 204	KINGS OF THE BLUES VOL. 3 (Arthur Big Boy Crudup/Furry Lewis/ Poor Joe Williams)	25
66	Holyground HG 111	THE LAST THING ON MY MIND (EP, 99 copies only)	90
59	Top Rank JKR 8008	LET'S GO NO. 1 (Jimmy Lee/Johnny Hines/Treetoppers)	35
59	Top Rank JKR 8012	LET'S GO NO. 2 (Johnny Hines/Billy Mack/Victors/Ted & Ray)	35
60	Philips BBE 12414/	LET'S MAKE LOVE - FILM SOUNDTRACK (Yves Montand/Marilyn Monroe/ Frankie Vaughan; stereo)	40
63	Embassy WEP 1104	LIVERPOOL BEAT (Typhoons/Mike Redway/Ray Pilgrim/Bobby Stevens)	10
57	London RE-D 1075	LONDON HIT PARADE NO. 1 (Tab Hunter/Hilltoppers/Pat Boone/ Fontane Sisters)	25
57	London RE-P 1096	LONDON HIT PARADE NO. 2 (Fats Domino/Slim Whitman/Ken Copeland/ Roy Brown)	100
58	London RE-D 1097	LONDON HIT PARADE NO. 3 (Pat Boone/Gale Storm/Tab Hunter/Jim Lowe)	25
58	London RE-D 1130	LONDON HIT PARADE NO. 4 (Pat Boone/Nick Todd/ Bonnie Guitar/Hilltoppers)	25
58	London RE-D 1136	LONDON TOPPERS NO. 2 (export issue; Pat Boone/Nick Todd/Tab Hunter/ Jim Lowe)	25
58	London RE-P 1137	LONDON TOPPERS NO. 3 (export issue; Slim Whitman/Fats Domino/ Ricky Nelson/Ernie Freeman)	60
58	London RE-D 1145	LONDON HIT PARADE NO. 5 (Pat Boone/Fontane Sisters/Frank De Rosa)	20

M

59	Jazz Collector JEL 2	THE MALE BLUES VOL. 1 (Georgia Slim/Walter Roland)	15
59	Jazz Collector JEL 4	THE MALE BLUES VOL. 3 (Blind Blake/Ramblin' Thomas)	15
59	Jazz Collector JEL 5	THE MALE BLUES VOL. 4 (Tall Tom/Pinewood Tom)	15
59	Jazz Collector JEL 8	THE MALE BLUES VOL. 5 (Blind Lemon Jefferson/Buddy Boy Hawkins)	15
60	Jazz Collector JEL 10	THE MALE BLUES VOL. 6 (Hound Head Henry/Frankie Jaxon)	15
60	Jazz Collector JEL 13	THE MALE BLUES VOL. 7 (Blind Lemon Jefferson/Ed Bell)	15
61	Jazz Collector JEL 24	THE MALE BLUES VOL. 8 (Blind Lemon Jefferson/Leadbelly)	15
69	Middle Earth MDE 201	MIDDLE EARTH SAMPLER (WRITING ON THE WALL: Aries/WOODEN O: Overture/ARCADIUM: Poor Lady) (promo only, 33rpm, no p/s)	80
60s	Jan & Dil TR 451	MORE DOWN HOME BLUES (Good Jelly Boss/Juke Boy Bonner/ Papa Lightfoot/Snooky Prior)	30

N

66	Tamla Motown TME 2014	NEW FACES FROM HITSVILLE (Jimmy Ruffin/Chris Clark & Lewis Sisters/ Tammi Terrell/Monitors)	300
57	Pye NEP 24052	NIXA HIT PARADE NO. 1 (Gary Miller/Pet Clark/Lonnie Donegan/John Frazer)	8
58	Pye NEP 24064	NIXA HIT PARADE NO. 2 (Pearl Carr & Teddy Johnson/Petula Clark/ Lonnie Donegan Skiffle Group/Colin Hicks & Cabin Boys)	10

O

65	Columbia SEG 8413	ON THE SCENE (Downliners Sect/Animals/Cherokees/Cheynes/ Georgie Fame/Yardbirds)	80
63	MGM MGM-EP 787	ORIGINAL HITS (Tommy Edwards/Johnny Ferguson/Jimmy Jones/ Conway Twitty)	35
63	London RE-K 1390	THE ORIGINAL HITS (Drifters/Ritchie Barrett/Coasters/Ben E. King)	55
65	Atlantic AET 6006	ORIGINAL HITS VOL. 2 (Barbara Lewis/Coasters/Solomon Burke/Drifters)	50
62	Ember EMB 4522	ORIGINAL RHYTHM AND BLUES HITS (Jesse Belvin/Ray Charles/ Linda Hayes/ Jimmy McCracklin/Johnny Moore Blazers)	75
55	Pye Jazz NJE 1043	ORIGINS OF SKIFFLE (Isla Cameron/Guy Carawan/Peggy Seeger)	20
58	Pye NSEP 85000	POPS GO STEREO (Marion Ryan/Tony Osborne Orch./Bill Shepherd Orch.)	20

R

67	Action ACT 002 EP	RAG GOES MAD AT THE MOJO (33rpm; Joe Cocker's Blues Band/ Tangerine Ayr Band/Pitiful Souls/Delroy Good Good Band)	50
56	Vogue EPV 1113	RHYTHM AND BLUES (Dominoes/Swallows)	350
60s	Range JRE 7002	RHYTHM AND BLUES (Sticks Herman/Tim Whitsett)	10
60s	Range JRE 7006	RHYTHM AND BLUES (Harry Lewis/Tommy Wills)	10
63	Stateside SE 1008	RHYTHM AND BLUES (Jimmy Reed/John Lee Hooker)	40
64	Stateside SE 1009	R&B CHARTMAKERS (Martha/Vandellas/Miracles/Marvin Gaye/Marvelettes)	100
64	Stateside SE 1018	R&B CHARTMAKERS NO. 2 (Miracles/Kim Weston/Supremes/Marvelettes)	125
64	Stateside SE 1022	R&B CHARTMAKERS NO. 3 (Marvin Gaye/Darnells/Eddie Holland/ Martha & Vandellas)	140
64	Stateside SE 1025	R&B CHARTMAKERS NO. 4 (Supremes/Eddie Holland/Temptations/ Contours)	110
60	Vogue EPV 1198	RHYTHM AND BLUES CONCERT (Helen Humes/Jimmy Witherspoon)	80
64	Pye Intl. NEP 44021	RHYTHM AND BLUES SHOWCASE VOL. 1 (Don & Bob/Dale Hawkins/ Clarence Henry/Larry Williams)	30
64	Pye Intl. NEP 44022	RHYTHM AND BLUES SHOWCASE VOL. 2 (Jimmy McCracklin/ Muddy Waters/Little Walter/Howlin' Wolf)	30
57	Vogue VE 170111	ROCK AND ROLL (Mister Google Eyes August/Louis Jones Rock & Roll Band/Walter Price Rock & Roll Band/Clarence Gatemouth Brown)	170
62	Capitol EAP1 20197	ROUND-UP (Tommy Collins/Farmer Boys/Ferlin Husky/Texas Bill Strength)	15
60	Top Rank JKP 2060	RUSHING FOR PERCUSSION (Preston Epps/Sandy Nelson)	20

S

60s	S.A.U.C.C. PR 5462	ST. ANDREWS UNIVERSITY CHARITIES CAMPAIGN (20th Century Sounds/ Steve Hall & Roosters/Black Ring; no p/s)	35
64	Lyntone LYN 738/739	SHEFFIELD UNIVERSITY RAG RECORD (flexidisc; Vantennas/ Dave Allen Band/ Addy Street Five/Los Caribos; die-cut sleeve)	40
55	Columbia SEG 7528	SHOUT FOR JOY (Pete Johnson/Albert Ammons/Meade Lux Lewis)	30
63	London RE-P 1403	SINGING THE BLUES (Ernie K-Doe/Showmen/Jesse Hill/Chris Kenner)	100
58	Decca DFE 6485	SIX FIVE SPECIAL (Jackie Dennis/Joan Regan/Diane Todd/Dickie Valentine)	40

			MINT VALUE £
66	Lyntone LYN 995	THE SOUND OF THE STARS (flexidisc with Disc And Music Echo; with mag & envelope/stamp)	20
65	Keele Rag/Lyntone	SOUNDS OF SAVILE (flexidisc; Hipster Image/London Apprentices/ Tom & Brennie; some in die-cut title sleeve)	80
60	Mercury ZEP 10088	SURPRISE PACKAGE (Ben Hewitt/Diamonds)	140
59	Top Rank JKR 8007	SWEET BEAT (Lee Allen Band/Fred Parris/Cindy Mann/Mellokings)	50

T

63	Oriole EP 7080	TAKE SIX (Mark Peters' Silhouettes/Ian & Zodiacs/Faron's Flamingos/Earl Preston & T.T.s/Rory Storm & Hurricanes/ Sonny Wade & Cascades)	70
59	Mercury ZEP 10015	TEAR IT UP (Boyd Bennett Orchestra/Red Prysock/Hi-Liters)	160
57	Mercury MEP 9522	TEEN-AGE ROCK (Red Prysock/Rusty Draper/Chuck Miller/Crew Cuts)	125
58	RCA RCX 111	TEENAGE TOPS (Ray Peterson/Jimmy Dell/Marlin Greene/Barry De Vorzon)	40
64	Ember EMB 4540	TEEN SCENE '64 (Dave Clark Five/Ray Singer/Washington D.C.s)	50
60	Heritage RE 102	THAT COUNTRY ROCK (with Walter Hawkins & William Moore, 99 copies only)	50
58	Brunswick OE 9425	THEY SOLD A MILLION NO. 9 (Bobby Helms/Four Aces/Jerry Lewis/ Kitty Kallen)	25
59	Brunswick OE 9427	THEY SOLD A MILLION NO. 11 (Ink Spots/Louis Jordan & His Tympany Five/ Mills Brothers/Weavers)	25
59	Brunswick OE 9431	THEY SOLD A MILLION NO. 15 (Four Aces/Bill Haley & His Comets)	20
63	Stateside SE 1004	TOP TEEN DANCES (Johnnie Morisette/Huey 'Piano' Smith & Clowns/ Al Brown's Tunetoppers/Spartans)	20
57	Parlophone R 4356	TOP TEN SPECIAL (Jim Dale/King Brothers/Vipers Skiffle Group)	15
65	Century 21 MA 105	T.V. CENTURY 21 THEMES (David Graham/Sylvia Anderson/Peter Dyneley/ Barry Gray Orchestra/Gary Miller/Eric Winstone Orchestra)	15
64	Decca DFE 8585	T.V. THEMES (Andrew Oldham Orchestra/Ted Heath Music/ Ron Grainer Music/Cyril Stapleton Orchestra)	40
62	Starlite STEP 31	TWIST OFF (Wayne Farmer/Medallions/Charles Perrywell/ Piano Slim/ Teenbeats/Dellos)	200
62	Starlite STEP 29	TWIST ON (Mighty Trojans/Dee Dee Gaudet/Dixie Lee/ Percy & The Rocking Aces)	125

V

70	Village Thing VTSX 1000	VILLAGE THING EP: Wizz Jones/Ian Anderson/Pigsty Light Orchestra	20

W

69	Apple CT 1	WALLS ICE CREAM PRESENTS (Mary Hopkin/Iveys/Jackie Lomax/ James Taylor; with/without p/s)	40
65	Liberty LEP 4036	WE SING THE BLUES (Jesse Hill/Ernie K. Doe/Aaron Neville/Benny Spellman)	65
64	Fontana TFE 18009	WITH GOD ON OUR SIDE (withdrawn; Bob Dylan/Joan Baez/Pete Seeger)	100
66	Chess CRE 6009	WITH THE BLUES (Eddie Boyd Blues Combo/Buddy Guy)	40

Y

64	Fontana TFE 18011	YE PLAYBOYS AND PLAYGIRLS (withdrawn; Bob Dylan/Joan Baez/ Pete Seeger)	100
68	Chess CRE 6026	YOUR CHESS REQUESTS (Fontella Bass/Tony Clarke/Mitty Collier/ Billy Stewart)	65

VARIOUS ARTISTS SINGLES & EPs 70s/80s/90s/00s

A

98	Twisted Nerve TN 003	ALL OAR NOTHING (10", p/s; Badly Drawn Boy/Mum & Dad/ Dakota Oak/ Sirconical/Andy Votel)	25
95	Sticky STICKY 16	AROUND THE WORLD WITH STICKY RECORDS (Rory Commodore [a.k.a. Tindersticks]/Boy Racer/Heck/Cornershop, picture disc, 700 only)	8
80	Deleted DEP 002	ANGST IN MY PANTS (2x7", fold-out numbered sleeve, Instant Automatons/ Door & The Window/Mic Woods/Midnight Circus/012/Digital Dinosaurs/ Missing Persons, etc)	15

B

83	Secret SHH 138	BACK ON THE STREET (p/s; Skin Disease/Angela Rippon's Bum/ Venom/ Strike/East End Badoes)	12
92	Rhythmic Tech. ART 1	NORT ROUTE (12")	20
87	Other OTH 6	BATTLEAXE (p/s; Black Riders/Holosade/Kes/Teacher's Pet)	30
78	Good Vibrations GOT 7	BATTLE OF THE BANDS (double pack, no'd p/s; Idiots/Rudi/Outcasts/Spider)	25
95	Ka-boom KA-BOOM 1	BIG BOLLOCKED BONFIRE BLOW-UP (Hood, et al.)	12
80	Vinyl Drip DRIP 001	BLACKPOOL ROX (p/s; Membranes/Section 25/Syntax/Kenneth Turner Set)	8
79	Skeleton SKL 002	THE BLANK TAPES VOL. 1 (folded p/s; Attempted Moustache/Junk Act/ Geisha Girls/Zorkie Twins)	8
81	Secret SHH 126	BOLLOCKS TO CHRISTMAS (p/s; Business/4-Skins/Gonads/Max Splodge)	30
80s	Secret	BRITANNIA WAIVES THE RULES (12", p/s; Exploited/Chron Gen/Infa Riot)	12
80	Crass 421984/5	BULLSHIT DETECTOR (12", p/s)	20

C

98	Twisted Nerve TNXMS 1	CHRISTMAS STOCKING FILLER (Badly Drawn Boy/Dakota Oak/ Sirconical/Mum & Dad/Elbow) (green vinyl in green wraparound sleeve or red vinyl in red sl.)	25
98	Twisted Nerve TNXM 025	CHRISTMAS STOCKING FILLER 2 (10", p/s; Andy Votel/D.O.T./ Lost Children's Desk/Misty Dixon/Cherrystones)	8
80s	No Future	A COUNTRY FIT FOR HEROES (12", p/s)	12
80s	No Future	A COUNTRY FIT FOR HEROES VOL. 2 (12", p/s)	20
94	Fierce Panda NING 02	CRAZED AND CONFUSED (p/s; Supergrass/Ash et al.)	15

D

71	Dandelion DS 7001	DANDELION (die-cut sleeve; Principal Edwards Magic Theatre/Stackwaddy/ Siren/The Way We Live)	15
92	Delirious DELIS 6	DELIRIOUS PRIME CUTS VOL. 1 (12"; The Moog/Hardcore Rhythm Team/ Justice And Mercy)	40
86	BBC ZRSL 193	DOCTOR WHO (cassette, holographic inlay; Dominic Glynn/Mankind/ BBC Radiophonic Workshop)	8
86	BBC 12RXL 193	DOCTOR WHO (12", holographic p/s; Dominic Glynn/Mankind/ BBC Radiophonic Workshop)	8

			MINT VALUE £
87	BBC RESL 193	DOCTOR WHO (p/s, reissue; Dominic Glynn/Mankind)	6
01	Trunk WWW 1	DIRTY FAN MAIL (7", white vinyl)	15

E

79	Fast Products FAST 9B	EARCOM 2 (12", p/s; Joy Division/Thursdays/Basczax)	12
97	Fat Cat 12FAT 003	8. 8.5, 9 (12", custom sleeve)	10
99	Lowlife LOW8	EASTER ISLAND (EP	25
78	Stiff FREEBIE 2	EXCERPTS FROM STIFF'S GREATEST HITS (promo only sampler, 33rpm)	10
96	Mo' Wax MWEX 001-010	EXCURSIONS (10 x 12", box set; the Prunes/IO/ Olde Scottish/David Caron/DJ Solo & DJ Aura/Midnight Funk Assoc./ Stasis/Solo feat. JT/Twig Bud/DJ Shadow)	30
99	Al Al 001	EXPERIMENTS IN COLOUR (12"; Normal/Cell/Fil)	20

F

78	Factory FAC 2	A FACTORY SAMPLE (double pack, p/s, in plastic bag, with 5 stickers; Joy Division/Cabaret Voltaire/Durutti Column/John Dowie)	200
95	555 5X555	5x555 (5x7" box set; Boyracer/Mike Nichols And His Excellency/Amy Linton & Stewart Anderson/Father/Hood)	30
91	Fontana FONT 1	THE FONTANA SINGLES BOX SET VOLUME 1 – HITS AND RARITIES (12-single box set, with 12 inserts)	30
91	Fontana FONT 2	THE FONTANA SINGLES BOX SET VOLUME 2 – HITS AND RARITIES (12-single box set, with 12 inserts)	30
79	Heartbeat PULSE 4	4 ALTERNATIVES (p/s; 48 Hours/Joe Public/Numbers/X-Certs)	15
80	Con (no cat. no.)	THE FOUR EPs (cassette; Mark Perry et al.)	15
96	Ché CHE 059	4 TRACK 3 BAND TOUR EP (p/s, Mogwai/Urusei Yatsura/Backwater, 50 only)	25
96	Mosquito MSQ 05	FRESH AS YOU FUCKIN' LIKE (12"; Paul Hannah/Russ Gabriel/ Steve Patton/ Cristian Vogel/Si Begg)	15

G

83	Mouth MOUTH 1	G-FORCE (Shady Deal/Dead Loss/Blythe Rocket/Egypt)	20
70	Village Thing VTSX 1000	THE GREAT WHITE DAP (Wizz Jones/Sun Also Rises/ Ian A. Anderson/ Pigsty Hill Light Orchestra)	20

H

80	Groucho Marxist	HA! HA! FUNNY POLIS (PAISLEY ROCKS AGAINST RACISM) (p/s; Defiant Pose/Fegs/Urban Enemies/XS Discharge)	20
71	Abreaction ABR 001	HART ROCK (Brass Alley/Yellow/Trilogy/Lucas Tyson) (no p/s)	20
90s	Sub Pop	HELTER SHELTER (box set, 4 x 7", Elastica/Gene)	12

I

78	Radar SAM 88	INTERNATIONAL ARTISTS (13th Floor Elevators/Red Crayola/ Lost & Found/Golden Dawn; Red Crayola Hope & Anchor gig freebie	12

L

79	Decca FR 13864	THE LONDON BOYS (p/s; David Bowie/Small Faces/Birds/Dobie Gray)	10
73	Ronco MR EP 001	LONG LIVE ROCK (no p/s; Billy Fury/Eugene Wallace/Wishful Thinking)	15

M

71	Track 2094 011	MAXI TRACK RECORD (John's Children/Crazy World Of Arthur Brown/ Thunderclap Newman/Jimi Hendrix; withdrawn blue sleeve crediting	125
71	Track 2094 011	MAXI TRACK RECORD (John's Children/Crazy World Of Arthur Brown/ Thunderclap Newman/Jimi Hendrix; red & white sleeve with press pack,	60
99	Twisted Nerve TN 009	MODERN MUSIC FOR MOTORCYCLES (10" EP, some on yellow vinyl; Dakota Oak/Alfie/Sirconical & Andy Votel/Mum & Dad/Badly Drawn Boy)	15
79	JSP JSP 4504	MORE BANDERA ROCKABILLIES (p/s)	12
95	Fierce Panda NING 15	MORTAL WOMBAT (double pack, p/s; Super Furry Animals/Baby Bird/ Panda/Mexican Pets/Harvey's Rabbit/Spare Snare)	8
75	Happy Time HT12	MUSIC FROM THUNDERBIRDS AND DOCTOR WHO (p/s)	8
80	EMI 12EMI 5074	MUTHA'S PRIDE (12", p/s; Wildfire/Quartz/White Spirit/Baby Jane)	20

N

98	Lowlife LOW6	98 Series Vol. 1 (EP)	30
98	Lowlife LOW7	98 Series Vol. 2 (EP)	25
80	Neutron NT 003	1980! THE FIRST FIFTEEN MINUTES EP (gatefold p/s with inserts; Vice Versa/Clock DVA/I'm So Hollow/Stunt Kites)	15

O

82	Neat NEAT 25	ONE TAKE NO DUBS (12", p/s; Black Rose/Hellanbach/Alien/Avenger)	12

P

90s	Fierce Panda NING 12CD	PANDEMONIUM (Easyworld, et al.) (250 only)	10
80s	A&M A&M PARTY 1/2/3/4/5/6	THE PARTY PARTY PACK (6 x 7", with picture sleeves, in PVC outer sleeve; Sting/Pauline Black/Dave Edmunds/Midge Ure /Modern Romance/Bad Manners/Chas & Dave/Bananarama/ Elvis Costello/Altered Images	50
80s	Pink & Black	PINK 'N' BLACK VOL 1 (p/s, re-issue of 1950's Rock 'n' Roll	10
97	V/VM VVMT4	PRIVILEGED FRAMES FOR REFERENCE (12" EP, p/s, 450 only)	15

R

93	Raptor RAP 1	RAPTOR PRESENTS . . . (12", p/s, 500 only; Ash/Buttlip/Marrow Bone/Fat)	40
82	Recommended RR-8.9	RECOMMENDED RECORDS SAMPLER (Peter Blegvad/Homosexuals/ Faust/ R. Stevie Moore; 1-sided, foldout p/s, clear vinyl, silk-screened PVC cover)	10
91	Ptolemaic Terrascope POT 8	RED FLIPPER (no p/s, Nurse With Wound/The Underworlde/Caravan Of Dreams)	20
94	Fierce Panda NING 03	RETURN TO SPLENDOUR (double pack in foldover p/s with insert in poly bag, 1,000 only; Bluetones et al.)	12
77	Rollercoaster RRCEP 00002	ROCKABILLY HOP (test pressings only)	12
83	Consett Music Project RD 1	ROCK AND DOLE (Obnoxious Tartus/Decade Waltz/Task Force/Hot Banana)	25
92	Melody Maker MMI	ROLLERCOASTER EP (CD, Blur/Jesus & Mary Chain/Dinosaur Jr./ My Bloody Valentine; 2,000 only)	12

S

95	Atol ATOL 02	S4C MAKES ME WANT TO SMOKE CRACK VOL. 1 (500 only, Catatonia et al.)	25
80	Sonic Int. S14283	SEX, VIOLENCE & ETERNAL TRUTH (oversized p/s, 250 pressed)	50

			MINT VALUE £
93	Duophonic DS 45-05/06	SHIMMIES IN SUPER 8 (double pack, 1 disc green vinyl, other white vinyl, numbered in poly bag, 800 with tri-foldout p/s, 400 also with sticker	35
95	Enraptured RAPT 4502	SILVER APPLES TRIBUTE (10", 12 in hand-drawn sleeve; Windy & Carl/ Scaredycat/Third Eye Foundation/Flowchart/Sabine	25
79	Groucho Marxist WH 1	SPECTACULAR COMMODITY (p/s; Mental Errors/Mod Cons/ Poems/Sneex/XS Discharge)	10
70s	Stiff BUY 1-10	STIFF BOX SET NO. 1 (10 x 7" box set)	35
70s	Stiff BUY 11-20	STIFF BOX SET NO. 2 (10 x 7" box set)	35
01	Edel 0128655ERESA	SUBSTITUTE EP : THE SONGS OF THE WHO (white vinyl, promo)	60

T

90s	Enraptured RAPT 4513	TERRASCOPE/TERRASTOCK (Bevis Frond/Damon & Naomi/ Flying Saucer Attack/Silver Apples)	12
83	White Noise WN 3	THIS IS WHITE NOISE (p/s; Skrewdriver/Brutal Attack/Die Hards/A.B.H.)	40
02	Warner Bros 50466 13441	TOP-DECK SKA 45'S BOX (8 x 7"s, coloured vinyl in cardboard box)	25
82	Total Noise TOT 1	TOTAL NOISE # 1 (Business/Blitz/Dead Generation/Gonads)	10
93	2 Tone CHSTT31	2 TONE EP	20
93	2 Tone CDCHSTT31	2 TONE EP (CD)	8
01	Trunk JBH 01	Theme To Screen Test (Marching There & back) (1-sided 7", 500 only)	20

U

80s	Fierce FRIGHT/SFTRI 38	AN UNHOLY MONTAGE (200 only [100 U.K./100 U.S.], coloured vinyl with numbered insert)	25

W

80	Fuck Off FEP 001	WEIRD NOISE (p/s, white labels; Danny & Dressmakers/The Door & The Window/Instant Automatons/012/Sell-Outs)	10
82	Bluurg FISH 1	WESSEX '82 (Subhumans/Pagans/Organized Chaos/The Heads)	12
77	MPL MPL 1	WE'VE MOVED! (Wings/Gene Vincent/Frank Sinatra et al., promo only excerpts sampler, with press pack)	350
84	Rather/Seventeen	WHAT A NICE WAY TO TURN SEVENTEEN NO. 2 (p/s; Swell Maps & others; with magazine)	12

Y

80s	Wonderful World Of WOW 1	YOU ARE NOT ALONE (p/s, with insert; Oi Polloi/Hex/Stalag 17/ Symbol Of Freedom)	15

UNTITLED EPs & SINGLES 50s - 00s

60s	Coxsone SCE 1	(no p/s, 33rpm; Gaylads/Hugh Godfrey/Glen & Dave/Roy Richards/ Cables/Richard Ace)	75
63	Embassy WEP 1086	(p/s; Mike Redway/Bud Ashton Group/Rory Pilgrim)	15
69	De Wolfe	(Lemon Dips, et al.)	30
73	Buddah 2011 164	(Shangri-La's/Tradewinds/Ad Libs)	6
94	Kennel Club VTDOG 10	(Strangelove/Tindersticks/God Machine/Breed (10", numbered, 1,500 only, free with Purr magazine issue 2)	10
98	Fat Cat 12FAT 008	REMIXES (12", custom sleeve; remixes of Fat Cat 12FAT 003 by Autechre et al.)	12
94	Kennel Club VTDOG 10	TINDERSTICKS: Girl On Death Row/STRANGELOVE: Wolf's Story/GOD MACHINE: The Devil Song/BREED: Diamonds Are Forever (10", numbered p/s)	10
96	SKAM MASK 1	UNTITLED (12", custom sleeve, 100 only; Freeform/Funkstorung/ Boards Of Canada/Jega)	150
97	SKAM MASK 2	UNTITLED (12", custom sleeve, 350 only; Hellinterface/ Funkstorung/Bola/ Jega/Intron)	75

VARIOUS ARTISTS LPs & COMPILATIONS (alphabetical by title)

A

70	ATP 102	THE ABBEY TAVERN	20
88	Woronzow WOO 6	ACID JAM (with insert)	18
69	Action ACLP 6005	ACTION PACKED SOUL	50
70s	Jem JEM	A DEAL A DAY	25
96	Ferox FERLP 1	ADVENTURES IN TECHNO SOUL (2-LP; Too Funk/Paul Hannah/Carl Craig et al.)	20
85	United Dairies UD 012	AN AFFLICTED MAN'S MUSICA BOX (3 different editions, 1st in gatefold sleeve)	75
75	Leader LEE 4056	A FINE HUNTING DAY - SONGS OF THE HOLME VALLEY BEAGLES (with book)	15
70	Pama PMP 2004	AFRICAN MELODY	70
71	Trojan TBL 166	AFRICA'S BLOOD (Lee Perry, et al.) (orange/white label)	20
70s	Contempo 2870 311	AFRO ROCK FESTIVAL	15
64	Decca LK 4606	AFTER SUNSET	150
66	Stateside SL 10172	AN ALBUM FULL OF SOUL	50
69	Key KL 002	ALIVE!	20
84	Creation CRELP 001	ALIVE IN THE LIVING ROOM	12
70	Talisman STAL 5013	ALL FOLK TOGETHER	20
84	Whaam! BIG 8	ALL FOR ART? AND ART FOR ALL	30
71	Utd. Artists UDX 201/202	ALL GOOD CLEAN FUN (2-LP)	15
83	Neat NEAT 102A/B	ALL HELL LET LOOSE	20
61	Blue Beat BBLP 801	ALL STARS - JAMAICAN BLUES	300
70	Speciality SPE 6609	ALL THE BLUES ALL THE TIME	22
58	Pye Nixa NJT 509	ALL THE WINNERS (10")	20
76	Riva RVLP 2	ALL THIS AND WORLD WAR TWO (2-LP, box set with booklet)	15
58	Parlophone PMD 1064	ALL TIME COUNTRY AND WESTERN HITS (10")	30
73	Polydor 2460 186	AMERICAN BLUES LEGENDS '73	15
63	Polydor LPHM 46 397	AMERICAN FOLK BLUES FESTIVAL (also stereo SLPHM 237 597)	15
70s	Rare Records 2	AMERICAN FOLK BLUES FESTIVAL 1962	25
64	Fontana TL 5204	AMERICAN FOLK BLUES FESTIVAL 1963	25
65	Fontana TL 5225	AMERICAN FOLK BLUES FESTIVAL 1964	25
66	Fontana TL 5286	AMERICAN FOLK BLUES FESTIVAL 1965	25
66	Fontana (S)TL 5389	AMERICAN FOLK BLUES FESTIVAL 1966 (mono/stereo)	22
70	CBS 63912	AMERICAN FOLK BLUES FESTIVAL 1969	20
80s	Pleasantly Surprised PS 2	THE ANGELS ARE COMING (2-cassette, with booklet)	25

			MINT VALUE £
83	No Future MPUNK 8	ANGELS WITH DIRTY FACES	18
60s	77' 77LA 12/13	ANGOLA PRISON SPIRITUALS	18
69	Immediate IMAL 03/04	ANTHOLOGY OF BRITISH BLUES VOLUME 1 (2-LP, gatefold sleeve)	30
69	Immediate IMAL 05/06	ANTHOLOGY OF BRITISH BLUES VOLUME 2 (2-LP, gatefold sleeve)	30
64	London HA-K/SH-K 8174	APOLLO SATURDAY NIGHT (mono/stereo)	60
93	Art ART 2CD	APPLIED RHYMIC TECHNOLOGY (CD)	30
93	Art ART 4CD	APPLIED RHYMIC TECHNOLOGY (CD)	20
80s	Ram RAMLP 001	THE ART OF SOLVING PROBLEMS (with poster & insert)	18
74	Ashanti SHAN 106	ASHANTI SHOWCASE	12
69	Atco 228 021	ATCO BLOCKBUSTERS	18
69	Atlantic 587/588 180	ATLANTIC BLOCKBUSTERS	20
65	Atlantic ATL 5020	ATLANTIC DISCOTHEQUE	40
60s	Atlantic AP 2	ATLANTIC IS SOUL	15
60s	Atlantic AC 3	ATLANTICLASSICS	25
67	Pye NPL 18198	AT LAST THE 1948 SHOW	15
90	Dover/PWL CCD 19	A TON OF HITS - THE HIT FACTORY VOL. 4 (2-CD)	25
64	Decca LK 4597	AT THE CAVERN	80
63	London HA-R 8133	AT THE HOOTENANNY - VOLUME 3	15
70	Beacon SBEAB 9	AUTHENTIC CHICAGO BLUES	20
57	London WB 91034	AUTHENTIC CARIBBEAN CALYPSOS (10" LP)	30
64	Stateside SL 10107	AUTHENTIC SKA	70
64	Stateside SL 10068	AUTHENTIC R & B	40
79	Heartbeat HB 1	AVON CALLING - THE BRISTOL COMPILATION (with poster)	25
80	K-Tel NE 1100	AXE ATTACK (early copies with demo of Iron Maiden's "Running Free")	15
85	Steeltrax JCI 7102	AXE ATTACK (LP)	18
80s	Flaccid FLAC 1	AYLESBURY GOES FLACCID	15
74	Deroy DER 1052	AYRSHIRE FOLK (LP, private pressing)	50

B

92	Chrysalis CHR TT 5012	BEST OF 2 TONE (LP)	40
70	Track 2407 001	BACKTRACK ONE	25
70	Track 2407 002	BACKTRACK TWO	12
70	Track 2407003	BACKTRACK THREE	15
70	Track 2407005	BACKTRACK FIVE	15
70	Track 2407 006	BACKTRACK SIX	15
70	Track 2407 007	BACKTRACK SEVEN	12
54	London AL 3535	BACKWOODS BLUES (10")	50
73	Incus INCUS 11	BALANCE (Ian Brighton, et al.)	60
62	Fontana 688 200 ZL	BALLIN'	18
79	JSP 1005	BANDERA ROCKABILLIES	15
68	Pama PMLP 4	BANG BANG LULU	30
69	Pama Economy ECO7	BANGARANG (LP)	45
73	BBC/Roundabout 17	BANG ON A DRUM	18
60	Melodisc 12-115	BANJO BREAKDOWN	15
59	Fontana TFR 6018	BARRELHOUSE, BOOGIE WOOGIE AND BLUES (10")	25
58	Vogue Coral LRA 10022	BARRELHOUSE PIANO (10" LP)	25
59	Vogue Coral LRA 10023	BARRELHOUSE PIANO VOLUME 2 (10" LP)	25
83	London CAVE 1	THE BATCAVE - YOUNG LIMBS AND NUMB HYMNS	12
71	Trojan TBL 167	BATTLE AXE	30
52	Capitol LC 6510	BATTLE OF THE BANDS (10" LP)	18
71	B&C BCM 103	BATTLE OF THE BANDS VOL. 1	15
64	Melodisc MLP 12-192	BATTLE OF THE GIANTS	20
53	MGM MGM-D 115	A BATTLE OF JAZZ: HOT VERSUS COOL (10")	30
71	BBC REC 118	BBC's FOLK ON TWO PRESENTS NORTHUMBRIAN FOLK	20
69	Beacon BEAB 1	BEACON BRINGS IT TO YOU	18
71	Revival RVS 1004	BEALE STREET MESS AROUND	12
84	Well Suspect SUSS 1	THE BEAT GENERATION AND THE ANGRY YOUNG MEN	20
86	Mercury WILD 1	BEAT RUNS WILD (Wet Wet Wet et al.)	25
87	Pink PINKY 15	BEAUTY (McCarthy et al.)	12
77	Impulse IS/BED/123	BEDROCK - ALTOGETHER BEDROCK LP (private pressing)	12
68	Elektra EUK 262	BEGIN HERE (also stereo EUKS 7262)	20
78	Rip Off ROLP 1	BELFAST ROCKS	35
71	Delmark DS 622	BELL'S BLUES HARP	15
68	Bell MBLL 102	BELL'S CELLAR OF SOUL VOLUME 1	30
69	Bell MBLL 107	BELL'S CELLAR OF SOUL VOLUME 2	30
69	Bell MBLL 117	BELL'S CELLAR OF SOUL VOLUME 3	30
69	Bell MBLL/SBLL 111	THE BEST FROM BELL	20
69	Bell MBLL/SBLL 124	THE BEST FROM BELL VOLUME 2	20
78	Stiff ODD 2	BE STIFF (TOUR '78 OFFICIAL RELEASE) (promo only)	15
78	Stiff DEAL 1	BE STIFF ROUTE '78 (with 16-page booklet & biographies, etc.)	15
70s	Storyville 671 188	THE BEST OF THE BLUES	15
65	Xtra XTRA 1031	THE BEST OF BRITISH FOLK	15
69	Pama SECO 18	THE BEST OF CAMEL	150
72	Paramount SPFL 286	BEST OF FILM MUSIC	15
76	Epic EPC 81224	THE BEST OF OKEH VOL. I	15
76	Epic EPC 81532	THE BEST OF OKEH VOL. II	15
69	President PTL 1016	THE BEST OF PRESIDENT VOLUME 1	12
69	President PTL 1036	THE BEST OF PRESIDENT VOLUME 2	12
93	Chrysalis	THE BEST OF 2 TONE	40
83	Statik STATLP 14	THE BEST OF YOUR SECRET'S SAFE WITH US	20
73	Attack ATLP 1011	BIG BAMBOO	30
60	Fontana TFL 5080	THE BIG BEAT!	55
85	Big Beat WIKM39	BIG BEAT BEACH PARTY	15
64	London HA-B 8199	THE BIG 'D' JAMBOREE	25
78	Giorno GPS	BIG EGO	20
69	Fontana SFXL 55	THE BIG FOLK	12
69	Minit MLL/MLS 40007E	THE BIG ONE	22

			MINT VALUE £
64	Capitol ST 2146	BIG SOUNDS OF THE DRAGS Vol 2	30
72	CBS 64844	THE BIG SUR FESTIVAL	18
70	Pama SECO 32	BIRTH CONTROL	30
80	Black Ark Intl. BALP 4001	BLACK ARK VOLUME 2	30
70	Matchbox SDX 207/8	BLACK DIAMOND EXPRESS TO HELL (2-LP)	25
60	Columbia 33SX 1244	BLACKPOOL NIGHTS	35
80	Form BB 1003	BLACK MAGIC DUB (LP)	100
58	HMV CLP 1167	BLACK SLACKS AND BOBBY SOCKS (LP)	300
70	Ember SE 8009	BLACK SOUL EXPLOSION	18
70	CBS 52796	BLACK WHITES AND BLUES	20
83	Quiet QLP 3	BLOOD ON THE ROQ! (withdrawn)	15
68	Coxsone CSP 1	BLUE BEAT SPECIAL	50
66	RCA Victor RD 7786	BLUEBIRD BLUES	20
63	Stateside SL 10021	THE BLUEGRASS HALL OF FAME	15
65	London HA-B 8227	BLUEGRASS HALL OF FAME VOL. 2	18
64	London HA-B 8118	BLUEGRASS SPECTACULAR	12
62	Columbia 33SX 1417	THE BLUES	60
64	Pye Intl. NPL 28030	BLUES VOL. 1	18
64	Pye Intl. NPL 28035	BLUES VOL. 2	18
64	Pye Intl. NPL 28045	BLUES VOL. 3	18
64	Chess CRL 4003	BLUES VOL. 4	18
65	Chess CRL 4512	BLUES VOL. 5	18
68	Immediate IMLP 014	BLUES ANYTIME VOL. 1	18
68	Immediate IMCP 015	BLUES ANYTIME VOL. 2	18
68	Immediate IMLP 019	BLUES ANYTIME VOL. 3	18
65	Fontana TFL 6048	THE BLUES AT NEWPORT 1964 PART 1	22
69	Saga FID 2165	BLUES AT SUNRISE	12
66	London HA-S 8265	THE BLUES CAME DOWN FROM MEMPHIS	80
73	Flyright LP 504	BLUES CAME TO CHAPEL HILL	15
65	Storyville SLP 176	BLUESCENE USA: VOLUME 1 - CHICAGO	18
65	Storyville SLP 177	BLUESCENE USA: VOLUME 2 - LOUISIANA BLUES	18
65	Storyville SLP 181	BLUESCENE USA: VOLUME 3 - BLUES ALL AROUND MY BED	18
67	Storyville SLP 180	BLUESCENE USA: VOLUME 4 - MISSISSIPPI BLUES	18
71	Python PLP-KM 17	BLUES - CHICAGO STYLE (LP)	45
60	Philips BBL 7369	BLUES FELL THIS MORNING	40
73	Polydor 2383 257	BLUES FOR MR. CRUMP	18
72	Transatlantic TRASAM 25	BLUES FOR YOUR POCKET	12
69	Chess CRLS 4558	BLUES FROM BIG BILL'S COPACABANA	35
69	Python PLP 6	BLUES FROM CHICAGO (99 copies only)	80
70	Python PLP 9	BLUES FROM CHICAGO VOL. 2 (99 copies only)	80
71	Python PLP 15	BLUES FROM CHICAGO VOL. 3 (99 copies only)	80
60s	Heritage 1004	BLUES FROM MAXWELL STREET (99 copies only)	80
71	Pye Intl. NPL 28142	BLUES FROM THE BAYOU	22
72	Saydisc SDM 226	BLUES FROM THE DELTA	25
71	Python PLP 21	BLUES FROM THE WINDY CITY (99 copies only)	80
77	Flyright LP 4713	BLUES FROM THE WINDY CITY	15
80	Kicking Mule SNKF 159	BLUES GUITAR WORKSHOP	15
63	Stateside SL 10076	BLUES HOOT (Lightning Hopkins)	35
57	Pye Nixa NJL 8	(ALAN LOMAX PRESENTS) BLUES IN THE MISSISSIPPI NIGHT	35
60s	Sunflower (no cat. no.)	BLUES IS MY COMPANION (99 copies only)	42
60s	Sunflower (no cat. no.)	BLUES KEEP FALLING (99 copies only)	80
69	Blue Horizon 7-66227	BLUES JAM AT CHESS (2-LP)	60
69	Immediate IMLP 024	BLUES LEFTOVERS	12
67	Saydisc Match. SDM 142	BLUES LIKE SHOWERS OF RAIN	70
68	Saydisc Match. SDM 167	BLUES LIKE SHOWERS OF RAIN VOLUME 2	70
65	Decca LK 4681	BLUES NOW	60
72	Blues Obscurities BOV 1	BLUES OBSCURITIES VOL. 1: SOUTHERN BLUES/ DARK MUDDY BOTTOM (plain cover with photocopied inserts)	40
72	Blues Obscurities BOV 2	BLUES OBSCURITIES VOL. 2: LONESOME HARMONICA	25
72	Blues Obscurities BOV 3	BLUES OBSCURITIES VOL. 3: WEST COAST BLUES	25
72	Blues Obscurities BOV 4	BLUES OBSCURITIES VOL. 4: ONE RAINY MORNING	25
72	Blues Obscurities BOV 5	BLUES OBSCURITIES VOL. 5: SOMETHING'S GONE WRONG	25
72	Blues Obscurities BOV 6	BLUES OBSCURITIES VOL. 6: COMING BACK HOME	25
72	Blues Obscurities BOV 7	BLUES OBSCURITIES VOL. 7	25
72	Blues Obscurities BOV 8	BLUES OBSCURITIES VOL. 8	25
72	Blues Obscurities BOV 9	BLUES OBSCURITIES VOL. 9	25
72	Blues Obscurities BOV 10	BLUES OBSCURITIES VOL. 10	25
74	London HA-U 8454	BLUES OBSCURITIES VOL. 1: DARK MUDDY BOTTOM (reissue)	15
74	London HA-U 8455	BLUES OBSCURITIES VOL. 2: LONESOME HARMONICA (reissue)	15
74	London HA-U 8456	BLUES OBSCURITIES VOL. 3: STRETCHIN' OUT	15
69	Mercury SMXL 77	BLUES PACKAGE '69	15
69	Highway 51 H 102	BLUES PEOPLE	40
68	Matchbox SDR 146	BLUES PIANO	20
72	Atlantic K 40404	BLUES PIANO - CHICAGO PLUS	20
68	Kokomo K 1001	A BLUES POTPOURRI (99 copies only)	60
71	Rarities (Tony's Records)	BLUES RARITIES VOL. 1 (2-LP)	25
69	Atlantic Special 590 019	THE BLUES ROLL ON (reissue of "Southern Folk Heritage: The Blues Roll On")	12
69	Poppy PYM 11001	BLUES ROOTS VOLUME ONE	25
66	Decca LK 4748	BLUES SOUTHSIDE CHICAGO	55
71	Python PLP 16	BLUES TODAY - SOUTHERN STYLE (99 copies only)	40
71	Polydor 2675 007	BOMBERS	12
65	Topic 12T 128	BONNY LASS COME O'ER THE BURN	12
55	London AL 3544	BOOGIE WOOGIE WITH THE BLUES (10")	50
69	Pama SECO 17	BOSS REGGAE	100
74	Eron 002	BOTH SIDES OF THE DOWNS (with insert)	25
80	Aardvark STEAL 2	BOUQUET OF STEEL (blue vinyl with 27-page booklet)	15

			MINT VALUE £
81	Bristol Recorder BR 002	THE BRISTOL RECORDER VOL. 2 (with magazine booklet)	15
68	Island ILP 966/ILPS 9066	BRITISH BLUE-EYED SOUL	75
67	Tamla Motown TML 11055	BRITISH MOTOWN CHARTBUSTERS (mono, flipback sleeve)	20
69	T. Motown STML 11055	BRITISH MOTOWN CHARTBUSTERS (stereo reissue, flipback sleeve)	20
68	T. Motown (S)TML 11082	BRITISH MOTOWN CHARTBUSTERS VOL. 2 (mono/stereo, flipback sleeve)	18
93	Hammer (no catalogue no.)	BRITISH OI! - WORKING CLASS ANTHEMS	12
87	See For Miles SEE 66	BRITISH PSYCHEDELIC TRIP 1	12
87	See For Miles SEE 206	BRITISH PSYCHEDELIC TRIP 4	12
70	Trojan TBL 106	BRIXTON CAT	35
64	Decca LK 4598	BRUM BEAT	85
64	Dial DLP 1	BRUM BEAT	50
79	Big Bear BRUM 1	BRUM BEAT - LIVE AT THE BARREL ORGAN (2-LP, with inserts)	20
80	MCA MCF 3074	BRUTE FORCE	20
70	Buddah 2349 008	BUDDAH IN MIND	12
72	Flyright LP 106	BULL CITY BLUES	15
81	Crass 421984/4	BULLSHIT DETECTIVE 1	15
82	Crass 221984/3	BULLSHIT DETECTIVE 2	15
83	Crass	BULLSHIT DETECTIVE 3	15
66	Decca LK 4734	BUMPER BUNDLE 16 HITS	25
77	Stiff SEEZ 2	A BUNCH OF STIFF RECORDS	15
79	Cherry Red ARED 2	BUSINESS UNUSUAL (with Zig Zag small labels catalogue)	30
81	Autumn AU 2	BUSTED AT OZ	20
84	Dambusters DAM 003	BUTTONS AND BOWS VOLUME 1 (2-LP)	30
84	Dambusters DAM 006	BUTTONS AND BOWS VOLUME 2 (2-LP)	30
69	BBC REB 39M	BRITISH PRIME MINISTERS 1924-1964 (LP)	15
98	Trunk BARKED 3	THE BATTLE OF BOSWORTH (LP)	20
		C	
50s	Melodisc MLP 507	CALYPSO CARNIVAL (10" LP)	18
72	Topic 12TS 219	CANNY NEWCASSEL (with booklet, blue label)	20
67	Bounty BY 6035	CAN'T KEEP FROM CRYING (TOPICAL BLUES ON THE DEATH OF PRESIDENT KENNEDY)	20
78	Capitol CAPS 1025	CAPITOL SOUL CASINO	12
50s	Parlophone CPMD 13	CARIBBEAN CALYPSO (10" LP, export issue)	25
81	Secret SEC 2	CARRY ON OI!	15
73	Nottingham Festival FEST 2	CASTLE ROCK	50
78	Nice NICE 1	CATCH A WAVE (2 x 10", gatefold sleeve)	30
90	Cerne CERNE 001/002/003	THE CERNE BOX SET (3-LP box set; Nurse With Wound/ Current 93/ Sol Invictus; with 3 inserts)	125
80	Quality QP 32/80	CHAMPIONS AGAIN: HIGHLIGHTS OF 1979-80 SEASON	20
71	Chess 6671 102	CHARLIE PARKER MEMORIAL CONCERT	12
60s	Columbia	CHARTBUSTERS USA	45
73	Checker 6445 150	CHESS GOLDEN DECADE VOL. 1: THE EARLY 50s	12
73	Checker 6445 151	CHESS GOLDEN DECADE VOL. 2: 1956 TAKE IT EASY GREASY	12
73	Checker 6445 152	CHESS GOLDEN DECADE VOL. 3: 1957 DIMESTORE PONYTAIL	12
74	Chess 6445 153	CHESS GOLDEN DECADE VOL. 4: 1958-1959 BOOK OF LOVE	12
74	Chess 6445 154	CHESS GOLDEN DECADE VOL. 5: 1959-1961 GOOD MORNING LITTLE SCHOOLGIRL	12
74	Chess 6445 202	CHESS GOLDEN DECADE VOL. 6: 1961-1962 TALKIN' TRASH	12
74	Chess 6445 203	CHESS GOLDEN DECADE VOL. 7: 1963-1965 HIGH HEEL SNEAKERS (gatefold sleeve)	15
74	Chess 6445 204	CHESS GOLDEN DECADE VOL. 8: 1965-1966 THE IN CROWD	12
78	Chess 9124 213	CHESS ROCKABILLIES	12
64	Chess CRL 4004	CHESS STORY VOL. 1	25
65	Chess CRL 4516	CHESS STORY VOL. 2	25
71	Vanguard VSD 79217	CHICAGO BLUES VOLUME 2	15
66	Fontana TFL 6068	CHICAGO/THE BLUES/TODAY	18
66	Fontana TFL 6069	CHICAGO/THE BLUES/TODAY VOLUME 2	18
66	Fontana TFL 6070	CHICAGO/THE BLUES/TODAY VOLUME 3	18
69	Vanguard SVRL 19020	CHICAGO/THE BLUES/TODAY VOLUME 1	20
69	Vanguard SVRL 19021	CHICAGO/THE BLUES/TODAY VOLUME 2	20
69	Vanguard SVRL 19022	CHICAGO/THE BLUES/TODAY VOLUME 3	18
68	Sunflower ET 1401	THE CHICAGO HOUSE BANDS (99 copies only)	40
69	Kokomo K 1005	CHICAGO SESSIONS VOLUME 1 (99 copies only)	50
70	Flyright LP 4700	CHICKEN STUFF	15
80	Relics LSD 1	CHOCOLATE SOUP FOR DIABETICS VOL. 1	15
81	Relics ACID 1	CHOCOLATE SOUP FOR DIABETICS VOL. 2 (gatefold sleeve)	15
83	Relics CSFD 3	CHOCOLATE SOUP FOR DIABETICS VOL. 3	12
84	MCA CHUNK 1	CHUNKS OF FUNK	20
58	Philips BBR 8112	CHRISTMAS (10")	12
73	United Artists UDX 205/6	CHRISTMAS AT THE PATTI (2 x 10", gatefold sleeve)	22
68	Chess CRLS 4541	CHRISTMAS DEDICATION	25
81	Ze/Island ILPS 7017	A CHRISTMAS RECORD (LP, initially white vinyl, then black)	12
63	London HA-U 8141	A CHRISTMAS GIFT FOR YOU (plum label, later black label)	100
78	Incus INCUS 33	CIRCADIAN RHYTHM	50
72	Specialty SNTF 5015	CITY BLUES	12
80s	White Elephant RIOCH 1	CITY WALLS - A SOUTHAMPTON COMPILATION (with insert)	12
70	Charisma CAS 1008	CLASSICAL HEADS	12
55	London AL 3559	CLASSIC JAZZ PIANO (10")	25
69	Atlantic 587 167	CLASSIC RHYTHM AND BLUES	12
70s	Waldo's DS 005	CLEANING UP THE MUSIC BIZ	12
85	Pusmort 0012-02	CLEANSE THE BACTERIA	20
72	Pegasus PS 1	CLOGS (FOLK SAMPLER) (with insert)	15
90s	Distronics ITCD 3	THE CLOSING PARTY - IN THE CITY LIVE UNSIGNED (CD)	50
72	Pegasus PS 2	CLUB FOLK VOLUME ONE	15
72	Pegasus PS 3	CLUB FOLK VOLUME TWO	15
72	Trojan TBL178	CLUB REGGAE 3	25

			MINT VALUE £
70	Trojan TTL 54	CLUB ROCK STEADY	25
68	W.I.R.L. ILP 965	CLUB ROCK STEADY '68	45
67	W.I.R.L. ILP 948	CLUB SKA '67	30
67	W.I.R.L. ILP 956	CLUB SKA '67 VOL. 2	35
70	Trojan TTL 48	CLUB SKA VOLUME ONE	20
70	Trojan TTL 51	CLUB SKA VOLUME TWO (Existence unconfirmed)	30
68	Island ILP 964	CLUB SOUL	50
84	Kent 022	CLUB SOUL	15
67	Elektra EUK 253	A COLD WIND BLOWS	15
65	Tamla Motown TML 11001	A COLLECTION OF 16 TAMLA MOTOWN HITS	40
67	Tamla Motown TML 11043	A COLLECTION OF 16 ORIGINAL BIG HITS VOL. 4	40
67	Tamla Motown TML 11050	A COLLECTION OF 16 ORIGINAL BIG HITS VOL. 5	40
68	T. Motown (S)TML 11074	A COLLECTION OF 16 ORIGINAL BIG HITS VOL. 6 (mono/stereo)	30
69	T. Motown (S)TML 11092	A COLLECTION OF 16 ORIGINAL BIG HITS VOL. 7 - THE MOTOWN SOUND	30
70	T. Motown (S)TML 11130	A COLLECTION OF 16 ORIGINAL BIG HITS VOL. 8	25
75	Chicago 202	COLLECTORS BLUES SERIES VOL. 1	15
75	Chicago 205	COLLECTORS BLUES SERIES VOL. 2	15
75	Chicago 210	COLLECTORS BLUES SERIES VOL. 3	15
75	Chicago 212	COLLECTORS BLUES SERIES VOL. 4	15
75	Chicago 213	COLLECTORS BLUES SERIES VOL. 5	15
54	London AL 3514	COLLECTORS' ITEMS VOLUME ONE (10")	18
54	London AL 3533	COLLECTORS' ITEMS VOLUME TWO (10")	18
56	London AL 3550	COLLECTORS' ITEMS VOLUME THREE (10")	18
86	Color Disc COLORS 4	COLOR SUPPLEMENT (400 only)	15
93	2-Tone CDCHRTT 5013	THE COMPACT 2-TONE STORY (4-CD, box set with book)	40
76	Incus INCUS 21	COMPANY 1	40
77	Incus INCUS 29	COMPANY 6	40
77	Incus INCUS 30	COMPANY 7	40
72	Apple STCX 3385	THE CONCERT FOR BANGLA DESH (3-LP box set, orange inside with BMI/ ASCAP label credits, with booklet, featuring Bob Dylan)	70
64	Decca LK 4664	CONVERSATION WITH THE BLUES	70
57	Tempo TAP 10	COOL MUSIC FOR A HOT NIGHT - MOOD MUSIC IN THE MODERN MANNER	150
72	Wicksteed WCKLP 02	CORBY CATCHMENT AREA (private pressing)	200
78	ABC ABCL 5247	COTTON PICKIN' ROCK	12
80s	Third Mind TMLP 09	COULD YOU WALK ON THE WATER	15
60	Storyville SLP 129	THE COUNTRY BLUES	20
73	Specialty SNTF 5014	COUNTRY BLUES	15
60s	Saydisc Roots RL 334	COUNTRY BLUES OBSCURITIES VOLUME 1	20
66	Stateside SL 10170	COUNTRY COUSINS	18
56	Brunswick LA 8729	COUNTRY FAVOURITES VOL. ONE (10")	30
81	No Future OI 3	COUNTRY FIT FOR HEROES	15
82	No Future 12 OI 23	COUNTY FIT FOR HEROES 2	18
59	Capitol T 1179	THE COUNTRY'S BEST	12
69	Pama ECO 2	CRAB - GREATEST HITS	60
80	Rabid/Absurd LAST 1	THE CRAP STOPS HERE	25
60	Fontana TFL 5103	THE CREAM OF 'TAKE IT FROM HERE' (also stereo SFL 534)	12
60s	Saydisc Roots RL 332	CREAM OF THE CROP	12
74	Eron 005	CRYPTADIA	15
79	Trojan TRLS 185	CREATION ROCKERS 5	15
79	Trojan TRLS 183	CREATION ROCKERS 3	18
77	Carib Gems CGDD 301	CARIB GEMS DISCO DISC	25

D

81	Two Tone CHRTT 5004	DANCE CRAZE	15
68	H. Note/B. Shot BSLP 5002	DANCING DOWN ORANGE STREET	80
84	Kent KENT 026	DANCING 'TIL DAWN	15
76	Dark Horse DH 1 (DHSAM 1)	DARK HORSE RECORDS '76 (promo only sampler, stickered sleeve & inner)	40
86	EMI EQ 5003	DAVE CLARK'S TIME (2-LP, with brochure and lyric inner, some with hologram)	30
90s	Nuphonic NUX 136LP	DAVID MANCUSO PRESENTS THE LOFT VOL. 1 (4 x 12" with booklet)	40
90s	Nuphonic NUX 154LP	DAVID MANCUSO PRESENTS THE LOFT VOL. 2 (4 x 12")	30
71	Dawn DNLB 3024	DAWN TAKEAWAY CONCERT	12
79	Dead Good DEAD 4	DEAD GOOD'S DEAD GOODS (unissued)	0
78	Virgin VD 2508	DEAD ON ARRIVAL (glow-in-the-dark vinyl with poster)	15
66	Highway 51 H 100	DECADE OF THE BLUES - THE 1950's (99 copies only)	75
66	Highway 51 H 104	DECADE OF THE BLUES - THE 1950's VOLUME 2 (99 copies only)	50
54	Decca LF 1160	DECCA SHOWCASE VOL. 3 (10")	15
55	Decca LF 1265	DECCA SHOWCASE VOL. 5 (10")	18
65	London HA-B 8249	DECK OF CARDS	12
71	United Artists UAS 29153	DEEPER INTO THE VAULTS	12
70	Polydor 2673 001	DEEP OVERGROUND POP	20
70	Stax SXATS 1037	THE DEEP SOUL OF STAX	22
71	Flyright LP 102	DEEP SOUTH COUNTRY BLUES	15
86	Decal LIK 9	DERAM DAYZE	15
68	Deram SML 1027	THE DERAM GOLDEN POPS SAMPLER	80
67	Island ILP 955	DERRICK HARRIOTT'S ROCK (SKA) STEADY PARTY	225
72	Trojan TTL 54	DERRICK HARRIOTT'S ROCKSTEADY PARTY (reissue - existence unconfirmed)	50
85	Yangki 01	DEVASTATE TO LIBERATE	15
89	Blast First BFDJ 1	DEVIL'S JUKEBOX (10 x 7" in numbered box, with booklet, 3,000 only)	20
79	Topic 12TS 349	DEVON TRADITION - AN ANTHOLOGY FROM TRADITIONAL SINGERS	12
73	London ZGU 131	DIMENSION DOLLS	15
70	Mercury 6641 006	DIMENSION OF MIRACLES	15 12
74	DIP DLP 5026	D.I.P. PRESENTS THE UPSETTER (Lee Perry et al.)	70
69	Minit MLL/MLS 40005	DIRT BLUES	25
70	BBC REC 65M	DISC A DAWN	20
57	RCA RC 2400	DISCTIONARY OF JAZZ (10")	12
67	Island ILP 943	DOCTOR SOUL	90
82	BBC 2-LP-22001	DOCTOR WHO COLLECTOR'S EDITION (2-LP, with poster)	30

			MINT VALUE £
80s	Pleasantly Surprised PS 12	DOCUMENT (cassette)	18
84	Hope Springs HOP 1	DON'T LET THE HOPE CLOSE DOWN	15
70	Python PLP	DOWNHOME BLUES (99 copies only)	90
70	Python PLP 14	DOWNHOME BLUES VOLUME 2 (99 copies only)	90
71	Python PLP 22	DOWNHOME BLUES VOLUME 3 (99 copies only)	90
71	Flyright LP 4703	DOWN IN HOGAN'S ALLEY	15
67	Down With The Game 200	DOWN WITH THE GAME VOLUME 1 (99 copies only)	55
67	Down With The Game 201	DOWN WITH THE GAME VOLUME 2 (99 copies only)	55
68	Down With The Game 203	DOWN WITH THE GAME VOLUME 3 (99 copies only)	55
68	Down With The Game 204	DOWN WITH THE GAME VOLUME 4 (99 copies only)	55
68	Down With The Game 205	DOWN WITH THE GAME VOLUME 5 (99 copies only)	55
68	Down With The Game 206	DOWN WITH THE GAME VOLUME 6 (99 copies only)	55
67	Island ILP 954	DR. KITCH	60
85	Capitol EG 26 0573 1-4	DREAM BABIES	15
72	Ember EMB 3413	A DROP OF THE HARD STUFF	12
59	Parlophone PMC 1101	DRUMBEAT (Adam Faith et al.)	55
60	Columbia SCX 3359	DRUM NIGHT AT BIRDLAND	12
68	Island ILP 976	THE DUKE AND THE PEACOCK	90
69	Trojan TTL 8	DUKE REID'S GOLDEN HITS	40
67	Island ILP 958	DUKE REID'S ROCK STEADY	350
70	Trojan TTL 53	DUKE REID'S ROCK STEADY (reissue, existence unconfirmed)	30
69	BBC REC 35S	DUNGEON FOLK	12
87	Manic Ears ACHE 3	DIGGING IN WATER (LP, featuring Disorder/Chaos UK/Oi Polloi..)	12
01	Trunk DFM 001 LP	DIRTY FAN MAIL (LP)	20

E

70	Matchbox SDR 199	EARLY BLUES VOLUME 1: SKOODLE-UM-SKOO	20
70	Matchbox SDR 206	EARLY FOLK BLUES VOLUME 2: HOMETOWN SKIFFLE	15
70	Middle Earth MDLS 20	EARTHED	30
80	Dead Good GOOD 1	EAST (with inner & stickered sleeve)	25
73	Southern Sound SD 200	EAST VERNON BLUES	30
63	Decca LK 4546	EDINBURGH FOLK FESTIVAL VOLUME 1	30
63	Decca LK 4563	EDINBURGH FOLK FESTIVAL VOLUME 2	30
55	Philips BBR 8046	EIGHT EVERGREENS (10")	15
75	Island/Transatlantic	ELECTRIC MUSE - THE STORY OF FOLK INTO ROCK (4-LP box set with booklet)	40
64	Turnabout TV340465	ELECTRONIC MUSIC	25
85	Push PUSH 001	ELEGANCE, CHARM AND DEADLY DANGER	25
80s	Master BBSLP 007	ELEMENTALS	20
83	Extract XX 001	THE ELEPHANT TABLE ALBUM (2-LP)	18
57	Philips BBR 8115	ELLA, LENA, BILLIE AND SARAH (10")	15
71	Island IDLP 1	EL PEA (pink rim label)	15
83	Psycho PSYCHO 1	ENDLESS JOURNEY VOL. 1 (numbered)	20
83	Psycho PSYCHO 3	ENDLESS JOURNEY VOL. 2 (numbered)	15
83	Psycho PSYCHO 19	ENDLESS JOURNEY VOL. 3 (numbered)	15
76	Topic 12T 296	ENGLISH COUNTRY MUSIC	12
88	MEK MEK 006	THE ENGLISH REBELS (with insert)	20
84	Street Sounds HBOX 1	ESSENTIAL ELECTRO (9 LP box set, 5000 only)	100
67	Speciality SPE 6601	EVERY DAY I HAVE THE BLUES	18
72	Blue Horizon 2683 007	THE EXCELLO STORY (2-LP)	120
68	Amal. AMGLP 2002	EXPLOSIVE ROCKSTEADY	85
87	Rot ASS 100	THE END OF AN ERA (LP)	15

F

67	Elektra EUK 259	FANTASTIC FOLK	15
64	Topic 12T 110	FAREWELL NANCY (blue label)	18
76	Lightning LIP 2	FAREWELL TO THE ROXY (2-LP)	18
76	Polydor 2475 605	A FEAST OF IRISH FOLK	12
68	Zeus CF 201	FESTIVAL AT TOWERSEY	50
63	Pye Intl. NPL 28033	FESTIVAL OF THE BLUES	30
60s	Melodisc MS 4	15 OLDIES BUT GOODIES	18
65	Sue ILP 920	50 MINUTES & 24 SECONDS OF RECORDED DYNAMITE!	100
85	L.A.Y.L.A.H. LAY 10	THE FIGHT IS ON (Nurse With Wound, Organum, et al.)	30
72	Warner Bros K 66013	FILLMORE: THE LAST DAYS (3-LP box set with poster & booklet)	35
72	CBS 63816	FILLMORE WEST	12
65	London HA-B 8205	FINGERS ON FIRE	15
60	HMV CLP 1358/CSD 1298	FINGS AIN'T WOT THEY USED TO BE	20
64	London HA-B 8117	FIRE ON THE STRINGS	15
69	Music Man	FIREPOINT - A COLLECTION OF FOLK BLUES	100
73	Spark SRLM 2003	FIREPOINT - A COLLECTION OF FOLK BLUES (reissue)	30
71	CBS 66311	THE FIRST GREAT ROCK FESTIVALS OF THE 70s: ISLE OF WIGHT AND ATLANTA (3-LP)	30
58	Esquire 20-091	THE FIRST MODERNS (10")	20
57	Esquire 20-089	THE FIRST NATIONAL SKIFFLE CONTEST (10")	80
56	Mercury MPT 7512	FIRST ROCK 'N' ROLL PARTY (10")	130
89	Confection LC 7871	FLAIR: THE OTHER WORLD OF BRITISH FOOTBALL (2-LP)	20
75	Chrysalis CHR 1081	FLASH FEARLESS V THE ZORG WOMEN PARTS 5 & 6 (Alice Cooper, Elkie Brooks, et al.)	12
80s	Alt. Tentacles VIRUS 22	FLEX YOUR HEAD	15
83	Kent KENT 007	FOR DANCERS ONLY	15
64	Blue Beat BBLP 803	FLY FLYING SKA	300
69	Atlantic 588 184	FLYING HIGH (record club edition)	15
76	Flams/Wounded WR 1068	FOLK AT THE CHEQUERS (private pressing)	15
64	Ember NR 5015	FOLK BLUES SONG FEST	20
69	World Rec. Club ST 890	FOLK FESTIVAL	15
76	Transatlantic TRA 324	FOLK FESTIVAL (2-LP)	15
60	Top Rank 35/070	FOLK FESTIVAL AT NEWPORT 1959 VOLUME 1	15

			MINT VALUE £
60	Top Rank 35/071	FOLK FESTIVAL AT NEWPORT 1959 VOLUME 2	15
60	Top Rank 35/072	FOLK FESTIVAL AT NEWPORT 1959 VOLUME 3	15
62	Fontana TFL 6000	FOLK FESTIVAL AT NEWPORT (VOL. 1)	18
62	Fontana TFL 6004	FOLK FESTIVAL AT NEWPORT (VOL. 2)	18
62	Fontana TFL 6009	FOLK FESTIVAL AT NEWPORT (VOL. 4)	18
63	Pye Intl. NPL 28033	FOLK FESTIVAL OF THE BLUES	20
73	Counterpoint CPT 3994	FOLK FROM McTAVISH'S KITCHENS	30
73	Windmill WMD	FOLK HERITAGE	30
73	Nottingham Festival FEST 1	FOLK NOTTINGHAM STYLE	200
65	Decca LK 4783	FOLK NOW	25
70	BBC REC 955	FOLK ON FRIDAY	18
71	Talisman STAL 5019	FOLK PHILOSOPHY	20
63	Golden Guinea GGL 0265	THE FOLK SCENE	15
66	Folkscene SSP 001	FOLK SCENE (LP, private pressing)	100
61	Topic 12T 157	THE FOLK SONGS OF BRITAIN - SONGS OF COURTSHIP	15
61	Topic 12T 158	THE FOLK SONGS OF BRITAIN VOL. 2 - SONGS OF SEDUCTION	15
61	Topic 12T 159	THE FOLK SONGS OF BRITAIN VOL. 3 - JACK OF ALL TRADES	15
61	Topic 12T 160	THE FOLK SONGS OF BRITAIN VOL. 4 - CHILD BALLADS 1	15
61	Topic 12T 161	THE FOLK SONGS OF BRITAIN VOL. 5 - CHILD BALLADS 2	15
61	Topic 12T 194	THE FOLK SONGS OF BRITAIN VOL. 6 - SAILORMEN AND SERVINGMAIDS	15 61
	Topic 12T 195	THE FOLK SONGS OF BRITAIN VOL. 7 - FAIR GAME AND FOUL	15
61	Topic 12T 196	THE FOLK SONGS OF BRITAIN VOL. 8 - A SOLDIER'S LIFE FOR ME	15
61	Topic 12T 197	THE FOLK SONGS OF BRITAIN VOL. 9 - SONGS OF CEREMONY	15
61	Topic 12T 198	THE FOLK SONGS OF BRITAIN VOL. 10 - SONGS OF ANIMAL	15
69	Topic	THE FOLK SONGS OF BRITAIN VOLS. 1-10 (10 x LP box set)	80
61	Topic TPS 201	TOPIC SAMPLER No. 6 - FOLK SONGS	12
57	HMV DLP 1143	FOLK SONG TODAY (SONGS AND BALLADS OF ENGLAND AND SCOTLAND) (10")	25
65	HMV CLP 1910	FOLKSOUND OF BRITAIN	18
71	Nicro K 220971	FOLK UPSTAIRS	80
63	Ember CEL 902	FOOL BRITANNIA	20
65	Decca LK 4695	FOURTEEN - THE LORD'S TAVERNERS' ALBUM	20
79	Pickwick PLD 8013	40 FOLK FAVOURITES (2-LP, limited edition)	18
70	Bamboo BLP 205	FREEDOM SOUNDS	50
81	Fresh FRESHLP 8	A FRESH SELECTION	12
72	Trojan TRL 51	FROM BAM BAM TO CHERRY OH BABY	15
70	Liberty LBS 83321	FROM THE BAYOU	15
70	Liberty LBS 83278	FROM THE VAULTS	15
83	New European BADVC 666	FROM TORTURE TO CONSCIENCE (with insert)	80
78	Virgon/Caroline C1521	FRONTLINE	12
71	Cutty Wren	FROST LANE	50
89	Sub Pop DAMP 104	FUCK ME, I'M RICH!	15
89	Unrest UNREST 14	FULL FORCE VOL. 3	15
70	Trojan TBL 137	FUNKY CHICKEN	18
70	Bamboo BLP 206	FUNKY REGGAE	40
82	Come Org. WDC 881021	FÜR ILSE KOCH (some on red vinyl; beware of bootlegs)	120
70	Ember	FUTURE STAR EXPLOSION	12
70	RCA Victor SF 8118	49 GREEK STREET (LP, featuring Synanthesia, Nadia Cattouse, Tin Angel & Keith Christmas)	50
76	Burning Sounds BS 1024	FUNNY FEELING (LP)	30
83	Greensleeves GREL 60	FORWARD	20
03	Trunk JBH 004 LP	FLEXI SEX (LP)	15
06	Trunk JBH 018 LP	FUZZY FELT FOLK (LP)	25
73	Eron ERON 001	FOLK IN SANDWICH (LP)	40

G

69	Pama ECO 4	GAS - GREATEST HITS	75
66	Doctor Bird DLM 5001	GAYFEET (Jamaican sleeve and UK pressed LP)	300
84	Kent KENT 021	GEMS	15
55	HMV DLP 1039	GENE NORMAN PRESENTS JUST JAZZ (10")	20
72	Chess 6641 047	GENESIS - THE BEGINNINGS OF ROCK (4-LP box set with booklet)	60
73	Chess 6641 125	GENESIS - MEMPHIS TO CHICAGO (4-LP box set with booklet)	60
75	Chess 6641 174	GENESIS - SWEET HOME CHICAGO (4-LP box set with booklet)	60
69	Kokomo K 1004	GEORGIA GUITARS 1927-1938 (99 copies only)	60
67	Coxsone CSL 8007	GET READY ROCK STEADY	130
60s	Riverside RLP 12-106	GIANTS OF BOOGIE WOOGIE	15
69	Pama SECO 20	A GIFT FROM PAMA	40
71	Wand WCS 1003	THE GIRLS WITH SOUL	15
80s	Sarah	GLASS ARCADE (The Field Mice/The Sea Urchins, et al.)	20
72	Revelation REV 1/2/3	GLASTONBURY FAYRE REVELATIONS - A MUSICAL ANTHOLOGY (3-LP, poster sleeve with booklets, pyramid & printed polythene bag)	140
66	Columbia SX 6062	GO!	70
80s	Touch & Go TG 11	GOD'S FAVOURITE DOG	20
95	Lissy's LISS 5	GODZ IS NOT A PUT ON (500 only, in hand-pressed sleeve; some with free 7")	30
72	Flyright LP 103	GOIN' AWAY WALKING	15
70	Python LP 1	GOIN' BACK TO CHICAGO (99 copies only)	80
70	Warner Bros WS 1874	GOING HOME	12
60s	Heritage 1003	GOING TO CALIFORNIA (99 copies only)	80
68	Decca LK 4931	GOIN' UP THE COUNTRY	20
69	Oliver & Boyd SBN 05 002118/9	THE GOLDEN BIRD (2-LP)	30
64	Columbia 33SX 1664	GOLDEN GOODIES VOL. 1	60
64	Columbia 33SX 1672	GOLDEN GOODIES VOL. 2	60
69	Roulette RCP 1000	GOLDEN GOODIES VOL. 1	20
69	Roulette RCP 1001	GOLDEN GOODIES VOL. 2	20
59	Philips BBL 7331	GOLDEN HITS	15
60	Philips BBL 7422	GOLDEN HITS VOL. 2	12

MINT VALUE £

61	Philips BBL 7581	GOLDEN HITS VOL. 3.	15
68	Allegro ALL885	GOLDEN HITS OF SOUL	20
57	Capitol T 830	THE GOLD RECORD (blue label)	15
75	Eron 004	GOOD FOLK OF KENT (with insert)	40
65	Atlantic ATL 5004	GOOD OLD FIFTIES	55
68	Elek. EUK 260/EUKS 7260	GOOD TIME MUSIC (U.K. version of "What's Shakin' ", gold or red label)	40
72	CBS 67234	GOSPEL SOUND (2-LP)	20
59	Brunswick LAT 8290	GOSPEL TRAIN	20
64	London HA-B 8172	GRAND OLE OPRY SPECTACULAR VOL. 1.	18
64	London HA-B 8173	GRAND OLE OPRY SPECTACULAR VOL. 2.	18
73	Greasy Truckers GT 4997	GREASY TRUCKERS - LIVE AT DINGWALLS DANCE HALL (2-LP with insert)	18
73	United Artists UDX 203/4	GREASY TRUCKERS PARTY (2-LP, gatefold sleeve)	20
72	Vanguard VSD 25/26	GREAT BLUESMEN (2-LP)	18
54	London AL 3530	THE GREAT BLUES SINGERS (10")	45
60s	Riverside RLP 12-121	THE GREAT BLUES SINGERS	25
70	Trojan TBL 111	GREATER JAMAICA	20
75	Brunswick BRLS 3006	GREATEST HITS	15
64	Stateside SL 10075	THE GREATEST GOSPEL SONGS OF OUR TIME	25
67	Doctor Bird DLM 5009	GREATEST JAMAICAN BEAT	150
70	Transatlantic TRASAM 17	GREAT SCOTS SAMPLER	20
70	Transatlantic TRASAM 21	GREAT SCOTS SAMPLER VOL. 2.	20
54	HMV DLP 1054	GREAT TRUMPET SOLOISTS (10").	25
85	Crashed METALPS 107	GREEN METAL	30
71	Bamboo BDLP 215	GROOVING WITH BAMBOO	50
69	Direction 8-63452	GROOVY BABY	15
63	Realm RM 149	GROUP BEAT '63	40
63	London HA-U 8086	GROUP OF GOODIES	55
64	World Record Club TP 444	GROUP '64.	20
78	Virgin VCL 5001	GUILLOTINE (10" mini-LP, with inner sleeve)	18
60s	Storyville SLP 166	GUITAR BLUES	20
73	Transatlantic TRA 271	GUITAR WORKSHOP (2-LP)	15
71	Sunnyland KS 102	GULF COAST BLUES (99 copies only)	40
69	Liberty LBX 3	GUTBUCKET	25
68	Island ILP 977	GUY STEVENS' TESTAMENT OF ROCK AND ROLL	60
71	Wand WCS 1002	THE GUYS WITH SOUL	20
69	BBC RESR 4	GANDHI - MAN ON TRIAL (LP)	15
84	Fashion FAD LP 001	GREAT BRITISH MCS	15
79	Bead Records BEAD 15	GROUPS IN FRONT OF PEOPLE (LP)	25
79	Bead Records BEAD 15	GROUPS IN FRONT OF PEOPLE 2 (LP)	25

H

80	Hackney Music Coll LP1	HACKNEY MUSIC COLLECTIVE	25
58	Oriole MG 20033	HAIL VARIETY!	15
70	Probe PSS 1	HANDLE WITH CARE	12
88	Hangman HANG 22-UP	HANGMAN SAMPLER.	20
88	HandMade (no cat. no.)	HANDMADE FILMS MUSIC - THE 10TH ANNIVERSARY (CD, promo only)	100
85	Anagram GRAM 23	HANG 11 (MUTANT SURF PUNKS)	20
68	Immediate IMLYIN 2	HAPPY TO BE PART OF THE INDUSTRY OF HUMAN HAPPINESS.	18
88	BPM BPLP2	HARDCORE ONE (LP)	30
77	VJM VLP 40	HARD LUCK BLUES	18
74	Decca DPA 3009/10	HARD UP HEROES 1963-68 (2-LP, gatefold sleeve)	20
57	London TKL 93119	HARLEM CONGREGATION	30
56	London AL 3553	HARLEM PIANO ROLL (10")	20
72	Carnival 2941 001	HARPIN' ON IT.	12
71	Harvest SHSS 3	HARVEST BAG	15
69	Harvest SPSLP 118	HARVEST SAMPLER OF THE INITIAL FOUR JUNE RELEASES (promo only)	150
63	Reprise R 50001	HAVE YOURSELF A MERRY LITTLE CHRISTMAS.	15
71	Sunnyland KS 101	HAVIN' A GOOD TIME - CHICAGO BLUES ANTHOLOGY (99 copies only)	50
66	Polydor 582 701	HEADLINE NEWS	15
71	Vertigo 6360 045	HEADS TOGETHER, FIRST ROUND (gatefold sleeve, swirl label)	18
94	Mo' Wax MWLP 026	HEADZ: A SOUNDTRACK OF EXPERIMENTAL BEATHEAD JAMS (3-LP)	25
96	Mo' Wax MW 061LP	HEADZ VOLUME 2A (4-LP)	25
90	Imaginary ILLUSION 016	HEAVEN AND HELL VOLUME 1: A TRIBUTE TO THE VELVET UNDERGROUND	70
81	Heavy Metal HMR LP 1	HEAVY METAL HEROES	30
82	Heavy Metal HMR LP 7	HEAVY METAL HEROES VOLUME 2.	25
84	Heavy Metal HMR LP 24	HEAVY METAL RECORDS (blue, clear & white vinyl, round sleeve).	15
68	Trojan TRL 6	HERE COMES THE DUKE	30
65	Pye NPL 18121	HERE COME THE GIRLS	15
85	Rock 'N' Dole RDR 2	HEROES.	15
80s	Temps Modernes LTMV:XI	HEURES SANS SOLEIL	20
69	Pama PSP 1002	HEY BOY HEY GIRL	40
58	Capitol T 926	HI-FI DRUMS	15
58	Melodisc MLP 518	HIGHLIFE: AUTHENTIC WEST AFRICAN MUSIC VOL. 1 (10")	12
58	Melodisc MLP 519	HIGHLIFE: AUTHENTIC WEST AFRICAN MUSIC VOL. 2 (10")	12
59	Parlophone PMD 1085	HIGHWAY TO HEAVEN (10")	20
52	Capitol LC 6508	THE HISTORY OF JAZZ - THE SOLID SOUTH	20
52	Capitol LC 6527	THE HISTORY OF JAZZ - THIS MODERN AGE	12
68	Atlantic 587 094	HISTORY OF RHYTHM AND BLUES - VOL. 1, THE ROOTS 1947-52.	15
68	Atlantic 587 095	HISTORY OF RHYTHM AND BLUES - VOL. 2, THE GOLDEN YEARS 1953-55	15
68	Atlantic 587 096	HISTORY OF RHYTHM AND BLUES - VOL. 3, ROCK 'N' ROLL 1956-57	15
68	Atlantic 587 097	HISTORY OF RHYTHM AND BLUES - VOL. 4, THE BIG BEAT 1958-60.	15
68	Atlantic 587 140	HISTORY OF RHYTHM AND BLUES - VOL. 5.	15
68	Atlantic 587 141	HISTORY OF RHYTHM AND BLUES - VOL. 6.	15
69	Bamboo BDLP 203	HISTORY OF SKA VOLUME ONE	200
64	Pye NPL 18108	THE HITMAKERS	20
65	Pye NPL 18115	THE HITMAKERS VOL. 2	20
65	Pye NPL 18116	THE HITMAKERS VOL. 3	20

Year	Label / Cat. No.	Title	MINT VALUE £
66	Pye NPL 18144	THE HITMAKERS VOL. 4	20
57	Pye Nixa NPT 19015	HIT PARADE OF 1956 (10")	18
59	Pye Nixa NPT 19032	HIT PARADE OF 1958	15
66	Marble Arch MAL 650	HITS FROM THE IVY LEAGUE, THE ROCKIN' BERRIES & THE SORROWS	12
77	Stiff FIST 1	HITS - GREATEST STIFFS (with 7", Max Wall's "England's Glory" [BUY 12])	12
65	Tamla Motown TML 11019	HITSVILLE U.S.A.	50
67	Stax 589 005	HIT THE ROAD STAX	30
81	United Dairies UD 05	HOISTING THE BLACK FLAG	35
55	Philips BBR 8048	HOLLYWOOD DANCE DATE (10")	12
62	Golden Guinea GGL 0129	HONEY HIT PARADE	12
74	Melodisc 12-216	HONEYS	35
52	Capitol LC 6544	HONKY TONK PIANO (10")	15
60s	Riverside RLP 8806	HONKY TONK TRAIN (with booklet)	22
65	Summit ATL 4150	HOOTENANNY AT THE BARGE	15
64	Stateside SL 10079	HOOTENANNY AT THE TROUBADOUR	18
63	Decca LK 4544	HOOTENANNY IN LONDON	15
84	Kent KENT 023	HOT CHILLS AND COLD THRILLS	15
71	Pama PMP 2006	HOT NUMBERS	40
71	Pama PMP 2009	HOT NUMBERS VOLUME TWO	30
77	WEA M 100	HOT PLATTER CORDON BLEU (available via Melody Maker)	20
70	Trojan TBL 128	HOT SHOTS OF REGGAE	12
72	Hot Wax SHW 5008	HOT WAX GREATEST HITS	15
69	Track 613 016	THE HOUSE THAT TRACK BUILT (gatefold sleeve)	30
80	Stark ST1	HOUSEHOLD SHOCKS	40
69	Blue Horizon PR 45/46	HOW BLUE CAN WE GET (2-LP, gatefold sleeve with insert)	40
84	Rot ASS 18	HAVE AROTTEN CHRISTMAS (LP)	25
08	Jonny JBH 025 LP	HEAR O ISRAEL (LP)	15

I

Year	Label / Cat. No.	Title	MINT VALUE £
69	Liberty LBL/LBS 83252	I ASKED FOR WATER ? AND SHE GAVE ME GASOLINE	80
88	Bam Caruso MARX 085	ILLUSIONS FROM THE CRACKLING VOID	15
90s	Dig The Fuzz DIG 013	ILLUSIONS OF ALICE IN BLACK (650 only, with booklet)	20
69	Immediate IMLYIN 1	IMMEDIATE LETS YOU IN	20
70	Highway 51 H-104	I'M YOUR COUNTRY MAN (99 copies only)	40
77	United Artists UAS 30101	IMPERIAL ROCKABILLIES	12
66	CBS/Denson Shoes	THE IN CROWD (shoe offer compilation)	25
69	Trojan TTL 15	INDEPENDENT JAMAICA	12
67	Fontana TL 5426	INDIAN MUSIC	12
79	Object Music OBJ 002	INDISCRETE MUSIC - DUBIOUS COLLABORATION (500 only)	15
84	Illuminated JAMS 39	THE INDUSTRIAL RECORDS STORY 1976-1981	35
84	United Dairies UD 015	IN FRACTURED SILENCE	35
95	RCA 74321 315501	IN FROM THE STORM - THE MUSIC OF JIMI HENDRIX (LP, picture disc)	15
69	T. Motown (S)TML 11124	IN LOVING MEMORY (TRIBUTE TO MRS LOUCYE G. WAKEFIELD)	60
70	Blue Horizon PR 37	IN OUR OWN WAY (OLDIES BUT GOODIES)	20
70	Ember EMB 34111	IN REGGAE TIME	15
80	Island IRSP3	INTENSIFIED VOLUME 2	12
66	Ember FA 2034	IRELAND'S GREATEST SOUNDS: FIVE TOP GROUPS FROM BELFAST'S MARITIME CLUB	70
64	Decca LK 4633	IRISH FOLK NIGHT	12
63	Topic 12T 86	THE IRON MUSE (blue label with lyric insert)	15
79	Rationale RATE 8	IRRATIONALE (cassette, in bag with booklet)	20
61	Oriole MG 20046	IT'S ALL HAPPENING HERE	35
64	Philips BL 7609	IT'S ALL OVER TOWN	15
85	Kent KENT 046	IT'S TORTURE	15
84	Sain 002	IT'S UNHEARD OF	150
81	TJM TJML 1	IDENTITY PARADE (LP)	15

J

Year	Label / Cat. No.	Title	MINT VALUE £
69	Amalgamated CSP 3	JACKPOT OF HITS	35
74	Atra ALP 001	JAH GUIDE - JAMAICA'S GREATEST HITS	20
71	Ashanti SHAN 102	JAMAICAN FOLK SINGERS	20
68	Blue Cat BCL 1	JAMAICAN MEMORIES	100
64	Atlantic 587 075	JAMAICA SKA (colour 'Dancers' sleeve)	50
67	Atlantic 587 075	JAMAICA SKA (reissue, orange sleeve)	30
60s	Whirl WHIRL 1	JAMAICA'S AMBASSADORS OF SONG	70
60s	Melodisc MLP 12-158	JAMAICA'S GREATEST	30
68	Flyright LP 3502	JAMBALAYA ON THE BAYOU - VOLUME 1	15
69	Flyright LP 3503	JAMBALAYA ON THE BAYOU - VOLUME 2	15
72	Utd. Artists UAS 60027/8	THE JAMES BOND COLLECTION (2-LP, with booklet)	25
72	Rolling Stones COC 39100	JAMMING WITH EDWARD	15
55	Columbia Clef 33CX 10008	JAM SESSION	15
61	HMV/Utd Artists CSD 1381	JAZZ ALIVE - A NIGHT AT THE HALF NOTE	12
56	Tempo TAP 5	JAZZ AT THE FLAMINGO	120
55	Columbia 33CX 10078	JAZZ AT THE PHILHARMONIC, 1955 VOL. 1	12
55	Columbia 33CX 10079	JAZZ AT THE PHILHARMONIC, 1955 VOL. 2	12
68	Columbia SLJS 1	JAZZ EXPLOSION	15
72	Decca ECS 2114	JAZZ IN BRITAIN 1968-1969	50
62	Parlophone PMC 1195	JAZZ IN THE MAKING	12
84	Streetsounds MUSIC 1	JAZZ JUICE	25
85	Streetsounds SOUND 1	JAZZ JUICE (reissue)	20
63	VJM LC 6	JAZZ PANORAMA OF THE SIXTIES	12
77	Decca DPA 3035/3036	THE JOE MEEK STORY (2-LP)	40
60	Top Rank 35/064	JOHN HAMMOND'S SPIRITUALS TO SWING VOLUME 1	15
60	Top Rank 35/065	JOHN HAMMOND'S SPIRITUALS TO SWING VOLUME 2	15
72	Vanguard VRS 8523/4	JOHN HAMMOND'S SPIRITUALS TO SWING: LEGENDARY CARNEGIE HALL CONCERTS OF 1938/9 (2-LP)	18
69	BBC REC 52S	JOHN PEEL PRESENTS TOP GEAR	40

			MINT VALUE £
70	BBC REC 68M	JOHN PEEL'S ARCHIVE THINGS	35
60	HMV CLP 1327	A JUG OF PUNCH (also issued as XLP 50003)	25
70s	Eric's ERICS 008	JUKEBOX AT ERIC'S	15
62	Embassy WLP 6052	JUKE BOX FAVOURITES	12
76	RCA RS 1066	JUMPING AT THE GO GO	18
77	Policy Wheel PW 459-1	JUMPING ON THE HILL	12
64	R&B JBL 1111	JUMP JAMAICA WAY	400
69	RCA Intl. INT 1014	JUST A LITTLE BIT OF SOUL	22
79	Kick KK 1	JUST FOR KICKS	35

K

59	Capitol T 1057	K.C. IN THE 30's	20
56	Vogue LAE 12028	KENTON'S SIDEMEN (Don Rendell, et al.)	60
81	White Witch	KENT ROCKS (200 only)	180
71	Jay Boy JSX 2009	KERBSIDE ENTERTAINERS	12
54	HMV DLP 1048	KEYBOARD KINGS OF JAZZ (10")	20
72	Key	KEY COLLECTION (with insert)	15
70	Trojan TBL 140	KING SIZE REGGAE	15
72	Sioux SLX 7502	KING OF THE ROAD	25
68	Polydor 623 273	KINGS OF RHYTHM AND BLUES	15
60s	Gryphon 13159	KINGS OF THE TWELVE STRING GUITAR	20
60s	Saydisc Roots RL 333	KINGS OF MEMPHIS TOWN 1927-1930	20
94	Mercury 522 476-1	KISS MY ASS (red, white or blue vinyl)	12
85	Rot ASS 21	KICK UP THE ARSE (LP)	15

L

79	The Label TRLP 002S	THE LABEL SOFA ('translumar defractor' 3D picture disc, stickered PVC sleeve)	35
83	Fetish FR 2011	THE LAST TESTAMENT (with inner, stickered sleeve)	18
87	Other OTH 10	LAST WARRIOR	18
68	Island ILP 986	LEAPING WITH MR LEE (by Bunny Lee All Stars)	300
80	Atra ATRA LP 1003	THE LEGENDS (Augustus Pablo et al.)	15
03	Ai AILP 004	LEISURE (100 copies only)	15
99	Jazzman 1	LE JAZZBEAT!	20
63	Polydor SLPHM 237 622	LET'S DO THE TWIST, HULLY GULLY, SLOP, SURF, LOCOMOTION, MONKEY	30
66	Neshoba N 11	LET'S GO DOWN SOUTH (99 copies only)	55
84	Cult 1	LET'S GET PISSED IT'S CHRISTMAS	15
58	Brunswick LAT 8271	LET'S HAVE A PARTY	30
73	Bell DUBL 9002/3	LET THE GOOD TIMES ROLL	15
81	Alt. Tentacles VIRUS 4	LET THEM EAT JELLYBEANS (with lyric poster)	20
74	Sonet SNTX 1	LEGACY OF THE BLUES SAMPLER	12
80s	Third Mind/Abstract	LIFE AT THE TOP	20
85	Riot City CITY 019	LIFE'S A RIOT WITH RIOT CITY RECORDS	20
68	Transatlantic TRASAM 2	LISTEN HERE!	12
81	NEMS NEL 6020	LIVE AND HEAVY	12
80	BUN 01	LIVE AT BUNJIES (gatefold sleeve with insert)	30
74	Key KL 021	LIVE AT SPREE	15
77	NEMS NEL 6013	LIVE AT THE VORTEX	15
65	Fontana TL 5240	LIVE AT THE WHISKEY A-GO-GO	40
68	Big Shot BBTL 4000	LIVE IT UP	75
64	Embassy WLP 6065	LIVERPOOL BEAT	15
65	Ember NR 5028	LIVERPOOL TODAY - LIVE AT THE CAVERN	40
64	CBS Realm RM 209	LIVIN' WITH THE BLUES	15
70	Trojan TBL 135	LOCH NESS MONSTER	15
87	4AD CAD 703D	LONELY IS AN EYESORE (cardboard pack with book)	30
87	4AD CADX 703	LONELY IS AN EYESORE (CD, LP & cassette, in wooden box with etching, screen print & video, 100 only)	700
71	Count Shelly SSLP 03	LOOK BEFORE YOU LEAP	60
91	Holyground HG 121	LOOSE ROUTES (2-LP, gatefold foldover sleeve)	30
65	Storyville 616002	LOUISIANA PRISON BLUES	15
69	Pama PSP 1001	A LOVELY DOZEN	40
96	Earth EARTHLP 001	LTJ BUKEM PRESENTS EARTH VOLUME 1 (5 LP box set, stickered box, 5 picture sleeves,5000 only)	35
97	Earth EARTHLP 002	LTJ BUKEM PRESENTS EARTH VOLUME 2 (5 LP box set, 5 picture sleeves)	25
98	Good Looking EARTH LP 003	LTJ BUKEM PRESENTS EARTH VOLUME 3 (5 LP box set)	25

M

76	Cornish Legend CLM 1	MADE IN CORNWALL (with insert)	25
58	Pye Nixa Jazz NJL 13	(LEONARD FEATHER PRESENTS) MAD THAD	12
79	Object Music OBJ 003	A MANCHESTER COLLECTION	25
70	Trojan TBL 129	MAN FROM CAROLINA	15
53	Brunswick LA 8567	MAN WITH A HORN (10" LP)	12
70	CBS 52798	MA RAINEY AND THE CLASSIC BLUES SINGERS	20
69	Marmalade 643 314	MARMALADE - 100% PROOF	15
72	Village Thing VTSAM 16	MATCHBOX DAYS	25
68	President PTL 1002	MAR-V-LUS SOUND OF R&B AND SOUL MUSIC	40
60s	Wudwink ISMF 107	MARY'S FOLK	200
78	CBS 82670	MAX'S KANSAS CITY	12
66	CBS Special Prod. WSR 853	McDONALDS ALL-STAR FAVOURITES	12
69	Liberty LBL/LBS 83190	ME AND THE DEVIL	75
87	Hangman HANG 4 UP	MEDWAY POWER HOUSE 1	20
87	Hangman HANG 8 UP	MEDWAY POWER HOUSE 2	20
88	Hangman HANG 17 UP	MEDWAY POWER HOUSE 3	25
78	Topic 12T 376	MELODEON GREATS - A COLLECTION OF MELODEON MASTERPIECES	15
64	London HA 8129	MEMORIES ARE MADE OF HITS VOL. 1	20
64	London HA 8130	MEMORIES ARE MADE OF HITS VOL. 2	20
64	London HA 8131	MEMORIES ARE MADE OF HITS VOL. 3	20
64	London HA 8138	MEMORIES ARE MADE OF HITS VOL. 4	20
64	London HA 8148	MEMORIES ARE MADE OF HITS VOL. 5	20

			MINT VALUE £
64	London HA 8171	MEMORIES ARE MADE OF HITS VOL. 6	20
64	London HA 8189	MEMORIES ARE MADE OF HITS VOL. 7	20
65	London HA 8213	MEMORIES ARE MADE OF HITS VOL. 8	20
69	Atco 228 023	MEMPHIS GOLD	15
54	Vogue Coral LVC 10008	MERRY CHRISTMAS (10")	15
69	T. Motown (S)TML 11126	MERRY CHRISTMAS FROM MOTOWN (mono/stereo)	40
67	Capitol T 9030	MERRY CHRISTMAS TO YOU	15
85	Neat NEAT 1014	METAL BATTLE	15
80	BBC REH 397	METAL EXPLOSION	20
82	Ebony EBON 1	METAL FATIGUE	12
80	EMI EMC 3318	METAL FOR MUTHAS	20
80	EMI EMC 3337	METAL FOR MUTHAS VOL. 2	12
97	Metalheadz METBOX 001	METALHEADZ (5 discs in circular tin, booklet)	30
82	Ebony EBON 8	METAL MANIAXE	15
87	Other OTH 9	METAL WARRIOR	50
60	RCA/Camden CDN 122	METRONOME ALL STARS	12
80	MGM 2315 394	THE MGM ROCKABILLY COLLECTION	12
56	Nixa Jazz Today NJL 3	MIDNIGHT AT NIXA	20
66	Atlantic 587 021	MIDNIGHT SOUL	20
69	Storyville 616 009	MIDNIGHT SPECIAL	15
62	Brunswick LAT 8401	MIDNIGHT JAMBOREE (also stereo STA 3061)	12
56	London AL 3554	MIDWESTERN JAZZ (10")	15
66	Xtra XTRA 1047	THE MIKE RAVEN BLUES SHOW	12
69	Transatlantic TRASAM 5	THE MIKE RAVEN BLUES SAMPLER	12
72	Polydor	MILL VALLEY JAM SESSION	12
60	Coral LVA 9126	MILLION-AIRS	18
80	Pipe PIPE 2	MINIATURES (with poster insert, 500 only)	15
80	Pipe PIPE 2	MINIATURES (cassette with mini-booklet insert, 100 only)	30
71	Trojan TBL 174	MISS LABBA LABBA REGGAE	30
60	Top Rank BUY 028	MR. BLUE	40
60s	Bounty BY 6025	MODERN CHICAGO BLUES	30
53	Capitol LC 6561	MODERN IDIOM (10")	15
55	HMV DLP 1022	MODERN JAZZ PIANO (10")	15
56	Tempo TAP 2	MODERN JAZZ SCENE 1956	100
53	Esquire 20-011	MODERN MIXTURE VOLUME ONE (10")	20
79	Bridge House BHLP 003	MODS MAYDAY '79 (original issue)	20
80	Polydor 2488810	MONSTERS OF ROCK	15
73	Stax STX 1029	MONTREUX FESTIVAL 1973	15
70	Trojan TTL 31	MOONLIGHT GROOVER	15
70	Liberty LBS 83377	MORE FROM THE VAULTS	15
62	HMV CLP 1583	MORE OF YOUR FAVOURITE TV AND RADIO THEMES	20
67	Atlantic 587088	MORE MIDNIGHT SOUL	15
68	Marble Arch MAL 813	MORE RHYTHM AND BLUES	12
65	private pressing	MORE SINGING AT THE COUNT HOUSE	30
72	Island HELP 5	MORRIS ON (black label with pink 'i')	18
80	Conventional CON 013	MOTHER OF A PUNK (cassette)	12
86	Iguana VYK LP 11	MOTOR CITY 9 (with booklet)	15
65	Tamla Motown TML 11007	THE MOTORTOWN REVUE LIVE	80
66	Tamla Motown TML 11027	THE MOTORTOWN REVUE IN PARIS	65
70	T. Motown (S)TML 11127	THE MOTORTOWN REVUE LIVE (mono/stereo)	20
69	T. Motown (S)TML 11121	MOTOWN CHARTBUSTERS VOL. 3 (original with flipback sleeve)	12
70	T. Motown STML 11162	MOTOWN CHARTBUSTERS VOL. 4 (original with flipback sleeve)	15
74	T. Motown STML 11270	MOTOWN CHARTBUSTERS VOL. 9 (green vinyl)	12
72	Tamla Motown STMA 8005	MOTOWN DISCO CLASSICS VOL. 2	15
66	Tamla Motown TML 11030	MOTOWN MAGIC	35
68	Tamla Motown TML 11064	MOTOWN MEMORIES (flipback sleeve)	60
68	Tamla Motown TML 11077	MOTOWN MEMORIES VOL. 2	60
70	T. Motown STML 11143	MOTOWN MEMORIES VOL. 3	60
72	Tamla Motown STML 11200	MOTOWN MEMORIES	12
80	Tamla Motown ZL 72032	MOTOWN MOD CLASSICS VOL. 1	12
80	Tamla Motown STML 12133	MOTOWN MOD CLASSICS VOL. 2	12
72	Tamla Motown TMSP 1130	THE MOTOWN STORY (5-LP box set)	20
83	Tamla Motown TMSP 6019	THE MOTOWN STORY - THE FIRST 25 YEARS (box set)	20
77	Mountain PSLP 200	MOUNTAIN ROCKS INTO '77 (Mountain label sampler, promo only)	20
84	Kent 013	MOVING ON UP	15
53	London AL 3503	MUGGY, TESCH AND THE CHICAGOANS (10")	15
57	Pye NJL 11	MURDERER'S HOME	20
71	Mushroom 100 MR 16	THE MUSHROOM FOLK SAMPLER	40
57	Brunswick LAT 8201	MUSIC FOR THE BOYFRIEND - HE REALLY DIGS ROCK'N'ROLL	100
57	Brunswick LAT 8202	MUSIC FOR THE BOYFRIEND - HE REALLY DIGS JAZZ	30
57	Brunswick LAT 8205	MUSIC FOR THE BOYFRIEND - THE FEMININE TOUCH	35
67	Argo RG 533	MUSIC FROM THE FAR NORTH (with foldout inner)	15
73	Charisma CADS 101	MUSIC FROM FREE CREEK (2-LP)	15
70	Disques Vogue VRLS 3043	LA MUSIQUE PROGRESSIVE	12
81	Ze ISSP 4001	MUTANT DISCO (3 x 12" box set, numbered, 2,000 only)	12
77	EMI NUT 4	MY GENERATION	15
89	Hangman HANG 35 UP	MEDWAY POWERHOUSE (LP)	30
78	Tartone TTL 010	MASTER MIX (LP)	25

N

73	Enterprise ESAM 100	THE NAME OF THE GAME	15
71	Eden LP 43	NAPTON FOLK CLUB (private pressing, 100 only)	35
62	London HA-B 8003	NASHVILLE SATURDAY NIGHT	18
63	London HA-B 8028	NASHVILLE STEEL GUITAR	18
69	Bamboo BLP 201	NATURAL REGGAE VOLUME ONE	50
70	Bamboo BLP 204	NATURAL REGGAE VOLUME TWO	60
81	4AD CAD 117	NATURES MORTES - STILL LIVES (export issue)	60

			MINT VALUE £
85	Musique Brut BRV 002	NECROPOLIS, AMPHIBIANS AND REPTILES: THE MUSIC OF ADOLF WOLFLI	20
70s	Bounty BY 6012	NEGRO FOLKLORE FROM TEXAS STATE PRISON	20
57	Vogue LAE 12033	NEGRO SPIRITUALS	28
61	World Records LH 12	NEGRO SPIRITUALS	15
87	Broken Flag BF V8	NEVER SAY WHEN	40
72	Atlantic K 20024	THE NEW AGE OF ATLANTIC	12
80	Logo MOGO 4011	NEW ELECTRIC WARRIORS	12
53	London AL 3509	NEW ORLEANS HORNS (10")	15
56	London AL 3557	NEW ORLEANS HORNS VOLUME 2 (10")	15
67	Ace Of Hearts AH 140	NEW ORLEANS MEMORIES	12
74	Flyright LP 4708	NEW ORLEANS R&B VOLUME 1	15
74	Flyright LP 4709	NEW ORLEANS R&B VOLUME 2	15
60s	77' 77LA 12/16	NEW ORLEANS TODAY	20
60s	77' 77LA 12/29	NEW ORLEANS TODAY VOL. 2	20
65	Fontana TFL 6038	NEWPORT BROADSIDE - TOPICAL SONGS AT THE NEWPORT FOLK FESTIVAL 1963	20
65	Fontana TFL 6041	NEWPORT FOLK FESTIVAL EVENING CONCERT VOL. 1	20
65	Fontana TFL 6050	NEWPORT FOLK FESTIVAL VOL. 1	12
57	Philips BBL 7147	NEWPORT JAZZ FESTIVAL	12
57	Philips BBL 7152	NEWPORT JAZZ FESTIVAL	12
58	London Jazz LTZ C15155	NEWPORT SPIRITUAL STARS	20
77	Vertigo 6300 902	NEW WAVE	15
72	Flyright LP 4706	NEW YORK CITY BLUES	12
55	London AL 3541	NEW YORK JAZZ OF THE ROARING TWENTIES (10")	15
72	Flyright LP 4707	NEW YORK RHYTHM AND BLUES	12
69	Island IWP(S) 6	NICE ENOUGH TO EAT (pink label)	12
57	Vanguard PPL 11004	A NIGHT AT THE APOLLO	15
69	Blue Horizon 7-63210	THE 1968 MEMPHIS COUNTRY BLUES FESTIVAL	25
83	DEL 306	19TH CAMBRIDGE FOLK FESTIVAL VOLUME 1	20
81	NMX	NMX: LIVE AT SHEFFIELD (cassette)	20
68	Spark SRLM 107	NO INTRODUCTION	30
69	Trojan TTL 14	NO MORE HEARTACHES	20
70	Polydor 545 017	NON STOP SOUL	30
69	Regal Starline SRS 5013	NO ONE'S GONNA CHANGE OUR WORLD	18
64	Concert Hall AM 2339	NORTHUMBRIAN MINSTRELS	15
60	Fontana TFL 5123	NOTHIN' BUT THE BLUES (gatefold sleeve)	60
71	CBS 66278	NOTHING BUT THE BLUES (2-LP, Blue Horizon pressings may also exist (£75))	60
82	See For Miles CM 112	NOT JUST BEAT MUSIC, 1965-70	12
79	Giorno GPS	THE NOVA CONVENTION	20
70	Decca Nova SPA 72	NOVA SAMPLER	20
70s	Warm PFLP 201	NOVA-VAGA	15
79	A&M AMLE 68505	NO WAVE ('pizza' picture disc)	15
79	A&M AMLE 68505	NO WAVE (orange, mauve or blue vinyl)	12
84	Virgin/EMI CDP 26 0408 2	NOW THAT'S WHAT I CALL MUSIC 4 (CD)	200
86	Virgin/EMI CDNOW 8	NOW THAT'S WHAT I CALL MUSIC 8 (CD)	35
87	Virgin/EMI CDNOW 9	NOW THAT'S WHAT I CALL MUSIC 9 (CD)	35
69	Pama ECO 6	NU BEAT - GREATEST HITS	60
73	Elektra K 62012	NUGGETS (Original Artyfacts From The First Psychedelic Era 1965-1968) (2-LP, gatefold sleeve)	45
86	Numa NUMA 1004	NUMA RECORDS YEAR 1 (with bonus Italian 12" "My Dying Machine")	15
90s	NWOBHM CD 002	NWOBHM - VOLUME 2 (CD)	30
90s	NWOBHM CD 003	NWOBHM - VOLUME 3 (CD)	30
81	Guardian Records	N E 1 (LP)	40

O

69	Liberty LBS 83234	OAKLAND BLUES	30
79	Rok ROK LP 001	ODD BODS, MODS AND SODS	75
58	Parlophone PMC 1072	OH BOY!	40
78	Raw RAWLP 2	OH NO IT'S MORE FROM RAW (Users/Killjoys et al.)	20
72	Music F. Pleasure MFP 1416	OH! WHAT A CARRY ON	15
80	EMI ZIT 1	OI! - THE ALBUM (initially mail-order only from Sounds magazine)	30
87	Link LP 23	OI! GLORIOUS OI!	15
84	Syndicate SYNLP 4	OI! OF SEX	15
83	Secret SEC 5	OI! OI! THAT'S YER LOT	15
60s	Melodisc MS 4	OLDIES BUT GOODIES	50
64	Stateside SL 10094	OLDIES R & B	70
60	Parlophone PMC 1127	OLD TIME MUSIC HALL	15
69	Transatlantic XTRA 1076	O LIVERPOOL WE LOVE YOU (Stan Kelly/Bill Shankley/Jimmy Tarbuck et al.)	40
68	Big Shot BBTL 4001	ONCE MORE	70
69	Marmalade 643 314	100% PROOF	15
86	Stateside/EMI SSL 6002	ONE MINIT AT A TIME	18
73	Charisma CLASS 3	ONE MORE CHANCE	12
63	Columbia 33SX 1536	ONE NIGHT STAND	40
63	Stateside SL 10065	ON STAGE LIVE!	65
69	Atco 228 009/010	ON STAGE - LIVE (2-LP)	25
73	Xtra XTRA 1133	ON THE ROAD AGAIN	20
83	Kent KENT 006	ON THE SOUL SIDE	15
64	Columbia 33SX 1662	ON THE SCENE	90
84	Kent KENT 20	ON THE UP BEAT	15
63	Stateside SL 10024	OPRY TIME IN TENNESSEE	18
67	Polydor 236 216	ORIGINAL AMERICAN FOLK BLUES FESTIVAL	18
64	Rio RLP 1	THE ORIGINAL COOL JAMAICAN SKA	130
70	Mercury SMCL 20182	ORIGINAL GOLDEN HITS OF THE GREAT BLUES SINGERS	20
73	Prince Buster PB 10	ORIGINAL GOLDEN OLDIES VOLUME 2	12
70	Mercury SMCL 20183	ORIGINAL GOLDEN RHYTHM AND BLUES HITS VOLUME 1	20
60	London HA-G 2308	THE ORIGINAL HITS	50
61	London HA-G 2339	THE ORIGINAL HITS VOL. 2	50

			MINT VALUE £
63	Golden Guinea GGL 0240	THE ORIGINAL HOOTENANNY	15
67	Ember SPE 6602	THE ORIGINAL SOUND OF DETROIT	18
68	United Artists ULP 1182	ORIGINAL SOUNDTRACKS OF HITS MUSIC	15
64	Vocalion VA 8017	ORIGINAL SURFIN' HITS	65
52	Vogue LDE 006	ORIGINATORS OF MODERN JAZZ (10")	15
75	Trailer LET SAM 2087	OUR FOLK MUSIC HERITAGE	12
62	London HA-U 2404	OUR SIGNIFICANT HITS	70
65	Ace Of Hearts AH 72	OUT CAME THE BLUES	15
67	Ace Of Hearts AH 158	OUT CAME THE BLUES VOLUME 2	15
83	Peninsula	OUT OF THE UNKNOWN	70

P

70	Golden Guinea GGL 0451	PADDY IS DEAD AND THE KIDS KNOW IT (LP)	150
64	Golden Guinea GGL 0268	PACKAGE TOUR	22
65	Blue Beat BBLP 804	PAIN IN MY BELLY	250
55	London HA-A 2001	THE PAJAMA GAME	15
67	Island ILP 945	PAKISTANI SOUL SESSION	75
61	Parlophone PMC 1134	PARADE OF THE POPS	15
85	LIL LP2	PARKSIDE STEELWORKS	60
68	Studio One SOL 9009	PARTY TIME IN JAMAICA	120
66	Decca LK 4824	PENTHOUSE MAGAZINE PRESENTS THE BEDSIDE BOND	40
83	Psycho PSYCHO 6	THE PERFUMED GARDEN	20
84	Psycho PSYCHO 15	THE PERFUMED GARDEN II	20
81	Cherry Red BRED 15	PERSPECTIVES AND DISTORTION (gatefold sleeve)	15
86	Streetsounds PHST 1986	THE PHILADELPHIA YEARS (14-LP box set)	80
72	Apple APCOR 24	PHIL SPECTOR'S CHRISTMAS ALBUM (reissue of "A Christmas Gift For You")	30
75	Warner Bros K 59010	PHIL SPECTOR'S CHRISTMAS ALBUM (2nd reissue, some with poster)	18
80	Phil Spector Intl. 2307 015	PHIL SPECTOR '74/'79	25
67	Riverside RLP 8809	PIANO BLUES 1927-1933	20
56	Vogue Coral LVA 9069	PIANO JAZZ - BARRELHOUSE AND BOOGIE WOOGIE	12
72	Flyright LP 104	PIEDMONT BLUES	15
60	HMV CLP 1362/XLP 50004	A PINCH OF SALT - BRITISH SEA SONGS OLD AND NEW	20
53	London AL 3506	PIONEERS OF BOOGIE WOOGIE (10")	40
54	London AL 3537	PIONEERS OF BOOGIE WOOGIE VOLUME TWO (10")	40
73	Trojan TBL 203	PIPELINE	15
80	Incus INCUS 37	PISA 1980: IMPROVISOR'S SYMPOSIUM	50
81	K-Tel NE 1134	THE PLATINUM ALBUM	12
70s	Flyright LP 4711	PLAY MY JUKEBOX	12
81	P. Surprised KLARK 002	PLEASANTLY SURPRISED - AN HOUR OF ELOQUENT SOUNDS (cassette)	20
71	Argo ZPR 264/5	POETRY AND JAZZ IN CONCERT 250	15
56	Mercury MPT	POP PARADE VOL. 1 (10")	15
56	Mercury MPT	POP PARADE VOL. 2 (10")	15
57	Mercury MPT 7519	POP PARADE VOL. 3 (10")	15
57	Mercury MPT 7523	POP PARADE VOL. 4 (10")	15
57	Mercury MPT 7525	POP PARADE VOL. 5 (10")	25
68	Polydor 236 517/8/9	POP PARTY! (3-LP in box)	20
83	Fall Out FALL 032	POSH HITS VOL. 1	15
65	Post War Blues PWB 1	POST WAR BLUES: CHICAGO (99 copies only)	45
66	Post War Blues PWB 2	POST WAR BLUES: MEMPHIS ON DOWN (99 copies only)	45
67	Post War Blues PWB 3	POST WAR BLUES: EASTERN AND GULF COAST STATES (99 copies only)	45
68	Post War Blues PWB 4	POST WAR BLUES: TEXAS (99 copies only)	45
68	Post War Blues PWB 5	POST WAR BLUES: DETROIT (99 copies only)	45
60s	Post War Blues PWB 6	POST WAR BLUES: WEST COAST (99 copies only)	45
60s	Post War Blues PWB 7	POST WAR BLUES: THE DEEP SOUTH (99 copies only)	45
69	Python PWBC 1	POST WAR COLLECTOR SERIES VOL. 1 (99 copies only)	80
63	Stateside SL 10046	PREACHIN' THE BLUES	25
80	4AD BAD 11	PRESAGES (mini-LP, green/pink or brown sleeve)	15
79	Preseli PRE 001	PRESELI FOLK (private pressing with insert)	30
70	Kokomo K 1006	PRE-WAR TEXAS BLUES (99 copies only)	45
60s	Jazz Collector JGN 1001	PRIMITIVE PIANO	20
87	A&M AMA 3906	PRINCE'S TRUST 10TH ANNIVERSARY BIRTHDAY PARTY (2-LP, some stickered, with Paul McCartney 7": "Long Tall Sally"/ "I Saw Her Standing There"	40
63	London HA-B 8062	PRISONERS' SONGS	20
90	United Dairies UD 134	PSILOTRIPITAKA (3-LP [UD 01, 03 & 04], with bonus LP "Registered Nurse" [UD 00], 1,000 only, some possibly in leather bag)	400
90	United Dairies UD 134CD	PSILOTRIPITAKA (3-CD [UD 01, 03 & 04], with bonus CD "Registered Nurse" [UD 00CD], 1,000 only, 30 in 'leather bondage bag')	400
91	Delerium DELP 005	PSYCHEDELIC SAUNA (2-LP, 500 numbered on multi-coloured vinyl)	18
81	Abstract AABT 100	PUNK AND DISORDERLY (red vinyl)	15
82	Anagram GRAM 001	PUNK AND DISORDERLY 2 (blue vinyl)	15
82	Anagram GRAM 005	PUNK AND DISORDERLY 2 (Multi-coloured vinyl)	20
82	Pax 7	PUNK DEAD?...NAH MATE	20
65	Sue ILP 919	PURE BLUES VOLUME ONE	60
83	Guardian GRC 2162	PURE OVERKILL	18
73	Purple TPSS 1	PURPLE PEOPLE	12
85	Color Disc COLORS 2	PURPLE TWILIGHT (400 only)	20
68	Island ILP 978	PUT IT ON, IT'S ROCK STEADY	40
71	Pye PSA 6	PYE SALES SAMPLER (sampler for Pye & Dawn releases; 99 copies only, with release sheet)	20
91	Sink Below SINK 2	PUNK'S NOT DREAD (LP, with inner)	15
88	On U Sound 37	PAY IT ALL BACK VOL 1	15
88	On U Sound 42	PAY IT ALL BACK VOL 2 (with booklet)	20
77	Uptempo UTLP 001	PRESENTING THE POSSE	30

Q

68	Stateside S(S)L 10209	A QUARTET OF SOUL	50
70	Trojan TBL 136	QUEEN OF THE WORLD	20
59	Vogue LAE 12031	THE QUINTET OF THE YEAR	15

			MINT VALUE £
		R	
54	London AL 3515	RAGTIME PIANO ROLL (10")	15
54	London AL 3523	RAGTIME PIANO ROLL VOLUME 2 (10")	15
55	London AL 3542	RAGTIME PIANO ROLL VOLUME 3 (10")	15
57	London AL 3563	RAGTIME PIANO ROLL VOLUME 4 (10")	15
81	Island ILPS 9705	RAIDERS OF THE LOST DUB (LP, withdrawn)	12
76	Phil Spector Intl. 2307 008	RARE MASTERS VOL. 1	15
76	Phil Spector Intl. 2307 009	RARE MASTERS VOL. 2	15
69	United Artists (S)UX 1214	RAVE	25
74	Mooncrest CREST 17	RAVE ON	12
73	Attack ATLP 1012	RAVE ON BROTHER	35
67	Ace Of Clubs ACL 1220	RAW BLUES (also stereo SCL 1220)	20
77	Raw RAWLP 1	RAW DEAL (black & white sleeve & red/blue label)	20
61	Pye NPL 18069	RAZZAMATAZZ AND ALL THAT JAZZ	30
83	Mean MNLP 82	READING ROCK VOL. 1 (2-LP)	20
64	Decca LK 4577	READY, STEADY, GO!	45
68	Pama PMLP 3	READY STEADY GO ROCKSTEADY	45
64	Decca LK 4634	READY, STEADY, WIN	75
65	Stateside SL 10112	THE REAL R & B	40
80s	Recloose Org. LOOSE 12	R.O. (RECLOOSE ORGANISATION) (picture disc with insert)	20
82	Recommended 104	RECOMMENDED SAMPLER	15
79	Destiny DS 10001	THE RECORD COLLECTOR	20
81	Recorder BR 003	RECORDER THREE	20
70	CBS 52797	RECORDING THE BLUES	22
65	Red Bird RB 20-102	RED BIRD GOLDIES	65
81	WEA K 58344	RED HOT ROCKABILLIES (with inner sleeve)	12
70	Trojan TBL 115	REGGAE FLIGHT 404	12
70	Pama Economy ECO 34	REGGAE FOR DAYS (LP)	100
68	Big Shot BIL 3000	REGGAE GIRL	100
69	Pama ECO 3	REGGAE HITS '69 VOL. 1	25
69	Pama ECO 11	REGGAE HITS VOL. 2	25
69	Pama PTP 1001	REGGAE HIT THE TOWN	25
68	Studio One SOL 9007	REGGAE IN THE GRASS	95
71	Trojan TBL 181	REGGAE JAMAICA	15
71	Trojan TBL 193	REGGAE JAMAICA VOL. 2	18
71	Bamboo BDLP 208	REGGAEMATIC SOUNDS	70
70	Trojan TBL 144	REGGAE MOVEMENT	15
72	Trojan TBL 189	REGGAE POWER 2	15
72	Trojan TBL	REGGAE REGGAE 2	30
69	Coxsone CSP 2	REGGAE SPECIAL	30
70	Trojan TBL 151	REGGAE STEADY GO	18
73	Trojan TRLS 54	REGGAE STRINGS	20
68	Coxsone CSL 8017	REGGAE TIME	100
72	Ashanti ANB 201	REGGAE TIME	15
71	Pama PMP 2012	REGGAE TO REGGAE	32
69	Pama PSP 1004	REGGAE TO UK WITH LOVE	150
80s	Ré 0101	RE RECORDS QUARTERLY VOL. No. 1 (with book)	15
72	Count Shelly CSLP 01	RETURN TO ME REGGAE	25
73	Count Shelly CSLP 02	RETURN TO ME REGGAE 2	25
64	Decca LK 4616	RHYTHM AND BLUES	80
67	Marble Arch MAL 726	RHYTHM AND BLUES	12
64	Golden Guinea GGL 0280	RHYTHM AND BLUES VOL	20
64	Golden Guinea GGL 0351	RHYTHM AND BLUES VOL. 2	12
69	Liberty LBL 83216	RHYTHM AND BLUES VOLUME 1: END OF AN ERA	20
70	Liberty LBL 83328	RHYTHM AND BLUES VOLUME 2: SWEET 'N' GREASY	20
64	Golden Guinea GGL 0293	RHYTHM AND BLUES ALL STARS	12
69	Minit MLL/MLS 40008E	RHYTHM AND BLUES CLASSICS	22
69	Minit MLL/MLS 40009E	RHYTHM AND BLUES CLASSICS VOL. 2	22
63	CBS Realm RM 101	R&B GREATS VOLUME 1	20
64	CBS Realm RM 175	R&B GREATS VOLUME 2	22
64	Mercury MCL 20019	RHYTHM AND BLUES PARTY	70
76	Philips 6436 028	RHYTHM AND BLUES PARTY (reissue)	15
70	Moodisc TBL 132	RHYTHM RULERS - MUDIES MOODS	20
73	Tamla Motown STML 11232	RIC TIC RELICS	20
68	Coxsone CSL 8015	RIDE ME DONKEY	110
69	Trojan TTL 18	RIDE YOUR DONKEY	20
85	Kent KENT 039	RIGHT BACK WHERE WE STARTED FROM	15
03	Dig The Fuzz DIG048	RIOT OF THE AMPHETAMINE GENERATION (400 copies only, with booklet)	40
82	Riot City ASSEMBLY 1	RIOTOUS ASSEMBLEY (red vinyl)	18
55	Vogue Coral LRA 10023	RIVERBOAT JAZZ (10" LP)	15
71	London SHU 8245	RIVERTOWN BLUES	20
61	London HA-A 2338	ROCK-A-HITS	95
57	London HB-C 1067	ROCK 'N' ROLL (10")	110
59	London HA-E 2180	ROCK AND ROLL FOREVER	95
60	HMV DLP 1204	ROCKET ALONG - NEW BALLADS ON OLD LINES (10")	20
70s	Flynight FLY 662	ROCKIN' ACCORDION	12
58	Decca LF 1300	ROCKIN' AT THE '2 I'S' (10")	60
59	London HA-E 2167	ROCKIN' TOGETHER	80
63	Philips BL 7583	ROCKING GUITARS (LP)	30
69	Decca LK 5002	ROCK STEADY	30
69	Pama PMLP 7	ROCKSTEADY COOL	60
68	Coxsone CSL 8013	ROCKSTEADY COXSONE STYLE	130
80	Guardian GRC 80	ROKSNAX	50
68	Atlantic Special 590 019	ROOTS OF THE BLUES	15
83	Cha Cha CHALP 016	ROOTS AND CULTURE	20
82	Guardian GRC 130	ROXCALIBUR	70

			MINT VALUE £
77	Harvest SHSP 4069	THE ROXY LONDON W.C.2 (JAN - APR 77) (with inner bag)	15
94	Mo' Wax MWLP 003	ROYALTIES OVERDUE (2-LP, coloured vinyl)	60
84	Bam Caruso KIRI 024	RUBBLE 1: THE PSYCHEDELIC SNARL (with 8-page insert; first 2000 with inner sleeve and lightshow labels)	20
86	Bam Caruso KIRI 025	RUBBLE 2: POP-SIKE PIPE DREAMS (with inner sleeve)	20
86	Bam Caruso KIRI 026	RUBBLE 3: NIGHTMARES IN WONDERLAND (with inner sleeve)	20
86	Bam Caruso KIRI 027	RUBBLE 4: THE 49 MINUTE TECHNICOLOUR DREAM (some with 4-page insert; first 2000 with inner sleeve and lightshow labels)	20
86	Bam Caruso KIRI 044	RUBBLE 5: THE ELECTRIC CRAYON SET (with inner sleeve)	15
86	Bam Caruso KIRI 049	RUBBLE 6: THE CLOUDS HAVE GROOVY FACES (with inner sleeve)	15
88	Bam Caruso KIRI 083	RUBBLE 7: PICTURES IN THE SKY (with inner sleeve)	15
91	Bam Caruso KIRI 051	RUBBLE 8: ALL THE COLOURS OF DARKNESS	15
85	Bam Caruso KIRI 065	RUBBLE 9: FROM THE HOUSE OF LORDS (1000 copies only)	18
91	Bam Caruso KIRI 079	RUBBLE 9: PLASTIC WILDERNESS	15
88	Bam Caruso KIRI 098	RUBBLE 10: PROFESSOR JORDAN'S MAGIC SOUND SHOW (with inner sleeve)	15
86	Bam Caruso KIRI 069	RUBBLE 11: ADVENTURES IN THE MIST (with inner sleeve)	20
86	Bam Caruso KIRI 070	RUBBLE 12: STAIRCASE TO NOWHERE (with inner sleeve)	20
89	Bam Caruso KIRI 102	RUBBLE 13: FREAK BEAT FANTOMS	20
88	Bam Caruso KIRI 106	RUBBLE 14: THE MAGIC ROCKING HORSE (with inner sleeve)	20
91	Bam Caruso KIRI 084	RUBBLE 15: 5000 SECONDS OVER TOYLAND	20
91	Bam Caruso KIRI 096	RUBBLE 16: GLASS ORCHID AFTERMATH	15
91	Bam Caruso KIRI 099	RUBBLE 17: A TRIP IN A PAINTED WORLD	20
92	Bam Caruso KIRI 101	RUBBLE 18: RAINBOW THYME WINDERS (unreleased, 25 test pressings only)	200
92	Bam Caruso KIRI 109	RUBBLE 19: EIDERDOWN MINDFOG (unreleased, 25 test pressings only)	200
90s	Bam Caruso KIRI 110	RUBBLE 20: THRICE UPON A TIME - NOTHING IS REAL (unreleased)	0
92	Forty NME 40 LP	RUBY TRAX (3-LP, box set)	40
92	Forty NME 40 CD	RUBY TRAX (3-CD)	30
81	Naive NAIVE 2	RUPERT PREACHING AT A PICNIC (handmade sleeve)	25
74	Cactus CTLP 104	RUPIE'S GEMS	20
69	Xtra XTRA 1035	RURAL BLUES (2-LP)	25
69	Liberty LBL 83213	RURAL BLUES VOLUME 1: GOIN' UP THE COUNTRY	20
69	Liberty LBL 83214	RURAL BLUES VOLUME 2: SATURDAY NIGHT FUNCTION	20
70	Liberty LBL 83329	RURAL BLUES VOLUME 3: DOWN HOME STOMP	20
01	Trunk/Second Coming SEC 001	RESURRECTION: THE AMPLIFIED BIBLE OF HEAVENLY GROOVES (LP)	30

S

70	Transworld SPLP 101	SAMANTHA PROMOTIONS (orange cover, private pressing, a few with poster)	500
70	Transworld SPLP 102	SAMANTHA PROMOTIONS (purple cover, private pressing, a few with poster)	500
78	Live And Love LAP 005	SATISFACTION IN DUB	50
60	Parlophone PMC 1130	SATURDAY CLUB	50
64	Decca LK 4583	SATURDAY CLUB	40
67	Atlantic Special 590 007	SATURDAY NIGHT AT THE APOLLO (reissue of "Apollo Saturday Night")	20
63	Brunswick LAT/STA 8520	SATURDAY NIGHT AT THE GRAND OLE OPRY	15
70	CBS 52799	SAVANNAH SYNCOPATORS	15
81	Suspect SU S3	SCENE OF THE CRIME	60
65	Columbia 33SX 1730	SCENE '65	125
69	Bamboo BDLP 202	A SCORCHA FROM BAMBOO	60
68	CBS 63288	SCREENING THE BLUES	20
95	Blue Eyed Dog VTDOG 12	SEARCH AND DISOBEY (2-LP, 10")	20
81	Airship AP 342	SEASIDE ROCK (2-LP, with insert)	20
81	Come Org. WDC 881008	THE SECOND COMING (various coloured vinyls)	30
84	Davies LP-D2 VOR 8	A SECRET LIVERPOOL (1-sided cardboard sleeve or 2-sided normal sleeve)	25
87	Cherry Red BRED 74	SEEDS I: POP (TV Personalities/Marine Girls, et al.)	20
68	Elektra EUK 261	SELECT ELEKTRA (also stereo EUKS 7261)	30
80	Kathedral KATH 1	SENT FROM COVENTRY (with booklet)	15
88	Sarah SARAH 587	SHADOW FACTORY (The Sea Urchins/14 Iced Bears, et al.)	18
68	Atlantic 587 109	SHAKE, RATTLE AND ROCK	25
74	Topic 12TS 234	SEA SHANTIES	12
78	GVR 201	THE SHANTY MEN	18
74	Eron 003	SHEPWAY FOLK (with insert)	30
84	Kent KENT 015	SHOES	15
78	Virgin VCL 5003	SHORT CIRCUIT - LIVE AT THE ELECTRIC CIRCUS (10"; orange, yellow, blue or black vinyl)	120
78	Virgin VCL 5003	SHORT CIRCUIT - LIVE AT THE ELECTRIC CIRCUS (10"; black vinyl with free John Dowie EP [VED 1004])	12
90	Horaces HRH 101	SHRINE - THE RAREST SOUL LABEL	12
87	ABC NOSE 15	SICK SICK SICK	12
76	Topic 12TS 281	THE SILVER BOW - SHETLAND FOLK FIDDLING VOL. 1	15
66	Chess CRL 4519	SING A SONG OF SOUL	40
57	RCA Camden CDN 147	SINGIN' THE BLUES	12
73	Sir Collins SCMW 001	SIR COLLINS MUSICAL WHEEL (LP)	40
79	Sire SMP 1	THE SIRE MACHINE TURNS YOU UP	12
57	Parlophone PMC 1047	SIX-FIVE SPECIAL	50
76	BBC REB 252	SIX-FIVE SPECIAL	12
71	Pama PMP 2015	16 DYNAMIC REGGAE HITS	30
66	Island ILP 930	SKA AT THE JAMAICA PLAYBOY CLUB (gatefold sleeve)	400
67	Coxsone CSL 8003	SKA-A-GO-GO	200
66	Doctor Bird DLM 5000	SKA-BOO-DA-BA	250
67	Studio One SOL 9000	SKA TO ROCKSTEADY	250
60s	Page One FOR 006	SKA'S THE LIMIT	15
68	Ace Of Clubs ACL 1250	SKIFFLE	30
80s	Kent KENT 052	SMART! 16 IMMACULATE CUTS TAILORED FOR STYLE	12
81	RSB 1	THE SNOOPIES ALBUM (THE LAST REMAINS OF A RICHMOND VENUE) (numbered, with booklet, 1,000 only)	20

			MINT VALUE £
83	Kent KENT 003	SLOW 'N' MOODY BLACK 'N' BLUESY	15
87	Countdown NXON 1	SMASHING TIME	15
67	Polydor 583 064	SOCK IT TO 'EM	15
60s	Solar	THE SOLAR BOX SET	40
70s	United Artists LBR 1007	SOLD ON SOUL	15
71	Bamboo BDLP 212	SOLID GOLD	50
66	Atlantic ATL 5048	SOLID GOLD SOUL	20
67	Atlantic 587 058	SOLID GOLD SOUL VOL. 2	20
75	Disco Demand DDLP 5002	SOLID SOUL SENSATIONS	18
81	Some Bizzare BZLP 1	THE SOME BIZZARE ALBUM	12
72	South. Preservation SPR 1	SOME COLD RAINY DAY	15
75	Flyright LP 114	SOME COLD RAINY DAY (reissue)	12
65	Lestar LLP 101	SOME FOLK IN LEICESTER (private pressing)	20
58	Decca LK 4292	SOMETHING NEW FROM AFRICA	18
70	Pama PMP 2003	SOMETHING SWEET FROM THE LADY	100
60	Topic 12001	SONGS AGAINST THE BOMB	12
72	Argo ZDA 147	SONGS AND MUSIC OF THE REDCOATS	15
77	Topic 12T 317	SONGS & SOUTHERN BREEZES – COUNTRY SINGERS FROM HAMPSHIRE & SUSSEX	15
77	private pressing	SONGS AT A SUSSEX FEAST	12
79	EMI NUT 18	SONGS LENNON AND McCARTNEY GAVE AWAY	12
67	Fontana STL 5436	SONGS OF GRIEF AND GLORY	12
69	Liberty LBX 4	SON OF GUTBUCKET	20
76	Harvest SHSM 2012	SON OF MORRIS ON	25
83	Syndicate SYNLP 3	SON OF OI!	15
72	Probe SPB 1061	SOUL BIBLE	15
84	Kent KENT 011	SOUL CLASS OF '66	15
69	Direction (S)PR 28	SOUL DIRECTION	25
69	Page One POS 608	SOULED AGAIN	20
69	Polydor 584 163	SOUL FEVER	20
60s	Minit MLL 40011E	SOUL FOOD	40
69	Soul City SCB 1	SOUL FROM THE CITY	45
70	Specialty SPE 6606	SOUL FROM THE VAULTS	15
74	Trojan TRL 65	SOULFUL REGGAE	12
70	Polydor 583 757	SOUL GOLD	18
72	Avco 6467 251	SOUL - IN THE BEGINNING	12
68	Trojan TRL 3	SOUL OF JAMAICA	35
68	Polydor Special 236 213	SOUL PARTY	20
69	Pama PMLP 8	SOUL SAUCE FROM PAMA	70
69	Polydor 236 554	SOUL SELLER	18
70s	United Artists UAL 229018	SOUL SENSATION	15
85	Kent KENT 041	SOUL SERENADE	15
66	Stateside SL 10186	SOUL SIXTEEN	45
66	Sue ILP 934	SOUL '66	60
67	CBS BPG 62965	SOUL SOUNDS	25
67	HMV CLP 3617	SOUL SOUNDS OF THE 60s	45
67	Stateside SL 10203	SOUL SUPPLY	50
86	SMP/Inferno SIMLP 4	SOUL TIME	12
69	Atlantic 218005	SOUL TOGETHER	15
73	Trojan TRLS 74	SOUL TO SOUL DJ CHOICE	20
65	Pye Intl. NPL 28061	THE SOUND OF BACHARACH	20
95	EMI EMI 8322 801	THE SOUND GALLERY	25
58	Fontana TFL 5025	THE SOUND OF JAZZ	15
68	President PTL 1008	THE SOUND OF SOUL	30
72	United Artists UAS 29215	SOUND OF THE CITY	12
79	Grapevine GRAL 1001	SOUND OF THE GRAPEVINE	20
64	Stateside SL 10077	THE SOUND OF THE R&B HITS	65
69	Joy JOY 125	SOUNDS LIKE SKA	12
70	Sentinel SENS 1001	SOUNDS LIKE WEST CORNWALL	20
78	Sonet SNTF 806	SOUTHEND ROCK	12
69	London HAK 8405	SOUTHERN COMFORT	125
83	Spectrum ASPEC 001	SOUTHERN COMFORT	75
80s	Spectrum ASPEC 003	SOUTHERN COMFORT 3	50
60s	Saydisc Roots RL 328	SOUTHERN SANCTIFIED SINGERS	15
61	London Jazz LTZ-K 15209	SOUTHERN FOLK HERITAGE VOLUME 1: SOUNDS OF THE SOUTH	20
61	London Jazz LTZ-K 15210	SOUTHERN FOLK HERITAGE VOLUME 2: BLUE RIDGE MOUNTAIN MUSIC	20
61	London Jazz LTZ-K 15211	SOUTHERN FOLK HERITAGE VOLUME 3: ROOTS OF THE BLUES	20
61	London Jazz LTZ-K 15209	SOUTHERN FOLK HERITAGE VOLUME 7: THE BLUES ROLL ON	20
54	London AL 3529	SOUTHSIDE CHICAGO JAZZ (10")	18
71	Python PLP 10	SOUTHSIDE CHICAGO (99 copies only)	80
70	CBS Special Prod. WSR 932	SPARKLING COLOUR (multicoloured vinyl)	12
58	Tempo TAP 17	SPEAK LOW - MORE MUSIC IN THE MODERN MANNER	150
69	BAF BAF001	SPECIAL BAF SOUNDS VOL. 1	30
73	Tempo TMP 9001	SPIN A MAGIC TUNE	20
57	Pye Nixa NPT 19019	SPIN WITH THE STARS - SELECTION NO. 2 (10")	18
57	Pye Nixa NPT 19021	SPIN WITH THE STARS - SELECTION NO. 3 (10")	18
65	Fontana TL 5243	SPIRITUAL AND GOSPEL FESTIVAL	20
59	Top Rank 35/064	SPIRITUALS TO SWING VOLUME 1	15
59	Top Rank 35/065	SPIRITUALS TO SWING VOLUME 2	15
82	WEA K 58415	A SPLASH OF COLOUR	15
62	Liberty LBY 1001	THE STARS OF LIBERTY	30
57	Decca LF 1299	STARS OF THE 6.5 SPECIAL (10")	50
84	Broken Flag BF V5	STATEMENT	40
85	Statik POL 274	STATIK COMPILATION ONE (2-LP)	20
04	Ai AILP 006	STATION (2-LP, clear vinyl, 1000 copies only)	15
69	Stax XATS 1007	STAX SOUL EXPLOSION	18

			MINT VALUE £
70s	Stax STXH 5004	THE STAX STORY (VOL. 1)	20
70s	Stax STXH 5005	THE STAX STORY (VOL. 1)	15
67	Stax 589 010	THE STAX/VOLT SHOW VOL. 1	20
67	Stax 589 011	THE STAX/VOLT SHOW VOL. 2	20
78	Stiff GET 1	STIFFS LIVE STIFFS	12
60	Topic 10T 59	STILL I LOVE HIM	12
69	CBS 66218	THE STORY OF THE BLUES (2-LP)	20
70	CBS 66232	THE STORY OF THE BLUES VOLUME 2 (2-LP)	20
94	Tenth Planet TP 010	THE STORY OF OAK RECORDS	25
94	Wooden Hill WHCD 007	THE STORY OF OAK RECORDS (CD)	18
70	Pama PMP 2002	STRAIGHTEN UP	50
71	Pama PMP 2007	STRAIGHTEN UP VOLUME TWO	20
71	Pama PMP 2014	STRAIGHTEN UP VOLUME THREE	20
72	Pama PMP 2017	STRAIGHTEN UP VOLUME FOUR	15
77	Beggars Banquet BEGA 1	STREETS	15
80s	Streetsounds	STREETSOUND ELECTRO (box set)	70
79	Open Eye OE LP 501	STREET TO STREET - A LIVERPOOL ALBUM	20
81	Open Eye OE LP 502	STREET TO STREET - A LIVERPOOL ALBUM VOL. 2	12
81	Decca SKIN 1	STRENGTH THROUGH OI!	50
85	Wonderful World WOWLP 3	STRENGTH THROUGH OI! (reissue)	20
80s	Private Pressing CFCEPI	STUFF THE NEIGHBOURS, PLAY IT LOUD (p/s, in poly bag, with fanzine)	12
86	Sub Pop SP 0010	SUB POP 100	20
81	Chick CHR 001	SUBWAY (clear vinyl)	15
98	Sorted SRLP 04	SUCTION PRINTS (handpainted or wraparound sleeve)	35
65	Sue ILP 919	SUE SAMPLER RECORD FOR CLUBS (promo, no sleeve, typed labels with detail sheet)	120
65	London HA-C 8239	THE SUE STORY	60
65	Sue ILP 925	THE SUE STORY!	55
69	United Artists UAS 29028	THE SUE STORY (reissue)	18
66	Sue ILP 933	THE SUE STORY VOL. 2	55
66	Sue ILP 938	THE SUE STORY VOL. 3	55
76	Giorno GPS	SUGAR, ALCOHOL & MEAT	20
82	CBS 22139	SUMMER MEANS FUN (2-LP)	20
75	Island ISS 1	SUMMER '75 (promo-only sampler)	15
66	Reprise R 5031	THE SUMMIT	30
86	Sun/Charly BOX 105	SUN RECORDS: THE BLUES YEARS (9-LP box with booklet)	60
81	Sunset Gun	SUNSET GUN (cassette with Sunset Gun fanzine)	15
68	Ember NR 5038	SUNSTROKE	20
73	Philips 6369 416	SUPER BLACK BLUES	20
69	Blue Horizon (S)PR 31	SUPER DUPER BLUES	15
68	Pye Intl. NPL 28107	SUPER SOUL	25
68	Chess SRL 4537	SUPER SUPER BLUES BAND	25
74	People PLEO 24	SUPER SWEET SOUL	15
64	Vocalion VA 8018	SURF BATTLE	60
86	Capitol EMS 1180	SURF CITY/DRAG CITY	25
88	Decal LIK 39	SURFERS STOMP	25
73	Pye/Disques Vogue HEN 1	SURPRISE PARTIE TOUS LES JEUNES	18
71	Blue Horizon 7-66263	SWAMP BLUES (2-LP)	75
68	Stateside S(S)L 10243	SWEET SOUL SOUNDS	50
68	Coxsone CSL 8018	SWING EASY	125
68	Saga FID 2136	SWINGING SAGA	15
58	Tempo TAP 21	SWINGIN' THE BLUES	25
93	Tenth Planet TP 002	SYDE TRYPS ONE (numbered, 500 only, with insert)	25
93	Tenth Planet TP 004	SYDE TRYPS TWO - FROM THERE TO UNCERTAINTY (numbered, 500 only, with insert)	25
93	Tenth Planet TP 006	SYDE TRYPS THREE (numbered, 500 only, with insert)	25
94	Tenth Planet TP 008	SYDE TRYPS FOUR (numbered, 500 only, with insert)	25
96	Tenth Planet TP 024	SYDE TRYPS SIX (numbered, gatefold sleeve, 1,000 only)	18
71	BBC RED 67 M	SINGING ALONG WITH THE GIRL GUIDES (LP)	15
72	BBC RESR 28M	SOME BRITISH ACCENTS AND DIALECTS (LP)	15
78	BBC REC 303	SCRAPBOOK OF 1977 (LP)	15
96	Trunk BARKED 1	THE SUPER SOUNDS OF BOSWORTH (LP)	50
96	Trunk BARKED 2	THE SUPER SOUNDS OF BOSWORTH 2 (LP, 750 only)	50

T

89	2-TONE CHR TT 5009	THE 2 TONE STORY (2-LP)	30
72	Rubber RUB 001	TAKE OFF YOUR HEAD AND LISTEN	15
71	A&M Mayfair AMLB 51029	TAKE ONE	12
78	Grapevine GRAL 1000	TALK OF THE GRAPEVINE	25
65	London HA-B 8250	THE TALL 12	12
67	London HA-B 8315	THE TALL 12 VOL. 2	12
85	Kent KENT 045	TEAR IN MY EYES	30
58	Capitol T 1009	TEENAGE ROCK (turquoise or 'rainbow' label)	55
63	Stateside SL 10020	TENNESSEE GUITAR	20
56	Nixa Jazz Today NJL 4	TENORAMA	100
77	Talisman STAL 1051	10 YEARS ON - THE UNIVERSAL FOLK CENTRE (LP)	20
70s	Fountain FV 205	TEXAS BLUES	18
69	Highway 51 H 103	TEXAS-LOUISIANA BLUES (99 copies only)	60
62	Ace Of Clubs ACL 1108	THANK YOUR LUCKY STARS	25
63	Golden Guinea GGL 0190	THANK YOUR LUCKY STARS	15
63	Decca LK 4554	THANK YOUR LUCKY STARS VOLUME 2	35
82	No Future PUNK 9	THERE IS NO FUTURE	18
72	Dandelion 2485 021	THERE IS SOME FUN GOING FORWARD (with poster)	18

			MINT VALUE £
82	Big Beat NED 3	THESE CATS AIN'T NOTHING BUT TRASH	20
69	Action ACLP 6009	THESE KIND OF BLUES VOL. 1	80
82	MCA MCA 6111	THE THING (LP)	20
81	TTFTC 001	THE THING FROM THE CRYPT (I NEARLY DIED LAUGHING)	15
87	Kent KENT 066	THINK SMART SOUL STRINGS	15
57	Tempo TAP 11	THIRD BRITISH FESTIVAL OF JAZZ	50
80s	Come Org. WDC 881021	33 FÜR ILSE KOCH (some on red vinyl)	70
68	Minit MLL/MLS 40002	THIRTY-THREE MINITS OF BLUES AND SOUL	45
83	2-Tone CHR TT 5007	THIS ARE 2-TONE (with free poster, green or pink sleeve)	15
64	Island ILP 910	THIS IS BLUE BEAT (unreleased, white labels may exist)	200
69	Island IWP 5	THIS IS THE BLUES	15
69	Chess CRL 4540	THIS IS CHESS	22
76	Loma/Warners K 56265	THIS IS LOMA VOL. 1	20
76	Loma/Warners K 56266	THIS IS LOMA VOL. 2	20
76	Loma/Warners K 56267	THIS IS LOMA VOL. 3	20
76	Loma/Warners K 56268	THIS IS LOMA VOL. 4	20
76	Loma/Warners K 56269	THIS IS LOMA VOL. 5	20
76	Loma/Warners K 56270	THIS IS LOMA VOL. 6	20
63	Oriole PS 40047	THIS IS MERSEYBEAT VOL. 1	70
63	Oriole PS 40048	THIS IS MERSEYBEAT VOL. 2	70
80	Grapevine GRAL 1002	THIS IS NORTHERN SOUL	30
69	Pama PSP 1003	THIS IS REGGAE	20
71	Pama PMP 2005	THIS IS REGGAE VOLUME TWO	20
71	Pama PMP 2008	THIS IS REGGAE VOLUME THREE	15
72	Pama PMP 2016	THIS IS REGGAE VOLUME FOUR	15
60s	Island IWP 3	THIS IS SUE!	25
60	Philips BBL 7356	THIS WONDERFUL WORLD OF JAZZ	12
63	RCA RD/SF 7608	THE THREE GREAT GUYS (Paul Anka, Sam Cooke & Neil Sedaka)	30
70	Saydisc Matchbox SDR182	THOSE CAKEWALKIN' BABIES FROM HOME	22
66	Allegro ALL 807	THUNDERBALL AND OTHER SECRET AGENT THEMES	15
69	Trojan TTL 7	TIGHTEN UP VOLUME TWO (pink Island label with different track listing & sleeve)	40
69	Parlophone PMC 7072	THAT TODDLIN' TOWN - CHICAGO (1926-1928)	12
71	CBS SPR 52	TOGETHER!	12
92	Too Pure SFRLP 119	TOO PURE - THE PEEL SESSIONS (LP, limited issue, custom sleeve)	20
64	Ember FA 2018	TOPS OF THE POPS	12
64	Golden Guinea GGL 0277	TOP 10 HITS, ORIGINAL ARTISTS	15
72	Studio 2 TWO 391	TOP TV THEMES AND COMMERCIALS	30
82	Zoo ZOO 4	TO THE SHORES OF LAKE PLACID (gatefold sleeve with 4-page booklet)	18
56	Tempo TAP 4	TOP TRUMPETS	50
55	Decca LK 4088	TRADITIONAL JAZZ AT THE ROYAL FESTIVAL HALL	15
55	Decca LK 4100	TRADITIONAL JAZZ AT THE ROYAL FESTIVAL HALL VOL. 2	15
60s	Fishers Music	TRANSAFRICK MUSICMAKERS	25
77	Free Reed FRRD 021/022	THE TRANSPORTS (2-LP, with book)	60
76	Eron 006	TRAVELLING FOLK (with insert)	25
70	RCA Intl. INTS 1175	TRAVELLING THIS LONESOME ROAD	12
61	77' LA 12-2	A TREASURY OF FIELD RECORDINGS VOLUME 1	35
61	77' LA 12-3	A TREASURY OF FIELD RECORDINGS VOLUME 2	35
61	Embassy WLP 6041	TRIBUTE TO CLIFF	15
60	Embassy WLP 6034	TRIBUTE TO ELVIS	15
64	Columbia 33SX 1635	TRIBUTE TO MICHAEL HOLLIDAY	25
69	Key KL 003	A TRIBUTE TO YOUTH PRAISE	20
80	Skeleton SKL LP 1	A TRIP TO THE DENTIST (with insert)	15
61	Parlophone PMC 1139	TRIPLE TREAT	25
71	Trojan TALL 1	TROJAN STORY (3xLP in fold-over sleeve)	20
50s	Esquire 32-036	TROMBONE BY THREE	12
71	Revival RVS 1007	TROUBLE IN MIND? (GEORGIA BLUES)	15
67	Riverside RLP 8802	TUB JUG WASHBOARD BANDS	15
74	Melodisc 12-193	12 BIG HITS	15
74	Melodisc 12-217	12 CARAT GOLD	20
60s	Envoy VOY 9159	12 STRING STORY	12
63	Fontana 688 0082L	12 STRING GUITAR: THE FOLK SINGERS	15
66	London HA-F/SH-F 8285	THE TWELVE-STRING STORY - GUITAR SOLOS	18
76	Lucky LYLP 5004	TWELVE TRIBES OF ISRAEL (LP)	200
73	Dragon DRLS 5003	20 DRAGON HITS	18
73	Trojan TRLS 81	20 EXPLOSIVE REGGAE HITS	18
79	Polydor POLS 1006	20 OF ANOTHER KIND	12
65	Ember EMB 3359	25 YEARS OF RHYTHM & BLUES HITS	45
89	WEA 241 690-1	TWIST & SHOUT - 12 ATLANTIC TRACKS PRODUCED BY PHIL SPECTOR (gatefold sleeve)	35
63	Philips BL 7578	TWIST AT THE STAR-CLUB, HAMBURG	80
89	Two Tone CHRTT 5009	TWO TONE STORY	30
82	Beat The System BTSLP 1	TOTAL ANARCHY (LP)	12
95	Dig The Fuzz DIG 001	THE TECHNICOLOUR MILKSHAKE VOL 1	30

U

68	BBC REC 28M	ULSTER'S FLOWERY VALE	15
69	Island ILP 993/ILPS 9093	THE UNFOLDING OF THE BOOK OF LIFE VOL. 1	45
72	Nevis NEV R 007	UNITY CREATES STRENGTH	25
69	Pama ECO 7	UNITY'S GREATEST	70
88	Unicorn PHZA 17	UNSUNG HEROES (red vinyl)	15
80	Safari UPP 1	UPPERS ON THE SOUTH DOWNS (original issue without Purple Hearts)	12
68	Atlantic 588 122	UPTOWN SOUL	20

			MINT VALUE £
77	Specialty SNTF 5023	URBAN BLUES	12
69	Liberty LBL 83215	URBAN BLUES VOLUME 1: BLUES UPTOWN	20
70	Liberty LBL 83327	URBAN BLUES VOLUME 2: NEW ORLEANS BOUNCE	20
72	Village Thing VTSAM 15	US	20
		V	
50s	Audubon AAM	VAUDEVILLE (10")	20
70	VJM VLP 30	VAUDEVILLE BLUES	15
78	Attrix RB 03	VAULTAGE '78 (TWO SIDES OF BRIGHTON) (originally hand-screened sleeve, later with insert)	20
71	Trojan TBL 175	VERSION GALORE VERSION TWO	15
73	Trojan TBL 200	VERSION GALORE VERSION THREE	12
72	Trojan TBL 182	VERSION TO VERSION	12
73	Trojan TBL 206	VERSION TO VERSION VOLUME THREE	12
70	Vertigo 6499 407/8	VERTIGO ANNUAL 1970 (2-LP, set no.: 6657 001)	30
87	BB BBLP 02	VINYL FRONTIER	12
		W	
70s	Object Music OBJ 007	WAITING ROOM	15
62	Columbia 33SX 1385	WAKEY WAKEY	20
85	Psycho PSYCHO 35	THE WAKING DREAM	15
64	Pye Intl. NPL 28041	WALKING BY MYSELF	40
64	Pye Intl. NPL 28044	WALKING THE BLUES	35
81	Phil Spector Intl. WOS 001	WALL OF SOUND (9-LP box set)	80
78	CBS WOW 100	THE WAR OF THE WORLDS (boxed 2-LP, book & poster)	18
78	Bridgehouse BHLP 001	A WEEKEND AT THE BRIDGEHOUSE E16 (with bonus 12" EP)	30
57	Rainbow Records	WEEKEND FILM STAR RECORD ALBUM (5 x 8" flexi 78s, mail order from Weekend magazine)	75
85	Music For Nations MFN 49	WELCOME TO THE METAL ZONE (2-LP)	18
59	Coral LVA 9096	WE LIKE GIRLS	25
59	Coral LVA 9098	WE LIKE GUYS	25
63	London HA-P 8061	WE SING THE BLUES	60
65	Liberty LBY 3051	WE SING THE BLUES	45
65	Sue ILP 921	WE SING THE BLUES!	45
72	Syndicate Chapter SC 005	WE THREE KINGS	15
70	Trojan TTL 34	WHAT AM I TO DO	30
68	Elektra EKS 7304	WHAT'S SHAKIN' (reissue of "Good Time Music")	15
80	S & T	WHERE THE HELL IS LEICESTER? (with bonus single & booklet)	25
86	Sunrise A40 111M	WHERE WOULD YOU RATHER BE TONIGHT?	25
83	Kamera KAM 14	THE WHIP (with insert)	20
79	London Bomp DHS-Z 3	WHO PUT THE BOMP? (2-LP, gatefold sleeve)	25
70	Trojan TBL 131	WHO YOU GONNA RUN TO	50
72	private pressing	WHOLLY GRAIL	25
74	Topic 12TS 227	WILD HILLS O'WANNIE - THE SMALL PIPES OF NORTHUMBRIA	12
61	Philips BBL 7430	WINNERS OF DOWNBEAT'S INTERNATIONAL CRITICS' POLL 1960	12
66	Dot DLP 3535	WIPE OUT	25
76	RCA RS 1085	WIZARD'S CONVENTION (with insert)	12
82	Womad WOMAD 001	WOMAD: RAINDROPS CLATTERING ON BANANA LEAVES	15
67	RCA Victor RD 7840	WOMEN OF THE BLUES	20
81	Stiff FREEB 3	WONDERFUL TIME OUT THERE (Xmas freebie)	12
81	Glass GLASS 010	THE WONDERFUL WORLD OF GLASS	15
87	Black Crow CRO 217 A	WOODY LIVES: A TRIBUTE TO WOODY GUTHRIE	15
96	Magna Carta MA 9010/2	WORKING MAN	15
63	London HA-P 8099	A WORLD OF BLUES	40
69	Decca (S)PA-R 14	THE WORLD OF BLUES POWER	12
70	Decca (S)PA 63	THE WORLD OF BLUES POWER VOL. 2	12
73	Decca SPA 263	THE WORLD OF BLUES POWER VOL. 3	12
69	Pama SECO 19	A WORLD OF BULLET	50
71	Decca SPA 156	WORLD OF CONTEMPORARY FOLK	12
71	Argo SPA-A 132	THE WORLD OF FOLK	15
73	Argo SPA-A 307	THE WORLD OF FOLK VOLUME 2	15
78	Yuk NE 1023	THE WORLD'S WORST RECORD SHOW (multi-coloured vinyl)	20
69	Decca (S)PA 34	WOWIE ZOWIE! - THE WORLD OF PROGRESSIVE MUSIC	12
09	Warp WARP 20	WARP 20 (5 x 10", 5-CD, booklet, box set)	150
73	Myrrh MST 6510	WHAT IS MYRRH? (LP)	12
		Y	
69	Island IWPS 2	YOU CAN ALL JOIN IN (pink label)	12
70	Trojan TBL 142	YOU CAN'T WINE	40
69	Trojan TTL 9	YOU LEFT ME STANDING	25
69	Young Blood SBYB 1	YOUNGBLOOD VOL. 1	15
71	Youngblood SBYB4	YOUNBLOOD VOL. 2	18
70	Pama ECO 35	YOUNG GIFTED AND BLACK	200
71	Bamboo BDLPS 211	YOUNG JAMAICAN GIRL	30
78	Stiff DEAL 1	YOU'RE EITHER ON THE TRAIN OR OFF THE TRAIN (promo only, with booklet)	12
62	HMV CLP 1565	YOUR FAVOURITE TV AND RADIO THEMES	20
63	HMV CLP 1676	YOUR FAVOURITE TV AND RADIO THEMES (VOL. 3)	20
63	HMV CLP 1762	YOUR FAVOURITE TV AND RADIO THEMES (VOL. 4)	20
66	HMV CLP 3521	YOUR FAVOURITE TV AND RADIO THEMES (VOL. 5)	20
71	Bamboo BDLP 211	YOUR JAMAICAN GIRL	80
82	Statik STATLP 7	YOUR SECRET'S SAFE WITH US (2-LP)	20
		Z	
84	Zulu ZULU 6	THE ZULU COMPILATION	20

MINT VALUE £

FILM & TV SOUNDTRACK LPs
(alphabetical by title, composers/artists in brackets)
(Only the first issues of soundtracks by the Beatles and Elvis Presley are listed below: for later repressings see their entries)

A

73	United Artists UAS 29451	ACROSS 110TH STREET (J.J. Johnson & Bobby Womack)	15
70	Paramount SPFL 260	THE ADVENTURERS (Antonio Carlos Jobim)	12
62	RCA RD 7512	ADVISE AND CONSENT (Jerry Fielding)	15
64	Parlophone PMC 1230	A HARD DAY'S NIGHT (Beatles) (LP, mono, 1st pressing, with The Parlophone Co. Ltd label rim copy & "Sold In The UK..." text)	80
64	Parlophone PCS 3058	A HARD DAY'S NIGHT (Beatles) (LP, stereo, 1st pressing, with "The Parlophone Co. Ltd" label rim copy & "Sold In The UK..." text; stereo, with mid-sized "stereo"	140
67	United Artists (S)ULP 1172	AFRICA ADDIO (Riz Ortolani/Jimmy Roselli)	20
66	United Artists (S)ULP 1151	AFTER THE FOX (Burt Bacharach/Hollies)	25
56	Nixa NPT 19010	ALEXANDER THE GREAT (Mario Nascimbene) (10"; beware of counterfeits)	75
69	MGM CS 8112	ALFRED THE GREAT (Ray Leppard)	150
72	Warner Bros K 56009	ALICE'S ADVENTURES IN WONDERLAND (John Barry) (gatefold sleeve)	12
79	20th Century T 593	ALIEN (Jerry Goldsmith)	12
61	Fontana (S)TFL 591	ALL NIGHT LONG (mono/stereo, Dave Brubeck/Johnny Dankworth, et al.)	25
65	Reprise R 6151	AMERICANIZATION OF EMILY (Johnny Mandel)	20
65	RCA RD 7732	THE AMOROUS ADVENTURES OF MOLL FLANDERS (John Addison)	35
57	Brunswick LAT 8175	ANASTASIA (Alfred Newman)	15
60	Philips SBBL 514	ANATOMY OF A MURDER (Duke Ellington)	12
76	BBC REB 236	ANGELS AND 15 OTHER BBC TV THEMES (Alan Parker, et al.)	15
72	Polydor 2383 109	ANTONY AND CLEOPATRA (John Scott) (foldout sleeve)	20
60	London HA-T 2287	THE APARTMENT (Adolph Deutsch)	18
79	Elektra K 62025	APOCALYPSE NOW (2-LP, music & dialogue)	18
69	CBS 70054	APRIL FOOLS (Marvin Hamlisch)	15
66	RCA Victor RD 7817	ARABESQUE (Henry Mancini)	15
54	HMV DLPC 1	AS LONG AS THEY'RE HAPPY (Jack Buchanan) (10")	50
87	Illegal ILP 017	ATHENS, GA. - INSIDE/OUT (R.E.M.)	12
67	Pye NPL 18198	AT LAST THE 1948 SHOW (TV soundtrack)	25
67	Marble Arch MAL 695	THE AVENGERS AND OTHER FAVOURITES (Laurie Johnson)	35
61	Fontana TFL 591	ALL NIGHT LONG (LP, mono, Dave Brubeck, Tubby Hayes, Johnny Dankworth et al.)	30
61	Fontana STFL 591	ALL NIGHT LONG (LP, stereo, Dave Brubeck, Tubby Hayes, Johnny Dankworth et al.)	40

B

66	Fontana TL 5306	BABY, THE RAIN MUST FALL (Elmer Bernstein)	30
62	Pye Intl. NPL 28020	BARABBAS (Mario Nascimbene)	15
68	Stateside (S)SL 10260	BARBARELLA (Bob Crewe/Charles Fox)	100
67	London HA-D 8337	BAREFOOT IN THE PARK (Neal Hefti)	30
75	Warner Bros K 56189	BARRY LYNDON (Leonard Rosenman)	12
66	Stateside S(S)L 10179	BATMAN (Nelson Riddle) (TV show music)	50
89	W.B./Paisley Park WX 281P	BATMAN (Prince) (picture disc, die-cut sleeve)	20
89	W.B./Paisley Park 925 978-2	BATMAN (Prince) (CD, picture disc in 'Bat' tin with booklet)	18
69	United Artists UAS 29019	BATTLE OF BRITAIN (Ron Goodwin)	12
66	Warner Bros W 1617	BATTLE OF THE BULGE (Benjamin Frankel)	25
60	Columbia 33SX 1225	BEAT GIRL (John Barry/Adam Faith)	70
57	London HAP 2056	BEAU JAMES (Joseph Lilley)	25
64	RCA Victor RD 7679	BECKET (dialogue only)	15
68	Decca LK 4923	BEDAZZLED (LP, mono, Peter Cook/Dudley Moore)	90
70	Island ILPS 9140	BE GLAD FOR THE SONG HAS NO ENDING (Incredible String Band)	15
60	Capitol W/SW 1435	BELLS ARE RINGING (André Previn) (mono/stereo)	15
73	Ronco RR 2006	THE BELSTONE FOX (Laurie Johnson) (gatefold sleeve)	12
60	MGM MGM-C(S) 802	BEN HUR (Miklos Rozsa) (box set with hardback book; mono/stereo)	15
70	Stateside SSL 10311	BEYOND THE VALLEY OF THE DOLLS (Stu Phillips/Strawberry Alarm Clock)	100
66	Stateside S(S)L 10188	THE BIBLE (Toshiro Mayuzumi)	15
59	London HA-T 2142	THE BIG COUNTRY (Jerome Moross) ('sun' cover)	12
68	MGM MGM-C(S) 8066	BIGGEST BUNDLE OF THEM ALL (Riz Ortolani/Eric Burdon)	20
86	MCA MCF 3328	BIGGLES (Stanislas/Deep Purple/Motley Crue et al.)	15
69	United Artists (S)ULP 1228	THE BIG GUNDOWN (Ennio Morricone)	15
67	United Artists (S)ULP 1183	BILLION DOLLAR BRAIN (Richard Rodney Bennett)	30
73	Polydor 2490 117	BLACK CAESAR (James Brown)	30
62	Stateside SL 10026	BLACK NATIVITY (Alex Bradford)	20
72	Pye NSPL 18376	BLOOMFIELD	15
66	MGM MGM-C(S) 8039	BLOW-UP (Herbie Hancock/Yardbirds)	80
68	Dot (S)LPD 508	BLUE (Manos Hadjidakis)	30
61	RCA RD 27238	BLUE HAWAII (Elvis Presley) (black/silver label, mono)	15
66	RCA RD 7795	BOEING BOEING (Neal Hefti)	20
62	RCA RD 7520	BONANZA (L.Greene, M. Langdon)	20
69	MCA MUPS 360	BOOM! (John Barry/Georgie Fame)	60
68	Warner Bros W 1742	BONNIE AND CLYDE (Charles Strouse)	20
70	Paramount SPFL 263	BORSALINO (Claude Bolling)	15
58	RCA RD 27054	BOTH ENDS OF THE CANDLE (Gogi Grant)	15
57	Brunswick LAT 8193	BOY ON A DOLPHIN (Hugo Friedhoffer)	30
80	MCA MCF 2013	BUCK ROGERS IN THE 25th CENTURY (Stu Phillips)	12
71	Capitol E-SW 621	THE BUGALOOS (LP)	18
72	Bell BELLS 209	THE BURGLARS (Ennio Morricone)	30
66	RCA RD 7791	BUNNY LAKE IS MISSING (Paul Glass/Zombies)	65
65	Liberty LBY 1246	BURKE'S LAW (Herschel/Burke/Gilbert) (TV series music)	15
63	RCA Victor RD 7580	BYE BYE BIRDIE (musical) (Charles Strouse; mono)	12
61	RCA SF 5115	BLUE HAWAII (Elvis Presley) (black/silver label, stereo)	30

			MINT VALUE £
63	RCA Victor SF 7580	BYE BYE BIRDIE (musical) (Charles Strouse; stereo)	15
80	Chrysalis CHR 1294	BABYLON (blue/white label)	20
05	Trunk JBH 016LP/PD	BOD: WORDS & MUSIC (LP 1-sided picture disc)	20
07	Trunk JBH 023 LP	BLOOD ON SATAN's CLAW (LP, 500 only)	20

C

56	Philips BBR 8104	CALAMITY JANE (Doris Day/Howard Keel) (10")	15
66	RCA Victor RD 7820	CALIFORNIA HOLIDAY (Elvis Presley) (black/red dot labels, mono)	20
66	RCA Victor SF 7820	CALIFORNIA HOLIDAY (Elvis Presley) (black/red dot labels, stereo)	30
69	Stateside (S)SL 10276	CANDY (Dave Grusin/Steppenwolf, et al.)	30
69	MCA MUPS 380	CAN HIERONYMUS MERKIN EVER FORGET MERCY HUMPPE AND FIND TRUE HAPPINESS? (Anthony Newley)	15
64	Philips SBL 7634	CAPTAIN FROM CASTILE (Robert Farnon)	12
60	Delyse DL 3057/DLS 6057	CAPTAIN HORATIO HORNBLOWER (Robert Farnon) (mono)	40
86	Virgin V 2401	CAPTIVE (The Edge et al.)	12
64	MGM MGM-C 984	THE CARPETBAGGERS (Elmer Bernstein)	12
64	London HA-A/SH-A 8219	THE CARPETBAGGERS (Elmer Bernstein)	12
67	RCA Victor RD/SF 7874	CASINO ROYALE (Burt Bacharach/Herb Alpert/Dusty Springfield) (mono/stereo)	50
66	United Artists (S)ULP 1140	CAST A GIANT SHADOW (Elmer Bernstein/Vince Hill)	18
71	Polydor 2383 035	CATCH MY SOUL (P.J. Proby/P.P. Arnold, et al.)	12
65	Columbia SX 1756	CATCH US IF YOU CAN (Dave Clark Five)	45
62	Fontana TFL 5170/STFL 585	CHANNEL THRILL: THE T.V. THRILLER THEMES (Johnny Gregory)	12
62	Warner Bros WS 8177	THE CHAPMAN REPORT (Leonard Rosenman)	15
63	RCA SF 7620	CHARADE (Henry Mancini)	20
63	MGM MGM-C 969	THE CHARGE IS MURDER (John Green)	20
68	United Artists SULP 1189	THE CHARGE OF THE LIGHT BRIGADE (John Addison/Manfred Mann)	18
83	Polydor BOX 1	CHARIOTS OF FIRE (Vangelis) (box set)	12
66	CBS (S)BPG 62665	THE CHASE (John Barry) (mono) (stereo copy is £30)	20
69	Polydor 583 736	CHE! (Lalo Schifrin)	15
67	Fontana TL 5417	CHIMES AT MIDNIGHT (Angelo Lavagnino)	30
74	ABC ABCL 5068	CHINATOWN (Jerry Goldsmith)	20
68	United Artists (S)ULP 1200	CHITTY CHITTY BANG BANG (Sherman Brothers) (gatefold sleeve)	12
68	RCA Victor RD/SF 7917	CLAMBAKE (Elvis Presley) (black/red dot labels, mono/stereo)	20
01	Trunk SOUP 001LP	THE CLANGERS (Vernon Elliot) (TV soundtrack, with knitted sleeve, 26 only)	100
01	Trunk SOUP 001LP	THE CLANGERS (Vernon Elliot) (TV soundtrack, without knitted sleeve)	20
74	Buddah BDLP 4010	CLAUDINE (Curtis Mayfield/Gladys Knight)	12
63	Stateside S(S)SL 10044	CLEOPATRA (Alex North)	15
72	Warner Bros K 46127	A CLOCKWORK ORANGE (Walter Carlos)	12
65	Fontana (S)TL 5259	THE COLLECTOR (Maurice Jarre)	25
78	MGM 2315 398	COMA (Jerry Goldsmith)	12
67	MGM MGM-C(S) 8058	THE COMEDIANS (Laurence Rosenthal)	15
72	Pye NSPL 18389	CONCERTO FOR HARRY - SOMETHING TO HIDE (Roy Budd)	35
75	Polydor 2383 350	CONFESSIONS OF A POP PERFORMER (Three's A Crowd/Ed Welch)	30
71	Philips 6332 033	CONTINENTAL CIRCUS (Gong)	60
62	Parlophone PMC 1194	THE COOL MIKADO (John Barry Seven/Frankie Howerd, et al.)	25
67	Brunswick AXA 4544	COUNTESS FROM HONG KONG (Charles Chaplin) (with booklet)	15
70	Capitol E-ST 640	CROMWELL (Frank Cordell)	15
70	Word WST 5550	THE CROSS & THE SWITCHBLADE (Ralph Carmichael)	25
77	EMI EMA 782	CROSS OF IRON (Ernest Gold) (gatefold sleeve)	15
80	CBS 70182	CRUISING (John Hiatt/Willy DeVille/Germs)	18
73	Buddah 2318 091	CURTIS IN CHICAGO (Curtis Mayfield/Impressions/Jerry Butler, Gene Chandler, Leroy Hutson) (TV soundtrack, gatefold sleeve)	15
68	Stateside (S)SL 10222	CUSTER OF THE WEST (Bernardo Segall)	35

D

81	2-Tone CHR TT 5004	DANCE CRAZE (with poster)	20
62	Fontana TFL 5184	DANGEROUS FRIENDSHIPS (Art Blakey, et. al.)	18
70	RCA SF 8138	DARLIN' LILI (Henry Mancini) (gatefold sleeve)	12
63	MGM MGM-C 952	DAVID AND LISA (Mark Lawrence/Victor Feldman All Stars)	15
74	Phase 4 Stereo PFS 4339	THE DAY OF THE LOCUST (John Barry)	12
67	Stateside (S)SL 10217	THE DAY THE FISH CAME OUT (Mikis Theodorakis)	15
68	Stateside (S)SL 10263	DEADFALL (John Barry/Shirley Bassey)	35
73	Columbia SCX 6550	DEAF SMITH AND JOHNNY EARS (Daniele Patucchi)	35
74	CBS 80546	DEATH WISH (Herbie Hancock)	15
68	Stateside (S)SL 10259	DECLINE AND FALL... OF A BIRDWATCHER (Ron Goodwin)	80
55	MGM MGM-C 755	DEEP IN MY HEART (Howard Keel/Vic Damone, et al.)	12
58	London HA-D 2111	DESIRE UNDER THE ELMS (Elmer Bernstein)	20
63	Colpix PXL 440	DIAMOND HEAD (John Williams)	15
76	Pye Intl. NSPL 28219	DIAMOND MERCENARIES (Georges Garvarentz)	15
76	Bradley BRADS 8002	DIAMONDS (Roy Budd)	50
71	United Artists UAS 29216	DIAMONDS ARE FOREVER (John Barry/Shirley Bassey)	20
59	Top Rank RX 3016	THE DIARY OF ANNE FRANK (Alfred Newman)	30
83	Ripple (no cat. no.)	DIGITAL DREAMS (Bill Wyman) (promo only)	50
68	MGM MGM-C(S) 8048	DIRTY DOZEN (Frank de Vol/Trini Lopez) (yellow label)	18
67	Stateside S(S)L 10214	DOCTOR DOLITTLE (Lionel Newman) (foldout sleeve)	12
62	Columbia 33SX 1446	DON'T KNOCK THE TWIST (Chubby Checker/Gene Chandler, et al.)	25
67	RCA Victor SF 7892	DOUBLE TROUBLE (Elvis Presley) (black/red dot labels, stereo) (Mono version RD7892 = £18)	25
67	CBS S 63189	DR. FAUSTUS (Mario Nascimbene)	75
65	United Artists (S)ULP 1097	DOCTOR NO (Monty Norman) (stereo)	40
69	Capitol EST 672	THE DOUBLE DECKERS (TV soundtrack)	30
87	Crammed MTM 14	DOWN BY LAW (John Lurie)	20
74	Studio Two TWO 500	DRACULA (HAMMER PRESENTS?) (Christopher Lee) (gatefold sleeve)	20
70	President PTLS 1068	DRAKE'S DREAM (Paul Jones)	20

			MINT VALUE £
90	Adventure ADVTCD 1001	THE DREAMSTONE (CD, Mike Batt, Ozzy Osbourne, Bonnie Tyler, Joe Brown, etc)	20
59	Parlophone PMCL 1101	DRUMBEAT (Adam Faith/John Barry Seven, et al.)	60
66	United Artists (S)ULP 1141	DUEL AT DIABLO (Neal Hefti)	18
58	Decca LF 1308	THE DUKE WORE JEANS (Tommy Steele) (10")	15
84	Polydor 422 8237-7	DUNE (Toto, 1 track by Brian Eno)	12
00	Trunk/Bonk XXX 1 LP	DEEP THROAT (LP)	40
04	Trunk JBH 011 LP	DAWN OF THE DEAD (LP, 500 only)	30
		E	
58	HMV DLP 1088	EDDIE FOY AND THE SEVEN LITTLE FOYS (10", Bob Hope/James Cagney)	30
54	Brunswick LAT 8040	THE EGYPTIAN (Alfred Newman)	25
67	Columbia S(C)X 6155	EL DORADO (Nelson Riddle)	25
63	Colpix PXL 459	ELIZABETH TAYLOR IN LONDON (John Barry) (stereo) (Mono = £35)	50
69	RCA Victor RD 8011	ELVIS ("TV Special", mono)	15
74	Warner Bros K 56084	EMMANUELLE (Pierre Bachelet)	12
76	Warner Bros K 56231	EMMANUELLE 2 (Francis Lai)	12
57	Vogue Coral LVA 9063	END AS A MAN (Kenyon Hopkins)	30
74	DJM DJLPS 431	ENGLAND MADE ME (John Scott)	12
74	Warner Bros K 46275	ENTER THE DRAGON (Lalo Schifrin)	20
84	Alt. Ten. VIRUS 30	ERASERHEAD (Fats Waller/Peter Ivers/et al.) (with insert)	20
76	EMI EMC 3148	ESCAPE FROM THE DARK (Ron Goodwin)	15
63	Parlophone PMC 1198	THE ESTABLISHMENT (Peter Cook, et al.)	20
83	MCA MCA 70000	E.T. - THE EXTRA TERRESTRIAL (John Williams) (box set, with booklet & poster)	30
67	Brunswick LAT 8678	AN EVENING WITH BORIS KARLOFF AND FRIENDS	40
74	Warner Bros K 56071	THE EXORCIST (Jack Nitzsche, et al.)	20
71	Ember NR 5057	EXPERIENCE - THE ORIGINAL SOUNDTRACK (Jimi Hendrix) (g/fold sleeve)	12
72	Deram SML 1095	EXTREEMS (Tony Klinger & Michael Lyons)	30
		F	
57	Capitol LCT 6139	A FACE IN THE CROWD (Tom Glazer) (10")	20
64	CBS (S)BPG 62277	FALL OF THE ROMAN EMPIRE (Dimitri Tiomkin)	20
67	Decca LK/SKL 4847	THE FAMILY WAY (Paul McCartney/George Martin) (mono/stereo)	100
60	Top Rank 30/003/4/5	FANTASIA (various classical pieces) (3-LP, with book)	30
58	Capitol LCT 6162	A FAREWELL TO ARMS (Mario Nascimbene)	15
67	MGM MGM-C(S) 8053	FAR FROM THE MADDING CROWD (Richard Rodney Bennett)	20
68	London HA-U/SH-U 8358	THE FASTEST GUITAR ALIVE (Roy Orbison)	25
67	Stateside S(S)L 10213	FATHOM (Johnny Dankworth)	40
73	Pye NSPL 18398	FEAR IS THE KEY (Roy Budd)	50
70	United Artists UAS 29118	FELLINI-SATYRICON (Nino Rota)	20
65	Columbia 33SX 1693	FERRY CROSS THE MERSEY (Gerry & Pacemakers/Cilla Black/Fourmost) (also stereo SCX 3544 = £35)	25
63	CBS SBPG 62148	55 DAYS AT PEKING (Dimitri Tiomkin/Andy Williams)	18
66	Columbia SX 6079	FINDERS KEEPERS (Cliff Richard) (with inner sleeve, mono) (stereo SCX 6079 = £15)	15
68	Warner Bros WF(S) 2550	FINIAN'S RAINBOW (Fred Astaire/Petula Clark et al.)	18
57	Brunswick LAT 8194	FIRE DOWN BELOW (Arthur Benjamin)	40
84	MCA MCF 3233	FIRESTARTER (Tangerine Dream)	12
78	United Artists UAS 30181	F-I-S-T (Bill Conti)	12
67	RCA Victor RD/SF 7875	A FISTFUL OF DOLLARS (Ennio Morricone)	20
72	United Artists UAS 29345	A FISTFUL OF DYNAMITE (Ennio Morricone)	40
71	CBS 70091	FIVE EASY PIECES (Tammy Wynette, et al.)	12
65	RCA Victor RD 7723	FLAMING STAR AND SUMMER KISSES (Elvis Presley) (mono only, black labels)	75
85	Heavy Metal HMI PD 29	FLASHPOINT (Tangerine Dream) (picture disc)	20
85	Heavy Metal HMXD 29	FLASHPOINT (Tangerine Dream) (CD, playable [most copies faulty])	50
68	Stateside SSL 10253	A FLEA IN HER EAR (Bronislau Kaper)	12
71	Decca SKL 5093	FLIGHT OF THE DOVES (Roy Budd/Dana)	12
61	Golden Guinea GGL 0092	THE FLINTSTONES (TV soundtrack)	15
62	Brunswick LAT 8392	FLOWER DRUM SONG (Nancy Kwan, et al.) (also stereo STA 3054)	15
64	Ace Of Clubs ACL 1166	FLYING CLIPPER (Riz Ortolani)	15
62	MGM MGM-C 882	THE 4 HORSEMEN OF THE APOCALYPSE (André Previn)	12
65	Ember NR 5029	FOUR IN THE MORNING (John Barry) (mono)	35
74	T. Motown STML 11269	FOXY BROWN (Willie Hutch)	15
66	RCA Victor RD 7793	FRANKIE AND JOHNNY (Elvis Presley) (black/red dot labels, mono) (Stereo SF 7793 = £30)	20
64	Fontana TL 5208	FREEDOM ROAD (Madeleine Bell, et al.) (TV production)	15
71	Paramount SPFL 269	FRIENDS (Elton John)	12
72	Fantasy FAN 9406	FRITZ THE CAT (Bo Diddley/Billie Holiday, et al.)	30
63	United Artists (S)ULP 1052	FROM RUSSIA WITH LOVE (John Barry/Matt Monroe) (mono/stereo)	25
60	London HA-T 2257	THE FUGITIVE KIND (Kenyon Hopkins)	30
67	RCA RD 7860	FUNERAL IN BERLIN (Konrad Elfers/Puppets)	25
63	RCA Victor RD/SF 7609	FUN IN ACAPULCO (Elvis Presley) (black/silver label, mono/stereo)	20
		G	
65	Liberty (S)LBY 1261	GENGHIS KHAN (Dusan Radic) (mono/stereo)	20
56	Vogue Coral LVA 9003	GENTLEMEN MARRY BRUNETTES (Robert Farnon)	30
53	MGM MGM-D 116	GENTLEMEN PREFER BLONDES (Marilyn Monroe, et al.) (10")	100
65	Mercury 20061 MCL	GENTLE RAIN (Luis Bonfa & Deodato)	15
98	Stella STELP 2	GET CHISHOLM! (David Beaumont, et al.)	12
70	RCA SF 8137	GETTING STRAIGHT (Ronald Stein)	15
57	Capitol LCT 6122	GIANT (Dimitri Tiomkin)	15
60	RCA RD 27192	G.I. BLUES (Elvis Presley) (black/silver label, mono) (stereo SF 507 = £25)	15
66	MGM MGM-C(S) 8034	GIRL FROM U.N.C.L.E. (Jerry Goldsmith & Teddy Randazzo)	60
65	RCA Victor RD 7714	GIRL HAPPY (Elvis Presley) (black/red dot labels, mono) (stereo SF 7714 = £30)	20
68	Polydor 583 714	GIRL ON A MOTORCYCLE (Les Reed)	40

			MINT VALUE £
63	RCA Victor RD 7534	GIRLS! GIRLS! GIRLS! (Elvis Presley) (black/silver labels, mono) (Stereo SF 7534 = £35)	15
66	United Artists SULP 1120	THE GLORY GUYS (Riz Ortolani)	30
72	Paramount SPFA 7003	THE GODFATHER (Nino Rota) (gatefold sleeve)	15
75	ABC ABCL 5128	THE GODFATHER - PART 2 (Nino Rota) (gatefold sleeve)	15
58	London HA-T 2125	GOD'S LITTLE ACRE (Elmer Bernstein)	25
72	Mother MO 4001	GOLD (MC5/David McWilliams, et al.)	35
74	Philips 9299 225	GOLD (Elmer Bernstein)	12
73	United Artists UAS 29576	THE GOLDEN VOYAGE OF SINBAD (Miklos Rozsa)	15
64	United Artists ULP 1076	GOLDFINGER (John Barry/Shirley Bassey) (mono) (Stereo, SULP 1076 = £30)	25
67	MGM CS 8056	GONE WITH THE WIND (Max Steiner)	12
64	Decca LK 4673	GONKS GO BEAT (Lulu/Nashville Teens/Graham Bond, et al.)	200
68	United Artists (S)ULP 1197	THE GOOD, THE BAD AND THE UGLY (Ennio Morricone)	15
61	HMV CSD 1386	GOODBYE AGAIN (Georges Auric)	12
65	Stateside SL 10126	GOODBYE CHARLIE (André Previn)	12
69	Warner Bros W(S) 1786	GOODBYE COLUMBUS (Charles Fox/Association)	18
70	DJM DJLPS 408	GOODBYE GEMINI (Christopher Gunning/Peddlers/Jackie Lee)	50
66	MGM MGM-CS 8037	GRAND PRIX (Maurice Jarre)	12
53	HMV ALP 1071	THE GREAT CARUSO (Mario Lanza)	12
63	United Artists (S)ULP 1041	THE GREAT ESCAPE (Elmer Bernstein) (mono/stereo)	15
77	Arista SPARTY 1013	THE GREATEST (Michael Masser/George Benson)	12
65	United Artists SULP 1093	THE GREATEST STORY EVER TOLD (Alfred Newman)	12
65	RCA RD 7759	THE GREAT RACE (Henry Mancini)	12
71	Pye NSPL 18373	GREAT SONGS AND THEMES FROM GREAT FILMS (Roy Budd)	40
75	MCA MCF 2707	THE GREAT WALDO PEPPER (Henry Mancini)	15
68	United Artists SULP 1220	GREAT WESTERN FILM THEMES (Various Artists)	15
70	Polydor 2384 021	GROUPIE GIRL (Opal Butterfly/English Rose, et al.)	40
67	RCA RD/SF 7899	GUNN (Henry Mancini)	18
69	RCA SF 8025	THE GURU (Ustad Vilayet Khan)	12
09	Trunk JBH 032 LP	G SPOTS (LP)	20

H

65	United Artists SULP 1106	THE HALLELUJAH TRAIL (Elmer Bernstein)	15
75	Contour 2870 437	THE HANGED MAN (Bullet) (TV soundtrack)	30
68	United Artists SULP 1204	HANG 'EM HIGH (Dominic Frontiere) (stereo/mono)	15
69	United Artists SULP 1231	HANNIBAL BROOKS (Francis Lai)	30
70	United Artists UAS 29084	THE HAPPY ENDING (Michel Legrand)	20
56	Philips BBL 7100	HAPPY HOLIDAY (Jo Stafford)	15
65	RCA Victor RD 7767	HAREM HOLIDAY (Elvis Presley) (black/red dot labels, mono) (stereo SF 7767 = £25)	18
65	Warner Bros W 1599	HARLOW (Neal Hefti)	25
66	United Artists (S)ULP 1154	HAWAII (Elmer Bernstein)	12
80s	PRT/Chips CHILP 1	HAWK THE SLAYER (Harry Robertson) (gatefold sleeve)	15
68	RCA RD/SF 8051	HEAD (Monkees) (mono/stereo)	90
73	Fantasy FT 516	HEAVY TRAFFIC (Chuck Berry/Sergio Mendes/et al.)	12
72	Reprise K 44168	THE HEIST (Quincy Jones/Little Richard)	15
74	Tamla Motown STML 11260	HELL UP IN HARLEM (Edwin Starr)	15
65	Parlophone PMC 1255	HELP! (Beatles) (1st pressing, with "The Gramophone Co. Ltd" & "Sold In The UK..." label text; mono, with "mono" in outline type on front cover)	90
65	Parlophone PCS 3071	HELP! (Beatles) (1st pressing, with "The Gramophone Co. Ltd" & "Sold In The UK..." label text; stereo, with "stereo" in outline type on front cover)	120
67	United Artists ULP 1186	HERE WE GO ROUND THE MULBERRY BUSH (Spencer Davis/Traffic/Andy Ellison) (mono) (stereo SULP 1186 = £35)	40
59	Capitol T 1160	HEY BOY! HEY GIRL! (Louis Prima/Keely Smith, et al.)	25
62	Columbia 33SX 1421	HEY, LET'S TWIST (Joey Dee, et al.)	20
83	A&R FILM 001	HIGH ROAD TO CHINA (John Barry)	15
70	Columbia SCX 6443	HIS LAND (Cliff Richard/Cliff Barrows)	20
67	United Artists ULP 1161	THE HONEY POT (John Addison)	15
59	London HA-T 2197	THE HORSE SOLDIERS (David Buttolph)	25
59	Philips BBL 7292	HOUSEBOAT (George Duning)	25
62	MGM MGM-C 915/CS 6061	HOW THE WEST WAS WON (Alfred Newman/Debbie Reynolds)	12
87	Silva Screen FILM 041	HOW TO GET AHEAD IN ADVERTISING/WITHNAIL & I	20
65	United Artists (S)ULP 1098	HOW TO MURDER YOUR WIFE (Neal Hefti)	25
68	CBS (S)BPG 63276	HOW TO SAVE A MARRIAGE AND RUIN YOUR LIFE (Michel Legrand/Ray Conniff)	12
72	Atlantic K 40371	HOW TO STEAL A DIAMOND IN FOUR UNEASY LESSONS (Quincy Jones)	15
66	Stateside S(S)L 10187	HOW TO STEAL A MILLION (John Williams)	25
61	Golden Guinea GGL 0069	HUCKLEBERRY HOUND (TV soundtrack)	12
67	RCA Victor RD/SF 7877	HURRY SUNDOWN (Hugo Montenegro)	25

I

69	MGM MGM-C(S) 8101	ICE STATION ZEBRA (Michel Legrand)	12
70	United Artists UAS 29044	IF IT'S TUESDAY THIS MUST BE BELGIUM (Walter Scharf)	15
67	Brunswick LAT/STA 8689	I'LL NEVER FORGET WHAT'S 'ISNAME (Francis Lai)	40
65	United Artists ULP 1105	I'LL TAKE SWEDEN (Bob Hope/Frankie Avalon, et al.)	15
68	RCA Victor RD/SF 7931	IN COLD BLOOD (Quincy Jones)	45
65	RCA RD 7707	IN HARM'S WAY (Jerry Goldsmith)	25
67	Stateside S(S)L 10207	IN LIKE FLINT (Jerry Goldsmith)	50
68	United Artists ULP 1201	INSPECTOR CLOUSEAU (Ken Thorne)	20
69	RCA Victor RD/SF 7990	INTERLUDE (Georges Delarue/Timi Yuro)	15
62	Colpix PXL 427	THE INTERNS (Leith Stevens)	18
67	United Artists (S)ULP 1181	IN THE HEAT OF THE NIGHT (Quincy Jones/Ray Charles)	25
65	CBS BPG 62530	THE IPCRESS FILE (John Barry) (mono only)	30
84	Illuminated JAMS 35	IN THE SHADOW OF THE SUN (Throbbing Gristle)	20
63	United Artists SULP 1051	IRMA LA DOUCE (Andre Previn)	12
66	CBS (S)BPG 62843	IS PARIS BURNING? (Maurice Jarre)	18

			MINT VALUE £
69	Paramount SPFL 256	THE ITALIAN JOB (Quincy Jones/Matt Monro)	100
63	RCA Victor RD 7565	IT HAPPENED AT THE WORLD'S FAIR (Elvis Presley) (black/silver label, mono) (stereo SF 7565 = £35)	18
63	Columbia 33SX 1533	IT'S ALL HAPPENING (Tommy Steele/Shane Fenton, et al.) (also stereo SCX 3486)	15
63	United Artists (S)ULP 1053	IT'S A MAD MAD MAD MAD WORLD (Ernest Gold)	20
62	Columbia 33SX 1412	IT'S TRAD, DAD! (Helen Shapiro/Gene Vincent, et al.)	12
65	Decca LK 4677	I'VE GOTTA HORSE (Billy Fury/Bachelors, et al.)	50
71	CBS 70083	I WALK THE LINE (Johnny Cash)	15
59	London LTZ-T 15160	I WANT TO LIVE (Johnny Mandel)	12
07	Trunk JBH 027 LP	IVOR THE ENGINE & POGLES WOOD (LP)	20

J

57	Capitol LCT 6140	THE JAMES DEAN STORY (Leith Stevens)	25
54	Brunswick LA 8671	JAZZ THEMES FROM "THE WILD ONE" (Leith Stevens) (10")	30
62	HMV CLP 1582	JESSICA (Mario Nascimbene)	15
77	Pye NSPH 28504	JESUS OF NAZARETH (Maurice Jarre) (gatefold sleeve)	15
73	Reprise K 64017	JIMI HENDRIX - SOUNDTRACK RECORDINGS FROM THE FILM (2-LP)	18
71	Mercury 6338 029	JOE (Bobby Scott/Jenny Butler)	20
64	United Artists ULP 1060	JOHNNY COOL (Billy May/Sammy Davis Jr.)	25
72	Reprise K 64015	JOURNEY THROUGH THE PAST (Neil Young) (2-LP, fold-out cover with inner sleeves)	25
77	Polydor/EG 2302 079	JUBILEE (Adam & Ants/Brian Eno, et al.)	20
61	HMV CLP 1545	JUDGEMENT AT NUREMBURG (Ernest Gold)	15
66	RCA RD 7788	JUDITH (Sol Kaplan)	12
67	Fontana (S)TL 5317	JULIET OF THE SPIRITS (Nino Rota)	30
63	Decca LK 4524	JUST FOR FUN (Tornados/Karl Denver, et al.)	40
64	Decca LK 4620	JUST FOR YOU (Applejacks/Merseybeats, et al.)	40
70	Monument LMO/SMO 5031	JUSTINE (Jerry Goldsmith)	15

K

71	MGM 2315 019	KELLY'S HEROES (Lalo Schifrin/Mike Curb)	25
66	United Artists (S)ULP 1139	KHARTOUM (Frank Cordell)	30
72	Polydor 2383 102	KIDNAPPED (Roy Budd/Mary Hopkin)	25
58	RCA RD 27088	KING CREOLE (Elvis Presley) (black/silver labels)	35
76	Reprise K 54090	KING KONG (John Barry) (with poster)	15
61	MGM MGM-CS 6043	KING OF KINGS (Miklos Rozsa)	20
58	Capitol LCT 6165	KINGS GO FORTH (Elmer Bernstein)	15
66	Fontana (S)TL 5302	KING RAT (John Barry)	18
64	RCA Victor RD 7645	KISSIN' COUSINS (Elvis Presley) (black/red dot labels, mono) (stereo SF 7645 = £30)	18
54	MGM MGM-C 753	KISS ME KATE (Howard Keel, et al.)	15
65	United Artists ULP 1104	THE KNACK (AND HOW TO GET IT) (John Barry)	30
54	Brunswick LA 8668	KNOCK ON WOOD (Danny Kaye) (10")	12
69	Stateside (S)SL 10277	KRAKATOA: EAST OF JAVA (Frank De Vol)	12
74	Warner Bros K 46271	KUNG FU (TV soundtrack) (with inner sleeve) (Jim Helms)	20
01	Trunk KES 001 LP	KES (LP - 1-sided)	40

L

61	RCA RD 27202	LA DOLCE VITA (Nino Rota) (gatefold sleeve)	50
63	Ace Of Hearts AH 70	THE LADY AND THE TRAMP (Peggy Lee)	20
69	Stateside S(S)L 10267	LADY IN CEMENT (Hugo Montenegro)	40
71	United Artists UAS 29120	THE LANDLORD (Al Kooper)	20
72	MGM 2315 072	THE LAST RUN (Jerry Goldsmith/Steve Lawrence)	25
80	Charisma CDS 4020	LARK RISE TO CANDLEFORD (A COUNTRY TAPESTRY)	12
73	United Artists UAS 29440	LAST TANGO IN PARIS (Gato Barbieri)	15
71	Probe SPB 1027	THE LAST VALLEY (John Barry) (mono, with insert) (stereo = £25)	18
85	United Artists 86002	LEGEND (Jerry Goldsmith)	25
71	M. F. Pleasure MFP 50034	THE LEGEND OF FRENCHIE KING (Francis Lai)	12
74	Warner Bros K 56085	THE LEGEND OF THE 7 GOLDEN VAMPIRES (James Bernard/Peter Cushing)	18
64	Stateside S(S)L 10058	THE LEOPARD (Nino Rota)	30
70	Apple PXS 1	LET IT BE (Beatles) (LP box set, 1st pressing, dark green label, red Apple logo on LP rear sleeve & white inner, with Get Back book housed in black card tray ['PXS1'] not listed on package)	250
70	Apple PCS 7096	LET IT BE (Beatles) (2nd pressing, green Apple logo on rear sleeve, plain white inner)	20
60	Philips BBL 7414/SBBL 592	LET'S MAKE LOVE (Marilyn Monroe/Yves Montand/Frankie Vaughan)	40
79	Warner Bros K 56751	LIFE OF BRIAN (Monty Python) (with inner sleeve)	12
64	Columbia SX 1626	LILIES OF THE FIELD (Jerry Goldsmith)	20
69	CBS 70049	THE LION IN WINTER (John Barry)	15
66	MGM MGM-CS 8029	THE LIQUIDATOR (Lalo Schifrin/Shirley Bassey)	40
73	United Artists UAS 29475	LIVE AND LET DIE (George Martin/Wings) (gatefold sleeve)	25
87	Warner Bros 925 616-1	THE LIVING DAYLIGHTS (John Barry)	12
76	MGM 2315 376	LOGAN'S RUN (Jerry Goldsmith)	25
62	MGM MGM-C 896	LOLITA (Nelson Riddle)	25
67	Polydor 583 014	LONG DUEL (Patrick John Scott/Vince Hill)	20
63	Stateside S(S)L 10045	THE LONGEST DAY (dialogue only)	20
83	CES CES 1001	THE LONG GOOD FRIDAY (Francis Monkman) (numbered sleeve with insert, black label print, 2,000 only)	60
83	CES CES 1001	THE LONG GOOD FRIDAY (Francis Monkman) (re-pressing, with insert, blue label print, 500 only)	50
84	CES CES 1001	THE LONG GOOD FRIDAY (Francis Monkman) (3rd pressing, with insert, blue label print, 5,000 only)	40
89	Silva Screen FILM 020	THE LONG GOOD FRIDAY (Francis Monkman) (reissue)	20
89	Silva Screen FILM 020	THE LONG GOOD FRIDAY (Francis Monkman) (CD)	25
70	CBS 70073	LOOT (Keith Mansfield/Steve Ellis)	50

			MINT VALUE £
65	Colpix PXL 521	LORD JIM (Bronislau Kaper)	15
69	Uni UNLS 103	LOST MAN (Quincy Jones)	25
70	CBS 70067	LOVE CIRCLE (Ennio Morricone)	50
57	RCA RC 24001	LOVING YOU (Elvis Presley) (10", silver spot label)	90

M

73	Tamla Motown STMA 8003	THE MACK (Willie Hutch)	15
69	RCA Victor SF 8017	MACKENNA'S GOLD (Quincy Jones/Jose Feliciano)	12
69	Warner Bros WS 1805	THE MADWOMAN OF CHAILLOT (Michael Lewis)	15
70	Pye Intl. NSPL 28133	THE MAGIC CHRISTIAN (Ken Thorne/Badfinger, et al.)	40
54	Brunswick LAT 8045	MAGNIFICENT OBSESSION (Frank Skinner)	30
65	MGM MGM-C 995	THE MAGNIFICENT SHOWMAN (Dimitri Tiomkin)	25
76	Atlantic K 50308	MAHONEY'S LAST STAND (Ronnie Lane & Ron Wood)	15
63	Ace Of Clubs ACL 1135	MAIGRET (Ron Grainer) (TV series music)	15
66	CBS SBPG 62525	MAJOR DUNDEE (Daniele Amfitheatrof/Mitch Miller)	15
67	United Artists SULP 1155	A MAN AND A WOMAN (Francis Lai)	12
66	Brunswick LAT/STA 8651	A MAN COULD GET KILLED (Bert Kaempfert)	15
67	RCA RB 6712/3	A MAN FOR ALL SEASONS (2-LP, dialogue only)	15
59	Top Rank 35/043	MAN FROM INTERPOL (Tony Crombie) (TV series music)	25
66	RCA Victor RD 7758	THE MAN FROM U.N.C.L.E. (Hugo Montenegro)	40
64	Stateside S(S)L 10087	MAN IN THE MIDDLE (Lionel Bart & John Barry)	30
56	Brunswick LAT 8101	THE MAN WITH THE GOLDEN ARM (Elmer Bernstein)	20
74	United Artists UAS 29671	THE MAN WITH THE GOLDEN GUN (John Barry/Lulu)	15
63	Stateside S(S)L 10048	MARILYN (Marilyn Monroe) (mono/stereo)	40
72	MCA MUPS 441	MARY QUEEN OF SCOTS (John Barry)	20
70	United Artists UAS 29122	MASTER OF THE ISLANDS (Henry Mancini)	15
69	Philips SBL 7876	MAYERLING (Francis Lai)	20
64	United Artists SULP 1059	McLINTOCK (Frank De Vol)	35
80	Polydor POLD 5034	McVICAR (Roger Daltrey) (some on clear vinyl)	15
71	Polydor 2383 043	MELODY (Bee Gees, Richard Hewson, et al.)	15
69	CBS 70061	ME, NATALIE (Henry Mancini/Rod McKuen)	12
57	London HA-P 2076	MEN IN WAR (Elmer Bernstein)	15
69	Bell BELL 6053	MERRY CHRISTMAS (David Frost/Billy Taylor)	20
65	MGM MGM-C 8001	MICKEY ONE (Stan Getz & Eddie Sauter) (with booklet, mono) (stereo MGM-CS 8001 = £25)	20
66	Mercury 20072 (S)MCL	MIRAGE (Quincy Jones)	25
61	HMV CLP 1481	THE MISFITS (Alex North)	25
68	Dot (S)LPD 503	MISSION: IMPOSSIBLE - MUSIC FROM THE TV SERIES (Lalo Schifrin)	40
54	Mercury 25181	MISS SADIE THOMPSON (George Duning) (10")	30
66	Fontana TL 5347	MODESTY BLAISE (Johnny Dankworth)	40
70	Paramount SPFL 259	THE MOLLY MAGUIRES (Henry Mancini)	15
80	BBC REB 384	MONKEY (Godiego) (TV soundtrack)	25
69	Paramount SPFL 255	MONTE CARLO OR BUST! (Ron Goodwin)	40
79	United Artists UAG 30247	MOONRAKER (John Barry/Shirley Bassey)	15
69	Columbia SCX 6346	MORE (Pink Floyd) (laminated flipback sleeve, 'couple facing west' photo on green-tinted rear sleeve)	50
70s	Columbia SCX 6346	MORE (Pink Floyd) (laminated non-flipback sleeve, 'couple facing west' photo on black-tinted rear sleeve)	45
70s	Columbia SCX 6346	MORE (Pink Floyd) (laminated non-flipback sleeve, 'couple facing east' photo on black-tinted rear sleeve)	50
72	Ember NR 5061	MORE EXPERIENCE (Jimi Hendrix)	12
69	Paramount SPFL 252	MORE 'MISSION: IMPOSSIBLE' (Lalo Schifrin)	40
60	MGM MGM-C(S) 857	MORE MUSIC FROM BEN-HUR (Miklos Rozsa)	15
66	RCA Victor RD 7832	MORE MUSIC FROM 'THE MAN FROM U.N.C.L.E.' (Hugo Montenegro)	45
62	MGM	MORE MUSIC FROM 'MUTINY ON THE BOUNTY' (Bronislau Kaper)	20
68	MGM CS8063	MORE THAN A MIRACLE (Piero Piccioni)	15
65	Columbia SX 6303	MRS BROWN YOU'VE GOT A LOVELY DAUGHTER (Hermans Hermits, mono, some with manuscript) (stereo SCX 6303 = £15)	12
67	RCA RD 7847	MURDERERS' ROW (Lalo Schifrin)	75
80	Unicorn Kachana KPM 7009	MUSIC FROM THE AVENGERS, THE NEW AVENGERS AND THE PROFESSIONALS	20
70	Harvest SHSP 4008	MUSIC FROM THE BODY (Ron Geesin & Roger Waters) (photos/green labels)	40
62	MGM MGM-CS 6060	MUTINY ON THE BOUNTY (Bronislau Kaper)	20
85	Cloud Nine CN 4002	MYSTERIOUS ISLAND (Bernard Herrman)	25

N

70	United Artists UAS 29108	NED KELLY (Shel Silverstein/Mick Jagger/Waylon Jennings)	35
72	Bell BELLS 202	NICHOLAS AND ALEXANDRA (Richard Rodney Bennet)	15
67	RCA RD 7848	NIGHT OF THE GENERALS (Maurice Jarre)	30
65	MGM MGM-C 994	NIGHT OF THE IGUANA (Benjamin Frankel)	15
69	United Artists (S)ULP 1235	THE NIGHT THEY RAIDED MINSKY'S (Charles Strouse)	20
62	Decca LK 4527	NINE HOURS TO RAMA (Malcolm Arnold)	100
68	Dot (S)LPD 507	NO WAY TO TREAT A LADY (American Breed)	20

O

72	Harvest SHSP 4020	OBSCURED BY CLOUDS (Pink Floyd) (rounded sleeve)	25
76	Phase 4 Stereo PF5 4381	OBSESSION (Bernard Herrman)	20
83	A&M AMLX 64967	OCTOPUSSY (John Barry/Rita Coolidge)	12
83	A&M 394 967-2	OCTOPUSSY (John Barry) (CD, withdrawn)	75
68	Dot (S)LPD 514	THE ODD COUPLE (Neal Hefti)	30
60	London HA-T 2220	ODDS AGAINST TOMORROW (John Lewis)	12
64	Stateside S(S)L 10056	OF LOVE AND DESIRE (Ronald Stein)	12
69	Paramount SPFL 251	OH! WHAT A LOVELY WAR (Alfred Ralston, et al.) (gatefold sleeve)	12
70	Starline SRS 5019	OLIVER IN THE OVERWORLD (Freddie Garrity)	12
57	Brunswick LAT 8226	OMAR KHAYYAM/THE MOUNTAIN (Victor Young/Daniele Amfitheatrof)	30
75	Fantasy FTA 3004	ONE FLEW OVER THE CUCKOO'S NEST (Jack Nitzsche) (gatefold sleeve)	15
69	United Artists UAS 29020	ON HER MAJESTY'S SECRET SERVICE (John Barry) (foldout sleeve)	40
59	Columbia 33SX 1208	ON THE BEACH (Ernest Gold)	12

			MINT VALUE £
70	Fontana SFJL 950	ORFEU NEGRO (BLACK ORPHEUS) (Luis Bonfa/Antonio Carlos Jobim)	15
69	RCA SF 8014	OTLEY (Stanley Myers/Don Partridge)	25
66	Stateside S(S)L 10174	OUR MAN FLINT (Jerry Goldsmith)	50
76	Warner Bros K 56286	THE OUTLAW JOSEY WALES (Jerry Fielding)	25
		P	
63	Warner Bros WM 8141	PALM SPRINGS WEEKEND (Frank Perkins)	20
74	EMI EMC 3020	PAPILLON (Jerry Goldsmith)	12
66	RCA Victor SF 7810	PARADISE, HAWAIIAN STYLE (Elvis Presley) (black/red dot labels, mono) (stereo SF 7810 = £30)	20
61	HMV CLP 1499	PARIS BLUES (Duke Ellington)	15
61	Warner Bros WS 8044	PARRISH (Max Steiner/George Creely)	20
70	Stateside SSL 10302	PATTON (Jerry Goldsmith)	12
65	Mercury 20063 SML	THE PAWNBROKER (Quincy Jones)	30
66	Philips (S)BL 7782	THE PEKING MEDALLION (Georges Garvarentz/Dusty Springfield)	20
67	Ember NR 5040	THE PENTHOUSE (John Hawksworth)	40
71	Pye NSPL 18365	PERCY (Kinks)	40
70	Warner Bros WS 2554	PERFORMANCE (First pressing, orange label, Mick Jagger/ Jack Nitzsche/Randy Newman, et al.)	45
71	CBS 64816	THE PERSUADERS (John Barry)	12
59	RCA RD 27123/SF 5033	PETER GUNN (Henry Mancini)	15
55	Philips BBL 7059	PETE KELLY'S BLUES (Sammy Cahn, Matty Matlock, et al.)	12
61	Ace Of Hearts AH 26	PETE KELLY'S BLUES (Peggy Lee, Ella Fitzgerald)	12
79	Gem GEM 102	PHANTASM (Fred Myrow & Malcolm Seagrave)	20
62	United Artists ULP 1016	PHAEDRA (Mikis Theodorakis)	12
56	Brunswick LAT 8120	PICNIC (George Duning)	20
68	Philips SBL 7858	PLAYTIME (Jacques Tati, Yan Tatore, Leo Petit)	35
70	Paramount SPFL 258	POOKIE (Fred Karlin/Sandpipers)	15
57	Capitol LCT 6141	THE PRIDE AND THE PASSION (Georges Antheil)	15
86	Bam Caruso WEBA 066	THE PRISONER (Ron Grainer, et al.) (fan club issue, gatefold sleeve with inner sleeve, booklet, membership form, map & poster)	40
66	HMV CLP/CSD 3623	PRIVILEGE (Paul Jones & Mike Leander)	30
69	RCA SF 8072	THE PRODUCERS (John Morris)	15
69	United Artists UAS 29005	A PROFESSIONAL GUN (Ennio Morricone)	25
67	RCA Victor RD/SF 7876	THE PROFESSIONALS (Maurice Jarre)	50
60	Contemporary LAC 12293	THE PROPER TIME (Shelly Manne)	15
68	Stateside S(S)L 10248	PRUDENCE AND THE PILL (Bernard Ebbinghouse)	25
75	Unicorn RHS 336	PSYCHO (Bernard Herrmann)	20
02	Trunk JBH002LP	PSYCHOMANIA	40
70	Warner Bros WS 2554	PERFORMANCE (Second pressing, green label, Mick Jagger/ Jack Nitzsche/Randy Newman, et al.)	35
		Q	
71	Sonet SNTF 622	QUIET DAYS IN CLICHY (Country Joe McDonald)	15
66	CBS (S)BPG 62869	THE QUILLER MEMORANDUM (John Barry/Matt Monro) (mono)	15
		R	
88	Silva Screen FILM 033	THE RAGGEDY RAWNEY (Michael Kamen)	12
71	Reprise K 44159	RAINBOW BRIDGE (Jimi Hendrix) (matt gatefold sleeve, 'steamboat' label)	20
75	Dart ARTS 65376	RANSOM (Jerry Goldsmith)	40
60	London HAD 2288	THE RAT RACE (Sam Butera & The Witnesses)	25
67	United Artists (S)ULP 1184	RED AND BLUE (Vanessa Redgrave)	40
72	Paramount SPFL 275	THE RED TENT (Ennio Morricone)	15
70	CBS 70068	THE REIVERS (John Williams)	12
76	United Artists UAS 30007	THE RETURN OF A MAN CALLED HORSE (Laurence Rosenthal)	12
75	RCA Red Seal RS 1010	THE RETURN OF THE PINK PANTHER (Henry Mancini)	15
69	United Artists ULP 1226	REVOLUTION (Quicksilver Messenger Service/Steve Miller, et al.)	20
70	United Artists UAS 29137	RIDER IN THE RAIN (Francis Lai)	20
68	MGM MGM-C(S) 8079	THE RISE AND FALL OF THE THIRD REICH (Lalo Schifrin)	28
53	Brunswick LA 8578	ROAD TO BALI (Bob Hope, Bing Crosby) (10")	30
62	Decca LKR 4427	THE ROAD TO HONG KONG (Robert Farnon/Bob Hope & Bing Crosby)	20
54	Brunswick LAT 8031	THE ROBE	15
67	Decca LK/SKL 4892	ROBBERY (Johnny Keating/Jackie Lee)	30
64	Reprise R 2021	ROBIN AND THE SEVEN HOODS (Nelson Riddle)	20
61	RCA RD 27233	ROCCO AND HIS BROTHERS (Nino Rota)	20
57	Mercury MPT 7527	ROCK ALL NIGHT (Platters, Norah Hayes, et al.) (10")	175
67	Polydor 583 013	JULES VERNE'S ROCKET TO THE MOON (John Scott)	100
57	Brunswick LAT 8162	ROCK, PRETTY BABY (Henry Mancini/Rod McKuen)	90
87	Ode RHVX 1	ROCKY HORROR BOX SET (Richard O'Brien) (4-LP box, with inserts, numbered)	20
87	Ode RHBXLP 1	ROCKY HORROR BOX SET (Richard O'Brien) (4-LP box, with different inserts to above)	20
75	Ode ODE 78332	THE ROCKY HORROR PICTURE SHOW (Richard O'Brien) (Original Soundtrack)	12
83	Ode OSVP 78332	THE ROCKY HORROR PICTURE SHOW ALBUM (picture disc)	15
87	Ode OSVP 21653	THE ROCKY HORROR PICTURE SHOW ALBUM (reissue, picture disc)	15
90	Ode RHBXCD 1	THE ROCKY HORROR PICTURE SHOW - 15TH ANNIVERSARY (Richard O'Brien, et al.) (4-CD box)	40
75	United Artists UAS 29865	ROLLERBALL (Andre Previn)	12
77	MCA MCF 2813	ROLLERCOASTER (Lalo Schifrin/Sparks)	12
68	Dot (S)LPD 519	ROSEMARY'S BABY (Kryzstophe Komeda)	40
65	Parlophone PMC 1262	ROTTEN TO THE CORE (New Jazz Voices)	20
64	RCA Victor RD 7678	ROUSTABOUT (Elvis Presley) (black/red dot labels, mono) (stereo SF 7678 = £25)	15
64	Capitol (S)T 1771	ROUTE 66 AND OTHER GREAT T.V. THEMES (Nelson Riddle) (TV show)	15
66	United Artists ULP 1147	THE RUSSIANS ARE COMING THE RUSSIANS ARE COMING (Johnny Mandel)	15
71	MGM 2315 028	RYAN'S DAUGHTER (Maurice Jarre) (gatefold sleeve)	12

MINT VALUE £

S

72	RCA SF 8211	SACCO AND VANZETTI (Ennio Morricone/Joan Baez)	12
53	Brunswick LA 8604	SALOMÉ (George Duning) (10")	50
68	United Artists SULP 1202	SALT AND PEPPER (Johnny Dankworth/Sammy Davis Jr)	15
67	Stateside S(S)L 10198	THE SAND PEBBLES (Jerry Goldsmith)	12
65	Mercury MCL 20065	THE SANDPIPER (Johnny Mandel)	15
68	United Artists (S)ULP 1190	THE SCALPHUNTERS (Elmer Bernstein)	15
78	Polydor 2480 429	SCOUSE THE MOUSE (Ringo Starr/Adam Faith, et al.) (some w/stickered sleeve & printed [not photocopied] competition insert)	130
78	Polydor 3194 429	SCOUSE THE MOUSE (Ringo Starr/Adam Faith, et al.) (cassette)	30
70	CBS 70077	SCROOGE (Leslie Bricusse) (musical, gatefold sleeve)	12
80	EMI EMC 3340	THE SEA WOLVES (Roy Budd/Matt Monroe)	12
62	Reprise R 2013	SERGEANTS 3 (Billy May)	30
73	Paramount SPFL 296	SERPICO (Mikis Theodorakis)	25
64	United Artists ULP 1072	THE 7th DAWN (Riz Ortolani)	15
74	United Artists UAS 29763	THE SEVENTH VOYAGE OF SINBAD (Bernard Hermann)	20
71	Stax 2659 007	SHAFT - ORIGINAL SOUNDTRACK (Isaac Hayes) (2-LP, gatefold sleeve)	15
73	Probe SPB 1077	SHAFT IN AFRICA (Johnny Pate/Four Tops)	30
72	MGM 2315 115	SHAFT'S BIG SCORE! (Gordon Parks/O.C. Smith/Isaac Hayes)	35
66	CBS BPG 62755	SHAKESPEARE WALLAH (Satyajit Ray)	15
68	Philips SBL 7867	SHALAKO (Robert Farnon)	15
80	Warner Bros K 56827	THE SHINING (Bela Bartok et al.)	25
69	MGM MGM-CS 8103	SHOES OF THE FISHERMAN (Alex North)	12
70	Stateside SSL 10307	THE SICILIAN CLAN (Ennio Morricone)	20
72	MCA MUPS 458	SILENT RUNNING (Pete Schikele/Joan Baez)	18
66	RCA RD 7792	THE SILENCERS (Elmer Bernstein/Vikki Carr)	30
58	Capitol T 929	SING, BOY, SING (Tommy Sands)	50
56	MGM D 140	SINGIN' IN THE RAIN/EASTER PARADE (Gene Kelly/Judy Garland) (10")	12
66	MGM MGM-C(S) 8011	THE SINGING NUN (Debbie Reynolds)	15
78	Charisma CAS 1139	SIR HENRY AT RAWLINSON END (Vivian Stanshall) (with insert)	20
64	United Artists ULP 1071	633 SQUADRON (Ron Goodwin)	20
69	RCA SF 8010	SKIDOO (Nilsson)	25
74	Polydor 2442 126	SLADE IN FLAME (Slade)	12
73	Polydor 2391 084	SLAUGHTER'S BIG RIP-OFF (James Brown)	30
66	Mercury MCL 20080	THE SLENDER THREAD (Quincy Jones)	20
73	CBS 70127	SLEUTH (John Addison)	12
69	NEMS 6-70059	THE SMASHING BIRD I USED TO KNOW (Bobby Richards)	20
68	Stateside S(S)L 10224	SMASHING TIME (John Addison)	30
73	PRT FBLP 8085	SMIKE	15
56	Pye Disneyland DPL 39003	SNOW WHITE AND THE SEVEN DWARFS (Disney Orchestra)	30
61	Philips BBL 7504	SNOW WHITE AND THE THREE STOOGES (Harry Harris)	12
70	Pye NSPL 18348	SOLDIER BLUE AND OTHER THEMES (Roy Budd)	40
60	London HA-T 2221	SOLOMON AND SHEBA (Mario Nascimbene)	75
59	Capitol LCT 6180	SOME CAME RUNNING (Elmer Bernstein)	18
59	London HA-T 2176	SOME LIKE IT HOT (Marilyn Monroe) (also stereo SAH-T 6040 = £80)	60
83	Liberty UASP 30226	SOME LIKE IT HOT (Marilyn Monroe) (picture disc)	15
67	RCA RD 7845	SONGS FROM THE SWINGER (Marty Paich/Ann-Margret)	30
74	Rapple/RCA APL1-0220	SON OF DRACULA (Ringo Starr/Harry Nilsson, fold-out sleeve)	15
65	CBS (S)BPG 62558	THE SONS OF KATIE ELDER (LP, mono, Elmer Bernstein/ Johnny Cash) (stereo SBPG 62558 = £25)	20
73	CBS 70123	SOUNDER (Taj Mahal)	12
69	RCA Victor SF 8024	THE SOUTHERN STAR (Matt Monro/Georges Garvarentz)	15
58	London HA-D 2079	SPANISH AFFAIR (Daniele Amfitheatrof)	50
61	Brunswick LAT 8363	SPARTACUS (Alex North) (gatefold sleeve)	20
68	RCA Victor SF 7957	SPEEDWAY (Elvis Presley/Nancy Sinatra) (black/red dot labels, mono) (stereo SF 7957 = £50)	30
53	Capitol CCL 7505	SPELLBOUND/THE RED HOUSE (Miklos Rosza) (10")	25
66	RCA RD 7787	THE SPY WHO CAME IN FROM THE COLD (Sol Kaplan)	20
77	United Artists UAG 30098	THE SPY WHO LOVED ME (Marvin Hamlisch/Carly Simon) (gatefold sleeve)	12
68	CBS 62919	THE SPY WITH THE COLD NOSE (Riz Ortolani)	35
66	Fontana TL 5354	STAGECOACH (Jerry Goldsmith)	25
79	CBS 70174	STAR TREK - THE MOTION PICTURE (Jerry Goldsmith)	12
77	20th C. BTD 541	STAR WARS (John Williams) (2-LP, with insert)	15
69	CBS 70062	STILETTO (Sid Ramin)	30
52	Capitol LC 6542	A STREET CAR NAMED DESIRE (Alex North) (10")	50
61	MGM MGM-C 864	THE SUBTERRANEANS (André Previn)	12
63	Columbia 33SX 1472	SUMMER HOLIDAY (Cliff Richard) (with inner sleeve, mono)	12
63	Columbia SCX 3462	SUMMER HOLIDAY (Cliff Richard) (first pressing, stereo, with inner sleeve, with green labels)	25
57	London HA-R 2077	THE SUN ALSO RISES (Hugo Friedhofer)	25
70	Avco Embassy 6466 002	SUNFLOWER (Henry Mancini)	12
55	HMV DLP 1104	SUN VALLEY SERENADE (Glenn Miller)	15
62	Golden Guinea GGL 0106	SUPERCAR - FLIGHT OF FANCY (Barry Gray/Edwin Astley)	60
72	Buddah 2318 065	SUPERFLY (Curtis Mayfield) (gatefold sleeve)	15
73	Buddah 2318 087	SUPER FLY T.N.T. (Osibisa)	15
64	Stateside SL 10089	SURF PARTY (Astronauts, Routers, et al.)	50
79	EMI EMC 3222	SUSPIRIA (Goblin)	40
69	MCA MUCS 133	SWEET CHARITY (Shirley MacLaine, et al.)	15
57	Brunswick LAT 8195	SWEET SMELL OF SUCCESS (Elmer Bernstein)	20
68	Stateside S(S)L 10250	THE SWEET RIDE (Pete Rugolo/Dusty Springfield)	15
68	CBS 70043	THE SWIMMER (Marvin Hamlisch)	25
65	MGM MGM-C 8012	THE SWINGIN' SET (Dave Clark Five/Animals, et al.)	30

			MINT VALUE £
66	Mercury 20057 SMCL	SYLVIA (David Raksin)	15
63	Columbia SCX 3462	SUMMER HOLIDAY (Cliff Richard) (second pressing, stereo, with blue/black labels)	18
		T	
70	Pye NSPL 18353	TAKE A GIRL LIKE YOU (Stanley Myers/Foundations)	30
73	EMI EMC 3016	TAKE ME HIGH (Cliff Richard) (some with poster)	20
67	RCA RB 6711	THE TAMING OF THE SHREW (dialogue only) (with insert)	12
57	Vogue Coral LVA 9070	TAMMY/INTERLUDE (Frank Skinner/Debbie Reynolds) (1 film per side)	30
63	United Artists ULP 1025	TARAS BULBA (Franz Waxman)	25
76	Arista ARTY 132	TAXI DRIVER (Bernard Herrman)	25
69	T. Motown (S)TML 11110	T.C.B. (Supremes/Temptations, et al.) (laminated gatefold sleeve)	12
58	London HA-D 2074-5	THE TEN COMMANDMENTS (Elmer Bernstein) (2-LP)	25
71	RCA Victor SF 8162	THAT'S THE WAY IT IS (Elvis Presley) (glossy or matt sleeve)	15
63	Parlophone PMC 1197	THAT WAS THE WEEK THAT WAS (Millicent Martin, et al.) (also stereo PCS 3040)	15
59	Coral LVA 9102	THEMES FROM HORROR MOVIES (Dick Jacobs)	15
70	United Artists UAS 29128	THEY CALL ME MISTER TIBBS (Quincy Jones)	60
69	Philips SBL 7898	THEY CAME TO ROB LAS VEGAS (Georges Gavarentz)	60
70	Stateside SSL 10305	THEY SHOOT HORSES, DON'T THEY? (John Green)	15
73	Elektra K 46239	THE THIEF WHO CAME TO DINNER (Henry Mancini)	15
82	MCA MCF 3148	THE THING (Ennio Morricone)	12
66	Verve VLP 9147	THIS PROPERTY IS CONDEMNED (Kenyon Hopkins)	35
68	United Artists SULP 1218	THE THOMAS CROWN AFFAIR (Michel Legrand/Noel Harrison)	35
68	Sunset SLS 50519	THE THOMAS CROWN AFFAIR (Michel Legrand, reissue)	20
65	Stateside SL 10136	THOSE MAGNIFICENT MEN IN THEIR FLYING MACHINES (Ron Goodwin)	20
54	Capitol LC 6665	THREE SAILORS AND A GIRL (Gordon MacRae, et al.) (10")	30
61	Golden Guinea GGL 0065	THREE WORLDS OF GULLIVER (Bernard Herrmann)	20
85	Cloud Nine CN 4003	THREE WORLDS OF GULLIVER (Bernard Herrmann) (reissue)	15
65	United Artists (S)ULP 1110	THUNDERBALL (John Barry) (mono/stereo)	25
67	United Artists (S)ULP 1159	THUNDERBIRDS ARE GO! (Barry Gray/ Cliff Richard & Shadows) (mono) (stereo = £120)	100
66	NPL 18154	TILL DEATH US DO PART (Warren Mitchell et al.)	15
69	Polydor 583 717	TILL DEATH DO US PART (Wilfred Burns)	15
72	RCA SF 8253	TIME FOR LOVING (Michel Legrand/Dusty Springfield, et al.)	12
63	MGM MGM-C 934	TO KILL A MOCKINGBIRD (Elmer Bernstein)	12
64	United Artists SULP 1062	TOM JONES (John Addison)	12
59	MGM MGM-C 772	TOM THUMB (Russ Tamblyn)	15
68	Instant INLP 002	TONITE LET'S ALL MAKE LOVE IN LONDON (Pink Floyd/Chris Farlowe, et al.)	100
70	RCA LSA 3008	TOOMORROW (with insert)	80
67	Fontana (S)TL 5446	TO SIR, WITH LOVE (Ron Grainer/ Lulu/Mindbenders)	35
69	Stateside S(S)L 10271	THE TOUCHABLES (Ken Thorne/Nirvana/Wynder K. Frog, et al.)	35
66	Polydor 582 004	THE TRAP (Ron Goodwin)	40
60	Pye Nonesuch PPLD 206	THE TRIAL OF LADY CHATTERLEY (drama/documentary)	12
67	United Artists ULP 1176	TRIPLE CROSS (Georges Garvarentz/Tony Allen)	25
82	CBS 70223	TRON (Wendy Carlos/Journey)	15
73	T. Motown STML 11225	TROUBLE MAN (Marvin Gaye)	20
74	Stax STXD 4001/2	TRUCK TURNER (Isaac Hayes) (2-LP)	15
70	Capitol E-ST 263	TRUE GRIT (Elmer Bernstein/Glen Campbell)	15
69	Polydor 583 728	TWISTED NERVE/LES BICYCLETTES DE BELSIZE (Les Reed/Barry Mason, Bernard Herrman)	100
69	Columbia S(C)X 6330	TWO CITIES (Jeff Wayne)	30
67	RCA RD/SF 7891	TWO FOR THE ROAD (Henry Mancini)	15
63	United Artists ULP 1027	TWO FOR THE SEESAW (André Previn)	15
71	United Artists UDF 50003	200 MOTELS (Frank Zappa) (2-LP, with booklet & poster)	35
70	MCA MKPS 2013	TWO MULES FOR SISTER SARA (Ennio Morricone)	30
62	Columbia 33SX 1482	TWO TICKETS TO PARIS (Joey Dee)	20
06	Trunk JBH 017 LP	THE TOMORROW PEOPLE (LP)	20
		U	
04	Trunk JBHO10LP	UFO (500 black/500 clear vinyl)	40
60	London HA-T 2258	THE UNFORGIVEN (Dimitri Tiomkin)	18
68	Fontana (S)TL 5460	UP THE JUNCTION (Manfred Mann)	50
70	Fontana 6852 005	UP THE JUNCTION (Manfred Mann) (reissue)	25
69	Stax (S)XATS 1005	UPTIGHT (Booker T & MGs)	15
		V	
73	Philips 6303 075	THE VALACHI PAPERS (Riz Ortolani)	25
68	Stateside (S)SL 10228	VALLEY OF THE DOLLS (André Previn/John Williams)	20
71	London SH-U 8420	VANISHING POINT (Delaney & Bonnie/Sam & Dave, et al.)	20
82	MGM 2315 437	VICTOR, VICTORIA (Henry Mancini)	15
63	Colpix PXL 516	THE VICTORS (Sol Kaplan/Frank Sinatra)	15
59	RCA SF 5092	VICTORY AT SEA (Richard Rogers)	12
85	Parlophone BOND 1	A VIEW TO A KILL (John Barry/Duran Duran)	12
58	London HAT 2118	THE VIKINGS (Mario Nascimbene)	40
68	Dot (S)LPD 515	VILLA RIDES (Maurice Jarre)	15
63	MGM MGM-C 951/CS 6074	THE VIPs (Miklos Rozsa)	20
66	United Artists (S)ULP 1126	VIVA MARIA! (Georges Delerue) (mono/stereo)	30
67	United Artists (S)ULP 1185	VIVRE POUR VIVRE (LIFE FOR LIFE) (Francis Lai)	12
		W	
60	Mercury MMC 14033	WAGON TRAIN (Stanley Wilson, et al.)	25
62	MGM MGM-C 891	WALK ON THE WILD SIDE (Elmer Bernstein)	15
66	Brunswick STA 8636	THE WAR LORD (Jerome Moross)	35
85	London YEAR 2	WATER	12
78	Satril SATL 4009	THE WATER MARGIN (Godiego) (TV soundtrack)	20

			MINT VALUE £
67	United Artists ULP 1173	THE WAY WEST (Bromislaw Kaper/Serendipity Singers)	12
67	Virtuoso TPLS 13010	WELLES RAISES KANE (Bernard Herrman)	30
64	Piccadilly N(S)PL 38011	WHAT A CRAZY WORLD (Joe Brown/Susan Maughan/Marty Wilde; mono/stereo)	22
64	Golden Guinea GGL 0272	WHAT A CRAZY WORLD (Joe Brown/Susan Maughan/Marty Wilde) (reissue)	12
64	Stateside SL 10090	WHAT A WAY TO GO! (Nelson Riddle)	12
66	RCA SF 7818	WHAT DID YOU DO IN THE WAR, DADDY? (Henry Mancini)	15
65	United Artists ULP 1096	WHAT'S NEW PUSSYCAT? (Burt Bacharach/Tom Jones/Manfred Mann, et al.)	20
66	MGM MGM-C(S) 8006	WHEN THE BOYS MEET THE GIRLS (Connie Francis/ Herman's Hermits) (mono/stereo)	15
69	MGM MGM-C(S) 8102	WHERE EAGLES DARE (Ron Goodwin)	12
69	Paramount SPFL 254	WHERE'S JACK? (Elmer Bernstein/Mary Hopkin)	12
66	United Artists (S)ULP 1166	WHIPLASH WILLIE (André Previn)	15
67	United Artists (S)ULP 1168	THE WHISPERERS (John Barry)	20
67	Warner Bros W 1656	WHO'S AFRAID OF VIRGINIA WOOLF? (Alex North)	25
98	Trunk BARKED 4	THE WICKER MAN (Giovanni) (2nd pressing, red vinyl with inserts)	60
57	London HA-N 2023	WILD BILL HICKOCK AND JINGLES ON THE SANTA FE TRAIL (TV s/track)	18
69	Warner Bros WS 1814	THE WILD BUNCH (Jerry Fielding) (red label original)	50
71	Warner Bros K 46035	THE WILD BUNCH (Jerry Fielding) (reissue)	15
78	A&M AMLH 64730	THE WILD GEESE (Roy Budd/Joan Armatrading)	15
68	Capitol (S)T 5099	WILD IN THE STREETS (Les Baxter/Gurus) (original issue, black label, rainbow rim)	25
71	MGM 2315 062	WILD ROVERS (Jerry Goldsmith)	20
83	Chrysalis CHR 1453	WILD STYLE (various artists)	20
71	Paramount SPFL 274	WILLY WONKA AND THE CHOCOLATE FACTORY (Leslie Bricusse)	15
75	Arista ARTY 111	THE WIND AND THE LION (Jerry Goldsmith)	15
87	Filmtrax MOMENT 110	WITHNAIL AND I (David Dundas)	25
57	MGM MGM-C 757	THE WIZARD OF OZ (Judy Garland, et al.)	40
67	Capitol (S)T 2800	WOMAN TIMES SEVEN (Riz Ortolani)	18
64	Columbia SX 1628	WONDERFUL LIFE (Cliff Richard) (gatefold sleeve with inner, also stereo SCX 3515 = £20)	12
63	Elstree Extra Range	SUMMER HOLIDAY (2-LP, full soundtrack recording, 80 copies only)	700
64	Elstree Extra Range	WONDERFUL LIFE (2-LP, full soundtrack recording, 150 copies only)	700
68	Apple (S)APCOR 1	WONDERWALL MUSIC (George Harrison) (with insert & black inner sleeve, mono/stereo)	250
70	Atlantic 2663 001	WOODSTOCK (Jimi Hendrix/Who/Joe Cocker, et al.) (3-LP in foldout sleeve with inners)	18
60	RCA RD 27198	THE WORLD OF SUZIE WONG (George Duning)	15
57	Brunswick LAT 8174	WRITTEN ON THE WIND/FOUR GIRLS IN TOWN (Frank Skinner)	25
98	Trunk BARKED 4	THE WICKER MAN (Giovanni) (1 st pressing, black vinyl)	40

Y

65	MGM MGM-C 997	THE YELLOW ROLLS-ROYCE (Riz Ortolani)	12
69	Apple PMC 7070	YELLOW SUBMARINE (Beatles) (1st pressing, laminated flipback sleeve with red lines above & below rear liner note & black inner; with "Sold In The UK..." label text, mono	200
69	Apple PCS 7070	YELLOW SUBMARINE (Beatles) (1st pressing, laminated flipback sleeve with red lines above & below rear liner note & black inner; with "Sold In The UK..." label text, stereo)	80
79	Warwick WW 5075	YESTERDAY'S HERO	12
61	Golden Guinea GGL 0081	YOGI BEAR TV SERIES (TV soundtrack)	12
69	CBS (S) 70045	YOU ARE WHAT YOU EAT (Tiny Tim/Electric Flag, et al.)	18
71	Ember NR 5055	YOU CAN'T HAVE EVERYTHING (Joe Parnello/Bobby Scott)	12
79	MCA MCF 2804	YOUNGBLOOD (War)	15
66	Philips (S)BL 7792	YOUNG GIRLS OF ROCHEFORT (Michel Legrand)	25
57	Brunswick LAT 8252	THE YOUNG LIONS (Hugo Friedhofer)	35
61	Columbia 33SX 1384	THE YOUNG ONES (Cliff Richard) (with inner sleeve, also stereo SCX 3397 = £30)	15
67	United Artists (S)ULP 1171	YOU ONLY LIVE TWICE (John Barry/Nancy Sinatra)	20
65	MGM MGM-CS 6081	YOUR CHEATIN' HEART (Hank Williams Jr.)	15
67	Kama Sutra KLP 402	YOU'RE A BIG BOY NOW (Lovin' Spoonful)	18

Z

70	MGM MGM CS 8120	ZABRISKIE POINT (Pink Floyd/Jerry Garcia/Kaleidoscope, et al.)	30
71	Probe SPB 1026	ZACHARIAH (Country Joe & Fish/James Gang, et al.)	12
69	Philips 600-287	ZITA	40
64	Ember NR 5012	ZULU (John Barry) (yellow/orange label, flipback sleeve)	20
65	Stateside SL10127	ZORBA THE GREEK (Nikis Theodoratis)	12

ORIGINAL STAGE SHOW & RADIO CAST RECORDING LPs

A-Z

60	Columbia SX 1211	ALADDIN (Bob Monkhouse)	15
59	Decca SKL 4136	BELLE - OR THE BALLAD OF DOCTOR CRIPPEN	15
65	Parlophone PMC 1238	BEYOND OUR KEN	15
63	Parlophone PMC 1190	BRIDGE ON THE RIVER WYE (also stereo PCS 3036)	15
56	HMV CLP 1064	BUCCANEER (Kenneth Williams)	30
61	HMV CSD 1366	BYE BYE BIRDIE (Studio cast including Sid James)	35
60s	Encore	CAN CAN	30
65	Pye N(S)PL 18408	THE CARD	30
67	Columbia S(C)X 6103	CINDERELLA (Cliff Richard/Shadows)	20
66	Decca LK/SKL 4810	COME SPY WITH ME (Barbara Windsor)	20
56	HMV CLP 1082	CRANKS (Anthony Newley)	40
60	HMV CLP 1375	NEW CRANKS (Bernard Cribbins)	40
75	Warner Bros K 56186	DAD'S ARMY	12
70	CBS 70063	DAMES AT SEA	18
58	Pye NPL 18016	EXPRESSO BONGO (Millicent Martin)	20

			MINT VALUE £
63	HMV CLP 1685	A FUNNY THING HAPPENED ON THE WAY TO THE FORUM (Frankie Howerd)	18
71	Columbia SCXA 9252	GONE WITH THE WIND (gatefold sleeve)	12
57	Oriole MG 20014	HARMONY CLOSE (Bernard Cribbins)	18
64	Pye NPL 18100/NSPL 83022	HIGH SPIRITS	15
64	Oriole PS 40062	INSTANT MARRIAGE	25
75	MCA MCF 2726	JEEVES	40
74	RSO 2394 141	JOHN, PAUL, GEORGE, RINGO AND BERT (with London cast)	20
58	Decca LK 4352	JOHNNY THE PRIEST	50
83	TER S1044	JOHNNY THE PRIEST (Limited Edition reissue)	20
73	Reflection RL 306	LONESOME STONE	20
61	Oriole MG 20054	MINE FAIR SADIE	15
60	World Record Club TP 151	OLIVER! (mono/stereo) (cast includes Steve Marriot)	12
61	HMV CLP 1459/CSD 1370	OLIVER! (mono/stereo) (Alma Cogan)	40
61	Decca LK 4393/SKL 4133	ONE OVER THE EIGHT (mono/stereo) (Kenneth Williams)	20
63	CBS 60005	ON THE TOWN	15
65	CBS BPG 62598	PASSION FLOWER HOTEL (mono only)	12
63	Parlophone PMC 1198	PETER COOK PRESENTS THE ESTABLISHMENT	15
69	Philips SBL 7916	PHIL THE FLUTER	15
59	Decca LK 4337	PIECES OF EIGHT (Kenneth Williams)	15
59	Decca SKL 4084	PIECES OF EIGHT (stereo) (Kenneth Williams)	20
60	Melodisc MLP 12-117	PREACHIN', PRAYIN', SINGIN' AND SHOUTIN' GOSPEL	12
75	UK UKAL 1015	THE ROCKY HORROR SHOW (London Cast)	12
58	Pye NPL 18011	SHARE MY LETTUCE (Kenneth Williams)	15
60s	Philips 632 303 BL	SPACE IS SO STARTLING	15
60	Fontana TFL 5103	TAKE IT FROM HERE (excerpts from radio show, also stereo STFL 534)	20
63	Parlophone PMC 1197	THAT WAS THE WEEK THAT WAS (also stereo PCS 3040)	12
69	Columbia S(C)X 6330	TWO CITIES (Jeff Wayne)	15
66	United Artists (S)ULP 1116	TWANG! (Lionel Bart)	25
65	HMV CLP 1834/CSD 1587	THE WAYWARD WAY	20
56	HMV DLP 1125	WILD GROWS THE HEATHER (10")	15
68	RCA SB 6792	THE YOUNG VISITORS	12

MUSIC LIBRARY LPs

Still comparatively little is known about the mysterious and often forgotten sub-genre of music known as "library", or rather non-commercial music pressed just for use in film, TV and radio. Since the mid-1990s collecting interest has peaked, dropped away and is now well on the rise again, as are prices for some of the rarer and more important pieces. Collectors also seem to favour early recordings by famous artists such as Jimmy Page or Tubby Hayes. Original pressing numbers and distribution still remain mysterious, most people guestimate that 500 to 1,000 copies for each library pressing is about the average, especially as we move towards the mid-1970s. Older and larger music companies such as De Wolfe originally issued recordings on ten inch (throughout the late 1960s) in incredibly short runs - maybe only 200-300 copies, and if these recordings proved commercially successful they were repressed later on twelve inch. Obviously the original smaller pressings are more desirable. But still pressing numbers and habits remain shrouded in mystery. It has to be noted that many international and desirable labels distributed their library recordings over here and these do turn up from time to time, however we only list original UK pressings in this price guide. Also, it's worth noting that for libraries such as Chappell and Conroy, not all LPs have titles, they simply list the artist names and track titles. In these cases we have just put down the LP catalogue numbers. One final note, all library records are still the property of the libraries companies that issued them and they can, at any time, ask for them back. This is all a little unlikely, but you have been warned.

AMPHONIC

73	AMPSLP1001	Moodsetter/Pacesetter	20

MUSIC LIBRARY APOLLO SOUNDS

71	APP 5012	Robin Jones - DENGA (blue label)	40
71	APP 5016	Robin Jones - EL MAJA (blue label)	50

MUSIC LIBRARY BOSWORTH

66	BLP 102	ELECTRONIC MUSIC (10")	40
67	BLP 104	ATONAL JAZZ STRUCTURES (10")	25
68	BLP 108	JAZZ DRAMATICS (10")	20
69	BLP 109	MODERN RHYTHM (10")	20
70	BLP 116	INDUSTRIAL ROCK (10")	15
70	BLP 118	MODERN DRAMATICS (10")	25
70	BLP 120	HARD AND FAST (10")	25
71	BLP 121	MISCELLANEA (10")	25
72	BLP 126	RHYTHMIC MOODS (10")	15
73	BLP 130	KEYBOARD PLUS	20
74	BLP 135	RHYTHM AT RANDOM	40
75	BLP 141	AMERICA '76	40
75	BLP 142	LET'S GO SOLO	15
75	BLP 143	MUSICAL COCKTAIL	20

MUSIC LIBRARY CHAPPELL

70	CIS 5001	BIG BAND SOUNDS VOL 1	12
70	CIS 5003	INDUSTRIAL SOUNDS VOL 2	25
70	CIS 5007	LIGHT ATMOSPHERE VOL 2	40
70	CIS 5008	MUSIC FOR DRAMA VOL 1 (John Barry etc)	30
70	CIS 5009	MUSIC FOR DRAMA VOL 2	25
70	CIS 5013	DANCE MUSIC VOLUME 1 (Night Club)	25
70	CIS 5023	JAZZ (SMALL GROUP) (John Barry etc)	30
70	CIS 5024	MUSIC FOR DRAMA VOL 3 (Robert Farnon)	30
75	CIS 5047	POP SOUNDS	40
70	672-677	672-677	25
70	678-682	678-682	20
71	1040	1040	15

MINT VALUE £

72	LPC 1045	Lee Mason	100
72	LPC 1051	Lee Mason	75
72	LPC 1052	Mark Duval	60
72	LPC 1053	Pop Sounds	30
73	LPC 1055	Electronic Music	25
73	LPC 1056	Cacavas / Hawksworth - Mark Duval	50
73	LPC 1058	Mark Duval	50
73	LPC 1059	Lee Mason	75
73	LPC 1060	Robert Farnon	20
73	LPC 1063	Roger Webb	30
73	LPC 1065	Rhythm'n'Brass - Mark Duval	80
73	LPC 1068	Dave Holland	30
73	LPC 1069	Light And Bright - Mark Duval	40
74	LPC 1070	Mark Duval	60
74	LPC 1711	Mark Duval	30
74	LPC 1075	Mark Duval	20
74	LPC 1076	Mark Duval	80
74	LPC 1077	Mark Duval	40

MUSIC LIBRARY CONROY

70	BMLP070	BMLP070	15
70	BMLP071	BMLP071	20
70	BMLP072	Electronic Percussion Points	25
70	BMLP074	Theme And Variation	20
70	BMLP080	Electroscope	30
71	BMLP089	BMLP089	20
72	BMLP090	BMLP090	25
72	BMLP092	London's Underground	75
73	BMLP093	BMLP093	80
73	BMLP097	BMLP097	30
74	BMLP101	Happy Moog	15
74	BMLP103	Clap Trap	25
74	BMLP114	Soft Sounds	30
75	BMLP115	Londons Underground 2	20
75	BMLP117	Sounds And Percussion	20
75	BMLP123	Electronic Sounds	30
75	BMLP124	Dramatic Tempi	75
75	BMLP128	Chromozones	35
75	BMLP131	On The Road	40
75	BMLP132	Sounds Funky	20
75	BMLP143	Feelings	150

MUSIC LIBRARY CONROY EUROBEATS SERIES

73	EURO 1	Silly Synthesisers	15
73	EURO 2	Ethnic / India	40
73	EURO 3	Modern baroque	20
73	EURO 4	Romantic backgrounds	50
73	EURO 5	Dramatic backgrounds	50
73	EURO 10	World At Work	507
73	EURO 11	Colla Voce	65

MUSIC LIBRARY DE WOLFE

65	DW LP2949	Band 8 (10")	60
65	DW LP2950	High Speed Jazz (10")	30
65	DW/LP2966	Mind On The Run (10")	60
66	DW/LP2968	Journey Into Sound (10")	40
66	DW LP2973	Abstractions Of The Industrial North (10")	80
66	DW LP2974	The Wild One (10") - (features Jimmy Page)	80
67	DW/LP2975	Town Beat (10")	20
67	DW/LP3022	Checkpoint (10")	20
67	DW/LP3040	Electric Banana (10")	100
67	DW/LP3066	Don't Lose Your Cool (10")	30
68	DW/LP3069	More Electric Banana (10")	80
68	DW/LP3088	Quietly With Johann (10")	20
69	DW/LP3114	Who's Gonna Buy? (The Lemon Dips) (10")	75
66	DW LP3115	Caribbean Sound (10")	20
69	DW/LP3123	Even More Electric Banana (10")	40
69	DW/LP3135	Electroshake Vol 2 (10")	25
69	DW/LP3136	Pop Sounds by The Cool (10")	40
70	DW/LP3154	Heavy Gravy (10")	25
71	DW/LP3182	Vocal Patterns	40
71	DW/LP3212	Moonshade	30
71	DW LP3214	Anglo Amercan Jazz	100
71	DW/LP3220	Afro-Rock	50
71	DW/LP3224	Little Bossa	30
71	DW/LP3227	Vocal Shades And Tones	100
72	DW/LP3243	Hogan, The Hawk And Dirty John Crown	40
73	DW/LP3285	Big Beat	60
74	DW/LP3318	Hard Hitter	40
75	DW/LP3324	Bite Hard	40
75	DW/LP3328	Rhythmes	60
76	DW/LP3347	A Rose For Dracula	25

MUSIC LIBRARY DE WOLFE "In Editions" Series

76	Timing 12	Conversations Between East And West	60
76	Timing 14	Cradle Of Time	30

MINT VALUE £

MUSIC LIBRARY FRANCIS, DAY & HUNTER

68	FDH 1018	Diplomatic Immunity	70

MUSIC LIBRARY HARMONIC

68	CBL618	FONTEYNS FOLK JAZZ (10")	30
69	CBL621 -	MORE BEAT (10")	20

MUSIC LIBRARY HUDSON

71	501 HMC	Rocking Tempo (Peter Merrick)	12
72	506 HMC	Mindbender (peter Merrick)	15
81	527 HMC	Headline (Barbara Moore)	12

MUSIC LIBRARY KPM

66	KPM/ACW1	Music For Your Movies	20
69	KPM1021	Light Jazz Feeling	30
69	KPM1027	Soul Organ Showcase (Alan Hawkshaw)	50
69	KPM1029	Colours In Rhythm	30
69	KPM1037	Flamboyant Themes	20
69	KPM1038	Flamboyant Themes 2	25
69	KPM1042	Jazz Graphics/Spy Set	25
69	KPM1043	Beat Incidental (Alan Hawkshaw/Keith Mansfield)	50
69	KPM1044	The Big Beat (Mohawks & Alan Hawkshaw)	80
69	KPM1046	Sounds In Percussion	20
69	KPM1049	Chorus And Orchestra (Syd Dale)	100
69	KPM1054	Native Africa	25
70	KPM1055	Dramatic Background	40
69	KPM1061	Impact And Action	20
69	KPM1063	Contemporary Colour (Syd Dale)	20
70	KPM1067	The Big Beat - Volume 2 (Alan Moorhouse)	80
70	KPM1070	Bugaloo In Brazil (Les Baxter)	40
70	KPM1071	The Brazillian Suite (Roger Duprat)	40
71	KPM1076	Speed And Excitement (Mansfield, Hawkshaw, Pearson)	35
72	KPM1079	Beat Industrial	40
72	KPM1080	Beat Incidental (Alan Hawkshaw)	50
72	KPM1084	Mediterranean Intrigue (Neil Ardley)	60
71	KPM1085	Electronic Music	50
71	KPM1086	Music For A Young Generation (Alan Hawkshaw)	50
71	KPM1087	Technical Viewpoint	50
71	KPM1088	Bass Guitar And Percussion - Volume 1	50
71	KPM1089	Bass Guitar And Percussion - Volume 2 (Herbie Flowers)	30
71	KPM1090	Bass Guitar And Percussion - Volume 3	30
71	KPM1091	Vibraphone Jazz Quartet	20
71	KPM1094	Accent on Percussion/Construction In Jazz	40
71	KPM1095	Theme Suites / Mustang (John Cameron/Keith Mansfield)	60
71	KPM1097	Jazzrock (John Cameron)	45
71	KPM1100	The Big Screen (Johnny Pearson)	20
72	KPM1102	Electrosound (Ron Geesin)	30
72	KPM1103	Electromusic	25
72	KPM1104	Electrosonic (Delia Derbyshire)	30
72	KPM1111	Brass Plus Moog	40
72	KPM1122	Move With The Times	25
72	KPM1124	Big Business (Keith Mansfield)	35
72	KPM1125	Voices In Harmony (John Cameron/Keith Mansfield)	20
73	KPM1126	Summer Songbirds	40
73	KPM1128	Counterpoint In Rhythm	40
73	KPM1130	Afro Rock (John Cameron/Alan Parker)	100
73	KPM1131	Trendsetters	25
74	KPM1136	Industrial Panorama (Johnny Pearson/Keith Mansfield)	35
75	KPM1160	Friends anf Lovers (Brian Bennett, David Lindup, Duncan Lamont etc)	30
74	KPM1161	Industry Volume 1	40
74	KPM1163	Rock Spectrum	30
74	KPM1165	Jazz Inclination	30
74	KPM1166	Piano Vibrartions	30
74	KPM1168	Drama	40
74	KPM1170	Sounds Of The Time	20
74	KPM1171	Impact (Keith Mansfield/Brian Bennett)	30
74	KPM1177	Hot Wax (Alan Hawkshaw/Brian Bennett)	30
77	KPM1183	Middle East Suite	40
77	KPM1191	Landscapes	15
77	KPM1196	Rock On	30
77	KPM1214	Pulse Of The City	15

MUSIC LIBRARY PEER INTERNATIONAL

70	PIL9006	My Thing	60
71	PIL9009	BIG HAMMER	60
72	PIL9013	Mindbender	150
73	PIL9023	Reggae For Real	75
74	PIL9026	Solar Flares	60
74	PIL9027	Electric Bazaar	40
75	PIL9028	Scoop!	25
76	PIL9029	5+4	25

			MINT VALUE £
77	PIL9037	Hit Man	25
77	PIL9038	Hangover	40
78	PIL9039	Lost Star	75

MUSIC LIBRARY PROGRAMME MUSIC

75	PM8	On The Side Of Angels	35
75	PM11	Music To Varnish Owls By	20
75	PM18 -	Ad-Version Therapy!	20

MUSIC LIBRARY REGENCY LINE

75	RL1001	Light Background Vol. 1	15
75	RL1002	Themes	15
75	RL1003	Rock	15
75	RL1004	Rock	15
75	RL1008	Synthesiser Spots	15
76	RL1013	Dramatic Moods	20
76	RL1019	The Detectives	25

MUSIC LIBRARY ROUGE

75	RMS 101	Skyboat	35
75	RMS 102	Sweet Soul	30
75	RMS 103	Interlace	35
75	RMS 104	The King And The Clown	40
75	RMS 105	Hi-Fly	40
75	RMS 106	Blackout	70
76	RMS 107	Return To Base	30
76	RMS 108	Cobra	35
77	RMS 109	Meal Ticket	25
77	RMS 110	Music Report	20
77	RMS 111	Kites "Electronic Music"	20
77	RMS 112	Let The Music Play	20
78	RMS 113	Hard As A Rock	20
78	RMS 114	Soft And Tender	20
78	RMS 115	Do It (Wally Waller Band - ex Pretty Things)	25
78	RMS 116	Faded Jeans	20
78	RMS 117	All About The Sea	15
78	RMS 118	Discos Like This	40
79	RMS 119	Pulses "Electronic Music"	25
79	RMS 120	Candover	25
79	RMS 121	Friday Girl	30
79	RMS 122	Robot Dancer	20
81	RMS 124	Country Grass	20
81	RMS 125	Making Tracks	20
81	RMS 126	Patterns	20
81	RMS 127	Dancing Grass	15
81	RMS 128	Impetus	15
81	RMS 129	Play On (by Patchwork)	20
81	RMS 130	Glass-Head	25
81	RMS 131	Superdoup	20
81	RMS 132	Sliced Apple	20
81	RMS 133	Pipsqueek	15
81	RMS 134	Whisper To The Moon	20
81	RMS 135	History Of Jazz	15
82	RMS 136	Telletext "Electronic" Music	30
82	RMS 137	Voyage Of Discovery	20
82	RMS 138	Movement	30
82	RMS 140	Instant Reggae (by Roots)	15
82	RMS 141	Hercules	12
82	RMS 142	Red Kite	20
82	RMS 143	New-Age	15
82	RMS 144	Remember	25
82	RMS 145	Drumatics	20
82	RMS 146	Eight Orchestral Sketches	15
83	RMS 147	Cutaway	20
83	RMS 148	Solarium	20
83	RMS 149	Some Shufflin'	15
83	RMS 150	Bass Moods Vol 1	15
83	RMS 151	Bass Moods Vol 2	15
83	RMS 152	Undercover	30
84	RMS 156	Frontrunner	15
84	RMS 157	Breakdance	15
84	RMS 158	Topsy Turvy	15
85	RMS 160	New-Outlook	15
85	RMS 165	Sound On Sound	15
86	RMS 166	Music Break	15
86	RMS 168	Audiotronics	15
86	RMS 169	Highlights (by Darryl Way)	15
87	RMS 173	Pace-Age	15
87	RMS 174	Breaking Ground	15

			MINT VALUE £
87	RMS 175	Changing Seasons	25
87	RMS 178	Kinetics (Alan Parker)	20

MUSIC LIBRARY STANDARD

00	ESL 103	Solo Guitar (Michael Chapman)	40
00	ESL 104	Electronic Music	100

MUSIC LIBRARY STUDIO G

70	LPSG1001	Beat Group	75
70	LPSG1002	Big Jazz & Big Beat	40
70	LPSG1008	Dramatic And Horror	20
80	LPSG4004	Abstract	15

MUSIC LIBRARY STUDIO ONE

71	SO7	MAURICE POP	15
73	SO14	PIERRE LAVIN POP BAND	30

MUSIC LIBRARY SYLVESTER

67	SMC/LP501	Jazz Waves (10")	15
67	SMC/LP502	Voices In The Wind (10")	20
67	SMC/LP503	Striptease (10")	15
67	SMC/LP504	Aquaplane (10")	15
67	SMC/LP505	And So On (10")	15
67	SMC/LP506	Tutti Flutti (10")	15
67	SMX/LP507	Go (10")	15
68	SMX/LP511	Rhythm For Ursula (10")	20
68	SMX/LP512	Exchanges (10")	80
68	SMX/LP516	Racing Tempo (10")	15
70	SMC/LP525	Jazz For Action	15
71	SMC/LP526	Post Combustion	15
71	SMC/LP527	Blue Cylinder	30
71	SMC/LP528	Chronoradial	20
71	SMC/LP529	Ultra Pop-Op	15

MUSIC LIBRARY THEMES

74	TIM1012	Synthesizer And Percussion	25
74	TIM1013	Breath Of Danger	40
74	TIM1015	Mystery Movie	20
75	TIM1018	The All American Powerhouse	20
76	TIM1021	The Voice Of Soul	40
76	TIM1022	The Sound Of Soul	50
76	TIM1024	Drama Suite - Part 1	100
76	TIM1025	The Drama Suite - Part II	100

SPORT RECORDINGS

77	Quality QP 23/77	BATTLE OF THE GIANTS: 1977 FA CUP FINAL – MANCHESTER UNITED V LIVERPOOL	12
78	Quality QP 26/78	BOBBY'S DAZZLERS: 1978 FA CUP FINAL - IPSWICH V ARSENAL	12
71	Quality QP 8/71	CHELSEA KINGS OF EUROPE: 1971 EUROPEAN CUP WINNERS CUP FINAL - CHELSEA V REAL MADRID	15
70	Quality QP 4/70	CHELSEA'S CUP:1970 FA CUP FINAL - CHELSEA V LEEDS	15
73	Quality QP 12/73	EUROPEAN CUP: THE MATCH 1968 - MANCHESTER UNITED V BENFICA	25
79	Quality QP 28/79	FOREST ARE MAGIC: 1979 LEAGUE CUP FINAL - FOREST V SOUTHAMPTON	12
80	Quality QP 33/80	FOREST'S EURO DOUBLE: 1979 EUROPEAN CUP FINAL V MALMÖ/ 1980 EUROPEAN CUP FINAL V HAMBURG	12
84	Quality HM 2	THE FRIENDLY FINAL: EVERTON V LIVERPOOL MILK CUP 1984	12
75	Quality QP 17/75	HAIL TO THE HAMMERS: 1975 FA CUP FINAL - WEST HAM V FULHAM	12
80	Quality QP 31/80	HAMMERS HEROES: 1980 FA CUP FINAL OFFICIAL SOUVENIR	12
76	Quality QP 18/76	LEAGUE CUP FINAL 1976: MANCHESTER CITY V NEWCASTLE UNITED	12
72	Quality QP 9/72	LEAGUE CUP FINAL 1972: CHELSEA V STOKE CITY	15
74	Quality QP 15/74	LIVERPOOL'S CUP: 1974 FA CUP FINAL - LIVERPOOL V NEWCASTLE	12
82	Quality QP 38/82	LIVERPOOL'S 1982 LEAGUE CUP DOUBLE: LIVERPOOL V SPURS	12
79	Quality QP 29/79	MATCH OF THE CENTURY: 1979 FA CUP FINAL – ARSENAL V MANCHESTER UNITED	15
71	Quality QP 7/71	1971 FA CUP FINAL: ARSENAL V LIVERPOOL	15
71	Quality QP 6/71	1971 LEAGUE CUP FINAL: SPURS V ASTON VILLA	15
72	BBC REC 122M	1972 FA CUP FINAL: LEEDS V ARSENAL	12
69	Quality QP 37/81	1969 FA CUP FINAL: MANCHESTER CITY V LEICESTER CITY	12
69	Quality QP 2/69	1969 HOME INTERNATIONAL TOURNAMENT: ENGLAND V SCOTLAND	12
73	Quality QP 15/74	SUNDERLAND'S CUP: 1973 FA CUP FINAL - SUNDERLAND V LEEDS	12
76	Quality QP 19/76	SUPER SAINTS: 1976 FA CUP FINAL - SOUTHAMPTON V MANCHESTER UNITED	15
81	Quality QP 37/81	VIVA EL KOP: THE STORY OF LIVERPOOL'S 1981 EUROPEAN CUP VICTORY	12
75	Quality QP 16/75	VIVA THE VILLA: 1975 FOOTBALL LEAGUE CUP FINAL	12
80	Quality QP 30/80	WOLVES CUP: 1980 FOOTBALL LEAGUE CUP	12
74	Quality QP 14/74	WONDERFUL WOLVES: 1974 LEAGUE CUP FINAL - WOLVERHAMPTON WANDERERS V MANCHESTER CITY	15
66	Centaur CPC 1234	WORLD CUP '66	40
81	Quality QP 35/81	YEAR OF THE COCKEREL: 1981 CENTENARY CUP FINAL	12

Sleeve Type A: coloured wavy lines with small box on front (left), large box on reverse (right).

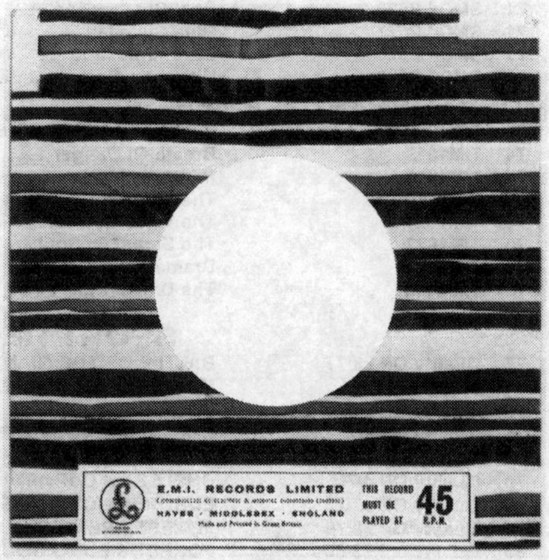

Sleeve Type B: coloured wavy lines without box on front (left), with large box on reverse (right).

Sleeve Type C: multicoloured shapes on front (left) and LP details on reverse (right).

Green sleeve Type 1: straight cut at top (left) and '6/- to 50/- record tokens' on reverse (right).

Green sleeve Type 1B: wavy cut at top (left) and '6/- to 50/- record tokens' on reverse (right).

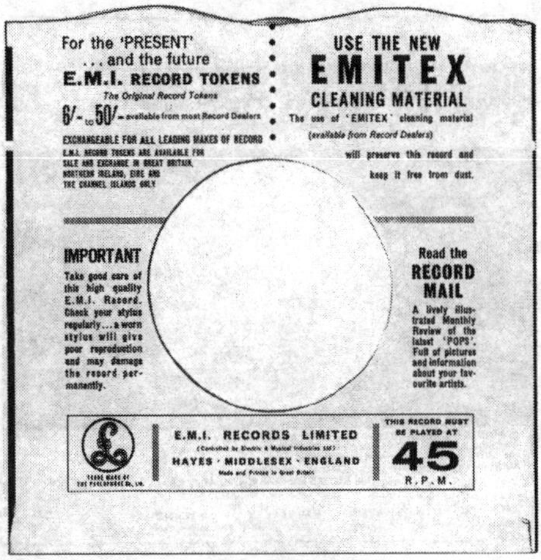

Green sleeve Type 2: rectangular box on front (left),'6/- to 50/- record tokens' on reverse (right).

Green sleeve Type 3: wavy cut at top (left) and 'Fran The Fan' advert on reverse (right).

Green sleeve Type 4: wavy cut at top (left) and 'Morphy-Richards offer' advert on reverse (right).

Green sleeve Type 5: straight cut at top (left), 'Fran The Fan, Dear Miss Brown' ad. on reverse (right).

Green sleeve Type 6: top wavy cut, front rectangular box (left), '6/- to 50/-' on reverse (right).

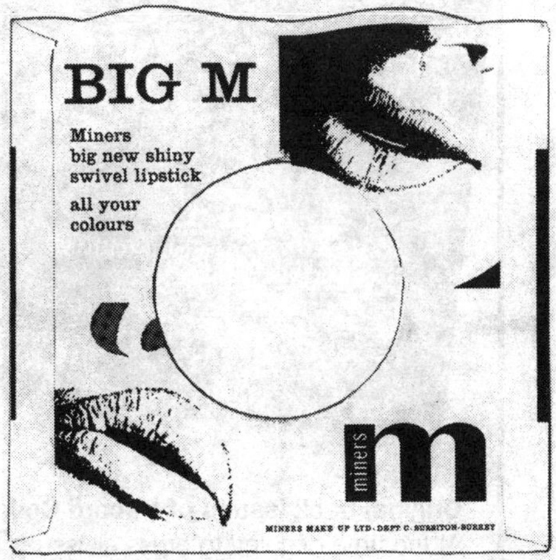

Green sleeve Type 7: wavy cut at top (left) and 'Big M' advert on reverse (right).

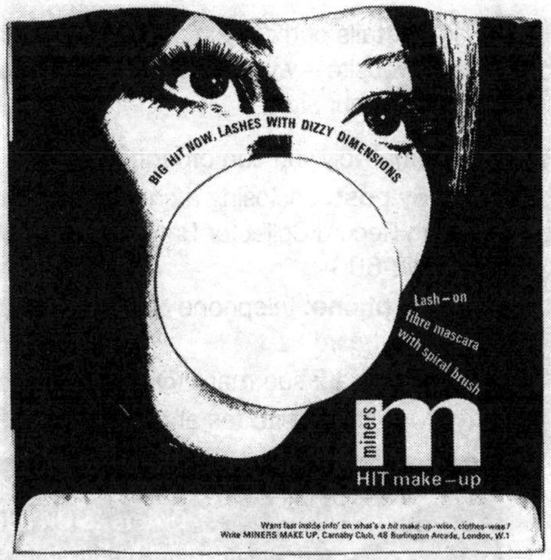

Green sleeve Type 8: wavy cut at top (left) and 'Hit make-up' advert on revesre (right).

RECORD COLLECTOR
BACK ISSUES

Original back issues of Record Collector are available to buy from us.
At the time of going to press all issues are available except for the following.
Nos. 1-31 Inc., 33-38 inc.,160, 170, 182, 183, 184, 208, 219, 290, 291, 294-298, 312, 329, 332, 338, 351, 354, 355, 372 & 375 ARE ALL OUT OF PRINT.

Full details of the main content for each issue, and up to date availability are on our website – **www.recordcollectormag.com**. You can order and pay by credit card on our site.

Alternatively you can order back copies in a number of ways:

- **By post:** enclosing a cheque payable to Diamond Publishing Limited, and sent to Record Collector Back Issues, Metropolis, 140 Wales Farm Road, London W3 6UG
- **By phone:** telephone Sue on +44 (0)20 8752 8193 paying by credit or debit card
- **By email:** sue.maritz@metropolis.co.uk
- Via the website (as above).

Cost per issue (including postage and packing)
Orders to UK addresses £4.90 each
Orders to European addresses £6.60 each
Orders to Rest of the World £8.40 each.